عقيدة المؤمنون

‘Aqeedatul Mu’minun

Published by
QAZI PUBLICATION
Ph.: 814-270-1422
e-mail: drmaqazi@hotmail.com
CC: qazima@gmail.com
URL: http://www.walqalam.media

First Edition: 9.22.2023

ISBN: 979-8-9900153-0-2 (hardcover)
ISBN: 979-8-9900153-1-9 (paperback)
ISBN: 979-8-9900153-4-0 (e-book)

This work incorporates quotes from The Translations of the meanings of Sahih Al-Bukhari (set ISBN: 9960-717-31-3) and the Quran Arabic English (ISBN 9780986136818). I am thankful to Dr. Mahmood A. Qazi and Talal Itani, the copyright holders, for graciously allowing me to use the English translations, They did not seek any compensation . إن شاء الله All of our efforts are entirely for Allah that the people may testify ;

"None has the right to be worshipped but Allah," With which will be opened blind eyes And deaf ears and enveloped hearts."
Sahih Al-Bukhari 2125

لاَ إِلَهَ إِلاَّ اللَّهُ. وَيَفْتَحُ بِهَا أَعْيُنًا عُمْيًا، وَآذَانًا صُمًّا، وَقُلُوبًا غُلْفًا.

بسم الله الرحمن الرحيم
الحمد لله رب العالمين والصلاة والسلام على سيدنا ونبينا محمد
وعلى آله وصحبه أجمعين

Preface

In my pursuit of seeking authentic traditions of Allah and His Messenger, I dedicated many years to reading and studying the Quran, along with entire collections of Hadith, to attain a clear understanding of our faith. I delved deeply into the lives of the Sahaba, which fueled my passion to explore every aspect of history before, during, and after the life of Muhammad (ﷺ). The works of esteemed scholars such as Al-Tabari, Ibn Ishaq, Ahmad, and Bukhari have been a significant source of inspiration and guidance in my journey.

Understanding the importance of these works is vital for nurturing a sound conviction in the declaration of faith: la ilaha illAllah, Muhammadur rasool Allah. However, the time and resources required to read and acquire these texts can often make this knowledge seem distant or unattainable for many.

Motivated by this inspiration and a desire to make this knowledge more accessible, I took on the project of organizing Quranic verses in the context of Aqeeda and arranging Hadith in chronological order to improve clarity and coherence. Additionally, I included brief biographies of notable Companions to provide context for each Hadith narrator. My goal is to compile this essential information into a single book format, offered at the most affordable price possible. I aspire for this work to be a valuable resource that helps all Muslims deepen their understanding of the Aqeeda of the Believers, emphasizing reliance on the Quran and authentic Hadith.

About Aqeedatul Mu'minun

Aqeedatul Mu'minun is a comprehensive resource presenting Al-Qur'an and Sahih Al-Bukhari through the lens of the foundational Islamic disciplines of 'Aqeedah (creed), Tarikh (history), and Musnad (hadith classification). By arranging ahadith chronologically and compiling a musnad for many influential Sahabah (Companions), it transforms vast bodies of knowledge into a system of accessible and interconnected insights. This methodical structure enables students, researchers, and lay readers alike to engage with authentic Islamic sources in a way that is both academically rigorous and spiritually enriching.

The title Aqeedatul Mu'minun-"The Believers' Creed"-reflects its aim to cultivate a holistic understanding of faith as both conviction and lived experience. The term 'Aqeedah, from 'aqada ("to tie" or "to bind"), symbolizes the firm bond between the believer and their certainty in Allah, His Angels, His Books, His Messengers, the Last Day, and His divine decree. This work seeks to illuminate not only what Muslims believe, but why those beliefs define their purpose and guide their conduct. Grounded in the Qur'an and the most authentic hadith collection, Aqeedatul Mu'minun invites readers to explore the intellectual and spiritual unity that forms the essence of Islam.

In Islamic study, understanding Tarikh-the historical context of revelation-is indispensable. Revelation descended over twenty-three years, addressing evolving circumstances within the early Muslim community. By integrating Tarikh into its analysis, Aqeedatul Mu'minun reveals the wisdom behind divine timing and the relevance of each command. This historical lens deepens comprehension and inspires reverence for the divine plan that shaped the Muslim ummah, guiding readers toward a nuanced grasp of Islam's moral and spiritual development during the lifetime of the Prophet Muhammad ﷺ and his Companions.

Central to this framework is the concept of Musnad. A musnad arranges ahadith by the Companion who transmitted them, echoing the meticulous efforts of the early muhaddithun (hadith scholars). Through this method, Aqeedatul Mu'minun enables readers to appreciate how each Companion conveyed the Prophet's ﷺ teachings and to recognize the human chain through which sacred knowledge was preserved. It bridges the modern student with the first custodians of the Sunnah, renewing awareness of the living continuity that connects believers to the Prophet ﷺ.

This work also emphasizes the harmony between 'Aqeedah (belief) and 'Amal (action). Faith, when grounded in knowledge, manifests in character, worship, and conduct. Aqeedatul Mu'minun demonstrates how sound belief naturally inspires righteous deeds, reaffirming that Islam is not an abstract doctrine but a dynamic faith that refines hearts and elevates conduct. By contextualizing narrations within creed and history, it revives the prophetic model of learning-one that unites understanding with transformation.

In an age of fragmented information, Aqeedatul Mu'minun stands as a disciplined effort to restore clarity and authenticity to the study of revelation. Its structured approach aligns with the methodology of Ahl al-'Ilm-the people of knowledge-who devoted their lives to preserving the Qur'an and Sunnah. With its scholarly precision and accessible organization, it serves as a valuable guide for students, educators, and seekers striving to deepen their understanding of Islam and strengthen their connection to the faith of the believers.

And say, "The truth has come, and falsehood has withered away; for falsehood is bound to wither away." – Surah Al-Isra 17:81

وَقُلْ جَآءَ ٱلْحَقُّ وَزَهَقَ ٱلْبَـٰطِلُ ۚ إِنَّ ٱلْبَـٰطِلَ كَانَ زَهُوقًا

No person to whom Allah has given the Scripture, and wisdom, and prophethood would ever say to the people, "Be my worshipers rather than Allah's." Rather, "Be people of the Lord, according to the Scripture you teach, and the teachings you learn." And he would never ask you to take angels and prophets as lords. Would he ask you to disbelieve after you have submitted? – Surah Al-Imran 3:79&80

مَا كَانَ لِبَشَرٍ أَن يُؤْتِيَهُ ٱللَّهُ ٱلْكِتَـٰبَ وَٱلْحُكْمَ وَٱلنُّبُوَّةَ ثُمَّ يَقُولَ لِلنَّاسِ كُونُوا۟ عِبَادًا لِّى مِن دُونِ ٱللَّهِ وَلَـٰكِن كُونُوا۟ رَبَّـٰنِيِّـۧنَ بِمَا كُنتُمْ تُعَلِّمُونَ ٱلْكِتَـٰبَ وَبِمَا كُنتُمْ تَدْرُسُونَ وَلَا يَأْمُرَكُمْ أَن تَتَّخِذُوا۟ ٱلْمَلَـٰٓئِكَةَ وَٱلنَّبِيِّـۧنَ أَرْبَابًا ۗ أَيَأْمُرُكُم بِٱلْكُفْرِ بَعْدَ إِذْ أَنتُم مُّسْلِمُونَ

.... It is incumbent on those who are present to convey this message (of mine) to those who are absent. May be that some of those to whom it will be conveyed will understand it better than those who have actually heard it." – Al-Bukhari 4406

... لِيُبَلِّغِ الشَّاهِدُ الْغَائِبَ، فَلَعَلَّ بَعْضَ مَنْ يُبَلِّغُهُ أَنْ يَكُونَ أَوْعَى لَهُ مِنْ بَعْضِ مَنْ سَمِعَهُ

On authority of Muhammad bin Sīrīn , that he said: 'Indeed this knowledge is faith, so carefully consider from whom you take your faith'. – Sahih Muslim Introduction 26

حَدَّثَنَا حَسَنُ بْنُ الرَّبِيعِ، حَدَّثَنَا حَمَّادُ بْنُ زَيْدٍ، عَنْ أَيُّوبَ، وَهِشَامٍ، عَنْ مُحَمَّدٍ، وَحَدَّثَنَا فُضَيْلٌ، عَنْ هِشَامٍ، قَالَ وَحَدَّثَنَا مَخْلَدُ بْنُ حُسَيْنٍ، عَنْ هِشَامٍ، عَنْ مُحَمَّدِ بْنِ سِيرِينَ، قَالَ إِنَّ هَذَا الْعِلْمَ دِينٌ فَانْظُرُوا عَمَّنْ تَأْخُذُونَ دِينَكُمْ

Uqba bin Aamir said: Learn before those who think (without proof), meaning those who speak with assumptions. Bukhari Volume 8 Chapter Learning about the Laws of inheritance. Pg 380

و قال عقبة بن عامر : تعلموا قبل الظانين ، يعني الذين يتكلمون بالظن

Sahl bin Hunaif said: O people, accuse your opinion over your religion. – Al-Bukhari 7308

قَالَ سَهْلُ بْنُ حُنَيْفٍ يَا أَيُّهَا النَّاسُ اتَّهِمُوا رَأْيَكُمْ عَلَى دِينِكُ

Shaykh Saalih al-Fawzaan, hafidhahullaah said: "As for the permissible form of blind-following (at-taqleedul-mubaah), then it is for the common person (aamee) who, if he does not follow the people of knowledge, then he will stray from the path

"وأما التقليد المباح فهو للعامي الذي إن لم يقلد أهل العلم ضل"

They want to extinguish Allah's light with their mouths, but Allah refuses except to complete His light, even though the disbelievers dislike it. – Surah At-Taubah 9:32

يُرِيدُونَ أَن يُطْفِـُٔوا۟ نُورَ ٱللَّهِ بِأَفْوَٰهِهِمْ وَيَأْبَى ٱللَّهُ إِلَّآ أَن يُتِمَّ نُورَهُۥ وَلَوْ كَرِهَ ٱلْكَـٰفِرُون

Index

Aqeedah

Tarikh

Musnad

Successor's

Sunnah

Appendix

بِسۡمِ ٱللَّهِ ٱلرَّحۡمَـٰنِ ٱلرَّحِيمِ

And the Messenger will say, "My Lord, my people have abandoned this (the) Quran." – Surah Al-Furqan 25:30

وَقَالَ ٱلرَّسُولُ يَـٰرَبِّ إِنَّ قَوۡمِى ٱتَّخَذُواْ هَـٰذَا ٱلۡقُرۡءَانَ مَهۡجُورًا

The Book of
Whenever they bring you an argument, but We bring you the Truth and the best tafsir.
وَلَا يَأْتُونَكَ بِمَثَلٍ إِلَّا جِئْنَـٰكَ بِٱلْحَقِّ وَأَحْسَنَ تَفْسِيرًا

This Quran could not have been produced by anyone other than Allah. In fact, it is a confirmation of what preceded it, and an elaboration of the Book. There is no doubt about it—it is from the Lord of the Universe. – Surah Yunus 10:37

وَمَا كَانَ هَٰذَا الْقُرْآنُ أَن يُفْتَرَىٰ مِن دُونِ اللَّهِ وَلَٰكِن تَصْدِيقَ الَّذِي بَيْنَ يَدَيْهِ وَتَفْصِيلَ الْكِتَابِ لَا رَيْبَ فِيهِ مِن رَّبِّ الْعَالَمِينَ

In their stories is a lesson for those who possess intelligence. This is not a fabricated tale, but a confirmation of what came before it, and a detailed explanation of all things, and guidance, and mercy for people who believe. – Surah Yusuf 12:111

لَقَدْ كَانَ فِي قَصَصِهِمْ عِبْرَةٌ لِّأُوْلِي ٱلْأَلْبَـٰبِ مَا كَانَ حَدِيثًا يُفْتَرَىٰ وَلَـٰكِن تَصْدِيقَ ٱلَّذِي بَيْنَ يَدَيْهِ وَتَفْصِيلَ كُلِّ شَيْءٍ وَهُدًى وَرَحْمَةً لِّقَوْمٍ يُؤْمِنُونَ

Whatever argument they come to you with, We provide you with the truth, and the best explanation. – Surah Al-Furqan 25:33

وَلَا يَأْتُونَكَ بِمَثَلٍ إِلَّا جِئْنَـٰكَ بِٱلْحَقِّ وَأَحْسَنَ تَفْسِيرًا

A messenger who recites to you Allah's Verses, clear and distinct, that he may bring those who believe and work righteousness from darkness into light. Whoever believes in Allah and acts with integrity, He will admit him into gardens beneath which rivers flow, therein to abide forever. Allah has given him an excellent provision. – Surah At-Talaq 65:11

رَّسُولًا يَتْلُوا۟ عَلَيْكُمْ ءَايَـٰتِ ٱللَّهِ مُبَيِّنَـٰتٍ لِّيُخْرِجَ ٱلَّذِينَ ءَامَنُوا۟ وَعَمِلُوا۟ ٱلصَّـٰلِحَـٰتِ مِنَ ٱلظُّلُمَـٰتِ إِلَى ٱلنُّورِ وَمَن يُؤْمِنۢ بِٱللَّهِ وَيَعْمَلْ صَـٰلِحًا يُدْخِلْهُ جَنَّـٰتٍ تَجْرِى مِن تَحْتِهَا ٱلْأَنْهَـٰرُ خَـٰلِدِينَ فِيهَآ أَبَدًا قَدْ أَحْسَنَ ٱللَّهُ لَهُۥ رِزْقًا

⸢It is⸣ a Book whose verses are perfectly explained—a Quran in Arabic for people who know, - Surah Al-Fussilat 41:3

كِتَـٰبٌ فُصِّلَتْ ءَايَـٰتُهُۥ قُرْءَانًا عَرَبِيًّا لِّقَوْمٍ يَعْلَمُونَ

Upon Us is its collection and its recitation. Then, when We have recited it, follow its recitation. Then upon Us is its explanation. – Surah Al-Qiyamah 75:17-19

إِنَّ عَلَيْنَا جَمْعَهُۥ وَقُرْءَانَهُۥ فَإِذَا قَرَأْنَـٰهُ فَٱتَّبِعْ قُرْءَانَهُۥ ثُمَّ إِنَّ عَلَيْنَا بَيَانَهُۥ

We made the day and night as two signs. So We made the sign of the night devoid of light, and We made the sign of the day ⸢perfectly⸣ bright, so that you may seek the bounty of your Lord and know the number of years and calculation ⸢of time⸣. And We have explained everything in detail. – Surah Al-Isra 17:12

وَجَعَلْنَا ٱلَّيْلَ وَٱلنَّهَارَ ءَايَتَيْنِ فَمَحَوْنَآ ءَايَةَ ٱلَّيْلِ وَجَعَلْنَآ ءَايَةَ ٱلنَّهَارِ مُبْصِرَةً لِّتَبْتَغُوا۟ فَضْلًا مِّن رَّبِّكُمْ وَلِتَعْلَمُوا۟ عَدَدَ ٱلسِّنِينَ وَٱلْحِسَابَ وَكُلَّ شَىْءٍ فَصَّلْنَـٰهُ تَفْصِيلًا

It is upon Us to guide. – Surah Al-Layl 92:12

إِنَّ عَلَيْنَا لَلْهُدَىٰ

Exalted is Allah, the True King. Do not be hasty with the Quran before its inspiration to you is concluded, and say, "My Lord, increase me in knowledge." – Surah Ta-Ha 20:114

فَتَعَٰلَى ٱللَّهُ ٱلْمَلِكُ ٱلْحَقُّ ۗ وَلَا تَعْجَلْ بِٱلْقُرْءَانِ مِن قَبْلِ أَن يُقْضَىٰٓ إِلَيْكَ وَحْيُهُۥ ۖ وَقُل رَّبِّ زِدْنِى عِلْمًا

(Allah) He will say, "Just as Our revelations came to you, and you forgot them, today you will be forgotten." – Surah Ta-Ha 20:126

قَالَ كَذَٰلِكَ أَتَتْكَ ءَايَٰتُنَا فَنَسِيتَهَا ۖ وَكَذَٰلِكَ ٱلْيَوْمَ تُنسَىٰ

Say, "O People of the Book, come to terms common between us and you: that we worship none but Allah, and that we associate nothing with Him, and that none of us takes others as lords besides Allah." And if they turn away, say, "Bear witness that we have submitted." – Surah Al-Imran 3:64

قُلْ يَٰٓأَهْلَ ٱلْكِتَٰبِ تَعَالَوْا۟ إِلَىٰ كَلِمَةٍ سَوَآءٍۭ بَيْنَنَا وَبَيْنَكُمْ أَلَّا نَعْبُدَ إِلَّا ٱللَّهَ وَلَا نُشْرِكَ بِهِۦ شَيْـًٔا وَلَا يَتَّخِذَ بَعْضُنَا بَعْضًا أَرْبَابًا مِّن
دُونِ ٱللَّهِ ۚ فَإِن تَوَلَّوْا۟ فَقُولُوا۟ ٱشْهَدُوا۟ بِأَنَّا مُسْلِمُونَ

A Scripture was revealed to you, so let there be no anxiety in your heart because of it. You are to warn with it—and a reminder for the believers. Follow what is revealed to you from your Lord, and do not follow other's beside Him. Little you recollect. – Surah Al-A'raf 7:2&3

كِتَٰبٌ أُنزِلَ إِلَيْكَ فَلَا يَكُن فِى صَدْرِكَ حَرَجٌ مِّنْهُ لِتُنذِرَ بِهِۦ وَذِكْرَىٰ لِلْمُؤْمِنِينَ
ٱتَّبِعُوا۟ مَآ أُنزِلَ إِلَيْكُم مِّن رَّبِّكُمْ وَلَا تَتَّبِعُوا۟ مِن دُونِهِۦٓ أَوْلِيَآءَ ۗ قَلِيلًا مَّا تَذَكَّرُونَ

Say, "Shall we invoke besides Allah something that can neither benefit us nor harm us, and turn back on our heels after Allah has guided us, like someone seduced by the devils and confused on earth, who has friends calling him to guidance: 'Come to us'?" Say, "The guidance of Allah is the guidance, and we are commanded to surrender to the Lord of the Universe." - Surah Al-An'am 6:71

قُلْ أَنَدْعُوا۟ مِن دُونِ ٱللَّهِ مَا لَا يَنفَعُنَا وَلَا يَضُرُّنَا وَنُرَدُّ عَلَىٰٓ أَعْقَابِنَا بَعْدَ إِذْ هَدَىٰنَا ٱللَّهُ كَٱلَّذِى ٱسْتَهْوَتْهُ ٱلشَّيَٰطِينُ فِى ٱلْأَرْضِ
حَيْرَانَ لَهُۥٓ أَصْحَٰبٌ يَدْعُونَهُۥٓ إِلَى ٱلْهُدَى ٱئْتِنَا ۗ قُلْ إِنَّ هُدَى ٱللَّهِ هُوَ ٱلْهُدَىٰ ۖ وَأُمِرْنَا لِنُسْلِمَ لِرَبِّ ٱلْعَٰلَمِينَ

Say, "I am forbidden from worshiping those you pray to besides Allah." Say, "I will not follow your desires; else I would be lost and not be of those guided." – Surah Al-An'am 6:56

قُلْ إِنِّى عَلَىٰ بَيِّنَةٍ مِّن رَّبِّى وَكَذَّبْتُم بِهِۦ ۚ مَا عِندِى مَا تَسْتَعْجِلُونَ بِهِۦٓ ۚ إِنِ ٱلْحُكْمُ إِلَّا لِلَّهِ ۖ يَقُصُّ ٱلْحَقَّ ۖ وَهُوَ خَيْرُ ٱلْفَٰصِلِينَ

O People of the Book! Our Messenger has come to you, clarifying for you much of what you kept hidden of the Book, and overlooking much. A light from Allah has come to you, and a clear Book. Allah guides with it whoever follows His approval to the ways of peace, and He brings them out of darkness into light, by His permission, and He guides them in a straight path. – Surah Al-Maidah 5:15&16

يَٰٓأَهْلَ ٱلْكِتَٰبِ قَدْ جَآءَكُمْ رَسُولُنَا يُبَيِّنُ لَكُمْ كَثِيرًا مِّمَّا كُنتُمْ تُخْفُونَ مِنَ ٱلْكِتَٰبِ وَيَعْفُوا۟ عَن كَثِيرٍ ۚ قَدْ جَآءَكُم مِّنَ ٱللَّهِ نُورٌ وَكِتَٰبٌ
مُّبِينٌ يَهْدِى بِهِ ٱللَّهُ مَنِ ٱتَّبَعَ رِضْوَٰنَهُۥ سُبُلَ ٱلسَّلَٰمِ وَيُخْرِجُهُم مِّنَ ٱلظُّلُمَٰتِ إِلَى ٱلنُّورِ بِإِذْنِهِۦ وَيَهْدِيهِمْ إِلَىٰ صِرَٰطٍ مُّسْتَقِيمٍ

We have revealed the Torah, wherein is guidance and light. The submissive prophets ruled the Jews according to it, so did the rabbis and the scholars, as they were required to protect Allah's Book, and were witnesses to it. So do not fear people, but fear Me. And do not sell My revelations for a cheap price. Those who do not rule according to what Allah revealed are the unbelievers. Surah Al-Ma`idah 5:44

إِنَّا أَنزَلْنَا ٱلتَّوْرَىٰةَ فِيهَا هُدًى وَنُورٌ ۚ يَحْكُمُ بِهَا ٱلنَّبِيُّونَ ٱلَّذِينَ أَسْلَمُوا۟ لِلَّذِينَ هَادُوا۟ وَٱلرَّبَّـٰنِيُّونَ وَٱلْأَحْبَارُ بِمَا ٱسْتُحْفِظُوا۟ مِن كِتَـٰبِ ٱللَّهِ وَكَانُوا۟ عَلَيْهِ شُهَدَآءَ ۚ فَلَا تَخْشَوُا۟ ٱلنَّاسَ وَٱخْشَوْنِ وَلَا تَشْتَرُوا۟ بِـَٔايَـٰتِى ثَمَنًا قَلِيلًا ۚ وَمَن لَّمْ يَحْكُم بِمَآ أَنزَلَ ٱللَّهُ فَأُو۟لَـٰٓئِكَ هُمُ ٱلْكَـٰفِرُونَ

So let the people of the Gospel rule according to what Allah revealed in it. Those who do not rule according to what Allah revealed are the sinners. And We revealed to you the Book, with truth, confirming the Scripture that preceded it, and superseding it. So judge between them according to what Allah revealed, and do not follow their desires if they differ from the truth that has come to you. For each of you We have assigned a law and a method. Had Allah willed, He could have made you a single nation, but He tests you through what He has given you. So compete in righteousness. To Allah is your return, all of you; then He will inform you of what you had disputed. And judge between them according to what Allah revealed, and do not follow their desires. And beware of them, lest they lure you away from some of what Allah has revealed to you. But if they turn away, know that Allah intends to strike them with some of their sins. In fact, a great many people are corrupt. Is it the laws of the time of ignorance that they desire? Who is better than Allah in judgment for people who are certain? – Surah Al-Maidah 5:47-50

وَلْيَحْكُمْ أَهْلُ ٱلْإِنجِيلِ بِمَآ أَنزَلَ ٱللَّهُ فِيهِ ۚ وَمَن لَّمْ يَحْكُم بِمَآ أَنزَلَ ٱللَّهُ فَأُو۟لَـٰٓئِكَ هُمُ ٱلْفَـٰسِقُونَ وَأَنزَلْنَآ إِلَيْكَ ٱلْكِتَـٰبَ بِٱلْحَقِّ مُصَدِّقًا لِّمَا بَيْنَ يَدَيْهِ مِنَ ٱلْكِتَـٰبِ وَمُهَيْمِنًا عَلَيْهِ ۖ فَٱحْكُم بَيْنَهُم بِمَآ أَنزَلَ ٱللَّهُ ۖ وَلَا تَتَّبِعْ أَهْوَآءَهُمْ عَمَّا جَآءَكَ مِنَ ٱلْحَقِّ ۚ لِكُلٍّ جَعَلْنَا مِنكُمْ شِرْعَةً وَمِنْهَاجًا ۚ وَلَوْ شَآءَ ٱللَّهُ لَجَعَلَكُمْ أُمَّةً وَٰحِدَةً وَلَـٰكِن لِّيَبْلُوَكُمْ فِى مَآ ءَاتَىٰكُمْ ۖ فَٱسْتَبِقُوا۟ ٱلْخَيْرَٰتِ ۚ إِلَى ٱللَّهِ مَرْجِعُكُمْ جَمِيعًا فَيُنَبِّئُكُم بِمَا كُنتُمْ فِيهِ تَخْتَلِفُونَ وَأَنِ ٱحْكُم بَيْنَهُم بِمَآ أَنزَلَ ٱللَّهُ وَلَا تَتَّبِعْ أَهْوَآءَهُمْ وَٱحْذَرْهُمْ أَن يَفْتِنُوكَ عَنۢ بَعْضِ مَآ أَنزَلَ ٱللَّهُ إِلَيْكَ ۖ فَإِن تَوَلَّوْا۟ فَٱعْلَمْ أَنَّمَا يُرِيدُ ٱللَّهُ أَن يُصِيبَهُم بِبَعْضِ ذُنُوبِهِمْ ۗ وَإِنَّ كَثِيرًا مِّنَ ٱلنَّاسِ لَفَـٰسِقُونَ أَفَحُكْمَ ٱلْجَـٰهِلِيَّةِ يَبْغُونَ ۚ وَمَنْ أَحْسَنُ مِنَ ٱللَّهِ حُكْمًا لِّقَوْمٍ يُوقِنُونَ

Narrated `Aisha: Allah's Messenge came to me, and I told him about the slave-girl (Barirah) Allah's Messenger said, "Buy and manumit her, for the Wala is for the one who manumits." In the evening the Prophet got up and glorified Allah as He deserved and then said, "Why do some people impose conditions which are not present in Allah's Book (Laws)? Whoever imposes such a condition as is not in Allah's Laws, then that condition is invalid even if he imposes one hundred conditions, for Allah's conditions are more binding and reliable." – Al-Bukhari 2155

حَدَّثَنَا أَبُو الْيَمَانِ، أَخْبَرَنَا شُعَيْبٌ، عَنِ الزُّهْرِيِّ، قَالَ عُرْوَةُ بْنُ الزُّبَيْرِ قَالَتْ عَائِشَةُ ـ رضى الله عنها دَخَلَ عَلَىَّ رَسُولُ اللَّهِ صلى الله عليه وسلم فَذَكَرْتُ لَهُ، فَقَالَ رَسُولُ اللَّهِ صلى الله عليه وسلم " اشْتَرِي وَأَعْتِقِي، فَإِنَّ الْوَلاَءَ لِمَنْ أَعْتَقَ ". ثُمَّ قَامَ النَّبِيُّ صلى الله عليه وسلم مِنَ الْعَشِيِّ، فَأَثْنَى عَلَى اللَّهِ بِمَا هُوَ أَهْلُهُ، ثُمَّ قَالَ " مَا بَالُ أُنَاسٍ يَشْتَرِطُونَ شُرُوطًا لَيْسَ فِي كِتَابِ اللَّهِ، مَنِ اشْتَرَطَ شَرْطًا لَيْسَ فِي كِتَابِ اللَّهِ فَهْوَ بَاطِلٌ، وَإِنِ اشْتَرَطَ مِائَةَ شَرْطٍ، شَرْطُ اللَّهِ أَحَقُّ وَأَوْثَقُ ".

O you who believe! Do not ask about things that would trouble you if disclosed to you. But if you were to ask about them while the Quran is being revealed, they will become obvious to you. Allah forgives that. Allah is Forgiving and Clement. – Surah Al-Maidah 5:101

يَـٰٓأَيُّهَا ٱلَّذِينَ ءَامَنُوا۟ لَا تَسْـَٔلُوا۟ عَنْ أَشْيَآءَ إِن تُبْدَ لَكُمْ تَسُؤْكُمْ وَإِن تَسْـَٔلُوا۟ عَنْهَا حِينَ يُنَزَّلُ ٱلْقُرْءَانُ تُبْدَ لَكُمْ عَفَا ٱللَّهُ عَنْهَا ۗ وَٱللَّهُ غَفُورٌ حَلِيمٌ

Whatever matter you differ about, its judgment rests with Allah. "Such is Allah, my Lord, in Whom I trust, and unto Him I repent." – Surah Ash-Shura 42:10

وَمَا ٱخْتَلَفْتُمْ فِيهِ مِن شَىْءٍ فَحُكْمُهُۥٓ إِلَى ٱللَّهِ ۚ ذَٰلِكُمُ ٱللَّهُ رَبِّى عَلَيْهِ تَوَكَّلْتُ وَإِلَيْهِ أُنِيبُ

O you who believe! Obey Allah and obey the Messenger and those in authority among you. And if you dispute over anything, refer it to Allah and the Messenger, if you believe in Allah and the Last Day. That is best, and a most excellent determination. – Surah An-Nisa 4:59

يَـٰٓأَيُّهَا ٱلَّذِينَ ءَامَنُوٓا۟ أَطِيعُوا۟ ٱللَّهَ وَأَطِيعُوا۟ ٱلرَّسُولَ وَأُو۟لِى ٱلْأَمْرِ مِنكُمْ ۖ فَإِن تَنَـٰزَعْتُمْ فِى شَىْءٍ فَرُدُّوهُ إِلَى ٱللَّهِ وَٱلرَّسُولِ إِن كُنتُمْ تُؤْمِنُونَ بِٱللَّهِ وَٱلْيَوْمِ ٱلْـَٔاخِرِ ۚ ذَٰلِكَ خَيْرٌ وَأَحْسَنُ تَأْوِيلًا

Or do they say, "He forged a lie about Allah." If Allah so willed, He could have sealed your heart. But Allah obliterates the false, and confirm the true by His Words. He knows what is in the hearts. – Surah Ash-Shura 42:24

أَمْ يَقُولُونَ ٱفْتَرَىٰ عَلَى ٱللَّهِ كَذِبًا ۖ فَإِن يَشَإِ ٱللَّهُ يَخْتِمْ عَلَىٰ قَلْبِكَ ۗ وَيَمْحُ ٱللَّهُ ٱلْبَـٰطِلَ وَيُحِقُّ ٱلْحَقَّ بِكَلِمَـٰتِهِۦٓ ۚ إِنَّهُۥ عَلِيمٌۢ بِذَاتِ ٱلصُّدُورِ

None argues against Allah's revelations except those who disbelieve. So do not be impressed by their activities in the land. – Surah Ghafir 40:4

مَا يُجَـٰدِلُ فِىٓ ءَايَـٰتِ ٱللَّهِ إِلَّا ٱلَّذِينَ كَفَرُوا۟ فَلَا يَغْرُرْكَ تَقَلُّبُهُمْ فِى ٱلْبِلَـٰدِ

Those who dispute regarding Allah's revelations without any authority having come to them— there is nothing in their hearts but the feeling of greatness, which they will never attain. So seek refuge in Allah; for He is the All-Hearing, the All-Seeing. – Surah Ghafir 40:56

إِنَّ ٱلَّذِينَ يُجَـٰدِلُونَ فِىٓ ءَايَـٰتِ ٱللَّهِ بِغَيْرِ سُلْطَـٰنٍ أَتَىٰهُمْ ۙ إِن فِى صُدُورِهِمْ إِلَّا كِبْرٌ مَّا هُم بِبَـٰلِغِيهِ ۚ فَٱسْتَعِذْ بِٱللَّهِ ۖ إِنَّهُۥ هُوَ ٱلسَّمِيعُ ٱلْبَصِيرُ

Say, "Allah knows best how long they stayed." His is the mystery of the heavens and the earth. By Him you see and hear. They have no guardian apart from Him, and He shares His Sovereignty with no one. – Surah Al-Kahf 18:26

قُلِ ٱللَّهُ أَعْلَمُ بِمَا لَبِثُوا۟ ۖ لَهُۥ غَيْبُ ٱلسَّمَـٰوَٰتِ وَٱلْأَرْضِ ۖ أَبْصِرْ بِهِۦ وَأَسْمِعْ ۚ مَا لَهُم مِّن دُونِهِۦ مِن وَلِىٍّ وَلَا يُشْرِكُ فِى حُكْمِهِۦٓ أَحَدًا

Say, "What thing is more solemn in testimony?" Say, "Allah is Witness between you and me. This Quran was revealed to me, that I may warn you with it, and whomever it may reach. Do you indeed testify that there are other gods with Allah?" Say, "I myself do not testify." Say, "He is but One God, and I am innocent of your idolatry." – Surah Al-An'am 6:19

قُلْ أَىُّ شَىْءٍ أَكْبَرُ شَهَـٰدَةً ۖ قُلِ ٱللَّهُ ۖ شَهِيدٌۢ بَيْنِى وَبَيْنَكُمْ ۚ وَأُوحِىَ إِلَىَّ هَـٰذَا ٱلْقُرْءَانُ لِأُنذِرَكُم بِهِۦ وَمَنۢ بَلَغَ ۚ أَئِنَّكُمْ لَتَشْهَدُونَ أَنَّ مَعَ ٱللَّهِ ءَالِهَةً أُخْرَىٰ ۚ قُل لَّآ أَشْهَدُ ۚ قُلْ إِنَّمَا هُوَ إِلَـٰهٌ وَٰحِدٌ وَإِنَّنِى بَرِىٓءٌ مِّمَّا تُشْرِكُونَ

And do not occupy yourself with what you have no knowledge of. The hearing, and the sight, and the brains—all these will be questioned. – Surah Al-Isra 17:36

وَلَا تَقْفُ مَا لَيْسَ لَكَ بِهِۦ عِلْمٌ ۚ إِنَّ ٱلسَّمْعَ وَٱلْبَصَرَ وَٱلْفُؤَادَ كُلُّ أُو۟لَـٰٓئِكَ كَانَ عَنْهُ مَسْـُٔولًا

Narrated `Abdullah bin `Amr: I heard the Prophet ﷺ saying, "Allah will not deprive you of knowledge after he has given it to you, but it will be taken away through the death of the religious learned men with their knowledge. Then there will remain ignorant people who, when consulted, will give verdicts according to their opinions whereby they will mislead others and go astray." – Al-Bukhari 7307

حَدَّثَنَا سَعِيدُ بْنُ تَلِيدٍ، حَدَّثَنِي ابْنُ وَهْبٍ، حَدَّثَنِي عَبْدُ الرَّحْمَنِ بْنُ شُرَيْحٍ، وَغَيْرُهُ، عَنْ أَبِي الأَسْوَدِ، عَنْ عُرْوَةَ، قَالَ حَجَّ عَلَيْنَا عَبْدُ اللَّهِ بْنُ عَمْرٍو فَسَمِعْتُهُ يَقُولُ سَمِعْتُ النَّبِيَّ صلى الله عليه وسلم يَقُولُ " إِنَّ اللَّهَ لاَ يَنْزِعُ الْعِلْمَ بَعْدَ أَنْ أَعْطَاهُمُوهُ انْتِزَاعًا، وَلَكِنْ يَنْتَزِعُهُ مِنْهُمْ مَعَ قَبْضِ الْعُلَمَاءِ بِعِلْمِهِمْ، فَيَبْقَى نَاسٌ جُهَّالٌ يُسْتَفْتَوْنَ فَيُفْتُونَ بِرَأْيِهِمْ، فَيُضِلُّونَ وَيَضِلُّونَ ". فَحَدَّثْتُ عَائِشَةَ زَوْجَ النَّبِيِّ صلى الله عليه وسلم ثُمَّ إِنَّ عَبْدَ اللَّهِ بْنَ عَمْرٍو حَجَّ بَعْدُ فَقَالَتْ يَا ابْنَ أُخْتِي انْطَلِقْ إِلَى عَبْدِ اللَّهِ

فَاسْتَثْبِتْ لِي مِنْهُ الَّذِي حَدَّثَنِي عَنْهُ. فَجِئْتُهُ فَسَأَلْتُهُ فَحَدَّثَنِي بِهِ كَنَحْوِ مَا حَدَّثَنِي، فَأَتَيْتُ عَائِشَةَ فَأَخْبَرْتُهَا فَعَجِبَتْ فَقَالَتْ وَاللَّهِ لَقَدْ حَفِظَ عَبْدُ اللَّهِ بْنُ عَمْرٍو

Narrated Al-A`mash: I asked Abu Wail, "Did you witness the battle of Siffin between `Ali and Muawiya?" He said, "Yes," and added, "Then I heard Sahl bin Hunaif saying, 'O people! Blame your personal opinions in your religion. No doubt, I remember myself on the day of Abi Jandal; if I had the power to refuse the order of Allah's Messenger ﷺ I would have refused it. We have never put our swords on our shoulders to get involved in a situation that might have been horrible for us, but those swords brought us to victory and peace, except this present situation.' "Abu Wail said, "I witnessed the battle of Siffin, and how nasty Siffin was!" – Al-Bukhari 7308
حَدَّثَنَا عَبْدَانُ، أَخْبَرَنَا أَبُو حَمْزَةَ، سَمِعْتُ الأَعْمَشَ، قَالَ سَأَلْتُ أَبَا وَائِلٍ هَلْ شَهِدْتَ صِفِّينَ قَالَ نَعَمْ. فَسَمِعْتُ سَهْلَ بْنَ حُنَيْفٍ، يَقُولُ ح وَحَدَّثَنَا مُوسَى بْنُ إِسْمَاعِيلَ، حَدَّثَنَا أَبُو عَوَانَةَ، عَنِ الأَعْمَشِ، عَنْ أَبِي وَائِلٍ، قَالَ قَالَ سَهْلُ بْنُ حُنَيْفٍ يَا أَيُّهَا النَّاسُ اتَّهِمُوا رَأْيَكُمْ عَلَى دِينِكُمْ، لَقَدْ رَأَيْتُنِي يَوْمَ أَبِي جَنْدَلٍ وَلَوْ أَسْتَطِيعُ أَنْ أَرُدَّ أَمْرَ رَسُولِ اللَّهِ صلى الله عليه وسلم لَرَدَدْتُهُ، وَمَا وَضَعْنَا سُيُوفَنَا عَلَى عَوَاتِقِنَا إِلَى أَمْرٍ يُفْظِعُنَا إِلاَّ أَسْهَلْنَ بِنَا إِلَى أَمْرٍ نَعْرِفُهُ غَيْرَ هَذَا الأَمْرِ. قَالَ وَقَالَ أَبُو وَائِلٍ شَهِدْتُ صِفِّينَ وَبِئْسَتْ صِفُّونَ

Say, "To Allah belongs the conclusive argument. Had He willed, He would have guided you all." – Surah Al-An'am 6:149
قُلْ فَلِلَّهِ ٱلْحُجَّةُ ٱلْبَـٰلِغَةُ ۖ فَلَوْ شَآءَ لَهَدَىٰكُمْ أَجْمَعِينَ

This is My path, straight, so follow it. And do not follow the other paths, lest they divert you from His path. All this He has enjoined upon you, that you may refrain from wrongdoing. – Surah Al-An'am 6:153
وَأَنَّ هَـٰذَا صِرَٰطِى مُسْتَقِيمًا فَٱتَّبِعُوهُ ۖ وَلَا تَتَّبِعُوا۟ ٱلسُّبُلَ فَتَفَرَّقَ بِكُمْ عَن سَبِيلِهِۦ ۚ ذَٰلِكُمْ وَصَّىٰكُم بِهِۦ لَعَلَّكُمْ تَتَّقُونَ

The Jews and the Christians will not approve of you, unless you follow their creed. Say, "Allah's guidance is the guidance." Should you follow their desires, after the knowledge that has come to you, you will have in Allah neither guardian nor helper. – Surah Al-Baqarah 2:120
وَلَن تَرْضَىٰ عَنكَ ٱلْيَهُودُ وَلَا ٱلنَّصَـٰرَىٰ حَتَّىٰ تَتَّبِعَ مِلَّتَهُمْ ۗ قُلْ إِنَّ هُدَى ٱللَّهِ هُوَ ٱلْهُدَىٰ ۗ وَلَئِنِ ٱتَّبَعْتَ أَهْوَآءَهُم بَعْدَ ٱلَّذِى جَآءَكَ مِنَ ٱلْعِلْمِ ۙ مَا لَكَ مِنَ ٱللَّهِ مِن وَلِىٍّ وَلَا نَصِيرٍ

So he began with their bags, before his brother's bag. Then he pulled it out of his brother's bag. Thus We devised a plan for Joseph; he could not have detained his brother under the king's law, unless Allah so willed. We elevate by degrees whomever We will; and above every person of knowledge, there is one more learned. – Surah Yusuf 12:76
فَبَدَأَ بِأَوْعِيَتِهِمْ قَبْلَ وِعَآءِ أَخِيهِ ثُمَّ ٱسْتَخْرَجَهَا مِن وِعَآءِ أَخِيهِ ۚ كَذَٰلِكَ كِدْنَا لِيُوسُفَ ۖ مَا كَانَ لِيَأْخُذَ أَخَاهُ فِى دِينِ ٱلْمَلِكِ إِلَّآ أَن يَشَآءَ ٱللَّهُ ۚ نَرْفَعُ دَرَجَـٰتٍ مَّن نَّشَآءُ ۗ وَفَوْقَ كُلِّ ذِى عِلْمٍ عَلِيمٌ

If you do not produce a miracle for them, they say, "Why don't you improvise one." Say, "I only follow what is inspired to me from my Lord." These are insights from your Lord, and guidance, and mercy, for a people who believe. – Surah Al-A'raf 7:203
وَإِذَا لَمْ تَأْتِهِم بِـَٔايَةٍ قَالُوا۟ لَوْلَا ٱجْتَبَيْتَهَا ۚ قُلْ إِنَّمَآ أَتَّبِعُ مَا يُوحَىٰٓ إِلَىَّ مِن رَّبِّى ۚ هَـٰذَا بَصَآئِرُ مِن رَّبِّكُمْ وَهُدًى وَرَحْمَةٌ لِّقَوْمٍ يُؤْمِنُونَ

It is Allah Who has raised the heavens without any visible support , and He then settled on the Throne of His majesty. He has made the sun and the moon subservient [to His laws], each ordained by Him, to run its course for an appointed time. He governs everything that exists.

He clearly explains these signs so that you may become certain that you are destined to meet your Lord [on Judgment Day]. – Surah Ar-Ra'd 13:2

ٱللَّهُ ٱلَّذِى رَفَعَ ٱلسَّمَٰوَٰتِ بِغَيْرِ عَمَدٍ تَرَوْنَهَا ۖ ثُمَّ ٱسْتَوَىٰ عَلَى ٱلْعَرْشِ ۖ وَسَخَّرَ ٱلشَّمْسَ وَٱلْقَمَرَ ۖ كُلٌّ يَجْرِى لِأَجَلٍ مُّسَمًّى ۚ يُدَبِّرُ
ٱلْأَمْرَ يُفَصِّلُ ٱلْـَٔايَٰتِ لَعَلَّكُم بِلِقَآءِ رَبِّكُمْ تُوقِنُونَ

It is He who revealed to you the Book. Some of its verses are definitive; they are the foundation of the Book, and others are unspecific. As for those in whose hearts is deviation, they follow the unspecific part, seeking descent, and seeking to derive an interpretation. But none knows its interpretation except Allah and those firmly rooted in knowledge say, "We believe in it; all is from our Lord." But none recollects except those with understanding. – Surah Al-Imran 3:7

هُوَ ٱلَّذِىٓ أَنزَلَ عَلَيْكَ ٱلْكِتَٰبَ مِنْهُ ءَايَٰتٌ مُّحْكَمَٰتٌ هُنَّ أُمُّ ٱلْكِتَٰبِ وَأُخَرُ مُتَشَٰبِهَٰتٌ ۖ فَأَمَّا ٱلَّذِينَ فِى قُلُوبِهِمْ زَيْغٌ فَيَتَّبِعُونَ مَا
تَشَٰبَهَ مِنْهُ ٱبْتِغَآءَ ٱلْفِتْنَةِ وَٱبْتِغَآءَ تَأْوِيلِهِۦ ۗ وَمَا يَعْلَمُ تَأْوِيلَهُۥٓ إِلَّا ٱللَّهُ ۗ وَٱلرَّٰسِخُونَ فِى ٱلْعِلْمِ يَقُولُونَ ءَامَنَّا بِهِۦ كُلٌّ مِّنْ عِندِ رَبِّنَا ۗ
وَمَا يَذَّكَّرُ إِلَّآ أُو۟لُوا۟ ٱلْأَلْبَٰبِ

And when Our clear revelations are recited to them, those who do not hope to meet Us say, "Bring a Quran other than this, or change it." Say, "It is not for me to change it of my own accord. I only follow what is revealed to me. I fear, if I disobeyed my Lord, the torment of a terrible Day." – Surah Yunus 10:15

وَإِذَا تُتْلَىٰ عَلَيْهِمْ ءَايَاتُنَا بَيِّنَٰتٍ قَالَ ٱلَّذِينَ لَا يَرْجُونَ لِقَآءَنَا ٱئْتِ بِقُرْءَانٍ غَيْرِ هَٰذَآ أَوْ بَدِّلْهُ ۚ قُلْ مَا يَكُونُ لِىٓ أَنْ أُبَدِّلَهُۥ مِن تِلْقَآئِ
نَفْسِىٓ ۖ إِنْ أَتَّبِعُ إِلَّا مَا يُوحَىٰٓ إِلَىَّ ۖ إِنِّىٓ أَخَافُ إِنْ عَصَيْتُ رَبِّى عَذَابَ يَوْمٍ عَظِيمٍ

Say, "Can any of your partners guide to the truth?" Say, "Allah guides to the truth. Is He who guides to the truth more worthy of being followed, or he who does not guide, unless he himself is guided? What is the matter with you? How do you judge?" – Surah Yunus 10:35

قُلْ هَلْ مِن شُرَكَآئِكُم مَّن يَهْدِىٓ إِلَى ٱلْحَقِّ ۚ قُلِ ٱللَّهُ يَهْدِى لِلْحَقِّ ۗ أَفَمَن يَهْدِىٓ إِلَى ٱلْحَقِّ أَحَقُّ أَن يُتَّبَعَ أَمَّن لَّا يَهِدِّىٓ إِلَّآ أَن يُهْدَىٰ ۖ
فَمَا لَكُمْ كَيْفَ تَحْكُمُونَ

And follow what is revealed to you, and be patient until Allah issues His judgment, for He is the Best of judges. – Surah Yunus 10:109

وَٱتَّبِعْ مَا يُوحَىٰٓ إِلَيْكَ وَٱصْبِرْ حَتَّىٰ يَحْكُمَ ٱللَّهُ ۚ وَهُوَ خَيْرُ ٱلْحَٰكِمِينَ

They were guided to purity of speech. They were guided to the path of the Most Praised. – Surah Al-Hajj 22:24

هُوَ ٱللَّهُ ٱلَّذِى لَآ إِلَٰهَ إِلَّا هُوَ ۖ عَٰلِمُ ٱلْغَيْبِ وَٱلشَّهَٰدَةِ ۖ هُوَ ٱلرَّحْمَٰنُ ٱلرَّحِيمُ

He said, "O my people, have you considered? What if I have clear evidence from my Lord, and He has given me good livelihood from Himself? I have no desire to do what I forbid you from doing. I desire nothing but reform, as far as I can. My success lies only with Allah. In Him I trust, and to Him I turn." – Surah Hud 11:88

قَالَ يَٰقَوْمِ أَرَءَيْتُمْ إِن كُنتُ عَلَىٰ بَيِّنَةٍ مِّن رَّبِّى وَرَزَقَنِى مِنْهُ رِزْقًا حَسَنًا ۚ وَمَآ أُرِيدُ أَنْ أُخَالِفَكُمْ إِلَىٰ مَآ أَنْهَىٰكُمْ عَنْهُ ۚ إِنْ أُرِيدُ إِلَّا
ٱلْإِصْلَٰحَ مَا ٱسْتَطَعْتُ ۚ وَمَا تَوْفِيقِىٓ إِلَّا بِٱللَّهِ ۚ عَلَيْهِ تَوَكَّلْتُ وَإِلَيْهِ أُنِيبُ

It is for Allah to point out the paths, but some of them are flawed. Had He willed, He could have guided you all. – Surah An-Nahl 16:9

وَعَلَى ٱللَّهِ قَصْدُ ٱلسَّبِيلِ وَمِنْهَا جَآئِرٌ ۚ وَلَوْ شَآءَ لَهَدَىٰكُمْ أَجْمَعِينَ

On the Day when We raise in every community a witness against them, from among them, and bring you as a witness against these. We have revealed to you the Book, as an explanation of all things, and guidance, and mercy and good news for those who submit. – Surah Al-Nahl 16:89

وَيَوْمَ نَبْعَثُ فِى كُلِّ أُمَّةٍ شَهِيدًا عَلَيْهِم مِّنْ أَنفُسِهِمْ ۖ وَجِئْنَا بِكَ شَهِيدًا عَلَىٰ هَٰٓؤُلَآءِ ۚ وَنَزَّلْنَا عَلَيْكَ ٱلْكِتَٰبَ تِبْيَٰنًا لِّكُلِّ شَىْءٍ وَهُدًى
وَرَحْمَةً وَبُشْرَىٰ لِلْمُسْلِمِينَ

Those who listen to the Word, and follow the best of it. These are they whom Allah has guided. These are they who possess intellect. –Surah Az-Zumar 39:18

ٱلَّذِينَ يَسْتَمِعُونَ ٱلْقَوْلَ فَيَتَّبِعُونَ أَحْسَنَهُۥٓ ۚ أُو۟لَٰٓئِكَ ٱلَّذِينَ هَدَىٰهُمُ ٱللَّهُ ۖ وَأُو۟لَٰٓئِكَ هُمْ أُو۟لُوا۟ ٱلْأَلْبَٰبِ

Have you seen him who chose his desire as his god? Would you be an agent for him? – Surah Al-Furqan 25:43

أَرَءَيْتَ مَنِ ٱتَّخَذَ إِلَٰهَهُۥ هَوَىٰهُ أَفَأَنتَ تَكُونُ عَلَيْهِ وَكِيلًا

Say, "Then bring a scripture from Allah, more conductive to guidance than both, and I will follow it, if you are truthful." – Surah Al-Qasas 28:49

قُلْ فَأْتُوا۟ بِكِتَٰبٍ مِّنْ عِندِ ٱللَّهِ هُوَ أَهْدَىٰ مِنْهُمَآ أَتَّبِعْهُ إِن كُنتُمْ صَٰدِقِينَ

So adhere to what is revealed to you. You are upon a straight path. – Surah Az-Zukhruf 43:43

فَٱسْتَمْسِكْ بِٱلَّذِىٓ أُوحِىَ إِلَيْكَ ۖ إِنَّكَ عَلَىٰ صِرَٰطٍ مُّسْتَقِيمٍ

Have you considered him who has taken his desire for his god? Allah has knowingly led him astray, and has sealed his hearing and his heart, and has placed a veil over his vision. Who will guide him after Allah? Will you not reflect? – Surah Al-Jathiyah 45:23

أَفَرَءَيْتَ مَنِ ٱتَّخَذَ إِلَٰهَهُۥ هَوَىٰهُ وَأَضَلَّهُ ٱللَّهُ عَلَىٰ عِلْمٍ وَخَتَمَ عَلَىٰ سَمْعِهِۦ وَقَلْبِهِۦ وَجَعَلَ عَلَىٰ بَصَرِهِۦ غِشَٰوَةً فَمَن يَهْدِيهِ مِنۢ
بَعْدِ ٱللَّهِ ۚ أَفَلَا تَذَكَّرُونَ

We are fully aware of what they say, and you are not a dictator over them. So remind by the Quran whoever fears My warning. – Surah Qaf 50:45

نَّحْنُ أَعْلَمُ بِمَا يَقُولُونَ ۖ وَمَآ أَنتَ عَلَيْهِم بِجَبَّارٍ ۖ فَذَكِّرْ بِٱلْقُرْءَانِ مَن يَخَافُ وَعِيدِ

O you who believe! Do not place your opinions above that of Allah and His Messenger, and fear Allah. Allah is Hearing and Knowing. – Surah Al-Hujurat 49:1

يَٰٓأَيُّهَا ٱلَّذِينَ ءَامَنُوا۟ لَا تُقَدِّمُوا۟ بَيْنَ يَدَىِ ٱللَّهِ وَرَسُولِهِۦ ۖ وَٱتَّقُوا۟ ٱللَّهَ ۚ إِنَّ ٱللَّهَ سَمِيعٌ عَلِيمٌ

We have revealed to you the Scripture, with the truth, so that you judge between people in accordance with what Allah has shown you. And do not be an advocate for the traitors.– Surah An-Nisa 4:105

إِنَّآ أَنزَلْنَآ إِلَيْكَ ٱلْكِتَٰبَ بِٱلْحَقِّ لِتَحْكُمَ بَيْنَ ٱلنَّاسِ بِمَآ أَرَىٰكَ ٱللَّهُ ۚ وَلَا تَكُن لِّلْخَآئِنِينَ خَصِيمًا

Have you not observed those who Claim that they believe in what was Revealed to you, and in what was Revealed before you, yet they seek Satanic sources for legislation, in Spite of being commanded to reject Them? Satan means to mislead them far away. And when it is said to them, "Come to what Allah has revealed, and to the Messenger," you see the hypocrites shunning you completely. – Surah An-Nisa 60&61

أَلَمۡ تَرَ إِلَى ٱلَّذِينَ يَزۡعُمُونَ أَنَّهُمۡ ءَامَنُواْ بِمَآ أُنزِلَ إِلَيۡكَ وَمَآ أُنزِلَ مِن قَبۡلِكَ يُرِيدُونَ أَن يَتَحَاكَمُوٓاْ إِلَى ٱلطَّٰغُوتِ وَقَدۡ أُمِرُوٓاْ أَن يَكۡفُرُواْ بِهِۦۖ وَيُرِيدُ ٱلشَّيۡطَٰنُ أَن يُضِلَّهُمۡ ضَلَٰلَۢا بَعِيدٗا وَإِذَا قِيلَ لَهُمۡ تَعَالَوۡاْ إِلَىٰ مَآ أَنزَلَ ٱللَّهُ وَإِلَى ٱلرَّسُولِ رَأَيۡتَ ٱلۡمُنَٰفِقِينَ يَصُدُّونَ عَنكَ صُدُودٗا

Say, "I am warning you through inspiration." But the deaf cannot hear the call when they are being warned. – Surah Al-Anbiya 21:45

قُلۡ إِنَّمَآ أُنذِرُكُم بِٱلۡوَحۡيِۚ وَلَا يَسۡمَعُ ٱلصُّمُّ ٱلدُّعَآءَ إِذَا مَا يُنذَرُونَ

In order to make Satan's suggestions a trial for those whose hearts are diseased, and those whose hearts are hardened. The wrongdoers are in profound discord. – Surah Al-Hajj 22:53

لِّيَجۡعَلَ مَا يُلۡقِي ٱلشَّيۡطَٰنُ فِتۡنَةٗ لِّلَّذِينَ فِي قُلُوبِهِم مَّرَضٞ وَٱلۡقَاسِيَةِ قُلُوبُهُمۡۗ وَإِنَّ ٱلظَّٰلِمِينَ لَفِي شِقَاقِۭ بَعِيدٖ

It is not for any believer, man or woman, when Allah and His Messenger have decided a matter, to have liberty of choice in their decision. Whoever disobeys Allah and His Messenger has gone far astray. – Surah Al-Ahzab 33:36

وَمَا كَانَ لِمُؤۡمِنٖ وَلَا مُؤۡمِنَةٍ إِذَا قَضَى ٱللَّهُ وَرَسُولُهُۥٓ أَمۡرًا أَن يَكُونَ لَهُمُ ٱلۡخِيَرَةُ مِنۡ أَمۡرِهِمۡۗ وَمَن يَعۡصِ ٱللَّهَ وَرَسُولَهُۥ فَقَدۡ ضَلَّ ضَلَٰلٗا مُّبِينٗا

There shall be no compulsion in religion; the right way has become distinct from the wrong way. Whoever renounces evil and believes in Allah has grasped the most trustworthy handle; which does not break. Allah is Hearing and Knowing. – Surah Al-Baqarah 2:256

لَآ إِكۡرَاهَ فِي ٱلدِّينِۖ قَد تَّبَيَّنَ ٱلرُّشۡدُ مِنَ ٱلۡغَيِّۚ فَمَن يَكۡفُرۡ بِٱلطَّٰغُوتِ وَيُؤۡمِنۢ بِٱللَّهِ فَقَدِ ٱسۡتَمۡسَكَ بِٱلۡعُرۡوَةِ ٱلۡوُثۡقَىٰ لَا ٱنفِصَامَ لَهَاۗ وَٱللَّهُ سَمِيعٌ عَلِيمٌ

Narrated Muawiya: Allah's Messenger ﷺ said, "If Allah wants to do good for somebody, he makes him comprehend the Religion (i.e. Islam), and Allah is the Giver and I am Al-Qasim (i.e. the distributor), and this (Muslim) nation will remain victorious over their opponents, till Allah's Order comes and they will still be victorious." – Al-Bukhari 3116

حَدَّثَنَا حِبَّانُ، أَخْبَرَنَا عَبْدُ اللَّهِ، عَنْ يُونُسَ، عَنِ الزُّهْرِيِّ، عَنْ حُمَيْدِ بْنِ عَبْدِ الرَّحْمَنِ، أَنَّهُ سَمِعَ مُعَاوِيَةَ، قَالَ قَالَ رَسُولُ اللَّهِ صلى الله عليه وسلم " مَنْ يُرِدِ اللَّهُ بِهِ خَيْرًا يُفَقِّهْهُ فِي الدِّينِ، وَاللَّهُ الْمُعْطِي وَأَنَا الْقَاسِمُ، وَلاَ تَزَالُ هَذِهِ الأُمَّةُ ظَاهِرِينَ عَلَى مَنْ خَالَفَهُمْ حَتَّى يَأْتِيَ أَمْرُ اللَّهِ وَهُمْ ظَاهِرُونَ ".

Narrated `Abdullah: When the Verse: 'It is those who believe and confuse not their belief with wrong (i.e., worshipping others besides Allah): (6.82) was revealed, it became very hard on the companions of the Prophet ﷺ and they said, "Who among us has not confused his belief with wrong (oppression)?" On that, Allah's Apostle said, "This is not meant (by the Verse). Don't you listen to Luqman's statement: 'Verily! Joining others in worship with Allah is a great wrong indeed.' (31.13) – Al-Bukhari 6918

حَدَّثَنَا قُتَيْبَةُ بْنُ سَعِيدٍ، حَدَّثَنَا جَرِيرٌ، عَنِ الأَعْمَشِ، عَنْ إِبْرَاهِيمَ، عَنْ عَلْقَمَةَ، عَنْ عَبْدِ اللَّهِ ـ رضى الله عنه ـ قَالَ لَمَّا نَزَلَتْ هَذِهِ الآيَةُ {الَّذِينَ آمَنُوا وَلَمْ يَلْبِسُوا إِيمَانَهُمْ بِظُلْمٍ} شَقَّ ذَلِكَ عَلَى أَصْحَابِ النَّبِيِّ صلى الله عليه وسلم وَقَالُوا أَيُّنَا لَمْ يَلْبِسْ إِيمَانَهُ بِظُلْمٍ فَقَالَ رَسُولُ اللَّهِ صلى الله عليه وسلم " إِنَّهُ لَيْسَ بِذَاكَ، أَلاَ تَسْمَعُونَ إِلَى قَوْلِ لُقْمَانَ {إِنَّ الشِّرْكَ لَظُلْمٌ عَظِيمٌ}".

Then Adam received words from his Lord, so He relented towards him. He is the Relenting, the Merciful. We said, "Go down from it, all of you. Yet whenever guidance comes to you from Me, then whoever follows My guidance—they have nothing to fear, nor shall they grieve. – Surah Al-Baqarah 2:37&38

فَتَلَقَّىٰٓ ءَادَمُ مِن رَّبِّهِۦ كَلِمَٰتٖ فَتَابَ عَلَيۡهِۚ إِنَّهُۥ هُوَ ٱلتَّوَّابُ ٱلرَّحِيمُ
قُلۡنَا ٱهۡبِطُواْ مِنۡهَا جَمِيعٗاۖ فَإِمَّا يَأۡتِيَنَّكُم مِّنِّي هُدٗى فَمَن تَبِعَ هُدَايَ فَلَا خَوۡفٌ عَلَيۡهِمۡ وَلَا هُمۡ يَحۡزَنُونَ

He said, "O Moses, I have chosen you over all people for My messages and for My Words. So take what I have given you, and be one of the thankful." And We inscribed for him in the Tablets all kinds of enlightenments, and decisive explanation of all things. "Hold fast to them, and exhort your people to adopt the best of them. I will show you the fate of the sinners."– Surah Al-A'raf 7:144&145

قَالَ يَـٰمُوسَىٰٓ إِنِّى ٱصْطَفَيْتُكَ عَلَى ٱلنَّاسِ بِرِسَـٰلَـٰتِى وَبِكَلَـٰمِى فَخُذْ مَآ ءَاتَيْتُكَ وَكُن مِّنَ ٱلشَّـٰكِرِينَ وَكَتَبْنَا لَهُۥ فِى ٱلْأَلْوَاحِ مِن كُلِّ شَىْءٍ مَّوْعِظَةً وَتَفْصِيلًا لِّكُلِّ شَىْءٍ فَخُذْهَا بِقُوَّةٍ وَأْمُرْ قَوْمَكَ يَأْخُذُوا۟ بِأَحْسَنِهَا سَأُو۟رِيكُمْ دَارَ ٱلْفَـٰسِقِينَ

So believe in Allah and His Messenger, and the Light which We sent down. Allah is Aware of everything you do.– Surah At-Taghabun 64:8

فَـَٔامِنُوا۟ بِٱللَّهِ وَرَسُولِهِۦ وَٱلنُّورِ ٱلَّذِىٓ أَنزَلْنَا ۚ وَٱللَّهُ بِمَا تَعْمَلُونَ خَبِيرٌ

Allah! There is no god except He, the Living, the Everlasting. Neither slumber overtakes Him, nor sleep. To Him belongs everything in the heavens and everything on earth. Who is he that can intercede with Him except with His permission? He knows what is before them, and what is behind them; and they cannot grasp any of His knowledge, except as He wills. His Throne extends over the heavens and the earth, and their preservation does not burden Him. He is the Most High, the Great.– Surah Al-Baqarah 2:255

ٱللَّهُ لَآ إِلَـٰهَ إِلَّا هُوَ ٱلْحَىُّ ٱلْقَيُّومُ ۚ لَا تَأْخُذُهُۥ سِنَةٌ وَلَا نَوْمٌ ۚ لَّهُۥ مَا فِى ٱلسَّمَـٰوَٰتِ وَمَا فِى ٱلْأَرْضِ ۗ مَن ذَا ٱلَّذِى يَشْفَعُ عِندَهُۥٓ إِلَّا بِإِذْنِهِۦ ۚ يَعْلَمُ مَا بَيْنَ أَيْدِيهِمْ وَمَا خَلْفَهُمْ ۖ وَلَا يُحِيطُونَ بِشَىْءٍ مِّنْ عِلْمِهِۦٓ إِلَّا بِمَا شَآءَ ۚ وَسِعَ كُرْسِيُّهُ ٱلسَّمَـٰوَٰتِ وَٱلْأَرْضَ ۖ وَلَا يَـُٔودُهُۥ حِفْظُهُمَا ۚ وَهُوَ ٱلْعَلِىُّ ٱلْعَظِيمُ

Narrated `Abdullah: Allah's Messenger ﷺ said, "The key of the Unseen are five: Verily with Allah (Alone) is the knowledge of the Hour He sends down the rain and knows what is in the wombs. No soul knows what it will earn tomorrow, and no soul knows in what land it will die. Verily, Allah is All-Knower, All-Aware." (31.34). – Sahih Al-Bukhari 4627

حَدَّثَنَا عَبْدُ الْعَزِيزِ بْنُ عَبْدِ اللَّهِ، حَدَّثَنَا إِبْرَاهِيمُ بْنُ سَعْدٍ، عَنِ ابْنِ شِهَابٍ، عَنْ سَالِمِ بْنِ عَبْدِ اللَّهِ، عَنْ أَبِيهِ، أَنَّ رَسُولَ اللَّهِ صلى الله عليه وسلم قَالَ " مَفَاتِحُ الْغَيْبِ خَمْسٌ إِنَّ اللَّهَ عِنْدَهُ عِلْمُ السَّاعَةِ، وَيُنَزِّلُ الْغَيْثَ، وَيَعْلَمُ مَا فِي الأَرْحَامِ، وَمَا تَدْرِي نَفْسٌ مَاذَا تَكْسِبُ غَدًا، وَمَا تَدْرِي نَفْسٌ بِأَىِّ أَرْضٍ تَمُوتُ، إِنَّ اللَّهَ عَلِيمٌ خَبِيرٌ "

Narrated Mu`adh bin Jabal: The Prophet ﷺ said, "O Mu`adh! Do you know what Allah's Right upon His slaves is?" I said, "Allah and His Apostle know best." The Prophet said, "To worship Him (Allah) Alone and to join none in worship with Him (Allah). Do you know what their right upon Him is?" I replied, "Allah and His Apostle know best." The Prophet ﷺ said, "Not to punish them (if they do so). – Sahih al-Bukhari 7373

حَدَّثَنَا مُحَمَّدُ بْنُ بَشَّارٍ، حَدَّثَنَا غُنْدَرٌ، حَدَّثَنَا شُعْبَةُ، عَنْ أَبِي حَصِينٍ، وَالأَشْعَثِ بْنِ سُلَيْمٍ، سَمِعَا الأَسْوَدَ بْنَ هِلاَلٍ، عَنْ مُعَاذِ بْنِ جَبَلٍ، قَالَ قَالَ النَّبِيُّ صلى الله عليه وسلم " يَا مُعَاذُ أَتَدْرِي مَا حَقُّ اللَّهِ عَلَى الْعِبَادِ ". قَالَ اللَّهُ وَرَسُولُهُ أَعْلَمُ. قَالَ " أَنْ يَعْبُدُوهُ وَلاَ يُشْرِكُوا بِهِ شَيْئًا، أَتَدْرِي مَا حَقُّهُمْ عَلَيْهِ ". قَالَ اللَّهُ وَرَسُولُهُ أَعْلَمُ. قَالَ " أَنْ لاَ يُعَذِّبَهُمْ "

Those who argue against Allah's revelations, without any proof having come to them—a heinous sin in the sight of Allah, and of those who believe. Thus Allah seals the heart of every proud bully.–Surah Ghafir40:35

ٱلَّذِينَ يُجَـٰدِلُونَ فِىٓ ءَايَـٰتِ ٱللَّهِ بِغَيْرِ سُلْطَـٰنٍ أَتَىٰهُمْ ۖ كَبُرَ مَقْتًا عِندَ ٱللَّهِ وَعِندَ ٱلَّذِينَ ءَامَنُوا۟ ۚ كَذَٰلِكَ يَطْبَعُ ٱللَّهُ عَلَىٰ كُلِّ قَلْبِ مُتَكَبِّرٍ جَبَّارٍ

Is he who stands upon evidence from his Lord, like someone whose evil deed is made to appear good to him? And they follow their own desires? – Surah Muhammad 47:14

أَفَمَن كَانَ عَلَىٰ بَيِّنَةٍ مِّن رَّبِّهِۦ كَمَن زُيِّنَ لَهُۥ سُوٓءُ عَمَلِهِۦ وَٱتَّبَعُوٓاْ أَهْوَآءَهُم

⌜Still⌝ there are some who dispute about Allah without knowledge, guidance, or an enlightening scripture, Surah Al-Hajj 22:8

وَمِنَ ٱلنَّاسِ مَن يُجَٰدِلُ فِى ٱللَّهِ بِغَيْرِ عِلْمٍ وَلَا هُدًى وَلَا كِتَٰبٍ مُّنِيرٍ

Who does more wrong than those who fabricate lies against Allah? They will be brought before their Lord, and the witnesses will say, "These are the ones who lied against their Lord." Surely Allah's condemnation is upon the wrongdoers, - Surah Hud 11:18

وَمَنْ أَظْلَمُ مِمَّنِ ٱفْتَرَىٰ عَلَى ٱللَّهِ كَذِبًا ۚ أُو۟لَٰٓئِكَ يُعْرَضُونَ عَلَىٰ رَبِّهِمْ وَيَقُولُ ٱلْأَشْهَٰدُ هَٰٓؤُلَآءِ ٱلَّذِينَ كَذَبُوا۟ عَلَىٰ رَبِّهِمْ ۚ أَلَا لَعْنَةُ ٱللَّهِ عَلَى ٱلظَّٰلِمِينَ

Do not falsely declare with your tongues, "This is lawful, and that is unlawful," ⌜only⌝ fabricating lies against Allah. Indeed, those who fabricate lies against Allah will never succeed. Surah An Nahl 16:116

وَلَا تَقُولُوا۟ لِمَا تَصِفُ أَلْسِنَتُكُمُ ٱلْكَذِبَ هَٰذَا حَلَٰلٌ وَهَٰذَا حَرَامٌ لِّتَفْتَرُوا۟ عَلَى ٱللَّهِ ٱلْكَذِبَ ۚ إِنَّ ٱلَّذِينَ يَفْتَرُونَ عَلَى ٱللَّهِ ٱلْكَذِبَ لَا يُفْلِحُونَ

Those with deviant hearts follow the elusive verses seeking ⌜to spread⌝ doubt through their ⌜false⌝ interpretations..... Surah Al-Imran 3:37

فَأَمَّا ٱلَّذِينَ فِى قُلُوبِهِمْ زَيْغٌ فَيَتَّبِعُونَ مَا تَشَٰبَهَ مِنْهُ ٱبْتِغَآءَ ٱلْفِتْنَةِ وَٱبْتِغَآءَ تَأْوِيلِهِ

Narrated Abu Sa`id Al-Khudri: The Prophet ﷺ said, "There will emerge from the East some people who will recite the Qur'an but it will not exceed their throats and who will go out of (renounce) the religion (Islam) as an arrow passes through the game, and they will never come back to it unless the arrow, comes back to the middle of the bow (by itself) (i.e., impossible). The people asked, "What will their signs be?" He said, "Their sign will be the habit of shaving (of their beards and their heads). (Fath-ul-Bari, Page 322, Vol. 17th) – Al-Bukhari 7562

حَدَّثَنَا أَبُو النُّعْمَانِ، حَدَّثَنَا مَهْدِيُّ بْنُ مَيْمُونٍ، سَمِعْتُ مُحَمَّدَ بْنَ سِيرِينَ، يُحَدِّثُ عَنْ مَعْبَدِ بْنِ سِيرِينَ، عَنْ أَبِي سَعِيدٍ الْخُدْرِيِّ ـ رضى الله عنه ـ عَنِ النَّبِيِّ صلى الله عليه وسلم قَالَ " يَخْرُجُ نَاسٌ مِنْ قِبَلِ الْمَشْرِقِ وَيَقْرَءُونَ الْقُرْآنَ لاَ يُجَاوِزُ تَرَاقِيَهُمْ، يَمْرُقُونَ مِنَ الدِّينِ كَمَا يَمْرُقُ السَّهْمُ مِنَ الرَّمِيَّةِ، ثُمَّ لاَ يَعُودُونَ فِيهِ حَتَّى يَعُودَ السَّهْمُ إِلَى فُوقِهِ ". قِيلَ مَا سِيمَاهُمْ. قَالَ " سِيمَاهُمُ التَّحْلِيقُ ". أَوْ قَالَ " التَّسْبِيدُ ".

The Book of **a Glorious Qur’an**
قُرۡءَانٌ مَّجِيدٌ.

If the Messenger ﷺ decided something, it was not permissible for any human being to suggest something other than Allāh’s Messenger’s ﷺ decision. On the day of (the battle of) Uhud, the Prophet ﷺ consulted his Companions whether they should stay at Al-Madina or go out (to meet the enemy), and they suggested that they should go out. When he had put on his armour and decided (to go out), they said, “You’d better stay.” But he ﷺ did not accept their (new) opinion after he ﷺ had decided (to go out) and said, “A Prophet should not put off his armour after he had put it on (for the battle) till Allāh decides the case.” The Prophet ﷺ also consulted ‘Ali and Usama concerning the false statement the liars had made about ‘Aishah. He listened to their opinions till Quranic Verses were revealed, whereupon the Prophet ﷺ flogged the slanderers and did not listen to their different opinions, but did what Allāh had ordered him to do. After the Prophet ﷺ, the Muslims used to consult the honest religious learned men in matters of law so that they might adopt the easiest of them, but if the Book (the Qur’an) or the Sunnah gave a clear, definite statement about a certain matter, they would not seek any other verdict. By that they used to adhere to the way of the Prophet. And Abū Bakr decided to fight those who refused to pay Zakāt. ‘Umar said to him, “How dare you fight them when Allah’s Messenger ﷺ said, I have been ordered to fight the people till they say: La ilaha illallah (none has the right to be worshipped but Allāh). And if they say: La ilaha illallah , then they would save their lives and properties from me, except for Allah’s Islāmic Laws (when they deserved a legal punishment) justly?’ “ Abū Bakr said, “By Allāh, I shall fight those who have separated what Allah’s Messenger ﷺ had put together!” Finally, ‘Umar yielded to Abu Bakr’s opinions, so Abū Bakr did not heed any counsel (in that matter) because he had the verdict of Allāh’s Messenger ﷺ concerning those people who made separation between Salāt (prayer) and Zakāt and intended to change the religion and its laws. The Qurra’ (religious Learned men), whether old or young, were Umar’s advisors, and he used to be very Cautious at the cases and matters dealt with By the Book of Allah (the Qur’an). – Al-Bukhari Vol.9 page 281-283

و شاور النبي أصحابه يوم احد في المقام و الخروج، فرأوا له الخروج، فلما لبس لأمته و عزم قالو : اقم، فلم يمل إليهم بعد العزم و قال : "لا ينبغي لنبي يلبس لأمته فيضعها حتى يحكم الله". و شاور عليا واسامة، فيما رمى به أهل الافك عاءشة، فسمع منهما حتى نزل القرآن فجلد الراحمين. و لم يلتفت إلى تنازعهم و لكن حكم بما أمره الله. و كانت الاءمة بعد النبي ﷺ يستشيرون الامناء من أهل العلم في الأمور المتاحة ليأخذوا باسهلها، فإذا و ضح الكتاب أو السنة لم يتعدوه إلى غيره اقتداء بالنبي ﷺ . ورأى ابو بكر قتال من منع الزكاة، فقال عمر : كيف تقاتل ؟ و قد قال رسول الله ﷺ : " أمرت أن تقاتل الناس حتى يقولوا : لا اله لا الله، فإذا قالوا : لا اله الا الله، عصموا مني دماءهم و اموالهم الا بحقها". فقال أبو بكر : و الله لا قاتلن من فرق بين ما جمع رسول الله ﷺ ، ثم تابعه بعد عمر . فلم يلتفت أبو بكر إلى مشورة إذ كان عنده حكم رسول الله ﷺ في الذين فرقوا بين الصلاة و الزكاة، وارادوا تبديل الدين وأحكامه. و قال النبي ﷺ : "من بدل دينه فاقتلوه". و كان القراء أصحاب مشورة عمر كهولا كانوا أو شبانا، و كان و قافا عند كتاب الله عز وجل.

Narrated `Uthman bin `Affan: The Prophet ﷺ said, “The most superior among you (Muslims) are those who learn the Qur’an and teach it.” – Al-Bukhari 5028

حَدَّثَنَا أَبُو نُعَيْمٍ، حَدَّثَنَا سُفْيَانُ، عَنْ عَلْقَمَةَ بْنِ مَرْثَدٍ، عَنْ أَبِي عَبْدِ الرَّحْمَنِ السُّلَمِيِّ، عَنْ عُثْمَانَ بْنِ عَفَّانَ، قَالَ قَالَ النَّبِيُّ صلى الله عليه وسلم " إِنَّ أَفْضَلَكُمْ مَنْ تَعَلَّمَ الْقُرْآنَ وَعَلَّمَهُ "

Narrated `Abdullah bin `Umar: Allah’s Messenger ﷺ said, “Not to wish to be the like except of two men. A man whom Allah has given the knowledge of the Book and he recites it during the hours of the night, and a man whom Allah has given wealth, and he spends it in charity during the night and the hours of the day." – Al-Bukhari 5025

حَدَّثَنَا أَبُو الْيَمَانِ، أَخْبَرَنَا شُعَيْبٌ، عَنِ الزُّهْرِيِّ، قَالَ حَدَّثَنِي سَالِمُ بْنُ عَبْدِ اللَّهِ، أَنَّ عَبْدَ اللَّهِ بْنَ عُمَرَ ـ رضى الله عنهما ـ قَالَ سَمِعْتُ رَسُولَ اللَّهِ صلى الله عليه وسلم يَقُولُ " لاَ حَسَدَ إِلاَّ عَلَى اثْنَتَيْنِ، رَجُلٌ آتَاهُ اللَّهُ الْكِتَابَ وَقَامَ بِهِ آنَاءَ اللَّيْلِ، وَرَجُلٌ أَعْطَاهُ اللَّهُ مَالاً فَهْوَ يَتَصَدَّقُ بِهِ آنَاءَ اللَّيْلِ وَالنَّهَارِ "

Narrated Sahl bin Sa`d: A lady came to the Prophet ﷺ and declared that she had decided to offer herself to Allah and His Apostle. The Prophet ﷺ said, "I am not in need of women." A man said (to the Prophet) "Please marry her to me." The Prophet ﷺ said (to him), "Give her a garment." The man said, "I cannot afford it." The Prophet said, "Give her anything, even if it were an iron ring." The man apologized again. The Prophet then asked him, "What do you know by heart of the Qur'an?" He replied, "I know such-and such portion of the Qur'an (by heart)." The Prophet ﷺ said, "Then I marry her to you for that much of the Qur'an which you know by heart." – Al-Bukhari 5029

حَدَّثَنَا عَمْرُو بْنُ عَوْنٍ، حَدَّثَنَا حَمَّادٌ، عَنْ أَبِي حَازِمٍ، عَنْ سَهْلِ بْنِ سَعْدٍ، قَالَ أَتَتِ النَّبِيَّ صلى الله عليه وسلم امْرَأَةٌ فَقَالَتْ إِنَّهَا قَدْ وَهَبَتْ نَفْسَهَا لِلَّهِ وَلِرَسُولِ اللَّهِ صلى الله عليه وسلم فَقَالَ " مَا لِي فِي النِّسَاءِ مِنْ حَاجَةٍ ". فَقَالَ رَجُلٌ زَوِّجْنِيهَا. قَالَ " أَعْطِهَا ثَوْبًا ". قَالَ لاَ أَجِدُ. قَالَ " أَعْطِهَا وَلَوْ خَاتَمًا مِنْ حَدِيدٍ ". فَاعْتَلَّ لَهُ. فَقَالَ " مَا مَعَكَ مِنَ الْقُرْآنِ ". قَالَ كَذَا وَكَذَا. قَالَ " فَقَدْ زَوَّجْتُكَهَا بِمَا مَعَكَ مِنَ الْقُرْآنِ ".

Narrated Jabir bin `Abdullah: The Prophet ﷺ collected every two martyrs of Uhud in one piece of cloth, then he would ask, "Which of them had (knew) more of the Qur'an?" When one of them was pointed out for him, he would put that one first in the grave and say, "I will be a witness on these on the Day of Resurrection." He ordered them to be buried with their blood on their bodies and they were neither washed nor was a funeral prayer offered for them. – Al-Bukhari 1343

حَدَّثَنَا عَبْدُ اللَّهِ بْنُ يُوسُفَ، حَدَّثَنَا اللَّيْثُ، قَالَ حَدَّثَنِي ابْنُ شِهَابٍ، عَنْ عَبْدِ الرَّحْمَنِ بْنِ كَعْبِ بْنِ مَالِكٍ، عَنْ جَابِرِ بْنِ عَبْدِ اللَّهِ ـ رضى الله عنهما ـ قَالَ كَانَ النَّبِيُّ صلى الله عليه وسلم يَجْمَعُ بَيْنَ الرَّجُلَيْنِ مِنْ قَتْلَى أُحُدٍ فِي ثَوْبٍ وَاحِدٍ ثُمَّ يَقُولُ " أَيُّهُمْ أَكْثَرُ أَخْذًا لِلْقُرْآنِ ". فَإِذَا أُشِيرَ لَهُ إِلَى أَحَدِهِمَا قَدَّمَهُ فِي اللَّحْدِ وَقَالَ " أَنَا شَهِيدٌ عَلَى هَؤُلاَءِ يَوْمَ الْقِيَامَةِ ". وَأَمَرَ بِدَفْنِهِمْ فِي دِمَائِهِمْ، وَلَمْ يُغَسَّلُوا وَلَمْ يُصَلِّ عَلَيْهِمْ

('Aishah, was led in the Salāt (prayer) by her slave Dhakwan who used to recite from the Mushaf [the written Qur'an (not from memory)]. Can an illegitimate boy A bedouin or a boy who has not reached the age of puberty lead the Şalāt? (It is Permissible according to) the statement of The Prophet , that the Imām should be a Person who knows the Qur`an more than the Others. – Al-Bukhari Vol.1 Pg 395

و كانت عائشة يومها عبدها ذكوان من المصحف ، وولد البغي والاعرابي والغلام الذي لم يحتلم لقول النبي : "يومهم اقروهم لكتاب الله" ، و لا يمنع العبر من الجماعة بغير علة .

Narrated `Amr bin Salama: We were at a place which was a thoroughfare for the people, and the caravans used to pass by us and we would ask them, "What is wrong with the people? What is wrong with the people? Who is that man?. They would say, "That man claims that Allah has sent him (as an Apostle), that he has been divinely inspired, that Allah has revealed to him such-and-such." I used to memorize that (Divine) Talk, and feel as if it was inculcated in my chest (i.e. mind) And the 'Arabs (other than Quraish) delayed their conversion to Islam till the Conquest (of Mecca). They used to say." "Leave him (i.e. Muhammad) and his people Quraish: if he overpowers them then he is a true Prophet. So, when Mecca was conquered, then every tribe rushed to embrace Islam, and my father hurried to embrace Islam before (the other members of) my tribe. When my father returned (from the Prophet) to his tribe, he said, "By Allah, I have come to you from the Prophet ﷺ for sure!" The Prophet ﷺ afterwards said to them, 'Offer such-and-such prayer at such-and-such time, and when the time for the prayer becomes due, then one of you should pronounce the Adhan (for the prayer), and let the one amongst you who knows Qur'an most should, lead the prayer." So they looked for such a person and found none who knew more Qur'an than I because of the Qur'anic material which I used to learn from the caravans. They therefore made me their Imam (to lead the prayer) and at that time I was a boy of six or seven years, wearing a Burda (i.e. a black square garment) proved to be very short for me (and my body became partly naked). A lady from the tribe said, "Won't you cover the anus of your reciter for us?" So they bought (a piece of cloth) and made a shirt for me. I had never been so happy with anything before as I was with that shirt. – Al-Bukhari 4302

حَدَّثَنَا سُلَيْمَانُ بْنُ حَرْبٍ، حَدَّثَنَا حَمَّادُ بْنُ زَيْدٍ، عَنْ أَيُّوبَ، عَنْ أَبِي قِلاَبَةَ، عَنْ عَمْرِو بْنِ سَلِمَةَ، قَالَ قَالَ لِي أَبُو قِلاَبَةَ أَلاَ تَلْقَاهُ فَتَسْأَلَهُ، قَالَ فَلَقِيتُهُ فَسَأَلْتُهُ فَقَالَ كُنَّا بِمَاءٍ مَمَرَّ النَّاسِ، وَكَانَ يَمُرُّ بِنَا الرُّكْبَانُ فَنَسْأَلُهُمْ مَا لِلنَّاسِ مَا لِلنَّاسِ مَا هَذَا الرَّجُلُ فَيَقُولُونَ يَزْعُمُ أَنَّ اللَّهَ أَرْسَلَهُ أَوْحَى إِلَيْهِ، أَوْ أَوْحَى اللَّهُ بِكَذَا‏.‏ فَكُنْتُ أَحْفَظُ ذَلِكَ الْكَلاَمَ، وَكَأَنَّمَا يُغْرَى فِي صَدْرِي، وَكَانَتِ الْعَرَبُ تَلَوَّمُ بِإِسْلاَمِهِمِ الْفَتْحَ، فَيَقُولُونَ اتْرُكُوهُ وَقَوْمَهُ، فَإِنَّهُ إِنْ ظَهَرَ عَلَيْهِمْ فَهْوَ نَبِيٌّ صَادِقٌ‏.‏ فَلَمَّا كَانَتْ وَقْعَةُ أَهْلِ الْفَتْحِ بَادَرَ كُلُّ قَوْمٍ بِإِسْلاَمِهِمْ، وَبَدَرَ أَبِي قَوْمِي بِإِسْلاَمِهِمْ، فَلَمَّا قَدِمَ قَالَ جِئْتُكُمْ وَاللَّهِ مِنْ عِنْدِ النَّبِيِّ صلى الله عليه وسلم حَقًّا فَقَالَ " صَلُّوا صَلاَةَ كَذَا فِي حِينِ كَذَا، وَصَلُّوا كَذَا فِي حِينِ كَذَا، فَإِذَا حَضَرَتِ الصَّلاَةُ، فَلْيُؤَذِّنْ أَحَدُكُمْ، وَلْيَؤُمَّكُمْ أَكْثَرُكُمْ قُرْآنًا ". فَنَظَرُوا فَلَمْ يَكُنْ أَحَدٌ أَكْثَرَ قُرْآنًا مِنِّي، لِمَا كُنْتُ أَتَلَقَّى مِنَ الرُّكْبَانِ، فَقَدَّمُونِي بَيْنَ أَيْدِيهِمْ، وَأَنَا ابْنُ سِتٍّ أَوْ سَبْعِ، سِنِينَ وَكَانَتْ عَلَىَّ بُرْدَةٌ، كُنْتُ إِذَا سَجَدْتُ تَقَلَّصَتْ عَنِّي، فَقَالَتِ امْرَأَةٌ مِنَ الْحَىِّ أَلاَ تُغَطُّوا عَنَّا اسْتَ قَارِئِكُمْ‏.‏ فَاشْتَرَوْا فَقَطَعُوا لِي قَمِيصًا، فَمَا فَرِحْتُ بِشَىْءٍ فَرَحِي بِذَلِكَ الْقَمِيصِ‏.‏

Narrated Ibn `Abbas: 'Uyaina bin Hisn bin Hudhaifa came and stayed with his nephew Al-Hurr bin Qais who was one of those whom `Umar used to keep near him, as the Qurra' (learned men knowing Qur'an by heart) were the people of `Umar's meetings and his advisors whether they were old or young. 'Uyaina said to his nephew, "O son of my brother! You have an approach to this chief, so get for me the permission to see him." Al-Hurr said, "I will get the permission for you to see him." So Al-Hurr asked the permission for 'Uyaina and `Umar admitted him. When 'Uyaina entered upon him, he said, "Beware! O the son of Al-Khattab! By Allah, you neither give us sufficient provision nor judge among us with justice." Thereupon `Umar became so furious that he intended to harm him, but Al-Hurr said, "O chief of the Believers! Allah said to His Prophet: "Hold to forgiveness; command what is right; and leave (don't punish) the foolish." (7.199) and this (i.e. 'Uyaina) is one of the foolish." By Allah, `Umar did not overlook that Verse when Al-Hurr recited it before him; he observed (the orders of) Allah's Book strictly. – Al-Bukhari 4642

حَدَّثَنَا أَبُو الْيَمَانِ، أَخْبَرَنَا شُعَيْبٌ، عَنِ الزُّهْرِيِّ، قَالَ أَخْبَرَنِي عُبَيْدُ اللَّهِ بْنُ عَبْدِ اللَّهِ بْنِ عُتْبَةَ، أَنَّ ابْنَ عَبَّاسٍ ـ رضى الله عنهما ـ قَالَ قَدِمَ عُيَيْنَةُ بْنُ حِصْنِ بْنِ حُذَيْفَةَ فَنَزَلَ عَلَى ابْنِ أَخِيهِ الْحُرِّ بْنِ قَيْسٍ، وَكَانَ مِنَ النَّفَرِ الَّذِينَ يُدْنِيهِمْ عُمَرُ، وَكَانَ الْقُرَّاءُ أَصْحَابَ مَجَالِسِ عُمَرَ وَمُشَاوَرَتِهِ كُهُولاً كَانُوا أَوْ شُبَّانًا‏.‏ فَقَالَ عُيَيْنَةُ لاِبْنِ أَخِيهِ يَا ابْنَ أَخِي، لَكَ وَجْهٌ عِنْدَ هَذَا الأَمِيرِ فَاسْتَأْذِنْ لِي عَلَيْهِ‏.‏ قَالَ سَأَسْتَأْذِنُ لَكَ عَلَيْهِ‏.‏ قَالَ ابْنُ عَبَّاسٍ فَاسْتَأْذَنَ الْحُرُّ لِعُيَيْنَةَ فَأَذِنَ لَهُ عُمَرُ، فَلَمَّا دَخَلَ عَلَيْهِ قَالَ هِيْ يَا ابْنَ الْخَطَّابِ، فَوَاللَّهِ مَا تُعْطِينَا الْجَزْلَ، وَلاَ تَحْكُمُ بَيْنَنَا بِالْعَدْلِ‏.‏ فَغَضِبَ عُمَرُ حَتَّى هَمَّ بِهِ، فَقَالَ لَهُ الْحُرُّ يَا أَمِيرَ الْمُؤْمِنِينَ إِنَّ اللَّهَ تَعَالَى قَالَ لِنَبِيِّهِ صلى الله عليه وسلم {خُذِ الْعَفْوَ وَأْمُرْ بِالْعُرْفِ وَأَعْرِضْ عَنِ الْجَاهِلِينَ} وَإِنَّ هَذَا مِنَ الْجَاهِلِينَ‏.‏ وَاللَّهِ مَا جَاوَزَهَا عُمَرُ حِينَ تَلاَهَا عَلَيْهِ، وَكَانَ وَقَّافًا عِنْدَ كِتَابِ اللَّهِ‏.‏

Narrated 'Aishah (ra) that Barira came to seek her help writing of emancipation and she had to pay five Uqiya (of gold) by five yearly installments. 'Aishah said to her, "Do you think that if I pay the whole sum at once, your masters will sell you to me, and I will free you and your Wala' will be for me." Barira went to her masters and told them about that offer. They said that they would not agree to it unless her Wala' would be for them. 'Aishah further said, "I went to Allah's Messenger ﷺ and told him about it." Allah Messenger ﷺ said to her, "Buy

Barira and manumit her and the Wala' will be for the liberator." Allah's Messenger ﷺ then got up and said, "What about those people who stipulate conditions that are not present in Allah's Laws? If anybody stipulates a condition which is not in Allah's Laws, then what he stipulates is invalid. Allah's Condition (Laws) are the truth and are more solid." – Al-Bukhari 2560

وَقَالَ اللَّيْثُ حَدَّثَنِي يُونُسُ، عَنِ ابْنِ شِهَابٍ، قَالَ عُرْوَةُ قَالَتْ عَائِشَةُ ـ رضى الله عنها ـ إِنَّ بَرِيرَةَ دَخَلَتْ عَلَيْهَا تَسْتَعِينُهَا فِي كِتَابَتِهَا وَعَلَيْهَا خَمْسَةُ أَوَاقٍ، نُجِّمَتْ عَلَيْهَا فِي خَمْسِ سِنِينَ، فَقَالَتْ لَهَا عَائِشَةُ وَنَفِسَتْ فِيهَا أَرَأَيْتِ إِنْ عَدَدْتُ لَهُمْ عَدَّةً وَاحِدَةً، أَيَبِيعُكِ أَهْلُكِ، فَأُعْتِقَكِ، فَيَكُونَ وَلاَؤُكِ لِي فَذَهَبَتْ بَرِيرَةُ إِلَى أَهْلِهَا، فَعَرَضَتْ ذَلِكَ عَلَيْهِمْ فَقَالُوا لاَ إِلاَّ أَنْ يَكُونَ لَنَا الْوَلاَءُ. قَالَتْ عَائِشَةُ فَدَخَلْتُ عَلَى رَسُولِ اللَّهِ صلى الله عليه وسلم فَذَكَرْتُ ذَلِكَ لَهُ. فَقَالَ لَهَا رَسُولُ اللَّهِ صلى الله عليه وسلم " اشْتَرِيهَا فَأَعْتِقِيهَا، فَإِنَّمَا الْوَلاَءُ لِمَنْ أَعْتَقَ ". ثُمَّ قَامَ رَسُولُ اللَّهِ صلى الله عليه وسلم فَقَالَ " مَا بَالُ رِجَالٍ يَشْتَرِطُونَ شُرُوطًا لَيْسَتْ فِي كِتَابِ اللَّهِ، مَنِ اشْتَرَطَ شَرْطًا لَيْسَ فِي كِتَابِ اللَّهِ فَهْوَ بَاطِلٌ، شَرْطُ اللَّهِ أَحَقُّ وَأَوْثَقُ "

In fact, it is clear signs in the hearts of those given knowledge. No one renounce Our signs except the unjust. – Surah Al-'Ankabut 29:49

بَلْ هُوَ ءَايَـٰتٌۢ بَيِّنَـٰتٌ فِى صُدُورِ ٱلَّذِينَ أُوتُوا۟ ٱلْعِلْمَ ۚ وَمَا يَجْحَدُ بِـَٔايَـٰتِنَآ إِلَّا ٱلظَّـٰلِمُونَ

O you who believe! When you are told to make room in your gatherings, make room; Allah will make room for you. And when you are told to disperse, disperse. Allah elevates those among you who believe, and those given knowledge, many steps. Allah is Aware of what you do. – Surah Al-Mujadilah 58:11

يَـٰٓأَيُّهَا ٱلَّذِينَ ءَامَنُوٓا۟ إِذَا قِيلَ لَكُمْ تَفَسَّحُوا۟ فِى ٱلْمَجَـٰلِسِ فَٱفْسَحُوا۟ يَفْسَحِ ٱللَّهُ لَكُمْ ۖ وَإِذَا قِيلَ ٱنشُزُوا۟ فَٱنشُزُوا۟ يَرْفَعِ ٱللَّهُ ٱلَّذِينَ ءَامَنُوا۟ مِنكُمْ وَٱلَّذِينَ أُوتُوا۟ ٱلْعِلْمَ دَرَجَـٰتٍ ۚ وَٱللَّهُ بِمَا تَعْمَلُونَ خَبِيرٌ

Those to whom We have given the Scripture follow it, as it ought to be followed—these believe in it. But as for those who reject it—these are the losers.– Surah Al-Baqarah 2:121

ٱلَّذِينَ ءَاتَيْنَـٰهُمُ ٱلْكِتَـٰبَ يَتْلُونَهُۥ حَقَّ تِلَاوَتِهِۦٓ أُو۟لَـٰٓئِكَ يُؤْمِنُونَ بِهِۦ ۗ وَمَن يَكْفُرْ بِهِۦ فَأُو۟لَـٰٓئِكَ هُمُ ٱلْخَـٰسِرُونَ

None argues against Allah's revelations except those who disbelieve. So do not be impressed by their activities in the land. – Surah Al-Ghafir 40:4

مَا يُجَـٰدِلُ فِىٓ ءَايَـٰتِ ٱللَّهِ إِلَّا ٱلَّذِينَ كَفَرُوا۟ فَلَا يَغْرُرْكَ تَقَلُّبُهُمْ فِى ٱلْبِلَـٰدِ

Narrated Abu Burda: That the Prophet ﷺ sent his (i.e. Abu Burda's) grandfather, Abu Musa and Mu`adh to Yemen and said to both of them "Facilitate things for the people (Be kind and lenient) and do not make things difficult (for people), and give them good tidings, and do not repulse them and both of you should obey each other." Abu Musa said, "O Allah's Prophet! In our land there is an alcoholic drink from barley called Al-Mizr, and another (prepared) from honey, called Al-Bit"' The Prophet ﷺ said, "All intoxicants are prohibited." Then both of them proceeded and Mu`adh asked Abu Musa, "How do you recite the Qur'an?" Abu Musa replied, "I recite it while I am standing, sitting or riding my riding animals, at intervals and piecemeal." Mu`adh said, "But I sleep and then get up. I sleep and hope for Allah's Reward for my sleep as I seek His Reward for my night prayer." Then he (i.e. Mu`adh) pitched a tent and they started visiting each other. Once Mu`adh paid a visit to Abu Musa and saw a chained man, Mu`adh asked, "What is this?" Abu Musa said, "(He was) a Jew who embraced Islam and has now turned apostate." Mu`adh said, "I will surely chop off his neck!" – Al-Bukhari 4344, 4345

حَدَّثَنَا مُسْلِمٌ، حَدَّثَنَا شُعْبَةُ، حَدَّثَنَا سَعِيدُ بْنُ أَبِي بُرْدَةَ، عَنْ أَبِيهِ، قَالَ بَعَثَ النَّبِيُّ صلى الله عليه وسلم جَدَّهُ أَبَا مُوسَى، وَمُعَاذًا إِلَى الْيَمَنِ فَقَالَ " يَسِّرَا وَلاَ تُعَسِّرَا، وَبَشِّرَا وَلاَ تُنَفِّرَا، وَتَطَاوَعَا ". فَقَالَ أَبُو مُوسَى يَا نَبِيَّ اللَّهِ، إِنَّ أَرْضَنَا بِهَا شَرَابٌ مِنَ الشَّعِيرِ الْمِزْرُ، وَشَرَابٌ مِنَ الْعَسَلِ الْبِتْعُ. فَقَالَ " كُلُّ مُسْكِرٍ حَرَامٌ ". فَانْطَلَقَا فَقَالَ مُعَاذٌ لأَبِي مُوسَى كَيْفَ تَقْرَأُ الْقُرْآنَ قَالَ

قَائِمًا وَقَاعِدًا وَعَلَى رَاحِلَتِهِ وَأَتَفَوَّقُهُ تَفَوُّقًا. قَالَ أَمَّا أَنَا فَأَنَامُ وَأَقُومُ، فَأَحْتَسِبُ نَوْمَتِي كَمَا أَحْتَسِبُ قَوْمَتِي، وَضَرَبَ فُسْطَاطًا، فَجَعَلاَ يَتَزَاوَرَانِ، فَزَارَ مُعَاذٌ أَبَا مُوسَى، فَإِذَا رَجُلٌ مُوثَقٌ، فَقَالَ مَا هَذَا فَقَالَ أَبُو مُوسَى يَهُودِيٌّ أَسْلَمَ ثُمَّ ارْتَدَّ. فَقَالَ مُعَاذٌ لأَضْرِبَنَّ عُنُقَهُ. تَابَعَهُ الْعَقَدِيُّ وَوَهْبٌ عَنْ شُعْبَةَ. وَقَالَ وَكِيعٌ وَالنَّضْرُ وَأَبُو دَاوُدَ عَنْ شُعْبَةَ، عَنْ سَعِيدٍ، عَنْ أَبِيهِ، عَنْ جَدِّهِ، عَنِ النَّبِيِّ صلى الله عليه وسلم. رَوَاهُ جَرِيرُ بْنُ عَبْدِ الْحَمِيدِ عَنِ الشَّيْبَانِيِّ عَنْ أَبِي بُرْدَةَ.

Narrated Ibn Abi Mulaika: There was a disagreement between them (i.e. Ibn `Abbas and Ibn Az-Zubair) so I went to Ibn `Abbas in the morning and said, "Do you want to fight against Ibn Zubair and thus make lawful what Allah has made unlawful (i.e. fighting in Meccas?" Ibn `Abbas said, "Allah forbid! Allah ordained that Ibn Zubair and Bani Umaiya would permit (fighting in Mecca), but by Allah, I will never regard it as permissible." Ibn `Abbas added. "The people asked me to take the oath of allegiance to Ibn AzZubair. I said, 'He is really entitled to assume authority for his father, Az-Zubair was the helper of the Prophet, his (maternal) grandfather, Abu Bakr was (the Prophet's) companion in the cave, his mother, Asma' was 'Dhatun-Nitaq', his aunt, `Aisha was the mother of the Believers, his paternal aunt, Khadija was the wife of the Prophet ﷺ, and the paternal aunt of the Prophet ﷺ was his grandmother. He himself Is pious and chaste In Islam, well versed In the Knowledge of the Qur'an. By Allah! (Really, I left my relatives, Bani Umaiya for his sake though) they are my close relatives, and if they should be my rulers, they are equally apt to be so and are descended from a noble family. – Al-Bukhari 4665

حَدَّثَنِي عَبْدُ اللَّهِ بْنُ مُحَمَّدٍ، قَالَ حَدَّثَنِي يَحْيَى بْنُ مَعِينٍ، حَدَّثَنَا حَجَّاجٌ، قَالَ ابْنُ جُرَيْجٍ قَالَ ابْنُ أَبِي مُلَيْكَةَ وَكَانَ بَيْنَهُمَا شَىْءٌ فَغَدَوْتُ عَلَى ابْنِ عَبَّاسٍ فَقُلْتُ أَتُرِيدُ أَنْ تُقَاتِلَ ابْنَ الزُّبَيْرِ، فَتُحِلَّ حَرَمَ اللَّهِ. فَقَالَ مَعَاذَ اللَّهِ، إِنَّ اللَّهَ كَتَبَ ابْنَ الزُّبَيْرِ وَبَنِي أُمَيَّةَ مُحِلِّينَ، وَإِنِّي وَاللَّهِ لاَ أُحِلُّهُ أَبَدًا. قَالَ قَالَ النَّاسُ بَايِعْ لاِبْنِ الزُّبَيْرِ. فَقُلْتُ وَأَيْنَ بِهَذَا الأَمْرِ عَنْهُ أَمَّا أَبُوهُ فَحَوَارِيُّ النَّبِيِّ صلى الله عليه وسلم، يُرِيدُ الزُّبَيْرَ، وَأَمَّا جَدُّهُ فَصَاحِبُ الْغَارِ، يُرِيدُ أَبَا بَكْرٍ، وَأُمُّهُ فَذَاتُ النِّطَاقِ، يُرِيدُ أَسْمَاءَ، وَأَمَّا خَالَتُهُ فَأُمُّ الْمُؤْمِنِينَ، يُرِيدُ عَائِشَةَ، وَأَمَّا عَمَّتُهُ فَزَوْجُ النَّبِيِّ صلى الله عليه وسلم، يُرِيدُ خَدِيجَةَ، وَأَمَّا عَمَّةُ النَّبِيِّ صلى الله عليه وسلم فَجَدَّتُهُ، يُرِيدُ صَفِيَّةَ، ثُمَّ عَفِيفٌ فِي الإِسْلاَمِ، قَارِئٌ لِلْقُرْآنِ. وَاللَّهِ إِنْ وَصَلُونِي وَصَلُونِي مِنْ قَرِيبٍ، وَإِنْ رَبُّونِي رَبَّنِي أَكْفَاءٌ كِرَامٌ، فَآثَرَ التُّوَيْتَاتِ وَالأُسَامَاتِ وَالْحُمَيْدَاتِ، يُرِيدُ أَبْطُنًا مِنْ بَنِي أَسَدٍ بَنِي تُوَيْتٍ وَبَنِي أُسَامَةَ وَبَنِي أَسَدٍ، إِنَّ ابْنَ أَبِي الْعَاصِ بَرَزَ يَمْشِي الْقُدَمِيَّةَ، يَعْنِي عَبْدَ الْمَلِكِ بْنَ مَرْوَانَ، وَإِنَّهُ لَوَّى ذَنَبَهُ، يَعْنِي ابْنَ الزُّبَيْرِ.

Narrated `Abdullah bin Mas`ud: Surat Bani-Israel, Al-Kahf (The Cave), Maryam, Taha, Al-Anbiya' (The prophets) are amongst my first earnings and my old property, and (in fact) they are my old property. – Al-Bukhari 4994

حَدَّثَنَا آدَمُ، حَدَّثَنَا شُعْبَةُ، عَنْ أَبِي إِسْحَاقَ، قَالَ سَمِعْتُ عَبْدَ الرَّحْمَنِ بْنَ يَزِيدَ، سَمِعْتُ ابْنَ مَسْعُودٍ، يَقُولُ فِي بَنِي إِسْرَائِيلَ وَالْكَهْفِ وَمَرْيَمَ وَطَهَ وَالأَنْبِيَاءِ إِنَّهُنَّ مِنَ الْعِتَاقِ الأُوَلِ وَهُنَّ مِنْ تِلاَدِي

Narrated Al-Hasan: The sister of Ma'qil bin Yasar was married to a man and then that man divorced her and remained away from her till her period of the 'Iddah expired. Then he demanded for her hand in marriage, but Ma'qil got angry out of pride and haughtiness and said, "He kept away from her when he could still retain her, and now he demands her hand again?" So Ma'qil disagreed to remarry her to him. Then Allah revealed: 'When you have divorced women and they have fulfilled the term of their prescribed period, do not prevent them from marrying their (former) husbands.' (2.232) So the Prophet ﷺ sent for Ma'qil and recited to him (Allah's order) and consequently Ma'qil gave up his pride and haughtiness and yielded to Allah's order. – Al-Bukhari 5331

وَحَدَّثَنِي مُحَمَّدُ بْنُ الْمُثَنَّى، حَدَّثَنَا عَبْدُ الأَعْلَى، حَدَّثَنَا سَعِيدٌ، عَنْ قَتَادَةَ، حَدَّثَنَا الْحَسَنُ، أَنَّ مَعْقِلَ بْنَ يَسَارٍ، كَانَتْ أُخْتُهُ تَحْتَ رَجُلٍ فَطَلَّقَهَا، ثُمَّ خَلَّى عَنْهَا حَتَّى انْقَضَتْ عِدَّتُهَا، ثُمَّ خَطَبَهَا فَحَمِيَ مَعْقِلٌ مِنْ ذَلِكَ أَنَفًا فَقَالَ خَلَّى عَنْهَا وَهْوَ يَقْدِرُ عَلَيْهَا، ثُمَّ يَخْطُبُهَا فَحَالَ بَيْنَهُ وَبَيْنَهَا، فَأَنْزَلَ اللَّهُ {وَإِذَا طَلَّقْتُمُ النِّسَاءَ فَبَلَغْنَ أَجَلَهُنَّ فَلاَ تَعْضُلُوهُنَّ} إِلَى آخِرِ الآيَةِ، فَدَعَاهُ رَسُولُ اللَّهِ صلى الله عليه وسلم فَقَرَأَ عَلَيْهِ، فَتَرَكَ الْحَمِيَّةَ وَاسْتَقَادَ لأَمْرِ اللَّهِ

Narrated Sahl: A woman came to the Prophet,, and presented herself to him (for marriage). He said, “I am not in need of women these days.” Then a man said, “O Allah’s Messengerﷺ ! Marry her to me.” The Prophetﷺ asked him, “What have you got?” He said, “I have got nothing.” The Prophetﷺ said, “Give her something, even an iron ring.” He said, “I have got nothing.” The Prophetﷺ asked (him), “How much of the Qur’an do you know (by heart)?” He said, “So much and so much.” The Prophetﷺ said, “I have married her to you for what you know of the Qur’an.” – Al-Bukhari 5141
حَدَّثَنَا أَبُو النُّعْمَانِ، حَدَّثَنَا حَمَّادُ بْنُ زَيْدٍ، عَنْ أَبِي حَازِمٍ، عَنْ سَهْلٍ، أَنَّ امْرَأَةً، أَتَتِ النَّبِيَّ صلى الله عليه وسلم فَعَرَضَتْ عَلَيْهِ نَفْسَهَا فَقَالَ " مَا لِي الْيَوْمَ فِي النِّسَاءِ مِنْ حَاجَةٍ ". فَقَالَ رَجُلٌ يَا رَسُولَ اللَّهِ زَوِّجْنِيهَا. قَالَ " مَا عِنْدَكَ ". قَالَ مَا عِنْدِي شَىْءٌ. قَالَ " أَعْطِهَا وَلَوْ خَاتَمًا مِنْ حَدِيدٍ ". قَالَ مَا عِنْدِي شَىْءٌ. قَالَ " فَمَا عِنْدَكَ مِنَ الْقُرْآنِ ". قَالَ عِنْدِي كَذَا وَكَذَا. قَالَ " فَقَدْ مَلَّكْتُكَهَا بِمَا مَعَكَ مِنَ الْقُرْآنِ ".

Narrated Usama bin Zaid: That Allah’s Messengerﷺ rode over a donkey covered with a Fadakiya (velvet sheet) and Usama was riding behind him. He was visiting Sa`d bin ‘Ubada (who was sick) in the dwelling place of Bani Al-Harith bin Al-Khazraj and this incident happened before the battle of Badr. They proceeded till they passed by a gathering in which `Abdullah bin Ubai bin Salul was present., and that was before `Abdullah bin Ubat embraced Islam. In that gathering there were Muslims, pagan idolators and Jews, and among the Muslims there was `Abdullah bin Rawaha. When a cloud of dust raised by (the movement of) the animal covered that gathering, `Abdullah bin Ubai covered his nose with his garment and said, “Do not cover us with dust.” Allah’s Messengerﷺ greeted them, stopped, dismounted and invited them to Allah (i.e. to embrace Islam) and recited to them the Holy Qur’an. On that `Abdullah bin Ubai bin Salul said to him, “O man! There is nothing better than what you say, if it is the truth. So do not trouble us with it in our gatherings, but if somebody comes to you, you can preach to him.” On that `Abdullah bin Rawaha said “Yes, O Allah’s Messengerﷺ! Call on us in our gathering, for we love that.” So the Muslims, the pagans and the Jews started abusing one another till they were about to fight with one another. Allah’s Messengerﷺ kept on quietening them till all of them became quiet, and then Allah’s Messengerﷺ rode his animal and proceeded till he entered upon Sa`d bin ‘Ubada. Allah’s Messengerﷺ said, “O Sa`d! Didn’t you hear what Abu Habab said?” (meaning `Abdullah bin Unbar). “He said so-and-so.” Sa`d bin Ubada said, “O Allah’s Messengerﷺ! Let my father be sacrificed for you! Excuse and forgive him for, by Him Who revealed to you the Book, Allah sent the Truth which was revealed to you at the time when the people of this town had decided to crown him (`Abdullah bin Ubai) as their ruler. So when Allah had prevented that with the Truth He had given you, he was choked by that, and that caused him to behave in such an impolite manner which you had noticed.” So Allah’s Messengerﷺ excused him. (It was the custom of) Allah’s Messengerﷺ and his companions to excuse the pagans and the people of the scripture (Christians and Jews) as Allah ordered them, and they used to be patient when annoyed (by them). Allah said: ‘You shall certainly hear much that will grieve you from those who received the Scripture before you.....and from the pagans (3.186) He also said: ‘Many of the people of the scripture wish that if they could turn you away as disbelievers after you have believed... (2.109) So Allah’s Messengerﷺ used to apply what Allah had ordered him by excusing them till he was allowed to fight against them. When Allah’s Messengerﷺ had fought the battle of Badr and Allah killed whomever He killed among the chiefs of the infidels and the nobles of Quraish, and Allah’s Messengerﷺ and his companions had returned with victory and booty, bringing with them some of the chiefs of the infidels and the nobles of the Quraish as captives. `Abdullah bin Ubai bin Salul and the pagan idolators who were with him, said, “This matter (Islam) has now brought out its face (triumphed), so give Allah's Messenger ﷺ the pledge of allegiance (for embracing Islam.)". Then they became Muslims. – Al-Bukhari 6207

حَدَّثَنَا أَبُو الْيَمَانِ، أَخْبَرَنَا شُعَيْبٌ، عَنِ الزُّهْرِيِّ، حَدَّثَنَا إِسْمَاعِيلُ، قَالَ حَدَّثَنِي أَخِي، عَنْ سُلَيْمَانَ، عَنْ مُحَمَّدِ بْنِ أَبِي عَتِيقٍ، عَنِ ابْنِ شِهَابٍ، عَنْ عُرْوَةَ بْنِ الزُّبَيْرِ، أَنَّ أُسَامَةَ بْنَ زَيْدٍ ـ رضى الله عنهما ـ أَخْبَرَهُ أَنَّ رَسُولَ اللَّهِ صلى الله عليه وسلم رَكِبَ عَلَى حِمَارٍ عَلَيْهِ قَطِيفَةٌ فَدَكِيَّةٌ وَأُسَامَةُ وَرَاءَهُ، يَعُودُ سَعْدَ بْنَ عُبَادَةَ فِي بَنِي حَارِثِ بْنِ الْخَزْرَجِ قَبْلَ وَقْعَةِ بَدْرٍ، فَسَارَا حَتَّى مَرَّا بِمَجْلِسٍ فِيهِ عَبْدُ اللَّهِ بْنُ أُبَىٍّ ابْنُ سَلُولَ، وَذَلِكَ قَبْلَ أَنْ يُسْلِمَ عَبْدُ اللَّهِ بْنُ أُبَىٍّ، فَإِذَا فِي الْمَجْلِسِ أَخْلاَطٌ مِنَ الْمُسْلِمِينَ وَالْمُشْرِكِينَ عَبَدَةِ الأَوْثَانِ وَالْيَهُودِ، وَفِي الْمُسْلِمِينَ عَبْدُ اللَّهِ بْنُ رَوَاحَةَ، فَلَمَّا غَشِيَتِ الْمَجْلِسَ عَجَاجَةُ الدَّابَّةِ خَمَّرَ ابْنُ أُبَىٍّ أَنْفَهُ بِرِدَائِهِ وَقَالَ لاَ تُغَبِّرُوا عَلَيْنَا. فَسَلَّمَ رَسُولُ اللَّهِ صلى الله عليه وسلم عَلَيْهِمْ، ثُمَّ وَقَفَ فَنَزَلَ فَدَعَاهُمْ إِلَى اللَّهِ وَقَرَأَ عَلَيْهِمُ الْقُرْآنَ، فَقَالَ لَهُ عَبْدُ اللَّهِ بْنُ أُبَىٍّ ابْنُ سَلُولَ أَيُّهَا الْمَرْءُ لاَ أَحْسَنَ مِمَّا تَقُولُ إِنْ كَانَ حَقًّا، فَلاَ تُؤْذِنَا بِهِ فِي مَجَالِسِنَا، فَمَنْ جَاءَكَ فَاقْصُصْ عَلَيْهِ. قَالَ عَبْدُ اللَّهِ بْنُ رَوَاحَةَ بَلَى يَا رَسُولَ اللَّهِ فَاغْشَنَا فِي مَجَالِسِنَا فَإِنَّا نُحِبُّ ذَلِكَ. فَاسْتَبَّ الْمُسْلِمُونَ وَالْمُشْرِكُونَ وَالْيَهُودُ حَتَّى كَادُوا يَتَثَاوَرُونَ فَلَمْ يَزَلْ رَسُولُ اللَّهِ صلى الله عليه وسلم يُخَفِّضُهُمْ حَتَّى سَكَتُوا، ثُمَّ رَكِبَ رَسُولُ اللَّهِ صلى الله عليه وسلم دَابَّتَهُ فَسَارَ حَتَّى دَخَلَ عَلَى سَعْدِ بْنِ عُبَادَةَ، فَقَالَ رَسُولُ اللَّهِ صلى الله عليه وسلم " أَىْ سَعْدُ أَلَمْ تَسْمَعْ مَا قَالَ أَبُو حُبَابٍ ـ يُرِيدُ عَبْدَ اللَّهِ بْنَ أُبَىٍّ ـ قَالَ كَذَا وَكَذَا ". فَقَالَ سَعْدُ بْنُ عُبَادَةَ أَىْ رَسُولَ اللَّهِ بِأَبِي أَنْتَ، اعْفُ عَنْهُ وَاصْفَحْ، فَوَالَّذِي أَنْزَلَ عَلَيْكَ الْكِتَابَ لَقَدْ جَاءَ اللَّهُ بِالْحَقِّ الَّذِي أَنْزَلَ عَلَيْكَ، وَلَقَدِ اصْطَلَحَ أَهْلُ هَذِهِ الْبَحْرَةِ عَلَى أَنْ يُتَوِّجُوهُ وَيُعَصِّبُوهُ بِالْعِصَابَةِ، فَلَمَّا رَدَّ اللَّهُ ذَلِكَ بِالْحَقِّ الَّذِي أَعْطَاكَ شَرِقَ بِذَلِكَ فَذَلِكَ فَعَلَ بِهِ مَا رَأَيْتَ. فَعَفَا عَنْهُ رَسُولُ اللَّهِ صلى الله عليه وسلم وَكَانَ رَسُولُ اللَّهِ صلى الله عليه وسلم وَأَصْحَابُهُ يَعْفُونَ عَنِ الْمُشْرِكِينَ وَأَهْلِ الْكِتَابِ كَمَا أَمَرَهُمُ اللَّهُ، وَيَصْبِرُونَ عَلَى الأَذَى، قَالَ اللَّهُ تَعَالَى {وَلَتَسْمَعُنَّ مِنَ الَّذِينَ أُوتُوا الْكِتَابَ} الآيَةَ، وَقَالَ {وَدَّ كَثِيرٌ مِنْ أَهْلِ الْكِتَابِ} فَكَانَ رَسُولُ اللَّهِ صلى الله عليه وسلم يَتَأَوَّلُ فِي الْعَفْوِ عَنْهُمْ مَا أَمَرَهُ اللَّهُ بِهِ حَتَّى أَذِنَ لَهُ فِيهِمْ، فَلَمَّا غَزَا رَسُولُ اللَّهِ صلى الله عليه وسلم بَدْرًا، فَقَتَلَ اللَّهُ بِهَا مَنْ قَتَلَ مِنْ صَنَادِيدِ الْكُفَّارِ، وَسَادَةِ قُرَيْشٍ، فَقَفَلَ رَسُولُ اللَّهِ صلى الله عليه وسلم وَأَصْحَابُهُ مَنْصُورِينَ غَانِمِينَ مَعَهُمْ أُسَارَى مِنْ صَنَادِيدِ الْكُفَّارِ وَسَادَةِ قُرَيْشٍ قَالَ ابْنُ أُبَىٍّ ابْنُ سَلُولَ، وَمَنْ مَعَهُ مِنَ الْمُشْرِكِينَ عَبَدَةِ الأَوْثَانِ هَذَا أَمْرٌ قَدْ تَوَجَّهَ فَبَايِعُوا رَسُولَ اللَّهِ صلى الله عليه وسلم عَلَى الإِسْلاَمِ فَأَسْلَمُوا.

Narrated Hudhaifa: Allah's Messenger ﷺ narrated to us two narrations, one of which I have seen (happening) and I am waiting for the other. He narrated that honesty was preserved in the roots of the hearts of men (in the beginning) and then they learnt it (honesty) from the Qur'an, and then they learnt it from the (Prophet's) Sunna (tradition). He also told us about its disappearance, saying, "A man will go to sleep whereupon honesty will be taken away from his heart, and only its trace will remain, resembling the traces of fire. He then will sleep whereupon the remainder of the honesty will also be taken away (from his heart) and its trace will resemble a blister which is raised over the surface of skin, when an ember touches one's foot; and in fact, this blister does not contain anything. So there will come a day when people will deal in business with each other but there will hardly be any trustworthy persons among them. Then it will be said that in such-and-such a tribe there is such-and-such person who is honest, and a man will be admired for his intelligence, good manners and strength, though indeed he will not have belief equal to a mustard seed in his heart." The narrator added: There came upon me a time when I did not mind dealing with anyone of you, for if he was a Muslim, his religion would prevent him from cheating; and if he was a Christian, his Muslim ruler would prevent him from cheating; but today I cannot deal except with so-and-so and so-and-so. (See Hadith No. 208, Vol. 9) – Al-Bukhari 6497

حَدَّثَنَا مُحَمَّدُ بْنُ كَثِيرٍ، أَخْبَرَنَا سُفْيَانُ، حَدَّثَنَا الأَعْمَشُ، عَنْ زَيْدِ بْنِ وَهْبٍ، حَدَّثَنَا حُذَيْفَةُ، قَالَ حَدَّثَنَا رَسُولُ اللَّهِ صلى الله عليه وسلم حَدِيثَيْنِ رَأَيْتُ أَحَدَهُمَا وَأَنَا أَنْتَظِرُ الآخَرَ، حَدَّثَنَا " أَنَّ الأَمَانَةَ نَزَلَتْ فِي جَذْرِ قُلُوبِ الرِّجَالِ، ثُمَّ عَلِمُوا مِنَ الْقُرْآنِ، ثُمَّ عَلِمُوا مِنَ السُّنَّةِ ". وَحَدَّثَنَا عَنْ رَفْعِهَا قَالَ " يَنَامُ الرَّجُلُ النَّوْمَةَ فَتُقْبَضُ الأَمَانَةُ مِنْ قَلْبِهِ، فَيَظَلُّ أَثَرُهَا مِثْلَ أَثَرِ الْوَكْتِ، ثُمَّ يَنَامُ النَّوْمَةَ فَتُقْبَضُ فَيَبْقَى أَثَرُهَا مِثْلَ الْمَجْلِ، كَجَمْرٍ دَحْرَجْتَهُ عَلَى رِجْلِكَ فَنَفِطَ، فَتَرَاهُ مُنْتَبِرًا، وَلَيْسَ فِيهِ شَىْءٌ، فَيُصْبِحُ النَّاسُ يَتَبَايَعُونَ فَلاَ يَكَادُ أَحَدٌ يُؤَدِّي الأَمَانَةَ، فَيُقَالُ إِنَّ فِي بَنِي فُلاَنٍ رَجُلاً أَمِينًا. وَيُقَالُ لِلرَّجُلِ مَا أَعْقَلَهُ وَمَا أَظْرَفَهُ وَمَا أَجْلَدَهُ. وَمَا فِي قَلْبِهِ مِثْقَالُ حَبَّةِ خَرْدَلٍ مِنْ إِيمَانٍ، وَلَقَدْ أَتَى عَلَىَّ زَمَانٌ وَمَا أُبَالِي أَيَّكُمْ بَايَعْتُ لَئِنْ كَانَ مُسْلِمًا رَدَّهُ الإِسْلاَمُ، وَإِنْ كَانَ نَصْرَانِيًّا رَدَّهُ عَلَىَّ سَاعِيهِ، فَأَمَّا الْيَوْمَ فَمَا كُنْتُ أُبَايِعُ إِلاَّ فُلاَنًا وَفُلاَنًا ". قَالَ الْفِرَبْرِيُّ قَالَ أَبُو جَعْفَرٍ حَدَّثْتُ أَبَا عَبْدِ اللَّهِ فَقَالَ سَمِعْتُ أَحْمَدَ بْنَ عَاصِمٍ يَقُولُ سَمِعْتُ أَبَا عُبَيْدٍ يَقُولُ قَالَ الأَصْمَعِيُّ وَأَبُو عَمْرٍو وَغَيْرُهُمَا جَذْرُ قُلُوبِ الرِّجَالِ الْجَذْرُ الأَصْلُ مِنْ كُلِّ شَىْءٍ، وَالْوَكْتُ أَثَرُ الشَّىْءِ الْيَسِيرُ مِنْهُ، وَالْمَجْلُ أَثَرُ الْعَمَلِ فِي الْكَفِّ إِذَا غَلُظَ

Narrated Ash-Shu`bi: I heard Abu Juhaifa saying, "I asked `Ali 'Have you got any Divine literature apart from the Qur'an?' (Once he said...apart from what the people have?) `Ali replied, 'By Him Who made the grain split (germinate) and created the soul, we have nothing except what is in the Qur'an and the ability (gift) of understanding Allah's Book which He may endow a man with and we have what is written in this paper.' I asked, 'What is written in this paper?' He replied, 'Al-`Aql (the regulation of Diya), about the ransom of captives, and the Judgment that a Muslim should not be killed in Qisas (equality in punishment) for killing a disbeliever." (See Hadith No. 283,Vol. 4) – Al-Bukhari 6903

حَدَّثَنَا صَدَقَةُ بْنُ الْفَضْلِ، أَخْبَرَنَا ابْنُ عُيَيْنَةَ، حَدَّثَنَا مُطَرِّفٌ، قَالَ سَمِعْتُ الشَّعْبِيَّ، قَالَ سَمِعْتُ أَبَا جُحَيْفَةَ، قَالَ سَأَلْتُ عَلِيًّا ـ رضى الله عنه ـ هَلْ عِنْدَكُمْ شَىْءٌ مَا لَيْسَ فِي الْقُرْآنِ وَقَالَ مَرَّةً مَا لَيْسَ عِنْدَ النَّاسِ فَقَالَ وَالَّذِي فَلَقَ الْحَبَّ وَبَرَأَ النَّسَمَةَ مَا عِنْدَنَا إِلاَّ مَا فِي الْقُرْآنِ، إِلاَّ فَهْمًا يُعْطَى رَجُلٌ فِي كِتَابِهِ، وَمَا فِي الصَّحِيفَةِ. قُلْتُ وَمَا فِي الصَّحِيفَةِ قَالَ الْعَقْلُ، وَفِكَاكُ الأَسِيرِ، وَأَنْ لاَ يُقْتَلَ مُسْلِمٌ بِكَافِرٍ.

Narrated Hudhaifa: Allah's Messenger ﷺ related to us, two prophetic narrations one of which I have seen fulfilled and I am waiting for the fulfillment of the other. The Prophet ﷺ told us that the virtue of honesty descended in the roots of men's hearts (from Allah) and then they learned it from the Qur'an and then they learned it from the Sunna (the Prophet's traditions). The Prophet ﷺ further told us how that honesty will be taken away: He said: "Man will go to sleep during which honesty will be taken away from his heart and only its trace will remain in his heart like the trace of a dark spot; then man will go to sleep, during which honesty will decrease further still, so that its trace will resemble the trace of blister as when an ember is dropped on one's foot which would make it swell, and one would see it swollen but there would be nothing inside. People would be carrying out their trade but hardly will there be a trustworthy person. It will be said, 'in such-and-such tribe there is an honest man,' and later it will be said about some man, 'What a wise, polite and strong man he is!' Though he will not have faith equal even to a mustard seed in his heart." No doubt, there came upon me a time when I did not mind dealing with anyone of you, for if he was a Muslim his Islam would compel him to pay me what is due to me, and if he was a Christian, the Muslim official would compel him to pay me what is due to me, but today I do not deal except with such-and-such person. – Al-Bukhari 7086

حَدَّثَنَا مُحَمَّدُ بْنُ كَثِيرٍ، أَخْبَرَنَا سُفْيَانُ، حَدَّثَنَا الأَعْمَشُ، عَنْ زَيْدِ بْنِ وَهْبٍ، حَدَّثَنَا حُذَيْفَةُ، قَالَ حَدَّثَنَا رَسُولُ اللَّهِ صلى الله عليه وسلم حَدِيثَيْنِ رَأَيْتُ أَحَدَهُمَا وَأَنَا أَنْتَظِرُ الآخَرَ حَدَّثَنَا " أَنَّ الأَمَانَةَ نَزَلَتْ فِي جَذْرِ قُلُوبِ الرِّجَالِ، ثُمَّ عَلِمُوا مِنَ الْقُرْآنِ، ثُمَّ عَلِمُوا مِنَ السُّنَّةِ ". وَحَدَّثَنَا عَنْ رَفْعِهَا قَالَ " يَنَامُ الرَّجُلُ النَّوْمَةَ فَتُقْبَضُ الأَمَانَةُ مِنْ قَلْبِهِ، فَيَظَلُّ أَثَرُهَا مِثْلَ أَثَرِ الْوَكْتِ، ثُمَّ يَنَامُ النَّوْمَةَ فَتُقْبَضُ فَيَبْقَى فِيهَا أَثَرُهَا مِثْلَ أَثَرِ الْمَجْلِ، كَجَمْرٍ دَحْرَجْتَهُ عَلَى رِجْلِكَ فَنَفِطَ، فَتَرَاهُ مُنْتَبِرًا وَلَيْسَ فِيهِ شَىْءٌ، وَيُصْبِحُ النَّاسُ يَتَبَايَعُونَ فَلاَ يَكَادُ أَحَدٌ يُؤَدِّي الأَمَانَةَ فَيُقَالُ إِنَّ فِي بَنِي فُلاَنٍ رَجُلاً أَمِينًا. وَيُقَالُ لِلرَّجُلِ مَا أَعْقَلَهُ، وَمَا أَظْرَفَهُ، وَمَا أَجْلَدَهُ، وَمَا فِي قَلْبِهِ مِثْقَالُ حَبَّةِ خَرْدَلٍ مِنْ إِيمَانٍ، وَلَقَدْ أَتَى عَلَىَّ زَمَانٌ، وَلاَ أُبَالِي أَيَّكُمْ بَايَعْتُ، لَئِنْ كَانَ مُسْلِمًا رَدَّهُ عَلَىَّ الإِسْلاَمُ، وَإِنْ كَانَ نَصْرَانِيًّا رَدَّهُ عَلَىَّ سَاعِيهِ، وَأَمَّا الْيَوْمَ فَمَا كُنْتُ أُبَايِعُ إِلاَّ فُلاَنًا وَفُلاَنًا "

Narrated Jabir bin `Abdullah: Allah's Messenger ﷺ used to shroud two martyrs of Uhud in one sheet and then say, "Which of them knew Qur'an more?" When one of the two was pointed out, he would put him first in the grave. Then he said, "I will be a witness for them on the Day of Resurrection." He ordered them to be buried with their blood (on their bodies). Neither was the funeral prayer offered for them, nor were they washed. Jabir added, "When my father was martyred, I started weeping and uncovering his face. The companions of the Prophet ﷺ stopped me from doing so but the Prophet ﷺ did not stop me. Then the Prophet said, '(O Jabir.) don't weep over him, for the angels kept on covering him with their wings till his body was carried away (for burial). – Al-Bukhari 4079, 4080

حَدَّثَنَا قُتَيْبَةُ بْنُ سَعِيدٍ، حَدَّثَنَا اللَّيْثُ، عَنِ ابْنِ شِهَابٍ، عَنْ عَبْدِ الرَّحْمَنِ بْنِ كَعْبِ بْنِ مَالِكٍ، أَنَّ جَابِرَ بْنَ عَبْدِ اللَّهِ ـ رضى الله عنهما ـ أَخْبَرَهُ أَنَّ رَسُولَ اللَّهِ صلى الله عليه وسلم كَانَ يَجْمَعُ بَيْنَ الرَّجُلَيْنِ مِنْ قَتْلَى أُحُدٍ فِي ثَوْبٍ وَاحِدٍ ثُمَّ يَقُولُ " أَيُّهُمْ أَكْثَرُ أَخْذًا لِلْقُرْآنِ ". فَإِذَا أُشِيرَ لَهُ إِلَى أَحَدٍ، قَدَّمَهُ فِي اللَّحْدِ، وَقَالَ " أَنَا شَهِيدٌ عَلَى هَؤُلاَءِ يَوْمَ الْقِيَامَةِ ". وَأَمَرَ بِدَفْنِهِمْ بِدِمَائِهِمْ، وَلَمْ يُصَلِّ عَلَيْهِمْ، وَلَمْ يُغَسَّلُوا. وَقَالَ أَبُو الْوَلِيدِ عَنْ شُعْبَةَ، عَنِ ابْنِ الْمُنْكَدِرِ، قَالَ سَمِعْتُ جَابِرًا، قَالَ لَمَّا قُتِلَ أَبِي جَعَلْتُ أَبْكِي وَأَكْشِفُ الثَّوْبَ عَنْ وَجْهِهِ،، فَجَعَلَ أَصْحَابُ النَّبِيِّ صلى الله عليه وسلم يَنْهَوْنِي وَالنَّبِيُّ صلى الله عليه وسلم لَمْ يَنْهَ، وَقَالَ النَّبِيُّ صلى الله عليه وسلم " لاَ تَبْكِيهِ أَوْ مَا تَبْكِيهِ، مَا زَالَتِ الْمَلاَئِكَةُ تُظِلُّهُ بِأَجْنِحَتِهَا حَتَّى رُفِعَ "

Narrated Ubaidullah bin `Abdullah bin `Utba: Ibn `Abbas said, “O Muslims? How do you ask the people of the Scriptures, though your Book (i.e. the Qur’an) which was revealed to His Prophet is the most recent information from Allah and you recite it, the Book that has not been distorted? Allah has revealed to you that the people of the scriptures have changed with their own hands what was revealed to them and they have said (as regards their changed Scriptures): This is from Allah, in order to get some worldly benefit thereby.” Ibn `Abbas added: “Isn’t the knowledge revealed to you sufficient to prevent you from asking them? By Allah I have never seen any one of them asking (Muslims) about what has been revealed to you.”. – Sahih Al-Bukhari 2685

حَدَّثَنَا يَحْيَى بْنُ بُكَيْرٍ، حَدَّثَنَا اللَّيْثُ، عَنْ يُونُسَ، عَنِ ابْنِ شِهَابٍ، عَنْ عُبَيْدِ اللَّهِ بْنِ عَبْدِ اللَّهِ بْنِ عُتْبَةَ، عَنِ ابْنِ عَبَّاسٍ ـ رضى الله عنهما ـ قَالَ يَا مَعْشَرَ الْمُسْلِمِينَ، كَيْفَ تَسْأَلُونَ أَهْلَ الْكِتَابِ، وَكِتَابُكُمُ الَّذِي أُنْزِلَ عَلَى نَبِيِّهِ صلى الله عليه وسلم أَحْدَثُ الأَخْبَارِ بِاللَّهِ، تَقْرَءُونَهُ لَمْ يُشَبْ، وَقَدْ حَدَّثَكُمُ اللَّهُ أَنَّ أَهْلَ الْكِتَابِ بَدَّلُوا مَا كَتَبَ اللَّهُ وَغَيَّرُوا بِأَيْدِيهِمُ الْكِتَابَ، فَقَالُوا هُوَ مِنْ عِنْدِ اللَّهِ، لِيَشْتَرُوا بِهِ ثَمَنًا قَلِيلاً أَفَلاَ يَنْهَاكُمْ مَا جَاءَكُمْ مِنَ الْعِلْمِ عَنْ مُسَاءَلَتِهِمْ، وَلاَ وَاللَّهِ مَا رَأَيْنَا مِنْهُمْ رَجُلاً قَطُّ يَسْأَلُكُمْ عَنِ الَّذِي أُنْزِلَ عَلَيْكُمْ

Narrated Ibn `Abbas :Some of the companions of the Prophet ﷺ passed by some people staying at a place where there was water, and one of those people had been stung by a scorpion. A man from those staying near the water, came and said to the companions of the Prophet, “Is there anyone among you who can do Ruqya as near the water there is a person who has been stung by a scorpion.” So one of the Prophet’s companions went to him and recited Surat-al-Fatiha for a sheep as his fees. The patient got cured and the man brought the sheep to his companions who disliked that and said, “You have taken wages for reciting Allah’s Book.” When they arrived at Medina, they said, ‘ O Allah’s Messenger ﷺ! (This person) has taken wages for reciting Allah’s Book” On that Allah’s Messenger ﷺ said, “You are most entitled to take wages for doing a Ruqya with Allah’s Book – .".Sahih Al-Bukhari 5737

حَدَّثَنِي سِيدَانُ بْنُ مُضَارِبٍ أَبُو مُحَمَّدٍ الْبَاهِلِيُّ، حَدَّثَنَا أَبُو مَعْشَرٍ الْبَصْرِيُّ ـ هُوَ صَدُوقٌ ـ يُوسُفُ بْنُ يَزِيدَ الْبَرَّاءُ قَالَ حَدَّثَنِي عُبَيْدُ اللَّهِ بْنُ الأَخْنَسِ أَبُو مَالِكٍ، عَنِ ابْنِ أَبِي مُلَيْكَةَ، عَنِ ابْنِ عَبَّاسٍ، أَنَّ نَفَرًا، مِنْ أَصْحَابِ النَّبِيِّ صلى الله عليه وسلم مَرُّوا بِمَاءٍ فِيهِمْ لَدِيغٌ ـ أَوْ سَلِيمٌ ـ فَعَرَضَ لَهُمْ رَجُلٌ مِنْ أَهْلِ الْمَاءِ فَقَالَ هَلْ فِيكُمْ مِنْ رَاقٍ إِنَّ فِي الْمَاءِ رَجُلاً لَدِيغًا أَوْ سَلِيمًا. فَانْطَلَقَ رَجُلٌ مِنْهُمْ فَقَرَأَ بِفَاتِحَةِ الْكِتَابِ عَلَى شَاءٍ، فَبَرَأَ، فَجَاءَ بِالشَّاءِ إِلَى أَصْحَابِهِ فَكَرِهُوا ذَلِكَ وَقَالُوا أَخَذْتَ عَلَى كِتَابِ اللَّهِ أَجْرًا. حَتَّى قَدِمُوا الْمَدِينَةَ فَقَالُوا يَا رَسُولَ اللَّهِ أَخَذَ عَلَى كِتَابِ اللَّهِ أَجْرًا. فَقَالَ رَسُولُ اللَّهِ صلى الله عليه وسلم " إِنَّ أَحَقَّ مَا أَخَذْتُمْ عَلَيْهِ أَجْرًا كِتَابُ اللَّهِ

And the statement of the Prophet ﷺ : The people of the Taurat (Torah) were given the Taurāt and they acted on it; and the people of the Injeel (Gospel) were given the Injeel and they acted on it; and you were given the Qur’ân and you acted on it.” And Abū Razīn said: ‘They recited it means, ‘They followed it (the Qur’an) and Acted on it as is required.’ Nobody can touch,’ means:’ nobody enjoys it and benefits by it except those who believe in it (i.e., the Qur’ân).’ And no one carries (acts on) it properly except a true believer as Allah says: “The likeness of those who were entrusted with the (obligation of the) Taurāt (Torah), (i.e., to obey its orders and to practice its Legal laws), but who subsequently failed in Those (obligations), is as the likeness of a donkey who carries huge burdens of books (but understands nothing from them). How Bad is the example (or the likeness) of the people who deny the Al-Ayāt (proofs, Evidences, verses, lessons, signs revelations, etc.) of Allah. And Allāh guides not the people who are Zālimūn (disbelievers, polytheists, wrongdoers, etc.) And the Prophetﷺ called Islám, Belief and As-Salat (the prayers) as a deed and actions. – Al-Bukhari Vol. 9 page 383&384

و قول النبي ﷺ : "اعطي أهل التوراة التورات فعملوا بها، واعطي أهل الانجيل الا نجيل فعملوا به، واعطيتم القران فعملتم به". و قال أبو رزين (يتلونه حق تلاوته) [البقرة : ١٢١] يعملون به حق عمله، يقال: (يتلى) [النساء: ١٢٧]: يقرا، حسن التلاوة: حسن القراءة للقران. (لا يمسه)[الواقعة:٧٩]: لا يجد طعمه و نفعه الا من امن بالقران، ولا تحمله بحقه الا الموقن، لقوله تعالى: (مثل الذين حملوا التوراة ثم لم يحملونها كمثل الحمار يحمل اسفارا بءس مثل القوم الذين كذبوا بايت الله و الله لا يهدي القوم الظالمين) [الجمعة : ٥] و سمى النبي ﷺ الاسلام والإيمان و الصلاة عملا، قال أبو هريرة: قال النبي ﷺ لبلال: "أخبرني بارجة عمل عملته في الاسلام؟" قال: ما عملت عملا أرجى عندي اني لم اتطهر الا صليت. و سءل: اي العمل افضل؟ قال : "ايمان با لله و رسوله، ثم الجهاد، ثم حبح مبرور".

The Book of
Allah Encompasses everything in knowledge
اللَّهَ قَدْ أَحَاطَ بِكُلِّ

He Is the First and the Last, and the Outer and the Inner, and He has knowledge of all things. It is He who created the heavens and the earth in six days, then settled over the Throne. He knows what penetrates into the earth, and what comes out of it, and what descends from the sky, and what ascends to it. And He is with you wherever you may be. Allah is Seeing of everything you do. – Surah Al-Hadid 57:3&4

هُوَ ٱلْأَوَّلُ وَٱلْـَٔاخِرُ وَٱلظَّـٰهِرُ وَٱلْبَاطِنُ ۖ وَهُوَ بِكُلِّ شَىْءٍ عَلِيمٌ هُوَ ٱلَّذِى خَلَقَ ٱلسَّمَـٰوَٰتِ وَٱلْأَرْضَ فِى سِتَّةِ أَيَّامٍ ثُمَّ ٱسْتَوَىٰ عَلَى ٱلْعَرْشِ ۚ يَعْلَمُ مَا يَلِجُ فِى ٱلْأَرْضِ وَمَا يَخْرُجُ مِنْهَا وَمَا يَنزِلُ مِنَ ٱلسَّمَآءِ وَمَا يَعْرُجُ فِيهَا ۖ وَهُوَ مَعَكُمْ أَيْنَ مَا كُنتُمْ ۚ وَٱللَّهُ بِمَا تَعْمَلُونَ بَصِيرٌ

Allah is He Who created seven heavens, and their like of earth. The command descends through them, so that you may know that Allah is Capable of everything, and that Allah Encompasses everything in knowledge. Surah At-Talaq 65:12

اللَّهُ الَّذِي خَلَقَ سَبْعَ سَمَاوَاتٍ وَمِنَ الْأَرْضِ مِثْلَهُنَّ يَتَنَزَّلُ الْأَمْرُ بَيْنَهُنَّ لِتَعْلَمُوا أَنَّ اللَّهَ عَلَىٰ كُلِّ شَيْءٍ قَدِيرٌ وَأَنَّ اللَّهَ قَدْ أَحَاطَ بِكُلِّ

Surely your god is Allah, the One besides whom there is no other god. He comprehends everything in knowledge. – Surah TaHa 20:98

إِنَّمَآ إِلَـٰهُكُمُ ٱللَّهُ ٱلَّذِى لَآ إِلَـٰهَ إِلَّا هُوَ ۚ وَسِعَ كُلَّ شَىْءٍ عِلْمًا

To Allah belongs what is in the heavens and what is on earth, and Allah encompasses everything. – Surah An-Nisa 4:126

وَلِلَّهِ مَا فِى ٱلسَّمَـٰوَٰتِ وَمَا فِى ٱلْأَرْضِ ۚ وَكَانَ ٱللَّهُ بِكُلِّ شَىْءٍ مُّحِيطًا

Allah! There is no god except He, the Living, the Everlasting. Neither slumber overtakes Him, nor sleep. To Him belongs everything in the heavens and everything on earth. Who is he that can intercede with Him except with His permission? He knows what is before them, and what is behind them; and they cannot grasp any of His knowledge, except as He wills. His Throne extends over the heavens and the earth, and their preservation does not burden Him. He is the Most High, the Great. – Surah Al-Baqarah 2:255

ٱللَّهُ لَآ إِلَـٰهَ إِلَّا هُوَ ٱلْحَىُّ ٱلْقَيُّومُ ۚ لَا تَأْخُذُهُۥ سِنَةٌ وَلَا نَوْمٌ ۚ لَّهُۥ مَا فِى ٱلسَّمَـٰوَٰتِ وَمَا فِى ٱلْأَرْضِ ۗ مَن ذَا ٱلَّذِى يَشْفَعُ عِندَهُۥٓ إِلَّا بِإِذْنِهِۦ ۚ يَعْلَمُ مَا بَيْنَ أَيْدِيهِمْ وَمَا خَلْفَهُمْ ۖ وَلَا يُحِيطُونَ بِشَىْءٍ مِّنْ عِلْمِهِۦٓ إِلَّا بِمَا شَآءَ ۚ وَسِعَ كُرْسِيُّهُ ٱلسَّمَـٰوَٰتِ وَٱلْأَرْضَ ۖ وَلَا يَـُٔودُهُۥ حِفْظُهُمَا ۚ وَهُوَ ٱلْعَلِىُّ ٱلْعَظِيمُ

The Book of

Allah raises those who have believed among you and those who have been given knowledge to high degrees.

يَرْفَعِ ٱللَّهُ ٱلَّذِينَ ءَامَنُوا۟ مِنكُمْ وَٱلَّذِينَ أُوتُوا۟ ٱلْعِلْمَ دَرَجَـٰتٍۢ

And We chose them knowingly over all other people.– Surah Ad-Dukhan 44:32
وَلَقَدِ ٱخْتَرْنَـٰهُمْ عَلَىٰ عِلْمٍ عَلَى ٱلْعَـٰلَمِينَ

Narrated Ibrahim: The companions of `Abdullah (bin Mas`ud) came to Abu Darda', (and before they arrived at his home), he looked for them and found them. Then he asked them,: 'Who among you can recite (Qur'an) as `Abdullah recites it?" They replied, "All of us." He asked, "Who among you knows it by heart?" They pointed at 'Alqama. Then he asked Alqama. "How did you hear `Abdullah bin Mas`ud reciting Surat Al-Lail (The Night)?" Alqama recited: 'By the male and the female.' Abu Ad-Darda said, "I testify that I heard me Prophet reciting it likewise, but these people want me to recite it:-- 'And by Him Who created male and female.' But by Allah, I will not follow them." – Al-Bukhari 4944
حَدَّثَنَا عُمَرُ، حَدَّثَنَا أَبِي، حَدَّثَنَا الأَعْمَشُ، عَنْ إِبْرَاهِيمَ، قَالَ قَدِمَ أَصْحَابُ عَبْدِ اللَّهِ عَلَى أَبِي الدَّرْدَاءِ فَطَلَبَهُمْ فَوَجَدَهُمْ فَقَالَ أَيُّكُمْ يَقْرَأُ عَلَى قِرَاءَةِ عَبْدِ اللَّهِ قَالَ كُلُّنَا. قَالَ فَأَيُّكُمْ يَحْفَظُ وَأَشَارُوا إِلَى عَلْقَمَةَ. قَالَ كَيْفَ سَمِعْتَهُ يَقْرَأُ {وَاللَّيْلِ إِذَا يَغْشَى}. قَالَ عَلْقَمَةُ {وَالذَّكَرِ وَالأُنْثَى}. قَالَ أَشْهَدُ أَنِّي سَمِعْتُ النَّبِيَّ صلى الله عليه وسلم يَقْرَأُ هَكَذَا، وَهَؤُلاَءِ يُرِيدُونِي عَلَى أَنْ أَقْرَأَ {وَمَا خَلَقَ الذَّكَرَ وَالأُنْثَى} وَاللَّهِ لاَ أُتَابِعُهُمْ

O you who believe! When you are told to make room in your gatherings, make room; Allah will make room for you. And when you are told to disperse, disperse. Allah elevates those among you who believe, and those given knowledge, many steps. Allah is Aware of what you do. – Surah Al-Mujadilah 58:11
يَـٰٓأَيُّهَا ٱلَّذِينَ ءَامَنُوٓا۟ إِذَا قِيلَ لَكُمْ تَفَسَّحُوا۟ فِى ٱلْمَجَـٰلِسِ فَٱفْسَحُوا۟ يَفْسَحِ ٱللَّهُ لَكُمْ ۖ وَإِذَا قِيلَ ٱنشُزُوا۟ فَٱنشُزُوا۟ يَرْفَعِ ٱللَّهُ ٱلَّذِينَ ءَامَنُوا۟ مِنكُمْ وَٱلَّذِينَ أُوتُوا۟ ٱلْعِلْمَ دَرَجَـٰتٍۢ ۚ وَٱللَّهُ بِمَا تَعْمَلُونَ خَبِيرٌۭ

Is he who worships devoutly during The watches of the night, prostrating Himself and standing up, mindful of The Hereafter, and placing his hope In the mercy of his Lord? Say, "Are Those who know and those who do Not know equal?" Only those Possessed of reason will remember. – Surah Az-Zumar 39:9
أَمَّنْ هُوَ قَـٰنِتٌ ءَانَآءَ ٱلَّيْلِ سَاجِدًۭا وَقَآئِمًۭا يَحْذَرُ ٱلْـَٔاخِرَةَ وَيَرْجُوا۟ رَحْمَةَ رَبِّهِۦ ۗ قُلْ هَلْ يَسْتَوِى ٱلَّذِينَ يَعْلَمُونَ وَٱلَّذِينَ لَا يَعْلَمُونَ ۗ إِنَّمَا يَتَذَكَّرُ أُو۟لُوا۟ ٱلْأَلْبَـٰبِ

These examples—We put them forward to the people; but none grasps them except the learned. – Surah Al-'Ankabut 29:43

وَتِلْكَ ٱلْأَمْثَـٰلُ نَضْرِبُهَا لِلنَّاسِ ۖ وَمَا يَعْقِلُهَآ إِلَّا ٱلْعَـٰلِمُونَ

Likewise, human beings, animals, and livestock come in various colors. From among His servants, the learned fear Allah. Allah is Almighty, Oft-Forgiving. -Surah Fatir 35:28
وَمِنَ ٱلنَّاسِ وَٱلدَّوَآبِّ وَٱلْأَنْعَـٰمِ مُخْتَلِفٌ أَلْوَٰنُهُۥ كَذَٰلِكَ ۗ إِنَّمَا يَخْشَى ٱللَّهَ مِنْ عِبَادِهِ ٱلْعُلَمَـٰٓؤُا۟ ۗ إِنَّ ٱللَّهَ عَزِيزٌ غَفُورٌ

Uqba bin Aamir said: Learn before those who think (without proof), meaning those who speak with assumptions . Bukhari Volume 8 Chapter Learning about the Laws of inheritance. Pg 380

و قال عقبة بن عامر : تعلموا قبل الظانين ، يعني الذين يتكلمون بالظن

Hasan bin ur-Rabī' narrated to us, Hammād bin Zayd narrated to us, on authority of Ayyūb and Hishām [bin Hassān], on authority of Muhammad [bin Sīrīn] ; and Fuḍayl [bin Īyāḍ] narrated to us on authority of Hishām [bin Hassān]; he said Mukhlad bin Husayn narrated to us, on authority of Hishām [bin Hassān], on authority of Muhammad bin Sīrīn , that he said: 'Indeed this knowledge is faith, so carefully consider from whom you take your faith'. – Sahih Muslim Introduction 26
حَدَّثَنَا حَسَنُ بْنُ الرَّبِيعِ، حَدَّثَنَا حَمَّادُ بْنُ زَيْدٍ، عَنْ أَيُّوبَ، وَهِشَامٍ، عَنْ مُحَمَّدٍ، وَحَدَّثَنَا فُضَيْلٌ، عَنْ هِشَامٍ، قَالَ وَحَدَّثَنَا مَخْلَدُ بْنُ حُسَيْنٍ، عَنْ هِشَامٍ، عَنْ مُحَمَّدِ بْنِ سِيرِينَ، قَالَ إِنَّ هَذَا الْعِلْمَ دِينٌ فَانْظُرُوا عَمَّنْ تَأْخُذُونَ دِينَكُمْ

Narrated `Abdullah bin `Amr bin Al-`As: I heard Allah's Messenger ﷺ saying, "Allah does not take away the knowledge, by taking it away from (the hearts of) the people, but takes it away by the death of the religious learned men till when none of the (religious learned men) remains, people will take as their leaders ignorant persons who when consulted will give their verdict without knowledge. So they will go astray and will lead the people astray." – Al-Bukhari 100
حَدَّثَنَا إِسْمَاعِيلُ بْنُ أَبِي أُوَيْسٍ، قَالَ حَدَّثَنِي مَالِكٌ، عَنْ هِشَامِ بْنِ عُرْوَةَ، عَنْ أَبِيهِ، عَنْ عَبْدِ اللَّهِ بْنِ عَمْرِو بْنِ الْعَاصِ، قَالَ سَمِعْتُ رَسُولَ اللَّهِ صلى الله عليه وسلم يَقُولُ " إِنَّ اللَّهَ لاَ يَقْبِضُ الْعِلْمَ انْتِزَاعًا، يَنْتَزِعُهُ مِنَ الْعِبَادِ، وَلَكِنْ يَقْبِضُ الْعِلْمَ بِقَبْضِ الْعُلَمَاءِ، حَتَّى إِذَا لَمْ يُبْقِ عَالِمًا، اتَّخَذَ النَّاسُ رُءُوسًا جُهَّالاً فَسُئِلُوا، فَأَفْتَوْا بِغَيْرِ عِلْمٍ، فَضَلُّوا وَأَضَلُّوا ".قَالَ الْفِرَبْرِيُّ حَدَّثَنَا عَبَّاسٌ قَالَ حَدَّثَنَا قُتَيْبَةُ حَدَّثَنَا جَرِيرٌ عَنْ هِشَامٍ نَحْوَهُ.

Narrated Ibrahim: Alaqama went to Sham and came to the mosque and offered a two-rak`at prayer, and invoked Allah: "O Allah! Bless me with a (pious) good companion." So he sat beside Abu Ad-Darda' who asked, "From where are you?" He said, "From the people of Kufa." Abu Darda' said, "Wasn't there among you the person who keeps the secrets (of the Prophet ﷺ which nobody knew except him (i.e., Hudhaifa (bin Al-Yaman). And isn't there among you the person whom Allah gave refuge from Satan through the request (tongue) of Allah's Messenger ﷺ ? (i.e., `Ammar). Isn't there among you the one who used to carry the Siwak and the cushion (or pillows (of the Prophets)? (i.e., Ibn Mas`ud). How did Ibn Mas`ud use to recite 'By the night as it conceals (the light)?" (Sura 92). 'Alqama said, "Wadhdhakari Wal Untha' (And by male and female.") Abu Ad-Darda added. 'These people continued to argue with me regarding it till they were about to cause me to have doubts although I heard it from Allah's Messenger ﷺ ." – Al-Bukhari 6278
حَدَّثَنَا يَحْيَى بْنُ جَعْفَرٍ، حَدَّثَنَا يَزِيدُ، عَنْ شُعْبَةَ، عَنْ مُغِيرَةَ، عَنْ إِبْرَاهِيمَ، عَنْ عَلْقَمَةَ، أَنَّهُ قَدِمَ الشَّأْمَ. وَحَدَّثَنَا أَبُو الْوَلِيدِ، حَدَّثَنَا شُعْبَةُ، عَنْ مُغِيرَةَ، عَنْ إِبْرَاهِيمَ، قَالَ ذَهَبَ عَلْقَمَةُ إِلَى الشَّأْمِ، فَأَتَى الْمَسْجِدَ فَصَلَّى رَكْعَتَيْنِ فَقَالَ اللَّهُمَّ ارْزُقْنِي جَلِيسًا. فَقَعَدَ إِلَى أَبِي الدَّرْدَاءِ فَقَالَ مِمَّنْ أَنْتَ قَالَ مِنْ أَهْلِ الْكُوفَةِ. قَالَ أَلَيْسَ فِيكُمْ صَاحِبُ السِّرِّ الَّذِي كَانَ لاَ يَعْلَمُهُ غَيْرُهُ ـ يَعْنِي حُذَيْفَةَ ـ أَلَيْسَ فِيكُمْ ـ أَوْ كَانَ فِيكُمُ ـ الَّذِي أَجَارَهُ اللَّهُ عَلَى لِسَانِ رَسُولِهِ صلى الله عليه وسلم مِنَ الشَّيْطَانِ ـ يَعْنِي عَمَّارًا ـ أَوَلَيْسَ فِيكُمْ صَاحِبُ السِّوَاكِ وَالْوِسَادِ ـ يَعْنِي ابْنَ مَسْعُودٍ ـ كَيْفَ كَانَ عَبْدُ اللَّهِ يَقْرَأُ {وَاللَّيْلِ إِذَا يَغْشَى}. قَالَ {وَالذَّكَرِ وَالأُنْثَى}. فَقَالَ مَا زَالَ هَؤُلاَءِ حَتَّى كَادُوا يُشَكِّكُونِي، وَقَدْ سَمِعْتُهَا مِنْ رَسُولِ اللَّهِ صلى الله عليه وسلم.

Narrated Mirdas Al-Aslami: The Prophet ﷺ said, "The righteous (pious people will depart (die) in succession one after the other, and there will remain (on the earth) useless people like the useless husk of barley seeds or bad dates.- Al-Bukhari 6434
حَدَّثَنِي يَحْيَى بْنُ حَمَّادٍ، حَدَّثَنَا أَبُو عَوَانَةَ، عَنْ بَيَانٍ، عَنْ قَيْسِ بْنِ أَبِي حَازِمٍ، عَنْ مِرْدَاسٍ الأَسْلَمِيِّ، قَالَ قَالَ النَّبِيُّ صلى الله عليه وسلم " يَذْهَبُ الصَّالِحُونَ الأَوَّلُ فَالأَوَّلُ، وَيَبْقَى حُفَالَةٌ كَحُفَالَةِ الشَّعِيرِ أَوِ التَّمْرِ، لاَ يُبَالِيهِمُ اللَّهُ بَالَةً ". قَالَ أَبُو عَبْدِ اللَّهِ يُقَالُ حُفَالَةٌ وَحُثَالَةٌ.

And We gave David and Solomon knowledge. They said, "Praise Allah, who has favored us over many of His believing servants." Surah An-Naml 27:15
وَلَقَدْ ءَاتَيْنَا دَاوُۥدَ وَسُلَيْمَـٰنَ عِلْمًا ۖ وَقَالَا ٱلْحَمْدُ لِلَّهِ ٱلَّذِى فَضَّلَنَا عَلَىٰ كَثِيرٍ مِّنْ عِبَادِهِ ٱلْمُؤْمِنِينَ

So he began with their bags, before his brother's bag. Then he pulled it out of his brother's bag. Thus We devised a plan for Joseph; he could not have detained his brother under the king's law, unless Allah so willed. We elevate by degrees whomever We will; and above every person of knowledge, there is one more learned.– Surah Yusuf 12:76

۞ فَبَدَأَ بِأَوْعِيَتِهِمْ قَبْلَ وِعَآءِ أَخِيهِ ثُمَّ ٱسْتَخْرَجَهَا مِن وِعَآءِ أَخِيهِ ۚ كَذَٰلِكَ كِدْنَا لِيُوسُفَ ۖ مَا كَانَ لِيَأْخُذَ أَخَاهُ فِى دِينِ ٱلْمَلِكِ إِلَّآ أَن يَشَآءَ ٱللَّهُ
نَرْفَعُ دَرَجَٰتٍ مَّن نَّشَآءُ ۗ وَفَوْقَ كُلِّ ذِى عِلْمٍ عَلِيمٌ

Among the people is he who argues about Allah without knowledge, and follows every defiant devil.– Surah Al-Hajj 22:3

وَمِنَ ٱلنَّاسِ مَن يُجَٰدِلُ فِى ٱللَّهِ بِغَيْرِ عِلْمٍ وَيَتَّبِعُ كُلَّ شَيْطَٰنٍ مَّرِيدٍ

And among the people is he who argues about Allah without knowledge, or guidance, or an enlightening scripture. Turning aside in contempt, to lead away from the path of Allah. He will have humiliation in this world, and on the Day of Resurrection We will make him taste the agony of burning.– Surah Al-Hajj 22:8&9

وَمِنَ ٱلنَّاسِ مَن يُجَٰدِلُ فِى ٱللَّهِ بِغَيْرِ عِلْمٍ وَلَا هُدًى وَلَا كِتَٰبٍ مُّنِيرٍ
ثَانِىَ عِطْفِهِۦ لِيُضِلَّ عَن سَبِيلِ ٱللَّهِ ۖ لَهُۥ فِى ٱلدُّنْيَا خِزْىٌ ۖ وَنُذِيقُهُۥ يَوْمَ ٱلْقِيَٰمَةِ عَذَابَ ٱلْحَرِيقِ

Say, "This is my way; I invite to Allah, based on clear knowledge—I and whoever follows me. Glory be to Allah; and I am not of the polytheists."- Surah Yusuf 12:108

قُلْ هَٰذِهِۦ سَبِيلِىٓ أَدْعُوٓا۟ إِلَى ٱللَّهِ ۚ عَلَىٰ بَصِيرَةٍ أَنَا۠ وَمَنِ ٱتَّبَعَنِى ۖ وَسُبْحَٰنَ ٱللَّهِ وَمَآ أَنَا۠ مِنَ ٱلْمُشْرِكِينَ

And among them are uneducated Who know the Scripture only through Hearsay, and they only speculate.- Surah Al-Baqarah 2:78

وَمِنْهُمْ أُمِّيُّونَ لَا يَعْلَمُونَ ٱلْكِتَٰبَ إِلَّآ أَمَانِىَّ وَإِنْ هُمْ إِلَّا يَظُنُّونَ

O you who believe! Do not approach the prayer while you are drunk, so that you know what you say; nor after sexual orgasm—unless you are travelling—until you have bathed. If you are sick, or traveling, or one of you comes from the toilet, or you have had intercourse with women, and cannot find water, find clean sand and wipe your faces and your hands with it. Allah is Pardoning and Forgiving.-Surah An-Nisa 4:43

يَٰٓأَيُّهَا ٱلَّذِينَ ءَامَنُوا۟ لَا تَقْرَبُوا۟ ٱلصَّلَوٰةَ وَأَنتُمْ سُكَٰرَىٰ حَتَّىٰ تَعْلَمُوا۟ مَا تَقُولُونَ وَلَا جُنُبًا إِلَّا عَابِرِى سَبِيلٍ حَتَّىٰ تَغْتَسِلُوا۟ ۚ وَإِن كُنتُم مَّرْضَىٰٓ
أَوْ عَلَىٰ سَفَرٍ أَوْ جَآءَ أَحَدٌ مِّنكُم مِّنَ ٱلْغَآئِطِ أَوْ لَٰمَسْتُمُ ٱلنِّسَآءَ فَلَمْ تَجِدُوا۟ مَآءً فَتَيَمَّمُوا۟ صَعِيدًا طَيِّبًا فَٱمْسَحُوا۟ بِوُجُوهِكُمْ وَأَيْدِيكُمْ ۗ إِنَّ ٱللَّهَ كَانَ
عَفُوًّا غَفُورًا

Among the Jews are some who take words out of context, and say, "We hear and we disobey", and "Hear without listening", and "Observe us," twisting with their tongues and slandering the religion. Had they said, "We hear and we obey", and "Listen", and "Give us your attention," it would have been better for them, and more upright. But Allah has cursed them for their disbelief; they do not believe except a little.- An-Nisa 4:46

۞ مِّنَ ٱلَّذِينَ هَادُوا۟ يُحَرِّفُونَ ٱلْكَلِمَ عَن مَّوَاضِعِهِۦ وَيَقُولُونَ سَمِعْنَا وَعَصَيْنَا وَٱسْمَعْ غَيْرَ مُسْمَعٍ وَرَٰعِنَا لَيًّۢا بِأَلْسِنَتِهِمْ وَطَعْنًا فِى ٱلدِّينِ
وَلَوْ أَنَّهُمْ قَالُوا۟ سَمِعْنَا وَأَطَعْنَا وَٱسْمَعْ وَٱنظُرْنَا لَكَانَ خَيْرًا لَّهُمْ وَأَقْوَمَ وَلَٰكِن لَّعَنَهُمُ ٱللَّهُ بِكُفْرِهِمْ فَلَا يُؤْمِنُونَ إِلَّا قَلِيلًا

And be not like those who say, "We hear," when they do not hear. The worst of animals to Allah are the deaf and dumb—those who do not reason. Had Allah recognized any good in them, He would have made them hear; and had He made them hear, they would have turned away defiantly. – Surah An-Anfal 8:21-23.

وَلَا تَكُونُوا۟ كَٱلَّذِينَ قَالُوا۟ سَمِعْنَا وَهُمْ لَا يَسْمَعُونَ إِنَّ شَرَّ ٱلدَّوَآبِّ عِندَ ٱللَّهِ ٱلصُّمُّ ٱلْبُكْمُ ٱلَّذِينَ لَا يَعْقِلُونَ وَلَوْ عَلِمَ ٱللَّهُ فِيهِمْ خَيْرًا لَّأَسْمَعَهُمْ ۖ وَلَوْ
أَسْمَعَهُمْ لَتَوَلَّوا۟ وَّهُم مُّعْرِضُونَ

Say, "My Lord has forbidden immoralities—both open and secret—and sin, and unjustified aggression, and that you associate with Allah anything for which He revealed no sanction, and that you say about Allah what you do not know."- Surah Al-A'raf 7:33
قُلْ إِنَّمَا حَرَّمَ رَبِّىَ ٱلْفَوَٰحِشَ مَا ظَهَرَ مِنْهَا وَمَا بَطَنَ وَٱلْإِثْمَ وَٱلْبَغْىَ بِغَيْرِ ٱلْحَقِّ وَأَن تُشْرِكُوا۟ بِٱللَّهِ مَا لَمْ يُنَزِّلْ بِهِۦ سُلْطَـٰنًا وَأَن تَقُولُوا۟ عَلَى ٱللَّهِ مَا لَا تَعْلَمُونَ

We gave the Children of Israel the Book, and wisdom, and prophecy; and We provided them with the good things; and We gave them advantage over all other people. – Surah Al-Jathiyah 45:16
وَلَقَدْ ءَاتَيْنَا بَنِىٓ إِسْرَٰٓءِيلَ ٱلْكِتَـٰبَ وَٱلْحُكْمَ وَٱلنُّبُوَّةَ وَرَزَقْنَـٰهُم مِّنَ ٱلطَّيِّبَـٰتِ وَفَضَّلْنَـٰهُمْ عَلَى ٱلْعَـٰلَمِينَ

The example of those who were entrusted with the Torah, but then failed to up hold it, is like the donkey carrying works of literature. Miserable is the example of the people who denounce Allah's revelations. Allah does not guide the wrongdoing people.-. – Surah Jumu'ah 62:5
مَثَلُ ٱلَّذِينَ حُمِّلُوا۟ ٱلتَّوْرَىٰةَ ثُمَّ لَمْ يَحْمِلُوهَا كَمَثَلِ ٱلْحِمَارِ يَحْمِلُ أَسْفَارًۢا ۚ بِئْسَ مَثَلُ ٱلْقَوْمِ ٱلَّذِينَ كَذَّبُوا۟ بِـَٔايَـٰتِ ٱللَّهِ ۚ وَٱللَّهُ لَا يَهْدِى ٱلْقَوْمَ ٱلظَّـٰلِمِينَ

Just as We sent to you a messenger from among you, who recites Our revelations to you, and purifies you, and teaches you the Book and wisdom, and teaches you what you did not know. – Surah Al-Baqarah 2:151
كَمَآ أَرْسَلْنَا فِيكُمْ رَسُولًا مِّنكُمْ يَتْلُوا۟ عَلَيْكُمْ ءَايَـٰتِنَا وَيُزَكِّيكُمْ وَيُعَلِّمُكُمُ ٱلْكِتَـٰبَ وَٱلْحِكْمَةَ وَيُعَلِّمُكُم مَّا لَمْ تَكُونُوا۟ تَعْلَمُونَ

It is He who sent among the unlettered a messenger from themselves; reciting His revelations to them, and purifying them, and teaching them the Scripture and wisdom; although they were in obvious error before that. – Surah Al-Jumu'ah 62:2
هُوَ ٱلَّذِى بَعَثَ فِى ٱلْأُمِّيِّـۧنَ رَسُولًا مِّنْهُمْ يَتْلُوا۟ عَلَيْهِمْ ءَايَـٰتِهِۦ وَيُزَكِّيهِمْ وَيُعَلِّمُهُمُ ٱلْكِتَـٰبَ وَٱلْحِكْمَةَ وَإِن كَانُوا۟ مِن قَبْلُ لَفِى ضَلَـٰلٍ مُّبِينٍ

Narrated Anas: Allah's Messenger ﷺ said, "From among the portents of the Hour are (the following): -1. Religious knowledge will be taken away (by the death of Religious learned men). -2. (Religious) ignorance will prevail. -3. Drinking of Alcoholic drinks (will be very common). -4. There will be prevalence of open illegal sexual intercourse.- Al-Bukhari 80
حَدَّثَنَا عِمْرَانُ بْنُ مَيْسَرَةَ، قَالَ حَدَّثَنَا عَبْدُ الْوَارِثِ، عَنْ أَبِي التَّيَّاحِ، عَنْ أَنَسٍ، قَالَ قَالَ رَسُولُ اللَّهِ صلى الله عليه وسلم " إِنَّ مِنْ أَشْرَاطِ السَّاعَةِ أَنْ يُرْفَعَ الْعِلْمُ، وَيَثْبُتَ الْجَهْلُ، وَيُشْرَبَ الْخَمْرُ، وَيَظْهَرَ الزِّنَا "

Allah bears witness that there is no god but He, as do the angels, and those endowed with knowledge—upholding justice. There is no god but He, the Mighty, the Wise. – Surah Al-Imran 3:18
شَهِدَ ٱللَّهُ أَنَّهُۥ لَآ إِلَـٰهَ إِلَّا هُوَ وَٱلْمَلَـٰٓئِكَةُ وَأُو۟لُوا۟ ٱلْعِلْمِ قَآئِمًۢا بِٱلْقِسْطِ ۚ لَآ إِلَـٰهَ إِلَّا هُوَ ٱلْعَزِيزُ ٱلْحَكِيمُ

Narrated `Abdullah (bin Mas`ud): By Allah other than Whom none has the right to be worshipped! There is no Sura revealed in Allah's Book but I know at what place it was revealed; and there is no Verse revealed in Allah's Book but I know about whom it was revealed. And if I know that there is somebody who knows Allah's Book better than I, and he is at a place that camels can reach, I would go to him. – Sahih Al-Bukhari 5002
حَدَّثَنَا عُمَرُ بْنُ حَفْصٍ، حَدَّثَنَا أَبِي، حَدَّثَنَا الأَعْمَشُ، حَدَّثَنَا مُسْلِمٌ، عَنْ مَسْرُوقٍ، قَالَ قَالَ عَبْدُ اللَّهِ ـ رضى الله عنه ـ وَاللَّهِ الَّذِي لاَ إِلَهَ غَيْرُهُ مَا أُنْزِلَتْ سُورَةٌ مِنْ كِتَابِ اللَّهِ إِلاَّ أَنَا أَعْلَمُ أَيْنَ أُنْزِلَتْ وَلاَ أُنْزِلَتْ آيَةٌ مِنْ كِتَابِ اللَّهِ إِلاَّ أَنَا أَعْلَمُ فِيمَ أُنْزِلَتْ، وَلَوْ أَعْلَمُ أَحَدًا أَعْلَمَ مِنِّي بِكِتَابِ اللَّهِ تُبَلِّغُهُ الإِبِلُ لَرَكِبْتُ إِلَيْهِ

The Book of

We have made clear to you the ayat that you may understand.

قَدْ بَيَّنَّا لَكُمُ الْآيَاتِ لَعَلَّكُمْ تَعْقِلُونَ

We never sent any messenger except in the language of his people, to make things clear for them. Allah leads astray whom He wills, and guides whom He wills. He is the Mighty, the Wise. – Surah Ibrahim 14:4

وَمَآ أَرْسَلْنَا مِن رَّسُولٍ إِلَّا بِلِسَانِ قَوْمِهِۦ لِيُبَيِّنَ لَهُمْ ۖ فَيُضِلُّ ٱللَّهُ مَن يَشَآءُ وَيَهْدِى مَن يَشَآءُ ۚ وَهُوَ ٱلْعَزِيزُ ٱلْحَكِيمُ

The idolaters say, "Had Allah willed, we would not have worshiped anything besides Him, neither us, nor our ancestors; nor would we have prohibited anything besides His prohibitions." Those before them did likewise. Are the messengers responsible for anything but clear communication? – Surah An-Nahl 16:35

وَقَالَ ٱلَّذِينَ أَشْرَكُوا۟ لَوْ شَآءَ ٱللَّهُ مَا عَبَدْنَا مِن دُونِهِۦ مِن شَىْءٍ نَّحْنُ وَلَآ ءَابَآؤُنَا وَلَا حَرَّمْنَا مِن دُونِهِۦ مِن شَىْءٍ ۚ كَذَٰلِكَ فَعَلَ ٱلَّذِينَ مِن قَبْلِهِمْ ۚ فَهَلْ عَلَى ٱلرُّسُلِ إِلَّا ٱلْبَلَٰغُ ٱلْمُبِينُ

Obey Allah and obey the Messenger, and be cautious. If you turn away—know that the duty of Our Messenger is clear communication. – Surah Al-Maidah 5:92

وَأَطِيعُوا۟ ٱللَّهَ وَأَطِيعُوا۟ ٱلرَّسُولَ وَٱحْذَرُوا۟ ۚ فَإِن تَوَلَّيْتُمْ فَٱعْلَمُوٓا۟ أَنَّمَا عَلَىٰ رَسُولِنَا ٱلْبَلَٰغُ ٱلْمُبِينُ

We revealed to you the Scripture only to clarify for them what they differ about, and guidance and mercy for people who believe. – Surah An-Nahl 16:64

وَمَآ أَنزَلْنَا عَلَيْكَ ٱلْكِتَٰبَ إِلَّا لِتُبَيِّنَ لَهُمُ ٱلَّذِى ٱخْتَلَفُوا۟ فِيهِ ۙ وَهُدًى وَرَحْمَةً لِّقَوْمٍ يُؤْمِنُونَ

Say, "Obey Allah and obey the Messenger." But if they turn away, then he is responsible for his obligations, and you are responsible for your obligations. And if you obey him, you will be guided. It is only incumbent on the Messenger to deliver the clarifying message. – Surah An-Nur 24:54

قُلْ أَطِيعُوا۟ ٱللَّهَ وَأَطِيعُوا۟ ٱلرَّسُولَ ۖ فَإِن تَوَلَّوْا۟ فَإِنَّمَا عَلَيْهِ مَا حُمِّلَ وَعَلَيْكُم مَّا حُمِّلْتُمْ ۖ وَإِن تُطِيعُوهُ تَهْتَدُوا۟ ۚ وَمَا عَلَى ٱلرَّسُولِ إِلَّا ٱلْبَلَٰغُ ٱلْمُبِينُ

If you disbelieve, communities before you have also disbelieved. The Messenger is only responsible for clear transmission. – Surah Al-'Ankabut 29:18

وَإِن تُكَذِّبُوا۟ فَقَدْ كَذَّبَ أُمَمٌ مِّن قَبْلِكُمْ ۖ وَمَا عَلَى ٱلرَّسُولِ إِلَّا ٱلْبَلَٰغُ ٱلْمُبِينُ

Before you, We sent messengers to their people. They came to them with clear proofs. Then We took revenge on those who sinned. It is incumbent on Us to help the believers. – Surah Ar-Rum 30:47

وَلَقَدْ أَرْسَلْنَا مِن قَبْلِكَ رُسُلًا إِلَىٰ قَوْمِهِمْ فَجَآءُوهُم بِٱلْبَيِّنَٰتِ فَٱنتَقَمْنَا مِنَ ٱلَّذِينَ أَجْرَمُوا۟ ۖ وَكَانَ حَقًّا عَلَيْنَا نَصْرُ ٱلْمُؤْمِنِينَ

And Our only duty is clear communication." – Surah Ya-Sin 36:17

وَمَا عَلَيْنَآ إِلَّا ٱلْبَلَٰغُ ٱلْمُبِينُ

Those who disbelieved will be driven to Hell in throngs. Until, when they have reached it, and its gates are opened, its keepers will say to them, "Did not messengers from among you come to you, reciting to you the revelations of your Lord, and warning you of the meeting of this

Day of yours?" They will say, "Yes, but the verdict of punishment is justified against the disbelievers." – Surah Az-Zumar 39:71

وَسِيقَ ٱلَّذِينَ كَفَرُوٓاْ إِلَىٰ جَهَنَّمَ زُمَرًا ۖ حَتَّىٰٓ إِذَا جَآءُوهَا فُتِحَتْ أَبْوَٰبُهَا وَقَالَ لَهُمْ خَزَنَتُهَآ أَلَمْ يَأْتِكُمْ رُسُلٌ مِّنكُمْ يَتْلُونَ عَلَيْكُمْ ءَايَـٰتِ رَبِّكُمْ وَيُنذِرُونَكُمْ لِقَآءَ يَوْمِكُمْ هَـٰذَا ۚ قَالُواْ بَلَىٰ وَلَـٰكِنْ حَقَّتْ كَلِمَةُ ٱلْعَذَابِ عَلَى ٱلْكَـٰفِرِينَ

So obey Allah, and obey the Messenger. But if you turn away—it is only incumbent on Our Messenger to deliver the clear message. – Surah At-Taghabun 64:12

وَأَطِيعُواْ ٱللَّهَ وَأَطِيعُواْ ٱلرَّسُولَ ۚ فَإِن تَوَلَّيْتُمْ فَإِنَّمَا عَلَىٰ رَسُولِنَا ٱلْبَلَـٰغُ ٱلْمُبِينُ

Narrated Muawiya: I heard Allah's Messenger ﷺ saying, "If Allah wants to do good to a person, He makes him comprehend the religion. I am just a distributor, but the grant is from Allah. (And remember) that this nation (true Muslims) will keep on following Allah's teachings strictly and they will not be harmed by any one going on a different path till Allah's order (Day of Judgment) is established." – Al-Bukhari 71

حَدَّثَنَا سَعِيدُ بْنُ عُفَيْرٍ، قَالَ حَدَّثَنَا ابْنُ وَهْبٍ، عَنْ يُونُسَ، عَنِ ابْنِ شِهَابٍ، قَالَ قَالَ حُمَيْدُ بْنُ عَبْدِ الرَّحْمَنِ سَمِعْتُ مُعَاوِيَةَ، خَطِيبًا يَقُولُ سَمِعْتُ النَّبِيَّ صلى الله عليه وسلم يَقُولُ " مَنْ يُرِدِ اللَّهُ بِهِ خَيْرًا يُفَقِّهْهُ فِي الدِّينِ، وَإِنَّمَا أَنَا قَاسِمٌ وَاللَّهُ يُعْطِي، وَلَنْ تَزَالَ هَذِهِ الأُمَّةُ قَائِمَةً عَلَى أَمْرِ اللَّهِ لاَ يَضُرُّهُمْ مَنْ خَالَفَهُمْ حَتَّى يَأْتِيَ أَمْرُ اللَّهِ ".

Narrated Abu Jamra: I was an interpreter between the people and Ibn `Abbas. Once Ibn `Abbas said that a delegation of the tribe of `Abdul Qais came to the Prophet ﷺ who asked them, "Who are the people (i.e. you)? (Or) who are the delegates?" They replied, "We are from the tribe of Rabi`a." Then the Prophet ﷺ said to them, "Welcome, O people (or said, "O delegation (of `Abdul Qais).") Neither will you have disgrace nor will you regret." They said, "We have come to you from a distant place and there is the tribe of the infidels of Mudar intervening between you and us and we cannot come to you except in the sacred month. So please order us to do something good (religious deeds) and that we may also inform our people whom we have left behind (at home) and that we may enter Paradise (by acting on them.)" The Prophet ordered them to do four things, and forbade them from four things. He ordered them to believe in Allah Alone, the Honorable the Majestic and said to them, "Do you know what is meant by believing in Allah Alone?" They replied, "Allah and His Apostle know better." Thereupon the Prophet ﷺ said, "(That means to testify that none has the right to be worshipped but Allah and that Muhammad is His Apostle, to offer prayers perfectly, to pay Zakat, to observe fasts during the month of Ramadan, (and) to pay Al-Khumus (one fifth of the booty to be given in Allah's cause)." Then he forbade them four things, namely Ad-Dubba.' Hantam, Muzaffat (and) An-Naqir or Muqaiyar (These were the names of pots in which alcoholic drinks used to be prepared). The Prophet ﷺ further said, "Memorize them (these instructions) and tell them to the people whom you have left behind." – Al-Bukhari 87

حَدَّثَنَا مُحَمَّدُ بْنُ بَشَّارٍ، قَالَ حَدَّثَنَا غُنْدَرٌ، قَالَ حَدَّثَنَا شُعْبَةُ، عَنْ أَبِي جَمْرَةَ، قَالَ كُنْتُ أُتَرْجِمُ بَيْنَ ابْنِ عَبَّاسٍ وَبَيْنَ النَّاسِ فَقَالَ إِنَّ وَفْدَ عَبْدِ الْقَيْسِ أَتَوُا النَّبِيَّ صلى الله عليه وسلم فَقَالَ " مَنِ الْوَفْدُ ـ أَوْ مَنِ الْقَوْمُ ". قَالُوا رَبِيعَةُ. فَقَالَ " مَرْحَبًا بِالْقَوْمِ ـ أَوْ بِالْوَفْدِ ـ غَيْرَ خَزَايَا وَلاَ نَدَامَى ". قَالُوا إِنَّا نَأْتِيكَ مِنْ شُقَّةٍ بَعِيدَةٍ، وَبَيْنَنَا وَبَيْنَكَ هَذَا الْحَىُّ مِنْ كُفَّارِ مُضَرَ، وَلاَ نَسْتَطِيعُ أَنْ نَأْتِيَكَ إِلاَّ فِي شَهْرٍ حَرَامٍ فَمُرْنَا بِأَمْرٍ نُخْبِرْ بِهِ مَنْ وَرَاءَنَا، نَدْخُلُ بِهِ الْجَنَّةَ. فَأَمَرَهُمْ بِأَرْبَعٍ، وَنَهَاهُمْ عَنْ أَرْبَعٍ أَمَرَهُمْ بِالإِيمَانِ بِاللَّهِ عَزَّ وَجَلَّ وَحْدَهُ. قَالَ " هَلْ تَدْرُونَ مَا الإِيمَانُ بِاللَّهِ وَحْدَهُ ". قَالُوا اللَّهُ وَرَسُولُهُ أَعْلَمُ. قَالَ " شَهَادَةُ أَنْ لاَ إِلَهَ إِلاَّ اللَّهُ وَأَنَّ مُحَمَّدًا رَسُولُ اللَّهِ، وَإِقَامُ الصَّلاَةِ، وَإِيتَاءُ الزَّكَاةِ، وَصَوْمُ رَمَضَانَ، وَتُعْطُوا الْخُمُسَ مِنَ الْمَغْنَمِ ". وَنَهَاهُمْ عَنِ الدُّبَّاءِ وَالْحَنْتَمِ وَالْمُزَفَّتِ. قَالَ شُعْبَةُ رُبَّمَا قَالَ النَّقِيرِ، وَرُبَّمَا قَالَ الْمُقَيَّرِ. قَالَ " احْفَظُوهُ وَأَخْبِرُوهُ مَنْ وَرَاءَكُمْ ".

Narrated Anas: Whenever the Prophet ﷺ spoke a sentence (said a thing), he used to repeat it thrice so that the people could understand it properly from him and whenever he asked permission to enter, (he knocked the door) thrice with greeting. – Al-Bukhari 95
حَدَّثَنَا عَبْدَةُ بْنُ عَبْدِ اللَّهِ، حَدَّثَنَا عَبْدُ الصَّمَدِ، قَالَ حَدَّثَنَا عَبْدُ اللَّهِ بْنُ الْمُثَنَّى، قَالَ حَدَّثَنَا ثُمَامَةُ بْنُ عَبْدِ اللَّهِ، عَنْ أَنَسٍ، عَنِ النَّبِيِّ صلى الله عليه وسلم أَنَّهُ كَانَ إِذَا تَكَلَّمَ بِكَلِمَةٍ أَعَادَهَا ثَلاَثًا حَتَّى تُفْهَمَ عَنْهُ، وَإِذَا أَتَى عَلَى قَوْمٍ فَسَلَّمَ عَلَيْهِمْ سَلَّمَ عَلَيْهِمْ ثَلاَثًا.

Narrated Ibn Abu Mulaika: Whenever `Aisha (the wife of the Prophet) heard anything which she did not understand, she used to ask again till she understood it completely. Aisha said: "Once the Prophet ﷺ said, "Whoever will be called to account (about his deeds on the Day of Resurrection) will surely be punished." I said, "Doesn't Allah say: "He surely will receive an easy reckoning." (84.8) The Prophet ﷺ replied, "This means only the presentation of the accounts but whoever will be argued about his account, will certainly be ruined." – Al-Bukhari 103
حَدَّثَنَا سَعِيدُ بْنُ أَبِي مَرْيَمَ، قَالَ أَخْبَرَنَا نَافِعُ بْنُ عُمَرَ، قَالَ حَدَّثَنِي ابْنُ أَبِي مُلَيْكَةَ، أَنَّ عَائِشَةَ، زَوْجَ النَّبِيِّ صلى الله عليه وسلم كَانَتْ لاَ تَسْمَعُ شَيْئًا لاَ تَعْرِفُهُ إِلاَّ رَاجَعَتْ فِيهِ حَتَّى تَعْرِفَهُ، وَأَنَّ النَّبِيَّ صلى الله عليه وسلم قَالَ " مَنْ حُوسِبَ عُذِّبَ ". قَالَتْ عَائِشَةُ فَقُلْتُ أَوَ لَيْسَ يَقُولُ اللَّهُ تَعَالَى {فَسَوْفَ يُحَاسَبُ حِسَابًا يَسِيرًا} قَالَتْ فَقَالَ " إِنَّمَا ذَلِكَ الْعَرْضُ، وَلَكِنْ مَنْ نُوقِشَ الْحِسَابَ يَهْلِكْ ".

And untie the knot from my tongue. So they can understand my speech. – Surah Ta-Ha 20:27&28
وَٱحْلُلْ عُقْدَةً مِّن لِّسَانِى يَفْقَهُوا۟ قَوْلِى

And 'Ali said, "You should preach to the people according to their mental caliber so that they may not convey wrong things about Allah and His Messenger ﷺ - Al-Bukhari Vol.1 page 130
و قال علي : حدثو الناس بما يعرفون اتحبون ان يكذب الله و رسوله

Narrated `Aisha: Allah's Messenger ﷺ said, "If anyone of you feels drowsy while praying he should go to bed (sleep) till his slumber is over because in praying while drowsy one does not know whether one is asking for forgiveness or for a bad thing for oneself." – Al-Bukhari 212
حَدَّثَنَا عَبْدُ اللَّهِ بْنُ يُوسُفَ، قَالَ أَخْبَرَنَا مَالِكٌ، عَنْ هِشَامٍ، عَنْ أَبِيهِ، عَنْ عَائِشَةَ، أَنَّ رَسُولَ اللَّهِ صلى الله عليه وسلم قَالَ " إِذَا نَعَسَ أَحَدُكُمْ وَهُوَ يُصَلِّي فَلْيَرْقُدْ حَتَّى يَذْهَبَ عَنْهُ النَّوْمُ، فَإِنَّ أَحَدَكُمْ إِذَا صَلَّى وَهُوَ نَاعِسٌ لاَ يَدْرِي لَعَلَّهُ يَسْتَغْفِرُ فَيَسُبَّ نَفْسَهُ ".

Narrated Anas: The Prophet ﷺ said, "If anyone of you feels drowsy while praying, he should sleep till he understands what he is saying (reciting). – Al-Bukhari 213
حَدَّثَنَا أَبُو مَعْمَرٍ، قَالَ حَدَّثَنَا عَبْدُ الْوَارِثِ، حَدَّثَنَا أَيُّوبُ، عَنْ أَبِي قِلاَبَةَ، عَنْ أَنَسٍ، عَنِ النَّبِيِّ صلى الله عليه وسلم قَالَ " إِذَا نَعَسَ أَحَدُكُمْ فِي الصَّلاَةِ فَلْيَنَمْ حَتَّى يَعْلَمَ مَا يَقْرَأُ "

Narrated Ibn `Abbas: (regarding the Verse):-- 'Neither say your prayer aloud, nor say it in a low tone.' (17.110) This Verse was revealed while Allah's Messenger ﷺ was hiding himself in Mecca, and when he raised his voice while reciting the Qur'an, the pagans would hear him and abuse the Qur'an and its Revealer and to the one who brought it. So Allah said:-- 'Neither say your prayer aloud, nor say it in a low tone.' (17.110) That is, 'Do not say your prayer so loudly that the pagans can hear you, nor say it in such a low tone that your companions do not hear you.' But seek a middle course between those (extremes), i.e., let your companions hear, but do not relate the Qur'an loudly, so that they may learn it from you. – Al-Bukhari 7490

حَدَّثَنَا مُسَدَّدٌ، عَنْ هُشَيْمٍ، عَنْ أَبِي بِشْرٍ، عَنْ سَعِيدِ بْنِ جُبَيْرٍ، عَنِ ابْنِ عَبَّاسٍ ـ رضى الله عنهما ـ {وَلاَ تَجْهَرْ بِصَلاَتِكَ وَلاَ تُخَافِتْ بِهَا} قَالَ أُنْزِلَتْ وَرَسُولُ اللَّهِ صلى الله عليه وسلم مُتَوَارٍ بِمَكَّةَ، فَكَانَ إِذَا رَفَعَ صَوْتَهُ سَمِعَ الْمُشْرِكُونَ فَسَبُّوا الْقُرْآنَ وَمَنْ أَنْزَلَهُ وَمَنْ جَاءَ بِهِ. وَقَالَ اللَّهُ تَعَالَى {وَلاَ تَجْهَرْ بِصَلاَتِكَ وَلاَ تُخَافِتْ بِهَا} لاَ تَجْهَرْ بِصَلاَتِكَ حَتَّى يَسْمَعَ الْمُشْرِكُونَ، وَلاَ تُخَافِتْ بِهَا عَنْ أَصْحَابِكَ فَلاَ تُسْمِعُهُمْ {وَابْتَغِ بَيْنَ ذَلِكَ سَبِيلاً} أَسْمِعْهُمْ وَلاَ تَجْهَرْ حَتَّى يَأْخُذُوا عَنْكَ الْقُرْآنَ

Umar bin Abdul 'AzIz said (to his Mu'adh-dhin i.e., call-maker), "Pronounce the Adhăn clearly and in a straight forward manner, otherwise we will dismiss you. – Al-Bukhari Vol.1 page 357

و قالعمر بن عبد عزيز : إذن اذانا سمحا ، و الا فاعتزلنا

Narrated Ibn Mas`ud: I heard the Prophet (ﷺ) saying, "There is no envy except in two: a person whom Allah has given wealth and he spends it in the right way, and a person whom Allah has given wisdom (i.e. religious knowledge) and he gives his decisions accordingly and teaches it to the others." – Sahih al-Bukhari 1409

حَدَّثَنَا مُحَمَّدُ بْنُ الْمُثَنَّى، حَدَّثَنَا يَحْيَى، عَنْ إِسْمَاعِيلَ، قَالَ حَدَّثَنِي قَيْسٌ، عَنِ ابْنِ مَسْعُودٍ ـ رضى الله عنه ـ قَالَ سَمِعْتُ النَّبِيَّ صلى الله عليه وسلم يَقُولُ " لاَ حَسَدَ إِلاَّ فِي اثْنَتَيْنِ رَجُلٌ آتَاهُ اللَّهُ مَالاً فَسَلَّطَهُ عَلَى هَلَكَتِهِ فِي الْحَقِّ، وَرَجُلٌ آتَاهُ اللَّهُ حِكْمَةً فَهْوَ يَقْضِي بِهَا وَيُعَلِّمُهَا ".

Narrated `Abdullah: I heard a man reciting a verse (of the Holy Qur'an) but I had heard the Prophetﷺ reciting it differently. So, I caught hold of the man by the hand and took him to Allah's Messengerﷺ who said, "Both of you are right." Shu`ba, the sub-narrator said, "I think he said to them, "Don't differ, for the nations before you differed and perished (because of their differences). " – Al-Bukhari 2410

حَدَّثَنَا أَبُو الْوَلِيدِ، حَدَّثَنَا شُعْبَةُ، قَالَ عَبْدُ الْمَلِكِ بْنُ مَيْسَرَةَ أَخْبَرَنِي قَالَ سَمِعْتُ النَّزَّالَ، سَمِعْتُ عَبْدَ اللَّهِ، يَقُولُ سَمِعْتُ رَجُلاً، قَرَأَ آيَةً سَمِعْتُ مِنَ النَّبِيِّ، صلى الله عليه وسلم خِلاَفَهَا، فَأَخَذْتُ بِيَدِهِ، فَأَتَيْتُ بِهِ رَسُولَ اللَّهِ صلى الله عليه وسلم فَقَالَ " كِلاَكُمَا مُحْسِنٌ ". قَالَ شُعْبَةُ أَظُنُّهُ قَالَ " لاَ تَخْتَلِفُوا فَإِنَّ مَنْ كَانَ قَبْلَكُمُ اخْتَلَفُوا فَهَلَكُوا ".

The hypocrites try to deceive Allah, but He is deceiving them. And when they stand for prayer, they stand lazily, showing off in front of people, and remembering Allah only a little. – Surah An-Nisa 4:142

إِنَّ ٱلْمُنَـٰفِقِينَ يُخَـٰدِعُونَ ٱللَّهَ وَهُوَ خَـٰدِعُهُمْ وَإِذَا قَامُوٓا۟ إِلَى ٱلصَّلَوٰةِ قَامُوا۟ كُسَالَىٰ يُرَآءُونَ ٱلنَّاسَ وَلَا يَذْكُرُونَ ٱللَّهَ إِلَّا قَلِيلًا

I gave these and their forefathers some enjoyment, until the truth and a manifest messenger came to them. – Surah Az-Zukhruf 43:29

بَلْ مَتَّعْتُ هَـٰٓؤُلَآءِ وَءَابَآءَهُمْ حَتَّىٰ جَآءَهُمُ ٱلْحَقُّ وَرَسُولٌ مُّبِينٌ

We made it easy in your tongue, in order to deliver good news to the righteous, and to warn with it a hostile people. – Surah Maryam 19:97

فَإِنَّمَا يَسَّرْنَـٰهُ بِلِسَانِكَ لِتُبَشِّرَ بِهِ ٱلْمُتَّقِينَ وَتُنذِرَ بِهِۦ قَوْمًا لُّدًّا

We have revealed it an Arabic Quran, so that you may understand. We narrate to you the most accurate history, by revealing to you this Quran. Although, prior to it, you were of the unaware. Surah Yusuf 12:2&3

إِنَّآ أَنزَلْنَـٰهُ قُرْءَٰنًا عَرَبِيًّا لَّعَلَّكُمْ تَعْقِلُونَ نَحْنُ نَقُصُّ عَلَيْكَ أَحْسَنَ ٱلْقَصَصِ بِمَآ أَوْحَيْنَآ إِلَيْكَ هَـٰذَا ٱلْقُرْءَانَ وَإِن كُنتَ مِن قَبْلِهِۦ لَمِنَ ٱلْغَـٰفِلِينَ

Narrated Sa`id: Um Khalid bint Khalid bin Sa`id said, "I came to Allah's Messenger ﷺ along with my father and I was wearing a yellow shirt. Allah's Messenger ﷺ said, "Sanah Sanah!"

(`Abdullah, the sub-narrator said, "It means, 'Nice, nice!' in the Ethiopian language.") Um Khalid added, "Then I started playing with the seal of Prophethood. My father admonished me. But Allah's Messenger ﷺ said (to my father), "Leave her," Allah's Messenger said, "May you live so long that your dress gets worn out, and you will mend it many times, and then wear another till it gets worn out (i.e. May Allah prolong your life)." (The sub-narrator, `Abdullah aid, "That garment (which she was wearing remained usable for a long period."). – Al-Bukhari 5993

حَدَّثَنَا حِبَّانُ، أَخْبَرَنَا عَبْدُ اللَّهِ، عَنْ خَالِدِ بْنِ سَعِيدٍ، عَنْ أَبِيهِ، عَنْ أُمِّ خَالِدٍ بِنْتِ خَالِدِ بْنِ سَعِيدٍ، قَالَتْ أَتَيْتُ رَسُولَ اللَّهِ صلى الله عليه وسلم مَعَ أَبِي وَعَلَىَّ قَمِيصٌ أَصْفَرُ، قَالَ رَسُولُ اللَّهِ صلى الله عليه وسلم " سَنَهْ سَنَهْ ". قَالَ عَبْدُ اللَّهِ وَهْىَ بِالْحَبَشِيَّةِ حَسَنَةٌ. قَالَتْ فَذَهَبْتُ أَلْعَبُ بِخَاتَمِ النُّبُوَّةِ، فَزَجَرَنِي أَبِي. قَالَ رَسُولُ اللَّهِ صلى الله عليه وسلم " دَعْهَا ". ثُمَّ قَالَ رَسُولُ اللَّهِ صلى الله عليه وسلم " أَبْلِي وَأَخْلِقِي، ثُمَّ أَبْلِي وَأَخْلِقِي، ثُمَّ أَبْلِي وَأَخْلِقِي ". قَالَ عَبْدُ اللَّهِ فَبَقِيَتْ حَتَّى ذَكَرَ. يَعْنِي مِنْ بَقَائِهَا

Narrated Abu Huraira: The Prophet ﷺ said, "The most awful (meanest) name in Allah's sight." Sufyan said more than once, "The most awful (meanest) name in Allah's sight is (that of) a man calling himself king of kings." Sufyan said, "Somebody else (i.e. other than Abu Az-Zinad, a sub-narrator) says: What is meant by 'The king of kings' is 'Shahan Shah.," – Al-Bukhari 6206

حَدَّثَنَا عَلِيُّ بْنُ عَبْدِ اللَّهِ، حَدَّثَنَا سُفْيَانُ، عَنْ أَبِي الزِّنَادِ، عَنِ الأَعْرَجِ، عَنْ أَبِي هُرَيْرَةَ، رِوَايَةً قَالَ " أَخْنَعُ اسْمٍ عِنْدَ اللَّهِ - وَقَالَ سُفْيَانُ غَيْرَ مَرَّةٍ أَخْنَعُ الأَسْمَاءِ عِنْدَ اللَّهِ - رَجُلٌ تَسَمَّى بِمَلِكِ الأَمْلاَكِ ". قَالَ سُفْيَانُ يَقُولُ غَيْرُهُ تَفْسِيرُهُ شَاهَانْ شَاهْ.

Narrated `Adi bin Hatim: The Prophet ﷺ said, "There will be none among you but will be talked to by Allah on the Day of Resurrection, without there being an interpreter between him and Him (Allah) . He will look and see nothing ahead of him, and then he will look (again for the second time) in front of him, and the Fire will confront him. So, whoever among you can save himself from the Fire, should do so even with one half of a date (in charity). – Al-Bukhari 6539

حَدَّثَنَا عُمَرُ بْنُ حَفْصٍ، حَدَّثَنَا أَبِي قَالَ، حَدَّثَنِي الأَعْمَشُ، قَالَ حَدَّثَنِي خَيْثَمَةُ، عَنْ عَدِيِّ بْنِ حَاتِمٍ، قَالَ قَالَ النَّبِيُّ صلى الله عليه وسلم " مَا مِنْكُمْ مِنْ أَحَدٍ إِلاَّ وَسَيُكَلِّمُهُ اللَّهُ يَوْمَ الْقِيَامَةِ، لَيْسَ بَيْنَ اللَّهِ وَبَيْنَهُ تُرْجُمَانٌ، ثُمَّ يَنْظُرُ فَلاَ يَرَى شَيْئًا قُدَّامَهُ، ثُمَّ يَنْظُرُ بَيْنَ يَدَيْهِ فَتَسْتَقْبِلُهُ النَّارُ، فَمَنِ اسْتَطَاعَ مِنْكُمْ أَنْ يَتَّقِيَ النَّارَ وَلَوْ بِشِقِّ تَمْرَةٍ ".

But how can they be reminded? An enlightening messenger has already come to them. – Surah Ad-Dukhan 44:13

أَنَّىٰ لَهُمُ ٱلذِّكْرَىٰ وَقَدْ جَآءَهُمْ رَسُولٌ مُّبِينٌ

Kharija bin Zaid bin Thabit said that Zaid bin Thabit said, "The Prophet ﷺ ordered me to learn the writing of the Jews. I even wrote letters for the Prophet ﷺ to the Jews and also read their letters when they wrote to him." And 'Umar said in the presence of 'Ali, 'Abdur-Rahman, and 'Uthman, "What is this woman saying?" (the woman was non-Arab) 'Abdur-Rahman bin Hatib said: "She is informing you about her companion who has committed illegal sexual intercourse with her." Abu Jamra said, "I was an interpreter between Ibn 'Abbas and the people." Some people said, "A ruler should have two interpreters." – Al-Bukhari 7195

وَقَالَ خَارِجَةُ بْنُ زَيْدِ بْنِ ثَابِتٍ عَنْ زَيْدِ بْنِ ثَابِتٍ أَنَّ النَّبِيَّ صلى الله عليه وسلم أَمَرَهُ أَنْ يَتَعَلَّمَ كِتَابَ الْيَهُودِ، حَتَّى كَتَبْتُ لِلنَّبِيِّ صلى الله عليه وسلم كُتُبَهُ، وَأَقْرَأْتُهُ كُتُبَهُمْ إِذَا كَتَبُوا إِلَيْهِ، وَقَالَ عُمَرُ وَعِنْدَهُ عَلِيٌّ وَعَبْدُ الرَّحْمَنِ وَعُثْمَانُ مَاذَا تَقُولُ هَذِهِ قَالَ عَبْدُ الرَّحْمَنِ بْنُ حَاطِبٍ فَقُلْتُ تُخْبِرُكَ بِصَاحِبِهِمَا الَّذِي صَنَعَ بِهِمَا. وَقَالَ أَبُو جَمْرَةَ كُنْتُ أُتَرْجِمُ بَيْنَ ابْنِ عَبَّاسٍ وَبَيْنَ النَّاسِ. وَقَالَ بَعْضُ النَّاسِ لاَ بُدَّ لِلْحَاكِمِ مِنْ مُتَرْجِمَيْنِ.

Narrated `Abdur-Rahman bin Abi Bakra's father: Once the Prophet ﷺ was riding his camel and a man was holding its rein. The Prophet ﷺ asked, "What is the day today?" We kept quiet, thinking that he might give that day another name. He said, "Isn't it the day of Nahr (slaughtering of the animals of sacrifice)" We replied, "Yes." He further asked, "Which month is this?" We again kept quiet, thinking that he might give it another name. Then he said, "Isn't it the month of Dhul-Hijja?" We replied, "Yes." He said, "Verily! Your blood, property and honor are sacred to one another (i.e. Muslims) like the sanctity of this day of yours, in this month of yours and in this city of yours. It is incumbent upon those who are present to inform those who are absent because those who are absent might comprehend (what I have said) better than the present audience." – Al-Bukhari 67

حَدَّثَنَا مُسَدَّدٌ، قَالَ حَدَّثَنَا بِشْرٌ، قَالَ حَدَّثَنَا ابْنُ عَوْنٍ، عَنِ ابْنِ سِيرِينَ، عَنْ عَبْدِ الرَّحْمَنِ بْنِ أَبِي بَكْرَةَ، عَنْ أَبِيهِ، ذَكَرَ النَّبِيَّ صلى الله عليه وسلم قَعَدَ عَلَى بَعِيرِهِ، وَأَمْسَكَ إِنْسَانٌ بِخِطَامِهِ ـ أَوْ بِزِمَامِهِ ـ قَالَ ‏"‏ أَىُّ يَوْمٍ هَذَا ‏"‏‏.‏ فَسَكَتْنَا حَتَّى ظَنَنَّا أَنَّهُ سَيُسَمِّيهِ سِوَى اسْمِهِ‏.‏ قَالَ ‏"‏ أَلَيْسَ يَوْمَ النَّحْرِ ‏"‏‏.‏ قُلْنَا بَلَى‏.‏ قَالَ ‏"‏ فَأَىُّ شَهْرٍ هَذَا ‏"‏‏.‏ فَسَكَتْنَا حَتَّى ظَنَنَّا أَنَّهُ سَيُسَمِّيهِ بِغَيْرِ اسْمِهِ‏.‏ فَقَالَ ‏"‏ أَلَيْسَ بِذِي الْحِجَّةِ ‏"‏‏.‏ قُلْنَا بَلَى‏.‏ قَالَ ‏"‏ فَإِنَّ دِمَاءَكُمْ وَأَمْوَالَكُمْ وَأَعْرَاضَكُمْ بَيْنَكُمْ حَرَامٌ كَحُرْمَةِ يَوْمِكُمْ هَذَا، فِي شَهْرِكُمْ هَذَا، فِي بَلَدِكُمْ هَذَا‏.‏ لِيُبَلِّغِ الشَّاهِدُ الْغَائِبَ، فَإِنَّ الشَّاهِدَ عَسَى أَنْ يُبَلِّغَ مَنْ هُوَ أَوْعَى لَهُ مِنْهُ ‏"

Narrated Anas: Whenever the Prophet ﷺ spoke a sentence (said a thing), he used to repeat it thrice so that the people could understand it properly from him and whenever he asked permission to enter, (he knocked the door) thrice with greeting. – Al-Bukhari 95

حَدَّثَنَا عَبْدَةُ بْنُ عَبْدِ اللَّهِ، حَدَّثَنَا عَبْدُ الصَّمَدِ، قَالَ حَدَّثَنَا عَبْدُ اللَّهِ بْنُ الْمُثَنَّى، قَالَ حَدَّثَنَا ثُمَامَةُ بْنُ عَبْدِ اللَّهِ، عَنْ أَنَسٍ، عَنِ النَّبِيِّ صلى الله عليه وسلم أَنَّهُ كَانَ إِذَا تَكَلَّمَ بِكَلِمَةٍ أَعَادَهَا ثَلاَثًا حَتَّى تُفْهَمَ عَنْهُ، وَإِذَا أَتَى عَلَى قَوْمٍ فَسَلَّمَ عَلَيْهِمْ سَلَّمَ عَلَيْهِمْ ثَلاَثًا‏.‏

Narrated Abu Huraira: Al-Hasan bin 'All took a date from the dates of the Sadaqa and put it in his mouth. The Prophet ﷺ said (to him) in Persian, "Kakh, kakh! (i.e. Don't you know that we do not eat the Sadaqa (i.e. what is given in charity) . -Al-Bukhari 3072

حَدَّثَنَا مُحَمَّدُ بْنُ بَشَّارٍ، حَدَّثَنَا غُنْدَرٌ، حَدَّثَنَا شُعْبَةُ، عَنْ مُحَمَّدِ بْنِ زِيَادٍ، عَنْ أَبِي هُرَيْرَةَ ـ رضى الله عنه أَنَّ الْحَسَنَ بْنَ عَلِيٍّ، أَخَذَ تَمْرَةً مِنْ تَمْرِ الصَّدَقَةِ، فَجَعَلَهَا فِي فِيهِ، فَقَالَ النَّبِيُّ صلى الله عليه وسلم بِالْفَارِسِيَّةِ ‏"‏ كَخٍ كَخٍ، أَمَا تَعْرِفُ أَنَّا لاَ نَأْكُلُ الصَّدَقَةَ ‏"‏

Narrated Aisha: Al Harith bin Hisham asked the Prophet, "How does the divine inspiration come to you?" He replied, "In all these ways: The Angel sometimes comes to me with a voice which resembles the sound of a ringing bell, and when this state abandons me, I remember what the Angel has said, and this type of Divine Inspiration is the hardest on me; and sometimes the Angel comes to me in the shape of a man and talks to me, and I understand and remember what he says." – Al-Bukhari 3215

حَدَّثَنَا فَرْوَةُ، حَدَّثَنَا عَلِيُّ بْنُ مُسْهِرٍ، عَنْ هِشَامِ بْنِ عُرْوَةَ، عَنْ أَبِيهِ، عَنْ عَائِشَةَ ـ رضى الله عنها ـ أَنَّ الْحَارِثَ بْنَ هِشَامٍ، سَأَلَ النَّبِيَّ صلى الله عليه وسلم كَيْفَ يَأْتِيكَ الْوَحْىُ قَالَ ‏"‏ كُلُّ ذَاكَ يَأْتِي الْمَلَكُ أَحْيَانًا فِي مِثْلِ صَلْصَلَةِ الْجَرَسِ، فَيَفْصِمُ عَنِّي وَقَدْ وَعَيْتُ مَا قَالَ، وَهْوَ أَشَدُّهُ عَلَىَّ، وَيَتَمَثَّلُ لِي الْمَلَكُ أَحْيَانًا رَجُلاً، فَيُكَلِّمُنِي فَأَعِي مَا يَقُولُ ‏"

Narrated `Aisha: The Prophet ﷺ used to talk so clearly that if somebody wanted to count the number of his words, he could do so. Narrated `Urwa bin Az-Zubair: `Aisha said, "Don't you wonder at Abu so-and-so who came and sat by my dwelling and started relating the traditions of Allah's Messenge ﷺ intending to let me hear that, while I was performing an optional prayer. He left before I finished my optional prayer. Had I found him still there. I would have said to him, 'Allah's Messenger ﷺ never talked so quickly & vaguely as you do.' " – Al-Bukhari 3567, 3568

حَدَّثَنِي الْحَسَنُ بْنُ صَبَّاحٍ الْبَزَّارُ، حَدَّثَنَا سُفْيَانُ، عَنِ الزُّهْرِيِّ، عَنْ عُرْوَةَ، عَنْ عَائِشَةَ ـ رضى الله عنها أَنَّ النَّبِيَّ صلى الله عليه وسلم كَانَ يُحَدِّثُ حَدِيثًا لَوْ عَدَّهُ الْعَادُّ لأَحْصَاهُ‏.‏ وَقَالَ اللَّيْثُ حَدَّثَنِي يُونُسُ، عَنِ ابْنِ شِهَابٍ، أَنَّهُ قَالَ أَخْبَرَنِي عُرْوَةُ بْنُ الزُّبَيْرِ، عَنْ عَائِشَةَ، أَنَّهَا قَالَتْ أَلاَ يُعْجِبُكَ أَبُو فُلاَنٍ جَاءَ فَجَلَسَ إِلَى جَانِبِ حُجْرَتِي يُحَدِّثُ عَنْ رَسُولِ اللَّهِ صلى الله عليه

وسلم، يُسْمِعُنِي ذَلِكَ وَكُنْتُ أُسَبِّحُ فَقَامَ قَبْلَ أَنْ أَقْضِيَ سُبْحَتِي، وَلَوْ أَدْرَكْتُهُ لَرَدَدْتُ عَلَيْهِ، إِنَّ رَسُولَ اللَّهِ صلى الله عليه وسلم لَمْ يَكُنْ يَسْرُدُ الْحَدِيثَ كَسَرْدِكُمْ.

Narrated Abu Musa: The Prophet ﷺ said, "Near the establishment of the Hour there will be days during which (religious) knowledge will be taken away (vanish) and general ignorance will spread, and there will be Al-Harj in abundance, and Al-Harj means killing." – Al-Bukhari 7064

حَدَّثَنَا عُمَرُ بْنُ حَفْصٍ، حَدَّثَنَا أَبِي، حَدَّثَنَا الأَعْمَشُ، حَدَّثَنَا شَقِيقٌ، قَالَ جَلَسَ عَبْدُ اللَّهِ وَأَبُو مُوسَى فَتَحَدَّثَا فَقَالَ أَبُو مُوسَى قَالَ النَّبِيُّ صلى الله عليه وسلم " إِنَّ بَيْنَ يَدَىِ السَّاعَةِ أَيَّامًا يُرْفَعُ فِيهَا الْعِلْمُ، وَيَنْزِلُ فِيهَا الْجَهْلُ، وَيَكْثُرُ فِيهَا الْهَرْجُ، وَالْهَرْجُ الْقَتْلُ ".

Narrated Abu Huraira: The people of the Book used to read the Torah in Hebrew and then explain it in Arabic to the Muslims. Allah's Messenger ﷺ said (to the Muslims). "Do not believe the people of the Book, nor disbelieve them, but say, 'We believe in Allah and whatever is revealed to us, and whatever is revealed to you.' " – Al-Bukhari 7362

حَدَّثَنِي مُحَمَّدُ بْنُ بَشَّارٍ، حَدَّثَنَا عُثْمَانُ بْنُ عُمَرَ، أَخْبَرَنَا عَلِيُّ بْنُ الْمُبَارَكِ، عَنْ يَحْيَى بْنِ أَبِي كَثِيرٍ، عَنْ أَبِي سَلَمَةَ، عَنْ أَبِي هُرَيْرَةَ، قَالَ كَانَ أَهْلُ الْكِتَابِ يَقْرَءُونَ التَّوْرَاةَ بِالْعِبْرَانِيَّةِ وَيُفَسِّرُونَهَا بِالْعَرَبِيَّةِ لأَهْلِ الإِسْلاَمِ فَقَالَ رَسُولُ اللَّهِ صلى الله عليه وسلم " لاَ تُصَدِّقُوا أَهْلَ الْكِتَابِ، وَلاَ تُكَذِّبُوهُمْ وَقُولُوا {آمَنَّا بِاللَّهِ وَمَا أُنْزِلَ إِلَيْنَا وَمَا أُنْزِلَ إِلَيْكُمْ} ". الآيَةَ

The Book of

The Sovereign, the Holy One, the Giver of Peace, the Giver of Security, the Guardian, the All-Mighty, the Irresistible, the Supreme.

ٱلْمَلِكُ ٱلْقُدُّوسُ ٱلسَّلَـٰمُ ٱلْمُؤْمِنُ ٱلْمُهَيْمِنُ ٱلْعَزِيزُ ٱلْجَبَّارُ ٱلْمُتَكَبِّرُ

It is Allah Who splits the grain and the seed. He brings the living from the dead, and He brings the dead from the living. Such is Allah. So how could you deviate? It is He Who breaks the dawn. And He made the night for rest, and the sun and the moon for calculation. Such is the disposition of the Almighty, the All-Knowing. And it is He Who created the stars for you, that you may be guided by them in the darkness of land and sea. We thus explain the revelations for people who know. And it is He who produced you from a single person, then a repository, then a depository. We have detailed the revelations for people who understand. And it is He who sends down water from the sky. With it We produce vegetation of all kinds, from which We bring greenery, from which We produce grains in clusters. And palm-trees with hanging clusters, and vineyards, and olives, and pomegranates—similar and dissimilar. Watch their fruits as they grow and ripen. Surely in this are signs for people who believe. Yet they attributed to Allah partners—the sprites—although He created them. And they invented for Him sons and daughters, without any knowledge. Glory be to Him. He is exalted, beyond what they describe. Originator of the heavens and the earth—how can He have a son when He never had a companion? He created all things, and He has knowledge of all things. Such is Allah, your Lord. There Is no god except He, the Creator of all things; so worship Him. He is responsible for everything. No vision can grasp Him, but His grasp is over all vision. He is the Subtle, the Expert. – Surah Al- An'am 6:95-103

إِنَّ ٱللَّهَ فَالِقُ ٱلْحَبِّ وَٱلنَّوَىٰ ۖ يُخْرِجُ ٱلْحَىَّ مِنَ ٱلْمَيِّتِ وَمُخْرِجُ ٱلْمَيِّتِ مِنَ ٱلْحَىِّ ۚ ذَٰلِكُمُ ٱللَّهُ ۖ فَأَنَّىٰ تُؤْفَكُونَ فَالِقُ ٱلْإِصْبَاحِ وَجَعَلَ ٱلَّيْلَ سَكَنًا وَٱلشَّمْسَ وَٱلْقَمَرَ حُسْبَانًا ۚ ذَٰلِكَ تَقْدِيرُ ٱلْعَزِيزِ ٱلْعَلِيمِ وَهُوَ ٱلَّذِى جَعَلَ لَكُمُ ٱلنُّجُومَ لِتَهْتَدُوا۟ بِهَا فِى ظُلُمَـٰتِ ٱلْبَرِّ وَٱلْبَحْرِ ۗ قَدْ فَصَّلْنَا ٱلْءَايَـٰتِ لِقَوْمٍ يَعْلَمُونَ وَهُوَ ٱلَّذِىٓ أَنشَأَكُم مِّن نَّفْسٍ وَٰحِدَةٍ فَمُسْتَقَرٌّ وَمُسْتَوْدَعٌ ۗ قَدْ فَصَّلْنَا ٱلْءَايَـٰتِ لِقَوْمٍ يَفْقَهُونَ وَهُوَ ٱلَّذِىٓ أَنزَلَ مِنَ ٱلسَّمَآءِ مَآءً فَأَخْرَجْنَا بِهِۦ نَبَاتَ كُلِّ شَىْءٍ فَأَخْرَجْنَا مِنْهُ خَضِرًا نُّخْرِجُ مِنْهُ حَبًّا مُّتَرَاكِبًا وَمِنَ ٱلنَّخْلِ مِن طَلْعِهَا قِنْوَانٌ دَانِيَةٌ وَجَنَّـٰتٍ مِّنْ أَعْنَابٍ وَٱلزَّيْتُونَ وَٱلرُّمَّانَ مُشْتَبِهًا وَغَيْرَ مُتَشَـٰبِهٍ ۗ ٱنظُرُوٓا۟ إِلَىٰ ثَمَرِهِۦٓ إِذَآ أَثْمَرَ وَيَنْعِهِۦٓ ۚ إِنَّ فِى ذَٰلِكُمْ لَـَٔايَـٰتٍ لِّقَوْمٍ يُؤْمِنُونَ وَجَعَلُوا۟ لِلَّهِ شُرَكَآءَ ٱلْجِنَّ وَخَلَقَهُمْ ۖ وَخَرَقُوا۟ لَهُۥ بَنِينَ وَبَنَـٰتٍۭ بِغَيْرِ عِلْمٍ ۚ سُبْحَـٰنَهُۥ وَتَعَـٰلَىٰ عَمَّا يَصِفُونَ بَدِيعُ ٱلسَّمَـٰوَٰتِ وَٱلْأَرْضِ ۖ أَنَّىٰ يَكُونُ لَهُۥ وَلَدٌ وَلَمْ تَكُن لَّهُۥ صَـٰحِبَةٌ ۖ وَخَلَقَ كُلَّ شَىْءٍ ۖ وَهُوَ بِكُلِّ شَىْءٍ عَلِيمٌ ذَٰلِكُمُ ٱللَّهُ رَبُّكُمْ ۖ لَآ إِلَـٰهَ إِلَّا هُوَ ۖ خَـٰلِقُ كُلِّ شَىْءٍ فَٱعْبُدُوهُ ۚ وَهُوَ عَلَىٰ كُلِّ شَىْءٍ وَكِيلٌ لَّا تُدْرِكُهُ ٱلْأَبْصَـٰرُ وَهُوَ يُدْرِكُ ٱلْأَبْصَـٰرَ ۖ وَهُوَ ٱللَّطِيفُ ٱلْخَبِيرُ

It Is He who shows you the lightening, causing fear and hope. And He produces the heavy clouds. The thunder praises His glory, and so do the angels, in awe of Him. And He sends the thunderbolts, striking with them whomever He wills. Yet they argue about Allah, while He is Tremendous in might. To Him belongs the call to truth. Those they call upon besides Him do not respond to them with anything—except as someone who stretches his hands towards water, so that it may reach his mouth, but it does not reach it. The prayers of the unbelievers are only in vain. To Allah prostrates everyone in the heavens and the earth, willingly or unwillingly, as do their shadows, in the morning and in the evening. Say, "Who is the Lord of the heavens and the earth?" Say, "Allah." Say, "Have you taken besides Him protectors, who have no power to profit or harm even themselves?" Say, "Are the blind and the seeing equal? Or are darkness and light equal? Or have they assigned to Allah associates, who created the likes of His creation, so that the creations seemed to them alike? Say, "Allah is the Creator of all things, and He is The One, the Irresistible." He sends down water from the sky, and riverbeds flow according to their capacity. The current carries swelling froth. And from what they heat in fire of ornaments or utensils comes a similar froth. Thus Allah exemplifies truth and falsehood. As for the froth, it is swept away, but what benefits the people remains in the ground. Thus Allah presents the analogies. – Surah Ar-Ra'd 13:12-17

هُوَ ٱلَّذِى يُرِيكُمُ ٱلْبَرْقَ خَوْفًا وَطَمَعًا وَيُنشِئُ ٱلسَّحَابَ ٱلثِّقَالَ وَيُسَبِّحُ ٱلرَّعْدُ بِحَمْدِهِۦ وَٱلْمَلَٰٓئِكَةُ مِنْ خِيفَتِهِۦ وَيُرْسِلُ ٱلصَّوَٰعِقَ فَيُصِيبُ بِهَا مَن يَشَآءُ وَهُمْ يُجَٰدِلُونَ فِى ٱللَّهِ وَهُوَ شَدِيدُ ٱلْمِحَالِ لَهُۥ دَعْوَةُ ٱلْحَقِّ ۖ وَٱلَّذِينَ يَدْعُونَ مِن دُونِهِۦ لَا يَسْتَجِيبُونَ لَهُم بِشَىْءٍ إِلَّا كَبَٰسِطِ كَفَّيْهِ إِلَى ٱلْمَآءِ لِيَبْلُغَ فَاهُ وَمَا هُوَ بِبَٰلِغِهِۦ ۚ وَمَا دُعَآءُ ٱلْكَٰفِرِينَ إِلَّا فِى ضَلَٰلٍ وَلِلَّهِ يَسْجُدُ مَن فِى ٱلسَّمَٰوَٰتِ وَٱلْأَرْضِ طَوْعًا وَكَرْهًا وَظِلَٰلُهُم بِٱلْغُدُوِّ وَٱلْءَاصَالِ قُلْ مَن رَّبُّ ٱلسَّمَٰوَٰتِ وَٱلْأَرْضِ قُلِ ٱللَّهُ ۚ قُلْ أَفَٱتَّخَذْتُم مِّن دُونِهِۦٓ أَوْلِيَآءَ لَا يَمْلِكُونَ لِأَنفُسِهِمْ نَفْعًا وَلَا ضَرًّا ۚ قُلْ هَلْ يَسْتَوِى ٱلْأَعْمَىٰ وَٱلْبَصِيرُ أَمْ هَلْ تَسْتَوِى ٱلظُّلُمَٰتُ وَٱلنُّورُ ۗ أَمْ جَعَلُوا۟ لِلَّهِ شُرَكَآءَ خَلَقُوا۟ كَخَلْقِهِۦ فَتَشَٰبَهَ ٱلْخَلْقُ عَلَيْهِمْ ۚ قُلِ ٱللَّهُ خَٰلِقُ كُلِّ شَىْءٍ وَهُوَ ٱلْوَٰحِدُ ٱلْقَهَّٰرُ أَنزَلَ مِنَ ٱلسَّمَآءِ مَآءً فَسَالَتْ أَوْدِيَةٌۢ بِقَدَرِهَا فَٱحْتَمَلَ ٱلسَّيْلُ زَبَدًا رَّابِيًا ۚ وَمِمَّا يُوقِدُونَ عَلَيْهِ فِى ٱلنَّارِ ٱبْتِغَآءَ حِلْيَةٍ أَوْ مَتَٰعٍ زَبَدٌ مِّثْلُهُۥ ۚ كَذَٰلِكَ يَضْرِبُ ٱللَّهُ ٱلْحَقَّ وَٱلْبَٰطِلَ ۚ فَأَمَّا ٱلزَّبَدُ فَيَذْهَبُ جُفَآءً ۖ وَأَمَّا مَا يَنفَعُ ٱلنَّاسَ فَيَمْكُثُ فِى ٱلْأَرْضِ ۚ كَذَٰلِكَ يَضْرِبُ ٱللَّهُ ٱلْأَمْثَالَ

How many a creature there is that does not carry its provision? Allah provides for them, and for you. He is the Hearer, the Knowledgeable. And if you asked them, "Who created the heavens and the earth and regulated the sun and the moon?" They would say, "Allah." Why then do they deviate? Allah expands the provision for whomever He wills of His servants, and restricts it. Allah is Cognizant of all things. And if you asked them, "Who sends water down from the sky, with which He revives the earth after it had died?" They would say, "Allah." Say, "Praise be to Allah." But most of them do not understand.- Surah Al-Ankabut 29:60-63

وَكَأَيِّن مِّن دَآبَّةٍ لَّا تَحْمِلُ رِزْقَهَا ٱللَّهُ يَرْزُقُهَا وَإِيَّاكُمْ ۚ وَهُوَ ٱلسَّمِيعُ ٱلْعَلِيمُ وَلَئِن سَأَلْتَهُم مَّنْ خَلَقَ ٱلسَّمَٰوَٰتِ وَٱلْأَرْضَ وَسَخَّرَ ٱلشَّمْسَ وَٱلْقَمَرَ لَيَقُولُنَّ ٱللَّهُ ۖ فَأَنَّىٰ يُؤْفَكُونَ ٱللَّهُ يَبْسُطُ ٱلرِّزْقَ لِمَن يَشَآءُ مِنْ عِبَادِهِۦ وَيَقْدِرُ لَهُۥٓ ۚ إِنَّ ٱللَّهَ بِكُلِّ شَىْءٍ عَلِيمٌ وَلَئِن سَأَلْتَهُم مَّن نَّزَّلَ مِنَ ٱلسَّمَآءِ مَآءً فَأَحْيَا بِهِ ٱلْأَرْضَ مِنۢ بَعْدِ مَوْتِهَا لَيَقُولُنَّ ٱللَّهُ ۚ قُلِ ٱلْحَمْدُ لِلَّهِ ۚ بَلْ أَكْثَرُهُمْ لَا يَعْقِلُونَ

Narrated `Abdullah bin `Umar: Whenever Allah's Messenger ﷺ returned from a Ghazwa, Hajj or `Umra, he used to say Takbir thrice at every elevation of the ground and then would say, "None has the right to be worshipped but Allah; He is One and has no partner. All the kingdoms is for Him, and all the praises are for Him, and He is Omnipotent. We are returning with repentance, worshipping, prostrating, and praising our Lord. He has kept up His promise and made His slave victorious, and He Alone defeated all the clans of (nonbelievers).- Al-Bukhari 1797

حَدَّثَنَا عَبْدُ اللَّهِ بْنُ يُوسُفَ، أَخْبَرَنَا مَالِكٌ، عَنْ نَافِعٍ، عَنْ عَبْدِ اللَّهِ بْنِ عُمَرَ ـ رضى الله عنهما ـ أَنَّ رَسُولَ اللَّهِ صلى الله عليه وسلم كَانَ إِذَا قَفَلَ مِنْ غَزْوٍ أَوْ حَجٍّ أَوْ عُمْرَةٍ يُكَبِّرُ عَلَى كُلِّ شَرَفٍ مِنَ الأَرْضِ ثَلاَثَ تَكْبِيرَاتٍ، ثُمَّ يَقُولُ " لاَ إِلَهَ إِلاَّ اللَّهُ وَحْدَهُ لاَ شَرِيكَ لَهُ، لَهُ الْمُلْكُ، وَلَهُ الْحَمْدُ، وَهُوَ عَلَى كُلِّ شَىْءٍ قَدِيرٌ، آيِبُونَ تَائِبُونَ عَابِدُونَ سَاجِدُونَ لِرَبِّنَا حَامِدُونَ، صَدَقَ اللَّهُ وَعْدَهُ وَنَصَرَ عَبْدَهُ وَهَزَمَ الأَحْزَابَ وَحْدَهُ

Narrated As-Sab bin Jath-thama: Allah's Messenger ﷺ said, No Hima except for Allah and His Apostle. We have been told that Allah's Apostle made a place called An-Naqi' as Hima, and `Umar made Ash-Sharaf and Ar-Rabadha Hima (for grazing the animals of Zakat).-Al-Bukhari 2370

حَدَّثَنَا يَحْيَى بْنُ بُكَيْرٍ، حَدَّثَنَا اللَّيْثُ، عَنْ يُونُسَ، عَنِ ابْنِ شِهَابٍ، عَنْ عُبَيْدِ اللَّهِ بْنِ عَبْدِ اللَّهِ بْنِ عُتْبَةَ، عَنِ ابْنِ عَبَّاسٍ ـ رضى الله عنهما ـ أَنَّ الصَّعْبَ بْنَ جَثَّامَةَ، قَالَ إِنَّ رَسُولَ اللَّهِ صلى الله عليه وسلم قَالَ " لاَ حِمَى إِلاَّ لِلَّهِ وَلِرَسُولِهِ ". وَقَالَ بَلَغَنَا أَنَّ النَّبِيَّ صلى الله عليه وسلم حَمَى النَّقِيعَ، وَأَنَّ عُمَرَ حَمَى السَّرَفَ

He is Allah. There is no god but He, the Knower of secrets and declarations. He is the Compassionate, the Merciful. He is Allah; besides Whom there is no god; the Sovereign, the

Holy, the PeaceGiver, the Faith-Giver, the Overseer, the Almighty, the Omnipotent, the Overwhelming. Glory be to Allah, beyond what they associate. He is Allah; the Creator, the Maker, the Designer. His are the Most Beautiful Names. Whatever is in the heavens and the earth glorifies Him. He is the Majestic, the Wise.- Surah Al-Hashr 59:22-24
هُوَ ٱللَّهُ ٱلَّذِى لَآ إِلَـٰهَ إِلَّا هُوَ ۖ عَـٰلِمُ ٱلْغَيْبِ وَٱلشَّهَـٰدَةِ ۖ هُوَ ٱلرَّحْمَـٰنُ ٱلرَّحِيمُ هُوَ ٱللَّهُ ٱلَّذِى لَآ إِلَـٰهَ إِلَّا هُوَ ٱلْمَلِكُ ٱلْقُدُّوسُ ٱلسَّلَـٰمُ ٱلْمُؤْمِنُ ٱلْمُهَيْمِنُ ٱلْعَزِيزُ ٱلْجَبَّارُ ٱلْمُتَكَبِّرُ ۚ سُبْحَـٰنَ ٱللَّهِ عَمَّا يُشْرِكُونَ هُوَ ٱللَّهُ ٱلَّذِى لَآ إِلَـٰهَ إِلَّا هُوَ ٱلْمَلِكُ ٱلْقُدُّوسُ ٱلسَّلَـٰمُ ٱلْمُؤْمِنُ ٱلْمُهَيْمِنُ ٱلْعَزِيزُ ٱلْجَبَّارُ ٱلْمُتَكَبِّرُ ۚ سُبْحَـٰنَ ٱللَّهِ عَمَّا يُشْرِكُونَ

Narrated Abu Huraira: Allah's Messenger ﷺ said, "The most awful name in Allah's sight on the Day of Resurrection, will be (that of) a man calling himself Malik Al-Amlak (the king of kings).-Al-Bukhari 6205
حَدَّثَنَا أَبُو الْيَمَانِ، أَخْبَرَنَا شُعَيْبٌ، حَدَّثَنَا أَبُو الزِّنَادِ، عَنِ الأَعْرَجِ، عَنْ أَبِي هُرَيْرَةَ، قَالَ قَالَ رَسُولُ اللَّهِ صلى الله عليه وسلم أَخْنَى الأَسْمَاءِ يَوْمَ الْقِيَامَةِ عِنْدَ اللَّهِ رَجُلٌ تَسَمَّى مَلِكَ الأَمْلاَكِ

Narrated Ibn `Abbas: Whenever the Prophet ﷺ offered the night (Tahajjud) prayer, he used to say, "O Allah! All the Praises are for You; You are the Light of the Heavens and the Earth. And all the Praises are for You; You are the Keeper of the Heavens and the Earth. All the Praises are for You; You are the Lord of the Heavens and the Earth and whatever is therein. You are the Truth, and Your Promise is the Truth, and Your Speech is the Truth, and meeting You is the Truth, and Paradise is the Truth and Hell (Fire) is the Truth and all the prophets are the Truth and the Hour is the Truth. O Allah! I surrender to You, and believe in You, and depend upon You, and repent to You, and in Your cause I fight and with Your orders I rule. So please forgive my past and future sins and those sins which I did in secret or in public. It is You Whom I worship, None has the right to be worshipped except You ." (See Hadith No. 329,Vol. 8) – Al-Bukhari 7499
حَدَّثَنَا مَحْمُودٌ، حَدَّثَنَا عَبْدُ الرَّزَّاقِ، أَخْبَرَنَا ابْنُ جُرَيْجٍ، أَخْبَرَنِي سُلَيْمَانُ الأَحْوَلُ، أَنَّ طَاوُسًا، أَخْبَرَهُ أَنَّهُ، سَمِعَ ابْنَ عَبَّاسٍ، يَقُولُ كَانَ النَّبِيُّ صلى الله عليه وسلم إِذَا تَهَجَّدَ مِنَ اللَّيْلِ قَالَ " اللَّهُمَّ لَكَ الْحَمْدُ أَنْتَ نُورُ السَّمَوَاتِ وَالأَرْضِ، وَلَكَ الْحَمْدُ أَنْتَ قَيِّمُ السَّمَوَاتِ وَالأَرْضِ، وَلَكَ الْحَمْدُ أَنْتَ رَبُّ السَّمَوَاتِ وَالأَرْضِ، وَمَنْ فِيهِنَّ أَنْتَ الْحَقُّ، وَوَعْدُكَ الْحَقُّ وَقَوْلُكَ الْحَقُّ، وَلِقَاؤُكَ الْحَقُّ، وَالْجَنَّةُ حَقٌّ، وَالنَّارُ حَقٌّ، وَالنَّبِيُّونَ حَقٌّ، وَالسَّاعَةُ حَقٌّ، اللَّهُمَّ لَكَ أَسْلَمْتُ، وَبِكَ آمَنْتُ، وَعَلَيْكَ تَوَكَّلْتُ، وَإِلَيْكَ أَنَبْتُ، وَبِكَ خَاصَمْتُ، وَإِلَيْكَ حَاكَمْتُ، فَاغْفِرْ لِي مَا قَدَّمْتُ وَمَا أَخَّرْتُ، وَمَا أَسْرَرْتُ وَمَا أَعْلَنْتُ، أَنْتَ إِلَهِي، لاَ إِلَهَ إِلاَّ أَنْتَ

It isIs He who initiates creation, and then repeats it, something easy for Him. His is the highest attribute, in the heavens and the earth. He is the Almighty, the Wise. – Surah Ar-Rum 30:27
وَهُوَ ٱلَّذِى يَبْدَؤُا۟ ٱلْخَلْقَ ثُمَّ يُعِيدُهُۥ وَهُوَ أَهْوَنُ عَلَيْهِ ۚ وَلَهُ ٱلْمَثَلُ ٱلْأَعْلَىٰ فِى ٱلسَّمَـٰوَٰتِ وَٱلْأَرْضِ ۚ وَهُوَ ٱلْعَزِيزُ ٱلْحَكِيمُ

Narrated Abu Musa: The Prophet ﷺ said, "The example of the one who celebrates the Praises of his Lord (Allah) in comparison to the one who does not celebrate the Praises of his Lord, is that of a living creature compared to a dead one.". – Sahih Al-Bukhari 6407
حَدَّثَنَا مُحَمَّدُ بْنُ الْعَلاَءِ، حَدَّثَنَا أَبُو أُسَامَةَ، عَنْ بُرَيْدِ بْنِ عَبْدِ اللَّهِ، عَنْ أَبِي بُرْدَةَ، عَنْ أَبِي مُوسَى ـ رضى الله عنه ـ قَالَ قَالَ النَّبِيُّ صلى الله عليه وسلم " مَثَلُ الَّذِي يَذْكُرُ رَبَّهُ وَالَّذِي لاَ يَذْكُرُ مَثَلُ الْحَيِّ وَالْمَيِّتِ "

Narrated Ibn `Abbas: When the Prophet ﷺ got up at night to offer the Tahajjud prayer, he used to say: Allahumma lakal-hamd. Anta qaiyyimus-samawati wal-ard wa man fihinna. Walakal-hamd, Laka mulkus-samawati wal-ard wa man fihinna. Walakal-hamd, anta nurus-samawati wal-ard. Wa lakal-hamd, anta-l-haq wa wa'duka-lhaq, wa liqa'uka Haq, wa qauluka Haq, wal-jannatu Han wan-naru Haq wannabiyuna Haq. Wa Muhammadun, sallal-lahu'alaihi wasallam, Haq, was-sa'atu Haq. Allahumma aslamtu Laka wabika amantu, wa 'Alaika

tawakkaltu, wa ilaika anabtu wa bika khasamtu, wa ilaika hakamtu faghfir li ma qaddamtu wama akh-khartu wama as-rartu wama'a lantu, anta-l-muqaddim wa anta-l-mu akh-khir, la ilaha illa anta (or la ilaha ghairuka). (O Allah! All the praises are for you, You are the Holder of the Heavens and the Earth, And whatever is in them. All the praises are for You; You have the possession of the Heavens and the Earth And whatever is in them. All the praises are for You; You are the Light of the Heavens and the Earth And all the praises are for You; You are the King of the Heavens and the Earth; And all the praises are for You; You are the Truth and Your Promise is the truth, And to meet You is true, Your Word is the truth And Paradise is true And Hell is true And all the Prophets (Peace be upon them) are true; And Muhammad is true, And the Day of Resurrection is true. O Allah ! I surrender (my will) to You; I believe in You and depend on You. And repent to You, And with Your help I argue (with my opponents, the non-believers) And I take You as a judge (to judge between us). Please forgive me my previous And future sins; And whatever I concealed or revealed And You are the One who make (some people) forward And (some) backward. There is none to be worshipped but you . Sufyan said that `Abdul Karim Abu Umaiya added to the above, 'Wala haula Wala quwata illa billah' (There is neither might nor power except with Allah). – Sahih al-Bukhari 1120
حَدَّثَنَا عَلِيُّ بْنُ عَبْدِ اللَّهِ، قَالَ حَدَّثَنَا سُفْيَانُ، قَالَ حَدَّثَنَا سُلَيْمَانُ بْنُ أَبِي مُسْلِمٍ، عَنْ طَاوُسٍ، سَمِعَ ابْنَ عَبَّاسٍ ـ رضى الله عنهما ـ قَالَ كَانَ النَّبِيُّ صلى الله عليه وسلم إِذَا قَامَ مِنَ اللَّيْلِ يَتَهَجَّدُ قَالَ " اللَّهُمَّ لَكَ الْحَمْدُ أَنْتَ قَيِّمُ السَّمَوَاتِ وَالأَرْضِ وَمَنْ فِيهِنَّ وَلَكَ الْحَمْدُ، لَكَ مُلْكُ السَّمَوَاتِ وَالأَرْضِ وَمَنْ فِيهِنَّ، وَلَكَ الْحَمْدُ أَنْتَ نُورُ السَّمَوَاتِ وَالأَرْضِ، وَلَكَ الْحَمْدُ أَنْتَ الْحَقُّ، وَوَعْدُكَ الْحَقُّ، وَلِقَاؤُكَ حَقٌّ، وَقَوْلُكَ حَقٌّ، وَالْجَنَّةُ حَقٌّ، وَالنَّارُ حَقٌّ، وَالنَّبِيُّونَ حَقٌّ، وَمُحَمَّدٌ صلى الله عليه وسلم حَقٌّ، وَالسَّاعَةُ حَقٌّ، اللَّهُمَّ لَكَ أَسْلَمْتُ، وَبِكَ آمَنْتُ وَعَلَيْكَ تَوَكَّلْتُ، وَإِلَيْكَ أَنَبْتُ، وَبِكَ خَاصَمْتُ، وَإِلَيْكَ حَاكَمْتُ، فَاغْفِرْ لِي مَا قَدَّمْتُ وَمَا أَخَّرْتُ، وَمَا أَسْرَرْتُ وَمَا أَعْلَنْتُ، أَنْتَ الْمُقَدِّمُ وَأَنْتَ الْمُؤَخِّرُ، لاَ إِلَهَ إِلاَّ أَنْتَ ـ أَوْ لاَ إِلَهَ غَيْرُكَ ـ ". قَالَ سُفْيَانُ وَزَادَ عَبْدُ الْكَرِيمِ أَبُو أُمَيَّةَ " وَلاَ حَوْلَ وَلاَ قُوَّةَ إِلاَّ بِاللَّهِ ". قَالَ سُفْيَانُ قَالَ سُلَيْمَانُ بْنُ أَبِي مُسْلِمٍ سَمِعَهُ مِنْ طَاوُسٍ عَنِ ابْنِ عَبَّاسٍ ـ رضى الله عنهما ـ عَنِ النَّبِيِّ صلى الله عليه وسلم.

Narrated 'Ubada bin As-Samit: The Prophet ﷺ Whoever gets up at night and says: -- 'La ilaha il-lallah Wahdahu la Sharika lahu Lahu-lmulk, waLahu-l-hamd wahuwa 'ala kullishai'in Qadir. Al hamdu lil-lahi wa subhanal-lahi wa la-ilaha il-lal-lah wa-l-lahu akbar wa la hawla Wala Quwata il-la-bil-lah.' (None has the right to be worshipped but Allah. He is the Only One and has no partners . For Him is the Kingdom and all the praises are due for Him. He is Omnipotent. All the praises are for Allah. All the glories are for Allah. And none has the right to be worshipped but Allah, And Allah is Great And there is neither Might nor Power Except with Allah). And then says: -- Allahumma, Ighfir li (O Allah! Forgive me). Or invokes (Allah), he will be responded to and if he performs ablution (and prays), his prayer will be accepted.". – Sahih al-Bukhari 1154
حَدَّثَنَا صَدَقَةُ بْنُ الْفَضْلِ، أَخْبَرَنَا الْوَلِيدُ، عَنِ الأَوْزَاعِيِّ، قَالَ حَدَّثَنِي عُمَيْرُ بْنُ هَانِئٍ، قَالَ حَدَّثَنِي جُنَادَةُ بْنُ أَبِي أُمَيَّةَ، حَدَّثَنِي عُبَادَةُ بْنُ الصَّامِتِ، عَنِ النَّبِيِّ صلى الله عليه وسلم قَالَ " مَنْ تَعَارَّ مِنَ اللَّيْلِ فَقَالَ لاَ إِلَهَ إِلاَّ اللَّهُ وَحْدَهُ لاَ شَرِيكَ لَهُ، لَهُ الْمُلْكُ، وَلَهُ الْحَمْدُ، وَهُوَ عَلَى كُلِّ شَىْءٍ قَدِيرٌ. الْحَمْدُ لِلَّهِ، وَسُبْحَانَ اللَّهِ، وَلاَ إِلَهَ إِلاَّ اللَّهُ، وَاللَّهُ أَكْبَرُ، وَلاَ حَوْلَ وَلاَ قُوَّةَ إِلاَّ بِاللَّهِ. ثُمَّ قَالَ اللَّهُمَّ اغْفِرْ لِي. أَوْ دَعَا اسْتُجِيبَ، فَإِنْ تَوَضَّأَ وَصَلَّى قُبِلَتْ صَلاَتُهُ ".

Narrated Jabir bin `Abdullah: The Prophet ﷺ used to teach us the way of doing Istikhara (Istikhara means to ask Allah to guide one to the right sort of action concerning any job or a deed), in all matters as he taught us the Suras of the Qur'an. He said, "If anyone of you thinks of doing any job he should offer a two rak`at prayer other than the compulsory ones and say (after the prayer): -- 'Allahumma inni astakhiruka bi'ilmika, Wa astaqdiruka bi-qudratika, Wa as'alaka min fadlika Al-`azlm Fa-innaka taqdiru Wala aqdiru, Wa ta'lamu Wala a'lamu, Wa anta 'allamu l-ghuyub. Allahumma, in kunta ta'lam anna hadha-lamra Khairun li fi dini wa ma'ashi wa'aqibati `Amri (or 'ajili `Amri wa'ajilihi) Faqdirhu wa yas-sirhu li thumma barik li

Fihi, Wa in kunta ta'lamu anna hadha-lamra shar-run li fi dini wa ma'ashi wa'aqibati `Amri (or fi'ajili `Amri wa ajilihi) Fasrifhu anni was-rifni anhu. Waqdir li al-khaira haithu kana Thumma ardini bihi.' (O Allah! I ask guidance from Your knowledge, And Power from Your Might and I ask for Your great blessings. You are capable and I am not. You know and I do not and You know the unseen. O Allah! If You know that this job is good for my religion and my subsistence and in my Hereafter—(or said: If it is better for my present and later needs)—Then You ordain it for me and make it easy for me to get, And then bless me in it, and if You know that this job is harmful to me In my religion and subsistence and in the Hereafter—(or said: If it is worse for my present and later needs)—Then keep it away from me and let me be away from it. And ordain for me whatever is good for me, And make me satisfied with it). The Prophetﷺ added that then the person should name (mention) his need. – Sahih al-Bukhari 1166

حَدَّثَنَا قُتَيْبَةُ، قَالَ حَدَّثَنَا عَبْدُ الرَّحْمَنِ بْنُ أَبِي الْمَوَالِي، عَنْ مُحَمَّدِ بْنِ الْمُنْكَدِرِ، عَنْ جَابِرِ بْنِ عَبْدِ اللَّهِ ـ رضى الله عنهما ـ قَالَ كَانَ رَسُولُ اللَّهِ صلى الله عليه وسلم يُعَلِّمُنَا الاِسْتِخَارَةَ فِي الأُمُورِ كَمَا يُعَلِّمُنَا السُّورَةَ مِنَ الْقُرْآنِ يَقُولُ " إِذَا هَمَّ أَحَدُكُمْ بِالأَمْرِ فَلْيَرْكَعْ رَكْعَتَيْنِ مِنْ غَيْرِ الْفَرِيضَةِ ثُمَّ لِيَقُلِ اللَّهُمَّ إِنِّي أَسْتَخِيرُكَ بِعِلْمِكَ وَأَسْتَقْدِرُكَ بِقُدْرَتِكَ، وَأَسْأَلُكَ مِنْ فَضْلِكَ الْعَظِيمِ، فَإِنَّكَ تَقْدِرُ وَلاَ أَقْدِرُ وَتَعْلَمُ وَلاَ أَعْلَمُ وَأَنْتَ عَلاَّمُ الْغُيُوبِ، اللَّهُمَّ إِنْ كُنْتَ تَعْلَمُ أَنَّ هَذَا الأَمْرَ خَيْرٌ لِي فِي دِينِي وَمَعَاشِي وَعَاقِبَةِ أَمْرِي ـ أَوْ قَالَ عَاجِلِ أَمْرِي وَآجِلِهِ ـ فَاقْدُرْهُ لِي وَيَسِّرْهُ لِي ثُمَّ بَارِكْ لِي فِيهِ، وَإِنْ كُنْتَ تَعْلَمُ أَنَّ هَذَا الأَمْرَ شَرٌّ لِي فِي دِينِي وَمَعَاشِي وَعَاقِبَةِ أَمْرِي ـ أَوْ قَالَ فِي عَاجِلِ أَمْرِي وَآجِلِهِ ـ فَاصْرِفْهُ عَنِّي وَاصْرِفْنِي عَنْهُ، وَاقْدُرْ لِي الْخَيْرَ حَيْثُ كَانَ ثُمَّ أَرْضِنِي بِهِ ـ قَالَ ـ وَيُسَمِّي حَاجَتَهُ ".

The Book of

Know you not that to Allah (Alone) belongs the dominion of the heavens and the earth!

أَلَمْ تَعْلَمْ أَنَّ ٱللَّهَ لَهُۥ مُلْكُ ٱلسَّمَـٰوَٰتِ وَٱلْأَرْضِ

His ﷺ statement: "The kingdom Belongs to none but Allah." So the Prophet ﷺ described Allāh as the Absolute King, the Only Real King. He also mentioned about the kings (saying): "(She said) Verily kings, when they enter a town, they despoil it..." (V.27:34) –Al-Bukhari Vol.8 page 116

كقوله "لا ملك الا الله" ، فوصفه بانتهاءالملك ، ثم ذكر الملوك ايصا فقال : "إِنَّ ٱلْمُلُوكَ إِذَا دَخَلُوا۟ قَرْيَةً أَفْسَدُوهَا"

Narrated Abu Huraira: I heard Allah's Messenger ﷺ saying, "Allah will hold the whole earth, and roll all the heavens up in His Right Hand, and then He will say, 'I am the King; where are the kings of the earth?"' – Al-Bukhari 4812

حَدَّثَنَا سَعِيدُ بْنُ عُفَيْرٍ، قَالَ حَدَّثَنِي اللَّيْثُ، قَالَ حَدَّثَنِي عَبْدُ الرَّحْمَنِ بْنُ خَالِدِ بْنِ مُسَافِرٍ، عَنِ ابْنِ شِهَابٍ، عَنْ أَبِي سَلَمَةَ، أَنَّ أَبَا هُرَيْرَةَ، قَالَ سَمِعْتُ رَسُولَ اللَّهِ صلى الله عليه وسلم يَقُولُ " يَقْبِضُ اللَّهُ الأَرْضَ، وَيَطْوِي السَّمَوَاتِ بِيَمِينِهِ، ثُمَّ يَقُولُ أَنَا الْمَلِكُ، أَيْنَ مُلُوكُ الأَرْضِ ".

Narrated Abu Huraira: Allah's Messenger ﷺ said, "The most awful name in Allah's sight on the Day of Resurrection, will be (that of) a man calling himself Malik Al-Amlak (the king of kings). - Al-Bukhari 6205

حَدَّثَنَا أَبُو الْيَمَانِ، أَخْبَرَنَا شُعَيْبٌ، حَدَّثَنَا أَبُو الزِّنَادِ، عَنِ الأَعْرَجِ، عَنْ أَبِي هُرَيْرَةَ، قَالَ قَالَ رَسُولُ اللَّهِ صلى الله عليه وسلم " أَخْنَى الأَسْمَاءِ يَوْمَ الْقِيَامَةِ عِنْدَ اللَّهِ رَجُلٌ تَسَمَّى مَلِكَ الأَمْلاَكِ "

Narrated Abu Huraira: Allah's Messenger ﷺ said, "(The Prophet) Abraham migrated with his wife Sarah till he reached a town where there was a king or a tyrant who sent a message, to Abraham, ordering him to send Sarah to him. So when Abraham had sent Sarah, the tyrant got up, intending to do evil with her, but she got up and performed ablution and prayed and said, 'O Allah ! If I have believed in You and in Your Apostle, then do not empower this oppressor over me.' So he (the king) had an epileptic fit and started moving his legs violently. " – Al-Bukhari 6950

حَدَّثَنَا أَبُو الْيَمَانِ، حَدَّثَنَا شُعَيْبٌ، حَدَّثَنَا أَبُو الزِّنَادِ، عَنِ الأَعْرَجِ، عَنْ أَبِي هُرَيْرَةَ، قَالَ قَالَ رَسُولُ اللَّهِ صلى الله عليه وسلم " هَاجَرَ إِبْرَاهِيمُ بِسَارَةَ، دَخَلَ بِهَا قَرْيَةً فِيهَا مَلِكٌ مِنَ الْمُلُوكِ أَوْ جَبَّارٌ مِنَ الْجَبَابِرَةِ، فَأَرْسَلَ إِلَيْهِ أَنْ أَرْسِلْ إِلَيَّ بِهَا. فَأَرْسَلَ بِهَا، فَقَامَ إِلَيْهَا فَقَامَتْ تَوَضَّأُ وَتُصَلِّي فَقَالَتِ اللَّهُمَّ إِنْ كُنْتُ آمَنْتُ بِكَ وَبِرَسُولِكَ فَلاَ تُسَلِّطْ عَلَىَّ الْكَافِرَ، فَغُطَّ حَتَّى رَكَضَ بِرِجْلِهِ ".

He merges the night into the day, and He merges the day into the night; and He regulates the sun and the moon, each running for a stated term. Such is Allah, your Lord; His is the sovereignty. As for those you call upon besides Him, they do not possess a speck. – Surah Fatir 35:13

يُولِجُ ٱلَّيْلَ فِى ٱلنَّهَارِ وَيُولِجُ ٱلنَّهَارَ فِى ٱلَّيْلِ وَسَخَّرَ ٱلشَّمْسَ وَٱلْقَمَرَ كُلٌّ يَجْرِى لِأَجَلٍ مُّسَمًّى ذَٰلِكُمُ ٱللَّهُ رَبُّكُمْ لَهُ ٱلْمُلْكُ وَٱلَّذِينَ تَدْعُونَ مِن دُونِهِۦ مَا يَمْلِكُونَ مِن قِطْمِيرٍ

To Him belongs the kingdom of the heavens and the earth. He gives life and causes death, and He has power over all things. – Surah Al-Hadid 57:2

لَهُۥ مُلْكُ ٱلسَّمَـٰوَٰتِ وَٱلْأَرْضِ يُحْىِۦ وَيُمِيتُ وَهُوَ عَلَىٰ كُلِّ شَىْءٍ قَدِيرٌ

To Him belongs the kingship of the heavens and the earth, and to Allah all matters are referred. – Surah Al-Hadid 57:5

لَّهُۥ مُلْكُ ٱلسَّمَـٰوَٰتِ وَٱلْأَرْضِ ۚ وَإِلَى ٱللَّهِ تُرْجَعُ ٱلْأُمُورُ

He created you from one person, then made from it its mate, and brought down livestock for you— eight kinds in pairs. He creates you in the wombs of your mothers, in successive formations, in a triple darkness. Such is Allah, your Lord. His is the kingdom. There is no god but He. So what made you deviate? – Surah Az-Zumar 39:6

خَلَقَكُم مِّن نَّفْسٍ وَٰحِدَةٍ ثُمَّ جَعَلَ مِنْهَا زَوْجَهَا وَأَنزَلَ لَكُم مِّنَ ٱلْأَنْعَـٰمِ ثَمَـٰنِيَةَ أَزْوَٰجٍ ۚ يَخْلُقُكُمْ فِى بُطُونِ أُمَّهَـٰتِكُمْ خَلْقًا مِّنۢ بَعْدِ خَلْقٍ فِى ظُلُمَـٰتٍ ثَلَـٰثٍ ۚ ذَٰلِكُمُ ٱللَّهُ رَبُّكُمْ لَهُ ٱلْمُلْكُ ۖ لَآ إِلَـٰهَ إِلَّا هُوَ ۖ فَأَنَّىٰ تُصْرَفُونَ

Everything in the heavens and the earth glorifies Allah the Sovereign, the Holy, the Almighty, the Wise. – Surah Al-Jumu'ah 62:1

يُسَبِّحُ لِلَّهِ مَا فِى ٱلسَّمَـٰوَٰتِ وَمَا فِى ٱلْأَرْضِ ٱلْمَلِكِ ٱلْقُدُّوسِ ٱلْعَزِيزِ ٱلْحَكِيمِ

The Day when they will emerge, nothing about them will be concealed from Allah. "To whom does the sovereignty belong today?" "To Allah, the One, the Irresistible." – Surah Ghafir 40:16

يَوْمَ هُم بَـٰرِزُونَ ۖ لَا يَخْفَىٰ عَلَى ٱللَّهِ مِنْهُمْ شَىْءٌ ۚ لِّمَنِ ٱلْمُلْكُ ٱلْيَوْمَ ۖ لِلَّهِ ٱلْوَٰحِدِ ٱلْقَهَّارِ

So Exalted is Allah, the Ruler, the Real. There is no god except He, the Lord of the Noble Throne. – Surah Al-Mu'minun 23:116

فَتَعَـٰلَى ٱللَّهُ ٱلْمَلِكُ ٱلْحَقُّ ۖ لَآ إِلَـٰهَ إِلَّا هُوَ رَبُّ ٱلْعَرْشِ ٱلْكَرِيمِ

Blessed is He in whose hand is the sovereignty, and Who has power over everything. – Surah Al-Mulk 67:1

تَبَـٰرَكَ ٱلَّذِى بِيَدِهِ ٱلْمُلْكُ وَهُوَ عَلَىٰ كُلِّ شَىْءٍ قَدِيرٌ

Narrated Jabir bin `Abdullah: As-Salami: Allah's Messenger ﷺ used to teach his companions to perform the prayer of Istikhara for each and every matter just as he used to teach them the Suras from the Qur'an He used to say, "If anyone of you intends to do some thing, he should offer a two rak`at prayer other than the compulsory prayers, and after finishing it, he should say: O Allah! I consult You, for You have all knowledge, and appeal to You to support me with Your Power and ask for Your Bounty, for You are able to do things while I am not, and You know while I do not; and You are the Knower of the Unseen. O Allah If You know It this matter (name your matter) is good for me both at present and in the future, (or in my religion), in my this life and in the Hereafter, then fulfill it for me and make it easy for me, and then bestow Your Blessings on me in that matter. O Allah! If You know that this matter is not good for me in my religion, in my this life and in my coming Hereafter (or at present or in the future), then divert me from it and choose for me what is good wherever it may be, and make me be pleased with it." (See Hadith No. 391, Vol. 8). – Sahih Al-Bukhari 7390

حَدَّثَنِي إِبْرَاهِيمُ بْنُ الْمُنْذِرِ، حَدَّثَنَا مَعْنُ بْنُ عِيسَى، حَدَّثَنِي عَبْدُ الرَّحْمَنِ بْنُ أَبِي الْمَوَالِي، قَالَ سَمِعْتُ مُحَمَّدَ بْنَ الْمُنْكَدِرِ، يُحَدِّثُ عَبْدَ اللَّهِ بْنَ الْحَسَنِ يَقُولُ أَخْبَرَنِي جَابِرُ بْنُ عَبْدِ اللَّهِ السَّلَمِيُّ، قَالَ كَانَ رَسُولُ اللَّهِ صلى الله عليه وسلم يُعَلِّمُ أَصْحَابَهُ الاِسْتِخَارَةَ فِي الأُمُورِ كُلِّهَا، كَمَا يُعَلِّمُ السُّورَةَ مِنَ الْقُرْآنِ يَقُولُ " إِذَا هَمَّ أَحَدُكُمْ بِالأَمْرِ فَلْيَرْكَعْ رَكْعَتَيْنِ مِنْ غَيْرِ الْفَرِيضَةِ ثُمَّ لِيَقُلِ اللَّهُمَّ إِنِّي أَسْتَخِيرُكَ بِعِلْمِكَ، وَأَسْتَقْدِرُكَ بِقُدْرَتِكَ، وَأَسْأَلُكَ مِنْ فَضْلِكَ، فَإِنَّكَ تَقْدِرُ وَلاَ أَقْدِرُ، وَتَعْلَمُ وَلاَ أَعْلَمُ، وَأَنْتَ عَلاَّمُ الْغُيُوبِ، اللَّهُمَّ فَإِنْ كُنْتَ تَعْلَمُ هَذَا الأَمْرَ - ثُمَّ تُسَمِّيهِ بِعَيْنِهِ - خَيْرًا لِي فِي عَاجِلِ أَمْرِي وَآجِلِهِ - قَالَ أَوْ فِي دِينِي وَمَعَاشِي وَعَاقِبَةِ أَمْرِي - فَاقْدُرْهُ لِي، وَيَسِّرْهُ لِي، ثُمَّ بَارِكْ لِي فِيهِ، اللَّهُمَّ وَإِنْ كُنْتَ تَعْلَمُ أَنَّهُ شَرٌّ لِي فِي دِينِي وَمَعَاشِي وَعَاقِبَةِ أَمْرِي - أَوْ قَالَ فِي عَاجِلِ أَمْرِي وَآجِلِهِ - فَاصْرِفْنِي عَنْهُ، وَاقْدُرْ لِيَ الْخَيْرَ حَيْثُ كَانَ، ثُمَّ رَضِّنِي بِهِ ".

Narrated `Abdullah :A (Jewish) Rabbi came to Allah's Messenger ﷺ and he said, "O Muhammad! We learn that Allah will put all the heavens on one finger, and the earths on one finger, and the trees on one finger, and the water and the dust on one finger, and all the other created beings on one finger. Then He will say, 'I am the King.' Thereupon the Prophet ﷺ smiled so that his pre-molar teeth became visible, and that was the confirmation of the Rabbi. Then Allah's Messenger ﷺ recited: 'They made not a just estimate of Allah such as is due to Him. And on the Day of Resurrection the whole of the earth will be grasped by His Hand and the heavens will be rolled up in His Right Hand. Glorified is He, and High is He above all that they associate as partners with Him.' (39.67). – Sahih Al-Bukhari 4811

حَدَّثَنَا آدَمُ، حَدَّثَنَا شَيْبَانُ، عَنْ مَنْصُورٍ، عَنْ إِبْرَاهِيمَ، عَنْ عَبِيدَةَ، عَنْ عَبْدِ اللَّهِ ـ رضى الله عنه ـ قَالَ جَاءَ حَبْرٌ مِنَ الأَحْبَارِ إِلَى رَسُولِ اللَّهِ صلى الله عليه وسلم فَقَالَ يَا مُحَمَّدُ، إِنَّا نَجِدُ أَنَّ اللَّهَ يَجْعَلُ السَّمَوَاتِ عَلَى إِصْبَعٍ وَالأَرَضِينَ عَلَى إِصْبَعٍ، وَالشَّجَرَ عَلَى إِصْبَعٍ، وَالْمَاءَ وَالثَّرَى عَلَى إِصْبَعٍ، وَسَائِرَ الْخَلاَئِقِ عَلَى إِصْبَعٍ، فَيَقُولُ أَنَا الْمَلِكُ. فَضَحِكَ النَّبِيُّ صلى الله عليه وسلم حَتَّى بَدَتْ نَوَاجِذُهُ تَصْدِيقًا لِقَوْلِ الْحَبْرِ ثُمَّ قَرَأَ رَسُولُ اللَّهِ صلى الله عليه وسلم {وَمَا قَدَرُوا اللَّهَ حَقَّ قَدْرِهِ وَالأَرْضُ جَمِيعًا قَبْضَتُهُ يَوْمَ الْقِيَامَةِ وَالسَّمَوَاتُ مَطْوِيَّاتٌ بِيَمِينِهِ سُبْحَانَهُ وَتَعَالَى عَمَّا يُشْرِكُونَ}

Narrated `Abdullah bin `Umar: The Talbiya of Allah's Messenge ﷺ r was : 'Labbaika Allahumma labbaik, Labbaika la sharika Laka labbaik, Inna-l-hamda wan-ni'mata Laka walmulk, La sharika Laka' (I respond to Your call O Allah, I respond to Your call, and I am obedient to Your orders, You have no partner, I respond to Your call All the praises and blessings are for You, All the sovereignty is for You, And You have no partners with you. – Sahih al-Bukhari 1549

حَدَّثَنَا عَبْدُ اللَّهِ بْنُ يُوسُفَ، أَخْبَرَنَا مَالِكٌ، عَنْ نَافِعٍ، عَنْ عَبْدِ اللَّهِ بْنِ عُمَرَ ـ رضى الله عنهما ـ أَنَّ تَلْبِيَةَ، رَسُولِ اللَّهِ صلى الله عليه وسلم لَبَّيْكَ اللَّهُمَّ لَبَّيْكَ، لَبَّيْكَ لاَ شَرِيكَ لَكَ لَبَّيْكَ، إِنَّ الْحَمْدَ وَالنِّعْمَةَ لَكَ وَالْمُلْكَ، لاَ شَرِيكَ لَكَ

The Book of
No calamity befalls on the earth or in yourselves but is inscribed in the Book before We bring it into existence.
مَآ أَصَابَ مِن مُّصِيبَةٍ فِى ٱلْأَرْضِ وَلَا فِىٓ أَنفُسِكُمْ إِلَّا فِى كِتَـٰبٍ مِّن قَبْلِ أَن نَّبْرَأَهَآ

Everything We created is precisely measured. – Surah Al-Qamar 54:49
إِنَّا كُلَّ شَىْءٍ خَلَقْنَـٰهُ بِقَدَرٍ

No disaster occurs except by Allah's leave. Whoever believes in Allah, He guides his heart. Allah is Aware of everything. . – Surah At-Taghabun 64:11
مَآ أَصَابَ مِن مُّصِيبَةٍ إِلَّا بِإِذْنِ ٱللَّهِ ۗ وَمَن يُؤْمِنۢ بِٱللَّهِ يَهْدِ قَلْبَهُۥ ۚ وَٱللَّهُ بِكُلِّ شَىْءٍ عَلِيمٌ

Narrated `Ali: While the Prophet ﷺ was in a funeral procession, he took a small stick and started scraping the earth with it and said, "There is none among you but has his place written for him, either in the Hell Fire or in Paradise." They (the people) said, "Allah's Messenger ﷺ ! Shall we depend on this (and leave work)?" He replied. "Carry on doing (good deeds), for everybody will find easy (to do) such deeds as will lead him to his destined place." The Prophet ﷺ then recited:-- 'As for him who gives (in charity) and keeps his duty to Allah, and believes in the Best Reward.'.....(92.5-10) – Al-Bukhari 4946
حَدَّثَنَا بِشْرُ بْنُ خَالِدٍ، أَخْبَرَنَا مُحَمَّدُ بْنُ جَعْفَرٍ، حَدَّثَنَا شُعْبَةُ، عَنْ سُلَيْمَانَ، عَنْ سَعْدِ بْنِ عُبَيْدَةَ، عَنْ أَبِي عَبْدِ الرَّحْمَنِ السُّلَمِيِّ، عَنْ عَلِيٍّ ـ رضى الله عنه ـ عَنِ النَّبِيِّ صلى الله عليه وسلم. أَنَّهُ كَانَ فِي جَنَازَةٍ فَأَخَذَ عُودًا يَنْكُتُ فِي الأَرْضِ فَقَالَ " مَا مِنْكُمْ مِنْ أَحَدٍ إِلاَّ وَقَدْ كُتِبَ مَقْعَدُهُ مِنَ النَّارِ أَوْ مِنَ الْجَنَّةِ ". قَالُوا يَا رَسُولَ اللَّهِ أَفَلاَ نَتَّكِلُ قَالَ " اعْمَلُوا فَكُلٌّ مُيَسَّرٌ {فَأَمَّا مَنْ أَعْطَى وَاتَّقَى * وَصَدَّقَ بِالْحُسْنَى} الآيَةَ. قَالَ شُعْبَةُ وَحَدَّثَنِي بِهِ مَنْصُورٌ فَلَمْ أُنْكِرْهُ مِنْ حَدِيثِ سُلَيْمَانَ".

"There is not one of us but has an assigned position. – Surah As-Saffat 37:164
إِلَّا مَنْ هُوَ صَالِ ٱلْجَحِيمِ وَمَا مِنَّآ إِلَّا لَهُۥ مَقَامٌ مَّعْلُومٌ

Narrated `Abdullah bin Mus'ud: Allah's Messenger ﷺ , the true and truly inspired said, "(The matter of the Creation of) a human being is put together in the womb of the mother in forty days, and then he becomes a clot of thick blood for a similar period, and then a piece of flesh for a similar period. Then Allah sends an angel who is ordered to write four things. He is ordered to write down his (i.e. the new creature's) deeds, his livelihood, his (date of) death, and whether he will be blessed or wretched (in religion). Then the soul is breathed into him. So, a man amongst you may do (good deeds till there is only a cubit between him and Paradise and then what has been written for him decides his behavior and he starts doing (evil) deeds characteristic of the people of the (Hell) Fire. And similarly a man amongst you may do (evil) deeds till there is only a cubit between him and the (Hell) Fire, and then what has been written for him decides his behavior, and he starts doing deeds characteristic of the people of Paradise." – Al-Bukhari 3208
حَدَّثَنَا الْحَسَنُ بْنُ الرَّبِيعِ، حَدَّثَنَا أَبُو الأَحْوَصِ، عَنِ الأَعْمَشِ، عَنْ زَيْدِ بْنِ وَهْبٍ، قَالَ عَبْدُ اللَّهِ حَدَّثَنَا رَسُولُ اللَّهِ صلى الله عليه وسلم وَهْوَ الصَّادِقُ الْمَصْدُوقُ قَالَ " إِنَّ أَحَدَكُمْ يُجْمَعُ خَلْقُهُ فِي بَطْنِ أُمِّهِ أَرْبَعِينَ يَوْمًا، ثُمَّ يَكُونُ عَلَقَةً مِثْلَ ذَلِكَ، ثُمَّ يَكُونُ مُضْغَةً مِثْلَ ذَلِكَ، ثُمَّ يَبْعَثُ اللَّهُ مَلَكًا، فَيُؤْمَرُ بِأَرْبَعِ كَلِمَاتٍ، وَيُقَالُ لَهُ اكْتُبْ عَمَلَهُ وَرِزْقَهُ وَأَجَلَهُ وَشَقِيٌّ أَوْ سَعِيدٌ. ثُمَّ يُنْفَخُ فِيهِ الرُّوحُ، فَإِنَّ الرَّجُلَ مِنْكُمْ لَيَعْمَلُ حَتَّى مَا يَكُونُ بَيْنَهُ وَبَيْنَ الْجَنَّةِ إِلاَّ ذِرَاعٌ، فَيَسْبِقُ عَلَيْهِ كِتَابُهُ، فَيَعْمَلُ بِعَمَلِ أَهْلِ النَّارِ، وَيَعْمَلُ حَتَّى مَا يَكُونُ بَيْنَهُ وَبَيْنَ النَّارِ إِلاَّ ذِرَاعٌ، فَيَسْبِقُ عَلَيْهِ الْكِتَابُ، فَيَعْمَلُ بِعَمَلِ أَهْلِ الْجَنَّةِ "

Allah abolishes whatever He wills, and He affirms. With Him is the source of the Scripture. – Surah Ar-Ra'd 13:39

يَمْحُوا۟ ٱللَّهُ مَا يَشَآءُ وَيُثْبِتُ ۖ وَعِندَهُۥٓ أُمُّ ٱلْكِتَـٰبِ

With Him are the keys of the unseen; none knows them except He. And He knows everything on land and in the sea. Not a leaf falls but He knows it; and there is not a single grain in the darkness of earth, nor is there anything wet or dry, but is in a clear record. – Surah Al-An'am 6:59

وَعِندَهُۥ مَفَاتِحُ ٱلْغَيْبِ لَا يَعْلَمُهَآ إِلَّا هُوَ ۚ وَيَعْلَمُ مَا فِى ٱلْبَرِّ وَٱلْبَحْرِ ۚ وَمَا تَسْقُطُ مِن وَرَقَةٍ إِلَّا يَعْلَمُهَا وَلَا حَبَّةٍ فِى ظُلُمَـٰتِ
ٱلْأَرْضِ وَلَا رَطْبٍ وَلَا يَابِسٍ إِلَّا فِى كِتَـٰبٍ مُّبِينٍ

You do not get into any situation, nor do you recite any Quran, nor do you do anything, but We are watching over you as you undertake it. Not even the weight of an atom, on earth or in the sky, escapes your Lord, nor is there anything smaller or larger, but is in a clear record. – Surah Yunus 10:61

وَمَا تَكُونُ فِى شَأْنٍ وَمَا تَتْلُوا۟ مِنْهُ مِن قُرْءَانٍ وَلَا تَعْمَلُونَ مِنْ عَمَلٍ إِلَّا كُنَّا عَلَيْكُمْ شُهُودًا إِذْ تُفِيضُونَ فِيهِ ۚ وَمَا يَعْزُبُ عَن
رَّبِّكَ مِن مِّثْقَالِ ذَرَّةٍ فِى ٱلْأَرْضِ وَلَا فِى ٱلسَّمَآءِ وَلَآ أَصْغَرَ مِن ذَٰلِكَ وَلَآ أَكْبَرَ إِلَّا فِى كِتَـٰبٍ مُّبِينٍ

No calamity occurs on earth, or in your souls, but it is in a Book, even before We make it happen. That is easy for Allah. – Surah Al-Hadid 57:22

مَآ أَصَابَ مِن مُّصِيبَةٍ فِى ٱلْأَرْضِ وَلَا فِىٓ أَنفُسِكُمْ إِلَّا فِى كِتَـٰبٍ مِّن قَبْلِ أَن نَّبْرَأَهَآ ۚ إِنَّ ذَٰلِكَ عَلَى ٱللَّهِ يَسِيرٌ

Do you not know that Allah knows everything in the heavens and the earth? This is in a book. That is easy for Allah. – Surah Al-Hajj 22:70

أَلَمْ تَعْلَمْ أَنَّ ٱللَّهَ يَعْلَمُ مَا فِى ٱلسَّمَآءِ وَٱلْأَرْضِ ۗ إِنَّ ذَٰلِكَ فِى كِتَـٰبٍ ۚ إِنَّ ذَٰلِكَ عَلَى ٱللَّهِ يَسِيرٌ

And will provide for him from where he never expected. Whoever relies on Allah—He will suffice him. Allah will accomplish His purpose. Allah has set a measure to all things. – Surah At-Talaq 65:3

وَيَرْزُقْهُ مِنْ حَيْثُ لَا يَحْتَسِبُ ۚ وَمَن يَتَوَكَّلْ عَلَى ٱللَّهِ فَهُوَ حَسْبُهُۥٓ ۚ إِنَّ ٱللَّهَ بَـٰلِغُ أَمْرِهِۦ ۚ قَدْ جَعَلَ ٱللَّهُ لِكُلِّ شَىْءٍ قَدْرًا

He to whom belongs the kingdom of the heavens and the earth, who took to Himself no son, who never had a partner in His kingship; who created everything and determined its measure. – Surah Al-Furqan 25:2

ٱلَّذِى لَهُۥ مُلْكُ ٱلسَّمَـٰوَٰتِ وَٱلْأَرْضِ وَلَمْ يَتَّخِذْ وَلَدًا وَلَمْ يَكُن لَّهُۥ شَرِيكٌ فِى ٱلْمُلْكِ وَخَلَقَ كُلَّ شَىْءٍ فَقَدَّرَهُۥ تَقْدِيرًا

It is He who created you. Some of you are unbelievers, and some of you are believers. And Allah perceives what you do. – Surah At-Taghabun 64:2

هُوَ ٱلَّذِى خَلَقَكُمْ فَمِنكُمْ كَافِرٌ وَمِنكُم مُّؤْمِنٌ ۚ وَٱللَّهُ بِمَا تَعْمَلُونَ بَصِيرٌ

If Allah afflicts you with harm, none can remove it except He. And if He wants good for you, none can repel His grace. He makes it reach whomever He wills of His servants. He is the Forgiver, the Merciful. Surah Yunus 10:107

وَإِن يَمْسَسْكَ ٱللَّهُ بِضُرٍّ فَلَا كَاشِفَ لَهُۥٓ إِلَّا هُوَ ۖ وَإِن يُرِدْكَ بِخَيْرٍ فَلَا رَآدَّ لِفَضْلِهِۦ ۚ يُصِيبُ بِهِۦ مَن يَشَآءُ مِنْ عِبَادِهِۦ ۚ وَهُوَ
ٱلْغَفُورُ ٱلرَّحِيمُ

The Originator of the heavens and the Earth. When He decrees something, He simply says to it, "Be!" and it is. – Surah Al-Baqarah 2:117

بَدِيعُ ٱلسَّمَـٰوَٰتِ وَٱلْأَرْضِ ۖ وَإِذَا قَضَىٰٓ أَمْرًا فَإِنَّمَا يَقُولُ لَهُۥ كُن فَيَكُونُ

Do they look for (nothing) except that Allah will come up to them in the overshadowings of mist, and the Angels? And the Command is accomplished and to Allah (all) the Commands are returned. – Surah Al-Baqarah 2:210

هَلْ يَنظُرُونَ إِلَّآ أَن يَأْتِيَهُمُ ٱللَّهُ فِى ظُلَلٍ مِّنَ ٱلْغَمَامِ وَٱلْمَلَـٰٓئِكَةُ وَقُضِىَ ٱلْأَمْرُ ۚ وَإِلَى ٱللَّهِ تُرْجَعُ ٱلْأُمُورُ

He is (The One) Who created you of clay, thereafter He decreed a term, and a term is stated in His Sight; thereafter you wrangle about that. – Surah Al-An'am 6:2

هُوَ ٱلَّذِى خَلَقَكُم مِّن طِينٍ ثُمَّ قَضَىٰٓ أَجَلًا ۖ وَأَجَلٌ مُّسَمًّى عِندَهُۥ ۖ ثُمَّ أَنتُمْ تَمْتَرُونَ

And if Allah were to hasten (quickly) to mankind evil as they would seek hastening of charity, their term would indeed be decreed to them. Yet We leave out the ones who do not hope for meeting with Us, in their inordinance blundering. Surah Yunus 10:11

وَلَوْ يُعَجِّلُ ٱللَّهُ لِلنَّاسِ ٱلشَّرَّ ٱسْتِعْجَالَهُم بِٱلْخَيْرِ لَقُضِىَ إِلَيْهِمْ أَجَلُهُمْ ۖ فَنَذَرُ ٱلَّذِينَ لَا يَرْجُونَ لِقَآءَنَا فِى طُغْيَـٰنِهِمْ يَعْمَهُونَ

No soul can ever die except by Allah's leave and at a term appointed….. – Surah Al-Imran 3:145

وَمَا كَانَ لِنَفْسٍ أَن تَمُوتَ إِلَّا بِإِذْنِ ٱللَّهِ كِتَـٰبًا مُّؤَجَّلًا ۗ

That is of the tidings of the Unseen that We reveal to you; in no way did you (yourself) know it, neither your people, even before this. So (endure) patiently; surely the (fair) end is for the pious. Surah Hud 11:49

تِلْكَ مِنْ أَنۢبَآءِ ٱلْغَيْبِ نُوحِيهَآ إِلَيْكَ ۖ مَا كُنتَ تَعْلَمُهَآ أَنتَ وَلَا قَوْمُكَ مِن قَبْلِ هَـٰذَا ۖ فَٱصْبِرْ ۖ إِنَّ ٱلْعَـٰقِبَةَ لِلْمُتَّقِينَ

The Book of
and that you must magnify Allah for having guided you so that you may be grateful to Him
وَلِتُكَبِّرُوا۟ ٱللَّهَ عَلَىٰ مَا هَدَىٰكُمْ وَلَعَلَّكُمْ تَشْكُرُونَ

Have you not seen how the ships sail through the sea, by the grace of Allah, to show you of His wonders? In that are signs for every persevering, thankful person. – Surah Luqman 31:31
أَلَمْ تَرَ أَنَّ ٱلْفُلْكَ تَجْرِى فِى ٱلْبَحْرِ بِنِعْمَتِ ٱللَّهِ لِيُرِيَكُم مِّنْ ءَايَـٰتِهِۦٓ ۚ إِنَّ فِى ذَٰلِكَ لَـَٔايَـٰتٍ لِّكُلِّ صَبَّارٍ شَكُورٍ

The two seas are not the same. One is fresh, sweet, good to drink, while the other is salty and bitter. Yet from each you eat tender meat, and extract jewelry which you wear. And you see the ships plowing through them, so that you may seek of His bounty, so that you may give thanks. – Surah Al-Fatir 35:12
وَمَا يَسْتَوِى ٱلْبَحْرَانِ هَـٰذَا عَذْبٌ فُرَاتٌ سَآئِغٌ شَرَابُهُۥ وَهَـٰذَا مِلْحٌ أُجَاجٌ ۖ وَمِن كُلٍّ تَأْكُلُونَ لَحْمًا طَرِيًّا وَتَسْتَخْرِجُونَ حِلْيَةً تَلْبَسُونَهَا ۖ وَتَرَى ٱلْفُلْكَ فِيهِ مَوَاخِرَ لِتَبْتَغُوا۟ مِن فَضْلِهِۦ وَلَعَلَّكُمْ تَشْكُرُونَ

If you disbelieve, Allah is Independent of you, yet He does not approve ingratitude on the part of His servants. And if you are thankful, He will approve that in you. No bearer of burden can bear the burden of another. Then to your Lord is your return; and He will inform you of what you used to do. He is aware of what the hearts contain. – Surah Az-Zumar 39:7
إِن تَكْفُرُوا۟ فَإِنَّ ٱللَّهَ غَنِىٌّ عَنكُمْ ۖ وَلَا يَرْضَىٰ لِعِبَادِهِ ٱلْكُفْرَ ۖ وَإِن تَشْكُرُوا۟ يَرْضَهُ لَكُمْ ۗ وَلَا تَزِرُ وَازِرَةٌ وِزْرَ أُخْرَىٰ ۗ ثُمَّ إِلَىٰ رَبِّكُم مَّرْجِعُكُمْ فَيُنَبِّئُكُم بِمَا كُنتُمْ تَعْمَلُونَ ۚ إِنَّهُۥ عَلِيمٌۢ بِذَاتِ ٱلصُّدُورِ

Narrated `Aisha: Whenever Allah's Messenger ﷺ paid a visit to a patient, or a patient was brought to him, he used to invoke Allah, saying, "Take away the disease, O the Lord of the people! Cure him as You are the One Who cures. There is no cure but Yours, a cure that leaves no disease." – Al-Bukhari 5675
حَدَّثَنَا مُوسَى بْنُ إِسْمَاعِيلَ، حَدَّثَنَا أَبُو عَوَانَةَ، عَنْ مَنْصُورٍ، عَنْ إِبْرَاهِيمَ، عَنْ مَسْرُوقٍ، عَنْ عَائِشَةَ ـ رضى الله عنها أَنَّ رَسُولَ اللَّهِ صلى الله عليه وسلم كَانَ إِذَا أَتَى مَرِيضًا ـ أَوْ أُتِيَ بِهِ ـ قَالَ " أَذْهِبِ الْبَاسَ رَبَّ النَّاسِ، اشْفِ وَأَنْتَ الشَّافِي لاَ شِفَاءَ إِلاَّ شِفَاؤُكَ، شِفَاءً لاَ يُغَادِرُ سَقَمًا ". قَالَ عَمْرُو بْنُ أَبِي قَيْسٍ وَإِبْرَاهِيمُ بْنُ طَهْمَانَ عَنْ مَنْصُورٍ عَنْ إِبْرَاهِيمَ وَأَبِي الضُّحَى إِذَا أُتِيَ بِالْمَرِيضِ، وَقَالَ جَرِيرٌ عَنْ مَنْصُورٍ عَنْ أَبِي الضُّحَى وَحْدَهُ، وَقَالَ إِذَا أَتَى مَرِيضًا.

Have they not seen that We created for them, of Our Handiwork, livestock that they own? And We subdued them for them. Some they ride, and some they eat. And they have in them other benefits, and drinks. Will they not give thanks? – Surah Ya-Sin 36:71-73
أَوَلَمْ يَرَوْا۟ أَنَّا خَلَقْنَا لَهُم مِّمَّا عَمِلَتْ أَيْدِينَآ أَنْعَـٰمًا فَهُمْ لَهَا مَـٰلِكُونَ وَذَلَّلْنَـٰهَا لَهُمْ فَمِنْهَا رَكُوبُهُمْ وَمِنْهَا يَأْكُلُونَ وَلَهُمْ فِيهَا مَنَـٰفِعُ وَمَشَارِبُ ۖ أَفَلَا يَشْكُرُونَ

Ramadan is the month in which the Quran was revealed. Guidance for humanity, and clear portents of guidance, and the Criterion. Whoever of you witnesses the month, shall fast it. But whoever is sick, or on a journey, then a number of other days. Allah desires ease for you, and does not desire hardship for you, that you may complete the number, and celebrate Allah for having guided you, so that you may be thankful. – Surah Al-Baqarah 2:185
شَهْرُ رَمَضَانَ ٱلَّذِىٓ أُنزِلَ فِيهِ ٱلْقُرْءَانُ هُدًى لِّلنَّاسِ وَبَيِّنَـٰتٍ مِّنَ ٱلْهُدَىٰ وَٱلْفُرْقَانِ ۚ فَمَن شَهِدَ مِنكُمُ ٱلشَّهْرَ فَلْيَصُمْهُ ۖ وَمَن كَانَ مَرِيضًا أَوْ عَلَىٰ سَفَرٍ فَعِدَّةٌ مِّنْ أَيَّامٍ أُخَرَ ۗ يُرِيدُ ٱللَّهُ بِكُمُ ٱلْيُسْرَ وَلَا يُرِيدُ بِكُمُ ٱلْعُسْرَ وَلِتُكْمِلُوا۟ ٱلْعِدَّةَ وَلِتُكَبِّرُوا۟ ٱللَّهَ عَلَىٰ مَا هَدَىٰكُمْ وَلَعَلَّكُمْ تَشْكُرُونَ

Narrated Al-Mughira: The Prophetﷺ used to stand (in the prayer) or pray till both his feet or legs swelled. He was asked why (he offered such an unbearable prayer) and he said, "should I not be a thankful slave." – Al-Bukhari 1130

حَدَّثَنَا أَبُو نُعَيْمٍ، قَالَ حَدَّثَنَا مِسْعَرٌ، عَنْ زِيَادٍ، قَالَ سَمِعْتُ الْمُغِيرَةَ ـ رضى الله عنه ـ يَقُولُ إِنْ كَانَ النَّبِيُّ صلى الله عليه وسلم لَيَقُومُ لِيُصَلِّيَ حَتَّى تَرِمُ قَدَمَاهُ أَوْ سَاقَاهُ، فَيُقَالُ لَهُ فَيَقُولُ " أَفَلاَ أَكُونُ عَبْدًا شَكُورًا "

You commit no error by seeking bounty from your Lord. When you disperse from Arafat, remember Allah at the Sacred Landmark. And remember Him as He has guided you. Although, before that, you were of those astray. – Surah Al-Baqarah 2:198

لَيْسَ عَلَيْكُمْ جُنَاحٌ أَن تَبْتَغُوا۟ فَضْلًا مِّن رَّبِّكُمْ ۚ فَإِذَآ أَفَضْتُم مِّنْ عَرَفَـٰتٍ فَٱذْكُرُوا۟ ٱللَّهَ عِندَ ٱلْمَشْعَرِ ٱلْحَرَامِ ۖ وَٱذْكُرُوهُ كَمَا هَدَىٰكُمْ وَإِن كُنتُم مِّن قَبْلِهِۦ لَمِنَ ٱلضَّآلِّينَ

To be ungrateful for what We have given them, and to enjoy themselves. They will surely come to know. – Surah Al-'Ankabut 29:66

لِيَكْفُرُوا۟ بِمَآ ءَاتَيْنَـٰهُمْ وَلِيَتَمَتَّعُوا۟ ۖ فَسَوْفَ يَعْلَمُونَ

When affliction touches the people, they call on their Lord, turning to Him in repentance. But then, when He gives them a taste of His mercy, some of them attribute partners to their Lord. To show ingratitude for what We have given them. Indulge yourselves—you will surely know.– Surah Ar-Rum 30:33&34

وَإِذَا مَسَّ ٱلنَّاسَ ضُرٌّ دَعَوْا۟ رَبَّهُم مُّنِيبِينَ إِلَيْهِ ثُمَّ إِذَآ أَذَاقَهُم مِّنْهُ رَحْمَةً إِذَا فَرِيقٌ مِّنْهُم بِرَبِّهِمْ يُشْرِكُونَ لِيَكْفُرُوا۟ بِمَآ ءَاتَيْنَـٰهُمْ ۚ فَتَمَتَّعُوا۟ فَسَوْفَ تَعْلَمُونَ

They made for him whatever he wished: sanctuaries, statues, bowls like pools, and heavy cauldrons. "O House of David, work with appreciation," but a few of My servants are appreciative. – Surah Saba' 34:13

يَعْمَلُونَ لَهُۥ مَا يَشَآءُ مِن مَّحَـٰرِيبَ وَتَمَـٰثِيلَ وَجِفَانٍ كَٱلْجَوَابِ وَقُدُورٍ رَّاسِيَـٰتٍ ۚ ٱعْمَلُوٓا۟ ءَالَ دَاوُۥدَ شُكْرًا ۚ وَقَلِيلٌ مِّنْ عِبَادِىَ ٱلشَّكُورُ

We thus penalized them for their ingratitude. Would We penalize any but the ungrateful? . – Surah Saba' 34:17

وَلَا تَقْرَبُوا۟ مَالَ ٱلْيَتِيمِ إِلَّا بِٱلَّتِى هِىَ أَحْسَنُ حَتَّىٰ يَبْلُغَ أَشُدَّهُۥ ۚ وَأَوْفُوا۟ بِٱلْعَهْدِ ۖ إِنَّ ٱلْعَهْدَ كَانَ مَسْـُٔولًا

The Compassionate. Has taught the Quran He created man And taught him clear expression. The sun and the moon move according to plan. And the stars and the trees prostrate themselves. And the sky, He raised; and He set up the balance. So do not transgress in the balance. But maintain the weights with justice, and do not violate the balance. And the earth, he set up for the creatures. In it are fruits, and palms in clusters. And grains in the blades, and fragrant plants. So which of your Lord's marvels will you deny? He created man from hard clay, like bricks. And created the jinn from a fusion of fire. So which of your Lord's marvels will you deny? Lord of the two Easts and Lord of the two Wests. So which of your Lord's marvels will you deny? He merged the two seas, converging together. Between them is a barrier, which they do not overrun. So which of your Lord's marvels will you deny? From them emerge pearls and coral. So which of your Lord's marvels will you deny? His are the ships, raised above the sea like landmarks. So which of your Lord's marvels will you deny? Everyone upon it is perishing. But will remain the Presence of your Lord, Full of Majesty and Splendor. So which of your Lord's marvels will you deny? Everyone in the heavens and the earth asks Him. Every day He is managing. So which of your Lord's marvels will you deny? We will attend to you, O prominent two. So which of your Lord's marvels will you deny? O society of jinn and humans! If you can pass through the bounds of the heavens and the earth, go ahead and pass. But you will not pass except with authorization. So which of your Lord's marvels will you deny? You will be bombarded with flares of fire and brass, and you will not succeed. So which of your Lord's marvels will you deny? When the sky splits apart, and becomes rose, like paint. So which of your Lord's marvels will you deny? On that Day, no human and no jinn will be asked about his sins. So which of your lord's marvels will you deny? The guilty will be recognized by their marks; they will be taken by the forelocks and the feet. So which of your Lord's marvels will you deny? This is Hell that the guilty denied. They circulate between it and between a seething bath. So which of your Lord's marvels will you deny? But for him who feared the standing of his Lord are two gardens. So which of your Lord's marvels will you deny? Full of varieties. So which of your Lord's marvels will you deny? In them are two flowing springs. So which of your Lord's marvels will you deny? In them are fruits of every kind, in pairs. So which of your Lord's marvels will you deny? Reclining on furnishings lined with brocade, and the fruits of the two gardens are near at hand. So which of your Lord's marvels will you deny? In them are maidens restraining their glances, untouched before by any man or jinn. So which of your Lord's marvels will you deny? As though they were rubies and corals. So which of your Lord's marvels will you deny? Is the reward of goodness anything but goodness? So which of your Lord's marvels will you deny? And beneath them are two gardens. So which of your Lord's marvels will you deny? Deep green. So which of your Lord's marvels will you deny? In them are two gushing springs. So which of your Lord's marvels will you deny? In them are fruits, and date-palms, and pomegranates. So which of your Lord's marvels will you deny? In them are good and beautiful ones. So which of your Lord's marvels will you deny? Companions, secluded in the tents. So which of your Lord's marvels will you deny? Whom no human has touched before, nor jinn. So which of your Lord's marvels will you deny? Reclining on green cushions, and exquisite carpets. So which of your Lord's marvels will you deny? Blessed be the name of your Lord, Full of Majesty and Splendor. . – Surah Ar-Rahman

ٱلرَّحۡمَـٰنُ عَلَّمَ ٱلۡقُرۡءَانَ خَلَقَ ٱلۡإِنسَـٰنَ عَلَّمَهُ ٱلۡبَيَانَ ٱلشَّمۡسُ وَٱلۡقَمَرُ بِحُسۡبَانٍ وَٱلنَّجۡمُ وَٱلشَّجَرُ يَسۡجُدَانِ وَٱلسَّمَآءَ رَفَعَهَا وَوَضَعَ ٱلۡمِيزَانَ أَلَّا تَطۡغَوۡاْ فِي ٱلۡمِيزَانِ وَأَقِيمُواْ ٱلۡوَزۡنَ بِٱلۡقِسۡطِ وَلَا تُخۡسِرُواْ ٱلۡمِيزَانَ وَٱلۡأَرۡضَ وَضَعَهَا لِلۡأَنَامِ فِيهَا فَـٰكِهَةٌ وَٱلنَّخۡلُ ذَاتُ ٱلۡأَكۡمَامِ وَٱلۡحَبُّ ذُو ٱلۡعَصۡفِ وَٱلرَّيۡحَانُ فَبِأَيِّ ءَالَآءِ رَبِّكُمَا تُكَذِّبَانِ خَلَقَ ٱلۡإِنسَـٰنَ مِن صَلۡصَـٰلٍ كَٱلۡفَخَّارِ وَخَلَقَ ٱلۡجَآنَّ مِن مَّارِجٍ مِّن نَّارٍ فَبِأَيِّ ءَالَآءِ رَبِّكُمَا تُكَذِّبَانِ رَبُّ ٱلۡمَشۡرِقَيۡنِ وَرَبُّ ٱلۡمَغۡرِبَيۡنِ فَبِأَيِّ ءَالَآءِ رَبِّكُمَا تُكَذِّبَانِ مَرَجَ ٱلۡبَحۡرَيۡنِ يَلۡتَقِيَانِ بَيۡنَهُمَا بَرۡزَخٌ لَّا يَبۡغِيَانِ فَبِأَيِّ ءَالَآءِ رَبِّكُمَا تُكَذِّبَانِ يَخۡرُجُ مِنۡهُمَا ٱللُّؤۡلُؤُ وَٱلۡمَرۡجَانُ فَبِأَيِّ ءَالَآءِ رَبِّكُمَا تُكَذِّبَانِ وَلَهُ ٱلۡجَوَارِ ٱلۡمُنشَـَٔاتُ فِي ٱلۡبَحۡرِ كَٱلۡأَعۡلَـٰمِ فَبِأَيِّ ءَالَآءِ رَبِّكُمَا تُكَذِّبَانِ كُلُّ مَنۡ عَلَيۡهَا فَانٍ وَيَبۡقَىٰ وَجۡهُ رَبِّكَ ذُو ٱلۡجَلَـٰلِ وَٱلۡإِكۡرَامِ فَبِأَيِّ ءَالَآءِ رَبِّكُمَا تُكَذِّبَانِ يَسۡـَٔلُهُۥ مَن فِي ٱلسَّمَـٰوَٰتِ وَٱلۡأَرۡضِۚ كُلَّ يَوۡمٍ هُوَ فِي شَأۡنٍ فَبِأَيِّ ءَالَآءِ رَبِّكُمَا تُكَذِّبَانِ سَنَفۡرُغُ لَكُمۡ أَيُّهَ ٱلثَّقَلَانِ فَبِأَيِّ ءَالَآءِ رَبِّكُمَا تُكَذِّبَانِ يَـٰمَعۡشَرَ ٱلۡجِنِّ وَٱلۡإِنسِ إِنِ ٱسۡتَطَعۡتُمۡ أَن تَنفُذُواْ مِنۡ أَقۡطَارِ ٱلسَّمَـٰوَٰتِ وَٱلۡأَرۡضِ فَٱنفُذُواْۚ لَا تَنفُذُونَ إِلَّا بِسُلۡطَـٰنٍ فَبِأَيِّ ءَالَآءِ رَبِّكُمَا تُكَذِّبَانِ يُرۡسَلُ عَلَيۡكُمَا شُوَاظٌ مِّن نَّارٍ وَنُحَاسٌ فَلَا تَنتَصِرَانِ فَبِأَيِّ ءَالَآءِ رَبِّكُمَا تُكَذِّبَانِ فَإِذَا ٱنشَقَّتِ ٱلسَّمَآءُ فَكَانَتۡ وَرۡدَةً كَٱلدِّهَانِ فَبِأَيِّ ءَالَآءِ رَبِّكُمَا تُكَذِّبَانِ فَيَوۡمَئِذٍ لَّا يُسۡـَٔلُ عَن ذَنۢبِهِۦٓ إِنسٌ وَلَا جَآنٌّ فَبِأَيِّ ءَالَآءِ رَبِّكُمَا تُكَذِّبَانِ يُعۡرَفُ ٱلۡمُجۡرِمُونَ بِسِيمَـٰهُمۡ فَيُؤۡخَذُ بِٱلنَّوَٰصِي وَٱلۡأَقۡدَامِ فَبِأَيِّ ءَالَآءِ رَبِّكُمَا تُكَذِّبَانِ هَـٰذِهِۦ جَهَنَّمُ ٱلَّتِي يُكَذِّبُ بِهَا ٱلۡمُجۡرِمُونَ يَطُوفُونَ بَيۡنَهَا وَبَيۡنَ حَمِيمٍ ءَانٍ فَبِأَيِّ ءَالَآءِ رَبِّكُمَا تُكَذِّبَانِ وَلِمَنۡ خَافَ مَقَامَ رَبِّهِۦ جَنَّتَانِ فَبِأَيِّ ءَالَآءِ رَبِّكُمَا تُكَذِّبَانِ ذَوَاتَآ أَفۡنَانٍ فَبِأَيِّ ءَالَآءِ رَبِّكُمَا تُكَذِّبَانِ فِيهِمَا عَيۡنَانِ تَجۡرِيَانِ فَبِأَيِّ ءَالَآءِ رَبِّكُمَا تُكَذِّبَانِ فِيهِمَا مِن كُلِّ فَـٰكِهَةٍ زَوۡجَانِ فَبِأَيِّ ءَالَآءِ رَبِّكُمَا تُكَذِّبَانِ مُتَّكِـِٔينَ عَلَىٰ فُرُشِۭ بَطَآئِنُهَا مِنۡ إِسۡتَبۡرَقٍۚ وَجَنَى ٱلۡجَنَّتَيۡنِ دَانٍ فَبِأَيِّ ءَالَآءِ رَبِّكُمَا تُكَذِّبَانِ فِيهِنَّ قَـٰصِرَٰتُ ٱلطَّرۡفِ لَمۡ يَطۡمِثۡهُنَّ إِنسٌ قَبۡلَهُمۡ وَلَا جَآنٌّ فَبِأَيِّ ءَالَآءِ رَبِّكُمَا تُكَذِّبَانِ كَأَنَّهُنَّ ٱلۡيَاقُوتُ وَٱلۡمَرۡجَانُ فَبِأَيِّ ءَالَآءِ رَبِّكُمَا تُكَذِّبَانِ هَلۡ جَزَآءُ ٱلۡإِحۡسَـٰنِ إِلَّا ٱلۡإِحۡسَـٰنُ فَبِأَيِّ ءَالَآءِ رَبِّكُمَا تُكَذِّبَانِ وَمِن دُونِهِمَا جَنَّتَانِ فَبِأَيِّ ءَالَآءِ رَبِّكُمَا تُكَذِّبَانِ مُدۡهَآمَّتَانِ فَبِأَيِّ ءَالَآءِ رَبِّكُمَا تُكَذِّبَانِ فِيهِمَا عَيۡنَانِ نَضَّاخَتَانِ فَبِأَيِّ ءَالَآءِ رَبِّكُمَا تُكَذِّبَانِ فِيهِمَا فَـٰكِهَةٌ وَنَخۡلٌ وَرُمَّانٌ فَبِأَيِّ ءَالَآءِ رَبِّكُمَا تُكَذِّبَانِ فِيهِنَّ خَيۡرَٰتٌ حِسَانٌ فَبِأَيِّ ءَالَآءِ رَبِّكُمَا تُكَذِّبَانِ حُورٌ مَّقۡصُورَٰتٌ فِي ٱلۡخِيَامِ فَبِأَيِّ ءَالَآءِ رَبِّكُمَا تُكَذِّبَانِ لَمۡ يَطۡمِثۡهُنَّ إِنسٌ قَبۡلَهُمۡ وَلَا جَآنٌّ فَبِأَيِّ ءَالَآءِ رَبِّكُمَا تُكَذِّبَانِ مُتَّكِـِٔينَ عَلَىٰ رَفۡرَفٍ خُضۡرٍ وَعَبۡقَرِيٍّ حِسَانٍ فَبِأَيِّ ءَالَآءِ رَبِّكُمَا تُكَذِّبَانِ تَبَـٰرَكَ ٱسۡمُ رَبِّكَ ذِي ٱلۡجَلَـٰلِ وَٱلۡإِكۡرَامِ

We guided him on the way, be he appreciative or unappreciative. – Surah Al-Insan 76:3
إِنَّا هَدَيْنَـٰهُ ٱلسَّبِيلَ إِمَّا شَاكِرًا وَإِمَّا كَفُورًا

Narrated Ibn 'Abbas: The Prophet ﷺ said: "I was shown the Hell-fire and that the majority of its dwellers were women who were ungrateful." It was asked, "Do they disbelieve in Allah?" (or are they ungrateful to Allah?) He replied, "They are ungrateful to their husbands and are ungrateful for the favors and the good (charitable deeds) done to them. If you have always been good (benevolent) to one of them and then she sees something in you (not of her liking), she will say, 'I have never received any good from you." – Al-Bukhari 29
حَدَّثَنَا عَبْدُ اللَّهِ بْنُ مَسْلَمَةَ، عَنْ مَالِكٍ، عَنْ زَيْدِ بْنِ أَسْلَمَ، عَنْ عَطَاءِ بْنِ يَسَارٍ، عَنِ ابْنِ عَبَّاسٍ، قَالَ قَالَ النَّبِيُّ صلى الله عليه وسلم " أُرِيتُ النَّارَ فَإِذَا أَكْثَرُ أَهْلِهَا النِّسَاءُ يَكْفُرْنَ ". قِيلَ أَيَكْفُرْنَ بِاللَّهِ قَالَ " يَكْفُرْنَ الْعَشِيرَ، وَيَكْفُرْنَ الإِحْسَانَ، لَوْ أَحْسَنْتَ إِلَى إِحْدَاهُنَّ الدَّهْرَ ثُمَّ رَأَتْ مِنْكَ شَيْئًا قَالَتْ مَا رَأَيْتُ مِنْكَ خَيْرًا قَطُّ ".

Have you not considered those who fled their homes, by the thousands, fearful of death? Allah said to them, "Die." Then He revived them. Allah is Gracious towards the people, but most people are not appreciative. – Surah Al-Baqarah 2:243
أَلَمْ تَرَ إِلَى ٱلَّذِينَ خَرَجُوا۟ مِن دِيَـٰرِهِمْ وَهُمْ أُلُوفٌ حَذَرَ ٱلْمَوْتِ فَقَالَ لَهُمُ ٱللَّهُ مُوتُوا۟ ثُمَّ أَحْيَـٰهُمْ ۚ إِنَّ ٱللَّهَ لَذُو فَضْلٍ عَلَى ٱلنَّاسِ وَلَـٰكِنَّ أَكْثَرَ ٱلنَّاسِ لَا يَشْكُرُونَ

Muhammad is no more than a messenger. Messengers have passed on before him. If he dies or gets killed, will you turn on your heels? He who turns on his heels will not harm Allah in any way. And Allah will reward the appreciative. – Surah Al-Imran 3:144
وَمَا مُحَمَّدٌ إِلَّا رَسُولٌ قَدْ خَلَتْ مِن قَبْلِهِ ٱلرُّسُلُ ۚ أَفَإِي۟ن مَّاتَ أَوْ قُتِلَ ٱنقَلَبْتُمْ عَلَىٰٓ أَعْقَـٰبِكُمْ ۚ وَمَن يَنقَلِبْ عَلَىٰ عَقِبَيْهِ فَلَن يَضُرَّ ٱللَّهَ شَيْـًٔا ۗ وَسَيَجْزِى ٱللَّهُ ٱلشَّـٰكِرِينَ

Narrated Ibn `Abbas: When the Prophet ﷺ came to Medina, he found (the Jews) fasting on the day of 'Ashura' (i.e. 10th of Muharram). They used to say: "This is a great day on which Allah saved Moses and drowned the folk of Pharaoh. Moses observed the fast on this day, as a sign of gratitude to Allah." The Prophet ﷺ said, "I am closer to Moses than they." So, he observed the fast (on that day) and ordered the Muslims to fast on it. – Sahih Al-Bukhari 3397
حَدَّثَنَا عَلِيُّ بْنُ عَبْدِ اللَّهِ، حَدَّثَنَا سُفْيَانُ، حَدَّثَنَا أَيُّوبُ السَّخْتِيَانِيُّ، عَنِ ابْنِ سَعِيدِ بْنِ جُبَيْرٍ، عَنْ أَبِيهِ، عَنِ ابْنِ عَبَّاسٍ ـ رضى الله عنهما أَنَّ النَّبِيَّ صلى الله عليه وسلم لَمَّا قَدِمَ الْمَدِينَةَ وَجَدَهُمْ يَصُومُونَ يَوْمًا، يَعْنِي عَاشُورَاءَ، فَقَالُوا هَذَا يَوْمٌ عَظِيمٌ، وَهْوَ يَوْمٌ نَجَّى اللَّهُ فِيهِ مُوسَى، وَأَغْرَقَ آلَ فِرْعَوْنَ، فَصَامَ مُوسَى شُكْرًا لِلَّهِ. فَقَالَ " أَنَا أَوْلَى بِمُوسَى مِنْهُمْ ". فَصَامَهُ وَأَمَرَ بِصِيَامِهِ

And when your Lord proclaimed: "If you give thanks, I will grant you increase; but if you are ungrateful, My punishment is severe." - Surah Ibrahim 14:7
وَإِذْ تَأَذَّنَ رَبُّكُمْ لَئِن شَكَرْتُمْ لَأَزِيدَنَّكُمْ ۖ وَلَئِن كَفَرْتُمْ إِنَّ عَذَابِى لَشَدِيدٌ

The Book of
Had it not been for the Grace of my Lord, I would certainly have been among those brought forth (to Hell).
وَلَوۡلَا نِعۡمَةُ رَبِّى لَكُنتُ مِنَ ٱلۡمُحۡضَرِينَ

O you who believe! Do not follow Satan's footsteps. Whoever follows Satan's footsteps—he advocates obscenity and immorality. Were it not for Allah's grace towards you, and His mercy, not one of you would have been pure, ever. But Allah purifies whomever He wills. Allah is All-Hearing, All-Knowing. – Surah An-Nur 24:21

إِنَّ ٱلَّذِينَ يُحِبُّونَ أَن تَشِيعَ ٱلۡفَـٰحِشَةُ فِى ٱلَّذِينَ ءَامَنُواْ لَهُمۡ عَذَابٌ أَلِيمٌ فِى ٱلدُّنۡيَا وَٱلۡأَاخِرَةِ ۚ وَٱللَّهُ يَعۡلَمُ وَأَنتُمۡ لَا تَعۡلَمُونَ وَلَوۡلَا فَضۡلُ ٱللَّهِ عَلَيۡكُمۡ وَرَحۡمَتُهُۥ وَأَنَّ ٱللَّهَ رَءُوفٌ رَّحِيمٌ وَلَوۡلَا فَضۡلُ ٱللَّهِ عَلَيۡكُمۡ وَرَحۡمَتُهُۥ وَأَنَّ ٱللَّهَ رَءُوفٌ رَّحِيمٌ

Except for those who repent, and believe, and do good deeds. These—Allah will replace their bad deeds with good deeds. Allah is ever Forgiving and Merciful. – Surah Al-Furqan 25:70

إِلَّا مَن تَابَ وَآمَنَ وَعَمِلَ عَمَلًا صَالِحًا فَأُولَٰئِكَ يُبَدِّلُ اللَّهُ سَيِّئَاتِهِمْ حَسَنَاتٍ وَكَانَ اللَّهُ غَفُورًا رَّحِيم

Were it not for the grace of my Lord, I would have been among the arraigned." (to Hell)." – Surah As-Saffat 37:57

وَلَوۡلَا نِعۡمَةُ رَبِّى لَكُنتُ مِنَ ٱلۡمُحۡضَرِينَ

Narrated Abu Huraira: Allah's Messenger ﷺ said, "The deeds of anyone of you will not save you (from the (Hell) Fire)." They said, "Even you (will not be saved by your deeds), O Allah's Messenge ﷺ?" He said, "No, even I (will not be saved) unless and until Allah bestows His Mercy on me. Therefore, do good deeds properly, sincerely and moderately, and worship Allah in the forenoon and in the afternoon and during a part of the night, and always adopt a middle, moderate, regular course whereby you will reach your target (Paradise). – Al-Bukhari 6463

حَدَّثَنَا آدَمُ، حَدَّثَنَا ابْنُ أَبِي ذِئْبٍ، عَنْ سَعِيدٍ الْمَقْبُرِيِّ، عَنْ أَبِي هُرَيْرَةَ ـ رضى الله عنه ـ قَالَ قَالَ رَسُولُ اللَّهِ صلى الله عليه وسلم " لَنْ يُنَجِّيَ أَحَدًا مِنْكُمْ عَمَلُهُ ". قَالُوا وَلاَ أَنْتَ يَا رَسُولَ اللَّهِ قَالَ " وَلاَ أَنَا، إِلاَّ أَنْ يَتَغَمَّدَنِي اللَّهُ بِرَحْمَةٍ، سَدِّدُوا وَقَارِبُوا، وَاغْدُوا وَرُوحُوا، وَشَىْءٌ مِنَ الدُّلْجَةِ. وَالْقَصْدَ الْقَصْدَ تَبْلُغُوا ".

Narrated `Aisha: The Prophet ﷺ said, "Do good deeds properly, sincerely and moderately, and receive good news because one's good deeds will not make him enter Paradise." They asked, "Even you, O Allah's Messenger ﷺ "?He said, "Even I, unless and until Allah bestows His pardon and Mercy on me." – Al-Bukhari 6467

حَدَّثَنَا عَلِيُّ بْنُ عَبْدِ اللَّهِ، حَدَّثَنَا مُحَمَّدُ بْنُ الزِّبْرِقَانِ، حَدَّثَنَا مُوسَى بْنُ عُقْبَةَ، عَنْ أَبِي سَلَمَةَ بْنِ عَبْدِ الرَّحْمَنِ، عَنْ عَائِشَةَ، عَنِ النَّبِيِّ صلى الله عليه وسلم قَالَ " سَدِّدُوا وَقَارِبُوا، وَأَبْشِرُوا، فَإِنَّهُ لاَ يُدْخِلُ أَحَدًا الْجَنَّةَ عَمَلُهُ ". قَالُوا وَلاَ، أَنْتَ يَا رَسُولَ اللَّهِ قَالَ " وَلاَ أَنَا إِلاَّ أَنْ يَتَغَمَّدَنِي اللَّهُ بِمَغْفِرَةٍ وَرَحْمَةٍ ". قَالَ أَظُنُّهُ عَنْ أَبِي النَّضْرِ عَنْ أَبِي سَلَمَةَ عَنْ عَائِشَةَ. وَقَالَ عَفَّانُ حَدَّثَنَا وُهَيْبٌ، عَنْ مُوسَى بْنِ عُقْبَةَ، قَالَ سَمِعْتُ أَبَا سَلَمَةَ، عَنْ عَائِشَةَ، عَنِ النَّبِيِّ صلى الله عليه وسلم " سَدِّدُوا وَأَبْشِرُوا ". وَقَالَ مُجَاهِدٌ {قَوْلاً سَدِيدًا} وَسَدَادًا صِدْقًا.

And when We let him taste a mercy from Us, after the adversity that had afflicted him, he will say, "This is mine, and I do not think that the Hour is coming; and even if I am returned to my Lord, I will have the very best with Him." We will inform those who disbelieve of what they did, and We will make them taste an awful punishment.– Surah Fussilat 41:50

وَلَئِنۡ أَذَقۡنَـٰهُ رَحۡمَةً مِّنَّا مِنۢ بَعۡدِ ضَرَّآءَ مَسَّتۡهُ لَيَقُولَنَّ هَـٰذَا لِى وَمَآ أَظُنُّ ٱلسَّاعَةَ قَآئِمَةً وَلَئِن رُّجِعۡتُ إِلَىٰ رَبِّىٓ إِنَّ لِى عِندَهُۥ لَلۡحُسۡنَىٰ ۚ فَلَنُنَبِّئَنَّ ٱلَّذِينَ كَفَرُواْ بِمَا عَمِلُواْ وَلَنُذِيقَنَّهُم مِّنۡ عَذَابٍ غَلِيظٍ

It is He who sent among the unlettered a messenger from themselves; reciting His revelations to them, and purifying them, and teaching them the Scripture and wisdom; although they were in obvious error before that. And others from them, who have not yet joined them. He is the Glorious, the Wise. – Surah Al-Jumu'ah 62:2&3

هُوَ ٱلَّذِى بَعَثَ فِى ٱلْأُمِّيِّـۧنَ رَسُولًا مِّنْهُمْ يَتْلُوا۟ عَلَيْهِمْ ءَايَـٰتِهِۦ وَيُزَكِّيهِمْ وَيُعَلِّمُهُمُ ٱلْكِتَـٰبَ وَٱلْحِكْمَةَ وَإِن كَانُوا۟ مِن قَبْلُ لَفِى ضَلَـٰلٍ مُّبِينٍ وَءَاخَرِينَ مِنْهُمْ لَمَّا يَلْحَقُوا۟ بِهِمْ ۚ وَهُوَ ٱلْعَزِيزُ ٱلْحَكِيمُ

That the People of the Book may know that they have no power whatsoever over Allah's grace, and that all grace is in Allah's hand; He gives it to whomever He wills. Allah is Possessor of Great Grace. – Surah Al-Hadid 57:29

لِّئَلَّا يَعْلَمَ أَهْلُ ٱلْكِتَـٰبِ أَلَّا يَقْدِرُونَ عَلَىٰ شَىْءٍ مِّن فَضْلِ ٱللَّهِ وَأَنَّ ٱلْفَضْلَ بِيَدِ ٱللَّهِ يُؤْتِيهِ مَن يَشَآءُ ۚ وَٱللَّهُ ذُو ٱلْفَضْلِ ٱلْعَظِيمِ

By the morning light. And the night as it settles. Your Lord did not abandon you, nor did He forget. The Hereafter is better for you than the First. And your Lord will give you, and you will be satisfied. Did He not find you orphaned, and sheltered you? And found you wandering, and guided you. And found you in need, and enriched you? Therefore, do not mistreat the orphan. Nor rebuff the seeker. But proclaim the blessings of your Lord. – Ad-Duha 93

وَٱلضُّحَىٰ وَٱلَّيْلِ إِذَا سَجَىٰ مَا وَدَّعَكَ رَبُّكَ وَمَا قَلَىٰ وَلَلْـَٔاخِرَةُ خَيْرٌ لَّكَ مِنَ ٱلْأُولَىٰ وَلَسَوْفَ يُعْطِيكَ رَبُّكَ فَتَرْضَىٰٓ أَلَمْ يَجِدْكَ يَتِيمًا فَـَٔاوَىٰ وَوَجَدَكَ ضَآلًّا فَهَدَىٰ وَوَجَدَكَ عَآئِلًا فَأَغْنَىٰ فَأَمَّا ٱلْيَتِيمَ فَلَا تَقْهَرْ وَأَمَّا ٱلسَّآئِلَ فَلَا تَنْهَرْ وَأَمَّا بِنِعْمَةِ رَبِّكَ فَحَدِّثْ

When some news of security or alarm comes their way, they broadcast it. But had they referred it to the Messenger, and to those in authority among them, those who can draw conclusions from it would have comprehended it. Were it not for Allah's blessing and mercy upon you, you would have followed the Devil, except for a few. – Surah An-Nisa 4:83

وَإِذَا جَآءَهُمْ أَمْرٌ مِّنَ ٱلْأَمْنِ أَوِ ٱلْخَوْفِ أَذَاعُوا۟ بِهِۦ ۖ وَلَوْ رَدُّوهُ إِلَى ٱلرَّسُولِ وَإِلَىٰٓ أُو۟لِى ٱلْأَمْرِ مِنْهُمْ لَعَلِمَهُ ٱلَّذِينَ يَسْتَنۢبِطُونَهُۥ مِنْهُمْ ۗ وَلَوْلَا فَضْلُ ٱللَّهِ عَلَيْكُمْ وَرَحْمَتُهُۥ لَٱتَّبَعْتُمُ ٱلشَّيْطَـٰنَ إِلَّا قَلِيلًا

Narrated Abu Sa`id Al-Khudri: Allah's Messenger ﷺ said, "Allah will say to the people of Paradise, 'O the people of Paradise!' They will say, 'Labbaik, O our Lord, and Sa`daik!' Allah will say, 'Are you pleased?" They will say, 'Why should we not be pleased since You have given us what You have not given to anyone of Your creation?' Allah will say, 'I will give you something better than that.' They will reply, 'O our Lord! And what is better than that?' Allah will say, 'I will bestow My pleasure and contentment upon you so that I will never be angry with you after for-ever.' " - Sahih al-Bukhari 6549

حَدَّثَنَا مُعَاذُ بْنُ أَسَدٍ، أَخْبَرَنَا عَبْدُ اللَّهِ، أَخْبَرَنَا مَالِكُ بْنُ أَنَسٍ، عَنْ زَيْدِ بْنِ أَسْلَمَ، عَنْ عَطَاءِ بْنِ يَسَارٍ، عَنْ أَبِي سَعِيدٍ الْخُدْرِيِّ، قَالَ قَالَ رَسُولُ اللَّهِ صلى الله عليه وسلم " إِنَّ اللَّهَ يَقُولُ لأَهْلِ الْجَنَّةِ يَا أَهْلَ الْجَنَّةِ‏.‏ يَقُولُونَ لَبَّيْكَ رَبَّنَا وَسَعْدَيْكَ‏.‏ فَيَقُولُ هَلْ رَضِيتُمْ فَيَقُولُونَ وَمَا لَنَا لاَ نَرْضَى وَقَدْ أَعْطَيْتَنَا مَا لَمْ تُعْطِ أَحَدًا مِنْ خَلْقِكَ‏.‏ فَيَقُولُ أَنَا أُعْطِيكُمْ أَفْضَلَ مِنْ ذَلِكَ‏.‏ قَالُوا يَا رَبِّ وَأَىُّ شَىْءٍ أَفْضَلُ مِنْ ذَلِكَ فَيَقُولُ أُحِلُّ عَلَيْكُمْ رِضْوَانِي فَلاَ أَسْخَطُ عَلَيْكُمْ بَعْدَهُ أَبَدًا "

And guide them away [from committing] evil deeds. You would be Merciful that Day to anyone you have guided away [from committing] evil deeds, and that is the supreme triumph." Surah Al-Ghafir 40:9

وَقِهِمُ ٱلسَّيِّـَٔاتِ ۚ وَمَن تَقِ ٱلسَّيِّـَٔاتِ يَوْمَئِذٍ فَقَدْ رَحِمْتَهُۥ ۚ وَذَٰلِكَ هُوَ ٱلْفَوْزُ ٱلْعَظِيمُ

So He may admit believing men and women into Gardens under which rivers flow—to stay there forever—and absolve them of their sins. And that is a supreme achievement in the sight of Allah. Surah Al-Fath 48:5

لِّيُدْخِلَ ٱلْمُؤْمِنِينَ وَٱلْمُؤْمِنَـٰتِ جَنَّـٰتٍ تَجْرِى مِن تَحْتِهَا ٱلْأَنْهَـٰرُ خَـٰلِدِينَ فِيهَا وَيُكَفِّرَ عَنْهُمْ سَيِّـَٔاتِهِمْ ۚ وَكَانَ ذَٰلِكَ عِندَ ٱللَّهِ فَوْزًا عَظِيمًا

The Book of

O Allah. Forgive me and bestow Your Mercy on me and let me join with the highest companions

اللَّهُمَّ اغْفِرْ لِي وَارْحَمْنِي وَأَلْحِقْنِي بِالرَّفِيقِ الأَعْلَى

O you who believe! When you journey in the way of Allah, investigate, and do not say to him who offers you peace, "You are not a believer," aspiring for the goods of this world. With Allah are abundant riches. You yourselves were like this before, and Allah bestowed favor on you; so investigate. Allah is well aware of what you do. – Surah An-Nisa 4:94
يَـٰٓأَيُّهَا ٱلَّذِينَ ءَامَنُوٓاْ إِذَا ضَرَبْتُمْ فِى سَبِيلِ ٱللَّهِ فَتَبَيَّنُواْ وَلَا تَقُولُواْ لِمَنْ أَلْقَىٰٓ إِلَيْكُمُ ٱلسَّلَـٰمَ لَسْتَ مُؤْمِنًا تَبْتَغُونَ عَرَضَ ٱلْحَيَوٰةِ ٱلدُّنْيَا فَعِندَ ٱللَّهِ مَغَانِمُ كَثِيرَةٌ ۚ كَذَٰلِكَ كُنتُم مِّن قَبْلُ فَمَنَّ ٱللَّهُ عَلَيْكُمْ فَتَبَيَّنُوٓاْ ۚ إِنَّ ٱللَّهَ كَانَ بِمَا تَعْمَلُونَ خَبِيرًا

Narrated Abu Huraira: Allah's Messenger ﷺ said, "The deeds of anyone of you will not save you (from the (Hell) Fire)." They said, "Even you (will not be saved by your deeds), O Allah's Messenger ﷺ ?" He said, "No, even I (will not be saved) unless and until Allah bestows His Mercy on me. Therefore, do good deeds properly, sincerely and moderately, and worship Allah in the forenoon and in the afternoon and during a part of the night, and always adopt a middle, moderate, regular course whereby you will reach your target (Paradise). – Al-Bukhari 6463
حَدَّثَنَا آدَمُ، حَدَّثَنَا ابْنُ أَبِي ذِئْبٍ، عَنْ سَعِيدٍ الْمَقْبُرِيِّ، عَنْ أَبِي هُرَيْرَةَ ـ رضى الله عنه ـ قَالَ قَالَ رَسُولُ اللَّهِ صلى الله عليه وسلم " لَنْ يُنَجِّيَ أَحَدًا مِنْكُمْ عَمَلُهُ ". قَالُوا وَلاَ أَنْتَ يَا رَسُولَ اللَّهِ قَالَ " وَلاَ أَنَا، إِلاَّ أَنْ يَتَغَمَّدَنِي اللَّهُ بِرَحْمَةٍ، سَدِّدُوا وَقَارِبُوا، وَاغْدُوا وَرُوحُوا، وَشَىْءٌ مِنَ الدُّلْجَةِ. وَالْقَصْدَ الْقَصْدَ تَبْلُغُوا ".

Narrated Abu Huraira: I heard Allah's Messenger ﷺ saying, "The good deeds of any person will not make him enter Paradise." (i.e., None can enter Paradise through his good deeds.) They (the Prophet's companions) said, 'Not even you, O Allah's Messenger ﷺ ?' He said, "Not even myself, unless Allah bestows His favor and mercy on me." So be moderate in your religious deeds and do the deeds that are within your ability: and none of you should wish for death, for if he is a good doer, he may increase his good deeds, and if he is an evil doer, he may repent to Allah." – Al-Bukhari 5673
حَدَّثَنَا أَبُو الْيَمَانِ، أَخْبَرَنَا شُعَيْبٌ، عَنِ الزُّهْرِيِّ، قَالَ أَخْبَرَنِي أَبُو عُبَيْدٍ، مَوْلَى عَبْدِ الرَّحْمَنِ بْنِ عَوْفٍ أَنَّ أَبَا هُرَيْرَةَ، قَالَ سَمِعْتُ رَسُولَ اللَّهِ صلى الله عليه وسلم يَقُولُ " لَنْ يُدْخِلَ أَحَدًا عَمَلُهُ الْجَنَّةَ ". قَالُوا وَلاَ أَنْتَ يَا رَسُولَ اللَّهِ قَالَ " لاَ، وَلاَ أَنَا إِلاَّ أَنْ يَتَغَمَّدَنِي اللَّهُ بِفَضْلٍ وَرَحْمَةٍ فَسَدِّدُوا وَقَارِبُوا وَلاَ يَتَمَنَّيَنَّ أَحَدُكُمُ الْمَوْتَ إِمَّا مُحْسِنًا فَلَعَلَّهُ أَنْ يَزْدَادَ خَيْرًا، وَإِمَّا مُسِيئًا فَلَعَلَّهُ أَنْ يَسْتَعْتِبَ "

That is Allah's grace, which He grants to whomever He wills. Allah is Possessor of limitless grace. – Surah Al-Jumu'ah 62:4

ذَٰلِكَ فَضْلُ ٱللَّهِ يُؤْتِيهِ مَن يَشَآءُ ۚ وَٱللَّهُ ذُو ٱلْفَضْلِ ٱلْعَظِيمِ

That the People of the Book may know that they have no power whatsoever over Allah's grace, and that all grace is in Allah's hand; He gives it to whomever He wills. Allah is Possessor of Great Grace. – Surah Al-Hadid 57:29
لِّئَلَّا يَعْلَمَ أَهْلُ ٱلْكِتَـٰبِ أَلَّا يَقْدِرُونَ عَلَىٰ شَىْءٍ مِّن فَضْلِ ٱللَّهِ ۙ وَأَنَّ ٱلْفَضْلَ بِيَدِ ٱللَّهِ يُؤْتِيهِ مَن يَشَآءُ ۚ وَٱللَّهُ ذُو ٱلْفَضْلِ

The Day when He gathers you for the Day of Gathering—that is the Day of Mutual Exchange. Whoever believes in Allah and acts with integrity, He will remit his misdeeds, and will admit him into gardens beneath which rivers flow, to dwell therein forever. That is the supreme achievement. Surah Al-Taghabun 64:9

يَوْمَ يَجْمَعُكُمْ لِيَوْمِ ٱلْجَمْعِ ۖ ذَٰلِكَ يَوْمُ ٱلتَّغَابُنِ ۗ وَمَن يُؤْمِنۢ بِٱللَّهِ وَيَعْمَلْ صَٰلِحًا يُكَفِّرْ عَنْهُ سَيِّـَٔاتِهِۦ وَيُدْخِلْهُ جَنَّٰتٍ تَجْرِى مِن تَحْتِهَا ٱلْأَنْهَٰرُ خَٰلِدِينَ فِيهَآ أَبَدًا ۚ ذَٰلِكَ ٱلْفَوْزُ ٱلْعَظِيمُ

....inside it there is mercy... Surah Al-Hadid 57:13

..... فِيهِ ٱلرَّحْمَةُ وَظَٰهِرُهُۥ .....

Narrated `Aisha: I heard the Prophetﷺ, who was resting against me, saying, "O Allah. Forgive me and bestow Your Mercy on me and let me join with the highest companions." - Al-Bukhari 5674

حَدَّثَنَا عَبْدُ اللَّهِ بْنُ أَبِي شَيْبَةَ، حَدَّثَنَا أَبُو أُسَامَةَ، عَنْ هِشَامٍ، عَنْ عَبَّادِ بْنِ عَبْدِ اللَّهِ بْنِ الزُّبَيْرِ، قَالَ سَمِعْتُ عَائِشَةَ ـ رضى الله عنها ـ قَالَتْ سَمِعْتُ النَّبِيَّ صلى الله عليه وسلم وَهْوَ مُسْتَنِدٌ إِلَىَّ يَقُولُ " اللَّهُمَّ اغْفِرْ لِي وَارْحَمْنِي وَأَلْحِقْنِي بِالرَّفِيقِ الأَعْلَى

Narrated Abu Huraira: The Prophetﷺ said, "None will enter Paradise but will be shown the place he would have occupied in the (Hell) Fire if he had rejected faith, so that he may be more thankful; and none will enter the (Hell) Fire but will be shown the place he would have occupied in Paradise if he had faith, so that may be a cause of sorrow for him.". – Sahih Al-Bukhari 6569

حَدَّثَنَا أَبُو الْيَمَانِ، أَخْبَرَنَا شُعَيْبٌ، حَدَّثَنَا أَبُو الزِّنَادِ، عَنِ الأَعْرَجِ، عَنْ أَبِي هُرَيْرَةَ، قَالَ النَّبِيُّ صلى الله عليه وسلم " لاَ يَدْخُلُ أَحَدٌ الْجَنَّةَ إِلاَّ أُرِيَ مَقْعَدَهُ مِنَ النَّارِ، لَوْ أَسَاءَ، لِيَزْدَادَ شُكْرًا، وَلاَ يَدْخُلُ النَّارَ أَحَدٌ إِلاَّ أُرِيَ مَقْعَدَهُ مِنَ الْجَنَّةِ، لَوْ أَحْسَنَ، لِيَكُونَ عَلَيْهِ حَسْرَةً ".

Narrated Abu Bakr As-Siddiq: I asked Allah's Messengerﷺ to teach me an invocation so that I may invoke Allah with it in my prayer. He told me to say, "Allahumma inni zalumtu nafsi zulman kathiran, Wala yaghfiru dh-dhunuba illa anta, fa ghfir li maghfiratan min `indika, wa r-hamni, innaka anta l-ghafuru r-rahim (O Allah! I have done great injustice to myself and none except You forgives sins, so bestow on me a forgiveness from You, and Have Mercy on me, You are the Forgiver, the Merciful). – Sahih Al-Bukhari 834

حَدَّثَنَا قُتَيْبَةُ بْنُ سَعِيدٍ، قَالَ حَدَّثَنَا اللَّيْثُ، عَنْ يَزِيدَ بْنِ أَبِي حَبِيبٍ، عَنْ أَبِي الْخَيْرِ، عَنْ عَبْدِ اللَّهِ بْنِ عَمْرٍو، عَنْ أَبِي بَكْرٍ الصِّدِّيقِ ـ رضى الله عنه ـ أَنَّهُ قَالَ لِرَسُولِ اللَّهِ صلى الله عليه وسلم عَلِّمْنِي دُعَاءً أَدْعُو بِهِ فِي صَلاَتِي. قَالَ " قُلِ اللَّهُمَّ إِنِّي ظَلَمْتُ نَفْسِي ظُلْمًا كَثِيرًا وَلاَ يَغْفِرُ الذُّنُوبَ إِلاَّ أَنْتَ، فَاغْفِرْ لِي مَغْفِرَةً مِنْ عِنْدِكَ، وَارْحَمْنِي إِنَّكَ أَنْتَ الْغَفُورُ الرَّحِيمُ "

Narrated Sa`id bin Jubair: `AbdurRahman bin Abza said, "Ask Ibn `Abbas about these two Qur'anic Verses: 'Nor kill such life as Allah has made sacred, Except for just cause.' (25.168) "And whoever kills a believer intentionally, his recompense is Hell. (4.93) So I asked Ibn `Abbas who said, "When the Verse that is in Sura-al-Furqan was revealed, the pagans of Mecca said, 'But we have slain such life as Allah has made sacred, and we have invoked other gods along with Allah, and we have also committed fornication.' So Allah revealed:-- 'Except those who repent, believe, and do good—(25.70) So this Verse was concerned with those people. As for the Verse in Surat-an-Nisa (4-93), it means that if a man, after understanding Islam and its laws and obligations, murders somebody, then his punishment is to dwell in the (Hell) Fire forever." Then I mentioned this to Mujahid who said, "Except the one who regrets (one's crime) . " – Sahih al-Bukhari 3855

حَدَّثَنَا عُثْمَانُ بْنُ أَبِي شَيْبَةَ، حَدَّثَنَا جَرِيرٌ، عَنْ مَنْصُورٍ، حَدَّثَنِي سَعِيدُ بْنُ جُبَيْرٍ، أَوْ قَالَ حَدَّثَنِي الْحَكَمُ، عَنْ سَعِيدِ بْنِ جُبَيْرٍ، قَالَ أَمَرَنِي عَبْدُ الرَّحْمَنِ بْنُ أَبْزَى قَالَ سَلِ ابْنَ عَبَّاسٍ عَنْ هَاتَيْنِ الآيَتَيْنِ، مَا أَمْرُهُمَا {وَلاَ تَقْتُلُوا النَّفْسَ الَّتِي حَرَّمَ اللَّهُ } {وَمَنْ يَقْتُلْ مُؤْمِنًا مُتَعَمِّدًا} فَسَأَلْتُ ابْنَ عَبَّاسٍ فَقَالَ لَمَّا أُنْزِلَتِ الَّتِي فِي الْفُرْقَانِ قَالَ مُشْرِكُو أَهْلِ مَكَّةَ فَقَدْ قَتَلْنَا النَّفْسَ الَّتِي حَرَّمَ اللَّهُ، وَدَعَوْنَا مَعَ اللَّهِ إِلَهًا آخَرَ، وَقَدْ أَتَيْنَا الْفَوَاحِشَ. فَأَنْزَلَ اللَّهُ {إِلاَّ مَنْ تَابَ وَآمَنَ} الآيَةَ فَهَذِهِ لأُولَئِكَ وَأَمَّا الَّتِي فِي النِّسَاءِ الرَّجُلُ إِذَا عَرَفَ الإِسْلاَمَ وَشَرَائِعَهُ، ثُمَّ قَتَلَ فَجَزَاؤُهُ جَهَنَّمُ. فَذَكَرْتُهُ لِمُجَاهِدٍ فَقَالَ إِلاَّ مَنْ نَدِمَ.

turning to your Lord ⌜alone⌝ with hope.
وَإِلَىٰ رَبِّكَ فَٱرْغَب

Say, "My worshipers who have transgressed against themselves do not despair of Allah's mercy, for Allah forgives all transgressions. He is the Ever-Forgiving, the Mercy-Giver." – Surah Az-Zumar 39:53
قُلْ يَـٰعِبَادِىَ ٱلَّذِينَ أَسْرَفُوا۟ عَلَىٰٓ أَنفُسِهِمْ لَا تَقْنَطُوا۟ مِن رَّحْمَةِ ٱللَّهِ ۚ إِنَّ ٱللَّهَ يَغْفِرُ ٱلذُّنُوبَ جَمِيعًا ۚ إِنَّهُۥ هُوَ ٱلْغَفُورُ ٱلرَّحِيمُ

..... And do not lose hope in the mercy of Allah, for no one loses hope in Allah's mercy except those with no faith. -Surah Yusuf 12:87
....وَلَا تَا۟يْـَٔسُوا۟ مِن رَّوْحِ ٱللَّهِ ۖ إِنَّهُۥ لَا يَا۟يْـَٔسُ مِن رَّوْحِ ٱللَّهِ إِلَّا ٱلْقَوْمُ ٱلْكَـٰفِرُونَ

He is the One Who sends down clear revelations to His servant to bring you out of darkness and into light. For indeed Allah is Ever Gracious and Most Merciful to you. – Surah Al-Hadid 57:9
هُوَ ٱلَّذِى يُنَزِّلُ عَلَىٰ عَبْدِهِۦٓ ءَايَـٰتٍۭ بَيِّنَـٰتٍ لِّيُخْرِجَكُم مِّنَ ٱلظُّلُمَـٰتِ إِلَى ٱلنُّورِ ۚ وَإِنَّ ٱللَّهَ بِكُمْ لَرَءُوفٌ رَّحِيمٌ

As for those who believe, do good, and have faith in what has been revealed to Muḥammad—which is the truth from their Lord—He will absolve them of their sins and improve their condition. – Surah Muhammad 47:2
وَٱلَّذِينَ ءَامَنُوا۟ وَعَمِلُوا۟ ٱلصَّـٰلِحَـٰتِ وَءَامَنُوا۟ بِمَا نُزِّلَ عَلَىٰ مُحَمَّدٍ وَهُوَ ٱلْحَقُّ مِن رَّبِّهِمْ ۙ كَفَّرَ عَنْهُمْ سَيِّـَٔاتِهِمْ وَأَصْلَحَ بَالَهُمْ

The Book of
those who believe not in the Hereafter
ٱلَّذِينَ لَا يُؤْمِنُونَ بِٱلْـَٔاخِرَةِ

And the human being says, "When I am dead, will I be brought back alive?" – Surah Maryam 19:66

وَيَقُولُ ٱلْإِنسَـٰنُ أَءِذَا مَا مِتُّ لَسَوْفَ أُخْرَجُ حَيًّا

They say, "After we have died, and become dust and bones, will we be resurrected? We were promised this before— we and our ancestors—these are nothing but legends of the ancients." – Surah Al-Mu'minun 23:82&83

قَالُوٓا۟ أَءِذَا مِتْنَا وَكُنَّا تُرَابًا وَعِظَـٰمًا أَءِنَّا لَمَبْعُوثُونَ لَقَدْ وُعِدْنَا نَحْنُ وَءَابَآؤُنَا هَـٰذَا مِن قَبْلُ إِنْ هَـٰذَآ إِلَّآ أَسَـٰطِيرُ ٱلْأَوَّلِينَ

And they say, "When we have become bones and fragments, shall we really be resurrected as a new creation?" – Surah Al-Isra 17:49

وَقَالُوٓا۟ أَءِذَا كُنَّا عِظَـٰمًا وَرُفَـٰتًا أَءِنَّا لَمَبْعُوثُونَ خَلْقًا جَدِيدًا

But the dignitaries of his people, those who disbelieved and denied the meeting of the Hereafter, and We had indulged them in the present life, said, "This is nothing but a human like you; he eats what you eat, and he drinks what you drink.If you obey a human being like yourselves, then you will be losers.Does he promise you that when you have died and become dust and bones, you will be brought out? – Surah Al-Mu'minun 23:33-35

وَقَالَ ٱلْمَلَأُ مِن قَوْمِهِ ٱلَّذِينَ كَفَرُوا۟ وَكَذَّبُوا۟ بِلِقَآءِ ٱلْـَٔاخِرَةِ وَأَتْرَفْنَـٰهُمْ فِى ٱلْحَيَوٰةِ ٱلدُّنْيَا مَا هَـٰذَآ إِلَّا بَشَرٌ مِّثْلُكُمْ يَأْكُلُ مِمَّا تَأْكُلُونَ مِنْهُ وَيَشْرَبُ مِمَّا تَشْرَبُونَ وَلَئِنْ أَطَعْتُم بَشَرًا مِّثْلَكُمْ إِنَّكُمْ إِذًا لَّخَـٰسِرُونَ أَيَعِدُكُمْ أَنَّكُمْ إِذَا مِتُّمْ وَكُنتُمْ تُرَابًا وَعِظَـٰمًا أَنَّكُم مُّخْرَجُونَ

And they came upon the city that was drenched by the terrible rain. Did they not see it? But they do not expect resurrection. – Surah Al-Furqan 25:40

وَلَقَدْ أَتَوْا۟ عَلَى ٱلْقَرْيَةِ ٱلَّتِىٓ أُمْطِرَتْ مَطَرَ ٱلسَّوْءِ ۚ أَفَلَمْ يَكُونُوا۟ يَرَوْنَهَا ۚ بَلْ كَانُوا۟ لَا يَرْجُونَ نُشُورًا

In fact, their knowledge of the Hereafter is confused. In fact, they are in doubt about it. In fact, they are blind to it. Those who disbelieve say, "When we have become dust, and our ancestors, shall we be brought out? – Surah An-Naml 27:66&67

بَلِ ٱدَّٰرَكَ عِلْمُهُمْ فِى ٱلْـَٔاخِرَةِ ۚ بَلْ هُمْ فِى شَكٍّ مِّنْهَا ۖ بَلْ هُم مِّنْهَا عَمُونَ وَقَالَ ٱلَّذِينَ كَفَرُوٓا۟ أَءِذَا كُنَّا تُرَٰبًا وَءَابَآؤُنَآ أَئِنَّا لَمُخْرَجُونَ

The Trumpet will be blown, then behold, they will rush from the tombs to their Lord. They will say, "Woe to us! Who resurrected us from our resting place?" This is what the Most Gracious had promised, and the messengers have spoken the truth." – Surah Ya-Sin 36:51&52

وَنُفِخَ فِى ٱلصُّورِ فَإِذَا هُم مِّنَ ٱلْأَجْدَاثِ إِلَىٰ رَبِّهِمْ يَنسِلُونَ قَالُوا۟ يَـٰوَيْلَنَا مَنۢ بَعَثَنَا مِن مَّرْقَدِنَا ۜ ۗ هَـٰذَا مَا وَعَدَ ٱلرَّحْمَـٰنُ وَصَدَقَ ٱلْمُرْسَلُونَ

And he produces arguments against Us, and he forgets his own creation. He says, "Who will revive the bones when they have decayed?" -Surah Ya-Sin 36:78

وَضَرَبَ لَنَا مَثَلًا وَنَسِىَ خَلْقَهُۥ ۖ قَالَ مَن يُحْىِ ٱلْعِظَـٰمَ وَهِىَ رَمِيمٌ

One of them will say, “I used to have a friend. Who used to say, “Are you of those who believe? That after we die and become dust and bones, we will be called to account?” He will say, “Will you have a look?” He will look, and will see him in the pit of Hell. He will say, “By Allah, you almost ruined me. Were it not for the grace of my Lord, I would have been among the arraigned.” – Surah As-Saffat 37:51-57

قَالَ قَآئِلٌ مِّنۡهُمۡ إِنِّى كَانَ لِى قَرِينٌ يَقُولُ أَءِنَّكَ لَمِنَ ٱلۡمُصَدِّقِينَ أَءِذَا مِتۡنَا وَكُنَّا تُرَابًا وَعِظَـٰمًا أَءِنَّا لَمَدِينُونَ قَالَ هَلۡ أَنتُم مُّطَّلِعُونَ فَٱطَّلَعَ فَرَءَاهُ فِى سَوَآءِ ٱلۡجَحِيمِ قَالَ تَٱللَّهِ إِن كِدتَّ لَتُرۡدِينِ وَلَوۡلَا نِعۡمَةُ رَبِّى لَكُنتُ مِنَ ٱلۡمُحۡضَرِينَ

Were We fatigued by the first creation? But they are in doubt of a new creation. – Surah Qaf 50:15

أَفَعَيِينَا بِٱلۡخَلۡقِ ٱلۡأَوَّلِۚ بَلۡ هُمۡ فِى لَبۡسٍ مِّنۡ خَلۡقٍ جَدِيدٍ

Narrate Aisha: Abu Bakr married a woman from the tribe of Bani Kalb, called Um Bakr. When Abu Bakr migrated to Medina, he divorced her and she was married by her cousin, the poet who said the following poem lamenting the infidels of Quraish: “What is there kept in the well, The well of Badr, (The owners of) the trays of Roasted camel humps? What is there kept in the well, The well of Badr, (The owners of) lady singers And friends of the honorable companions; who used to drink (wine) together, Um Bakr greets us With the greeting of peace, But can I find peace After my people have gone? The Apostle tells us that We shall live again, But what sort of life will owls and skulls live?: - Al-Bukhari 3921

حَدَّثَنَا أَصْبَغُ، حَدَّثَنَا ابْنُ وَهْبٍ، عَنْ يُونُسَ، عَنِ ابْنِ شِهَابٍ، عَنْ عُرْوَةَ بْنِ الزُّبَيْرِ، عَنْ عَائِشَةَ، أَنَّ أَبَا بَكْرٍ ـ رضى الله عنه ـ تَزَوَّجَ امْرَأَةً مِنْ كَلْبٍ يُقَالُ لَهَا أُمُّ بَكْرٍ، فَلَمَّا هَاجَرَ أَبُو بَكْرٍ طَلَّقَهَا، فَتَزَوَّجَهَا ابْنُ عَمِّهَا، هَذَا الشَّاعِرُ الَّذِي قَالَ هَذِهِ الْقَصِيدَةَ، رَثَى كُفَّارَ قُرَيْشٍ وَمَاذَا بِالْقَلِيبِ قَلِيبِ بَدْرٍ مِنَ الشِّيزَى تُزَيَّنُ بِالسَّنَامِ وَمَاذَا بِالْقَلِيبِ، قَلِيبِ بَدْرٍ مِنَ الْقَيْنَاتِ وَالشَّرْبِ الْكِرَامِ تُحَيِّي بِالسَّلاَمَةِ أُمُّ بَكْرٍ وَهَلْ لِي بَعْدَ قَوْمِي مِنْ سَلاَمِ يُحَدِّثُنَا الرَّسُولُ بِأَنْ سَنَحْيَا وَكَيْفَ حَيَاةُ أَصْدَاءٍ وَهَامِ

If only you could see, when they are stationed before their Lord. He will say, “Is this not real?” They will say, “Yes indeed, by our Lord.” He will say, “Then taste the torment for having disbelieved.” – Surah Al-An’am 6:30

وَلَوۡ تَرَىٰٓ إِذۡ وُقِفُواْ عَلَىٰ رَبِّهِمۡۚ قَالَ أَلَيۡسَ هَـٰذَا بِٱلۡحَقِّۚ قَالُواْ بَلَىٰ وَرَبِّنَاۚ قَالَ فَذُوقُواْ ٱلۡعَذَابَ بِمَا كُنتُمۡ تَكۡفُرُونَ

Should you wonder—the real wonder is their saying: “When we have become dust, will we be in a new creation?” Those are they who defied their Lord. Those are they who will have yokes around their necks. Those are the inhabitants of the Fire, where they will remain forever.– Surah Ar-Ra’d 13:5

وَإِن تَعۡجَبۡ فَعَجَبٌ قَوۡلُهُمۡ أَءِذَا كُنَّا تُرَٰبًا أَءِنَّا لَفِي خَلۡقٍ جَدِيدٍۗ أُوْلَـٰٓئِكَ ٱلَّذِينَ كَفَرُواْ بِرَبِّهِمۡۖ وَأُوْلَـٰٓئِكَ ٱلۡأَغۡلَـٰلُ فِيٓ أَعۡنَاقِهِمۡۖ وَأُوْلَـٰٓئِكَ أَصۡحَـٰبُ ٱلنَّارِۖ هُمۡ فِيهَا خَـٰلِدُونَ

And because the Hour is coming— there is no doubt about it—and because Allah will resurrect those in the graves. – Surah Al-Hajj 22:7

وَأَنَّ ٱلسَّاعَةَ ءَاتِيَةٌ لَّا رَيۡبَ فِيهَا وَأَنَّ ٱللَّهَ يَبۡعَثُ مَن فِى ٱلۡقُبُورِ

As for those who do not believe in the Hereafter. We made their deeds appear good to them, so they wander aimlessly.– Surah An-Naml 27:4

إِنَّ ٱلَّذِينَ لَا يُؤۡمِنُونَ بِٱلۡءَاخِرَةِ زَيَّنَّا لَهُمۡ أَعۡمَـٰلَهُمۡ فَهُمۡ يَعۡمَهُونَ

Those who disbelieve say, “When we have become dust, and our ancestors, shall we be brought out?– Surah An-Naml 27:67

وَيَقُولُونَ مَتَىٰ هَـٰذَا ٱلۡوَعۡدُ إِن كُنتُمۡ صَـٰدِقِينَ

And they say, “This is nothing but plain magic. When we have died and become dust and bones, shall we be resurrected?– Surah As-Saffat 37:15&16

وَقَالُوٓا۟ إِنْ هَـٰذَآ إِلَّا سِحْرٌ مُّبِينٌ أَءِذَا مِتْنَا وَكُنَّا تُرَابًا وَعِظَـٰمًا أَءِنَّا لَمَبْعُوثُونَ

How can you deny Allah, when you were dead and He gave you life, then He will put you to death, then He will bring you to life, then to Him you will be returned?. - Surah Al-Baqarah 2:28

كَيْفَ تَكْفُرُونَ بِٱللَّهِ وَكُنتُمْ أَمْوَٰتًا فَأَحْيَـٰكُمْ ۖ ثُمَّ يُمِيتُكُمْ ثُمَّ يُحْيِيكُمْ ثُمَّ إِلَيْهِ تُرْجَعُونَ

On the Day when the Quake quakes. And is followed by the Successor. Hearts on that Day will be pounding.Their sights downcast. They say, “Are we to be restored to the original condition? When we have become hollow bones?” They say, “This is a losing proposition.” But it will be only a single nudge. And they will be awake. - Surah An-Nazi’at 79:6-14

يَوْمَ تَرْجُفُ ٱلرَّاجِفَةُ تَتْبَعُهَا ٱلرَّادِفَةُ قُلُوبٌ يَوْمَئِذٍ وَاجِفَةٌ أَبْصَـٰرُهَا خَـٰشِعَةٌ يَقُولُونَ أَءِنَّا لَمَرْدُودُونَ فِى ٱلْحَافِرَةِ أَءِذَا كُنَّا عِظَـٰمًا نَّخِرَةً قَالُوا۟ تِلْكَ إِذًا كَرَّةٌ خَاسِرَةٌ فَإِنَّمَا هِىَ زَجْرَةٌ وَٰحِدَةٌ فَإِذَا هُم بِٱلسَّاهِرَةِ

Narrated Abu Sa`id Al-Khudri: Allah’s Messenger ﷺ said, “Allah will say to the people of Paradise, ‘O the people of Paradise!’ They will say, ‘Labbaik, O our Lord, and Sa`daik!’ Allah will say, ‘Are you pleased?” They will say, ‘Why should we not be pleased since You have given us what You have not given to anyone of Your creation?’ Allah will say, ‘I will give you something better than that.’ They will reply, ‘O our Lord! And what is better than that?’ Allah will say, ‘I will bestow My pleasure and contentment upon you so that I will never be angry with you after for-ever.’ “ – Al-Bukhari 6549

حَدَّثَنَا مُعَاذُ بْنُ أَسَدٍ، أَخْبَرَنَا عَبْدُ اللَّهِ، أَخْبَرَنَا مَالِكُ بْنُ أَنَسٍ، عَنْ زَيْدِ بْنِ أَسْلَمَ، عَنْ عَطَاءِ بْنِ يَسَارٍ، عَنْ أَبِي سَعِيدٍ الْخُدْرِيِّ، قَالَ قَالَ رَسُولُ اللَّهِ صلى الله عليه وسلم " إِنَّ اللَّهَ يَقُولُ لأَهْلِ الْجَنَّةِ يَا أَهْلَ الْجَنَّةِ. يَقُولُونَ لَبَّيْكَ رَبَّنَا وَسَعْدَيْكَ. فَيَقُولُ هَلْ رَضِيتُمْ فَيَقُولُونَ وَمَا لَنَا لاَ نَرْضَى وَقَدْ أَعْطَيْتَنَا مَا لَمْ تُعْطِ أَحَدًا مِنْ خَلْقِكَ. فَيَقُولُ أَنَا أُعْطِيكُمْ أَفْضَلَ مِنْ ذَلِكَ. قَالُوا يَا رَبِّ وَأَىُّ شَىْءٍ أَفْضَلُ مِنْ ذَلِكَ فَيَقُولُ أُحِلُّ عَلَيْكُمْ رِضْوَانِي فَلاَ أَسْخَطُ عَلَيْكُمْ بَعْدَهُ أَبَدًا "

Have you not considered him who argued with Abraham about his Lord, because Allah had given him sovereignty? Abraham said, “My Lord is He who gives life and causes death.” He said, “I give life and cause death.” Abraham said, “Allah brings the sun from the East, so bring it from the West,” so the blasphemer was confounded. Allah people. Does not guide the wrongdoing Or like him who passed by a town collapsed on its foundations. He said, “How can Allah revive this after its demise?” Thereupon Allah caused him to die for a hundred years, and then resurrected him. He said, “For how long have you tarried?” a day, or part of a day.” He said, “No. You have tarried for a hundred years. Now look at your food and your drink—it has not spoiled—and look at your donkey. We will make you a wonder for mankind. And look at the bones, how We arrange them, and then clothe them with flesh.” So when it became clear to him, he said, “I know that Allah has power over all things.” And when Abraham said, “My Lord, show me how You give life to the dead.” He said, “Have you not believed?” He said, “Yes, but to put my heart at ease.” He said, “Take four birds, and incline them to yourself, then place a part on each hill, then call to them; and they will come rushing to you. And know that Allah is Powerful and Wise.”” – Surah Al-Baqarah 2:258-260

أَلَمْ تَرَ إِلَى ٱلَّذِى حَآجَّ إِبْرَٰهِـۧمَ فِى رَبِّهِۦٓ أَنْ ءَاتَىٰهُ ٱللَّهُ ٱلْمُلْكَ إِذْ قَالَ إِبْرَٰهِـۧمُ رَبِّىَ ٱلَّذِى يُحْىِۦ وَيُمِيتُ قَالَ أَنَا۠ أُحْىِۦ وَأُمِيتُ ۖ قَالَ إِبْرَٰهِـۧمُ فَإِنَّ ٱللَّهَ يَأْتِى بِٱلشَّمْسِ مِنَ ٱلْمَشْرِقِ فَأْتِ بِهَا مِنَ ٱلْمَغْرِبِ فَبُهِتَ ٱلَّذِى كَفَرَ ۗ وَٱللَّهُ لَا يَهْدِى ٱلْقَوْمَ ٱلظَّـٰلِمِينَ أَوْ كَٱلَّذِى مَرَّ عَلَىٰ قَرْيَةٍ وَهِىَ خَاوِيَةٌ عَلَىٰ عُرُوشِهَا قَالَ أَنَّىٰ يُحْىِۦ هَـٰذِهِ ٱللَّهُ بَعْدَ مَوْتِهَا ۖ فَأَمَاتَهُ ٱللَّهُ مِا۟ئَةَ عَامٍ ثُمَّ بَعَثَهُۥ ۖ قَالَ كَمْ لَبِثْتَ ۖ قَالَ لَبِثْتُ يَوْمًا أَوْ بَعْضَ يَوْمٍ ۖ قَالَ بَل لَّبِثْتَ مِا۟ئَةَ عَامٍ فَٱنظُرْ إِلَىٰ طَعَامِكَ وَشَرَابِكَ لَمْ يَتَسَنَّهْ ۖ وَٱنظُرْ إِلَىٰ حِمَارِكَ وَلِنَجْعَلَكَ

ءَايَةً لِّلنَّاسِ وَٱنظُرْ إِلَى ٱلْعِظَامِ كَيْفَ نُنشِزُهَا ثُمَّ نَكْسُوهَا لَحْمًا ۚ فَلَمَّا تَبَيَّنَ لَهُۥ قَالَ أَعْلَمُ أَنَّ ٱللَّهَ عَلَىٰ كُلِّ شَىْءٍ قَدِيرٌ وَإِذْ قَالَ
إِبْرَٰهِـۧمُ رَبِّ أَرِنِى كَيْفَ تُحْىِ ٱلْمَوْتَىٰ قَالَ أَوَلَمْ تُؤْمِن قَالَ بَلَىٰ وَلَـٰكِن لِّيَطْمَئِنَّ قَلْبِى قَالَ فَخُذْ أَرْبَعَةً مِّنَ ٱلطَّيْرِ فَصُرْهُنَّ
إِلَيْكَ ثُمَّ ٱجْعَلْ عَلَىٰ كُلِّ جَبَلٍ مِّنْهُنَّ جُزْءًا ثُمَّ ٱدْعُهُنَّ يَأْتِينَكَ سَعْيًا ۚ وَٱعْلَمْ أَنَّ ٱللَّهَ عَزِيزٌ حَكِيمٌ

Tell those who believe to forgive those who do not hope for the Days of Allah. He will fully recompense people for whatever they have earned.– Surah Al-Jathiyah 45:14
قُل لِّلَّذِينَ ءَامَنُوا۟ يَغْفِرُوا۟ لِلَّذِينَ لَا يَرْجُونَ أَيَّامَ ٱللَّهِ لِيَجْزِىَ قَوْمًۢا بِمَا كَانُوا۟ يَكْسِبُونَ

Those who do not hope to meet Us, and are content with the worldly life, and are at ease in it, and those who pay no heed to Our signs. – Surah Yunus 10:7
إِنَّ ٱلَّذِينَ لَا يَرْجُونَ لِقَآءَنَا وَرَضُوا۟ بِٱلْحَيَوٰةِ ٱلدُّنْيَا وَٱطْمَأَنُّوا۟ بِهَا وَٱلَّذِينَ هُمْ عَنْ ءَايَـٰتِنَا غَـٰفِلُونَ

And when Our clear revelations are recited to them, those who do not hope to meet Us say, "Bring a Quran other than this, or change it." Say, "It is not for me to change it of my own accord. I only follow what is revealed to me. I fear, if I disobeyed my Lord, the torment of a terrible Day." – Surah Yunus 10:15
وَإِذَا تُتْلَىٰ عَلَيْهِمْ ءَايَاتُنَا بَيِّنَـٰتٍ قَالَ ٱلَّذِينَ لَا يَرْجُونَ لِقَآءَنَا ٱئْتِ بِقُرْءَانٍ غَيْرِ هَـٰذَآ أَوْ بَدِّلْهُ ۚ قُلْ مَا يَكُونُ لِىٓ أَنْ أُبَدِّلَهُۥ مِن
تِلْقَآئِ نَفْسِىٓ ۖ إِنْ أَتَّبِعُ إِلَّا مَا يُوحَىٰٓ إِلَىَّ ۖ إِنِّىٓ أَخَافُ إِنْ عَصَيْتُ رَبِّى عَذَابَ يَوْمٍ عَظِيمٍ

Those who disbelieved in Allah's signs and His encounter—these have despaired of My mercy. For them is a painful torment. – Surah Al-Ankabut 29:23
وَالَّذِينَ كَفَرُوا بِآيَاتِ اللَّهِ وَلِقَائِهِ أُولَٰئِكَ يَئِسُوا مِن رَّحْمَتِي وَأُولَٰئِكَ لَهُمْ عَذَابٌ أَلِيم

Tell those who believe to forgive those who do not hope for the Days of Allah. He will fully recompense people for whatever they have earned. – Surah Al-Jathiyah 45:14
قُل لِّلَّذِينَ آمَنُوا يَغْفِرُوا لِلَّذِينَ لَا يَرْجُونَ أَيَّامَ اللَّهِ لِيَجْزِيَ قَوْمًا بِمَا كَانُوا يَكْسِبُون

O you who believe! Do not befriend people with whom Allah has become angry, and have despaired of the Hereafter, as the faithless have despaired of the occupants of the graves. – Surah Al-Mutahinah 60:13
يَـٰٓأَيُّهَا ٱلَّذِينَ ءَامَنُوا۟ لَا تَتَوَلَّوْا۟ قَوْمًا غَضِبَ ٱللَّهُ عَلَيْهِمْ قَدْ يَئِسُوا۟ مِنَ ٱلْـَٔاخِرَةِ كَمَا يَئِسَ ٱلْكُفَّارُ مِنْ أَصْحَـٰبِ ٱلْقُبُورِ

The Book of
whoever believes in Allah and the Last Day and do righteous good deeds shall have their reward with their Lord
مَنْ ءَامَنَ بِٱللَّهِ وَٱلْيَوْمِ ٱلْءَاخِرِ وَعَمِلَ صَٰلِحًا فَلَهُمْ أَجْرُهُمْ عِندَ رَبِّهِمْ

Surely, those who say: "Our Lord is Allah," and then go straight, the angels will descend upon them: "Do not fear, and do not grieve, but rejoice in the news of the Garden which you were promised. We are your allies in this life and in the Hereafter, wherein you will have whatever your souls desire, and you will have therein whatever you call for.- Surah Al-Fussilat 41:30&31
إِنَّ ٱلَّذِينَ قَالُواْ رَبُّنَا ٱللَّهُ ثُمَّ ٱسْتَقَٰمُواْ تَتَنَزَّلُ عَلَيْهِمُ ٱلْمَلَٰٓئِكَةُ أَلَّا تَخَافُواْ وَلَا تَحْزَنُواْ وَأَبْشِرُواْ بِٱلْجَنَّةِ ٱلَّتِى كُنتُمْ تُوعَدُونَ نَحْنُ
أَوْلِيَآؤُكُمْ فِى ٱلْحَيَوٰةِ ٱلدُّنْيَا وَفِى ٱلْءَاخِرَةِ ۖ وَلَكُمْ فِيهَا مَا تَشْتَهِىٓ أَنفُسُكُمْ وَلَكُمْ فِيهَا مَا تَدَّعُونَ

As for those who believed and did good deeds—they will be delighted in meadows.– Surah Ar-Rum 30:15

فَأَمَّا ٱلَّذِينَ ءَامَنُواْ وَعَمِلُواْ ٱلصَّٰلِحَٰتِ فَهُمْ فِى رَوْضَةٍ يُحْبَرُونَ

The inhabitants of Paradise, on that Day, will be happily busy. They and their spouses, in shades, reclining on couches.They will have therein fruits. They will have whatever they call for.Peace—a saying from a Most Merciful Lord – Surah Ya-Sin 36:55-58
إِنَّ أَصْحَٰبَ ٱلْجَنَّةِ ٱلْيَوْمَ فِى شُغُلٍ فَٰكِهُونَ هُمْ وَأَزْوَٰجُهُمْ فِى ظِلَٰلٍ عَلَى ٱلْأَرَآئِكِ مُتَّكِـُٔونَ لَهُمْ فِيهَا فَٰكِهَةٌ وَلَهُم مَّا يَدَّعُونَ سَلَٰمٌ
قَوْلًا مِّن رَّبٍّ رَّحِيمٍ

Except for Allah sincere servants. For them is a known provision. Fruits; and they will be honored. In the Gardens of Bliss. On furnishings, facing one another. They will be offered a cup of pure drink. White; a delight to those who drink. Never polluted, and never intoxicating. With them will be bashful women with lovely eyes. As if they were closely guarded pearls. – Surah As-Saffat 37:40-49
إِلَّا عِبَادَ ٱللَّهِ ٱلْمُخْلَصِينَ أُوْلَٰٓئِكَ لَهُمْ رِزْقٌ مَّعْلُومٌ فَوَٰكِهُ وَهُم مُّكْرَمُونَ فِى جَنَّٰتِ ٱلنَّعِيمِ عَلَىٰ سُرُرٍ مُّتَقَٰبِلِينَ يُطَافُ عَلَيْهِم
بِكَأْسٍ مِّن مَّعِينٍ بَيْضَآءَ لَذَّةٍ لِّلشَّٰرِبِينَ لَا فِيهَا غَوْلٌ وَلَا هُمْ عَنْهَا يُنزَفُونَ وَعِندَهُمْ قَٰصِرَٰتُ ٱلطَّرْفِ عِينٌ كَأَنَّهُنَّ بَيْضٌ
مَّكْنُونٌ

Say, "Shall I inform you of something better than that? For those who are righteous, with their Lord are Gardens beneath which rivers flow, where they will remain forever, and purified spouses, and acceptance from Allah." Allah is Observant of the servants. – Surah Al-Imran 3:15
قُلْ أَؤُنَبِّئُكُم بِخَيْرٍ مِّن ذَٰلِكُمْ ۚ لِلَّذِينَ ٱتَّقَوْاْ عِندَ رَبِّهِمْ جَنَّٰتٌ تَجْرِى مِن تَحْتِهَا ٱلْأَنْهَٰرُ خَٰلِدِينَ فِيهَا وَأَزْوَٰجٌ مُّطَهَّرَةٌ وَرِضْوَٰنٌ
مِّنَ ٱللَّهِ ۗ وَٱللَّهُ بَصِيرٌۢ بِٱلْعِبَادِ

Narrated Abu Huraira: The Prophetﷺ said, "Allah said, "I have prepared for My righteous slaves (such excellent things) as no eye has ever seen, nor an ear has ever heard nor a human heart can ever think of.' " – Al-Bukhari 7498
حَدَّثَنَا مُعَاذُ بْنُ أَسَدٍ، أَخْبَرَنَا عَبْدُ اللَّهِ، أَخْبَرَنَا مَعْمَرٌ، عَنْ هَمَّامِ بْنِ مُنَبِّهٍ، عَنْ أَبِي هُرَيْرَةَ ـ رضى الله عنه ـ عَنِ النَّبِيِّ صلى
الله عليه وسلم قَالَ " قَالَ اللَّهُ أَعْدَدْتُ لِعِبَادِي الصَّالِحِينَ مَا لاَ عَيْنٌ رَأَتْ، وَلاَ أُذُنٌ سَمِعَتْ، وَلاَ خَطَرَ عَلَى قَلْبِ بَشَرٍ "

Narrated Abu Sa`id Al-Khudri: The Prophetﷺ said, "Allah will say to the people of Paradise, "O the people of Paradise!" They will say, 'Labbaik, O our Lord, and Sa`daik, and all the good is in Your Hands!' Allah will say, "Are you satisfied?' They will say, 'Why shouldn't we be satisfied, O our Lord as You have given us what You have not given to any of Your created beings?' He will say, 'Shall I not give you something better than that?' They will say, 'O our Lord! What else could be better than that?' He will say, 'I bestow My Pleasure on you and will never be angry with you after that.' " – Al-Bukhari 7518

حَدَّثَنَا يَحْيَى بْنُ سُلَيْمَانَ، حَدَّثَنِي ابْنُ وَهْبٍ، قَالَ حَدَّثَنِي مَالِكٌ، عَنْ زَيْدِ بْنِ أَسْلَمَ، عَنْ عَطَاءِ بْنِ يَسَارٍ، عَنْ أَبِي سَعِيدٍ الْخُدْرِيِّ ـ رضى الله عنه ـ قَالَ قَالَ النَّبِيُّ صلى الله عليه وسلم " إِنَّ اللَّهَ يَقُولُ لأَهْلِ الْجَنَّةِ يَا أَهْلَ الْجَنَّةِ. فَيَقُولُونَ لَبَّيْكَ رَبَّنَا وَسَعْدَيْكَ وَالْخَيْرُ فِي يَدَيْكَ. فَيَقُولُ هَلْ رَضِيتُمْ فَيَقُولُونَ وَمَا لَنَا لاَ نَرْضَى يَا رَبِّ وَقَدْ أَعْطَيْتَنَا مَا لَمْ تُعْطِ أَحَدًا مِنْ خَلْقِكَ. فَيَقُولُ أَلاَ أُعْطِيكُمْ أَفْضَلَ مِنْ ذَلِكَ. فَيَقُولُونَ يَا رَبِّ وَأَىُّ شَىْءٍ أَفْضَلُ مِنْ ذَلِكَ فَيَقُولُ أُحِلُّ عَلَيْكُمْ رِضْوَانِي فَلاَ أَسْخَطُ عَلَيْكُمْ بَعْدَهُ أَبَدًا "

The Book of
Has not the news reached you of those who disbelieved aforetime? And so they tasted the evil result of their disbelief, and theirs will be a painful torment.
أَلَمْ يَأْتِكُمْ نَبَؤُا۟ ٱلَّذِينَ كَفَرُوا۟ مِن قَبْلُ فَذَاقُوا۟ وَبَالَ أَمْرِهِمْ وَلَهُمْ عَذَابٌ

"Those whose efforts in this world are misguided, while they assume that they are doing well." It is they who rejected the communications of their Lord, and the encounter with Him. So their works are in vain. And on the Day of Resurrection, We will consider them of no weight. – Surah Al-Khaf 18:104&105
ٱلَّذِينَ ضَلَّ سَعْيُهُمْ فِى ٱلْحَيَوٰةِ ٱلدُّنْيَا وَهُمْ يَحْسَبُونَ أَنَّهُمْ يُحْسِنُونَ صُنْعًا أُو۟لَـٰٓئِكَ ٱلَّذِينَ كَفَرُوا۟ بِـَٔايَـٰتِ رَبِّهِمْ وَلِقَآئِهِۦ فَحَبِطَتْ أَعْمَـٰلُهُمْ فَلَا نُقِيمُ لَهُمْ يَوْمَ ٱلْقِيَـٰمَةِ وَزْنًا

Those who reject Our revelations—We will scorch them in a Fire. Every time their skins are cooked, We will replace them with other skins, so they will experience the suffering. Allah is Most Powerful, Most Wise. – Surah An-Nisa 4:56
إِنَّ ٱلَّذِينَ كَفَرُوا۟ بِـَٔايَـٰتِنَا سَوْفَ نُصْلِيهِمْ نَارًا كُلَّمَا نَضِجَتْ جُلُودُهُم بَدَّلْنَـٰهُمْ جُلُودًا غَيْرَهَا لِيَذُوقُوا۟ ٱلْعَذَابَ ۗ إِنَّ ٱللَّهَ كَانَ عَزِيزًا حَكِيمًا

For those who reject their Lord, there is the torment of Hell. What an evil destination! – Surah Al-Mulk 67:6
وَلِلَّذِينَ كَفَرُوا۟ بِرَبِّهِمْ عَذَابُ جَهَنَّمَ ۖ وَبِئْسَ ٱلْمَصِيرُ

Has the news not reached you, of those who disbelieved before? They tasted the ill consequences of their conduct, and a painful torment awaits them. That is because their messengers came to them with clear explanations, but they said, "Are human beings going to guide us?" So they disbelieved and turned away. But Allah is in no need. Allah is Independent and Praiseworthy. Those who disbelieve claim that they will not be resurrected. Say, "Yes indeed, by my Lord, you will be resurrected; then you will be informed of everything you did; and that is easy for Allah." – Surah At-Taghabun 64:5-7
أَلَمْ يَأْتِكُمْ نَبَؤُا۟ ٱلَّذِينَ كَفَرُوا۟ مِن قَبْلُ فَذَاقُوا۟ وَبَالَ أَمْرِهِمْ وَلَهُمْ عَذَابٌ أَلِيمٌ ذَٰلِكَ بِأَنَّهُۥ كَانَت تَّأْتِيهِمْ رُسُلُهُم بِٱلْبَيِّنَـٰتِ فَقَالُوٓا۟ أَبَشَرٌ يَهْدُونَنَا فَكَفَرُوا۟ وَتَوَلَّوا۟ ۚ وَّٱسْتَغْنَى ٱللَّهُ ۚ وَٱللَّهُ غَنِىٌّ حَمِيدٌ زَعَمَ ٱلَّذِينَ كَفَرُوٓا۟ أَن لَّن يُبْعَثُوا۟ ۚ قُلْ بَلَىٰ وَرَبِّى لَتُبْعَثُنَّ ثُمَّ لَتُنَبَّؤُنَّ بِمَا عَمِلْتُمْ ۚ وَذَٰلِكَ عَلَى ٱللَّهِ يَسِيرٌ

As for those who are miserable, they will be in the Fire. They will have therein sighing and wailing. — Surah Hud 11:106
فَأَمَّا ٱلَّذِينَ شَقُوا۟ فَفِى ٱلنَّارِ لَهُمْ فِيهَا زَفِيرٌ وَشَهِيقٌ

Awaiting them is Hell, and they will be left to drink oozing pus, which they will sip with difficulty, and can hardly swallow. Death will overwhelm them from every side, yet they will not ⌜be able to⌝ die. Awaiting them still is harsher torment.– Surah Ibrahim 14:16-17
مِّن وَرَآئِهِۦ جَهَنَّمُ وَيُسْقَىٰ مِن مَّآءٍ صَدِيدٍ. يَتَجَرَّعُهُۥ وَلَا يَكَادُ يُسِيغُهُۥ وَيَأْتِيهِ ٱلْمَوْتُ مِن كُلِّ مَكَانٍ وَمَا هُوَ بِمَيِّتٍ ۖ وَمِن وَرَآئِهِۦ عَذَابٌ غَلِيظٌ

Here are two adversaries feuding regarding their Lord. As for those who disbelieve, garments of fire will be tailored for them, and scalding water will be poured over their heads. Melting

their insides and their skins. And they will have maces of iron. Whenever they try to escape the gloom, they will be driven back to it: "Taste the suffering of burning." – Surah Al-Hajj 22:19-22
هَٰذَانِ خَصْمَانِ ٱخْتَصَمُوا۟ فِى رَبِّهِمْ ۖ فَٱلَّذِينَ كَفَرُوا۟ قُطِّعَتْ لَهُمْ ثِيَابٌ مِّن نَّارٍ يُصَبُّ مِن فَوْقِ رُءُوسِهِمُ ٱلْحَمِيمُ. يُصْهَرُ بِهِۦ مَا فِى بُطُونِهِمْ وَٱلْجُلُودُ. وَلَهُم مَّقَٰمِعُ مِنْ حَدِيدٍ. كُلَّمَآ أَرَادُوٓا۟ أَن يَخْرُجُوا۟ مِنْهَا مِنْ غَمٍّ أُعِيدُوا۟ فِيهَا وَذُوقُوا۟ عَذَابَ ٱلْحَرِيقِ

Roasting in a scorching Fire. Given to drink from a flaming spring. The Overwhelming They will have no food except thorns. Nor ,nourishes neither That satisfies hunger. – Surah Al-Ghashiyah 88:4-7
تَصْلَىٰ نَارًا حَامِيَةً.تُسْقَىٰ مِنْ عَيْنٍ ءَانِيَةٍ.لَّيْسَ لَهُمْ طَعَامٌ إِلَّا مِن ضَرِيعٍ.لَّا يُسْمِنُ وَلَا يُغْنِى مِن جُوعٍ

They will taste therein neither coolness, nor drink. Except boiling water, and freezing hail. A fitting requital.– Surah An-Naba 78:24-26
لَّا يَذُوقُونَ فِيهَا بَرْدًا وَلَا شَرَابًا.إِلَّا حَمِيمًا وَغَسَّاقًا.جَزَآءً وِفَاقًا

Those who call the Book a lie, and what We sent Our messengers with—they will surely know.. their around are yokes the When necks, and they will be dragged by the chains. E in then ,water boiling the Into Fire they will be consumed. – Surah Ghafir 40:70-72
ٱلَّذِينَ كَذَّبُوا۟ بِٱلْكِتَٰبِ وَبِمَآ أَرْسَلْنَا بِهِۦ رُسُلَنَا ۖ فَسَوْفَ يَعْلَمُونَ.إِذِ ٱلْأَغْلَٰلُ فِىٓ أَعْنَٰقِهِمْ وَٱلسَّلَٰسِلُ يُسْحَبُونَ.فِى ٱلْحَمِيمِ ثُمَّ فِى ٱلنَّارِ يُسْجَرُونَ

And say, "The truth is from your Lord. Whoever wills—let him believe. And whoever wills—let him disbelieve". We have prepared for the unjust a Fire, whose curtains will hem them in. And when they cry for relief, they will be relieved with water like molten brass, which scalds the What a miserable drink, and what a terrible place. – Surah Al-Kahfi 18:29
وَقُلِ ٱلْحَقُّ مِن رَّبِّكُمْ ۖ فَمَن شَآءَ فَلْيُؤْمِن وَمَن شَآءَ فَلْيَكْفُرْ ۚ إِنَّآ أَعْتَدْنَا لِلظَّٰلِمِينَ نَارًا أَحَاطَ بِهِمْ سُرَادِقُهَا ۚ وَإِن يَسْتَغِيثُوا۟ يُغَاثُوا۟ بِمَآءٍ كَٱلْمُهْلِ يَشْوِى ٱلْوُجُوهَ ۚ بِئْسَ ٱلشَّرَابُ وَسَآءَتْ مُرْتَفَقًا

And do not obey the disbelievers and the hypocrites
وَلَا تُطِعِ ٱلْكَٰفِرِينَ وَٱلْمُنَٰفِقِينَ

O you Prophet, be pious to Allah, and do not obey the disbelievers and the hypocrites; surely Allah as been Ever-Knowing, Ever-Wise. – Surah Al-Azhab 33:1
يَٰٓأَيُّهَا ٱلنَّبِىُّ ٱتَّقِ ٱللَّهَ وَلَا تُطِعِ ٱلْكَٰفِرِينَ وَٱلْمُنَٰفِقِينَ ۗ إِنَّ ٱللَّهَ كَانَ عَلِيمًا حَكِيمًا

And do not obey the disbelievers and the hypocrites; and disregard their hurt, and put your trust in Allah; and Allah suffices as an Ever-Trusted Trustee. – Surah Al-Azhab 33:48
وَلَا تُطِعِ ٱلْكَٰفِرِينَ وَٱلْمُنَٰفِقِينَ وَدَعْ أَذَىٰهُمْ وَتَوَكَّلْ عَلَى ٱللَّهِ ۚ وَكَفَىٰ بِٱللَّهِ وَكِيلًا

Then do not obey the unbelievers. They wish that you compromise, So they too can compromise. And do not obey any worthless contemptible swearer Surah Al-Qalam 68:8-10
فَلَا تُطِعِ ٱلْمُكَذِّبِينَ وَدُّوا۟ لَوْ تُدْهِنُ فَيُدْهِنُونَ وَلَا تُطِعْ كُلَّ حَلَّافٍ مَّهِينٍ

So await your Lord's Judgment with patience; and do not obey a sinner or a denier of the truth from among them. – Surah Al-Insan 76:24
فَٱصْبِرْ لِحُكْمِ رَبِّكَ وَلَا تُطِعْ مِنْهُمْ ءَاثِمًا أَوْ كَفُورًا

O you who have believed, in case you obey the ones who have disbelieved, they will turn you back on your heels; so you turn over, losers. – Surah Al-Imran 3:149
يَـٰٓأَيُّهَا ٱلَّذِينَ ءَامَنُوٓا۟ إِن تُطِيعُوا۟ ٱلَّذِينَ كَفَرُوا۟ يَرُدُّوكُمْ عَلَىٰٓ أَعْقَـٰبِكُمْ فَتَنقَلِبُوا۟ خَـٰسِرِينَ

The Book of
Obey Allah and His Messenger
أَطِيعُوا۟ ٱللَّهَ وَرَسُولَهُۥ

We did not send any messenger except to be obeyed by Allah's leave. Had they, when they wronged themselves, come to you, and prayed for Allah's forgiveness, and the Messenger had prayed for their forgiveness, they would have found Allah Relenting and Merciful. But no, by your Lord, they will not believe until they call you to arbitrate in their disputes, and then find within themselves no resentment regarding your decisions, and submit themselves completely. – Surah An-Nisa 4:64&65
وَمَآ أَرْسَلْنَا مِن رَّسُولٍ إِلَّا لِيُطَاعَ بِإِذْنِ ٱللَّهِ ۚ وَلَوْ أَنَّهُمْ إِذ ظَّلَمُوٓا۟ أَنفُسَهُمْ جَآءُوكَ فَٱسْتَغْفَرُوا۟ ٱللَّهَ وَٱسْتَغْفَرَ لَهُمُ ٱلرَّسُولُ لَوَجَدُوا۟ ٱللَّهَ تَوَّابًا رَّحِيمًا فَلَا وَرَبِّكَ لَا يُؤْمِنُونَ حَتَّىٰ يُحَكِّمُوكَ فِيمَا شَجَرَ بَيْنَهُمْ ثُمَّ لَا يَجِدُوا۟ فِىٓ أَنفُسِهِمْ حَرَجًا مِّمَّا قَضَيْتَ وَيُسَلِّمُوا۟ تَسْلِيمًا

The Desert-Arabs say, "We have believed." Say, "You have not believed; but say, 'We have submitted,' for faith has not yet entered into your hearts. But if you obey Allah and His Messenger, He will not diminish any of your deeds. Allah is Forgiving and Merciful."– Surah Al-Hujurat 49:14
قَالَتِ ٱلْأَعْرَابُ ءَامَنَّا ۖ قُل لَّمْ تُؤْمِنُوا۟ وَلَـٰكِن قُولُوٓا۟ أَسْلَمْنَا وَلَمَّا يَدْخُلِ ٱلْإِيمَـٰنُ فِى قُلُوبِكُمْ ۖ وَإِن تُطِيعُوا۟ ٱللَّهَ وَرَسُولَهُۥ لَا يَلِتْكُم مِّنْ أَعْمَـٰلِكُمْ شَيْـًٔا ۚ إِنَّ ٱللَّهَ غَفُورٌ رَّحِيمٌ

So believe in Allah and His Messenger, and the Light which We sent down. Allah is Aware of everything you do. – Surah At-Taghabun 64:8
فَـَٔامِنُوا۟ بِٱللَّهِ وَرَسُولِهِۦ وَٱلنُّورِ ٱلَّذِىٓ أَنزَلْنَا ۚ وَٱللَّهُ بِمَا تَعْمَلُونَ خَبِيرٌ

Narrated `Aisha: The Prophet ﷺ did something as it was allowed from the religious point of view but some people refrained from it. When the Prophet ﷺ heard of that he, after glorifying and praising Allah, said, "Why do some people refrain from doing something which I do? By Allah, I know Allah more than they." – Al-Bukhari 7301
حَدَّثَنَا عُمَرُ بْنُ حَفْصٍ، حَدَّثَنَا أَبِي، حَدَّثَنَا الأَعْمَشُ، حَدَّثَنَا مُسْلِمٌ، عَنْ مَسْرُوقٍ، قَالَ قَالَتْ عَائِشَةُ ـ رَضِيَ الله عنها ـ صَنَعَ النَّبِيُّ صلى الله عليه وسلم شَيْئًا تَرَخَّصَ وَتَنَزَّهَ عَنْهُ قَوْمٌ، فَبَلَغَ ذَلِكَ النَّبِيَّ صلى الله عليه وسلم فَحَمِدَ اللَّهَ ثُمَّ قَالَ " مَا بَالُ أَقْوَامٍ يَتَنَزَّهُونَ عَنِ الشَّىْءِ أَصْنَعُهُ، فَوَاللَّهِ إِنِّي أَعْلَمُهُمْ بِاللَّهِ، وَأَشَدُّهُمْ لَهُ خَشْيَةً "

Narrated Abu Huraira: The Prophet ﷺ said, "Leave me as I leave you, for the people who were before you were ruined because of their questions and their differences over their prophets. So, if I forbid you to do something, then keep away from it. And if I order you to do something, then do of it as much as you can." – Al-Bukhari 7288
حَدَّثَنَا إِسْمَاعِيلُ، حَدَّثَنِي مَالِكٌ، عَنْ أَبِي الزِّنَادِ، عَنِ الأَعْرَجِ، عَنْ أَبِي هُرَيْرَةَ، عَنِ النَّبِيِّ صلى الله عليه وسلم قَالَ " دَعُونِي مَا تَرَكْتُكُمْ، إِنَّمَا هَلَكَ مَنْ كَانَ قَبْلَكُمْ بِسُؤَالِهِمْ وَاخْتِلاَفِهِمْ عَلَى أَنْبِيَائِهِمْ، فَإِذَا نَهَيْتُكُمْ عَنْ شَىْءٍ فَاجْتَنِبُوهُ، وَإِذَا أَمَرْتُكُمْ بِأَمْرٍ فَأْتُوا مِنْهُ مَا اسْتَطَعْتُمْ "

Narrated `Abdullah bin Hisham: We were with the Prophetﷺ and he was holding the hand of `Umar bin Al-Khattab. `Umar said to Him, "O Allah's Messengerﷺ ! You are dearer to me than everything except my own self." The Prophet ﷺ said, "No, by Him in Whose Hand my soul is, (you will not have complete faith) till I am dearer to you than your own self." Then `Umar said to him, "However, now, by Allah, you are dearer to me than my own self." The Prophetﷺ said, "Now, O `Umar, (now you are a believer). – Al-Bukhari 6632
حَدَّثَنَا يَحْيَى بْنُ سُلَيْمَانَ، قَالَ حَدَّثَنِي ابْنُ وَهْبٍ، قَالَ أَخْبَرَنِي حَيْوَةُ، قَالَ حَدَّثَنِي أَبُو عَقِيلٍ، زُهْرَةُ بْنُ مَعْبَدٍ أَنَّهُ سَمِعَ جَدَّهُ عَبْدَ اللَّهِ بْنَ هِشَامٍ، قَالَ كُنَّا مَعَ النَّبِيِّ صلى الله عليه وسلم وَهُوَ آخِذٌ بِيَدِ عُمَرَ بْنِ الْخَطَّابِ فَقَالَ لَهُ عُمَرُ يَا رَسُولَ اللَّهِ لأَنْتَ أَحَبُّ إِلَىَّ مِنْ كُلِّ شَىْءٍ إِلاَّ مِنْ نَفْسِي. فَقَالَ النَّبِيُّ صلى الله عليه وسلم " لاَ وَالَّذِي نَفْسِي بِيَدِهِ حَتَّى أَكُونَ أَحَبَّ إِلَيْكَ مِنْ نَفْسِكَ ". فَقَالَ لَهُ عُمَرُ فَإِنَّهُ الآنَ وَاللَّهِ لأَنْتَ أَحَبُّ إِلَىَّ مِنْ نَفْسِي. فَقَالَ النَّبِيُّ صلى الله عليه وسلم " الآنَ يَا عُمَرُ ".

O you who believe! Obey Allah and His Messenger, and do not turn away from him when you hear. And be not like those who say, "We hear," when they do not hear. Surah Al-Anfal 8:20&21
يَـٰٓأَيُّهَا ٱلَّذِينَ ءَامَنُوٓاْ أَطِيعُواْ ٱللَّهَ وَرَسُولَهُۥ وَلَا تَوَلَّوْاْ عَنْهُ وَأَنتُمْ تَسْمَعُونَ وَلَا تَكُونُواْ كَٱلَّذِينَ قَالُواْ سَمِعْنَا وَهُمْ لَا يَسْمَعُونَ

O you who believe! Do not betray Allah and the Messenger, nor betray your trusts, while you know. Surah Al-Anfal 8:27
يَـٰٓأَيُّهَا ٱلَّذِينَ ءَامَنُواْ لَا تَخُونُواْ ٱللَّهَ وَٱلرَّسُولَ وَتَخُونُوٓاْ أَمَـٰنَـٰتِكُمْ وَأَنتُمْ تَعْلَمُونَ

O you who believe! Do not place your opinions above that of Allah and His Messenger, and fear Allah. Allah is Hearing and Knowing.– Surah Al-Hujurat 49:1
يَـٰٓأَيُّهَا ٱلَّذِينَ ءَامَنُواْ لَا تُقَدِّمُواْ بَيْنَ يَدَىِ ٱللَّهِ وَرَسُولِهِۦ ۖ وَٱتَّقُواْ ٱللَّهَ ۚ إِنَّ ٱللَّهَ سَمِيعٌ عَلِيمٌ

Narrated Anas: The Prophetﷺ said, "Whoever possesses the following three qualities will have the sweetness (delight) of faith: 1) The one to whom Allah and His Apostle becomes dearer than anything else. 2) Who loves a person and he loves him only for Allah's sake. 3) Who hates to revert to Atheism (disbelief) as he hates to be thrown into the fire." – Al-Bukhari 16
حَدَّثَنَا مُحَمَّدُ بْنُ الْمُثَنَّى، قَالَ حَدَّثَنَا عَبْدُ الْوَهَّابِ الثَّقَفِيُّ، قَالَ حَدَّثَنَا أَيُّوبُ، عَنْ أَبِي قِلاَبَةَ، عَنْ أَنَسٍ، عَنِ النَّبِيِّ صلى الله عليه وسلم قَالَ " ثَلاَثٌ مَنْ كُنَّ فِيهِ وَجَدَ حَلاَوَةَ الإِيمَانِ أَنْ يَكُونَ اللَّهُ وَرَسُولُهُ أَحَبَّ إِلَيْهِ مِمَّا سِوَاهُمَا، وَأَنْ يُحِبَّ الْمَرْءَ لاَ يُحِبُّهُ إِلاَّ لِلَّهِ، وَأَنْ يَكْرَهَ أَنْ يَعُودَ فِي الْكُفْرِ كَمَا يَكْرَهُ أَنْ يُقْذَفَ فِي النَّارِ ".

These are the bounds set by Allah. Whoever obeys Allah and His Messenger, He will admit him into Gardens beneath which rivers flow, to abide therein forever. That is the great attainment. But whoever disobeys Allah and His Messenger, and oversteps His bounds, He will admit him into a Fire, wherein he abides forever, and he will have a shameful punishment. – Surah An-Nisa 4:13&14
تِلْكَ حُدُودُ ٱللَّهِ ۚ وَمَن يُطِعِ ٱللَّهَ وَرَسُولَهُۥ يُدْخِلْهُ جَنَّـٰتٍ تَجْرِى مِن تَحْتِهَا ٱلْأَنْهَـٰرُ خَـٰلِدِينَ فِيهَا ۚ وَذَٰلِكَ ٱلْفَوْزُ ٱلْعَظِيمُ وَمَن يَعْصِ ٱللَّهَ وَرَسُولَهُۥ وَيَتَعَدَّ حُدُودَهُۥ يُدْخِلْهُ نَارًا خَـٰلِدًا فِيهَا وَلَهُۥ عَذَابٌ مُّهِينٌ

O you who believe! Obey Allah and obey the Messenger and those in authority among you. And if you dispute over anything, refer it to Allah and the Messenger, if you believe in Allah and the Last Day. That is best, and a most excellent determination. – Surah An-Nisa 4:59
يَـٰٓأَيُّهَا ٱلَّذِينَ ءَامَنُوٓاْ أَطِيعُواْ ٱللَّهَ وَأَطِيعُواْ ٱلرَّسُولَ وَأُوْلِى ٱلْأَمْرِ مِنكُمْ ۖ فَإِن تَنَـٰزَعْتُمْ فِى شَىْءٍ فَرُدُّوهُ إِلَى ٱللَّهِ وَٱلرَّسُولِ إِن كُنتُمْ تُؤْمِنُونَ بِٱللَّهِ وَٱلْيَوْمِ ٱلْـَٔاخِرِ ۚ ذَٰلِكَ خَيْرٌ وَأَحْسَنُ تَأْوِيلًا

Whoever obeys Allah and the Messenger—these are with those whom Allah has blessed—among the prophets, and the sincere, I martyrs, and the upright. Excellent are those as companions.–Surah An-Nisa 4:69

وَمَن يُطِعِ ٱللَّهَ وَٱلرَّسُولَ فَأُو۟لَـٰٓئِكَ مَعَ ٱلَّذِينَ أَنْعَمَ ٱللَّهُ عَلَيْهِم مِّنَ ٱلنَّبِيِّـۧنَ وَٱلصِّدِّيقِينَ وَٱلشُّهَدَآءِ وَٱلصَّـٰلِحِينَ ۚ وَحَسُنَ أُو۟لَـٰٓئِكَ رَفِيقًا

They ask you (O Muhammad) about the spoils of war. Say: "The spoils are for Allah and the Messenger." So fear Allah and adjust all matters of difference among you, and obey Allah and His Messenger (Muhammad), if you are believers. – Surah Al-Anfal 8:1

يَسْـَٔلُونَكَ عَنِ ٱلْأَنفَالِ ۖ قُلِ ٱلْأَنفَالُ لِلَّهِ وَٱلرَّسُولِ ۖ فَٱتَّقُوا۟ ٱللَّهَ وَأَصْلِحُوا۟ ذَاتَ بَيْنِكُمْ ۖ وَأَطِيعُوا۟ ٱللَّهَ وَرَسُولَهُۥٓ إِن كُنتُم مُّؤْمِنِينَ

That is because they opposed Allah and His Messenger. Whoever opposes Allah and His Messenger Allah is severe in retribution. Surah Al-Anfal 8:13

ذَٰلِكَ بِأَنَّهُمْ شَآقُّوا۟ ٱللَّهَ وَرَسُولَهُۥ ۚ وَمَن يُشَاقِقِ ٱللَّهَ وَرَسُولَهُۥ فَإِنَّ ٱللَّهَ شَدِيدُ ٱلْعِقَابِ

And obey Allah and His Messenger, and do not dispute, lest you falter and lose your courage. And be steadfast. Allah is with the steadfast. – Surah Al-Anfal 8:46

وَأَطِيعُوا۟ ٱللَّهَ وَرَسُولَهُۥ وَلَا تَنَـٰزَعُوا۟ فَتَفْشَلُوا۟ وَتَذْهَبَ رِيحُكُمْ ۖ وَٱصْبِرُوٓا۟ ۚ إِنَّ ٱللَّهَ مَعَ ٱلصَّـٰبِرِينَ

The believing men and believing women are friends of one another. They advocate virtue, forbid evil, perform the prayers, practice charityand obey Allah and His Messenger. These Allah will have mercy on them. Allah is Noble and Wise.– Surah At-Taubah 9:71

وَٱلْمُؤْمِنُونَ وَٱلْمُؤْمِنَـٰتُ بَعْضُهُمْ أَوْلِيَآءُ بَعْضٍ ۚ يَأْمُرُونَ بِٱلْمَعْرُوفِ وَيَنْهَوْنَ عَنِ ٱلْمُنكَرِ وَيُقِيمُونَ ٱلصَّلَوٰةَ وَيُؤْتُونَ ٱلزَّكَوٰةَ
وَيُطِيعُونَ ٱللَّهَ وَرَسُولَهُۥٓ ۚ أُو۟لَـٰٓئِكَ سَيَرْحَمُهُمُ ٱللَّهُ ۗ إِنَّ ٱللَّهَ عَزِيزٌ حَكِيمٌ

The response of the believers, when they are called to Allah and His Messenger in order to judge between them, is to say, "We hear and we obey." These are the successful. Whoever obeys Allah and His Messenger, and fears Allah, and is conscious of Him—these are the winners.– Surah An-Nur 24:51&52

إِنَّمَا كَانَ قَوْلَ ٱلْمُؤْمِنِينَ إِذَا دُعُوٓا۟ إِلَى ٱللَّهِ وَرَسُولِهِۦ لِيَحْكُمَ بَيْنَهُمْ أَن يَقُولُوا۟ سَمِعْنَا وَأَطَعْنَا ۚ وَأُو۟لَـٰٓئِكَ هُمُ ٱلْمُفْلِحُونَ وَمَن يُطِعِ
ٱللَّهَ وَرَسُولَهُۥ وَيَخْشَ ٱللَّهَ وَيَتَّقْهِ فَأُو۟لَـٰٓئِكَ هُمُ ٱلْفَآئِزُونَ

And settle in your homes; and do not display yourselves, as in the former days of ignorance. And perform the prayer, and give regular charity, and obey Allah and His Messenger. Allah desires to remove all impurity from you, O People of the Household, and to purify you thoroughly.– Surah Al-Ahzab 33:33

وَقَرْنَ فِى بُيُوتِكُنَّ وَلَا تَبَرَّجْنَ تَبَرُّجَ ٱلْجَـٰهِلِيَّةِ ٱلْأُولَىٰ ۖ وَأَقِمْنَ ٱلصَّلَوٰةَ وَءَاتِينَ ٱلزَّكَوٰةَ وَأَطِعْنَ ٱللَّهَ وَرَسُولَهُۥٓ ۚ إِنَّمَا يُرِيدُ ٱللَّهُ
لِيُذْهِبَ عَنكُمُ ٱلرِّجْسَ أَهْلَ ٱلْبَيْتِ وَيُطَهِّرَكُمْ تَطْهِيرًا

It is not for any believer, man or woman, when Allah and His Messenger have decided a matter, to have liberty of choice in their decision. Whoever disobeys Allah and His Messenger has gone far astray.– Surah Al-Ahzab 33:36

وَمَا كَانَ لِمُؤْمِنٍ وَلَا مُؤْمِنَةٍ إِذَا قَضَى ٱللَّهُ وَرَسُولُهُۥٓ أَمْرًا أَن يَكُونَ لَهُمُ ٱلْخِيَرَةُ مِنْ أَمْرِهِمْ ۗ وَمَن يَعْصِ ٱللَّهَ وَرَسُولَهُۥ فَقَدْ ضَلَّ ضَلَـٰلًا مُّبِينًا

He will rectify your conduct for you, and will forgive you your sins. Whoever obeys Allah and His Messenger has won a great victory.– Surah Al-Ahzab 33:71

يُصْلِحْ لَكُمْ أَعْمَـٰلَكُمْ وَيَغْفِرْ لَكُمْ ذُنُوبَكُمْ ۗ وَمَن يُطِعِ ٱللَّهَ وَرَسُولَهُۥ فَقَدْ فَازَ فَوْزًا عَظِيمًا

There is no blame on the blind, nor any blame on the lame, nor any blame on the sick. Whoever obeys Allah and His Messenger—He will. Admit him into gardens beneath which rivers flow; but whoever turns away—He will punish him with a painful punishment.– Surah Al-Fath 48:17

لَّيْسَ عَلَى ٱلْأَعْمَىٰ حَرَجٌ وَلَا عَلَى ٱلْأَعْرَجِ حَرَجٌ وَلَا عَلَى ٱلْمَرِيضِ حَرَجٌ ۗ وَمَن يُطِعِ ٱللَّهَ وَرَسُولَهُۥ يُدْخِلْهُ جَنَّـٰتٍ تَجْرِى مِن تَحْتِهَا ٱلْأَنْهَـٰرُ ۖ وَمَن يَتَوَلَّ يُعَذِّبْهُ عَذَابًا أَلِيمًا

Except for a proclamation from Allah and His messages. He who defies Allah and His Messenger—for him is the Fire of Hell, in which they will dwell forever."– Surah Al-Jinn 72:23

إِلَّا بَلَـٰغًا مِّنَ ٱللَّهِ وَرِسَـٰلَـٰتِهِۦ ۚ وَمَن يَعْصِ ٱللَّهَ وَرَسُولَهُۥ فَإِنَّ لَهُۥ نَارَ جَهَنَّمَ خَـٰلِدِينَ فِيهَآ أَبَدًا

On that Day, those who disbelieved and disobeyed the Messenger will wish that the earth were leveled over them. They will conceal nothing from Allah.– Surah An-Nisa 4:42

يَوْمَئِذٍ يَوَدُّ ٱلَّذِينَ كَفَرُوا۟ وَعَصَوُا۟ ٱلرَّسُولَ لَوْ تُسَوَّىٰ بِهِمُ ٱلْأَرْضُ وَلَا يَكْتُمُونَ ٱللَّهَ حَدِيثًا

Whoever obeys the Messenger is obeying Allah. And whoever turns away—We did not send you as a watcher over them.– Surah An-Nisa 4:80

مَّن يُطِعِ ٱلرَّسُولَ فَقَدْ أَطَاعَ ٱللَّهَ ۖ وَمَن تَوَلَّىٰ فَمَآ أَرْسَلْنَـٰكَ عَلَيْهِمْ حَفِيظًا

What Allah gave as booty (Fai') to His Messenger (Muhammad) from the people of the townships, – it is for Allah, His Messenger (Muhammad), the kindred (of Messenger Muhammad), the orphans, Al-Masakin (the poor), and the wayfarer, in order that it may not become a fortune used by the rich among you. And whatsoever the Messenger (Muhammad) gives you, take it, and whatsoever he forbids you, abstain (from it) , and fear Allah. Verily, Allah is Severe in punishment. Surah Al-Hashr 59:7

مَّآ أَفَآءَ ٱللَّهُ عَلَىٰ رَسُولِهِۦ مِنْ أَهْلِ ٱلْقُرَىٰ فَلِلَّهِ وَلِلرَّسُولِ وَلِذِى ٱلْقُرْبَىٰ وَٱلْيَتَـٰمَىٰ وَٱلْمَسَـٰكِينِ وَٱبْنِ ٱلسَّبِيلِ كَىْ لَا يَكُونَ دُولَةًۢ بَيْنَ ٱلْأَغْنِيَآءِ مِنكُمْ ۚ وَمَآ ءَاتَىٰكُمُ ٱلرَّسُولُ فَخُذُوهُ وَمَا نَهَىٰكُمْ عَنْهُ فَٱنتَهُوا۟ ۚ وَٱتَّقُوا۟ ٱللَّهَ ۖ إِنَّ ٱللَّهَ شَدِيدُ ٱلْعِقَابِ

O you who believe [in Musa (Moses) (i.e. Jews) and 'Iesa (Jesus) (i.e. Christians)]! Fear Allah, and believe too in His Messenger (Muhammad), He will give you a double portion of His Mercy, and He will give you a light by which you shall walk (straight), and He will forgive you. And Allah is Oft-Forgiving, Most Merciful. – Surah Al-Hadid 57:28

يَـٰٓأَيُّهَا ٱلَّذِينَ ءَامَنُوا۟ ٱتَّقُوا۟ ٱللَّهَ وَءَامِنُوا۟ بِرَسُولِهِۦ يُؤْتِكُمْ كِفْلَيْنِ مِن رَّحْمَتِهِۦ وَيَجْعَل لَّكُمْ نُورًا تَمْشُونَ بِهِۦ وَيَغْفِرْ لَكُمْ ۚ وَٱللَّهُ غَفُورٌ رَّحِيمٌ

Narrated Abu Bakra: The Prophetﷺ said, "Time has come back to its original state which it had on the day Allah created the Heavens and the Earth. The year is twelve months, four of which are sacred, three of them are in succession, namely Dhul-Qa'da, Dhul Hijja and Muharram, (the fourth being) Rajab Mudar which is between Juma'da (ath-thamj and Sha'ban. The Prophetﷺ then asked, "Which month is this?" We said, "Allah and his Apostle know better." He kept silent so long that we thought that he would call it by a name other than its real name. He said, "Isn't it the month of Dhul-Hijja?" We said, "Yes." He said, "Which town is this?" We said, "Allah and His Apostle know better." He kept silent so long that we thought that he would call it, a name other than its real name. He said, "isn't it the town (of Mecca)?" We replied, "Yes." He said, "What day is today?" We replied, "Allah and His Apostle know better." He kept silent so long that we thought that he would call it by a name other than its real name. He said, "Isn't it the day of Nahr?" We replied, "Yes." He then said, "Your blood, properties and honor are as sacred to one another as this day of yours in this town of yours in this month of yours. You will meet your Lord, and He will ask you about your deeds.

Beware! Do not go astray after me by cutting the necks of each other. It is incumbent upon those who are present to convey this message to those who are absent, for some of those to whom it is conveyed may comprehend it better than some of those who have heard it directly." (Muhammad, the sub-narrator, on mentioning this used to say: The Prophet then said, "No doubt! Haven't I delivered (Allah's) Message (to you)? Haven't I delivered Allah's message (to you)?". – Sahih al-Bukhari 5550

حَدَّثَنَا مُحَمَّدُ بْنُ سَلاَمٍ، حَدَّثَنَا عَبْدُ الْوَهَّابِ، حَدَّثَنَا أَيُّوبُ، عَنْ مُحَمَّدٍ، عَنِ ابْنِ أَبِي بَكْرَةَ، عَنْ أَبِي بَكْرَةَ ـ رضى الله عنه ـ عَنِ النَّبِيِّ صلى الله عليه وسلم قَالَ " الزَّمَانُ قَدِ اسْتَدَارَ كَهَيْئَتِهِ يَوْمَ خَلَقَ اللَّهُ السَّمَوَاتِ وَالأَرْضَ، السَّنَةُ اثْنَا عَشَرَ شَهْرًا، مِنْهَا أَرْبَعَةٌ حُرُمٌ، ثَلاَثٌ مُتَوَالِيَاتٌ ذُو الْقَعْدَةِ وَذُو الْحِجَّةِ وَالْمُحَرَّمُ، وَرَجَبُ مُضَرَ الَّذِي بَيْنَ جُمَادَى وَشَعْبَانَ، أَىُّ شَهْرٍ هَذَا ". قُلْنَا اللَّهُ وَرَسُولُهُ أَعْلَمُ. فَسَكَتَ حَتَّى ظَنَنَّا أَنَّهُ سَيُسَمِّيهِ بِغَيْرِ اسْمِهِ، قَالَ " أَلَيْسَ ذَا الْحِجَّةِ ". قُلْنَا بَلَى. قَالَ " أَىُّ بَلَدٍ هَذَا ". قُلْنَا اللَّهُ وَرَسُولُهُ أَعْلَمُ. فَسَكَتَ حَتَّى ظَنَنَّا أَنَّهُ سَيُسَمِّيهِ بِغَيْرِ اسْمِهِ، قَالَ " أَلَيْسَ الْبَلْدَةَ ". قُلْنَا بَلَى. قَالَ " فَأَىُّ يَوْمٍ هَذَا ". قُلْنَا اللَّهُ وَرَسُولُهُ أَعْلَمُ، فَسَكَتَ حَتَّى ظَنَنَّا أَنَّهُ سَيُسَمِّيهِ بِغَيْرِ اسْمِهِ قَالَ " أَلَيْسَ يَوْمَ النَّحْرِ ". قُلْنَا بَلَى. قَالَ " فَإِنَّ دِمَاءَكُمْ وَأَمْوَالَكُمْ ـ قَالَ مُحَمَّدٌ وَأَحْسِبُهُ قَالَ ـ وَأَعْرَاضَكُمْ عَلَيْكُمْ حَرَامٌ كَحُرْمَةِ يَوْمِكُمْ هَذَا، فِي بَلَدِكُمْ هَذَا فِي شَهْرِكُمْ، وَسَتَلْقَوْنَ رَبَّكُمْ فَيَسْأَلُكُمْ عَنْ أَعْمَالِكُمْ، أَلاَ فَلاَ تَرْجِعُوا بَعْدِي ضُلاَّلاً، يَضْرِبُ بَعْضُكُمْ رِقَابَ بَعْضٍ، أَلاَ لِيُبَلِّغِ الشَّاهِدُ الْغَائِبَ، فَلَعَلَّ بَعْضَ مَنْ يَبْلُغُهُ أَنْ يَكُونَ أَوْعَى لَهُ مِنْ بَعْضِ مَنْ سَمِعَهُ ـ وَكَانَ مُحَمَّدٌ إِذَا ذَكَرَهُ قَالَ صَدَقَ النَّبِيُّ صلى الله عليه وسلم ثُمَّ قَالَ ـ أَلاَ هَلْ بَلَّغْتُ أَلاَ هَلْ بَلَّغْتُ ".

Narrated Zaid bin Khalid Al-Juhani: The Prophet ﷺ led us in the Fajr prayer at Hudaibiya after a rainy night. On completion of the prayer, he faced the people and said, "Do you know what your Lord has said (revealed)?" The people replied, "Allah and His Apostle know better." He said, "Allah has said, 'In this morning some of my slaves remained as true believers and some became non-believers; whoever said that the rain was due to the Blessings and the Mercy of Allah had belief in Me and he disbelieves in the stars, and whoever said that it rained because of a particular star had no belief in Me but believes in that star.'" – Sahih al-Bukhari 846

حَدَّثَنَا عَبْدُ اللَّهِ بْنُ مَسْلَمَةَ، عَنْ مَالِكٍ، عَنْ صَالِحِ بْنِ كَيْسَانَ، عَنْ عُبَيْدِ اللَّهِ بْنِ عَبْدِ اللَّهِ بْنِ عُتْبَةَ بْنِ مَسْعُودٍ، عَنْ زَيْدِ بْنِ خَالِدٍ الْجُهَنِيِّ، أَنَّهُ قَالَ صَلَّى لَنَا رَسُولُ اللَّهِ صلى الله عليه وسلم صَلاَةَ الصُّبْحِ بِالْحُدَيْبِيَةِ عَلَى إِثْرِ سَمَاءٍ كَانَتْ مِنَ اللَّيْلَةِ، فَلَمَّا انْصَرَفَ أَقْبَلَ عَلَى النَّاسِ فَقَالَ " هَلْ تَدْرُونَ مَاذَا قَالَ رَبُّكُمْ ". قَالُوا اللَّهُ وَرَسُولُهُ أَعْلَمُ. قَالَ " أَصْبَحَ مِنْ عِبَادِي مُؤْمِنٌ بِي وَكَافِرٌ، فَأَمَّا مَنْ قَالَ مُطِرْنَا بِفَضْلِ اللَّهِ وَرَحْمَتِهِ فَذَلِكَ مُؤْمِنٌ بِي وَكَافِرٌ بِالْكَوْكَبِ، وَأَمَّا مَنْ قَالَ بِنَوْءِ كَذَا وَكَذَا فَذَلِكَ كَافِرٌ بِي وَمُؤْمِنٌ بِالْكَوْكَبِ ".

Narrated Abu Huraira: "Allah's Messenger ﷺ said, "By Him in Whose Hands my life is, none of you will have faith till he loves me more than his father and his children." – Al-Bukhari 14

حَدَّثَنَا أَبُو الْيَمَانِ، قَالَ أَخْبَرَنَا شُعَيْبٌ، قَالَ حَدَّثَنَا أَبُو الزِّنَادِ، عَنِ الأَعْرَجِ، عَنْ أَبِي هُرَيْرَةَ ـ رضى الله عنه ـ أَنَّ رَسُولَ اللَّهِ صلى الله عليه وسلم قَالَ " فَوَالَّذِي نَفْسِي بِيَدِهِ لاَ يُؤْمِنُ أَحَدُكُمْ حَتَّى أَكُونَ أَحَبَّ إِلَيْهِ مِنْ وَالِدِهِ وَوَلَدِهِ ".

Narrated `Abdullah bin Hisham :We were with the Prophet ﷺ and he was holding the hand of `Umar bin Al-Khattab. `Umar said to Him, "O Allah's Messenger ﷺ ! You are dearer to me than everything except my own self." The Prophet ﷺ said, "No, by Him in Whose Hand my soul is, (you will not have complete faith) till I am dearer to you than your own self." Then `Umar said to him, "However, now, by Allah, you are dearer to me than my own self." The Prophet ﷺ said, "Now, O `Umar, (now you are a believer). – Sahih al-Bukhari 6632

حَدَّثَنَا يَحْيَى بْنُ سُلَيْمَانَ، قَالَ حَدَّثَنِي ابْنُ وَهْبٍ، قَالَ أَخْبَرَنِي حَيْوَةُ، قَالَ حَدَّثَنِي أَبُو عَقِيلٍ، زُهْرَةُ بْنُ مَعْبَدٍ أَنَّهُ سَمِعَ جَدَّهُ عَبْدَ اللَّهِ بْنَ هِشَامٍ، قَالَ كُنَّا مَعَ النَّبِيِّ صلى الله عليه وسلم وَهْوَ آخِذٌ بِيَدِ عُمَرَ بْنِ الْخَطَّابِ فَقَالَ لَهُ عُمَرُ يَا رَسُولَ اللَّهِ لأَنْتَ أَحَبُّ إِلَيَّ مِنْ كُلِّ شَىْءٍ إِلاَّ مِنْ نَفْسِي. فَقَالَ النَّبِيُّ صلى الله عليه وسلم " لاَ وَالَّذِي نَفْسِي بِيَدِهِ حَتَّى أَكُونَ أَحَبَّ إِلَيْكَ مِنْ نَفْسِكَ ". فَقَالَ لَهُ عُمَرُ فَإِنَّهُ الآنَ وَاللَّهِ لأَنْتَ أَحَبُّ إِلَيَّ مِنْ نَفْسِي. فَقَالَ النَّبِيُّ صلى الله عليه وسلم " الآنَ يَا عُمَرُ ".

Say (O Muhammad), "in case you (really) love Allah, then closely follow me, (and) Allah will love you and forgive you your guilty (deeds); and Allah is Ever-Forgiving, Ever-Merciful." – Surah Al-Imran 3:31

قُلْ إِن كُنتُمْ تُحِبُّونَ ٱللَّهَ فَٱتَّبِعُونِى يُحْبِبْكُمُ ٱللَّهُ وَيَغْفِرْ لَكُمْ ذُنُوبَكُمْ ۗ وَٱللَّهُ غَفُورٌ رَّحِيمٌ

Narrated Ibn `Umar: At Mina, the Prophet ﷺ said, "Do you know what is the day today?" The people replied, "Allah and His Apostle know it better." He said, "It is the forbidden (sacred) day. And do you know what town is this?" They replied, "Allah and His Apostle know it better." He said, "This is the forbidden (Sacred) town (Mecca). And do you know which month is this?" The people replied, "Allah and His Apostle know it better." He said, "This is the forbidden (sacred) month." The Prophet ﷺ added, "No doubt, Allah made your blood, your properties, and your honor sacred to one another like the sanctity of this day of yours in this month of yours in this town of yours." Narrated Ibn `Umar: On the Day of Nahr (10th of Dhul-Hijja), the Prophet ﷺ stood in between the Jamrat during his Hajj which he performed (as in the previous Hadith) and said, "This is the greatest Day (i.e. 10th of Dhul-Hijjah)." The Prophet ﷺ started saying repeatedly, "O Allah! Be Witness (I have conveyed Your Message)." He then bade the people farewell. The people said, "This Is Hajjat-al-Wada.") – Sahih al-Bukhari 1742

حَدَّثَنَا مُحَمَّدُ بْنُ الْمُثَنَّى، حَدَّثَنَا يَزِيدُ بْنُ هَارُونَ، أَخْبَرَنَا عَاصِمُ بْنُ مُحَمَّدِ بْنِ زَيْدٍ، عَنْ أَبِيهِ، عَنِ ابْنِ عُمَرَ ـ رضى الله عنهما ـ قَالَ قَالَ النَّبِيُّ صلى الله عليه وسلم بِمِنًى " أَتَدْرُونَ أَىُّ يَوْمٍ هَذَا ". قَالُوا اللَّهُ وَرَسُولُهُ أَعْلَمُ. فَقَالَ " فَإِنَّ هَذَا يَوْمٌ حَرَامٌ، أَفَتَدْرُونَ أَىُّ بَلَدٍ هَذَا ". قَالُوا اللَّهُ وَرَسُولُهُ أَعْلَمُ. قَالَ " بَلَدٌ حَرَامٌ، أَفَتَدْرُونَ أَىُّ شَهْرٍ هَذَا ". قَالُوا اللَّهُ وَرَسُولُهُ أَعْلَمُ. قَالَ " شَهْرٌ حَرَامٌ ـ قَالَ ـ فَإِنَّ اللَّهَ حَرَّمَ عَلَيْكُمْ دِمَاءَكُمْ وَأَمْوَالَكُمْ وَأَعْرَاضَكُمْ، كَحُرْمَةِ يَوْمِكُمْ هَذَا، فِي شَهْرِكُمْ هَذَا، فِي بَلَدِكُمْ هَذَا ". وَقَالَ هِشَامُ بْنُ الْغَازِ أَخْبَرَنِي نَافِعٌ عَنِ ابْنِ عُمَرَ ـ رضى الله عنهما ـ وَقَفَ النَّبِيُّ صلى الله عليه وسلم يَوْمَ النَّحْرِ بَيْنَ الْجَم

Narrated Abu Dhar: The Prophet ﷺ asked me at sunset, "Do you know where the sun goes (at the time of sunset)?" I replied, "Allah and His Apostle know better." He said, "It goes (i.e. travels) till it prostrates Itself underneath the Throne and takes the permission to rise again, and it is permitted and then (a time will come when) it will be about to prostrate itself but its prostration will not be accepted, and it will ask permission to go on its course but it will not be permitted, but it will be ordered to return whence it has come and so it will rise in the west. And that is the interpretation of the Statement of Allah: "And the sun Runs its fixed course For a term (decreed). That is The Decree of (Allah) The Exalted in Might, The All-Knowing." (36.38). – Sahih Al-Bukhari 3199

حَدَّثَنَا مُحَمَّدُ بْنُ يُوسُفَ، حَدَّثَنَا سُفْيَانُ، عَنِ الأَعْمَشِ، عَنْ إِبْرَاهِيمَ التَّيْمِيِّ، عَنْ أَبِيهِ، عَنْ أَبِي ذَرٍّ ـ رضى الله عنه ـ قَالَ قَالَ النَّبِيُّ صلى الله عليه وسلم لأَبِي ذَرٍّ حِينَ غَرَبَتِ الشَّمْسُ " تَدْرِي أَيْنَ تَذْهَبُ ". قُلْتُ اللَّهُ وَرَسُولُهُ أَعْلَمُ. قَالَ " فَإِنَّهَا تَذْهَبُ حَتَّى تَسْجُدَ تَحْتَ الْعَرْشِ، فَتَسْتَأْذِنَ فَيُؤْذَنَ لَهَا، وَيُوشِكُ أَنْ تَسْجُدَ فَلاَ يُقْبَلَ مِنْهَا، وَتَسْتَأْذِنَ فَلاَ يُؤْذَنَ لَهَا، يُقَالُ لَهَا ارْجِعِي مِنْ حَيْثُ جِئْتِ. فَتَطْلُعُ مِنْ مَغْرِبِهَا، فَذَلِكَ قَوْلُهُ تَعَالَى {وَالشَّمْسُ تَجْرِي لِمُسْتَقَرٍّ لَهَا ذَلِكَ تَقْدِيرُ الْعَزِيزِ الْعَلِيمِ}".

Narrated Abu Huraira: Allah's Messenger ﷺ said, "Whoever obeys me, obeys Allah, and whoever disobeys me, disobeys Allah, and whoever obeys the ruler I appoint, obeys me, and whoever disobeys him, disobeys me." – Sahih al-Bukhari 7137

حَدَّثَنَا عَبْدَانُ، أَخْبَرَنَا عَبْدُ اللَّهِ، عَنْ يُونُسَ، عَنِ الزُّهْرِيِّ، أَخْبَرَنِي أَبُو سَلَمَةَ بْنُ عَبْدِ الرَّحْمَنِ، أَنَّهُ سَمِعَ أَبَا هُرَيْرَةَ ـ رضى الله عنه ـ أَنَّ رَسُولَ اللَّهِ صلى الله عليه وسلم قَالَ " مَنْ أَطَاعَنِي فَقَدْ أَطَاعَ اللَّهَ، وَمَنْ عَصَانِي فَقَدْ عَصَى اللَّهَ، وَمَنْ أَطَاعَ أَمِيرِي فَقَدْ أَطَاعَنِي، وَمَنْ عَصَى أَمِيرِي فَقَدْ عَصَانِي "

Wahab bin Munabbih was asked. "Isn't The saying: La ilaha illallah (none has the right to be worshipped but Allāh)'. The key of Paradise?" He replied in the affirmative, and said, "There is no key without tooth, and if You have the key which has teeth, it will open It for you, and if it is without teeth then it will not open It for you." Sahih Al-Bukhari vol 2. Pg.196

و قيل لوهب بن منبه : أليس مفتاح الجنة ؟ لا اله الا الله قال : بلى، و لكن ليس مفتاح الا له اسنان، فإن جت بمفتاح له اسنان فتح لك و الا لم يفتح لك .

The Book of
And most of them believe not in Allah except that they attribute partners unto Him
وَمَا يُؤْمِنُ أَكْثَرُهُم بِٱللَّهِ إِلَّا وَهُم مُّشْرِكُونَ

And the Day whereon We shall gather them all together, then We shall say to those who did set partners in worship with Us: "Stop at your place! You and your partners (whom you had worshipped in the worldly life)." Then We shall separate them, and their (Allah's so-called) partners shall say: "It was not us that you used to worship." – Surah Yunus 10:28
وَيَوْمَ نَحْشُرُهُمْ جَمِيعًا ثُمَّ نَقُولُ لِلَّذِينَ أَشْرَكُوا۟ مَكَانَكُمْ أَنتُمْ وَشُرَكَآؤُكُمْ ۚ فَزَيَّلْنَا بَيْنَهُمْ ۖ وَقَالَ شُرَكَآؤُهُم مَّا كُنتُمْ إِيَّانَا تَعْبُدُونَ

Say: "Is there of your (Allah's so-called) partners one that guides to the truth?" Say: "It is Allah Who guides to the truth. Is then He, Who gives guidance to the truth, more worthy to be followed, or he who finds not guidance (himself) unless he is guided? Then, what is the matter with you? How judge you?"– Surah Yunus 10:35
قُلْ هَلْ مِن شُرَكَآئِكُم مَّن يَهْدِىٓ إِلَى ٱلْحَقِّ ۚ قُلِ ٱللَّهُ يَهْدِى لِلْحَقِّ ۗ أَفَمَن يَهْدِىٓ إِلَى ٱلْحَقِّ أَحَقُّ أَن يُتَّبَعَ أَمَّن لَّا يَهِدِّىٓ إِلَّآ أَن يُهْدَىٰ ۖ فَمَا لَكُمْ كَيْفَ تَحْكُمُونَ

No doubt! Verily, to Allah belongs whosoever is in the heavens and whosoever is in the earth. And those who worship and invoke others besides Allah, in fact they follow not the (Allah's so-called) partners, they follow only a conjecture and they only invent lies. – Surah Yunus 10:66
أَلَآ إِنَّ لِلَّهِ مَن فِى ٱلسَّمَٰوَٰتِ وَمَن فِى ٱلْأَرْضِ ۗ وَمَا يَتَّبِعُ ٱلَّذِينَ يَدْعُونَ مِن دُونِ ٱللَّهِ شُرَكَآءَ ۚ إِن يَتَّبِعُونَ إِلَّا ٱلظَّنَّ وَإِنْ هُمْ إِلَّا يَخْرُصُونَ

And most of them believe not in Allah except that they attribute partners unto Him [i.e. they are Mushrikun -polytheists – see Verse 6: 121]. – Surah Yusuf 12:106
وَمَا يُؤْمِنُ أَكْثَرُهُم بِٱللَّهِ إِلَّا وَهُم مُّشْرِكُونَ

And they set up rivals to Allah, to mislead (men) from His Path! Say: "Enjoy (your brief life)! But certainly, your destination is the (Hell) Fire!" – Surah Ibrahim 14:30
وَجَعَلُوا۟ لِلَّهِ أَندَادًا لِّيُضِلُّوا۟ عَن سَبِيلِهِۦ ۗ قُلْ تَمَتَّعُوا۟ فَإِنَّ مَصِيرَكُمْ إِلَى ٱلنَّارِ

And they have taken (for worship) aliha (gods) besides Allah, that they might give them honour, power and glory (and also protect them from Allah's Punishment etc.). Nay, but they (the so-called gods) will deny their worship of them, and become opponents to them (on the Day of Resurrection). – Surah Maryam 19:81&82
وَٱتَّخَذُوا۟ مِن دُونِ ٱللَّهِ ءَالِهَةً لِّيَكُونُوا۟ لَهُمْ عِزًّا كَلَّا ۚ سَيَكْفُرُونَ بِعِبَادَتِهِمْ وَيَكُونُونَ عَلَيْهِمْ ضِدًّا

And when Our Clear Verses are recited to them, you will notice a denial on the faces of the disbelievers! They are nearly ready to attack with violence those who recite Our Verses to them. Say: "Shall I tell you of something worse than that? The Fire (of Hell) which Allah has promised to those who disbelieve, and worst indeed is that destination!" O mankind! A similitude has been coined, so listen to it (carefully): Verily! Those on whom you call besides Allah, cannot create (even) a fly, even though they combine together for the purpose. And if the fly snatched away a thing from them, they would have no power to release it from the fly. So weak are (both) the seeker and the sought. They have not estimated Allah His Rightful Estimate; Verily, Allah is All-Strong, All-Mighty. – Surah Al-Hajj 22:72-74

وَإِذَا تُتْلَىٰ عَلَيْهِمْ ءَايَـٰتُنَا بَيِّنَـٰتٍ تَعْرِفُ فِى وُجُوهِ ٱلَّذِينَ كَفَرُوا۟ ٱلْمُنكَرَ ۖ يَكَادُونَ يَسْطُونَ بِٱلَّذِينَ يَتْلُونَ عَلَيْهِمْ ءَايَـٰتِنَا ۗ قُلْ أَفَأُنَبِّئُكُم
بِشَرٍّ مِّن ذَٰلِكُمُ ۗ ٱلنَّارُ وَعَدَهَا ٱللَّهُ ٱلَّذِينَ كَفَرُوا۟ ۖ وَبِئْسَ ٱلْمَصِيرُ يَـٰٓأَيُّهَا ٱلنَّاسُ ضُرِبَ مَثَلٌ فَٱسْتَمِعُوا۟ لَهُۥٓ ۚ إِنَّ ٱلَّذِينَ تَدْعُونَ مِن
دُونِ ٱللَّهِ لَن يَخْلُقُوا۟ ذُبَابًا وَلَوِ ٱجْتَمَعُوا۟ لَهُۥ ۖ وَإِن يَسْلُبْهُمُ ٱلذُّبَابُ شَيْـًٔا لَّا يَسْتَنقِذُوهُ مِنْهُ ۚ ضَعُفَ ٱلطَّالِبُ وَٱلْمَطْلُوبُ مَا قَدَرُوا۟
ٱللَّهَ حَقَّ قَدْرِهِۦٓ ۗ إِنَّ ٱللَّهَ لَقَوِىٌّ عَزِيزٌ

And when Allah Alone is mentioned, the hearts of those who believe not in the Hereafter are filled with disgust (from the Oneness of Allah) and when those (whom they obey or worship) besides Him [like all false deities other than Allah, it may be a Messenger like 'Iesa (Jesus) – son of Maryam (Mary), 'Uzair (Ezra), an angel, a pious man, a jinn, or any other creature even idols, graves of religious people, saints, priests, monks, etc.] are mentioned, behold, they rejoice!– Surah Az-Zumar 39:45

وَإِذَا ذُكِرَ ٱللَّهُ وَحْدَهُ ٱشْمَأَزَّتْ قُلُوبُ ٱلَّذِينَ لَا يُؤْمِنُونَ بِٱلْـَٔاخِرَةِ ۖ وَإِذَا ذُكِرَ ٱلَّذِينَ مِن دُونِهِۦٓ إِذَا هُمْ يَسْتَبْشِرُونَ

(It will be said): "This is because, when Allah Alone was invoked (in worship, etc.) you disbelieved, but when partners were joined to Him, you believed! So the judgement is only with Allah, the Most High, the Most Great!"—the Most High, All-Great." – Surah Ghafir 40:12

ذَٰلِكُم بِأَنَّهُۥٓ إِذَا دُعِىَ ٱللَّهُ وَحْدَهُۥ كَفَرْتُمْ ۖ وَإِن يُشْرَكْ بِهِۦ تُؤْمِنُوا۟ ۚ فَٱلْحُكْمُ لِلَّهِ ٱلْعَلِىِّ ٱلْكَبِيرِ

And (remember) the Day when He will call to them, and say: "Where are My (so-called) partners whom you used to assert?" Those about whom the Word will have come true (to be punished) will say: "Our Lord! These are they whom we led astray. We led them astray, as we were astray ourselves. We declare our innocence (from them) before You. It was not us they worshipped." And it will be said (to them): "Call upon your (so-called) partners (of Allah), and they will call upon them, but they will give no answer to them, and they will see the torment. (They will then wish) if only they had been guided!– Surah Al-Qasas 28:62-64

وَيَوْمَ يُنَادِيهِمْ فَيَقُولُ أَيْنَ شُرَكَآءِىَ ٱلَّذِينَ كُنتُمْ تَزْعُمُونَ قَالَ ٱلَّذِينَ حَقَّ عَلَيْهِمُ ٱلْقَوْلُ رَبَّنَا هَـٰٓؤُلَآءِ ٱلَّذِينَ أَغْوَيْنَآ أَغْوَيْنَـٰهُمْ كَمَا
غَوَيْنَا ۖ تَبَرَّأْنَآ إِلَيْكَ ۖ مَا كَانُوٓا۟ إِيَّانَا يَعْبُدُونَ وَقِيلَ ٱدْعُوا۟ شُرَكَآءَكُمْ فَدَعَوْهُمْ فَلَمْ يَسْتَجِيبُوا۟ لَهُمْ وَرَأَوُا۟ ٱلْعَذَابَ ۚ لَوْ أَنَّهُمْ كَانُوا۟
يَهْتَدُونَ

The likeness of those who take Auliya' (protectors and helpers) other than Allah is as the likeness of a spider, who builds (for itself) a house, but verily, the frailest (weakest) of houses is the spider's house; if they but knew.. – Surah Al-'Ankabut 29:41

مَثَلُ ٱلَّذِينَ ٱتَّخَذُوا۟ مِن دُونِ ٱللَّهِ أَوْلِيَآءَ كَمَثَلِ ٱلْعَنكَبُوتِ ٱتَّخَذَتْ بَيْتًا ۖ وَإِنَّ أَوْهَنَ ٱلْبُيُوتِ لَبَيْتُ ٱلْعَنكَبُوتِ ۖ لَوْ كَانُوا۟ يَعْلَمُونَ

He sets forth for you a parable from your ownselves, – Do you have partners among those whom your right hands possess (i.e your slaves) to share as equals in the wealth We have bestowed on you? Whom you fear as you fear each other? Thus do We explain the signs in detail to a people who have sense.– Surah Ar-Rum 30:28

ضَرَبَ لَكُم مَّثَلًا مِّنْ أَنفُسِكُمْ ۖ هَل لَّكُم مِّن مَّا مَلَكَتْ أَيْمَـٰنُكُم مِّن شُرَكَآءَ فِى مَا رَزَقْنَـٰكُمْ فَأَنتُمْ فِيهِ سَوَآءٌ تَخَافُونَهُمْ كَخِيفَتِكُمْ
أَنفُسَكُمْ ۚ كَذَٰلِكَ نُفَصِّلُ ٱلْـَٔايَـٰتِ لِقَوْمٍ يَعْقِلُونَ

See you not those who dispute about the Ayat (proofs, evidences, verses, lessons, signs, revelations, etc.) of Allah? How are they turning away (from the truth, i.e. Islamic Monotheism to the falsehood of polytheism)? Those who deny the Book (this Qur'an), and that with which We sent Our Messengers (i.e. to worship none but Allah Alone sincerely, and to reject all false deities and to confess resurrection after the death for recompense) they will come to know (when they will be cast into the Fire of Hell). When iron collars will be rounded over their necks, and the chains, they shall be dragged along. In the boiling water, then they will be burned in the Fire. Then it will be said to them: “Where are (all) those whom you used to join in worship as partners– Surah Ghafir 40:69-73

أَلَمْ تَرَ إِلَى ٱلَّذِينَ يُجَٰدِلُونَ فِىٓ ءَايَٰتِ ٱللَّهِ أَنَّىٰ يُصْرَفُونَ ٱلَّذِينَ كَذَّبُوا۟ بِٱلْكِتَٰبِ وَبِمَآ أَرْسَلْنَا بِهِۦ رُسُلَنَا ۖ فَسَوْفَ يَعْلَمُونَ
إِذِ ٱلْأَغْلَٰلُ فِىٓ أَعْنَٰقِهِمْ وَٱلسَّلَٰسِلُ يُسْحَبُونَ فِى ٱلْحَمِيمِ ثُمَّ فِى ٱلنَّارِ يُسْجَرُونَ ثُمَّ قِيلَ لَهُمْ أَيْنَ مَا كُنتُمْ تُشْرِكُونَ

Narrated `Abdullah: Allah’s Messenger ﷺ said a sentence and I said another. He said, “Whoever dies while he is setting up rivals along with Allah (i.e. worshipping others along with Allah) shall be admitted into the (Hell) Fire.” And I said the other: “Whoever dies while he is not setting up rivals along with Allah (i.e. worshipping none except Allah) shall be admitted into Paradise.” – Al-Bukhari 6683

حَدَّثَنَا مُوسَى بْنُ إِسْمَاعِيلَ، حَدَّثَنَا عَبْدُ الْوَاحِدِ، حَدَّثَنَا الأَعْمَشُ، عَنْ شَقِيقٍ، عَنْ عَبْدِ اللَّهِ ـ رضى الله عنه ـ قَالَ قَالَ رَسُولُ اللَّهِ صلى الله عليه وسلم كَلِمَةً وَقُلْتُ أُخْرَى " مَنْ مَاتَ يَجْعَلُ لِلَّهِ نِدًّا أُدْخِلَ النَّارَ ". وَقُلْتُ أُخْرَى مَنْ مَاتَ لاَ يَجْعَلُ لِلَّهِ نِدًّا أُدْخِلَ الْجَنَّةَ

Say (O Muhammad): “O people of the Scripture (Jews and Christians): Come to a word that is just between us and you, that we worship none but Allah, and that we associate no partners with Him, and that none of us shall take others as lords besides Allah. Then, if they turn away, say: “Bear witness that we are Muslims.” – Surah Al-Imran 3:64

قُلْ يَٰٓأَهْلَ ٱلْكِتَٰبِ تَعَالَوْا۟ إِلَىٰ كَلِمَةٍ سَوَآءٍۭ بَيْنَنَا وَبَيْنَكُمْ أَلَّا نَعْبُدَ إِلَّا ٱللَّهَ وَلَا نُشْرِكَ بِهِۦ شَيْـًٔا وَلَا يَتَّخِذَ بَعْضُنَا بَعْضًا أَرْبَابًا مِّن دُونِ ٱللَّهِ ۚ فَإِن تَوَلَّوْا۟ فَقُولُوا۟ ٱشْهَدُوا۟ بِأَنَّا مُسْلِمُونَ

Worship Allah and join none with Him in worship, and do good to parents, kinsfolk, orphans, Al-Masakin (the poor), the neighbour who is near of kin, the neighbour who is a stranger, the companion by your side, the wayfarer (you meet), and those (slaves) whom your right hands possess. Verily, Allah does not like such as are proud and boastful; — Surah An-Nisa 4:36

وَٱعْبُدُوا۟ ٱللَّهَ وَلَا تُشْرِكُوا۟ بِهِۦ شَيْـًٔا ۖ وَبِٱلْوَٰلِدَيْنِ إِحْسَٰنًا وَبِذِى ٱلْقُرْبَىٰ وَٱلْيَتَٰمَىٰ وَٱلْمَسَٰكِينِ وَٱلْجَارِ ذِى ٱلْقُرْبَىٰ وَٱلْجَارِ ٱلْجُنُبِ وَٱلصَّاحِبِ بِٱلْجَنۢبِ وَٱبْنِ ٱلسَّبِيلِ وَمَا مَلَكَتْ أَيْمَٰنُكُمْ ۗ إِنَّ ٱللَّهَ لَا يُحِبُّ مَن كَانَ مُخْتَالًا فَخُورًا

Say (O Muhammad): “Shall we invoke others besides Allah (false deities), that can do us neither good nor harm, and shall we turn on our heels after Allah has guided us (to true Monotheism)? – like one whom the Shayatin (devils) have made to go astray, confused (wandering) through the earth, his companions calling him to guidance (saying): ‘Come to us.’ ” Say: “Verily, Allah’s Guidance is the only guidance, and we have been commanded to submit (ourselves) to the Lord of the ‘Alamin (mankind, jinns and all that exists); - Surah Al-An’am 6:71

قُلْ أَنَدْعُوا۟ مِن دُونِ ٱللَّهِ مَا لَا يَنفَعُنَا وَلَا يَضُرُّنَا وَنُرَدُّ عَلَىٰٓ أَعْقَابِنَا بَعْدَ إِذْ هَدَىٰنَا ٱللَّهُ كَٱلَّذِى ٱسْتَهْوَتْهُ ٱلشَّيَٰطِينُ فِى ٱلْأَرْضِ حَيْرَانَ لَهُۥٓ أَصْحَٰبٌ يَدْعُونَهُۥٓ إِلَى ٱلْهُدَى ٱئْتِنَا ۗ قُلْ إِنَّ هُدَى ٱللَّهِ هُوَ ٱلْهُدَىٰ ۖ وَأُمِرْنَا لِنُسْلِمَ لِرَبِّ ٱلْعَٰلَمِينَ

Eat not (O believers) of that (meat) on which Allah’s Name has not been pronounced (at the time of the slaughtering of the animal), for sure it is Fisq (a sin and disobedience of Allah). And certainly, the Shayatin (devils) do inspire their friends (from mankind) to dispute with you, and if you obey them [by making Al-Maytatah (a dead animal) legal by eating it], then you would indeed be Mushrikun (polytheists) [because they (devils and their friends) made lawful to you to eat that which Allah has made unlawful to eat and you obeyed them by considering it lawful to eat, and by doing so you worshipped them, and to worship others besides Allah is polytheism]. – Surah Al-An’am 6:121

وَلَا تَأْكُلُوا۟ مِمَّا لَمْ يُذْكَرِ ٱسْمُ ٱللَّهِ عَلَيْهِ وَإِنَّهُۥ لَفِسْقٌ ۗ وَإِنَّ ٱلشَّيَٰطِينَ لَيُوحُونَ إِلَىٰٓ أَوْلِيَآئِهِمْ لِيُجَٰدِلُوكُمْ ۖ وَإِنْ أَطَعْتُمُوهُمْ إِنَّكُمْ لَمُشْرِكُونَ

And (remember) when Luqman said to his son when he was advising him: "O my son! Join not in worship others with Allah. Verily! Joining others in worship with Allah is a great Zulm (wrong) indeed. – Surah Luqman 31:13

وَإِذْ قَالَ لُقْمَـٰنُ لِٱبْنِهِۦ وَهُوَ يَعِظُهُۥ يَـٰبُنَىَّ لَا تُشْرِكْ بِٱللَّهِ ۖ إِنَّ ٱلشِّرْكَ لَظُلْمٌ عَظِيمٌ

Narrated `Abdullah: When the Verse: 'It is those who believe and confuse not their belief with wrong (i.e., worshipping others besides Allah): (6.82) was revealed, it became very hard on the companions of the Prophet ﷺ and they said, "Who among us has not confused his belief with wrong (oppression)?" On that, Allah's Apostle said, "This is not meant (by the Verse). Don't you listen to Luqman's statement: 'Verily! Joining others in worship with Allah is a great wrong indeed.' (31.13) – Al-Bukhari 6918

حَدَّثَنَا قُتَيْبَةُ بْنُ سَعِيدٍ، حَدَّثَنَا جَرِيرٌ، عَنِ الأَعْمَشِ، عَنْ إِبْرَاهِيمَ، عَنْ عَلْقَمَةَ، عَنْ عَبْدِ اللَّهِ ـ رضى الله عنه ـ قَالَ لَمَّا نَزَلَتْ هَذِهِ الآيَةُ {الَّذِينَ آمَنُوا وَلَمْ يَلْبِسُوا إِيمَانَهُمْ بِظُلْمٍ} شَقَّ ذَلِكَ عَلَى أَصْحَابِ النَّبِيِّ صلى الله عليه وسلم وَقَالُوا أَيُّنَا لَمْ يَلْبِسْ إِيمَانَهُ بِظُلْمٍ فَقَالَ رَسُولُ اللَّهِ صلى الله عليه وسلم " إِنَّهُ لَيْسَ بِذَاكَ، أَلاَ تَسْمَعُونَ إِلَى قَوْلِ لُقْمَانَ {إِنَّ الشِّرْكَ لَظُلْمٌ عَظِيمٌ}".

And of mankind are some who take (for worship) others besides Allah as rivals (to Allah). They love them as they love Allah. But those who believe, love Allah more (than anything else). If only, those who do wrong could see, when they will see the torment, that all power belongs to Allah and that Allah is Severe in punishment. When those who were followed, disown (declare themselves innocent of) those who followed (them), and they see the torment, then all their relations will be cut off from them. And those who followed will say: "If only we had one more chance to return (to the worldly life), we would disown (declare ourselves as innocent from) them as they have disowned (declared themselves as innocent from) us." Thus Allah will show them their deeds as regrets for them. And they will never get out of the Fire . – Surah Al-Baqarah 2:165-167

وَمِنَ ٱلنَّاسِ مَن يَتَّخِذُ مِن دُونِ ٱللَّهِ أَندَادًا يُحِبُّونَهُمْ كَحُبِّ ٱللَّهِ ۖ وَٱلَّذِينَ ءَامَنُوٓا۟ أَشَدُّ حُبًّا لِّلَّهِ ۗ وَلَوْ يَرَى ٱلَّذِينَ ظَلَمُوٓا۟ إِذْ يَرَوْنَ ٱلْعَذَابَ أَنَّ ٱلْقُوَّةَ لِلَّهِ جَمِيعًا وَأَنَّ ٱللَّهَ شَدِيدُ ٱلْعَذَابِ إِذْ تَبَرَّأَ ٱلَّذِينَ ٱتُّبِعُوا۟ مِنَ ٱلَّذِينَ ٱتَّبَعُوا۟ وَرَأَوُا۟ ٱلْعَذَابَ وَتَقَطَّعَتْ بِهِمُ ٱلْأَسْبَابُ وَقَالَ ٱلَّذِينَ ٱتَّبَعُوا۟ لَوْ أَنَّ لَنَا كَرَّةً فَنَتَبَرَّأَ مِنْهُمْ كَمَا تَبَرَّءُوا۟ مِنَّا ۗ كَذَٰلِكَ يُرِيهِمُ ٱللَّهُ أَعْمَـٰلَهُمْ حَسَرَٰتٍ عَلَيْهِمْ ۖ وَمَا هُم بِخَـٰرِجِينَ مِنَ ٱلنَّارِ

Ah! Woe to me! Would that I had never taken so-and-so as a friend! "He indeed led me astray from the Reminder (this Qur'an) after it had come to me. And Shaitan (Satan) is ever a deserter to man in the hour of need." And the Messenger (Muhammad) will say: "O my Lord! Verily, my people deserted this Qur'an (neither listened to it, nor acted on its laws and orders)." – Surah Al-Furqan 25:28-30

يَـٰوَيْلَتَىٰ لَيْتَنِى لَمْ أَتَّخِذْ فُلَانًا خَلِيلًا لَّقَدْ أَضَلَّنِى عَنِ ٱلذِّكْرِ بَعْدَ إِذْ جَآءَنِى ۗ وَكَانَ ٱلشَّيْطَـٰنُ لِلْإِنسَـٰنِ خَذُولًا وَقَالَ ٱلرَّسُولُ يَـٰرَبِّ إِنَّ قَوْمِى ٱتَّخَذُوا۟ هَـٰذَا ٱلْقُرْءَانَ مَهْجُورًا

They (Jews and Christians) took their rabbis and their monks to be their lords besides Allah (by obeying them in things which they made lawful or unlawful according to their own desires without being ordered by Allah), and (they also took as their Lord) Messiah, son of Maryam (Mary), while they (Jews and Christians) were commanded [in the Taurat (Torah) and the Injeel (Gospel) to worship none but One Ilah (God – Allah) La ilaha illa Huwa (none has the right to be worshipped but He). Praise and glory be to Him, (far above is He) from having the partners they associate (with Him)." – Surah At-Taubah 9:31

ٱتَّخَذُوٓا۟ أَحْبَارَهُمْ وَرُهْبَـٰنَهُمْ أَرْبَابًا مِّن دُونِ ٱللَّهِ وَٱلْمَسِيحَ ٱبْنَ مَرْيَمَ وَمَآ أُمِرُوٓا۟ إِلَّا لِيَعْبُدُوٓا۟ إِلَـٰهًا وَٰحِدًا ۖ لَّآ إِلَـٰهَ إِلَّا هُوَ ۚ سُبْحَـٰنَهُۥ عَمَّا يُشْرِكُونَ

Say (O Muhammad): "Who is the Lord of the heavens and the earth?" Say: "(It is) Allah." Say: "Have you then taken (for worship) Auliya' (protectors, etc.) other than Him, such as have no power either for benefit or for harm to themselves?" Say: "Is the blind equal to the one who sees? Or darkness equal to light? Or do they assign to Allah partners who created the like of His creation, so that the creation (which they made and His creation) seemed alike to them." Say: "Allah is the Creator of all things, He is the One, the Irresistible." He sends down water (rain) from the sky, and the valleys flow according to their measure, but the flood bears away the foam that mounts up to the surface, and (also) from that (ore) which they heat in the fire in order to make ornaments or utensils, rises a foam like unto it, thus does Allah (by parables) show forth truth and falsehood . Then, as for the foam it passes away as scum upon the banks, while that which is for the good of mankind remains in the earth. Thus Allah sets forth parables (for the truth and falsehood, i.e. Belief and disbelief). For those who answered their Lord's Call [believed in the Oneness of Allah and followed His Messenger Muhammad i.e. Islamic Monotheism] is Al-Husna (i.e. Paradise). But those who answered not His Call (disbelieved in the Oneness of Allah and followed not His Messenger Muhammad), if they had all that is in the earth together with its like, they would offer it in order to save themselves (from the torment, it will be in vain). For them there will be the terrible reckoning. Their dwelling place will be Hell; – and worst indeed is that place for rest. Shall he then who knows that what has been revealed unto you (O Muhammad) from your Lord is the truth be like him who is blind? But it is only the men of understanding that pay heed. Those who fulfill the Covenant of Allah and break not the Mithaq (bond, treaty, covenant); Those who join that which Allah has commanded to be joined (i.e. they are good to their relatives and do not sever the bond of kinship), fear their Lord, and dread the terrible reckoning (i.e. abstain from all kinds of sins and evil deeds which Allah has forbidden and perform all kinds of good deeds which Allah has ordained). And those who remain patient, seeking their Lord's Countenance, perform As-Salat (Iqamat-as-Salat), and spend out of that which We have bestowed on them, secretly and openly, and defend evil with good, for such there is a good end; - Surah Ar-Ra'd 13:16-22

قُلْ مَن رَّبُّ ٱلسَّمَٰوَٰتِ وَٱلْأَرْضِ قُلِ ٱللَّهُ قُلْ أَفَٱتَّخَذْتُم مِّن دُونِهِۦٓ أَوْلِيَآءَ لَا يَمْلِكُونَ لِأَنفُسِهِمْ نَفْعًا وَلَا ضَرًّا قُلْ هَلْ يَسْتَوِى ٱلْأَعْمَىٰ وَٱلْبَصِيرُ
أَمْ هَلْ تَسْتَوِى ٱلظُّلُمَٰتُ وَٱلنُّورُ أَمْ جَعَلُوا۟ لِلَّهِ شُرَكَآءَ خَلَقُوا۟ كَخَلْقِهِۦ فَتَشَٰبَهَ ٱلْخَلْقُ عَلَيْهِمْ قُلِ ٱللَّهُ خَٰلِقُ كُلِّ شَىْءٍ وَهُوَ ٱلْوَٰحِدُ ٱلْقَهَّٰرُ أَنزَلَ
مِنَ ٱلسَّمَآءِ مَآءً فَسَالَتْ أَوْدِيَةٌۢ بِقَدَرِهَا فَٱحْتَمَلَ ٱلسَّيْلُ زَبَدًا رَّابِيًا وَمِمَّا يُوقِدُونَ عَلَيْهِ فِى ٱلنَّارِ ٱبْتِغَآءَ حِلْيَةٍ أَوْ مَتَٰعٍ زَبَدٌ مِّثْلُهُۥ كَذَٰلِكَ يَضْرِبُ
ٱللَّهُ ٱلْحَقَّ وَٱلْبَٰطِلَ فَأَمَّا ٱلزَّبَدُ فَيَذْهَبُ جُفَآءً وَأَمَّا مَا يَنفَعُ ٱلنَّاسَ فَيَمْكُثُ فِى ٱلْأَرْضِ كَذَٰلِكَ يَضْرِبُ ٱللَّهُ ٱلْأَمْثَالَ لِلَّذِينَ ٱسْتَجَابُوا۟ لِرَبِّهِمُ
ٱلْحُسْنَىٰ وَٱلَّذِينَ لَمْ يَسْتَجِيبُوا۟ لَهُۥ لَوْ أَنَّ لَهُم مَّا فِى ٱلْأَرْضِ جَمِيعًا وَمِثْلَهُۥ مَعَهُۥ لَٱفْتَدَوْا۟ بِهِۦٓ أُو۟لَٰٓئِكَ لَهُمْ سُوٓءُ ٱلْحِسَابِ وَمَأْوَىٰهُمْ جَهَنَّمُ
وَبِئْسَ ٱلْمِهَادُ أَفَمَن يَعْلَمُ أَنَّمَآ أُنزِلَ إِلَيْكَ مِن رَّبِّكَ ٱلْحَقُّ كَمَنْ هُوَ أَعْمَىٰٓ إِنَّمَا يَتَذَكَّرُ أُو۟لُوا۟ ٱلْأَلْبَٰبِ ٱلَّذِينَ يُوفُونَ بِعَهْدِ ٱللَّهِ وَلَا يَنقُضُونَ
ٱلْمِيثَٰقَ وَٱلَّذِينَ يَصِلُونَ مَآ أَمَرَ ٱللَّهُ بِهِۦٓ أَن يُوصَلَ وَيَخْشَوْنَ رَبَّهُمْ وَيَخَافُونَ سُوٓءَ ٱلْحِسَابِ وَٱلَّذِينَ صَبَرُوا۟ ٱبْتِغَآءَ وَجْهِ رَبِّهِمْ وَأَقَامُوا۟
ٱلصَّلَوٰةَ وَأَنفَقُوا۟ مِمَّا رَزَقْنَٰهُمْ سِرًّا وَعَلَانِيَةً وَيَدْرَءُونَ بِٱلْحَسَنَةِ ٱلسَّيِّئَةَ أُو۟لَٰٓئِكَ لَهُمْ عُقْبَى ٱلدَّارِ

And if the truth had been in accordance with their desires, verily, the heavens and the earth, and whosoever is therein would have been corrupted! Nay, We have brought them their reminder, but they turn away from their reminder.– Surah Al-Mu'minun 23:71

وَلَوِ ٱتَّبَعَ ٱلْحَقُّ أَهْوَآءَهُمْ لَفَسَدَتِ ٱلسَّمَٰوَٰتُ وَٱلْأَرْضُ وَمَن فِيهِنَّ بَلْ أَتَيْنَٰهُم بِذِكْرِهِمْ فَهُمْ عَن ذِكْرِهِم مُّعْرِضُونَ

Do then those who disbelieve think that they can take My slaves [i.e., the angels, Allah's Messengers, 'Iesa (Jesus), son of Maryam (Mary), etc.] as Auliya' (lords, gods, protectors, etc.) besides Me? Verily, We have prepared Hell as an entertainment for the disbelievers (in the Oneness of Allah Islamic Monotheism). Say (O Muhammad): "Shall We tell you the greatest losers in respect of (their) deeds?. "Those whose efforts have been wasted in this life while they thought that they were acquiring good by their deeds!– Surah Al-Khaf 18:102-104

أَفَحَسِبَ ٱلَّذِينَ كَفَرُوٓا۟ أَن يَتَّخِذُوا۟ عِبَادِى مِن دُونِىٓ أَوْلِيَآءَ إِنَّآ أَعْتَدْنَا جَهَنَّمَ لِلْكَٰفِرِينَ نُزُلًا قُلْ هَلْ نُنَبِّئُكُم بِٱلْأَخْسَرِينَ أَعْمَٰلًا ٱلَّذِينَ ضَلَّ
سَعْيُهُمْ فِى ٱلْحَيَوٰةِ ٱلدُّنْيَا وَهُمْ يَحْسَبُونَ أَنَّهُمْ يُحْسِنُونَ صُنْعًا

Their intercession does not avail anything
لَا تُغۡنِى شَفَـٰعَتُهُمۡ شَيۡـًٔا

Allah is (The One) Who created the heavens and the earth, and whatever is between them in six days; thereafter He leveled Himself upon the Throne. (How He did so is beyond human understanding) In no way do you have, apart from Him, any patron nor any intercessor. Will you then not remind yourselves. – Surah As-Sajdah 32:4
ٱللَّهُ ٱلَّذِى خَلَقَ ٱلسَّمَـٰوَٰتِ وَٱلۡأَرۡضَ وَمَا بَيۡنَهُمَا فِى سِتَّةِ أَيَّامٍ ثُمَّ ٱسۡتَوَىٰ عَلَى ٱلۡعَرۡشِۖ مَا لَكُم مِّن دُونِهِۦ مِن وَلِىٍّ وَلَا شَفِيعٍۚ أَفَلَا تَتَذَكَّرُونَ

Shall I take to myself, apart from Him, gods whose intercession, in case The All-Merciful wills any adversity to me, will not avail me anything, nor will they rescue me. – Surah Ya Sin 36:23
ءَأَتَّخِذُ مِن دُونِهِۦٓ ءَالِهَةً إِن يُرِدۡنِ ٱلرَّحۡمَـٰنُ بِضُرٍّ لَّا تُغۡنِ عَنِّى شَفَـٰعَتُهُمۡ شَيۡـًٔا وَلَا يُنقِذُونِ

Or even have they taken to themselves constant intercessors apart from Allah? Say, "And (even) if they do not possess (any power) for anything, nor do they consider?"
39:44 Say, (This is addressed to the Prophet) "To Allah is intercession all together. To Him is the Kingdom of the heavens and the earth; thereafter to Him you will be returned." – Surah Az-Zumar 39:43&44
أَمِ ٱتَّخَذُواْ مِن دُونِ ٱللَّهِ شُفَعَآءَۚ قُلۡ أَوَلَوۡ كَانُواْ لَا يَمۡلِكُونَ شَيۡـًٔا وَلَا يَعۡقِلُونَ قُل لِّلَّهِ ٱلشَّفَـٰعَةُ جَمِيعًاۖ لَّهُۥ مُلۡكُ ٱلسَّمَـٰوَٰتِ وَٱلۡأَرۡضِۖ ثُمَّ إِلَيۡهِ تُرۡجَعُونَ

And warn them of the Imminent Day, when the hearts are at the throats, choking them. The unjust will have no dependable friend and no intercessor [who is] obeyed. – Surah Ghafir 40:18
وَأَنذِرۡهُمۡ يَوۡمَ ٱلۡـَٔازِفَةِ إِذِ ٱلۡقُلُوبُ لَدَى ٱلۡحَنَاجِرِ كَـٰظِمِينَۚ مَا لِلظَّـٰلِمِينَ مِنۡ حَمِيمٍ وَلَا شَفِيعٍ يُطَاعُ

And the ones they invoke, apart from Him, do not possess (the power) of intercession, excepting him who witnesses to the Truth, and they know it. – Surah Az-Zukhruf 43:86
وَلَا يَمۡلِكُ ٱلَّذِينَ يَدۡعُونَ مِن دُونِهِ ٱلشَّفَـٰعَةَ إِلَّا مَن شَهِدَ بِٱلۡحَقِّ وَهُمۡ يَعۡلَمُونَ

And how many an Angel (there is) in the heavens whose intercession does not avail anything except even after Allah gives permission to whomever He decides and He is satisfied. – Surah An-Najm 53:26

وَكَم مِّن مَّلَكٍ فِى ٱلسَّمَـٰوَٰتِ لَا تُغۡنِى شَفَـٰعَتُهُمۡ شَيۡـًٔا إِلَّا مِنۢ بَعۡدِ أَن يَأۡذَنَ ٱللَّهُ لِمَن يَشَآءُ وَيَرۡضَىٰٓ

The Imminent is imminent Apart from Allah, none can lift it off. – Surah An-Najm 53:57&58
أَزِفَتِ ٱلۡـَٔازِفَةُ لَيۡسَ لَهَا مِن دُونِ ٱللَّهِ كَاشِفَةٌ

And that (certain) men of the humankind used to take refuge with (certain) men of the jinn; so they increased them in confusion. – Surah Al-Jinn 72:6
وَأَنَّهُۥ كَانَ رِجَالٌ مِّنَ ٱلۡإِنسِ يَعُوذُونَ بِرِجَالٍ مِّنَ ٱلۡجِنِّ فَزَادُوهُمۡ رَهَقًا

So in no way will the intercession of the intercessors profit them. – Surah Al-Mudathir 74:48
فَمَا تَنفَعُهُمۡ شَفَـٰعَةُ ٱلشَّـٰفِعِينَ

And beware of a day when no Soul can benefit another Soul, nor will any intercession be accepted on its behalf, nor will any ransom be accepted from it; nor will they be helped. – Surah Al-Baqarah 2:48

وَٱتَّقُواْ يَوۡمٗا لَّا تَجۡزِي نَفۡسٌ عَن نَّفۡسٖ شَيۡـٔٗا وَلَا يُقۡبَلُ مِنۡهَا شَفَٰعَةٞ وَلَا يُؤۡخَذُ مِنۡهَا عَدۡلٞ وَلَا هُمۡ يُنصَرُونَ

And beware of a day when no Soul stands in for another. Ransom will not be accepted, nor will intercession benefit any of them, nor will any be helped. – Surah Al-Baqarah 2:123

وَٱتَّقُواْ يَوۡمٗا لَّا تَجۡزِي نَفۡسٌ عَن نَّفۡسٖ شَيۡـٔٗا وَلَا يُقۡبَلُ مِنۡهَا عَدۡلٞ وَلَا تَنفَعُهَا شَفَٰعَةٞ وَلَا هُمۡ يُنصَرُونَ

And in case Allah touches you with an adversity, then none (can) lift it off except He, and in case He touches you with charity, (i.e., benefit, welfare) then He is Ever-Determiner over everything. – Surah Al-An'am 6:17

وَإِن يَمۡسَسۡكَ ٱللَّهُ بِضُرّٖ فَلَا كَاشِفَ لَهُۥٓ إِلَّا هُوَۖ وَإِن يَمۡسَسۡكَ بِخَيۡرٖ فَهُوَ عَلَىٰ كُلِّ شَيۡءٖ قَدِيرٞ

Say, "Have you seen (for) yourselves, in case the torment of Allah comes up to you or the Hour comes up to you, will you invoke any other than Allah, in case you are (truly) sincere?" – Surah Al-An'am 6:40

قُلۡ أَرَءَيۡتَكُمۡ إِنۡ أَتَىٰكُمۡ عَذَابُ ٱللَّهِ أَوۡ أَتَتۡكُمُ ٱلسَّاعَةُ أَغَيۡرَ ٱللَّهِ تَدۡعُونَ إِن كُنتُمۡ صَٰدِقِينَ

And that they surmised, as you also surmised
وَأَنَّهُمۡ ظَنُّواْ كَمَا ظَنَنتُمۡ

And in no way do they have any knowledge thereof. Decidedly they closely follow (nothing) except surmise, and surely surmise does not avail anything against the Truth So veer away from him who turns back from Our Remembrance and is not willing (to seek anything) except the present life (Literally: the lowly life, i.e., the life of this world) That is their attainment of knowledge. Surely your Lord is He Who knows best the ones who have erred away from His way, and He knows best the ones who are guided And to Allah belongs whatever is in the heavens and whatever is in the earth that He may recompense the ones who have done odious (deeds) for what they have done and recompense the ones who have done fair (deeds) with the fairest reward The ones who avoid the great (kinds) of vice and obscenities, except lesser offences; surely your Lord is Ever-Embracing in (His) forgiveness. He knows you best, as He brought you into being from the earth, and as you were embryos in your mothers' bellies; so do not (consider) yourselves cleansed; (only) He knows best him who is pious Have you (The Prophet) then seen him who turns away And gives little and (then) parsimoniously Does he have in his presence the knowledge of the Unseen, so he sees Or even has he not been fully informed of what is in the Scrolls of Musa (Moses) And Ibrahim, (Abraham) who constantly fulfilled the Message That no encumbered self will be encumbered with the encumbrance of another And that man will have nothing except that for which he has endeavored (to achieve) And that his endeavor will eventually be seen. – Surah An-Najm 53:28-40

وَمَا لَهُم بِهِۦ مِنۡ عِلۡمٍۖ إِن يَتَّبِعُونَ إِلَّا ٱلظَّنَّۖ وَإِنَّ ٱلظَّنَّ لَا يُغۡنِي مِنَ ٱلۡحَقِّ شَيۡـٔٗا فَأَعۡرِضۡ عَن مَّن تَوَلَّىٰ عَن ذِكۡرِنَا وَلَمۡ يُرِدۡ
إِلَّا ٱلۡحَيَوٰةَ ٱلدُّنۡيَا ذَٰلِكَ مَبۡلَغُهُم مِّنَ ٱلۡعِلۡمِۚ إِنَّ رَبَّكَ هُوَ أَعۡلَمُ بِمَن ضَلَّ عَن سَبِيلِهِۦ وَهُوَ أَعۡلَمُ بِمَنِ ٱهۡتَدَىٰ وَلِلَّهِ مَا فِي ٱلسَّمَٰوَٰتِ
وَمَا فِي ٱلۡأَرۡضِ لِيَجۡزِيَ ٱلَّذِينَ أَسَٰٓـُٔواْ بِمَا عَمِلُواْ وَيَجۡزِيَ ٱلَّذِينَ أَحۡسَنُواْ بِٱلۡحُسۡنَى ٱلَّذِينَ يَجۡتَنِبُونَ كَبَٰٓئِرَ ٱلۡإِثۡمِ وَٱلۡفَوَٰحِشَ إِلَّا
ٱللَّمَمَۚ إِنَّ رَبَّكَ وَٰسِعُ ٱلۡمَغۡفِرَةِۚ هُوَ أَعۡلَمُ بِكُمۡ إِذۡ أَنشَأَكُم مِّنَ ٱلۡأَرۡضِ وَإِذۡ أَنتُمۡ أَجِنَّةٞ فِي بُطُونِ أُمَّهَٰتِكُمۡۖ فَلَا تُزَكُّوٓاْ أَنفُسَكُمۡۖ هُوَ

أَعْلَمُ بِمَنِ ٱتَّقَىٰٓ أَفَرَءَيْتَ ٱلَّذِى تَوَلَّىٰ وَأَعْطَىٰ قَلِيلًا وَأَكْدَىٰٓ أَعِندَهُۥ عِلْمُ ٱلْغَيْبِ فَهُوَ يَرَىٰٓ أَمْ لَمْ يُنَبَّأْ بِمَا فِى صُحُفِ مُوسَىٰ
وَإِبْرَٰهِيمَ ٱلَّذِى وَفَّىٰٓ أَلَّا تَزِرُ وَازِرَةٌ وِزْرَ أُخْرَىٰ وَأَن لَّيْسَ لِلْإِنسَـٰنِ إِلَّا مَا سَعَىٰ وَأَنَّ سَعْيَهُۥ سَوْفَ يُرَىٰ

And that (certain) men of the humankind used to take refuge with (certain) men of the jinn; so they increased them in oppression And that they surmised, as you (The pronoun is plural) also surmised, that Allah would never make anyone to rise again And that we contacted the heaven, yet we found it filled with very strict guards and flaming (meteors) And that we used to sit (there) on seats for (over)hearing; yet whoever listens now finds a flaming (meteor) (closely) observing him And that we do not realize whether evil is willed for whoever are in the earth, or whether their Lord wills for them rectitude And that among us are the righteous, and among us are lesser than that; (i.e., besides that) we have been of discrete roads And that we surmised that we can never defy Allah in the earth, and we can never defy Him by escaping And that as soon as we heard the guidance, we believed in it; so whoever believes in his Lord, then he fears neither depreciation nor oppression And that among us are the Muslims, and among us are the inequitable. So whoever have surrendered (to Allah), then those are they who earnestly sought rectitude And as for the inequitable, then they are firewood for Hell." And that if they had gone straight on the right mode (of life), indeed We would have made them to drink copious water That We may tempt them therein; and whoever veers away from the Remembrance of his Lord, He will insert him into a mounting torment And that the mosques belong to Allah; so do not invoke, along with Allah, anyone And that as soon as the bondman of Allah rose up invoking Him, they almost densely packed upon him Say, "Surely I invoke only my Lord, and I do not associate with Him anyone." Say, "Surely I possess (no power) over you, either for harm or for rectitude." Say, "Surely never can anyone give me neighborly (protection) from Allah, and never can I find, apart from Him, any shielding. – Surah Al-Jinn 72:6-22

وَأَنَّهُۥ كَانَ رِجَالٌ مِّنَ ٱلْإِنسِ يَعُوذُونَ بِرِجَالٍ مِّنَ ٱلْجِنِّ فَزَادُوهُمْ رَهَقًا وَأَنَّهُمْ ظَنُّوا۟ كَمَا ظَنَنتُمْ أَن لَّن يَبْعَثَ ٱللَّهُ أَحَدًا وَأَنَّا
لَمَسْنَا ٱلسَّمَآءَ فَوَجَدْنَـٰهَا مُلِئَتْ حَرَسًا شَدِيدًا وَشُهُبًا وَأَنَّا كُنَّا نَقْعُدُ مِنْهَا مَقَـٰعِدَ لِلسَّمْعِ ۖ فَمَن يَسْتَمِعِ ٱلْـَٔانَ يَجِدْ لَهُۥ شِهَابًا رَّصَدًا
وَأَنَّا لَا نَدْرِىٓ أَشَرٌّ أُرِيدَ بِمَن فِى ٱلْأَرْضِ أَمْ أَرَادَ بِهِمْ رَبُّهُمْ رَشَدًا وَأَنَّا مِنَّا ٱلصَّـٰلِحُونَ وَمِنَّا دُونَ ذَٰلِكَ ۖ كُنَّا طَرَآئِقَ قِدَدًا وَأَنَّا
ظَنَنَّآ أَن لَّن نُّعْجِزَ ٱللَّهَ فِى ٱلْأَرْضِ وَلَن نُّعْجِزَهُۥ هَرَبًا وَأَنَّا لَمَّا سَمِعْنَا ٱلْهُدَىٰٓ ءَامَنَّا بِهِۦ ۖ فَمَن يُؤْمِنۢ بِرَبِّهِۦ فَلَا يَخَافُ بَخْسًا وَلَا
رَهَقًا وَأَنَّا مِنَّا ٱلْمُسْلِمُونَ وَمِنَّا ٱلْقَـٰسِطُونَ ۖ فَمَنْ أَسْلَمَ فَأُو۟لَـٰٓئِكَ تَحَرَّوْا۟ رَشَدًا وَأَمَّا ٱلْقَـٰسِطُونَ فَكَانُوا۟ لِجَهَنَّمَ حَطَبًا وَأَلَّوِ ٱسْتَقَـٰمُوا۟
عَلَى ٱلطَّرِيقَةِ لَأَسْقَيْنَـٰهُم مَّآءً غَدَقًا لِّنَفْتِنَهُمْ فِيهِ ۚ وَمَن يُعْرِضْ عَن ذِكْرِ رَبِّهِۦ يَسْلُكْهُ عَذَابًا صَعَدًا وَأَنَّ ٱلْمَسَـٰجِدَ لِلَّهِ فَلَا تَدْعُوا۟
مَعَ ٱللَّهِ أَحَدًا وَأَنَّهُۥ لَمَّا قَامَ عَبْدُ ٱللَّهِ يَدْعُوهُ كَادُوا۟ يَكُونُونَ عَلَيْهِ لِبَدًا قُلْ إِنَّمَآ أَدْعُوا۟ رَبِّى وَلَآ أُشْرِكُ بِهِۦٓ أَحَدًا قُلْ إِنِّى لَآ أَمْلِكُ
لَكُمْ ضَرًّا وَلَا رَشَدًا قُلْ إِنِّى لَن يُجِيرَنِى مِنَ ٱللَّهِ أَحَدٌ وَلَنْ أَجِدَ مِن دُونِهِۦ مُلْتَحَدًا

Or even do you reckon that the Companions of the Cave and Ar-Raqim (It is the name of a leaden plate, on which were written the names of the seven sleepers) were among Our signs a wonder As the young men (Literally: the pages) took (their) abode in the cave, (and) so they said, "Our Lord, bring us mercy from very close to You, and dispose for us rectitude in our Command." (i.e., in Your Command to us; our: in our affair Then We struck upon their ears for a (great) number of years in the cave Thereafter We made them to rise again that We might know whichever of the two parties would best enumerate the span they had lingered We, Ever We, narrate to you their tidings with the truth. Surely they were young men who believed in their Lord, and We increased them in guidance And We braced (Literally: tied upon their hearts) their hearts as they rose up and said, "Our Lord is The Lord of the heavens and the earth; we will never invoke any god, apart from Him, for indeed, we had already spoken unjudiciously These our people have taken to themselves (other) gods apart from Him. Had they come up with a most evident all-binding authority concerning their belief in them? So, who is more unjust than he who fabricates against Allah a lie And as you have kept apart from them and what they worship excepting Allah, so take (your) abode in the cave, (then) your Lord will spread for you of His mercy and will dispose for you a convenient (place) of your Command." (i.e., the command of Allah to you; or: your affair And you might have seen the sun when it rose, declining from their cave towards the right; and when it set, it went past them towards the left while they were in a broad fissure of (the cave). That was one of the signs of Allah. Whomever Allah guides, then he is right-guided, and whomever He leads away into error, then you will never find for him a right-minded patron And you would have reckoned that they were awake (as) they were lying down, and We turned them about towards the right and towards the left, and their dog stretching out his two fore-legs (Literally: his two arms) on the threshold. If you had viewed them, indeed you would have turned away from them in flight and indeed been filled with horror of them And thus We made them rise again that they might ask one another (Literally: among themselves). A speaker from among them said, "How long have you lingered?" They said, "We have lingered a day, or part (Literally: some "part" of a day) of a day." (others) said, "Your Lord knows best how long you have lingered. So send one of you forth with this money to the city, then let him look for whichever of them has the purest (Literally: most cleansed) food, so let him come up to you with a provision thereof, and let him be courteous, and definitely let no man be aware of your (presence) Surely in case they get the better of you, they will stone you or bring you back to their creed, and (then) you will never prosper at all." And thus We made the (people of the city) discover them that they might know that the promise of Allah is true and that the Hour, there is no suspicion about it. As they were contending among themselves their command, (The Command of Allah concerning Resurrection; or: their affair) (then) they said, "Build over them a structure; their Lord knows them best." (But) the ones who prevailed over their Command (Literally: overcame them in their Command; or: in their affair) said, "Indeed we will definitely build (Literally: take to ourselves) over them a mosque." – Surah Al-Khaf 18:9-21

أَمۡ حَسِبۡتَ أَنَّ أَصۡحَٰبَ ٱلۡكَهۡفِ وَٱلرَّقِيمِ كَانُواْ مِنۡ ءَايَٰتِنَا عَجَبًا إِذۡ أَوَى ٱلۡفِتۡيَةُ إِلَى ٱلۡكَهۡفِ فَقَالُواْ رَبَّنَآ ءَاتِنَا مِن لَّدُنكَ رَحۡمَةً وَهَيِّئۡ لَنَا مِنۡ أَمۡرِنَا رَشَدًا فَضَرَبۡنَا عَلَىٰٓ ءَاذَانِهِمۡ فِي ٱلۡكَهۡفِ سِنِينَ عَدَدًا ثُمَّ بَعَثۡنَٰهُمۡ لِنَعۡلَمَ أَيُّ ٱلۡحِزۡبَيۡنِ أَحۡصَىٰ لِمَا لَبِثُوٓاْ أَمَدًا نَّحۡنُ نَقُصُّ عَلَيۡكَ نَبَأَهُم بِٱلۡحَقِّۚ إِنَّهُمۡ فِتۡيَةٌ ءَامَنُواْ بِرَبِّهِمۡ وَزِدۡنَٰهُمۡ هُدًى وَرَبَطۡنَا عَلَىٰ قُلُوبِهِمۡ إِذۡ قَامُواْ فَقَالُواْ رَبُّنَا رَبُّ ٱلسَّمَٰوَٰتِ وَٱلۡأَرۡضِ لَن نَّدۡعُوَاْ مِن دُونِهِۦٓ إِلَٰهٗاۖ لَّقَدۡ قُلۡنَآ إِذٗا شَطَطًا هَٰٓؤُلَآءِ قَوۡمُنَا ٱتَّخَذُواْ مِن دُونِهِۦٓ ءَالِهَةٗۖ لَّوۡلَا يَأۡتُونَ عَلَيۡهِم بِسُلۡطَٰنِۭ بَيِّنٖۖ فَمَنۡ أَظۡلَمُ مِمَّنِ ٱفۡتَرَىٰ عَلَى ٱللَّهِ كَذِبٗا وَإِذِ ٱعۡتَزَلۡتُمُوهُمۡ وَمَا يَعۡبُدُونَ إِلَّا ٱللَّهَ فَأۡوُۥٓاْ إِلَى ٱلۡكَهۡفِ يَنشُرۡ لَكُمۡ رَبُّكُم مِّن رَّحۡمَتِهِۦ وَيُهَيِّئۡ لَكُم مِّنۡ أَمۡرِكُم مِّرۡفَقٗا وَتَرَى ٱلشَّمۡسَ إِذَا طَلَعَت تَّزَٰوَرُ عَن كَهۡفِهِمۡ ذَاتَ ٱلۡيَمِينِ وَإِذَا غَرَبَت تَّقۡرِضُهُمۡ ذَاتَ ٱلشِّمَالِ وَهُمۡ فِي فَجۡوَةٖ مِّنۡهُۚ ذَٰلِكَ مِنۡ ءَايَٰتِ ٱللَّهِۗ مَن يَهۡدِ ٱللَّهُ فَهُوَ ٱلۡمُهۡتَدِۖ وَمَن يُضۡلِلۡ فَلَن تَجِدَ لَهُۥ وَلِيّٗا مُّرۡشِدٗا وَتَحۡسَبُهُمۡ أَيۡقَاظٗا وَهُمۡ رُقُودٞۚ وَنُقَلِّبُهُمۡ ذَاتَ ٱلۡيَمِينِ وَذَاتَ ٱلشِّمَالِۖ وَكَلۡبُهُم بَٰسِطٞ ذِرَاعَيۡهِ بِٱلۡوَصِيدِۚ لَوِ ٱطَّلَعۡتَ عَلَيۡهِمۡ لَوَلَّيۡتَ مِنۡهُمۡ فِرَارٗا وَلَمُلِئۡتَ مِنۡهُمۡ رُعۡبٗا وَكَذَٰلِكَ بَعَثۡنَٰهُمۡ لِيَتَسَآءَلُواْ بَيۡنَهُمۡۚ قَالَ قَآئِلٞ مِّنۡهُمۡ كَمۡ لَبِثۡتُمۡۖ قَالُواْ لَبِثۡنَا يَوۡمًا أَوۡ بَعۡضَ يَوۡمٖۚ قَالُواْ رَبُّكُمۡ أَعۡلَمُ بِمَا لَبِثۡتُمۡ فَٱبۡعَثُوٓاْ أَحَدَكُم بِوَرِقِكُمۡ هَٰذِهِۦٓ إِلَى ٱلۡمَدِينَةِ فَلۡيَنظُرۡ أَيُّهَآ أَزۡكَىٰ طَعَامٗا فَلۡيَأۡتِكُم بِرِزۡقٖ مِّنۡهُ وَلۡيَتَلَطَّفۡ وَلَا يُشۡعِرَنَّ بِكُمۡ أَحَدًا إِنَّهُمۡ إِن يَظۡهَرُواْ عَلَيۡكُمۡ يَرۡجُمُوكُمۡ أَوۡ يُعِيدُوكُمۡ فِي مِلَّتِهِمۡ وَلَن تُفۡلِحُوٓاْ إِذًا أَبَدٗا وَكَذَٰلِكَ أَعۡثَرۡنَا عَلَيۡهِمۡ لِيَعۡلَمُوٓاْ أَنَّ وَعۡدَ ٱللَّهِ حَقّٞ وَأَنَّ ٱلسَّاعَةَ لَا رَيۡبَ فِيهَآ إِذۡ يَتَنَٰزَعُونَ بَيۡنَهُمۡ أَمۡرَهُمۡۖ فَقَالُواْ ٱبۡنُواْ عَلَيۡهِم بُنۡيَٰنٗاۖ رَّبُّهُمۡ أَعۡلَمُ بِهِمۡۚ قَالَ ٱلَّذِينَ غَلَبُواْ عَلَىٰٓ أَمۡرِهِمۡ لَنَتَّخِذَنَّ عَلَيۡهِم مَّسۡجِدٗا

O you who have believed, surely many of the religious learned men and monks indeed eat (up) the riches of mankind untruthfully and bar from the way of Allah; and (so do) the ones who hoard gold and silver and do not expend them in the way of Allah. Then give them the tidings of a painful torment. – Surah At-Taubah 9:34

يَٰٓأَيُّهَا ٱلَّذِينَ ءَامَنُوٓاْ إِنَّ كَثِيرٗا مِّنَ ٱلۡأَحۡبَارِ وَٱلرُّهۡبَانِ لَيَأۡكُلُونَ أَمۡوَٰلَ ٱلنَّاسِ بِٱلۡبَٰطِلِ وَيَصُدُّونَ عَن سَبِيلِ ٱللَّهِۗ وَٱلَّذِينَ يَكۡنِزُونَ ٱلذَّهَبَ وَٱلۡفِضَّةَ وَلَا يُنفِقُونَهَا فِي سَبِيلِ ٱللَّهِ فَبَشِّرۡهُم بِعَذَابٍ أَلِيمٖ

The Book of
.....Then those who disbelieved in their Lord equate others with Him. – Surah Al-An'am 6:1
....ثُمَّ ٱلَّذِينَ كَفَرُوا۟ بِرَبِّهِمۡ يَعۡدِلُونَ

Have you not considered those who were given a share of the Book? They believe in superstition and evil powers, and say of those who disbelieve, "These are better guided on the way than the believers." – Surah An-Nisa 4:51

أَلَمۡ تَرَ إِلَى ٱلَّذِينَ أُوتُوا۟ نَصِيبًا مِّنَ ٱلۡكِتَٰبِ يُؤۡمِنُونَ بِٱلۡجِبۡتِ وَٱلطَّٰغُوتِ وَيَقُولُونَ لِلَّذِينَ كَفَرُوا۟ هَٰٓؤُلَآءِ أَهۡدَىٰ مِنَ ٱلَّذِينَ ءَامَنُوا۟ سَبِيلًا

Have you not observed those who claim that they believe in what was revealed to you, and in what was revealed before you, yet they seek Satanic sources for legislation, in spite of being commanded to reject them? Satan means to mislead them far away. And when it is said to them, "Come to what Allah has revealed, and to the Messenger," you see the hypocrites shunning you comp letely.– Surah An-Nisa 4:60&61

أَلَمۡ تَرَ إِلَى ٱلَّذِينَ يَزۡعُمُونَ أَنَّهُمۡ ءَامَنُوا۟ بِمَآ أُنزِلَ إِلَيۡكَ وَمَآ أُنزِلَ مِن قَبۡلِكَ يُرِيدُونَ أَن يَتَحَاكَمُوٓا۟ إِلَى ٱلطَّٰغُوتِ وَقَدۡ أُمِرُوٓا۟ أَن يَكۡفُرُوا۟ بِهِۦۖ وَيُرِيدُ ٱلشَّيۡطَٰنُ أَن يُضِلَّهُمۡ ضَلَٰلَۢا بَعِيدًا وَإِذَا قِيلَ لَهُمۡ تَعَالَوۡا۟ إِلَىٰ مَآ أَنزَلَ ٱللَّهُ وَإِلَى ٱلرَّسُولِ رَأَيۡتَ ٱلۡمُنَٰفِقِينَ يَصُدُّونَ عَنكَ صُدُودًا

Praise be to Allah, Who created the heavens and the earth, and made the darkness and the light. Yet those who disbelieve ascribe equals to their Lord.– Surah Al-An'am 6:1

ٱلۡحَمۡدُ لِلَّهِ ٱلَّذِي خَلَقَ ٱلسَّمَٰوَٰتِ وَٱلۡأَرۡضَ وَجَعَلَ ٱلظُّلُمَٰتِ وَٱلنُّورَۖ ثُمَّ ٱلَّذِينَ كَفَرُوا۟ بِرَبِّهِمۡ يَعۡدِلُونَ

Say, "I am forbidden from worshiping those you pray to besides Allah." Say, "I will not follow your desires; else I would be lost and not be of those guided."– Surah Al-An'am 6:56

قُلۡ إِنِّي نُهِيتُ أَنۡ أَعۡبُدَ ٱلَّذِينَ تَدۡعُونَ مِن دُونِ ٱللَّهِۚ قُل لَّآ أَتَّبِعُ أَهۡوَآءَكُمۡ قَدۡ ضَلَلۡتُ إِذٗا وَمَآ أَنَا۠ مِنَ ٱلۡمُهۡتَدِينَ

Follow what is revealed to you from your Lord, and do not follow other masters beside Him. Little you recollect. – Surah Al-A'raf 7:3

ٱتَّبِعُوا۟ مَآ أُنزِلَ إِلَيۡكُم مِّن رَّبِّكُمۡ وَلَا تَتَّبِعُوا۟ مِن دُونِهِۦٓ أَوۡلِيَآءَۗ قَلِيلٗا مَّا تَذَكَّرُونَ

Or do you think that you will be left alone, without Allah identifying which of you will strive, and take no supporters apart from Allah, His Messenger, and the believers? Allah is well Aware of what you do. – Surah At-Taubah 9:16

أَمۡ حَسِبۡتُمۡ أَن تُتۡرَكُوا۟ وَلَمَّا يَعۡلَمِ ٱللَّهُ ٱلَّذِينَ جَٰهَدُوا۟ مِنكُمۡ وَلَمۡ يَتَّخِذُوا۟ مِن دُونِ ٱللَّهِ وَلَا رَسُولِهِۦ وَلَا ٱلۡمُؤۡمِنِينَ وَلِيجَةٗۚ وَٱللَّهُ خَبِيرُۢ بِمَا تَعۡمَلُونَ

They have taken their rabbis and their priests as lords instead of Allah, as well as the Messiah son of Mary. Although they were commanded to worship none but The One God. There is no god except He. Glory be to Him; High above what they associate with Him.– Surah At-Taubah 9:31

ٱتَّخَذُوٓا۟ أَحۡبَارَهُمۡ وَرُهۡبَٰنَهُمۡ أَرۡبَابٗا مِّن دُونِ ٱللَّهِ وَٱلۡمَسِيحَ ٱبۡنَ مَرۡيَمَ وَمَآ أُمِرُوٓا۟ إِلَّا لِيَعۡبُدُوٓا۟ إِلَٰهٗا وَٰحِدٗاۖ لَّآ إِلَٰهَ إِلَّا هُوَۚ سُبۡحَٰنَهُۥ عَمَّا يُشۡرِكُونَ

Postponement is an increase in disbelief—by which those who disbelieve are led astray. They allow it one year, and forbid it another year, in order to conform to the number made sacred by Allah, thus permitting what Allah has forbidden. The evil of their deeds seems good to them. Allah does not guide the disbelieving people.– Surah At-Taubah 9:37
إِنَّمَا ٱلنَّسِىٓءُ زِيَادَةٌ فِى ٱلْكُفْرِ ۖ يُضَلُّ بِهِ ٱلَّذِينَ كَفَرُوا۟ يُحِلُّونَهُۥ عَامًا وَيُحَرِّمُونَهُۥ عَامًا لِّيُوَاطِـُٔوا۟ عِدَّةَ مَا حَرَّمَ ٱللَّهُ فَيُحِلُّوا۟ مَا حَرَّمَ ٱللَّهُ ۚ زُيِّنَ لَهُمْ سُوٓءُ أَعْمَـٰلِهِمْ ۗ وَٱللَّهُ لَا يَهْدِى ٱلْقَوْمَ ٱلْكَـٰفِرِينَ

He said, "Your prayer has been answered, so go straight, and do not follow the– Surah Yunus 10:89
قَالَ قَدْ أُجِيبَت دَّعْوَتُكُمَا فَٱسْتَقِيمَا وَلَا تَتَّبِعَآنِّ سَبِيلَ ٱلَّذِينَ لَا يَعْلَمُونَ

Say, "O people, if you are in doubt about my religion—I do not serve those you serve apart from Allah. But I serve Allah, the one who will terminate your lives. And I was commanded to be of the believers." – Surah Yunus 10:104
قُلْ يَـٰٓأَيُّهَا ٱلنَّاسُ إِن كُنتُمْ فِى شَكٍّ مِّن دِينِى فَلَآ أَعْبُدُ ٱلَّذِينَ تَعْبُدُونَ مِن دُونِ ٱللَّهِ وَلَـٰكِنْ أَعْبُدُ ٱللَّهَ ٱلَّذِى يَتَوَفَّىٰكُمْ ۖ وَأُمِرْتُ أَنْ أَكُونَ مِنَ ٱلْمُؤْمِنِينَ

We never sent a messengerbefore you, or a prophet, but when he had a desire Satan interfered in his wishes. But Allah nullifies what Satan interjects, and Allah affirms His revelations. Allah is Omniscient and Wise.In order to make Satan's suggestions a trial for those whose hearts are diseased, and those whose hearts are hardened. The wrongdoers are in profound discord– Surah Al-Hajj 22:52&53
وَمَآ أَرْسَلْنَا مِن قَبْلِكَ مِن رَّسُولٍ وَلَا نَبِىٍّ إِلَّآ إِذَا تَمَنَّىٰٓ أَلْقَى ٱلشَّيْطَـٰنُ فِىٓ أُمْنِيَّتِهِۦ فَيَنسَخُ ٱللَّهُ مَا يُلْقِى ٱلشَّيْطَـٰنُ ثُمَّ يُحْكِمُ ٱللَّهُ ءَايَـٰتِهِۦ ۗ وَٱللَّهُ عَلِيمٌ حَكِيمٌ لِّيَجْعَلَ مَا يُلْقِى ٱلشَّيْطَـٰنُ فِتْنَةً لِّلَّذِينَ فِى قُلُوبِهِم مَّرَضٌ وَٱلْقَاسِيَةِ قُلُوبُهُمْ ۗ وَإِنَّ ٱلظَّـٰلِمِينَ لَفِى شِقَاقٍۭ بَعِيدٍ

Narrated Anas: The Prophet ﷺ said, "Some of my companions will come to me at my Lake Fount, and after I recognize them, they will then be taken away from me, whereupon I will say, 'My companions!' Then it will be said, 'You do not know what they innovated (new things) in the religion after you." – Al-Bukhari 6582
حَدَّثَنَا مُسْلِمُ بْنُ إِبْرَاهِيمَ، حَدَّثَنَا وُهَيْبٌ، حَدَّثَنَا عَبْدُ الْعَزِيزِ، عَنْ أَنَسٍ، عَنِ النَّبِيِّ صلى الله عليه وسلم قَالَ " لَيَرِدَنَّ عَلَىَّ نَاسٌ مِنْ أَصْحَابِي الْحَوْضَ، حَتَّى عَرَفْتُهُمُ اخْتُلِجُوا دُونِي، فَأَقُولُ أَصْحَابِي. فَيَقُولُ لاَ تَدْرِي مَا أَحْدَثُوا بَعْدَكَ "

Narrated Abu Hazim from Sahl bin Sa`d: The Prophet ﷺ said, "I am your predecessor (forerunner) at the Lake-Fount, and whoever will pass by there, he will drink from it and whoever will drink from it, he will never be thirsty. There will come to me some people whom I will recognize, and they will recognize me, but a barrier will be placed between me and them." – Al-Bukhari 6583
حَدَّثَنَا سَعِيدُ بْنُ أَبِي مَرْيَمَ، حَدَّثَنَا مُحَمَّدُ بْنُ مُطَرِّفٍ، حَدَّثَنِي أَبُو حَازِمٍ، عَنْ سَهْلِ بْنِ سَعْدٍ، قَالَ قَالَ النَّبِيُّ صلى الله عليه وسلم " إِنِّي فَرَطُكُمْ عَلَى الْحَوْضِ، مَنْ مَرَّ عَلَىَّ شَرِبَ، وَمَنْ شَرِبَ لَمْ يَظْمَأْ أَبَدًا، لَيَرِدَنَّ عَلَىَّ أَقْوَامٌ أَعْرِفُهُمْ وَيَعْرِفُونِي، ثُمَّ يُحَالُ بَيْنِي وَبَيْنَهُمْ ".

Narrated Abu Huraira: The Prophet ﷺ said, "Leave me as I leave you, for the people who were before you were ruined because of their questions and their differences over their prophets. So, if I forbid you to do something, then keep away from it. And if I order you to do something, then do of it as much as you can." – Al-Bukhari 7288
حَدَّثَنَا إِسْمَاعِيلُ، حَدَّثَنِي مَالِكٌ، عَنْ أَبِي الزِّنَادِ، عَنِ الأَعْرَجِ، عَنْ أَبِي هُرَيْرَةَ، عَنِ النَّبِيِّ صلى الله عليه وسلم قَالَ " دَعُونِي مَا تَرَكْتُكُمْ، إِنَّمَا هَلَكَ مَنْ كَانَ قَبْلَكُمْ بِسُؤَالِهِمْ وَاخْتِلاَفِهِمْ عَلَى أَنْبِيَائِهِمْ، فَإِذَا نَهَيْتُكُمْ عَنْ شَىْءٍ فَاجْتَنِبُوهُ، وَإِذَا أَمَرْتُكُمْ بِأَمْرٍ فَأْتُوا مِنْهُ مَا اسْتَطَعْتُمْ "

Narrated Fatima bint Al-Mundhir: Asma' bint Abi Bakr As-Siddiq said, "I went to 'Aishah and the people were offering Salat. I asked her, 'What is wrong with the people ?' She pointed towards the sky with her head. I asked her, 'Is there a sign ?' 'Aishah nodded with her head meaning 'Yes'." Asma' added, "Allah's Messengerﷺ prolonged the Salat to such an extent that I fainted. There was a waterskin by my side and I opened it and poured some water on my head. When Allah's Messengerﷺ finished Salat, and the solar eclipse had cleared, the Prophetﷺ addressed the people and praised Allah as He deserves and said, 'Amma ba'du'." Asma' further said, "Some Ansari women started talking, so I turned to them in order to make them quiet. I asked 'Aishah what the Prophetﷺ had said. 'Aishah said: 'He said, 'I have seen things at this place of mine which were never shown to me before; (I have seen) even Paradise and Hell. And, no doubt it has been revealed to me that you (people) will be put in trial in your graves like or nearly like the trial of Masih Ad-Dajjal. (The angels) will come to everyone of you and ask him, 'What do you know about this man (Prophet Muhammadﷺ ?" (The faithful believer or firm believer (Hisham was in doubt which word the Prophet ﷺ used), will say, 'He is Allah's Messengerﷺ and he is Muhammad who came to us with clear evidences and guidance. So we believed him, accepted his teachings and followed and trusted his teaching.' Then the angels will tell him to sleep (in peace) as they have come to know that he was a believer. But the hypocrite or a doubtful person (Hisham is not sure as to which word the Prophetﷺ used), will be asked what he knew about this man (Prophet Muhammedﷺ .) He will say, 'I do not know but I heard the people saying something (about him) so I said the same' " Hisham added, "Fatima told me that she remembered that narration completely by heart except that she said about the hypocrite or a doubtful person that he will be punished severely." – Al-Bukhari 922

وَقَالَ مَحْمُودٌ حَدَّثَنَا أَبُو أُسَامَةَ، قَالَ حَدَّثَنَا هِشَامُ بْنُ عُرْوَةَ، قَالَ أَخْبَرَتْنِي فَاطِمَةُ بِنْتُ الْمُنْذِرِ، عَنْ أَسْمَاءَ بِنْتِ أَبِي بَكْرٍ، قَالَتْ دَخَلْتُ عَلَى عَائِشَةَ ـ رضى الله عنها ـ وَالنَّاسُ يُصَلُّونَ قُلْتُ مَا شَأْنُ النَّاسِ فَأَشَارَتْ بِرَأْسِهَا إِلَى السَّمَاءِ. فَقُلْتُ آيَةٌ فَأَشَارَتْ بِرَأْسِهَا أَىْ نَعَمْ. قَالَتْ فَأَطَالَ رَسُولُ اللَّهِ صلى الله عليه وسلم جِدًّا حَتَّى تَجَلاَّنِي الْغَشْىُ وَإِلَى جَنْبِي قِرْبَةٌ فِيهَا مَاءٌ فَفَتَحْتُهَا فَجَعَلْتُ أَصُبُّ مِنْهَا عَلَى رَأْسِي، فَانْصَرَفَ رَسُولُ اللَّهِ صلى الله عليه وسلم وَقَدْ تَجَلَّتِ الشَّمْسُ، فَخَطَبَ النَّاسَ، وَحَمِدَ اللَّهَ بِمَا هُوَ أَهْلُهُ ثُمَّ قَالَ " أَمَّا بَعْدُ ". قَالَتْ وَلَغِطَ نِسْوَةٌ مِنَ الأَنْصَارِ، فَانْكَفَأْتُ إِلَيْهِنَّ لأُسَكِّتَهُنَّ فَقُلْتُ لِعَائِشَةَ مَا قَالَ قَالَتْ قَالَ " مَا مِنْ شَىْءٍ لَمْ أَكُنْ أُرِيتُهُ إِلاَّ قَدْ رَأَيْتُهُ فِي مَقَامِي هَذَا حَتَّى الْجَنَّةَ وَالنَّارَ، وَإِنَّهُ قَدْ أُوحِيَ إِلَىَّ أَنَّكُمْ تُفْتَنُونَ فِي الْقُبُورِ مِثْلَ ـ أَوْ قَرِيبَ مِنْ ـ فِتْنَةِ الْمَسِيحِ الدَّجَّالِ، يُؤْتَى أَحَدُكُمْ، فَيُقَالُ لَهُ مَا عِلْمُكَ بِهَذَا الرَّجُلِ فَأَمَّا الْمُؤْمِنُ ـ أَوْ قَالَ الْمُوقِنُ شَكَّ هِشَامٌ ـ فَيَقُولُ هُوَ رَسُولُ اللَّهِ، هُوَ مُحَمَّدٌ صلى الله عليه وسلم جَاءَنَا بِالْبَيِّنَاتِ وَالْهُدَى فَآمَنَّا وَأَجَبْنَا وَاتَّبَعْنَا وَصَدَّقْنَا. فَيُقَالُ لَهُ نَمْ صَالِحًا، قَدْ كُنَّا نَعْلَمُ إِنْ كُنْتَ لَتُؤْمِنُ بِهِ. وَأَمَّا الْمُنَافِقُ ـ أَوْ قَالَ الْمُرْتَابُ شَكَّ هِشَامٌ ـ فَيُقَالُ لَهُ مَا عِلْمُكَ بِهَذَا الرَّجُلِ فَيَقُولُ لاَ أَدْرِي، سَمِعْتُ النَّاسَ يَقُولُونَ شَيْئًا فَقُلْتُهُ ". قَالَ هِشَامٌ فَلَقَدْ قَالَتْ لِي فَاطِمَةُ فَأَوْعَيْتُهُ، غَيْرَ أَنَّهَا ذَكَرَتْ مَا يُغَلِّظُ عَلَيْهِ.

So do not obey the disbelievers, but strive against them with it, a mighty struggle.– Surah Al-Furqan 25:52

فَلَا تُطِعِ ٱلْكَٰفِرِينَ وَجَٰهِدْهُم بِهِۦ جِهَادًا كَبِيرًا

And do not obey the command of the extravagant. And ,earth on turmoil spread Who do not reform."– Surah Ash-Shu'ara 26:151&152

وَلَا تُطِيعُوٓا۟ أَمْرَ ٱلْمُسْرِفِينَ ٱلَّذِينَ يُفْسِدُونَ فِى ٱلْأَرْضِ وَلَا يُصْلِحُونَ

Say, "O People of the Scripture! Do not exaggerate in your religion beyond the truth; and do not follow the opinions of people who went astray before, and misled many, and themselves strayed off the balanced way."– Surah Al-Maidah 5:77

قُلْ يَٰٓأَهْلَ ٱلْكِتَٰبِ لَا تَغْلُوا۟ فِى دِينِكُمْ غَيْرَ ٱلْحَقِّ وَلَا تَتَّبِعُوٓا۟ أَهْوَآءَ قَوْمٍ قَدْ ضَلُّوا۟ مِن قَبْلُ وَأَضَلُّوا۟ كَثِيرًا وَضَلُّوا۟ عَن سَوَآءِ ٱلسَّبِيلِ

Narrated Sa`d: I was one of (the first) seven (who had embraced Islam) with Allah's Messenger ﷺ and we had nothing to eat then, except the leaves of the Habala or Hubula tree, so that our stool used to be similar to that of sheep. Now the tribe of Bani Asad wants to teach me Islam; I would be a loser and all my efforts would be in vain (if I learn Islam anew from them). – Al-Bukhari 5412

حَدَّثَنَا عَبْدُ اللَّهِ بْنُ مُحَمَّدٍ، حَدَّثَنَا وَهْبُ بْنُ جَرِيرٍ، حَدَّثَنَا شُعْبَةُ، عَنْ إِسْمَاعِيلَ، عَنْ قَيْسٍ، عَنْ سَعْدٍ، قَالَ رَأَيْتُنِي سَابِعَ سَبْعَةٍ مَعَ النَّبِيِّ صلى الله عليه وسلم مَا لَنَا طَعَامٌ إِلاَّ وَرَقُ الْحُبْلَةِ ـ أَوِ الْحَبَلَةِ ـ حَتَّى يَضَعَ أَحَدُنَا مَا تَضَعُ الشَّاةُ، ثُمَّ أَصْبَحَتْ بَنُو أَسَدٍ تُعَزِّرُنِي عَلَى الإِسْلاَمِ، خَسِرْتُ إِذًا وَضَلَّ سَعْيِي

And We sent Moses with Our signs and a clear mandate. To Pharaoh and his nobles, but they followed the command of Pharaoh, and the command of Pharaoh was not wise. – Surah Hud 11:96&97

وَلَقَدْ أَرْسَلْنَا مُوسَىٰ بِـَٔايَٰتِنَا وَسُلْطَٰنٍ مُّبِينٍ إِلَىٰ فِرْعَوْنَ وَمَلَإِي۟هِۦ فَٱتَّبَعُوٓا۟ أَمْرَ فِرْعَوْنَ ۖ وَمَآ أَمْرُ فِرْعَوْنَ بِرَشِيدٍ

Say, "O People of the Scripture, why do you hinder from Allah's path those who believe, seeking to distort it, even though you are witnesses? Allah is not unaware of what you do." O you who believe! If you obey a party of those who were given the Scripture, they will turn you, after your belief, into disbelievers.– Surah Al-Imran 3:99&100

قُلْ يَٰٓأَهْلَ ٱلْكِتَٰبِ لِمَ تَصُدُّونَ عَن سَبِيلِ ٱللَّهِ مَنْ ءَامَنَ تَبْغُونَهَا عِوَجًا وَأَنتُمْ شُهَدَآءُ ۗ وَمَا ٱللَّهُ بِغَٰفِلٍ عَمَّا تَعْمَلُونَ يَٰٓأَيُّهَا ٱلَّذِينَ ءَامَنُوٓا۟ إِن تُطِيعُوا۟ فَرِيقًا مِّنَ ٱلَّذِينَ أُوتُوا۟ ٱلْكِتَٰبَ يَرُدُّوكُم بَعْدَ إِيمَٰنِكُمْ كَٰفِرِينَ

O you who believe! If you obey those who disbelieve, they will turn you back on your heels, and you end up losers. Allah is your Master, and He is the Best of Helpers.– Surah Al-Imran 3:149&150

يَٰٓأَيُّهَا ٱلَّذِينَ ءَامَنُوٓا۟ إِن تُطِيعُوا۟ ٱلَّذِينَ كَفَرُوا۟ يَرُدُّوكُمْ عَلَىٰٓ أَعْقَٰبِكُمْ فَتَنقَلِبُوا۟ خَٰسِرِينَ بَلِ ٱللَّهُ مَوْلَىٰكُمْ ۖ وَهُوَ خَيْرُ ٱلنَّٰصِرِينَ

The Day when their faces are flipped into the Fire, they will say, "If only we had obeyed Allah and obeyed the Messenger." And they will say, "Lord, we have obeyed our superiors and our dignitaries, but they led us away from the way– Surah Al-Ahzab 33:66&67

يَوْمَ تُقَلَّبُ وُجُوهُهُمْ فِى ٱلنَّارِ يَقُولُونَ يَٰلَيْتَنَآ أَطَعْنَا ٱللَّهَ وَأَطَعْنَا ٱلرَّسُولَا۠ وَقَالُوا۟ رَبَّنَآ إِنَّآ أَطَعْنَا سَادَتَنَا وَكُبَرَآءَنَا فَأَضَلُّونَا ٱلسَّبِيلَا۠

And in no way does the invocation of the disbelievers go anywhere except in error

وَمَا دُعَآءُ ٱلْكَٰفِرِينَ إِلَّا فِى ضَلَٰلٍ

(Such) is the likeness of the ones who have disbelieved in their Lord: their deeds are like ashes on which the wind blows severely upon a tempestuous day; they are unable (to do) anything with whatever they have earned. That is the far error itself - Surah Ibrahim 14:18

مَّثَلُ ٱلَّذِينَ كَفَرُوا۟ بِرَبِّهِمْ ۖ أَعْمَٰلُهُمْ كَرَمَادٍ ٱشْتَدَّتْ بِهِ ٱلرِّيحُ فِى يَوْمٍ عَاصِفٍ ۖ لَّا يَقْدِرُونَ مِمَّا كَسَبُوا۟ عَلَىٰ شَىْءٍ ۚ ذَٰلِكَ هُوَ ٱلضَّلَٰلُ ٱلْبَعِيدُ

To Him is the call of Truth. And the ones upon whom they invoke, apart from Him, do not respond to them in anything, except it is as one who stretches out his hands to water that it may reach his mouth; and in no way will it reach it. And in no way does the invocation of the disbelievers go anywhere except in error. – Surah Ar-Ra'd 13:14
لَهُۥ دَعْوَةُ ٱلْحَقِّ ۖ وَٱلَّذِينَ يَدْعُونَ مِن دُونِهِۦ لَا يَسْتَجِيبُونَ لَهُم بِشَىْءٍ إِلَّا كَبَـٰسِطِ كَفَّيْهِ إِلَى ٱلْمَآءِ لِيَبْلُغَ فَاهُ وَمَا هُوَ بِبَـٰلِغِهِۦ ۚ وَمَا دُعَآءُ ٱلْكَـٰفِرِينَ إِلَّا فِى ضَلَـٰلٍ

They will say, "And did your Messengers not come up to you with the supreme evidence (s)?" They will say, "Yes indeed." They will say, "Then do you invoke!" And in no way is the invocation of the disbelievers in anything except in error – Surah Al-Ghafir 40:50
قَالُوٓا۟ أَوَلَمْ تَكُ تَأْتِيكُمْ رُسُلُكُم بِٱلْبَيِّنَـٰتِ ۖ قَالُوا۟ بَلَىٰ ۚ قَالُوا۟ فَٱدْعُوا۟ ۗ وَمَا دُعَـٰٓؤُا۟ ٱلْكَـٰفِرِينَ إِلَّا فِى ضَلَـٰلٍ

The Book of
Friends on that Day will be foes one to another except Al-Muttaqun
ٱلۡأَخِلَّآءُ يَوۡمَئِذِۭ بَعۡضُهُمۡ لِبَعۡضٍ عَدُوٌّ إِلَّا ٱلۡمُتَّقِينَ

Then how will it be, when We bring a witness from every community, and We bring you as a witness against these? – Surah An-Nisa 4:41
فَكَيۡفَ إِذَا جِئۡنَا مِن كُلِّ أُمَّةِۭ بِشَهِيدٖ وَجِئۡنَا بِكَ عَلَىٰ هَٰٓؤُلَآءِ شَهِيدٗا

We have entrusted the human being with the care of his parents. His mother carried him through hardship upon hardship, weaning him in two years. So give thanks to Me, and to your parents. To Me is the destination. But if they strive to have you associate with Me something of which you have no knowledge, do not obey them. But keep them company in this life, in kindness, and follow the path of him who turns to Me. Then to Me is your return; and I will inform you of what you used to do. – Surah Luqman 31:14&15
وَوَصَّيۡنَا ٱلۡإِنسَٰنَ بِوَٰلِدَيۡهِ حَمَلَتۡهُ أُمُّهُۥ وَهۡنًا عَلَىٰ وَهۡنٖ وَفِصَٰلُهُۥ فِي عَامَيۡنِ أَنِ ٱشۡكُرۡ لِي وَلِوَٰلِدَيۡكَ إِلَيَّ ٱلۡمَصِيرُ وَإِن جَٰهَدَاكَ عَلَىٰٓ أَن تُشۡرِكَ بِي مَا لَيۡسَ لَكَ بِهِۦ عِلۡمٞ فَلَا تُطِعۡهُمَاۖ وَصَاحِبۡهُمَا فِي ٱلدُّنۡيَا مَعۡرُوفٗاۖ وَٱتَّبِعۡ سَبِيلَ مَنۡ أَنَابَ إِلَيَّۚ ثُمَّ إِلَيَّ مَرۡجِعُكُمۡ فَأُنَبِّئُكُم بِمَا كُنتُمۡ تَعۡمَلُونَ

Narrated Abu Huraira: Some (cooked) meat was brought to Allah Apostle and the meat of a forearm was presented to him as he used to like it. He ate a morsel of it and said, "I will be the chief of all the people on the Day of Resurrection. Do you know the reason for it? Allah will gather all the human being of early generations as well as late generation on one plain so that the announcer will be able to make them all-hear his voice and the watcher will be able to see all of them. The sun will come so close to the people that they will suffer such distress and trouble as they will not be able to bear or stand. Then the people will say, 'Don't you see to what state you have reached? Won't you look for someone who can intercede for you with your Lord' Some people will say to some others, 'Go to Adam.' So they will go to Adam and say to him. 'You are the father of mankind; Allah created you with His Own Hand, and breathed into you of His Spirit (meaning the spirit which he created for you); and ordered the angels to prostrate before you; so (please) intercede for us with your Lord. Don't you see in what state we are? Don't you see what condition we have reached?' Adam will say, 'Today my Lord has become angry as He has never become before, nor will ever become thereafter. He forbade me (to eat of the fruit of) the tree, but I disobeyed Him . Myself! Myself! Myself! (I am preoccuied with my own problems). Go to someone else; go to Noah.' So they will go to Noah and say (to him), 'O Noah! You are the first (of Allah's Messengers) to the people of the earth, and Allah has named you a thankful slave; please intercede for us with your Lord. Don't you see in what state we are?' He will say.' Today my Lord has become angry as He has never become nor will ever become thereafter. I had (in the world) the right to make one definitely accepted invocation, and I made it against my nation. Myself! Myself! Myself! Go to someone else; go to Abraham.' They will go to Abraham and say, 'O Abraham! You are Allah's Messenger ﷺ and His Khalil from among the people of the earth; so please intercede for us with your Lord. Don't you see in what state we are?' He will say to them, 'My Lord has today become angry as He has never become before, nor will ever become thereafter. I had told three lies (Abu Haiyan (the sub-narrator) mentioned them in the Hadith) Myself! Myself! Myself! Go to someone else; go to Moses.' The people will then go to Moses and say, 'O

Moses! You art Allah's Messenger ﷺ and Allah gave you superiority above the others with this message and with His direct Talk to you; (please) intercede for us with your Lord Don't you see in what state we are?' Moses will say, 'My Lord has today become angry as He has never become before, nor will become thereafter, I killed a person whom I had not been ordered to kill. Myself! Myself! Myself! Go to someone else; go to Jesus.' So they will go to Jesus and say, 'O Jesus! You are Allah's Messenger ﷺ and His Word which He sent to Mary, and a superior soul created by Him, and you talked to the people while still young in the cradle. Please intercede for us with your Lord. Don't you see in what state we are?' Jesus will say. 'My Lord has today become angry as He has never Become before nor will ever become thereafter. Jesus will not mention any sin, but will say, 'Myself! Myself! Myself! Go to someone else; go to Muhammad.' So they will come to me and say, 'O Muhammad ! You are Allah's Messenger and the last of the prophets, and Allah forgave your early and late sins. (Please) intercede for us with your Lord. Don't you see in what state we are?" The Prophet ﷺ added, "Then I will go beneath Allah's Throne and fall in prostration before my Lord. And then Allah will guide me to such praises and glorification to Him as He has never guided anybody else before me. Then it will be said, 'O Muhammad Raise your head. Ask, and it will be granted. Intercede and It (your intercession) will be accepted.' So I will raise my head and Say, 'My followers, O my Lord! My followers, O my Lord'. It will be said, 'O Muhammad! Let those of your followers who have no accounts, enter through such a gate of the gates of Paradise as lies on the right; and they will share the other gates with the people." The Prophet ﷺ further said, "By Him in Whose Hand my soul is, the distance between every two gate-posts of Paradise is like the distance between Mecca and Busra (in Sham). – Al-Bukhari 4712

حَدَّثَنَا مُحَمَّدُ بْنُ مُقَاتِلٍ، أَخْبَرَنَا عَبْدُ اللَّهِ، أَخْبَرَنَا أَبُو حَيَّانَ التَّيْمِيُّ، عَنْ أَبِي زُرْعَةَ بْنِ عَمْرِو بْنِ جَرِيرٍ، عَنْ أَبِي هُرَيْرَةَ ـ رضى الله عنه ـ قَالَ أُتِيَ رَسُولُ اللَّهِ صلى الله عليه وسلم بِلَحْمٍ، فَرُفِعَ إِلَيْهِ الذِّرَاعُ، وَكَانَتْ تُعْجِبُهُ، فَنَهَسَ مِنْهَا نَهْسَةً ثُمَّ قَالَ " أَنَا سَيِّدُ النَّاسِ يَوْمَ الْقِيَامَةِ، وَهَلْ تَدْرُونَ مِمَّ ذَلِكَ يُجْمَعُ النَّاسُ الأَوَّلِينَ وَالآخِرِينَ فِي صَعِيدٍ وَاحِدٍ، يُسْمِعُهُمُ الدَّاعِي، وَيَنْفُذُهُمُ الْبَصَرُ، وَتَدْنُو الشَّمْسُ، فَيَبْلُغُ النَّاسَ مِنَ الْغَمِّ وَالْكَرْبِ مَا لاَ يُطِيقُونَ وَلاَ يَحْتَمِلُونَ فَيَقُولُ النَّاسُ أَلاَ تَرَوْنَ مَا قَدْ بَلَغَكُمْ أَلاَ تَنْظُرُونَ مَنْ يَشْفَعُ لَكُمْ إِلَى رَبِّكُمْ فَيَقُولُ بَعْضُ النَّاسِ لِبَعْضٍ عَلَيْكُمْ بِآدَمَ فَيَأْتُونَ آدَمَ عليه السلام فَيَقُولُونَ لَهُ أَنْتَ أَبُو الْبَشَرِ خَلَقَكَ اللَّهُ بِيَدِهِ. وَنَفَخَ فِيكَ مِنْ رُوحِهِ، وَأَمَرَ الْمَلاَئِكَةَ فَسَجَدُوا لَكَ، اشْفَعْ لَنَا إِلَى رَبِّكَ، أَلاَ تَرَى إِلَى مَا نَحْنُ فِيهِ أَلاَ تَرَى إِلَى مَا قَدْ بَلَغَنَا فَيَقُولُ آدَمُ إِنَّ رَبِّي قَدْ غَضِبَ الْيَوْمَ غَضَبًا لَمْ يَغْضَبْ قَبْلَهُ مِثْلَهُ وَلَنْ يَغْضَبَ بَعْدَهُ مِثْلَهُ، وَإِنَّهُ نَهَانِي عَنِ الشَّجَرَةِ فَعَصَيْتُهُ، نَفْسِي نَفْسِي نَفْسِي، اذْهَبُوا إِلَى غَيْرِي، اذْهَبُوا إِلَى نُوحٍ، فَيَأْتُونَ نُوحًا فَيَقُولُونَ يَا نُوحُ إِنَّكَ أَنْتَ أَوَّلُ الرُّسُلِ إِلَى أَهْلِ الأَرْضِ، وَقَدْ سَمَّاكَ اللَّهُ عَبْدًا شَكُورًا اشْفَعْ لَنَا إِلَى رَبِّكَ، أَلاَ تَرَى إِلَى مَا نَحْنُ فِيهِ فَيَقُولُ إِنَّ رَبِّي عَزَّ وَجَلَّ قَدْ غَضِبَ الْيَوْمَ غَضَبًا لَمْ يَغْضَبْ قَبْلَهُ مِثْلَهُ، وَلَنْ يَغْضَبَ بَعْدَهُ مِثْلَهُ، وَإِنَّهُ قَدْ كَانَتْ لِي دَعْوَةٌ دَعَوْتُهَا عَلَى قَوْمِي نَفْسِي نَفْسِي نَفْسِي اذْهَبُوا إِلَى غَيْرِي، اذْهَبُوا إِلَى إِبْرَاهِيمَ، فَيَأْتُونَ إِبْرَاهِيمَ، فَيَقُولُونَ يَا إِبْرَاهِيمُ، أَنْتَ نَبِيُّ اللَّهِ وَخَلِيلُهُ مِنْ أَهْلِ الأَرْضِ اشْفَعْ لَنَا إِلَى رَبِّكَ أَلاَ تَرَى إِلَى مَا نَحْنُ فِيهِ فَيَقُولُ لَهُمْ إِنَّ رَبِّي قَدْ غَضِبَ الْيَوْمَ غَضَبًا لَمْ يَغْضَبْ قَبْلَهُ مِثْلَهُ وَلَنْ يَغْضَبَ بَعْدَهُ مِثْلَهُ، وَإِنِّي قَدْ كُنْتُ كَذَبْتُ ثَلاَثَ كَذَبَاتٍ ـ فَذَكَرَهُنَّ أَبُو حَيَّانَ فِي الْحَدِيثِ ـ نَفْسِي نَفْسِي نَفْسِي، اذْهَبُوا إِلَى غَيْرِي اذْهَبُوا إِلَى مُوسَى، فَيَأْتُونَ مُوسَى، فَيَقُولُونَ يَا مُوسَى أَنْتَ رَسُولُ اللَّهِ، فَضَّلَكَ اللَّهُ بِرِسَالَتِهِ وَبِكَلاَمِهِ عَلَى النَّاسِ، اشْفَعْ لَنَا إِلَى رَبِّكَ أَلاَ تَرَى إِلَى مَا نَحْنُ فِيهِ فَيَقُولُ إِنَّ رَبِّي قَدْ غَضِبَ الْيَوْمَ غَضَبًا لَمْ يَغْضَبْ قَبْلَهُ مِثْلَهُ، وَلَنْ يَغْضَبَ بَعْدَهُ مِثْلَهُ، وَإِنِّي قَدْ قَتَلْتُ نَفْسًا لَمْ أُومَرْ بِقَتْلِهَا، نَفْسِي نَفْسِي نَفْسِي، اذْهَبُوا إِلَى غَيْرِي، اذْهَبُوا إِلَى عِيسَى، فَيَأْتُونَ عِيسَى فَيَقُولُونَ يَا عِيسَى أَنْتَ رَسُولُ اللَّهِ وَكَلِمَتُهُ أَلْقَاهَا إِلَى مَرْيَمَ وَرُوحٌ مِنْهُ، وَكَلَّمْتَ النَّاسَ فِي الْمَهْدِ صَبِيًّا اشْفَعْ لَنَا أَلاَ تَرَى إِلَى مَا نَحْنُ فِيهِ فَيَقُولُ عِيسَى إِنَّ رَبِّي قَدْ غَضِبَ الْيَوْمَ غَضَبًا لَمْ يَغْضَبْ قَبْلَهُ مِثْلَهُ، وَلَنْ يَغْضَبَ بَعْدَهُ مِثْلَهُ ـ وَلَمْ يَذْكُرْ ذَنْبًا ـ نَفْسِي نَفْسِي نَفْسِي، اذْهَبُوا إِلَى غَيْرِي اذْهَبُوا إِلَى مُحَمَّدٍ صلى الله عليه وسلم فَيَأْتُونَ مُحَمَّدًا صلى الله عليه وسلم فَيَقُولُونَ يَا مُحَمَّدُ أَنْتَ رَسُولُ اللَّهِ وَخَاتَمُ الأَنْبِيَاءِ، وَقَدْ غَفَرَ اللَّهُ لَكَ مَا تَقَدَّمَ مِنْ ذَنْبِكَ وَمَا تَأَخَّرَ، اشْفَعْ لَنَا إِلَى رَبِّكَ أَلاَ تَرَى إِلَى مَا نَحْنُ فِيهِ فَأَنْطَلِقُ فَآتِي تَحْتَ الْعَرْشِ، فَأَقَعُ سَاجِدًا لِرَبِّي عَزَّ وَجَلَّ ثُمَّ يَفْتَحُ اللَّهُ عَلَىَّ مِنْ مَحَامِدِهِ وَحُسْنِ الثَّنَاءِ عَلَيْهِ شَيْئًا لَمْ يَفْتَحْهُ عَلَى أَحَدٍ قَبْلِي ثُمَّ يُقَالُ يَا مُحَمَّدُ ارْفَعْ رَأْسَكَ، سَلْ تُعْطَهْ، وَاشْفَعْ تُشَفَّعْ، فَأَرْفَعُ رَأْسِي، فَأَقُولُ أُمَّتِي يَا رَبِّ، أُمَّتِي يَا رَبِّ فَيُقَالُ يَا مُحَمَّدُ أَدْخِلْ مِنْ أُمَّتِكَ مَنْ لاَ حِسَابَ عَلَيْهِمْ مِنَ الْبَابِ الأَيْمَنِ مِنْ أَبْوَابِ الْجَنَّةِ وَهُمْ شُرَكَاءُ النَّاسِ فِيمَا سِوَى ذَلِكَ مِنَ الأَبْوَابِ، ثُمَّ قَالَ وَالَّذِي نَفْسِي بِيَدِهِ إِنَّ مَا بَيْنَ الْمِصْرَاعَيْنِ مِنْ مَصَارِيعِ الْجَنَّةِ كَمَا بَيْنَ مَكَّةَ وَحِمْيَرَ، أَوْ كَمَا بَيْنَ مَكَّةَ وَبُصْرَى ".

The Day when a person will flee from his brother. And his mother and his father. And his consort and his children. Every one of them, on that Day, will have enough to preoccupy him. – Surah 'Abasa 80:34-37

يَوْمَ يَفِرُّ ٱلْمَرْءُ مِنْ أَخِيهِ وَأُمِّهِۦ وَأَبِيهِ وَصَـٰحِبَتِهِۦ وَبَنِيهِ لِكُلِّ ٱمْرِئٍ مِّنْهُمْ يَوْمَئِذٍ شَأْنٌ يُغْنِيهِ

On the Day when you will see it: every nursing mother will discard her infant, and every pregnant woman will abort her load, and you will see the people drunk, even though they are not drunk—but the punishment of Allah is severe. . – Surah Al-Hajj 22:2
يَوْمَ تَرَوْنَهَا تَذْهَلُ كُلُّ مُرْضِعَةٍ عَمَّآ أَرْضَعَتْ وَتَضَعُ كُلُّ ذَاتِ حَمْلٍ حَمْلَهَا وَتَرَى ٱلنَّاسَ سُكَٰرَىٰ وَمَا هُم بِسُكَٰرَىٰ وَلَٰكِنَّ عَذَابَ ٱللَّهِ شَدِيدٌ

On the Day when you will see it: every nursing mother will discard her infant, and every pregnant woman will abort her load, and you will see the people drunk, even though they are not drunk—but the punishment of Allah is severe. They will be shown each other. The criminal wishes he would be redeemed from the punishment of that Day by his children. And his spouse, and his brother. And his family that sheltered him. And everyone on earth, in order to save him. – Surah Al-Ma'arij 70:10-14
وَلَا يَسْـَٔلُ حَمِيمٌ حَمِيمًا يُبَصَّرُونَهُمْ يَوَدُّ ٱلْمُجْرِمُ لَوْ يَفْتَدِى مِنْ عَذَابِ يَوْمِئِذٍۭ بِبَنِيهِ وَصَٰحِبَتِهِۦ وَأَخِيهِ وَفَصِيلَتِهِ ٱلَّتِى تُـْٔوِيهِ وَمَن فِى ٱلْأَرْضِ جَمِيعًا ثُمَّ يُنجِيهِ

You will not find a people who believe in Allah and the Last Day, loving those who oppose Allah and His Messenger, even if they were their parents, or their children, or their siblings, or their close relatives. These—He has inscribed faith in their hearts, and has supported them with a spirit from Him. And He will admit them into Gardens beneath which rivers flow, wherein they will dwell forever. Allah is pleased with them, and they are pleased with Him. These are the partisans of Allah. Indeed, it is Allah's partisans who are the successful.– Surah Al-Mujadilah 58:22
لَّا تَجِدُ قَوْمًا يُؤْمِنُونَ بِٱللَّهِ وَٱلْيَوْمِ ٱلْءَاخِرِ يُوَآدُّونَ مَنْ حَآدَّ ٱللَّهَ وَرَسُولَهُۥ وَلَوْ كَانُوٓا۟ ءَابَآءَهُمْ أَوْ أَبْنَآءَهُمْ أَوْ إِخْوَٰنَهُمْ أَوْ عَشِيرَتَهُمْ أُو۟لَٰٓئِكَ كَتَبَ فِى قُلُوبِهِمُ ٱلْإِيمَٰنَ وَأَيَّدَهُم بِرُوحٍ مِّنْهُ وَيُدْخِلُهُمْ جَنَّٰتٍ تَجْرِى مِن تَحْتِهَا ٱلْأَنْهَٰرُ خَٰلِدِينَ فِيهَا رَضِىَ ٱللَّهُ عَنْهُمْ وَرَضُوا۟ عَنْهُ أُو۟لَٰٓئِكَ حِزْبُ ٱللَّهِ أَلَآ إِنَّ حِزْبَ ٱللَّهِ هُمُ ٱلْمُفْلِحُونَ

On that Day, friends will be enemies of one another, except for the righteous.- Surah Az-Zukhruf 43:67
ٱلْأَخِلَّآءُ يَوْمَئِذٍۭ بَعْضُهُمْ لِبَعْضٍ عَدُوٌّ إِلَّا ٱلْمُتَّقِينَ

Neither your relatives nor your children will benefit you on the Day of Resurrection. He will separate between you. Allah is Observant of what you do. – Surah Al-Mumtahanah 60:3
لَن تَنفَعَكُمْ أَرْحَامُكُمْ وَلَآ أَوْلَٰدُكُمْ يَوْمَ ٱلْقِيَٰمَةِ يَفْصِلُ بَيْنَكُمْ وَٱللَّهُ بِمَا تَعْمَلُونَ بَصِيرٌ

O you who believe! Among your wives and your children are enemies to you, so beware of them. But if you pardon, and overlook, and forgive— Allah is Forgiver and Merciful. Your possessions and your children are a test, but with Allah is a splendid reward. – Surah At-Taghabun 64:14&15
يَٰٓأَيُّهَا ٱلَّذِينَ ءَامَنُوٓا۟ إِنَّ مِنْ أَزْوَٰجِكُمْ وَأَوْلَٰدِكُمْ عَدُوًّا لَّكُمْ فَٱحْذَرُوهُمْ وَإِن تَعْفُوا۟ وَتَصْفَحُوا۟ وَتَغْفِرُوا۟ فَإِنَّ ٱللَّهَ غَفُورٌ رَّحِيمٌ إِنَّمَآ أَمْوَٰلُكُمْ وَأَوْلَٰدُكُمْ فِتْنَةٌ وَٱللَّهُ عِندَهُۥٓ أَجْرٌ عَظِيمٌ

Say, "If your parents, and your children, and your siblings, and your spouses, and your relatives, and the wealth you have acquired, and a business you worry about, and homes you love, are more dear to you than Allah, and His Messenger, and the struggle in His cause, then wait until Allah executes His judgment." Allah does not guide the sinful people. – Surah At-Taubah 9:24
قُلْ إِن كَانَ ءَابَآؤُكُمْ وَأَبْنَآؤُكُمْ وَإِخْوَٰنُكُمْ وَأَزْوَٰجُكُمْ وَعَشِيرَتُكُمْ وَأَمْوَٰلٌ ٱقْتَرَفْتُمُوهَا وَتِجَٰرَةٌ تَخْشَوْنَ كَسَادَهَا وَمَسَٰكِنُ تَرْضَوْنَهَآ أَحَبَّ إِلَيْكُم مِّنَ ٱللَّهِ وَرَسُولِهِۦ وَجِهَادٍ فِى سَبِيلِهِۦ فَتَرَبَّصُوا۟ حَتَّىٰ يَأْتِىَ ٱللَّهُ بِأَمْرِهِۦ وَٱللَّهُ لَا يَهْدِى ٱلْقَوْمَ ٱلْفَٰسِقِينَ

O you who believe! Let neither your possessions nor your children distract you from the remembrance of Allah. Whoever does that—these are the losers. – Surah Al-Munafiqun 63:9

يَـٰٓأَيُّهَا ٱلَّذِينَ ءَامَنُوا۟ لَا تُلْهِكُمْ أَمْوَٰلُكُمْ وَلَآ أَوْلَـٰدُكُمْ عَن ذِكْرِ ٱللَّهِ ۚ وَمَن يَفْعَلْ ذَٰلِكَ فَأُو۟لَـٰٓئِكَ هُمُ ٱلْخَـٰسِرُونَ

Allah illustrates an example of those who disbelieve: the wife of Noah and the wife of Lot. They were under two of Our righteous servants, but they betrayed them. They availed them nothing against Allah, and it was said, "Enter the Fire with those who are entering." – Surah At-Tahrim 66:10

ضَرَبَ ٱللَّهُ مَثَلًا لِّلَّذِينَ كَفَرُوا۟ ٱمْرَأَتَ نُوحٍ وَٱمْرَأَتَ لُوطٍ ۖ كَانَتَا تَحْتَ عَبْدَيْنِ مِنْ عِبَادِنَا صَـٰلِحَيْنِ فَخَانَتَاهُمَا فَلَمْ يُغْنِيَا عَنْهُمَا مِنَ ٱللَّهِ شَيْـًٔا
وَقِيلَ ٱدْخُلَا ٱلنَّارَ مَعَ ٱلدَّٰخِلِينَ

Like the devil, when he says to the human being, "Disbelieve." But when he has disbelieved, he says, "I am innocent of you; I fear Allah, the Lord of the Worlds." – Surah Al-Hashr 59:16

كَمَثَلِ ٱلشَّيْطَـٰنِ إِذْ قَالَ لِلْإِنسَـٰنِ ٱكْفُرْ فَلَمَّا كَفَرَ قَالَ إِنِّى بَرِىٓءٌ مِّنكَ إِنِّىٓ أَخَافُ ٱللَّهَ رَبَّ ٱلْعَـٰلَمِينَ

They will emerge before Allah, altogether. The weak will say to those who were proud, "We were your followers, can you protect us at all against Allah's punishment?" They will say, "Had Allah guided us, we would have guided you. It is the same for us; whether we mourn, or are patient; there is no asylum for us." – Surah Ibrahim 14:21

وَبَرَزُوا۟ لِلَّهِ جَمِيعًا فَقَالَ ٱلضُّعَفَـٰٓؤُا۟ لِلَّذِينَ ٱسْتَكْبَرُوٓا۟ إِنَّا كُنَّا لَكُمْ تَبَعًا فَهَلْ أَنتُم مُّغْنُونَ عَنَّا مِنْ عَذَابِ ٱللَّهِ مِن شَىْءٍ ۚ قَالُوا۟ لَوْ هَدَىٰنَا ٱللَّهُ لَهَدَيْنَـٰكُمْ ۖ
سَوَآءٌ عَلَيْنَآ أَجَزِعْنَآ أَمْ صَبَرْنَا مَا لَنَا مِن مَّحِيصٍ

Those who disbelieve say, "We will never believe in this Quran, nor in what came before it." If you could only see the wrongdoers, captive before their Lord, throwing back allegations at one another. Those who were oppressed will say to those who were arrogant, "Were it not for you, we would have been believers." Those who were arrogant will say to those who were oppressed, "Was it us who turned you away from guidance when it came to you? No indeed, you yourselves were sinful." And those who were oppressed will say to those who were arrogant, "It was your scheming by night and day; as you instructed us to reject Allah, and to set up rivals to Him." They will hide their remorse when they see the retribution. We will put yokes around the necks of those who disbelieved. Will they be repaid for anything other than what they used to do? – Surah Saba 34:31-33

وَقَالَ ٱلَّذِينَ كَفَرُوا۟ لَن نُّؤْمِنَ بِهَـٰذَا ٱلْقُرْءَانِ وَلَا بِٱلَّذِى بَيْنَ يَدَيْهِ ۗ وَلَوْ تَرَىٰٓ إِذِ ٱلظَّـٰلِمُونَ مَوْقُوفُونَ عِندَ رَبِّهِمْ يَرْجِعُ بَعْضُهُمْ إِلَىٰ بَعْضٍ ٱلْقَوْلَ
يَقُولُ ٱلَّذِينَ ٱسْتُضْعِفُوا۟ لِلَّذِينَ ٱسْتَكْبَرُوا۟ لَوْلَآ أَنتُمْ لَكُنَّا مُؤْمِنِينَ قَالَ ٱلَّذِينَ ٱسْتَكْبَرُوا۟ لِلَّذِينَ ٱسْتُضْعِفُوٓا۟ أَنَحْنُ صَدَدْنَـٰكُمْ عَنِ ٱلْهُدَىٰ بَعْدَ إِذْ
جَآءَكُم ۖ بَلْ كُنتُم مُّجْرِمِينَ وَقَالَ ٱلَّذِينَ ٱسْتُضْعِفُوا۟ لِلَّذِينَ ٱسْتَكْبَرُوا۟ بَلْ مَكْرُ ٱلَّيْلِ وَٱلنَّهَارِ إِذْ تَأْمُرُونَنَآ أَن نَّكْفُرَ بِٱللَّهِ وَنَجْعَلَ لَهُۥٓ أَندَادًا ۚ وَأَسَرُّوا۟
ٱلنَّدَامَةَ لَمَّا رَأَوُا۟ ٱلْعَذَابَ وَجَعَلْنَا ٱلْأَغْلَـٰلَ فِىٓ أَعْنَاقِ ٱلَّذِينَ كَفَرُوا۟ ۚ هَلْ يُجْزَوْنَ إِلَّا مَا كَانُوا۟ يَعْمَلُونَ

As they quarrel in the Fire, the weak will say to those who were arrogant, "We were followers of yours; will you then spare us a portion of the Fire?" – Surah Ghafir 40:47

وَإِذْ يَتَحَآجُّونَ فِى ٱلنَّارِ فَيَقُولُ ٱلضُّعَفَـٰٓؤُا۟ لِلَّذِينَ ٱسْتَكْبَرُوٓا۟ إِنَّا كُنَّا لَكُمْ تَبَعًا فَهَلْ أَنتُم مُّغْنُونَ عَنَّا نَصِيبًا مِّنَ ٱلنَّارِ

And on the Day He will say, "Call out My associates whom you asserted." So they will call on them, yet they will not respond to them; and We will make a chasm between them. Surah Al-Kahf 18:52

ويوم يقول نادوا شركاءى ٱلذين زعمتم فدعوهم فلم يستجيبوا لهم وجعلنا بينهم موبقا

A Muslim is a brother of another Muslim
الْمُسْلِمُ أَخُو الْمُسْلِمِ

O you who have believed, let not any people scoff at (another) people who may be more charitable than they; neither let women scoff (other) women who may be more charitable (i.e., better) than they. And do not defame one another, (Literally: do not defame yourselves) nor revile one another by nicknames. Miserable is the name, evident immorality, after belief! And whoever does not repent, then those are they who are the unjust O you who have believed, avoid much surmise; surely some surmise is a vice. And do not spy on each other, (Literally: some of you on some others) nor backbite one another; would any of you love to eat the flesh of his brother dead? So you would hate it! And be pious to Allah; surely Allah is Superbly Relenting, Ever-Merciful - Surah Al-Hujurat 49:11&12

يَٰٓأَيُّهَا ٱلَّذِينَ ءَامَنُواْ لَا يَسْخَرْ قَوْمٌ مِّن قَوْمٍ عَسَىٰٓ أَن يَكُونُواْ خَيْرًا مِّنْهُمْ وَلَا نِسَآءٌ مِّن نِّسَآءٍ عَسَىٰٓ أَن يَكُنَّ خَيْرًا مِّنْهُنَّ وَلَا تَلْمِزُوٓاْ أَنفُسَكُمْ وَلَا تَنَابَزُواْ بِٱلْأَلْقَٰبِ بِئْسَ ٱلِٱسْمُ ٱلْفُسُوقُ بَعْدَ ٱلْإِيمَٰنِ وَمَن لَّمْ يَتُبْ فَأُوْلَٰٓئِكَ هُمُ ٱلظَّٰلِمُونَ يَٰٓأَيُّهَا ٱلَّذِينَ ءَامَنُواْ ٱجْتَنِبُواْ كَثِيرًا مِّنَ ٱلظَّنِّ إِنَّ بَعْضَ ٱلظَّنِّ إِثْمٌ وَلَا تَجَسَّسُواْ وَلَا يَغْتَب بَّعْضُكُم بَعْضًا أَيُحِبُّ أَحَدُكُمْ أَن يَأْكُلَ لَحْمَ أَخِيهِ مَيْتًا فَكَرِهْتُمُوهُ وَٱتَّقُواْ ٱللَّهَ إِنَّ ٱللَّهَ تَوَّابٌ رَّحِيمٌ

Narrated `Abdullah bin `Umar: Allah's Messenger ﷺ said, "A Muslim is a brother of another Muslim. So he should neither oppress him nor hand him over to an oppressor. And whoever fulfilled the needs of his brother, Allah will fulfill his needs." - Sahih al-Bukhari 6951

حَدَّثَنَا يَحْيَى بْنُ بُكَيْرٍ، حَدَّثَنَا اللَّيْثُ، عَنْ عُقَيْلٍ، عَنِ ابْنِ شِهَابٍ، أَنَّ سَالِمًا، أَخْبَرَهُ أَنَّ عَبْدَ اللَّهِ بْنَ عُمَرَ ـ رضى الله عنهما ـ أَخْبَرَهُ أَنَّ رَسُولَ اللَّهِ صلى الله عليه وسلم قَالَ " الْمُسْلِمُ أَخُو الْمُسْلِمِ، لاَ يَظْلِمُهُ، وَلاَ يُسْلِمُهُ، وَمَنْ كَانَ فِي حَاجَةِ أَخِيهِ، كَانَ اللَّهُ فِي حَاجَتِهِ ".

Narrated Anas bin Malik: Allah's Messenger ﷺ said, "Do not hate one another, and do not be jealous of one another, and do not desert each other, and O, Allah's worshipers! Be brothers. Lo! It is not permissible for any Muslim to desert (not talk to) his brother (Muslim) for more than three days." - Sahih al-Bukhari 6065

حَدَّثَنَا أَبُو الْيَمَانِ، أَخْبَرَنَا شُعَيْبٌ، عَنِ الزُّهْرِيِّ، قَالَ حَدَّثَنِي أَنَسُ بْنُ مَالِكٍ ـ رضى الله عنه ـ أَنَّ رَسُولَ اللَّهِ صلى الله عليه وسلم قَالَ " لاَ تَبَاغَضُوا، وَلاَ تَحَاسَدُوا، وَلاَ تَدَابَرُوا، وَكُونُوا عِبَادَ اللَّهِ إِخْوَانًا، وَلاَ يَحِلُّ لِمُسْلِمٍ أَنْ يَهْجُرَ أَخَاهُ فَوْقَ ثَلاَثَةِ أَيَّامٍ "

Narrated Abu Huraira: Allah's Messenger ﷺ said, "Beware of suspicion, for suspicion is the worst of false tales. And do not look for the others' faults, and do not do spying on one another, and do not practice Najsh, and do not be jealous of one another and do not hate one another, and do not desert (stop talking to) one another. And O, Allah's worshipers! Be brothers!". – Sahih al-Bukhari 6066

حَدَّثَنَا عَبْدُ اللَّهِ بْنُ يُوسُفَ، أَخْبَرَنَا مَالِكٌ، عَنْ أَبِي الزِّنَادِ، عَنِ الأَعْرَجِ، عَنْ أَبِي هُرَيْرَةَ ـ رضى الله عنه ـ أَنَّ رَسُولَ اللَّهِ صلى الله عليه وسلم قَالَ " إِيَّاكُمْ وَالظَّنَّ، فَإِنَّ الظَّنَّ أَكْذَبُ الْحَدِيثِ، وَلاَ تَحَسَّسُوا، وَلاَ تَجَسَّسُوا، وَلاَ تَنَاجَشُوا، وَلاَ تَحَاسَدُوا، وَلاَ تَبَاغَضُوا، وَلاَ تَدَابَرُوا، وَكُونُوا عِبَادَ اللَّهِ إِخْوَانًا ".

Narrated An-Nu`man bin Bashir: Allah's Messenger ((ﷺsaid, "You see the believers as regards their being merciful among themselves and showing love among themselves and being kind, resembling one body, so that, if any part of the body is not well then the whole body shares the sleeplessness (insomnia) and fever with it.". – Sahih al-Bukhari 6011

حَدَّثَنَا أَبُو نُعَيْمٍ، حَدَّثَنَا زَكَرِيَّاءُ، عَنْ عَامِرٍ، قَالَ سَمِعْتُهُ يَقُولُ سَمِعْتُ النُّعْمَانَ بْنَ بَشِيرٍ، يَقُولُ قَالَ رَسُولُ اللَّهِ صلى الله عليه وسلم " تَرَى الْمُؤْمِنِينَ فِي تَرَاحُمِهِمْ وَتَوَادِّهِمْ وَتَعَاطُفِهِمْ كَمَثَلِ الْجَسَدِ إِذَا اشْتَكَى عُضْوًا تَدَاعَى لَهُ سَائِرُ جَسَدِهِ بِالسَّهَرِ وَالْحُمَّى "

Narrated Jarir bin Abdullah: I gave the pledge of allegiance to Allah's Messenger ﷺ for the following: 1 Offer prayers perfectly 2 Pay the Zakat (obligatory charity) 3 And be sincere and true to every Muslim. – Sahih al-Bukhari 57

حَدَّثَنَا مُسَدَّدٌ، قَالَ حَدَّثَنَا يَحْيَى، عَنْ إِسْمَاعِيلَ، قَالَ حَدَّثَنِي قَيْسُ بْنُ أَبِي حَازِمٍ، عَنْ جَرِيرِ بْنِ عَبْدِ اللَّهِ، قَالَ بَايَعْتُ رَسُولَ اللَّهِ صلى الله عليه وسلم عَلَى إِقَامِ الصَّلاَةِ، وَإِيتَاءِ الزَّكَاةِ، وَالنُّصْحِ لِكُلِّ مُسْلِمٍ.

Narrated Abu Musa: The Prophet ﷺ said, "A faithful believer to a faithful believer is like the bricks of a wall, enforcing each other." While (saying that) the Prophet ﷺ clasped his hands, by interlacing his fingers. – Sahih al-Bukhari 481

حَدَّثَنَا خَلاَّدُ بْنُ يَحْيَى، قَالَ حَدَّثَنَا سُفْيَانُ، عَنْ أَبِي بُرْدَةَ بْنِ عَبْدِ اللَّهِ بْنِ أَبِي بُرْدَةَ، عَنْ جَدِّهِ، عَنْ أَبِي مُوسَى، عَنِ النَّبِيِّ صلى الله عليه وسلم قَالَ " إِنَّ الْمُؤْمِنَ لِلْمُؤْمِنِ كَالْبُنْيَانِ، يَشُدُّ بَعْضُهُ بَعْضًا ". وَشَبَّكَ أَصَابِعَهُ.

The Book of
I shall indeed adorn the path of error for them (mankind) on the earth
لَأُزَيِّنَنَّ لَهُمْ فِى ٱلْأَرْضِ

And I will mislead them, and I will entice them, and I will prompt them to slit the ears of cattle, and I will prompt them to alter the creation of Allah." Whoever takes Satan as a lord, instead of Allah, has surely suffered a profound loss. – Surah An-Nisa 4:119

وَلَأُضِلَّنَّهُمْ وَلَأُمَنِّيَنَّهُمْ وَلَءَامُرَنَّهُمْ فَلَيُبَتِّكُنَّ ءَاذَانَ ٱلْأَنْعَـٰمِ وَلَءَامُرَنَّهُمْ فَلَيُغَيِّرُنَّ خَلْقَ ٱللَّهِ وَمَن يَتَّخِذِ ٱلشَّيْطَـٰنَ وَلِيًّا مِّن دُونِ ٱللَّهِ فَقَدْ خَسِرَ خُسْرَانًا مُّبِينًا

It was decreed for him, that whoever follows him—he will misguide him, and lead him to the torment of the Blaze. Surah Al-Hajj 22:4

كُتِبَ عَلَيْهِ أَنَّهُۥ مَن تَوَلَّاهُ فَأَنَّهُۥ يُضِلُّهُۥ وَيَهْدِيهِ إِلَىٰ عَذَابِ ٱلسَّعِيرِ

[Iblis (Satan)] said, "My Lord, since You have lured me away, I will glamorize for them on earth, and I will lure them all away." - Surah Al-Hujr 15:39

قَالَ رَبِّ بِمَآ أَغْوَيْتَنِى لَأُزَيِّنَنَّ لَهُمْ فِى ٱلْأَرْضِ وَلَأُغْوِيَنَّهُمْ أَجْمَعِينَ

[Iblis (Satan)] said, "Do You see this one whom You have honored more than me? If You reprieve me until the Day of Resurrection, I will bring his descendants under my sway, except for a few." Surah Al-Isra 17:62

قَالَ أَرَءَيْتَكَ هَـٰذَا ٱلَّذِى كَرَّمْتَ عَلَىَّ لَئِنْ أَخَّرْتَنِ إِلَىٰ يَوْمِ ٱلْقِيَـٰمَةِ لَأَحْتَنِكَنَّ ذُرِّيَّتَهُۥٓ إِلَّا قَلِيلًا

The Book of
And of mankind there is he whose speech may please you
وَمِنَ ٱلنَّاسِ مَن يُعْجِبُكَ قَوْلُهُۥ

Likewise, We have assigned for every prophet an enemy—human and jinn devils—inspiring one another with fancy words in order to deceive. But had your Lord willed, they would not have done it. So leave them to their fabrications. – Surah Al-An'am 6:112
وَكَذَٰلِكَ جَعَلْنَا لِكُلِّ نَبِيٍّ عَدُوًّا شَيَٰطِينَ ٱلْإِنسِ وَٱلْجِنِّ يُوحِى بَعْضُهُمْ إِلَىٰ بَعْضٍ زُخْرُفَ ٱلْقَوْلِ غُرُورًا ۚ وَلَوْ شَآءَ رَبُّكَ مَا فَعَلُوهُ ۖ فَذَرْهُمْ وَمَا يَفْتَرُونَ

How? Whenever they overcome you, they respect neither kinship nor treaty with you. They satisfy you with lip service, but their hearts refuse, and most of them are immoral. They traded away Allah's revelations for a cheap price, so they barred others from His path. How evil is what they did. Towards a believer they respect neither kinship nor treaty. These are the transgressors. – Surah At-Taubah 9:8-10
كَيْفَ وَإِن يَظْهَرُوا۟ عَلَيْكُمْ لَا يَرْقُبُوا۟ فِيكُمْ إِلًّا وَلَا ذِمَّةً ۚ يُرْضُونَكُم بِأَفْوَٰهِهِمْ وَتَأْبَىٰ قُلُوبُهُمْ وَأَكْثَرُهُمْ فَٰسِقُونَ ٱشْتَرَوْا۟ بِـَٔايَٰتِ ٱللَّهِ ثَمَنًا قَلِيلًا فَصَدُّوا۟ عَن سَبِيلِهِۦٓ ۚ إِنَّهُمْ سَآءَ مَا كَانُوا۟ يَعْمَلُونَ لَا يَرْقُبُونَ فِى مُؤْمِنٍ إِلًّا وَلَا ذِمَّةً ۚ وَأُو۟لَٰٓئِكَ هُمُ ٱلْمُعْتَدُونَ

Am I not better than this miserable wretch, who can barely express himself? Why are bracelets of gold not dropped on him, or they angels came with him in procession?" Thus he fooled his people, and they obeyed him. They were wicked people. – Surah Az-Zukhruf 43:52-54
أَمْ أَنَا۠ خَيْرٌ مِّنْ هَٰذَا ٱلَّذِى هُوَ مَهِينٌ وَلَا يَكَادُ يُبِينُ فَلَوْلَآ أُلْقِىَ عَلَيْهِ أَسْوِرَةٌ مِّن ذَهَبٍ أَوْ جَآءَ مَعَهُ ٱلْمَلَٰٓئِكَةُ مُقْتَرِنِينَ فَٱسْتَخَفَّ قَوْمَهُۥ فَأَطَاعُوهُ ۚ إِنَّهُمْ كَانُوا۟ قَوْمًا فَٰسِقِينَ

Narrated Ibn `Umar: Two men came from the east and delivered speeches, and the Prophet ﷺ said, "Some eloquent speech has the influence of magic." (e.g., some people refuse to do something and then a good eloquent speaker addresses them and then they agree to do that very thing after his speech) – Al-Bukhari 5146
حَدَّثَنَا قَبِيصَةُ، حَدَّثَنَا سُفْيَانُ، عَنْ زَيْدِ بْنِ أَسْلَمَ، قَالَ سَمِعْتُ ابْنَ عُمَرَ، يَقُولُ جَاءَ رَجُلاَنِ مِنَ الْمَشْرِقِ فَخَطَبَا فَقَالَ النَّبِيُّ صلى الله عليه وسلم " إِنَّ مِنَ الْبَيَانِ لَسِحْرًا ".

Narrated Um Salama: Once Allah's Messenger ﷺ said, "You people present your cases to me and some of you may be more eloquent and persuasive in presenting their argument. So, if I give some one's right to another (wrongly) because of the latter's (tricky) presentation of the case, I am really giving him a piece of fire; so he should not take it." – Al-Bukhari 2680
حَدَّثَنَا عَبْدُ اللَّهِ بْنُ مَسْلَمَةَ، عَنْ مَالِكٍ، عَنْ هِشَامِ بْنِ عُرْوَةَ، عَنْ أَبِيهِ، عَنْ زَيْنَبَ، عَنْ أُمِّ سَلَمَةَ ـ رضى الله عنها ـ أَنَّ رَسُولَ اللَّهِ صلى الله عليه وسلم قَالَ " إِنَّكُمْ تَخْتَصِمُونَ إِلَىَّ، وَلَعَلَّ بَعْضَكُمْ أَلْحَنُ بِحُجَّتِهِ مِنْ بَعْضٍ، فَمَنْ قَضَيْتُ لَهُ بِحَقِّ أَخِيهِ شَيْئًا بِقَوْلِهِ، فَإِنَّمَا أَقْطَعُ لَهُ قِطْعَةً مِنَ النَّارِ فَلاَ يَأْخُذْهَا ".

Among the people is he whose speech about the worldly life impresses you, and he calls Allah to witness what is in his heart, while he is the most hostile of adversaries. When he gains power, he strives to spread corruption on earth, destroying properties and lives. Allah does not like corruption. – Surah Al-Baqarah 2:204&205
وَمِنَ ٱلنَّاسِ مَن يُعْجِبُكَ قَوْلُهُۥ فِى ٱلْحَيَوٰةِ ٱلدُّنْيَا وَيُشْهِدُ ٱللَّهَ عَلَىٰ مَا فِى قَلْبِهِۦ وَهُوَ أَلَدُّ ٱلْخِصَامِ وَإِذَا تَوَلَّىٰ سَعَىٰ فِى ٱلْأَرْضِ لِيُفْسِدَ فِيهَا وَيُهْلِكَ ٱلْحَرْثَ وَٱلنَّسْلَ ۗ وَٱللَّهُ لَا يُحِبُّ ٱلْفَسَادَ

Is He who is watchful over the deeds of every soul? Yet they ascribe associates to Allah. Say, "Name them! Or are you informing Him of something on earth He does not know, or is it a show of words?" In fact, the scheming of those who disbelieve is made to appear good to them, and they are averted from the path. Whomever Allah misguides has no guide. .– Surah Ar-Ra'd 13:33

أَفَمَنْ هُوَ قَآئِمٌ عَلَىٰ كُلِّ نَفْسٍۭ بِمَا كَسَبَتْ ۗ وَجَعَلُوا۟ لِلَّهِ شُرَكَآءَ قُلْ سَمُّوهُمْ ۚ أَمْ تُنَبِّـُٔونَهُۥ بِمَا لَا يَعْلَمُ فِى ٱلْأَرْضِ أَم بِظَـٰهِرٍ مِّنَ ٱلْقَوْلِ ۗ بَلْ زُيِّنَ لِلَّذِينَ كَفَرُوا۟ مَكْرُهُمْ وَصُدُّوا۟ عَنِ ٱلسَّبِيلِ ۗ وَمَن يُضْلِلِ ٱللَّهُ فَمَا لَهُۥ مِنْ هَادٍ

Narrated Abu Huraira: Allah's Messenger ﷺ said, "The Hour will not be established (1) till two big groups fight each other whereupon there will be a great number of casualties on both sides and they will be following one and the same religious doctrine, (2) till about thirty Dajjals (liars) appear, and each one of them will claim that he is Allah's Messenger ﷺ (3) ,till the religious knowledge is taken away (by the death of Religious scholars) (4) earthquakes will increase in number (5) time will pass quickly, (6) afflictions will appear, (7) Al-Harj, (i.e., killing) will increase, (8) till wealth will be in abundance ---- so abundant that a wealthy person will worry lest nobody should accept his Zakat, and whenever he will present it to someone, that person (to whom it will be offered) will say, 'I am not in need of it, (9) till the people compete with one another in constructing high buildings, (10) till a man when passing by a grave of someone will say, 'Would that I were in his place (11) and till the sun rises from the West. So when the sun will rise and the people will see it (rising from the West) they will all believe (embrace Islam) but that will be the time when: (As Allah said,) 'No good will it do to a soul to believe then, if it believed not before, nor earned good (by deeds of righteousness) through its Faith.' (6.158) And the Hour will be established while two men spreading a garment in front of them but they will not be able to sell it, nor fold it up; and the Hour will be established when a man has milked his she-camel and has taken away the milk but he will not be able to drink it; and the Hour will be established before a man repairing a tank (for his livestock) is able to water (his animals) in it; and the Hour will be established when a person has raised a morsel (of food) to his mouth but will not be able to eat it." – Al-Bukhari 7121

حَدَّثَنَا أَبُو الْيَمَانِ، أَخْبَرَنَا شُعَيْبٌ، حَدَّثَنَا أَبُو الزِّنَادِ، عَنْ عَبْدِ الرَّحْمَنِ، عَنْ أَبِي هُرَيْرَةَ، أَنَّ رَسُولَ اللَّهِ صلى الله عليه وسلم قَالَ " لاَ تَقُومُ السَّاعَةُ حَتَّى تَقْتَتِلَ فِئَتَانِ عَظِيمَتَانِ، يَكُونُ بَيْنَهُمَا مَقْتَلَةٌ عَظِيمَةٌ، دَعْوَتُهُمَا وَاحِدَةٌ، وَحَتَّى يُبْعَثَ دَجَّالُونَ كَذَّابُونَ، قَرِيبٌ مِنْ ثَلاَثِينَ، كُلُّهُمْ يَزْعُمُ أَنَّهُ رَسُولُ اللَّهِ، وَحَتَّى يُقْبَضَ الْعِلْمُ، وَتَكْثُرَ الزَّلاَزِلُ، وَيَتَقَارَبَ الزَّمَانُ، وَتَظْهَرَ الْفِتَنُ، وَيَكْثُرَ الْهَرْجُ وَهْوَ الْقَتْلُ، وَحَتَّى يَكْثُرَ فِيكُمُ الْمَالُ فَيَفِيضَ، حَتَّى يُهِمَّ رَبَّ الْمَالِ مَنْ يَقْبَلُ صَدَقَتَهُ، وَحَتَّى يَعْرِضَهُ فَيَقُولَ الَّذِي يَعْرِضُهُ عَلَيْهِ لاَ أَرَبَ لِي بِهِ. وَحَتَّى يَتَطَاوَلَ النَّاسُ فِي الْبُنْيَانِ، وَحَتَّى يَمُرَّ الرَّجُلُ بِقَبْرِ الرَّجُلِ فَيَقُولُ يَا لَيْتَنِي مَكَانَهُ. وَحَتَّى تَطْلُعَ الشَّمْسُ مِنْ مَغْرِبِهَا، فَإِذَا طَلَعَتْ وَرَآهَا النَّاسُ ـ يَعْنِي ـ آمَنُوا أَجْمَعُونَ، فَذَلِكَ حِينَ لاَ يَنْفَعُ نَفْسًا إِيمَانُهَا لَمْ تَكُنْ آمَنَتْ مِنْ قَبْلُ، أَوْ كَسَبَتْ فِي إِيمَانِهَا خَيْرًا، وَلَتَقُومَنَّ السَّاعَةُ وَقَدْ نَشَرَ الرَّجُلاَنِ ثَوْبَهُمَا بَيْنَهُمَا، فَلاَ يَتَبَايَعَانِهِ وَلاَ يَطْوِيَانِهِ، وَلَتَقُومَنَّ السَّاعَةُ وَقَدِ انْصَرَفَ الرَّجُلُ بِلَبَنِ لِقْحَتِهِ فَلاَ يَطْعَمُهُ، وَلَتَقُومَنَّ السَّاعَةُ وَهْوَ يُلِيطُ حَوْضَهُ فَلاَ يَسْقِي فِيهِ، وَلَتَقُومَنَّ السَّاعَةُ وَقَدْ رَفَعَ أُكْلَتَهُ إِلَى فِيهِ فَلاَ يَطْعَمُهَا ".

The Prophet ﷺ said, "Perhaps some of you are more eloquent and persuasive in presenting their arguments than their opponents." Tăwûs, Ibrahim and Shuraih said, "A clear, just evidence (produced by the plaintiff) is more valid than a false oath (taken by the defendant).' – Al-Bukhari vol.3 page 494

و قال نبي ﷺ : لعل بعضكم الحن بحخته من بعض. و قال طاوس و ابراهيم و شريح البينة العادلة أحق من اليمين ألفاخرة

They will mislead you far away from Allah's Path
يُضِلُّوكَ عَن سَبِيلِ ٱللَّهِ

Once he entered the city, unnoticed by its people. He found in it two men fighting—one of his own sect, and one from his enemies. The one of his sect solicited his assistance against the one from his enemies; so Moses punched him, and put an end to him. He said, "This is of Satan's doing; he is an enemy that openly misleads." He said, "My Lord, I have wronged myself, so forgive me." So He forgave him. He is the Forgiver, the Merciful. He said, "My Lord, in as much as you have favored me, I will never be a supporter of the criminals." The next morning, he went about in the city, fearful and vigilant, when the man who had sought his assistance the day before was shouting out to him. Moses said to him, "You are clearly a troublemaker." – Surah Al-Qasas 28:15-18

ٱلْمَدِينَةَ عَلَىٰ حِينِ غَفْلَةٍ مِّنْ أَهْلِهَا فَوَجَدَ فِيهَا رَجُلَيْنِ يَقْتَتِلَانِ هَٰذَا مِن شِيعَتِهِۦ وَهَٰذَا مِنْ عَدُوِّهِۦ فَٱسْتَغَٰثَهُ ٱلَّذِى مِن شِيعَتِهِۦ عَلَى ٱلَّذِى مِنْ عَدُوِّهِۦ فَوَكَزَهُۥ مُوسَىٰ فَقَضَىٰ عَلَيْهِ قَالَ هَٰذَا مِنْ عَمَلِ ٱلشَّيْطَٰنِ إِنَّهُۥ عَدُوٌّ مُّضِلٌّ مُّبِينٌ قَالَ رَبِّ إِنِّى ظَلَمْتُ نَفْسِى فَٱغْفِرْ لِى فَغَفَرَ لَهُۥٓ إِنَّهُۥ هُوَ ٱلْغَفُورُ ٱلرَّحِيمُ قَالَ رَبِّ بِمَآ أَنْعَمْتَ عَلَىَّ فَلَنْ أَكُونَ ظَهِيرًا لِّلْمُجْرِمِينَ فَأَصْبَحَ فِى ٱلْمَدِينَةِ خَآئِفًا يَتَرَقَّبُ فَإِذَا ٱلَّذِى ٱسْتَنصَرَهُۥ بِٱلْأَمْسِ يَسْتَصْرِخُهُۥ قَالَ لَهُۥ مُوسَىٰٓ إِنَّكَ لَغَوِىٌّ مُّبِينٌ

Noah said, "My Lord, do not leave of the unbelievers a single dweller on earth. If You leave them, they will mislead your servants, and will breed only wicked unbelievers. – Surah Nuh 71:26&27

وَقَالَ نُوحٌ رَّبِّ لَا تَذَرْ عَلَى ٱلْأَرْضِ مِنَ ٱلْكَٰفِرِينَ دَيَّارًا إِنَّكَ إِن تَذَرْهُمْ يُضِلُّوا۟ عِبَادَكَ وَلَا يَلِدُوٓا۟ إِلَّا فَاجِرًا كَفَّارًا

If you were to obey most of those on earth, they would divert you from Allah's path. They follow nothing but assumptions, and they only conjecture. – Surah Al-An'am 6:116

وَإِن تُطِعْ أَكْثَرَ مَن فِى ٱلْأَرْضِ يُضِلُّوكَ عَن سَبِيلِ ٱللَّهِ إِن يَتَّبِعُونَ إِلَّا ٱلظَّنَّ وَإِنْ هُمْ إِلَّا يَخْرُصُونَ

When some adversity touches the human being, he prays to his Lord, repenting to Him. But then, when He confers on him a grace of His, he forgets what he was praying for before, and he attributes rivals to Allah, in order to lead astray from His way. Say, "Enjoy your disbelief for a little while; you will be among the inmates of the Fire." – Surah Az-Zumar 39:8

وَإِذَا مَسَّ ٱلْإِنسَٰنَ ضُرٌّ دَعَا رَبَّهُۥ مُنِيبًا إِلَيْهِ ثُمَّ إِذَا خَوَّلَهُۥ نِعْمَةً مِّنْهُ نَسِىَ مَا كَانَ يَدْعُوٓا۟ إِلَيْهِ مِن قَبْلُ وَجَعَلَ لِلَّهِ أَندَادًا لِّيُضِلَّ عَن سَبِيلِهِۦ قُلْ تَمَتَّعْ بِكُفْرِكَ قَلِيلًا إِنَّكَ مِنْ أَصْحَٰبِ ٱلنَّارِ

So let them carry their loads complete on the Day of Resurrection, and some of the loads of those they misguided without knowledge. Evil is what they carry. – Surah An-Nahl 16:25

لِيَحْمِلُوٓا۟ أَوْزَارَهُمْ كَامِلَةً يَوْمَ ٱلْقِيَٰمَةِ وَمِنْ أَوْزَارِ ٱلَّذِينَ يُضِلُّونَهُم بِغَيْرِ عِلْمٍ أَلَا سَآءَ مَا يَزِرُونَ

And among the people is he who argues about Allah without knowledge, or guidance, or an enlightening scripture. Turning aside in contempt, to lead away from the path of Allah. He will have humiliation in this world, and on the Day of Resurrection We will make him taste the agony of burning. – Surah Al-Hajj 22:8&9

وَمِنَ ٱلنَّاسِ مَن يُجَٰدِلُ فِى ٱللَّهِ بِغَيْرِ عِلْمٍ وَلَا هُدًى وَلَا كِتَٰبٍ مُّنِيرٍ ثَانِىَ عِطْفِهِۦ لِيُضِلَّ عَن سَبِيلِ ٱللَّهِ لَهُۥ فِى ٱلدُّنْيَا خِزْىٌ وَنُذِيقُهُۥ يَوْمَ ٱلْقِيَٰمَةِ عَذَابَ ٱلْحَرِيقِ

We will certainly test you, until We know those among you who strive, and those who are steadfast, and We will test your reactions. Those who disbelieve, and hinder from the path of Allah, and oppose the Messenger after guidance has become clear to them—they will not hurt Allah in the least, but He will nullify their deeds. – Surah Muhammad 47:31&32

وَلَنَبْلُوَنَّكُمْ حَتَّىٰ نَعْلَمَ ٱلْمُجَٰهِدِينَ مِنكُمْ وَٱلصَّٰبِرِينَ وَنَبْلُوَا۟ أَخْبَارَكُمْ إِنَّ ٱلَّذِينَ كَفَرُوا۟ وَصَدُّوا۟ عَن سَبِيلِ ٱللَّهِ وَشَآقُّوا۟ ٱلرَّسُولَ مِنۢ بَعْدِ مَا تَبَيَّنَ لَهُمُ ٱلْهُدَىٰ لَن يَضُرُّوا۟ ٱللَّهَ شَيْـًٔا وَسَيُحْبِطُ أَعْمَٰلَهُمْ

(Samiri) said, "I saw what they did not see, so I grasped a handful from the Messenger's traces, and I flung it away. Thus my soul prompted me." – Surah TaHa 20:96
قَالَ بَصُرْتُ بِمَا لَمْ يَبْصُرُوا بِهِۦ فَقَبَضْتُ قَبْضَةً مِّنْ أَثَرِ ٱلرَّسُولِ فَنَبَذْتُهَا وَكَذَٰلِكَ سَوَّلَتْ لِى نَفْسِى

Were it not for Allah's grace towards you, and His mercy, a faction of them would have managed to mislead you. But they only mislead themselves, and they cannot harm you in any way. Allah has revealed to you the Scripture and wisdom, and has taught you what you did not know. Allah's goodness towards you is great. – Surah An-Nisa 4:113
وَلَوْلَا فَضْلُ ٱللَّهِ عَلَيْكَ وَرَحْمَتُهُۥ لَهَمَّت طَّآئِفَةٌ مِّنْهُمْ أَن يُضِلُّوكَ وَمَا يُضِلُّونَ إِلَّآ أَنفُسَهُمْ وَمَا يَضُرُّونَكَ مِن شَىْءٍ وَأَنزَلَ ٱللَّهُ عَلَيْكَ ٱلْكِتَٰبَ وَٱلْحِكْمَةَ وَعَلَّمَكَ مَا لَمْ تَكُن تَعْلَمُ وَكَانَ فَضْلُ ٱللَّهِ عَلَيْكَ عَظِيمًا

And whomever Allah guides, for him there is no misleader. Is Allah not Powerful and Vengeful? –Surah Az-Zumar 39:37
وَمَن يَهْدِ ٱللَّهُ فَمَا لَهُۥ مِن مُّضِلٍّ أَلَيْسَ ٱللَّهُ بِعَزِيزٍ ذِى ٱنتِقَامٍ

The Book of
Beware from giving a false statement
لا و قول الزور

Narrated `Ali: The Prophet ﷺ said, "Do not tell a lie against me for whoever tells a lie against me (intentionally) then he will surely enter the Hell-fire." – Al-Bukhari 106
حَدَّثَنَا عَلِيُّ بْنُ الْجَعْدِ، قَالَ أَخْبَرَنَا شُعْبَةُ، قَالَ أَخْبَرَنِي مَنْصُورٌ، قَالَ سَمِعْتُ رِبْعِيَّ بْنَ حِرَاشٍ، يَقُولُ سَمِعْتُ عَلِيًّا، يَقُولُ قَالَ النَّبِيُّ صلى الله عليه وسلم " لاَ تَكْذِبُوا عَلَىَّ، فَإِنَّهُ مَنْ كَذَبَ عَلَىَّ فَلْيَلِجِ النَّارَ ".

But Satan whispered to them, to reveal to them their nakedness, which was invisible to them. He said, "Your Lord has only forbidden you this tree, lest you become angels, or become immortals." And he swore to them, "I am a sincere advisor to you." – Surah Al-A'raf 7:20&21
فَوَسْوَسَ لَهُمَا ٱلشَّيْطَٰنُ لِيُبْدِىَ لَهُمَا مَا وُۥرِىَ عَنْهُمَا مِن سَوْءَٰتِهِمَا وَقَالَ مَا نَهَىٰكُمَا رَبُّكُمَا عَنْ هَٰذِهِ ٱلشَّجَرَةِ إِلَّآ أَن تَكُونَا مَلَكَيْنِ أَوْ تَكُونَا مِنَ ٱلْخَٰلِدِينَ وَقَاسَمَهُمَآ إِنِّى لَكُمَا لَمِنَ ٱلنَّٰصِحِينَ

Like the devil, when he says to the human being, "Disbelieve." But when he has disbelieved, he says, "I am innocent of you; I fear Allah, the Lord of the Worlds." – Surah Al-Hashr 59:16
كَمَثَلِ ٱلشَّيْطَٰنِ إِذْ قَالَ لِلْإِنسَٰنِ ٱكْفُرْ فَلَمَّا كَفَرَ قَالَ إِنِّى بَرِىٓءٌ مِّنكَ إِنِّىٓ أَخَافُ ٱللَّهَ رَبَّ ٱلْعَٰلَمِينَ

Narrated Anas bin Malik: Allah's Messenger ﷺ mentioned the greatest sins or he was asked about the greatest sins. He said, "To join partners in worship with Allah; to kill a soul which Allah has forbidden to kill; and to be undutiful or unkind to one's parents." The Prophet ﷺ added, "Shall I inform you of the biggest of the great sins? That is the forged statement or the false witness." Shu`ba (the sub-narrator) states that most probably the Prophet said, "the false witness." – Al-Bukhari 5977
حَدَّثَنِي مُحَمَّدُ بْنُ الْوَلِيدِ، حَدَّثَنَا مُحَمَّدُ بْنُ جَعْفَرٍ، حَدَّثَنَا شُعْبَةُ، قَالَ حَدَّثَنِي عُبَيْدُ اللَّهِ بْنُ أَبِي بَكْرٍ، قَالَ سَمِعْتُ أَنَسَ بْنَ مَالِكٍ ـ رضى الله عنه ـ قَالَ ذَكَرَ رَسُولُ اللَّهِ صلى الله عليه وسلم الْكَبَائِرَ، أَوْ سُئِلَ عَنِ الْكَبَائِرِ فَقَالَ " الشِّرْكُ بِاللَّهِ، وَقَتْلُ النَّفْسِ، وَعُقُوقُ الْوَالِدَيْنِ ". فَقَالَ " أَلاَ أُنَبِّئُكُمْ بِأَكْبَرِ الْكَبَائِرِ ـ قَالَ ـ قَوْلُ الزُّورِ ـ أَوْ قَالَ ـ شَهَادَةُ الزُّورِ ". قَالَ شُعْبَةُ وَأَكْثَرُ ظَنِّي أَنَّهُ قَالَ " شَهَادَةُ الزُّورِ ".

Narrated Samura bin Jundub: The Prophet ﷺ said, "I saw (in a dream), two men came to me." Then the Prophet ﷺ narrated the story (saying), "They said, 'The person, the one whose cheek you saw being torn away (from the mouth to the ear) was a liar and used to tell lies and the people would report those lies on his authority till they spread all over the world. So he will be punished like that till the Day of Resurrection."' – Al-Bukhari 6096

حَدَّثَنَا مُوسَى بْنُ إِسْمَاعِيلَ، حَدَّثَنَا جَرِيرٌ، حَدَّثَنَا أَبُو رَجَاءٍ، عَنْ سَمُرَةَ بْنِ جُنْدُبٍ ـ رضى الله عنه ـ قَالَ قَالَ النَّبِيُّ صلى الله عليه وسلم " رَأَيْتُ رَجُلَيْنِ أَتَيَانِي قَالاَ الَّذِي رَأَيْتَهُ يُشَقُّ شِدْقُهُ فَكَذَّابٌ يَكْذِبُ بِالْكَذْبَةِ تُحْمَلُ عَنْهُ حَتَّى تَبْلُغَ الآفَاقَ فَيُصْنَعُ بِهِ إِلَى يَوْمِ الْقِيَامَةِ "

Narrated Bishr: As above (No. 290) adding: The Prophet ﷺ was reclining (leaning) and then he sat up saying, "And I warn you against giving a false statement." And he kept on saying that warning so much so that we said, "Would that he had stopped." – Al-Bukhari 6274

حَدَّثَنَا مُسَدَّدٌ، حَدَّثَنَا بِشْرٌ، مِثْلَهُ، وَكَانَ مُتَّكِئًا فَجَلَسَ فَقَالَ " أَلاَ وَقَوْلُ الزُّورِ ". فَمَا زَالَ يُكَرِّرُهَا حَتَّى قُلْنَا لَيْتَهُ سَكَتَ

Narrated `Aisha: Some people asked Allah's Messenger ﷺ about the fore-tellers. Allah's Messenger ﷺ said to them, "They are nothing." The people said, 'O Allah's Messenger ﷺ! Sometimes they tell something which comes out to be true." Allah's Messenger ﷺ said, "That word which comes to be true is what a jinx snatches away by stealing and then pours it in the ear of his fore-teller with a sound similar to the cackle of a hen, and then they add to it one-hundred lies." – Al-Bukhari 6213

حَدَّثَنَا مُحَمَّدُ بْنُ سَلاَمٍ، أَخْبَرَنَا مَخْلَدُ بْنُ يَزِيدَ، أَخْبَرَنَا ابْنُ جُرَيْجٍ، قَالَ ابْنُ شِهَابٍ أَخْبَرَنِي يَحْيَى بْنُ عُرْوَةَ، أَنَّهُ سَمِعَ عُرْوَةَ، يَقُولُ قَالَتْ عَائِشَةُ سَأَلَ أُنَاسٌ رَسُولَ اللَّهِ صلى الله عليه وسلم عَنِ الْكُهَّانِ فَقَالَ لَهُمْ رَسُولُ اللَّهِ صلى الله عليه وسلم " لَيْسُوا بِشَىْءٍ ". قَالُوا يَا رَسُولَ اللَّهِ فَإِنَّهُمْ يُحَدِّثُونَ أَحْيَانًا بِالشَّىْءِ يَكُونُ حَقًّا. فَقَالَ رَسُولُ اللَّهِ صلى الله عليه وسلم " تِلْكَ الْكَلِمَةُ مِنَ الْحَقِّ يَخْطَفُهَا الْجِنِّيُّ، فَيَقُرُّهَا فِي أُذُنِ وَلِيِّهِ قَرَّ الدَّجَاجَةِ، فَيَخْلِطُونَ فِيهَا أَكْثَرَ مِنْ مِائَةِ كَذْبَةٍ ".

Narrated Abu Bakra: Allah's Messenger ﷺ said thrice, "Shall I not inform you of the biggest of the great sins?" We said, "Yes, O Allah's Messenger ﷺ "He said, "To join partners in worship with Allah: to be undutiful to one's parents." The Prophet ﷺ sat up after he had been reclining and added, "And I warn you against giving forged statement and a false witness; I warn you against giving a forged statement and a false witness." The Prophet kept on saying that warning till we thought that he would not stop. – Al-Bukhari 5976 (also #2654)

حَدَّثَنِي إِسْحَاقُ، حَدَّثَنَا خَالِدٌ الْوَاسِطِيُّ، عَنِ الْجُرَيْرِيِّ، عَنْ عَبْدِ الرَّحْمَنِ بْنِ أَبِي بَكْرَةَ، عَنْ أَبِيهِ ـ رضى الله عنه ـ قَالَ قَالَ رَسُولُ اللَّهِ صلى الله عليه وسلم " أَلاَ أُنَبِّئُكُمْ بِأَكْبَرِ الْكَبَائِرِ ". قُلْنَا بَلَى يَا رَسُولَ اللَّهِ. قَالَ " الإِشْرَاكُ بِاللَّهِ، وَعُقُوقُ الْوَالِدَيْنِ ". وَكَانَ مُتَّكِئًا فَجَلَسَ فَقَالَ " أَلاَ وَقَوْلُ الزُّورِ وَشَهَادَةُ الزُّورِ، أَلاَ وَقَوْلُ الزُّورِ وَشَهَادَةُ الزُّورِ ". فَمَا زَالَ يَقُولُهَا حَتَّى قُلْتُ لاَ يَسْكُتُ

Narrated 'Abdullah bin 'Amr: The Prophet ﷺ said, "Whoever has the following four (characteristics) will be a pure hypocrite and whoever has one of the following four characteristics will have one characteristic of hypocrisy unless and until he gives it up. 1) Whenever he is entrusted, he betrays. 2) Whenever he speaks, he tells a lie. 3) Whenever he makes a covenant, he proves treacherous. 4) Whenever he quarrels, he behaves in a very imprudent, evil and insulting manner." – Al-Bukhari 34

حَدَّثَنَا قَبِيصَةُ بْنُ عُقْبَةَ، قَالَ حَدَّثَنَا سُفْيَانُ، عَنِ الأَعْمَشِ، عَنْ عَبْدِ اللَّهِ بْنِ مُرَّةَ، عَنْ مَسْرُوقٍ، عَنْ عَبْدِ اللَّهِ بْنِ عَمْرٍو، أَنَّ النَّبِيَّ صلى الله عليه وسلم قَالَ " أَرْبَعٌ مَنْ كُنَّ فِيهِ كَانَ مُنَافِقًا خَالِصًا، وَمَنْ كَانَتْ فِيهِ خَصْلَةٌ مِنْهُنَّ كَانَتْ فِيهِ خَصْلَةٌ مِنَ النِّفَاقِ حَتَّى يَدَعَهَا إِذَا اؤْتُمِنَ خَانَ وَإِذَا حَدَّثَ كَذَبَ وَإِذَا عَاهَدَ غَدَرَ، وَإِذَا خَاصَمَ فَجَرَ ". تَابَعَهُ شُعْبَةُ عَنِ الأَعْمَشِ.

Say, "My Lord has forbidden immoralities—both open and secret—and sin, and unjustified aggression, and that you associate with Allah anything for which He revealed no sanction, and that you say about Allah what you do not know." – Surah Al-A'raf 7:33

قُلْ إِنَّمَا حَرَّمَ رَبِّيَ ٱلْفَوَٰحِشَ مَا ظَهَرَ مِنْهَا وَمَا بَطَنَ وَٱلْإِثْمَ وَٱلْبَغْىَ بِغَيْرِ ٱلْحَقِّ وَأَن تُشْرِكُوا۟ بِٱللَّهِ مَا لَمْ يُنَزِّلْ بِهِۦ سُلْطَـٰنًا وَأَن تَقُولُوا۟ عَلَى ٱللَّهِ مَا لَا تَعْلَمُونَ

Narrated Masruq: We came upon `Abdullah bin Mas`ud and he said "O people! If somebody knows something, he can say it, but if he does not know it, he should say, "Allah knows better,' for it is a sign of having knowledge to say about something which one does not know, 'Allah knows better.' Allah said to His Prophet: 'Say (O Muhammad !) No wage do I ask of You for this (Qur'an) nor am I one of the pretenders (a person who pretends things which do not exist).' (38.86) Now I will tell you about Ad- Dukhan (the smoke), Allah's Messenger ﷺ invited the Quraish to embrace Islam, but they delayed their response. So he said, "O Allah! Help me against them by sending on them seven years of famine similar to the seven years of famine of Joseph." So the famine year overtook them and everything was destroyed till they ate dead animals and skins. People started imagining to see smoke between them and the sky because of severe hunger. Allah said: 'Then watch you for the Day that the sky will bring forth a kind of smoke plainly visible, covering the people. . . This is painful torment.' (44.10-11) (So they invoked Allah) "Our Lord! Remove the punishment from us really we are believers." How can there be an (effectual) reminder for them when an Apostle, explaining things clearly, has already come to them? Then they had turned away from him and said: 'One taught (by a human being), a madman?' 'We shall indeed remove punishment for a while, but truly, you will revert (to disbelief).' (44.12-15) Will the punishment be removed on the Day of Resurrection?" `Abdullah added, "The punishment was removed from them for a while but they reverted to disbelief, so Allah destroyed them on the Day of Badr. Allah said: 'The day We shall seize you with a mighty grasp. We will indeed (then) exact retribution." (44.16) – Al-Bukhari 4809

حَدَّثَنَا قُتَيْبَةُ، حَدَّثَنَا جَرِيرٌ، عَنِ الأَعْمَشِ، عَنْ أَبِي الضُّحَى، عَنْ مَسْرُوقٍ، قَالَ دَخَلْنَا عَلَى عَبْدِ اللَّهِ بْنِ مَسْعُودٍ، قَالَ يَا أَيُّهَا النَّاسُ مَنْ عَلِمَ شَيْئًا فَلْيَقُلْ بِهِ، وَمَنْ لَمْ يَعْلَمْ فَلْيَقُلِ اللَّهُ أَعْلَمُ، فَإِنَّ مِنَ الْعِلْمِ أَنْ يَقُولَ لِمَا لاَ يَعْلَمُ اللَّهُ أَعْلَمُ، قَالَ اللَّهُ عَزَّ وَجَلَّ لِنَبِيِّهِ صلى الله عليه وسلم {قُلْ مَا أَسْأَلُكُمْ عَلَيْهِ مِنْ أَجْرٍ وَمَا أَنَا مِنَ الْمُتَكَلِّفِينَ} وَسَأُحَدِّثُكُمْ عَنِ الدُّخَانِ إِنَّ رَسُولَ اللَّهِ صلى الله عليه وسلم دَعَا قُرَيْشًا إِلَى الإِسْلاَمِ فَأَبْطَئُوا عَلَيْهِ فَقَالَ " اللَّهُمَّ أَعِنِّي عَلَيْهِمْ بِسَبْعٍ كَسَبْعِ يُوسُفَ "، فَأَخَذَتْهُمْ سَنَةٌ فَحَصَّتْ كُلَّ شَىْءٍ حَتَّى أَكَلُوا الْمَيْتَةَ وَالْجُلُودَ حَتَّى جَعَلَ الرَّجُلُ يَرَى بَيْنَهُ وَبَيْنَ السَّمَاءِ دُخَانًا مِنَ الْجُوعِ، قَالَ اللَّهُ عَزَّ وَجَلَّ {فَارْتَقِبْ يَوْمَ تَأْتِي السَّمَاءُ بِدُخَانٍ مُبِينٍ * يَغْشَى النَّاسَ هَذَا عَذَابٌ أَلِيمٌ} قَالَ فَدَعَوْا {رَبَّنَا اكْشِفْ عَنَّا الْعَذَابَ إِنَّا مُؤْمِنُونَ * أَنَّى لَهُمُ الذِّكْرَى وَقَدْ جَاءَهُمْ رَسُولٌ مُبِينٌ * ثُمَّ تَوَلَّوْا عَنْهُ وَقَالُوا مُعَلَّمٌ مَجْنُونٌ * إِنَّا كَاشِفُو الْعَذَابِ قَلِيلاً إِنَّكُمْ عَائِدُونَ} أَفَيُكْشَفُ الْعَذَابُ يَوْمَ الْقِيَامَةِ قَالَ فَكُشِفَ ثُمَّ عَادُوا فِي كُفْرِهِمْ، فَأَخَذَهُمُ اللَّهُ يَوْمَ بَدْرٍ قَالَ اللَّهُ تَعَالَى {يَوْمَ نَبْطِشُ الْبَطْشَةَ الْكُبْرَى إِنَّا مُنْتَقِمُونَ}.

The Prophet ﷺ said : "Beware from giving a false statement." And he kept on repeating it. Ibn Umar said that the Prophet says thrice, "Haven't I conveyed Allah's Message (to you?)" – Al-Bukhari Vol.1 page 112

فقال : "ا لا و قول الزور" فما زال يذكرها. و قال ابن عمر : قال النبي : "هل بلغت"؟ ثلاثا .

Narrated Asma: Some lady said, "O Allah's Messenger ﷺ ! My husband has another wife, so it is sinful of me to claim that he has given me what he has not given me (in order to tease her)?" Allah's Messenger ﷺ said, The one who pretends that he has been given what he has not been given, is just like the (false) one who wears two garments of falsehood.". – Sahih Al-Bukhari 5219

حَدَّثَنَا سُلَيْمَانُ بْنُ حَرْبٍ، حَدَّثَنَا حَمَّادُ بْنُ زَيْدٍ، عَنْ هِشَامٍ، عَنْ فَاطِمَةَ، عَنْ أَسْمَاءَ، عَنِ النَّبِيِّ صلى الله عليه وسلم. حَدَّثَنِي مُحَمَّدُ بْنُ الْمُثَنَّى، حَدَّثَنَا يَحْيَى، عَنْ هِشَامٍ، حَدَّثَتْنِي فَاطِمَةُ، عَنْ أَسْمَاءَ، أَنَّ امْرَأَةً، قَالَتْ يَا رَسُولَ اللَّهِ إِنَّ لِي ضَرَّةً، فَهَلْ عَلَىَّ جُنَاحٌ إِنْ تَشَبَّعْتُ مِنْ زَوْجِي غَيْرَ الَّذِي يُعْطِينِي فَقَالَ رَسُولُ اللَّهِ صلى الله عليه وسلم " الْمُتَشَبِّعُ بِمَا لَمْ يُعْطَ كَلاَبِسِ ثَوْبَىْ زُورٍ "

˹Still˺ there are some who dispute about Allah without knowledge, guidance, or an enlightening scripture, Surah Al-Hajj 22:8

وَمِنَ ٱلنَّاسِ مَن يُجَـٰدِلُ فِى ٱللَّهِ بِغَيْرِ عِلْمٍ وَلَا هُدًى وَلَا كِتَـٰبٍ مُّنِيرٍ

Who does more wrong than those who fabricate lies against Allah? They will be brought before their Lord, and the witnesses will say, "These are the ones who lied against their Lord." Surely Allah's condemnation is upon the wrongdoers, - Surah Hud 11:18

وَمَنْ أَظْلَمُ مِمَّنِ ٱفْتَرَىٰ عَلَى ٱللَّهِ كَذِبًا ۚ أُو۟لَـٰٓئِكَ يُعْرَضُونَ عَلَىٰ رَبِّهِمْ وَيَقُولُ ٱلْأَشْهَـٰدُ هَـٰٓؤُلَآءِ ٱلَّذِينَ كَذَبُوا۟ عَلَىٰ رَبِّهِمْ ۚ أَلَا لَعْنَةُ ٱللَّهِ عَلَى ٱلظَّـٰلِمِينَ

Do not falsely declare with your tongues, "This is lawful, and that is unlawful," ⌜only⌝ fabricating lies against Allah. Indeed, those who fabricate lies against Allah will never succeed. Surah An Nahl 16:116

وَلَا تَقُولُوا۟ لِمَا تَصِفُ أَلْسِنَتُكُمُ ٱلْكَذِبَ هَـٰذَا حَلَـٰلٌ وَهَـٰذَا حَرَامٌ لِّتَفْتَرُوا۟ عَلَى ٱللَّهِ ٱلْكَذِبَ ۚ إِنَّ ٱلَّذِينَ يَفْتَرُونَ عَلَى ٱللَّهِ ٱلْكَذِبَ لَا يُفْلِحُونَ

And do not make Allah an object for your oaths (i.e., idle oaths) (as an excuse) against being and pious

وَلَا تَجْعَلُوا۟ ٱللَّهَ عُرْضَةً لِّأَيْمَـٰنِكُمْ أَن تَبَرُّوا۟ وَتَتَّقُوا۟

Allah does not take you to task for an idleness in your oaths, but He takes you to task for whatever contracts you have made by oaths. So the expiation thereof is the feeding of ten indigent persons with the average of that wherewith you feed your own families; or their raiment; or the freeing of a neck. (i.e., a slave) Yet, for him who does not find the (means), then (the expiation is) the fasting for three days. That is the expiation of your oaths when you have sworn; and keep your oaths. Thus Allah makes evident to you His signs, that possibly you would thank (Him) – Surah Al-Ma'idah 5:89

لَا يُؤَاخِذُكُمُ ٱللَّهُ بِٱللَّغْوِ فِىٓ أَيْمَـٰنِكُمْ وَلَـٰكِن يُؤَاخِذُكُم بِمَا عَقَّدتُّمُ ٱلْأَيْمَـٰنَ ۖ فَكَفَّـٰرَتُهُۥٓ إِطْعَامُ عَشَرَةِ مَسَـٰكِينَ مِنْ أَوْسَطِ مَا تُطْعِمُونَ أَهْلِيكُمْ أَوْ كِسْوَتُهُمْ أَوْ تَحْرِيرُ رَقَبَةٍ ۖ فَمَن لَّمْ يَجِدْ فَصِيَامُ ثَلَـٰثَةِ أَيَّامٍ ۚ ذَ‌ٰلِكَ كَفَّـٰرَةُ أَيْمَـٰنِكُمْ إِذَا حَلَفْتُمْ ۚ وَٱحْفَظُوٓا۟ أَيْمَـٰنَكُمْ ۚ كَذَ‌ٰلِكَ يُبَيِّنُ ٱللَّهُ لَكُمْ ءَايَـٰتِهِۦ لَعَلَّكُمْ تَشْكُرُونَ

And do not make Allah an object for your oaths (i.e., idle oaths) (as an excuse) against being and pious, and acting righteously (Or: reconciling) among mankind, and Allah is Ever-Hearing, Ever-Knowing. – Surah Al-Baqarah 2:224

وَلَا تَجْعَلُوا۟ ٱللَّهَ عُرْضَةً لِّأَيْمَـٰنِكُمْ أَن تَبَرُّوا۟ وَتَتَّقُوا۟ وَتُصْلِحُوا۟ بَيْنَ ٱلنَّاسِ ۗ وَٱللَّهُ سَمِيعٌ عَلِيمٌ

Narrated `Aisha: Abu Bakr As-Siddiq had never broken his oaths till Allah revealed the expiation for the oaths. Then he said, "If I take an oath to do something and later on I find something else better than the first one, then I do what is better and make expiation for my oath.". – Sahih al-Bukhari 6621

حَدَّثَنَا مُحَمَّدُ بْنُ مُقَاتِلٍ أَبُو الْحَسَنِ، أَخْبَرَنَا عَبْدُ اللَّهِ، أَخْبَرَنَا هِشَامُ بْنُ عُرْوَةَ، عَنْ أَبِيهِ، عَنْ عَائِشَةَ، أَنَّ أَبَا بَكْرٍ ـ رضى الله عنه ـ لَمْ يَكُنْ يَحْنَثُ فِي يَمِينٍ قَطُّ، حَتَّى أَنْزَلَ اللَّهُ كَفَّارَةَ الْيَمِينِ وَقَالَ لاَ أَحْلِفُ عَلَى يَمِينٍ فَرَأَيْتُ غَيْرَهَا خَيْرًا مِنْهَا، إِلاَّ أَتَيْتُ الَّذِي هُوَ خَيْرٌ، وَكَفَّرْتُ عَنْ يَمِينِي

It was narrated from Muhammad bin Az-Zubair, from his father, from a man from the inhabitants of Al-Basrah, who said: "I accompanied 'Imran bin Husain, who said: 'I heard the Messenger of Allah say: Vows are of two types: A vow that is made to do an act of obedience to Allah; that is for Allah and must be fulfilled, and a vow that is made to do an act of disobedience to Allah; that is for Shaitan and should not be fulfilled, and its expiation is the expiation for an oath.'". – Sunan an-Nasa'I 3845

أَخْبَرَنِي مُحَمَّدُ بْنُ وَهْبٍ، قَالَ حَدَّثَنَا مُحَمَّدُ بْنُ سَلَمَةَ، قَالَ حَدَّثَنِي ابْنُ إِسْحَاقَ، عَنْ مُحَمَّدِ بْنِ الزُّبَيْرِ، عَنْ أَبِيهِ، عَنْ رَجُلٍ، مِنْ أَهْلِ الْبَصْرَةِ قَالَ صَحِبْتُ عِمْرَانَ بْنَ حُصَيْنٍ قَالَ سَمِعْتُ رَسُولَ اللَّهِ صلى الله عليه وسلم يَقُولُ " النَّذْرُ نَذْرَانِ فَمَا كَانَ مِنْ نَذْرٍ فِي طَاعَةِ اللَّهِ فَذَلِكَ لِلَّهِ وَفِيهِ الْوَفَاءُ وَمَا كَانَ مِنْ نَذْرٍ فِي مَعْصِيَةِ اللَّهِ فَذَلِكَ لِلشَّيْطَانِ وَلاَ وَفَاءَ فِيهِ وَيُكَفِّرُهُ مَا يُكَفِّرُ الْيَمِينَ

Humaid b. ‘Abd al-Rahman b. ‘Auf reported that his mother Umm Kulthum daughter of ‘Uqba b. Abu Mu’ait, and she was one amongst the first emigrants who pledged allegiance to Allah’s Apostle ﷺ, as saying that she heard Allah’s Messenger ﷺ as saying: A liar is not one who tries to bring reconciliation amongst people and speaks good (in order to avert dispute), or he conveys good. Ibn Shihab said he did not hear that exemption was granted in anything what the people speak as lie but in three cases: in battle, for bringing reconciliation amongst persons and the narration of the words of the husband to his wife, and the narration of the words of a wife to her husband (in a twisted form in order to bring reconciliation between them). – Sahih Muslim 2605 a

حَدَّثَنِي حَرْمَلَةُ بْنُ يَحْيَى، أَخْبَرَنَا ابْنُ وَهْبٍ، أَخْبَرَنِي يُونُسُ، عَنِ ابْنِ شِهَابٍ، أَخْبَرَنِي حُمَيْدُ بْنُ عَبْدِ الرَّحْمَنِ بْنِ عَوْفٍ، أَنَّ أُمَّهُ أُمَّ كُلْثُومٍ بِنْتَ عُقْبَةَ بْنِ أَبِي مُعَيْطٍ، وَكَانَتْ، مِنَ الْمُهَاجِرَاتِ الأُوَلِ اللاَّتِي بَايَعْنَ النَّبِيَّ صلى الله عليه وسلم أَخْبَرَتْهُ أَنَّهَا سَمِعَتْ رَسُولَ اللَّهِ صلى الله عليه وسلم وَهُوَ يَقُولُ " لَيْسَ الْكَذَّابُ الَّذِي يُصْلِحُ بَيْنَ النَّاسِ وَيَقُولُ خَيْرًا وَيَنْمِي خَيْرًا " . قَالَ ابْنُ شِهَابٍ وَلَمْ أَسْمَعْ يُرَخَّصُ فِي شَىْءٍ مِمَّا يَقُولُ النَّاسُ كَذِبٌ إِلاَّ فِي ثَلاَثٍ الْحَرْبُ وَالإِصْلاَحُ بَيْنَ النَّاسِ وَحَدِيثُ الرَّجُلِ امْرَأَتَهُ وَحَدِيثُ الْمَرْأَةِ زَوْجَهَا

Yes indeed, (but) whoever fulfils his covenant and is pious (to Allah)
بَلَىٰ مَنْ أَوْفَىٰ بِعَهْدِهِۦ وَٱتَّقَىٰ

And do not be as she who breaks her yarn, even after it is strongly spun, (Literally: powerfully spun) into strands, by taking to yourselves your oaths fraudulently among yourselves, one nation being more numerous than another nation. Surely, Allah only tries you thereby; and indeed He will definitely make evident to you upon the Day of the Resurrection that wherein you used to differ And if Allah had (so) decided, indeed He would have made you one nation; but He leads into error whomever He decides to, and He guides whomever He decides to; and indeed you will definitely be questioned about whatever you were doing And do not take to yourselves your oaths fraudulently among yourselves for that a foot should slide back after firm (steadiness) and you should taste the odious (reward) for that you barred from the way of Allah; and – Surah An-Nahl 16:92-94

وَلَا تَكُونُواْ كَٱلَّتِي نَقَضَتْ غَزْلَهَا مِنۢ بَعْدِ قُوَّةٍ أَنكَٰثًا تَتَّخِذُونَ أَيْمَٰنَكُمْ دَخَلَۢا بَيْنَكُمْ أَن تَكُونَ أُمَّةٌ هِيَ أَرْبَىٰ مِنْ أُمَّةٍۚ إِنَّمَا يَبْلُوكُمُ ٱللَّهُ بِهِۦۚ وَلَيُبَيِّنَنَّ لَكُمْ يَوْمَ ٱلْقِيَٰمَةِ مَا كُنتُمْ فِيهِ تَخْتَلِفُونَ وَلَوْ شَآءَ ٱللَّهُ لَجَعَلَكُمْ أُمَّةً وَٰحِدَةً وَلَٰكِن يُضِلُّ مَن يَشَآءُ وَيَهْدِي مَن يَشَآءُۚ وَلَتُسْـَٔلُنَّ عَمَّا كُنتُمْ تَعْمَلُونَ وَلَا تَتَّخِذُوٓاْ أَيْمَٰنَكُمْ دَخَلَۢا بَيْنَكُمْ فَتَزِلَّ قَدَمُۢ بَعْدَ ثُبُوتِهَا وَتَذُوقُواْ ٱلسُّوٓءَ بِمَا صَدَدتُّمْ عَن سَبِيلِ ٱللَّهِۖ وَلَكُمْ عَذَابٌ عَظِيمٌ

Yes indeed, (but) whoever fulfils his covenant and is pious (to Allah), then surely Allah loves the pious – Surah Al-Imran 3:76

بَلَىٰۚ مَنْ أَوْفَىٰ بِعَهْدِهِۦ وَٱتَّقَىٰ فَإِنَّ ٱللَّهَ يُحِبُّ ٱلْمُتَّقِينَ

Among the believers are men who are sincere to what they covenanted with Allah. So, of them are (they) who have accomplished their life-time. (i.e., fuilled their vows by) And of them are (they) who are still waiting, and in no way have they exchanged the least exchanges – Surah Al-Azhab 33:23

مِّنَ ٱلْمُؤْمِنِينَ رِجَالٌ صَدَقُواْ مَا عَٰهَدُواْ ٱللَّهَ عَلَيْهِۖ فَمِنْهُم مَّن قَضَىٰ نَحْبَهُۥ وَمِنْهُم مَّن يَنتَظِرُۖ وَمَا بَدَّلُواْ تَبْدِيلًا

The Book of
But those who disbelieve, for them is destruction, and (Allah) will make their deeds vain
وَٱلَّذِينَ كَفَرُوا۟ فَتَعْسًا لَّهُمْ وَأَضَلَّ أَعْمَـٰلَهُمْ

O you who believe! Do not take the Jews and the Christians as allies; some of them are allies of one another. Whoever of you allies himself with them is one of them. Allah does not guide the wrongdoing people. You will see those in whose hearts is sickness racing towards them. They say, "We fear the wheel of fate may turn against us." But perhaps Allah will bring about victory, or some event of His making; thereupon they will regret what they concealed within themselves. Those who believe will say, "Are these the ones who swore by Allah with their strongest oaths that they are with you?" Their works have failed, so they became losers. – Surah Al-Maidah 5:51-53

يَـٰٓأَيُّهَا ٱلَّذِينَ ءَامَنُوا۟ لَا تَتَّخِذُوا۟ ٱلْيَهُودَ وَٱلنَّصَـٰرَىٰٓ أَوْلِيَآءَ ۘ بَعْضُهُمْ أَوْلِيَآءُ بَعْضٍ ۚ وَمَن يَتَوَلَّهُم مِّنكُمْ فَإِنَّهُۥ مِنْهُمْ ۗ إِنَّ ٱللَّهَ لَا يَهْدِى ٱلْقَوْمَ ٱلظَّـٰلِمِينَ فَتَرَى ٱلَّذِينَ فِى قُلُوبِهِم مَّرَضٌ يُسَـٰرِعُونَ فِيهِمْ يَقُولُونَ نَخْشَىٰٓ أَن تُصِيبَنَا دَآئِرَةٌ ۚ فَعَسَى ٱللَّهُ أَن يَأْتِىَ بِٱلْفَتْحِ أَوْ أَمْرٍ مِّنْ عِندِهِۦ فَيُصْبِحُوا۟ عَلَىٰ مَآ أَسَرُّوا۟ فِىٓ أَنفُسِهِمْ نَـٰدِمِينَ وَيَقُولُ ٱلَّذِينَ ءَامَنُوٓا۟ أَهَـٰٓؤُلَآءِ ٱلَّذِينَ أَقْسَمُوا۟ بِٱللَّهِ جَهْدَ أَيْمَـٰنِهِمْ ۙ إِنَّهُمْ لَمَعَكُمْ ۚ حَبِطَتْ أَعْمَـٰلُهُمْ فَأَصْبَحُوا۟ خَـٰسِرِينَ

Narrated Sa`d: I was one of (the first) seven (who had embraced Islam) with Allah's Messenger ﷺ and we had nothing to eat then, except the leaves of the Habala or Hubula tree, so that our stool used to be similar to that of sheep. Now the tribe of Bani Asad wants to teach me Islam; I would be a loser and all my efforts would be in vain (if I learn Islam anew from them). – Al-Bukhari 5412

حَدَّثَنَا عَبْدُ اللَّهِ بْنُ مُحَمَّدٍ، حَدَّثَنَا وَهْبُ بْنُ جَرِيرٍ، حَدَّثَنَا شُعْبَةُ، عَنْ إِسْمَاعِيلَ، عَنْ قَيْسٍ، عَنْ سَعْدٍ، قَالَ رَأَيْتُنِي سَابِعَ سَبْعَةٍ مَعَ النَّبِيِّ صلى الله عليه وسلم مَا لَنَا طَعَامٌ إِلاَّ وَرَقُ الْحُبْلَةِ ـ أَوِ الْحَبَلَةِ ـ حَتَّى يَضَعَ أَحَدُنَا مَا تَضَعُ الشَّاةُ، ثُمَّ أَصْبَحَتْ بَنُو أَسَدٍ تُعَزِّرُنِي عَلَى الإِسْلاَمِ، خَسِرْتُ إِذًا وَضَلَّ سَعْيِي

Do those who disbelieve think that they can take My servants for masters instead of Me? We have prepared Hell for the hospitality of the faithless. Say, "Shall We inform you of the greatest losers in their works?" Those whose efforts in this world are misguided, while they assume that they are doing well." It is they who rejected the communications of their Lord, and the encounter with Him. So their works are in vain. And on the Day of Resurrection, We will consider them of no weight. – Surah Al-Khaf 18: 102-105

أَفَحَسِبَ ٱلَّذِينَ كَفَرُوٓا۟ أَن يَتَّخِذُوا۟ عِبَادِى مِن دُونِىٓ أَوْلِيَآءَ ۚ إِنَّآ أَعْتَدْنَا جَهَنَّمَ لِلْكَـٰفِرِينَ نُزُلًا قُلْ هَلْ نُنَبِّئُكُم بِٱلْأَخْسَرِينَ أَعْمَـٰلًا ٱلَّذِينَ ضَلَّ سَعْيُهُمْ فِى ٱلْحَيَوٰةِ ٱلدُّنْيَا وَهُمْ يَحْسَبُونَ أَنَّهُمْ يُحْسِنُونَ صُنْعًا أُو۟لَـٰٓئِكَ ٱلَّذِينَ كَفَرُوا۟ بِـَٔايَـٰتِ رَبِّهِمْ وَلِقَآئِهِۦ فَحَبِطَتْ أَعْمَـٰلُهُمْ فَلَا نُقِيمُ لَهُمْ يَوْمَ ٱلْقِيَـٰمَةِ وَزْنًا

Those who do not expect to meet Us say, "If only the angels were sent down to us, or we could see our Lord." They have grown arrogant within themselves, and have become excessively defiant. On the Day when they see the angels—there will be no good news for sinners on that Day; and they will say, "A protective refuge." We will proceed to the works they did, and will turn them into scattered dust. – Surah Al-Furqan 25:21-23

وَقَالَ ٱلَّذِينَ لَا يَرْجُونَ لِقَآءَنَا لَوْلَآ أُنزِلَ عَلَيْنَا ٱلْمَلَـٰٓئِكَةُ أَوْ نَرَىٰ رَبَّنَا ۗ لَقَدِ ٱسْتَكْبَرُوا۟ فِىٓ أَنفُسِهِمْ وَعَتَوْ عُتُوًّا كَبِيرًا يَوْمَ يَرَوْنَ ٱلْمَلَـٰٓئِكَةَ لَا بُشْرَىٰ يَوْمَئِذٍ لِّلْمُجْرِمِينَ وَيَقُولُونَ حِجْرًا مَّحْجُورًا وَقَدِمْنَآ إِلَىٰ مَا عَمِلُوا۟ مِنْ عَمَلٍ فَجَعَلْنَـٰهُ هَبَآءً مَّنثُورًا

We will certainly test you, until We know those among you who strive, and those who are steadfast, and We will test your reactions. Those who disbelieve, and hinder from the path of Allah, and oppose the Messenger after guidance has become clear to them—they will not hurt Allah in the least, but He will nullify their deeds. O you who believe! Obey Allah, and obey the Messenger, and do not let your deeds go to waste. – Surah Muhammad 47:31-33

وَلَنَبْلُوَنَّكُمْ حَتَّىٰ نَعْلَمَ ٱلْمُجَـٰهِدِينَ مِنكُمْ وَٱلصَّـٰبِرِينَ وَنَبْلُوَا۟ أَخْبَارَكُمْ إِنَّ ٱلَّذِينَ كَفَرُوا۟ وَصَدُّوا۟ عَن سَبِيلِ ٱللَّهِ وَشَآقُّوا۟ ٱلرَّسُولَ مِنۢ بَعْدِ مَا تَبَيَّنَ لَهُمُ ٱلْهُدَىٰ لَن يَضُرُّوا۟ ٱللَّهَ شَيْـًٔا وَسَيُحْبِطُ أَعْمَـٰلَهُمْ يَـٰٓأَيُّهَا ٱلَّذِينَ ءَامَنُوٓا۟ أَطِيعُوا۟ ٱللَّهَ وَأَطِيعُوا۟ ٱلرَّسُولَ وَلَا تُبْطِلُوٓا۟ أَعْمَـٰلَكُمْ

I will turn away from My revelations those who behave proudly on earth without justification. Even if they see every sign, they will not believe in it; and if they see the path of rectitude, they will not adopt it for a path; and if they see the path of error, they will adopt it for a path. That is because they denied Our revelations, and paid no attention to them. Those who deny Our revelations and the meeting of the Hereafter— their deeds will come to nothing. Will they be repaid except according to what they used to do? Surah Al-A'raf 7:146&147

سَأَصْرِفُ عَنْ ءَايَـٰتِىَ ٱلَّذِينَ يَتَكَبَّرُونَ فِى ٱلْأَرْضِ بِغَيْرِ ٱلْحَقِّ وَإِن يَرَوْا۟ كُلَّ ءَايَةٍ لَّا يُؤْمِنُوا۟ بِهَا وَإِن يَرَوْا۟ سَبِيلَ ٱلرُّشْدِ لَا يَتَّخِذُوهُ سَبِيلًا وَإِن يَرَوْا۟ سَبِيلَ ٱلْغَىِّ يَتَّخِذُوهُ سَبِيلًا ذَٰلِكَ بِأَنَّهُمْ كَذَّبُوا۟ بِـَٔايَـٰتِنَا وَكَانُوا۟ عَنْهَا غَـٰفِلِينَ وَٱلَّذِينَ كَذَّبُوا۟ بِـَٔايَـٰتِنَا وَلِقَآءِ ٱلْـَٔاخِرَةِ حَبِطَتْ أَعْمَـٰلُهُمْ هَلْ يُجْزَوْنَ إِلَّا مَا كَانُوا۟ يَعْمَلُونَ

Like those before you. They were more powerful than you, and had more wealth and children. They enjoyed their share, and you enjoyed your share, as those before you enjoyed their share. And you indulged, as they indulged. It is they whose works will fail in this world and in the Hereafter. It is they who are the losers. – Surah At-Taubah 9:69

كَٱلَّذِينَ مِن قَبْلِكُمْ كَانُوٓا۟ أَشَدَّ مِنكُمْ قُوَّةً وَأَكْثَرَ أَمْوَٰلًا وَأَوْلَـٰدًا فَٱسْتَمْتَعُوا۟ بِخَلَـٰقِهِمْ فَٱسْتَمْتَعْتُم بِخَلَـٰقِكُمْ كَمَا ٱسْتَمْتَعَ ٱلَّذِينَ مِن قَبْلِكُم بِخَلَـٰقِهِمْ وَخُضْتُمْ كَٱلَّذِى خَاضُوٓا۟ أُو۟لَـٰٓئِكَ حَبِطَتْ أَعْمَـٰلُهُمْ فِى ٱلدُّنْيَا وَٱلْـَٔاخِرَةِ وَأُو۟لَـٰٓئِكَ هُمُ ٱلْخَـٰسِرُونَ

Whoever desires the worldly life and its glitter—We will fully recompense them for their deeds therein, and therein they will not be defrauded. These—they will have nothing but the Fire in the Hereafter. Their deeds are in vain therein, and their works are null. – Surah Hud 11:15&16

مَن كَانَ يُرِيدُ ٱلْحَيَوٰةَ ٱلدُّنْيَا وَزِينَتَهَا نُوَفِّ إِلَيْهِمْ أَعْمَـٰلَهُمْ فِيهَا وَهُمْ فِيهَا لَا يُبْخَسُونَ أُو۟لَـٰٓئِكَ ٱلَّذِينَ لَيْسَ لَهُمْ فِى ٱلْـَٔاخِرَةِ إِلَّا ٱلنَّارُ وَحَبِطَ مَا صَنَعُوا۟ فِيهَا وَبَـٰطِلٌ مَّا كَانُوا۟ يَعْمَلُونَ

It was revealed to you, and to those before you, that if you idolize, your works will be in vain, and you will be of the losers. – Surah Az-Zumar 39:65

وَلَقَدْ أُوحِىَ إِلَيْكَ وَإِلَى ٱلَّذِينَ مِن قَبْلِكَ لَئِنْ أَشْرَكْتَ لَيَحْبَطَنَّ عَمَلُكَ وَلَتَكُونَنَّ مِنَ ٱلْخَـٰسِرِينَ

Those who disbelieve and repel from the path of Allah—He nullifies their works. . – Surah Muhammad 47:1

ٱلَّذِينَ كَفَرُوا۟ وَصَدُّوا۟ عَن سَبِيلِ ٱللَّهِ أَضَلَّ أَعْمَـٰلَهُمْ

But as for those who disbelieve, for them is perdition, and He will waste their deeds. – Surah Muhammad 47:8

وَٱلَّذِينَ كَفَرُوا۟ فَتَعْسًا لَّهُمْ وَأَضَلَّ أَعْمَـٰلَهُمْ

Among the people are those who say, "We believe in Allah and in the Last Day," but they are not believers. They seek to deceive Allah and those who believe, but they deceive none but themselves, though they are not aware. In their hearts is sickness, and Allah has increased their sickness. They will have a painful punishment because of their denial. And when it is said to them, "Do not make trouble on earth," they say, "We are only reformers." In fact, they are the troublemakers, but they are not aware. And when it is said to them, "Believe as the people have believed," they say, "Shall we believe as the fools have believed?" In fact, it is they who are the fools, but they do not know. And when they come across those who believe, they say, "We believe"; but when they are alone with their devils, they say, "We are with you; we were only ridiculing." It is Allah who ridicules them, and leaves them bewildered in their transgression. Those are they who have bartered error for guidance; but their trade does not profit them, and they are not guided. – Surah Al-Baqarah 2:8-16

وَمِنَ ٱلنَّاسِ مَن يَقُولُ ءَامَنَّا بِٱللَّهِ وَبِٱلْيَوْمِ ٱلْءَاخِرِ وَمَا هُم بِمُؤْمِنِينَ يُخَٰدِعُونَ ٱللَّهَ وَٱلَّذِينَ ءَامَنُواْ وَمَا يَخْدَعُونَ إِلَّآ أَنفُسَهُمْ وَمَا
يَشْعُرُونَ فِى قُلُوبِهِم مَّرَضٌ فَزَادَهُمُ ٱللَّهُ مَرَضًاۖ وَلَهُمْ عَذَابٌ أَلِيمٌۢ بِمَا كَانُواْ يَكْذِبُونَ وَإِذَا قِيلَ لَهُمْ لَا تُفْسِدُواْ فِى ٱلْأَرْضِ قَالُوٓاْ
إِنَّمَا نَحْنُ مُصْلِحُونَ أَلَآ إِنَّهُمْ هُمُ ٱلْمُفْسِدُونَ وَلَٰكِن لَّا يَشْعُرُونَ وَإِذَا قِيلَ لَهُمْ ءَامِنُواْ كَمَآ ءَامَنَ ٱلنَّاسُ قَالُوٓاْ أَنُؤْمِنُ كَمَآ ءَامَنَ
ٱلسُّفَهَآءُۗ أَلَآ إِنَّهُمْ هُمُ ٱلسُّفَهَآءُ وَلَٰكِن لَّا يَعْلَمُونَ وَإِذَا لَقُواْ ٱلَّذِينَ ءَامَنُواْ قَالُوٓاْ ءَامَنَّا وَإِذَا خَلَوْاْ إِلَىٰ شَيَٰطِينِهِمْ قَالُوٓاْ إِنَّا مَعَكُمْ إِنَّمَا
نَحْنُ مُسْتَهْزِءُونَ ٱللَّهُ يَسْتَهْزِئُ بِهِمْ وَيَمُدُّهُمْ فِى طُغْيَٰنِهِمْ يَعْمَهُونَ أُوْلَٰٓئِكَ ٱلَّذِينَ ٱشْتَرَوُاْ ٱلضَّلَٰلَةَ بِٱلْهُدَىٰ فَمَا رَبِحَت تِّجَٰرَتُهُمْ
وَمَا كَانُواْ مُهْتَدِينَ

Being stingy towards you. And when fear approaches, you see them staring at you—their eyes rolling—like someone fainting at death. Then, when panic is over, they whip you with sharp tongues. They resent you any good. These have never believed, so Allah has nullified their works; a matter easy for Allah. – Surah Al-Ahzab 33:19

أَشِحَّةً عَلَيْكُمْۖ فَإِذَا جَآءَ ٱلْخَوْفُ رَأَيْتَهُمْ يَنظُرُونَ إِلَيْكَ تَدُورُ أَعْيُنُهُمْ كَٱلَّذِى يُغْشَىٰ عَلَيْهِ مِنَ ٱلْمَوْتِۖ فَإِذَا ذَهَبَ ٱلْخَوْفُ سَلَقُوكُم
بِأَلْسِنَةٍ حِدَادٍ أَشِحَّةً عَلَى ٱلْخَيْرِۚ أُوْلَٰٓئِكَ لَمْ يُؤْمِنُواْ فَأَحْبَطَ ٱللَّهُ أَعْمَٰلَهُمْۚ وَكَانَ ذَٰلِكَ عَلَى ٱللَّهِ يَسِيرًا

On the Day when the hypocritical men and hypocritical women will say to those who believed, "Wait for us; let us absorb some of your light." It will be said, "Go back behind you, and seek light." A wall will be raised between them, in which is a door; within it is mercy, and outside it is agony. They will call to them, "Were we not with you?" They will say, "Yes, but you cheated your souls, and waited, and doubted, and became deluded by wishful thinking, until the command of Allah arrived; and arrogance deceived you regarding Allah." –Surah Hadid 57:13&14

يَوْمَ يَقُولُ ٱلْمُنَٰفِقُونَ وَٱلْمُنَٰفِقَٰتُ لِلَّذِينَ ءَامَنُواْ ٱنظُرُونَا نَقْتَبِسْ مِن نُّورِكُمْ قِيلَ ٱرْجِعُواْ وَرَآءَكُمْ فَٱلْتَمِسُواْ نُورًاۖ فَضُرِبَ بَيْنَهُم
بِسُورٍ لَّهُۥ بَابٌۢ بَاطِنُهُۥ فِيهِ ٱلرَّحْمَةُ وَظَٰهِرُهُۥ مِن قِبَلِهِ ٱلْعَذَابُ يُنَادُونَهُمْ أَلَمْ نَكُن مَّعَكُمْۖ قَالُواْ بَلَىٰ وَلَٰكِنَّكُمْ فَتَنتُمْ أَنفُسَكُمْ
وَتَرَبَّصْتُمْ وَٱرْتَبْتُمْ وَغَرَّتْكُمُ ٱلْأَمَانِىُّ حَتَّىٰ جَآءَ أَمْرُ ٱللَّهِ وَغَرَّكُم بِٱللَّهِ ٱلْغَرُورُ

And We made a covenant with you, and raised the Mount above you: "Take what We have given you firmly, and listen." They said, "We hear and disobey." And their hearts became filled with the love of the calf because of their disbelief. Say, "Wretched is what your faith commands you to do, if you are believers." – Surah Al-Baqarah 2:93

وَإِذْ أَخَذْنَا مِيثَٰقَكُمْ وَرَفَعْنَا فَوْقَكُمُ ٱلطُّورَ خُذُواْ مَآ ءَاتَيْنَٰكُم بِقُوَّةٍ وَٱسْمَعُواْۖ قَالُواْ سَمِعْنَا وَعَصَيْنَا وَأُشْرِبُواْ فِى قُلُوبِهِمُ ٱلْعِجْلَ
بِكُفْرِهِمْۚ قُلْ بِئْسَمَا يَأْمُرُكُم بِهِۦٓ إِيمَٰنُكُمْ إِن كُنتُم مُّؤْمِنِينَ

The hypocrites try to deceive Allah, but He is deceiving them. And when they stand for prayer, they stand lazily, showing off in front of people, and remembering Allah only a little. – Surah An-Nisa 4:142

إِنَّ ٱلْمُنَٰفِقِينَ يُخَٰدِعُونَ ٱللَّهَ وَهُوَ خَٰدِعُهُمْ وَإِذَا قَامُوٓاْ إِلَى ٱلصَّلَوٰةِ قَامُواْ كُسَالَىٰ يُرَآءُونَ ٱلنَّاسَ وَلَا يَذْكُرُونَ ٱللَّهَ إِلَّا قَلِيلًا

Those who disbelieve in Allah and His messengers, and want to separate between Allah and His messengers, and say, "We believe in some, and reject some," and wish to take a path in between. These are the unbelievers, truly. We have prepared for the unbelievers a shameful punishment. – Surah An-Nisa 4:150&151

إِنَّ ٱلَّذِينَ يَكۡفُرُونَ بِٱللَّهِ وَرُسُلِهِۦ وَيُرِيدُونَ أَن يُفَرِّقُواْ بَيۡنَ ٱللَّهِ وَرُسُلِهِۦ وَيَقُولُونَ نُؤۡمِنُ بِبَعۡضٖ وَنَكۡفُرُ بِبَعۡضٖ وَيُرِيدُونَ أَن يَتَّخِذُواْ بَيۡنَ ذَٰلِكَ سَبِيلًا أُوْلَٰٓئِكَ هُمُ ٱلۡكَٰفِرُونَ حَقّٗاۚ وَأَعۡتَدۡنَا لِلۡكَٰفِرِينَ عَذَابٗا مُّهِينٗا

What prevents the acceptance of their contributions is nothing but the fact that they disbelieved in Allah and His Messenger, and that they do not approach the prayer except lazily, and that they do not spend except grudgingly. – Surah At-Taubah 9:54

وَمَا مَنَعَهُمۡ أَن تُقۡبَلَ مِنۡهُمۡ نَفَقَٰتُهُمۡ إِلَّآ أَنَّهُمۡ كَفَرُواْ بِٱللَّهِ وَبِرَسُولِهِۦ وَلَا يَأۡتُونَ ٱلصَّلَوٰةَ إِلَّا وَهُمۡ كُسَالَىٰ وَلَا يُنفِقُونَ إِلَّا وَهُمۡ كَٰرِهُونَ

O you who believe! Why do you say what you do not do? It is most hateful to Allah that you say what you do not do. – Surah As-Saffat 61:2&3

يَٰٓأَيُّهَا ٱلَّذِينَ ءَامَنُواْ لِمَ تَقُولُونَ مَا لَا تَفۡعَلُونَ كَبُرَ مَقۡتًا عِندَ ٱللَّهِ أَن تَقُولُواْ مَا لَا تَفۡعَلُونَ

When the hypocrites come to you, they say, "We bear witness that you are Allah's Messenger." Allah knows that you are His Messenger, and Allah bears witness that the hypocrites are liars. They treat their oaths as a cover, and so they repel others from Allah's path. Evil is what they do. That is because they believed, and then disbelieved; so their hearts were sealed, and they cannot understand. When you see them, their appearance impresses you. And when they speak, you listen to what they say. They are like propped-up timber. They think every shout is aimed at them. They are the enemy, so beware of them. Allah condemns them; how deluded they are! And when it is said to them, "Come, the Messenger of Allah will ask forgiveness for you," they bend their heads, and you see them turning away arrogantly. It is the same for them, whether you ask forgiveness for them, or do not ask forgiveness for them; Allah will not forgive them. Allah does not guide the sinful people. It is they who say: "Do not spend anything on those who side with Allah's Messenger, unless they have dispersed." To Allah belong the treasures of the heavens and the earth, but the hypocrites do not understand. They say, "If we return to the City, the more powerful therein will evict the weak." But power belongs to Allah, and His Messenger, and the believers; but the hypocrites do not know. O you who believe! Let neither your possessions nor your children distract you from the remembrance of Allah. Whoever does that—these are the losers. And give from what We have provided for you, before death approaches one of you, and he says, "My Lord, if only You would delay me for a short while, so that I may be charitable, and be one of the righteous." But Allah will not delay a soul when its time has come. Allah is Informed of what you do. – Surah Al-Munafiqun 63

إِذَا جَآءَكَ ٱلۡمُنَٰفِقُونَ قَالُواْ نَشۡهَدُ إِنَّكَ لَرَسُولُ ٱللَّهِۗ وَٱللَّهُ يَعۡلَمُ إِنَّكَ لَرَسُولُهُۥ وَٱللَّهُ يَشۡهَدُ إِنَّ ٱلۡمُنَٰفِقِينَ لَكَٰذِبُونَ ٱتَّخَذُوٓاْ أَيۡمَٰنَهُمۡ جُنَّةٗ فَصَدُّواْ عَن سَبِيلِ ٱللَّهِۚ إِنَّهُمۡ سَآءَ مَا كَانُواْ يَعۡمَلُونَ ذَٰلِكَ بِأَنَّهُمۡ ءَامَنُواْ ثُمَّ كَفَرُواْ فَطُبِعَ عَلَىٰ قُلُوبِهِمۡ فَهُمۡ لَا يَفۡقَهُونَ وَإِذَا رَأَيۡتَهُمۡ تُعۡجِبُكَ أَجۡسَامُهُمۡۖ وَإِن يَقُولُواْ تَسۡمَعۡ لِقَوۡلِهِمۡۖ كَأَنَّهُمۡ خُشُبٞ مُّسَنَّدَةٞۖ يَحۡسَبُونَ كُلَّ صَيۡحَةٍ عَلَيۡهِمۡۚ هُمُ ٱلۡعَدُوُّ فَٱحۡذَرۡهُمۡۚ قَٰتَلَهُمُ ٱللَّهُۖ أَنَّىٰ يُؤۡفَكُونَ وَإِذَا قِيلَ لَهُمۡ تَعَالَوۡاْ يَسۡتَغۡفِرۡ لَكُمۡ رَسُولُ ٱللَّهِ لَوَّوۡاْ رُءُوسَهُمۡ وَرَأَيۡتَهُمۡ يَصُدُّونَ وَهُم مُّسۡتَكۡبِرُونَ سَوَآءٌ عَلَيۡهِمۡ أَسۡتَغۡفَرۡتَ لَهُمۡ أَمۡ لَمۡ تَسۡتَغۡفِرۡ لَهُمۡ لَن يَغۡفِرَ ٱللَّهُ لَهُمۡۚ إِنَّ ٱللَّهَ لَا يَهۡدِي ٱلۡقَوۡمَ ٱلۡفَٰسِقِينَ هُمُ ٱلَّذِينَ يَقُولُونَ لَا تُنفِقُواْ عَلَىٰ مَنۡ عِندَ رَسُولِ ٱللَّهِ حَتَّىٰ يَنفَضُّواْۗ وَلِلَّهِ خَزَآئِنُ ٱلسَّمَٰوَٰتِ وَٱلۡأَرۡضِ وَلَٰكِنَّ ٱلۡمُنَٰفِقِينَ لَا يَفۡقَهُونَ يَقُولُونَ لَئِن رَّجَعۡنَآ إِلَى ٱلۡمَدِينَةِ لَيُخۡرِجَنَّ ٱلۡأَعَزُّ مِنۡهَا ٱلۡأَذَلَّۚ وَلِلَّهِ ٱلۡعِزَّةُ وَلِرَسُولِهِۦ وَلِلۡمُؤۡمِنِينَ وَلَٰكِنَّ ٱلۡمُنَٰفِقِينَ لَا يَعۡلَمُونَ يَٰٓأَيُّهَا ٱلَّذِينَ ءَامَنُواْ لَا تُلۡهِكُمۡ أَمۡوَٰلُكُمۡ وَلَآ أَوۡلَٰدُكُمۡ عَن ذِكۡرِ ٱللَّهِۚ وَمَن يَفۡعَلۡ ذَٰلِكَ فَأُوْلَٰٓئِكَ هُمُ ٱلۡخَٰسِرُونَ وَأَنفِقُواْ مِن مَّا رَزَقۡنَٰكُم مِّن قَبۡلِ أَن يَأۡتِيَ أَحَدَكُمُ ٱلۡمَوۡتُ فَيَقُولَ رَبِّ لَوۡلَآ أَخَّرۡتَنِيٓ إِلَىٰٓ أَجَلٖ قَرِيبٖ فَأَصَّدَّقَ وَأَكُن مِّنَ ٱلصَّٰلِحِينَ وَلَن يُؤَخِّرَ ٱللَّهُ نَفۡسًا إِذَا جَآءَ أَجَلُهَاۚ وَٱللَّهُ خَبِيرُۢ بِمَا تَعۡمَلُونَ

Narrated Ka`b: The Prophetﷺ said, "The example of a believer is that of a fresh tender plant, which the wind bends It sometimes and some other time it makes it straight. And the example of a hypocrite is that of a pine tree which keeps straight till once it is uprooted suddenly. – Al-Bukhari 5643

حَدَّثَنَا مُسَدَّدٌ، حَدَّثَنَا يَحْيَى، عَنْ سُفْيَانَ، عَنْ سَعْدٍ، عَنْ عَبْدِ اللَّهِ بْنِ كَعْبٍ، عَنْ أَبِيهِ، عَنِ النَّبِيِّ صلى الله عليه وسلم قَالَ " مَثَلُ الْمُؤْمِنِ كَالْخَامَةِ مِنَ الزَّرْعِ تُفَيِّئُهَا الرِّيحُ مَرَّةً، وَتَعْدِلُهَا مَرَّةً، وَمَثَلُ الْمُنَافِقِ كَالأَرْزَةِ لاَ تَزَالُ حَتَّى يَكُونَ انْجِعَافُهَا مَرَّةً وَاحِدَةً ". وَقَالَ زَكَرِيَّاءُ حَدَّثَنِي سَعْدٌ، حَدَّثَنَا ابْنُ كَعْبٍ، عَنْ أَبِيهِ، كَعْبٍ عَنِ النَّبِيِّ صلى الله عليه وسلم.

Narrated Fatima bint Al-Mundhir: Asma' bint Abi Bakr As-Siddiq said, "I went to 'Aishah and the people were offering Salat. I asked her, 'What is wrong with the people ?' She pointed towards the sky with her head. I asked her, 'Is there a sign ?' 'Aishah nodded with her head meaning 'Yes'." Asma' added, "Allah's Messenger ﷺ prolonged the Salat to such an extent that I fainted. There was a waterskin by my side and I opened it and poured some water on my head. When Allah's Messenger ﷺ finished Salat, and the solar eclipse had cleared, the Prophet ﷺ addressed the people and praised Allah as He deserves and said, 'Amma ba'du'." Asma' further said, "Some Ansari women started talking, so I turned to them in order to make them quiet. I asked 'Aishah what the Prophet ﷺ had said. 'Aishah said: 'He said, 'I have seen things at this place of mine which were never shown to me before; (I have seen) even Paradise and Hell. And, no doubt it has been revealed to me that you (people) will be put in trial in your graves like or nearly like the trial of Masih Ad-Dajjal. (The angels) will come to everyone of you and ask him, 'What do you know about this man (Prophet Muhammad ﷺ ?") The faithful believer or firm believer (Hisham was In doubt Ih word the Prophet ﷺ used), will say, 'He is Allah's Messenger ﷺ and he is Muhammad ﷺ who came to us with clear evidences and guidance. So we believed him, accepted his teachings and followed and trusted his teaching.' Then the angels will tell him to sleep (in peace) as they have come to know that he was a believer. But the hypocrite or a doubtful person (Hisham is not sure as to which word the Prophet ﷺ used), will be asked what he knew about this man (Prophet Muhammed ﷺ .) He will say, 'I do not know but I heard the people saying something (about him) so I said the same' " Hisham added, "Fatima told me that she remembered that narration completely by heart except that she said about the hypocrite or a doubtful person that he will be punished severely." – Al-Bukhari 922

وَقَالَ مَحْمُودٌ حَدَّثَنَا أَبُو أُسَامَةَ، قَالَ حَدَّثَنَا هِشَامُ بْنُ عُرْوَةَ، قَالَ أَخْبَرَتْنِي فَاطِمَةُ بِنْتُ الْمُنْذِرِ، عَنْ أَسْمَاءَ بِنْتِ أَبِي بَكْرٍ، قَالَتْ دَخَلْتُ عَلَى عَائِشَةَ ـ رضى الله عنها ـ وَالنَّاسُ يُصَلُّونَ قُلْتُ مَا شَأْنُ النَّاسِ فَأَشَارَتْ بِرَأْسِهَا إِلَى السَّمَاءِ. فَقُلْتُ آيَةٌ فَأَشَارَتْ بِرَأْسِهَا أَىْ نَعَمْ. قَالَتْ فَأَطَالَ رَسُولُ اللَّهِ صلى الله عليه وسلم جِدًّا حَتَّى تَجَلاَّنِي الْغَشْىُ وَإِلَى جَنْبِي قِرْبَةٌ فِيهَا مَاءٌ فَفَتَحْتُهَا فَجَعَلْتُ أَصُبُّ مِنْهَا عَلَى رَأْسِي، فَانْصَرَفَ رَسُولُ اللَّهِ صلى الله عليه وسلم وَقَدْ تَجَلَّتِ الشَّمْسُ، فَخَطَبَ النَّاسَ، وَحَمِدَ اللَّهَ بِمَا هُوَ أَهْلُهُ ثُمَّ قَالَ " أَمَّا بَعْدُ ". قَالَتْ وَلَغِطَ نِسْوَةٌ مِنَ الأَنْصَارِ، فَانْكَفَأْتُ إِلَيْهِنَّ لأُسَكِّتَهُنَّ فَقُلْتُ لِعَائِشَةَ مَا قَالَ قَالَتْ قَالَ " مَا مِنْ شَىْءٍ لَمْ أَكُنْ أُرِيتُهُ إِلاَّ قَدْ رَأَيْتُهُ فِي مَقَامِي هَذَا حَتَّى الْجَنَّةَ وَالنَّارَ، وَإِنَّهُ قَدْ أُوحِيَ إِلَىَّ أَنَّكُمْ تُفْتَنُونَ فِي الْقُبُورِ مِثْلَ ـ أَوْ قَرِيبَ مِنْ ـ فِتْنَةِ الْمَسِيحِ الدَّجَّالِ، يُؤْتَى أَحَدُكُمْ، فَيُقَالُ لَهُ مَا عِلْمُكَ بِهَذَا الرَّجُلِ فَأَمَّا الْمُؤْمِنُ ـ أَوْ قَالَ الْمُوقِنُ شَكَّ هِشَامٌ ـ فَيَقُولُ هُوَ رَسُولُ اللَّهِ، هُوَ مُحَمَّدٌ صلى الله عليه وسلم جَاءَنَا بِالْبَيِّنَاتِ وَالْهُدَى فَآمَنَّا وَأَجَبْنَا وَاتَّبَعْنَا وَصَدَّقْنَا. فَيُقَالُ لَهُ نَمْ صَالِحًا، قَدْ كُنَّا نَعْلَمُ إِنْ كُنْتَ لَتُؤْمِنُ بِهِ. وَأَمَّا الْمُنَافِقُ ـ أَوْ قَالَ الْمُرْتَابُ شَكَّ هِشَامٌ ـ فَيُقَالُ لَهُ مَا عِلْمُكَ بِهَذَا الرَّجُلِ فَيَقُولُ لاَ أَدْرِي، سَمِعْتُ النَّاسَ يَقُولُونَ شَيْئًا فَقُلْتُهُ ". قَالَ هِشَامٌ فَلَقَدْ قَالَتْ لِي فَاطِمَةُ فَأَوْعَيْتُهُ، غَيْرَ أَنَّهَا ذَكَرَتْ مَا يُغَلِّظُ عَلَيْهِ.

The Book of

He (Allah) has ordained for you the same religion (Islam) which He ordained for Nuh

شَرَعَ لَكُم مِّنَ ٱلدِّينِ مَا وَصَّىٰ بِهِۦ نُوحًا

Those who believe, and those who are Jewish, and the Christians, and the Sabeans—any who believe in Allah and the Last Day, and act righteously—will have their reward with their Lord; they have nothing to fear, nor will they grieve. – Surah Al-Baqarah 2:62

إِنَّ ٱلَّذِينَ ءَامَنُوا۟ وَٱلَّذِينَ هَادُوا۟ وَٱلنَّصَـٰرَىٰ وَٱلصَّـٰبِـِٔينَ مَنْ ءَامَنَ بِٱللَّهِ وَٱلْيَوْمِ ٱلْءَاخِرِ وَعَمِلَ صَـٰلِحًا فَلَهُمْ أَجْرُهُمْ عِندَ رَبِّهِمْ وَلَا خَوْفٌ عَلَيْهِمْ وَلَا هُمْ يَحْزَنُونَ

Who is more unjust than him who forbids the remembrance of Allah's name in places of worship, and contributes to their ruin? These ought not to enter them except in fear. For them is disgrace in this world, and for them is a terrible punishment in the Hereafter. – Surah Al-Baqarah 2:114

وَمَنْ أَظْلَمُ مِمَّن مَّنَعَ مَسَـٰجِدَ ٱللَّهِ أَن يُذْكَرَ فِيهَا ٱسْمُهُۥ وَسَعَىٰ فِى خَرَابِهَآ ۚ أُو۟لَـٰٓئِكَ مَا كَانَ لَهُمْ أَن يَدْخُلُوهَآ إِلَّا خَآئِفِينَ ۚ لَهُمْ فِى ٱلدُّنْيَا خِزْىٌ وَلَهُمْ فِى ٱلْءَاخِرَةِ عَذَابٌ عَظِيمٌ

And they say, "Be Jews or Christians, and you will be guided." Say, "Rather, the religion of Abraham, the Monotheist; he was not an idolater." Say, "We believe in Allah; and in what was revealed to us; and in what was revealed to Abraham, and Ishmael, and Isaac, and Jacob, and the Patriarchs; and in what was given to Moses and Jesus; and in what was given to the prophets— from their Lord. We make no distinction between any of them, and to Him we surrender." – Surah Al-Baqarah 2:135&136

وَقَالُوا۟ كُونُوا۟ هُودًا أَوْ نَصَـٰرَىٰ تَهْتَدُوا۟ ۗ قُلْ بَلْ مِلَّةَ إِبْرَٰهِـۧمَ حَنِيفًا ۖ وَمَا كَانَ مِنَ ٱلْمُشْرِكِينَ قُولُوٓا۟ ءَامَنَّا بِٱللَّهِ وَمَآ أُنزِلَ إِلَيْنَا وَمَآ أُنزِلَ إِلَىٰٓ إِبْرَٰهِـۧمَ وَإِسْمَـٰعِيلَ وَإِسْحَـٰقَ وَيَعْقُوبَ وَٱلْأَسْبَاطِ وَمَآ أُوتِىَ مُوسَىٰ وَعِيسَىٰ وَمَآ أُوتِىَ ٱلنَّبِيُّونَ مِن رَّبِّهِمْ لَا نُفَرِّقُ بَيْنَ أَحَدٍ مِّنْهُمْ وَنَحْنُ لَهُۥ مُسْلِمُونَ

He (Allah) has ordained for you the same religion (Islam) which He ordained for Nuh, and that which We have inspired in you, and that which We ordained for Ibrahim, Musa and 'Iesa saying you should establish religion, and make no divisions in it. Surah Ash-Shura 42:13

شَرَعَ لَكُم مِّنَ ٱلدِّينِ مَا وَصَّىٰ بِهِۦ نُوحًا وَٱلَّذِىٓ أَوْحَيْنَآ إِلَيْكَ وَمَا وَصَّيْنَا بِهِۦٓ إِبْرَٰهِيمَ وَمُوسَىٰ وَعِيسَىٰٓ ۖ أَنْ أَقِيمُوا۟ ٱلدِّينَ وَلَا تَتَفَرَّقُوا۟ فِيهِ

Narrated `Abdullah bin `Umar: `Umar bin Al-Khattab set out with Allah's Messenger ﷺ, and a group of his companions to Ibn Saiyad. They found him playing with the boys in the fort or near the Hillocks of Bani Maghala. Ibn Saiyad was nearing his puberty at that time, and he did not notice the arrival of the Prophet ﷺ till Allah's Apostle stroked him on the back with his hand and said, "Do you testify that I am Allah's Messenger ﷺ?" Ibn Saiyad looked at him and said, "I testify that you are the Apostle of the unlettered ones (illiterates)". Then Ibn Saiyad said to the Prophets . "Do you testify that I am Allah's Messenger ﷺ ?" The Prophet denied that, saying, "I believe in Allah and all His Apostles," and then said to Ibn Saiyad, "What do you see?" Ibn Saiyad said, "True people and liars visit me." The Prophet ﷺ said, "You have been confused as to this matter." Allah's Messenger ﷺ added, "I have kept something for you (in my mind)." Ibn Saiyad said, "Ad-Dukh." The Prophet ﷺ said, "Ikhsa (you should be ashamed) for you can not cross your limits." `Umar said, "O Allah's Messenger ﷺ !" Allow me to chop off h is neck." Allah's Apostle said (to `Umar). "Should this person be him (i.e. Ad-Dajjal) then you cannot over-power him; and should he be someone else, then it will be no use your killing him." `Abdullah bin `Umar added: Later on Allah's Messenger ﷺ and Ubai bin Ka`b Al-Ansari (once again) went to the garden in which Ibn Saiyad was present. When Allah's Messenger ﷺ entered the garden, he started hiding behind the trunks of the date-palms intending to hear something from Ibn Saiyad before the latter could see him. Ibn Saiyad was Lying on his bed, covered with a velvet sheet from where his mumur were heard. Ibn Saiyad's mother saw the Prophet and said, "O Saf (the nickname of Ibn Saiyad)! Here is Muhammad!" Ibn Saiyad stopped his murmuring. The Prophet ﷺ said, "If his mother had kept quiet, then I would have learnt more about him." `Abdullah added: Allah's Messenger ﷺ stood up before the people (delivering a sermon), and after praising and glorifying Allah as He deserved, he mentioned the Ad-Dajjal saying, "I warn you against him, and there has been no prophet but warned his followers against him. Noah warned his followers against him but I am telling you about him, something which no prophet has told his people of, and that is: Know that he is blind in one eye where as Allah is not so." – Al-Bukhari 6173-6175

حَدَّثَنَا أَبُو الْيَمَانِ، أَخْبَرَنَا شُعَيْبٌ، عَنِ الزُّهْرِيِّ، قَالَ أَخْبَرَنِي سَالِمُ بْنُ عَبْدِ اللَّهِ، أَنَّ عَبْدَ اللَّهِ بْنَ عُمَرَ، أَخْبَرَهُ أَنَّ عُمَرَ بْنَ الْخَطَّابِ انْطَلَقَ مَعَ رَسُولِ اللَّهِ صلى الله عليه وسلم فِي رَهْطٍ مِنْ أَصْحَابِهِ قِبَلَ ابْنِ صَيَّادٍ، حَتَّى وَجَدَهُ يَلْعَبُ مَعَ الْغِلْمَانِ فِي أُطُمِ بَنِي مَغَالَةَ، وَقَدْ قَارَبَ ابْنُ صَيَّادٍ يَوْمَئِذٍ الْحُلُمَ، فَلَمْ يَشْعُرْ حَتَّى ضَرَبَ رَسُولُ اللَّهِ صلى الله عليه وسلم ظَهْرَهُ بِيَدِهِ ثُمَّ قَالَ " أَتَشْهَدُ أَنِّي رَسُولُ اللَّهِ ". فَنَظَرَ إِلَيْهِ فَقَالَ أَشْهَدُ أَنَّكَ رَسُولُ الأُمِّيِّينَ. ثُمَّ قَالَ ابْنُ صَيَّادٍ أَتَشْهَدُ أَنِّي رَسُولُ اللَّهِ فَرَضَّهُ النَّبِيُّ صلى الله عليه وسلم ثُمَّ قَالَ " آمَنْتُ بِاللَّهِ وَرُسُلِهِ ". ثُمَّ قَالَ لاِبْنِ صَيَّادٍ " مَاذَا تَرَى ". قَالَ يَأْتِينِي صَادِقٌ وَكَاذِبٌ. قَالَ رَسُولُ اللَّهِ صلى الله عليه وسلم " خُلِّطَ عَلَيْكَ الأَمْرُ ". قَالَ رَسُولُ اللَّهِ صلى الله عليه وسلم " إِنِّي خَبَأْتُ لَكَ خَبِيئًا ". قَالَ هُوَ الدُّخُ. قَالَ " اخْسَأْ، فَلَنْ تَعْدُوَ قَدْرَكَ ". قَالَ عُمَرُ يَا رَسُولَ اللَّهِ أَتَأْذَنُ لِي فِيهِ أَضْرِبْ عُنُقَهُ. قَالَ رَسُولُ اللَّهِ صلى الله عليه وسلم " إِنْ يَكُنْ هُوَ لاَ تُسَلَّطُ عَلَيْهِ، وَإِنْ لَمْ يَكُنْ هُوَ فَلاَ خَيْرَ لَكَ فِي قَتْلِهِ ". قَالَ سَالِمٌ فَسَمِعْتُ عَبْدَ اللَّهِ بْنَ عُمَرَ، يَقُولُ انْطَلَقَ بَعْدَ ذَلِكَ رَسُولُ اللَّهِ صلى الله عليه وسلم وَأُبَىُّ بْنُ كَعْبٍ الأَنْصَارِيُّ يَؤُمَّانِ النَّخْلَ الَّتِي فِيهَا ابْنُ صَيَّادٍ، حَتَّى إِذَا دَخَلَ رَسُولُ اللَّهِ صلى الله عليه وسلم طَفِقَ رَسُولُ اللَّهِ صلى الله عليه وسلم يَتَّقِي بِجُذُوعِ النَّخْلِ، وَهْوَ يَخْتِلُ أَنْ يَسْمَعَ مِنِ ابْنِ صَيَّادٍ شَيْئًا قَبْلَ أَنْ يَرَاهُ، وَابْنُ صَيَّادٍ مُضْطَجِعٌ عَلَى فِرَاشِهِ فِي قَطِيفَةٍ لَهُ فِيهَا رَمْرَمَةٌ أَوْ زَمْزَمَةٌ، فَرَأَتْ أُمُّ ابْنِ صَيَّادٍ النَّبِيَّ صلى الله عليه وسلم وَهْوَ يَتَّقِي بِجُذُوعِ النَّخْلِ، فَقَالَتْ لاِبْنِ صَيَّادٍ أَىْ صَافِ ـ وَهْوَ اسْمُهُ ـ هَذَا مُحَمَّدٌ. فَتَنَاهَى ابْنُ صَيَّادٍ. قَالَ رَسُولُ اللَّهِ صلى الله عليه وسلم " لَوْ تَرَكَتْهُ بَيَّنَ ". قَالَ سَالِمٌ قَالَ عَبْدُ اللَّهِ قَامَ رَسُولُ اللَّهِ صلى الله عليه وسلم فِي النَّاسِ فَأَثْنَى عَلَى اللَّهِ بِمَا هُوَ أَهْلُهُ، ثُمَّ ذَكَرَ الدَّجَّالَ فَقَالَ " إِنِّي أُنْذِرُكُمُوهُ، وَمَا مِنْ نَبِيٍّ إِلاَّ وَقَدْ أَنْذَرَ قَوْمَهُ، لَقَدْ أَنْذَرَهُ نُوحٌ قَوْمَهُ، وَلَكِنِّي سَأَقُولُ لَكُمْ فِيهِ قَوْلاً لَمْ يَقُلْهُ نَبِيٌّ لِقَوْمِهِ، تَعْلَمُونَ أَنَّهُ أَعْوَرُ، وَأَنَّ اللَّهَ لَيْسَ بِأَعْوَرَ ".
قَالَ أَبُو عَبْدِ اللَّهِ خَسَأْتُ الْكَلْبَ بَعَّدْتُهُ خَاسِئِينَ مُبْعَدِينَ

Narrated Abu Sa`id: The Prophet ﷺ said, "Do not prefer some prophets to others." – Al-Bukhari 6916

حَدَّثَنَا أَبُو نُعَيْمٍ، حَدَّثَنَا سُفْيَانُ، عَنْ عَمْرِو بْنِ يَحْيَى، عَنْ أَبِيهِ، عَنْ أَبِي سَعِيدٍ، عَنِ النَّبِيِّ صلى الله عليه وسلم قَالَ " لاَ تُخَيِّرُوا بَيْنَ الأَنْبِيَاءِ "

Narrated Abu Sa`id Al-Khudri: A Jew whose face had been slapped (by someone), came to the Prophet ﷺ and said, "O Muhammad! A man from your Ansari companions slapped me. " The Prophet ﷺ said, "Call him". They called him and the Prophet ﷺ asked him, "Why did you slap his face?" He said, "O Allah's Messenger ﷺ ! While I was passing by the Jews, I heard him saying, 'By Him Who chose Moses above all the human beings.' I said (protestingly), 'Even above Muhammad?' So I became furious and slapped him." The Prophet ﷺ said, "Do not give me preference to other prophets, for the people will become unconscious on the Day of Resurrection and I will be the first to gain conscious, and behold, I will Find Moses holding one of the pillars of the Throne (of Allah). Then I will not know whether he has become conscious before me or he has been exempted because of his unconsciousness at the mountain (during his worldly life) which he received." – Al-Bukhari 6917

حَدَّثَنَا مُحَمَّدُ بْنُ يُوسُفَ، حَدَّثَنَا سُفْيَانُ، عَنْ عَمْرِو بْنِ يَحْيَى الْمَازِنِيِّ، عَنْ أَبِيهِ، عَنْ أَبِي سَعِيدٍ الْخُدْرِيِّ، قَالَ جَاءَ رَجُلٌ مِنَ
الْيَهُودِ إِلَى النَّبِيِّ صلى الله عليه وسلم قَدْ لُطِمَ وَجْهُهُ فَقَالَ يَا مُحَمَّدُ إِنَّ رَجُلاً مِنْ أَصْحَابِكَ مِنَ الأَنْصَارِ لَطَمَ فِي وَجْهِي.
قَالَ " ادْعُوهُ ". فَدَعَوْهُ. قَالَ " لِمَ لَطَمْتَ وَجْهَهُ ". قَالَ يَا رَسُولَ اللَّهِ إِنِّي مَرَرْتُ بِالْيَهُودِ فَسَمِعْتُهُ يَقُولُ وَالَّذِي اصْطَفَى
مُوسَى عَلَى الْبَشَرِ. قَالَ قُلْتُ وَعَلَى مُحَمَّدٍ صلى الله عليه وسلم قَالَ فَأَخَذَتْنِي غَضْبَةٌ فَلَطَمْتُهُ. قَالَ " لاَ تُخَيِّرُونِي مِنْ بَيْنِ
الأَنْبِيَاءِ فَإِنَّ النَّاسَ يَصْعَقُونَ يَوْمَ الْقِيَامَةِ فَأَكُونُ أَوَّلَ مَنْ يُفِيقُ، فَإِذَا أَنَا بِمُوسَى آخِذٌ بِقَائِمَةٍ مِنْ قَوَائِمِ الْعَرْشِ، فَلاَ أَدْرِي أَفَاقَ
قَبْلِي أَمْ جُزِيَ بِصَعْقَةِ الطُّورِ ".

And those who believe in what was revealed to you, and in what was revealed before you, and are certain of the Hereafter. – Surah Al-Baqarah 2:4

وَٱلَّذِينَ يُؤْمِنُونَ بِمَآ أُنزِلَ إِلَيْكَ وَمَآ أُنزِلَ مِن قَبْلِكَ وَبِٱلْـَٔاخِرَةِ هُمْ يُوقِنُونَ

Who would forsake the religion of Abraham, except he who fools himself? We chose him in this world, and in the Hereafter he will be among the righteous. – Surah Al-Baqarah 2:130

وَمَن يَرْغَبُ عَن مِّلَّةِ إِبْرَٰهِـۧمَ إِلَّا مَن سَفِهَ نَفْسَهُۥ ۚ وَلَقَدِ ٱصْطَفَيْنَـٰهُ فِى ٱلدُّنْيَا ۖ وَإِنَّهُۥ فِى ٱلْـَٔاخِرَةِ لَمِنَ ٱلصَّـٰلِحِينَ

Say, "We believe in Allah, and in what was revealed to us; and in what was revealed to Abraham, and Ishmael, and Isaac, and Jacob, and the Patriarchs; and in what was given to Moses, and Jesus, and the prophets from their Lord. We make no distinction between any of them, and to Him we submit." – Surah Al-Imran 3:84

قُلْ ءَامَنَّا بِٱللَّهِ وَمَآ أُنزِلَ عَلَيْنَا وَمَآ أُنزِلَ عَلَىٰٓ إِبْرَٰهِيمَ وَإِسْمَـٰعِيلَ وَإِسْحَـٰقَ وَيَعْقُوبَ وَٱلْأَسْبَاطِ وَمَآ أُوتِىَ مُوسَىٰ وَعِيسَىٰ
وَٱلنَّبِيُّونَ مِن رَّبِّهِمْ لَا نُفَرِّقُ بَيْنَ أَحَدٍ مِّنْهُمْ وَنَحْنُ لَهُۥ مُسْلِمُونَ

And do not argue with the People of the Scripture except in the best manner possible, except those who do wrong among them. And say, "We believe in what was revealed to us, and in what was revealed to you; and our God and your God is One; and to Him we are submissive." – Surah Al-'Ankabut 29:46

وَلَا تُجَـٰدِلُوٓا۟ أَهْلَ ٱلْكِتَـٰبِ إِلَّا بِٱلَّتِى هِىَ أَحْسَنُ إِلَّا ٱلَّذِينَ ظَلَمُوا۟ مِنْهُمْ ۖ وَقُولُوٓا۟ ءَامَنَّا بِٱلَّذِىٓ أُنزِلَ إِلَيْنَا وَأُنزِلَ إِلَيْكُمْ وَإِلَـٰهُنَا
وَإِلَـٰهُكُمْ وَٰحِدٌ وَنَحْنُ لَهُۥ مُسْلِمُونَ

Narrated Abu Huraira: Allah's Messenger ﷺ said, "We are more liable to be in doubt than Abraham when he said, 'My Lord! Show me how You give life to the dead." . He (i.e. Allah) slid: 'Don't you believe then?' He (i.e. Abraham) said: "Yes, but (I ask) in order to be stronger in Faith." (2.260) And may Allah send His Mercy on Lot! He wished to have a powerful support. If I were to stay in prison for such a long time as Joseph did I would have accepted the offer (of freedom without insisting on having my guiltless less declared). – Al-Bukhari 3372

حَدَّثَنَا أَحْمَدُ بْنُ صَالِحٍ، حَدَّثَنَا ابْنُ وَهْبٍ، قَالَ أَخْبَرَنِي يُونُسُ، عَنِ ابْنِ شِهَابٍ، عَنْ أَبِي سَلَمَةَ بْنِ عَبْدِ الرَّحْمَنِ، وَسَعِيدِ بْنِ
الْمُسَيَّبِ، عَنْ أَبِي هُرَيْرَةَ ـ رضى الله عنه ـ أَنَّ رَسُولَ اللَّهِ صلى الله عليه وسلم قَالَ " نَحْنُ أَحَقُّ مِنْ إِبْرَاهِيمَ إِذْ قَالَ {رَبِّ
أَرِنِي كَيْفَ تُحْيِي الْمَوْتَى قَالَ أَوَلَمْ تُؤْمِنْ قَالَ بَلَى وَلَكِنْ لِيَطْمَئِنَّ قَلْبِي} وَيَرْحَمُ اللَّهُ لُوطًا، لَقَدْ كَانَ يَأْوِي إِلَى رُكْنٍ شَدِيدٍ وَلَوْ
لَبِثْتُ فِي السِّجْنِ طُولَ مَا لَبِثَ يُوسُفُ لأَجَبْتُ الدَّاعِيَ "

Muhammad is the Messenger of Allah. Those with him are stern against the disbelievers, yet compassionate amongst themselves. You see them kneeling, prostrating, seeking blessings from Allah and approval. Their marks are on their faces from the effects of prostration. Such is their description in the Torah, and their description in the Gospel: like a plant that sprouts, becomes strong, grows thick, and rests on its stem, impressing the farmers. Through them He enrages the disbelievers. Allah has promised those among them who believe and do good deeds forgiveness and a great reward. – Surah Al-Fath 48:29

مُّحَمَّدٌ رَّسُولُ ٱللَّهِۚ وَٱلَّذِينَ مَعَهُۥٓ أَشِدَّآءُ عَلَى ٱلۡكُفَّارِ رُحَمَآءُ بَيۡنَهُمۡۖ تَرَىٰهُمۡ رُكَّعٗا سُجَّدٗا يَبۡتَغُونَ فَضۡلٗا مِّنَ ٱللَّهِ وَرِضۡوَٰنٗاۖ سِيمَاهُمۡ فِي وُجُوهِهِم مِّنۡ أَثَرِ ٱلسُّجُودِۚ ذَٰلِكَ مَثَلُهُمۡ فِي ٱلتَّوۡرَىٰةِۚ وَمَثَلُهُمۡ فِي ٱلۡإِنجِيلِ كَزَرۡعٍ أَخۡرَجَ شَطۡـَٔهُۥ فَـَٔازَرَهُۥ فَٱسۡتَغۡلَظَ فَٱسۡتَوَىٰ عَلَىٰ سُوقِهِۦ يُعۡجِبُ ٱلزُّرَّاعَ لِيَغِيظَ بِهِمُ ٱلۡكُفَّارَۗ وَعَدَ ٱللَّهُ ٱلَّذِينَ ءَامَنُواْ وَعَمِلُواْ ٱلصَّٰلِحَٰتِ مِنۡهُم مَّغۡفِرَةٗ وَأَجۡرًا عَظِيمَۢا

Narrated Jabir bin `Abdullah: The Prophet ﷺ said, "My similitude in comparison with the other prophets is that of a man who has built a house completely and excellently except for a place of one brick. When the people enter the house, they admire its beauty and say: 'But for the place of this brick (how splendid the house will be)!" – Al-Bukhari 3534

حَدَّثَنَا مُحَمَّدُ بْنُ سِنَانٍ، حَدَّثَنَا سَلِيمٌ، حَدَّثَنَا سَعِيدُ بْنُ مِينَاءَ، عَنْ جَابِرِ بْنِ عَبْدِ اللَّهِ ـ رضى الله عنهما ـ قَالَ قَالَ النَّبِيُّ صلى الله عليه وسلم " مَثَلِي وَمَثَلُ الأَنْبِيَاءِ كَرَجُلٍ بَنَى دَارًا فَأَكْمَلَهَا وَأَحْسَنَهَا، إِلاَّ مَوْضِعَ لَبِنَةٍ، فَجَعَلَ النَّاسُ يَدْخُلُونَهَا وَيَتَعَجَّبُونَ، وَيَقُولُونَ لَوْلاَ مَوْضِعُ اللَّبِنَةِ ".

Narrated Mujahid: That he asked Ibn `Abbas, "Is there a prostration Surat-al-Sa`d?" (38.24) Ibn `Abbas said, "Yes," and then recited: "We gave...So follow their guidance." (6.85,90) Then he said, "He (David ) is one them (i.e. those prophets)." Mujahid narrated: I asked Ibn `Abbas (regarding the above Verse). He said, "Your Prophet (Muhammad) was one of those who were ordered to follow them." – Al-Bukhari 4632

حَدَّثَنِي إِبْرَاهِيمُ بْنُ مُوسَى، أَخْبَرَنَا هِشَامٌ، أَنَّ ابْنَ جُرَيْجٍ، أَخْبَرَهُمْ قَالَ أَخْبَرَنِي سُلَيْمَانُ الأَحْوَلُ، أَنَّ مُجَاهِدًا، أَخْبَرَهُ أَنَّهُ، سَأَلَ ابْنَ عَبَّاسٍ أَفِي " ص " سَجْدَةٌ فَقَالَ نَعَمْ. ثُمَّ تَلاَ {وَوَهَبْنَا} إِلَى قَوْلِهِ {فَبِهُدَاهُمُ اقْتَدِهْ} ثُمَّ قَالَ هُوَ مِنْهُمْ. زَادَ يَزِيدُ بْنُ هَارُونَ وَمُحَمَّدُ بْنُ عُبَيْدٍ وَسَهْلُ بْنُ يُوسُفَ عَنِ الْعَوَّامِ عَنْ مُجَاهِدٍ قُلْتُ لاِبْنِ عَبَّاسٍ فَقَالَ نَبِيُّكُمْ صلى الله عليه وسلم مِمَّنْ أُمِرَ أَنْ يَقْتَدِيَ بِهِمْ.

The Book of
Actions Before Revelation
الأفعال قبل الوحي

And they swore by Allah with their solemn oaths, that if a warner came to them, they would be more guided than any other people. Yet when a warner came to them, it only increased them in aversion. Priding themselves on earth, and scheming evil. But evil scheming overwhelms none but its authors. Do they expect anything but the precedent of the ancients? You will not find any change in Allah's practice, and you will not find any substitute to Allah's practice. – Surah Fatir 35:42&43
وَأَقْسَمُواْ بِٱللَّهِ جَهْدَ أَيْمَـٰنِهِمْ لَئِن جَآءَهُمْ نَذِيرٌ لَّيَكُونُنَّ أَهْدَىٰ مِنْ إِحْدَى ٱلْأُمَمِۖ فَلَمَّا جَآءَهُمْ نَذِيرٌ مَّا زَادَهُمْ إِلَّا نُفُورًا ٱسْتِكْبَارًا فِى ٱلْأَرْضِ وَمَكْرَ ٱلسَّيِّئِۚ وَلَا يَحِيقُ ٱلْمَكْرُ ٱلسَّيِّئُ إِلَّا بِأَهْلِهِۦۚ فَهَلْ يَنظُرُونَ إِلَّا سُنَّتَ ٱلْأَوَّلِينَۚ فَلَن تَجِدَ لِسُنَّتِ ٱللَّهِ تَبْدِيلًاۖ وَلَن تَجِدَ لِسُنَّتِ ٱللَّهِ تَحْوِيلًا

This nation of yours is one nation, and I am your Lord, so fear Me. But they tore themselves into sects; each party happy with what they have. So leave them in their bewilderment until a time. – Surah Al-Mu'Minun 23:52-54
وَإِنَّ هَـٰذِهِۦٓ أُمَّتُكُمْ أُمَّةً وَٰحِدَةً وَأَنَا۠ رَبُّكُمْ فَٱتَّقُونِ فَتَقَطَّعُوٓاْ أَمْرَهُم بَيْنَهُمْ زُبُرًاۖ كُلُّ حِزْبٍ بِمَا لَدَيْهِمْ فَرِحُونَ فَذَرْهُمْ فِى غَمْرَتِهِمْ حَتَّىٰ حِينٍ

Narrated `Aisha: Allah's Messenger ﷺ said, " I know whether you are angry or pleased." I said, "How do you know that, Allah's Messenger ﷺ " ? He said, "When you are pleased, you say, "Yes, by the Lord of Muhammad,' but when you are angry, you say, 'No, by the Lord of Abraham!' " I said, "Yes, I do not leave, except your name." – Al-Bukhari 6078
حَدَّثَنَا مُحَمَّدٌ، أَخْبَرَنَا عَبْدَةُ، عَنْ هِشَامِ بْنِ عُرْوَةَ، عَنْ أَبِيهِ، عَنْ عَائِشَةَ ـ رضى الله عنها ـ قَالَتْ قَالَ رَسُولُ اللَّهِ صلى الله عليه وسلم " إِنِّي لأَعْرِفُ غَضَبَكِ وَرِضَاكِ ". قَالَتْ قُلْتُ وَكَيْفَ تَعْرِفُ ذَاكَ يَا رَسُولَ اللَّهِ قَالَ " إِنَّكِ إِذَا كُنْتِ رَاضِيَةً قُلْتِ بَلَى وَرَبِّ مُحَمَّدٍ. وَإِذَا كُنْتِ سَاخِطَةً قُلْتِ لاَ وَرَبِّ إِبْرَاهِيمَ ". قَالَتْ قُلْتُ أَجَلْ لَسْتُ أُهَاجِرُ إِلاَّ اسْمَكَ

He prescribed for you the same religion He enjoined upon Noah, and what We inspired to you, and what We enjoined upon Abraham, and Moses, and Jesus: "You shall uphold the religion, and be not divided therein." As for the idolaters, what you call them to is outrageous to them. Allah chooses to Himself whom He wills, and He guides to Himself whoever repents. – Surah Ash-Shura 42:13
شَرَعَ لَكُم مِّنَ ٱلدِّينِ مَا وَصَّىٰ بِهِۦ نُوحًا وَٱلَّذِىٓ أَوْحَيْنَآ إِلَيْكَ وَمَا وَصَّيْنَا بِهِۦٓ إِبْرَٰهِيمَ وَمُوسَىٰ وَعِيسَىٰٓۖ أَنْ أَقِيمُواْ ٱلدِّينَ وَلَا تَتَفَرَّقُواْ فِيهِۚ كَبُرَ عَلَى ٱلْمُشْرِكِينَ مَا تَدْعُوهُمْ إِلَيْهِۚ ٱللَّهُ يَجْتَبِىٓ إِلَيْهِ مَن يَشَآءُ وَيَهْدِىٓ إِلَيْهِ مَن يُنِيبُ

Narrated Jabir bin `Abdullah: The Prophet ﷺ said, "My similitude in comparison with the other prophets is that of a man who has built a house completely and excellently except for a place of one brick. When the people enter the house, they admire its beauty and say: 'But for the place of this brick (how splendid the house will be)!" – Al-Bukhari 3534
حَدَّثَنَا مُحَمَّدُ بْنُ سِنَانٍ، حَدَّثَنَا سَلِيمٌ، حَدَّثَنَا سَعِيدُ بْنُ مِينَاءَ، عَنْ جَابِرِ بْنِ عَبْدِ اللَّهِ ـ رضى الله عنهما ـ قَالَ قَالَ النَّبِيُّ صلى الله عليه وسلم " مَثَلِي وَمَثَلُ الأَنْبِيَاءِ كَرَجُلٍ بَنَى دَارًا فَأَكْمَلَهَا وَأَحْسَنَهَا، إِلاَّ مَوْضِعَ لَبِنَةٍ، فَجَعَلَ النَّاسُ يَدْخُلُونَهَا وَيَتَعَجَّبُونَ، وَيَقُولُونَ لَوْلاَ مَوْضِعُ اللَّبِنَةِ "

Narrated Mujahid: I asked Ibn `Abbas, "Should we perform a prostration on reciting Surat-Sa`d?" He recited (the Sura) including: 'And among his progeny, David, Solomon..(up to)...so

follow their guidance (6.84-91) And then he said, “Your Prophet is amongst those people who have been ordered to follow them (i.e. the preceding apostles). – Al-Bukhari 3421
حَدَّثَنَا مُحَمَّدٌ، حَدَّثَنَا سَهْلُ بْنُ يُوسُفَ، قَالَ سَمِعْتُ الْعَوَّامَ، عَنْ مُجَاهِدٍ، قَالَ قُلْتُ لاِبْنِ عَبَّاسٍ أَسْجُدُ فِي {ص} فَقَرَأَ {وَمِنْ ذُرِّيَّتِهِ دَاوُدَ وَسُلَيْمَانَ} حَتَّى أَتَى {فَبِهُدَاهُمُ اقْتَدِهْ} فَقَالَ نَبِيُّكُمْ صلى الله عليه وسلم مِمَّنْ أُمِرَ أَنْ يَقْتَدِيَ بِهِمْ.

Narrated `Aisha: The Prophet ﷺ returned to Khadija while his heart was beating rapidly. She took him to Waraqa bin Naufal who was a Christian convert and used to read the Gospels in Arabic Waraqa asked (the Prophet), “What do you see?” When he told him, Waraqa said, “That is the same angel whom Allah sent to the Prophet) Moses. Should I live till you receive the Divine Message, I will support you strongly.” – Al-Bukhari 3392
حَدَّثَنَا عَبْدُ اللَّهِ بْنُ يُوسُفَ، حَدَّثَنَا اللَّيْثُ، قَالَ حَدَّثَنِي عُقَيْلٌ، عَنِ ابْنِ شِهَابٍ، سَمِعْتُ عُرْوَةَ، قَالَ قَالَتْ عَائِشَةُ ـ رضى الله عنها فَرَجَعَ النَّبِيُّ صلى الله عليه وسلم إِلَى خَدِيجَةَ يَرْجُفُ فُؤَادُهُ، فَانْطَلَقَتْ بِهِ إِلَى وَرَقَةَ بْنِ نَوْفَلٍ، وَكَانَ رَجُلاً تَنَصَّرَ يَقْرَأُ الإِنْجِيلَ بِالْعَرَبِيَّةِ. فَقَالَ وَرَقَةُ مَاذَا تَرَى فَأَخْبَرَهُ. فَقَالَ وَرَقَةُ هَذَا النَّامُوسُ الَّذِي أَنْزَلَ اللَّهُ عَلَى مُوسَى، وَإِنْ أَدْرَكَنِي يَوْمُكَ أَنْصُرْكَ نَصْرًا مُؤَزَّرًا. النَّامُوسُ صَاحِبُ السِّرِّ الَّذِي يُطْلِعُهُ بِمَا يَسْتُرُهُ عَنْ غَيْرِهِ

Narrated `Abdullah bin `Amr: The Prophet ﷺ said, “Convey (my teachings) to the people even if it were a single sentence, and tell others the stories of Bani Israel, for it is not sinful to do so. And whoever tells a lie on me intentionally, will surely take his place in the (Hell) Fire.” – Al-Bukhari 3461
حَدَّثَنَا أَبُو عَاصِمٍ الضَّحَّاكُ بْنُ مَخْلَدٍ، أَخْبَرَنَا الأَوْزَاعِيُّ، حَدَّثَنَا حَسَّانُ بْنُ عَطِيَّةَ، عَنْ أَبِي كَبْشَةَ، عَنْ عَبْدِ اللَّهِ بْنِ عَمْرٍو، أَنَّ النَّبِيَّ صلى الله عليه وسلم قَالَ " بَلِّغُوا عَنِّي وَلَوْ آيَةً، وَحَدِّثُوا عَنْ بَنِي إِسْرَائِيلَ وَلاَ حَرَجَ، وَمَنْ كَذَبَ عَلَىَّ مُتَعَمِّدًا فَلْيَتَبَوَّأْ مَقْعَدَهُ مِنَ النَّارِ ".

Narrated Ibn `Abbas: Allah’s Messenger ﷺ used to let his hair hang down while the infidels used to part their hair. The people of the Scriptures were used to letting their hair hang down and Allah’s Messenger ﷺ liked to follow the people of the Scriptures in the matters about which he was not instructed otherwise. Then Allah’s Messenger ﷺ parted his hair. – Al-Bukhari 3558
حَدَّثَنَا يَحْيَى بْنُ بُكَيْرٍ، حَدَّثَنَا اللَّيْثُ، عَنْ يُونُسَ، عَنِ ابْنِ شِهَابٍ، قَالَ أَخْبَرَنِي عُبَيْدُ اللَّهِ بْنُ عَبْدِ اللَّهِ، عَنِ ابْنِ عَبَّاسٍ ـ رضى الله عنهما أَنَّ رَسُولَ اللَّهِ صلى الله عليه وسلم كَانَ يَسْدِلُ شَعَرَهُ، وَكَانَ الْمُشْرِكُونَ يَفْرُقُونَ رُءُوسَهُمْ فَكَانَ أَهْلُ الْكِتَابِ يَسْدِلُونَ رُءُوسَهُمْ، وَكَانَ رَسُولُ اللَّهِ صلى الله عليه وسلم يُحِبُّ مُوَافَقَةَ أَهْلِ الْكِتَابِ فِيمَا لَمْ يُؤْمَرْ فِيهِ بِشَىْءٍ، ثُمَّ فَرَقَ رَسُولُ اللَّهِ صلى الله عليه وسلم رَأْسَهُ

Narrated Abu As-Sawar Al-Adawi: `Imran bin Husain said: The Prophet ﷺ said, “Haya’ (pious shyness from committing religeous indiscretions) does not bring anything except good.” Thereupon Bashir bin Ka`b said, ‘It is written in the wisdom paper: Haya’ leads to solemnity; Haya’ leads to tranquility (peace of mind).” `Imran said to him, “I am narrating to you the saying of Allah’s Messenger ﷺ and you are speaking about your pap”r”(wisdom book)?” – Al-Bukhari 6117
حَدَّثَنَا آدَمُ، حَدَّثَنَا شُعْبَةُ، عَنْ قَتَادَةَ، عَنْ أَبِي السَّوَّارِ الْعَدَوِيِّ، قَالَ سَمِعْتُ عِمْرَانَ بْنَ حُصَيْنٍ، قَالَ قَالَ النَّبِيُّ صلى الله عليه وسلم " الْحَيَاءُ لاَ يَأْتِي إِلاَّ بِخَيْرٍ ". فَقَالَ بُشَيْرُ بْنُ كَعْبٍ مَكْتُوبٌ فِي الْحِكْمَةِ إِنَّ مِنَ الْحَيَاءِ وَقَارًا، وَإِنَّ مِنَ الْحَيَاءِ سَكِينَةً. فَقَالَ لَهُ عِمْرَانُ أُحَدِّثُكَ عَنْ رَسُولِ اللَّهِ صلى الله عليه وسلم وَتُحَدِّثُنِي عَنْ صَحِيفَتِكَ.

Narrated Abu Mas`ud: The Prophet ﷺ said, ‘One of the sayings of the early Prophets which the people have got is: If you don’t feel ashamed (from Haya’: pious shyness from committing religeous indiscretions) do whatever you like.” (See Hadith No 690, 691, Vol 4) – Al-Bukhari 6120

حَدَّثَنَا أَحْمَدُ بْنُ يُونُسَ، حَدَّثَنَا زُهَيْرٌ، حَدَّثَنَا مَنْصُورٌ، عَنْ رِبْعِيِّ بْنِ حِرَاشٍ، حَدَّثَنَا أَبُو مَسْعُودٍ، قَالَ قَالَ النَّبِيُّ صلى الله عليه وسلم " إِنَّ مِمَّا أَدْرَكَ النَّاسُ مِنْ كَلاَمِ النُّبُوَّةِ الأُولَى إِذَا لَمْ تَسْتَحِي فَاصْنَعْ مَا شِئْتَ ".

Narrated `Aisha: Two old ladies from among the Jewish ladies entered upon me and said' "The dead are punished in their graves," but I thought they were telling a lie and did not believe them in the beginning. When they went away and the Prophet ﷺ entered upon me, I said, "O Allah's Messenger ﷺ ! Two old ladies.." and told him the whole story. He said, "They told the truth; the dead are really punished, to the extent that all the animals hear (the sound resulting from) their punishment." Since then I always saw him seeking refuge with Allah from the punishment of the grave in his prayers. – Al-Bukhari 6366

حَدَّثَنَا عُثْمَانُ بْنُ أَبِي شَيْبَةَ، حَدَّثَنَا جَرِيرٌ، عَنْ مَنْصُورٍ، عَنْ أَبِي وَائِلٍ، عَنْ مَسْرُوقٍ، عَنْ عَائِشَةَ، قَالَتْ دَخَلَتْ عَلَىَّ عَجُوزَانِ مِنْ عُجُزِ يَهُودِ الْمَدِينَةِ فَقَالَتَا لِي إِنَّ أَهْلَ الْقُبُورِ يُعَذَّبُونَ فِي قُبُورِهِمْ، فَكَذَّبْتُهُمَا، وَلَمْ أُنْعِمْ أَنْ أُصَدِّقَهُمَا، فَخَرَجَتَا وَدَخَلَ عَلَىَّ النَّبِيُّ صلى الله عليه وسلم فَقُلْتُ لَهُ يَا رَسُولَ اللَّهِ إِنَّ عَجُوزَيْنِ وَذَكَرْتُ لَهُ، فَقَالَ " صَدَقَتَا، إِنَّهُمْ يُعَذَّبُونَ عَذَابًا تَسْمَعُهُ الْبَهَائِمُ كُلُّهَا ". فَمَا رَأَيْتُهُ بَعْدُ فِي صَلاَةٍ إِلاَّ تَعَوَّذَ مِنْ عَذَابِ الْقَبْرِ

And strive for Allah, with the striving due to Him. He has chosen you, and has not burdened you in religion—the faith of your father Abraham. It is he who named you Muslims before, and in this. So that the Messenger may be a witness over you, and you may be witnesses over the people. So pray regularly, and give regular charity, and cleave to Allah. He is your Protector. What an excellent Protector, and what an excellent Helper. – Surah Al-Hajj 22:78

وَجَٰهِدُوا۟ فِى ٱللَّهِ حَقَّ جِهَادِهِۦ ۚ هُوَ ٱجْتَبَىٰكُمْ وَمَا جَعَلَ عَلَيْكُمْ فِى ٱلدِّينِ مِنْ حَرَجٍ ۚ مِّلَّةَ أَبِيكُمْ إِبْرَٰهِيمَ ۚ هُوَ سَمَّىٰكُمُ ٱلْمُسْلِمِينَ مِن قَبْلُ وَفِى هَٰذَا لِيَكُونَ ٱلرَّسُولُ شَهِيدًا عَلَيْكُمْ وَتَكُونُوا۟ شُهَدَآءَ عَلَى ٱلنَّاسِ ۚ فَأَقِيمُوا۟ ٱلصَّلَوٰةَ وَءَاتُوا۟ ٱلزَّكَوٰةَ وَٱعْتَصِمُوا۟ بِٱللَّهِ هُوَ مَوْلَىٰكُمْ ۖ فَنِعْمَ ٱلْمَوْلَىٰ وَنِعْمَ ٱلنَّصِيرُ

Say, "We believe in Allah, and in what was revealed to us; and in what was revealed to Abraham, and Ishmael, and Isaac, and Jacob, and the Patriarchs; and in what was given to Moses, and Jesus, and the prophets from their Lord. We make no distinction between any of them, and to Him we submit." Whoever seeks other than Islam as a religion, it will not be accepted from him, and in the Hereafter he will be among the losers. – Surah Al-Imran 3:84&85

قُلْ ءَامَنَّا بِٱللَّهِ وَمَآ أُنزِلَ عَلَيْنَا وَمَآ أُنزِلَ عَلَىٰٓ إِبْرَٰهِيمَ وَإِسْمَٰعِيلَ وَإِسْحَٰقَ وَيَعْقُوبَ وَٱلْأَسْبَاطِ وَمَآ أُوتِىَ مُوسَىٰ وَعِيسَىٰ وَٱلنَّبِيُّونَ مِن رَّبِّهِمْ لَا نُفَرِّقُ بَيْنَ أَحَدٍ مِّنْهُمْ وَنَحْنُ لَهُۥ مُسْلِمُونَ وَمَن يَبْتَغِ غَيْرَ ٱلْإِسْلَٰمِ دِينًا فَلَن يُقْبَلَ مِنْهُ وَهُوَ فِى ٱلْءَاخِرَةِ مِنَ ٱلْخَٰسِرِينَ

Muhammad is the Messenger of Allah. Those with him are stern against the disbelievers, yet compassionate amongst themselves. You see them kneeling, prostrating, seeking blessings from Allah and approval. Their marks are on their faces from the effects of prostration. Such is their description in the Torah, and their description in the Gospel: like a plant that sprouts, becomes strong, grows thick, and rests on its stem, impressing the farmers. Through them He enrages the disbelievers. Allah has promised those among them who believe and do good deeds forgiveness and a great reward. .– Surah Al-Fath 48:29

مُّحَمَّدٌ رَّسُولُ ٱللَّهِ ۚ وَٱلَّذِينَ مَعَهُۥٓ أَشِدَّآءُ عَلَى ٱلْكُفَّارِ رُحَمَآءُ بَيْنَهُمْ ۖ تَرَىٰهُمْ رُكَّعًا سُجَّدًا يَبْتَغُونَ فَضْلًا مِّنَ ٱللَّهِ وَرِضْوَٰنًا ۖ سِيمَاهُمْ فِى وُجُوهِهِم مِّنْ أَثَرِ ٱلسُّجُودِ ۚ ذَٰلِكَ مَثَلُهُمْ فِى ٱلتَّوْرَىٰةِ ۚ وَمَثَلُهُمْ فِى ٱلْإِنجِيلِ كَزَرْعٍ أَخْرَجَ شَطْـَٔهُۥ فَـَٔازَرَهُۥ فَٱسْتَغْلَظَ فَٱسْتَوَىٰ عَلَىٰ سُوقِهِۦ يُعْجِبُ ٱلزُّرَّاعَ لِيَغِيظَ بِهِمُ ٱلْكُفَّارَ ۗ وَعَدَ ٱللَّهُ ٱلَّذِينَ ءَامَنُوا۟ وَعَمِلُوا۟ ٱلصَّٰلِحَٰتِ مِنْهُم مَّغْفِرَةً وَأَجْرًا عَظِيمًۢا

Then the angels called out to him, as he stood praying in the sanctuary: "Allah gives you good news of John; confirming a Word from Allah, and honorable, and moral, and a prophet; one of the upright." – Surah Al-Imran 3:39

فَنَادَتْهُ ٱلْمَلَٰٓئِكَةُ وَهُوَ قَآئِمٌ يُصَلِّى فِى ٱلْمِحْرَابِ أَنَّ ٱللَّهَ يُبَشِّرُكَ بِيَحْيَىٰ مُصَدِّقًۢا بِكَلِمَةٍ مِّنَ ٱللَّهِ وَسَيِّدًا وَحَصُورًا وَنَبِيًّا مِّنَ ٱلصَّٰلِحِينَ

The Book of
But never you will find in (the) way (of) Allah any change
فَلَن تَجِدَ لِسُنَّتِ ٱللَّهِ تَبْدِيلًا

He has ordained for you ˹believers˺ the Way which He decreed for Noah, and what We have revealed to you ˹O Prophet˺ and what We decreed for Abraham, Moses, and Jesus, ˹commanding:˺ "Uphold the faith, and make no divisions in it." What you call the polytheists to is unbearable for them. Allah chooses for Himself whoever He wills, and guides to Himself whoever turns ˹to Him˺. -Surah Ash-Shura 42:13

شَرَعَ لَكُم مِّنَ ٱلدِّينِ مَا وَصَّىٰ بِهِۦ نُوحًا وَٱلَّذِىٓ أَوْحَيْنَآ إِلَيْكَ وَمَا وَصَّيْنَا بِهِۦٓ إِبْرَٰهِيمَ وَمُوسَىٰ وَعِيسَىٰٓ ۖ أَنْ أَقِيمُوا۟ ٱلدِّينَ وَلَا تَتَفَرَّقُوا۟ فِيهِ ۚ كَبُرَ عَلَى ٱلْمُشْرِكِينَ مَا تَدْعُوهُمْ إِلَيْهِ ۚ ٱللَّهُ يَجْتَبِىٓ إِلَيْهِ مَن يَشَآءُ وَيَهْدِىٓ إِلَيْهِ مَن يُنِيبُ

Narrated Hisham Ibn `Urwa from his father who said: While I was a youngster, I asked `Aisha the wife of the Prophet. "What about the meaning of the Statement of Allah; "Verily! (the mountains) As-Safa and Al Marwa, are among the symbols of Allah. So, it is not harmful if those who perform Hajj or `Umra of the House (Ka`ba at Mecca) to perform the going (Tawaf) between them? (2.158) I understand (from that) that there is no harm if somebody does not perform the Tawaf between them." `Aisha replied, "No, for if it were as you are saying, then the recitation would have been like this: 'It is not harmful not to perform Tawaf between them.' This verse was revealed in connection with the Ansar who used to assume the Ihram for the idol Manat which was put beside a place called Qudaid and those people thought it not right to perform the Tawaf of As- Safa and Al-Marwa. When Islam came, they asked Allah's Messenger ﷺ about that, and Allah revealed:-- "Verily! (the mountains) As-Safa and Al-Marwa Are among the symbols of Allah. So, it is not harmful of those who perform Hajj or `Umra of the House (Ka`ba at Mecca) to perform the going (Tawaf) between them." (2.158) Sufyan and Abu Muawiya added from Hisham (from `Aisha): "The Hajj or `Umra of the person who does not perform the going (Tawaf) between As-Safa and Al-Marwa is incomplete in Allah's sight. – Al-Bukhari 1790

حَدَّثَنَا عَبْدُ اللَّهِ بْنُ يُوسُفَ، أَخْبَرَنَا مَالِكٌ، عَنْ هِشَامِ بْنِ عُرْوَةَ، عَنْ أَبِيهِ، أَنَّهُ قَالَ قُلْتُ لِعَائِشَةَ ـ رضى الله عنها ـ زَوْجِ النَّبِيِّ صلى الله عليه وسلم وَأَنَا يَوْمَئِذٍ حَدِيثُ السِّنِّ أَرَأَيْتِ قَوْلَ اللَّهِ تَبَارَكَ وَتَعَالَى {إِنَّ الصَّفَا وَالْمَرْوَةَ مِنْ شَعَائِرِ اللَّهِ فَمَنْ حَجَّ الْبَيْتَ أَوِ اعْتَمَرَ فَلاَ جُنَاحَ عَلَيْهِ أَنْ يَطَّوَّفَ بِهِمَا} فَلاَ أُرَى عَلَى أَحَدٍ شَيْئًا أَنْ لاَ يَطَّوَّفَ بِهِمَا. فَقَالَتْ عَائِشَةُ كَلاَّ، لَوْ كَانَتْ كَمَا تَقُولُ كَانَتْ فَلاَ جُنَاحَ عَلَيْهِ أَنْ لاَ يَطَّوَّفَ بِهِمَا. إِنَّمَا أُنْزِلَتْ هَذِهِ الآيَةُ فِي الأَنْصَارِ كَانُوا يُهِلُّونَ لِمَنَاةَ، وَكَانَتْ مَنَاةُ حَذْوَ قُدَيْدٍ، وَكَانُوا يَتَحَرَّجُونَ أَنْ يَطُوفُوا بَيْنَ الصَّفَا وَالْمَرْوَةِ، فَلَمَّا جَاءَ الإِسْلاَمُ سَأَلُوا رَسُولَ اللَّهِ صلى الله عليه وسلم عَنْ ذَلِكَ، فَأَنْزَلَ اللَّهُ تَعَالَى {إِنَّ الصَّفَا وَالْمَرْوَةَ مِنْ شَعَائِرِ اللَّهِ فَمَنْ حَجَّ الْبَيْتَ أَوِ اعْتَمَرَ فَلاَ جُنَاحَ عَلَيْهِ أَنْ يَطَّوَّفَ بِهِمَا}. زَادَ سُفْيَانُ وَأَبُو مُعَاوِيَةَ عَنْ هِشَامٍ مَا أَتَمَّ اللَّهُ حَجَّ امْرِئٍ وَلاَ عُمْرَتَهُ لَمْ يَطُفْ بَيْنَ الصَّفَا وَالْمَرْوَةِ.

Narrated Ibn `Abbas: When the Prophet ﷺ arrived at Medina he found that the Jews observed fast on the day of 'Ashura'. They were asked the reason for the fast. They replied, "This is the day when Allah caused Moses and the children of Israel to have victory over Pharaoh, so we fast on this day as a sign of glorifying it." Allah's Messenger ﷺ said, "We are closer to Moses than you." Then he ordered that fasting on this day should be observed. – Al-Bukhari 3943

حَدَّثَنَا زِيَادُ بْنُ أَيُّوبَ، حَدَّثَنَا هُشَيْمٌ، حَدَّثَنَا أَبُو بِشْرٍ، عَنْ سَعِيدِ بْنِ جُبَيْرٍ، عَنِ ابْنِ عَبَّاسٍ ـ رضى الله عنهما ـ قَالَ لَمَّا قَدِمَ النَّبِيُّ صلى الله عليه وسلم الْمَدِينَةَ وَجَدَ الْيَهُودَ يَصُومُونَ عَاشُورَاءَ، فَسُئِلُوا عَنْ ذَلِكَ، فَقَالُوا هَذَا الْيَوْمُ الَّذِي أَظْفَرَ اللَّهُ فِيهِ مُوسَى وَبَنِي إِسْرَائِيلَ عَلَى فِرْعَوْنَ، وَنَحْنُ نَصُومُهُ تَعْظِيمًا لَهُ، فَقَالَ رَسُولُ اللَّهِ صلى الله عليه وسلم " نَحْنُ أَوْلَى بِمُوسَى مِنْكُمْ ". ثُمَّ أَمَرَ بِصَوْمِهِ

Narrated Abu Raja Al-Utaridi: We used to worship stones, and when we found a better stone than the first one, we would throw the first one and take the latter, but if we could not get a stone then we would collect some earth (i.e. soil) and then bring a sheep and milk that sheep over it, and perform the Tawaf around it. When the month of Rajab came, we used (to stop the military actions), calling this month the iron remover, for we used to remove and throw away the iron parts of every spear and arrow in the month of Rajab. Abu Raja' added: When the Prophetﷺ sent with (Allah's) Message, I was a boy working as a shepherd of my family camels. When we heard the news about the appearance of the Prophet, we ran to the fire, i.e. to Musailima al-Kadhdhab. – Al-Bukhari 4376, 4377

حَدَّثَنَا الصَّلْتُ بْنُ مُحَمَّدٍ، قَالَ سَمِعْتُ مَهْدِيَّ بْنَ مَيْمُونٍ، قَالَ سَمِعْتُ أَبَا رَجَاءٍ الْعُطَارِدِيَّ، يَقُولُ كُنَّا نَعْبُدُ الْحَجَرَ، فَإِذَا وَجَدْنَا حَجَرًا هُوَ أَخْيَرُ مِنْهُ أَلْقَيْنَاهُ وَأَخَذْنَا الآخَرَ، فَإِذَا لَمْ نَجِدْ حَجَرًا جَمَعْنَا جُثْوَةً مِنْ تُرَابٍ، ثُمَّ جِئْنَا بِالشَّاةِ فَحَلَبْنَاهُ عَلَيْهِ، ثُمَّ طُفْنَا بِهِ، فَإِذَا دَخَلَ شَهْرُ رَجَبٍ قُلْنَا مُنَصِّلُ الأَسِنَّةِ. فَلاَ نَدَعُ رُمْحًا فِيهِ حَدِيدَةٌ وَلاَ سَهْمًا فِيهِ حَدِيدَةٌ إِلاَّ نَزَعْنَاهُ وَأَلْقَيْنَاهُ شَهْرَ رَجَبٍ. وَسَمِعْتُ أَبَا رَجَاءٍ، يَقُولُ كُنْتُ يَوْمَ بُعِثَ النَّبِيُّ صلى الله عليه وسلم غُلاَمًا أَرْعَى الإِبِلَ عَلَى أَهْلِي، فَلَمَّا سَمِعْنَا بِخُرُوجِهِ فَرَرْنَا إِلَى النَّارِ إِلَى مُسَيْلِمَةَ الْكَذَّابِ.

Narrated `Abdullah: When the Prophetﷺ entered Mecca on the day of the Conquest, there were 360 idols around the Ka`ba. The Prophetﷺ started striking them with a stick he had in his hand and was saying, "Truth has come and Falsehood will neither start nor will it reappear. – Al-Bukhari 4287

حَدَّثَنَا صَدَقَةُ بْنُ الْفَضْلِ، أَخْبَرَنَا ابْنُ عُيَيْنَةَ، عَنِ ابْنِ أَبِي نَجِيحٍ، عَنْ مُجَاهِدٍ، عَنْ أَبِي مَعْمَرٍ، عَنْ عَبْدِ اللَّهِ ـ رضى الله عنه ـ قَالَ دَخَلَ النَّبِيُّ صلى الله عليه وسلم مَكَّةَ يَوْمَ الْفَتْحِ وَحَوْلَ الْبَيْتِ سِتُّونَ وَثَلاَثُمِائَةِ نُصُبٍ، فَجَعَلَ يَطْعُنُهَا بِعُودٍ فِي يَدِهِ وَيَقُولُ " جَاءَ الْحَقُّ وَزَهَقَ الْبَاطِلُ، جَاءَ الْحَقُّ، وَمَا يُبْدِئُ الْبَاطِلُ وَمَا يُعِيدُ "

Then the angels called out to him, as he stood praying in the sanctuary: "Allah gives you good news of John; confirming a Word from Allah, and honorable, and moral, and a prophet; one of the upright." – Surah Al-Imran 3:39

فَنَادَتْهُ ٱلْمَلَـٰٓئِكَةُ وَهُوَ قَآئِمٌ يُصَلِّى فِى ٱلْمِحْرَابِ أَنَّ ٱللَّهَ يُبَشِّرُكَ بِيَحْيَىٰ مُصَدِّقًۢا بِكَلِمَةٍ مِّنَ ٱللَّهِ وَسَيِّدًا وَحَصُورًا وَنَبِيًّا مِّنَ ٱلصَّـٰلِحِينَ

And has made me blessed wherever I may be; and has enjoined on me prayer and charity, so long as I live. – Surah Mariyam 19:31

وَجَعَلَنِى مُبَارَكًا أَيْنَ مَا كُنتُ وَأَوْصَـٰنِى بِٱلصَّلَوٰةِ وَٱلزَّكَوٰةِ مَا دُمْتُ حَيًّا

Narrated Al-Awwam: I asked Mujahid regarding the prostration in Surat Sa`d. He said, "I asked Ibn `Abbas, 'What evidence makes you prostrate?' He said, "Don't you recite:--'And among his progeny, David and Solomon..(6.84). Those are they whom Allah had guided. So follow their guidance.' (6.90) So David was the one of those prophets whom Prophet (Muhammad) was ordered to follow. David prostrated, so Allah's Messengerﷺ (Muhammad) performed this prostration too.'. – Sahih Al-Bukhari 4807

حَدَّثَنِي مُحَمَّدُ بْنُ عَبْدِ اللَّهِ، حَدَّثَنَا مُحَمَّدُ بْنُ عُبَيْدٍ الطَّنَافِسِيُّ، عَنِ الْعَوَّامِ، قَالَ سَأَلْتُ مُجَاهِدًا عَنْ سَجْدَةٍ، ص فَقَالَ سَأَلْتُ ابْنَ عَبَّاسٍ مِنْ أَيْنَ سَجَدْتَ فَقَالَ أَوَمَا تَقْرَأُ {وَمِنْ ذُرِّيَّتِهِ دَاوُدَ وَسُلَيْمَانَ} {أُولَئِكَ الَّذِينَ هَدَى اللَّهُ فَبِهُدَاهُمُ اقْتَدِهْ} فَكَانَ دَاوُدُ مِمَّنْ أُمِرَ نَبِيُّكُمْ صلى الله عليه وسلم أَنْ يَقْتَدِيَ بِهِ، فَسَجَدَهَا رَسُولُ اللَّهِ صلى الله عليه وسلم. {عُجَابٌ} عَجِيبٌ. الْقِطُّ الصَّحِيفَةُ هُوَ هَا هُنَا صَحِيفَةُ الْحَسَنَاتِ. وَقَالَ مُجَاهِدٌ {فِي عِزَّةٍ} مُعَازِّينَ. {الْمِلَّةِ الآخِرَةِ} مِلَّةُ قُرَيْشٍ. الاِخْتِلاَقُ الْكَذِبُ. الأَسْبَابُ طُرُقُ السَّمَاءِ فِي أَبْوَابِهَا {جُنْدٌ مَا هُنَالِكَ مَهْزُومٌ} يَعْنِي قُرَيْشًا {أُولَئِكَ الأَحْزَابُ} الْقُرُونُ الْمَاضِيَةُ. {فَوَاقٍ} رُجُوعٍ. {قِطَّنَا} عَذَابَنَا {اتَّخَذْنَاهُمْ سُخْرِيًّا} أَحَطْنَا بِهِمْ أَتْرَابٌ أَمْثَالٌ. وَقَالَ ابْنُ عَبَّاسٍ الأَيْدُ الْقُوَّةُ فِي الْعِبَادَةِ الأَبْصَارُ الْبَصَرُ فِي أَمْرِ اللَّهِ، {حُبَّ الْخَيْرِ عَنْ ذِكْرِ رَبِّي} مِنْ ذِكْرٍ. {طَفِقَ مَسْحًا} يَمْسَحُ أَعْرَافَ الْخَيْلِ وَعَرَاقِيبَهَا. {الأَصْفَادِ} الْوَثَاقِ.

This is in the former scriptures .The Scriptures of Abraham and Moses – Surah A'la 87:18&19

إِنَّ هَـٰذَا لَفِى ٱلصُّحُفِ ٱلْأُولَىٰ صُحُفِ إِبْرَٰهِيمَ وَمُوسَىٰ.

The Book of
they have abandoned a good part of the Message that was sent to them
فَنَسُواْ حَظًّا مِّمَّا ذُكِّرُواْ

Narrated Zaid bin Wahab: I passed by a place called Ar-Rabadha and by chance I met Abu Dhar and asked him, "What has brought you to this place?" He said, "I was in Sham and differed with Muawiya on the meaning of (the following verses of the Qur'an): 'They who hoard up gold and silver and spend them not in the way of Allah.' (9.34). Muawiya said, 'This verse is revealed regarding the people of the scriptures." I said, It was revealed regarding us and also the people of the scriptures." So we had a quarrel and Mu'awiya sent a complaint against me to `Uthman. `Uthman wrote to me to come to Medina, and I came to Medina. Many people came to me as if they had not seen me before. So I told this to `Uthman who said to me, "You may depart and live nearby if you wish." That was the reason for my being here for even If an Ethiopian had been nominated as my ruler, I would have obeyed him . – Al-Bukhari 1406

حَدَّثَنَا عَلِيٌّ، سَمِعَ هُشَيْمًا، أَخْبَرَنَا حُصَيْنٌ، عَنْ زَيْدِ بْنِ وَهْبٍ، قَالَ مَرَرْتُ بِالرَّبَذَةِ فَإِذَا أَنَا بِأَبِي، ذَرٍّ ـ رضى الله عنه ـ فَقُلْتُ لَهُ مَا أَنْزَلَكَ مَنْزِلَكَ هَذَا قَالَ كُنْتُ بِالشَّأْمِ، فَاخْتَلَفْتُ أَنَا وَمُعَاوِيَةُ فِي الَّذِينَ يَكْنِزُونَ الذَّهَبَ وَالْفِضَّةَ وَلاَ يُنْفِقُونَهَا فِي سَبِيلِ اللَّهِ. قَالَ مُعَاوِيَةُ نَزَلَتْ فِي أَهْلِ الْكِتَابِ. فَقُلْتُ نَزَلَتْ فِينَا وَفِيهِمْ. فَكَانَ بَيْنِي وَبَيْنَهُ فِي ذَاكَ، وَكَتَبَ إِلَى عُثْمَانَ ـ رضى الله عنه ـ يَشْكُونِي، فَكَتَبَ إِلَىَّ عُثْمَانُ أَنِ اقْدَمِ الْمَدِينَةَ. فَقَدِمْتُهَا فَكَثُرَ عَلَىَّ النَّاسُ حَتَّى كَأَنَّهُمْ لَمْ يَرَوْنِي قَبْلَ ذَلِكَ، فَذَكَرْتُ ذَاكَ لِعُثْمَانَ فَقَالَ لِي إِنْ شِئْتَ تَنَحَّيْتَ فَكُنْتَ قَرِيبًا. فَذَاكَ الَّذِي أَنْزَلَنِي هَذَا الْمَنْزِلَ، وَلَوْ أَمَّرُوا عَلَىَّ حَبَشِيًّا لَسَمِعْتُ وَأَطَعْتُ.

And from those who say, "We are Christians," We received their pledge, but they neglected some of what they were reminded of. So We provoked enmity and hatred among them until the Day of Resurrection; Allah will then inform them of what they used to craft. – Surah Al-Maidah 5:14

وَمِنَ ٱلَّذِينَ قَالُوٓاْ إِنَّا نَصَٰرَىٰٓ أَخَذْنَا مِيثَٰقَهُمْ فَنَسُواْ حَظًّا مِّمَّا ذُكِّرُواْ بِهِۦ فَأَغْرَيْنَا بَيْنَهُمُ ٱلْعَدَاوَةَ وَٱلْبَغْضَآءَ إِلَىٰ يَوْمِ ٱلْقِيَٰمَةِۚ وَسَوْفَ يُنَبِّئُهُمُ ٱللَّهُ بِمَا كَانُواْ يَصْنَعُونَ

Have you not considered those who were given a share of the Book? They believe in superstition and evil powers, and say of those who disbelieve, "These are better guided on the way than the believers." – Surah An-Nisa 4:51

أَلَمْ تَرَ إِلَى ٱلَّذِينَ أُوتُواْ نَصِيبًا مِّنَ ٱلْكِتَٰبِ يُؤْمِنُونَ بِٱلْجِبْتِ وَٱلطَّٰغُوتِ وَيَقُولُونَ لِلَّذِينَ كَفَرُواْ هَٰٓؤُلَآءِ أَهْدَىٰ مِنَ ٱلَّذِينَ ءَامَنُواْ سَبِيلًا

Is it not time for those who believe to surrender their hearts to the remembrance of Allah, and to the truth that has come down, and not be like those who were given the Book previously, but time became prolonged for them, so their hearts hardened, and many of them are sinners? – Surah Al-Hadid 57:16

أَلَمْ يَأْنِ لِلَّذِينَ ءَامَنُوٓاْ أَن تَخْشَعَ قُلُوبُهُمْ لِذِكْرِ ٱللَّهِ وَمَا نَزَلَ مِنَ ٱلْحَقِّ وَلَا يَكُونُواْ كَٱلَّذِينَ أُوتُواْ ٱلْكِتَٰبَ مِن قَبْلُ فَطَالَ عَلَيْهِمُ ٱلْأَمَدُ فَقَسَتْ قُلُوبُهُمْۖ وَكَثِيرٌ مِّنْهُمْ فَٰسِقُونَ

And when it is said to them, "Come, the Messenger of Allah will ask forgiveness for you," they bend their heads, and you see them turning away arrogantly. – Surah Al-Jumu'ah 62:5

مَثَلُ ٱلَّذِينَ حُمِّلُواْ ٱلتَّوْرَىٰةَ ثُمَّ لَمْ يَحْمِلُوهَا كَمَثَلِ ٱلْحِمَارِ يَحْمِلُ أَسْفَارًۢاۚ بِئْسَ مَثَلُ ٱلْقَوْمِ ٱلَّذِينَ كَذَّبُواْ بِـَٔايَٰتِ ٱللَّهِۚ وَٱللَّهُ لَا يَهْدِي ٱلْقَوْمَ ٱلظَّٰلِمِينَ

Narrated `Abdullah bin `Amr: The Prophetﷺ said, "Convey (my teachings) to the people even if it were a single sentence, and tell others the stories of Bani Israel (which have been taught to you), for it is not sinful to do so. And whoever tells a lie on me intentionally, will surely take his place in the (Hell) Fire.". – Sahih Al-Bukhari 3461

حَدَّثَنَا أَبُو عَاصِمٍ الضَّحَّاكُ بْنُ مَخْلَدٍ، أَخْبَرَنَا الأَوْزَاعِيُّ، حَدَّثَنَا حَسَّانُ بْنُ عَطِيَّةَ، عَنْ أَبِي كَبْشَةَ، عَنْ عَبْدِ اللَّهِ بْنِ عَمْرٍو، أَنَّ النَّبِيَّ صلى الله عليه وسلم قَالَ " بَلِّغُوا عَنِّي وَلَوْ آيَةً، وَحَدِّثُوا عَنْ بَنِي إِسْرَائِيلَ وَلاَ حَرَجَ، وَمَنْ كَذَبَ عَلَىَّ مُتَعَمِّدًا فَلْيَتَبَوَّأْ مَقْعَدَهُ مِنَ النَّارِ ".

The Book of
Allah guides whom He wills
ٱللَّهُ يَهْدِى مَن يَشَآءُ

Had your Lord willed, everyone on earth would have believed. Will you compel people to become believers? No soul can believe except by Allah's leave; and He lays disgrace upon those who refuse to understand. .–Surah Yunus 10:99&100

وَلَوْ شَآءَ رَبُّكَ لَـَٔامَنَ مَن فِى ٱلْأَرْضِ كُلُّهُمْ جَمِيعًا ۚ أَفَأَنتَ تُكْرِهُ ٱلنَّاسَ حَتَّىٰ يَكُونُوا۟ مُؤْمِنِينَ

But most people, for all your eagerness, will not believe. — Surah Yusuf 12:103

وَمَآ أَكْثَرُ ٱلنَّاسِ وَلَوْ حَرَصْتَ بِمُؤْمِنِينَ

Even if We opened for them a gateway into the sky, and they began to ascend through it. They would still say, "Our eyes are hallucinating; in fact, we are people bewitched." – Surah Al:Hijr 15:14&15

وَلَوْ فَتَحْنَا عَلَيْهِم بَابًا مِّنَ ٱلسَّمَآءِ فَظَلُّوا۟ فِيهِ يَعْرُجُونَ لَقَالُوٓا۟ إِنَّمَا سُكِّرَتْ أَبْصَـٰرُنَا بَلْ نَحْنُ قَوْمٌ مَّسْحُورُونَ

Even though you may be concerned about their guidance, Allah does not guide those who misguide. And they will have no saviors. – Surah An-Nahl 16:37

إِن تَحْرِصْ عَلَىٰ هُدَىٰهُمْ فَإِنَّ ٱللَّهَ لَا يَهْدِى مَن يُضِلُّ ۖ وَمَا لَهُم مِّن نَّـٰصِرِينَ

Allah is the Light of the heavens and the earth. The allegory of His light is that of a pillar on which is a lamp. The lamp is within a glass. The glass is like a brilliant planet, fueled by a blessed tree, an olive tree, neither eastern nor western. Its oil would almost illuminate, even if no fire has touched it. Light upon Light. Allah guides to His light whomever He wills. Allah thus cites the parables for the people. Allah is cognizant of everything. – Surah An-Nur 24:35

ٱللَّهُ نُورُ ٱلسَّمَـٰوَٰتِ وَٱلْأَرْضِ ۚ مَثَلُ نُورِهِۦ كَمِشْكَوٰةٍ فِيهَا مِصْبَاحٌ ۖ ٱلْمِصْبَاحُ فِى زُجَاجَةٍ ۖ ٱلزُّجَاجَةُ كَأَنَّهَا كَوْكَبٌ دُرِّىٌّ يُوقَدُ مِن شَجَرَةٍ مُّبَـٰرَكَةٍ زَيْتُونَةٍ لَّا شَرْقِيَّةٍ وَلَا غَرْبِيَّةٍ يَكَادُ زَيْتُهَا يُضِىٓءُ وَلَوْ لَمْ تَمْسَسْهُ نَارٌ ۚ نُّورٌ عَلَىٰ نُورٍ ۗ يَهْدِى ٱللَّهُ لِنُورِهِۦ مَن يَشَآءُ ۚ وَيَضْرِبُ ٱللَّهُ ٱلْأَمْثَـٰلَ لِلنَّاسِ ۗ وَٱللَّهُ بِكُلِّ شَىْءٍ عَلِيمٌ

Perhaps you will destroy yourself with grief, because they do not become believers. – Surah Ash-Shu'ara 26:3

لَعَلَّكَ بَـٰخِعٌ نَّفْسَكَ أَلَّا يَكُونُوا۟ مُؤْمِنِينَ

And whomever Allah guides, for him there is no misleader. Is Allah not Powerful and Vengeful? – Surah Az-Zumar 39: 37

وَمَن يَهْدِ ٱللَّهُ فَمَا لَهُۥ مِن مُّضِلٍّ ۗ أَلَيْسَ ٱللَّهُ بِعَزِيزٍ ذِى ٱنتِقَامٍ

What of him whose evil deed was made attractive to him, and so he regards it as good? Allah leads astray whomever He wills, and He guides whomever He wills. Therefore, do not waste yourself sorrowing over them. Allah knows exactly what they do. – Surah Fatir 35:8
أَفَمَن زُيِّنَ لَهُۥ سُوٓءُ عَمَلِهِۦ فَرَءَاهُ حَسَنًاۖ فَإِنَّ ٱللَّهَ يُضِلُّ مَن يَشَآءُ وَيَهۡدِي مَن يَشَآءُۖ فَلَا تَذۡهَبۡ نَفۡسُكَ عَلَيۡهِمۡ حَسَرَٰتٍۚ إِنَّ ٱللَّهَ
عَلِيمُۢ بِمَا يَصۡنَعُونَ

Whose seal is musk— and for this let (all) those strive who want to strive (i.e. hasten earnestly to the obedience of Allah). – Surah Al-Mutaffifin 83:26

خِتَٰمُهُۥ مِسۡكٞۚ وَفِي ذَٰلِكَ فَلۡيَتَنَافَسِ ٱلۡمُتَنَٰفِسُونَ

There shall be no compulsion in religion; the right way has become distinct from the wrong way. Whoever renounces evil and believes in Allah has grasped the most trustworthy handle; which does not break. Allah is Hearing and Knowing. – Surah Al-Baqarah 2:256
لَآ إِكۡرَاهَ فِي ٱلدِّينِۖ قَد تَّبَيَّنَ ٱلرُّشۡدُ مِنَ ٱلۡغَيِّۚ فَمَن يَكۡفُرۡ بِٱلطَّٰغُوتِ وَيُؤۡمِنۢ بِٱللَّهِ فَقَدِ ٱسۡتَمۡسَكَ بِٱلۡعُرۡوَةِ ٱلۡوُثۡقَىٰ لَا ٱنفِصَامَ لَهَاۗ
وَٱللَّهُ سَمِيعٌ عَلِيمٌ

Had Allah recognized any good in them, He would have made them hear; and had He made them hear, they would have turned away defiantly. – Surah Al-Anfal 8:23
وَلَوۡ عَلِمَ ٱللَّهُ فِيهِمۡ خَيۡرٗا لَّأَسۡمَعَهُمۡۖ وَلَوۡ أَسۡمَعَهُمۡ لَتَوَلَّواْ وَّهُم مُّعۡرِضُونَ

But if they turn away—We did not send you as a guardian over them. Your only duty is communication. Whenever We let man taste mercy from Us, he rejoices in it; but when misfortune befalls them, as a consequence of what their hands have perpetrated, man turns blasphemous. – Surah Ash-Shura 42:48
فَإِنۡ أَعۡرَضُواْ فَمَآ أَرۡسَلۡنَٰكَ عَلَيۡهِمۡ حَفِيظًاۖ إِنۡ عَلَيۡكَ إِلَّا ٱلۡبَلَٰغُۗ وَإِنَّآ إِذَآ أَذَقۡنَا ٱلۡإِنسَٰنَ مِنَّا رَحۡمَةٗ فَرِحَ بِهَاۖ وَإِن تُصِبۡهُمۡ سَيِّئَةُۢ بِمَا
قَدَّمَتۡ أَيۡدِيهِمۡ فَإِنَّ ٱلۡإِنسَٰنَ كَفُورٞ

So remind. You are only a reminder. You have no control over them. – Surah Al-Ghashiyah 88:21&22

فَذَكِّرۡ إِنَّمَآ أَنتَ مُذَكِّرٞ لَّسۡتَ عَلَيۡهِم بِمُصَيۡطِرٍ

We sent down enlightening revelations, and Allah guides whomever He wills to a straight path. – Surah An-Nur 24:46

لَّقَدۡ أَنزَلۡنَآ ءَايَٰتٖ مُّبَيِّنَٰتٖۚ وَٱللَّهُ يَهۡدِي مَن يَشَآءُ إِلَىٰ صِرَٰطٖ مُّسۡتَقِيمٖ

I will turn away from My revelations those who behave proudly on earth without justification. Even if they see every sign, they will not believe in it; and if they see the path of rectitude, they will not adopt it for a path; and if they see the path of error, they will adopt it for a path. That is because they denied Our revelations, and paid no attention to them. – Surah Al-A'raf 7:146
سَأَصۡرِفُ عَنۡ ءَايَٰتِيَ ٱلَّذِينَ يَتَكَبَّرُونَ فِي ٱلۡأَرۡضِ بِغَيۡرِ ٱلۡحَقِّ وَإِن يَرَوۡاْ كُلَّ ءَايَةٖ لَّا يُؤۡمِنُواْ بِهَا وَإِن يَرَوۡاْ سَبِيلَ ٱلرُّشۡدِ لَا
يَتَّخِذُوهُ سَبِيلٗا وَإِن يَرَوۡاْ سَبِيلَ ٱلۡغَيِّ يَتَّخِذُوهُ سَبِيلٗاۚ ذَٰلِكَ بِأَنَّهُمۡ كَذَّبُواْ بِـَٔايَٰتِنَا وَكَانُواْ عَنۡهَا غَٰفِلِينَ

If you find their rejection hard to bear, then if you can, seek a tunnel into the earth, or a stairway into the heaven, and bring them a sign. Had Allah willed, He could have gathered them to guidance. So do not be of the ignorant. – Surah Al-An'am 6:35

وَإِن كَانَ كَبُرَ عَلَيۡكَ إِعۡرَاضُهُمۡ فَإِنِ ٱسۡتَطَعۡتَ أَن تَبۡتَغِيَ نَفَقٗا فِي ٱلۡأَرۡضِ أَوۡ سُلَّمٗا فِي ٱلسَّمَآءِ فَتَأۡتِيَهُم بِـَٔايَةٖۚ وَلَوۡ شَآءَ ٱللَّهُ لَجَمَعَهُمۡ عَلَى ٱلۡهُدَىٰۚ فَلَا تَكُونَنَّ مِنَ ٱلۡجَٰهِلِينَ

Their guidance is not your responsibility, but Allah guides whom He wills. Any charity you give is for your own good. Any charity you give shall be for the sake of Allah. Any charity you give will be repaid to you in full, and you will not be wronged. – Surah Al-Baqarah 2:272
لَّيۡسَ عَلَيۡكَ هُدَىٰهُمۡ وَلَٰكِنَّ ٱللَّهَ يَهۡدِي مَن يَشَآءُۗ وَمَا تُنفِقُواْ مِنۡ خَيۡرٖ فَلِأَنفُسِكُمۡۚ وَمَا تُنفِقُونَ إِلَّا ٱبۡتِغَآءَ وَجۡهِ ٱللَّهِۚ وَمَا تُنفِقُواْ مِنۡ خَيۡرٖ يُوَفَّ إِلَيۡكُمۡ وَأَنتُمۡ لَا تُظۡلَمُونَ

Whoever disbelieves—let not his disbelief sadden you. To Us is their return. Then We will inform them of what they did. Allah knows what lies within the hearts. – Surah Luqman 31:23
وَمَن كَفَرَ فَلَا يَحۡزُنكَ كُفۡرُهُۥٓۚ إِلَيۡنَا مَرۡجِعُهُمۡ فَنُنَبِّئُهُم بِمَا عَمِلُوٓاْۚ إِنَّ ٱللَّهَ عَلِيمُۢ بِذَاتِ ٱلصُّدُورِ

What is the matter with you, divided into two factions regarding the hypocrites, when Allah Himself has overwhelmed them on account of what they did? Do you want to guide those whom Allah has led astray? Whomever Allah leads astray—you will never find for him a way. – Surah An-Nisa 4:88
فَمَا لَكُمۡ فِي ٱلۡمُنَٰفِقِينَ فِئَتَيۡنِ وَٱللَّهُ أَرۡكَسَهُم بِمَا كَسَبُوٓاْۚ أَتُرِيدُونَ أَن تَهۡدُواْ مَنۡ أَضَلَّ ٱللَّهُۖ وَمَن يُضۡلِلِ ٱللَّهُ فَلَن تَجِدَ لَهُۥ سَبِيلٗا

"My advice will not benefit you, much as I may want to advise you, if Allah desires to confound you. He is your Lord, and to Him you will be returned." – Surah Hud 11:34
وَلَا يَنفَعُكُمۡ نُصۡحِيٓ إِنۡ أَرَدتُّ أَنۡ أَنصَحَ لَكُمۡ إِن كَانَ ٱللَّهُ يُرِيدُ أَن يُغۡوِيَكُمۡۚ هُوَ رَبُّكُمۡ وَإِلَيۡهِ تُرۡجَعُونَ

And upon Allah is the responsibility to explain the Straight Path (i.e. Islamic Monotheism for mankind i.e. to show them legal and illegal, good and evil things, etc. so, whosoever accepts the guidance, it will be for his own benefit and whosoever goes astray, it will be for his own destruction), but there are ways that turn aside (such as Paganism, Judaism, Christianity, etc.). And had He willed, He would have guided you all (mankind). – Surah An-Nahl 16:9
وَعَلَى ٱللَّهِ قَصۡدُ ٱلسَّبِيلِ وَمِنۡهَا جَآئِرٞۚ وَلَوۡ شَآءَ لَهَدَىٰكُمۡ أَجۡمَعِينَ

You warn only him who follows the Message, and fears the Most Gracious inwardly. So give him good news of forgiveness, and a generous reward. – Surah Ya-Sin 36:11
إِنَّمَا تُنذِرُ مَنِ ٱتَّبَعَ ٱلذِّكۡرَ وَخَشِيَ ٱلرَّحۡمَٰنَ بِٱلۡغَيۡبِۖ فَبَشِّرۡهُ بِمَغۡفِرَةٖ وَأَجۡرٖ كَرِيمٍ

And He united their hearts. Had you spent everything on earth, you would not have united their hearts, but Allah united them together. He is Mighty and Wise. – Surah Al-Anfal 8:63
وَأَلَّفَ بَيۡنَ قُلُوبِهِمۡۚ لَوۡ أَنفَقۡتَ مَا فِي ٱلۡأَرۡضِ جَمِيعٗا مَّآ أَلَّفۡتَ بَيۡنَ قُلُوبِهِمۡ وَلَٰكِنَّ ٱللَّهَ أَلَّفَ بَيۡنَهُمۡۚ إِنَّهُۥ عَزِيزٌ حَكِيمٞ

The Book of

And whosoever strives, he strives only for himself.

وَمَن جَـٰهَدَ فَإِنَّمَا يُجَـٰهِدُ لِنَفْسِهِ

Whoever is guided—is guided for his own good. And whoever goes astray—goes astray to his detriment. No burdened soul carries the burdens of another, nor do We ever punish until We have sent a messenger. – Surah Al-Isra 17:15

مَّنِ ٱهْتَدَىٰ فَإِنَّمَا يَهْتَدِى لِنَفْسِهِۦ ۖ وَمَن ضَلَّ فَإِنَّمَا يَضِلُّ عَلَيْهَا ۚ وَلَا تَزِرُ وَازِرَةٌ وِزْرَ أُخْرَىٰ ۗ وَمَا كُنَّا مُعَذِّبِينَ حَتَّىٰ نَبْعَثَ رَسُولًا

No burdened soul can carry the burden of another. Even if one weighted down calls for help with its burden, nothing can be lifted from it, even if they were related. You are to warn those who fear their Lord inwardly, and perform the prayer. He who purifies himself purifies himself for his own good. To Allah is the ultimate return. – Surah Fatir 35:18

وَلَا تَزِرُ وَازِرَةٌ وِزْرَ أُخْرَىٰ ۚ وَإِن تَدْعُ مُثْقَلَةٌ إِلَىٰ حِمْلِهَا لَا يُحْمَلْ مِنْهُ شَىْءٌ وَلَوْ كَانَ ذَا قُرْبَىٰٓ ۗ إِنَّمَا تُنذِرُ ٱلَّذِينَ يَخْشَوْنَ رَبَّهُم بِٱلْغَيْبِ وَأَقَامُوا۟ ٱلصَّلَوٰةَ ۚ وَمَن تَزَكَّىٰ فَإِنَّمَا يَتَزَكَّىٰ لِنَفْسِهِۦ ۚ وَإِلَى ٱللَّهِ ٱلْمَصِيرُ

Whoever acts righteously does so for himself; and whoever works evil does so against himself. Your Lord is not unjust to the servants. – Surah Fussilat 41:46

مَّنْ عَمِلَ صَـٰلِحًا فَلِنَفْسِهِۦ ۖ وَمَنْ أَسَآءَ فَعَلَيْهَا ۗ وَمَا رَبُّكَ بِظَلَّـٰمٍ لِّلْعَبِيدِ

Whoever strives, strives only for himself. Allah is Independent of the beings. – Surah Al-'Ankabut 29:6

وَمَن جَـٰهَدَ فَإِنَّمَا يُجَـٰهِدُ لِنَفْسِهِۦٓ ۚ إِنَّ ٱللَّهَ لَغَنِىٌّ عَنِ ٱلْعَـٰلَمِينَ

On the Day when man will remind himself (of) whatever he has endeavored (to achieve) – Surah An-Nazi'at 79:35

يَوْمَ يَتَذَكَّرُ الْإِنسَانُ مَا سَعَىٰ

Surely the Hour is coming up-I would almost conceal it-that every self may be recompensed for whatever it endeavors (to achieve). – Surah TaHa 20:15

إِنَّ ٱلسَّاعَةَ ءَاتِيَةٌ أَكَادُ أُخْفِيهَا لِتُجْزَىٰ كُلُّ نَفْسٍۭ بِمَا تَسْعَىٰ

And whoever is willing (to gain) the Hereafter and diligently endeavors after it as he should (endeavor), being a believer, then those, their endeavor is to be thanked. – Surah Al-Isra 17:19

وَمَنْ أَرَادَ ٱلْـَٔاخِرَةَ وَسَعَىٰ لَهَا سَعْيَهَا وَهُوَ مُؤْمِنٌ فَأُو۟لَـٰٓئِكَ كَانَ سَعْيُهُم مَّشْكُورًا

"This is a reward for you. Your efforts are well appreciated.". – Surah Al-Insan 76:22

إِنَّ هَـٰذَا كَانَ لَكُمْ جَزَآءً وَكَانَ سَعْيُكُم مَّشْكُورًا

Indeed We will definitely guide them to Our ways
لَنَهۡدِيَنَّهُمۡ سُبُلَنَاۚ

And the ones who have striven in (our way), (Literally: in us) indeed We will definitely guide them to Our ways; and surely Allah is indeed with the fair-doers – Surah Al-Ankabut 29:69
وَٱلَّذِينَ جَٰهَدُواْ فِينَا لَنَهۡدِيَنَّهُمۡ سُبُلَنَاۚ وَإِنَّ ٱللَّهَ لَمَعَ ٱلۡمُحۡسِنِينَ

So, as for the ones who believed in Allah and firmly adhered to Him, then He will soon cause them to enter into a mercy from Him, and Grace, and will guide them to Him on a straight Path – Surah An-Nisa 4:175
فَأَمَّا ٱلَّذِينَ ءَامَنُواْ بِٱللَّهِ وَٱعۡتَصَمُواْ بِهِۦ فَسَيُدۡخِلُهُمۡ فِي رَحۡمَةٖ مِّنۡهُ وَفَضۡلٖ وَيَهۡدِيهِمۡ إِلَيۡهِ صِرَٰطٗا مُّسۡتَقِيمٗا

And Allah increases the ones who have been guided in guidance. And the enduring things, the deeds of righteousness, are more charitable from the Providence of your Lord in requital and more charitable for turning back – Surah Maryam 19:76
وَيَزِيدُ ٱللَّهُ ٱلَّذِينَ ٱهۡتَدَوۡاْ هُدٗىۗ وَٱلۡبَٰقِيَٰتُ ٱلصَّٰلِحَٰتُ خَيۡرٌ عِندَ رَبِّكَ ثَوَابٗا وَخَيۡرٞ مَّرَدًّا

The believers are those whose hearts tremble with awe whenever God is mentioned, and whose faith is strengthened whenever His revelations are recited and who place their trust in their Lord; - Surah Al-Anfal 8:2
إِنَّمَا ٱلۡمُؤۡمِنُونَ ٱلَّذِينَ إِذَا ذُكِرَ ٱللَّهُ وَجِلَتۡ قُلُوبُهُمۡ وَإِذَا تُلِيَتۡ عَلَيۡهِمۡ ءَايَٰتُهُۥ زَادَتۡهُمۡ إِيمَٰنٗا وَعَلَىٰ رَبِّهِمۡ يَتَوَكَّلُونَ

Those who were told by others, “People have gathered [an army] to fight you So fear them.” This instead increased their faith, and they said, “It is sufficient for us to be on Allah’s side. He is the best of protectors. – Surah Al-Imran 3:173
ٱلَّذِينَ قَالَ لَهُمُ ٱلنَّاسُ إِنَّ ٱلنَّاسَ قَدۡ جَمَعُواْ لَكُمۡ فَٱخۡشَوۡهُمۡ فَزَادَهُمۡ إِيمَٰنٗا وَقَالُواْ حَسۡبُنَا ٱللَّهُ وَنِعۡمَ ٱلۡوَكِيلُ

And (the ones) who have been guided (aright), (He) increases them in guidance and brings them their piety. – Surah Muhammad 47:17
وَٱلَّذِينَ ٱهۡتَدَوۡاْ زَادَهُمۡ هُدٗى وَءَاتَىٰهُمۡ تَقۡوَىٰهُمۡ

The Book of

On that Day will man remember, but how will that remembrance (then) avail him?

يَوْمَئِذٍ يَتَذَكَّرُ ٱلْإِنسَـٰنُ وَأَنَّىٰ لَهُ ٱلذِّكْرَىٰ

But repentance is not available for those who commit evils, until when death approaches one of them, he says, "Now I repent," nor for those who die as disbelievers. These—Wehave prepared for them a painful torment. – Surah An-Nisa 4:18

وَلَيْسَتِ ٱلتَّوْبَةُ لِلَّذِينَ يَعْمَلُونَ ٱلسَّيِّـَٔاتِ حَتَّىٰٓ إِذَا حَضَرَ أَحَدَهُمُ ٱلْمَوْتُ قَالَ إِنِّى تُبْتُ ٱلْـَٔـٰنَ وَلَا ٱلَّذِينَ يَمُوتُونَ وَهُمْ كُفَّارٌ ۚ أُو۟لَـٰٓئِكَ أَعْتَدْنَا لَهُمْ عَذَابًا أَلِيمًا

If only you could see, when they are made to stand before the Fire; they will say, "If only we could be sent back, and not reject the revelations of our Lord, and be among the faithful." – Surah Al-An'am 6:27

وَلَوْ تَرَىٰٓ إِذْ وُقِفُوا۟ عَلَى ٱلنَّارِ فَقَالُوا۟ يَـٰلَيْتَنَا نُرَدُّ وَلَا نُكَذِّبَ بِـَٔايَـٰتِ رَبِّنَا وَنَكُونَ مِنَ ٱلْمُؤْمِنِينَ

Are they waiting for anything but for the angels to come to them, or for your Lord to arrive, or for some of your Lord's signs to come? On the Day when some of your Lord's signs come, no soul will benefit from its faith unless it had believed previously, or had earned goodness through its faith. Say, "Wait, we too are waiting." – Surah Al-An'am 6:158

هَلْ يَنظُرُونَ إِلَّآ أَن تَأْتِيَهُمُ ٱلْمَلَـٰٓئِكَةُ أَوْ يَأْتِىَ رَبُّكَ أَوْ يَأْتِىَ بَعْضُ ءَايَـٰتِ رَبِّكَ ۗ يَوْمَ يَأْتِى بَعْضُ ءَايَـٰتِ رَبِّكَ لَا يَنفَعُ نَفْسًا إِيمَـٰنُهَا لَمْ تَكُنْ ءَامَنَتْ مِن قَبْلُ أَوْ كَسَبَتْ فِىٓ إِيمَـٰنِهَا خَيْرًا ۗ قُلِ ٱنتَظِرُوٓا۟ إِنَّا مُنتَظِرُونَ

Are they waiting for anything but its fulfillment? The Day its fulfillment comes true, those who disregarded it before will say, "The messengers of our Lord did come with the truth. Have we any intercessors to intercede for us? Or, could we be sent back, to behave differently from the way we behaved before?" They ruined their souls, and what they used to invent has failed them. – Surah Al-A'raf 7:53

هَلْ يَنظُرُونَ إِلَّا تَأْوِيلَهُۥ ۚ يَوْمَ يَأْتِى تَأْوِيلُهُۥ يَقُولُ ٱلَّذِينَ نَسُوهُ مِن قَبْلُ قَدْ جَآءَتْ رُسُلُ رَبِّنَا بِٱلْحَقِّ فَهَل لَّنَا مِن شُفَعَآءَ فَيَشْفَعُوا۟ لَنَآ أَوْ نُرَدُّ فَنَعْمَلَ غَيْرَ ٱلَّذِى كُنَّا نَعْمَلُ ۚ قَدْ خَسِرُوٓا۟ أَنفُسَهُمْ وَضَلَّ عَنْهُم مَّا كَانُوا۟ يَفْتَرُونَ

"Then, when it falls, will you believe in it? Now? When before you tried to hasten it?" Then it will be said to those who did wrong, "Taste the torment of eternity. Will you be rewarded except for what you used to do?" - Surah Yunus 10:51&52

أَثُمَّ إِذَا مَا وَقَعَ ءَامَنتُم بِهِۦٓ ۚ ءَآلْـَٔـٰنَ وَقَدْ كُنتُم بِهِۦ تَسْتَعْجِلُونَ ثُمَّ قِيلَ لِلَّذِينَ ظَلَمُوا۟ ذُوقُوا۟ عَذَابَ ٱلْخُلْدِ هَلْ تُجْزَوْنَ إِلَّا بِمَا كُنتُمْ تَكْسِبُونَ

On the Day when We raise up a witness from every community— those who disbelieved will not be permitted, nor will they be excused. – Surah An-Nahl 16:84

وَيَوْمَ نَبْعَثُ مِن كُلِّ أُمَّةٍ شَهِيدًا ثُمَّ لَا يُؤْذَنُ لِلَّذِينَ كَفَرُوا۟ وَلَا هُمْ يُسْتَعْتَبُونَ

On that Day, the sinners' excuses will not benefit them, nor will they be excused. – Surah Ar-Rum 30:57

فَيَوْمَئِذٍ لَّا يَنفَعُ ٱلَّذِينَ ظَلَمُوا۟ مَعْذِرَتُهُمْ وَلَا هُمْ يُسْتَعْتَبُونَ

Say, "On the day of victory, the faith of those who disbelieved will be of no avail to them, and they will not be granted respite." – Surah As-Sajdah 32:29

قُلۡ يَوۡمَ ٱلۡفَتۡحِ لَا يَنفَعُ ٱلَّذِينَ كَفَرُوٓاْ إِيمَـٰنُهُمۡ وَلَا هُمۡ يُنظَرُونَ

And they will scream therein, "Our Lord, let us out, and we will act righteously, differently from the way we used to act." Did We not give you a life long enough, in which anyone who wanted to understand would have understood? And the warner did come to you. So taste. The evildoers will have no helper. – Surah Fatir 35:37

وَهُمۡ يَصۡطَرِخُونَ فِيهَا رَبَّنَآ أَخۡرِجۡنَا نَعۡمَلۡ صَـٰلِحًا غَيۡرَ ٱلَّذِى كُنَّا نَعۡمَلُۚ أَوَ لَمۡ نُعَمِّرۡكُم مَّا يَتَذَكَّرُ فِيهِ مَن تَذَكَّرَ وَجَآءَكُمُ ٱلنَّذِيرُۖ فَذُوقُواْ فَمَا لِلظَّـٰلِمِينَ مِن نَّصِيرٍ

And on that Day, Hell is brought forward. On that Day, man will remember, but how will remembrance avail him? He will say, "If only I had forwarded for my life." – Al-Fajr 89:23&24

وَجِاْىٓءَ يَوۡمَئِذِۭ بِجَهَنَّمَۚ يَوۡمَئِذٍ يَتَذَكَّرُ ٱلۡإِنسَـٰنُ وَأَنَّىٰ لَهُ ٱلذِّكۡرَىٰ يَقُولُ يَـٰلَيۡتَنِى قَدَّمۡتُ لِحَيَاتِى

And they say, "We have believed in it." But how can they attain it from a distant place?– Surah Saba 34:52

وَقَالُوٓاْ ءَامَنَّا بِهِۦ وَأَنَّىٰ لَهُمُ ٱلتَّنَاوُشُ مِن مَّكَانِۭ بَعِيدٍ

"Our Lord, lift the torment from us, we are believers." But how can they be reminded? An enlightening messenger has already come to them. – Surah Ad-Dukhan 44:12&13

رَّبَّنَا ٱكۡشِفۡ عَنَّا ٱلۡعَذَابَ إِنَّا مُؤۡمِنُونَ أَنَّىٰ لَهُمُ ٱلذِّكۡرَىٰ وَقَدۡ جَآءَهُمۡ رَسُولٌ مُّبِينٌ

Are they just waiting until the Hour comes to them suddenly? Its tokens have already come. But how will they be reminded when it has come to them? – Surah Muhammad 47:18

فَهَلۡ يَنظُرُونَ إِلَّا ٱلسَّاعَةَ أَن تَأۡتِيَهُم بَغۡتَةًۖ فَقَدۡ جَآءَ أَشۡرَاطُهَاۚ فَأَنَّىٰ لَهُمۡ إِذَا جَآءَتۡهُمۡ ذِكۡرَىٰهُمۡ

The Day when their faces are flipped into the Fire, they will say, "If only we had obeyed Allah and obeyed the Messenger." Surah Al-Ahzab 33:66

يَوۡمَ تُقَلَّبُ وُجُوهُهُمۡ فِى ٱلنَّارِ يَقُولُونَ يَـٰلَيۡتَنَآ أَطَعۡنَا ٱللَّهَ وَأَطَعۡنَا ٱلرَّسُولَا

The Book of

Surely, We have sent down to you the Book (this Qur'an) in truth that you might judge between men by that which Allah has shown you

إِنَّآ أَنزَلْنَآ إِلَيْكَ ٱلْكِتَـٰبَ بِٱلْحَقِّ لِتَحْكُمَ بَيْنَ ٱلنَّاسِ بِمَآ أَرَىٰكَ ٱللَّهُ ۚ

Humanity used to be one community; then Allah sent the prophets, bringing good news and giving warnings. And He sent down with them the Scripture, with the truth, to judge between people regarding their differences. But none differed over it except those who were given it—after the proofs had come to them—out of mutual envy between them. Then Allah guided those who believed to the truth they had disputed, in accordance with His will. Allah guides whom He wills to a straight path. Surah Al-Baqarah 2:213

كَانَ ٱلنَّاسُ أُمَّةً وَٰحِدَةً فَبَعَثَ ٱللَّهُ ٱلنَّبِيِّـۧنَ مُبَشِّرِينَ وَمُنذِرِينَ وَأَنزَلَ مَعَهُمُ ٱلْكِتَـٰبَ بِٱلْحَقِّ لِيَحْكُمَ بَيْنَ ٱلنَّاسِ فِيمَا ٱخْتَلَفُوا۟ فِيهِ ۚ وَمَا ٱخْتَلَفَ فِيهِ إِلَّا ٱلَّذِينَ أُوتُوهُ مِنۢ بَعْدِ مَا جَآءَتْهُمُ ٱلْبَيِّنَـٰتُ بَغْيًۢا بَيْنَهُمْ ۖ فَهَدَى ٱللَّهُ ٱلَّذِينَ ءَامَنُوا۟ لِمَا ٱخْتَلَفُوا۟ فِيهِ مِنَ ٱلْحَقِّ بِإِذْنِهِۦ ۗ وَٱللَّهُ يَهْدِى مَن يَشَآءُ إِلَىٰ صِرَٰطٍ مُّسْتَقِيمٍ

We have revealed to you the Scripture, with the truth, so that you judge between people in accordance with what Allah has shown you. And do not be an advocate for the traitors. – Surah An-Nisa 4:105

إِنَّآ أَنزَلْنَآ إِلَيْكَ ٱلْكِتَـٰبَ بِٱلْحَقِّ لِتَحْكُمَ بَيْنَ ٱلنَّاسِ بِمَآ أَرَىٰكَ ٱللَّهُ ۚ وَلَا تَكُن لِّلْخَآئِنِينَ خَصِيمًا

We have revealed the Torah, wherein is guidance and light. The submissive prophets ruled the Jews according to it, so did the rabbis and the scholars, as they were required to protect Allah's Book, and were witnesses to it. So do not fear people, but fear Me. And do not sell My revelations for a cheap price. Those who do not rule according to what Allah revealed are the unbelievers. – Surah Al-Maidah 5:44

إِنَّآ أَنزَلْنَا ٱلتَّوْرَىٰةَ فِيهَا هُدًى وَنُورٌ ۚ يَحْكُمُ بِهَا ٱلنَّبِيُّونَ ٱلَّذِينَ أَسْلَمُوا۟ لِلَّذِينَ هَادُوا۟ وَٱلرَّبَّـٰنِيُّونَ وَٱلْأَحْبَارُ بِمَا ٱسْتُحْفِظُوا۟ مِن كِتَـٰبِ ٱللَّهِ وَكَانُوا۟ عَلَيْهِ شُهَدَآءَ ۚ فَلَا تَخْشَوُا۟ ٱلنَّاسَ وَٱخْشَوْنِ وَلَا تَشْتَرُوا۟ بِـَٔايَـٰتِى ثَمَنًا قَلِيلًا ۚ وَمَن لَّمْ يَحْكُم بِمَآ أَنزَلَ ٱللَّهُ فَأُو۟لَـٰٓئِكَ هُمُ ٱلْكَـٰفِرُونَ

And We revealed to you the Book, with truth, confirming the Scripture that preceded it, and superseding it. So judge between them according to what Allah revealed, and do not follow their desires if they differ from the truth that has come to you. For each of you We have assigned a law and a method. Had Allah willed, He could have made you a single nation, but He tests you through what He has given you. So compete in righteousness. To Allah is your return, all of you; then He will inform you of what you had disputed. And judge between them according to what Allah revealed, and do not follow their desires. And beware of them, lest they lure you away from some of what Allah has revealed to you. But if they turn away, know that Allah intends to strike them with some of their sins. In fact, a great many people are corrupt. – Surah Al-Maidah 5:48&49

وَأَنزَلْنَآ إِلَيْكَ ٱلْكِتَـٰبَ بِٱلْحَقِّ مُصَدِّقًا لِّمَا بَيْنَ يَدَيْهِ مِنَ ٱلْكِتَـٰبِ وَمُهَيْمِنًا عَلَيْهِ ۖ فَٱحْكُم بَيْنَهُم بِمَآ أَنزَلَ ٱللَّهُ ۖ وَلَا تَتَّبِعْ أَهْوَآءَهُمْ عَمَّا جَآءَكَ مِنَ ٱلْحَقِّ ۚ لِكُلٍّ جَعَلْنَا مِنكُمْ شِرْعَةً وَمِنْهَاجًا ۚ وَلَوْ شَآءَ ٱللَّهُ لَجَعَلَكُمْ أُمَّةً وَٰحِدَةً وَلَـٰكِن لِّيَبْلُوَكُمْ فِى مَآ ءَاتَىٰكُمْ ۖ فَٱسْتَبِقُوا۟ ٱلْخَيْرَٰتِ ۚ إِلَى ٱللَّهِ مَرْجِعُكُمْ جَمِيعًا فَيُنَبِّئُكُم بِمَا كُنتُمْ فِيهِ تَخْتَلِفُونَ وَأَنِ ٱحْكُم بَيْنَهُم بِمَآ أَنزَلَ ٱللَّهُ وَلَا تَتَّبِعْ أَهْوَآءَهُمْ وَٱحْذَرْهُمْ أَن يَفْتِنُوكَ عَنۢ بَعْضِ مَآ أَنزَلَ ٱللَّهُ إِلَيْكَ ۖ فَإِن تَوَلَّوْا۟ فَٱعْلَمْ أَنَّمَا يُرِيدُ ٱللَّهُ أَن يُصِيبَهُم بِبَعْضِ ذُنُوبِهِمْ ۗ وَإِنَّ كَثِيرًا مِّنَ ٱلنَّاسِ لَفَـٰسِقُونَ

"Shall I seek a judge other than Allah, when He is the One who revealed to you the Book, explained in detail?" Those to whom We gave the Book know that it is the truth revealed from your Lord. So do not be of those who doubt. – Surah Al-An'am 6:114

أَفَغَيْرَ ٱللَّهِ أَبْتَغِى حَكَمًا وَهُوَ ٱلَّذِىٓ أَنزَلَ إِلَيْكُمُ ٱلْكِتَـٰبَ مُفَصَّلًا ۚ وَٱلَّذِينَ ءَاتَيْنَـٰهُمُ ٱلْكِتَـٰبَ يَعْلَمُونَ أَنَّهُۥ مُنَزَّلٌ مِّن رَّبِّكَ بِٱلْحَقِّ ۖ فَلَا تَكُونَنَّ مِنَ ٱلْمُمْتَرِينَ

And strive for Allah, with the striving due to Him. He has chosen you, and has not burdened you in religion—the faith of your father Abraham. It is he who named you Muslims before, and in this. So that the Messenger may be a witness over you, and you may be witnesses over the people. So pray regularly, and give regular charity, and cleave to Allah. He is your Protector. What an excellent Protector, and what an excellent Helper. – Surah Al-Hajj 22:78

وَجَـٰهِدُوا۟ فِى ٱللَّهِ حَقَّ جِهَادِهِۦ ۚ هُوَ ٱجْتَبَىٰكُمْ وَمَا جَعَلَ عَلَيْكُمْ فِى ٱلدِّينِ مِنْ حَرَجٍ ۚ مِّلَّةَ أَبِيكُمْ إِبْرَٰهِيمَ ۚ هُوَ سَمَّىٰكُمُ ٱلْمُسْلِمِينَ مِن قَبْلُ وَفِى هَـٰذَا لِيَكُونَ ٱلرَّسُولُ شَهِيدًا عَلَيْكُمْ وَتَكُونُوا۟ شُهَدَآءَ عَلَى ٱلنَّاسِ ۚ فَأَقِيمُوا۟ ٱلصَّلَوٰةَ وَءَاتُوا۟ ٱلزَّكَوٰةَ وَٱعْتَصِمُوا۟ بِٱللَّهِ هُوَ مَوْلَىٰكُمْ ۖ فَنِعْمَ ٱلْمَوْلَىٰ وَنِعْمَ ٱلنَّصِيرُ

They (hypocrites) say, "We have believed in Allah and the Messenger, and we obey," but some of them turn away afterwards. These are not believers. And when they are called to Allah and His Messenger, in order to judge between them, some of them refuse. But if justice is on their side, they accept it willingly. Is there sickness in their hearts? Or are they suspicious? Or do they fear that Allah may do them injustice? Or His Messenger? In fact, they themselves are the unjust. The response of the believers, when they are called to Allah and His Messenger in order to judge between them, is to say, "We hear and we obey." These are the successful. – Surah An-Nur 24:47-51

وَيَقُولُونَ ءَامَنَّا بِٱللَّهِ وَبِٱلرَّسُولِ وَأَطَعْنَا ثُمَّ يَتَوَلَّىٰ فَرِيقٌ مِّنْهُم مِّنۢ بَعْدِ ذَٰلِكَ ۚ وَمَآ أُو۟لَـٰٓئِكَ بِٱلْمُؤْمِنِينَ وَإِذَا دُعُوٓا۟ إِلَى ٱللَّهِ وَرَسُولِهِۦ لِيَحْكُمَ بَيْنَهُمْ إِذَا فَرِيقٌ مِّنْهُم مُّعْرِضُونَ وَإِن يَكُن لَّهُمُ ٱلْحَقُّ يَأْتُوٓا۟ إِلَيْهِ مُذْعِنِينَ أَفِى قُلُوبِهِم مَّرَضٌ أَمِ ٱرْتَابُوٓا۟ أَمْ يَخَافُونَ أَن يَحِيفَ ٱللَّهُ عَلَيْهِمْ وَرَسُولُهُۥ ۚ بَلْ أُو۟لَـٰٓئِكَ هُمُ ٱلظَّـٰلِمُونَ إِنَّمَا كَانَ قَوْلَ ٱلْمُؤْمِنِينَ إِذَا دُعُوٓا۟ إِلَى ٱللَّهِ وَرَسُولِهِۦ لِيَحْكُمَ بَيْنَهُمْ أَن يَقُولُوا۟ سَمِعْنَا وَأَطَعْنَا ۚ وَأُو۟لَـٰٓئِكَ هُمُ ٱلْمُفْلِحُونَ

The Book of

And Allah bears witness that the hypocrites are liars indeed.

وَٱللَّهُ يَشْهَدُ إِنَّ ٱلْمُنَـٰفِقِينَ لَكَـٰذِبُونَ

Have you considered him who denies the religion? It is he who mistreats the orphan. And does not encourage the feeding of the poor. So woe to those who pray. Those who are heedless of their prayers. Those who put on the appearance. And withhold the assistance. Surah Al-Ma'un 107

أَرَءَيْتَ ٱلَّذِى يُكَذِّبُ بِٱلدِّينِ فَذَٰلِكَ ٱلَّذِى يَدُعُّ ٱلْيَتِيمَ وَلَا يَحُضُّ عَلَىٰ طَعَامِ ٱلْمِسْكِينِ فَوَيْلٌ لِّلْمُصَلِّينَ ٱلَّذِينَ هُمْ عَن صَلَاتِهِمْ سَاهُونَ ٱلَّذِينَ هُمْ يُرَآءُونَ وَيَمْنَعُونَ ٱلْمَاعُونَ

Among the people are those who say, "We believe in Allah and in the Last Day," but they are not believers. They seek to deceive Allah and those who believe, but they deceive none but themselves, though they are not aware. In their hearts is sickness, and Allah has increased their sickness. They will have a painful punishment because of their denial. And when it is said to them, "Do not make trouble on earth," they say, "We are only reformers." In fact, they are the troublemakers, but they are not aware. – Surah Al-Baqarah 2:8-12

وَمِنَ ٱلنَّاسِ مَن يَقُولُ ءَامَنَّا بِٱللَّهِ وَبِٱلْيَوْمِ ٱلْـَٔاخِرِ وَمَا هُم بِمُؤْمِنِينَ يُخَـٰدِعُونَ ٱللَّهَ وَٱلَّذِينَ ءَامَنُوا۟ وَمَا يَخْدَعُونَ إِلَّآ أَنفُسَهُمْ وَمَا يَشْعُرُونَ فِى قُلُوبِهِم مَّرَضٌ فَزَادَهُمُ ٱللَّهُ مَرَضًا ۖ وَلَهُمْ عَذَابٌ أَلِيمٌۢ بِمَا كَانُوا۟ يَكْذِبُونَ وَإِذَا قِيلَ لَهُمْ لَا تُفْسِدُوا۟ فِى ٱلْأَرْضِ قَالُوٓا۟ إِنَّمَا نَحْنُ مُصْلِحُونَ أَلَآ إِنَّهُمْ هُمُ ٱلْمُفْسِدُونَ وَلَـٰكِن لَّا يَشْعُرُونَ

Among the people is he whose speech about the worldly life impresses you, and he calls Allah to witness what is in his heart, while he is the most hostile of adversaries. When he gains power, he strives to spread corruption on earth, destroying properties and lives. Allah does not like corruption. – Surah Al-Baqarah 2:204&205

وَمِنَ ٱلنَّاسِ مَن يُعْجِبُكَ قَوْلُهُۥ فِى ٱلْحَيَوٰةِ ٱلدُّنْيَا وَيُشْهِدُ ٱللَّهَ عَلَىٰ مَا فِى قَلْبِهِۦ وَهُوَ أَلَدُّ ٱلْخِصَامِ وَإِذَا تَوَلَّىٰ سَعَىٰ فِى ٱلْأَرْضِ لِيُفْسِدَ فِيهَا وَيُهْلِكَ ٱلْحَرْثَ وَٱلنَّسْلَ ۗ وَٱللَّهُ لَا يُحِبُّ ٱلْفَسَادَ

It is He who revealed to you the Book. Some of its verses are definitive; they are the foundation of the Book, and others are unspecific. As for those in whose hearts is deviation, they follow the unspecific part, seeking descent, and seeking to derive an interpretation. But none knows its interpretation except Allah and those firmly rooted in knowledge say, "We believe in it; all is from our Lord." But none recollects except those with understanding. – Surah Al-Imran 3:7

هُوَ ٱلَّذِىٓ أَنزَلَ عَلَيْكَ ٱلْكِتَـٰبَ مِنْهُ ءَايَـٰتٌ مُّحْكَمَـٰتٌ هُنَّ أُمُّ ٱلْكِتَـٰبِ وَأُخَرُ مُتَشَـٰبِهَـٰتٌ ۖ فَأَمَّا ٱلَّذِينَ فِى قُلُوبِهِمْ زَيْغٌ فَيَتَّبِعُونَ مَا تَشَـٰبَهَ مِنْهُ ٱبْتِغَآءَ ٱلْفِتْنَةِ وَٱبْتِغَآءَ تَأْوِيلِهِۦ ۗ وَمَا يَعْلَمُ تَأْوِيلَهُۥٓ إِلَّا ٱللَّهُ ۗ وَٱلرَّٰسِخُونَ فِى ٱلْعِلْمِ يَقُولُونَ ءَامَنَّا بِهِۦ كُلٌّ مِّنْ عِندِ رَبِّنَا ۗ وَمَا يَذَّكَّرُ إِلَّآ أُو۟لُوا۟ ٱلْأَلْبَـٰبِ

Narrated Mirdas Al-Aslami: The Prophetﷺ said, "The righteous (pious people will depart (die) in succession one after the other, and there will remain (on the earth) useless people like the useless husk of barley seeds or bad dates. – Al-Bukhari 6434

حَدَّثَنِي يَحْيَى بْنُ حَمَّادٍ، حَدَّثَنَا أَبُو عَوَانَةَ، عَنْ بَيَانٍ، عَنْ قَيْسِ بْنِ أَبِي حَازِمٍ، عَنْ مِرْدَاسٍ الأَسْلَمِيِّ، قَالَ قَالَ النَّبِيُّ صلى الله عليه وسلم " يَذْهَبُ الصَّالِحُونَ الأَوَّلُ فَالأَوَّلُ، وَيَبْقَى حُفَالَةٌ كَحُفَالَةِ الشَّعِيرِ أَوِ التَّمْرِ، لاَ يُبَالِيهِمُ اللَّهُ بَالَةً ". قَالَ أَبُو عَبْدِ اللَّهِ يُقَالُ حُفَالَةٌ وَحُثَالَةٌ.

Narrated 'Abdullah bin 'Amr: The Prophet ﷺ said, "Whoever has the following four (characteristics) will be a pure hypocrite and whoever has one of the following four characteristics will have one characteristic of hypocrisy unless and until he gives it up. Whenever he is entrusted, he betrays. 2) Whenever he speaks, he tells a lie. 3) Whenever he makes a covenant, he proves treacherous. 4) Whenever he quarrels, he behaves in a very imprudent, evil and insulting manner." – Al-Bukhari 34

حَدَّثَنَا قَبِيصَةُ بْنُ عُقْبَةَ، قَالَ حَدَّثَنَا سُفْيَانُ، عَنِ الأَعْمَشِ، عَنْ عَبْدِ اللَّهِ بْنِ مُرَّةَ، عَنْ مَسْرُوقٍ، عَنْ عَبْدِ اللَّهِ بْنِ عَمْرٍو، أَنَّ النَّبِيَّ صلى الله عليه وسلم قَالَ " أَرْبَعٌ مَنْ كُنَّ فِيهِ كَانَ مُنَافِقًا خَالِصًا، وَمَنْ كَانَتْ فِيهِ خَصْلَةٌ مِنْهُنَّ كَانَتْ فِيهِ خَصْلَةٌ مِنَ النِّفَاقِ حَتَّى يَدَعَهَا إِذَا اؤْتُمِنَ خَانَ وَإِذَا حَدَّثَ كَذَبَ وَإِذَا عَاهَدَ غَدَرَ، وَإِذَا خَاصَمَ فَجَرَ ". تَابَعَهُ شُعْبَةُ عَنِ الأَعْمَشِ.

Have you not observed those who claim that they believe in what was revealed to you, and in what was revealed before you, yet they seek Satanic sources for legislation, in spite of being commanded to reject them? Satan – Surah An-Nisa 4:60

أَلَمْ تَرَ إِلَى ٱلَّذِينَ يَزْعُمُونَ أَنَّهُمْ ءَامَنُوا۟ بِمَآ أُنزِلَ إِلَيْكَ وَمَآ أُنزِلَ مِن قَبْلِكَ يُرِيدُونَ أَن يَتَحَاكَمُوٓا۟ إِلَى ٱلطَّـٰغُوتِ وَقَدْ أُمِرُوٓا۟ أَن يَكْفُرُوا۟ بِهِۦ وَيُرِيدُ ٱلشَّيْطَـٰنُ أَن يُضِلَّهُمْ ضَلَـٰلًۢا بَعِيدًا

Among you is he who lags behind. Then, when a calamity befalls you, he says, "Allah has favored me, that I was not martyred with them." But when some bounty from Allah comes to you, he says—as if no affection existed between you and him—"If only I had been with them, I would have achieved a great victory." Let those who sell the life of this world for the Hereafter fight in the cause of Allah. Whoever fights in the cause of Allah, and then is killed, or achieves victory, We will grant hAnd why would you not fight in the cause of Allah, and the helpless men, and women, and children, cry out, "Our Lord, deliver us from this town whose people are oppressive, and appoint for us from Your Presence a Protector, and appoint for us from Your Presence a Victor." Those who believe fight in the cause of Allah, while those who disbelieve fight in the cause of Evil. So fight the allies of the Devil. Surely the strategy of the Devil is weak. Have you not considered those who were told, "Restrain your hands, and perform your prayers, and spend in regular charity"? But when fighting was ordained for them, a faction of them feared the people as Allah is ought to be feared, or even more. And they said, "Our Lord, why did You ordain fighting for us? If only You would postpone it for us for a short while." Say, "The enjoyments of this life are brief, but the Hereafter is better for the righteous, and you will not be wronged one bit." Wherever you may be, death will catch up with you, even if you were in fortified towers. When a good fortune comes their way, they say, "This is from Allah." But when a misfortune befalls them, they say, "This is from you." Say, "All is from Allah." So what is the matter with these people, that they hardly understand a thing? – Surah An-Nisa 4:72-78

وَإِنَّ مِنكُمْ لَمَن لَّيُبَطِّئَنَّ فَإِنْ أَصَـٰبَتْكُم مُّصِيبَةٌ قَالَ قَدْ أَنْعَمَ ٱللَّهُ عَلَىَّ إِذْ لَمْ أَكُن مَّعَهُمْ شَهِيدًا وَلَئِنْ أَصَـٰبَكُمْ فَضْلٌ مِّنَ ٱللَّهِ لَيَقُولَنَّ كَأَن لَّمْ تَكُنۢ بَيْنَكُمْ وَبَيْنَهُۥ مَوَدَّةٌ يَـٰلَيْتَنِى كُنتُ مَعَهُمْ فَأَفُوزَ فَوْزًا عَظِيمًا فَلْيُقَـٰتِلْ فِى سَبِيلِ ٱللَّهِ ٱلَّذِينَ يَشْرُونَ ٱلْحَيَوٰةَ ٱلدُّنْيَا بِٱلْءَاخِرَةِ ۚ وَمَن يُقَـٰتِلْ فِى سَبِيلِ ٱللَّهِ فَيُقْتَلْ أَوْ يَغْلِبْ فَسَوْفَ نُؤْتِيهِ أَجْرًا عَظِيمًا وَمَا لَكُمْ لَا تُقَـٰتِلُونَ فِى سَبِيلِ ٱللَّهِ وَٱلْمُسْتَضْعَفِينَ مِنَ ٱلرِّجَالِ وَٱلنِّسَآءِ وَٱلْوِلْدَٰنِ ٱلَّذِينَ يَقُولُونَ رَبَّنَآ أَخْرِجْنَا مِنْ هَـٰذِهِ ٱلْقَرْيَةِ ٱلظَّالِمِ أَهْلُهَا وَٱجْعَل لَّنَا مِن لَّدُنكَ وَلِيًّا وَٱجْعَل لَّنَا مِن لَّدُنكَ نَصِيرًا ٱلَّذِينَ ءَامَنُوا۟ يُقَـٰتِلُونَ فِى سَبِيلِ ٱللَّهِ ۖ وَٱلَّذِينَ كَفَرُوا۟ يُقَـٰتِلُونَ فِى سَبِيلِ ٱلطَّـٰغُوتِ فَقَـٰتِلُوٓا۟ أَوْلِيَآءَ ٱلشَّيْطَـٰنِ ۖ إِنَّ كَيْدَ ٱلشَّيْطَـٰنِ كَانَ ضَعِيفًا أَلَمْ تَرَ إِلَى ٱلَّذِينَ قِيلَ لَهُمْ كُفُّوٓا۟ أَيْدِيَكُمْ وَأَقِيمُوا۟ ٱلصَّلَوٰةَ وَءَاتُوا۟ ٱلزَّكَوٰةَ فَلَمَّا كُتِبَ عَلَيْهِمُ ٱلْقِتَالُ إِذَا فَرِيقٌ مِّنْهُمْ يَخْشَوْنَ ٱلنَّاسَ كَخَشْيَةِ ٱللَّهِ أَوْ أَشَدَّ خَشْيَةً ۚ وَقَالُوا۟ رَبَّنَا لِمَ كَتَبْتَ عَلَيْنَا ٱلْقِتَالَ لَوْلَآ أَخَّرْتَنَآ إِلَىٰٓ أَجَلٍ قَرِيبٍ ۗ قُلْ مَتَـٰعُ ٱلدُّنْيَا قَلِيلٌ وَٱلْءَاخِرَةُ خَيْرٌ لِّمَنِ ٱتَّقَىٰ وَلَا تُظْلَمُونَ فَتِيلًا أَيْنَمَا تَكُونُوا۟ يُدْرِككُّمُ ٱلْمَوْتُ وَلَوْ كُنتُمْ فِى بُرُوجٍ مُّشَيَّدَةٍ ۗ وَإِن تُصِبْهُمْ حَسَنَةٌ يَقُولُوا۟ هَـٰذِهِۦ مِنْ عِندِ ٱللَّهِ ۖ وَإِن تُصِبْهُمْ سَيِّئَةٌ يَقُولُوا۟ هَـٰذِهِۦ مِنْ عِندِكَ ۚ قُلْ كُلٌّ مِّنْ عِندِ ٱللَّهِ ۖ فَمَالِ هَـٰٓؤُلَآءِ ٱلْقَوْمِ لَا يَكَادُونَ يَفْقَهُونَ حَدِيثًا

They traded away Allah's revelations for a cheap price, so they barred others from His path. How evil is what they did. Towards a believer they respect neither kinship nor treaty. These are the transgressors. – Surah At-Taubah 9:9&10

ٱشْتَرَوْا۟ بِـَٔايَـٰتِ ٱللَّهِ ثَمَنًا قَلِيلًا فَصَدُّوا۟ عَن سَبِيلِهِۦٓ ۚ إِنَّهُمْ سَآءَ مَا كَانُوا۟ يَعْمَلُونَ لَا يَرْقُبُونَ فِى مُؤْمِنٍ إِلًّا وَلَا ذِمَّةً ۚ وَأُو۟لَـٰٓئِكَ
هُمُ ٱلْمُعْتَدُونَ

When the hypocrites come to you, they say, "We bear witness that you are Allah's Messenger." Allah knows that you are His Messenger, and Allah bears witness that the hypocrites are liars. They treat their oaths as a cover, and so they repel others from Allah's path. Evil is what they do. That is because they believed, and then disbelieved; so their hearts were sealed, and they cannot understand. When you see them, their appearance impresses you. And when they speak, you listen to what they say. They are like propped-up timber. They think every shout is aimed at them. They are the enemy, so beware of them. Allah condemns them; how deluded they are! And when it is said to them, "Come, the Messenger of Allah will ask forgiveness for you," they bend their heads, and you see them turning away arrogantly. It is the same for them, whether you ask forgiveness for them, or do not ask forgiveness for them; Allah will not forgive them. Allah does not guide the sinful people. It is they who say: "Do not spend anything on those who side with Allah's Messenger, unless they have dispersed." To Allah belong the treasures of the heavens and the earth, but the hypocrites do not understand. They say, "If we return to the City, the more powerful therein will evict the weak." But power belongs to Allah, and His Messenger, and the believers; but the hypocrites do not know. O you who believe! Let neither your possessions nor your children distract you from the remembrance of Allah. Whoever does that—these are the losers. And give from what We have provided for you, before death approaches one of you, and he says, "My Lord, if only You would delay me for a short while, so that I may be charitable, and be one of the righteous." But Allah will not delay a soul when its time has come. Allah is Informed of what you do. – Surah Al-Munafiqun

إِذَا جَآءَكَ ٱلْمُنَـٰفِقُونَ قَالُوا۟ نَشْهَدُ إِنَّكَ لَرَسُولُ ٱللَّهِ ۗ وَٱللَّهُ يَعْلَمُ إِنَّكَ لَرَسُولُهُۥ وَٱللَّهُ يَشْهَدُ إِنَّ ٱلْمُنَـٰفِقِينَ لَكَـٰذِبُونَ ٱتَّخَذُوٓا۟ أَيْمَـٰنَهُمْ
جُنَّةً فَصَدُّوا۟ عَن سَبِيلِ ٱللَّهِ ۚ إِنَّهُمْ سَآءَ مَا كَانُوا۟ يَعْمَلُونَ ذَٰلِكَ بِأَنَّهُمْ ءَامَنُوا۟ ثُمَّ كَفَرُوا۟ فَطُبِعَ عَلَىٰ قُلُوبِهِمْ فَهُمْ لَا يَفْقَهُونَ وَإِذَا
رَأَيْتَهُمْ تُعْجِبُكَ أَجْسَامُهُمْ ۖ وَإِن يَقُولُوا۟ تَسْمَعْ لِقَوْلِهِمْ ۖ كَأَنَّهُمْ خُشُبٌ مُّسَنَّدَةٌ ۖ يَحْسَبُونَ كُلَّ صَيْحَةٍ عَلَيْهِمْ ۚ هُمُ ٱلْعَدُوُّ فَٱحْذَرْهُمْ ۚ قَـٰتَلَهُمُ
ٱللَّهُ ۖ أَنَّىٰ يُؤْفَكُونَ وَإِذَا قِيلَ لَهُمْ تَعَالَوْا۟ يَسْتَغْفِرْ لَكُمْ رَسُولُ ٱللَّهِ لَوَّوْا۟ رُءُوسَهُمْ وَرَأَيْتَهُمْ يَصُدُّونَ وَهُم مُّسْتَكْبِرُونَ سَوَآءٌ عَلَيْهِمْ
أَسْتَغْفَرْتَ لَهُمْ أَمْ لَمْ تَسْتَغْفِرْ لَهُمْ لَن يَغْفِرَ ٱللَّهُ لَهُمْ ۚ إِنَّ ٱللَّهَ لَا يَهْدِى ٱلْقَوْمَ ٱلْفَـٰسِقِينَ هُمُ ٱلَّذِينَ يَقُولُونَ لَا تُنفِقُوا۟ عَلَىٰ مَنْ عِندَ
رَسُولِ ٱللَّهِ حَتَّىٰ يَنفَضُّوا۟ ۗ وَلِلَّهِ خَزَآئِنُ ٱلسَّمَـٰوَٰتِ وَٱلْأَرْضِ وَلَـٰكِنَّ ٱلْمُنَـٰفِقِينَ لَا يَفْقَهُونَ يَقُولُونَ لَئِن رَّجَعْنَآ إِلَى ٱلْمَدِينَةِ
لَيُخْرِجَنَّ ٱلْأَعَزُّ مِنْهَا ٱلْأَذَلَّ ۚ وَلِلَّهِ ٱلْعِزَّةُ وَلِرَسُولِهِۦ وَلِلْمُؤْمِنِينَ وَلَـٰكِنَّ ٱلْمُنَـٰفِقِينَ لَا يَعْلَمُونَ يَـٰٓأَيُّهَا ٱلَّذِينَ ءَامَنُوا۟ لَا تُلْهِكُمْ أَمْوَٰلُكُمْ
وَلَآ أَوْلَـٰدُكُمْ عَن ذِكْرِ ٱللَّهِ ۚ وَمَن يَفْعَلْ ذَٰلِكَ فَأُو۟لَـٰٓئِكَ هُمُ ٱلْخَـٰسِرُونَ وَأَنفِقُوا۟ مِن مَّا رَزَقْنَـٰكُم مِّن قَبْلِ أَن يَأْتِىَ أَحَدَكُمُ ٱلْمَوْتُ
فَيَقُولَ رَبِّ لَوْلَآ أَخَّرْتَنِىٓ إِلَىٰٓ أَجَلٍ قَرِيبٍ فَأَصَّدَّقَ وَأَكُن مِّنَ ٱلصَّـٰلِحِينَ وَلَن يُؤَخِّرَ ٱللَّهُ نَفْسًا إِذَا جَآءَ أَجَلُهَا ۚ وَٱللَّهُ خَبِيرٌۢ بِمَا
تَعْمَلُونَ

Surely the hypocrites try to deceive Allah, and He is deceiving them; and when they rise up for prayer, they rise up lazily, showing off to (other) men, and they do not remember Allah except a little. – Surah An-Nisa 4:142

إِنَّ ٱلْمُنَـٰفِقِينَ يُخَـٰدِعُونَ ٱللَّهَ وَهُوَ خَـٰدِعُهُمْ وَإِذَا قَامُوٓا۟ إِلَى ٱلصَّلَوٰةِ قَامُوا۟ كُسَالَىٰ يُرَآءُونَ ٱلنَّاسَ وَلَا يَذْكُرُونَ ٱللَّهَ إِلَّا قَلِيلًا

The Book of
Therefore withdraw from him who turns away from Our Reminder
فَأَعۡرِضۡ عَن مَّن تَوَلَّىٰ عَن ذِكۡرِنَا

So leave alone those who take their religion for play and pastime, and whom the worldly life has deceived. But remind with it, lest a soul becomes damned on account of what it has earned. It has no helper or intercessor besides Allah. Even if it offers every equivalent, none will be accepted from it. These are the ones who are delivered to perdition by their actions. They will have a drink of scalding water, and a painful punishment, because they used to disbelieve. – Surah Al-An'am 6:70

وَذَرِ ٱلَّذِينَ ٱتَّخَذُواْ دِينَهُمۡ لَعِبٗا وَلَهۡوٗا وَغَرَّتۡهُمُ ٱلۡحَيَوٰةُ ٱلدُّنۡيَاۚ وَذَكِّرۡ بِهِۦٓ أَن تُبۡسَلَ نَفۡسُۢ بِمَا كَسَبَتۡ لَيۡسَ لَهَا مِن دُونِ ٱللَّهِ وَلِيّٞ وَلَا شَفِيعٞ وَإِن تَعۡدِلۡ كُلَّ عَدۡلٖ لَّا يُؤۡخَذۡ مِنۡهَآۗ أُوْلَٰٓئِكَ ٱلَّذِينَ أُبۡسِلُواْ بِمَا كَسَبُواْۖ لَهُمۡ شَرَابٞ مِّنۡ حَمِيمٖ وَعَذَابٌ أَلِيمُۢ بِمَا كَانُواْ يَكۡفُرُونَ

They are those whom Allah knows what is in their hearts. So ignore them, and admonish them, and say to them concerning themselves penetrating words. – Surah An-Nisa 4:63

أُوْلَٰٓئِكَ ٱلَّذِينَ يَعۡلَمُ ٱللَّهُ مَا فِي قُلُوبِهِمۡ فَأَعۡرِضۡ عَنۡهُمۡ وَعِظۡهُمۡ وَقُل لَّهُمۡ فِيٓ أَنفُسِهِمۡ قَوۡلَۢا بَلِيغٗا

What is the matter with you, divided into two factions regarding the hypocrites, when Allah Himself has overwhelmed them on account of what they did? Do you want to guide those whom Allah has led astray? Whomever Allah leads astray—you will never find for him a way. – Surah An-Nisa 4:88

فَمَا لَكُمۡ فِي ٱلۡمُنَٰفِقِينَ فِئَتَيۡنِ وَٱللَّهُ أَرۡكَسَهُم بِمَا كَسَبُوٓاْۚ أَتُرِيدُونَ أَن تَهۡدُواْ مَنۡ أَضَلَّ ٱللَّهُۖ وَمَن يُضۡلِلِ ٱللَّهُ فَلَن تَجِدَ لَهُۥ سَبِيلٗا

They will swear to you by Allah, when you return to them, that you may leave them alone. So leave them alone. They are a disgrace, and their destiny is Hell; a reward for what they used to earn.– Surah At-Taubah 9:95

سَيَحۡلِفُونَ بِٱللَّهِ لَكُمۡ إِذَا ٱنقَلَبۡتُمۡ إِلَيۡهِمۡ لِتُعۡرِضُواْ عَنۡهُمۡۖ فَأَعۡرِضُواْ عَنۡهُمۡۖ إِنَّهُمۡ رِجۡسٞۖ وَمَأۡوَىٰهُمۡ جَهَنَّمُ جَزَآءَۢ بِمَا كَانُواْ يَكۡسِبُونَ

And do not obey the blasphemers and the hypocrites, and ignore their insults, and rely on Allah. Allah is a sufficient protector. – Surah Al-Azhab 33:48

وَلَا تُطِعِ ٱلۡكَٰفِرِينَ وَٱلۡمُنَٰفِقِينَ وَدَعۡ أَذَىٰهُمۡ وَتَوَكَّلۡ عَلَى ٱللَّهِۚ وَكَفَىٰ بِٱللَّهِ وَكِيلٗا

.....Do not obey anyone whose heart We have made oblivious of Our remembrance, who follows his own whims and desires, and who abandons all that is good. – Surah Al-Kahf 18:28

وَلَا تُطِعۡ مَنۡ أَغۡفَلۡنَا قَلۡبَهُۥ عَن ذِكۡرِنَا وَٱتَّبَعَ هَوَىٰهُ وَكَانَ أَمۡرُهُۥ فُرُطٗا

Narrated Hudhaifa bin Al-Yaman: The people used to ask Allah's Messenger ﷺ about the good but I used to ask him about the evil lest I should be overtaken by them. So I said, "O Allah's Messenger ﷺ ! We were living in ignorance and in an (extremely) worst atmosphere, then Allah brought to us this good (i.e., Islam); will there be any evil after this good?" He said, "Yes." I said, 'Will there be any good after that evil?" He replied, "Yes, but it will be tainted (not pure.)" I asked, "What will be its taint?" He replied, "(There will be) some people who will guide others not according to my tradition? You will approve of some of their deeds and disapprove of some others." I asked, "Will there be any evil after that good?" He replied, "Yes, (there will be) some people calling at the gates of the (Hell) Fire, and whoever will respond to their call, will be thrown by them into the (Hell) Fire." I said, "O Allah s Apostle! Will you describe them to us?" He said, "They will be from our own people and will speak our language." I said, "What do you order me to do if such a state should take place in my life?" He said, "Stick to the group of Muslims and their Imam (ruler)." I said, "If there is neither a group of Muslims nor an Imam (ruler)?" He said, "Then turn away from all those sects even if you were to bite (eat) the roots of a tree till death overtakes you while you are in that state." – Al-Bukhari 7084

حَدَّثَنَا مُحَمَّدُ بْنُ الْمُثَنَّى، حَدَّثَنَا الْوَلِيدُ بْنُ مُسْلِمٍ، حَدَّثَنَا ابْنُ جَابِرٍ، حَدَّثَنِي بُسْرُ بْنُ عُبَيْدِ اللَّهِ الْحَضْرَمِيُّ، أَنَّهُ سَمِعَ أَبَا إِدْرِيسَ الْخَوْلاَنِيَّ، أَنَّهُ سَمِعَ حُذَيْفَةَ بْنَ الْيَمَانِ، يَقُولُ كَانَ النَّاسُ يَسْأَلُونَ رَسُولَ اللَّهِ صلى الله عليه وسلم عَنِ الْخَيْرِ، وَكُنْتُ أَسْأَلُهُ عَنِ الشَّرِّ، مَخَافَةَ أَنْ يُدْرِكَنِي فَقُلْتُ يَا رَسُولَ اللَّهِ إِنَّا كُنَّا فِي جَاهِلِيَّةٍ وَشَرٍّ فَجَاءَنَا اللَّهُ بِهَذَا الْخَيْرِ، فَهَلْ بَعْدَ هَذَا الْخَيْرِ مِنْ شَرٍّ قَالَ " نَعَمْ ". قُلْتُ وَهَلْ بَعْدَ ذَلِكَ الشَّرِّ مِنْ خَيْرٍ قَالَ " نَعَمْ، وَفِيهِ دَخَنٌ ". قُلْتُ وَمَا دَخَنُهُ قَالَ " قَوْمٌ يَهْدُونَ بِغَيْرِ هَدْيِي، تَعْرِفُ مِنْهُمْ وَتُنْكِرُ ". قُلْتُ فَهَلْ بَعْدَ ذَلِكَ الْخَيْرِ مِنْ شَرٍّ قَالَ " نَعَمْ، دُعَاةٌ عَلَى أَبْوَابِ جَهَنَّمَ، مَنْ أَجَابَهُمْ إِلَيْهَا قَذَفُوهُ فِيهَا ". قُلْتُ يَا رَسُولَ اللَّهِ صِفْهُمْ لَنَا. قَالَ " هُمْ مِنْ جِلْدَتِنَا، وَيَتَكَلَّمُونَ بِأَلْسِنَتِنَا ". قُلْتُ فَمَا تَأْمُرُنِي إِنْ أَدْرَكَنِي ذَلِكَ قَالَ " تَلْزَمُ جَمَاعَةَ الْمُسْلِمِينَ وَإِمَامَهُمْ ". قُلْتُ فَإِنْ لَمْ يَكُنْ لَهُمْ جَمَاعَةٌ وَلاَ إِمَامٌ قَالَ " فَاعْتَزِلْ تِلْكَ الْفِرَقَ كُلَّهَا، وَلَوْ أَنْ تَعَضَّ بِأَصْلِ شَجَرَةٍ، حَتَّى يُدْرِكَكَ الْمَوْتُ، وَأَنْتَ عَلَى ذَلِكَ "

They profess obedience, but when they leave your presence, some of them conspire something contrary to what you said. But Allah writes down what they conspire. So avoid them, and put your trust in Allah. Allah is Guardian enough. – Surah An-Nisa 4:81

وَيَقُولُونَ طَاعَةٌ فَإِذَا بَرَزُوا۟ مِنْ عِندِكَ بَيَّتَ طَآئِفَةٌ مِّنْهُمْ غَيْرَ ٱلَّذِى تَقُولُ ۖ وَٱللَّهُ يَكْتُبُ مَا يُبَيِّتُونَ ۖ فَأَعْرِضْ عَنْهُمْ وَتَوَكَّلْ عَلَى ٱللَّهِ ۚ وَكَفَىٰ بِٱللَّهِ وَكِيلًا

Allah will not leave the believers as you are, without distinguishing the wicked from the sincere. Nor will Allah inform you of the future, but Allah elects from among His messengers whom He wills. So believe in Allah and His messengers. If you believe and practice piety, you will have a splendid reward. – Surah Al-Imran 3:179

مَّا كَانَ ٱللَّهُ لِيَذَرَ ٱلْمُؤْمِنِينَ عَلَىٰ مَآ أَنتُمْ عَلَيْهِ حَتَّىٰ يَمِيزَ ٱلْخَبِيثَ مِنَ ٱلطَّيِّبِ ۗ وَمَا كَانَ ٱللَّهُ لِيُطْلِعَكُمْ عَلَى ٱلْغَيْبِ وَلَـٰكِنَّ ٱللَّهَ يَجْتَبِى مِن رُّسُلِهِۦ مَن يَشَآءُ ۖ فَـَٔامِنُوا۟ بِٱللَّهِ وَرُسُلِهِۦ ۚ وَإِن تُؤْمِنُوا۟ وَتَتَّقُوا۟ فَلَكُمْ أَجْرٌ عَظِيمٌ

Narrated Ibn `Umar: The 'Prophet said, "It is obligatory for one to listen to and obey (the ruler's orders) unless these orders involve one disobedience (to Allah); but if an act of disobedience (to Allah) is imposed, he should not listen to or obey it." – Al-Bukhari 2955

حَدَّثَنَا مُسَدَّدٌ، حَدَّثَنَا يَحْيَى، عَنْ عُبَيْدِ اللَّهِ، قَالَ حَدَّثَنِي نَافِعٌ، عَنِ ابْنِ عُمَرَ ـ رضى الله عنهما ـ عَنِ النَّبِيِّ صلى الله عليه وسلم. وَحَدَّثَنِي مُحَمَّدُ بْنُ صَبَّاحٍ، حَدَّثَنَا إِسْمَاعِيلُ بْنُ زَكَرِيَّاءَ، عَنْ عُبَيْدِ اللَّهِ، عَنْ نَافِعٍ، عَنِ ابْنِ عُمَرَ ـ رضى الله عنهما ـ عَنِ النَّبِيِّ صلى الله عليه وسلم قَالَ " السَّمْعُ وَالطَّاعَةُ حَقٌّ، مَا لَمْ يُؤْمَرْ بِالْمَعْصِيَةِ، فَإِذَا أُمِرَ بِمَعْصِيَةٍ فَلاَ سَمْعَ وَلاَ طَاعَةَ

Narrated `Abdullah bin `Amr bin Al-`As: I heard Allah's Messenger ﷺ saying, "Allah does not take away the knowledge, by taking it away from (the hearts of) the people, but takes it away by the death of the religious learned men till when none of the (religious learned men) remains, people will take as their leaders ignorant persons who when consulted will give their verdict without knowledge. So they will go astray and will lead the people astray." – Al-Bukhari 100

حَدَّثَنَا إِسْمَاعِيلُ بْنُ أَبِي أُوَيْسٍ، قَالَ حَدَّثَنِي مَالِكٌ، عَنْ هِشَامِ بْنِ عُرْوَةَ، عَنْ أَبِيهِ، عَنْ عَبْدِ اللَّهِ بْنِ عَمْرِو بْنِ الْعَاصِ، قَالَ سَمِعْتُ رَسُولَ اللَّهِ صلى الله عليه وسلم يَقُولُ " إِنَّ اللَّهَ لاَ يَقْبِضُ الْعِلْمَ انْتِزَاعًا، يَنْتَزِعُهُ مِنَ الْعِبَادِ، وَلَكِنْ يَقْبِضُ الْعِلْمَ بِقَبْضِ الْعُلَمَاءِ، حَتَّى إِذَا لَمْ يُبْقِ عَالِمًا، اتَّخَذَ النَّاسُ رُءُوسًا جُهَّالاً فَسُئِلُوا، فَأَفْتَوْا بِغَيْرِ عِلْمٍ، فَضَلُّوا وَأَضَلُّوا "

So avoid him who has turned away from Our remembrance, and desires nothing but the present life. – Surah An-Najm 53:29

فَأَعْرِضْ عَن مَّن تَوَلَّىٰ عَن ذِكْرِنَا وَلَمْ يُرِدْ إِلَّا ٱلْحَيَوٰةَ ٱلدُّنْيَا

Anas said: When you visit a Muslim who is not suspicious, then eat of his food and drink of his drink. – Bukhari Vol.7 page 225
و قال أنس : إذا دخلت على مسلم لا يتهم فكل من طعامه و اشرب من شرابه

He said, "Your prayer has been answered, so go straight, and do not follow the path of those who do not know." – Surah Yunus 10:89
قَالَ قَدْ أُجِيبَت دَّعْوَتُكُمَا فَٱسْتَقِيمَا وَلَا تَتَّبِعَآنِّ سَبِيلَ ٱلَّذِينَ لَا يَعْلَمُونَ

Then We set you upon a pathway of faith, so follow it, and do not follow the inclinations of those who do not know. – Surah Al-Jathiyah 45:18
ثُمَّ جَعَلْنَـٰكَ عَلَىٰ شَرِيعَةٍ مِّنَ ٱلْأَمْرِ فَٱتَّبِعْهَا وَلَا تَتَّبِعْ أَهْوَآءَ ٱلَّذِينَ لَا يَعْلَمُونَ

This is My path, straight, so follow it. And do not follow the other paths, lest they divert you from His path. All this He has enjoined upon you, that you may refrain from wrongdoing. – Surah Al-An'am 6:153
وَأَنَّ هَـٰذَا صِرَٰطِى مُسْتَقِيمًا فَٱتَّبِعُوهُ ۖ وَلَا تَتَّبِعُوا۟ ٱلسُّبُلَ فَتَفَرَّقَ بِكُمْ عَن سَبِيلِهِۦ ۚ ذَٰلِكُمْ وَصَّىٰكُم بِهِۦ لَعَلَّكُمْ تَتَّقُونَ

And do not occupy yourself with what you have no knowledge of. The hearing, and the sight, and the brains—all these will be questioned. – Surah Al-Isra 17:36
وَلَا تَقْفُ مَا لَيْسَ لَكَ بِهِۦ عِلْمٌ ۚ إِنَّ ٱلسَّمْعَ وَٱلْبَصَرَ وَٱلْفُؤَادَ كُلُّ أُو۟لَـٰٓئِكَ كَانَ عَنْهُ مَسْـُٔولًا

Have you considered those who befriended a people with whom Allah has become angry? They are not of you, nor of them. And they swear to a lie while they know. Allah has prepared for them a terrible punishment. Evil is what they used to do. They took their oaths as a screen, and prevented others from Allah's path. They will have a shameful punishment. Neither their possessions nor their children will avail them anything against Allah. These are the inhabitants of the Fire, dwelling therein forever. On the Day when Allah will resurrect them altogether—they will swear to Him, as they swear to you, thinking that they are upon something. Indeed, they themselves are the liars. Satan has taken hold of them, and so has caused them to forget the remembrance of Allah. These are the partisans of Satan. Indeed, it is Satan's partisans who are the losers. Those who oppose Allah and His Messenger are among the lowliest. Allah has written: "I will certainly prevail, I and My messengers." Allah is Strong and Mighty. You will not find a people who believe in Allah and the Last Day, loving those who oppose Allah and His Messenger, even if they were their parents, or their children, or their siblings, or their close relatives. These—He has inscribed faith in their hearts, and has supported them with a spirit from Him. And He will admit them into Gardens beneath which rivers flow, wherein they will dwell forever. Allah is pleased with them, and they are pleased with Him. These are the partisans of Allah. Indeed, it is Allah's partisans who are the successful. – Surah Al-Mujadilah 58:14-22
أَلَمْ تَرَ إِلَى ٱلَّذِينَ تَوَلَّوْا۟ قَوْمًا غَضِبَ ٱللَّهُ عَلَيْهِم مَّا هُم مِّنكُمْ وَلَا مِنْهُمْ وَيَحْلِفُونَ عَلَى ٱلْكَذِبِ وَهُمْ يَعْلَمُونَ أَعَدَّ ٱللَّهُ لَهُمْ عَذَابًا
شَدِيدًا ۖ إِنَّهُمْ سَآءَ مَا كَانُوا۟ يَعْمَلُونَ ٱتَّخَذُوٓا۟ أَيْمَـٰنَهُمْ جُنَّةً فَصَدُّوا۟ عَن سَبِيلِ ٱللَّهِ فَلَهُمْ عَذَابٌ مُّهِينٌ لَّن تُغْنِىَ عَنْهُمْ أَمْوَٰلُهُمْ وَلَآ
أَوْلَـٰدُهُم مِّنَ ٱللَّهِ شَيْـًٔا ۚ أُو۟لَـٰٓئِكَ أَصْحَـٰبُ ٱلنَّارِ ۖ هُمْ فِيهَا خَـٰلِدُونَ يَوْمَ يَبْعَثُهُمُ ٱللَّهُ جَمِيعًا فَيَحْلِفُونَ لَهُۥ كَمَا يَحْلِفُونَ لَكُمْ ۖ وَيَحْسَبُونَ
أَنَّهُمْ عَلَىٰ شَىْءٍ ۚ أَلَآ إِنَّهُمْ هُمُ ٱلْكَـٰذِبُونَ ٱسْتَحْوَذَ عَلَيْهِمُ ٱلشَّيْطَـٰنُ فَأَنسَىٰهُمْ ذِكْرَ ٱللَّهِ ۚ أُو۟لَـٰٓئِكَ حِزْبُ ٱلشَّيْطَـٰنِ ۚ أَلَآ إِنَّ حِزْبَ
ٱلشَّيْطَـٰنِ هُمُ ٱلْخَـٰسِرُونَ إِنَّ ٱلَّذِينَ يُحَآدُّونَ ٱللَّهَ وَرَسُولَهُۥٓ أُو۟لَـٰٓئِكَ فِى ٱلْأَذَلِّينَ كَتَبَ ٱللَّهُ لَأَغْلِبَنَّ أَنَا۠ وَرُسُلِىٓ ۚ إِنَّ ٱللَّهَ قَوِىٌّ عَزِيزٌ
لَّا تَجِدُ قَوْمًا يُؤْمِنُونَ بِٱللَّهِ وَٱلْيَوْمِ ٱلْـَٔاخِرِ يُوَآدُّونَ مَنْ حَآدَّ ٱللَّهَ وَرَسُولَهُۥ وَلَوْ كَانُوٓا۟ ءَابَآءَهُمْ أَوْ أَبْنَآءَهُمْ أَوْ إِخْوَٰنَهُمْ أَوْ

عَشِيرَتَهُمْۚ أُوْلَـٰٓئِكَ كَتَبَ فِى قُلُوبِهِمُ ٱلْإِيمَـٰنَ وَأَيَّدَهُم بِرُوحٍ مِّنْهُۖ وَيُدْخِلُهُمْ جَنَّـٰتٍ تَجْرِى مِن تَحْتِهَا ٱلْأَنْهَـٰرُ خَـٰلِدِينَ فِيهَاۚ رَضِىَ ٱللَّهُ عَنْهُمْ وَرَضُواْ عَنْهُۚ أُوْلَـٰٓئِكَ حِزْبُ ٱللَّهِۚ أَلَآ إِنَّ حِزْبَ ٱللَّهِ هُمُ ٱلْمُفْلِحُونَ

And do not argue on behalf of those who deceive themselves. Allah does not love the deceitful sinner. – Surah An-Nisa 4:107

وَلَا تُجَـٰدِلْ عَنِ ٱلَّذِينَ يَخْتَانُونَ أَنفُسَهُمْۚ إِنَّ ٱللَّهَ لَا يُحِبُّ مَن كَانَ خَوَّانًا أَثِيمًا

O Prophet (Muhammad)! Strive against the disbelievers and the hypocrites, and be stern with them. Their abode is Hell—what a miserable destination! – Surah At-Taubah 9:73

يَـٰٓأَيُّهَا ٱلنَّبِىُّ جَـٰهِدِ ٱلْكُفَّارَ وَٱلْمُنَـٰفِقِينَ وَٱغْلُظْ عَلَيْهِمْۚ وَمَأْوَىٰهُمْ جَهَنَّمُۖ وَبِئْسَ ٱلْمَصِيرُ

And endure patiently what they say, and withdraw from them politely. – Surah Al-Muzzamil 73:10

وَٱصْبِرْ عَلَىٰ مَا يَقُولُونَ وَٱهْجُرْهُمْ هَجْرًا جَمِيلًا

And I will withdraw from you, and from what you pray to instead of Allah. And I will pray to my Lord, and I hope I will not be disappointed in my prayer to my Lord." – Surah Mariyam 19:48

وَأَعْتَزِلُكُمْ وَمَا تَدْعُونَ مِن دُونِ ٱللَّهِ وَأَدْعُواْ رَبِّى عَسَىٰٓ أَلَّآ أَكُونَ بِدُعَآءِ رَبِّى شَقِيًّا

O you who believe! The polytheists are polluted, so let them not approach the Sacred Mosque after this year of theirs. And if you fear poverty, Allah will enrich you from His grace, if He wills. Allah is Aware and Wise.– Surah At-Taubah 9:28

يَـٰٓأَيُّهَا ٱلَّذِينَ ءَامَنُوٓاْ إِنَّمَا ٱلْمُشْرِكُونَ نَجَسٌ فَلَا يَقْرَبُواْ ٱلْمَسْجِدَ ٱلْحَرَامَ بَعْدَ عَامِهِمْ هَـٰذَاۚ وَإِنْ خِفْتُمْ عَيْلَةً فَسَوْفَ يُغْنِيكُمُ ٱللَّهُ مِن فَضْلِهِۦٓ إِن شَآءَۚ إِنَّ ٱللَّهَ عَلِيمٌ حَكِيمٌ

Just as We sent down to the separatists. Those who made the Quran obsolete. By your Lord, we will question them all. About what they used to do. So proclaim openly what you are commanded, and turn away from the polytheists. – Surah Al-Hijr 15:90-94

كَمَآ أَنزَلْنَا عَلَى ٱلْمُقْتَسِمِينَ ٱلَّذِينَ جَعَلُواْ ٱلْقُرْءَانَ عِضِينَ فَوَرَبِّكَ لَنَسْـَٔلَنَّهُمْ أَجْمَعِينَ عَمَّا كَانُواْ يَعْمَلُونَ فَٱصْدَعْ بِمَا تُؤْمَرُ وَأَعْرِضْ عَنِ ٱلْمُشْرِكِينَ

Follow what was revealed to you from your Lord. There is no god but He. And turn away from the polytheists. – Surah Al-An'am 6:106

ٱتَّبِعْ مَآ أُوحِىَ إِلَيْكَ مِن رَّبِّكَۖ لَآ إِلَـٰهَ إِلَّا هُوَۖ وَأَعْرِضْ عَنِ ٱلْمُشْرِكِينَ

So avoid him who has turned away from Our remembrance, and desires nothing but the present life. – Surah An-Najm 53:29

فَأَعْرِضْ عَن مَّن تَوَلَّىٰ عَن ذِكْرِنَا وَلَمْ يُرِدْ إِلَّا ٱلْحَيَوٰةَ ٱلدُّنْيَا

The Book of
Allah is the Wali of those who believe
ٱللَّهُ وَلِيُّ ٱلَّذِينَ ءَامَنُوا۟

They used not to prevent one another from the wrongs they used to commit. Evil is what they used to do. You will see many of them befriending those who disbelieve. Terrible is what their souls prompts them to do. The wrath of Allah fell upon them, and in the torment they will remain. Had they believed in Allah and the Prophet, and in what was revealed to him, they would not have befriended them. But many of them are immoral. – Surah Al-Maidah 5:79-81

كَانُوا۟ لَا يَتَنَاهَوْنَ عَن مُّنكَرٍ فَعَلُوهُ ۚ لَبِئْسَ مَا كَانُوا۟ يَفْعَلُونَ تَرَىٰ كَثِيرًا مِّنْهُمْ يَتَوَلَّوْنَ ٱلَّذِينَ كَفَرُوا۟ ۚ لَبِئْسَ مَا قَدَّمَتْ لَهُمْ أَنفُسُهُمْ أَن سَخِطَ ٱللَّهُ عَلَيْهِمْ وَفِى ٱلْعَذَابِ هُمْ خَـٰلِدُونَ وَلَوْ كَانُوا۟ يُؤْمِنُونَ بِٱللَّهِ وَٱلنَّبِىِّ وَمَآ أُنزِلَ إِلَيْهِ مَا ٱتَّخَذُوهُمْ أَوْلِيَآءَ وَلَـٰكِنَّ كَثِيرًا مِّنْهُمْ فَـٰسِقُونَ

Follow what was revealed to you from your Lord. There is no god but He. And turn away from the polytheists. – Surah Al-An'am 6:106

ٱتَّبِعْ مَآ أُوحِىَ إِلَيْكَ مِن رَّبِّكَ ۖ لَآ إِلَـٰهَ إِلَّا هُوَ ۖ وَأَعْرِضْ عَنِ ٱلْمُشْرِكِينَ

You did not expect the Scripture to be transmitted to you, except as mercy from your Lord. Therefore, do not be a supporter of the disbelievers. – Surah Al-Qasas 28:86

وَمَا كُنتَ تَرْجُوٓا۟ أَن يُلْقَىٰٓ إِلَيْكَ ٱلْكِتَـٰبُ إِلَّا رَحْمَةً مِّن رَّبِّكَ ۖ فَلَا تَكُونَنَّ ظَهِيرًا لِّلْكَـٰفِرِينَ

Narrated Aishah (ra): I heard the Prophet ﷺ, "Souls are like recruited troops: Those who are like qualities are inclined to each other, but those who have dissimilar qualities, differ." – Al-Bukhari 3336

قَالَ قَالَ اللَّيْثُ عَنْ يَحْيَى بْنِ سَعِيدٍ، عَنْ عَمْرَةَ، عَنْ عَائِشَةَ، رضى الله عنها قَالَتْ سَمِعْتُ النَّبِيَّ صلى الله عليه وسلم يَقُولُ " الأَرْوَاحُ جُنُودٌ مُجَنَّدَةٌ، فَمَا تَعَارَفَ مِنْهَا ائْتَلَفَ، وَمَا تَنَاكَرَ مِنْهَا اخْتَلَفَ ". وَقَالَ يَحْيَى بْنُ أَيُّوبَ حَدَّثَنِي يَحْيَى بْنُ سَعِيدٍ بِهَذَا

O you who believe! Do not befriend outsiders who never cease to wish you harm. They love to see you suffer. Hatred has already appeared from their mouths, but what their hearts conceal is worse. We have made the messages clear for you, if you understand. – Surah Al-Imran 3:118

يَـٰٓأَيُّهَا ٱلَّذِينَ ءَامَنُوا۟ لَا تَتَّخِذُوا۟ بِطَانَةً مِّن دُونِكُمْ لَا يَأْلُونَكُمْ خَبَالًا وَدُّوا۟ مَا عَنِتُّمْ قَدْ بَدَتِ ٱلْبَغْضَآءُ مِنْ أَفْوَٰهِهِمْ وَمَا تُخْفِى صُدُورُهُمْ أَكْبَرُ ۚ قَدْ بَيَّنَّا لَكُمُ ٱلْـَٔايَـٰتِ ۖ إِن كُنتُمْ تَعْقِلُونَ

Neither your relatives nor your children will benefit you on the Day of Resurrection. He will separate between you. Allah is Observant of what you do. You have had an excellent example in Abraham and those with him; when they said to their people, "We are quit of you, and what you worship apart from Allah. We denounce you. Enmity and hatred has surfaced between us and you, forever, until you believe in Allah alone." Except for the words of Abraham to his father, "I will ask forgiveness for you, though I have no power from Allah to do anything for you." "Our Lord, in You we trust, and to You we repent, and to You is the ultimate resort. – Surah Muntahanah 60:3&4

لَن تَنفَعَكُمْ أَرْحَامُكُمْ وَلَآ أَوْلَـٰدُكُمْ ۚ يَوْمَ ٱلْقِيَـٰمَةِ يَفْصِلُ بَيْنَكُمْ ۚ وَٱللَّهُ بِمَا تَعْمَلُونَ بَصِيرٌ قَدْ كَانَتْ لَكُمْ أُسْوَةٌ حَسَنَةٌ فِىٓ إِبْرَٰهِيمَ وَٱلَّذِينَ مَعَهُۥٓ إِذْ قَالُوا۟ لِقَوْمِهِمْ إِنَّا بُرَءَٰٓؤُا۟ مِنكُمْ وَمِمَّا تَعْبُدُونَ مِن دُونِ ٱللَّهِ كَفَرْنَا بِكُمْ وَبَدَا بَيْنَنَا وَبَيْنَكُمُ ٱلْعَدَٰوَةُ وَٱلْبَغْضَآءُ أَبَدًا

حَتَّىٰ تُؤْمِنُوا۟ بِٱللَّهِ وَحْدَهُۥٓ إِلَّا قَوْلَ إِبْرَٰهِيمَ لِأَبِيهِ لَأَسْتَغْفِرَنَّ لَكَ وَمَآ أَمْلِكُ لَكَ مِنَ ٱللَّهِ مِن شَىْءٍ ۖ رَّبَّنَا عَلَيْكَ تَوَكَّلْنَا وَإِلَيْكَ أَنَبْنَا
وَإِلَيْكَ ٱلْمَصِيرُ

Perhaps Allah will plant affection between you and those of them you consider enemies. Allah is Capable. Allah is Forgiving and Merciful. As for those who have not fought against you for your religion, nor expelled you from your homes, Allah does not prohibit you from dealing with them kindly and equitably. Allah loves the equitable. But Allah prohibits you from befriending those who fought against you over your religion, and expelled you from your homes, and aided in your expulsion. Whoever takes them for friends—these are the wrongdoers. O you who believe! When believing women come to you emigrating, test them. Allah is Aware of their faith. And if you find them to be faithful, do not send them back to the unbelievers. They are not lawful for them, nor are they lawful for them. But give them what they have spent. You are not at fault if you marry them, provided you give them their compensation. And do not hold on to ties with unbelieving women, but demand what you have spent, and let them demand what they have spent. This is the rule of Allah; He rules among you. Allah is Knowing and Wise. If any of your wives desert you to the unbelievers, and you decide to penalize them, give those whose wives have gone away the equivalent of what they had spent. And fear Allah, in whom you are believers. O prophet! If believing women come to you, pledging allegiance to you, on condition that they will not associate anything with Allah, nor steal, nor commit adultery, nor kill their children, nor commit perjury as to parenthood, nor disobey you in anything righteous, accept their allegiance and ask Allah's forgiveness for them. Allah is Forgiving and Merciful. O you who believe! Do not befriend people with whom Allah has become angry, and have despaired of the Hereafter, as the faithless have despaired of the occupants of the graves . Surah Al-Mumtahanah 60:7-13

عَسَى ٱللَّهُ أَن يَجْعَلَ بَيْنَكُمْ وَبَيْنَ ٱلَّذِينَ عَادَيْتُم مِّنْهُم مَّوَدَّةً ۚ وَٱللَّهُ قَدِيرٌ ۚ وَٱللَّهُ غَفُورٌ رَّحِيمٌ لَّا يَنْهَىٰكُمُ ٱللَّهُ عَنِ ٱلَّذِينَ لَمْ يُقَٰتِلُوكُمْ
فِى ٱلدِّينِ وَلَمْ يُخْرِجُوكُم مِّن دِيَٰرِكُمْ أَن تَبَرُّوهُمْ وَتُقْسِطُوٓا۟ إِلَيْهِمْ ۚ إِنَّ ٱللَّهَ يُحِبُّ ٱلْمُقْسِطِينَ إِنَّمَا يَنْهَىٰكُمُ ٱللَّهُ عَنِ ٱلَّذِينَ قَٰتَلُوكُمْ فِى
ٱلدِّينِ وَأَخْرَجُوكُم مِّن دِيَٰرِكُمْ وَظَٰهَرُوا۟ عَلَىٰٓ إِخْرَاجِكُمْ أَن تَوَلَّوْهُمْ ۚ وَمَن يَتَوَلَّهُمْ فَأُو۟لَٰٓئِكَ هُمُ ٱلظَّٰلِمُونَ يَٰٓأَيُّهَا ٱلَّذِينَ ءَامَنُوٓا۟ إِذَا
جَآءَكُمُ ٱلْمُؤْمِنَٰتُ مُهَٰجِرَٰتٍ فَٱمْتَحِنُوهُنَّ ۖ ٱللَّهُ أَعْلَمُ بِإِيمَٰنِهِنَّ ۖ فَإِنْ عَلِمْتُمُوهُنَّ مُؤْمِنَٰتٍ فَلَا تَرْجِعُوهُنَّ إِلَى ٱلْكُفَّارِ ۖ لَا هُنَّ حِلٌّ لَّهُمْ
وَلَا هُمْ يَحِلُّونَ لَهُنَّ ۖ وَءَاتُوهُم مَّآ أَنفَقُوا۟ ۚ وَلَا جُنَاحَ عَلَيْكُمْ أَن تَنكِحُوهُنَّ إِذَآ ءَاتَيْتُمُوهُنَّ أُجُورَهُنَّ ۚ وَلَا تُمْسِكُوا۟ بِعِصَمِ ٱلْكَوَافِرِ
وَسْـَٔلُوا۟ مَآ أَنفَقْتُمْ وَلْيَسْـَٔلُوا۟ مَآ أَنفَقُوا۟ ۚ ذَٰلِكُمْ حُكْمُ ٱللَّهِ ۖ يَحْكُمُ بَيْنَكُمْ ۚ وَٱللَّهُ عَلِيمٌ حَكِيمٌ وَإِن فَاتَكُمْ شَىْءٌ مِّنْ أَزْوَٰجِكُمْ إِلَى ٱلْكُفَّارِ
فَعَاقَبْتُمْ فَـَٔاتُوا۟ ٱلَّذِينَ ذَهَبَتْ أَزْوَٰجُهُم مِّثْلَ مَآ أَنفَقُوا۟ ۚ وَٱتَّقُوا۟ ٱللَّهَ ٱلَّذِىٓ أَنتُم بِهِۦ مُؤْمِنُونَ يَٰٓأَيُّهَا ٱلنَّبِىُّ إِذَا جَآءَكَ ٱلْمُؤْمِنَٰتُ
يُبَايِعْنَكَ عَلَىٰٓ أَن لَّا يُشْرِكْنَ بِٱللَّهِ شَيْـًٔا وَلَا يَسْرِقْنَ وَلَا يَزْنِينَ وَلَا يَقْتُلْنَ أَوْلَٰدَهُنَّ وَلَا يَأْتِينَ بِبُهْتَٰنٍ يَفْتَرِينَهُۥ بَيْنَ أَيْدِيهِنَّ
وَأَرْجُلِهِنَّ وَلَا يَعْصِينَكَ فِى مَعْرُوفٍ ۙ فَبَايِعْهُنَّ وَٱسْتَغْفِرْ لَهُنَّ ٱللَّهَ ۖ إِنَّ ٱللَّهَ غَفُورٌ رَّحِيمٌ يَٰٓأَيُّهَا ٱلَّذِينَ ءَامَنُوا۟ لَا تَتَوَلَّوْا۟ قَوْمًا
غَضِبَ ٱللَّهُ عَلَيْهِمْ قَدْ يَئِسُوا۟ مِنَ ٱلْءَاخِرَةِ كَمَا يَئِسَ ٱلْكُفَّارُ مِنْ أَصْحَٰبِ ٱلْقُبُورِ

Wavering in between, neither with these, nor with those. Whomever Allah sends astray, you will never find for him a way. O you who believe! Do not befriend disbelievers rather than believers. Do you want to give Allah a clear case against you? – Surah An-Nisa 4:143&144

مُّذَبْذَبِينَ بَيْنَ ذَٰلِكَ لَآ إِلَىٰ هَٰٓؤُلَآءِ وَلَآ إِلَىٰ هَٰٓؤُلَآءِ ۚ وَمَن يُضْلِلِ ٱللَّهُ فَلَن تَجِدَ لَهُۥ سَبِيلًا يَٰٓأَيُّهَا ٱلَّذِينَ ءَامَنُوا۟ لَا تَتَّخِذُوا۟ ٱلْكَٰفِرِينَ
أَوْلِيَآءَ مِن دُونِ ٱلْمُؤْمِنِينَ ۚ أَتُرِيدُونَ أَن تَجْعَلُوا۟ لِلَّهِ عَلَيْكُمْ سُلْطَٰنًا مُّبِينًا

Believers are not to take disbelievers for friends instead of believers. Whoever does that has nothing to do with Allah, unless it is to protect your own selves against them. Allah warns you to beware of Him. To Allah is the destiny. – Surah Al-Imran 3:28

لَّا يَتَّخِذِ ٱلْمُؤْمِنُونَ ٱلْكَٰفِرِينَ أَوْلِيَآءَ مِن دُونِ ٱلْمُؤْمِنِينَ ۖ وَمَن يَفْعَلْ ذَٰلِكَ فَلَيْسَ مِنَ ٱللَّهِ فِى شَىْءٍ إِلَّآ أَن تَتَّقُوا۟ مِنْهُمْ تُقَىٰةً
وَيُحَذِّرُكُمُ ٱللَّهُ نَفْسَهُۥ ۗ وَإِلَى ٱللَّهِ ٱلْمَصِيرُ

Allah is the Lord of those who believe; He brings them out of darkness and into light. As for those who disbelieve, their lords are the evil ones; they bring them out of light and into darkness—these are the inmates of the Fire, in which they will abide forever. – Surah Al-Baqarah 2:257

ٱللَّهُ وَلِيُّ ٱلَّذِينَ ءَامَنُوا۟ يُخْرِجُهُم مِّنَ ٱلظُّلُمَـٰتِ إِلَى ٱلنُّورِ ۖ وَٱلَّذِينَ كَفَرُوٓا۟ أَوْلِيَآؤُهُمُ ٱلطَّـٰغُوتُ يُخْرِجُونَهُم مِّنَ ٱلنُّورِ إِلَى ٱلظُّلُمَـٰتِ ۗ أُو۟لَـٰٓئِكَ أَصْحَـٰبُ ٱلنَّارِ ۖ هُمْ فِيهَا خَـٰلِدُونَ

And trust none except those who follow your religion." Say, "Guidance is Allah's guidance. If someone is given the like of what you were given, or they argue with you before your Lord, say, "All grace is in Allah's hand; He gives it to whomever He wills." Allah is Bounteous and Knowing. – Surah Al-Imran 3:73

وَلَا تُؤْمِنُوٓا۟ إِلَّا لِمَن تَبِعَ دِينَكُمْ قُلْ إِنَّ ٱلْهُدَىٰ هُدَى ٱللَّهِ أَن يُؤْتَىٰٓ أَحَدٌ مِّثْلَ مَآ أُوتِيتُمْ أَوْ يُحَآجُّوكُمْ عِندَ رَبِّكُمْ ۗ قُلْ إِنَّ ٱلْفَضْلَ بِيَدِ ٱللَّهِ يُؤْتِيهِ مَن يَشَآءُ ۗ وَٱللَّهُ وَٰسِعٌ عَلِيمٌ

Inform the hypocrites that they will have a painful punishment. Those who ally themselves with the disbelievers instead of the believers. Do they seek glory in them? All glory belongs to Allah. – Surah An-Nisa 4:138&139

بَشِّرِ ٱلْمُنَـٰفِقِينَ بِأَنَّ لَهُمْ عَذَابًا أَلِيمًا ٱلَّذِينَ يَتَّخِذُونَ ٱلْكَـٰفِرِينَ أَوْلِيَآءَ مِن دُونِ ٱلْمُؤْمِنِينَ ۚ أَيَبْتَغُونَ عِندَهُمُ ٱلْعِزَّةَ فَإِنَّ ٱلْعِزَّةَ لِلَّهِ جَمِيعًا

O you who believe! Do not take the Jews and the Christians as allies; some of them are allies of one another. Whoever of you allies himself with them is one of them. Allah does not guide the wrongdoing people. – Surah Al-Maidah 5:51

يَـٰٓأَيُّهَا ٱلَّذِينَ ءَامَنُوا۟ لَا تَتَّخِذُوا۟ ٱلْيَهُودَ وَٱلنَّصَـٰرَىٰٓ أَوْلِيَآءَ ۘ بَعْضُهُمْ أَوْلِيَآءُ بَعْضٍ ۚ وَمَن يَتَوَلَّهُم مِّنكُمْ فَإِنَّهُۥ مِنْهُمْ ۗ إِنَّ ٱللَّهَ لَا يَهْدِى ٱلْقَوْمَ ٱلظَّـٰلِمِينَ

Your allies are Allah, and His Messenger, and those who believe—those who pray regularly, and give charity, and bow down. Whoever allies himself with Allah, and His Messenger, and those who believe—surely the Party of Allah is the victorious. O you who believe! Do not befriend those who take your religion in mockery and as a sport, be they from among those who were given the Scripture before you, or the disbelievers. And obey Allah, if you are believers. – Surah Al-Maidah 5:55-57

إِنَّمَا وَلِيُّكُمُ ٱللَّهُ وَرَسُولُهُۥ وَٱلَّذِينَ ءَامَنُوا۟ ٱلَّذِينَ يُقِيمُونَ ٱلصَّلَوٰةَ وَيُؤْتُونَ ٱلزَّكَوٰةَ وَهُمْ رَٰكِعُونَ وَمَن يَتَوَلَّ ٱللَّهَ وَرَسُولَهُۥ وَٱلَّذِينَ ءَامَنُوا۟ فَإِنَّ حِزْبَ ٱللَّهِ هُمُ ٱلْغَـٰلِبُونَ يَـٰٓأَيُّهَا ٱلَّذِينَ ءَامَنُوا۟ لَا تَتَّخِذُوا۟ ٱلَّذِينَ ٱتَّخَذُوا۟ دِينَكُمْ هُزُوًا وَلَعِبًا مِّنَ ٱلَّذِينَ أُوتُوا۟ ٱلْكِتَـٰبَ مِن قَبْلِكُمْ وَٱلْكُفَّارَ أَوْلِيَآءَ ۚ وَٱتَّقُوا۟ ٱللَّهَ إِن كُنتُم مُّؤْمِنِينَ

O you who believe! Do not ally yourselves with your parents and your siblings if they prefer disbelief to belief. Whoever of you allies himself with them—these are the wrongdoers. – Surah At-Taubah 9:23

يَـٰٓأَيُّهَا ٱلَّذِينَ ءَامَنُوا۟ لَا تَتَّخِذُوٓا۟ ءَابَآءَكُمْ وَإِخْوَٰنَكُمْ أَوْلِيَآءَ إِنِ ٱسْتَحَبُّوا۟ ٱلْكُفْرَ عَلَى ٱلْإِيمَـٰنِ ۚ وَمَن يَتَوَلَّهُم مِّنكُمْ فَأُو۟لَـٰٓئِكَ هُمُ ٱلظَّـٰلِمُونَ

The believing men and believing women are friends of one another. They advocate virtue, forbid evil, perform the prayers, practice charity,and obey Allah and His Messenger. These—Allah will have mercy on them. Allah is Noble and Wise. – Surah At-Taubah 9:71

وَٱلْمُؤْمِنُونَ وَٱلْمُؤْمِنَـٰتُ بَعْضُهُمْ أَوْلِيَآءُ بَعْضٍ ۚ يَأْمُرُونَ بِٱلْمَعْرُوفِ وَيَنْهَوْنَ عَنِ ٱلْمُنكَرِ وَيُقِيمُونَ ٱلصَّلَوٰةَ وَيُؤْتُونَ ٱلزَّكَوٰةَ وَيُطِيعُونَ ٱللَّهَ وَرَسُولَهُۥٓ ۚ أُو۟لَـٰٓئِكَ سَيَرْحَمُهُمُ ٱللَّهُ ۗ إِنَّ ٱللَّهَ عَزِيزٌ حَكِيمٌ

And so it sailed with them amidst waves like hills. And Noah called to his son, who had kept away, "O my son! Embark with us, and do not be with the disbelievers." – Surah Hud 11:42

وَهِىَ تَجْرِى بِهِمْ فِى مَوْجٍ كَٱلْجِبَالِ وَنَادَىٰ نُوحٌ ٱبْنَهُۥ وَكَانَ فِى مَعْزِلٍ يَـٰبُنَىَّ ٱرْكَب مَّعَنَا وَلَا تَكُن مَّعَ ٱلْكَـٰفِرِينَ

He said, “O Noah, he is not of your family. It is an unrighteous deed. So do not ask Me about something you know nothing about. I admonish you, lest you be one of the ignorant.” – Surah Hud 11:46

قَالَ يَٰنُوحُ إِنَّهُۥ لَيۡسَ مِنۡ أَهۡلِكَۖ إِنَّهُۥ عَمَلٌ غَيۡرُ صَٰلِحٖۖ فَلَا تَسۡـَٔلۡنِ مَا لَيۡسَ لَكَ بِهِۦ عِلۡمٌۖ إِنِّيٓ أَعِظُكَ أَن تَكُونَ مِنَ ٱلۡجَٰهِلِينَ

“Except for the family of Lot; we will save them all.” “Except for his wife.” We have determined that she will be of those who lag behind. – Surah Al-Hijr 15:59&60

إِلَّآ ءَالَ لُوطٍ إِنَّا لَمُنَجُّوهُمۡ أَجۡمَعِينَ إِلَّا ٱمۡرَأَتَهُۥ قَدَّرۡنَآ إِنَّهَا لَمِنَ ٱلۡغَٰبِرِينَ

O you who believe! Be conscious of Allah, and be with the sincere. . – Surah At-Taubah 9:119

يَٰٓأَيُّهَا ٱلَّذِينَ ءَامَنُواْ ٱتَّقُواْ ٱللَّهَ وَكُونُواْ مَعَ ٱلصَّٰدِقِينَ

Narrated Abu Musa: Allah’s Messenger ﷺ said, “The example of a good companion (who sits with you) in comparison with a bad one, is like that of the musk seller and the blacksmith’s bellows (or furnace); from the first you would either buy musk or enjoy its good smell while the bellows would either burn your clothes or your house, or you get a bad nasty smell thereof.” – Al-Bukhari 2101

حَدَّثَنِي مُوسَى بْنُ إِسْمَاعِيلَ، حَدَّثَنَا عَبْدُ الْوَاحِدِ، حَدَّثَنَا أَبُو بُرْدَةَ بْنُ عَبْدِ اللَّهِ، قَالَ سَمِعْتُ أَبَا بُرْدَةَ بْنَ أَبِي مُوسَى، عَنْ أَبِيهِ ـ رضى الله عنه ـ قَالَ قَالَ رَسُولُ اللَّهِ صلى الله عليه وسلم " مَثَلُ الْجَلِيسِ الصَّالِحِ وَالْجَلِيسِ السَّوْءِ كَمَثَلِ صَاحِبِ الْمِسْكِ، وَكِيرِ الْحَدَّادِ، لاَ يَعْدَمُكَ مِنْ صَاحِبِ الْمِسْكِ إِمَّا تَشْتَرِيهِ، أَوْ تَجِدُ رِيحَهُ، وَكِيرُ الْحَدَّادِ يُحْرِقُ بَدَنَكَ أَوْ ثَوْبَكَ أَوْ تَجِدُ مِنْهُ رِيحًا خَبِيثَةً "

Narrated Abu Huraira: Some (cooked) meat was brought to Allah Apostle and the meat of a forearm was presented to him as he used to like it. He ate a morsel of it and said, “I will be the chief of all the people on the Day of Resurrection. Do you know the reason for it? Allah will gather all the human being of early generations as well as late generation on one plain so that the announcer will be able to make them all-hear his voice and the watcher will be able to see all of them. The sun will come so close to the people that they will suffer such distress and trouble as they will not be able to bear or stand. Then the people will say, ‘Don’t you see to what state you have reached? Won’t you look for someone who can intercede for you with your Lord’ Some people will say to some others, ‘Go to Adam.’ So they will go to Adam and say to him. ‘You are the father of mankind; Allah created you with His Own Hand, and breathed into you of His Spirit (meaning the spirit which he created for you); and ordered the angels to prostrate before you; so (please) intercede for us with your Lord. Don’t you see in what state we are? Don’t you see what condition we have reached?’ Adam will say, ‘Today my Lord has become angry as He has never become before, nor will ever become thereafter. He forbade me (to eat of the fruit of) the tree, but I disobeyed Him . Myself! Myself! Myself! (I am preoccuied with my own problems). Go to someone else; go to Noah.’ So they will go to Noah and say (to him), ‘O Noah! You are the first (of Allah’s Messengers) to the people of the earth, and Allah has named you a thankful slave; please intercede for us with your Lord. Don’t you see in what state we are?’ He will say.’ Today my Lord has become angry as He has never become nor will ever become thereafter. I had (in the world) the right to make one definitely accepted invocation, and I made it against my nation. Myself! Myself! Myself! Go to someone else; go to Abraham.’ They will go to Abraham and say, ‘O Abraham! You are Allah’s Messenger ﷺ and His Khalil from among the people of the earth; so please intercede for us with your Lord. Don’t you see in what state we are?’ He will say to them, ‘My Lord has today become angry as He has never become before, nor will ever become thereafter. I had told three lies (Abu Haiyan (the sub-narrator) mentioned them in the Hadith) Myself! Myself! Myself! Go to someone else; go to Moses.’ The people will then go to Moses and say, ‘O Moses! You art Allah’s Messenger ﷺ and Allah gave you superiority above the others with this message and with His direct Talk to you; (please) intercede for us with your Lord Don't you see in what state we are?' Moses will say, 'My Lord has today become angry as He has never become before, nor will become thereafter, I killed a person whom I had not been ordered to kill. Myself! Myself! Myself! Go to someone else; go to Jesus.' So they will go to Jesus and say, 'O Jesus! You are Allah's Messenger ﷺ and His Word which He sent to Mary, and a superior soul created by Him, and you talked to the people while still young in the cradle. Please intercede for us with your Lord. Don't you see in what state we are?' Jesus will say. 'My Lord has today become angry as He has never become before nor will ever become thereafter. Jesus will not mention any sin, but will say, 'Myself! Myself! Myself! Go to someone else; go to Muhammad.' So they will come to me and say, 'O Muhammad ! You are Allah's Messenger ﷺ and the last of the prophets, and Allah forgave your early and late sins. (Please) intercede for us with your Lord. Don't you see in what state we are?" The Prophet ﷺ added, "Then I will go beneath Allah's Throne and fall in prostration before my Lord. And then Allah will guide me to such praises and glorification to Him as He has never guided anybody else before me. Then it will be said, 'O Muhammad Raise your head. Ask, and it will be granted. Intercede and It (your intercession) will be accepted.' So I will raise my head and Say, 'My followers, O my Lord! My followers, O my Lord'. It will be said, 'O Muhammad! Let those of your followers who have no accounts, enter through such a gate of the gates of Paradise as lies on the right; and they will share the other gates with the people." The Prophet ﷺ further said, "By Him in Whose Hand my soul is, the distance between every two gate-posts of Paradise is like the distance between Mecca and Busra (in Sham). – Sahih Al-Bukhari 4712

حَدَّثَنَا مُحَمَّدُ بْنُ مُقَاتِلٍ، أَخْبَرَنَا عَبْدُ اللَّهِ، أَخْبَرَنَا أَبُو حَيَّانَ التَّيْمِيُّ، عَنْ أَبِي زُرْعَةَ بْنِ عَمْرِو بْنِ جَرِيرٍ، عَنْ أَبِي هُرَيْرَةَ ـ رضى الله عنه ـ قَالَ أُتِيَ رَسُولُ اللَّهِ صلى الله عليه وسلم بِلَحْمٍ، فَرُفِعَ إِلَيْهِ الذِّرَاعُ، وَكَانَتْ تُعْجِبُهُ، فَنَهَسَ مِنْهَا نَهْسَةً ثُمَّ قَالَ " أَنَا سَيِّدُ النَّاسِ يَوْمَ الْقِيَامَةِ، وَهَلْ تَدْرُونَ مِمَّ ذَلِكَ يُجْمَعُ النَّاسُ الأَوَّلِينَ وَالآخِرِينَ فِي صَعِيدٍ وَاحِدٍ، يُسْمِعُهُمُ الدَّاعِي، وَيَنْفُذُهُمُ الْبَصَرُ، وَتَدْنُو الشَّمْسُ، فَيَبْلُغُ النَّاسَ مِنَ الْغَمِّ وَالْكَرْبِ مَا لاَ يُطِيقُونَ وَلاَ يَحْتَمِلُونَ فَيَقُولُ النَّاسُ أَلاَ تَرَوْنَ مَا قَدْ بَلَغَكُمْ أَلاَ تَنْظُرُونَ مَنْ يَشْفَعُ لَكُمْ إِلَى رَبِّكُمْ فَيَقُولُ بَعْضُ النَّاسِ لِبَعْضٍ عَلَيْكُمْ بِآدَمَ فَيَأْتُونَ آدَمَ عليه السلام فَيَقُولُونَ لَهُ أَنْتَ أَبُو الْبَشَرِ خَلَقَكَ اللَّهُ بِيَدِهِ. وَنَفَخَ فِيكَ مِنْ رُوحِهِ، وَأَمَرَ الْمَلاَئِكَةَ فَسَجَدُوا لَكَ، اشْفَعْ لَنَا إِلَى رَبِّكَ، أَلاَ تَرَى إِلَى مَا نَحْنُ فِيهِ أَلاَ تَرَى إِلَى مَا قَدْ بَلَغَنَا فَيَقُولُ آدَمُ إِنَّ رَبِّي قَدْ غَضِبَ الْيَوْمَ غَضَبًا لَمْ يَغْضَبْ قَبْلَهُ مِثْلَهُ وَلَنْ يَغْضَبَ بَعْدَهُ مِثْلَهُ، وَإِنَّهُ نَهَانِي عَنِ الشَّجَرَةِ فَعَصَيْتُهُ، نَفْسِي نَفْسِي نَفْسِي، اذْهَبُوا إِلَى غَيْرِي، اذْهَبُوا إِلَى نُوحٍ، فَيَأْتُونَ نُوحًا فَيَقُولُونَ يَا نُوحُ إِنَّكَ أَنْتَ أَوَّلُ الرُّسُلِ إِلَى أَهْلِ الأَرْضِ، وَقَدْ سَمَّاكَ اللَّهُ عَبْدًا شَكُورًا اشْفَعْ لَنَا إِلَى رَبِّكَ، أَلاَ تَرَى إِلَى مَا نَحْنُ فِيهِ فَيَقُولُ إِنَّ رَبِّي عَزَّ وَجَلَّ قَدْ غَضِبَ الْيَوْمَ غَضَبًا لَمْ يَغْضَبْ قَبْلَهُ مِثْلَهُ، وَلَنْ يَغْضَبَ بَعْدَهُ مِثْلَهُ، وَإِنَّهُ قَدْ كَانَتْ لِي دَعْوَةٌ دَعَوْتُهَا عَلَى قَوْمِي نَفْسِي نَفْسِي نَفْسِي اذْهَبُوا إِلَى غَيْرِي، اذْهَبُوا إِلَى إِبْرَاهِيمَ، فَيَأْتُونَ إِبْرَاهِيمَ، فَيَقُولُونَ يَا إِبْرَاهِيمُ، أَنْتَ نَبِيُّ اللَّهِ وَخَلِيلُهُ مِنْ أَهْلِ الأَرْضِ اشْفَعْ لَنَا إِلَى رَبِّكَ أَلاَ تَرَى إِلَى مَا نَحْنُ فِيهِ فَيَقُولُ لَهُمْ إِنَّ رَبِّي قَدْ غَضِبَ الْيَوْمَ غَضَبًا لَمْ يَغْضَبْ قَبْلَهُ مِثْلَهُ وَلَنْ يَغْضَبَ بَعْدَهُ مِثْلَهُ، وَإِنِّي قَدْ كُنْتُ كَذَبْتُ ثَلاَثَ كَذَبَاتٍ ـ فَذَكَرَهُنَّ أَبُو حَيَّانَ فِي الْحَدِيثِ ـ نَفْسِي نَفْسِي نَفْسِي، اذْهَبُوا إِلَى غَيْرِي اذْهَبُوا إِلَى مُوسَى، فَيَأْتُونَ مُوسَى، فَيَقُولُونَ يَا مُوسَى أَنْتَ رَسُولُ اللَّهِ، فَضَّلَكَ اللَّهُ بِرِسَالَتِهِ وَبِكَلاَمِهِ عَلَى النَّاسِ، اشْفَعْ لَنَا إِلَى رَبِّكَ أَلاَ تَرَى إِلَى مَا نَحْنُ فِيهِ فَيَقُولُ إِنَّ رَبِّي قَدْ غَضِبَ الْيَوْمَ غَضَبًا لَمْ يَغْضَبْ قَبْلَهُ مِثْلَهُ، وَلَنْ يَغْضَبَ بَعْدَهُ مِثْلَهُ، وَإِنِّي قَدْ قَتَلْتُ نَفْسًا لَمْ أُومَرْ بِقَتْلِهَا، نَفْسِي نَفْسِي نَفْسِي، اذْهَبُوا إِلَى غَيْرِي، اذْهَبُوا إِلَى عِيسَى، فَيَأْتُونَ عِيسَى فَيَقُولُونَ يَا عِيسَى أَنْتَ رَسُولُ اللَّهِ وَكَلِمَتُهُ أَلْقَاهَا إِلَى مَرْيَمَ وَرُوحٌ مِنْهُ، وَكَلَّمْتَ النَّاسَ فِي الْمَهْدِ صَبِيًّا اشْفَعْ لَنَا أَلاَ تَرَى إِلَى مَا نَحْنُ فِيهِ فَيَقُولُ عِيسَى إِنَّ رَبِّي قَدْ غَضِبَ الْيَوْمَ غَضَبًا لَمْ يَغْضَبْ قَبْلَهُ مِثْلَهُ، وَلَنْ يَغْضَبَ بَعْدَهُ مِثْلَهُ ـ وَلَمْ يَذْكُرْ ذَنْبًا ـ نَفْسِي نَفْسِي نَفْسِي، اذْهَبُوا إِلَى غَيْرِي اذْهَبُوا إِلَى مُحَمَّدٍ صلى الله عليه وسلم فَيَأْتُونَ مُحَمَّدًا صلى الله عليه وسلم فَيَقُولُونَ يَا مُحَمَّدُ أَنْتَ رَسُولُ اللَّهِ وَخَاتَمُ الأَنْبِيَاءِ، وَقَدْ غَفَرَ اللَّهُ لَكَ مَا تَقَدَّمَ مِنْ ذَنْبِكَ وَمَا تَأَخَّرَ، اشْفَعْ لَنَا إِلَى رَبِّكَ أَلاَ تَرَى إِلَى مَا نَحْنُ فِيهِ فَأَنْطَلِقُ فَآتِي تَحْتَ الْعَرْشِ، فَأَقَعُ سَاجِدًا لِرَبِّي عَزَّ وَجَلَّ ثُمَّ يَفْتَحُ اللَّهُ عَلَىَّ مِنْ مَحَامِدِهِ وَحُسْنِ الثَّنَاءِ عَلَيْهِ شَيْئًا لَمْ يَفْتَحْهُ عَلَى أَحَدٍ قَبْلِي ثُمَّ يُقَالُ يَا مُحَمَّدُ ارْفَعْ رَأْسَكَ، سَلْ تُعْطَهْ، وَاشْفَعْ تُشَفَّعْ، فَأَرْفَعُ رَأْسِي، فَأَقُولُ أُمَّتِي يَا رَبِّ، أُمَّتِي يَا رَبِّ فَيُقَالُ يَا مُحَمَّدُ أَدْخِلْ مِنْ أُمَّتِكَ مَنْ لاَ حِسَابَ عَلَيْهِمْ مِنَ الْبَابِ الأَيْمَنِ مِنْ أَبْوَابِ الْجَنَّةِ وَهُمْ شُرَكَاءُ النَّاسِ فِيمَا سِوَى ذَلِكَ مِنَ الأَبْوَابِ، ثُمَّ قَالَ وَالَّذِي نَفْسِي بِيَدِهِ إِنَّ مَا بَيْنَ الْمِصْرَاعَيْنِ مِنْ مَصَارِيعِ الْجَنَّةِ كَمَا بَيْنَ مَكَّةَ وَحِمْيَرَ، أَوْ كَمَا بَيْنَ مَكَّةَ وَبُصْرَى ".

And on Allah let the believers then put their trust.
مَوْلَىٰنَاۚ وَعَلَى ٱللَّهِ فَلْيَتَوَكَّلِ ٱلْمُؤْمِنُونَ

The Lord of the east and the west; there is no god except He; so take Him to yourself for an Ever-Trusted Trustee. – Surah Al-Muzammil 73:9

رَّبُّ ٱلْمَشْرِقِ وَٱلْمَغْرِبِ لَآ إِلَـٰهَ إِلَّا هُوَ فَٱتَّخِذْهُ وَكِيلًا

Allah! There is no god except He. And in Allah let the believers then put their trust. – Surah At-Taughabun 64:13

ٱللَّهُ لَآ إِلَـٰهَ إِلَّا هُوَۚ وَعَلَى ٱللَّهِ فَلْيَتَوَكَّلِ ٱلْمُؤْمِنُونَ

Surely private conference is only of Ash-Shaytan, (The ever-Vicious (one), i.e., the Devil) that the ones who have believed may feel grieved; and he will not harm them anything, except by the permission of Allah, and in Allah then let the believers put their trust. – Surah Al-Mujadilah 58:10

إِنَّمَا ٱلنَّجْوَىٰ مِنَ ٱلشَّيْطَـٰنِ لِيَحْزُنَ ٱلَّذِينَ ءَامَنُوا۟ وَلَيْسَ بِضَآرِّهِمْ شَيْـًٔا إِلَّا بِإِذْنِ ٱللَّهِۚ وَعَلَى ٱللَّهِ فَلْيَتَوَكَّلِ ٱلْمُؤْمِنُونَ

And indeed in case you ask them, "Who created the heavens and the earth?" indeed they will definitely say Allah." Say, (This is addressed to the Ptopet) "Have you seen then the ones you invoke apart from Allah. In case Allah ever wills some adversity for me, will they lift off His adversity? Or (in case) He wills (some) mercy for me, will they hold back His mercy?" Say, (This is addressed to the Ptophet) " Allah is enough (Reckoner) for me; on Him do (all) the trusting ones put their trust." – Surah Az-Zumar 39:38

وَلَئِن سَأَلْتَهُم مَّنْ خَلَقَ ٱلسَّمَـٰوَٰتِ وَٱلْأَرْضَ لَيَقُولُنَّ ٱللَّهُۚ قُلْ أَفَرَءَيْتُم مَّا تَدْعُونَ مِن دُونِ ٱللَّهِ إِنْ أَرَادَنِىَ ٱللَّهُ بِضُرٍّ هَلْ هُنَّ كَـٰشِفَـٰتُ ضُرِّهِۦٓ أَوْ أَرَادَنِى بِرَحْمَةٍ هَلْ هُنَّ مُمْسِكَـٰتُ رَحْمَتِهِۦۚ قُلْ حَسْبِىَ ٱللَّهُۖ عَلَيْهِ يَتَوَكَّلُ ٱلْمُتَوَكِّلُونَ

And do not obey the disbelievers and the hypocrites; and disregard their hurt, and put your trust in Allah; and Allah suffices as an Ever-Trusted Trustee. – Surah Al-Ahzab 33:48

وَلَا تُطِعِ ٱلْكَـٰفِرِينَ وَٱلْمُنَـٰفِقِينَ وَدَعْ أَذَىٰهُمْ وَتَوَكَّلْ عَلَى ٱللَّهِۚ وَكَفَىٰ بِٱللَّهِ وَكِيلًا

Say, "Never will anything afflict us except what Allah has prescribed for us; He is our Supreme Patronizer; and on Allah let the believers then put their trust." – Surah At-Taubah 9:51

قُل لَّن يُصِيبَنَآ إِلَّا مَا كَتَبَ ٱللَّهُ لَنَا هُوَ مَوْلَىٰنَاۚ وَعَلَى ٱللَّهِ فَلْيَتَوَكَّلِ ٱلْمُؤْمِنُونَ

Surely the believers are only the ones who, when Allah is mentioned, their hearts tremble and when His ayat (Signs or verses) are recited to them, they increase them in belief, and in their Lord they put their trust. – Surah Al-Anfal 8:2

إِنَّمَا ٱلْمُؤْمِنُونَ ٱلَّذِينَ إِذَا ذُكِرَ ٱللَّهُ وَجِلَتْ قُلُوبُهُمْ وَإِذَا تُلِيَتْ عَلَيْهِمْ ءَايَـٰتُهُۥ زَادَتْهُمْ إِيمَـٰنًا وَعَلَىٰ رَبِّهِمْ يَتَوَكَّلُونَ

Said two men of the ones that feared Allah) (and) whom Allah had favored, "Enter in upon them (by) the gate. So, when you enter it, then surely you will be overcoming them. And so put all your trust in Allah in case you are believers." – Surah Al-Ma'idah 5:23

قَالَ رَجُلَانِ مِنَ ٱلَّذِينَ يَخَافُونَ أَنْعَمَ ٱللَّهُ عَلَيْهِمَا ٱدْخُلُوا۟ عَلَيْهِمُ ٱلْبَابَ فَإِذَا دَخَلْتُمُوهُ فَإِنَّكُمْ غَـٰلِبُونَۚ وَعَلَى ٱللَّهِ فَتَوَكَّلُوٓا۟ إِن كُنتُم مُّؤْمِنِينَ

O you who have believed, remember the favor of Allah upon you as a (certain) people designed to stretch against you their hands, so He restrained their hands from you. And be pious to Allah, and in Allah let the believers then put their trust. – Surah Al-Ma'idah 5:11
يَـٰٓأَيُّهَا ٱلَّذِينَ ءَامَنُواْ ٱذْكُرُواْ نِعْمَتَ ٱللَّهِ عَلَيْكُمْ إِذْ هَمَّ قَوْمٌ أَن يَبْسُطُوٓاْ إِلَيْكُمْ أَيْدِيَهُمْ فَكَفَّ أَيْدِيَهُمْ عَنكُمْ ۖ وَٱتَّقُواْ ٱللَّهَ ۚ وَعَلَى ٱللَّهِ فَلْيَتَوَكَّلِ ٱلْمُؤْمِنُونَ

In case Allah grants you victory, then none can overcome you, (Literally: none can be your over comer) and in case He abandons you, who then can give you victory after Him? And in (Literally: on) Allah let the believers put their trust. – Surah Al-Imran 3:160
إِن يَنصُرْكُمُ ٱللَّهُ فَلَا غَالِبَ لَكُمْ ۖ وَإِن يَخْذُلْكُمْ فَمَن ذَا ٱلَّذِى يَنصُرُكُم مِّنۢ بَعْدِهِۦ ۗ وَعَلَى ٱللَّهِ فَلْيَتَوَكَّلِ ٱلْمُؤْمِنُونَ

(Remember) as two sections of you were about to be disheartened, and Allah is their Ever-Patronizing Patron; and on Allah let the believers then put their trust. – Surah Al-Imran 3:122
إِذْ هَمَّت طَّآئِفَتَانِ مِنكُمْ أَن تَفْشَلَا وَٱللَّهُ وَلِيُّهُمَا ۗ وَعَلَى ٱللَّهِ فَلْيَتَوَكَّلِ ٱلْمُؤْمِنُونَ

Their Messengers said to them, "Decidedly we are nothing except mortals like you; but Allah bestows His Bounty to whomever He decides of His bondmen. And in no way could we come up to you with an all- binding authority except by the permission of Allah, and in (Literally: on) Allah let the believers then put their trust. – Surah Ibrahim 14:11
قَالَتْ لَهُمْ رُسُلُهُمْ إِن نَّحْنُ إِلَّا بَشَرٌ مِّثْلُكُمْ وَلَـٰكِنَّ ٱللَّهَ يَمُنُّ عَلَىٰ مَن يَشَآءُ مِنْ عِبَادِهِۦ ۖ وَمَا كَانَ لَنَآ أَن نَّأْتِيَكُم بِسُلْطَـٰنٍ إِلَّا بِإِذْنِ ٱللَّهِ ۚ وَعَلَى ٱللَّهِ فَلْيَتَوَكَّلِ ٱلْمُؤْمِنُونَ

The Book of
whoever kills a believer intentionally, his recompense is Hell
وَمَن يَقۡتُلۡ مُؤۡمِنٗا مُّتَعَمِّدٗا فَجَزَآؤُهُۥ جَهَنَّمُ

Those who tempt the believers, men and women, then do not repent; for them is the punishment of Hell; for them is the punishment of Burning. – Surah Al-Buruj 85:10
إِنَّ ٱلَّذِينَ فَتَنُواْ ٱلۡمُؤۡمِنِينَ وَٱلۡمُؤۡمِنَٰتِ ثُمَّ لَمۡ يَتُوبُواْ فَلَهُمۡ عَذَابُ جَهَنَّمَ وَلَهُمۡ عَذَابُ ٱلۡحَرِيقِ

O you who believe! If a troublemaker brings you any news, investigate, lest you harm people out of ignorance, and you become regretful for what you have done.– Surah Al-Hujurat 49:6
يَٰٓأَيُّهَا ٱلَّذِينَ ءَامَنُوٓاْ إِن جَآءَكُمۡ فَاسِقُۢ بِنَبَإٖ فَتَبَيَّنُوٓاْ أَن تُصِيبُواْ قَوۡمَۢا بِجَهَٰلَةٖ فَتُصۡبِحُواْ عَلَىٰ مَا فَعَلۡتُمۡ نَٰدِمِينَ

If two groups of believers fight each other, reconcile between them. But if one group aggresses against the other, fight the aggressing group until it complies with Allah's command. Once it has complied, reconcile between them with justice, and be equitable. Allah loves the equitable.The believers are brothers, so reconcile betweenyour brothers, and remain conscious of Allah, so that you may receive mercy. O you who believe! No people shall ridicule other people, for they may be better than they. Nor shall any women ridicule other women, for they may be better than they. Nor shall you slander one another, nor shall you insult one another with names. Evil is the return to wickedness after having attained faith. Whoever does not repent—these are the wrongdoers.O you who believe! Avoid most suspicion—some suspicion is sinful. And do not spy on one another, nor backbite one another. Would any of you like to eat the flesh of his dead brother? You would detest it. So remain mindful of Allah. Allah is Most Relenting, Most Merciful. – Surah Al-Hujurat 49:9-12
وَإِن طَآئِفَتَانِ مِنَ ٱلۡمُؤۡمِنِينَ ٱقۡتَتَلُواْ فَأَصۡلِحُواْ بَيۡنَهُمَاۖ فَإِنۢ بَغَتۡ إِحۡدَىٰهُمَا عَلَى ٱلۡأُخۡرَىٰ فَقَٰتِلُواْ ٱلَّتِي تَبۡغِي حَتَّىٰ تَفِيٓءَ إِلَىٰٓ أَمۡرِ ٱللَّهِۚ فَإِن فَآءَتۡ فَأَصۡلِحُواْ بَيۡنَهُمَا بِٱلۡعَدۡلِ وَأَقۡسِطُوٓاْۖ إِنَّ ٱللَّهَ يُحِبُّ ٱلۡمُقۡسِطِينَ إِنَّمَا ٱلۡمُؤۡمِنُونَ إِخۡوَةٞ فَأَصۡلِحُواْ بَيۡنَ أَخَوَيۡكُمۡۚ وَٱتَّقُواْ ٱللَّهَ لَعَلَّكُمۡ تُرۡحَمُونَ يَٰٓأَيُّهَا ٱلَّذِينَ ءَامَنُواْ لَا يَسۡخَرۡ قَوۡمٞ مِّن قَوۡمٍ عَسَىٰٓ أَن يَكُونُواْ خَيۡرٗا مِّنۡهُمۡ وَلَا نِسَآءٞ مِّن نِّسَآءٍ عَسَىٰٓ أَن يَكُنَّ خَيۡرٗا مِّنۡهُنَّۖ وَلَا تَلۡمِزُوٓاْ أَنفُسَكُمۡ وَلَا تَنَابَزُواْ بِٱلۡأَلۡقَٰبِۖ بِئۡسَ ٱلِٱسۡمُ ٱلۡفُسُوقُ بَعۡدَ ٱلۡإِيمَٰنِۚ وَمَن لَّمۡ يَتُبۡ فَأُوْلَٰٓئِكَ هُمُ ٱلظَّٰلِمُونَ يَٰٓأَيُّهَا ٱلَّذِينَ ءَامَنُواْ ٱجۡتَنِبُواْ كَثِيرٗا مِّنَ ٱلظَّنِّ إِنَّ بَعۡضَ ٱلظَّنِّ إِثۡمٞۖ وَلَا تَجَسَّسُواْ وَلَا يَغۡتَب بَّعۡضُكُم بَعۡضًاۚ أَيُحِبُّ أَحَدُكُمۡ أَن يَأۡكُلَ لَحۡمَ أَخِيهِ مَيۡتٗا فَكَرِهۡتُمُوهُۚ وَٱتَّقُواْ ٱللَّهَۚ إِنَّ ٱللَّهَ تَوَّابٞ رَّحِيمٞ

Never should a believer kill another believer, unless by error. Anyone who kills a believer by error must set free a believing slave, and pay compensation to the victim's family, unless they remit it as charity. If the victim belonged to a people who are hostile to you, but is abeliever, then the compensation is to free a believing slave. If he belonged to a people with whom you have a treaty, then compensation should be handed over to his family, and a believing slave set free. Anyone who lacks the means must fast for twobconsecutive months, by way of repentance to Allah. Allah is All Knowing, Most Wise.Whoever kills a believer deliberately, the penalty for him is Hell,where he will remain forever. And Allah will be angry with him, and will curse him, and will prepare for him a terrible punishment. O you who believe! When you journey in the way of Allah, investigate, and do not say to him who offers you peace, "You are not a believer," aspiring for the goods of this world. With Allah are abundant riches. You yourselves were like this before, and Allah bestowed favor on you; so investigate. Allah is well aware of what you do.– Surah An-Nisa 4:92-94
وَمَا كَانَ لِمُؤۡمِنٍ أَن يَقۡتُلَ مُؤۡمِنًا إِلَّا خَطَـٔٗاۚ وَمَن قَتَلَ مُؤۡمِنًا خَطَـٔٗا فَتَحۡرِيرُ رَقَبَةٖ مُّؤۡمِنَةٖ وَدِيَةٞ مُّسَلَّمَةٌ إِلَىٰٓ أَهۡلِهِۦٓ إِلَّآ أَن يَصَّدَّقُواْۚ فَإِن كَانَ مِن قَوۡمٍ عَدُوّٖ لَّكُمۡ وَهُوَ مُؤۡمِنٞ فَتَحۡرِيرُ رَقَبَةٖ مُّؤۡمِنَةٖۖ وَإِن كَانَ مِن قَوۡمِۢ بَيۡنَكُمۡ وَبَيۡنَهُم مِّيثَٰقٞ فَدِيَةٞ مُّسَلَّمَةٌ إِلَىٰٓ أَهۡلِهِۦ وَتَحۡرِيرُ رَقَبَةٖ مُّؤۡمِنَةٖۖ فَمَن لَّمۡ يَجِدۡ فَصِيَامُ شَهۡرَيۡنِ مُتَتَابِعَيۡنِ تَوۡبَةٗ مِّنَ ٱللَّهِۗ وَكَانَ ٱللَّهُ عَلِيمًا حَكِيمٗا وَمَن يَقۡتُلۡ مُؤۡمِنٗا

مُّتَعَمِّدًا فَجَزَآؤُهُۥ جَهَنَّمُ خَٰلِدًا فِيهَا وَغَضِبَ ٱللَّهُ عَلَيْهِ وَلَعَنَهُۥ وَأَعَدَّ لَهُۥ عَذَابًا عَظِيمًا يَٰٓأَيُّهَا ٱلَّذِينَ ءَامَنُوٓاْ إِذَا ضَرَبْتُمْ فِى سَبِيلِ ٱللَّهِ فَتَبَيَّنُواْ وَلَا تَقُولُواْ لِمَنْ أَلْقَىٰٓ إِلَيْكُمُ ٱلسَّلَٰمَ لَسْتَ مُؤْمِنًا تَبْتَغُونَ عَرَضَ ٱلْحَيَوٰةِ ٱلدُّنْيَا فَعِندَ ٱللَّهِ مَغَانِمُ كَثِيرَةٌ كَذَٰلِكَ كُنتُم مِّن قَبْلُ فَمَنَّ ٱللَّهُ عَلَيْكُمْ فَتَبَيَّنُوٓاْ إِنَّ ٱللَّهَ كَانَ بِمَا تَعْمَلُونَ خَبِيرًا

Those who perpetrated the slander are a band of you. Do not consider it bad for you, but it is good for you. Each person among them bears his share in the sin. As for him who played the major role—for him is a terrible punishment Why, when you heard about it, the believing men and women did not think well of one another, and say, "This is an obvious lie"? Why did they not bring four witnesses to testify to it? If they fail to bring the witnesses, then in Allah's sight, they are liars.– Surah An-Nur 24:11-13

إِنَّ ٱلَّذِينَ جَآءُو بِٱلْإِفْكِ عُصْبَةٌ مِّنكُمْ لَا تَحْسَبُوهُ شَرًّا لَّكُم بَلْ هُوَ خَيْرٌ لَّكُمْ لِكُلِّ ٱمْرِي مِّنْهُم مَّا ٱكْتَسَبَ مِنَ ٱلْإِثْمِ وَٱلَّذِى تَوَلَّىٰ كِبْرَهُۥ مِنْهُمْ لَهُۥ عَذَابٌ عَظِيمٌ لَّوْلَآ إِذْ سَمِعْتُمُوهُ ظَنَّ ٱلْمُؤْمِنُونَ وَٱلْمُؤْمِنَٰتُ بِأَنفُسِهِمْ خَيْرًا وَقَالُواْ هَٰذَآ إِفْكٌ مُّبِينٌ لَّوْلَا جَآءُو عَلَيْهِ بِأَرْبَعَةِ شُهَدَآءَ فَإِذْ لَمْ يَأْتُواْ بِٱلشُّهَدَآءِ فَأُوْلَٰٓئِكَ عِندَ ٱللَّهِ هُمُ ٱلْكَٰذِبُونَ

Narrated Abu Musa: Some people asked Allah's Messenger ﷺ, "Whose Islam is the best? i.e. (Who is a very good Muslim)?" He replied, "One who avoids harming the Muslims with his tongue and hands." – Al-Bukhari 11

حَدَّثَنَا سَعِيدُ بْنُ يَحْيَى بْنِ سَعِيدٍ الْقُرَشِيُّ، قَالَ حَدَّثَنَا أَبِي قَالَ، حَدَّثَنَا أَبُو بُرْدَةَ بْنُ عَبْدِ اللَّهِ بْنِ أَبِي بُرْدَةَ، عَنْ أَبِي بُرْدَةَ، عَنْ أَبِي مُوسَى ـ رضى الله عنه ـ قَالَ قَالُوا يَا رَسُولَ اللَّهِ أَىُّ الإِسْلاَمِ أَفْضَلُ قَالَ " مَنْ سَلِمَ الْمُسْلِمُونَ مِنْ لِسَانِهِ وَيَدِهِ "

Being stingy towards you. And when fear approaches, you see them staring at you—their eyes rolling—like someone fainting at death. Then, when panic is over, they whip you with sharp tongues. They resent you any good. These have never believed, so Allah has nullified their works; a matter easy for Allah. – Surah Al-Ahzab 33:19

أَشِحَّةً عَلَيْكُمْ فَإِذَا جَآءَ ٱلْخَوْفُ رَأَيْتَهُمْ يَنظُرُونَ إِلَيْكَ تَدُورُ أَعْيُنُهُمْ كَٱلَّذِى يُغْشَىٰ عَلَيْهِ مِنَ ٱلْمَوْتِ فَإِذَا ذَهَبَ ٱلْخَوْفُ سَلَقُوكُم بِأَلْسِنَةٍ حِدَادٍ أَشِحَّةً عَلَى ٱلْخَيْرِ أُوْلَٰٓئِكَ لَمْ يُؤْمِنُواْ فَأَحْبَطَ ٱللَّهُ أَعْمَٰلَهُمْ وَكَانَ ذَٰلِكَ عَلَى ٱللَّهِ يَسِيرًا

And We made a covenant with you: "You shall not shed the blood of your own, nor shall you evict your own from your homes." You agreed, and were all witnesses. But here you are, killing your own, and expelling a group of your own from their homes—conspiring against them in wrongdoing and hostility. And if they come to you as captives, you ransom them, although it was forbidden to you. Is it that you believe in part of the Scripture, and disbelieve in part? What is the reward for those among you who do that but humiliation in this life? And on the Day of Resurrection, they will be assigned to the most severe torment. Allah is not unaware of what you do.– Surah Al-Baqarah 2:84&85

وَإِذْ أَخَذْنَا مِيثَٰقَكُمْ لَا تَسْفِكُونَ دِمَآءَكُمْ وَلَا تُخْرِجُونَ أَنفُسَكُم مِّن دِيَٰرِكُمْ ثُمَّ أَقْرَرْتُمْ وَأَنتُمْ تَشْهَدُونَ ثُمَّ أَنتُمْ هَٰٓؤُلَآءِ تَقْتُلُونَ أَنفُسَكُمْ وَتُخْرِجُونَ فَرِيقًا مِّنكُم مِّن دِيَٰرِهِمْ تَظَٰهَرُونَ عَلَيْهِم بِٱلْإِثْمِ وَٱلْعُدْوَٰنِ وَإِن يَأْتُوكُمْ أُسَٰرَىٰ تُفَٰدُوهُمْ وَهُوَ مُحَرَّمٌ عَلَيْكُمْ إِخْرَاجُهُمْ أَفَتُؤْمِنُونَ بِبَعْضِ ٱلْكِتَٰبِ وَتَكْفُرُونَ بِبَعْضٍ فَمَا جَزَآءُ مَن يَفْعَلُ ذَٰلِكَ مِنكُمْ إِلَّا خِزْىٌ فِى ٱلْحَيَوٰةِ ٱلدُّنْيَا وَيَوْمَ ٱلْقِيَٰمَةِ يُرَدُّونَ إِلَىٰٓ أَشَدِّ ٱلْعَذَابِ وَمَا ٱللَّهُ بِغَٰفِلٍ عَمَّا تَعْمَلُونَ

Narrated Anas bin Malik: Allah's Messenger ﷺ mentioned the greatest sins or he was asked about the greatest sins. He said, "To join partners in worship with Allah; to kill a soul which Allah has forbidden to kill; and to be undutiful or unkind to one's parents." The Prophet ﷺ added, "Shall I inform you of the biggest of the great sins? That is the forged statement or the false witness." Shu`ba (the sub-narrator) states that most probably the Prophet said, "the false witness." – Al-Bukhari 5977

حَدَّثَنِي مُحَمَّدُ بْنُ الْوَلِيدِ، حَدَّثَنَا مُحَمَّدُ بْنُ جَعْفَرٍ، حَدَّثَنَا شُعْبَةُ، قَالَ حَدَّثَنِي عُبَيْدُ اللَّهِ بْنُ أَبِي بَكْرٍ، قَالَ سَمِعْتُ أَنَسَ بْنَ مَالِكٍ ـ رضى الله عنه ـ قَالَ ذَكَرَ رَسُولُ اللَّهِ صلى الله عليه وسلم الْكَبَائِرَ، أَوْ سُئِلَ عَنِ الْكَبَائِرِ فَقَالَ " الشِّرْكُ بِاللَّهِ، وَقَتْلُ النَّفْسِ،

وَعُقُوقُ الْوَالِدَيْنِ ". فَقَالَ " أَلاَ أُنَبِّئُكُمْ بِأَكْبَرِ الْكَبَائِرِ ـ قَالَ ـ قَوْلُ الزُّورِ ـ أَوْ قَالَ ـ شَهَادَةُ الزُّورِ ". قَالَ شُعْبَةُ وَأَكْثَرُ ظَنِّي أَنَّهُ قَالَ " شَهَادَةُ الزُّورِ ".

Narrated Jarir: The Prophet ﷺ said to me during Hajjat-al-Wada`, "Let the people keep quiet and listen." Then he said (addressing the people), "Beware! Do not renegade as disbelievers after me by striking (cutting) the necks of one another." – Al-Bukhari 7080
حَدَّثَنَا سُلَيْمَانُ بْنُ حَرْبٍ، حَدَّثَنَا شُعْبَةُ، عَنْ عَلِيِّ بْنِ مُدْرِكٍ، سَمِعْتُ أَبَا زُرْعَةَ بْنَ عَمْرِو بْنِ جَرِيرٍ، عَنْ جَدِّهِ، جَرِيرٍ قَالَ قَالَ لِي رَسُولُ اللَّهِ صلى الله عليه وسلم فِي حَجَّةِ الْوَدَاعِ " اسْتَنْصِتِ النَّاسَ ". ثُمَّ قَالَ " لاَ تَرْجِعُوا بَعْدِي كُفَّارًا، يَضْرِبُ بَعْضُكُمْ رِقَابَ بَعْضٍ ".

Narrated Ibn `Umar: The Prophet ﷺ said, "Every betrayer will have a flag which will be fixed on the Day of Resurrection, and the flag's prominence will be made in order to show the betrayal he committed." – Al-Bukhari 3188
حَدَّثَنَا سُلَيْمَانُ بْنُ حَرْبٍ، حَدَّثَنَا حَمَّادٌ، عَنْ أَيُّوبَ، عَنْ نَافِعٍ، عَنِ ابْنِ عُمَرَ ـ رضى الله عنهما ـ قَالَ سَمِعْتُ النَّبِيَّ صلى الله عليه وسلم يَقُولُ " لِكُلِّ غَادِرٍ لِوَاءٌ يُنْصَبُ لِغَدْرَتِهِ "

Narrated Usama bin Zaid: Allah's Messenger ﷺ sent us towards Al-Huruqa, and in the morning we attacked them and defeated them. I and an Ansari man followed a man from among them and when we took him over, he said, "La ilaha illal-Lah." On hearing that, the Ansari man stopped, but I killed him by stabbing him with my spear. When we returned, the Prophet ﷺ came to know about that and he said, "O Usama! Did you kill him after he had said "La ilaha ilal-Lah?" I said, "But he said so only to save himself." The Prophet ﷺ kept on repeating that so often that I wished I had not embraced Islam before that day. – Sahih Al-Bukhari 4269
حَدَّثَنِي عَمْرُو بْنُ مُحَمَّدٍ، حَدَّثَنَا هُشَيْمٌ، أَخْبَرَنَا حُصَيْنٌ، أَخْبَرَنَا أَبُو ظَبْيَانَ، قَالَ سَمِعْتُ أُسَامَةَ بْنَ زَيْدٍ ـ رضى الله عنهما ـ يَقُولُ بَعَثَنَا رَسُولُ اللَّهِ صلى الله عليه وسلم إِلَى الْحُرَقَةِ، فَصَبَّحْنَا الْقَوْمَ فَهَزَمْنَاهُمْ وَلَحِقْتُ أَنَا وَرَجُلٌ مِنَ الأَنْصَارِ رَجُلاً مِنْهُمْ، فَلَمَّا غَشِينَاهُ قَالَ لاَ إِلَهَ إِلاَّ اللَّهُ. فَكَفَّ الأَنْصَارِيُّ، فَطَعَنْتُهُ بِرُمْحِي حَتَّى قَتَلْتُهُ، فَلَمَّا قَدِمْنَا بَلَغَ النَّبِيَّ صلى الله عليه وسلم فَقَالَ " يَا أُسَامَةُ أَقَتَلْتَهُ بَعْدَ مَا قَالَ لاَ إِلَهَ إِلاَّ اللَّهُ " قُلْتُ كَانَ مُتَعَوِّذًا. فَمَا زَالَ يُكَرِّرُهَا حَتَّى تَمَنَّيْتُ أَنِّي لَمْ أَكُنْ أَسْلَمْتُ قَبْلَ ذَلِكَ الْيَوْمِ.

Narrated Abu Musa: The Prophet ﷺ said, "A believer to another believer is like a building whose different parts enforce each other." The Prophet ﷺ then clasped his hands with the fingers interlaced. (At that time) the Prophet ﷺ was sitting and a man came and begged or asked for something. The Prophet ﷺ faced us and said, "Help and recommend him and you will receive the reward for it, and Allah will bring about what He will through His Prophet's tongue.". – Sahih Al-Bukhari 6026, 6027
حَدَّثَنَا مُحَمَّدُ بْنُ يُوسُفَ، حَدَّثَنَا سُفْيَانُ، عَنْ أَبِي بُرْدَةَ، بُرَيْدِ بْنِ أَبِي بُرْدَةَ قَالَ أَخْبَرَنِي جَدِّي أَبُو بُرْدَةَ، عَنْ أَبِيهِ أَبِي مُوسَى، عَنِ النَّبِيِّ صلى الله عليه وسلم قَالَ " الْمُؤْمِنُ لِلْمُؤْمِنِ كَالْبُنْيَانِ، يَشُدُّ بَعْضُهُ بَعْضًا ". ثُمَّ شَبَّكَ بَيْنَ أَصَابِعِهِ. وَكَانَ النَّبِيُّ صلى الله عليه وسلم جَالِسًا إِذْ جَاءَ رَجُلٌ يَسْأَلُ أَوْ طَالِبُ حَاجَةٍ أَقْبَلَ عَلَيْنَا بِوَجْهِهِ فَقَالَ " اشْفَعُوا فَلْتُؤْجَرُوا، وَلْيَقْضِ اللَّهُ عَلَى لِسَانِ نَبِيِّهِ مَا شَاءَ "

Narrated Al-Ahnaf bin Qais: While I was going to help this man ('Ali Ibn Abi Talib), Abu Bakra met me and asked, "Where are you going?" I replied, "I am going to help that person." He said, "Go back for I have heard Allah's Messenger ﷺ saying, 'When two Muslims fight (meet) each other with their swords, both the murderer as well as the murdered will go to the Hell-fire.' I said, 'O Allah's Messenger ﷺ ! It is all right for the murderer but what about the murdered one?' Allah's Messenger ﷺ replied, "He surely had the intention to kill his companion."

حَدَّثَنَا عَبْدُ الرَّحْمَنِ بْنُ الْمُبَارَكِ، حَدَّثَنَا حَمَّادُ بْنُ زَيْدٍ، حَدَّثَنَا أَيُّوبُ، وَيُونُسُ، عَنِ الْحَسَنِ، عَنِ الأَحْنَفِ بْنِ قَيْسٍ، قَالَ ذَهَبْتُ لأَنْصُرَ هَذَا الرَّجُلَ، فَلَقِيَنِي أَبُو بَكْرَةَ فَقَالَ أَيْنَ تُرِيدُ قُلْتُ أَنْصُرُ هَذَا الرَّجُلَ. قَالَ ارْجِعْ فَإِنِّي سَمِعْتُ رَسُولَ اللَّهِ صلى الله عليه وسلم يَقُولُ " إِذَا الْتَقَى الْمُسْلِمَانِ بِسَيْفَيْهِمَا فَالْقَاتِلُ وَالْمَقْتُولُ فِي النَّارِ ". فَقُلْتُ يَا رَسُولَ اللَّهِ هَذَا الْقَاتِلُ فَمَا بَالُ الْمَقْتُولِ قَالَ " إِنَّهُ كَانَ حَرِيصًا عَلَى قَتْلِ صَاحِبِهِ "

O you who believe! If a troublemaker brings you any news, investigate, lest you harm people out of ignorance, and you become regretful for what you have done. And know that among you is the Messenger of Allah. Had he obeyed you in many things, you would have suffered hardship. But Allah has given you the love of faith, and adorned it in your hearts, and made disbelief, mischief, and rebellion hateful to you. These are the rightly guided. A Grace and Favor from Allah. Allah is Knowing and Wise. If two groups of believers fight each other, reconcile between them. But if one group aggresses against the other, fight the aggressing group until it complies with Allah's command. Once it has complied, reconcile between them with justice, and be equitable. Allah loves the equitable. The believers are brothers, so reconcile between your brothers, and remain conscious of Allah, so that you may receive mercy. O you who believe! No people shall ridicule other people, for they may be better than they. Nor shall any women ridicule other women, for they may be better than they. Nor shall you slander one another, nor shall you insult one another with names. Evil is the return to wickedness after having attained faith. Whoever does not repent— these are the wrongdoers. O you who believe! Avoid most suspicion—some suspicion is sinful. And do not spy on one another, nor backbite one another. Would any of you like to eat the flesh of his dead brother? You would detest it. So remain mindful of Allah. Allah is Most Relenting, Most Merciful. – Surah Al-Hujurat 49:7-12

وَٱعْلَمُوٓا۟ أَنَّ فِيكُمْ رَسُولَ ٱللَّهِ ۚ لَوْ يُطِيعُكُمْ فِى كَثِيرٍ مِّنَ ٱلْأَمْرِ لَعَنِتُّمْ وَلَـٰكِنَّ ٱللَّهَ حَبَّبَ إِلَيْكُمُ ٱلْإِيمَـٰنَ وَزَيَّنَهُۥ فِى قُلُوبِكُمْ وَكَرَّهَ إِلَيْكُمُ ٱلْكُفْرَ وَٱلْفُسُوقَ وَٱلْعِصْيَانَ ۚ أُو۟لَـٰٓئِكَ هُمُ ٱلرَّٰشِدُونَ فَضْلًا مِّنَ ٱللَّهِ وَنِعْمَةً ۚ وَٱللَّهُ عَلِيمٌ حَكِيمٌ وَإِن طَآئِفَتَانِ مِنَ ٱلْمُؤْمِنِينَ ٱقْتَتَلُوا۟ فَأَصْلِحُوا۟ بَيْنَهُمَا ۖ فَإِنۢ بَغَتْ إِحْدَىٰهُمَا عَلَى ٱلْأُخْرَىٰ فَقَـٰتِلُوا۟ ٱلَّتِى تَبْغِى حَتَّىٰ تَفِىٓءَ إِلَىٰٓ أَمْرِ ٱللَّهِ ۚ فَإِن فَآءَتْ فَأَصْلِحُوا۟ بَيْنَهُمَا بِٱلْعَدْلِ وَأَقْسِطُوٓا۟ ۖ إِنَّ ٱللَّهَ يُحِبُّ ٱلْمُقْسِطِينَ إِنَّمَا ٱلْمُؤْمِنُونَ إِخْوَةٌ فَأَصْلِحُوا۟ بَيْنَ أَخَوَيْكُمْ ۚ وَٱتَّقُوا۟ ٱللَّهَ لَعَلَّكُمْ تُرْحَمُونَ يَـٰٓأَيُّهَا ٱلَّذِينَ ءَامَنُوا۟ لَا يَسْخَرْ قَوْمٌ مِّن قَوْمٍ عَسَىٰٓ أَن يَكُونُوا۟ خَيْرًا مِّنْهُمْ وَلَا نِسَآءٌ مِّن نِّسَآءٍ عَسَىٰٓ أَن يَكُنَّ خَيْرًا مِّنْهُنَّ ۖ وَلَا تَلْمِزُوٓا۟ أَنفُسَكُمْ وَلَا تَنَابَزُوا۟ بِٱلْأَلْقَـٰبِ ۖ بِئْسَ ٱلِٱسْمُ ٱلْفُسُوقُ بَعْدَ ٱلْإِيمَـٰنِ ۚ وَمَن لَّمْ يَتُبْ فَأُو۟لَـٰٓئِكَ هُمُ ٱلظَّـٰلِمُونَ يَـٰٓأَيُّهَا ٱلَّذِينَ ءَامَنُوا۟ ٱجْتَنِبُوا۟ كَثِيرًا مِّنَ ٱلظَّنِّ إِنَّ بَعْضَ ٱلظَّنِّ إِثْمٌ ۖ وَلَا تَجَسَّسُوا۟ وَلَا يَغْتَب بَّعْضُكُم بَعْضًا ۚ أَيُحِبُّ أَحَدُكُمْ أَن يَأْكُلَ لَحْمَ أَخِيهِ مَيْتًا فَكَرِهْتُمُوهُ ۚ وَٱتَّقُوا۟ ٱللَّهَ ۚ إِنَّ ٱللَّهَ تَوَّابٌ رَّحِيمٌ

The Book of
Say, "O My servants who have transgressed against themselves
قُلْ يَـٰعِبَادِىَ ٱلَّذِينَ أَسْرَفُوا۟ عَلَىٰٓ

Narrated Abu Huraira: The Prophet ﷺ said, "Religion is very easy and whoever overburdens himself in his religion will not be able to continue in that way. So you should not be extremists, but try to be near to perfection and receive the good tidings that you will be rewarded; and gain strength by worshipping in the mornings, the afternoons, and during the last hours of the nights." (See Fath-ul-Bari, Page 102, Vol 1). – Sahih Al-Bukhari 39

حَدَّثَنَا عَبْدُ السَّلاَمِ بْنُ مُطَهَّرٍ، قَالَ حَدَّثَنَا عُمَرُ بْنُ عَلِيٍّ، عَنْ مَعْنِ بْنِ مُحَمَّدٍ الْغِفَارِيِّ، عَنْ سَعِيدِ بْنِ أَبِي سَعِيدٍ الْمَقْبُرِيِّ، عَنْ أَبِي هُرَيْرَةَ، عَنِ النَّبِيِّ صلى الله عليه وسلم قَالَ " إِنَّ الدِّينَ يُسْرٌ، وَلَنْ يُشَادَّ الدِّينَ أَحَدٌ إِلاَّ غَلَبَهُ، فَسَدِّدُوا وَقَارِبُوا وَأَبْشِرُوا، وَاسْتَعِينُوا بِالْغَدْوَةِ وَالرَّوْحَةِ وَشَىْءٍ مِنَ الدُّلْجَةِ ".

Narrated `Aisha: That during the Mina days, Abu Bakr came to her, while there where two girls with her, beating drums, and the Prophet ﷺ was (lying) covering himself with his garment. Abu Bakr rebuked the two girls, but the Prophet ﷺ uncovered his face and said, "O Abu Bakr! Leave them, for these are the days of Id (festival)." Those days were the days of Mina-. `Aisha added, "I was being screened by the Prophet ﷺ while I was watching the Ethiopians playing in the Mosque. `Umar rebuked them, but the Prophet ﷺ said, "Leave them, O Bani Arfida! Play. (for) you are safe." – Al-Bukhari 3529, 3530

حَدَّثَنَا يَحْيَى بْنُ بُكَيْرٍ، حَدَّثَنَا اللَّيْثُ، عَنْ عُقَيْلٍ، عَنِ ابْنِ شِهَابٍ، عَنْ عُرْوَةَ، عَنْ عَائِشَةَ، أَنَّ أَبَا بَكْرٍ ـ رضى الله عنه ـ دَخَلَ عَلَيْهَا وَعِنْدَهَا جَارِيَتَانِ فِي أَيَّامِ مِنًى تُدَفِّفَانِ وَتَضْرِبَانِ، وَالنَّبِيُّ صلى الله عليه وسلم مُتَغَشٍّ بِثَوْبِهِ، فَانْتَهَرَهُمَا أَبُو بَكْرٍ، فَكَشَفَ النَّبِيُّ صلى الله عليه وسلم عَنْ وَجْهِهِ، فَقَالَ " دَعْهُمَا يَا أَبَا بَكْرٍ، فَإِنَّهَا أَيَّامُ عِيدٍ، وَتِلْكَ الأَيَّامُ أَيَّامُ مِنًى ". وَقَالَتْ عَائِشَةُ رَأَيْتُ النَّبِيَّ صلى الله عليه وسلم يَسْتُرُنِي، وَأَنَا أَنْظُرُ إِلَى الْحَبَشَةِ، وَهُمْ يَلْعَبُونَ فِي الْمَسْجِدِ فَزَجَرَهُمْ {عُمَرُ} فَقَالَ النَّبِيُّ صلى الله عليه وسلم " دَعْهُمْ أَمْنًا بَنِي أَرْفَدَةَ ". يَعْنِي مِنَ الأَمْنِ.

Narrated Subaia bint Al-Harith: That she was married to Sad bin Khaula who was from the tribe of Bani 'Amr bin Luai, and was one of those who fought the Badr battle. He died while she wa pregnant during Hajjat-ul-Wada.' Soon after his death, she gave birth to a child. When she completed the term of deliver (i.e. became clean), she prepared herself for suitors. Abu As-Sanabil bin Bu'kak, a man from the tribe of Bani Abd-ud-Dal called on her and said to her, "What! I see you dressed up for the people to ask you in marriage. Do you want to marry By Allah, you are not allowed to marry unless four months and ten days have elapsed (after your husband's death)." Subai'a in her narration said, "When he (i.e. Abu As-Sanabil) said this to me. I put on my dress in the evening and went to Allah's Messenger ﷺ and asked him about this problem. He gave the verdict that I was free to marry as I had already given birth to my child and ordered me to marry if I wished." – Al-Bukhari 3991

وَقَالَ اللَّيْثُ حَدَّثَنِي يُونُسُ، عَنِ ابْنِ شِهَابٍ، قَالَ حَدَّثَنِي عُبَيْدُ اللَّهِ بْنُ عَبْدِ اللَّهِ بْنِ عُتْبَةَ، أَنَّ أَبَاهُ، كَتَبَ إِلَى عُمَرَ بْنِ عَبْدِ اللَّهِ بْنِ الأَرْقَمِ الزُّهْرِيِّ، يَأْمُرُهُ أَنْ يَدْخُلَ، عَلَى سُبَيْعَةَ بِنْتِ الْحَارِثِ الأَسْلَمِيَّةِ، فَيَسْأَلَهَا عَنْ حَدِيثِهَا وَعَنْ مَا قَالَ لَهَا رَسُولُ اللَّهِ صلى الله عليه وسلم حِينَ اسْتَفْتَتْهُ، فَكَتَبَ عُمَرُ بْنُ عَبْدِ اللَّهِ بْنِ الأَرْقَمِ إِلَى عَبْدِ اللَّهِ بْنِ عُتْبَةَ يُخْبِرُهُ أَنَّ سُبَيْعَةَ بِنْتَ الْحَارِثِ أَخْبَرَتْهُ أَنَّهَا كَانَتْ تَحْتَ سَعْدِ ابْنِ خَوْلَةَ، وَهْوَ مِنْ بَنِي عَامِرِ بْنِ لُؤَىٍّ، وَكَانَ مِمَّنْ شَهِدَ بَدْرًا، فَتُوُفِّيَ عَنْهَا فِي حَجَّةِ الْوَدَاعِ وَهْىَ حَامِلٌ، فَلَمْ تَنْشَبْ أَنْ وَضَعَتْ حَمْلَهَا بَعْدَ وَفَاتِهِ، فَلَمَّا تَعَلَّتْ مِنْ نِفَاسِهَا تَجَمَّلَتْ لِلْخُطَّابِ، فَدَخَلَ عَلَيْهَا أَبُو السَّنَابِلِ بْنُ بَعْكَكٍ ـ رَجُلٌ مِنْ بَنِي عَبْدِ الدَّارِ ـ فَقَالَ لَهَا مَا لِي أَرَاكِ تَجَمَّلْتِ لِلْخُطَّابِ تُرَجِّينَ النِّكَاحَ فَإِنَّكِ وَاللَّهِ مَا أَنْتِ بِنَاكِحٍ حَتَّى تَمُرَّ عَلَيْكِ أَرْبَعَةُ أَشْهُرٍ وَعَشْرٌ. قَالَتْ سُبَيْعَةُ فَلَمَّا قَالَ لِي ذَلِكَ جَمَعْتُ عَلَىَّ ثِيَابِي حِينَ أَمْسَيْتُ، وَأَتَيْتُ رَسُولَ اللَّهِ صلى الله عليه وسلم فَسَأَلْتُهُ عَنْ ذَلِكَ، فَأَفْتَانِي بِأَنِّي قَدْ حَلَلْتُ حِينَ وَضَعْتُ حَمْلِي، وَأَمَرَنِي بِالتَّزَوُّجِ إِنْ بَدَا لِي. تَابَعَهُ أَصْبَغُ عَنِ ابْنِ وَهْبٍ عَنْ يُونُسَ. وَقَالَ اللَّيْثُ حَدَّثَنِي يُونُسُ، عَنِ ابْنِ شِهَابٍ، وَسَأَلْنَاهُ، فَقَالَ أَخْبَرَنِي مُحَمَّدُ بْنُ عَبْدِ الرَّحْمَنِ بْنِ ثَوْبَانَ، مَوْلَى بَنِي عَامِرِ بْنِ لُؤَىٍّ أَنَّ مُحَمَّدَ بْنَ إِيَاسِ بْنِ الْبُكَيْرِ، وَكَانَ، أَبُوهُ شَهِدَ بَدْرًا أَخْبَرَهُ.

Narrated Ka`b: The Prophetﷺ said, "The example of a believer is that of a fresh tender plant, which the wind bends It sometimes and some other time it makes it straight. And the example of a hypocrite is that of a pine tree which keeps straight till once it is uprooted suddenly. – Al-Bukhari 5643

حَدَّثَنَا مُسَدَّدٌ، حَدَّثَنَا يَحْيَى، عَنْ سُفْيَانَ، عَنْ سَعْدٍ، عَنْ عَبْدِ اللَّهِ بْنِ كَعْبٍ، عَنْ أَبِيهِ، عَنِ النَّبِيِّ صلى الله عليه وسلم قَالَ " مَثَلُ الْمُؤْمِنِ كَالْخَامَةِ مِنَ الزَّرْعِ تُفَيِّئُهَا الرِّيحُ مَرَّةً، وَتَعْدِلُهَا مَرَّةً، وَمَثَلُ الْمُنَافِقِ كَالأَرْزَةِ لاَ تَزَالُ حَتَّى يَكُونَ انْجِعَافُهَا مَرَّةً وَاحِدَةً ". وَقَالَ زَكَرِيَّاءُ حَدَّثَنِي سَعْدٌ، حَدَّثَنَا ابْنُ كَعْبٍ، عَنْ أَبِيهِ، كَعْبٍ عَنِ النَّبِيِّ صلى الله عليه وسلم.

Narrated Abu Huraira: I heard Allah's Messengerﷺ saying, "The good deeds of any person will not make him enter Paradise." (i.e., None can enter Paradise through his good deeds.) They (the Prophet's companions) said, 'Not even you, O Allah's Messengerﷺ ?' He said, "Not even myself, unless Allah bestows His favor and mercy on me." So be moderate in your religious deeds and do the deeds that are within your ability: and none of you should wish for death, for if he is a good doer, he may increase his good deeds, and if he is an evil doer, he may repent to Allah." – Al-Bukhari 5673

حَدَّثَنَا أَبُو الْيَمَانِ، أَخْبَرَنَا شُعَيْبٌ، عَنِ الزُّهْرِيِّ، قَالَ أَخْبَرَنِي أَبُو عُبَيْدٍ، مَوْلَى عَبْدِ الرَّحْمَنِ بْنِ عَوْفٍ أَنَّ أَبَا هُرَيْرَةَ، قَالَ سَمِعْتُ رَسُولَ اللَّهِ صلى الله عليه وسلم يَقُولُ " لَنْ يُدْخِلَ أَحَدًا عَمَلُهُ الْجَنَّةَ ". قَالُوا وَلاَ أَنْتَ يَا رَسُولَ اللَّهِ قَالَ " لاَ، وَلاَ أَنَا إِلاَّ أَنْ يَتَغَمَّدَنِي اللَّهُ بِفَضْلٍ وَرَحْمَةٍ فَسَدِّدُوا وَقَارِبُوا وَلاَ يَتَمَنَّيَنَّ أَحَدُكُمُ الْمَوْتَ إِمَّا مُحْسِنًا فَلَعَلَّهُ أَنْ يَزْدَادَ خَيْرًا، وَإِمَّا مُسِيئًا فَلَعَلَّهُ أَنْ يَسْتَعْتِبَ "

Narrated Al-Azraq bin Qais: We were in the city of Al-Ahwaz on the bank of a river which had dried up. Then Abu Barza Al- Aslami came riding a horse and he started praying and let his horse loose. The horse ran away, so Abu Barza interrupted his prayer and went after the horse till he caught it and brought it, and then he offered his prayer. There was a man amongst us who was (from the Khawari) having a different opinion. He came saying. "Look at this old man! He left his prayer because of a horse." On that Abu Barza came to us and said, "Since the time I left Allah's Messengerﷺ , nobody has admonished me; My house is very far from this place, and if I had carried on praying and left my horse, I could not have reached my house till night." Then Abu Barza mentioned that he had been in the company of the Prophet, and that he had seen his leniency. – Al-Bukhari 6127

حَدَّثَنَا أَبُو النُّعْمَانِ، حَدَّثَنَا حَمَّادُ بْنُ زَيْدٍ، عَنِ الأَزْرَقِ بْنِ قَيْسٍ، قَالَ كُنَّا عَلَى شَاطِئِ نَهْرٍ بِالأَهْوَازِ قَدْ نَضَبَ عَنْهُ الْمَاءُ، فَجَاءَ أَبُو بَرْزَةَ الأَسْلَمِيُّ عَلَى فَرَسٍ، فَصَلَّى وَخَلَّى فَرَسَهُ، فَانْطَلَقَتِ الْفَرَسُ، فَتَرَكَ صَلاَتَهُ وَتَبِعَهَا حَتَّى أَدْرَكَهَا، فَأَخَذَهَا ثُمَّ جَاءَ فَقَضَى صَلاَتَهُ، وَفِينَا رَجُلٌ لَهُ رَأْىٌ، فَأَقْبَلَ يَقُولُ انْظُرُوا إِلَى هَذَا الشَّيْخِ تَرَكَ صَلاَتَهُ مِنْ أَجْلِ فَرَسٍ. فَأَقْبَلَ فَقَالَ مَا عَنَّفَنِي أَحَدٌ مُنْذُ فَارَقْتُ رَسُولَ اللَّهِ صلى الله عليه وسلم وَقَالَ إِنَّ مَنْزِلِي مُتَرَاخٍ فَلَوْ صَلَّيْتُ وَتَرَكْتُ لَمْ آتِ أَهْلِي إِلَى اللَّيْلِ. وَذَكَرَ أَنَّهُ صَحِبَ النَّبِيَّ صلى الله عليه وسلم فَرَأَى مِنْ تَيْسِيرِهِ

Narrated Salim's father: The Prophetﷺ sent Khalid bin Al-Walid to the tribe of Jadhima and Khalid invited them to Islam but they could not express themselves by saying, "Aslamna (i.e. we have embraced Islam)," but they started saying "Saba'na! Saba'na (i.e. we have come out of one religion to another)." Khalid kept on killing (some of) them and taking (some of) them as captives and gave every one of us his Captive. When there came the day then Khalid ordered that each man (i.e. Muslim soldier) should kill his captive, I said, "By Allah, I will not kill my captive, and none of my companions will kill his captive." When we reached the Prophet, we mentioned to him the whole story. On that, the Prophetﷺ raised both his hands and said twice, "O Allah! I am free from what Khalid has done." – Al-Bukhari 4339 (also see Al-Bukhari 7189)

حَدَّثَنِي مَحْمُودٌ، حَدَّثَنَا عَبْدُ الرَّزَّاقِ، أَخْبَرَنَا مَعْمَرٌ، وَحَدَّثَنِي نُعَيْمٌ، أَخْبَرَنَا عَبْدُ اللَّهِ، أَخْبَرَنَا مَعْمَرٌ، عَنِ الزُّهْرِيِّ، عَنْ سَالِمٍ، عَنْ أَبِيهِ، قَالَ بَعَثَ النَّبِيُّ صلى الله عليه وسلم خَالِدَ بْنَ الْوَلِيدِ إِلَى بَنِي جَذِيمَةَ، فَدَعَاهُمْ إِلَى الإِسْلاَمِ فَلَمْ يُحْسِنُوا أَنْ يَقُولُوا أَسْلَمْنَا. فَجَعَلُوا يَقُولُونَ صَبَأْنَا، صَبَأْنَا. فَجَعَلَ خَالِدٌ يَقْتُلُ مِنْهُمْ وَيَأْسِرُ، وَدَفَعَ إِلَى كُلِّ رَجُلٍ مِنَّا أَسِيرَهُ، حَتَّى إِذَا كَانَ يَوْمٌ أَمَرَ خَالِدٌ أَنْ يَقْتُلَ كُلُّ رَجُلٍ مِنَّا أَسِيرَهُ فَقُلْتُ وَاللَّهِ لاَ أَقْتُلُ أَسِيرِي، وَلاَ يَقْتُلُ رَجُلٌ مِنْ أَصْحَابِي أَسِيرَهُ، حَتَّى قَدِمْنَا عَلَى النَّبِيِّ صلى الله عليه وسلم فَذَكَرْنَاهُ، فَرَفَعَ النَّبِيُّ صلى الله عليه وسلم يَدَهُ فَقَالَ " اللَّهُمَّ إِنِّي أَبْرَأُ إِلَيْكَ مِمَّا صَنَعَ خَالِدٌ ". مَرَّتَيْنِ

And when it is said to them, "Believe in what Allah has revealed," they say, "We believe in what was revealed to us," and they reject anything beyond that, although it is the truth which confirms what they have. Say, "Why did you kill Allah's prophets before, if you were believers?"– Surah Al-Baqarah 2:91

وَإِذَا قِيلَ لَهُمْ ءَامِنُوا۟ بِمَآ أَنزَلَ ٱللَّهُ قَالُوا۟ نُؤْمِنُ بِمَآ أُنزِلَ عَلَيْنَا وَيَكْفُرُونَ بِمَا وَرَآءَهُۥ وَهُوَ ٱلْحَقُّ مُصَدِّقًا لِّمَا مَعَهُمْ ۗ قُلْ فَلِمَ تَقْتُلُونَ أَنۢبِيَآءَ ٱللَّهِ مِن قَبْلُ إِن كُنتُم مُّؤْمِنِينَ

Narrated Jabir bin `Abdullah :A funeral procession passed in front of us and the Prophet ﷺ stood up and we too stood up. We said, 'O Allah's Messenger ﷺ ! This is the funeral procession of a Jew." He said, "Whenever you see a funeral procession, you should stand up – .".Sahih Al-Bukhari 1311

حَدَّثَنَا مُعَاذُ بْنُ فَضَالَةَ، حَدَّثَنَا هِشَامٌ، عَنْ يَحْيَى، عَنْ عُبَيْدِ اللَّهِ بْنِ مِقْسَمٍ، عَنْ جَابِرِ بْنِ عَبْدِ اللَّهِ ـ رضى الله عنهما ـ قَالَ مَرَّ بِنَا جَنَازَةٌ فَقَامَ لَهَا النَّبِيُّ صلى الله عليه وسلم وَقُمْنَا بِهِ. فَقُلْنَا يَا رَسُولَ اللَّهِ، إِنَّهَا جَنَازَةُ يَهُودِيٍّ. قَالَ " إِذَا رَأَيْتُمُ الْجَنَازَةَ فَقُومُوا ".يقُومَانِ لِلْجِنَازَةِ.

Narrated Jabir bin `Abdullah: Allah's Messenger ﷺ was on a journey and saw a crowd of people, and a man was being shaded (by them). He asked, "What is the matter?" They said, "He (the man) is fasting." The Prophet ﷺ said, "It is not righteousness that you fast on a journey." – Al-Bukhari 1946

حَدَّثَنَا آدَمُ، حَدَّثَنَا شُعْبَةُ، حَدَّثَنَا مُحَمَّدُ بْنُ عَبْدِ الرَّحْمَنِ الأَنْصَارِيُّ، قَالَ سَمِعْتُ مُحَمَّدَ بْنَ عَمْرِو بْنِ الْحَسَنِ بْنِ عَلِيٍّ، عَنْ جَابِرِ بْنِ عَبْدِ اللَّهِ ـ رضى الله عنهم ـ قَالَ كَانَ رَسُولُ اللَّهِ صلى الله عليه وسلم فِي سَفَرٍ، فَرَأَى زِحَامًا، وَرَجُلاً قَدْ ظُلِّلَ عَلَيْهِ، فَقَالَ " مَا هَذَا ". فَقَالُوا صَائِمٌ. فَقَالَ " لَيْسَ مِنَ الْبِرِّ الصَّوْمُ فِي السَّفَرِ ".

Narrated Anas bin Malik: A group of three men came to the houses of the wives of the Prophet ﷺ asking how the Prophet ﷺ worshipped (Allah), and when they were informed about that, they considered their worship insufficient and said, "Where are we from the Prophet ﷺ as his past and future sins have been forgiven." Then one of them said, "I will offer the prayer throughout the night forever." The other said, "I will fast throughout the year and will not break my fast." The third said, "I will keep away from the women and will not marry forever." Allah's Messenger ﷺ came to them and said, "Are you the same people who said so-and-so? By Allah, I am more submissive to Allah and more afraid of Him than you; yet I fast and break my fast, I do sleep and I also marry women. So he who does not follow my tradition in religion, is not from me (not one of my followers). – Al-Bukhari 5063

حَدَّثَنَا سَعِيدُ بْنُ أَبِي مَرْيَمَ، أَخْبَرَنَا مُحَمَّدُ بْنُ جَعْفَرٍ، أَخْبَرَنَا حُمَيْدُ بْنُ أَبِي حُمَيْدٍ الطَّوِيلُ، أَنَّهُ سَمِعَ أَنَسَ بْنَ مَالِكٍ ـ رضى الله عنه ـ يَقُولُ جَاءَ ثَلاَثَةُ رَهْطٍ إِلَى بُيُوتِ أَزْوَاجِ النَّبِيِّ صلى الله عليه وسلم يَسْأَلُونَ عَنْ عِبَادَةِ النَّبِيِّ صلى الله عليه وسلم فَلَمَّا أُخْبِرُوا كَأَنَّهُمْ تَقَالُّوهَا فَقَالُوا وَأَيْنَ نَحْنُ مِنَ النَّبِيِّ صلى الله عليه وسلم قَدْ غُفِرَ لَهُ مَا تَقَدَّمَ مِنْ ذَنْبِهِ وَمَا تَأَخَّرَ. قَالَ أَحَدُهُمْ أَمَّا أَنَا فَإِنِّي أُصَلِّي اللَّيْلَ أَبَدًا. وَقَالَ آخَرُ أَنَا أَصُومُ الدَّهْرَ وَلاَ أُفْطِرُ. وَقَالَ آخَرُ أَنَا أَعْتَزِلُ النِّسَاءَ فَلاَ أَتَزَوَّجُ أَبَدًا. فَجَاءَ رَسُولُ اللَّهِ صلى الله عليه وسلم فَقَالَ " أَنْتُمُ الَّذِينَ قُلْتُمْ كَذَا وَكَذَا أَمَا وَاللَّهِ إِنِّي لأَخْشَاكُمْ لِلَّهِ وَأَتْقَاكُمْ لَهُ، لَكِنِّي أَصُومُ وَأُفْطِرُ، وَأُصَلِّي وَأَرْقُدُ وَأَتَزَوَّجُ النِّسَاءَ، فَمَنْ رَغِبَ عَنْ سُنَّتِي فَلَيْسَ مِنِّي ".

Narrated `Ali: Allah's Messengerﷺ sent me, Az-Zubair bin Al-Awwam and Abu Marthad Al-Ghanawi, and all of us were horsemen, and he said, "Proceed till you reach Rawdat Khakh, where there is a woman from the pagans carrying a letter sent by Hatib bin Abi Balta'a to the pagans (of Mecca)." So we overtook her while she was proceeding on her camel at the same place as Allah's Messengerﷺ told us. We said (to her) "Where is the letter which is with you?" She said, "I have no letter with me." So we made her camel kneel down and searched her mount (baggage etc) but could not find anything. My two companions said, "We do not see any letter." I said, "I know that Allah's Messenger ﷺ did not tell a lie. By Allah, if you (the lady) do not bring out the letter, I will strip you of your clothes' When she noticed that I was serious, she put her hand into the knot of her waist sheet, for she was tying a sheet round herself, and brought out the letter. So we proceeded to Allah's Messengerﷺ with the letter. The Prophetﷺ said (to Habib), "What made you o what you have done, O Hatib?" Hatib replied, "I have done nothing except that I believe in Allah and His Apostle, and I have not changed or altered (my religion). But I wanted to do the favor to the people (pagans of Mecca) through which Allah might protect my family and my property, as there is none among your companions but has someone in Mecca through whom Allah protects his property (against harm). The Prophetﷺ said, "Habib has told you the truth, so do not say to him (anything) but good." `Umar bin Al-Khattab said, "Verily he has betrayed Allah, His Apostle, and the believers! Allow me to chop his neck off!" The Prophetﷺ said, "O `Umar! What do you know; perhaps Allah looked upon the Badr warriors and said, 'Do whatever you like, for I have ordained that you will be in Paradise.'" On that `Umar wept and said, "Allah and His Apostle know best." – Al-Bukhari 6259

حَدَّثَنَا يُوسُفُ بْنُ بُهْلُولٍ، حَدَّثَنَا ابْنُ إِدْرِيسَ، قَالَ حَدَّثَنِي حُصَيْنُ بْنُ عَبْدِ الرَّحْمَنِ، عَنْ سَعْدِ بْنِ عُبَيْدَةَ، عَنْ أَبِي عَبْدِ الرَّحْمَنِ السُّلَمِيِّ، عَنْ عَلِيٍّ ـ رضى الله عنه ـ قَالَ بَعَثَنِي رَسُولُ اللَّهِ صلى الله عليه وسلم وَالزُّبَيْرَ بْنَ الْعَوَّامِ وَأَبَا مَرْثَدٍ الْغَنَوِيَّ وَكُلُّنَا فَارِسٌ فَقَالَ " انْطَلِقُوا حَتَّى تَأْتُوا رَوْضَةَ خَاخٍ، فَإِنَّ بِهَا امْرَأَةً مِنَ الْمُشْرِكِينَ مَعَهَا صَحِيفَةٌ مِنْ حَاطِبِ بْنِ أَبِي بَلْتَعَةَ إِلَى الْمُشْرِكِينَ ". قَالَ فَأَدْرَكْنَاهَا تَسِيرُ عَلَى جَمَلٍ لَهَا حَيْثُ قَالَ لَنَا رَسُولُ اللَّهِ صلى الله عليه وسلم قَالَ قُلْنَا أَيْنَ الْكِتَابُ الَّذِي مَعَكِ قَالَتْ مَا مَعِي كِتَابٌ. فَأَنَخْنَا بِهَا، فَابْتَغَيْنَا فِي رَحْلِهَا فَمَا وَجَدْنَا شَيْئًا، قَالَ صَاحِبَاىَ مَا نَرَى كِتَابًا. قَالَ قُلْتُ لَقَدْ عَلِمْتُ مَا كَذَبَ رَسُولُ اللَّهِ صلى الله عليه وسلم وَالَّذِي يُحْلَفُ بِهِ لَتُخْرِجِنَّ الْكِتَابَ أَوْ لأُجَرِّدَنَّكِ. قَالَ فَلَمَّا رَأَتِ الْجِدَّ مِنِّي أَهْوَتْ بِيَدِهَا إِلَى حُجْزَتِهَا وَهْىَ مُحْتَجِزَةٌ بِكِسَاءٍ فَأَخْرَجَتِ الْكِتَابَ ـ قَالَ ـ فَانْطَلَقْنَا بِهِ إِلَى رَسُولِ اللَّهِ صلى الله عليه وسلم فَقَالَ " مَا حَمَلَكَ يَا حَاطِبُ عَلَى مَا صَنَعْتَ ". قَالَ مَا بِي إِلاَّ أَنْ أَكُونَ مُؤْمِنًا بِاللَّهِ وَرَسُولِهِ، وَمَا غَيَّرْتُ وَلاَ بَدَّلْتُ، أَرَدْتُ أَنْ تَكُونَ لِي عِنْدَ الْقَوْمِ يَدٌ يَدْفَعُ اللَّهُ بِهَا عَنْ أَهْلِي وَمَالِي، وَلَيْسَ مِنْ أَصْحَابِكَ هُنَاكَ إِلاَّ وَلَهُ مَنْ يَدْفَعُ اللَّهُ بِهِ عَنْ أَهْلِهِ وَمَالِهِ. قَالَ " صَدَقَ فَلاَ تَقُولُوا لَهُ إِلاَّ خَيْرًا ". قَالَ فَقَالَ عُمَرُ بْنُ الْخَطَّابِ إِنَّهُ قَدْ خَانَ اللَّهَ وَرَسُولَهُ وَالْمُؤْمِنِينَ، فَدَعْنِي فَأَضْرِبَ عُنُقَهُ. قَالَ فَقَالَ " يَا عُمَرُ وَمَا يُدْرِيكَ لَعَلَّ اللَّهَ قَدِ اطَّلَعَ عَلَى أَهْلِ بَدْرٍ فَقَالَ اعْمَلُوا مَا شِئْتُمْ فَقَدْ وَجَبَتْ لَكُمُ الْجَنَّةُ قَالَ فَدَمَعَتْ عَيْنَا عُمَرَ وَقَالَ اللَّهُ وَرَسُولُهُ أَعْلَمُ.

Ibn Abbas chained 'Ikrima to teach him the Quran, The Prophet's Sunnah, and the knowledge of Fara'id. – Al-Bukhari Vol.3 page 347

و قيد ابن عباس عكرمة على تعلم القرآن و السنن و الفراعض

Narrated Sahl bin Sa`d: Allah's Messengerﷺ said, "The people will remain on the right path as long as they hasten the breaking of the fast." – Al-Bukhari 1957

حَدَّثَنَا عَبْدُ اللَّهِ بْنُ يُوسُفَ، أَخْبَرَنَا مَالِكٌ، عَنْ أَبِي حَازِمٍ، عَنْ سَهْلِ بْنِ سَعْدٍ، أَنَّ رَسُولَ اللَّهِ صلى الله عليه وسلم قَالَ " لاَ يَزَالُ النَّاسُ بِخَيْرٍ مَا عَجَّلُوا الْفِطْرَ ".

Narrated `Abdullah: I heard a man reciting a verse (of the Holy Qur'an) but I had heard the Prophetﷺ reciting it differently. So, I caught hold of the man by the hand and took him to Allah's Messengerﷺ who said, "Both of you are right." Shu`ba, the sub-narrator said, "I think he said to them, "Don't differ, for the nations before you differed and perished (because of their differences). " – Al-Bukhari 2410

حَدَّثَنَا أَبُو الْوَلِيدِ، حَدَّثَنَا شُعْبَةُ، قَالَ عَبْدُ الْمَلِكِ بْنُ مَيْسَرَةَ أَخْبَرَنِي قَالَ سَمِعْتُ النَّزَّالَ، سَمِعْتُ عَبْدَ اللَّهِ، يَقُولُ سَمِعْتُ رَجُلاً، قَرَأَ آيَةً سَمِعْتُ مِنَ النَّبِيِّ، صلى الله عليه وسلم خِلاَفَهَا، فَأَخَذْتُ بِيَدِهِ، فَأَتَيْتُ بِهِ رَسُولَ اللَّهِ صلى الله عليه وسلم فَقَالَ " كِلاَكُمَا مُحْسِنٌ ". قَالَ شُعْبَةُ أَظُنُّهُ قَالَ " لاَ تَخْتَلِفُوا فَإِنَّ مَنْ كَانَ قَبْلَكُمُ اخْتَلَفُوا فَهَلَكُوا ".

Those who carry the Throne, and those around it, glorify their Lord with praise, and believe in Him, and ask for forgiveness for those who believe: "Our Lord, You have encompassed everything in mercy and knowledge; so forgive those who repent and follow Your path, and protect them from the agony of the Blaze. – Surah Ghafir 40:7

ٱلَّذِينَ يَحْمِلُونَ ٱلْعَرْشَ وَمَنْ حَوْلَهُۥ يُسَبِّحُونَ بِحَمْدِ رَبِّهِمْ وَيُؤْمِنُونَ بِهِۦ وَيَسْتَغْفِرُونَ لِلَّذِينَ ءَامَنُوا۟ ۖ رَبَّنَا وَسِعْتَ كُلَّ شَىْءٍ رَّحْمَةً وَعِلْمًا فَٱغْفِرْ لِلَّذِينَ تَابُوا۟ وَٱتَّبَعُوا۟ سَبِيلَكَ وَقِهِمْ عَذَابَ ٱلْجَحِيمِ

Ibn Shihab was asked, "If one of those with whom Muslims have made a covenant bewitches people, will he be sentenced to death?" He replied, "We have been informed that Allah's Messenger was bewitched, yet he did not kill the magician who was from the People of the Scriptures." – Al-Bukhari Vol.4 page 254

و قال ابن وهب : أخبرني يونس، عن ابن شهاب، سءل : أعلى من سحر من أهل العهد قيل ؟ قال : بلغنا أن رسول الله صلى الله عليه وسلم قد صنع له ذلك فلم يقتل من صنعه و كان من أهل الكتاب.

Narrated `Abdullah bin `Amr bin Al-As: The Prophet ﷺ said to me, "I have been informed that you pray all the nights and observe fast all the days; is this true?" I replied, "Yes." He said, "If you do so, your eyes will become weak and you will get bored. So fast three days a month, for this will be the fasting of a whole year, or equal to the fasting of a whole year." I said, "I find myself able to fast more." He said, "Then fast like the fasting of (the Prophet) David who used to fast on alternate days and would not flee on facing the enemy." – Al-Bukhari 3419

حَدَّثَنَا خَلاَّدُ بْنُ يَحْيَى، حَدَّثَنَا مِسْعَرٌ، حَدَّثَنَا حَبِيبُ بْنُ أَبِي ثَابِتٍ، عَنْ أَبِي الْعَبَّاسِ، عَنْ عَبْدِ اللَّهِ بْنِ عَمْرِو بْنِ الْعَاصِ، قَالَ قَالَ لِي رَسُولُ اللَّهِ صلى الله عليه وسلم " أَلَمْ أُنَبَّأْ أَنَّكَ تَقُومُ اللَّيْلَ وَتَصُومُ ". فَقُلْتُ نَعَمْ. فَقَالَ " فَإِنَّكَ إِذَا فَعَلْتَ ذَلِكَ هَجَمَتِ الْعَيْنُ وَنَفِهَتِ النَّفْسُ، صُمْ مِنْ كُلِّ شَهْرٍ ثَلاَثَةَ أَيَّامٍ، فَذَلِكَ صَوْمُ الدَّهْرِ ـ أَوْ كَصَوْمِ الدَّهْرِ ". قُلْتُ إِنِّي أَجِدُ بِي ـ قَالَ مِسْعَرٌ يَعْنِي ـ قُوَّةً. قَالَ " فَصُمْ صَوْمَ دَاوُدَ ـ عَلَيْهِ السَّلاَمُ ـ وَكَانَ يَصُومُ يَوْمًا، وَيُفْطِرُ يَوْمًا، وَلاَ يَفِرُّ إِذَا لاَقَى "

Narrated Abu Huraira: While some Ethiopians were playing in the presence of the Prophet, `Umar came in, picked up a stone and hit them with it. On that the Prophet ﷺ said, "O `Umar! Allow them (to play)." Ma`mar (the subnarrator) added that they were playing in the Mosque. – Al-Bukhari 2901

حَدَّثَنَا إِبْرَاهِيمُ بْنُ مُوسَى، أَخْبَرَنَا هِشَامٌ، عَنْ مَعْمَرٍ، عَنِ الزُّهْرِيِّ، عَنِ ابْنِ الْمُسَيَّبِ، عَنْ أَبِي هُرَيْرَةَ ـ رضى الله عنه ـ قَالَ بَيْنَا الْحَبَشَةُ يَلْعَبُونَ عِنْدَ النَّبِيِّ صلى الله عليه وسلم بِحِرَابِهِمْ دَخَلَ عُمَرُ، فَأَهْوَى إِلَى الْحَصَى فَحَصَبَهُمْ بِهَا. فَقَالَ " دَعْهُمْ يَا عُمَرُ ". وَزَادَ عَلِيٌّ حَدَّثَنَا عَبْدُ الرَّزَّاقِ أَخْبَرَنَا مَعْمَرٌ فِي الْمَسْجِدِ.

Narrated `Aisha: Allah's Messenger ﷺ came to my house while two girls were singing beside me the songs of Bu'ath (a story about the war between the two tribes of the Ansar, i.e. Khazraj and Aus, before Islam.) The Prophet ﷺ reclined on the bed and turned his face to the other side. Abu Bakr came and scolded me and said protestingly, "Instrument of Satan in the presence of Allah's Messenger ﷺ "?Allah's Messenger ﷺ turned his face towards him and said, "Leave them." When Abu Bakr became inattentive, I waved the two girls to go away and they left. It was the day of `Id when negroes used to play with leather shields and spears. Either I requested Allah's Messenger ﷺ or he himself asked me whether I would like to see the display. I replied in the affirmative. Then he let me stand behind him and my cheek was touching his cheek and he was saying, "Carry on, O Bani Arfida (i.e. negroes)!" When I got tired, he asked me if that was enough. I replied in the affirmative and he told me to leave. – Al-Bukhari 2906, 2907

حَدَّثَنَا إِسْمَاعِيلُ، قَالَ حَدَّثَنِي ابْنُ وَهْبٍ، قَالَ عَمْرٌو حَدَّثَنِي أَبُو الأَسْوَدِ، عَنْ عُرْوَةَ، عَنْ عَائِشَةَ ـ رضى الله عنها ـ دَخَلَ عَلَىَّ رَسُولُ اللَّهِ صلى الله عليه وسلم وَعِنْدِي جَارِيَتَانِ تُغَنِّيَانِ بِغِنَاءِ بُعَاثَ، فَاضْطَجَعَ عَلَى الْفِرَاشِ وَحَوَّلَ وَجْهَهُ، فَدَخَلَ أَبُو بَكْرٍ فَانْتَهَرَنِي وَقَالَ مِزْمَارَةُ الشَّيْطَانِ عِنْدَ رَسُولِ اللَّهِ صلى الله عليه وسلم. فَأَقْبَلَ عَلَيْهِ رَسُولُ اللَّهِ صلى الله عليه وسلم فَقَالَ " دَعْهُمَا ". فَلَمَّا غَفَلَ غَمَزْتُهُمَا فَخَرَجَتَا. قَالَتْ وَكَانَ يَوْمُ عِيدٍ يَلْعَبُ السُّودَانُ بِالدَّرَقِ وَالْحِرَابِ، فَإِمَّا سَأَلْتُ رَسُولَ اللَّهِ صلى الله عليه وسلم وَإِمَّا قَالَ " تَشْتَهِينَ تَنْظُرِينَ ". فَقَالَتْ نَعَمْ. فَأَقَامَنِي وَرَاءَهُ خَدِّي عَلَى خَدِّهِ وَيَقُولُ " دُونَكُمْ بَنِي أَرْفِدَةَ حَتَّى إِذَا مَلِلْتُ قَالَ " حَسْبُكِ ". قُلْتُ نَعَمْ. قَالَ " فَاذْهَبِي ". قَالَ أَحْمَدُ عَنِ ابْنِ وَهْبٍ، فَلَمَّا غَفَلَ.

Narrated Jabir bin `Abdullah :We were in a Ghazwa and a man from the emigrants kicked an Ansari (on the buttocks with his foot). The Ansari man said, "O the Ansari! (Help!)" The emigrant said, "O the emigrants! (Help)." When Allah's Messenger ﷺ heard that, he said, "What is that?" They said, "A man from the emigrants kicked a man from the Ansar (on the buttocks his foot). On that the Ansar said, 'O the Ansar!' and the emigrant said, 'O the emigrants!" The Prophet ﷺ said' "Leave it (that call) for it Is a detestable thing." The number of Ansar was larger (than that of the emigrants) at the time when the Prophet ﷺ came to Medina, but later the number of emigrants increased. `Abdullah bin Ubai said, "Have they, (the emigrants) done so? By Allah, if we return to Medina, surely, the more honorable will expel therefrom the meaner," `Umar bin Al-Khattab said, "O Allah's Messenger ﷺ ! Let me chop off the head of this hypocrite!" The Prophet said, "Leave him, lest the people say Muhammad kills his companions – ":Al-Bukhari 4907

حَدَّثَنَا الْحُمَيْدِيُّ، حَدَّثَنَا سُفْيَانُ، قَالَ حَفِظْنَاهُ مِنْ عَمْرِو بْنِ دِينَارٍ قَالَ سَمِعْتُ جَابِرَ بْنَ عَبْدِ اللَّهِ ـ رضى الله عنهما ـ يَقُولُ كُنَّا فِي غَزَاةٍ فَكَسَعَ رَجُلٌ مِنَ الْمُهَاجِرِينَ رَجُلاً مِنَ الأَنْصَارِ فَقَالَ الأَنْصَارِيُّ يَا لَلأَنْصَارِ. وَقَالَ الْمُهَاجِرِيُّ يَا لَلْمُهَاجِرِينَ. فَسَمَّعَهَا اللَّهُ رَسُولَهُ صلى الله عليه وسلم قَالَ " مَا هَذَا ". فَقَالُوا كَسَعَ رَجُلٌ مِنَ الْمُهَاجِرِينَ رَجُلاً مِنَ الأَنْصَارِ فَقَالَ الأَنْصَارِيُّ يَا لَلأَنْصَارِ. وَقَالَ الْمُهَاجِرِيُّ يَالَلْمُهَاجِرِينَ. فَقَالَ النَّبِيُّ صلى الله عليه وسلم " دَعُوهَا فَإِنَّهَا مُنْتِنَةٌ ". قَالَ جَابِرٌ وَكَانَتِ الأَنْصَارُ حِينَ قَدِمَ النَّبِيُّ صلى الله عليه وسلم أَكْثَرَ، ثُمَّ كَثُرَ الْمُهَاجِرُونَ بَعْدُ، فَقَالَ عَبْدُ اللَّهِ بْنُ أُبَىٍّ أَوَقَدْ فَعَلُوا، وَاللَّهِ لَئِنْ رَجَعْنَا إِلَى الْمَدِينَةِ لَيُخْرِجَنَّ الأَعَزُّ مِنْهَا الأَذَلَّ. فَقَالَ عُمَرُ بْنُ الْخَطَّابِ رضى الله عنه دَعْنِي يَا رَسُولَ اللَّهِ أَضْرِبْ عُنُقَ هَذَا الْمُنَافِقِ. قَالَ النَّبِيُّ صلى الله عليه وسلم " دَعْهُ لاَ يَتَحَدَّثُ النَّاسُ أَنَّ مُحَمَّدًا يَقْتُلُ أَصْحَابَهُ ".

Know that there is no god but Allah, and ask forgiveness for your sin, and for the believing men and believing women. Allah knows your movements, and your resting-place. – Surah Muhammad 47:19

فَٱعْلَمْ أَنَّهُۥ لَآ إِلَـٰهَ إِلَّا ٱللَّهُ وَٱسْتَغْفِرْ لِذَنۢبِكَ وَلِلْمُؤْمِنِينَ وَٱلْمُؤْمِنَـٰتِ ۗ وَٱللَّهُ يَعْلَمُ مُتَقَلَّبَكُمْ وَمَثْوَىٰكُمْ

And We gave them precise rulings. They fell into dispute only after knowledge came to them, out of mutual rivalry. Your Lord will judge between them on the Day of Resurrection regarding the things they differed about.– Surah Al-Jathiyah 45:17

وَءَاتَيْنَـٰهُم بَيِّنَـٰتٍ مِّنَ ٱلْأَمْرِ ۖ فَمَا ٱخْتَلَفُوٓا۟ إِلَّا مِنۢ بَعْدِ مَا جَآءَهُمُ ٱلْعِلْمُ بَغْيًۢا بَيْنَهُمْ ۚ إِنَّ رَبَّكَ يَقْضِى بَيْنَهُمْ يَوْمَ ٱلْقِيَـٰمَةِ فِيمَا كَانُوا۟ فِيهِ يَخْتَلِفُونَ

And endure patiently what they say, and withdraw from them politely.– Surah Al-Muzzamil 73:10

وَٱصْبِرْ عَلَىٰ مَا يَقُولُونَ وَٱهْجُرْهُمْ هَجْرًا جَمِيلًا

Narrated `Itban bin Malik: Who was one of the companions of Allah's Messenger ﷺ and one of the Ansar's who took part in the battle of Badr: I came to Allah's Messenger ﷺ and said, "O Allah's Messenger ﷺ I have weak eyesight and I lead my people in prayers. When it rains the water flows in the valley between me and my people so I cannot go to their mosque to lead them in prayer. O Allah's Messenger ﷺ ! I wish you would come to my house and pray in it so that I could take that place as a Musalla. Allah's Messenger ﷺ said. "Allah willing, I will do so." Next day after the sun rose high, Allah's Messenger ﷺ and Abu Bakr came and Allah's Messenger ﷺ asked for permission to enter. I gave him permission and he did not sit on entering the house but said to me, "Where do you like me to pray?" I pointed to a place in my house. So Allah's Messenger ﷺ stood there and said, 'Allahu Akbar', and we all got up and aligned behind him and offered a two-rak`at prayer and ended it with Taslim. We requested him to stay for a meal called "Khazira" which we had prepared for him. Many members of our family gathered in the house and one of them said, "Where is Malik bin Al-Dukhaishin or Ibn Al-Dukhshun?" One of them replied, "He is a hypocrite and does not love Allah and His Apostle." Hearing that, Allah's Messenger ﷺ said, "Do not say so. Haven't you seen that he said, 'None has the right to be worshipped but Allah' for Allah's sake only?" He said, "Allah and His Apostle know better. We have seen him helping and advising hypocrites." Allah's Messenger ﷺ said, "Allah has forbidden the (Hell) fire for those who say, 'None has the right to be worshipped but Allah' for Allah's sake only." – Al-Bukhari 425

حَدَّثَنَا سَعِيدُ بْنُ عُفَيْرٍ، قَالَ حَدَّثَنِي اللَّيْثُ، قَالَ حَدَّثَنِي عُقَيْلٌ، عَنِ ابْنِ شِهَابٍ، قَالَ أَخْبَرَنِي مَحْمُودُ بْنُ الرَّبِيعِ الأَنْصَارِيُّ، أَنَّ عِتْبَانَ بْنَ مَالِكٍ ـ وَهُوَ مِنْ أَصْحَابِ رَسُولِ اللَّهِ صلى الله عليه وسلم مِمَّنْ شَهِدَ بَدْرًا مِنَ الأَنْصَارِ ـ أَنَّهُ أَتَى رَسُولَ اللَّهِ صلى الله عليه وسلم فَقَالَ يَا رَسُولَ اللَّهِ، قَدْ أَنْكَرْتُ بَصَرِي، وَأَنَا أُصَلِّي لِقَوْمِي، فَإِذَا كَانَتِ الأَمْطَارُ سَالَ الْوَادِي الَّذِي بَيْنِي وَبَيْنَهُمْ، لَمْ أَسْتَطِعْ أَنْ آتِيَ مَسْجِدَهُمْ فَأُصَلِّيَ بِهِمْ، وَوَدِدْتُ يَا رَسُولَ اللَّهِ أَنَّكَ تَأْتِينِي فَتُصَلِّيَ فِي بَيْتِي، فَأَتَّخِذَهُ مُصَلًّى. قَالَ فَقَالَ لَهُ رَسُولُ اللَّهِ صلى الله عليه وسلم " سَأَفْعَلُ إِنْ شَاءَ اللَّهُ ". قَالَ عِتْبَانُ فَغَدَا رَسُولُ اللَّهِ صلى الله عليه وسلم وَأَبُو بَكْرٍ حِينَ ارْتَفَعَ النَّهَارُ، فَاسْتَأْذَنَ رَسُولُ اللَّهِ صلى الله عليه وسلم فَأَذِنْتُ لَهُ، فَلَمْ يَجْلِسْ حَتَّى دَخَلَ الْبَيْتَ ثُمَّ قَالَ " أَيْنَ تُحِبُّ أَنْ أُصَلِّيَ مِنْ بَيْتِكَ ". قَالَ فَأَشَرْتُ لَهُ إِلَى نَاحِيَةٍ مِنَ الْبَيْتِ، فَقَامَ رَسُولُ اللَّهِ صلى الله عليه وسلم فَكَبَّرَ، فَقُمْنَا فَصَفَّنَا، فَصَلَّى رَكْعَتَيْنِ ثُمَّ سَلَّمَ، قَالَ وَحَبَسْنَاهُ عَلَى خَزِيرَةٍ صَنَعْنَاهَا لَهُ. قَالَ فَثَابَ فِي الْبَيْتِ رِجَالٌ مِنْ أَهْلِ الدَّارِ ذَوُو عَدَدٍ فَاجْتَمَعُوا، فَقَالَ قَائِلٌ مِنْهُمْ أَيْنَ مَالِكُ بْنُ الدُّخَيْشِنِ أَوِ ابْنُ الدُّخْشُنِ فَقَالَ بَعْضُهُمْ ذَلِكَ مُنَافِقٌ لاَ يُحِبُّ اللَّهَ وَرَسُولَهُ. فَقَالَ رَسُولُ اللَّهِ صلى الله عليه وسلم " لاَ تَقُلْ ذَلِكَ، أَلاَ تَرَاهُ قَدْ قَالَ لاَ إِلَهَ إِلاَّ اللَّهُ. يُرِيدُ بِذَلِكَ وَجْهَ اللَّهِ ". قَالَ اللَّهُ وَرَسُولُهُ أَعْلَمُ. قَالَ فَإِنَّا نَرَى وَجْهَهُ وَنَصِيحَتَهُ إِلَى الْمُنَافِقِينَ. قَالَ رَسُولُ اللَّهِ صلى الله عليه وسلم " فَإِنَّ اللَّهَ قَدْ حَرَّمَ عَلَى النَّارِ مَنْ قَالَ لاَ إِلَهَ إِلاَّ اللَّهُ. يَبْتَغِي بِذَلِكَ وَجْهَ اللَّهِ ". قَالَ ابْنُ شِهَابٍ ثُمَّ سَأَلْتُ الْحُصَيْنَ بْنَ مُحَمَّدٍ الأَنْصَارِيَّ ـ وَهْوَ أَحَدُ بَنِي سَالِمٍ وَهُوَ مِنْ سَرَاتِهِمْ ـ عَنْ حَدِيثِ مَحْمُودِ بْنِ الرَّبِيعِ، فَصَدَّقَهُ بِذَلِكَ

Narrated Anas bin Malik: The Prophet ﷺ came to some of his wives among whom there was Um Sulaim, and said, "May Allah be merciful to you, O Anjasha! Drive the camels slowly, as they are carrying glass vessels!" Abu Qalaba said, "The Prophet ﷺ said a sentence (i.e. the above metaphor) which, had anyone of you said it, you would have admonished him for it". – Al-Bukhari 6149

حَدَّثَنَا مُسَدَّدٌ، حَدَّثَنَا إِسْمَاعِيلُ، حَدَّثَنَا أَيُّوبُ، عَنْ أَبِي قِلاَبَةَ، عَنْ أَنَسِ بْنِ مَالِكٍ ـ رضى الله عنه ـ قَالَ أَتَى النَّبِيُّ صلى الله عليه وسلم عَلَى بَعْضِ نِسَائِهِ وَمَعَهُنَّ أُمُّ سُلَيْمٍ فَقَالَ " وَيْحَكَ يَا أَنْجَشَةُ، رُوَيْدَكَ سَوْقًا بِالْقَوَارِيرِ ". قَالَ أَبُو قِلاَبَةَ فَتَكَلَّمَ النَّبِيُّ صلى الله عليه وسلم بِكَلِمَةٍ، لَوْ تَكَلَّمَ بَعْضُكُمْ لَعِبْتُمُوهَا عَلَيْهِ قَوْلُهُ " سَوْقَكَ بِالْقَوَارِيرِ "

Narrated Abu Huraira: The Prophet ﷺ said twice, "(O you people) Be cautious! Do not practice Al-Wisal." The people said to him, "But you practice Al-Wisal?" The Prophet ﷺ replied, "My Lord gives me food and drink during my sleep. Do that much of deeds which is within your ability." – Al-Bukhari 1966

حَدَّثَنَا يَحْيَى، حَدَّثَنَا عَبْدُ الرَّزَّاقِ، عَنْ مَعْمَرٍ، عَنْ هَمَّامٍ، أَنَّهُ سَمِعَ أَبَا هُرَيْرَةَ ـ رضى الله عنه ـ عَنِ النَّبِيِّ صلى الله عليه وسلم قَالَ " إِيَّاكُمْ وَالْوِصَالَ ". مَرَّتَيْنِ قِيلَ إِنَّكَ تُوَاصِلُ. قَالَ " إِنِّي أَبِيتُ يُطْعِمُنِي رَبِّي وَيَسْقِينِ، فَاكْلَفُوا مِنَ الْعَمَلِ مَا تُطِيقُونَ "

Narrated Anas bin Malik: The Prophet ﷺ said, "Facilitate things to people (concerning religious matters), and do not make it hard for them and give them good tidings and do not make them run away (from Islam). – Al-Bukhari 69

حَدَّثَنَا مُحَمَّدُ بْنُ بَشَّارٍ، قَالَ حَدَّثَنَا يَحْيَى بْنُ سَعِيدٍ، قَالَ حَدَّثَنَا شُعْبَةُ، قَالَ حَدَّثَنِي أَبُو التَّيَّاحِ، عَنْ أَنَسٍ، عَنِ النَّبِيِّ صلى الله عليه وسلم قَالَ " يَسِّرُوا وَلاَ تُعَسِّرُوا، وَبَشِّرُوا وَلاَ تُنَفِّرُوا ".

Narrated `Abdullah bin `Amr bin Al `Aas: Allah's Messenger ﷺ stopped (for a while near the Jimar) at Mina during his last Hajj for the people and they were asking him questions. A man came and said, "I forgot and got my head shaved before slaughtering the Hadi (sacrificing animal)." The Prophet ﷺ said, "There is no harm, go and do the slaughtering now." Then another person came and said, "I forgot and slaughtered (the camel) before Rami (throwing of the pebbles) at the Jamra." The Prophet ﷺ said, "Do the Rami now and there is no harm." The narrator added: So on that day, when the Prophet ﷺ was asked about anything (as regards the ceremonies of Hajj) performed before or after its due time, his reply was: "Do it (now) and there is no harm." – Al-Bukhari 83

حَدَّثَنَا إِسْمَاعِيلُ، قَالَ حَدَّثَنِي مَالِكٌ، عَنِ ابْنِ شِهَابٍ، عَنْ عِيسَى بْنِ طَلْحَةَ بْنِ عُبَيْدِ اللَّهِ، عَنْ عَبْدِ اللَّهِ بْنِ عَمْرِو بْنِ الْعَاصِ، أَنَّ رَسُولَ اللَّهِ صلى الله عليه وسلم وَقَفَ فِي حَجَّةِ الْوَدَاعِ بِمِنًى لِلنَّاسِ يَسْأَلُونَهُ، فَجَاءَهُ رَجُلٌ فَقَالَ لَمْ أَشْعُرْ فَحَلَقْتُ قَبْلَ أَنْ أَذْبَحَ. فَقَالَ " اذْبَحْ وَلاَ حَرَجَ ". فَجَاءَ آخَرُ فَقَالَ لَمْ أَشْعُرْ، فَنَحَرْتُ قَبْلَ أَنْ أَرْمِيَ. قَالَ " ارْمِ وَلاَ حَرَجَ ". فَمَا سُئِلَ النَّبِيُّ صلى الله عليه وسلم عَنْ شَىْءٍ قُدِّمَ وَلاَ أُخِّرَ إِلاَّ قَالَ افْعَلْ وَلاَ حَرَجَ

And We made a covenant with you: "You shall not shed the blood of your own, nor shall you evict your own from your homes." You agreed, and were all witnesses. But here you are, killing your own, and expelling a group of your own from their homes—conspiring against them in wrongdoing and hostility. And if they come to you as captives, you ransom them, although it was forbidden to you. Is it that you believe in part of the Scripture, and disbelieve in part? What is the reward for those among you who do that but humiliation in this life? And on the Day of Resurrection, they will be assigned to the most severe torment. Allah is not unaware of what you do.. – Surah Al-Baqarah 2:84&85

وَإِذْ أَخَذْنَا مِيثَـٰقَكُمْ لَا تَسْفِكُونَ دِمَآءَكُمْ وَلَا تُخْرِجُونَ أَنفُسَكُم مِّن دِيَـٰرِكُمْ ثُمَّ أَقْرَرْتُمْ وَأَنتُمْ تَشْهَدُونَ ثُمَّ أَنتُمْ هَـٰٓؤُلَآءِ تَقْتُلُونَ أَنفُسَكُمْ وَتُخْرِجُونَ فَرِيقًا مِّنكُم مِّن دِيَـٰرِهِمْ تَظَـٰهَرُونَ عَلَيْهِم بِٱلْإِثْمِ وَٱلْعُدْوَٰنِ وَإِن يَأْتُوكُمْ أُسَـٰرَىٰ تُفَـٰدُوهُمْ وَهُوَ مُحَرَّمٌ عَلَيْكُمْ إِخْرَاجُهُمْ ۚ أَفَتُؤْمِنُونَ بِبَعْضِ ٱلْكِتَـٰبِ وَتَكْفُرُونَ بِبَعْضٍ ۚ فَمَا جَزَآءُ مَن يَفْعَلُ ذَٰلِكَ مِنكُمْ إِلَّا خِزْىٌ فِى ٱلْحَيَوٰةِ ٱلدُّنْيَا ۖ وَيَوْمَ ٱلْقِيَـٰمَةِ يُرَدُّونَ إِلَىٰٓ أَشَدِّ ٱلْعَذَابِ ۗ وَمَا ٱللَّهُ بِغَـٰفِلٍ عَمَّا تَعْمَلُونَ

Narrated Ibn `Umar: The Prophet ﷺ sent (an army unit under the command of) Khalid bin Al-Walid to fight against the tribe of Bani Jadhima and those people could not express themselves by saying, "Aslamna," but they said, "Saba'na! Saba'na! " Khalid kept on killing some of them and taking some others as captives, and he gave a captive to everyone of us and ordered everyone of us to kill his captive. I said, "By Allah, I shall not kill my captive and none of my companions shall kill his captive!" Then we mentioned that to the Prophet ﷺ and he said, "O Allah! I am free from what Khalid bin Al-Walid has done," and repeated it twice. – Al-Bukhari 7189

حَدَّثَنَا مَحْمُودٌ، حَدَّثَنَا عَبْدُ الرَّزَّاقِ، أَخْبَرَنَا مَعْمَرٌ، عَنِ الزُّهْرِيِّ، عَنْ سَالِمٍ، عَنِ ابْنِ عُمَرَ، بَعَثَ النَّبِيُّ صلى الله عليه وسلم خَالِدًا ح وَحَدَّثَنِي نُعَيْمٌ أَخْبَرَنَا عَبْدُ اللَّهِ أَخْبَرَنَا مَعْمَرٌ عَنِ الزُّهْرِيِّ عَنْ سَالِمٍ عَنْ أَبِيهِ قَالَ بَعَثَ النَّبِيُّ صلى الله عليه وسلم خَالِدَ بْنَ الْوَلِيدِ إِلَى بَنِي جَذِيمَةَ فَلَمْ يُحْسِنُوا أَنْ يَقُولُوا أَسْلَمْنَا. فَقَالُوا صَبَأْنَا صَبَأْنَا، فَجَعَلَ خَالِدٌ يَقْتُلُ وَيَأْسِرُ، وَدَفَعَ إِلَى كُلِّ

رَجُلٌ مِنَّا أَسِيرَهُ، فَأَمَرَ كُلَّ رَجُلٍ مِنَّا أَنْ يَقْتُلَ أَسِيرَهُ، فَقُلْتُ وَاللَّهِ لاَ أَقْتُلُ أَسِيرِي وَلاَ يَقْتُلُ رَجُلٌ مِنْ أَصْحَابِي أَسِيرَهُ. فَذَكَرْنَا ذَلِكَ لِلنَّبِيِّ صلى الله عليه وسلم فَقَالَ " اللَّهُمَّ إِنِّي أَبْرَأُ إِلَيْكَ مِمَّا صَنَعَ خَالِدُ بْنُ الْوَلِيدِ "، مَرَّتَيْنِ

We are fully aware of what they say, and you are not a dictator over them. So remind by the Quran whoever fears My warning. – Surah Qaf 50:45
نَّحْنُ أَعْلَمُ بِمَا يَقُولُونَ ۖ وَمَآ أَنتَ عَلَيْهِم بِجَبَّارٍ ۖ فَذَكِّرْ بِٱلْقُرْءَانِ مَن يَخَافُ وَعِيدِ

Narrated Ma'rur: I saw Abu Dhar wearing a Burd (garment) and his slave too was wearing a Burd, so I said (to Abu Dhar), "If you take this (Burda of your slave) and wear it (along with yours), you will have a nice suit (costume) and you may give him another garment." Abu Dhar said, "There was a quarrel between me and another man whose mother was a non-Arab and I called her bad names. The man mentioned (complained about) me to the Prophet. The Prophet ﷺ said, "Did you abuse so-and-so?" I said, "Yes" He said, "Did you call his mother bad names?" I said, "Yes". He said, "You still have the traits of (the Pre-Islamic period of) ignorance." I said. "(Do I still have ignorance) even now in my old age?" He said, "Yes, they (slaves or servants) are your brothers, and Allah has put them under your command. So the one under whose hand Allah has put his brother, should feed him of what he eats, and give him dresses of what he wears, and should not ask him to do a thing beyond his capacity. And if at all he asks him to do a hard task, he should help him therein." – Al-Bukhari 6050
حَدَّثَنَا عُمَرُ بْنُ حَفْصٍ، حَدَّثَنَا أَبِي، حَدَّثَنَا الأَعْمَشُ، عَنِ الْمَعْرُورِ، عَنْ أَبِي ذَرٍّ، قَالَ رَأَيْتُ عَلَيْهِ بُرْدًا وَعَلَى غُلاَمِهِ بُرْدًا فَقُلْتُ لَوْ أَخَذْتَ هَذَا فَلَبِسْتَهُ كَانَتْ حُلَّةً، وَأَعْطَيْتَهُ ثَوْبًا آخَرَ. فَقَالَ كَانَ بَيْنِي وَبَيْنَ رَجُلٍ كَلاَمٌ، وَكَانَتْ أُمُّهُ أَعْجَمِيَّةً، فَنِلْتُ مِنْهَا فَذَكَرَنِي إِلَى النَّبِيِّ صلى الله عليه وسلم فَقَالَ لِي " أَسَابَبْتَ فُلاَنًا ". قُلْتُ نَعَمْ. قَالَ " أَفَنِلْتَ مِنْ أُمِّهِ ". قُلْتُ نَعَمْ. قَالَ " إِنَّكَ امْرُؤٌ فِيكَ جَاهِلِيَّةٌ ". قُلْتُ عَلَى حِينِ سَاعَتِي هَذِهِ مِنْ كِبَرِ السِّنِّ قَالَ " نَعَمْ، هُمْ إِخْوَانُكُمْ، جَعَلَهُمُ اللَّهُ تَحْتَ أَيْدِيكُمْ، فَمَنْ جَعَلَ اللَّهُ أَخَاهُ تَحْتَ يَدِهِ فَلْيُطْعِمْهُ مِمَّا يَأْكُلُ، وَلْيُلْبِسْهُ مِمَّا يَلْبَسُ، وَلاَ يُكَلِّفُهُ مِنَ الْعَمَلِ مَا يَغْلِبُهُ، فَإِنْ كَلَّفَهُ مَا يَغْلِبُهُ فَلْيُعِنْهُ عَلَيْهِ

Narrated Jabir bin `Abdullah: We were in a Ghazwa (Sufyan once said, in an army) and a man from the emigrants kicked an Ansari man (on the buttocks with his foot). The Ansari man said, "O the Ansar! (Help!)" and the emigrant said. "O the emigrants! (Help!) Allah's Messenger ﷺ heard that and said, "What is this call for, which is characteristic of the period of ignorance?" They said, "O Allah's Messenger ﷺ ! A man from the emigrants kicked one of the Ansar (on the buttocks with his foot)." Allah's Messenger ﷺ said, "Leave it (that call) as is a detestable thing." `Abdullah bin Ubai heard that and said, 'Have the (the emigrants) done so? By Allah, if we return Medina, surely, the more honorable will expel therefrom the meaner." When this statement reached the Prophet. `Umar got up an, said, "O Allah's Messenger ﷺ ! Let me chop off the head of this hypocrite (`Abdullah bin Ubai)!" The Prophet ﷺ said "Leave him, lest the people say that Muhammad kills his companions." The Ansar were then more in number than the emigrants when the latter came to Medina, but later on the emigrant increased. – Al-Bukhari 4905
حَدَّثَنَا عَلِيٌّ، حَدَّثَنَا سُفْيَانُ، قَالَ عَمْرٌو سَمِعْتُ جَابِرَ بْنَ عَبْدِ اللَّهِ ـ رضى الله عنهما ـ قَالَ كُنَّا فِي غَزَاةٍ ـ قَالَ سُفْيَانُ مَرَّةً فِي جَيْشٍ ـ فَكَسَعَ رَجُلٌ مِنَ الْمُهَاجِرِينَ رَجُلاً مِنَ الأَنْصَارِ فَقَالَ الأَنْصَارِيُّ يَا لَلأَنْصَارِ. وَقَالَ الْمُهَاجِرِيُّ يَا لَلْمُهَاجِرِينَ. فَسَمِعَ ذَاكَ رَسُولُ اللَّهِ صلى الله عليه وسلم فَقَالَ " مَا بَالُ دَعْوَى جَاهِلِيَّةٍ " قَالُوا يَا رَسُولَ اللَّهِ كَسَعَ رَجُلٌ مِنَ الْمُهَاجِرِينَ رَجُلاً مِنَ الأَنْصَارِ. فَقَالَ " دَعُوهَا فَإِنَّهَا مُنْتِنَةٌ ". فَسَمِعَ بِذَلِكَ عَبْدُ اللَّهِ بْنُ أُبَىٍّ فَقَالَ فَعَلُوهَا، أَمَا وَاللَّهِ لَئِنْ رَجَعْنَا إِلَى الْمَدِينَةِ لَيُخْرِجَنَّ الأَعَزُّ مِنْهَا الأَذَلَّ. فَبَلَغَ النَّبِيَّ صلى الله عليه وسلم فَقَامَ عُمَرُ فَقَالَ يَا رَسُولَ اللَّهِ دَعْنِي أَضْرِبْ عُنُقَ هَذَا الْمُنَافِقِ. فَقَالَ النَّبِيُّ صلى الله عليه وسلم " دَعْهُ لاَ يَتَحَدَّثُ النَّاسُ أَنَّ مُحَمَّدًا يَقْتُلُ أَصْحَابَهُ " وَكَانَتِ الأَنْصَارُ أَكْثَرَ مِنَ الْمُهَاجِرِينَ حِينَ قَدِمُوا الْمَدِينَةَ، ثُمَّ إِنَّ الْمُهَاجِرِينَ كَثُرُوا بَعْدُ. قَالَ سُفْيَانُ فَحَفِظْتُهُ مِنْ عَمْرٍو قَالَ عَمْرٌو سَمِعْتُ جَابِرًا كُنَّا مَعَ النَّبِيِّ صلى الله عليه وسلم

Narrated Al-Miqdad bin `Amr Al-Kindi: An ally of Bani Zuhra who took part in the battle of Badr with the Prophet, that he said, “O Allah’s Apostle! If I meet an unbeliever and we have a fight, and he strikes my hand with the sword and cuts it off, and then takes refuge from me under a tree, and says, ‘I have surrendered to Allah (i.e. embraced Islam),’ may I kill him after he has said so?” Allah’s Messenger ﷺ said, “Do not kill him.” Al- Miqdad said, “But O Allah’s Messenger ﷺ ! He had chopped off one of my hands and he said that after he had cut it off. May I kill him?” The Prophet ﷺ said. “Do not kill him for if you kill him, he would be in the position in which you had been before you kill him, and you would be in the position in which he was before he said the sentence.” The Prophet ﷺ also said to Al-Miqdad, “If a faithful believer conceals his faith (Islam) from the disbelievers, and then when he declares his Islam, you kill him, (you will be sinful). Remember that you were also concealing your faith (Islam) at Mecca before.” – Al-Bukhari 6865, 6866

حَدَّثَنَا عَبْدَانُ، حَدَّثَنَا عَبْدُ اللَّهِ، حَدَّثَنَا يُونُسُ، عَنِ الزُّهْرِيِّ، حَدَّثَنَا عَطَاءُ بْنُ يَزِيدَ، أَنَّ عُبَيْدَ اللَّهِ بْنَ عَدِيٍّ، حَدَّثَهُ أَنَّ الْمِقْدَادَ بْنَ عَمْرٍو الْكِنْدِيَّ حَلِيفَ بَنِي زُهْرَةَ حَدَّثَهُ وَكَانَ، شَهِدَ بَدْرًا مَعَ النَّبِيِّ صلى الله عليه وسلم أَنَّهُ قَالَ يَا رَسُولَ اللَّهِ إِنْ لَقِيتُ كَافِرًا فَاقْتَتَلْنَا، فَضَرَبَ يَدِي بِالسَّيْفِ فَقَطَعَهَا، ثُمَّ لاَذَ بِشَجَرَةٍ وَقَالَ أَسْلَمْتُ لِلَّهِ. آقْتُلُهُ بَعْدَ أَنْ قَالَهَا قَالَ رَسُولُ اللَّهِ صلى الله عليه وسلم " لاَ تَقْتُلْهُ ". قَالَ يَا رَسُولَ اللَّهِ فَإِنَّهُ طَرَحَ إِحْدَى يَدَىَّ، ثُمَّ قَالَ بَعْدَ مَا قَطَعَهَا، آقْتُلُهُ قَالَ " لاَ تَقْتُلْهُ، فَإِنْ قَتَلْتَهُ فَإِنَّهُ بِمَنْزِلَتِكَ قَبْلَ أَنْ تَقْتُلَهُ، وَأَنْتَ بِمَنْزِلَتِهِ قَبْلَ أَنْ يَقُولَ كَلِمَتَهُ الَّتِي قَالَ ". وَقَالَ حَبِيبُ بْنُ أَبِي عَمْرَةَ عَنْ سَعِيدٍ، عَنِ ابْنِ عَبَّاسٍ، قَالَ قَالَ النَّبِيُّ صلى الله عليه وسلم لِلْمِقْدَادِ " إِذَا كَانَ رَجُلٌ مُؤْمِنٌ يُخْفِي إِيمَانَهُ مَعَ قَوْمٍ كُفَّارٍ، فَأَظْهَرَ إِيمَانَهُ، فَقَتَلْتَهُ، فَكَذَلِكَ كُنْتَ أَنْتَ تُخْفِي إِيمَانَكَ بِمَكَّةَ مِنْ قَبْلُ "

There shall be no compulsion in religion; the right way has become distinct from the wrong way. Whoever renounces evil and believes in Allah has grasped the most trustworthy handle; which does not break. Allah is Hearing and Knowing.– Surah Al-Baqarah 2:256

لَآ إِكۡرَاهَ فِى ٱلدِّينِۖ قَد تَّبَيَّنَ ٱلرُّشۡدُ مِنَ ٱلۡغَىِّۚ فَمَن يَكۡفُرۡ بِٱلطَّـٰغُوتِ وَيُؤۡمِنۢ بِٱللَّهِ فَقَدِ ٱسۡتَمۡسَكَ بِٱلۡعُرۡوَةِ ٱلۡوُثۡقَىٰ لَا ٱنفِصَامَ لَهَاۗ وَٱللَّهُ سَمِيعٌ عَلِيمٌ

Tell those who believe to forgive those who do not hope for the Days of Allah. He will fully recompense people for whatever they have earned. – Surah Al-Jathiyah 45:14

قُل لِّلَّذِينَ ءَامَنُواْ يَغۡفِرُواْ لِلَّذِينَ لَا يَرۡجُونَ أَيَّامَ ٱللَّهِ لِيَجۡزِىَ قَوۡمَۢا بِمَا كَانُواْ يَكۡسِبُونَ

Narrated Abu Wail: Abu Musa Al-Ash`ari used to lay great stress on the question of urination and he used to say, “If anyone from Bani Israel happened to soil his clothes with urine, he used to cut that portion away.” Hearing that, Hudhaifa said to Abu Wail, “I wish he (Abu Musa) didn’t (lay great stress on that matter).” Hudhaifa added, “Allah’s Messenger ﷺ went to the dumps of some people and urinated while standing.” – Sahih al-Bukhari 226

حَدَّثَنَا مُحَمَّدُ بْنُ عَرْعَرَةَ، قَالَ حَدَّثَنَا شُعْبَةُ، عَنْ مَنْصُورٍ، عَنْ أَبِي وَائِلٍ، قَالَ كَانَ أَبُو مُوسَى الأَشْعَرِيُّ يُشَدِّدُ فِي الْبَوْلِ وَيَقُولُ إِنَّ بَنِي إِسْرَائِيلَ كَانَ إِذَا أَصَابَ ثَوْبَ أَحَدِهِمْ قَرَضَهُ. فَقَالَ حُذَيْفَةُ لَيْتَهُ أَمْسَكَ، أَتَى رَسُولُ اللَّهِ صلى الله عليه وسلم سُبَاطَةَ قَوْمٍ فَبَالَ قَائِمًا.

You will follow the ways of those nations who were before you inch by inch

لَتَتَّبِعُنَّ سَنَنَ مَنْ كَانَ قَبْلَكُمْ شِبْرًا شِبْرًا

Narrated Abu Sa`id Al-Khudri: The Prophet ﷺ said, “You will follow the ways of those nations who were before you, span by span and cubit by cubit (i.e., inch by inch) so much so that even if they entered a hole of a mastigure, you would follow them.” We said, “O Allah’s

Messenger ﷺ! (Do you mean) the Jews and the Christians?" He said, "Whom else?" – Sahih Al-Bukhari 7320

حَدَّثَنَا مُحَمَّدُ بْنُ عَبْدِ الْعَزِيزِ، حَدَّثَنَا أَبُو عُمَرَ الصَّنْعَانِيُّ ـ مِنَ الْيَمَنِ ـ عَنْ زَيْدِ بْنِ أَسْلَمَ، عَنْ عَطَاءِ بْنِ يَسَارٍ، عَنْ أَبِي سَعِيدٍ الْخُدْرِيِّ، عَنِ النَّبِيِّ صلى الله عليه وسلم قَالَ " لَتَتْبَعُنَّ سَنَنَ مَنْ كَانَ قَبْلَكُمْ شِبْرًا شِبْرًا وَذِرَاعًا بِذِرَاعٍ، حَتَّى لَوْ دَخَلُوا جُحْرَ ضَبٍّ تَبِعْتُمُوهُمْ ". قُلْنَا يَا رَسُولَ اللَّهِ الْيَهُودُ وَالنَّصَارَى قَالَ " فَمَنْ "

And the Jews have said, "The Nasara (i.e. the Christians) do not (stand) on anything, " and the Nasara have said, "The Jews do not (stand) on anything, " and they recite the Book. Thus the ones who do not know have said the like of their saying. So, Allah will judge between them on the Day of the Resurrection wherein they used to differ. Surah Al-Baqarah 2:113

وَقَالَتِ ٱلْيَهُودُ لَيْسَتِ ٱلنَّصَـٰرَىٰ عَلَىٰ شَىْءٍ وَقَالَتِ ٱلنَّصَـٰرَىٰ لَيْسَتِ ٱلْيَهُودُ عَلَىٰ شَىْءٍ وَهُمْ يَتْلُونَ ٱلْكِتَـٰبَ ۗ كَذَٰلِكَ قَالَ ٱلَّذِينَ لَا يَعْلَمُونَ مِثْلَ قَوْلِهِمْ ۚ فَٱللَّهُ يَحْكُمُ بَيْنَهُمْ يَوْمَ ٱلْقِيَـٰمَةِ فِيمَا كَانُوا۟ فِيهِ يَخْتَلِفُونَ

And they say, "None will enter Heaven unless he is a Jew or a Christian." These are their wishes. Say, "Produce your proof, if you are truthful." – Surah Al-Baqarah 2:111

وَقَالُوا۟ لَن يَدْخُلَ ٱلْجَنَّةَ إِلَّا مَن كَانَ هُودًا أَوْ نَصَـٰرَىٰ ۗ تِلْكَ أَمَانِيُّهُمْ ۗ قُلْ هَاتُوا۟ بُرْهَـٰنَكُمْ إِن كُنتُمْ صَـٰدِقِينَ

Humanity used to be one community; then Allah sent the prophets, bringing good news and giving warnings. And He sent down with them the Scripture, with the truth, to judge between people regarding their differences. But none differed over it except those who were given it—after the proofs had come to them—out of mutual envy between them. Then Allah guided those who believed to the truth they had disputed, in accordance with His will. Allah guides whom He wills to a straight path. – Surah Al-Baqarah 2:213

كَانَ ٱلنَّاسُ أُمَّةً وَٰحِدَةً فَبَعَثَ ٱللَّهُ ٱلنَّبِيِّـۧنَ مُبَشِّرِينَ وَمُنذِرِينَ وَأَنزَلَ مَعَهُمُ ٱلْكِتَـٰبَ بِٱلْحَقِّ لِيَحْكُمَ بَيْنَ ٱلنَّاسِ فِيمَا ٱخْتَلَفُوا۟ فِيهِ ۚ وَمَا ٱخْتَلَفَ فِيهِ إِلَّا ٱلَّذِينَ أُوتُوهُ مِنۢ بَعْدِ مَا جَآءَتْهُمُ ٱلْبَيِّنَـٰتُ بَغْيًۢا بَيْنَهُمْ ۖ فَهَدَى ٱللَّهُ ٱلَّذِينَ ءَامَنُوا۟ لِمَا ٱخْتَلَفُوا۟ فِيهِ مِنَ ٱلْحَقِّ بِإِذْنِهِۦ ۗ وَٱللَّهُ يَهْدِى مَن يَشَآءُ إِلَىٰ صِرَٰطٍ مُّسْتَقِيمٍ

But for their violation of their covenant, and their denial of Allah's revelations, and their killing of the prophets unjustly, and their saying, "Our minds are closed." In fact, Allah has sealed them for their disbelief, so they do not believe, except for a few. And for their faithlessness, and their saying against Mary a monstrous slander. And for their saying, "We have killed the Messiah, Jesus, the son of Mary, the Messenger of Allah." In fact, they did not kill him, nor did they crucify him, but it appeared to them as if they did. Indeed, those who differ about him are in doubt about it. They have no knowledge of it, except the following of assumptions. Certainly, they did not kill him. – Surah An-Nisa 4:155-157

فَبِمَا نَقْضِهِم مِّيثَـٰقَهُمْ وَكُفْرِهِم بِـَٔايَـٰتِ ٱللَّهِ وَقَتْلِهِمُ ٱلْأَنۢبِيَآءَ بِغَيْرِ حَقٍّ وَقَوْلِهِمْ قُلُوبُنَا غُلْفٌۢ ۚ بَلْ طَبَعَ ٱللَّهُ عَلَيْهَا بِكُفْرِهِمْ فَلَا يُؤْمِنُونَ إِلَّا قَلِيلًا وَبِكُفْرِهِمْ وَقَوْلِهِمْ عَلَىٰ مَرْيَمَ بُهْتَـٰنًا عَظِيمًا وَقَوْلِهِمْ إِنَّا قَتَلْنَا ٱلْمَسِيحَ عِيسَى ٱبْنَ مَرْيَمَ رَسُولَ ٱللَّهِ وَمَا قَتَلُوهُ وَمَا صَلَبُوهُ وَلَـٰكِن شُبِّهَ لَهُمْ ۚ وَإِنَّ ٱلَّذِينَ ٱخْتَلَفُوا۟ فِيهِ لَفِى شَكٍّ مِّنْهُ ۚ مَا لَهُم بِهِۦ مِنْ عِلْمٍ إِلَّا ٱتِّبَاعَ ٱلظَّنِّ ۚ وَمَا قَتَلُوهُ يَقِينًۢا

They became divided only after knowledge came to them, out of resentment among themselves. Were it not for a predetermined decision from your Lord, judgment would have been pronounced between them. Indeed, those who were made to inherit the Book after them are in grave doubt about it. – Surah Ash-Shura 42:14

وَمَا تَفَرَّقُوٓا۟ إِلَّا مِنۢ بَعْدِ مَا جَآءَهُمُ ٱلْعِلْمُ بَغْيًۢا بَيْنَهُمْ ۚ وَلَوْلَا كَلِمَةٌ سَبَقَتْ مِن رَّبِّكَ إِلَىٰٓ أَجَلٍ مُّسَمًّى لَّقُضِىَ بَيْنَهُمْ ۚ وَإِنَّ ٱلَّذِينَ أُورِثُوا۟ ٱلْكِتَـٰبَ مِنۢ بَعْدِهِمْ لَفِى شَكٍّ مِّنْهُ مُرِيبٍ

And We made a covenant with you: "You shall not shed the blood of your own, nor shall you evict your own from your homes." You agreed, and were all witnesses. But here you are, killing your own, and expelling a group of your own from their homes—conspiring against them in wrongdoing and hostility. And if they come to you as captives, you ransom them, although it was forbidden to you. Is it that you believe in part of the Scripture, and disbelieve in part? What is the reward for those among you who do that but humiliation in this life? And on the Day of Resurrection, they will be assigned to the most severe torment. Allah is not unaware of what you do. – Surah Al-Baqarah 2:84&85

كُمْ ثُمَّ أَقْرَرْتُمْ وَأَنتُمْ تَشْهَدُونَ ثُمَّ أَنتُمْ هَٰٓؤُلَآءِ تَقْتُلُونَ أَنفُسَكُمْ وَتُخْرِجُونَ فَرِيقًا مِّنكُم مِّن دِيَٰرِهِمْ تَظَٰهَرُونَ عَلَيْهِم بِٱلْإِثْمِ
وَٱلْعُدْوَٰنِ وَإِن يَأْتُوكُمْ أُسَٰرَىٰ تُفَٰدُوهُمْ وَهُوَ مُحَرَّمٌ عَلَيْكُمْ إِخْرَاجُهُمْ ۚ أَفَتُؤْمِنُونَ بِبَعْضِ ٱلْكِتَٰبِ وَتَكْفُرُونَ بِبَعْضٍ ۚ فَمَا جَزَآءُ مَن
يَفْعَلُ ذَٰلِكَ مِنكُمْ إِلَّا خِزْىٌ فِى ٱلْحَيَوٰةِ ٱلدُّنْيَا ۖ وَيَوْمَ ٱلْقِيَٰمَةِ يُرَدُّونَ إِلَىٰٓ أَشَدِّ ٱلْعَذَابِ ۗ وَمَا ٱللَّهُ بِغَٰفِلٍ عَمَّا تَعْمَلُونَ

As for those who defy Allah's revelations, and kill the prophets unjustly, and kill those who advocate justice among the people—promise them a painful retribution. – Surah Al-Imran 3:21

إِنَّ ٱلَّذِينَ يَكْفُرُونَ بِـَٔايَٰتِ ٱللَّهِ وَيَقْتُلُونَ ٱلنَّبِيِّـۧنَ بِغَيْرِ حَقٍّ وَيَقْتُلُونَ ٱلَّذِينَ يَأْمُرُونَ بِٱلْقِسْطِ مِنَ ٱلنَّاسِ فَبَشِّرْهُم بِعَذَابٍ أَلِيمٍ

Of those who divided their religion, and became sects; each faction pleased with what they have. – Surah Ar-Rum 30:32 [1]

مِنَ ٱلَّذِينَ فَرَّقُوا۟ دِينَهُمْ وَكَانُوا۟ شِيَعًا ۖ كُلُّ حِزْبٍۭ بِمَا لَدَيْهِمْ فَرِحُونَ

Say, " you who follow Judaism, if you claim that out of all people you alone are friends of Allah, then wish for death if you are truthful." – Surah Al-Jumu'ah 62:6

قُلْ يَٰٓأَيُّهَا ٱلَّذِينَ هَادُوٓا۟ إِن زَعَمْتُمْ أَنَّكُمْ أَوْلِيَآءُ لِلَّهِ مِن دُونِ ٱلنَّاسِ فَتَمَنَّوُا۟ ٱلْمَوْتَ إِن كُنتُمْ صَٰدِقِينَ

Those are the Messengers; We have graced some of them over some others; of them (there are some) to whom Allah spoke, and some He raised in degrees. And We brought Isa son of Maryam (Jesus son of Mary) the supreme evidences and aided him with the Spirit of Holiness. (The Angel Jibril) And if Allah had (so) decided, the ones who (came) after them would not have fought against each other, after the supreme evidences had come to them. But they differed among themselves. So of them are the ones who believed, and of them are the ones who disbelieved. And if Allah had (so) decided, they would not have fought against each other; but Allah performs whatever He wills. – Surah Al-Baqarah 2:253

تِلْكَ ٱلرُّسُلُ فَضَّلْنَا بَعْضَهُمْ عَلَىٰ بَعْضٍ ۘ مِّنْهُم مَّن كَلَّمَ ٱللَّهُ ۖ وَرَفَعَ بَعْضَهُمْ دَرَجَٰتٍ ۚ وَءَاتَيْنَا عِيسَى ٱبْنَ مَرْيَمَ ٱلْبَيِّنَٰتِ وَأَيَّدْنَٰهُ
بِرُوحِ ٱلْقُدُسِ ۗ وَلَوْ شَآءَ ٱللَّهُ مَا ٱقْتَتَلَ ٱلَّذِينَ مِنۢ بَعْدِهِم مِّنۢ بَعْدِ مَا جَآءَتْهُمُ ٱلْبَيِّنَٰتُ وَلَٰكِنِ ٱخْتَلَفُوا۟ فَمِنْهُم مَّنْ ءَامَنَ وَمِنْهُم مَّن
كَفَرَ ۚ وَلَوْ شَآءَ ٱللَّهُ مَا ٱقْتَتَلُوا۟ وَلَٰكِنَّ ٱللَّهَ يَفْعَلُ مَا يُرِيدُ

(The ones) who have disbelieved among the population of the Book (Or: family of the Book; i.e., the Jews and Christians) and the associators (Those who associate others with Allah) could not have left off (erring) until the Supreme Evidence came up to them A Messenger from Allah, reciting Scrolls purified Therein are ever-upright Books And in no way did the ones

---

[1] "Do not make your da'wah to a particular group, but to Islam in general…". – Shaykh Muhammad ibn Salih al-'Uthaymeen
"There is no doubt that the name Muslim is better than all these names, and more complete…". – Shaykh al-Islam Ibn Taymiyyah
"I do not say I am Salafi to create a new group. I say it to clarify that I follow the way of the Salaf. But if you ask what name the Muslim should use, then I say: the name Allah gave us is 'Muslim'. That is enough." – al-Albani

to whom the Book was brought (become) disunited, except ever after the Supreme Evidence came up to them. – Surah Al-Baiyinah 98:1-4

لَمْ يَكُنِ الَّذِينَ كَفَرُوا مِنْ أَهْلِ الْكِتَابِ وَالْمُشْرِكِينَ مُنفَكِّينَ حَتَّىٰ تَأْتِيَهُمُ الْبَيِّنَةُ رَسُولٌ مِّنَ اللَّهِ يَتْلُو صُحُفًا مُّطَهَّرَةً فِيهَا كُتُبٌ قَيِّمَةٌ وَمَا تَفَرَّقَ الَّذِينَ أُوتُوا الْكِتَابَ إِلَّا مِن بَعْدِ مَا جَاءَتْهُمُ الْبَيِّنَةُ

Then We sent in their wake Our messengers, and followed up with Jesus son of Mary, and We gave him the Gospel, and instilled in the hearts of those who followed him compassion and mercy. But as for the monasticism which they invented—We did not ordain it for them—only to seek Allah's approval. But they did not observe it with its due observance. So We gave those of them who believed their reward, but many of them are sinful. O you who believe! Fear Allah, and believe in His Messenger: He will give you a double portion of His mercy, and will give you a light by which you walk, and will forgive you. Allah is Forgiving and Merciful. That the People of the Book may know that they have no power whatsoever over Allah's grace, and that all grace is in Allah's hand; He gives it to whomever He wills. Allah is Possessor of Great Grace. – Surah Al-Hadid 57:27-29

ثُمَّ قَفَّيْنَا عَلَىٰ ءَاثَٰرِهِم بِرُسُلِنَا وَقَفَّيْنَا بِعِيسَى ٱبْنِ مَرْيَمَ وَءَاتَيْنَٰهُ ٱلْإِنجِيلَ وَجَعَلْنَا فِى قُلُوبِ ٱلَّذِينَ ٱتَّبَعُوهُ رَأْفَةً وَرَحْمَةً وَرَهْبَانِيَّةً ٱبْتَدَعُوهَا مَا كَتَبْنَٰهَا عَلَيْهِمْ إِلَّا ٱبْتِغَآءَ رِضْوَٰنِ ٱللَّهِ فَمَا رَعَوْهَا حَقَّ رِعَايَتِهَا فَـَٔاتَيْنَا ٱلَّذِينَ ءَامَنُوا۟ مِنْهُمْ أَجْرَهُمْ وَكَثِيرٌ مِّنْهُمْ فَٰسِقُونَ يَٰٓأَيُّهَا ٱلَّذِينَ ءَامَنُوا۟ ٱتَّقُوا۟ ٱللَّهَ وَءَامِنُوا۟ بِرَسُولِهِۦ يُؤْتِكُمْ كِفْلَيْنِ مِن رَّحْمَتِهِۦ وَيَجْعَل لَّكُمْ نُورًا تَمْشُونَ بِهِۦ وَيَغْفِرْ لَكُمْ وَٱللَّهُ غَفُورٌ رَّحِيمٌ لِّئَلَّا يَعْلَمَ أَهْلُ ٱلْكِتَٰبِ أَلَّا يَقْدِرُونَ عَلَىٰ شَىْءٍ مِّن فَضْلِ ٱللَّهِ وَأَنَّ ٱلْفَضْلَ بِيَدِ ٱللَّهِ يُؤْتِيهِ مَن يَشَآءُ وَٱللَّهُ ذُو ٱلْفَضْلِ ٱلْعَظِيمِ

They have taken their rabbis and their priests as lords instead of Allah, as well as the Messiah son of Mary. Although they were commanded to worship none but The One God. There is no god except He. Glory be to Him; High above what they associate with Him. – Surah At-Taubah 9:31

ٱتَّخَذُوٓا۟ أَحْبَارَهُمْ وَرُهْبَٰنَهُمْ أَرْبَابًا مِّن دُونِ ٱللَّهِ وَٱلْمَسِيحَ ٱبْنَ مَرْيَمَ وَمَآ أُمِرُوٓا۟ إِلَّا لِيَعْبُدُوٓا۟ إِلَٰهًا وَٰحِدًا لَّآ إِلَٰهَ إِلَّا هُوَ سُبْحَٰنَهُۥ عَمَّا يُشْرِكُونَ

Those who believe, and those who are Jewish, and the Christians, and the Sabeans—any who believe in Allah and the Last Day, and act righteously—will have their reward with their Lord; they have nothing to fear, nor will they grieve. – Surah Al-Baqarah 2:62

إِنَّ ٱلَّذِينَ ءَامَنُوا۟ وَٱلَّذِينَ هَادُوا۟ وَٱلنَّصَٰرَىٰ وَٱلصَّٰبِـِٔينَ مَنْ ءَامَنَ بِٱللَّهِ وَٱلْيَوْمِ ٱلْءَاخِرِ وَعَمِلَ صَٰلِحًا فَلَهُمْ أَجْرُهُمْ عِندَ رَبِّهِمْ وَلَا خَوْفٌ عَلَيْهِمْ وَلَا هُمْ يَحْزَنُونَ

It is Allah who named you Muslims before, and in this (Quran). – Surah Al-Hajj 22:78

...هُوَ سَمَّىٰكُمُ ٱلْمُسْلِمِينَ مِن قَبْلُ وَفِى هَٰذَا...

Whoever kills a believer deliberately, the penalty for him is Hell, where he will remain forever. And Allah will be angry with him, and will curse him, and will prepare for him a terrible punishment. – Surah An-Nisa 4:93

وَمَن يَقْتُلْ مُؤْمِنًا مُّتَعَمِّدًا فَجَزَآؤُهُۥ جَهَنَّمُ خَٰلِدًا فِيهَا وَغَضِبَ ٱللَّهُ عَلَيْهِ وَلَعَنَهُۥ وَأَعَدَّ لَهُۥ عَذَابًا عَظِيمًا

Is it not time for those who believe to surrender their hearts to the remembrance of Allah, and to the truth that has come down, and not be like those who were given the Book previously, but time became prolonged for them, so their hearts hardened, and many of them are sinners? – Surah Al-Hadid 57:16

أَلَمْ يَأْنِ لِلَّذِينَ ءَامَنُوٓا۟ أَن تَخْشَعَ قُلُوبُهُمْ لِذِكْرِ ٱللَّهِ وَمَا نَزَلَ مِنَ ٱلْحَقِّ وَلَا يَكُونُوا۟ كَٱلَّذِينَ أُوتُوا۟ ٱلْكِتَٰبَ مِن قَبْلُ فَطَالَ عَلَيْهِمُ ٱلْأَمَدُ فَقَسَتْ قُلُوبُهُمْ وَكَثِيرٌ مِّنْهُمْ فَٰسِقُونَ

Narrated Usama bin Zaid: Allah's Messenger ﷺ sent us towards Al-Huruqa, and in the morning we attacked them and defeated them. I and an Ansari man followed a man from among them and when we took him over, he said, "La ilaha illal-Lah." On hearing that, the Ansari man stopped, but I killed him by stabbing him with my spear. When we returned, the Prophetﷺ came to know about that and he said, "O Usama! Did you kill him after he had said "La ilaha ilal-Lah?" I said, "But he said so only to save himself." The Prophetﷺ kept on repeating that so often that I wished I had not embraced Islam before that day. – Sahih Al-Bukhari 4269

حَدَّثَنِي عَمْرُو بْنُ مُحَمَّدٍ، حَدَّثَنَا هُشَيْمٌ، أَخْبَرَنَا حُصَيْنٌ، أَخْبَرَنَا أَبُو ظَبْيَانَ، قَالَ سَمِعْتُ أُسَامَةَ بْنَ زَيْدٍ ـ رضى الله عنهما ـ يَقُولُ بَعَثَنَا رَسُولُ اللَّهِ صلى الله عليه وسلم إِلَى الْحُرَقَةِ، فَصَبَّحْنَا الْقَوْمَ فَهَزَمْنَاهُمْ وَلَحِقْتُ أَنَا وَرَجُلٌ مِنَ الأَنْصَارِ رَجُلاً مِنْهُمْ، فَلَمَّا غَشِينَاهُ قَالَ لاَ إِلَهَ إِلاَّ اللَّهُ. فَكَفَّ الأَنْصَارِيُّ، فَطَعَنْتُهُ بِرُمْحِي حَتَّى قَتَلْتُهُ، فَلَمَّا قَدِمْنَا بَلَغَ النَّبِيَّ صلى الله عليه وسلم فَقَالَ " يَا أُسَامَةُ أَقَتَلْتَهُ بَعْدَ مَا قَالَ لاَ إِلَهَ إِلاَّ اللَّهُ " قُلْتُ كَانَ مُتَعَوِّذًا. فَمَا زَالَ يُكَرِّرُهَا حَتَّى تَمَنَّيْتُ أَنِّي لَمْ أَكُنْ أَسْلَمْتُ قَبْلَ ذَلِكَ الْيَوْمِ.

Narrated `Umar: I heard the Prophetﷺ saying, "Do not exaggerate in praising me as the Christians praised the son of Mary, for I am only a Slave. So, call me the Slave of Allah and His Apostle.". – Al-Bukhari 3445

حَدَّثَنَا الْحُمَيْدِيُّ، حَدَّثَنَا سُفْيَانُ، قَالَ سَمِعْتُ الزُّهْرِيَّ، يَقُولُ أَخْبَرَنِي عُبَيْدُ اللَّهِ بْنُ عَبْدِ اللَّهِ، عَنِ ابْنِ عَبَّاسٍ، سَمِعَ عُمَرَ ـ رضى الله عنه ـ يَقُولُ عَلَى الْمِنْبَرِ سَمِعْتُ النَّبِيَّ صلى الله عليه وسلم يَقُولُ " لاَ تُطْرُونِي كَمَا أَطْرَتِ النَّصَارَى ابْنَ مَرْيَمَ، فَإِنَّمَا أَنَا عَبْدُهُ، فَقُولُوا عَبْدُ اللَّهِ وَرَسُولُهُ ".

Narrated Abu Wail: Abu Musa Al-Ash`ari used to lay great stress on the question of urination and he used to say, "If anyone from Bani Israel happened to soil his clothes with urine, he used to cut that portion away." Hearing that, Hudhaifa said to Abu Wail, "I wish he (Abu Musa) didn't (lay great stress on that matter)." Hudhaifa added, "Allah's Messenger went to the dumps of some people and urinated while standing." – Sahih al-Bukhari 226

حَدَّثَنَا مُحَمَّدُ بْنُ عَرْعَرَةَ، قَالَ حَدَّثَنَا شُعْبَةُ، عَنْ مَنْصُورٍ، عَنْ أَبِي وَائِلٍ، قَالَ كَانَ أَبُو مُوسَى الأَشْعَرِيُّ يُشَدِّدُ فِي الْبَوْلِ وَيَقُولُ إِنَّ بَنِي إِسْرَائِيلَ كَانَ إِذَا أَصَابَ ثَوْبَ أَحَدِهِمْ قَرَضَهُ. فَقَالَ حُذَيْفَةُ لَيْتَهُ أَمْسَكَ، أَتَى رَسُولُ اللَّهِ صلى الله عليه وسلم سُبَاطَةَ قَوْمٍ فَبَالَ قَائِمًا.

Narrated Mu`adha: A woman asked `Aisha, "Should I offer the prayers that which I did not offer because of menses" `Aisha said, "Are you from the Huraura' (a town in Iraq?) We were with the Prophetﷺ and used to get our periods but he never ordered us to offer them (the Prayers missed during menses)." `Aisha perhaps said, "We did not offer them." Bukhari 321

حَدَّثَنَا مُوسَى بْنُ إِسْمَاعِيلَ، قَالَ حَدَّثَنَا هَمَّامٌ، قَالَ حَدَّثَنَا قَتَادَةُ، قَالَ حَدَّثَتْنِي مُعَاذَةُ، أَنَّ امْرَأَةً، قَالَتْ لِعَائِشَةَ أَتَجْزِي إِحْدَانَا صَلاَتَهَا إِذَا طَهُرَتْ فَقَالَتْ أَحَرُورِيَّةٌ أَنْتِ كُنَّا نَحِيضُ مَعَ النَّبِيِّ صلى الله عليه وسلم فَلاَ يَأْمُرُنَا بِهِ. أَوْ قَالَتْ فَلاَ نَفْعَلُهُ.

And among them are uneducated who know the Scripture only through hearsay, and they only speculate. Surah Al-Baqarah 2:78

وَمِنْهُمْ أُمِّيُّونَ لَا يَعْلَمُونَ ٱلْكِتَـٰبَ إِلَّآ أَمَانِىَّ وَإِنْ هُمْ إِلَّا يَظُنُّونَ

Aisha Said, "A woman from Bani Makhzumiya committed a theft and the people said, 'Who can intercede with the Prophetﷺ for her?' So nobody dared speak to him (i.e. the Prophet) but Usama bin Zaid spoke to him. The Prophet said, 'If a reputable man amongst the children of Bani Israel committed a theft, they used to forgive him, but if a poor man committed a theft, they would cut his hand. But I would cut even the hand of Fatima (i.e. the daughter of the Prophet) if she committed a theft." – Sahih al-Bukhari 3733

حَدَّثَنَا عَلِيٌّ، حَدَّثَنَا سُفْيَانُ، قَالَ ذَهَبْتُ أَسْأَلُ الزُّهْرِيَّ عَنْ حَدِيثِ الْمَخْزُومِيَّةِ، فَصَاحَ بِي، قُلْتُ لِسُفْيَانَ فَلَمْ تَحْتَمِلْهُ عَنْ أَحَدٍ قَالَ وَجَدْتُهُ فِي كِتَابٍ كَانَ كَتَبَهُ أَيُّوبُ بْنُ مُوسَى عَنِ الزُّهْرِيِّ عَنْ عُرْوَةَ عَنْ عَائِشَةَ ـ رضى الله عنها أَنَّ امْرَأَةً مِنْ بَنِي مَخْزُومٍ سَرَقَتْ، فَقَالُوا مَنْ يُكَلِّمُ فِيهَا النَّبِيَّ صلى الله عليه وسلم فَلَمْ يَجْتَرِئْ أَحَدٌ أَنْ يُكَلِّمَهُ، فَكَلَّمَهُ أُسَامَةُ بْنُ زَيْدٍ، فَقَالَ " إِنَّ بَنِي إِسْرَائِيلَ كَانَ إِذَا سَرَقَ فِيهِمُ الشَّرِيفُ تَرَكُوهُ، وَإِذَا سَرَقَ الضَّعِيفُ قَطَعُوهُ، لَوْ كَانَتْ فَاطِمَةُ لَقَطَعْتُ يَدَهَا ".

Have you not considered those who claim purity for themselves? Rather, Allah purifies whom He wills, and they will not be wronged in the least. – Surah An-Nisa 4:49

أَلَمْ تَرَ إِلَى ٱلَّذِينَ يُزَكُّونَ أَنفُسَهُمۚ بَلِ ٱللَّهُ يُزَكِّى مَن يَشَآءُ وَلَا يُظْلَمُونَ فَتِيلًا

....We took their covenant, but they forgot a portion of that of which they had been reminded. So We stirred up among them enmity and hatred until the Day of Resurrection. And Allah will inform them about what they used to do. – Surah Al-Ma'idah 5:14
أَخَذْنَا مِيثَـٰقَهُمْ فَنَسُوا۟ حَظًّا مِّمَّا ذُكِّرُوا۟ بِهِۦ فَأَغْرَيْنَا بَيْنَهُمُ ٱلْعَدَاوَةَ وَٱلْبَغْضَآءَ إِلَىٰ يَوْمِ ٱلْقِيَـٰمَةِ ۚ وَسَوْفَ يُنَبِّئُهُمُ ٱللَّهُ بِمَا كَانُوا۟ يَصْنَعُونَ

.........they are only following their guess, and they only tell lies. – Surah Yunus 10:66
إِن يَتَّبِعُونَ إِلَّا ٱلظَّنَّ وَإِنْ هُمْ إِلَّا يَخْرُصُونَ

And Haya is a part of faith
الْحَيَاءُ شُعْبَةٌ مِنَ الإِيمَانِ

Then, one of the two women came walking toward him shyly and said, "My father would like to pay you for having watered [our flock] for us." So, when Moses came to him and told him his story, he said, "Don't be afraid. You have escaped from those oppressive people.". – Surah Al-Qasas 28:25
فَجَآءَتْهُ إِحْدَىٰهُمَا تَمْشِى عَلَى ٱسْتِحْيَآءٍ قَالَتْ إِنَّ أَبِى يَدْعُوكَ لِيَجْزِيَكَ أَجْرَ مَا سَقَيْتَ لَنَا ۚ فَلَمَّا جَآءَهُۥ وَقَصَّ عَلَيْهِ ٱلْقَصَصَ قَالَ لَا تَخَفْ ۖ نَجَوْتَ مِنَ ٱلْقَوْمِ ٱلظَّـٰلِمِينَ

Narrated Abu Sa`id Al-Khudri: The Prophet ﷺ was more shy than a virgin in her separate room. And if he saw a thing which he disliked, we would recognize that (feeling) in his face. – Sahih al-Bukhari 6102
حَدَّثَنَا عَبْدَانُ، أَخْبَرَنَا عَبْدُ اللَّهِ، أَخْبَرَنَا شُعْبَةُ، عَنْ قَتَادَةَ، سَمِعْتُ عَبْدَ اللَّهِ ـ هُوَ ابْنُ أَبِي عُتْبَةَ مَوْلَى أَنَسٍ ـ عَنْ أَبِي سَعِيدٍ الْخُدْرِيِّ، قَالَ كَانَ النَّبِيُّ صلى الله عليه وسلم أَشَدَّ حَيَاءً مِنَ الْعَذْرَاءِ فِي خِدْرِهَا، فَإِذَا رَأَى شَيْئًا يَكْرَهُهُ عَرَفْنَاهُ فِي وَجْهِهِ

Narrated Abu Huraira: The Prophet ﷺ said, "Faith (Belief) consists of more than sixty branches (i.e. parts). And Haya (This term "Haya" covers a large number of concepts which are to be taken together; amongst them are self respect, modesty, bashfulness, and scruple, etc.) is a part of faith.". – Sahih al-Bukhari 9
حَدَّثَنَا عَبْدُ اللَّهِ بْنُ مُحَمَّدٍ، قَالَ حَدَّثَنَا أَبُو عَامِرٍ الْعَقَدِيُّ، قَالَ حَدَّثَنَا سُلَيْمَانُ بْنُ بِلاَلٍ، عَنْ عَبْدِ اللَّهِ بْنِ دِينَارٍ، عَنْ أَبِي صَالِحٍ، عَنْ أَبِي هُرَيْرَةَ ـ رضى الله عنه ـ عَنِ النَّبِيِّ صلى الله عليه وسلم قَالَ " الإِيمَانُ بِضْعٌ وَسِتُّونَ شُعْبَةً، وَالْحَيَاءُ شُعْبَةٌ مِنَ الإِيمَانِ "

Narrated 'Abdullah (bin 'Umar): Once Allah's Messenger ﷺ passed by an Ansari (man) who was admonishing his brother regarding Haya'. On that Allah's Messenger ﷺ said, "Leave him as Haya' is a part of faith." (See Hadith 9). – Sahih al-Bukhari 24
حَدَّثَنَا عَبْدُ اللَّهِ بْنُ يُوسُفَ، قَالَ أَخْبَرَنَا مَالِكُ بْنُ أَنَسٍ، عَنِ ابْنِ شِهَابٍ، عَنْ سَالِمِ بْنِ عَبْدِ اللَّهِ، عَنْ أَبِيهِ، أَنَّ رَسُولَ اللَّهِ صلى الله عليه وسلم مَرَّ عَلَى رَجُلٍ مِنَ الأَنْصَارِ وَهُوَ يَعِظُ أَخَاهُ فِي الْحَيَاءِ، فَقَالَ رَسُولُ اللَّهِ صلى الله عليه وسلم " دَعْهُ فَإِنَّ الْحَيَاءَ مِنَ الإِيمَانِ ".

It was narrated that Abu Hurairah said: "The Messenger of Allah ﷺ said: 'Faith has seventy-odd branches, the most virtuous of which is La ilaha illallah (there is none worthy of worship except Allah) and the least of which is removing something harmful from the road. And modesty (Al-Haya') is a branch of faith.'". – Sunan an-Nasa'I 5005
أَخْبَرَنَا أَحْمَدُ بْنُ سُلَيْمَانَ، قَالَ حَدَّثَنَا أَبُو دَاوُدَ، عَنْ سُفْيَانَ، قَالَ وَحَدَّثَنَا أَبُو نُعَيْمٍ، قَالَ حَدَّثَنَا سُفْيَانُ، عَنْ سُهَيْلٍ، عَنْ عَبْدِ اللَّهِ بْنِ دِينَارٍ، عَنْ أَبِي صَالِحٍ، عَنْ أَبِي هُرَيْرَةَ، قَالَ قَالَ رَسُولُ اللَّهِ صلى الله عليه وسلم " الإِيمَانُ بِضْعٌ وَسَبْعُونَ شُعْبَةً أَفْضَلُهَا لاَ إِلَهَ إِلاَّ اللَّهُ وَأَوْضَعُهَا إِمَاطَةُ الأَذَى عَنِ الطَّرِيقِ وَالْحَيَاءُ شُعْبَةٌ مِنَ الإِيمَانِ "

The Book of
Truly! Allah is with the patient ones
إِنَّ ٱللَّهَ مَعَ ٱلصَّـٰبِرِينَ

Whether We show you some of what We have promised them, or We cause you to die—your duty is to inform, and Ours is the reckoning. – Surah Ar-Ra'd 13:40
وَإِن مَّا نُرِيَنَّكَ بَعْضَ ٱلَّذِى نَعِدُهُمْ أَوْ نَتَوَفَّيَنَّكَ فَإِنَّمَا عَلَيْكَ ٱلْبَلَـٰغُ وَعَلَيْنَا ٱلْحِسَابُ

Those who believe, and those who are Jewish, and the Sabeans, and the Christians, and the Zoroastrians, and the Polytheists—Allah will judge between them on the Day of Resurrection. Allah is witness to all things.– Surah Al-Hajj 22:17
إِنَّ ٱلَّذِينَ ءَامَنُوا۟ وَٱلَّذِينَ هَادُوا۟ وَٱلصَّـٰبِـِٔينَ وَٱلنَّصَـٰرَىٰ وَٱلْمَجُوسَ وَٱلَّذِينَ أَشْرَكُوٓا۟ إِنَّ ٱللَّهَ يَفْصِلُ بَيْنَهُمْ يَوْمَ ٱلْقِيَـٰمَةِ ۚ إِنَّ ٱللَّهَ عَلَىٰ كُلِّ شَىْءٍ شَهِيدٌ

O you who believe! You are responsible for your own souls. He who has strayed cannot harm you if you are guided. To Allah is you return, all of you, and He will inform you of what you used to do. – Surah Al-Maidah 5:105
يَـٰٓأَيُّهَا ٱلَّذِينَ ءَامَنُوا۟ عَلَيْكُمْ أَنفُسَكُمْ ۖ لَا يَضُرُّكُم مَّن ضَلَّ إِذَا ٱهْتَدَيْتُمْ ۚ إِلَى ٱللَّهِ مَرْجِعُكُمْ جَمِيعًا فَيُنَبِّئُكُم بِمَا كُنتُمْ تَعْمَلُونَ

O you who believe! Fear Allah,and let every soul consider what it has forwarded for the morrow, and fear Allah. Allah is Aware of what you do – Al-Hashr 59:18
يَـٰٓأَيُّهَا ٱلَّذِينَ ءَامَنُوا۟ ٱتَّقُوا۟ ٱللَّهَ وَلْتَنظُرْ نَفْسٌ مَّا قَدَّمَتْ لِغَدٍ ۖ وَٱتَّقُوا۟ ٱللَّهَ ۚ إِنَّ ٱللَّهَ خَبِيرٌۢ بِمَا تَعْمَلُونَ

Do not insult what they invoke besides Allah or they will insult Allah spitefully out of ignorance. This is how We have made each people's deeds appealing to them. Then to their Lord is their return, and He will inform them of what they used to do. – Surah Al-An'am 6:108
وَلَا تَسُبُّوا۟ ٱلَّذِينَ يَدْعُونَ مِن دُونِ ٱللَّهِ فَيَسُبُّوا۟ ٱللَّهَ عَدْوًۢا بِغَيْرِ عِلْمٍ ۗ كَذَٰلِكَ زَيَّنَّا لِكُلِّ أُمَّةٍ عَمَلَهُمْ ثُمَّ إِلَىٰ رَبِّهِم مَّرْجِعُهُمْ فَيُنَبِّئُهُم بِمَا كَانُوا۟ يَعْمَلُونَ

If some of you do believe in what I have been sent with while others do not, then be patient until Allah judges between us. He is the Best of Judges." – Surah Al-A'raf 7:87
وَإِن كَانَ طَآئِفَةٌ مِّنكُمْ ءَامَنُوا۟ بِٱلَّذِىٓ أُرْسِلْتُ بِهِۦ وَطَآئِفَةٌ لَّمْ يُؤْمِنُوا۟ فَٱصْبِرُوا۟ حَتَّىٰ يَحْكُمَ ٱللَّهُ بَيْنَنَا ۚ وَهُوَ خَيْرُ ٱلْحَـٰكِمِينَ

We would surely be fabricating a lie against Allah if we were to return to your faith after Allah has saved us from it. It does not befit us to return to it unless it is the Will of Allah, our Lord. Our Lord has encompassed everything in ⌜His⌝ knowledge. In Allah we trust. Our Lord! Judge between us and our people with truth. You are the best of those who judge." – Surah Al-A'raf 7:89
قَدِ ٱفْتَرَيْنَا عَلَى ٱللَّهِ كَذِبًا إِنْ عُدْنَا فِى مِلَّتِكُم بَعْدَ إِذْ نَجَّىٰنَا ٱللَّهُ مِنْهَا ۚ وَمَا يَكُونُ لَنَآ أَن نَّعُودَ فِيهَآ إِلَّآ أَن يَشَآءَ ٱللَّهُ رَبُّنَا ۚ وَسِعَ رَبُّنَا كُلَّ شَىْءٍ عِلْمًا ۚ عَلَى ٱللَّهِ تَوَكَّلْنَا ۚ رَبَّنَا ٱفْتَحْ بَيْنَنَا وَبَيْنَ قَوْمِنَا بِٱلْحَقِّ وَأَنتَ خَيْرُ ٱلْفَـٰتِحِينَ

You ⌜O Prophet⌝ have no say in the matter. It is up to Allah to turn to them in mercy or punish them, for indeed they are wrongdoers. – Surah Al-Imran 3:128
لَيْسَ لَكَ مِنَ ٱلْأَمْرِ شَىْءٌ أَوْ يَتُوبَ عَلَيْهِمْ أَوْ يُعَذِّبَهُمْ فَإِنَّهُمْ ظَـٰلِمُونَ

"My Master is Allah, He Who sent down the Book, and He takes care of the righteous." Those you call upon besides Him cannot help you, nor can they help themselves. And if you call them to guidance, they will not hear. And you see them looking at you, yet they do not see. Be tolerant, and command decency, and avoid the ignorant. Those who are righteous—when an impulse from Satan strikes them, they remind themselves, and immediately see clearly. And when a suggestion from Satan assails you, take refuge with Allah. He is Hearing and Knowing. But their brethren lead them relentlessly into error, and they never stop short. If you do not produce a miracle for them, they say, “Why don’t you improvise one.” Say, “I only follow what is inspired to me from my Lord.” These are insights from your Lord, and guidance, and mercy, for a people who believe. – Surah Al-A’raf 7:196-203

إِنَّ وَلِـِّۧيَ ٱللَّهُ ٱلَّذِى نَزَّلَ ٱلْكِتَـٰبَ ۖ وَهُوَ يَتَوَلَّى ٱلصَّـٰلِحِينَ وَٱلَّذِينَ تَدْعُونَ مِن دُونِهِۦ لَا يَسْتَطِيعُونَ نَصْرَكُمْ وَلَآ أَنفُسَهُمْ يَنصُرُونَ وَإِن تَدْعُوهُمْ إِلَى ٱلْهُدَىٰ لَا يَسْمَعُوا۟ ۖ وَتَرَىٰهُمْ يَنظُرُونَ إِلَيْكَ وَهُمْ لَا يُبْصِرُونَ خُذِ ٱلْعَفْوَ وَأْمُرْ بِٱلْعُرْفِ وَأَعْرِضْ عَنِ ٱلْجَـٰهِلِينَ وَإِمَّا يَنزَغَنَّكَ مِنَ ٱلشَّيْطَـٰنِ نَزْغٌ فَٱسْتَعِذْ بِٱللَّهِ ۚ إِنَّهُۥ سَمِيعٌ عَلِيمٌ إِنَّ ٱلَّذِينَ ٱتَّقَوْا۟ إِذَا مَسَّهُمْ طَـٰٓئِفٌ مِّنَ ٱلشَّيْطَـٰنِ تَذَكَّرُوا۟ فَإِذَا هُم مُّبْصِرُونَ وَإِخْوَٰنُهُمْ يَمُدُّونَهُمْ فِى ٱلْغَىِّ ثُمَّ لَا يُقْصِرُونَ وَإِذَا لَمْ تَأْتِهِم بِـَٔايَةٍ قَالُوا۟ لَوْلَا ٱجْتَبَيْتَهَا ۚ قُلْ إِنَّمَآ أَتَّبِعُ مَا يُوحَىٰٓ إِلَىَّ مِن رَّبِّى ۚ هَـٰذَا بَصَآئِرُ مِن رَّبِّكُمْ وَهُدًى وَرَحْمَةٌ لِّقَوْمٍ يُؤْمِنُونَ

Whether We show you some of what We have promised them, or We cause you to die—your duty is to inform, and Ours is the reckoning. Do they not see how We deal with the earth, diminishing it at its edges? Allah judges; and nothing can hold back His judgment. And He is quick to settle accounts. – Surah Ar-Ra’d 13:40&41

وَإِن مَّا نُرِيَنَّكَ بَعْضَ ٱلَّذِى نَعِدُهُمْ أَوْ نَتَوَفَّيَنَّكَ فَإِنَّمَا عَلَيْكَ ٱلْبَلَـٰغُ وَعَلَيْنَا ٱلْحِسَابُ أَوَلَمْ يَرَوْا۟ أَنَّا نَأْتِى ٱلْأَرْضَ نَنقُصُهَا مِنْ أَطْرَافِهَا ۚ وَٱللَّهُ يَحْكُمُ لَا مُعَقِّبَ لِحُكْمِهِۦ ۚ وَهُوَ سَرِيعُ ٱلْحِسَابِ

“Peace be upon you, because you endured patiently. How excellent is the Final Home.” – Surah Ar’Rad 13:24

سَلَـٰمٌ عَلَيْكُم بِمَا صَبَرْتُمْ ۚ فَنِعْمَ عُقْبَى ٱلدَّارِ

The command of Allah has come, so do not rush it. Glory be to Him; exalted above what they associate. – Surah Al-Nahl 16:1

أَتَىٰٓ أَمْرُ ٱللَّهِ فَلَا تَسْتَعْجِلُوهُ ۚ سُبْحَـٰنَهُۥ وَتَعَـٰلَىٰ عَمَّا يُشْرِكُونَ

With the truth We sent it down, and with the truth it descended. We sent you only as a bearer of good news and a warner. – Surah Al-Isra 17:105

وَبِٱلْحَقِّ أَنزَلْنَـٰهُ وَبِٱلْحَقِّ نَزَلَ ۗ وَمَآ أَرْسَلْنَـٰكَ إِلَّا مُبَشِّرًا وَنَذِيرًا

So do not hurry against them. We are counting for them a countdown. – Surah Al-Maryam 19:84

فَلَا تَعْجَلْ عَلَيْهِمْ ۖ إِنَّمَا نَعُدُّ لَهُمْ عَدًّا

And do not corrupt on earth after its reformation, and pray to Him with fear and hope. Allah’s mercy is close to the doers of good. – Surah Al-A’raf 7:56

وَلَا تُفْسِدُوا۟ فِى ٱلْأَرْضِ بَعْدَ إِصْلَـٰحِهَا وَٱدْعُوهُ خَوْفًا وَطَمَعًا ۚ إِنَّ رَحْمَتَ ٱللَّهِ قَرِيبٌ مِّنَ ٱلْمُحْسِنِينَ

Narrated `Abdullah and Abu Musa: The Prophetﷺ said, “Near the establishment of the Hour there will be days during which Religious ignorance will spread, knowledge will be taken away (vanish) and there will be much Al-Harj, and Al- Harj means killing – ".Al-Bukhari 7062, 7063

حَدَّثَنَا عُبَيْدُ اللَّهِ بْنُ مُوسَى، عَنِ الأَعْمَشِ، عَنْ شَقِيقٍ، قَالَ كُنْتُ مَعَ عَبْدِ اللَّهِ وَأَبِي مُوسَى فَقَالاَ قَالَ النَّبِيُّ صلى الله عليه وسلم " إِنَّ بَيْنَ يَدَىِ السَّاعَةِ لأَيَّامًا يَنْزِلُ فِيهَا الْجَهْلُ، وَيُرْفَعُ فِيهَا الْعِلْمُ، وَيَكْثُرُ فِيهَا الْهَرْجُ، وَالْهَرْجُ الْقَتْلُ ".

When we have died and become dust and bones, shall we be resurrected? And our ancestors of old?" Say, "Yes indeed, and you will be totally subdued." It will be a single nudge, and they will be staring. They will say, "Woe to us. This is the Day of Judgment." "This is the Day of Separation which you used to deny. – Surah As-Saffat 37:16-21

أَءِذَا مِتْنَا وَكُنَّا تُرَابًا وَعِظَـٰمًا أَءِنَّا لَمَبْعُوثُونَ أَوَ ءَابَآؤُنَا ٱلْأَوَّلُونَ قُلْ نَعَمْ وَأَنتُمْ دَٰخِرُونَ فَإِنَّمَا هِىَ زَجْرَةٌ وَٰحِدَةٌ فَإِذَا هُمْ يَنظُرُونَ وَقَالُوا۟ يَـٰوَيْلَنَا هَـٰذَا يَوْمُ ٱلدِّينِ هَـٰذَا يَوْمُ ٱلْفَصْلِ ٱلَّذِى كُنتُم بِهِۦ تُكَذِّبُونَ

They said, "Shall we believe in you, when it is the lowliest who follow you?" He said, "What do I know about what they do? Their account rests only with my Lord, if you have sense. And I am not about to drive away the believers. I am only a clear warner." – Surah Ash-Shu'ara 26:111-115

قَالُوٓا۟ أَنُؤْمِنُ لَكَ وَٱتَّبَعَكَ ٱلْأَرْذَلُونَ قَالَ وَمَا عِلْمِى بِمَا كَانُوا۟ يَعْمَلُونَ إِنْ حِسَابُهُمْ إِلَّا عَلَىٰ رَبِّى ۖ لَوْ تَشْعُرُونَ وَمَآ أَنَا۠ بِطَارِدِ ٱلْمُؤْمِنِينَ إِنْ أَنَا۠ إِلَّا نَذِيرٌ مُّبِينٌ

Pardon them, and say, "Peace." They will come to know. Surah Az-Zukhruf 43:89

فَٱصْفَحْ عَنْهُمْ وَقُلْ سَلَـٰمٌ ۚ فَسَوْفَ يَعْلَمُونَ

Abundance distracts you. Until you visit the graveyards. Indeed, you will know. Certainly, you will know. If you knew with knowledge of certainty. You would see the Inferno. Then you will see it with the eye of certainty. Then, on that Day, you will be questioned about the Bliss. – Surah At-Takathur

أَلْهَىٰكُمُ ٱلتَّكَاثُرُ حَتَّىٰ زُرْتُمُ ٱلْمَقَابِرَ كَلَّا سَوْفَ تَعْلَمُونَ ثُمَّ كَلَّا سَوْفَ تَعْلَمُونَ كَلَّا لَوْ تَعْلَمُونَ عِلْمَ ٱلْيَقِينِ لَتَرَوُنَّ ٱلْجَحِيمَ ثُمَّ لَتَرَوُنَّهَا عَيْنَ ٱلْيَقِينِ ثُمَّ لَتُسْـَٔلُنَّ يَوْمَئِذٍ عَنِ ٱلنَّعِيمِ

So be patient, as the messengers with resolve were patient, and do not be hasty regarding them. On the Day when they witness what they are promised, it will seem as if they had lasted only for an hour of a day. A proclamation: Will any be destroyed except the sinful people? – Surah Al-Ahqaf 46:35

فَٱصْبِرْ كَمَا صَبَرَ أُو۟لُوا۟ ٱلْعَزْمِ مِنَ ٱلرُّسُلِ وَلَا تَسْتَعْجِل لَّهُمْ ۚ كَأَنَّهُمْ يَوْمَ يَرَوْنَ مَا يُوعَدُونَ لَمْ يَلْبَثُوٓا۟ إِلَّا سَاعَةً مِّن نَّهَارٍ ۚ بَلَـٰغٌ ۚ فَهَلْ يُهْلَكُ إِلَّا ٱلْقَوْمُ ٱلْفَـٰسِقُونَ

Those who believe, and those who are Jewish, and the Sabeans, and the Christians, and the Zoroastrians, and the Polytheists—Allah will judge between them on the Day of Resurrection. Allah is witness to all things. Do you not realize that to Allah prostrates everyone in the heavens and everyone on earth, and the sun, and the moon, and the stars, and the mountains, and the trees, and the animals, and many of the people? But many are justly deserving of punishment. Whomever Allah shames, there is none to honor him. Allah does whatever He wills. – Surah Al-Hajj 22:17&18

إِنَّ ٱلَّذِينَ ءَامَنُوا۟ وَٱلَّذِينَ هَادُوا۟ وَٱلصَّـٰبِـِٔينَ وَٱلنَّصَـٰرَىٰ وَٱلْمَجُوسَ وَٱلَّذِينَ أَشْرَكُوٓا۟ إِنَّ ٱللَّهَ يَفْصِلُ بَيْنَهُمْ يَوْمَ ٱلْقِيَـٰمَةِ ۚ إِنَّ ٱللَّهَ عَلَىٰ كُلِّ شَىْءٍ شَهِيدٌ أَلَمْ تَرَ أَنَّ ٱللَّهَ يَسْجُدُ لَهُۥ مَن فِى ٱلسَّمَـٰوَٰتِ وَمَن فِى ٱلْأَرْضِ وَٱلشَّمْسُ وَٱلْقَمَرُ وَٱلنُّجُومُ وَٱلْجِبَالُ وَٱلشَّجَرُ وَٱلدَّوَآبُّ وَكَثِيرٌ مِّنَ ٱلنَّاسِ ۖ وَكَثِيرٌ حَقَّ عَلَيْهِ ٱلْعَذَابُ ۗ وَمَن يُهِنِ ٱللَّهُ فَمَا لَهُۥ مِن مُّكْرِمٍ ۚ إِنَّ ٱللَّهَ يَفْعَلُ مَا يَشَآءُ

As for those who take masters other than Him: Allah is in charge of them, and you are not responsible for them. – Surah Ash-Shura 42:6

وَٱلَّذِينَ ٱتَّخَذُوا۟ مِن دُونِهِۦٓ أَوْلِيَآءَ ٱللَّهُ حَفِيظٌ عَلَيْهِمْ وَمَآ أَنتَ عَلَيْهِم بِوَكِيلٍ

So be patient, with sweet patience. They see it distant. But We see it near. On the Day when the sky will be like molten brass. And the mountains will be like tufted wool. No friend will care about his friend. They will be shown each other. The criminal wishes he would be redeemed from the punishment of that Day by his children. And his spouse, and his brother. And his family that sheltered him. And everyone on earth, in order to save him. - Surah Al-Ma'arij 70:5-14

فَٱصْبِرْ صَبْرًا جَمِيلًا إِنَّهُمْ يَرَوْنَهُۥ بَعِيدًا وَنَرَىٰهُ قَرِيبًا يَوْمَ تَكُونُ ٱلسَّمَآءُ كَٱلْمُهْلِ وَتَكُونُ ٱلْجِبَالُ كَٱلْعِهْنِ وَلَا يَسْـَٔلُ حَمِيمٌ حَمِيمًا يُبَصَّرُونَهُمْ يَوَدُّ ٱلْمُجْرِمُ لَوْ يَفْتَدِى مِنْ عَذَابِ يَوْمِئِذٍۭ بِبَنِيهِ وَصَٰحِبَتِهِۦ وَأَخِيهِ وَفَصِيلَتِهِ ٱلَّتِى تُـْٔوِيهِ وَمَن فِى ٱلْأَرْضِ جَمِيعًا ثُمَّ يُنجِيهِ

And follow what is revealed to you, and be patient until Allah issues His judgment, for He is the Best of judges. – Surah Yunus 10:109

وَٱتَّبِعْ مَا يُوحَىٰٓ إِلَيْكَ وَٱصْبِرْ حَتَّىٰ يَحْكُمَ ٱللَّهُ وَهُوَ خَيْرُ ٱلْحَٰكِمِينَ

Narrated Abu Sa`id: Some people from the Ansar asked Allah's Messenger ﷺ (to give them something) and he gave to everyone of them, who asked him, until all that he had was finished. When everything was finished and he had spent all that was in his hand, he said to them, '"(Know) that if I have any wealth, I will not withhold it from you (to keep for somebody else); And (know) that he who refrains from begging others (or doing prohibited deeds), Allah will make him contented and not in need of others; and he who remains patient, Allah will bestow patience upon him, and he who is satisfied with what he has, Allah will make him self-sufficient. And there is no gift better and vast (you may be given) than patience.". – Sahih Al-Bukhari 6470

حَدَّثَنَا أَبُو الْيَمَانِ، أَخْبَرَنَا شُعَيْبٌ، عَنِ الزُّهْرِيِّ، قَالَ أَخْبَرَنِي عَطَاءُ بْنُ يَزِيدَ، أَنَّ أَبَا سَعِيدٍ، أَخْبَرَهُ أَنَّ أُنَاسًا مِنَ الأَنْصَارِ سَأَلُوا رَسُولَ اللَّهِ صلى الله عليه وسلم فَلَمْ يَسْأَلْهُ أَحَدٌ مِنْهُمْ إِلاَّ أَعْطَاهُ حَتَّى نَفِدَ مَا عِنْدَهُ فَقَالَ لَهُمْ حِينَ نَفِدَ كُلُّ شَىْءٍ أَنْفَقَ بِيَدَيْهِ " مَا يَكُنْ عِنْدِي مِنْ خَيْرٍ لاَ أَدَّخِرْهُ عَنْكُمْ، وَإِنَّهُ مَنْ يَسْتَعِفَّ يُعِفُّهُ اللَّهُ، وَمَنْ يَتَصَبَّرْ يُصَبِّرْهُ اللَّهُ، وَمَنْ يَسْتَغْنِ يُغْنِهِ اللَّهُ، وَلَنْ تُعْطَوْا عَطَاءً خَيْرًا وَأَوْسَعَ مِنَ الصَّبْرِ "

The Book of
This, your Ummah is one religion
إِنَّ هَٰذِهِۦٓ أُمَّتُكُمْ أُمَّةً وَٰحِدَةً

Turning towards Him—and be conscious of Him, and perform the prayer, and do not be of the idolaters. Of those who divided their religion, and became sects; each faction pleased with what they have. – Surah Ar-Rum 30:31&32

مُنِيبِينَ إِلَيْهِ وَٱتَّقُوهُ وَأَقِيمُوا۟ ٱلصَّلَوٰةَ وَلَا تَكُونُوا۟ مِنَ ٱلْمُشْرِكِينَ مِنَ ٱلَّذِينَ فَرَّقُوا۟ دِينَهُمْ وَكَانُوا۟ شِيَعًا ۖ كُلُّ حِزْبٍۭ بِمَا لَدَيْهِمْ فَرِحُونَ

He prescribed for you the same religion He enjoined upon Noah, and what We inspired to you, and what We enjoined upon Abraham, and Moses, and Jesus: "You shall uphold the religion, and be not divided therein." As for the idolaters, what you call them to is outrageous to them. Allah chooses to Himself whom He wills, and He guides to Himself whoever repents. – Surah Ash-Shura 42:13

شَرَعَ لَكُم مِّنَ ٱلدِّينِ مَا وَصَّىٰ بِهِۦ نُوحًا وَٱلَّذِىٓ أَوْحَيْنَآ إِلَيْكَ وَمَا وَصَّيْنَا بِهِۦٓ إِبْرَٰهِيمَ وَمُوسَىٰ وَعِيسَىٰٓ ۖ أَنْ أَقِيمُوا۟ ٱلدِّينَ وَلَا تَتَفَرَّقُوا۟ فِيهِ ۚ كَبُرَ عَلَى ٱلْمُشْرِكِينَ مَا تَدْعُوهُمْ إِلَيْهِ ۚ ٱللَّهُ يَجْتَبِىٓ إِلَيْهِ مَن يَشَآءُ وَيَهْدِىٓ إِلَيْهِ مَن يُنِيبُ

Then We sent in their wake Our messengers, and followed up with Jesus son of Mary, and We gave him the Gospel, and instilled in the hearts of those who followed him compassion and mercy. But as for the monasticism which they invented—We did not ordain it for them—only to seek Allah's approval. But they did not observe it with its due observance. So We gave those of them who believed their reward, but many of them are sinful. O you who believe! Fear Allah, and believe in His Messenger: He will give you a double portion of His mercy, and will give you a light by which you walk, and will forgive you. Allah is Forgiving and Merciful. That the People of the Book may know that they have no power whatsoever over Allah's grace, and that all grace is in Allah's hand; He gives it to whomever He wills. Allah is Possessor of Great Grace. – Surah Al-Hadid 57:27-29

ثُمَّ قَفَّيْنَا عَلَىٰٓ ءَاثَٰرِهِم بِرُسُلِنَا وَقَفَّيْنَا بِعِيسَى ٱبْنِ مَرْيَمَ وَءَاتَيْنَٰهُ ٱلْإِنجِيلَ ۖ وَجَعَلْنَا فِى قُلُوبِ ٱلَّذِينَ ٱتَّبَعُوهُ رَأْفَةً وَرَحْمَةً وَرَهْبَانِيَّةً ٱبْتَدَعُوهَا مَا كَتَبْنَٰهَا عَلَيْهِمْ إِلَّا ٱبْتِغَآءَ رِضْوَٰنِ ٱللَّهِ فَمَا رَعَوْهَا حَقَّ رِعَايَتِهَا ۖ فَـَٔاتَيْنَا ٱلَّذِينَ ءَامَنُوا۟ مِنْهُمْ أَجْرَهُمْ ۖ وَكَثِيرٌ مِّنْهُمْ فَٰسِقُونَ يَٰٓأَيُّهَا ٱلَّذِينَ ءَامَنُوا۟ ٱتَّقُوا۟ ٱللَّهَ وَءَامِنُوا۟ بِرَسُولِهِۦ يُؤْتِكُمْ كِفْلَيْنِ مِن رَّحْمَتِهِۦ وَيَجْعَل لَّكُمْ نُورًا تَمْشُونَ بِهِۦ وَيَغْفِرْ لَكُمْ ۚ وَٱللَّهُ غَفُورٌ رَّحِيمٌ لِّئَلَّا يَعْلَمَ أَهْلُ ٱلْكِتَٰبِ أَلَّا يَقْدِرُونَ عَلَىٰ شَىْءٍ مِّن فَضْلِ ٱللَّهِ ۙ وَأَنَّ ٱلْفَضْلَ بِيَدِ ٱللَّهِ يُؤْتِيهِ مَن يَشَآءُ ۚ وَٱللَّهُ ذُو ٱلْفَضْلِ ٱلْعَظِيمِ

Then, out of every sect, We will snatch those most defiant to the Most Merciful. – Surah Maryam 19:69

ثُمَّ لَنَنزِعَنَّ مِن كُلِّ شِيعَةٍ أَيُّهُمْ أَشَدُّ عَلَى ٱلرَّحْمَٰنِ عِتِيًّا

This community of yours is one community, and I am your Lord, so worship Me. But they splintered themselves into factions. They will all return to Us. Whoever does righteous deeds, and is a believer, his effort will not be denied. We are writing it down for him. – Surah Al-Anbiya 21:92-94

إِنَّ هَٰذِهِۦٓ أُمَّتُكُمْ أُمَّةً وَٰحِدَةً وَأَنَا۠ رَبُّكُمْ فَٱعْبُدُونِ وَتَقَطَّعُوٓا۟ أَمْرَهُم بَيْنَهُمْ ۖ كُلٌّ إِلَيْنَا رَٰجِعُونَ فَمَن يَعْمَلْ مِنَ ٱلصَّٰلِحَٰتِ وَهُوَ مُؤْمِنٌ فَلَا كُفْرَانَ لِسَعْيِهِۦ وَإِنَّا لَهُۥ كَٰتِبُونَ

Pharaoh exalted himself in the land, and divided its people into factions. He persecuted a group of them, slaughtering their sons, while sparing their daughters. He was truly a corrupter. – Surah Al-Qasas 28:4
إِنَّ فِرْعَوْنَ عَلَا فِى ٱلْأَرْضِ وَجَعَلَ أَهْلَهَا شِيَعًا يَسْتَضْعِفُ طَآئِفَةً مِّنْهُمْ يُذَبِّحُ أَبْنَآءَهُمْ وَيَسْتَحْىِۦ نِسَآءَهُمْ ۚ إِنَّهُۥ كَانَ مِنَ ٱلْمُفْسِدِينَ

Humanity used to be one community; then Allah sent the prophets, bringing good news and giving warnings. And He sent down with them the Scripture, with the truth, to judge between people regarding their differences. But none differed over it except those who were given it—after the proofs had come to them—out of mutual envy between them. Then Allah guided those who believed to the truth they had disputed, in accordance with His will. Allah guides whom He wills to a straight path. – Surah Al-Baqarah 2:213
كَانَ ٱلنَّاسُ أُمَّةً وَٰحِدَةً فَبَعَثَ ٱللَّهُ ٱلنَّبِيِّـۧنَ مُبَشِّرِينَ وَمُنذِرِينَ وَأَنزَلَ مَعَهُمُ ٱلْكِتَٰبَ بِٱلْحَقِّ لِيَحْكُمَ بَيْنَ ٱلنَّاسِ فِيمَا ٱخْتَلَفُوا۟ فِيهِ ۚ وَمَا ٱخْتَلَفَ فِيهِ إِلَّا ٱلَّذِينَ أُوتُوهُ مِنۢ بَعْدِ مَا جَآءَتْهُمُ ٱلْبَيِّنَٰتُ بَغْيًۢا بَيْنَهُمْ ۖ فَهَدَى ٱللَّهُ ٱلَّذِينَ ءَامَنُوا۟ لِمَا ٱخْتَلَفُوا۟ فِيهِ مِنَ ٱلْحَقِّ بِإِذْنِهِۦ ۗ وَٱللَّهُ يَهْدِى مَن يَشَآءُ إِلَىٰ صِرَٰطٍ مُّسْتَقِيمٍ

And hold fast to the rope of Allah, altogether, and do not become divided. And remember Allah's blessings upon you; how you were enemies, and He reconciled your hearts, and by His grace you became brethren. And you were on the brink of a pit of fire, and He saved you from it. Allah thus clarifies His revelations for you, so that you may be guided. – Surah Al-Imran 3:103
وَٱعْتَصِمُوا۟ بِحَبْلِ ٱللَّهِ جَمِيعًا وَلَا تَفَرَّقُوا۟ ۚ وَٱذْكُرُوا۟ نِعْمَتَ ٱللَّهِ عَلَيْكُمْ إِذْ كُنتُمْ أَعْدَآءً فَأَلَّفَ بَيْنَ قُلُوبِكُمْ فَأَصْبَحْتُم بِنِعْمَتِهِۦٓ إِخْوَٰنًا وَكُنتُمْ عَلَىٰ شَفَا حُفْرَةٍ مِّنَ ٱلنَّارِ فَأَنقَذَكُم مِّنْهَا ۗ كَذَٰلِكَ يُبَيِّنُ ٱللَّهُ لَكُمْ ءَايَٰتِهِۦ لَعَلَّكُمْ تَهْتَدُونَ

Allah will not leave the believers as you are, without distinguishing the wicked from the sincere. Nor will Allah inform you of the future, but Allah elects from among His messengers whom He wills. So believe in Allah and His messengers. If you believe and practice piety, you will have a splendid reward. – Surah Al-Imran 3:179
مَّا كَانَ ٱللَّهُ لِيَذَرَ ٱلْمُؤْمِنِينَ عَلَىٰ مَآ أَنتُمْ عَلَيْهِ حَتَّىٰ يَمِيزَ ٱلْخَبِيثَ مِنَ ٱلطَّيِّبِ ۗ وَمَا كَانَ ٱللَّهُ لِيُطْلِعَكُمْ عَلَى ٱلْغَيْبِ وَلَٰكِنَّ ٱللَّهَ يَجْتَبِى مِن رُّسُلِهِۦ مَن يَشَآءُ ۖ فَـَٔامِنُوا۟ بِٱللَّهِ وَرُسُلِهِۦ ۚ وَإِن تُؤْمِنُوا۟ وَتَتَّقُوا۟ فَلَكُمْ أَجْرٌ عَظِيمٌ

But the various factions differed among themselves. So woe to those who disbelieve from the scene of a tremendous Day. – Surah Al-Maryam 19:37
فَٱخْتَلَفَ ٱلْأَحْزَابُ مِنۢ بَيْنِهِمْ ۖ فَوَيْلٌ لِّلَّذِينَ كَفَرُوا۟ مِن مَّشْهَدِ يَوْمٍ عَظِيمٍ

This nation of yours is one nation, and I am your Lord, so fear Me. But they tore themselves into sects; each party happy with what they have. – Surah Al-Mu'minun 23:52&53
فَتَقَطَّعُوٓا۟ أَمْرَهُم بَيْنَهُمْ زُبُرًا ۖ كُلُّ حِزْبٍۭ بِمَا لَدَيْهِمْ فَرِحُونَ فَذَرْهُمْ فِى غَمْرَتِهِمْ حَتَّىٰ حِينٍ

Narrated Ibn `Abbas: The Prophet ﷺ said, "One should not say that I am better than Jonah (i.e. Yunus) bin Matta." So, he mentioned his father Matta. The Prophet ﷺ mentioned the night of his Ascension and said, "The prophet Moses was brown, a tall person as if from the people of the tribe of Shanu'a. Jesus was a curly-haired man of moderate height." He also mentioned Malik, the gate-keeper of the (Hell) Fire, and Ad-Dajjal. – Sahih al-Bukhari 3395, 3396
حَدَّثَنِي مُحَمَّدُ بْنُ بَشَّارٍ، حَدَّثَنَا غُنْدَرٌ، حَدَّثَنَا شُعْبَةُ، عَنْ قَتَادَةَ، قَالَ سَمِعْتُ أَبَا الْعَالِيَةِ، حَدَّثَنَا ابْنُ عَمِّ، نَبِيِّكُمْ ـ يَعْنِي ابْنَ عَبَّاسٍ ـ عَنِ النَّبِيِّ صلى الله عليه وسلم قَالَ " لاَ يَنْبَغِي لِعَبْدٍ أَنْ يَقُولَ أَنَا خَيْرٌ مِنْ يُونُسَ بْنِ مَتَّى ". وَنَسَبَهُ إِلَى أَبِيهِ. وَذَكَرَ

النَّبِيُّ صلى الله عليه وسلم لَيْلَةَ أُسْرِيَ بِهِ فَقَالَ " مُوسَى آدَمُ طُوَالٌ كَأَنَّهُ مِنْ رِجَالِ شَنُوءَةَ ". وَقَالَ " عِيسَى جَعْدٌ مَرْبُوعٌ ". وَذَكَرَ مَالِكًا خَازِنَ النَّارِ، وَذَكَرَ الدَّجَّالَ.

Narrated Abu Huraira: Allah's Messenger ﷺ was asked, "Who are the most honorable of the people?" The Prophet ﷺ said, "The most honorable of them in Allah's Sight are those who keep their duty to Allah and fear Him. They said, "We do not ask you about that." He said, "Then the most honorable of the people is Joseph, Allah's prophet, the son of Allah's prophet, the son of Allah's prophet, the son of Allah's Khalil i.e. Abraham) They said, "We do not ask you about that." The Prophet ﷺ said, Do you ask about (the virtues of the ancestry of the Arabs?" They said, "Yes," He said, "Those who were the best amongst you in the PreIslamic Period are the best amongst you in Islam if they comprehend (the Islamic religion).. – Sahih al-Bukhari 4689

حَدَّثَنِي مُحَمَّدٌ، أَخْبَرَنَا عَبْدَةُ، عَنْ عُبَيْدِ اللَّهِ، عَنْ سَعِيدِ بْنِ أَبِي سَعِيدٍ، عَنْ أَبِي هُرَيْرَةَ ـ رضى الله عنه ـ قَالَ سُئِلَ رَسُولُ اللَّهِ صلى الله عليه وسلم أَىُّ النَّاسِ أَكْرَمُ قَالَ " أَكْرَمُهُمْ عِنْدَ اللَّهِ أَتْقَاهُمْ ". قَالُوا لَيْسَ عَنْ هَذَا نَسْأَلُكَ. قَالَ " فَأَكْرَمُ النَّاسِ يُوسُفُ نَبِيُّ اللَّهِ ابْنُ نَبِيِّ اللَّهِ ابْنِ نَبِيِّ اللَّهِ ابْنِ خَلِيلِ اللَّهِ ". قَالُوا لَيْسَ عَنْ هَذَا نَسْأَلُكَ. قَالَ " فَعَنْ مَعَادِنِ الْعَرَبِ تَسْأَلُونِي ". قَالُوا نَعَمْ. قَالَ " فَخِيَارُكُمْ فِي الْجَاهِلِيَّةِ خِيَارُكُمْ فِي الإِسْلاَمِ إِذَا فَقِهُوا ". تَابَعَهُ أَبُو أُسَامَةَ عَنْ عُبَيْدِ اللَّهِ.

Narrated Abu Huraira: Two persons, a Muslim and a Jew, quarreled. The Muslim said, "By Him Who gave Muhammad superiority over all the people! The Jew said, "By Him Who gave Moses superiority over all the people!" At that the Muslim raised his hand and slapped the Jew on the face. The Jew went to the Prophet and informed him of what had happened between him and the Muslim. The Prophet ﷺ sent for the Muslim and asked him about it. The Muslim informed him of the event. The Prophet ﷺ said, "Do not give me superiority over Moses, for on the Day of Resurrection all the people will fall unconscious and I will be one of them, but I will. Be the first to gain consciousness, and will see Moses standing and holding the side of the Throne (of Allah). I will not know whether (Moses) has also fallen unconscious and got up before me, or Allah has exempted him from that stroke.". – Sahih al-Bukhari 2411

حَدَّثَنَا يَحْيَى بْنُ قَزَعَةَ، حَدَّثَنَا إِبْرَاهِيمُ بْنُ سَعْدٍ، عَنِ ابْنِ شِهَابٍ، عَنْ أَبِي سَلَمَةَ، وَعَبْدِ الرَّحْمَنِ الأَعْرَجِ، عَنْ أَبِي هُرَيْرَةَ ـ رضى الله عنه ـ قَالَ اسْتَبَّ رَجُلاَنِ رَجُلٌ مِنَ الْمُسْلِمِينَ وَرَجُلٌ مِنَ الْيَهُودِ، قَالَ الْمُسْلِمُ وَالَّذِي اصْطَفَى مُحَمَّدًا عَلَى الْعَالَمِينَ، فَقَالَ الْيَهُودِيُّ وَالَّذِي اصْطَفَى مُوسَى عَلَى الْعَالَمِينَ. فَرَفَعَ الْمُسْلِمُ يَدَهُ عِنْدَ ذَلِكَ فَلَطَمَ وَجْهَ الْيَهُودِيِّ، فَذَهَبَ الْيَهُودِيُّ إِلَى النَّبِيِّ صلى الله عليه وسلم فَأَخْبَرَهُ بِمَا كَانَ مِنْ أَمْرِهِ وَأَمْرِ الْمُسْلِمِ، فَدَعَا النَّبِيُّ صلى الله عليه وسلم الْمُسْلِمَ فَسَأَلَهُ عَنْ ذَلِكَ، فَأَخْبَرَهُ فَقَالَ النَّبِيُّ صلى الله عليه وسلم " لاَ تُخَيِّرُونِي عَلَى مُوسَى، فَإِنَّ النَّاسَ يَصْعَقُونَ يَوْمَ الْقِيَامَةِ، فَأَصْعَقُ مَعَهُمْ، فَأَكُونُ أَوَّلَ مَنْ يُفِيقُ، فَإِذَا مُوسَى بَاطِشٌ جَانِبَ الْعَرْشِ، فَلاَ أَدْرِي أَكَانَ فِيمَنْ صَعِقَ فَأَفَاقَ قَبْلِي، أَوْ كَانَ مِمَّنِ اسْتَثْنَى اللَّهُ ".

Narrated `Abdullah bin `Amr: Allah's Messenger ﷺ was informed that I had taken an oath to fast daily and to pray (every night) all the night throughout my life (so Allah's Messenger ﷺ came to me and asked whether it was correct): I replied, "Let my parents be sacrificed for you! I said so." The Prophet ﷺ said, "You can not do that. So, fast for few days and give it up for few days, offer Salat (prayer) and sleep. Fast three days a month as the reward of good deeds is multiplied ten times and that will be equal to one year of fasting." The Prophet ﷺ said to me, "Fast one day and give up fasting for two days." I replied, "I can do better than that." The Prophet ﷺ said to me, "Fast one day and give up fasting for a day and that is the fasting of Prophet David and that is the best fasting." I said, "I have the power to fast better (more) than that." The Prophet ﷺ said, "There is no better fasting than that.". – Sahih al-Bukhari 1976

حَدَّثَنَا أَبُو الْيَمَانِ، أَخْبَرَنَا شُعَيْبٌ، عَنِ الزُّهْرِيِّ، قَالَ أَخْبَرَنِي سَعِيدُ بْنُ الْمُسَيَّبِ، وَأَبُو سَلَمَةَ بْنُ عَبْدِ الرَّحْمَنِ أَنَّ عَبْدَ اللَّهِ بْنَ عَمْرٍو، قَالَ أُخْبِرَ رَسُولُ اللَّهِ صلى الله عليه وسلم أَنِّي أَقُولُ وَاللَّهِ لأَصُومَنَّ النَّهَارَ، وَلأَقُومَنَّ اللَّيْلَ، مَا عِشْتُ. فَقُلْتُ لَهُ قَدْ

قُلْتُهُ بِأَبِي أَنْتَ وَأُمِّي. قَالَ " فَإِنَّكَ لاَ تَسْتَطِيعُ ذَلِكَ، فَصُمْ وَأَفْطِرْ، وَقُمْ وَنَمْ، وَصُمْ مِنَ الشَّهْرِ ثَلاَثَةَ أَيَّامٍ، فَإِنَّ الْحَسَنَةَ بِعَشْرِ أَمْثَالِهَا، وَذَلِكَ مِثْلُ صِيَامِ الدَّهْرِ ". قُلْتُ إِنِّي أُطِيقُ أَفْضَلَ مِنْ ذَلِكَ. قَالَ " فَصُمْ يَوْمًا وَأَفْطِرْ يَوْمَيْنِ ". قُلْتُ إِنِّي أُطِيقُ أَفْضَلَ مِنْ ذَلِكَ. قَالَ " فَصُمْ يَوْمًا وَأَفْطِرْ يَوْمًا، فَذَلِكَ صِيَامُ دَاوُدَ ـ عَلَيْهِ السَّلاَمُ ـ وَهْوَ أَفْضَلُ الصِّيَامِ ". فَقُلْتُ إِنِّي أُطِيقُ أَفْضَلَ مِنْ ذَلِكَ. فَقَالَ النَّبِيُّ صلى الله عليه وسلم " لاَ أَفْضَلَ مِنْ ذَلِكَ ".

Narrated `Abdullah bin `Amr: The Prophet ﷺ said, "Convey (my teachings) to the people even if it were a single sentence, and tell others the stories of Bani Israel (which have been taught to you), for it is not sinful to do so. And whoever tells a lie on me intentionally, will surely take his place in the (Hell) Fire.". – Sahih al-Bukhari 3461

حَدَّثَنَا أَبُو عَاصِمٍ الضَّحَّاكُ بْنُ مَخْلَدٍ، أَخْبَرَنَا الأَوْزَاعِيُّ، حَدَّثَنَا حَسَّانُ بْنُ عَطِيَّةَ، عَنْ أَبِي كَبْشَةَ، عَنْ عَبْدِ اللَّهِ بْنِ عَمْرٍو، أَنَّ النَّبِيَّ صلى الله عليه وسلم قَالَ " بَلِّغُوا عَنِّي وَلَوْ آيَةً، وَحَدِّثُوا عَنْ بَنِي إِسْرَائِيلَ وَلاَ حَرَجَ، وَمَنْ كَذَبَ عَلَىَّ مُتَعَمِّدًا فَلْيَتَبَوَّأْ مَقْعَدَهُ مِنَ النَّارِ ".

Narrated Abu Huraira: I heard Allah's Messenger ﷺ saying, "I am the nearest of all the people to the son of Mary, and all the prophets are paternal brothers, and there has been no prophet between me and him (i.e. Jesus) – .Sahih al-Bukhari 3442

حَدَّثَنَا أَبُو الْيَمَانِ، أَخْبَرَنَا شُعَيْبٌ، عَنِ الزُّهْرِيِّ، قَالَ أَخْبَرَنِي أَبُو سَلَمَةَ، أَنَّ أَبَا هُرَيْرَةَ ـ رضى الله عنه ـ قَالَ سَمِعْتُ رَسُولَ اللَّهِ صلى الله عليه وسلم يَقُولُ " أَنَا أَوْلَى النَّاسِ بِابْنِ مَرْيَمَ، وَالأَنْبِيَاءُ أَوْلاَدُ عَلاَّتٍ، لَيْسَ بَيْنِي وَبَيْنَهُ نَبِيٌّ ".

The believers, both men, and women support each other....... Surah At-Taubah 9:71

وَٱلْمُؤْمِنُونَ وَٱلْمُؤْمِنَـٰتُ بَعْضُهُمْ أَوْلِيَآءُ بَعْضٍۢ

Narrated `Abdullah bin `Umar: Allah's Messenger ﷺ said, "A Muslim is a brother of another Muslim. So he should neither oppress him nor hand him over to an oppressor. And whoever fulfilled the needs of his brother, Allah will fulfill his needs.". - Sahih al-Bukhari 6951

حَدَّثَنَا يَحْيَى بْنُ بُكَيْرٍ، حَدَّثَنَا اللَّيْثُ، عَنْ عُقَيْلٍ، عَنِ ابْنِ شِهَابٍ، أَنَّ سَالِمًا، أَخْبَرَهُ أَنَّ عَبْدَ اللَّهِ بْنَ عُمَرَ ـ رضى الله عنهما ـ أَخْبَرَهُ أَنَّ رَسُولَ اللَّهِ صلى الله عليه وسلم قَالَ " الْمُسْلِمُ أَخُو الْمُسْلِمِ، لاَ يَظْلِمُهُ، وَلاَ يُسْلِمُهُ، وَمَنْ كَانَ فِي حَاجَةِ أَخِيهِ، كَانَ اللَّهُ فِي حَاجَتِهِ ".

Narrated Anas bin Malik: Allah's Messenger ﷺ said, "Do not hate one another, and do not be jealous of one another, and do not desert each other, and O, Allah's worshipers! Be brothers. Lo! It is not permissible for any Muslim to desert (not talk to) his brother (Muslim) for more than three days." - Sahih al-Bukhari 6065

حَدَّثَنَا أَبُو الْيَمَانِ، أَخْبَرَنَا شُعَيْبٌ، عَنِ الزُّهْرِيِّ، قَالَ حَدَّثَنِي أَنَسُ بْنُ مَالِكٍ ـ رضى الله عنه ـ أَنَّ رَسُولَ اللَّهِ صلى الله عليه وسلم قَالَ " لاَ تَبَاغَضُوا، وَلاَ تَحَاسَدُوا، وَلاَ تَدَابَرُوا، وَكُونُوا عِبَادَ اللَّهِ إِخْوَانًا، وَلاَ يَحِلُّ لِمُسْلِمٍ أَنْ يَهْجُرَ أَخَاهُ فَوْقَ ثَلاَثَةِ أَيَّامٍ "

Narrated Abu Musa: The Prophet ﷺ said, "A faithful believer to a faithful believer is like the bricks of a wall, enforcing each other." While (saying that) the Prophet ﷺ clasped his hands, by interlacing his fingers. – Sahih al-Bukhari 481

حَدَّثَنَا خَلاَّدُ بْنُ يَحْيَى، قَالَ حَدَّثَنَا سُفْيَانُ، عَنْ أَبِي بُرْدَةَ بْنِ عَبْدِ اللَّهِ بْنِ أَبِي بُرْدَةَ، عَنْ جَدِّهِ، عَنْ أَبِي مُوسَى، عَنِ النَّبِيِّ صلى الله عليه وسلم قَالَ " إِنَّ الْمُؤْمِنَ لِلْمُؤْمِنِ كَالْبُنْيَانِ، يَشُدُّ بَعْضُهُ بَعْضًا ". وَشَبَّكَ أَصَابِعَهُ.

Narrated Abu Aiyub Al-Ansari: Allah's Messenger ﷺ said, "It is not lawful for a man to desert his brother Muslim for more than three nights. (It is unlawful for them that) when they meet, one of them turns his face away from the other, and the other turns his face from the former, and the better of the two will be the one who greets the other first.". – Sahih al-Bukhari 6077

حَدَّثَنَا عَبْدُ اللَّهِ بْنُ يُوسُفَ، أَخْبَرَنَا مَالِكٌ، عَنِ ابْنِ شِهَابٍ، عَنْ عَطَاءِ بْنِ يَزِيدَ اللَّيْثِيِّ، عَنْ أَبِي أَيُّوبَ الأَنْصَارِيِّ، أَنَّ رَسُولَ اللَّهِ صلى الله عليه وسلم قَالَ " لاَ يَحِلُّ لِرَجُلٍ أَنْ يَهْجُرَ أَخَاهُ فَوْقَ ثَلاَثِ لَيَالٍ، يَلْتَقِيَانِ فَيُعْرِضُ هَذَا وَيُعْرِضُ هَذَا، وَخَيْرُهُمَا الَّذِي يَبْدَأُ بِالسَّلاَمِ "

Surely the believers are only brothers; so make a reconciliation between your two brothers, and be pious to Allah, that possibly you would be granted mercy – Surah Al-Hujurat 49:10

إِنَّمَا ٱلْمُؤْمِنُونَ إِخْوَةٌ فَأَصْلِحُوا۟ بَيْنَ أَخَوَيْكُمْ ۚ وَٱتَّقُوا۟ ٱللَّهَ لَعَلَّكُمْ تُرْحَمُونَ

Humaid b. 'Abd al-Rahman b. 'Auf reported that his mother Umm Kulthum daughter of 'Uqba b. Abu Mu'ait, and she was one amongst the first emigrants who pledged allegiance to Allah's Apostle ﷺ, as saying that she heard Allah's Messenger ﷺ as saying: A liar is not one who tries to bring reconciliation amongst people and speaks good (in order to avert dispute), or he conveys good. Ibn Shihab said he did not hear that exemption was granted in anything what the people speak as lie but in three cases: in battle, for bringing reconciliation amongst persons and the narration of the words of the husband to his wife, and the narration of the words of a wife to her husband (in a twisted form in order to bring reconciliation between them). – Sahih Muslim 2605 a

حَدَّثَنِي حَرْمَلَةُ بْنُ يَحْيَى، أَخْبَرَنَا ابْنُ وَهْبٍ، أَخْبَرَنِي يُونُسُ، عَنِ ابْنِ شِهَابٍ، أَخْبَرَنِي حُمَيْدُ بْنُ عَبْدِ الرَّحْمَنِ بْنِ عَوْفٍ، أَنَّ أُمَّهُ أُمَّ كُلْثُومٍ بِنْتَ عُقْبَةَ بْنِ أَبِي مُعَيْطٍ، وَكَانَتْ، مِنَ الْمُهَاجِرَاتِ الأُوَلِ اللاَّتِي بَايَعْنَ النَّبِيَّ صلى الله عليه وسلم أَخْبَرَتْهُ أَنَّهَا سَمِعَتْ رَسُولَ اللَّهِ صلى الله عليه وسلم وَهُوَ يَقُولُ " لَيْسَ الْكَذَّابُ الَّذِي يُصْلِحُ بَيْنَ النَّاسِ وَيَقُولُ خَيْرًا وَيَنْمِي خَيْرًا " . قَالَ ابْنُ شِهَابٍ وَلَمْ أَسْمَعْ يُرَخَّصُ فِي شَىْءٍ مِمَّا يَقُولُ النَّاسُ كَذِبٌ إِلاَّ فِي ثَلاَثٍ الْحَرْبُ وَالإِصْلاَحُ بَيْنَ النَّاسِ وَحَدِيثُ الرَّجُلِ امْرَأَتَهُ وَحَدِيثُ الْمَرْأَةِ زَوْجَهَا.

Cling firmly to what we bring you and listen

خُذُوا۟ مَآ ءَاتَيْنَـٰكُم بِقُوَّةٍ وَٱسْمَعُوا۟ ۖ

When We made a covenant with you and raised the mountain above you, [We said], "Hold fast to what We give you, and remember what is in it, so that you may be mindful of Allah. – Surah Al-Baqarah 2:63

وَإِذْ أَخَذْنَا مِيثَـٰقَكُمْ وَرَفَعْنَا فَوْقَكُمُ ٱلطُّورَ خُذُوا۟ مَآ ءَاتَيْنَـٰكُم بِقُوَّةٍ وَٱذْكُرُوا۟ مَا فِيهِ لَعَلَّكُمْ تَتَّقُونَ

And when We made a covenant with you and raised the mountain above you, saying, "Cling firmly to what we bring you and listen," they said, "We listened and disobeyed." Then, in their unbelief, their hearts were filled with the [worship of the] calf. Say, "It is dreadful what your faith commands you to do if you are in fact believers.". – Surah Al-Baqarah 2:93

وَإِذْ أَخَذْنَا مِيثَـٰقَكُمْ وَرَفَعْنَا فَوْقَكُمُ ٱلطُّورَ خُذُوا۟ مَآ ءَاتَيْنَـٰكُم بِقُوَّةٍ وَٱسْمَعُوا۟ ۖ قَالُوا۟ سَمِعْنَا وَعَصَيْنَا وَأُشْرِبُوا۟ فِى قُلُوبِهِمُ ٱلْعِجْلَ بِكُفْرِهِمْ ۚ قُلْ بِئْسَمَا يَأْمُرُكُم بِهِۦٓ إِيمَـٰنُكُمْ إِن كُنتُم مُّؤْمِنِينَ

We inscribed everything for him in the Tablets, which taught and clearly explained everything. [We said,] "Hold on to them with [all your] strength, and tell your people to hold fast to those most excellent teachings." I will show you the fate of the disobedient people. – Surah Al-A'raf 7:145

وَكَتَبْنَا لَهُۥ فِى ٱلْأَلْوَاحِ مِن كُلِّ شَىْءٍ مَّوْعِظَةً وَتَفْصِيلًا لِّكُلِّ شَىْءٍ فَخُذْهَا بِقُوَّةٍ وَأْمُرْ قَوْمَكَ يَأْخُذُوا۟ بِأَحْسَنِهَا ۚ سَأُو۟رِيكُمْ دَارَ ٱلْفَـٰسِقِينَ

And (remember) as We agitated the mountain above them as if it were an overshadowing (awning) and they expected it was going to fall down on them: "Take powerfully what We have brought you, and remember what is in it, that possibly you would be pious." - Surah Al-A'raf 7:171

وَإِذْ نَتَقْنَا ٱلْجَبَلَ فَوْقَهُمْ كَأَنَّهُۥ ظُلَّةٌ وَظَنُّوٓا۟ أَنَّهُۥ وَاقِعٌۢ بِهِمْ خُذُوا۟ مَآ ءَاتَيْنَـٰكُم بِقُوَّةٍ وَٱذْكُرُوا۟ مَا فِيهِ لَعَلَّكُمْ تَتَّقُونَ

The Book of
And Allah likes not prideful boasters
وَٱللَّهُ لَا يُحِبُّ كُلَّ مُخْتَالٍ فَخُورٍ

And cite for them the parable of two men. To one of them We gave two gardens of vine, and We surrounded them with palm-trees, and We placed between them crops.Both gardens produced their harvest in full, and suffered no loss. And We made a river flow through them. And thus he had abundant fruits. He said to his friend, as he conversed with him, "I am wealthier than you, and greater in manpower." And he entered his garden, wronging himself. He said, "I do not think this will ever perish.""And I do not think the Hour is coming. And even if I am returned to my Lord, I will find something better than this in return." His friend said to him, as he conversed with him, "Are you being ungrateful to Him who created you from dust, Then from a sperm-drop, then evolved you into a man? But as for me, He is Allah, my Lord, and I never associate with my Lord anyone. When you entered your garden, why did you not say, "As Allah wills; there is no power except through Allah"? Although you see me inferior to you in wealth and children. Perhaps my Lord will give me something better than your garden, and release upon it thunderbolts from the sky, so it becomes barren waste. Or its water will sink into the ground, and you will be unable to draw it." And ruin closed in on his crops, and so he began wringing his hands over what he had invested in it, as it lays fallen upon its trellises. And he was saying, "I wish I never associated anyone with my Lord." He had no faction to help him besides Allah, and he was helpless. – Surah Al-Khaf 18:32-43

وَٱضْرِبْ لَهُم مَّثَلًا رَّجُلَيْنِ جَعَلْنَا لِأَحَدِهِمَا جَنَّتَيْنِ مِنْ أَعْنَـٰبٍ وَحَفَفْنَـٰهُمَا بِنَخْلٍ وَجَعَلْنَا بَيْنَهُمَا زَرْعًا كِلْتَا ٱلْجَنَّتَيْنِ ءَاتَتْ أُكُلَهَا وَلَمْ تَظْلِم مِّنْهُ شَيْـًٔا وَفَجَّرْنَا خِلَـٰلَهُمَا نَهَرًا وَكَانَ لَهُۥ ثَمَرٌ فَقَالَ لِصَـٰحِبِهِۦ وَهُوَ يُحَاوِرُهُۥٓ أَنَا۠ أَكْثَرُ مِنكَ مَالًا وَأَعَزُّ نَفَرًا وَدَخَلَ جَنَّتَهُۥ وَهُوَ ظَالِمٌ لِّنَفْسِهِۦ قَالَ مَآ أَظُنُّ أَن تَبِيدَ هَـٰذِهِۦٓ أَبَدًا وَمَآ أَظُنُّ ٱلسَّاعَةَ قَآئِمَةً وَلَئِن رُّدِدتُّ إِلَىٰ رَبِّى لَأَجِدَنَّ خَيْرًا مِّنْهَا مُنقَلَبًا قَالَ لَهُۥ صَاحِبُهُۥ وَهُوَ يُحَاوِرُهُۥٓ أَكَفَرْتَ بِٱلَّذِى خَلَقَكَ مِن تُرَابٍ ثُمَّ مِن نُّطْفَةٍ ثُمَّ سَوَّىٰكَ رَجُلًا لَّـٰكِنَّا۠ هُوَ ٱللَّهُ رَبِّى وَلَآ أُشْرِكُ بِرَبِّىٓ أَحَدًا وَلَوْلَآ إِذْ دَخَلْتَ جَنَّتَكَ قُلْتَ مَا شَآءَ ٱللَّهُ لَا قُوَّةَ إِلَّا بِٱللَّهِ إِن تَرَنِ أَنَا۠ أَقَلَّ مِنكَ مَالًا وَوَلَدًا فَعَسَىٰ رَبِّىٓ أَن يُؤْتِيَنِ خَيْرًا مِّن جَنَّتِكَ وَيُرْسِلَ عَلَيْهَا حُسْبَانًا مِّنَ ٱلسَّمَآءِ فَتُصْبِحَ صَعِيدًا زَلَقًا أَوْ يُصْبِحَ مَآؤُهَا غَوْرًا فَلَن تَسْتَطِيعَ لَهُۥ طَلَبًا وَأُحِيطَ بِثَمَرِهِۦ فَأَصْبَحَ يُقَلِّبُ كَفَّيْهِ عَلَىٰ مَآ أَنفَقَ فِيهَا وَهِىَ خَاوِيَةٌ عَلَىٰ عُرُوشِهَا وَيَقُولُ يَـٰلَيْتَنِى لَمْ أُشْرِكْ بِرَبِّىٓ أَحَدًا وَلَمْ تَكُن لَّهُۥ فِئَةٌ يَنصُرُونَهُۥ مِن دُونِ ٱللَّهِ وَمَا كَانَ مُنتَصِرًا

Quaroon belonged to the clan of Moses, but he oppressed them. We had given him treasures, the keys of which would weigh down a group of strong men. His people said to him, "Do not exult; Allah does not love the exultant. But seek, with what Allah has given you, the Home of the Hereafter, and do not neglect your share of this world. And be charitable, as Allah has been charitable to you. And do not seek corruption in the land. Allah does not like the seekers of corruption." He said, "I was given all this on account of knowledge I possess." Did he not know that Allah destroyed many generations before him, who were stronger than he, and possessed greater riches? But the guilty will not be asked about their sins. And he went out before his people in his splendor. Those who desired the worldly life said, "If only we possessed the likes of what Quaroon was given. He is indeed very fortunate." But those who were given knowledge said, "Woe to you! The reward of Allah is better for those who believe and do righteous deeds." Yet none attains it except the steadfast. So We caused the earth to cave in on him and his mansion. He had no company to save him from Allah, and he could not defend himself. Those who had wished they were in his position the day before were saying, "Indeed, it is Allah who spreads the bounty to whomever He wills of His servants, and restricts it. Had Allah not been gracious to us, He would have caved in on us. No wonder the ungrateful never prosper." That Home of the Hereafter—We assign it for those who seek no superiority on earth, nor corruption. And the outcome is for the cautious. (pious – see V.2:2). – Surah Al-Qasas 28:76-83

إِنَّ قَـٰرُونَ كَانَ مِن قَوْمِ مُوسَىٰ فَبَغَىٰ عَلَيْهِمْ ۖ وَءَاتَيْنَـٰهُ مِنَ ٱلْكُنُوزِ مَآ إِنَّ مَفَاتِحَهُۥ لَتَنُوٓأُ بِٱلْعُصْبَةِ أُو۟لِى ٱلْقُوَّةِ إِذْ قَالَ لَهُۥ قَوْمُهُۥ لَا تَفْرَحْ ۖ إِنَّ ٱللَّهَ لَا يُحِبُّ ٱلْفَرِحِينَ وَٱبْتَغِ فِيمَآ ءَاتَىٰكَ ٱللَّهُ ٱلدَّارَ ٱلْـَٔاخِرَةَ ۖ وَلَا تَنسَ نَصِيبَكَ مِنَ ٱلدُّنْيَا ۖ وَأَحْسِن كَمَآ أَحْسَنَ ٱللَّهُ إِلَيْكَ ۖ وَلَا تَبْغِ ٱلْفَسَادَ فِى ٱلْأَرْضِ ۖ إِنَّ ٱللَّهَ لَا يُحِبُّ ٱلْمُفْسِدِينَ قَالَ إِنَّمَآ أُوتِيتُهُۥ عَلَىٰ عِلْمٍ عِندِىٓ ۚ أَوَلَمْ يَعْلَمْ أَنَّ ٱللَّهَ قَدْ أَهْلَكَ مِن قَبْلِهِۦ مِنَ ٱلْقُرُونِ مَنْ هُوَ أَشَدُّ مِنْهُ قُوَّةً وَأَكْثَرُ جَمْعًا ۚ وَلَا يُسْـَٔلُ عَن ذُنُوبِهِمُ ٱلْمُجْرِمُونَ فَخَرَجَ عَلَىٰ قَوْمِهِۦ فِى زِينَتِهِۦ ۖ قَالَ ٱلَّذِينَ يُرِيدُونَ ٱلْحَيَوٰةَ ٱلدُّنْيَا يَـٰلَيْتَ لَنَا مِثْلَ مَآ أُوتِىَ قَـٰرُونُ إِنَّهُۥ لَذُو حَظٍّ عَظِيمٍ وَقَالَ ٱلَّذِينَ أُوتُوا۟ ٱلْعِلْمَ وَيْلَكُمْ ثَوَابُ ٱللَّهِ خَيْرٌ لِّمَنْ ءَامَنَ وَعَمِلَ صَـٰلِحًا وَلَا يُلَقَّىٰهَآ إِلَّا ٱلصَّـٰبِرُونَ فَخَسَفْنَا بِهِۦ وَبِدَارِهِ ٱلْأَرْضَ فَمَا كَانَ لَهُۥ مِن فِئَةٍ يَنصُرُونَهُۥ مِن دُونِ ٱللَّهِ وَمَا كَانَ مِنَ ٱلْمُنتَصِرِينَ وَأَصْبَحَ ٱلَّذِينَ تَمَنَّوْا۟ مَكَانَهُۥ بِٱلْأَمْسِ يَقُولُونَ وَيْكَأَنَّ ٱللَّهَ يَبْسُطُ ٱلرِّزْقَ لِمَن يَشَآءُ مِنْ عِبَادِهِۦ وَيَقْدِرُ ۖ لَوْلَآ أَن مَّنَّ ٱللَّهُ عَلَيْنَا لَخَسَفَ بِنَا ۖ وَيْكَأَنَّهُۥ لَا يُفْلِحُ ٱلْكَـٰفِرُونَ تِلْكَ ٱلدَّارُ ٱلْـَٔاخِرَةُ نَجْعَلُهَا لِلَّذِينَ لَا يُرِيدُونَ عُلُوًّا فِى ٱلْأَرْضِ وَلَا فَسَادًا ۚ وَٱلْعَـٰقِبَةُ لِلْمُتَّقِينَ

The Prophet ﷺ said, "Eat, drink, wear clothes and give alms without extravagance and without conciet." – Al-Bukhari Vol.7 page 373

و قال النبى صلى الله عليه وسلم : "كلوا و اشربوا و البسوا ما شاءت ، ما اخطاتك اثنتان : سرف أو مخيلة

Narrated Ibn `Abbas: I brought water to `Uthman bin `Affan to perform the ablution while he was sitting on his seat. He performed the ablution in a perfect way and said, "I saw the Prophet ﷺ performing the ablution in this place and he performed it in a perfect way and said, "Whoever performs the ablution as I have done this time and then proceeds to the mosque and offers a two-rak`at prayer and then sits there (waiting for the compulsory congregational prayers), then all his past sins will be forgiven." The Prophet ﷺ further added, "Do not be conceited (thinking that your sins will be forgiven because of your prayer). – Al-Bukhari 6433

حَدَّثَنَا سَعْدُ بْنُ حَفْصٍ، حَدَّثَنَا شَيْبَانُ، عَنْ يَحْيَى، عَنْ مُحَمَّدِ بْنِ إِبْرَاهِيمَ الْقُرَشِيِّ، قَالَ أَخْبَرَنِي مُعَاذُ بْنُ عَبْدِ الرَّحْمَنِ، أَنَّ ابْنَ أَبَانَ، أَخْبَرَهُ قَالَ أَتَيْتُ عُثْمَانَ بِطَهُورٍ وَهْوَ جَالِسٌ عَلَى الْمَقَاعِدِ، فَتَوَضَّأَ فَأَحْسَنَ الْوُضُوءَ ثُمَّ قَالَ رَأَيْتُ النَّبِيَّ صلى الله عليه وسلم تَوَضَّأَ وَهْوَ فِي هَذَا الْمَجْلِسِ، فَأَحْسَنَ الْوُضُوءَ ثُمَّ قَالَ ‏"‏ مَنْ تَوَضَّأَ مِثْلَ هَذَا الْوُضُوءِ، ثُمَّ أَتَى الْمَسْجِدَ فَرَكَعَ رَكْعَتَيْنِ، ثُمَّ جَلَسَ، غُفِرَ لَهُ مَا تَقَدَّمَ مِنْ ذَنْبِهِ ‏"‏‏.‏ قَالَ وَقَالَ النَّبِيُّ صلى الله عليه وسلم ‏"‏ لاَ تَغْتَرُّوا ‏"‏‏.‏

Narrated Abu Aiyub: The Prophet ﷺ said, "It is not lawful for a Muslim to desert (not to speak to) his brother Muslim for more than three days while meeting, one turns his face to one side and the other turns his face to the other side. Lo! The better of the two is the one who starts greeting the other." – Al-Bukhari 6237

حَدَّثَنَا عَلِيُّ بْنُ عَبْدِ اللَّهِ، حَدَّثَنَا سُفْيَانُ، عَنِ الزُّهْرِيِّ، عَنْ عَطَاءِ بْنِ يَزِيدَ اللَّيْثِيِّ، عَنْ أَبِي أَيُّوبَ ـ رضى الله عنه ـ عَنِ النَّبِيِّ صلى الله عليه وسلم قَالَ ‏"‏ لاَ يَحِلُّ لِمُسْلِمٍ أَنْ يَهْجُرَ أَخَاهُ فَوْقَ ثَلاَثٍ، يَلْتَقِيَانِ فَيَصُدُّ هَذَا، وَيَصُدُّ هَذَا، وَخَيْرُهُمَا الَّذِي يَبْدَأُ بِالسَّلاَمِ ‏"‏‏.‏ وَذَكَرَ سُفْيَانُ أَنَّهُ سَمِعَهُ مِنْهُ ثَلاَثَ مَرَّاتٍ‏.‏

When adversity touches the human being, he calls on Us. But then, when We favor him with a blessing from Us, he says, "I have attained this by virtue of my knowledge." However, it is a test, but most of them do not know. – Surah Az-Zumar 39:49

فَإِذَا مَسَّ ٱلْإِنسَـٰنَ ضُرٌّ دَعَانَا ثُمَّ إِذَا خَوَّلْنَـٰهُ نِعْمَةً مِّنَّا قَالَ إِنَّمَآ أُوتِيتُهُۥ عَلَىٰ عِلْمٍ ۚ بَلْ هِىَ فِتْنَةٌ وَلَـٰكِنَّ أَكْثَرَهُمْ لَا يَعْلَمُونَ

Have you considered him who has taken his desire for his god? Allah has knowingly led him astray, and has sealed his hearing and his heart, and has placed a veil over his vision. Who will guide him after Allah? Will you not reflect? –Surah Al-Jathiyah 45:23

أَفَرَءَيْتَ مَنِ ٱتَّخَذَ إِلَـٰهَهُۥ هَوَىٰهُ وَأَضَلَّهُ ٱللَّهُ عَلَىٰ عِلْمٍ وَخَتَمَ عَلَىٰ سَمْعِهِۦ وَقَلْبِهِۦ وَجَعَلَ عَلَىٰ بَصَرِهِۦ غِشَـٰوَةً فَمَن يَهْدِيهِ مِنۢ بَعْدِ ٱللَّهِ ۚ أَفَلَا تَذَكَّرُونَ

Have you seen him who chose his desire as his god? Would you be an agent for him? – Surah Al-Furqan 25:43

أَرَءَيْتَ مَنِ ٱتَّخَذَ إِلَـٰهَهُۥ هَوَىٰهُ أَفَأَنتَ تَكُونُ عَلَيْهِ وَكِيلًا

Narrated Anas: The Prophet ﷺ had a she camel called Al Adba which could not be excelled in a race. (Humaid, a sub narrator said, "Or could hardly be excelled.") Once a bedouin came riding a camel below six years of age which surpasses it (i.e. Al-`Adba') in the race. The Muslims felt it so much that the Prophet ﷺ noticed their distress. He then said, "It is Allah's Law that He brings down whatever rises high in the world." – Al-Bukhari 2872

حَدَّثَنَا مَالِكُ بْنُ إِسْمَاعِيلَ، حَدَّثَنَا زُهَيْرٌ، عَنْ حُمَيْدٍ، عَنْ أَنَسٍ ـ رضى الله عنه ـ قَالَ كَانَ لِلنَّبِيِّ صلى الله عليه وسلم نَاقَةٌ تُسَمَّى الْعَضْبَاءَ لاَ تُسْبَقُ ـ قَالَ حُمَيْدٌ أَوْ لاَ تَكَادُ تُسْبَقُ ـ فَجَاءَ أَعْرَابِيٌّ عَلَى قَعُودٍ فَسَبَقَهَا، فَشَقَّ ذَلِكَ عَلَى الْمُسْلِمِينَ، حَتَّى عَرَفَهُ فَقَالَ " حَقٌّ عَلَى اللَّهِ أَنْ لاَ يَرْتَفِعَ شَىْءٌ مِنَ الدُّنْيَا إِلاَّ وَضَعَهُ ". طَوَّلَهُ مُوسَى عَنْ حَمَّادٍ عَنْ ثَابِتٍ عَنْ أَنَسٍ عَنِ النَّبِيِّ صلى الله عليه وسلم

And do not treat people with arrogance, nor walk proudly on earth. Allah does not love the arrogant showoffs. – Surah Luqman 31:18

وَلَا تُصَعِّرْ خَدَّكَ لِلنَّاسِ وَلَا تَمْشِ فِى ٱلْأَرْضِ مَرَحًا ۖ إِنَّ ٱللَّهَ لَا يُحِبُّ كُلَّ مُخْتَالٍ فَخُورٍ

Am I not better than this miserable wretch, who can barely express himself? Why are bracelets of gold not dropped on him, or they angels came with him in procession?" Thus he fooled his people, and they obeyed him. They were wicked people. – Surah Az-Zukhruf 43:52-54

أَمْ أَنَا۠ خَيْرٌ مِّنْ هَـٰذَا ٱلَّذِى هُوَ مَهِينٌ وَلَا يَكَادُ يُبِينُ فَلَوْلَآ أُلْقِىَ عَلَيْهِ أَسْوِرَةٌ مِّن ذَهَبٍ أَوْ جَآءَ مَعَهُ ٱلْمَلَـٰٓئِكَةُ مُقْتَرِنِينَ فَٱسْتَخَفَّ قَوْمَهُۥ فَأَطَاعُوهُ ۚ إِنَّهُمْ كَانُوا۟ قَوْمًا فَـٰسِقِينَ

Narrated Haritha bin Wahb Al-Khuza`i: I heard the Prophet ﷺ saying. "May I tell you of the people of Paradise? Every weak and poor obscure person whom the people look down upon but his oath is fulfilled by Allah when he takes an oath to do something. And may I inform you of the people of the Hell-Fire? They are all those violent, arrogant and stubborn people." – Al-Bukhari 4918

حَدَّثَنَا أَبُو نُعَيْمٍ، حَدَّثَنَا سُفْيَانُ، عَنْ مَعْبَدِ بْنِ خَالِدٍ، قَالَ سَمِعْتُ حَارِثَةَ بْنَ وَهْبٍ الْخُزَاعِيَّ، قَالَ سَمِعْتُ النَّبِيَّ صلى الله عليه وسلم يَقُولُ " أَلاَ أُخْبِرُكُمْ بِأَهْلِ الْجَنَّةِ كُلُّ ضَعِيفٍ مُتَضَعِّفٍ لَوْ أَقْسَمَ عَلَى اللَّهِ لأَبَرَّهُ، أَلاَ أُخْبِرُكُمْ بِأَهْلِ النَّارِ كُلُّ عُتُلٍّ جَوَّاظٍ مُسْتَكْبِرٍ "

No calamity occurs on earth, or in your souls, but it is in a Book, even before We make it happen. That is easy for Allah. That you may not sorrow over what eludes you, nor exult over what He has given you. Allah does not love the proud snob. - Surah Al-Hadid 57:22&23

مَآ أَصَابَ مِن مُّصِيبَةٍ فِى ٱلْأَرْضِ وَلَا فِىٓ أَنفُسِكُمْ إِلَّا فِى كِتَـٰبٍ مِّن قَبْلِ أَن نَّبْرَأَهَآ ۚ إِنَّ ذَٰلِكَ عَلَى ٱللَّهِ يَسِيرٌ لِّكَيْلَا تَأْسَوْا۟ عَلَىٰ
مَا فَاتَكُمْ وَلَا تَفْرَحُوا۟ بِمَآ ءَاتَىٰكُمْ ۗ وَٱللَّهُ لَا يُحِبُّ كُلَّ مُخْتَالٍ فَخُورٍ

Narrated `Abdullah bin `Umar: Allah's Messenger ﷺ said, "Whoever drags his clothes (on the ground) out of pride and arrogance, Allah will not look at him on the Day of Resurrection." – Sahih Al-Bukhari 5791

حَدَّثَنَا مَطَرُ بْنُ الْفَضْلِ، حَدَّثَنَا شَبَابَةُ، حَدَّثَنَا شُعْبَةُ، قَالَ لَقِيتُ مُحَارِبَ بْنَ دِثَارٍ عَلَى فَرَسٍ وَهْوَ يَأْتِي مَكَانَهُ الَّذِي يَقْضِي فِيهِ فَسَأَلْتُهُ عَنْ هَذَا الْحَدِيثِ فَحَدَّثَنِي فَقَالَ سَمِعْتُ عَبْدَ اللَّهِ بْنَ عُمَرَ ـ رضى الله عنهما ـ يَقُولُ قَالَ رَسُولُ اللَّهِ صلى الله عليه وسلم " مَنْ جَرَّ ثَوْبَهُ مَخِيلَةً، لَمْ يَنْظُرِ اللَّهُ إِلَيْهِ يَوْمَ الْقِيَامَةِ ". فَقُلْتُ لِمُحَارِبٍ أَذَكَرَ إِزَارَهُ قَالَ مَا خَصَّ إِزَارًا وَلاَ قَمِيصًا. تَابَعَهُ جَبَلَةُ بْنُ سُحَيْمٍ وَزَيْدُ بْنُ أَسْلَمَ وَزَيْدُ بْنُ عَبْدِ اللَّهِ عَنِ ابْنِ عُمَرَ عَنِ النَّبِيِّ صلى الله عليه وسلم. وَقَالَ اللَّيْثُ عَنْ نَافِعٍ

عَنِ ابْنِ عُمَرَ مِثْلَهُ. وَتَابَعَهُ مُوسَى بْنُ عُقْبَةَ وَعُمَرُ بْنُ مُحَمَّدٍ وَقُدَامَةُ بْنُ مُوسَى عَنْ سَالِمٍ عَنِ ابْنِ عُمَرَ عَنِ النَّبِيِّ صلى الله عليه وسلم " مَنْ جَرَّ ثَوْبَهُ ".

Narrated Abu Huraira: Allah's Messenger ﷺ said, "The main source of disbelief is in the east. Pride and arrogance are characteristics of the owners of horses and camels, and those bedouins who are busy with their camels and pay no attention to Religion; while modesty and gentleness are the characteristics of the owners of sheep.". – Sahih Al-Bukhari 3301

حَدَّثَنَا عَبْدُ اللَّهِ بْنُ يُوسُفَ، أَخْبَرَنَا مَالِكٌ، عَنْ أَبِي الزِّنَادِ، عَنِ الأَعْرَجِ، عَنْ أَبِي هُرَيْرَةَ ـ رضى الله عنه ـ أَنَّ رَسُولَ اللَّهِ صلى الله عليه وسلم قَالَ " رَأْسُ الْكُفْرِ نَحْوَ الْمَشْرِقِ، وَالْفَخْرُ وَالْخُيَلاَءُ فِي أَهْلِ الْخَيْلِ وَالإِبِلِ، وَالْفَدَّادِينَ أَهْلِ الْوَبَرِ، وَالسَّكِينَةُ فِي أَهْلِ الْغَنَمِ "

Narrated Abu Huraira: The Prophet ﷺ said, "Paradise and the Fire (Hell) argued, and the Fire (Hell) said, "I have been given the privilege of receiving the arrogant and the tyrants.' Paradise said, 'What is the matter with me? Why do only the weak and the humble among the people enter me?' On that, Allah said to Paradise. 'You are My Mercy which I bestow on whoever I wish of my servants.' Then Allah said to the (Hell) Fire, 'You are my (means of) punishment by which I punish whoever I wish of my slaves. And each of you will have its fill.' As for the Fire (Hell), it will not be filled till Allah puts His Foot over it whereupon it will say, 'Qati! Qati!' At that time it will be filled, and Its different parts will come closer to each other; and Allah will not wrong any of His created beings. As regards Paradise, Allah will create a new creation to fill it with.". – Sahih Al-Bukhari 4850

حَدَّثَنَا عَبْدُ اللَّهِ بْنُ مُحَمَّدٍ، حَدَّثَنَا عَبْدُ الرَّزَّاقِ، أَخْبَرَنَا مَعْمَرٌ، عَنْ هَمَّامٍ، عَنْ أَبِي هُرَيْرَةَ، رضى الله عنه قَالَ قَالَ النَّبِيُّ صلى الله عليه وسلم " تَحَاجَّتِ الْجَنَّةُ وَالنَّارُ فَقَالَتِ النَّارُ أُوثِرْتُ بِالْمُتَكَبِّرِينَ وَالْمُتَجَبِّرِينَ. وَقَالَتِ الْجَنَّةُ مَا لِي لاَ يَدْخُلُنِي إِلاَّ ضُعَفَاءُ النَّاسِ وَسَقَطُهُمْ. قَالَ اللَّهُ تَبَارَكَ وَتَعَالَى لِلْجَنَّةِ أَنْتِ رَحْمَتِي أَرْحَمُ بِكِ مَنْ أَشَاءُ مِنْ عِبَادِي. وَقَالَ لِلنَّارِ إِنَّمَا أَنْتِ عَذَابٌ أُعَذِّبُ بِكِ مَنْ أَشَاءُ مِنْ عِبَادِي. وَلِكُلِّ وَاحِدَةٍ مِنْهُمَا مِلْؤُهَا، فَأَمَّا النَّارُ فَلاَ تَمْتَلِئُ حَتَّى يَضَعَ رِجْلَهُ فَتَقُولُ قَطٍ قَطٍ قَطٍ. فَهُنَالِكَ تَمْتَلِئُ وَيُزْوَى بَعْضُهَا إِلَى بَعْضٍ، وَلاَ يَظْلِمُ اللَّهُ ـ عَزَّ وَجَلَّ ـ مِنْ خَلْقِهِ أَحَدًا، وَأَمَّا الْجَنَّةُ فَإِنَّ اللَّهَ عَزَّ وَجَلَّ يُنْشِئُ لَهَا خَلْقًا "

Narrated Haritha bin Wahb Al-Khuza`i: I heard the Prophet ﷺ saying. "May I tell you of the people of Paradise? Every weak and poor obscure person whom the people look down upon but his oath is fulfilled by Allah when he takes an oath to do something. And may I inform you of the people of the Hell-Fire? They are all those violent, arrogant and stubborn people." - Sahih Al-Bukhari 4918

حَدَّثَنَا أَبُو نُعَيْمٍ، حَدَّثَنَا سُفْيَانُ، عَنْ مَعْبَدِ بْنِ خَالِدٍ، قَالَ سَمِعْتُ حَارِثَةَ بْنَ وَهْبٍ الْخُزَاعِيَّ، قَالَ سَمِعْتُ النَّبِيَّ صلى الله عليه وسلم يَقُولُ " أَلاَ أُخْبِرُكُمْ بِأَهْلِ الْجَنَّةِ كُلُّ ضَعِيفٍ مُتَضَعِّفٍ لَوْ أَقْسَمَ عَلَى اللَّهِ لأَبَرَّهُ، أَلاَ أُخْبِرُكُمْ بِأَهْلِ النَّارِ كُلُّ عُتُلٍّ جَوَّاظٍ مُسْتَكْبِرٍ "

Narrated Abu Huraira: Allah's Messenger ﷺ said, "Keeping horses may be a source of reward to some (man), a shelter to another (i.e. means of earning one's living), or a burden to a third. He to whom the horse will be a source of reward is the one who keeps it in Allah's Cause (prepare it for holy battles) and ties it by a long rope in a pasture (or a garden). He will get a reward equal to what its long rope allows it to eat in the pasture or the garden, and if that horse breaks its rope and crosses one or two hills, then all its footsteps and its dung will be counted as good deeds for its owner; and if it passes by a river and drinks from it, then that will also be regarded as a good deed for its owner even if he has had no intention of watering it then. Horses are a shelter from poverty to the second person who keeps horses for earning his living so as not to ask others, and at the same time he gives Allah's right (i.e. rak`at) (from the wealth he earns through using them in trading etc.,) and does not overburden them. He who keeps horses just out of pride and for showing off and as a means of harming the Muslims, his horses will be a source of sins to him." When Allah's Messenger ﷺ was asked about donkeys, he replied, "Nothing particular was revealed to me regarding them except the general unique verse which is applicable to everything: "Whoever does goodness equal to the weight of an atom (or small ant) shall see it (its reward) on the Day of Resurrection.". – Sahih Al-Bukhari 2371

حَدَّثَنَا عَبْدُ اللَّهِ بْنُ يُوسُفَ، أَخْبَرَنَا مَالِكُ بْنُ أَنَسٍ، عَنْ زَيْدِ بْنِ أَسْلَمَ، عَنْ أَبِي صَالِحٍ السَّمَّانِ، عَنْ أَبِي هُرَيْرَةَ ـ رضى الله عنه ـ أَنَّ رَسُولَ اللَّهِ صلى الله عليه وسلم قَالَ " الْخَيْلُ لِرَجُلٍ أَجْرٌ، وَلِرَجُلٍ سِتْرٌ، وَعَلَى رَجُلٍ وِزْرٌ، فَأَمَّا الَّذِي لَهُ أَجْرٌ فَرَجُلٌ رَبَطَهَا فِي سَبِيلِ اللَّهِ، فَأَطَالَ بِهَا فِي مَرْجٍ أَوْ رَوْضَةٍ، فَمَا أَصَابَتْ فِي طِيَلِهَا ذَلِكَ مِنَ الْمَرْجِ أَوِ الرَّوْضَةِ كَانَتْ لَهُ حَسَنَاتٍ، وَلَوْ أَنَّهُ انْقَطَعَ طِيَلُهَا فَاسْتَنَّتْ شَرَفًا أَوْ شَرَفَيْنِ كَانَتْ آثَارُهَا وَأَرْوَاثُهَا حَسَنَاتٍ لَهُ، وَلَوْ أَنَّهَا مَرَّتْ بِنَهَرٍ فَشَرِبَتْ مِنْهُ وَلَمْ يُرِدْ أَنْ يَسْقِيَ كَانَ ذَلِكَ حَسَنَاتٍ لَهُ، فَهِيَ لِذَلِكَ أَجْرٌ، وَرَجُلٌ رَبَطَهَا تَغَنِّيًا وَتَعَفُّفًا ثُمَّ لَمْ يَنْسَ حَقَّ اللَّهِ فِي رِقَابِهَا وَلاَ ظُهُورِهَا، فَهِيَ لِذَلِكَ سِتْرٌ، وَرَجُلٌ رَبَطَهَا فَخْرًا وَرِيَاءً وَنِوَاءً لأَهْلِ الإِسْلاَمِ، فَهِيَ عَلَى ذَلِكَ وِزْرٌ ". وَسُئِلَ رَسُولُ اللَّهِ صلى الله عليه وسلم عَنِ الْحُمُرِ فَقَالَ " مَا أُنْزِلَ عَلَىَّ فِيهَا شَىْءٌ إِلاَّ هَذِهِ الآيَةُ الْجَامِعَةُ الْفَاذَّةُ {مَنْ يَعْمَلْ مِثْقَالَ ذَرَّةٍ خَيْرًا يَرَهُ * وَمَنْ يَعْمَلْ مِثْقَالَ ذَرَّةٍ شَرًّا يَرَهُ }

The Book of
So whoever does righteous good deeds while he is a believer, his efforts will not be rejected.
فَمَن يَعْمَلْ مِنَ ٱلصَّـٰلِحَـٰتِ وَهُوَ مُؤْمِنٌ فَلَا كُفْرَانَ لِسَعْيِهِۦ

Whoever commits a sin will be repaid only with its like. But whoever works righteousness, whether male or female, and is a believer—these will enter Paradise, where they will be provided for without account. – Surah Al-Ghafir 40:40

مَنْ عَمِلَ سَيِّئَةً فَلَا يُجْزَىٰٓ إِلَّا مِثْلَهَا ۖ وَمَنْ عَمِلَ صَـٰلِحًا مِّن ذَكَرٍ أَوْ أُنثَىٰ وَهُوَ مُؤْمِنٌ فَأُو۟لَـٰٓئِكَ يَدْخُلُونَ ٱلْجَنَّةَ يُرْزَقُونَ فِيهَا بِغَيْرِ حِسَابٍ

And I am Forgiving towards him who repents, believes, acts righteously, and then remains guided. – Surah TaHa 20:82

إِنِّى لَغَفَّارٌ لِّمَن تَابَ وَءَامَنَ وَعَمِلَ صَـٰلِحًا ثُمَّ ٱهْتَدَىٰ

But whoever has done righteous deeds, while being a believer—will fear neither injustice, nor grievance. – Surah TaHa 20:112

وَمَن يَعْمَلْ مِنَ ٱلصَّـٰلِحَـٰتِ وَهُوَ مُؤْمِنٌ فَلَا يَخَافُ ظُلْمًا وَلَا هَضْمًا

But whoever works righteousness, whether male or female, and is a believer— those will enter Paradise, and will not be wronged a whit. – Surah An-Nisa 4:124

وَمَن يَعْمَلْ مِنَ ٱلصَّـٰلِحَـٰتِ مِن ذَكَرٍ أَوْ أُنثَىٰ وَهُوَ مُؤْمِنٌ فَأُو۟لَـٰٓئِكَ يَدْخُلُونَ ٱلْجَنَّةَ وَلَا يُظْلَمُونَ نَقِيرًا

As for those who believe and lead a righteous life—We will not waste the reward of those who work righteousness. – Surah Al-Khaf 18:30

إِنَّ ٱلَّذِينَ ءَامَنُوا۟ وَعَمِلُوا۟ ٱلصَّـٰلِحَـٰتِ إِنَّا لَا نُضِيعُ أَجْرَ مَنْ أَحْسَنَ عَمَلًا

Those who believe and do righteous deeds—We will remit their sins, and We will reward them according to the best of what they used to do. – Surah Ankabut 29:7
وَٱلَّذِينَ ءَامَنُوا۟ وَعَمِلُوا۟ ٱلصَّـٰلِحَـٰتِ لَنُكَفِّرَنَّ عَنْهُمْ سَيِّـَٔاتِهِمْ وَلَنَجْزِيَنَّهُمْ أَحْسَنَ ٱلَّذِى كَانُوا۟ يَعْمَلُونَ

And He answers those who believe and do good deeds, and He increases them of His grace. But the disbelievers will suffer a terrible punishment.– Surah Ash-Shura 42:26
وَيَسْتَجِيبُ ٱلَّذِينَ ءَامَنُوا۟ وَعَمِلُوا۟ ٱلصَّـٰلِحَـٰتِ وَيَزِيدُهُم مِّن فَضْلِهِۦ ۚ وَٱلْكَـٰفِرُونَ لَهُمْ عَذَابٌ شَدِيدٌ

The Day when He gathers you for the Day of Gathering—that is the Day of Mutual Exchange. Whoever believes in Allah and acts with integrity, He will remit his misdeeds, and will admit him into gardens beneath which rivers flow, to dwell therein forever. That is the supreme achievement. – Surah At-Taghabun 64:9
يَوْمَ يَجْمَعُكُمْ لِيَوْمِ ٱلْجَمْعِ ۖ ذَٰلِكَ يَوْمُ ٱلتَّغَابُنِ ۗ وَمَن يُؤْمِنۢ بِٱللَّهِ وَيَعْمَلْ صَـٰلِحًا يُكَفِّرْ عَنْهُ سَيِّـَٔاتِهِۦ وَيُدْخِلْهُ جَنَّـٰتٍ تَجْرِى مِن تَحْتِهَا ٱلْأَنْهَـٰرُ خَـٰلِدِينَ فِيهَآ أَبَدًا ۚ ذَٰلِكَ ٱلْفَوْزُ ٱلْعَظِيمُ

In fact, whoever submits himself to Allah, and is a doer of good, will have his reward with his Lord—they have nothing to fear, nor shall they grieve. – Surah Al-Baqarah 2:112
بَلَىٰ مَنْ أَسْلَمَ وَجْهَهُۥ لِلَّهِ وَهُوَ مُحْسِنٌ فَلَهُۥٓ أَجْرُهُۥ عِندَ رَبِّهِۦ وَلَا خَوْفٌ عَلَيْهِمْ وَلَا هُمْ يَحْزَنُونَ

They believe in Allah and the Last Day, and advocate righteousness and forbid evil, and are quick to do good deeds. These are among the righteous. Whatever good they do, they will not be denied it. Allah knows the righteous. – Surah Al-Imran 3:114&115
يُؤْمِنُونَ بِٱللَّهِ وَٱلْيَوْمِ ٱلْـَٔاخِرِ وَيَأْمُرُونَ بِٱلْمَعْرُوفِ وَيَنْهَوْنَ عَنِ ٱلْمُنكَرِ وَيُسَـٰرِعُونَ فِى ٱلْخَيْرَٰتِ ۖ وَأُو۟لَـٰٓئِكَ مِنَ ٱلصَّـٰلِحِينَ وَمَا يَفْعَلُوا۟ مِنْ خَيْرٍ فَلَن يُكْفَرُوهُ ۗ وَٱللَّهُ عَلِيمٌۢ بِٱلْمُتَّقِينَ

Narrated Abu Sa`id: A bedouin came to the Prophetﷺ and asked him about emigration. The Prophetﷺ said to him, "May Allah be merciful to you. The matter of emigration is difficult. Have you got some camels?" He replied in the affirmative. The Prophetﷺ asked him, "Do you pay their Zakat?" He replied in the affirmative. He asked, "Do you lend them so that their milk may be utilized by others?" The bedouin said, "Yes." The Prophetﷺ asked, "Do you milk them on the day off watering them?" He replied, "Yes." The Prophetﷺ said, "Do good deeds beyond the merchants (or the sea) and Allah will never disregard any of your deeds." (See Hadith No. 260, Vol. 5) – Al-Bukhari 2633
وَقَالَ مُحَمَّدُ بْنُ يُوسُفَ حَدَّثَنَا الأَوْزَاعِيُّ، حَدَّثَنِي الزُّهْرِيُّ، حَدَّثَنِي عَطَاءُ بْنُ يَزِيدَ، حَدَّثَنِي أَبُو سَعِيدٍ، قَالَ جَاءَ أَعْرَابِيٌّ إِلَى النَّبِيِّ صلى الله عليه وسلم فَسَأَلَهُ عَنِ الْهِجْرَةِ، فَقَالَ " وَيْحَكَ إِنَّ الْهِجْرَةَ شَأْنُهَا شَدِيدٌ فَهَلْ لَكَ مِنْ إِبِلٍ " قَالَ نَعَمْ. قَالَ " فَتُعْطِي صَدَقَتَهَا ". قَالَ نَعَمْ. قَالَ " فَهَلْ تَمْنَحُ مِنْهَا شَيْئًا ". قَالَ نَعَمْ. قَالَ " فَتَحْلُبُهَا يَوْمَ وِرْدِهَا ". قَالَ نَعَمْ. قَالَ " فَاعْمَلْ مِنْ وَرَاءِ الْبِحَارِ، فَإِنَّ اللَّهَ لَنْ يَتِرَكَ مِنْ عَمَلِكَ شَيْئًا "

Whoever does righteous deeds, and is a believer, his effort will not be denied. We are writing it down for him – Surah Al-Anbiya 21:94
فَمَن يَعْمَلْ مِنَ ٱلصَّـٰلِحَـٰتِ وَهُوَ مُؤْمِنٌ فَلَا كُفْرَانَ لِسَعْيِهِۦ وَإِنَّا لَهُۥ كَـٰتِبُونَ

Narrated Hudhaifa bin Al-Yaman: The people used to ask Allah's Messengerﷺ about the good but I used to ask him about the evil lest I should be overtaken by them. So I said, "O Allah's Messengerﷺ! We were living in ignorance and in an (extremely) worst atmosphere, then Allah brought to us this good (i.e., Islam); will there be any evil after this good?" He said, "Yes." I said, 'Will there be any good after that evil?" He replied, "Yes, but it will be tainted (not pure.)'' I asked, "What will be its taint?" He replied, "(There will be) some people who will guide others not according to my tradition? You will approve of some of their deeds and disapprove of some others." I asked, "Will there be any evil after that good?" He replied, "Yes, (there will be) some people calling at the gates of the (Hell) Fire, and whoever will respond to their call, will be thrown by them into the (Hell) Fire." I said, "O Allah s Apostle! Will you describe them to us?" He said, "They will be from our own people and will speak our language." I said, "What do you order me to do if such a state should take place in my life?" He said, "Stick to the group of Muslims and their Imam (ruler)." I said, "If there is neither a group of Muslims nor an Imam (ruler)?" He said, "Then turn away from all those sects even if you were to bite (eat) the roots of a tree till death overtakes you while you are in that state.". – Sahih Al-Bukhari 7084

حَدَّثَنَا مُحَمَّدُ بْنُ الْمُثَنَّى، حَدَّثَنَا الْوَلِيدُ بْنُ مُسْلِمٍ، حَدَّثَنَا ابْنُ جَابِرٍ، حَدَّثَنِي بُسْرُ بْنُ عُبَيْدِ اللَّهِ الْحَضْرَمِيُّ، أَنَّهُ سَمِعَ أَبَا إِدْرِيسَ الْخَوْلاَنِيَّ، أَنَّهُ سَمِعَ حُذَيْفَةَ بْنَ الْيَمَانِ، يَقُولُ كَانَ النَّاسُ يَسْأَلُونَ رَسُولَ اللَّهِ صلى الله عليه وسلم عَنِ الْخَيْرِ، وَكُنْتُ أَسْأَلُهُ عَنِ الشَّرِّ، مَخَافَةَ أَنْ يُدْرِكَنِي فَقُلْتُ يَا رَسُولَ اللَّهِ إِنَّا كُنَّا فِي جَاهِلِيَّةٍ وَشَرٍّ فَجَاءَنَا اللَّهُ بِهَذَا الْخَيْرِ، فَهَلْ بَعْدَ هَذَا الْخَيْرِ مِنْ شَرٍّ قَالَ " نَعَمْ ". قُلْتُ وَهَلْ بَعْدَ ذَلِكَ الشَّرِّ مِنْ خَيْرٍ قَالَ " نَعَمْ، وَفِيهِ دَخَنٌ ". قُلْتُ وَمَا دَخَنُهُ قَالَ " قَوْمٌ يَهْدُونَ بِغَيْرِ هَدْيِي، تَعْرِفُ مِنْهُمْ وَتُنْكِرُ ". قُلْتُ فَهَلْ بَعْدَ ذَلِكَ الْخَيْرِ مِنْ شَرٍّ قَالَ " نَعَمْ، دُعَاةٌ عَلَى أَبْوَابِ جَهَنَّمَ، مَنْ أَجَابَهُمْ إِلَيْهَا قَذَفُوهُ فِيهَا ". قُلْتُ يَا رَسُولَ اللَّهِ صِفْهُمْ لَنَا. قَالَ " هُمْ مِنْ جِلْدَتِنَا، وَيَتَكَلَّمُونَ بِأَلْسِنَتِنَا ". قُلْتُ فَمَا تَأْمُرُنِي إِنْ أَدْرَكَنِي ذَلِكَ قَالَ " تَلْزَمُ جَمَاعَةَ الْمُسْلِمِينَ وَإِمَامَهُمْ ". قُلْتُ فَإِنْ لَمْ يَكُنْ لَهُمْ جَمَاعَةٌ وَلاَ إِمَامٌ قَالَ " فَاعْتَزِلْ تِلْكَ الْفِرَقَ كُلَّهَا، وَلَوْ أَنْ تَعَضَّ بِأَصْلِ شَجَرَةٍ، حَتَّى يُدْرِكَكَ الْمَوْتُ، وَأَنْتَ عَلَى ذَلِكَ "

The Book of

There is a piece of flesh in the body if it becomes good (reformed) the whole body becomes good

وَإِنَّ فِي الْجَسَدِ مُضْغَةً إِذَا صَلَحَتْ صَلَحَ الْجَسَدُ كُلُّهُ

Narrated An-Nu'man bin Bashir: I heard Allah's Messenger ﷺ saying, 'Both legal and illegal things are evident but in between them there are doubtful (suspicious) things and most of the people have no knowledge about them. So whoever saves himself from these suspicious things saves his religion and his honor. And whoever indulges in these suspicious things is like a shepherd who grazes (his animals) near the Hima (private pasture) of someone else and at any moment he is liable to get in it. (O people!) Beware! Every king has a Hima and the Hima of Allah on the earth is His illegal (forbidden) things. Beware! There is a piece of flesh in the body if it becomes good (reformed) the whole body becomes good but if it gets spoilt the whole body gets spoilt and that is the Heart. – Sahih al-Bukhari 52

حَدَّثَنَا أَبُو نُعَيْمٍ، حَدَّثَنَا زَكَرِيَّاءُ، عَنْ عَامِرٍ، قَالَ سَمِعْتُ النُّعْمَانَ بْنَ بَشِيرٍ، يَقُولُ سَمِعْتُ رَسُولَ اللَّهِ صلى الله عليه وسلم يَقُولُ " الْحَلاَلُ بَيِّنٌ وَالْحَرَامُ بَيِّنٌ، وَبَيْنَهُمَا مُشَبَّهَاتٌ لاَ يَعْلَمُهَا كَثِيرٌ مِنَ النَّاسِ، فَمَنِ اتَّقَى الْمُشَبَّهَاتِ اسْتَبْرَأَ لِدِينِهِ وَعِرْضِهِ، وَمَنْ وَقَعَ فِي الشُّبُهَاتِ كَرَاعٍ يَرْعَى حَوْلَ الْحِمَى، يُوشِكُ أَنْ يُوَاقِعَهُ. أَلاَ وَإِنَّ لِكُلِّ مَلِكٍ حِمًى، أَلاَ إِنَّ حِمَى اللَّهِ فِي أَرْضِهِ مَحَارِمُهُ، أَلاَ وَإِنَّ فِي الْجَسَدِ مُضْغَةً إِذَا صَلَحَتْ صَلَحَ الْجَسَدُ كُلُّهُ، وَإِذَا فَسَدَتْ فَسَدَ الْجَسَدُ كُلُّهُ. أَلاَ وَهِيَ الْقَلْبُ ".

Narrated Abu Huraira: Allah's Messenger ﷺ said, "The deeds of anyone of you will not save you (from the (Hell) Fire)." They said, "Even you (will not be saved by your deeds), O Allah's Messenger ﷺ ?" He said, "No, even I (will not be saved) unless and until Allah bestows His Mercy on me. Therefore, do good deeds properly, sincerely and moderately, and worship Allah in the forenoon and in the afternoon and during a part of the night, and always adopt a middle, moderate, regular course whereby you will reach your target (Paradise). – Sahih al-Bukhari 6463

حَدَّثَنَا آدَمُ، حَدَّثَنَا ابْنُ أَبِي ذِئْبٍ، عَنْ سَعِيدٍ الْمَقْبُرِيِّ، عَنْ أَبِي هُرَيْرَةَ ـ رضى الله عنه ـ قَالَ قَالَ رَسُولُ اللَّهِ صلى الله عليه وسلم " لَنْ يُنَجِّيَ أَحَدًا مِنْكُمْ عَمَلُهُ ". قَالُوا وَلاَ أَنْتَ يَا رَسُولَ اللَّهِ قَالَ " وَلاَ أَنَا، إِلاَّ أَنْ يَتَغَمَّدَنِي اللَّهُ بِرَحْمَةٍ، سَدِّدُوا وَقَارِبُوا، وَاغْدُوا وَرُوحُوا، وَشَىْءٌ مِنَ الدُّلْجَةِ. وَالْقَصْدَ الْقَصْدَ تَبْلُغُوا ".

Righteousness is not a matter of turning your faces eastward or westward. Rather, righteousness is believing in Allah and the Last Day and the angels and the Book and the prophets; giving money for the love of Him to relatives, orphans, disabled persons , stranded travelers, beggars, and to free slaves; performing prayers and paying the purifying alms; keeping promises, and enduring misery and hard times in the time of threat. It is they who prove themselves true, and it is they who are mindful of Allah. – Surah Al-Baqarah 2:177

لَّيْسَ ٱلْبِرَّ أَن تُوَلُّوا۟ وُجُوهَكُمْ قِبَلَ ٱلْمَشْرِقِ وَٱلْمَغْرِبِ وَلَـٰكِنَّ ٱلْبِرَّ مَنْ ءَامَنَ بِٱللَّهِ وَٱلْيَوْمِ ٱلْـَٔاخِرِ وَٱلْمَلَـٰٓئِكَةِ وَٱلْكِتَـٰبِ وَٱلنَّبِيِّـۧنَ وَءَاتَى ٱلْمَالَ عَلَىٰ حُبِّهِۦ ذَوِى ٱلْقُرْبَىٰ وَٱلْيَتَـٰمَىٰ وَٱلْمَسَـٰكِينَ وَٱبْنَ ٱلسَّبِيلِ وَٱلسَّآئِلِينَ وَفِى ٱلرِّقَابِ وَأَقَامَ ٱلصَّلَوٰةَ وَءَاتَى ٱلزَّكَوٰةَ وَٱلْمُوفُونَ بِعَهْدِهِمْ إِذَا عَـٰهَدُوا۟ ۖ وَٱلصَّـٰبِرِينَ فِى ٱلْبَأْسَآءِ وَٱلضَّرَّآءِ وَحِينَ ٱلْبَأْسِ ۗ أُو۟لَـٰٓئِكَ ٱلَّذِينَ صَدَقُوا۟ ۖ وَأُو۟لَـٰٓئِكَ هُمُ ٱلْمُتَّقُونَ

Allah will not take you to task for idleness in your oaths, but He will take you to task for whatever your hearts have earned; and Allah is Ever-Forgiving, Ever-Forbearing . Surah Al-Baqarah 2:225

لَّا يُؤَاخِذُكُمُ ٱللَّهُ بِٱللَّغْوِ فِىٓ أَيْمَـٰنِكُمْ وَلَـٰكِن يُؤَاخِذُكُم بِمَا كَسَبَتْ قُلُوبُكُمْ ۗ وَٱللَّهُ غَفُورٌ حَلِيمٌ

Children of Adam, We have sent down clothes to you to cover your nakedness and as a thing of beauty, but the garment of Taqwa of Allah is the best of all. These are blessings from Allah so that you may remember. – Surah Al-A'raf 7:26

يَـٰبَنِىٓ ءَادَمَ قَدْ أَنزَلْنَا عَلَيْكُمْ لِبَاسًا يُوَٰرِى سَوْءَٰتِكُمْ وَرِيشًا ۖ وَلِبَاسُ ٱلتَّقْوَىٰ ذَٰلِكَ خَيْرٌ ۚ ذَٰلِكَ مِنْ ءَايَـٰتِ ٱللَّهِ لَعَلَّهُمْ يَذَّكَّرُونَ

.... And whoever keeps it (his testimony) back, then surely his heart is vicious; and Allah is Ever-Knowing of whatever you do. Surah Al-Baqarah 2:283

وَمَن يَكْتُمْهَا فَإِنَّهُۥٓ ءَاثِمٌ قَلْبُهُۥ ۗ وَٱللَّهُ بِمَا تَعْمَلُونَ عَلِيمٌ

O you who have believed, respond to Allah and to the Messenger when He calls you to that which enlivens you; and know that Allah interposes between a person and his heart, and that to Him you will be mustered. – Surah Al-Anfal 8:24

يَـٰٓأَيُّهَا ٱلَّذِينَ ءَامَنُوا۟ ٱسْتَجِيبُوا۟ لِلَّهِ وَلِلرَّسُولِ إِذَا دَعَاكُمْ لِمَا يُحْيِيكُمْ ۖ وَٱعْلَمُوٓا۟ أَنَّ ٱللَّهَ يَحُولُ بَيْنَ ٱلْمَرْءِ وَقَلْبِهِۦ وَأَنَّهُۥٓ إِلَيْهِ
تُحْشَرُونَ

In no way is there any affliction that afflicts, except it be by the permission of Allah. And whoever believes in Allah, He will guide his heart; and Allah is Ever-Knowing of everything – Surah At-Taghabun 64:11

مَآ أَصَابَ مِن مُّصِيبَةٍ إِلَّا بِإِذْنِ ٱللَّهِ ۗ وَمَن يُؤْمِنۢ بِٱللَّهِ يَهْدِ قَلْبَهُۥ ۚ وَٱللَّهُ بِكُلِّ شَىْءٍ عَلِيمٌ

Allah will not take you to task for idleness in your oaths, but He will take you to task for whatever your hearts have earned; and Allah is Ever-Forgiving, Ever-Forbearing – Surah Al-Baqarah 2:225

لَّا يُؤَاخِذُكُمُ ٱللَّهُ بِٱللَّغْوِ فِىٓ أَيْمَـٰنِكُمْ وَلَـٰكِن يُؤَاخِذُكُم بِمَا كَسَبَتْ قُلُوبُكُمْ ۗ وَٱللَّهُ غَفُورٌ حَلِيمٌ

The Pilgrimage is (in) months well-known; so, whoever ordains (upon himself) the Pilgrimage in them, then there shall be no lying with (womenfolk), nor evident immorality, nor disputing in the Pilgrimage. And whatever charity you perform, Allah knows it. And sustain yourselves; so, the most charitable sustenance is piety; and be pious to Me, O (you) endowed with intellects. – Surah Al-Baqarah 2:197

ٱلْحَجُّ أَشْهُرٌ مَّعْلُومَـٰتٌ ۚ فَمَن فَرَضَ فِيهِنَّ ٱلْحَجَّ فَلَا رَفَثَ وَلَا فُسُوقَ وَلَا جِدَالَ فِى ٱلْحَجِّ ۗ وَمَا تَفْعَلُوا۟ مِنْ خَيْرٍ يَعْلَمْهُ ٱللَّهُ ۗ
وَتَزَوَّدُوا۟ فَإِنَّ خَيْرَ ٱلزَّادِ ٱلتَّقْوَىٰ ۚ وَٱتَّقُونِ يَـٰٓأُو۟لِى ٱلْأَلْبَـٰبِ

They ask you concerning the new moons (Literally: crescents). Say, "They are fixed times for mankind, and (for) the Pilgrimage." And benignancy is not to come up to the homes from their backs; but benignancy is for man to be pious; and come up to the homes by their doors, and be pious towards Allah, so that possibly you would prosper – Surah Al-Baqarah 2:189

يَسْـَٔلُونَكَ عَنِ ٱلْأَهِلَّةِ ۖ قُلْ هِىَ مَوَٰقِيتُ لِلنَّاسِ وَٱلْحَجِّ ۗ وَلَيْسَ ٱلْبِرُّ بِأَن تَأْتُوا۟ ٱلْبُيُوتَ مِن ظُهُورِهَا وَلَـٰكِنَّ ٱلْبِرَّ مَنِ ٱتَّقَىٰ ۗ وَأْتُوا۟
ٱلْبُيُوتَ مِنْ أَبْوَٰبِهَا ۚ وَٱتَّقُوا۟ ٱللَّهَ لَعَلَّكُمْ تُفْلِحُونَ

It is neither their meat nor their blood that reaches Allah: what reaches Him is your piety. Thus, He has made them subject to you So that you may glorify Allah for having guided you. And give good news to those who do their best at whatever they do. – Surah Al-Hajj 22:37

لَن يَنَالَ ٱللَّهَ لُحُومُهَا وَلَا دِمَآؤُهَا وَلَـٰكِن يَنَالُهُ ٱلتَّقْوَىٰ مِنكُمْ ۚ كَذَٰلِكَ سَخَّرَهَا لَكُمْ لِتُكَبِّرُوا۟ ٱللَّهَ عَلَىٰ مَا هَدَىٰكُمْ ۗ وَبَشِّرِ ٱلْمُحْسِنِينَ

The Book of
Now the tribe of Bani Asad wants to teach me Islam; I would be a loser and all my efforts would be in vain.
ثُمَّ أَصْبَحَتْ بَنُو أَسَدٍ تُعَزِّرُنِي عَلَى الإِسْلاَمِ، خَسِرْتُ إِذًا وَضَلَّ سَعْيِي

And of mankind, there are some (hypocrites) who say: "We believe in Allah and the Last Day" while in fact they believe not. They (think to) deceive Allah and those who believe, while they only deceive themselves, and perceive (it) not! In their hearts is a disease (of doubt and hypocrisy) and Allah has increased their disease. A painful torment is theirs because they used to tell lies.. And when it is said to them: "Make not mischief on the earth," they say: "We are only peacemakers.". Verily! They are the ones who make mischief, but they perceive not. And when it is said to them (hypocrites): "Believe as the people (followers of Muhammad Peace be upon him , Al-Ansar and Al-Muhajirun) have believed," they say: "Shall we believe as the fools have believed?" Verily, they are the fools, but they know not. And when they meet those who believe, they say: "We believe," but when they are alone with their Shayatin (devils – polytheists, hypocrites, etc.), they say: "Truly, we are with you; verily, we were but mocking." Allah mocks at them and gives them increase in their wrong-doings to wander blindly. These are they who have purchased error for guidance, so their commerce was profitless. And they were not guided. – Surah Al-Baqarah 2:8-16
وَمِنَ ٱلنَّاسِ مَن يَقُولُ ءَامَنَّا بِٱللَّهِ وَبِٱلْيَوْمِ ٱلْءَاخِرِ وَمَا هُم بِمُؤْمِنِينَ يُخَـٰدِعُونَ ٱللَّهَ وَٱلَّذِينَ ءَامَنُوا۟ وَمَا يَخْدَعُونَ إِلَّآ أَنفُسَهُمْ وَمَا يَشْعُرُونَ فِى قُلُوبِهِم مَّرَضٌ فَزَادَهُمُ ٱللَّهُ مَرَضًا ۖ وَلَهُمْ عَذَابٌ أَلِيمٌۢ بِمَا كَانُوا۟ يَكْذِبُونَ وَإِذَا قِيلَ لَهُمْ لَا تُفْسِدُوا۟ فِى ٱلْأَرْضِ قَالُوٓا۟ إِنَّمَا نَحْنُ مُصْلِحُونَ أَلَآ إِنَّهُمْ هُمُ ٱلْمُفْسِدُونَ وَلَـٰكِن لَّا يَشْعُرُونَ وَإِذَا قِيلَ لَهُمْ ءَامِنُوا۟ كَمَآ ءَامَنَ ٱلنَّاسُ قَالُوٓا۟ أَنُؤْمِنُ كَمَآ ءَامَنَ ٱلسُّفَهَآءُ ۗ أَلَآ إِنَّهُمْ هُمُ ٱلسُّفَهَآءُ وَلَـٰكِن لَّا يَعْلَمُونَ وَإِذَا لَقُوا۟ ٱلَّذِينَ ءَامَنُوا۟ قَالُوٓا۟ ءَامَنَّا وَإِذَا خَلَوْا۟ إِلَىٰ شَيَـٰطِينِهِمْ قَالُوٓا۟ إِنَّا مَعَكُمْ إِنَّمَا نَحْنُ مُسْتَهْزِءُونَ ٱللَّهُ يَسْتَهْزِئُ بِهِمْ وَيَمُدُّهُمْ فِى طُغْيَـٰنِهِمْ يَعْمَهُونَ أُو۟لَـٰٓئِكَ ٱلَّذِينَ ٱشْتَرَوُا۟ ٱلضَّلَـٰلَةَ بِٱلْهُدَىٰ فَمَا رَبِحَت تِّجَـٰرَتُهُمْ وَمَا كَانُوا۟ مُهْتَدِينَ

Those who believe will say, "Are these the ones who swore by Allah with their strongest oaths that they are with you?" Their works have failed, so they became losers. – Surah Al-Maidah 5:53
وَيَقُولُ ٱلَّذِينَ ءَامَنُوٓا۟ أَهَـٰٓؤُلَآءِ ٱلَّذِينَ أَقْسَمُوا۟ بِٱللَّهِ جَهْدَ أَيْمَـٰنِهِمْ ۙ إِنَّهُمْ لَمَعَكُمْ ۚ حَبِطَتْ أَعْمَـٰلُهُمْ فَأَصْبَحُوا۟ خَـٰسِرِينَ

Do those who disbelieve think that they can take My servants for masters instead of Me? We have prepared Hell for the hospitality of the faithless. Say, "Shall We inform you of the greatest losers in their works?""Those whose efforts in this world are misguided, while they assume that they are doing well." It is they who rejected the communications of their Lord, and the encounter with Him. So their works are in vain. And on the Day of Resurrection, We will consider them of no weight.– Surah Al-Khaf 18:102-105
أَفَحَسِبَ ٱلَّذِينَ كَفَرُوٓا۟ أَن يَتَّخِذُوا۟ عِبَادِى مِن دُونِىٓ أَوْلِيَآءَ ۚ إِنَّآ أَعْتَدْنَا جَهَنَّمَ لِلْكَـٰفِرِينَ نُزُلًا قُلْ هَلْ نُنَبِّئُكُم بِٱلْأَخْسَرِينَ أَعْمَـٰلًا ٱلَّذِينَ ضَلَّ سَعْيُهُمْ فِى ٱلْحَيَوٰةِ ٱلدُّنْيَا وَهُمْ يَحْسَبُونَ أَنَّهُمْ يُحْسِنُونَ صُنْعًا أُو۟لَـٰٓئِكَ ٱلَّذِينَ كَفَرُوا۟ بِـَٔايَـٰتِ رَبِّهِمْ وَلِقَآئِهِۦ فَحَبِطَتْ أَعْمَـٰلُهُمْ فَلَا نُقِيمُ لَهُمْ يَوْمَ ٱلْقِيَـٰمَةِ وَزْنًا

Those who do not expect to meet Us say, "If only the angels were sent down to us, or we could see our Lord." They have grown arrogant within themselves, and have become excessively defiant. On the Day when they see the angels—there will be no good news for

sinners on that Day; and they will say, “A protective refuge.” We will proceed to the works they did, and will turn them into scattered dust.– Surah Al-Furqan 25:21-23
وَقَالَ ٱلَّذِينَ لَا يَرۡجُونَ لِقَآءَنَا لَوۡلَآ أُنزِلَ عَلَيۡنَا ٱلۡمَلَٰٓئِكَةُ أَوۡ نَرَىٰ رَبَّنَاۗ لَقَدِ ٱسۡتَكۡبَرُواْ فِيٓ أَنفُسِهِمۡ وَعَتَوۡ عُتُوّٗا كَبِيرٗا يَوۡمَ يَرَوۡنَ ٱلۡمَلَٰٓئِكَةَ لَا بُشۡرَىٰ يَوۡمَئِذٖ لِّلۡمُجۡرِمِينَ وَيَقُولُونَ حِجۡرٗا مَّحۡجُورٗا وَقَدِمۡنَآ إِلَىٰ مَا عَمِلُواْ مِنۡ عَمَلٖ فَجَعَلۡنَٰهُ هَبَآءٗ مَّنثُورًا

Narrated Sa`d: I was one of (the first) seven (who had embraced Islam) with Allah’s Messenger ﷺ and we had nothing to eat then, except the leaves of the Habala or Hubula tree, so that our stool used to be similar to that of sheep. Now the tribe of Bani Asad wants to teach me Islam; I would be a loser and all my efforts would be in vain (if I learn Islam anew from them). – Al-Bukhari 5412
حَدَّثَنَا عَبْدُ اللَّهِ بْنُ مُحَمَّدٍ، حَدَّثَنَا وَهْبُ بْنُ جَرِيرٍ، حَدَّثَنَا شُعْبَةُ، عَنْ إِسْمَاعِيلَ، عَنْ قَيْسٍ، عَنْ سَعْدٍ، قَالَ رَأَيْتُنِي سَابِعَ سَبْعَةٍ مَعَ النَّبِيِّ صلى الله عليه وسلم مَا لَنَا طَعَامٌ إِلاَّ وَرَقُ الْحُبْلَةِ ـ أَوِ الْحَبَلَةِ ـ حَتَّى يَضَعَ أَحَدُنَا مَا تَضَعُ الشَّاةُ، ثُمَّ أَصْبَحَتْ بَنُو أَسَدٍ تُعَزِّرُنِي عَلَى الإِسْلاَمِ، خَسِرْتُ إِذًا وَضَلَّ سَعْيِي.

We will certainly test you, until We know those among you who strive, and those who are steadfast, and We will test your reactions.Those who disbelieve, and hinder from the path of Allah, and oppose the Messenger after guidance has become clear to them—they will not hurt Allah in the least, but He will nullify their deeds. O you who believe! Obey Allah, and obey the Messenger, and do not let your deeds go to waste.– Surah Muhammad 47:31-33
وَلَنَبۡلُوَنَّكُمۡ حَتَّىٰ نَعۡلَمَ ٱلۡمُجَٰهِدِينَ مِنكُمۡ وَٱلصَّٰبِرِينَ وَنَبۡلُوَاْ أَخۡبَارَكُمۡ إِنَّ ٱلَّذِينَ كَفَرُواْ وَصَدُّواْ عَن سَبِيلِ ٱللَّهِ وَشَآقُّواْ ٱلرَّسُولَ مِنۢ بَعۡدِ مَا تَبَيَّنَ لَهُمُ ٱلۡهُدَىٰ لَن يَضُرُّواْ ٱللَّهَ شَيۡـٔٗا وَسَيُحۡبِطُ أَعۡمَٰلَهُمۡ يَٰٓأَيُّهَا ٱلَّذِينَ ءَامَنُوٓاْ أَطِيعُواْ ٱللَّهَ وَأَطِيعُواْ ٱلرَّسُولَ وَلَا تُبۡطِلُوٓاْ أَعۡمَٰلَكُمۡ

The Book of

Verily, those who believe not in the Hereafter, We have made their deeds fair-seeming to them

إِنَّ ٱلَّذِينَ لَا يُؤْمِنُونَ بِٱلْـَٔاخِرَةِ زَيَّنَّا لَهُمْ أَعْمَـٰلَهُمْ

Narrated Ghailan: Anas said "You people do (bad) deeds (commit sins) which seem in your eyes as tiny (minute) than hair while we used to consider those (very deeds) during the life-time of the Prophet ﷺ as destructive sins." – Al-Bukhari 6492

حَدَّثَنَا أَبُو الْوَلِيدِ، حَدَّثَنَا مَهْدِيٌّ، عَنْ غَيْلاَنَ، عَنْ أَنَسٍ ـ رضى الله عنه ـ قَالَ إِنَّكُمْ لَتَعْمَلُونَ أَعْمَالاً هِيَ أَدَقُّ فِي أَعْيُنِكُمْ مِنَ الشَّعَرِ، إِنْ كُنَّا نَعُدُّهَا عَلَى عَهْدِ النَّبِيِّ صلى الله عليه وسلم الْمُوبِقَاتِ. قَالَ أَبُو عَبْدِ اللَّهِ يَعْنِي بِذَلِكَ الْمُهْلِكَاتِ.

If only, when Our calamity came upon them, they humbled themselves. But their hearts hardened, and Satan made their deeds appear good to them..– Surah Al-An'am 6:43

فَلَوْلَآ إِذْ جَآءَهُم بَأْسُنَا تَضَرَّعُوا۟ وَلَـٰكِن قَسَتْ قُلُوبُهُمْ وَزَيَّنَ لَهُمُ ٱلشَّيْطَـٰنُ مَا كَانُوا۟ يَعْمَلُونَ

Do not insult those they call upon besides Allah, lest they insult Allah out of hostility and ignorance. We made attractive to every community their deeds. Then to their Lord is their return, and He will inform them of what they used to do – Surah Al-An'am 6:108

وَلَا تَسُبُّوا۟ ٱلَّذِينَ يَدْعُونَ مِن دُونِ ٱللَّهِ فَيَسُبُّوا۟ ٱللَّهَ عَدْوًۢا بِغَيْرِ عِلْمٍۢ ۗ كَذَٰلِكَ زَيَّنَّا لِكُلِّ أُمَّةٍ عَمَلَهُمْ ثُمَّ إِلَىٰ رَبِّهِم مَّرْجِعُهُمْ فَيُنَبِّئُهُم بِمَا كَانُوا۟ يَعْمَلُونَ

Likewise, their idols entice many idolaters to kill their children, in order to lead them to their ruin, and confuse them in their religion. Had Allah willed, they would not have done it; so leave them to their fraud. – Surah Al-An'am 6:137

وَكَذَٰلِكَ زَيَّنَ لِكَثِيرٍ مِّنَ ٱلْمُشْرِكِينَ قَتْلَ أَوْلَـٰدِهِمْ شُرَكَآؤُهُمْ لِيُرْدُوهُمْ وَلِيَلْبِسُوا۟ عَلَيْهِمْ دِينَهُمْ ۖ وَلَوْ شَآءَ ٱللَّهُ مَا فَعَلُوهُ ۖ فَذَرْهُمْ وَمَا يَفْتَرُونَ

Satan made their deeds appear good to them, and said, "You cannot be defeated by any people today,and I am at your side." But when the two armies came in sight of one another, he turned on his heels, and said, "I am innocent of you; I see what you do not see; I fear Allah; Allah is severe in punishment."– Surah Al-Anfal 8:48

وَإِذْ زَيَّنَ لَهُمُ ٱلشَّيْطَـٰنُ أَعْمَـٰلَهُمْ وَقَالَ لَا غَالِبَ لَكُمُ ٱلْيَوْمَ مِنَ ٱلنَّاسِ وَإِنِّى جَارٌ لَّكُمْ ۖ فَلَمَّا تَرَآءَتِ ٱلْفِئَتَانِ نَكَصَ عَلَىٰ عَقِبَيْهِ وَقَالَ إِنِّى بَرِىٓءٌ مِّنكُمْ إِنِّىٓ أَرَىٰ مَا لَا تَرَوْنَ إِنِّىٓ أَخَافُ ٱللَّهَ ۚ وَٱللَّهُ شَدِيدُ ٱلْعِقَابِ

Postponement is an increase in disbelief—by which those who disbelieve are led astray. They allow it one year, and forbid it another year, in order to conform to the number made sacred by Allah, thus permitting what Allah has forbidden.The evil of their deeds seems good to them. Allah does not guide the disbelieving people..– Surah At-Taubah 9:37

إِنَّمَا ٱلنَّسِىٓءُ زِيَادَةٌ فِى ٱلْكُفْرِ ۖ يُضَلُّ بِهِ ٱلَّذِينَ كَفَرُوا۟ يُحِلُّونَهُۥ عَامًا وَيُحَرِّمُونَهُۥ عَامًا لِّيُوَاطِـُٔوا۟ عِدَّةَ مَا حَرَّمَ ٱللَّهُ فَيُحِلُّوا۟ مَا حَرَّمَ ٱللَّهُ ۚ زُيِّنَ لَهُمْ سُوٓءُ أَعْمَـٰلِهِمْ ۗ وَٱللَّهُ لَا يَهْدِى ٱلْقَوْمَ ٱلْكَـٰفِرِينَ

Whenever adversity touches the human being, he prays to Us reclining on his side, or sitting, or standing. But when We have he passes on his way as if he had never invoked Us for a harm that touched him! Thus it seems fair to the Musrifun that which they used to do. – Surah Yunus 10:12

وَإِذَا مَسَّ ٱلْإِنسَـٰنَ ٱلضُّرُّ دَعَانَا لِجَنۢبِهِۦٓ أَوْ قَاعِدًا أَوْ قَآئِمًا فَلَمَّا كَشَفْنَا عَنْهُ ضُرَّهُۥ مَرَّ كَأَن لَّمْ يَدْعُنَآ إِلَىٰ ضُرٍّ مَّسَّهُۥ ۚ كَذَٰلِكَ زُيِّنَ لِلْمُسْرِفِينَ مَا كَانُوا۟ يَعْمَلُونَ

Is He who is watchful over the deeds of every soul? Yet they ascribe associates to Allah. Say, "Name them! Or are you informing Him of something on earth He does not know, or is it a show of words?" In fact, the scheming of those who disbelieve is made to appear good to them, and they are averted from the path. Whomever Allah misguides has no guide. – Surah Ar-Ra'd 13:33

أَفَمَنْ هُوَ قَآئِمٌ عَلَىٰ كُلِّ نَفْسٍ بِمَا كَسَبَتْ ۗ وَجَعَلُوا۟ لِلَّهِ شُرَكَآءَ قُلْ سَمُّوهُمْ ۚ أَمْ تُنَبِّـُٔونَهُۥ بِمَا لَا يَعْلَمُ فِى ٱلْأَرْضِ أَم بِظَـٰهِرٍ مِّنَ ٱلْقَوْلِ ۗ بَلْ زُيِّنَ لِلَّذِينَ كَفَرُوا۟ مَكْرُهُمْ وَصُدُّوا۟ عَنِ ٱلسَّبِيلِ ۗ وَمَن يُضْلِلِ ٱللَّهُ فَمَا لَهُۥ مِنْ هَادٍ

By Allah, We sent messengers to communities before you, but Satan made their deeds appear alluring to them. He is their master today, and they will have a painful punishment. – Surah An-Nahl 16:63

تَٱللَّهِ لَقَدْ أَرْسَلْنَآ إِلَىٰٓ أُمَمٍ مِّن قَبْلِكَ فَزَيَّنَ لَهُمُ ٱلشَّيْطَـٰنُ أَعْمَـٰلَهُمْ فَهُوَ وَلِيُّهُمُ ٱلْيَوْمَ وَلَهُمْ عَذَابٌ أَلِيمٌ

As for those who do not believe in the Hereafter: We made their deeds appear good to them, so they wander aimlessly.– Surah An-Naml 27:4

إِنَّ ٱلَّذِينَ لَا يُؤْمِنُونَ بِٱلْـَٔاخِرَةِ زَيَّنَّا لَهُمْ أَعْمَـٰلَهُمْ فَهُمْ يَعْمَهُونَ

I found her and her people worshiping the sun, instead of Allah. Satan made their conduct appear good to them, and diverted them from the path, so they are not guided. — Surah An-Naml 27:24

وَجَدتُّهَا وَقَوْمَهَا يَسْجُدُونَ لِلشَّمْسِ مِن دُونِ ٱللَّهِ وَزَيَّنَ لَهُمُ ٱلشَّيْطَـٰنُ أَعْمَـٰلَهُمْ فَصَدَّهُمْ عَنِ ٱلسَّبِيلِ فَهُمْ لَا يَهْتَدُونَ

And Aad and Thamood. It has become clear to you from their dwellings. Satan embellished for them their deeds, barring them from the path, even though they could see. – Surah Al-Ankabut 29:38

وَعَادًا وَثَمُودَا۟ وَقَد تَّبَيَّنَ لَكُم مِّن مَّسَـٰكِنِهِمْ ۖ وَزَيَّنَ لَهُمُ ٱلشَّيْطَـٰنُ أَعْمَـٰلَهُمْ فَصَدَّهُمْ عَنِ ٱلسَّبِيلِ وَكَانُوا۟ مُسْتَبْصِرِينَ

Those who disbelieve will suffer a harsh punishment, but those who believe and do righteous deeds will have forgiveness and a great reward. What of him whose evil deed was made attractive to him, and so he regards it as good? Allah leads astray whomever He wills, and He guides whomever He wills. Therefore, do not waste yourself sorrowing over them. Allah knows exactly what they do. –Surah Fatir 35:7&8

ٱلَّذِينَ كَفَرُوا۟ لَهُمْ عَذَابٌ شَدِيدٌ ۖ وَٱلَّذِينَ ءَامَنُوا۟ وَعَمِلُوا۟ ٱلصَّـٰلِحَـٰتِ لَهُم مَّغْفِرَةٌ وَأَجْرٌ كَبِيرٌ. أَفَمَن زُيِّنَ لَهُۥ سُوٓءُ عَمَلِهِۦ فَرَءَاهُ حَسَنًا ۖ فَإِنَّ ٱللَّهَ يُضِلُّ مَن يَشَآءُ وَيَهْدِى مَن يَشَآءُ ۖ فَلَا تَذْهَبْ نَفْسُكَ عَلَيْهِمْ حَسَرَٰتٍ ۚ إِنَّ ٱللَّهَ عَلِيمٌۢ بِمَا يَصْنَعُونَ

And Pharaoh said, "O Hamaan, build me a tower, that I may reach the pathways. The pathways of the heavens, so that I may glance at the God of Moses; though I think he is lying." Thus Pharaoh's evil deeds were made to appear good to him, and he was averted from the path. Pharaoh's guile was only in defeat. – Surah Ghafir 40:36&37

وَقَالَ فِرْعَوْنُ يَـٰهَـٰمَـٰنُ ٱبْنِ لِى صَرْحًا لَّعَلِّىٓ أَبْلُغُ ٱلْأَسْبَـٰبَ أَسْبَـٰبَ ٱلسَّمَـٰوَٰتِ فَأَطَّلِعَ إِلَىٰٓ إِلَـٰهِ مُوسَىٰ وَإِنِّى لَأَظُنُّهُۥ كَـٰذِبًا ۚ وَكَذَٰلِكَ زُيِّنَ لِفِرْعَوْنَ سُوٓءُ عَمَلِهِۦ وَصُدَّ عَنِ ٱلسَّبِيلِ ۚ وَمَا كَيْدُ فِرْعَوْنَ إِلَّا فِى تَبَابٍ

We had assigned companions for them, who glamorized to them what was in front of them, and what was behind them. And the Word proved true against them in communities of jinn and humans that have passed away before them. They were losers. – Surah Al-Fussilat 41:25

وَقَيَّضْنَا لَهُمْ قُرَنَآءَ فَزَيَّنُوا۟ لَهُم مَّا بَيْنَ أَيْدِيهِمْ وَمَا خَلْفَهُمْ وَحَقَّ عَلَيْهِمُ ٱلْقَوْلُ فِىٓ أُمَمٍ قَدْ خَلَتْ مِن قَبْلِهِم مِّنَ ٱلْجِنِّ وَٱلْإِنسِ ۖ إِنَّهُمْ كَانُوا۟ خَـٰسِرِينَ

The Book of

None feels secure from the Plan of Allah except the people who are the losers.

فَلَا يَأْمَنُ مَكْرَ ٱللَّهِ إِلَّا ٱلْقَوْمُ ٱلْخَـٰسِرُونَ

And when the servant of Allah got up calling on Him, they almost fell on him in a mass. Say, "I pray only to my Lord, and I never associate anyone with Him." Say, "It is not in my power to harm you, nor to bring you to right conduct." Say, "No one can protect me from Allah, and I will not find any refuge except with Him. Except for a proclamation from Allah and His messages. He who defies Allah and His Messenger—for him is the Fire of Hell, in which they will dwell forever." – Surah Al-Jinn 72:19-23

وَأَنَّهُۥ لَمَّا قَامَ عَبْدُ ٱللَّهِ يَدْعُوهُ كَادُوا۟ يَكُونُونَ عَلَيْهِ لِبَدًا قُلْ إِنَّمَآ أَدْعُوا۟ رَبِّى وَلَآ أُشْرِكُ بِهِۦٓ أَحَدًا قُلْ إِنِّى لَآ أَمْلِكُ لَكُمْ ضَرًّا وَلَا رَشَدًا قُلْ إِنِّى لَن يُجِيرَنِى مِنَ ٱللَّهِ أَحَدٌ وَلَنْ أَجِدَ مِن دُونِهِۦ مُلْتَحَدًا إِلَّا بَلَـٰغًا مِّنَ ٱللَّهِ وَرِسَـٰلَـٰتِهِۦ ۚ وَمَن يَعْصِ ٱللَّهَ وَرَسُولَهُۥ فَإِنَّ لَهُۥ نَارَ جَهَنَّمَ خَـٰلِدِينَ فِيهَآ أَبَدًا

He who, I hope, will forgive my sins on the Day of the Reckoning." – Surah Ash-Shu'ara 26:82

وَٱلَّذِىٓ أَطْمَعُ أَن يَغْفِرَ لِى خَطِيٓـَٔتِى يَوْمَ ٱلدِّينِ

Our Lord, do not make us a target for those who disbelieve, and forgive us, our Lord. You are indeed the Mighty and Wise." – Surah Al-Mumtahanah 60:5

رَبَّنَا لَا تَجْعَلْنَا فِتْنَةً لِّلَّذِينَ كَفَرُوا۟ وَٱغْفِرْ لَنَا رَبَّنَآ ۖ إِنَّكَ أَنتَ ٱلْعَزِيزُ ٱلْحَكِيمُ

If Allah were to hold mankind for their injustices, He would not leave upon it a single creature, but He postpones them until an appointed time. Then, when their time arrives, they will not delay it by one hour, nor will they advance it. – Surah An-Nahl 16:61

وَلَوْ يُؤَاخِذُ ٱللَّهُ ٱلنَّاسَ بِظُلْمِهِم مَّا تَرَكَ عَلَيْهَا مِن دَآبَّةٍ وَلَـٰكِن يُؤَخِّرُهُمْ إِلَىٰٓ أَجَلٍ مُّسَمًّى ۖ فَإِذَا جَآءَ أَجَلُهُمْ لَا يَسْتَـْٔخِرُونَ سَاعَةً وَلَا يَسْتَقْدِمُونَ

Say, "If the Final Home with Allah is yours alone, to the exclusion of all other people, then wish for death if you are sincere." – Surah Al-Baqarah 2:94

قُلْ إِن كَانَتْ لَكُمُ ٱلدَّارُ ٱلْـَٔاخِرَةُ عِندَ ٱللَّهِ خَالِصَةً مِّن دُونِ ٱلنَّاسِ فَتَمَنَّوُا۟ ٱلْمَوْتَ إِن كُنتُمْ صَـٰدِقِينَ

Their Lord's punishment Is not to be taken for granted. — Surah Al-Ma'arij 70:28

إِنَّ عَذَابَ رَبِّهِمْ غَيْرُ مَأْمُونٍ

Narrated Al-Harith bin Suwaid: `Abdullah bin Mas`ud related to us two narrations: One from the Prophet ﷺ and the other from himself, saying: A believer sees his sins as if he were sitting under a mountain which, he is afraid, may fall on him; whereas the wicked person considers his sins as flies passing over his nose and he just drives them away like this." Abu Shihab (the sub-narrator) moved his hand over his nose in illustration. (Ibn Mas`ud added): Allah's Messenger ﷺ said, "Allah is more pleased with the repentance of His slave than a man who encamps at a place where his life is jeopardized, but he has his riding beast carrying his food and water. He then rests his head and sleeps for a short while and wakes to find his riding beast gone. (He starts looking for it) and suffers from severe heat and thirst or what Allah wished (him to suffer from). He then says, 'I will go back to my place.' He returns and sleeps again, and then (getting up), he raises his head to find his riding beast standing beside him." – Al-Bukhari 6308

حَدَّثَنَا أَحْمَدُ بْنُ يُونُسَ، حَدَّثَنَا أَبُو شِهَابٍ، عَنِ الأَعْمَشِ، عَنْ عُمَارَةَ بْنِ عُمَيْرٍ، عَنِ الْحَارِثِ بْنِ سُوَيْدٍ، حَدَّثَنَا عَبْدُ اللَّهِ، حَدِيثَيْنِ أَحَدُهُمَا عَنِ النَّبِيِّ صلى الله عليه وسلم وَالآخَرُ عَنْ نَفْسِهِ، قَالَ " إِنَّ الْمُؤْمِنَ يَرَى ذُنُوبَهُ كَأَنَّهُ قَاعِدٌ تَحْتَ جَبَلٍ يَخَافُ أَنْ يَقَعَ عَلَيْهِ، وَإِنَّ الْفَاجِرَ يَرَى ذُنُوبَهُ كَذُبَابٍ مَرَّ عَلَى أَنْفِهِ ". فَقَالَ بِهِ هَكَذَا قَالَ أَبُو شِهَابٍ بِيَدِهِ فَوْقَ أَنْفِهِ. ثُمَّ قَالَ " لَلَّهُ أَفْرَحُ بِتَوْبَةِ عَبْدِهِ مِنْ رَجُلٍ نَزَلَ مَنْزِلاً، وَبِهِ مَهْلَكَةٌ، وَمَعَهُ رَاحِلَتُهُ عَلَيْهَا طَعَامُهُ وَشَرَابُهُ، فَوَضَعَ رَأْسَهُ فَنَامَ نَوْمَةً، فَاسْتَيْقَظَ وَقَدْ ذَهَبَتْ رَاحِلَتُهُ، حَتَّى اشْتَدَّ عَلَيْهِ الْحَرُّ وَالْعَطَشُ أَوْ مَا شَاءَ اللَّهُ، قَالَ أَرْجِعُ إِلَى مَكَانِي. فَرَجَعَ فَنَامَ نَوْمَةً، ثُمَّ رَفَعَ رَأْسَهُ، فَإِذَا رَاحِلَتُهُ عِنْدَهُ ". تَابَعَهُ أَبُو عَوَانَةَ وَجَرِيرٌ عَنِ الأَعْمَشِ. وَقَالَ أَبُو أُسَامَةَ حَدَّثَنَا الأَعْمَشُ حَدَّثَنَا عُمَارَةُ سَمِعْتُ الْحَارِثَ. وَقَالَ شُعْبَةُ وَأَبُو مُسْلِمٍ عَنِ الأَعْمَشِ عَنْ إِبْرَاهِيمَ التَّيْمِيِّ عَنِ الْحَارِثِ بْنِ سُوَيْدٍ. وَقَالَ أَبُو مُعَاوِيَةَ حَدَّثَنَا الأَعْمَشُ عَنْ عُمَارَةَ عَنِ الأَسْوَدِ عَنْ عَبْدِ اللَّهِ وَعَنْ إِبْرَاهِيمَ التَّيْمِيِّ عَنِ الْحَارِثِ بْنِ سُوَيْدٍ عَنْ عَبْدِ اللَّهِ

Narrated Qais bin 'Ubada: I was sitting in a gathering in which there was Sa`d bin Malik and Ibn `Umar. `Abdullah bin Salam passed in front of them and they said, "This man is from the people of Paradise." I said to `Abdullah bin Salam, "They said so-and-so." He replied, "Subhan Allah! They ought not to have said things of which they have no knowledge, but I saw (in a dream) that a post was fixed in a green garden. At the top of the post there was a handhold and below it there was a servant. I was asked to climb (the post). So I climbed it till I got hold of the handhold." Then I narrated this dream to Allah's Messenger ﷺ .Allah's Apostle said, "`Abdullah will die while still holding the firm reliable handhold (i.e., Islam). – Al-Bukhari 7010

حَدَّثَنَا عَبْدُ اللَّهِ بْنُ مُحَمَّدٍ الْجُعْفِيُّ، حَدَّثَنَا حَرَمِيُّ بْنُ عُمَارَةَ، حَدَّثَنَا قُرَّةُ بْنُ خَالِدٍ، عَنْ مُحَمَّدِ بْنِ سِيرِينَ، قَالَ قَالَ قَيْسُ بْنُ عُبَادٍ كُنْتُ فِي حَلْقَةٍ فِيهَا سَعْدُ بْنُ مَالِكٍ وَابْنُ عُمَرَ فَمَرَّ عَبْدُ اللَّهِ بْنُ سَلاَمٍ فَقَالُوا هَذَا رَجُلٌ مِنْ أَهْلِ الْجَنَّةِ. فَقُلْتُ لَهُ إِنَّهُمْ قَالُوا كَذَا وَكَذَا. قَالَ سُبْحَانَ اللَّهِ مَا كَانَ يَنْبَغِي لَهُمْ أَنْ يَقُولُوا مَا لَيْسَ لَهُمْ بِهِ عِلْمٌ، إِنَّمَا رَأَيْتُ كَأَنَّمَا عَمُودٌ وُضِعَ فِي رَوْضَةٍ خَضْرَاءَ، فَنُصِبَ فِيهَا وَفِي رَأْسِهَا عُرْوَةٌ وَفِي أَسْفَلِهَا مِنْصَفٌ ـ وَالْمِنْصَفُ الْوَصِيفُ ـ فَقِيلَ ارْقَهْ. فَرَقِيتُ حَتَّى أَخَذْتُ بِالْعُرْوَةِ. فَقَصَصْتُهَا عَلَى رَسُولِ اللَّهِ صلى الله عليه وسلم فَقَالَ رَسُولُ اللَّهِ صلى الله عليه وسلم " يَمُوتُ عَبْدُ اللَّهِ وَهْوَ آخِذٌ بِالْعُرْوَةِ الْوُثْقَى ".

Do they feel safe from Allah's plan? None feel safe from Allah's plan except the losing people. – Surah Al-A'raf 7:99

أَفَأَمِنُوا۟ مَكْرَ ٱللَّهِ ۚ فَلَا يَأْمَنُ مَكْرَ ٱللَّهِ إِلَّا ٱلْقَوْمُ ٱلْخَـٰسِرُونَ

Narrated Abu Musa: The sun eclipsed and the Prophet ﷺ got up, being afraid that it might be the Hour (i.e. Day of Judgment). He went to the Mosque and offered the prayer with the longest Qiyam, bowing and prostration that I had ever seen him doing. Then he said, "These signs which Allah sends do not occur because of the life or death of somebody, but Allah makes His worshipers afraid by them. So when you see anything thereof, proceed to remember Allah, invoke Him and ask for His forgiveness." Sahih al-Bukhari 1059

حَدَّثَنَا مُحَمَّدُ بْنُ الْعَلاَءِ، قَالَ حَدَّثَنَا أَبُو أُسَامَةَ، عَنْ بُرَيْدِ بْنِ عَبْدِ اللَّهِ، عَنْ أَبِي بُرْدَةَ، عَنْ أَبِي مُوسَى، قَالَ خَسَفَتِ الشَّمْسُ، فَقَامَ النَّبِيُّ صلى الله عليه وسلم فَزِعًا، يَخْشَى أَنْ تَكُونَ السَّاعَةُ، فَأَتَى الْمَسْجِدَ، فَصَلَّى بِأَطْوَلِ قِيَامٍ وَرُكُوعٍ وَسُجُودٍ رَأَيْتُهُ قَطُّ يَفْعَلُهُ وَقَالَ " هَذِهِ الآيَاتُ الَّتِي يُرْسِلُ اللَّهُ لاَ تَكُونُ لِمَوْتِ أَحَدٍ وَلاَ لِحَيَاتِهِ، وَلَكِنْ يُخَوِّفُ اللَّهُ بِهِ عِبَادَهُ، فَإِذَا رَأَيْتُمْ شَيْئًا مِنْ ذَلِكَ فَافْزَعُوا إِلَى ذِكْرِهِ وَدُعَائِهِ وَاسْتِغْفَارِهِ ".

Narrated Anas: Whenever a strong wind blew, anxiety appeared on the face of the Prophet (fearing that wind might be a sign of Allah's wrath). – Sahih al-Bukhari 1034

حَدَّثَنَا سَعِيدُ بْنُ أَبِي مَرْيَمَ، قَالَ أَخْبَرَنَا مُحَمَّدُ بْنُ جَعْفَرٍ، قَالَ أَخْبَرَنِي حُمَيْدٌ، أَنَّهُ سَمِعَ أَنَسًا، يَقُولُ كَانَتِ الرِّيحُ الشَّدِيدَةُ إِذَا هَبَّتْ عُرِفَ ذَلِكَ فِي وَجْهِ النَّبِيِّ صلى الله عليه وسلم.

And Ibrāhīm At-Taimi said, "When I compare my talks with my deeds (then I find that my deeds are deficient compared with my talks), I am afraid, my deeds deny what I talk." And

Ibn Abī Mulaika _said, "I met and thirty Companions of the Prophet each of them was afraid of becoming a hypocrite and none of them said that he was as strong in belief as the angel Jibril (Gabriel) or Mikãel (Michael)." And Al-Hasan (Al-Başrī) said, "It is only a faithful believer who dreads hypocrisy and only a hypocrite who considers himself safe (is not afraid of hypocrisy)." And one should be afraid, not to persist in hypocrisy and disobedience of Allah (by committing sins) without repenting to Allah immediately, as is referred to in the Statement of Allah : "And (they) do not persist in what (wrong) they have done, while they know." (V.3:135). – Sahihl Al-Bukhari vol 1 pg . 79

و قال إبراهيم آلتيمي: ما عرضت قولي على عملي الا خشيت أن أكون مكذبا، و قال ابن أبي مليكة : أدركت ثلاثين من أصحاب النبي كلهم يخاف النفاق على نفسه، ما منهم احد يقول إنه على إيمان جبريل و ميكايل، و يذكر عن الحسن : ما خلفه الا مؤمن و لا امنه الا منافق. و ما يحذر من الإصرار على القاتل و العصيان من غير توبه لقول الله عز وجل : (و لم يصلوا على ما فعلوا و هم يعلمون) [آل عمران : ١٣٥]

Those who disbelieve in it ˹ask to˺ hasten it ˹mockingly˺. But the believers are fearful of it, knowing that it is the truth. Surely those who dispute about the Hour have gone far astray. Surah Ash-Shura 42:18

يَسْتَعْجِلُ بِهَا ٱلَّذِينَ لَا يُؤْمِنُونَ بِهَا ۖ وَٱلَّذِينَ ءَامَنُوا۟ مُشْفِقُونَ مِنْهَا وَيَعْلَمُونَ أَنَّهَا ٱلْحَقُّ ۗ أَلَآ إِنَّ ٱلَّذِينَ يُمَارُونَ فِى ٱلسَّاعَةِ لَفِى ضَلَـٰلٍۭ بَعِيدٍ

Say, "I am not the first messenger ever sent, nor do I know what will happen to me or you. I only follow what is revealed to me. And I am only sent with a clear warning." Surah Al-Ahqaf 46:9

قُلْ مَا كُنتُ بِدْعًا مِّنَ ٱلرُّسُلِ وَمَآ أَدْرِى مَا يُفْعَلُ بِى وَلَا بِكُمْ ۖ إِنْ أَتَّبِعُ إِلَّا مَا يُوحَىٰٓ إِلَىَّ وَمَآ أَنَا۠ إِلَّا نَذِيرٌ مُّبِينٌ

They will say, "Before ˹this reward˺ we used to be in awe ˹of Allah˺ in the midst of our people. Surah At-Tur 52:26

قَالُوٓا۟ إِنَّا كُنَّا قَبْلُ فِىٓ أَهْلِنَا مُشْفِقِينَ

Those they call upon are themselves seeking means of access to their Lord, vying to be nearer, and hoping for His mercy, and fearing His punishment. The punishment of your Lord is to be dreaded. – Surah Al-Isra 17:57

أُو۟لَـٰٓئِكَ ٱلَّذِينَ يَدْعُونَ يَبْتَغُونَ إِلَىٰ رَبِّهِمُ ٱلْوَسِيلَةَ أَيُّهُمْ أَقْرَبُ وَيَرْجُونَ رَحْمَتَهُۥ وَيَخَافُونَ عَذَابَهُۥٓ ۚ إِنَّ عَذَابَ رَبِّكَ كَانَ مَحْذُورًا

And do not corrupt on earth after its reformation, and pray to Him with fear and hope. Allah's mercy is close to the doers of good. Surah Al-A'raf 7:56

وَلَا تُفْسِدُوا۟ فِى ٱلْأَرْضِ بَعْدَ إِصْلَـٰحِهَا وَٱدْعُوهُ خَوْفًا وَطَمَعًا ۚ إِنَّ رَحْمَتَ ٱللَّهِ قَرِيبٌ مِّنَ ٱلْمُحْسِنِينَ

Their sides shun their beds, as they pray to their Lord, out of reverence and hope; and from Our provisions to them, they give. – Surah Sajdah 32:16

تَتَجَافَىٰ جُنُوبُهُمْ عَنِ ٱلْمَضَاجِعِ يَدْعُونَ رَبَّهُمْ خَوْفًا وَطَمَعًا وَمِمَّا رَزَقْنَـٰهُمْ يُنفِقُونَ

Do they then feel secure that there will not come up to them an Enveloper of the torment of Allah, or that the Hour will not come to them suddently and they are not aware. – Surah Yusuf 12:107

أَفَأَمِنُوٓا۟ أَن تَأْتِيَهُمْ غَـٰشِيَةٌ مِّنْ عَذَابِ ٱللَّهِ أَوْ تَأْتِيَهُمُ ٱلسَّاعَةُ بَغْتَةً وَهُمْ لَا يَشْعُرُونَ

The Book of

And that none of us shall take others as lords besides Allah.

وَلَا يَتَّخِذَ بَعْضُنَا بَعْضًا أَرْبَابًا مِّن دُونِ ٱللَّهِ

Narrated Fatima bint Al-Mundhir: Asma' bint Abi Bakr As-Siddiq said, "I went to 'Aishah and the people were offering Salat. I asked her, 'What is wrong with the people ?' She pointed towards the sky with her head. I asked her, 'Is there a sign ?' 'Aishah nodded with her head meaning 'Yes'." Asma' added, "Allah's Messengerﷺ prolonged the Salat to such an extent that I fainted. There was a waterskin by my side and I opened it and poured some water on my head. When Allah's Messengerﷺ finished Salat, and the solar eclipse had cleared, the Prophetﷺ addressed the people and praised Allah as He deserves and said, 'Amma ba'du'." Asma' further said, "Some Ansari women started talking, so I turned to them in order to make them quiet. I asked 'Aishah what the Prophetﷺ had said. 'Aishah said: 'He said, 'I have seen things at this place of mine which were never shown to me before; (I have seen) even Paradise and Hell. And, no doubt it has been revealed to me that you (people) will be put in trial in your graves like or nearly like the trial of Masih Ad-Dajjal. (The angels) will come to everyone of you and ask him, 'What do you know about this man (Prophet Muhammadﷺ)?" The faithful believer or firm believer (Hisham was In doubt Ih word the Prophetﷺ used), will say, 'He is Allah's Messengerﷺ and he is Muhammadﷺ who came to us with clear evidences and guidance. So we believed him, accepted his teachings and followed and trusted his teaching.' Then the angels will tell him to sleep (in peace) as they have come to know that he was a believer. But the hypocrite or a doubtful person (Hisham is not sure as to which word the Prophetﷺ used), will be asked what he knew about this man (Prophet Muhammedﷺ .(He will say, 'I do not know but I heard the people saying something (about him) so I said the same' " Hisham added, "Fatima told me that she remembered that narration completely by heart except that she said about the hypocrite or a doubtful person that he will be punished severely." – Al-Bukhari 922

وَقَالَ مَحْمُودٌ حَدَّثَنَا أَبُو أُسَامَةَ، قَالَ حَدَّثَنَا هِشَامُ بْنُ عُرْوَةَ، قَالَ أَخْبَرَتْنِي فَاطِمَةُ بِنْتُ الْمُنْذِرِ، عَنْ أَسْمَاءَ بِنْتِ أَبِي بَكْرٍ، قَالَتْ دَخَلْتُ عَلَى عَائِشَةَ ـ رضى الله عنها ـ وَالنَّاسُ يُصَلُّونَ قُلْتُ مَا شَأْنُ النَّاسِ فَأَشَارَتْ بِرَأْسِهَا إِلَى السَّمَاءِ. فَقُلْتُ آيَةٌ فَأَشَارَتْ بِرَأْسِهَا أَىْ نَعَمْ. قَالَتْ فَأَطَالَ رَسُولُ اللَّهِ صلى الله عليه وسلم جِدًّا حَتَّى تَجَلاَّنِي الْغَشْىُ وَإِلَى جَنْبِي قِرْبَةٌ فِيهَا مَاءٌ فَفَتَحْتُهَا فَجَعَلْتُ أَصُبُّ مِنْهَا عَلَى رَأْسِي، فَانْصَرَفَ رَسُولُ اللَّهِ صلى الله عليه وسلم وَقَدْ تَجَلَّتِ الشَّمْسُ، فَخَطَبَ النَّاسَ، وَحَمِدَ اللَّهَ بِمَا هُوَ أَهْلُهُ ثُمَّ قَالَ " أَمَّا بَعْدُ ". قَالَتْ وَلَغِطَ نِسْوَةٌ مِنَ الأَنْصَارِ، فَانْكَفَأْتُ إِلَيْهِنَّ لأُسَكِّتَهُنَّ فَقُلْتُ لِعَائِشَةَ مَا قَالَ قَالَتْ قَالَ " مَا مِنْ شَىْءٍ لَمْ أَكُنْ أُرِيتُهُ إِلاَّ قَدْ رَأَيْتُهُ فِي مَقَامِي هَذَا حَتَّى الْجَنَّةَ وَالنَّارَ، وَإِنَّهُ قَدْ أُوحِيَ إِلَىَّ أَنَّكُمْ تُفْتَنُونَ فِي الْقُبُورِ مِثْلَ ـ أَوْ قَرِيبَ مِنْ ـ فِتْنَةِ الْمَسِيحِ الدَّجَّالِ، يُؤْتَى أَحَدُكُمْ، فَيُقَالُ لَهُ مَا عِلْمُكَ بِهَذَا الرَّجُلِ فَأَمَّا الْمُؤْمِنُ ـ أَوْ قَالَ الْمُوقِنُ شَكَّ هِشَامٌ ـ فَيَقُولُ هُوَ رَسُولُ اللَّهِ، هُوَ مُحَمَّدٌ صلى الله عليه وسلم جَاءَنَا بِالْبَيِّنَاتِ وَالْهُدَى فَآمَنَّا وَأَجَبْنَا وَاتَّبَعْنَا وَصَدَّقْنَا. فَيُقَالُ لَهُ نَمْ صَالِحًا، قَدْ كُنَّا نَعْلَمُ إِنْ كُنْتَ لَتُؤْمِنُ بِهِ. وَأَمَّا الْمُنَافِقُ ـ أَوْ قَالَ الْمُرْتَابُ شَكَّ هِشَامٌ ـ فَيُقَالُ لَهُ مَا عِلْمُكَ بِهَذَا الرَّجُلِ فَيَقُولُ لاَ أَدْرِي، سَمِعْتُ النَّاسَ يَقُولُونَ شَيْئًا فَقُلْتُهُ ". قَالَ هِشَامٌ فَلَقَدْ قَالَتْ لِي فَاطِمَةُ فَأَوْعَيْتُهُ، غَيْرَ أَنَّهَا ذَكَرَتْ مَا يُغَلِّظُ عَلَيْهِ.

Narrated Kharija bin Zaid bin Thabit: Um Al-`Ala', an Ansari woman who gave the pledge of allegiance to the Prophet ﷺ said to me, "The emigrants were distributed amongst us by drawing lots and we got in our share `Uthman bin Maz'un. We made him stay with us in our house. Then he suffered from a disease which proved fatal when he died and was given a bath and was shrouded in his clothes, Allah's Messengerﷺ came I said, 'May Allah be merciful to you, O Abu As-Sa'ib! I testify that Allah has honored you'. The Prophetﷺ said, 'How do you know that Allah has honored him?' I replied, 'O Allah's Messengerﷺ ! Let my father be sacrificed for you! On whom else shall Allah bestow His honor?' The Prophetﷺ said, 'No doubt, death came to him. By Allah, I too wish him good, but by Allah, I do not know what Allah will do with me though I am Allah's Messenger ﷺ'. By Allah, I never attested the piety of anyone after that." Al-Laith also narrated as above. – Al-Bukhari 1243

حَدَّثَنَا يَحْيَى بْنُ بُكَيْرٍ، حَدَّثَنَا اللَّيْثُ، عَنْ عُقَيْلٍ، عَنِ ابْنِ شِهَابٍ، قَالَ أَخْبَرَنِي خَارِجَةُ بْنُ زَيْدِ بْنِ ثَابِتٍ، أَنَّ أُمَّ الْعَلاَءِ ـ امْرَأَةً مِنَ الأَنْصَارِ ـ بَايَعَتِ النَّبِيَّ صلى الله عليه وسلم أَخْبَرَتْهُ أَنَّهُ اقْتُسِمَ الْمُهَاجِرُونَ قُرْعَةً فَطَارَ لَنَا عُثْمَانُ بْنُ مَظْعُونٍ، فَأَنْزَلْنَاهُ فِي أَبْيَاتِنَا، فَوَجِعَ وَجَعَهُ الَّذِي تُوُفِّيَ فِيهِ، فَلَمَّا تُوُفِّيَ وَغُسِّلَ وَكُفِّنَ فِي أَثْوَابِهِ، دَخَلَ رَسُولُ اللَّهِ صلى الله عليه وسلم فَقُلْتُ رَحْمَةُ اللَّهِ عَلَيْكَ أَبَا السَّائِبِ، فَشَهَادَتِي عَلَيْكَ لَقَدْ أَكْرَمَكَ اللَّهُ. فَقَالَ النَّبِيُّ صلى الله عليه وسلم " وَمَا يُدْرِيكِ أَنَّ اللَّهَ قَدْ أَكْرَمَهُ ". فَقُلْتُ بِأَبِي أَنْتَ يَا رَسُولَ اللَّهِ فَمَنْ يُكْرِمُهُ اللَّهُ فَقَالَ " أَمَّا هُوَ فَقَدْ جَاءَهُ الْيَقِينُ، وَاللَّهِ إِنِّي لأَرْجُو لَهُ الْخَيْرَ، وَاللَّهِ مَا أَدْرِي ـ وَأَنَا رَسُولُ اللَّهِ ـ مَا يُفْعَلُ بِي ". قَالَتْ فَوَاللَّهِ لاَ أُزَكِّي أَحَدًا بَعْدَهُ أَبَدًا.
حَدَّثَنَا سَعِيدُ بْنُ عُفَيْرٍ، حَدَّثَنَا اللَّيْثُ، مِثْلَهُ. وَقَالَ نَافِعُ بْنُ يَزِيدَ عَنْ عُقَيْلٍ، مَا يُفْعَلُ بِهِ وَتَابَعَهُ شُعَيْبٌ وَعَمْرُو بْنُ دِينَارٍ وَمَعْمَرٌ

Narrated `Aisha: When the Prophet ﷺ became ill, some of his wives talked about a church which they had seen in Ethiopia and it was called Mariya. Um Salma and Um Habiba had been to Ethiopia, and both of them narrated its (the Church's) beauty and the pictures it contained. The Prophet ﷺ raised his head and said, "Those are the people who, whenever a pious man dies amongst them, make a place of worship at his grave and then they make those pictures in it. Those are the worst creatures in the Sight of Allah." – Al-Bukhari 1341

حَدَّثَنَا إِسْمَاعِيلُ، قَالَ حَدَّثَنِي مَالِكٌ، عَنْ هِشَامٍ، عَنْ أَبِيهِ، عَنْ عَائِشَةَ ـ رضى الله عنها ـ قَالَتْ لَمَّا اشْتَكَى النَّبِيُّ صلى الله عليه وسلم ذَكَرَتْ بَعْضُ نِسَائِهِ كَنِيسَةً رَأَيْنَهَا بِأَرْضِ الْحَبَشَةِ، يُقَالُ لَهَا مَارِيَةُ، وَكَانَتْ أُمُّ سَلَمَةَ وَأُمُّ حَبِيبَةَ ـ رضى الله عنهما ـ أَتَتَا أَرْضَ الْحَبَشَةِ، فَذَكَرَتَا مِنْ حُسْنِهَا وَتَصَاوِيرَ فِيهَا، فَرَفَعَ رَأْسَهُ فَقَالَ " أُولَئِكَ إِذَا مَاتَ مِنْهُمُ الرَّجُلُ الصَّالِحُ بَنَوْا عَلَى قَبْرِهِ مَسْجِدًا، ثُمَّ صَوَّرُوا فِيهِ تِلْكَ الصُّورَةَ، أُولَئِكَ شِرَارُ الْخَلْقِ عِنْدَ اللَّهِ ".

Narrated Abu Bakra: A man praised another man in front of the Prophet ﷺ. The Prophet ﷺ said to him, "Woe to you, you have cut off your companion's neck, you have cut off your companion's neck," repeating it several times and then added, "Whoever amongst you has to praise his brother should say, 'I think that he is so and so, and Allah knows exactly the truth, and I do not confirm anybody's good conduct before Allah, but I think him so and so,' if he really knows what he says about him." - Al-Bukhari 2662

حَدَّثَنَا مُحَمَّدُ بْنُ سَلاَمٍ أَخْبَرَنَا عَبْدُ الْوَهَّابِ حَدَّثَنَا خَالِدٌ الْحَذَّاءُ عَنْ عَبْدِ الرَّحْمَنِ بْنِ أَبِي بَكْرَةَ عَنْ أَبِيهِ قَالَ أَثْنَى رَجُلٌ عَلَى رَجُلٍ عِنْدَ النَّبِيِّ صَلَّى اللَّهُ عَلَيْهِ وَسَلَّمَ فَقَالَ وَيْلَكَ قَطَعْتَ عُنُقَ صَاحِبِكَ قَطَعْتَ عُنُقَ صَاحِبِكَ مِرَارًا ثُمَّ قَالَ مَنْ كَانَ مِنْكُمْ مَادِحًا أَخَاهُ لَا مَحَالَةَ فَلْيَقُلْ أَحْسِبُ فُلَانًا وَاللَّهُ حَسِيبُهُ وَلَا أُزَكِّي عَلَى اللَّهِ أَحَدًا أَحْسِبُهُ كَذَا وَكَذَا إِنْ كَانَ يَعْلَمُ ذَلِكَ مِنْهُ

Narrated Abu Musa Al-Ash`ari: The Prophet ﷺ heard someone praising another & exaggerating in his praise. The Prophet ﷺ said, "You have ruined or cut the man's back (by praising him so much). – Al-Bukhari 2663

حَدَّثَنَا مُحَمَّدُ بْنُ صَبَّاحٍ، حَدَّثَنَا إِسْمَاعِيلُ بْنُ زَكَرِيَّاءَ، حَدَّثَنَا بُرَيْدُ بْنُ عَبْدِ اللَّهِ، عَنْ أَبِي بُرْدَةَ، عَنْ أَبِي مُوسَى ـ رضى الله عنه ـ قَالَ سَمِعَ النَّبِيُّ صلى الله عليه وسلم رَجُلاً يُثْنِي عَلَى رَجُلٍ، وَيُطْرِيهِ فِي مَدْحِهِ فَقَالَ " أَهْلَكْتُمْ ـ أَوْ قَطَعْتُمْ ـ ظَهْرَ الرَّجُلِ ".

Narrated Sahl bin Sa`d As-Sa`idi: Allah's Messenger ﷺ and the pagans faced each other and started fighting. When Allah's Messenger ﷺ returned to his camp and when the pagans returned to their camp, somebody talked about a man amongst the companions of Allah's Messenger ﷺ who would follow and kill with his sword any pagan going alone. He said, "Nobody did his job (i.e. fighting) so properly today as that man." Allah's Messenger ﷺ said, "Indeed, he is amongst the people of the (Hell) Fire." A man amongst the people said, "I shall accompany him (to watch what he does)" Thus he accompanied him, and wherever he stood, he would stand with him, and wherever he ran, he would run with him. Then the (brave) man got wounded seriously and he decided to bring about his death quickly. He planted the blade of the sword in the ground directing its sharp end towards his chest between his two breasts. Then he leaned on the sword and killed himself. The other man came to Allah's Messenger ﷺ and said, "I testify that you are Allah's Messenger ﷺ ". The Prophet ﷺ asked, "What has happened?" He replied, "(It is about) the man whom you had described as one of the people of the (Hell) Fire. The people were greatly surprised at what you said, and I said, 'I will find out his reality for you.' So, I came out seeking him. He got severely wounded, and hastened to die by slanting the blade of his sword in the ground directing its sharp end towards his chest between his two breasts. Then he eased on his sword and killed himself." When Allah's Messenger ﷺ said, "A man may seem to the people as if he were practising the deeds of the people of Paradise while in fact he is from the people of the Hell) Fire, another may seem to the people as if he were practicing the deeds of the people of Hell (Fire), while in fact he is from the people of Paradise." – Al-Bukhari 2898

حَدَّثَنَا قُتَيْبَةُ، حَدَّثَنَا يَعْقُوبُ بْنُ عَبْدِ الرَّحْمَنِ، عَنْ أَبِي حَازِمٍ، عَنْ سَهْلِ بْنِ سَعْدٍ السَّاعِدِيِّ ـ رضى الله عنه أَنَّ رَسُولَ اللَّهِ صلى الله عليه وسلم الْتَقَى هُوَ وَالْمُشْرِكُونَ فَاقْتَتَلُوا، فَلَمَّا مَالَ رَسُولُ اللَّهِ صلى الله عليه وسلم إِلَى عَسْكَرِهِ، وَمَالَ الآخَرُونَ إِلَى عَسْكَرِهِمْ، وَفِي أَصْحَابِ رَسُولِ اللَّهِ صلى الله عليه وسلم رَجُلٌ لاَ يَدَعُ لَهُمْ شَاذَّةً وَلاَ فَاذَّةً إِلاَّ اتَّبَعَهَا يَضْرِبُهَا بِسَيْفِهِ، فَقَالَ مَا أَجْزَأَ مِنَّا الْيَوْمَ أَحَدٌ كَمَا أَجْزَأَ فُلاَنٌ. فَقَالَ رَسُولُ اللَّهِ صلى الله عليه وسلم " أَمَا إِنَّهُ مِنْ أَهْلِ النَّارِ ". فَقَالَ رَجُلٌ مِنَ الْقَوْمِ أَنَا صَاحِبُهُ. قَالَ فَخَرَجَ مَعَهُ كُلَّمَا وَقَفَ وَقَفَ مَعَهُ، وَإِذَا أَسْرَعَ أَسْرَعَ مَعَهُ قَالَ فَجُرِحَ الرَّجُلُ جُرْحًا شَدِيدًا، فَاسْتَعْجَلَ الْمَوْتَ، فَوَضَعَ نَصْلَ سَيْفِهِ بِالأَرْضِ وَذُبَابَهُ بَيْنَ ثَدْيَيْهِ، ثُمَّ تَحَامَلَ عَلَى سَيْفِهِ، فَقَتَلَ نَفْسَهُ، فَخَرَجَ الرَّجُلُ إِلَى رَسُولِ اللَّهِ صلى الله عليه وسلم فَقَالَ أَشْهَدُ أَنَّكَ رَسُولُ اللَّهِ. قَالَ " وَمَا ذَاكَ ". قَالَ الرَّجُلُ الَّذِي ذَكَرْتَ آنِفًا أَنَّهُ مِنْ أَهْلِ النَّارِ، فَأَعْظَمَ النَّاسُ ذَلِكَ. فَقُلْتُ أَنَا لَكُمْ بِهِ. فَخَرَجْتُ فِي طَلَبِهِ، ثُمَّ جُرِحَ جُرْحًا شَدِيدًا، فَاسْتَعْجَلَ الْمَوْتَ، فَوَضَعَ نَصْلَ سَيْفِهِ فِي الأَرْضِ وَذُبَابَهُ بَيْنَ ثَدْيَيْهِ، ثُمَّ تَحَامَلَ عَلَيْهِ، فَقَتَلَ نَفْسَهُ. فَقَالَ رَسُولُ اللَّهِ صلى الله عليه وسلم عِنْدَ ذَلِكَ " إِنَّ الرَّجُلَ لَيَعْمَلُ عَمَلَ أَهْلِ الْجَنَّةِ فِيمَا يَبْدُو لِلنَّاسِ، وَهْوَ مِنْ أَهْلِ النَّارِ، وَإِنَّ الرَّجُلَ لَيَعْمَلُ عَمَلَ أَهْلِ النَّارِ فِيمَا يَبْدُو لِلنَّاسِ، وَهْوَ مِنْ أَهْلِ الْجَنَّةِ "

Narrated `Umar: I heard the Prophet ﷺ saying, "Do not exaggerate in praising me as the Christians praised the son of Mary, for I am only a Slave. So, call me the Slave of Allah and His Apostle." – Al-Bukhari 3445

حَدَّثَنَا الْحُمَيْدِيُّ، حَدَّثَنَا سُفْيَانُ، قَالَ سَمِعْتُ الزُّهْرِيَّ، يَقُولُ أَخْبَرَنِي عُبَيْدُ اللَّهِ بْنُ عَبْدِ اللَّهِ، عَنِ ابْنِ عَبَّاسٍ، سَمِعَ عُمَرَ ـ رضى الله عنه ـ يَقُولُ عَلَى الْمِنْبَرِ سَمِعْتُ النَّبِيَّ صلى الله عليه وسلم يَقُولُ " لاَ تُطْرُونِي كَمَا أَطْرَتِ النَّصَارَى ابْنَ مَرْيَمَ، فَإِنَّمَا أَنَا عَبْدُهُ، فَقُولُوا عَبْدُ اللَّهِ وَرَسُولُهُ ".

Those who avoid gross sins and indecencies—except for minor lapses—your Lord is of Vast Forgiveness. He knows you well, ever since He created you from the earth, and ever since you were embryos in your mothers' wombs. So do not acclaim your own virtue; He is fully aware of the righteous. – Surah An-Najm 53:32

ٱلَّذِينَ يَجْتَنِبُونَ كَبَٰٓئِرَ ٱلْإِثْمِ وَٱلْفَوَٰحِشَ إِلَّا ٱللَّمَمَ ۚ إِنَّ رَبَّكَ وَٰسِعُ ٱلْمَغْفِرَةِ ۚ هُوَ أَعْلَمُ بِكُمْ إِذْ أَنشَأَكُم مِّنَ ٱلْأَرْضِ وَإِذْ أَنتُمْ أَجِنَّةٌ فِى بُطُونِ أُمَّهَٰتِكُمْ ۖ فَلَا تُزَكُّوٓا۟ أَنفُسَكُمْ ۖ هُوَ أَعْلَمُ بِمَنِ ٱتَّقَىٰٓ

Narrated Abu Huraira: Zainab's original name was "Barrah," but it was said' "By that she is giving herself the prestige of piety." So the Prophet ﷺ changed her name to Zainab. – Al-Bukhari 6192

حَدَّثَنَا صَدَقَةُ بْنُ الْفَضْلِ، أَخْبَرَنَا مُحَمَّدُ بْنُ جَعْفَرٍ، عَنْ شُعْبَةَ، عَنْ عَطَاءِ بْنِ أَبِي مَيْمُونَةَ، عَنْ أَبِي رَافِعٍ، عَنْ أَبِي هُرَيْرَةَ، أَنَّ زَيْنَبَ، كَانَ اسْمُهَا بَرَّةَ، فَقِيلَ تُزَكِّي نَفْسَهَا. فَسَمَّاهَا رَسُولُ اللَّهِ صلى الله عليه وسلم زَيْنَبَ

Narrated Sa'd: Allah's Messenger ﷺ distributed (Zakat) amongst (a group of) people while I was sitting there but Allah's Messenger ﷺ left a man whom I thought the best of the lot. I asked, "O Allah's Messenger ﷺ ! Why have you left that person? By Allah I regard him as a faithful believer." The Prophet ﷺ commented: "Or merely a Muslim." I remained quiet for a while, but could not help repeating my question because of what I knew about him. And then asked Allah's Messenger ﷺ," Why have you left so and so? By Allah! He is a faithful believer." The Prophet ﷺ again said, "Or merely a Muslim." And I could not help repeating my question because of what I knew about him. Then the Prophet ﷺ said, "O Sa'd! I give to a person while another is dearer to me, for fear that he might be thrown on his face in the Fire by Allah." – Al-Bukhari 27

حَدَّثَنَا أَبُو الْيَمَانِ، قَالَ أَخْبَرَنَا شُعَيْبٌ، عَنِ الزُّهْرِيِّ، قَالَ أَخْبَرَنِي عَامِرُ بْنُ سَعْدِ بْنِ أَبِي وَقَّاصٍ، عَنْ سَعْدٍ، رضى الله عنه أَنَّ رَسُولَ اللَّهِ صلى الله عليه وسلم أَعْطَى رَهْطًا وَسَعْدٌ جَالِسٌ، فَتَرَكَ رَسُولُ اللَّهِ صلى الله عليه وسلم رَجُلاً هُوَ أَعْجَبُهُمْ إِلَىَّ فَقُلْتُ يَا رَسُولَ اللَّهِ مَا لَكَ عَنْ فُلاَنٍ فَوَاللَّهِ إِنِّي لأَرَاهُ مُؤْمِنًا. فَقَالَ " أَوْ مُسْلِمًا ". فَسَكَتُّ قَلِيلاً، ثُمَّ غَلَبَنِي مَا أَعْلَمُ مِنْهُ فَعُدْتُ لِمَقَالَتِي فَقُلْتُ مَا لَكَ عَنْ فُلاَنٍ فَوَاللَّهِ إِنِّي لأَرَاهُ مُؤْمِنًا فَقَالَ " أَوْ مُسْلِمًا ". ثُمَّ غَلَبَنِي مَا أَعْلَمُ مِنْهُ فَعُدْتُ لِمَقَالَتِي وَعَادَ رَسُولُ اللَّهِ صلى الله عليه وسلم ثُمَّ قَالَ " يَا سَعْدُ، إِنِّي لأُعْطِي الرَّجُلَ وَغَيْرُهُ أَحَبُّ إِلَىَّ مِنْهُ، خَشْيَةَ أَنْ يَكُبَّهُ اللَّهُ فِي النَّارِ ". وَرَوَاهُ يُونُسُ وَصَالِحٌ وَمَعْمَرٌ وَابْنُ أَخِي الزُّهْرِيِّ عَنِ الزُّهْرِيِّ.

So it was, that We caused them to be discovered, that they would know that the promise of Allah is true, and that of the Hour there is no doubt. As they were disputing their case among themselves, they said, "Build over them a building." Their Lord knows best about them. Those who prevailed over their case said, "We will set up over them a place of worship." – Surah Al-Khaf 18:21

وَكَذَٰلِكَ أَعْثَرْنَا عَلَيْهِمْ لِيَعْلَمُوٓا۟ أَنَّ وَعْدَ ٱللَّهِ حَقٌّ وَأَنَّ ٱلسَّاعَةَ لَا رَيْبَ فِيهَآ إِذْ يَتَنَـٰزَعُونَ بَيْنَهُمْ أَمْرَهُمْ ۖ فَقَالُوا۟ ٱبْنُوا۟ عَلَيْهِم بُنْيَـٰنًا ۖ رَّبُّهُمْ أَعْلَمُ بِهِمْ ۚ قَالَ ٱلَّذِينَ غَلَبُوا۟ عَلَىٰٓ أَمْرِهِمْ لَنَتَّخِذَنَّ عَلَيْهِم مَّسْجِدًا

Say, "O People of the Book, come to terms common between us and you: that we worship none but Allah, and that we associate nothing with Him, and that none of us takes others as lords besides Allah." And if they turn away, say, "Bear witness that we have submitted." – Suarh Al-Imran 3:64

قُلْ يَـٰٓأَهْلَ ٱلْكِتَـٰبِ تَعَالَوْا۟ إِلَىٰ كَلِمَةٍ سَوَآءٍۭ بَيْنَنَا وَبَيْنَكُمْ أَلَّا نَعْبُدَ إِلَّا ٱللَّهَ وَلَا نُشْرِكَ بِهِۦ شَيْـًٔا وَلَا يَتَّخِذَ بَعْضُنَا بَعْضًا أَرْبَابًا مِّن دُونِ ٱللَّهِ ۚ فَإِن تَوَلَّوْا۟ فَقُولُوا۟ ٱشْهَدُوا۟ بِأَنَّا مُسْلِمُونَ

Narrated Abu Huraira: I heard Allah's Messenger ﷺ saying, "The good deeds of any person will not make him enter Paradise." (i.e., None can enter Paradise through his good deeds.) They (the Prophet's companions) said, 'Not even you, O Allah's Messenger ﷺ?' He said, "Not even myself, unless Allah bestows His favor and mercy on me." So be moderate in your religious deeds and do the deeds that are within your ability: and none of you should wish for death, for if he is a good doer, he may increase his good deeds, and if he is an evil doer, he may repent to Allah." – Al-Bukhari 5673

حَدَّثَنَا أَبُو الْيَمَانِ، أَخْبَرَنَا شُعَيْبٌ، عَنِ الزُّهْرِيِّ، قَالَ أَخْبَرَنِي أَبُو عُبَيْدٍ، مَوْلَى عَبْدِ الرَّحْمَنِ بْنِ عَوْفٍ أَنَّ أَبَا هُرَيْرَةَ، قَالَ سَمِعْتُ رَسُولَ اللَّهِ صلى الله عليه وسلم يَقُولُ " لَنْ يُدْخِلَ أَحَدًا عَمَلُهُ الْجَنَّةَ ". قَالُوا وَلاَ أَنْتَ يَا رَسُولَ اللَّهِ قَالَ " لاَ، وَلاَ أَنَا إِلاَّ أَنْ يَتَغَمَّدَنِي اللَّهُ بِفَضْلٍ وَرَحْمَةٍ فَسَدِّدُوا وَقَارِبُوا وَلاَ يَتَمَنَّيَنَّ أَحَدُكُمُ الْمَوْتَ إِمَّا مُحْسِنًا فَلَعَلَّهُ أَنْ يَزْدَادَ خَيْرًا، وَإِمَّا مُسِيئًا فَلَعَلَّهُ أَنْ يَسْتَعْتِبَ "

The Book of
Kneel along with Ar-Raki'un
ٱرْكَعُوا۟ مَعَ ٱلرَّٰكِعِينَ

As for those who disbelieve, they are allies of one another. Unless you do this, there will be turmoil in the land, and much corruption. – Surah Al-Anfal 8:73
وَٱلَّذِينَ كَفَرُوا۟ بَعْضُهُمْ أَوْلِيَآءُ بَعْضٍ ۚ إِلَّا تَفْعَلُوهُ تَكُن فِتْنَةٌ فِى ٱلْأَرْضِ وَفَسَادٌ كَبِيرٌ

And attend to your prayers, and practice regular charity, and kneel with those who kneel. – Surah Al-Baqarah 2:43
وَأَقِيمُوا۟ ٱلصَّلَوٰةَ وَءَاتُوا۟ ٱلزَّكَوٰةَ وَٱرْكَعُوا۟ مَعَ ٱلرَّٰكِعِينَ

Do not marry idolatresses, unless they have believed. A believing maid is better than an idolatress, even if you like her. And do not marry idolaters, unless they have believed. A believing servant is better than an idolater, even if you like him. These call to the Fire, but Allah calls to the Garden and to forgiveness, by His leave. He makes clear His communications to the people, that they may be mindful. – Surah Al-Baqarah 2:221
وَلَا تَنكِحُوا۟ ٱلْمُشْرِكَٰتِ حَتَّىٰ يُؤْمِنَّ ۚ وَلَأَمَةٌ مُّؤْمِنَةٌ خَيْرٌ مِّن مُّشْرِكَةٍ وَلَوْ أَعْجَبَتْكُمْ ۗ وَلَا تُنكِحُوا۟ ٱلْمُشْرِكِينَ حَتَّىٰ يُؤْمِنُوا۟ ۚ وَلَعَبْدٌ مُّؤْمِنٌ خَيْرٌ مِّن مُّشْرِكٍ وَلَوْ أَعْجَبَكُمْ ۗ أُو۟لَٰٓئِكَ يَدْعُونَ إِلَى ٱلنَّارِ ۖ وَٱللَّهُ يَدْعُوٓا۟ إِلَى ٱلْجَنَّةِ وَٱلْمَغْفِرَةِ بِإِذْنِهِۦ ۖ وَيُبَيِّنُ ءَايَٰتِهِۦ لِلنَّاسِ لَعَلَّهُمْ يَتَذَكَّرُونَ

Narrated `Abdullah: That he heard a man reciting a Quranic Verse which he had heard the Prophetﷺ reciting in a different way. So he took that man to the Prophet (and told him the story). The Prophetﷺ said, "Both of you are reciting in a correct way, so carry on reciting." The Prophetﷺ further added, "The nations which were before you were destroyed (by Allah) because they differed." – Al-Bukhari 5062
حَدَّثَنَا سُلَيْمَانُ بْنُ حَرْبٍ، حَدَّثَنَا شُعْبَةُ، عَنْ عَبْدِ الْمَلِكِ بْنِ مَيْسَرَةَ، عَنِ النَّزَّالِ بْنِ سَبْرَةَ، عَنْ عَبْدِ اللَّهِ، أَنَّهُ سَمِعَ رَجُلاً، يَقْرَأُ آيَةً، سَمِعَ النَّبِيَّ صلى الله عليه وسلم خِلاَفَهَا، فَأَخَذْتُ بِيَدِهِ فَانْطَلَقْتُ بِهِ إِلَى النَّبِيِّ صلى الله عليه وسلم فَقَالَ " كِلاَكُمَا مُحْسِنٌ فَاقْرَآ ـ أَكْبَرُ عِلْمِي قَالَ ـ فَإِنَّ مَنْ كَانَ قَبْلَكُمُ اخْتَلَفُوا فَأَهْلَكَهُمْ ".

And hold fast to the rope of Allah, altogether, and do not become divided. And remember Allah's blessings upon you; how you were enemies, and He reconciled your hearts, and by His grace you became brethren. And you were on the brink of a pit of fire, and He saved you from it. Allah thus clarifies His revelations for you, so that you may be guided. – Surah Al-Imran 3:103
وَٱعْتَصِمُوا۟ بِحَبْلِ ٱللَّهِ جَمِيعًا وَلَا تَفَرَّقُوا۟ ۚ وَٱذْكُرُوا۟ نِعْمَتَ ٱللَّهِ عَلَيْكُمْ إِذْ كُنتُمْ أَعْدَآءً فَأَلَّفَ بَيْنَ قُلُوبِكُمْ فَأَصْبَحْتُم بِنِعْمَتِهِۦٓ إِخْوَٰنًا وَكُنتُمْ عَلَىٰ شَفَا حُفْرَةٍ مِّنَ ٱلنَّارِ فَأَنقَذَكُم مِّنْهَا ۗ كَذَٰلِكَ يُبَيِّنُ ٱللَّهُ لَكُمْ ءَايَٰتِهِۦ لَعَلَّكُمْ تَهْتَدُونَ

The hypocrites will be in the lowest level of the Fire, and you will find no helper for them. Except those who repent, and reform, and hold fast to Allah, and dedicate their religion to Allah alone. These are with the believers; and Allah will give the believers a great reward. – Surah An-Nisa 4:145&146
إِنَّ ٱلْمُنَٰفِقِينَ فِى ٱلدَّرْكِ ٱلْأَسْفَلِ مِنَ ٱلنَّارِ وَلَن تَجِدَ لَهُمْ نَصِيرًا إِلَّا ٱلَّذِينَ تَابُوا۟ وَأَصْلَحُوا۟ وَٱعْتَصَمُوا۟ بِٱللَّهِ وَأَخْلَصُوا۟ دِينَهُمْ لِلَّهِ فَأُو۟لَٰٓئِكَ مَعَ ٱلْمُؤْمِنِينَ ۖ وَسَوْفَ يُؤْتِ ٱللَّهُ ٱلْمُؤْمِنِينَ أَجْرًا عَظِيمًا

Narrated Abu Huraira: The Prophetﷺ said, "Beware of suspicion (about others), as suspicion is the falsest talk, and do not spy upon each other, and do not listen to the evil talk of the

people about others' affairs, and do not have enmity with one another, but be brothers. And none should ask for the hand of a girl who is already engaged to his (Muslim) brother, but one should wait till the first suitor marries her or leaves her." – Al-Bukhari 5143, 5144
حَدَّثَنَا يَحْيَى بْنُ بُكَيْرٍ، حَدَّثَنَا اللَّيْثُ، عَنْ جَعْفَرِ بْنِ رَبِيعَةَ، عَنِ الأَعْرَجِ، قَالَ قَالَ أَبُو هُرَيْرَةَ يَأْثُرُ عَنِ النَّبِيِّ صلى الله عليه وسلم قَالَ " إِيَّاكُمْ وَالظَّنَّ، فَإِنَّ الظَّنَّ أَكْذَبُ الْحَدِيثِ، وَلاَ تَجَسَّسُوا، وَلاَ تَحَسَّسُوا، وَلاَ تَبَاغَضُوا، وَكُونُوا إِخْوَانًا ". وَلاَ يَخْطُبُ الرَّجُلُ عَلَى خِطْبَةِ أَخِيهِ حَتَّى يَنْكِحَ أَوْ يَتْرُكَ

Narrated Jabir bin `Abdullah: We were in a Ghazwa and a man from the emigrants kicked an Ansari (on the buttocks with his foot). The Ansari man said, "O the Ansari! (Help!)" The emigrant said, "O the emigrants! (Help)." When Allah's Messenger ﷺ heard that, he said, "What is that?" They said, "A man from the emigrants kicked a man from the Ansar (on the buttocks his foot). On that the Ansar said, 'O the Ansar!' and the emigrant said, 'O the emigrants!" The Prophet ﷺ said "Leave it (that call) for it Is a detestable thing." The number of Ansar was larger (than that of the emigrants) at the time when the Prophet ﷺ came to Medina, but later the number of emigrants increased. `Abdullah bin Ubai said, "Have they, (the emigrants) done so? By Allah, if we return to Medina, surely, the more honorable will expel therefrom the meaner," `Umar bin Al-Khattab said, "O Allah's Messenger ﷺ ! Let me chop off the head of this hypocrite!" The Prophet said, "Leave him, lest the people say Muhammad kills his companions:" – Al-Bukhari 4907
حَدَّثَنَا الْحُمَيْدِيُّ، حَدَّثَنَا سُفْيَانُ، قَالَ حَفِظْنَاهُ مِنْ عَمْرِو بْنِ دِينَارٍ قَالَ سَمِعْتُ جَابِرَ بْنَ عَبْدِ اللَّهِ ـ رضى الله عنهما ـ يَقُولُ كُنَّا فِي غَزَاةٍ فَكَسَعَ رَجُلٌ مِنَ الْمُهَاجِرِينَ رَجُلاً مِنَ الأَنْصَارِ فَقَالَ الأَنْصَارِيُّ يَا لَلأَنْصَارِ. وَقَالَ الْمُهَاجِرِيُّ يَا لَلْمُهَاجِرِينَ. فَسَمَّعَهَا اللَّهُ رَسُولَهُ صلى الله عليه وسلم قَالَ " مَا هَذَا ". فَقَالُوا كَسَعَ رَجُلٌ مِنَ الْمُهَاجِرِينَ رَجُلاً مِنَ الأَنْصَارِ فَقَالَ الأَنْصَارِيُّ يَا لَلأَنْصَارِ. وَقَالَ الْمُهَاجِرِيُّ يَالَلْمُهَاجِرِينَ. فَقَالَ النَّبِيُّ صلى الله عليه وسلم " دَعُوهَا فَإِنَّهَا مُنْتِنَةٌ ". قَالَ جَابِرٌ وَكَانَتِ الأَنْصَارُ حِينَ قَدِمَ النَّبِيُّ صلى الله عليه وسلم أَكْثَرَ، ثُمَّ كَثُرَ الْمُهَاجِرُونَ بَعْدُ، فَقَالَ عَبْدُ اللَّهِ بْنُ أُبَىٍّ أَوَقَدْ فَعَلُوا، وَاللَّهِ لَئِنْ رَجَعْنَا إِلَى الْمَدِينَةِ لَيُخْرِجَنَّ الأَعَزُّ مِنْهَا الأَذَلَّ. فَقَالَ عُمَرُ بْنُ الْخَطَّابِ رضى الله عنه دَعْنِي يَا رَسُولَ اللَّهِ أَضْرِبْ عُنُقَ هَذَا الْمُنَافِقِ. قَالَ النَّبِيُّ صلى الله عليه وسلم " دَعْهُ لاَ يَتَحَدَّثُ النَّاسُ أَنَّ مُحَمَّدًا يَقْتُلُ أَصْحَابَهُ "

Narrated Salama bin Al-Akwa`: The Prophet ﷺ passed by some persons of the tribe of Aslam practicing archery (i.e. the throwing of arrows) Allah's Messenger ﷺ said, "O offspring of Ishmael! Practice archery (i.e. arrow throwing) as your father was a great archer (i.e. arrow-thrower). I am with (on the side of) the son of so-and-so-." Hearing that, one of the two teams stopped throwing. Allah's Messenger ﷺ asked them, ' Why are you not throwing?" They replied, "O Allah's Messenger ﷺ ! How shall we throw when you are with the opposite team?" He said, "Throw, for I am with you all." – Al-Bukhari 3373
حَدَّثَنَا قُتَيْبَةُ بْنُ سَعِيدٍ، حَدَّثَنَا حَاتِمٌ، عَنْ يَزِيدَ بْنِ أَبِي عُبَيْدٍ، عَنْ سَلَمَةَ بْنِ الأَكْوَعِ ـ رضى الله عنه ـ قَالَ مَرَّ النَّبِيُّ صلى الله عليه وسلم عَلَى نَفَرٍ مِنْ أَسْلَمَ يَنْتَضِلُونَ، فَقَالَ رَسُولُ اللَّهِ صلى الله عليه وسلم " ارْمُوا بَنِي إِسْمَاعِيلَ، فَإِنَّ أَبَاكُمْ كَانَ رَامِيًا، وَأَنَا مَعَ بَنِي فُلاَنٍ ". قَالَ فَأَمْسَكَ أَحَدُ الْفَرِيقَيْنِ بِأَيْدِيهِمْ، فَقَالَ رَسُولُ اللَّهِ صلى الله عليه وسلم " مَا لَكُمْ لاَ تَرْمُونَ ". فَقَالُوا يَا رَسُولَ اللَّهِ، نَرْمِي وَأَنْتَ مَعَهُمْ قَالَ " ارْمُوا وَأَنَا مَعَكُمْ كُلِّكُمْ ".

And obey Allah and His Messenger, and do not dispute, lest you falter and lose your courage. And be steadfast. Allah is with the steadfast. – Surah Al-Anfal 8:46
وَأَطِيعُوا۟ ٱللَّهَ وَرَسُولَهُۥ وَلَا تَنَـٰزَعُوا۟ فَتَفْشَلُوا۟ وَتَذْهَبَ رِيحُكُمْ ۖ وَٱصْبِرُوٓا۟ ۚ إِنَّ ٱللَّهَ مَعَ ٱلصَّـٰبِرِينَ

And He united their hearts. Had you spent everything on earth, you would not have united their hearts, but Allah united them together. He is Mighty and Wise. – Surah Al-Anfal 8:63
وَأَلَّفَ بَيْنَ قُلُوبِهِمْ ۚ لَوْ أَنفَقْتَ مَا فِى ٱلْأَرْضِ جَمِيعًا مَّآ أَلَّفْتَ بَيْنَ قُلُوبِهِمْ وَلَـٰكِنَّ ٱللَّهَ أَلَّفَ بَيْنَهُمْ ۚ إِنَّهُۥ عَزِيزٌ حَكِيمٌ

And We will remove all ill-feelings from their hearts—brothers and sisters, on couches facing one another. – Surah Al-Hijr 15:47

وَنَزَعْنَا مَا فِى صُدُورِهِم مِّنْ غِلٍّ إِخْوَٰنًا عَلَىٰ سُرُرٍ مُّتَقَـٰبِلِينَ

"I was commanded to worship the Lord of this town, who has sanctified it, and to Whom everything belongs; and I was commanded to be of those who submit. – Surah Al-Naml 27:91

إِنَّمَآ أُمِرْتُ أَنْ أَعْبُدَ رَبَّ هَـٰذِهِ ٱلْبَلْدَةِ ٱلَّذِى حَرَّمَهَا وَلَهُۥ كُلُّ شَىْءٍ ۖ وَأُمِرْتُ أَنْ أَكُونَ مِنَ ٱلْمُسْلِمِينَ

Narrated Abu Musa: The Prophet ﷺ said, "I saw in a dream that I moved a sword and its blade got broken, and that symbolized the casualties which the believers suffered on the day of Uhud. Then I moved it again, and it became as perfect as it had been, and that symbolized the Conquest (of Mecca) which Allah helped us to achieve, and the union of all the believers. I (also) saw cows in the dream, and what Allah does is always beneficial. Those cows appeared to symbolize the faithful believers (who were martyred) on the day of Uhud." – Al-Bukhari 4081

حَدَّثَنَا مُحَمَّدُ بْنُ الْعَلاَءِ، حَدَّثَنَا أَبُو أُسَامَةَ، عَنْ بُرَيْدِ بْنِ عَبْدِ اللَّهِ بْنِ أَبِي بُرْدَةَ، عَنْ جَدِّهِ أَبِي بُرْدَةَ، عَنْ أَبِي مُوسَى ـ رضى الله عنه ـ أُرَى عَنِ النَّبِيِّ صلى الله عليه وسلم قَالَ " رَأَيْتُ فِي رُؤْيَاىَ أَنِّي هَزَزْتُ سَيْفًا فَانْقَطَعَ صَدْرُهُ، فَإِذَا هُوَ مَا أُصِيبَ مِنَ الْمُؤْمِنِينَ يَوْمَ أُحُدٍ، ثُمَّ هَزَزْتُهُ أُخْرَى فَعَادَ أَحْسَنَ مَا كَانَ، فَإِذَا هُوَ مَا جَاءَ بِهِ اللَّهُ مِنَ الْفَتْحِ وَاجْتِمَاعِ الْمُؤْمِنِينَ، وَرَأَيْتُ فِيهَا بَقَرًا وَاللَّهُ خَيْرٌ، فَإِذَا هُمُ الْمُؤْمِنُونَ يَوْمَ أُحُدٍ ".

Narrated Ubaida: Ali said (to the people of 'Iraq), "Judge as you used to judge, for I hate differences (and I do my best) till the people unite as one group, or I die as my companions have died." – Al-Bukhari 3707

حَدَّثَنَا عَلِيُّ بْنُ الْجَعْدِ، أَخْبَرَنَا شُعْبَةُ، عَنْ أَيُّوبَ، عَنِ ابْنِ سِيرِينَ، عَنْ عَبِيدَةَ، عَنْ عَلِيٍّ ـ رضى الله عنه ـ قَالَ اقْضُوا كَمَا كُنْتُمْ تَقْضُونَ، فَإِنِّي أَكْرَهُ الاِخْتِلاَفَ حَتَّى يَكُونَ لِلنَّاسِ جَمَاعَةٌ، أَوْ أَمُوتَ كَمَا مَاتَ أَصْحَابِي. فَكَانَ ابْنُ سِيرِينَ يَرَى أَنَّ عَامَّةَ مَا يُرْوَى عَلَى عَلِيٍّ الْكَذِبُ.

So pay no attention to whoever turns away from Our message and desires only this worldly life. Surah An-Najm 53:29

فَأَعْرِضْ عَن مَّن تَوَلَّىٰ عَن ذِكْرِنَا وَلَمْ يُرِدْ إِلَّا ٱلْحَيَوٰةَ ٱلدُّنْيَا

The Book of
emigrate for the sake of my Lord
مُهَاجِرٌ إِلَىٰ رَبِّىٓ

"And deliver us, by Your mercy, from the disbelieving people." And We inspired Moses and his brother, "Settle your people in Egypt, and make your homes places of worship, and perform the prayer, and give good news to the believers." – Surah Yunus 10:86&87
وَنَجِّنَا بِرَحْمَتِكَ مِنَ ٱلْقَوْمِ ٱلْكَـٰفِرِينَ وَأَوْحَيْنَآ إِلَىٰ مُوسَىٰ وَأَخِيهِ أَن تَبَوَّءَا لِقَوْمِكُمَا بِمِصْرَ بُيُوتًا وَٱجْعَلُوا۟ بُيُوتَكُمْ قِبْلَةً وَأَقِيمُوا۟ ٱلصَّلَوٰةَ وَبَشِّرِ ٱلْمُؤْمِنِينَ

Those who believed, and those who migrated and fought for the sake of Allah—those look forward to Allah's mercy. Allah is Forgiving and Merciful. – Surah Al-Baqarah 2:218
إِنَّ ٱلَّذِينَ ءَامَنُوا۟ وَٱلَّذِينَ هَاجَرُوا۟ وَجَـٰهَدُوا۟ فِى سَبِيلِ ٱللَّهِ أُو۟لَـٰٓئِكَ يَرْجُونَ رَحْمَتَ ٱللَّهِ وَٱللَّهُ غَفُورٌ رَّحِيمٌ

Then Lot believed in him, and said, "I am emigrating to my Lord. He is the Noble, the Wise." – Surah Al-'Ankabut 29:26
فَـَٔامَنَ لَهُۥ لُوطٌ وَقَالَ إِنِّى مُهَاجِرٌ إِلَىٰ رَبِّىٓ ۖ إِنَّهُۥ هُوَ ٱلْعَزِيزُ ٱلْحَكِيمُ

Narrated 'Amir bin Sa`d bin Abi Waqqas: That his father said, "In the year of the last Hajj of the Prophet ﷺ I became seriously ill and the Prophet ﷺ used to visit me inquiring about my health. I told him, 'I am reduced to this state because of illness and I am wealthy and have no inheritors except a daughter, (In this narration the name of 'Amir bin Sa`d is mentioned and in fact it is a mistake; the narrator is `Aisha bint Sa`d bin Abi Waqqas). Should I give two-thirds of my property in charity?' He said, 'No.' I asked, 'Half?' He said, 'No.' then he added, 'Onethird, and even one-third is much. You'd better leave your inheritors wealthy rather than leaving them poor, begging others. You will get a reward for whatever you spend for Allah's sake, even for what you put in your wife's mouth.' I said, 'O Allah's Messenger ﷺ ! Will I be left alone after my companions have gone?' He said, 'If you are left behind, whatever good deeds you will do will upgrade you and raise you high. And perhaps you will have a long life so that some people will be benefited by you while others will be harmed by you. O Allah! Complete the emigration of my companions and do not turn them renegades.' But Allah's Messenger ﷺ felt sorry for poor Sa`d bin Khaula as he died in Mecca." {but Sa`d bin Abi Waqqas lived long after the Prophet ﷺ.} – Al-Bukhari 1295 (also see Al-Bukhari #6373)
حَدَّثَنَا عَبْدُ اللَّهِ بْنُ يُوسُفَ، أَخْبَرَنَا مَالِكٌ، عَنِ ابْنِ شِهَابٍ، عَنْ عَامِرِ بْنِ سَعْدِ بْنِ أَبِي وَقَّاصٍ، عَنْ أَبِيهِ ـ رضى الله عنه ـ قَالَ كَانَ رَسُولُ اللَّهِ صلى الله عليه وسلم يَعُودُنِي عَامَ حَجَّةِ الْوَدَاعِ مِنْ وَجَعٍ اشْتَدَّ بِي فَقُلْتُ إِنِّي قَدْ بَلَغَ بِي مِنَ الْوَجَعِ وَأَنَا ذُو مَالٍ، وَلاَ يَرِثُنِي إِلاَّ ابْنَةٌ، أَفَأَتَصَدَّقُ بِثُلُثَىْ مَالِي قَالَ " لاَ ". فَقُلْتُ بِالشَّطْرِ فَقَالَ " لاَ " ثُمَّ قَالَ " الثُّلُثُ وَالثُّلْثُ كَبِيرٌ ـ أَوْ كَثِيرٌ ـ إِنَّكَ أَنْ تَذَرَ وَرَثَتَكَ أَغْنِيَاءَ خَيْرٌ مِنْ أَنْ تَذَرَهُمْ عَالَةً يَتَكَفَّفُونَ النَّاسَ، وَإِنَّكَ لَنْ تُنْفِقَ نَفَقَةً تَبْتَغِي بِهَا وَجْهَ اللَّهِ إِلاَّ أُجِرْتَ بِهَا، حَتَّى مَا تَجْعَلُ فِي فِي امْرَأَتِكَ ". فَقُلْتُ يَا رَسُولَ اللَّهِ، أُخَلَّفُ بَعْدَ أَصْحَابِي قَالَ " إِنَّكَ لَنْ تُخَلَّفَ فَتَعْمَلَ عَمَلاً صَالِحًا إِلاَّ ازْدَدْتَ بِهِ دَرَجَةً وَرِفْعَةً، ثُمَّ لَعَلَّكَ أَنْ تُخَلَّفَ حَتَّى يَنْتَفِعَ بِكَ أَقْوَامٌ وَيُضَرَّ بِكَ آخَرُونَ، اللَّهُمَّ أَمْضِ لأَصْحَابِي هِجْرَتَهُمْ، وَلاَ تَرُدَّهُمْ عَلَى أَعْقَابِهِمْ، لَكِنِ الْبَائِسُ سَعْدُ ابْنُ خَوْلَةَ، يَرْثِي لَهُ رَسُولُ اللَّهِ صلى الله عليه وسلم أَنْ مَاتَ بِمَكَّةَ ".

Narrated Qais: When Abu Huraira accompanied by his slave set out intending to embrace Islam they lost each other on the way. The slave then came while Abu Huraira was sitting with the Prophet. The Prophet ﷺ said, "O Abu Huraira! Your slave has come back." Abu Huraira said, "Indeed, I would like you to witness that I have manumitted him." That happened at the time when Abu Huraira recited (the following poetic verse):-- 'What a long tedious tiresome night! Nevertheless, it has delivered us From the land of Kufr (disbelief). – Al-Bukhari 2530

حَدَّثَنَا مُحَمَّدُ بْنُ عَبْدِ اللَّهِ بْنِ نُمَيْرٍ، عَنْ مُحَمَّدِ بْنِ بِشْرٍ، عَنْ إِسْمَاعِيلَ، عَنْ قَيْسٍ، عَنْ أَبِي هُرَيْرَةَ ـ رضى الله عنه ـ أَنَّهُ لَمَّا أَقْبَلَ يُرِيدُ الإِسْلاَمَ وَمَعَهُ غُلاَمُهُ، ضَلَّ كُلُّ وَاحِدٍ مِنْهُمَا مِنْ صَاحِبِهِ، فَأَقْبَلَ بَعْدَ ذَلِكَ وَأَبُو هُرَيْرَةَ جَالِسٌ مَعَ النَّبِيِّ صلى الله عليه وسلم فَقَالَ النَّبِيُّ صلى الله عليه وسلم " يَا أَبَا هُرَيْرَةَ، هَذَا غُلاَمُكَ قَدْ أَتَاكَ ". فَقَالَ أَمَا إِنِّي أُشْهِدُكَ أَنَّهُ حُرٌّ. قَالَ فَهُوَ حِينَ يَقُولُ يَا لَيْلَةً مِنْ طُولِهَا وَعَنَائِهَا عَلَى أَنَّهَا مِنْ دَارَةِ الْكُفْرِ نَجَّتِ

Narrated Ibn `Umar: When the Prophetﷺ passed by Al-Hijr, he said, "Do not enter the dwelling places of those people who were unjust to themselves unless you enter in a weeping state lest the same calamity as of theirs should befall you." Then he covered his head and made his speed fast till he crossed the valley. – Al-Bukhari 4419

حَدَّثَنَا عَبْدُ اللَّهِ بْنُ مُحَمَّدٍ الْجُعْفِيُّ، حَدَّثَنَا عَبْدُ الرَّزَّاقِ، أَخْبَرَنَا مَعْمَرٌ، عَنِ الزُّهْرِيِّ، عَنْ سَالِمٍ، عَنِ ابْنِ عُمَرَ ـ رضى الله عنهما ـ قَالَ لَمَّا مَرَّ النَّبِيُّ صلى الله عليه وسلم بِالْحِجْرِ قَالَ " لاَ تَدْخُلُوا مَسَاكِنَ الَّذِينَ ظَلَمُوا أَنْفُسَهُمْ، أَنْ يُصِيبَكُمْ مَا أَصَابَهُمْ إِلاَّ أَنْ تَكُونُوا بَاكِينَ ". ثُمَّ قَنَّعَ رَأْسَهُ وَأَسْرَعَ السَّيْرَ حَتَّى أَجَازَ الْوَادِيَ

Narrated `Aisha: There was a black slave girl belonging to an 'Arab tribe and they manumitted her but she remained with them. The slave girl said, "Once one of their girls (of that tribe) came out wearing a red leather scarf decorated with precious stones. It fell from her or she placed it somewhere. A kite passed by that place, saw it Lying there and mistaking it for a piece of meat, flew away with it. Those people searched for it but they did not find it. So they accused me of stealing it and started searching me and even searched my private parts." The slave girl further said, "By Allah! While I was standing (in that state) with those people, the same kite passed by them and dropped the red scarf and it fell amongst them. I told them, 'This is what you accused me of and I was innocent and now this is it.' " `Aisha added: That slave girl came to Allah's Messengerﷺ and embraced Islam. She had a tent or a small room with a low roof in the mosque. Whenever she called on me, she had a talk with me and whenever she sat with me, she would recite the following: "The day of the scarf (band) was one of the wonders of our Lord, verily He rescued me from the disbelievers' town. `Aisha added: "Once I asked her, 'What is the matter with you? Whenever you sit with me, you always recite these poetic verses.' On that she told me the whole story. " – Al-Bukhari 439

حَدَّثَنَا عُبَيْدُ بْنُ إِسْمَاعِيلَ، قَالَ حَدَّثَنَا أَبُو أُسَامَةَ، عَنْ هِشَامٍ، عَنْ أَبِيهِ، عَنْ عَائِشَةَ، أَنَّ وَلِيدَةً، كَانَتْ سَوْدَاءَ لِحَىٍّ مِنَ الْعَرَبِ، فَأَعْتَقُوهَا، فَكَانَتْ مَعَهُمْ قَالَتْ فَخَرَجَتْ صَبِيَّةٌ لَهُمْ عَلَيْهَا وِشَاحٌ أَحْمَرُ مِنْ سُيُورٍ قَالَتْ فَوَضَعَتْهُ أَوْ وَقَعَ مِنْهَا، فَمَرَّتْ بِهِ حُدَيَّاةٌ وَهْوَ مُلْقًى، فَحَسِبَتْهُ لَحْمًا فَخَطَفَتْهُ قَالَتْ فَالْتَمَسُوهُ فَلَمْ يَجِدُوهُ قَالَتْ فَاتَّهَمُونِي بِهِ قَالَتْ فَطَفِقُوا يُفَتِّشُونَ حَتَّى فَتَّشُوا قُبُلَهَا قَالَتْ وَاللَّهِ إِنِّي لَقَائِمَةٌ مَعَهُمْ، إِذْ مَرَّتِ الْحُدَيَّاةُ فَأَلْقَتْهُ قَالَتْ فَوَقَعَ بَيْنَهُمْ قَالَتْ فَقُلْتُ هَذَا الَّذِي اتَّهَمْتُمُونِي بِهِ ـ زَعَمْتُمْ ـ وَأَنَا مِنْهُ بَرِيئَةٌ، وَهُوَ ذَا هُوَ قَالَتْ فَجَاءَتْ إِلَى رَسُولِ اللَّهِ صلى الله عليه وسلم فَأَسْلَمَتْ. قَالَتْ عَائِشَةُ فَكَانَ لَهَا خِبَاءٌ فِي الْمَسْجِدِ أَوْ حِفْشٌ قَالَتْ فَكَانَتْ تَأْتِينِي فَتَحَدَّثُ عِنْدِي قَالَتْ فَلاَ تَجْلِسُ عِنْدِي مَجْلِسًا إِلاَّ قَالَتْ وَيَوْمَ الْوِشَاحِ مِنْ أَعَاجِيبِ رَبِّنَا أَلاَ إِنَّهُ مِنْ بَلْدَةِ الْكُفْرِ أَنْجَانِي قَالَتْ عَائِشَةُ فَقُلْتُ لَهَا مَا شَأْنُكِ لاَ تَقْعُدِينَ مَعِي مَقْعَدًا إِلاَّ قُلْتِ هَذَا قَالَتْ فَحَدَّثَتْنِي بِهَذَا الْحَدِيثِ

Narrated `Abdullah bin `Umar: Allah's Messengerﷺ said, "Do not enter (the places) of these people where Allah's punishment had fallen unless you do so weeping. If you do not weep, do not enter (the places of these people) because Allah's curse and punishment which fell upon them may fall upon you." – Al-Bukhari 433

حَدَّثَنَا إِسْمَاعِيلُ بْنُ عَبْدِ اللَّهِ، قَالَ حَدَّثَنِي مَالِكٌ، عَنْ عَبْدِ اللَّهِ بْنِ دِينَارٍ، عَنْ عَبْدِ اللَّهِ بْنِ عُمَرَ ـ رضى الله عنهما ـ أَنَّ رَسُولَ اللَّهِ صلى الله عليه وسلم قَالَ " لاَ تَدْخُلُوا عَلَى هَؤُلاَءِ الْمُعَذَّبِينَ إِلاَّ أَنْ تَكُونُوا بَاكِينَ، فَإِنْ لَمْ تَكُونُوا بَاكِينَ فَلاَ تَدْخُلُوا عَلَيْهِمْ، لاَ يُصِيبُكُمْ مَا أَصَابَهُمْ "

Narrated Abu Musa: Allah's Messengerﷺ said. "My example and the example of the message with which Allah has sent me is like that of a man who came to some people and said, "I have seen with my own eyes the enemy forces, and I am a naked warner (to you) so save yourself, save yourself! A group of them obeyed him and went out at night, slowly and stealthily and were safe, while another group did not believe him and thus the army took them in the morning and destroyed them." – Al-Bukhari 6482

حَدَّثَنَا مُحَمَّدُ بْنُ الْعَلاَءِ، حَدَّثَنَا أَبُو أُسَامَةَ، عَنْ بُرَيْدِ بْنِ عَبْدِ اللَّهِ بْنِ أَبِي بُرْدَةَ، عَنْ أَبِي بُرْدَةَ، عَنْ أَبِي مُوسَى، قَالَ قَالَ رَسُولُ اللَّهِ صلى الله عليه وسلم " مَثَلِي وَمَثَلُ مَا بَعَثَنِي اللَّهُ كَمَثَلِ رَجُلٍ أَتَى قَوْمًا فَقَالَ رَأَيْتُ الْجَيْشَ بِعَيْنَىَّ، وَإِنِّي أَنَا النَّذِيرُ الْعُرْيَانُ فَالنَّجَا النَّجَاءَ. فَأَطَاعَتْهُ طَائِفَةٌ فَأَدْلَجُوا عَلَى مَهْلِهِمْ فَنَجَوْا، وَكَذَّبَتْهُ طَائِفَةٌ فَصَبَّحَهُمُ الْجَيْشُ فَاجْتَاحَهُمْ ".

Those who believed, and emigrated, and struggled in Allah's cause with their possessions and their persons, and those who provided shelter and support—these are allies of one another. As for those who believed, but did not emigrate, you owe them no protection, until they have emigrated. But if they ask you for help in religion, you must come to their aid, except against a people with whom you have a treaty. Allah is Seeing of what you do. As for those who disbelieve, they are allies of one another. Unless you do this, there will be turmoil in the land, and much corruption. – Surah Al-Anfal 8:72&73

إِنَّ ٱلَّذِينَ ءَامَنُوا۟ وَهَاجَرُوا۟ وَجَـٰهَدُوا۟ بِأَمْوَٰلِهِمْ وَأَنفُسِهِمْ فِى سَبِيلِ ٱللَّهِ وَٱلَّذِينَ ءَاوَوا۟ وَّنَصَرُوٓا۟ أُو۟لَـٰٓئِكَ بَعْضُهُمْ أَوْلِيَآءُ بَعْضٍ ۚ وَٱلَّذِينَ ءَامَنُوا۟ وَلَمْ يُهَاجِرُوا۟ مَا لَكُم مِّن وَلَـٰيَتِهِم مِّن شَىْءٍ حَتَّىٰ يُهَاجِرُوا۟ ۚ وَإِنِ ٱسْتَنصَرُوكُمْ فِى ٱلدِّينِ فَعَلَيْكُمُ ٱلنَّصْرُ إِلَّا عَلَىٰ قَوْمٍۭ بَيْنَكُمْ وَبَيْنَهُم مِّيثَـٰقٌ ۗ وَٱللَّهُ بِمَا تَعْمَلُونَ بَصِيرٌ وَٱلَّذِينَ كَفَرُوا۟ بَعْضُهُمْ أَوْلِيَآءُ بَعْضٍ ۚ إِلَّا تَفْعَلُوهُ تَكُن فِتْنَةٌ فِى ٱلْأَرْضِ وَفَسَادٌ كَبِيرٌ

O My servants who have believed: My earth is vast, so worship Me alone. – Surah Al-'Akabut 29:56

يَـٰعِبَادِىَ ٱلَّذِينَ ءَامَنُوٓا۟ إِنَّ أَرْضِى وَٰسِعَةٌ فَإِيَّـٰىَ فَٱعْبُدُونِ

Narrated `Abdullah bin `Umar: The people landed at the land of Thamud called Al-Hijr along with Allah's Messenger ﷺ and they took water from its well for drinking and kneading the dough with it as well. (When Allah's Messenger ﷺ heard about it) he ordered them to pour out the water they had taken from its wells and feed the camels with the dough, and ordered them to take water from the well whence the she-camel (of Prophet Salih) used to drink. – Al-Bukhari 3379

حَدَّثَنَا إِبْرَاهِيمُ بْنُ الْمُنْذِرِ، حَدَّثَنَا أَنَسُ بْنُ عِيَاضٍ، عَنْ عُبَيْدِ اللَّهِ، عَنْ نَافِعٍ، أَنَّ عَبْدَ اللَّهِ بْنَ عُمَرَ ـ رضى الله عنهما ـ أَخْبَرَهُ أَنَّ النَّاسَ نَزَلُوا مَعَ رَسُولِ اللَّهِ صلى الله عليه وسلم أَرْضَ ثَمُودَ الْحِجْرَ، فَاسْتَقَوْا مِنْ بِئْرِهَا، وَاعْتَجَنُوا بِهِ، فَأَمَرَهُمْ رَسُولُ اللَّهِ صلى الله عليه وسلم أَنْ يُهَرِيقُوا مَا اسْتَقَوْا مِنْ بِئْرِهَا، وَأَنْ يَعْلِفُوا الإِبِلَ الْعَجِينَ، وَأَمَرَهُمْ أَنْ يَسْتَقُوا مِنَ الْبِئْرِ الَّتِي كَانَ تَرِدُهَا النَّاقَةُ. تَابَعَهُ أُسَامَةُ عَنْ نَافِعٍ.

Narrated Abu Burda: When I came to Medina. I met `Abdullah bin Salam. He said, "Will you come to me so that I may serve you with Sawiq (i.e. powdered barley) and dates, and let you enter a (blessed) house that in which the Prophet ﷺ entered?" Then he added, "You are In a country where the practice of Riba (i.e. usury) is prevalent; so if somebody owe you something and he sends you a present of a load of chopped straw or a load of barley or a load of provender then do not take it, as it is Riba." – Al-Bukhari 3814

حَدَّثَنَا سُلَيْمَانُ بْنُ حَرْبٍ، حَدَّثَنَا شُعْبَةُ، عَنْ سَعِيدِ بْنِ أَبِي بُرْدَةَ، عَنْ أَبِيهِ، أَتَيْتُ الْمَدِينَةَ فَلَقِيتُ عَبْدَ اللَّهِ بْنَ سَلاَمٍ ـ رضى الله عنه ـ فَقَالَ أَلاَ تَجِيءُ فَأُطْعِمَكَ سَوِيقًا وَتَمْرًا، وَتَدْخُلَ فِي بَيْتٍ ثُمَّ قَالَ إِنَّكَ بِأَرْضٍ الرِّبَا بِهَا فَاشٍ، إِذَا كَانَ لَكَ عَلَى رَجُلٍ حَقٌّ فَأَهْدَى إِلَيْكَ حِمْلَ تِبْنٍ، أَوْ حِمْلَ شَعِيرٍ، أَوْ حِمْلَ قَتٍّ، فَلاَ تَأْخُذْهُ، فَإِنَّهُ رِبًا. وَلَمْ يَذْكُرِ النَّضْرُ وَأَبُو دَاوُدَ وَوَهْبٌ عَنْ شُعْبَةَ الْبَيْتَ.

Narrated Al-Harith bin Suwaid: `Abdullah bin Mas`ud related to us two narrations: One from the Prophet ﷺ and the other from himself, saying: A believer sees his sins as if he were sitting

under a mountain which, he is afraid, may fall on him; whereas the wicked person considers his sins as flies passing over his nose and he just drives them away like this." Abu Shihab (the sub-narrator) moved his hand over his nose in illustration. (Ibn Mas`ud added): Allah's Messenger ﷺ said, "Allah is more pleased with the repentance of His slave than a man who encamps at a place where his life is jeopardized, but he has his riding beast carrying his food and water. He then rests his head and sleeps for a short while and wakes to find his riding beast gone. (He starts looking for it) and suffers from severe heat and thirst or what Allah wished (him to suffer from). He then says, 'I will go back to my place.' He returns and sleeps again, and then (getting up), he raises his head to find his riding beast standing beside him."
– Al-Bukhari 6308

حَدَّثَنَا أَحْمَدُ بْنُ يُونُسَ، حَدَّثَنَا أَبُو شِهَابٍ، عَنِ الأَعْمَشِ، عَنْ عُمَارَةَ بْنِ عُمَيْرٍ، عَنِ الْحَارِثِ بْنِ سُوَيْدٍ، حَدَّثَنَا عَبْدُ اللَّهِ، حَدِيثَيْنِ أَحَدُهُمَا عَنِ النَّبِيِّ صلى الله عليه وسلم وَالآخَرُ عَنْ نَفْسِهِ، قَالَ " إِنَّ الْمُؤْمِنَ يَرَى ذُنُوبَهُ كَأَنَّهُ قَاعِدٌ تَحْتَ جَبَلٍ يَخَافُ أَنْ يَقَعَ عَلَيْهِ، وَإِنَّ الْفَاجِرَ يَرَى ذُنُوبَهُ كَذُبَابٍ مَرَّ عَلَى أَنْفِهِ ". فَقَالَ بِهِ هَكَذَا قَالَ أَبُو شِهَابٍ بِيَدِهِ فَوْقَ أَنْفِهِ. ثُمَّ قَالَ " لَلَّهُ أَفْرَحُ بِتَوْبَةِ عَبْدِهِ مِنْ رَجُلٍ نَزَلَ مَنْزِلاً، وَبِهِ مَهْلَكَةٌ، وَمَعَهُ رَاحِلَتُهُ عَلَيْهَا طَعَامُهُ وَشَرَابُهُ، فَوَضَعَ رَأْسَهُ فَنَامَ نَوْمَةً، فَاسْتَيْقَظَ وَقَدْ ذَهَبَتْ رَاحِلَتُهُ، حَتَّى اشْتَدَّ عَلَيْهِ الْحَرُّ وَالْعَطَشُ أَوْ مَا شَاءَ اللَّهُ، قَالَ أَرْجِعُ إِلَى مَكَانِي. فَرَجَعَ فَنَامَ نَوْمَةً، ثُمَّ رَفَعَ رَأْسَهُ، فَإِذَا رَاحِلَتُهُ عِنْدَهُ ". تَابَعَهُ أَبُو عَوَانَةَ وَجَرِيرٌ عَنِ الأَعْمَشِ. وَقَالَ أَبُو أُسَامَةَ حَدَّثَنَا الأَعْمَشُ حَدَّثَنَا عُمَارَةُ سَمِعْتُ الْحَارِثَ. وَقَالَ شُعْبَةُ وَأَبُو مُسْلِمٍ عَنِ الأَعْمَشِ عَنْ إِبْرَاهِيمَ التَّيْمِيِّ عَنِ الْحَارِثِ بْنِ سُوَيْدٍ. وَقَالَ أَبُو مُعَاوِيَةَ حَدَّثَنَا الأَعْمَشُ عَنْ عُمَارَةَ عَنِ الأَسْوَدِ عَنْ عَبْدِ اللَّهِ وَعَنْ إِبْرَاهِيمَ التَّيْمِيِّ عَنِ الْحَارِثِ بْنِ سُوَيْدٍ عَنْ عَبْدِ اللَّهِ

Narrated Muhammad bin `Abdur-Rahman Abu Al-Aswad: The people of Medina were forced to prepare an army (to fight against the people of Sham during the caliphate of `Abdullah bin Az-Zubair at Mecca), and I was enlisted in it; Then I met `Ikrima, the freed slave of Ibn `Abbas, and informed him (about it), and he forbade me strongly to do so (i.e. to enlist in that army), and then said, "Ibn `Abbas informed me that some Muslim people were with the pagans, increasing the number of the pagans against Allah's Messenger ﷺ .An arrow used to be shot which would hit one of them (the Muslims in the company of the pagans) and kill him, or he would be struck and killed (with a sword)." Then Allah revealed:-- "Verily! As for those whom the angels take (in death) while they are wronging themselves (by staying among the disbelievers)" (4.97) Abu AlAswad also narrated it. – Al-Bukhari 4596

حَدَّثَنَا عَبْدُ اللَّهِ بْنُ يَزِيدَ الْمُقْرِئُ، حَدَّثَنَا حَيْوَةُ، وَغَيْرُهُ، قَالاَ حَدَّثَنَا مُحَمَّدُ بْنُ عَبْدِ الرَّحْمَنِ أَبُو الأَسْوَدِ، قَالَ قُطِعَ عَلَى أَهْلِ الْمَدِينَةِ بَعْثٌ فَاكْتُتِبْتُ فِيهِ، فَلَقِيتُ عِكْرِمَةَ مَوْلَى ابْنِ عَبَّاسٍ فَأَخْبَرْتُهُ، فَنَهَانِي عَنْ ذَلِكَ أَشَدَّ النَّهْىِ، ثُمَّ قَالَ أَخْبَرَنِي ابْنُ عَبَّاسٍ أَنَّ نَاسًا مِنَ الْمُسْلِمِينَ كَانُوا مَعَ الْمُشْرِكِينَ يُكَثِّرُونَ سَوَادَ الْمُشْرِكِينَ عَلَى رَسُولِ اللَّهِ صلى الله عليه وسلم يَأْتِي السَّهْمُ فَيُرْمَى بِهِ، فَيُصِيبُ أَحَدَهُمْ فَيَقْتُلُهُ أَوْ يُضْرَبُ فَيُقْتَلُ، فَأَنْزَلَ اللَّهُ {إِنَّ الَّذِينَ تَوَفَّاهُمُ الْمَلاَئِكَةُ ظَالِمِي أَنْفُسِهِمْ} الآيَةَ. رَوَاهُ اللَّيْثُ عَنْ أَبِي الأَسْوَدِ

The Book of
Flee with his religion to Allah and His Prophet ﷺ
يَفِرُّ أَحَدُهُمْ بِدِينِهِ إِلَى اللَّهِ وَإِلَى رَسُولِهِ صلى الله عليه وسلم

Narrated Zaid bin Wahab :I passed by a place called Ar-Rabadha and by chance I met Abu Dhar and asked him, "What has brought you to this place?" He said, "I was in Sham and differed with Muawiya on the meaning of (the following verses of the Qur'an): 'They who hoard up gold and silver and spend them not in the way of Allah.' (9.34). Muawiya said, 'This verse is revealed regarding the people of the scriptures." I said, It was revealed regarding us and also the people of the scriptures." So we had a quarrel and Mu'awiya sent a complaint against me to `Uthman. `Uthman wrote to me to come to Medina, and I came to Medina. Many people came to me as if they had not seen me before. So I told this to `Uthman who said to me, "You may depart and live nearby if you wish." That was the reason for my being here for even if an Ethiopian had been nominated as my ruler, I would have obeyed him -. Sahih Al-Bukhari 1406

حَدَّثَنَا عَلِيٌّ، سَمِعَ هُشَيْمًا، أَخْبَرَنَا حُصَيْنٌ، عَنْ زَيْدِ بْنِ وَهْبٍ، قَالَ مَرَرْتُ بِالرَّبَذَةِ فَإِذَا أَنَا بِأَبِي، ذَرٍّ ـ رضى الله عنه ـ فَقُلْتُ لَهُ مَا أَنْزَلَكَ مَنْزِلَكَ هَذَا قَالَ كُنْتُ بِالشَّأْمِ، فَاخْتَلَفْتُ أَنَا وَمُعَاوِيَةُ فِي الَّذِينَ يَكْنِزُونَ الذَّهَبَ وَالْفِضَّةَ وَلاَ يُنْفِقُونَهَا فِي سَبِيلِ اللَّهِ. قَالَ مُعَاوِيَةُ نَزَلَتْ فِي أَهْلِ الْكِتَابِ. فَقُلْتُ نَزَلَتْ فِينَا وَفِيهِمْ. فَكَانَ بَيْنِي وَبَيْنَهُ فِي ذَاكَ، وَكَتَبَ إِلَى عُثْمَانَ ـ رضى الله عنه ـ يَشْكُونِي، فَكَتَبَ إِلَىَّ عُثْمَانُ أَنِ اقْدَمِ الْمَدِينَةَ. فَقَدِمْتُهَا فَكَثُرَ عَلَىَّ النَّاسُ حَتَّى كَأَنَّهُمْ لَمْ يَرَوْنِي قَبْلَ ذَلِكَ، فَذَكَرْتُ ذَاكَ لِعُثْمَانَ فَقَالَ لِي إِنْ شِئْتَ تَنَحَّيْتَ فَكُنْتَ قَرِيبًا. فَذَاكَ الَّذِي أَنْزَلَنِي هَذَا الْمَنْزِلَ، وَلَوْ أَمَّرُوا عَلَىَّ حَبَشِيًّا لَسَمِعْتُ وَأَطَعْتُ.

You will not find a people who believe in Allah and the Last Day, loving those who oppose Allah and His Messenger, even if they were their parents, or their children, or their siblings, or their close relatives. These—He has inscribed faith in their hearts, and has supported them with a spirit from Him. And He will admit them into Gardens beneath which rivers flow, wherein they will dwell forever. Allah is pleased with them, and they are pleased with Him. These are the partisans of Allah. Indeed, it is Allah's partisans who are the successful. – Surah Al-Mujadilah 58:22

لَّا تَجِدُ قَوْمًا يُؤْمِنُونَ بِٱللَّهِ وَٱلْيَوْمِ ٱلْـَٔاخِرِ يُوَآدُّونَ مَنْ حَآدَّ ٱللَّهَ وَرَسُولَهُۥ وَلَوْ كَانُوٓا۟ ءَابَآءَهُمْ أَوْ أَبْنَآءَهُمْ أَوْ إِخْوَٰنَهُمْ أَوْ عَشِيرَتَهُمْ ۚ أُو۟لَـٰٓئِكَ كَتَبَ فِى قُلُوبِهِمُ ٱلْإِيمَـٰنَ وَأَيَّدَهُم بِرُوحٍ مِّنْهُ ۖ وَيُدْخِلُهُمْ جَنَّـٰتٍ تَجْرِى مِن تَحْتِهَا ٱلْأَنْهَـٰرُ خَـٰلِدِينَ فِيهَا ۚ رَضِىَ ٱللَّهُ عَنْهُمْ وَرَضُوا۟ عَنْهُ ۚ أُو۟لَـٰٓئِكَ حِزْبُ ٱللَّهِ ۚ أَلَآ إِنَّ حِزْبَ ٱللَّهِ هُمُ ٱلْمُفْلِحُونَ

Narrated Ibn `Umar: Allah's Messenger ﷺ said, "Do not enter the ruined dwellings of those who were unjust to themselves unless (you enter) weeping, lest you should suffer the same punishment as was inflicted upon them." – Al-Bukhari 3381

حَدَّثَنِي عَبْدُ اللَّهِ، حَدَّثَنَا وَهْبٌ، حَدَّثَنَا أَبِي، سَمِعْتُ يُونُسَ، عَنِ الزُّهْرِيِّ، عَنْ سَالِمٍ، أَنَّ ابْنَ عُمَرَ، قَالَ قَالَ رَسُولُ اللَّهِ صلى الله عليه وسلم " لاَ تَدْخُلُوا مَسَاكِنَ الَّذِينَ ظَلَمُوا أَنْفُسَهُمْ إِلاَّ أَنْ تَكُونُوا بَاكِينَ، أَنْ يُصِيبَكُمْ مِثْلُ مَا أَصَابَهُمْ "

Narrated `Abdullah bin `Umar: The people landed at the land of Thamud called Al-Hijr along with Allah's Messenger ﷺ and they took water from its well for drinking and kneading the dough with it as well. (When Allah's Messenger ﷺ heard about it) he ordered them to pour out the water they had taken from its wells and feed the camels with the dough, and ordered them to take water from the well whence the she-camel (of Prophet Salih) used to drink. – Al-Bukhari 3379

حَدَّثَنَا إِبْرَاهِيمُ بْنُ الْمُنْذِرِ، حَدَّثَنَا أَنَسُ بْنُ عِيَاضٍ، عَنْ عُبَيْدِ اللَّهِ، عَنْ نَافِعٍ، أَنَّ عَبْدَ اللَّهِ بْنَ عُمَرَ ـ رضى الله عنهما ـ أَخْبَرَهُ أَنَّ النَّاسَ نَزَلُوا مَعَ رَسُولِ اللَّهِ صلى الله عليه وسلم أَرْضَ ثَمُودَ الْحِجْرَ، فَاسْتَقَوْا مِنْ بِئْرِهَا، وَاعْتَجَنُوا بِهِ، فَأَمَرَهُمْ رَسُولُ اللَّهِ صلى الله عليه وسلم أَنْ يُهَرِيقُوا مَا اسْتَقَوْا مِنْ بِئْرِهَا، وَأَنْ يَعْلِفُوا الإِبِلَ الْعَجِينَ، وَأَمَرَهُمْ أَنْ يَسْتَقُوا مِنَ الْبِئْرِ الَّتِي كَانَ تَرِدُهَا النَّاقَةُ. تَابَعَهُ أُسَامَةُ عَنْ نَافِعٍ.

Then there are those who establish a mosque to cause harm, and disbelief, and disunity among the believers, and as an outpost for those who fight Allah and His Messenger. They will swear: "Our intentions are nothing but good." But Allah bears witness that they are liars. Do not stand in it, ever. A mosque founded upon piety from the first day is worthier of your standing in it. In it are men who love to be purified. Allah loves those who purify themselves. – Surah At-Taubah 9:107&108

وَٱلَّذِينَ ٱتَّخَذُواْ مَسْجِدًا ضِرَارًا وَكُفْرًا وَتَفْرِيقًا بَيْنَ ٱلْمُؤْمِنِينَ وَإِرْصَادًا لِّمَنْ حَارَبَ ٱللَّهَ وَرَسُولَهُۥ مِن قَبْلُ وَلَيَحْلِفُنَّ إِنْ أَرَدْنَآ إِلَّا ٱلْحُسْنَىٰ وَٱللَّهُ يَشْهَدُ إِنَّهُمْ لَكَـٰذِبُونَ لَا تَقُمْ فِيهِ أَبَدًا لَّمَسْجِدٌ أُسِّسَ عَلَى ٱلتَّقْوَىٰ مِنْ أَوَّلِ يَوْمٍ أَحَقُّ أَن تَقُومَ فِيهِ فِيهِ رِجَالٌ يُحِبُّونَ أَن يَتَطَهَّرُواْ وَٱللَّهُ يُحِبُّ ٱلْمُطَّهِّرِينَ

Neither your relatives nor your children will benefit you on the Day of Resurrection. He will separate between you. Allah is Observant of what you do. – Surah Al-Mumtahanah 60:3

يَـٰٓأَيُّهَا ٱلَّذِينَ ءَامَنُواْ لَا تَتَوَلَّوْاْ قَوْمًا غَضِبَ ٱللَّهُ عَلَيْهِمْ قَدْ يَئِسُواْ مِنَ ٱلْءَاخِرَةِ كَمَا يَئِسَ ٱلْكُفَّارُ مِنْ أَصْحَـٰبِ ٱلْقُبُورِ

Narrated Abu Said Al-Khudri: Allah's Messenger ﷺ said, "A time will soon come when the best property of a Muslim will be sheep which he will take on the top of mountains and the places of rainfall (valleys) so as to flee with his religion from afflictions." – Al-Bukhari 19

حَدَّثَنَا عَبْدُ اللَّهِ بْنُ مَسْلَمَةَ، عَنْ مَالِكٍ، عَنْ عَبْدِ الرَّحْمَنِ بْنِ عَبْدِ اللَّهِ بْنِ عَبْدِ الرَّحْمَنِ بْنِ أَبِي صَعْصَعَةَ، عَنْ أَبِيهِ، عَنْ أَبِي سَعِيدٍ الْخُدْرِيِّ، أَنَّهُ قَالَ قَالَ رَسُولُ اللَّهِ صلى الله عليه وسلم " يُوشِكُ أَنْ يَكُونَ خَيْرَ مَالِ الْمُسْلِمِ غَنَمٌ يَتْبَعُ بِهَا شَعَفَ الْجِبَالِ وَمَوَاقِعَ الْقَطْرِ، يَفِرُّ بِدِينِهِ مِنَ الْفِتَنِ ".

Moses said: "I have taken refuge with my Lord and your Lord from everyone who waxes arrogant and does not believe in the Day of Reckoning." Surah Al-Ghafir 40:27

وَقَالَ مُوسَىٰٓ إِنِّى عُذْتُ بِرَبِّى وَرَبِّكُم مِّن كُلِّ مُتَكَبِّرٍ لَّا يُؤْمِنُ بِيَوْمِ ٱلْحِسَابِ

Lord, I have settled some of my children in an uncultivated valley,
رَّبَّنَآ إِنِّىٓ أَسْكَنتُ مِن ذُرِّيَّتِى بِوَادٍ غَيْرِ ذِى زَرْعٍ

As the young men (Literally: the pages) took (their) abode in the cave, (and) so they said, "Our Lord, bring us mercy from very close to You, and dispose for us rectitude in our Command." (i.e., in Your Command to us; our: in our affair. – Surah Al-Khaf 18:10

إِذْ أَوَى ٱلْفِتْيَةُ إِلَى ٱلْكَهْفِ فَقَالُواْ رَبَّنَآ ءَاتِنَا مِن لَّدُنكَ رَحْمَةً وَهَيِّئْ لَنَا مِنْ أَمْرِنَا رَشَدًا

Lord, I have settled some of my children in an uncultivated valley, close to Your Sacred Sanctuary so that, oh our Lord, they might establish prayer. Make some people's hearts drawn towards them, and provide them with sustenance, so that they may be grateful. "Our Lord, You truly know all that we may hide [in our hearts], as well as all that we bring into the open: for nothing, on Earth or in heaven, remains hidden from God. All praise is due to God, who has granted me, Ishmael and Isaac, in my old age. My Lord hears all prayer. – Surah Ibrahim 14:37-39

رَّبَّنَآ إِنِّىٓ أَسْكَنتُ مِن ذُرِّيَّتِى بِوَادٍ غَيْرِ ذِى زَرْعٍ عِندَ بَيْتِكَ ٱلْمُحَرَّمِ رَبَّنَا لِيُقِيمُواْ ٱلصَّلَوٰةَ فَٱجْعَلْ أَفْـِٔدَةً مِّنَ ٱلنَّاسِ تَهْوِىٓ إِلَيْهِمْ وَٱرْزُقْهُم مِّنَ ٱلثَّمَرَٰتِ لَعَلَّهُمْ يَشْكُرُونَ رَبَّنَآ إِنَّكَ تَعْلَمُ مَا نُخْفِى وَمَا نُعْلِنُ وَمَا يَخْفَىٰ عَلَى ٱللَّهِ مِن شَىْءٍ فِى ٱلْأَرْضِ وَلَا فِى ٱلسَّمَآءِ ٱلْحَمْدُ لِلَّهِ ٱلَّذِى وَهَبَ لِى عَلَى ٱلْكِبَرِ إِسْمَـٰعِيلَ وَإِسْحَـٰقَ إِنَّ رَبِّى لَسَمِيعُ ٱلدُّعَآءِ

Narrated 'Aisha (the mother of the faithful believers): The commencement of the Divine Inspiration to Allah's Messenger ﷺ was in the form of good dreams which came true like bright daylight, and then the love of seclusion was bestowed upon him. He used to go in seclusion in the cave of Hira where he used to worship (Allah alone) continuously for many days before his desire to see his family. He used to take with him the journey food for the stay and then come back to (his wife) Khadija to take his food likewise again till suddenly the Truth descended upon him while he was in the cave of Hira. The angel came to him and asked him to read. The Prophetﷺ replied, "I do not know how to read." The Prophetﷺ added, "The angel caught me (forcefully) and pressed me so hard that I could not bear it any more. He then released me and again asked me to read and I replied, 'I do not know how to read.' Thereupon he caught me again and pressed me a second time till I could not bear it any more. He then released me and again asked me to read but again I replied, 'I do not know how to read (or what shall I read)?' Thereupon he caught me for the third time and pressed me, and then released me and said, 'Read in the name of your Lord, who has created (all that exists), created man from a clot. Read! And your Lord is the Most Generous." (96.1, 96.2, 96.3) Then Allah's Messengerﷺ returned with the Inspiration and with his heart beating severely. Then he went to Khadija bint Khuwailid and said, "Cover me! Cover me!" They covered him till his fear was over and after that he told her everything that had happened and said, "I fear that something may happen to me." Khadija replied, "Never! By Allah, Allah will never disgrace you. You keep good relations with your kith and kin, help the poor and the destitute, serve your guests generously and assist the deserving calamity-afflicted ones." Khadija then accompanied him to her cousin Waraqa bin Naufal bin Asad bin 'Abdul 'Uzza, who, during the pre-Islamic Period became a Christian and used to write the writing with Hebrew letters. He would write from the Gospel in Hebrew as much as Allah wished him to write. He was an old man and had lost his eyesight. Khadija said to Waraqa, "Listen to the story of your nephew, O my cousin!" Waraqa asked, "O my nephew! What have you seen?" Allah's Messengerﷺ described whatever he had seen. Waraqa said, "This is the same one who keeps the secrets (angel Gabriel) whom Allah had sent to Moses. I wish I were young and could live up to the time when your people would turn you out." Allah's Messengerﷺ asked, "Will they drive me out?" Waraqa replied in the affirmative and said, "Anyone (man) who came with something similar to what you have brought was treated with hostility; and if I should remain alive till the day when you will be turned out then I would support you strongly." But after a few days Waraqa died and the Divine Inspiration was also paused for a while. – Sahih al-Bukhari 3

حَدَّثَنَا يَحْيَى بْنُ بُكَيْرٍ، قَالَ حَدَّثَنَا اللَّيْثُ، عَنْ عُقَيْلٍ، عَنِ ابْنِ شِهَابٍ، عَنْ عُرْوَةَ بْنِ الزُّبَيْرِ، عَنْ عَائِشَةَ أُمِّ الْمُؤْمِنِينَ، أَنَّهَا قَالَتْ أَوَّلُ مَا بُدِئَ بِهِ رَسُولُ اللَّهِ صلى الله عليه وسلم مِنَ الْوَحْىِ الرُّؤْيَا الصَّالِحَةُ فِي النَّوْمِ، فَكَانَ لاَ يَرَى رُؤْيَا إِلاَّ جَاءَتْ مِثْلَ فَلَقِ الصُّبْحِ، ثُمَّ حُبِّبَ إِلَيْهِ الْخَلاَءُ، وَكَانَ يَخْلُو بِغَارِ حِرَاءٍ فَيَتَحَنَّثُ فِيهِ ـ وَهُوَ التَّعَبُّدُ ـ اللَّيَالِيَ ذَوَاتِ الْعَدَدِ قَبْلَ أَنْ يَنْزِعَ إِلَى أَهْلِهِ، وَيَتَزَوَّدُ لِذَلِكَ، ثُمَّ يَرْجِعُ إِلَى خَدِيجَةَ، فَيَتَزَوَّدُ لِمِثْلِهَا، حَتَّى جَاءَهُ الْحَقُّ وَهُوَ فِي غَارِ حِرَاءٍ، فَجَاءَهُ الْمَلَكُ فَقَالَ اقْرَأْ. قَالَ " مَا أَنَا بِقَارِئٍ ". قَالَ " فَأَخَذَنِي فَغَطَّنِي حَتَّى بَلَغَ مِنِّي الْجَهْدَ، ثُمَّ أَرْسَلَنِي فَقَالَ اقْرَأْ. قُلْتُ مَا أَنَا بِقَارِئٍ. فَأَخَذَنِي فَغَطَّنِي الثَّانِيَةَ حَتَّى بَلَغَ مِنِّي الْجَهْدَ، ثُمَّ أَرْسَلَنِي فَقَالَ اقْرَأْ. فَقُلْتُ مَا أَنَا بِقَارِئٍ. فَأَخَذَنِي فَغَطَّنِي الثَّالِثَةَ، ثُمَّ أَرْسَلَنِي فَقَالَ {اقْرَأْ بِاسْمِ رَبِّكَ الَّذِي خَلَقَ * خَلَقَ الإِنْسَانَ مِنْ عَلَقٍ * اقْرَأْ وَرَبُّكَ الأَكْرَمُ} ". فَرَجَعَ بِهَا رَسُولُ اللَّهِ صلى الله عليه وسلم يَرْجُفُ فُؤَادُهُ، فَدَخَلَ عَلَى خَدِيجَةَ بِنْتِ خُوَيْلِدٍ رضى الله عنها فَقَالَ " زَمِّلُونِي زَمِّلُونِي ". فَزَمَّلُوهُ حَتَّى ذَهَبَ عَنْهُ الرَّوْعُ، فَقَالَ لِخَدِيجَةَ وَأَخْبَرَهَا الْخَبَرَ " لَقَدْ خَشِيتُ عَلَى نَفْسِي ". فَقَالَتْ خَدِيجَةُ كَلاَّ وَاللَّهِ مَا يُخْزِيكَ اللَّهُ أَبَدًا، إِنَّكَ لَتَصِلُ الرَّحِمَ، وَتَحْمِلُ الْكَلَّ، وَتَكْسِبُ الْمَعْدُومَ، وَتَقْرِي الضَّيْفَ، وَتُعِينُ عَلَى نَوَائِبِ الْحَقِّ. فَانْطَلَقَتْ بِهِ خَدِيجَةُ حَتَّى أَتَتْ بِهِ وَرَقَةَ بْنَ نَوْفَلِ بْنِ أَسَدِ بْنِ عَبْدِ الْعُزَّى ابْنَ عَمِّ خَدِيجَةَ ـ وَكَانَ امْرَأً تَنَصَّرَ فِي الْجَاهِلِيَّةِ، وَكَانَ يَكْتُبُ الْكِتَابَ الْعِبْرَانِيَّ، فَيَكْتُبُ مِنَ الإِنْجِيلِ بِالْعِبْرَانِيَّةِ مَا شَاءَ اللَّهُ أَنْ يَكْتُبَ، وَكَانَ شَيْخًا كَبِيرًا قَدْ عَمِيَ ـ فَقَالَتْ لَهُ خَدِيجَةُ يَا ابْنَ عَمِّ اسْمَعْ مِنَ ابْنِ أَخِيكَ. فَقَالَ لَهُ وَرَقَةُ يَا ابْنَ أَخِي مَاذَا تَرَى فَأَخْبَرَهُ رَسُولُ اللَّهِ صلى الله عليه وسلم خَبَرَ مَا رَأَى. فَقَالَ لَهُ وَرَقَةُ هَذَا النَّامُوسُ الَّذِي نَزَّلَ اللَّهُ عَلَى مُوسَى صلى الله عليه وسلم يَا لَيْتَنِي فِيهَا جَذَعًا، لَيْتَنِي أَكُونُ حَيًّا إِذْ يُخْرِجُكَ قَوْمُكَ. فَقَالَ رَسُولُ اللَّهِ صلى الله عليه وسلم " أَوَمُخْرِجِيَّ هُمْ ". قَالَ نَعَمْ، لَمْ يَأْتِ رَجُلٌ قَطُّ بِمِثْلِ مَا جِئْتَ بِهِ إِلاَّ عُودِيَ، وَإِنْ يُدْرِكْنِي يَوْمُكَ أَنْصُرْكَ نَصْرًا مُؤَزَّرًا. ثُمَّ لَمْ يَنْشَبْ وَرَقَةُ أَنْ تُوُفِّيَ وَفَتَرَ الْوَحْىُ.

.......Anas added: There were graves of pagans in it and some of it was unleveled and there were some date-palm trees in it. The Prophet ﷺ ordered that the graves of the pagans be dug out and the unleveled land be level led and the date-palm trees be cut down . (So all that was done). They aligned these cut date-palm trees towards the Qibla of the mosque (as a wall) and they also built two stone side-walls (of the mosque). His companions brought the stones while reciting some poetic verses. The Prophet ﷺ was with them and he kept on saying, "There is no goodness except that of the Hereafter, O Allah! So please forgive the Ansars and the emigrants. " – Sahih Al-Bukhari 428

فَقَالَ أَنَسٌ فَكَانَ فِيهِ مَا أَقُولُ لَكُمْ، قُبُورُ الْمُشْرِكِينَ، وَفِيهِ خَرِبٌ، وَفِيهِ نَخْلٌ، فَأَمَرَ النَّبِيُّ صلى الله عليه وسلم بِقُبُورِ الْمُشْرِكِينَ فَنُبِشَتْ، ثُمَّ بِالْخَرِبِ فَسُوِّيَتْ، وَبِالنَّخْلِ فَقُطِعَ، فَصَفُّوا النَّخْلَ قِبْلَةَ الْمَسْجِدِ، وَجَعَلُوا عِضَادَتَيْهِ الْحِجَارَةَ، وَجَعَلُوا يَنْقُلُونَ الصَّخْرَ، وَهُمْ يَرْتَجِزُونَ، وَالنَّبِيُّ صلى الله عليه وسلم مَعَهُمْ وَهُوَ يَقُولُ " اللَّهُمَّ لاَ خَيْرَ إِلاَّ خَيْرُ الآخِرَهْ فَاغْفِرْ لِلأَنْصَارِ وَالْمُهَاجِرَهْ "

.......They would dearly wish that you renounce your faith. – Surah Al-Mumtahinah 60:2

وَوَدُّوا۟ لَوْ تَكْفُرُونَ

And in no way did they seek vengeance on them except that they believed in Allah, The Ever-Mighty, The Ever-Praiseworthy. Surah Al-Buruj 85:8

وَمَا نَقَمُوا مِنْهُمْ إِلَّا أَن يُؤْمِنُوا بِاللَّهِ الْعَزِيزِ الْحَمِيدِ

And in no way do you take vengeance upon us except that we have believed in the signs of our Lord as soon they came to us. Our Lord, pour out upon us patience and take us to Yourself as Muslims." – Surah Al-A'raf 7:126

وَمَا تَنقِمُ مِنَّآ إِلَّآ أَنْ ءَامَنَّا بِـَٔايَـٰتِ رَبِّنَا لَمَّا جَآءَتْنَا ۚ رَبَّنَآ أَفْرِغْ عَلَيْنَا صَبْرًا وَتَوَفَّنَا مُسْلِمِينَ

And the ones who disbelieved said to their Messengers, "Indeed we will definitely drive you out of our land or indeed you will definitely go back to our creed." Then their Lord revealed to them, "Indeed We will definitely cause the unjust to perish. – Surah Ibrahim 14:13

وَقَالَ ٱلَّذِينَ كَفَرُوا۟ لِرُسُلِهِمْ لَنُخْرِجَنَّكُم مِّنْ أَرْضِنَآ أَوْ لَتَعُودُنَّ فِى مِلَّتِنَا ۖ فَأَوْحَىٰٓ إِلَيْهِمْ رَبُّهُمْ لَنُهْلِكَنَّ ٱلظَّـٰلِمِينَ

(Those) who have been driven out of their homes untruthfully (i.e., without right) except that they say, "Our Lord is Allah."..... – Surah Al-Hajj 22:40

ٱلَّذِينَ أُخْرِجُوا۟ مِن دِيَـٰرِهِم بِغَيْرِ حَقٍّ إِلَّآ أَن يَقُولُوا۟ رَبُّنَا ٱللَّهُ

The Book of

Certainly, there has been in them an excellent example for you to follow, for those who look forward to Allah and the Last Day.

لَقَدْ كَانَ لَكُمْ فِيهِمْ أُسْوَةٌ حَسَنَةٌ لِّمَن كَانَ يَرْجُواْ ٱللَّهَ

Narrated Salama bin Al-Akwa`: That he visited Al-Hajjaj (bin Yusuf). Al-Hajjaj said, "O son of Al-Akwa`! You have turned on your heels (i.e., deserted Islam) by staying (in the desert) with the bedouins." Salama replied, "No, but Allah's Messenger ﷺ allowed me to stay with the bedouin in the desert." Narrated Yazid bin Abi Ubaid: When `Uthman bin `Affan was killed (martyred), Salama bin Al-Akwa` went out to a place called Ar- Rabadha and married there and begot children, and he stayed there till a few nights before his death when he came to Medina. – Al-Bukhari 7087

حَدَّثَنَا قُتَيْبَةُ بْنُ سَعِيدٍ، حَدَّثَنَا حَاتِمٌ، عَنْ يَزِيدَ بْنِ أَبِي عُبَيْدٍ، عَنْ سَلَمَةَ بْنِ الأَكْوَعِ، أَنَّهُ دَخَلَ عَلَى الْحَجَّاجِ فَقَالَ يَا ابْنَ الأَكْوَعِ ارْتَدَدْتَ عَلَى عَقِبَيْكَ تَعَرَّبْتَ قَالَ لاَ وَلَكِنَّ رَسُولَ اللَّهِ صلى الله عليه وسلم أَذِنَ لِي فِي الْبَدْوِ. وَعَنْ يَزِيدَ بْنِ أَبِي عُبَيْدٍ قَالَ لَمَّا قُتِلَ عُثْمَانُ بْنُ عَفَّانَ خَرَجَ سَلَمَةُ بْنُ الأَكْوَعِ إِلَى الرَّبَذَةِ، وَتَزَوَّجَ هُنَاكَ امْرَأَةً وَوَلَدَتْ لَهُ أَوْلاَدًا، فَلَمْ يَزَلْ بِهَا حَتَّى قَبْلَ أَنْ يَمُوتَ بِلَيَالٍ، فَنَزَلَ الْمَدِينَةَ

Narrated Zaid bin Wahab: I passed by a place called Ar-Rabadha and by chance I met Abu Dhar and asked him, "What has brought you to this place?" He said, "I was in Sham and differed with Muawiya on the meaning of (the following verses of the Qur'an): 'They who hoard up gold and silver and spend them not in the way of Allah.' (9.34). Muawiya said, 'This verse is revealed regarding the people of the scriptures." I said, It was revealed regarding us and also the people of the scriptures." So we had a quarrel and Mu'awiya sent a complaint against me to `Uthman. `Uthman wrote to me to come to Medina, and I came to Medina. Many people came to me as if they had not seen me before. So I told this to `Uthman who said to me, "You may depart and live nearby if you wish." That was the reason for my being here for even if an Ethiopian had been nominated as my ruler, I would have obeyed him .- Sahih Al-Bukhari 1406

حَدَّثَنَا عَلِيٌّ، سَمِعَ هُشَيْمًا، أَخْبَرَنَا حُصَيْنٌ، عَنْ زَيْدِ بْنِ وَهْبٍ، قَالَ مَرَرْتُ بِالرَّبَذَةِ فَإِذَا أَنَا بِأَبِي، ذَرٍّ ـ رضى الله عنه ـ فَقُلْتُ لَهُ مَا أَنْزَلَكَ مَنْزِلَكَ هَذَا قَالَ كُنْتُ بِالشَّأْمِ، فَاخْتَلَفْتُ أَنَا وَمُعَاوِيَةُ فِي الَّذِينَ يَكْنِزُونَ الذَّهَبَ وَالْفِضَّةَ وَلاَ يُنْفِقُونَهَا فِي سَبِيلِ اللَّهِ. قَالَ مُعَاوِيَةُ نَزَلَتْ فِي أَهْلِ الْكِتَابِ. فَقُلْتُ نَزَلَتْ فِينَا وَفِيهِمْ. فَكَانَ بَيْنِي وَبَيْنَهُ فِي ذَاكَ، وَكَتَبَ إِلَى عُثْمَانَ ـ رضى الله عنه ـ يَشْكُونِي، فَكَتَبَ إِلَىَّ عُثْمَانُ أَنِ اقْدَمِ الْمَدِينَةَ. فَقَدِمْتُهَا فَكَثُرَ عَلَىَّ النَّاسُ حَتَّى كَأَنَّهُمْ لَمْ يَرَوْنِي قَبْلَ ذَلِكَ، فَذَكَرْتُ ذَاكَ لِعُثْمَانَ فَقَالَ لِي إِنْ شِئْتَ تَنَحَّيْتَ فَكُنْتَ قَرِيبًا. فَذَاكَ الَّذِي أَنْزَلَنِي هَذَا الْمَنْزِلَ، وَلَوْ أَمَّرُوا عَلَىَّ حَبَشِيًّا لَسَمِعْتُ وَأَطَعْتُ.

Recall that Abraham said, "O my Lord, make this land peaceful, and keep me and my sons from worshiping idols." "My Lord, they have led many people astray. Whoever follows me belongs with me; and whoever disobeys me—You are Forgiving and Merciful. "Our Lord, I have settled some of my offspring in a valley of no vegetation, by Your Sacred House, our Lord, so that they may perform the prayers. So make the hearts of some people incline towards them, and provide them with fruits, that they may be thankful." – Surah Ibrahim 14:35-37

وَإِذْ قَالَ إِبْرَٰهِيمُ رَبِّ ٱجْعَلْ هَٰذَا ٱلْبَلَدَ ءَامِنًا وَٱجْنُبْنِى وَبَنِىَّ أَن نَّعْبُدَ ٱلْأَصْنَامَ رَبِّ إِنَّهُنَّ أَضْلَلْنَ كَثِيرًا مِّنَ ٱلنَّاسِ فَمَن تَبِعَنِى فَإِنَّهُۥ مِنِّى وَمَنْ عَصَانِى فَإِنَّكَ غَفُورٌ رَّحِيمٌ رَّبَّنَآ إِنِّىٓ أَسْكَنتُ مِن ذُرِّيَّتِى بِوَادٍ غَيْرِ ذِى زَرْعٍ عِندَ بَيْتِكَ ٱلْمُحَرَّمِ رَبَّنَا لِيُقِيمُوا۟ ٱلصَّلَوٰةَ فَٱجْعَلْ أَفْـِٔدَةً مِّنَ ٱلنَّاسِ تَهْوِىٓ إِلَيْهِمْ وَٱرْزُقْهُم مِّنَ ٱلثَّمَرَٰتِ لَعَلَّهُمْ يَشْكُرُونَ

Narrated Anas bin Malik: When Allah's Messenger ﷺ arrived at Medina, he alighted at the upper part of Medina among the people called Bani `Amr bin `Auf and he stayed with them for fourteen nights. Then he sent for the chiefs of Bani An-Najjar, and they came, carrying their swords. As if I am just now looking at Allah's Messenger ﷺ on his she-camel with Abu Bakr riding behind him (on the same camel) and the chiefs of Bani An- Najjar around him till he dismounted in the courtyard of Abu Aiyub's home. The Prophet ﷺ used to offer the prayer wherever the prayer was due, and he would pray even in sheepfolds. Then he ordered that the mosque be built. He sent for the chiefs of Banu An-Najjar, and when they came, he said, "O Banu An-Najjar! Suggest to me the price of this garden of yours." They replied "No! By Allah, we do not demand its price except from Allah." In that garden there were the (following) things that I will tell you: Graves of pagans, unleveled land with holes and pits etc., and date-palm trees. Allah's Messenger ﷺ ordered that the graves of the pagans be dug up and, the unleveled land be leveled and the date-palm trees be cut down. The trunks of the trees were arranged so as to form the wall facing the Qibla. The Stone pillars were built at the sides of its gate. The companions of the Prophet ﷺ were carrying the stones and reciting some lyrics, and Allah's Messenger ﷺ . . was with them and they were saying, "O Allah! There is no good Excel the good of the Hereafter, so bestow victory on the Ansar and the Emigrants. " – Al-Bukhari 3932

حَدَّثَنَا مُسَدَّدٌ، حَدَّثَنَا عَبْدُ الْوَارِثِ، وَحَدَّثَنَا إِسْحَاقُ بْنُ مَنْصُورٍ، أَخْبَرَنَا عَبْدُ الصَّمَدِ، قَالَ سَمِعْتُ أَبِي يُحَدِّثُ، حَدَّثَنَا أَبُو التَّيَّاحِ، يَزِيدُ بْنُ حُمَيْدٍ الضُّبَعِيُّ قَالَ حَدَّثَنِي أَنَسُ بْنُ مَالِكٍ ـ رضى الله عنه ـ قَالَ لَمَّا قَدِمَ رَسُولُ اللَّهِ صلى الله عليه وسلم الْمَدِينَةَ، نَزَلَ فِي عُلْوِ الْمَدِينَةِ فِي حَىٍّ يُقَالُ لَهُمْ بَنُو عَمْرِو بْنِ عَوْفٍ ـ قَالَ ـ فَأَقَامَ فِيهِمْ أَرْبَعَ عَشْرَةَ لَيْلَةً، ثُمَّ أَرْسَلَ إِلَى مَلإِ بَنِي النَّجَّارِ ـ قَالَ ـ فَجَاءُوا مُتَقَلِّدِي سُيُوفِهِمْ، قَالَ وَكَأَنِّي أَنْظُرُ إِلَى رَسُولِ اللَّهِ صلى الله عليه وسلم عَلَى رَاحِلَتِهِ، وَأَبُو بَكْرٍ رِدْفَهُ، وَمَلأُ بَنِي النَّجَّارِ حَوْلَهُ حَتَّى أَلْقَى بِفِنَاءِ أَبِي أَيُّوبَ، قَالَ فَكَانَ يُصَلِّي حَيْثُ أَدْرَكَتْهُ الصَّلاَةُ، وَيُصَلِّي فِي مَرَابِضِ الْغَنَمِ، قَالَ ثُمَّ إِنَّهُ أَمَرَ بِبِنَاءِ الْمَسْجِدِ، فَأَرْسَلَ إِلَى مَلإِ بَنِي النَّجَّارِ، فَجَاءُوا فَقَالَ " يَا بَنِي النَّجَّارِ، ثَامِنُونِي حَائِطَكُمْ هَذَا ". فَقَالُوا لاَ، وَاللَّهِ لاَ نَطْلُبُ ثَمَنَهُ إِلاَّ إِلَى اللَّهِ. قَالَ فَكَانَ فِيهِ مَا أَقُولُ لَكُمْ كَانَتْ فِيهِ قُبُورُ الْمُشْرِكِينَ، وَكَانَتْ فِيهِ خِرَبٌ، وَكَانَ فِيهِ نَخْلٌ، فَأَمَرَ رَسُولُ اللَّهِ صلى الله عليه وسلم بِقُبُورِ الْمُشْرِكِينَ فَنُبِشَتْ، وَبِالْخِرَبِ فَسُوِّيَتْ، وَبِالنَّخْلِ فَقُطِعَ، قَالَ فَصَفُّوا النَّخْلَ قِبْلَةَ الْمَسْجِدِ ـ قَالَ ـ وَجَعَلُوا عِضَادَتَيْهِ حِجَارَةً. قَالَ قَالَ جَعَلُوا يَنْقُلُونَ ذَاكَ الصَّخْرَ وَهُمْ يَرْتَجِزُونَ، وَرَسُولُ اللَّهِ صلى الله عليه وسلم مَعَهُمْ يَقُولُونَ اللَّهُمَّ إِنَّهُ لاَ خَيْرَ إِلاَّ خَيْرُ الآخِرَهْ فَانْصُرِ الأَنْصَارَ وَالْمُهَاجِرَهْ

And he elevated his parents on the throne, and they fell prostrate before him. He said, "Father, this is the fulfillment of my vision of long ago. My Lord has made it come true. He has blessed me, when he released me from prison, and brought you out of the wilderness, after the devil had sown conflict between me and my brothers. My Lord is Most Kind towards whomever He wills. He is the Allknowing, the Most Wise." – Surah Yusuf 12:100

وَرَفَعَ أَبَوَيْهِ عَلَى ٱلْعَرْشِ وَخَرُّواْ لَهُۥ سُجَّدًاۖ وَقَالَ يَٰٓأَبَتِ هَٰذَا تَأْوِيلُ رُءْيَٰىَ مِن قَبْلُ قَدْ جَعَلَهَا رَبِّى حَقًّاۖ وَقَدْ أَحْسَنَ بِىٓ إِذْ أَخْرَجَنِى مِنَ ٱلسِّجْنِ وَجَآءَ بِكُم مِّنَ ٱلْبَدْوِ مِنۢ بَعْدِ أَن نَّزَغَ ٱلشَّيْطَٰنُ بَيْنِى وَبَيْنَ إِخْوَتِىٓۚ إِنَّ رَبِّى لَطِيفٌ لِّمَا يَشَآءُۚ إِنَّهُۥ هُوَ ٱلْعَلِيمُ ٱلْحَكِيمُ

"But if you believe me not, then keep away from me and leave me alone." – Surah Ad-Dukhan 44:21

وَإِن لَّمْ تُؤْمِنُواْ لِى فَٱعْتَزِلُونِ

The Book of
Pharaoh Ramesses II
الفرعون رمسيس الثاني

He (Pharaoh) said, "I am your Lord, the most high." – Surah An-Nazi'at 79:24
فَقَالَ أَنَا رَبُّكُمُ الأَعْلَىٰ

Pharaoh proclaimed among his people, saying, "O my people, do I not own the Kingdom of Egypt, and these rivers flow beneath me? Do you not see? Am I not better than this miserable wretch, who can barely express himself? Why are bracelets of gold not dropped on him, or they angels came with him in procession?" Thus he fooled his people, and they obeyed him. They were wicked people. – Surah Az-Zukhruf 43:51-54
وَنَادَىٰ فِرْعَوْنُ فِى قَوْمِهِۦ قَالَ يَـٰقَوْمِ أَلَيْسَ لِى مُلْكُ مِصْرَ وَهَـٰذِهِ ٱلْأَنْهَـٰرُ تَجْرِى مِن تَحْتِىٓ ۖ أَفَلَا تُبْصِرُونَ أَمْ أَنَا۠ خَيْرٌ مِّنْ هَـٰذَا ٱلَّذِى هُوَ مَهِينٌ وَلَا يَكَادُ يُبِينُ فَلَوْلَآ أُلْقِىَ عَلَيْهِ أَسْوِرَةٌ مِّن ذَهَبٍ أَوْ جَآءَ مَعَهُ ٱلْمَلَـٰٓئِكَةُ مُقْتَرِنِينَ فَٱسْتَخَفَّ قَوْمَهُۥ فَأَطَاعُوهُ ۚ إِنَّهُمْ كَانُوا۟ قَوْمًا فَـٰسِقِينَ

And recall that We delivered you from the people of Pharaoh. They inflicted on you terrible persecution, killing your sons and sparing your women. Therein was a tremendous trial from your Lord. – Surah Al-Baqarah 2:49
وَإِذْ نَجَّيْنَـٰكُم مِّنْ ءَالِ فِرْعَوْنَ يَسُومُونَكُمْ سُوٓءَ ٱلْعَذَابِ يُذَبِّحُونَ أَبْنَآءَكُمْ وَيَسْتَحْيُونَ نِسَآءَكُمْ ۚ وَفِى ذَٰلِكُم بَلَآءٌ مِّن رَّبِّكُمْ عَظِيمٌ

Moses said to his people, "Remember Allah's blessings upon you, as He delivered you from the people of Pharaoh, who inflicted on you terrible suffering, slaughtering your sons while sparing your daughters. In that was a serious trial from your Lord." - Surah Ibrahim 14:6
وَإِذْ قَالَ مُوسَىٰ لِقَوْمِهِ ٱذْكُرُوا۟ نِعْمَةَ ٱللَّهِ عَلَيْكُمْ إِذْ أَنجَىٰكُم مِّنْ ءَالِ فِرْعَوْنَ يَسُومُونَكُمْ سُوٓءَ ٱلْعَذَابِ وَيُذَبِّحُونَ أَبْنَآءَكُمْ وَيَسْتَحْيُونَ نِسَآءَكُمْ ۚ وَفِى ذَٰلِكُم بَلَآءٌ مِّن رَّبِّكُمْ عَظِيمٌ

Pharaoh exalted himself in the land, and divided its people into factions. He persecuted a group of them, slaughtering their sons, while sparing their daughters. He was truly a corrupter. – Surah Al-Qasas 28:4
إِنَّ فِرْعَوْنَ عَلَا فِى ٱلْأَرْضِ وَجَعَلَ أَهْلَهَا شِيَعًا يَسْتَضْعِفُ طَآئِفَةً مِّنْهُمْ يُذَبِّحُ أَبْنَآءَهُمْ وَيَسْتَحْىِۦ نِسَآءَهُمْ ۚ إِنَّهُۥ كَانَ مِنَ ٱلْمُفْسِدِينَ

He said, "If you accept any god other than me, I will make you a prisoner." – Surah Ash-Shu'ara 26:29
قَالَ لَئِنِ ٱتَّخَذْتَ إِلَـٰهًا غَيْرِى لَأَجْعَلَنَّكَ مِنَ ٱلْمَسْجُونِينَ

When the magicians arrived, they said to Pharaoh, "Is there a reward for us, if we are the winners?" He said, "Yes, and you will be among those favored."
Surah Ash-Shu'ara 26:41&42
فلمّا جاءَ السّحرةُ قالوا لِفِرْعَوْنَ ائِنّ لنا لاجْرًا إن كُنّا نَحْنُ الغَٰلِبِينَ قَالَ نَعَمْ وَإِنَّكُمْ إِذًا لَّمِنَ ٱلْمُقَرَّبِينَ

He said, "Did you believe in Him before I have given you permission? He must be your chief, who taught you magic. You will soon know. I will cut off your hands and feet on opposite sides, and I will crucify you all." – Surah Ash-Shu'ara 26:49
قَالَ ءَامَنتُمْ لَهُۥ قَبْلَ أَنْ ءَاذَنَ لَكُمْ ۖ إِنَّهُۥ لَكَبِيرُكُمُ ٱلَّذِى عَلَّمَكُمُ ٱلسِّحْرَ فَلَسَوْفَ تَعْلَمُونَ ۚ لَأُقَطِّعَنَّ أَيْدِيَكُمْ وَأَرْجُلَكُم مِّنْ خِلَـٰفٍ وَلَأُصَلِّبَنَّكُمْ أَجْمَعِينَ

The magicians came to Pharaoh, and said, "Surely there is a reward for us, if we are the victors." He said, "Yes, and you will be among my favorites." Surah Al-A'raf 7:113&114
وَجَآءَ ٱلسَّحَرَةُ فِرْعَوْنَ قَالُوٓا۟ إِنَّ لَنَا لَأَجْرًا إِن كُنَّا نَحْنُ ٱلْغَـٰلِبِينَ قَالَ نَعَمْ وَإِنَّكُمْ لَمِنَ ٱلْمُقَرَّبِينَ

Pharaoh said, "Did you believe in Him before I have given you permission? This is surely a conspiracy you schemed in the city, in order to expel its people from it. You will surely know." "I will cut off your hands and your feet on opposite sides; then I will crucify you all." – Surah Al-A'raf 7123&124
قَالَ فِرْعَوْنُ ءَامَنتُم بِهِۦ قَبْلَ أَنْ ءَاذَنَ لَكُمْ ۖ إِنَّ هَـٰذَا لَمَكْرٌ مَّكَرْتُمُوهُ فِى ٱلْمَدِينَةِ لِتُخْرِجُوا۟ مِنْهَآ أَهْلَهَا ۖ فَسَوْفَ تَعْلَمُونَ لَأُقَطِّعَنَّ أَيْدِيَكُمْ وَأَرْجُلَكُم مِّنْ خِلَـٰفٍ ثُمَّ لَأُصَلِّبَنَّكُمْ أَجْمَعِينَ

The chiefs of Pharaoh's people said, "Will you let Moses and his people cause trouble in the land, and forsake you and your gods?" He said, "We will kill their sons, and spare their women. We have absolute power over them."
Surah Al-A'raf 7:127
وَقَالَ ٱلْمَلَأُ مِن قَوْمِ فِرْعَوْنَ أَتَذَرُ مُوسَىٰ وَقَوْمَهُۥ لِيُفْسِدُوا۟ فِى ٱلْأَرْضِ وَيَذَرَكَ وَءَالِهَتَكَ ۚ قَالَ سَنُقَتِّلُ أَبْنَآءَهُمْ وَنَسْتَحْىِۦ نِسَآءَهُمْ وَإِنَّا فَوْقَهُمْ قَـٰهِرُونَ

Pharaoh said, "Leave me to kill Moses, and let him appeal to his Lord. I fear he may change your religion, or spread disorder in the land." – Surah Ghafir 40:26
وَقَالَ فِرْعَوْنُ ذَرُونِىٓ أَقْتُلْ مُوسَىٰ وَلْيَدْعُ رَبَّهُۥٓ ۖ إِنِّىٓ أَخَافُ أَن يُبَدِّلَ دِينَكُمْ أَوْ أَن يُظْهِرَ فِى ٱلْأَرْضِ ٱلْفَسَادَ

A believing man from Pharaoh's family, who had concealed his faith, said, "Are you going to kill a man for saying, `My Lord is Allah,' and he has brought you clear proofs from your Lord? If he is a liar, his lying will rebound upon him; but if he is truthful, then some of what he promises you will befall you. Allah does not guide the extravagant imposter. O my people! Yours is the dominion today, supreme in the land; but who will help us against Allah's might, should it fall upon us?" Pharaoh said, "I do not show you except what I see, and I do not guide you except to the path of prudence." The one who had believed said, "O my people, I fear for you the like of the day of the confederates. Like the fate of the people of Noah, and Aad, and Thamood, and those after them. Allah wants no injustice for the servants. O my people, I fear for you the Day of Calling Out. The Day when you will turn and flee, having no defender against Allah. Whomever Allah misguides has no guide." Joseph had come to you with clear revelations, but you continued to doubt what he came to you with. Until, when he perished, you said, "Allah will never send a messenger after him." Thus Allah leads astray the outrageous skeptic. Those who argue against Allah's revelations, without any proof having come to them—a heinous sin in the sight of Allah, and of those who believe. Thus Allah seals the heart of every proud bully. – Surah Ghafir 40:28-35
وَقَالَ رَجُلٌ مُّؤْمِنٌ مِّنْ ءَالِ فِرْعَوْنَ يَكْتُمُ إِيمَـٰنَهُۥٓ أَتَقْتُلُونَ رَجُلًا أَن يَقُولَ رَبِّىَ ٱللَّهُ وَقَدْ جَآءَكُم بِٱلْبَيِّنَـٰتِ مِن رَّبِّكُمْ ۖ وَإِن يَكُ كَـٰذِبًا فَعَلَيْهِ كَذِبُهُۥ ۖ وَإِن يَكُ صَادِقًا يُصِبْكُم بَعْضُ ٱلَّذِى يَعِدُكُمْ ۖ إِنَّ ٱللَّهَ لَا يَهْدِى مَنْ هُوَ مُسْرِفٌ كَذَّابٌ يَـٰقَوْمِ لَكُمُ ٱلْمُلْكُ ٱلْيَوْمَ ظَـٰهِرِينَ فِى ٱلْأَرْضِ فَمَن يَنصُرُنَا مِنۢ بَأْسِ ٱللَّهِ إِن جَآءَنَا ۚ قَالَ فِرْعَوْنُ مَآ أُرِيكُمْ إِلَّا مَآ أَرَىٰ وَمَآ أَهْدِيكُمْ إِلَّا سَبِيلَ ٱلرَّشَادِ وَقَالَ ٱلَّذِىٓ ءَامَنَ يَـٰقَوْمِ إِنِّىٓ أَخَافُ عَلَيْكُم مِّثْلَ يَوْمِ ٱلْأَحْزَابِ مِثْلَ دَأْبِ قَوْمِ نُوحٍ وَعَادٍ وَثَمُودَ وَٱلَّذِينَ مِنۢ بَعْدِهِمْ ۚ وَمَا ٱللَّهُ يُرِيدُ ظُلْمًا لِّلْعِبَادِ وَيَـٰقَوْمِ إِنِّىٓ أَخَافُ عَلَيْكُمْ يَوْمَ ٱلتَّنَادِ يَوْمَ تُوَلُّونَ مُدْبِرِينَ مَا لَكُم مِّنَ ٱللَّهِ مِنْ عَاصِمٍ ۗ وَمَن يُضْلِلِ ٱللَّهُ فَمَا لَهُۥ مِنْ هَادٍ وَلَقَدْ جَآءَكُمْ يُوسُفُ مِن قَبْلُ بِٱلْبَيِّنَـٰتِ فَمَا زِلْتُمْ فِى شَكٍّ مِّمَّا جَآءَكُم بِهِۦ ۖ حَتَّىٰٓ إِذَا هَلَكَ قُلْتُمْ لَن يَبْعَثَ ٱللَّهُ مِنۢ بَعْدِهِۦ رَسُولًا ۚ كَذَٰلِكَ يُضِلُّ ٱللَّهُ مَنْ هُوَ مُسْرِفٌ مُّرْتَابٌ ٱلَّذِينَ يُجَـٰدِلُونَ فِىٓ ءَايَـٰتِ ٱللَّهِ بِغَيْرِ سُلْطَـٰنٍ أَتَىٰهُمْ ۖ كَبُرَ مَقْتًا عِندَ ٱللَّهِ وَعِندَ ٱلَّذِينَ ءَامَنُوا۟ ۚ كَذَٰلِكَ يَطْبَعُ ٱللَّهُ عَلَىٰ كُلِّ قَلْبِ مُتَكَبِّرٍ جَبَّارٍ

So Allah protected him from the evils of their scheming, while a terrible torment besieged Pharaoh's clan. The Fire. They will be exposed to it morning and evening. And on the Day the Hour takes place: "Admit the clan of Pharaoh to the most intense agony." – Surah Ghafir 40:45&46

فَوَقَىٰهُ ٱللَّهُ سَيِّـَٔاتِ مَا مَكَرُوا۟ ۖ وَحَاقَ بِـَٔالِ فِرْعَوْنَ سُوٓءُ ٱلْعَذَابِ ٱلنَّارُ يُعْرَضُونَ عَلَيْهَا غُدُوًّا وَعَشِيًّا ۖ وَيَوْمَ تَقُومُ ٱلسَّاعَةُ أَدْخِلُوٓا۟ ءَالَ فِرْعَوْنَ أَشَدَّ ٱلْعَذَابِ

But none believed in Moses except some children of his people, for fear that Pharaoh and his chiefs would persecute them. Pharaoh was high and mighty in the land. He was a tyrant. – Surah Yunus 10:83

فَمَآ ءَامَنَ لِمُوسَىٰٓ إِلَّا ذُرِّيَّةٌ مِّن قَوْمِهِۦ عَلَىٰ خَوْفٍ مِّن فِرْعَوْنَ وَمَلَإِي۟هِمْ أَن يَفْتِنَهُمْ ۚ وَإِنَّ فِرْعَوْنَ لَعَالٍ فِى ٱلْأَرْضِ وَإِنَّهُۥ لَمِنَ ٱلْمُسْرِفِينَ

We have believed in our Lord, so that He may forgive us our sins, and the magic you have compelled us to practice. Allah is Better, and more Lasting." – Surah TaHa 20:73

إِنَّآ ءَامَنَّا بِرَبِّنَا لِيَغْفِرَ لَنَا خَطَـٰيَـٰنَا وَمَآ أَكْرَهْتَنَا عَلَيْهِ مِنَ ٱلسِّحْرِ ۗ وَٱللَّهُ خَيْرٌ وَأَبْقَىٰٓ

[Pharaoh] said, "This messenger who has been sent to you is really mad." – Surah Ash-Shu'ara 26:27

قَالَ إِنَّ رَسُولَكُمُ ٱلَّذِىٓ أُرْسِلَ إِلَيْكُمْ لَمَجْنُونٌ

The chiefs who disbelieved among his people
ٱلْمَلَؤُا۟ ٱلَّذِينَ كَفَرُوا۟ مِن قَوْمِهِ

Then said the chiefs who disbelieved among his people, "In no way is this anything except a mortal like yourselves, who would like to be graced with (superiority) (Literally: assume graciousness) over you. And if Allah had (so) decided, He would indeed have sent down Angels. In no way did we hear of this among our earliest fathers. – Surah Al-Mu'minun 23:24

فَقَالَ ٱلْمَلَؤُا۟ ٱلَّذِينَ كَفَرُوا۟ مِن قَوْمِهِۦ مَا هَـٰذَآ إِلَّا بَشَرٌ مِّثْلُكُمْ يُرِيدُ أَن يَتَفَضَّلَ عَلَيْكُمْ وَلَوْ شَآءَ ٱللَّهُ لَأَنزَلَ مَلَـٰٓئِكَةً مَّا سَمِعْنَا بِهَـٰذَا فِىٓ ءَابَآئِنَا ٱلْأَوَّلِينَ

And (the ones) who were deemed weak will say to (the ones) who waxed proud, "No indeed, (but) (it was your) scheming night and day-time as you commanded us to disbelieve in Allah and make up compeers to Him." .... Surah Saba 34:33

وَقَالَ ٱلَّذِينَ ٱسْتُضْعِفُوا۟ لِلَّذِينَ ٱسْتَكْبَرُوا۟ بَلْ مَكْرُ ٱلَّيْلِ وَٱلنَّهَارِ إِذْ تَأْمُرُونَنَآ أَن نَّكْفُرَ بِٱللَّهِ وَنَجْعَلَ لَهُۥٓ أَندَادًا ۚ

And the chiefs among them went off, (saying), "Go on! (Or: March on!) And endure (patiently) with your gods; surely this indeed is a thing willfully (designed). – Surah Sad 38:6

وَٱنطَلَقَ ٱلْمَلَأُ مِنْهُمْ أَنِ ٱمْشُوا۟ وَٱصْبِرُوا۟ عَلَىٰٓ ءَالِهَتِكُمْ ۖ إِنَّ هَـٰذَا لَشَىْءٌ يُرَادُ

The chiefs who disbelieved among his people said, "Surely we see you indeed in foolishness, and surely we indeed expect that you are one of the liars." – Surah Al-A'raf 7:66

قَالَ ٱلْمَلَأُ ٱلَّذِينَ كَفَرُوا۟ مِن قَوْمِهِۦٓ إِنَّا لَنَرَىٰكَ فِى سَفَاهَةٍ وَإِنَّا لَنَظُنُّكَ مِنَ ٱلْكَـٰذِبِينَ

Indeed We have already sent N?h to his people; so he said "O my people! Worship Allah. In no way do you have any god other than He. Surely I fear for you the torment of a tremendous

Day." The chiefs of his people said, "Surely we indeed see you in evident error." – Surah Al-A'raf 7:59&60

لَقَدْ أَرْسَلْنَا نُوحًا إِلَىٰ قَوْمِهِۦ فَقَالَ يَٰقَوْمِ ٱعْبُدُوا۟ ٱللَّهَ مَا لَكُم مِّنْ إِلَٰهٍ غَيْرُهُۥٓ إِنِّىٓ أَخَافُ عَلَيْكُمْ عَذَابَ يَوْمٍ عَظِيمٍ قَالَ ٱلْمَلَأُ مِن
قَوْمِهِۦٓ إِنَّا لَنَرَىٰكَ فِى ضَلَٰلٍ مُّبِينٍ

And remember as He made you successors even after c?d and located you in the earth, taking to your selves palaces of its plains, and hewing (its) mountains into homes; so remember the boons of Allah, and do not perpetrate (mischief) in the earth as corruptors The chiefs who waxed proud from among his people said to whomever were deemed weak, to whomever of them believed, "Do you know that Salih is an Emissary from his Lord?" They said, "Surely in whatever he has been sent with, we are believers." The ones who waxed proud said, "Surely in that which you believe, we are disbelievers." – Surah Al-A'raf 7:74-76

وَٱذْكُرُوٓا۟ إِذْ جَعَلَكُمْ خُلَفَآءَ مِنۢ بَعْدِ عَادٍ وَبَوَّأَكُمْ فِى ٱلْأَرْضِ تَتَّخِذُونَ مِن سُهُولِهَا قُصُورًا وَتَنْحِتُونَ ٱلْجِبَالَ بُيُوتًا ۖ فَٱذْكُرُوٓا۟
ءَالَآءَ ٱللَّهِ وَلَا تَعْثَوْا۟ فِى ٱلْأَرْضِ مُفْسِدِينَ قَالَ ٱلْمَلَأُ ٱلَّذِينَ ٱسْتَكْبَرُوا۟ مِن قَوْمِهِۦ لِلَّذِينَ ٱسْتُضْعِفُوا۟ لِمَنْ ءَامَنَ مِنْهُمْ أَتَعْلَمُونَ أَنَّ
صَٰلِحًا مُّرْسَلٌ مِّن رَّبِّهِۦ ۚ قَالُوٓا۟ إِنَّا بِمَآ أُرْسِلَ بِهِۦ مُؤْمِنُونَ قَالَ ٱلَّذِينَ ٱسْتَكْبَرُوٓا۟ إِنَّا بِٱلَّذِىٓ ءَامَنتُم بِهِۦ كَٰفِرُونَ

And the chiefs of the people of Firaawn said, "Will you leave Musa (Moses) and his people corrupt in the earth, and leave you and your gods behind?" He said, "We will soon massacre their sons and (spare) alive their women, and surely above them we are vanquishers." Surah Al-A'raf 7:90

وَقَالَ ٱلْمَلَأُ مِن قَوْمِ فِرْعَوْنَ أَتَذَرُ مُوسَىٰ وَقَوْمَهُۥ لِيُفْسِدُوا۟ فِى ٱلْأَرْضِ وَيَذَرَكَ وَءَالِهَتَكَ ۚ قَالَ سَنُقَتِّلُ أَبْنَآءَهُمْ وَنَسْتَحْىِۦ نِسَآءَهُمْ
وَإِنَّا فَوْقَهُمْ قَٰهِرُونَ

And the chiefs of the people of Firaawn said, "Will you leave Musa (Moses) and his people corrupt in the earth, and leave you and your gods behind?" He said, "We will soon massacre their sons and (spare) alive their women, and surely above them we are vanquishers." Surah Al-A'raf 7:127

وَقَالَ ٱلْمَلَأُ مِن قَوْمِ فِرْعَوْنَ أَتَذَرُ مُوسَىٰ وَقَوْمَهُۥ لِيُفْسِدُوا۟ فِى ٱلْأَرْضِ وَيَذَرَكَ وَءَالِهَتَكَ ۚ قَالَ سَنُقَتِّلُ أَبْنَآءَهُمْ وَنَسْتَحْىِۦ نِسَآءَهُمْ
وَإِنَّا فَوْقَهُمْ قَٰهِرُونَ

And the chiefs who disbelieved from among his people said, "Indeed in case you (ever) follow Shuaayb, lo, surely in that case you will indeed be losers." – Surah Al-A'raf 7:90

وَقَالَ ٱلْمَلَأُ ٱلَّذِينَ كَفَرُوا۟ مِن قَوْمِهِۦ لَئِنِ ٱتَّبَعْتُمْ شُعَيْبًا إِنَّكُمْ إِذًا لَّخَٰسِرُونَ

So, the chiefs of the ones who disbelieved of his people said, "In no way do we see you except a mortal like ourselves, and in no way do we see that anyone has closely followed you except the ones who are the most decrepit of us, inconsiderately (i.e., without considering; literally: readily declared opinion). And in no way do we see you have over us any grace (Superiority) No indeed, we expect that you are liars." – Surah Hud 11:27

فَقَالَ ٱلْمَلَأُ ٱلَّذِينَ كَفَرُوا۟ مِن قَوْمِهِۦ مَا نَرَىٰكَ إِلَّا بَشَرًا مِّثْلَنَا وَمَا نَرَىٰكَ ٱتَّبَعَكَ إِلَّا ٱلَّذِينَ هُمْ أَرَاذِلُنَا بَادِىَ ٱلرَّأْىِ وَمَا نَرَىٰ لَكُمْ
عَلَيْنَا مِن فَضْلٍۭ بَلْ نَظُنُّكُمْ كَٰذِبِينَ

And he was working out (i.e., making) the Ship (s) (Arabic fulk "ship" can mean singular or plural) and whenever (some) chiefs of his people passed by him, they scoffed at him. He said, "In case you scoff at us, surely we will scoff at you, as you scoff. – Surah Hud 11:38

وَيَصْنَعُ ٱلْفُلْكَ وَكُلَّمَا مَرَّ عَلَيْهِ مَلَأٌ مِّن قَوْمِهِۦ سَخِرُوا۟ مِنْهُ ۚ قَالَ إِن تَسْخَرُوا۟ مِنَّا فَإِنَّا نَسْخَرُ مِنكُمْ كَمَا تَسْخَرُونَ

But the leaders among his people, who denied the truth and denied the encounter with the Hereafter, and to whom We had given ease and plenty in this worldly, life said, "This is only a man like you, who eats what you eat and drinks what you drink and, if you should obey a human being like yourselves, you would then fail. Does he promise you that when you have died and become dust and bones that you will be brought forth [to a new life]? – Surah Al-Mu'minun 23:33-35

وَقَالَ ٱلْمَلَأُ مِن قَوْمِهِ ٱلَّذِينَ كَفَرُوا۟ وَكَذَّبُوا۟ بِلِقَآءِ ٱلْءَاخِرَةِ وَأَتْرَفْنَـٰهُمْ فِى ٱلْحَيَوٰةِ ٱلدُّنْيَا مَا هَـٰذَآ إِلَّا بَشَرٌ مِّثْلُكُمْ يَأْكُلُ مِمَّا تَأْكُلُونَ
مِنْهُ وَيَشْرَبُ مِمَّا تَشْرَبُونَ وَلَئِنْ أَطَعْتُم بَشَرًا مِّثْلَكُمْ إِنَّكُمْ إِذًا لَّخَـٰسِرُونَ أَيَعِدُكُمْ أَنَّكُمْ إِذَا مِتُّمْ وَكُنتُمْ تُرَابًا وَعِظَـٰمًا أَنَّكُم

And the ones who disbelieved said to their Messengers
وَقَالَ ٱلَّذِينَ كَفَرُوا۟ لِرُسُلِهِمْ

(And some said): "He is only a man possessed: wait (and have patience) with him for a time." – Surah Al-Mu'minun 23:25

إِنْ هُوَ إِلَّا رَجُلٌۢ بِهِۦ جِنَّةٌ فَتَرَبَّصُوا۟ بِهِۦ حَتَّىٰ حِينٍ

Thereafter we sent Our Messengers intermittently. Whenever its Messenger came to a nation, they cried lies to him. Then We caused some of them to follow others, and We made them (as) discourses, so far away (are gone) a people that do not believe. Surah Al-Mu'minun 23:44

ثُمَّ أَرْسَلْنَا رُسُلَنَا تَتْرَا ۖ كُلَّ مَا جَآءَ أُمَّةً رَّسُولُهَا كَذَّبُوهُ ۚ فَأَتْبَعْنَا بَعْضَهُم بَعْضًا وَجَعَلْنَـٰهُمْ أَحَادِيثَ ۚ فَبُعْدًا لِّقَوْمٍ لَّا يُؤْمِنُونَ

Or do they say, "There is madness in him"? No indeed, he has come to them with the Truth, and most of them hate the Truth. (Literally: are haters of the Truth. – Surah Al-Mu'minun 23:70

أَمْ يَقُولُونَ بِهِۦ جِنَّةٌۢ ۚ بَلْ جَآءَهُم بِٱلْحَقِّ وَأَكْثَرُهُمْ لِلْحَقِّ كَـٰرِهُونَ

Or, "Why hasn't he been given a treasure?" Or, "Why does he not have a garden from which he eats?" And the unjust say, "The man you follow is simply bewitched." – Surah Al-Furqan 25:8

أَوْ يُلْقَىٰٓ إِلَيْهِ كَنزٌ أَوْ تَكُونُ لَهُۥ جَنَّةٌ يَأْكُلُ مِنْهَا ۚ وَقَالَ ٱلظَّـٰلِمُونَ إِن تَتَّبِعُونَ إِلَّا رَجُلًا مَّسْحُورًا

And when Our ayat (Verses, signs) are recited to them, supremely evident (signs), they say, "In no way is this (anything) except a man who is willing to bar you from what your fathers were worshiping." And they say, "In no way is this (anything) except fabricated falsehood." And the ones who disbelieved say to the Truth, as soon as it has come to them, "Decidedly this is (nothing) except an evident sorcery." – Surah Saba 34:43

وَإِذَا تُتْلَىٰ عَلَيْهِمْ ءَايَـٰتُنَا بَيِّنَـٰتٍ قَالُوا۟ مَا هَـٰذَآ إِلَّا رَجُلٌ يُرِيدُ أَن يَصُدَّكُمْ عَمَّا كَانَ يَعْبُدُ ءَابَآؤُكُمْ وَقَالُوا۟ مَا هَـٰذَآ إِلَّآ إِفْكٌ مُّفْتَرًى ۚ
وَقَالَ الَّذِينَ كَفَرُوا لِلحَقِّ لَمَّا جَاءَهُمْ إِنْ هَـٰذَا إِلا سِحْرٌ مُّبِينٌ

And they said, "Shall we surely be leaving indeed our gods for a mad poet?" – Surah As-Saffat 37:36

وَيَقُولُونَ أَئِنَّا لَتَارِكُوٓا۟ ءَالِهَتِنَا لِشَاعِرٍ مَّجْنُونٍۭ

The people of Nuh (Noah) before them cried lies and the (allied) parties even after them; and every nation designed against their Messenger to take him (away), and disputed with untruth that they might rebut thereby the Truth. Then I took them (away); so how was (My) punishment. Surah Ghafir 40:5
كَذَّبَتْ قَبْلَهُمْ قَوْمُ نُوحٍ وَٱلْأَحْزَابُ مِنْ بَعْدِهِمْ ۖ وَهَمَّتْ كُلُّ أُمَّةٍ بِرَسُولِهِمْ لِيَأْخُذُوهُ ۖ وَجَـٰدَلُوا۟ بِٱلْبَـٰطِلِ لِيُدْحِضُوا۟ بِهِ ٱلْحَقَّ فَأَخَذْتُهُمْ ۖ فَكَيْفَ كَانَ عِقَابِ

(Yet) thereafter they turned away from him and said, "A man taught (by others), a madman!" – Surah Ad-Dukhan 44:14
ثُمَّ تَوَلَّوْا۟ عَنْهُ وَقَالُوا۟ مُعَلَّمٌ مَّجْنُونٌ

Or even do they say, "He is a poet for whom we await the uncertainty (i.e., the calamity of death; literally: the suspicion of fortune or fate) of fortune?" – Surah At-Tur 52:30
أَمْ يَقُولُونَ شَاعِرٌ نَّتَرَبَّصُ بِهِۦ رَيْبَ ٱلْمَنُونِ

Has the Remembrance been cast upon him (alone) from among us? No indeed, (but) he is an insolent liar." – Surah Al-Qamar 54:25
أَءُلْقِىَ ٱلذِّكْرُ عَلَيْهِ مِنۢ بَيْنِنَا بَلْ هُوَ كَذَّابٌ أَشِرٌ

And the ones who disbelieved said to their Messengers, "Indeed we will definitely drive you out of our land or indeed you will definitely go back to our creed." Then their Lord revealed to them, "Indeed We will definitely cause the unjust to perish. – Surah Ibrahim 14:13
وَقَالَ ٱلَّذِينَ كَفَرُوا۟ لِرُسُلِهِمْ لَنُخْرِجَنَّكُم مِّنْ أَرْضِنَآ أَوْ لَتَعُودُنَّ فِى مِلَّتِنَا ۖ فَأَوْحَىٰٓ إِلَيْهِمْ رَبُّهُمْ لَنُهْلِكَنَّ ٱلظَّـٰلِمِينَ

And they said, "O you upon whom the Remembrance is being sent down, surely you are indeed a madman. – Surah Al-Hijr 15:6
وَقَالُوا۟ يَـٰٓأَيُّهَا ٱلَّذِى نُزِّلَ عَلَيْهِ ٱلذِّكْرُ إِنَّكَ لَمَجْنُونٌ

And when it is said to them, "What has your Lord sent down?" they say, "Myths of the earliest (people)." – Surah An-Nahl 16:24
وَإِذَا قِيلَ لَهُم مَّاذَآ أَنزَلَ رَبُّكُمْ قَالُوٓا۟ أَسَـٰطِيرُ ٱلْأَوَّلِينَ

He has Legislated (Shara'a) for you as the religion
شَرَعَ لَكُم مِّنَ ٱلدِّينِ

Thereafter We have made you upon a Law of the Command; (i.e., a religion from our command to Jibril (Gabriel) so follow it closely, and do not ever follow the prejudices of the ones who do not know. – Surah Al-Jathiyah 45:18
ثُمَّ جَعَلْنَـٰكَ عَلَىٰ شَرِيعَةٍ مِّنَ ٱلْأَمْرِ فَٱتَّبِعْهَا وَلَا تَتَّبِعْ أَهْوَآءَ ٱلَّذِينَ لَا يَعْلَمُونَ

He has legislated for you as the religion what He enjoined on Nuh, (Noah) and that which We have revealed to you, (The Prophet) and what We have enjoined on Ibrahim and Musa and Isa (Abraham, Moses and Jesus, respectively) (saying), "Keep up the religion and do not be disunited therein." Greatly (detested) to the associators (i.e., those who associate others with Allah) is that to which you call them. Allah selects to Himself whomever He decides and guides to Himself whomever turns penitent. – Surah Ash-Shura 42:13

شَرَعَ لَكُم مِّنَ ٱلدِّينِ مَا وَصَّىٰ بِهِۦ نُوحًا وَٱلَّذِىٓ أَوْحَيْنَآ إِلَيْكَ وَمَا وَصَّيْنَا بِهِۦٓ إِبْرَٰهِيمَ وَمُوسَىٰ وَعِيسَىٰٓ ۖ أَنْ أَقِيمُوا۟ ٱلدِّينَ وَلَا تَتَفَرَّقُوا۟ فِيهِ ۚ كَبُرَ عَلَى ٱلْمُشْرِكِينَ مَا تَدْعُوهُمْ إِلَيْهِ ۚ ٱللَّهُ يَجْتَبِىٓ إِلَيْهِ مَن يَشَآءُ وَيَهْدِىٓ إِلَيْهِ مَن يُنِيبُ

Surely the ones who disbelieve in Allah and His Messengers and would make a distinction between Allah and His Messengers, and say, "We believe in some, and disbelieve in some (others), " and would take to themselves a way in-between, (Literally: a way between that; i.e. away between this and that) Those are they (who are) truly the disbelievers; and We have readied for the disbelievers a degrading torment And the ones who have believed in Allah and His Messengers and have made no distinction between any of them, those He will eventually bring them their rewards, and Allah has been Ever-Forgiving, Ever-Merciful The population of the Book (Or: Family of the Book, i.e., the Jews and Christians) ask you to (keep) (Moses) bringing down upon them a Book from the heaven; yet they already asked Musa far greater than that; So they said, "Show us Allah openly." Then the stunning (thunderbolt) took them for their injustice. Thereafter they took to themselves the Calf, even after the supreme evidences came to them, yet We were clement (towards them) for that, and We brought M?s'a an evident all-binding authority And We raised above them the Tur, (Mount) (taking) compact with them. And We said to them, "Enter in at the gate, constantly prostrating." And We said to them, "Do not be aggressors on the Sabbath, " (Mount) and We took from them a solemn compact So, for their breaking of their compact, and their disbelieving in the signs of Allah, and their killing of the Prophesiers (i.e. prophets) untruthfully and their saying, "Our hearts are encased." No indeed, (but) Allah has stamped upon them for their disbelief; so they do not believe except a few And for their disbelief and their speaking against Maryam (Mary) a tremendous all-malicious (calumny) And for their saying, "Surely we killed the Masih, Isa son of Maryam, (The Messiah, Jesus son of Mary) the Messenger of Allah." And in no way did they kill him, and in no way did they crucify him, but a resemblance of him was presented to them (i.e. the matter was made obscure for them through mutual resemblance). And surely the ones who differed about him are indeed in doubt about him. (Or: it, "that") In no way do they have any knowledge about him except the close following of surmise, and in no way did they kill him of a certainty No indeed, Allah raised him up to Him; and Allah has been Ever-Mighty, Ever-Wise And decidedly there is not one of the population of the Book (Or: Family of the Book, i.e., the Jews and Christians) but will indeed definitely believe in him before his death, and on the Day of the Resurrection he will be a witness against them So, for the injustice (on the part) of (the ones) who have Judaized, We have prohibited them good things that were lawful to them, and for their barring from the way of Allah many (people) And for their taking riba, (Usury and other tyoes of unlawful) and they were already forbidden it, and eating (up) the riches of mankind untruthfully; (Literally: with untruth) and We have readied for the disbelievers among them a painful torment But the ones of them who are firmly established in knowledge and the believers believe in what has been sent down to you, and what was sent down even before you, and (the ones who) regularly keeping up the prayer, and bringing the Zakat, (i.e., pay the poor-dues) and believing in Allah and the Last Day, for those We will soon bring a magnificent reward Surely We have revealed to you as We revealed to Nuh, (Noah) and the Prophets (even) after him, and We revealed to Ibrahim, and Shuaayb, and Ishaq, and Yaaqub, and the Grandsons, and Isa, and Ayyub, and Yunus, and Harun, and Sulayman, (Abraham, Ishmael, Isaac, Jacob, the Tribes, Jesus, Job, Jonah, Aaron, Solomon, respectively) and We brought Dawud (David) a Scripture (Zabur, said to be the psalms) And Messengers We have already narrated to you (about) even before and Messengers We have not narrated to you (about); and to Musa (Moses) Allah spoke long, (eloquent) speech Messengers (who are) constant bearers of good tidings and constant warners lest mankind should have argument against Allah after the Messengers; and Allah has been Ever-Mighty, Ever-Wise But Allah bears witness to what He has sent down to you. He has sent it down with His knowledge; and the Angels (also) bear witness; and Allah suffices as Ever-Witnessing. – Surah An-Nisa 4:150-166

إِنَّ ٱلَّذِينَ يَكۡفُرُونَ بِٱللَّهِ وَرُسُلِهِۦ وَيُرِيدُونَ أَن يُفَرِّقُواْ بَيۡنَ ٱللَّهِ وَرُسُلِهِۦ وَيَقُولُونَ نُؤۡمِنُ بِبَعۡضٖ وَنَكۡفُرُ بِبَعۡضٖ وَيُرِيدُونَ أَن يَتَّخِذُواْ بَيۡنَ ذَٰلِكَ سَبِيلًا أُوْلَٰٓئِكَ هُمُ ٱلۡكَٰفِرُونَ حَقّٗاۚ وَأَعۡتَدۡنَا لِلۡكَٰفِرِينَ عَذَابٗا مُّهِينٗا وَٱلَّذِينَ ءَامَنُواْ بِٱللَّهِ وَرُسُلِهِۦ وَلَمۡ يُفَرِّقُواْ بَيۡنَ أَحَدٖ مِّنۡهُمۡ أُوْلَٰٓئِكَ سَوۡفَ يُؤۡتِيهِمۡ أُجُورَهُمۡۚ وَكَانَ ٱللَّهُ غَفُورٗا رَّحِيمٗا يَسۡـَٔلُكَ أَهۡلُ ٱلۡكِتَٰبِ أَن تُنَزِّلَ عَلَيۡهِمۡ كِتَٰبٗا مِّنَ ٱلسَّمَآءِۚ فَقَدۡ سَأَلُواْ مُوسَىٰٓ أَكۡبَرَ مِن ذَٰلِكَ فَقَالُوٓاْ أَرِنَا ٱللَّهَ جَهۡرَةٗ فَأَخَذَتۡهُمُ ٱلصَّٰعِقَةُ بِظُلۡمِهِمۡۚ ثُمَّ ٱتَّخَذُواْ ٱلۡعِجۡلَ مِنۢ بَعۡدِ مَا جَآءَتۡهُمُ ٱلۡبَيِّنَٰتُ فَعَفَوۡنَا عَن ذَٰلِكَۚ وَءَاتَيۡنَا مُوسَىٰ سُلۡطَٰنٗا مُّبِينٗا وَرَفَعۡنَا فَوۡقَهُمُ ٱلطُّورَ بِمِيثَٰقِهِمۡ وَقُلۡنَا لَهُمُ ٱدۡخُلُواْ ٱلۡبَابَ سُجَّدٗا وَقُلۡنَا لَهُمۡ لَا تَعۡدُواْ فِي ٱلسَّبۡتِ وَأَخَذۡنَا مِنۡهُم مِّيثَٰقًا غَلِيظٗا فَبِمَا نَقۡضِهِم مِّيثَٰقَهُمۡ وَكُفۡرِهِم بِـَٔايَٰتِ ٱللَّهِ وَقَتۡلِهِمُ ٱلۡأَنۢبِيَآءَ بِغَيۡرِ حَقّٖ وَقَوۡلِهِمۡ قُلُوبُنَا غُلۡفُۢۚ بَلۡ طَبَعَ ٱللَّهُ عَلَيۡهَا بِكُفۡرِهِمۡ فَلَا يُؤۡمِنُونَ إِلَّا قَلِيلٗا وَبِكُفۡرِهِمۡ وَقَوۡلِهِمۡ عَلَىٰ مَرۡيَمَ بُهۡتَٰنًا عَظِيمٗا وَقَوۡلِهِمۡ إِنَّا قَتَلۡنَا ٱلۡمَسِيحَ عِيسَى ٱبۡنَ مَرۡيَمَ رَسُولَ ٱللَّهِ وَمَا قَتَلُوهُ وَمَا صَلَبُوهُ وَلَٰكِن شُبِّهَ لَهُمۡۚ وَإِنَّ ٱلَّذِينَ ٱخۡتَلَفُواْ فِيهِ لَفِي شَكّٖ مِّنۡهُۚ مَا لَهُم بِهِۦ مِنۡ عِلۡمٍ إِلَّا ٱتِّبَاعَ ٱلظَّنِّۚ وَمَا قَتَلُوهُ يَقِينَۢا بَل رَّفَعَهُ ٱللَّهُ إِلَيۡهِۚ وَكَانَ ٱللَّهُ عَزِيزًا حَكِيمٗا وَإِن مِّنۡ أَهۡلِ ٱلۡكِتَٰبِ إِلَّا لَيُؤۡمِنَنَّ بِهِۦ قَبۡلَ مَوۡتِهِۦۖ وَيَوۡمَ ٱلۡقِيَٰمَةِ يَكُونُ عَلَيۡهِمۡ شَهِيدٗا فَبِظُلۡمٖ مِّنَ ٱلَّذِينَ هَادُواْ حَرَّمۡنَا عَلَيۡهِمۡ طَيِّبَٰتٍ أُحِلَّتۡ لَهُمۡ وَبِصَدِّهِمۡ عَن سَبِيلِ ٱللَّهِ كَثِيرٗا وَأَخۡذِهِمُ ٱلرِّبَوٰاْ وَقَدۡ نُهُواْ عَنۡهُ وَأَكۡلِهِمۡ أَمۡوَٰلَ ٱلنَّاسِ بِٱلۡبَٰطِلِۚ وَأَعۡتَدۡنَا لِلۡكَٰفِرِينَ مِنۡهُمۡ عَذَابًا أَلِيمٗا لَّٰكِنِ ٱلرَّٰسِخُونَ فِي ٱلۡعِلۡمِ مِنۡهُمۡ وَٱلۡمُؤۡمِنُونَ يُؤۡمِنُونَ بِمَآ أُنزِلَ إِلَيۡكَ وَمَآ أُنزِلَ مِن قَبۡلِكَۚ وَٱلۡمُقِيمِينَ ٱلصَّلَوٰةَۚ وَٱلۡمُؤۡتُونَ ٱلزَّكَوٰةَ وَٱلۡمُؤۡمِنُونَ بِٱللَّهِ وَٱلۡيَوۡمِ ٱلۡأٓخِرِ أُوْلَٰٓئِكَ سَنُؤۡتِيهِمۡ أَجۡرًا عَظِيمًا إِنَّآ أَوۡحَيۡنَآ إِلَيۡكَ كَمَآ أَوۡحَيۡنَآ إِلَىٰ نُوحٖ وَٱلنَّبِيِّـۧنَ مِنۢ بَعۡدِهِۦۚ وَأَوۡحَيۡنَآ إِلَىٰٓ إِبۡرَٰهِيمَ وَإِسۡمَٰعِيلَ وَإِسۡحَٰقَ وَيَعۡقُوبَ وَٱلۡأَسۡبَاطِ وَعِيسَىٰ وَأَيُّوبَ وَيُونُسَ وَهَٰرُونَ وَسُلَيۡمَٰنَۚ وَءَاتَيۡنَا دَاوُۥدَ زَبُورٗا وَرُسُلٗا قَدۡ قَصَصۡنَٰهُمۡ عَلَيۡكَ مِن قَبۡلُ وَرُسُلٗا لَّمۡ نَقۡصُصۡهُمۡ عَلَيۡكَۚ وَكَلَّمَ ٱللَّهُ مُوسَىٰ تَكۡلِيمٗا رُّسُلٗا مُّبَشِّرِينَ وَمُنذِرِينَ لِئَلَّا يَكُونَ لِلنَّاسِ عَلَى ٱللَّهِ حُجَّةُۢ بَعۡدَ ٱلرُّسُلِۚ وَكَانَ ٱللَّهُ عَزِيزًا حَكِيمٗا لَّٰكِنِ ٱللَّهُ يَشۡهَدُ بِمَآ أَنزَلَ إِلَيۡكَۖ أَنزَلَهُۥ بِعِلۡمِهِۦۖ وَٱلۡمَلَ

......Pharaoh said, “I show you only what I see, and I am guiding you along the right path.” – Surah Ghafir 40:29

فِرۡعَوۡنُ مَآ أُرِيكُمۡ إِلَّا مَآ أَرَىٰ وَمَآ أَهۡدِيكُمۡ إِلَّا سَبِيلَ ٱلرَّشَادِ

To Pharaoh and his inner circle, but they followed Pharaoh’s orders, and Pharaoh’s orders were misguided. – Surah Al-Hud 11:29

إِلَىٰ فِرۡعَوۡنَ وَمَلَإِيْهِۦ فَٱتَّبَعُوٓاْ أَمۡرَ فِرۡعَوۡنَۖ وَمَآ أَمۡرُ فِرۡعَوۡنَ بِرَشِيدٖ

And We have sent down to you the Book with the Truth, sincerely verifying whatever of the Book that was before it, (Literally: between its two hands) and Supremely Hegemonic over it. So judge between them according to what Allah has sent down, and do not ever follow their prejudices away from the Truth that has come to you. To every one of you We have made a legislation and a program. And if Allah had so decided, He would indeed have made you one nation; but (He did not) that He may try you in what He has brought you. So race with each other in the charitable (deeds); to Allah will be your return, altogether; so He will fully inform you of that wherein you used to differ. – Surah Al-Ma’idah 5:48

وَأَنزَلۡنَآ إِلَيۡكَ ٱلۡكِتَٰبَ بِٱلۡحَقِّ مُصَدِّقٗا لِّمَا بَيۡنَ يَدَيۡهِ مِنَ ٱلۡكِتَٰبِ وَمُهَيۡمِنًا عَلَيۡهِۖ فَٱحۡكُم بَيۡنَهُم بِمَآ أَنزَلَ ٱللَّهُۖ وَلَا تَتَّبِعۡ أَهۡوَآءَهُمۡ عَمَّا جَآءَكَ مِنَ ٱلۡحَقِّۚ لِكُلّٖ جَعَلۡنَا مِنكُمۡ شِرۡعَةٗ وَمِنۡهَاجٗاۚ وَلَوۡ شَآءَ ٱللَّهُ لَجَعَلَكُمۡ أُمَّةٗ وَٰحِدَةٗ وَلَٰكِن لِّيَبۡلُوَكُمۡ فِي مَآ ءَاتَىٰكُمۡۖ فَٱسۡتَبِقُواْ ٱلۡخَيۡرَٰتِۚ إِلَى ٱللَّهِ مَرۡجِعُكُمۡ جَمِيعٗا فَيُنَبِّئُكُم بِمَا كُنتُمۡ فِيهِ تَخۡتَلِفُونَ

And We made them leaders calling to the Fire; and on the Day of the Resurrection they will not be vindicated. – Surah Al-Qasas 28:41

وَجَعَلۡنَٰهُمۡ أَئِمَّةٗ يَدۡعُونَ إِلَى ٱلنَّارِۖ وَيَوۡمَ ٱلۡقِيَٰمَةِ لَا يُنصَرُونَ

And thus We make the unjust ones patrons of each other, for whatever they were earning. – Surah Al-An'am 6:129

وَكَذَٰلِكَ نُوَلِّى بَعْضَ ٱلظَّـٰلِمِينَ بَعْضًۢا بِمَا كَانُوا۟ يَكْسِبُونَ

That Allah may discriminate the wicked from the good, and set up the wicked one upon another; (Literally: make some of them upon some "others") (and) so accumulate them up altogether, and then set them up in Hell; those are they (who are) the losers. – Surah Al-Anfal 8:37

لِيَمِيزَ ٱللَّهُ ٱلْخَبِيثَ مِنَ ٱلطَّيِّبِ وَيَجْعَلَ ٱلْخَبِيثَ بَعْضَهُۥ عَلَىٰ بَعْضٍ فَيَرْكُمَهُۥ جَمِيعًا فَيَجْعَلَهُۥ فِى جَهَنَّمَ ۚ أُو۟لَـٰٓئِكَ هُمُ ٱلْخَـٰسِرُونَ

That they may carry their encumbrances complete on the Day of the Resurrection and (some) of the encumbrances of the ones that they lead into error without (any) knowledge. Verily odious is that with which they encumber themselves. – Surah An-Nahl 16:25

لِيَحْمِلُوٓا۟ أَوْزَارَهُمْ كَامِلَةً يَوْمَ ٱلْقِيَـٰمَةِ وَمِنْ أَوْزَارِ ٱلَّذِينَ يُضِلُّونَهُم بِغَيْرِ عِلْمٍ ۗ أَلَا سَآءَ مَا يَزِرُونَ

Do not incline towards those who do evil, lest the fire touches you. You will [then] have no one to protect you from Allah, nor will you be helped. – Surah Hud 11:113

وَلَا تَرْكَنُوٓا۟ إِلَى ٱلَّذِينَ ظَلَمُوا۟ فَتَمَسَّكُمُ ٱلنَّارُ وَمَا لَكُم مِّن دُونِ ٱللَّهِ مِنْ أَوْلِيَآءَ ثُمَّ لَا تُنصَرُونَ

The Book of

Obedience is required only in what is good

إِنَّمَا الطَّاعَةُ فِي الْمَعْرُوفِ

Narrated `Abdullah: The Prophetﷺ said, "A Muslim has to listen to and obey (the order of his ruler) whether he likes it or not, as long as his orders involve not one in disobedience (to Allah), but if an act of disobedience (to Allah) is imposed one should not listen to it or obey it. (See Hadith No. 203, Vol. 4) – Al-Bukhari 7144

حَدَّثَنَا مُسَدَّدٌ، حَدَّثَنَا يَحْيَى بْنُ سَعِيدٍ، عَنْ عُبَيْدِ اللَّهِ، حَدَّثَنِي نَافِعٌ، عَنْ عَبْدِ اللَّهِ ـ رضى الله عنه ـ عَنِ النَّبِيِّ صلى الله عليه وسلم قَالَ " السَّمْعُ وَالطَّاعَةُ عَلَى الْمَرْءِ الْمُسْلِمِ، فِيمَا أَحَبَّ وَكَرِهَ، مَا لَمْ يُؤْمَرْ بِمَعْصِيَةٍ، فَإِذَا أُمِرَ بِمَعْصِيَةٍ فَلاَ سَمْعَ وَلاَ طَاعَةَ ".

Narrated Qais bin Abi Hazim: Abu Bakr went to a lady from the Ahmas tribe called Zainab bint Al-Muhajir and found that she refused to speak. He asked, "Why does she not speak." The people said, "She has intended to perform Hajj without speaking." He said to her, "Speak, for it is illegal not to speak, as it is an action of the pre-islamic period of ignorance. So she spoke and said, "Who are you?" He said, "A man from the Emigrants." She asked, "Which Emigrants?" He replied, "From Quraish." She asked, "From what branch of Quraish are you?" He said, "You ask too many questions; I am Abu Bakr." She said, "How long shall we enjoy this good order (i.e. Islamic religion) which Allah has brought after the period of ignorance?" He said, "You will enjoy it as long as your Imams keep on abiding by its rules and regulations." She asked, "What are the Imams?" He said, "Were there not heads and chiefs of your nation who used to order the people and they used to obey them?" She said, "Yes." He said, "So they (i.e. the Imams) are those whom I meant." – Al-Bukhari 3834

حَدَّثَنَا أَبُو النُّعْمَانِ، حَدَّثَنَا أَبُو عَوَانَةَ، عَنْ بَيَانٍ أَبِي بِشْرٍ، عَنْ قَيْسِ بْنِ أَبِي حَازِمٍ، قَالَ دَخَلَ أَبُو بَكْرٍ عَلَى امْرَأَةٍ مِنْ أَحْمَسَ يُقَالُ لَهَا زَيْنَبُ، فَرَآهَا لاَ تَكَلَّمُ، فَقَالَ مَا لَهَا لاَ تَكَلَّمُ قَالُوا حَجَّتْ مُصْمِتَةً. قَالَ لَهَا تَكَلَّمِي، فَإِنَّ هَذَا لاَ يَحِلُّ، هَذَا مِنْ عَمَلِ الْجَاهِلِيَّةِ. فَتَكَلَّمَتْ، فَقَالَتْ مَنْ أَنْتَ قَالَ امْرُؤٌ مِنَ الْمُهَاجِرِينَ. قَالَتْ أَىُّ الْمُهَاجِرِينَ قَالَ مِنْ قُرَيْشٍ. قَالَتْ مِنْ أَىِّ قُرَيْشٍ أَنْتَ قَالَ إِنَّكِ لَسَئُولٌ أَنَا أَبُو بَكْرٍ. قَالَتْ مَا بَقَاؤُنَا عَلَى هَذَا الأَمْرِ الصَّالِحِ الَّذِي جَاءَ اللَّهُ بِهِ بَعْدَ الْجَاهِلِيَّةِ قَالَ بَقَاؤُكُمْ عَلَيْهِ مَا اسْتَقَامَتْ بِكُمْ أَئِمَّتُكُمْ. قَالَتْ وَمَا الأَئِمَّةُ قَالَ أَمَا كَانَ لِقَوْمِكِ رُءُوسٌ وَأَشْرَافٌ يَأْمُرُونَهُمْ فَيُطِيعُونَهُمْ قَالَتْ بَلَى. قَالَ فَهُمْ أُولَئِكَ عَلَى النَّاسِ

We have revealed the Torah, wherein is guidance and light. The submissive prophets ruled the Jews according to it, so did the rabbis and the scholars, as they were required to protect Allah's Book, and were witnesses to it. So do not fear people, but fear Me. And do not sell My revelations for a cheap price. Those who do not rule according to what Allah revealed are the unbelievers. – Surah Al-Maidah 5:44

إِنَّآ أَنزَلْنَا ٱلتَّوْرَىٰةَ فِيهَا هُدًى وَنُورٌ ۚ يَحْكُمُ بِهَا ٱلنَّبِيُّونَ ٱلَّذِينَ أَسْلَمُوا۟ لِلَّذِينَ هَادُوا۟ وَٱلرَّبَّـٰنِيُّونَ وَٱلْأَحْبَارُ بِمَا ٱسْتُحْفِظُوا۟ مِن كِتَـٰبِ ٱللَّهِ وَكَانُوا۟ عَلَيْهِ شُهَدَآءَ ۚ فَلَا تَخْشَوُا۟ ٱلنَّاسَ وَٱخْشَوْنِ وَلَا تَشْتَرُوا۟ بِـَٔايَـٰتِى ثَمَنًا قَلِيلًا ۚ وَمَن لَّمْ يَحْكُم بِمَآ أَنزَلَ ٱللَّهُ فَأُو۟لَـٰٓئِكَ هُمُ ٱلْكَـٰفِرُونَ

Narrated `Aisha: Allah's Messengerﷺ came to me and I told him about the slave-girl (Barirah) Allah's Messengerﷺ said, "Buy and manumit her, for the Wala is for the one who manumits." In the evening the Prophetﷺ got up and glorified Allah as He deserved and then said, "Why do some people impose conditions which are not present in Allah's Book (Laws)? Whoever imposes such a condition as is not in Allah's Laws, then that condition is invalid even if he imposes one hundred conditions, for Allah's conditions are more binding and reliable." – Al-Bukhari 2155

حَدَّثَنَا أَبُو الْيَمَانِ، أَخْبَرَنَا شُعَيْبٌ، عَنِ الزُّهْرِيِّ، قَالَ عُرْوَةُ بْنُ الزُّبَيْرِ قَالَتْ عَائِشَةُ ـ رضى الله عنها دَخَلَ عَلَىَّ رَسُولُ اللَّهِ صلى الله عليه وسلم فَذَكَرْتُ لَهُ، فَقَالَ رَسُولُ اللَّهِ صلى الله عليه وسلم " اشْتَرِي وَأَعْتِقِي، فَإِنَّ الْوَلاَءَ لِمَنْ أَعْتَقَ ". ثُمَّ قَامَ النَّبِيُّ صلى الله عليه وسلم مِنَ الْعَشِيِّ، فَأَثْنَى عَلَى اللَّهِ بِمَا هُوَ أَهْلُهُ، ثُمَّ قَالَ " مَا بَالُ أُنَاسٍ يَشْتَرِطُونَ شُرُوطًا لَيْسَ فِي كِتَابِ اللَّهِ، مَنِ اشْتَرَطَ شَرْطًا لَيْسَ فِي كِتَابِ اللَّهِ فَهْوَ بَاطِلٌ، وَإِنِ اشْتَرَطَ مِائَةَ شَرْطٍ، شَرْطُ اللَّهِ أَحَقُّ وَأَوْثَقُ ".

Narrated `Ali: The Prophet ﷺ sent a Sariya under the command of a man from the Ansar and ordered the soldiers to obey him. He (i.e. the commander) became angry and said "Didn't the Prophet ﷺ order you to obey me!" They replied, "Yes." He said, "Collect fire-wood for me." So they collected it. He said, "Make a fire." When they made it, he said, "Enter it (i.e. the fire)." So they intended to do that and started holding each other and saying, "We run towards (i.e. take refuge with) the Prophet ﷺ from the fire." They kept on saying that till the fire was extinguished and the anger of the commander abated. When that news reached the Prophet ﷺ he said, "If they had entered it (i.e. the fire), they would not have come out of it till the Day of Resurrection. Obedience (to somebody) is required when he enjoins what is good.". – Sahih Al-Bukhari 4340

حَدَّثَنَا مُسَدَّدٌ، حَدَّثَنَا عَبْدُ الْوَاحِدِ، حَدَّثَنَا الأَعْمَشُ، قَالَ حَدَّثَنِي سَعْدُ بْنُ عُبَيْدَةَ، عَنْ أَبِي عَبْدِ الرَّحْمَنِ، عَنْ عَلِيٍّ ـ رضى الله عنه ـ قَالَ بَعَثَ النَّبِيُّ صلى الله عليه وسلم سَرِيَّةً فَاسْتَعْمَلَ رَجُلاً مِنَ الأَنْصَارِ، وَأَمَرَهُمْ أَنْ يُطِيعُوهُ، فَغَضِبَ فَقَالَ أَلَيْسَ أَمَرَكُمُ النَّبِيُّ صلى الله عليه وسلم أَنْ تُطِيعُونِي. قَالُوا بَلَى. قَالَ فَاجْمَعُوا لِي حَطَبًا. فَجَمَعُوا، فَقَالَ أَوْقِدُوا نَارًا. فَأَوْقَدُوهَا، فَقَالَ ادْخُلُوهَا. فَهَمُّوا، وَجَعَلَ بَعْضُهُمْ يُمْسِكُ بَعْضًا، وَيَقُولُونَ فَرَرْنَا إِلَى النَّبِيِّ صلى الله عليه وسلم مِنَ النَّارِ. فَمَا زَالُوا حَتَّى خَمَدَتِ النَّارُ، فَسَكَنَ غَضَبُهُ، فَبَلَغَ النَّبِيَّ صلى الله عليه وسلم فَقَالَ " لَوْ دَخَلُوهَا مَا خَرَجُوا مِنْهَا إِلَى يَوْمِ الْقِيَامَةِ، الطَّاعَةُ فِي الْمَعْرُوفِ "

Narrated `Abdullah bin `Amr bin Al-`As: I heard Allah's Messenger ﷺ saying, "Allah does not take away the knowledge, by taking it away from (the hearts of) the people, but takes it away by the death of the religious learned men till when none of the (religious learned men) remains, people will take as their leaders ignorant persons who when consulted will give their verdict without knowledge. So they will go astray and will lead the people astray." – Al-Bukhari 100

حَدَّثَنَا إِسْمَاعِيلُ بْنُ أَبِي أُوَيْسٍ، قَالَ حَدَّثَنِي مَالِكٌ، عَنْ هِشَامِ بْنِ عُرْوَةَ، عَنْ أَبِيهِ، عَنْ عَبْدِ اللَّهِ بْنِ عَمْرِو بْنِ الْعَاصِ، قَالَ سَمِعْتُ رَسُولَ اللَّهِ صلى الله عليه وسلم يَقُولُ " إِنَّ اللَّهَ لاَ يَقْبِضُ الْعِلْمَ انْتِزَاعًا، يَنْتَزِعُهُ مِنَ الْعِبَادِ، وَلَكِنْ يَقْبِضُ الْعِلْمَ بِقَبْضِ الْعُلَمَاءِ، حَتَّى إِذَا لَمْ يُبْقِ عَالِمًا، اتَّخَذَ النَّاسُ رُءُوسًا جُهَّالاً فَسُئِلُوا، فَأَفْتَوْا بِغَيْرِ عِلْمٍ، فَضَلُّوا وَأَضَلُّوا ".
قَالَ الْفِرَبْرِيُّ حَدَّثَنَا عَبَّاسٌ قَالَ حَدَّثَنَا قُتَيْبَةُ حَدَّثَنَا جَرِيرٌ عَنْ هِشَامٍ نَحْوَهُ

And He united their hearts. Had you spent everything on earth, you would not have united their hearts, but Allah united them together. He is Mighty and Wise. – Surah Al-Anfal 8:63

وَأَلَّفَ بَيْنَ قُلُوبِهِمْ ۚ لَوْ أَنفَقْتَ مَا فِى ٱلْأَرْضِ جَمِيعًا مَّآ أَلَّفْتَ بَيْنَ قُلُوبِهِمْ وَلَـٰكِنَّ ٱللَّهَ أَلَّفَ بَيْنَهُمْ ۚ إِنَّهُۥ عَزِيزٌ حَكِيمٌ

Narrated `Ali: The Prophet ﷺ, sent an army and appointed some man their commander The man made a fire and then said (to the soldiers), "Enter it." Some of them intended to enter it while some others said, 'We have run away from it (i.e., embraced Islam to save ourselves from the 'fire')." They mentioned that to the Prophet, and he said about people who had intended to enter the fire. ''If they had entered it, they would have remained In it till the Day of Resurrection.'' Then he said to others, "No obedience for evil deeds, obedience is required only in what is good .". – Sahih Al-Bukhari 7257

حَدَّثَنَا مُحَمَّدُ بْنُ بَشَّارٍ، حَدَّثَنَا غُنْدَرٌ، حَدَّثَنَا شُعْبَةُ، عَنْ زُبَيْدٍ، عَنْ سَعْدِ بْنِ عُبَيْدَةَ، عَنْ أَبِي عَبْدِ الرَّحْمَنِ، عَنْ عَلِيٍّ ـ رضى الله عنه ـ أَنَّ النَّبِيَّ صلى الله عليه وسلم بَعَثَ جَيْشًا وَأَمَّرَ عَلَيْهِمْ رَجُلاً، فَأَوْقَدَ نَارًا وَقَالَ ادْخُلُوهَا. فَأَرَادُوا أَنْ يَدْخُلُوهَا،

وَقَالَ آخَرُونَ إِنَّمَا فَرَرْنَا مِنْهَا، فَذَكَرُوا لِلنَّبِيِّ صلى الله عليه وسلم فَقَالَ لِلَّذِينَ أَرَادُوا أَنْ يَدْخُلُوهَا " لَوْ دَخَلُوهَا لَمْ يَزَالُوا
فِيهَا إِلَى يَوْمِ الْقِيَامَةِ ". وَقَالَ لِلآخَرِينَ " لاَ طَاعَةَ فِي مَعْصِيَةٍ، إِنَّمَا الطَّاعَةُ فِي الْمَعْرُوفِ ".

The believing men and believing women are friends of one another. They advocate virtue, forbid evil, perform the prayers, practice charity, and obey Allah and His Messenger. These—Allah will have mercy on them. Allah is Noble and Wise. – Surah At-Taubah 9:71
وَٱلْمُؤْمِنُونَ وَٱلْمُؤْمِنَٰتُ بَعْضُهُمْ أَوْلِيَآءُ بَعْضٍۢ ۚ يَأْمُرُونَ بِٱلْمَعْرُوفِ وَيَنْهَوْنَ عَنِ ٱلْمُنكَرِ وَيُقِيمُونَ ٱلصَّلَوٰةَ وَيُؤْتُونَ ٱلزَّكَوٰةَ
وَيُطِيعُونَ ٱللَّهَ وَرَسُولَهُۥٓ ۚ أُو۟لَٰٓئِكَ سَيَرْحَمُهُمُ ٱللَّهُ ۗ إِنَّ ٱللَّهَ عَزِيزٌ حَكِيمٌ

He is The One Who made you succeeding each other in the earth. So whoever disbelieves, then his disbelief will be against him
هُوَ ٱلَّذِى جَعَلَكُمْ خَلَٰٓئِفَ فِى ٱلْأَرْضِ ۚ فَمَن كَفَرَ فَعَلَيْهِ كُفْرُهُۥ

He is The One Who made you succeeding each other in the earth. So whoever disbelieves, then his disbelief will be against him; and their disbelief increases the disbelievers (in nothing) except detestation in the Reckoning of their Lord, and their disbelief increases the disbelievers (in nothing) except in greater loss. – Surah Al-Fatir 35:39
هُوَ ٱلَّذِى جَعَلَكُمْ خَلَٰٓئِفَ فِى ٱلْأَرْضِ ۚ فَمَن كَفَرَ فَعَلَيْهِ كُفْرُهُۥ ۖ وَلَا يَزِيدُ ٱلْكَٰفِرِينَ كُفْرُهُمْ عِندَ رَبِّهِمْ إِلَّا مَقْتًا ۖ وَلَا يَزِيدُ ٱلْكَٰفِرِينَ
كُفْرُهُمْ إِلَّا خَسَارًا

And your Lord is The Ever-Affluent, (Literally: The Ever-Rich) The Owner of (the) mercy. In case He decides, He (can) put you away, and cause whatever He decides to succeed even after you, as He brought you from the offspring of another people. – Surah Al-An'am 6:133
وَرَبُّكَ ٱلْغَنِىُّ ذُو ٱلرَّحْمَةِ ۚ إِن يَشَأْ يُذْهِبْكُمْ وَيَسْتَخْلِفْ مِنۢ بَعْدِكُم مَّا يَشَآءُ كَمَآ أَنشَأَكُم مِّن ذُرِّيَّةِ قَوْمٍ ءَاخَرِينَ

Say, "O Allah, (The Arabic word has the supplication suffix umma) Possessor of the Kingship, You bring the kingship to whomever You decide, and You draw (Literally: pluck out) the kingship from whomever You decide, and You render mighty whomever You decide, and You humiliate whomever You decide. In Your Hand is (the) Charity; (i.e., the choicest) surely You are Ever-Determiner over everything. – Surah Al-Imran 3:26
قُلِ ٱللَّهُمَّ مَٰلِكَ ٱلْمُلْكِ تُؤْتِى ٱلْمُلْكَ مَن تَشَآءُ وَتَنزِعُ ٱلْمُلْكَ مِمَّن تَشَآءُ وَتُعِزُّ مَن تَشَآءُ وَتُذِلُّ مَن تَشَآءُ ۖ بِيَدِكَ ٱلْخَيْرُ ۖ إِنَّكَ عَلَىٰ كُلِّ
شَىْءٍ قَدِيرٌ

Is not He (Most Charitable) Who answers the constrained person when he invokes Him, and lifts off odious (happenings) and makes you successors of the earth? Is there a god with Allah? Little is that of which you are mindful. - An-Naml 27:62
أَمَّن يُجِيبُ ٱلْمُضْطَرَّ إِذَا دَعَاهُ وَيَكْشِفُ ٱلسُّوٓءَ وَيَجْعَلُكُمْ خُلَفَآءَ ٱلْأَرْضِ ۗ أَءِلَٰهٌ مَّعَ ٱللَّهِ ۚ قَلِيلًا مَّا تَذَكَّرُونَ

And He is (The One) Who made you succeeding each other (in) the earth, and has raised some of you above others (Literally: above "some" others) in degrees, that He may try you in what He has brought you. Surely your Lord is swift in punishment, and surely He is indeed Ever-Forgiving, Ever-Merciful. - Surah Al-An'am 6:165
وَهُوَ ٱلَّذِى جَعَلَكُمْ خَلَٰٓئِفَ ٱلْأَرْضِ وَرَفَعَ بَعْضَكُمْ فَوْقَ بَعْضٍ دَرَجَٰتٍ لِّيَبْلُوَكُمْ فِى مَآ ءَاتَىٰكُمْ ۗ إِنَّ رَبَّكَ سَرِيعُ ٱلْعِقَابِ وَإِنَّهُۥ
لَغَفُورٌ رَّحِيمٌۢ

.....if Allah had not so willed, he could not have detained his brother as a penalty under the king's law..... – Surah Yusuf 12:76
مَا كَانَ لِيَأۡخُذَ أَخَاهُ فِي دِينِ ٱلۡمَلِكِ إِلَّآ أَن يَشَآءَ ٱللَّهُۚ

And she in whose home he was solicited him, (Literally: she solicited him about himself) and bolted the doors (on them), and said, "Come! Everything is ready for you." (i.e., take me) He said, " Allah be my refuge! Surely he is my lord (i.e., your husband is my lord) who has given me the fairest of lodging. Surely the unjust (ones) do not prosper." – Surah Yusuf 12:23
وَرَٰوَدَتۡهُ ٱلَّتِي هُوَ فِي بَيۡتِهَا عَن نَّفۡسِهِۦ وَغَلَّقَتِ ٱلۡأَبۡوَٰبَ وَقَالَتۡ هَيۡتَ لَكَۚ قَالَ مَعَاذَ ٱللَّهِۖ إِنَّهُۥ رَبِّيٓ أَحۡسَنَ مَثۡوَايَۖ إِنَّهُۥ لَا يُفۡلِحُ ٱلظَّٰلِمُونَ

And the king said, "Come up with him (i.e., Bring him) to me!" Then as soon as the messenger came to him, he (Yusuf) said, "Return to your lord and so ask him, What about the women folk who severely cut (The Arabic verb from implies an action that is done repeatedly or to high degree or to a great extent) their hands? Surely my Lord is Ever-Knowing of their scheming.". – Surah Yusuf 12:50
وَقَالَ ٱلۡمَلِكُ ٱئۡتُونِي بِهِۦۖ فَلَمَّا جَآءَهُ ٱلرَّسُولُ قَالَ ٱرۡجِعۡ إِلَىٰ رَبِّكَ فَسۡـَٔلۡهُ مَا بَالُ ٱلنِّسۡوَةِ ٱلَّٰتِي قَطَّعۡنَ أَيۡدِيَهُنَّۚ إِنَّ رَبِّي بِكَيۡدِهِنَّ عَلِيمٞ

O (you) two companions of the prison! As for one of you, he will give his lord wine to drink; and as for the other, then he will be crucified (and) so birds will eat of his head. The Command is decreed of which you (both) ask for pronouncement And he said to the one of the two (that) he expected would be delivered, "Mention me in the presence of your lord." (But) then Ash-Shaytan (The all-vicious (one), i.e., the Devil) caused him to forget mentioning (him to) his lord; so he lingered in the prison for several years – Surah Yusuf 12:41&42
يَٰصَٰحِبَيِ ٱلسِّجۡنِ أَمَّآ أَحَدُكُمَا فَيَسۡقِي رَبَّهُۥ خَمۡرٗاۖ وَأَمَّا ٱلۡأٓخَرُ فَيُصۡلَبُ فَتَأۡكُلُ ٱلطَّيۡرُ مِن رَّأۡسِهِۦۚ قُضِيَ ٱلۡأَمۡرُ ٱلَّذِي فِيهِ تَسۡتَفۡتِيَانِ وَقَالَ لِلَّذِي ظَنَّ أَنَّهُۥ نَاجٖ مِّنۡهُمَا ٱذۡكُرۡنِي عِندَ رَبِّكَ فَأَنسَىٰهُ ٱلشَّيۡطَٰنُ ذِكۡرَ رَبِّهِۦ فَلَبِثَ فِي ٱلسِّجۡنِ بِضۡعَ سِنِينَ

Until, when he reached the setting of the sun, he found it [as if] setting in a dark, muddy spring, and nearby he found Some people. We said, "O Zul-Qarnayn, either cause [them] to suffer or treat them with kindness." – Surah Al-Khaf 18:86
حَتَّىٰٓ إِذَا بَلَغَ مَغۡرِبَ ٱلشَّمۡسِ وَجَدَهَا تَغۡرُبُ فِي عَيۡنٍ حَمِئَةٖ وَوَجَدَ عِندَهَا قَوۡمٗاۗ قُلۡنَا يَٰذَا ٱلۡقَرۡنَيۡنِ إِمَّآ أَن تُعَذِّبَ وَإِمَّآ أَن تَتَّخِذَ فِيهِمۡ حُسۡنٗا

Narrated Usaid bin Hudair: A man came to the Prophet ((ﷺand said, "O Allah's Messenger (!(ﷺYou appointed such-and-such person and you did not appoint me?" The Prophet ((ﷺ said, "After me you will see rulers not giving you your right (but you should give them their right) and be patient till you meet me.". – Sahih al-Bukhari 7057
حَدَّثَنَا مُحَمَّدُ بْنُ عَرْعَرَةَ، حَدَّثَنَا شُعْبَةُ، عَنْ قَتَادَةَ، عَنْ أَنَسِ بْنِ مَالِكٍ، عَنْ أُسَيْدِ بْنِ حُضَيْرٍ، أَنَّ رَجُلاً، أَتَى النَّبِيَّ صلى الله عليه وسلم فَقَالَ يَا رَسُولَ اللَّهِ اسْتَعْمَلْتَ فُلاَنًا وَلَمْ تَسْتَعْمِلْنِي. قَالَ " إِنَّكُمْ سَتَرَوْنَ بَعْدِي أَثَرَةً، فَاصْبِرُوا حَتَّى تَلْقَوْنِي ".

So await your Lord's Judgment with patience
فَٱصْبِرْ لِحُكْمِ رَبِّكَ

And (suffer) yourself to (endure) patiently with the ones who invoke their Lord in the early morning and nightfall, willing to seek His Face, and do not let your eyes go past them, (i.e., overlook them) willing (to gain) the adornment of the present life; (Literally: the lowly life, i.e., the life of this world) and do not obey him whose heart We have made heedless of Our Remembrance, and who closely follows his own prejudices, and to whom the Command (i.e., the Command of Allah to him, or: his affair) has been all excess (i.e., He has been most disbelieving) – Surah Al-Khaf 18:28
وَٱصْبِرْ نَفْسَكَ مَعَ ٱلَّذِينَ يَدْعُونَ رَبَّهُم بِٱلْغَدَوٰةِ وَٱلْعَشِيِّ يُرِيدُونَ وَجْهَهُۥ وَلَا تَعْدُ عَيْنَاكَ عَنْهُمْ تُرِيدُ زِينَةَ ٱلْحَيَوٰةِ ٱلدُّنْيَا وَلَا تُطِعْ مَنْ أَغْفَلْنَا قَلْبَهُۥ عَن ذِكْرِنَا وَٱتَّبَعَ هَوَىٰهُ وَكَانَ أَمْرُهُۥ فُرُطًا

So do not go along with the unbelievers, but strove hard against them with this [Qur'an). – Surah Al-Furqan 25:52

فَلَا تُطِعِ ٱلْكَـٰفِرِينَ وَجَـٰهِدْهُم بِهِۦ جِهَادًا كَبِيرًا

And do not obey the command of the extravagant – Surah Ash-Shu'ara 26:51
وَلَا تُطِيعُوٓا۟ أَمْرَ ٱلْمُسْرِفِينَ

So do not obey the beliers They would like (if) you would dissimulate, then they would dissimulate And do not obey every most contemptible (person), constantly swearing Constantly slandering, ever-walking about with detraction Constant preventer of charity, constantly-vicious transgressor Coarse-grained, and of spurious parentage after all (Literally: after that For that he has (Literally: for that he owns) wealth and sons When Our ayat (Verses, signs) are recited to him, he says, "Myths of the earliest (people)." – Surah Al-Qalam 68:8-15
فَلَا تُطِعِ ٱلْمُكَذِّبِينَ وَدُّوا۟ لَوْ تُدْهِنُ فَيُدْهِنُونَ وَلَا تُطِعْ كُلَّ حَلَّافٍ مَّهِينٍ هَمَّازٍ مَّشَّآءٍۭ بِنَمِيمٍ مَّنَّاعٍ لِّلْخَيْرِ مُعْتَدٍ أَثِيمٍ عُتُلٍّۭ بَعْدَ ذَٰلِكَ زَنِيمٍ أَن كَانَ ذَا مَالٍ وَبَنِينَ إِذَا تُتْلَىٰ عَلَيْهِ ءَايَـٰتُنَا قَالَ أَسَـٰطِيرُ ٱلْأَوَّلِينَ

So await your Lord's Judgment with patience; and do not obey a sinner or a denier of the truth from among them. – Surah Al-Insan 76:24

فَٱصْبِرْ لِحُكْمِ رَبِّكَ وَلَا تُطِعْ مِنْهُمْ ءَاثِمًا أَوْ كَفُورًا

.... Surely the Hour is indeed coming up, so pardon, with becoming pardoning. – Surah Al-Hujr 15:85

وَإِنَّ ٱلسَّاعَةَ لَـَٔاتِيَةٌ فَٱصْفَحِ ٱلصَّفْحَ ٱلْجَمِيلَ

So be patient for your Lord's judgment, and do not be like the fellow of the whale who called out in despair. – Surah Al-Qalam 68:48
فَٱصْبِرْ لِحُكْمِ رَبِّكَ وَلَا تَكُن كَصَاحِبِ ٱلْحُوتِ إِذْ نَادَىٰ وَهُوَ مَكْظُومٌ

And to your Lord (endure) patiently So when Trumpet is sounded (Literally: trumpeted) – Surah Al-Mudathir 74:7&8

وَلِرَبِّكَ فَٱصْبِرْ فَإِذَا نُقِرَ فِى ٱلنَّاقُورِ

Look how We have graced some of them over the others
ٱنظُرْ كَيْفَ فَضَّلْنَا بَعْضَهُمْ عَلَىٰ بَعْضٍ

He torments whomever He decides, and He has mercy on whomever He decides. And to Him you will be turned over. – Surah Al-'Ankabut 29:21

يُعَذِّبُ مَن يَشَآءُ وَيَرْحَمُ مَن يَشَآءُ ۖ وَإِلَيْهِ تُقْلَبُونَ

There are, on Earth, neighboring plots, gardens of vineyards, crops, date palm trees sharing the same root, or alone. They are all watered with the same water, yet We make Some better tasting than others. Surely there are signs in all of this for people who use their reason. – Surah Ar-Ra'd 13:4

وَفِى ٱلْأَرْضِ قِطَعٌ مُّتَجَـٰوِرَٰتٌ وَجَنَّـٰتٌ مِّنْ أَعْنَـٰبٍ وَزَرْعٌ وَنَخِيلٌ صِنْوَانٌ وَغَيْرُ صِنْوَانٍ يُسْقَىٰ بِمَآءٍ وَٰحِدٍ وَنُفَضِّلُ بَعْضَهَا عَلَىٰ بَعْضٍ فِى ٱلْأُكُلِ ۚ إِنَّ فِى ذَٰلِكَ لَـَٔايَـٰتٍ لِّقَوْمٍ يَعْقِلُونَ

And Allah has graced some of you over others (Literally: over some "others") in provision; so in no way will the ones who have been graced turn back their provision to the ones whom their right hands possess, so that they may be equal therein. Then, do they repudiate the favor of Allah. – Surah An-Nahl 16:71

وَٱللَّهُ فَضَّلَ بَعْضَكُمْ عَلَىٰ بَعْضٍ فِى ٱلرِّزْقِ ۚ فَمَا ٱلَّذِينَ فُضِّلُوا۟ بِرَآدِّى رِزْقِهِمْ عَلَىٰ مَا مَلَكَتْ أَيْمَـٰنُهُمْ فَهُمْ فِيهِ سَوَآءٌ ۚ أَفَبِنِعْمَةِ ٱللَّهِ يَجْحَدُونَ

Is it they who divide the mercy of your Lord? We have divided among them their subsistence in the present life (Literally: the lowly life, i.e., the life of this world) and raised some of them above (some) others in degrees, that some of them may take to themselves (some) others in subjection; and the mercy of your Lord is more charitable (i.e., better) than whatever they heap (Literally: gather) together – Surah Az-Zukhruf 43:32

أَهُمْ يَقْسِمُونَ رَحْمَتَ رَبِّكَ ۚ نَحْنُ قَسَمْنَا بَيْنَهُم مَّعِيشَتَهُمْ فِى ٱلْحَيَوٰةِ ٱلدُّنْيَا ۚ وَرَفَعْنَا بَعْضَهُمْ فَوْقَ بَعْضٍ دَرَجَـٰتٍ لِّيَتَّخِذَ بَعْضُهُم بَعْضًا سُخْرِيًّا ۗ وَرَحْمَتُ رَبِّكَ خَيْرٌ مِّمَّا يَجْمَعُونَ

To Allah (belongs) whatever is in the heavens and whatever is in the earth; and in case you display whatever is in yourselves or conceal it, Allah makes reckoning with you for it. So He forgives whomever He decides, and torments whomever He decides, and Allah is Ever-Determiner over everything. – Surah Al-Baqarah 2:284

لِّلَّهِ مَا فِى ٱلسَّمَـٰوَٰتِ وَمَا فِى ٱلْأَرْضِ ۗ وَإِن تُبْدُوا۟ مَا فِىٓ أَنفُسِكُمْ أَوْ تُخْفُوهُ يُحَاسِبْكُم بِهِ ٱللَّهُ ۖ فَيَغْفِرُ لِمَن يَشَآءُ وَيُعَذِّبُ مَن يَشَآءُ ۗ وَٱللَّهُ عَلَىٰ كُلِّ شَىْءٍ قَدِيرٌ

Do you not know that to Allah belongs the Kingdom of the heavens and the earth? He torments whomever He decides and forgives whomever He decides; and Allah is Ever-Determiner over everything. – Surah Al-Ma'idah 5:40

أَلَمْ تَعْلَمْ أَنَّ ٱللَّهَ لَهُۥ مُلْكُ ٱلسَّمَـٰوَٰتِ وَٱلْأَرْضِ يُعَذِّبُ مَن يَشَآءُ وَيَغْفِرُ لِمَن يَشَآءُ ۗ وَٱللَّهُ عَلَىٰ كُلِّ شَىْءٍ قَدِيرٌ

Look how We have graced some of them over the others, (Literally: over some "others") and indeed the Hereafter is greater in degrees and greater with marked graciousness. – Al-Isra 17:21

ٱنظُرْ كَيْفَ فَضَّلْنَا بَعْضَهُمْ عَلَىٰ بَعْضٍ ۚ وَلَلْـَٔاخِرَةُ أَكْبَرُ دَرَجَـٰتٍ وَأَكْبَرُ تَفْضِيلًا

They said, "By Allah! Indeed, Allah has already preferred you above us, and decidedly we were indeed sinners." – Surah Yusuf 12:91

قَالُوا۟ تَٱللَّهِ لَقَدْ ءَاثَرَكَ ٱللَّهُ عَلَيْنَا وَإِن كُنَّا لَخَـٰطِـِٔينَ

Book of

And the chief deceiver deceived you about Allah

وَغَرَّكُم بِٱللَّهِ ٱلْغَرُورُ

But Satan whispered to him. He said, “O Adam, shall I show you the Tree of Immortality, and a kingdom that never decays?” – Surah Ta-Ha 20:120

فَوَسْوَسَ إِلَيْهِ ٱلشَّيْطَٰنُ قَالَ يَٰٓـَٔادَمُ هَلْ أَدُلُّكَ عَلَىٰ شَجَرَةِ ٱلْخُلْدِ وَمُلْكٍ لَّا يَبْلَىٰ

Adorned for the people is the love of desires, such as women, and children, and piles upon piles of gold and silver, and branded horses, and livestock, and fields. These are the conveniences of the worldly life, but with Allah lies the finest resort. – Surah Al-Imran 3:14

زُيِّنَ لِلنَّاسِ حُبُّ ٱلشَّهَوَٰتِ مِنَ ٱلنِّسَآءِ وَٱلْبَنِينَ وَٱلْقَنَٰطِيرِ ٱلْمُقَنطَرَةِ مِنَ ٱلذَّهَبِ وَٱلْفِضَّةِ وَٱلْخَيْلِ ٱلْمُسَوَّمَةِ وَٱلْأَنْعَٰمِ وَٱلْحَرْثِ ۗ ذَٰلِكَ مَتَٰعُ
ٱلْحَيَوٰةِ ٱلدُّنْيَا ۖ وَٱللَّهُ عِندَهُۥ حُسْنُ ٱلْمَـَٔابِ

I am sending them a gift, and will see what the envoys bring back.” When he came to Solomon, he said, “Are you supplying me with money? What Allah has given me is better than what He has given you. It is you who delight in your gift. – Surah An-Naml 27:35&36

وَإِنِّى مُرْسِلَةٌ إِلَيْهِم بِهَدِيَّةٍ فَنَاظِرَةٌۢ بِمَ يَرْجِعُ ٱلْمُرْسَلُونَ فَلَمَّا جَآءَ سُلَيْمَٰنَ قَالَ أَتُمِدُّونَنِ بِمَالٍ فَمَآ ءَاتَىٰنِۦَ ٱللَّهُ خَيْرٌ مِّمَّآ ءَاتَىٰكُم بَلْ أَنتُم بِهَدِيَّتِكُمْ
تَفْرَحُونَ

And those who spend their money to be seen by people, and believe neither in Allah nor in the Last Day. Whoever has Satan as a companion—what an evil companion. – Surah An-Nisa 4:38

وَٱلَّذِينَ يُنفِقُونَ أَمْوَٰلَهُمْ رِئَآءَ ٱلنَّاسِ وَلَا يُؤْمِنُونَ بِٱللَّهِ وَلَا بِٱلْيَوْمِ ٱلْـَٔاخِرِ ۗ وَمَن يَكُنِ ٱلشَّيْطَٰنُ لَهُۥ قَرِينًا فَسَآءَ قَرِينًا

O Children of Adam! Do not let Satan seduce you, as he drove your parents out of the Garden, stripping them of their garments, to show them their nakedness. He sees you, him and his clan, from where you cannot see them. We have made the devils friends of those who do not believe. – Surah Al-A’raf 7:27

يَٰبَنِىٓ ءَادَمَ لَا يَفْتِنَنَّكُمُ ٱلشَّيْطَٰنُ كَمَآ أَخْرَجَ أَبَوَيْكُم مِّنَ ٱلْجَنَّةِ يَنزِعُ عَنْهُمَا لِبَاسَهُمَا لِيُرِيَهُمَا سَوْءَٰتِهِمَآ ۗ إِنَّهُۥ يَرَىٰكُمْ هُوَ وَقَبِيلُهُۥ مِنْ حَيْثُ لَا
تَرَوْنَهُمْ ۗ إِنَّا جَعَلْنَا ٱلشَّيَٰطِينَ أَوْلِيَآءَ لِلَّذِينَ لَا يُؤْمِنُونَ

Moses said, “Our Lord, you have given Pharaoh and his chiefs splendor and wealth in the worldly life. Our Lord, for them to lead away from Your path. Our Lord, obliterate their wealth, and harden their hearts, they will not believe until they see the painful torment.” – Surah Yunus 10:88

وَقَالَ مُوسَىٰ رَبَّنَآ إِنَّكَ ءَاتَيْتَ فِرْعَوْنَ وَمَلَأَهُۥ زِينَةً وَأَمْوَٰلًا فِى ٱلْحَيَوٰةِ ٱلدُّنْيَا رَبَّنَا لِيُضِلُّوا۟ عَن سَبِيلِكَ ۖ رَبَّنَا ٱطْمِسْ عَلَىٰٓ أَمْوَٰلِهِمْ وَٱشْدُدْ
عَلَىٰ قُلُوبِهِمْ فَلَا يُؤْمِنُوا۟ حَتَّىٰ يَرَوُا۟ ٱلْعَذَابَ ٱلْأَلِيمَ

Satan promises you poverty, and urges you to immorality; but Allah promises you forgiveness from Himself, and grace. Allah is Embracing and Knowing. – Surah Al-Baqarah 2:268

ٱلشَّيْطَٰنُ يَعِدُكُمُ ٱلْفَقْرَ وَيَأْمُرُكُم بِٱلْفَحْشَآءِ ۖ وَٱللَّهُ يَعِدُكُم مَّغْفِرَةً مِّنْهُ وَفَضْلًا ۗ وَٱللَّهُ وَٰسِعٌ عَلِيمٌ

[Fir’aun (Pharaoh)] He said, “Did you believe in him before I have given you permission? He must be your chief, who has taught you magic. I will cut off your hands and your feet on alternate sides, and I will crucify you on the trunks of the palm-trees. Then you will know which of us is more severe in punishment, and more lasting.” They said, “We will not prefer you to the proofs that have come to us, and Him who created us. So issue whatever judgment you wish to issue. You can only rule in this lowly life. We have believed in our Lord, so that He may forgive us our sins, and the magic you have compelled us to practice. Allah is Better, and more Lasting." – Surah Ta-Ha 20:71-73

قَالَ ءَامَنتُمْ لَهُۥ قَبْلَ أَنْ ءَاذَنَ لَكُمْ ۖ إِنَّهُۥ لَكَبِيرُكُمُ ٱلَّذِى عَلَّمَكُمُ ٱلسِّحْرَ ۖ فَلَأُقَطِّعَنَّ أَيْدِيَكُمْ وَأَرْجُلَكُم مِّنْ خِلَٰفٍ وَلَأُصَلِّبَنَّكُمْ فِى جُذُوعِ ٱلنَّخْلِ وَلَتَعْلَمُنَّ أَيُّنَآ أَشَدُّ عَذَابًا وَأَبْقَىٰ قَالُوا۟ لَن نُّؤْثِرَكَ عَلَىٰ مَا جَآءَنَا مِنَ ٱلْبَيِّنَٰتِ وَٱلَّذِى فَطَرَنَا ۖ فَٱقْضِ مَآ أَنتَ قَاضٍ ۖ إِنَّمَا تَقْضِى هَٰذِهِ ٱلْحَيَوٰةَ ٱلدُّنْيَآ إِنَّآ ءَامَنَّا بِرَبِّنَا لِيَغْفِرَ لَنَا خَطَٰيَٰنَا وَمَآ أَكْرَهْتَنَا عَلَيْهِ مِنَ ٱلسِّحْرِ ۗ وَٱللَّهُ خَيْرٌ وَأَبْقَىٰٓ

Yet whenever they come across some business, or some entertainment, they scramble towards it, and leave you standing. Say, "What is with Allah is better than entertainment and business; and Allah is the Best of providers." – Surah Al-Jumu'ah 62:11

وَإِذَا رَأَوْا۟ تِجَٰرَةً أَوْ لَهْوًا ٱنفَضُّوٓا۟ إِلَيْهَا وَتَرَكُوكَ قَآئِمًا ۚ قُلْ مَا عِندَ ٱللَّهِ خَيْرٌ مِّنَ ٱللَّهْوِ وَمِنَ ٱلتِّجَٰرَةِ ۚ وَٱللَّهُ خَيْرُ ٱلرَّٰزِقِينَ

And recall when you said, "O Moses, we cannot endure one kind of food, so call to your Lord to produce for us of what the earth grows: of its herbs, and its cucumbers, and its garlic, and its lentils, and its onions." He said, "Would you substitute worse for better? Go down to Egypt, where you will have what you asked for." They were struck with humiliation and poverty, and incurred wrath from Allah. That was because they rejected Allah's revelations and wrongfully killed the prophets. That was because they disobeyed and transgressed. – Surah Al-Baqarah 2:61

وَإِذْ قُلْتُمْ يَٰمُوسَىٰ لَن نَّصْبِرَ عَلَىٰ طَعَامٍ وَٰحِدٍ فَٱدْعُ لَنَا رَبَّكَ يُخْرِجْ لَنَا مِمَّا تُنۢبِتُ ٱلْأَرْضُ مِنۢ بَقْلِهَا وَقِثَّآئِهَا وَفُومِهَا وَعَدَسِهَا وَبَصَلِهَا ۖ قَالَ أَتَسْتَبْدِلُونَ ٱلَّذِى هُوَ أَدْنَىٰ بِٱلَّذِى هُوَ خَيْرٌ ۚ ٱهْبِطُوا۟ مِصْرًا فَإِنَّ لَكُم مَّا سَأَلْتُمْ ۗ وَضُرِبَتْ عَلَيْهِمُ ٱلذِّلَّةُ وَٱلْمَسْكَنَةُ وَبَآءُو بِغَضَبٍ مِّنَ ٱللَّهِ ۗ ذَٰلِكَ بِأَنَّهُمْ كَانُوا۟ يَكْفُرُونَ بِـَٔايَٰتِ ٱللَّهِ وَيَقْتُلُونَ ٱلنَّبِيِّۦنَ بِغَيْرِ ٱلْحَقِّ ۗ ذَٰلِكَ بِمَا عَصَوا۟ وَّكَانُوا۟ يَعْتَدُونَ

And they followed what the devils taught during the reign of Solomon. It was not Solomon who disbelieved, but it was the devils who disbelieved. They taught the people witchcraft and what was revealed inBabylon to the two angels Harut and Marut. They did not teach anybody until they had said, "We are a test, so do not lose faith." But they learned from them the means to cause separation between man and his wife. But they cannot harm anyone except with Allah's permission. And they learned what would harm them and not benefit them. Yet they knew that whoever deals in it will have no share in the Hereafter. Miserable is what they sold their souls for, if they only knew.– Surah Al-Baqarah 2:102

وَٱتَّبَعُوا۟ مَا تَتْلُوا۟ ٱلشَّيَٰطِينُ عَلَىٰ مُلْكِ سُلَيْمَٰنَ ۖ وَمَا كَفَرَ سُلَيْمَٰنُ وَلَٰكِنَّ ٱلشَّيَٰطِينَ كَفَرُوا۟ يُعَلِّمُونَ ٱلنَّاسَ ٱلسِّحْرَ وَمَآ أُنزِلَ عَلَى ٱلْمَلَكَيْنِ بِبَابِلَ هَٰرُوتَ وَمَٰرُوتَ ۚ وَمَا يُعَلِّمَانِ مِنْ أَحَدٍ حَتَّىٰ يَقُولَآ إِنَّمَا نَحْنُ فِتْنَةٌ فَلَا تَكْفُرْ ۖ فَيَتَعَلَّمُونَ مِنْهُمَا مَا يُفَرِّقُونَ بِهِۦ بَيْنَ ٱلْمَرْءِ وَزَوْجِهِۦ ۚ وَمَا هُم بِضَآرِّينَ بِهِۦ مِنْ أَحَدٍ إِلَّا بِإِذْنِ ٱللَّهِ ۚ وَيَتَعَلَّمُونَ مَا يَضُرُّهُمْ وَلَا يَنفَعُهُمْ ۚ وَلَقَدْ عَلِمُوا۟ لَمَنِ ٱشْتَرَىٰهُ مَا لَهُۥ فِى ٱلْءَاخِرَةِ مِنْ خَلَٰقٍ ۚ وَلَبِئْسَ مَا شَرَوْا۟ بِهِۦٓ أَنفُسَهُمْ ۚ لَوْ كَانُوا۟ يَعْلَمُونَ

But Satan whispered to them, to reveal to them their nakedness, which was invisible to them. He said, "Your Lord has only forbidden you this tree, lest you become angels, or become immortals." And he swore to them, "I am a sincere advisor to you." So he lured them with deceit. And when they tasted the tree, their nakedness became evident to them, and they began covering themselves with the leaves of the Garden. And their Lord called out to them, "Did I not forbid you from this tree, and say to you that Satan is a sworn enemy to you?" – Surah Al-A'raf 7:20-22

فَوَسْوَسَ لَهُمَا ٱلشَّيْطَٰنُ لِيُبْدِىَ لَهُمَا مَا وُۥرِىَ عَنْهُمَا مِن سَوْءَٰتِهِمَا وَقَالَ مَا نَهَىٰكُمَا رَبُّكُمَا عَنْ هَٰذِهِ ٱلشَّجَرَةِ إِلَّآ أَن تَكُونَا مَلَكَيْنِ أَوْ تَكُونَا مِنَ ٱلْخَٰلِدِينَ وَقَاسَمَهُمَآ إِنِّى لَكُمَا لَمِنَ ٱلنَّٰصِحِينَ فَدَلَّىٰهُمَا بِغُرُورٍ ۚ فَلَمَّا ذَاقَا ٱلشَّجَرَةَ بَدَتْ لَهُمَا سَوْءَٰتُهُمَا وَطَفِقَا يَخْصِفَانِ عَلَيْهِمَا مِن وَرَقِ ٱلْجَنَّةِ ۖ وَنَادَىٰهُمَا رَبُّهُمَآ أَلَمْ أَنْهَكُمَا عَن تِلْكُمَا ٱلشَّجَرَةِ وَأَقُل لَّكُمَآ إِنَّ ٱلشَّيْطَٰنَ لَكُمَا عَدُوٌّ مُّبِينٌ

Narrated `Adi bin Hatim: While I was sitting with Allah's Messenger ﷺ two person came to him; one of them complained about his poverty and the other complained about the prevalence of robberies. Allah's Messenger ﷺ said, "As regards stealing and robberies, there will shortly come a time when a caravan will go to Mecca (from Medina) without any guard. And regarding poverty, The Hour (Day of Judgment) will not be established till one of you wanders about with his object of charity and will not find anybody to accept it And (no doubt) each one of you will stand in front of Allah and there will be neither a curtain nor an interpreter between him and Allah, and Allah will ask him, 'Did not I give you wealth?' He will reply in the affirmative. Allah will further ask, 'Didn't send a messenger to you?' And again that person will reply in the affirmative Then he will look to his right and he will see nothing but Hell-fire, and then he will look to his left and will see nothing but Hell-fire. And so, any (each one) of you should save himself from the fire even by giving half of a date-fruit (in charity). And if you do not find a hall datefruit, then (you can do it through saying) a good pleasant word (to your brethren). (See Hadith No. 793 Vol. 4). – Al-Bukhari 1413

حَدَّثَنَا عَبْدُ اللَّهِ بْنُ مُحَمَّدٍ، حَدَّثَنَا أَبُو عَاصِمٍ النَّبِيلُ، أَخْبَرَنَا سَعْدَانُ بْنُ بِشْرٍ، حَدَّثَنَا أَبُو مُجَاهِدٍ، حَدَّثَنَا مُحِلُّ بْنُ خَلِيفَةَ الطَّائِيُّ، قَالَ سَمِعْتُ عَدِيَّ بْنَ حَاتِمٍ ـ رضى الله عنه ـ يَقُولُ كُنْتُ عِنْدَ رَسُولِ اللَّهِ صلى الله عليه وسلم فَجَاءَهُ رَجُلاَنِ أَحَدُهُمَا يَشْكُو الْعَيْلَةَ، وَالآخَرُ يَشْكُو قَطْعَ السَّبِيلِ، فَقَالَ رَسُولُ اللَّهِ صلى الله عليه وسلم " أَمَّا قَطْعُ السَّبِيلِ فَإِنَّهُ لاَ يَأْتِي عَلَيْكَ إِلاَّ قَلِيلٌ حَتَّى تَخْرُجَ الْعِيرُ إِلَى مَكَّةَ بِغَيْرِ خَفِيرٍ، وَأَمَّا الْعَيْلَةُ فَإِنَّ السَّاعَةَ لاَ تَقُومُ حَتَّى يَطُوفَ أَحَدُكُمْ بِصَدَقَتِهِ لاَ يَجِدُ مَنْ يَقْبَلُهَا مِنْهُ، ثُمَّ لَيَقِفَنَّ أَحَدُكُمْ بَيْنَ يَدَىِ اللَّهِ لَيْسَ بَيْنَهُ وَبَيْنَهُ حِجَابٌ وَلاَ تُرْجُمَانٌ يُتَرْجِمُ لَهُ، ثُمَّ لَيَقُولَنَّ لَهُ أَلَمْ أُوتِكَ مَالاً فَلَيَقُولَنَّ بَلَى. ثُمَّ لَيَقُولَنَّ أَلَمْ أُرْسِلْ إِلَيْكَ رَسُولاً فَلَيَقُولَنَّ بَلَى. فَيَنْظُرُ عَنْ يَمِينِهِ فَلاَ يَرَى إِلاَّ النَّارَ، ثُمَّ يَنْظُرُ عَنْ شِمَالِهِ فَلاَ يَرَى إِلاَّ النَّارَ، فَلْيَتَّقِيَنَّ أَحَدُكُمُ النَّارَ وَلَوْ بِشِقِّ تَمْرَةٍ، فَإِنْ لَمْ يَجِدْ فَبِكَلِمَةٍ طَيِّبَةٍ "

"And entice whomever of them you can with your voice, and rally against them your cavalry and your infantry, and share with them in wealth and children, and make promises to them." But Satan promises them nothing but delusion. – Surah Al-Isra 17:64

وَٱسْتَفْزِزْ مَنِ ٱسْتَطَعْتَ مِنْهُم بِصَوْتِكَ وَأَجْلِبْ عَلَيْهِم بِخَيْلِكَ وَرَجِلِكَ وَشَارِكْهُمْ فِى ٱلْأَمْوَٰلِ وَٱلْأَوْلَٰدِ وَعِدْهُمْ ۚ وَمَا يَعِدُهُمُ ٱلشَّيْطَٰنُ إِلَّا غُرُورًا

O Prophet (Muhammad)! Say to your wives, "If you desire the life of this world and its finery, then let me compensate you, and release you kindly. – Surah Al-Azhab 33:28

يَٰٓأَيُّهَا ٱلنَّبِىُّ قُل لِّأَزْوَٰجِكَ إِن كُنتُنَّ تُرِدْنَ ٱلْحَيَوٰةَ ٱلدُّنْيَا وَزِينَتَهَا فَتَعَالَيْنَ أُمَتِّعْكُنَّ وَأُسَرِّحْكُنَّ سَرَاحًا جَمِيلًا

[Iblis (Satan)] He said, "My Lord, since You have lured me away, I will glamorize for them on earth, and I will lure them all away." "Except for Your sincere servants among them." – Surah Al-Hijr 15:39&40

قَالَ رَبِّ بِمَآ أَغْوَيْتَنِى لَأُزَيِّنَنَّ لَهُمْ فِى ٱلْأَرْضِ وَلَأُغْوِيَنَّهُمْ أَجْمَعِينَ إِلَّا عِبَادَكَ مِنْهُمُ ٱلْمُخْلَصِينَ

Narrated Abu Dhar: While I was walking with the Prophet ﷺ in the Harra of Medina, Uhud came in sight. The Prophet ﷺ said, "O Abu Dhar!" I said, "Labbaik, O Allah's Messenger ﷺ !" He said, "I would not like to have gold equal to this mountain of Uhud, unless nothing of it, not even a single Dinar of it remains with me for more than three days, except something which I will keep for repaying debts. I would have spent all of it (distributed it) amongst Allah's Slaves like this, and like this, and like this." The Prophet ﷺ pointed out with his hand towards his right, his left and his back (while illustrating it). He proceeded with his walk and said, "The rich are in fact the poor (little rewarded) on the Day of Resurrection except those who spend their wealth like this, and like this, and like this, to their right, left and back, but such people are few in number." Then he said to me, "Stay at your place and do not leave it till I come back." Then he proceeded in the darkness of the night till he went out of sight, and then I heard a loud voice, and was afraid that something might have happened to the Prophet ﷺ 1. intended to go to him, but I remembered what he had said to me, i.e. 'Don't leave your place till I come back to you,' so I remained at my place till he came back to me. I said, "O Allah's Messenger ﷺ !" I heard a voice and I was afraid." So I mentioned the whole story to him. He said, "Did you hear it?" I replied, "Yes." He said, "It was Gabriel who came to me and said, 'Whoever died without joining others in worship with Allah, will enter Paradise.' I asked (Gabriel), 'Even if he had committed theft or committed illegal sexual intercourse? Gabriel said, 'Yes, even if he had committed theft or committed illegal sexual intercourse." – Al-Bukhari 6444 (also See Al-Bukhari 6258 & 2388)

حَدَّثَنَا الْحَسَنُ بْنُ الرَّبِيعِ، حَدَّثَنَا أَبُو الأَحْوَصِ، عَنِ الأَعْمَشِ، عَنْ زَيْدِ بْنِ وَهْبٍ، قَالَ قَالَ أَبُو ذَرٍّ كُنْتُ أَمْشِي مَعَ النَّبِيِّ صلى الله عليه وسلم فِي حَرَّةِ الْمَدِينَةِ فَاسْتَقْبَلَنَا أُحُدٌ فَقَالَ " يَا أَبَا ذَرٍّ ". قُلْتُ لَبَّيْكَ يَا رَسُولَ اللَّهِ. قَالَ " مَا يَسُرُّنِي أَنَّ عِنْدِي مِثْلَ أُحُدٍ هَذَا ذَهَبًا، تَمْضِي عَلَىَّ ثَالِثَةٌ وَعِنْدِي مِنْهُ دِينَارٌ، إِلاَّ شَيْئًا أَرْصِدُهُ لِدَيْنٍ، إِلاَّ أَنْ أَقُولَ بِهِ فِي عِبَادِ اللَّهِ هَكَذَا وَهَكَذَا وَهَكَذَا ". عَنْ يَمِينِهِ وَعَنْ شِمَالِهِ وَمِنْ خَلْفِهِ. ثُمَّ مَشَى فَقَالَ " إِنَّ الأَكْثَرِينَ هُمُ الأَقَلُّونَ يَوْمَ الْقِيَامَةِ إِلاَّ مَنْ قَالَ هَكَذَا وَهَكَذَا وَهَكَذَا ـ عَنْ يَمِينِهِ وَعَنْ شِمَالِهِ وَمِنْ خَلْفِهِ ـ وَقَلِيلٌ مَا هُمْ ". ثُمَّ قَالَ لِي " مَكَانَكَ لاَ تَبْرَحْ حَتَّى آتِيَكَ ". ثُمَّ انْطَلَقَ فِي سَوَادِ اللَّيْلِ حَتَّى تَوَارَى فَسَمِعْتُ صَوْتًا قَدِ ارْتَفَعَ، فَتَخَوَّفْتُ أَنْ يَكُونَ قَدْ عَرَضَ لِلنَّبِيِّ صلى الله عليه وسلم فَأَرَدْتُ أَنْ آتِيَهُ فَذَكَرْتُ قَوْلَهُ لِي " لاَ تَبْرَحْ حَتَّى آتِيَكَ " فَلَمْ أَبْرَحْ حَتَّى أَتَانِي، قُلْتُ يَا رَسُولَ اللَّهِ لَقَدْ سَمِعْتُ صَوْتًا تَخَوَّفْتُ، فَذَكَرْتُ لَهُ فَقَالَ " وَهَلْ سَمِعْتَهُ ". قُلْتُ نَعَمْ. قَالَ " ذَاكَ جِبْرِيلُ أَتَانِي فَقَالَ مَنْ مَاتَ مِنْ أُمَّتِكَ لاَ يُشْرِكُ بِاللَّهِ شَيْئًا دَخَلَ الْجَنَّةَ ". قُلْتُ وَإِنْ زَنَى وَإِنْ سَرَقَ قَالَ " وَإِنْ زَنَى وَإِنْ سَرَقَ ".

Narrated `Imran bin Husain: The Prophet ﷺ said, "I looked into Paradise and found that the majority of its dwellers were the poor people, and I looked into the (Hell) Fire and found that the majority of its dwellers were women." – Al-Bukhari 6449

حَدَّثَنَا أَبُو الْوَلِيدِ، حَدَّثَنَا سَلْمُ بْنُ زَرِيرٍ، حَدَّثَنَا أَبُو رَجَاءٍ، عَنْ عِمْرَانَ بْنِ حُصَيْنٍ ـ رضى الله عنهما ـ عَنِ النَّبِيِّ صلى الله عليه وسلم قَالَ " اطَّلَعْتُ فِي الْجَنَّةِ فَرَأَيْتُ أَكْثَرَ أَهْلِهَا الْفُقَرَاءَ، وَاطَّلَعْتُ فِي النَّارِ فَرَأَيْتُ أَكْثَرَ أَهْلِهَا النِّسَاءَ ". تَابَعَهُ أَيُّوبُ وَعَوْفٌ، وَقَالَ صَخْرٌ وَحَمَّادُ بْنُ نَجِيحٍ عَنْ أَبِي رَجَاءٍ عَنِ ابْنِ عَبَّاسٍ.

Narrated Abu Huraira: Allah's Messenger ﷺ said, "The (Hell) Fire is surrounded by all kinds of desires and passions, while Paradise is surrounded by all kinds of disliked undesirable things." – Al-Bukhari 6487

حَدَّثَنَا إِسْمَاعِيلُ، قَالَ حَدَّثَنِي مَالِكٌ، عَنْ أَبِي الزِّنَادِ، عَنِ الأَعْرَجِ، عَنْ أَبِي هُرَيْرَةَ، أَنَّ رَسُولَ اللَّهِ صلى الله عليه وسلم قَالَ " حُجِبَتِ النَّارُ بِالشَّهَوَاتِ، وَحُجِبَتِ الْجَنَّةُ بِالْمَكَارِهِ "

But they were succeeded by generations who lost the prayers and followed their appetites. They will meet perdition. – Surah Al-Maryam 19:59

فَخَلَفَ مِنۢ بَعْدِهِمْ خَلْفٌ أَضَاعُوا۟ ٱلصَّلَوٰةَ وَٱتَّبَعُوا۟ ٱلشَّهَوَٰتِ ۖ فَسَوْفَ يَلْقَوْنَ غَيًّا

Narrated Haritha bin Wahb: I heard the Prophet ﷺ saying, "Shall I tell you of the people of Paradise? They comprise every poor humble person, and if he swears by Allah to do something, Allah will fulfill it; while the people of the fire comprise every violent, cruel arrogant person." – Al-Bukhari 6657

حَدَّثَنَا مُحَمَّدُ بْنُ الْمُثَنَّى، حَدَّثَنِي غُنْدَرٌ، حَدَّثَنَا شُعْبَةُ، عَنْ مَعْبَدِ بْنِ خَالِدٍ، سَمِعْتُ حَارِثَةَ بْنَ وَهْبٍ، قَالَ سَمِعْتُ النَّبِيَّ صلى الله عليه وسلم يَقُولُ " أَلاَ أَدُلُّكُمْ عَلَى أَهْلِ الْجَنَّةِ، كُلُّ ضَعِيفٍ مُتَضَعِّفٍ، لَوْ أَقْسَمَ عَلَى اللَّهِ لأَبَرَّهُ، وَأَهْلِ النَّارِ كُلُّ جَوَّاظٍ عُتُلٍّ مُسْتَكْبِرٍ "

Narrated Ibn `Abbas: I heard the Prophet ﷺ saying, "If the son of Adam (the human being) had two valleys of money, he would wish for a third, for nothing can fill the belly of Adam's son except dust, and Allah forgives him who repents to Him." – Al-Bukhari 6436

حَدَّثَنَا أَبُو عَاصِمٍ، عَنِ ابْنِ جُرَيْجٍ، عَنْ عَطَاءٍ، قَالَ سَمِعْتُ ابْنَ عَبَّاسٍ ـ رضى الله عنهما ـ يَقُولُ سَمِعْتُ النَّبِيَّ صلى الله عليه وسلم يَقُولُ " لَوْ كَانَ لاِبْنِ آدَمَ وَادِيَانِ مِنْ مَالٍ لاَبْتَغَى ثَالِثًا، وَلاَ يَمْلأُ جَوْفَ ابْنِ آدَمَ إِلاَّ التُّرَابُ، وَيَتُوبُ اللَّهُ عَلَى مَنْ تَابَ "

Narrated `Uqba bin Al-Harith: I offered the `Asr prayer with the Prophet ﷺ and after finishing the prayer with Taslim he got up quickly and went to some of his wives and then came out. He noticed the signs of astonishment on the faces of the people caused by his speed. He then said, "I remembered while I was in my prayer that a piece of gold was Lying in my house and I disliked that it should remain with us throughout the night, and so I have ordered it to be distributed." – Al-Bukhari 1221

حَدَّثَنَا إِسْحَاقُ بْنُ مَنْصُورٍ، حَدَّثَنَا رَوْحٌ، حَدَّثَنَا عُمَرُ ـ هُوَ ابْنُ سَعِيدٍ ـ قَالَ أَخْبَرَنِي ابْنُ أَبِي مُلَيْكَةَ، عَنْ عُقْبَةَ بْنِ الْحَارِثِ ـ رضى الله عنه ـ قَالَ صَلَّيْتُ مَعَ النَّبِيِّ صلى الله عليه وسلم الْعَصْرَ، فَلَمَّا سَلَّمَ قَامَ سَرِيعًا دَخَلَ عَلَى بَعْضِ نِسَائِهِ، ثُمَّ خَرَجَ وَرَأَى مَا فِي وُجُوهِ الْقَوْمِ مِنْ تَعَجُّبِهِمْ لِسُرْعَتِهِ فَقَالَ " ذَكَرْتُ وَأَنَا فِي الصَّلاَةِ تِبْرًا عِنْدَنَا، فَكَرِهْتُ أَنْ يُمْسِيَ أَوْ يَبِيتَ عِنْدَنَا فَأَمَرْتُ بِقِسْمَتِهِ "

O people! The promise of Allah is true; so let not the lowly life seduce you, and let not the Tempter tempt you away from Allah. Satan is an enemy to you, so treat him as an enemy. He only invites his gang to be among the inmates of the Inferno. – Surah Fatir 35:5&6

يَٰٓأَيُّهَا ٱلنَّاسُ إِنَّ وَعْدَ ٱللَّهِ حَقٌّۖ فَلَا تَغُرَّنَّكُمُ ٱلْحَيَوٰةُ ٱلدُّنْيَاۖ وَلَا يَغُرَّنَّكُم بِٱللَّهِ ٱلْغَرُورُ .إِنَّ ٱلشَّيْطَٰنَ لَكُمْ عَدُوٌّ فَٱتَّخِذُوهُ عَدُوًّاۚ إِنَّمَا يَدْعُواْ حِزْبَهُۥ لِيَكُونُواْ مِنْ أَصْحَٰبِ ٱلسَّعِيرِ

Narrated Abu Huraira The Prophetﷺ said, "Let the slave of Dinar and Dirham of Quantify and Khamisa (i.e. money and luxurious clothes) perish for he is pleased if these things are given to him, and if not, he is displeased!"–Al-Bukhari 2886

حَدَّثَنَا يَحْيَى بْنُ يُوسُفَ، أَخْبَرَنَا أَبُو بَكْرٍ، عَنْ أَبِي حَصِينٍ، عَنْ أَبِي صَالِحٍ، عَنْ أَبِي هُرَيْرَةَ ـ رضى الله عنه ـ عَنِ النَّبِيِّ صلى الله عليه وسلم قَالَ " تَعِسَ عَبْدُ الدِّينَارِ وَالدِّرْهَمِ وَالْقَطِيفَةِ وَالْخَمِيصَةِ، إِنْ أُعْطِيَ رَضِيَ، وَإِنْ لَمْ يُعْطَ لَمْ يَرْضَ ". لَمْ يَرْفَعْهُ إِسْرَائِيلُ عَنْ أَبِي حَصِينٍ

"O David, We made you a ruler in the land, so judge between the people with justice, and do not follow desire, lest it diverts you from Allah's path. Those who stray from Allah's path will have a painful punishment, for having ignored the Day of Account." – Surah Sad 38:26

يَٰدَاوُۥدُ إِنَّا جَعَلْنَٰكَ خَلِيفَةً فِى ٱلْأَرْضِ فَٱحْكُم بَيْنَ ٱلنَّاسِ بِٱلْحَقِّ وَلَا تَتَّبِعِ ٱلْهَوَىٰ فَيُضِلَّكَ عَن سَبِيلِ ٱللَّهِۚ إِنَّ ٱلَّذِينَ يَضِلُّونَ عَن سَبِيلِ ٱللَّهِ لَهُمْ عَذَابٌ شَدِيدٌۢ بِمَا نَسُواْ يَوْمَ ٱلْحِسَابِ

Narrated Ibn `Umar: Umar saw a silken cloak being sold in the market and he brought it to Allah's Messengerﷺ and said, "O Allah's Messengerﷺ ! Buy this cloak and adorn yourself with it on the `Id festivals and on meeting the delegations." Allah's Messengerﷺ replied, "This is the dress for the one who will have no share in the Hereafter (or, this is worn by one who will have no share in the Hereafter)." After sometime had passed, Allah's Messengerﷺ sent a silken cloak to `Umar. `Umar took it and brought it to Allah's Messengerﷺ and said, "O Allah's Messengerﷺ ! You have said that this is the dress of that who will have no share in the Hereafter (or, this is worn by one who will have no share in the Hereafter), yet you have sent me this!" The Prophetﷺ said," I have sent it) so that you may sell it or fulfill with it some of your needs."–Al-Bukhari 3054

حَدَّثَنَا يَحْيَى بْنُ بُكَيْرٍ، حَدَّثَنَا اللَّيْثُ، عَنْ عُقَيْلٍ، عَنِ ابْنِ شِهَابٍ، عَنْ سَالِمِ بْنِ عَبْدِ اللَّهِ، أَنَّ ابْنَ عُمَرَ ـ رضى الله عنهما ـ قَالَ وَجَدَ عُمَرُ حُلَّةَ إِسْتَبْرَقٍ تُبَاعُ فِي السُّوقِ فَأَتَى بِهَا رَسُولَ اللَّهِ صلى الله عليه وسلم فَقَالَ يَا رَسُولَ اللَّهِ، ابْتَعْ هَذِهِ الْحُلَّةَ فَتَجَمَّلْ بِهَا لِلْعِيدِ وَلِلْوُفُودِ. فَقَالَ رَسُولُ اللَّهِ صلى الله عليه وسلم " إِنَّمَا هَذِهِ لِبَاسُ مَنْ لاَ خَلاَقَ لَهُ، أَوْ إِنَّمَا يَلْبَسُ هَذِهِ مَنْ لاَ خَلاَقَ لَهُ ". فَلَبِثَ مَا شَاءَ اللَّهُ ثُمَّ أَرْسَلَ إِلَيْهِ النَّبِيُّ صلى الله عليه وسلم بِجُبَّةِ دِيبَاجٍ، فَأَقْبَلَ بِهَا عُمَرُ حَتَّى أَتَى بِهَا رَسُولَ اللَّهِ صلى الله عليه وسلم فَقَالَ يَا رَسُولَ اللَّهِ، قُلْتَ " إِنَّمَا هَذِهِ لِبَاسُ مَنْ لاَ خَلاَقَ لَهُ أَوْ إِنَّمَا يَلْبَسُ هَذِهِ مَنْ لاَ خَلاَقَ لَهُ ". ثُمَّ أَرْسَلْتَ إِلَيَّ بِهَذِهِ فَقَالَ " تَبِيعُهَا، أَوْ تُصِيبُ بِهَا بَعْضَ حَاجَتِكَ ".

Narrated Al-Bara bin Azib: Allah's Messengerﷺ was given a silken garment, and its beauty and delicacy astonished the people. On that, Allah's Messengerﷺ said, "No doubt, the handkerchiefs of Sa`d bin Mu`adh in Paradise are better than this."–Al-Bukhari 3249

حَدَّثَنَا مُسَدَّدٌ، حَدَّثَنَا يَحْيَى بْنُ سَعِيدٍ، عَنْ سُفْيَانَ، قَالَ حَدَّثَنِي أَبُو إِسْحَاقَ، قَالَ سَمِعْتُ الْبَرَاءَ بْنَ عَازِبٍ ـ رضى الله عنهما ـ قَالَ أُتِيَ رَسُولُ اللَّهِ صلى الله عليه وسلم بِثَوْبٍ مِنْ حَرِيرٍ، فَجَعَلُوا يَعْجَبُونَ مِنْ حُسْنِهِ وَلِينِهِ، فَقَالَ رَسُولُ اللَّهِ صلى الله عليه وسلم " لَمَنَادِيلُ سَعْدِ بْنِ مُعَاذٍ فِي الْجَنَّةِ أَفْضَلُ مِنْ هَذَا "

Narrated Mus`ab bin Sa`d: Once Sa`d (bin Abi Waqqas) thought that he was superior to those who were below him in rank. On that the Prophetﷺ said, "You gain no victory or livelihood except through (the blessings and invocations of) the poor amongst you."–Al-Bukhari 2896

حَدَّثَنَا سُلَيْمَانُ بْنُ حَرْبٍ، حَدَّثَنَا مُحَمَّدُ بْنُ طَلْحَةَ، عَنْ طَلْحَةَ، عَنْ مُصْعَبِ بْنِ سَعْدٍ، قَالَ رَأَى سَعْدٌ ـ رضى الله عنه ـ أَنَّ لَهُ فَضْلاً عَلَى مَنْ دُونَهُ، فَقَالَ النَّبِيُّ صلى الله عليه وسلم " هَلْ تُنْصَرُونَ وَتُرْزَقُونَ إِلاَّ بِضُعَفَائِكُمْ "

Narrated Um Salama: (the wife of the Prophet) Allah's Messenger ﷺ said, "He who drinks in silver utensils is only filling his `Abdomen with Hell Fire."–Al-Bukhari 5634

حَدَّثَنَا إِسْمَاعِيلُ، قَالَ حَدَّثَنِي مَالِكُ بْنُ أَنَسٍ، عَنْ نَافِعٍ، عَنْ زَيْدِ بْنِ عَبْدِ اللَّهِ بْنِ عُمَرَ، عَنْ عَبْدِ اللَّهِ بْنِ عَبْدِ الرَّحْمَنِ بْنِ أَبِي بَكْرٍ الصِّدِّيقِ، عَنْ أُمِّ سَلَمَةَ، زَوْجِ النَّبِيِّ صلى الله عليه وسلم أَنَّ رَسُولَ اللَّهِ صلى الله عليه وسلم قَالَ " الَّذِي يَشْرَبُ فِي إِنَاءِ الْفِضَّةِ إِنَّمَا يُجَرْجِرُ فِي بَطْنِهِ نَارَ جَهَنَّمَ "

Narrated Um Salama: (One night) the Prophet ﷺ woke up and said, "Subhan Allah ! How many treasures have been (disclosed) sent down! And how many afflictions have been descended! Who will go and wake the sleeping lady occupants up of these dwellings (for praying)?" (He meant by this his wives.) The Prophet ﷺ added, "A well-dressed soul (person) in this world may be naked in the "Hereafter." `Umar said, "I asked the Prophet, 'Have you divorced your wives?' He said, 'No.' I said, 'Allahu Akbar.'"–Al-Bukhari 6218

حَدَّثَنَا أَبُو الْيَمَانِ، أَخْبَرَنَا شُعَيْبٌ، عَنِ الزُّهْرِيِّ، حَدَّثَتْنِي هِنْدُ بِنْتُ الْحَارِثِ، أَنَّ أُمَّ سَلَمَةَ ـ رضى الله عنها ـ قَالَتِ اسْتَيْقَظَ النَّبِيُّ صلى الله عليه وسلم فَقَالَ " سُبْحَانَ اللَّهِ مَاذَا أُنْزِلَ مِنَ الْخَزَائِنِ، وَمَاذَا أُنْزِلَ مِنَ الْفِتَنِ، مَنْ يُوقِظُ صَوَاحِبَ الْحُجَرِ ـ يُرِيدُ بِهِ أَزْوَاجَهُ ـ حَتَّى يُصَلِّينَ، رُبَّ كَاسِيَةٍ فِي الدُّنْيَا، عَارِيَةٍ فِي الآخِرَةِ ". وَقَالَ ابْنُ أَبِي ثَوْرٍ عَنِ ابْنِ عَبَّاسٍ، عَنْ عُمَرَ، قَالَ قُلْتُ لِلنَّبِيِّ صلى الله عليه وسلم طَلَّقْتَ نِسَاءَكَ قَالَ " لاَ ". قُلْتُ اللَّهُ أَكْبَرُ.

Narrated `Amr bin `Auf: (An ally of the tribe of Bani 'Amir bin Lu'ai and one of those who had witnessed the battle of Badr with Allah's Messenger ﷺ) Allah's Messenger ﷺ sent Abu 'Ubaida bin AlJarrah to Bahrain to collect the Jizya tax. Allah's Messenger ﷺ had concluded a peace treaty with the people of Bahrain and appointed Al 'Ala bin Al-Hadrami as their chief; Abu Ubaida arrived from Bahrain with the money. The Ansar heard of Abu 'Ubaida's arrival which coincided with the Fajr (morning) prayer led by Allah's Messenger ﷺ . When the Prophet ﷺ finished the prayer, they came to him. Allah's Messenger ﷺ smiled when he saw them and said, "I think you have heard of the arrival of Abu 'Ubaida and that he has brought something." They replied, "Yes, O Allah's Messenger ﷺ " !He said, "Have the good news, and hope for what will please you. By Allah, I am not afraid that you will become poor, but I am afraid that worldly wealth will be given to you in abundance as it was given to those (nations) before you, and you will start competing each other for it as the previous nations competed for it, and then it will divert you (from good) as it diverted them."–Al-Bukhari 6425

حَدَّثَنَا إِسْمَاعِيلُ بْنُ عَبْدِ اللَّهِ، قَالَ حَدَّثَنِي إِسْمَاعِيلُ بْنُ إِبْرَاهِيمَ بْنِ عُقْبَةَ، عَنْ مُوسَى بْنِ عُقْبَةَ، قَالَ ابْنُ شِهَابٍ حَدَّثَنِي عُرْوَةُ بْنُ الزُّبَيْرِ، أَنَّ الْمِسْوَرَ بْنَ مَخْرَمَةَ، أَخْبَرَهُ أَنَّ عَمْرَو بْنَ عَوْفٍ وَهُوَ حَلِيفٌ لِبَنِي عَامِرِ بْنِ لُؤَىٍّ كَانَ شَهِدَ بَدْرًا مَعَ رَسُولِ اللَّهِ صلى الله عليه وسلم أَخْبَرَهُ أَنَّ رَسُولَ اللَّهِ صلى الله عليه وسلم بَعَثَ أَبَا عُبَيْدَةَ بْنَ الْجَرَّاحِ إِلَى الْبَحْرَيْنِ يَأْتِي بِجِزْيَتِهَا، وَكَانَ رَسُولُ اللَّهِ صلى الله عليه وسلم هُوَ صَالَحَ أَهْلَ الْبَحْرَيْنِ، وَأَمَّرَ عَلَيْهِمُ الْعَلاَءَ بْنَ الْحَضْرَمِيِّ، فَقَدِمَ أَبُو عُبَيْدَةَ بِمَالٍ مِنَ الْبَحْرَيْنِ، فَسَمِعَتِ الأَنْصَارُ بِقُدُومِهِ فَوَافَتْهُ صَلاَةَ الصُّبْحِ مَعَ رَسُولِ اللَّهِ صلى الله عليه وسلم فَلَمَّا انْصَرَفَ تَعَرَّضُوا لَهُ فَتَبَسَّمَ حِينَ رَآهُمْ وَقَالَ " أَظُنُّكُمْ سَمِعْتُمْ بِقُدُومِ أَبِي عُبَيْدَةَ، وَأَنَّهُ جَاءَ بِشَىْءٍ ". قَالُوا أَجَلْ يَا رَسُولَ اللَّهِ. قَالَ " فَأَبْشِرُوا وَأَمِّلُوا مَا يَسُرُّكُمْ، فَوَاللَّهِ مَا الْفَقْرَ أَخْشَى عَلَيْكُمْ، وَلَكِنْ أَخْشَى عَلَيْكُمْ أَنْ تُبْسَطَ عَلَيْكُمُ الدُّنْيَا، كَمَا بُسِطَتْ عَلَى مَنْ كَانَ قَبْلَكُمْ، فَتَنَافَسُوهَا كَمَا تَنَافَسُوهَا وَتُلْهِيَكُمْ كَمَا أَلْهَتْهُمْ ".

Narrated Ibn `Abbas: Musailama-al-Kadhdhab (i.e. the liar) came in the life-time of Allah's Messenger ﷺ with many of his people (to Medina) and said, "If Muhammad makes me his successor, I will follow him." Allah's Messenger ﷺ went up to him with Thabit bin Qais bin Shams; and Allah's Messenger ﷺ was carrying a piece of a datepalm leaf in his hand. He stood before Musailama (and his companions) and said, "If you asked me even this piece (of a leaf), I would not give it to you. You cannot avoid the fate you are destined to, by Allah. If you reject Islam, Allah will destroy you. I think that you are most probably the same person whom I have seen in the dream." Abu Huraira told me that Allah's Messenger ﷺ; said, "While I was sleeping, I saw (in a dream) two gold bracelets round my arm, and that worried me too much. Then I was instructed divinely in my dream, to blow them off and so I blew them off, and they flew away. I interpreted the two bracelets as symbols of two liars who would appear after me. And so one of them was Al-Ansi and the other was Musailama Al-Kadhdhab from Al-Yamama."–Al-Bukhari 3620, 3621

حَدَّثَنَا أَبُو الْيَمَانِ، أَخْبَرَنَا شُعَيْبٌ، عَنْ عَبْدِ اللَّهِ بْنِ أَبِي حُسَيْنٍ، حَدَّثَنَا نَافِعُ بْنُ جُبَيْرٍ، عَنِ ابْنِ عَبَّاسٍ ـ رضى الله عنهما ـ قَالَ قَدِمَ مُسَيْلِمَةُ الْكَذَّابُ عَلَى عَهْدِ رَسُولِ اللَّهِ صلى الله عليه وسلم فَجَعَلَ يَقُولُ إِنْ جَعَلَ لِي مُحَمَّدٌ الأَمْرَ مِنْ بَعْدِهِ تَبِعْتُهُ. وَقَدِمَهَا فِي بَشَرٍ كَثِيرٍ مِنْ قَوْمِهِ، فَأَقْبَلَ إِلَيْهِ رَسُولُ اللَّهِ صلى الله عليه وسلم وَمَعَهُ ثَابِتُ بْنُ قَيْسِ بْنِ شَمَّاسٍ، وَفِي يَدِ رَسُولِ اللَّهِ صلى الله عليه وسلم قِطْعَةُ جَرِيدٍ، حَتَّى وَقَفَ عَلَى مُسَيْلِمَةَ فِي أَصْحَابِهِ فَقَالَ " لَوْ سَأَلْتَنِي هَذِهِ الْقِطْعَةَ مَا أَعْطَيْتُكَهَا، وَلَنْ تَعْدُوَ أَمْرَ اللَّهِ فِيكَ، وَلَئِنْ أَدْبَرْتَ لَيَعْقِرَنَّكَ اللَّهُ، وَإِنِّي لأَرَاكَ الَّذِي أُرِيتُ فِيكَ مَا رَأَيْتُ ". فَأَخْبَرَنِي أَبُو هُرَيْرَةَ، أَنَّ رَسُولَ اللَّهِ صلى الله عليه وسلم قَالَ " بَيْنَمَا أَنَا نَائِمٌ رَأَيْتُ فِي يَدَىَّ سِوَارَيْنِ مِنْ ذَهَبٍ، فَأَهَمَّنِي شَأْنُهُمَا، فَأُوحِيَ إِلَيَّ فِي الْمَنَامِ أَنِ انْفُخْهُمَا، فَنَفَخْتُهُمَا فَطَارَا فَأَوَّلْتُهُمَا كَذَّابَيْنِ يَخْرُجَانِ بَعْدِي ". فَكَانَ أَحَدُهُمَا الْعَنْسِيَّ وَالآخَرُ مُسَيْلِمَةَ الْكَذَّابَ صَاحِبَ الْيَمَامَةِ

Indeed, the human being is ungrateful to his Lord. And he bears witness to that. And he is fierce in his love of wealth. Does he not know? When the contents of the graves are scattered around. – Surah Al- Adiyat 100:6-9

إِنَّ ٱلْإِنسَٰنَ لِرَبِّهِۦ لَكَنُودٌ وَإِنَّهُۥ عَلَىٰ ذَٰلِكَ لَشَهِيدٌ وَإِنَّهُۥ لِحُبِّ ٱلْخَيْرِ لَشَدِيدٌ أَفَلَا يَعْلَمُ إِذَا بُعْثِرَ مَا فِى ٱلْقُبُورِ

Woe to every slanderer backbiter. Who gathers wealth and counts it over. Thinking that his wealth has made him immortal. – Surah Al-Humazah 104:1-3

وَيْلٌ لِّكُلِّ هُمَزَةٍ لُّمَزَةٍ.ٱلَّذِى جَمَعَ مَالًا وَعَدَّدَهُۥ.يَحْسَبُ أَنَّ مَالَهُۥٓ أَخْلَدَهُۥ

Narrated `Abdullah: The Prophet ﷺ said, "The best people are those of my generation, and then those who will come after them (the next generation), and then those who will come after them (i.e. the next generation), and then after them, there will come people whose witness will precede their oaths, and whose oaths will precede their witness."–Al-Bukhari 6429

حَدَّثَنَا عَبْدَانُ، عَنْ أَبِي حَمْزَةَ، عَنِ الأَعْمَشِ، عَنْ إِبْرَاهِيمَ، عَنْ عَبِيدَةَ، عَنْ عَبْدِ اللَّهِ ـ رضى الله عنه ـ عَنِ النَّبِيِّ صلى الله عليه وسلم قَالَ " خَيْرُ النَّاسِ قَرْنِي، ثُمَّ الَّذِينَ يَلُونَهُمْ، ثُمَّ الَّذِينَ يَلُونَهُمْ، ثُمَّ يَجِيءُ مِنْ بَعْدِهِمْ قَوْمٌ تَسْبِقُ شَهَادَتُهُمْ أَيْمَانَهُمْ وَأَيْمَانُهُمْ شَهَادَتَهُمْ ".

Narrated Zahdam bin Mudarrib: Imran bin Husain said: The Prophet ﷺ said, "The best people are my contemporaries [i.e., the present (my) generation] and then those who come after them (i.e., the next generation)." `Imran added: I am not sure whether the Prophet ﷺ repeated the statement twice after his first saying. The Prophet ﷺ added, "And after them there will come people who will bear witness, though they will not be asked to give their witness; and they will be treacherous and nobody will trust them, and they will make vows, but will not fulfill them, and fatness will appear among them."–Al-Bukhari 6428

حَدَّثَنِي مُحَمَّدُ بْنُ بَشَّارٍ، حَدَّثَنَا غُنْدَرٌ، حَدَّثَنَا شُعْبَةُ، قَالَ سَمِعْتُ أَبَا جَمْرَةَ، قَالَ حَدَّثَنِي زَهْدَمُ بْنُ مُضَرِّبٍ، قَالَ سَمِعْتُ عِمْرَانَ بْنَ حُصَيْنٍ ـ رضى الله عنهما ـ عَنِ النَّبِيِّ صلى الله عليه وسلم قَالَ " خَيْرُكُمْ قَرْنِي، ثُمَّ الَّذِينَ يَلُونَهُمْ، ثُمَّ الَّذِينَ يَلُونَهُمْ ". قَالَ عِمْرَانُ فَمَا أَدْرِي قَالَ النَّبِيُّ صلى الله عليه وسلم بَعْدَ قَوْلِهِ مَرَّتَيْنِ أَوْ ثَلاَثًا " ثُمَّ يَكُونُ بَعْدَهُمْ قَوْمٌ يَشْهَدُونَ وَلاَ يُسْتَشْهَدُونَ، وَيَخُونُونَ وَلاَ يُؤْتَمَنُونَ، وَيَنْذِرُونَ وَلاَ يَفُونَ وَيَظْهَرُ فِيهِمُ السِّمَنُ "

Narrated Rabi bin Hirash :Uqba bin `Amr said to Hudhaifa, "Won't you relate to us of what you have heard from Allah's Apostle ?" He said, "I heard him saying, "When Al-Dajjal appears, he will have fire and water along with him. What the people will consider as cold water, will be fire that will burn (things). So, if anyone of you comes across this, he should fall in the thing which will appear to him as fire, for in reality, it will be fresh cold water." Hudhaifa added, "I also heard him saying, 'From among the people preceding your generation, there was a man whom the angel of death visited to capture his soul. (So his soul was captured) and he was asked if he had done any good deed.' He replied, 'I don't remember any good

deed.' He was asked to think it over. He said, 'I do not remember, except that I used to trade with the people in the world and I used to give a respite to the rich and forgive the poor (among my debtors). So Allah made him enter Paradise." Hudhaifa further said, "I also heard him saying, 'Once there was a man on his death-bed, who, losing every hope of surviving said to his family: When I die, gather for me a large heap of wood and make a fire (to burn me). When the fire eats my meat and reaches my bones, and when the bones burn, take and crush them into powder and wait for a windy day to throw it (i.e. the powder) over the sea. They did so, but Allah collected his particles and asked him: Why did you do so? He replied: For fear of You. So Allah forgave him." `Uqba bin `Amr said, "I heard him saying that the Israeli used to dig the grave of the dead (to steal their shrouds). – Sahih al-Bukhari 3450 - 3452
حَدَّثَنَا مُوسَى بْنُ إِسْمَاعِيلَ، حَدَّثَنَا أَبُو عَوَانَةَ، حَدَّثَنَا عَبْدُ الْمَلِكِ، عَنْ رِبْعِيِّ بْنِ حِرَاشٍ، قَالَ قَالَ عُقْبَةُ بْنُ عَمْرٍو لِحُذَيْفَةَ أَلاَ تُحَدِّثُنَا مَا سَمِعْتَ مِنْ رَسُولِ اللَّهِ صلى الله عليه وسلم قَالَ إِنِّي سَمِعْتُهُ يَقُولُ " إِنَّ مَعَ الدَّجَّالِ إِذَا خَرَجَ مَاءً وَنَارًا، فَأَمَّا الَّذِي يَرَى النَّاسُ أَنَّهَا النَّارُ فَمَاءٌ بَارِدٌ، وَأَمَّا الَّذِي يَرَى النَّاسُ أَنَّهُ مَاءٌ بَارِدٌ فَنَارٌ تُحْرِقُ، فَمَنْ أَدْرَكَ مِنْكُمْ فَلْيَقَعْ فِي الَّذِي يَرَى أَنَّهَا نَارٌ، فَإِنَّهُ عَذْبٌ بَارِدٌ ". قَالَ حُذَيْفَةُ وَسَمِعْتُهُ يَقُولُ " إِنَّ رَجُلاً كَانَ فِيمَنْ كَانَ قَبْلَكُمْ أَتَاهُ الْمَلَكُ لِيَقْبِضَ رُوحَهُ فَقِيلَ لَهُ هَلْ عَمِلْتَ مِنْ خَيْرٍ قَالَ مَا أَعْلَمُ، قِيلَ لَهُ انْظُرْ. قَالَ مَا أَعْلَمُ شَيْئًا غَيْرَ أَنِّي كُنْتُ أُبَايِعُ النَّاسَ فِي الدُّنْيَا وَأُجَازِيهِمْ، فَأُنْظِرُ الْمُوسِرَ، وَأَتَجَاوَزُ عَنِ الْمُعْسِرِ. فَأَدْخَلَهُ اللَّهُ الْجَنَّةَ ". فَقَالَ وَسَمِعْتُهُ يَقُولُ " إِنَّ رَجُلاً حَضَرَهُ الْمَوْتُ، فَلَمَّا يَئِسَ مِنَ الْحَيَاةِ أَوْصَى أَهْلَهُ إِذَا أَنَا مُتُّ فَاجْمَعُوا لِي حَطَبًا كَثِيرًا وَأَوْقِدُوا فِيهِ نَارًا حَتَّى إِذَا أَكَلَتْ لَحْمِي، وَخَلَصَتْ إِلَى عَظْمِي، فَامْتَحَشْتُ، فَخُذُوهَا فَاطْحَنُوهَا، ثُمَّ انْظُرُوا يَوْمًا رَاحًا فَاذْرُوهُ فِي الْيَمِّ. فَفَعَلُوا، فَجَمَعَهُ فَقَالَ لَهُ لِمَ فَعَلْتَ ذَلِكَ قَالَ مِنْ خَشْيَتِكَ. فَغَفَرَ اللَّهُ لَهُ ". قَالَ عُقْبَةُ بْنُ عَمْرٍو، وَأَنَا سَمِعْتُهُ يَقُولُ ذَاكَ، وَكَانَ نَبَّاشًا.وسلم.

Narrated Abu Huraira: Allah's Messenger ﷺ said, "The Hour will not be established (1) till two big groups fight each other whereupon there will be a great number of casualties on both sides and they will be following one and the same religious doctrine, (2) till about thirty Dajjals (liars) appear, and each one of them will claim that he is Allah's Messenger ﷺ (3) ,till the religious knowledge is taken away (by the death of Religious scholars) (4) earthquakes will increase in number (5) time will pass quickly, (6) afflictions will appear, (7) Al-Harj, (i.e., killing) will increase, (8) till wealth will be in abundance ---- so abundant that a wealthy person will worry lest nobody should accept his Zakat, and whenever he will present it to someone, that person (to whom it will be offered) will say, 'I am not in need of it, (9) till the people compete with one another in constructing high buildings, (10) till a man when passing by a grave of someone will say, 'Would that I were in his place (11) and till the sun rises from the West. So when the sun will rise and the people will see it (rising from the West) they will all believe (embrace Islam) but that will be the time when: (As Allah said,) 'No good will it do to a soul to believe then, if it believed not before, nor earned good (by deeds of righteousness) through its Faith.' (6.158) And the Hour will be established while two men spreading a garment in front of them but they will not be able to sell it, nor fold it up; and the Hour will be established when a man has milked his she-camel and has taken away the milk but he will not be able to drink it; and the Hour will be established before a man repairing a tank (for his livestock) is able to water (his animals) in it; and the Hour will be established when a person has raised a morsel (of food) to his mouth but will not be able to eat it."–Al-Bukhari 7121
حَدَّثَنَا أَبُو الْيَمَانِ، أَخْبَرَنَا شُعَيْبٌ، حَدَّثَنَا أَبُو الزِّنَادِ، عَنْ عَبْدِ الرَّحْمَنِ، عَنْ أَبِي هُرَيْرَةَ، أَنَّ رَسُولَ اللَّهِ صلى الله عليه وسلم قَالَ " لاَ تَقُومُ السَّاعَةُ حَتَّى تَقْتَتِلَ فِئَتَانِ عَظِيمَتَانِ، يَكُونُ بَيْنَهُمَا مَقْتَلَةٌ عَظِيمَةٌ، دَعْوَتُهُمَا وَاحِدَةٌ، وَحَتَّى يُبْعَثَ دَجَّالُونَ كَذَّابُونَ، قَرِيبٌ مِنْ ثَلاَثِينَ، كُلُّهُمْ يَزْعُمُ أَنَّهُ رَسُولُ اللَّهِ، وَحَتَّى يُقْبَضَ الْعِلْمُ، وَتَكْثُرَ الزَّلاَزِلُ، وَيَتَقَارَبَ الزَّمَانُ، وَتَظْهَرَ الْفِتَنُ، وَيَكْثُرَ الْهَرْجُ وَهْوَ الْقَتْلُ، وَحَتَّى يَكْثُرَ فِيكُمُ الْمَالُ فَيَفِيضَ، حَتَّى يُهِمَّ رَبَّ الْمَالِ مَنْ يَقْبَلُ صَدَقَتَهُ، وَحَتَّى يَعْرِضَهُ فَيَقُولَ الَّذِي يَعْرِضُهُ عَلَيْهِ لاَ أَرَبَ لِي بِهِ. وَحَتَّى يَتَطَاوَلَ النَّاسُ فِي الْبُنْيَانِ، وَحَتَّى يَمُرَّ الرَّجُلُ بِقَبْرِ الرَّجُلِ فَيَقُولُ يَا لَيْتَنِي مَكَانَهُ. وَحَتَّى تَطْلُعَ الشَّمْسُ مِنْ مَغْرِبِهَا، فَإِذَا طَلَعَتْ وَرَآهَا النَّاسُ ـ يَعْنِي ـ آمَنُوا أَجْمَعُونَ، فَذَلِكَ حِينَ لاَ يَنْفَعُ نَفْسًا إِيمَانُهَا لَمْ تَكُنْ آمَنَتْ مِنْ قَبْلُ، أَوْ كَسَبَتْ فِي إِيمَانِهَا خَيْرًا، وَلَتَقُومَنَّ السَّاعَةُ وَقَدْ نَشَرَ الرَّجُلاَنِ ثَوْبَهُمَا بَيْنَهُمَا، فَلاَ يَتَبَايَعَانِهِ وَلاَ

يَطْوِيَانِهِ، وَلَتَقُومَنَّ السَّاعَةُ وَقَدِ انْصَرَفَ الرَّجُلُ بِلَبَنِ لِقْحَتِهِ فَلاَ يَطْعَمُهُ، وَلَتَقُومَنَّ السَّاعَةُ وَهْوَ يُلِيطُ حَوْضَهُ فَلاَ يَسْقِي فِيهِ، وَلَتَقُومَنَّ السَّاعَةُ وَقَدْ رَفَعَ أُكْلَتَهُ إِلَى فِيهِ فَلاَ يَطْعَمُهَا "

Narrated `Aisha: (the wife of the Prophet) Allah's Messenger ﷺ used to invoke Allah in the prayer saying "Allahumma inni a`udhu bika min `adhabi l-qabr, wa a`udhu bika min fitnati l-masihi d-dajjal, wa a`udhu bika min fitnati l-mahya wa fitnati l-mamat. Allahumma inni a`udhu bika mina l-ma'thami wa l-maghram. (O Allah, I seek refuge with You from the punishment of the grave, from the afflictions of the imposter- Messiah, and from the afflictions of life and death. O Allah, I seek refuge with You from sins and from debt)." Somebody said to him, "Why do you so frequently seek refuge with Allah from being in debt?" The Prophet ﷺ replied, "A person in debt tells lies whenever he speaks, and breaks promises whenever he makes (them)." - Sahih al-Bukhari 832
حَدَّثَنَا أَبُو الْيَمَانِ، قَالَ أَخْبَرَنَا شُعَيْبٌ، عَنِ الزُّهْرِيِّ، قَالَ أَخْبَرَنَا عُرْوَةُ بْنُ الزُّبَيْرِ، عَنْ عَائِشَةَ، زَوْجِ النَّبِيِّ صلى الله عليه وسلم أَخْبَرَتْهُ أَنَّ رَسُولَ اللَّهِ صلى الله عليه وسلم كَانَ يَدْعُو فِي الصَّلاَةِ " اللَّهُمَّ إِنِّي أَعُوذُ بِكَ مِنْ عَذَابِ الْقَبْرِ وَأَعُوذُ بِكَ مِنْ فِتْنَةِ الْمَسِيحِ الدَّجَّالِ، وَأَعُوذُ بِكَ مِنْ فِتْنَةِ الْمَحْيَا وَفِتْنَةِ الْمَمَاتِ، اللَّهُمَّ إِنِّي أَعُوذُ بِكَ مِنَ الْمَأْثَمِ وَالْمَغْرَمِ ". فَقَالَ لَهُ قَائِلٌ مَا أَكْثَرَ مَا تَسْتَعِيذُ مِنَ الْمَغْرَمِ فَقَالَ " إِنَّ الرَّجُلَ إِذَا غَرِمَ حَدَّثَ فَكَذَبَ، وَوَعَدَ فَأَخْلَفَ ".

Satan has taken hold of them, causing them to forget the remembrance of Allah. They are the party of Satan. Surely Satan's party is bound to lose. – Surah Al-Mujadilah 58:19
ٱسْتَحْوَذَ عَلَيْهِمُ ٱلشَّيْطَـٰنُ فَأَنسَىٰهُمْ ذِكْرَ ٱللَّهِ ۚ أُو۟لَـٰٓئِكَ حِزْبُ ٱلشَّيْطَـٰنِ ۚ أَلَآ إِنَّ حِزْبَ ٱلشَّيْطَـٰنِ هُمُ ٱلْخَـٰسِرُونَ

And whoever turns a blind eye to the Reminder of the Most Compassionate, We place at the disposal of each a devilish one as their close associate, - Surah Az-Zukhruf 43:36
وَمَن يَعْشُ عَن ذِكْرِ ٱلرَّحْمَـٰنِ نُقَيِّضْ لَهُۥ شَيْطَـٰنًا فَهُوَ لَهُۥ قَرِينٌ

Satan wants to provoke strife and hatred among you through intoxicants and gambling, and to prevent you from the remembrance of Allah, and from prayer. Will you not desist? – Surah Al-Ma'idah 5:91
إِنَّمَا يُرِيدُ ٱلشَّيْطَـٰنُ أَن يُوقِعَ بَيْنَكُمُ ٱلْعَدَٰوَةَ وَٱلْبَغْضَآءَ فِى ٱلْخَمْرِ وَٱلْمَيْسِرِ وَيَصُدَّكُمْ عَن ذِكْرِ ٱللَّهِ وَعَنِ ٱلصَّلَوٰةِ ۖ فَهَلْ أَنتُم مُّنتَهُونَ

So he misled them both by delusion..... – Surah Al-A'raf 7:22
فَدَلَّىٰهُمَا بِغُرُورٍ....

And when everything will have been decided, Satan will say: "Behold, Allah promised you something that was bound to come true! I, too, held out [all manner of] promises to you -but I deceived you. Yet I had no power at all over you: I but called you-and you responded unto me. Hence, blame not me, but blame yourselves. It is not for me to respond to your cries, nor for you to respond to mine: for, behold, I have [always] refused to admit that there was any truth in your erstwhile belief that I had a share in Allah's divinity." Verily, for all evildoers there is grievous suffering in store. – Surah Ibrahim 14:22
وَقَالَ ٱلشَّيْطَـٰنُ لَمَّا قُضِىَ ٱلْأَمْرُ إِنَّ ٱللَّهَ وَعَدَكُمْ وَعْدَ ٱلْحَقِّ وَوَعَدتُّكُمْ فَأَخْلَفْتُكُمْ ۖ وَمَا كَانَ لِىَ عَلَيْكُم مِّن سُلْطَـٰنٍ إِلَّآ أَن دَعَوْتُكُمْ فَٱسْتَجَبْتُمْ لِى ۖ فَلَا تَلُومُونِى وَلُومُوٓا۟ أَنفُسَكُم ۖ مَّآ أَنَا۠ بِمُصْرِخِكُمْ وَمَآ أَنتُم بِمُصْرِخِىَّ ۖ إِنِّى كَفَرْتُ بِمَآ أَشْرَكْتُمُونِ مِن قَبْلُ ۗ إِنَّ ٱلظَّـٰلِمِينَ لَهُمْ عَذَابٌ أَلِيمٌ

And indeed I will definitely lead them into error, and indeed I will definitely arouse (vain) covetings in them, and indeed I will definitely command them (and) so indeed they will definitely cut off the cattle's ears; (One of the superstitions of the pagans) and indeed I will definitely command them (and) so indeed they will definitely change the creation of Allah."

And whoever takes Ash-Shaytan (An all-vicious one, i.e., satan) to himself for a constant patron apart from Allah, then he has already suffered (Literally: lost) evidently the greatest loss. – Surah An-Nisa 4:119
وَلَأُضِلَّنَّهُمْ وَلَأُمَنِّيَنَّهُمْ وَلَءَامُرَنَّهُمْ فَلَيُبَتِّكُنَّ ءَاذَانَ ٱلْأَنْعَٰمِ وَلَءَامُرَنَّهُمْ فَلَيُغَيِّرُنَّ خَلْقَ ٱللَّهِ ۚ وَمَن يَتَّخِذِ ٱلشَّيْطَٰنَ وَلِيًّا مِّن دُونِ ٱللَّهِ فَقَدْ خَسِرَ خُسْرَانًا مُّبِينًا

People, be conscious of your Lord and fear a Day when no father will be able to rescue his son, nor will a son be able to rescue his father at all. Allah's promise [of resurrection] is the Truth, so do not let this worldly life deceive you, nor deceptive thoughts about Allah delude you. – Surah Luqman 31:33
يَٰٓأَيُّهَا ٱلنَّاسُ ٱتَّقُوا۟ رَبَّكُمْ وَٱخْشَوْا۟ يَوْمًا لَّا يَجْزِى وَالِدٌ عَن وَلَدِهِۦ وَلَا مَوْلُودٌ هُوَ جَازٍ عَن وَالِدِهِۦ شَيْـًٔا ۚ إِنَّ وَعْدَ ٱللَّهِ حَقٌّ ۖ فَلَا تَغُرَّنَّكُمُ ٱلْحَيَوٰةُ ٱلدُّنْيَا وَلَا يَغُرَّنَّكُم بِٱللَّهِ ٱلْغَرُورُ

Then as soon as Talut (Saul) departed with the hosts, he said, "Surely Allah will be trying you with a river; so whoever drinks of it, then he is not of me, and whoever does not taste (Literally: does not feed on it) it, then surely he is of me, excepting him who scoops up (a scoop) with his hand." Then they drank of it except a few of them.... – Surah Al-Baqarah 2:249
فَلَمَّا فَصَلَ طَالُوتُ بِٱلْجُنُودِ قَالَ إِنَّ ٱللَّهَ مُبْتَلِيكُم بِنَهَرٍ فَمَن شَرِبَ مِنْهُ فَلَيْسَ مِنِّى وَمَن لَّمْ يَطْعَمْهُ فَإِنَّهُۥ مِنِّىٓ إِلَّا مَنِ ٱغْتَرَفَ غُرْفَةًۢ بِيَدِهِۦ ۚ فَشَرِبُوا۟ مِنْهُ إِلَّا قَلِيلًا مِّنْهُمْ ۚ

Iblis
بْلِيسَ

And indeed We already created you, thereafter We fashioned you, thereafter We said to the Angels, "Prostrate to Adam;" so they prostrated, except Iblis; he was not of the prostrators Said He, "What prevented you from prostrating as I commanded you?" Said he, "I am more charitable (i.e. better) than he. You created me of fire, and You created him of clay." Said He, "Then get down (out of) it; so, in no way is it for you to be proud therein; then go out; surely you are among the belittled." Said he, "Respite me to the Day they are made to rise again." Said He, "Surely you are among the ones respited." Said he, "So, for that You caused me to be misguided, indeed I will definitely sit (i.e., in ambush) for them (on) Your straight Path Thereafter indeed I will definitely come up to them from before them (Literally: between their hands) and from behind them, and from their right (hands), and from their left (hands); and You will not find most of them thankful." Said He, "Go out of it, reproved and regretfully rejected. Indeed whoever of them will follow you, indeed I will definitely fill Hell from among you all together." And O Adam, dwell, you and your spouse, in the Garden (and) so eat of where you (both) decide; and do not draw near this tree, (or) then (both of) you will be of the unjust." Then Ash-Shaytan (The all-vicious, i.e., the Devil) whispered to them (both) to display to them that which was overlaid (i.e., hidden) from them of their shameful parts; and he said, "In no way has your Lord forbidden you from this tree except that you should become (two) angels or become of the ones eternally (abiding)." And he swore to both of them, "Surely I am indeed for you both one of your honest (Literally: one of the honest advisers) advisers." So he misled them both by delusion; (Or: caused their fall) then, as soon as they (both) tasted the tree, their shameful parts appeared to them, and they took to splicing upon themselves (some of) the leaves of the Garden. And their Lord called out to them, "Did I not forbid you from that tree and say to you both, surely Satan is for you both an evident enemy?" They both said, "Our Lord, we have done an injustice to ourselves; and in case You do not forgive us and have mercy on us, indeed we (both) will definitely be among the losers." Said He, "Get down (all of you), some of you an enemy to (some) others; and in the earth there is for you a repository and an enjoyment for a while." Said He, "Therein you will live, and therein you will die, and there from you will be brought out." O Seed (Or: sons) of Adam! We have readily sent down on you a garment to overlay your shameful parts, and a vesture; (Fine clothes; or feathers) and the garment of piety, that is the most charitable; (i.e., better) that is of the signs of Allah, that possibly they would constantly remember O Seeds (Or: sons) of Adam! Definitely do not let Ash-Shaytan (The All-vicious, i.e., the Devil) tempt you just as he brought your parents (Literally: your two feathers) out of the Garden, plucking out from them (both) their garments to show them their shameful parts. Surely he sees you, he and his (dependent) tribe, from where you do not see them. Surely We have made Ash-Shayatin (The all-vicious ones, i.e., the devils) patrons of the ones who do not believe And when they perform an obscenity, they say, "We found our fathers (performing) it, and Allah has commanded us to (perform) it." Say, "Surely Allah does not command obscenity; do you say against Allah that which you do not know?" Say, "My Lord has commanded equity; and set your faces upright at every mosque and Invoke Him, making the religion His faithfully; just as He began you, so you will go back (to Him) A group He has guided, and errancy has come true against (another) group." Surely they have taken to themselves Ash-Shayatin (The all-vicious ones, i.e., the devils) for patrons, apart from Allah, and they reckon that they are (right) guided. Surah Al-A'raf 7:11-30

فَسَجَدُوٓاْ إِلَّآ إِبۡلِيسَ لَمۡ يَكُن مِّنَ ٱلسَّٰجِدِينَ قَالَ مَا مَنَعَكَ أَلَّا تَسۡجُدَ إِذۡ أَمَرۡتُكَۖ قَالَ أَنَا۠ خَيۡرٞ مِّنۡهُ خَلَقۡتَنِي مِن نَّارٖ وَخَلَقۡتَهُۥ مِن
طِينٖ قَالَ فَٱهۡبِطۡ مِنۡهَا فَمَا يَكُونُ لَكَ أَن تَتَكَبَّرَ فِيهَا فَٱخۡرُجۡ إِنَّكَ مِنَ ٱلصَّٰغِرِينَ قَالَ أَنظِرۡنِيٓ إِلَىٰ يَوۡمِ يُبۡعَثُونَ قَالَ إِنَّكَ مِنَ
ٱلۡمُنظَرِينَ قَالَ فَبِمَآ أَغۡوَيۡتَنِي لَأَقۡعُدَنَّ لَهُمۡ صِرَٰطَكَ ٱلۡمُسۡتَقِيمَ ثُمَّ لَأٓتِيَنَّهُم مِّنۢ بَيۡنِ أَيۡدِيهِمۡ وَمِنۡ خَلۡفِهِمۡ وَعَنۡ أَيۡمَٰنِهِمۡ وَعَن
شَمَآئِلِهِمۡۖ وَلَا تَجِدُ أَكۡثَرَهُمۡ شَٰكِرِينَ قَالَ ٱخۡرُجۡ مِنۡهَا مَذۡءُومٗا مَّدۡحُورٗاۖ لَّمَن تَبِعَكَ مِنۡهُمۡ لَأَمۡلَأَنَّ جَهَنَّمَ مِنكُمۡ أَجۡمَعِينَ وَيَٰٓـَٔادَمُ
ٱسۡكُنۡ أَنتَ وَزَوۡجُكَ ٱلۡجَنَّةَ فَكُلَا مِنۡ حَيۡثُ شِئۡتُمَا وَلَا تَقۡرَبَا هَٰذِهِ ٱلشَّجَرَةَ فَتَكُونَا مِنَ ٱلظَّٰلِمِينَ فَوَسۡوَسَ لَهُمَا ٱلشَّيۡطَٰنُ لِيُبۡدِيَ
لَهُمَا مَا وُۥرِيَ عَنۡهُمَا مِن سَوۡءَٰتِهِمَا وَقَالَ مَا نَهَىٰكُمَا رَبُّكُمَا عَنۡ هَٰذِهِ ٱلشَّجَرَةِ إِلَّآ أَن تَكُونَا مَلَكَيۡنِ أَوۡ تَكُونَا مِنَ ٱلۡخَٰلِدِينَ
وَقَاسَمَهُمَآ إِنِّي لَكُمَا لَمِنَ ٱلنَّٰصِحِينَ فَدَلَّىٰهُمَا بِغُرُورٖۚ فَلَمَّا ذَاقَا ٱلشَّجَرَةَ بَدَتۡ لَهُمَا سَوۡءَٰتُهُمَا وَطَفِقَا يَخۡصِفَانِ عَلَيۡهِمَا مِن وَرَقِ
ٱلۡجَنَّةِۖ وَنَادَىٰهُمَا رَبُّهُمَآ أَلَمۡ أَنۡهَكُمَا عَن تِلۡكُمَا ٱلشَّجَرَةِ وَأَقُل لَّكُمَآ إِنَّ ٱلشَّيۡطَٰنَ لَكُمَا عَدُوّٞ مُّبِينٞ قَالَا رَبَّنَا ظَلَمۡنَآ أَنفُسَنَا وَإِن لَّمۡ
تَغۡفِرۡ لَنَا وَتَرۡحَمۡنَا لَنَكُونَنَّ مِنَ ٱلۡخَٰسِرِينَ قَالَ ٱهۡبِطُواْ بَعۡضُكُمۡ لِبَعۡضٍ عَدُوّٞۖ وَلَكُمۡ فِي ٱلۡأَرۡضِ مُسۡتَقَرّٞ وَمَتَٰعٌ إِلَىٰ حِينٖ قَالَ فِيهَا
تَحۡيَوۡنَ وَفِيهَا تَمُوتُونَ وَمِنۡهَا تُخۡرَجُونَ يَٰبَنِيٓ ءَادَمَ قَدۡ أَنزَلۡنَا عَلَيۡكُمۡ لِبَاسٗا يُوَٰرِي سَوۡءَٰتِكُمۡ وَرِيشٗاۖ وَلِبَاسُ ٱلتَّقۡوَىٰ ذَٰلِكَ خَيۡرٞۚ
ذَٰلِكَ مِنۡ ءَايَٰتِ ٱللَّهِ لَعَلَّهُمۡ يَذَّكَّرُونَ يَٰبَنِيٓ ءَادَمَ لَا يَفۡتِنَنَّكُمُ ٱلشَّيۡطَٰنُ كَمَآ أَخۡرَجَ أَبَوَيۡكُم مِّنَ ٱلۡجَنَّةِ يَنزِعُ عَنۡهُمَا لِبَاسَهُمَا لِيُرِيَهُمَا
سَوۡءَٰتِهِمَآۚ إِنَّهُۥ يَرَىٰكُمۡ هُوَ وَقَبِيلُهُۥ مِنۡ حَيۡثُ لَا تَرَوۡنَهُمۡۗ إِنَّا جَعَلۡنَا ٱلشَّيَٰطِينَ أَوۡلِيَآءَ لِلَّذِينَ لَا يُؤۡمِنُونَ وَإِذَا فَعَلُواْ فَٰحِشَةٗ قَالُواْ
وَجَدۡنَا عَلَيۡهَآ ءَابَآءَنَا وَٱللَّهُ أَمَرَنَا بِهَاۗ قُلۡ إِنَّ ٱللَّهَ لَا يَأۡمُرُ بِٱلۡفَحۡشَآءِۖ أَتَقُولُونَ عَلَى ٱللَّهِ مَا لَا تَعۡلَمُونَ قُلۡ أَمَرَ رَبِّي بِٱلۡقِسۡطِۖ
وَأَقِيمُواْ وُجُوهَكُمۡ عِندَ كُلِّ مَسۡجِدٖ وَٱدۡعُوهُ مُخۡلِصِينَ لَهُ ٱلدِّينَۚ كَمَا بَدَأَكُمۡ تَعُودُونَ فَرِيقًا هَدَىٰ وَفَرِيقًا حَقَّ عَلَيۡهِمُ ٱلضَّلَٰلَةُۚ إِنَّهُمُ
ٱتَّخَذُواْ ٱلشَّيَٰطِينَ أَوۡلِيَآءَ مِن دُونِ ٱللَّهِ وَيَحۡسَبُونَ أَنَّهُم مُّهۡتَدُونَ

Said he, "O my people! There is no errancy in me; but I am a Messenger from The Lord of the worlds I constantly proclaim to you the Messages of my Lord, and I advise you (sincerely), and I know from Allah what you do not know And do you wonder that a Remembrance from your Lord has come to you by means (Literally: upon a man) of a man among you, that he may warn you, and that you may be pious, and that possibly you would be granted mercy?" So they cried him lies; then We delivered him, and the ones with him, in the ship (s), and We drowned (the ones) who cried lies to Our signs; surely they were a wilfully blind people And to Aad (We sent) their brother H?d; he said, "O my people! Worship Allah! In no way do you have any god other than He. Will you then not be pious?" – Surah Al-A'raf 7:61-65

قَالَ يَٰقَوْمِ لَيْسَ بِى ضَلَٰلَةٌ وَلَٰكِنِّى رَسُولٌ مِّن رَّبِّ ٱلْعَٰلَمِينَ أُبَلِّغُكُمْ رِسَٰلَٰتِ رَبِّى وَأَنصَحُ لَكُمْ وَأَعْلَمُ مِنَ ٱللَّهِ مَا لَا تَعْلَمُونَ أَوَعَجِبْتُمْ أَن جَآءَكُمْ ذِكْرٌ مِّن رَّبِّكُمْ عَلَىٰ رَجُلٍ مِّنكُمْ لِيُنذِرَكُمْ وَلِتَتَّقُوا۟ وَلَعَلَّكُمْ تُرْحَمُونَ فَكَذَّبُوهُ فَأَنجَيْنَٰهُ وَٱلَّذِينَ مَعَهُۥ فِى ٱلْفُلْكِ وَأَغْرَقْنَا ٱلَّذِينَ كَذَّبُوا۟ بِـَٔايَٰتِنَآ ۚ إِنَّهُمْ كَانُوا۟ قَوْمًا عَمِينَ وَإِلَىٰ عَادٍ أَخَاهُمْ هُودًا ۗ قَالَ يَٰقَوْمِ ٱعْبُدُوا۟ ٱللَّهَ مَا لَكُم مِّنْ إِلَٰهٍ غَيْرُهُۥٓ ۚ أَفَلَا تَتَّقُونَ

And (remember) as We said to the Angels, “Prostrate (yourselves) to Adam”, so they prostrated (themselves) except Iblis: He refused and waxed proud, and he was (one) of the disbelievers. – Surah Al-Baqarah 2:34
وَإِذْ قُلْنَا لِلْمَلَٰٓئِكَةِ ٱسْجُدُوا۟ لِءَادَمَ فَسَجَدُوٓا۟ إِلَّآ إِبْلِيسَ أَبَىٰ وَٱسْتَكْبَرَ وَكَانَ مِنَ ٱلْكَٰفِرِينَ

And as your Lord said to the Angels, “Surely I am creating a mortal of dry clay of mud modeled So, when I have molded him and breathed into him of My Spirit, fall down to him prostrating!” So the Angels prostrated themselves, all of them together Except Iblis; he refused to be among the prostrate Said He, “O Iblis, what about you, that you are not among the prostrate?” Said he, “Indeed I did not have to prostrate myself to a mortal whom You created of dry clay of mud modeled.” Said He, “Then get out (Literally: go out) of it; so, surely you are outcast And surely the curse will be upon you till the Day of Doom.” Said he, “Lord! Then respite me till the Day they will be made to rise again.” Said He, “Then surely you are among the respited To the Day of a known time.” Said he, “Lord! For (the fact) that You misguided me, indeed I will definitely adorn for them (i.e., make “evil” attractive to them) in the earth; and indeed I will definitely misguide them all together Excepting Your bondmen among them, who are most faithful.” Said He, “This is for Me a straight Path Surely over My bondmen you will have no all-binding authority, except the ones who closely follow you of the misguided ones.” And surely Hell will be indeed their promised (abode) all together It has seven gates; and each gate has an appointed part (Literally: divided) Surely the pious will be amidst Gardens and Springs.” “Enter them, in peace, secure!” And We will draw out from them whatever rancor may be in their breasts; as brethren they will be upon settees facing one another No toil will touch them therein, and in no way will they be made to go out of it Fully inform My bondmen that I, Ever I, am The Ever-Forgiving, The Ever-Merciful And that My torment is the (most) painful torment. – Surah Al-Hijr 15:28-50
فَإِذَا سَوَّيْتُهُۥ وَنَفَخْتُ فِيهِ مِن رُّوحِى فَقَعُوا۟ لَهُۥ سَٰجِدِينَ فَسَجَدَ ٱلْمَلَٰٓئِكَةُ كُلُّهُمْ أَجْمَعُونَ إِلَّآ إِبْلِيسَ أَبَىٰٓ أَن يَكُونَ مَعَ ٱلسَّٰجِدِينَ قَالَ يَٰٓإِبْلِيسُ مَا لَكَ أَلَّا تَكُونَ مَعَ ٱلسَّٰجِدِينَ قَالَ لَمْ أَكُن لِّأَسْجُدَ لِبَشَرٍ خَلَقْتَهُۥ مِن صَلْصَٰلٍ مِّنْ حَمَإٍ مَّسْنُونٍ قَالَ فَٱخْرُجْ مِنْهَا فَإِنَّكَ رَجِيمٌ وَإِنَّ عَلَيْكَ ٱللَّعْنَةَ إِلَىٰ يَوْمِ ٱلدِّينِ قَالَ رَبِّ فَأَنظِرْنِىٓ إِلَىٰ يَوْمِ يُبْعَثُونَ قَالَ فَإِنَّكَ مِنَ ٱلْمُنظَرِينَ إِلَىٰ يَوْمِ ٱلْوَقْتِ ٱلْمَعْلُومِ قَالَ رَبِّ بِمَآ أَغْوَيْتَنِى لَأُزَيِّنَنَّ لَهُمْ فِى ٱلْأَرْضِ وَلَأُغْوِيَنَّهُمْ أَجْمَعِينَ إِلَّا عِبَادَكَ مِنْهُمُ ٱلْمُخْلَصِينَ قَالَ هَٰذَا صِرَٰطٌ عَلَىَّ مُسْتَقِيمٌ إِنَّ عِبَادِى لَيْسَ لَكَ عَلَيْهِمْ سُلْطَٰنٌ إِلَّا مَنِ ٱتَّبَعَكَ مِنَ ٱلْغَاوِينَ وَإِنَّ جَهَنَّمَ لَمَوْعِدُهُمْ أَجْمَعِينَ لَهَا سَبْعَةُ أَبْوَٰبٍ لِّكُلِّ بَابٍ مِّنْهُمْ جُزْءٌ مَّقْسُومٌ إِنَّ ٱلْمُتَّقِينَ فِى جَنَّٰتٍ وَعُيُونٍ ٱدْخُلُوهَا بِسَلَٰمٍ ءَامِنِينَ وَنَزَعْنَا مَا فِى صُدُورِهِم مِّنْ غِلٍّ إِخْوَٰنًا عَلَىٰ سُرُرٍ مُّتَقَٰبِلِينَ لَا يَمَسُّهُمْ فِيهَا نَصَبٌ وَمَا هُم مِّنْهَا بِمُخْرَجِينَ نَبِّئْ عِبَادِىٓ أَنِّىٓ أَنَا ٱلْغَفُورُ ٱلرَّحِيمُ وَأَنَّ عَذَابِى هُوَ ٱلْعَذَابُ ٱلْأَلِيمُ

And as We said to the Angels, “Prostrate yourselves to Adam.” So they prostrated themselves, except Iblis; he refused Then We said, “O Adam, surely this is an enemy to you and to your spouse; so definitely do not let him drive you both out of the Garden, so that you (The Arabic pronoun here is singular) be wretched.” – Surah TaHa 20:116&117
وَإِذْ قُلْنَا لِلْمَلَٰٓئِكَةِ ٱسْجُدُوا۟ لِءَادَمَ فَسَجَدُوٓا۟ إِلَّآ إِبْلِيسَ أَبَىٰ فَقُلْنَا يَٰٓـَٔادَمُ إِنَّ هَٰذَا عَدُوٌّ لَّكَ وَلِزَوْجِكَ فَلَا يُخْرِجَنَّكُمَا مِنَ ٱلْجَنَّةِ فَتَشْقَىٰٓ

So the angels fell prostrate, all of them Except for Satan. He was too proud, and one of the faithless He said, ‘O Satan, what prevented you from prostrating before what I created with My Own hands? Are you too proud, or were you one of the exalted?’ – Surah Sad 38:73-75
فَسَجَدَ ٱلْمَلَٰٓئِكَةُ كُلُّهُمْ أَجْمَعُونَ إِلَّآ إِبْلِيسَ ٱسْتَكْبَرَ وَكَانَ مِنَ ٱلْكَٰفِرِينَ قَالَ يَٰٓإِبْلِيسُ مَا مَنَعَكَ أَن تَسْجُدَ لِمَا خَلَقْتُ بِيَدَىَّ ۖ أَسْتَكْبَرْتَ أَمْ كُنتَ مِنَ ٱلْعَالِينَ

Narrated `Abdullah: Allah's Messenger ﷺ said to us, "You will see after me, selfishness (on the part of other people) and other matters that you will disapprove of." They asked, "What do you order us to do, O Allah's Messenger ﷺ ? Under such circumstances)?" He said, "Pay their rights to them (to the rulers) and ask your right from Allah." - Sahih al-Bukhari 7052
حَدَّثَنَا مُسَدَّدٌ، حَدَّثَنَا يَحْيَى بْنُ سَعِيدٍ، حَدَّثَنَا الأَعْمَشُ، حَدَّثَنَا زَيْدُ بْنُ وَهْبٍ، سَمِعْتُ عَبْدَ اللَّهِ، قَالَ قَالَ لَنَا رَسُولُ اللَّهِ صلى الله عليه وسلم " إِنَّكُمْ سَتَرَوْنَ بَعْدِي أَثَرَةً وَأُمُورًا تُنْكِرُونَهَا". قَالُوا فَمَا تَأْمُرُنَا يَا رَسُولَ اللَّهِ قَالَ " أَدُّوا إِلَيْهِمْ حَقَّهُمْ وَسَلُوا اللَّهَ حَقَّكُمْ "

The life of this world is only diversion and amusement
وَمَا هَٰذِهِ ٱلْحَيَوٰةُ ٱلدُّنْيَآ إِلَّا لَهْوٌ وَلَعِبٌ

So surely you will not make the dead to hear, nor will you make the deaf to hear the call when they turn away, withdrawing And in no way will you (even) be a guide to the blind out of their errancy; decidedly you will not make any to hear except for the ones who believe in Our signs, and so they are Muslims (i.e., those that surrender to Allah) – Surah Ar-Rum 30:52&53
فَإِنَّكَ لَا تُسْمِعُ ٱلْمَوْتَىٰ وَلَا تُسْمِعُ ٱلصُّمَّ ٱلدُّعَآءَ إِذَا وَلَّوْا۟ مُدْبِرِينَ وَمَآ أَنتَ بِهَٰدِ ٱلْعُمْىِ عَن ضَلَٰلَتِهِمْ إِن تُسْمِعُ إِلَّا مَن يُؤْمِنُ بِـَٔايَٰتِنَا فَهُم مُّسْلِمُونَ

And in no way are the living and the dead equal. Surely Allah makes to hear whomever He decides; and in no way can you ever make (the ones) in the tombs to hear. – Surah Fatir 35:22
وَمَا يَسْتَوِى ٱلْأَحْيَآءُ وَلَا ٱلْأَمْوَٰتُ إِنَّ ٱللَّهَ يُسْمِعُ مَن يَشَآءُ وَمَآ أَنتَ بِمُسْمِعٍ مَّن فِى ٱلْقُبُورِ

But you shall not be able to make your voice reach the spiritually dead nor shall you be able to make it reach the worthless who counsel deaf nor do they open their hearts' ears when they turn their backs Nor shall you be able to guide those who lack intellectual or spiritual perception and their minds' eyes are blind nor can you extricate them or disengage out of the entangled wood of error. You can only influence those who listen to you and give credence to Our revelations and to Our authoritative divine signs with hearts impressed with the image of religious and spiritual virtues, for such persons have indeed conformed to Islam. – Surah An-Naml 27-80&81
إِنَّكَ لَا تُسْمِعُ ٱلْمَوْتَىٰ وَلَا تُسْمِعُ ٱلصُّمَّ ٱلدُّعَآءَ إِذَا وَلَّوْا۟ مُدْبِرِينَ وَمَآ أَنتَ بِهَٰدِى ٱلْعُمْىِ عَن ضَلَٰلَتِهِمْ إِن تُسْمِعُ إِلَّا مَن يُؤْمِنُ بِـَٔايَٰتِنَا فَهُم مُّسْلِمُونَ

The likeness of them is as the likeness of one who set to kindle a fire; so, as soon as it illuminated whatever is around him, Allah went away with their light, (i.e., took away their light)and left them in darkness (es) (where) they do not behold (anything) Deaf, dumb, blind, so they will not return – Surah Al-Baqarah 2:17&18
أُو۟لَٰٓئِكَ ٱلَّذِينَ ٱشْتَرَوُا۟ ٱلضَّلَٰلَةَ بِٱلْهُدَىٰ فَمَا رَبِحَت تِّجَٰرَتُهُمْ وَمَا كَانُوا۟ مُهْتَدِينَ مَثَلُهُمْ كَمَثَلِ ٱلَّذِى ٱسْتَوْقَدَ نَارًا فَلَمَّآ أَضَآءَتْ مَا حَوْلَهُۥ ذَهَبَ ٱللَّهُ بِنُورِهِمْ وَتَرَكَهُمْ فِى ظُلُمَٰتٍ لَّا يُبْصِرُونَ

Narrated Abu Musa: The Prophet ﷺ said, "The example of the one who celebrates the Praises of his Lord (Allah) in comparison to the one who does not celebrate the Praises of his Lord, is that of a living creature compared to a dead one.". – Sahih al-Bukhari 6407
حَدَّثَنَا مُحَمَّدُ بْنُ الْعَلاَءِ، حَدَّثَنَا أَبُو أُسَامَةَ، عَنْ بُرَيْدِ بْنِ عَبْدِ اللَّهِ، عَنْ أَبِي بُرْدَةَ، عَنْ أَبِي مُوسَى ـ رضى الله عنه ـ قَالَ قَالَ النَّبِيُّ صلى الله عليه وسلم " مَثَلُ الَّذِي يَذْكُرُ رَبَّهُ وَالَّذِي لاَ يَذْكُرُ مَثَلُ الْحَىِّ وَالْمَيِّتِ "

The life of this world is only diversion and amusement, whereas the real life is in the Hereafter. If they only knew. – Surah Al-Ankabut 29:64

وَمَا هَٰذِهِ ٱلْحَيَوٰةُ ٱلدُّنْيَآ إِلَّا لَهْوٌ وَلَعِبٌ ۚ وَإِنَّ ٱلدَّارَ ٱلْءَاخِرَةَ لَهِىَ ٱلْحَيَوَانُ ۚ لَوْ كَانُوا۟ يَعْلَمُونَ

Know that the life of this world is just a game; recreation, glitter, boasting to one another and rivalry in wealth and children. It is like a rain that helps plants grow, pleasing the growers, but then it dries up and you see it turn yellow, then it becomes stubble. There is severe punishment in the Hereafter, as well as forgiveness from God and [His] approval. The life of this world is only an illusion. – Surah Al-Hadid 57:20

ٱعْلَمُوٓا۟ أَنَّمَا ٱلْحَيَوٰةُ ٱلدُّنْيَا لَعِبٌ وَلَهْوٌ وَزِينَةٌ وَتَفَاخُرٌۢ بَيْنَكُمْ وَتَكَاثُرٌ فِى ٱلْأَمْوَٰلِ وَٱلْأَوْلَٰدِ ۖ كَمَثَلِ غَيْثٍ أَعْجَبَ ٱلْكُفَّارَ نَبَاتُهُۥ ثُمَّ يَهِيجُ فَتَرَىٰهُ مُصْفَرًّا ثُمَّ يَكُونُ حُطَٰمًا ۖ وَفِى ٱلْءَاخِرَةِ عَذَابٌ شَدِيدٌ وَمَغْفِرَةٌ مِّنَ ٱللَّهِ وَرِضْوَٰنٌ ۚ وَمَا ٱلْحَيَوٰةُ ٱلدُّنْيَآ إِلَّا مَتَٰعُ ٱلْغُرُورِ

Had We So willed, We could have used those [messages] to raise him high, but he always clung to the Earth and followed his own desires. He was like a dog who pants with his tongue hanging out whether you drive him away or leave him alone. That's the image of those who reject Our messages. Tell this story So that they might reflect on it. – Surah Al-A'raf 7:176

وَلَوْ شِئْنَا لَرَفَعْنَٰهُ بِهَا وَلَٰكِنَّهُۥٓ أَخْلَدَ إِلَى ٱلْأَرْضِ وَٱتَّبَعَ هَوَىٰهُ ۚ فَمَثَلُهُۥ كَمَثَلِ ٱلْكَلْبِ إِن تَحْمِلْ عَلَيْهِ يَلْهَثْ أَوْ تَتْرُكْهُ يَلْهَث ۚ ذَّٰلِكَ مَثَلُ ٱلْقَوْمِ ٱلَّذِينَ كَذَّبُوا۟ بِـَٔايَٰتِنَا ۚ فَٱقْصُصِ ٱلْقَصَصَ لَعَلَّهُمْ يَتَفَكَّرُونَ

And do you think that most of them hear or understand? They are just like cattle; indeed, they are [even] more lost. – Surah Al-Furqan 25:44

أَمْ تَحْسَبُ أَنَّ أَكْثَرَهُمْ يَسْمَعُونَ أَوْ يَعْقِلُونَ ۚ إِنْ هُمْ إِلَّا كَٱلْأَنْعَٰمِ ۖ بَلْ هُمْ أَضَلُّ سَبِيلًا

Surely the Tree of Az-Zaqqum Is the food of the constantly vicious
إِنَّ شَجَرَتَ ٱلزَّقُّومِ طَعَامُ ٱلْأَثِيمِ

Is this a more charitable (i.e., better) hospitality, or even the Tree of Az-Zaqqum Surely We have made it as a temptation (Or: trial) for the unjust Surely it is a tree that comes out (Literally: goes out) in the root of Hell-Fire Its spathes are as the heads of Shayatun. (Ever-vicious (ones), i.e., devils Then surely they will indeed be eating of it, and so of it they will be filling their bellies Thereafter on top of it surely they will have indeed an admixture of scalding (water) Thereafter surely their return indeed is to Hell-Fire Surely they came upon their fathers erring So they are made to hurry in their tracks And indeed before them already erred away most of the earliest (people) – Surah As-Saffat 37:62-71

أَذَٰلِكَ خَيْرٌ نُّزُلًا أَمْ شَجَرَةُ ٱلزَّقُّومِ إِنَّا جَعَلْنَٰهَا فِتْنَةً لِّلظَّٰلِمِينَ إِنَّهَا شَجَرَةٌ تَخْرُجُ فِىٓ أَصْلِ ٱلْجَحِيمِ طَلْعُهَا كَأَنَّهُۥ رُءُوسُ ٱلشَّيَٰطِينِ فَإِنَّهُمْ لَءَاكِلُونَ مِنْهَا فَمَالِـُٔونَ مِنْهَا ٱلْبُطُونَ ثُمَّ إِنَّ لَهُمْ عَلَيْهَا لَشَوْبًا مِّنْ حَمِيمٍ ثُمَّ إِنَّ مَرْجِعَهُمْ لَإِلَى ٱلْجَحِيمِ إِنَّهُمْ أَلْفَوْا۟ ءَابَآءَهُمْ ضَآلِّينَ فَهُمْ عَلَىٰٓ ءَاثَٰرِهِمْ يُهْرَعُونَ وَلَقَدْ ضَلَّ قَبْلَهُمْ أَكْثَرُ ٱلْأَوَّلِينَ

Indeed you will eat of the trees of Zaqqum So you will be filling therewith (your) bellies Then you will be drinking thermeon of scalding water So you will be drinking (like) the drinking of diseased camels wandering with thirst." This is their hospitality on the Day of Doom. – Surah Al-Waqi'ah 56:52-56

لَءَاكِلُونَ مِن شَجَرٍ مِّن زَقُّومٍ فَمَالِـُٔونَ مِنْهَا ٱلْبُطُونَ فَشَٰرِبُونَ عَلَيْهِ مِنَ ٱلْحَمِيمِ فَشَٰرِبُونَ شُرْبَ ٱلْهِيمِ هَٰذَا نُزُلُهُمْ يَوْمَ ٱلدِّينِ

Surely the Tree of Az-Zaqqum Is the food of the constantly vicious Like molten metal, it boils in the bellies As the boiling of scalding water "Take him, then thrust him into the (deepest) level of Hell-Fire Thereafter pour above his head of the torment of scalding (water) Taste! Surely you, (only) you are (i.e., you used to think that you were mighty) the constantly mighty, the constantly honorable – Surah Ad-Dukhan 44:43-49
إِنَّ شَجَرَتَ ٱلزَّقُّومِ طَعَامُ ٱلْأَثِيمِ كَٱلْمُهْلِ يَغْلِى فِى ٱلْبُطُونِ كَغَلْىِ ٱلْحَمِيمِ خُذُوهُ فَٱعْتِلُوهُ إِلَىٰ سَوَآءِ ٱلْجَحِيمِ ثُمَّ صُبُّوا۟ فَوْقَ
رَأْسِهِۦ مِنْ عَذَابِ ٱلْحَمِيمِ ذُقْ إِنَّكَ أَنتَ ٱلْعَزِيزُ ٱلْكَرِيمُ

We have already told you [Muhammad] that your Lord knows all about human beings. The vision that We showed you is only a trial and temptation for men and so is the cursed tree in the Qur'an. We put Our fear in them, but this only increases their tyranny. – Surah Al-Isra 17:60
وَإِذْ قُلْنَا لَكَ إِنَّ رَبَّكَ أَحَاطَ بِٱلنَّاسِ ۚ وَمَا جَعَلْنَا ٱلرُّءْيَا ٱلَّتِىٓ أَرَيْنَـٰكَ إِلَّا فِتْنَةً لِّلنَّاسِ وَٱلشَّجَرَةَ ٱلْمَلْعُونَةَ فِى ٱلْقُرْءَانِ ۚ وَنُخَوِّفُهُمْ فَمَا
يَزِيدُهُمْ إِلَّا طُغْيَـٰنًا كَبِيرًا

"Do you bring me wealth when what Allah has given me is better than what He has given you? – Surah An-Naml 27:36
أَتُمِدُّونَنِ بِمَالٍ فَمَآ ءَاتَىٰنِۦَ ٱللَّهُ خَيْرٌ مِّمَّآ ءَاتَىٰكُم بَلْ أَنتُم بِهَدِيَّتِكُمْ تَفْرَحُونَ

The remainder of Allah is most charitable for you, in case you are believers; and in no way am I a constant preserver over you." – Surah Hud 11:86
بَقِيَّتُ ٱللَّهِ خَيْرٌ لَّكُمْ إِن كُنتُم مُّؤْمِنِينَ ۚ وَمَآ أَنَا۠ عَلَيْكُم بِحَفِيظٍ

And indeed in case you are killed in the way of Allah or die, indeed forgiveness from Allah and mercy are more charitable than whatever they (heap) together. – Surah Al-Imran 3:157
وَلَئِن قُتِلْتُمْ فِى سَبِيلِ ٱللَّهِ أَوْ مُتُّمْ لَمَغْفِرَةٌ مِّنَ ٱللَّهِ وَرَحْمَةٌ خَيْرٌ مِّمَّا يَجْمَعُونَ

He brings (the) Wisdom to whomever He decides; and whoever is brought (the) Wisdom, then he has been brought much charity (i.e., benefit); and in no way does anyone constantly remember except the ones endowed with intellects. – Surah Al-Baqarah 2:269
يُؤْتِى ٱلْحِكْمَةَ مَن يَشَآءُ ۚ وَمَن يُؤْتَ ٱلْحِكْمَةَ فَقَدْ أُوتِىَ خَيْرًا كَثِيرًا ۗ وَمَا يَذَّكَّرُ إِلَّآ أُو۟لُوا۟ ٱلْأَلْبَـٰبِ

O you mankind, there has already come to you an admonition from your Lord, and a cure for what is in the breasts Say, "By the Grace of Allah, and by His mercy; so with that let them exult; it is more charitable (i.e., better) than whatever they (heap) together. (Literally: whatever they gather. – Surah Yunus 10:57&58
يَـٰٓأَيُّهَا ٱلنَّاسُ قَدْ جَآءَتْكُم مَّوْعِظَةٌ مِّن رَّبِّكُمْ وَشِفَآءٌ لِّمَا فِى ٱلصُّدُورِ وَهُدًى وَرَحْمَةٌ لِّلْمُؤْمِنِينَ قُلْ بِفَضْلِ ٱللَّهِ وَبِرَحْمَتِهِۦ فَبِذَٰلِكَ
فَلْيَفْرَحُوا۟ هُوَ خَيْرٌ مِّمَّا يَجْمَعُونَ

So he came out, in his splendor, before his people. Those who desired this worldly life said, "How we wish to have been given like what Korah had been given; he is truly a most fortunate man." But those who had been given knowledge said, "You are wrong! God's reward is better for him who believes and does good deeds; only those with great patience will obtain this." – Surah Al-Qasas 28:79&80
فَخَرَجَ عَلَىٰ قَوْمِهِۦ فِى زِينَتِهِۦ ۖ قَالَ ٱلَّذِينَ يُرِيدُونَ ٱلْحَيَوٰةَ ٱلدُّنْيَا يَـٰلَيْتَ لَنَا مِثْلَ مَآ أُوتِىَ قَـٰرُونُ إِنَّهُۥ لَذُو حَظٍّ عَظِيمٍ وَقَالَ
ٱلَّذِينَ أُوتُوا۟ ٱلْعِلْمَ وَيْلَكُمْ ثَوَابُ ٱللَّهِ خَيْرٌ لِّمَنْ ءَامَنَ وَعَمِلَ صَـٰلِحًا وَلَا يُلَقَّىٰهَآ إِلَّا ٱلصَّـٰبِرُونَ

Narrated 'Usama bin Zaid: I asked, "O Allah's Messenger ﷺ ! Where will you stay in Mecca? Will you stay in your house in Mecca?" He replied, "Has `Aqil left any property or house?" `Aqil along with Talib had inherited the property of Abu Talib. Jafar and `Ali did not inherit anything as they were Muslims and the other two were non-believers. `Umar bin Al-Khattab used to say, "A believer cannot inherit (anything from an) infidel." Ibn Shihab, (a sub-narrator) said, "They (`Umar and others) derived the above verdict from Allah's Statement: "Verily! Those who believed and Emigrated and strove with their life And property in Allah's Cause, And those who helped (the emigrants) And gave them their places to live in, These are (all) allies to one another." (8.72) – Sahih al-Bukhari 1588

حَدَّثَنَا أَصْبَغُ، قَالَ أَخْبَرَنِي ابْنُ وَهْبٍ، عَنْ يُونُسَ، عَنِ ابْنِ شِهَابٍ، عَنْ عَلِيِّ بْنِ حُسَيْنٍ، عَنْ عَمْرِو بْنِ عُثْمَانَ، عَنْ أُسَامَةَ بْنِ زَيْدٍ ـ رضى الله عنهما ـ أَنَّهُ قَالَ يَا رَسُولَ اللَّهِ، أَيْنَ تَنْزِلُ فِي دَارِكَ بِمَكَّةَ‏.‏ فَقَالَ ‏"‏ وَهَلْ تَرَكَ عَقِيلٌ مِنْ رِبَاعٍ أَوْ دُورٍ ‏"‏‏.‏ وَكَانَ عَقِيلٌ وَرِثَ أَبَا طَالِبٍ هُوَ وَطَالِبٌ وَلَمْ يَرِثْهُ جَعْفَرٌ وَلاَ عَلِيٌّ ـ رضى الله عنهما ـ شَيْئًا لأَنَّهُمَا كَانَا مُسْلِمَيْنِ، وَكَانَ عَقِيلٌ وَطَالِبٌ كَافِرَيْنِ، فَكَانَ عُمَرُ بْنُ الْخَطَّابِ ـ رضى الله عنه ـ يَقُولُ لاَ يَرِثُ الْمُؤْمِنُ الْكَافِرَ‏.‏ قَالَ ابْنُ شِهَابٍ وَكَانُوا يَتَأَوَّلُونَ قَوْلَ اللَّهِ تَعَالَى ‏{‏إِنَّ الَّذِينَ آمَنُوا وَهَاجَرُوا وَجَاهَدُوا بِأَمْوَالِهِمْ وَأَنْفُسِهِمْ فِي سَبِيلِ اللَّهِ وَالَّذِينَ آوَوْا وَنَصَرُوا أُولَئِكَ بَعْضُهُمْ أَوْلِيَاءُ بَعْضٍ‏}‏ الآيَةَ‏.‏

Narrated `Abdullah bin `Umar: The people landed at the land of Thamud called Al-Hijr along with Allah's Messenger ﷺ and they took water from its well for drinking and kneading the dough with it as well. (When Allah's Messenger ﷺ heard about it) he ordered them to pour out the water they had taken from its wells and feed the camels with the dough, and ordered them to take water from the well whence the she-camel (of Prophet Salih) used to drink. – Sahih al-Bukhari 3379

حَدَّثَنَا إِبْرَاهِيمُ بْنُ الْمُنْذِرِ، حَدَّثَنَا أَنَسُ بْنُ عِيَاضٍ، عَنْ عُبَيْدِ اللَّهِ، عَنْ نَافِعٍ، أَنَّ عَبْدَ اللَّهِ بْنَ عُمَرَ ـ رضى الله عنهما ـ أَخْبَرَهُ أَنَّ النَّاسَ نَزَلُوا مَعَ رَسُولِ اللَّهِ صلى الله عليه وسلم أَرْضَ ثَمُودَ الْحِجْرَ، فَاسْتَقَوْا مِنْ بِئْرِهَا، وَاعْتَجَنُوا بِهِ، فَأَمَرَهُمْ رَسُولُ اللَّهِ صلى الله عليه وسلم أَنْ يُهَرِيقُوا مَا اسْتَقَوْا مِنْ بِئْرِهَا، وَأَنْ يَعْلِفُوا الإِبِلَ الْعَجِينَ، وَأَمَرَهُمْ أَنْ يَسْتَقُوا مِنَ الْبِئْرِ الَّتِي كَانَ تَرِدُهَا النَّاقَةُ‏.‏ تَابَعَهُ أُسَامَةُ عَنْ نَافِعٍ‏.‏

Then as soon as Talut (Saul) departed with the hosts, he said, "Surely Allah will be trying you with a river; so whoever drinks of it, then he is not of me, and whoever does not taste (Literally: does not feed on it) it, then surely he is of me, excepting him who scoops up (a scoop) with his hand." Then they drank of it except a few of them. Then, as soon as he passed over it, he and the ones who believed with him, they said, "We have no capability today against Jalut (Goliath) and his hosts." (But) the ones who expect that they will be meeting Allah said, "How often a little community has overcome a much (larger) community by the permission of Allah; and Allah is with the patient." – Surah Al-Baqarah 2:249

فَلَمَّا فَصَلَ طَالُوتُ بِٱلْجُنُودِ قَالَ إِنَّ ٱللَّهَ مُبْتَلِيكُم بِنَهَرٍ فَمَن شَرِبَ مِنْهُ فَلَيْسَ مِنِّي وَمَن لَّمْ يَطْعَمْهُ فَإِنَّهُۥ مِنِّىٓ إِلَّا مَنِ ٱغْتَرَفَ غُرْفَةًۢ بِيَدِهِۦ ۚ فَشَرِبُوا۟ مِنْهُ إِلَّا قَلِيلًا مِّنْهُمْ ۚ فَلَمَّا جَاوَزَهُۥ هُوَ وَٱلَّذِينَ ءَامَنُوا۟ مَعَهُۥ قَالُوا۟ لَا طَاقَةَ لَنَا ٱلْيَوْمَ بِجَالُوتَ وَجُنُودِهِۦ ۚ قَالَ ٱلَّذِينَ يَظُنُّونَ أَنَّهُم مُّلَـٰقُوا۟ ٱللَّهِ كَم مِّن فِئَةٍ قَلِيلَةٍ غَلَبَتْ فِئَةً كَثِيرَةًۢ بِإِذْنِ ٱللَّهِ ۗ وَٱللَّهُ مَعَ ٱلصَّـٰبِرِينَ

The Book of
Let not your properties or your children divert you from the remembrance of Allah.
لَا تُلْهِكُمْ أَمْوَٰلُكُمْ وَلَآ أَوْلَـٰدُكُمْ عَن ذِكْرِ ٱللَّهِ

Narrated Abu Sa`id Al-Khudri: Allah's Messenger ﷺ said, "The thing I am afraid of most for your sake, is the worldly blessings which Allah will bring forth to you." It was said, "What are the blessings of this world?" The Prophet ﷺ said, "The pleasures of the world." A man said, "Can the good bring forth evil?" The Prophet ﷺ kept quiet for a while till we thought that he was being inspired divinely. Then he started removing the sweat from his forehead and said," Where is the questioner?" That man said, "I (am present)." Abu Sa`id added: We thanked the man when the result (of his question) was such. The Prophet ﷺ said, "Good never brings forth but good. This wealth (of the world) is (like) green and sweet (fruit), and all the vegetation which grows on the bank of a stream either kills or nearly kills the animal that eats too much of it, except the animal that eats the Khadira (a kind of vegetation). Such an animal eats till its stomach is full and then it faces the sun and starts ruminating and then it passes out dung and urine and goes to eat again. This worldly wealth is (like) sweet (fruit), and if a person earns it (the wealth) in a legal way and spends it properly, then it is an excellent helper, and whoever earns it in an illegal way, he will be like the one who eats but is never satisfied." – Al-Bukhari 6427

حَدَّثَنَا إِسْمَاعِيلُ، قَالَ حَدَّثَنِي مَالِكٌ، عَنْ زَيْدِ بْنِ أَسْلَمَ، عَنْ عَطَاءِ بْنِ يَسَارٍ، عَنْ أَبِي سَعِيدٍ، قَالَ قَالَ رَسُولُ اللَّهِ صلى الله عليه وسلم " إِنَّ أَكْثَرَ مَا أَخَافُ عَلَيْكُمْ مَا يُخْرِجُ اللَّهُ لَكُمْ مِنْ بَرَكَاتِ الأَرْضِ ". قِيلَ وَمَا بَرَكَاتُ الأَرْضِ قَالَ " زَهْرَةُ الدُّنْيَا ". فَقَالَ لَهُ رَجُلٌ هَلْ يَأْتِي الْخَيْرُ بِالشَّرِّ فَصَمَتَ النَّبِيُّ صلى الله عليه وسلم حَتَّى ظَنَنَّا أَنَّهُ يُنْزَلُ عَلَيْهِ، ثُمَّ جَعَلَ يَمْسَحُ عَنْ جَبِينِهِ فَقَالَ " أَيْنَ السَّائِلُ ". قَالَ أَنَا. قَالَ أَبُو سَعِيدٍ لَقَدْ حَمِدْنَاهُ حِينَ طَلَعَ ذَلِكَ. قَالَ " لاَ يَأْتِي الْخَيْرُ إِلاَّ بِالْخَيْرِ، إِنَّ هَذَا الْمَالَ خَضِرَةٌ حُلْوَةٌ، وَإِنَّ كُلَّ مَا أَنْبَتَ الرَّبِيعُ يَقْتُلُ حَبَطًا أَوْ يُلِمُّ، إِلاَّ آكِلَةَ الْخَضِرَةِ، أَكَلَتْ حَتَّى إِذَا امْتَدَّتْ خَاصِرَتَاهَا اسْتَقْبَلَتِ الشَّمْسَ، فَاجْتَرَّتْ وَثَلَطَتْ وَبَالَتْ، ثُمَّ عَادَتْ فَأَكَلَتْ، وَإِنَّ هَذَا الْمَالَ حُلْوَةٌ، مَنْ أَخَذَهُ بِحَقِّهِ وَوَضَعَهُ فِي حَقِّهِ، فَنِعْمَ الْمَعُونَةُ هُوَ، وَمَنْ أَخَذَهُ بِغَيْرِ حَقِّهِ، كَانَ الَّذِي يَأْكُلُ وَلاَ يَشْبَعُ ".

Narrated Abu Huraira: Allah's Messenger ﷺ said, "Soon the river "Euphrates" will disclose the treasure (the mountain) of gold, so whoever will be present at that time should not take anything of it." Al-A'raj narrated from Abii Huraira that the Prophet ﷺ said the same but he said, "It (Euphrates) will uncover a mountain of gold (under it). – Al-Bukhari 7119

حَدَّثَنَا عَبْدُ اللَّهِ بْنُ سَعِيدٍ الْكِنْدِيُّ، حَدَّثَنَا عُقْبَةُ بْنُ خَالِدٍ، حَدَّثَنَا عُبَيْدُ اللَّهِ، عَنْ خُبَيْبِ بْنِ عَبْدِ الرَّحْمَنِ، عَنْ جَدِّهِ، حَفْصِ بْنِ عَاصِمٍ عَنْ أَبِي هُرَيْرَةَ، قَالَ قَالَ رَسُولُ اللَّهِ صلى الله عليه وسلم " يُوشِكُ الْفُرَاتُ أَنْ يَحْسِرَ عَنْ كَنْزٍ مِنْ ذَهَبٍ، فَمَنْ حَضَرَهُ فَلاَ يَأْخُذْ مِنْهُ شَيْئًا ". قَالَ عُقْبَةُ وَحَدَّثَنَا عُبَيْدُ اللَّهِ، حَدَّثَنَا أَبُو الزِّنَادِ، عَنِ الأَعْرَجِ، عَنْ أَبِي هُرَيْرَةَ، عَنِ النَّبِيِّ صلى الله عليه وسلم مِثْلَهُ إِلاَّ أَنَّهُ قَالَ " يَحْسِرُ عَنْ جَبَلٍ مِنْ ذَهَبٍ "

O you who believe! Let neither your possessions nor your children distract you from the remembrance of Allah. Whoever does that—these are the losers. – Surah Al-Munafiqun 63:9

يَـٰٓأَيُّهَا ٱلَّذِينَ ءَامَنُوا۟ لَا تُلْهِكُمْ أَمْوَٰلُكُمْ وَلَآ أَوْلَـٰدُكُمْ عَن ذِكْرِ ٱللَّهِ وَمَن يَفْعَلْ ذَٰلِكَ فَأُو۟لَـٰٓئِكَ هُمُ ٱلْخَـٰسِرُونَ

Narrated Al-Bara' bin 'Azib: Allah's Messenger ﷺ ordered us to do seven (things): to visit the sick, to follow the funeral processions, to say Tashmit to a sneezer, to help the weak, to help the oppressed ones, to propagate As-Salam (greeting), and to help others to fulfill their oaths (if it is not sinful). He forbade us to drink from silver utensils, to wear gold rings, to ride on silken saddles, to wear silk clothes, Dibaj (thick silk cloth), Qassiy and Istabraq (two kinds of silk). (See Hadith No. 539, Vol. 7) – Al-Bukhari 6235

حَدَّثَنَا قُتَيْبَةُ، حَدَّثَنَا جَرِيرٌ، عَنِ الشَّيْبَانِيِّ، عَنْ أَشْعَثَ بْنِ أَبِي الشَّعْثَاءِ، عَنْ مُعَاوِيَةَ بْنِ سُوَيْدِ بْنِ مُقَرِّنٍ، عَنِ الْبَرَاءِ بْنِ عَازِبٍ ـ رضى الله عنهما ـ قَالَ أَمَرَنَا رَسُولُ اللَّهِ صلى الله عليه وسلم بِسَبْعٍ بِعِيَادَةِ الْمَرِيضِ، وَاتِّبَاعِ الْجَنَائِزِ، وَتَشْمِيتِ الْعَاطِسِ، وَنَصْرِ الضَّعِيفِ، وَعَوْنِ الْمَظْلُومِ، وَإِفْشَاءِ السَّلاَمِ، وَإِبْرَارِ الْمُقْسِمِ، وَنَهَى عَنِ الشُّرْبِ فِي الْفِضَّةِ، وَنَهَانَا عَنْ تَخَتُّمِ الذَّهَبِ، وَعَنْ رُكُوبِ الْمَيَاثِرِ، وَعَنْ لُبْسِ الْحَرِيرِ، وَالدِّيبَاجِ، وَالْقَسِّيِّ، وَالإِسْتَبْرَقِ.

Narrated Anas: To the best of my knowledge, the Prophetﷺ did not take his meals in a big tray at all, nor did he ever eat well-baked thin bread, nor did he ever eat at a dining table. – Al-Bukhari 5386

حَدَّثَنَا عَلِيُّ بْنُ عَبْدِ اللَّهِ، حَدَّثَنَا مُعَاذُ بْنُ هِشَامٍ، قَالَ حَدَّثَنِي أَبِي، عَنْ يُونُسَ ـ قَالَ عَلِيٌّ هُوَ الإِسْكَافُ ـ عَنْ قَتَادَةَ، عَنْ أَنَسٍ، رضى الله عنه قَالَ مَا عَلِمْتُ النَّبِيَّ صلى الله عليه وسلم أَكَلَ عَلَى سُكُرُّجَةٍ قَطُّ، وَلاَ خُبِزَ لَهُ مُرَقَّقٌ قَطُّ، وَلاَ أَكَلَ عَلَى خِوَانٍ. قِيلَ لِقَتَادَةَ فَعَلَى مَا كَانُوا يَأْكُلُونَ قَالَ عَلَى السُّفَرِ

Narrated Qais bin Abi Hazim: We went to pay a visit to Khabbab (who was sick) and he had been branded (cauterized) at seven places in his body. He said, "Our companions who died (during the lifetime of the Prophet) left (this world) without having their rewards reduced through enjoying the pleasures of this life, but we have got (so much) wealth that we find no way to spend It except on the construction of buildings Had the Prophet not forbidden us to wish for death, I would have wished for it.' We visited him for the second time while he was building a wall. He said, A Muslim is rewarded (in the Hereafter) for whatever he spends except for something that he spends on building." – Al-Bukhari 5672

حَدَّثَنَا آدَمُ، حَدَّثَنَا شُعْبَةُ، عَنْ إِسْمَاعِيلَ بْنِ أَبِي خَالِدٍ، عَنْ قَيْسِ بْنِ أَبِي حَازِمٍ، قَالَ دَخَلْنَا عَلَى خَبَّابٍ نَعُودُهُ وَقَدِ اكْتَوَى سَبْعَ كَيَّاتٍ فَقَالَ إِنَّ أَصْحَابَنَا الَّذِينَ سَلَفُوا مَضَوْا وَلَمْ تَنْقُصْهُمُ الدُّنْيَا وَإِنَّا أَصَبْنَا مَا لاَ نَجِدُ لَهُ مَوْضِعًا إِلاَّ التُّرَابَ وَلَوْلاَ أَنَّ النَّبِيَّ صلى الله عليه وسلم نَهَانَا أَنْ نَدْعُوَ بِالْمَوْتِ لَدَعَوْتُ بِهِ، ثُمَّ أَتَيْنَاهُ مَرَّةً أُخْرَى وَهْوَ يَبْنِي حَائِطًا لَهُ فَقَالَ إِنَّ الْمُسْلِمَ لَيُوجَرُ فِي كُلِّ شَىْءٍ يُنْفِقُهُ إِلاَّ فِي شَىْءٍ يَجْعَلُهُ فِي هَذَا التُّرَابِ.

Narrated Um Salama: (the wife of the Prophet) Allah's Messengerﷺ said, "He who drinks in silver utensils is only filling his `Abdomen with Hell Fire." – Al-Bukhari 5634

حَدَّثَنَا إِسْمَاعِيلُ، قَالَ حَدَّثَنِي مَالِكُ بْنُ أَنَسٍ، عَنْ نَافِعٍ، عَنْ زَيْدِ بْنِ عَبْدِ اللَّهِ بْنِ عُمَرَ، عَنْ عَبْدِ اللَّهِ بْنِ عَبْدِ الرَّحْمَنِ بْنِ أَبِي بَكْرٍ الصِّدِّيقِ، عَنْ أُمِّ سَلَمَةَ، زَوْجِ النَّبِيِّ صلى الله عليه وسلم أَنَّ رَسُولَ اللَّهِ صلى الله عليه وسلم قَالَ " الَّذِي يَشْرَبُ فِي إِنَاءِ الْفِضَّةِ إِنَّمَا يُجَرْجِرُ فِي بَطْنِهِ نَارَ جَهَنَّمَ "

Narrated Um Salama: (One night) the Prophetﷺ woke up and said, "Subhan Allah ! How many treasures have been (disclosed) sent down! And how many afflictions have been descended! Who will go and wake the sleeping ladyoccupants up of these dwellings (for praying)?" (He meant by this his wives.) The Prophetﷺ added, "A well-dressed soul (person) in this world may be naked in the "Hereafter." `Umar said, "I asked the Prophet, 'Have you divorced your wives?' He said, 'No.' I said, 'Allahu Akbar.' " – Al-Bukhari 6218

حَدَّثَنَا أَبُو الْيَمَانِ، أَخْبَرَنَا شُعَيْبٌ، عَنِ الزُّهْرِيِّ، حَدَّثَتْنِي هِنْدُ بِنْتُ الْحَارِثِ، أَنَّ أُمَّ سَلَمَةَ ـ رضى الله عنها ـ قَالَتِ اسْتَيْقَظَ النَّبِيُّ صلى الله عليه وسلم فَقَالَ " سُبْحَانَ اللَّهِ مَاذَا أُنْزِلَ مِنَ الْخَزَائِنِ، وَمَاذَا أُنْزِلَ مِنَ الْفِتَنِ، مَنْ يُوقِظُ صَوَاحِبَ الْحُجَرِ ـ يُرِيدُ بِهِ أَزْوَاجَهُ ـ حَتَّى يُصَلِّينَ، رُبَّ كَاسِيَةٍ فِي الدُّنْيَا، عَارِيَةٍ فِي الآخِرَةِ ". وَقَالَ ابْنُ أَبِي ثَوْرٍ عَنِ ابْنِ عَبَّاسٍ، عَنْ عُمَرَ، قَالَ قُلْتُ لِلنَّبِيِّ صلى الله عليه وسلم طَلَّقْتَ نِسَاءَكَ قَالَ " لاَ ". قُلْتُ اللَّهُ أَكْبَرُ.

And We granted David, Solomon, an excellent servant. He was penitent. When the beautiful horses were paraded before him in the evening. He said, "I have preferred the love of niceties to the remembrance of my Lord—until it disappeared behind the veil. Bring them back to me." And he began caressing their legs and necks. We tested Solomon, and placed a body on his throne; then he repented. He said, "My Lord, forgive me, and grant me a kingdom never to be attained by anyone after me. You are the Giver." – Surah Sad 38:30-35

وَوَهَبْنَا لِدَاوُۥدَ سُلَيْمَـٰنَ ۚ نِعْمَ ٱلْعَبْدُ ۖ إِنَّهُۥٓ أَوَّابٌ إِذْ عُرِضَ عَلَيْهِ بِٱلْعَشِىِّ ٱلصَّـٰفِنَـٰتُ ٱلْجِيَادُ فَقَالَ إِنِّىٓ أَحْبَبْتُ حُبَّ ٱلْخَيْرِ عَن ذِكْرِ رَبِّى حَتَّىٰ تَوَارَتْ بِٱلْحِجَابِ رُدُّوهَا عَلَىَّ ۖ فَطَفِقَ مَسْحًۢا بِٱلسُّوقِ وَٱلْأَعْنَاقِ وَلَقَدْ فَتَنَّا سُلَيْمَـٰنَ وَأَلْقَيْنَا عَلَىٰ كُرْسِيِّهِۦ جَسَدًا ثُمَّ أَنَابَ قَالَ رَبِّ ٱغْفِرْ لِى وَهَبْ لِى مُلْكًا لَّا يَنۢبَغِى لِأَحَدٍ مِّنۢ بَعْدِىٓ ۖ إِنَّكَ أَنتَ ٱلْوَهَّابُ

Narrated `Uqba bin Al-Harith: I offered the `Asr prayer with the Prophet ﷺ and after finishing the prayer with Taslim he got up quickly and went to some of his wives and then came out. He noticed the signs of astonishment on the faces of the people caused by his speed. He then said, "I remembered while I was in my prayer that a piece of gold was Lying in my house and I disliked that it should remain with us throughout the night, and so I have ordered it to be distributed." – Al-Bukhari 1221

حَدَّثَنَا إِسْحَاقُ بْنُ مَنْصُورٍ، حَدَّثَنَا رَوْحٌ، حَدَّثَنَا عُمَرُ ـ هُوَ ابْنُ سَعِيدٍ ـ قَالَ أَخْبَرَنِي ابْنُ أَبِي مُلَيْكَةَ، عَنْ عُقْبَةَ بْنِ الْحَارِثِ ـ رضى الله عنه ـ قَالَ صَلَّيْتُ مَعَ النَّبِيِّ صلى الله عليه وسلم الْعَصْرَ، فَلَمَّا سَلَّمَ قَامَ سَرِيعًا دَخَلَ عَلَى بَعْضِ نِسَائِهِ، ثُمَّ خَرَجَ وَرَأَى مَا فِي وُجُوهِ الْقَوْمِ مِنْ تَعَجُّبِهِمْ لِسُرْعَتِهِ فَقَالَ " ذَكَرْتُ وَأَنَا فِي الصَّلاَةِ تِبْرًا عِنْدَنَا، فَكَرِهْتُ أَنْ يُمْسِيَ أَوْ يَبِيتَ عِنْدَنَا فَأَمَرْتُ بِقِسْمَتِهِ "

Narrated Al-Bara' bin `Azib: Allah's Messenger ﷺ ordered us to do seven things and forbade us to do other seven. He ordered us: to follow the funeral procession. To visit the sick, to accept invitations, to help the oppressed, to fulfill the oaths, to return the greeting and to reply to the sneezer: (saying, "May Allah be merciful on you," provided the sneezer says, "All the praises are for Allah,"). He forbade us to use silver utensils and dishes and to wear golden rings, silk (clothes), Dibaj (pure silk cloth), Qissi and Istabraq (two kinds of silk cloths). – Al-Bukhari 1239

حَدَّثَنَا أَبُو الْوَلِيدِ، حَدَّثَنَا شُعْبَةُ، عَنِ الأَشْعَثِ، قَالَ سَمِعْتُ مُعَاوِيَةَ بْنَ سُوَيْدِ بْنِ مُقَرِّنٍ، عَنِ الْبَرَاءِ ـ رضى الله عنه ـ قَالَ أَمَرَنَا النَّبِيُّ صلى الله عليه وسلم بِسَبْعٍ، وَنَهَانَا عَنْ سَبْعٍ أَمَرَنَا بِاتِّبَاعِ الْجَنَائِزِ، وَعِيَادَةِ الْمَرِيضِ، وَإِجَابَةِ الدَّاعِي، وَنَصْرِ الْمَظْلُومِ، وَإِبْرَارِ الْقَسَمِ، وَرَدِّ السَّلاَمِ، وَتَشْمِيتِ الْعَاطِسِ. وَنَهَانَا عَنْ آنِيَةِ الْفِضَّةِ، وَخَاتَمِ الذَّهَبِ، وَالْحَرِيرِ، وَالدِّيبَاجِ، وَالْقَسِّيِّ، وَالإِسْتَبْرَقِ

Narrated Qatada: We used to go to Anas bin Malik and see his baker standing (preparing the bread). Anas said, "Eat. I have not known that the Prophet ﷺ ever saw a thin well-baked loaf of bread till he died, and he never saw a roasted sheep with his eyes." – Al-Bukhari 6457

حَدَّثَنَا هُدْبَةُ بْنُ خَالِدٍ، حَدَّثَنَا هَمَّامُ بْنُ يَحْيَى، حَدَّثَنَا قَتَادَةُ، قَالَ كُنَّا نَأْتِي أَنَسَ بْنَ مَالِكٍ وَخَبَّازُهُ قَائِمٌ وَقَالَ كُلُوا فَمَا أَعْلَمُ النَّبِيَّ صلى الله عليه وسلم رَأَى رَغِيفًا مُرَقَّقًا، حَتَّى لَحِقَ بِاللَّهِ، وَلاَ رَأَى شَاةً سَمِيطًا بِعَيْنِهِ قَطُّ

Narrated Sahl bin Sa`d As-Sa`id: A man passed by Allah's Messenger ﷺ and the Prophet ﷺ asked a man sitting beside him, "What is your opinion about this (passer-by)?" He replied, "This (passer-by) is from the noble class of people. By Allah, if he should ask for a lady's hand in marriage, he ought to be given her in marriage, and if he intercedes for somebody, his intercession will be accepted. Allah's Messenger ﷺ kept quiet, and then another man passed by and Allah's Messenger ﷺ asked the same man (his companion) again, "What is your opinion about this (second) one?" He said, "O Allah's Messenger ﷺ ! This person is one of the poor Muslims. If he should ask a lady's hand in marriage, no-one will accept him, and if he intercedes for somebody, no one will accept his intercession, and if he talks, no-one will listen to his talk." Then Allah's Messenger ﷺ said, "This (poor man) is better than such a large number of the first type (i.e. rich men) as to fill the earth." – Al-Bukhari 6447

حَدَّثَنَا إِسْمَاعِيلُ، قَالَ حَدَّثَنِي عَبْدُ الْعَزِيزِ بْنُ أَبِي حَازِمٍ، عَنْ أَبِيهِ، عَنْ سَهْلِ بْنِ سَعْدٍ السَّاعِدِيِّ، أَنَّهُ قَالَ مَرَّ رَجُلٌ عَلَى رَسُولِ اللَّهِ صلى الله عليه وسلم فَقَالَ لِرَجُلٍ عِنْدَهُ جَالِسٍ " مَا رَأْيُكَ فِي هَذَا ". فَقَالَ رَجُلٌ مِنْ أَشْرَافِ النَّاسِ، هَذَا وَاللَّهِ حَرِيٌّ إِنْ خَطَبَ أَنْ يُنْكَحَ، وَإِنْ شَفَعَ أَنْ يُشَفَّعَ. قَالَ فَسَكَتَ رَسُولُ اللَّهِ صلى الله عليه وسلم ثُمَّ مَرَّ رَجُلٌ فَقَالَ لَهُ رَسُولُ اللَّهِ صلى الله عليه وسلم " مَا رَأْيُكَ فِي هَذَا ". فَقَالَ يَا رَسُولَ اللَّهِ هَذَا رَجُلٌ مِنْ فُقَرَاءِ الْمُسْلِمِينَ، هَذَا حَرِيٌّ إِنْ خَطَبَ أَنْ لاَ

يُنْكَحَ، وَإِنْ شَفَعَ أَنْ لاَ يُشَفَّعَ، وَإِنْ قَالَ أَنْ لاَ يُسْمَعَ لِقَوْلِهِ. فَقَالَ رَسُولُ اللَّهِ صلى الله عليه وسلم " هَذَا خَيْرٌ مِنْ مِلْءِ الأَرْضِ مِثْلَ هَذَا "

Narrated Al-Bara 'bin `Azib: A piece of silken cloth was given to the Prophetﷺ as a present and the people handed it over amongst themselves and were astonished at its beauty and softness. Allah's Messengerﷺ said, "Are you astonished at it?" They said, "Yes, O Allah's Messengerﷺ !" He said, "By Him in Whose Hand my soul is, the handkerchiefs of Sa`d in Paradise are better than it." – Al-Bukhari 6640
حَدَّثَنَا مُحَمَّدٌ، حَدَّثَنَا أَبُو الأَحْوَصِ، عَنْ أَبِي إِسْحَاقَ، عَنِ الْبَرَاءِ بْنِ عَازِبٍ، قَالَ أُهْدِيَ إِلَى النَّبِيِّ صلى الله عليه وسلم سَرَقَةٌ مِنْ حَرِيرٍ، فَجَعَلَ النَّاسُ يَتَدَاوَلُونَهَا بَيْنَهُمْ، وَيَعْجَبُونَ مِنْ حُسْنِهَا وَلِينِهَا، فَقَالَ رَسُولُ اللَّهِ صلى الله عليه وسلم " أَتَعْجَبُونَ مِنْهَا ". قَالُوا نَعَمْ يَا رَسُولَ اللَّهِ. قَالَ " وَالَّذِي نَفْسِي بِيَدِهِ لَمَنَادِيلُ سَعْدٍ فِي الْجَنَّةِ خَيْرٌ مِنْهَا ". لَمْ يَقُلْ شُعْبَةُ وَإِسْرَائِيلُ عَنْ أَبِي إِسْحَاقَ " وَالَّذِي نَفْسِي بِيَدِهِ ".

Narrated `Aisha: Hind bint `Utba bin Rabi`a said, "O Allah 's Apostle! (Before I embraced Islam), there was no family on the surface of the earth, I wish to have degraded more than I did your family. But today there is no family whom I wish to have honored more than I did yours." Allah's Messengerﷺ said, "I thought similarly, by Him in Whose Hand Muhammad's soul is!" Hind said, "O Allah's Messengerﷺ ! (My husband) Abu Sufyan is a miser. Is it sinful of me to feed my children from his property?" The Prophet said, "No, unless you take it for your needs what is just and reasonable." – Al-Bukhari 6641
حَدَّثَنَا يَحْيَى بْنُ بُكَيْرٍ، حَدَّثَنَا اللَّيْثُ، عَنْ يُونُسَ، عَنِ ابْنِ شِهَابٍ، حَدَّثَنِي عُرْوَةُ بْنُ الزُّبَيْرِ، أَنَّ عَائِشَةَ ـ رضى الله عنها ـ قَالَتْ إِنَّ هِنْدَ بِنْتَ عُتْبَةَ بْنِ رَبِيعَةَ قَالَتْ يَا رَسُولَ اللَّهِ مَا كَانَ مِمَّا عَلَى ظَهْرِ الأَرْضِ أَهْلُ أَخْبَاءٍ ـ أَوْ خِبَاءٍ ـ أَحَبَّ إِلَىَّ أَنْ يَذِلُّوا مِنْ أَهْلِ أَخْبَائِكَ ـ أَوْ خِبَائِكَ، شَكَّ يَحْيَى ـ ثُمَّ مَا أَصْبَحَ الْيَوْمَ أَهْلُ أَخْبَاءٍ ـ أَوْ خِبَاءٍ ـ أَحَبَّ إِلَىَّ مِنْ أَنْ يَعِزُّوا مِنْ أَهْلِ أَخْبَائِكَ أَوْ خِبَائِكَ. قَالَ رَسُولُ اللَّهِ صلى الله عليه وسلم " وَأَيْضًا وَالَّذِي نَفْسُ مُحَمَّدٍ بِيَدِهِ ". قَالَتْ يَا رَسُولَ اللَّهِ إِنَّ أَبَا سُفْيَانَ رَجُلٌ مِسِّيكٌ، فَهَلْ عَلَىَّ حَرَجٌ أَنْ أُطْعِمَ مِنَ الَّذِي لَهُ قَالَ " لاَ إِلاَّ بِالْمَعْرُوفِ "

Narrated Ibn `Umar: Allah's Messengerﷺ had a gold ring made for himself, and he used to wear it with the stone towards the inner part of his hand. Consequently, the people had similar rings made for themselves. Afterwards the Prophet; sat on the pulpit and took it off, saying, "I used to wear this ring and keep its stone towards the palm of my hand." He then threw it away and said, "By Allah, I will never wear it." Therefore all the people threw away their rings as well. – Al-Bukhari 6651
حَدَّثَنَا قُتَيْبَةُ، حَدَّثَنَا اللَّيْثُ، عَنْ نَافِعٍ، عَنِ ابْنِ عُمَرَ ـ رضى الله عنهما ـ أَنَّ رَسُولَ اللَّهِ صلى الله عليه وسلم اصْطَنَعَ خَاتَمًا مِنْ ذَهَبٍ وَكَانَ يَلْبَسُهُ، فَيَجْعَلُ فَصَّهُ فِي بَاطِنِ كَفِّهِ، فَصَنَعَ النَّاسُ خَوَاتِيمَ ثُمَّ إِنَّهُ جَلَسَ عَلَى الْمِنْبَرِ فَنَزَعَهُ، فَقَالَ " إِنِّي كُنْتُ أَلْبَسُ هَذَا الْخَاتِمَ وَأَجْعَلُ فَصَّهُ مِنْ دَاخِلٍ ". فَرَمَى بِهِ ثُمَّ قَالَ " وَاللَّهِ لاَ أَلْبَسُهُ أَبَدًا ". فَنَبَذَ النَّاسُ خَوَاتِيمَهُمْ

Narrated Ka`b bin Malik: In the last part of his narration about the three who remained behind (from the battle of Tabuk). (I said) "As a proof of my true repentance (for not joining the Holy battle of Tabuk), I shall give up all my property for the sake of Allah and His Apostle (as an expiation for that sin)." The Prophetﷺ said (to me), "Keep some of your wealth, for that is better for you." – Al-Bukhari 6690
حَدَّثَنَا أَحْمَدُ بْنُ صَالِحٍ، حَدَّثَنَا ابْنُ وَهْبٍ، أَخْبَرَنِي يُونُسُ، عَنِ ابْنِ شِهَابٍ، أَخْبَرَنِي عَبْدُ الرَّحْمَنِ، عَنْ عَبْدِ اللَّهِ بْنِ كَعْبِ بْنِ مَالِكٍ، وَكَانَ، قَائِدَ كَعْبٍ مِنْ بَنِيهِ حِينَ عَمِيَ ـ قَالَ سَمِعْتُ كَعْبَ بْنَ مَالِكٍ، فِي حَدِيثِهِ {ۚعَلَى الثَّلاَثَةِ الَّذِينَ خُلِّفُوا} قَالَ فِي آخِرِ حَدِيثِهِ إِنَّ مِنْ تَوْبَتِي أَنِّي أَنْخَلِعُ مِنْ مَالِي صَدَقَةً إِلَى اللَّهِ وَرَسُولِهِ. فَقَالَ النَّبِيُّ صلى الله عليه وسلم " أَمْسِكْ عَلَيْكَ بَعْضَ مَالِكَ فَهْوَ خَيْرٌ لَكَ ".

Narrated Ibn `Abbas: The Prophetﷺ saw a dead sheep which had been given in charity to a freed slave-girl of Maimuna, the wife of the Prophetﷺ . The Prophetﷺ said, "Why don't you get the benefit of its hide?" They said, "It is dead." He replied, "Only to eat (its meat) is illegal." – Al-Bukhari 1492

حَدَّثَنَا سَعِيدُ بْنُ عُفَيْرٍ، حَدَّثَنَا ابْنُ وَهْبٍ، عَنْ يُونُسَ، عَنِ ابْنِ شِهَابٍ، حَدَّثَنِي عُبَيْدُ اللَّهِ بْنُ عَبْدِ اللَّهِ، عَنِ ابْنِ عَبَّاسٍ ـ رضى الله عنهما ـ قَالَ وَجَدَ النَّبِيُّ صلى الله عليه وسلم شَاةً مَيِّتَةً أُعْطِيَتْهَا مَوْلاَةٌ لِمَيْمُونَةَ مِنَ الصَّدَقَةِ، قَالَ النَّبِيُّ صلى الله عليه وسلم " هَلاَّ انْتَفَعْتُمْ بِجِلْدِهَا ". قَالُوا إِنَّهَا مَيْتَةٌ. قَالَ " إِنَّمَا حَرُمَ أَكْلُهَا "

Narrated `Ali: The Prophet ﷺ sent me to supervise the (slaughtering of) Budn (Hadi camels) and ordered me to distribute their meat, and then he ordered me to distribute their covering sheets and skins. 'All added, "The Prophet ﷺ ordered me to supervise the slaughtering (of the Budn) and not to give anything (of their bodies) to the butcher as wages for slaughtering." – Al-Bukhari 1716

حَدَّثَنَا مُحَمَّدُ بْنُ كَثِيرٍ، أَخْبَرَنَا سُفْيَانُ، قَالَ أَخْبَرَنِي ابْنُ أَبِي نَجِيحٍ، عَنْ مُجَاهِدٍ، عَنْ عَبْدِ الرَّحْمَنِ بْنِ أَبِي لَيْلَى، عَنْ عَلِيٍّ ـ رضى الله عنه ـ قَالَ بَعَثَنِي النَّبِيُّ صلى الله عليه وسلم فَقُمْتُ عَلَى الْبُدْنِ، فَأَمَرَنِي فَقَسَمْتُ لُحُومَهَا، ثُمَّ أَمَرَنِي فَقَسَمْتُ جِلاَلَهَا وَجُلُودَهَا. قَالَ سُفْيَانُ وَحَدَّثَنِي عَبْدُ الْكَرِيمِ، عَنْ مُجَاهِدٍ، عَنْ عَبْدِ الرَّحْمَنِ بْنِ أَبِي لَيْلَى، عَنْ عَلِيٍّ ـ رضى الله عنه ـ قَالَ أَمَرَنِي النَّبِيُّ صلى الله عليه وسلم أَنْ أَقُومَ عَلَى الْبُدْنِ، وَلاَ أُعْطِيَ عَلَيْهَا شَيْئًا فِي جِزَارَتِهَا

Narrated Abu Huraira: The Prophet ﷺ said, "Let the slave of Dinar and Dirham of Quantify and Khamisa (i.e. money and luxurious clothes) perish for he is pleased if these things are given to him, and if not, he is displeased!" – Al-Bukhari 2886

حَدَّثَنَا يَحْيَى بْنُ يُوسُفَ، أَخْبَرَنَا أَبُو بَكْرٍ، عَنْ أَبِي حَصِينٍ، عَنْ أَبِي صَالِحٍ، عَنْ أَبِي هُرَيْرَةَ ـ رضى الله عنه ـ عَنِ النَّبِيِّ صلى الله عليه وسلم قَالَ " تَعِسَ عَبْدُ الدِّينَارِ وَالدِّرْهَمِ وَالْقَطِيفَةِ وَالْخَمِيصَةِ، إِنْ أُعْطِيَ رَضِيَ، وَإِنْ لَمْ يُعْطَ لَمْ يَرْضَ ". لَمْ يَرْفَعْهُ إِسْرَائِيلُ عَنْ أَبِي حَصِينٍ

Narrated Ibn `Umar: `Umar saw a silken cloak being sold in the market and he brought it to Allah's Messenger ﷺ and said, "O Allah's Messenger ﷺ ! Buy this cloak and adorn yourself with it on the `Id festivals and on meeting the delegations." Allah's Messenger ﷺ replied, "This is the dress for the one who will have no share in the Hereafter (or, this is worn by one who will have no share in the Hereafter)." After sometime had passed, Allah's Messenger ﷺ sent a silken cloak to `Umar. `Umar took it and brought it to Allah's Messenger ﷺ and said, "O Allah's Messenger ﷺ ! You have said that this is the dress of that who will have no share in the Hereafter (or, this is worn by one who will have no share in the Hereafter), yet you have sent me this!" The Prophet ﷺ said," I have sent it) so that you may sell it or fulfill with it some of your needs." – Al-Bukhari 3054

حَدَّثَنَا يَحْيَى بْنُ بُكَيْرٍ، حَدَّثَنَا اللَّيْثُ، عَنْ عُقَيْلٍ، عَنِ ابْنِ شِهَابٍ، عَنْ سَالِمِ بْنِ عَبْدِ اللَّهِ، أَنَّ ابْنَ عُمَرَ ـ رضى الله عنهما ـ قَالَ وَجَدَ عُمَرُ حُلَّةَ إِسْتَبْرَقٍ تُبَاعُ فِي السُّوقِ فَأَتَى بِهَا رَسُولَ اللَّهِ صلى الله عليه وسلم فَقَالَ يَا رَسُولَ اللَّهِ، ابْتَعْ هَذِهِ الْحُلَّةَ فَتَجَمَّلْ بِهَا لِلْعِيدِ وَلِلْوُفُودِ. فَقَالَ رَسُولُ اللَّهِ صلى الله عليه وسلم " إِنَّمَا هَذِهِ لِبَاسُ مَنْ لاَ خَلاَقَ لَهُ، أَوْ إِنَّمَا يَلْبَسُ هَذِهِ مَنْ لاَ خَلاَقَ لَهُ ". فَلَبِثَ مَا شَاءَ اللَّهُ ثُمَّ أَرْسَلَ إِلَيْهِ النَّبِيُّ صلى الله عليه وسلم بِجُبَّةِ دِيبَاجٍ، فَأَقْبَلَ بِهَا عُمَرُ حَتَّى أَتَى بِهَا رَسُولَ اللَّهِ صلى الله عليه وسلم فَقَالَ يَا رَسُولَ اللَّهِ، قُلْتَ " إِنَّمَا هَذِهِ لِبَاسُ مَنْ لاَ خَلاَقَ لَهُ أَوْ إِنَّمَا يَلْبَسُ هَذِهِ مَنْ لاَ خَلاَقَ لَهُ ". ثُمَّ أَرْسَلْتَ إِلَىَّ بِهَذِهِ فَقَالَ " تَبِيعُهَا، أَوْ تُصِيبُ بِهَا بَعْضَ حَاجَتِكَ "

Narrated `Imran bin Husain: The Prophet ﷺ said, "I looked at Paradise and found poor people forming the majority of its inhabitants; and I looked at Hell and saw that the majority of its inhabitants were women." – Al-Bukhari 3241

حَدَّثَنَا أَبُو الْوَلِيدِ، حَدَّثَنَا سَلْمُ بْنُ زَرِيرٍ، حَدَّثَنَا أَبُو رَجَاءٍ، عَنْ عِمْرَانَ بْنِ حُصَيْنٍ، عَنِ النَّبِيِّ صلى الله عليه وسلم قَالَ " اطَّلَعْتُ فِي الْجَنَّةِ فَرَأَيْتُ أَكْثَرَ أَهْلِهَا الْفُقَرَاءَ، وَاطَّلَعْتُ فِي النَّارِ فَرَأَيْتُ أَكْثَرَ أَهْلِهَا النِّسَاءَ "

"O David, We made you a ruler in the land, so judge between the people with justice, and do not follow desire, lest it diverts you from Allah's path. Those who stray from Allah's path will have a painful punishment, for having ignored the Day of Account." – Surah Sad 38:26

يَـٰدَاوُۥدُ إِنَّا جَعَلْنَـٰكَ خَلِيفَةً فِى ٱلْأَرْضِ فَٱحْكُم بَيْنَ ٱلنَّاسِ بِٱلْحَقِّ وَلَا تَتَّبِعِ ٱلْهَوَىٰ فَيُضِلَّكَ عَن سَبِيلِ ٱللَّهِ ۚ إِنَّ ٱلَّذِينَ يَضِلُّونَ عَن سَبِيلِ ٱللَّهِ لَهُمْ عَذَابٌ شَدِيدٌۢ بِمَا نَسُوا۟ يَوْمَ ٱلْحِسَابِ

Narrated Abu Dhar: Once, while I was in the company of the Prophet, he saw the mountain of Uhud and said, "I would not like to have this mountain turned into gold for me unless nothing of it, not even a single Dinar remains of it with me for more than three days (i.e. I will spend all of it in Allah's Cause), except that Dinar which I will keep for repaying debts." Then he said, "Those who are rich in this world would have little reward in the Hereafter except those who spend their money here and there (in Allah's Cause), and they are few in number." Then he ordered me to stay at my place and went not far away. I heard a voice and intended to go to him but I remembered his order, "Stay at your place till I return." On his return I said, "O Allah's Messenger ﷺ ! (What was) that noise which I heard?" He said, "Did you hear anything?" I said, "Yes." He said, "Gabriel came and said to me, 'Whoever amongst your followers dies, worshipping none along with Allah, will enter Paradise.' " I said, "Even if he did such-and-such things (i.e. even if he stole or committed illegal sexual intercourse)" He said, "Yes." – Al-Bukhari 2388 & 6268

حَدَّثَنَا أَحْمَدُ بْنُ يُونُسَ، حَدَّثَنَا أَبُو شِهَابٍ، عَنِ الأَعْمَشِ، عَنْ زَيْدِ بْنِ وَهْبٍ، عَنْ أَبِي ذَرٍّ ـ رضى الله عنه ـ قَالَ كُنْتُ مَعَ النَّبِيِّ صلى الله عليه وسلم فَلَمَّا أَبْصَرَ ـ يَعْنِي أُحُدًا ـ قَالَ " مَا أُحِبُّ أَنَّهُ يُحَوَّلُ لِي ذَهَبًا يَمْكُثُ عِنْدِي مِنْهُ دِينَارٌ فَوْقَ ثَلاَثٍ، إِلاَّ دِينَارًا أُرْصِدُهُ لِدَيْنٍ ". ثُمَّ قَالَ " إِنَّ الأَكْثَرِينَ هُمُ الأَقَلُّونَ، إِلاَّ مَنْ قَالَ بِالْمَالِ هَكَذَا وَهَكَذَا ". وَأَشَارَ أَبُو شِهَابٍ بَيْنَ يَدَيْهِ وَعَنْ يَمِينِهِ وَعَنْ شِمَالِهِ ـ وَقَلِيلٌ مَا هُمْ ـ وَقَالَ مَكَانَكَ. وَتَقَدَّمَ غَيْرَ بَعِيدٍ، فَسَمِعْتُ صَوْتًا، فَأَرَدْتُ أَنْ آتِيَهُ، ثُمَّ ذَكَرْتُ قَوْلَهُ مَكَانَكَ حَتَّى آتِيَكَ، فَلَمَّا جَاءَ قُلْتُ يَا رَسُولَ اللَّهِ، الَّذِي سَمِعْتُ أَوْ قَالَ الصَّوْتُ الَّذِي سَمِعْتُ قَالَ " وَهَلْ سَمِعْتَ ". قُلْتُ نَعَمْ. قَالَ " أَتَانِي جِبْرِيلُ ـ عَلَيْهِ السَّلاَمُ ـ فَقَالَ مَنْ مَاتَ مِنْ أُمَّتِكَ لاَ يُشْرِكُ بِاللَّهِ شَيْئًا دَخَلَ الْجَنَّةَ ". قُلْتُ وَإِنْ فَعَلَ كَذَا وَكَذَا قَالَ " نَعَمْ "

Narrated Abu Huraira: Allah's Messenger ﷺ said, "A woman called her son while he was in his hermitage and said, 'O Juraij' He said, 'O Allah, my mother (is calling me) and (I am offering) my prayer (what shall I do)?' She again said, 'O Juraij!' He said again, 'O Allah ! My mother (is calling me) and (I am offering) my prayer (what shall I do)?' She again said, 'O Juraij' He again said, 'O Allah! My mother (is calling me) and (I am offering) my prayer. (What shall I do?)' She said, 'O Allah! Do not let Juraij die till he sees the faces of prostitutes.' A shepherdess used to come by his hermitage for grazing her sheep and she gave birth to a child. She was asked whose child that was, and she replied that it was from Juraij and that he had come out from his hermitage. Juraij said, 'Where is that woman who claims that her child is from me?' (When she was brought to him along with the child), Juraij asked the child, 'O Babus, who is your father?' The child replied, 'The shepherd.' " (See Hadith No 662. Vol 3). – Sahih al-Bukhari 1206

وَقَالَ اللَّيْثُ حَدَّثَنِي جَعْفَرٌ، عَنْ عَبْدِ الرَّحْمَنِ بْنِ هُرْمُزَ، قَالَ قَالَ أَبُو هُرَيْرَةَ ـ رضى الله عنه ـ قَالَ رَسُولُ اللَّهِ صلى الله عليه وسلم " نَادَتِ امْرَأَةٌ ابْنَهَا، وَهْوَ فِي صَوْمَعَةٍ قَالَتْ يَا جُرَيْجُ. قَالَ اللَّهُمَّ أُمِّي وَصَلاَتِي. قَالَتْ يَا جُرَيْجُ. قَالَ اللَّهُمَّ أُمِّي وَصَلاَتِي. قَالَتْ يَا جُرَيْجُ. قَالَ اللَّهُمَّ أُمِّي وَصَلاَتِي. قَالَتِ اللَّهُمَّ لاَ يَمُوتُ جُرَيْجٌ حَتَّى يَنْظُرَ فِي وَجْهِ الْمَيَامِيسِ. وَكَانَتْ تَأْوِي إِلَى صَوْمَعَتِهِ رَاعِيَةٌ تَرْعَى الْغَنَمَ فَوَلَدَتْ فَقِيلَ لَهَا مِمَّنْ هَذَا الْوَلَدُ قَالَتْ مِنْ جُرَيْجٍ نَزَلَ مِنْ صَوْمَعَتِهِ. قَالَ جُرَيْجٌ أَيْنَ هَذِهِ الَّتِي تَزْعُمُ أَنَّ وَلَدَهَا لِي قَالَ يَا بَابُوسُ مَنْ أَبُوكَ قَالَ رَاعِي الْغَنَمِ ".

But you took them (in) mockery until they made you forget My remembrance, and you used (to) at them laugh. – Surah Al-Mu'mimun 23:110

فَٱتَّخَذْتُمُوهُمْ سِخْرِيًّا حَتَّىٰٓ أَنسَوْكُمْ ذِكْرِى وَكُنتُم مِّنْهُمْ تَضْحَكُونَ

And who does more wrong than those who, when reminded of their Lord's revelations, turn away from them and forget what their own hands have done? We have certainly cast veils over their hearts—leaving them unable to comprehend this ⌜Quran⌝—and deafness in their ears. And if you ⌜O Prophet⌝ invite them to ⌜true⌝ guidance, they will never be ⌜rightly⌝ guided. – Surah Al-Kahf 18:57

وَمَنۡ أَظۡلَمُ مِمَّن ذُكِّرَ بِـَٔايَٰتِ رَبِّهِۦ فَأَعۡرَضَ عَنۡهَا وَنَسِيَ مَا قَدَّمَتۡ يَدَاهُۚ إِنَّا جَعَلۡنَا عَلَىٰ قُلُوبِهِمۡ أَكِنَّةً أَن يَفۡقَهُوهُ وَفِيٓ ءَاذَانِهِمۡ وَقۡرٗاۖ وَإِن تَدۡعُهُمۡ إِلَى ٱلۡهُدَىٰ فَلَن يَهۡتَدُوٓاْ إِذًا أَبَدٗا

Surely the losers are they who lose their (own) selves and their own families on the Day of the Resurrection

إِنَّ ٱلۡخَٰسِرِينَ ٱلَّذِينَ خَسِرُوٓاْ أَنفُسَهُمۡ وَأَهۡلِيهِمۡ يَوۡمَ ٱلۡقِيَٰمَةِۗ

Say, "To whom (belongs) whatever is in the heavens and the earth?" Say, "To Allah." He has prescribed for Himself (the) mercy. Indeed He will definitely gather you to the Day of the Resurrection; there is no suspicion about it. The ones who have lost their (own) selves; so they do not believe. – Surah Al-An'am 6:12

قُل لِّمَن مَّا فِي ٱلسَّمَٰوَٰتِ وَٱلۡأَرۡضِۖ قُل لِّلَّهِۚ كَتَبَ عَلَىٰ نَفۡسِهِ ٱلرَّحۡمَةَۚ لَيَجۡمَعَنَّكُمۡ إِلَىٰ يَوۡمِ ٱلۡقِيَٰمَةِ لَا رَيۡبَ فِيهِۚ ٱلَّذِينَ خَسِرُوٓاْ أَنفُسَهُمۡ فَهُمۡ لَا يُؤۡمِنُونَ

And you will see them set before (the Fire), submissive in humbleness, looking with the furtive (Literally: concealed) glance. And the ones who have believed will say, "Surely the losers are they who lose their (own) selves and their own families on the Day of the Resurrection. Verily the unjust are surely in perpetual torment." – Surah Ash-Shura 42:45

وَتَرَىٰهُمۡ يُعۡرَضُونَ عَلَيۡهَا خَٰشِعِينَ مِنَ ٱلذُّلِّ يَنظُرُونَ مِن طَرۡفٍ خَفِيّٖۗ وَقَالَ ٱلَّذِينَ ءَامَنُوٓاْ إِنَّ ٱلۡخَٰسِرِينَ ٱلَّذِينَ خَسِرُوٓاْ أَنفُسَهُمۡ وَأَهۡلِيهِمۡ يَوۡمَ ٱلۡقِيَٰمَةِۗ أَلَآ إِنَّ ٱلظَّٰلِمِينَ فِي عَذَابٖ مُّقِيمٖ

Then they will not be able to make any testament, nor will they return to their families. – Surah Ya Sin 36:50

فَلَا يَسۡتَطِيعُونَ تَوۡصِيَةٗ وَلَآ إِلَىٰٓ أَهۡلِهِمۡ يَرۡجِعُونَ

So worship whatever you decide on, apart from Him." Say, "Surely the losers are they who lose their (own) selves and their own families on the Day of the Resurrection. Verily that is the evident, all-deserved loss.". – Surah Az-Zumar 39:15

فَٱعۡبُدُواْ مَا شِئۡتُم مِّن دُونِهِۦۗ قُلۡ إِنَّ ٱلۡخَٰسِرِينَ ٱلَّذِينَ خَسِرُوٓاْ أَنفُسَهُمۡ وَأَهۡلِيهِمۡ يَوۡمَ ٱلۡقِيَٰمَةِۗ أَلَا ذَٰلِكَ هُوَ ٱلۡخُسۡرَانُ ٱلۡمُبِينُ

....do not slacken in Remembrance of Me...

....وَلَا تَنِيَا فِي ذِكۡرِي ....

Surely the ones who are pious, when a visitation of Ash-Shaytan (the all-vicious (one), i.e., the Devil) touches them, remind themselves, then, only then are they (clear) beholders. Surah Al-A'raf 7:201

إِنَّ ٱلَّذِينَ ٱتَّقَوۡاْ إِذَا مَسَّهُمۡ طَٰٓئِفٞ مِّنَ ٱلشَّيۡطَٰنِ تَذَكَّرُواْ فَإِذَا هُم مُّبۡصِرُونَ

....take hold of the Book with steadfastness... - Surah Maryam 19:12

....خُذِ ٱلۡكِتَٰبَ بِقُوَّةٖ.....

.....and establish prayer for My remembrance...... Surah TaHa 20:19

....وَأَقِمِ ٱلصَّلَوٰةَ لِذِكۡرِيٓ ....

Said (Allah) He, "Thus it is. Our signs came up to you, yet you forgot them; and thus today you are forgotten." – Surah TaHa 20:126

قَالَ كَذَٰلِكَ أَتَتْكَ ءَايَـٰتُنَا فَنَسِيتَهَا ۖ وَكَذَٰلِكَ ٱلْيَوْمَ تُنسَىٰ

And whoever is blinded from remembrance of the Most Merciful – We appoint for him a devil, and he is to him a companion. Surah Az-Zukhruf 43:36

وَمَن يَعْشُ عَن ذِكْرِ ٱلرَّحْمَـٰنِ نُقَيِّضْ لَهُۥ شَيْطَـٰنًا فَهُوَ لَهُۥ قَرِينٌ

So in no way will the intercession of the intercessors profit them Then what is it with them that they are veering away from the Reminder. – Surah Al-Mudathir 74:48&49

فَمَا تَنفَعُهُمْ شَفَـٰعَةُ ٱلشَّـٰفِعِينَ فَمَا لَهُمْ عَنِ ٱلتَّذْكِرَةِ مُعْرِضِينَ

Satan has taken hold of them, causing them to forget the remembrance of Allah. They are the party of Satan. Surely Satan's party is bound to lose. – Surah Al-Mujadilah 58:19

ٱسْتَحْوَذَ عَلَيْهِمُ ٱلشَّيْطَـٰنُ فَأَنسَىٰهُمْ ذِكْرَ ٱللَّهِ ۚ أُو۟لَـٰٓئِكَ حِزْبُ ٱلشَّيْطَـٰنِ ۚ أَلَآ إِنَّ حِزْبَ ٱلشَّيْطَـٰنِ هُمُ ٱلْخَـٰسِرُونَ

And do not be like those who forgot Allah, so He made them forget themselves. It is they who are ˹truly˺ rebellious. – Surah Al-Hashr 59:19

وَلَا تَكُونُوا۟ كَٱلَّذِينَ نَسُوا۟ ٱللَّهَ فَأَنسَىٰهُمْ أَنفُسَهُمْ ۚ أُو۟لَـٰٓئِكَ هُمُ ٱلْفَـٰسِقُونَ

Indeed he readily made me err away from the Remembrance after it had come to me." And Ash-Shaytan (i.e., dwelling habitation) has been constantly abandoning man. – Surah Al-Furqan 25:29

لَّقَدْ أَضَلَّنِى عَنِ ٱلذِّكْرِ بَعْدَ إِذْ جَآءَنِى ۗ وَكَانَ ٱلشَّيْطَـٰنُ لِلْإِنسَـٰنِ خَذُولًا

The Book of
His Grace is in His Hand to bestow it on whomsoever He wills
ٱلۡفَضۡلَ بِيَدِ ٱللَّهِ يُؤۡتِيهِ مَن يَشَآءُ

Miserable is what they sold their souls for—rejecting what Allah has revealed, out of resentment that Allah would send down His grace upon whomever He chooses from among His servants. Thus they incurred wrath upon wrath. And there is a demeaning punishment for the disbelievers. – Surah Al-Baqarah 2:90
بِئۡسَمَا ٱشۡتَرَوۡاْ بِهِۦٓ أَنفُسَهُمۡ أَن يَكۡفُرُواْ بِمَآ أَنزَلَ ٱللَّهُ بَغۡيًا أَن يُنَزِّلَ ٱللَّهُ مِن فَضۡلِهِۦ عَلَىٰ مَن يَشَآءُ مِنۡ عِبَادِهِۦۖ فَبَآءُو بِغَضَبٍ عَلَىٰ غَضَبٍۚ وَلِلۡكَٰفِرِينَ عَذَابٌ مُّهِينٌ

It is never the wish of the disbelievers from among the People of the Book, nor of the polytheists, that any good should be sent down to you from your Lord. But Allah chooses for His mercy whomever He wills. Allah is Possessor of Sublime Grace. – Surah Al-Baqarah 2:105
مَّا يَوَدُّ ٱلَّذِينَ كَفَرُواْ مِنۡ أَهۡلِ ٱلۡكِتَٰبِ وَلَا ٱلۡمُشۡرِكِينَ أَن يُنَزَّلَ عَلَيۡكُم مِّنۡ خَيۡرٖ مِّن رَّبِّكُمۡۚ وَٱللَّهُ يَخۡتَصُّ بِرَحۡمَتِهِۦ مَن يَشَآءُۚ وَٱللَّهُ ذُو ٱلۡفَضۡلِ ٱلۡعَظِيمِ

Have you not considered those who claim purity for themselves? Rather, Allah purifies whom He wills, and they will not be wronged in the least. – Surah An-Nisa 4:49
أَلَمۡ تَرَ إِلَى ٱلَّذِينَ يُزَكُّونَ أَنفُسَهُمۚ بَلِ ٱللَّهُ يُزَكِّي مَن يَشَآءُ وَلَا يُظۡلَمُونَ فَتِيلًا

Race towards forgiveness from your Lord; and a Garden as vast as the heavens and the earth, prepared for those who believe in Allah and His messengers. That is the grace of Allah; He bestows it on whomever He wills. Allah is the Possessor of Immense Grace. – Surah Al-Hadid 57:21
سَابِقُوٓاْ إِلَىٰ مَغۡفِرَةٖ مِّن رَّبِّكُمۡ وَجَنَّةٍ عَرۡضُهَا كَعَرۡضِ ٱلسَّمَآءِ وَٱلۡأَرۡضِ أُعِدَّتۡ لِلَّذِينَ ءَامَنُواْ بِٱللَّهِ وَرُسُلِهِۦۚ ذَٰلِكَ فَضۡلُ ٱللَّهِ يُؤۡتِيهِ مَن يَشَآءُۚ وَٱللَّهُ ذُو ٱلۡفَضۡلِ ٱلۡعَظِيمِ

That the People of the Book may know that they have no power whatsoever over Allah's grace, and that all grace is in Allah's hand; He gives it to whomever He wills. Allah is Possessor of Great Grace. – Surah Al-Hadid 57:29
لِّئَلَّا يَعۡلَمَ أَهۡلُ ٱلۡكِتَٰبِ أَلَّا يَقۡدِرُونَ عَلَىٰ شَيۡءٖ مِّن فَضۡلِ ٱللَّهِ وَأَنَّ ٱلۡفَضۡلَ بِيَدِ ٱللَّهِ يُؤۡتِيهِ مَن يَشَآءُۚ وَٱللَّهُ ذُو ٱلۡفَضۡلِ ٱلۡعَظِيمِ

And others from them, who have not yet joined them. He is the Glorious, the Wise. That is Allah's grace, which He grants to whomever He wills. Allah is Possessor of limitless grace. – Surah Al-Jumu'ah 62:3&4
وَءَاخَرِينَ مِنۡهُمۡ لَمَّا يَلۡحَقُواْ بِهِمۡۚ وَهُوَ ٱلۡعَزِيزُ ٱلۡحَكِيمُ ذَٰلِكَ فَضۡلُ ٱللَّهِ يُؤۡتِيهِ مَن يَشَآءُۚ وَٱللَّهُ ذُو ٱلۡفَضۡلِ ٱلۡعَظِيمِ

He is high above [all] ranks, the Lord of the Throne. He confers the Spirit by His command on whoever He wills of His worshipers to warn of the Day when they will meet Him. Surah Al-Ghafir 40:15
رَفِيعُ ٱلدَّرَجَٰتِ ذُو ٱلۡعَرۡشِ يُلۡقِي ٱلرُّوحَ مِنۡ أَمۡرِهِۦ عَلَىٰ مَن يَشَآءُ مِنۡ عِبَادِهِۦ لِيُنذِرَ يَوۡمَ ٱلتَّلَاقِ

So, whomever Allah wills to guide, He expands his breast to Islam
فَمَن يُرِدِ ٱللَّهُ أَن يَهْدِيَهُۥ يَشْرَحْ صَدْرَهُۥ لِلْإِسْلَٰمِ

And in no way were they commanded anything except to worship Allah, making the religion His faithfully (and) unswerving, and to keep up prayer, and bring the Zakat; (i.e., pay the poor-dues) and that is the Religion most upright – Surah Al-Baiyinah 98:5
وَمَا أُمِرُوا إِلَّا لِيَعْبُدُوا اللَّهَ مُخْلِصِينَ لَهُ الدِّينَ حُنَفَاءَ وَيُقِيمُوا الصَّلَاةَ وَيُؤْتُوا الزَّكَاةَ وَذَٰلِكَ دِينُ الْقَيِّمَةِ

And that you should worship Me? This is a straight Path. – Surah Ya-Sin 36:61
وَأَنِ ٱعْبُدُونِىۚ هَٰذَا صِرَٰطٌ مُّسْتَقِيمٌ

For, behold, it is We who have bestowed this revelation upon thee from on high, setting forth the truth: so worship Him, sincere in thy faith in Him alone Is it not to Allah alone that all sincere faith is due? And yet, they who take for their protectors aught beside Him [are wont to say], "We worship them for no other reason than that they bring us nearer to Allah." Behold, Allah will judge between them [on Resurrection Day] with regard to all wherein they differ [from the truth]: for, verily, Allah does not grace with His guidance anyone who is bent on lying [to himself and is] stubbornly ingrate – Surah Az-Zumar 39:2&3
إِنَّآ أَنزَلْنَآ إِلَيْكَ ٱلْكِتَٰبَ بِٱلْحَقِّ فَٱعْبُدِ ٱللَّهَ مُخْلِصًا لَّهُ ٱلدِّينَ أَلَا لِلَّهِ ٱلدِّينُ ٱلْخَالِصُ وَٱلَّذِينَ ٱتَّخَذُوا۟ مِن دُونِهِۦٓ أَوْلِيَآءَ مَا نَعْبُدُهُمْ إِلَّا لِيُقَرِّبُونَآ إِلَى ٱللَّهِ زُلْفَىٰٓ إِنَّ ٱللَّهَ يَحْكُمُ بَيْنَهُمْ فِى مَا هُمْ فِيهِ يَخْتَلِفُونَ إِنَّ ٱللَّهَ لَا يَهْدِى مَنْ هُوَ كَٰذِبٌ كَفَّارٌ

Surely Allah, Ever He, is my Lord and your Lord; so worship Him. This is a straight Path.". – Surah Az-Zukhruf 43:64
إِنَّ ٱللَّهَ هُوَ رَبِّى وَرَبُّكُمْ فَٱعْبُدُوهُۚ هَٰذَا صِرَٰطٌ مُّسْتَقِيمٌ

So, whomever Allah wills to guide, He expands his breast to Islam; and whomever He wills to lead into error, He makes his breast straitened, restricted, as if he were laboriously climbing up in the heaven. Thus Allah sets (Literally: makes) abomination upon (the ones) who do not believe And this is the Path of your Lord, straight; We have already expounded the signs to a people who constantly remember – Surah Al-An'am 6:125&126
فَمَن يُرِدِ ٱللَّهُ أَن يَهْدِيَهُۥ يَشْرَحْ صَدْرَهُۥ لِلْإِسْلَٰمِ وَمَن يُرِدْ أَن يُضِلَّهُۥ يَجْعَلْ صَدْرَهُۥ ضَيِّقًا حَرَجًا كَأَنَّمَا يَصَّعَّدُ فِى ٱلسَّمَآءِ كَذَٰلِكَ يَجْعَلُ ٱللَّهُ ٱلرِّجْسَ عَلَى ٱلَّذِينَ لَا يُؤْمِنُونَ وَهَٰذَا صِرَٰطُ رَبِّكَ مُسْتَقِيمًا قَدْ فَصَّلْنَا ٱلْءَايَٰتِ لِقَوْمٍ يَذَّكَّرُونَ

So, as for the ones who believed in Allah and firmly adhered to Him, then He will soon cause them to enter into a mercy from Him, and Grace, and will guide them to Him on a straight Path – Surah An-Nisa 4:175
فَأَمَّا ٱلَّذِينَ ءَامَنُوا۟ بِٱللَّهِ وَٱعْتَصَمُوا۟ بِهِۦ فَسَيُدْخِلُهُمْ فِى رَحْمَةٍ مِّنْهُ وَفَضْلٍ وَيَهْدِيهِمْ إِلَيْهِ صِرَٰطًا مُّسْتَقِيمًا

And the ones who have striven in (our way), (Literally: in us) indeed We will definitely guide them to Our ways; and surely Allah is indeed with the fair-doers – Surah Al-Ankabut 29:69
وَالَّذِينَ جَٰهَدُوا فِينَا لَنَهْدِيَنَّهُمْ سُبُلَنَا وَإِنَّ اللَّهَ لَمَعَ الْمُحْسِنِينَ

The Book of
The year of the Elephant
ام الفيل

Have you not considered how your Lord dealt with the People of the Elephant? Did He not make their plan go wrong? He sent against them swarms of birds. Throwing at them rocks of baked clay. Leaving them like chewed-up leaves. . - Surah Al-Fil 105

أَلَمْ تَرَ كَيْفَ فَعَلَ رَبُّكَ بِأَصْحَـٰبِ ٱلْفِيلِ أَلَمْ يَجْعَلْ كَيْدَهُمْ فِى تَضْلِيلٍ وَأَرْسَلَ عَلَيْهِمْ طَيْرًا أَبَابِيلَ تَرْمِيهِم بِحِجَارَةٍ مِّن سِجِّيلٍ فَجَعَلَهُمْ كَعَصْفٍ مَّأْكُولٍ

Narrated Abu Huraira: In the year of the Conquest of Mecca, the tribe of Khuza`a killed a man from the tribe of Bam Laith in revenge for a killed person belonging to them in the Pre-Islamic Period of Ignorance. So Allah's Apostle got up saying, "Allah held back the (army having) elephants from Mecca, but He let His Apostle and the believers overpower the infidels (of Mecca). Beware! (Mecca is a sanctuary)! Verily! Fighting in Mecca was not permitted for anybody before me, nor will it be permitted for anybody after me; It was permitted for me only for a while (an hour or so) of that day. No doubt! It is at this moment a sanctuary; its thorny shrubs should not be uprooted; its trees should not be cut down; and its Luqata (fallen things) should not be picked up except by the one who would look for its owner. And if somebody is killed, his closest relative has the right to choose one of two things, i.e., either the Blood money or retaliation by having the killer killed." Then a man from Yemen, called Abu Shah, stood up and said, "Write that for me, O Allah's Messenger ﷺ !" Allah's Messenger ﷺ said (to his companions), "Write that for Abu Shah." Then another man from Quraish got up, saying, "O Allah's Messenger ﷺ ! Except Al- Idhkhir (a special kind of grass) as we use it in our houses and for graves." Allah's Messenger ﷺ said, "Except Al-idhkkir.". – Sahih Al-Bukhari 6880

حَدَّثَنَا أَبُو نُعَيْمٍ، حَدَّثَنَا شَيْبَانُ، عَنْ يَحْيَى، عَنْ أَبِي سَلَمَةَ، عَنْ أَبِي هُرَيْرَةَ، أَنَّ خُزَاعَةَ، قَتَلُوا رَجُلاً. وَقَالَ عَبْدُ اللَّهِ بْنُ رَجَاءٍ حَدَّثَنَا حَرْبٌ عَنْ يَحْيَى حَدَّثَنَا أَبُو سَلَمَةَ حَدَّثَنَا أَبُو هُرَيْرَةَ أَنَّهُ عَامَ فَتْحِ مَكَّةَ قَتَلَتْ خُزَاعَةُ رَجُلاً مِنْ بَنِي لَيْثٍ بِقَتِيلٍ لَهُمْ فِي الْجَاهِلِيَّةِ، فَقَامَ رَسُولُ اللَّهِ صلى الله عليه وسلم فَقَالَ " إِنَّ اللَّهَ حَبَسَ عَنْ مَكَّةَ الْفِيلَ وَسَلَّطَ عَلَيْهِمْ رَسُولَهُ وَالْمُؤْمِنِينَ، أَلاَ وَإِنَّهَا لَمْ تَحِلَّ لأَحَدٍ قَبْلِي، وَلاَ تَحِلُّ لأَحَدٍ بَعْدِي، أَلاَ وَإِنَّمَا أُحِلَّتْ لِي سَاعَةً مِنْ نَهَارٍ، أَلاَ وَإِنَّهَا سَاعَتِي هَذِهِ حَرَامٌ لاَ يُخْتَلَى شَوْكُهَا، وَلاَ يُعْضَدُ شَجَرُهَا، وَلاَ يَلْتَقِطُ سَاقِطَتَهَا إِلاَّ مُنْشِدٌ، وَمَنْ قُتِلَ لَهُ قَتِيلٌ فَهْوَ بِخَيْرِ النَّظَرَيْنِ إِمَّا يُودَى وَإِمَّا يُقَادُ ". فَقَامَ رَجُلٌ مِنْ أَهْلِ الْيَمَنِ يُقَالُ لَهُ أَبُو شَاهٍ فَقَالَ اكْتُبْ لِي يَا رَسُولَ اللَّهِ. فَقَالَ رَسُولُ اللَّهِ صلى الله عليه وسلم " اكْتُبُوا لأَبِي شَاهٍ ". ثُمَّ قَامَ رَجُلٌ مِنْ قُرَيْشٍ فَقَالَ يَا رَسُولَ اللَّهِ إِلاَّ الإِذْخِرَ، فَإِنَّمَا نَجْعَلُهُ فِي بُيُوتِنَا وَقُبُورِنَا. فَقَالَ رَسُولُ اللَّهِ صلى الله عليه وسلم " إِلاَّ الإِذْخِرَ ". وَتَابَعَهُ عُبَيْدُ اللَّهِ عَنْ شَيْبَانَ فِي الْفِيلِ، قَالَ بَعْضُهُمْ عَنْ أَبِي نُعَيْمٍ الْقَتْلَ. وَقَالَ عُبَيْدُ اللَّهِ إِمَّا أَنْ يُقَادَ أَهْلُ الْقَتِيلِ.

The Book of
Muhammadﷺ
محمد ﷺ

And We have sent you to mankind (as) a Messenger
وَأَرْسَلْنَـٰكَ لِلنَّاسِ رَسُولاً

Say, "O you mankind, surely I am the Messenger of Allah to you altogether, to Whom belongs the Kingdom of the heavens and the earth. There is no god except He. He gives life and causes to die. So believe in Allah and His Messenger, the Prophet the illiterate one who believes in Allah and His Speeches, and follow him closely that possibly you would be guided." – Surah Al-A'raf 7:158

قُلْ يَـٰٓأَيُّهَا ٱلنَّاسُ إِنِّى رَسُولُ ٱللَّهِ إِلَيْكُمْ جَمِيعًا ٱلَّذِى لَهُۥ مُلْكُ ٱلسَّمَـٰوَٰتِ وَٱلْأَرْضِ ۖ لَآ إِلَـٰهَ إِلَّا هُوَ يُحْىِۦ وَيُمِيتُ ۖ فَـَٔامِنُوا۟ بِٱللَّهِ وَرَسُولِهِ ٱلنَّبِىِّ ٱلْأُمِّىِّ ٱلَّذِى يُؤْمِنُ بِٱللَّهِ وَكَلِمَـٰتِهِۦ وَٱتَّبِعُوهُ لَعَلَّكُمْ تَهْتَدُونَ

Whatever fair (thing) alights upon (Literally: afflicts) you, then it is from Allah, and whatever odious (thing) afflicts you, then it is from yourself; and We have sent you to mankind (as) a Messenger; and Allah suffices as Ever-Witnessing – Surah An-Nisa 4:79

مَّآ أَصَابَكَ مِنْ حَسَنَةٍ فَمِنَ ٱللَّهِ ۖ وَمَآ أَصَابَكَ مِن سَيِّئَةٍ فَمِن نَّفْسِكَ ۚ وَأَرْسَلْنَـٰكَ لِلنَّاسِ رَسُولاً ۚ وَكَفَىٰ بِٱللَّهِ شَهِيدًا

But it is only a Reminder to all people – Surah Al-Qalam 68:52

وَمَا هُوَ إِلَّا ذِكْرٌ لِّلْعَـٰلَمِينَ

And in no way have We sent you except as a constant bearer of good tidings and a constant warner to the whole of mankind; but most of mankind do not know – Surah Saba 34:28

وَمَآ أَرْسَلْنَـٰكَ إِلَّا كَآفَّةً لِّلنَّاسِ بَشِيرًا وَنَذِيرًا وَلَـٰكِنَّ أَكْثَرَ ٱلنَّاسِ لَا يَعْلَمُونَ

Muhammad the Messenger of Allah and those with him are tough on the unbelievers, yet compassionate to one another. You see them kneeling and bowing down, seeking Allah's blessings and His approval. Their faces bear the mark of their prostrations. Such is their example in the Torah. And their description in the Gospel is like a plant that sprouts, becoming strong, grows thick, and rises on its stem to the delight of the farmer. Through them Allah infuriates the unbelievers. Allah has promised forgiveness and a great reward to those among them, who believe and do good deeds. – Surah Al-Fath 48:29 [2]

---

[2] (Prostration Mark)

Narrated Abu Huraira: ....when Allah has finished the judgments among His slaves, and intends to take out of the Fire whoever He wishes to take out from among those who used to testify that none had the right to be worshipped but Allah. We will order the angels to take them out and the angels will know them by the mark of the traces of prostration (on their foreheads) for Allah banned the f ire to consume the traces of prostration on the body of Adam's son......... Sahih al-Bukhari 6573

حَتَّى إِذَا فَرَغَ اللَّهُ مِنَ الْقَضَاءِ بَيْنَ عِبَادِهِ، وَأَرَادَ أَنْ يُخْرِجَ مِنَ النَّارِ مَنْ أَرَادَ أَنْ يُخْرِجَ، مِمَّنْ كَانَ يَشْهَدُ أَنْ لاَ إِلَهَ إِلاَّ اللَّهُ، أَمَرَ الْمَلاَئِكَةَ أَنْ يُخْرِجُوهُمْ، فَيَعْرِفُونَهُمْ بِعَلاَمَةِ آثَارِ السُّجُودِ، وَحَرَّمَ اللَّهُ عَلَى النَّارِ أَنْ تَأْكُلَ مِنِ ابْنِ آدَمَ أَثَرَ السُّجُودِ

مُحَمَّدٌ رَّسُولُ ٱللَّهِ ۚ وَٱلَّذِينَ مَعَهُۥٓ أَشِدَّآءُ عَلَى ٱلْكُفَّارِ رُحَمَآءُ بَيْنَهُمْ ۖ تَرَىٰهُمْ رُكَّعًا سُجَّدًا يَبْتَغُونَ فَضْلًا مِّنَ ٱللَّهِ وَرِضْوَٰنًا ۖ سِيمَاهُمْ فِى وُجُوهِهِم مِّنْ أَثَرِ ٱلسُّجُودِ ۚ ذَٰلِكَ مَثَلُهُمْ فِى ٱلتَّوْرَىٰةِ ۚ وَمَثَلُهُمْ فِى ٱلْإِنجِيلِ كَزَرْعٍ أَخْرَجَ شَطْـَٔهُۥ فَـَٔازَرَهُۥ فَٱسْتَغْلَظَ فَٱسْتَوَىٰ عَلَىٰ سُوقِهِۦ يُعْجِبُ ٱلزُّرَّاعَ لِيَغِيظَ بِهِمُ ٱلْكُفَّارَ ۗ وَعَدَ ٱللَّهُ ٱلَّذِينَ ءَامَنُوا۟ وَعَمِلُوا۟ ٱلصَّـٰلِحَـٰتِ مِنْهُم مَّغْفِرَةً وَأَجْرًا عَظِيمًۢا

O prophet! We have sent you as a witness, and a bearer of good news, and a warner. Surah Al-Ahzab 33:45

يَـٰٓأَيُّهَا ٱلنَّبِىُّ إِنَّآ أَرْسَلْنَـٰكَ شَـٰهِدًا وَمُبَشِّرًا وَنَذ .

We sent you only as a herald of good news and a warner. – Surah Al-Furqan 25:56

وَمَآ أَرْسَلْنَـٰكَ إِلَّا مُبَشِّرًا وَنَذِيرًا

You are just a warner for whoever dreads it. – Surah An-Nazi'at 79:45

إِنَّمَآ أَنتَ مُنذِرُ مَن يَخْشَىٰهَا

Narrated Ata bin Yasar: I met `Abdullah bin `Amr bin Al-`As and asked him, "Tell me about the description of Allah's Messenger ﷺ which is mentioned in Torah (i.e. Old Testament.") He replied, 'Yes. By Allah, he is described in Torah with some of the qualities attributed to him in the Qur'an as follows: "O Prophet ! We have sent you as a witness (for Allah's True religion) And a giver of glad tidings (to the faithful believers), And a warner (to the unbelievers) And guardian of the illiterates. You are My slave and My messenger (i.e. Apostle). I have named you "Al-Mutawakkil" (who depends upon Allah). You are neither discourteous, harsh Nor a noisemaker in the markets And you do not do evil to those Who do evil to you, but you deal With them with forgiveness and kindness. Allah will not let him (the Prophet) Die till he makes straight the crooked people by making them say: "None has the right to be worshipped but Allah," With which will be opened blind eyes And deaf ears and enveloped hearts." – Al-Bukhari 2125

حَدَّثَنَا مُحَمَّدُ بْنُ سِنَانٍ، حَدَّثَنَا فُلَيْحٌ، حَدَّثَنَا هِلاَلٌ، عَنْ عَطَاءِ بْنِ يَسَارٍ، قَالَ لَقِيتُ عَبْدَ اللَّهِ بْنَ عَمْرِو بْنِ الْعَاصِ ـ رضى الله عنهما ـ قُلْتُ أَخْبِرْنِي عَنْ صِفَةِ، رَسُولِ اللَّهِ صلى الله عليه وسلم فِي التَّوْرَاةِ‏.‏ قَالَ أَجَلْ، وَاللَّهِ إِنَّهُ لَمَوْصُوفٌ فِي التَّوْرَاةِ بِبَعْضِ صِفَتِهِ فِي الْقُرْآنِ يَا أَيُّهَا النَّبِيُّ إِنَّا أَرْسَلْنَاكَ شَاهِدًا وَمُبَشِّرًا وَنَذِيرًا، وَحِرْزًا لِلأُمِّيِّينَ، أَنْتَ عَبْدِي وَرَسُولِي سَمَّيْتُكَ الْمُتَوَكِّلَ، لَيْسَ بِفَظٍّ وَلاَ غَلِيظٍ وَلاَ سَخَّابٍ فِي الأَسْوَاقِ، وَلاَ يَدْفَعُ بِالسَّيِّئَةِ السَّيِّئَةَ وَلَكِنْ يَعْفُو وَيَغْفِرُ، وَلَنْ يَقْبِضَهُ اللَّهُ حَتَّى يُقِيمَ بِهِ الْمِلَّةَ الْعَوْجَاءَ بِأَنْ يَقُولُوا لاَ إِلَهَ إِلاَّ اللَّهُ‏.‏ وَيَفْتَحُ بِهَا أَعْيُنًا عُمْيًا، وَآذَانًا صُمًّا، وَقُلُوبًا غُلْفًا‏.‏ تَابَعَهُ عَبْدُ الْعَزِيزِ بْنُ أَبِي سَلَمَةَ عَنْ هِلاَلٍ‏.‏ وَقَالَ سَعِيدٌ عَنْ هِلاَلٍ عَنْ عَطَاءٍ عَنِ ابْنِ سَلاَمٍ‏.‏ غُلْفٌ كُلُّ شَىْءٍ فِي غِلاَفٍ، سَيْفٌ أَغْلَفُ، وَقَوْسٌ غَلْفَاءُ، وَرَجُلٌ أَغْلَفُ إِذَا لَمْ يَكُنْ مَخْتُونًا

Nor were you by the side of the Mount when We proclaimed. Rather, it was a mercy from your Lord, that you may warn people who received no warner before you, so that they may take heed. Otherwise, if a calamity befell them as a result of what their hands have perpetrated, they would say, "Our Lord, if only You had sent us a messenger, we would have followed Your revelations, and been among the believers." – Surah Al-Qasas 28:46&47

فَلَمَّا جَآءَهُم مُّوسَىٰ بِـَٔايَـٰتِنَا بَيِّنَـٰتٍ قَالُوا۟ مَا هَـٰذَآ إِلَّا سِحْرٌ مُّفْتَرًى وَمَا سَمِعْنَا بِهَـٰذَا فِىٓ ءَابَآئِنَا ٱلْأَوَّلِينَ وَقَالَ مُوسَىٰ رَبِّىٓ أَعْلَمُ بِمَن جَآءَ بِٱلْهُدَىٰ مِنْ عِندِهِۦ وَمَن تَكُونُ لَهُۥ عَـٰقِبَةُ ٱلدَّارِ ۖ إِنَّهُۥ لَا يُفْلِحُ ٱلظَّـٰلِمُونَ

We sent you only universally to all people, a herald and warner, but most people do not know. .–Surah Saba 34:28

وَمَآ أَرْسَلْنَـٰكَ إِلَّا كَآفَّةً لِّلنَّاسِ بَشِيرًا وَنَذِيرًا وَلَـٰكِنَّ أَكْثَرَ ٱلنَّاسِ لَا يَعْلَمُونَ

Be tolerant, and command decency, and avoid the ignorant. And when a suggestion from Satan assails you, take refuge with Allah. He is Hearing and Knowing. Al-A'raf 7:199&200
خُذِ ٱلْعَفْوَ وَأْمُرْ بِٱلْعُرْفِ وَأَعْرِضْ عَنِ ٱلْجَـٰهِلِينَ.أَوَلَمْ يَهْدِ لِلَّذِينَ يَرِثُونَ ٱلْأَرْضَ مِنۢ بَعْدِ أَهْلِهَآ أَن لَّوْ نَشَآءُ أَصَبْنَـٰهُم بِذُنُوبِهِمْ ۚ وَنَطْبَعُ عَلَىٰ قُلُوبِهِمْ فَهُمْ لَا يَسْمَعُونَ

So remind. You are only a reminder. You have no control over them. – Surah Al-Ghashiyah 88:21&22

فَذَكِّرْ إِنَّمَآ أَنتَ مُذَكِّرٌ.لَّسْتَ عَلَيْهِم بِمُصَيْطِرٍ

But if they turn away—We did not send you as a guardian over them. Your only duty is communication. Whenever We let man taste mercy from Us, he rejoices in it; but when misfortune befalls them, as a consequence of what their hands have perpetrated, man turns blasphemous. – Surah Ash-Shuraa 42:48
فَإِنْ أَعْرَضُوا۟ فَمَآ أَرْسَلْنَـٰكَ عَلَيْهِمْ حَفِيظًا ۖ إِنْ عَلَيْكَ إِلَّا ٱلْبَلَـٰغُ ۗ وَإِنَّآ إِذَآ أَذَقْنَا ٱلْإِنسَـٰنَ مِنَّا رَحْمَةً فَرِحَ بِهَا ۖ وَإِن تُصِبْهُمْ سَيِّئَةٌۢ بِمَا قَدَّمَتْ أَيْدِيهِمْ فَإِنَّ ٱلْإِنسَـٰنَ كَفُورٌ

We are fully aware of what they say, and you are not a dictator over them. So remind by the Quran whoever fears My warning. – Surah Qaf 50:45
نَّحْنُ أَعْلَمُ بِمَا يَقُولُونَ ۖ وَمَآ أَنتَ عَلَيْهِم بِجَبَّارٍ ۖ فَذَكِّرْ بِٱلْقُرْءَانِ مَن يَخَافُ وَعِيدِ

With the truth We sent it down, and with the truth it descended. We sent you only as a bearer of good news and a warner. –Surah Al-Isra 17:105
وَبِٱلْحَقِّ أَنزَلْنَـٰهُ وَبِٱلْحَقِّ نَزَلَ ۗ وَمَآ أَرْسَلْنَـٰكَ إِلَّا مُبَشِّرًا وَنَذِيرًا

Tell those who believe to forgive those who do not hope for the Days of Allah. He will fully recompense people for whatever they have earned. – Surah Al-Jathiyah 45:14
قُل لِّلَّذِينَ ءَامَنُوا۟ يَغْفِرُوا۟ لِلَّذِينَ لَا يَرْجُونَ أَيَّامَ ٱللَّهِ لِيَجْزِىَ قَوْمًۢا بِمَا كَانُوا۟ يَكْسِبُونَ

.....a mercy to mankind
رَحْمَةً لِّلْعَـٰلَمِينَ....

The servants of the Merciful are those who walk the earth in humility, and when the ignorant address them, they say, "Peace." – Surah Al-Furqan 25:63
وَعِبَادُ ٱلرَّحْمَـٰنِ ٱلَّذِينَ يَمْشُونَ عَلَى ٱلْأَرْضِ هَوْنًا وَإِذَا خَاطَبَهُمُ ٱلْجَـٰهِلُونَ قَالُوا۟ سَلَـٰمًا

Narrated 'Aisha (the mother of the faithful believers): The commencement of the Divine Inspiration to Allah's Messenger ﷺ was in the form of good dreams which came true like bright daylight, and then the love of seclusion was bestowed upon him. He used to go in seclusion in the cave of Hira where he used to worship (Allah alone) continuously for many days before his desire to see his family. He used to take with him the journey food for the stay and then come back to (his wife) Khadija to take his food likewise again till suddenly the Truth descended upon him while he was in the cave of Hira. The angel came to him and asked him to read. The Prophet ﷺ replied, "I do not know how to read." The Prophet ﷺ added, "The angel caught me (forcefully) and pressed me so hard that I could not bear it any more. He then released me and again asked me to read and I replied, 'I do not know how to read.' Thereupon he caught me again and pressed me a second time till I could not bear it any more. He then released me and again asked me to read but again I replied, 'I do not know how to read (or what shall I read)?' Thereupon he caught me for the third time and pressed me, and then released me and said, 'Read in the name of your Lord, who has created (all that exists), created man from a clot. Read! And your Lord is the Most Generous." (96.1, 96.2, 96.3) Then Allah's Messenger ﷺ returned with the Inspiration and with his heart beating severely. Then he went to Khadija bint Khuwailid and said, "Cover me! Cover me!" They covered him till his fear was over and after that he told her everything that had happened and said, "I fear that something may happen to me." Khadija replied, "Never! By Allah, Allah will never disgrace you. You keep good relations with your kith and kin, help the poor and the destitute, serve your guests generously and assist the deserving calamity-afflicted ones." Khadija then accompanied him to her cousin Waraqa bin Naufal bin Asad bin 'Abdul 'Uzza, who, during the pre-Islamic Period became a Christian and used to write the writing with Hebrew letters. He would write from the Gospel in Hebrew as much as Allah wished him to write. He was an old man and had lost his eyesight. Khadija said to Waraqa, "Listen to the story of your nephew, O my cousin!" Waraqa asked, "O my nephew! What have you seen?" Allah's Messenger ﷺ described whatever he had seen. Waraqa said, "This is the same one who keeps the secrets (angel Gabriel) whom Allah had sent to Moses. I wish I were young and could live up to the time when your people would turn you out." Allah's Messenger ﷺ asked, "Will they drive me out?" Waraqa replied in the affirmative and said, "Anyone (man) who came with something similar to what you have brought was treated with hostility; and if I should remain alive till the day when you will be turned out then I would support you strongly." But after a few days Waraqa died and the Divine Inspiration was also paused for a while. – Al-Bukhari 3

حَدَّثَنَا يَحْيَى بْنُ بُكَيْرٍ، قَالَ حَدَّثَنَا اللَّيْثُ، عَنْ عُقَيْلٍ، عَنِ ابْنِ شِهَابٍ، عَنْ عُرْوَةَ بْنِ الزُّبَيْرِ، عَنْ عَائِشَةَ أُمِّ الْمُؤْمِنِينَ، أَنَّهَا قَالَتْ أَوَّلُ مَا بُدِئَ بِهِ رَسُولُ اللَّهِ صلى الله عليه وسلم مِنَ الْوَحْىِ الرُّؤْيَا الصَّالِحَةُ فِي النَّوْمِ، فَكَانَ لاَ يَرَى رُؤْيَا إِلاَّ جَاءَتْ مِثْلَ فَلَقِ الصُّبْحِ، ثُمَّ حُبِّبَ إِلَيْهِ الْخَلاَءُ، وَكَانَ يَخْلُو بِغَارِ حِرَاءٍ فَيَتَحَنَّثُ فِيهِ ـ وَهُوَ التَّعَبُّدُ ـ اللَّيَالِيَ ذَوَاتِ الْعَدَدِ قَبْلَ أَنْ يَنْزِعَ إِلَى أَهْلِهِ، وَيَتَزَوَّدُ لِذَلِكَ، ثُمَّ يَرْجِعُ إِلَى خَدِيجَةَ، فَيَتَزَوَّدُ لِمِثْلِهَا، حَتَّى جَاءَهُ الْحَقُّ وَهُوَ فِي غَارِ حِرَاءٍ، فَجَاءَهُ الْمَلَكُ فَقَالَ اقْرَأْ. قَالَ " مَا أَنَا بِقَارِئٍ ". قَالَ " فَأَخَذَنِي فَغَطَّنِي حَتَّى بَلَغَ مِنِّي الْجَهْدَ، ثُمَّ أَرْسَلَنِي فَقَالَ اقْرَأْ. قُلْتُ مَا أَنَا بِقَارِئٍ. فَأَخَذَنِي فَغَطَّنِي الثَّانِيَةَ حَتَّى بَلَغَ مِنِّي الْجَهْدَ، ثُمَّ أَرْسَلَنِي فَقَالَ اقْرَأْ. فَقُلْتُ مَا أَنَا بِقَارِئٍ. فَأَخَذَنِي فَغَطَّنِي الثَّالِثَةَ، ثُمَّ أَرْسَلَنِي فَقَالَ {اقْرَأْ بِاسْمِ رَبِّكَ الَّذِي خَلَقَ * خَلَقَ الإِنْسَانَ مِنْ عَلَقٍ * اقْرَأْ وَرَبُّكَ الأَكْرَمُ} ". فَرَجَعَ بِهَا رَسُولُ اللَّهِ صلى الله عليه وسلم يَرْجُفُ فُؤَادُهُ، فَدَخَلَ عَلَى خَدِيجَةَ بِنْتِ خُوَيْلِدٍ رضى الله عنها فَقَالَ " زَمِّلُونِي زَمِّلُونِي ". فَزَمَّلُوهُ حَتَّى ذَهَبَ عَنْهُ الرَّوْعُ، فَقَالَ لِخَدِيجَةَ وَأَخْبَرَهَا الْخَبَرَ " لَقَدْ خَشِيتُ عَلَى نَفْسِي ". فَقَالَتْ خَدِيجَةُ كَلاَّ وَاللَّهِ مَا يُخْزِيكَ اللَّهُ أَبَدًا، إِنَّكَ لَتَصِلُ الرَّحِمَ، وَتَحْمِلُ الْكَلَّ، وَتَكْسِبُ الْمَعْدُومَ، وَتَقْرِي الضَّيْفَ، وَتُعِينُ عَلَى نَوَائِبِ الْحَقِّ. فَانْطَلَقَتْ بِهِ خَدِيجَةُ حَتَّى أَتَتْ بِهِ وَرَقَةَ بْنَ نَوْفَلِ بْنِ أَسَدِ بْنِ عَبْدِ الْعُزَّى ابْنَ عَمِّ خَدِيجَةَ ـ وَكَانَ امْرَأً تَنَصَّرَ فِي الْجَاهِلِيَّةِ، وَكَانَ يَكْتُبُ الْكِتَابَ الْعِبْرَانِيَّ، فَيَكْتُبُ مِنَ الإِنْجِيلِ بِالْعِبْرَانِيَّةِ مَا شَاءَ اللَّهُ أَنْ يَكْتُبَ، وَكَانَ شَيْخًا كَبِيرًا قَدْ عَمِيَ ـ فَقَالَتْ لَهُ خَدِيجَةُ يَا ابْنَ عَمِّ اسْمَعْ مِنَ ابْنِ أَخِيكَ. فَقَالَ لَهُ وَرَقَةُ يَا ابْنَ أَخِي مَاذَا تَرَى فَأَخْبَرَهُ رَسُولُ اللَّهِ صلى الله عليه وسلم خَبَرَ مَا رَأَى. فَقَالَ لَهُ وَرَقَةُ هَذَا النَّامُوسُ الَّذِي نَزَّلَ اللَّهُ عَلَى مُوسَى صلى الله عليه وسلم يَا لَيْتَنِي فِيهَا جَذَعًا، لَيْتَنِي أَكُونُ حَيًّا إِذْ يُخْرِجُكَ قَوْمُكَ. فَقَالَ رَسُولُ اللَّهِ صلى الله عليه وسلم " أَوَمُخْرِجِيَّ هُمْ ". قَالَ نَعَمْ، لَمْ يَأْتِ رَجُلٌ قَطُّ بِمِثْلِ مَا جِئْتَ بِهِ إِلاَّ عُودِيَ، وَإِنْ يُدْرِكْنِي يَوْمُكَ أَنْصُرْكَ نَصْرًا مُؤَزَّرًا. ثُمَّ لَمْ يَنْشَبْ وَرَقَةُ أَنْ تُوُفِّيَ وَفَتَرَ الْوَحْىُ.

Narrated Jabir bin `Abdullah: I fell ill, Allah's Messenger ﷺ and Abu Bakr came to visit me on foot. The Prophet ﷺ came to me while I was unconscious. Allah's Messenger ﷺ performed ablution and poured the Remaining water of his ablution over me whereupon I became conscious and said, 'O Allah's Messenger ﷺ ! How should I spend my wealth? Or how should I deal with my wealth?" But the Prophet ﷺ did not give me any reply till the Verse of the laws of inheritance was revealed. – Al-Bukhari 7309

حَدَّثَنَا عَلِيُّ بْنُ عَبْدِ اللَّهِ، حَدَّثَنَا سُفْيَانُ، قَالَ سَمِعْتُ ابْنَ الْمُنْكَدِرِ، يَقُولُ سَمِعْتُ جَابِرَ بْنَ عَبْدِ اللَّهِ، يَقُولُ مَرِضْتُ فَجَاءَنِي رَسُولُ اللَّهِ صلى الله عليه وسلم يَعُودُنِي وَأَبُو بَكْرٍ وَهُمَا مَاشِيَانِ، فَأَتَانِي وَقَدْ أُغْمِيَ عَلَىَّ فَتَوَضَّأَ رَسُولُ اللَّهِ صلى الله عليه وسلم ثُمَّ صَبَّ وَضُوءَهُ عَلَىَّ فَأَفَقْتُ فَقُلْتُ يَا رَسُولَ اللَّهِ ـ وَرُبَّمَا قَالَ سُفْيَانُ فَقُلْتُ أَىْ رَسُولَ اللَّهِ ـ كَيْفَ أَقْضِي فِي مَالِي كَيْفَ أَصْنَعُ فِي مَالِي قَالَ فَمَا أَجَابَنِي بِشَىْءٍ حَتَّى نَزَلَتْ آيَةُ الْمِيرَاثِ

Narrated Anas: I served the Prophet ﷺ for ten years, and he never said to me, "Uf" (a minor harsh word denoting impatience) and never blamed me by saying, "Why did you do so or why didn't you do so?" – Al-Bukhari 6038

حَدَّثَنَا مُوسَى بْنُ إِسْمَاعِيلَ، سَمِعَ سَلاَّمَ بْنَ مِسْكِينٍ، قَالَ سَمِعْتُ ثَابِتًا، يَقُولُ حَدَّثَنَا أَنَسٌ ـ رضى الله عنه ـ قَالَ خَدَمْتُ النَّبِيَّ صلى الله عليه وسلم عَشْرَ سِنِينَ، فَمَا قَالَ لِي أُفٍّ. وَلاَ لِمَ صَنَعْتَ وَلاَ أَلاَّ صَنَعْتَ.

Narrated Al-Aswad: I asked `Aisha what did the Prophet ﷺ use to do at home. She replied. "He used to keep himself busy serving his family and when it was time for the prayer, he would get up for prayer." – Al-Bukhari 6039

حَدَّثَنَا حَفْصُ بْنُ عُمَرَ، حَدَّثَنَا شُعْبَةُ، عَنِ الْحَكَمِ، عَنْ إِبْرَاهِيمَ، عَنِ الأَسْوَدِ، قَالَ سَأَلْتُ عَائِشَةَ مَا كَانَ النَّبِيُّ صلى الله عليه وسلم يَصْنَعُ فِي أَهْلِهِ قَالَتْ كَانَ فِي مِهْنَةِ أَهْلِهِ، فَإِذَا حَضَرَتِ الصَّلاَةُ قَامَ إِلَى الصَّلاَةِ.

Narrated Anas bin Malik: A group of three men came to the houses of the wives of the Prophet ﷺ asking how the Prophet ﷺ worshipped (Allah), and when they were informed about that, they considered their worship insufficient and said, "Where are we from the Prophet ﷺ as his past and future sins have been forgiven." Then one of them said, "I will offer the prayer throughout the night forever." The other said, "I will fast throughout the year and will not break my fast." The third said, "I will keep away from the women and will not marry forever." Allah's Messenger ﷺ came to them and said, "Are you the same people who said so-and-so? By Allah, I am more submissive to Allah and more afraid of Him than you; yet I fast and break my fast, I do sleep and I also marry women. So he who does not follow my tradition in religion, is not from me (not one of my followers). – Al-Bukhari 5063

حَدَّثَنَا سَعِيدُ بْنُ أَبِي مَرْيَمَ، أَخْبَرَنَا مُحَمَّدُ بْنُ جَعْفَرٍ، أَخْبَرَنَا حُمَيْدُ بْنُ أَبِي حُمَيْدٍ الطَّوِيلُ، أَنَّهُ سَمِعَ أَنَسَ بْنَ مَالِكٍ ـ رضى الله عنه ـ يَقُولُ جَاءَ ثَلاَثَةُ رَهْطٍ إِلَى بُيُوتِ أَزْوَاجِ النَّبِيِّ صلى الله عليه وسلم يَسْأَلُونَ عَنْ عِبَادَةِ النَّبِيِّ صلى الله عليه وسلم فَلَمَّا أُخْبِرُوا كَأَنَّهُمْ تَقَالُّوهَا فَقَالُوا وَأَيْنَ نَحْنُ مِنَ النَّبِيِّ صلى الله عليه وسلم قَدْ غُفِرَ لَهُ مَا تَقَدَّمَ مِنْ ذَنْبِهِ وَمَا تَأَخَّرَ. قَالَ أَحَدُهُمْ أَمَّا أَنَا فَإِنِّي أُصَلِّي اللَّيْلَ أَبَدًا. وَقَالَ آخَرُ أَنَا أَصُومُ الدَّهْرَ وَلاَ أُفْطِرُ. وَقَالَ آخَرُ أَنَا أَعْتَزِلُ النِّسَاءَ فَلاَ أَتَزَوَّجُ أَبَدًا. فَجَاءَ رَسُولُ اللَّهِ صلى الله عليه وسلم فَقَالَ " أَنْتُمُ الَّذِينَ قُلْتُمْ كَذَا وَكَذَا أَمَا وَاللَّهِ إِنِّي لأَخْشَاكُمْ لِلَّهِ وَأَتْقَاكُمْ لَهُ، لَكِنِّي أَصُومُ وَأُفْطِرُ، وَأُصَلِّي وَأَرْقُدُ وَأَتَزَوَّجُ النِّسَاءَ، فَمَنْ رَغِبَ عَنْ سُنَّتِي فَلَيْسَ مِنِّي ".

Narrated Muhammad bin Jubair bin Mut`im: My father said, "(Before Islam) I was looking for my camel .." The same narration is told by a different sub-narrator. Jubair bin Mut`im said, "My camel was lost and I went out in search of it on the day of `Arafat, and I saw the Prophet ﷺ standing in `Arafat. I said to myself: By Allah he is from the Hums (literally: strictly religious, Quraish were called so, as they used to say, 'We are the people of Allah we shall not go out of the sanctuary). What has brought him here?" – Al-Bukhari 1664

حَدَّثَنَا عَلِيُّ بْنُ عَبْدِ اللَّهِ، حَدَّثَنَا سُفْيَانُ، حَدَّثَنَا عَمْرٌو، حَدَّثَنَا مُحَمَّدُ بْنُ جُبَيْرِ بْنِ مُطْعِمٍ، عَنْ أَبِيهِ، كُنْتُ أَطْلُبُ بَعِيرًا لِي.
وَحَدَّثَنَا مُسَدَّدٌ، حَدَّثَنَا سُفْيَانُ، عَنْ عَمْرٍو، سَمِعَ مُحَمَّدَ بْنَ جُبَيْرٍ، عَنْ أَبِيهِ، جُبَيْرِ بْنِ مُطْعِمٍ قَالَ أَضْلَلْتُ بَعِيرًا لِي، فَذَهَبْتُ أَطْلُبُهُ يَوْمَ عَرَفَةَ، فَرَأَيْتُ النَّبِيَّ صلى الله عليه وسلم وَاقِفًا بِعَرَفَةَ، فَقُلْتُ هَذَا وَاللَّهِ مِنَ الْحُمْسِ فَمَا شَأْنُهُ هَا هُنَا

Narrated Abu Huraira :The Prophet ﷺ said, "None of you should point out towards his Muslim brother with a weapon, for he does not know, Satan may tempt him to hit him and thus he would fall into a pit of fire (Hell) – "Sahih al-Bukhari 7072

حَدَّثَنَا مُحَمَّدٌ، أَخْبَرَنَا عَبْدُ الرَّزَّاقِ، عَنْ مَعْمَرٍ، عَنْ هَمَّامٍ، سَمِعْتُ أَبَا هُرَيْرَةَ، عَنِ النَّبِيِّ صلى الله عليه وسلم قَالَ " لاَ يُشِيرُ أَحَدُكُمْ عَلَى أَخِيهِ بِالسِّلاَحِ، فَإِنَّهُ لاَ يَدْرِي لَعَلَّ الشَّيْطَانَ يَنْزِعُ فِي يَدِهِ، فَيَقَعُ فِي حُفْرَةٍ مِنَ النَّارِ ".

Narrated `Abdullah bin Mulaika: `Aisha said that the Jews came to the Prophet ﷺ and said, "As-Samu 'Alaikum" (death be on you). `Aisha said (to them), "(Death) be on you, and may Allah curse you and shower His wrath upon you!" The Prophet ﷺ said, "Be calm, O `Aisha ! You should be kind and lenient, and beware of harshness and Fuhsh (i.e. bad words)." She said (to the Prophet), "Haven't you heard what they (Jews) have said?" He said, "Haven't you heard what I have said (to them)? I said the same to them, and my invocation against them will be accepted while theirs against me will be rejected (by Allah). " – Al-Bukhari 6030

حَدَّثَنَا مُحَمَّدُ بْنُ سَلاَمٍ، أَخْبَرَنَا عَبْدُ الْوَهَّابِ، عَنْ أَيُّوبَ، عَنْ عَبْدِ اللَّهِ بْنِ أَبِي مُلَيْكَةَ، عَنْ عَائِشَةَ ـ رضى الله عنها أَنَّ يَهُودَ، أَتَوُا النَّبِيَّ صلى الله عليه وسلم فَقَالُوا السَّامُ عَلَيْكُمْ. فَقَالَتْ عَائِشَةُ عَلَيْكُمْ، وَلَعَنَكُمُ اللَّهُ، وَغَضِبَ اللَّهُ عَلَيْكُمْ. قَالَ " مَهْلاً يَا عَائِشَةُ، عَلَيْكِ بِالرِّفْقِ، وَإِيَّاكِ وَالْعُنْفَ وَالْفُحْشَ ". قَالَتْ أَوَلَمْ تَسْمَعْ مَا قَالُوا قَالَ " أَوَلَمْ تَسْمَعِي مَا قُلْتُ رَدَدْتُ عَلَيْهِمْ، فَيُسْتَجَابُ لِي فِيهِمْ، وَلاَ يُسْتَجَابُ لَهُمْ فِيَّ ".

Narrated Ma'rur: I saw Abu Dhar wearing a Burd (garment) and his slave too was wearing a Burd, so I said (to Abu Dhar), "If you take this (Burda of your slave) and wear it (along with yours), you will have a nice suit (costume) and you may give him another garment." Abu Dhar said, "There was a quarrel between me and another man whose mother was a non-Arab and I called her bad names. The man mentioned (complained about) me to the Prophet. The Prophet ﷺ said, "Did you abuse so-and-so?" I said, "Yes" He said, "Did you call his mother bad names?" I said, "Yes". He said, "You still have the traits of (the Pre-Islamic period of) ignorance." I said. "(Do I still have ignorance) even now in my old age?" He said, "Yes, they (slaves or servants) are your brothers, and Allah has put them under your command. So the one under whose hand Allah has put his brother, should feed him of what he eats, and give him dresses of what he wears, and should not ask him to do a thing beyond his capacity. And if at all he asks him to do a hard task, he should help him therein." – Al-Bukhari 6050

حَدَّثَنَا عُمَرُ بْنُ حَفْصٍ، حَدَّثَنَا أَبِي، حَدَّثَنَا الأَعْمَشُ، عَنِ الْمَعْرُورِ، عَنْ أَبِي ذَرٍّ، قَالَ رَأَيْتُ عَلَيْهِ بُرْدًا وَعَلَى غُلاَمِهِ بُرْدًا فَقُلْتُ لَوْ أَخَذْتَ هَذَا فَلَبِسْتَهُ كَانَتْ حُلَّةً، وَأَعْطَيْتَهُ ثَوْبًا آخَرَ. فَقَالَ كَانَ بَيْنِي وَبَيْنَ رَجُلٍ كَلاَمٌ، وَكَانَتْ أُمُّهُ أَعْجَمِيَّةً، فَنِلْتُ مِنْهَا فَذَكَرَنِي إِلَى النَّبِيِّ صلى الله عليه وسلم فَقَالَ لِي " أَسَابَبْتَ فُلاَنًا ". قُلْتُ نَعَمْ. قَالَ " أَفَنِلْتَ مِنْ أُمِّهِ ". قُلْتُ نَعَمْ. قَالَ " إِنَّكَ امْرُؤٌ فِيكَ جَاهِلِيَّةٌ ". قُلْتُ عَلَى حِينِ سَاعَتِي هَذِهِ مِنْ كِبَرِ السِّنِّ قَالَ " نَعَمْ، هُمْ إِخْوَانُكُمْ، جَعَلَهُمُ اللَّهُ تَحْتَ أَيْدِيكُمْ، فَمَنْ جَعَلَ اللَّهُ أَخَاهُ تَحْتَ يَدِهِ فَلْيُطْعِمْهُ مِمَّا يَأْكُلُ، وَلْيُلْبِسْهُ مِمَّا يَلْبَسُ، وَلاَ يُكَلِّفُهُ مِنَ الْعَمَلِ مَا يَغْلِبُهُ، فَإِنْ كَلَّفَهُ مَا يَغْلِبُهُ فَلْيُعِنْهُ عَلَيْهِ

Narrated Anas bin Malik: The Prophet ﷺ was not one who would abuse (others) or say obscene words, or curse (others), and if he wanted to admonish anyone of us, he used to say: "What is wrong with him, his forehead be dusted!" – Al-Bukhari 6031

حَدَّثَنَا أَصْبَغُ، قَالَ أَخْبَرَنِي ابْنُ وَهْبٍ، أَخْبَرَنَا أَبُو يَحْيَى، هُوَ فُلَيْحُ بْنُ سُلَيْمَانَ عَنْ هِلاَلِ بْنِ أُسَامَةَ، عَنْ أَنَسِ بْنِ مَالِكٍ ـ رضى الله عنه ـ قَالَ لَمْ يَكُنِ النَّبِيُّ صلى الله عليه وسلم سَبَّابًا وَلاَ فَحَّاشًا وَلاَ لَعَّانًا، كَانَ يَقُولُ لأَحَدِنَا عِنْدَ الْمَعْتِبَةِ " مَا لَهُ، تَرِبَ جَبِينُهُ ".

Narrated Anas bin Malik: The Prophet ﷺ used to mix with us to the extent that he would say to a younger brother of mine, 'O Aba `Umair! What did the Nughair (a kind of bird) do?" – Al-Bukhari 6129

حَدَّثَنَا آدَمُ، حَدَّثَنَا شُعْبَةُ، حَدَّثَنَا أَبُو التَّيَّاحِ، قَالَ سَمِعْتُ أَنَسَ بْنَ مَالِكٍ ـ رضى الله عنه ـ يَقُولُ إِنْ كَانَ النَّبِيُّ صلى الله عليه وسلم لَيُخَالِطُنَا حَتَّى يَقُولَ لأَخٍ لِي صَغِيرٍ " يَا أَبَا عُمَيْرٍ مَا فَعَلَ النُّغَيْرُ ".

Narrated Ibn 'Abbas: Allah's Messenger ﷺ was the most generous of all the people, and he used to reach the peak in generosity in the month of Ramadan when Gabriel met him. Gabriel used to meet him every night of Ramadan to teach him the Qur'an. Allah's Messenger ﷺ was the most generous person, even more generous than the strong uncontrollable wind (in readiness and haste to do charitable deeds). – Al-Bukhari 6

حَدَّثَنَا عَبْدَانُ، قَالَ أَخْبَرَنَا عَبْدُ اللَّهِ، قَالَ أَخْبَرَنَا يُونُسُ، عَنِ الزُّهْرِيِّ، ح وَحَدَّثَنَا بِشْرُ بْنُ مُحَمَّدٍ، قَالَ أَخْبَرَنَا عَبْدُ اللَّهِ، قَالَ أَخْبَرَنَا يُونُسُ، وَمَعْمَرٌ، عَنِ الزُّهْرِيِّ، نَحْوَهُ قَالَ أَخْبَرَنِي عُبَيْدُ اللَّهِ بْنُ عَبْدِ اللَّهِ، عَنِ ابْنِ عَبَّاسٍ، قَالَ كَانَ رَسُولُ اللَّهِ صلى الله عليه وسلم أَجْوَدَ النَّاسِ، وَكَانَ أَجْوَدُ مَا يَكُونُ فِي رَمَضَانَ حِينَ يَلْقَاهُ جِبْرِيلُ، وَكَانَ يَلْقَاهُ فِي كُلِّ لَيْلَةٍ مِنْ رَمَضَانَ فَيُدَارِسُهُ الْقُرْآنَ، فَلَرَسُولُ اللَّهِ صلى الله عليه وسلم أَجْوَدُ بِالْخَيْرِ مِنَ الرِّيحِ الْمُرْسَلَةِ

Righteousness does not consist of turning your faces towards the East and the West. But righteous is he who believes in Allah, and the Last Day, and the angels, and the Scripture, and the prophets. Who gives money, though dear, to near relatives, and orphans, and the needy, and the homeless, and the beggars, and for the freeing of slaves; those who perform the prayers, and pay the obligatory charity, and fulfill their promise when they promise, and patiently persevere in the face of persecution, hardship, and in the time of conflict. These are the sincere; these are the pious. – Surah Al-Baqarah 2:177

لَّيْسَ ٱلْبِرَّ أَن تُوَلُّوا۟ وُجُوهَكُمْ قِبَلَ ٱلْمَشْرِقِ وَٱلْمَغْرِبِ وَلَـٰكِنَّ ٱلْبِرَّ مَنْ ءَامَنَ بِٱللَّهِ وَٱلْيَوْمِ ٱلْـَٔاخِرِ وَٱلْمَلَـٰٓئِكَةِ وَٱلْكِتَـٰبِ وَٱلنَّبِيِّـۧنَ وَءَاتَى ٱلْمَالَ عَلَىٰ حُبِّهِۦ ذَوِى ٱلْقُرْبَىٰ وَٱلْيَتَـٰمَىٰ وَٱلْمَسَـٰكِينَ وَٱبْنَ ٱلسَّبِيلِ وَٱلسَّآئِلِينَ وَفِى ٱلرِّقَابِ وَأَقَامَ ٱلصَّلَوٰةَ وَءَاتَى ٱلزَّكَوٰةَ وَٱلْمُوفُونَ بِعَهْدِهِمْ إِذَا عَـٰهَدُوا۟ ۖ وَٱلصَّـٰبِرِينَ فِى ٱلْبَأْسَآءِ وَٱلضَّرَّآءِ وَحِينَ ٱلْبَأْسِ ۗ أُو۟لَـٰٓئِكَ ٱلَّذِينَ صَدَقُوا۟ ۖ وَأُو۟لَـٰٓئِكَ هُمُ ٱلْمُتَّقُونَ

Narrated 'Aisha: Whenever Allah's Messenger ﷺ was given the choice of one of two matters he would choose the easier of the two as long as it was not sinful to do so, but if it was sinful, he would not approach it. Allah's Apostle never took revenge over anybody for his own sake but (he did) only when Allah's legal bindings were outraged, in which case he would take revenge for Allah's sake." (See Hadith No. 760. Vol. 4) – Al-Bukhari 6126

حَدَّثَنَا عَبْدُ اللَّهِ بْنُ مَسْلَمَةَ، عَنْ مَالِكٍ، عَنِ ابْنِ شِهَابٍ، عَنْ عُرْوَةَ، عَنْ عَائِشَةَ ـ رضى الله عنها ـ أَنَّهَا قَالَتْ مَا خُيِّرَ رَسُولُ اللَّهِ صلى الله عليه وسلم بَيْنَ أَمْرَيْنِ قَطُّ إِلاَّ أَخَذَ أَيْسَرَهُمَا، مَا لَمْ يَكُنْ إِثْمًا، فَإِنْ كَانَ إِثْمًا كَانَ أَبْعَدَ النَّاسِ مِنْهُ، وَمَا انْتَقَمَ رَسُولُ اللَّهِ صلى الله عليه وسلم لِنَفْسِهِ فِي شَىْءٍ قَطُّ، إِلاَّ أَنْ تُنْتَهَكَ حُرْمَةُ اللَّهِ، فَيَنْتَقِمَ بِهَا لِلَّهِ.

Narrated Jabir bin 'Abdullah: The Prophet ﷺ said, "War is deceit." – Al-Bukhari 3030

حَدَّثَنَا صَدَقَةُ بْنُ الْفَضْلِ، أَخْبَرَنَا ابْنُ عُيَيْنَةَ، عَنْ عَمْرٍو، سَمِعَ جَابِرَ بْنَ عَبْدِ اللَّهِ ـ رضى الله عنهما ـ قَالَ قَالَ النَّبِيُّ صلى الله عليه وسلم " الْحَرْبُ خُدْعَةٌ ".

Narrated Abu Huraira: The Prophet ﷺ said: "Do not wish to meet the enemy, but when you meet face) the enemy, be patient." – Al-Bukhari 3026

وَقَالَ أَبُو عَامِرٍ حَدَّثَنَا مُغِيرَةُ بْنُ عَبْدِ الرَّحْمَنِ، عَنْ أَبِي الزِّنَادِ، عَنِ الأَعْرَجِ، عَنْ أَبِي هُرَيْرَةَ ـ رضى الله عنه ـ عَنِ النَّبِيِّ صلى الله عليه وسلم قَالَ " لاَ تَمَنَّوْا لِقَاءَ الْعَدُوِّ، فَإِذَا لَقِيتُمُوهُمْ فَاصْبِرُوا "

Narrated 'Abdullah bin Ka'b: I heard Ka'b bin Malik talking after his failure to join (the Ghazwa of) Tabuk. He said, "When I greeted Allah's Messenger ﷺ whose face was glittering with happiness, for whenever Allah's Messenger ﷺ was happy, his face used to glitter, as if it was a piece of the moon, and we used to recognize it (i.e. his happiness) from his face.". – Sahih Al-Bukhari 3556

حَدَّثَنَا يَحْيَى بْنُ بُكَيْرٍ، حَدَّثَنَا اللَّيْثُ، عَنْ عُقَيْلٍ، عَنِ ابْنِ شِهَابٍ، عَنْ عَبْدِ الرَّحْمَنِ بْنِ عَبْدِ اللَّهِ بْنِ كَعْبٍ، أَنَّ عَبْدَ اللَّهِ بْنَ كَعْبٍ، قَالَ سَمِعْتُ كَعْبَ بْنَ مَالِكٍ، يُحَدِّثُ حِينَ تَخَلَّفَ عَنْ تَبُوكَ، قَالَ فَلَمَّا سَلَّمْتُ عَلَى رَسُولِ اللَّهِ صلى الله عليه وسلم وَهْوَ يَبْرُقُ وَجْهُهُ مِنَ السُّرُورِ، وَكَانَ رَسُولُ اللَّهِ صلى الله عليه وسلم إِذَا سُرَّ اسْتَنَارَ وَجْهُهُ، حَتَّى كَأَنَّهُ قِطْعَةُ قَمَرٍ، وَكُنَّا نَعْرِفُ ذَلِكَ مِنْهُ

Narrated Abu Huraira: A Arab urinated in the mosque, and the people rushed to beat him. Allah's Messenger ﷺ ordered them to leave him and pour a bucket or a tumbler (full) of water over the place where he has passed urine. The Prophet then said, " You have been sent to make things easy (for the people) and you have not been sent to make things difficult for them.". – Sahih Al-Bukhari 6128

حَدَّثَنَا أَبُو الْيَمَانِ، أَخْبَرَنَا شُعَيْبٌ، عَنِ الزُّهْرِيِّ، ح وَقَالَ اللَّيْثُ حَدَّثَنِي يُونُسُ، عَنِ ابْنِ شِهَابٍ، أَخْبَرَنِي عُبَيْدُ اللَّهِ بْنُ عَبْدِ اللَّهِ بْنِ عُتْبَةَ، أَنَّ أَبَا هُرَيْرَةَ، أَخْبَرَهُ أَنَّ أَعْرَابِيًّا بَالَ فِي الْمَسْجِدِ، فَثَارَ إِلَيْهِ النَّاسُ لِيَقَعُوا بِهِ فَقَالَ لَهُمْ رَسُولُ اللَّهِ صلى الله عليه وسلم " دَعُوهُ، وَأَهْرِيقُوا عَلَى بَوْلِهِ ذَنُوبًا مِنْ مَاءٍ ـ أَوْ سَجْلاً مِنْ مَاءٍ ـ فَإِنَّمَا بُعِثْتُمْ مُيَسِّرِينَ، وَلَمْ تُبْعَثُوا مُعَسِّرِينَ ".

Narrated Abu Musa: The Prophet ﷺ said, "Near the establishment of the Hour there will be days during which (religious) knowledge will be taken away (vanish) and general ignorance will spread, and there will be Al-Harj in abundance, and Al-Harj means killing." – Sahih al-Bukhari 7064

حَدَّثَنَا عُمَرُ بْنُ حَفْصٍ، حَدَّثَنَا أَبِي، حَدَّثَنَا الأَعْمَشُ، حَدَّثَنَا شَقِيقٌ، قَالَ جَلَسَ عَبْدُ اللَّهِ وَأَبُو مُوسَى فَتَحَدَّثَا فَقَالَ أَبُو مُوسَى قَالَ النَّبِيُّ صلى الله عليه وسلم " إِنَّ بَيْنَ يَدَىِ السَّاعَةِ أَيَّامًا يُرْفَعُ فِيهَا الْعِلْمُ، وَيَنْزِلُ فِيهَا الْجَهْلُ، وَيَكْثُرُ فِيهَا الْهَرْجُ، وَالْهَرْجُ الْقَتْلُ ".

Narrated `Abdullah bin `Amr: Allah's Messenger (ﷺ) neither talked in an insulting manner nor did he ever speak evil intentionally. He used to say, "The most beloved to me amongst you is the one who has the best character and manners." He added, " Learn the Qur'an from (any of these) four persons. `Abdullah bin Mas`ud, Salim the freed slave of Abu Hudhaifa, Ubai bin Ka`b, and Mu`adh bin Jabal." – Sahih al-Bukhari 3759, 3760

حَدَّثَنَا حَفْصُ بْنُ عُمَرَ، حَدَّثَنَا شُعْبَةُ، عَنْ سُلَيْمَانَ، قَالَ سَمِعْتُ أَبَا وَائِلٍ، قَالَ سَمِعْتُ مَسْرُوقًا، قَالَ قَالَ عَبْدُ اللَّهِ بْنُ عَمْرٍو إِنَّ رَسُولَ اللَّهِ صلى الله عليه وسلم لَمْ يَكُنْ فَاحِشًا وَلاَ مُتَفَحِّشًا وَقَالَ " إِنَّ مِنْ أَحَبِّكُمْ إِلَىَّ أَحْسَنَكُمْ أَخْلاَقًا ". وَقَالَ " اسْتَقْرِئُوا الْقُرْآنَ مِنْ أَرْبَعَةٍ مِنْ عَبْدِ اللَّهِ بْنِ مَسْعُودٍ، وَسَالِمٍ مَوْلَى أَبِي حُذَيْفَةَ، وَأُبَىِّ بْنِ كَعْبٍ، وَمُعَاذِ بْنِ جَبَلٍ ".

Hidayah
هداية

Narrated 'Abdullah bin 'Abbas: Abu Sufyan bin Harb informed me that Heraclius had sent a messenger to him while he had been accompanying a caravan from Quraish. They were merchants doing business in Sham (Syria, Palestine, Lebanon and Jordan), at the time when Allah's Messenger ﷺ had truce with Abu Sufyan and Quraish infidels. So Abu Sufyan and his companions went to Heraclius at Ilya (Jerusalem). Heraclius called them in the court and he had all the senior Roman dignitaries around him. He called for his translator who, translating Heraclius's question said to them, "Who amongst you is closely related to that man who claims to be a Prophet?" Abu Sufyan replied, "I am the nearest relative to him (amongst the group)." Heraclius said, "Bring him (Abu Sufyan) close to me and make his companions stand behind him." Abu Sufyan added, Heraclius told his translator to tell my companions that he wanted to put some questions to me regarding that man (The Prophet) and that if I told a lie they (my companions) should contradict me." Abu Sufyan added, "By Allah! Had I not been afraid of my companions labeling me a liar, I would not have spoken the truth about the Prophet. The first question he asked me about him was: 'What is his family status amongst you?' I replied, 'He belongs to a good (noble) family amongst us.' Heraclius further asked, 'Has anybody amongst you ever claimed the same (i.e. to be a Prophet) before him?' I replied,

'No.' He said, 'Was anybody amongst his ancestors a king?' I replied, 'No.' Heraclius asked, 'Do the nobles or the poor follow him?' I replied, 'It is the poor who follow him.' He said, 'Are his followers increasing decreasing (day by day)?' I replied, 'They are increasing.' He then asked, 'Does anybody amongst those who embrace his religion become displeased and renounce the religion afterwards?' I replied, 'No.' Heraclius said, 'Have you ever accused him of telling lies before his claim (to be a Prophet)?' I replied, 'No. ' Heraclius said, 'Does he break his promises?' I replied, 'No. We are at truce with him but we do not know what he will do in it.' I could not find opportunity to say anything against him except that. Heraclius asked, 'Have you ever had a war with him?' I replied, 'Yes.' Then he said, 'What was the outcome of the battles?' I replied, 'Sometimes he was victorious and sometimes we.' Heraclius said, 'What does he order you to do?' I said, 'He tells us to worship Allah and Allah alone and not to worship anything along with Him, and to renounce all that our ancestors had said. He orders us to pray, to speak the truth, to be chaste and to keep good relations with our Kith and kin.' Heraclius asked the translator to convey to me the following, I asked you about his family and your reply was that he belonged to a very noble family. In fact all the Apostles come from noble families amongst their respective peoples. I questioned you whether anybody else amongst you claimed such a thing, your reply was in the negative. If the answer had been in the affirmative, I would have thought that this man was following the previous man's statement. Then I asked you whether anyone of his ancestors was a king. Your reply was in the negative, and if it had been in the affirmative, I would have thought that this man wanted to take back his ancestral kingdom. I further asked whether he was ever accused of telling lies before he said what he said, and your reply was in the negative. So I wondered how a person who does not tell a lie about others could ever tell a lie about Allah. I, then asked you whether the rich people followed him or the poor. You replied that it was the poor who followed him. And in fact all the Apostle have been followed by this very class of people. Then I asked you whether his followers were increasing or decreasing. You replied that they were increasing, and in fact this is the way of true faith, till it is complete in all respects. I further asked you whether there was anybody, who, after embracing his religion, became displeased and discarded his religion. Your reply was in the negative, and in fact this is (the sign of) true faith, when its delight enters the hearts and mixes with them completely. I asked you whether he had ever betrayed. You replied in the negative and likewise the Apostles never betray. Then I asked you what he ordered you to do. You replied that he ordered you to worship Allah and Allah alone and not to worship any thing along with Him and forbade you to worship idols and ordered you to pray, to speak the truth and to be chaste. If what you have said is true, he will very soon occupy this place underneath my feet and I knew it (from the scriptures) that he was going to appear but I did not know that he would be from you, and if I could reach him definitely, I would go immediately to meet him and if I were with him, I would certainly wash his feet.' Heraclius then asked for the letter addressed by Allah's Apostle Which was delivered by Dihya to the Governor of Busra, who forwarded it to Heraclius to read. The contents of the letter were as follows: "In the name of Allah the Beneficent, the Merciful (This letter is) from Muhammad the slave of Allah and His Apostle to Heraclius the ruler of Byzantine. Peace be upon him, who follows the right path. Furthermore I invite you to Islam, and if you become a Muslim you will be safe, and Allah will double your reward, and if you reject this invitation of Islam you will be committing a sin of Arisiyin (tillers, farmers i.e. your people). And (Allah's Statement.'O people of the scripture! Come to a word common to you and us that we worship none but Allah and that we associate nothing in worship with Him, and that none of us shall take others as Lords beside Allah.

Then, if they turn away, say: Bear witness that we are Muslims (those who have surrendered to Allah).' (3:64). Abu Sufyan then added, "When Heraclius had finished his speech and had read the letter, there was a great hue and cry in the Royal Court. So we were turned out of the court. I told my companions that the question of Ibn-Abi-Kabsha) (the Prophet ﷺ Muhammad) has become so prominent that even the King of Bani Al-Asfar (Byzantine) is afraid of him. Then I started to become sure that he (the Prophet) would be the conqueror in the near future till I embraced Islam (i.e. Allah guided me to it).".The sub narrator adds, "Ibn An-Natur was the Governor of Ilya' (Jerusalem) and Heraclius was the head of the Christians of Sham. Ibn An-Natur narrates that once while Heraclius was visiting ilya' (Jerusalem), he got up in the morning with a sad mood. Some of his priests asked him why he was in that mood? Heraclius was a foreteller and an astrologer. He replied, 'At night when I looked at the stars, I saw that the leader of those who practice circumcision had appeared (become the conqueror). Who are they who practice circumcision?' The people replied, 'Except the Jews nobody practices circumcision, so you should not be afraid of them (Jews). 'Just Issue orders to kill every Jew present in the country.' While they were discussing it, a messenger sent by the king of Ghassan to convey the news of Allah's Messenger ﷺ to Heraclius was brought in. Having heard the news, he (Heraclius) ordered the people to go and see whether the messenger of Ghassan was circumcised. The people, after seeing him, told Heraclius that he was circumcised. Heraclius then asked him about the Arabs. The messenger replied, 'Arabs also practice circumcision.' (After hearing that) Heraclius remarked that sovereignty of the 'Arabs had appeared. Heraclius then wrote a letter to his friend in Rome who was as good as Heraclius in knowledge. Heraclius then left for Homs. (a town in Syrian and stayed there till he received the reply of his letter from his friend who agreed with him in his opinion about the emergence of the Prophet ﷺ and the fact that he was a Prophet. On that Heraclius invited all the heads of the Byzantines to assemble in his palace at Homs. When they assembled, he ordered that all the doors of his palace be closed. Then he came out and said, 'O Byzantines! If success is your desire and if you seek right guidance and want your empire to remain then give a pledge of allegiance to this Prophet (i.e. embrace Islam).' (On hearing the views of Heraclius) the people ran towards the gates of the palace like onagers but found the doors closed. Heraclius realized their hatred towards Islam and when he lost the hope of their embracing Islam, he ordered that they should be brought back in audience. (When they returned) he said, 'What already said was just to test the strength of your conviction and I have seen it.' The people prostrated before him and became pleased with him, and this was the end of Heraclius's story (in connection with his faith). Bukhari 7

حَدَّثَنَا أَبُو الْيَمَانِ الْحَكَمُ بْنُ نَافِعٍ، قَالَ أَخْبَرَنَا شُعَيْبٌ، عَنِ الزُّهْرِيِّ، قَالَ أَخْبَرَنِي عُبَيْدُ اللَّهِ بْنُ عَبْدِ اللَّهِ بْنِ عُتْبَةَ بْنِ مَسْعُودٍ، أَنَّ عَبْدَ اللَّهِ بْنَ عَبَّاسٍ، أَخْبَرَهُ أَنَّ أَبَا سُفْيَانَ بْنَ حَرْبٍ أَخْبَرَهُ أَنَّ هِرَقْلَ أَرْسَلَ إِلَيْهِ فِي رَكْبٍ مِنْ قُرَيْشٍ ـ وَكَانُوا تُجَّارًا بِالشَّأْمِ ـ فِي الْمُدَّةِ الَّتِي كَانَ رَسُولُ اللَّهِ صلى الله عليه وسلم مَادَّ فِيهَا أَبَا سُفْيَانَ وَكُفَّارَ قُرَيْشٍ، فَأَتَوْهُ وَهُمْ بِإِيلِيَاءَ فَدَعَاهُمْ فِي مَجْلِسِهِ، وَحَوْلَهُ عُظَمَاءُ الرُّومِ ثُمَّ دَعَاهُمْ وَدَعَا بِتَرْجُمَانِهِ فَقَالَ أَيُّكُمْ أَقْرَبُ نَسَبًا بِهَذَا الرَّجُلِ الَّذِي يَزْعُمُ أَنَّهُ نَبِيٌّ فَقَالَ أَبُو سُفْيَانَ فَقُلْتُ أَنَا أَقْرَبُهُمْ نَسَبًا. فَقَالَ أَدْنُوهُ مِنِّي، وَقَرِّبُوا أَصْحَابَهُ، فَاجْعَلُوهُمْ عِنْدَ ظَهْرِهِ. ثُمَّ قَالَ لِتَرْجُمَانِهِ قُلْ لَهُمْ إِنِّي سَائِلٌ هَذَا عَنْ هَذَا الرَّجُلِ، فَإِنْ كَذَبَنِي فَكَذِّبُوهُ. فَوَاللَّهِ لَوْلاَ الْحَيَاءُ مِنْ أَنْ يَأْثِرُوا عَلَىَّ كَذِبًا لَكَذَبْتُ عَنْهُ، ثُمَّ كَانَ أَوَّلَ مَا سَأَلَنِي عَنْهُ أَنْ قَالَ كَيْفَ نَسَبُهُ فِيكُمْ قُلْتُ هُوَ فِينَا ذُو نَسَبٍ. قَالَ فَهَلْ قَالَ هَذَا الْقَوْلَ مِنْكُمْ أَحَدٌ قَطُّ قَبْلَهُ قُلْتُ لاَ. قَالَ فَهَلْ كَانَ مِنْ آبَائِهِ مِنْ مَلِكٍ قُلْتُ لاَ. قَالَ فَأَشْرَافُ النَّاسِ يَتَّبِعُونَهُ أَمْ ضُعَفَاؤُهُمْ فَقُلْتُ بَلْ ضُعَفَاؤُهُمْ. قَالَ أَيَزِيدُونَ أَمْ يَنْقُصُونَ قُلْتُ بَلْ يَزِيدُونَ. قَالَ فَهَلْ يَرْتَدُّ أَحَدٌ مِنْهُمْ سَخْطَةً لِدِينِهِ بَعْدَ أَنْ يَدْخُلَ فِيهِ قُلْتُ لاَ. قَالَ فَهَلْ كُنْتُمْ تَتَّهِمُونَهُ بِالْكَذِبِ قَبْلَ أَنْ يَقُولَ مَا قَالَ قُلْتُ لاَ. قَالَ فَهَلْ يَغْدِرُ قُلْتُ لاَ، وَنَحْنُ مِنْهُ فِي مُدَّةٍ لاَ نَدْرِي مَا هُوَ فَاعِلٌ فِيهَا. قَالَ وَلَمْ تُمْكِنِّي كَلِمَةٌ أُدْخِلُ فِيهَا شَيْئًا غَيْرُ هَذِهِ الْكَلِمَةِ. قَالَ فَهَلْ قَاتَلْتُمُوهُ قُلْتُ نَعَمْ. قَالَ فَكَيْفَ كَانَ قِتَالُكُمْ إِيَّاهُ قُلْتُ الْحَرْبُ بَيْنَنَا وَبَيْنَهُ سِجَالٌ، يَنَالُ مِنَّا وَنَنَالُ مِنْهُ. قَالَ مَاذَا يَأْمُرُكُمْ قُلْتُ يَقُولُ اعْبُدُوا اللَّهَ وَحْدَهُ، وَلاَ تُشْرِكُوا بِهِ شَيْئًا، وَاتْرُكُوا مَا يَقُولُ آبَاؤُكُمْ، وَيَأْمُرُنَا بِالصَّلاَةِ وَالصِّدْقِ وَالْعَفَافِ وَالصِّلَةِ. فَقَالَ لِلتَّرْجُمَانِ قُلْ لَهُ سَأَلْتُكَ عَنْ نَسَبِهِ، فَذَكَرْتَ أَنَّهُ فِيكُمْ ذُو نَسَبٍ، فَكَذَلِكَ الرُّسُلُ تُبْعَثُ فِي نَسَبِ قَوْمِهَا، وَسَأَلْتُكَ هَلْ قَالَ أَحَدٌ مِنْكُمْ هَذَا الْقَوْلَ فَذَكَرْتَ أَنْ لاَ، فَقُلْتُ لَوْ كَانَ أَحَدٌ قَالَ هَذَا الْقَوْلَ قَبْلَهُ لَقُلْتُ رَجُلٌ يَأْتَسِي بِقَوْلٍ قِيلَ قَبْلَهُ، وَسَأَلْتُكَ

هَلْ كَانَ مِنْ آبَائِهِ مِنْ مَلِكٍ فَذَكَرْتَ أَنْ لاَ، قُلْتُ فَلَوْ كَانَ مِنْ آبَائِهِ مِنْ مَلِكٍ قُلْتُ رَجُلٌ يَطْلُبُ مُلْكَ أَبِيهِ، وَسَأَلْتُكَ هَلْ كُنْتُمْ تَتَّهِمُونَهُ بِالْكَذِبِ قَبْلَ أَنْ يَقُولَ مَا قَالَ فَذَكَرْتَ أَنْ لاَ، فَقَدْ أَعْرِفُ أَنَّهُ لَمْ يَكُنْ لِيَذَرَ الْكَذِبَ عَلَى النَّاسِ وَيَكْذِبَ عَلَى اللَّهِ، وَسَأَلْتُكَ أَشْرَافُ النَّاسِ اتَّبَعُوهُ أَمْ ضُعَفَاؤُهُمْ فَذَكَرْتَ أَنَّ ضُعَفَاءَهُمُ اتَّبَعُوهُ، وَهُمْ أَتْبَاعُ الرُّسُلِ، وَسَأَلْتُكَ أَيَزِيدُونَ أَمْ يَنْقُصُونَ فَذَكَرْتَ أَنَّهُمْ يَزِيدُونَ، وَكَذَلِكَ أَمْرُ الإِيمَانِ حَتَّى يَتِمَّ، وَسَأَلْتُكَ أَيَرْتَدُّ أَحَدٌ سَخْطَةً لِدِينِهِ بَعْدَ أَنْ يَدْخُلَ فِيهِ فَذَكَرْتَ أَنْ لاَ، وَكَذَلِكَ الإِيمَانُ حِينَ تُخَالِطُ بَشَاشَتُهُ الْقُلُوبَ، وَسَأَلْتُكَ هَلْ يَغْدِرُ فَذَكَرْتَ أَنْ لاَ، وَكَذَلِكَ الرُّسُلُ لاَ تَغْدِرُ، وَسَأَلْتُكَ بِمَا يَأْمُرُكُمْ، فَذَكَرْتَ أَنَّهُ يَأْمُرُكُمْ أَنْ تَعْبُدُوا اللَّهَ، وَلاَ تُشْرِكُوا بِهِ شَيْئًا، وَيَنْهَاكُمْ عَنْ عِبَادَةِ الأَوْثَانِ، وَيَأْمُرُكُمْ بِالصَّلاَةِ وَالصِّدْقِ وَالْعَفَافِ. فَإِنْ كَانَ مَا تَقُولُ حَقًّا فَسَيَمْلِكُ مَوْضِعَ قَدَمَىَّ هَاتَيْنِ، وَقَدْ كُنْتُ أَعْلَمُ أَنَّهُ خَارِجٌ، لَمْ أَكُنْ أَظُنُّ أَنَّهُ مِنْكُمْ، فَلَوْ أَنِّي أَعْلَمُ أَنِّي أَخْلُصُ إِلَيْهِ لَتَجَشَّمْتُ لِقَاءَهُ، وَلَوْ كُنْتُ عِنْدَهُ لَغَسَلْتُ عَنْ قَدَمِهِ. ثُمَّ دَعَا بِكِتَابِ رَسُولِ اللَّهِ صلى الله عليه وسلم الَّذِي بَعَثَ بِهِ دِحْيَةُ إِلَى عَظِيمِ بُصْرَى، فَدَفَعَهُ إِلَى هِرَقْلَ فَقَرَأَهُ فَإِذَا فِيهِ بِسْمِ اللَّهِ الرَّحْمَنِ الرَّحِيمِ. مِنْ مُحَمَّدٍ عَبْدِ اللَّهِ وَرَسُولِهِ إِلَى هِرَقْلَ عَظِيمِ الرُّومِ. سَلاَمٌ عَلَى مَنِ اتَّبَعَ الْهُدَى، أَمَّا بَعْدُ فَإِنِّي أَدْعُوكَ بِدِعَايَةِ الإِسْلاَمِ، أَسْلِمْ تَسْلَمْ، يُؤْتِكَ اللَّهُ أَجْرَكَ مَرَّتَيْنِ، فَإِنْ تَوَلَّيْتَ فَإِنَّ عَلَيْكَ إِثْمَ الأَرِيسِيِّينَ وَ{يَا أَهْلَ الْكِتَابِ تَعَالَوْا إِلَى كَلِمَةٍ سَوَاءٍ بَيْنَنَا وَبَيْنَكُمْ أَنْ لاَ نَعْبُدَ إِلاَّ اللَّهَ وَلاَ نُشْرِكَ بِهِ شَيْئًا وَلاَ يَتَّخِذَ بَعْضُنَا بَعْضًا أَرْبَابًا مِنْ دُونِ اللَّهِ فَإِنْ تَوَلَّوْا فَقُولُوا اشْهَدُوا بِأَنَّا مُسْلِمُونَ} قَالَ أَبُو سُفْيَانَ فَلَمَّا قَالَ مَا قَالَ، وَفَرَغَ مِنْ قِرَاءَةِ الْكِتَابِ كَثُرَ عِنْدَهُ الصَّخَبُ، وَارْتَفَعَتِ الأَصْوَاتُ وَأُخْرِجْنَا، فَقُلْتُ لأَصْحَابِي حِينَ أُخْرِجْنَا لَقَدْ أَمِرَ أَمْرُ ابْنِ أَبِي كَبْشَةَ، إِنَّهُ يَخَافُهُ مَلِكُ بَنِي الأَصْفَرِ. فَمَا زِلْتُ مُوقِنًا أَنَّهُ سَيَظْهَرُ حَتَّى أَدْخَلَ اللَّهُ عَلَيَّ الإِسْلاَمَ. وَكَانَ ابْنُ النَّاظُورِ صَاحِبُ إِيلِيَاءَ وَهِرَقْلَ سُقُفًّا عَلَى نَصَارَى الشَّأْمِ، يُحَدِّثُ أَنَّ هِرَقْلَ حِينَ قَدِمَ إِيلِيَاءَ أَصْبَحَ يَوْمًا خَبِيثَ النَّفْسِ، فَقَالَ بَعْضُ بَطَارِقَتِهِ قَدِ اسْتَنْكَرْنَا هَيْئَتَكَ. قَالَ ابْنُ النَّاظُورِ وَكَانَ هِرَقْلُ حَزَّاءً يَنْظُرُ فِي النُّجُومِ، فَقَالَ لَهُمْ حِينَ سَأَلُوهُ إِنِّي رَأَيْتُ اللَّيْلَةَ حِينَ نَظَرْتُ فِي النُّجُومِ مَلِكَ الْخِتَانِ قَدْ ظَهَرَ، فَمَنْ يَخْتَتِنُ مِنْ هَذِهِ الأُمَّةِ قَالُوا لَيْسَ يَخْتَتِنُ إِلاَّ الْيَهُودُ فَلاَ يُهِمَّنَّكَ شَأْنُهُمْ وَاكْتُبْ إِلَى مَدَايِنِ مُلْكِكَ، فَيَقْتُلُوا مَنْ فِيهِمْ مِنَ الْيَهُودِ. فَبَيْنَمَا هُمْ عَلَى أَمْرِهِمْ أُتِيَ هِرَقْلُ بِرَجُلٍ أَرْسَلَ بِهِ مَلِكُ غَسَّانَ، يُخْبِرُ عَنْ خَبَرِ رَسُولِ اللَّهِ صلى الله عليه وسلم فَلَمَّا اسْتَخْبَرَهُ هِرَقْلُ قَالَ اذْهَبُوا فَانْظُرُوا أَمُخْتَتِنٌ هُوَ أَمْ لاَ. فَنَظَرُوا إِلَيْهِ، فَحَدَّثُوهُ أَنَّهُ مُخْتَتِنٌ، وَسَأَلَهُ عَنِ الْعَرَبِ فَقَالَ هُمْ يَخْتَتِنُونَ. فَقَالَ هِرَقْلُ هَذَا مَلِكُ هَذِهِ الأُمَّةِ قَدْ ظَهَرَ. ثُمَّ كَتَبَ هِرَقْلُ إِلَى صَاحِبٍ لَهُ بِرُومِيَةَ، وَكَانَ نَظِيرَهُ فِي الْعِلْمِ، وَسَارَ هِرَقْلُ إِلَى حِمْصَ، فَلَمْ يَرِمْ حِمْصَ حَتَّى أَتَاهُ كِتَابٌ مِنْ صَاحِبِهِ يُوَافِقُ رَأْىَ هِرَقْلَ عَلَى خُرُوجِ النَّبِيِّ صلى الله عليه وسلم وَأَنَّهُ نَبِيٌّ، فَأَذِنَ هِرَقْلُ لِعُظَمَاءِ الرُّومِ فِي دَسْكَرَةٍ لَهُ بِحِمْصَ ثُمَّ أَمَرَ بِأَبْوَابِهَا فَغُلِّقَتْ، ثُمَّ اطَّلَعَ فَقَالَ يَا مَعْشَرَ الرُّومِ، هَلْ لَكُمْ فِي الْفَلاَحِ وَالرُّشْدِ وَأَنْ يَثْبُتَ مُلْكُكُمْ فَتُبَايِعُوا هَذَا النَّبِيَّ، فَحَاصُوا حَيْصَةَ حُمُرِ الْوَحْشِ إِلَى الأَبْوَابِ، فَوَجَدُوهَا قَدْ غُلِّقَتْ، فَلَمَّا رَأَى هِرَقْلُ نَفْرَتَهُمْ، وَأَيِسَ مِنَ الإِيمَانِ قَالَ رُدُّوهُمْ عَلَىَّ. وَقَالَ إِنِّي قُلْتُ مَقَالَتِي آنِفًا أَخْتَبِرُ بِهَا شِدَّتَكُمْ عَلَى دِينِكُمْ، فَقَدْ رَأَيْتُ. فَسَجَدُوا لَهُ وَرَضُوا عَنْهُ، فَكَانَ ذَلِكَ آخِرَ شَأْنِ هِرَقْلَ. رَوَاهُ صَالِحُ بْنُ كَيْسَانَ وَيُونُسُ وَمَعْمَرٌ عَنِ الزُّهْرِيِّ.

Narrated Jarir bin Abdullah: I gave the pledge of allegiance to Allah's Messenger ﷺ for the following: Offer prayers perfectly. 2)Pay the Zakat (obligatory charity) . 3) And be sincere and true to every Muslim. – Al-Bukhari 57

حَدَّثَنَا مُسَدَّدٌ، قَالَ حَدَّثَنَا يَحْيَى، عَنْ إِسْمَاعِيلَ، قَالَ حَدَّثَنِي قَيْسُ بْنُ أَبِي حَازِمٍ، عَنْ جَرِيرِ بْنِ عَبْدِ اللَّهِ، قَالَ بَايَعْتُ رَسُولَ اللَّهِ صلى الله عليه وسلم عَلَى إِقَامِ الصَّلاَةِ، وَإِيتَاءِ الزَّكَاةِ، وَالنُّصْحِ لِكُلِّ مُسْلِمٍ.

Narrated Ibn `Abbas: The Prophet ﷺ sent Mu`adh to Yemen and said, "Invite the people to testify that none has the right to be worshipped but Allah and I am Allah's Messenger ﷺ ,and if they obey you to do so, then teach them that Allah has enjoined on them five prayers in every day and night (in twenty-four hours), and if they obey you to do so, then teach them that Allah has made it obligatory for them to pay the Zakat from their property and it is to be taken from the wealthy among them and given to the poor." – Al-Bukhari 1395

حَدَّثَنَا أَبُو عَاصِمٍ الضَّحَّاكُ بْنُ مَخْلَدٍ، عَنْ زَكَرِيَّاءَ بْنِ إِسْحَاقَ، عَنْ يَحْيَى بْنِ عَبْدِ اللَّهِ بْنِ صَيْفِيٍّ، عَنْ أَبِي مَعْبَدٍ، عَنِ ابْنِ عَبَّاسٍ ـ رضى الله عنهما ـ أَنَّ النَّبِيَّ صلى الله عليه وسلم بَعَثَ مُعَاذًا ـ رضى الله عنه ـ إِلَى الْيَمَنِ فَقَالَ " ادْعُهُمْ إِلَى شَهَادَةِ أَنْ لاَ إِلَهَ إِلاَّ اللَّهُ، وَأَنِّي رَسُولُ اللَّهِ، فَإِنْ هُمْ أَطَاعُوا لِذَلِكَ فَأَعْلِمْهُمْ أَنَّ اللَّهَ قَدِ افْتَرَضَ عَلَيْهِمْ خَمْسَ صَلَوَاتٍ فِي كُلِّ يَوْمٍ وَلَيْلَةٍ، فَإِنْ هُمْ أَطَاعُوا لِذَلِكَ فَأَعْلِمْهُمْ أَنَّ اللَّهَ افْتَرَضَ عَلَيْهِمْ صَدَقَةً فِي أَمْوَالِهِمْ، تُؤْخَذُ مِنْ أَغْنِيَائِهِمْ وَتُرَدُّ عَلَى فُقَرَائِهِمْ

Narrated Abu Burda: From his father from his grandfather that the Prophet ﷺ said, "Every Muslim has to give in charity." The people asked, "O Allah's Prophet! If someone has nothing to give, what will he do?" He said, "He should work with his hands and benefit himself and also give in charity (from what he earns)." The people further asked, "If he cannot find even that?" He replied, "He should help the needy who appeal for help." Then the people asked,

"If he cannot do that?" He replied, "Then he should perform good deeds and keep away from evil deeds and this will be regarded as charitable deeds." – Al-Bukhari 1445

حَدَّثَنَا مُسْلِمُ بْنُ إِبْرَاهِيمَ، حَدَّثَنَا شُعْبَةُ، حَدَّثَنَا سَعِيدُ بْنُ أَبِي بُرْدَةَ، عَنْ أَبِيهِ، عَنْ جَدِّهِ، عَنِ النَّبِيِّ صلى الله عليه وسلم قَالَ " عَلَى كُلِّ مُسْلِمٍ صَدَقَةٌ ". فَقَالُوا يَا نَبِيَّ اللَّهِ فَمَنْ لَمْ يَجِدْ قَالَ " يَعْمَلُ بِيَدِهِ فَيَنْفَعُ نَفْسَهُ وَيَتَصَدَّقُ ". قَالُوا فَإِنْ لَمْ يَجِدْ قَالَ " يُعِينُ ذَا الْحَاجَةِ الْمَلْهُوفَ ". قَالُوا فَإِنْ لَمْ يَجِدْ. قَالَ " فَلْيَعْمَلْ بِالْمَعْرُوفِ، وَلْيُمْسِكْ عَنِ الشَّرِّ فَإِنَّهَا لَهُ صَدَقَةٌ "

Narrated Abu Mas`ud Al-Ansari: Whenever Allah's Messenger ﷺ ordered us to give in charity, we used to go to the market and work as porters and get a Mudd (a special measure of grain) and then give it in charity. (Those were the days of poverty) and today some of us have one hundred thousand. – Al-Bukhari 1416

حَدَّثَنَا سَعِيدُ بْنُ يَحْيَى، حَدَّثَنَا أَبِي، حَدَّثَنَا الأَعْمَشُ، عَنْ شَقِيقٍ، عَنْ أَبِي مَسْعُودٍ الأَنْصَارِيِّ ـ رضى الله عنه ـ قَالَ كَانَ رَسُولُ اللَّهِ صلى الله عليه وسلم إِذَا أَمَرَنَا بِالصَّدَقَةِ انْطَلَقَ أَحَدُنَا إِلَى السُّوقِ فَتَحَامَلَ فَيُصِيبُ الْمُدَّ، وَإِنَّ لِبَعْضِهِمُ الْيَوْمَ لَمِائَةَ أَلْفٍ

Narrated Abu Jamra: I used to sit with Ibn 'Abbas and he made me sit on his sitting place. He requested me to stay with him in order that he might give me a share from his property. So I stayed with him for two months. Once he told (me) that when the delegation of the tribe of 'Abdul Qais came to the Prophet, the Prophet ﷺ asked them, "Who are the people (i.e. you)? (Or) who are the delegate?" They replied, "We are from the tribe of Rabi'a." Then the Prophet ﷺ said to them, "Welcome! O people (or O delegation of 'Abdul Qais)! Neither will you have disgrace nor will you regret." They said, "O Allah's Messenger ﷺ ! We cannot come to you except in the sacred month and there is the Infidel tribe of Mudar intervening between you and us. So please order us to do something good (religious deeds) so that we may inform our people whom we have left behind (at home), and that we may enter Paradise (by acting on them)." Then they asked about drinks (what is legal and what is illegal). The Prophet ﷺ ordered them to do four things and forbade them from four things. He ordered them to believe in Allah Alone and asked them, "Do you know what is meant by believing in Allah Alone?" They replied, "Allah and His Apostle know better." Thereupon the Prophet ﷺ said, "It means: To testify that none has the right to be worshipped but Allah and Muhammad is Allah's Messenger ﷺ 2) To offer prayers perfectly 3)To pay the Zakat (obligatory charity) 4) To observe fast during the month of Ramadan. 5)And to pay Al-Khumus (one fifth of the booty to be given in Allah's Cause). Then he forbade them four things, namely, Hantam, Dubba,' Naqir Ann Muzaffat or Muqaiyar; (These were the names of pots in which Alcoholic drinks were prepared) (The Prophet ﷺ mentioned the container of wine and he meant the wine itself). The Prophet ﷺ further said (to them): "Memorize them (these instructions) and convey them to the people whom you have left behind." – Al-Bukhari 53

حَدَّثَنَا عَلِيُّ بْنُ الْجَعْدِ، قَالَ أَخْبَرَنَا شُعْبَةُ، عَنْ أَبِي جَمْرَةَ، قَالَ كُنْتُ أَقْعُدُ مَعَ ابْنِ عَبَّاسٍ، يُجْلِسُنِي عَلَى سَرِيرِهِ فَقَالَ أَقِمْ عِنْدِي حَتَّى أَجْعَلَ لَكَ سَهْمًا مِنْ مَالِي، فَأَقَمْتُ مَعَهُ شَهْرَيْنِ، ثُمَّ قَالَ إِنَّ وَفْدَ عَبْدِ الْقَيْسِ لَمَّا أَتَوُا النَّبِيَّ صلى الله عليه وسلم قَالَ " مَنِ الْقَوْمُ أَوْ مَنِ الْوَفْدُ ". قَالُوا رَبِيعَةُ. قَالَ " مَرْحَبًا بِالْقَوْمِ ـ أَوْ بِالْوَفْدِ ـ غَيْرَ خَزَايَا وَلاَ نَدَامَى ". فَقَالُوا يَا رَسُولَ اللَّهِ، إِنَّا لاَ نَسْتَطِيعُ أَنْ نَأْتِيَكَ إِلاَّ فِي شَهْرِ الْحَرَامِ، وَبَيْنَنَا وَبَيْنَكَ هَذَا الْحَىُّ مِنْ كُفَّارِ مُضَرَ، فَمُرْنَا بِأَمْرٍ فَصْلٍ، نُخْبِرْ بِهِ مَنْ وَرَاءَنَا، وَنَدْخُلْ بِهِ الْجَنَّةَ. وَسَأَلُوهُ عَنِ الأَشْرِبَةِ. فَأَمَرَهُمْ بِأَرْبَعٍ، وَنَهَاهُمْ عَنْ أَرْبَعٍ، أَمَرَهُمْ بِالإِيمَانِ بِاللَّهِ وَحْدَهُ. قَالَ " أَتَدْرُونَ مَا الإِيمَانُ بِاللَّهِ وَحْدَهُ ". قَالُوا اللَّهُ وَرَسُولُهُ أَعْلَمُ. قَالَ " شَهَادَةُ أَنْ لاَ إِلَهَ إِلاَّ اللَّهُ وَأَنَّ مُحَمَّدًا رَسُولُ اللَّهِ، وَإِقَامُ الصَّلاَةِ، وَإِيتَاءُ الزَّكَاةِ، وَصِيَامُ رَمَضَانَ، وَأَنْ تُعْطُوا مِنَ الْمَغْنَمِ الْخُمُسَ ". وَنَهَاهُمْ عَنْ أَرْبَعٍ عَنِ الْحَنْتَمِ وَالدُّبَّاءِ وَالنَّقِيرِ وَالْمُزَفَّتِ. وَرُبَّمَا قَالَ الْمُقَيَّرِ. وَقَالَ " احْفَظُوهُنَّ وَأَخْبِرُوا بِهِنَّ مَنْ وَرَاءَكُمْ ".

The Book of

Onset of Revelation

بداية الوحي

Narrated `Abdullah: Allah's Messenger ﷺ said that he met Zaid bin `Amr Nufail at a place near Baldah and this had happened before Allah's Messenger ﷺ received the Divine Inspiration. Allah's Messenger ﷺ presented a dish of meat (that had been offered to him by the pagans) to Zaid bin `Amr, but Zaid refused to eat of it and then said (to the pagans), "I do not eat of what you slaughter on your stonealtars (Ansabs) nor do I eat except that on which Allah's Name has been mentioned on slaughtering." – Al-Bukhari 5499

حَدَّثَنَا مُعَلَّى بْنُ أَسَدٍ، حَدَّثَنَا عَبْدُ الْعَزِيزِ ـ يَعْنِي ابْنَ الْمُخْتَارِ ـ أَخْبَرَنَا مُوسَى بْنُ عُقْبَةَ، قَالَ أَخْبَرَنِي سَالِمٌ، أَنَّهُ سَمِعَ عَبْدَ اللَّهِ، يُحَدِّثُ عَنْ رَسُولِ اللَّهِ صلى الله عليه وسلم أَنَّهُ لَقِيَ زَيْدَ بْنَ عَمْرِو بْنِ نُفَيْلٍ بِأَسْفَلِ بَلْدَحٍ، وَذَاكَ قَبْلَ أَنْ يُنْزَلَ عَلَى رَسُولِ اللَّهِ صلى الله عليه وسلم الْوَحْىُ، فَقَدَّمَ إِلَيْهِ رَسُولُ اللَّهِ صلى الله عليه وسلم سُفْرَةً فِيهَا لَحْمٌ، فَأَبَى أَنْ يَأْكُلَ مِنْهَا، ثُمَّ قَالَ إِنِّي لاَ آكُلُ مِمَّا تَذْبَحُونَ عَلَى أَنْصَابِكُمْ، وَلاَ آكُلُ إِلاَّ مِمَّا ذُكِرَ اسْمُ اللَّهِ عَلَيْهِ

Narrated Muhammad bin Jubair bin Mut`im: My father said, "(Before Islam) I was looking for my camel .." The same narration is told by a different sub-narrator. Jubair bin Mut`im said, "My camel was lost and I went out in search of it on the day of `Arafat, and I saw the Prophet ﷺ standing in `Arafat. I said to myself: By Allah he is from the Hums (literally: strictly religious, Quraish were called so, as they used to say, 'We are the people of Allah we shall not go out of the sanctuary). What has brought him here?" – Al-Bukhari 1664

حَدَّثَنَا عَلِيُّ بْنُ عَبْدِ اللَّهِ، حَدَّثَنَا سُفْيَانُ، حَدَّثَنَا عَمْرٌو، حَدَّثَنَا مُحَمَّدُ بْنُ جُبَيْرِ بْنِ مُطْعِمٍ، عَنْ أَبِيهِ، كُنْتُ أَطْلُبُ بَعِيرًا لِي. وَحَدَّثَنَا مُسَدَّدٌ، حَدَّثَنَا سُفْيَانُ، عَنْ عَمْرٍو، سَمِعَ مُحَمَّدَ بْنَ جُبَيْرٍ، عَنْ أَبِيهِ، جُبَيْرِ بْنِ مُطْعِمٍ قَالَ أَضْلَلْتُ بَعِيرًا لِي، فَذَهَبْتُ أَطْلُبُهُ يَوْمَ عَرَفَةَ، فَرَأَيْتُ النَّبِيَّ صلى الله عليه وسلم وَاقِفًا بِعَرَفَةَ، فَقُلْتُ هَذَا وَاللَّهِ مِنَ الْحُمْسِ فَمَا شَأْنُهُ هَا هُنَا

Narrated Al-Miswar bin Makhrama: `Ali demanded the hand of the daughter of Abu Jahl. Fatima heard of this and went to Allah's Messenger ﷺ saying, "Your people think that you do not become angry for the sake of your daughters as `Ali is now going to marry the daughter of Abu Jahl. "On that Allah's Messenger ﷺ got up and after his recitation of Tashah-hud. I heard him saying, "Then after! I married one of my daughters to Abu Al-`As bin Al- Rabi` (the husband of Zainab, the daughter of the Prophet ﷺ) before Islam and he proved truthful in whatever he said to me. No doubt, Fatima Is a part of me, I hate to see her being troubled. By Allah, the daughter of Allah's Messenger ﷺ and the daughter of Allah's Enemy cannot be the wives of one man." So `Ali gave up that engagement. 'Al-Miswar further said: I heard the Prophet ﷺ talking and he mentioned a son-in-law of his belonging to the tribe of Bani `Abd-Shams. He highly praised him concerning that relationship and said (whenever) he spoke to me, he spoke the truth, and whenever he promised me, he fulfilled his promise." – Sahih al-Bukhari 3729

حَدَّثَنَا أَبُو الْيَمَانِ، أَخْبَرَنَا شُعَيْبٌ، عَنِ الزُّهْرِيِّ، قَالَ حَدَّثَنِي عَلِيُّ بْنُ حُسَيْنٍ، أَنَّ الْمِسْوَرَ بْنَ مَخْرَمَةَ، قَالَ إِنَّ عَلِيًّا خَطَبَ بِنْتَ أَبِي جَهْلٍ، فَسَمِعَتْ بِذَلِكَ، فَاطِمَةُ، فَأَتَتْ رَسُولَ اللَّهِ صلى الله عليه وسلم فَقَالَتْ يَزْعُمُ قَوْمُكَ أَنَّكَ لاَ تَغْضَبُ لِبَنَاتِكَ، هَذَا عَلِيٌّ نَاكِحٌ بِنْتَ أَبِي جَهْلٍ، فَقَامَ رَسُولُ اللَّهِ صلى الله عليه وسلم فَسَمِعْتُهُ حِينَ تَشَهَّدَ يَقُولُ " أَمَّا بَعْدُ أَنْكَحْتُ أَبَا الْعَاصِ بْنَ الرَّبِيعِ، فَحَدَّثَنِي وَصَدَقَنِي، وَإِنَّ فَاطِمَةَ بَضْعَةٌ مِنِّي، وَإِنِّي أَكْرَهُ أَنْ يَسُوءَهَا، وَاللَّهِ لاَ تَجْتَمِعُ بِنْتُ رَسُولِ اللَّهِ صلى الله عليه وسلم وَبِنْتُ عَدُوِّ اللَّهِ عِنْدَ رَجُلٍ وَاحِدٍ ". فَتَرَكَ عَلِيٌّ الْخِطْبَةَ. وَزَادَ مُحَمَّدُ بْنُ عَمْرِو بْنِ حَلْحَلَةَ عَنِ ابْنِ شِهَابٍ عَنْ عَلِيٍّ عَنْ مِسْوَرٍ، سَمِعْتُ النَّبِيَّ صلى الله عليه وسلم وَذَكَرَ صِهْرًا لَهُ مِنْ بَنِي عَبْدِ شَمْسٍ فَأَثْنَى عَلَيْهِ فِي مُصَاهَرَتِهِ إِيَّاهُ فَأَحْسَنَ قَالَ " حَدَّثَنِي فَصَدَقَنِي، وَوَعَدَنِي فَوَفَى لِي ".

Narrated Abu Huraira: When Allah revealed the Verse: "Warn your nearest kinsmen," Allah's Messenger ﷺ got up and said, "O people of Quraish (or said similar words)! Buy (i.e. save) yourselves (from the Hellfire) as I cannot save you from Allah's Punishment; O Bani `Abd Manaf! I cannot save you from Allah's Punishment, O Safiya, the Aunt of Allah's Messenger ﷺ ! I cannot save you from Allah's Punishment; O Fatima bint Muhammad! Ask me anything from my wealth, but I cannot save you from Allah's Punishment." – Al-Bukhari 2753
حَدَّثَنَا أَبُو الْيَمَانِ، أَخْبَرَنَا شُعَيْبٌ، عَنِ الزُّهْرِيِّ، قَالَ أَخْبَرَنِي سَعِيدُ بْنُ الْمُسَيَّبِ، وَأَبُو سَلَمَةَ بْنُ عَبْدِ الرَّحْمَنِ أَنَّ أَبَا هُرَيْرَةَ ـ رضى الله عنه ـ قَالَ قَامَ رَسُولُ اللَّهِ صلى الله عليه وسلم حِينَ أَنْزَلَ اللَّهُ عَزَّ وَجَلَّ {وَأَنْذِرْ عَشِيرَتَكَ الأَقْرَبِينَ} قَالَ " يَا مَعْشَرَ قُرَيْشٍ ـ أَوْ كَلِمَةً نَحْوَهَا ـ اشْتَرُوا أَنْفُسَكُمْ، لاَ أُغْنِي عَنْكُمْ مِنَ اللَّهِ شَيْئًا، يَا بَنِي عَبْدِ مَنَافٍ لاَ أُغْنِي عَنْكُمْ مِنَ اللَّهِ شَيْئًا، يَا عَبَّاسُ بْنَ عَبْدِ الْمُطَّلِبِ لاَ أُغْنِي عَنْكَ مِنَ اللَّهِ شَيْئًا، وَيَا صَفِيَّةُ عَمَّةَ رَسُولِ اللَّهِ لاَ أُغْنِي عَنْكِ مِنَ اللَّهِ شَيْئًا، وَيَا فَاطِمَةُ بِنْتَ مُحَمَّدٍ سَلِينِي مَا شِئْتِ مِنْ مَالِي لاَ أُغْنِي عَنْكِ مِنَ اللَّهِ شَيْئًا ". تَابَعَهُ أَصْبَغُ عَنِ ابْنِ وَهْبٍ عَنْ يُونُسَ عَنِ ابْنِ شِهَابٍ

Narrated Yahya bin Abi Kathir: I asked Aba Salama bin `Abdur-Rahman about the first Sura revealed of the Qur'an. He replied "O you, wrapped-up (i.e. Al Muddaththir)." I said, "They say it was, 'Read, in the Name of your Lord Who created,' (i.e. Surat Al-`Alaq (the Clot)." On that, Abu Salama said, "I asked Jabir bin `Abdullah about that, saying the same as you have said, whereupon he said, 'I will not tell you except what Allah's Messenger ﷺ had told us. Allah's Messenger ﷺ said, "I was in seclusion in the cave of Hiram', and after I completed the limited period of my seclusion. I came down (from the cave) and heard a voice calling me. I looked to my right, but saw nothing. Then I looked up and saw something. So I went to Khadija (the Prophet's wife) and told her to wrap me up and pour cold water on me. So they wrapped me up and poured cold water on me." Then, 'O you, (Muhammad) wrapped up! Arise and warn,' (Surat Al Muddaththir) was revealed." (74.1) – Al-Bukhari 4922
حَدَّثَنَا يَحْيَى، حَدَّثَنَا وَكِيعٌ، عَنْ عَلِيِّ بْنِ الْمُبَارَكِ، عَنْ يَحْيَى بْنِ أَبِي كَثِيرٍ، سَأَلْتُ أَبَا سَلَمَةَ بْنَ عَبْدِ الرَّحْمَنِ عَنْ أَوَّلِ، مَا نَزَلَ مِنَ الْقُرْآنِ. قَالَ {يَا أَيُّهَا الْمُدَّثِّرُ} قُلْتُ يَقُولُونَ {اقْرَأْ بِاسْمِ رَبِّكَ الَّذِي خَلَقَ} فَقَالَ أَبُو سَلَمَةَ سَأَلْتُ جَابِرَ بْنَ عَبْدِ اللَّهِ رضى الله عنهما عَنْ ذَلِكَ وَقُلْتُ لَهُ مِثْلَ الَّذِي قُلْتَ فَقَالَ جَابِرٌ لاَ أُحَدِّثُكَ إِلاَّ مَا حَدَّثَنَا رَسُولُ اللَّهِ صلى الله عليه وسلم قَالَ " جَاوَرْتُ بِحِرَاءٍ، فَلَمَّا قَضَيْتُ جِوَارِي هَبَطْتُ فَنُودِيتُ فَنَظَرْتُ عَنْ يَمِينِي فَلَمْ أَرَ شَيْئًا، وَنَظَرْتُ عَنْ شِمَالِي فَلَمْ أَرَ شَيْئًا، وَنَظَرْتُ أَمَامِي فَلَمْ أَرَ شَيْئًا، وَنَظَرْتُ خَلْفِي فَلَمْ أَرَ شَيْئًا، فَرَفَعْتُ رَأْسِي فَرَأَيْتُ شَيْئًا، فَأَتَيْتُ خَدِيجَةَ فَقُلْتُ دَثِّرُونِي وَصُبُّوا عَلَىَّ مَاءً بَارِدًا ـ قَالَ ـ فَدَثَّرُونِي وَصَبُّوا عَلَىَّ مَاءً بَارِدًا قَالَ فَنَزَلَتْ {يَا أَيُّهَا الْمُدَّثِّرُ * قُمْ فَأَنْذِرْ * وَرَبَّكَ فَكَبِّرْ} ".

O you covered up ⌜in your clothes⌝! Arise and warn ⌜all⌝. Revere your Lord ⌜alone⌝. Purify your garments. ⌜Continue to⌝ shun idols. Surah Al-Mudathir 74:1-5
يَـٰٓأَيُّهَا ٱلْمُدَّثِّرُ قُمْ فَأَنذِرْ وَرَبَّكَ فَكَبِّرْ وَثِيَابَكَ فَطَهِّرْ وَٱلرُّجْزَ فَٱهْجُرْ

Narrated Jabir bin `Abdullah: While Allah's Messenger ﷺ was carrying stones (along) with the people of Mecca for (the building of) the Ka`ba wearing an Izar (waist-sheet cover), his uncle Al-`Abbas said to him, "O my nephew! (It would be better) if you take off your Izar and put it over your shoulders underneath the stones." So he took off his Izar and put it over his shoulders, but he fell unconscious and since then he had never been seen naked. - Al-Bukhari 364
حَدَّثَنَا مَطَرُ بْنُ الْفَضْلِ، قَالَ حَدَّثَنَا رَوْحٌ، قَالَ حَدَّثَنَا زَكَرِيَّاءُ بْنُ إِسْحَاقَ، حَدَّثَنَا عَمْرُو بْنُ دِينَارٍ، قَالَ سَمِعْتُ جَابِرَ بْنَ عَبْدِ اللَّهِ، يُحَدِّثُ أَنَّ رَسُولَ اللَّهِ صلى الله عليه وسلم كَانَ يَنْقُلُ مَعَهُمُ الْحِجَارَةَ لِلْكَعْبَةِ وَعَلَيْهِ إِزَارُهُ. فَقَالَ لَهُ الْعَبَّاسُ عَمُّهُ يَا ابْنَ أَخِي، لَوْ حَلَلْتَ إِزَارَكَ فَجَعَلْتَ عَلَى مَنْكِبَيْكَ دُونَ الْحِجَارَةِ. قَالَ فَحَلَّهُ فَجَعَلَهُ عَلَى مَنْكِبَيْهِ، فَسَقَطَ مَغْشِيًّا عَلَيْهِ، فَمَا رُئِيَ بَعْدَ ذَلِكَ عُرْيَانًا صلى الله عليه وسلم.

Seclusion in the cave of Hira
جَاوَرْتُ بِحِرَاءٍ

Narrated Yahya bin Abi Kathir: I asked Aba Salama bin `Abdur-Rahman about the first Sura revealed of the Qur'an. He replied "O you, wrapped-up (i.e. Al Muddaththir)." I said, "They say it was, 'Read, in the Name of your Lord Who created,' (i.e. Surat Al-`Alaq (the Clot)." On that, Abu Salama said, "I asked Jabir bin `Abdullah about that, saying the same as you have said, whereupon he said, 'I will not tell you except what Allah's Messenger ﷺ had told us. Allah's Messenger ﷺ said, "I was in seclusion in the cave of Hiram', and after I completed the limited period of my seclusion. I came down (from the cave) and heard a voice calling me. I looked to my right, but saw nothing. Then I looked up and saw something. So I went to Khadija (the Prophet's wife) and told her to wrap me up and pour cold water on me. So they wrapped me up and poured cold water on me." Then, 'O you, (Muhammad) wrapped up! Arise and warn,' (Surat Al Muddaththir) was revealed." (74.1) – Sahih al-Bukhari 4922
حَدَّثَنَا يَحْيَى، حَدَّثَنَا وَكِيعٌ، عَنْ عَلِيِّ بْنِ الْمُبَارَكِ، عَنْ يَحْيَى بْنِ أَبِي كَثِيرٍ، سَأَلْتُ أَبَا سَلَمَةَ بْنَ عَبْدِ الرَّحْمَنِ عَنْ أَوَّلِ، مَا نَزَلَ مِنَ الْقُرْآنِ. قَالَ {يَا أَيُّهَا الْمُدَّثِّرُ} قُلْتُ يَقُولُونَ {اقْرَأْ بِاسْمِ رَبِّكَ الَّذِي خَلَقَ} فَقَالَ أَبُو سَلَمَةَ سَأَلْتُ جَابِرَ بْنَ عَبْدِ اللَّهِ رضى الله عنهما عَنْ ذَلِكَ وَقُلْتُ لَهُ مِثْلَ الَّذِي قُلْتَ فَقَالَ جَابِرٌ لاَ أُحَدِّثُكَ إِلاَّ مَا حَدَّثَنَا رَسُولُ اللَّهِ صلى الله عليه وسلم قَالَ " جَاوَرْتُ بِحِرَاءٍ، فَلَمَّا قَضَيْتُ جِوَارِي هَبَطْتُ فَنُودِيتُ فَنَظَرْتُ عَنْ يَمِينِي فَلَمْ أَرَ شَيْئًا، وَنَظَرْتُ عَنْ شِمَالِي فَلَمْ أَرَ شَيْئًا، وَنَظَرْتُ أَمَامِي فَلَمْ أَرَ شَيْئًا، وَنَظَرْتُ خَلْفِي فَلَمْ أَرَ شَيْئًا، فَرَفَعْتُ رَأْسِي فَرَأَيْتُ شَيْئًا، فَأَتَيْتُ خَدِيجَةَ فَقُلْتُ دَثِّرُونِي وَصُبُّوا عَلَىَّ مَاءً بَارِدًا ـ قَالَ ـ فَدَثَّرُونِي وَصَبُّوا عَلَىَّ مَاءً بَارِدًا قَالَ فَنَزَلَتْ {يَا أَيُّهَا الْمُدَّثِّرُ * قُمْ فَأَنْذِرْ * وَرَبَّكَ فَكَبِّرْ} "

Narrated 'Aisha (the mother of the faithful believers): The commencement of the Divine Inspiration to Allah's Messenger ﷺ was in the form of good dreams which came true like bright daylight, and then the love of seclusion was bestowed upon him. He used to go in seclusion in the cave of Hira where he used to worship (Allah alone) continuously for many days before his desire to see his family. He used to take with him the journey food for the stay and then come back to (his wife) Khadija to take his food likewise again till suddenly the Truth descended upon him while he was in the cave of Hira. The angel came to him and asked him to read. The Prophet ﷺ replied, "I do not know how to read." The Prophet ﷺ added, "The angel caught me (forcefully) and pressed me so hard that I could not bear it any more. He then released me and again asked me to read and I replied, 'I do not know how to read.' Thereupon he caught me again and pressed me a second time till I could not bear it any more. He then released me and again asked me to read but again I replied, 'I do not know how to read (or what shall I read)?' Thereupon he caught me for the third time and pressed me, and then released me and said, 'Read in the name of your Lord, who has created (all that exists), created man from a clot. Read! And your Lord is the Most Generous." (96.1, 96.2, 96.3) Then Allah's Messenger ﷺ returned with the Inspiration and with his heart beating severely. Then he went to Khadija bint Khuwailid and said, "Cover me! Cover me!" They covered him till his fear was over and after that he told her everything that had happened and said, "I fear that something may happen to me." Khadija replied, "Never! By Allah, Allah will never disgrace you. You keep good relations with your kith and kin, help the poor and the destitute, serve your guests generously and assist the deserving calamity-afflicted ones." Khadija then accompanied him to her cousin Waraqa bin Naufal bin Asad bin 'Abdul 'Uzza, who, during the pre-Islamic Period became a Christian and used to write the writing with Hebrew letters. He would write from the Gospel in Hebrew as much as Allah wished him to write. He was an old man and had lost his eyesight. Khadija said to Waraqa, "Listen to the story of your nephew, O my cousin!" Waraqa asked, "O my nephew! What have you seen?" Allah's Messenger ﷺ

described whatever he had seen. Waraqa said, "This is the same one who keeps the secrets (angel Gabriel) whom Allah had sent to Moses. I wish I were young and could live up to the time when your people would turn you out." Allah's Messenger ﷺ asked, "Will they drive me out?" Waraqa replied in the affirmative and said, "Anyone (man) who came with something similar to what you have brought was treated with hostility; and if I should remain alive till the day when you will be turned out then I would support you strongly." But after a few days Waraqa died and the Divine Inspiration was also paused for a while. - Sahih Al-Bukhari 3

حَدَّثَنَا يَحْيَى بْنُ بُكَيْرٍ، قَالَ حَدَّثَنَا اللَّيْثُ، عَنْ عُقَيْلٍ، عَنِ ابْنِ شِهَابٍ، عَنْ عُرْوَةَ بْنِ الزُّبَيْرِ، عَنْ عَائِشَةَ أُمِّ الْمُؤْمِنِينَ، أَنَّهَا قَالَتْ أَوَّلُ مَا بُدِئَ بِهِ رَسُولُ اللَّهِ صلى الله عليه وسلم مِنَ الْوَحْىِ الرُّؤْيَا الصَّالِحَةُ فِي النَّوْمِ، فَكَانَ لاَ يَرَى رُؤْيَا إِلاَّ جَاءَتْ مِثْلَ فَلَقِ الصُّبْحِ، ثُمَّ حُبِّبَ إِلَيْهِ الْخَلاَءُ، وَكَانَ يَخْلُو بِغَارِ حِرَاءٍ فَيَتَحَنَّثُ فِيهِ ـ وَهُوَ التَّعَبُّدُ ـ اللَّيَالِيَ ذَوَاتِ الْعَدَدِ قَبْلَ أَنْ يَنْزِعَ إِلَى أَهْلِهِ، وَيَتَزَوَّدُ لِذَلِكَ، ثُمَّ يَرْجِعُ إِلَى خَدِيجَةَ، فَيَتَزَوَّدُ لِمِثْلِهَا، حَتَّى جَاءَهُ الْحَقُّ وَهُوَ فِي غَارِ حِرَاءٍ، فَجَاءَهُ الْمَلَكُ فَقَالَ اقْرَأْ‏.‏ قَالَ ‏"‏ مَا أَنَا بِقَارِئٍ ‏"‌‏.‏ قَالَ ‏"‏ فَأَخَذَنِي فَغَطَّنِي حَتَّى بَلَغَ مِنِّي الْجَهْدَ، ثُمَّ أَرْسَلَنِي فَقَالَ اقْرَأْ‏.‏ قُلْتُ مَا أَنَا بِقَارِئٍ‏.‏ فَأَخَذَنِي فَغَطَّنِي الثَّانِيَةَ حَتَّى بَلَغَ مِنِّي الْجَهْدَ، ثُمَّ أَرْسَلَنِي فَقَالَ اقْرَأْ‏.‏ فَقُلْتُ مَا أَنَا بِقَارِئٍ‏.‏ فَأَخَذَنِي فَغَطَّنِي الثَّالِثَةَ، ثُمَّ أَرْسَلَنِي فَقَالَ {اقْرَأْ بِاسْمِ رَبِّكَ الَّذِي خَلَقَ * خَلَقَ الإِنْسَانَ مِنْ عَلَقٍ * اقْرَأْ وَرَبُّكَ الأَكْرَمُ} ‏"‏‏.‏ فَرَجَعَ بِهَا رَسُولُ اللَّهِ صلى الله عليه وسلم يَرْجُفُ فُؤَادُهُ، فَدَخَلَ عَلَى خَدِيجَةَ بِنْتِ خُوَيْلِدٍ رضى الله عنها فَقَالَ ‏"‏ زَمِّلُونِي زَمِّلُونِي ‏"‏‏.‏ فَزَمَّلُوهُ حَتَّى ذَهَبَ عَنْهُ الرَّوْعُ، فَقَالَ لِخَدِيجَةَ وَأَخْبَرَهَا الْخَبَرَ ‏"‏ لَقَدْ خَشِيتُ عَلَى نَفْسِي ‏"‏‏.‏ فَقَالَتْ خَدِيجَةُ كَلاَّ وَاللَّهِ مَا يُخْزِيكَ اللَّهُ أَبَدًا، إِنَّكَ لَتَصِلُ الرَّحِمَ، وَتَحْمِلُ الْكَلَّ، وَتَكْسِبُ الْمَعْدُومَ، وَتَقْرِي الضَّيْفَ، وَتُعِينُ عَلَى نَوَائِبِ الْحَقِّ‏.‏ فَانْطَلَقَتْ بِهِ خَدِيجَةُ حَتَّى أَتَتْ بِهِ وَرَقَةَ بْنَ نَوْفَلِ بْنِ أَسَدِ بْنِ عَبْدِ الْعُزَّى ابْنَ عَمِّ خَدِيجَةَ ـ وَكَانَ امْرَأً تَنَصَّرَ فِي الْجَاهِلِيَّةِ، وَكَانَ يَكْتُبُ الْكِتَابَ الْعِبْرَانِيَّ، فَيَكْتُبُ مِنَ الإِنْجِيلِ بِالْعِبْرَانِيَّةِ مَا شَاءَ اللَّهُ أَنْ يَكْتُبَ، وَكَانَ شَيْخًا كَبِيرًا قَدْ عَمِيَ ـ فَقَالَتْ لَهُ خَدِيجَةُ يَا ابْنَ عَمِّ اسْمَعْ مِنَ ابْنِ أَخِيكَ‏.‏ فَقَالَ لَهُ وَرَقَةُ يَا ابْنَ أَخِي مَاذَا تَرَى فَأَخْبَرَهُ رَسُولُ اللَّهِ صلى الله عليه وسلم خَبَرَ مَا رَأَى‏.‏ فَقَالَ لَهُ وَرَقَةُ هَذَا النَّامُوسُ الَّذِي نَزَّلَ اللَّهُ عَلَى مُوسَى صلى الله عليه وسلم يَا لَيْتَنِي فِيهَا جَذَعًا، لَيْتَنِي أَكُونُ حَيًّا إِذْ يُخْرِجُكَ قَوْمُكَ‏.‏ فَقَالَ رَسُولُ اللَّهِ صلى الله عليه وسلم ‏"‏ أَوَمُخْرِجِيَّ هُمْ ‏"‏‏.‏ قَالَ نَعَمْ، لَمْ يَأْتِ رَجُلٌ قَطُّ بِمِثْلِ مَا جِئْتَ بِهِ إِلاَّ عُودِيَ، وَإِنْ يُدْرِكْنِي يَوْمُكَ أَنْصُرْكَ نَصْرًا مُؤَزَّرًا‏.‏ ثُمَّ لَمْ يَنْشَبْ وَرَقَةُ أَنْ تُوُفِّيَ وَفَتَرَ الْوَحْىُ‏

Ascension of As-Safa
صعود الصفا

Narrated Ibn `Abbas: When the Verse:-- 'And warn your tribe of near kindred.' (26.214) was revealed. Allah's Messenger ﷺ went out, and when he had ascended As-Safa mountain, he shouted, "O Sabahah!" The people said, "Who is that?" "Then they gathered around him, whereupon he said, "Do you see? If I inform you that cavalrymen are proceeding up the side of this mountain, will you believe me?" They said, "We have never heard you telling a lie." Then he said, "I am a plain warner to you of a coming severe punishment." Abu Lahab said, "May you perish! You gathered us only for this reason? " Then Abu Lahab went away. So the "Surat:--ul—LAHAB" 'Perish the hands of Abu Lahab!' (111.1) was revealed – .Sahih al-Bukhari 4971

حَدَّثَنَا يُوسُفُ بْنُ مُوسَى، حَدَّثَنَا أَبُو أُسَامَةَ، حَدَّثَنَا الأَعْمَشُ، حَدَّثَنَا عَمْرُو بْنُ مُرَّةَ، عَنْ سَعِيدِ بْنِ جُبَيْرٍ، عَنِ ابْنِ عَبَّاسٍ ـ رضى الله عنهما ـ قَالَ لَمَّا نَزَلَتْ {وَأَنْذِرْ عَشِيرَتَكَ الأَقْرَبِينَ} وَرَهْطَكَ مِنْهُمُ الْمُخْلَصِينَ، خَرَجَ رَسُولُ اللَّهِ صلى الله عليه وسلم حَتَّى صَعِدَ الصَّفَا فَهَتَفَ ‏"‏ يَا صَبَاحَاهْ ‏"‏‏.‏ فَقَالُوا مَنْ هَذَا، فَاجْتَمَعُوا إِلَيْهِ‏.‏ فَقَالَ ‏"‏ أَرَأَيْتُمْ إِنْ أَخْبَرْتُكُمْ أَنَّ خَيْلاً تَخْرُجُ مِنْ سَفْحِ هَذَا الْجَبَلِ أَكُنْتُمْ مُصَدِّقِيَّ ‏"‏‏.‏ قَالُوا مَا جَرَّبْنَا عَلَيْكَ كَذِبًا‏.‏ قَالَ ‏"‏ فَإِنِّي نَذِيرٌ لَكُمْ بَيْنَ يَدَىْ عَذَابٍ شَدِيدٍ ‏"‏‏.‏ قَالَ أَبُو لَهَبٍ تَبًّا لَكَ مَا جَمَعْتَنَا إِلاَّ لِهَذَا ثُمَّ قَامَ فَنَزَلَتْ {تَبَّتْ يَدَا أَبِي لَهَبٍ وَتَبَّ} وَقَدْ تَبَّ هَكَذَا قَرَأَهَا الأَعْمَشُ يَوْمَئِذٍ‏.‏

Surah Al-Masad
سورة المسد

Condemned are the hands of Abee Lahab, and he is condemned. His wealth did not avail him, nor did what he acquired. He will burn in a Flaming Fire. And his wife—the firewood carrier. Around her neck is a rope of thorns. – Surah Al-Masad

تَبَّتْ يَدَا أَبِي لَهَبٍ وَتَبَّ مَا أَغْنَىٰ عَنْهُ مَالُهُ وَمَا كَسَبَ سَيَصْلَىٰ نَارًا ذَاتَ لَهَبٍ وَامْرَأَتُهُ حَمَّالَةَ الْحَطَبِ فِي جِيدِهَا حَبْلٌ مِنْ مَسَدٍ

Cave at Mina
كهف منى

Narrated `Abdullah: While we were in the company of the Prophet ﷺ in a cave at Mina, when Surat-wal-Mursalat were revealed and he recited it and I heard it (directly) from his mouth as soon as he recited its revelation. Suddenly a snake sprang at us and the Prophet ﷺ said (ordered us): "Kill it." We ran to kill it but it escaped quickly. The Prophet ﷺ said, "It has escaped your evil and you too have escaped its evil. – Sahih al-Bukhari 1830

حَدَّثَنَا عُمَرُ بْنُ حَفْصِ بْنِ غِيَاثٍ، حَدَّثَنَا أَبِي، حَدَّثَنَا الأَعْمَشُ، قَالَ حَدَّثَنِي إِبْرَاهِيمُ، عَنِ الأَسْوَدِ، عَنْ عَبْدِ اللَّهِ ـ رضى الله عنه ـ قَالَ بَيْنَمَا نَحْنُ مَعَ النَّبِيِّ صلى الله عليه وسلم فِي غَارٍ بِمِنًى، إِذْ نَزَلَ عَلَيْهِ {وَالْمُرْسَلاَتِ} وَإِنَّهُ لَيَتْلُوهَا، وَإِنِّي لأَتَلَقَّاهَا مِنْ فِيهِ، وَإِنَّ فَاهُ لَرَطْبٌ بِهَا، إِذْ وَثَبَتْ عَلَيْنَا حَيَّةٌ فَقَالَ النَّبِيُّ صلى الله عليه وسلم " اقْتُلُوهَا ". فَابْتَدَرْنَاهَا، فَذَهَبَتْ، فَقَالَ النَّبِيُّ صلى الله عليه وسلم " وُقِيَتْ شَرَّكُمْ كَمَا وُقِيتُمْ شَرَّهَا "

And (by) the emissaries in a (continual) series with benevolence Then (by) tempests (storming) tempestuously And (by) the spreaders spreading Then (by) the ones who separate with a (distinct) separation Then (by) the ones casting a Remembrance Excusing or warning Surely that which you are promised is indeed befalling So when the stars will be obliterate And when the heaven will be riven And when the mountains will be crushed And when the Messengers' (time) is fixed To whichever Day is (this) term appointed To the Day of Verdict And what makes you realize what the Day of Verdict is Upon that Day woe to the beliers Did We not cause the earliest people to perish Thereafter We make the later generations follow them up Thus We perform against the criminals Upon that Day woe to the beliers Did We not create you of a contemptible water Then We made it in an established reposing Till a known (term) determined So We determined; so Excellent the Determiners are We Upon that Day woe to the beliers Have We not made the earth a receptacle For the living and the dead And We made therein lofty anchorages, (i.e., mountains) and We made you to drink water grateful (to taste) Upon that Day woe to the beliers Go off to what you used to cry as lies Go off to a three-pronged (Literally: comprising three prongs) shade With no plenteous shade and of no avail against the flames Surely it throws up sparks like palace (s) (Or: dry faggots) As if they were yellow (heaps) of cables (Or: golden herds) Upon that Day woe to the beliers This is the Day they will not pronounce (a word) Nor be permitted to, then excuse themselves Upon that Day woe to the beliers This is the Day of Verdict: We have gathered you and the earliest (people) So, if (ever) you have any plotting, then plot against Me Upon that Day woe to the beliers Surely the pious will be in shades and springs And such fruits as they crave "Eat and drink, rejoicing with wholesome appetite, for whatever you were doing." Thus surely We recompense the fair-doers Upon that Day woe to the beliers "Eat and enjoy (your life) a little: surely you are criminals" Upon that Day woe to the beliers And when it is said to them, "Bow down!" They do not bow down Upon that Day woe to the beliers. So, in whichever discourse after (this) do they believe. – Surah Al-Mursalat

وَٱلْمُرْسَلَٰتِ عُرْفًا فَٱلْعَٰصِفَٰتِ عَصْفًا وَٱلنَّٰشِرَٰتِ نَشْرًا فَٱلْفَٰرِقَٰتِ فَرْقًا فَٱلْمُلْقِيَٰتِ ذِكْرًا عُذْرًا أَوْ نُذْرًا إِنَّمَا تُوعَدُونَ لَوَٰقِعٌ فَإِذَا ٱلنُّجُومُ طُمِسَتْ وَإِذَا ٱلسَّمَآءُ فُرِجَتْ وَإِذَا ٱلْجِبَالُ نُسِفَتْ وَإِذَا ٱلرُّسُلُ أُقِّتَتْ لِأَىِّ يَوْمٍ أُجِّلَتْ لِيَوْمِ ٱلْفَصْلِ وَمَآ أَدْرَىٰكَ مَا يَوْمُ ٱلْفَصْلِ وَيْلٌ يَوْمَئِذٍ لِّلْمُكَذِّبِينَ أَلَمْ نُهْلِكِ ٱلْأَوَّلِينَ ثُمَّ نُتْبِعُهُمُ ٱلْءَاخِرِينَ كَذَٰلِكَ نَفْعَلُ بِٱلْمُجْرِمِينَ وَيْلٌ يَوْمَئِذٍ لِّلْمُكَذِّبِينَ أَلَمْ نَخْلُقكُّم مِّن مَّآءٍ مَّهِينٍ فَجَعَلْنَٰهُ فِى قَرَارٍ مَّكِينٍ إِلَىٰ قَدَرٍ مَّعْلُومٍ فَقَدَرْنَا فَنِعْمَ ٱلْقَٰدِرُونَ وَيْلٌ يَوْمَئِذٍ لِّلْمُكَذِّبِينَ أَلَمْ نَجْعَلِ ٱلْأَرْضَ كِفَاتًا أَحْيَآءً وَأَمْوَٰتًا وَجَعَلْنَا فِيهَا رَوَٰسِىَ شَٰمِخَٰتٍ وَأَسْقَيْنَٰكُم مَّآءً فُرَاتًا وَيْلٌ يَوْمَئِذٍ لِّلْمُكَذِّبِينَ ٱنطَلِقُوٓا۟ إِلَىٰ مَا كُنتُم بِهِۦ تُكَذِّبُونَ ٱنطَلِقُوٓا۟ إِلَىٰ ظِلٍّ ذِى ثَلَٰثِ شُعَبٍ لَّا ظَلِيلٍ وَلَا يُغْنِى مِنَ ٱللَّهَبِ إِنَّهَا تَرْمِى بِشَرَرٍ كَٱلْقَصْرِ كَأَنَّهُۥ جِمَٰلَتٌ صُفْرٌ وَيْلٌ يَوْمَئِذٍ لِّلْمُكَذِّبِينَ هَٰذَا يَوْمُ لَا يَنطِقُونَ وَلَا يُؤْذَنُ لَهُمْ فَيَعْتَذِرُونَ وَيْلٌ يَوْمَئِذٍ لِّلْمُكَذِّبِينَ هَٰذَا يَوْمُ ٱلْفَصْلِ جَمَعْنَٰكُمْ وَٱلْأَوَّلِينَ فَإِن كَانَ لَكُمْ كَيْدٌ فَكِيدُونِ وَيْلٌ يَوْمَئِذٍ لِّلْمُكَذِّبِينَ إِنَّ ٱلْمُتَّقِينَ فِى ظِلَٰلٍ وَعُيُونٍ وَفَوَٰكِهَ مِمَّا يَشْتَهُونَ كُلُوا۟ وَٱشْرَبُوا۟ هَنِيٓـًٔا بِمَا كُنتُمْ تَعْمَلُونَ إِنَّا كَذَٰلِكَ نَجْزِى ٱلْمُحْسِنِينَ وَيْلٌ يَوْمَئِذٍ لِّلْمُكَذِّبِينَ كُلُوا۟ وَتَمَتَّعُوا۟ قَلِيلًا إِنَّكُم مُّجْرِمُونَ وَيْلٌ يَوْمَئِذٍ لِّلْمُكَذِّبِينَ وَإِذَا قِيلَ لَهُمُ ٱرْكَعُوا۟ لَا يَرْكَعُونَ وَيْلٌ يَوْمَئِذٍ لِّلْمُكَذِّبِينَ فَبِأَىِّ حَدِيثٍ بَعْدَهُۥ يُؤْمِنُونَ

The Book
Boycott of Bani Hashim
مقاطعة بني هاشم

Narrated Jubair bin Mut`im: `Uthman bin `Affan went (to the Prophet) and said, "O Allah's Messenger ﷺ! You gave property to Bani Al-Muttalib and did not give us, although we and they are of the same degree of relationship to you." The Prophet ﷺ said, "Only Bani Hashim and Bani Al Muttalib are one thing (as regards family status). – Sahih al-Bukhari 3502

حَدَّثَنَا يَحْيَى بْنُ بُكَيْرٍ، حَدَّثَنَا اللَّيْثُ، عَنْ عُقَيْلٍ، عَنِ ابْنِ شِهَابٍ، عَنِ ابْنِ الْمُسَيَّبِ، عَنْ جُبَيْرِ بْنِ مُطْعِمٍ، قَالَ مَشَيْتُ أَنَا وَعُثْمَانُ بْنُ عَفَّانَ،، فَقَالَ يَا رَسُولَ اللَّهِ أَعْطَيْتَ بَنِي الْمُطَّلِبِ وَتَرَكْتَنَا، وَإِنَّمَا نَحْنُ وَهُمْ مِنْكَ بِمَنْزِلَةٍ وَاحِدَةٍ. فَقَالَ النَّبِيُّ صلى الله عليه وسلم " إِنَّمَا بَنُو هَاشِمٍ وَبَنُو الْمُطَّلِبِ شَىْءٌ وَاحِدٌ ".

Narrated Abu Huraira: When Allah's Messenger ﷺ intended to enter Mecca he said, "Our destination tomorrow, if Allah wished, will be Khaif Bani Kinana where (the pagans) had taken the oath of Kufr." (Against the Prophet ﷺ i.e. to be loyal to heathenism by boycotting Bani Hashim, the Prophet's folk) (See Hadith 3882). – Sahih al-Bukhari 1589

حَدَّثَنَا أَبُو الْيَمَانِ، أَخْبَرَنَا شُعَيْبٌ، عَنِ الزُّهْرِيِّ، قَالَ حَدَّثَنِي أَبُو سَلَمَةَ، أَنَّ أَبَا هُرَيْرَةَ ـ رضى الله عنه ـ قَالَ قَالَ رَسُولُ اللَّهِ صلى الله عليه وسلم حِينَ أَرَادَ قُدُومَ مَكَّةَ " مَنْزِلُنَا غَدًا إِنْ شَاءَ اللَّهُ بِخَيْفِ بَنِي كِنَانَةَ حَيْثُ تَقَاسَمُوا عَلَى الْكُفْرِ ".

Narrated Abu Huraira: On the Day of Nahr at Mina, the Prophet ﷺ said, "Tomorrow we shall stay at Khaif Bani Kinana where the pagans had taken the oath of Kufr (heathenism)." He meant (by that place) Al-Muhassab where the Quraish tribe and Bani Kinana concluded a contract against Bani Hashim and Bani `Abdul-Muttalib or Bani Al-Muttalib that they would not intermarry with them or deal with them in business until they handed over the Prophet ﷺ to them. – Sahih al-Bukhari 1590

حَدَّثَنَا الْحُمَيْدِيُّ، حَدَّثَنَا الْوَلِيدُ، حَدَّثَنَا الأَوْزَاعِيُّ، قَالَ حَدَّثَنِي الزُّهْرِيُّ، عَنْ أَبِي سَلَمَةَ، عَنْ أَبِي هُرَيْرَةَ ـ رضى الله عنه ـ قَالَ قَالَ النَّبِيُّ صلى الله عليه وسلم مِنَ الْغَدِ يَوْمَ النَّحْرِ وَهُوَ بِمِنًى " نَحْنُ نَازِلُونَ غَدًا بِخَيْفِ بَنِي كِنَانَةَ حَيْثُ تَقَاسَمُوا عَلَى الْكُفْرِ ". يَعْنِي ذَلِكَ الْمُحَصَّبَ، وَذَلِكَ أَنَّ قُرَيْشًا وَكِنَانَةَ تَحَالَفَتْ عَلَى بَنِي هَاشِمٍ وَبَنِي عَبْدِ الْمُطَّلِبِ، أَوْ بَنِي الْمُطَّلِبِ أَنْ لاَ يُنَاكِحُوهُمْ، وَلاَ يُبَايِعُوهُمْ حَتَّى يُسْلِمُوا إِلَيْهِمُ النَّبِيَّ صلى الله عليه وسلم. وَقَالَ سَلاَمَةُ عَنْ عُقَيْلٍ وَيَحْيَى بْنُ الضَّحَّاكِ عَنِ الأَوْزَاعِيِّ أَخْبَرَنِي ابْنُ شِهَابٍ وَقَالاَ بَنِي هَاشِمٍ وَبَنِي الْمُطَّلِبِ. قَالَ أَبُو عَبْدِ اللَّهِ بَنِي الْمُطَّلِبِ أَشْبَهُ.

It was narrated that Jubair bin Mut'im said: "When the Messenger of Allah distributed the share for his relatives to Banu Hashim and BanuA-Muttalib, I came to himwith 'Uthman bin 'Affan and we said: 'O Messenger of Allah, no one denies the virtue of Banu Hashim because of the relationship between you and them. But how come you have given (a share) to Banu Al-Muttalib and not to us? They and we share the same degree of relationship to you. 'The Messenger of Allah said: "They did not abandon me during the Jahiliyyah or in Islam. Banu Hashim and Banu Al-Muttalib are the same thing, and he interlaced his fingers." - Sunan an-Nasa'I 4137

أَخْبَرَنَا مُحَمَّدُ بْنُ الْمُثَنَّى، قَالَ حَدَّثَنَا يَزِيدُ بْنُ هَارُونَ، قَالَ أَنْبَأَنَا مُحَمَّدُ بْنُ إِسْحَاقَ، عَنِ الزُّهْرِيِّ، عَنْ سَعِيدِ بْنِ الْمُسَيَّبِ، عَنْ جُبَيْرِ بْنِ مُطْعِمٍ، قَالَ لَمَّا قَسَمَ رَسُولُ اللَّهِ صلى الله عليه وسلم سَهْمَ ذِي الْقُرْبَى بَيْنَ بَنِي هَاشِمٍ وَبَنِي الْمُطَّلِبِ أَتَيْتُهُ أَنَا وَعُثْمَانُ بْنُ عَفَّانَ فَقُلْنَا يَا رَسُولَ اللَّهِ هَؤُلاَءِ بَنُو هَاشِمٍ لاَ نُنْكِرُ فَضْلَهُمْ لِمَكَانِكَ الَّذِي جَعَلَكَ اللَّهُ بِهِ مِنْهُمْ أَرَأَيْتَ بَنِي الْمُطَّلِبِ أَعْطَيْتَهُمْ وَمَنَعْتَنَا فَإِنَّمَا نَحْنُ وَهُمْ مِنْكَ بِمَنْزِلَةٍ . فَقَالَ رَسُولُ اللَّهِ صلى الله عليه وسلم " إِنَّهُمْ لَمْ يُفَارِقُونِي فِي جَاهِلِيَّةٍ وَلاَ إِسْلاَمٍ إِنَّمَا بَنُو هَاشِمٍ وَبَنُو الْمُطَّلِبِ شَىْءٌ وَاحِدٌ " . وَشَبَّكَ بَيْنَ أَصَابِعِهِ.

Splitting of the Moon
انْشِقَاقَ الْقَمَرِ

Narrated Anas: That the Meccan people requested Allah's Messenger ﷺ to show them a miracle, and so he showed them the splitting of the moon. – Sahih al-Bukhari 3637
حَدَّثَنِي عَبْدُ اللَّهِ بْنُ مُحَمَّدٍ، حَدَّثَنَا يُونُسُ، حَدَّثَنَا شَيْبَانُ، عَنْ قَتَادَةَ، عَنْ أَنَسِ بْنِ مَالِكٍ. وَقَالَ لِي خَلِيفَةُ حَدَّثَنَا يَزِيدُ بْنُ زُرَيْعٍ، حَدَّثَنَا سَعِيدٌ، عَنْ قَتَادَةَ، عَنْ أَنَسِ بْنِ مَالِكٍ ـ رضى الله عنه ـ أَنَّهُ حَدَّثَهُمْ أَنَّ أَهْلَ مَكَّةَ سَأَلُوا رَسُولَ اللَّهِ صلى الله عليه وسلم أَنْ يُرِيَهُمْ آيَةً، فَأَرَاهُمُ انْشِقَاقَ الْقَمَرِ

Narrated `Abdullah: Allah sent (the Prophet) Muhammad and said:-- 'Say, No wage do I ask of you for this (Qur'an) nor am I one of the pretenders (i.e. a person who pretends things which do not exist). (38.68) When Allah's Messenger ﷺ saw Quraish standing against him, he said, "O Allah! Help me against them by afflicting them with seven years of famine similar to the seven years (of famine) of Joseph. So they were afflicted with a year of drought that destroyed everything, and they ate bones and hides. (One of them said), "And they ate hides and dead animals, and (it seemed to them that) something like smoke was coming out of the earth. So Abu Sufyan came to the Prophet ﷺ and said, "O Muhammad! Your people are on the verge of destruction! Please invoke Allah to relieve them." So the Prophet ﷺ invoked Allah for them (and the famine disappeared). He said to them. "You will revert (to heathenism) after that." `Abdullah then recited: 'Then watch you for the Day that the sky will bring forth a kind of smoke plainly visible.......but truly you will revert (to disbelief).' He added, "Will the punishment be removed from them in the Hereafter? The smoke and the grasp and the Al-Lizam have all passed." One of the sub-narrater said, "The splitting of the moon." And another said, "The defeat of the Romans (has passed). – Sahih al-Bukhari 4824
حَدَّثَنَا بِشْرُ بْنُ خَالِدٍ، أَخْبَرَنَا مُحَمَّدٌ، عَنْ شُعْبَةَ، عَنْ سُلَيْمَانَ، وَمَنْصُورٍ، عَنْ أَبِي الضُّحَى، عَنْ مَسْرُوقٍ، قَالَ قَالَ عَبْدُ اللَّهِ إِنَّ اللَّهَ بَعَثَ مُحَمَّدًا صلى الله عليه وسلم وَقَالَ {قُلْ مَا أَسْأَلُكُمْ عَلَيْهِ مِنْ أَجْرٍ وَمَا أَنَا مِنَ الْمُتَكَلِّفِينَ} فَإِنَّ رَسُولَ اللَّهِ صلى الله عليه وسلم لَمَّا رَأَى قُرَيْشًا اسْتَعْصَوْا عَلَيْهِ فَقَالَ " اللَّهُمَّ أَعِنِّي عَلَيْهِمْ بِسَبْعٍ كَسَبْعِ يُوسُفَ ". فَأَخَذَتْهُمُ السَّنَةُ حَتَّى حَصَّتْ كُلَّ شَىْءٍ حَتَّى أَكَلُوا الْعِظَامَ وَالْجُلُودَ ـ فَقَالَ أَحَدُهُمْ حَتَّى أَكَلُوا الْجُلُودَ وَالْمَيْتَةَ ـ وَجَعَلَ يَخْ

Surah Al-Qamar
سورة القمر

The Hour has drawn near and the moon was split ˹in two˺. Yet, whenever they see a sign, they turn away, saying, "Same old magic!" They rejected ˹the truth˺ and followed their own desires—and every matter will be settled— even though the stories ˹of destroyed nations˺ that have already come to them are a sufficient deterrent. ˹This Quran is˺ profound ˹in˺ wisdom, but warnings are of no benefit ˹to them˺. So turn away from them ˹O Prophet˺. ˹And wait for˺ the Day ˹when˺ the caller will summon ˹them˺ for something horrifying. – Surah Al-Qamar 54:1-6
ٱقْتَرَبَتِ ٱلسَّاعَةُ وَٱنشَقَّ ٱلْقَمَرُ وَإِن يَرَوْا۟ ءَايَةً يُعْرِضُوا۟ وَيَقُولُوا۟ سِحْرٌ مُّسْتَمِرٌّ وَكَذَّبُوا۟ وَٱتَّبَعُوٓا۟ أَهْوَآءَهُمْ وَكُلُّ أَمْرٍ مُّسْتَقِرٌّ وَلَقَدْ جَآءَهُم مِّنَ ٱلْأَنۢبَآءِ مَا فِيهِ مُزْدَجَرٌ حِكْمَةٌۢ بَٰلِغَةٌ فَمَا تُغْنِ ٱلنُّذُرُ فَتَوَلَّ عَنْهُمْ يَوْمَ يَدْعُ ٱلدَّاعِ إِلَىٰ شَىْءٍ نُّكُرٍ

Surah Al-Jin
سورة الجن

Narrated Ibn `Abbas: Allah's Messenger ﷺ went out along with a group of his companions towards `Ukaz Market. At that time something intervened between the devils and the news of the Heaven, and flames were sent down upon them, so the devils returned. Their fellow-devils said, "What is wrong with you? " They said, "Something has intervened between us and the news of the Heaven, and fires (flames) have been shot at us." Their fellow-devils said, "Nothing has intervened between you and the news of the Heaven, but an important event has happened. Therefore, travel all over the world, east and west, and try to find out what has happened." And so they set out and travelled all over the world, east and west, looking for that thing which intervened between them and the news of the Heaven. Those of the devils who had set out towards Tihama, went to Allah's Messenger ﷺ at Nakhla (a place between Mecca and Taif) while he was on his way to `Ukaz Market. (They met him) while he was offering the Fajr prayer with his companions. When they heard the Holy Qur'an being recited (by Allah's Messenger ﷺ ,) they listened to it and said (to each other). This is the thing which has intervened between you and the news of the Heavens." Then they returned to their people and said, "O our people! We have really heard a wonderful recital (Qur'an). It gives guidance to the right, and we have believed therein. We shall not join in worship, anybody with our Lord." (See 72.1-2) Then Allah revealed to His Prophet (Surat al- Jinn): 'Say: It has been revealed to me that a group (3 to 9) of Jinns listened (to the Qur'an).' (72.1) The statement of the Jinns was revealed to him . – Sahih al-Bukhari 4921

حَدَّثَنَا مُوسَى بْنُ إِسْمَاعِيلَ، حَدَّثَنَا أَبُو عَوَانَةَ، عَنْ أَبِي بِشْرٍ، عَنْ سَعِيدِ بْنِ جُبَيْرٍ، عَنِ ابْنِ عَبَّاسٍ، قَالَ انْطَلَقَ رَسُولُ اللَّهِ صلى الله عليه وسلم فِي طَائِفَةٍ مِنْ أَصْحَابِهِ عَامِدِينَ إِلَى سُوقِ عُكَاظٍ، وَقَدْ حِيلَ بَيْنَ الشَّيَاطِينِ وَبَيْنَ خَبَرِ السَّمَاءِ، وَأُرْسِلَتْ عَلَيْهِمُ الشُّهُبُ فَرَجَعَتِ الشَّيَاطِينُ فَقَالُوا مَا لَكُمْ فَقَالُوا حِيلَ بَيْنَنَا وَبَيْنَ خَبَرِ السَّمَاءِ وَأُرْسِلَتْ عَلَيْنَا الشُّهُبُ. قَالَ مَا حَالَ بَيْنَكُمْ وَبَيْنَ خَبَرِ السَّمَاءِ إِلاَّ مَا حَدَثَ، فَاضْرِبُوا مَشَارِقَ الأَرْضِ وَمَغَارِبَهَا فَانْظُرُوا مَا هَذَا الأَمْرُ الَّذِي حَدَثَ. فَانْطَلَقُوا فَضَرَبُوا مَشَارِقَ الأَرْضِ وَمَغَارِبَهَا يَنْظُرُونَ مَا هَذَا الأَمْرُ الَّذِي حَالَ بَيْنَهُمْ وَبَيْنَ خَبَرِ السَّمَاءِ. قَالَ فَانْطَلَقَ الَّذِينَ تَوَجَّهُوا نَحْوَ تِهَامَةَ إِلَى رَسُولِ اللَّهِ صلى الله عليه وسلم بِنَخْلَةَ، وَهْوَ عَامِدٌ إِلَى سُوقِ عُكَاظٍ، وَهْوَ يُصَلِّي بِأَصْحَابِهِ صَلاَةَ الْفَجْرِ، فَلَمَّا سَمِعُوا الْقُرْآنَ تَسَمَّعُوا لَهُ فَقَالُوا هَذَا الَّذِي حَالَ بَيْنَكُمْ وَبَيْنَ خَبَرِ السَّمَاءِ. فَهُنَالِكَ رَجَعُوا إِلَى قَوْمِهِمْ فَقَالُوا يَا قَوْمَنَا إِنَّا سَمِعْنَا قُرْآنًا عَجَبًا يَهْدِي إِلَى الرُّشْدِ فَآمَنَّا بِهِ، وَلَنْ نُشْرِكَ بِرَبِّنَا أَحَدًا. وَأَنْزَلَ اللَّهُ عَزَّ وَجَلَّ عَلَى نَبِيِّهِ صلى الله عليه وسلم {قُلْ أُوحِيَ إِلَيَّ أَنَّهُ اسْتَمَعَ نَفَرٌ مِنَ الْجِنِّ} وَإِنَّمَا أُوحِيَ إِلَيْهِ قَوْلُ الْجِنِّ.

The Book
Ām al-Ḥuzn [3]
عام الحزن

Passing of Khadijah
وفاة السيدة خديجة

Narrated Hisham's father: Khadija died three years before the Prophetﷺ departed to Medina. He stayed there for two years or so and then he married `Aisha when she was a girl of six years of age, and he consumed that marriage when she was nine years old. – Al-Bukhari 3896

حَدَّثَنِي عُبَيْدُ بْنُ إِسْمَاعِيلَ، حَدَّثَنَا أَبُو أُسَامَةَ، عَنْ هِشَامٍ، عَنْ أَبِيهِ، قَالَ تُوُفِّيَتْ خَدِيجَةُ قَبْلَ مَخْرَجِ النَّبِيِّ صلى الله عليه وسلم إِلَى الْمَدِينَةِ بِثَلاَثِ سِنِينَ، فَلَبِثَ سَنَتَيْنِ أَوْ قَرِيبًا مِنْ ذَلِكَ، وَنَكَحَ عَائِشَةَ وَهْىَ بِنْتُ سِتِّ سِنِينَ، ثُمَّ بَنَى بِهَا وَهْىَ بِنْتُ تِسْعِ سِنِينَ.

Narrated `Ali: I heard the Prophetﷺ saying, "Mary, the daughter of `Imran, was the best among the women (of the world of her time) and Khadija is the best amongst the women. (of this nation). – Al-Bukhari 3432

حَدَّثَنِي أَحْمَدُ بْنُ أَبِي رَجَاءٍ، حَدَّثَنَا النَّضْرُ، عَنْ هِشَامٍ، قَالَ أَخْبَرَنِي أَبِي قَالَ، سَمِعْتُ عَبْدَ اللَّهِ بْنَ جَعْفَرٍ، قَالَ سَمِعْتُ عَلِيًّا ـ رضى الله عنه ـ يَقُولُ سَمِعْتُ النَّبِيَّ صلى الله عليه وسلم يَقُولُ " خَيْرُ نِسَائِهَا مَرْيَمُ ابْنَةُ عِمْرَانَ، وَخَيْرُ نِسَائِهَا خَدِيجَةُ "

Narrated Isma`il: I asked `Abdullah bin Abi `Aufa, "Did the Prophetﷺ give glad tidings to Khadija?" He said, "Yes, of a palace of Qasab (in Paradise) where there will be neither any noise nor any fatigue." – Al-Bukhari 3819

حَدَّثَنَا مُسَدَّدٌ، حَدَّثَنَا يَحْيَى، عَنْ إِسْمَاعِيلَ، قَالَ قُلْتُ لِعَبْدِ اللَّهِ بْنِ أَبِي أَوْفَى ـ رضى الله عنهما ـ بَشَّرَ النَّبِيُّ صلى الله عليه وسلم خَدِيجَةَ قَالَ نَعَمْ بِبَيْتٍ مِنْ قَصَبٍ، لاَ صَخَبَ فِيهِ وَلاَ نَصَبَ.

Narrated `Aisha: I never felt so jealous of any wife of Allah's Messengerﷺ as I did of Khadija because Allah's Messengerﷺ used to remember and praise her too often and because it was revealed to Allah's Messengerﷺ that he should give her (Khadija) the glad tidings of her having a palace of Qasab in Paradise . – Al-Bukhari 5229

حَدَّثَنِي أَحْمَدُ بْنُ أَبِي رَجَاءٍ، حَدَّثَنَا النَّضْرُ، عَنْ هِشَامٍ، قَالَ أَخْبَرَنِي أَبِي، عَنْ عَائِشَةَ، أَنَّهَا قَالَتْ مَا غِرْتُ عَلَى امْرَأَةٍ لِرَسُولِ اللَّهِ صلى الله عليه وسلم كَمَا غِرْتُ عَلَى خَدِيجَةَ، لِكَثْرَةِ ذِكْرِ رَسُولِ اللَّهِ صلى الله عليه وسلم إِيَّاهَا وَثَنَائِهِ عَلَيْهَا، وَقَدْ أُوحِيَ إِلَى رَسُولِ اللَّهِ صلى الله عليه وسلم أَنْ يُبَشِّرَهَا بِبَيْتٍ لَهَا فِي الْجَنَّةِ مِنْ قَصَبٍ

Narrated 'Aisha: Once Hala bint Khuwailid, Khadija's sister, asked the permission of the Prophetﷺ to enter. On that, the Prophetﷺ remembered the way Khadija used to ask permission, and that upset him. He said, "O Allah! Hala!" So I became jealous and said, "What makes you remember an old woman amongst the old women of Quraish an old woman (with a teethless mouth) of red gums who died long ago, and in whose place Allah has given you somebody better than her?" – Al-Bukhari 3821

---

[3] A Islamic term for; the Year of Sorrow for Muhammad

وَقَالَ إِسْمَاعِيلُ بْنُ خَلِيلٍ أَخْبَرَنَا عَلِيُّ بْنُ مُسْهِرٍ، عَنْ هِشَامٍ، عَنْ أَبِيهِ، عَنْ عَائِشَةَ ـ رضى الله عنها ـ قَالَتِ اسْتَأْذَنَتْ هَالَةُ بِنْتُ خُوَيْلِدٍ أُخْتُ خَدِيجَةَ عَلَى رَسُولِ اللَّهِ صلى الله عليه وسلم، فَعَرَفَ اسْتِئْذَانَ خَدِيجَةَ فَارْتَاعَ لِذَلِكَ، فَقَالَ " اللَّهُمَّ هَالَةَ ". قَالَتْ فَغِرْتُ فَقُلْتُ مَا تَذْكُرُ مِنْ عَجُوزٍ مِنْ عَجَائِزِ قُرَيْشٍ، حَمْرَاءِ الشِّدْقَيْنِ، هَلَكَتْ فِي الدَّهْرِ، قَدْ، أَبْدَلَكَ اللَّهُ خَيْرًا مِنْهَا

Narrated Isma`il: `Abdullah bin Abu `Aufa said: "Allah's Messenger ﷺ performed `Umra and we too performed `Umra along with him. When he entered Mecca he performed the Tawaf (of Ka`ba) and we too performed it along with him, and then he came to the As-Safa and Al-Marwa (i.e. performed the Sai) and we also came to them along with him. We were shielding him from the people of Mecca lest they may hit him with an arrow." A friend of his asked him (i.e. `Abdullah bin `Aufa), "Did the Prophet ﷺ enter the Ka`ba (during that `Umra)?" He replied in the negative. Then he said, "What did he (the Prophet ﷺ) say about Khadija?" He (Abdullah bin `Aufa) said, "(He said) 'Give Khadija the good tidings that she will have a palace made of Qasab in Paradise and there will be neither noise nor any trouble in it." – Al-Bukhari 1791, 1792

حَدَّثَنَا إِسْحَاقُ بْنُ إِبْرَاهِيمَ، عَنْ جَرِيرٍ، عَنْ إِسْمَاعِيلَ، عَنْ عَبْدِ اللَّهِ بْنِ أَبِي أَوْفَى، قَالَ اعْتَمَرَ رَسُولُ اللَّهِ صلى الله عليه وسلم وَاعْتَمَرْنَا مَعَهُ فَلَمَّا دَخَلَ مَكَّةَ طَافَ وَطُفْنَا مَعَهُ، وَأَتَى الصَّفَا وَالْمَرْوَةَ وَأَتَيْنَاهَا مَعَهُ، وَكُنَّا نَسْتُرُهُ مِنْ أَهْلِ مَكَّةَ أَنْ يَرْمِيَهُ أَحَدٌ. فَقَالَ لَهُ صَاحِبٌ لِي أَكَانَ دَخَلَ الْكَعْبَةَ قَالَ لاَ. قَالَ فَحَدِّثْنَا مَا، قَالَ لِخَدِيجَةَ. قَالَ " بَشِّرُوا خَدِيجَةَ بِبَيْتٍ فِي الْجَنَّةِ مِنْ قَصَبٍ لاَ صَخَبَ فِيهِ وَلاَ نَصَبَ "

Narrated `Ali: The Prophet ﷺ said, "The best of the world's women is Mary (at her lifetime), and the best of the world's women is Khadija (at her lifetime). – Sahih Al-Bukhari 3815

حَدَّثَنِي مُحَمَّدٌ، أَخْبَرَنَا عَبْدَةُ، عَنْ هِشَامِ بْنِ عُرْوَةَ، عَنْ أَبِيهِ، قَالَ سَمِعْتُ عَبْدَ اللَّهِ بْنَ جَعْفَرٍ، قَالَ سَمِعْتُ عَلِيًّا ـ رضى الله عنه ـ يَقُولُ سَمِعْتُ رَسُولَ اللَّهِ صلى الله عليه وسلم يَقُولُ ح حَدَّثَنِي صَدَقَةُ أَخْبَرَنَا عَبْدَةُ عَنْ هِشَامٍ عَنْ أَبِيهِ قَالَ سَمِعْتُ عَبْدَ اللَّهِ بْنَ جَعْفَرٍ عَنْ عَلِيٍّ ـ رضى الله عنهم ـ عَنِ النَّبِيِّ صلى الله عليه وسلم قَالَ " خَيْرُ نِسَائِهَا مَرْيَمُ، وَخَيْرُ نِسَائِهَا خَدِيجَةُ

Narrated `Aisha: I did not feel jealous of any of the wives of the Prophet ﷺ as much as I did of Khadija though I did not see her, but the Prophet ﷺ used to mention her very often, and when ever he slaughtered a sheep, he would cut its parts and send them to the women friends of Khadija. When I sometimes said to him, "(You treat Khadija in such a way) as if there is no woman on earth except Khadija," he would say, "Khadija was such-and-such, and from her I had children.". – Sahih Al-Bukhari 3818

حَدَّثَنِي عُمَرُ بْنُ مُحَمَّدِ بْنِ حَسَنٍ، حَدَّثَنَا أَبِي، حَدَّثَنَا حَفْصٌ، عَنْ هِشَامٍ، عَنْ أَبِيهِ، عَنْ عَائِشَةَ ـ رضى الله عنها ـ قَالَتْ مَا غِرْتُ عَلَى أَحَدٍ مِنْ نِسَاءِ النَّبِيِّ صلى الله عليه وسلم مَا غِرْتُ عَلَى خَدِيجَةَ، وَمَا رَأَيْتُهَا، وَلَكِنْ كَانَ النَّبِيُّ صلى الله عليه وسلم يُكْثِرُ ذِكْرَهَا، وَرُبَّمَا ذَبَحَ الشَّاةَ، ثُمَّ يُقَطِّعُهَا أَعْضَاءً، ثُمَّ يَبْعَثُهَا فِي صَدَائِقِ خَدِيجَةَ، فَرُبَّمَا قُلْتُ لَهُ كَأَنَّهُ لَمْ يَكُنْ فِي الدُّنْيَا امْرَأَةٌ إِلاَّ خَدِيجَةُ. فَيَقُولُ إِنَّهَا كَانَتْ وَكَانَتْ، وَكَانَ لِي مِنْهَا وَلَدٌ.

Narrated Hisham's father: Khadija died three years before the Prophet ﷺ departed to Medina. He stayed there for two years or so and then he married `Aisha when she was a girl of six years of age, and he consumed that marriage when she was nine years old. – Sahih al-Bukhari 3896

حَدَّثَنِي عُبَيْدُ بْنُ إِسْمَاعِيلَ، حَدَّثَنَا أَبُو أُسَامَةَ، عَنْ هِشَامٍ، عَنْ أَبِيهِ، قَالَ تُوُفِّيَتْ خَدِيجَةُ قَبْلَ مَخْرَجِ النَّبِيِّ صلى الله عليه وسلم إِلَى الْمَدِينَةِ بِثَلاَثِ سِنِينَ، فَلَبِثَ سَنَتَيْنِ أَوْ قَرِيبًا مِنْ ذَلِكَ، وَنَكَحَ عَائِشَةَ وَهْىَ بِنْتُ سِتِّ سِنِينَ، ثُمَّ بَنَى بِهَا وَهْىَ بِنْتُ تِسْعِ سِنِينَ.

Passing of Abu Talib
وفاة أبي طالب

Narrated Sa`id bin Al-Musaiyab from his father: When the time of the death of Abu Talib approached, Allah's Messenger ﷺ went to him and found Abu Jahl bin Hisham and `Abdullah bin Abi Umaiya bin Al-Mughira by his side. Allah's Messenger ﷺ said to Abu Talib, "O uncle! Say: None has the right to be worshipped but Allah, a sentence with which I shall be a witness (i.e. argue) for you before Allah. Abu Jahl and `Abdullah bin Abi Umaiya said, "O Abu Talib! Are you going to denounce the religion of `Abdul Muttalib?" Allah's Messenger ﷺ kept on inviting Abu Talib to say it (i.e. 'None has the right to be worshipped but Allah') while they (Abu Jahl and `Abdullah) kept on repeating their statement till Abu Talib said as his last statement that he was on the religion of `Abdul Muttalib and refused to say, 'None has the right to be worshipped but Allah.' Then Allah's Messenger ﷺ said, "I will keep on asking Allah's forgiveness for you unless I am forbidden (by Allah) to do so." So Allah revealed (the verse) concerning him (i.e. It is not fitting for the Prophet ﷺ and those who believe that they should invoke (Allah) for forgiveness for pagans even though they be of kin, after it has become clear to them that they are companions of the fire (9.113). – Al-Bukhari 1360

حَدَّثَنَا إِسْحَاقُ، أَخْبَرَنَا يَعْقُوبُ بْنُ إِبْرَاهِيمَ، قَالَ حَدَّثَنِي أَبِي، عَنْ صَالِحٍ، عَنِ ابْنِ شِهَابٍ، قَالَ أَخْبَرَنِي سَعِيدُ بْنُ الْمُسَيَّبِ، عَنْ أَبِيهِ، أَنَّهُ أَخْبَرَهُ أَنَّهُ، لَمَّا حَضَرَتْ أَبَا طَالِبٍ الْوَفَاةُ جَاءَهُ رَسُولُ اللَّهِ صلى الله عليه وسلم فَوَجَدَ عِنْدَهُ أَبَا جَهْلِ بْنَ هِشَامٍ، وَعَبْدَ اللَّهِ بْنَ أَبِي أُمَيَّةَ بْنِ الْمُغِيرَةِ، قَالَ رَسُولُ اللَّهِ صلى الله عليه وسلم لأَبِي طَالِبٍ " يَا عَمِّ، قُلْ لاَ إِلَهَ إِلاَّ اللَّهُ، كَلِمَةً أَشْهَدُ لَكَ بِهَا عِنْدَ اللَّهِ ". فَقَالَ أَبُو جَهْلٍ وَعَبْدُ اللَّهِ بْنُ أَبِي أُمَيَّةَ يَا أَبَا طَالِبٍ، أَتَرْغَبُ عَنْ مِلَّةِ عَبْدِ الْمُطَّلِبِ فَلَمْ يَزَلْ رَسُولُ اللَّهِ صلى الله عليه وسلم يَعْرِضُهَا عَلَيْهِ، وَيَعُودَانِ بِتِلْكَ الْمَقَالَةِ، حَتَّى قَالَ أَبُو طَالِبٍ آخِرَ مَا كَلَّمَهُمْ هُوَ عَلَى مِلَّةِ عَبْدِ الْمُطَّلِبِ، وَأَبَى أَنْ يَقُولَ لاَ إِلَهَ إِلاَّ اللَّهُ. فَقَالَ رَسُولُ اللَّهِ صلى الله عليه وسلم " أَمَا وَاللَّهِ لأَسْتَغْفِرَنَّ لَكَ، مَا لَمْ أُنْهَ عَنْكَ ". فَأَنْزَلَ اللَّهُ تَعَالَى فِيهِ {مَا كَانَ لِلنَّبِيِّ} الآيَةَ

Narrated Al-Musaiyab: When Abu Talib was on his death bed, Allah's Messenger ﷺ came to him and found with him, Abu Jahl and `Abdullah bin Abi Umaiya bin Al-Mughira. Allah's Messenger ﷺ said, "O uncle! Say: None has the right to be worshipped except Allah, a sentence with which I will defend you before Allah." On that Abu Jahl and `Abdullah bin Abi Umaiya said to Abu Talib, "Will you now leave the religion of `Abdul Muttalib?" Allah's Messenger ﷺ kept on inviting him to say that sentence while the other two kept on repeating their sentence before him till Abu Talib said as the last thing he said to them, "I am on the religion of `Abdul Muttalib," and refused to say: None has the right to be worshipped except Allah. On that Allah's Messenger ﷺ said, "By Allah, I will keep on asking Allah's forgiveness for you unless I am forbidden (by Allah) to do so." So Allah revealed:-- 'It is not fitting for the Prophet ﷺ and those who believe that they should invoke (Allah) for forgiveness for pagans.' (9.113) And then Allah revealed especially about Abu Talib:--'Verily! You (O, Muhammad) guide not whom you like, but Allah guides whom He will.' (28.56) – Al-Bukhari 4772

حَدَّثَنَا أَبُو الْيَمَانِ، أَخْبَرَنَا شُعَيْبٌ، عَنِ الزُّهْرِيِّ، قَالَ أَخْبَرَنِي سَعِيدُ بْنُ الْمُسَيَّبِ، عَنْ أَبِيهِ، قَالَ لَمَّا حَضَرَتْ أَبَا طَالِبٍ الْوَفَاةُ جَاءَهُ رَسُولُ اللَّهِ صلى الله عليه وسلم فَوَجَدَ عِنْدَهِ أَبَا جَهْلٍ وَعَبْدَ اللَّهِ بْنَ أَبِي أُمَيَّةَ بْنِ الْمُغِيرَةِ، فَقَالَ " أَىْ عَمِّ قُلْ لاَ إِلَهَ إِلاَّ اللَّهُ، كَلِمَةً أُحَاجُّ لَكَ بِهَا عِنْدَ اللَّهِ ". فَقَالَ أَبُو جَهْلٍ وَعَبْدُ اللَّهِ بْنُ أَبِي أُمَيَّةَ أَتَرْغَبُ عَنْ مِلَّةِ عَبْدِ الْمُطَّلِبِ فَلَمْ يَزَلْ رَسُولُ اللَّهِ صلى الله عليه وسلم يعرِضها عليهِ، وَيُعِيدانِهِ بِتِلْكَ المَقالةِ حَتى قَالَ أبو طالِبٍ اخِرَ مَا كَلمَهُمْ عَلى مِلةِ عَبْدِ المُطلِبِ، وَأَبَى أَنْ يَقُولَ لاَ إِلَهَ إِلاَّ اللَّهُ. قَالَ قَالَ رَسُولُ اللَّهِ صلى الله عليه وسلم " وَاللَّهِ لأَسْتَغْفِرَنَّ لَكَ مَا لَمْ أُنْهَ عَنْكَ ". فَأَنْزَلَ اللَّهُ {مَا كَانَ لِلنَّبِيِّ وَالَّذِينَ آمَنُوا أَنْ يَسْتَغْفِرُوا لِلْمُشْرِكِينَ} وَأَنْزَلَ اللَّهُ فِي أَبِي طَالِبٍ، فَقَالَ لِرَسُولِ اللَّهِ صلى الله عليه وسلم {إِنَّكَ لاَ تَهْدِي مَنْ أَحْبَبْتَ وَلَكِنَّ اللَّهَ يَهْدِي مَنْ يَشَاءُ}. قَالَ ابْنُ عَبَّاسٍ {أُولِي الْقُوَّةِ} لاَ يَرْفَعُهَا الْعُصْبَةُ مِنَ الرِّجَالِ. {لَتَنُوءُ} لَتُثْقِلُ. {فَارِغًا} إِلاَّ مِنْ ذِكْرِ مُوسَى. {الْفَرِحِينَ} الْمَرِحِينَ. {قُصِّيهِ} اتَّبِعِي أَثَرَهُ، وَقَدْ يَكُونُ أَنْ يَقُصَّ الْكَلاَمَ {نَحْنُ نَقُصُّ عَلَيْكَ}. {عَنْ جُنُبٍ} عَنْ بُعْدٍ عَنْ جَنَابَةٍ وَاحِدٌ، وَعَنِ اجْتِنَابٍ أَيْضًا، يَبْطِشُ وَيَبْطُشُ. {يَأْتَمِرُونَ} يَتَشَاوَرُونَ. الْعُدْوَانُ وَالْعَدَاءُ وَالتَّعَدِّي وَاحِدٌ. {آنَسَ} أَبْصَرَ. الْجِذْوَةُ قِطْعَةٌ غَلِيظَةٌ مِنَ الْخَشَبِ، لَيْسَ فِيهَا لَهَبٌ، وَالشِّهَابُ فِيهِ لَهَبٌ. وَالْحَيَّاتُ أَجْنَاسٌ الْجَانُّ وَالأَفَاعِي

وَالأَسَاوِدُ. {رِدْءًا} مُعِينًا. قَالَ ابْنُ عَبَّاسٍ {يُصَدِّقُنِي} وَقَالَ غَيْرُهُ {سَنَشُدُّ} سَنُعِينُكَ كُلَّمَا عَزَّزْتَ شَيْئًا فَقَدْ جَعَلْتَ لَهُ عَضُدًا. مَقْبُوحِينَ مُهْلَكِينَ. {وَصَّلْنَا} بَيَّنَّاهُ وَأَتْمَمْنَاهُ. {يُجْبَى} يُجْلَبُ. {بَطِرَتْ} أَشِرَتْ. {فِي أُمِّهَا رَسُولاً} أُمُّ الْقُرَى مَكَّةُ وَمَا حَوْلَهَا. {تُكِنُّ} تُخْفِي. أَكْنَنْتُ الشَّىْءَ أَخْفَيْتُهُ، وَكَنَنْتُهُ أَخْفَيْتُهُ وَأَظْهَرْتُهُ. {وَيْكَأَنَّ اللَّهَ} مِثْلُ أَلَمْ تَرَ أَنَّ اللَّهَ {يَبْسُطُ الرِّزْقَ لِمَنْ يَشَاءُ وَيَقْدِرُ} يُوَسِّعُ عَلَيْهِ وَيُضَيِّقُ عَلَيْهِ.

Narrated Al-Musaiyab: When Abu Talib's death approached, the Prophet ﷺ went to him while Abu Jahl and `Abdullah bin Abi Umaiya were present with him. The Prophet ﷺ said, "O uncle, say: None has the right to be worshipped except Allah, so that I may argue for your case with it before Allah." On that, Abu Jahl and `Abdullah bin Abu Umaiya said, "O Abu Talib! Do you want to renounce `Abdul Muttalib's religion?" Then the Prophet said, "I will keep on asking (Allah for) forgiveness for you unless I am forbidden to do so." Then there was revealed:-- 'It is not fitting for the Prophet ﷺ and those who believe that they should invoke (Allah) for forgiveness for pagans even though they be of kin, after it has become clear to them that they are companions of the Fire.' (9.113) – Al-Bukhari 4675

حَدَّثَنَا إِسْحَاقُ بْنُ إِبْرَاهِيمَ، حَدَّثَنَا عَبْدُ الرَّزَّاقِ، أَخْبَرَنَا مَعْمَرٌ، عَنِ الزُّهْرِيِّ، عَنْ سَعِيدِ بْنِ الْمُسَيَّبِ، عَنْ أَبِيهِ، قَالَ لَمَّا حَضَرَتْ أَبَا طَالِبٍ الْوَفَاةُ دَخَلَ عَلَيْهِ النَّبِيُّ صلى الله عليه وسلم وَعِنْدَهُ أَبُو جَهْلٍ وَعَبْدُ اللَّهِ بْنُ أَبِي أُمَيَّةَ، فَقَالَ النَّبِيُّ صلى الله عليه وسلم " أَىْ عَمِّ قُلْ لاَ إِلَهَ إِلاَّ اللَّهُ. أُحَاجُّ لَكَ بِهَا عِنْدَ اللَّهِ ". فَقَالَ أَبُو جَهْلٍ وَعَبْدُ اللَّهِ بْنُ أَبِي أُمَيَّةَ يَا أَبَا طَالِبٍ، أَتَرْغَبُ عَنْ مِلَّةِ عَبْدِ الْمُطَّلِبِ. فَقَالَ النَّبِيُّ صلى الله عليه وسلم " لأَسْتَغْفِرَنَّ لَكَ مَا لَمْ أُنْهَ عَنْكَ ". فَنَزَلَتْ {مَا كَانَ لِلنَّبِيِّ وَالَّذِينَ آمَنُوا أَنْ يَسْتَغْفِرُوا لِلْمُشْرِكِينَ وَلَوْ كَانُوا أُولِي قُرْبَى مِنْ بَعْدِ مَا تَبَيَّنَ لَهُمْ أَنَّهُمْ أَصْحَابُ الْجَحِيمِ}

Narrated Al-Abbas bin `Abdul Muttalib: That he said to the Prophet ﷺ" You have not been of any avail to your uncle (Abu Talib) (though) by Allah, he used to protect you and used to become angry on your behalf." The Prophet ﷺ said, "He is in a shallow fire, and had It not been for me, he would have been in the bottom of the (Hell) Fire.". – Al-Bukhari 3883

حَدَّثَنَا مُسَدَّدٌ، حَدَّثَنَا يَحْيَى، عَنْ سُفْيَانَ، حَدَّثَنَا عَبْدُ الْمَلِكِ، حَدَّثَنَا عَبْدُ اللَّهِ بْنُ الْحَارِثِ، حَدَّثَنَا الْعَبَّاسُ بْنُ عَبْدِ الْمُطَّلِبِ ـ رضى الله عنه ـ قَالَ لِلنَّبِيِّ صلى الله عليه وسلم مَا أَغْنَيْتَ عَنْ عَمِّكَ فَإِنَّهُ كَانَ يَحُوطُكَ وَيَغْضَبُ لَكَ. قَالَ " هُوَ فِي ضَحْضَاحٍ مِنْ نَارٍ، وَلَوْلاَ أَنَا لَكَانَ فِي الدَّرَكِ الأَسْفَلِ مِنَ النَّارِ ".

Narrated Abu Sa`id Al-Khudri: That he heard the Prophet ﷺ when somebody mentioned his uncle (i.e. Abu Talib), saying, "Perhaps my intercession will be helpful to him on the Day of Resurrection so that he may be put in a shallow fire reaching only up to his ankles. His brain will boil from it." Narrated Yazid: (as above, Hadith 224) using the words: "will make his brain boil." – Al-Bukhari 3885

حَدَّثَنَا عَبْدُ اللَّهِ بْنُ يُوسُفَ، حَدَّثَنَا اللَّيْثُ، حَدَّثَنَا ابْنُ الْهَادِ، عَنْ عَبْدِ اللَّهِ بْنِ خَبَّابٍ، عَنْ أَبِي سَعِيدٍ الْخُدْرِيِّ ـ رضى الله عنه ـ أَنَّهُ سَمِعَ النَّبِيَّ صلى الله عليه وسلم وَذُكِرَ عِنْدَهُ عَمُّهُ فَقَالَ " لَعَلَّهُ تَنْفَعُهُ شَفَاعَتِي يَوْمَ الْقِيَامَةِ، فَيُجْعَلُ فِي ضَحْضَاحٍ مِنَ النَّارِ، يَبْلُغُ كَعْبَيْهِ، يَغْلِي مِنْهُ دِمَاغُهُ ". حَدَّثَنَا إِبْرَاهِيمُ بْنُ حَمْزَةَ حَدَّثَنَا ابْنُ أَبِي حَازِمٍ وَالدَّرَاوَرْدِيُّ عَنْ يَزِيدَ بِهَذَا، وَقَالَ تَغْلِي مِنْهُ أُمُّ دِمَاغِهِ.

The Book of
Al-Hijrat Al'uwlaa
الهجرة الأولى

Narrated 'Aisha: (the wife of the Prophet) I never remembered my parents believing in any religion other than the true religion (i.e. Islam), and (I don't remember) a single day passing without our being visited by Allah's Messengerﷺ in the morning and in the evening. When the Muslims were put to test (i.e. troubled by the pagans), Abu Bakr set out migrating to the land of Ethiopia, and when he reached Bark-al-Ghimad, Ibn Ad-Daghina, the chief of the tribe of Qara, met him and said, "O Abu Bakr! Where are you going?" Abu Bakr replied, "My people have turned me out (of my country), so I want to wander on the earth and worship my Lord." Ibn Ad-Daghina said, "O Abu Bakr! A man like you should not leave his home-land, nor should he be driven out, because you help the destitute, earn their livings, and you keep good relations with your Kith and kin, help the weak and poor, entertain guests generously, and help the calamity-stricken persons. Therefore I am your protector. Go back and worship your Lord in your town." So Abu Bakr returned and Ibn Ad-Daghina accompanied him. In the evening Ibn Ad-Daghina visited the nobles of Quraish and said to them. "A man like Abu Bakr should not leave his homeland, nor should he be driven out. Do you (i.e. Quraish) drive out a man who helps the destitute, earns their living, keeps good relations with his Kith and kin, helps the weak and poor, entertains guests generously and helps the calamity-stricken persons?" So the people of Quraish could not refuse Ibn Ad-Daghina's protection, and they said to Ibn Ad-Daghina, "Let Abu Bakr worship his Lord in his house. He can pray and recite there whatever he likes, but he should not hurt us with it, and should not do it publicly, because we are afraid that he may affect our women and children." Ibn Ad-Daghina told Abu Bakr of all that. Abu Bakr stayed in that state, worshipping his Lord in his house. He did not pray publicly, nor did he recite Quran outside his house. Then a thought occurred to Abu Bakr to build a mosque in front of his house, and there he used to pray and recite the Quran. The women and children of the pagans began to gather around him in great number. They used to wonder at him and look at him. Abu Bakr was a man who used to weep too much, and he could not help weeping on reciting the Quran. That situation scared the nobles of the pagans of Quraish, so they sent for Ibn Ad-Daghina. When he came to them, they said, "We accepted your protection of Abu Bakr on condition that he should worship his Lord in his house, but he has violated the conditions and he has built a mosque in front of his house where he prays and recites the Quran publicly. We are now afraid that he may affect our women and children unfavorably. So, prevent him from that. If he likes to confine the worship of his Lord to his house, he may do so, but if he insists on doing that openly, ask him to release you from your obligation to protect him, for we dislike to break our pact with you, but we deny Abu Bakr the right to announce his act publicly." Ibn Ad-Daghina went to Abu- Bakr and said, ("O Abu Bakr!) You know well what contract I have made on your behalf; now, you are either to abide by it, or else release me from my obligation of protecting you, because I do not want the 'Arabs hear that my people have dishonored a contract I have made on behalf of another man." Abu Bakr replied, "I release you from your pact to protect me, and am pleased with the protection from Allah." At that time the Prophetﷺ was in Mecca, and he said to the Muslims, "In a dream I have been shown your migration place, a land of date palm trees, between two mountains, the two stony tracts." So, some people migrated to Medina, and most of those people who had previously migrated to the land of Ethiopia, returned to

Medina. Abu Bakr also prepared to leave for Medina, but Allah's Messenger ﷺ said to him, "Wait for a while, because I hope that I will be allowed to migrate also." Abu Bakr said, "Do you indeed expect this? Let my father be sacrificed for you!" The Prophet ﷺ said, "Yes." So Abu Bakr did not migrate for the sake of Allah's Messenger ﷺ in order to accompany him. He fed two she-camels he possessed with the leaves of As-Samur tree that fell on being struck by a stick for four months. One day, while we were sitting in Abu Bakr's house at noon, someone said to Abu Bakr, "This is Allah's Messenger ﷺ with his head covered coming at a time at which he never used to visit us before." Abu Bakr said, "May my parents be sacrificed for him. By Allah, he has not come at this hour except for a great necessity." So Allah's Messenger ﷺ came and asked permission to enter, and he was allowed to enter. When he entered, he said to Abu Bakr. "Tell everyone who is present with you to go away." Abu Bakr replied, "There are none but your family. May my father be sacrificed for you, O Allah's Messenger ﷺ !" The Prophet ﷺ said, "I have been given permission to migrate." Abu Bakr said, "Shall I accompany you? May my father be sacrificed for you, O Allah's Messenger ﷺ !" Allah's Messenger ﷺ said, "Yes." Abu Bakr said, "O Allah's Messenger ﷺ ! May my father be sacrificed for you, take one of these two she-camels of mine." Allah's Messenger ﷺ replied, "(I will accept it) with payment." So we prepared the baggage quickly and put some journey food in a leather bag for them. Asma, Abu Bakr's daughter, cut a piece from her waist belt and tied the mouth of the leather bag with it, and for that reason she was named Dhat-un-Nitaqain (i.e. the owner of two belts). Then Allah's Messenger ﷺ and Abu Bakr reached a cave on the mountain of Thaur and stayed there for three nights. 'Abdullah bin Abi Bakr who was intelligent and a sagacious youth, used to stay (with them) aver night. He used to leave them before day break so that in the morning he would be with Quraish as if he had spent the night in Mecca. He would keep in mind any plot made against them, and when it became dark he would (go and) inform them of it. 'Amir bin Fuhaira, the freed slave of Abu Bakr, used to bring the milch sheep (of his master, Abu Bakr) to them a little while after nightfall in order to rest the sheep there. So they always had fresh milk at night, the milk of their sheep, and the milk which they warmed by throwing heated stones in it. 'Amir bin Fuhaira would then call the herd away when it was still dark (before daybreak). He did the same in each of those three nights. Allah's Messenger ﷺ and Abu Bakr had hired a man from the tribe of Bani Ad-Dail from the family of Bani Abd bin Adi as an expert guide, and he was in alliance with the family of Al-'As bin Wail As-Sahmi and he was on the religion of the infidels of Quraish. The Prophet ﷺ and Abu Bakr trusted him and gave him their two she-camels and took his promise to bring their two she camels to the cave of the mountain of Thaur in the morning after three nights later. And (when they set out), 'Amir bin Fuhaira and the guide went along with them and the guide led them along the sea-shore. – Al-Bukhari 3905 (Also Bukhari 5807)

حَدَّثَنَا يَحْيَى بْنُ بُكَيْرٍ، حَدَّثَنَا اللَّيْثُ، عَنْ عُقَيْلٍ، قَالَ ابْنُ شِهَابٍ فَأَخْبَرَنِي عُرْوَةُ بْنُ الزُّبَيْرِ، أَنَّ عَائِشَةَ ـ رضى الله عنها ـ زَوْجَ النَّبِيِّ صلى الله عليه وسلم قَالَتْ لَمْ أَعْقِلْ أَبَوَىَّ قَطُّ إِلاَّ وَهُمَا يَدِينَانِ الدِّينَ، وَلَمْ يَمُرَّ عَلَيْنَا يَوْمٌ إِلاَّ يَأْتِينَا فِيهِ رَسُولُ اللَّهِ صلى الله عليه وسلم طَرَفَىِ النَّهَارِ بُكْرَةً وَعَشِيَّةً، فَلَمَّا ابْتُلِيَ الْمُسْلِمُونَ خَرَجَ أَبُو بَكْرٍ مُهَاجِرًا نَحْوَ أَرْضِ الْحَبَشَةِ، حَتَّى بَلَغَ بَرْكَ الْغِمَادِ لَقِيَهُ ابْنُ الدَّغِنَةِ وَهْوَ سَيِّدُ الْقَارَةِ. فَقَالَ أَيْنَ تُرِيدُ يَا أَبَا بَكْرٍ فَقَالَ أَبُو بَكْرٍ أَخْرَجَنِي قَوْمِي، فَأُرِيدُ أَنْ أَسِيحَ فِي الأَرْضِ وَأَعْبُدَ رَبِّي. قَالَ ابْنُ الدَّغِنَةِ فَإِنَّ مِثْلَكَ يَا أَبَا بَكْرٍ لاَ يَخْرُجُ وَلاَ يُخْرَجُ، إِنَّكَ تَكْسِبُ الْمَعْدُومَ، وَتَصِلُ الرَّحِمَ وَتَحْمِلُ الْكَلَّ، وَتَقْرِي الضَّيْفَ، وَتُعِينُ عَلَى نَوَائِبِ الْحَقِّ، فَأَنَا لَكَ جَارٌ، ارْجِعْ وَاعْبُدْ رَبَّكَ بِبَلَدِكَ. فَرَجَعَ وَارْتَحَلَ مَعَهُ ابْنُ الدَّغِنَةِ، فَطَافَ ابْنُ الدَّغِنَةِ عَشِيَّةً فِي أَشْرَافِ قُرَيْشٍ، فَقَالَ لَهُمْ إِنَّ أَبَا بَكْرٍ لاَ يَخْرُجُ مِثْلُهُ وَلاَ يُخْرَجُ، أَتُخْرِجُونَ رَجُلاً يَكْسِبُ الْمَعْدُومَ، وَيَصِلُ الرَّحِمَ، وَيَحْمِلُ الْكَلَّ، وَيَقْرِي الضَّيْفَ، وَيُعِينُ عَلَى نَوَائِبِ الْحَقِّ فَلَمْ تُكَذِّبْ قُرَيْشٌ بِجِوَارِ ابْنِ الدَّغِنَةِ، وَقَالُوا لاِبْنِ الدَّغِنَةِ مُرْ أَبَا بَكْرٍ فَلْيَعْبُدْ رَبَّهُ فِي دَارِهِ، فَلْيُصَلِّ فِيهَا وَلْيَقْرَأْ مَا شَاءَ، وَلاَ يُؤْذِينَا بِذَلِكَ، وَلاَ يَسْتَعْلِنْ بِهِ، فَإِنَّا نَخْشَى أَنْ يَفْتِنَ نِسَاءَنَا وَأَبْنَاءَنَا. فَقَالَ ذَلِكَ ابْنُ الدَّغِنَةِ لأَبِي بَكْرٍ، فَلَبِثَ أَبُو بَكْرٍ بِذَلِكَ يَعْبُدُ رَبَّهُ فِي دَارِهِ، وَلاَ يَسْتَعْلِنُ بِصَلاَتِهِ، وَلاَ يَقْرَأُ فِي غَيْرِ دَارِهِ، ثُمَّ بَدَا لأَبِي بَكْرٍ فَابْتَنَى مَسْجِدًا بِفِنَاءِ دَارِهِ وَكَانَ يُصَلِّي فِيهِ وَيَقْرَأُ الْقُرْآنَ، فَيَنْقَذِفُ عَلَيْهِ نِسَاءُ الْمُشْرِكِينَ وَأَبْنَاؤُهُمْ، وَهُمْ يَعْجَبُونَ مِنْهُ، وَيَنْظُرُونَ إِلَيْهِ، وَكَانَ أَبُو بَكْرٍ رَجُلاً بَكَّاءً، لاَ يَمْلِكُ عَيْنَيْهِ إِذَا قَرَأَ الْقُرْآنَ،

وَأَفْزَعَ ذَلِكَ أَشْرَافَ قُرَيْشٍ مِنَ الْمُشْرِكِينَ، فَأَرْسَلُوا إِلَى ابْنِ الدَّغِنَةِ، فَقَدِمَ عَلَيْهِمْ. فَقَالُوا إِنَّا كُنَّا أَجَرْنَا أَبَا بَكْرٍ بِجِوَارِكَ، عَلَى أَنْ يَعْبُدَ رَبَّهُ فِي دَارِهِ، فَقَدْ جَاوَزَ ذَلِكَ، فَابْتَنَى مَسْجِدًا بِفِنَاءِ دَارِهِ، فَأَعْلَنَ بِالصَّلاَةِ وَالْقِرَاءَةِ فِيهِ، وَإِنَّا قَدْ خَشِينَا أَنْ يَفْتِنَ نِسَاءَنَا وَأَبْنَاءَنَا فَانْهَهُ، فَإِنْ أَحَبَّ أَنْ يَقْتَصِرَ عَلَى أَنْ يَعْبُدَ رَبَّهُ فِي دَارِهِ فَعَلَ، وَإِنْ أَبَى إِلاَّ أَنْ يُعْلِنَ بِذَلِكَ فَسَلْهُ أَنْ يَرُدَّ إِلَيْكَ ذِمَّتَكَ، فَإِنَّا قَدْ كَرِهْنَا أَنْ نُخْفِرَكَ، وَلَسْنَا مُقِرِّينَ لأَبِي بَكْرٍ الاِسْتِعْلاَنَ. قَالَتْ عَائِشَةُ فَأَتَى ابْنُ الدَّغِنَةِ إِلَى أَبِي بَكْرٍ فَقَالَ قَدْ عَلِمْتَ الَّذِي عَاقَدْتُ لَكَ عَلَيْهِ، فَإِمَّا أَنْ تَقْتَصِرَ عَلَى ذَلِكَ، وَإِمَّا أَنْ تَرْجِعَ إِلَىَّ ذِمَّتِي، فَإِنِّي لاَ أُحِبُّ أَنْ تَسْمَعَ الْعَرَبُ أَنِّي أُخْفِرْتُ فِي رَجُلٍ عَقَدْتُ لَهُ. فَقَالَ أَبُو بَكْرٍ فَإِنِّي أَرُدُّ إِلَيْكَ جِوَارَكَ وَأَرْضَى بِجِوَارِ اللَّهِ عَزَّ وَجَلَّ. وَالنَّبِيُّ صلى الله عليه وسلم يَوْمَئِذٍ بِمَكَّةَ، فَقَالَ النَّبِيُّ صلى الله عليه وسلم لِلْمُسْلِمِينَ " إِنِّي أُرِيتُ دَارَ هِجْرَتِكُمْ ذَاتَ نَخْلٍ بَيْنَ لاَبَتَيْنِ ". وَهُمَا الْحَرَّتَانِ، فَهَاجَرَ مَنْ هَاجَرَ قِبَلَ الْمَدِينَةِ، وَرَجَعَ عَامَّةُ مَنْ كَانَ هَاجَرَ بِأَرْضِ الْحَبَشَةِ إِلَى الْمَدِينَةِ، وَتَجَهَّزَ أَبُو بَكْرٍ قِبَلَ الْمَدِينَةِ، فَقَالَ لَهُ رَسُولُ اللَّهِ صلى الله عليه وسلم " عَلَى رِسْلِكَ، فَإِنِّي أَرْجُو أَنْ يُؤْذَنَ لِي ". فَقَالَ أَبُو بَكْرٍ وَهَلْ تَرْجُو ذَلِكَ بِأَبِي أَنْتَ قَالَ " نَعَمْ ". فَحَبَسَ أَبُو بَكْرٍ نَفْسَهُ عَلَى رَسُولِ اللَّهِ صلى الله عليه وسلم لِيَصْحَبَهُ، وَعَلَفَ رَاحِلَتَيْنِ كَانَتَا عِنْدَهُ وَرَقَ السَّمُرِ وَهْوَ الْخَبَطُ أَرْبَعَةَ أَشْهُرٍ. قَالَ ابْنُ شِهَابٍ قَالَ عُرْوَةُ قَالَتْ عَائِشَةُ فَبَيْنَمَا نَحْنُ يَوْمًا جُلُوسٌ فِي بَيْتِ أَبِي بَكْرٍ فِي نَحْرِ الظَّهِيرَةِ قَالَ قَائِلٌ لأَبِي بَكْرٍ هَذَا رَسُولُ اللَّهِ صلى الله عليه وسلم مُتَقَنِّعًا ـ فِي سَاعَةٍ لَمْ يَكُنْ يَأْتِينَا فِيهَا ـ فَقَالَ أَبُو بَكْرٍ فِدَاءٌ لَهُ أَبِي وَأُمِّي، وَاللَّهِ مَا جَاءَ بِهِ فِي هَذِهِ السَّاعَةِ إِلاَّ أَمْرٌ. قَالَتْ فَجَاءَ رَسُولُ اللَّهِ صلى الله عليه وسلم فَاسْتَأْذَنَ، فَأُذِنَ لَهُ فَدَخَلَ، فَقَالَ النَّبِيُّ صلى الله عليه وسلم لأَبِي بَكْرٍ " أَخْرِجْ مَنْ عِنْدَكَ ". فَقَالَ أَبُو بَكْرٍ إِنَّمَا هُمْ أَهْلُكَ بِأَبِي أَنْتَ يَا رَسُولَ اللَّهِ. قَالَ " فَإِنِّي قَدْ أُذِنَ لِي فِي الْخُرُوجِ ". فَقَالَ أَبُو بَكْرٍ الصَّحَابَةُ بِأَبِي أَنْتَ يَا رَسُولَ اللَّهِ. قَالَ رَسُولُ اللَّهِ صلى الله عليه وسلم " نَعَمْ ". قَالَ أَبُو بَكْرٍ فَخُذْ بِأَبِي أَنْتَ يَا رَسُولَ اللَّهِ إِحْدَى رَاحِلَتَىَّ هَاتَيْنِ. قَالَ رَسُولُ اللَّهِ صلى الله عليه وسلم " بِالثَّمَنِ ". قَالَتْ عَائِشَةُ فَجَهَّزْنَاهُمَا أَحَثَّ الْجِهَازِ، وَصَنَعْنَا لَهُمَا سُفْرَةً فِي جِرَابٍ، فَقَطَعَتْ أَسْمَاءُ بِنْتُ أَبِي بَكْرٍ قِطْعَةً مِنْ نِطَاقِهَا فَرَبَطَتْ بِهِ عَلَى فَمِ الْجِرَابِ، فَبِذَلِكَ سُمِّيَتْ ذَاتَ النِّطَاقِ ـ قَالَتْ ـ ثُمَّ لَحِقَ رَسُولُ اللَّهِ صلى الله عليه وسلم وَأَبُو بَكْرٍ بِغَارٍ فِي جَبَلِ ثَوْرٍ فَكَمَنَا فِيهِ ثَلاَثَ لَيَالٍ، يَبِيتُ عِنْدَهُمَا عَبْدُ اللَّهِ بْنُ أَبِي بَكْرٍ وَهْوَ غُلاَمٌ شَابٌّ ثَقِفٌ لَقِنٌ، فَيُدْلِجُ مِنْ عِنْدِهِمَا بِسَحَرٍ، فَيُصْبِحُ مَعَ قُرَيْشٍ بِمَكَّةَ كَبَائِتٍ، فَلاَ يَسْمَعُ أَمْرًا يُكْتَادَانِ بِهِ إِلاَّ وَعَاهُ، حَتَّى يَأْتِيَهُمَا بِخَبَرِ ذَلِكَ حِينَ يَخْتَلِطُ الظَّلاَمُ، وَيَرْعَى عَلَيْهِمَا عَامِرُ بْنُ فُهَيْرَةَ مَوْلَى أَبِي بَكْرٍ مِنْحَةً مِنْ غَنَمٍ، فَيُرِيحُهَا عَلَيْهِمَا حِينَ يَذْهَبُ سَاعَةٌ مِنَ الْعِشَاءِ، فَيَبِيتَانِ فِي رِسْلٍ وَهْوَ لَبَنُ مِنْحَتِهِمَا وَرَضِيفِهِمَا، حَتَّى يَنْعِقَ بِهَا عَامِرُ بْنُ فُهَيْرَةَ بِغَلَسٍ، يَفْعَلُ ذَلِكَ فِي كُلِّ لَيْلَةٍ مِنْ تِلْكَ اللَّيَالِي الثَّلاَثِ، وَاسْتَأْجَرَ رَسُولُ اللَّهِ صلى الله عليه وسلم وَأَبُو بَكْرٍ رَجُلاً مِنْ بَنِي الدِّيلِ، وَهْوَ مِنْ بَنِي عَبْدِ بْنِ عَدِيٍّ هَادِيًا خِرِّيتًا ـ وَالْخِرِّيتُ الْمَاهِرُ بِالْهِدَايَةِ ـ قَدْ غَمَسَ حِلْفًا فِي آلِ الْعَاصِ بْنِ وَائِلٍ السَّهْمِيِّ، وَهْوَ عَلَى دِينِ كُفَّارِ قُرَيْشٍ فَأَمِنَاهُ، فَدَفَعَا إِلَيْهِ رَاحِلَتَيْهِمَا، وَوَاعَدَاهُ غَارَ ثَوْرٍ بَعْدَ ثَلاَثِ لَيَالٍ بِرَاحِلَتَيْهِمَا صُبْحَ ثَلاَثٍ، وَانْطَلَقَ مَعَهُمَا عَامِرُ بْنُ فُهَيْرَةَ وَالدَّلِيلُ فَأَخَذَ بِهِمْ طَرِيقَ السَّوَاحِلِ

So when the Prophet ﷺ came, she said, "O Allah's Prophet `Umar has said so-and-so." He said (to Asma'), "What did you say to him?" Asma's aid, "I told him so-and-so." The Prophet ﷺ said, "He (i.e. `Umar) has not got more right than you people over me, as he and his companions have (the reward of) only one migration, and you, the people of the boat, have (the reward of) two migrations." Asma' later on said, "I saw Abu Musa and the other people of the boat coming to me in successive groups, asking me about this narration,, and to them nothing in the world was more cheerful and greater than what the Prophet ﷺ had said about them." Narrated Abu Burda: Asma' said, "I saw Abu Musa requesting me to repeat this narration again and again." – Al-Bukhari 4231

فَلَمَّا جَاءَ النَّبِيُّ صلى الله عليه وسلم قَالَتْ يَا نَبِيَّ اللَّهِ إِنَّ عُمَرَ قَالَ كَذَا وَكَذَا. قَالَ " فَمَا قُلْتِ لَهُ ". قَالَتْ قُلْتُ لَهُ كَذَا وَكَذَا. قَالَ " لَيْسَ بِأَحَقَّ بِي مِنْكُمْ، وَلَهُ وَلأَصْحَابِهِ هِجْرَةٌ وَاحِدَةٌ، وَلَكُمْ أَنْتُمْ أَهْلَ السَّفِينَةِ هِجْرَتَانِ ". قَالَتْ فَلَقَدْ رَأَيْتُ أَبَا مُوسَى وَأَصْحَابَ السَّفِينَةِ يَأْتُونِي أَرْسَالاً، يَسْأَلُونِي عَنْ هَذَا الْحَدِيثِ، مَا مِنَ الدُّنْيَا شَىْءٌ هُمْ بِهِ أَفْرَحُ وَلاَ أَعْظَمُ فِي أَنْفُسِهِمْ مِمَّا قَالَ لَهُمُ النَّبِيُّ صلى الله عليه وسلم . قَالَ أَبُو بُرْدَةَ قَالَتْ أَسْمَاءُ فَلَقَدْ رَأَيْتُ أَبَا مُوسَى وَإِنَّهُ لَيَسْتَعِيدُ هَذَا الْحَدِيثَ مِنِّي

The Event of Isra and Miraj
حادثة الإسراء والمعراج

Glory to Him who journeyed His servant by night, from the Sacred Mosque, to the Farthest Mosque, whose precincts We have blessed, in order to show him of Our wonders. He is the Listener, the Beholder. – Surah Al-Isra 17:1

سُبْحَٰنَ ٱلَّذِىٓ أَسْرَىٰ بِعَبْدِهِۦ لَيْلًا مِّنَ ٱلْمَسْجِدِ ٱلْحَرَامِ إِلَى ٱلْمَسْجِدِ ٱلْأَقْصَا ٱلَّذِى بَٰرَكْنَا حَوْلَهُۥ لِنُرِيَهُۥ مِنْ ءَايَٰتِنَآ ۚ إِنَّهُۥ هُوَ ٱلسَّمِيعُ ٱلْبَصِيرُ

Narrated Anas bin Malik: The night Allah's Messenger ﷺ was taken for a journey from the sacred mosque (of Mecca) Al-Ka`ba: Three persons came to him (in a dreamy while he was sleeping in the Sacred Mosque before the Divine Inspiration was revealed to Him. One of them said, "Which of them is he?" The middle (second) angel said, "He is the best of them." The last (third) angle said, "Take the best of them." Only that much happened on that night and he did not see them till they came on another night, i.e. after The Divine Inspiration was revealed to him. (Fath-ul-Bari Page 258, Vol. 17) and he saw them, his eyes were asleep but his heart was not----and so is the case with the prophets: their eyes sleep while their hearts do not sleep. So those angels did not talk to him till they carried him and placed him beside the well of Zamzam. From among them Gabriel took charge of him. Gabriel cut open (the part of his body) between his throat and the middle of his chest (heart) and took all the material out of his chest and `Abdomen and then washed it with Zamzam water with his own hands till he cleansed the inside of his body, and then a gold tray containing a gold bowl full of belief and wisdom was brought and then Gabriel stuffed his chest and throat blood vessels with it and then closed it (the chest). He then ascended with him to the heaven of the world and knocked on one of its doors. The dwellers of the Heaven asked, 'Who is it?' He said, "Gabriel." They said, "Who is accompanying you?" He said, "Muhammad." They said, "Has he been called?" He said, "Yes" They said, "He is welcomed." So the dwellers of the Heaven became pleased with his arrival, and they did not know what Allah would do to the Prophet ﷺ on earth unless Allah informed them. The Prophet ﷺ met Adam over the nearest Heaven. Gabriel said to the Prophet, "He is your father; greet him." The Prophet ﷺ greeted him and Adam returned his greeting and said, "Welcome, O my Son! O what a good son you are!" Behold, he saw two flowing rivers, while he was in the nearest sky. He asked, "What are these two rivers, O Gabriel?" Gabriel said, "These are the sources of the Nile and the Euphrates." Then Gabriel took him around that Heaven and behold, he saw another river at the bank of which there was a palace built of pearls and emerald. He put his hand into the river and found its mud like musk Adhfar. He asked, "What is this, O Gabriel?" Gabriel said, "This is the Kauthar which your Lord has kept for you." Then Gabriel ascended (with him) to the second Heaven and the angels asked the same questions as those on the first Heaven, i.e., "Who is it?" Gabriel replied, "Gabriel". They asked, "Who is accompanying you?" He said, "Muhammad." They asked, "Has he been sent for?" He said, "Yes." Then they said, "He is welcomed." Then he (Gabriel) ascended with the Prophet ﷺ to the third Heaven, and the angels said the same as the angels of the first and the second Heavens had said. Then he ascended with him to the fourth Heaven and they said the same; and then he ascended with him to the fifth Heaven and they said the same; and then he ascended with him to the sixth Heaven and they said the same; then he ascended with him to the seventh Heaven and they said the same. On each Heaven there were prophets whose names he had mentioned and of whom I remember Idris on the second Heaven, Aaron on the fourth Heavens another prophet whose name I don't remember, on the fifth Heaven, Abraham on the sixth Heaven, and Moses on the seventh Heaven because of his privilege of talking to Allah directly. Moses said (to Allah), "O Lord! I thought that none would be raised up above me." But Gabriel ascended with him (the Prophet) for a distance above that, the distance of which only Allah knows, till he reached the Lote Tree (beyond which none may pass) and then the Irresistible, the Lord of Honor and Majesty approached and came closer till he (Gabriel) was about two bow lengths or (even) nearer. (It is said that it was Gabriel who approached and came closer to the Prophet. (Fate Al-Bari Page 263, 264, Vol. 17). Among the things which Allah revealed to him then, was: “Fifty prayers were enjoined on his followers in a day and a night.” Then the Prophetﷺ descended till he met Moses, and then Moses stopped him and asked, “O Muhammad ! What did your Lord en join upon you?” The Prophetﷺ replied,” He enjoined upon me to perform fifty prayers in a day and a night.” Moses said, “Your followers cannot do that; Go back so that your Lord may reduce it for you and for them.” So the Prophetﷺ turned to Gabriel as if he wanted to consult him about that issue. Gabriel told him of his opinion, saying, “Yes, if you wish.” So Gabriel ascended with him to the Irresistible and said while he was in his place, “O Lord, please lighten our burden as my followers cannot do that.” So Allah deducted for him ten prayers where upon he returned to Moses who stopped him again and kept on sending him back to his Lord till the enjoined prayers were reduced to only five prayers. Then Moses stopped him when the prayers had been reduced to five and said, “O Muhammad! By Allah, I tried to persuade my nation, Bani Israel to do less than this, but they could not do it and gave it up. However, your followers are weaker in body, heart, sight and hearing, so return to your Lord so that He may lighten your burden.” The Prophetﷺ turned towards Gabriel for advice and Gabriel did not disapprove of that. So he ascended with him for the fifth time. The Prophetﷺ said, “O Lord, my followers are weak in their bodies, hearts, hearing and constitution, so lighten our burden.” On that the Irresistible said, “O Muhammad!” the Prophet replied, “Labbaik and Sa`daik.” Allah said, “The Word that comes from Me does not change, so it will be as I enjoined on you in the Mother of the Book.” Allah added, “Every good deed will be rewarded as ten times so it is fifty (prayers) in the Mother of the Book (in reward) but you are to perform only five (in practice).” The Prophetﷺ returned to Moses who asked, “What have you done?” He said, “He has lightened our burden: He has given us for every good deed a tenfold reward.” Moses said, “By Allah! I tried to make Bani Israel observe less than that, but they gave it up. So go back to your Lord that He may lighten your burden further.” Allah’s Messengerﷺ said, “O Moses! By Allah, I feel shy of returning too many times to my Lord.” On that Gabriel said, “Descend in Allah’s Name.” The Prophetﷺ then woke while he was in the Sacred Mosque (at Mecca). – Al-Bukhari 7517

حَدَّثَنَا عَبْدُ الْعَزِيزِ بْنُ عَبْدِ اللَّهِ، حَدَّثَنِي سُلَيْمَانُ، عَنْ شَرِيكِ بْنِ عَبْدِ اللَّهِ، أَنَّهُ قَالَ سَمِعْتُ ابْنَ مَالِكٍ، يَقُولُ لَيْلَةَ أُسْرِيَ بِرَسُولِ اللَّهِ صلى الله عليه وسلم مِنْ مَسْجِدِ الْكَعْبَةِ أَنَّهُ جَاءَهُ ثَلاَثَةُ نَفَرٍ قَبْلَ أَنْ يُوحَى إِلَيْهِ وَهْوَ نَائِمٌ فِي الْمَسْجِدِ الْحَرَامِ، فَقَالَ أَوَّلُهُمْ أَيُّهُمْ هُوَ فَقَالَ أَوْسَطُهُمْ هُوَ خَيْرُهُمْ. فَقَالَ آخِرُهُمْ خُذُوا خَيْرَهُمْ. فَكَانَتْ تِلْكَ اللَّيْلَةَ، فَلَمْ يَرَهُمْ حَتَّى أَتَوْهُ لَيْلَةً أُخْرَى فِيمَا يَرَى قَلْبُهُ، وَتَنَامُ عَيْنُهُ وَلاَ يَنَامُ قَلْبُهُ وَكَذَلِكَ الأَنْبِيَاءُ تَنَامُ أَعْيُنُهُمْ وَلاَ تَنَامُ قُلُوبُهُمْ، فَلَمْ يُكَلِّمُوهُ حَتَّى احْتَمَلُوهُ فَوَضَعُوهُ عِنْدَ بِئْرِ زَمْزَمَ فَتَوَلاَّهُ مِنْهُمْ جِبْرِيلُ فَشَقَّ جِبْرِيلُ مَا بَيْنَ نَحْرِهِ إِلَى لَبَّتِهِ حَتَّى فَرَغَ مِنْ صَدْرِهِ وَجَوْفِهِ، فَغَسَلَهُ مِنْ مَاءِ زَمْزَمَ بِيَدِهِ، حَتَّى أَنْقَى جَوْفَهُ، ثُمَّ أُتِيَ بِطَسْتٍ مِنْ ذَهَبٍ فِيهِ تَوْرٌ مِنْ ذَهَبٍ مَحْشُوًّا إِيمَانًا وَحِكْمَةً، فَحَشَا بِهِ صَدْرَهُ وَلَغَادِيدَهُ - يَعْنِي عُرُوقَ حَلْقِهِ - ثُمَّ أَطْبَقَهُ ثُمَّ عَرَجَ بِهِ إِلَى السَّمَاءِ الدُّنْيَا فَضَرَبَ بَابًا مِنْ أَبْوَابِهَا فَنَادَاهُ أَهْلُ السَّمَاءِ مَنْ هَذَا فَقَالَ جِبْرِيلُ. قَالُوا وَمَنْ مَعَكَ قَالَ مَعِي مُحَمَّدٌ. قَالَ وَقَدْ بُعِثَ قَالَ نَعَمْ. قَالُوا فَمَرْحَبًا بِهِ وَأَهْلاً. فَيَسْتَبْشِرُ بِهِ أَهْلُ السَّمَاءِ، لاَ يَعْلَمُ أَهْلُ السَّمَاءِ بِمَا يُرِيدُ اللَّهُ بِهِ فِي الأَرْضِ حَتَّى يُعْلِمَهُمْ، فَوَجَدَ فِي السَّمَاءِ الدُّنْيَا آدَمَ فَقَالَ لَهُ جِبْرِيلُ هَذَا أَبُوكَ فَسَلِّمْ عَلَيْهِ. فَسَلَّمَ عَلَيْهِ وَرَدَّ عَلَيْهِ آدَمُ وَقَالَ مَرْحَبًا وَأَهْلاً بِابْنِي، نِعْمَ الاِبْنُ أَنْتَ. فَإِذَا هُوَ فِي السَّمَاءِ الدُّنْيَا بِنَهَرَيْنِ يَطَّرِدَانِ فَقَالَ مَا هَذَانِ النَّهَرَانِ يَا جِبْرِيلُ قَالَ هَذَا النِّيلُ وَالْفُرَاتُ عُنْصُرُهُمَا. ثُمَّ مَضَى بِهِ فِي السَّمَاءِ فَإِذَا هُوَ بِنَهَرٍ آخَرَ عَلَيْهِ قَصْرٌ مِنْ لُؤْلُؤٍ وَزَبَرْجَدٍ فَضَرَبَ يَدَهُ فَإِذَا هُوَ مِسْكٌ قَالَ مَا هَذَا يَا جِبْرِيلُ قَالَ هَذَا الْكَوْثَرُ الَّذِي خَبَأَ لَكَ رَبُّكَ. ثُمَّ عَرَجَ إِلَى السَّمَاءِ الثَّانِيَةِ فَقَالَتِ الْمَلاَئِكَةُ لَهُ مِثْلَ مَا قَالَتْ لَهُ الأُولَى مَنْ هَذَا قَالَ جِبْرِيلُ، قَالُوا وَمَنْ مَعَكَ قَالَ مُحَمَّدٌ صلى الله عليه وسلم. قَالُوا وَقَدْ بُعِثَ إِلَيْهِ قَالَ نَعَمْ. قَالُوا مَرْحَبًا بِهِ وَأَهْلاً. ثُمَّ عَرَجَ بِهِ إِلَى السَّمَاءِ الثَّالِثَةِ وَقَالُوا لَهُ مِثْلَ مَا قَالَتِ الأُولَى وَالثَّانِيَةُ، ثُمَّ عَرَجَ بِهِ إِلَى الرَّابِعَةِ فَقَالُوا لَهُ مِثْلَ ذَلِكَ، ثُمَّ عَرَجَ بِهِ إِلَى السَّمَاءِ الْخَامِسَةِ فَقَالُوا مِثْلَ ذَلِكَ، ثُمَّ عَرَجَ بِهِ إِلَى السَّمَاءِ السَّادِسَةِ فَقَالُوا لَهُ مِثْلَ ذَلِكَ، ثُمَّ عَرَجَ بِهِ إِلَى السَّمَاءِ السَّابِعَةِ فَقَالُوا لَهُ مِثْلَ ذَلِكَ، كُلُّ سَمَاءٍ فِيهَا أَنْبِيَاءُ قَدْ سَمَّاهُمْ فَأَوْعَيْتُ مِنْهُمْ إِدْرِيسَ فِي الثَّانِيَةِ، وَهَارُونَ فِي الرَّابِعَةِ، وَآخَرَ فِي الْخَامِسَةِ لَمْ أَحْفَظِ اسْمَهُ، وَإِبْرَاهِيمَ فِي السَّادِسَةِ، وَمُوسَى فِي السَّابِعَةِ بِتَفْضِيلِ كَلاَمِ اللَّهِ، فَقَالَ مُوسَى رَبِّ لَمْ أَظُنَّ أَنْ يُرْفَعَ عَلَىَّ أَحَدٌ. ثُمَّ عَلاَ بِهِ فَوْقَ ذَلِكَ بِمَا لاَ يَعْلَمُهُ إِلاَّ اللَّهُ، حَتَّى جَاءَ سِدْرَةَ الْمُنْتَهَى وَدَنَا الْجَبَّارُ رَبُّ الْعِزَّةِ فَتَدَلَّى حَتَّى كَانَ مِنْهُ قَابَ قَوْسَيْنِ أَوْ أَدْنَى فَأَوْحَى اللَّهُ فِيمَا أَوْحَى إِلَيْهِ خَمْسِينَ صَلاَةً عَلَى أُمَّتِكَ كُلَّ يَوْمٍ وَلَيْلَةٍ. ثُمَّ هَبَطَ حَتَّى بَلَغَ مُوسَى فَاحْتَبَسَهُ مُوسَى فَقَالَ يَا مُحَمَّدُ مَاذَا عَهِدَ إِلَيْكَ رَبُّكَ قَالَ عَهِدَ إِلَىَّ خَمْسِينَ صَلاَةً كُلَّ يَوْمٍ وَلَيْلَةٍ. قَالَ إِنَّ أُمَّتَكَ لاَ تَسْتَطِيعُ ذَلِكَ

فَارْجِعْ فَلْيُخَفِّفْ عَنْكَ رَبُّكَ وَعَنْهُمْ. فَالْتَفَتَ النَّبِيُّ صلى الله عليه وسلم إِلَى جِبْرِيلَ كَأَنَّهُ يَسْتَشِيرُهُ فِي ذَلِكَ، فَأَشَارَ إِلَيْهِ جِبْرِيلُ أَنْ نَعَمْ إِنْ شِئْتَ. فَعَلاَ بِهِ إِلَى الْجَبَّارِ فَقَالَ وَهْوَ مَكَانَهُ يَا رَبِّ خَفِّفْ عَنَّا، فَإِنَّ أُمَّتِي لاَ تَسْتَطِيعُ هَذَا. فَوَضَعَ عَنْهُ عَشْرَ صَلَوَاتٍ ثُمَّ رَجَعَ إِلَى مُوسَى فَاحْتَبَسَهُ، فَلَمْ يَزَلْ يُرَدِّدُهُ مُوسَى إِلَى رَبِّهِ حَتَّى صَارَتْ إِلَى خَمْسِ صَلَوَاتٍ، ثُمَّ احْتَبَسَهُ مُوسَى عِنْدَ الْخَمْسِ فَقَالَ يَا مُحَمَّدُ وَاللَّهِ لَقَدْ رَاوَدْتُ بَنِي إِسْرَائِيلَ قَوْمِي عَلَى أَدْنَى مِنْ هَذَا فَضَعُفُوا فَتَرَكُوهُ فَأُمَّتُكَ أَضْعَفُ أَجْسَادًا وَقُلُوبًا وَأَبْدَانًا وَأَبْصَارًا وَأَسْمَاعًا، فَارْجِعْ فَلْيُخَفِّفْ عَنْكَ رَبُّكَ، كُلَّ ذَلِكَ يَلْتَفِتُ النَّبِيُّ صلى الله عليه وسلم إِلَى جِبْرِيلَ لِيُشِيرَ عَلَيْهِ وَلاَ يَكْرَهُ ذَلِكَ جِبْرِيلُ، فَرَفَعَهُ عِنْدَ الْخَامِسَةِ فَقَالَ يَا رَبِّ إِنَّ أُمَّتِي ضُعَفَاءُ أَجْسَادُهُمْ وَقُلُوبُهُمْ وَأَسْمَاعُهُمْ وَأَبْدَانُهُمْ فَخَفِّفْ عَنَّا فَقَالَ الْجَبَّارُ يَا مُحَمَّدُ. قَالَ لَبَّيْكَ وَسَعْدَيْكَ. قَالَ إِنَّهُ لاَ يُبَدَّلُ الْقَوْلُ لَدَىَّ، كَمَا فَرَضْتُ عَلَيْكَ فِي أُمِّ الْكِتَابِ ـ قَالَ ـ فَكُلُّ حَسَنَةٍ بِعَشْرِ أَمْثَالِهَا، فَهْىَ خَمْسُونَ فِي أُمِّ الْكِتَابِ وَهْىَ خَمْسٌ عَلَيْكَ. فَرَجَعَ إِلَى مُوسَى فَقَالَ كَيْفَ فَعَلْتَ فَقَالَ خَفَّفَ عَنَّا أَعْطَانَا بِكُلِّ حَسَنَةٍ عَشْرَ أَمْثَالِهَا. قَالَ مُوسَى قَدْ وَاللَّهِ رَاوَدْتُ بَنِي إِسْرَائِيلَ عَلَى أَدْنَى مِنْ ذَلِكَ فَتَرَكُوهُ، ارْجِعْ إِلَى رَبِّكَ فَلْيُخَفِّفْ عَنْكَ أَيْضًا. قَالَ رَسُولُ اللَّهِ صلى الله عليه وسلم يَا مُوسَى قَدْ وَاللَّهِ اسْتَحْيَيْتُ مِنْ رَبِّي مِمَّا اخْتَلَفْتُ إِلَيْهِ. قَالَ فَاهْبِطْ بِاسْمِ اللَّهِ. قَالَ وَاسْتَيْقَظَ وَهْوَ فِي مَسْجِدِ الْحَرَامِ.

Surah Al-Kauthar
سورة الكوثر

Narrated Anas bin Malik: The Prophet ﷺ said: "While I was walking in Paradise (on the night of Mi'raj), I saw a river, on the two banks of which there were tents made of hollow pearls. I asked, "What is this, O Gabriel?' He said, 'That is the Kauthar which Your Lord has given to you.' Behold! Its scent or its mud was sharp smelling musk!" (The sub-narrator, Hudba is in doubt as to the correct expression.) – Al-Bukhari 6581

حَدَّثَنَا أَبُو الْوَلِيدِ، حَدَّثَنَا هَمَّامٌ، عَنْ قَتَادَةَ، عَنْ أَنَسٍ، عَنِ النَّبِيِّ صلى الله عليه وسلم. وَحَدَّثَنَا هُدْبَةُ بْنُ خَالِدٍ، حَدَّثَنَا هَمَّامٌ، حَدَّثَنَا قَتَادَةُ، حَدَّثَنَا أَنَسُ بْنُ مَالِكٍ، عَنِ النَّبِيِّ صلى الله عليه وسلم قَالَ " بَيْنَمَا أَنَا أَسِيرُ فِي الْجَنَّةِ إِذَا أَنَا بِنَهَرٍ حَافَتَاهُ قِبَابُ الدُّرِّ الْمُجَوَّفِ قُلْتُ مَا هَذَا يَا جِبْرِيلُ قَالَ هَذَا الْكَوْثَرُ الَّذِي أَعْطَاكَ رَبُّكَ. فَإِذَا طِينُهُ ـ أَوْ طِيبُهُ ـ مِسْكٌ أَذْفَرُ ". شَكَّ هُدْبَةُ

It was narrated that Anas in Malik said: "One day when he-the Prophet ﷺ - was still among us, he took a nap, then he raised his head, smiling. We said to him: 'Why are you smiling, O Messenger of Allah?' He said: 'Just now this Surah was revealed to me: In the Name of Allah, the Most Gracious, the Most Merciful. Verily, We have granted you (O Muahmmad) Al-Kawthar. Therefore turn in prayer to your Lord and sacrifice (to Him only). For he who hates you, he will be cut off.' Then he said: 'Do you know what Al-Kawthar is?' We said: 'Allah and His Messenger know best.' He said: 'It is a river that my Lord has promised me in Paradise. Its vessels are more than the number of the stars. My Ummah will come to me, then a man among them will be pulled away and I will say: "O Lord, he is one of my Ummah" and He will say to me: 'You do not know what he did after you were gone." - Sunan an-Nasa'I 904

أَخْبَرَنَا عَلِيُّ بْنُ حُجْرٍ، قَالَ حَدَّثَنَا عَلِيُّ بْنُ مُسْهِرٍ، عَنِ الْمُخْتَارِ بْنِ فُلْفُلٍ، عَنْ أَنَسِ بْنِ مَالِكٍ، قَالَ بَيْنَمَا ذَاتَ يَوْمٍ بَيْنَ أَظْهُرِنَا – يُرِيدُ النَّبِيَّ صلى الله عليه وسلم – إِذْ أَغْفَى إِغْفَاءَةً ثُمَّ رَفَعَ رَأْسَهُ مُتَبَسِّمًا فَقُلْنَا لَهُ مَا أَضْحَكَكَ يَا رَسُولَ اللَّهِ قَالَ " نَزَلَتْ عَلَىَّ آنِفًا سُورَةٌ بِسْمِ اللَّهِ الرَّحْمَنِ الرَّحِيمِ { إِنَّا أَعْطَيْنَاكَ الْكَوْثَرَ * فَصَلِّ لِرَبِّكَ وَانْحَرْ * إِنَّ شَانِئَكَ هُوَ الأَبْتَرُ } " . ثُمَّ قَالَ " هَلْ تَدْرُونَ مَا الْكَوْثَرُ " . قُلْنَا اللَّهُ وَرَسُولُهُ أَعْلَمُ . قَالَ " فَإِنَّهُ نَهْرٌ وَعَدَنِيهِ رَبِّي فِي الْجَنَّةِ آنِيَتُهُ أَكْثَرُ مِنْ عَدَدِ الْكَوَاكِبِ تَرِدُهُ عَلَىَّ أُمَّتِي فَيُخْتَلَجُ الْعَبْدُ مِنْهُمْ فَأَقُولُ يَا رَبِّ إِنَّهُ مِنْ أُمَّتِي . فَيَقُولُ لِي إِنَّكَ لاَ تَدْرِي مَا أَحْدَثَ بَعْدَكَ " .

Narrated Ibn `Abbas: The Prophet ﷺ said, "On the night of my Ascent to the Heaven, I saw Moses who was a tall brown curlyhaired man as if he was one of the men of Shan'awa tribe, and I saw Jesus, a man of medium height and moderate complexion inclined to the red and white colors and of lank hair. I also saw Malik, the gate-keeper of the (Hell) Fire and Ad-Dajjal amongst the signs which Allah showed me." (The Prophet then recited the Holy Verse): "So be not you in doubt of meeting him' when you met Moses during the night of Mi'raj over the heavens" (32.23) Narrated Anas and Abu Bakra: "The Prophet ﷺ said, "The angels will guard Medina from Ad-Dajjal (who will not be able to enter the city of Medina). – Al-Bukhari 3239

حَدَّثَنَا مُحَمَّدُ بْنُ بَشَّارٍ، حَدَّثَنَا غُنْدَرٌ، حَدَّثَنَا شُعْبَةُ، عَنْ قَتَادَةَ. وَقَالَ لِي خَلِيفَةُ حَدَّثَنَا يَزِيدُ بْنُ زُرَيْعٍ، حَدَّثَنَا سَعِيدٌ، عَنْ قَتَادَةَ، عَنْ أَبِي الْعَالِيَةِ، حَدَّثَنَا ابْنُ عَمِّ، نَبِيِّكُمْ يَعْنِي ابْنَ عَبَّاسٍ ـ رضى الله عنهما ـ عَنِ النَّبِيِّ صلى الله عليه وسلم قَالَ " رَأَيْتُ لَيْلَةَ أُسْرِيَ بِي مُوسَى رَجُلاً آدَمَ طُوَالاً جَعْدًا، كَأَنَّهُ مِنْ رِجَالِ شَنُوءَةَ، وَرَأَيْتُ عِيسَى رَجُلاً مَرْبُوعًا مَرْبُوعَ الْخَلْقِ إِلَى الْحُمْرَةِ وَالْبَيَاضِ، سَبْطَ الرَّأْسِ، وَرَأَيْتُ مَالِكًا خَازِنَ النَّارِ ". وَالدَّجَّالَ فِي آيَاتٍ أَرَاهُنَّ اللَّهُ إِيَّاهُ، فَلاَ تَكُنْ فِي مِرْيَةٍ مِنْ لِقَائِهِ. قَالَ أَنَسٌ وَأَبُو بَكْرَةَ عَنِ النَّبِيِّ صلى الله عليه وسلم " تَحْرُسُ الْمَلاَئِكَةُ الْمَدِينَةَ مِنَ الدَّجَّالِ ".

Narrated Anas bin Malik that Abu Dhar said: Allah's Messenger ﷺ said, "The roof of my house was made open while I was at Makkah (on the night of Mi'raj) and Jibril descended. He opened up my chest and washed it with the water of Zamzam. The he brought the golden tray full of Wisdom and Belief and poured it in my chest and then closed it. The he took hold of my hand and ascended to the nearest heaven. Jibril told the gatekeeper of the nearest heaven to open the gate. The gatekeeper asked, "Who is it?" Jibril replied, "I am Jibril." (See Hadith No. 349 Vol.1) – Al-Bukhari 1636

وَقَالَ عَبْدَانُ أَخْبَرَنَا عَبْدُ اللَّهِ، أَخْبَرَنَا يُونُسُ، عَنِ الزُّهْرِيِّ، قَالَ أَنَسُ بْنُ مَالِكٍ كَانَ أَبُو ذَرٍّ ـ رضى الله عنه ـ يُحَدِّثُ أَنَّ رَسُولَ اللَّهِ صلى الله عليه وسلم قَالَ " فُرِجَ سَقْفِي وَأَنَا بِمَكَّةَ، فَنَزَلَ جِبْرِيلُ ـ عَلَيْهِ السَّلاَمُ ـ فَفَرَجَ صَدْرِي، ثُمَّ غَسَلَهُ بِمَاءِ زَمْزَمَ، ثُمَّ جَاءَ بِطَسْتٍ مِنْ ذَهَبٍ مُمْتَلِئٍ حِكْمَةً وَإِيمَانًا، فَأَفْرَغَهَا فِي صَدْرِي، ثُمَّ أَطْبَقَهُ، ثُمَّ أَخَذَ بِيَدِي فَعَرَجَ إِلَى السَّمَاءِ الدُّنْيَا. قَالَ جِبْرِيلُ لِخَازِنِ السَّمَاءِ الدُّنْيَا افْتَحْ. قَالَ مَنْ هَذَا قَالَ جِبْرِيلُ ".

By the star as it goes down. Your friend has not gone astray, nor has he erred. Nor does he speak out of desire.It is but a revelation revealed. Taught to him by the Extremely Powerful. The one of vigor. He settled. While he was at the highest horizon. Then he came near, and hovered around. He was within two bows' length, or closer. Then He revealed to His servant what He revealed. The heart did not lie about what it saw. Will you dispute with him concerning what he saw? He saw him on another descent. At the Lotus Tree of the Extremity. Near which is the Garden of Repose. As there covered the Lotus Tree what covered it. The sight did not waver, nor did it exceed. He saw some of the Great Signs of his Lord. – Surah An-Najm 53:1-18

وَٱلنَّجْمِ إِذَا هَوَىٰ مَا ضَلَّ صَاحِبُكُمْ وَمَا غَوَىٰ وَمَا يَنطِقُ عَنِ ٱلْهَوَىٰٓ إِنْ هُوَ إِلَّا وَحْىٌ يُوحَىٰ عَلَّمَهُۥ شَدِيدُ ٱلْقُوَىٰ ذُو مِرَّةٍ فَٱسْتَوَىٰ وَهُوَ بِٱلْأُفُقِ ٱلْأَعْلَىٰ ثُمَّ دَنَا فَتَدَلَّىٰ فَكَانَ قَابَ قَوْسَيْنِ أَوْ أَدْنَىٰ فَأَوْحَىٰٓ إِلَىٰ عَبْدِهِۦ مَآ أَوْحَىٰ مَا كَذَبَ ٱلْفُؤَادُ مَا رَأَىٰٓ أَفَتُمَٰرُونَهُۥ عَلَىٰ مَا يَرَىٰ وَلَقَدْ رَءَاهُ نَزْلَةً أُخْرَىٰ عِندَ سِدْرَةِ ٱلْمُنتَهَىٰ عِندَهَا جَنَّةُ ٱلْمَأْوَىٰٓ إِذْ يَغْشَى ٱلسِّدْرَةَ مَا يَغْشَىٰ مَا زَاغَ ٱلْبَصَرُ وَمَا طَغَىٰ لَقَدْ رَأَىٰ مِنْ ءَايَٰتِ رَبِّهِ ٱلْكُبْرَىٰٓ

Narrated Jabir bin `Abdullah: That he heard Allah's Messenger ﷺ saying, "When the people of Quraish did not believe me (i.e. the story of my Night Journey), I stood up in Al-Hijr and Allah displayed Jerusalem in front of me, and I began describing it to them while I was looking at it." – Sahih al-Bukhari 3886

حَدَّثَنَا يَحْيَى بْنُ بُكَيْرٍ، حَدَّثَنَا اللَّيْثُ، عَنْ عُقَيْلٍ، عَنِ ابْنِ شِهَابٍ، حَدَّثَنِي أَبُو سَلَمَةَ بْنُ عَبْدِ الرَّحْمَنِ، سَمِعْتُ جَابِرَ بْنَ عَبْدِ اللَّهِ ـ رضى الله عنهما ـ أَنَّهُ سَمِعَ رَسُولَ اللَّهِ صلى الله عليه وسلم يَقُولُ " لَمَّا كَذَّبَنِي قُرَيْشٌ قُمْتُ فِي الْحِجْرِ، فَجَلاَ اللَّهُ لِي بَيْتَ الْمَقْدِسِ، فَطَفِقْتُ أُخْبِرُهُمْ عَنْ آيَاتِهِ وَأَنَا أَنْظُرُ إِلَيْهِ

The Book of

The Day of Bu'ath, Migration to Yathrib

معركة بُعاث والهجرة إلى يثرب

The nephew of Suraqa bin Ju'sham said that his father informed him that he heard Suraqa bin Ju'sham saying, "The messengers of the heathens of Quraish came to us declaring that they had assigned for the persons why would kill or arrest Allah's Messenger ﷺ and Abu Bakr, a reward equal to their bloodmoney. While I was sitting in one of the gatherings of my tribe. Bani Mudlij, a man from them came to us and stood up while we were sitting, and said, "O Suraqa! No doubt, I have just seen some people far away on the seashore, and I think they are Muhammad and his companions." Suraqa added, "I too realized that it must have been they. But I said 'No, it is not they, but you have seen so-and-so, and so-and-so whom we saw set out.' I stayed in the gathering for a while and then got up and left for my home. And ordered my slave-girl to get my horse which was behind a hillock, and keep it ready for me. Then I took my spear and left by the back door of my house dragging the lower end of the spear on the ground and keeping it low. Then I reached my horse, mounted it and made it gallop. When I approached them (i.e. Muhammad and Abu Bakr), my horse stumbled and I fell down from it, Then I stood up, got hold of my quiver and took out the divining arrows and drew lots as to whether I should harm them (i.e. the Prophet ﷺ and Abu Bakr) or not, and the lot which I disliked came out. But I remounted my horse and let it gallop, giving no importance to the divining arrows. When I heard the recitation of the Quran by Allah's Messenger ﷺ who did not look hither and thither while Abu Bakr was doing it often, suddenly the forelegs of my horse sank into the ground up to the knees, and I fell down from it. Then I rebuked it and it got up but could hardly take out its forelegs from the ground, and when it stood up straight again, its fore-legs caused dust to rise up in the sky like smoke. Then again I drew lots with the divining arrows, and the lot which I disliked, came out. So I called upon them to feel secure. They stopped, and I remounted my horse and went to them. When I saw how I had been hampered from harming them, it came to my mind that the cause of Allah's Messenger ﷺ (i.e. Islam) will become victorious. So I said to him, "Your people have assigned a reward equal to the bloodmoney for your head." Then I told them all the plans the people of Mecca had made concerning them. Then I offered them some journey food and goods but they refused to take anything and did not ask for anything, but the Prophet ﷺ said, "Do not tell others about us." Then I requested him to write for me a statement of security and peace. He ordered 'Amr bin Fuhaira who wrote it for me on a parchment, and then Allah's Messenger ﷺ proceeded on his way. Narrated 'Urwa bin Az-Zubair: Allah's Messenger ﷺ met Az-Zubair in a caravan of Muslim merchants who were returning from Sham. Az-Zubair provided Allah's Messenger ﷺ and Abu Bakr with white clothes to wear. When the Muslims of Medina heard the news of the departure of Allah's Messenger ﷺ from Mecca (towards Medina), they started going to the Harra every morning . They would wait for him till the heat of the noon forced them to return. One day, after waiting for a long while, they returned home, and when they went into their houses, a Jew climbed up the roof of one of the forts of his people to look for some thing, and he saw Allah's Messenger ﷺ and his companions dressed in white clothes, emerging out of the desert mirage. The Jew could not help shouting at "he top of his voice, "O you 'Arabs! Here is your great man whom you have been waiting for!" So all the Muslims rushed to their arms and received Allah's Messenger ﷺ on the summit of Harra. The Prophet ﷺ turned with them to the right and alighted at the quarters of Bani

'Amr bin 'Auf, and this was on Monday in the month of Rabi-ul-Awal. Abu Bakr stood up, receiving the people while Allah's Messenger ﷺ sat down and kept silent. Some of the Ansar who came and had not seen Allah's Messenger ﷺ before, began greeting Abu Bakr, but when the sunshine fell on Allah's Messenger ﷺ and Abu Bakr came forward and shaded him with his sheet only then the people came to know Allah's Messenger ﷺ . Allah's Messenger ﷺ stayed with Bani 'Amr bin 'Auf for ten nights and established the mosque (mosque of Quba) which was founded on piety. Allah's Messenger ﷺ prayed in it and then mounted his she-camel and proceeded on, accompanied by the people till his she-camel knelt down at (the place of) the Mosque of Allah's Messenger ﷺ at Medina. Some Muslims used to pray there in those days, and that place was a yard for drying dates belonging to Suhail and Sahl, the orphan boys who were under the guardianship of 'Asad bin Zurara. When his she-camel knelt down, Allah's Messenger ﷺ said, "This place, Allah willing, will be our abiding place." Allah's Messenger ﷺ then called the two boys and told them to suggest a price for that yard so that he might take it as a mosque. The two boys said, "No, but we will give it as a gift, O Allah's Messenger ﷺ !" Allah's Messenger ﷺ then built a mosque there. The Prophet ﷺ himself started carrying unburnt bricks for its building and while doing so, he was saying "This load is better than the load of Khaibar, for it is more pious in the Sight of Allah and purer and better rewardable." He was also saying, "O Allah! The actual reward is the reward in the Hereafter, so bestow Your Mercy on the Ansar and the Emigrants." Thus the Prophet ﷺ recited (by way of proverb) the poem of some Muslim poet whose name is unknown to me. (Ibn Shibab said, "In the Hadiths it does not occur that Allah's Apostle Recited a complete poetic verse other than this one.") – Sahih al-Bukhari 3906

قَالَ ابْنُ شِهَابٍ وَأَخْبَرَنِي عَبْدُ الرَّحْمَنِ بْنُ مَالِكٍ الْمُدْلِجِيُّ ـ وَهْوَ ابْنُ أَخِي سُرَاقَةَ بْنِ مَالِكِ بْنِ جُعْشُمٍ ـ أَنَّ أَبَاهُ، أَخْبَرَهُ أَنَّهُ، سَمِعَ سُرَاقَةَ بْنَ جُعْشُمٍ، يَقُولُ جَاءَنَا رُسُلُ كُفَّارِ قُرَيْشٍ يَجْعَلُونَ فِي رَسُولِ اللَّهِ صلى الله عليه وسلم وَأَبِي بَكْرٍ دِيَةَ كُلِّ وَاحِدٍ مِنْهُمَا، مَنْ قَتَلَهُ أَوْ أَسَرَهُ، فَبَيْنَمَا أَنَا جَالِسٌ فِي مَجْلِسٍ مِنْ مَجَالِسِ قَوْمِي بَنِي مُدْلِجٍ أَقْبَلَ رَجُلٌ مِنْهُمْ حَتَّى قَامَ عَلَيْنَا وَنَحْنُ جُلُوسٌ، فَقَالَ يَا سُرَاقَةُ، إِنِّي قَدْ رَأَيْتُ آنِفًا أَسْوِدَةً بِالسَّاحِلِ ـ أُرَاهَا مُحَمَّدًا وَأَصْحَابَهُ. قَالَ سُرَاقَةُ فَعَرَفْتُ أَنَّهُمْ هُمْ، فَقُلْتُ لَهُ إِنَّهُمْ لَيْسُوا بِهِمْ، وَلَكِنَّكَ رَأَيْتَ فُلاَنًا وَفُلاَنًا انْطَلَقُوا بِأَعْيُنِنَا. ثُمَّ لَبِثْتُ فِي الْمَجْلِسِ سَاعَةً، ثُمَّ قُمْتُ فَدَخَلْتُ فَأَمَرْتُ جَارِيَتِي أَنْ تَخْرُجَ بِفَرَسِي وَهْىَ مِنْ وَرَاءِ أَكَمَةٍ فَتَحْبِسَهَا عَلَىَّ، وَأَخَذْتُ رُمْحِي، فَخَرَجْتُ بِهِ مِنْ ظَهْرِ الْبَيْتِ، فَحَطَطْتُ بِزُجِّهِ الأَرْضَ، وَخَفَضْتُ عَالِيَهُ حَتَّى أَتَيْتُ فَرَسِي فَرَكِبْتُهَا، فَرَفَعْتُهَا تُقَرِّبُ بِي حَتَّى دَنَوْتُ مِنْهُمْ، فَعَثَرَتْ بِي فَرَسِي، فَخَرَرْتُ عَنْهَا فَقُمْتُ، فَأَهْوَيْتُ يَدِي إِلَى كِنَانَتِي فَاسْتَخْرَجْتُ مِنْهَا الأَزْلاَمَ، فَاسْتَقْسَمْتُ بِهَا أَضُرُّهُمْ أَمْ لاَ فَخَرَجَ الَّذِي أَكْرَهُ، فَرَكِبْتُ فَرَسِي، وَعَصَيْتُ الأَزْلاَمَ، تُقَرِّبُ بِي حَتَّى إِذَا سَمِعْتُ قِرَاءَةَ رَسُولِ اللَّهِ صلى الله عليه وسلم وَهْوَ لاَ يَلْتَفِتُ، وَأَبُو بَكْرٍ يُكْثِرُ الاِلْتِفَاتَ سَاخَتْ يَدَا فَرَسِي فِي الأَرْضِ حَتَّى بَلَغَتَا الرُّكْبَتَيْنِ، فَخَرَرْتُ عَنْهَا ثُمَّ زَجَرْتُهَا فَنَهَضَتْ، فَلَمْ تَكَدْ تُخْرِجُ يَدَيْهَا، فَلَمَّا اسْتَوَتْ قَائِمَةً، إِذَا لأَثَرِ يَدَيْهَا عُثَانٌ سَاطِعٌ فِي السَّمَاءِ مِثْلُ الدُّخَانِ، فَاسْتَقْسَمْتُ بِالأَزْلاَمِ، فَخَرَجَ الَّذِي أَكْرَهُ، فَنَادَيْتُهُمْ بِالأَمَانِ فَوَقَفُوا، فَرَكِبْتُ فَرَسِي حَتَّى جِئْتُهُمْ، وَوَقَعَ فِي نَفْسِي حِينَ لَقِيتُ مَا لَقِيتُ مِنَ الْحَبْسِ عَنْهُمْ أَنْ سَيَظْهَرُ أَمْرُ رَسُولِ اللَّهِ صلى الله عليه وسلم فَقُلْتُ لَهُ إِنَّ قَوْمَكَ قَدْ جَعَلُوا فِيكَ الدِّيَةَ. وَأَخْبَرْتُهُمْ أَخْبَارَ مَا يُرِيدُ النَّاسُ بِهِمْ، وَعَرَضْتُ عَلَيْهِمِ الزَّادَ وَالْمَتَاعَ، فَلَمْ يَرْزَآنِي وَلَمْ يَسْأَلاَنِي إِلاَّ أَنْ قَالَ أَخْفِ عَنَّا. فَسَأَلْتُهُ أَنْ يَكْتُبَ لِي كِتَابَ أَمْنٍ، فَأَمَرَ عَامِرَ بْنَ فُهَيْرَةَ، فَكَتَبَ فِي رُقْعَةٍ مِنْ أَدِيمٍ، ثُمَّ مَضَى رَسُولُ اللَّهِ صلى الله عليه وسلم. قَالَ ابْنُ شِهَابٍ فَأَخْبَرَنِي عُرْوَةُ بْنُ الزُّبَيْرِ أَنَّ رَسُولَ اللَّهِ صلى الله عليه وسلم لَقِيَ الزُّبَيْرَ فِي رَكْبٍ مِنَ الْمُسْلِمِينَ كَانُوا تِجَارًا قَافِلِينَ مِنَ الشَّأْمِ، فَكَسَا الزُّبَيْرُ رَسُولَ اللَّهِ صلى الله عليه وسلم وَأَبَا بَكْرٍ ثِيَابَ بَيَاضٍ، وَسَمِعَ الْمُسْلِمُونَ بِالْمَدِينَةِ مَخْرَجَ رَسُولِ اللَّهِ صلى الله عليه وسلم مِنْ مَكَّةَ، فَكَانُوا يَغْدُونَ كُلَّ غَدَاةٍ إِلَى الْحَرَّةِ فَيَنْتَظِرُونَهُ، حَتَّى يَرُدَّهُمْ حَرُّ الظَّهِيرَةِ، فَانْقَلَبُوا يَوْمًا بَعْدَ مَا أَطَالُوا انْتِظَارَهُمْ، فَلَمَّا أَوَوْا إِلَى بُيُوتِهِمْ، أَوْفَى رَجُلٌ مِنْ يَهُودَ عَلَى أُطُمٍ مِنْ آطَامِهِمْ لأَمْرٍ يَنْظُرُ إِلَيْهِ، فَبَصُرَ بِرَسُولِ اللَّهِ صلى الله عليه وسلم وَأَصْحَابِهِ مُبَيَّضِينَ يَزُولُ بِهِمُ السَّرَابُ، فَلَمْ يَمْلِكِ الْيَهُودِيُّ أَنْ قَالَ بِأَعْلَى صَوْتِهِ يَا مَعَاشِرَ الْعَرَبِ هَذَا جَدُّكُمُ الَّذِي تَنْتَظِرُونَ. فَثَارَ الْمُسْلِمُونَ إِلَى السِّلاَحِ، فَتَلَقَّوْا رَسُولَ اللَّهِ صلى الله عليه وسلم بِظَهْرِ الْحَرَّةِ، فَعَدَلَ بِهِمْ ذَاتَ الْيَمِينِ حَتَّى نَزَلَ بِهِمْ فِي بَنِي عَمْرِو بْنِ عَوْفٍ، وَذَلِكَ يَوْمَ الاِثْنَيْنِ مِنْ شَهْرِ رَبِيعٍ الأَوَّلِ، فَقَامَ أَبُو بَكْرٍ لِلنَّاسِ، وَجَلَسَ رَسُولُ اللَّهِ صلى الله عليه وسلم صَامِتًا، فَطَفِقَ مَنْ جَاءَ مِنَ الأَنْصَارِ مِمَّنْ لَمْ يَرَ رَسُولَ اللَّهِ صلى الله عليه وسلم يُحَيِّي أَبَا بَكْرٍ، حَتَّى أَصَابَتِ الشَّمْسُ رَسُولَ اللَّهِ صلى الله عليه وسلم فَأَقْبَلَ أَبُو بَكْرٍ حَتَّى ظَلَّلَ عَلَيْهِ بِرِدَائِهِ، فَعَرَفَ النَّاسُ رَسُولَ اللَّهِ صلى الله عليه وسلم عِنْدَ ذَلِكَ، فَلَبِثَ رَسُولُ اللَّهِ صلى الله عليه وسلم فِي بَنِي عَمْرِو بْنِ عَوْفٍ بِضْعَ عَشْرَةَ لَيْلَةً وَأُسِّسَ الْمَسْجِدُ الَّذِي أُسِّسَ عَلَى التَّقْوَى، وَصَلَّى فِيهِ رَسُولُ اللَّهِ صلى الله عليه وسلم، ثُمَّ رَكِبَ رَاحِلَتَهُ فَسَارَ يَمْشِي مَعَهُ النَّاسُ حَتَّى بَرَكَتْ عِنْدَ مَسْجِدِ الرَّسُولِ صلى الله عليه وسلم بِالْمَدِينَةِ، وَهْوَ يُصَلِّي فِيهِ يَوْمَئِذٍ رِجَالٌ مِنَ الْمُسْلِمِينَ، وَكَانَ مِرْبَدًا لِلتَّمْرِ لِسُهَيْلٍ وَسَهْلٍ غُلاَمَيْنِ يَتِيمَيْنِ فِي حَجْرِ أَسْعَدَ بْنِ

زُرَارَةَ، فَقَالَ رَسُولُ اللَّهِ صلى الله عليه وسلم حِينَ بَرَكَتْ بِهِ رَاحِلَتُهُ " هَذَا إِنْ شَاءَ اللَّهُ الْمَنْزِلُ ". ثُمَّ دَعَا رَسُولُ اللَّهِ صلى الله عليه وسلم الْغُلاَمَيْنِ، فَسَاوَمَهُمَا بِالْمِرْبَدِ لِيَتَّخِذَهُ مَسْجِدًا، فَقَالاَ لاَ بَلْ نَهَبُهُ لَكَ يَا رَسُولَ اللَّهِ، ثُمَّ بَنَاهُ مَسْجِدًا، وَطَفِقَ رَسُولُ اللَّهِ صلى الله عليه وسلم يَنْقُلُ مَعَهُمُ اللَّبِنَ فِي بُنْيَانِهِ، وَيَقُولُ وَهُوَ يَنْقُلُ اللَّبِنَ " هَذَا الْحِمَالُ لاَ حِمَالَ خَيْبَرْ هَذَا أَبَرُّ رَبَّنَا وَأَطْهَرْ ". وَيَقُولُ " اللَّهُمَّ إِنَّ الأَجْرَ أَجْرُ الآخِرَهْ فَارْحَمِ الأَنْصَارَ وَالْمُهَاجِرَهْ ". فَتَمَثَّلَ بِشِعْرِ رَجُلٍ مِنَ الْمُسْلِمِينَ لَمْ يُسَمَّ لِي. قَالَ ابْنُ شِهَابٍ وَلَمْ يَبْلُغْنَا فِي الأَحَادِيثِ أَنَّ رَسُولَ اللَّهِ صلى الله عليه وسلم تَمَثَّلَ بِبَيْتِ شِعْرٍ تَامٍّ غَيْرِ هذه الآيات

Narrated Abu Bakr: I said to the Prophet ﷺ while I was in the Cave. “If any of them should look under his feet, he would see us.” He said, “O Abu Bakr! What do you think of two (persons) the third of whom is Allah?” – Sahih al-Bukhari 3653
حَدَّثَنَا مُحَمَّدُ بْنُ سِنَانٍ، حَدَّثَنَا هَمَّامٌ، عَنْ ثَابِتٍ، عَنْ أَنَسٍ، عَنْ أَبِي بَكْرٍ ـ رضى الله عنه ـ قَالَ قُلْتُ لِلنَّبِيِّ صلى الله عليه وسلم وَأَنَا فِي الْغَارِ لَوْ أَنَّ أَحَدَهُمْ نَظَرَ تَحْتَ قَدَمَيْهِ لأَبْصَرَنَا. فَقَالَ " مَا ظَنُّكَ يَا أَبَا بَكْرٍ بِاثْنَيْنِ اللَّهُ ثَالِثُهُمَا ".

Narrated Anas bin Malik: Allah’s Messenger ﷺ arrived at Medina with Abu Bakr, riding behind him on the same camel. Abu Bakr was an elderly man known to the people, while Allah’s Messenger ﷺ was a youth that was unknown. Thus, if a man met Abu Bakr, he would say, “O Abu Bakr! Who is this man in front of you?” Abu Bakr would say, “This man shows me the Way,” One would think that Abu Bakr meant the road, while in fact, Abu Bakr meant the way of virtue and good. Then Abu Bakr looked behind and saw a horse-rider pursuing them. He said, “O Allah’s Messenger ﷺ ! This is a horse-rider pursuing us.” The Prophet ﷺ looked behind and said, “O Allah! Cause him to fall down.” So the horse threw him down and got up neighing. After that the rider, Suraqa said, “O Allah’s Prophet! Order me whatever you want.” The Prophet said, “Stay where you are and do not allow anybody to reach us.” So, in the first part of the day Suraqa was an enemy of Allah’s Prophet and in the last part of it, he was a protector. Then Allah’s Apostle alighted by the side of the Al-Harra and sent a message to the Ansar, and they came to Allah’s Prophet and Abu Bakr, and having greeted them, they said, “Ride (your she-camels) safe and obeyed.” Allah’s Messenger ﷺ and Abu Bakr rode and the Ansar, carrying their arms, surrounded them. The news that Allah’s Prophet had come circulated in Medina. The people came out and were eagerly looking and saying “Allah’s Prophet has come! Allah’s Prophet has come! So the Prophet ﷺ went on till he alighted near the house of Abu Ayub. While the Prophet ﷺ was speaking with the family members of Abu Ayub, `Abdullah bin Salam heard the news of his arrival while he himself was picking the dates for his family from his family garden. He hurried to the Prophet ﷺ carrying the dates which he had collected for his family from the garden. He listened to Allah’s Prophet and then went home. Then Allah’s Prophet said, “Which is the nearest of the houses of our kith and kin?” Abu Ayub replied, “Mine, O Allah’s Prophet! This is my house and this Is my gate.” The Prophet ﷺ said, “Go and prepare a place for our midday rest.” Abu Ayub said, “Get up (both of you) with Allah’s Blessings.” So when Allah’s Prophet went into the house, `Abdullah bin Salam came and said “I testify that you (i.e. Muhammad) are Apostle of Allah and that you have come with the Truth. The Jews know well that I am their chief and the son of their chief and the most learned amongst them and the son of the most learned amongst them. So send for them (i.e. Jews) and ask them about me before they know that I have embraced Islam, for if they know that they will say about me things which are not correct.” So Allah’s Messenger ﷺ sent for them, and they came and entered. Allah’s Messenger ﷺ said to them, “O (the group of) Jews! Woe to you: be afraid of Allah. By Allah except Whom none has the right to be worshipped, you people know for certain, that I am Apostle of Allah and that I have come to you with the Truth, so embrace Islam.” The Jews replied, “We do not know this.” So they said this to the Prophet and he repeated it thrice. Then he said, “What sort of a man is `Abdullah bin Salam amongst you?” They said, “He is our chief and the son of our chief and the most learned man, and the son of the most learned amongst us." He said, "What would you think if he should embrace Islam?" They said, "Allah forbid! He can not embrace Islam." He said, " What would you think if he should embrace Islam?" They said, "Allah forbid! He can not embrace Islam." He said, "What would you think if he should embrace Islam?" They said, "Allah forbid! He can not embrace Islam." He said, "O Ibn Salam! Come out to them." He came out and said, "O (the group of) Jews! Be afraid of Allah except Whom none has the right to be worshipped. You know for certain that he is Apostle of Allah and that he has brought a True Religion!' They said, "You tell a lie." On that Allah's Messenger ﷺ turned them out. – Sahih al-Bukhari 3911

حَدَّثَنِي مُحَمَّدٌ، حَدَّثَنَا عَبْدُ الصَّمَدِ، حَدَّثَنَا أَبِي، حَدَّثَنَا عَبْدُ الْعَزِيزِ بْنُ صُهَيْبٍ، حَدَّثَنَا أَنَسُ بْنُ مَالِكٍ ـ رضى الله عنه ـ قَالَ أَقْبَلَ نَبِيُّ اللَّهِ صلى الله عليه وسلم إِلَى الْمَدِينَةِ وَهْوَ مُرْدِفٌ أَبَا بَكْرٍ، وَأَبُو بَكْرٍ شَيْخٌ يُعْرَفُ، وَنَبِيُّ اللَّهِ صلى الله عليه وسلم شَابٌّ لاَ يُعْرَفُ، قَالَ فَيَلْقَى الرَّجُلُ أَبَا بَكْرٍ فَيَقُولُ يَا أَبَا بَكْرٍ، مَنْ هَذَا الرَّجُلُ الَّذِي بَيْنَ يَدَيْكَ فَيَقُولُ هَذَا الرَّجُلُ يَهْدِينِي السَّبِيلَ. قَالَ فَيَحْسِبُ الْحَاسِبُ أَنَّهُ إِنَّمَا يَعْنِي الطَّرِيقَ، وَإِنَّمَا يَعْنِي سَبِيلَ الْخَيْرِ، فَالْتَفَتَ أَبُو بَكْرٍ، فَإِذَا هُوَ بِفَارِسٍ قَدْ لَحِقَهُمْ، فَقَالَ يَا رَسُولَ اللَّهِ، هَذَا فَارِسٌ قَدْ لَحِقَ بِنَا. فَالْتَفَتَ نَبِيُّ اللَّهِ صلى الله عليه وسلم فَقَالَ " اللَّهُمَّ اصْرَعْهُ ". فَصَرَعَهُ الْفَرَسُ، ثُمَّ قَامَتْ تُحَمْحِمُ فَقَالَ يَا نَبِيَّ اللَّهِ مُرْنِي بِمَا شِئْتَ. قَالَ " فَقِفْ مَكَانَكَ، لاَ تَتْرُكَنَّ أَحَدًا يَلْحَقُ بِنَا ". قَالَ فَكَانَ أَوَّلَ النَّهَارِ جَاهِدًا عَلَى نَبِيِّ اللَّهِ صلى الله عليه وسلم، وَكَانَ آخِرَ النَّهَارِ مَسْلَحَةً لَهُ، فَنَزَلَ رَسُولُ اللَّهِ صلى الله عليه وسلم جَانِبَ الْحَرَّةِ، ثُمَّ بَعَثَ إِلَى الأَنْصَارِ، فَجَاءُوا إِلَى نَبِيِّ اللَّهِ صلى الله عليه وسلم فَسَلَّمُوا عَلَيْهِمَا، وَقَالُوا ارْكَبَا آمِنَيْنِ مُطَاعَيْنِ. فَرَكِبَ نَبِيُّ اللَّهِ صلى الله عليه وسلم وَأَبُو بَكْرٍ، وَحَفُّوا دُونَهُمَا بِالسِّلاَحِ، فَقِيلَ فِي الْمَدِينَةِ جَاءَ نَبِيُّ اللَّهِ، جَاءَ نَبِيُّ اللَّهِ صلى الله عليه وسلم. فَأَشْرَفُوا يَنْظُرُونَ وَيَقُولُونَ جَاءَ نَبِيُّ اللَّهِ، جَاءَ نَبِيُّ اللَّهِ. فَأَقْبَلَ يَسِيرُ حَتَّى نَزَلَ جَانِبَ دَارِ أَبِي أَيُّوبَ، فَإِنَّهُ لَيُحَدِّثُ أَهْلَهُ، إِذْ سَمِعَ بِهِ عَبْدُ اللَّهِ بْنُ سَلاَمٍ وَهْوَ فِي نَخْلٍ لأَهْلِهِ يَخْتَرِفُ لَهُمْ، فَعَجِلَ أَنْ يَضَعَ الَّذِي يَخْتَرِفُ لَهُمْ فِيهَا، فَجَاءَ وَهْىَ مَعَهُ، فَسَمِعَ مِنْ نَبِيِّ اللَّهِ صلى الله عليه وسلم ثُمَّ رَجَعَ إِلَى أَهْلِهِ، فَقَالَ نَبِيُّ اللَّهِ صلى الله عليه وسلم " أَىُّ بُيُوتِ أَهْلِنَا أَقْرَبُ ". فَقَالَ أَبُو أَيُّوبَ أَنَا يَا نَبِيَّ اللَّهِ، هَذِهِ دَارِي، وَهَذَا بَابِي. قَالَ " فَانْطَلِقْ فَهَيِّئْ لَنَا مَقِيلاً ". قَالَ قُومَا عَلَى بَرَكَةِ اللَّهِ. فَلَمَّا جَاءَ نَبِيُّ اللَّهِ صلى الله عليه وسلم جَاءَ عَبْدُ اللَّهِ بْنُ سَلاَمٍ فَقَالَ أَشْهَدُ أَنَّكَ رَسُولُ اللَّهِ، وَأَنَّكَ جِئْتَ بِحَقٍّ، وَقَدْ عَلِمَتْ يَهُودُ أَنِّي سَيِّدُهُمْ وَابْنُ سَيِّدِهِمْ، وَأَعْلَمُهُمْ وَابْنُ أَعْلَمِهِمْ، فَادْعُهُمْ فَاسْأَلْهُمْ عَنِّي قَبْلَ أَنْ يَعْلَمُوا أَنِّي قَدْ أَسْلَمْتُ، فَإِنَّهُمْ إِنْ يَعْلَمُوا أَنِّي قَدْ أَسْلَمْتُ قَالُوا فِيَّ مَا لَيْسَ فِيَّ. فَأَرْسَلَ نَبِيُّ اللَّهِ صلى الله عليه وسلم فَأَقْبَلُوا فَدَخَلُوا عَلَيْهِ. فَقَالَ لَهُمْ رَسُولُ اللَّهِ صلى الله عليه وسلم " يَا مَعْشَرَ الْيَهُودِ، وَيْلَكُمُ اتَّقُوا اللَّهَ، فَوَاللَّهِ الَّذِي لاَ إِلَهَ إِلاَّ هُوَ إِنَّكُمْ لَتَعْلَمُونَ أَنِّي رَسُولُ اللَّهِ حَقًّا، وَأَنِّي جِئْتُكُمْ بِحَقٍّ فَأَسْلِمُوا ". قَالُوا مَا نَعْلَمُهُ. قَالُوا لِلنَّبِيِّ صلى الله عليه وسلم قَالَهَا ثَلاَثَ مِرَارٍ. قَالَ " فَأَىُّ رَجُلٍ فِيكُمْ عَبْدُ اللَّهِ بْنُ سَلاَمٍ ". قَالُوا ذَاكَ سَيِّدُنَا وَابْنُ سَيِّدِنَا، وَأَعْلَمُنَا وَابْنُ أَعْلَمِنَا. قَالَ " أَفَرَأَيْتُمْ إِنْ أَسْلَمَ ". قَالُوا حَاشَا لِلَّهِ، مَا كَانَ لِيُسْلِمَ. قَالَ " أَفَرَأَيْتُمْ إِنْ أَسْلَمَ ". قَالُوا حَاشَا لِلَّهِ، مَا كَانَ لِيُسْلِمَ. قَالَ " يَا ابْنَ سَلاَمٍ، اخْرُجْ عَلَيْهِمْ ". فَخَرَجَ فَقَالَ يَا مَعْشَرَ الْيَهُودِ، اتَّقُوا اللَّهَ، فَوَاللَّهِ الَّذِي لاَ إِلَهَ إِلاَّ هُوَ إِنَّكُمْ لَتَعْلَمُونَ أَنَّهُ رَسُولُ اللَّهِ، وَأَنَّهُ جَاءَ بِحَقٍّ. فَقَالُوا كَذَبْتَ. فَأَخْرَجَهُمْ رَسُولُ اللَّهِ صلى الله عليه وسلم.

Narrated Anas: When the news of the arrival of the Prophet ﷺ at Medina reached `Abdullah bin Salam, he went to him to ask him about certain things, He said, "I am going to ask you about three things which only a Prophet can answer: What is the first sign of The Hour? What is the first food which the people of Paradise will eat? Why does a child attract the similarity to his father or to his mother?" The Prophet ﷺ replied, "Gabriel has just now informed me of that." Ibn Salam said, "He (i.e. Gabriel) is the enemy of the Jews amongst the angels. The Prophet ﷺ said, "As for the first sign of The Hour, it will be a fire that will collect the people from the East to the West. As for the first meal which the people of Paradise will eat, it will be the caudate (extra) lobe of the fish-liver. As for the child, if the man's discharge proceeds the woman's discharge, the child attracts the similarity to the man, and if the woman's discharge proceeds the man's, then the child attracts the similarity to the woman." On this, `Abdullah bin Salam said, "I testify that None has the right to be worshipped except Allah, and that you are the Messenger of Allah." And added, "O Allah's Messenger ﷺ ! Jews invent such lies as make one astonished, so please ask them about me before they know about my conversion to Islam . " The Jews came, and the Prophet ﷺ said, "What kind of man is `Abdullah bin Salam among you?" They replied, "The best of us and the son of the best of us and the most superior among us, and the son of the most superior among us. "The Prophet ﷺ said,

"What would you think if `Abdullah bin Salam should embrace Islam?" They said, "May Allah protect him from that." The Prophetﷺ repeated his question and they gave the same answer. Then `Abdullah came out to them and said, "I testify that None has the right to be worshipped except Allah and that Muhammad is the Messenger of Allah!" On this, the Jews said, "He is the most wicked among us and the son of the most wicked among us." So they degraded him. On this, he (i.e. `Abdullah bin Salam) said, "It is this that I was afraid of, O Allah's Messenger. – Sahih al-Bukhari 3938

حَدَّثَنِي حَامِدُ بْنُ عُمَرَ، عَنْ بِشْرِ بْنِ الْمُفَضَّلِ، حَدَّثَنَا حُمَيْدٌ، حَدَّثَنَا أَنَسٌ، أَنَّ عَبْدَ اللَّهِ بْنَ سَلاَمٍ، بَلَغَهُ مَقْدَمُ النَّبِيِّ صلى الله عليه وسلم الْمَدِينَةَ، فَأَتَاهُ يَسْأَلُهُ عَنْ أَشْيَاءَ، فَقَالَ إِنِّي سَائِلُكَ عَنْ ثَلاَثٍ لاَ يَعْلَمُهُنَّ إِلاَّ نَبِيٌّ مَا أَوَّلُ أَشْرَاطِ السَّاعَةِ وَمَا أَوَّلُ طَعَامٍ يَأْكُلُهُ أَهْلُ الْجَنَّةِ وَمَا بَالُ الْوَلَدِ يَنْزِعُ إِلَى أَبِيهِ أَوْ إِلَى أُمِّهِ قَالَ " أَخْبَرَنِي بِهِ جِبْرِيلُ آنِفًا ". قَالَ ابْنُ سَلاَمٍ ذَاكَ عَدُوُّ الْيَهُودِ مِنَ الْمَلاَئِكَةِ. قَالَ " أَمَّا أَوَّلُ أَشْرَاطِ السَّاعَةِ فَنَارٌ تَحْشُرُهُمْ مِنَ الْمَشْرِقِ إِلَى الْمَغْرِبِ، وَأَمَّا أَوَّلُ طَعَامٍ يَأْكُلُهُ أَهْلُ الْجَنَّةِ، فَزِيَادَةُ كَبِدِ الْحُوتِ، وَأَمَّا الْوَلَدُ، فَإِذَا سَبَقَ مَاءُ الرَّجُلِ مَاءَ الْمَرْأَةِ نَزَعَ الْوَلَدَ، وَإِذَا سَبَقَ مَاءُ الْمَرْأَةِ مَاءَ الرَّجُلِ نَزَعَتِ الْوَلَدَ ". قَالَ أَشْهَدُ أَنْ لاَ إِلَهَ إِلاَّ اللَّهُ وَأَنَّكَ رَسُولُ اللَّهِ. قَالَ يَا رَسُولَ اللَّهِ، إِنَّ الْيَهُودَ قَوْمٌ بُهُتٌ، فَاسْأَلْهُمْ عَنِّي قَبْلَ أَنْ يَعْلَمُوا بِإِسْلاَمِي، فَجَاءَتِ الْيَهُودُ فَقَالَ النَّبِيُّ صلى الله عليه وسلم " أَىُّ رَجُلٍ عَبْدُ اللَّهِ بْنُ سَلاَمٍ فِيكُمْ ". قَالُوا خَيْرُنَا وَابْنُ خَيْرِنَا وَأَفْضَلُنَا وَابْنُ أَفْضَلِنَا. فَقَالَ النَّبِيُّ صلى الله عليه وسلم " أَرَأَيْتُمْ إِنْ أَسْلَمَ عَبْدُ اللَّهِ بْنُ سَلاَمٍ ". قَالُوا أَعَاذَهُ اللَّهُ مِنْ ذَلِكَ. فَأَعَادَ عَلَيْهِمْ، فَقَالُوا مِثْلَ ذَلِكَ، فَخَرَجَ إِلَيْهِمْ عَبْدُ اللَّهِ فَقَالَ أَشْهَدُ أَنْ لاَ إِلَهَ إِلاَّ اللَّهُ وَأَنَّ مُحَمَّدًا رَسُولُ اللَّهِ. قَالُوا شَرُّنَا وَابْنُ شَرِّنَا. وَتَنَقَّصُوهُ. قَالَ هَذَا كُنْتُ أَخَافُ يَا رَسُولَ اللَّهِ.

Narrated Anas bin Malik: When Allah's Messengerﷺ arrived at Medina, he alighted at the upper part of Medina among the people called Bani `Amr bin `Auf and he stayed with them for fourteen nights. Then he sent for the chiefs of Bani An-Najjar, and they came, carrying their swords. As if I am just now looking at Allah's Messenger on his she-camel with Abu Bakr riding behind him (on the same camel) and the chiefs of Bani An- Najjar around him till he dismounted in the courtyard of Abu Aiyub's home. The Prophetﷺ used to offer the prayer wherever the prayer was due, and he would pray even in sheepfolds. Then he ordered that the mosque be built. He sent for the chiefs of Banu An-Najjar, and when they came, he said, "O Banu An-Najjar! Suggest to me the price of this garden of yours." They replied "No! By Allah, we do not demand its price except from Allah." In that garden there were the (following) things that I will tell you: Graves of pagans, unleveled land with holes and pits etc., and date-palm trees. Allah's Messengerﷺ ordered that the graves of the pagans be dug up and, the unleveled land be leveled and the date-palm trees be cut down. The trunks of the trees were arranged so as to form the wall facing the Qibla. The Stone pillars were built at the sides of its gate. The companions of the Prophetﷺ were carrying the stones and reciting some lyrics, and Allah's Messengerﷺ was with them and they were saying, "O Allah! There is no good Excel the good of the Hereafter, so bestow victory on the Ansar and the Emigrants. ". – Al-Bukhari 3932 also Bukhari 2774

حَدَّثَنَا مُسَدَّدٌ، حَدَّثَنَا عَبْدُ الْوَارِثِ. وَحَدَّثَنَا إِسْحَاقُ بْنُ مَنْصُورٍ، أَخْبَرَنَا عَبْدُ الصَّمَدِ، قَالَ سَمِعْتُ أَبِي يُحَدِّثُ، حَدَّثَنَا أَبُو التَّيَّاحِ، يَزِيدُ بْنُ حُمَيْدٍ الضُّبَعِيُّ قَالَ حَدَّثَنِي أَنَسُ بْنُ مَالِكٍ ـ رضى الله عنه ـ قَالَ لَمَّا قَدِمَ رَسُولُ اللَّهِ صلى الله عليه وسلم الْمَدِينَةَ، نَزَلَ فِي عُلْوِ الْمَدِينَةِ فِي حَىٍّ يُقَالُ لَهُمْ بَنُو عَمْرِو بْنِ عَوْفٍ ـ قَالَ ـ فَأَقَامَ فِيهِمْ أَرْبَعَ عَشْرَةَ لَيْلَةً، ثُمَّ أَرْسَلَ إِلَى مَلإِ بَنِي النَّجَّارِ ـ قَالَ ـ فَجَاءُوا مُتَقَلِّدِي سُيُوفِهِمْ، قَالَ وَكَأَنِّي أَنْظُرُ إِلَى رَسُولِ اللَّهِ صلى الله عليه وسلم عَلَى رَاحِلَتِهِ، وَأَبُو بَكْرٍ رِدْفُهُ، وَمَلأُ بَنِي النَّجَّارِ حَوْلَهُ حَتَّى أَلْقَى بِفِنَاءِ أَبِي أَيُّوبَ، قَالَ فَكَانَ يُصَلِّي حَيْثُ أَدْرَكَتْهُ الصَّلاَةُ، وَيُصَلِّي فِي مَرَابِضِ الْغَنَمِ، قَالَ ثُمَّ إِنَّهُ أَمَرَ بِبِنَاءِ الْمَسْجِدِ، فَأَرْسَلَ إِلَى مَلإِ بَنِي النَّجَّارِ، فَجَاءُوا فَقَالَ " يَا بَنِي النَّجَّارِ، ثَامِنُونِي حَائِطَكُمْ هَذَا ". فَقَالُوا لاَ، وَاللَّهِ لاَ نَطْلُبُ ثَمَنَهُ إِلاَّ إِلَى اللَّهِ. قَالَ فَكَانَ فِيهِ مَا أَقُولُ لَكُمْ كَانَتْ فِيهِ قُبُورُ الْمُشْرِكِينَ، وَكَانَتْ فِيهِ خِرَبٌ، وَكَانَ فِيهِ نَخْلٌ، فَأَمَرَ رَسُولُ اللَّهِ صلى الله عليه وسلم بِقُبُورِ الْمُشْرِكِينَ فَنُبِشَتْ، وَبِالْخِرَبِ فَسُوِّيَتْ، وَبِالنَّخْلِ فَقُطِعَ، قَالَ فَصَفُّوا النَّخْلَ قِبْلَةَ الْمَسْجِدِ ـ قَالَ ـ وَجَعَلُوا عِضَادَتَيْهِ حِجَارَةً. قَالَ قَالَ جَعَلُوا يَنْقُلُونَ ذَاكَ الصَّخْرَ وَهُمْ يَرْتَجِزُونَ، وَرَسُولُ اللَّهِ صلى الله عليه وسلم مَعَهُمْ يَقُولُونَ اللَّهُمَّ إِنَّهُ لاَ خَيْرَ إِلاَّ خَيْرُ الآخِرَهْ فَانْصُرِ الأَنْصَارَ وَالْمُهَاجِرَهْ

Narrated `Aisha: When Allah's Messenger ﷺ reached Medina, Abu Bakr and Bilal became ill. When Abu Bakr's fever got worse, he would recite (this poetic verse): "Everybody is staying alive with his People, yet Death is nearer to him than His shoe laces." And Bilal, when his fever deserted him, would recite: "Would that I could stay overnight in A valley wherein I would be Surrounded by Idhkhir and Jalil (kinds of goodsmelling grass). Would that one day I could Drink the water of the Majanna, and Would that (The two mountains) Shama and Tafil would appear to me!" The Prophet ﷺ said, "O Allah! Curse Shaiba bin Rabi`a and `Utba bin Rabi`a and Umaiya bin Khalaf as they turned us out of our land to the land of epidemics." Allah's Messenger ﷺ then said, "O Allah! Make us love Medina as we love Mecca or even more than that. O Allah! Give blessings in our Sa and our Mudd (measures symbolizing food) and make the climate of Medina suitable for us, and divert its fever towards Aljuhfa." Aisha added: When we reached Medina, it was the most unhealthy of Allah's lands, and the valley of Bathan (the valley of Medina) used to flow with impure colored water. Al-Bukhari 1889

حَدَّثَنَا عُبَيْدُ بْنُ إِسْمَاعِيلَ، حَدَّثَنَا أَبُو أُسَامَةَ، عَنْ هِشَامٍ، عَنْ أَبِيهِ، عَنْ عَائِشَةَ ـ رضى الله عنها ـ قَالَتْ لَمَّا قَدِمَ رَسُولُ اللَّهِ صلى الله عليه وسلم الْمَدِينَةَ وُعِكَ أَبُو بَكْرٍ وَبِلاَلٌ، فَكَانَ أَبُو بَكْرٍ إِذَا أَخَذَتْهُ الْحُمَّى يَقُولُ كُلُّ امْرِئٍ مُصَبَّحٌ فِي أَهْلِهِ وَالْمَوْتُ أَدْنَى مِنْ شِرَاكِ نَعْلِهِ وَكَانَ بِلاَلٌ إِذَا أُقْلِعَ عَنْهُ الْحُمَّى يَرْفَعُ عَقِيرَتَهُ يَقُولُ أَلاَ لَيْتَ شِعْرِي هَلْ أَبِيتَنَّ لَيْلَةً بِوَادٍ وَحَوْلِي إِذْخِرٌ وَجَلِيلُ وَهَلْ أَرِدَنْ يَوْمًا مِيَاهَ مَجَنَّةٍ وَهَلْ يَبْدُوَنْ لِ

Narrated Sahl bin Sa`d: The Prophet's companions did not take as a starting date for the Muslim calendar, the day, the Prophet ﷺ had been sent as an Apostle or the day of his death, but the day of his arrival at Medina. – Sahih al-Bukhari 3934

حَدَّثَنَا عَبْدُ اللَّهِ بْنُ مَسْلَمَةَ، حَدَّثَنَا عَبْدُ الْعَزِيزِ، عَنْ أَبِيهِ، عَنْ سَهْلِ بْنِ سَعْدٍ، قَالَ مَا عَدُّوا مِنْ مَبْعَثِ النَّبِيِّ صلى الله عليه وسلم وَلاَ مِنْ وَفَاتِهِ، مَا عَدُّوا إِلاَّ مِنْ مَقْدَمِهِ الْمَدِينَةَ.

Narrated Al-Bara bin Azib: The first people who came to us (in Medina) were Mus`ab bin `Umar and Ibn Um Maktum who were teaching Qur'an to the people. Then their came Bilal. Sa`d and `Ammar bin Yasir. After that `Umar bin Al-Khattab came along with twenty other companions of the Prophet. Later on the Prophet ﷺ himself (to Medina) and I had never seen the people of Medina so joyful as they were on the arrival of Allah's Apostle, for even the slave girls were saying, "Allah's Messenger ﷺ has arrived!" And before his arrival I had read the Sura starting with:-- "Glorify the Name of your Lord, the Most High" (87.1) together with other Suras of Al-Mufassal. – Sahih al-Bukhari 3925

حَدَّثَنَا مُحَمَّدُ بْنُ بَشَّارٍ، حَدَّثَنَا غُنْدَرٌ، حَدَّثَنَا شُعْبَةُ، عَنْ أَبِي إِسْحَاقَ، قَالَ سَمِعْتُ الْبَرَاءَ بْنَ عَازِبٍ ـ رضى الله عنهما ـ قَالَ أَوَّلُ مَنْ قَدِمَ عَلَيْنَا مُصْعَبُ بْنُ عُمَيْرٍ وَابْنُ أُمِّ مَكْتُومٍ، وَكَانَا يُقْرِئَانِ النَّاسَ، فَقَدِمَ بِلاَلٌ وَسَعْدٌ وَعَمَّارُ بْنُ يَاسِرٍ، ثُمَّ قَدِمَ عُمَرُ بْنُ الْخَطَّابِ فِي عِشْرِينَ مِنْ أَصْحَابِ النَّبِيِّ صلى الله عليه وسلم ثُمَّ قَدِمَ النَّبِيُّ صلى الله عليه وسلم، فَمَا رَأَيْتُ أَهْلَ الْمَدِينَةِ فَرِحُوا بِشَىْءٍ فَرَحَهُمْ بِرَسُولِ اللَّهِ صلى الله عليه وسلم، حَتَّى جَعَلَ الإِمَاءُ يَقُلْنَ قَدِمَ رَسُولُ اللَّهِ صلى الله عليه وسلم فَمَا قَدِمَ حَتَّى قَرَأْتُ {سَبِّحِ اسْمَ رَبِّكَ الأَعْلَى} فِي سُوَرٍ مِنَ الْمُفَصَّلِ.

Narrated `Abdullah bin Mas`ud: Sa`d bin Mu`adh came to Mecca with the intention of performing `Umra, and stayed at the house of Umaiya bin Khalaf Abi Safwan, for Umaiya himself used to stay at Sa`d's house when he passed by Medina on his way to Sham. Umaiya said to Sa`d, "Will you wait till midday when the people are (at their homes), then you may go and perform the Tawaf round the Ka`ba?" So, while Sa`d was going around the Ka`ba, Abu Jahl came and asked, "Who is that who is performing Tawaf?" Sa`d replied, "I am Sa`d." Abu Jahl said, "Are you circumambulating the Ka`ba safely although you have given refuge to Muhammad and his companions?" Sa`d said, "Yes," and they started quarreling. Umaiya said to Sa`d, "Don't shout at Abi-l-Hakam (i.e. Abu Jahl), for he is chief of the valley (of Mecca)."

Sa`d then said (to Abu Jahl). 'By Allah, if you prevent me from performing the Tawaf of the Ka`ba, I will spoil your trade with Sham." Umaiya kept on saying to Sa`d, "Don't raise your voice." And kept on taking hold of him. Sa`d became furious and said, (to Umaiya), "Be away from me, for I have heard Muhammad saying that he will kill you." Umaiiya said, "Will he kill me?" Sa`d said, "Yes,." Umaiya said, "By Allah! When Muhammad says a thing, he never tells a lie." Umaiya went to his wife and said to her, "Do you know what my brother from Yathrib (i.e. Medina) has said to me?" She said, "What has he said?" He said, "He claims that he has heard Muhammad claiming that he will kill me." She said, By Allah! Muhammad never tells a lie." So when the infidels started to proceed for Badr (Battle) and declared war (against the Muslims), his wife said to him, "Don't you remember what your brother from Yathrib told you?" Umaiya decided not to go but Abu Jahl said to him, "You are from the nobles of the valley (of Mecca), so you should accompany us for a day or two." He went with them and thus Allah got him killed. – Sahih al-Bukhari 3632

حَدَّثَنِي أَحْمَدُ بْنُ إِسْحَاقَ، حَدَّثَنَا عُبَيْدُ اللَّهِ بْنُ مُوسَى، حَدَّثَنَا إِسْرَائِيلُ، عَنْ أَبِي إِسْحَاقَ، عَنْ عَمْرِو بْنِ مَيْمُونٍ، عَنْ عَبْدِ اللَّهِ بْنِ مَسْعُودٍ ـ رضى الله عنه ـ قَالَ انْطَلَقَ سَعْدُ بْنُ مُعَاذٍ مُعْتَمِرًا ـ قَالَ ـ فَنَزَلَ عَلَى أُمَيَّةَ بْنِ خَلَفٍ أَبِي صَفْوَانَ، وَكَانَ أُمَيَّةُ إِذَا انْطَلَقَ إِلَى الشَّأْمِ فَمَرَّ بِالْمَدِينَةِ نَزَلَ عَلَى سَعْدٍ، فَقَالَ أُمَيَّةُ لِسَعْدٍ انْتَظِرْ حَتَّى إِذَا انْتَصَفَ النَّهَارُ، وَغَفَلَ النَّاسُ انْطَلَقْتُ فَطُفْتُ، فَبَيْنَا سَعْدٌ يَطُوفُ إِذَا أَبُو جَهْلٍ فَقَالَ مَنْ هَذَا الَّذِي يَطُوفُ بِالْكَعْبَةِ فَقَالَ سَعْدٌ أَنَا سَعْدٌ. فَقَالَ أَبُو جَهْلٍ تَطُوفُ بِالْكَعْبَةِ آمِنًا، وَقَدْ آوَيْتُمْ مُحَمَّدًا وَأَصْحَابَهُ فَقَالَ نَعَمْ. فَتَلاَحَيَا بَيْنَهُمَا. فَقَالَ أُمَيَّةُ لِسَعْدٍ لاَ تَرْفَعْ صَوْتَكَ عَلَى أَبِي الْحَكَمِ، فَإِنَّهُ سَيِّدُ أَهْلِ الْوَادِي. ثُمَّ قَالَ سَعْدٌ وَاللَّهِ لَئِنْ مَنَعْتَنِي أَنْ أَطُوفَ بِالْبَيْتِ لأَقْطَعَنَّ مَتْجَرَكَ بِالشَّأْمِ. قَالَ فَجَعَلَ أُمَيَّةُ يَقُولُ لِسَعْدٍ لاَ تَرْفَعْ صَوْتَكَ. وَجَعَلَ يُمْسِكُهُ، فَغَضِبَ سَعْدٌ فَقَالَ دَعْنَا عَنْكَ، فَإِنِّي سَمِعْتُ مُحَمَّدًا صلى الله عليه وسلم يَزْعُمُ أَنَّهُ قَاتِلُكَ. قَالَ إِيَّاىَ قَالَ نَعَمْ. قَالَ وَاللَّهِ مَا يَكْذِبُ مُحَمَّدٌ إِذَا حَدَّثَ. فَرَجَعَ إِلَى امْرَأَتِهِ، فَقَالَ أَمَا تَعْلَمِينَ مَا قَالَ لِي أَخِي الْيَثْرِبِيُّ قَالَتْ وَمَا قَالَ قَالَ زَعَمَ أَنَّهُ سَمِعَ مُحَمَّدًا يَزْعُمُ أَنَّهُ قَاتِلِي. قَالَتْ فَوَاللَّهِ مَا يَكْذِبُ مُحَمَّدٌ. قَالَ فَلَمَّا خَرَجُوا إِلَى بَدْرٍ، وَجَاءَ الصَّرِيخُ قَالَتْ لَهُ امْرَأَتُهُ أَمَا ذَكَرْتَ مَا قَالَ لَكَ أَخُوكَ الْيَثْرِبِيُّ قَالَ فَأَرَادَ أَنْ لاَ يَخْرُجَ، فَقَالَ لَهُ أَبُو جَهْلٍ إِنَّكَ مِنْ أَشْرَافِ الْوَادِي، فَسِرْ يَوْمًا أَوْ يَوْمَيْنِ، فَسَارَ مَعَهُمْ فَقَتَلَهُ اللَّهُ.

Narrated Usama bin Zaid: That Allah's Messenger ﷺ rode over a donkey covered with a Fadakiya (velvet sheet) and Usama was riding behind him. He was visiting Sa`d bin 'Ubada (who was sick) in the dwelling place of Bani Al-Harith bin Al-Khazraj and this incident happened before the battle of Badr. They proceeded till they passed by a gathering in which `Abdullah bin Ubai bin Salul was present., and that was before `Abdullah bin Ubat embraced Islam. In that gathering there were Muslims, pagan idolators and Jews, and among the Muslims there was `Abdullah bin Rawaha. When a cloud of dust raised by (the movement of) the animal covered that gathering, `Abdullah bin Ubai covered his nose with his garment and said, "Do not cover us with dust." Allah's Messenger ﷺ greeted them, stopped, dismounted and invited them to Allah (i.e. to embrace Islam) and recited to them the Holy Qur'an. On that `Abdullah bin Ubai bin Salul said to him, "O man! There is nothing better than what you say, if it is the truth. So do not trouble us with it in our gatherings, but if somebody comes to you, you can preach to him." On that `Abdullah bin Rawaha said "Yes, O Allah's Messenger ﷺ ! Call on us in our gathering, for we love that." So the Muslims, the pagans and the Jews started abusing one another till they were about to fight with one another. Allah's Messenger kept on quietening them till all of them became quiet, and then Allah's Messenger ﷺ rode his animal and proceeded till he entered upon Sa`d bin 'Ubada. Allah's Messenger ﷺ said, "O Sa`d! Didn't you hear what Abu Habab said?" (meaning `Abdullah bin Unbar). "He said so-and-so." Sa`d bin Ubada said, "O Allah's Messenger ﷺ ! Let my father be sacrificed for you ! Excuse and forgive him for, by Him Who revealed to you the Book, Allah sent the Truth which was revealed to you at the time when the people of this town had decided to crown him (`Abdullah bin Ubai) as their ruler. So when Allah had prevented that with the Truth He had given you, he was choked by that, and that caused him to behave in such an impolite manner which you had noticed." So Allah's Messenger ﷺ excused him. (It was the custom of) Allah's Messenger ﷺ and his companions to excuse the pagans and the people of the scripture (Christians and Jews) as Allah ordered them, and they used to be patient when annoyed (by them). Allah said: 'You shall certainly hear much that will grieve you from those who received the Scripture before you.....and from the pagans (3.186) He also said: 'Many of the people of the scripture wish that if they could turn you away as disbelievers after you have believed. .... (2.109) So Allah's Messenger ﷺ used to apply what Allah had ordered him by excusing them till he was allowed to fight against them. When Allah's Messenger ﷺ had fought the battle of Badr and Allah killed whomever He killed among the chiefs of the infidels and the nobles of Quraish, and Allah's Messenger ﷺ and his companions had returned with victory and booty, bringing with them some of the chiefs of the infidels and the nobles of the Quraish as captives. `Abdullah bin Ubai bin Salul and the pagan idolators who were with him, said, "This matter (Islam) has now brought out its face (triumphed), so give Allah's Messenger ﷺ the pledge of allegiance (for embracing Islam.)". Then they became Muslims. – Al-Bukhari 6207 also 6254

حَدَّثَنَا أَبُو الْيَمَانِ، أَخْبَرَنَا شُعَيْبٌ، عَنِ الزُّهْرِيِّ، حَدَّثَنَا إِسْمَاعِيلُ، قَالَ حَدَّثَنِي أَخِي، عَنْ سُلَيْمَانَ، عَنْ مُحَمَّدِ بْنِ أَبِي عَتِيقٍ، عَنِ ابْنِ شِهَابٍ، عَنْ عُرْوَةَ بْنِ الزُّبَيْرِ، أَنَّ أُسَامَةَ بْنَ زَيْدٍ ـ رضى الله عنهما ـ أَخْبَرَهُ أَنَّ رَسُولَ اللَّهِ صلى الله عليه وسلم رَكِبَ عَلَى حِمَارٍ عَلَيْهِ قَطِيفَةٌ فَدَكِيَّةٌ وَأُسَامَةُ وَرَاءَهُ، يَعُودُ سَعْدَ بْنَ عُبَادَةَ فِي بَنِي حَارِثِ بْنِ الْخَزْرَجِ قَبْلَ وَقْعَةِ بَدْرٍ، فَسَارَا حَتَّى مَرَّا بِمَجْلِسٍ فِيهِ عَبْدُ اللَّهِ بْنُ أُبَىٍّ ابْنُ سَلُولَ، وَذَلِكَ قَبْلَ أَنْ يُسْلِمَ عَبْدُ اللَّهِ بْنُ أُبَىٍّ، فَإِذَا فِي الْمَجْلِسِ أَخْلاَطٌ مِنَ الْمُسْلِمِينَ وَالْمُشْرِكِينَ عَبَدَةِ الأَوْثَانِ وَالْيَهُودِ، وَفِي الْمُسْلِمِينَ عَبْدُ اللَّهِ بْنُ رَوَاحَةَ، فَلَمَّا غَشِيَتِ الْمَجْلِسَ عَجَاجَةُ الدَّابَّةِ خَمَّرَ ابْنُ أُبَىٍّ أَنْفَهُ بِرِدَائِهِ وَقَالَ لاَ تُغَبِّرُوا عَلَيْنَا. فَسَلَّمَ رَسُولُ اللَّهِ صلى الله عليه وسلم عَلَيْهِمْ، ثُمَّ وَقَفَ فَنَزَلَ فَدَعَاهُمْ إِلَى اللَّهِ وَقَرَأَ عَلَيْهِمُ الْقُرْآنَ، فَقَالَ لَهُ عَبْدُ اللَّهِ بْنُ أُبَىٍّ ابْنُ سَلُولَ أَيُّهَا الْمَرْءُ لاَ أَحْسَنَ مِمَّا تَقُولُ إِنْ كَانَ حَقًّا، فَلاَ تُؤْذِنَا بِهِ فِي مَجَالِسِنَا، فَمَنْ جَاءَكَ فَاقْصُصْ عَلَيْهِ. قَالَ عَبْدُ اللَّهِ بْنُ رَوَاحَةَ بَلَى يَا رَسُولَ اللَّهِ فَاغْشَنَا فِي مَجَالِسِنَا فَإِنَّا نُحِبُّ ذَلِكَ. فَاسْتَبَّ الْمُسْلِمُونَ وَالْمُشْرِكُونَ وَالْيَهُودُ حَتَّى كَادُوا يَتَثَاوَرُونَ فَلَمْ يَزَلْ رَسُولُ اللَّهِ صلى الله عليه وسلم يُخَفِّضُهُمْ حَتَّى سَكَتُوا، ثُمَّ رَكِبَ رَسُولُ اللَّهِ صلى الله عليه وسلم دَابَّتَهُ فَسَارَ حَتَّى دَخَلَ عَلَى سَعْدِ بْنِ عُبَادَةَ، فَقَالَ رَسُولُ اللَّهِ صلى الله عليه وسلم " أَىْ سَعْدُ أَلَمْ تَسْمَعْ مَا قَالَ أَبُو حُبَابٍ ـ يُرِيدُ عَبْدَ اللَّهِ بْنَ أُبَىٍّ ـ قَالَ كَذَا وَكَذَا ". فَقَالَ سَعْدُ بْنُ عُبَادَةَ أَىْ رَسُولَ اللَّهِ بِأَبِي أَنْتَ، اعْفُ عَنْهُ وَاصْفَحْ، فَوَالَّذِي أَنْزَلَ عَلَيْكَ الْكِتَابَ لَقَدْ جَاءَ اللَّهُ بِالْحَقِّ الَّذِي أَنْزَلَ عَلَيْكَ، وَلَقَدِ اصْطَلَحَ أَهْلُ هَذِهِ الْبَحْرَةِ عَلَى أَنْ يُتَوِّجُوهُ وَيُعَصِّبُوهُ بِالْعِصَابَةِ، فَلَمَّا رَدَّ اللَّهُ ذَلِكَ بِالْحَقِّ الَّذِي أَعْطَاكَ شَرِقَ بِذَلِكَ فَذَلِكَ فَعَلَ بِهِ مَا رَأَيْتَ. فَعَفَا عَنْهُ رَسُولُ اللَّهِ صلى الله عليه وسلم وَكَانَ رَسُولُ اللَّهِ صلى الله عليه وسلم وَأَصْحَابُهُ يَعْفُونَ عَنِ الْمُشْرِكِينَ وَأَهْلِ الْكِتَابِ كَمَا أَمَرَهُمُ اللَّهُ، وَيَصْبِرُونَ عَلَى الأَذَى، قَالَ اللَّهُ تَعَالَى {وَلَتَسْمَعُنَّ مِنَ الَّذِينَ أُوتُوا الْكِتَابَ} الآيَةَ، وَقَالَ {وَدَّ كَثِيرٌ مِنْ أَهْلِ الْكِتَابِ} فَكَانَ رَسُولُ اللَّهِ صلى الله عليه وسلم يَتَأَوَّلُ فِي الْعَفْوِ عَنْهُمْ مَا أَمَرَهُ اللَّهُ بِهِ حَتَّى أَذِنَ لَهُ فِيهِمْ، فَلَمَّا غَزَا رَسُولُ اللَّهِ صلى الله عليه وسلم بَدْرًا، فَقَتَلَ اللَّهُ بِهَا مَنْ قَتَلَ مِنْ صَنَادِيدِ الْكُفَّارِ، وَسَادَةِ قُرَيْشٍ، فَقَفَلَ رَسُولُ اللَّهِ صلى الله عليه وسلم وَأَصْحَابُهُ مَنْصُورِينَ غَانِمِينَ مَعَهُمْ أُسَارَى مِنْ صَنَادِيدِ الْكُفَّارِ وَسَادَةِ قُرَيْشٍ قَالَ ابْنُ أُبَىٍّ ابْنُ سَلُولَ، وَمَنْ مَعَهُ مِنَ الْمُشْرِكِينَ عَبَدَةِ الأَوْثَانِ هَذَا أَمْرٌ قَدْ تَوَجَّهَ فَبَايِعُوا رَسُولَ اللَّهِ صلى الله عليه وسلم عَلَى الإِسْلاَمِ فَأَسْلَمُوا.

Narrated Ibn `Abbas: When the Prophet ﷺ arrived at Medina he found that the Jews observed fast on the day of 'Ashura'. They were asked the reason for the fast. They replied, "This is the day when Allah caused Moses and the children of Israel to have victory over Pharaoh, so we fast on this day as a sign of glorifying it." Allah's Messenger ﷺ said, "We are closer to Moses than you." Then he ordered that fasting on this day should be observed. – Sahih al-Bukhari 3943

حَدَّثَنَا زِيَادُ بْنُ أَيُّوبَ، حَدَّثَنَا هُشَيْمٌ، حَدَّثَنَا أَبُو بِشْرٍ، عَنْ سَعِيدِ بْنِ جُبَيْرٍ، عَنِ ابْنِ عَبَّاسٍ ـ رضى الله عنهما ـ قَالَ لَمَّا قَدِمَ النَّبِيُّ صلى الله عليه وسلم الْمَدِينَةَ وجد الْيهود يصومون عاشوراء، فسئلوا عن ذلك، فقالوا هَذَا الْيَوْمُ الَّذِي أظْفَرَ اللَّهُ فِيهِ مُوسَى وَبَنِي إِسْرَائِيلَ عَلَى فِرْعَوْنَ، وَنَحْنُ نَصُومُهُ تَعْظِيمًا لَهُ، فَقَالَ رَسُولُ اللَّهِ صلى الله عليه وسلم " نَحْنُ أَوْلَى بِمُوسَى مِنْكُمْ ". ثُمَّ أَمَرَ بِصَوْمِهِ.

Narrated `Aisha: Allah's Messenger ﷺ came to my house while two girls were singing beside me the songs of Bu'ath (a story about the war between the two tribes of the Ansar, i.e. Khazraj and Aus, before Islam.) The Prophet ﷺ reclined on the bed and turned his face to the other side. Abu Bakr came and scolded me and said protestingly, "Instrument of Satan in the presence of Allah's Messenger ﷺ?" Allah's Messenger ﷺ turned his face towards him and said, "Leave them." When Abu Bakr became inattentive, I waved the two girls to go away and they left. It was the day of `Id when negroes used to play with leather shields and spears. Either I requested Allah's Messenger ﷺ or he himself asked me whether I would like to see the display. I replied in the affirmative. Then he let me stand behind him and my cheek was touching his cheek and he was saying, "Carry on, O Bani Arfida (i.e. negroes)!" When I got tired, he asked me if that was enough. I replied in the affirmative and he told me to leave. – Al-Bukhari 2906, 2907

حَدَّثَنَا إِسْمَاعِيلُ، قَالَ حَدَّثَنِي ابْنُ وَهْبٍ، قَالَ عَمْرٌو حَدَّثَنِي أَبُو الأَسْوَدِ، عَنْ عُرْوَةَ، عَنْ عَائِشَةَ ـ رضى الله عنها ـ دَخَلَ عَلَيَّ رَسُولُ اللَّهِ صلى الله عليه وسلم وَعِنْدِي جَارِيَتَانِ تُغَنِّيَانِ بِغِنَاءِ بُعَاثَ، فَاضْطَجَعَ عَلَى الْفِرَاشِ وَحَوَّلَ وَجْهَهُ، فَدَخَلَ أَبُو بَكْرٍ فَانْتَهَرَنِي وَقَالَ مِزْمَارَةُ الشَّيْطَانِ عِنْدَ رَسُولِ اللَّهِ صلى الله عليه وسلم. فَأَقْبَلَ عَلَيْهِ رَسُولُ اللَّهِ صلى الله عليه وسلم فَقَالَ " دَعْهُمَا ". فَلَمَّا غَفَلَ غَمَزْتُهُمَا فَخَرَجَتَا. قَالَتْ وَكَانَ يَوْمُ عِيدٍ يَلْعَبُ السُّودَانُ بِالدَّرَقِ وَالْحِرَابِ، فَإِمَّا سَأَلْتُ رَسُولَ اللَّهِ صلى الله عليه وسلم وَإِمَّا قَالَ " تَشْتَهِينَ تَنْظُرِينَ ". فَقَالَتْ نَعَمْ. فَأَقَامَنِي وَرَاءَهُ خَدِّي عَلَى خَدِّهِ وَيَقُولُ " دُونَكُمْ بَنِي أَرْفِدَةَ ". حَتَّى إِذَا مَلِلْتُ قَالَ " حَسْبُكِ ". قُلْتُ نَعَمْ. قَالَ " فَاذْهَبِي ". قَالَ أَحْمَدُ عَنِ ابْنِ وَهْبٍ، فَلَمَّا غَفَلَ.

Narrated Abu Musa: The news of the migration of the Prophet (from Mecca to Medina) reached us while we were in Yemen. So we set out as emigrants towards him. We were (three) I and my two brothers. I was the youngest of them, and one of the two was Abu Burda, and the other, Abu Ruhm, and our total number was either 53 or 52 men from my people. We got on board a boat and our boat took us to Negus in Ethiopia. There we met Ja`far bin Abi Talib and stayed with him. Then we all came (to Medina) and met the Prophet ﷺ at the time of the conquest of Khaibar. Some of the people used to say to us, namely the people of the ship, "We have migrated before you." Asma' bint 'Umais who was one of those who had come with us, came as a visitor to Hafsa, the wife the Prophet ﷺ. She had migrated along with those other Muslims who migrated to Negus. `Umar came to Hafsa while Asma' bint 'Umais was with her. `Umar, on seeing Asma,' said, "Who is this?" She said, "Asma' bint 'Umais," `Umar said, "Is she the Ethiopian? Is she the sea-faring lady?" Asma' replied, "Yes." `Umar said, "We have migrated before you (people of the boat), so we have got more right than you over Allah's Messenger ﷺ" on that Asma' became angry and said, "No, by Allah, while you were with Allah's Messenger ﷺ who was feeding the hungry ones amongst you, and advised the ignorant ones amongst you, we were in the far-off hated land of Ethiopia, and all that was for the sake of Allah's Messenger ﷺ. By Allah, I will neither eat any food nor drink anything till I inform Allah's Messenger ﷺ of all that you have said. There we were harmed and frightened. I will mention this to the Prophet ﷺ and will not tell a lie or curtail your saying or add something to it." – Al-Bukhari 4230

حَدَّثَنِي مُحَمَّدُ بْنُ الْعَلاَءِ، حَدَّثَنَا أَبُو أُسَامَةَ، حَدَّثَنَا بُرَيْدُ بْنُ عَبْدِ اللَّهِ، عَنْ أَبِي بُرْدَةَ، عَنْ أَبِي مُوسَى ـ رضى الله عنه ـ قَالَ بَلَغَنَا مَخْرَجُ النَّبِيِّ صلى الله عليه وسلم وَنَحْنُ بِالْيَمَنِ، فَخَرَجْنَا مُهَاجِرِينَ إِلَيْهِ أَنَا، وَأَخَوَانِ لِي أَنَا أَصْغَرُهُمْ، أَحَدُهُمَا أَبُو بُرْدَةَ، وَالآخَرُ أَبُو رُهْمٍ ـ إِمَّا قَالَ بِضْعٌ وَإِمَّا قَالَ ـ فِي ثَلاَثَةٍ وَخَمْسِينَ أَوِ اثْنَيْنِ وَخَمْسِينَ رَجُلاً مِنْ قَوْمِي، فَرَكِبْنَا سَفِينَةً، فَأَلْقَتْنَا سَفِينَتُنَا إِلَى النَّجَاشِيِّ بِالْحَبَشَةِ، فَوَافَقْنَا جَعْفَرَ بْنَ أَبِي طَالِبٍ فَأَقَمْنَا مَعَهُ حَتَّى قَدِمْنَا جَمِيعًا، فَوَافَقْنَا النَّبِيَّ صلى الله عليه وسلم حِينَ افْتَتَحَ خَيْبَرَ، وَكَانَ أُنَاسٌ مِنَ النَّاسِ يَقُولُونَ لَنَا ـ يَعْنِي لأَهْلِ السَّفِينَةِ ـ سَبَقْنَاكُمْ بِالْهِجْرَةِ، وَدَخَلَتْ أَسْمَاءُ بِنْتُ عُمَيْسٍ، وَهْىَ مِمَّنْ قَدِمَ مَعَنَا، عَلَى حَفْصَةَ زَوْجِ النَّبِيِّ صلى الله عليه وسلم زَائِرَةً، وَقَدْ كَانَتْ هَاجَرَتْ إِلَى النَّجَاشِيِّ فِيمَنْ هَاجَرَ، فَدَخَلَ عُمَرُ عَلَى حَفْصَةَ وَأَسْمَاءُ عِنْدَهَا، فَقَالَ عُمَرُ حِينَ رَأَى أَسْمَاءَ مَنْ هَذِهِ قَالَتْ أَسْمَاءُ بِنْتُ عُمَيْسٍ. قَالَ عُمَرُ الْحَبَشِيَّةُ هَذِهِ الْبَحْرِيَّةُ هَذِهِ قَالَتْ أَسْمَاءُ نَعَمْ. قَالَ سَبَقْنَاكُمْ بِالْهِجْرَةِ، فَنَحْنُ أَحَقُّ بِرَسُولِ اللَّهِ صلى الله عليه وسلم مِنْكُمْ. فَغَضِبَتْ وَقَالَتْ كَلاَّ وَاللَّهِ، كُنْتُمْ مَعَ رَسُولِ اللَّهِ صلى الله عليه وسلم يُطْعِمُ جَائِعَكُمْ، وَيَعِظُ جَاهِلَكُمْ، وَكُنَّا فِي دَارِ أَوْ فِي أَرْضِ الْبُعَدَاءِ الْبُغَضَاءِ بِالْحَبَشَةِ، وَذَلِكَ فِي اللَّهِ وَفِي رَسُولِهِ صلى الله عليه وسلم وَايْمُ اللَّهِ، لاَ أَطْعَمُ طَعَامًا، وَلاَ أَشْرَبُ شَرَابًا حَتَّى أَذْكُرَ مَا قُلْتَ لِرَسُولِ اللَّهِ صلى الله عليه وسلم وَنَحْنُ كُنَّا نُؤْذَى وَنُخَافُ، وَسَأَذْكُرُ ذَلِكَ لِلنَّبِيِّ صلى الله عليه وسلم وَأَسْأَلُهُ، وَاللَّهِ لاَ أَكْذِبُ وَلاَ أَزِيغُ وَلاَ أَزِيدُ عَلَيْهِ

Marriage with Aisha
الزواج من عائشة

Narrated Hisham's father: Khadija died three years before the Prophet ﷺ departed to Medina. He stayed there for two years or so and then he married `Aisha when she was a girl of six years of age, and he consumed that marriage when she was nine years old. – Sahih al-Bukhari 3896

حَدَّثَنِي عُبَيْدُ بْنُ إِسْمَاعِيلَ، حَدَّثَنَا أَبُو أُسَامَةَ، عَنْ هِشَامٍ، عَنْ أَبِيهِ، قَالَ تُوُفِّيَتْ خَدِيجَةُ قَبْلَ مَخْرَجِ النَّبِيِّ صلى الله عليه وسلم إِلَى الْمَدِينَةِ بِثَلاَثِ سِنِينَ، فَلَبِثَ سَنَتَيْنِ أَوْ قَرِيبًا مِنْ ذَلِكَ، وَنَكَحَ عَائِشَةَ وَهْىَ بِنْتُ سِتِّ سِنِينَ، ثُمَّ بَنَى بِهَا وَهْىَ بِنْتُ تِسْعِ سِنِينَ.

Narrated 'Urwa: The Prophet ﷺ asked Abu Bakr for `Aisha's hand in marriage. Abu Bakr said "But I am your brother." The Prophet ﷺ said, "You are my brother in Allah's religion and His Book, but she (Aisha) is lawful for me to marry.". – Sahih al-Bukhari 5081

حَدَّثَنَا عَبْدُ اللَّهِ بْنُ يُوسُفَ، حَدَّثَنَا اللَّيْثُ، عَنْ يَزِيدَ، عَنْ عِرَاكٍ، عَنْ عُرْوَةَ، أَنَّ النَّبِيَّ صلى الله عليه وسلم خَطَبَ عَائِشَةَ إِلَى أَبِي بَكْرٍ فَقَالَ لَهُ أَبُو بَكْرٍ إِنَّمَا أَنَا أَخُوكَ، فَقَالَ " أَنْتَ أَخِي فِي دِينِ اللَّهِ وَكِتَابِهِ وَهْىَ لِي حَلاَلٌ "

Narrated Aisha: The Prophet ﷺ engaged me when I was a girl of six (years). We went to Medina and stayed at the home of Bani-al-Harith bin Khazraj. Then I got ill and my hair fell down. Later on my hair grew (again) and my mother, Um Ruman, came to me while I was playing in a swing with some of my girl friends. She called me, and I went to her, not knowing what she wanted to do to me. She caught me by the hand and made me stand at the door of the house. I was breathless then, and when my breathing became Allright, she took some water and rubbed my face and head with it. Then she took me into the house. There in the house I saw some Ansari women who said, "Best wishes and Allah's Blessing and a good luck." Then she entrusted me to them and they prepared me (for the marriage). Unexpectedly Allah's Apostle came to me in the forenoon and my mother handed me over to him, and at that time I was a girl of nine years of age. – Sahih al-Bukhari 3894

حَدَّثَنِي فَرْوَةُ بْنُ أَبِي الْمَغْرَاءِ، حَدَّثَنَا عَلِيُّ بْنُ مُسْهِرٍ، عَنْ هِشَامٍ، عَنْ أَبِيهِ، عَنْ عَائِشَةَ ـ رضى الله عنها ـ قَالَتْ تَزَوَّجَنِي النَّبِيُّ صلى الله عليه وسلم وَأَنَا بِنْتُ سِتِّ سِنِينَ، فَقَدِمْنَا الْمَدِينَةَ فَنَزَلْنَا فِي بَنِي الْحَارِثِ بْنِ خَزْرَجٍ، فَوُعِكْتُ فَتَمَرَّقَ شَعَرِي فَوَفَى جُمَيْمَةً، فَأَتَتْنِي أُمِّي أُمُّ رُومَانَ وَإِنِّي لَفِي أُرْجُوحَةٍ وَمَعِي صَوَاحِبُ لِي، فَصَرَخَتْ بِي فَأَتَيْتُهَا لاَ أَدْرِي مَا تُرِيدُ بِي فَأَخَذَتْ بِيَدِي حَتَّى أَوْقَفَتْنِي عَلَى بَابِ الدَّارِ، وَإِنِّي لأُنْهِجُ، حَتَّى سَكَنَ بَعْضُ نَفَسِي، ثُمَّ أَخَذَتْ شَيْئًا مِنْ مَاءٍ فَمَسَحَتْ بِهِ وَجْهِي وَرَأْسِي ثُمَّ أَدْخَلَتْنِي الدَّارَ فَإِذَا نِسْوَةٌ مِنَ الأَنْصَارِ فِي الْبَيْتِ فَقُلْنَ عَلَى الْخَيْرِ وَالْبَرَكَةِ، وَعَلَى خَيْرِ طَائِرٍ. فَأَسْلَمَتْنِي إِلَيْهِنَّ فَأَصْلَحْنَ مِنْ شَأْنِي، فَلَمْ يَرُعْنِي إِلاَّ رَسُولُ اللَّهِ صلى الله عليه وسلم ضُحًى، فَأَسْلَمَتْنِي إِلَيْهِ، وَأَنَا يَوْمَئِذٍ بِنْتُ تِسْعِ سِنِينَ.

Narrated `Aisha: That the Prophet ﷺ said to her, "You have been shown to me twice in my dream. I saw you pictured on a piece of silk and some-one said (to me). 'This is your wife.' When I uncovered the picture, I saw that it was yours. I said, 'If this is from Allah, it will be done." – Sahih al-Bukhari 3895

حَدَّثَنَا مُعَلًّى، حَدَّثَنَا وُهَيْبٌ، عَنْ هِشَامِ بْنِ عُرْوَةَ، عَنْ أَبِيهِ، عَنْ عَائِشَةَ ـ رضى الله عنها ـ أَنَّ النَّبِيَّ صلى الله عليه وسلم قَالَ لَهَا " أُرِيتُكِ فِي الْمَنَامِ مَرَّتَيْنِ، أَرَى أَنَّكِ فِي سَرَقَةٍ مِنْ حَرِيرٍ وَيَقُولُ هَذِهِ امْرَأَتُكَ فَاكْشِفْ عَنْهَا فَإِذَا هِيَ أَنْتِ فَأَقُولُ إِنْ يَكُ هَذَا مِنْ عِنْدِ اللَّهِ يُمْضِهِ "

Narrated 'Urwah: It was narrated from 'Urwah, that 'Aishah said: "The Messenger of Allah married me in Shawwal and my marriage was consummated in Shawwal." –'Aishah liked for her women's marriages to be consummated in Shawwal –"and which of his wives was more beloved to him than me?" – Sunan an-Nasa'I 3236

أَخْبَرَنَا عُبَيْدُ اللَّهِ بْنُ سَعِيدٍ، قَالَ حَدَّثَنَا يَحْيَى، عَنْ سُفْيَانَ، قَالَ حَدَّثَنَا إِسْمَاعِيلُ بْنُ أُمَيَّةَ، عَنْ عَبْدِ اللَّهِ بْنِ عُرْوَةَ، عَنْ عُرْوَةَ، عَنْ عَائِشَةَ، قَالَتْ تَزَوَّجَنِي رَسُولُ اللَّهِ صلى الله عليه وسلم فِي شَوَّالٍ وَأُدْخِلْتُ عَلَيْهِ فِي شَوَّالٍ وَكَانَتْ عَائِشَةُ تُحِبُّ أَنْ تُدْخِلَ نِسَاءَهَا فِي شَوَّالٍ فَأَىُّ نِسَائِهِ كَانَتْ أَحْظَى عِنْدَهُ مِنِّي

The Book of
Al-Aqaba Pledge
بيعة العقبة

Narrated `Aisha: The day of Bu'ath (i.e. Day of fighting between the two tribes of the Ansar, the Aus and Khazraj) was brought about by Allah for the good of His Apostle so that when Allah's Messenger ﷺ reached (Medina), the tribes of Medina had already divided and their chiefs had been killed and wounded. So Allah had brought about the battle for the good of His Apostle in order that they (i.e. the Ansar) might embrace Islam. – Al-Bukhari 3777 [4]

---

[4] Muhammad drafted the Constitution of Medina shortly after the pledges of al-Aqabah to establish the first Islamic government in Medina
This is a prescript of Muhammad, the Prophet and Messenger of God (to operate) between the faithful and the followers of Islam ("Muslims") from among the Quraish and the people of Madina and those who may be under them, may join them and take part in wars in their company.
They shall constitute a separate political unit (Ummat) as distinguished from all the people (of the world).
The emigrants from the Quraish shall be (responsible) for their own ward; and shall pay their blood money in mutual collaboration and shall secure the release of their own prisoners by paying their ransom from themselves so that the mutual dealings between the believers be in accordance with the principles of goodness and justice.
And Banu 'Awf shall be responsible for their own ward and shall pay their blood money in mutual collaboration, and every group shall secure the release of its own prisoners by paying their ransom from themselves so that the dealings between the believers be in accordance with the principles of goodness and justice.
And Banu Al-Harith-ibn-Khazraj shall be responsible for their own ward and shall pay their blood-money in mutual collaboration and every group shall secure the release of its own prisoners by paying their ransom from themselves, so that the dealings between the believers be in accordance with the principles of goodness and justice.
And Banu Sa'ida shall be responsible for their own ward, and shall pay their blood-money in mutual collaboration and every group shall secure the release of its own prisoners by paying their ransom from themselves, so that the dealings between the believers be in accordance with the principles of goodness and justice.
And Banu Jusham shall be responsible for their own ward and shall pay their blood-money in mutual collaboration and every group shall secure the release of its own prisoners by paying their ransom so that the dealings between the believers be in accordance with the principles of goodness and justice.
And Banu an-Najjar shall be responsible for their own ward and shall pay their blood-money in mutual collaboration and every group shall secure the release of its own prisoners by paying their ransom so that the dealings between the believers be in accordance with the principles of goodness and justice.

And Banu 'Amr-ibn-'Awf shall be responsible for their own ward and shall pay their blood-money in mutual collaboration and every group shall secure the release of its own prisoners by paying their ransom, so that the dealings between the believers be in accordance with the principles of goodness and justice.

And Banu-al-Nabit shall be responsible for their own ward and shall pay their blood-money in mutual collaboration and every group shall secure the release of its own prisoners by paying their ransom so that the dealings between the believers be in accordance with the principles of goodness and justice.

And Banu-al-Aws shall be responsible for their own ward and shall pay their blood-money in mutual collaboration and every group shall secure the release of its own prisoners by paying their ransom, so that the dealings between the believers be in accordance with the principles of goodness and justice.

And the believers shall not leave any one, hard-pressed with debts, without affording him some relief, in order that the dealings between the believers be in accordance with the principles of goodness and justice.

Also no believer shall enter into a contract of clientage with one who is already in such a contract with another believer.

And the hands of pious believers shall be raised against every such person as rises in rebellion or attempts to acquire anything by force or is guilty of any sin or excess or attempts to spread mischief among the believers ; their hands shall be raised all together against such a person, even if he be a son to any one of them.

A Believer will not kill a Believer [in retaliation] for a non-Believer and will not aid a non-Believer against a Believer.

The protection (dhimmah) of Allah is one, the least of them [i.e., the Believers] is entitled to grant protection (yujīr) that is binding for all of them. The Believers are each other's allies (mawālī) to the exclusion of other people.

And that those who will follow us among the Jews, will have help and equality. Neither shall they be oppressed nor will any help be given against them.

And the peace of the believers shall be one. If there be any war in the way of God, no believer shall be under any peace (with the enemy) apart from other believers, unless it (this peace) be the same and equally binding on all.

And all those detachments that will fight on our side will be relieved by turns.

And the believers as a body shall take blood vengeance in the way of God.

And undoubtedly pious believers are the best and in the rightest course.

And that no associator (non-Muslim subject) shall give any protection to the life and property of a Quraishite, nor shall he come in the way of any believer in this matter.

And if any one intentionally murders a believer, and it is proved, he shall be killed in retaliation, unless the heir of the murdered person be satisfied with blood-money. And all believers shall actually stand for this ordinance and nothing else shall be proper for them to do.

And it shall not be lawful for any one, who has agreed to carry out the provisions laid down in this code and has affixed his faith in God and the Day of Judgment, to give help or protection to any murderer, and if he gives any help or protection to such a person, God"s curse and wrath shall be on him on the Day of Resurrection, and no money or compensation shall be accepted from such a person.

And that whenever you differ about anything, refer it to God and to Muhammad
And the Jews shall share with the believers the expenses of war so long as they fight in conjunction,
And the Jews of Banu 'Awf shall be considered as one community (Ummat) along with the believers—for the Jews their religion, and for the Muslims theirs, be one client or patron. But whoever does wrong or commits treachery brings evil only on himself and his household.
And the Jews of Banu-an-Najjar shall have the same rights as the Jews of Banu 'Awf.
And the Jews of Banu-al-Harith shall have the same rights as the Jews of Banu 'Awf.
And the Jews of Banu Sa'ida shall have the same rights as the Jews of Banu 'Awf
And the Jews of Banu Jusham shall have the same rights as the Jews of Banu 'Awf.
And the Jews of Banu al-Aws shall have the same rights as the Jews of Banu 'Awf.
And the Jews of Banu Tha'laba shall have the same rights as the Jews of Banu 'Awf. But whoever does wrong or commits treachery brings evil only on himself and his household.
And Jafna, who are a branch of the Tha'laba tribe, shall have the same rights as the mother tribes.
And Banu-ash-Shutaiba shall have the same rights as the Jews of Banu 'Awf; and they shall be faithful to, and not violators of, treaty.
And the mawlas (clients) of Tha'laba shall have the same rights as those of the original members of it.
And the sub-branches of the Jewish tribes shall have the same rights as the mother tribes.
And that none of them shall go out to fight as a soldier of the Muslim army, without the per-mission of Muhammad.
And no obstruction shall be placed in the way of any one"s retaliation for beating or injuries; and whoever sheds blood brings it upon himself and his household, except he who has been wronged, and Allah demands the most righteous fulfillment of this [treaty].
And the Jews shall bear the burden of their expenses and the Muslims theirs.
And if any one fights against the people of this code, their (i.e., of the Jews and Muslims) mutual help shall come into operation, and there shall be friendly counsel and sincere behaviour between them; and faithfulness and no breach of covenant.
And the Jews shall be bearing their own expenses so long as they shall be fighting in conjunction with the believers.
And the Valley of Yathrib (Madina) shall be a Haram (sacred place) for the people of this code.
The clients (mawla) shall have the same treatment as the original persons (i.e., persons accepting clientage). He shall neither be harmed nor shall he himself break the covenant.
And no refuge shall be given to any one without the permission of the people of the place (i.e., the refugee shall have no right of giving refuge to others).
And that if any murder or quarrel takes place among the people of this code, from which any trouble may be feared, it shall be referred to God and God's Messenger, Muhammad; and God will be with him who will be most particular about what is written in this code and act on it most faithfully.
The Quraish shall be given no protection nor shall they who help them.
And they (i.e., Jews and Muslims) shall have each other's help in the event of any force invading Yathrib.

حَدَّثَنِي عُبَيْدُ بْنُ إِسْمَاعِيلَ، حَدَّثَنَا أَبُو أُسَامَةَ، عَنْ هِشَامٍ، عَنْ أَبِيهِ، عَنْ عَائِشَةَ ـ رضى الله عنها ـ قَالَتْ كَانَ يَوْمُ بُعَاثَ يَوْمًا قَدَّمَهُ اللَّهُ لِرَسُولِهِ صلى الله عليه وسلم فَقَدِمَ رَسُولُ اللَّهِ صلى الله عليه وسلم وَقَدِ افْتَرَقَ مَلَؤُهُمْ، وَقُتِلَتْ سَرَوَاتُهُمْ، وَجُرِّحُوا، فَقَدَّمَهُ اللَّهُ لِرَسُولِهِ صلى الله عليه وسلم فِي دُخُولِهِمْ فِي الإِسْلاَمِ.

Narrated `Aisha: The day of Bu'ath was a day (i.e. battle) which Allah caused to take place just before the mission of His Apostle so that when Allah's Messenger ﷺ came to Medina, they (the tribes) had divided (into hostile groups) and their nobles had been killed; and all that facilitated their conversion to Islam. – Al-Bukhari 3930

حَدَّثَنَا عُبَيْدُ اللَّهِ بْنُ سَعِيدٍ، حَدَّثَنَا أَبُو أُسَامَةَ، عَنْ هِشَامٍ، عَنْ أَبِيهِ، عَنْ عَائِشَةَ ـ رضى الله عنها ـ قَالَتْ كَانَ يَوْمُ بُعَاثٍ يَوْمًا قَدَّمَهُ اللَّهُ عَزَّ وَجَلَّ لِرَسُولِهِ صلى الله عليه وسلم، فَقَدِمَ رَسُولُ اللَّهِ صلى الله عليه وسلم الْمَدِينَةَ وَقَدِ افْتَرَقَ مَلَؤُهُمْ، وَقُتِلَتْ سَرَاتُهُمْ فِي دُخُولِهِمْ فِي الإِسْلاَمِ.

Narrated `Abdullah bin Ka`b bin Malik: Who, from among Ka`b's sons, was the guide of Ka`b when he became blind: I heard Ka`b bin Malik narrating the story of (the Ghazwa of) Tabuk in which he failed to take part. Ka`b said, "I did not remain behind Allah's Messenger ﷺ in any Ghazwa that he fought except the Ghazwa of Tabuk, and I failed to take part in the Ghazwa of Badr, but Allah did not admonish anyone who had not participated in it, for in fact, Allah's Messenger ﷺ had gone out in search of the caravan of Quraish till Allah made them (i.e. the Muslims) and their enemy meet without any appointment. I witnessed the night of Al-`Aqaba (pledge) with Allah's Messenger ﷺ when we pledged for Islam, and I would not exchange it for the Badr battle although the Badr battle is more popular amongst the people than It (i.e. Al-`Aqaba pledge). Sahih Al-Bukhari 4418

حَدَّثَنَا اللَّيْثُ، عَنْ عُقَيْلٍ، عَنِ ابْنِ شِهَابٍ، عَنْ عَبْدِ الرَّحْمَنِ بْنِ عَبْدِ اللَّهِ بْنِ كَعْبِ بْنِ مَالِكٍ، أَنَّ عَبْدَ اللَّهِ بْنَ كَعْبِ بْنِ مَالِكٍ ـ وَكَانَ قَائِدَ كَعْبٍ مِنْ بَنِيهِ حِينَ عَمِيَ ـ قَالَ سَمِعْتُ كَعْبَ بْنَ مَالِكٍ، يُحَدِّثُ حِينَ تَخَلَّفَ عَنْ قِصَّةِ، تَبُوكَ قَالَ كَعْبٌ لَمْ أَتَخَلَّفْ عَنْ رَسُولِ اللَّهِ صلى الله عليه وسلم فِي غَزْوَةٍ غَزَاهَا إِلاَّ فِي غَزْوَةِ تَبُوكَ، غَيْرَ أَنِّي كُنْتُ تَخَلَّفْتُ فِي غَزْوَةِ بَدْرٍ، وَلَمْ يُعَاتِبْ أَحَدًا تَخَلَّفَ، عَنْهَا إِنَّمَا خَرَجَ رَسُولُ اللَّهِ صلى الله عليه وسلم يُرِيدُ عِيرَ قُرَيْشٍ، حَتَّى جَمَعَ اللَّهُ بَيْنَهُمْ وَبَيْنَ عَدُوِّهِمْ عَلَى غَيْرِ مِيعَادٍ وَلَقَدْ شَهِدْتُ مَعَ رَسُولِ اللَّهِ صلى الله عليه وسلم لَيْلَةَ الْعَقَبَةِ حِينَ تَوَاثَقْنَا عَلَى الإِسْلاَمِ، وَمَا أُحِبُّ أَنَّ لِي بِهَا مَشْهَدَ بَدْرٍ، وَإِنْ كَانَتْ بَدْرٌ أَذْكَرَ فِي النَّاسِ مِنْهَا، كَانَ مِنْ خَبَرِي أَنِّي لَمْ أَكُنْ قَطُّ أَقْوَى وَلاَ أَيْسَرَ حِينَ تَخَلَّفْتُ عَنْهُ فِي تِلْكَ الْغَزْوَةِ،

Narrated 'Ubada bin As Samit: I was one of the Naqibs who gave the ('Aqaba) Pledge of Allegiance to Allah's Messenger ﷺ . We gave the pledge of allegiance to him that we would not worship anything other than Allah, would not steal, would not commit illegal sexual intercourse, would not kill a person whose killing Allah has made illegal except rightfully, would not rob each other, and we would not be promised Paradise jf we did the above sins,

---

And if they (i.e., the Jews) are invited to any peace, they also shall offer peace and shall be a party to it; and if they invite the believers to some such affairs, it shall be their (Muslims) duty as well to reciprocate the dealings, excepting that any one makes a religious war.
On every group shall rest the responsibility of (repulsing) the enemy from the place which faces its part of the city.
And the Jews of the tribe of al-Aws, clients as well as original members, shall have the same rights as the people of this code: and shall behave sincerely and faithfully towards the latter, not perpetrating any breach of covenant. As one shall sow so shall he reap. And God is with him who will most sincerely and faithfully carry out the provisions of this code.
And this prescript shall not be of any avail to any oppressor or breaker of covenant. And one shall have security whether one goes out to a campaign or remains in Madina, or else it will be an oppression and breach of covenant. And God is the Protector of him who performs the obligations with faithfulness and care, as also His Messenger Muhammad

then if we committed one of the above sins, Allah will give His Judgment concerning it. – Al-Bukhari 3893

حَدَّثَنَا قُتَيْبَةُ، حَدَّثَنَا اللَّيْثُ، عَنْ يَزِيدَ بْنِ أَبِي حَبِيبٍ، عَنْ أَبِي الْخَيْرِ، عَنِ الصُّنَابِحِيِّ، عَنْ عُبَادَةَ بْنِ الصَّامِتِ ـ رضى الله عنه ـ أَنَّهُ قَالَ إِنِّي مِنَ النُّقَبَاءِ الَّذِينَ بَايَعُوا رَسُولَ اللَّهِ صلى الله عليه وسلم. وَقَالَ بَايَعْنَاهُ عَلَى أَنْ لاَ نُشْرِكَ بِاللَّهِ شَيْئًا، وَلاَ نَسْرِقَ، وَلاَ نَزْنِيَ، وَلاَ نَقْتُلَ النَّفْسَ الَّتِي حَرَّمَ اللَّهُ، وَلاَ نَنْتَهِبَ، وَلاَ نَعْصِيَ بِالْجَنَّةِ إِنْ فَعَلْنَا ذَلِكَ، فَإِنْ غَشِينَا مِنْ ذَلِكَ شَيْئًا كَانَ قَضَاءُ ذَلِكَ إِلَى اللَّهِ.

Narrated Jabir bin `Abdullah: I was present with my two maternal uncles at Al-`Aqaba (where the pledge of allegiance was given). (Ibn 'Uyaina said, "One of the two was Al-Bara' bin Marur.") – Al-Bukhari 3890

حَدَّثَنَا عَلِيُّ بْنُ عَبْدِ اللَّهِ، حَدَّثَنَا سُفْيَانُ، قَالَ كَانَ عَمْرٌو يَقُولُ سَمِعْتُ جَابِرَ بْنَ عَبْدِ اللَّهِ ـ رضى الله عنهما ـ يَقُولُ شَهِدَ بِي خَالاَىَ الْعَقَبَةَ. قَالَ أَبُو عَبْدِ اللَّهِ قَالَ ابْنُ عُيَيْنَةَ أَحَدُهُمَا الْبَرَاءُ بْنُ مَعْرُورٍ

Narrated Mu`adh bin Rifa`a bin Rafi`: Rifa`a was one of the warriors of Badr while (his father) Rafi` was one of the people of Al-`Aqaba (i.e. those who gave the pledge of allegiance at Al-`Aqaba). Rafi` used to say to his son, "I would not have been happier if I had taken part in the Badr battle instead of taking part in the 'Aqaba pledge.". – Sahih Al-Bukhari 3993

حَدَّثَنَا سُلَيْمَانُ بْنُ حَرْبٍ، حَدَّثَنَا حَمَّادٌ، عَنْ يَحْيَى، عَنْ مُعَاذِ بْنِ رِفَاعَةَ بْنِ رَافِعٍ،، وَكَانَ، رِفَاعَةُ مِنْ أَهْلِ بَدْرٍ، وَكَانَ رَافِعٌ مِنْ أَهْلِ الْعَقَبَةِ، فَكَانَ يَقُولُ لاِبْنِهِ مَا يَسُرُّنِي أَنِّي شَهِدْتُ بَدْرًا بِالْعَقَبَةِ قَالَ سَأَلَ جِبْرِيلُ النَّبِيَّ صلى الله عليه وسلم. بِهَذَا.

Narrated `Abdullah bin Ka`b: Who was Ka`b's guide when Ka`b turned blind: I heard Ka`b bin Malik narrating: When he remained behind (i.e. did not Join) the Prophet ﷺ in the Ghazwa of Tabuk. Ibn Bukair, in his narration stated that Ka`b said, " I witnessed the Al-`Aqaba pledge of allegiance at night with the Prophet ﷺ when we jointly agreed to support Islam with all our efforts I would not like to have attended the Badr battle instead of that 'Aqaba pledge although Badr is more well-known than it, amongst the people." – Sahih al-Bukhari 3889

حَدَّثَنَا يَحْيَى بْنُ بُكَيْرٍ، حَدَّثَنَا اللَّيْثُ، عَنْ عُقَيْلٍ، عَنِ ابْنِ شِهَابٍ، حَدَّثَنَا أَحْمَدُ بْنُ صَالِحٍ، حَدَّثَنَا عَنْبَسَةُ، حَدَّثَنَا يُونُسُ، عَنِ ابْنِ شِهَابٍ، قَالَ أَخْبَرَنِي عَبْدُ الرَّحْمَنِ بْنُ عَبْدِ اللَّهِ بْنِ كَعْبِ بْنِ مَالِكٍ، أَنَّ عَبْدَ اللَّهِ بْنَ كَعْبٍ ـ وَكَانَ قَائِدَ كَعْبٍ حِينَ عَمِيَ ـ قَالَ سَمِعْتُ كَعْبَ بْنَ مَالِكٍ يُحَدِّثُ حِينَ تَخَلَّفَ عَنِ النَّبِيِّ صلى الله عليه وسلم فِي غَزْوَةِ تَبُوكَ. بِطُولِهِ، قَالَ ابْنُ بُكَيْرٍ فِي حَدِيثِهِ وَلَقَدْ شَهِدْتُ مَعَ النَّبِيِّ صلى الله عليه وسلم لَيْلَةَ الْعَقَبَةِ حِينَ تَوَاثَقْنَا عَلَى الإِسْلاَمِ، وَمَا أُحِبُّ أَنَّ لِي بِهَا مَشْهَدَ بَدْرٍ وَإِنْ كَانَتْ بَدْرٌ، أَذْكَرَ فِي النَّاسِ مِنْهَا

Narrated 'Ubada bin As-Samit: Who had taken part in the battle of Badr with Allah's Messenger ﷺ and had been amongst his companions on the night of Al-`Aqaba Pledge: Allah's Messenger ﷺ, surrounded by a group of his companions said, "Come along and give me the pledge of allegiance that you will not worship anything besides Allah, will not steal, will not commit illegal sexual intercourse will not kill your children, will not utter; slander, invented by yourself, and will not disobey me if I order you to do something good. Whoever among you will respect and fulfill this pledge, will be rewarded by Allah. And if one of you commits any of these sins and is punished In this world then that will be his expiation for it, and if one of you commits any of these sins and Allah screens his sin, then his matter, will rest with Allah: If He will, He will punish him and if He will,. He will excuse him." So I gave the pledge of allegiance to him for these conditions. – Sahih al-Bukhari 3892

حَدَّثَنِي إِسْحَاقُ بْنُ مَنْصُورٍ، أَخْبَرَنَا يَعْقُوبُ بْنُ إِبْرَاهِيمَ، حَدَّثَنَا ابْنُ أَخِي ابْنِ شِهَابٍ، عَنْ عَمِّهِ، قَالَ أَخْبَرَنِي أَبُو إِدْرِيسَ، عَائِذُ اللَّهِ أَنَّ عُبَادَةَ بْنَ الصَّامِتِ ـ مِنَ الَّذِينَ شَهِدُوا بَدْرًا مَعَ رَسُولِ اللَّهِ صلى الله عليه وسلم ـ وَمِنْ أَصْحَابِهِ لَيْلَةَ الْعَقَبَةِ ـ أَخْبَرَهُ أَنَّ رَسُولَ اللَّهِ صلى الله عليه وسلم قَالَ وَحَوْلَهُ عِصَابَةٌ مِنْ أَصْحَابِهِ " تَعَالَوْا بَايِعُونِي عَلَى أَنْ لاَ تُشْرِكُوا بِاللَّهِ شَيْئًا، وَلاَ تَسْرِقُوا، وَلاَ تَزْنُوا، وَلاَ تَقْتُلُوا أَوْلاَدَكُمْ، وَلاَ تَأْتُونَ بِبُهْتَانٍ تَفْتَرُونَهُ بَيْنَ أَيْدِيكُمْ وَأَرْجُلِكُمْ، وَلاَ تَعْصُونِي فِي مَعْرُوفٍ، فَمَنْ وَفَى مِنْكُمْ فَأَجْرُهُ عَلَى اللَّهِ، وَمَنْ أَصَابَ مِنْ ذَلِكَ شَيْئًا فَعُوقِبَ بِهِ فِي الدُّنْيَا فَهْوَ لَهُ كَفَّارَةٌ، وَمَنْ أَصَابَ مِنْ ذَلِكَ شَيْئًا فَسَتَرَهُ اللَّهُ فَأَمْرُهُ إِلَى اللَّهِ، إِنْ شَاءَ عَاقَبَهُ، وَإِنْ شَاءَ عَفَا عَنْهُ ". قَالَ فَبَايَعْتُهُ عَلَى ذَلِكَ.

Then he ordered that fasting on this day (Ashura') should be observed
ثُمَّ أَمَرَ بِصَوْمِهِ

Narrated Ibn `Abbas: When the Prophet ﷺ arrived at Medina he found that the Jews observed fast on the day of 'Ashura'. They were asked the reason for the fast. They replied, "This is the day when Allah caused Moses and the children of Israel to have victory over Pharaoh, so we fast on this day as a sign of glorifying it." Allah's Messenger ﷺ said, "We are closer to Moses than you." Then he ordered that fasting on this day should be observed – .Sahih al-Bukhari 3943 [5]

حَدَّثَنَا زِيَادُ بْنُ أَيُّوبَ، حَدَّثَنَا هُشَيْمٌ، حَدَّثَنَا أَبُو بِشْرٍ، عَنْ سَعِيدِ بْنِ جُبَيْرٍ، عَنِ ابْنِ عَبَّاسٍ ـ رضى الله عنهما ـ قَالَ لَمَّا قَدِمَ النَّبِيُّ صلى الله عليه وسلم الْمَدِينَةَ وَجَدَ الْيَهُودَ يَصُومُونَ عَاشُورَاءَ، فَسُئِلُوا عَنْ ذَلِكَ، فَقَالُوا هَذَا الْيَوْمُ الَّذِي أَظْفَرَ اللَّهُ فِيهِ مُوسَى وَبَنِي إِسْرَائِيلَ عَلَى فِرْعَوْنَ، وَنَحْنُ نَصُومُهُ تَعْظِيمًا لَهُ، فَقَالَ رَسُولُ اللَّهِ صلى الله عليه وسلم " نَحْنُ أَوْلَى بِمُوسَى مِنْكُمْ ". ثُمَّ أَمَرَ بِصَوْمِهِ.

Narrated Salama bin Al-Akwa`: The Prophet ﷺ ordered a man from the tribe of Bani Aslam to announce amongst the people that whoever had eaten should fast the rest of the day, and whoever had not eaten should continue his fast, as that day was the day of 'Ashura' . – Sahih al-Bukhari 2007

حَدَّثَنَا الْمَكِّيُّ بْنُ إِبْرَاهِيمَ، حَدَّثَنَا يَزِيدُ، عَنْ سَلَمَةَ بْنِ الأَكْوَعِ ـ رضى الله عنه ـ قَالَ أَمَرَ النَّبِيُّ صلى الله عليه وسلم رَجُلاً مِنْ أَسْلَمَ أَنْ أَذِّنْ فِي النَّاسِ " أَنَّ مَنْ كَانَ أَكَلَ فَلْيَصُمْ بَقِيَّةَ يَوْمِهِ، وَمَنْ لَمْ يَكُنْ أَكَلَ فَلْيَصُمْ، فَإِنَّ الْيَوْمَ يَوْمُ عَاشُورَاءَ ".

Narrated Ibn `Abbas: When the Prophet ﷺ came to Medina, he found (the Jews) fasting on the day of 'Ashura' (i.e. 10th of Muharram). They used to say: "This is a great day on which Allah saved Moses and drowned the folk of Pharaoh. Moses observed the fast on this day, as a sign of gratitude to Allah." The Prophet ﷺ said, "I am closer to Moses than they." So, he observed the fast (on that day) and ordered the Muslims to fast on it. – Sahih al-Bukhari 3397

حَدَّثَنَا عَلِيُّ بْنُ عَبْدِ اللَّهِ، حَدَّثَنَا سُفْيَانُ، حَدَّثَنَا أَيُّوبُ السَّخْتِيَانِيُّ، عَنِ ابْنِ سَعِيدِ بْنِ جُبَيْرٍ، عَنْ أَبِيهِ، عَنِ ابْنِ عَبَّاسٍ ـ رضى الله عنهما أَنَّ النَّبِيَّ صلى الله عليه وسلم لَمَّا قَدِمَ الْمَدِينَةَ وَجَدَهُمْ يَصُومُونَ يَوْمًا، يَعْنِي عَاشُورَاءَ، فَقَالُوا هَذَا يَوْمٌ عَظِيمٌ، وَهْوَ يَوْمٌ نَجَّى اللَّهُ فِيهِ مُوسَى، وَأَغْرَقَ آلَ فِرْعَوْنَ، فَصَامَ مُوسَى شُكْرًا لِلَّهِ. فَقَالَ " أَنَا أَوْلَى بِمُوسَى مِنْهُمْ ". فَصَامَهُ وَأَمَرَ بِصِيَامِهِ.

[5] The command to fast 'Ashura was issued during the Prophet's time in Medina, likely in 1 AH (623 CE). Ramadan having been revealed the following year 2AH.

The Book of
Buwat
بوات

Ibn Ishaq said: The first thing the Prophet invaded was Al-Abwa, then Buwat, then Al-Ushayrah. – Sahih Al-Bukhari Volume 5 page 176

قال ابن إسحاق: اول ما غزا النبي الابواء ، ثم بواط ، ثم العشيرة.

......Jabir said: This is why you should apply scent to your mosques. It is reported on the same authority: We set out along with Allah's Messenger ﷺ on an expedition of Buwat. He (the Holy Prophet) was in search of al-Majdi b. 'Amr al-Juhani. (We had so meagre equipment) that five. Six or seven of us had one camel to ride and so we mounted it turn by turn. Once there wan. The turn of an Ansari to ride upon the camel. He made it kneel down to ride over it (and after having. Mounted it), he tried to raise it up but it hesitated. So he said. May there be curse of Allah upon you! Thereupon Allah's Messenger ﷺ said: Who is there to curse his camel? He said: Allah's Messenger, it' is I. Thereupon he said: Get down from the camel and let us not have in our company the cursed one. Don't curse your own selves, nor your children. Nor your belongings. There is the possibility that your curse may synchronies with the time when Allah is about to confer upon you what you demand and thus your prayer may be readily responded. ...... – Sahih Muslim 3006-3014

..... فَقَالَ جَابِرٌ فَمِنْ هُنَاكَ جَعَلْتُمُ الْخَلُوقَ فِي مَسَاجِدِكُمْ . سِرْنَا مَعَ رَسُولِ اللَّهِ صلى الله عليه وسلم فِي غَزْوَةِ بَطْنِ بُوَاطٍ وَهُوَ يَطْلُبُ الْمَجْدِيَّ بْنَ عَمْرٍو الْجُهَنِيَّ وَكَانَ النَّاضِحُ يَعْتَقِبُهُ مِنَّا الْخَمْسَةُ وَالسِّتَّةُ وَالسَّبْعَةُ فَدَارَتْ عُقْبَةُ رَجُلٍ مِنَ الأَنْصَارِ عَلَى نَاضِحٍ لَهُ فَأَنَاخَهُ فَرَكِبَهُ ثُمَّ بَعَثَهُ فَتَلَدَّنَ عَلَيْهِ بَعْضَ التَّلَدُّنِ فَقَالَ لَهُ شَأْ لَعَنَكَ اللَّهُ . فَقَالَ رَسُولُ اللَّهِ صلى الله عليه وسلم " مَنْ هَذَا اللاَّعِنُ بَعِيرَهُ " . قَالَ أَنَا يَا رَسُولَ اللَّهِ . قَالَ " انْزِلْ عَنْهُ فَلاَ تَصْحَبْنَا بِمَلْعُونٍ لاَ تَدْعُوا عَلَى أَنْفُسِكُمْ وَلاَ تَدْعُوا عَلَى أَوْلاَدِكُمْ وَلاَ تَدْعُوا عَلَى أَمْوَالِكُمْ لاَ تُوَافِقُوا مِنَ اللَّهِ سَاعَةً يُسْأَلُ فِيهَا عَطَاءٌ فَيَسْتَجِيبُ لَكُمْ " ...

The Book of
Al-'Ushayrah
الْعُسَيْرَةُ

Narrated Abu 'Is-haq: Once, while I was sitting beside Zaid bin Al-Arqam, he was asked, "How many Ghazwat did the Prophet undertake?" Zaid replied, "Nineteen." They said, "In how many Ghazwat did you join him?" He replied, "Seventeen." I asked, "Which of these was the first?" He replied, "Al-`Ashira or Al- `Ashiru." – Al-Bukhari 3949

حَدَّثَنِي عَبْدُ اللَّهِ بْنُ مُحَمَّدٍ، حَدَّثَنَا وَهْبٌ، حَدَّثَنَا شُعْبَةُ، عَنْ أَبِي إِسْحَاقَ، كُنْتُ إِلَى جَنْبِ زَيْدِ بْنِ أَرْقَمَ، فَقِيلَ لَهُ كَمْ غَزَا النَّبِيُّ صلى الله عليه وسلم مِنْ غَزْوَةٍ قَالَ تِسْعَ عَشْرَةَ. قِيلَ كَمْ غَزَوْتَ أَنْتَ مَعَهُ قَالَ سَبْعَ عَشْرَةَ. قُلْتُ فَأَيُّهُمْ كَانَتْ أَوَّلَ قَالَ الْعُسَيْرَةُ أَوِ الْعُشَيْرُ. فَذَكَرْتُ لِقَتَادَةَ فَقَالَ الْعُشَيْرُ.

Ramadan was revealed, fasting in Ramadan became an obligation
نَزَلَ رَمَضَانُ كَانَ رَمَضَانُ الْفَرِيضَةَ

Narrated Aisha: During the Pre-lslamic Period of ignorance the Quraish used to observe fasting on the day of 'Ashura', and the Prophet ﷺ himself used to observe fasting on it too. But when he came to Medina, he fasted on that day and ordered the Muslims to fast on it. When (the order of compulsory fasting in) Ramadan was revealed, fasting in Ramadan became an obligation, and fasting on 'Ashura' was given up, and who ever wished to fast (on it) did so, and whoever did not wish to fast on it, did not fast – .Sahih al-Bukhari 4504 [6]
حَدَّثَنِي مُحَمَّدُ بْنُ الْمُثَنَّى، حَدَّثَنَا يَحْيَى، حَدَّثَنَا هِشَامٌ، قَالَ أَخْبَرَنِي أَبِي، عَنْ عَائِشَةَ ـ رضى الله عنها ـ قَالَتْ كَانَ يَوْمُ عَاشُورَاءَ تَصُومُهُ قُرَيْشٌ فِي الْجَاهِلِيَّةِ، وَكَانَ النَّبِيُّ صلى الله عليه وسلم يَصُومُهُ، فَلَمَّا قَدِمَ الْمَدِينَةَ صَامَهُ وَأَمَرَ بِصِيَامِهِ، فَلَمَّا نَزَلَ رَمَضَانُ كَانَ رَمَضَانُ الْفَرِيضَةَ، وَتُرِكَ عَاشُورَاءُ، فَكَانَ مَنْ شَاءَ صَامَهُ، وَمَنْ شَاءَ لَمْ يَصُمْهُ.

Narrated `Aisha: Allah's Messenger ﷺ ordered (the Muslims) to fast on the day of 'Ashura', and when fasting in the month of Ramadan was prescribed, it became optional for one to fast on that day ('Ashura') or not – .Sahih al-Bukhari 2001
حَدَّثَنَا أَبُو الْيَمَانِ، أَخْبَرَنَا شُعَيْبٌ، عَنِ الزُّهْرِيِّ، قَالَ أَخْبَرَنِي عُرْوَةُ بْنُ الزُّبَيْرِ، أَنَّ عَائِشَةَ ـ رضى الله عنها ـ قَالَتْ كَانَ رَسُولُ اللَّهِ صلى الله عليه وسلم أَمَرَ بِصِيَامِ يَوْمِ عَاشُورَاءَ، فَلَمَّا فُرِضَ رَمَضَانُ كَانَ مَنْ شَاءَ صَامَ، وَمَنْ شَاءَ أَفْطَرَ.

---

[6] Revealed: In Sha'ban 2 AH (~Feb/March 624 CE)
First Ramadan fasting observed: In Ramadan 2 AH (~March/April 624 CE)
Battle of Badr: Took place in Ramadan 17, 2 AH, during that same month.

The Book of
Ghazwa of Badr
غزوة بدر

Had gone out to meet the caravans of (Quraish), but Allah caused them (i.e. Muslims) to meet their enemy unexpectedly.
يُرِيدُ عِيرَ قُرَيْشٍ، حَتَّى جَمَعَ اللَّهُ بَيْنَهُمْ وَبَيْنَ عَدُوِّهِمْ عَلَى غَيْرِ مِيعَادٍ

If you fear treachery on the part of a people, break off with them in a like manner. Allah does not like the treacherous. – Surah Al-Anfal 8:58
وَإِمَّا تَخَافَنَّ مِن قَوْمٍ خِيَانَةً فَٱنۢبِذْ إِلَيْهِمْ عَلَىٰ سَوَآءٍ ۚ إِنَّ ٱللَّهَ لَا يُحِبُّ ٱلْخَآئِنِينَ

Narrated Sa`id bin Jubair: I asked Ibn `Abbas regarding Surat-al-Anfal. He said, "It was revealed in connection with the Battle of Badr." – Al-Bukhari 4645
حَدَّثَنِي مُحَمَّدُ بْنُ عَبْدِ الرَّحِيمِ، حَدَّثَنَا سَعِيدُ بْنُ سُلَيْمَانَ، أَخْبَرَنَا هُشَيْمٌ، أَخْبَرَنَا أَبُو بِشْرٍ، عَنْ سَعِيدِ بْنِ جُبَيْرٍ، قَالَ قُلْتُ لاِبْنِ عَبَّاسٍ ـ رضى الله عنهما ـ سُورَةُ الأَنْفَالِ قَالَ نَزَلَتْ فِي بَدْرٍ. الشَّوْكَةُ الْحَدُّ {مُرْدَفِينَ} فَوْجًا بَعْدَ فَوْجٍ، رَدِفَنِي وَأَرْدَفَنِي جَاءَ بَعْدِي {ذُوقُوا} بَاشِرُوا وَجَرِّبُوا وَلَيْسَ هَذَا مِنْ ذَوْقِ الْفَمِ {فَيَرْكُمَهُ} يَجْمَعُهُ. {شَرِّدْ} فَرِّقْ {وَإِنْ جَنَحُوا} طَلَبُوا {يُثْخِنَ} يَغْلِبَ. وَقَالَ مُجَاهِدٌ {مُكَاءً} إِدْخَالُ أَصَابِعِهِمْ فِي أَفْوَاهِهِمْ وَ{تَصْدِيَةً} الصَّفِيرُ {لِيُثْبِتُوكَ} لِيَحْبِسُوكَ.

Narrated Ka`b bin Malik: I never failed to join Allah's Messenger ﷺ in any of his Ghazawat except in the Ghazwa of Tabuk. However, I did not take part in the Ghazwa of Badr, but none who failed to take part in it, was blamed, for Allah's Messenger ﷺ had gone out to meet the caravans of (Quraish, but Allah caused them (i.e. Muslims) to meet their enemy unexpectedly (with no previous intention) . – Sahih Al-Bukhari 3951
حَدَّثَنِي يَحْيَى بْنُ بُكَيْرٍ، حَدَّثَنَا اللَّيْثُ، عَنْ عُقَيْلٍ، عَنِ ابْنِ شِهَابٍ، عَنْ عَبْدِ الرَّحْمَنِ بْنِ عَبْدِ اللَّهِ بْنِ كَعْبٍ، أَنَّ عَبْدَ اللَّهِ بْنَ كَعْبٍ، قَالَ سَمِعْتُ كَعْبَ بْنَ مَالِكٍ ـ رضى الله عنه ـ يَقُولُ لَمْ أَتَخَلَّفْ عَنْ رَسُولِ اللَّهِ صلى الله عليه وسلم فِي غَزْوَةٍ غَزَاهَا إِلاَّ فِي غَزْوَةِ تَبُوكَ، غَيْرَ أَنِّي تَخَلَّفْتُ عَنْ غَزْوَةِ بَدْرٍ، وَلَمْ يُعَاتَبْ أَحَدٌ تَخَلَّفَ عَنْهَا، إِنَّمَا خَرَجَ رَسُولُ اللَّهِ صلى الله عليه وسلم يُرِيدُ عِيرَ قُرَيْشٍ، حَتَّى جَمَعَ اللَّهُ بَيْنَهُمْ وَبَيْنَ عَدُوِّهِمْ عَلَى غَيْرِ مِيعَادٍ

Narrated Ibn `Abbas: The Prophet ﷺ , while in a tent (on the day of the battle of Badr) said, "O Allah! I ask you the fulfillment of Your Covenant and Promise. O Allah! If You wish (to destroy the believers) You will never be worshipped after today." Abu Bakr caught him by the hand and said, "This is sufficient, O Allah's Apostle! You have asked Allah pressingly." The Prophet ﷺ was clad in his armor at that time. He went out, saying to me: "There multitude will be put to flight and they will show their backs. Nay, but the Hour is their appointed time (for their full recompense) and that Hour will be more grievous and more bitter (than their worldly failure)." (54.45-46) Khalid said that was on the day of the battle of Badr. – Al-Bukhari 2915
حَدَّثَنِي مُحَمَّدُ بْنُ الْمُثَنَّى، حَدَّثَنَا عَبْدُ الْوَهَّابِ، حَدَّثَنَا خَالِدٌ، عَنْ عِكْرِمَةَ، عَنِ ابْنِ عَبَّاسٍ ـ رضى الله عنهما ـ قَالَ قَالَ النَّبِيُّ صلى الله عليه وسلم وَهْوَ فِي قُبَّةٍ " اللَّهُمَّ إِنِّي أَنْشُدُكَ عَهْدَكَ وَوَعْدَكَ، اللَّهُمَّ إِنْ شِئْتَ لَمْ تُعْبَدْ بَعْدَ الْيَوْمِ ". فَأَخَذَ أَبُو بَكْرٍ بِيَدِهِ فَقَالَ حَسْبُكَ يَا رَسُولَ اللَّهِ، فَقَدْ أَلْحَحْتَ عَلَى رَبِّكَ، وَهْوَ فِي الدِّرْعِ، فَخَرَجَ وَهْوَ يَقُولُ {سَيُهْزَمُ الْجَمْعُ وَيُوَلُّونَ الدُّبُرَ * بَلِ السَّاعَةُ مَوْعِدُهُمْ وَالسَّاعَةُ أَدْهَى وَأَمَرُّ }. وَقَالَ وُهَيْبٌ حَدَّثَنَا خَالِدٌ يَوْمَ بَدْرٍ

Narrated `Abdur-Rahman bin `Auf: I got an agreement written between me and Umaiya bin Khalaf that Umaiya would look after my property (or family) in Mecca and I would look after his in Medina. When I mentioned the word 'Ar64 Rahman' in the documents, Umaiya said, "I do not know 'Ar-Rahman.' Write down to me your name, (with which you called yourself) in the Pre-Islamic Period of Ignorance." So, I wrote my name ' `Abdu `Amr'. On the day (of the battle) of Badr, when all the people went to sleep, I went up the hill to protect him. Bilal(1) saw him (i.e. Umaiya) and went to a gathering of Ansar and said, "(Here is) Umaiya bin Khalaf! Woe to me if he escapes!" So, a group of Ansar went out with Bilal to follow us (`Abdur-Rahman and Umaiya). Being afraid that they would catch us, I left Umaiya's son for them to keep them busy but the Ansar killed the son and insisted on following us. Umaiya was a fat man, and when they approached us, I told him to kneel down, and he knelt, and I laid myself on him to protect him, but the Ansar killed him by passing their swords underneath me, and one of them injured my foot with his sword. (The sub narrator said, " `Abdur-Rahman used to show us the trace of the wound on the back of his foot.") – Al-Bukhari 2301

حَدَّثَنَا عَبْدُ الْعَزِيزِ بْنُ عَبْدِ اللَّهِ، قَالَ حَدَّثَنِي يُوسُفُ بْنُ الْمَاجِشُونِ، عَنْ صَالِحِ بْنِ إِبْرَاهِيمَ بْنِ عَبْدِ الرَّحْمَنِ بْنِ عَوْفٍ، عَنْ أَبِيهِ، عَنْ جَدِّهِ عَبْدِ الرَّحْمَنِ بْنِ عَوْفٍ ـ رضى الله عنه ـ قَالَ كَاتَبْتُ أُمَيَّةَ بْنَ خَلَفٍ كِتَابًا بِأَنْ يَحْفَظَنِي فِي صَاغِيَتِي بِمَكَّةَ، وَأَحْفَظَهُ فِي صَاغِيَتِهِ بِالْمَدِينَةِ، فَلَمَّا ذَكَرْتُ الرَّحْمَنَ قَالَ لاَ أَعْرِفُ الرَّحْمَنَ، كَاتِبْنِي بِاسْمِكَ الَّذِي كَانَ فِي الْجَاهِلِيَّةِ. فَكَاتَبْتُهُ عَبْدُ عَمْرٍو فَلَمَّا كَانَ فِي يَوْمِ بَدْرٍ خَرَجْتُ إِلَى جَبَلٍ لأُحْرِزَهُ حِينَ نَامَ النَّاسُ فَأَبْصَرَهُ بِلاَلٌ فَخَرَجَ حَتَّى وَقَفَ عَلَى مَجْلِسٍ مِنَ الأَنْصَارِ فَقَالَ أُمَيَّةُ بْنُ خَلَفٍ، لاَ نَجَوْتُ إِنْ نَجَا أُمَيَّةُ. فَخَرَجَ مَعَهُ فَرِيقٌ مِنَ الأَنْصَارِ فِي آثَارِنَا، فَلَمَّا خَشِيتُ أَنْ يَلْحَقُونَا خَلَّفْتُ لَهُمُ ابْنَهُ، لأَشْغَلَهُمْ فَقَتَلُوهُ ثُمَّ أَبَوْا حَتَّى يَتْبَعُونَا، وَكَانَ رَجُلاً ثَقِيلاً، فَلَمَّا أَدْرَكُونَا قُلْتُ لَهُ ابْرُكْ. فَبَرَكَ، فَأَلْقَيْتُ عَلَيْهِ نَفْسِي لأَمْنَعَهُ، فَتَخَلَّلُوهُ بِالسُّيُوفِ مِنْ تَحْتِي، حَتَّى قَتَلُوهُ، وَأَصَابَ أَحَدُهُمْ رِجْلِي بِسَيْفِهِ، وَكَانَ عَبْدُ الرَّحْمَنِ بْنُ عَوْفٍ يُرِينَا ذَلِكَ الأَثَرَ فِي ظَهْرِ قَدَمِهِ. قَالَ أَبُو عَبْد اللَّهِ سَمِعَ يُوسُفُ صَالِحًا وَإِبْرَاهِيمُ أَبَاهُ

When two groups among you almost faltered, but Allah was their Protector. So in Allah let the believers put their trust. Allah had given you victory at Badr, when you were weak. So fear Allah, that you may be thankful. When you said to the believers, "Is it not enough for you that your Lord has reinforced you with three thousand angels, sent down?" It is; but if you persevere and remain cautious, and they attack you suddenly, your Lord will reinforce you with five thousand angels, well trained. – Surah Al-Imran 3:122-125

إِذْ هَمَّت طَّآئِفَتَانِ مِنكُمْ أَن تَفْشَلَا وَٱللَّهُ وَلِيُّهُمَا ۗ وَعَلَى ٱللَّهِ فَلْيَتَوَكَّلِ ٱلْمُؤْمِنُونَ وَلَقَدْ نَصَرَكُمُ ٱللَّهُ بِبَدْرٍ وَأَنتُمْ أَذِلَّةٌ ۖ فَٱتَّقُوا۟ ٱللَّهَ لَعَلَّكُمْ تَشْكُرُونَ إِذْ تَقُولُ لِلْمُؤْمِنِينَ أَلَن يَكْفِيَكُمْ أَن يُمِدَّكُمْ رَبُّكُم بِثَلَٰثَةِ ءَالَٰفٍ مِّنَ ٱلْمَلَٰٓئِكَةِ مُنزَلِينَ بَلَىٰٓ ۚ إِن تَصْبِرُوا۟ وَتَتَّقُوا۟ وَيَأْتُوكُم مِّن فَوْرِهِمْ هَٰذَا يُمْدِدْكُمْ رَبُّكُم بِخَمْسَةِ ءَالَٰفٍ مِّنَ ٱلْمَلَٰٓئِكَةِ مُسَوِّمِينَ

Narrated Ibn `Abbas: The Prophet ﷺ said on the day (of the battle) of Badr, "This is Gabriel holding the head of his horse and equipped with arms for the battle. – Al-Bukhari 3995

حَدَّثَنِي إِبْرَاهِيمُ بْنُ مُوسَى، أَخْبَرَنَا عَبْدُ الْوَهَّابِ، حَدَّثَنَا خَالِدٌ، عَنْ عِكْرِمَةَ، عَنِ ابْنِ عَبَّاسٍ ـ رضى الله عنهما ـ أَنَّ النَّبِيَّ صلى الله عليه وسلم قَالَ يَوْمَ بَدْرٍ " هَذَا جِبْرِيلُ آخِذٌ بِرَأْسِ فَرَسِهِ ـ عَلَيْهِ أَدَاةُ الْحَرْبِ "

Narrated `Abdullah (bin Masud): On the day of Badr, Al-Miqdad said, "O Allah's Messenger ﷺ ! We do not say to you as the children of Israel said to Moses, 'Go you and your Lord and fight you two; we are sitting here, (5.24) but (we say), "Proceed, and we are with you." That seemed to delight Allah's Messenger ﷺ greatly. – Al-Bukhari 4609

حَدَّثَنَا أَبُو نُعَيْمٍ، حَدَّثَنَا إِسْرَائِيلُ، عَنْ مُخَارِقٍ، عَنْ طَارِقِ بْنِ شِهَابٍ، سَمِعْتُ ابْنَ مَسْعُودٍ ـ رضى الله عنه ـ قَالَ شَهِدْتُ مِنَ الْمِقْدَادِ ح وَحَدَّثَنِي حَمْدَانُ بْنُ عُمَرَ حَدَّثَنَا أَبُو النَّضْرِ حَدَّثَنَا الأَشْجَعِيُّ عَنْ سُفْيَانَ عَنْ مُخَارِقٍ عَنْ طَارِقٍ عَنْ عَبْدِ اللَّهِ قَالَ قَالَ الْمِقْدَادُ يَوْمَ بَدْرٍ يَا رَسُولَ اللَّهِ إِنَّا لاَ نَقُولُ لَكَ كَمَا قَالَتْ بَنُو إِسْرَائِيلَ لِمُوسَى {فَاذْهَبْ أَنْتَ وَرَبُّكَ فَقَاتِلاَ إِنَّا هَا هُنَا قَاعِدُونَ} وَلَكِنِ امْضِ وَنَحْنُ مَعَكَ. فَكَأَنَّهُ سُرِّيَ عَنْ رَسُولِ اللَّهِ صلى الله عليه وسلم. وَرَوَاهُ وَكِيعٌ عَنْ سُفْيَانَ عَنْ مُخَارِقٍ عَنْ طَارِقٍ أَنَّ الْمِقْدَادَ قَالَ ذَلِكَ لِلنَّبِيِّ صلى الله عليه وسلم

Narrated Al-Bara: The companions of (the Prophet) Muhammad who took part in Badr, told me that their number was that of Saul's (i.e. Talut's) companions who crossed the river (of Jordan) with him and they were over three-hundred-and-ten men. By Allah, none crossed the river with him but a believer. (See Qur'an 2:249) – Al-Bukhari 3957

حَدَّثَنَا عَمْرُو بْنُ خَالِدٍ، حَدَّثَنَا زُهَيْرٌ، حَدَّثَنَا أَبُو إِسْحَاقَ، قَالَ سَمِعْتُ الْبَرَاءَ ـ رضى الله عنه ـ يَقُولُ حَدَّثَنِي أَصْحَابُ، مُحَمَّدٍ صلى الله عليه وسلم مِمَّنْ شَهِدَ بَدْرًا أَنَّهُمْ كَانُوا عِدَّةَ أَصْحَابِ طَالُوتَ الَّذِينَ جَازُوا مَعَهُ النَّهَرَ، بِضْعَةَ عَشَرَ وَثَلاَثَمِائَةٍ. قَالَ الْبَرَاءُ لاَ وَاللَّهِ مَا جَاوَزَ مَعَهُ النَّهَرَ إِلاَّ مُؤْمِنٌ

Narrated Abu Usaid: On the day (of the battle) of Badr when we stood in rows against (the army of) Quraish and they stood in rows against us, the Prophet ﷺ said, "When they do come near you, throw arrows at them."–Al-Bukhari 2900

حَدَّثَنَا أَبُو نُعَيْمٍ، حَدَّثَنَا عَبْدُ الرَّحْمَنِ بْنُ الْغَسِيلِ، عَنْ حَمْزَةَ بْنِ أَبِي أُسَيْدٍ، عَنْ أَبِيهِ، قَالَ قَالَ النَّبِيُّ صلى الله عليه وسلم يَوْمَ بَدْرٍ حِينَ صَفَفْنَا لِقُرَيْشٍ وَصَفُّوا لَنَا " إِذَا أَكْثَبُوكُمْ فَعَلَيْكُمْ بِالنَّبْلِ ".

Narrated Abu Usaid: On the day of (the battle of) Badr, Allah's Messenger ﷺ said to us, "When your enemy comes near to you (i.e. overcome you by sheer number), shoot at them but use your arrows sparingly."–Al-Bukhari 3985

حَدَّثَنِي مُحَمَّدُ بْنُ عَبْدِ الرَّحِيمِ، حَدَّثَنَا أَبُو أَحْمَدَ الزُّبَيْرِيُّ، حَدَّثَنَا عَبْدُ الرَّحْمَنِ بْنُ الْغَسِيلِ، عَنْ حَمْزَةَ بْنِ أَبِي أُسَيْدٍ، وَالْمُنْذِرِ بْنِ أَبِي أُسَيْدٍ، عَنْ أَبِي أُسَيْدٍ ـ رضى الله عنه ـ قَالَ قَالَ لَنَا رَسُولُ اللَّهِ صلى الله عليه وسلم يَوْمَ بَدْرٍ " إِذَا أَكْثَبُوكُمْ ـ يَعْنِي كَثَرُوكُمْ ـ فَارْمُوهُمْ، وَاسْتَبْقُوا نَبْلَكُمْ "

Narrated `Abdur-Rahman bin `Auf: While I was fighting in the front file on the day (of the battle) of Badr, suddenly I looked behind and saw on my right and left two young boys and did not feel safe by standing between them. Then one of them asked me secretly so that his companion may not hear, "O Uncle! Show me Abu Jahl." I said, "O nephew! What will you do to him?" He said, "I have promised Allah that if I see him (i.e. Abu Jahl), I will either kill him or be killed before I kill him." then the other said the same to me secretly so that his companion should not hear. I would not have been pleased to be in between two other men instead of them. Then I pointed him (i.e. Abu Jahl) out to them. Both of them attacked him like two hawks till they knocked him down. Those two boys were the sons of 'Afra' (i.e. an Ansari woman).–Al-Bukhari 3988

حَدَّثَنِي يَعْقُوبُ، حَدَّثَنَا إِبْرَاهِيمُ بْنُ سَعْدٍ، عَنْ أَبِيهِ، عَنْ جَدِّهِ، قَالَ قَالَ عَبْدُ الرَّحْمَنِ بْنُ عَوْفٍ إِنِّي لَفِي الصَّفِّ يَوْمَ بَدْرٍ إِذِ الْتَفَتُّ، فَإِذَا عَنْ يَمِينِي وَعَنْ يَسَارِي فَتَيَانِ حَدِيثَا السِّنِّ، فَكَأَنِّي لَمْ آمَنْ بِمَكَانِهِمَا، إِذْ قَالَ لِي أَحَدُهُمَا سِرًّا مِنْ صَاحِبِهِ يَا عَمِّ أَرِنِي أَبَا جَهْلٍ. فَقُلْتُ يَا ابْنَ أَخِي، وَمَا تَصْنَعُ بِهِ قَالَ عَاهَدْتُ اللَّهَ إِنْ رَأَيْتُهُ أَنْ أَقْتُلَهُ أَوْ أَمُوتَ دُونَهُ. فَقَالَ لِي الآخَرُ سِرًّا مِنْ صَاحِبِهِ مِثْلَهُ قَالَ فَمَا سَرَّنِي أَنِّي بَيْنَ رَجُلَيْنِ مَكَانَهُمَا، فَأَشَرْتُ لَهُمَا إِلَيْهِ، فَشَدَّا عَلَيْهِ مِثْلَ الصَّقْرَيْنِ حَتَّى ضَرَبَاهُ، وَهُمَا ابْنَا عَفْرَاءَ.

Narrated `Urwa: Az-Zubair said, "I met Ubaida bin Sa`id bin Al-As on the day (of the battle) of Badr and he was covered with armor; so much that only his eyes were visible. He was surnamed Abu Dhat-al-Karish. He said (proudly), 'I am Abu-al-Karish.' I attacked him with the spear and pierced his eye and he died. I put my foot over his body to pull (that spear) out, but even then I had to use a great force to take it out as its both ends were bent." `Urwa said, "Later on Allah's Messenger ﷺ asked Az-Zubair for the spear and he gave it to him. When Allah's Messenger ﷺ died, Az-Zubair took it back. After that Abu Bakr demanded it and he gave it to him, and when Abu Bakr died, Az-Zubair took it back. `Umar then demanded it from him and he gave it to him. When `Umar died, Az-Zubair took it back, and then `Uthman demanded it from him and he gave it to him. When `Uthman was martyred, the spear remained with `Ali's offspring. Then `Abdullah bin Az-Zubair demanded it back, and it remained with him till he was martyred.–Al-Bukhari 3998

حَدَّثَنِي عُبَيْدُ بْنُ إِسْمَاعِيلَ، حَدَّثَنَا أَبُو أُسَامَةَ، عَنْ هِشَامِ بْنِ عُرْوَةَ، عَنْ أَبِيهِ، قَالَ قَالَ الزُّبَيْرُ لَقِيتُ يَوْمَ بَدْرٍ عُبَيْدَةَ بْنَ سَعِيدِ بْنِ الْعَاصِ وَهْوَ مُدَجَّجٌ لاَ يُرَى مِنْهُ إِلاَّ عَيْنَاهُ، وَهْوَ يُكْنَى أَبُو ذَاتِ الْكَرِشِ، فَقَالَ أَنَا أَبُو ذَاتِ الْكَرِشِ. فَحَمَلْتُ عَلَيْهِ بِالْعَنَزَةِ، فَطَعَنْتُهُ فِي عَيْنِهِ فَمَاتَ. قَالَ هِشَامٌ فَأُخْبِرْتُ أَنَّ الزُّبَيْرَ قَالَ لَقَدْ وَضَعْتُ رِجْلِي عَلَيْهِ ثُمَّ تَمَطَّأْتُ، فَكَانَ الْجَهْدَ أَنْ نَزَعْتُهَا وَقَدِ انْثَنَى طَرَفَاهَا. قَالَ عُرْوَةُ فَسَأَلَهُ إِيَّاهَا رَسُولُ اللَّهِ صلى الله عليه وسلم فَأَعْطَاهُ، فَلَمَّا قُبِضَ رَسُولُ اللَّهِ صلى الله عليه وسلم أَخَذَهَا، ثُمَّ طَلَبَهَا أَبُو بَكْرٍ فَأَعْطَاهُ، فَلَمَّا قُبِضَ أَبُو بَكْرٍ سَأَلَهَا إِيَّاهُ عُمَرُ فَأَعْطَاهُ إِيَّاهَا، فَلَمَّا قُبِضَ عُمَرُ أَخَذَهَا، ثُمَّ طَلَبَهَا عُثْمَانُ مِنْهُ فَأَعْطَاهُ إِيَّاهَا، فَلَمَّا قُتِلَ عُثْمَانُ وَقَعَتْ عِنْدَ آلِ عَلِيٍّ، فَطَلَبَهَا عَبْدُ اللَّهِ بْنُ الزُّبَيْرِ، فَكَانَتْ عِنْدَهُ حَتَّى قُتِلَ

Narrated Abu 'Is-haq: A man asked Al-Bara' and I was listening, "Did `Ali take part in (the battle of) Badr?" Al-Bara' said, "(Yes). He even met (his enemies) in a duel and was clad in two armors (one over the other).–Al-Bukhari 3970

حَدَّثَنِي أَحْمَدُ بْنُ سَعِيدٍ أَبُو عَبْدِ اللَّهِ، حَدَّثَنَا إِسْحَاقُ بْنُ مَنْصُورٍ، حَدَّثَنَا إِبْرَاهِيمُ بْنُ يُوسُفَ، عَنْ أَبِيهِ، عَنْ أَبِي إِسْحَاقَ، سَأَلَ رَجُلٌ الْبَرَاءَ وَأَنَا أَسْمَعُ، قَالَ أَشَهِدَ عَلِيٌّ بَدْرًا قَالَ بَارَزَ وَظَاهَرَ.

Narrated Qais bin Ubad: `Ali said, "I will be the first to kneel before the Beneficent on the Day of Resurrection because of the dispute." Qais said; This Verse: 'These two opponents (believers and disbelievers dispute with each other about their Lord,' (22.19) was revealed in connection with those who came out for the Battle of Badr, i.e. `Ali, Hamza, 'Ubaida, Shaiba bin Rabi`a, `Utba bin Rabi`a and Al-Walid bin `Utba.–Al-Bukhari 4744

حَدَّثَنَا حَجَّاجُ بْنُ مِنْهَالٍ، حَدَّثَنَا مُعْتَمِرُ بْنُ سُلَيْمَانَ، قَالَ سَمِعْتُ أَبِي قَالَ، حَدَّثَنَا أَبُو مِجْلَزٍ، عَنْ قَيْسِ بْنِ عُبَادٍ، عَنْ عَلِيِّ بْنِ أَبِي طَالِبٍ ـ رضى الله عنه ـ قَالَ أَنَا أَوَّلُ، مَنْ يَجْثُو بَيْنَ يَدَىِ الرَّحْمَنِ لِلْخُصُومَةِ يَوْمَ الْقِيَامَةِ. قَالَ قَيْسٌ وَفِيهِمْ نَزَلَتْ {هَذَانِ خَصْمَانِ اخْتَصَمُوا فِي رَبِّهِمْ} قَالَ هُمُ الَّذِينَ بَارَزُوا يَوْمَ بَدْرٍ عَلِيٌّ وَحَمْزَةُ وَعُبَيْدَةُ وَشَيْبَةُ بْنُ رَبِيعَةَ وَعُتْبَةُ بْنُ رَبِيعَةَ وَالْوَلِيدُ بْنُ عُتْبَةَ

Narrated Anas: The Prophetﷺ said, "Who will go and see what has happened to Abu Jahl?" Ibn Mas`ud went and found that the two sons of 'Afra had struck him fatally (and he was in his last breaths). `Abdullah bin Mas`ud said, "Are you Abu Jahl?" And took him by the beard. Abu Jahl said, "Can there be a man superior to one you have killed or one whom his own folk have killed?"–Al-Bukhari 3962 also Bukhari 3963

حَدَّثَنَا أَحْمَدُ بْنُ يُونُسَ، حَدَّثَنَا زُهَيْرٌ، حَدَّثَنَا سُلَيْمَانُ التَّيْمِيُّ، أَنَّ أَنَسًا، حَدَّثَهُمْ قَالَ قَالَ النَّبِيُّ صلى الله عليه وسلم ح وَحَدَّثَنِي عَمْرُو بْنُ خَالِدٍ حَدَّثَنَا زُهَيْرٌ عَنْ سُلَيْمَانَ التَّيْمِيِّ عَنْ أَنَسٍ ـ رضى الله عنه ـ قَالَ قَالَ النَّبِيُّ صلى الله عليه وسلم " مَنْ يَنْظُرُ مَا صَنَعَ أَبُو جَهْلٍ " فَانْطَلَقَ ابْنُ مَسْعُودٍ، فَوَجَدَهُ قَدْ ضَرَبَهُ ابْنَا عَفْرَاءَ حَتَّى بَرَدَ قَالَ آأَنْتَ أَبُو جَهْلٍ قَالَ فَأَخَذَ بِلِحْيَتِهِ. قَالَ وَهَلْ فَوْقَ رَجُلٍ قَتَلْتُمُوهُ أَوْ رَجُلٍ قَتَلَهُ قَوْمُهُ؟ قَالَ أَحْمَدُ بْنُ يُونُسَ أَنْتَ أَبُو جَهْلٍ

Narrated Jabir bin `Abdullah: When it was the day (of the battle) of Badr, prisoners of war were brought including Al-Abbas who was undressed. The Prophetﷺ looked for a shirt for him. It was found that the shirt of `Abdullah bin Ubai would do, so the Prophetﷺ let him wear it. That was the reason why the Prophetﷺ took off and gave his own shirt to `Abdullah. (The narrator adds, "He had done the Prophetﷺ some favor for which the Prophet liked to reward him.")– Al-Bukhari 3008

حَدَّثَنَا عَبْدُ اللَّهِ بْنُ مُحَمَّدٍ، حَدَّثَنَا ابْنُ عُيَيْنَةَ، عَنْ عَمْرٍو، سَمِعَ جَابِرَ بْنَ عَبْدِ اللَّهِ ـ رضى الله عنهما ـ قَالَ لَمَّا كَانَ يَوْمَ بَدْرٍ أُتِيَ بِأُسَارَى، وَأُتِيَ بِالْعَبَّاسِ وَلَمْ يَكُنْ عَلَيْهِ ثَوْبٌ، فَنَظَرَ النَّبِيُّ صلى الله عليه وسلم لَهُ قَمِيصًا فَوَجَدُوا قَمِيصَ عَبْدِ اللَّهِ بْنِ أُبَىٍّ يَقْدُرُ عَلَيْهِ، فَكَسَاهُ النَّبِيُّ صلى الله عليه وسلم إِيَّاهُ، فَلِذَلِكَ نَزَعَ النَّبِيُّ صلى الله عليه وسلم قَمِيصَهُ الَّذِي أَلْبَسَهُ. قَالَ ابْنُ عُيَيْنَةَ كَانَتْ لَهُ عِنْدَ النَّبِيِّ صلى الله عليه وسلم يَدٌ فَأَحَبَّ أَنْ يُكَافِئَهُ.

Narrated Jubair bin Mut`im: The Prophetﷺ talked about war prisoners of Badr saying, "Had Al-Mut`im bin Adi been alive and interceded with me for these mean people, I would have freed them for his sake."–Al-Bukhari 3139 also Bukhari 4023

حَدَّثَنَا إِسْحَاقُ بْنُ مَنْصُورٍ، أَخْبَرَنَا عَبْدُ الرَّزَّاقِ، أَخْبَرَنَا مَعْمَرٌ، عَنِ الزُّهْرِيِّ، عَنْ مُحَمَّدِ بْنِ جُبَيْرٍ، عَنْ أَبِيهِ ـ رضى الله عنه ـ أَنَّ النَّبِيَّ صلى الله عليه وسلم قَالَ فِي أُسَارَى بَدْرٍ " لَوْ كَانَ الْمُطْعِمُ بْنُ عَدِيٍّ حَيًّا، ثُمَّ كَلَّمَنِي فِي هَؤُلاَءِ النَّتْنَى، لَتَرَكْتُهُمْ لَهُ "

Narrated Abu Talha: On the day of Badr, the Prophetﷺ ordered that the corpses of twenty four leaders of Quraish should be thrown into one of the dirty dry wells of Badr. (It was a habit of the Prophetﷺ that whenever he conquered some people, he used to stay at the battle-field for three nights. So, on the third day of the battle of Badr, he ordered that his she-camel be saddled, then he set out, and his companions followed him saying among themselves." "Definitely he (i.e. the Prophet) is proceeding for some great purpose." When he halted at the edge of the well, he addressed the corpses of the Quraish infidels by their names and their fathers' names, "O so-and-so, son of so-and-so and O so-and-so, son of so-andso! Would it have pleased you if you had obeyed Allah and His Apostle? We have found true what our Lord promised us. Have you too found true what your Lord promised you? "`Umar said, "O Allah's Messengerﷺ ! You are speaking to bodies that have no souls!" Allah's Messengerﷺ said, "By Him in Whose Hand Muhammad's soul is, you do not hear, what I say better than they do." (Qatada said, "Allah brought them to life (again) to let them hear him, to reprimand them and slight them and take revenge over them and caused them to feel remorseful and regretful.")–Al-Bukhari 3976

حَدَّثَنِي عَبْدُ اللَّهِ بْنُ مُحَمَّدٍ، سَمِعَ رَوْحَ بْنَ عُبَادَةَ، حَدَّثَنَا سَعِيدُ بْنُ أَبِي عَرُوبَةَ، عَنْ قَتَادَةَ، قَالَ ذَكَرَ لَنَا أَنَسُ بْنُ مَالِكٍ عَنْ أَبِي طَلْحَةَ، أَنَّ نَبِيَّ اللَّهِ صلى الله عليه وسلم أَمَرَ يَوْمَ بَدْرٍ بِأَرْبَعَةٍ وَعِشْرِينَ رَجُلاً مِنْ صَنَادِيدِ قُرَيْشٍ فَقُذِفُوا فِي طَوِيٍّ مِنْ أَطْوَاءِ بَدْرٍ خَبِيثٍ مُخْبِثٍ، وَكَانَ إِذَا ظَهَرَ عَلَى قَوْمٍ أَقَامَ بِالْعَرْصَةِ ثَلاَثَ لَيَالٍ، فَلَمَّا كَانَ بِبَدْرٍ الْيَوْمَ الثَّالِثَ، أَمَرَ بِرَاحِلَتِهِ فَشُدَّ عَلَيْهَا رَحْلُهَا، ثُمَّ مَشَى وَاتَّبَعَهُ أَصْحَابُهُ وَقَالُوا مَا نُرَى يَنْطَلِقُ إِلاَّ لِبَعْضِ حَاجَتِهِ، حَتَّى قَامَ عَلَى شَفَةِ الرَّكِيِّ، فَجَعَلَ يُنَادِيهِمْ بِأَسْمَائِهِمْ وَأَسْمَاءِ آبَائِهِمْ " يَا فُلاَنُ بْنَ فُلاَنٍ، وَيَا فُلاَنُ بْنَ فُلاَنٍ، أَيَسُرُّكُمْ أَنَّكُمْ أَطَعْتُمُ اللَّهَ وَرَسُولَهُ فَإِنَّا قَدْ وَجَدْنَا مَا وَعَدَنَا رَبُّنَا حَقًّا، فَهَلْ وَجَدْتُمْ مَا وَعَدَ رَبُّكُمْ حَقًّا ". قَالَ فَقَالَ عُمَرُ يَا رَسُولَ اللَّهِ، مَا تُكَلِّمُ مِنْ أَجْسَادٍ لاَ أَرْوَاحَ لَهَا فَقَالَ رَسُولُ اللَّهِ صلى الله عليه وسلم " وَالَّذِي نَفْسُ مُحَمَّدٍ بِيَدِهِ، مَا أَنْتُمْ بِأَسْمَعَ لِمَا أَقُولُ مِنْهُمْ ". قَالَ قَتَادَةُ أَحْيَاهُمُ اللَّهُ حَتَّى أَسْمَعَهُمْ قَوْلَهُ تَوْبِيخًا وَتَصْغِيرًا وَنَقِيمَةً وَحَسْرَةً وَنَدَمًا.

Narrated Rifaa: (who was one of the Badr warriors) Gabriel came to the Prophetﷺ and said, "How do you look upon the warriors of Badr among yourselves?" The Prophetﷺ said, "As the best of the Muslims." Or said a similar statement. On that, Gabriel said, "And so are the Angels who participated in the Badr (battle).–Al-Bukhari 3992

حَدَّثَنِي إِسْحَاقُ بْنُ إِبْرَاهِيمَ، أَخْبَرَنَا جَرِيرٌ، عَنْ يَحْيَى بْنِ سَعِيدٍ، عَنْ مُعَاذِ بْنِ رِفَاعَةَ بْنِ رَافِعٍ الزُّرَقِيِّ، عَنْ أَبِيهِ ـ وَكَانَ أَبُوهُ مِنْ أَهْلِ بَدْرٍ ـ قَالَ جَاءَ جِبْرِيلُ إِلَى النَّبِيِّ صلى الله عليه وسلم فَقَالَ " مَا تَعُدُّونَ أَهْلَ بَدْرٍ فِيكُمْ قَالَ مِنْ أَفْضَلِ الْمُسْلِمِينَ ـ أَوْ كَلِمَةً نَحْوَهَا ـ قَالَ وَكَذَلِكَ مَنْ شَهِدَ بَدْرًا مِنَ الْمَلاَئِكَةِ "

Narrated Ibn `Abbas: Not equal are those believers who sat (at home) and did not join the Badr battle and those who joined the Badr battle.–Al-Bukhari 4595 also Bukhari 3954

حَدَّثَنَا إِبْرَاهِيمُ بْنُ مُوسَى، أَخْبَرَنَا هِشَامٌ، أَنَّ ابْنَ جُرَيْجٍ، أَخْبَرَهُمْ ح، وَحَدَّثَنِي إِسْحَاقُ، أَخْبَرَنَا عَبْدُ الرَّزَّاقِ، أَخْبَرَنَا ابْنُ جُرَيْجٍ، أَخْبَرَنِي عَبْدُ الْكَرِيمِ، أَنَّ مِقْسَمًا، مَوْلَى عَبْدِ اللَّهِ بْنِ الْحَارِثِ أَخْبَرَهُ أَنَّ ابْنَ عَبَّاسٍ ـ رضى الله عنهما ـ أَخْبَرَهُ {لاَ يَسْتَوِي الْقَاعِدُونَ مِنَ الْمُؤْمِنِينَ} عَنْ بَدْرٍ وَالْخَارِجُونَ إِلَى بَدْرٍ.

Narrated Qais: The Badr warriors were given five thousand (Dirhams) each, yearly. `Umar said, "I will surely give them more than what I will give to others."–Al-Bukhari 4022

حَدَّثَنَا إِسْحَاقُ بْنُ إِبْرَاهِيمَ، سَمِعَ مُحَمَّدَ بْنَ فُضَيْلٍ، عَنْ إِسْمَاعِيلَ، عَنْ قَيْسٍ، كَانَ عَطَاءُ الْبَدْرِيِّينَ خَمْسَةَ آلاَفٍ خَمْسَةَ آلاَفٍ. وَقَالَ عُمَرُ لأُفَضِّلَنَّهُمْ عَلَى مَنْ بَعْدَهُمْ

Narrated Husain bin `Ali: `Ali bin Abi Talib said: “I got a she-camel as my share of the war booty on the day (of the battle) of Badr, and Allah’s Messengerﷺ gave me another she-camel. I let both of them kneel at the door of one of the Ansar, intending to carry Idhkhir on them to sell it and use its price for my wedding banquet on marrying Fatima. A goldsmith from Bani Qainqa’ was with me. Hamza bin `Abdul-Muttalib was in that house drinking wine and a lady singer was reciting: “O Hamza! (Kill) the (two) fat old she camels (and serve them to your guests). So Hamza took his sword and went towards the two she-camels and cut off their humps and opened their flanks and took a part of their livers.” (I said to Ibn Shihab, “Did he take part of the humps?” He replied, “He cut off their humps and carried them away.”) `Ali further said, “When I saw that dreadful sight, I went to the Prophetﷺ and told him the news. The Prophetﷺ came out in the company of Zaid bin Haritha who was with him then, and I too went with them. He went to Hamza and spoke harshly to him. Hamza looked up and said, ‘Aren’t you only the slaves of my forefathers?’ The Prophetﷺ retreated and went out. This incident happened before the prohibition of drinking.”–Al-Bukhari 2375 also Bukhari 4003

حَدَّثَنَا إِبْرَاهِيمُ بْنُ مُوسَى، أَخْبَرَنَا هِشَامٌ، أَنَّ ابْنَ جُرَيْجٍ، أَخْبَرَهُمْ قَالَ أَخْبَرَنِي ابْنُ شِهَابٍ، عَنْ عَلِيِّ بْنِ حُسَيْنِ بْنِ عَلِيٍّ، عَنْ أَبِيهِ، حُسَيْنِ بْنِ عَلِيٍّ عَنْ عَلِيِّ بْنِ أَبِي طَالِبٍ ـ رضى الله عنهم ـ أَنَّهُ قَالَ أَصَبْتُ شَارِفًا مَعَ رَسُولِ اللَّهِ صلى الله عليه وسلم فِي مَغْنَمٍ يَوْمَ بَدْرٍ قَالَ وَأَعْطَانِي رَسُولُ اللَّهِ صلى الله عليه وسلم شَارِفًا أُخْرَى، فَأَنَخْتُهُمَا يَوْمًا عِنْدَ باب رَجُلٍ مِنَ الأَنْصَارِ، وَأَنَا أُرِيدُ أَنْ أَحْمِلَ عَلَيْهِمَا إِذْخِرًا لأَبِيعَهُ، وَمَعِي صَائِغٌ مِنْ بَنِي قَيْنُقَاعَ فَأَسْتَعِينَ بِهِ عَلَى وَلِيمَةِ فَاطِمَةَ، وَحَمْزَةُ بْنُ عَبْدِ الْمُطَّلِبِ يَشْرَبُ فِي ذَلِكَ الْبَيْتِ مَعَهُ قَيْنَةٌ، فَقَالَتْ أَلاَ يَا حَمْزَ لِلشُّرُفِ النِّوَاءِ. فَثَارَ إِلَيْهِمَا حَمْزَةُ بِالسَّيْفِ، فَجَبَّ أَسْنِمَتَهُمَا، وَبَقَرَ خَوَاصِرَهُمَا، ثُمَّ أَخَذَ مِنْ أَكْبَادِهِمَا. قُلْتُ لاِبْنِ شِهَابٍ وَمِنَ السَّنَامِ قَالَ قَدْ جَبَّ أَسْنِمَتَهُمَا فَذَهَبَ بِهَا. قَالَ ابْنُ شِهَابٍ قَالَ عَلِيٌّ ـ رضى الله عنه ـ فَنَظَرْتُ إِلَى مَنْظَرٍ أَفْظَعَنِي فَأَتَيْتُ نَبِيَّ اللَّهِ صلى الله عليه وسلم وَعِنْدَهُ زَيْدُ بْنُ حَارِثَةَ فَأَخْبَرْتُهُ الْخَبَرَ فَخَرَجَ وَمَعَهُ زَيْدٌ، فَانْطَلَقْتُ مَعَهُ، فَدَخَلَ عَلَى حَمْزَةَ فَتَغَيَّظَ عَلَيْهِ فَرَفَعَ حَمْزَةُ بَصَرَهُ وَقَالَ هَلْ أَنْتُمْ إِلاَّ عَبِيدٌ لآبَائِي فَرَجَعَ رَسُولُ اللَّهِ صلى الله عليه وسلم يُقَهْقِرُ حَتَّى خَرَجَ عَنْهُمْ، وَذَلِكَ قَبْلَ تَحْرِيمِ الْخَمْرِ

Narrated Nafi: Ibn ‘Umar was once told that Said bin Zaid bin ‘Amr bin Nufail, one of the Badr warriors, had fallen ill on a Friday. Ibn ‘Umar rode to him late in the forenoon. The time of the Friday prayer approached and Ibn ‘Umar did not take part in the Friday prayer.–Al-Bukhari 3990

حَدَّثَنَا قُتَيْبَةُ، حَدَّثَنَا لَيْثٌ، عَنْ يَحْيَى، عَنْ نَافِعٍ، أَنَّ ابْنَ عُمَرَ ـ رضى الله عنهما ـ ذُكِرَ لَهُ أَنَّ سَعِيدَ بْنَ زَيْدِ بْنِ عَمْرِو بْنِ نُفَيْلٍ ـ وَكَانَ بَدْرِيًّا ـ مَرِضَ فِي يَوْمِ جُمُعَةٍ فَرَكِبَ إِلَيْهِ بَعْدَ أَنْ تَعَالَى النَّهَارُ وَاقْتَرَبَتِ الْجُمُعَةُ، وَتَرَكَ الْجُمُعَةَ

Narrated Ibn `Abbas: Abu Talha, a companion of Allah’s Messengerﷺ and one of those who fought at Badr together with Allah’s Apostle told me that Allah’s Messengerﷺ said. “Angels do not enter a house in which there is a dog or a picture” He meant the images of creatures that have souls.–Al-Bukhari 4002

حَدَّثَنَا إِبْرَاهِيمُ بْنُ مُوسَى، أَخْبَرَنَا هِشَامٌ، عَنْ مَعْمَرٍ، عَنِ الزُّهْرِيِّ. حَدَّثَنَا إِسْمَاعِيلُ، قَالَ حَدَّثَنِي أَخِي، عَنْ سُلَيْمَانَ، عَنْ مُحَمَّدِ بْنِ أَبِي عَتِيقٍ، عَنِ ابْنِ شِهَابٍ، عَنْ عُبَيْدِ اللَّهِ بْنِ عَبْدِ اللَّهِ بْنِ عُتْبَةَ بْنِ مَسْعُودٍ، أَنَّ ابْنَ عَبَّاسٍ ـ رضى الله عنهما ـ قَالَ أَخْبَرَنِي أَبُو طَلْحَةَ ـ رضى الله عنه ـ صَاحِبُ رَسُولِ اللَّهِ صلى الله عليه وسلم وَكَانَ قَدْ شَهِدَ بَدْرًا مَعَ رَسُولِ اللَّهِ صلى الله عليه وسلم أَنَّهُ قَالَ " لاَ تَدْخُلُ الْمَلاَئِكَةُ بَيْتًا فِيهِ كَلْبٌ وَلاَ صُورَةٌ ". يُرِيدُ التَّمَاثِيلَ الَّتِي فِيهَا الأَرْوَاحُ

Narrated Ibn `Abbas: `Umar said, “When the Prophetﷺ died I said to Abu Bakr, ‘Let us go to our Ansari brethren.’ We met two pious men from them, who had fought in the battle of Badr.” When I mentioned this to `Urwa bin Az-Zubair, he said, “Those two pious men were ‘Uwaim bin Sa`ida and Manbin Adi.”–Al-Bukhari 4021

حَدَّثَنَا مُوسَى، حَدَّثَنَا عَبْدُ الْوَاحِدِ، حَدَّثَنَا مَعْمَرٌ، عَنِ الزُّهْرِيِّ، عَنْ عُبَيْدِ اللَّهِ بْنِ عَبْدِ اللَّهِ، حَدَّثَنِي ابْنُ عَبَّاسٍ، عَنْ عُمَرَ ـ رضى الله عنهم ـ لَمَّا تُوُفِّيَ النَّبِيُّ صلى الله عليه وسلم قُلْتُ لأَبِي بَكْرٍ انْطَلِقْ بِنَا إِلَى إِخْوَانِنَا مِنَ الأَنْصَارِ. فَلَقِينَا مِنْهُمْ رَجُلاَنِ صَالِحَانِ شَهِدَا بَدْرًا. فَحَدَّثْتُ عُرْوَةَ بْنَ الزُّبَيْرِ فَقَالَ هُمَا عُوَيْمُ بْنُ سَاعِدَةَ، وَمَعْنُ بْنُ عَدِيٍّ.

Narrated `Itban bin Malik: who was one of the companions of Allah's Messenger ﷺ and one of the Ansar's who took part in the battle of Badr: I came to Allah's Messenger ﷺ and said, "O Allah's Messenger ﷺ I have weak eyesight and I lead my people in prayers. When it rains the water flows in the valley between me and my people so I cannot go to their mosque to lead them in prayer. O Allah's Messenger ﷺ! I wish you would come to my house and pray in it so that I could take that place as a Musalla. Allah's Messenger ﷺ said. "Allah willing, I will do so." Next day after the sun rose high, Allah's Messenger ﷺ and Abu Bakr came and Allah's Messenger ﷺ asked for permission to enter. I gave him permission and he did not sit on entering the house but said to me, "Where do you like me to pray?" I pointed to a place in my house. So Allah's Messenger ﷺ stood there and said, 'Allahu Akbar', and we all got up and aligned behind him and offered a two-rak`at prayer and ended it with Taslim. We requested him to stay for a meal called "Khazira" which we had prepared for him. Many members of our family gathered in the house and one of them said, "Where is Malik bin Al-Dukhaishin or Ibn Al-Dukhshun?" One of them replied, "He is a hypocrite and does not love Allah and His Apostle." Hearing that, Allah's Messenger ﷺ said, "Do not say so. Haven't you seen that he said, 'None has the right to be worshipped but Allah' for Allah's sake only?" He said, "Allah and His Apostle know better. We have seen him helping and advising hypocrites." Allah's Messenger ﷺ said, "Allah has forbidden the (Hell) fire for those who say, 'None has the right to be worshipped but Allah' for Allah's sake only."–Al-Bukhari 425

حَدَّثَنَا سَعِيدُ بْنُ عُفَيْرٍ، قَالَ حَدَّثَنِي اللَّيْثُ، قَالَ حَدَّثَنِي عُقَيْلٌ، عَنِ ابْنِ شِهَابٍ، قَالَ أَخْبَرَنِي مَحْمُودُ بْنُ الرَّبِيعِ الأَنْصَارِيُّ، أَنَّ عِتْبَانَ بْنَ مَالِكٍ ـ وَهُوَ مِنْ أَصْحَابِ رَسُولِ اللَّهِ صلى الله عليه وسلم مِمَّنْ شَهِدَ بَدْرًا مِنَ الأَنْصَارِ ـ أَنَّهُ أَتَى رَسُولَ اللَّهِ صلى الله عليه وسلم فَقَالَ يَا رَسُولَ اللَّهِ، قَدْ أَنْكَرْتُ بَصَرِي، وَأَنَا أُصَلِّي لِقَوْمِي، فَإِذَا كَانَتِ الأَمْطَارُ سَالَ الْوَادِي الَّذِي بَيْنِي وَبَيْنَهُمْ، لَمْ أَسْتَطِعْ أَنْ آتِيَ مَسْجِدَهُمْ فَأُصَلِّيَ بِهِمْ، وَوَدِدْتُ يَا رَسُولَ اللَّهِ أَنَّكَ تَأْتِينِي فَتُصَلِّيَ فِي بَيْتِي، فَأَتَّخِذَهُ مُصَلًّى. قَالَ فَقَالَ لَهُ رَسُولُ اللَّهِ صلى الله عليه وسلم " سَأَفْعَلُ إِنْ شَاءَ اللَّهُ ". قَالَ عِتْبَانُ فَغَدَا رَسُولُ اللَّهِ صلى الله عليه وسلم وَأَبُو بَكْرٍ حِينَ ارْتَفَعَ النَّهَارُ، فَاسْتَأْذَنَ رَسُولُ اللَّهِ صلى الله عليه وسلم فَأَذِنْتُ لَهُ، فَلَمْ يَجْلِسْ حَتَّى دَخَلَ الْبَيْتَ ثُمَّ قَالَ " أَيْنَ تُحِبُّ أَنْ أُصَلِّيَ مِنْ بَيْتِكَ ". قَالَ فَأَشَرْتُ لَهُ إِلَى نَاحِيَةٍ مِنَ الْبَيْتِ، فَقَامَ رَسُولُ اللَّهِ صلى الله عليه وسلم فَكَبَّرَ، فَقُمْنَا فَصَفَّنَا، فَصَلَّى رَكْعَتَيْنِ ثُمَّ سَلَّمَ، قَالَ وَحَبَسْنَاهُ عَلَى خَزِيرَةٍ صَنَعْنَاهَا لَهُ. قَالَ فَثَابَ فِي الْبَيْتِ رِجَالٌ مِنْ أَهْلِ الدَّارِ ذَوُو عَدَدٍ فَاجْتَمَعُوا، فَقَالَ قَائِلٌ مِنْهُمْ أَيْنَ مَالِكُ بْنُ الدُّخَيْشِنِ أَوِ ابْنُ الدُّخْشُنِ فَقَالَ بَعْضُهُمْ ذَلِكَ مُنَافِقٌ لاَ يُحِبُّ اللَّهَ وَرَسُولَهُ. فَقَالَ رَسُولُ اللَّهِ صلى الله عليه وسلم " لاَ تَقُلْ ذَلِكَ، أَلاَ تَرَاهُ قَدْ قَالَ لاَ إِلَهَ إِلاَّ اللَّهُ. يُرِيدُ بِذَلِكَ وَجْهَ اللَّهِ ". قَالَ اللَّهُ وَرَسُولُهُ أَعْلَمُ. قَالَ فَإِنَّا نَرَى وَجْهَهُ وَنَصِيحَتَهُ إِلَى الْمُنَافِقِينَ. قَالَ رَسُولُ اللَّهِ صلى الله عليه وسلم " فَإِنَّ اللَّهَ قَدْ حَرَّمَ عَلَى النَّارِ مَنْ قَالَ لاَ إِلَهَ إِلاَّ اللَّهُ. يَبْتَغِي بِذَلِكَ وَجْهَ اللَّهِ ". قَالَ ابْنُ شِهَابٍ ثُمَّ سَأَلْتُ الْحُصَيْنَ بْنَ مُحَمَّدٍ الأَنْصَارِيَّ ـ وَهْوَ أَحَدُ بَنِي سَالِمٍ وَهُوَ مِنْ سَرَاتِهِمْ ـ عَنْ حَدِيثِ مَحْمُودِ بْنِ الرَّبِيعِ، فَصَدَّقَهُ بِذَلِكَ

Narrated Anas bin Malik: Um Ar-Rubai'bint Al-Bara', the mother of Hartha bin Suraqa came to the Prophet ﷺ and said, "O Allah's Prophet! Will you tell me about Hartha?" Hartha has been killed (i.e. martyred) on the day of Badr with an arrow thrown by an unidentified person. She added, "If he is in Paradise, I will be patient; otherwise, I will weep bitterly for him." He said, "O mother of Hartha! There are Gardens in Paradise and your son got the Firdausal-ala (i.e. the best place in Paradise).–Al-Bukhari 2809 also Bukhari 3982

حَدَّثَنَا مُحَمَّدُ بْنُ عَبْدِ اللَّهِ، حَدَّثَنَا حُسَيْنُ بْنُ مُحَمَّدٍ أَبُو أَحْمَدَ، حَدَّثَنَا شَيْبَانُ، عَنْ قَتَادَةَ، حَدَّثَنَا أَنَسُ بْنُ مَالِكٍ، أَنَّ أُمَّ الرُّبَيِّعِ بِنْتَ الْبَرَاءِ، وَهْىَ أُمُّ حَارِثَةَ بْنِ سُرَاقَةَ أَتَتِ النَّبِيَّ صلى الله عليه وسلم فَقَالَتْ يَا نَبِيَّ اللَّهِ، أَلاَ تُحَدِّثُنِي عَنْ حَارِثَةَ وَكَانَ قُتِلَ يَوْمَ بَدْرٍ أَصَابَهُ سَهْمٌ غَرْبٌ، فَإِنْ كَانَ فِي الْجَنَّةِ، صَبَرْتُ، وَإِنْ كَانَ غَيْرَ ذَلِكَ اجْتَهَدْتُ عَلَيْهِ فِي الْبُكَاءِ. قَالَ " يَا أُمَّ حَارِثَةَ، إِنَّهَا جِنَانٌ فِي الْجَنَّةِ، وَإِنَّ ابْنَكِ أَصَابَ الْفِرْدَوْسَ الأَعْلَى ".

Narrated `Aisha: (the wife of the Prophet) Abu Hudhaifa, one of those who fought the battle of Badr, with Allah's Apostle adopted Salim as his son and married his niece Hind bint Al-Wahd bin `Utba to him' and Salim was a freed slave of an Ansari woman. Allah's Messenger ﷺ also adopted Zaid as his son. In the PreIslamic period of ignorance the custom was that, if one adopted a son, the people would call him by the name of the adopted-father whom he would inherit as well, till Allah revealed: "Call them (adopted sons) By (the names of) their fathers." (33.5)–Al-Bukhari 4000

حَدَّثَنَا يَحْيَى بْنُ بُكَيْرٍ، حَدَّثَنَا اللَّيْثُ، عَنْ عُقَيْلٍ، عَنِ ابْنِ شِهَابٍ، أَخْبَرَنِي عُرْوَةُ بْنُ الزُّبَيْرِ، عَنْ عَائِشَةَ ـ رضى الله عنها ـ زَوْجِ النَّبِيِّ صلى الله عليه وسلم أَنَّ أَبَا حُذَيْفَةَ وَكَانَ مِمَّنْ شَهِدَ بَدْرًا مَعَ رَسُولِ اللَّهِ صلى الله عليه وسلم تَبَنَّى سَالِمًا، وَأَنْكَحَهُ بِنْتَ أَخِيهِ هِنْدَ بِنْتَ الْوَلِيدِ بْنِ عُتْبَةَ ـ وَهْوَ مَوْلًى لاِمْرَأَةٍ مِنَ الأَنْصَارِ ـ كَمَا تَبَنَّى رَسُولُ اللَّهِ صلى الله عليه وسلم زَيْدًا، وَكَانَ مَنْ تَبَنَّى رَجُلاً فِي الْجَاهِلِيَّةِ دَعَاهُ النَّاسُ إِلَيْهِ، وَوَرِثَ مِنْ مِيرَاثِهِ حَتَّى أَنْزَلَ اللَّهُ تَعَالَى {ادْعُوهُمْ لآبَائِهِمْ} فَجَاءَتْ سَهْلَةُ النَّبِيَّ صلى الله عليه وسلم، فَذَكَرَ الْحَدِيثَ.

Narrated `Ali: Allah's Messenger ﷺ sent me, Abu Marthad and Az-Zubair, and all of us were riding horses, and said, "Go till you reach Raudat-Khakh where there is a pagan woman carrying a letter from Hatib bin Abi Balta' a to the pagans of Mecca." So we found her riding her camel at the place which Allah's Messenger ﷺ had mentioned. We said (to her),"(Give us) the letter." She said, "I have no letter." Then we made her camel kneel down and we searched her, but we found no letter. Then we said, "Allah's Messenger ﷺ had not told us a lie, certainly. Take out the letter, otherwise we will strip you naked." When she saw that we were determined, she put her hand below her waist belt, for she had tied her cloak round her waist, and she took out the letter, and we brought her to Allah's Messenger ﷺ Then `Umar said, "O Allah's Apostle! (This Hatib) has betrayed Allah, His Apostle and the believers! Let me cut off his neck!" The Prophet asked Hatib, "What made you do this?" Hatib said, "By Allah, I did not intend to give up my belief in Allah and His Apostle but I wanted to have some influence among the (Mecca) people so that through it, Allah might protect my family and property. There is none of your companions but has some of his relatives there through whom Allah protects his family and property." The Prophet ﷺ said, "He has spoken the truth; do no say to him but good." `Umar said, "He as betrayed Allah, His Apostle and the faithful believers. Let me cut off his neck!" The Prophet ﷺ said, "Is he not one of the Badr warriors? May be Allah looked at the Badr warriors and said, 'Do whatever you like, as I have granted Paradise to you, or said, 'I have forgiven you."' On this, tears came out of `Umar's eyes, and he said, "Allah and His Apostle know better."–Al-Bukhari 3983

حَدَّثَنِي إِسْحَاقُ بْنُ إِبْرَاهِيمَ، أَخْبَرَنَا عَبْدُ اللَّهِ بْنُ إِدْرِيسَ، قَالَ سَمِعْتُ حُصَيْنَ بْنَ عَبْدِ الرَّحْمَنِ، عَنْ سَعْدِ بْنِ عُبَيْدَةَ، عَنْ أَبِي عَبْدِ الرَّحْمَنِ السُّلَمِيِّ، عَنْ عَلِيٍّ ـ رضى الله عنه ـ قَالَ بَعَثَنِي رَسُولُ اللَّهِ صلى الله عليه وسلم وَأَبَا مَرْثَدٍ وَالزُّبَيْرَ وَكُلُّنَا فَارِسٌ قَالَ " انْطَلِقُوا حَتَّى تَأْتُوا رَوْضَةَ خَاخٍ، فَإِنَّ بِهَا امْرَأَةً مِنَ الْمُشْرِكِينَ، مَعَهَا كِتَابٌ مِنْ حَاطِبِ بْنِ أَبِي بَلْتَعَةَ إِلَى الْمُشْرِكِينَ ". فَأَدْرَكْنَاهَا تَسِيرُ عَلَى بَعِيرٍ لَهَا حَيْثُ قَالَ رَسُولُ اللَّهِ صلى الله عليه وسلم فَقُلْنَا الْكِتَابُ. فَقَالَتْ مَا مَعَنَا كِتَابٌ. فَأَنَخْنَاهَا فَالْتَمَسْنَا فَلَمْ نَرَ كِتَابًا، فَقُلْنَا مَا كَذَبَ رَسُولُ اللَّهِ صلى الله عليه وسلم، لَتُخْرِجِنَّ الْكِتَابَ أَوْ لَنُجَرِّدَنَّكِ. فَلَمَّا رَأَتِ الْجِدَّ أَهْوَتْ إِلَى حُجْزَتِهَا وَهْىَ مُحْتَجِزَةٌ بِكِسَاءٍ فَأَخْرَجَتْهُ، فَانْطَلَقْنَا بِهَا إِلَى رَسُولِ اللَّهِ صلى الله عليه وسلم فَقَالَ عُمَرُ يَا رَسُولَ اللَّهِ، قَدْ خَانَ اللَّهَ وَرَسُولَهُ وَالْمُؤْمِنِينَ، فَدَعْنِي فَلأَضْرِبْ عُنُقَهُ. فَقَالَ النَّبِيُّ صلى الله عليه وسلم " مَا حَمَلَكَ عَلَى مَا صَنَعْتَ ". قَالَ حَاطِبٌ وَاللَّهِ مَا بِي أَنْ لاَ أَكُونَ مُؤْمِنًا بِاللَّهِ وَرَسُولِهِ صلى الله عليه وسلم أَرَدْتُ أَنْ يَكُونَ لِي عِنْدَ الْقَوْمِ يَدٌ يَدْفَعُ اللَّهُ بِهَا عَنْ أَهْلِي وَمَالِي، وَلَيْسَ أَحَدٌ مِنْ أَصْحَابِكَ إِلاَّ لَهُ هُنَاكَ مِنْ عَشِيرَتِهِ مَنْ يَدْفَعُ اللَّهُ بِهِ عَنْ أَهْلِهِ وَمَالِهِ. فَقَالَ النَّبِيُّ صلى الله عليه وسلم " صَدَقَ، وَلاَ تَقُولُوا لَهُ إِلاَّ خَيْرًا ". فَقَالَ عُمَرُ إِنَّهُ قَدْ خَانَ اللَّهَ وَرَسُولَهُ وَالْمُؤْمِنِينَ، فَدَعْنِي فَلأَضْرِبَ عُنُقَهُ. فَقَالَ " أَلَيْسَ مِنْ أَهْلِ بَدْرٍ ". فَقَالَ " لَعَلَّ اللَّهَ اطَّلَعَ إِلَى أَهْلِ بَدْرٍ فَقَالَ اعْمَلُوا مَا شِئْتُمْ فَقَدْ وَجَبَتْ لَكُمُ الْجَنَّةُ، أَوْ فَقَدْ غَفَرْتُ لَكُمْ ". فَدَمَعَتْ عَيْنَا عُمَرَ وَقَالَ اللَّهُ وَرَسُولُهُ أَعْلَمُ

Narrated Abu Sa`id Al-Khudri: that once he was not present (at the time of `Id-al-Adha) and when he came. Some meat was presented to him. And the people said (to him), 'This is the meat of our sacrifices" He said. 'Take it away; I shall not taste it. (In his narration) Abu Sa`id added: I got up and went to my brother, Abu Qatada (who was his maternal brother and was one of the warriors of the battle of Badr) and mentioned that to him He Sa`d. 'A new verdict was given in your absence (i.e., meat of sacrifices was allowed to be stored and eaten later on).–Al-Bukhari 5568

حَدَّثَنَا إِسْمَاعِيلُ، قَالَ حَدَّثَنِي سُلَيْمَانُ، عَنْ يَحْيَى بْنِ سَعِيدٍ، عَنِ الْقَاسِمِ، أَنَّ ابْنَ خَبَّابٍ، أَخْبَرَهُ أَنَّهُ، سَمِعَ أَبَا سَعِيدٍ، يُحَدِّثُ أَنَّهُ كَانَ غَائِبًا، فَقَدِمَ فَقُدِّمَ إِلَيْهِ لَحْمٌ. قَالَ وَهَذَا مِنْ لَحْمِ ضَحَايَانَا. فَقَالَ أَخِّرُوهُ لاَ أَذُوقُهُ. قَالَ ثُمَّ قُمْتُ فَخَرَجْتُ حَتَّى آتِيَ أَخِي قَتَادَةَ ـ وَكَانَ أَخَاهُ لأُمِّهِ، وَكَانَ بَدْرِيًّا ـ فَذَكَرْتُ ذَلِكَ لَهُ فَقَالَ إِنَّهُ قَدْ حَدَثَ بَعْدَكَ أَمْرٌ.

Narrated 'Ubada bin As-Samit: Who had taken part in the battle of Badr with Allah's Messenger ﷺ and had been amongst his companions on the night of Al-`Aqaba Pledge: Allah's Messenger ﷺ, surrounded by a group of his companions said, "Come along and give me the pledge of allegiance that you will not worship anything besides Allah, will not steal, will not commit illegal sexual intercourse will not kill your children, will not utter; slander, invented by yourself, and will not disobey me if I order you to do something good. Whoever among you will respect and fulfill this pledge, will be rewarded by Allah. And if one of you commits any of these sins and is punished in this world then that will be his expiation for it, and if one of you commits any of these sins and Allah screens his sin, then his matter, will rest with Allah: If He will, He will punish him and if He will,. He will excuse him." So I gave the pledge of allegiance to him for these conditions.–Al-Bukhari 3892

حَدَّثَنِي إِسْحَاقُ بْنُ مَنْصُورٍ، أَخْبَرَنَا يَعْقُوبُ بْنُ إِبْرَاهِيمَ، حَدَّثَنَا ابْنُ أَخِي ابْنِ شِهَابٍ، عَنْ عَمِّهِ، قَالَ أَخْبَرَنِي أَبُو إِدْرِيسَ، عَائِذُ اللَّهِ أَنَّ عُبَادَةَ بْنَ الصَّامِتِ ـ مِنَ الَّذِينَ شَهِدُوا بَدْرًا مَعَ رَسُولِ اللَّهِ صلى الله عليه وسلم ـ وَمِنْ أَصْحَابِهِ لَيْلَةَ الْعَقَبَةِ ـ أَخْبَرَهُ أَنَّ رَسُولَ اللَّهِ صلى الله عليه وسلم قَالَ وَحَوْلَهُ عِصَابَةٌ مِنْ أَصْحَابِهِ " تَعَالَوْا بَايِعُونِي عَلَى أَنْ لاَ تُشْرِكُوا بِاللَّهِ شَيْئًا، وَلاَ تَسْرِقُوا، وَلاَ تَزْنُوا، وَلاَ تَقْتُلُوا أَوْلاَدَكُمْ، وَلاَ تَأْتُونَ بِبُهْتَانٍ تَفْتَرُونَهُ بَيْنَ أَيْدِيكُمْ وَأَرْجُلِكُمْ، وَلاَ تَعْصُونِي فِي مَعْرُوفٍ، فَمَنْ وَفَى مِنْكُمْ فَأَجْرُهُ عَلَى اللَّهِ، وَمَنْ أَصَابَ مِنْ ذَلِكَ شَيْئًا فَعُوقِبَ بِهِ فِي الدُّنْيَا فَهْوَ لَهُ كَفَّارَةٌ، وَمَنْ أَصَابَ مِنْ ذَلِكَ شَيْئًا فَسَتَرَهُ اللَّهُ فَأَمْرُهُ إِلَى اللَّهِ، إِنْ شَاءَ عَاقَبَهُ، وَإِنْ شَاءَ عَفَا عَنْهُ ". قَالَ فَبَايَعْتُهُ عَلَى ذَلِكَ.

Narrated Az-Zuhri: I heard `Urwa bin Az-Zubair talking to `Umar bin `Abdul `Aziz during the latter's Governorship (at Medina), he said, "Al-Mughira bin Shu`ba delayed the `Asr prayer when he was the ruler of Al-Kufa. On that, Abu Mas`ud. `Uqba bin `Amr Al-Ansari, the grand-father of Zaid bin Hasan, who was one of the Badr warriors, came in and said, (to Al-Mughira), 'You know that Gabriel came down and offered the prayer and Allah's Messenger ﷺ prayed five prescribed prayers, and Gabriel said (to the Prophet ﷺ)", I have been ordered to do so (i.e. offer these five prayers at these fixed stated hours of the day).–Al-Bukhari 4007

حَدَّثَنَا أَبُو الْيَمَانِ، أَخْبَرَنَا شُعَيْبٌ، عَنِ الزُّهْرِيِّ، سَمِعْتُ عُرْوَةَ بْنَ الزُّبَيْرِ، يُحَدِّثُ عُمَرَ بْنَ عَبْدِ الْعَزِيزِ فِي إِمَارَتِهِ أَخَّرَ الْمُغِيرَةُ بْنُ شُعْبَةَ الْعَصْرَ وَهْوَ أَمِيرُ الْكُوفَةِ، فَدَخَلَ أَبُو مَسْعُودٍ عُقْبَةُ بْنُ عَمْرٍو الأَنْصَارِيُّ جَدُّ زَيْدِ بْنِ حَسَنٍ شَهِدَ بَدْرًا فَقَالَ لَقَدْ عَلِمْتَ نَزَلَ جِبْرِيلُ فَصَلَّى فَصَلَّى رَسُولُ اللَّهِ صلى الله عليه وسلم خَمْسَ صَلَوَاتٍ ثُمَّ قَالَ هَكَذَا أُمِرْتُ. كَذَلِكَ كَانَ بَشِيرُ بْنُ أَبِي مَسْعُودٍ يُحَدِّثُ عَنْ أَبِيهِ.

Narrated Al-Bara: I and Ibn `Umar were considered too young to take part in the battle of Badr.–Al-Bukhari 3955

حَدَّثَنَا مُسْلِمٌ، حَدَّثَنَا شُعْبَةُ، عَنْ أَبِي إِسْحَاقَ، عَنِ الْبَرَاءِ، قَالَ اسْتُصْغِرْتُ أَنَا وَابْنُ، عُمَرَ

Narrated Ibn `Umar: `Uthman did not join the Badr battle because he was married to one of the daughters of Allah's Apostle and she was ill. So, the Prophet ﷺ said to him. "You will get a reward and a share (from the war booty) similar to the reward and the share of one who has taken part in the Badr battle."–Al-Bukhari 3130 also Bukhari 3698& 4066

حَدَّثَنَا مُوسَى، حَدَّثَنَا أَبُو عَوَانَةَ، حَدَّثَنَا عُثْمَانُ بْنُ مَوْهَبٍ، عَنِ ابْنِ عُمَرَ ـ رضى الله عنهما ـ قَالَ إِنَّمَا تَغَيَّبَ عُثْمَانُ عَنْ بَدْرٍ، فَإِنَّهُ كَانَتْ تَحْتَهُ بِنْتُ رَسُولِ اللَّهِ صلى الله عليه وسلم وَكَانَتْ مَرِيضَةً. فَقَالَ لَهُ النَّبِيُّ صلى الله عليه وسلم " إِنَّ لَكَ أَجْرَ رَجُلٍ مِمَّنْ شَهِدَ بَدْرًا وَسَهْمَهُ ".

Narrated Ka`b bin Malik: I never failed to join Allah's Messenger ﷺ in any of his Ghazawat except in the Ghazwa of Tabuk. However, I did not take part in the Ghazwa of Badr, but none who failed to take part in it, was blamed, for Allah's Messenger ﷺ had gone out to meet the caravans of (Quraish, but Allah caused them (i.e. Muslims) to meet their enemy unexpectedly (with no previous intention) .–Al-Bukhari 3951 also Bukhari 4677

حَدَّثَنِي يَحْيَى بْنُ بُكَيْرٍ، حَدَّثَنَا اللَّيْثُ، عَنْ عُقَيْلٍ، عَنِ ابْنِ شِهَابٍ، عَنْ عَبْدِ الرَّحْمَنِ بْنِ عَبْدِ اللَّهِ بْنِ كَعْبٍ، أَنَّ عَبْدَ اللَّهِ بْنَ كَعْبٍ، قَالَ سَمِعْتُ كَعْبَ بْنَ مَالِكٍ ـ رضى الله عنه ـ يَقُولُ لَمْ أَتَخَلَّفْ عَنْ رَسُولِ اللَّهِ صلى الله عليه وسلم فِي غَزْوَةٍ غَزَاهَا إِلاَّ فِي غَزْوَةِ تَبُوكَ، غَيْرَ أَنِّي تَخَلَّفْتُ عَنْ غَزْوَةِ بَدْرٍ، وَلَمْ يُعَاتَبْ أَحَدٌ تَخَلَّفَ عَنْهَا، إِنَّمَا خَرَجَ رَسُولُ اللَّهِ صلى الله عليه وسلم يُرِيدُ عِيرَ قُرَيْشٍ، حَتَّى جَمَعَ اللَّهُ بَيْنَهُمْ وَبَيْنَ عَدُوِّهِمْ عَلَى غَيْرِ مِيعَادٍ.

Narrated Mu`adh bin Rifa`a bin Rafi`: Rifa`a was one of the warriors of Badr while (his father) Rafi` was one of the people of Al-`Aqaba (i.e. those who gave the pledge of allegiance at Al-`Aqaba). Rafi` used to say to his son, "I would not have been happier if I had taken part in the Badr battle instead of taking part in the 'Aqaba pledge."–Al-Bukhari 3993

حَدَّثَنَا سُلَيْمَانُ بْنُ حَرْبٍ، حَدَّثَنَا حَمَّادٌ، عَنْ يَحْيَى، عَنْ مُعَاذِ بْنِ رِفَاعَةَ بْنِ رَافِعٍ،، وَكَانَ، رِفَاعَةُ مِنْ أَهْلِ بَدْرٍ، وَكَانَ رَافِعٌ مِنْ أَهْلِ الْعَقَبَةِ، فَكَانَ يَقُولُ لاِبْنِهِ مَا يَسُرُّنِي أَنِّي شَهِدْتُ بَدْرًا بِالْعَقَبَةِ قَالَ سَأَلَ جِبْرِيلُ النَّبِيَّ صلى الله عليه وسلم. بِهَذَا

Narrated `Abdullah bin Ka`b: Who was Ka`b's guide when Ka`b turned blind: I heard Ka`b bin Malik narrating: When he remained behind (i.e. did not Join) the Prophet ﷺ in the Ghazwa of Tabuk. Ibn Bukair, in his narration stated that Ka`b said, " I witnessed the Al-`Aqaba pledge of allegiance at night with the Prophet ﷺ when we jointly agreed to support Islam with all our efforts I would not like to have attended the Badr battle instead of that 'Aqaba pledge although Badr is more well-known than it, amongst the people."–Al-Bukhari 3889

حَدَّثَنَا يَحْيَى بْنُ بُكَيْرٍ، حَدَّثَنَا اللَّيْثُ، عَنْ عُقَيْلٍ، عَنِ ابْنِ شِهَابٍ، حَدَّثَنَا أَحْمَدُ بْنُ صَالِحٍ، حَدَّثَنَا عَنْبَسَةُ، حَدَّثَنَا يُونُسُ، عَنِ ابْنِ شِهَابٍ، قَالَ أَخْبَرَنِي عَبْدُ الرَّحْمَنِ بْنُ عَبْدِ اللَّهِ بْنِ كَعْبِ بْنِ مَالِكٍ، أَنَّ عَبْدَ اللَّهِ بْنَ كَعْبٍ ـ وَكَانَ قَائِدَ كَعْبٍ حِينَ عَمِيَ ـ قَالَ سَمِعْتُ كَعْبَ بْنَ مَالِكٍ يُحَدِّثُ حِينَ تَخَلَّفَ عَنِ النَّبِيِّ صلى الله عليه وسلم فِي غَزْوَةِ تَبُوكَ. بِطُولِهِ، قَالَ ابْنُ بُكَيْرٍ فِي حَدِيثِهِ وَلَقَدْ شَهِدْتُ مَعَ النَّبِيِّ صلى الله عليه وسلم لَيْلَةَ الْعَقَبَةِ حِينَ تَوَاثَقْنَا عَلَى الإِسْلاَمِ، وَمَا أُحِبُّ أَنَّ لِي بِهَا مَشْهَدَ بَدْرٍ وَإِنْ كَانَتْ بَدْرٌ، أَذْكَرَ فِي النَّاسِ مِنْهَا.

Narrated Usama bin Zaid: That Allah's Messenger ﷺ rode over a donkey covered with a Fadakiya (velvet sheet) and Usama was riding behind him. He was visiting Sa`d bin 'Ubada (who was sick) in the dwelling place of Bani Al-Harith bin Al-Khazraj and this incident happened before the battle of Badr. They proceeded till they passed by a gathering in which `Abdullah bin Ubai bin Salul was present., and that was before `Abdullah bin Ubat embraced Islam. In that gathering there were Muslims, pagan idolators and Jews, and among the Muslims there was `Abdullah bin Rawaha. When a cloud of dust raised by (the movement of) the animal covered that gathering, `Abdullah bin Ubai covered his nose with his garment and said, "Do not cover us with dust." Allah's Messenger ﷺ greeted them, stopped, dismounted and invited them to Allah (i.e. to embrace Islam) and recited to them the Holy Qur'an. On that `Abdullah bin Ubai bin Salul said to him, "O man! There is nothing better than what you say, if it is the truth. So do not trouble us with it in our gatherings, but if somebody comes to you, you can preach to him." On that `Abdullah bin Rawaha said "Yes, O Allah's Messenger ﷺ ! Call on us in our gathering, for we love that." So the Muslims, the pagans and the Jews started abusing one another till they were about to fight with one another. Allah's Messenger ﷺ kept on quietening them till all of them became quiet, and then Allah's Messenger ﷺ rode his animal and proceeded till he entered upon Sa`d bin 'Ubada. Allah's Messenger ﷺ said, "O Sa`d! Didn't you hear what Abu Habab said?" (meaning `Abdullah bin Unbar). "He said so-and-so." Sa`d bin Ubada said, "O Allah's Messenger ﷺ ! Let my father be sacrificed for you ! Excuse and forgive him for, by Him Who revealed to you the Book, Allah sent the Truth which was revealed to you at the time when the people of this town had decided to crown him (`Abdullah bin Ubai) as their ruler. So when Allah had prevented that with the Truth He had given you, he was choked by that, and that caused him to behave in such an impolite manner which you had noticed." So Allah's Messenger ﷺ excused him. (It was the custom of) Allah's Messenger ﷺ and his companions to excuse the pagans and the people of the scripture (Christians and Jews) as Allah ordered them, and they used to be patient when annoyed (by them). Allah said: 'You shall certainly hear much that will grieve you from those who received the Scripture before you.....and from the pagans (3.186) He also said: 'Many of the people of the scripture wish that if they could turn you away as disbelievers after you have believed. .... (2.109) So Allah's Messenger ﷺ used to apply what Allah had ordered him by excusing them till he was allowed to fight against them. When Allah's Messenger ﷺ had fought the battle of Badr and Allah killed whomever He killed among the chiefs of the infidels and the nobles of Quraish, and Allah's Messenger ﷺ and his companions had returned with victory and booty, bringing with them some of the chiefs of the infidels and the nobles of the Quraish as captives. `Abdullah bin Ubai bin Salul and the pagan idolators who were with him, said, "This matter (Islam) has now brought out its face (triumphed), so give Allah's Messenger ﷺ the pledge of allegiance (for embracing Islam.)". Then they became Muslims.– Al-Bukhari 6207

حَدَّثَنَا أَبُو الْيَمَانِ، أَخْبَرَنَا شُعَيْبٌ، عَنِ الزُّهْرِيِّ، حَدَّثَنَا إِسْمَاعِيلُ، قَالَ حَدَّثَنِي أَخِي، عَنْ سُلَيْمَانَ، عَنْ مُحَمَّدِ بْنِ أَبِي عَتِيقٍ، عَنِ ابْنِ شِهَابٍ، عَنْ عُرْوَةَ بْنِ الزُّبَيْرِ، أَنَّ أُسَامَةَ بْنَ زَيْدٍ ـ رضى الله عنهما ـ أَخْبَرَهُ أَنَّ رَسُولَ اللَّهِ صلى الله عليه وسلم رَكِبَ عَلَى حِمَارٍ عَلَيْهِ قَطِيفَةٌ فَدَكِيَّةٌ وَأُسَامَةُ وَرَاءَهُ، يَعُودُ سَعْدَ بْنَ عُبَادَةَ فِي بَنِي حَارِثِ بْنِ الْخَزْرَجِ قَبْلَ وَقْعَةِ بَدْرٍ، فَسَارَا حَتَّى مَرَّا بِمَجْلِسٍ فِيهِ عَبْدُ اللَّهِ بْنُ أُبَىٍّ ابْنُ سَلُولَ، وَذَلِكَ قَبْلَ أَنْ يُسْلِمَ عَبْدُ اللَّهِ بْنُ أُبَىٍّ، فَإِذَا فِي الْمَجْلِسِ أَخْلاَطٌ مِنَ الْمُسْلِمِينَ وَالْمُشْرِكِينَ عَبَدَةِ الأَوْثَانِ وَالْيَهُودِ، وَفِي الْمُسْلِمِينَ عَبْدُ اللَّهِ بْنُ رَوَاحَةَ، فَلَمَّا غَشِيَتِ الْمَجْلِسَ عَجَاجَةُ الدَّابَّةِ خَمَّرَ ابْنُ أُبَىٍّ أَنْفَهُ بِرِدَائِهِ وَقَالَ لاَ تُغَبِّرُوا عَلَيْنَا. فَسَلَّمَ رَسُولُ اللَّهِ صلى الله عليه وسلم عَلَيْهِمْ، ثُمَّ وَقَفَ فَنَزَلَ فَدَعَاهُمْ إِلَى اللَّهِ وَقَرَأَ عَلَيْهِمُ الْقُرْآنَ، فَقَالَ لَهُ عَبْدُ اللَّهِ بْنُ أُبَىٍّ ابْنُ سَلُولَ أَيُّهَا الْمَرْءُ لاَ أَحْسَنَ مِمَّا تَقُولُ إِنْ كَانَ حَقًّا، فَلاَ تُؤْذِنَا بِهِ فِي مَجَالِسِنَا، فَمَنْ جَاءَكَ فَاقْصُصْ عَلَيْهِ. قَالَ عَبْدُ اللَّهِ بْنُ رَوَاحَةَ بَلَى يَا رَسُولَ اللَّهِ فَاغْشَنَا فِي مَجَالِسِنَا فَإِنَّا نُحِبُّ ذَلِكَ. فَاسْتَبَّ الْمُسْلِمُونَ وَالْمُشْرِكُونَ وَالْيَهُودُ حَتَّى كَادُوا يَتَثَاوَرُونَ فَلَمْ يَزَلْ رَسُولُ اللَّهِ صلى الله عليه وسلم يُخَفِّضُهُمْ حَتَّى سَكَتُوا، ثُمَّ رَكِبَ رَسُولُ اللَّهِ صلى الله عليه وسلم دَابَّتَهُ فَسَارَ حَتَّى دَخَلَ عَلَى سَعْدِ بْنِ عُبَادَةَ، فَقَالَ رَسُولُ اللَّهِ صلى الله عليه وسلم " أَىْ سَعْدُ أَلَمْ تَسْمَعْ مَا قَالَ أَبُو حُبَابٍ ـ يُرِيدُ عَبْدَ اللَّهِ بْنَ أُبَىٍّ ـ قَالَ كَذَا وَكَذَا ". فَقَالَ سَعْدُ بْنُ عُبَادَةَ أَىْ رَسُولَ اللَّهِ بِأَبِي أَنْتَ، اعْفُ عَنْهُ وَاصْفَحْ، فَوَالَّذِي أَنْزَلَ عَلَيْكَ الْكِتَابَ لَقَدْ جَاءَ اللَّهُ بِالْحَقِّ الَّذِي أَنْزَلَ عَلَيْكَ، وَلَقَدِ اصْطَلَحَ أَهْلُ هَذِهِ الْبَحْرَةِ عَلَى أَنْ يُتَوِّجُوهُ وَيُعَصِّبُوهُ بِالْعِصَابَةِ، فَلَمَّا رَدَّ اللَّهُ ذَلِكَ بِالْحَقِّ الَّذِي أَعْطَاكَ شَرِقَ بِذَلِكَ فَذَلِكَ فَعَلَ بِهِ مَا رَأَيْتَ. فَعَفَا عَنْهُ رَسُولُ اللَّهِ صلى الله عليه وسلم وَكَانَ رَسُولُ اللَّهِ صلى الله عليه وسلم وَأَصْحَابُهُ يَعْفُونَ عَنِ الْمُشْرِكِينَ وَأَهْلِ الْكِتَابِ كَمَا أَمَرَهُمُ اللَّهُ، وَيَصْبِرُونَ عَلَى الأَذَى، قَالَ اللَّهُ تَعَالَى {وَلَتَسْمَعُنَّ مِنَ الَّذِينَ أُوتُوا الْكِتَابَ} الآيَةَ، وَقَالَ {وَدَّ كَثِيرٌ مِنْ أَهْلِ الْكِتَابِ} فَكَانَ رَسُولُ اللَّهِ صلى الله عليه وسلم يَتَأَوَّلُ فِي الْعَفْوِ عَنْهُمْ مَا أَمَرَهُ اللَّهُ بِهِ حَتَّى أَذِنَ لَهُ فِيهِمْ، فَلَمَّا غَزَا رَسُولُ اللَّهِ صلى الله عليه وسلم بَدْرًا، فَقَتَلَ اللَّهُ بِهَا مَنْ قَتَلَ مِنْ صَنَادِيدِ الْكُفَّارِ، وَسَادَةِ قُرَيْشٍ، فَقَفَلَ رَسُولُ اللَّهِ صلى الله عليه وسلم وَأَصْحَابُهُ مَنْصُورِينَ غَانِمِينَ مَعَهُمْ أُسَارَى مِنْ صَنَادِيدِ الْكُفَّارِ وَسَادَةِ قُرَيْشٍ قَالَ ابْنُ أُبَىٍّ ابْنُ سَلُولَ، وَمَنْ مَعَهُ مِنَ الْمُشْرِكِينَ عَبَدَةِ الأَوْثَانِ هَذَا أَمْرٌ قَدْ تَوَجَّهَ فَبَايِعُوا رَسُولَ اللَّهِ صلى الله عليه وسلم عَلَى الإِسْلاَمِ فَأَسْلَمُوا

Narrated Abu Musa:That the Prophet ﷺ said, "The good is what Allah gave us later on (after Uhud), and the reward of truthfulness is what Allah gave us after the day (of the battle) of Badr."–Al-Bukhari 3987

حَدَّثَنِي مُحَمَّدُ بْنُ الْعَلاَءِ، حَدَّثَنَا أَبُو أُسَامَةَ، عَنْ بُرَيْدٍ، عَنْ جَدِّهِ أَبِي بُرْدَةَ، عَنْ أَبِي مُوسَى،، أُرَاهُ عَنِ النَّبِيِّ صلى الله عليه وسلم قَالَ " وَإِذَا الْخَيْرُ مَا جَاءَ اللَّهُ بِهِ مِنَ الْخَيْرِ بَعْدُ، وَثَوَابُ الصِّدْقِ الَّذِي آتَانَا بَعْدَ يَوْمِ بَدْرٍ "

Narrated `Abdullah: Five things have passed, i.e. the smoke, the defeat of the Romans, the splitting of the moon, Al-Batsha (the defeat of the infidels in the battle of Badr) and Al-Lizam (the punishment)'.–Al-Bukhari 4820

حَدَّثَنَا عَبْدَانُ، عَنْ أَبِي حَمْزَةَ، عَنِ الأَعْمَشِ، عَنْ مُسْلِمٍ، عَنْ مَسْرُوقٍ، عَنْ عَبْدِ اللَّهِ، قَالَ مَضَى خَمْسٌ الدُّخَانُ وَالرُّومُ وَالْقَمَرُ وَالْبَطْشَةُ وَاللِّزَامُ

Narrate Aisha: Abu Bakr married a woman from the tribe of Bani Kalb, called Um Bakr. When Abu Bakr migrated to Medina, he divorced her and she was married by her cousin, the poet who said the following poem lamenting the infidels of Quraish: "What is there kept in the well, The well of Badr, (The owners of) the trays of Roasted camel humps? What is there kept in the well, The well of Badr, (The owners of) lady singers And friends of the honorable companions; who used to drink (wine) together, Um Bakr greets us With the greeting of peace, But can I find peace After my people have gone? The Apostle tells us that We shall live again, But what sort of life will owls and skulls live?:–Al-Bukhari 3921

حَدَّثَنَا أَصْبَغُ، حَدَّثَنَا ابْنُ وَهْبٍ، عَنْ يُونُسَ، عَنِ ابْنِ شِهَابٍ، عَنْ عُرْوَةَ بْنِ الزُّبَيْرِ، عَنْ عَائِشَةَ، أَنَّ أَبَا بَكْرٍ ـ رضى الله عنه ـ تَزَوَّجَ امْرَأَةً مِنْ كَلْبٍ يُقَالُ لَهَا أُمُّ بَكْرٍ، فَلَمَّا هَاجَرَ أَبُو بَكْرٍ طَلَّقَهَا، فَتَزَوَّجَهَا ابْنُ عَمِّهَا، هَذَا الشَّاعِرُ الَّذِي قَالَ هَذِهِ الْقَصِيدَةَ، رَثَى كُفَّارَ قُرَيْشٍ وَمَاذَا بِالْقَلِيبِ قَلِيبِ بَدْرٍ مِنَ الشِّيزَى تُزَيَّنُ بِالسَّنَامِ وَمَاذَا بِالْقَلِيبِ، قَلِيبِ بَدْرٍ مِنَ الْقَيْنَاتِ وَالشَّرْبِ الْكِرَامِ تُحَيِّي بِالسَّلاَمَةِ أُمُّ بَكْرٍ وَهَلْ لِي بَعْدَ قَوْمِي مِنْ سَلاَمِ يُحَدِّثُنَا الرَّسُولُ بِأَنْ سَنَحْيَا وَكَيْفَ حَيَاةُ أَصْدَاءٍ وَهَامِ

Narrated Aisha: With the start of the last ten days of Ramadan, the Prophet ﷺ used to tighten his waist belt (i.e. work hard) and used to pray all the night, and used to keep his family awake for the prayers.–Al-Bukhari 2024

حَدَّثَنَا عَلِيُّ بْنُ عَبْدِ اللَّهِ، حَدَّثَنَا سُفْيَانُ، عَنْ أَبِي يَعْفُورٍ، عَنْ أَبِي الضُّحَى، عَنْ مَسْرُوقٍ، عَنْ عَائِشَةَ ـ رضى الله عنها ـ قَالَتْ كَانَ النَّبِيُّ صلى الله عليه وسلم إِذَا دَخَلَ الْعَشْرُ شَدَّ مِئْزَرَهُ، وَأَحْيَا لَيْلَهُ، وَأَيْقَظَ أَهْلَهُ

Narrated Al-Bara' bin `Azib: On the day of Uhud the Prophet ﷺ appointed `Abdullah bin Jubair as chief of the archers, and seventy among us were injured and martyred. On the day (of the battle) of Badr, the Prophet ﷺ and his companions had inflicted 140 casualties on the pagans, 70 were taken prisoners, and 70 were killed. Abu Sufyan said, "This is a day of (revenge) for the day of Badr and the issue of war is undecided ."–Al-Bukhari 3986

حَدَّثَنِي عَمْرُو بْنُ خَالِدٍ، حَدَّثَنَا زُهَيْرٌ، حَدَّثَنَا أَبُو إِسْحَاقَ، قَالَ سَمِعْتُ الْبَرَاءَ بْنَ عَازِبٍ ـ رضى الله عنهما ـ قَالَ جَعَلَ النَّبِيُّ صلى الله عليه وسلم عَلَى الرُّمَاةِ يَوْمَ أُحُدٍ عَبْدَ اللَّهِ بْنَ جُبَيْرٍ، فَأَصَابُوا مِنَّا سَبْعِينَ، وَكَانَ النَّبِيُّ صلى الله عليه وسلم وَأَصْحَابُهُ أَصَابُوا مِنَ الْمُشْرِكِينَ يَوْمَ بَدْرٍ أَرْبَعِينَ وَمِائَةً سَبْعِينَ أَسِيرًا وَسَبْعِينَ قَتِيلاً. قَالَ أَبُو سُفْيَانَ يَوْمٌ بِيَوْمِ بَدْرٍ، وَالْحَرْبُ سِجَالٌ.

Marriage with Hafsa bint Umar occurred a month before Al-Uhud
وكان زواجه من حفصة بنت عمر قبل غزوة أحد بشهر.

Narrated `Abdullah bin `Umar: `Umar bin Al-Khattab said, "When Hafsa bint `Umar became a widow after the death of (her husband) Khunais bin Hudhafa As-Sahmi who had been one of the companions of the Prophet, and he died at Medina. I went to `Uthman bin `Affan and presented Hafsa (for marriage) to him. He said, "I will think it over.' I waited for a few days, then he met me and said, 'It seems that it is not possible for me to marry at present.' " `Umar further said, "I met Abu Bakr As-Siddique and said to him, 'If you wish, I will marry my daughter Hafsa to you." Abu Bakr kept quiet and did not say anything to me in reply. I became more angry with him than with `Uthman. I waited for a few days and then Allah's Messenger ﷺ asked for her hand, and I gave her in marriage to him. Afterwards I met Abu Bakr who said, 'Perhaps you became angry with me when you presented Hafsa to me and I did not give you a reply?' I said, 'Yes.' Abu Bakr said, 'Nothing stopped me to respond to your offer except that I knew that Allah's Apostle had mentioned her, and I never wanted to let out the secret of Allah's Messenger ﷺ . And if Allah's Apostle had refused her, I would have accepted her.' " – Sahih al-Bukhari 5122

حَدَّثَنَا عَبْدُ الْعَزِيزِ بْنُ عَبْدِ اللَّهِ، حَدَّثَنَا إِبْرَاهِيمُ بْنُ سَعْدٍ، عَنْ صَالِحِ بْنِ كَيْسَانَ، عَنِ ابْنِ شِهَابٍ، قَالَ أَخْبَرَنِي سَالِمُ بْنُ عَبْدِ اللَّهِ، أَنَّهُ سَمِعَ عَبْدَ اللَّهِ بْنَ عُمَرَ ـ رضى الله عنهما ـ يُحَدِّثُ أَنَّ عُمَرَ بْنَ الْخَطَّابِ حِينَ تَأَيَّمَتْ حَفْصَةُ بِنْتُ عُمَرَ مِنْ خُنَيْسِ بْنِ حُذَافَةَ السَّهْمِيِّ ـ وَكَانَ مِنْ أَصْحَابِ رَسُولِ اللَّهِ صلى الله عليه وسلم فَتُوُفِّيَ بِالْمَدِينَةِ ـ فَقَالَ عُمَرُ بْنُ الْخَطَّابِ أَتَيْتُ عُثْمَانَ بْنَ عَفَّانَ فَعَرَضْتُ عَلَيْهِ حَفْصَةَ فَقَالَ سَأَنْظُرُ فِي أَمْرِي. فَلَبِثْتُ لَيَالِيَ ثُمَّ لَقِيَنِي فَقَالَ قَدْ بَدَا لِي أَنْ لاَ أَتَزَوَّجَ يَوْمِي هَذَا. قَالَ عُمَرُ فَلَقِيتُ أَبَا بَكْرٍ الصِّدِّيقَ فَقُلْتُ إِنْ شِئْتَ زَوَّجْتُكَ حَفْصَةَ بِنْتَ عُمَرَ. فَصَمَتَ أَبُو بَكْرٍ فَلَمْ يَرْجِعْ إِلَىَّ شَيْئًا، وَكُنْتُ أَوْجَدَ عَلَيْهِ مِنِّي عَلَى عُثْمَانَ، فَلَبِثْتُ لَيَالِيَ ثُمَّ خَطَبَهَا رَسُولُ اللَّهِ صلى الله عليه وسلم فَأَنْكَحْتُهَا إِيَّاهُ، فَلَقِيَنِي أَبُو بَكْرٍ فَقَالَ لَعَلَّكَ وَجَدْتَ عَلَىَّ حِينَ عَرَضْتَ عَلَىَّ حَفْصَةَ فَلَمْ أَرْجِعْ إِلَيْكَ شَيْئًا. قَالَ عُمَرُ قُلْتُ نَعَمْ. قَالَ أَبُو بَكْرٍ فَإِنَّهُ لَمْ يَمْنَعْنِي أَنْ أَرْجِعَ إِلَيْكَ فِيمَا عَرَضْتَ عَلَىَّ إِلاَّ أَنِّي كُنْتُ عَلِمْتُ أَنَّ رَسُولَ اللَّهِ صلى الله عليه وسلم قَدْ ذَكَرَهَا، فَلَمْ أَكُنْ لأُفْشِيَ سِرَّ رَسُولِ اللَّهِ صلى الله عليه وسلم وَلَوْ تَرَكَهَا رَسُولُ اللَّهِ صلى الله عليه وسلم قَبِلْتُهَا.

The Book of
Ghazwa of Uhud
غزوة أحد

Narrated Abu Musa: The Prophet ﷺ said, "I saw in a dream that I was migrating from Mecca to a land where there were date palm trees. I thought that it might be the land of Al-Yamama or Hajar, but behold, it turned out to be Yathrib (i.e. Medina). And I saw cows (being slaughtered) there, but the reward given by Allah is better (than worldly benefits). Behold, those cows proved to symbolize the believers (who were killed) on the Day (of the battle) of Uhud, and the good (which I saw in the dream) was the good and the reward and the truth which Allah bestowed upon us after the Badr battle. (or the Battle of Uhud) and that was the victory bestowed by Allah in the Battle of Khaibar and the conquest of Mecca) . – Al-Bukhari 7035

حَدَّثَنِي مُحَمَّدُ بْنُ الْعَلاَءِ، حَدَّثَنَا أَبُو أُسَامَةَ، عَنْ بُرَيْدٍ، عَنْ جَدِّهِ أَبِي بُرْدَةَ، عَنْ أَبِي مُوسَى، أُرَاهُ عَنِ النَّبِيِّ صلى الله عليه وسلم قَالَ " رَأَيْتُ فِي الْمَنَامِ أَنِّي أُهَاجِرُ مِنْ مَكَّةَ إِلَى أَرْضٍ بِهَا نَخْلٌ، فَذَهَبَ وَهَلِي إِلَى أَنَّهَا الْيَمَامَةُ أَوْ هَجَرٌ، فَإِذَا هِيَ

الْمَدِينَةُ يَثْرِبُ، وَرَأَيْتُ فِيهَا بَقَرًا وَاللَّهُ خَيْرٌ، فَإِذَا هُمُ الْمُؤْمِنُونَ يَوْمَ أُحُدٍ، وَإِذَا الْخَيْرُ مَا جَاءَ اللَّهُ مِنَ الْخَيْرِ وَثَوَابِ الصِّدْقِ الَّذِي أَتَانَا اللَّهُ بِهِ بَعْدَ يَوْمِ بَدْرٍ ".

⌜Remember, O Prophet,⌝ when you left your home in the early morning to position the believers in the battlefield. And Allah is All-Hearing, All-Knowing. – Surah Al-Imran 3:121
وَإِذْ غَدَوْتَ مِنْ أَهْلِكَ تُبَوِّئُ ٱلْمُؤْمِنِينَ مَقَٰعِدَ لِلْقِتَالِ ۗ وَٱللَّهُ سَمِيعٌ عَلِيمٌ

Narrated Ibn `Umar: Allah's Messenger ﷺ called me to present myself in front of him or the eve of the battle of Uhud, while I was fourteen years of age at that time, and he did not allow me to take part in that battle, but he called me in front of him on the eve of the battle of the Trench when I was fifteen years old, and he allowed me (to join the battle)." Nafi` said, "I went to `Umar bin `Abdul `Aziz who was Caliph at that time and related the above narration to him, He said, "This age (fifteen) is the limit between childhood and manhood," and wrote to his governors to give salaries to those who reached the age of fifteen. – Al-Bukhari 2664
حَدَّثَنَا عُبَيْدُ اللَّهِ بْنُ سَعِيدٍ، حَدَّثَنَا أَبُو أُسَامَةَ، قَالَ حَدَّثَنِي عُبَيْدُ اللَّهِ، قَالَ حَدَّثَنِي نَافِعٌ، قَالَ حَدَّثَنِي ابْنُ عُمَرَ ـ رضى الله عنهما ـ أَنَّ رَسُولَ اللَّهِ صلى الله عليه وسلم عَرَضَهُ يَوْمَ أُحُدٍ وَهْوَ ابْنُ أَرْبَعَ عَشْرَةَ سَنَةً، فَلَمْ يُجِزْنِي، ثُمَّ عَرَضَنِي يَوْمَ الْخَنْدَقِ وَأَنَا ابْنُ خَمْسَ عَشْرَةَ فَأَجَازَنِي. قَالَ نَافِعٌ فَقَدِمْتُ عَلَى عُمَرَ بْنِ عَبْدِ الْعَزِيزِ وَهْوَ خَلِيفَةٌ، فَحَدَّثْتُهُ هَذَا الْحَدِيثَ، فَقَالَ إِنَّ هَذَا لَحَدٌّ بَيْنَ الصَّغِيرِ وَالْكَبِيرِ. وَكَتَبَ إِلَى عُمَّالِهِ أَنْ يَفْرِضُوا لِمَنْ بَلَغَ خَمْسَ عَشْرَةَ.

Narrated Jabir bin `Abdullah: On the day of the battle of Uhud, a man came to the Prophet ﷺ and said, "Can you tell me where I will be if I should get martyred?" The Prophet ﷺ replied, "In Paradise." The man threw away some dates he was carrying in his hand, and fought till he was martyred . – Al-Bukhari 4046
حَدَّثَنَا عَبْدُ اللَّهِ بْنُ مُحَمَّدٍ، حَدَّثَنَا سُفْيَانُ، عَنْ عَمْرٍو، سَمِعَ جَابِرَ بْنَ عَبْدِ اللَّهِ ـ رضى الله عنهما ـ قَالَ قَالَ رَجُلٌ لِلنَّبِيِّ صلى الله عليه وسلم يَوْمَ أُحُدٍ أَرَأَيْتَ إِنْ قُتِلْتُ فَأَيْنَ أَنَا قَالَ " فِي الْجَنَّةِ " فَأَلْقَى تَمَرَاتٍ فِي يَدِهِ، ثُمَّ قَاتَلَ حَتَّى قُتِلَ.

Narrated Al-Bara bin Azib: The Prophet ﷺ appointed `Abdullah bin Jubair as the commander of the infantry men (archers) who were fifty on the day (of the battle) of Uhud. He instructed them, "Stick to your place, and don't leave it even if you see birds snatching us, till I send for you; and if you see that we have defeated the infidels and made them flee, even then you should not leave your place till I send for you." Then the infidels were defeated. By Allah, I saw the women fleeing lifting up their clothes revealing their leg-bangles and their legs. So, the companions of `Abdullah bin Jubair said, "The booty! O people, the booty ! Your companions have become victorious, what are you waiting for now?" `Abdullah bin Jubair said, "Have you forgotten what Allah's Messenger ﷺ said to you?" They replied, "By Allah! We will go to the people (i.e. the enemy) and collect our share from the war booty." But when they went to them, they were forced to turn back defeated. At that time Allah's Messenger ﷺ in their rear was calling them back. Only twelve men remained with the Prophet ﷺ and the infidels martyred seventy men from us. On the day (of the battle) of Badr, the Prophet ﷺ and his companions had caused the 'Pagans to lose 140 men, seventy of whom were captured and seventy were killed. Then Abu Sufyan asked thrice, "Is Muhammad present amongst these people?" The Prophet ﷺ ordered his companions not to answer him. Then he asked thrice, "Is the son of Abu Quhafa present amongst these people?" He asked again thrice, "Is the son of Al-Khattab present amongst these people?" He then returned to his companions and said, "As for these (men), they have been killed." `Umar could not control himself and said (to Abu Sufyan), "You told a lie, by Allah! O enemy of Allah! All those you have mentioned are alive, and the thing which will make you unhappy is still there." Abu Sufyan said, "Our victory today is a counterbalance to yours in the battle of Badr, and in war (the victory) is always undecided and is shared in turns by the belligerents, and you will find some of your (killed) men mutilated, but I did not urge my men to do so, yet I do not feel sorry for their deed" After that he started reciting cheerfully, "O Hubal, be high! (1) On that the Prophet ﷺ said (to his companions), "Why don't you answer him back?" They said, "O Allah's Messenger ﷺ What shall we say?" He said, "Say, Allah is Higher and more Sublime." (Then) Abu Sufyan said, "We have the (idol) Al `Uzza, and you have no `Uzza." The Prophet said (to his companions), "Why don't you answer him back?" They asked, "O Allah's Messenger ﷺ ! What shall we say?" He said, "Says Allah is our Helper and you have no helper.". – Al-Bukhari 3039 also Bukhari 4043 & 3986

حَدَّثَنَا عَمْرُو بْنُ خَالِدٍ، حَدَّثَنَا زُهَيْرٌ، حَدَّثَنَا أَبُو إِسْحَاقَ، قَالَ سَمِعْتُ الْبَرَاءَ بْنَ عَازِبٍ ـ رضى الله عنهما ـ يُحَدِّثُ قَالَ جَعَلَ النَّبِيُّ صلى الله عليه وسلم عَلَى الرَّجَّالَةِ يَوْمَ أُحُدٍ ـ وَكَانُوا خَمْسِينَ رَجُلاً ـ عَبْدَ اللَّهِ بْنَ جُبَيْرٍ فَقَالَ " إِنْ رَأَيْتُمُونَا تَخْطَفُنَا الطَّيْرُ، فَلاَ تَبْرَحُوا مَكَانَكُمْ هَذَا حَتَّى أُرْسِلَ إِلَيْكُمْ، وَإِنْ رَأَيْتُمُونَا هَزَمْنَا الْقَوْمَ وَأَوْطَأْنَاهُمْ فَلاَ تَبْرَحُوا حَتَّى أُرْسِلَ إِلَيْكُمْ " فَهَزَمُوهُمْ. قَالَ فَأَنَا وَاللَّهِ رَأَيْتُ النِّسَاءَ يَشْتَدِدْنَ قَدْ بَدَتْ خَلاَخِلُهُنَّ وَأَسْوُقُهُنَّ رَافِعَاتٍ ثِيَابَهُنَّ، فَقَالَ أَصْحَابُ عَبْدِ اللَّهِ بْنِ جُبَيْرٍ الْغَنِيمَةَ ـ أَىْ قَوْمِ ـ الْغَنِيمَةَ، ظَهَرَ أَصْحَابُكُمْ فَمَا تَنْتَظِرُونَ فَقَالَ عَبْدُ اللَّهِ بْنُ جُبَيْرٍ أَنَسِيتُمْ مَا قَالَ لَكُمْ رَسُولُ اللَّهِ صلى الله عليه وسلم قَالُوا وَاللَّهِ لَنَأْتِيَنَّ النَّاسَ فَلَنُصِيبَنَّ مِنَ الْغَنِيمَةِ. فَلَمَّا أَتَوْهُمْ صُرِفَتْ وُجُوهُهُمْ فَأَقْبَلُوا مُنْهَزِمِينَ، فَذَاكَ إِذْ يَدْعُوهُمُ الرَّسُولُ فِي أُخْرَاهُمْ، فَلَمْ يَبْقَ مَعَ النَّبِيِّ صلى الله عليه وسلم غَيْرُ اثْنَىْ عَشَرَ رَجُلاً، فَأَصَابُوا مِنَّا سَبْعِينَ، وَكَانَ النَّبِيُّ صلى الله عليه وسلم وَأَصْحَابُهُ أَصَابَ مِنَ الْمُشْرِكِينَ يَوْمَ بَدْرٍ أَرْبَعِينَ وَمِائَةً سَبْعِينَ أَسِيرًا وَسَبْعِينَ قَتِيلاً، فَقَالَ أَبُو سُفْيَانَ أَفِي الْقَوْمِ مُحَمَّدٌ ثَلاَثَ مَرَّاتٍ، فَنَهَاهُمُ النَّبِيُّ صلى الله عليه وسلم أَنْ يُجِيبُوهُ ثُمَّ قَالَ أَفِي الْقَوْمِ ابْنُ أَبِي قُحَافَةَ ثَلاَثَ مَرَّاتٍ، ثُمَّ قَالَ أَفِي الْقَوْمِ ابْنُ الْخَطَّابِ ثَلاَثَ مَرَّاتٍ، ثُمَّ رَجَعَ إِلَى أَصْحَابِهِ فَقَالَ أَمَّا هَؤُلاَءِ فَقَدْ قُتِلُوا. فَمَا مَلَكَ عُمَرُ نَفْسَهُ فَقَالَ كَذَبْتَ وَاللَّهِ يَا عَدُوَّ اللَّهِ، إِنَّ الَّذِينَ عَدَدْتَ لأَحْيَاءٌ كُلُّهُمْ، وَقَدْ بَقِيَ لَكَ مَا يَسُوؤُكَ. قَالَ يَوْمٌ بِيَوْمِ بَدْرٍ، وَالْحَرْبُ سِجَالٌ، إِنَّكُمْ سَتَجِدُونَ فِي الْقَوْمِ مُثْلَةً لَمْ آمُرْ بِهَا وَلَمْ تَسُؤْنِي، ثُمَّ أَخَذَ يَرْتَجِزُ أُعْلُ هُبَلْ، أُعْلُ هُبَلْ. قَالَ النَّبِيُّ صلى الله عليه وسلم " أَلاَ تُجِيبُوا لَهُ ". قَالُوا يَا رَسُولَ اللَّهِ، مَا نَقُولُ قَالَ " قُولُوا اللَّهُ أَعْلَى وَأَجَلُّ ". قَالَ إِنَّ لَنَا الْعُزَّى وَلاَ عُزَّى لَكُمْ. فَقَالَ النَّبِيُّ صلى الله عليه وسلم " أَلاَ تُجِيبُوا لَهُ ". قَالَ قَالُوا يَا رَسُولَ اللَّهِ، مَا نَقُولُ قَالَ " قُولُوا اللَّهُ مَوْلاَنَا وَلاَ مَوْلَى لَكُمْ ".

Narrated `Uthman bin Mauhab: A man came to perform the Hajj to (Allah's) House. Seeing some people sitting, he said, "Who are these sitting people?" Somebody said, "They are the people of Quraish." He said, "Who is the old man?" They said, "Ibn `Umar." He went to him and said, "I want to ask you about something; will you tell me about it? I ask you with the respect due to the sanctity of this (Sacred) House, do you know that `Uthman bin `Affan fled on the day of Uhud?" Ibn `Umar said, "Yes." He said, "Do you know that he (i.e. `Uthman) was absent from the Badr (battle) and did not join it?" Ibn `Umar said, "Yes." He said, "Do you know that he failed to be present at the Ridwan Pledge of allegiance (i.e. Pledge of allegiance at Hudaibiya) and did not witness it?" Ibn `Umar replied, "Yes," He then said, "Allahu- Akbar!" Ibn `Umar said, "Come along; I will inform you and explain to you what you have asked. As for the flight (of `Uthman) on the day of Uhud, I testify that Allah forgave him. As regards his absence from the Badr (battle), he was married to the daughter of Allah's Messenger ﷺ and she was ill, so the Prophet ﷺ said to him, 'You will have such reward as a man who has fought the Badr battle will get, and will also have the same share of the booty.' As for his absence from the Ridwan Pledge of allegiance if there had been anybody more respected by the Meccans than `Uthman bin `Affan, the Prophet would surely have sent that man instead of `Uthman. So the Prophet ﷺ sent him (i.e. `Uthman to Mecca) and the Ridwan Pledge of allegiance took place after `Uthman had gone to Mecca. The Prophet raised his right hand saying. 'This is the hand of `Uthman,' and clapped it over his other hand and said, "This is for `Uthman.'" Ibn `Umar then said (to the man), "Go now, after taking this information." – Al-Bukhari 4066 also Bukhari 4062

حَدَّثَنَا عَبْدَانُ، أَخْبَرَنَا أَبُو حَمْزَةَ، عَنْ عُثْمَانَ بْنِ مَوْهَبٍ، قَالَ جَاءَ رَجُلٌ حَجَّ الْبَيْتَ فَرَأَى قَوْمًا جُلُوسًا فَقَالَ مَنْ هَؤُلاَءِ الْقُعُودُ قَالُوا هَؤُلاَءِ قُرَيْشٌ. قَالَ مَنِ الشَّيْخُ قَالُوا ابْنُ عُمَرَ. فَأَتَاهُ فَقَالَ إِنِّي سَائِلُكَ عَنْ شَىْءٍ أَتُحَدِّثُنِي، قَالَ أَنْشُدُكَ بِحُرْمَةِ هَذَا

الْبَيْتِ أَتَعْلَمُ أَنَّ عُثْمَانَ بْنَ عَفَّانَ فَرَّ يَوْمَ أُحُدٍ قَالَ نَعَمْ. قَالَ فَتَعْلَمُهُ تَغَيَّبَ عَنْ بَدْرٍ فَلَمْ يَشْهَدْهَا قَالَ نَعَمْ. قَالَ فَتَعْلَمُ أَنَّهُ تَخَلَّفَ عَنْ بَيْعَةِ الرِّضْوَانِ فَلَمْ يَشْهَدْهَا قَالَ نَعَمْ. قَالَ فَكَبَّرَ. قَالَ ابْنُ عُمَرَ تَعَالَ لأُخْبِرَكَ وَلأُبَيِّنَ لَكَ عَمَّا سَأَلْتَنِي عَنْهُ، أَمَّا فِرَارُهُ يَوْمَ أُحُدٍ فَأَشْهَدُ أَنَّ اللَّهَ عَفَا عَنْهُ، وَأَمَّا تَغَيُّبُهُ عَنْ بَدْرٍ فَإِنَّهُ كَانَ تَحْتَهُ بِنْتُ رَسُولِ اللَّهِ صلى الله عليه وسلم وَكَانَتْ مَرِيضَةً، فَقَالَ لَهُ النَّبِيُّ صلى الله عليه وسلم " إِنَّ لَكَ أَجْرَ رَجُلٍ مِمَّنْ شَهِدَ بَدْرًا وَسَهْمَهُ ". وَأَمَّا تَغَيُّبُهُ عَنْ بَيْعَةِ الرِّضْوَانِ فَإِنَّهُ لَوْ كَانَ أَحَدٌ أَعَزَّ بِبَطْنِ مَكَّةَ مِنْ عُثْمَانَ بْنِ عَفَّانَ لَبَعَثَهُ مَكَانَهُ، فَبَعَثَ عُثْمَانَ، وَكَانَ بَيْعَةُ الرِّضْوَانِ بَعْدَ مَا ذَهَبَ عُثْمَانُ إِلَى مَكَّةَ فَقَالَ النَّبِيُّ صلى الله عليه وسلم بِيَدِهِ الْيُمْنَى " هَذِهِ يَدُ عُثْمَانَ ". فَضَرَبَ بِهَا عَلَى يَدِهِ فَقَالَ " هَذِهِ لِعُثْمَانَ ". اذْهَبْ بِهَذَا الآنَ مَعَكَ

Narrated Zaid bin Thabit: Regarding the Verse:-- "Then what is the matter with you that you are divided into two parties about the hypocrites?" (4.88) Some of the companions of the Prophet ﷺ returned from the battle of Uhud (i.e. refused to fight) whereupon the Muslims got divided into two parties; one of them was in favor of their execution and the other was not in favour of it. So there ware revealed: "Then what is the matter with you that you are divided into two parties about the hypocrites?" (4.88). Then the Prophet ﷺ said "It (i.e. Medina) is aTayyaboh (good), it expels impurities as the fire expels the impurities of silver." – Al-Bukhari 4589

حَدَّثَنِي مُحَمَّدُ بْنُ بَشَّارٍ، حَدَّثَنَا غُنْدَرٌ، وَعَبْدُ الرَّحْمَنِ، قَالاَ حَدَّثَنَا شُعْبَةُ، عَنْ عَدِيٍّ، عَنْ عَبْدِ اللَّهِ بْنِ يَزِيدَ، عَنْ زَيْدِ بْنِ ثَابِتٍ ـ رضى الله عنه ـ {فَمَا لَكُمْ فِي الْمُنَافِقِينَ فِئَتَيْنِ} رَجَعَ نَاسٌ مِنْ أَصْحَابِ النَّبِيِّ صلى الله عليه وسلم مِنْ أُحُدٍ، وَكَانَ النَّاسُ فِيهِمْ فِرْقَتَيْنِ فَرِيقٌ يَقُولُ اقْتُلْهُمْ. وَفَرِيقٌ يَقُولُ لاَ فَنَزَلَتْ {فَمَا لَكُمْ فِي الْمُنَافِقِينَ فِئَتَيْنِ} وَقَالَ " إِنَّهَا طَيْبَةُ تَنْفِي الْخَبَثَ كَمَا تَنْفِي النَّارُ خَبَثَ الْفِضَّةِ "

Those of you who turned back on the day when the two armies clashed—it was Satan who caused them to backslide, on account of some of what they have earned. But Allah has forgiven them. Allah is Forgiving and Prudent. - Surah Al-Imran 3:155

إِنَّ ٱلَّذِينَ تَوَلَّوْا۟ مِنكُمْ يَوْمَ ٱلْتَقَى ٱلْجَمْعَانِ إِنَّمَا ٱسْتَزَلَّهُمُ ٱلشَّيْطَـٰنُ بِبَعْضِ مَا كَسَبُوا۟ ۖ وَلَقَدْ عَفَا ٱللَّهُ عَنْهُمْ ۗ إِنَّ ٱللَّهَ غَفُورٌ حَلِيمٌ

Narrated Mu'tamir's father: `Uthman said that on the day of the battle of Uhud, none remained with the Prophet ﷺ but Talha and Sa`d. – Al-Bukhari 4060, 4061

حَدَّثَنَا مُوسَى بْنُ إِسْمَاعِيلَ، عَنْ مُعْتَمِرٍ، عَنْ أَبِيهِ، قَالَ زَعَمَ أَبُو عُثْمَانَ أَنَّهُ لَمْ يَبْقَ مَعَ النَّبِيِّ صلى الله عليه وسلم فِي بَعْضِ تِلْكَ الأَيَّامِ الَّتِي يُقَاتِلُ فِيهِنَّ غَيْرُ طَلْحَةَ وَسَعْدٍ. عَنْ حَدِيثِهِمَا

Narrated Anas: On the day of the battle of Uhud, the people ran away, leaving the Prophet ﷺ ,but Abu- Talha was shielding the Prophet ﷺ with his shield in front of him. Abu Talha was a strong, experienced archer who used to keep his arrow bow strong and well stretched. On that day he broke two or three arrow bows. If any man passed by carrying a quiver full of arrows, the Prophet ﷺ would say to him, "Empty it in front of Abu Talha." When the Prophet ﷺ stated looking at the enemy by raising his head, Abu Talha said, "O Allah's Prophet! Let my parents be sacrificed for your sake! Please don't raise your head and make it visible, lest an arrow of the enemy should hit you. Let my neck and chest be wounded instead of yours." (On that day) I saw `Aisha, the daughter of Abu Bakr and Um Sulaim both lifting their dresses up so that I was able to see the ornaments of their legs, and they were carrying the water skins of their arms to pour the water into the mouths of the thirsty people and then go back and fill them and come to pour the water into the mouths of the people again. (On that day) Abu Talha's sword fell from his hand twice or thrice. – Al-Bukhari 3811

حَدَّثَنَا أَبُو مَعْمَرٍ، حَدَّثَنَا عَبْدُ الْوَارِثِ، حَدَّثَنَا عَبْدُ الْعَزِيزِ، عَنْ أَنَسٍ ـ رضى الله عنه ـ قَالَ لَمَّا كَانَ يَوْمُ أُحُدٍ انْهَزَمَ النَّاسُ عَنِ النَّبِيِّ صلى الله عليه وسلم وَأَبُو طَلْحَةَ بَيْنَ يَدَيِ النَّبِيِّ صلى الله عليه وسلم مُجَوِّبٌ بِهِ عَلَيْهِ بِحَجَفَةٍ لَهُ، وَكَانَ أَبُو طَلْحَةَ رَجُلاً رَامِيًا شَدِيدَ الْقِدِّ، يَكْسِرُ يَوْمَئِذٍ قَوْسَيْنِ أَوْ ثَلاَثًا، وَكَانَ الرَّجُلُ يَمُرُّ مَعَهُ الْجَعْبَةُ مِنَ النَّبْلِ فَيَقُولُ انْشُرْهَا لأَبِي طَلْحَةَ. فَأَشْرَفَ النَّبِيُّ صلى الله عليه وسلم يَنْظُرُ إِلَى الْقَوْمِ، فَيَقُولُ أَبُو طَلْحَةَ يَا نَبِيَّ اللَّهِ بِأَبِي أَنْتَ وَأُمِّي، لاَ تُشْرِفْ يُصِيبُكَ سَهْمٌ

مِنْ سِهَامِ الْقَوْمِ، نَحْرِي دُونَ نَحْرِكَ. وَلَقَدْ رَأَيْتُ عَائِشَةَ بِنْتَ أَبِي بَكْرٍ وَأُمَّ سُلَيْمٍ وَإِنَّهُمَا لَمُشَمِّرَتَانِ، أَرَى خَدَمَ سُوقِهِمَا، تُنْقِزَانِ الْقِرَبَ عَلَى مُتُونِهِمَا، تُفْرِغَانِهِ فِي أَفْوَاهِ الْقَوْمِ، ثُمَّ تَرْجِعَانِ فَتَمْلآنِهَا، ثُمَّ تَجِيآنِ فَتُفْرِغَانِهِ فِي أَفْوَاهِ الْقَوْمِ، وَلَقَدْ وَقَعَ السَّيْفُ مِنْ يَدَىْ أَبِي طَلْحَةَ إِمَّا مَرَّتَيْنِ، وَإِمَّا ثَلاَثًا

Narrated Abu Talha: Slumber overtook us during the battle of Uhud while we were in the front files. My sword would fall from my hand and I would pick it up, and again it would fall down and I would pick it up again. – Al-Bukhari 4562

حَدَّثَنَا إِسْحَاقُ بْنُ إِبْرَاهِيمَ بْنِ عَبْدِ الرَّحْمَنِ أَبُو يَعْقُوبَ، حَدَّثَنَا حُسَيْنُ بْنُ مُحَمَّدٍ، حَدَّثَنَا شَيْبَانُ، عَنْ قَتَادَةَ، حَدَّثَنَا أَنَسٌ، أَنَّ أَبَا طَلْحَةَ، قَالَ غَشِيَنَا النُّعَاسُ وَنَحْنُ فِي مَصَافِّنَا يَوْمَ أُحُدٍ ـ قَالَ ـ فَجَعَلَ سَيْفِي يَسْقُطُ مِنْ يَدِي وَآخُذُهُ، وَيَسْقُطُ وَآخُذُهُ

Narrated `Ali: I never heard Allah's Messenger ﷺ saying, "Let my father and mother be sacrificed for you," except for Sa`d (bin Abi Waqqas). I heard him saying, "Throw! (arrows), Let my father and mother be sacrificed for you !" (The sub-narrator added, "I think that was in the battle of Uhud."). – Al-Bukhari 6184

حَدَّثَنَا مُسَدَّدٌ، حَدَّثَنَا يَحْيَى، عَنْ سُفْيَانَ، حَدَّثَنِي سَعْدُ بْنُ إِبْرَاهِيمَ، عَنْ عَبْدِ اللَّهِ بْنِ شَدَّادٍ، عَنْ عَلِيٍّ ـ رضى الله عنه ـ قَالَ مَا سَمِعْتُ رَسُولَ اللَّهِ صلى الله عليه وسلم يُفَدِّي أَحَدًا غَيْرَ سَعْدٍ، سَمِعْتُهُ يَقُولُ " ارْمِ فَدَاكَ أَبِي وَأُمِّي ". أَظُنُّهُ يَوْمَ أُحُدٍ

Narrated Sa`d: On the day of the battle of Uhud the Prophet ﷺ mentioned for me both his parents (i.e. saying, "Let my parents be sacrificed for you."). – Al-Bukhari 3725

حَدَّثَنِي مُحَمَّدُ بْنُ الْمُثَنَّى، حَدَّثَنَا عَبْدُ الْوَهَّابِ، قَالَ سَمِعْتُ يَحْيَى، قَالَ سَمِعْتُ سَعِيدَ بْنَ الْمُسَيَّبِ، قَالَ سَمِعْتُ سَعْدًا، يَقُولُ جَمَعَ لِي النَّبِيُّ صلى الله عليه وسلم أَبَوَيْهِ يَوْمَ أُحُدٍ.

Narrated Sa`d: On the day of the battle of Uhud, on the right and on the left of the Prophet ﷺ were two men wearing white clothes, and I had neither seen them before, nor did I see them afterwards. – Al-Bukhari 5826

حَدَّثَنَا إِسْحَاقُ بْنُ إِبْرَاهِيمَ الْحَنْظَلِيُّ، أَخْبَرَنَا مُحَمَّدُ بْنُ بِشْرٍ، حَدَّثَنَا مِسْعَرٌ، عَنْ سَعْدِ بْنِ إِبْرَاهِيمَ، عَنْ أَبِيهِ، عَنْ سَعْدٍ، قَالَ رَأَيْتُ بِشِمَالِ النَّبِيِّ صلى الله عليه وسلم وَبِيَمِينِهِ رَجُلَيْنِ عَلَيْهِمَا ثِيَابٌ بِيضٌ يَوْمَ أُحُدٍ، مَا رَأَيْتُهُمَا قَبْلُ وَلاَ بَعْدُ.

Narrated Sahl bin Saud As-Sa`idi: When the helmet broke on the head of the Prophet ﷺ and his face became covered with blood and his incisor tooth broke (i.e. during the battle of Uhud), `Ali used to bring water in his shield while Fatima was washing the blood off his face. When Fatima saw that the bleeding increased because of the water, she took a mat (of palm leaves), burnt it, and stuck it (the burnt ashes) on the wound of Allah's Apostle, whereupon the bleeding stopped. – Al-Bukhari 5722

حَدَّثَنِي سَعِيدُ بْنُ عُفَيْرٍ، حَدَّثَنَا يَعْقُوبُ بْنُ عَبْدِ الرَّحْمَنِ الْقَارِيُّ، عَنْ أَبِي حَازِمٍ، عَنْ سَهْلِ بْنِ سَعْدٍ السَّاعِدِيِّ، قَالَ لَمَّا كُسِرَتْ عَلَى رَأْسِ رَسُولِ اللَّهِ صلى الله عليه وسلم الْبَيْضَةُ، وَأُدْمِيَ وَجْهُهُ، وَكُسِرَتْ رَبَاعِيَتُهُ، وَكَانَ عَلِيٌّ يَخْتَلِفُ بِالْمَاءِ فِي الْمِجَنِّ، وَجَاءَتْ فَاطِمَةُ تَغْسِلُ عَنْ وَجْهِهِ الدَّمَ، فَلَمَّا رَأَتْ فَاطِمَةُ ـ عَلَيْهَا السَّلاَمُ ـ الدَّمَ يَزِيدُ عَلَى الْمَاءِ كَثْرَةً عَمَدَتْ إِلَى حَصِيرٍ فَأَحْرَقَتْهَا وَأَلْصَقَتْهَا عَلَى جُرْحِ رَسُولِ اللَّهِ صلى الله عليه وسلم فَرَقَأَ الدَّمُ.

Narrated Jabir: When the time of the Battle of Uhud approached, my father called me at night and said, "I think that I will be the first amongst the companions of the Prophet ﷺ to be martyred. I do not leave anyone after me dearer to me than you, except Allah's Messenger's ﷺ soul and I owe some debt and you should repay it and treat your sisters favorably (nicely and politely)." So in the morning he was the first to be martyred and was buried along with another (martyr). I did not like to leave him with the other (martyr) so I took him out of the grave after six months of his burial and he was in the same condition as he was on the day of burial, except a slight change near his ear. – Al-Bukhari 1351. [7]

حَدَّثَنَا مُسَدَّدٌ، أَخْبَرَنَا بِشْرُ بْنُ الْمُفَضَّلِ، حَدَّثَنَا حُسَيْنٌ الْمُعَلِّمُ، عَنْ عَطَاءٍ، عَنْ جَابِرٍ ـ رضى الله عنه ـ قَالَ لَمَّا حَضَرَ أُحُدٌ دَعَانِي أَبِي مِنَ اللَّيْلِ فَقَالَ مَا أُرَانِي إِلاَّ مَقْتُولاً فِي أَوَّلِ مَنْ يُقْتَلُ مِنْ أَصْحَابِ النَّبِيِّ صلى الله عليه وسلم، وَإِنِّي لاَ أَتْرُكُ بَعْدِي أَعَزَّ عَلَىَّ مِنْكَ، غَيْرَ نَفْسِ رَسُولِ اللَّهِ صلى الله عليه وسلم، فَإِنَّ عَلَىَّ دَيْنًا فَاقْضِ، وَاسْتَوْصِ بِأَخَوَاتِكَ خَيْرًا.
فَأَصْبَحْنَا فَكَانَ أَوَّلَ قَتِيلٍ، وَدُفِنَ مَعَهُ آخَرُ فِي قَبْرٍ، ثُمَّ لَمْ تَطِبْ نَفْسِي أَنْ أَتْرُكَهُ مَعَ الآخَرِ فَاسْتَخْرَجْتُهُ بَعْدَ سِتَّةِ أَشْهُرٍ، فَإِذَا هُوَ كَيَوْمِ وَضَعْتُهُ هُنَيَّةً غَيْرَ أُذُنِهِ.

Narrated Jabir bin `Abdullah: On the day of the Battle of Uhud, my father was brought and he had been mutilated (in battle) and was placed in front of Allah's Messenge ﷺ and a sheet was over him. I went intending to uncover my father but my people forbade me; again I wanted to uncover him but my people forbade me. Allah's Messenger ﷺ gave his order and he was shifted away. At that time he heard the voice of a crying woman and asked, "Who is this?" They said, "It is the daughter or the sister of `Amr." He said, "Why does she weep? (or let her stop weeping), for the angels had been shading him with their wings till he (i.e. the body of the martyr) was shifted away." – Al-Bukhari 1293

حَدَّثَنَا عَلِيُّ بْنُ عَبْدِ اللَّهِ، حَدَّثَنَا سُفْيَانُ، حَدَّثَنَا ابْنُ الْمُنْكَدِرِ، قَالَ سَمِعْتُ جَابِرَ بْنَ عَبْدِ اللَّهِ ـ رضى الله عنهما ـ قَالَ جِيءَ بِأَبِي يَوْمَ أُحُدٍ، قَدْ مُثِّلَ بِهِ حَتَّى وُضِعَ بَيْنَ يَدَىْ رَسُولِ اللَّهِ صلى الله عليه وسلم وَقَدْ سُجِّيَ ثَوْبًا فَذَهَبْتُ أُرِيدُ أَنْ أَكْشِفَ عَنْهُ فَنَهَانِي قَوْمِي، ثُمَّ ذَهَبْتُ أَكْشِفُ عَنْهُ فَنَهَانِي قَوْمِي، فَأَمَرَ رَسُولُ اللَّهِ صلى الله عليه وسلم فَرُفِعَ فَسَمِعَ صَوْتَ صَائِحَةٍ فَقَالَ " مَنْ هَذِهِ ". فَقَالُوا ابْنَةُ عَمْرٍو أَوْ أُخْتُ عَمْرٍو. قَالَ " فَلِمَ تَبْكِي أَوْ لاَ تَبْكِي فَمَا زَالَتِ الْمَلاَئِكَةُ تُظِلُّهُ بِأَجْنِحَتِهَا حَتَّى رُفِعَ "

Narrated Jabir bin `Abdullah: My father was martyred on the day (of the battle) of Uhud, and he was in debt. His creditors demanded their rights persistently. I went to the Prophet (and informed him about it). He told them to take the fruits of my garden and exempt my father from the debts but they refused to do so. So, the Prophet did not give them my garden and told me that he would come to me the next morning. He came to us early in the morning and wandered among the date-palms and invoked Allah to bless their fruits. I then plucked the dates and paid the creditors, and there remained some of the dates for us. – Al-Bukhari 2395

حَدَّثَنَا عَبْدَانُ، أَخْبَرَنَا عَبْدُ اللَّهِ، أَخْبَرَنَا يُونُسُ، عَنِ الزُّهْرِيِّ، قَالَ حَدَّثَنِي ابْنُ كَعْبِ بْنِ مَالِكٍ، أَنَّ جَابِرَ بْنَ عَبْدِ اللَّهِ ـ رضى الله عنهما ـ أَخْبَرَهُ أَنَّ أَبَاهُ قُتِلَ يَوْمَ أُحُدٍ شَهِيدًا، وَعَلَيْهِ دَيْنٌ فَاشْتَدَّ الْغُرَمَاءُ فِي حُقُوقِهِمْ، فَأَتَيْتُ النَّبِيَّ صلى الله عليه وسلم فَسَأَلَهُمْ أَنْ يَقْبَلُوا تَمْرَ حَائِطِي وَيُحَلِّلُوا أَبِي فَأَبَوْا، فَلَمْ يُعْطِهِمِ النَّبِيُّ صلى الله عليه وسلم حَائِطِي، وَقَالَ " سَنَغْدُو عَلَيْكَ ".
فَغَدَا عَلَيْنَا حِينَ أَصْبَحَ، فَطَافَ فِي النَّخْلِ، وَدَعَا فِي ثَمَرِهَا بِالْبَرَكَةِ، فَجَدَدْتُهَا فَقَضَيْتُهُمْ، وَبَقِيَ لَنَا مِنْ تَمْرِهَا

Narrated `Aisha: On the day (of the battle) of Uhud when the pagans were defeated, Satan shouted, "O slaves of Allah! Beware of the forces at your back," and on that the Muslims of the front files fought with the Muslims of the back files (thinking they were pagans). Hudhaifa looked back to see his father "Al-Yaman," (being attacked by the Muslims). He shouted, "O Allah's Slaves! My father! My father!" By Allah, they did not stop till they killed him. Hudhaifa said, "May Allah forgive you." `Urwa said that Hudhaifa continued to do good (invoking Allah to forgive the killer of his father till he met Allah (i.e. died). – Al-Bukhari 3290 also Bukhari 6883 , 4065 , 3824

حَدَّثَنَا زَكَرِيَّاءُ بْنُ يَحْيَى، حَدَّثَنَا أَبُو أُسَامَةَ، قَالَ هِشَامٌ أَخْبَرَنَا عَنْ أَبِيهِ، عَنْ عَائِشَةَ ـ رضى الله عنها قَالَتْ لَمَّا كَانَ يَوْمَ أُحُدٍ هُزِمَ الْمُشْرِكُونَ فَصَاحَ إِبْلِيسُ أَىْ عِبَادَ اللَّهِ أُخْرَاكُمْ. فَرَجَعَتْ أُولاَهُمْ فَاجْتَلَدَتْ هِيَ وَأُخْرَاهُمْ، فَنَظَرَ حُذَيْفَةُ فَإِذَا هُوَ بِأَبِيهِ الْيَمَانِ فَقَالَ أَىْ عِبَادَ اللَّهِ أَبِي أَبِي. فَوَاللَّهِ مَا احْتَجَزُوا حَتَّى قَتَلُوهُ، فَقَالَ حُذَيْفَةُ غَفَرَ اللَّهُ لَكُمْ. قَالَ عُرْوَةُ فَمَا زَالَتْ فِي حُذَيْفَةَ مِنْهُ بَقِيَّةُ خَيْرٍ حَتَّى لَحِقَ بِاللَّهِ

[7] (Jabir bin Abdullah fulfilled his father's request and married a matron to assist with his younger sisters Bukhari 4052 . Jabir also paid his father's debt see Bukhari 3580)

Narrated Anas: My uncle Anas bin An-Nadr was absent from the Battle of Badr. He said, "O Allah's Messenger ﷺ ! I was absent from the first battle you fought against the pagans. (By Allah) if Allah gives me a chance to fight the pagans, no doubt. Allah will see how (bravely) I will fight." On the day of Uhud when the Muslims turned their backs and fled, he said, "O Allah! I apologize to You for what these (i.e. his companions) have done, and I denounce what these (i.e. the pagans) have done." Then he advanced and Sa`d bin Mu`adh met him. He said "O Sa`d bin Mu`adh ! By the Lord of An-Nadr, Paradise! I am smelling its aroma coming from before (the mountain of) Uhud," Later on Sa`d said, "O Allah's Apostle! I cannot achieve or do what he (i.e. Anas bin An-Nadr) did. We found more than eighty wounds by swords and arrows on his body. We found him dead and his body was mutilated so badly that none except his sister could recognize him by his fingers." We used to think that the following Verse was revealed concerning him and other men of his sort: "Among the believers are men who have been true to their covenant with Allah.........." (33.23) His sister Ar-Rubbaya' broke a front tooth of a woman and Allah's Messenger ﷺ ordered for retaliation. On that Anas (bin An-Nadr) said, "O Allah's Messenger ﷺ ! By Him Who has sent you with the Truth, my sister's tooth shall not be broken." Then the opponents of Anas's sister accepted the compensation and gave up the claim of retaliation. So Allah's Messenger ﷺ said, "There are some people amongst Allah's slaves whose oaths are fulfilled by Allah when they take them." – Al-Bukhari 2805, 2806 also Bukhari 4048

حَدَّثَنَا مُحَمَّدُ بْنُ سَعِيدٍ الْخُزَاعِيُّ، حَدَّثَنَا عَبْدُ الأَعْلَى، عَنْ حُمَيْدٍ، قَالَ سَأَلْتُ أَنَسًا. حَدَّثَنَا عَمْرُو بْنُ زُرَارَةَ، حَدَّثَنَا زِيَادٌ، قَالَ حَدَّثَنِي حُمَيْدٌ الطَّوِيلُ، عَنْ أَنَسٍ ـ رضى الله عنه ـ قَالَ غَابَ عَمِّي أَنَسُ بْنُ النَّضْرِ عَنْ قِتَالِ بَدْرٍ فَقَالَ يَا رَسُولَ اللَّهِ، غِبْتُ عَنْ أَوَّلِ قِتَالٍ قَاتَلْتَ الْمُشْرِكِينَ، لَئِنِ اللَّهُ أَشْهَدَنِي قِتَالَ الْمُشْرِكِينَ لَيَرَيَنَّ اللَّهُ مَا أَصْنَعُ، فَلَمَّا كَانَ يَوْمُ أُحُدٍ وَانْكَشَفَ الْمُسْلِمُونَ قَالَ " اللَّهُمَّ إِنِّي أَعْتَذِرُ إِلَيْكَ مِمَّا صَنَعَ هَؤُلاَءِ ـ يَعْنِي أَصْحَابَهُ ـ وَأَبْرَأُ إِلَيْكَ مِمَّا صَنَعَ هَؤُلاَءِ " ـ يَعْنِي الْمُشْرِكِينَ ـ ثُمَّ تَقَدَّمَ، فَاسْتَقْبَلَهُ سَعْدُ بْنُ مُعَاذٍ، فَقَالَ يَا سَعْدُ بْنَ مُعَاذٍ، الْجَنَّةَ، وَرَبِّ النَّضْرِ إِنِّي أَجِدُ رِيحَهَا مِنْ دُونِ أُحُدٍ. قَالَ سَعْدٌ فَمَا اسْتَطَعْتُ يَا رَسُولَ اللَّهِ مَا صَنَعَ. قَالَ أَنَسٌ فَوَجَدْنَا بِهِ بِضْعًا وَثَمَانِينَ ضَرْبَةً بِالسَّيْفِ أَوْ طَعْنَةً بِرُمْحٍ أَوْ رَمْيَةً بِسَهْمٍ، وَوَجَدْنَاهُ قَدْ قُتِلَ وَقَدْ مَثَّلَ بِهِ الْمُشْرِكُونَ، فَمَا عَرَفَهُ أَحَدٌ إِلاَّ أُخْتُهُ بِبَنَانِهِ. قَالَ أَنَسٌ كُنَّا نُرَى أَوْ نَظُنُّ أَنَّ هَذِهِ الآيَةَ نَزَلَتْ فِيهِ وَفِي أَشْبَاهِهِ {مِنَ الْمُؤْمِنِينَ رِجَالٌ صَدَقُوا مَا عَاهَدُوا اللَّهَ عَلَيْهِ} إِلَى آخِرِ الآيَةِ. وَقَالَ إِنَّ أُخْتَهُ وَهْىَ تُسَمَّى الرُّبَيِّعَ كَسَرَتْ ثَنِيَّةَ امْرَأَةٍ فَأَمَرَ رَسُولُ اللَّهِ صلى الله عليه وسلم بِالْقِصَاصِ، فَقَالَ أَنَسٌ يَا رَسُولَ اللَّهِ، وَالَّذِي بَعَثَكَ بِالْحَقِّ لاَ تُكْسَرُ ثَنِيَّتُهَا. فَرَضُوا بِالأَرْشِ وَتَرَكُوا الْقِصَاصَ، فَقَالَ رَسُولُ اللَّهِ صلى الله عليه وسلم " إِنَّ مِنْ عِبَادِ اللَّهِ مَنْ لَوْ أَقْسَمَ عَلَى اللَّهِ لأَبَرَّهُ ".

Narrated Khabbab: We emigrated with the Prophet ﷺ in Allah's cause, and so our reward was then surely incumbent on Allah. Some of us died and they did not take anything from their rewards in this world, and amongst them was Mustab bin `Umar; and the others were those who got their rewards. Mustab bin `Umar was martyred on the day of the Battle of Uhud and we could get nothing except his Burd to shroud him in. And when we covered his head his feet became bare and vice versa. So the Prophet ﷺ ordered us to cover his head only and to put idhkhir (a kind of shrub) over his feet. – Al-Bukhari 1276 also Bukhari 3897 & 3914

حَدَّثَنَا عُمَرُ بْنُ حَفْصِ بْنِ غِيَاثٍ، حَدَّثَنَا أَبِي، حَدَّثَنَا الأَعْمَشُ، حَدَّثَنَا شَقِيقٌ، حَدَّثَنَا خَبَّابٌ ـ رضى الله عنه ـ قَالَ هَاجَرْنَا مَعَ النَّبِيِّ صلى الله عليه وسلم نَلْتَمِسُ وَجْهَ اللَّهِ، فَوَقَعَ أَجْرُنَا عَلَى اللَّهِ، فَمِنَّا مَنْ مَاتَ لَمْ يَأْكُلْ مِنْ أَجْرِهِ شَيْئًا مِنْهُمْ مُصْعَبُ بْنُ عُمَيْرٍ، وَمِنَّا مَنْ أَيْنَعَتْ لَهُ ثَمَرَتُهُ فَهْوَ يَهْدِبُهَا. قُتِلَ يَوْمَ أُحُدٍ، فَلَمْ نَجِدْ مَا نُكَفِّنُهُ إِلاَّ بُرْدَةً إِذَا غَطَّيْنَا بِهَا رَأْسَهُ خَرَجَتْ رِجْلاَهُ، وَإِذَا غَطَّيْنَا رِجْلَيْهِ خَرَجَ رَأْسُهُ، فَأَمَرَنَا النَّبِيُّ صلى الله عليه وسلم أَنْ نُغَطِّيَ رَأْسَهُ، وَأَنْ نَجْعَلَ عَلَى رِجْلَيْهِ مِنَ الإِذْخِرِ.

Narrated Jabir bin `Abdullah: Allah's Messenger ﷺ used to shroud two martyrs of Uhud in one sheet and then say, "Which of them knew Qur'an more?" When one of the two was pointed out, he would put him first in the grave. Then he said, "I will be a witness for them on the Day of Resurrection." He ordered them to be buried with their blood (on their bodies). Neither was the funeral prayer offered for them, nor were they washed. Jabir added, "When my father was martyred, I started weeping and uncovering his face. The companions of the Prophetﷺ stopped me from doing so but the Prophetﷺ did not stop me. Then the Prophet said, '(O Jabir.) don't weep over him, for the angels kept on covering him with their wings till his body was carried away (for burial). – Al-Bukhari 4079, 4080 also Bukhari 1346

حَدَّثَنَا قُتَيْبَةُ بْنُ سَعِيدٍ، حَدَّثَنَا اللَّيْثُ، عَنِ ابْنِ شِهَابٍ، عَنْ عَبْدِ الرَّحْمَنِ بْنِ كَعْبِ بْنِ مَالِكٍ، أَنَّ جَابِرَ بْنَ عَبْدِ اللَّهِ ـ رضى الله عنهما ـ أَخْبَرَهُ أَنَّ رَسُولَ اللَّهِ صلى الله عليه وسلم كَانَ يَجْمَعُ بَيْنَ الرَّجُلَيْنِ مِنْ قَتْلَى أُحُدٍ فِي ثَوْبٍ وَاحِدٍ ثُمَّ يَقُولُ " أَيُّهُمْ أَكْثَرُ أَخْذًا لِلْقُرْآنِ ". فَإِذَا أُشِيرَ لَهُ إِلَى أَحَدٍ، قَدَّمَهُ فِي اللَّحْدِ، وَقَالَ " أَنَا شَهِيدٌ عَلَى هَؤُلاَءِ يَوْمَ الْقِيَامَةِ ". وَأَمَرَ بِدَفْنِهِمْ بِدِمَائِهِمْ، وَلَمْ يُصَلِّ عَلَيْهِمْ، وَلَمْ يُغَسِّلُوا. وَقَالَ أَبُو الْوَلِيدِ عَنْ شُعْبَةَ، عَنِ ابْنِ الْمُنْكَدِرِ، قَالَ سَمِعْتُ جَابِرًا، قَالَ لَمَّا قُتِلَ أَبِي جَعَلْتُ أَبْكِي وَأَكْشِفُ الثَّوْبَ عَنْ وَجْهِهِ، فَجَعَلَ أَصْحَابُ النَّبِيِّ صلى الله عليه وسلم يَنْهَوْنِي وَالنَّبِيُّ صلى الله عليه وسلم لَمْ يَنْهَ، وَقَالَ النَّبِيُّ صلى الله عليه وسلم " لاَ تَبْكِيهِ أَوْ مَا تَبْكِيهِ، مَا زَالَتِ الْمَلاَئِكَةُ تُظِلُّهُ بِأَجْنِحَتِهَا حَتَّى رُفِعَ ".

Narrated `Uqba bin 'Amir: The Prophetﷺ went out and offered the funeral prayer for the martyrs of the (battle of) Uhud and then ascended the pulpit and said, "I am your predecessor and I am a witness against you. By Allah, I am now looking at my Tank-lake (Al-Kauthar) and I have been given the keys of the treasures of the earth (or the keys of the earth). By Allah! I am not afraid that after me you will worship others besides Allah, but I am afraid that you will start competing for (the pleasures of) this world.". – Al-Bukhari 6426

حَدَّثَنَا قُتَيْبَةُ بْنُ سَعِيدٍ، حَدَّثَنَا اللَّيْثُ، عَنْ يَزِيدَ بْنِ أَبِي حَبِيبٍ، عَنْ أَبِي الْخَيْرِ، عَنْ عُقْبَةَ بْنِ عَامِرٍ، أَنَّ رَسُولَ اللَّهِ صلى الله عليه وسلم خَرَجَ يَوْمًا فَصَلَّى عَلَى أَهْلِ أُحُدٍ صَلاَتَهُ عَلَى الْمَيِّتِ، ثُمَّ انْصَرَفَ إِلَى الْمِنْبَرِ فَقَالَ " إِنِّي فَرَطُكُمْ وَأَنَا شَهِيدٌ عَلَيْكُمْ، وَإِنِّي وَاللَّهِ لأَنْظُرُ إِلَى حَوْضِي الآنَ، وَإِنِّي قَدْ أُعْطِيتُ مَفَاتِيحَ خَزَائِنِ الأَرْضِ ـ أَوْ مَفَاتِيحَ الأَرْضِ ـ وَإِنِّي وَاللَّهِ مَا أَخَافُ عَلَيْكُمْ أَنْ تُشْرِكُوا بَعْدِي، وَلَكِنِّي أَخَافُ عَلَيْكُمْ أَنْ تَنَافَسُوا فِيهَا "

What befell you on the day the two armies clashed was with Allah's permission; that He may know the believers. - Surah Al-Imran 3:166

وَمَآ أَصَـٰبَكُمْ يَوْمَ ٱلْتَقَى ٱلْجَمْعَانِ فَبِإِذْنِ ٱللَّهِ وَلِيَعْلَمَ ٱلْمُؤْمِنِينَ

Narrated Anas: The alcoholic drink which was spilled was Al-Fadikh. I used to offer alcoholic drinks to the people at the residence of Abu Talha. Then the order of prohibiting Alcoholic drinks was revealed, and the Prophet ordered somebody to announce that: Abu Talha said to me, "Go out and see what this voice (this announcement) is." I went out and (on coming back) said, "This is somebody announcing that alcoholic beverages have been prohibited." Abu Talha said to me, "Go and spill it (I.e. the wine)," Then it (alcoholic drinks) was seen flowing through the streets of Medina. At that time the wine was Al-Fadikh. The people said, "Some people (Muslims) were killed (during the battle of Uhud) while wine was in their stomachs." So Allah revealed: "On those who believe and do good deeds there is no blame for what they ate (in the past)." (5.93) – Al-Bukhari 4620

حَدَّثَنَا أَبُو النُّعْمَانِ، حَدَّثَنَا حَمَّادُ بْنُ زَيْدٍ، حَدَّثَنَا ثَابِتٌ، عَنْ أَنَسٍ ـ رضى الله عنه ـ أَنَّ الْخَمْرَ، الَّتِي أُهْرِيقَتِ الْفَضِيخُ. وَزَادَنِي مُحَمَّدٌ عَنْ أَبِي النُّعْمَانِ قَالَ كُنْتُ سَاقِيَ الْقَوْمِ فِي مَنْزِلِ أَبِي طَلْحَةَ فَنَزَلَ تَحْرِيمُ الْخَمْرِ، فَأَمَرَ مُنَادِيًا فَنَادَى. فَقَالَ أَبُو طَلْحَةَ اخْرُجْ فَانْظُرْ مَا هَذَا الصَّوْتُ قَالَ فَخَرَجْتُ فَقُلْتُ هَذَا مُنَادٍ يُنَادِي أَلاَ إِنَّ الْخَمْرَ قَدْ حُرِّمَتْ. فَقَالَ لِي اذْهَبْ فَأَهْرِقْهَا. قَالَ فَجَرَتْ فِي سِكَكِ الْمَدِينَةِ. قَالَ وَكَانَتْ خَمْرُهُمْ يَوْمَئِذٍ الْفَضِيخَ فَقَالَ بَعْضُ الْقَوْمِ قُتِلَ قَوْمٌ وَهْىَ فِي بُطُونِهِمْ قَالَ فَأَنْزَلَ اللَّهُ {لَيْسَ عَلَى الَّذِينَ آمَنُوا وَعَمِلُوا الصَّالِحَاتِ جُنَاحٌ فِيمَا طَعِمُوا}

Narrated Tha`laba bin Abi Malik: `Umar bin Al-Khattab distributed woolen clothes amongst some women of Medina, and a nice woolen garment remained. Some of those who were sitting with him, said, "O chief of the believers! Give it to the daughter of Allah's Messengerﷺ who is with you," and by that, they meant Um Kulthum, the daughter of `Ali. `Umar said, "Um Salit has got more right than she." Um Salit was amongst those Ansari women who had given the pledge of allegiance to Allah's Messenger ﷺ.' Umar added, "She (i.e. Um Salit) used to carry the filled water skins for us on the day of the battle of Uhud.". – Al-Bukhari 4071

حَدَّثَنَا يَحْيَى بْنُ بُكَيْرٍ، حَدَّثَنَا اللَّيْثُ، عَنْ يُونُسَ، عَنِ ابْنِ شِهَابٍ، وَقَالَ ثَعْلَبَةُ بْنُ أَبِي مَالِكٍ إِنَّ عُمَرَ بْنَ الْخَطَّابِ ـ رضى الله عنه ـ قَسَمَ مُرُوطًا بَيْنَ نِسَاءٍ مِنْ نِسَاءِ أَهْلِ الْمَدِينَةِ، فَبَقِيَ مِنْهَا مِرْطٌ جَيِّدٌ، فَقَالَ لَهُ بَعْضُ مَنْ عِنْدَهُ يَا أَمِيرَ الْمُؤْمِنِينَ أَعْطِ هَذَا بِنْتَ رَسُولِ اللَّهِ صلى الله عليه وسلم الَّتِي عِنْدَكَ. يُرِيدُونَ أُمَّ كُلْثُومٍ بِنْتَ عَلِيٍّ. فَقَالَ عُمَرُ أُمُّ سَلِيطٍ أَحَقُّ بِهِ. وَأُمُّ سَلِيطٍ مِنْ نِسَاءِ الأَنْصَارِ مِمَّنْ بَايَعَ رَسُولَ اللَّهِ صلى الله عليه وسلم، قَالَ عُمَرُ فَإِنَّهَا كَانَتْ تُزْفِرُ لَنَا الْقِرَبَ يَوْمَ أُحُدٍ

Narrated Jafar bin `Amr bin Umaiya: I went out with 'Ubaidullah bin `Adi Al-Khaiyar. When we reached Hims (i.e. a town in Syria), 'Ubaidullah bin `Adi said (to me), "Would you like to see Wahshi so that we may ask him about the killing of Hamza?" I replied, "Yes." Wahshi used to live in Hims. We enquired about him and somebody said to us, "He is that in the shade of his palace, as if he were a full water skin." So we went up to him, and when we were at a short distance from him, we greeted him and he greeted us in return. 'Ubaidullah was wearing his turban and Wahshi could not see except his eyes and feet. 'Ubaidullah said, "O Wahshi! Do you know me?" Wahshi looked at him and then said, "No, by Allah! But I know that `Adi bin Al-Khiyar married a woman called Um Qital, the daughter of Abu Al-Is, and she delivered a boy for him at Mecca, and I looked for a wet nurse for that child. (Once) I carried that child along with his mother and then I handed him over to her, and your feet resemble that child's feet." Then 'Ubaidullah uncovered his face and said (to Wahshi), "Will you tell us (the story of) the killing of Hamza?" Wahshi replied "Yes, Hamza killed Tuaima bin `Adi bin Al-Khaiyar at Badr (battle) so my master, Jubair bin Mut`im said to me, 'If you kill Hamza in revenge for my uncle, then you will be set free." When the people set out (for the battle of Uhud) in the year of 'Ainain ..'Ainain is a mountain near the mountain of Uhud, and between it and Uhud there is a valley.. I went out with the people for the battle. When the army aligned for the fight, Siba' came out and said, 'Is there any (Muslim) to accept my challenge to a duel?' Hamza bin `Abdul Muttalib came out and said, 'O Siba'. O Ibn Um Anmar, the one who circumcises other ladies! Do you challenge Allah and His Apostle?' Then Hamza attacked and killed him, causing him to be non-extant like the bygone yesterday. I hid myself under a rock, and when he (i.e. Hamza) came near me, I threw my spear at him, driving it into his umbilicus so that it came out through his buttocks, causing him to die. When all the people returned to Mecca, I too returned with them. I stayed in (Mecca) till Islam spread in it (i.e. Mecca). Then I left for Taif, and when the people (of Taif) sent their messengers to Allah's Messenger ﷺ, I was told that the Prophet ﷺ did not harm the messengers; So I too went out with them till I reached Allah's Messenger ﷺ. When he saw me, he said, 'Are you Wahshi?' I said, 'Yes.' He said, 'Was it you who killed Hamza?' I replied, 'What happened is what you have been told of.' He said, 'Can you hide your face from me?' So I went out when Allah's Messenger ﷺ died, and Musailamah Al-Kadhdhab appeared (claiming to be a prophet). I said, 'I will go out to Musailamah so that I may kill him, and make amends for killing Hamza. So I went out with the people (to fight Musailamah and his followers) and then famous events took place concerning that battle. Suddenly I saw a man (i.e. Musailamah) standing near a gap in a wall. He looked like an ash-colored camel and his hair was dishevelled. So I threw my spear at him, driving it into his chest in between his breasts till it passed out through his shoulders, and then an Ansari man attacked him and struck him on the head with a sword. `Abdullah bin `Umar said, 'A slave girl on the roof of a house said: Alas! The chief of the believers (i.e. Musailamah) has been killed by a black slave." – Al-Bukhari 4072

حَدَّثَنِي أَبُو جَعْفَرٍ، مُحَمَّدُ بْنُ عَبْدِ اللَّهِ حَدَّثَنَا حُجَيْنُ بْنُ الْمُثَنَّى، حَدَّثَنَا عَبْدُ الْعَزِيزِ بْنُ عَبْدِ اللَّهِ بْنِ أَبِي سَلَمَةَ، عَنْ عَبْدِ اللَّهِ بْنِ الْفَضْلِ، عَنْ سُلَيْمَانَ بْنِ يَسَارٍ، عَنْ جَعْفَرِ بْنِ عَمْرِو بْنِ أُمَيَّةَ الضَّمْرِيِّ، قَالَ خَرَجْتُ مَعَ عُبَيْدِ اللَّهِ بْنِ عَدِيِّ بْنِ الْخِيَارِ، فَلَمَّا قَدِمْنَا حِمْصَ قَالَ لِي عُبَيْدُ اللَّهِ هَلْ لَكَ فِي وَحْشِيٍّ نَسْأَلُهُ عَنْ قَتْلِ حَمْزَةَ قُلْتُ نَعَمْ. وَكَانَ وَحْشِيٌّ يَسْكُنُ حِمْصَ فَسَأَلْنَا عَنْهُ

فَقِيلَ لَنَا هُوَ ذَاكَ فِي ظِلِّ قَصْرِهِ، كَأَنَّهُ حَمِيتٌ. قَالَ فَجِئْنَا حَتَّى وَقَفْنَا عَلَيْهِ بِيَسِيرٍ، فَسَلَّمْنَا، فَرَدَّ السَّلاَمَ، قَالَ وَعُبَيْدُ اللَّهِ مُعْتَجِرٌ بِعِمَامَتِهِ، مَا يَرَى وَحْشِيٌّ إِلاَّ عَيْنَيْهِ وَرِجْلَيْهِ، فَقَالَ عُبَيْدُ اللَّهِ يَا وَحْشِيُّ أَتَعْرِفُنِي قَالَ فَنَظَرَ إِلَيْهِ ثُمَّ قَالَ لاَ وَاللَّهِ إِلاَّ أَنِّي أَعْلَمُ أَنَّ عَدِيَّ بْنَ الْخِيَارِ تَزَوَّجَ امْرَأَةً يُقَالُ لَهَا أُمُّ قِتَالٍ بِنْتُ أَبِي الْعِيصِ، فَوَلَدَتْ لَهُ غُلاَمًا بِمَكَّةَ، فَكُنْتُ أَسْتَرْضِعُ لَهُ، فَحَمَلْتُ ذَلِكَ الْغُلاَمَ مَعَ أُمِّهِ، فَنَاوَلْتُهَا إِيَّاهُ، فَلَكَأَنِّي نَظَرْتُ إِلَى قَدَمَيْكَ. قَالَ فَكَشَفَ عُبَيْدُ اللَّهِ عَنْ وَجْهِهِ ثُمَّ قَالَ أَلاَ تُخْبِرُنَا بِقَتْلِ حَمْزَةَ قَالَ نَعَمْ، إِنَّ حَمْزَةَ قَتَلَ طُعَيْمَةَ بْنَ عَدِيِّ بْنِ الْخِيَارِ بِبَدْرٍ، فَقَالَ لِي مَوْلاَىَ جُبَيْرُ بْنُ مُطْعِمٍ إِنْ قَتَلْتَ حَمْزَةَ بِعَمِّي فَأَنْتَ حُرٌّ، قَالَ فَلَمَّا أَنْ خَرَجَ النَّاسُ عَامَ عَيْنَيْنِ ـ وَعَيْنَيْنِ جَبَلٌ بِحِيَالِ أُحُدٍ، بَيْنَهُ وَبَيْنَهُ وَادٍ ـ خَرَجْتُ مَعَ النَّاسِ إِلَى الْقِتَالِ، فَلَمَّا اصْطَفُّوا لِلْقِتَالِ خَرَجَ سِبَاعٌ فَقَالَ هَلْ مِنْ مُبَارِزٍ قَالَ فَخَرَجَ إِلَيْهِ حَمْزَةُ بْنُ عَبْدِ الْمُطَّلِبِ فَقَالَ يَا سِبَاعُ يَا ابْنَ أُمِّ أَنْمَارٍ مُقَطِّعَةِ الْبُظُورِ، أَتُحَادُّ اللَّهَ وَرَسُولَهُ صلى الله عليه وسلم قَالَ ثُمَّ شَدَّ عَلَيْهِ فَكَانَ كَأَمْسِ الذَّاهِبِ ـ قَالَ ـ وَكَمَنْتُ لِحَمْزَةَ تَحْتَ صَخْرَةٍ فَلَمَّا دَنَا مِنِّي رَمَيْتُهُ بِحَرْبَتِي، فَأَضَعُهَا فِي ثُنَّتِهِ حَتَّى خَرَجَتْ مِنْ بَيْنِ وَرِكَيْهِ ـ قَالَ ـ فَكَانَ ذَاكَ الْعَهْدَ بِهِ، فَلَمَّا رَجَعَ النَّاسُ رَجَعْتُ مَعَهُمْ فَأَقَمْتُ بِمَكَّةَ، حَتَّى فَشَا فِيهَا الإِسْلاَمُ، ثُمَّ خَرَجْتُ إِلَى الطَّائِفِ، فَأَرْسَلُوا إِلَى رَسُولِ اللَّهِ صلى الله عليه وسلم رَسُولاً، فَقِيلَ لِي إِنَّهُ لاَ يَهِيجُ الرُّسُلَ ـ قَالَ ـ فَخَرَجْتُ مَعَهُمْ حَتَّى قَدِمْتُ عَلَى رَسُولِ اللَّهِ صلى الله عليه وسلم فَلَمَّا رَآنِي قَالَ " آنْتَ وَحْشِيٌّ ". قُلْتُ نَعَمْ. قَالَ " أَنْتَ قَتَلْتَ حَمْزَةَ ". قُلْتُ قَدْ كَانَ مِنَ الأَمْرِ مَا بَلَغَكَ. قَالَ " فَهَلْ تَسْتَطِيعُ أَنْ تُغَيِّبَ وَجْهَكَ عَنِّي ". قَالَ فَخَرَجْتُ، فَلَمَّا قُبِضَ رَسُولُ اللَّهِ صلى الله عليه وسلم فَخَرَجَ مُسَيْلِمَةُ الْكَذَّابُ قُلْتُ لأَخْرُجَنَّ إِلَى مُسَيْلِمَةَ لَعَلِّي أَقْتُلُهُ فَأُكَافِئَ بِهِ حَمْزَةَ ـ قَالَ ـ فَخَرَجْتُ مَعَ النَّاسِ، فَكَانَ مِنْ أَمْرِهِ مَا كَانَ ـ قَالَ ـ فَإِذَا رَجُلٌ قَائِمٌ فِي ثَلْمَةِ جِدَارٍ، كَأَنَّهُ جَمَلٌ أَوْرَقُ ثَائِرُ الرَّأْسِ ـ قَالَ ـ فَرَمَيْتُهُ بِحَرْبَتِي، فَأَضَعُهَا بَيْنَ ثَدْيَيْهِ حَتَّى خَرَجَتْ مِنْ بَيْنِ كَتِفَيْهِ ـ قَالَ ـ وَوَثَبَ إِلَيْهِ رَجُلٌ مِنَ الأَنْصَارِ، فَضَرَبَهُ بِالسَّيْفِ عَلَى هَامَتِهِ. قَالَ قَالَ عَبْدُ اللَّهِ بْنُ الْفَضْلِ فَأَخْبَرَنِي سُلَيْمَانُ بْنُ يَسَارٍ أَنَّهُ سَمِعَ عَبْدَ اللَّهِ بْنَ عُمَرَ يَقُولُ فَقَالَتْ جَارِيَةٌ عَلَى ظَهْرِ بَيْتٍ وَا أَمِيرَ الْمُؤْمِنِينَ، قَتَلَهُ الْعَبْدُ الأَسْوَدُ

Narrated Qatada: We do not know of any tribe amongst the 'Arab tribes who lost more martyrs than Al-Ansar, and they will have superiority on the Day of Resurrection. Anas bin Malik told us that seventy from the Ansar were martyred on the day of Uhud, and seventy on the day (of the battle of) Bir Ma'una, and seventy on the day of Al-Yamama. Anas added, "The battle of Bir Ma'una took place during the lifetime of Allah's Messengerﷺ and the battle of Al-Yamama, during the caliphate of Abu Bakr, and it was the day when Musailamah Al-Kadhdhab was killed.". – Al-Bukhari 4078

حَدَّثَنِي عَمْرُو بْنُ عَلِيٍّ، حَدَّثَنَا مُعَاذُ بْنُ هِشَامٍ، قَالَ حَدَّثَنِي أَبِي، عَنْ قَتَادَةَ، قَالَ مَا نَعْلَمُ حَيًّا مِنْ أَحْيَاءِ الْعَرَبِ أَكْثَرَ شَهِيدًا أَعَزَّ يَوْمَ الْقِيَامَةِ مِنَ الأَنْصَارِ. قَالَ قَتَادَةُ وَحَدَّثَنَا أَنَسُ بْنُ مَالِكٍ أَنَّهُ قُتِلَ مِنْهُمْ يَوْمَ أُحُدٍ سَبْعُونَ، وَيَوْمَ بِئْرِ مَعُونَةَ سَبْعُونَ، وَيَوْمَ الْيَمَامَةِ سَبْعُونَ، قَالَ وَكَانَ بِئْرُ مَعُونَةَ عَلَى عَهْدِ رَسُولِ اللَّهِ صلى الله عليه وسلم، وَيَوْمُ الْيَمَامَةِ عَلَى عَهْدِ أَبِي بَكْرٍ يَوْمَ مُسَيْلِمَةَ الْكَذَّابِ

Narrated Abu Musa: The Prophetﷺ said, "I saw in a dream that I moved a sword and its blade got broken, and that symbolized the casualties which the believers suffered on the day of Uhud. Then I moved it again, and it became as perfect as it had been, and that symbolized the Conquest (of Mecca) which Allah helped us to achieve, and the union of all the believers. I (also) saw cows in the dream, and what Allah does is always beneficial. Those cows appeared to symbolize the faithful believers (who were martyred) on the day of Uhud.". – Al-Bukhari 4081

حَدَّثَنَا مُحَمَّدُ بْنُ الْعَلاَءِ، حَدَّثَنَا أَبُو أُسَامَةَ، عَنْ بُرَيْدِ بْنِ عَبْدِ اللَّهِ بْنِ أَبِي بُرْدَةَ، عَنْ جَدِّهِ أَبِي بُرْدَةَ، عَنْ أَبِي مُوسَى ـ رضى الله عنه ـ أُرَى عَنِ النَّبِيِّ صلى الله عليه وسلم قَالَ " رَأَيْتُ فِي رُؤْيَاىَ أَنِّي هَزَزْتُ سَيْفًا فَانْقَطَعَ صَدْرُهُ، فَإِذَا هُوَ مَا أُصِيبَ مِنَ الْمُؤْمِنِينَ يَوْمَ أُحُدٍ، ثُمَّ هَزَزْتُهُ أُخْرَى فَعَادَ أَحْسَنَ مَا كَانَ، فَإِذَا هُوَ مَا جَاءَ بِهِ اللَّهُ مِنَ الْفَتْحِ وَاجْتِمَاعِ الْمُؤْمِنِينَ، وَرَأَيْتُ فِيهَا بَقَرًا وَاللَّهُ خَيْرٌ، فَإِذَا هُمُ الْمُؤْمِنُونَ يَوْمَ أُحُدٍ ".

Narrated 'Aisha: That she asked the Prophetﷺ, Have you encountered a day harder than the day of the battle) of Uhud?" The Prophetﷺ replied, "Your tribes have troubled me a lot, and the worse trouble was the trouble on the day of 'Aqaba when I presented myself to Ibn `Abd-Yalail bin `Abd-Kulal and he did not respond to my demand. So I departed, overwhelmed with excessive sorrow, and proceeded on, and could not relax till I found myself at Qarnath-Tha-alib where I lifted my head towards the sky to see a cloud shading me unexpectedly. I looked up and saw Gabriel in it. He called me saying, 'Allah has heard your people's saying to you, and what they have replied back to you, Allah has sent the Angel of the Mountains to you so that you may order him to do whatever you wish to these people.' The Angel of the Mountains called and greeted me, and then said, "O Muhammad! Order what you wish. If you like, I will let Al-Akh-Shabain (i.e. two mountains) fall on them." The Prophetﷺ said, "No but I hope that Allah will let them beget children who will worship Allah Alone, and will worship None besides Him.". – Sahih Al-Bukhari 3231

حَدَّثَنَا عَبْدُ اللَّهِ بْنُ يُوسُفَ، أَخْبَرَنَا ابْنُ وَهْبٍ، قَالَ أَخْبَرَنِي يُونُسُ، عَنِ ابْنِ شِهَابٍ، قَالَ حَدَّثَنِي عُرْوَةُ، أَنَّ عَائِشَةَ ـ رضى الله عنها ـ زَوْجَ النَّبِيِّ صلى الله عليه وسلم حَدَّثَتْهُ أَنَّهَا قَالَتْ لِلنَّبِيِّ صلى الله عليه وسلم هَلْ أَتَى عَلَيْكَ يَوْمٌ كَانَ أَشَدَّ مِنْ يَوْمِ أُحُدٍ قَالَ " لَقَدْ لَقِيتُ مِنْ قَوْمِكِ مَا لَقِيتُ، وَكَانَ أَشَدُّ مَا لَقِيتُ مِنْهُمْ يَوْمَ الْعَقَبَةِ، إِذْ عَرَضْتُ نَفْسِي عَلَى ابْنِ عَبْدِ يَالِيلَ بْنِ عَبْدِ كُلاَلٍ، فَلَمْ يُجِبْنِي إِلَى مَا أَرَدْتُ، فَانْطَلَقْتُ وَأَنَا مَهْمُومٌ عَلَى وَجْهِي، فَلَمْ أَسْتَفِقْ إِلاَّ وَأَنَا بِقَرْنِ الثَّعَالِبِ، فَرَفَعْتُ رَأْسِي، فَإِذَا أَنَا بِسَحَابَةٍ قَدْ أَظَلَّتْنِي، فَنَظَرْتُ فَإِذَا فِيهَا جِبْرِيلُ فَنَادَانِي فَقَالَ إِنَّ اللَّهَ قَدْ سَمِعَ قَوْلَ قَوْمِكَ لَكَ وَمَا رَدُّوا عَلَيْكَ، وَقَدْ بَعَثَ إِلَيْكَ مَلَكَ الْجِبَالِ لِتَأْمُرَهُ بِمَا شِئْتَ فِيهِمْ، فَنَادَانِي مَلَكُ الْجِبَالِ، فَسَلَّمَ عَلَىَّ ثُمَّ قَالَ يَا مُحَمَّدُ، فَقَالَ ذَلِكَ فِيمَا شِئْتَ، إِنْ شِئْتَ أَنْ أُطْبِقَ عَلَيْهِمِ الأَخْشَبَيْنِ، فَقَالَ النَّبِيُّ صلى الله عليه وسلم بَلْ أَرْجُو أَنْ يُخْرِجَ اللَّهُ مِنْ أَصْلاَبِهِمْ مَنْ يَعْبُدُ اللَّهَ وَحْدَهُ لاَ يُشْرِكُ بِهِ شَيْئًا

Never think of those martyred in the cause of Allah as dead. In fact, they are alive with their Lord, well provided for— Surah Al-Imran 3:169

وَلَا تَحْسَبَنَّ ٱلَّذِينَ قُتِلُوا۟ فِى سَبِيلِ ٱللَّهِ أَمْوَٰتًۢا ۚ بَلْ أَحْيَآءٌ عِندَ رَبِّهِمْ يُرْزَقُونَ

Hind bint Abī Umayyah ibn al-Mughīrah al-Makhzūmiyyah; Umm Salama
هِنْدُ بِنْتُ أَبِي أُمَيَّةَ بْنِ الْمُغِيرَةِ الْمَخْزُومِيَّةُ، وَهِيَ أُمُّ سَلَمَةَ

She reported God's messenger as saying, "If any Muslim who suffers some calamity says what God has commanded him, 'We belong to God and to Him do we return ; O God, reward me for my affliction and give me something better than it in exchange for it,' God will give him something better than it in exchange." When Abu Salama died she said, "What Muslim is better than Abu Salama whose family was the first to emigrate to God's messenger? "(He and his wife, Umm Salama, were among those who emigrated to Abyssinia. Abu Salama died of wounds received at the battle of Uhud, and the Prophet later married Umm Salama.) She then said the words, and God gave her God's messenger in exchange. – Mishkat al-Masabih 1618 - Muslim transmitted it.

وَعَنْ أُمِّ سَلَمَةَ قَالَتْ: قَالَ رَسُولُ اللَّهِ صَلَّى اللَّهُ عَلَيْهِ وَسَلَّمَ: " مَا مِنْ مُسْلِمٍ تُصِيبُهُ مُصِيبَةٌ فَيَقُولُ مَا أَمَرَهُ اللَّهُ بِهِ: (إِنَّا لِلَّهِ وَإِنَّا إِلَيْهِ رَاجِعُونَ) اللَّهُمَّ أَجِرْنِي فِي مُصِيبَتِي وَاخْلُفْ لِي خَيْرًا مِنْهَا إِلَّا أَخْلَفَ اللَّهُ لَهُ خَيْرًا مِنْهَا ". فَلَمَّا مَاتَ أَبُو سَلَمَةَ قَالَت: أَيُّ الْمُسْلِمِينَ خَيْرٌ مِنْ أَبِي سَلَمَةَ؟ أَوَّلُ بَيْتٍ هَاجَرَ إِلَى رَسُولِ اللَّهِ صَلَّى اللَّهُ عَلَيْهِ وَسَلَّمَ ثُمَّ إِنِّي قُلْتُهَا فَأَخْلَفَ اللَّهُ لِي رَسُولَ اللَّهِ صَلَّى اللَّهُ عَلَيْهِ وَسَلَّمَ. رَوَاهُ مُسلم

Umm Salama reported: When Abu Salama died I said: I am a stranger in a strange land; I shall weep for him in a manner that would be talked of. I made preparation for weeping for him when a woman from the upper side of the city came there who intended to help me (in weeping). She happened to come across the Messenger of Allahﷺ and he said: Do you intend to bring the devil into a house from which Allah has twice driven him out? I (Umm Salama), therefore, refrained from weeping and I did not weep. – Sahih Muslim 922

وَحَدَّثَنَا أَبُو بَكْرِ بْنُ أَبِي شَيْبَةَ، وَابْنُ، نُمَيْرٍ وَإِسْحَاقُ بْنُ إِبْرَاهِيمَ كُلُّهُمْ عَنِ ابْنِ، عُيَيْنَةَ – قَالَ ابْنُ نُمَيْرٍ حَدَّثَنَا سُفْيَانُ، - عَنِ ابْنِ أَبِي نَجِيحٍ، عَنْ أَبِيهِ، عَنْ عُبَيْدِ بْنِ عُمَيْرٍ، قَالَ قَالَتْ أُمُّ سَلَمَةَ لَمَّا مَاتَ أَبُو سَلَمَةَ قُلْتُ غَرِيبٌ وَفِي أَرْضِ غُرْبَةٍ لأَبْكِيَنَّهُ بُكَاءً يُتَحَدَّثُ عَنْهُ . فَكُنْتُ قَدْ تَهَيَّأْتُ لِلْبُكَاءِ عَلَيْهِ إِذْ أَقْبَلَتِ امْرَأَةٌ مِنَ الصَّعِيدِ تُرِيدُ أَنْ تُسْعِدَنِي فَاسْتَقْبَلَهَا رَسُولُ اللَّهِ صلى الله عليه وسلم وَقَالَ " أَتُرِيدِينَ أَنْ تُدْخِلِي الشَّيْطَانَ بَيْتًا أَخْرَجَهُ اللَّهُ مِنْهُ " . مَرَّتَيْنِ فَكَفَفْتُ عَنِ الْبُكَاءِ فَلَمْ أَبْكِ .

Umm Salama reported Allah's Messenger ﷺ as saying: Whenever you visit the sick or the dead, supplicate for good because angels say" Amen" to whatever you say. She added: When Abu Salama died, I went to the Messenger of Allah ﷺ and said: Messenger of Allah, Abu Salama has died. He told me to recite:" O Allah! Forgive me and him (Abu Salama) and give me a better substitute than he." So I said (this), and Allah gave me in exchange Muhammad, who is better for me than him (Abu Salama). – Sahih Muslim 919
حَدَّثَنَا أَبُو بَكْرِ بْنُ أَبِي شَيْبَةَ، وَأَبُو كُرَيْبٍ قَالاَ حَدَّثَنَا أَبُو مُعَاوِيَةَ، عَنِ الأَعْمَشِ، عَنْ شَقِيقٍ، عَنْ أُمِّ سَلَمَةَ، قَالَتْ قَالَ رَسُولُ اللَّهِ صلى الله عليه وسلم " إِذَا حَضَرْتُمُ الْمَرِيضَ أَوِ الْمَيِّتَ فَقُولُوا خَيْرًا فَإِنَّ الْمَلاَئِكَةَ يُؤَمِّنُونَ عَلَى مَا تَقُولُونَ " . قَالَتْ فَلَمَّا مَاتَ أَبُو سَلَمَةَ أَتَيْتُ النَّبِيَّ صلى الله عليه وسلم فَقُلْتُ يَا رَسُولَ اللَّهِ إِنَّ أَبَا سَلَمَةَ قَدْ مَاتَ قَالَ " قُولِي اللَّهُمَّ اغْفِرْ لِي وَلَهُ وَأَعْقِبْنِي مِنْهُ عُقْبَى حَسَنَةً " . قَالَتْ فَقُلْتُ فَأَعْقَبَنِي اللَّهُ مَنْ هُوَ خَيْرٌ لِي مِنْهُ مُحَمَّدًا صلى الله عليه وسلم

Narrated Zainab bint Salama: Um Habiba said to Allah's Messenger ﷺ "We have heard that you want to marry Durra bint Abu-Salama." Allah's Messenger ﷺ said, "Can she be married along with Um Salama (her mother)? Even if I have not married Um Salama, she would not be lawful for me to marry, for her father is my foster brother.". – Sahih al-Bukhari 5123
حَدَّثَنَا قُتَيْبَةُ، حَدَّثَنَا اللَّيْثُ، عَنْ يَزِيدَ بْنِ أَبِي حَبِيبٍ، عَنْ عِرَاكِ بْنِ مَالِكٍ، أَنَّ زَيْنَبَ ابْنَةَ أَبِي سَلَمَةَ، أَخْبَرَتْهُ أَنَّ أُمَّ حَبِيبَةَ قَالَتْ لِرَسُولِ اللَّهِ صلى الله عليه وسلم إِنَّا قَدْ تَحَدَّثْنَا أَنَّكَ نَاكِحٌ دُرَّةَ بِنْتَ أَبِي سَلَمَةَ. فَقَالَ رَسُولُ اللَّهِ صلى الله عليه وسلم " أَعَلَى أُمِّ سَلَمَةَ لَوْ لَمْ أَنْكِحْ أُمَّ سَلَمَةَ مَا حَلَّتْ لِي، إِنَّ أَبَاهَا أَخِي مِنَ الرَّضَاعَةِ ".

Narrated Um Salama: I said, "O Allah's Messenger ﷺ ! Shall I get a reward (in the Hereafter) if I spend on the children of Abu Salama and do not leave them like this and like this (i.e., poor) but treat them like my children?" The Prophet said, "Yes, you will be rewarded for that which you will spend on them.". – Sahih al-Bukhari 5369
حَدَّثَنَا مُوسَى بْنُ إِسْمَاعِيلَ، حَدَّثَنَا وُهَيْبٌ، أَخْبَرَنَا هِشَامٌ، عَنْ أَبِيهِ، عَنْ زَيْنَبَ ابْنَةِ أَبِي سَلَمَةَ، عَنْ أُمِّ سَلَمَةَ، قُلْتُ يَا رَسُولَ اللَّهِ هَلْ لِي مِنْ أَجْرٍ فِي بَنِي أَبِي سَلَمَةَ أَنْ أُنْفِقَ عَلَيْهِمْ، وَلَسْتُ بِتَارِكَتِهِمْ هَكَذَا وَهَكَذَا، إِنَّمَا هُمْ بَنِيَّ. قَالَ " نَعَمْ لَكِ أَجْرُ مَا أَنْفَقْتِ عَلَيْهِمْ "

Hind bint Utbah
هند بنت عتبة

Narrated `Aisha: Hind bint `Utba bin Rabi`a said, "O Allah's Apostle! (Before I embraced Islam), there was no family on the surface of the earth, I wish to have degraded more than I did your family. But today there is no family whom I wish to have honored more than I did yours." Allah's Messenger ﷺ said, "I thought similarly, by Him in Whose Hand Muhammad's soul is!" Hind said, "O Allah's Messenger ﷺ ! (My husband) Abu Sufyan is a miser. Is it sinful of me to feed my children from his property?" The Prophet said, "No, unless you take it for your needs what is just and reasonable.". – Sahih al-Bukhari 6641
حَدَّثَنَا يَحْيَى بْنُ بُكَيْرٍ، حَدَّثَنَا اللَّيْثُ، عَنْ يُونُسَ، عَنِ ابْنِ شِهَابٍ، حَدَّثَنِي عُرْوَةُ بْنُ الزُّبَيْرِ، أَنَّ عَائِشَةَ ـ رضى الله عنها ـ قَالَتْ إِنَّ هِنْدَ بِنْتَ عُتْبَةَ بْنِ رَبِيعَةَ قَالَتْ يَا رَسُولَ اللَّهِ مَا كَانَ مِمَّا عَلَى ظَهْرِ الأَرْضِ أَهْلُ أَخْبَاءٍ ـ أَوْ خِبَاءٍ ـ أَحَبَّ إِلَيَّ أَنْ يَذِلُّوا مِنْ أَهْلِ أَخْبَائِكَ ـ أَوْ خِبَائِكَ، شكَ يحيى ـ ثُمَّ مَا أَصبح اليومَ أهلُ أخباءٍ ـ أو خِباءٍ ـ أحَبَّ إليَّ مِن أن يَعِزُّوا مِن أهلِ أَخْبَائِكَ أَوْ خِبَائِكَ. قَالَ رَسُولُ اللَّهِ صلى الله عليه وسلم " وَأَيْضًا وَالَّذِي نَفْسُ مُحَمَّدٍ بِيَدِهِ ". قَالَتْ يَا رَسُولَ اللَّهِ إِنَّ أَبَا سُفْيَانَ رَجُلٌ مِسِّيكٌ، فَهَلْ عَلَيَّ حَرَجٌ أَنْ أُطْعِمَ مِنَ الَّذِي لَهُ قَالَ " لاَ إِلاَّ بِالْمَعْرُوفِ ".

Narrated 'Aishah: It was narrated from 'Aishah the wife of the Prophet, and Umm Salamah the wife of the Prophet that Abu Hudhaifah bin 'Utbah bin Rabi'ah bin Abd Shams –who was one of those who had been present at Badr with the Messenger of Allah—adopted Salim –

who was the freed slave of an Ansari woman—as the Messenger of Allah had adopted Zaid bin Harithah. Abu Hudhaifah bin 'Utbah married Salim to his brother's daughter Hind bint Al-Walid bin 'Utbah bin Rabi'ah. Hind bint Al-Walid bin 'Utbah was one of the first Muhajir women, and at that time she was one of the best single women of the Quraish. When Allah, the Mighty and Sublime, revealed the following concerning Zaid bin Harithah: "Call them by (the names of) their fathers, that is more just with Allah. But if you know not their fathers' (names, call them) your brothers in Faith and Mawalikum (your freed slaves).' Each of them went back to being called after his father, and if a person's father was unknown, he was named after his former masters. – Sunan an-Nasa'I 3224

أَخْبَرَنَا مُحَمَّدُ بْنُ نَصْرٍ، قَالَ حَدَّثَنَا أَيُّوبُ بْنُ سُلَيْمَانَ بْنِ بِلاَلٍ، قَالَ حَدَّثَنِي أَبُو بَكْرِ بْنُ أَبِي أُوَيْسٍ، عَنْ سُلَيْمَانَ بْنِ بِلاَلٍ، قَالَ قَالَ يَحْيَى – يَعْنِي ابْنَ سَعِيدٍ – وَأَخْبَرَنِي ابْنُ شِهَابٍ، قَالَ حَدَّثَنِي عُرْوَةُ بْنُ الزُّبَيْرِ، وَابْنُ عَبْدِ اللَّهِ بْنِ رَبِيعَةَ، عَنْ عَائِشَةَ، زَوْجِ النَّبِيِّ صلى الله عليه وسلم وَأُمِّ سَلَمَةَ زَوْجِ النَّبِيِّ صلى الله عليه وسلم أَنَّ أَبَا حُذَيْفَةَ بْنَ عُتْبَةَ بْنِ رَبِيعَةَ بْنِ عَبْدِ شَمْسٍ – وَكَانَ مِمَّنْ شَهِدَ بَدْرًا مَعَ رَسُولِ اللَّهِ صلى الله عليه وسلم – تَبَنَّى سَالِمًا وَهُوَ مَوْلًى لاِمْرَأَةٍ مِنَ الأَنْصَارِ كَمَا تَبَنَّى رَسُولُ اللَّهِ صلى الله عليه وسلم زَيْدَ بْنَ حَارِثَةَ وَأَنْكَحَ أَبُو حُذَيْفَةَ بْنُ عُتْبَةَ سَالِمًا ابْنَةَ أَخِيهِ هِنْدَ ابْنَةَ الْوَلِيدِ بْنِ عُتْبَةَ بْنِ رَبِيعَةَ وَكَانَتْ هِنْدُ بِنْتُ الْوَلِيدِ بْنِ عُتْبَةَ مِنَ الْمُهَاجِرَاتِ الأُوَلِ وَهِيَ يَوْمَئِذٍ مِنْ أَفْضَلِ أَيَامَى قُرَيْشٍ فَلَمَّا أَنْزَلَ اللَّهُ عَزَّ وَجَلَّ فِي زَيْدِ بْنِ حَارِثَةَ { ادْعُوهُمْ لآبَائِهِمْ هُوَ أَقْسَطُ عِنْدَ اللَّهِ } رُدَّ كُلُّ أَحَدٍ يَنْتَمِي مِنْ أُولَئِكَ إِلَى أَبِيهِ فَإِنْ لَمْ يَكُنْ يُعْلَمُ أَبُوهُ رُدَّ إِلَى مَوَالِيهِ .

Narrated Aisha, Ummul Mu'minin: When Hind, daughter of Utbah, said: Prophet of Allah, accept my allegiance, he replied; I shall not accept your allegiance till you make a difference to the palms of your hands; for they look like the paws of a beast of prey. – Sunan Abi Dawud 4165

حَدَّثَنَا مُسْلِمُ بْنُ إِبْرَاهِيمَ، حَدَّثَتْنِي غِبْطَةُ بِنْتُ عَمْرٍو الْمُجَاشِعِيَّةُ، قَالَتْ حَدَّثَتْنِي عَمَّتِي أُمُّ الْحَسَنِ، عَنْ جَدَّتِهَا، عَنْ عَائِشَةَ، رضى الله عنها أَنَّ هِنْدًا بِنْتَ عُتْبَةَ، قَالَتْ يَا نَبِيَّ اللَّهِ بَايِعْنِي . قَالَ " لاَ أُبَايِعُكِ حَتَّى تُغَيِّرِي كَفَّيْكِ كَأَنَّهُمَا كَفَّا سَبُعٍ "

Narrated `Aisha: Hind (bint `Utba) said to the Prophe ﷺ "Abu Sufyan is a miserly man and I need to take some money of his wealth." The Prophet ﷺ said, "Take reasonably what is sufficient for you and your children " – Sahih al-Bukhari 7180 [8]

حَدَّثَنَا مُحَمَّدُ بْنُ كَثِيرٍ، أَخْبَرَنَا سُفْيَانُ، عَنْ هِشَامٍ، عَنْ أَبِيهِ، عَنْ عَائِشَةَ ـ رضى الله عنها ـ أَنَّ هِنْدَ، قَالَتْ لِلنَّبِيِّ صلى الله عليه وسلم إِنَّ أَبَا سُفْيَانَ رَجُلٌ شَحِيحٌ، فَأَحْتَاجُ أَنْ آخُذَ مِنْ مَالِهِ. قَالَ " خُذِي مَا يَكْفِيكِ وَوَلَدَكِ بِالْمَعْرُوفِ

[8] • Connection to Status: Abu Sufyan's wife, Hind bint Utbah, may have adopted the name Umm Salama to align herself with the respected figures in the early Muslim community, especially considering the prominence of Umm Salama (Hind bint Abu Umayyah). This would have been a way to assert her credibility and status.

• "Hind bint Abī Umayyah ibn al-Mughīrah al-Makhzūmiyyah; she is Umm Salama, the wife of the Prophet – ".ﷺIbn Sa'd, Ṭabaqāt al-Kubrá, vol. 8

هِنْدُ بِنْتُ أَبِي أُمَيَّةَ بْنِ الْمُغِيرَةِ الْمَخْزُومِيَّةُ، وَهِيَ أُمُّ سَلَمَةَ زَوْجُ النَّبِيِّ ﷺ

The Book of
Bir Ma'una
بئر معونـة

The Messenger of God declined to accept it, saying, "Abu Bara', I do not accept presents from polytheists, so become a Muslim if you want me to accept it." Then he expounded Islam to him, explained its advantages for him and God's promises to the believers, and recited the Qur'an to him. He did not accept Islam, but was not far from doing so, saying, "Muhammad, this matter of yours to which you call me is good and beautiful. If you were to send some of your companions to the people of Najd to call them to your religion, I would hope that they would respond to you." The Messenger of God said, "I fear that the people of Najd would do them some harm." Abu Bara' replied, "I will guarantee their protection, so send them to call people to your religion." The Messenger of God thereupon sent al-Mundhir b. `Amr [Tabari Volume 7, p. 151] [9]

فأبى رسول الله صلى الله عليه وسلم أن يقبلها وقال: يا أبا براء، إني لا أقبل هدية من مشرك، فأسلم إن أردت أن أقبلها منك. ثم عرض عليه الإسلام، وبَيَّن له فضله، وما وعد الله المؤمنين، وتلا عليه القرآن. فلم يسلم، ولم يبعد من ذلك، وقال: يا محمد، إن أمرك هذا الذي تدعو إليه حسن جميل، فلو بعثت رجالاً من أصحابك إلى أهل نجد يدعونهم إلى دينك، رجوت أن يستجيبوا لك. فقال رسول الله صلى الله عليه وسلم: إني أخاف عليهم أهل نجد. فقال أبو براء: أنا جار لهم، فابعثهم يدعون الناس إلى دينك. فبعث رسول الله صلى الله عليه وسلم المنذر بن عمرو"

Narrated `Aisha: Abu Bakr asked the Prophet ﷺ to allow him to go out (of Mecca) when he was greatly annoyed (by the infidels). But the Prophet ﷺ said to him, "Wait." Abu Bakr said, O Allah's Messenger ﷺ ! Do you hope that you will be allowed (to migrate)?" Allah's Messenger ﷺ replied, "I hope so." So Abu Bakr waited for him till one day Allah's Messenger ﷺ came at noon time and addressed him saying "Let whoever is present with you, now leave you." Abu Bakr said, "None is present but my two daughters." The Prophet ﷺ said, "Have you noticed that I have been allowed to go out (to migrate)?" Abu Bakr said, "O Allah's Apostle, I would like to accompany you." The Prophet ﷺ said, "You will accompany me." Abu Bakr said, "O Allah's Messenger ﷺ ! I have got two she-camels which I had prepared and kept ready for (our) going out." So he gave one of the two (she-camels) to the Prophet ﷺ and it was Al-Jad`a . They both rode and proceeded till they reached the Cave at the mountain of Thaur where they hid themselves. Amir bin Fuhaira was the slave of `Abdullah bin at-Tufail bin Sakhbara `Aisha's brother from her mother's side. Abu Bakr had a milch she-camel. Amir used to go with it (i.e. the milch she-camel) in the afternoon and come back to them before noon by setting out towards them in the early morning when it was still dark and then he would take it to the pasture so that none of the shepherds would be aware of his job. When the Prophet (and Abu Bakr) went away (from the Cave), he (i.e. 'Amir) too went along with them and they both used to make him ride at the back of their camels in turns till they reached Medina. 'Amir bin Fuhaira was martyred on the day of Bir Ma'una. Narrated `Urwa: When those (Muslims) at Bir Ma'una were martyred and `Amr bin Umaiya Ad- Damri was taken prisoner, 'Amir bin at-Tufail, pointing at a killed person, asked `Amr, "Who is this?" `Amr bin Umaiya said to him, "He is 'Amir bin Fuhaira." 'Amir bin at-Tufail said, "I saw him lifted to the sky after

[9] Tabari, The History of al-Tabari Vol. 7: The Foundation of the Community Muhammad, pg. 151
1987, ISBN 088706346

he was killed till I saw the sky between him and the earth, and then he was brought down upon the earth. Then the news of the killed Muslims reached the Prophetﷺ and he announced the news of their death saying, "Your companions (of Bir Ma'una) have been killed, and they have asked their Lord saying, 'O our Lord! Inform our brothers about us as we are pleased with You and You are pleased with us." So Allah informed them (i.e. the Prophetﷺ and his companions) about them (i.e. martyrs of Bir Mauna). On that day, `Urwa bin Asma bin As-Salt who was one of them, was killed, and `Urwa (bin Az- Zubair) was named after `Urwa bin Asma and Mundhir (bin AzZubair) was named after Mundhir bin `Amr (who had also been martyred on that day). – Al-Bukhari 4093

حَدَّثَنَا عُبَيْدُ بْنُ إِسْمَاعِيلَ، حَدَّثَنَا أَبُو أُسَامَةَ، عَنْ هِشَامٍ، عَنْ أَبِيهِ، عَنْ عَائِشَةَ ـ رضى الله عنها ـ قَالَتِ اسْتَأْذَنَ النَّبِيَّ صلى الله عليه وسلم أَبُو بَكْرٍ فِي الْخُرُوجِ حِينَ اشْتَدَّ عَلَيْهِ الأَذَى، فَقَالَ لَهُ " أَقِمْ ". فَقَالَ يَا رَسُولَ اللَّهِ أَتَطْمَعُ أَنْ يُؤْذَنَ لَكَ، فَكَانَ رَسُولُ اللَّهِ صلى الله عليه وسلم يَقُولُ " إِنِّي لأَرْجُو ذَلِكَ " قَالَتْ فَانْتَظَرَهُ أَبُو بَكْرٍ فَأَتَاهُ رَسُولُ اللَّهِ صلى الله عليه وسلم ذَاتَ يَوْمٍ ظُهْرًا فَنَادَاهُ فَقَالَ " أَخْرِجْ مَنْ عِنْدَكَ ". فَقَالَ أَبُو بَكْرٍ إِنَّمَا هُمَا ابْنَتَاىَ. فَقَالَ " أَشَعَرْتَ أَنَّهُ قَدْ أُذِنَ لِي فِي الْخُرُوجِ ". فَقَالَ يَا رَسُولَ اللَّهِ الصُّحْبَةُ. فَقَالَ النَّبِيُّ صلى الله عليه وسلم " الصُّحْبَةُ ". قَالَ يَا رَسُولَ اللَّهِ عِنْدِي نَاقَتَانِ قَدْ كُنْتُ أَعْدَدْتُهُمَا لِلْخُرُوجِ. فَأَعْطَى النَّبِيَّ صلى الله عليه وسلم إِحْدَاهُمَا وَهْىَ الْجَدْعَاءُ، فَرَكِبَا فَانْطَلَقَا حَتَّى أَتَيَا الْغَارَ، وَهْوَ بِثَوْرٍ، فَتَوَارَيَا فِيهِ، فَكَانَ عَامِرُ بْنُ فُهَيْرَةَ غُلاَمًا لِعَبْدِ اللَّهِ بْنِ الطُّفَيْلِ بْنِ سَخْبَرَةَ أَخُو عَائِشَةَ لأُمِّهَا، وَكَانَتْ لأَبِي بَكْرٍ مِنْحَةٌ، فَكَانَ يَرُوحُ بِهَا وَيَغْدُو عَلَيْهِمْ، وَيُصْبِحُ فَيَدَّلِجُ إِلَيْهِمَا ثُمَّ يَسْرَحُ، فَلاَ يَفْطُنُ بِهِ أَحَدٌ مِنَ الرِّعَاءِ، فَلَمَّا خَرَجَ خَرَجَ مَعَهُمَا يُعْقِبَانِهِ حَتَّى قَدِمَا الْمَدِينَةَ، فَقُتِلَ عَامِرُ بْنُ فُهَيْرَةَ يَوْمَ بِئْرِ مَعُونَةَ. وَعَنْ أَبِي أُسَامَةَ قَالَ قَالَ هِشَامُ بْنُ عُرْوَةَ فَأَخْبَرَنِي أَبِي قَالَ لَمَّا قُتِلَ الَّذِينَ بِبِئْرِ مَعُونَةَ وَأُسِرَ عَمْرُو بْنُ أُمَيَّةَ الضَّمْرِيُّ قَالَ لَهُ عَامِرُ بْنُ الطُّفَيْلِ مَنْ هَذَا فَأَشَارَ إِلَى قَتِيلٍ، فَقَالَ لَهُ عَمْرُو بْنُ أُمَيَّةَ هَذَا عَامِرُ بْنُ فُهَيْرَةَ. فَقَالَ لَقَدْ رَأَيْتُهُ بَعْدَ مَا قُتِلَ رُفِعَ إِلَى السَّمَاءِ حَتَّى إِنِّي لأَنْظُرُ إِلَى السَّمَاءِ بَيْنَهُ وَبَيْنَ الأَرْضِ، ثُمَّ وُضِعَ. فَأَتَى النَّبِيَّ صلى الله عليه وسلم خَبَرُهُمْ فَنَعَاهُمْ فَقَالَ " إِنَّ أَصْحَابَكُمْ قَدْ أُصِيبُوا، وَإِنَّهُمْ قَدْ سَأَلُوا رَبَّهُمْ، فَقَالُوا رَبَّنَا أَخْبِرْ عَنَّا إِخْوَانَنَا بِمَا رَضِينَا عَنْكَ وَرَضِيتَ عَنَّا. فَأَخْبَرَهُمْ عَنْهُمْ ". وَأُصِيبَ يَوْمَئِذٍ فِيهِمْ عُرْوَةُ بْنُ أَسْمَاءَ بْنِ الصَّلْتِ، فَسُمِّيَ عُرْوَةُ بِهِ، وَمُنْذِرُ بْنُ عَمْرٍو سُمِّيَ بِهِ مُنْذِرًا

Narrated `Abdul `Aziz: Anas said, "The Prophetﷺ sent seventy men, called Al-Qurra 'for some purpose. The two groups of Bani Sulaim called Ri'l and Dhakwan, appeared to them near a well called Bir Ma'una. The people (i.e. Al- Qurra) said, 'By Allah, we have not come to harm you, but we are passing by you on our way to do something for the Prophet.' But (the infidels) killed them. The Prophetﷺ therefore invoked evil upon them for a month during the morning prayer. That was the beginning of Al Qunut and we used not to say Qunut before that." A man asked Anas about Al-Qunut, "Is it to be said after the Bowing (in the prayer) or after finishing the Recitation (i.e. before Bowing)?" Anas replied, "No, but (it is to be said) after finishing the Recitation.". – Al-Bukhari 4088

حَدَّثَنَا أَبُو مَعْمَرٍ، حَدَّثَنَا عَبْدُ الْوَارِثِ، حَدَّثَنَا عَبْدُ الْعَزِيزِ، عَنْ أَنَسٍ ـ رضى الله عنه ـ قَالَ بَعَثَ النَّبِيُّ صلى الله عليه وسلم سَبْعِينَ رَجُلاً لِحَاجَةٍ يُقَالُ لَهُمُ الْقُرَّاءُ، فَعَرَضَ لَهُمْ حَيَّانِ مِنْ بَنِي سُلَيْمٍ رِعْلٌ وَذَكْوَانُ، عِنْدَ بِئْرٍ يُقَالُ لَهَا بِئْرُ مَعُونَةَ، فَقَالَ الْقَوْمُ وَاللَّهِ مَا إِيَّاكُمْ أَرَدْنَا، إِنَّمَا نَحْنُ مُجْتَازُونَ فِي حَاجَةٍ لِلنَّبِيِّ صلى الله عليه وسلم، فَقَتَلُوهُمْ فَدَعَا النَّبِيُّ صلى الله عليه وسلم عَلَيْهِمْ شَهْرًا فِي صَلاَةِ الْغَدَاةِ، وَذَلِكَ بَدْءُ الْقُنُوتِ وَمَا كُنَّا نَقْنُتُ. قَالَ عَبْدُ الْعَزِيزِ وَسَأَلَ رَجُلٌ أَنَسًا عَنِ الْقُنُوتِ أَبَعْدَ الرُّكُوعِ، أَوْ عِنْدَ فَرَاغٍ مِنَ الْقِرَاءَةِ قَالَ لاَ بَلْ عِنْدَ فَرَاغٍ مِنَ الْقِرَاءَةِ

Narrated Anas bin Malik: (The tribes of) Ril, Dhakwan, 'Usaiya and Bani Lihyan asked Allah's Messengerﷺ to provide them with some men to support them against their enemy. He therefore provided them with seventy men from the Ansar whom we used to call Al-Qurra' in their lifetime. They used to collect wood by daytime and pray at night. When they were at the well of Ma'una, the infidels killed them by betraying them. When this news reached the Prophetﷺ , he said Al-Qunut for one month In the morning prayer, invoking evil upon some of the 'Arab tribes, upon Ril, Dhakwan, 'Usaiya and Bani Libyan. We used to read a verse of the Qur'an revealed in their connection, but later the verse was cancelled. It was: "convey to our people on our behalf the information that we have met our Lord, and He is pleased with us, and has made us pleased." (Anas bin Malik added Allah's Prophet said Qunut for one month in the morning prayer, invoking evil upon some of the 'Arab tribes (namely), Ril, Dhakwan, Usaiya, and Bani Libyan. (Anas added Those seventy Ansari men were killed at the well of Mauna. – Al-Bukhari 4090 also 3064 & 2801

حَدَّثَنِي عَبْدُ الأَعْلَى بْنُ حَمَّادٍ، حَدَّثَنَا يَزِيدُ بْنُ زُرَيْعٍ، حَدَّثَنَا سَعِيدٌ، عَنْ قَتَادَةَ، عَنْ أَنَسِ بْنِ مَالِكٍ ـ رضى الله عنه ـ أَنَّ رِعْلاً، وَذَكْوَانَ وَعُصَيَّةَ وَبَنِي لَحْيَانَ اسْتَمَدُّوا رَسُولَ اللَّهِ صلى الله عليه وسلم عَلَى عَدُوٍّ، فَأَمَدَّهُمْ بِسَبْعِينَ مِنَ الأَنْصَارِ، كُنَّا نُسَمِّيهِمُ الْقُرَّاءَ فِي زَمَانِهِمْ، كَانُوا يَحْتَطِبُونَ بِالنَّهَارِ وَيُصَلُّونَ بِاللَّيْلِ، حَتَّى كَانُوا بِبِئْرِ مَعُونَةَ قَتَلُوهُمْ، وَغَدَرُوا بِهِمْ، فَبَلَغَ النَّبِيَّ صلى الله عليه وسلم، فَقَنَتَ شَهْرًا يَدْعُو فِي الصُّبْحِ عَلَى أَحْيَاءٍ مِنْ أَحْيَاءِ الْعَرَبِ، عَلَى رِعْلٍ وَذَكْوَانَ وَعُصَيَّةَ وَبَنِي لَحْيَانَ. قَالَ أَنَسٌ فَقَرَأْنَا فِيهِمْ قُرْآنًا ثُمَّ إِنَّ ذَلِكَ رُفِعَ بَلِّغُوا عَنَّا قَوْمَنَا، أَنَّا لَقِينَا رَبَّنَا، فَرَضِيَ عَنَّا وَأَرْضَانَا. وَعَنْ قَتَادَةَ عَنْ أَنَسِ بْنِ مَالِكٍ حَدَّثَهُ أَنَّ نَبِيَّ اللَّهِ صلى الله عليه وسلم قَنَتَ شَهْرًا فِي صَلاَةِ الصُّبْحِ يَدْعُو عَلَى أَحْيَاءٍ مِنْ أَحْيَاءِ الْعَرَبِ، عَلَى رِعْلٍ وَذَكْوَانَ وَعُصَيَّةَ وَبَنِي لَحْيَانَ. زَادَ خَلِيفَةُ حَدَّثَنَا ابْنُ زُرَيْعٍ، حَدَّثَنَا سَعِيدٌ، عَنْ قَتَادَةَ، حَدَّثَنَا أَنَسٌ، أَنَّ أُولَئِكَ السَّبْعِينَ، مِنَ الأَنْصَارِ قُتِلُوا بِبِئْرِ مَعُونَةَ، قُرْآنًا كِتَابًا. نَحْوَهُ.

Narrated Anas: That the Prophet ﷺ sent his uncle, the brother of Um Sulaim at the head of seventy riders. The chief of the pagans, 'Amir bin at-Tufail proposed three suggestions (to the Prophet ﷺ) saying, "Choose one of three alternatives: (1) that the bedouins will be under your command and the townspeople will be under my command; (2) or that I will be your successor, (3) or otherwise I will attack you with two thousand from Bani Ghatafan." But 'Amir was infected with plague in the House of Um so-and-so. He said, "Shall I stay in the house of a lady from the family of so-and-so after having a (swelled) gland like that she-camel? Get me my horse." So he died on the back of his horse. Then Haram, the brother of Um Sulaim and a lame man along with another man from so-and-so (tribe) went towards the pagans (i.e. the tribe of 'Amir). Haram said (to his companions), "Stay near to me, for I will go to them. If they (i.e. infidels) should give me protection, you will be near to me, and if they should kill me, then you should go back to your companions. Then Haram went to them and said, "Will you give me protection so as to convey the message of Allah's Messenger ﷺ ?" So, he started talking to them' but they signalled to a man (to kill him) and he went behind him and stabbed him (with a spear). He (i.e. Haram) said, "Allahu Akbar! I have succeeded, by the Lord of the Ka`ba!" The companion of Haram was pursued by the infidels, and then they (i.e. Haram's companions) were all killed except the lame man who was at the top of a mountain. Then Allah revealed to us a verse that was among the cancelled ones later on. It was: 'We have met our Lord and He is pleased with us and has made us pleased.' (After this event) the Prophet ﷺ invoked evil on the infidels every morning for 30 days. He invoked evil upon the (tribes of) Ril, Dhakwan, Bani Lihyan and Usaiya who disobeyed Allah and His Apostle. – Al-Bukhari 4091

حَدَّثَنَا مُوسَى بْنُ إِسْمَاعِيلَ، حَدَّثَنَا هَمَّامٌ، عَنْ إِسْحَاقَ بْنِ عَبْدِ اللَّهِ بْنِ أَبِي طَلْحَةَ، قَالَ حَدَّثَنِي أَنَسٌ، أَنَّ النَّبِيَّ صلى الله عليه وسلم بَعَثَ خَالَهُ أَخٌ لأُمِّ سُلَيْمٍ فِي سَبْعِينَ رَاكِبًا، وَكَانَ رَئِيسَ الْمُشْرِكِينَ عَامِرُ بْنُ الطُّفَيْلِ خَيَّرَ بَيْنَ ثَلاَثِ خِصَالٍ فَقَالَ يَكُونُ لَكَ أَهْلُ السَّهْلِ، وَلِي أَهْلُ الْمَدَرِ، أَوْ أَكُونُ خَلِيفَتَكَ، أَوْ أَغْزُوكَ بِأَهْلِ غَطَفَانَ بِأَلْفٍ وَأَلْفٍ، فَطُعِنَ عَامِرٌ فِي بَيْتِ أُمِّ فُلاَنٍ فَقَالَ غُدَّةٌ كَغُدَّةِ الْبَكْرِ فِي بَيْتِ امْرَأَةٍ مِنْ آلِ فُلاَنٍ ائْتُونِي بِفَرَسِي. فَمَاتَ عَلَى ظَهْرِ فَرَسِهِ، فَانْطَلَقَ حَرَامٌ أَخُو أُمِّ سُلَيْمٍ هُوَ {وَ} رَجُلٌ أَعْرَجُ وَرَجُلٌ مِنْ بَنِي فُلاَنٍ قَالَ كُونَا قَرِيبًا حَتَّى آتِيَهُمْ، فَإِنْ آمَنُونِي كُنْتُمْ، وَإِنْ قَتَلُونِي أَتَيْتُمْ أَصْحَابَكُمْ. فَقَالَ أَتُؤْمِنُونِي أُبَلِّغْ رِسَالَةَ رَسُولِ اللَّهِ صلى الله عليه وسلم. فَجَعَلَ يُحَدِّثُهُمْ وَأَوْمَئُوا إِلَى رَجُلٍ، فَأَتَاهُ مِنْ خَلْفِهِ فَطَعَنَهُ ـ قَالَ هَمَّامٌ أَحْسِبُهُ حَتَّى أَنْفَذَهُ ـ بِالرُّمْحِ، قَالَ اللَّهُ أَكْبَرُ، فُزْتُ وَرَبِّ الْكَعْبَةِ، فَلُحِقَ الرَّجُلُ، فَقُتِلُوا كُلُّهُمْ غَيْرَ الأَعْرَجِ كَانَ فِي رَأْسِ جَبَلٍ، فَأَنْزَلَ اللَّهُ عَلَيْنَا، ثُمَّ كَانَ مِنَ الْمَنْسُوخِ إِنَّا قَدْ لَقِينَا رَبَّنَا فَرَضِيَ عَنَّا وَأَرْضَانَا. فَدَعَا النَّبِيُّ صلى الله عليه وسلم عَلَيْهِمْ ثَلاَثِينَ صَبَاحًا، عَلَى رِعْلٍ وَذَكْوَانَ وَبَنِي لَحْيَانَ وَعُصَيَّةَ، الَّذِينَ عَصَوُا اللَّهَ وَرَسُولَهُ صلى الله عليه وسلم.

Narrated Abu Huraira: Allah's Messenger ﷺ sent a Sariya of ten men as spies under the leadership of `Asim bin Thabit al-Ansari, the grandfather of `Asim bin `Umar Al-Khattab. They proceeded till they reached Hadaa, a place between 'Usfan, and Mecca, and their news reached a branch of the tribe of Hudhail called Bani Lihyan. About two-hundred men, who were all archers, hurried to follow their tracks till they found the place where they had eaten dates they had brought with them from Medina. They said, "These are the dates of Yathrib (i.e. Medina), "and continued following their tracks When `Asim and his companions saw their pursuers, they went up a high place and the infidels circled them. The infidels said to them, "Come down and surrender, and we promise and guarantee you that we will not kill any one of you" `Asim bin Thabit; the leader of the Sariya said, "By Allah! I will not come down to be under the protection of infidels. O Allah! Convey our news to Your Prophet. Then the infidels threw arrows at them till they martyred `Asim along with six other men, and three men came down accepting their promise and convention, and they were Khubaib-al-Ansari and Ibn Dathina and another man So, when the infidels captured them, they undid the strings of their bows and tied them. Then the third (of the captives) said, "This is the first betrayal. By Allah! I will not go with you. No doubt these, namely the martyred, have set a good example to us." So, they dragged him and tried to compel him to accompany them, but as he refused, they killed him. They took Khubaid and Ibn Dathina with them and sold them (as slaves) in Mecca (and all that took place) after the battle of Badr. Khubaib was bought by the sons of Al-Harith bin 'Amir bin Naufal bin `Abd Manaf. It was Khubaib who had killed Al-Harith bin 'Amir on the day (of the battle of) Badr. So, Khubaib remained a prisoner with those people. Narrated Az-Zuhri: 'Ubaidullah bin 'Iyyad said that the daughter of Al-Harith had told him, "When those people gathered (to kill Khubaib) he borrowed a razor from me to shave his pubes and I gave it to him. Then he took a son of mine while I was unaware when he came upon him. I saw him placing my son on his thigh and the razor was in his hand. I got scared so much that Khubaib noticed the agitation on my face and said, 'Are you afraid that I will kill him? No, I will never do so.' By Allah, I never saw a prisoner better than Khubaib. By Allah, one day I saw him eating of a bunch of grapes in his hand while he was chained in irons, and there was no fruit at that time in Mecca." The daughter of Al-Harith used to say, "It was a boon Allah bestowed upon Khubaib." When they took him out of the Sanctuary (of Mecca) to kill him outside its boundaries, Khubaib requested them to let him offer two rak`at (prayer). They allowed him and he offered Two rak`at and then said, "Hadn't I been afraid that you would think that I was afraid (of being killed), I would have prolonged the prayer. O Allah, kill them all with no exception." (He then recited the poetic verse):-- "I being martyred as a Muslim, Do not mind how I am killed in Allah's Cause, For my killing is for Allah's Sake, And if Allah wishes, He will bless the amputated parts of a torn body" Then the son of Al Harith killed him. So, it was Khubaib who set the tradition for any Muslim sentenced to death in captivity, to offer a two-rak`at prayer (before being killed). Allah fulfilled the invocation of `Asim bin Thabit on that very day on which he was martyred. The Prophet ﷺ informed his companions of their news and what had happened to them. Later on when some infidels from Quraish were informed that `Asim had been killed, they sent some people to fetch a part of his body (i.e. his head) by which he would be recognized. (That was because) `Asim had killed one of their chiefs on the day (of the battle) of Badr. So, a swarm of wasps, resembling a shady cloud, were sent to hover over `Asim and protect him from their messenger and thus they could not cut off anything from his flesh. – Al-Bukhari 3045

حَدَّثَنَا أَبُو الْيَمَانِ، أَخْبَرَنَا شُعَيْبٌ، عَنِ الزُّهْرِيِّ، قَالَ أَخْبَرَنِي عَمْرُو بْنُ أَبِي سُفْيَانَ بْنِ أَسِيدِ بْنِ جَارِيَةَ الثَّقَفِيُّ ـ وَهْوَ حَلِيفٌ لِبَنِي زُهْرَةَ وَكَانَ مِنْ أَصْحَابِ أَبِي هُرَيْرَةَ ـ أَنَّ أَبَا هُرَيْرَةَ ـ رضى الله عنه ـ قَالَ بَعَثَ رَسُولُ اللَّهِ صلى الله عليه وسلم عَشَرَةَ رَهْطٍ سَرِيَّةً عَيْنًا، وَأَمَّرَ عَلَيْهِمْ عَاصِمَ بْنَ ثَابِتٍ الأَنْصَارِيَّ جَدَّ عَاصِمِ بْنِ عُمَرَ، فَانْطَلَقُوا حَتَّى إِذَا كَانُوا بِالْهَدَأَةِ وَهْوَ بَيْنَ عُسْفَانَ وَمَكَّةَ ذُكِرُوا لِحَيٍّ مِنْ هُذَيْلٍ يُقَالُ لَهُمْ بَنُو لِحْيَانَ، فَنَفَرُوا لَهُمْ قَرِيبًا مِنْ مِائَتَىْ رَجُلٍ، كُلُّهُمْ رَامٍ، فَاقْتَصُّوا آثَارَهُمْ حَتَّى وَجَدُوا مَأْكَلَهُمْ تَمْرًا تَزَوَّدُوهُ مِنَ الْمَدِينَةِ فَقَالُوا هَذَا تَمْرُ يَثْرِبَ. فَاقْتَصُّوا آثَارَهُمْ، فَلَمَّا رَآهُمْ عَاصِمٌ وَأَصْحَابُهُ لَجَئُوا إِلَى فَدْفَدٍ، وَأَحَاطَ بِهِمُ الْقَوْمُ فَقَالُوا لَهُمُ انْزِلُوا وَأَعْطُونَا بِأَيْدِيكُمْ، وَلَكُمُ الْعَهْدُ وَالْمِيثَاقُ، وَلاَ نَقْتُلُ مِنْكُمْ أَحَدًا. قَالَ عَاصِمُ بْنُ

ثَابِتٍ أَمِيرُ السَّرِيَّةِ أَمَّا أَنَا فَوَاللَّهِ لاَ أَنْزِلُ الْيَوْمَ فِي ذِمَّةِ كَافِرٍ، اللَّهُمَّ أَخْبِرْ عَنَّا نَبِيَّكَ. فَرَمَوْهُمْ بِالنَّبْلِ، فَقَتَلُوا عَاصِمًا فِي سَبْعَةٍ، فَنَزَلَ إِلَيْهِمْ ثَلاَثَةُ رَهْطٍ بِالْعَهْدِ وَالْمِيثَاقِ، مِنْهُمْ خُبَيْبٌ الأَنْصَارِيُّ وَابْنُ دَثِنَةَ وَرَجُلٌ آخَرُ، فَلَمَّا اسْتَمْكَنُوا مِنْهُمْ أَطْلَقُوا أَوْتَارَ قِسِيِّهِمْ فَأَوْثَقُوهُمْ فَقَالَ الرَّجُلُ الثَّالِثُ هَذَا أَوَّلُ الْغَدْرِ، وَاللَّهِ لاَ أَصْحَبُكُمْ، إِنَّ فِي هَؤُلاَءِ لأُسْوَةً. يُرِيدُ الْقَتْلَى، فَجَرَّرُوهُ وَعَالَجُوهُ عَلَى أَنْ يَصْحَبَهُمْ فَأَبَى فَقَتَلُوهُ، فَانْطَلَقُوا بِخُبَيْبٍ وَابْنِ دَثِنَةَ حَتَّى بَاعُوهُمَا بِمَكَّةَ بَعْدَ وَقْعَةِ بَدْرٍ، فَابْتَاعَ خُبَيْبًا بَنُو الْحَارِثِ بْنِ عَامِرِ بْنِ نَوْفَلِ بْنِ عَبْدِ مَنَافٍ، وَكَانَ خُبَيْبٌ هُوَ قَتَلَ الْحَارِثَ بْنَ عَامِرٍ يَوْمَ بَدْرٍ، فَلَبِثَ خُبَيْبٌ عِنْدَهُمْ أَسِيرًا، فَأَخْبَرَنِي عُبَيْدُ اللَّهِ بْنُ عِيَاضٍ أَنَّ بِنْتَ الْحَارِثِ أَخْبَرَتْهُ أَنَّهُمْ حِينَ اجْتَمَعُوا اسْتَعَارَ مِنْهَا مُوسَى يَسْتَحِدُّ بِهَا فَأَعَارَتْهُ، فَأَخَذَ ابْنًا لِي وَأَنَا غَافِلَةٌ حِينَ أَتَاهُ قَالَتْ فَوَجَدْتُهُ مُجْلِسَهُ عَلَى فَخِذِهِ وَالْمُوسَى بِيَدِهِ، فَفَزِعْتُ فَزْعَةً عَرَفَهَا خُبَيْبٌ فِي وَجْهِي فَقَالَ تَخْشَيْنَ أَنْ أَقْتُلَهُ مَا كُنْتُ لأَفْعَلَ ذَلِكَ. وَاللَّهِ مَا رَأَيْتُ أَسِيرًا قَطُّ خَيْرًا مِنْ خُبَيْبٍ، وَاللَّهِ لَقَدْ وَجَدْتُهُ يَوْمًا يَأْكُلُ مِنْ قِطْفِ عِنَبٍ فِي يَدِهِ، وَإِنَّهُ لَمُوثَقٌ فِي الْحَدِيدِ، وَمَا بِمَكَّةَ مِنْ ثَمَرٍ وَكَانَتْ تَقُولُ إِنَّهُ لَرِزْقٌ مِنَ اللَّهِ رَزَقَهُ خُبَيْبًا، فَلَمَّا خَرَجُوا مِنَ الْحَرَمِ لِيَقْتُلُوهُ فِي الْحِلِّ، قَالَ لَهُمْ خُبَيْبٌ ذَرُونِي أَرْكَعْ رَكْعَتَيْنِ. فَتَرَكُوهُ، فَرَكَعَ رَكْعَتَيْنِ ثُمَّ قَالَ لَوْلاَ أَنْ تَظُنُّوا أَنَّ مَا بِي جَزَعٌ لَطَوَّلْتُهَا اللَّهُمَّ أَحْصِهِمْ عَدَدًا. وَلَسْتُ أُبَالِي حِينَ أُقْتَلُ مُسْلِمًا عَلَى أَيِّ شِقٍّ كَانَ لِلَّهِ مَصْرَعِي وَذَلِكَ فِي ذَاتِ الإِلَهِ وَإِنْ يَشَأْ يُبَارِكْ عَلَى أَوْصَالِ شِلْوٍ مُمَزَّعِ فَقَتَلَهُ ابْنُ الْحَارِثِ، فَكَانَ خُبَيْبٌ هُوَ سَنَّ الرَّكْعَتَيْنِ لِكُلِّ امْرِئٍ مُسْلِمٍ قُتِلَ صَبْرًا، فَاسْتَجَابَ اللَّهُ لِعَاصِمِ بْنِ ثَابِتٍ يَوْمَ أُصِيبَ، فَأَخْبَرَ النَّبِيُّ صلى الله عليه وسلم أَصْحَابَهُ خَبَرَهُمْ وَمَا أُصِيبُوا، وَبَعَثَ نَاسٌ مِنْ كُفَّارِ قُرَيْشٍ إِلَى عَاصِمٍ حِينَ حُدِّثُوا أَنَّهُ قُتِلَ لِيُؤْتَوْا بِشَىْءٍ مِنْهُ يُعْرَفُ، وَكَانَ قَدْ قَتَلَ رَجُلاً مِنْ عُظَمَائِهِمْ يَوْمَ بَدْرٍ، فَبُعِثَ عَلَى عَاصِمٍ مِثْلُ الظُّلَّةِ مِنَ الدَّبْرِ، فَحَمَتْهُ مِنْ رُسُلِهِمْ، فَلَمْ يَقْدِرُوا عَلَى أَنْ يَقْطَعَ مِنْ لَحْمِهِ شَيْئًا

Narrated Qatada: We do not know of any tribe amongst the ‘Arab tribes who lost more martyrs than Al-Ansar, and they will have superiority on the Day of Resurrection. Anas bin Malik told us that seventy from the Ansar were martyred on the day of Uhud, and seventy on the day (of the battle of) Bir Ma’una, and seventy on the day of Al-Yamama. Anas added, “The battle of Bir Ma’una took place during the lifetime of Allah’s Messenger ﷺ and the battle of Al-Yamama, during the caliphate of Abu Bakr, and it was the day when Musailamah Al-Kadhdhab was killed.” – Al-Bukhari 4078

حَدَّثَنِي عَمْرُو بْنُ عَلِيٍّ، حَدَّثَنَا مُعَاذُ بْنُ هِشَامٍ، قَالَ حَدَّثَنِي أَبِي، عَنْ قَتَادَةَ، قَالَ مَا نَعْلَمُ حَيًّا مِنْ أَحْيَاءِ الْعَرَبِ أَكْثَرَ شَهِيدًا أَعَزَّ يَوْمَ الْقِيَامَةِ مِنَ الأَنْصَارِ. قَالَ قَتَادَةُ وَحَدَّثَنَا أَنَسُ بْنُ مَالِكٍ أَنَّهُ قُتِلَ مِنْهُمْ يَوْمَ أُحُدٍ سَبْعُونَ، وَيَوْمَ بِئْرِ مَعُونَةَ سَبْعُونَ، وَيَوْمَ الْيَمَامَةِ سَبْعُونَ، قَالَ وَكَانَ بِئْرُ مَعُونَةَ عَلَى عَهْدِ رَسُولِ اللَّهِ صلى الله عليه وسلم، وَيَوْمُ الْيَمَامَةِ عَلَى عَهْدِ أَبِي بَكْرٍ يَوْمَ مُسَيْلِمَةَ الْكَذَّابِ

The Book of
Al-Raji
الراجي

Narrated Abu Huraira: Allah's Messenger ﷺ sent a Sariya of ten men as spies under the leadership of `Asim bin Thabit al-Ansari, the grandfather of `Asim bin `Umar Al-Khattab. They proceeded till they reached Hadaa, a place between 'Usfan, and Mecca, and their news reached a branch of the tribe of Hudhail called Bani Lihyan. About two-hundred men, who were all archers, hurried to follow their tracks till they found the place where they had eaten dates they had brought with them from Medina. They said, "These are the dates of Yathrib (i.e. Medina), "and continued following their tracks When `Asim and his companions saw their pursuers, they went up a high place and the infidels circled them. The infidels said to them, "Come down and surrender, and we promise and guarantee you that we will not kill any one of you" `Asim bin Thabit; the leader of the Sariya said, "By Allah! I will not come down to be under the protection of infidels. O Allah! Convey our news to Your Prophet. Then the infidels threw arrows at them till they martyred `Asim along with six other men, and three men came down accepting their promise and convention, and they were Khubaib-al-Ansari and Ibn Dathina and another man So, when the infidels captured them, they undid the strings of their bows and tied them. Then the third (of the captives) said, "This is the first betrayal. By Allah! I will not go with you. No doubt these, namely the martyred, have set a good example to us." So, they dragged him and tried to compel him to accompany them, but as he refused, they killed him. They took Khubaid and Ibn Dathina with them and sold them (as slaves) in Mecca (and all that took place) after the battle of Badr. Khubaib was bought by the sons of Al-Harith bin 'Amir bin Naufal bin `Abd Manaf. It was Khubaib who had killed Al-Harith bin 'Amir on the day (of the battle of) Badr. So, Khubaib remained a prisoner with those people. Narrated Az-Zuhri: 'Ubaidullah bin 'Iyyad said that the daughter of Al-Harith had told him, "When those people gathered (to kill Khubaib) he borrowed a razor from me to shave his pubes and I gave it to him. Then he took a son of mine while I was unaware when he came upon him. I saw him placing my son on his thigh and the razor was in his hand. I got scared so much that Khubaib noticed the agitation on my face and said, 'Are you afraid that I will kill him? No, I will never do so.' By Allah, I never saw a prisoner better than Khubaib. By Allah, one day I saw him eating of a bunch of grapes in his hand while he was chained in irons, and there was no fruit at that time in Mecca." The daughter of Al-Harith used to say, "It was a boon Allah bestowed upon Khubaib." When they took him out of the Sanctuary (of Mecca) to kill him outside its boundaries, Khubaib requested them to let him offer two rak`at (prayer). They allowed him and he offered Two rak`at and then said, "Hadn't I been afraid that you would think that I was afraid (of being killed), I would have prolonged the prayer. O Allah, kill them all with no exception." (He then recited the poetic verse):-- "I being martyred as a Muslim, Do not mind how I am killed in Allah's Cause, For my killing is for Allah's Sake, And if Allah wishes, He will bless the amputated parts of a torn body" Then the son of Al Harith killed him. So, it was Khubaib who set the tradition for any Muslim sentenced to death in captivity, to offer a two-rak`at prayer (before being killed). Allah fulfilled the invocation of `Asim bin Thabit on that very day on which he was martyred. The Prophet ﷺ informed his companions of their news and what had happened to them. Later on when some infidels from Quraish were informed that `Asim had been killed, they sent some people to fetch a part of his body (i.e. his head) by which he would be recognized. (That was because) `Asim had killed one of their chiefs on the day (of the battle) of Badr. So, a swarm of wasps, resembling a shady cloud, were sent to hover over `Asim and protect him from their messenger and thus they could not cut off anything from his flesh. - Al-Bukhari 3045 & 3989

حَدَّثَنَا أَبُو الْيَمَانِ، أَخْبَرَنَا شُعَيْبٌ، عَنِ الزُّهْرِيِّ، قَالَ أَخْبَرَنِي عَمْرُو بْنُ أَبِي سُفْيَانَ بْنِ أَسِيدِ بْنِ جَارِيَةَ الثَّقَفِيُّ ـ وَهْوَ حَلِيفٌ لِبَنِي زُهْرَةَ وَكَانَ مِنْ أَصْحَابِ أَبِي هُرَيْرَةَ ـ أَنَّ أَبَا هُرَيْرَةَ ـ رضى الله عنه ـ قَالَ بَعَثَ رَسُولُ اللَّهِ صلى الله عليه وسلم عَشَرَةَ رَهْطٍ سَرِيَّةً عَيْنًا، وَأَمَّرَ عَلَيْهِمْ عَاصِمَ بْنَ ثَابِتٍ الأَنْصَارِيَّ جَدَّ عَاصِمِ بْنِ عُمَرَ، فَانْطَلَقُوا حَتَّى إِذَا كَانُوا بِالْهَدَأَةِ وَهْوَ بَيْنَ عُسْفَانَ وَمَكَّةَ ذُكِرُوا لِحَيٍّ مِنْ هُذَيْلٍ يُقَالُ لَهُمْ بَنُو لِحْيَانَ، فَنَفَرُوا لَهُمْ قَرِيبًا مِنْ مِائَتَىْ رَجُلٍ، كُلُّهُمْ رَامٍ، فَاقْتَصُّوا آثَارَهُمْ حَتَّى وَجَدُوا مَأْكَلَهُمْ تَمْرًا تَزَوَّدُوهُ مِنَ الْمَدِينَةِ فَقَالُوا هَذَا تَمْرُ يَثْرِبَ. فَاقْتَصُّوا آثَارَهُمْ، فَلَمَّا رَآهُمْ عَاصِمٌ وَأَصْحَابُهُ لَجَئُوا إِلَى فَدْفَدٍ، وَأَحَاطَ بِهِمُ الْقَوْمُ فَقَالُوا لَهُمُ انْزِلُوا وَأَعْطُونَا بِأَيْدِيكُمْ، وَلَكُمُ الْعَهْدُ وَالْمِيثَاقُ، وَلاَ نَقْتُلُ مِنْكُمْ أَحَدًا. قَالَ عَاصِمُ بْنُ ثَابِتٍ أَمِيرُ السَّرِيَّةِ أَمَّا أَنَا فَوَاللَّهِ لاَ أَنْزِلُ الْيَوْمَ فِي ذِمَّةِ كَافِرٍ، اللَّهُمَّ أَخْبِرْ عَنَّا نَبِيَّكَ. فَرَمَوْهُمْ بِالنَّبْلِ، فَقَتَلُوا عَاصِمًا فِي سَبْعَةٍ، فَنَزَلَ إِلَيْهِمْ ثَلاَثَةُ رَهْطٍ بِالْعَهْدِ وَالْمِيثَاقِ، مِنْهُمْ خُبَيْبٌ الأَنْصَارِيُّ وَابْنُ دَثِنَةَ وَرَجُلٌ آخَرُ، فَلَمَّا اسْتَمْكَنُوا مِنْهُمْ أَطْلَقُوا أَوْتَارَ قِسِيِّهِمْ فَأَوْثَقُوهُمْ فَقَالَ الرَّجُلُ الثَّالِثُ هَذَا أَوَّلُ الْغَدْرِ، وَاللَّهِ لاَ أَصْحَبُكُمْ، إِنَّ فِي هَؤُلاَءِ لأُسْوَةً. يُرِيدُ الْقَتْلَى، فَجَرَّرُوهُ وَعَالَجُوهُ عَلَى أَنْ يَصْحَبَهُمْ فَأَبَى فَقَتَلُوهُ، فَانْطَلَقُوا بِخُبَيْبٍ وَابْنِ دَثِنَةَ حَتَّى بَاعُوهُمَا بِمَكَّةَ بَعْدَ وَقْعَةِ بَدْرٍ، فَابْتَاعَ خُبَيْبًا بَنُو الْحَارِثِ بْنِ عَامِرِ بْنِ نَوْفَلِ بْنِ عَبْدِ مَنَافٍ، وَكَانَ خُبَيْبٌ هُوَ قَتَلَ الْحَارِثَ بْنَ عَامِرٍ يَوْمَ بَدْرٍ، فَلَبِثَ خُبَيْبٌ عِنْدَهُمْ أَسِيرًا، فَأَخْبَرَنِي عُبَيْدُ اللَّهِ بْنُ عِيَاضٍ أَنَّ بِنْتَ الْحَارِثِ أَخْبَرَتْهُ أَنَّهُمْ حِينَ اجْتَمَعُوا اسْتَعَارَ مِنْهَا مُوسَى يَسْتَحِدُّ بِهَا فَأَعَارَتْهُ، فَأَخَذَ ابْنًا لِي وَأَنَا غَافِلَةٌ حِينَ أَتَاهُ قَالَتْ فَوَجَدْتُهُ مُجْلِسَهُ عَلَى فَخِذِهِ وَالْمُوسَى بِيَدِهِ، فَفَزِعْتُ فَزْعَةً عَرَفَهَا خُبَيْبٌ فِي وَجْهِي فَقَالَ تَخْشَيْنَ أَنْ أَقْتُلَهُ مَا كُنْتُ لأَفْعَلَ ذَلِكَ. وَاللَّهِ مَا رَأَيْتُ أَسِيرًا قَطُّ خَيْرًا مِنْ خُبَيْبٍ، وَاللَّهِ لَقَدْ وَجَدْتُهُ يَوْمًا يَأْكُلُ مِنْ قِطْفِ عِنَبٍ فِي يَدِهِ، وَإِنَّهُ لَمُوثَقٌ فِي الْحَدِيدِ، وَمَا بِمَكَّةَ مِنْ ثَمَرٍ وَكَانَتْ تَقُولُ إِنَّهُ لَرِزْقٌ مِنَ اللَّهِ رَزَقَهُ خُبَيْبًا، فَلَمَّا خَرَجُوا مِنَ الْحَرَمِ لِيَقْتُلُوهُ فِي الْحِلِّ، قَالَ لَهُمْ خُبَيْبٌ ذَرُونِي أَرْكَعْ رَكْعَتَيْنِ. فَتَرَكُوهُ، فَرَكَعَ رَكْعَتَيْنِ ثُمَّ قَالَ لَوْلاَ أَنْ تَظُنُّوا أَنَّ مَا بِي جَزَعٌ لَطَوَّلْتُهَا اللَّهُمَّ أَحْصِهِمْ عَدَدًا. وَلَسْتُ أُبَالِي حِينَ أُقْتَلُ مُسْلِمًا عَلَى أَىِّ شِقٍّ كَانَ لِلَّهِ مَصْرَعِي وَذَلِكَ فِي ذَاتِ الإِلَهِ وَإِنْ يَشَأْ يُبَارِكْ عَلَى أَوْصَالِ شِلْوٍ مُمَزَّعِ فَقَتَلَهُ ابْنُ الْحَارِثِ، فَكَانَ خُبَيْبٌ هُوَ سَنَّ الرَّكْعَتَيْنِ لِكُلِّ امْرِئٍ مُسْلِمٍ قُتِلَ صَبْرًا، فَاسْتَجَابَ اللَّهُ لِعَاصِمِ بْنِ ثَابِتٍ يَوْمَ أُصِيبَ، فَأَخْبَرَ النَّبِيُّ صلى الله عليه وسلم أَصْحَابَهُ خَبَرَهُمْ وَمَا أُصِيبُوا، وَبَعَثَ نَاسٌ مِنْ كُفَّارِ قُرَيْشٍ إِلَى عَاصِمٍ حِينَ حُدِّثُوا أَنَّهُ قُتِلَ لِيُؤْتَوْا بِشَىْءٍ مِنْهُ يُعْرَفُ، وَكَانَ قَدْ قَتَلَ رَجُلاً مِنْ عُظَمَائِهِمْ يَوْمَ بَدْرٍ، فَبُعِثَ عَلَى عَاصِمٍ مِثْلُ الظُّلَّةِ مِنَ الدَّبْرِ، فَحَمَتْهُ مِنْ رَسُولِهِمْ، فَلَمْ يَقْدِرُوا عَلَى أَنْ يَقْطَعَ مِنْ لَحْمِهِ شَيْئًا

Anas reported that the Messenger of Allah ﷺ observed Qunut for one month invoking curse upon some tribes of Arabia (those who were responsible for the murders in Bi'r Ma'una and Raji'), but then abandoned it. – Sahih Muslim 677 j

حَدَّثَنَا مُحَمَّدُ بْنُ الْمُثَنَّى، حَدَّثَنَا عَبْدُ الرَّحْمَنِ، حَدَّثَنَا هِشَامٌ، عَنْ قَتَادَةَ، عَنْ أَنَسٍ، أَنَّ رَسُولَ اللَّهِ صلى الله عليه وسلم قَنَتَ شَهْرًا يَدْعُو عَلَى أَحْيَاءٍ مِنْ أَحْيَاءِ الْعَرَبِ ثُمَّ تَرَكَهُ .

The Book of
So famine overtook them for one year
فَأَخَذَتْهُمْ سَنَةٌ حَصَّتْ كُلَّ شَىْءٍ

Narrated Masruq: One day I went to Ibn Mas`ud who said, "When Quraish delayed in embracing Islam, the Prophet ﷺ I invoked Allah to curse them, so they were afflicted with a (famine) year because of which many of them died and they ate the carcasses and Abu Sufyan came to the Prophet ﷺ and said, 'O Muhammad! You came to order people to keep good relation with kith and kin and your nation is being destroyed, so invoke Allah? So the Prophet ﷺ recited the Holy verses of Sirat-Ad-Dukhan: 'Then watch you For the day that The sky will Bring forth a kind Of smoke Plainly visible.' (44.10) When the famine was taken off, the people renegade once again as nonbelievers. The statement of Allah, (in Sura "Ad-Dukhan"-44) refers to that: 'On the day when We shall seize You with a mighty grasp.' (44.16) And that was what happened on the day of the battle of Badr." Asbath added on the authority of Mansur, "Allah's Messenger ﷺ prayed for them and it rained heavily for seven days. So the people complained of the excessive rain. The Prophet ﷺ said, 'O Allah! (Let it rain) around us and not on us.' So the clouds dispersed over his head and it rained over the surroundings.". – Al-Bukhari 1020

حَدَّثَنَا مُحَمَّدُ بْنُ كَثِيرٍ، عَنْ سُفْيَانَ، حَدَّثَنَا مَنْصُورٌ، وَالأَعْمَشُ، عَنْ أَبِي الضُّحَى، عَنْ مَسْرُوقٍ، قَالَ أَتَيْتُ ابْنَ مَسْعُودٍ فَقَالَ إِنَّ قُرَيْشًا أَبْطَئُوا عَنِ الإِسْلاَمِ،، فَدَعَا عَلَيْهِمُ النَّبِيُّ صلى الله عليه وسلم فَأَخَذَتْهُمْ سَنَةٌ حَتَّى هَلَكُوا فِيهَا وَأَكَلُوا الْمَيْتَةَ وَالْعِظَامَ، فَجَاءَهُ أَبُو سُفْيَانَ فَقَالَ يَا مُحَمَّدُ، جِئْتَ تَأْمُرُ بِصِلَةِ الرَّحِمِ، وَإِنَّ قَوْمَكَ هَلَكُوا، فَادْعُ اللَّهَ. فَقَرَأَ {فَارْتَقِبْ يَوْمَ تَأْتِي السَّمَاءُ بِدُخَانٍ مُبِينٍ} ثُمَّ عَادُوا إِلَى كُفْرِهِمْ فَذَلِكَ قَوْلُهُ تَعَالَى {يَوْمَ نَبْطِشُ الْبَطْشَةَ الْكُبْرَى} يَوْمَ بَدْرٍ. قَالَ وَزَادَ أَسْبَاطٌ عَنْ مَنْصُورٍ فَدَعَا رَسُولُ اللَّهِ صلى الله عليه وسلم، فَسُقُوا الْغَيْثَ، فَأَطْبَقَتْ عَلَيْهِمْ سَبْعًا، وَشَكَا النَّاسُ كَثْرَةَ الْمَطَرِ فَقَالَ " اللَّهُمَّ حَوَالَيْنَا وَلاَ عَلَيْنَا ". فَانْحَدَرَتِ السَّحَابَةُ عَنْ رَأْسِهِ، فَسُقُوا النَّاسُ حَوْلَهُمْ.

Narrated Masruq: We were with `Abdullah and he said, "When the Prophet ﷺ saw the refusal of the people to accept Islam he said, "O Allah! Send (famine) years on them for (seven years) like the seven years (of famine during the time) of (Prophet) Joseph." So famine overtook them for one year and destroyed every kind of life to such an extent that the people started eating hides, carcasses and rotten dead animals. Whenever one of them looked towards the sky, he would (imagine himself to) see smoke because of hunger. So Abu Sufyan went to the Prophet ﷺ and said, "O Muhammad! You order people to obey Allah and to keep good relations with kith and kin. No doubt the people of your tribe are dying, so please pray to Allah for them." So Allah revealed: "Then watch you For the day that The sky will bring forth a kind Of smoke Plainly visible ... Verily! You will return (to disbelief) On the day when We shall seize You with a mighty grasp. (44.10-16) Ibn Mas`ud added, "Al-Batsha (i.e. grasp) happened in the battle of Badr and no doubt smoke, Al-Batsha, Al-Lizam, and the verse of Surat Ar-Rum have all passed . – Al-Bukhari 1007

حَدَّثَنَا عُثْمَانُ بْنُ أَبِي شَيْبَةَ، قَالَ حَدَّثَنَا جَرِيرٌ، عَنْ مَنْصُورٍ، عَنْ أَبِي الضُّحَى، عَنْ مَسْرُوقٍ، قَالَ كُنَّا عِنْدَ عَبْدِ اللَّهِ فَقَالَ إِنَّ النَّبِيَّ صلى الله عليه وسلم لَمَّا رَأَى مِنَ النَّاسِ إِدْبَارًا قَالَ " اللَّهُمَّ سَبْعٌ كَسَبْعِ يُوسُفَ ". فَأَخَذَتْهُمْ سَنَةٌ حَصَّتْ كُلَّ شَىْءٍ حَتَّى أَكَلُوا الْجُلُودَ وَالْمَيْتَةَ وَالْجِيَفَ، وَيَنْظُرَ أَحَدُهُمْ إِلَى السَّمَاءِ فَيَرَى الدُّخَانَ مِنَ الْجُوعِ، فَأَتَاهُ أَبُو سُفْيَانَ فَقَالَ يَا مُحَمَّدُ إِنَّكَ تَأْمُرُ بِطَاعَةِ اللَّهِ وَبِصِلَةِ الرَّحِمِ وَإِنَّ قَوْمَكَ قَدْ هَلَكُوا، فَادْعُ اللَّهَ لَهُمْ قَالَ اللَّهُ تَعَالَى {فَارْتَقِبْ يَوْمَ تَأْتِي السَّمَاءُ بِدُخَانٍ مُبِينٍ} إِلَى قَوْلِهِ {عَائِدُونَ * يَوْمَ نَبْطِشُ الْبَطْشَةَ الْكُبْرَى} فَالْبَطْشَةُ يَوْمَ بَدْرٍ، وَقَدْ مَضَتِ الدُّخَانُ وَالْبَطْشَةُ وَاللِّزَامُ وَآيَةُ الرُّومِ.

Narrated `Abdullah: It (i.e., the imagined smoke) was because, when the Quraish refused to obey the Prophet, he asked Allah to afflict them with years of famine similar to those of (Prophet) Joseph. So they were stricken with famine and fatigue, so much so that they ate even bones. A man would look towards the sky and imagine seeing something like smoke between him and the sky because of extreme fatigue. So Allah revealed:-- 'Then watch you for the Day that the sky will bring forth a kind of smoke plainly visible, covering the people; this is a painfull of torment.' (44.10-11) Then someone (Abu Sufyan) came to Allah's Messenger ﷺ and said, "O Allah's Messenger ﷺ ! Invoke Allah to send rain for the tribes of Mudar for they are on the verge of destruction." On that the Prophet ﷺ said (astonishingly) "Shall I invoke Allah) for the tribes of Mudar? Verily, you are a brave man!" But the Prophet prayed for rain and it rained for them. Then the Verse was revealed. 'But truly you will return (to disbelief).' (44.15) (When the famine was over and) they restored prosperity and welfare, they reverted to their ways (of heathenism) whereupon Allah revealed: 'On the Day when We shall seize you with a Mighty Grasp. We will indeed (then) exact retribution.' (44.16) The narrator said, "That was the day of the Battle of Badr.". – Al-Bukhari 4821

حَدَّثَنَا يَحْيَى، حَدَّثَنَا أَبُو مُعَاوِيَةَ، عَنِ الأَعْمَشِ، عَنْ مُسْلِمٍ، عَنْ مَسْرُوقٍ، قَالَ قَالَ عَبْدُ اللَّهِ إِنَّمَا كَانَ هَذَا لأَنَّ قُرَيْشًا لَمَّا اسْتَعْصَوْا عَلَى النَّبِيِّ صلى الله عليه وسلم دَعَا عَلَيْهِمْ بِسِنِينَ كَسِنِي يُوسُفَ، فَأَصَابَهُمْ قَحْطٌ وَجَهْدٌ حَتَّى أَكَلُوا الْعِظَامَ، فَجَعَلَ الرَّجُلُ يَنْظُرُ إِلَى السَّمَاءِ فَيَرَى مَا بَيْنَهُ وَبَيْنَهَا كَهَيْئَةِ الدُّخَانِ مِنَ الْجَهْدِ، فَأَنْزَلَ اللَّهُ تَعَالَى {فَارْتَقِبْ يَوْمَ تَأْتِي السَّمَاءُ بِدُخَانٍ مُبِينٍ * يَغْشَى النَّاسَ هَذَا عَذَابٌ أَلِيمٌ} قَالَ فَأُتِيَ رَسُولُ اللَّهِ صلى الله عليه وسلم فَقِيلَ يَا رَسُولَ اللَّهِ اسْتَسْقِ اللَّهَ لِمُضَرَ، فَإِنَّهَا قَدْ هَلَكَتْ. قَالَ " لِمُضَرَ إِنَّكَ لَجَرِيءٌ ". فَاسْتَسْقَى فَسُقُوا. فَنَزَلَتْ {إِنَّكُمْ عَائِدُونَ} فَلَمَّا أَصَابَتْهُمُ الرَّفَاهِيَةُ عَادُوا إِلَى حَالِهِمْ حِينَ أَصَابَتْهُمُ الرَّفَاهِيَةُ. فَأَنْزَلَ اللَّهُ عَزَّ وَجَلَّ {يَوْمَ نَبْطِشُ الْبَطْشَةَ الْكُبْرَى إِنَّا مُنْتَقِمُونَ} قَالَ يَعْنِي يَوْمَ بَدْرٍ.

Narrated `Abdullah: Allah sent (the Prophet) Muhammad and said:-- 'Say, No wage do I ask of you for this (Qur'an) nor am I one of the pretenders (i.e. a person who pretends things which do not exist). (38.68) When Allah's Messenger ﷺ saw Quraish standing against him, he said, "O Allah! Help me against them by afflicting them with seven years of famine similar to the seven years (of famine) of Joseph. So they were afflicted with a year of drought that destroyed everything, and they ate bones and hides. (One of them said), "And they ate hides and dead animals, and (it seemed to them that) something like smoke was coming out of the earth. So Abu Sufyan came to the Prophet ﷺ and said, "O Muhammad! Your people are on the verge of destruction! Please invoke Allah to relieve them." So the Prophet ﷺ invoked Allah for them (and the famine disappeared). He said to them. "You will revert (to heathenism) after that." `Abdullah then recited: 'Then watch you for the Day that the sky will bring forth a kind of smoke plainly visible.......but truly you will revert (to disbelief).' He added, "Will the punishment be removed from them in the Hereafter? The smoke and the grasp and the Al-Lizam have all passed." One of the sub-narrater said, "The splitting of the moon." And another said, "The defeat of the Romans (has passed). – Al-Bukhari 4824

حَدَّثَنَا بِشْرُ بْنُ خَالِدٍ، أَخْبَرَنَا مُحَمَّدٌ، عَنْ شُعْبَةَ، عَنْ سُلَيْمَانَ، وَمَنْصُورٍ، عَنْ أَبِي الضُّحَى، عَنْ مَسْرُوقٍ، قَالَ قَالَ عَبْدُ اللَّهِ إِنَّ اللَّهَ بَعَثَ مُحَمَّدًا صلى الله عليه وسلم وَقَالَ {قُلْ مَا أَسْأَلُكُمْ عَلَيْهِ مِنْ أَجْرٍ وَمَا أَنَا مِنَ الْمُتَكَلِّفِينَ} فَإِنَّ رَسُولَ اللَّهِ صلى الله عليه وسلم لَمَّا رَأَى قُرَيْشًا اسْتَعْصَوْا عَلَيْهِ فَقَالَ " اللَّهُمَّ أَعِنِّي عَلَيْهِمْ بِسَبْعٍ كَسَبْعِ يُوسُفَ ". فَأَخَذَتْهُمُ السَّنَةُ حَتَّى حَصَّتْ كُلَّ شَىْءٍ حَتَّى أَكَلُوا الْعِظَامَ وَالْجُلُودَ ـ فَقَالَ أَحَدُهُمْ حَتَّى أَكَلُوا الْجُلُودَ وَالْمَيْتَةَ ـ وَجَعَلَ يَخْرُجُ مِنَ الأَرْضِ كَهَيْئَةِ الدُّخَانِ فَأَتَاهُ أَبُو سُفْيَانَ فَقَالَ أَىْ مُحَمَّدُ إِنَّ قَوْمَكَ قَدْ هَلَكُوا فَادْعُ اللَّهَ أَنْ يَكْشِفَ عَنْهُمْ فَدَعَا ثُمَّ قَالَ " تَعُودُوا بَعْدَ هَذَا ". فِي حَدِيثِ مَنْصُورٍ ثُمَّ قَرَأَ {فَارْتَقِبْ يَوْمَ تَأْتِي السَّمَاءُ بِدُخَانٍ مُبِينٍ} إِلَى {عَائِدُونَ} أَيُكْشَفُ عَذَابُ الآخِرَةِ فَقَدْ مَضَى الدُّخَانُ وَالْبَطْشَةُ وَاللِّزَامُ وَقَالَ أَحَدُهُمُ الْقَمَرُ وَقَالَ الآخَرُ الرُّومُ.

The Book of
Ghazwat Nadir
غزوة نادر

Narrated Ibn `Umar: Bani An-Nadir and Bani Quraiza fought (against the Prophet ﷺ violating their peace treaty), so the Prophet exiled Bani An-Nadir and allowed Bani Quraiza to remain at their places (in Medina) taking nothing from them till they fought against the Prophet ﷺ again) . He then killed their men and distributed their women, children and property among the Muslims, but some of them came to the Prophet ﷺ and he granted them safety, and they embraced Islam. He exiled all the Jews from Medina. They were the Jews of Bani Qainuqa', the tribe of `Abdullah bin Salam and the Jews of Bani Haritha and all the other Jews of Medina. – Sahih Al-Bukhari 4028

حَدَّثَنَا إِسْحَاقُ بْنُ نَصْرٍ، حَدَّثَنَا عَبْدُ الرَّزَّاقِ، أَخْبَرَنَا ابْنُ جُرَيْجٍ، عَنْ مُوسَى بْنِ عُقْبَةَ، عَنْ نَافِعٍ، عَنِ ابْنِ عُمَرَ ـ رضى الله عنهما ـ قَالَ حَارَبَتِ النَّضِيرُ وَقُرَيْظَةُ، فَأَجْلَى بَنِي النَّضِيرِ، وَأَقَرَّ قُرَيْظَةَ وَمَنَّ عَلَيْهِمْ، حَتَّى حَارَبَتْ قُرَيْظَةُ فَقَتَلَ رِجَالَهُمْ وَقَسَمَ نِسَاءَهُمْ وَأَوْلاَدَهُمْ وَأَمْوَالَهُمْ بَيْنَ الْمُسْلِمِينَ إِلاَّ بَعْضَهُمْ لَحِقُوا بِالنَّبِيِّ صلى الله عليه وسلم فَآمَنَهُمْ وَأَسْلَمُوا، وَأَجْلَى يَهُودَ الْمَدِينَةِ كُلَّهُمْ بَنِي قَيْنُقَاعَ وَهُمْ رَهْطُ عَبْدِ اللَّهِ بْنِ سَلاَمٍ وَيَهُودَ بَنِي حَارِثَةَ، وَكُلَّ يَهُودِ الْمَدِينَةِ.

Surah Al-Hashr
سورة الحشر

Narrated Ibn `Umar: Allah's Messenger ﷺ had the date-palm trees of Bani Al-Nadir burnt and cut down at a place called Al- Buwaira. Allah then revealed: "What you cut down of the date-palm trees (of the enemy) Or you left them standing on their stems. It was by Allah's Permission." (59.5) – Sahih al-Bukhari 4031

حَدَّثَنَا آدَمُ، حَدَّثَنَا اللَّيْثُ، عَنْ نَافِعٍ، عَنِ ابْنِ عُمَرَ ـ رضى الله عنهما ـ قَالَ حَرَّقَ رَسُولُ اللَّهِ صلى الله عليه وسلم نَخْلَ بَنِي النَّضِيرِ وَقَطَعَ وَهْىَ الْبُوَيْرَةُ فَنَزَلَتْ {مَا قَطَعْتُمْ مِنْ لِينَةٍ أَوْ تَرَكْتُمُوهَا قَائِمَةً عَلَى أُصُولِهَا فَبِإِذْنِ اللَّهِ}

Whatever Allah restored to His Messenger from the inhabitants of the villages belongs to Allah, and to the Messenger, and to the relatives, and to the orphans, and to the poor, and to the wayfarer; so that it may not circulate solely between the wealthy among you. Whatever the Messenger gives you, accept it; and whatever he forbids you, abstain from it. And fear Allah. Allah is severe in punishment. To the poor refugees who were driven out of their homes and their possessions, as they sought the favor of Allah and His approval, and came to the aid of Allah and His Messenger. These are the sincere. And those who, before them, had settled in the homeland, and had accepted faith. They love those who emigrated to them, and find no hesitation in their hearts in helping them. They give them priority over themselves, even if they themselves are needy. Whoever is protected from his natural greed—it is they who are the successful. – Surah Al-Hashr 59:7-9

مَّآ أَفَآءَ ٱللَّهُ عَلَىٰ رَسُولِهِۦ مِنْ أَهْلِ ٱلْقُرَىٰ فَلِلَّهِ وَلِلرَّسُولِ وَلِذِى ٱلْقُرْبَىٰ وَٱلْيَتَـٰمَىٰ وَٱلْمَسَـٰكِينِ وَٱبْنِ ٱلسَّبِيلِ كَىْ لَا يَكُونَ دُولَةًۢ بَيْنَ ٱلْأَغْنِيَآءِ مِنكُمْ ۚ وَمَآ ءَاتَىٰكُمُ ٱلرَّسُولُ فَخُذُوهُ وَمَا نَهَىٰكُمْ عَنْهُ فَٱنتَهُوا۟ ۚ وَٱتَّقُوا۟ ٱللَّهَ ۖ إِنَّ ٱللَّهَ شَدِيدُ ٱلْعِقَابِ لِلْفُقَرَآءِ ٱلْمُهَـٰجِرِينَ ٱلَّذِينَ أُخْرِجُوا۟ مِن دِيَـٰرِهِمْ وَأَمْوَٰلِهِمْ يَبْتَغُونَ فَضْلًا مِّنَ ٱللَّهِ وَرِضْوَٰنًا وَيَنصُرُونَ ٱللَّهَ وَرَسُولَهُۥٓ ۚ أُو۟لَـٰٓئِكَ هُمُ ٱلصَّـٰدِقُونَ وَٱلَّذِينَ تَبَوَّءُو ٱلدَّارَ وَٱلْإِيمَـٰنَ مِن قَبْلِهِمْ يُحِبُّونَ مَنْ هَاجَرَ إِلَيْهِمْ وَلَا يَجِدُونَ فِى صُدُورِهِمْ حَاجَةً مِّمَّآ أُوتُوا۟ وَيُؤْثِرُونَ عَلَىٰٓ أَنفُسِهِمْ وَلَوْ كَانَ بِهِمْ خَصَاصَةٌ ۚ وَمَن يُوقَ شُحَّ نَفْسِهِۦ فَأُو۟لَـٰٓئِكَ هُمُ ٱلْمُفْلِحُونَ

Narrated Abu Sa'id Al-Khudri: Some people (i.e. the Jews of Bani bin Quraiza) agreed to accept the verdict of Sa`d bin Mu`adh so the Prophet ﷺ sent for him (i.e. Sa`d bin Mu`adh). He came riding a donkey, and when he approached the Mosque, the Prophet ﷺ said, "Get up for the best amongst you." Or said, "Get up for your chief." Then the Prophet ﷺ said, "O Sa`d! These people have agreed to accept your verdict." Sa`d said, "I judge that their warriors should be killed and their children and women should be taken as captives." The Prophet said, "You have given a judgment similar to Allah's Judgment (or the King's judgment). – Sahih Al-Bukhari 3804

حَدَّثَنَا مُحَمَّدُ بْنُ عَرْعَرَةَ، حَدَّثَنَا شُعْبَةُ، عَنْ سَعْدِ بْنِ إِبْرَاهِيمَ، عَنْ أَبِي أُمَامَةَ بْنِ سَهْلِ بْنِ حُنَيْفٍ، عَنْ أَبِي سَعِيدٍ الْخُدْرِيِّ ـ رضى الله عنه ـ أَنَّ أُنَاسًا نَزَلُوا عَلَى حُكْمِ سَعْدِ بْنِ مُعَاذٍ، فَأَرْسَلَ إِلَيْهِ فَجَاءَ عَلَى حِمَارٍ، فَلَمَّا بَلَغَ قَرِيبًا مِنَ الْمَسْجِدِ قَالَ النَّبِيُّ صلى الله عليه وسلم " قُومُوا إِلَى خَيْرِكُمْ أَوْ سَيِّدِكُمْ ". فَقَالَ " يَا سَعْدُ، إِنَّ هَؤُلاَءِ نَزَلُوا عَلَى حُكْمِكَ ". قَالَ فَإِنِّي أَحْكُمُ فِيهِمْ أَنْ تُقْتَلَ مُقَاتِلَتُهُمْ وَتُسْبَى ذَرَارِيُّهُمْ. قَالَ " حَكَمْتَ بِحُكْمِ اللَّهِ، أَوْ بِحُكْمِ الْمَلِكِ "

Narrated Anas bin Malik: People used to give some of their datepalms to the Prophet (as a gift), till he conquered Bani Quraiza and Bani An-Nadir, whereupon he started returning their favors. – Sahih Al-Bukhari 3128

حَدَّثَنَا عَبْدُ اللَّهِ بْنُ أَبِي الأَسْوَدِ، حَدَّثَنَا مُعْتَمِرٌ، عَنْ أَبِيهِ، قَالَ سَمِعْتُ أَنَسَ بْنَ مَالِكٍ ـ رضى الله عنه ـ يَقُولُ كَانَ الرَّجُلُ يَجْعَلُ لِلنَّبِيِّ صلى الله عليه وسلم النَّخَلاَتِ حَتَّى افْتَتَحَ قُرَيْظَةَ وَالنَّضِيرَ، فَكَانَ بَعْدَ ذَلِكَ يَرُدُّ عَلَيْهِمْ

Narrated Anas: Some (of the Ansar) used to present date palm trees to the Prophet ﷺ till Banu Quraiza and Banu An- Nadir were conquered (then he returned to the people their date palms). My people ordered me to ask the Prophet ﷺ to return some or all the date palms they had given to him, but the Prophet ﷺ had given those trees to Um Aiman. On that, Um Aiman came and put the garment around my neck and said, "No, by Him except Whom none has the right to be worshipped, he will not return those trees to you as he (i.e. the Prophet ﷺ) has given them to me." The Prophet ﷺ go said (to her), "Return those trees and I will give you so much (instead of them)." But she kept on refusing, saying, "No, by Allah," till he gave her ten times the number of her date palms. – Sahih Al-Bukhari 4120

حَدَّثَنَا ابْنُ أَبِي الأَسْوَدِ، حَدَّثَنَا مُعْتَمِرٌ، وَحَدَّثَنِي خَلِيفَةُ، حَدَّثَنَا مُعْتَمِرٌ، قَالَ سَمِعْتُ أَبِي، عَنْ أَنَسٍ ـ رضى الله عنه ـ قَالَ كَانَ الرَّجُلُ يَجْعَلُ لِلنَّبِيِّ صلى الله عليه وسلم النَّخَلاَتِ حَتَّى افْتَتَحَ قُرَيْظَةَ وَالنَّضِيرَ، وَإِنَّ أَهْلِي أَمَرُونِي أَنْ آتِيَ النَّبِيَّ صلى الله عليه وسلم فَأَسْأَلَهُ الَّذِينَ كَانُوا أَعْطَوْهُ أَوْ بَعْضَهُ. وَكَانَ النَّبِيُّ صلى الله عليه وسلم قَدْ أَعْطَاهُ أُمَّ أَيْمَنَ، فَجَاءَتْ أُمُّ أَيْمَنَ فَجَعَلَتِ الثَّوْبَ فِي عُنُقِي تَقُولُ كَلاَّ وَالَّذِي لاَ إِلَهَ إِلاَّ هُوَ لاَ يُعْطِيكَهُمْ وَقَدْ أَعْطَانِيهَا، أَوْ كَمَا قَالَتْ، وَالنَّبِيُّ صلى الله عليه وسلم يَقُولُ " لَكِ كَذَا ". وَتَقُولُ كَلاَّ وَاللَّهِ. حَتَّى أَعْطَاهَا، حَسِبْتُ أَنَّهُ قَالَ " عَشَرَةَ أَمْثَالِهِ ". أَوْ كَمَا قَالَ.

Narrated Ibn `Umar: The Prophet ﷺ burnt the date-palm trees of Bani An-Nadir. Hassan bin Thabit said the following poetic Verses about this event:-- "the terrible burning of Al-Buwaira Has been received indifferently By the nobles of Bani Luai (The masters and nobles of Quraish)." Abu Sufyan bin Al-Harith (i.e. the Prophet's cousin who was still a disbeliever then) replied to Hassan, saying in poetic verses:-- "May Allah bless that burning And set all its (i.e. Medina's) Parts on burning fire. You will see who is far from it (i.e. Al-Buwaira) And which of our lands will be Harmed by it (i.e. the burning of Al- Buwaira). – Sahih al-Bukhari 4032

حَدَّثَنِي إِسْحَاقُ، أَخْبَرَنَا حَبَّانُ، أَخْبَرَنَا جُوَيْرِيَةُ بْنُ أَسْمَاءَ، عَنْ نَافِعٍ، عَنِ ابْنِ عُمَرَ ـ رضى الله عنهما أَنَّ النَّبِيَّ صلى الله عليه وسلم حَرَّقَ نَخْلَ بَنِي النَّضِيرِ قَالَ وَلَهَا يَقُولُ حَسَّانُ بْنُ ثَابِتٍ وَهَانَ عَلَى سَرَاةِ بَنِي لُؤَيٍّ حَرِيقٌ بِالْبُوَيْرَةِ مُسْتَطِيرُ قَالَ فَأَجَابَهُ أَبُو سُفْيَانَ بْنُ الْحَارِثِ أَدَامَ اللَّهُ ذَلِكَ مِنْ صَنِيعٍ وَحَرَّقَ فِي نَوَاحِيهَا السَّعِيرُ سَتَعْلَمُ أَيُّنَا مِنْهَا بِنُزْهٍ وَتَعْلَمُ أَىَّ أَرْضَيْنَا تَضِيرُ

Marriage with Zainab bint Jahsh
زواجه من زينب بنت جحش

Narrated Thabit: The marriage of Zainab bint Jahash was mentioned in the presence of Anas and he said, "I did not see the Prophet ﷺ giving a better banquet on marrying any of his wives than the one he gave on marrying Zainab. He then gave a banquet with one sheep." – Sahih al-Bukhari 5171

حَدَّثَنَا مُسَدَّدٌ، حَدَّثَنَا حَمَّادُ بْنُ زَيْدٍ، عَنْ ثَابِتٍ، قَالَ ذُكِرَ تَزْوِيجُ زَيْنَبَ ابْنَةِ جَحْشٍ عِنْدَ أَنَسٍ فَقَالَ مَا رَأَيْتُ النَّبِيَّ صلى الله عليه وسلم أَوْلَمَ عَلَى أَحَدٍ مِنْ نِسَائِهِ مَا أَوْلَمَ عَلَيْهَا أَوْلَمَ بِشَاةٍ.

Narrated Anas bin Malik: I of all the people know best this verse of Al-Hijab. When Allah's Messenger ﷺ married Zainab bint Jahsh she was with him in the house and he prepared a meal and invited the people (to it). They sat down (after finishing their meal) and started chatting. So the Prophet ﷺ went out and then returned several times while they were still sitting and talking. So Allah revealed the Verse: 'O you who believe! Enter not the Prophet's houses until leave is given to you for a meal, (and then) not (so early as) to wait for its preparation .....ask them from behind a screen.' (33.53) So the screen was set up and the people went away. – Sahih al-Bukhari 4792

حَدَّثَنَا سُلَيْمَانُ بْنُ حَرْبٍ، حَدَّثَنَا حَمَّادُ بْنُ زَيْدٍ، عَنْ أَيُّوبَ، عَنْ أَبِي قِلاَبَةَ، قَالَ أَنَسُ بْنُ مَالِكٍ أَنَا أَعْلَمُ النَّاسِ، بِهَذِهِ الآيَةِ آيَةِ الْحِجَابِ، لَمَّا أُهْدِيَتْ زَيْنَبُ إِلَى رَسُولِ اللَّهِ صلى الله عليه وسلم كَانَتْ مَعَهُ فِي الْبَيْتِ، صَنَعَ طَعَامًا، وَدَعَا الْقَوْمَ، فَقَعَدُوا يَتَحَدَّثُونَ، فَجَعَلَ النَّبِيُّ صلى الله عليه وسلم يَخْرُجُ، ثُمَّ يَرْجِعُ، وَهُمْ قُعُودٌ يَتَحَدَّثُونَ، فَأَنْزَلَ اللَّهُ تَعَالَى {يَا أَيُّهَا الَّذِينَ آمَنُوا لاَ تَدْخُلُوا بُيُوتَ النَّبِيِّ إِلاَّ أَنْ يُؤْذَنَ لَكُمْ إِلَى طَعَامٍ غَيْرَ نَاظِرِينَ إِنَاهُ} إِلَى قَوْلِهِ {مِنْ وَرَاءِ حِجَابٍ} فَضُرِبَ الْحِجَابُ، وَقَامَ الْقَوْمُ

O you who have believed, do not enter the homes of the Prophet except (when you are permitted in for food, without waiting for its dueness. (i.e., its hour, its time) But when you are invited, then enter. So, when you have had food, then disperse yourselves, neither (announcing yourselves) into familiar discourse. Surely that (Literally: those) hurts the Prophet, so he (feels) shy before you; and Allah does not shy from the truth. And when you ask (his wives) for any article, then ask them from behind a curtain; that is purer for your hearts and their hearts. And in no way should you hurt the Messenger of Allah, nor marry his spouses even after him at all. Surely that would, in the Reckoning of Allah, be a monstrous (thing) – Surah Al-Ahzab 33:53

يَٰٓأَيُّهَا ٱلَّذِينَ ءَامَنُوا۟ لَا تَدْخُلُوا۟ بُيُوتَ ٱلنَّبِيِّ إِلَّآ أَن يُؤْذَنَ لَكُمْ إِلَىٰ طَعَامٍ غَيْرَ نَٰظِرِينَ إِنَىٰهُ وَلَٰكِنْ إِذَا دُعِيتُمْ فَٱدْخُلُوا۟ فَإِذَا طَعِمْتُمْ فَٱنتَشِرُوا۟ وَلَا مُسْتَـْٔنِسِينَ لِحَدِيثٍ إِنَّ ذَٰلِكُمْ كَانَ يُؤْذِى ٱلنَّبِىَّ فَيَسْتَحْىِۦ مِنكُمْ وَٱللَّهُ لَا يَسْتَحْىِۦ مِنَ ٱلْحَقِّ وَإِذَا سَأَلْتُمُوهُنَّ مَتَٰعًا فَسْـَٔلُوهُنَّ مِن وَرَآءِ حِجَابٍ ذَٰلِكُمْ أَطْهَرُ لِقُلُوبِكُمْ وَقُلُوبِهِنَّ وَمَا كَانَ لَكُمْ أَن تُؤْذُوا۟ رَسُولَ ٱللَّهِ وَلَآ أَن تَنكِحُوٓا۟ أَزْوَٰجَهُۥ مِنۢ بَعْدِهِۦٓ أَبَدًا إِنَّ ذَٰلِكُمْ كَانَ عِندَ ٱللَّهِ عَظِيمًا

Narrated Anas bin Malik: The Verse of Al-Hijab (veiling of women) was revealed in connection with Zainab bint Jahsh. (On the day of her marriage with him) the Prophet ﷺ gave a wedding banquet with bread and meat; and she used to boast before other wives of the Prophet ﷺ and used to say, "Allah married me (to the Prophet ﷺ in the Heavens." – Sahih al-Bukhari 7421

حَدَّثَنَا خَلاَّدُ بْنُ يَحْيَى، حَدَّثَنَا عِيسَى بْنُ طَهْمَانَ، قَالَ سَمِعْتُ أَنَسَ بْنَ مَالِكٍ ـ رضى الله عنه ـ يَقُولُ نَزَلَتْ آيَةُ الْحِجَابِ فِي زَيْنَبَ بِنْتِ جَحْشٍ وَأَطْعَمَ عَلَيْهَا يَوْمَئِذٍ خُبْزًا وَلَحْمًا وَكَانَتْ تَفْخَرُ عَلَى نِسَاءِ النَّبِيِّ صلى الله عليه وسلم وَكَانَتْ تَقُولُ إِنَّ اللَّهَ أَنْكَحَنِي فِي السَّمَاءِ

Narrated Anas: The Prophet ﷺ offered a wedding banquet on the occasion of his marriage to Zainab, and provided a good meal for the Muslims. Then he went out as was his custom on marrying, he came to the dwelling places of the mothers of the Believers (i.e. his wives) invoking good (on them), and they were invoking good (on him). Then he departed (and came back) and saw two men (still sitting there). So he left again. I do not remember whether I informed him or he was informed (by somebody else) of their departure).b- Sahih al-Bukhari 5154

حَدَّثَنَا مُسَدَّدٌ، حَدَّثَنَا يَحْيَى، عَنْ حُمَيْدٍ، عَنْ أَنَسٍ، قَالَ أَوْلَمَ النَّبِيُّ صلى الله عليه وسلم بِزَيْنَبَ فَأَوْسَعَ الْمُسْلِمِينَ خَيْرًا فَخَرَجَ - كَمَا يَصْنَعُ إِذَا تَزَوَّجَ - فَأَتَى حُجَرَ أُمَّهَاتِ الْمُؤْمِنِينَ يَدْعُو وَيَدْعُونَ {لَهُ} ثُمَّ انْصَرَفَ فَرَأَى رَجُلَيْنِ فَرَجَعَ لاَ أَدْرِي آخْبَرْتُهُ أَوْ أُخْبِرَ بِخُرُوجِهِمَا

Narrated Anas: When Allah's Messenger ﷺ married Zainab bint Jahsh, he made the people eat meat and bread to their fill (by giving a Walima banquet). Then he went out to the dwelling places of the mothers of the believers (his wives), as he used to do in the morning of his marriage. He would greet them and invoke good on them, and they (too) would return his greeting and invoke good on him. When he returned to his house, he found two men talking to each other; and when he saw them, he went out of his house again. When those two men saw Allah's Messenger ﷺ : going out of his house, they quickly got up (and departed). I do not remember whether I informed him of their departure, or he was informed (by somebody else). So he returned, and when he entered the house, he lowered the curtain between me and him. Then the Verse of Al-Hijab was revealed. – Sahih al-Bukhari 4794

حَدَّثَنَا إِسْحَاقُ بْنُ مَنْصُورٍ، أَخْبَرَنَا عَبْدُ اللَّهِ بْنُ بَكْرٍ السَّهْمِيُّ، حَدَّثَنَا حُمَيْدٌ، عَنْ أَنَسٍ - رضى الله عنه - قَالَ أَوْلَمَ رَسُولُ اللَّهِ صلى الله عليه وسلم حِينَ بَنَى بِزَيْنَبَ ابْنَةِ جَحْشٍ فَأَشْبَعَ النَّاسَ خُبْزًا وَلَحْمًا ثُمَّ خَرَجَ إِلَى حُجَرِ أُمَّهَاتِ الْمُؤْمِنِينَ كَمَا كَانَ يَصْنَعُ صَبِيحَةَ بِنَائِهِ فَيُسَلِّمُ عَلَيْهِنَّ وَيَدْعُو لَهُنَّ وَيُسَلِّمْنَ عَلَيْهِ وَيَدْعُونَ لَهُ فَلَمَّا رَجَعَ إِلَى بَيْتِهِ رَأَى رَجُلَيْنِ جَرَى بِهِمَا الْحَدِيثُ، فَلَمَّا رَآهُمَا رَجَعَ عَنْ بَيْتِهِ، فَلَمَّا رَأَى الرَّجُلاَنِ نَبِيَّ اللَّهِ صلى الله عليه وسلم رَجَعَ عَنْ بَيْتِهِ وَثَبَا مُسْرِعَيْنِ، فَمَا أَدْرِي أَنَا أَخْبَرْتُهُ بِخُرُوجِهِمَا أَمْ أُخْبِرَ فَرَجَعَ حَتَّى دَخَلَ الْبَيْتَ، وَأَرْخَى السِّتْرَ بَيْنِي وَبَيْنَهُ وَأُنْزِلَتْ آيَةُ الْحِجَابِ. وَقَالَ ابْنُ أَبِي مَرْيَمَ أَخْبَرَنَا يَحْيَى حَدَّثَنِي حُمَيْدٌ سَمِعَ أَنَسًا عَنِ النَّبِيِّ صلى الله عليه وسلم

Assassination of Ka`b bin Al-Ashraf & Abu Rafi`
اغتيال كعب بن الأشرف وأبي رافع

Narrated Jabir bin `Abdullah: Allah's Messenger ﷺ said, "Who is willing to kill Ka`b bin Al-Ashraf who has hurt Allah and His Apostle?" Thereupon Muhammad bin Maslama got up saying, "O Allah's Messenger ﷺ ! Would you like that I kill him?" The Prophet ﷺ said, "Yes," Muhammad bin Maslama said, "Then allow me to say a (false) thing (i.e. to deceive Ka`b). "The Prophet ﷺ said, "You may say it." Then Muhammad bin Maslama went to Ka`b and said, "That man (i.e. Muhammad demands Sadaqa (i.e. Zakat) from us, and he has troubled us, and I have come to borrow something from you." On that, Ka`b said, "By Allah, you will get tired of him!" Muhammad bin Maslama said, "Now as we have followed him, we do not want to leave him unless and until we see how his end is going to be. Now we want you to lend us a camel load or two of food." (Some difference between narrators about a camel load or two.) Ka`b said, "Yes, (I will lend you), but you should mortgage something to me." Muhammad bin Mas-lama and his companion said, "What do you want?" Ka`b replied, "Mortgage your women to me." They said, "How can we mortgage our women to you and you are the most handsome of the 'Arabs?" Ka`b said, "Then mortgage your sons to me." They said, "How can we mortgage our sons to you? Later they would be abused by the people's saying that so-and-so has been mortgaged for a camel load of food. That would cause us great disgrace, but we will mortgage our arms to you." Muhammad bin Maslama and his companion promised Ka`b that Muhammad would return to him. He came to Ka`b at night along with Ka`b's foster brother, Abu Na'ila. Ka`b invited them to come into his fort, and then he went down to them. His wife asked him, "Where are you going at this time?" Ka`b replied, "None but Muhammad bin Maslama and my (foster) brother Abu Na'ila have come." His wife said, "I hear a voice as if dropping blood is from him, Ka`b said. "They are none but my brother Muhammad bin Maslama and my foster brother Abu Naila. A generous man should respond to a call at night even if invited to be killed." Muhammad bin Maslama went with two men. (Some narrators mention the men as 'Abu bin Jabr. Al Harith bin Aus and `Abbad bin Bishr). So Muhammad bin Maslama went in together with two men, and sail to them, "When Ka`b comes, I will touch his hair and smell it, and when you see that I have got hold of his head, strip him. I will let you smell his head." Ka`b bin Al-Ashraf came down to them wrapped in his clothes, and diffusing perfume. Muhammad bin Maslama said. " have never smelt a better scent than this. Ka`b replied. "I have got the best 'Arab women who know how to use the high class of perfume." Muhammad bin Maslama requested Ka`b "Will you allow me to smell your head?" Ka`b said, "Yes." Muhammad smelt it and made his companions smell it as well. Then he requested Ka`b again, "Will you let me (smell your head)?" Ka`b said, "Yes." When Muhammad got a strong hold of him, he said (to his companions), "Get at him!" So they killed him and went to the Prophet ﷺ and informed him. (Abu Rafi`) was killed after Ka`b bin Al-Ashraf." – Sahih al-Bukhari 4037

حَدَّثَنَا عَلِيُّ بْنُ عَبْدِ اللَّهِ، حَدَّثَنَا سُفْيَانُ، قَالَ عَمْرٌو سَمِعْتُ جَابِرَ بْنَ عَبْدِ اللَّهِ ـ رضى الله عنهما ـ يَقُولُ قَالَ رَسُولُ اللَّهِ صلى الله عليه وسلم " مَنْ لِكَعْبِ بْنِ الأَشْرَفِ فَإِنَّهُ قَدْ آذَى اللَّهَ وَرَسُولَهُ ". فَقَامَ مُحَمَّدُ بْنُ مَسْلَمَةَ فَقَالَ يَا رَسُولَ اللَّهِ أَتُحِبُّ أَنْ أَقْتُلَهُ قَالَ " نَعَمْ ". قَالَ فَأْذَنْ لِي أَنْ أَقُولَ شَيْئًا. قَالَ " قُلْ ". فَأَتَاهُ مُحَمَّدُ بْنُ مَسْلَمَةَ فَقَالَ إِنَّ هَذَا الرَّجُلَ قَدْ سَأَلَنَا صَدَقَةً، وَإِنَّهُ قَدْ عَنَّانَا، وَإِنِّي قَدْ أَتَيْتُكَ أَسْتَسْلِفُكَ. قَالَ وَأَيْضًا وَاللَّهِ لَتَمَلُّنَّهُ قَالَ إِنَّا قَدِ اتَّبَعْنَاهُ فَلاَ نُحِبُّ أَنْ نَدَعَهُ حَتَّى نَنْظُرَ إِلَى أَىِّ شَىْءٍ يَصِيرُ شَأْنُهُ، وَقَدْ أَرَدْنَا أَنْ تُسْلِفَنَا وَسْقًا، أَوْ وَسْقَيْنِ ـ وَحَدَّثَنَا عَمْرٌو غَيْرَ مَرَّةٍ، فَلَمْ يَذْكُرْ وَسْقًا أَوْ وَسْقَيْنِ أَوْ فَقُلْتُ لَهُ فِيهِ وَسْقًا أَوْ وَسْقَيْنِ فَقَالَ أُرَى فِيهِ وَسْقًا أَوْ وَسْقَيْنِ ـ فَقَالَ نَعَمِ ارْهَنُونِي. قَالُوا أَىَّ شَىْءٍ تُرِيدُ قَالَ فَارْهَنُونِي نِسَاءَكُمْ. قَالُوا كَيْفَ نَرْهَنُكَ نِسَاءَنَا وَأَنْتَ أَجْمَلُ الْعَرَبِ قَالَ فَارْهَنُونِي أَبْنَاءَكُمْ. قَالُوا كَيْفَ نَرْهَنُكَ أَبْنَاءَنَا فَيُسَبُّ أَحَدُهُمْ، فَيُقَالُ رُهِنَ بِوَسْقٍ أَوْ وَسْقَيْنِ. هَذَا عَارٌ عَلَيْنَا، وَلَكِنَّا نَرْهَنُكَ اللأْمَةَ ـ قَالَ سُفْيَانُ يَعْنِي السِّلاَحَ ـ فَوَاعَدَهُ أَنْ يَأْتِيَهُ، فَجَاءَهُ لَيْلاً وَمَعَهُ أَبُو نَائِلَةَ وَهْوَ أَخُو كَعْبٍ مِنَ الرَّضَاعَةِ، فَدَعَاهُمْ إِلَى الْحِصْنِ، فَنَزَلَ إِلَيْهِمْ فَقَالَتْ لَهُ امْرَأَتُهُ أَيْنَ تَخْرُجُ هَذِهِ السَّاعَةَ فَقَالَ إِنَّمَا هُوَ مُحَمَّدُ بْنُ مَسْلَمَةَ، وَأَخِي أَبُو نَائِلَةَ ـ وَقَالَ غَيْرُ عَمْرٍو قَالَتْ أَسْمَعُ صَوْتًا كَأَنَّهُ يَقْطُرُ مِنْهُ الدَّمُ. قَالَ إِنَّمَا هُوَ أَخِي مُحَمَّدُ بْنُ مَسْلَمَةَ وَرَضِيعِي أَبُو نَائِلَةَ ـ إِنَّ الْكَرِيمَ لَوْ دُعِيَ إِلَى طَعْنَةٍ بِلَيْلٍ لأَجَابَ قَالَ وَيُدْخِلُ مُحَمَّدُ بْنُ مَسْلَمَةَ مَعَهُ رَجُلَيْنِ ـ قِيلَ لِسُفْيَانَ سَمَّاهُمْ عَمْرٌو قَالَ سَمَّى بَعْضَهُمْ قَالَ عَمْرٌو جَاءَ مَعَهُ بِرَجُلَيْنِ وَقَالَ غَيْرُ عَمْرٍو أَبُو عَبْسِ بْنُ جَبْرٍ، وَالْحَارِثُ بْنُ أَوْسٍ وَعَبَّادُ بْنُ بِشْرٍ قَالَ عَمْرٌو وَجَاءَ مَعَهُ بِرَجُلَيْنِ ـ فَقَالَ إِذَا مَا جَاءَ فَإِنِّي قَائِلٌ بِشَعَرِهِ فَأَشَمُّهُ، فَإِذَا رَأَيْتُمُونِي اسْتَمْكَنْتُ مِنْ رَأْسِهِ فَدُونَكُمْ فَاضْرِبُوهُ. وَقَالَ مَرَّةً ثُمَّ أُشِمُّكُمْ. فَنَزَلَ إِلَيْهِمْ مُتَوَشِّحًا وَهْوَ يَنْفَحُ مِنْهُ رِيحُ الطِّيبِ، فَقَالَ مَا رَأَيْتُ كَالْيَوْمِ رِيحًا ـ أَىْ أَطْيَبَ ـ وَقَالَ غَيْرُ عَمْرٍو قَالَ عِنْدِي أَعْطَرُ نِسَاءِ الْعَرَبِ وَأَكْمَلُ الْعَرَبِ قَالَ عَمْرٌو فَقَالَ أَتَأْذَنُ لِي أَنْ أَشَمَّ رَأْسَكَ قَالَ نَعَمْ، فَشَمَّهُ، ثُمَّ أَشَمَّ أَصْحَابَهُ ثُمَّ قَالَ أَتَأْذَنُ لِي قَالَ نَعَمْ. فَلَمَّا اسْتَمْكَنَ مِنْهُ قَالَ دُونَكُمْ. فَقَتَلُوهُ ثُمَّ أَتَوُا النَّبِيَّ صلى الله عليه وسلم فَأَخْبَرُوهُ

Narrated Al-Bara: Allah's Messenger ﷺ sent `Abdullah bin 'Atik and `Abdullah bin `Utba with a group of men to Abu Rafi` (to kill him). They proceeded till they approached his castle, whereupon `Abdullah bin Atik said to them, "Wait (here), and in the meantime I will go and see." `Abdullah said later on, "I played a trick in order to enter the castle. By chance, they lost a donkey of theirs and came out carrying a flaming light to search for it. I was afraid that they would recognize me, so I covered my head and legs and pretended to answer the call to nature. The gatekeeper called, 'Whoever wants to come in, should come in before I close the gate.' So I went in and hid myself in a stall of a donkey near the gate of the castle. They took their supper with Abu Rafi` and had a chat till late at night. Then they went back to their homes. When the voices vanished and I no longer detected any movement, I came out. I had seen where the gate-keeper had kept the key of the castle in a hole in the wall. I took it and unlocked the gate of the castle, saying to myself, 'If these people should notice me, I will run away easily.' Then I locked all the doors of their houses from outside while they were inside, and ascended to Abu Rafi` by a staircase. I saw the house in complete darkness with its light off, and I could not know where the man was. So I called, 'O Abu Rafi`!' He replied, 'Who is it?' I proceeded towards the voice and hit him. He cried loudly but my blow was futile. Then I came to him, pretending to help him, saying with a different tone of my voice, ' What is wrong with you, O Abu Rafi`?' He said, 'Are you not surprised? Woe on your mother! A man has come to me and hit me with a sword!' So again I aimed at him and hit him, but the blow proved futile again, and on that Abu Rafi` cried loudly and his wife got up. I came again and changed my voice as if I were a helper, and found Abu Rafi` lying straight on his back, so I drove the sword into his belly and bent on it till I heard the sound of a bone break. Then I came out, filled with astonishment and went to the staircase to descend, but I fell down from it and got my leg dislocated. I bandaged it and went to my companions limping. I said (to them), 'Go and tell Allah's Messenger ﷺ of this good news, but I will not leave (this place) till I hear the news of his (i.e. Abu Rafi`'s) death.' When dawn broke, an announcer of death got over the wall and announced, 'I convey to you the news of Abu Rafi`'s death.' I got up and proceeded without feeling any pain till I caught up with my companions before they reached the Prophet ﷺ to whom I conveyed the good news." – Sahih al-Bukhari 4040

حَدَّثَنَا أَحْمَدُ بْنُ عُثْمَانَ، حَدَّثَنَا شُرَيْحٌ ـ هُوَ ابْنُ مَسْلَمَةَ ـ حَدَّثَنَا إِبْرَاهِيمُ بْنُ يُوسُفَ، عَنْ أَبِيهِ، عَنْ أَبِي إِسْحَاقَ، قَالَ سَمِعْتُ الْبَرَاءَ ـ رضى الله عنه ـ قَالَ بَعَثَ رَسُولُ اللَّهِ صلى الله عليه وسلم إِلَى أَبِي رَافِعٍ عَبْدَ اللَّهِ بْنَ عَتِيكٍ وَعَبْدَ اللَّهِ بْنَ عُتْبَةَ فِي نَاسٍ مَعَهُمْ، فَانْطَلَقُوا حَتَّى دَنَوْا مِنَ الْحِصْنِ، فَقَالَ لَهُمْ عَبْدُ اللَّهِ بْنُ عَتِيكٍ امْكُثُوا أَنْتُمْ حَتَّى أَنْطَلِقَ أَنَا فَأَنْظُرَ. قَالَ فَتَلَطَّفْتُ أَنْ أَدْخُلَ الْحِصْنَ، فَفَقَدُوا حِمَارًا لَهُمْ ـ قَالَ ـ فَخَرَجُوا بِقَبَسٍ يَطْلُبُونَهُ ـ قَالَ ـ فَخَشِيتُ أَنْ أُعْرَفَ ـ قَالَ ـ فَغَطَّيْتُ رَأْسِي كَأَنِّي أَقْضِي حَاجَةً، ثُمَّ نَادَى صَاحِبُ الْبَابِ مَنْ أَرَادَ أَنْ يَدْخُلَ فَلْيَدْخُلْ قَبْلَ أَنْ أُغْلِقَهُ. فَدَخَلْتُ ثُمَّ اخْتَبَأْتُ فِي مَرْبِطِ حِمَارٍ عِنْدَ بَابِ الْحِصْنِ، فَتَعَشَّوْا عِنْدَ أَبِي رَافِعٍ وَتَحَدَّثُوا حَتَّى ذَهَبَتْ سَاعَةٌ مِنَ اللَّيْلِ، ثُمَّ رَجَعُوا إِلَى بُيُوتِهِمْ، فَلَمَّا هَدَأَتِ الأَصْوَاتُ وَلاَ أَسْمَعُ حَرَكَةً خَرَجْتُ ـ قَالَ ـ وَرَأَيْتُ صَاحِبَ الْبَابِ حَيْثُ وَضَعَ مِفْتَاحَ الْحِصْنِ، فِي كَوَّةٍ فَأَخَذْتُهُ فَفَتَحْتُ بِهِ بَابَ الْحِصْنِ. قَالَ قُلْتُ إِنْ نَذِرَ بِي الْقَوْمُ انْطَلَقْتُ عَلَى مَهَلٍ، ثُمَّ عَمَدْتُ إِلَى أَبْوَابِ بُيُوتِهِمْ، فَغَلَّقْتُهَا عَلَيْهِمْ مِنْ ظَاهِرٍ، ثُمَّ صَعِدْتُ إِلَى أَبِي رَافِعٍ فِي سُلَّمٍ، فَإِذَا الْبَيْتُ مُظْلِمٌ قَدْ طَفِئَ سِرَاجُهُ، فَلَمْ أَدْرِ أَيْنَ الرَّجُلُ، فَقُلْتُ يَا أَبَا رَافِعٍ. قَالَ مَنْ هَذَا قَالَ فَعَمَدْتُ نَحْوَ الصَّوْتِ فَأَضْرِبُهُ، وَصَاحَ فَلَمْ تُغْنِ شَيْئًا ـ قَالَ ـ ثُمَّ جِئْتُ كَأَنِّي أُغِيثُهُ فَقُلْتُ مَا لَكَ يَا أَبَا رَافِعٍ وَغَيَّرْتُ صَوْتِي. فَقَالَ أَلاَ أُعْجِبُكَ لأُمِّكَ الْوَيْلُ، دَخَلَ عَلَىَّ رَجُلٌ فَضَرَبَنِي بِالسَّيْفِ. قَالَ فَعَمَدْتُ لَهُ أَيْضًا فَأَضْرِبُهُ أُخْرَى فَلَمْ تُغْنِ شَيْئًا، فَصَاحَ وَقَامَ أَهْلُهُ، قَالَ ثُمَّ جِئْتُ وَغَيَّرْتُ صَوْتِي كَهَيْئَةِ الْمُغِيثِ، فَإِذَا هُوَ مُسْتَلْقٍ عَلَى ظَهْرِهِ، فَأَضَعُ السَّيْفَ فِي بَطْنِهِ ثُمَّ أَنْكَفِئُ عَلَيْهِ حَتَّى سَمِعْتُ صَوْتَ الْعَظْمِ، ثُمَّ خَرَجْتُ دَهِشًا حَتَّى أَتَيْتُ السُّلَّمَ أُرِيدُ أَنْ أَنْزِلَ، فَأَسْقُطُ مِنْهُ فَانْخَلَعَتْ رِجْلِي فَعَصَبْتُهَا، ثُمَّ أَتَيْتُ أَصْحَابِي أَحْجُلُ فَقُلْتُ انْطَلِقُوا فَبَشِّرُوا رَسُولَ اللَّهِ صلى الله عليه وسلم فَإِنِّي لاَ أَبْرَحُ حَتَّى أَسْمَعَ النَّاعِيَةَ، فَلَمَّا كَانَ فِي وَجْهِ الصُّبْحِ صَعِدَ النَّاعِيَةُ فَقَالَ أَنْعَى أَبَا رَافِعٍ. قَالَ فَقُمْتُ أَمْشِي مَا بِي قَلَبَةٌ، فَأَدْرَكْتُ أَصْحَابِي قَبْلَ أَنْ يَأْتُوا النَّبِيَّ صلى الله عليه وسلم فَبَشَّرْتُهُ

The Book of
Ghazwat Khandaq
غزوة خندق

Narrated Jabir bin `Abdullah: When the Prophetﷺ called the people (Sadqa, a sub-narrator, said, 'Most likely that happened on the day of Al-Khandaq) Az-Zubair responded to the call (i.e. to act as a scout). The Prophet) called the people again and Az-Zubair responded to the call. The Prophetﷺ then said, "Every prophet had a disciple and my disciple is Zubair bin Al-`Awwam." – Sahih Al-Bukhari 2847

حَدَّثَنَا صَدَقَةُ، أَخْبَرَنَا ابْنُ عُيَيْنَةَ، حَدَّثَنَا ابْنُ الْمُنْكَدِرِ، سَمِعَ جَابِرَ بْنَ عَبْدِ اللَّهِ ـ رضى الله عنهما ـ قَالَ نَدَبَ النَّبِيُّ صلى الله عليه وسلم النَّاسَ ـ قَالَ صَدَقَةُ أَظُنُّهُ ـ يَوْمَ الْخَنْدَقِ فَانْتَدَبَ الزُّبَيْرُ، ثُمَّ نَدَبَ فَانْتَدَبَ الزُّبَيْرُ، ثُمَّ نَدَبَ النَّاسَ فَانْتَدَبَ الزُّبَيْرُ فَقَالَ النَّبِيُّ صلى الله عليه وسلم " إِنَّ لِكُلِّ نَبِيٍّ حَوَارِيًّا، وَإِنَّ حَوَارِيَّ الزُّبَيْرُ بْنُ الْعَوَّامِ "

Narrated Ibn `Umar: That the Prophetﷺ inspected him on the day of Uhud while he was fourteen years old, and the Prophetﷺ did not allow him to take part in the battle. He was inspected again by the Prophetﷺ on the day of Al- Khandaq (i.e. battle of the Trench) while he was fifteen years old, and the Prophetﷺ allowed him to take Part in the battle. – Sahih Al-Bukhari 4097

حَدَّثَنَا يَعْقُوبُ بْنُ إِبْرَاهِيمَ، حَدَّثَنَا يَحْيَى بْنُ سَعِيدٍ، عَنْ عُبَيْدِ اللَّهِ، قَالَ أَخْبَرَنِي نَافِعٌ، عَنِ ابْنِ عُمَرَ ـ رضى الله عنهما أَنَّ النَّبِيَّ صلى الله عليه وسلم عَرَضَهُ يَوْمَ أُحُدٍ وَهْوَ ابْنُ أَرْبَعَ عَشْرَةَ فَلَمْ يُجِزْهُ، وَعَرَضَهُ يَوْمَ الْخَنْدَقِ وَهْوَ ابْنُ خَمْسَ عَشْرَةَ فَأَجَازَهُ.

Narrated Jabir: We were digging (the trench) on the day of (Al-Khandaq (i.e. Trench) and we came across a big solid rock. We went to the Prophetﷺ and said, "Here is a rock appearing across the trench." He said, "I am coming down." Then he got up, and a stone was tied to his belly for we had not eaten anything for three days. So the Prophetﷺ took the spade and struck the big solid rock and it became like sand. I said, "O Allah's Messengerﷺ ! Allow me to go home." (When the Prophetﷺ allowed me) I said to my wife, "I saw the Prophetﷺ in a state that I cannot treat lightly. Have you got something (for him to eat?" She replied, "I have barley and a she goat." So I slaughtered the she-kid and she ground the barley; then we put the meat in the earthenware cooking pot. Then I came to the Prophetﷺ when the dough had become soft and fermented and (the meat in) the pot over the stone trivet had nearly been well-cooked, and said, "I have got a little food prepared, so get up O Allah's Messengerﷺ , you and one or two men along with you (for the food)." The Prophetﷺ asked, "How much is that food?" I told him about it. He said, "It is abundant and good. Tell your wife not to remove the earthenware pot from the fire and not to take out any bread from the oven till I reach there." Then he said (to all his companions), "Get up." So the Muhajirn (i.e. Emigrants) and the Ansar got up. When I came to my wife, I said, "Allah's Mercy be upon you! The Prophet came along with the Muhajirin and the Ansar and those who were present with them." She said, "Did the Prophetﷺ ask you (how much food you had)?" I replied, "Yes." Then the Prophetﷺ said, "Enter and do not throng." The Prophetﷺ started cutting the bread (into pieces) and put the cooked meat over it. He covered the earthenware pot and the oven whenever he took something out of them. He would give the food to his companions and take the meat out of the pot. He went on cutting the bread and scooping the meat (for his companions) till they all ate their fill, and even then, some food remained. Then the Prophetﷺ said (to my wife), "Eat and present to others as the people are struck with hunger." – Sahih Al-Bukhari 4101

حَدَّثَنَا خَلاَّدُ بْنُ يَحْيَى، حَدَّثَنَا عَبْدُ الْوَاحِدِ بْنُ أَيْمَنَ، عَنْ أَبِيهِ، قَالَ أَتَيْتُ جَابِرًا ـ رضى الله عنه ـ فَقَالَ إِنَّا يَوْمَ الْخَنْدَقِ نَحْفِرُ فَعَرَضَتْ كُدْيَةٌ شَدِيدَةٌ، فَجَاءُوا النَّبِيَّ صلى الله عليه وسلم فَقَالُوا هَذِهِ كُدْيَةٌ عَرَضَتْ فِي الْخَنْدَقِ، فَقَالَ " أَنَا نَازِلٌ ". ثُمَّ قَامَ وَبَطْنُهُ مَعْصُوبٌ بِحَجَرٍ، وَلَبِثْنَا ثَلاَثَةَ أَيَّامٍ لاَ نَذُوقُ ذَوَاقًا، فَأَخَذَ النَّبِيُّ صلى الله عليه وسلم الْمِعْوَلَ فَضَرَبَ، فَعَادَ كَثِيبًا أَهْيَلَ أَوْ أَهْيَمَ، فَقُلْتُ يَا رَسُولَ اللَّهِ ائْذَنْ لِي إِلَى الْبَيْتِ. فَقُلْتُ لاِمْرَأَتِي رَأَيْتُ بِالنَّبِيِّ صلى الله عليه وسلم شَيْئًا، مَا كَانَ فِي ذَلِكَ صَبْرٌ، فَعِنْدَكِ شَىْءٌ قَالَتْ عِنْدِي شَعِيرٌ وَعَنَاقٌ. فَذَبَحْتُ الْعَنَاقَ وَطَحَنَتِ الشَّعِيرَ، حَتَّى جَعَلْنَا اللَّحْمَ فِي الْبُرْمَةِ، ثُمَّ جِئْتُ النَّبِيَّ صلى الله عليه وسلم وَالْعَجِينُ قَدِ انْكَسَرَ، وَالْبُرْمَةُ بَيْنَ الأَثَافِيِّ قَدْ كَادَتْ أَنْ تَنْضَجَ فَقُلْتُ طُعَيِّمٌ لِي، فَقُمْ أَنْتَ يَا رَسُولَ اللَّهِ وَرَجُلٌ أَوْ رَجُلاَنِ. قَالَ " كَمْ هُوَ ". فَذَكَرْتُ لَهُ، قَالَ " كَثِيرٌ طَيِّبٌ ". قَالَ " قُلْ لَهَا لاَ تَنْزِعُ الْبُرْمَةَ وَلاَ الْخُبْزَ مِنَ التَّنُّورِ حَتَّى آتِيَ ". فَقَالَ " قُومُوا ". فَقَامَ الْمُهَاجِرُونَ وَالأَنْصَارُ، فَلَمَّا دَخَلَ عَلَى امْرَأَتِهِ قَالَ وَيْحَكِ جَاءَ النَّبِيُّ صلى الله عليه وسلم بِالْمُهَاجِرِينَ وَالأَنْصَارِ وَمَنْ مَعَهُمْ. قَالَتْ هَلْ سَأَلَكَ قُلْتُ نَعَمْ. فَقَالَ " ادْخُلُوا وَلاَ تَضَاغَطُوا ". فَجَعَلَ يَكْسِرُ الْخُبْزَ وَيَجْعَلُ عَلَيْهِ اللَّحْمَ، وَيُخَمِّرُ الْبُرْمَةَ وَالتَّنُّورَ إِذَا أَخَذَ مِنْهُ، وَيُقَرِّبُ إِلَى أَصْحَابِهِ ثُمَّ يَنْزِعُ، فَلَمْ يَزَلْ يَكْسِرُ الْخُبْزَ وَيَغْرِفُ حَتَّى شَبِعُوا وَبَقِيَ بَقِيَّةٌ قَالَ " كُلِي هَذَا وَأَهْدِي، فَإِنَّ النَّاسَ أَصَابَتْهُمْ مَجَاعَةٌ "

Narrated `Aisha: As regards the following Qur'anic Verse:-- "When they came on you from above and from below you (from east and west of the valley) and when the eyes grew wild and the hearts reached up to the throats....." (33.10) That happened on the day of Al-Khandaq (i.e. Trench). – Sahih Al-Bukhari 4103

حَدَّثَنِي عُثْمَانُ بْنُ أَبِي شَيْبَةَ، حَدَّثَنَا عَبْدَةُ، عَنْ هِشَامٍ، عَنْ أَبِيهِ، عَنْ عَائِشَةَ، رضى الله عنها {إِذْ جَاءُوكُمْ مِنْ فَوْقِكُمْ وَمِنْ أَسْفَلَ مِنْكُمْ وَإِذْ زَاغَتِ الأَبْصَارُ} قَالَتْ كَانَ ذَاكَ يَوْمَ الْخَنْدَقِ.

O you who believe! Remember Allah's blessings upon you, when forces came against you, and We sent against them a wind, and forces you did not see. Allah is Observant of what you do. When they came upon you, from above you, and from beneath you; and the eyes became dazed, and the hearts reached the throats, and you harbored doubts about Allah. There and then the believers were tested, and were shaken most severely. When the hypocrites and those in whose hearts is sickness said, "Allah and His Messenger promised us nothing but illusion." And when a group of them said, "O people of Yathrib, you cannot make a stand, so retreat." And a faction of them asked the Prophet to excuse them, saying, "Our homes are exposed," although they were not exposed. They only wanted to flee. Had it been invaded from its sides, and they were asked to dissent, they would have done so with little hesitation. Although they had made a pledged to Allah, in the past, that they will not turn their backs. A pledge to Allah is a responsibility. Say, "Flight will not benefit you, if you flee from death or killing, even then you will be given only brief enjoyment." Say, "Who is it who will shield you from Allah, if He intends adversity for you, or intends mercy for you?" Besides Allah, they will find for themselves neither friend nor helper. Allah already knows the hinderers among you, and those who say to their brethren, "Come and join us." Rarely do they mobilize for battle. Being stingy towards you. And when fear approaches, you see them staring at you—their eyes rolling—like someone fainting at death. Then, when panic is over, they whip you with sharp tongues. They resent you any good. These have never believed, so Allah has nullified their works; a matter easy for Allah. They assumed that the confederates had not withdrawn. But were the confederates to advance, they would wish they were in the desert with the Bedouins, inquiring about your news. And if they were among you, they would have done little fighting. You have an excellent example in the Messenger of Allah; for anyone who seeks Allah and the Last Day, and remembers Allah frequently. And when the believers saw the confederates, they said, "This is what Allah and His messenger have promised us; and Allah and His messenger have told the truth." And it only increased them in faith and submission. Of the believers are men who are true to what they pledged to Allah. Some of them have fulfilled their vows; and some are still waiting, and never wavering. That Allah may reward the truthful for their truthfulness; and punish the hypocrites, if He wills, or pardon them.

Allah is Forgiving and Merciful. Allah repelled the disbelievers in their rage; they gained no advantage. Allah thus spared the believers combat. Allah is Strong and Mighty. And He brought down from their strongholds those of the People of the Book who backed them, and He threw terror into their hearts. Some of them you killed, and others you took captive. And He made you inherit their land, and their homes, and their possessions, and a region you have never stepped on. Allah has power over all things. – Surah Al-Ahzab 33:9-27

ٱشْتَرَوْا۟ بِـَٔايَـٰتِ ٱللَّهِ ثَمَنًا قَلِيلًا فَصَدُّوا۟ عَن سَبِيلِهِۦٓ ۚ إِنَّهُمْ سَآءَ مَا كَانُوا۟ يَعْمَلُونَ لَا يَرْقُبُونَ فِى مُؤْمِنٍ إِلًّا وَلَا ذِمَّةً ۚ وَأُو۟لَـٰٓئِكَ
هُمُ ٱلْمُعْتَدُونَ فَإِن تَابُوا۟ وَأَقَامُوا۟ ٱلصَّلَوٰةَ وَءَاتَوُا۟ ٱلزَّكَوٰةَ فَإِخْوَٰنُكُمْ فِى ٱلدِّينِ ۗ وَنُفَصِّلُ ٱلْـَٔايَـٰتِ لِقَوْمٍ يَعْلَمُونَ وَإِن نَّكَثُوٓا۟ أَيْمَـٰنَهُم
مِّنۢ بَعْدِ عَهْدِهِمْ وَطَعَنُوا۟ فِى دِينِكُمْ فَقَـٰتِلُوٓا۟ أَئِمَّةَ ٱلْكُفْرِ ۙ إِنَّهُمْ لَآ أَيْمَـٰنَ لَهُمْ لَعَلَّهُمْ يَنتَهُونَ أَلَا تُقَـٰتِلُونَ قَوْمًا نَّكَثُوٓا۟ أَيْمَـٰنَهُمْ وَهَمُّوا۟
بِإِخْرَاجِ ٱلرَّسُولِ وَهُم بَدَءُوكُمْ أَوَّلَ مَرَّةٍ ۚ أَتَخْشَوْنَهُمْ ۚ فَٱللَّهُ أَحَقُّ أَن تَخْشَوْهُ إِن كُنتُم مُّؤْمِنِينَ قَـٰتِلُوهُمْ يُعَذِّبْهُمُ ٱللَّهُ بِأَيْدِيكُمْ وَيُخْزِهِمْ
وَيَنصُرْكُمْ عَلَيْهِمْ وَيَشْفِ صُدُورَ قَوْمٍ مُّؤْمِنِينَ وَيُذْهِبْ غَيْظَ قُلُوبِهِمْ ۗ وَيَتُوبُ ٱللَّهُ عَلَىٰ مَن يَشَآءُ ۗ وَٱللَّهُ عَلِيمٌ حَكِيمٌ أَمْ حَسِبْتُمْ أَن
تُتْرَكُوا۟ وَلَمَّا يَعْلَمِ ٱللَّهُ ٱلَّذِينَ جَـٰهَدُوا۟ مِنكُمْ وَلَمْ يَتَّخِذُوا۟ مِن دُونِ ٱللَّهِ وَلَا رَسُولِهِۦ وَلَا ٱلْمُؤْمِنِينَ وَلِيجَةً ۚ وَٱللَّهُ خَبِيرٌۢ بِمَا تَعْمَلُونَ
مَا كَانَ لِلْمُشْرِكِينَ أَن يَعْمُرُوا۟ مَسَـٰجِدَ ٱللَّهِ شَـٰهِدِينَ عَلَىٰٓ أَنفُسِهِم بِٱلْكُفْرِ ۚ أُو۟لَـٰٓئِكَ حَبِطَتْ أَعْمَـٰلُهُمْ وَفِى ٱلنَّارِ هُمْ خَـٰلِدُونَ إِنَّمَا
يَعْمُرُ مَسَـٰجِدَ ٱللَّهِ مَنْ ءَامَنَ بِٱللَّهِ وَٱلْيَوْمِ ٱلْـَٔاخِرِ وَأَقَامَ ٱلصَّلَوٰةَ وَءَاتَى ٱلزَّكَوٰةَ وَلَمْ يَخْشَ إِلَّا ٱللَّهَ ۖ فَعَسَىٰٓ أُو۟لَـٰٓئِكَ أَن يَكُونُوا۟ مِنَ
ٱلْمُهْتَدِينَ ۞ أَجَعَلْتُمْ سِقَايَةَ ٱلْحَآجِّ وَعِمَارَةَ ٱلْمَسْجِدِ ٱلْحَرَامِ كَمَنْ ءَامَنَ بِٱللَّهِ وَٱلْيَوْمِ ٱلْـَٔاخِرِ وَجَـٰهَدَ فِى سَبِيلِ ٱللَّهِ ۚ لَا يَسْتَوُۥنَ عِندَ
ٱللَّهِ ۗ وَٱللَّهُ لَا يَهْدِى ٱلْقَوْمَ ٱلظَّـٰلِمِينَ ٱلَّذِينَ ءَامَنُوا۟ وَهَاجَرُوا۟ وَجَـٰهَدُوا۟ فِى سَبِيلِ ٱللَّهِ بِأَمْوَٰلِهِمْ وَأَنفُسِهِمْ أَعْظَمُ دَرَجَةً عِندَ ٱللَّهِ ۚ
وَأُو۟لَـٰٓئِكَ هُمُ ٱلْفَآئِزُونَ يُبَشِّرُهُمْ رَبُّهُم بِرَحْمَةٍ مِّنْهُ وَرِضْوَٰنٍ وَجَنَّـٰتٍ لَّهُمْ فِيهَا نَعِيمٌ مُّقِيمٌ خَـٰلِدِينَ فِيهَآ أَبَدًا ۚ إِنَّ ٱللَّهَ عِندَهُۥٓ أَجْرٌ
عَظِيمٌ يَـٰٓأَيُّهَا ٱلَّذِينَ ءَامَنُوا۟ لَا تَتَّخِذُوٓا۟ ءَابَآءَكُمْ وَإِخْوَٰنَكُمْ أَوْلِيَآءَ إِنِ ٱسْتَحَبُّوا۟ ٱلْكُفْرَ عَلَى ٱلْإِيمَـٰنِ ۚ وَمَن يَتَوَلَّهُم مِّنكُمْ فَأُو۟لَـٰٓئِكَ هُمُ
ٱلظَّـٰلِمُونَ قُلْ إِن كَانَ ءَابَآؤُكُمْ وَأَبْنَآؤُكُمْ وَإِخْوَٰنُكُمْ وَأَزْوَٰجُكُمْ وَعَشِيرَتُكُمْ وَأَمْوَٰلٌ ٱقْتَرَفْتُمُوهَا وَتِجَـٰرَةٌ تَخْشَوْنَ كَسَادَهَا
وَمَسَـٰكِنُ تَرْضَوْنَهَآ أَحَبَّ إِلَيْكُم مِّنَ ٱللَّهِ وَرَسُولِهِۦ وَجِهَادٍ فِى سَبِيلِهِۦ فَتَرَبَّصُوا۟ حَتَّىٰ يَأْتِىَ ٱللَّهُ بِأَمْرِهِۦ ۗ وَٱللَّهُ لَا يَهْدِى ٱلْقَوْمَ
ٱلْفَـٰسِقِينَ لَقَدْ نَصَرَكُمُ ٱللَّهُ فِى مَوَاطِنَ كَثِيرَةٍ ۙ وَيَوْمَ حُنَيْنٍ ۙ إِذْ أَعْجَبَتْكُمْ كَثْرَتُكُمْ فَلَمْ تُغْنِ عَنكُمْ شَيْـًٔا وَضَاقَتْ عَلَيْكُمُ ٱلْأَرْضُ بِمَا
رَحُبَتْ ثُمَّ وَلَّيْتُم مُّدْبِرِينَ ثُمَّ أَنزَلَ ٱللَّهُ سَكِينَتَهُۥ عَلَىٰ رَسُولِهِۦ وَعَلَى ٱلْمُؤْمِنِينَ وَأَنزَلَ جُنُودًا لَّمْ تَرَوْهَا وَعَذَّبَ ٱلَّذِينَ كَفَرُوا۟ ۚ
وَذَٰلِكَ جَزَآءُ ٱلْكَـٰفِرِينَ ثُمَّ يَتُوبُ ٱللَّهُ مِنۢ بَعْدِ ذَٰلِكَ عَلَىٰ مَن يَشَآءُ ۗ وَٱللَّهُ غَفُورٌ رَّحِيمٌ

Narrated Anas bin Malik: On the day of the battle of the Trench (i.e. Ghazwat-ul-Khandaq) the Ansar used to say, "We are those who have given the pledge of allegiance to Muhammad for Jihad (i.e. holy fighting) as long as we live." The Prophet ﷺ, replied to them, "O Allah! There is no life except the life of the Hereafter; so please honor the Ansar and the Emigrants." - Sahih al-Bukhari 3796

حَدَّثَنَا آدَمُ، حَدَّثَنَا شُعْبَةُ، عَنْ حُمَيْدٍ الطَّوِيلِ، سَمِعْتُ أَنَسَ بْنَ مَالِكٍ ـ رضى الله عنه ـ قَالَ كَانَتِ الأَنْصَارُ يَوْمَ الْخَنْدَقِ تَقُولُ
نَحْنُ الَّذِينَ بَايَعُوا مُحَمَّدَا عَلَى الْجِهَادِ مَا حَيِينَا أَبَدَا فَأَجَابَهُمُ اللَّهُمَّ لاَ عَيْشَ إِلاَّ عَيْشُ الآخِرَهْ فَأَكْرِمِ الأَنْصَارَ وَالْمُهَاجِرَهْ

Narrated Anas: The Prophet ﷺ went out on a cold morning while the Muhajirin (emigrants) and the Ansar were digging the trench. The Prophet ﷺ then said, "O Allah! The real goodness is the goodness of the Here after, so please forgive the Ansar and the Muhajirin." They replied, "We are those who have given the Pledge of allegiance to Muhammad for to observe Jihad as long as we remain alive.". – Sahih Al-Bukhari 7201

حَدَّثَنَا عَمْرُو بْنُ عَلِيٍّ، حَدَّثَنَا خَالِدُ بْنُ الْحَارِثِ، حَدَّثَنَا حُمَيْدٌ، عَنْ أَنَسٍ ـ رضى الله عنه ـ خَرَجَ النَّبِيُّ صلى الله عليه وسلم
فِي غَدَاةٍ بَارِدَةٍ وَالْمُهَاجِرُونَ وَالأَنْصَارُ يَحْفِرُونَ الْخَنْدَقَ فَقَالَ " اللَّهُمَّ إِنَّ الْخَيْرَ خَيْرُ الآخِرَهْ فَاغْفِرْ لِلأَنْصَارِ وَالْمُهَاجِرَهْ "
فَأَجَابُوا نَحْنُ الَّذِينَ بَايَعُوا مُحَمَّدَا عَلَى الْجِهَادِ مَا بَقِينَا أَبَدَا

Narrated Al-Bara: When it was the day of Al-Ahzab (i.e. the clans) and Allah's Messenger ﷺ dug the trench, I saw him carrying earth out of the trench till dust made the skin of his `Abdomen out of my sight and he was a hairy man. I heard him reciting the poetic verses composed by Ibn Rawaha while he was carrying the earth, "O Allah! Without You we would not have been guided, nor would we have given in charity, nor would we have prayed. So, (O Allah), please send Sakina (i.e. calmness) upon us and make our feet firm if we meet the enemy, as they have rebelled against us. And if they intend affliction (i.e. want to frighten us, and fight against us) then we would not (flee but withstand them)." The Prophetﷺ would then prolong his voice at the last words. – Sahih Al-Bukhari 4106

حَدَّثَنِي أَحْمَدُ بْنُ عُثْمَانَ، حَدَّثَنَا شُرَيْحُ بْنُ مَسْلَمَةَ، قَالَ حَدَّثَنِي إِبْرَاهِيمُ بْنُ يُوسُفَ، قَالَ حَدَّثَنِي أَبِي، عَنْ أَبِي إِسْحَاقَ، قَالَ سَمِعْتُ الْبَرَاءَ، يُحَدِّثُ قَالَ لَمَّا كَانَ يَوْمُ الأَحْزَابِ، وَخَنْدَقَ رَسُولُ اللَّهِ صلى الله عليه وسلم رَأَيْتُهُ يَنْقُلُ مِنْ تُرَابِ الْخَنْدَقِ حَتَّى وَارَى عَنِّي الْغُبَارُ جِلْدَةَ بَطْنِهِ، وَكَانَ كَثِيرَ الشَّعَرِ، فَسَمِعْتُهُ يَرْتَجِزُ بِكَلِمَاتِ ابْنِ رَوَاحَةَ، وَهْوَ يَنْقُلُ مِنَ التُّرَابِ يَقُولُ اللَّهُمَّ لَوْلاَ أَنْتَ مَا اهْتَدَيْنَا وَلاَ تَصَدَّقْنَا وَلاَ صَلَّيْنَا فَأَنْزِلَنْ سَكِينَةً عَلَيْنَا وَثَبِّتِ الأَقْدَامَ إِنْ لاَقَيْنَا إِنَّ الأُلَى قَدْ بَغَوْا عَلَيْنَا وَإِنْ أَرَادُوا فِتْنَةً أَبَيْنَا قَالَ ثُمَّ يَمُدُّ صَوْتَهُ بِآخِرِهَا

Narrated Jabir: `Umar came cursing the disbelievers (of Quraish) on the day of Al-Khandaq (the battle of Trench) and said, "I could not offer the `Asr prayer till the sun had set. Then we went to Buthan and he offered the (`Asr) prayer after sunset and then he offered the Maghrib prayer. – Sahih Al-Bukhari 598 .

حَدَّثَنَا مُسَدَّدٌ، قَالَ حَدَّثَنَا يَحْيَى، عَنْ هِشَامٍ، قَالَ حَدَّثَنَا يَحْيَى ـ هُوَ ابْنُ أَبِي كَثِيرٍ ـ عَنْ أَبِي سَلَمَةَ، عَنْ جَابِرٍ، قَالَ جَعَلَ عُمَرُ يَوْمَ الْخَنْدَقِ يَسُبُّ كُفَّارَهُمْ وَقَالَ مَا كِدْتُ أُصَلِّي الْعَصْرَ حَتَّى غَرَبَتْ. قَالَ فَنَزَلْنَا بُطْحَانَ، فَصَلَّى بَعْدَ مَا غَرَبَتِ الشَّمْسُ، ثُمَّ صَلَّى الْمَغْرِبَ.

Narrated `Ali: On the day of Al-Khandaq (i.e. Trench), the Prophetﷺ said '(Let) Allah fill their (i.e. the infidels') houses and graves with fire just as they have prevented us from offering the Middle Prayer (i.e. `Asr prayer) till the sun had set.". – Sahih Al-Bukhari 4111 .

حَدَّثَنَا إِسْحَاقُ، حَدَّثَنَا رَوْحٌ، حَدَّثَنَا هِشَامٌ، عَنْ مُحَمَّدٍ، عَنْ عَبِيدَةَ، عَنْ عَلِيٍّ ـ رضى الله عنه ـ عَنِ النَّبِيِّ صلى الله عليه وسلم أَنَّهُ قَالَ يَوْمَ الْخَنْدَقِ " مَلأَ اللَّهُ عَلَيْهِمْ بُيُوتَهُمْ وَقُبُورَهُمْ نَارًا كَمَا شَغَلُونَا عَنْ صَلاَةِ الْوُسْطَى حَتَّى غَابَتِ الشَّمْسُ ".

Narrated `Aisha: Sa`d was wounded on the day of Khandaq (i.e. Trench) when a man from Quraish, called Hibban bin Al-`Araqa hit him (with an arrow). The man was Hibban bin Qais from (the tribe of) Bani Mais bin 'Amir bin Lu'ai who shot an arrow at Sa`d's medial arm vein (or main artery of the arm). The Prophetﷺ pitched a tent (for Sa`d) in the Mosque so that he might be near to the Prophetﷺ to visit. When the Prophet returned from the (battle) of Al-Khandaq (i.e. Trench) and laid down his arms and took a bath Gabriel came to him while he (i.e. Gabriel) was shaking the dust off his head, and said, "You have laid down the arms?" By Allah, I have not laid them down. Go out to them (to attack them)." The Prophetﷺ said, "Where?" Gabriel pointed towards Bani Quraiza. So Allah's Messengerﷺ went to them (i.e. Banu Quraiza) (i.e. besieged them). They then surrendered to the Prophet's judgment but he directed them to Sa`d to give his verdict concerning them. Sa`d said, "I give my judgment that their warriors should be killed, their women and children should be taken as captives, and their properties distributed." Narrated Hisham: My father informed me that `Aisha said, "Sa`d said, "O Allah! You know that there is nothing more beloved to me than to fight in Your Cause against those who disbelieved Your Apostle and turned him out (of Mecca). O Allah! I think you have put to an end the fight between us and them (i.e. Quraish infidels). And if there still remains any fight with the Quraish (infidels), then keep me alive till I fight against them for Your Sake. But if you have brought the war to an end, then let this wound burst and cause my death thereby.' So blood gushed from the wound. There was a tent in the Mosque belonging to Banu Ghifar who were surprised by the blood flowing towards them. They said, 'O people of the tent! What is this thing which is coming to us from your side?' Behold! Blood was flowing profusely out of Sa`d's wound. Sa`d then died because of that." – Sahih Al-Bukhari 4122

حَدَّثَنَا زَكَرِيَّاءُ بْنُ يَحْيَى، حَدَّثَنَا عَبْدُ اللَّهِ بْنُ نُمَيْرٍ، حَدَّثَنَا هِشَامٌ، عَنْ أَبِيهِ، عَنْ عَائِشَةَ ـ رضى الله عنها ـ قَالَتْ أُصِيبَ سَعْدٌ يَوْمَ الْخَنْدَقِ، رَمَاهُ رَجُلٌ مِنْ قُرَيْشٍ يُقَالُ لَهُ حِبَّانُ ابْنُ الْعَرِقَةِ، رَمَاهُ فِي الأَكْحَلِ، فَضَرَبَ النَّبِيُّ صلى الله عليه وسلم خَيْمَةً فِي الْمَسْجِدِ لِيَعُودَهُ مِنْ قَرِيبٍ، فَلَمَّا رَجَعَ رَسُولُ اللَّهِ صلى الله عليه وسلم مِنَ الْخَنْدَقِ وَضَعَ السِّلاَحَ وَاغْتَسَلَ، فَأَتَاهُ جِبْرِيلُ ـ

عَلَيْهِ السَّلاَمُ - وَهْوَ يَنْفُضُ رَأْسَهُ مِنَ الْغُبَارِ فَقَالَ قَدْ وَضَعْتَ السِّلاَحَ وَاللَّهِ مَا وَضَعْتُهُ، اخْرُجْ إِلَيْهِمْ. قَالَ النَّبِيُّ صلى الله عليه وسلم " فَأَيْنَ ". فَأَشَارَ إِلَى بَنِي قُرَيْظَةَ، فَأَتَاهُمْ رَسُولُ اللَّهِ صلى الله عليه وسلم فَنَزَلُوا عَلَى حُكْمِهِ، فَرَدَّ الْحُكْمَ إِلَى سَعْدٍ، قَالَ فَإِنِّي أَحْكُمُ فِيهِمْ أَنْ تُقْتَلَ الْمُقَاتِلَةُ، وَأَنْ تُسْبَى النِّسَاءُ وَالذُّرِّيَّةُ، وَأَنْ تُقْسَمَ أَمْوَالُهُمْ. قَالَ هِشَامٌ فَأَخْبَرَنِي أَبِي عَنْ عَائِشَةَ أَنَّ سَعْدًا قَالَ اللَّهُمَّ إِنَّكَ تَعْلَمُ أَنَّهُ لَيْسَ أَحَدٌ أَحَبَّ إِلَيَّ أَنْ أُجَاهِدَهُمْ فِيكَ مِنْ قَوْمٍ كَذَّبُوا رَسُولَكَ صلى الله عليه وسلم وَأَخْرَجُوهُ، اللَّهُمَّ فَإِنِّي أَظُنُّ أَنَّكَ قَدْ وَضَعْتَ الْحَرْبَ بَيْنَنَا وَبَيْنَهُمْ، فَإِنْ كَانَ بَقِيَ مِنْ حَرْبِ قُرَيْشٍ شَىْءٌ، فَأَبْقِنِي لَهُ حَتَّى أُجَاهِدَهُمْ فِيكَ، وَإِنْ كُنْتَ وَضَعْتَ الْحَرْبَ فَافْجُرْهَا، وَاجْعَلْ مَوْتَتِي فِيهَا. فَانْفَجَرَتْ مِنْ لَبَّتِهِ، فَلَمْ يَرُعْهُمْ وَفِي الْمَسْجِدِ خَيْمَةٌ مِنْ بَنِي غِفَارٍ إِلاَّ الدَّمُ يَسِيلُ إِلَيْهِمْ فَقَالُوا يَا أَهْلَ الْخَيْمَةِ مَا هَذَا الَّذِي يَأْتِينَا مِنْ قِبَلِكُمْ فَإِذَا سَعْدٌ يَغْذُو جُرْحُهُ دَمًا، فَمَاتَ مِنْهَا رضى الله عنه.

Narrated Jabir: I heard the Prophet ﷺ saying, "The Throne (of Allah) shook at the death of Sa`d bin Mu`adh." Through another group of narrators, Jabir added, "I heard the Prophet ﷺ :saying, 'The Throne of the Beneficent shook because of the death of Sa`d bin Mu`adh." – Al-Bukhari 3803

حَدَّثَنِي مُحَمَّدُ بْنُ الْمُثَنَّى، حَدَّثَنَا فَضْلُ بْنُ مُسَاوِرٍ، خَتَنُ أَبِي عَوَانَةَ حَدَّثَنَا أَبُو عَوَانَةَ، عَنِ الأَعْمَشِ، عَنْ أَبِي سُفْيَانَ، عَنْ جَابِرٍ - رضى الله عنه - سَمِعْتُ النَّبِيَّ صلى الله عليه وسلم يَقُولُ " اهْتَزَّ الْعَرْشُ لِمَوْتِ سَعْدِ بْنِ مُعَاذٍ ". وَعَنِ الأَعْمَشِ حَدَّثَنَا أَبُو صَالِحٍ عَنْ جَابِرٍ عَنِ النَّبِيِّ صلى الله عليه وسلم مِثْلَهُ. فَقَالَ رَجُلٌ لِجَابِرٍ فَإِنَّ الْبَرَاءَ يَقُولُ اهْتَزَّ السَّرِيرُ. فَقَالَ إِنَّهُ كَانَ بَيْنَ هَذَيْنِ الْحَيَّيْنِ ضَغَائِنُ، سَمِعْتُ النَّبِيَّ صلى الله عليه وسلم يَقُولُ " اهْتَزَّ عَرْشُ الرَّحْمَنِ لِمَوْتِ سَعْدِ بْنِ مُعَاذٍ "

Narrated `Aisha: When Allah's Messenger ﷺ returned on the day (of the battle) of Al-Khandaq (i.e. Trench), he put down his arms and took a bath. Then Gabriel whose head was covered with dust, came to him saying, "You have put down your arms! By Allah, I have not put down my arms yet." Allah's Messenger ﷺ said, "Where (to go now)?" Gabriel said, "This way," pointing towards the tribe of Bani Quraiza. So Allah's Messenger ﷺ went out towards them . – Al-Bukhari 2813

حَدَّثَنَا مُحَمَّدٌ، أَخْبَرَنَا عَبْدَةُ، عَنْ هِشَامِ بْنِ عُرْوَةَ، عَنْ أَبِيهِ، عَنْ عَائِشَةَ - رضى الله عنها أَنَّ رَسُولَ اللَّهِ صلى الله عليه وسلم لَمَّا رَجَعَ يَوْمَ الْخَنْدَقِ وَوَضَعَ السِّلاَحَ وَاغْتَسَلَ، فَأَتَاهُ جِبْرِيلُ وَقَدْ عَصَبَ رَأْسَهُ الْغُبَارُ فَقَالَ وَضَعْتَ السِّلاَحَ، فَوَاللَّهِ مَا وَضَعْتُهُ. فَقَالَ رَسُولُ اللَّهِ صلى الله عليه وسلم " فَأَيْنَ ". قَالَ هَا هُنَا. وَأَوْمَأَ إِلَى بَنِي قُرَيْظَةَ. قَالَتْ فَخَرَجَ إِلَيْهِمْ رَسُولُ اللَّهِ صلى الله عليه وسلم

Narrated `Aisha: Fatima and Al-`Abbas came to Abu Bakr, claiming their inheritance of the Prophet's land of Fadak and his share from Khaibar. Abu Bakr said, "I heard the Prophet ﷺ sayng, 'Our property is not inherited, and whatever we leave is to be given in charity. But the family of Muhammad can take their sustenance from this property.' By Allah, I would love to do good to the Kith and kin of Allah's Apostle rather than to my own Kith and kin." - Sahih al-Bukhari 4035, 4036

حَدَّثَنَا إِبْرَاهِيمُ بْنُ مُوسَى، أَخْبَرَنَا هِشَامٌ، أَخْبَرَنَا مَعْمَرٌ، عَنِ الزُّهْرِيِّ، عَنْ عُرْوَةَ، عَنْ عَائِشَةَ، أَنَّ فَاطِمَةَ - عَلَيْهَا السَّلاَمُ - وَالْعَبَّاسَ أَتَيَا أَبَا بَكْرٍ يَلْتَمِسَانِ مِيرَاثَهُمَا، أَرْضَهُ مِنْ فَدَكٍ، وَسَهْمَهُ مِنْ خَيْبَرَ. فَقَالَ أَبُو بَكْرٍ سَمِعْتُ النَّبِيَّ صلى الله عليه وسلم يَقُولُ " لاَ نُورَثُ، مَا تَرَكْنَا صَدَقَةٌ، إِنَّمَا يَأْكُلُ آلُ مُحَمَّدٍ فِي هَذَا الْمَالِ ". وَاللَّهِ لَقَرَابَةُ رَسُولِ اللَّهِ صلى الله عليه وسلم أَحَبُّ إِلَيَّ أَنْ أَصِلَ مِنْ قَرَابَتِي

At-Takhyîry
التخيير

O you Prophet, say to your spouses, "In case you would (like) the present life (Literally: the lowly life, i.e., the life of this world) and its adornment, then come, and I will allow you (the necessary) enjoyment and will release you a becoming release And in case you would (like) Allah and His Messenger and the Last Home, then surely Allah has prepared for the fair-doers among you a magnificent reward." – Surah Al-Ahzab 33:28&29

يَـٰٓأَيُّهَا ٱلنَّبِىُّ قُل لِّأَزْوَٰجِكَ إِن كُنتُنَّ تُرِدْنَ ٱلْحَيَوٰةَ ٱلدُّنْيَا وَزِينَتَهَا فَتَعَالَيْنَ أُمَتِّعْكُنَّ وَأُسَرِّحْكُنَّ سَرَاحًا جَمِيلًا وَإِن كُنتُنَّ تُرِدْنَ ٱللَّهَ وَرَسُولَهُۥ وَٱلدَّارَ ٱلْـَٔاخِرَةَ فَإِنَّ ٱللَّهَ أَعَدَّ لِلْمُحْسِنَـٰتِ مِنكُنَّ أَجْرًا عَظِيمًا

Narrated `Aisha: (the wife of the Prophet) when Allah's Messenger ﷺ was ordered to give option to his wives, he started with me, saying, "I am going to mention to you something, but you shall not hasten (to give your reply) unless you consult your parents." The Prophet ﷺ knew that my parents would not order me to leave him. Then he said, "Allah says: 'O Prophet (Muhammad)! Say to your wives: If you desire the life of this world and its glitter........a great reward." (33.28-29) I said, "Then why I consult my parents? Verily, I seek Allah, His Apostle and the Home of the Hereafter." Then all the other wives of the Prophet ﷺ did the same as I did. – Sahih al-Bukhari 4786

وَقَالَ اللَّيْثُ حَدَّثَنِي يُونُسُ، عَنِ ابْنِ شِهَابٍ، قَالَ أَخْبَرَنِي أَبُو سَلَمَةَ بْنُ عَبْدِ الرَّحْمَنِ، أَنَّ عَائِشَةَ، زَوْجَ النَّبِيِّ صلى الله عليه وسلم قَالَتْ لَمَّا أُمِرَ رَسُولُ اللَّهِ صلى الله عليه وسلم بِتَخْيِيرِ أَزْوَاجِهِ بَدَأَ بِي فَقَالَ " إِنِّي ذَاكِرٌ لَكِ أَمْرًا فَلاَ عَلَيْكِ أَنْ لاَ تَعْجَلِي حَتَّى تَسْتَأْمِرِي أَبَوَيْكِ ". قَالَتْ وَقَدْ عَلِمَ أَنَّ أَبَوَىَّ لَمْ يَكُونَا يَأْمُرَانِي بِفِرَاقِهِ، قَالَتْ ثُمَّ قَالَ " إِنَّ اللَّهَ جَلَّ ثَنَاؤُهُ قَالَ {يَا أَيُّهَا النَّبِيُّ قُلْ لأَزْوَاجِكَ إِنْ كُنْتُنَّ تُرِدْنَ الْحَيَاةَ الدُّنْيَا وَزِينَتَهَا} إِلَى {أَجْرًا عَظِيمًا} ". قَالَتْ فَقُلْتُ فَفِي أَىِّ هَذَا أَسْتَأْمِرُ أَبَوَىَّ فَإِنِّي أُرِيدُ اللَّهَ وَرَسُولَهُ وَالدَّارَ الآخِرَةَ، قَالَتْ ثُمَّ فَعَلَ أَزْوَاجُ النَّبِيِّ صلى الله عليه وسلم مِثْلَ مَا فَعَلْتُ. تَابَعَهُ مُوسَى بْنُ أَعْيَنَ عَنْ مَعْمَرٍ عَنِ الزُّهْرِيِّ قَالَ أَخْبَرَنِي أَبُو سَلَمَةَ. وَقَالَ عَبْدُ الرَّزَّاقِ وَأَبُو سُفْيَانَ الْمَعْمَرِيُّ عَنْ مَعْمَرٍ عَنِ الزُّهْرِيِّ عَنْ عُرْوَةَ عَنْ عَائِشَةَ.

It was narrated that 'Aishah, the wife of the Prophet, said: "When the Messenger of Allah was commanded to give his wives the choice, he started with me and said: 'I am going to say something to you and you do not have to rush (to make a decision) until you consult your parents.'" She said: "He knew that my parents would never tell me to leave him." She said: "Then he recited this Verse: 'O Prophet! Say to your wives: If you desire the life of this world, and its glitter, then come! I will make a provision for you and set you free in a handsome manner.' I said: 'Do I need to consult my parents concerning this? I desire Allah, the Mighty and Sublime, and His Messenger, and the home of the Hereafter.'" 'Aishah said: "Then the wives of the Prophet all did the same as I did, and that was not counted as a divorce, when the Messenger of Allah gave them the choice and they chose him." – Sunan an-Nasa'I 3439

أَخْبَرَنَا يُونُسُ بْنُ عَبْدِ الأَعْلَى، قَالَ حَدَّثَنَا ابْنُ وَهْبٍ، قَالَ أَنْبَأَنَا يُونُسُ بْنُ يَزِيدَ، وَمُوسَى بْنُ عَلِيٍّ، عَنِ ابْنِ شِهَابٍ، قَالَ أَخْبَرَنِي أَبُو سَلَمَةَ بْنُ عَبْدِ الرَّحْمَنِ، أَنَّ عَائِشَةَ، زَوْجَ النَّبِيِّ صلى الله عليه وسلم قَالَتْ لَمَّا أُمِرَ رَسُولُ اللَّهِ بِتَخْيِيرِ أَزْوَاجِهِ بَدَأَ بِي فَقَالَ " إِنِّي ذَاكِرٌ لَكِ أَمْرًا فَلاَ عَلَيْكِ أَنْ لاَ تُعَجِّلِي حَتَّى تَسْتَأْمِرِي أَبَوَيْكِ " . قَالَتْ قَدْ عَلِمَ أَنَّ أَبَوَاىَ لَمْ يَكُونَا لِيَأْمُرَانِي بِفِرَاقِهِ ـ قَالَتْ ـ ثُمَّ تَلاَ هَذِهِ الآيَةَ { يَا أَيُّهَا النَّبِيُّ قُلْ لأَزْوَاجِكَ إِنْ كُنْتُنَّ تُرِدْنَ الْحَيَاةَ الدُّنْيَا } إِلَى قَوْلِهِ { جَمِيلاً } فَقُلْتُ أَفِي هَذَا أَسْتَأْمِرُ أَبَوَىَّ فَإِنِّي أُرِيدُ اللَّهَ عَزَّ وَجَلَّ وَرَسُولَهُ وَالدَّارَ الآخِرَةَ ـ قَالَتْ عَائِشَةُ ـ ثُمَّ فَعَلَ أَزْوَاجُ النَّبِيِّ صلى الله عليه وسلم مِثْلَ مَا فَعَلْتُ وَلَمْ يَكُنْ ذَلِكَ حِينَ قَالَ لَهُنَّ رَسُولُ اللَّهِ صلى الله عليه وسلم وَاخْتَرْنَهُ طَلاَقًا مِنْ أَجْلِ أَنَّهُنَّ اخْتَرْنَهُ .

The Book of
Dhat-ur-Riqa
ذات الرقة

Narrated Abu Burda: Abu Musa said, "We went out in the company of the Prophet ﷺ for a Ghazwa and we were six persons having one camel which we rode in rotation. So, (due to excessive walking) our feet became thin and my feet became thin and my nail dropped, and we used to wrap our feet with the pieces of cloth, and for this reason, the Ghazwa was named Dhat-ur-Riqa as we wrapped our feet with rags." When Abu- Musa narrated this (Hadith), he felt regretful to do so and said, as if he disliked to have disclosed a good deed of his. – Sahih Al-Bukhari 4128

حَدَّثَنَا مُحَمَّدُ بْنُ الْعَلاَءِ، حَدَّثَنَا أَبُو أُسَامَةَ، عَنْ بُرَيْدِ بْنِ عَبْدِ اللَّهِ بْنِ أَبِي بُرْدَةَ، عَنْ أَبِي بُرْدَةَ، عَنْ أَبِي مُوسَى ـ رضى الله عنه ـ قَالَ خَرَجْنَا مَعَ النَّبِيِّ صلى الله عليه وسلم فِي غَزَاةٍ وَنَحْنُ سِتَّةُ نَفَرٍ بَيْنَنَا بَعِيرٌ نَعْتَقِبُهُ، فَنَقِبَتْ أَقْدَامُنَا وَنَقِبَتْ قَدَمَاىَ وَسَقَطَتْ أَظْفَارِي، وَكُنَّا نَلُفُّ عَلَى أَرْجُلِنَا الْخِرَقَ، فَسُمِّيَتْ غَزْوَةَ ذَاتِ الرِّقَاعِ، لِمَا كُنَّا نَعْصِبُ مِنَ الْخِرَقِ عَلَى أَرْجُلِنَا، وَحَدَّثَ أَبُو مُوسَى بِهَذَا، ثُمَّ كَرِهَ ذَاكَ، قَالَ مَا كُنْتُ أَصْنَعُ بِأَنْ أَذْكُرَهُ. كَأَنَّهُ كَرِهَ أَنْ يَكُونَ شَىْءٌ مِنْ عَمَلِهِ أَفْشَاهُ.

Jabir added: "The Prophet ﷺ set out for the battle of Dhat-ur-Riqa' at a place called Nakhl and he met a group of people from Ghatafan, but there was no clash (between them); the people were afraid of each other and the Prophet ﷺ offered the two raka'at of the Fear prayer." Narrated Salama: "I fought in the company of the Prophet ﷺ on the day of al-Qarad." – Sahih Al-Bukhari 4127

وَقَالَ ابْنُ إِسْحَاقَ سَمِعْتُ وَهْبَ بْنَ كَيْسَانَ، سَمِعْتُ جَابِرًا، خَرَجَ النَّبِيُّ صلى الله عليه وسلم إِلَى ذَاتِ الرِّقَاعِ مِنْ نَخْلٍ فَلَقِيَ جَمْعًا مِنْ غَطَفَانَ، فَلَمْ يَكُنْ قِتَالٌ، وَأَخَافَ النَّاسُ بَعْضُهُمْ بَعْضًا فَصَلَّى النَّبِيُّ صلى الله عليه وسلم رَكْعَتَىِ الْخَوْفِ. وَقَالَ يَزِيدُ عَنْ سَلَمَةَ غَزَوْتُ مَعَ النَّبِيِّ صلى الله عليه وسلم يَوْمَ الْقَرَدِ.

(through another group of narrators) Jabir said: "We were in the company of the Prophet (during the battle of) Dhat-ur-Riqa', and we came across a shady tree and we left it for the Prophet (to take rest under its shade). A man from the pagans came while the Prophet's sword was hanging on the tree. He took it out of its sheath secretly and said (to the Prophet ﷺ), 'Are you afraid of me?' The Prophet ﷺ said, 'No.' He said, 'Who can save you from me?' The Prophet ﷺ said, Allah.' The companions of the Prophet ﷺ threatened him, then the Iqama for the prayer was announced and the Prophet ﷺ offered a two rak`at Fear prayer with one of the two batches, and that batch went aside and he offered two rak`a-t with the other batch. So the Prophet ﷺ offered four rak`at but the people offered two rak`at only." (The subnarrator) Abu Bishr added, "The man was Ghaurath bin Al-Harith and the battle was waged against Muharib Khasafa." – Sahih Al-Bukhari 4136

وَقَالَ أَبَانُ حَدَّثَنَا يَحْيَى بْنُ أَبِي كَثِيرٍ، عَنْ أَبِي سَلَمَةَ، عَنْ جَابِرٍ، قَالَ كُنَّا مَعَ النَّبِيِّ صلى الله عليه وسلم بِذَاتِ الرِّقَاعِ، فَإِذَا أَتَيْنَا عَلَى شَجَرَةٍ ظَلِيلَةٍ تَرَكْنَاهَا لِلنَّبِيِّ صلى الله عليه وسلم، فَجَاءَ رَجُلٌ مِنَ الْمُشْرِكِينَ وَسَيْفُ النَّبِيِّ صلى الله عليه وسلم مُعَلَّقٌ بِالشَّجَرَةِ فَاخْتَرَطَهُ فَقَالَ تَخَافُنِي قَالَ " لاَ ". قَالَ فَمَنْ يَمْنَعُكَ مِنِّي قَالَ " اللَّهُ ". فَتَهَدَّدَهُ أَصْحَابُ النَّبِيِّ صلى الله عليه وسلم، وَأُقِيمَتِ الصَّلاَةُ فَصَلَّى بِطَائِفَةٍ رَكْعَتَيْنِ، ثُمَّ تَأَخَّرُوا، وَصَلَّى بِالطَّائِفَةِ الأُخْرَى رَكْعَتَيْنِ، وَكَانَ لِلنَّبِيِّ صلى الله عليه وسلم أَرْبَعٌ وَلِلْقَوْمِ رَكْعَتَيْنِ. وَقَالَ مُسَدَّدٌ عَنْ أَبِي عَوَانَةَ عَنْ أَبِي بِشْرٍ اسْمُ الرَّجُلِ غَوْرَثُ بْنُ الْحَارِثِ، وَقَاتَلَ فِيهَا مُحَارِبَ خَصَفَةَ

Narrated Salih bin Khawwat: Concerning those who witnessed the Fear Prayer that was performed in the battle of Dhat-ur-Riqa' in the company of Allah's Messenger ﷺ ;One batch lined up behind him while another batch (lined up) facing the enemy. The Prophet ﷺ led the batch that was with him in one rak`a, and he stayed in the standing posture while that batch completed their (two rak`at) prayer by themselves and went away, lining in the face of the enemy, while the other batch came and he (i.e. the Prophet) offered his remaining rak`a with them, and then, kept on sitting till they completed their prayer by themselves, and he then finished his prayer with Taslim along with them. – Sahih Al-Bukhari 4129

حَدَّثَنَا قُتَيْبَةُ بْنُ سَعِيدٍ، عَنْ مَالِكٍ، عَنْ يَزِيدَ بْنِ رُومَانَ، عَنْ صَالِحِ بْنِ خَوَّاتٍ، عَمَّنْ شَهِدَ رَسُولَ اللَّهِ صلى الله عليه وسلم يَوْمَ ذَاتِ الرِّقَاعِ صَلَّى صَلاَةَ الْخَوْفِ أَنَّ طَائِفَةً صَفَّتْ مَعَهُ، وَطَائِفَةٌ وُجَاهَ الْعَدُوِّ، فَصَلَّى بِالَّتِي مَعَهُ رَكْعَةً، ثُمَّ ثَبَتَ قَائِمًا، وَأَتَمُّوا لأَنْفُسِهِمْ ثُمَّ انْصَرَفُوا، فَصَفُّوا وُجَاهَ الْعَدُوِّ، وَجَاءَتِ الطَّائِفَةُ الأُخْرَى فَصَلَّى بِهِمِ الرَّكْعَةَ الَّتِي بَقِيَتْ مِنْ صَلاَتِهِ، ثُمَّ ثَبَتَ جَالِسًا، وَأَتَمُّوا لأَنْفُسِهِمْ، ثُمَّ سَلَّمَ بِهِمْ

Narrated Jabir bin Abdullah (ra): The Prophet ﷺ led his Companions in the Fear Prayer in the seventh Ghazwa i.e. the Ghazwa of Dhat-ur-Riqa. Ibn Abbas said, "The Prophet ﷺ offered the Fear Prayer at a place called Dhi-Qarad." - Sahih Al-Bukhari 4125

وَقَالَ عَبْدُ اللَّهِ بْنُ رَجَاءٍ أَخْبَرَنَا عِمْرَانُ الْقَطَّانُ، عَنْ يَحْيَى بْنِ أَبِي كَثِيرٍ، عَنْ أَبِي سَلَمَةَ، عَنْ جَابِرِ بْنِ عَبْدِ اللَّهِ ـ رضى الله عنهما أَنَّ النَّبِيَّ صلى الله عليه وسلم صَلَّى بِأَصْحَابِهِ فِي الْخَوْفِ فِي غَزْوَةِ السَّابِعَةِ غَزْوَةِ ذَاتِ الرِّقَاعِ. قَالَ ابْنُ عَبَّاسٍ صَلَّى النَّبِيُّ صلى الله عليه وسلم الْخَوْفَ بِذِي قَرَدٍ

Narrated Shu'aib: I asked Az-Zuhri, "Did the Prophet ﷺ ever offer the Fear Prayer?" Az-Zuhri said, "I was told by Salim that `Abdullah bin `Umar I had said, 'I took part in a holy battle with Allah's Messenger ﷺ in Najd. We faced the enemy and arranged ourselves in rows. Then Allah's Messenger ﷺ stood up to lead the prayer and one party stood to pray with him while the other faced the enemy. Allah's Messenger ﷺ and the former party bowed and performed two prostrations. Then that party left and took the place of those who had not prayed. Allah's Messenger ﷺ prayed one rak`a (with the latter) and performed two prostrations and finished his prayer with Taslim. Then everyone of them bowed once and performed two prostrations individually.' " – Sahih al-Bukhari 942

حَدَّثَنَا أَبُو الْيَمَانِ، قَالَ أَخْبَرَنَا شُعَيْبٌ، عَنِ الزُّهْرِيِّ، قَالَ سَأَلْتُهُ هَلْ صَلَّى النَّبِيُّ صلى الله عليه وسلم يَعْنِي صَلاَةَ الْخَوْفِ قَالَ أَخْبَرَنِي سَالِمٌ أَنَّ عَبْدَ اللَّهِ بْنَ عُمَرَ ـ رضى الله عنهما ـ قَالَ غَزَوْتُ مَعَ رَسُولِ اللَّهِ صلى الله عليه وسلم قِبَلَ نَجْدٍ، فَوَازَيْنَا الْعَدُوَّ فَصَافَفْنَا لَهُمْ فَقَامَ رَسُولُ اللَّهِ صلى الله عليه وسلم يُصَلِّي لَنَا فَقَامَتْ طَائِفَةٌ مَعَهُ تُصَلِّي، وَأَقْبَلَتْ طَائِفَةٌ عَلَى الْعَدُوِّ وَرَكَعَ رَسُولُ اللَّهِ صلى الله عليه وسلم بِمَنْ مَعَهُ، وَسَجَدَ سَجْدَتَيْنِ، ثُمَّ انْصَرَفُوا مَكَانَ الطَّائِفَةِ الَّتِي لَمْ تُصَلِّ، فَجَاءُوا، فَرَكَعَ رَسُولُ اللَّهِ صلى الله عليه وسلم بِهِمْ رَكْعَةً، وَسَجَدَ سَجْدَتَيْنِ ثُمَّ سَلَّمَ، فَقَامَ كُلُّ وَاحِدٍ مِنْهُمْ فَرَكَعَ لِنَفْسِهِ رَكْعَةً وَسَجَدَ سَجْدَتَيْنِ.

And Jābir stated, "The Prophet ﷺ was in the battle of Dhāt-ur-Riqã and a person was shot with an arrow and he bled profusely, but he bowed and prostrated and continued his Şalāt. " Bukhari Vol.1 pg 154

و يذكر عن جابر أن النبي ﷺ كان في غزوة ذات الرقاع فرمي رجل بسهم فنزفه الدم، فركع و سجد،و مض في صلاته

The Book of
Retribution of Mustaliq
غزوة المريسيع

Narrated Ibn `Aun: I wrote a letter to Nafi` and Nafi` wrote in reply to my letter that the Prophet ﷺ had suddenly attacked Bani Mustaliq without warning while they were heedless and their cattle were being watered at the places of water. Their fighting men were killed and their women and children were taken as captives; the Prophet ﷺ got Juwairiya on that day. Nafi` said that Ibn `Umar had told him the above narration and that Ibn `Umar was in that army. – Al-Bukhari 2541

حَدَّثَنَا عَلِيُّ بْنُ الْحَسَنِ، أَخْبَرَنَا عَبْدُ اللَّهِ، أَخْبَرَنَا ابْنُ عَوْنٍ، قَالَ كَتَبْتُ إِلَى نَافِعٍ فَكَتَبَ إِلَىَّ أَنَّ النَّبِيَّ صلى الله عليه وسلم أَغَارَ عَلَى بَنِي الْمُصْطَلِقِ وَهُمْ غَارُّونَ وَأَنْعَامُهُمْ تُسْقَى عَلَى الْمَاءِ، فَقَتَلَ مُقَاتِلَتَهُمْ، وَسَبَى ذَرَارِيَّهُمْ، وَأَصَابَ يَوْمَئِذٍ جُوَيْرِيَةَ. حَدَّثَنِي بِهِ عَبْدُ اللَّهِ بْنُ عُمَرَ، وَكَانَ فِي ذَلِكَ الْجَيْشِ.

Narrated Ibn Muhairiz: I saw Abu Sa`id and asked him about coitus interruptus. Abu Sa`id said, "We went with Allah's Apostle, in the Ghazwa of Bani Al-Mustaliq and we captured some of the 'Arabs as captives, and the long separation from our wives was pressing us hard and we wanted to practice coitus interruptus. We asked Allah's Messenger ﷺ (whether it was permissible). He said, "It is better for you not to do so. No soul, (that which Allah has) destined to exist, up to the Day of Resurrection, but will definitely come, into existence." – Sahih Al-Bukhari 2542

حَدَّثَنَا عَبْدُ اللَّهِ بْنُ يُوسُفَ، أَخْبَرَنَا مَالِكٌ، عَنْ رَبِيعَةَ بْنِ أَبِي عَبْدِ الرَّحْمَنِ، عَنْ مُحَمَّدِ بْنِ يَحْيَى بْنِ حَبَّانَ، عَنِ ابْنِ مُحَيْرِيزٍ، قَالَ رَأَيْتُ أَبَا سَعِيدٍ ـ رضى الله عنه ـ فَسَأَلْتُهُ فَقَالَ خَرَجْنَا مَعَ رَسُولِ اللَّهِ صلى الله عليه وسلم فِي غَزْوَةِ بَنِي الْمُصْطَلِقِ فَأَصَبْنَا سَبْيًا مِنْ سَبْىِ الْعَرَبِ، فَاشْتَهَيْنَا النِّسَاءَ فَاشْتَدَّتْ عَلَيْنَا الْعُزْبَةُ وَأَحْبَبْنَا الْعَزْلَ، فَسَأَلْنَا رَسُولَ اللَّهِ صلى الله عليه وسلم فَقَالَ " مَا عَلَيْكُمْ أَنْ لاَ تَفْعَلُوا، مَا مِنْ نَسَمَةٍ كَائِنَةٍ إِلَى يَوْمِ الْقِيَامَةِ إِلاَّ وَهْىَ كَائِنَةٌ "

Narrated Ibn Muhairiz: I entered the Mosque and saw Abu Sa`id Al-Khudri and sat beside him and asked him about Al-Azl (i.e. coitus interruptus). Abu Sa`id said, "We went out with Allah's Messenger ﷺ for the Ghazwa of Banu Al-Mustaliq and we received captives from among the Arab captives and we desired women and celibacy became hard on us and we loved to do coitus interruptus. So when we intended to do coitus interrupt us, we said, 'How can we do coitus interruptus before asking Allah's Messenger ﷺ who is present among us?" We asked (him) about it and he said, 'It is better for you not to do so, for if any soul (till the Day of Resurrection) is predestined to exist, it will exist." – Sahih Al-Bukhari 4138

حَدَّثَنَا قُتَيْبَةُ بْنُ سَعِيدٍ، أَخْبَرَنَا إِسْمَاعِيلُ بْنُ جَعْفَرٍ، عَنْ رَبِيعَةَ بْنِ أَبِي عَبْدِ الرَّحْمَنِ، عَنْ مُحَمَّدِ بْنِ يَحْيَى بْنِ حَبَّانَ، عَنِ ابْنِ مُحَيْرِيزٍ، أَنَّهُ قَالَ دَخَلْتُ الْمَسْجِدَ فَرَأَيْتُ أَبَا سَعِيدٍ الْخُدْرِيَّ فَجَلَسْتُ إِلَيْهِ فَسَأَلْتُهُ عَنِ الْعَزْلِ،، قَالَ أَبُو سَعِيدٍ خَرَجْنَا مَعَ رَسُولِ اللَّهِ صلى الله عليه وسلم فِي غَزْوَةِ بَنِي الْمُصْطَلِقِ، فَأَصَبْنَا سَبْيًا مِنْ سَبْىِ الْعَرَبِ، فَاشْتَهَيْنَا النِّسَاءَ وَاشْتَدَّتْ عَلَيْنَا الْعُزْبَةُ، وَأَحْبَبْنَا الْعَزْلَ، فَأَرَدْنَا أَنْ نَعْزِلَ، وَقُلْنَا نَعْزِلُ وَرَسُولُ اللَّهِ صلى الله عليه وسلم بَيْنَ أَظْهُرِنَا قَبْلَ أَنْ نَسْأَلَهُ فَسَأَلْنَاهُ عَنْ ذَلِكَ فَقَالَ " مَا عَلَيْكُمْ أَنْ لاَ تَفْعَلُوا، مَا مِنْ نَسَمَةٍ كَائِنَةٍ إِلَى يَوْمِ الْقِيَامَةِ إِلاَّ وَهْىَ كَائِنَةٌ "

Narrated Abu Aiyub from Juwairiya bint Al-Harith: The Prophet ﷺ visited her (Juwairiya) on a Friday and she was fasting. He asked her, "Did you fast yesterday?" She said, "No." He said, "Do you intend to fast tomorrow?" She said, "No." He said, "Then break your fast." Through another series of narrators, Abu Aiyub is reported to have said, "He ordered her and she broke her fast.". – Sahih Al-Bukhari 1986 . [10]

حَدَّثَنَا مُسَدَّدٌ، حَدَّثَنَا يَحْيَى، عَنْ شُعْبَةَ، ح. وَحَدَّثَنِي مُحَمَّدٌ، حَدَّثَنَا غُنْدَرٌ، حَدَّثَنَا شُعْبَةُ، عَنْ قَتَادَةَ، عَنْ أَبِي أَيُّوبَ، عَنْ جُوَيْرِيَةَ بِنْتِ الْحَارِثِ ـ رضى الله عنها ـ أَنَّ النَّبِيَّ صلى الله عليه وسلم دَخَلَ عَلَيْهَا يَوْمَ الْجُمُعَةِ وَهْىَ صَائِمَةٌ فَقَالَ " أَصُمْتِ أَمْسِ ". قَالَتْ لاَ. قَالَ " تُرِيدِينَ أَنْ تَصُومِي غَدًا ". قَالَتْ لاَ. قَالَ " فَأَفْطِرِي ".
وَقَالَ حَمَّادُ بْنُ الْجَعْدِ سَمِعَ قَتَادَةَ حَدَّثَنِي أَبُو أَيُّوبَ أَنَّ جُوَيْرِيَةَ حَدَّثَتْهُ فَأَمَرَهَا فَأَفْطَرَتْ.

---

[10] Based on the following statement of Muhammad I placed 1986 at the time of his proposal with Juwairiya Narrated Abu Huraira: The Prophet ﷺ said, "A woman should not fast except with her husband's permission if he is at home (staying with her). – Sahih Al-Bukhari 5192

حَدَّثَنَا مُحَمَّدُ بْنُ مُقَاتِلٍ، أَخْبَرَنَا عَبْدُ اللَّهِ، أَخْبَرَنَا مَعْمَرٌ، عَنْ هَمَّامِ بْنِ مُنَبِّهٍ، عَنْ أَبِي هُرَيْرَةَ، عَنِ النَّبِيِّ صلى الله عليه وسلم " لاَ تَصُومُ الْمَرْأَةُ وَبَعْلُهَا شَاهِدٌ إِلاَّ بِإِذْنِهِ ".

The Book of

The slander (Ifk) against Aishah

التهمة (افك) على عائشة

Narrated `Aisha: Whenever Allah's Messenger ﷺ intended to go on a journey, he used to draw lots amongst his wives, and Allah's Messenger ﷺ used to take with him the one on whom lot fell. He drew lots amongst us during one of the Ghazwat which he fought. The lot fell on me and so I proceeded with Allah's Messenger ﷺ after Allah's order of veiling (the women) had been revealed. I was carried (on the back of a camel) in my howdah and carried down while still in it (when we came to a halt). So we went on till Allah's Messenger ﷺ had finished from that Ghazwa of his and returned. When we approached the city of Medina he announced at night that it was time for departure. So when they announced the news of departure, I got up and went away from the army camps, and after finishing from the call of nature, I came back to my riding animal. I touched my chest to find that my necklace which was made of Zifar beads (i.e. Yemenite beads partly black and partly white) was missing. So I returned to look for my necklace and my search for it detained me. (In the meanwhile) the people who used to carry me on my camel, came and took my howdah and put it on the back of my camel on which I used to ride, as they considered that I was in it. In those days women were light in weight for they did not get fat, and flesh did not cover their bodies in abundance as they used to eat only a little food. Those people therefore, disregarded the lightness of the howdah while lifting and carrying it; and at that time I was still a young girl. They made the camel rise and all of them left (along with it). I found my necklace after the army had gone. Then I came to their camping place to find no call maker of them, nor one who would respond to the call. So I intended to go to the place where I used to stay, thinking that they would miss me and come back to me (in my search). While I was sitting in my resting place, I was overwhelmed by sleep and slept. Safwan bin Al-Muattal As-Sulami Adh-Dhakwani was behind the army. When he reached my place in the morning, he saw the figure of a sleeping person and he recognized me on seeing me as he had seen me before the order of compulsory veiling (was prescribed). So I woke up when he recited Istirja' (i.e. "Inna li l-lahi wa inna llaihi raji'un") as soon as he recognized me. I veiled my face with my head cover at once, and by Allah, we did not speak a single word, and I did not hear him saying any word besides his Istirja'. He dismounted from his camel and made it kneel down, putting his leg on its front legs and then I got up and rode on it. Then he set out leading the camel that was carrying me till we overtook the army in the extreme heat of midday while they were at a halt (taking a rest). (Because of the event) some people brought destruction upon themselves and the one who spread the Ifk (i.e. slander) more, was `Abdullah bin Ubai Ibn Salul." (Urwa said, "The people propagated the slander and talked about it in his (i.e. `Abdullah's) presence and he confirmed it and listened to it and asked about it to let it prevail." `Urwa also added, "None was mentioned as members of the slanderous group besides (`Abdullah) except Hassan bin Thabit and Mistah bin Uthatha and Hamna bint Jahsh along with others about whom I have no knowledge, but they were a group as Allah said. It is said that the one who carried most of the slander was `Abdullah bin Ubai bin Salul." `Urwa added, "`Aisha disliked to have Hassan abused in her presence and she used to say, 'It was he who said: My father and his (i.e. my father's) father and my honor are all for the protection of Muhammad's honor from you."). `Aisha added, "After we returned to Medina, I became ill for a month. The people were propagating the forged statements of the slanderers while I was unaware of anything of all that, but I felt that in my present ailment, I was not receiving the same kindness from Allah's Messenger ﷺ as I used to receive when I got sick. (But now) Allah's Messenger ﷺ would only come, greet me and say,' How is that (lady)?' and leave. That roused my doubts, but I did not discover the evil (i.e. slander) till I went out after my convalescence, I went out with Um Mistah to Al-Manasi' where we used to answer the call of nature and we used not to go out (to answer the call of nature) except at night, and that was before we had latrines near our houses. And this habit of our concerning evacuating the bowels, was similar to the habits of the old 'Arabs living in the deserts, for it would be troublesome for us to take latrines near our houses. So I and Um Mistah who was the daughter of Abu Ruhm bin Al-Muttalib bin `Abd Manaf, whose mother was the daughter of Sakhr bin 'Amir and the aunt of Abu Bakr As-Siddiq and whose son was Mistah bin Uthatha bin `Abbas bin Al-Muttalib, went out. I and Um Mistah returned to my house after we finished answering the call of nature. Um Mistah stumbled by getting her foot entangled in her covering sheet and on that she said, 'Let Mistah be ruined!' I said, 'What a hard word you have said. Do you abuse a man who took part in the battle of Badr?' On that she said, 'O you Hantah! Didn't you hear what he (i.e. Mistah) said? 'I said, 'What did he say?' Then she told me the slander of the people of Ifk. So my ailment was aggravated, and when I reached my home, Allah's Messenger ﷺ came to me, and after greeting me, said, 'How is that (lady)?' I said, 'Will you allow me to go to my parents?' as I wanted to be sure about the news through them. Allah's Apostle allowed me (and I went to my parents) and asked my mother, 'O mother! What are the people talking about?' She said, 'O my daughter! Don't worry, for scarcely is there a charming woman who is loved by her husband and whose husband has other wives besides herself that they (i.e. women) would find faults with her.' I said, 'Subhan-Allah! (I testify the uniqueness of Allah). Are the people really talking in this way?' I kept on weeping that night till dawn I could neither stop weeping nor sleep then in the morning again, I kept on weeping. When the Divine Inspiration was delayed. Allah's Messenger ﷺ called `Ali bin Abi Talib and Usama bin Zaid to ask and consult them about divorcing me. Usama bin Zaid said what he knew of my innocence, and the respect he preserved in himself for me. Usama said, '(O Allah's Messenger ﷺ!) She is your wife and we do not know anything except good about her.' `Ali bin Abi Talib said, 'O Allah's Messenger ﷺ! Allah does not put you in difficulty and there are plenty of women other than she, yet, ask the maid-servant who will tell you the truth.' On that Allah's Messenger ﷺ called Barira (i.e. the maid-servant) and said, 'O Barira! Did you ever see anything which aroused your suspicion?' Barira said to him, 'By Him Who has sent you with the Truth. I have never seen anything in her (i.e. Aisha) which I would conceal, except that she is a young girl who sleeps leaving the dough of her family exposed so that the domestic goats come and eat it.' So, on that day, Allah's Messenger ﷺ got up on the pulpit and complained about `Abdullah bin Ubai (bin Salul) before his companions, saying, 'O you Muslims! Who will relieve me from that man who has hurt me with his evil statement about my family? By Allah, I know nothing except good about my family and they have blamed a man about whom I know nothing except good and he used never to enter my home except with me.' Sa`d bin Mu`adh the brother of Banu `Abd Al-Ashhal got up and said, 'O Allah's Messenger ﷺ! I will relieve you from him; if he is from the tribe of Al-Aus, then I will chop his head off, and if he is from our brothers, i.e. Al-Khazraj, then order us, and we will fulfill your order.' On that, a man from Al-Khazraj got up. Um Hassan, his cousin, was from his branch tribe, and he was Sa`d bin Ubada, chief of Al-Khazraj. Before this incident, he was a pious man, but his love for his tribe goaded him into saying to Sa`d (bin Mu`adh). 'By Allah, you have told a lie; you shall not and cannot kill him. If he belonged to you[11]r people, you would not wish him to be killed.' On that, Usaid bin Hudair who was the cousin of Sa`d (bin Mu`adh) got up and said to Sa`d bin 'Ubada, 'By Allah! You are a liar! We will surely kill him, and you are a hypocrite arguing on the behalf of hypocrites.' On this, the two tribes of Al-Aus and Al Khazraj got so much excited that they were about to fight while Allah's Messenger ﷺ was standing on the pulpit. Allah's Messenger ﷺ kept on quietening them till they became silent and so did he. All that day I kept on weeping with my tears never ceasing, and I could never sleep. In the morning my parents were with me and I wept for two nights and a day with my tears never ceasing and I could never sleep till I thought that my liver would burst from weeping. So, while my parents were sitting with me and I was weeping, an Ansari woman asked me to grant her admittance. I allowed her to come in, and when she came in, she sat down and started weeping with me. While we were in this state, Allah's Messenger ﷺ came, greeted us and sat down. He had never sat with me since that day of the slander. A month had elapsed and no Divine Inspiration came to him about my case. Allah's Apostle then recited Tashah-hud and then said, 'Amma Badu, O `Aisha! I have been informed so-andso about you; if you are innocent, then soon Allah will reveal your innocence, and if you have committed a sin, then repent to Allah and ask Him for forgiveness for when a slave confesses his sins and asks Allah for forgiveness, Allah accepts his repentance.' (continued...) (continuing... 1): -5.462:... ... When Allah's Messenger ﷺ finished his speech, my tears ceased flowing completely that I no longer felt a single drop of tear flowing. I said to my father, 'Reply to Allah's Messenger ﷺ on my behalf concerning what he has said.' My father said, 'By Allah, I do not know what to say to Allah's Messenger ﷺ .' Then I said to my mother, 'Reply to Allah's Messenger ﷺ on my behalf concerning what he has said.' She said, 'By Allah, I do not know what to say to Allah's Messenger ﷺ.' In spite of the fact that I was a young girl and had a little knowledge of Qur'an, I said, 'By Allah, no doubt I know that you heard this (slanderous) speech so that it has been planted in your hearts (i.e. minds) and you have taken it as a truth. Now if I tell you that I am innocent, you will not believe me, and if confess to you about it, and Allah knows that I am innocent, you will surely believe me. By Allah, I find no similitude for me and you except that of Joseph's father when he said, '(For me) patience in the most fitting against that which you assert; it is Allah (Alone) Whose Help can be sought.' Then I turned to the other side and lay on my bed; and Allah knew then that I was innocent and hoped that Allah would reveal my innocence. But, by Allah, I never thought that Allah would reveal about my case, Divine Inspiration, that would be recited (forever) as I considered myself too unworthy to be talked of by Allah with something of my concern, but I hoped that Allah's Messenger ﷺ might have a dream in which Allah would prove my innocence. But, by Allah, before Allah's Messenger ﷺ left his seat and before any of the household left, the Divine inspiration came to Allah's Messenger ﷺ. So there overtook him the same hard condition which used to overtake him, (when he used to be inspired Divinely). The sweat was dropping from his body like pearls though it was a wintry day and that was because of the weighty statement which was being revealed to him. When that state of Allah's Messenger ﷺ was over, he got up smiling, and the first word he said was, 'O `Aisha! Allah has declared your innocence!' Then my Mother said to me, 'Get up and go to him (i.e. Allah's Messenger ﷺ). I replied, 'By Allah, I will not go to him, and I praise none but Allah. So Allah revealed the ten Verses:- - "Verily! They who spread the slander Are a gang, among you............" (24.11-20) Allah revealed those Qur'anic Verses to declare my innocence. Abu Bakr As-Siddiq who used to disburse money for Mistah bin Uthatha because of his relationship to him and his poverty, said, 'By Allah, I will never give to Mistah bin Uthatha anything after what he has said about Aisha.' Then Allah revealed:-- "And let not those among you who are good and wealthy swear not to give (any sort of help) to their kinsmen, those in need, and those who have left their homes for Allah's cause, let them pardon and forgive. Do you not love that Allah should forgive you? And Allah is oft-Forgiving Most Merciful." (24.22) Abu Bakr As-Siddiq said, 'Yes, by Allah, I would like that Allah forgive me.' And went on giving Mistah the money he used to give him before. He also added, 'By Allah, I will never deprive him of it at all.' Aisha further said:." Allah's Messenger ﷺ also asked Zainab bint Jahsh (i.e. his wife) about my case. He said to Zainab, 'What do you know and what did you see?" She replied, "O Allah's Messenger ﷺ! I refrain from claiming falsely that I have heard or seen anything. By Allah, I know nothing except good (about `Aisha).' From amongst the wives of the Prophet ﷺ Zainab was my peer (in beauty and in the love she received from the Prophet) but Allah saved her from that evil because of her piety. Her sister Hamna, started struggling on her behalf and she was destroyed along with those who were destroyed. The man who was blamed said, 'Subhan-Allah! By Him in Whose Hand my soul is, I have never uncovered the cover (i.e. veil) of any female.' Later on the man was martyred in Allah's Cause.". – Sahih Al-Bukhari 4141 [12]

حَدَّثَنَا عَبْدُ الْعَزِيزِ بْنُ عَبْدِ اللَّهِ، حَدَّثَنَا إِبْرَاهِيمُ بْنُ سَعْدٍ، عَنْ صَالِحٍ، عَنِ ابْنِ شِهَابٍ، قَالَ حَدَّثَنِي عُرْوَةُ بْنُ الزُّبَيْرِ، وَسَعِيدُ بْنُ الْمُسَيَّبِ، وَعَلْقَمَةُ بْنُ وَقَّاصٍ، وَعُبَيْدُ اللَّهِ بْنُ عَبْدِ اللَّهِ بْنِ عُتْبَةَ بْنِ مَسْعُودٍ، عَنْ عَائِشَةَ، رضى الله عنها زَوْجِ النَّبِيِّ صلى الله عليه وسلم حِينَ قَالَ لَهَا أَهْلُ الإِفْكِ مَا قَالُوا، وَكُلُّهُمْ حَدَّثَنِي طَائِفَةً مِنْ حَدِيثِهَا، وَبَعْضُهُمْ كَانَ أَوْعَى لِحَدِيثِهَا مِنْ بَعْضٍ وَأَثْبَتَ لَهُ اقْتِصَاصًا، وَقَدْ وَعَيْتُ عَنْ كُلِّ رَجُلٍ مِنْهُمُ الْحَدِيثَ الَّذِي حَدَّثَنِي عَنْ عَائِشَةَ، وَبَعْضُ حَدِيثِهِمْ يُصَدِّقُ بَعْضًا، وَإِنْ كَانَ بَعْضُهُمْ أَوْعَى لَهُ مِنْ بَعْضٍ، قَالُوا قَالَتْ عَائِشَةُ كَانَ رَسُولُ اللَّهِ صلى الله عليه وسلم إِذَا أَرَادَ سَفَرًا أَقْرَعَ بَيْنَ أَزْوَاجِهِ، فَأَيُّهُنَّ خَرَجَ سَهْمُهَا، خَرَجَ بِهَا رَسُولُ اللَّهِ صلى الله عليه وسلم مَعَهُ، قَالَتْ عَائِشَةُ فَأَقْرَعَ بَيْنَنَا فِي غَزْوَةٍ غَزَاهَا فَخَرَجَ فِيهَا سَهْمِي، فَخَرَجْتُ مَعَ رَسُولِ اللَّهِ صلى الله عليه وسلم بَعْدَ مَا أُنْزِلَ الْحِجَابُ، فَكُنْتُ أُحْمَلُ فِي هَوْدَجِي وَأُنْزَلُ فِيهِ، فَسِرْنَا حَتَّى إِذَا فَرَغَ رَسُولُ اللَّهِ صلى الله عليه وسلم مِنْ غَزْوَتِهِ تِلْكَ وَقَفَلَ، دَنَوْنَا مِنَ الْمَدِينَةِ قَافِلِينَ، آذَنَ لَيْلَةً بِالرَّحِيلِ، فَقُمْتُ حِينَ آذَنُوا بِالرَّحِيلِ فَمَشَيْتُ حَتَّى جَاوَزْتُ الْجَيْشَ، فَلَمَّا قَضَيْتُ شَأْنِي أَقْبَلْتُ إِلَى رَحْلِي، فَلَمَسْتُ صَدْرِي، فَإِذَا عِقْدٌ لِي مِنْ جَزْعِ ظَفَارِ قَدِ انْقَطَعَ، فَرَجَعْتُ فَالْتَمَسْتُ عِقْدِي، فَحَبَسَنِي ابْتِغَاؤُهُ، قَالَتْ وَأَقْبَلَ الرَّهْطُ الَّذِينَ كَانُوا يُرَحِّلُونِي فَاحْتَمَلُوا هَوْدَجِي، فَرَحَلُوهُ عَلَى بَعِيرِي الَّذِي كُنْتُ أَرْكَبُ عَلَيْهِ، وَهُمْ يَحْسِبُونَ أَنِّي فِيهِ، وَكَانَ النِّسَاءُ إِذْ ذَاكَ خِفَافًا لَمْ يَهْبُلْنَ وَلَمْ يَغْشَهُنَّ اللَّحْمُ، إِنَّمَا يَأْكُلْنَ الْعُلْقَةَ مِنَ الطَّعَامِ، فَلَمْ يَسْتَنْكِرِ الْقَوْمُ خِفَّةَ الْهَوْدَجِ حِينَ رَفَعُوهُ وَحَمَلُوهُ، وَكُنْتُ جَارِيَةً حَدِيثَةَ السِّنِّ، فَبَعَثُوا الْجَمَلَ فَسَارُوا، وَوَجَدْتُ عِقْدِي بَعْدَ مَا اسْتَمَرَّ الْجَيْشُ، فَجِئْتُ مَنَازِلَهُمْ وَلَيْسَ بِهَا مِنْهُمْ دَاعٍ وَلاَ مُجِيبٌ، فَتَيَمَّمْتُ مَنْزِلِي الَّذِي كُنْتُ بِهِ، وَظَنَنْتُ أَنَّهُمْ سَيَفْقِدُونِي فَيَرْجِعُونَ إِلَىَّ، فَبَيْنَا أَنَا جَالِسَةٌ فِي مَنْزِلِي غَلَبَتْنِي عَيْنِي فَنِمْتُ، وَكَانَ صَفْوَانُ بْنُ الْمُعَطَّلِ السُّلَمِيُّ ثُمَّ الذَّكْوَانِيُّ مِنْ وَرَاءِ الْجَيْشِ، فَأَصْبَحَ عِنْدَ مَنْزِلِي فَرَأَى سَوَادَ إِنْسَانٍ نَائِمٍ، فَعَرَفَنِي حِينَ رَآنِي، وَكَانَ رَآنِي قَبْلَ الْحِجَابِ، فَاسْتَيْقَظْتُ بِاسْتِرْجَاعِهِ حِينَ عَرَفَنِي، فَخَمَّرْتُ وَجْهِي بِجِلْبَابِي، وَاللَّهِ مَا تَكَلَّمْنَا بِكَلِمَةٍ وَلاَ سَمِعْتُ مِنْهُ كَلِمَةً غَيْرَ اسْتِرْجَاعِهِ، وَهَوَى حَتَّى أَنَاخَ رَاحِلَتَهُ، فَوَطِئَ عَلَى يَدِهَا، فَقُمْتُ إِلَيْهَا فَرَكِبْتُهَا، فَانْطَلَقَ يَقُودُ بِي الرَّاحِلَةَ حَتَّى أَتَيْنَا الْجَيْشَ مُوغِرِينَ فِي نَحْرِ الظَّهِيرَةِ، وَهُمْ نُزُولٌ ـ قَالَتْ ـ فَهَلَكَ {فِيَّ} مَنْ هَلَكَ، وَكَانَ الَّذِي تَوَلَّى كِبْرَ الإِفْكِ عَبْدَ اللَّهِ بْنَ أُبَىٍّ ابْنَ سَلُولَ. قَالَ عُرْوَةُ أُخْبِرْتُ أَنَّهُ كَانَ يُشَاعُ وَيُتَحَدَّثُ بِهِ عِنْدَهُ، فَيُقِرُّهُ وَيَسْتَمِعُهُ وَيَسْتَوْشِيهِ. وَقَالَ عُرْوَةُ أَيْضًا لَمْ يُسَمَّ مِنْ أَهْلِ الإِفْكِ أَيْضًا إِلاَّ حَسَّانُ بْنُ ثَابِتٍ، وَمِسْطَحُ بْنُ أُثَاثَةَ، وَحَمْنَةُ بِنْتُ جَحْشٍ فِي نَاسٍ آخَرِينَ، لاَ عِلْمَ لِي بِهِمْ، غَيْرَ أَنَّهُمْ عُصْبَةٌ ـ كَمَا قَالَ اللَّهُ تَعَالَى ـ وَإِنَّ كُبْرَ ذَلِكَ يُقَالُ عَبْدُ اللَّهِ بْنُ أُبَىٍّ ابْنُ سَلُولَ. قَالَ عُرْوَةُ كَانَتْ عَائِشَةُ تَكْرَهُ أَنْ يُسَبَّ عِنْدَهَا حَسَّانُ، وَتَقُولُ إِنَّهُ الَّذِي قَالَ : فَإِنَّ أَبِي وَوَالِدَهُ وَعِرْضِي لِعِرْضِ مُحَمَّدٍ مِنْكُمْ وِقَاءُ

قَالَتْ عَائِشَةُ فَقَدِمْنَا الْمَدِينَةَ فَاشْتَكَيْتُ حِينَ قَدِمْتُ شَهْرًا، وَالنَّاسُ يُفِيضُونَ فِي قَوْلِ أَصْحَابِ الإِفْكِ، لاَ أَشْعُرُ بِشَىْءٍ مِنْ ذَلِكَ، وَهْوَ يَرِيبُنِي فِي وَجَعِي أَنِّي لاَ أَعْرِفُ مِنْ رَسُولِ اللَّهِ صلى الله عليه وسلم اللُّطْفَ الَّذِي كُنْتُ أَرَى مِنْهُ حِينَ أَشْتَكِي، إِنَّمَا يَدْخُلُ عَلَىَّ رَسُولُ اللَّهِ صلى الله عليه وسلم فَيُسَلِّمُ ثُمَّ يَقُولُ " كَيْفَ تِيكُمْ " ثُمَّ يَنْصَرِفُ، فَذَلِكَ يَرِيبُنِي وَلاَ أَشْعُرُ بِالشَّرِّ، حَتَّى خَرَجْتُ حِينَ نَقَهْتُ، فَخَرَجْتُ مَعَ أُمِّ مِسْطَحٍ قِبَلَ الْمَنَاصِعِ، وَكَانَ مُتَبَرَّزَنَا، وَكُنَّا لاَ نَخْرُجُ إِلاَّ لَيْلاً إِلَى لَيْلٍ، وَذَلِكَ قَبْلَ

---

[12] Al-Bukhari Vol.5 page 278 : 'Ibn Ishaq said, "It took place in the 6th year (of the Hijrah)" Musa bin Uqba said, "It was in the 4th year [of the forged statement against 'Aishah which was during the Al-Muraisi (Battle of Mustaliq)]."

أَنْ نَتَّخِذَ الْكُنُفَ قَرِيبًا مِنْ بُيُوتِنَا. قَالَتْ وَأَمْرُنَا أَمْرُ الْعَرَبِ الأُوَلِ فِي الْبَرِّيَّةِ قِبَلَ الْغَائِطِ، وَكُنَّا نَتَأَذَّى بِالْكُنُفِ أَنْ نَتَّخِذَهَا عِنْدَ بُيُوتِنَا، قَالَتْ فَانْطَلَقْتُ أَنَا وَأُمُّ مِسْطَحٍ وَهْىَ ابْنَةُ أَبِي رُهْمِ بْنِ الْمُطَّلِبِ بْنِ عَبْدِ مَنَافٍ، وَأُمُّهَا بِنْتُ صَخْرِ بْنِ عَامِرٍ خَالَةُ أَبِي بَكْرٍ الصِّدِّيقِ، وَابْنُهَا مِسْطَحُ بْنُ أُثَاثَةَ بْنِ عَبَّادِ بْنِ الْمُطَّلِبِ، فَأَقْبَلْتُ أَنَا وَأُمُّ مِسْطَحٍ قِبَلَ بَيْتِي، حِينَ فَرَغْنَا مِنْ شَأْنِنَا، فَعَثَرَتْ أُمُّ مِسْطَحٍ فِي مِرْطِهَا فَقَالَتْ تَعِسَ مِسْطَحٌ. فَقُلْتُ لَهَا بِئْسَ مَا قُلْتِ، أَتَسُبِّينَ رَجُلاً شَهِدَ بَدْرًا فَقَالَتْ أَىْ هَنْتَاهْ وَلَمْ تَسْمَعِي مَا قَالَ قَالَتْ وَقُلْتُ مَا قَالَ فَأَخْبَرَتْنِي بِقَوْلِ أَهْلِ الإِفْكِ ـ قَالَتْ ـ فَازْدَدْتُ مَرَضًا عَلَى مَرَضِي، فَلَمَّا رَجَعْتُ إِلَى بَيْتِي دَخَلَ عَلَىَّ رَسُولُ اللَّهِ صلى الله عليه وسلم فَسَلَّمَ ثُمَّ قَالَ " كَيْفَ تِيكُمْ ". فَقُلْتُ لَهُ أَتَأْذَنُ لِي أَنْ آتِيَ أَبَوَىَّ قَالَتْ وَأُرِيدُ أَنْ أَسْتَيْقِنَ الْخَبَرَ مِنْ قِبَلِهِمَا، قَالَتْ فَأَذِنَ لِي رَسُولُ اللَّهِ صلى الله عليه وسلم، فَقُلْتُ لأُمِّي يَا أُمَّتَاهْ مَاذَا يَتَحَدَّثُ النَّاسُ قَالَتْ يَا بُنَيَّةُ هَوِّنِي عَلَيْكِ، فَوَاللَّهِ لَقَلَّمَا كَانَتِ امْرَأَةٌ قَطُّ وَضِيئَةً عِنْدَ رَجُلٍ يُحِبُّهَا لَهَا ضَرَائِرُ إِلاَّ كَثَّرْنَ عَلَيْهَا. قَالَتْ فَقُلْتُ سُبْحَانَ اللَّهِ أَوَلَقَدْ تَحَدَّثَ النَّاسُ بِهَذَا قَالَتْ فَبَكَيْتُ تِلْكَ اللَّيْلَةَ، حَتَّى أَصْبَحْتُ لاَ يَرْقَأُ لِي دَمْعٌ، وَلاَ أَكْتَحِلُ بِنَوْمٍ، ثُمَّ أَصْبَحْتُ أَبْكِي ـ قَالَتْ ـ وَدَعَا رَسُولُ اللَّهِ صلى الله عليه وسلم عَلِيَّ بْنَ أَبِي طَالِبٍ وَأُسَامَةَ بْنَ زَيْدٍ حِينَ اسْتَلْبَثَ الْوَحْىُ يَسْأَلُهُمَا وَيَسْتَشِيرُهُمَا فِي فِرَاقِ أَهْلِهِ ـ قَالَتْ ـ فَأَمَّا أُسَامَةُ فَأَشَارَ عَلَى رَسُولِ اللَّهِ صلى الله عليه وسلم بِالَّذِي يَعْلَمُ مِنْ بَرَاءَةِ أَهْلِهِ، وَبِالَّذِي يَعْلَمُ لَهُمْ فِي نَفْسِهِ، فَقَالَ أُسَامَةُ أَهْلَكَ وَلاَ نَعْلَمُ إِلاَّ خَيْرًا. وَأَمَّا عَلِيٌّ فَقَالَ يَا رَسُولَ اللَّهِ لَمْ يُضَيِّقِ اللَّهُ عَلَيْكَ، وَالنِّسَاءُ سِوَاهَا كَثِيرٌ، وَسَلِ الْجَارِيَةَ تَصْدُقْكَ. قَالَتْ فَدَعَا رَسُولُ اللَّهِ صلى الله عليه وسلم بَرِيرَةَ فَقَالَ " أَىْ بَرِيرَةُ هَلْ رَأَيْتِ مِنْ شَىْءٍ يَرِيبُكِ ". قَالَتْ لَهُ بَرِيرَةُ وَالَّذِي بَعَثَكَ بِالْحَقِّ مَا رَأَيْتُ عَلَيْهَا أَمْرًا قَطُّ أَغْمِصُهُ، غَيْرَ أَنَّهَا جَارِيَةٌ حَدِيثَةُ السِّنِّ تَنَامُ عَنْ عَجِينِ أَهْلِهَا، فَتَأْتِي الدَّاجِنُ فَتَأْكُلُهُ ـ قَالَتْ ـ فَقَامَ رَسُولُ اللَّهِ صلى الله عليه وسلم مِنْ يَوْمِهِ، فَاسْتَعْذَرَ مِنْ عَبْدِ اللَّهِ بْنِ أُبَىٍّ وَهْوَ عَلَى الْمِنْبَرِ فَقَالَ " يَا مَعْشَرَ الْمُسْلِمِينَ مَنْ يَعْذِرُنِي مِنْ رَجُلٍ قَدْ بَلَغَنِي عَنْهُ أَذَاهُ فِي أَهْلِي، وَاللَّهِ مَا عَلِمْتُ عَلَى أَهْلِي إِلاَّ خَيْرًا، وَلَقَدْ ذَكَرُوا رَجُلاً مَا عَلِمْتُ عَلَيْهِ إِلاَّ خَيْرًا، وَمَا يَدْخُلُ عَلَى أَهْلِي إِلاَّ مَعِي ". قَالَتْ فَقَامَ سَعْدُ بْنُ مُعَاذٍ أَخُو بَنِي عَبْدِ الأَشْهَلِ فَقَالَ أَنَا يَا رَسُولَ اللَّهِ أَعْذِرُكَ، فَإِنْ كَانَ مِنَ الأَوْسِ ضَرَبْتُ عُنُقَهُ، وَإِنْ كَانَ مِنْ إِخْوَانِنَا مِنَ الْخَزْرَجِ أَمَرْتَنَا فَفَعَلْنَا أَمْرَكَ. قَالَتْ فَقَامَ رَجُلٌ مِنَ الْخَزْرَجِ، وَكَانَتْ أُمُّ حَسَّانَ بِنْتَ عَمِّهِ مِنْ فَخِذِهِ، وَهْوَ سَعْدُ بْنُ عُبَادَةَ، وَهْوَ سَيِّدُ الْخَزْرَجِ ـ قَالَتْ ـ وَكَانَ قَبْلَ ذَلِكَ رَجُلاً صَالِحًا، وَلَكِنِ احْتَمَلَتْهُ الْحَمِيَّةُ فَقَالَ لِسَعْدٍ كَذَبْتَ لَعَمْرُ اللَّهِ لاَ تَقْتُلُهُ، وَلاَ تَقْدِرُ عَلَى قَتْلِهِ، وَلَوْ كَانَ مِنْ رَهْطِكَ مَا أَحْبَبْتَ أَنْ يُقْتَلَ. فَقَامَ أُسَيْدُ بْنُ حُضَيْرٍ ـ وَهْوَ ابْنُ عَمِّ سَعْدٍ ـ فَقَالَ لِسَعْدِ بْنِ عُبَادَةَ كَذَبْتَ لَعَمْرُ اللَّهِ لَنَقْتُلَنَّهُ، فَإِنَّكَ مُنَافِقٌ تُجَادِلُ عَنِ الْمُنَافِقِينَ. قَالَتْ فَثَارَ الْحَيَّانِ الأَوْسُ وَالْخَزْرَجُ حَتَّى هَمُّوا أَنْ يَقْتَتِلُوا، وَرَسُولُ اللَّهِ صلى الله عليه وسلم قَائِمٌ عَلَى الْمِنْبَرِ ـ قَالَتْ ـ فَلَمْ يَزَلْ رَسُولُ اللَّهِ صلى الله عليه وسلم يُخَفِّضُهُمْ حَتَّى سَكَتُوا وَسَكَتَ ـ قَالَتْ ـ فَبَكَيْتُ يَوْمِي ذَلِكَ كُلَّهُ، لاَ يَرْقَأُ لِي دَمْعٌ، وَلاَ أَكْتَحِلُ بِنَوْمٍ ـ قَالَتْ ـ وَأَصْبَحَ أَبَوَاىَ عِنْدِي، وَقَدْ بَكَيْتُ لَيْلَتَيْنِ وَيَوْمًا، لاَ يَرْقَأُ لِي دَمْعٌ، وَلاَ أَكْتَحِلُ بِنَوْمٍ، حَتَّى إِنِّي لأَظُنُّ أَنَّ الْبُكَاءَ فَالِقٌ كَبِدِي، فَبَيْنَا أَبَوَاىَ جَالِسَانِ عِنْدِي وَأَنَا أَبْكِي فَاسْتَأْذَنَتْ عَلَىَّ امْرَأَةٌ مِنَ الأَنْصَارِ، فَأَذِنْتُ لَهَا، فَجَلَسَتْ تَبْكِي مَعِي ـ قَالَتْ ـ فَبَيْنَا نَحْنُ عَلَى ذَلِكَ دَخَلَ رَسُولُ اللَّهِ صلى الله عليه وسلم عَلَيْنَا، فَسَلَّمَ ثُمَّ جَلَسَ ـ قَالَتْ ـ وَلَمْ يَجْلِسْ عِنْدِي مُنْذُ قِيلَ مَا قِيلَ قَبْلَهَا، وَقَدْ لَبِثَ شَهْرًا لاَ يُوحَى إِلَيْهِ فِي شَأْنِي بِشَىْءٍ ـ قَالَتْ ـ فَتَشَهَّدَ رَسُولُ اللَّهِ صلى الله عليه وسلم حِينَ جَلَسَ ثُمَّ قَالَ " أَمَّا بَعْدُ، يَا عَائِشَةُ إِنَّهُ بَلَغَنِي عَنْكِ كَذَا وَكَذَا، فَإِنْ كُنْتِ بَرِيئَةً، فَسَيُبَرِّئُكِ اللَّهُ، وَإِنْ كُنْتِ أَلْمَمْتِ بِذَنْبٍ، فَاسْتَغْفِرِي اللَّهَ وَتُوبِي إِلَيْهِ، فَإِنَّ الْعَبْدَ إِذَا اعْتَرَفَ ثُمَّ تَابَ تَابَ اللَّهُ عَلَيْهِ ". قَالَتْ فَلَمَّا قَضَى رَسُولُ اللَّهِ صلى الله عليه وسلم مَقَالَتَهُ قَلَصَ دَمْعِي حَتَّى مَا أُحِسُّ مِنْهُ قَطْرَةً، فَقُلْتُ لأَبِي أَجِبْ رَسُولَ اللَّهِ صلى الله عليه وسلم عَنِّي فِيمَا قَالَ. فَقَالَ أَبِي وَاللَّهِ مَا أَدْرِي مَا أَقُولُ لِرَسُولِ اللَّهِ صلى الله عليه وسلم. فَقُلْتُ لأُمِّي أَجِيبِي رَسُولَ اللَّهِ صلى الله عليه وسلم فِيمَا قَالَ. قَالَتْ أُمِّي وَاللَّهِ مَا أَدْرِي مَا أَقُولُ لِرَسُولِ اللَّهِ صلى الله عليه وسلم. فَقُلْتُ وَأَنَا جَارِيَةٌ حَدِيثَةُ السِّنِّ لاَ أَقْرَأُ مِنَ الْقُرْآنِ كَثِيرًا إِنِّي وَاللَّهِ لَقَدْ عَلِمْتُ لَقَدْ سَمِعْتُمْ هَذَا الْحَدِيثَ حَتَّى اسْتَقَرَّ فِي أَنْفُسِكُمْ وَصَدَّقْتُمْ بِهِ، فَلَئِنْ قُلْتُ لَكُمْ إِنِّي بَرِيئَةٌ لاَ تُصَدِّقُونِي، وَلَئِنِ اعْتَرَفْتُ لَكُمْ بِأَمْرٍ، وَاللَّهُ يَعْلَمُ أَنِّي مِنْهُ بَرِيئَةٌ لَتُصَدِّقُنِّي، فَوَاللَّهِ لاَ أَجِدُ لِي وَلَكُمْ مَثَلاً إِلاَّ أَبَا يُوسُفَ حِينَ قَالَ {فَصَبْرٌ جَمِيلٌ وَاللَّهُ الْمُسْتَعَانُ عَلَى مَا تَصِفُونَ} ثُمَّ تَحَوَّلْتُ وَاضْطَجَعْتُ عَلَى فِرَاشِي، وَاللَّهُ يَعْلَمُ أَنِّي حِينَئِذٍ بَرِيئَةٌ، وَأَنَّ اللَّهَ مُبَرِّئِي بِبَرَاءَتِي وَلَكِنْ وَاللَّهِ مَا كُنْتُ أَظُنُّ أَنَّ اللَّهَ مُنْزِلٌ فِي شَأْنِي وَحْيًا يُتْلَى، لَشَأْنِي فِي نَفْسِي كَانَ أَحْقَرَ مِنْ أَنْ يَتَكَلَّمَ اللَّهُ فِيَّ بِأَمْرٍ، وَلَكِنْ كُنْتُ أَرْجُو أَنْ يَرَى رَسُولُ اللَّهِ صلى الله عليه وسلم فِي النَّوْمِ رُؤْيَا يُبَرِّئُنِي اللَّهُ بِهَا، فَوَاللَّهِ مَا رَامَ رَسُولُ اللَّهِ صلى الله عليه وسلم مَجْلِسَهُ، وَلاَ خَرَجَ أَحَدٌ مِنْ أَهْلِ الْبَيْتِ، حَتَّى أُنْزِلَ عَلَيْهِ، فَأَخَذَهُ مَا كَانَ يَأْخُذُهُ مِنَ الْبُرَحَاءِ، حَتَّى إِنَّهُ لَيَتَحَدَّرُ مِنْهُ مِنَ الْعَرَقِ مِثْلُ الْجُمَانِ وَهْوَ فِي يَوْمٍ شَاتٍ، مِنْ ثِقَلِ الْقَوْلِ الَّذِي أُنْزِلَ عَلَيْهِ ـ قَالَتْ ـ فَسُرِّيَ عَنْ رَسُولِ اللَّهِ صلى الله عليه وسلم وَهْوَ يَضْحَكُ، فَكَانَتْ أَوَّلَ كَلِمَةٍ تَكَلَّمَ بِهَا أَنْ قَالَ " يَا عَائِشَةُ أَمَّا اللَّهُ فَقَدْ بَرَّأَكِ ". قَالَتْ فَقَالَتْ لِي أُمِّي قُومِي إِلَيْهِ. فَقُلْتُ وَاللَّهِ لاَ أَقُومُ إِلَيْهِ، فَإِنِّي لاَ أَحْمَدُ إِلاَّ اللَّهَ عَزَّ وَجَلَّ ـ قَالَتْ ـ وَأَنْزَلَ اللَّهُ تَعَالَى {إِنَّ الَّذِينَ جَاءُوا بِالإِفْكِ} الْعَشْرَ الآيَاتِ، ثُمَّ أَنْزَلَ اللَّهُ هَذَا فِي بَرَاءَتِي. قَالَ أَبُو بَكْرٍ الصِّدِّيقُ ـ وَكَانَ يُنْفِقُ عَلَى مِسْطَحِ بْنِ أُثَاثَةَ لِقَرَابَتِهِ مِنْهُ وَفَقْرِهِ ـ وَاللَّهِ لاَ أُنْفِقُ عَلَى مِسْطَحٍ شَيْئًا أَبَدًا بَعْدَ الَّذِي قَالَ لِعَائِشَةَ مَا قَالَ. فَأَنْزَلَ اللَّهُ { وَلاَ يَأْتَلِ أُولُو الْفَضْلِ مِنْكُمْ} إِلَى قَوْلِهِ {غَفُورٌ رَحِيمٌ} قَالَ أَبُو بَكْرٍ الصِّدِّيقُ بَلَى وَاللَّهِ إِنِّي لأُحِبُّ أَنْ يَغْفِرَ اللَّهُ لِي فَرَجَعَ إِلَى مِسْطَحٍ النَّفَقَةَ الَّتِي كَانَ يُنْفِقُ عَلَيْهِ وَقَالَ وَاللَّهِ لَا أَنْزِعُهَا مِنْهُ أَبَدًا قَالَتْ عَائِشَةُ وَكَانَ رَسُولُ اللَّهِ صَلَّى اللَّهُ عَلَيْهِ وَسَلَّمَ سَأَلَ زَيْنَبَ بِنْتَ جَحْشٍ عَنْ أَمْرِي فَقَالَ لِزَيْنَبَ مَاذَا عَلِمْتِ أَوْ رَأَيْتِ فَقَالَتْ يَا رَسُولَ اللَّهِ أَحْمِي سَمْعِي وَبَصَرِي وَاللَّهِ مَا عَلِمْتُ إِلَّا خَيْرًا قَالَتْ عَائِشَةُ وَهِيَ الَّتِي كَانَتْ تُسَامِينِي مِنْ أَزْوَاجِ النَّبِيِّ صَلَّى اللَّهُ عَلَيْهِ وَسَلَّمَ فَعَصَمَهَا اللَّهُ بِالْوَرَعِ قَالَتْ وَطَفِقَتْ أُخْتُهَا حَمْنَةُ تُحَارِبُ لَهَا فَهَلَكَتْ فِيمَنْ هَلَكَ قَالَ ابْنُ شِهَابٍ فَهَذَا الَّذِي بَلَغَنِي مِنْ حَدِيثِ هَؤُلَاءِ الرَّهْطِ ثُمَّ قَالَ عُرْوَةُ قَالَتْ عَائِشَةُ وَاللَّهِ إِنَّ الرَّجُلَ الَّذِي قِيلَ لَهُ مَا قِيلَ لَيَقُولُ سُبْحَانَ اللَّهِ فَوَالَّذِي نَفْسِي بِيَدِهِ مَا كَشَفْتُ مِنْ كَنَفِ أُنْثَى قَطُّ قَالَتْ ثُمَّ قُتِلَ بَعْدَ ذَلِكَ فِي سَبِيلِ اللَّهِ

Narrated Az-Zuhri: Al-Walid bin `Abdul Malik said to me, "Have you heard that `Ali' was one of those who slandered `Aisha?" I replied, "No, but two men from your people (named) Abu Salama bin `Abdur-Rahman and Abu Bakr bin `Abdur-Rahman bin Al-Harith have informed me that Aisha told them that `Ali remained silent about her case.". – Sahih Al-Bukhari 4142

حَدَّثَنِي عَبْدُ اللَّهِ بْنُ مُحَمَّدٍ، قَالَ أَمْلَى عَلَيَّ هِشَامُ بْنُ يُوسُفَ مِنْ حِفْظِهِ أَخْبَرَنَا مَعْمَرٌ، عَنِ الزُّهْرِيِّ، قَالَ قَالَ لِي الْوَلِيدُ بْنُ عَبْدِ الْمَلِكِ أَبَلَغَكَ أَنَّ عَلِيًّا، كَانَ فِيمَنْ قَذَفَ عَائِشَةَ قُلْتُ لاَ. وَلَكِنْ قَدْ أَخْبَرَنِي رَجُلاَنِ مِنْ قَوْمِكَ أَبُو سَلَمَةَ بْنُ عَبْدِ الرَّحْمَنِ وَأَبُو بَكْرِ بْنُ عَبْدِ الرَّحْمَنِ بْنِ الْحَارِثِ أَنَّ عَائِشَةَ ـ رضى الله عنها ـ قَالَتْ لَهُمَا كَانَ عَلِيٌّ مُسَلِّمًا فِي شَأْنِهَا. فَرَاجَعُوهُ فَلَمْ يَرْجِعْ وَقَالَ مُسَلِّمًا بِلاَ شَكٍّ فِيهِ وَعَلَيْهِ كَانَ فِي أَصْلِ الْعَتِيقِ كَذَلِكَ

Those who perpetrated the slander are a band of you. Do not consider it bad for you, but it is good for you. Each person among them bears his share in the sin. As for him who played the major role—for him is a terrible punishment. Why, when you heard about it, the believing men and women did not think well of one another, and say, "This is an obvious lie"? Why did they not bring four witnesses to testify to it? If they fail to bring the witnesses, then in Allah's sight, they are liars. Were it not for Allah's favor upon you, and His mercy, in this world and the Hereafter, you would have suffered a great punishment for what you have ventured into. When you rumored it with your tongues, and spoke with your mouths what you had no knowledge of, and you considered it trivial; but according to Allah, it is serious. When you heard it, you should have said, "It is not for us to repeat this. By Your glory, this is a serious slander." Allah cautions you never to return to the like of it, if you are believers. Allah explains the Verses to you. Allah is Knowing and Wise. Those who love to see immorality spread among the believers—for them is a painful punishment, in this life and in the Hereafter. Allah knows, and you do not know. Were it not for Allah's grace upon you, and His mercy, and that Allah is Clement and Merciful. O you who believe! Do not follow Satan's footsteps. Whoever follows Satan's footsteps—he advocates obscenity and immorality. Were it not for Allah's grace towards you, and His mercy, not one of you would have been pure, ever. But Allah purifies whomever He wills. Allah is All-Hearing, All-Knowing. – Surah An-Nur 24:11-21

إِنَّ ٱلَّذِينَ جَآءُو بِٱلْإِفْكِ عُصْبَةٌ مِّنكُمْ لَا تَحْسَبُوهُ شَرًّا لَّكُم بَلْ هُوَ خَيْرٌ لَّكُمْ لِكُلِّ ٱمْرِئٍ مِّنْهُم مَّا ٱكْتَسَبَ مِنَ ٱلْإِثْمِ وَٱلَّذِى تَوَلَّىٰ كِبْرَهُۥ مِنْهُمْ لَهُۥ عَذَابٌ عَظِيمٌ لَّوْلَآ إِذْ سَمِعْتُمُوهُ ظَنَّ ٱلْمُؤْمِنُونَ وَٱلْمُؤْمِنَٰتُ بِأَنفُسِهِمْ خَيْرًا وَقَالُوا۟ هَٰذَآ إِفْكٌ مُّبِينٌ لَّوْلَا جَآءُو عَلَيْهِ بِأَرْبَعَةِ شُهَدَآءَ فَإِذْ لَمْ يَأْتُوا۟ بِٱلشُّهَدَآءِ فَأُو۟لَٰٓئِكَ عِندَ ٱللَّهِ هُمُ ٱلْكَٰذِبُونَ وَلَوْلَا فَضْلُ ٱللَّهِ عَلَيْكُمْ وَرَحْمَتُهُۥ فِى ٱلدُّنْيَا وَٱلْءَاخِرَةِ لَمَسَّكُمْ فِى مَآ أَفَضْتُمْ فِيهِ عَذَابٌ عَظِيمٌ إِذْ تَلَقَّوْنَهُۥ بِأَلْسِنَتِكُمْ وَتَقُولُونَ بِأَفْوَاهِكُم مَّا لَيْسَ لَكُم بِهِۦ عِلْمٌ وَتَحْسَبُونَهُۥ هَيِّنًا وَهُوَ عِندَ ٱللَّهِ عَظِيمٌ وَلَوْلَآ إِذْ سَمِعْتُمُوهُ قُلْتُم مَّا يَكُونُ لَنَآ أَن نَّتَكَلَّمَ بِهَٰذَا سُبْحَٰنَكَ هَٰذَا بُهْتَٰنٌ عَظِيمٌ يَعِظُكُمُ ٱللَّهُ أَن تَعُودُوا۟ لِمِثْلِهِۦٓ أَبَدًا إِن كُنتُم مُّؤْمِنِينَ وَيُبَيِّنُ ٱللَّهُ لَكُمُ ٱلْءَايَٰتِ وَٱللَّهُ عَلِيمٌ حَكِيمٌ إِنَّ ٱلَّذِينَ يُحِبُّونَ أَن تَشِيعَ ٱلْفَٰحِشَةُ فِى ٱلَّذِينَ ءَامَنُوا۟ لَهُمْ عَذَابٌ أَلِيمٌ فِى ٱلدُّنْيَا وَٱلْءَاخِرَةِ وَٱللَّهُ يَعْلَمُ وَأَنتُمْ لَا تَعْلَمُونَ وَلَوْلَا فَضْلُ ٱللَّهِ عَلَيْكُمْ وَرَحْمَتُهُۥ وَأَنَّ ٱللَّهَ رَءُوفٌ رَّحِيمٌ يَٰٓأَيُّهَا ٱلَّذِينَ ءَامَنُوا۟ لَا تَتَّبِعُوا۟ خُطُوَٰتِ ٱلشَّيْطَٰنِ وَمَن يَتَّبِعْ خُطُوَٰتِ ٱلشَّيْطَٰنِ فَإِنَّهُۥ يَأْمُرُ بِٱلْفَحْشَآءِ وَٱلْمُنكَرِ وَلَوْلَا فَضْلُ ٱللَّهِ عَلَيْكُمْ وَرَحْمَتُهُۥ مَا زَكَىٰ مِنكُم مِّنْ أَحَدٍ أَبَدًا وَلَٰكِنَّ ٱللَّهَ يُزَكِّى مَن يَشَآءُ وَٱللَّهُ سَمِيعٌ عَلِيمٌ

Those of you who have affluence and means should not refuse to give to the relatives, and the needy, and the emigrants for the sake of Allah. And let them pardon, and let them overlook. Do you not love for Allah to pardon you? Allah is All-Forgiving, Most Merciful. – Surah An-Nur 24:22

وَلَا يَأْتَلِ أُو۟لُوا۟ ٱلْفَضْلِ مِنكُمْ وَٱلسَّعَةِ أَن يُؤْتُوٓا۟ أُو۟لِى ٱلْقُرْبَىٰ وَٱلْمَسَٰكِينَ وَٱلْمُهَٰجِرِينَ فِى سَبِيلِ ٱللَّهِ وَلْيَعْفُوا۟ وَلْيَصْفَحُوٓا۟ أَلَا تُحِبُّونَ أَن يَغْفِرَ ٱللَّهُ لَكُمْ وَٱللَّهُ غَفُورٌ رَّحِيمٌ

Narrated Az-Zuhri: I heard `Urwa bin Az-Zubair, Sa`id bin Al-Musaiyab, 'Alqama bin Waqqas and 'Ubaidullah bin `Abdullah bin `Uqba relating from `Aisha, the wife of the Prophet ﷺ the narration of the people (i.e. the liars) who spread the slander against her and they said what they said, and how Allah revealed her innocence. Each of them related to me a portion of that narration. (They said that `Aisha said), ''Then Allah revealed the ten Verses starting with:- -'Verily! Those who spread the slander..' (24.11-21) All these verses were in proof of my innocence. Abu Bakr As-Siddiq who used to provide for Mistah some financial aid because of his relation to him, said, "By Allah, I will never give anything (in charity) to Mistah, after what he has said about `Aisha" Then Allah revealed:-- 'And let not those among you who are good and are wealthy swear not to give (any sort of help) to their kins men....' (24.22) On that, Abu Bakr said, "Yes, by Allah, I like that Allah should forgive me." And then resumed giving Mistah the aid he used to give him and said, "By Allah! I will never withhold it from him." – Sahih Al-Bukhari 6679

حَدَّثَنَا عَبْدُ الْعَزِيزِ، حَدَّثَنَا إِبْرَاهِيمُ، عَنْ صَالِحٍ، عَنِ ابْنِ شِهَابٍ، ح وَحَدَّثَنَا الْحَجَّاجُ، حَدَّثَنَا عَبْدُ اللَّهِ بْنُ عُمَرَ النُّمَيْرِيُّ، حَدَّثَنَا يُونُسُ بْنُ يَزِيدَ الأَيْلِيُّ، قَالَ سَمِعْتُ الزُّهْرِيَّ، قَالَ سَمِعْتُ عُرْوَةَ بْنَ الزُّبَيْرِ، وَسَعِيدَ بْنَ الْمُسَيَّبِ، وَعَلْقَمَةَ بْنَ وَقَّاصٍ، وَعُبَيْدَ اللَّهِ بْنَ عَبْدِ اللَّهِ بْنِ عُتْبَةَ، عَنْ حَدِيثِ، عَائِشَةَ زَوْجِ النَّبِيِّ صلى الله عليه وسلم حِينَ قَالَ لَهَا أَهْلُ الإِفْكِ مَا قَالُوا، فَبَرَّأَهَا اللَّهُ مِمَّا قَالُوا ـ كُلٌّ حَدَّثَنِي طَائِفَةً مِنَ الْحَدِيثِ ـ فَأَنْزَلَ اللَّهُ {إِنَّ الَّذِينَ جَاءُوا بِالإِفْكِ} الْعَشْرَ الآيَاتِ كُلَّهَا فِي بَرَاءَتِي. فَقَالَ أَبُو بَكْرٍ الصِّدِّيقُ ـ وَكَانَ يُنْفِقُ عَلَى مِسْطَحٍ لِقَرَابَتِهِ مِنْهُ ـ وَاللَّهِ لاَ أُنْفِقُ عَلَى مِسْطَحٍ شَيْئًا أَبَدًا، بَعْدَ الَّذِي قَالَ لِعَائِشَةَ. فَأَنْزَلَ اللَّهُ {وَلاَ يَأْتَلِ أُولُو الْفَضْلِ مِنْكُمْ وَالسَّعَةِ أَنْ يُؤْتُوا أُولِي الْقُرْبَى} الآيَةَ. قَالَ أَبُو بَكْرٍ بَلَى وَاللَّهِ إِنِّي لأُحِبُّ أَنْ يَغْفِرَ اللَّهُ لِي. فَرَجَعَ إِلَى مِسْطَحٍ النَّفَقَةَ الَّتِي كَانَ يُنْفِقُ عَلَيْهِ وَقَالَ وَاللَّهِ لاَ أَنْزِعُهَا عَنْهُ أَبَدًا

The Book of
Al-Hudaybia
الْحُدَيْبِيَة

Narrated Al-Miswar bin Makhrama and Marwan bin Al-Hakam: (one of them said more than his friend): The Prophet ﷺ set out in the company of more than one thousand of his companions in the year of Al-Hudaibiya, and when he reached Dhul-Hulaifa, he garlanded his Hadi (i.e. sacrificing animal), assumed the state of Ihram for `Umra from that place and sent a spy of his from Khuzi'a (tribe). The Prophet ﷺ proceeded on till he reached (a village called) Ghadir-al-Ashtat. There his spy came and said, "The Quraish (infidels) have collected a great number of people against you, and they have collected against you the Ethiopians, and they will fight with you, and will stop you from entering the Ka`ba and prevent you." The Prophet ﷺ said, "O people! Give me your opinion. Do you recommend that I should destroy the families and offspring of those who want to stop us from the Ka`ba? If they should come to us (for peace) then Allah will destroy a spy from the pagans, or otherwise we will leave them in a miserable state." On that Abu Bakr said, "O Allah Apostle! You have come with the intention of visiting this House (i.e. Ka`ba) and you do not want to kill or fight anybody. So proceed to it, and whoever should stop us from it, we will fight him." On that the Prophet ﷺ said, "Proceed on, in the Name of Allah !" – Sahih Al-Bukhari 4178, 4179

حَدَّثَنَا عَبْدُ اللَّهِ بْنُ مُحَمَّدٍ، حَدَّثَنَا سُفْيَانُ، قَالَ سَمِعْتُ الزُّهْرِيَّ، حِينَ حَدَّثَ هَذَا الْحَدِيثَ،، حَفِظْتُ بَعْضَهُ، وَثَبَّتَنِي مَعْمَرٌ عَنْ عُرْوَةَ بْنِ الزُّبَيْرِ، عَنِ الْمِسْوَرِ بْنِ مَخْرَمَةَ، وَمَرْوَانَ بْنِ الْحَكَمِ، يَزِيدُ أَحَدُهُمَا عَلَى صَاحِبِهِ قَالاَ خَرَجَ النَّبِيُّ صلى الله عليه وسلم عَامَ الْحُدَيْبِيَةِ فِي بِضْعَ عَشْرَةَ مِائَةً مِنْ أَصْحَابِهِ، فَلَمَّا أَتَى ذَا الْحُلَيْفَةِ قَلَّدَ الْهَدْىَ، وَأَشْعَرَهُ، وَأَحْرَمَ مِنْهَا بِعُمْرَةٍ، وَبَعَثَ عَيْنًا لَهُ مِنْ خُزَاعَةَ، وَسَارَ النَّبِيُّ صلى الله عليه وسلم حَتَّى كَانَ بِغَدِيرِ الأَشْطَاطِ، أَتَاهُ عَيْنُهُ قَالَ إِنَّ قُرَيْشًا جَمَعُوا لَكَ جُمُوعًا، وَقَدْ جَمَعُوا لَكَ الأَحَابِيشَ، وَهُمْ مُقَاتِلُوكَ وَصَادُّوكَ عَنِ الْبَيْتِ وَمَانِعُوكَ. فَقَالَ " أَشِيرُوا أَيُّهَا النَّاسُ عَلَىَّ، أَتَرَوْنَ أَنْ أَمِيلَ إِلَى عِيَالِهِمْ وَذَرَارِيِّ هَؤُلاَءِ الَّذِينَ يُرِيدُونَ أَنْ يَصُدُّونَا عَنِ الْبَيْتِ، فَإِنْ يَأْتُونَا كَانَ اللَّهُ عَزَّ وَجَلَّ قَدْ قَطَعَ عَيْنًا مِنَ الْمُشْرِكِينَ، وَإِلاَّ تَرَكْنَاهُمْ مَحْرُوبِينَ ". قَالَ أَبُو بَكْرٍ يَا رَسُولَ اللَّهِ، خَرَجْتَ عَامِدًا لِهَذَا الْبَيْتِ، لاَ تُرِيدُ قَتْلَ أَحَدٍ وَلاَ حَرْبَ أَحَدٍ، فَتَوَجَّهْ لَهُ، فَمَنْ صَدَّنَا عَنْهُ قَاتَلْنَاهُ. قَالَ " امْضُوا عَلَى اسْمِ اللَّهِ ".

Narrated Zaid bin Khalid Al-Juhani: The Prophet ﷺ led us in the Fajr prayer at Hudaibiya after a rainy night. On completion of the prayer, he faced the people and said, "Do you know what your Lord has said (revealed)?" The people replied, "Allah and His Apostle know better." He said, "Allah has said, 'In this morning some of my slaves remained as true believers and some became non-believers; whoever said that the rain was due to the Blessings and the Mercy of Allah had belief in Me and he disbelieves in the stars, and whoever said that it rained because of a particular star had no belief in Me but believes in that star.' ". – Sahih Al-Bukhari 846

حَدَّثَنَا عَبْدُ اللَّهِ بْنُ مَسْلَمَةَ، عَنْ مَالِكٍ، عَنْ صَالِحِ بْنِ كَيْسَانَ، عَنْ عُبَيْدِ اللَّهِ بْنِ عَبْدِ اللَّهِ بْنِ عُتْبَةَ بْنِ مَسْعُودٍ، عَنْ زَيْدِ بْنِ خَالِدٍ الْجُهَنِيِّ، أَنَّهُ قَالَ صَلَّى لَنَا رَسُولُ اللَّهِ صلى الله عليه وسلم صَلاَةَ الصُّبْحِ بِالْحُدَيْبِيَةِ عَلَى إِثْرِ سَمَاءٍ كَانَتْ مِنَ اللَّيْلَةِ، فَلَمَّا انْصَرَفَ أَقْبَلَ عَلَى النَّاسِ فَقَالَ " هَلْ تَدْرُونَ مَاذَا قَالَ رَبُّكُمْ ". قَالُوا اللَّهُ وَرَسُولُهُ أَعْلَمُ. قَالَ " أَصْبَحَ مِنْ عِبَادِي مُؤْمِنٌ بِي وَكَافِرٌ، فَأَمَّا مَنْ قَالَ مُطِرْنَا بِفَضْلِ اللَّهِ وَرَحْمَتِهِ فَذَلِكَ مُؤْمِنٌ بِي وَكَافِرٌ بِالْكَوْكَبِ، وَأَمَّا مَنْ قَالَ بِنَوْءِ كَذَا وَكَذَا فَذَلِكَ كَافِرٌ بِي وَمُؤْمِنٌ بِالْكَوْكَبِ ".

Narrated Qatada: I asked Anas (about the Prophet's `Umra) and he replied, "The Prophet ﷺ performed `Umra when the pagans made him return, and Umra of al-Hudaibiya (the next year), and another `Umra in Dhi-l-Qa'da, and another `Umra in combination with his Hajj.". – Sahih Al-Bukhari 1779

حَدَّثَنَا أَبُو الْوَلِيدِ، هِشَامُ بْنُ عَبْدِ الْمَلِكِ حَدَّثَنَا هَمَّامٌ، عَنْ قَتَادَةَ، قَالَ سَأَلْتُ أَنَسًا ـ رضى الله عنه ـ فَقَالَ اعْتَمَرَ النَّبِيُّ صلى الله عليه وسلم حَيْثُ رَدُّوهُ، وَمِنَ الْقَابِلِ عُمْرَةَ الْحُدَيْبِيَةِ، وَعُمْرَةً فِي ذِي الْقَعْدَةِ وَعُمْرَةً مَعَ حَجَّتِهِ.

Narrated Ka`b bin Ujra: We were in the company of Allah's Messenger ﷺ at Al-Hudaibiya in the state of Ihram and the pagans did not allow us to proceed (to the Ka`ba). I had thick hair and lice started falling on my face. The Prophet ﷺ passed by me and said, "Are the lice of your head troubling you?" I replied, Yes." (The sub-narrator added, "Then the following Divine Verse was revealed:-- "And if anyone of you is ill or has an ailment in his scalp, (necessitating shaving) must pay a ransom (Fida) of either fasting or feeding the poor, Or offering a sacrifice." (2.196). – Sahih Al-Bukhari 4191

حَدَّثَنِي مُحَمَّدُ بْنُ هِشَامٍ أَبُو عَبْدِ اللَّهِ، حَدَّثَنَا هُشَيْمٌ، عَنْ أَبِي بِشْرٍ، عَنْ مُجَاهِدٍ، عَنْ عَبْدِ الرَّحْمَنِ بْنِ أَبِي لَيْلَى، عَنْ كَعْبِ بْنِ عُجْرَةَ، قَالَ كُنَّا مَعَ رَسُولِ اللَّهِ صلى الله عليه وسلم بِالْحُدَيْبِيَةِ وَنَحْنُ مُحْرِمُونَ، وَقَدْ حَصَرَنَا الْمُشْرِكُونَ ـ قَالَ ـ وَكَانَتْ لِي وَفْرَةٌ فَجَعَلَتِ الْهَوَامُّ تَسَّاقَطُ عَلَى وَجْهِي، فَمَرَّ بِي النَّبِيُّ صلى الله عليه وسلم فَقَالَ " أَيُؤْذِيكَ هَوَامُّ رَأْسِكَ ". قُلْتُ نَعَمْ. قَالَ وَأُنْزِلَتْ هَذِهِ الآيَةُ {فَمَنْ كَانَ مِنْكُمْ مَرِيضًا أَوْ بِهِ أَذًى مِنْ رَأْسِهِ فَفِدْيَةٌ مِنْ صِيَامٍ أَوْ صَدَقَةٍ أَوْ نُسُكٍ}

Narrated `Abdullah bin Abu Qatada: That his father said "We proceeded with the Prophet ﷺ in the year of Al-Hudaibiya and his companions assumed Ihram but I did not. We were informed that some enemies were at Ghaiqa and so we went on towards them. My companions saw an onager and some of them started laughing among themselves. I looked and saw it. I chased it with my horse and stabbed and caught it. I wanted some help from my companions but they refused. (I slaughtered it all alone). We all ate from it (i.e. its meat). Then I followed Allah's Messenger ﷺ lest we should be left behind. At times I urged my horse to run at a galloping speed and at other times at an ordinary slow speed. On the way I met a man from the tribe of Bani Ghifar at midnight. I asked him where he had left Allah's Messenger ﷺ. The man replied that he had left the Prophet ﷺ at a place called Ta'hun and he had the intention of having the midday rest at As-Suqya. So, I followed Allah's Messenger ﷺ till I reached him and said, "O Allah's Messenger ﷺ ! I have been sent by my companions who send you their greetings and compliments and ask for Allah's Mercy and Blessings upon you. They were afraid lest the enemy might intervene between you and them; so please wait for them." So he did. Then I said, "O Allah's Messenger ﷺ ! We have hunted an onager and have some of it (i.e. its meat) left over." Allah's Messenger ﷺ told his companions to eat the meat although all of them were in a state of Ihram.". – Sahih Al-Bukhari 1822

حَدَّثَنَا سَعِيدُ بْنُ الرَّبِيعِ، حَدَّثَنَا عَلِيُّ بْنُ الْمُبَارَكِ، عَنْ يَحْيَى، عَنْ عَبْدِ اللَّهِ بْنِ أَبِي قَتَادَةَ، أَنَّ أَبَاهُ، حَدَّثَهُ قَالَ انْطَلَقْنَا مَعَ النَّبِيِّ صلى الله عليه وسلم عَامَ الْحُدَيْبِيَةِ فَأَحْرَمَ أَصْحَابُهُ، وَلَمْ أُحْرِمْ، فَأُنْبِئْنَا بِعَدُوٍّ بِغَيْقَةَ فَتَوَجَّهْنَا نَحْوَهُمْ، فَبَصُرَ أَصْحَابِي بِحِمَارِ وَحْشٍ، فَجَعَلَ بَعْضُهُمْ يَضْحَكُ إِلَى بَعْضٍ، فَنَظَرْتُ فَرَأَيْتُهُ فَحَمَلْتُ عَلَيْهِ الْفَرَسَ، فَطَعَنْتُهُ، فَأَثْبَتُّهُ، فَاسْتَعَنْتُهُمْ، فَأَبَوْا أَنْ يُعِينُونِي، فَأَكَلْنَا مِنْهُ، ثُمَّ لَحِقْتُ بِرَسُولِ اللَّهِ صلى الله عليه وسلم وَخَشِينَا أَنْ نُقْتَطَعَ، أَرْفَعُ فَرَسِي شَأْوًا، وَأَسِيرُ عَلَيْهِ شَأْوًا، فَلَقِيتُ رَجُلاً مِنْ بَنِي غِفَارٍ فِي جَوْفِ اللَّيْلِ فَقُلْتُ أَيْنَ تَرَكْتَ رَسُولَ اللَّهِ صلى الله عليه وسلم فَقَالَ تَرَكْتُهُ بِتَعْهَنَ وَهُوَ قَائِلٌ السُّقْيَا. فَلَحِقْتُ بِرَسُولِ اللَّهِ صلى الله عليه وسلم حَتَّى أَتَيْتُهُ فَقُلْتُ يَا رَسُولَ اللَّهِ، إِنَّ أَصْحَابَكَ أَرْسَلُوا يَقْرَءُونَ عَلَيْكَ السَّلاَمَ وَرَحْمَةَ اللَّهِ وَبَرَكَاتِهِ، وَإِنَّهُمْ قَدْ خَشُوا أَنْ يَقْتَطِعَهُمُ الْعَدُوُّ دُونَكَ، فَانْظُرْهُمْ، فَفَعَلَ فَقُلْتُ يَا رَسُولَ اللَّهِ، إِنَّا اصَّدْنَا حِمَارَ وَحْشٍ، وَإِنَّ عِنْدَنَا فَاضِلَةً. فَقَالَ رَسُولُ اللَّهِ صلى الله عليه وسلم لأَصْحَابِهِ " كُلُوا ". وَهُمْ مُحْرِمُونَ

Treaty of Al-Hudaybia
صُلح الْحُدَيْبِيَة

Narrated Al-Bara bin `Azib: When Allah's Messenger ﷺ concluded a peace treaty with the people of Hudaibiya, `Ali bin Abu Talib wrote the document and he mentioned in it, "Muhammad, Allah's Messenger ﷺ ." The pagans said, "Don't write: 'Muhammad, Allah's Messenger ﷺ ,' for if you were an apostle we would not fight with you." Allah's Apostle asked `Ali to rub it out, but `Ali said, "I will not be the person to rub it out." Allah's Messenger ﷺ rubbed it out and made peace with them on the condition that the Prophet ﷺ and his

companions would enter Mecca and stay there for three days, and that they would enter with their weapons in cases. – Sahih Al-Bukhari 2698
حَدَّثَنَا مُحَمَّدُ بْنُ بَشَّارٍ، حَدَّثَنَا غُنْدَرٌ، حَدَّثَنَا شُعْبَةُ، عَنْ أَبِي إِسْحَاقَ، قَالَ سَمِعْتُ الْبَرَاءَ بْنَ عَازِبٍ ـ رضى الله عنهما ـ قَالَ لَمَّا صَالَحَ رَسُولُ اللَّهِ صلى الله عليه وسلم أَهْلَ الْحُدَيْبِيَةِ كَتَبَ عَلِيٌّ بَيْنَهُمْ كِتَابًا فَكَتَبَ مُحَمَّدٌ رَسُولُ اللَّهِ صلى الله عليه وسلم. فَقَالَ الْمُشْرِكُونَ لاَ تَكْتُبْ مُحَمَّدٌ رَسُولُ اللَّهِ، لَوْ كُنْتَ رَسُولاً لَمْ نُقَاتِلْكَ. فَقَالَ لِعَلِيٍّ " امْحُهُ ". فَقَالَ عَلِيٌّ مَا أَنَا بِالَّذِي أَمْحَاهُ. فَمَحَاهُ رَسُولُ اللَّهِ صلى الله عليه وسلم بِيَدِهِ، وَصَالَحَهُمْ عَلَى أَنْ يَدْخُلَ هُوَ وَأَصْحَابُهُ ثَلاَثَةَ أَيَّامٍ، وَلاَ يَدْخُلُوهَا إِلاَّ بِجُلُبَّانِ السِّلاَحِ، فَسَأَلُوهُ مَا جُلُبَّانُ السِّلاَحِ فَقَالَ الْقِرَابُ بِمَا فِيهِ

Narrated Al-Bara' bin 'Azib (ra): On the day of Hudaibiya, the Prophet ﷺ, the Prophet ﷺ made a peace treaty with the Al-Mushrikun on three conditions: 1) The Prophet ﷺ would return to them any person from Al-Mushrikun (polytheists, idolaters, pagans). 2) Al-Mushrikun pagans would not return any of the Muslims going to them, and 3) The Prophet ﷺ and his companions would come to Makkah the following year and would stay there for three days and would enter with their weapons in cases, e.g., swords, arrows, bows, etc. Abu Jandal came hopping, his legs being chained, but the Prophet ﷺ returned him to Al-Mushrikun. – Sahih Al-Bukhari 2700
وَقَالَ مُوسَى بْنُ مَسْعُودٍ حَدَّثَنَا سُفْيَانُ بْنُ سَعِيدٍ، عَنْ أَبِي إِسْحَاقَ، عَنِ الْبَرَاءِ بْنِ عَازِبٍ ـ رضى الله عنهما ـ قَالَ صَالَحَ النَّبِيُّ صلى الله عليه وسلم الْمُشْرِكِينَ يَوْمَ الْحُدَيْبِيَةِ عَلَى ثَلاَثَةِ أَشْيَاءَ عَلَى أَنَّ مَنْ أَتَاهُ مِنَ الْمُشْرِكِينَ رَدَّهُ إِلَيْهِمْ، وَمَنْ أَتَاهُمْ مِنَ الْمُسْلِمِينَ لَمْ يَرُدُّوهُ، وَعَلَى أَنْ يَدْخُلَهَا مِنْ قَابِلٍ وَيُقِيمَ بِهَا ثَلاَثَةَ أَيَّامٍ، وَلاَ يَدْخُلَهَا إِلاَّ بِجُلُبَّانِ السِّلاَحِ السَّيْفِ وَالْقَوْسِ وَنَحْوِهِ. فَجَاءَ أَبُو جَنْدَلٍ يَحْجُلُ فِي قُيُودِهِ فَرَدَّهُ إِلَيْهِمْ. قَالَ لَمْ يَذْكُرْ مُؤَمَّلٌ عَنْ سُفْيَانَ أَبَا جَنْدَلٍ وَقَالَ إِلاَّ بِجُلُبِ السِّلاَحِ.

Al-Fath Al-Mubin, Ridwan Pledge
الفتح المبين، بيعة الرضوان

Narrated Al-Bara: Do you (people) consider the conquest of Mecca, the Victory (referred to in the Qur'an 48:1). Was the conquest of Mecca a victory? We really consider that the actual Victory was the Ar-Ridwan Pledge of allegiance which we gave on the day of Al-Hudaibiya (to the Prophet) . On the day of Al-Hudaibiya we were fourteen hundred men along with the Prophet ﷺ Al-Hudaibiya was a well, the water of which we used up leaving not a single drop of water in it. When the Prophet ﷺ was informed of that, he came and sat on its edge. Then he asked for a utensil of water, performed ablution from it, rinsed (his mouth), invoked (Allah), and poured the remaining water into the well. We stayed there for a while and then the well brought forth what we required of water for ourselves and our riding animals. – Sahih Al-Bukhari 4150
حَدَّثَنَا عُبَيْدُ اللَّهِ بْنُ مُوسَى، عَنْ إِسْرَائِيلَ، عَنْ أَبِي إِسْحَاقَ، عَنِ الْبَرَاءِ ـ رضى الله عنه ـ قَالَ تَعُدُّونَ أَنْتُمُ الْفَتْحَ فَتْحَ مَكَّةَ، وَقَدْ كَانَ فَتْحُ مَكَّةَ فَتْحًا، وَنَحْنُ نَعُدُّ الْفَتْحَ بَيْعَةَ الرِّضْوَانِ يَوْمَ الْحُدَيْبِيَةِ. كُنَّا مَعَ النَّبِيِّ صلى الله عليه وسلم أَرْبَعَ عَشْرَةَ مِائَةً، وَالْحُدَيْبِيَةُ بِئْرٌ فَنَزَحْنَاهَا، فَلَمْ نَتْرُكْ فِيهَا قَطْرَةً، فَبَلَغَ ذَلِكَ النَّبِيَّ صلى الله عليه وسلم فَأَتَاهَا، فَجَلَسَ عَلَى شَفِيرِهَا، ثُمَّ دَعَا بِإِنَاءٍ مِنْ مَاءٍ فَتَوَضَّأَ ثُمَّ مَضْمَضَ وَدَعَا، ثُمَّ صَبَّهُ فِيهَا فَتَرَكْنَاهَا غَيْرَ بَعِيدٍ ثُمَّ إِنَّهَا أَصْدَرَتْنَا مَا شِئْنَا نَحْنُ وَرِكَابَنَا

Indeed, We have granted you a clear triumph ˹O Prophet˺ - Surah Al-Fath 48:1
إِنَّا فَتَحْنَا لَكَ فَتْحًا مُّبِينًا

Indeed, Allah was pleased with the believers when they pledged allegiance to you ˹O Prophet˺ under the tree. He knew what was in their hearts, so He sent down serenity upon them and rewarded them with a victory at hand, - Surah Al-Fath 48:18
لَّقَدْ رَضِىَ ٱللَّهُ عَنِ ٱلْمُؤْمِنِينَ إِذْ يُبَايِعُونَكَ تَحْتَ ٱلشَّجَرَةِ فَعَلِمَ مَا فِى قُلُوبِهِمْ فَأَنزَلَ ٱلسَّكِينَةَ عَلَيْهِمْ وَأَثَـٰبَهُمْ فَتْحًا قَرِيبًا

Narrated Jabir bin `Abdullah: On the day of Al-Hudaibiya, Allah's Messenger ﷺ said to us' "You are the best people on the earth!" We were 1400 then. If I could see now, I would have shown you the place of the Tree (beneath which we gave the Pledge of Allegiance)." Salim said, "Our number was 1400." - Sahih Al-Bukhari 4154

حَدَّثَنَا عَلِيٌّ، حَدَّثَنَا سُفْيَانُ، قَالَ عَمْرٌو سَمِعْتُ جَابِرَ بْنَ عَبْدِ اللَّهِ ـ رضى الله عنهما ـ قَالَ قَالَ لَنَا رَسُولُ اللَّهِ صلى الله عليه وسلم يَوْمَ الْحُدَيْبِيَةِ " أَنْتُمْ خَيْرُ أَهْلِ الأَرْضِ ". وَكُنَّا أَلْفًا وَأَرْبَعَمِائَةٍ، وَلَوْ كُنْتُ أُبْصِرُ الْيَوْمَ لأَرَيْتُكُمْ مَكَانَ الشَّجَرَةِ. تَابَعَهُ الأَعْمَشُ سَمِعَ سَالِمًا سَمِعَ جَابِرًا أَلْفًا وَأَرْبَعَمِائَةٍ

Narrated Al-Bara bin Azib: That they were in the company of Allah's Messenger ﷺ on the day of Al-Hudaibiya and their number was 1400 or more. They camped at a well and drew its water till it was dried. When they informed Allah's Apostle of that, he came and sat over its edge and said, "Bring me a bucket of its water." When it was brought, he spat and invoked (Allah) and said, "Leave it for a while." Then they quenched their thirst and watered their riding animals (from that well) till they departed. – Sahih Al-Bukhari 4151

حَدَّثَنِي فَضْلُ بْنُ يَعْقُوبَ، حَدَّثَنَا الْحَسَنُ بْنُ مُحَمَّدِ بْنِ أَعْيَنَ أَبُو عَلِيٍّ الْحَرَّانِيُّ، حَدَّثَنَا زُهَيْرٌ، حَدَّثَنَا أَبُو إِسْحَاقَ، قَالَ أَنْبَأَنَا الْبَرَاءُ بْنُ عَازِبٍ ـ رضى الله عنهما أَنَّهُمْ كَانُوا مَعَ رَسُولِ اللَّهِ صلى الله عليه وسلم يَوْمَ الْحُدَيْبِيَةِ أَلْفًا وَأَرْبَعَمِائَةٍ أَوْ أَكْثَرَ، فَنَزَلُوا عَلَى بِئْرٍ فَنَزَحُوهَا، فَأَتَوْا رَسُولَ اللَّهِ صلى الله عليه وسلم فَأَتَى الْبِئْرَ، وَقَعَدَ عَلَى شَفِيرِهَا ثُمَّ قَالَ " ائْتُونِي بِدَلْوٍ مِنْ مَائِهَا ". فَأُتِيَ بِهِ فَبَصَقَ فَدَعَا ثُمَّ قَالَ " دَعُوهَا سَاعَةً ". فَأَرْوَوْا أَنْفُسَهُمْ وَرِكَابَهُمْ حَتَّى ارْتَحَلُوا.

Narrated Yazid bin Ubaid: Salama said, "I gave the Pledge of allegiance (Al-Ridwan) to Allah's Messenger ﷺ and then I moved to the shade of a tree. When the number of people around the Prophet ﷺ diminished, he said, 'O Ibn Al-Akwa` ! Will you not give to me the pledge of Allegiance?' I replied, 'O Allah's Messenger ﷺ ! I have already given to you the pledge of Allegiance.' He said, 'Do it again.' So I gave the pledge of allegiance for the second time." I asked 'O Abu Muslim! For what did you give he pledge of Allegiance on that day?" He replied, "We gave the pledge of Allegiance for death.". – Sahih Al-Bukhari 2960

حَدَّثَنَا الْمَكِّيُّ بْنُ إِبْرَاهِيمَ، حَدَّثَنَا يَزِيدُ بْنُ أَبِي عُبَيْدٍ، عَنْ سَلَمَةَ ـ رضى الله عنه ـ قَالَ بَايَعْتُ النَّبِيَّ صلى الله عليه وسلم ثُمَّ عَدَلْتُ إِلَى ظِلِّ الشَّجَرَةِ، فَلَمَّا خَفَّ النَّاسُ قَالَ " يَا ابْنَ الأَكْوَعِ، أَلاَ تُبَايِعُ ". قَالَ قُلْتُ قَدْ بَايَعْتُ يَا رَسُولَ اللَّهِ. قَالَ " وَأَيْضًا فَبَايَعْتُهُ الثَّانِيَةَ. فَقُلْتُ لَهُ يَا أَبَا مُسْلِمٍ، عَلَى أَيِّ شَىْءٍ كُنْتُمْ تُبَايِعُونَ يَوْمَئِذٍ قَالَ عَلَى الْمَوْتِ

Narrated Sa`id bin Al-Musaiyab: That his father said, "I saw the Tree (of the Ar-Ridwan Pledge of allegiance and when I returned to it later, I was not able to recognize it. (The sub—narrator MahmiJd said, Al-Musaiyab said, 'Then; forgot it (i.e., the Tree).)" – Sahih Al-Bukhari 4162

حَدَّثَنِي مُحَمَّدُ بْنُ رَافِعٍ، حَدَّثَنَا شَبَابَةُ بْنُ سَوَّارٍ أَبُو عَمْرٍو الْفَزَارِيُّ، حَدَّثَنَا شُعْبَةُ، عَنْ قَتَادَةَ، عَنْ سَعِيدِ بْنِ الْمُسَيَّبِ، عَنْ أَبِيهِ، قَالَ لَقَدْ رَأَيْتُ الشَّجَرَةَ، ثُمَّ أَتَيْتُهَا بَعْدُ فَلَمْ أَعْرِفْهَا. قَالَ مَحْمُودٌ ثُمَّ أُنْسِيتُهَا بَعْدُ

Narrated Al-Miswar bin Makhrama and Marwan: (whose narrations attest each other) Allah's Messenger ﷺ set out at the time of Al-Hudaibiya (treaty), and when they proceeded for a distance, he said, "Khalid bin Al-Walid leading the cavalry of Quraish constituting the front of the army, is at a place called Al-Ghamim, so take the way on the right." By Allah, Khalid did not perceive the arrival of the Muslims till the dust arising from the march of the Muslim army reached him, and then he turned back hurriedly to inform Quraish. The Prophet ﷺ went on advancing till he reached the Thaniya (i.e. a mountainous way) through which one would go to them (i.e. people of Quraish). The she-camel of the Prophet ﷺ sat down. The people tried their best to cause the she-camel to get up but in vain, so they said, "Al-Qaswa' (i.e. the she-camel's name) has become stubborn! Al-Qaswa' has become stubborn!" The Prophet ﷺ said, "Al-Qaswa' has not become stubborn, for stubbornness is not her habit, but she was stopped by Him Who stopped the elephant." Then he said, "By the Name of Him in Whose

Hands my soul is, if they (i.e. the Quraish infidels) ask me anything which will respect the ordinances of Allah, I will grant it to them." The Prophet ﷺ then rebuked the she-camel and she got up. The Prophet ﷺ changed his way till he dismounted at the farthest end of Al-Hudaibiya at a pit (i.e. well) containing a little water which the people used in small amounts, and in a short while the people used up all its water and complained to Allah's Messenger ﷺ ; of thirst. The Prophet ﷺ took an arrow out of his arrow-case and ordered them to put the arrow in that pit. By Allah, the water started and continued sprouting out till all the people quenched their thirst and returned with satisfaction. While they were still in that state, Budail bin Warqa-al- Khuza`I came with some persons from his tribe Khuza`a and they were the advisers of Allah's Messenger ﷺ who would keep no secret from him and were from the people of Tihama. Budail said, "I left Ka`b bin Luai and 'Amir bin Luai residing at the profuse water of Al-Hudaibiya and they had milch camels (or their women and children) with them, and will wage war against you, and will prevent you from visiting the Ka`ba." Allah's Messenger ﷺ said, "We have not come to fight anyone, but to perform the `Umra. No doubt, the war has weakened Quraish and they have suffered great losses, so if they wish, I will conclude a truce with them, during which they should refrain from interfering between me and the people (i.e. the 'Arab infidels other than Quraish), and if I have victory over those infidels, Quraish will have the option to embrace Islam as the other people do, if they wish; they will at least get strong enough to fight. But if they do not accept the truce, by Allah in Whose Hands my life is, I will fight with them defending my Cause till I get killed, but (I am sure) Allah will definitely make His Cause victorious." Budail said, "I will inform them of what you have said." So, he set off till he reached Quraish and said, "We have come from that man (i.e. Muhammad) whom we heard saying something which we will disclose to you if you should like." Some of the fools among Quraish shouted that they were not in need of this information, but the wiser among them said, "Relate what you heard him saying." Budail said, "I heard him saying so-and-so," relating what the Prophet ﷺ had told him. `Urwa bin Mas`ud got up and said, "O people! Aren't you the sons? They said, "Yes." He added, "Am I not the father?" They said, "Yes." He said, "Do you mistrust me?" They said, "No." He said, "Don't you know that I invited the people of `Ukaz for your help, and when they refused I brought my relatives and children and those who obeyed me (to help you)?" They said, "Yes." He said, "Well, this man (i.e. the Prophet) has offered you a reasonable proposal, you'd better accept it and allow me to meet him." They said, "You may meet him." So, he went to the Prophet ﷺ and started talking to him. The Prophet ﷺ told him almost the same as he had told Budail. Then `Urwa said, "O Muhammad! Won't you feel any scruple in extirpating your relations? Have you ever heard of anyone amongst the Arabs extirpating his relatives before you? On the other hand, if the reverse should happen, (nobody will aid you, for) by Allah, I do not see (with you) dignified people, but people from various tribes who would run away leaving you alone." Hearing that, Abu Bakr abused him and said, "Do you say we would run and leave the Prophet ﷺ alone?" `Urwa said, "Who is that man?" They said, "He is Abu Bakr." `Urwa said to Abu Bakr, "By Him in Whose Hands my life is, were it not for the favor which you did to me and which I did not compensate, I would retort on you." `Urwa kept on talking to the Prophet ﷺ and seizing the Prophet's beard as he was talking while Al-Mughira bin Shu`ba was standing near the head of the Prophet, holding a sword and wearing a helmet. Whenever `Urwa stretched his hand towards the beard of the Prophet, Al-Mughira would hit his hand with the handle of the sword and say (to `Urwa), "Remove your hand from the beard of Allah's Messenger ﷺ` ".Urwa raised his head and asked, "Who is that?" The people said, "He is Al-Mughira bin Shu`ba." `Urwa said, "O treacherous! Am I not doing my best to prevent evil consequences of your treachery?" Before embracing Islam Al-Mughira was in the company of some people. He killed them and took their property and came (to Medina) to embrace Islam. The Prophet ﷺ said (to him, "As regards your Islam, I accept it, but as for the property I do not take anything of it. (As it was taken through treason). `Urwa then started looking at the Companions of the Prophet. By Allah, whenever Allah's Messenger ﷺ spat, the spittle would fall in the hand of one of them (i.e. the Prophet's companions) who would rub it on his face and skin; if he ordered them they would carry his orders immediately; if he performed ablution, they would struggle to take the remaining water; and when they spoke to him, they would lower their voices and would not look at his face constantly out of respect. `Urwa returned to his people and said, "O people! By Allah, I have been to the kings and to Caesar, Khosrau and An- Najashi, yet I have never seen any of them respected by his courtiers as much as Muhammad is respected by his companions. By Allah, if he spat, the spittle would fall in the hand of one of them (i.e. the Prophet's companions) who would rub it on his face and skin; if he ordered them, they would carry out his order immediately; if he performed ablution, they would struggle to take the remaining water; and when they spoke, they would lower their voices and would not look at his face constantly out of respect." `Urwa added, "No doubt, he has presented to you a good reasonable offer, so please accept it." A man from the tribe of Bani Kinana said, "Allow me to go to him," and they allowed him, and when he approached the Prophet and his companions, Allah's Messenger ﷺ said, "He is so-and-so who belongs to the tribe that respects the Budn (i.e. camels of the sacrifice). So, bring the Budn in front of him." So, the Budn were brought before him and the people received him while they were reciting Talbiya. When he saw that scene, he said, "Glorified be Allah! It is not fair to prevent these people from visiting the Ka`ba." When he returned to his people, he said, 'I saw the Budn garlanded (with colored knotted ropes) and marked (with stabs on their backs). I do not think it is advisable to prevent them from visiting the Ka`ba." Another person called Mikraz bin Hafs got up and sought their permission to go to Muhammad, and they allowed him, too. When he approached the Muslims, the Prophet ﷺ said, "Here is Mikraz and he is a vicious man." Mikraz started talking to the Prophet and as he was talking, Suhail bin `Amr came. When Suhail bin `Amr came, the Prophet ﷺ said, "Now the matter has become easy." Suhail said to the Prophet "Please conclude a peace treaty with us." So, the Prophet ﷺ called the clerk and said to him, "Write: By the Name of Allah, the most Beneficent, the most Merciful." Suhail said, "As for 'Beneficent,' by Allah, I do not know what it means. So write: By Your Name O Allah, as you used to write previously." The Muslims said, "By Allah, we will not write except: By the Name of Allah, the most Beneficent, the most Merciful." The Prophet ﷺ said, "Write: By Your Name O Allah." Then he dictated, "This is the peace treaty which Muhammad, Allah's Messenger ﷺ has concluded." Suhail said, "By Allah, if we knew that you are Allah's Messenger ﷺ we would not prevent you from visiting the Ka`ba, and would not fight with you. So, write: "Muhammad bin `Abdullah." The Prophet ﷺ said, "By Allah! I am Apostle of Allah even if you people do not believe me. Write: Muhammad bin `Abdullah." (Az-Zuhri said, "The Prophet ﷺ accepted all those things, as he had already said that he would accept everything they would demand if it respects the ordinance of Allah, (i.e. by letting him and his companions perform `Umra.)" The Prophet ﷺ said to Suhail, "On the condition that you allow us to visit the House (i.e. Ka`ba) so that we may perform Tawaf around it." Suhail said, "By Allah, we will not (allow you this year) so as not to give chance to the 'Arabs to say that we have yielded to you, but we will allow you next year." So, the Prophet ﷺ got that written. Then Suhail said, "We also stipulate that you should return to us whoever comes to you from us, even if he embraced your religion." The Muslims said,

"Glorified be Allah! How will such a person be returned to the pagans after he has become a Muslim? While they were in this state Abu- Jandal bin Suhail bin `Amr came from the valley of Mecca staggering with his fetters and fell down amongst the Muslims. Suhail said, "O Muhammad! This is the very first term with which we make peace with you, i.e. you shall return Abu Jandal to me." The Prophet said, "The peace treaty has not been written yet." Suhail said, "I will never allow you to keep him." The Prophet said, "Yes, do." He said, "I won't do.: Mikraz said, "We allow you (to keep him)." Abu Jandal said, "O Muslims! Will I be returned to the pagans though I have come as a Muslim? Don't you see how much I have suffered?" (continued...) (continuing... 1): -3.891:... ... Abu Jandal had been tortured severely for the Cause of Allah. `Umar bin Al-Khattab said, "I went to the Prophet and said, 'Aren't you truly the Messenger of Allah?' The Prophet said, 'Yes, indeed.' I said, 'Isn't our Cause just and the cause of the enemy unjust?' He said, 'Yes.' I said, 'Then why should we be humble in our religion?' He said, 'I am Allah's Messenger and I do not disobey Him, and He will make me victorious.' I said, 'Didn't you tell us that we would go to the Ka`ba and perform Tawaf around it?' He said, 'Yes, but did I tell you that we would visit the Ka`ba this year?' I said, 'No.' He said, 'So you will visit it and perform Tawaf around it?' " `Umar further said, "I went to Abu Bakr and said, 'O Abu Bakr! Isn't he truly Allah's Prophet?' He replied, 'Yes.' I said, 'Then why should we be humble in our religion?' He said, 'Indeed, he is Allah's Messenger and he does not disobey his Lord, and He will make him victorious. Adhere to him as, by Allah, he is on the right.' I said, 'Was he not telling us that we would go to the Ka`ba and perform Tawaf around it?' He said, 'Yes, but did he tell you that you would go to the Ka`ba this year?' I said, 'No.' He said, "You will go to Ka`ba and perform Tawaf around it." (Az-Zuhri said, " `Umar said, 'I performed many good deeds as expiation for the improper questions I asked them.' ") When the writing of the peace treaty was concluded, Allah's Messenger said to his companions, "Get up and' slaughter your sacrifices and get your head shaved." By Allah none of them got up, and the Prophet repeated his order thrice. When none of them got up, he left them and went to Um Salama and told her of the people's attitudes towards him. Um Salama said, "O the Prophet of Allah! Do you want your order to be carried out? Go out and don't say a word to anybody till you have slaughtered your sacrifice and call your barber to shave your head." So, the Prophet went out and did not talk to anyone of them till he did that, i.e. slaughtered the sacrifice and called his barber who shaved his head. Seeing that, the companions of the Prophet got up, slaughtered their sacrifices, and started shaving the heads of one another, and there was so much rush that there was a danger of killing each other. Then some believing women came (to the Prophet)"; and Allah revealed the following Divine Verses:-- "O you who believe, when the believing women come to you as emigrants examine them . . ." (60.10) `Umar then divorced two wives of his who were infidels. Later on Muawiya bin Abu Sufyan married one of them, and Safwan bin Umaiya married the other. When the Prophet returned to Medina, Abu Basir, a new Muslim convert from Quraish came to him. The Infidels sent in his pursuit two men who said (to the Prophet)", Abide by the promise you gave us." So, the Prophet handed him over to them. They took him out (of the City) till they reached Dhul-Hulaifa where they dismounted to eat some dates they had with them. Abu Basir said to one of them, "By Allah, O so-and-so, I see you have a fine sword." The other drew it out (of the scabbard) and said, "By Allah, it is very fine and I have tried it many times." Abu Basir said, "Let me have a look at it." When the other gave it to him, he hit him with it till he died, and his companion ran away till he came to Medina and entered the Mosque running. When Allah's Messenger saw him he said, "This man appears to have been frightened." When he reached the

Prophet ﷺ he said, "My companion has been murdered and I would have been murdered too." Abu Basir came and said, "O Allah's Messenger ﷺ ,by Allah, Allah has made you fulfill your obligations by your returning me to them (i.e. the Infidels), but Allah has saved me from them." The Prophet ﷺ said, "Woe to his mother! What excellent war kindler he would be, should he only have supporters." When Abu Basir heard that he understood that the Prophet ﷺ would return him to them again, so he set off till he reached the seashore. Abu Jandal bin Suhail got himself released from them (i.e. infidels) and joined Abu Basir. So, whenever a man from Quraish embraced Islam he would follow Abu Basir till they formed a strong group. By Allah, whenever they heard about a caravan of Quraish heading towards Sham, they stopped it and attacked and killed them (i.e. infidels) and took their properties. The people of Quraish sent a message to the Prophet ﷺ requesting him for the Sake of Allah and Kith and kin to send for (i.e. Abu Basir and his companions) promising that whoever (amongst them) came to the Prophet ﷺ would be secure. So the Prophet ﷺ sent for them (i.e. Abu Basir's companions) and Allah I revealed the following Divine Verses: "And it is He Who Has withheld their hands from you and your hands From them in the midst of Mecca, After He made you the victorious over them. ... the unbelievers had pride and haughtiness, in their hearts ... the pride and haughtiness of the time of ignorance." (48.24-26) And their pride and haughtiness was that they did not confess (write in the treaty) that he (i.e. Muhammad) was the Prophet of Allah and refused to write: "In the Name of Allah, the most Beneficent, the Most Merciful," and they (the mushriks) prevented them (the Muslims) from visiting the House (the Ka`bah). – Sahih Al-Bukhari 2731, 2732

حَدَّثَنِي عَبْدُ اللَّهِ بْنُ مُحَمَّدٍ، حَدَّثَنَا عَبْدُ الرَّزَّاقِ، أَخْبَرَنَا مَعْمَرٌ، قَالَ أَخْبَرَنِي الزُّهْرِيُّ، قَالَ أَخْبَرَنِي عُرْوَةُ بْنُ الزُّبَيْرِ، عَنِ الْمِسْوَرِ بْنِ مَخْرَمَةَ، وَمَرْوَانَ، يُصَدِّقُ كُلُّ وَاحِدٍ مِنْهُمَا حَدِيثَ صَاحِبِهِ قَالَ خَرَجَ رَسُولُ اللَّهِ صلى الله عليه وسلم زَمَنَ الْحُدَيْبِيَةِ، حَتَّى كَانُوا بِبَعْضِ الطَّرِيقِ قَالَ النَّبِيُّ صلى الله عليه وسلم " إِنَّ خَالِدَ بْنَ الْوَلِيدِ بِالْغَمِيمِ فِي خَيْلٍ لِقُرَيْشٍ طَلِيعَةً فَخُذُوا ذَاتَ الْيَمِينِ ". فَوَاللَّهِ مَا شَعَرَ بِهِمْ خَالِدٌ حَتَّى إِذَا هُمْ بِقَتَرَةِ الْجَيْشِ، فَانْطَلَقَ يَرْكُضُ نَذِيرًا لِقُرَيْشٍ، وَسَارَ النَّبِيُّ صلى الله عليه وسلم حَتَّى إِذَا كَانَ بِالثَّنِيَّةِ الَّتِي يُهْبَطُ عَلَيْهِمْ مِنْهَا، بَرَكَتْ بِهِ رَاحِلَتُهُ. فَقَالَ النَّاسُ حَلْ حَلْ. فَأَلَحَّتْ، فَقَالُوا خَلأَتِ الْقَصْوَاءُ، خَلأَتِ الْقَصْوَاءُ. فَقَالَ النَّبِيُّ صلى الله عليه وسلم " مَا خَلأَتِ الْقَصْوَاءُ، وَمَا ذَاكَ لَهَا بِخُلُقٍ، وَلَكِنْ حَبَسَهَا حَابِسُ الْفِيلِ، ثُمَّ قَالَ وَالَّذِي نَفْسِي بِيَدِهِ لاَ يَسْأَلُونِي خُطَّةً يُعَظِّمُونَ فِيهَا حُرُمَاتِ اللَّهِ إِلاَّ أَعْطَيْتُهُمْ إِيَّاهَا ". ثُمَّ زَجَرَهَا فَوَثَبَتْ، قَالَ فَعَدَلَ عَنْهُمْ حَتَّى نَزَلَ بِأَقْصَى الْحُدَيْبِيَةِ، عَلَى ثَمَدٍ قَلِيلِ الْمَاءِ يَتَبَرَّضُهُ النَّاسُ تَبَرُّضًا، فَلَمْ يُلَبِّثْهُ النَّاسُ حَتَّى نَزَحُوهُ، وَشُكِيَ إِلَى رَسُولِ اللَّهِ صلى الله عليه وسلم الْعَطَشُ، فَانْتَزَعَ سَهْمًا مِنْ كِنَانَتِهِ، ثُمَّ أَمَرَهُمْ أَنْ يَجْعَلُوهُ فِيهِ، فَوَاللَّهِ مَا زَالَ يَجِيشُ لَهُمْ بِالرِّيِّ حَتَّى صَدَرُوا عَنْهُ، فَبَيْنَمَا هُمْ كَذَلِكَ، إِذْ جَاءَ بُدَيْلُ بْنُ وَرْقَاءَ الْخُزَاعِيُّ فِي نَفَرٍ مِنْ قَوْمِهِ مِنْ خُزَاعَةَ، وَكَانُوا عَيْبَةَ نُصْحِ رَسُولِ اللَّهِ صلى الله عليه وسلم مِنْ أَهْلِ تِهَامَةَ، فَقَالَ إِنِّي تَرَكْتُ كَعْبَ بْنَ لُؤَيٍّ وَعَامِرَ بْنَ لُؤَيٍّ نَزَلُوا أَعْدَادَ مِيَاهِ الْحُدَيْبِيَةِ، وَمَعَهُمُ الْعُوذُ الْمَطَافِيلُ، وَهُمْ مُقَاتِلُوكَ وَصَادُّوكَ عَنِ الْبَيْتِ. فَقَالَ رَسُولُ اللَّهِ صلى الله عليه وسلم " إِنَّا لَمْ نَجِئْ لِقِتَالِ أَحَدٍ، وَلَكِنَّا جِئْنَا مُعْتَمِرِينَ، وَإِنَّ قُرَيْشًا قَدْ نَهِكَتْهُمُ الْحَرْبُ، وَأَضَرَّتْ بِهِمْ، فَإِنْ شَاءُوا مَادَدْتُهُمْ مُدَّةً، وَيُخَلُّوا بَيْنِي وَبَيْنَ النَّاسِ، فَإِنْ أَظْهَرْ فَإِنْ شَاءُوا أَنْ يَدْخُلُوا فِيمَا دَخَلَ فِيهِ النَّاسُ فَعَلُوا، وَإِلاَّ فَقَدْ جَمُّوا، وَإِنْ هُمْ أَبَوْا فَوَالَّذِي نَفْسِي بِيَدِهِ، لأُقَاتِلَنَّهُمْ عَلَى أَمْرِي هَذَا حَتَّى تَنْفَرِدَ سَالِفَتِي، وَلَيُنْفِذَنَّ اللَّهُ أَمْرَهُ ". فَقَالَ بُدَيْلٌ سَأُبَلِّغُهُمْ مَا تَقُولُ. قَالَ فَانْطَلَقَ حَتَّى أَتَى قُرَيْشًا قَالَ إِنَّا قَدْ جِئْنَاكُمْ مِنْ هَذَا الرَّجُلِ، وَسَمِعْنَاهُ يَقُولُ قَوْلاً، فَإِنْ شِئْتُمْ أَنْ نَعْرِضَهُ عَلَيْكُمْ فَعَلْنَا، فَقَالَ سُفَهَاؤُهُمْ لاَ حَاجَةَ لَنَا أَنْ تُخْبِرَنَا عَنْهُ بِشَىْءٍ. وَقَالَ ذَوُو الرَّأْىِ مِنْهُمْ هَاتِ مَا سَمِعْتَهُ يَقُولُ. قَالَ سَمِعْتُهُ يَقُولُ كَذَا وَكَذَا، فَحَدَّثَهُمْ بِمَا قَالَ النَّبِيُّ صلى الله عليه وسلم. فَقَامَ عُرْوَةُ بْنُ مَسْعُودٍ فَقَالَ أَىْ قَوْمِ أَلَسْتُمْ بِالْوَالِدِ قَالُوا بَلَى. قَالَ أَوَلَسْتُ بِالْوَلَدِ قَالُوا بَلَى. قَالَ فَهَلْ تَتَّهِمُونِي. قَالُوا لاَ. قَالَ أَلَسْتُمْ تَعْلَمُونَ أَنِّي اسْتَنْفَرْتُ أَهْلَ عُكَاظٍ، فَلَمَّا بَلَّحُوا عَلَىَّ جِئْتُكُمْ بِأَهْلِي وَوَلَدِي وَمَنْ أَطَاعَنِي قَالُوا بَلَى. قَالَ فَإِنَّ هَذَا قَدْ عَرَضَ لَكُمْ خُطَّةَ رُشْدٍ، اقْبَلُوهَا وَدَعُونِي آتِهِ. قَالُوا ائْتِهِ. فَأَتَاهُ فَجَعَلَ يُكَلِّمُ النَّبِيَّ صلى الله عليه وسلم فَقَالَ النَّبِيُّ صلى الله عليه وسلم نَحْوًا مِنْ قَوْلِهِ لِبُدَيْلٍ، فَقَالَ عُرْوَةُ عِنْدَ ذَلِكَ أَىْ مُحَمَّدُ، أَرَأَيْتَ إِنِ اسْتَأْصَلْتَ أَمْرَ قَوْمِكَ هَلْ سَمِعْتَ بِأَحَدٍ مِنَ الْعَرَبِ اجْتَاحَ أَهْلَهُ قَبْلَكَ وَإِنْ تَكُنِ الأُخْرَى، فَإِنِّي وَاللَّهِ لأَرَى وُجُوهًا، وَإِنِّي لأَرَى أَوْشَابًا مِنَ النَّاسِ خَلِيقًا أَنْ يَفِرُّوا وَيَدَعُوكَ. فَقَالَ لَهُ أَبُو بَكْرٍ امْصُصْ بَظْرَ اللاَّتِ، أَنَحْنُ نَفِرُّ عَنْهُ وَنَدَعُهُ فَقَالَ مَنْ ذَا قَالُوا أَبُو بَكْرٍ. قَالَ أَمَا وَالَّذِي نَفْسِي بِيَدِهِ لَوْلاَ يَدٌ كَانَتْ لَكَ عِنْدِي لَمْ أَجْزِكَ بِهَا لأَجَبْتُكَ. قَالَ وَجَعَلَ يُكَلِّمُ النَّبِيَّ صلى الله عليه وسلم فَكُلَّمَا تَكَلَّمَ أَخَذَ بِلِحْيَتِهِ، وَالْمُغِيرَةُ بْنُ شُعْبَةَ قَائِمٌ عَلَى رَأْسِ النَّبِيِّ صلى الله عليه وسلم وَمَعَهُ السَّيْفُ وَعَلَيْهِ الْمِغْفَرُ، فَكُلَّمَا أَهْوَى عُرْوَةُ بِيَدِهِ إِلَى لِحْيَةِ النَّبِيِّ صلى الله عليه وسلم ضَرَبَ يَدَهُ بِنَعْلِ السَّيْفِ، وَقَالَ لَهُ أَخِّرْ يَدَكَ عَنْ لِحْيَةِ رَسُولِ اللَّهِ صلى الله عليه وسلم.
فَرَفَعَ عُرْوَةُ رَأْسَهُ فَقَالَ مَنْ هَذَا قَالُوا الْمُغِيرَةُ بْنُ شُعْبَةَ. فَقَالَ أَىْ غُدَرُ، أَلَسْتُ أَسْعَى فِي غَدْرَتِكَ وَكَانَ الْمُغِيرَةُ صَحِبَ قَوْمًا فِي الْجَاهِلِيَّةِ، فَقَتَلَهُمْ، وَأَخَذَ أَمْوَالَهُمْ، ثُمَّ جَاءَ فَأَسْلَمَ فَقَالَ النَّبِيُّ صلى الله عليه وسلم " أَمَّا الإِسْلاَمَ فَأَقْبَلُ، وَأَمَّا الْمَالَ فَلَسْتُ

مِنْهُ فِي شَيْءٍ ". ثُمَّ إِنَّ عُرْوَةَ جَعَلَ يَرْمُقُ أَصْحَابَ النَّبِيِّ صلى الله عليه وسلم بِعَيْنَيْهِ. قَالَ فَوَاللَّهِ مَا تَنَخَّمَ رَسُولُ اللَّهِ صلى الله عليه وسلم نُخَامَةً إِلاَّ وَقَعَتْ فِي كَفِّ رَجُلٍ مِنْهُمْ فَدَلَكَ بِهَا وَجْهَهُ وَجِلْدَهُ، وَإِذَا أَمَرَهُمُ ابْتَدَرُوا أَمْرَهُ، وَإِذَا تَوَضَّأَ كَادُوا يَقْتَتِلُونَ عَلَى وَضُوئِهِ، وَإِذَا تَكَلَّمَ خَفَضُوا أَصْوَاتَهُمْ عِنْدَهُ، وَمَا يُحِدُّونَ إِلَيْهِ النَّظَرَ تَعْظِيمًا لَهُ، فَرَجَعَ عُرْوَةُ إِلَى أَصْحَابِهِ، فَقَالَ أَىْ قَوْمِ، وَاللَّهِ لَقَدْ وَفَدْتُ عَلَى الْمُلُوكِ، وَوَفَدْتُ عَلَى قَيْصَرَ وَكِسْرَى وَالنَّجَاشِيِّ وَاللَّهِ إِنْ رَأَيْتُ مَلِكًا قَطُّ، يُعَظِّمُهُ أَصْحَابُهُ مَا يُعَظِّمُ أَصْحَابُ مُحَمَّدٍ صلى الله عليه وسلم مُحَمَّدًا، وَاللَّهِ إِنْ تَنَخَّمَ نُخَامَةً إِلاَّ وَقَعَتْ فِي كَفِّ رَجُلٍ مِنْهُمْ، فَدَلَكَ بِهَا وَجْهَهُ وَجِلْدَهُ، وَإِذَا أَمَرَهُمُ ابْتَدَرُوا أَمْرَهُ وَإِذَا تَوَضَّأَ كَادُوا يَقْتَتِلُونَ عَلَى وَضُوئِهِ، وَإِذَا تَكَلَّمَ خَفَضُوا أَصْوَاتَهُمْ عِنْدَهُ، وَمَا يُحِدُّونَ إِلَيْهِ النَّظَرَ تَعْظِيمًا لَهُ، وَإِنَّهُ قَدْ عَرَضَ عَلَيْكُمْ خُطَّةَ رُشْدٍ، فَاقْبَلُوهَا. فَقَالَ رَجُلٌ مِنْ بَنِي كِنَانَةَ دَعُونِي آتِيهِ. فَقَالُوا ائْتِهِ. فَلَمَّا أَشْرَفَ عَلَى النَّبِيِّ صلى الله عليه وسلم وَأَصْحَابِهِ، قَالَ رَسُولُ اللَّهِ صلى الله عليه وسلم " هَذَا فُلاَنٌ، وَهْوَ مِنْ قَوْمٍ يُعَظِّمُونَ الْبُدْنَ فَابْعَثُوهَا لَهُ ". فَبُعِثَتْ لَهُ وَاسْتَقْبَلَهُ النَّاسُ يُلَبُّونَ، فَلَمَّا رَأَى ذَلِكَ قَالَ سُبْحَانَ اللَّهِ مَا يَنْبَغِي لِهَؤُلاَءِ أَنْ يُصَدُّوا عَنِ الْبَيْتِ، فَلَمَّا رَجَعَ إِلَى أَصْحَابِهِ قَالَ رَأَيْتُ الْبُدْنَ قَدْ قُلِّدَتْ وَأُشْعِرَتْ، فَمَا أَرَى أَنْ يُصَدُّوا عَنِ الْبَيْتِ. فَقَامَ رَجُلٌ مِنْهُمْ يُقَالُ لَهُ مِكْرَزُ بْنُ حَفْصٍ. فَقَالَ دَعُونِي آتِيهِ. فَقَالُوا ائْتِهِ. فَلَمَّا أَشْرَفَ عَلَيْهِمْ قَالَ النَّبِيُّ صلى الله عليه وسلم " هَذَا مِكْرَزٌ وَهْوَ رَجُلٌ فَاجِرٌ ". فَجَعَلَ يُكَلِّمُ النَّبِيَّ صلى الله عليه وسلم، فَبَيْنَمَا هُوَ يُكَلِّمُهُ إِذْ جَاءَ سُهَيْلُ بْنُ عَمْرٍو. قَالَ مَعْمَرٌ فَأَخْبَرَنِي أَيُّوبُ عَنْ عِكْرِمَةَ، أَنَّهُ لَمَّا جَاءَ سُهَيْلُ بْنُ عَمْرٍو قَالَ النَّبِيُّ صلى الله عليه وسلم " لَقَدْ سَهُلَ لَكُمْ مِنْ أَمْرِكُمْ ". قَالَ مَعْمَرٌ قَالَ الزُّهْرِيُّ فِي حَدِيثِهِ فَجَاءَ سُهَيْلُ بْنُ عَمْرٍو فَقَالَ هَاتِ، اكْتُبْ بَيْنَنَا وَبَيْنَكُمْ كِتَابًا، فَدَعَا النَّبِيُّ صلى الله عليه وسلم الْكَاتِبَ، فَقَالَ النَّبِيُّ صلى الله عليه وسلم " بِسْمِ اللَّهِ الرَّحْمَنِ الرَّحِيمِ ". قَالَ سُهَيْلٌ أَمَّا الرَّحْمَنُ فَوَاللَّهِ مَا أَدْرِي مَا هُوَ وَلَكِنِ اكْتُبْ بِاسْمِكَ اللَّهُمَّ. كَمَا كُنْتَ تَكْتُبُ. فَقَالَ الْمُسْلِمُونَ وَاللَّهِ لاَ نَكْتُبُهَا إِلاَّ بِسْمِ اللَّهِ الرَّحْمَنِ الرَّحِيمِ. فَقَالَ النَّبِيُّ صلى الله عليه وسلم " اكْتُبْ بِاسْمِكَ اللَّهُمَّ ". ثُمَّ قَالَ " هَذَا مَا قَاضَى عَلَيْهِ مُحَمَّدٌ رَسُولُ اللَّهِ ". فَقَالَ سُهَيْلٌ وَاللَّهِ لَوْ كُنَّا نَعْلَمُ أَنَّكَ رَسُولُ اللَّهِ مَا صَدَدْنَاكَ عَنِ الْبَيْتِ وَلاَ قَاتَلْنَاكَ، وَلَكِنِ اكْتُبْ مُحَمَّدُ بْنُ عَبْدِ اللَّهِ. فَقَالَ النَّبِيُّ صلى الله عليه وسلم " وَاللَّهِ إِنِّي لَرَسُولُ اللَّهِ وَإِنْ كَذَّبْتُمُونِي. اكْتُبْ مُحَمَّدُ بْنُ عَبْدِ اللَّهِ ". قَالَ الزُّهْرِيُّ وَذَلِكَ لِقَوْلِهِ " لاَ يَسْأَلُونِي خُطَّةً يُعَظِّمُونَ فِيهَا حُرُمَاتِ اللَّهِ إِلاَّ أَعْطَيْتُهُمْ إِيَّاهَا ". فَقَالَ لَهُ النَّبِيُّ صلى الله عليه وسلم " عَلَى أَنْ تُخَلُّوا بَيْنَنَا وَبَيْنَ الْبَيْتِ فَنَطُوفَ بِهِ ". فَقَالَ سُهَيْلٌ وَاللَّهِ لاَ تَتَحَدَّثُ الْعَرَبُ أَنَّا أُخِذْنَا ضُغْطَةً وَلَكِنْ ذَلِكَ مِنَ الْعَامِ الْمُقْبِلِ فَكَتَبَ. فَقَالَ سُهَيْلٌ وَعَلَى أَنَّهُ لاَ يَأْتِيكَ مِنَّا رَجُلٌ، وَإِنْ كَانَ عَلَى دِينِكَ، إِلاَّ رَدَدْتَهُ إِلَيْنَا. قَالَ الْمُسْلِمُونَ سُبْحَانَ اللَّهِ كَيْفَ يُرَدُّ إِلَى الْمُشْرِكِينَ وَقَدْ جَاءَ مُسْلِمًا فَبَيْنَمَا هُمْ كَذَلِكَ إِذْ دَخَلَ أَبُو جَنْدَلِ بْنُ سُهَيْلِ بْنِ عَمْرٍو يَرْسُفُ فِي قُيُودِهِ، وَقَدْ خَرَجَ مِنْ أَسْفَلِ مَكَّةَ، حَتَّى رَمَى بِنَفْسِهِ بَيْنَ أَظْهُرِ الْمُسْلِمِينَ. فَقَالَ سُهَيْلٌ هَذَا يَا مُحَمَّدُ أَوَّلُ مَا أُقَاضِيكَ عَلَيْهِ أَنْ تَرُدَّهُ إِلَيَّ. فَقَالَ النَّبِيُّ صلى الله عليه وسلم " إِنَّا لَمْ نَقْضِ الْكِتَابَ بَعْدُ ". قَالَ فَوَاللَّهِ إِذًا لَمْ أُصَالِحْكَ عَلَى شَىْءٍ أَبَدًا. قَالَ النَّبِيُّ صلى الله عليه وسلم " فَأَجِزْهُ لِي ". قَالَ مَا أَنَا بِمُجِيزِهِ لَكَ. قَالَ " بَلَى، فَافْعَلْ ". قَالَ مَا أَنَا بِفَاعِلٍ. قَالَ مِكْرَزٌ بَلْ قَدْ أَجَزْنَاهُ لَكَ. قَالَ أَبُو جَنْدَلٍ أَىْ مَعْشَرَ الْمُسْلِمِينَ، أُرَدُّ إِلَى الْمُشْرِكِينَ وَقَدْ جِئْتُ مُسْلِمًا أَلاَ تَرَوْنَ مَا قَدْ لَقِيتُ وَكَانَ قَدْ عُذِّبَ عَذَابًا شَدِيدًا فِي اللَّهِ. قَالَ فَقَالَ عُمَرُ بْنُ الْخَطَّابِ فَأَتَيْتُ نَبِيَّ اللَّهِ صلى الله عليه وسلم فَقُلْتُ أَلَسْتَ نَبِيَّ اللَّهِ حَقًّا قَالَ " بَلَى ". قُلْتُ أَلَسْنَا عَلَى الْحَقِّ وَعَدُوُّنَا عَلَى الْبَاطِلِ قَالَ " بَلَى ". قُلْتُ فَلِمَ نُعْطِي الدَّنِيَّةَ فِي دِينِنَا إِذًا قَالَ " إِنِّي رَسُولُ اللَّهِ، وَلَسْتُ أَعْصِيهِ وَهْوَ نَاصِرِي ". قُلْتُ أَوَلَيْسَ كُنْتَ تُحَدِّثُنَا أَنَّا سَنَأْتِي الْبَيْتَ فَنَطُوفُ بِهِ قَالَ " بَلَى، فَأَخْبَرْتُكَ أَنَّا نَأْتِيهِ الْعَامَ ". قَالَ قُلْتُ لاَ. قَالَ " فَإِنَّكَ آتِيهِ وَمُطَّوِّفٌ بِهِ ". قَالَ فَأَتَيْتُ أَبَا بَكْرٍ فَقُلْتُ يَا أَبَا بَكْرٍ، أَلَيْسَ هَذَا نَبِيَّ اللَّهِ حَقًّا قَالَ بَلَى. قُلْتُ أَلَسْنَا عَلَى الْحَقِّ وَعَدُوُّنَا عَلَى الْبَاطِلِ قَالَ بَلَى. قُلْتُ فَلِمَ نُعْطِي الدَّنِيَّةَ فِي دِينِنَا إِذًا قَالَ أَيُّهَا الرَّجُلُ، إِنَّهُ لَرَسُولُ اللَّهِ صلى الله عليه وسلم وَلَيْسَ يَعْصِي رَبَّهُ وَهْوَ نَاصِرُهُ، فَاسْتَمْسِكْ بِغَرْزِهِ، فَوَاللَّهِ إِنَّهُ عَلَى الْحَقِّ. قُلْتُ أَلَيْسَ كَانَ يُحَدِّثُنَا أَنَّا سَنَأْتِي الْبَيْتَ وَنَطُوفُ بِهِ قَالَ بَلَى، أَفَأَخْبَرَكَ أَنَّكَ تَأْتِيهِ الْعَامَ قُلْتُ لاَ. قَالَ فَإِنَّكَ آتِيهِ وَمُطَّوِّفٌ بِهِ. قَالَ الزُّهْرِيِّ قَالَ عُمَرُ فَعَمِلْتُ لِذَلِكَ أَعْمَالاً. قَالَ فَلَمَّا فَرَغَ مِنْ قَضِيَّةِ الْكِتَابِ قَالَ رَسُولُ اللَّهِ صلى الله عليه وسلم لأَصْحَابِهِ " قُومُوا فَانْحَرُوا، ثُمَّ احْلِقُوا ". قَالَ فَوَاللَّهِ مَا قَامَ مِنْهُمْ رَجُلٌ حَتَّى قَالَ ذَلِكَ ثَلاَثَ مَرَّاتٍ، فَلَمَّا لَمْ يَقُمْ مِنْهُمْ أَحَدٌ دَخَلَ عَلَى أُمِّ سَلَمَةَ، فَذَكَرَ لَهَا مَا لَقِيَ مِنَ النَّاسِ. فَقَالَتْ أُمُّ سَلَمَةَ يَا نَبِيَّ اللَّهِ، أَتُحِبُّ ذَلِكَ اخْرُجْ ثُمَّ لاَ تُكَلِّمْ أَحَدًا مِنْهُمْ كَلِمَةً حَتَّى تَنْحَرَ بُدْنَكَ، وَتَدْعُوَ حَالِقَكَ فَيَحْلِقَكَ. فَخَرَجَ فَلَمْ يُكَلِّمْ أَحَدًا مِنْهُمْ، حَتَّى فَعَلَ ذَلِكَ نَحَرَ بُدْنَهُ، وَدَعَا حَالِقَهُ فَحَلَقَهُ. فَلَمَّا رَأَوْا ذَلِكَ، قَامُوا فَنَحَرُوا، وَجَعَلَ بَعْضُهُمْ يَحْلِقُ بَعْضًا، حَتَّى كَادَ بَعْضُهُمْ يَقْتُلُ بَعْضًا غَمًّا، ثُمَّ جَاءَهُ نِسْوَةٌ مُؤْمِنَاتٌ فَأَنْزَلَ اللَّهُ تَعَالَى {يَا أَيُّهَا الَّذِينَ آمَنُوا إِذَا جَاءَكُمُ الْمُؤْمِنَاتُ مُهَاجِرَاتٍ فَامْتَحِنُوهُنَّ} حَتَّى بَلَغَ {بِعِصَمِ الْكَوَافِرِ} فَطَلَّقَ عُمَرُ يَوْمَئِذٍ امْرَأَتَيْنِ كَانَتَا لَهُ فِي الشِّرْكِ، فَتَزَوَّجَ إِحْدَاهُمَا مُعَاوِيَةُ بْنُ أَبِي سُفْيَانَ، وَالأُخْرَى صَفْوَانُ بْنُ أُمَيَّةَ، ثُمَّ رَجَعَ النَّبِيُّ صلى الله عليه وسلم إِلَى الْمَدِينَةِ، فَجَاءَهُ أَبُو بَصِيرٍ ـ رَجُلٌ مِنْ قُرَيْشٍ ـ وَهْوَ مُسْلِمٌ فَأَرْسَلُوا فِي طَلَبِهِ رَجُلَيْنِ، فَقَالُوا الْعَهْدَ الَّذِي جَعَلْتَ لَنَا. فَدَفَعَهُ إِلَى الرَّجُلَيْنِ، فَخَرَجَا بِهِ حَتَّى بَلَغَا ذَا الْحُلَيْفَةِ، فَنَزَلُوا يَأْكُلُونَ مِنْ تَمْرٍ لَهُمْ، فَقَالَ أَبُو بَصِيرٍ لأَحَدِ الرَّجُلَيْنِ وَاللَّهِ إِنِّي لأَرَى سَيْفَكَ هَذَا يَا فُلاَنُ جَيِّدًا. فَاسْتَلَّهُ الآخَرُ فَقَالَ أَجَلْ، وَاللَّهِ إِنَّهُ لَجَيِّدٌ، لَقَدْ جَرَّبْتُ بِهِ ثُمَّ جَرَّبْتُ. فَقَالَ أَبُو بَصِيرٍ أَرِنِي أَنْظُرْ إِلَيْهِ، فَأَمْكَنَهُ مِنْهُ، فَضَرَبَهُ حَتَّى بَرَدَ، وَفَرَّ الآخَرُ حَتَّى أَتَى الْمَدِينَةَ، فَدَخَلَ الْمَسْجِدَ يَعْدُو. فَقَالَ رَسُولُ اللَّهِ صلى الله عليه وسلم حِينَ رَآهُ " لَقَدْ رَأَى هَذَا ذُعْرًا ". فَلَمَّا انْتَهَى إِلَى النَّبِيِّ صلى الله عليه وسلم قَالَ قُتِلَ وَاللَّهِ صَاحِبِي وَإِنِّي لَمَقْتُولٌ، فَجَاءَ أَبُو بَصِيرٍ فَقَالَ يَا نَبِيَّ اللَّهِ، قَدْ وَاللَّهِ أَوْفَى اللَّهُ ذِمَّتَكَ، قَدْ رَدَدْتَنِي إِلَيْهِمْ ثُمَّ أَنْجَانِي اللَّهُ مِنْهُمْ. قَالَ النَّبِيُّ صلى الله عليه وسلم " وَيْلُ أُمِّهِ مِسْعَرَ حَرْبٍ، لَوْ كَانَ لَهُ أَحَدٌ ". فَلَمَّا سَمِعَ ذَلِكَ عَرَفَ أَنَّهُ سَيَرُدُّهُ إِلَيْهِمْ، فَخَرَجَ حَتَّى أَتَى سِيفَ الْبَحْرِ. قَالَ وَيَنْفَلِتُ مِنْهُمْ أَبُو جَنْدَلِ بْنُ سُهَيْلٍ، فَلَحِقَ بِأَبِي بَصِيرٍ، فَجَعَلَ لاَ يَخْرُجُ مِنْ قُرَيْشٍ رَجُلٌ قَدْ أَسْلَمَ إِلاَّ لَحِقَ بِأَبِي بَصِيرٍ، حَتَّى اجْتَمَعَتْ مِنْهُمْ عِصَابَةٌ، فَوَاللَّهِ مَا يَسْمَعُونَ بِعِيرٍ خَرَجَتْ لِقُرَيْشٍ إِلَى الشَّأْمِ إِلاَّ اعْتَرَضُوا لَهَا، فَقَتَلُوهُمْ، وَأَخَذُوا أَمْوَالَهُمْ، فَأَرْسَلَتْ قُرَيْشٌ إِلَى النَّبِيِّ صلى الله عليه وسلم تُنَاشِدُهُ بِاللَّهِ وَالرَّحِمِ لَمَّا أَرْسَلَ، فَمَنْ أَتَاهُ فَهْوَ آمِنٌ، فَأَرْسَلَ النَّبِيُّ صلى الله عليه وسلم إِلَيْهِمْ،

فَأَنْزَلَ اللَّهُ تَعَالَى {وَهُوَ الَّذِي كَفَّ أَيْدِيَهُمْ عَنْكُمْ وَأَيْدِيَكُمْ عَنْهُمْ بِبَطْنِ مَكَّةَ مِنْ بَعْدِ أَنْ أَظْفَرَكُمْ عَلَيْهِمْ} حَتَّى بَلَغَ {الْحَمِيَّةَ حَمِيَّةَ الْجَاهِلِيَّةِ} وَكَانَتْ حَمِيَّتُهُمْ أَنَّهُمْ لَمْ يُقِرُّوا أَنَّهُ نَبِيُّ اللَّهِ، وَلَمْ يُقِرُّوا بِبِسْمِ اللَّهِ الرَّحْمَنِ الرَّحِيمِ، وَحَالُوا بَيْنَهُمْ وَبَيْنَ الْبَيْتِ

Umra a Year after Hudaybia
العمرة سنة بعد الحديبية

And He is (The One) Who restrained their hands from you, and your hands from them, in the hollow (Literally: the belly, i.e., the midst of makkah) of Makkah, even after He had made you to win over them; and Allah has been Ever-Beholding whatever you do They are (the ones) who disbelieved and barred you from the Inviolable Mosque and (barred) the consecrated offering (also) from reaching its lawful destination. And had it not been for (some) believing men and (some) believing women whom you did not know, (for fear) that you should trample (i.e., kill them) them, and so dishonor would afflict you on their account without (your) knowing it, that Allah may cause whomever He decides to enter into His mercy. If they (i.e., believers and disbelivers) had been made clearly distinct, indeed We would have tormented the ones who disbelieved among them with a painful torment – Surah Al-Fath 48:24&25
وَهُوَ ٱلَّذِى كَفَّ أَيْدِيَهُمْ عَنكُمْ وَأَيْدِيَكُمْ عَنْهُم بِبَطْنِ مَكَّةَ مِنۢ بَعْدِ أَنْ أَظْفَرَكُمْ عَلَيْهِمْۚ وَكَانَ ٱللَّهُ بِمَا تَعْمَلُونَ بَصِيرًا هُمُ ٱلَّذِينَ كَفَرُوا۟ وَصَدُّوكُمْ عَنِ ٱلْمَسْجِدِ ٱلْحَرَامِ وَٱلْهَدْىَ مَعْكُوفًا أَن يَبْلُغَ مَحِلَّهُۥۚ وَلَوْلَا رِجَالٌ مُّؤْمِنُونَ وَنِسَآءٌ مُّؤْمِنَٰتٌ لَّمْ تَعْلَمُوهُمْ أَن تَطَـُٔوهُمْ فَتُصِيبَكُم مِّنْهُم مَّعَرَّةٌۢ بِغَيْرِ عِلْمٍۖ لِّيُدْخِلَ ٱللَّهُ فِى رَحْمَتِهِۦ مَن يَشَآءُۚ لَوْ تَزَيَّلُوا۟ لَعَذَّبْنَا ٱلَّذِينَ كَفَرُوا۟ مِنْهُمْ عَذَابًا أَلِيمًا

Narrated Tariq bin `Abdur-Rahman: When I set out for Hajj, I passed by some people offering a prayer, I asked, "What is this mosque?" They said, "This is the Tree where Allah's Messenger ﷺ took the Ar-Ridwan Pledge of allegiance. Then I went to Sa`id bin Musaiyab and informed him about it. Sa`id said, "My father said that he was amongst those who had given the Pledge of allegiance to Allah's Messenger ﷺ beneath the Tree. He (i.e. my father) said, "When we set out the following year, we forgot the Tree and were unable to recognize it. "Then Sa`id said (perhaps ironically) "The companions of the Prophet ﷺ could not recognize it; nevertheless, you do recognize it; therefore you have a better knowledge." – Sahih Al-Bukhari 4163
حَدَّثَنَا مَحْمُودٌ، حَدَّثَنَا عُبَيْدُ اللَّهِ، عَنْ إِسْرَائِيلَ، عَنْ طَارِقِ بْنِ عَبْدِ الرَّحْمَنِ، قَالَ انْطَلَقْتُ حَاجًّا فَمَرَرْتُ بِقَوْمٍ يُصَلُّونَ قُلْتُ مَا هَذَا الْمَسْجِدُ قَالُوا هَذِهِ الشَّجَرَةُ، حَيْثُ بَايَعَ رَسُولُ اللَّهِ صلى الله عليه وسلم بَيْعَةَ الرُّضْوَانِ. فَأَتَيْتُ سَعِيدَ بْنَ الْمُسَيَّبِ فَأَخْبَرْتُهُ فَقَالَ سَعِيدٌ حَدَّثَنِي أَبِي أَنَّهُ كَانَ فِيمَنْ بَايَعَ رَسُولَ اللَّهِ صلى الله عليه وسلم تَحْتَ الشَّجَرَةِ، قَالَ فَلَمَّا خَرَجْنَا مِنَ الْعَامِ الْمُقْبِلِ نَسِينَاهَا، فَلَمْ نَقْدِرْ عَلَيْهَا. فَقَالَ سَعِيدٌ إِنَّ أَصْحَابَ مُحَمَّدٍ صلى الله عليه وسلم لَمْ يَعْلَمُوهَا وَعَلِمْتُمُوهَا أَنْتُمْ، فَأَنْتُمْ أَعْلَمُ

Narrated Al-Musaiyab: I met Al-Bara bin `Azib and said (to him). "May you live prosperously! You enjoyed the company of the Prophet ﷺ and gave him the Pledge of allegiance (of Al-Hudaibiya) under the Tree." On that, Al- Bara' said, "O my nephew! You do not know what we have done after him (i.e. his death). – Sahih Al-Bukhari 4170
حَدَّثَنِي أَحْمَدُ بْنُ إِشْكَابٍ، حَدَّثَنَا مُحَمَّدُ بْنُ فُضَيْلٍ، عَنِ الْعَلاَءِ بْنِ الْمُسَيَّبِ، عَنْ أَبِيهِ، قَالَ لَقِيتُ الْبَرَاءَ بْنَ عَازِبٍ ـ رضى الله عنهما ـ فَقُلْتُ طُوبَى لَكَ صَحِبْتَ النَّبِيَّ صلى الله عليه وسلم وَبَايَعْتَهُ تَحْتَ الشَّجَرَةِ. فَقَالَ يَا ابْنَ أَخِي إِنَّكَ لاَ تَدْرِي مَا أَحْدَثْنَا بَعْدَهُ.

Narrated Mirdas Al-Aslami: Who was among those (who had given the Pledge of allegiance) under the Tree: Pious people will die in succession, and there will remain the dregs of society who will be like the useless residues of dates and barley and Allah will pay no attention to them. – Sahih Al-Bukhari 4156

حَدَّثَنَا إِبْرَاهِيمُ بْنُ مُوسَى، أَخْبَرَنَا عِيسَى، عَنْ إِسْمَاعِيلَ، عَنْ قَيْسٍ، أَنَّهُ سَمِعَ مِرْدَاسًا الأَسْلَمِيَّ، يَقُولُ ـ وَكَانَ مِنْ أَصْحَابِ الشَّجَرَةِ ـ يُقْبَضُ الصَّالِحُونَ الأَوَّلُ فَالأَوَّلُ، وَتَبْقَى حُفَالَةٌ كَحُفَالَةِ التَّمْرِ وَالشَّعِيرِ، لاَ يَعْبَأُ اللَّهُ بِهِمْ شَيْئًا

Narrated Ibn `Umar: When we reached (Hudaibiya) in the next year (of the treaty of Hudaibiya), not even two men amongst us agreed unanimously as to which was the tree under which we had given the pledge of allegiance, and that was out of Allah's Mercy. (The sub narrator asked Naf'I, "For what did the Prophet ﷺ take their pledge of allegiance, was it for death?" Naf'I replied "No, but he took their pledge of allegiance for patience."). – Sahih Al-Bukhari 2958

حَدَّثَنَا مُوسَى بْنُ إِسْمَاعِيلَ، حَدَّثَنَا جُوَيْرِيَةُ، عَنْ نَافِعٍ، قَالَ قَالَ ابْنُ عُمَرَ ـ رضى الله عنهما ـ رَجَعْنَا مِنَ الْعَامِ الْمُقْبِلِ فَمَا اجْتَمَعَ مِنَّا اثْنَانِ عَلَى الشَّجَرَةِ الَّتِي بَايَعْنَا تَحْتَهَا، كَانَتْ رَحْمَةً مِنَ اللَّهِ. فَسَأَلْتُ نَافِعًا عَلَى أَيِّ شَىْءٍ بَايَعَهُمْ عَلَى الْمَوْتِ قَالَ لاَ، بَايَعَهُمْ عَلَى الصَّبْرِ

Narrated Ibn Abi `Aufa: When Allah's Messenger ﷺ performed the `Umra (which he performed in the year following the treaty of Al-Hudaibiya) we were screening Allah's Messenger ﷺ from the infidels and their boys lest they should harm him. – Sahih Al-Bukhari 4255

حَدَّثَنَا عَلِيُّ بْنُ عَبْدِ اللَّهِ، حَدَّثَنَا سُفْيَانُ، عَنْ إِسْمَاعِيلَ بْنِ أَبِي خَالِدٍ، سَمِعَ ابْنَ أَبِي أَوْفَى، يَقُولُ لَمَّا اعْتَمَرَ رَسُولُ اللَّهِ صلى الله عليه وسلم سَتَرْنَاهُ مِنْ غِلْمَانِ الْمُشْرِكِينَ وَمِنْهُمْ، أَنْ يُؤْذُوا رَسُولَ اللَّهِ صلى الله عليه وسلم.

Narrated Ibn `Abbas: The Prophet ﷺ hastened in going around the Ka`ba and between the Safa and Marwa in order to show the pagans his strength. Ibn `Abbas added, "When the Prophet ﷺ arrived (at Mecca) in the year of peace (following that of Al-Hudaibiya treaty with the pagans of Mecca), he (ordered his companions) to do Ramal in order to show their strength to the pagans and the pagans were watching (the Muslims) from (the hill of) Quaiqan. – Sahih Al-Bukhari 4257

حَدَّثَنِي مُحَمَّدٌ، عَنْ سُفْيَانَ بْنِ عُيَيْنَةَ، عَنْ عَمْرٍو، عَنْ عَطَاءٍ، عَنِ ابْنِ عَبَّاسٍ ـ رضى الله عنهما ـ قَالَ إِنَّمَا سَعَى النَّبِيُّ صلى الله عليه وسلم بِالْبَيْتِ وَبَيْنَ الصَّفَا وَالْمَرْوَةِ لِيُرِيَ الْمُشْرِكِينَ قُوَّتَهُ

Narrated Asma 'bint Abi Bakr: During the period of the peace treaty of Quraish with Allah's Messenger ﷺ, my mother, accompanied by her father, came to visit me, and she was a pagan. I consulted Allah's Messenger ﷺ, " O Allah's Messenger ﷺ ! My mother has come to me and she desires to receive a reward from me, shall I keep good relation with her?" He said, "Yes, keep good relation with her.". – Sahih Al-Bukhari 3183

حَدَّثَنَا قُتَيْبَةُ بْنُ سَعِيدٍ، حَدَّثَنَا حَاتِمٌ، عَنْ هِشَامِ بْنِ عُرْوَةَ، عَنْ أَبِيهِ، عَنْ أَسْمَاءَ ابْنَةِ أَبِي بَكْرٍ ـ رضى الله عنهما ـ قَالَتْ قَدِمَتْ عَلَىَّ أُمِّي وَهْىَ مُشْرِكَةٌ فِي عَهْدِ قُرَيْشٍ، إِذْ عَاهَدُوا رَسُولَ اللَّهِ صلى الله عليه وسلم وَمُدَّتِهِمْ، مَعَ أَبِيهَا، فَاسْتَفْتَتْ رَسُولَ اللَّهِ صلى الله عليه وسلم فَقَالَتْ يَا رَسُولَ اللَّهِ، إِنَّ أُمِّي قَدِمَتْ عَلَىَّ، وَهْىَ رَاغِبَةٌ، أَفَأَصِلُهَا قَالَ " نَعَمْ، صِلِيهَا "

Narrated Abu Wail: We were in Siffin and Sahl bin Hunaif got up and said, "O people! Blame yourselves! We were with the Prophet ﷺ on the day of Hudaibiya, and if we had been called to fight, we would have fought. But `Umar bin Al Khatab came and said, 'O Allah's Messenger ﷺ ! Aren't we in the right and our opponents in the wrongs' Allah's Messenger ﷺ said, 'Yes.' `Umar said, 'Aren't our killed persons in Paradise and their's in Hell?' He said, 'Yes.' `Umar said, 'Then why should we accept hard terms in matters concerning our religion? Shall we return before Allah judges between us and them?' Allah's Messenger ﷺ said, 'O Ibn Al-Khattab! I am the Messenger of Allah and Allah will never degrade me. Then `Umar went to Abu Bakr and told him the same as he had told the Prophet. On that Abu Bakr said (to `Umar). 'He is the Messenger of Allah and Allah will never degrade him.' Then Surat-al-Fath (i.e.

Victory) was revealed and Allah's Messenger ﷺ recited it to the end in front of `Umar. On that `Umar asked, 'O Allah's Messenger ﷺ ! Was it (i.e. the Hudaibiya Treaty) a victory?' Allah's Messenger ﷺ said, "Yes". – Sahih Al-Bukhari 3182

حَدَّثَنَا عَبْدُ اللَّهِ بْنُ مُحَمَّدٍ، حَدَّثَنَا يَحْيَى بْنُ آدَمَ، حَدَّثَنَا يَزِيدُ بْنُ عَبْدِ الْعَزِيزِ، عَنْ أَبِيهِ، حَدَّثَنَا حَبِيبُ بْنُ أَبِي ثَابِتٍ، قَالَ حَدَّثَنِي أَبُو وَائِلٍ، قَالَ كُنَّا بِصِفِّينَ فَقَامَ سَهْلُ بْنُ حُنَيْفٍ فَقَالَ أَيُّهَا النَّاسُ اتَّهِمُوا أَنْفُسَكُمْ فَإِنَّا كُنَّا مَعَ رَسُولِ اللَّهِ صلى الله عليه وسلم يَوْمَ الْحُدَيْبِيَةِ، وَلَوْ نَرَى قِتَالاً لَقَاتَلْنَا، فَجَاءَ عُمَرُ بْنُ الْخَطَّابِ فَقَالَ يَا رَسُولَ اللَّهِ، أَلَسْنَا عَلَى الْحَقِّ وَهُمْ عَلَى الْبَاطِلِ فَقَالَ " بَلَى ". فَقَالَ أَلَيْسَ قَتْلاَنَا فِي الْجَنَّةِ وَقَتْلاَهُمْ فِي النَّارِ قَالَ " بَلَى ". قَالَ فَعَلَى مَا نُعْطِي الدَّنِيَّةَ فِي دِينِنَا أَنَرْجِعُ وَلَمَّا يَحْكُمِ اللَّهُ بَيْنَنَا وَبَيْنَهُمْ فَقَالَ " ابْنَ الْخَطَّابِ، إِنِّي رَسُولُ اللَّهِ، وَلَنْ يُضَيِّعَنِي اللَّهُ أَبَدًا ". فَانْطَلَقَ عُمَرُ إِلَى أَبِي بَكْرٍ فَقَالَ لَهُ مِثْلَ مَا قَالَ لِلنَّبِيِّ صلى الله عليه وسلم فَقَالَ إِنَّهُ رَسُولُ اللَّهِ، وَلَنْ يُضَيِّعَهُ اللَّهُ أَبَدًا. فَنَزَلَتْ سُورَةُ الْفَتْحِ، فَقَرَأَهَا رَسُولُ اللَّهِ صلى الله عليه وسلم عَلَى عُمَرَ إِلَى آخِرِهَا. فَقَالَ عُمَرُ يَا رَسُولَ اللَّهِ، أَوَفَتْحٌ هُوَ قَالَ " نَعَمْ "

Narrated `Uthman: (the son of Muhib) An Egyptian who came and performed the Hajj to the Ka`ba saw some people sitting. He enquire, "Who are these people?" Somebody said, "They are the tribe of Quraish." He said, "Who is the old man sitting amongst them?" The people replied, "He is `Abdullah bin `Umar." He said, "O Ibn `Umar! I want to ask you about something; please tell me about it. Do you know that `Uthman fled away on the day (of the battle) of Uhud?" Ibn `Umar said, "Yes." The (Egyptian) man said, "Do you know that `Uthman was absent on the day (of the battle) of Badr and did not join it?" Ibn `Umar said, "Yes." The man said, "Do you know that he failed to attend the Ar Ridwan pledge and did not witness it (i.e. Hudaibiya pledge of allegiance)?" Ibn `Umar said, "Yes." The man said, "Allahu Akbar!" Ibn `Umar said, "Let me explain to you (all these three things). As for his flight on the day of Uhud, I testify that Allah has excused him and forgiven him; and as for his absence from the battle of Badr, it was due to the fact that the daughter of Allah's Messenger ﷺ was his wife and she was sick then. Allah's Messenger ﷺ said to him, "You will receive the same reward and share (of the booty) as anyone of those who participated in the battle of Badr (if you stay with her).' As for his absence from the Ar-Ridwan pledge of allegiance, had there been any person in Mecca more respectable than `Uthman (to be sent as a representative). Allah's Messenger ﷺ would have sent him instead of him. No doubt, Allah's Messenger ﷺ had sent him, and the incident of the Ar-Ridwan pledge of Allegiance happened after `Uthman had gone to Mecca. Allah's Messenger ﷺ held out his right hand saying, 'This is `Uthman's hand.' He stroke his (other) hand with it saying, 'This (pledge of allegiance) is on the behalf of `Uthman.' Then Ibn `Umar said to the man, 'Bear (these) excuses in mind with you.' Sahih Al-Bukhari 3698

حَدَّثَنَا مُوسَى بْنُ إِسْمَاعِيلَ، حَدَّثَنَا أَبُو عَوَانَةَ، حَدَّثَنَا عُثْمَانُ ـ هُوَ ابْنُ مَوْهَبٍ ـ قَالَ جَاءَ رَجُلٌ مَنْ أَهْلِ مِصْرَ حَجَّ الْبَيْتَ فَرَأَى قَوْمًا جُلُوسًا، فَقَالَ مَنْ هَؤُلاَءِ الْقَوْمُ قَالَ هَؤُلاَءِ قُرَيْشٌ. قَالَ فَمَنِ الشَّيْخُ فِيهِمْ قَالُوا عَبْدُ اللَّهِ بْنُ عُمَرَ. قَالَ يَا ابْنَ عُمَرَ إِنِّي سَائِلُكَ عَنْ شَىْءٍ فَحَدِّثْنِي هَلْ تَعْلَمُ أَنَّ عُثْمَانَ فَرَّ يَوْمَ أُحُدٍ قَالَ نَعَمْ. قَالَ تَعْلَمُ أَنَّهُ تَغَيَّبَ عَنْ بَدْرٍ وَلَمْ يَشْهَدْ قَالَ نَعَمْ. قَالَ تَعْلَمُ أَنَّهُ تَغَيَّبَ عَنْ بَيْعَةِ الرُّضْوَانِ فَلَمْ يَشْهَدْهَا قَالَ نَعَمْ. قَالَ اللَّهُ أَكْبَرُ. قَالَ ابْنُ عُمَرَ تَعَالَ أُبَيِّنْ لَكَ أَمَّا فِرَارُهُ يَوْمَ أُحُدٍ فَأَشْهَدُ أَنَّ اللَّهَ عَفَا عَنْهُ وَغَفَرَ لَهُ، وَأَمَّا تَغَيُّبُهُ عَنْ بَدْرٍ، فَإِنَّهُ كَانَتْ تَحْتَهُ بِنْتُ رَسُولِ اللَّهِ صلى الله عليه وسلم وَكَانَتْ مَرِيضَةً، فَقَالَ لَهُ رَسُولُ اللَّهِ صلى الله عليه وسلم " إِنَّ لَكَ أَجْرَ رَجُلٍ مِمَّنْ شَهِدَ بَدْرًا وَسَهْمَهُ ". وَأَمَّا تَغَيُّبُهُ عَنْ بَيْعَةِ الرُّضْوَانِ فَلَوْ كَانَ أَحَدٌ أَعَزَّ بِبَطْنِ مَكَّةَ مِنْ عُثْمَانَ لَبَعَثَهُ مَكَانَهُ فَبَعَثَ رَسُولُ اللَّهِ صلى الله عليه وسلم عُثْمَانَ وَكَانَتْ بَيْعَةُ الرُّضْوَانِ بَعْدَ مَا ذَهَبَ عُثْمَانُ إِلَى مَكَّةَ، فَقَالَ رَسُولُ اللَّهِ صلى الله عليه وسلم بِيَدِهِ الْيُمْنَى " هَذِهِ يَدُ عُثْمَانَ ". فَضَرَبَ بِهَا عَلَى يَدِهِ، فَقَالَ " هَذِهِ لِعُثْمَانَ ". فَقَالَ لَهُ ابْنُ عُمَرَ اذْهَبْ بِهَا الآنَ مَعَكَ

Narrated Haritha bin Wahab: The Prophet ﷺ led us in the prayer at Mina during the peace period by offering two rak`at. – Sahih al-Bukhari 1083

حَدَّثَنَا أَبُو الْوَلِيدِ، قَالَ حَدَّثَنَا شُعْبَةُ، أَنْبَأَنَا أَبُو إِسْحَاقَ، قَالَ سَمِعْتُ حَارِثَةَ بْنَ وَهْبٍ، قَالَ صَلَّى بِنَا النَّبِيُّ صلى الله عليه وسلم آمَنَ مَا كَانَ بِمِنًى رَكْعَتَيْنِ

The Book of
Māriyyah al-Qibṭiyyah
مارية القبط

It was narrated from Anas, that the Messenger of Allah had a female slave with whom he had intercourse, but 'Aishah and Hafsah would not leave him alone until he said that she was forbidden for him. Then Allah, the Mighty and Sublime, revealed: "O Prophet! Why do you forbid (for yourself) that which Allah has allowed to you.' Until the end of the Verse. – Sunan an-Nasa'I 3959

أَخْبَرَنِي إِبْرَاهِيمُ بْنُ يُونُسَ بْنِ مُحَمَّدٍ، حَرَمِيٌّ – هُوَ لَقَبُهُ – قَالَ حَدَّثَنَا أَبِي قَالَ، حَدَّثَنَا حَمَّادُ بْنُ سَلَمَةَ، عَنْ ثَابِتٍ، عَنْ أَنَسٍ، أَنَّ رَسُولَ اللَّهِ صلى الله عليه وسلم كَانَتْ لَهُ أَمَةٌ يَطَؤُهَا فَلَمْ تَزَلْ بِهِ عَائِشَةُ وَحَفْصَةُ حَتَّى حَرَّمَهَا عَلَى نَفْسِهِ فَأَنْزَلَ اللَّهُ عَزَّ وَجَلَّ { يَا أَيُّهَا النَّبِيُّ لِمَ تُحَرِّمُ مَا أَحَلَّ اللَّهُ لَكَ } إِلَى آخِرِ الآيَةِ

It was narrated that Ibn`Abbas said: "Mention was made of the mother of Ibrahim in the presence of the Messenger of Allahﷺ, and he said: 'Her son set her free.'". – Sunan Ibn Majah 2516

حَدَّثَنَا أَحْمَدُ بْنُ يُوسُفَ، حَدَّثَنَا أَبُو عَاصِمٍ، حَدَّثَنَا أَبُو بَكْرٍ يَعْنِي النَّهْشَلِيَّ، عَنِ الْحُسَيْنِ بْنِ عَبْدِ اللَّهِ، عَنْ عِكْرِمَةَ، عَنِ ابْنِ عَبَّاسٍ، قَالَ ذُكِرَتْ أُمُّ إِبْرَاهِيمَ عِنْدَ رَسُولِ اللَّهِ صلى الله عليه وسلم . فَقَالَ " أَعْتَقَهَا وَلَدُهَا "

I make you witness that I my concubine (surriyyati) is now forbidden unto me. [13]
أشهدك أن سريتي علي حرام

Surah At-Taḥrīm
سورة التحريم

O prophet! Why do you prohibit what Allah has permitted for you, seeking to please your wives? Allah is Forgiving and Merciful. Allah has decreed for you the dissolution of your oaths. Allah is your Master. He is the All-Knowing, the Most Wise. The Prophet told something in confidence to one of his wives. But when she disclosed it, and Allah made it known to him; he communicated part of it, and he avoided another part. Then, when he informed her of it, she said, "Who informed you of this?" He said, "The All-Knowing, the All-Informed, informed me." If you repent to Allah, then your hearts have listened. But if you band together against him, then Allah is his Ally, as is Gabriel, and the righteous believers. In addition, the angels will assist him. Perhaps, if he divorces you, his Lord will give him in exchange wives better than you: submissive, believing, obedient, penitent, devout, fasting—previously married, or virgins. – Surah At-Tahrim 66:1-5

يَٰٓأَيُّهَا ٱلنَّبِيُّ لِمَ تُحَرِّمُ مَآ أَحَلَّ ٱللَّهُ لَكَۖ تَبۡتَغِي مَرۡضَاتَ أَزۡوَٰجِكَۚ وَٱللَّهُ غَفُورٞ رَّحِيمٞ قَدۡ فَرَضَ ٱللَّهُ لَكُمۡ تَحِلَّةَ أَيۡمَٰنِكُمۡۚ وَٱللَّهُ مَوۡلَىٰكُمۡۖ وَهُوَ ٱلۡعَلِيمُ ٱلۡحَكِيمُ وَإِذۡ أَسَرَّ ٱلنَّبِيُّ إِلَىٰ بَعۡضِ أَزۡوَٰجِهِۦ حَدِيثٗا فَلَمَّا نَبَّأَتۡ بِهِۦ وَأَظۡهَرَهُ ٱللَّهُ عَلَيۡهِ عَرَّفَ بَعۡضَهُۥ وَأَعۡرَضَ عَنۢ

---

[13] Reported by Ibn 'Abbas: Al-Tabari, Ibn Jarir, Jami' al-Bayan fi Tafsir al-Qur'an, (Beirut: al-Resalah Publishers, 2000) Vol.23, 477-478; al-Baihaqi, Abu Bakr, al-Sunan al-Kubra, (Beirut: DKI, 2003) Hadith 15075; Ibn al-Jawzi, Abu al-Farj, al-Tahqiq fi Ahadith al-Khilaf, (Beirut: DKI, 1415 AH) Vol.2, 379; It comes through an isnad involving 'Atiyah al-'Awfi and his descendants. Though criticized otherwise, the tafsir reports through this isnad are accepted since they are known to have been transmitted in writing. See, al-Turifi, 'Abdul 'Aziz, al-Taqrir fi Asanid al-Tafsir, (Riyadh: Dar al-Minhaj, 2011) 67-68

بَعْضٍۖ فَلَمَّا نَبَّأَهَا بِهِۦ قَالَتْ مَنْ أَنۢبَأَكَ هَٰذَاۖ قَالَ نَبَّأَنِيَ ٱلْعَلِيمُ ٱلْخَبِيرُ إِن تَتُوبَآ إِلَى ٱللَّهِ فَقَدْ صَغَتْ قُلُوبُكُمَاۖ وَإِن تَظَٰهَرَا عَلَيْهِ فَإِنَّ ٱللَّهَ هُوَ مَوْلَىٰهُ وَجِبْرِيلُ وَصَٰلِحُ ٱلْمُؤْمِنِينَۖ وَٱلْمَلَٰٓئِكَةُ بَعْدَ ذَٰلِكَ ظَهِيرٌ عَسَىٰ رَبُّهُۥٓ إِن طَلَّقَكُنَّ أَن يُبْدِلَهُۥٓ أَزْوَٰجًا خَيْرًا مِّنكُنَّ مُسْلِمَٰتٍ مُّؤْمِنَٰتٍ قَٰنِتَٰتٍ تَٰٓئِبَٰتٍ عَٰبِدَٰتٍ سَٰٓئِحَٰتٍ ثَيِّبَٰتٍ وَأَبْكَارًا

Narrated `Abdullah bin `Abbas: I had been eager to ask `Umar about the two ladies from among the wives of the Prophetﷺ regarding whom Allah said (in the Qur'an saying): If you two (wives of the Prophetﷺ namely Aisha and Hafsa) turn in repentance to Allah your hearts are indeed so inclined (to oppose what the Prophetﷺ likes) (66.4), till performed the Hajj along with `Umar (and on our way back from Hajj) he went aside (to answer the call of nature) and I also went aside along with him carrying a tumbler of water. When he had answered the call of nature and returned. I poured water on his hands from the tumbler and he performed ablution. I said, "O Chief of the believers! ' Who were the two ladies from among the wives of the Prophetﷺ to whom Allah said: 'If you two return in repentance (66.4)? He said, "I am astonished at your question, O Ibn `Abbas. They were Aisha and Hafsa." Then `Umar went on relating the narration and said. "I and an Ansari neighbor of mine from Bani Umaiya bin Zaid who used to live in `Awali Al-Medina, used to visit the Prophetﷺ in turns. He used to go one day, and I another day. When I went I would bring him the news of what had happened that day regarding the instructions and orders and when he went, he used to do the same for me. We, the people of Quraish, used to have authority over women, but when we came to live with the Ansar, we noticed that the Ansari women had the upper hand over their men, so our women started acquiring the habits of the Ansari women. Once I shouted at my wife and she paid me back in my coin and I disliked that she should answer me back. She said, 'Why do you take it ill that I retort upon you? By Allah, the wives of the Prophetﷺ retort upon him, and some of them may not speak with him for the whole day till night.' What she said scared me and I said to her, 'Whoever amongst them does so, will be a great loser.' Then I dressed myself and went to Hafsa and asked her, 'Does any of you keep Allah's Messengerﷺ angry all the day long till night?' She replied in the affirmative. I said, 'She is a ruined losing person (and will never have success)! Doesn't she fear that Allah may get angry for the anger of Allah's Messenger and thus she will be ruined? Don't ask Allah's Messenger too many things, and don't retort upon him in any case, and don't desert him. Demand from me whatever you like, and don't be tempted to imitate your neighbor (i.e. `Aisha) in her behavior towards the Prophet), for she (i.e. Aisha) is more beautiful than you, and more beloved to Allah's Messengerﷺ. In those days it was rumored that Ghassan, (a tribe living in Sham) was getting prepared their horses to invade us. My companion went (to the Prophetﷺ on the day of his turn, went and returned to us at night and knocked at my door violently, asking whether I was sleeping. I was scared (by the hard knocking) and came out to him. He said that a great thing had happened. I asked him: What is it? Have Ghassan come? He replied that it was worse and more serious than that, and added that Allah's Apostle had divorced all his wives. I said, Hafsa is a ruined loser! I expected that would happen some day.' So I dressed myself and offered the Fajr prayer with the Prophet. Then the Prophetﷺ entered an upper room and stayed there alone. I went to Hafsa and found her weeping. I asked her, 'Why are you weeping? Didn't I warn you? Have Allah's Messengerﷺ divorced you all?' She replied, 'I don't know. He is there in the upper room.' I then went out and came to the pulpit and found a group of people around it and some of them were weeping. Then I sat with them for some time, but could not endure the situation. So I went to the upper room where the Prophetﷺ was and requested to a black slave of his: "Will you get the permission of (Allah's Apostle) for `Umar (to enter)? The slave went in, talked to the Prophetﷺ about it and came out saying, 'I mentioned you to him but he did not reply.' So, I went and sat with the people who were sitting by the pulpit, but I could not bear the situation, so I went to the slave again and said: "Will you get he permission for `Umar? He went in and brought the same reply as before. When I was leaving, behold, the slave called me saying, "Allah's Messenger ﷺ has granted you permission." So, I entered upon the Prophet and saw him lying on a mat without wedding on it, and the mat had left its mark on the body of the Prophet, and he was leaning on a leather pillow stuffed with palm fires. I greeted him and while still standing, I said: "Have you divorced your wives?' He raised his eyes to me and replied in the negative. And then while still standing, I said chatting: "Will you heed what I say, 'O Allah's Messenger ﷺ! We, the people of Quraish used to have the upper hand over our women (wives), and when we came to the people whose women had the upper hand over them..." `Umar told the whole story (about his wife). "On that the Prophet ﷺ smiled." `Umar further said, "I then said, 'I went to Hafsa and said to her: Do not be tempted to imitate your companion (`Aisha) for she is more beautiful than you and more beloved to the Prophet.' The Prophet ﷺ smiled again. When I saw him smiling, I sat down and cast a glance at the room, and by Allah, I couldn't see anything of importance but three hides. I said (to Allah's Messenger ﷺ!) "Invoke Allah to make your followers prosperous for the Persians and the Byzantines have been made prosperous and given worldly luxuries, though they do not worship Allah?' The Prophet ﷺ was leaning then (and on hearing my speech he sat straight) and said, 'O Ibn Al-Khattab! Do you have any doubt (that the Hereafter is better than this world)? These people have been given rewards of their good deeds in this world only.' I asked the Prophet ﷺ. 'Please ask Allah's forgiveness for me. The Prophet ﷺ did not go to his wives because of the secret which Hafsa had disclosed to `Aisha, and he said that he would not go to his wives for one month as he was angry with them when Allah admonished him (for his oath that he would not approach Maria). When twenty-nine days had passed, the Prophet ﷺ went to Aisha first of all. She said to him, 'You took an oath that you would not come to us for one month, and today only twenty-nine days have passed, as I have been counting them day by day.' The Prophet ﷺ said, 'The month is also of twenty-nine days.' That month consisted of twenty-nine days. Aisha said, 'When the Divine revelation of Choice was revealed, the Prophet ﷺ started with me, saying to me, 'I am telling you something, but you need not hurry to give the reply till you can consult your parents." `Aisha knew that her parents would not advise her to part with the Prophet ﷺ. The Prophet ﷺ said that Allah had said: 'O Prophet! Say To your wives; If you desire The life of this world And its glitter, ... then come! I will make a provision for you and set you free In a handsome manner. But if you seek Allah And His Apostle, and The Home of the Hereafter, then Verily, Allah has prepared For the good-doers amongst you A great reward.' (33.28) `Aisha said, 'Am I to consult my parents about this? I indeed prefer Allah, His Apostle, and the Home of the Hereafter.' After that the Prophet ﷺ gave the choice to his other wives and they also gave the same reply as `Aisha did.". – Sahih al-Bukhari 2468

حَدَّثَنَا يَحْيَى بْنُ بُكَيْرٍ، حَدَّثَنَا اللَّيْثُ، عَنْ عُقَيْلٍ، عَنِ ابْنِ شِهَابٍ، قَالَ أَخْبَرَنِي عُبَيْدُ اللَّهِ بْنُ عَبْدِ اللَّهِ بْنِ أَبِي ثَوْرٍ، عَنْ عَبْدِ اللَّهِ بْنِ عَبَّاسٍ ـ رضى الله عنهما ـ قَالَ لَمْ أَزَلْ حَرِيصًا عَلَى أَنْ أَسْأَلَ عُمَرَ ـ رضى الله عنه ـ عَنِ الْمَرْأَتَيْنِ مِنْ أَزْوَاجِ النَّبِيِّ صلى الله عليه وسلم اللَّتَيْنِ قَالَ اللَّهُ لَهُمَا {إِنْ تَتُوبَا إِلَى اللَّهِ فَقَدْ صَغَتْ قُلُوبُكُمَا} فَحَجَجْتُ مَعَهُ فَعَدَلَ وَعَدَلْتُ مَعَهُ بِالإِدَاوَةِ، فَتَبَرَّزَ حَتَّى جَاءَ، فَسَكَبْتُ عَلَى يَدَيْهِ مِنَ الإِدَاوَةِ، فَتَوَضَّأَ فَقُلْتُ يَا أَمِيرَ الْمُؤْمِنِينَ مَنِ الْمَرْأَتَانِ مِنْ أَزْوَاجِ النَّبِيِّ صلى الله عليه وسلم اللَّتَانِ قَالَ لَهُمَا {إِنْ تَتُوبَا إِلَى اللَّهِ} فَقَالَ وَاعَجَبِي لَكَ يَا ابْنَ عَبَّاسٍ عَائِشَةُ وَحَفْصَةُ، ثُمَّ اسْتَقْبَلَ عُمَرُ الْحَدِيثَ يَسُوقُهُ، فَقَالَ إِنِّي كُنْتُ وَجَارٌ لِي مِنَ الأَنْصَارِ فِي بَنِي أُمَيَّةَ بْنِ زَيْدٍ، وَهْىَ مِنْ عَوَالِي الْمَدِينَةِ، وَكُنَّا نَتَنَاوَبُ النُّزُولَ عَلَى النَّبِيِّ صلى الله عليه وسلم فَيَنْزِلُ يَوْمًا وَأَنْزِلُ يَوْمًا، فَإِذَا نَزَلْتُ جِئْتُهُ مِنْ خَبَرِ ذَلِكَ الْيَوْمِ مِنَ الأَمْرِ وَغَيْرِهِ، وَإِذَا نَزَلَ فَعَلَ مِثْلَهُ، وَكُنَّا مَعْشَرَ قُرَيْشٍ نَغْلِبُ النِّسَاءَ، فَلَمَّا قَدِمْنَا عَلَى الأَنْصَارِ إِذَا هُمْ قَوْمٌ تَغْلِبُهُمْ نِسَاؤُهُمْ، فَطَفِقَ نِسَاؤُنَا يَأْخُذْنَ مِنْ أَدَبِ نِسَاءِ الأَنْصَارِ، فَصِحْتُ عَلَى امْرَأَتِي، فَرَاجَعَتْنِي، فَأَنْكَرْتُ أَنْ تُرَاجِعَنِي، فَقَالَتْ وَلِمَ تُنْكِرُ أَنْ أُرَاجِعَكَ فَوَاللَّهِ إِنَّ أَزْوَاجَ النَّبِيِّ صلى الله عليه وسلم لَيُرَاجِعْنَهُ، وَإِنَّ إِحْدَاهُنَّ لَتَهْجُرُهُ الْيَوْمَ حَتَّى اللَّيْلِ. فَأَفْزَعَنِي، فَقُلْتُ خَابَتْ مَنْ فَعَلَ مِنْهُنَّ بِعَظِيمٍ. ثُمَّ جَمَعْتُ عَلَىَّ ثِيَابِي، فَدَخَلْتُ عَلَى حَفْصَةَ فَقُلْتُ أَىْ حَفْصَةُ، أَتُغَاضِبُ إِحْدَاكُنَّ رَسُولَ اللَّهِ صلى الله عليه وسلم الْيَوْمَ حَتَّى

اللَّيْلِ فَقَالَتْ نَعَمْ. فَقُلْتُ خَابَتْ وَخَسِرَتْ، أَفَتَأْمَنُ أَنْ يَغْضَبَ اللَّهُ لِغَضَبِ رَسُولِهِ صلى الله عليه وسلم فَتَهْلِكِينَ لاَ تَسْتَكْثِرِي عَلَى رَسُولِ اللَّهِ صلى الله عليه وسلم وَلاَ تُرَاجِعِيهِ فِي شَىْءٍ وَلاَ تَهْجُرِيهِ، وَاسْأَلِينِي مَا بَدَا لَكِ، وَلاَ يَغُرَّنَّكِ أَنْ كَانَتْ ج ارَتُكِ هِيَ أَوْضَأَ مِنْكِ وَأَحَبَّ إِلَى رَسُولِ اللَّهِ صلى الله عليه وسلم - يُرِيدُ عَائِشَةَ - وَكُنَّا تَحَدَّثْنَا أَنَّ غَسَّانَ تُنْعِلُ النِّعَالَ لِغَزْوِنَا، فَنَزَلَ صَاحِبِي يَوْمَ نَوْبَتِهِ فَرَجَعَ عِشَاءً، فَضَرَبَ بَابِي ضَرْبًا شَدِيدًا، وَقَالَ أَنَائِمٌ هُوَ فَفَزِعْتُ فَخَرَجْتُ إِلَيْهِ. وَقَالَ حَدَثَ أَمْرٌ عَظِيمٌ. قُلْتُ مَا هُوَ أَجَاءَتْ غَسَّانُ قَالَ لاَ، بَلْ أَعْظَمُ مِنْهُ وَأَطْوَلُ، طَلَّقَ رَسُولُ اللَّهِ صلى الله عليه وسلم نِسَاءَهُ. قَالَ قَدْ خَابَتْ حَفْصَةُ وَخَسِرَتْ، كُنْتُ أَظُنُّ أَنَّ هَذَا يُوشِكُ أَنْ يَكُونَ، فَجَمَعْتُ عَلَىَّ ثِيَابِي، فَصَلَّيْتُ صَلاَةَ الْفَجْرِ مَعَ النَّبِيِّ صلى الله عليه وسلم فَدَخَلَ مَشْرُبَةً لَهُ فَاعْتَزَلَ فِيهَا، فَدَخَلْتُ عَلَى حَفْصَةَ، فَإِذَا هِيَ تَبْكِي. قُلْتُ مَا يُبْكِيكِ أَوَلَمْ أَكُنْ حَذَّرْتُكِ أَطَلَّقَكُنَّ رَسُولُ اللَّهِ صلى الله عليه وسلم قَالَتْ لاَ أَدْرِي هُوَ ذَا فِي الْمَشْرُبَةِ. فَخَرَجْتُ، فَجِئْتُ الْمِنْبَرَ، فَإِذَا حَوْلَهُ رَهْطٌ يَبْكِي بَعْضُهُمْ، فَجَلَسْتُ مَعَهُمْ قَلِيلاً ثُمَّ غَلَبَنِي مَا أَجِدُ، فَجِئْتُ الْمَشْرُبَةَ الَّتِي هُوَ فِيهَا فَقُلْتُ لِغُلاَمٍ لَهُ أَسْوَدَ اسْتَأْذِنْ لِعُمَرَ. فَدَخَلَ، فَكَلَّمَ النَّبِيَّ صلى الله عليه وسلم ثُمَّ خَرَجَ، فَقَالَ ذَكَرْتُكَ لَهُ، فَصَمَتَ، فَانْصَرَفْتُ حَتَّى جَلَسْتُ مَعَ الرَّهْطِ الَّذِينَ عِنْدَ الْمِنْبَرِ، ثُمَّ غَلَبَنِي مَا أَجِدُ فَجِئْتُ، فَذَكَرَ مِثْلَهُ، فَجَلَسْتُ مَعَ الرَّهْطِ الَّذِينَ عِنْدَ الْمِنْبَرِ، ثُمَّ غَلَبَنِي مَا أَجِدُ فَجِئْتُ الْغُلاَمَ. فَقُلْتُ اسْتَأْذِنْ لِعُمَرَ. فَذَكَرَ مِثْلَهُ، فَلَمَّا وَلَّيْتُ مُنْصَرِفًا، فَإِذَا الْغُلاَمُ يَدْعُونِي قَالَ أَذِنَ لَكَ رَسُولُ اللَّهِ صلى الله عليه وسلم. فَدَخَلْتُ عَلَيْهِ، فَإِذَا هُوَ مُضْطَجِعٌ عَلَى رِمَالِ حَصِيرٍ لَيْسَ بَيْنَهُ وَبَيْنَهُ فِرَاشٌ، قَدْ أَثَّرَ الرِّمَالُ بِجَنْبِهِ، مُتَّكِئٌ عَلَى وِسَادَةٍ مِنْ أَدَمٍ حَشْوُهَا لِيفٌ، فَسَلَّمْتُ عَلَيْهِ، ثُمَّ قُلْتُ وَأَنَا قَائِمٌ طَلَّقْتَ نِسَاءَكَ فَرَفَعَ بَصَرَهُ إِلَىَّ، فَقَالَ " لاَ ". ثُمَّ قُلْتُ - وَأَنَا قَائِمٌ أَسْتَأْنِسُ يَا رَسُولَ اللَّهِ، لَوْ رَأَيْتَنِي، وَكُنَّا مَعْشَرَ قُرَيْشٍ نَغْلِبُ النِّسَاءَ، فَلَمَّا قَدِمْنَا عَلَى قَوْمٍ تَغْلِبُهُمْ نِسَاؤُهُمْ، فَذَكَرَهُ، فَتَبَسَّمَ النَّبِيُّ صلى الله عليه وسلم، ثُمَّ قُلْتُ لَوْ رَأَيْتَنِي، وَدَخَلْتُ عَلَى حَفْصَةَ، فَقُلْتُ لاَ يَغُرَّنَّكِ أَنْ كَانَتْ جَارَتُكِ هِيَ أَوْضَأَ مِنْكِ وَأَحَبَّ إِلَى النَّبِيِّ صلى الله عليه وسلم - يُرِيدُ عَائِشَةَ - فَتَبَسَّمَ أُخْرَى، فَجَلَسْتُ حِينَ رَأَيْتُهُ تَبَسَّمَ، ثُمَّ رَفَعْتُ بَصَرِي فِي بَيْتِهِ، فَوَاللَّهِ مَا رَأَيْتُ فِيهِ شَيْئًا يَرُدُّ الْبَصَرَ غَيْرَ أَهَبَةٍ ثَلاَثَةٍ. فَقُلْتُ ادْعُ اللَّهَ فَلْيُوَسِّعْ عَلَى أُمَّتِكَ، فَإِنَّ فَارِسَ وَالرُّومَ وُسِّعَ عَلَيْهِمْ وَأُعْطُوا الدُّنْيَا، وَهُمْ لاَ يَعْبُدُونَ اللَّهَ، وَكَانَ مُتَّكِئًا. فَقَالَ " أَوَفِي شَكٍّ أَنْتَ يَا ابْنَ الْخَطَّابِ أُولَئِكَ قَوْمٌ عُجِّلَتْ لَهُمْ طَيِّبَاتُهُمْ فِي الْحَيَاةِ الدُّنْيَا ". فَقُلْتُ يَا رَسُولَ اللَّهِ اسْتَغْفِرْ لِي. فَاعْتَزَلَ النَّبِيُّ صلى الله عليه وسلم مِنْ أَجْلِ ذَلِكَ الْحَدِيثِ حِينَ أَفْشَتْهُ حَفْصَةُ إِلَى عَائِشَةَ، وَكَانَ قَدْ قَالَ " مَا أَنَا بِدَاخِلٍ عَلَيْهِنَّ شَهْرًا ". مِنْ شِدَّةِ مَوْجَدَتِهِ عَلَيْهِنَّ حِينَ عَاتَبَهُ اللَّهُ. فَلَمَّا مَضَتْ تِسْعٌ وَعِشْرُونَ دَخَلَ عَلَى عَائِشَةَ فَبَدَأَ بِهَا، فَقَالَتْ لَهُ عَائِشَةُ إِنَّكَ أَقْسَمْتَ أَنْ لاَ تَدْخُلَ عَلَيْنَا شَهْرًا، وَإِنَّا أَصْبَحْنَا لِتِسْعٍ وَعِشْرِينَ لَيْلَةً، أَعُدُّهَا عَدًّا. فَقَالَ النَّبِيُّ صلى الله عليه وسلم " الشَّهْرُ تِسْعٌ وَعِشْرُونَ ". وَكَانَ ذَلِكَ الشَّهْرُ تِسْعٌ وَعِشْرُونَ. قَالَتْ عَائِشَةُ فَأُنْزِلَتْ آيَةُ التَّخْيِيرِ فَبَدَأَ بِي أَوَّلَ امْرَأَةٍ، فَقَالَ " إِنِّي ذَاكِرٌ لَكِ أَمْرًا، وَلاَ عَلَيْكِ أَنْ لاَ تَعْجَلِي حَتَّى تَسْتَأْمِرِي أَبَوَيْكِ ". قَالَتْ قَدْ أَعْلَمُ أَنَّ أَبَوَىَّ لَمْ يَكُونَا يَأْمُرَانِي بِفِرَاقِكَ. ثُمَّ قَالَ " إِنَّ اللَّهَ قَالَ {يَا أَيُّهَا النَّبِيُّ قُلْ لأَزْوَاجِكَ} إِلَى قَوْلِهِ { عَظِيمًا} ". قُلْتُ أَفِي هَذَا أَسْتَأْمِرُ أَبَوَىَّ فَإِنِّي أُرِيدُ اللَّهَ وَرَسُولَهُ وَالدَّارَ الآخِرَةَ. ثُمَّ خَيَّرَ نِسَاءَهُ، فَقُلْنَ مِثْلَ مَا قَالَتْ عَائِشَةُ.

The Book of **Ghazwat of Khaybar** غَزْوَة خَيْبَر

Narrated Salama bin Al-Akwa`: We went out to Khaibar in the company of the Prophet. While we were proceeding at night, a man from the group said to 'Amir, "O 'Amir! Won't you let us hear your poetry?" 'Amir was a poet, so he got down and started reciting for the people poetry that kept pace with the camels' footsteps, saying:-- "O Allah! Without You we Would not have been guided On the right path Neither would be have given In charity, nor would We have prayed. So please forgive us, what we have committed (i.e. our defects); let all of us Be sacrificed for Your Cause And send Sakina (i.e. calmness) Upon us to make our feet firm When we meet our enemy, and If they will call us towards An unjust thing, We will refuse. The infidels have made a hue and Cry to ask others' help Against us." The Prophet ﷺ on that, asked, "Who is that (camel) driver (reciting poetry)?" The people said, "He is 'Amir bin Al-Akwa`." Then the Prophet ﷺ said, "May Allah bestow His Mercy on him." A man amongst the people said, "O Allah's Prophet! Has (martyrdom) been granted to him. Would that you let us enjoy his company longer." Then we reached and besieged Khaibar till we were afflicted with severe hunger. Then Allah helped the Muslims conquer it (i.e. Khaibar). In the evening of the day of the conquest of the city, the Muslims made huge fires. The Prophet ﷺ said, "What are these fires? For cooking what, are you making the fire?" The people replied, "(For cooking) meat." He asked, "What kind of meat?" They (i.e. people) said, "The meat of donkeys." The Prophet ﷺ said, "Throw away the meat and break the pots!" Some man said, "O Allah's Messenger ﷺ ! Shall we throw away the meat and wash the pots instead?" He said, "(Yes, you can do) that too." So when the army files were arranged in rows (for the clash), 'Amir's sword was short and he aimed at the leg of a Jew to strike it, but the sharp blade of the sword returned to him and injured his own knee, and that caused him to die. When they returned from the battle, Allah's Messenger ﷺ saw me (in a sad mood). He took my hand and said, "What is bothering you?" I replied, "Let my father and mother be sacrificed for you! The people say that the deeds of 'Amir are lost." The Prophet ﷺ said, "Whoever says so, is mistaken, for 'Amir has got a double reward." The Prophet raised two fingers and added, "He (i.e. Amir) was a persevering struggler in the Cause of Allah and there are few 'Arabs who achieved the like of (good deeds) 'Amir had done.". – Sahih Al-Bukhari 4196

حَدَّثَنَا عَبْدُ اللَّهِ بْنُ مَسْلَمَةَ، حَدَّثَنَا حَاتِمُ بْنُ إِسْمَاعِيلَ، عَنْ يَزِيدَ بْنِ أَبِي عُبَيْدٍ، عَنْ سَلَمَةَ بْنِ الأَكْوَعِ ـ رضى الله عنه ـ قَالَ خَرَجْنَا مَعَ النَّبِيِّ صلى الله عليه وسلم إِلَى خَيْبَرَ فَسِرْنَا لَيْلاً، فَقَالَ رَجُلٌ مِنَ الْقَوْمِ لِعَامِرٍ يَا عَامِرُ أَلاَ تُسْمِعُنَا مِنْ هُنَيْهَاتِكَ. وَكَانَ عَامِرٌ رَجُلاً شَاعِرًا فَنَزَلَ يَحْدُو بِالْقَوْمِ يَقُولُ: اللَّهُمَّ لَوْلاَ أَنْتَ مَا اهْتَدَيْنَا وَلاَ تَصَدَّقْنَا وَلاَ صَلَّيْنَ فَاغْفِرْ فِدَاءً لَكَ مَا أَبْقَيْنَا وَثَبِّتِ الأَقْدَامَ إِنْ لاَقَيْنَا وَأَلْقِيَنْ سَكِينَةً عَلَيْنَا إِنَّا إِذَا صِيحَ بِنَا أَبَيْنَا وَبِالصِّيَاحِ عَوَّلُوا عَلَيْنَا

فَقَالَ رَسُولُ اللَّهِ صلى الله عليه وسلم " مَنْ هَذَا السَّائِقُ ". قَالُوا عَامِرُ بْنُ الأَكْوَعِ. قَالَ " يَرْحَمُهُ اللَّهُ ". قَالَ رَجُلٌ مِنَ الْقَوْمِ وَجَبَتْ يَا نَبِيَّ اللَّهِ، لَوْلاَ أَمْتَعْتَنَا بِهِ. فَأَتَيْنَا خَيْبَرَ، فَحَاصَرْنَاهُمْ حَتَّى أَصَابَتْنَا مَخْمَصَةٌ شَدِيدَةٌ، ثُمَّ إِنَّ اللَّهَ تَعَالَى فَتَحَهَا عَلَيْهِمْ، فَلَمَّا أَمْسَى النَّاسُ مَسَاءَ الْيَوْمِ الَّذِي فُتِحَتْ عَلَيْهِمْ أَوْقَدُوا نِيرَانًا كَثِيرَةً، فَقَالَ النَّبِيُّ صلى الله عليه وسلم " مَا هَذِهِ النِّيرَانُ عَلَى أَىِّ شَىْءٍ تُوقِدُونَ ". قَالُوا عَلَى لَحْمٍ. قَالَ " عَلَى أَىِّ لَحْمٍ ". قَالُوا لَحْمِ حُمُرِ الإِنْسِيَّةِ. قَالَ النَّبِيُّ صلى الله عليه وسلم " أَهْرِيقُوهَا وَاكْسِرُوهَا ". فَقَالَ رَجُلٌ يَا رَسُولَ اللَّهِ أَوْ نُهَرِيقُهَا وَنَغْسِلُهَا قَالَ " أَوْ ذَاكَ ". فَلَمَّا تَصَافَّ الْقَوْمُ كَانَ سَيْفُ عَامِرٍ قَصِيرًا فَتَنَاوَلَ بِهِ سَاقَ يَهُودِيٍّ لِيَضْرِبَهُ، وَيَرْجِعُ ذُبَابُ سَيْفِهِ، فَأَصَابَ عَيْنَ رُكْبَةِ عَامِرٍ، فَمَاتَ مِنْهُ قَالَ فَلَمَّا قَفَلُوا، قَالَ سَلَمَةُ رَآنِي رَسُولُ اللَّهِ صلى الله عليه وسلم وَهْوَ آخِذٌ بِيَدِي، قَالَ " مَا لَكَ ". قُلْتُ لَهُ فِدَاكَ أَبِي وَأُمِّي، زَعَمُوا أَنَّ عَامِرًا حَبِطَ عَمَلُهُ. قَالَ النَّبِيُّ صلى الله عليه وسلم " كَذَبَ مَنْ قَالَهُ، إِنَّ لَهُ لأَجْرَيْنِ ـ وَجَمَعَ بَيْنَ إِصْبَعَيْهِ ـ إِنَّهُ لَجَاهِدٌ مُجَاهِدٌ قَلَّ عَرَبِيٌّ مَشَى بِهَا مِثْلَهُ ". حَدَّثَنَا قُتَيْبَةُ حَدَّثَنَا حَاتِمٌ قَالَ " نَشَأَ بِهَا "

Narrated Humaid: Anas bin Malik said, "Whenever the Prophet ﷺ went out with us to fight (in Allah's cause) against any nation, he never allowed us to attack till morning and he would wait and see: if he heard Adhan he would postpone the attack and if he did not hear Adhan he would attack them." Anas added, "We reached Khaibar at night and in the morning when he did not hear the Adhan for the prayer, he (the Prophet) rode and I rode behind Abi Talha and my foot was touching that of the Prophet. The inhabitants of Khaibar came out with their baskets and spades and when they saw the Prophet ﷺ they shouted 'Muhammad! By Allah, Muhammad and his army.' When Allah's Messenger ﷺ saw them, he said, "Allahu-Akbar! Allahu-Akbar! Khaibar is ruined. Whenever we approach a (hostile) nation (to fight), then evil will be the morning of those who have been warned.". – Sahih Al-Bukhari 610

حَدَّثَنَا قُتَيْبَةُ بْنُ سَعِيدٍ، قَالَ حَدَّثَنَا إِسْمَاعِيلُ بْنُ جَعْفَرٍ، عَنْ حُمَيْدٍ، عَنْ أَنَسِ بْنِ مَالِكٍ، أَنَّ النَّبِيَّ صلى الله عليه وسلم كَانَ إِذَا غَزَا بِنَا قَوْمًا لَمْ يَكُنْ يَغْزُو بِنَا حَتَّى يُصْبِحَ وَيَنْظُرَ، فَإِنْ سَمِعَ أَذَانًا كَفَّ عَنْهُمْ، وَإِنْ لَمْ يَسْمَعْ أَذَانًا أَغَارَ عَلَيْهِمْ، قَالَ فَخَرَجْنَا إِلَى خَيْبَرَ فَانْتَهَيْنَا إِلَيْهِمْ لَيْلاً، فَلَمَّا أَصْبَحَ وَلَمْ يَسْمَعْ أَذَانًا رَكِبَ وَرَكِبْتُ خَلْفَ أَبِي طَلْحَةَ، وَإِنَّ قَدَمِي لَتَمَسُّ قَدَمَ النَّبِيِّ صلى الله عليه وسلم. قَالَ فَخَرَجُوا إِلَيْنَا بِمَكَاتِلِهِمْ وَمَسَاحِيهِمْ فَلَمَّا رَأَوُا النَّبِيَّ صلى الله عليه وسلم قَالُوا مُحَمَّدٌ وَاللَّهِ، مُحَمَّدٌ وَالْخَمِيسُ. قَالَ فَلَمَّا رَآهُمْ رَسُولُ اللَّهِ صلى الله عليه وسلم قَالَ " اللَّهُ أَكْبَرُ، اللَّهُ أَكْبَرُ، خَرِبَتْ خَيْبَرُ، إِنَّا إِذَا نَزَلْنَا بِسَاحَةِ قَوْمٍ فَسَاءَ صَبَاحُ الْمُنْذَرِينَ "

Narrated Anas: The Prophet ﷺ offered the Fajr Prayer near Khaibar when it was still dark and then said, "Allahu-Akbar! Khaibar is destroyed, for whenever we approach a (hostile) nation (to fight), then evil will be the morning for those who have been warned." Then the inhabitants of Khaibar came out running on the roads. The Prophet ﷺ had their warriors killed, their offspring and woman taken as captives. Safiya was amongst the captives, She first came in the share of Dahya Alkali but later on she belonged to the Prophet . The Prophet ﷺ made her manumission as her 'Mahr'. – Sahih Al-Bukhari 4200

حَدَّثَنَا سُلَيْمَانُ بْنُ حَرْبٍ، حَدَّثَنَا حَمَّادُ بْنُ زَيْدٍ، عَنْ ثَابِتٍ، عَنْ أَنَسٍ ـ رضى الله عنه ـ قَالَ صَلَّى النَّبِيُّ صلى الله عليه وسلم الصُّبْحَ قَرِيبًا مِنْ خَيْبَرَ بِغَلَسٍ ثُمَّ قَالَ " اللَّهُ أَكْبَرُ خَرِبَتْ خَيْبَرُ، إِنَّا إِذَا نَزَلْنَا بِسَاحَةِ قَوْمٍ، فَسَاءَ صَبَاحُ الْمُنْذَرِينَ ". فَخَرَجُوا يَسْعَوْنَ فِي السِّكَكِ، فَقَتَلَ النَّبِيُّ صلى الله عليه وسلم الْمُقَاتِلَةَ، وَسَبَى الذُّرِّيَّةَ، وَكَانَ فِي السَّبْىِ صَفِيَّةُ، فَصَارَتْ إِلَى دِحْيَةَ الْكَلْبِيِّ، ثُمَّ صَارَتْ إِلَى النَّبِيِّ صلى الله عليه وسلم، فَجَعَلَ عِتْقَهَا صَدَاقَهَا. فَقَالَ عَبْدُ الْعَزِيزِ بْنُ صُهَيْبٍ لِثَابِتٍ يَا أَبَا مُحَمَّدٍ آنْتَ قُلْتَ لأَنَسٍ مَا أَصْدَقَهَا فَحَرَّكَ ثَابِتٌ رَأْسَهُ تَصْدِيقًا لَهُ

Narrated `Abdullah bin Mughaffal: While we were besieging the fort of Khaibar, a person threw a leather container containing fat, and I ran to take it, but when I turned I saw the Prophet (standing behind), so I felt embarrassed in front of him. – Sahih Al-Bukhari 3153

حَدَّثَنَا أَبُو الْوَلِيدِ، حَدَّثَنَا شُعْبَةُ، عَنْ حُمَيْدِ بْنِ هِلاَلٍ، عَنْ عَبْدِ اللَّهِ بْنِ مُغَفَّلٍ ـ رضى الله عنه ـ قَالَ كُنَّا مُحَاصِرِينَ قَصْرَ خَيْبَرَ، فَرَمَى إِنْسَانٌ بِجِرَابٍ فِيهِ شَحْمٌ، فَنَزَوْتُ لآخُذَهُ، فَالْتَفَتُّ فَإِذَا النَّبِيُّ صلى الله عليه وسلم فَاسْتَحْيَيْتُ مِنْهُ

Narrated Salama: `Ali remained behind the Prophet ﷺ during the Ghazwa of Khaibar as he was suffering from eye trouble. He then said, "(How can) I remain behind the Prophet ﷺ ", and followed him. So when he slept on the night of the conquest of Khaibar, the Prophet ﷺ said, "I will give the flag tomorrow, or tomorrow the flag will be taken by a man who is loved by Allah and His Apostle , and (Khaibar) will be conquered through him, (with Allah's help)" While every one of us was hopeful to have the flag, it was said, "Here is `Ali" and the Prophet ﷺ gave him the flag and Khaibar was conquered through him (with Allah's Help). – Sahih Al-Bukhari 4209

حَدَّثَنَا عَبْدُ اللَّهِ بْنُ مَسْلَمَةَ، حَدَّثَنَا حَاتِمٌ، عَنْ يَزِيدَ بْنِ أَبِي عُبَيْدٍ، عَنْ سَلَمَةَ، رضى الله عنه قَالَ كَانَ عَلِيٌّ ـ رضى الله عنه ـ تَخَلَّفَ عَنِ النَّبِيِّ صلى الله عليه وسلم فِي خَيْبَرَ، وَكَانَ رَمِدًا فَقَالَ أَنَا أَتَخَلَّفُ عَنِ النَّبِيِّ صلى الله عليه وسلم فَلَحِقَ، فَلَمَّا بِتْنَا اللَّيْلَةَ الَّتِي فُتِحَتْ قَالَ " لأُعْطِيَنَّ الرَّايَةَ غَدًا ـ أَوْ لَيَأْخُذَنَّ الرَّايَةَ غَدًا ـ رَجُلٌ يُحِبُّهُ اللَّهُ وَرَسُولُهُ، يُفْتَحُ عَلَيْهِ ". فَنَحْنُ نَرْجُوهَا فَقِيلَ هَذَا عَلِيٌّ، فَأَعْطَاهُ فَفُتِحَ عَلَيْهِ

Narrated Yazid bin Abi Ubaid: I saw the trace of a wound in Salama's leg. I said to him, "O Abu Muslim! What is this wound?" He said, "This was inflicted on me on the day of Khaibar and the people said, 'Salama has been wounded.' Then I went to the Prophet ﷺ and he puffed his saliva in it (i.e. the wound) thrice., and since then I have not had any pain in it till this hour.". – Sahih Al-Bukhari 4206

حَدَّثَنَا الْمَكِّيُّ بْنُ إِبْرَاهِيمَ، حَدَّثَنَا يَزِيدُ بْنُ أَبِي عُبَيْدٍ، قَالَ رَأَيْتُ أَثَرَ ضَرْبَةٍ فِي سَاقِ سَلَمَةَ، فَقُلْتُ يَا أَبَا مُسْلِمٍ، مَا هَذِهِ الضَّرْبَةُ قَالَ هَذِهِ ضَرْبَةٌ أَصَابَتْنِي يَوْمَ خَيْبَرَ، فَقَالَ النَّاسُ أُصِيبَ سَلَمَةُ. فَأَتَيْتُ النَّبِيَّ صلى الله عليه وسلم فَنَفَثَ فِيهِ ثَلاَثَ نَفَثَاتٍ، فَمَا اشْتَكَيْتُهَا حَتَّى السَّاعَةِ.

Narrated Abu Huraira: We witnessed (the battle of) Khaibar. Allah's Messenger ﷺ said about one of those who were with him and who claimed to be a Muslim. "This (man) is from the dwellers of the Hell-Fire." When the battle started, that fellow fought so violently and bravely that he received plenty of wounds. Some of the people were about to doubt (the Prophet's statement), but the man, feeling the pain of his wounds, put his hand into his quiver and took out of it, some arrows with which he slaughtered himself (i.e. committed suicide). Then some men amongst the Muslims came hurriedly and said, "O Allah's Apostle! Allah has made your statement true so-and-so has committed suicide. "The Prophet ﷺ said, "O so-and-so! Get up and make an announcement that none but a believer will enter Paradise and that Allah may support the religion with an unchaste (evil) wicked man. – Sahih Al-Bukhari 4203

حَدَّثَنَا أَبُو الْيَمَانِ، أَخْبَرَنَا شُعَيْبٌ، عَنِ الزُّهْرِيِّ، قَالَ أَخْبَرَنِي سَعِيدُ بْنُ الْمُسَيَّبِ، أَنَّ أَبَا هُرَيْرَةَ ـ رضى الله عنه ـ قَالَ شَهِدْنَا خَيْبَرَ، فَقَالَ رَسُولُ اللَّهِ صلى الله عليه وسلم لِرَجُلٍ مِمَّنْ مَعَهُ يَدَّعِي الإِسْلاَمَ " هَذَا مِنْ أَهْلِ النَّارِ ". فَلَمَّا حَضَرَ الْقِتَالُ قَاتَلَ الرَّجُلُ أَشَدَّ الْقِتَالِ، حَتَّى كَثُرَتْ بِهِ الْجِرَاحَةُ، فَكَادَ بَعْضُ النَّاسِ يَرْتَابُ، فَوَجَدَ الرَّجُلُ أَلَمَ الْجِرَاحَةِ، فَأَهْوَى بِيَدِهِ إِلَى كِنَانَتِهِ، فَاسْتَخْرَجَ مِنْهَا أَسْهُمًا، فَنَحَرَ بِهَا نَفْسَهُ، فَاشْتَدَّ رِجَالٌ مِنَ الْمُسْلِمِينَ، فَقَالُوا يَا رَسُولَ اللَّهِ، صَدَّقَ اللَّهُ حَدِيثَكَ، انْتَحَرَ فُلاَنٌ فَقَتَلَ نَفْسَهُ. فَقَالَ " قُمْ يَا فُلاَنُ فَأَذِّنْ أَنَّهُ لاَ يَدْخُلُ الْجَنَّةَ إِلاَّ مُؤْمِنٌ، إِنَّ اللَّهَ يُؤَيِّدُ الدِّينَ بِالرَّجُلِ الْفَاجِرِ ". تَابَعَهُ مَعْمَرٌ عَنِ الزُّهْرِيِّ

Narrated `Ali: Allah's Messenger ﷺ prohibited Al-Mut'a marriage and the eating of donkey's meat in the year of the Khaibar battle. – Sahih Al-Bukhari 5523

حَدَّثَنَا عَبْدُ اللَّهِ بْنُ يُوسُفَ، أَخْبَرَنَا مَالِكٌ، عَنِ ابْنِ شِهَابٍ، عَنْ عَبْدِ اللَّهِ، وَالْحَسَنِ، ابْنَىْ مُحَمَّدِ بْنِ عَلِيٍّ عَنْ أَبِيهِمَا، عَنْ عَلِيٍّ ـ رضى الله عنهم ـ قَالَ نَهَى رَسُولُ اللَّهِ صلى الله عليه وسلم عَنِ الْمُتْعَةِ عَامَ خَيْبَرَ وَلُحُومِ حُمُرِ الإِنْسِيَّةِ

Narrated Jabir bin `Abdullah: The Prophet ﷺ prohibited the eating of donkey's meat on the day of the battle of Khaibar, and allowed the eating of horse flesh. – Sahih Al-Bukhari 5524

حَدَّثَنَا سُلَيْمَانُ بْنُ حَرْبٍ، حَدَّثَنَا حَمَّادٌ، عَنْ عَمْرٍو، عَنْ مُحَمَّدِ بْنِ عَلِيٍّ، عَنْ جَابِرِ بْنِ عَبْدِ اللَّهِ، قَالَ نَهَى النَّبِيُّ صلى الله عليه وسلم يَوْمَ خَيْبَرَ عَنْ لُحُومِ الْحُمُرِ، وَرَخَّصَ فِي لُحُومِ الْخَيْلِ.

Narrated Ibn `Abbas: I do not know whether the Prophet ﷺ forbade the eating of donkey-meat (temporarily) because they were the beasts of burden for the people, and he disliked that their means of transportation should be lost, or he forbade it on the day of Khaibar permanently. – Sahih Al-Bukhari 4227

حَدَّثَنِي مُحَمَّدُ بْنُ أَبِي الْحُسَيْنِ، حَدَّثَنَا عُمَرُ بْنُ حَفْصٍ، حَدَّثَنَا أَبِي، عَنْ عَاصِمٍ، عَنْ عَامِرٍ، عَنِ ابْنِ عَبَّاسٍ ـ رضى الله عنهما ـ قَالَ لاَ أَدْرِي أَنَهَى عَنْهُ رَسُولُ اللَّهِ صلى الله عليه وسلم مِنْ أَجْلِ أَنَّهُ كَانَ حَمُولَةَ النَّاسِ، فَكَرِهَ أَنْ تَذْهَبَ حَمُولَتُهُمْ، أَوْ حَرَّمَهُ فِي يَوْمِ خَيْبَرَ، لَحْمَ الْحُمُرِ الأَهْلِيَّةِ.

Narrated Ibn Abi `Aufa: We were afflicted with hunger during the besiege of Khaibar, and when it was the day of (the battle of) Khaibar, we slaughtered the donkeys and when the pots got boiling (with their meat). Allah's Apostle made an announcement that all the pots should be upset and that nobody should eat anything of the meat of the donkeys. We thought that the Prophetﷺ prohibited that because the Khumus had not been taken out of the booty (i.e. donkeys); other people said, "He prohibited eating them for ever." The sub-narrator added, "I asked Sa`id bin Jubair who said, 'He has made the eating of donkeys' meat illegal for ever."). – Al-Bukhari 3155

حَدَّثَنَا مُوسَى بْنُ إِسْمَاعِيلَ، حَدَّثَنَا عَبْدُ الْوَاحِدِ، حَدَّثَنَا الشَّيْبَانِيُّ، قَالَ سَمِعْتُ ابْنَ أَبِي أَوْفَى ـ رضى الله عنهما ـ يَقُولُ أَصَابَتْنَا مَجَاعَةٌ لَيَالِيَ خَيْبَرَ، فَلَمَّا كَانَ يَوْمُ خَيْبَرَ وَقَعْنَا فِي الْحُمُرِ الأَهْلِيَّةِ، فَانْتَحَرْنَاهَا فَلَمَّا غَلَتِ الْقُدُورُ، نَادَى مُنَادِي رَسُولِ اللَّهِ صلى الله عليه وسلم اكْفَئُوا الْقُدُورَ، فَلاَ تَطْعَمُوا مِنْ لُحُومِ الْحُمُرِ شَيْئًا. قَالَ عَبْدُ اللَّهِ فَقُلْنَا إِنَّمَا نَهَى النَّبِيُّ صلى الله عليه وسلم لأَنَّهَا لَمْ تُخَمَّسْ. قَالَ وَقَالَ آخَرُونَ حَرَّمَهَا الْبَتَّةَ. وَسَأَلْتُ سَعِيدَ بْنَ جُبَيْرٍ فَقَالَ حَرَّمَهَا الْبَتَّةَ

Narrated `Amr: I said to Jabir bin Zaid, "The people claim that Allah's Messengerﷺ forbade the eating of donkey's meat." He said, "Al-Hakam bin `Amr Al-Ghifari used to say so when he was with us, but Ibn `Abbas, the great religious learned man, refused to give a final verdict and recited:-- 'Say: I find not in that which has been inspired to me anything forbidden to be eaten by one who wishes to eat it, unless it be carrion, blood poured forth or the flesh of swine...' (6.145). – Sahih Al-Bukhari 5529

حَدَّثَنَا عَلِيُّ بْنُ عَبْدِ اللَّهِ، حَدَّثَنَا سُفْيَانُ، قَالَ عَمْرٌو قُلْتُ لِجَابِرِ بْنِ زَيْدٍ يَزْعُمُونَ أَنَّ رَسُولَ اللَّهِ صلى الله عليه وسلم نَهَى عَنْ حُمُرِ الأَهْلِيَّةِ فَقَالَ قَدْ كَانَ يَقُولُ ذَاكَ الْحَكَمُ بْنُ عَمْرٍو الْغِفَارِيُّ عِنْدَنَا بِالْبَصْرَةِ، وَلَكِنْ أَبَى ذَاكَ الْبَحْرُ ابْنُ عَبَّاسٍ وَقَرَأَ {قُلْ لاَ أَجِدُ فِيمَا أُوحِيَ إِلَيَّ مُحَرَّمًا}

Narrated Ibn `Umar: During the holy battle of Khaibar the Prophetﷺ said, "Whoever ate from this plant (i.e. garlic) should not enter our mosque.". – Sahih Al-Bukhari 853

حَدَّثَنَا مُسَدَّدٌ، قَالَ حَدَّثَنَا يَحْيَى، عَنْ عُبَيْدِ اللَّهِ، قَالَ حَدَّثَنِي نَافِعٌ، عَنِ ابْنِ عُمَرَ ـ رضى الله عنهما ـ أَنَّ النَّبِيَّ صلى الله عليه وسلم قَالَ فِي غَزْوَةِ خَيْبَرَ " مَنْ أَكَلَ مِنْ هَذِهِ الشَّجَرَةِ ـ يَعْنِي الثُّومَ ـ فَلاَ يَقْرَبَنَّ مَسْجِدَنَا ".

Narrated `Aisha: When Khaibar was conquered, we said, "Now we will eat our fill of dates!". – Sahih Al-Bukhari 4242

حَدَّثَنِي مُحَمَّدُ بْنُ بَشَّارٍ، حَدَّثَنَا حَرَمِيٌّ، حَدَّثَنَا شُعْبَةُ، قَالَ أَخْبَرَنِي عُمَارَةُ، عَنْ عِكْرِمَةَ، عَنْ عَائِشَةَ ـ رضى الله عنها ـ قَالَتْ وَلَمَّا فُتِحَتْ خَيْبَرُ قُلْنَا الآنَ نَشْبَعُ مِنَ التَّمْرِ.

Narrated Ibn `Umar: On the day of Khaibar, Allah's Messengerﷺ divided (the war booty of Khaibar) with the ratio of two shares for the horse and one-share for the foot soldier. (The sub-narrator, Nafi` explained this, saying, "If a man had a horse, he was given three shares and if he had no horse, then he was given one share."). – Sahih Al-Bukhari 4228

حَدَّثَنَا الْحَسَنُ بْنُ إِسْحَاقَ، حَدَّثَنَا مُحَمَّدُ بْنُ سَابِقٍ، حَدَّثَنَا زَائِدَةُ، عَنْ عُبَيْدِ اللَّهِ بْنِ عُمَرَ، عَنْ نَافِعٍ، عَنِ ابْنِ عُمَرَ ـ رضى الله عنهما ـ قَالَ قَسَمَ رَسُولُ اللَّهِ صلى الله عليه وسلم يَوْمَ خَيْبَرَ لِلْفَرَسِ سَهْمَيْنِ، وَلِلرَّاجِلِ سَهْمًا. قَالَ فَسَّرَهُ نَافِعٌ فَقَالَ إِذَا كَانَ مَعَ الرَّجُلِ فَرَسٌ فَلَهُ ثَلاَثَةُ أَسْهُمٍ، فَإِنْ لَمْ يَكُنْ لَهُ فَرَسٌ فَلَهُ سَهْمٌ.

Narrated `Abdullah bin `Umar: The Prophetﷺ concluded a contract with the people of Khaibar to utilize the land on the condition that half the products of fruits or vegetation would be their share. The Prophetﷺ used to give his wives one hundred Wasqs each, eighty Wasqs of dates and twenty Wasqs of barley. (When `Umar became the Caliph) he gave the wives of the Prophetﷺ the option of either having the land and water as their shares, or carrying on the previous practice. Some of them chose the land and some chose the Wasqs, and `Aisha chose the land. – Sahih Al-Bukhari 2328

حَدَّثَنَا إِبْرَاهِيمُ بْنُ الْمُنْذِرِ، حَدَّثَنَا أَنَسُ بْنُ عِيَاضٍ، عَنْ عُبَيْدِ اللَّهِ، عَنْ نَافِعٍ، أَنَّ عَبْدَ اللَّهِ بْنَ عُمَرَ ـ رضى الله عنهما ـ أَخْبَرَهُ أَنَّ النَّبِيَّ صلى الله عليه وسلم عَامَلَ خَيْبَرَ بِشَطْرِ مَا يَخْرُجُ مِنْهَا مِنْ ثَمَرٍ أَوْ زَرْعٍ، فَكَانَ يُعْطِي أَزْوَاجَهُ مِائَةَ وَسْقٍ ثَمَانُونَ

وَسْقَ تَمْرٍ وَعِشْرُونَ وَسْقَ شَعِيرٍ، فَقَسَمَ عُمَرُ خَيْبَرَ، فَخَيَّرَ أَزْوَاجَ النَّبِيِّ صلى الله عليه وسلم أَنْ يُقْطِعَ لَهُنَّ مِنَ الْمَاءِ وَالأَرْضِ، أَوْ يُمْضِيَ لَهُنَّ، فَمِنْهُنَّ مَنِ اخْتَارَ الأَرْضَ وَمِنْهُنَّ مَنِ اخْتَارَ الْوَسْقَ، وَكَانَتْ عَائِشَةُ اخْتَارَتِ الأَرْضَ.

Narrated Ibn Shihab Az-Zuhri: Anas bin Malik said, "When the emigrants came Medina, they had nothing whereas the Ansar had land and property. The Ansar gave them their land on condition that the emigrants would give them half the yearly yield and work on the land and provide the necessaries for cultivation." His (i.e. Anas's mother who was also the mother of `Abdullah bin Abu Talha, gave some date-palms to Allah' Apostle who gave them to his freed slave-girl (Um Aiman) who was also the mother of Usama bin Zaid. When the Prophet ﷺ finished from the fighting against the people of Khaibar and returned to Medina, the emigrants returned to the Ansar the fruit gifts which the Ansar had given them. The Prophet ﷺ also returned to Anas's mother the date-palms. Allah's Messenger ﷺ gave Um Aiman other trees from his garden in lieu of the old gift. – Sahih Al-Bukhari 2630

حَدَّثَنَا عَبْدُ اللَّهِ بْنُ يُوسُفَ، أَخْبَرَنَا ابْنُ وَهْبٍ، حَدَّثَنَا يُونُسُ، عَنِ ابْنِ شِهَابٍ، عَنْ أَنَسِ بْنِ مَالِكٍ ـ رضى الله عنه ـ قَالَ لَمَّا قَدِمَ الْمُهَاجِرُونَ الْمَدِينَةَ مِنْ مَكَّةَ وَلَيْسَ بِأَيْدِيهِمْ ـ يَعْنِي شَيْئًا ـ وَكَانَتِ الأَنْصَارُ أَهْلَ الأَرْضِ وَالْعَقَارِ، فَقَاسَمَهُمُ الأَنْصَارُ عَلَى أَنْ يُعْطُوهُمْ ثِمَارَ أَمْوَالِهِمْ كُلَّ عَامٍ وَيَكْفُوهُمُ الْعَمَلَ وَالْمَئُونَةَ، وَكَانَتْ أُمُّهُ أُمُّ أَنَسٍ أُمُّ سُلَيْمٍ كَانَتْ أُمَّ عَبْدِ اللَّهِ بْنِ أَبِي طَلْحَةَ، فَكَانَتْ أَعْطَتْ أُمُّ أَنَسٍ رَسُولَ اللَّهِ صلى الله عليه وسلم عِذَاقًا فَأَعْطَاهُنَّ النَّبِيُّ صلى الله عليه وسلم أُمَّ أَيْمَنَ مَوْلاَتَهُ أُمَّ أُسَامَةَ بْنِ زَيْدٍ. قَالَ ابْنُ شِهَابٍ فَأَخْبَرَنِي أَنَسُ بْنُ مَالِكٍ أَنَّ النَّبِيَّ صلى الله عليه وسلم لَمَّا فَرَغَ مِنْ قَتْلِ أَهْلِ خَيْبَرَ فَانْصَرَفَ إِلَى الْمَدِينَةِ، رَدَّ الْمُهَاجِرُونَ إِلَى الأَنْصَارِ مَنَائِحَهُمُ الَّتِي كَانُوا مَنَحُوهُمْ مِنْ ثِمَارِهِمْ فَرَدَّ النَّبِيُّ صلى الله عليه وسلم إِلَى أُمِّهِ عِذَاقَهَا، وَأَعْطَى رَسُولُ اللَّهِ صلى الله عليه وسلم أُمَّ أَيْمَنَ مَكَانَهُنَّ مِنْ حَائِطِهِ. وَقَالَ أَحْمَدُ بْنُ شَبِيبٍ أَخْبَرَنَا أَبِي عَنْ يُونُسَ بِهَذَا، وَقَالَ مَكَانَهُنَّ مِنْ خَالِصِهِ

Narrated Jubair bin Mut`im: `Uthman bin `Affan and I went to the Prophet ﷺ and said, "You had given Banu Al-Muttalib from the Khumus of Khaibar's booty and left us in spite of the fact that we and Banu Al-Muttalib are similarly related to you." The Prophet ﷺ said, "Banu Hashim and Banu Al-Muttalib only are one and the same." So the Prophet ﷺ did not give anything to Banu `Abd Shams and Banu Nawfal. – Sahih Al-Bukhari 4229

حَدَّثَنَا يَحْيَى بْنُ بُكَيْرٍ، حَدَّثَنَا اللَّيْثُ، عَنْ يُونُسَ، عَنِ ابْنِ شِهَابٍ، عَنْ سَعِيدِ بْنِ الْمُسَيَّبِ، أَنَّ جُبَيْرَ بْنَ مُطْعِمٍ، أَخْبَرَهُ قَالَ مَشَيْتُ أَنَا وَعُثْمَانُ بْنُ عَفَّانَ، إِلَى النَّبِيِّ صلى الله عليه وسلم فَقُلْنَا أَعْطَيْتَ بَنِي الْمُطَّلِبِ مِنْ خُمْسِ خَيْبَرَ، وَتَرَكْتَنَا، وَنَحْنُ بِمَنْزِلَةٍ وَاحِدَةٍ مِنْكَ. فَقَالَ " إِنَّمَا بَنُو هَاشِمٍ وَبَنُو الْمُطَّلِبِ شَىْءٌ وَاحِدٌ ". قَالَ جُبَيْرٌ وَلَمْ يَقْسِمِ النَّبِيُّ صلى الله عليه وسلم لِبَنِي عَبْدِ شَمْسٍ وَبَنِي نَوْفَلٍ شَيْئًا

Whatever Allah restored to His Messenger from the inhabitants of the villages belongs to Allah, and to the Messenger, and to the relatives, and to the orphans, and to the poor, and to the wayfarer; so that it may not circulate solely between the wealthy among you. Whatever the Messenger gives you, accept it; and whatever he forbids you, abstain from it. And fear Allah. Allah is severe in punishment. To the poor refugees who were driven out of their homes and their possessions, as they sought the favor of Allah and His approval, and came to the aid of Allah and His Messenger. These are the sincere. - Surah Al-Hashr 59:7&8

مَّآ أَفَآءَ ٱللَّهُ عَلَىٰ رَسُولِهِۦ مِنْ أَهْلِ ٱلْقُرَىٰ فَلِلَّهِ وَلِلرَّسُولِ وَلِذِى ٱلْقُرْبَىٰ وَٱلْيَتَـٰمَىٰ وَٱلْمَسَـٰكِينِ وَٱبْنِ ٱلسَّبِيلِ كَىْ لَا يَكُونَ دُولَةًۢ بَيْنَ ٱلْأَغْنِيَآءِ مِنكُمْ ۚ وَمَآ ءَاتَىٰكُمُ ٱلرَّسُولُ فَخُذُوهُ وَمَا نَهَىٰكُمْ عَنْهُ فَٱنتَهُوا۟ ۚ وَٱتَّقُوا۟ ٱللَّهَ ۖ إِنَّ ٱللَّهَ شَدِيدُ ٱلْعِقَابِ لِلْفُقَرَآءِ ٱلْمُهَـٰجِرِينَ ٱلَّذِينَ أُخْرِجُوا۟ مِن دِيَـٰرِهِمْ وَأَمْوَٰلِهِمْ يَبْتَغُونَ فَضْلًا مِّنَ ٱللَّهِ وَرِضْوَٰنًا وَيَنصُرُونَ ٱللَّهَ وَرَسُولَهُۥٓ ۚ أُو۟لَـٰٓئِكَ هُمُ ٱلصَّـٰدِقُونَ

Jabir added, "We were with the Prophet ﷺ at Nakhl and he offered the Fear prayer." Abu Huraira said, "I offered the Fear prayer with the Prophet ﷺ during the Ghazwa (i.e. the battle) of Najd." Abu Huraira came to the Prophet ﷺ during the day of Khaibar. – Al-Bukhari 4137

وَقَالَ أَبُو الزُّبَيْرِ عَنْ جَابِرٍ، كُنَّا مَعَ النَّبِيِّ صلى الله عليه وسلم بِنَخْلٍ فَصَلَّى الْخَوْفَ. وَقَالَ أَبُو هُرَيْرَةَ صَلَّيْتُ مَعَ النَّبِيِّ صلى الله عليه وسلم غَزْوَةَ نَجْدٍ صَلاَةَ الْخَوْفِ. وَإِنَّمَا جَاءَ أَبُو هُرَيْرَةَ إِلَى النَّبِيِّ صلى الله عليه وسلم أَيَّامَ خَيْبَرَ.

Narrated Abu Huraira: I went to Allah's Messengerﷺ while he was at Khaibar after it had fallen in the Muslims' hands. I said, "O Allah's Messengerﷺ ! Give me a share (from the land of Khaibar)." One of the sons of Sa'id bin Al-'As said, "O Allah's Messengerﷺ ! Do not give him a share." I said, "This is the murderer of Ibn Qauqal." The son of Said bin Al-As said, "Strange! A Wabr (i.e. guinea pig) who has come down to us from the mountain of Qaduim (i.e. grazing place of sheep) blames me for killing a Muslim who was given superiority by Allah because of me, and Allah did not disgrace me at his hands (i.e. was not killed as an infidel)." (The sub-narrator said "I do not know whether the Prophetﷺ gave him a share or not."). – Sahih Al-Bukhari 2827

حَدَّثَنَا الْحُمَيْدِيُّ، حَدَّثَنَا سُفْيَانُ، حَدَّثَنَا الزُّهْرِيُّ، قَالَ أَخْبَرَنِي عَنْبَسَةُ بْنُ سَعِيدٍ، عَنْ أَبِي هُرَيْرَةَ ـ رضى الله عنه ـ قَالَ أَتَيْتُ رَسُولَ اللَّهِ صلى الله عليه وسلم وَهْوَ بِخَيْبَرَ بَعْدَ مَا افْتَتَحُوهَا، فَقُلْتُ يَا رَسُولَ اللَّهِ أَسْهِمْ لِي. فَقَالَ بَعْضُ بَنِي سَعِيدِ بْنِ الْعَاصِ لاَ تُسْهِمْ لَهُ يَا رَسُولَ اللَّهِ. فَقَالَ أَبُو هُرَيْرَةَ هَذَا قَاتِلُ ابْنِ قَوْقَلٍ. فَقَالَ ابْنُ سَعِيدِ بْنِ الْعَاصِ وَاعَجَبًا لِوَبْرٍ تَدَلَّى عَلَيْنَا مِنْ قَدُومِ ضَأْنٍ، يَنْعَى عَلَىَّ قَتْلَ رَجُلٍ مُسْلِمٍ أَكْرَمَهُ اللَّهُ عَلَى يَدَىَّ وَلَمْ يُهِنِّي عَلَى يَدَيْهِ. قَالَ فَلاَ أَدْرِي أَسْهَمَ لَهُ أَمْ لَمْ يُسْهِمْ لَهُ. قَالَ سُفْيَانُ وَحَدَّثَنِيهِ السَّعِيدِيُّ عَنْ جَدِّهِ عَنْ أَبِي هُرَيْرَةَ. قَالَ أَبُو عَبْدِ اللَّهِ السَّعِيدِيُّ عَمْرُو بْنُ يَحْيَى بْنِ سَعِيدِ بْنِ عَمْرِو بْنِ سَعِيدِ بْنِ الْعَاصِ

Abu Sa`id and Abu Huraira said: "The Prophetﷺ made the brother of Bani Adi from the Ansar as the ruler of Khaibar. – Sahih Al-Bukhari 4246, 4247

وَقَالَ عَبْدُ الْعَزِيزِ بْنُ مُحَمَّدٍ عَنْ عَبْدِ الْمَجِيدِ، عَنْ سَعِيدٍ، أَنَّ أَبَا سَعِيدٍ، وَأَبَا، هُرَيْرَةَ حَدَّثَاهُ أَنَّ النَّبِيَّ صلى الله عليه وسلم بَعَثَ أَخَا بَنِي عَدِيٍّ مِنَ الأَنْصَارِ إِلَى خَيْبَرَ فَأَمَّرَهُ عَلَيْهَا. وَعَنْ عَبْدِ الْمَجِيدِ عَنْ أَبِي صَالِحٍ السَّمَّانِ عَنْ أَبِي هُرَيْرَةَ وَأَبِي سَعِيدٍ مِثْلَهُ.

Narrated Abu Sa`id Al-Khudri and Abu Huraira: Allah's Messengerﷺ appointed somebody as a governor of Khaibar. That governor brought to him an excellent kind of dates (from Khaibar). The Prophetﷺ asked, "Are all the dates of Khaibar like this?" He replied, "By Allah, no, O Allah's Messengerﷺ ! But we barter one Sa of this (type of dates) for two Sas of dates of ours and two Sas of it for three of ours." Allah's Messengerﷺ said, "Do not do so (as that is a kind of usury) but sell the mixed dates (of inferior quality) for money, and then buy good dates with that money.". – Sahih Al-Bukhari 2201, 2202

حَدَّثَنَا قُتَيْبَةُ، عَنْ مَالِكٍ، عَنْ عَبْدِ الْمَجِيدِ بْنِ سُهَيْلِ بْنِ عَبْدِ الرَّحْمَنِ، عَنْ سَعِيدِ بْنِ الْمُسَيَّبِ، عَنْ أَبِي سَعِيدٍ الْخُدْرِيِّ، وَعَنْ أَبِي هُرَيْرَةَ ـ رضى الله عنهما ـ أَنَّ رَسُولَ اللَّهِ صلى الله عليه وسلم اسْتَعْمَلَ رَجُلاً عَلَى خَيْبَرَ، فَجَاءَهُ بِتَمْرٍ جَنِيبٍ، فَقَالَ رَسُولُ اللَّهِ صلى الله عليه وسلم " أَكُلُّ تَمْرِ خَيْبَرَ هَكَذَا ". قَالَ لاَ وَاللَّهِ يَا رَسُولَ اللَّهِ، إِنَّا لَنَأْخُذُ الصَّاعَ مِنْ هَذَا بِالصَّاعَيْنِ، وَالصَّاعَيْنِ بِالثَّلاَثَةِ. فَقَالَ رَسُولُ اللَّهِ صلى الله عليه وسلم " لاَ تَفْعَلْ، بِعِ الْجَمْعَ بِالدَّرَاهِمِ، ثُمَّ ابْتَعْ بِالدَّرَاهِمِ جَنِيبًا"

Narrated Ibn `Umar : During the holy battle of Khaibar the Prophetﷺ said, "Whoever ate from this plant (i.e. garlic) should not enter our mosque." – Sahih al-Bukhari 853

حَدَّثَنَا مُسَدَّدٌ، قَالَ حَدَّثَنَا يَحْيَى، عَنْ عُبَيْدِ اللَّهِ، قَالَ حَدَّثَنِي نَافِعٌ، عَنِ ابْنِ عُمَرَ ـ رضى الله عنهما ـ أَنَّ النَّبِيَّ صلى الله عليه وسلم قَالَ فِي غَزْوَةِ خَيْبَرَ " مَنْ أَكَلَ مِنْ هَذِهِ الشَّجَرَةِ ـ يَعْنِي الثُّومَ ـ فَلاَ يَقْرَبَنَّ مَسْجِدَنَا "

Narrated Ibn `Umar:On the day of Khaiber, Allah's Messengerﷺ forbade the eating of garlic and the meat of donkeys. – Sahih al-Bukhari 4215

حَدَّثَنِي عُبَيْدُ بْنُ إِسْمَاعِيلَ، عَنْ أَبِي أُسَامَةَ، عَنْ عُبَيْدِ اللَّهِ، عَنْ نَافِعٍ، وَسَالِمٍ، عَنِ ابْنِ عُمَرَ ـ رضى الله عنهما ـ أَنَّ رَسُولَ اللَّهِ صلى الله عليه وسلم نَهَى يَوْمَ خَيْبَرَ عَنْ أَكْلِ الثُّومِ، وَعَنْ لُحُومِ الْحُمُرِ الأَهْلِيَّةِ. نَهَى عَنْ أَكْلِ الثُّومِ هُوَ عَنْ نَافِعٍ وَحْدَهُ. وَلُحُومُ الْحُمُرِ الأَهْلِيَّةِ عَنْ سَالِمٍ

And He brought down (the ones) of the population of the Book (Or: Family of the Book, i.e., the Jews and christians) who backed them from their bastions, and hurled horror in their hearts; a group you killed and (another) group you (made) captive And He caused you to inherit their land, and their residences and their riches, and a land you have not trodden; and Allah has been Ever-Determiner over everything. Surah Al-Ahzab 33:26&27

وَأَنزَلَ ٱلَّذِينَ ظَـٰهَرُوهُم مِّنْ أَهْلِ ٱلْكِتَـٰبِ مِن صَيَاصِيهِمْ وَقَذَفَ فِى قُلُوبِهِمُ ٱلرُّعْبَ فَرِيقًا تَقْتُلُونَ وَتَأْسِرُونَ فَرِيقًا وَأَوْرَثَكُمْ أَرْضَهُمْ وَدِيَـٰرَهُمْ وَأَمْوَ ٰلَهُمْ وَأَرْضًا لَّمْ تَطَـُٔوهَا ۚ وَكَانَ ٱللَّهُ عَلَىٰ كُلِّ شَىْءٍ قَدِيرًا

Marriage with Safiyya bint Huyayy
زواج صفية بنت حيي

Narrated `Abdul `Aziz: Anas said, 'When Allah's Messenger ﷺ invaded Khaibar, we offered the Fajr prayer there (early in the morning) when it was still dark. The Prophet ﷺ rode and Abu Talha rode too and I was riding behind Abu Talha. The Prophet ﷺ passed through the lane of Khaibar quickly and my knee was touching the thigh of the Prophet ﷺ. He uncovered his thigh and I saw the whiteness of the thigh of the Prophet. When he entered the town, he said, 'Allahu Akbar! Khaibar is ruined. Whenever we approach near a (hostile) nation (to fight) then evil will be the morning of those who have been warned.' He repeated this thrice. The people came out for their jobs and some of them said, 'Muhammad (has come).' (Some of our companions added, "With his army.") We conquered Khaibar, took the captives, and the booty was collected. Dihya came and said, 'O Allah's Prophet! Give me a slave girl from the captives.' The Prophet said, 'Go and take any slave girl.' He took Safiya bint Huyai. A man came to the Prophet ﷺ and said, 'O Allah's Messenger ﷺ! You gave Safiya bint Huyai to Dihya and she is the chief mistress of the tribes of Quraidha and An-Nadir and she befits none but you.' So the Prophet said, 'Bring him along with her.' So Dihya came with her and when the Prophet ﷺ saw her, he said to Dihya, 'Take any slave girl other than her from the captives.' Anas added: The Prophet ﷺ then manumitted her and married her." Thabit asked Anas, "O Abu Hamza! What did the Prophet ﷺ pay her (as Mahr)?" He said, "Her self was her Mahr for he manumitted her and then married her." Anas added, "While on the way, Um Sulaim dressed her for marriage (ceremony) and at night she sent her as a bride to the Prophet ﷺ. So the Prophet was a bridegroom and he said, 'Whoever has anything (food) should bring it.' He spread out a leather sheet (for the food) and some brought dates and others cooking butter. (I think he (Anas) mentioned As-Sawaq). So they prepared a dish of Hais (a kind of meal). And that was Walima (the marriage banquet) of Allah's Messenger ﷺ." – Sahih al-Bukhari 371

حَدَّثَنَا يَعْقُوبُ بْنُ إِبْرَاهِيمَ، قَالَ حَدَّثَنَا إِسْمَاعِيلُ ابْنُ عُلَيَّةَ، قَالَ حَدَّثَنَا عَبْدُ الْعَزِيزِ بْنُ صُهَيْبٍ، عَنْ أَنَسٍ، أَنَّ رَسُولَ اللَّهِ صلى الله عليه وسلم غَزَا خَيْبَرَ، فَصَلَّيْنَا عِنْدَهَا صَلاَةَ الْغَدَاةِ بِغَلَسٍ، فَرَكِبَ نَبِيُّ اللَّهِ صلى الله عليه وسلم وَرَكِبَ أَبُو طَلْحَةَ، وَأَنَا رَدِيفُ أَبِي طَلْحَةَ، فَأَجْرَى نَبِيُّ اللَّهِ صلى الله عليه وسلم فِي زُقَاقِ خَيْبَرَ، وَإِنَّ رُكْبَتِي لَتَمَسُّ فَخِذَ نَبِيِّ اللَّهِ صلى الله عليه وسلم، ثُمَّ حَسَرَ الإِزَارَ عَنْ فَخِذِهِ حَتَّى إِنِّي أَنْظُرُ إِلَى بَيَاضِ فَخِذِ نَبِيِّ اللَّهِ صلى الله عليه وسلم، فَلَمَّا دَخَلَ الْقَرْيَةَ قَالَ " اللَّهُ أَكْبَرُ، خَرِبَتْ خَيْبَرُ، إِنَّا إِذَا نَزَلْنَا بِسَاحَةِ قَوْمٍ فَسَاءَ صَبَاحُ الْمُنْذَرِينَ ". قَالَهَا ثَلاَثًا. قَالَ وَخَرَجَ الْقَوْمُ إِلَى أَعْمَالِهِمْ فَقَالُوا مُحَمَّدٌ ـ قَالَ عَبْدُ الْعَزِيزِ وَقَالَ بَعْضُ أَصْحَابِنَا ـ وَالْخَمِيسُ. يَعْنِي الْجَيْشَ، قَالَ فَأَصَبْنَاهَا عَنْوَةً، فَجُمِعَ السَّبْىُ، فَجَاءَ دِحْيَةُ فَقَالَ يَا نَبِيَّ اللَّهِ، أَعْطِنِي جَارِيَةً مِنَ السَّبْىِ. قَالَ " اذْهَبْ فَخُذْ جَارِيَةً ". فَأَخَذَ صَفِيَّةَ بِنْتَ حُيَىٍّ، فَجَاءَ رَجُلٌ إِلَى النَّبِيِّ صلى الله عليه وسلم فَقَالَ يَا نَبِيَّ اللَّهِ، أَعْطَيْتَ دِحْيَةَ صَفِيَّةَ بِنْتَ حُيَىٍّ سَيِّدَةَ قُرَيْظَةَ وَالنَّضِيرِ، لاَ تَصْلُحُ إِلاَّ لَكَ. قَالَ " ادْعُوهُ بِهَا ". فَجَاءَ بِهَا، فَلَمَّا نَظَرَ إِلَيْهَا النَّبِيُّ صلى الله عليه وسلم قَالَ " خُذْ جَارِيَةً مِنَ السَّبْىِ غَيْرَهَا ". قَالَ فَأَعْتَقَهَا النَّبِيُّ صلى الله عليه وسلم وَتَزَوَّجَهَا. فَقَالَ لَهُ ثَابِتٌ يَا أَبَا حَمْزَةَ، مَا أَصْدَقَهَا قَالَ نَفْسَهَا، أَعْتَقَهَا وَتَزَوَّجَهَا، حَتَّى إِذَا كَانَ بِالطَّرِيقِ جَهَّزَتْهَا لَهُ أُمُّ سُلَيْمٍ فَأَهْدَتْهَا لَهُ مِنَ اللَّيْلِ، فَأَصْبَحَ النَّبِيُّ صلى الله عليه وسلم عَرُوسًا فَقَالَ " مَنْ كَانَ عِنْدَهُ شَىْءٌ فَلْيَجِئْ بِهِ ". وَبَسَطَ نِطَعًا، فَجَعَلَ الرَّجُلُ يَجِيءُ بِالتَّمْرِ، وَجَعَلَ الرَّجُلُ يَجِيءُ بِالسَّمْنِ ـ قَالَ وَأَحْسِبُهُ قَدْ ذَكَرَ السَّوِيقَ ـ قَالَ فَحَاسُوا حَيْسًا، فَكَانَتْ وَلِيمَةَ رَسُولِ اللَّهِ صلى الله عليه وسلم.

Narrated Anas: The Prophet ﷺ halted to consummate his marriage with Safiyya. I invited the Muslims to his wedding banquet. He ordered that leather dining sheets be spread. Then dates, dried yoghurt and butter were put on those sheets. Anas added: The Prophet ﷺ consummated his marriage with Safiyya (during a journey) whereupon Hais (sweet dish) was served on a leather dining sheet. – Sahih al-Bukhari 5387

حَدَّثَنَا ابْنُ أَبِي مَرْيَمَ، أَخْبَرَنَا مُحَمَّدُ بْنُ جَعْفَرٍ، أَخْبَرَنِي حُمَيْدٌ، أَنَّهُ سَمِعَ أَنَسًا، يَقُولُ قَامَ النَّبِيُّ صلى الله عليه وسلم يَبْنِي بِصَفِيَّةَ فَدَعَوْتُ الْمُسْلِمِينَ إِلَى وَلِيمَتِهِ أَمَرَ بِالأَنْطَاعِ فَبُسِطَتْ فَأُلْقِيَ عَلَيْهَا التَّمْرُ وَالأَقِطُ وَالسَّمْنُ. وَقَالَ عَمْرٌو عَنْ أَنَسٍ بَنَى بِهَا النَّبِيُّ صلى الله عليه وسلم ثُمَّ صَنَعَ حَيْسًا فِي نِطَعٍ.

After they had covered a portion of the way suddenly the foot of the she-camel slipped and both the Prophet ﷺ and the woman (i.e., his wife, Safiya) fell down.

فَلَمَّا كَانُوا بِبَعْضِ الطَّرِيقِ عَثَرَتِ النَّاقَةُ، فَصُرِعَ النَّبِيُّ صلى الله عليه وسلم وَالْمَرْأَةُ

Narrated Anas bin Malik: Once the Prophet ﷺ was on one of his journeys, and the driver of the camels started chanting (to let the camels go fast). The Prophet ﷺ said to him. "(Take care) Drive slowly with the glass vessels, O Anjasha! Waihaka (May Allah be Merciful to you). – Sahih al-Bukhari 6209

حَدَّثَنَا آدَمُ، حَدَّثَنَا شُعْبَةُ، عَنْ ثَابِتٍ الْبُنَانِيِّ، عَنْ أَنَسِ بْنِ مَالِكٍ، قَالَ كَانَ النَّبِيُّ صلى الله عليه وسلم فِي مَسِيرٍ لَهُ فَحَدَا الْحَادِي، فَقَالَ النَّبِيُّ صلى الله عليه وسلم " ارْفُقْ يَا أَنْجَشَةُ، وَيْحَكَ، بِالْقَوَارِيرِ "

Narrated Anas bin Malik: That he and Abu Talha were coming in the company of the Prophet (towards Medina), while Safiya (the Prophet's wife) was riding behind him on his she-camel. After they had covered a portion of the way suddenly the foot of the she-camel slipped and both the Prophet ﷺ and the woman (i.e., his wife, Safiya) fell down. Abu Talha jumped quickly off his camel and came to the Prophet (saying.) "O Allah's Messenger ﷺ ! Let Allah sacrifice me for you! Have you received any injury?" The Prophet ﷺ said, "No, but take care of the woman (my wife)." Abu Talha covered his face with his garment and went towards her and threw his garment over her. Then the woman got up and Abu Talha prepared their she-camel (by tightening its saddle, etc.) and both of them (the Prophet ﷺ and Safiya) mounted it. Then all of them proceeded and when they approached near Medina, or saw Medina, the Prophet ﷺ said, "Ayibun, taibun, `abidun, liRabbina hamidun (We are coming back (to Medina) with repentance, worshiping (our Lord) and celebrating His (our Lord's) praises". The Prophet ﷺ continued repeating these words till he entered the city of Medina. – Sahih al-Bukhari 6185

حَدَّثَنَا عَلِيُّ بْنُ عَبْدِ اللَّهِ، حَدَّثَنَا بِشْرُ بْنُ الْمُفَضَّلِ، حَدَّثَنَا يَحْيَى بْنُ أَبِي إِسْحَاقَ، عَنْ أَنَسِ بْنِ مَالِكٍ، أَنَّهُ أَقْبَلَ هُوَ وَأَبُو طَلْحَةَ مَعَ النَّبِيِّ صلى الله عليه وسلم وَمَعَ النَّبِيِّ صلى الله عليه وسلم صَفِيَّةُ، مُرْدِفُهَا عَلَى رَاحِلَتِهِ، فَلَمَّا كَانُوا بِبَعْضِ الطَّرِيقِ عَثَرَتِ النَّاقَةُ، فَصُرِعَ النَّبِيُّ صلى الله عليه وسلم وَالْمَرْأَةُ، وَأَنَّ أَبَا طَلْحَةَ ـ قَالَ أَحْسِبُ ـ اقْتَحَمَ عَنْ بَعِيرِهِ، فَأَتَى رَسُولَ اللَّهِ صلى الله عليه وسلم فَقَالَ يَا نَبِيَّ اللَّهِ جَعَلَنِي اللَّهُ فِدَاكَ، هَلْ أَصَابَكَ مِنْ شَىْءٍ. قَالَ " لاَ وَلَكِنْ عَلَيْكَ بِالْمَرْأَةِ ". فَأَلْقَى أَبُو طَلْحَةَ ثَوْبَهُ عَلَى وَجْهِهِ فَقَصَدَ قَصْدَهَا، فَأَلْقَى ثَوْبَهُ عَلَيْهَا فَقَامَتِ الْمَرْأَةُ، فَشَدَّ لَهُمَا عَلَى رَاحِلَتِهِمَا فَرَكِبَا، فَسَارُوا حَتَّى إِذَا كَانُوا بِظَهْرِ الْمَدِينَةِ ـ أَوْ قَالَ أَشْرَفُوا عَلَى الْمَدِينَةِ ـ قَالَ النَّبِيُّ صلى الله عليه وسلم " آيِبُونَ تَائِبُونَ، عَابِدُونَ لِرَبِّنَا حَامِدُونَ ". فَلَمْ يَزَلْ يَقُولُهَا حَتَّى دَخَلَ الْمَدِينَةَ.

Lubaid bin Asam
لبيد بن أعصم

Narrated `Aisha: The Prophet ﷺ continued for such-and-such period imagining that he has slept (had sexual relations) with his wives, and in fact he did not. One day he said, to me, "O `Aisha! Allah has instructed me regarding a matter about which I had asked Him. There came to me two men, one of them sat near my feet and the other near my head. The one near my feet, asked the one near my head (pointing at me), 'What is wrong with this man? The latter replied, 'He is under the effect of magic.' The first one asked, 'Who had worked magic on him?' The other replied, 'Lubaid bin Asam.' The first one asked, 'What material (did he use)?' The other replied, 'The skin of the pollen of a male date tree with a comb and the hair stuck to it, kept under a stone in the well of Dharwan."' Then the Prophet ﷺ went to that well and said, "This is the same well which was shown to me in the dream. The tops of its date-palm trees look like the heads of the devils, and its water looks like the Henna infusion." Then the Prophet ﷺ ordered that those things be taken out. I said, "O Allah's Messenger ﷺ ! Won't you disclose (the magic object)?" The Prophet ﷺ said, "Allah has cured me and I hate to circulate the evil among the people." `Aisha added, "(The magician) Lubaid bin Asam was a man from Bani Zuraiq, an ally of the Jews." – Sahih al-Bukhari 6063

حَدَّثَنَا الْحُمَيْدِيُّ، حَدَّثَنَا سُفْيَانُ، حَدَّثَنَا هِشَامُ بْنُ عُرْوَةَ، عَنْ أَبِيهِ، عَنْ عَائِشَةَ ـ رضى الله عنها ـ قَالَتْ مَكَثَ النَّبِيُّ صلى الله عليه وسلم كَذَا وَكَذَا يُخَيَّلُ إِلَيْهِ أَنَّهُ يَأْتِي أَهْلَهُ وَلاَ يَأْتِي، قَالَتْ عَائِشَةُ فَقَالَ لِي ذَاتَ يَوْمٍ " يَا عَائِشَةُ إِنَّ اللَّهَ أَفْتَانِي فِي أَمْرٍ اسْتَفْتَيْتُهُ فِيهِ، أَتَانِي رَجُلاَنِ، فَجَلَسَ أَحَدُهُمَا عِنْدَ رِجْلَىَّ وَالآخَرُ عِنْدَ رَأْسِي، فَقَالَ الَّذِي عِنْدَ رِجْلَىَّ لِلَّذِي عِنْدَ رَأْسِي مَا بَالُ الرَّجُلِ قَالَ مَطْبُوبٌ. يَعْنِي مَسْحُورًا. قَالَ وَمَنْ طَبَّهُ قَالَ لَبِيدُ بْنُ أَعْصَمَ. قَالَ وَفِيمَ قَالَ فِي جُفِّ طَلْعَةِ ذَكَرٍ فِي مُشْطٍ وَمُشَاقَةٍ، تَحْتَ رَعُوفَةٍ فِي بِئْرِ ذَرْوَانَ ". فَجَاءَ النَّبِيُّ صلى الله عليه وسلم فَقَالَ " هَذِهِ الْبِئْرُ الَّتِي أُرِيتُهَا كَأَنَّ رُءُوسَ نَخْلِهَا رُءُوسُ الشَّيَاطِينِ، وَكَأَنَّ مَاءَهَا نُقَاعَةُ الْحِنَّاءِ ". فَأَمَرَ بِهِ النَّبِيُّ صلى الله عليه وسلم فَأُخْرِجَ. قَالَتْ عَائِشَةُ فَقُلْتُ يَا رَسُولَ اللَّهِ فَهَلاَّ ـ تَعْنِي ـ تَنَشَّرْتَ فَقَالَ النَّبِيُّ صلى الله عليه وسلم " أَمَّا اللَّهُ فَقَدْ شَفَانِي، وَأَمَّا أَنَا فَأَكْرَهُ أَنْ أُثِيرَ عَلَى النَّاسِ شَرًّا ". قَالَتْ وَلَبِيدُ بْنُ أَعْصَمَ رَجُلٌ مِنْ بَنِي زُرَيْقٍ حَلِيفٌ لِيَهُودَ.

Narrated Abu Huraira: When Khaibar was conquered, a roasted poisoned sheep was presented to the Prophet ﷺ as a gift (by the Jews). The Prophet ﷺ ordered, "Let all the Jews who have been here, be assembled before me." The Jews were collected and the Prophet ﷺ said (to them), "I am going to ask you a question. Will you tell the truth?" They said, "Yes." The Prophet ﷺ asked, "Who is your father?" They replied, "So-and-so." He said, "You have told a lie; your father is so-and-so." They said, "You are right." He said, "Will you now tell me the truth, if I ask you about something?" They replied, "Yes, O Abu Al-Qasim; and if we should tell a lie, you can realize our lie as you have done regarding our father." On that he asked, "Who are the people of the (Hell) Fire?" They said, "We shall remain in the (Hell) Fire for a short period, and after that you will replace us." The Prophet ﷺ said, "You may be cursed and humiliated in it! By Allah, we shall never replace you in it." Then he asked, "Will you now tell me the truth if I ask you a question?" They said, "Yes, O Abu Al-Qasim." He asked, "Have you poisoned this sheep?" They said, "Yes." He asked, "What made you do so?" They said, "We wanted to know if you were a liar in which case we would get rid of you, and if you are a prophet then the poison would not harm you." Sahih Al-Bukhari 3169

حَدَّثَنَا عَبْدُ اللَّهِ بْنُ يُوسُفَ، حَدَّثَنَا اللَّيْثُ، قَالَ حَدَّثَنِي سَعِيدٌ، عَنْ أَبِي هُرَيْرَةَ ـ رضى الله عنه ـ قَالَ لَمَّا فُتِحَتْ خَيْبَرُ أُهْدِيَتْ لِلنَّبِيِّ صلى الله عليه وسلم شَاةٌ فِيهَا سُمٌّ فَقَالَ النَّبِيُّ صلى الله عليه وسلم " اجْمَعُوا إِلَىَّ مَنْ كَانَ هَا هُنَا مِنْ يَهُودَ ". فَجُمِعُوا لَهُ فَقَالَ " إِنِّي سَائِلُكُمْ عَنْ شَىْءٍ فَهَلْ أَنْتُمْ صَادِقِيَّ عَنْهُ ". فَقَالُوا نَعَمْ. قَالَ لَهُمُ النَّبِيُّ صلى الله عليه وسلم " مَنْ أَبُوكُمْ ". قَالُوا فُلاَنٌ. فَقَالَ " كَذَبْتُمْ، بَلْ أَبُوكُمْ فُلاَنٌ ". قَالُوا صَدَقْتَ. قَالَ " فَهَلْ أَنْتُمْ صَادِقِيَّ عَنْ شَىْءٍ إِنْ سَأَلْتُ عَنْهُ " فَقَالُوا نَعَمْ يَا

أَبَا الْقَاسِمِ، وَإِنْ كَذَبْنَا عَرَفْتَ كَذِبَنَا كَمَا عَرَفْتَهُ فِي أَبِينَا. فَقَالَ لَهُمْ " مَنْ أَهْلُ النَّارِ ". قَالُوا نَكُونُ فِيهَا يَسِيرًا ثُمَّ تَخْلُفُونَا فِيهَا. فَقَالَ النَّبِيُّ صلى الله عليه وسلم " اخْسَئُوا فِيهَا، وَاللَّهِ لاَ نَخْلُفُكُمْ فِيهَا أَبَدًا - ثُمَّ قَالَ - هَلْ أَنْتُمْ صَادِقِيَّ عَنْ شَىْءٍ إِنْ سَأَلْتُكُمْ عَنْهُ ". فَقَالُوا نَعَمْ يَا أَبَا الْقَاسِمِ. قَالَ " هَلْ جَعَلْتُمْ فِي هَذِهِ الشَّاةِ سُمًّا ". قَالُوا نَعَمْ. قَالَ " مَا حَمَلَكُمْ عَلَى ذَلِكَ ". قَالُوا أَرَدْنَا إِنْ كُنْتَ كَاذِبًا نَسْتَرِيحُ، وَإِنْ كُنْتَ نَبِيًّا لَمْ يَضُرَّكَ

It was narrated that 'Uqbah bin 'Amir said: "I was walking with the Messenger of Allah [SAW] and he said: "O 'Uqbah, say!' I said: 'What should I say, O Messenger of Allah?' He did not answer me, then h esaid: 'O 'Uqbah, say!' I said: 'What should I say, O Messenger of Allah?' But he did not answer me. I said: 'O Allah, make him answer me.' He said: 'O 'Uqbah, say!' I said: 'What should I say, O Messenger of Allah?' He said: 'Say: I seek refuge with (Allah) the Lord of the daybreak...' So I recited it until I came to the end. Then he said: 'Say,' and I said: 'What should I say, O Messenger of Allah?' He said: 'Say: I seek refuge with (Allah) the Lord of mankind...,' so I recited it until I came to the end. Then the Messenger of Allah [SAW] said: 'No one who asks has ever asked by means of anything like them, and no one who seeks refuge has ever sought refuge with anything like them.'" – Sunan an-Nasa'I 5438

أَخْبَرَنَا قُتَيْبَةُ، قَالَ حَدَّثَنَا اللَّيْثُ، عَنِ ابْنِ عَجْلاَنَ، عَنْ سَعِيدٍ الْمَقْبُرِيِّ، عَنْ عُقْبَةَ بْنِ عَامِرٍ، قَالَ كُنْتُ أَمْشِي مَعَ رَسُولِ اللَّهِ صلى الله عليه وسلم فَقَالَ " يَا عُقْبَةُ قُلْ " . فَقُلْتُ مَاذَا أَقُولُ يَا رَسُولَ اللَّهِ فَسَكَتَ عَنِّي ثُمَّ قَالَ " يَا عُقْبَةُ قُلْ " . قُلْتُ مَاذَا أَقُولُ يَا رَسُولَ اللَّهِ فَسَكَتَ عَنِّي فَقُلْتُ اللَّهُمَّ ارْدُدْهُ عَلَىَّ فَقَالَ " يَا عُقْبَةُ قُلْ " . قُلْتُ مَاذَا أَقُولُ يَا رَسُولَ اللَّهِ فَقَالَ " { قُلْ أَعُوذُ بِرَبِّ الْفَلَقِ } فَقَرَأْتُهَا حَتَّى أَتَيْتُ عَلَى آخِرِهَا ثُمَّ قَالَ " قُلْ " . قُلْتُ مَاذَا أَقُولُ يَا رَسُولَ اللَّهِ قَالَ " { قُلْ أَعُوذُ بِرَبِّ النَّاسِ } " . فَقَرَأْتُهَا حَتَّى أَتَيْتُ عَلَى آخِرِهَا ثُمَّ قَالَ رَسُولُ اللَّهِ صلى الله عليه وسلم عِنْدَ ذَلِكَ " مَا سَأَلَ سَائِلٌ بِمِثْلِهِمَا وَلاَ اسْتَعَاذَ مُسْتَعِيذٌ بِمِثْلِهِمَا " .

Surah Al-Falaq and Surah An-Nas
سورة الفلق و سورة الناس

Say, "I take refuge with the Lord of Daybreak. From the evil of what He created. And from the evil of the darkness as it gathers. And from the evil of those who practice sorcery. And from the evil of an envious when he envies." - Surah Al-Falaq

قُلْ أَعُوذُ بِرَبِّ الْفَلَقِ مِنْ شَرِّ مَا خَلَقَ وَمِنْ شَرِّ غَاسِقٍ إِذَا وَقَبَ وَمِنْ شَرِّ النَّفَّاثَاتِ فِي الْعُقَدِ وَمِنْ شَرِّ حَاسِدٍ إِذَا حَسَدَ

Say, "I seek refuge in the Lord of mankind. The King of mankind. The God of mankind. From the evil of the sneaky whisperer. Who whispers into the hearts of people. From among jinn and among people." – Surah An-Nas

قُلْ أَعُوذُ بِرَبِّ النَّاسِ مَلِكِ النَّاسِ إِلَٰهِ النَّاسِ مِنْ شَرِّ الْوَسْوَاسِ الْخَنَّاسِ الَّذِي يُوَسْوِسُ فِي صُدُورِ النَّاسِ مِنَ الْجِنَّةِ وَالنَّاسِ

The Book of **Retribution of Mu'tah** قصاص مؤتة

Narrated Anas: The Prophetﷺ had informed the people about the death of Zaid, Ja`far and Ibn Rawaha before the news of their death reached them. He said with his eyes flowing with tears, "Zaid took the flag and was martyred; then Ja`far took the flag and was martyred, and then Ibn Rawaha took the flag and was martyred. Finally the flag was taken by one of Allah's Swords (i.e. Khalid bin Al-Walid) and Allah gave them (i.e. the Muslims) victory.". – Sahih Al-Bukhari 3757

حَدَّثَنَا أَحْمَدُ بْنُ وَاقِدٍ، حَدَّثَنَا حَمَّادُ بْنُ زَيْدٍ، عَنْ أَيُّوبَ، عَنْ حُمَيْدِ بْنِ هِلاَلٍ، عَنْ أَنَسٍ ـ رضى الله عنه أَنَّ النَّبِيَّ صلى الله عليه وسلم نَعَى زَيْدًا وَجَعْفَرًا وَابْنَ رَوَاحَةَ لِلنَّاسِ قَبْلَ أَنْ يَأْتِيَهُمْ خَبَرُهُمْ، فَقَالَ " أَخَذَ الرَّايَةَ زَيْدٌ فَأُصِيبَ، ثُمَّ أَخَذَ جَعْفَرٌ فَأُصِيبَ، ثُمَّ أَخَذَ ابْنُ رَوَاحَةَ فَأُصِيبَ ـ وَعَيْنَاهُ تَذْرِفَانِ ـ حَتَّى أَخَذَ سَيْفٌ مِنْ سُيُوفِ اللَّهِ حَتَّى فَتَحَ اللَّهُ عَلَيْهِمْ "

Narrated Nafi`: Ibn `Umar informed me that on the day (of Mu'tah) he stood beside Ja`far who was dead (i.e. killed in the battle), and he counted fifty wounds in his body, caused by stabs or strokes, and none of those wounds was in his back. – Sahih Al-Bukhari 4260

حَدَّثَنَا أَحْمَدُ، حَدَّثَنَا ابْنُ وَهْبٍ، عَنْ عَمْرٍو، عَنِ ابْنِ أَبِي هِلاَلٍ، قَالَ وَأَخْبَرَنِي نَافِعٌ، أَنَّ ابْنَ عُمَرَ، أَخْبَرَهُ أَنَّهُ، وَقَفَ عَلَى جَعْفَرٍ يَوْمَئِذٍ وَهْوَ قَتِيلٌ، فَعَدَدْتُ بِهِ خَمْسِينَ بَيْنَ طَعْنَةٍ وَضَرْبَةٍ، لَيْسَ مِنْهَا شَىْءٌ فِي دُبُرِهِ. يَعْنِي فِي ظَهْرِهِ.

Narrated Khalid bin Al-Walid: On the day of Mu'tah, nine swords were broken in my hand and only a Yemenite sword of mine remained in my hand. – Sahih Al-Bukhari 4266

حَدَّثَنِي مُحَمَّدُ بْنُ الْمُثَنَّى، حَدَّثَنَا يَحْيَى، عَنْ إِسْمَاعِيلَ، قَالَ حَدَّثَنِي قَيْسٌ، قَالَ سَمِعْتُ خَالِدَ بْنَ الْوَلِيدِ، يَقُولُ لَقَدْ دُقَّ فِي يَدِي يَوْمَ مُوتَةَ تِسْعَةُ أَسْيَافٍ، وَصَبَرَتْ فِي يَدِي صَفِيحَةٌ لِي يَمَانِيَةٌ

Narrated Anas bin Malik: The Prophetﷺ had informed us of the death of Ja`far and Zaid before the news of their death reached us, and his eyes were shedding tears. – Sahih Al-Bukhari 3630

حَدَّثَنَا سُلَيْمَانُ بْنُ حَرْبٍ، حَدَّثَنَا حَمَّادُ بْنُ زَيْدٍ، عَنْ أَيُّوبَ، عَنْ حُمَيْدِ بْنِ هِلاَلٍ، عَنْ أَنَسِ بْنِ مَالِكٍ ـ رضى الله عنه ـ أَنَّ النَّبِيَّ صلى الله عليه وسلم نَعَى جَعْفَرًا وَزَيْدًا قَبْلَ أَنْ يَجِيءَ خَبَرُهُمْ، وَعَيْنَاهُ تَذْرِفَانِ

Narrated Aisha: When the news of the martyrdom of Zaid bin Haritha, Ja`far and `Abdullah bin Rawaha came, the Prophet sat down looking sad, and I was looking through the chink of the door. A man came and said, "O Allah's Messengerﷺ ! The women of Ja`far," and then he mentioned their crying . The Prophet (p.b.u.h) ordered him to stop them from crying. The man went and came back and said, "I tried to stop them but they disobeyed." The Prophet (p.b.u.h) ordered him for the second time to forbid them. He went again and came back and said, "They did not listen to me, (or "us": the sub-narrator Muhammad bin Haushab is in doubt as to which is right). " (`Aisha added: The Prophetﷺ said, "Put dust in their mouths." I said (to that man), "May Allah stick your nose in the dust (i.e. humiliate you)." By Allah, you could not (stop the women from crying) to fulfill the order, besides you did not relieve Allah's Apostle from fatigue." – Sahih al-Bukhari 1305

حَدَّثَنَا مُحَمَّدُ بْنُ عَبْدِ اللَّهِ بْنِ حَوْشَبٍ، حَدَّثَنَا عَبْدُ الْوَهَّابِ، حَدَّثَنَا يَحْيَى بْنُ سَعِيدٍ، قَالَ أَخْبَرَتْنِي عَمْرَةُ، قَالَتْ سَمِعْتُ عَائِشَةَ ـ رضى الله عنها ـ تَقُولُ لَمَّا جَاءَ قَتْلُ زَيْدِ بْنِ حَارِثَةَ وَجَعْفَرٍ وَعَبْدِ اللَّهِ بْنِ رَوَاحَةَ، جَلَسَ النَّبِيُّ صلى الله عليه وسلم يُعْرَفُ فِيهِ الْحُزْنُ، وَأَنَا أَطَّلِعُ مِنْ شَقِّ الْبَابِ، فَأَتَاهُ رَجُلٌ فَقَالَ يَا رَسُولَ اللَّهِ إِنَّ نِسَاءَ جَعْفَرٍ وَذَكَرَ بُكَاءَهُنَّ فَأَمَرَهُ بِأَنْ يَنْهَاهُنَّ، فَذَهَبَ الرَّجُلُ ثُمَّ أَتَى فَقَالَ قَدْ نَهَيْتُهُنَّ، وَذَكَرَ أَنَّهُنَّ لَمْ يُطِعْنَهُ، فَأَمَرَهُ الثَّانِيَةَ أَنْ يَنْهَاهُنَّ، فَذَهَبَ، ثُمَّ أَتَى، فَقَالَ وَاللَّهِ لَقَدْ غَلَبْنَنِي أَوْ غَلَبْنَنَا الشَّكُّ مِنْ مُحَمَّدِ بْنِ حَوْشَبٍ ـ فَزَعَمَتْ أَنَّ النَّبِيَّ صلى الله عليه وسلم قَالَ " فَاحْثُ فِي أَفْوَاهِهِنَّ التُّرَابَ ". فَقُلْتُ أَرْغَمَ اللَّهُ أَنْفَكَ، فَوَاللَّهِ مَا أَنْتَ بِفَاعِلٍ وَمَا تَرَكْتَ رَسُولَ اللَّهِ صلى الله عليه وسلم مِنَ الْعَنَاءِ.

The Book of
Conquest of Mecca
عَامَ الْفَتْحِ

Narrated Nafi` from `Abdullah: Allah's Messenger ﷺ came to Mecca through its higher region on the day of the Conquest (of Mecca) riding his she-camel on which Usama was riding behind him. Bilal and `Uthman bin Talha, one of the servants of the Ka`ba, were also accompanying him till he made his camel kneel in the mosque and ordered the latter to bring the key of the Ka`ba. He opened the door of the Ka`ba and Allah's Messenger ﷺ entered in the company of Usama, Bilal and `Uthman, and stayed in it for a long period. When he came out, the people rushed to it, and `Abdullah bin `Umar was the first to enter it and found Bilal standing behind the door. He asked Bilal, "Where did the Prophet ﷺ offer his prayer?" He pointed to the place where he had offered his prayer. `Abdullah said, "I forgot to ask him how many rak`at he had performed.". – Sahih Al-Bukhari 2988

حَدَّثَنَا يَحْيَى بْنُ بُكَيْرٍ، حَدَّثَنَا اللَّيْثُ، قَالَ يُونُسُ أَخْبَرَنِي نَافِعٌ، عَنْ عَبْدِ اللَّهِ ـ رضى الله عنه أَنَّ رَسُولَ اللَّهِ صلى الله عليه وسلم أَقْبَلَ يَوْمَ الْفَتْحِ مِنْ أَعْلَى مَكَّةَ عَلَى رَاحِلَتِهِ، مُرْدِفًا أُسَامَةَ بْنَ زَيْدٍ وَمَعَهُ بِلاَلٌ وَمَعَهُ عُثْمَانُ بْنُ طَلْحَةَ مِنَ الْحَجَبَةِ، حَتَّى أَنَاخَ فِي الْمَسْجِدِ، فَأَمَرَهُ أَنْ يَأْتِيَ بِمِفْتَاحِ الْبَيْتِ، فَفَتَحَ وَدَخَلَ رَسُولُ اللَّهِ صلى الله عليه وسلم وَمَعَهُ أُسَامَةُ وَبِلاَلٌ وَعُثْمَانُ، فَمَكَثَ فِيهَا نَهَارًا طَوِيلاً ثُمَّ خَرَجَ، فَاسْتَبَقَ النَّاسُ، وَكَانَ عَبْدُ اللَّهِ بْنُ عُمَرَ أَوَّلَ مَنْ دَخَلَ، فَوَجَدَ بِلاَلاً وَرَاءَ الْبَابِ قَائِمًا، فَسَأَلَهُ أَيْنَ صَلَّى رَسُولُ اللَّهِ صلى الله عليه وسلم فَأَشَارَ لَهُ إِلَى الْمَكَانِ الَّذِي صَلَّى فِيهِ، قَالَ عَبْدُ اللَّهِ فَنَسِيتُ أَنْ أَسْأَلَهُ كَمْ صَلَّى مِنْ سَجْدَةٍ

Narrated `Aisha: During the year of the Conquest (of Mecca), the Prophet ﷺ entered Mecca through Kada which was at the upper part of Mecca. – Sahih Al-Bukhari 4290

حَدَّثَنَا الْهَيْثَمُ بْنُ خَارِجَةَ، حَدَّثَنَا حَفْصُ بْنُ مَيْسَرَةَ، عَنْ هِشَامِ بْنِ عُرْوَةَ، عَنْ أَبِيهِ، أَنَّ عَائِشَةَ ـ رضى الله عنها ـ أَخْبَرَتْهُ أَنَّ النَّبِيَّ صلى الله عليه وسلم دَخَلَ عَامَ الْفَتْحِ مِنْ كَدَاءٍ الَّتِي بِأَعْلَى مَكَّةَ. تَابَعَهُ أَبُو أُسَامَةَ وَوُهَيْبٌ فِي كَدَاءٍ.

Narrated Anas bin Malik: In the year of the conquest of Mecca the Prophet ﷺ entered Mecca, wearing a helmet on his head. – Sahih Al-Bukhari 5808

حَدَّثَنَا أَبُو الْوَلِيدِ، حَدَّثَنَا مَالِكٌ، عَنِ الزُّهْرِيِّ، عَنْ أَنَسٍ ـ رضى الله عنه ـ أَنَّ النَّبِيَّ صلى الله عليه وسلم دَخَلَ مَكَّةَ عَامَ الْفَتْحِ وَعَلَى رَأْسِهِ الْمِغْفَرُ

Narrated Anas bin Malik: Allah's Messenger ﷺ entered Mecca in the year of its Conquest wearing an Arabian helmet on his head and when the Prophet ﷺ took it off, a person came and said, "Ibn Khatal is holding the covering of the Ka`ba (taking refuge in the Ka`ba)." The Prophet ﷺ said, "Kill him.". – Sahih Al-Bukhari 1846

حَدَّثَنَا عَبْدُ اللَّهِ بْنُ يُوسُفَ، أَخْبَرَنَا مَالِكٌ، عَنِ ابْنِ شِهَابٍ، عَنْ أَنَسِ بْنِ مَالِكٍ ـ رضى الله عنه ـ أَنَّ رَسُولَ اللَّهِ صلى الله عليه وسلم دَخَلَ عَامَ الْفَتْحِ، وَعَلَى رَأْسِهِ الْمِغْفَرُ، فَلَمَّا نَزَعَهُ جَاءَ رَجُلٌ، فَقَالَ إِنَّ ابْنَ خَطَلٍ مُتَعَلِّقٌ بِأَسْتَارِ الْكَعْبَةِ. فَقَالَ " اقْتُلُوهُ "

Narrated `Abdullah: When the Prophet ﷺ entered Mecca on the day of the Conquest, there were 360 idols around the Ka`ba. The Prophet ﷺ started striking them with a stick he had in his hand and was saying, "Truth has come and Falsehood will neither start nor will it reappear. – Sahih Al-Bukhari 4287

حَدَّثَنَا صَدَقَةُ بْنُ الْفَضْلِ، أَخْبَرَنَا ابْنُ عُيَيْنَةَ، عَنِ ابْنِ أَبِي نَجِيحٍ، عَنْ مُجَاهِدٍ، عَنْ أَبِي مَعْمَرٍ، عَنْ عَبْدِ اللَّهِ ـ رضى الله عنه ـ قَالَ دَخَلَ النَّبِيُّ صلى الله عليه وسلم مَكَّةَ يَوْمَ الْفَتْحِ وَحَوْلَ الْبَيْتِ سِتُّونَ وَثَلاَثُمِائَةِ نُصُبٍ، فَجَعَلَ يَطْعُنُهَا بِعُودٍ فِي يَدِهِ وَيَقُولُ " جَاءَ الْحَقُّ وَزَهَقَ الْبَاطِلُ، جَاءَ الْحَقُّ، وَمَا يُبْدِئُ الْبَاطِلُ وَمَا يُعِيدُ "

Narrated `Abdullah bin Mughaffal: On the Day of the Conquest of Mecca, the Prophet ﷺ recited Surat Al-Fath in a vibrating and pleasant voice. (Muawaiya, the subnarrator said, "If I could imitate the recitation of the Prophet ﷺ I would do so."). – Sahih Al-Bukhari 4835

حَدَّثَنَا مُسْلِمُ بْنُ إِبْرَاهِيمَ، حَدَّثَنَا شُعْبَةُ، حَدَّثَنَا مُعَاوِيَةُ بْنُ قُرَّةَ، عَنْ عَبْدِ اللَّهِ بْنِ مُغَفَّلٍ، قَالَ قَرَأَ النَّبِيُّ صلى الله عليه وسلم يَوْمَ فَتْحِ مَكَّةَ سُورَةَ الْفَتْحِ فَرَجَّعَ فِيهَا. قَالَ مُعَاوِيَةُ لَوْ شِئْتُ أَنْ أَحْكِيَ لَكُمْ قِرَاءَةَ النَّبِيِّ صلى الله عليه وسلم لَفَعَلْتُ.

Narrated Sa`id: Abu Shuraih said, "When `Amr bin Sa`id was sending the troops to Mecca (to fight `Abdullah bin Az- Zubair) I said to him, 'O chief! Allow me to tell you what the Prophet ﷺ said on the day following the conquests of Mecca. My ears heard and my heart comprehended, and I saw him with my own eyes, when he said it. He glorified and praised Allah and then said, "Allah and not the people has made Mecca a sanctuary. So anybody who has belief in Allah and the Last Day (i.e. a Muslim) should neither shed blood in it nor cut down its trees. If anybody argues that fighting is allowed in Mecca as Allah's Messenger ﷺ did fight (in Mecca), tell him that Allah gave permission to His Apostle, but He did not give it to you. The Prophet ﷺ added: Allah allowed me only for a few hours on that day (of the conquest) and today (now) its sanctity is the same (valid) as it was before. So it is incumbent upon those who are present to convey it (this information) to those who are absent." Abu-Shuraih was asked, "What did `Amr reply?" He said `Amr said, "O Abu Shuraih! I know better than you (in this respect). Mecca does not give protection to one who disobeys (Allah) or runs after committing murder, or theft (and takes refuge in Mecca). – Sahih Al-Bukhari 104

حَدَّثَنَا عَبْدُ اللَّهِ بْنُ يُوسُفَ، قَالَ حَدَّثَنِي اللَّيْثُ، قَالَ حَدَّثَنِي سَعِيدٌ، عَنْ أَبِي شُرَيْحٍ، أَنَّهُ قَالَ لِعَمْرِو بْنِ سَعِيدٍ وَهُوَ يَبْعَثُ الْبُعُوثَ إِلَى مَكَّةَ ائْذَنْ لِي أَيُّهَا الأَمِيرُ أُحَدِّثْكَ قَوْلاً قَامَ بِهِ النَّبِيُّ صلى الله عليه وسلم الْغَدَ مِنْ يَوْمِ الْفَتْحِ، سَمِعَتْهُ أُذُنَاىَ وَوَعَاهُ قَلْبِي، وَأَبْصَرَتْهُ عَيْنَاىَ، حِينَ تَكَلَّمَ بِهِ، حَمِدَ اللَّهَ وَأَثْنَى عَلَيْهِ ثُمَّ قَالَ " إِنَّ مَكَّةَ حَرَّمَهَا اللَّهُ، وَلَمْ يُحَرِّمْهَا النَّاسُ، فَلاَ يَحِلُّ لاِمْرِئٍ يُؤْمِنُ بِاللَّهِ وَالْيَوْمِ الآخِرِ أَنْ يَسْفِكَ بِهَا دَمًا، وَلاَ يَعْضِدَ بِهَا شَجَرَةً، فَإِنْ أَحَدٌ تَرَخَّصَ لِقِتَالِ رَسُولِ اللَّهِ صلى الله عليه وسلم فِيهَا فَقُولُوا إِنَّ اللَّهَ قَدْ أَذِنَ لِرَسُولِهِ، وَلَمْ يَأْذَنْ لَكُمْ. وَإِنَّمَا أَذِنَ لِي فِيهَا سَاعَةً مِنْ نَهَارٍ، ثُمَّ عَادَتْ حُرْمَتُهَا الْيَوْمَ كَحُرْمَتِهَا بِالأَمْسِ، وَلْيُبَلِّغِ الشَّاهِدُ الْغَائِبَ ". فَقِيلَ لأَبِي شُرَيْحٍ مَا قَالَ عَمْرٌو قَالَ أَنَا أَعْلَمُ مِنْكَ يَا أَبَا شُرَيْحٍ، لاَ يُعِيذُ عَاصِيًا، وَلاَ فَارًّا بِدَمٍ، وَلاَ فَارًّا بِخَرْبَةٍ

Narrated Jabir bin `Abdullah: I heard Allah's Messenger ﷺ ,in the year of the Conquest of Mecca, saying, "Allah and His Apostle made illegal the trade of alcohol, dead animals, pigs and idols." The people asked, "O Allah's Messenger ﷺ ! What about the fat of dead animals, for it was used for greasing the boats and the hides; and people use it for lights?" He said, "No, it is illegal." Allah's Messenger ﷺ further said, "May Allah curse the Jews, for Allah made the fat (of animals) illegal for them, yet they melted the fat and sold it and ate its price.". – Sahih Al-Bukhari 2236

حَدَّثَنَا قُتَيْبَةُ، حَدَّثَنَا اللَّيْثُ، عَنْ يَزِيدَ بْنِ أَبِي حَبِيبٍ، عَنْ عَطَاءِ بْنِ أَبِي رَبَاحٍ، عَنْ جَابِرِ بْنِ عَبْدِ اللَّهِ ـ رضى الله عنهما ـ أَنَّهُ سَمِعَ رَسُولَ اللَّهِ صلى الله عليه وسلم يَقُولُ عَامَ الْفَتْحِ، وَهُوَ بِمَكَّةَ " إِنَّ اللَّهَ وَرَسُولَهُ حَرَّمَ بَيْعَ الْخَمْرِ وَالْمَيْتَةِ وَالْخِنْزِيرِ وَالأَصْنَامِ ". فَقِيلَ يَا رَسُولَ اللَّهِ، أَرَأَيْتَ شُحُومَ الْمَيْتَةِ فَإِنَّهَا يُطْلَى بِهَا السُّفُنُ، وَيُدْهَنُ بِهَا الْجُلُودُ، وَيَسْتَصْبِحُ بِهَا النَّاسُ. فَقَالَ " لاَ، هُوَ حَرَامٌ ". ثُمَّ قَالَ رَسُولُ اللَّهِ صلى الله عليه وسلم عِنْدَ ذَلِكَ " قَاتَلَ اللَّهُ الْيَهُودَ، إِنَّ اللَّهَ لَمَّا حَرَّمَ شُحُومَهَا جَمَلُوهُ ثُمَّ بَاعُوهُ فَأَكَلُوا ثَمَنَهُ ". قَالَ أَبُو عَاصِمٍ حَدَّثَنَا عَبْدُ الْحَمِيدِ، حَدَّثَنَا يَزِيدُ، كَتَبَ إِلَىَّ عَطَاءٌ سَمِعْتُ جَابِرًا ـ رضى الله عنه ـ عَنِ النَّبِيِّ صلى الله عليه وسلم.

Narrated Az-Zuhri: While we were in the company of the Ibn Al-Musaiyab, Sunain Abi Jamila informed us (a Hadith), Abu Jamila said that he lived during the lifetime of the Prophet ﷺ and that he had accompanied him (to Mecca) during the year of the Conquest (of Mecca). – Sahih Al-Bukhari 4301

حَدَّثَنِي إِبْرَاهِيمُ بْنُ مُوسَى، أَخْبَرَنَا هِشَامٌ، عَنْ مَعْمَرٍ، عَنِ الزُّهْرِيِّ، عَنْ سُنَيْنٍ أَبِي جَمِيلَةَ، قَالَ أَخْبَرَنَا وَنَحْنُ، مَعَ ابْنِ الْمُسَيَّبِ قَالَ وَزَعَمَ أَبُو جَمِيلَةَ أَنَّهُ أَدْرَكَ النَّبِيَّ صلى الله عليه وسلم، وَخَرَجَ مَعَهُ عَامَ الْفَتْحِ.

Narrated Hisham's father: When Allah's Messenger ﷺ set out (towards Mecca) during the year of the Conquest (of Mecca) and this news reached (the infidels of Quraish), Abu Sufyan, Hakim bin Hizam and Budail bin Warqa came out to gather information about Allah's Messenger ﷺ , They proceeded on their way till they reached a place called Marr-az-Zahran (which is near Mecca). Behold! There they saw many fires as if they were the fires of `Arafat. Abu Sufyan said, "What is this? It looked like the fires of `Arafat." Budail bin Warqa' said, "Banu `Amr are less in number than that." Some of the guards of Allah's Messenger ﷺ saw them and took them over, caught them and brought them to Allah's Messenger ﷺ .Abu Sufyan embraced Islam. When the Prophet ﷺ proceeded, he said to Al-Abbas, "Keep Abu Sufyan standing at the top of the mountain so that he would look at the Muslims. So Al-`Abbas kept him standing (at that place) and the tribes with the Prophet ﷺ started passing in front of Abu Sufyan in military batches. A batch passed and Abu Sufyan said, "O `Abbas Who are these?" `Abbas said, "They are (Banu) Ghifar." Abu Sufyan said, I have got nothing to do with Ghifar." Then (a batch of the tribe of) Juhaina passed by and he said similarly as above. Then (a batch of the tribe of) Sa`d bin Huzaim passed by and he said similarly as above. Then (Banu) Sulaim passed by and he said similarly as above. Then came a batch, the like of which Abu Sufyan had not seen. He said, "Who are these?" `Abbas said, "They are the Ansar headed by Sa`d bin Ubada, the one holding the flag." Sa`d bin Ubada said, "O Abu Sufyan! Today is the day of a great battle and today (what is prohibited in) the Ka`ba will be permissible." Abu Sufyan said., "O `Abbas! How excellent the day of destruction is! "Then came another batch (of warriors) which was the smallest of all the batches, and in it there was Allah's Messenger ﷺ and his companions and the flag of the Prophet ﷺ was carried by Az-Zubair bin Al Awwam. When Allah's Messenger ﷺ passed by Abu Sufyan, the latter said, (to the Prophet), "Do you know what Sa`d bin 'Ubada said?" The Prophet ﷺ said, "What did he say?" Abu Sufyan said, "He said so-and-so." The Prophet ﷺ said, "Sa`d told a lie, but today Allah will give superiority to the Ka`ba and today the Ka`ba will be covered with a (cloth) covering." Allah's Messenger ﷺ ordered that his flag be fixed at Al-Hajun. Narrated `Urwa: Nafi` bin Jubair bin Mut`im said, "I heard Al-Abbas saying to Az-Zubair bin Al- `Awwam, 'O Abu `Abdullah ! Did Allah's Messenger ﷺ order you to fix the flag here?' " Allah's Messenger ﷺ ordered Khalid bin Al-Walid to enter Mecca from its upper part from Ka'da while the Prophet ﷺ himself entered from Kuda. Two men from the cavalry of Khalid bin Al-Wahd named Hubaish bin Al-Ash'ar and Kurz bin Jabir Al-Fihri were martyred on that day. – Sahih Al-Bukhari 4280

حَدَّثَنَا عُبَيْدُ بْنُ إِسْمَاعِيلَ، حَدَّثَنَا أَبُو أُسَامَةَ، عَنْ هِشَامٍ، عَنْ أَبِيهِ، قَالَ لَمَّا سَارَ رَسُولُ اللَّهِ صلى الله عليه وسلم عَامَ الْفَتْحِ فَبَلَغَ ذَلِكَ قُرَيْشًا، خَرَجَ أَبُو سُفْيَانَ بْنُ حَرْبٍ وَحَكِيمُ بْنُ حِزَامٍ وَبُدَيْلُ بْنُ وَرْقَاءَ يَلْتَمِسُونَ الْخَبَرَ عَنْ رَسُولِ اللَّهِ صلى الله عليه وسلم فَأَقْبَلُوا يَسِيرُونَ حَتَّى أَتَوْا مَرَّ الظَّهْرَانِ، فَإِذَا هُمْ بِنِيرَانٍ كَأَنَّهَا نِيرَانُ عَرَفَةَ، فَقَالَ أَبُو سُفْيَانَ مَا هَذِهِ لَكَأَنَّهَا نِيرَانُ عَرَفَةَ. فَقَالَ بُدَيْلُ بْنُ وَرْقَاءَ نِيرَانُ بَنِي عَمْرٍو. فَقَالَ أَبُو سُفْيَانَ عَمْرٌو أَقَلُّ مِنْ ذَلِكَ. فَرَآهُمْ نَاسٌ مِنْ حَرَسِ رَسُولِ اللَّهِ صلى الله عليه وسلم فَأَدْرَكُوهُمْ فَأَخَذُوهُمْ، فَأَتَوْا بِهِمْ رَسُولَ اللَّهِ صلى الله عليه وسلم فَأَسْلَمَ أَبُو سُفْيَانَ، فَلَمَّا سَارَ قَالَ لِلْعَبَّاسِ " احْبِسْ أَبَا سُفْيَانَ عِنْدَ حَطْمِ الْخَيْلِ حَتَّى يَنْظُرَ إِلَى الْمُسْلِمِينَ ". فَحَبَسَهُ الْعَبَّاسُ، فَجَعَلَتِ الْقَبَائِلُ تَمُرُّ مَعَ النَّبِيِّ صلى الله عليه وسلم تَمُرُّ كَتِيبَةً كَتِيبَةً عَلَى أَبِي سُفْيَانَ، فَمَرَّتْ كَتِيبَةٌ قَالَ يَا عَبَّاسُ مَنْ هَذِهِ قَالَ هَذِهِ غِفَارُ. قَالَ مَا لِي وَلِغِفَارَ ثُمَّ مَرَّتْ جُهَيْنَةُ، قَالَ مِثْلَ ذَلِكَ، ثُمَّ مَرَّتْ سَعْدُ بْنُ هُذَيْمٍ، فَقَالَ مِثْلَ ذَلِكَ، وَمَرَّتْ سُلَيْمُ، فَقَالَ مِثْلَ ذَلِكَ، حَتَّى أَقْبَلَتْ كَتِيبَةٌ لَمْ يَرَ مِثْلَهَا، قَالَ مَنْ هَذِهِ قَالَ هَؤُلاَءِ الأَنْصَارُ عَلَيْهِمْ سَعْدُ بْنُ عُبَادَةَ مَعَهُ الرَّايَةُ. فَقَالَ سَعْدُ بْنُ عُبَادَةَ يَا أَبَا سُفْيَانَ الْيَوْمُ يَوْمُ الْمَلْحَمَةِ، الْيَوْمَ تُسْتَحَلُّ الْكَعْبَةُ. فَقَالَ أَبُو سُفْيَانَ يَا عَبَّاسُ حَبَّذَا يَوْمُ الذِّمَارِ. ثُمَّ جَاءَتْ كَتِيبَةٌ، وَهْىَ أَقَلُّ الْكَتَائِبِ، فِيهِمْ رَسُولُ اللَّهِ صلى الله عليه وسلم وَأَصْحَابُهُ، وَرَايَةُ النَّبِيِّ صلى الله عليه وسلم مَعَ الزُّبَيْرِ بْنِ الْعَوَّامِ، فَلَمَّا مَرَّ رَسُولُ اللَّهِ صلى الله عليه وسلم بِأَبِي سُفْيَانَ قَالَ أَلَمْ تَعْلَمْ مَا قَالَ سَعْدُ بْنُ عُبَادَةَ قَالَ " مَا قَالَ ". قَالَ كَذَا وَكَذَا. فَقَالَ " كَذَبَ سَعْدٌ، وَلَكِنْ هَذَا يَوْمٌ يُعَظِّمُ اللَّهُ فِيهِ الْكَعْبَةَ، وَيَوْمٌ تُكْسَى فِيهِ الْكَعْبَةُ ". قَالَ وَأَمَرَ رَسُولُ اللَّهِ صلى الله عليه وسلم أَنْ تُرْكَزَ رَايَتُهُ بِالْحَجُونِ. قَالَ عُرْوَةُ وَأَخْبَرَنِي نَافِعُ بْنُ جُبَيْرِ بْنِ مُطْعِمٍ قَالَ سَمِعْتُ الْعَبَّاسَ يَقُولُ لِلزُّبَيْرِ بْنِ الْعَوَّامِ يَا أَبَا عَبْدِ اللَّهِ، هَا هُنَا أَمَرَكَ رَسُولُ اللَّهِ صلى

الله عليه وسلم أَنْ تَرْكُزَ الرَّايَةَ، قَالَ وَأَمَرَ رَسُولُ اللَّهِ صلى الله عليه وسلم يَوْمَئِذٍ خَالِدَ بْنَ الْوَلِيدِ أَنْ يَدْخُلَ مِنْ أَعْلَى مَكَّةَ مِنْ كَدَاءٍ، وَدَخَلَ النَّبِيُّ صلى الله عليه وسلم مِنْ كُدًا، فَقُتِلَ مِنْ خَيْلِ خَالِدٍ يَوْمَئِذٍ رَجُلاَنِ حُبَيْشُ بْنُ الأَشْعَرِ وَكُرْزُ بْنُ جَابِرٍ الْفِهْرِيُّ

Narrated Anas: On the day of the Conquest of Mecca, when the Prophet ﷺ had given (from the booty) the Quraish, the Ansar said, "By Allah, this is indeed very strange: While our swords are still dribbling with the blood of Quraish, our war booty are distributed amongst them." When this news reached the Prophet ﷺ he called the Ansar and said, "What is this news that has reached me from you?" They used not to tell lies, so they replied, "What has reached you is true." He said, "Doesn't it please you that the people take the booty to their homes and you take Allah's Messenger ﷺ to your homes? If the Ansar took their way through a valley or a mountain pass, I would take the Ansar's valley or a mountain pass.". – Sahih Al-Bukhari 3778

حَدَّثَنَا أَبُو الْوَلِيدِ، حَدَّثَنَا شُعْبَةُ، عَنْ أَبِي التَّيَّاحِ، قَالَ سَمِعْتُ أَنَسًا ـ رضى الله عنه ـ يَقُولُ قَالَتِ الأَنْصَارُ يَوْمَ فَتْحِ مَكَّةَ ـ وَأَعْطَى قُرَيْشًا ـ وَاللَّهِ إِنَّ هَذَا لَهُوَ الْعَجَبُ، إِنَّ سُيُوفَنَا تَقْطُرُ مِنْ دِمَاءِ قُرَيْشٍ، وَغَنَائِمُنَا تُرَدُّ عَلَيْهِمْ. فَبَلَغَ ذَلِكَ النَّبِيَّ صلى الله عليه وسلم فَدَعَا الأَنْصَارَ قَالَ فَقَالَ " مَا الَّذِي بَلَغَنِي عَنْكُمْ ". وَكَانُوا لاَ يَكْذِبُونَ. فَقَالُوا هُوَ الَّذِي بَلَغَكَ. قَالَ " أَوَلاَ تَرْضَوْنَ أَنْ يَرْجِعَ النَّاسُ بِالْغَنَائِمِ إِلَى بُيُوتِهِمْ، وَتَرْجِعُونَ بِرَسُولِ اللَّهِ صلى الله عليه وسلم إِلَى بُيُوتِكُمْ لَوْ سَلَكَتِ الأَنْصَارُ وَادِيًا أَوْ شِعْبًا، لَسَلَكْتُ وَادِيَ الأَنْصَارِ أَوْ شِعْبَهُمْ ".

Narrated `Amr bin `Uthman: Usama bin Zaid said during the Conquest (of Mecca), "O Allah's Messenger ﷺ ! Where will we encamp tomorrow?" The Prophet ﷺ said, "But has `Aqil left for us any house to lodge in?" He then added, "No believer will inherit an infidel's property, and no infidel will inherit the property of a believer." Az- Zuhri was asked, "Who inherited Abu Talib?" Az-Zuhri replied, "Ail and Talib inherited him.". – Sahih Al-Bukhari 4282, 4283

حَدَّثَنَا سُلَيْمَانُ بْنُ عَبْدِ الرَّحْمَنِ، حَدَّثَنَا سَعْدَانُ بْنُ يَحْيَى، حَدَّثَنَا مُحَمَّدُ بْنُ أَبِي حَفْصَةَ، عَنِ الزُّهْرِيِّ، عَنْ عَلِيِّ بْنِ حُسَيْنٍ، عَنْ عَمْرِو بْنِ عُثْمَانَ، عَنْ أُسَامَةَ بْنِ زَيْدٍ، أَنَّهُ قَالَ زَمَنَ الْفَتْحِ يَا رَسُولَ اللَّهِ، أَيْنَ تَنْزِلُ غَدًا قَالَ النَّبِيُّ صلى الله عليه وسلم " وَهَلْ تَرَكَ لَنَا عَقِيلٌ مِنْ مَنْزِلٍ ". ثُمَّ قَالَ " لاَ يَرِثُ الْمُؤْمِنُ الْكَافِرَ، وَلاَ يَرِثُ الْكَافِرُ الْمُؤْمِنَ ". قِيلَ لِلزُّهْرِيِّ وَمَنْ وَرِثَ أَبَا طَالِبٍ قَالَ وَرِثَهُ عَقِيلٌ وَطَالِبٌ. قَالَ مَعْمَرٌ عَنِ الزُّهْرِيِّ أَيْنَ تَنْزِلُ غَدًا. فِي حَجَّتِهِ، وَلَمْ يَقُلْ يُونُسُ حَجَّتِهِ وَلاَ زَمَنَ الْفَتْحِ.

Narrated `Aisha: `Utba bin Abi Waqqas authorized his brother Sa`d to take the son of the slave-girl of Zam`a into his custody. `Utba said (to him). "He is my son." When Allah's Messenger ﷺ arrived in Mecca during the Conquest (of Mecca), Sa`d bin Abi Waqqas took the son of the slave-girl of Zam`a and took him to the Prophet ﷺ 'Abd bin Zam`a too came along with him. Sa`d said. "This is the son of my brother and the latter has informed me that he is his son." `Abd bin Zam`a said, "O Allah's Messenger ﷺ ! This is my brother who is the son of the slave-girl of Zam`a and was born on his (i.e. Zam'as) bed.' Allah's Apostle looked at the son of the slave-girl of Zam`a and noticed that he, of all the people had the greatest resemblance to `Utba bin Abi Waqqas. Allah's Messenger ﷺ then said (to `Abd), " He is yours; he is your brother, O `Abd bin Zam`a, he was born on the bed (of your father)." (At the same time) Allah's Messenger ﷺ said (to his wife Sauda), "Veil yourself before him (i.e. the son of the slave girl) O Sauda," because of the resemblance he noticed between him and `Utba bin Abi Waqqas. Allah's Apostle added, "The boy is for the bed (i.e. for the owner of the bed where he was born), and stone is for the adulterer." (Ibn Shihab said, "Abu Huraira used to say that (i.e. the last statement of the Prophet in the above Hadith 596, publicly."). – Sahih Al-Bukhari 4303

حَدَّثَنِي عَبْدُ اللَّهِ بْنُ مَسْلَمَةَ، عَنْ مَالِكٍ، عَنِ ابْنِ شِهَابٍ، عَنْ عُرْوَةَ بْنِ الزُّبَيْرِ، عَنْ عَائِشَةَ ـ رضى الله عنها ـ عَنِ النَّبِيِّ صلى الله عليه وسلم. وَقَالَ اللَّيْثُ حَدَّثَنِي يُونُسُ عَنِ ابْنِ شِهَابٍ أَخْبَرَنِي عُرْوَةُ بْنُ الزُّبَيْرِ أَنَّ عَائِشَةَ قَالَتْ كَانَ عُتْبَةُ بْنُ أَبِي

وَقَّاصٍ عَهِدَ إِلَى أَخِيهِ سَعْدٍ أَنْ يَقْبِضَ ابْنَ وَلِيدَةِ زَمْعَةَ، وَقَالَ عُتْبَةُ إِنَّهُ ابْنِي. فَلَمَّا قَدِمَ رَسُولُ اللَّهِ صلى الله عليه وسلم مَكَّةَ فِي الْفَتْحِ أَخَذَ سَعْدُ بْنُ أَبِي وَقَّاصٍ ابْنَ وَلِيدَةِ زَمْعَةَ، فَأَقْبَلَ بِهِ إِلَى رَسُولِ اللَّهِ صلى الله عليه وسلم، وَأَقْبَلَ مَعَهُ عَبْدُ بْنُ زَمْعَةَ، فَقَالَ سَعْدُ بْنُ أَبِي وَقَّاصٍ هَذَا ابْنُ أَخِي، عَهِدَ إِلَيَّ أَنَّهُ ابْنُهُ. قَالَ عَبْدُ بْنُ زَمْعَةَ يَا رَسُولَ اللَّهِ، هَذَا أَخِي، هَذَا ابْنُ زَمْعَةَ، وُلِدَ عَلَى فِرَاشِهِ. فَنَظَرَ رَسُولُ اللَّهِ صلى الله عليه وسلم إِلَى ابْنِ وَلِيدَةِ زَمْعَةَ، فَإِذَا أَشْبَهُ النَّاسِ بِعُتْبَةَ بْنِ أَبِي وَقَّاصٍ، فَقَالَ رَسُولُ اللَّهِ صلى الله عليه وسلم " هُوَ لَكَ، هُوَ أَخُوكَ يَا عَبْدُ بْنَ زَمْعَةَ ". مِنْ أَجْلِ أَنَّهُ وُلِدَ عَلَى فِرَاشِهِ، وَقَالَ رَسُولُ اللَّهِ صلى الله عليه وسلم " احْتَجِبِي مِنْهُ يَا سَوْدَةُ ". لِمَا رَأَى مِنْ شَبَهِ عُتْبَةَ بْنِ أَبِي وَقَّاصٍ. قَالَ ابْنُ شِهَابٍ قَالَتْ عَائِشَةُ قَالَ رَسُولُ اللَّهِ صلى الله عليه وسلم " الْوَلَدُ لِلْفِرَاشِ وَلِلْعَاهِرِ الْحَجَرُ ". وَقَالَ ابْنُ شِهَابٍ وَكَانَ أَبُو هُرَيْرَةَ يَصِيحُ بِذَلِكَ

Narrated `Urwa bin Az-Zubair: A lady committed theft during the lifetime of Allah's Messenger ﷺ in the Ghazwa of Al-Fath, (i.e. Conquest of Mecca). Her folk went to Usama bin Zaid to intercede for her (with the Prophet). When Usama interceded for her with Allah's Messenger ﷺ , the color of the face of Allah's Messenger ﷺ changed and he said, "Do you intercede with me in a matter involving one of the legal punishments prescribed by Allah?" Usama said, "O Allah's Messenger ﷺ ! Ask Allah's Forgiveness for me." So in the afternoon, Allah's Apostle got up and addressed the people. He praised Allah as He deserved and then said, "Amma ba'du ! The nations prior to you were destroyed because if a noble amongst them stole, they used to excuse him, and if a poor person amongst them stole, they would apply (Allah's) Legal Punishment to him. By Him in Whose Hand Muhammad's soul is, if Fatima, the daughter of Muhammad stole, I would cut her hand." Then Allah's Messenger ﷺ gave his order in the case of that woman and her hand was cut off. Afterwards her repentance proved sincere and she got married. `Aisha said, "That lady used to visit me and I used to convey her demands to Allah's Messenger ﷺ – ". Al-Bukhari 4304

حَدَّثَنَا مُحَمَّدُ بْنُ مُقَاتِلٍ، أَخْبَرَنَا عَبْدُ اللَّهِ، أَخْبَرَنِي يُونُسُ، عَنِ الزُّهْرِيِّ، قَالَ أَخْبَرَنِي عُرْوَةُ بْنُ الزُّبَيْرِ، أَنَّ امْرَأَةً، سَرَقَتْ فِي عَهْدِ رَسُولِ اللَّهِ صلى الله عليه وسلم فِي غَزْوَةِ الْفَتْحِ، فَفَزِعَ قَوْمُهَا إِلَى أُسَامَةَ بْنِ زَيْدٍ يَسْتَشْفِعُونَهُ، قَالَ عُرْوَةُ فَلَمَّا كَلَّمَهُ أُسَامَةُ فِيهَا تَلَوَّنَ وَجْهُ رَسُولِ اللَّهِ صلى الله عليه وسلم فَقَالَ " أَتُكَلِّمُنِي فِي حَدٍّ مِنْ حُدُودِ اللَّهِ ". قَالَ أُسَامَةُ اسْتَغْفِرْ لِي يَا رَسُولَ اللَّهِ. فَلَمَّا كَانَ الْعَشِيُّ قَامَ رَسُولُ اللَّهِ صلى الله عليه وسلم خَطِيبًا، فَأَثْنَى عَلَى اللَّهِ بِمَا هُوَ أَهْلُهُ ثُمَّ قَالَ " أَمَّا بَعْدُ، فَإِنَّمَا أَهْلَكَ النَّاسَ قَبْلَكُمْ أَنَّهُمْ كَانُوا إِذَا سَرَقَ فِيهِمُ الشَّرِيفُ تَرَكُوهُ، وَإِذَا سَرَقَ فِيهِمِ الضَّعِيفُ أَقَامُوا عَلَيْهِ الْحَدَّ، وَالَّذِي نَفْسُ مُحَمَّدٍ بِيَدِهِ، لَوْ أَنَّ فَاطِمَةَ بِنْتَ مُحَمَّدٍ سَرَقَتْ لَقَطَعْتُ يَدَهَا ". ثُمَّ أَمَرَ رَسُولُ اللَّهِ صلى الله عليه وسلم بِتِلْكَ الْمَرْأَةِ، فَقُطِعَتْ يَدُهَا، فَحَسُنَتْ تَوْبَتُهَا بَعْدَ ذَلِكَ وَتَزَوَّجَتْ. قَالَتْ عَائِشَةُ فَكَانَتْ تَأْتِي بَعْدَ ذَلِكَ فَأَرْفَعُ حَاجَتَهَا إِلَى رَسُولِ اللَّهِ صلى الله عليه وسلم

Narrated Um Hani: (the daughter of Abu Talib) I visited Allah's Messenger ﷺ in the year of the Conquest of Mecca and found him taking a bath, and his daughter, Fatima was screening him. When I greeted him, he said, "Who is it?" I replied, "I am Um Hani, the daughter of Abu Talib." He said, "Welcome, O Um Hani ! " When the Prophet ﷺ had finished his bath, he stood up and offered eight rak`at of prayer while he was wrapped in a single garment. When he had finished his prayer, I said, "O Allah's Messenger ﷺ ! My maternal brother assumes (or claims) that he will murder some man whom I have given shelter, i.e., so-and-so bin Hubaira." Allah's Messenger ﷺ said, "O Um Hani! We shelter him whom you have sheltered." Um Hani added, "That happened in the forenoon.". – Sahih Al-Bukhari 6158

حَدَّثَنَا عَبْدُ اللَّهِ بْنُ مَسْلَمَةَ، عَنْ مَالِكٍ، عَنْ أَبِي النَّضْرِ، مَوْلَى عُمَرَ بْنِ عُبَيْدِ اللَّهِ أَنَّ أَبَا مُرَّةَ، مَوْلَى أُمِّ هَانِئٍ بِنْتِ أَبِي طَالِبٍ أَخْبَرَهُ أَنَّهُ، سَمِعَ أُمَّ هَانِئٍ بِنْتَ أَبِي طَالِبٍ، تَقُولُ ذَهَبْتُ إِلَى رَسُولِ اللَّهِ صلى الله عليه وسلم عَامَ الْفَتْحِ فَوَجَدْتُهُ يَغْتَسِلُ، وَفَاطِمَةُ ابْنَتُهُ تَسْتُرُهُ، فَسَلَّمْتُ عَلَيْهِ، فَقَالَ " مَنْ هَذِهِ ". فَقُلْتُ أَنَا أُمُّ هَانِئٍ بِنْتُ أَبِي طَالِبٍ. فَقَالَ " مَرْحَبًا بِأُمِّ هَانِئٍ ". فَلَمَّا فَرَغَ مِنْ غَسْلِهِ قَامَ فَصَلَّى ثَمَانِيَ رَكَعَاتٍ، مُلْتَحِفًا فِي ثَوْبٍ وَاحِدٍ، فَلَمَّا انْصَرَفَ قُلْتُ يَا رَسُولَ اللَّهِ زَعَمَ ابْنُ أُمِّي أَنَّهُ قَاتِلٌ رَجُلاً قَدْ أَجَرْتُهُ فُلاَنُ بْنُ هُبَيْرَةَ. فَقَالَ رَسُولُ اللَّهِ صلى الله عليه وسلم " قَدْ أَجَرْنَا مَنْ أَجَرْتِ يَا أُمَّ هَانِئٍ ". قَالَتْ أُمُّ هَانِئٍ وَذَاكَ ضُحًى.

Narrated Abu `Uthman An-Nahdi: Mujashi (bin Mas`ud) took his brother Mujalid bin Musud to the Prophet ﷺ and said, "This is Mujalid and he will give a pledge of allegiance to you for

migration." The Prophet ﷺ said, "There is no migration after the Conquest of Mecca, but I will take his pledge of allegiance for Islam.". – Sahih Al-Bukhari 3078, 3079
حَدَّثَنَا إِبْرَاهِيمُ بْنُ مُوسَى، أَخْبَرَنَا يَزِيدُ بْنُ زُرَيْعٍ، عَنْ خَالِدٍ، عَنْ أَبِي عُثْمَانَ النَّهْدِيِّ، عَنْ مُجَاشِعِ بْنِ مَسْعُودٍ، قَالَ جَاءَ مُجَاشِعٌ بِأَخِيهِ مُجَالِدِ بْنِ مَسْعُودٍ إِلَى النَّبِيِّ صلى الله عليه وسلم فَقَالَ هَذَا مُجَالِدٌ يُبَايِعُكَ عَلَى الْهِجْرَةِ. فَقَالَ " لاَ هِجْرَةَ بَعْدَ فَتْحِ مَكَّةَ، وَلَكِنْ أُبَايِعُهُ عَلَى الإِسْلاَمِ "

Narrated Ibn `Abbas: `Umar used to make me sit with the elderly men who had fought in the Battle of Badr. Some of them felt it (did not like that) and said to `Umar "Why do you bring in this boy to sit with us while we have sons like him?" `Umar replied, "Because of what you know of his position (i.e. his religious knowledge.)" One day `Umar called me and made me sit in the gathering of those people; and I think that he called me just to show them. (my religious knowledge). `Umar then asked them (in my presence). "What do you say about the interpretation of the Statement of Allah: 'When comes Help of Allah (to you O, Muhammad against your enemies) and the conquest (of Mecca).' (110.1) Some of them said, "We are ordered to praise Allah and ask for His forgiveness when Allah's Help and the conquest (of Mecca) comes to us." Some others kept quiet and did not say anything. On that, `Umar asked me, "Do you say the same, O Ibn `Abbas?" I replied, "No." He said, 'What do you say then?" I replied, "That is the sign of the death of Allah's Messenger ﷺ which Allah informed him of. Allah said:-- '(O Muhammad) When comes the Help of Allah (to you against your enemies) and the conquest (of Mecca) (which is the sign of your death). You should celebrate the praises of your Lord and ask for His Forgiveness, and He is the One Who accepts the repentance and forgives.' (110.3) On that `Umar said, "I do not know anything about it other than what you have said.". – Sahih Al-Bukhari 4970
حَدَّثَنَا مُوسَى بْنُ إِسْمَاعِيلَ، حَدَّثَنَا أَبُو عَوَانَةَ، عَنْ أَبِي بِشْرٍ، عَنْ سَعِيدِ بْنِ جُبَيْرٍ، عَنِ ابْنِ عَبَّاسٍ، قَالَ كَانَ عُمَرُ يُدْخِلُنِي مَعَ أَشْيَاخِ بَدْرٍ، فَكَأَنَّ بَعْضَهُمْ وَجَدَ فِي نَفْسِهِ فَقَالَ لِمَ تُدْخِلُ هَذَا مَعَنَا وَلَنَا أَبْنَاءٌ مِثْلُهُ فَقَالَ عُمَرُ إِنَّهُ مِنْ حَيْثُ عَلِمْتُمْ. فَدَعَا ذَاتَ يَوْمٍ ـ فَأَدْخَلَهُ مَعَهُمْ ـ فَمَا رُئِيتُ أَنَّهُ دَعَانِي يَوْمَئِذٍ إِلاَّ لِيُرِيَهُمْ. قَالَ مَا تَقُولُونَ فِي قَوْلِ اللَّهِ تَعَالَى {إِذَا جَاءَ نَصْرُ اللَّهِ وَالْفَتْحُ} فَقَالَ بَعْضُهُمْ أُمِرْنَا نَحْمَدُ اللَّهَ وَنَسْتَغْفِرُهُ، إِذَا نُصِرْنَا وَفُتِحَ عَلَيْنَا. وَسَكَتَ بَعْضُهُمْ فَلَمْ يَقُلْ شَيْئًا فَقَالَ لِي أَكَذَاكَ تَقُولُ يَا ابْنَ عَبَّاسٍ فَقُلْتُ لاَ. قَالَ فَمَا تَقُولُ قُلْتُ هُوَ أَجَلُ رَسُولِ اللَّهِ صلى الله عليه وسلم أَعْلَمَهُ لَهُ، قَالَ {إِذَا جَاءَ نَصْرُ اللَّهِ وَالْفَتْحُ} وَذَلِكَ عَلاَمَةُ أَجَلِكَ {فَسَبِّحْ بِحَمْدِ رَبِّكَ وَاسْتَغْفِرْهُ إِنَّهُ كَانَ تَوَّابًا}. فَقَالَ عُمَرُ مَا أَعْلَمُ مِنْهَا إِلاَّ مَا تَقُولُ

The Book of
Ghazwat of Hunain
غَزْوَةُ حُنَيْنٍ

Narrated Ibn `Abbas: Allah's Messenger ﷺ set out towards Hunain in the month of Ramadan and some of the people were fasting while some others were not fasting, and when the Prophet ﷺ mounted his she-camel, he asked for a tumbler of milk or water and put it on the palm of his hand or on his she-camel and then the people looked at him; and those who were not fasting told those who were fasting, to break their fast (i.e. as the Prophet ﷺ had done so). – All-Bukhari 4277

حَدَّثَنِي عَيَّاشُ بْنُ الْوَلِيدِ، حَدَّثَنَا عَبْدُ الأَعْلَى، حَدَّثَنَا خَالِدٌ، عَنْ عِكْرِمَةَ، عَنِ ابْنِ عَبَّاسٍ، قَالَ خَرَجَ النَّبِيُّ صلى الله عليه وسلم فِي رَمَضَانَ إِلَى حُنَيْنٍ، وَالنَّاسُ مُخْتَلِفُونَ فَصَائِمٌ وَمُفْطِرٌ، فَلَمَّا اسْتَوَى عَلَى رَاحِلَتِهِ دَعَا بِإِنَاءٍ مِنْ لَبَنٍ أَوْ مَاءٍ، فَوَضَعَهُ عَلَى رَاحَتِهِ أَوْ عَلَى رَاحِلَتِهِ، ثُمَّ نَظَرَ إِلَى النَّاسِ فَقَالَ الْمُفْطِرُونَ لِلصُّوَّامِ أَفْطِرُوا.

Narrated Abu Huraira: Allah's Messenger ﷺ ,while going out for the battle of Hunain, said, "Tomorrow Allah willing, we will encamp at Khaif Bani Kinana where the pagans(of Quraish) took the oath of Kufr (against the Prophet ﷺ i.e. to be loyal to heathenism, by boycotting Banu Hashim, the Prophet's folk. (See Hadith 1589). – Sahih Al-Bukhari 3882

حَدَّثَنَا عَبْدُ الْعَزِيزِ بْنُ عَبْدِ اللَّهِ، قَالَ حَدَّثَنِي إِبْرَاهِيمُ بْنُ سَعْدٍ، عَنِ ابْنِ شِهَابٍ، عَنْ أَبِي سَلَمَةَ بْنِ عَبْدِ الرَّحْمَنِ، عَنْ أَبِي هُرَيْرَةَ ـ رضى الله عنه ـ قَالَ قَالَ رَسُولُ اللَّهِ صلى الله عليه وسلم حِينَ أَرَادَ حُنَيْنًا " مَنْزِلُنَا غَدًا إِنْ شَاءَ اللَّهُ بِخَيْفِ بَنِي كِنَانَةَ، حَيْثُ تَقَاسَمُوا عَلَى الْكُفْرِ ".

Narrated Abu Huraira: When Allah's Messenger ﷺ intended to carry on the Ghazwa of Hunain, he said, "Tomorrow, if Allah wished, our encamping) plaice will be Khaif Bani Kinana where (the infidels) took an oath to be loyal to Heathenism.". – Sahih Al-Bukhari 4285

حَدَّثَنَا مُوسَى بْنُ إِسْمَاعِيلَ، حَدَّثَنَا إِبْرَاهِيمُ بْنُ سَعْدٍ، أَخْبَرَنَا ابْنُ شِهَابٍ، عَنْ أَبِي سَلَمَةَ، عَنْ أَبِي هُرَيْرَةَ ـ رضى الله عنه ـ قَالَ قَالَ رَسُولُ اللَّهِ صلى الله عليه وسلم حِينَ أَرَادَ حُنَيْنًا " مَنْزِلُنَا غَدًا إِنْ شَاءَ اللَّهُ بِخَيْفِ بَنِي كِنَانَةَ، حَيْثُ تَقَاسَمُوا عَلَى الْكُفْرِ "

Narrated Anas: When it was the day of (the battle of) Hunain, the Prophet ﷺ confronted the tribe of Hawazin while there were ten-thousand (men) besides the Tulaqa' (i.e. those who had embraced Islam on the day of the Conquest of Mecca) with the Prophet. When they (i.e. Muslims) fled, the Prophet ﷺ said, "O the group of Ansari" They replied, "Labbaik, O Allah's Messenger ﷺ and Sadaik! We are under your command." Then the Prophet ﷺ got down (from his mule) and said, "I am Allah's Slave and His Apostle." Then the pagans were defeated. The Prophet ﷺ distributed the war booty amongst the Tulaqa and Muhajirin (i.e. Emigrants) and did not give anything to the Ansar. So the Ansar spoke (i.e. were dissatisfied) and he called them and made them enter a leather tent and said, Won't you be pleased that the people take the sheep and camels, and you take Allah's Messenger ﷺ along with you?" The Prophet ﷺ added, "If the people took their way through a valley and the Ansar took their way through a mountain pass, then I would choose a mountain pass of the Ansar.". – Sahih Al-Bukhari 4333

حَدَّثَنَا عَلِيُّ بْنُ عَبْدِ اللَّهِ، حَدَّثَنَا أَزْهَرُ، عَنِ ابْنِ عَوْنٍ، أَنْبَأَنَا هِشَامُ بْنُ زَيْدِ بْنِ أَنَسٍ، عَنْ أَنَسٍ ـ رضى الله عنه ـ قَالَ لَمَّا كَانَ يَوْمَ حُنَيْنٍ الْتَقَى هَوَازِنُ وَمَعَ النَّبِيِّ صلى الله عليه وسلم عَشَرَةُ آلاَفٍ وَالطُّلَقَاءُ فَأَدْبَرُوا قَالَ " يَا مَعْشَرَ الأَنْصَارِ ". قَالُوا لَبَّيْكَ يَا رَسُولَ اللَّهِ وَسَعْدَيْكَ، لَبَّيْكَ نَحْنُ بَيْنَ يَدَيْكَ، فَنَزَلَ النَّبِيُّ صلى الله عليه وسلم فَقَالَ " أَنَا عَبْدُ اللَّهِ وَرَسُولُهُ ". فَانْهَزَمَ الْمُشْرِكُونَ، فَأَعْطَى الطُّلَقَاءَ وَالْمُهَاجِرِينَ وَلَمْ يُعْطِ الأَنْصَارَ شَيْئًا فَقَالُوا، فَدَعَاهُمْ فَأَدْخَلَهُمْ فِي قُبَّةٍ فَقَالَ " أَمَا تَرْضَوْنَ أَنْ

يَذْهَبَ النَّاسُ بِالشَّاةِ وَالْبَعِيرِ، وَتَذْهَبُونَ بِرَسُولِ اللَّهِ صلى الله عليه وسلم "، فَقَالَ النَّبِيُّ صلى الله عليه وسلم "لَوْ سَلَكَ النَّاسُ وَادِيًا وَسَلَكَتِ الأَنْصَارُ شِعْبًا لاَخْتَرْتُ شِعْبَ الأَنْصَارِ"

Narrated Abu Qatada: We set out in the company of Allah's Messenger ﷺ on the day (of the battle) of Hunain. When we faced the enemy, the Muslims retreated and I saw a pagan throwing himself over a Muslim. I turned around and came upon him from behind and hit him on the shoulder with the sword He (i.e. the pagan) came towards me and seized me so violently that I felt as if it were death itself, but death overtook him and he released me. I followed `Umar bin Al Khattab and asked (him), "What is wrong with the people (fleeing)?" He replied, "This is the Will of Allah," After the people returned, the Prophet ﷺ sat and said, "Anyone who has killed an enemy and has a proof of that, will posses his spoils." I got up and said, "Who will be a witness for me?" and then sat down. The Prophet ﷺ again said, "Anyone who has killed an enemy and has proof of that, will possess his spoils." I (again) got up and said, "Who will be a witness for me?" and sat down. Then the Prophet ﷺ said the same for the third time. I again got up, and Allah's Messenger ﷺ said, "O Abu Qatada! What is your story?" Then I narrated the whole story to him. A man (got up and) said, "O Allah's Messenger ﷺ ! He is speaking the truth, and the spoils of the killed man are with me. So please compensate him on my behalf." On that Abu Bakr As-Siddiq said, "No, by Allah, he (i.e. Allah's Messenger ﷺ) will not agree to give you the spoils gained by one of Allah's Lions who fights on the behalf of Allah and His Apostle." The Prophet ﷺ said, "Abu Bakr has spoken the truth." So, Allah's Messenger ﷺ gave the spoils to me. I sold that armor (i.e. the spoils) and with its price I bought a garden at Bani Salima, and this was my first property which I gained after my conversion to Islam. – Sahih Al-Bukhari 3142

حَدَّثَنَا عَبْدُ اللَّهِ بْنُ مَسْلَمَةَ، عَنْ مَالِكٍ، عَنْ يَحْيَى بْنِ سَعِيدٍ، عَنِ ابْنِ أَفْلَحَ، عَنْ أَبِي مُحَمَّدٍ، مَوْلَى أَبِي قَتَادَةَ عَنْ أَبِي قَتَادَةَ ـ رضى الله عنه ـ قَالَ خَرَجْنَا مَعَ رَسُولِ اللَّهِ صلى الله عليه وسلم عَامَ حُنَيْنٍ، فَلَمَّا الْتَقَيْنَا كَانَتْ لِلْمُسْلِمِينَ جَوْلَةٌ، فَرَأَيْتُ رَجُلاً مِنَ الْمُشْرِكِينَ عَلاَ رَجُلاً مِنَ الْمُسْلِمِينَ، فَاسْتَدَرْتُ حَتَّى أَتَيْتُهُ مِنْ وَرَائِهِ حَتَّى ضَرَبْتُهُ بِالسَّيْفِ عَلَى حَبْلِ عَاتِقِهِ، فَأَقْبَلَ عَلَىَّ فَضَمَّنِي ضَمَّةً وَجَدْتُ مِنْهَا رِيحَ الْمَوْتِ، ثُمَّ أَدْرَكَهُ الْمَوْتُ فَأَرْسَلَنِي، فَلَحِقْتُ عُمَرَ بْنَ الْخَطَّابِ فَقُلْتُ مَا بَالُ النَّاسِ قَالَ أَمْرُ اللَّهِ، ثُمَّ إِنَّ النَّاسَ رَجَعُوا، وَجَلَسَ النَّبِيُّ صلى الله عليه وسلم فَقَالَ " مَنْ قَتَلَ قَتِيلاً لَهُ عَلَيْهِ بَيِّنَةٌ فَلَهُ سَلَبُهُ ". فَقُمْتُ فَقُلْتُ مَنْ يَشْهَدُ لِي ثُمَّ جَلَسْتُ ثُمَّ قَالَ " مَنْ قَتَلَ قَتِيلاً لَهُ عَلَيْهِ بَيِّنَةٌ فَلَهُ سَلَبُهُ " فَقُمْتُ فَقُلْتُ مَنْ يَشْهَدُ لِي ثُمَّ جَلَسْتُ، ثُمَّ قَالَ الثَّالِثَةَ مِثْلَهُ فَقَالَ رَجُلٌ صَدَقَ يَا رَسُولَ اللَّهِ، وَسَلَبُهُ عِنْدِي فَأَرْضِهِ عَنِّي. فَقَالَ أَبُو بَكْرٍ الصِّدِّيقُ ـ رضى الله عنه لاَهَا اللَّهِ إِذًا يَعْمِدُ إِلَى أَسَدٍ مِنْ أُسْدِ اللَّهِ يُقَاتِلُ عَنِ اللَّهِ وَرَسُولِهِ صلى الله عليه وسلم يُعْطِيكَ سَلَبَهُ. فَقَالَ النَّبِيُّ صلى الله عليه وسلم " صَدَقَ ". فَأَعْطَاهُ فَبِعْتُ الدِّرْعَ، فَابْتَعْتُ بِهِ مَخْرِفًا فِي بَنِي سَلِمَةَ، فَإِنَّهُ لأَوَّلُ مَالٍ تَأَثَّلْتُهُ فِي الإِسْلاَمِ

Narrated Abu Musa: When the Prophet ﷺ had finished from the battle of Hunain, he sent Abu Amir at the head of an army to Autas He (i.e. Abu Amir) met Duraid bin As Summa and Duraid was killed and Allah defeated his companions. The Prophet ﷺ sent me with Abu 'Amir. Abu Amir was shot at his knee with an arrow which a man from Jushm had shot and fixed into his knee. I went to him and said, "O Uncle! Who shot you?" He pointed me out (his killer) saying, "That is my killer who shot me (with an arrow)." So I headed towards him and overtook him, and when he saw me, he fled, and I followed him and started saying to him, "Won't you be ashamed? Won't you stop?" So that person stopped, and we exchanged two hits with the swords and I killed him. Then I said to Abu 'Amir. "Allah has killed your killer." He said, "Take out this arrow" So I removed it, and water oozed out of the wound. He then said, "O son of my brother! Convey my compliments to the Prophet ﷺ and request him to ask Allah's Forgiveness for me." Abu Amir made me his successor in commanding the people (i.e. troops). He survived for a short while and then died. (Later) I returned and entered upon the Prophet ﷺ at his house, and found him lying in a bed made of stalks of date-palm leaves knitted with ropes, and on it there was bedding. The strings of the bed had their traces over his back and sides. Then I told the Prophetﷺ about our and Abu Amir's news and how he had said "Tell him to ask for Allah's Forgiveness for me." The Prophetﷺ asked for water, performed ablution and then raised hands, saying, "O Allah's Forgive `Ubaid, Abu Amir." At that time I saw the whiteness of the Prophet's armpits. The Prophetﷺ then said, "O Allah, make him (i.e. Abu Amir) on the Day of Resurrection, superior to many of Your human creatures." I said, "Will you ask Allah's Forgiveness for me?" (On that) the Prophetﷺ said, "O Allah, forgive the sins of `Abdullah bin Qais and admit him to a nice entrance (i.e. paradise) on the Day of Resurrection." Abu Burda said, "One of the prayers was for Abu 'Amir and the other was for Abu Musa (i.e. `Abdullah bin Qais). – Sahih Al-Bukhari 4323

حَدَّثَنَا مُحَمَّدُ بْنُ الْعَلاَءِ، حَدَّثَنَا أَبُو أُسَامَةَ، عَنْ بُرَيْدِ بْنِ عَبْدِ اللَّهِ، عَنْ أَبِي بُرْدَةَ، عَنْ أَبِي مُوسَى ـ رضى الله عنه ـ قَالَ لَمَّا فَرَغَ النَّبِيُّ صلى الله عليه وسلم مِنْ حُنَيْنٍ بَعَثَ أَبَا عَامِرٍ عَلَى جَيْشٍ إِلَى أَوْطَاسٍ فَلَقِيَ دُرَيْدَ بْنَ الصِّمَّةِ، فَقُتِلَ دُرَيْدٌ وَهَزَمَ اللَّهُ أَصْحَابَهُ. قَالَ أَبُو مُوسَى وَبَعَثَنِي مَعَ أَبِي عَامِرٍ فَرُمِيَ أَبُو عَامِرٍ فِي رُكْبَتِهِ، رَمَاهُ جُشَمِيٌّ بِسَهْمٍ فَأَثْبَتَهُ فِي رُكْبَتِهِ، فَانْتَهَيْتُ إِلَيْهِ فَقُلْتُ يَا عَمِّ مَنْ رَمَاكَ فَأَشَارَ إِلَى أَبِي مُوسَى فَقَالَ ذَاكَ قَاتِلِي الَّذِي رَمَانِي. فَقَصَدْتُ لَهُ فَلَحِقْتُهُ فَلَمَّا رَآنِي وَلَّى فَاتَّبَعْتُهُ وَجَعَلْتُ أَقُولُ لَهُ أَلاَ تَسْتَحِي، أَلاَ تَثْبُتُ. فَكَفَّ فَاخْتَلَفْنَا ضَرْبَتَيْنِ بِالسَّيْفِ فَقَتَلْتُهُ ثُمَّ قُلْتُ لأَبِي عَامِرٍ قَتَلَ اللَّهُ صَاحِبَكَ. قَالَ فَانْزِعْ هَذَا السَّهْمَ فَنَزَعْتُهُ فَنَزَا مِنْهُ الْمَاءُ. قَالَ يَا ابْنَ أَخِي أَقْرِئِ النَّبِيَّ صلى الله عليه وسلم السَّلاَمَ، وَقُلْ لَهُ اسْتَغْفِرْ لِي. وَاسْتَخْلَفَنِي أَبُو عَامِرٍ عَلَى النَّاسِ، فَمَكُثَ يَسِيرًا ثُمَّ مَاتَ، فَرَجَعْتُ فَدَخَلْتُ عَلَى النَّبِيِّ صلى الله عليه وسلم فِي بَيْتِهِ عَلَى سَرِيرٍ مُرْمَلٍ وَعَلَيْهِ فِرَاشٌ قَدْ أَثَّرَ رِمَالُ السَّرِيرِ بِظَهْرِهِ وَجَنْبَيْهِ، فَأَخْبَرْتُهُ بِخَبَرِنَا وَخَبَرِ أَبِي عَامِرٍ، وَقَالَ قُلْ لَهُ اسْتَغْفِرْ لِي، فَدَعَا بِمَاءٍ فَتَوَضَّأَ ثُمَّ رَفَعَ يَدَيْهِ فَقَالَ " اللَّهُمَّ اغْفِرْ لِعُبَيْدٍ أَبِي عَامِرٍ ". وَرَأَيْتُ بَيَاضَ إِبْطَيْهِ ثُمَّ قَالَ " اللَّهُمَّ اجْعَلْهُ يَوْمَ الْقِيَامَةِ فَوْقَ كَثِيرٍ مِنْ خَلْقِكَ مِنَ النَّاسِ ". فَقُلْتُ وَلِي فَاسْتَغْفِرْ. فَقَالَ " اللَّهُمَّ اغْفِرْ لِعَبْدِ اللَّهِ بْنِ قَيْسٍ ذَنْبَهُ وَأَدْخِلْهُ يَوْمَ الْقِيَامَةِ مُدْخَلاً كَرِيمًا ". قَالَ أَبُو بُرْدَةَ إِحْدَاهُمَا لأَبِي عَامِرٍ وَالأُخْرَى لأَبِي مُوسَى

Narrated Anas Bin Malik: When it was the day (of the battle) of Hunain, the tributes of Hawazin and Ghatafan and others, along with their animals and offspring (and wives) came to fight against the Prophetﷺ The Prophetﷺ had with him, ten thousand men and some of the Tulaqa. The companions fled, leaving the Prophetﷺ alone. The Prophet then made two calls which were clearly distinguished from each other. He turned right and said, "O the group of Ansar!" They said, "Labbaik, O Allah's Messengerﷺ ! Rejoice, for we are with you!" Then he turned left and said, "O the group of Ansar!" They said, "Labbaik! O Allah's Messengerﷺ ! Rejoice, for we are with you!" The Prophetﷺ at that time, was riding on a white mule; then he dismounted and said, "I am Allah's Slave and His Apostle." The infidels then were defeated, and on that day the Prophetﷺ gained a large amount of booty which he distributed amongst the Muhajirin and the Tulaqa and did not give anything to the Ansar. The Ansar said, "When there is a difficulty, we are called, but the booty is given to other than us." The news reached the Prophetﷺ and he gathered them in a leather tent and said, "What is this news reaching me from you, O the group of Ansar?" They kept silent, He added," O the group of Ansar! Won't you be happy that the people take the worldly things and you take Allah's Messengerﷺ to your homes reserving him for yourself?" They said, "Yes." Then the Prophet said, "If the people took their way through a valley, and the Ansar took their way through a mountain pass, surely, I would take the Ansar's mountain pass." Hisham said, "O Abu Hamza (i.e. Anas)! Did you witness that? " He replied, "And how could I be absent from him?". – Sahih Al-Bukhari 4337

حَدَّثَنَا مُحَمَّدُ بْنُ بَشَّارٍ، حَدَّثَنَا مُعَاذُ بْنُ مُعَاذٍ، حَدَّثَنَا ابْنُ عَوْنٍ، عَنْ هِشَامِ بْنِ زَيْدِ بْنِ أَنَسِ بْنِ مَالِكٍ، عَنْ أَنَسِ بْنِ مَالِكٍ ـ رضى الله عنه ـ قَالَ لَمَّا كَانَ يَوْمُ حُنَيْنٍ أَقْبَلَتْ هَوَازِنُ وَغَطَفَانُ وَغَيْرُهُمْ بِنَعَمِهِمْ وَذَرَارِيِّهِمْ، وَمَعَ النَّبِيِّ صلى الله عليه وسلم عَشَرَةُ آلاَفٍ وَمِنَ الطُّلَقَاءِ، فَأَدْبَرُوا عَنْهُ حَتَّى بَقِيَ وَحْدَهُ، فَنَادَى يَوْمَئِذٍ نِدَاءَيْنِ لَمْ يَخْلِطْ بَيْنَهُمَا، الْتَفَتَ عَنْ يَمِينِهِ، فَقَالَ " يَا مَعْشَرَ الأَنْصَارِ ". قَالُوا لَبَّيْكَ يَا رَسُولَ اللَّهِ، أَبْشِرْ نَحْنُ مَعَكَ. ثُمَّ الْتَفَتَ عَنْ يَسَارِهِ، فَقَالَ " يَا مَعْشَرَ الأَنْصَارِ ". قَالُوا لَبَّيْكَ يَا رَسُولَ اللَّهِ، أَبْشِرْ نَحْنُ مَعَكَ. وَهْوَ عَلَى بَغْلَةٍ بَيْضَاءَ، فَنَزَلَ فَقَالَ " أَنَا عَبْدُ اللَّهِ وَرَسُولُهُ "، فَانْهَزَمَ الْمُشْرِكُونَ، فَأَصَابَ يَوْمَئِذٍ غَنَائِمَ كَثِيرَةً، فَقَسَمَ فِي الْمُهَاجِرِينَ وَالطُّلَقَاءِ وَلَمْ يُعْطِ الأَنْصَارَ شَيْئًا، فَقَالَتِ الأَنْصَارُ إِذَا كَانَتْ شَدِيدَةٌ فَنَحْنُ نُدْعَى، وَيُعْطَى الْغَنِيمَةَ غَيْرُنَا. فَبَلَغَهُ ذَلِكَ، فَجَمَعَهُمْ فِي قُبَّةٍ، فَقَالَ " يَا مَعْشَرَ الأَنْصَارِ مَا حَدِيثٌ بَلَغَنِي عَنْكُمْ ". فَسَكَتُوا

فَقَالَ " يَا مَعْشَرَ الأَنْصَارِ أَلاَ تَرْضَوْنَ أَنْ يَذْهَبَ النَّاسُ بِالدُّنْيَا، وَتَذْهَبُونَ بِرَسُولِ اللَّهِ صلى الله عليه وسلم تَحُوزُونَهُ إِلَى بُيُوتِكُمْ ". قَالُوا بَلَى. فَقَالَ رَسُولُ اللَّهِ صلى الله عليه وسلم " لَوْ سَلَكَ النَّاسُ وَادِيًا، وَسَلَكَتِ الأَنْصَارُ شِعْبًا لأَخَذْتُ شِعْبَ الأَنْصَارِ ". فَقَالَ هِشَامٌ يَا أَبَا حَمْزَةَ، وَأَنْتَ شَاهِدٌ ذَاكَ قَالَ وَأَيْنَ أَغِيبُ عَنْهُ

Narrated Isma`il: I saw (a healed scar of) blow over the hand of Ibn Abi `Aufa who said, "I received that blow in the battle of Hunain in the company of the Prophet." I said, "Did you take part in the battle of Hunain?" He replied, "Yes (and in other battles) before it.". – Sahih Al-Bukhari 4314

حَدَّثَنَا مُحَمَّدُ بْنُ عَبْدِ اللَّهِ بْنِ نُمَيْرٍ، حَدَّثَنَا يَزِيدُ بْنُ هَارُونَ، أَخْبَرَنَا إِسْمَاعِيلُ، رَأَيْتُ بِيَدِ ابْنِ أَبِي أَوْفَى ضَرْبَةً، قَالَ ضُرِبْتُهَا مَعَ النَّبِيِّ صلى الله عليه وسلم يَوْمَ حُنَيْنٍ. قُلْتُ شَهِدْتَ حُنَيْنًا قَالَ قَبْلَ ذَلِكَ.

Narrated Nafi`: `Umar bin Al-Khattab said, "O Allah's Messenger ﷺ ! I vowed to observe I`tikaf for one day during the PreIslamic period." The Prophet ﷺ ordered him to fulfill his vow. `Umar gained two lady captives from the war prisoners of Hunain and he left them in some of the houses at Mecca. When Allah's Messenger ﷺ freed the captives of Hunain without ransom, they came out walking in the streets. `Umar said (to his son), "O `Abdullah! See what is the matter." `Abdullah replied, "Allah's Messenger ﷺ has freed the captives without ransom." He said (to him), "Go and set free those two slave girls." (Nafi` added Allah's Apostle did not perform the `Umra from Al-Jarana, and if he had performed the `Umra, it would not have been hidden from `Abdullah. – Sahih Al-Bukhari 3144

حَدَّثَنَا أَبُو النُّعْمَانِ، حَدَّثَنَا حَمَّادُ بْنُ زَيْدٍ، عَنْ أَيُّوبَ، عَنْ نَافِعٍ، أَنَّ عُمَرَ بْنَ الْخَطَّابِ ـ رضى الله عنه ـ قَالَ يَا رَسُولَ اللَّهِ إِنَّهُ كَانَ عَلَىَّ اعْتِكَافُ يَوْمٍ فِي الْجَاهِلِيَّةِ، فَأَمَرَهُ أَنْ يَفِيَ بِهِ. قَالَ وَأَصَابَ عُمَرُ جَارِيَتَيْنِ مِنْ سَبْىِ حُنَيْنٍ، فَوَضَعَهُمَا فِي بَعْضِ بُيُوتِ مَكَّةَ ـ قَالَ ـ فَمَنَّ رَسُولُ اللَّهِ صلى الله عليه وسلم عَلَى سَبْىِ حُنَيْنٍ، فَجَعَلُوا يَسْعَوْنَ فِي السِّكَكِ فَقَالَ عُمَرُ يَا عَبْدَ اللَّهِ، انْظُرْ مَا هَذَا فَقَالَ مَنَّ رَسُولُ اللَّهِ صلى الله عليه وسلم عَلَى السَّبْىِ. قَالَ اذْهَبْ فَأَرْسِلِ الْجَارِيَتَيْنِ. قَالَ نَافِعٌ وَلَمْ يَعْتَمِرْ رَسُولُ اللَّهِ صلى الله عليه وسلم مِنَ الْجِعْرَانَةِ وَلَوِ اعْتَمَرَ لَمْ يَخْفَ عَلَى عَبْدِ اللَّهِ. وَزَادَ جَرِيرُ بْنُ حَازِمٍ عَنْ أَيُّوبَ عَنْ نَافِعٍ عَنِ ابْنِ عُمَرَ قَالَ مِنَ الْخُمُسِ. وَرَوَاهُ مَعْمَرٌ عَنْ أَيُّوبَ عَنْ نَافِعٍ عَنِ ابْنِ عُمَرَ فِي النَّذْرِ وَلَمْ يَقُلْ يَوْمَ.

Narrated Muhammad bin Jubair: Jubair bin Mut`im told me that while he was in the company of Allah's Messenger ﷺ with the people returning from Hunain, some people (Bedouins) caught hold of the Prophet ﷺ and started begging of him so much so that he had to stand under a (kind of thorny tree (i.e. Samurah) and his cloak was snatched away. The Prophet ﷺ stopped and said, "Give me my cloak. If I had as many camels as these thorny trees, I would have distributed them amongst you and you will not find me a miser or a liar or a coward.". – Sahih Al-Bukhari 2821

حَدَّثَنَا أَبُو الْيَمَانِ، أَخْبَرَنَا شُعَيْبٌ، عَنِ الزُّهْرِيِّ، قَالَ أَخْبَرَنِي عُمَرُ بْنُ مُحَمَّدِ بْنِ جُبَيْرِ بْنِ مُطْعِمٍ، أَنَّ مُحَمَّدَ بْنَ جُبَيْرٍ، قَالَ أَخْبَرَنِي جُبَيْرُ بْنُ مُطْعِمٍ، أَنَّهُ بَيْنَمَا هُوَ يَسِيرُ مَعَ رَسُولِ اللَّهِ صلى الله عليه وسلم وَمَعَهُ النَّاسُ، مُقْفَلَهُ مِنْ حُنَيْنٍ، فَعَلِقَهُ النَّاسُ يَسْأَلُونَهُ حَتَّى اضْطَرُّوهُ إِلَى سَمُرَةٍ فَخَطِفَتْ رِدَاءَهُ، فَوَقَفَ النَّبِيُّ صلى الله عليه وسلم فَقَالَ " أَعْطُونِي رِدَائِي، لَوْ كَانَ لِي عَدَدُ هَذِهِ الْعِضَاهِ نَعَمًا لَقَسَمْتُهُ بَيْنَكُمْ، ثُمَّ لاَ تَجِدُونِي بَخِيلاً وَلاَ كَذُوبًا وَلاَ جَبَانًا "

Narrated `Abdullah: When it was the day of Hunain, Prophet favored some people over some others (in the distribution of the booty). He gave Al-Aqra' one-hundred camels and gave Uyaina the same, and also gave other people (of Quraish). A man said, "Allah's Pleasure was not the aim, in this distribution." I said, "I will inform the Prophet (about your statement)." The Prophet ﷺ said, "May Allah bestow Mercy on Moses, for he was troubled more this but he remained patient." - Sahih Al-Bukhari 4336

حَدَّثَنَا قُتَيْبَةُ بْنُ سَعِيدٍ، حَدَّثَنَا جَرِيرٌ، عَنْ مَنْصُورٍ، عَنْ أَبِي وَائِلٍ، عَنْ عَبْدِ اللَّهِ ـ رضى الله عنه ـ قَالَ لَمَّا كَانَ يَوْمُ حُنَيْنٍ آثَرَ النَّبِيُّ صلى الله عليه وسلم نَاسًا، أَعْطَى الأَقْرَعَ مِائَةً مِنَ الإِبِلِ، وَأَعْطَى عُيَيْنَةَ مِثْلَ ذَلِكَ، وَأَعْطَى نَاسًا، فَقَالَ رَجُلٌ مَا أُرِيدَ بِهَذِهِ الْقِسْمَةِ وَجْهُ اللَّهِ. فَقُلْتُ لأُخْبِرَنَّ النَّبِيَّ صلى الله عليه وسلم قَالَ " رَحِمَ اللَّهُ مُوسَى. قَدْ أُوذِيَ بِأَكْثَرَ مِنْ هَذَا فَصَبَرَ "

Narrated `Abdullah bin Zaid bin `Asim: When Allah gave to His Apostle the war booty on the day of Hunain, he distributed that booty amongst those whose hearts have been (recently) reconciled (to Islam), but did not give anything to the Ansar. So they seemed to have felt angry and sad as they did not get the same as other people had got. The Prophet ﷺ then delivered a sermon before them, saying, "O, the assembly of Ansar! Didn't I find you astray, and then Allah guided you on the Right Path through me? You were divided into groups, and Allah brought you together through me; you were poor and Allah made you rich through me." Whatever the Prophet ﷺ said , they (i.e. the Ansar) said, "Allah and his Apostle have more favours to do." The Prophet ﷺ said, "What stops you from answering the Messenger of Allah?" But whatever he said to them, they replied, "Allah and His Apostle have more favours to do." The Prophet ﷺ then said, "If you wish you could say: 'You came to us in such-and-such state (at Medina).' Wouldn't you be willing to see the people go away with sheep and camels while you go with the Prophet ﷺ to your homes? But for the migration, I would have been one of the Ansar, and if the people took their way through a valley or mountain pass, I would select the valley or mountain pass of the Ansar. The Ansar are Shiar (i.e. those clothes which are in direct contact with the body and worn inside the other garments), and the people are Dithar (i.e. those clothes which are not in direct contact with the body and are worn over other garments). No doubt, you will see other people favoured over you, so you should be patient till you meet me at the Tank (of Kauthar). – Al-Bukhari 4330

حَدَّثَنَا مُوسَى بْنُ إِسْمَاعِيلَ، حَدَّثَنَا وُهَيْبٌ، حَدَّثَنَا عَمْرُو بْنُ يَحْيَى، عَنْ عَبَّادِ بْنِ تَمِيمٍ، عَنْ عَبْدِ اللَّهِ بْنِ زَيْدِ بْنِ عَاصِمٍ، قَالَ لَمَّا أَفَاءَ اللَّهُ عَلَى رَسُولِهِ صلى الله عليه وسلم يَوْمَ حُنَيْنٍ قَسَمَ فِي النَّاسِ فِي الْمُؤَلَّفَةِ قُلُوبُهُمْ، وَلَمْ يُعْطِ الأَنْصَارَ شَيْئًا، فَكَأَنَّهُمْ وَجَدُوا إِذْ لَمْ يُصِبْهُمْ مَا أَصَابَ النَّاسَ فَخَطَبَهُمْ فَقَالَ " يَا مَعْشَرَ الأَنْصَارِ أَلَمْ أَجِدْكُمْ ضُلاَّلاً فَهَدَاكُمُ اللَّهُ بِي، وَكُنْتُمْ مُتَفَرِّقِينَ فَأَلَّفَكُمُ اللَّهُ بِي وَعَالَةً، فَأَغْنَاكُمُ اللَّهُ بِي ". كُلَّمَا قَالَ شَيْئًا قَالُوا اللَّهُ وَرَسُولُهُ أَمَنُّ. قَالَ " مَا يَمْنَعُكُمْ أَنْ تُجِيبُوا رَسُولَ اللَّهِ صلى الله عليه وسلم ". قَالَ كُلَّمَا قَالَ شَيْئًا قَالُوا اللَّهُ وَرَسُولُهُ أَمَنُّ. قَالَ " لَوْ شِئْتُمْ قُلْتُمْ جِئْتَنَا كَذَا وَكَذَا. أَتَرْضَوْنَ أَنْ يَذْهَبَ النَّاسُ بِالشَّاةِ وَالْبَعِيرِ، وَتَذْهَبُونَ بِالنَّبِيِّ صلى الله عليه وسلم إِلَى رِحَالِكُمْ، لَوْلاَ الْهِجْرَةُ لَكُنْتُ امْرَأً مِنَ الأَنْصَارِ، وَلَوْ سَلَكَ النَّاسُ وَادِيًا وَشِعْبًا لَسَلَكْتُ وَادِيَ الأَنْصَارِ وَشِعْبَهَا، الأَنْصَارُ شِعَارٌ وَالنَّاسُ دِثَارٌ، إِنَّكُمْ سَتَلْقَوْنَ بَعْدِي أَثَرَةً فَاصْبِرُوا حَتَّى تَلْقَوْنِي عَلَى الْحَوْضِ ".

Narrated Abu Qatada: We set out with Allah's Messenger ﷺ in the year of Hunain, (the Prophet ﷺ gave me an armor). I sold that armor and bought a garden in the region of the tribe of Bani Salama and that was the first property I got after embracing Islam. – Sahih Al-Bukhari 2100

حَدَّثَنَا عَبْدُ اللَّهِ بْنُ مَسْلَمَةَ، عَنْ مَالِكٍ، عَنْ يَحْيَى بْنِ سَعِيدٍ، عَنِ ابْنِ أَفْلَحَ، عَنْ أَبِي مُحَمَّدٍ، مَوْلَى أَبِي قَتَادَةَ عَنْ أَبِي قَتَادَةَ ـ رضى الله عنه ـ قَالَ خَرَجْنَا مَعَ رَسُولِ اللَّهِ صلى الله عليه وسلم عَامَ حُنَيْنٍ، فَأَعْطَاهُ ـ يَعْنِي دِرْعًا ـ فَبِعْتُ الدِّرْعَ، فَابْتَعْتُ بِهِ مَخْرَفًا فِي بَنِي سَلِمَةَ، فَإِنَّهُ لأَوَّلُ مَالٍ تَأَثَّلْتُهُ فِي الإِسْلاَمِ.

The Book of
Sieged of the people of Ta'if
أَهْلَ الطَّائِفِ فَلَمْ يَفْتَحْهَا

Narrated Um Salama: That while the Prophetﷺ was with her, there was an effeminate man in the house. The effeminate man said to Um Salama's brother, `Abdullah bin Abi Umaiyya, "If Allah should make you conquer Ta'if tomorrow, I recommend that you take the daughter of Ghailan (in marriage) for (she is so fat) that she shows four folds of flesh when facing you and eight when she turns her back." Thereupon the Prophetﷺ said (to us), "This (effeminate man) should not enter upon you (anymore). – Sahih Al-Bukhari 5235

حَدَّثَنَا عُثْمَانُ بْنُ أَبِي شَيْبَةَ، حَدَّثَنَا عَبْدَةُ، عَنْ هِشَامِ بْنِ عُرْوَةَ، عَنْ أَبِيهِ، عَنْ زَيْنَبَ ابْنَةِ أَمِّ سَلَمَةَ، عَنْ أَمِّ سَلَمَةَ، أَنَّ النَّبِيَّ صلى الله عليه وسلم كَانَ عِنْدَهَا وَفِي الْبَيْتِ مُخَنَّثٌ، فَقَالَ الْمُخَنَّثُ لأَخِي أَمِّ سَلَمَةَ عَبْدِ اللَّهِ بْنِ أَبِي أُمَيَّةَ إِنْ فَتَحَ اللَّهُ عَلَيْكُمُ الطَّائِفَ غَدًا أَدُلُّكَ عَلَى ابْنَةِ غَيْلاَنَ، فَإِنَّهَا تُقْبِلُ بِأَرْبَعٍ وَتُدْبِرُ بِثَمَانٍ. فَقَالَ النَّبِيُّ صلى الله عليه وسلم " لاَ يَدْخُلَنَّ هَذَا عَلَيْكُنَّ "

Narrated `Abdullah bin `Umar: The Prophetﷺ besieged the people of Ta'if, but he did not conquer it. He said, "Tomorrow, if Allah will, we will return home. On this the Muslims said, "Then we return without conquering it?" He said, 'Then carry on fighting tomorrow." The next day many of them were injured. The Prophetﷺ said, "If Allah will, we will return home tomorrow." It seemed that statement pleased them whereupon Allah's Apostle smiled. – Sahih Al-Bukhari 7480

حَدَّثَنَا عَبْدُ اللَّهِ بْنُ مُحَمَّدٍ، حَدَّثَنَا ابْنُ عُيَيْنَةَ، عَنْ عَمْرٍو، عَنْ أَبِي الْعَبَّاسِ، عَنْ عَبْدِ اللَّهِ بْنِ عُمَرَ، قَالَ حَاصَرَ النَّبِيُّ صلى الله عليه وسلم أَهْلَ الطَّائِفِ فَلَمْ يَفْتَحْهَا فَقَالَ " إِنَّا قَافِلُونَ إِنْ شَاءَ اللَّهُ ". فَقَالَ الْمُسْلِمُونَ نَقْفُلُ وَلَمْ نَفْتَحْ. قَالَ " فَاغْدُوا عَلَى الْقِتَالِ ". فَغَدَوْا فَأَصَابَتْهُمْ جِرَاحَاتٌ. قَالَ النَّبِيُّ صلى الله عليه وسلم " إِنَّا قَافِلُونَ غَدًا إِنْ شَاءَ اللَّهُ "، فَكَأَنَّ ذَلِكَ أَعْجَبَهُمْ فَتَبَسَّمَ رَسُولُ اللَّهِ صلى الله عليه وسلم

Narrated `Abdullah bin `Umar: When Allah Apostle was in Ta'if (trying to conquer it), he said to his companions, "Tomorrow we will return (to Medina), if Allah wills." Some of the companions of Allah's Messengerﷺ said, "We will not leave till we conquer it." The Prophetﷺ said, "Therefore, be ready to fight tomorrow." On the following day, they (Muslims) fought fiercely (with the people of Ta'if) and suffered many wounds. Then Allah's Messengerﷺ said, "Tomorrow we will return (to Medina), if Allah wills." His companions kept quiet this time. Allah's Messengerﷺ then smiled. – Sahih Al-Bukhari 6086

حَدَّثَنَا قُتَيْبَةُ بْنُ سَعِيدٍ، حَدَّثَنَا سُفْيَانُ، عَنْ عَمْرٍو، عَنْ أَبِي الْعَبَّاسِ، عَنْ عَبْدِ اللَّهِ بْنِ عَمْرٍو، قَالَ لَمَّا كَانَ رَسُولُ اللَّهِ صلى الله عليه وسلم بِالطَّائِفِ قَالَ " إِنَّا قَافِلُونَ غَدًا إِنْ شَاءَ اللَّهُ ". فَقَالَ نَاسٌ مِنْ أَصْحَابِ رَسُولِ اللَّهِ صلى الله عليه وسلم لاَ نَبْرَحُ أَوْ نَفْتَحَهَا. فَقَالَ النَّبِيُّ صلى الله عليه وسلم " فَاغْدُوا عَلَى الْقِتَالِ ". قَالَ فَغَدَوْا فَقَاتَلُوهُمْ قِتَالاً شَدِيدًا وَكَثُرَ فِيهِمُ الْجِرَاحَاتُ فَقَالَ رَسُولُ اللَّهِ صلى الله عليه وسلم " إِنَّا قَافِلُونَ غَدًا إِنْ شَاءَ اللَّهُ ". قَالَ فَسَكَتُوا فَضَحِكَ رَسُولُ اللَّهِ صلى الله عليه وسلم. قَالَ الْحُمَيْدِيُّ حَدَّثَنَا سُفْيَانُ بِالْخَبَرِ كُلِّهِ.

Call them after their fathers; that is more equitable with Allah. But if you do not know their fathers, then your brethren in faith and your friends. There is no blame on you if you err therein, barring what your hearts premeditates. Allah is Forgiving and Merciful. – Surah Al-Ahzab 33:5

ٱدْعُوهُمْ لِءَابَآئِهِمْ هُوَ أَقْسَطُ عِندَ ٱللَّهِ ۚ فَإِن لَّمْ تَعْلَمُوٓا۟ ءَابَآءَهُمْ فَإِخْوَٰنُكُمْ فِى ٱلدِّينِ وَمَوَٰلِيكُمْ ۚ وَلَيْسَ عَلَيْكُمْ جُنَاحٌ فِيمَآ أَخْطَأْتُم بِهِۦ وَلَٰكِن مَّا تَعَمَّدَتْ قُلُوبُكُمْ ۚ وَكَانَ ٱللَّهُ غَفُورًا رَّحِيمًا

Narrated Abu `Uthman: I heard from Sa`d, the first man who has thrown an arrow in Allah's Cause, and from Abu Bakra who jumped over the wall of the Ta'if Fort along with a few persons and came to the Prophet. They both said, "We heard the Prophet ﷺ saying, " If somebody claims to be the son of somebody other than his father knowingly, he will be denied Paradise (i.e. he will not enter Paradise).' " Narrated Ma`mar from `Asim from Abu Al-`Aliya or Abu `Uthman An-Nahdi who said. "I heard Sa`d and Abu Bakra narrating from the Prophet." `Asim said, "I said (to him), 'Very trustworthy persons have narrated to you.' He said, 'Yes, one of them was the first to throw an arrow in Allah's Cause and the other came to the Prophet ﷺ in a group of thirty-three persons from Ta'if.'. – Sahih Al-Bukhari 4326, 4327

حَدَّثَنَا مُحَمَّدُ بْنُ بَشَّارٍ، حَدَّثَنَا غُنْدَرٌ، حَدَّثَنَا شُعْبَةُ، عَنْ عَاصِمٍ، قَالَ سَمِعْتُ أَبَا عُثْمَانَ، قَالَ سَمِعْتُ سَعْدًا ـ وَهْوَ أَوَّلُ مَنْ رَمَى بِسَهْمٍ فِي سَبِيلِ اللَّهِ ـ وَأَبَا بَكْرَةَ ـ وَكَانَ تَسَوَّرَ حِصْنَ الطَّائِفِ فِي أُنَاسٍ ـ فَجَاءَ إِلَى النَّبِيِّ صلى الله عليه وسلم فَقَالاَ سَمِعْنَا النَّبِيَّ صلى الله عليه وسلم يَقُولُ " مَنِ ادَّعَى إِلَى غَيْرِ أَبِيهِ وَهْوَ يَعْلَمُ فَالْجَنَّةُ عَلَيْهِ حَرَامٌ ". وَقَالَ هِشَامٌ وَأَخْبَرَنَا مَعْمَرٌ، عَنْ عَاصِمٍ، عَنْ أَبِي الْعَالِيَةِ، أَوْ أَبِي عُثْمَانَ النَّهْدِيِّ قَالَ سَمِعْتُ سَعْدًا، وَأَبَا، بَكْرَةَ عَنِ النَّبِيِّ صلى الله عليه وسلم. قَالَ عَاصِمٌ قُلْتُ لَقَدْ شَهِدَ عِنْدَكَ رَجُلاَنِ حَسْبُكَ بِهِمَا. قَالَ أَجَلْ أَمَّا أَحَدُهُمَا فَأَوَّلُ مَنْ رَمَى بِسَهْمٍ فِي سَبِيلِ اللَّهِ، وَأَمَّا الآخَرُ فَنَزَلَ إِلَى النَّبِيِّ صلى الله عليه وسلم ثَالِثَ ثَلاَثَةٍ وَعِشْرِينَ مِنَ الطَّائِفِ

Narrated Marwan and Al-Miswar bin Makhrama: When the delegates of the tribe of Hawazin came to the Prophet ﷺ and they requested him to return their properties and captives. The Prophet ﷺ stood up and said to them, "I have other people with me in this matter (as you see) and the most beloved statement to me is the true one; you may choose either the properties or the prisoners as I have delayed their distribution." The Prophet ﷺ had waited for them for more than ten days since his arrival from Ta'if. So, when it became evident to them that the Prophet ﷺ was not going to return them except one of the two, they said, "We choose our prisoners." The Prophet got up amongst the people and glorified and praised Allah as He deserved and said, "Then after, these brethren of yours have come to us with repentance, and I see it logical to return them the captives. So, whoever amongst you likes to do that as a favor, then he can do it, and whoever of you likes to stick to his share till we recompense him from the very first war booty which Allah will give us, then he can do so (i.e. give up the present captives)." The people unanimously said, "We do that (return the captives) willingly." The Prophet ﷺ said, "We do not know which of you has agreed to it and which have not, so go back and let your leaders forward us your decision." So, all the people then went back and discussed the matter with their leaders who returned and informed the Prophet ﷺ that all the people had willingly given their consent to return the captives. This is what has reached us about the captives of Hawazin. Narrated Anas that `Abbas said to the Prophet, "I paid for my ransom and `Aqil's ransom.". – Al-Bukhari 2539

حَدَّثَنَا ابْنُ أَبِي مَرْيَمَ، قَالَ أَخْبَرَنِي اللَّيْثُ، عَنْ عُقَيْلٍ، عَنِ ابْنِ شِهَابٍ، ذَكَرَ عُرْوَةُ أَنَّ مَرْوَانَ، وَالْمِسْوَرَ بْنَ مَخْرَمَةَ، أَخْبَرَاهُ أَنَّ النَّبِيَّ صلى الله عليه وسلم قَامَ حِينَ جَاءَهُ وَفْدُ هَوَازِنَ، فَسَأَلُوهُ أَنْ يَرُدَّ إِلَيْهِمْ أَمْوَالَهُمْ وَسَبْيَهُمْ فَقَالَ " إِنَّ مَعِي مَنْ تَرَوْنَ، وَأَحَبُّ الْحَدِيثِ إِلَيَّ أَصْدَقُهُ، فَاخْتَارُوا إِحْدَى الطَّائِفَتَيْنِ إِمَّا الْمَالَ، وَإِمَّا السَّبْىَ، وَقَدْ كُنْتُ اسْتَأْنَيْتُ بِهِمْ ". وَكَانَ النَّبِيُّ صلى الله عليه وسلم انْتَظَرَهُمْ بِضْعَ عَشْرَةَ لَيْلَةً حِينَ قَفَلَ مِنَ الطَّائِفِ، فَلَمَّا تَبَيَّنَ لَهُمْ أَنَّ النَّبِيَّ صلى الله عليه وسلم غَيْرُ رَادٍّ إِلَيْهِمْ إِلاَّ إِحْدَى الطَّائِفَتَيْنِ قَالُوا فَإِنَّا نَخْتَارُ سَبْيَنَا. فَقَامَ النَّبِيُّ صلى الله عليه وسلم فِي النَّاسِ، فَأَثْنَى عَلَى اللَّهِ بِمَا هُوَ أَهْلُهُ، ثُمَّ قَالَ " أَمَّا بَعْدُ فَإِنَّ إِخْوَانَكُمْ جَاءُونَا تَائِبِينَ، وَإِنِّي رَأَيْتُ أَنْ أَرُدَّ إِلَيْهِمْ سَبْيَهُمْ، فَمَنْ أَحَبَّ مِنْكُمْ أَنْ يُطَيِّبَ ذَلِكَ فَلْيَفْعَلْ، وَمَنْ أَحَبَّ أَنْ يَكُونَ عَلَى حَظِّهِ حَتَّى نُعْطِيَهُ إِيَّاهُ مِنْ أَوَّلِ مَا يُفِيءُ اللَّهُ عَلَيْنَا فَلْيَفْعَلْ ". فَقَالَ النَّاسُ طَيَّبْنَا ذَلِكَ. قَالَ " إِنَّا لاَ نَدْرِي مَنْ أَذِنَ مِنْكُمْ مِمَّنْ لَمْ يَأْذَنْ فَارْجِعُوا حَتَّى يَرْفَعَ إِلَيْنَا عُرَفَاؤُكُمْ أَمْرَكُمْ ". فَرَجَعَ النَّاسُ، فَكَلَّمَهُمْ عُرَفَاؤُهُمْ، ثُمَّ رَجَعُوا إِلَى النَّبِيِّ صلى الله عليه وسلم فَأَخْبَرُوهُ أَنَّهُمْ طَيَّبُوا وَأَذِنُوا، فَهَذَا الَّذِي بَلَغَنَا عَنْ سَبْىِ هَوَازِنَ. وَقَالَ أَنَسٌ قَالَ عَبَّاسٌ لِلنَّبِيِّ صلى الله عليه وسلم فَادَيْتُ نَفْسِي، وَفَادَيْتُ عَقِيلاً.

The Book of
Ghazwat of Tabuk
غزوة تبوك

Narrated Ka`b bin Malik: Whenever Allah's Messenger ﷺ intended to carry out a Ghazwa, he would use an equivocation to conceal his real destination till it was the Ghazwa of Tabuk which Allah's Messenger ﷺ carried out in very hot weather. As he was going to face a very long journey through a wasteland and was to meet and attack a large number of enemies. So, he made the situation clear to the Muslims so that they might prepare themselves accordingly and get ready to conquer their enemy. The Prophet ﷺ informed them of the destination he was heading for.. – Sahih Al-Bukhari 2948

وَحَدَّثَنِي أَحْمَدُ بْنُ مُحَمَّدٍ، أَخْبَرَنَا عَبْدُ اللَّهِ، أَخْبَرَنَا يُونُسُ، عَنِ الزُّهْرِيِّ، قَالَ أَخْبَرَنِي عَبْدُ الرَّحْمَنِ بْنُ عَبْدِ اللَّهِ بْنِ كَعْبِ بْنِ مَالِكٍ، قَالَ سَمِعْتُ كَعْبَ بْنَ مَالِكٍ ـ رضى الله عنه ـ يَقُولُ كَانَ رَسُولُ اللَّهِ صلى الله عليه وسلم قَلَّمَا يُرِيدُ غَزْوَةً يَغْزُوهَا إِلاَّ وَرَّى بِغَيْرِهَا، حَتَّى كَانَتْ غَزْوَةُ تَبُوكَ، فَغَزَاهَا رَسُولُ اللَّهِ صلى الله عليه وسلم فِي حَرٍّ شَدِيدٍ، وَاسْتَقْبَلَ سَفَرًا بَعِيدًا وَمَفَازًا، وَاسْتَقْبَلَ غَزْوَ عَدُوٍّ كَثِيرٍ، فَجَلَّى لِلْمُسْلِمِينَ أَمْرَهُمْ، لِيَتَأَهَّبُوا أُهْبَةَ عَدُوِّهِمْ، وَأَخْبَرَهُمْ بِوَجْهِهِ الَّذِي يُرِيدُ

Narrated Abu Musa: My Companions sent me to Allah's Messenger ﷺ to ask him for some animals to ride on as they were accompanying him in the army of Al-Usra, and that was the Ghazwa (Battle) of Tabuk, I said, "O Allah's Prophet! My companions have sent me to you to provide them with means of transportation." He said, "By Allah! I will not make you ride anything." It happened that when I reached him, he was in an angry mood, and I didn't notice it. So I returned in a sad mood because of the refusal the Prophet ﷺ and for the fear that the Prophet ﷺ might have become 'angry with me. So I returned to my companions and informed them of what the Prophet ﷺ had said. Only a short while had passed when I heard Bilal calling, "O `Abdullah bin Qais!" I replied to his call. Bilal said, "Respond to Allah's Messenger ﷺ who is calling you." When I went to him (i.e. the Prophet), he said, "Take these two camels tied together and also these two camels tied together,"' referring to six camels he had brought them from Sa`d at that time. The Prophet ﷺ added, "Take them to your companions and say, 'Allah (or Allah's Messenger ﷺ) allows you to ride on these,' so ride on them." So I took those camels to them and said, "The Prophet ﷺ allows you to ride on these (camels) but by Allah, I will not leave you till some of you proceed with me to somebody who heard the statement of Allah's Messenger ﷺ .Do not think that I narrate to you a thing which Allah's Messenger ﷺ has not said." They said to me, "We consider you truthful, and we will do what you like." The sub-narrator added: So Abu Musa proceeded along with some of them till they came to those who have heard the statement of Allah's Messenger ﷺ wherein he denied them (some animals to ride on) and (his statement) whereby he gave them the same. So these people told them the same information as Abu Musa had told them. – Sahih Al-Bukhari 4415

حَدَّثَنِي مُحَمَّدُ بْنُ الْعَلاَءِ، حَدَّثَنَا أَبُو أُسَامَةَ، عَنْ بُرَيْدِ بْنِ عَبْدِ اللَّهِ بْنِ أَبِي بُرْدَةَ، عَنْ أَبِي بُرْدَةَ، عَنْ أَبِي مُوسَى ـ رضى الله عنه ـ قَالَ أَرْسَلَنِي أَصْحَابِي إِلَى رَسُولِ اللَّهِ صلى الله عليه وسلم أَسْأَلُهُ الْحُمْلاَنَ لَهُمْ، إِذْ هُمْ مَعَهُ فِي جَيْشِ الْعُسْرَةِ وَهْىَ غَزْوَةُ تَبُوكَ فَقُلْتُ يَا نَبِيَّ اللَّهِ، إِنَّ أَصْحَابِي أَرْسَلُونِي إِلَيْكَ لِتَحْمِلَهُمْ فَقَالَ " وَاللَّهِ لاَ أَحْمِلُكُمْ عَلَى شَىْءٍ ". وَوَافَقْتُهُ وَهْوَ غَضْبَانُ وَلاَ أَشْعُرُ، وَرَجَعْتُ حَزِينًا مِنْ مَنْعِ النَّبِيِّ صلى الله عليه وسلم، وَمِنْ مَخَافَةِ أَنْ يَكُونَ النَّبِيُّ صلى الله عليه وسلم وَجَدَ فِي نَفْسِهِ عَلَىَّ، فَرَجَعْتُ إِلَى أَصْحَابِي فَأَخْبَرْتُهُمُ الَّذِي قَالَ النَّبِيُّ صلى الله عليه وسلم، فَلَمْ أَلْبَثْ إِلاَّ سُوَيْعَةً إِذْ سَمِعْتُ بِلاَلاً يُنَادِي أَىْ عَبْدَ اللَّهِ بْنَ قَيْسٍ. فَأَجَبْتُهُ، فَقَالَ أَجِبْ رَسُولَ اللَّهِ صلى الله عليه وسلم يَدْعُوكَ، فَلَمَّا أَتَيْتُهُ، قَالَ " خُذْ هَذَيْنِ الْقَرِينَيْنِ ـ وَهَذَيْنِ الْقَرِينَيْنِ لِسِتَّةِ أَبْعِرَةٍ ابْتَاعَهُنَّ حِينَئِذٍ مِنْ سَعْدٍ ـ فَانْطَلِقْ بِهِنَّ إِلَى أَصْحَابِكَ فَقُلْ إِنَّ اللَّهَ ـ أَوْ قَالَ إِنَّ رَسُولَ اللَّهِ صلى الله عليه وسلم ـ يَحْمِلُكُمْ عَلَى هَؤُلاَءِ فَارْكَبُوهُنَّ ". فَانْطَلَقْتُ إِلَيْهِمْ بِهِنَّ، فَقُلْتُ إِنَّ النَّبِيَّ صلى الله عليه وسلم يَحْمِلُكُمْ عَلَى هَؤُلاَءِ وَلَكِنِّي وَاللَّهِ لاَ أَدَعُكُمْ حَتَّى يَنْطَلِقَ مَعِي بَعْضُكُمْ إِلَى مَنْ سَمِعَ مَقَالَةَ رَسُولِ اللَّهِ صلى الله عليه وسلم لاَ تَظُنُّوا أَنِّي حَدَّثْتُكُمْ شَيْئًا لَمْ يَقُلْهُ رَسُولُ اللَّهِ صلى الله عليه وسلم فَقَالُوا لِي إِنَّكَ عِنْدَنَا لَمُصَدَّقٌ، وَلَنَفْعَلَنَّ مَا أَحْبَبْتَ. فَانْطَلَقَ

أَبُو مُوسَى بِنَفَرٍ مِنْهُمْ حَتَّى أَتَوُا الَّذِينَ سَمِعُوا قَوْلَ رَسُولِ اللَّهِ صلى الله عليه وسلم مَنْعَهُ إِيَّاهُمْ، ثُمَّ إِعْطَاءَهُمْ بَعْدُ، فَحَدَّثُوهُمْ بِمِثْلِ مَا حَدَّثَهُمْ بِهِ أَبُو مُوسَى

Narrated Sa`d: Allah's Messenger ﷺ set out for Tabuk. Appointing `Ali as his deputy (in Medina). `Ali said, "Do you want to leave me with the children and women?" The Prophet ﷺ said, "Will you not be pleased that you will be to me like Aaron to Moses? But there will be no prophet after me.". – Sahih Al-Bukhari 4416

حَدَّثَنَا مُسَدَّدٌ، حَدَّثَنَا يَحْيَى، عَنْ شُعْبَةَ، عَنِ الْحَكَمِ، عَنْ مُصْعَبِ بْنِ سَعْدٍ، عَنْ أَبِيهِ، أَنَّ رَسُولَ اللَّهِ صلى الله عليه وسلم خَرَجَ إِلَى تَبُوكَ، وَاسْتَخْلَفَ عَلِيًّا فَقَالَ أَتُخَلِّفُنِي فِي الصِّبْيَانِ وَالنِّسَاءِ قَالَ " أَلاَ تَرْضَى أَنْ تَكُونَ مِنِّي بِمَنْزِلَةِ هَارُونَ مِنْ مُوسَى إِلاَّ أَنَّهُ لَيْسَ نَبِيٌّ بَعْدِي ". وَقَالَ أَبُو دَاوُدَ حَدَّثَنَا شُعْبَةُ عَنِ الْحَكَمِ سَمِعْتُ مُصْعَبًا.

Narrated Ka`b bin Malik: The Prophet ﷺ set out on Thursday for the Ghazwa of Tabuk and he used to prefer to set out (i.e. travel) on Thursdays. – Sahih Al-Bukhari 2950

حَدَّثَنِي عَبْدُ اللَّهِ بْنُ مُحَمَّدٍ، حَدَّثَنَا هِشَامٌ، أَخْبَرَنَا مَعْمَرٌ، عَنِ الزُّهْرِيِّ، عَنْ عَبْدِ الرَّحْمَنِ بْنِ كَعْبِ بْنِ مَالِكٍ، عَنْ أَبِيهِ ـ رضى الله عنه ـ أَنَّ النَّبِيَّ صلى الله عليه وسلم خَرَجَ يَوْمَ الْخَمِيسِ فِي غَزْوَةِ تَبُوكَ، وَكَانَ يُحِبُّ أَنْ يَخْرُجَ يَوْمَ الْخَمِيسِ.

Narrated Ibn `Umar: When Allah's Messenger ﷺ landed at Al-Hijr during the Ghazwa of Tabuk, he ordered his companions not to drink water from its well or reserve water from it. They said, "We have already kneaded the dough with its water. And also filled our bags with its water." On that, the Prophet ﷺ ordered them to throw away the dough and pour out the water. – Sahih Al-Bukhari 3378

حَدَّثَنَا مُحَمَّدُ بْنُ مِسْكِينٍ أَبُو الْحَسَنِ، حَدَّثَنَا يَحْيَى بْنُ حَسَّانَ بْنِ حَيَّانَ أَبُو زَكَرِيَّاءَ، حَدَّثَنَا سُلَيْمَانُ، عَنْ عَبْدِ اللَّهِ بْنِ دِينَارٍ، عَنِ ابْنِ عُمَرَ ـ رضى الله عنهما أَنَّ رَسُولَ اللَّهِ صلى الله عليه وسلم لَمَّا نَزَلَ الْحِجْرَ فِي غَزْوَةِ تَبُوكَ أَمَرَهُمْ أَنْ لاَ يَشْرَبُوا مِنْ بِئْرِهَا، وَلاَ يَسْتَقُوا مِنْهَا فَقَالُوا قَدْ عَجَنَّا مِنْهَا، وَاسْتَقَيْنَا. فَأَمَرَهُمْ أَنْ يَطْرَحُوا ذَلِكَ الْعَجِينَ وَيُهَرِيقُوا ذَلِكَ الْمَاءَ. وَيُرْوَى عَنْ سَبْرَةَ بْنِ مَعْبَدٍ وَأَبِي الشُّمُوسِ أَنَّ النَّبِيَّ صلى الله عليه وسلم أَمَرَ بِإِلْقَاءِ الطَّعَامِ. وَقَالَ أَبُو ذَرٍّ عَنِ النَّبِيِّ صلى الله عليه وسلم " مَنِ اعْتَجَنَ بِمَائِهِ "

Narrated `Urwa bin Al-Mughira: Al-Mughira bin Shu`ba, said, "The Prophet ﷺ went out to answer the call of nature and (when he had finished) I got up to pour water for him." I think that he said that the event had taken place during the Ghazwa of Tabuk. Al-Mughira added. "The Prophet ﷺ washed his face, and when he wanted to wash his forearms, the sleeves of his cloak became tight over them, so he took them out from underneath the cloak and then he washed them (i.e. his forearms) and passed wet hands over his Khuffs (socks made from thick fabric or leather).". – Sahih Al-Bukhari 4421

حَدَّثَنَا يَحْيَى بْنُ بُكَيْرٍ، عَنِ اللَّيْثِ، عَنْ عَبْدِ الْعَزِيزِ بْنِ أَبِي سَلَمَةَ، عَنْ سَعْدِ بْنِ إِبْرَاهِيمَ، عَنْ نَافِعِ بْنِ جُبَيْرٍ، عَنْ عُرْوَةَ بْنِ الْمُغِيرَةِ، عَنْ أَبِيهِ الْمُغِيرَةِ بْنِ شُعْبَةَ، قَالَ ذَهَبَ النَّبِيُّ صلى الله عليه وسلم لِبَعْضِ حَاجَتِهِ، فَقُمْتُ أَسْكُبُ عَلَيْهِ الْمَاءَ ـ لاَ أَعْلَمُهُ إِلاَّ قَالَ فِي غَزْوَةِ تَبُوكَ ـ فَغَسَلَ وَجْهَهُ، وَذَهَبَ يَغْسِلُ ذِرَاعَيْهِ فَضَاقَ عَلَيْهِ كُمُّ الْجُبَّةِ، فَأَخْرَجَهُمَا مِنْ تَحْتِ جُبَّتِهِ فَغَسَلَهُمَا ثُمَّ مَسَحَ عَلَى خُفَّيْهِ.

Narrated Abu Humaid As-Sa`idi: We took part in the holy battle of Tabuk in the company of the Prophet ﷺ and when we arrived at the Wadi-al-Qura, there was a woman in her garden. The Prophet ﷺ asked his companions to estimate the amount of the fruits in the garden, and Allah's Messenger ﷺ estimated it at ten Awsuq (One Wasaq = 60 Sa's) and 1 Sa'= 3 kg. approximately). The Prophet ﷺ said to that lady, "Check what your garden will yield." When we reached Tabuk, the Prophet ﷺ said, "There will be a strong wind tonight and so no one should stand and whoever has a camel, should fasten it." So we fastened our camels. A strong wind blew at night and a man stood up and he was blown away to a mountain called Taiy,

The King of Aila sent a white mule and a sheet for wearing to the Prophetﷺ as a present, and wrote to the Prophetﷺ that his people would stay in their place (and will pay Jizya taxation.) (1) When the Prophetﷺ reached Wadi-al- Qura he asked that woman how much her garden had yielded. She said, "Ten Awsuq," and that was what Allah's Messengerﷺ had estimated. Then the Prophetﷺ said, "I want to reach Medina quickly, and whoever among you wants to accompany me, should hurry up." The sub-narrator Ibn Bakkar said something which meant: When the Prophetﷺ saw Medina he said, "This is Taba." And when he saw the mountain of Uhud, he said, "This mountain loves us and we love it. Shall I tell you of the best amongst the Ansar?" They replied in the affirmative. He said, "The family of Bani-n-Najjar, and then the family of Bani Sa`ida or Bani Al-Harith bin Al-Khazraj. (The above-mentioned are the best) but there is goodness in all the families of Ansar.". – Sahih Al-Bukhari 1481, 1482
حَدَّثَنَا سَهْلُ بْنُ بَكَّارٍ، حَدَّثَنَا وُهَيْبٌ، عَنْ عَمْرِو بْنِ يَحْيَى، عَنْ عَبَّاسٍ السَّاعِدِيِّ، عَنْ أَبِي حُمَيْدٍ السَّاعِدِيِّ، قَالَ غَزَوْنَا مَعَ النَّبِيِّ صلى الله عليه وسلم غَزْوَةَ تَبُوكَ فَلَمَّا جَاءَ وَادِيَ الْقُرَى إِذَا امْرَأَةٌ فِي حَدِيقَةٍ لَهَا فَقَالَ النَّبِيُّ صلى الله عليه وسلم لأَصْحَابِهِ " اخْرُصُوا ". وَخَرَصَ رَسُولُ اللَّهِ صلى الله عليه وسلم عَشَرَةَ أَوْسُقٍ فَقَالَ لَهَا " أَحْصِي مَا يَخْرُجُ مِنْهَا ". فَلَمَّا أَتَيْنَا تَبُوكَ قَالَ " أَمَا إِنَّهَا سَتَهُبُّ اللَّيْلَةَ رِيحٌ شَدِيدَةٌ فَلاَ يَقُومَنَّ أَحَدٌ، وَمَنْ كَانَ مَعَهُ بَعِيرٌ فَلْيَعْقِلْهُ ". فَعَقَلْنَاهَا وَهَبَّتْ رِيحٌ شَدِيدَةٌ فَقَامَ رَجُلٌ فَأَلْقَتْهُ بِجَبَلِ طَيِّئٍ ـ وَأَهْدَى مَلِكُ أَيْلَةَ لِلنَّبِيِّ صلى الله عليه وسلم بَغْلَةً بَيْضَاءَ، وَكَسَاهُ بُرْدًا وَكَتَبَ لَهُ بِبَحْرِهِمْ ـ فَلَمَّا أَتَى وَادِيَ الْقُرَى قَالَ لِلْمَرْأَةِ " كَمْ جَاءَ حَدِيقَتُكِ ". قَالَتْ عَشَرَةَ أَوْسُقٍ خَرْصَ رَسُولِ اللَّهِ صلى الله عليه وسلم فَقَالَ النَّبِيُّ صلى الله عليه وسلم " إِنِّي مُتَعَجِّلٌ إِلَى الْمَدِينَةِ، فَمَنْ أَرَادَ مِنْكُمْ أَنْ يَتَعَجَّلَ مَعِي فَلْيَتَعَجَّلْ ". فَلَمَّا ـ قَالَ ابْنُ بَكَّارٍ كَلِمَةً مَعْنَاهَا ـ أَشْرَفَ عَلَى الْمَدِينَةِ قَالَ " هَذِهِ طَابَةُ ". فَلَمَّا رَأَى أُحُدًا قَالَ " هَذَا جُبَيْلٌ يُحِبُّنَا وَنُحِبُّهُ، أَلاَ أُخْبِرُكُمْ بِخَيْرِ دُورِ الأَنْصَارِ ". قَالُوا بَلَى. قَالَ " دُورُ بَنِي النَّجَّارِ، ثُمَّ دُورُ بَنِي عَبْدِ الأَشْهَلِ، ثُمَّ دُورُ بَنِي سَاعِدَةَ، أَوْ دُورُ بَنِي الْحَارِثِ بْنِ الْخَزْرَجِ، وَفِي كُلِّ دُورِ الأَنْصَارِ ـ يَعْنِي ـ خَيْرًا ". وَقَالَ سُلَيْمَانُ بْنُ بِلاَلٍ حَدَّثَنِي عَمْرٌو، " ثُمَّ دَارُ بَنِي الْحَارِثِ، ثُمَّ بَنِي سَاعِدَةَ ". وَقَالَ سُلَيْمَانُ عَنْ سَعْدِ بْنِ سَعِيدٍ، عَنْ عُمَارَةَ بْنِ غَزِيَّةَ، عَنْ عَبَّاسٍ، عَنْ أَبِيهِ، عَنِ النَّبِيِّ صلى الله عليه وسلم قَالَ " أُحُدٌ جَبَلٌ يُحِبُّنَا وَنُحِبُّهُ ". قَالَ أَبُو عَبْدِ اللَّهِ كُلُّ بُسْتَانٍ عَلَيْهِ حَائِطٌ فَهْوَ حَدِيقَةٌ، وَمَا لَمْ يَكُنْ عَلَيْهِ حَائِطٌ لَمْ يَقُلْ حَدِيقَةٌ.

Narrated `Auf bin Mali: I went to the Prophetﷺ during the Ghazwa of Tabuk while he was sitting in a leather tent. He said, "Count six signs that indicate the approach of the Hour: my death, the conquest of Jerusalem, a plague that will afflict you (and kill you in great numbers) as the plague that afflicts sheep, the increase of wealth to such an extent that even if one is given one hundred Dinars, he will not be satisfied; then an affliction which no Arab house will escape, and then a truce between you and Bani Al-Asfar (i.e. the Byzantines) who will betray you and attack you under eighty flags. Under each flag will be twelve thousand soldiers. – Sahih Al-Bukhari 3176
حَدَّثَنَا الْحُمَيْدِيُّ، حَدَّثَنَا الْوَلِيدُ بْنُ مُسْلِمٍ، حَدَّثَنَا عَبْدُ اللَّهِ بْنُ الْعَلاَءِ بْنِ زَبْرٍ، قَالَ سَمِعْتُ بُسْرَ بْنَ عُبَيْدِ اللَّهِ، أَنَّهُ سَمِعَ أَبَا إِدْرِيسَ، قَالَ سَمِعْتُ عَوْفَ بْنَ مَالِكٍ، قَالَ أَتَيْتُ النَّبِيَّ صلى الله عليه وسلم فِي غَزْوَةِ تَبُوكَ، وَهْوَ فِي قُبَّةٍ مِنْ أَدَمٍ فَقَالَ " اعْدُدْ سِتًّا بَيْنَ يَدَىِ السَّاعَةِ، مَوْتِي، ثُمَّ فَتْحُ بَيْتِ الْمَقْدِسِ، ثُمَّ مُوتَانٌ يَأْخُذُ فِيكُمْ كَقُعَاصِ الْغَنَمِ، ثُمَّ اسْتِفَاضَةُ الْمَالِ حَتَّى يُعْطَى الرَّجُلُ مِائَةَ دِينَارٍ فَيَظَلُّ سَاخِطًا، ثُمَّ فِتْنَةٌ لاَ يَبْقَى بَيْتٌ مِنَ الْعَرَبِ إِلاَّ دَخَلَتْهُ، ثُمَّ هُدْنَةٌ تَكُونُ بَيْنَكُمْ وَبَيْنَ بَنِي الأَصْفَرِ فَيَغْدِرُونَ، فَيَأْتُونَكُمْ تَحْتَ ثَمَانِينَ غَايَةً، تَحْتَ كُلِّ غَايَةٍ اثْنَا عَشَرَ أَلْفًا ".

Narrated As-Saib: I remember I went out with the boys to Thaniyat-ul-Wada` to receive the Prophetﷺ when he returned from the Ghazwa of Tabuk. – Sahih Al-Bukhari 4427
حَدَّثَنَا عَبْدُ اللَّهِ بْنُ مُحَمَّدٍ، حَدَّثَنَا سُفْيَانُ، عَنِ الزُّهْرِيِّ، عَنِ السَّائِبِ، أَذْكُرُ أَنِّي خَرَجْتُ مَعَ الصِّبْيَانِ نَتَلَقَّى النَّبِيَّ صلى الله عليه وسلم إِلَى ثَنِيَّةِ الْوَدَاعِ مَقْدَمَهُ مِنْ غَزْوَةِ تَبُوكَ

Narrated Anas bin Malik: Allah's Messengerﷺ returned from the Ghazwa of Tabuk, and when he approached Medina, he said, "There are some people in Medina who were with you all the time, you did not travel any portion of the journey nor crossed any valley, but they were with you they (i.e. the people) said, "O Allah's Messengerﷺ ! Even though they were at

Medina?" He said, "Yes, because they were stopped by a genuine excuse.". – Sahih Al-Bukhari 4423

حَدَّثَنَا أَحْمَدُ بْنُ مُحَمَّدٍ، أَخْبَرَنَا عَبْدُ اللَّهِ، أَخْبَرَنَا حُمَيْدٌ الطَّوِيلُ، عَنْ أَنَسِ بْنِ مَالِكٍ ـ رضى الله عنه ـ أَنَّ رَسُولَ اللَّهِ صلى الله عليه وسلم رَجَعَ مِنْ غَزْوَةِ تَبُوكَ فَدَنَا مِنَ الْمَدِينَةِ فَقَالَ " إِنَّ بِالْمَدِينَةِ أَقْوَامًا مَا سِرْتُمْ مَسِيرًا وَلاَ قَطَعْتُمْ وَادِيًا إِلاَّ كَانُوا مَعَكُمْ قَالُوا يَا رَسُولَ اللَّهِ وَهُمْ بِالْمَدِينَةِ قَالَ " وَهُمْ بِالْمَدِينَةِ، حَبَسَهُمُ الْعُذْرُ ".

Narrated Abu Humaid: We returned in the company of the Prophet ﷺ from the Ghazwa of Tabuk, and when we looked upon Medina, the Prophet ﷺ said, "This is Taba (i.e. Medina), and this is Uhud, a mountain that loves us and is loved by us.". – Sahih Al-Bukhari 4422

حَدَّثَنَا خَالِدُ بْنُ مَخْلَدٍ، حَدَّثَنَا سُلَيْمَانُ، قَالَ حَدَّثَنِي عَمْرُو بْنُ يَحْيَى، عَنْ عَبَّاسِ بْنِ سَهْلِ بْنِ سَعْدٍ، عَنْ أَبِي حُمَيْدٍ، قَالَ أَقْبَلْنَا مَعَ النَّبِيِّ صلى الله عليه وسلم مِنْ غَزْوَةِ تَبُوكَ حَتَّى إِذَا أَشْرَفْنَا عَلَى الْمَدِينَةِ قَالَ " هَذِهِ طَابَةُ، وَهَذَا أُحُدٌ، جَبَلٌ يُحِبُّنَا وَنُحِبُّهُ "

Except for those among the polytheists with whom you had made a treaty, and did not violate any of its terms, nor aided anyone against you. So fulfill the treaty with them to the end of its term. Allah loves the righteous. Surah At-Taubah 9:4

إِلَّا ٱلَّذِينَ عَـٰهَدتُّم مِّنَ ٱلْمُشْرِكِينَ ثُمَّ لَمْ يَنقُصُوكُمْ شَيْـًٔا وَلَمْ يُظَـٰهِرُوا۟ عَلَيْكُمْ أَحَدًا فَأَتِمُّوٓا۟ إِلَيْهِمْ عَهْدَهُمْ إِلَىٰ مُدَّتِهِمْ ۚ إِنَّ ٱللَّهَ يُحِبُّ ٱلْمُتَّقِينَ

Narrated Humaid bin `Abdur-Rahman: Abu Huraira said that Abu Bakr sent him during the Hajj in which Abu Bakr was made the chief of the pilgrims by Allah's Messenger ﷺ before (the year of) Hajjat al-Wada` in a group (of announcers) to announce before the people; 'No pagan shall perform the Hajj after this year, and none shall perform the Tawaf around the Ka`ba in a naked state. Humaid used to say The Day of Nahr is the day of Al- Hajj Al-Akbar (the Greatest Day) because of the narration of Abu Huraira. – Sahih al-Bukhari 4657

حَدَّثَنَا إِسْحَاقُ، حَدَّثَنَا يَعْقُوبُ بْنُ إِبْرَاهِيمَ، حَدَّثَنَا أَبِي، عَنْ صَالِحٍ، عَنِ ابْنِ شِهَابٍ، أَنَّ حُمَيْدَ بْنَ عَبْدِ الرَّحْمَنِ، أَخْبَرَهُ أَنَّ أَبَا هُرَيْرَةَ أَخْبَرَهُ أَنَّ أَبَا بَكْرٍ ـ رضى الله عنه ـ بَعَثَهُ فِي الْحَجَّةِ الَّتِي أَمَّرَهُ رَسُولُ اللَّهِ صلى الله عليه وسلم عَلَيْهَا قَبْلَ حَجَّةِ الْوَدَاعِ فِي رَهْطٍ يُؤَذِّنُ فِي النَّاسِ أَنْ لاَ يَحُجَّنَّ بَعْدَ الْعَامِ مُشْرِكٌ وَلاَ يَطُوفَ بِالْبَيْتِ عُرْيَانٌ. فَكَانَ حُمَيْدٌ يَقُولُ يَوْمُ النَّحْرِ يَوْمُ الْحَجِّ الأَكْبَرِ. مِنْ أَجْلِ حَدِيثِ أَبِي هُرَيْرَةَ.

How? Whenever they overcome you, they respect neither kinship nor treaty with you. They satisfy you with lip service, but their hearts refuse, and most of them are immoral. – Surah At-Taubah 9:8

كَيْفَ وَإِن يَظْهَرُوا۟ عَلَيْكُمْ لَا يَرْقُبُوا۟ فِيكُمْ إِلًّا وَلَا ذِمَّةً ۚ يُرْضُونَكُم بِأَفْوَٰهِهِمْ وَتَأْبَىٰ قُلُوبُهُمْ وَأَكْثَرُهُمْ فَـٰسِقُونَ

O you who believe! The polytheists are polluted, so let them not approach the Sacred Mosque after this year of theirs. And if you fear poverty, Allah will enrich you from His grace, if He wills. Allah is Aware and Wise. – Surah At-Tawbah 9:28

يَـٰٓأَيُّهَا ٱلَّذِينَ ءَامَنُوٓا۟ إِنَّمَا ٱلْمُشْرِكُونَ نَجَسٌ فَلَا يَقْرَبُوا۟ ٱلْمَسْجِدَ ٱلْحَرَامَ بَعْدَ عَامِهِمْ هَـٰذَا ۚ وَإِنْ خِفْتُمْ عَيْلَةً فَسَوْفَ يُغْنِيكُمُ ٱللَّهُ مِن فَضْلِهِۦٓ إِن شَآءَ ۚ إِنَّ ٱللَّهَ عَلِيمٌ حَكِيمٌ

The Book of

Ibrāhīm ibn Muḥammad

إِبْرَاهِيم ٱبْن مُحَمَّد

Narrated Isma`il: I asked Abi `Aufa, "Did you see Ibrahim, the son of the Prophet ﷺ?" He said, "Yes, but he died in his early childhood. Had there been a Prophet after Muhammad then his son would have lived, but there is no Prophet after him.". – Sahih al-Bukhari 6194

حَدَّثَنَا ابْنُ نُمَيْرٍ، حَدَّثَنَا مُحَمَّدُ بْنُ بِشْرٍ، حَدَّثَنَا إِسْمَاعِيلُ، قُلْتُ لاِبْنِ أَبِي أَوْفَى رَأَيْتَ إِبْرَاهِيمَ ابْنَ النَّبِيِّ صلى الله عليه وسلم قَالَ مَاتَ صَغِيرًا، وَلَوْ قُضِيَ أَنْ يَكُونَ بَعْدَ مُحَمَّدٍ صلى الله عليه وسلم نَبِيٌّ عَاشَ ابْنُهُ، وَلَكِنْ لاَ نَبِيَّ بَعْدَهُ.

Narrated Anas bin Malik: We went with Allah's Messenger ﷺ to the blacksmith Abu Saif, and he was the husband of the wet-nurse of Ibrahim (the son of the Prophet). Allah's Messenger ﷺ took Ibrahim and kissed him and smelled him and later we entered Abu Saif's house and at that time Ibrahim was in his last breaths, and the eyes of Allah's Messenger ﷺ started shedding tears. `Abdur Rahman bin `Auf said, "O Allah's Apostle, even you are weeping!" He said, "O Ibn `Auf, this is mercy." Then he wept more and said, "The eyes are shedding tears and the heart is grieved, and we will not say except what pleases our Lord, O Ibrahim ! Indeed we are grieved by your separation.". – Sahih al-Bukhari 1303

حَدَّثَنَا الْحَسَنُ بْنُ عَبْدِ الْعَزِيزِ، حَدَّثَنَا يَحْيَى بْنُ حَسَّانَ، حَدَّثَنَا قُرَيْشٌ ـ هُوَ ابْنُ حَيَّانَ ـ عَنْ ثَابِتٍ، عَنْ أَنَسِ بْنِ مَالِكٍ ـ رضى الله عنه ـ قَالَ دَخَلْنَا مَعَ رَسُولِ اللَّهِ صلى الله عليه وسلم عَلَى أَبِي سَيْفٍ الْقَيْنِ ـ وَكَانَ ظِئْرًا لإِبْرَاهِيمَ ـ عَلَيْهِ السَّلاَمُ ـ فَأَخَذَ رَسُولُ اللَّهِ صلى الله عليه وسلم إِبْرَاهِيمَ فَقَبَّلَهُ وَشَمَّهُ، ثُمَّ دَخَلْنَا عَلَيْهِ بَعْدَ ذَلِكَ، وَإِبْرَاهِيمُ يَجُودُ بِنَفْسِهِ، فَجَعَلَتْ عَيْنَا رَسُولِ اللَّهِ صلى الله عليه وسلم تَذْرِفَانِ. فَقَالَ لَهُ عَبْدُ الرَّحْمَنِ بْنُ عَوْفٍ ـ رضى الله عنه ـ وَأَنْتَ يَا رَسُولَ اللَّهِ فَقَالَ " يَا ابْنَ عَوْفٍ إِنَّهَا رَحْمَةٌ ". ثُمَّ أَتْبَعَهَا بِأُخْرَى فَقَالَ صلى الله عليه وسلم " إِنَّ الْعَيْنَ تَدْمَعُ، وَالْقَلْبَ يَحْزَنُ، وَلاَ نَقُولُ إِلاَّ مَا يَرْضَى رَبُّنَا، وَإِنَّا بِفِرَاقِكَ يَا إِبْرَاهِيمُ لَمَحْزُونُونَ ". رَوَاهُ مُوسَى عَنْ سُلَيْمَانَ بْنِ الْمُغِيرَةِ عَنْ ثَابِتٍ عَنْ أَنَسٍ ـ رضى الله عنه ـ عَنِ النَّبِيِّ صلى الله عليه وسلم

Once solar eclipse occurred during the lifetime of Allah's Messenger ﷺ

خَسَفَتِ الشَّمْسُ عَلَى عَهْدِ رَسُولِ اللَّهِ صلى الله عليه وسلم

Narrated Al-Mughira bin Shu`ba: On the day of Ibrahim's death, the sun eclipsed and the people said that the eclipse was due to the death of Ibrahim (the son of the Prophet). Allah's Messenger ﷺ said, "The sun and the moon are two signs amongst the signs of Allah. They do not eclipse because of someone's death or life. So when you see them, invoke Allah and pray till the eclipse is clear.". – Sahih al-Bukhari 1060

حَدَّثَنَا أَبُو الْوَلِيدِ، قَالَ حَدَّثَنَا زَائِدَةُ، قَالَ حَدَّثَنَا زِيَادُ بْنُ عِلاَقَةَ، قَالَ سَمِعْتُ الْمُغِيرَةَ بْنَ شُعْبَةَ، يَقُولُ انْكَسَفَتِ الشَّمْسُ يَوْمَ مَاتَ إِبْرَاهِيمُ، فَقَالَ النَّاسُ انْكَسَفَتْ لِمَوْتِ إِبْرَاهِيمَ. فَقَالَ رَسُولُ اللَّهِ صلى الله عليه وسلم " إِنَّ الشَّمْسَ وَالْقَمَرَ آيَتَانِ مِنْ آيَاتِ اللَّهِ، لاَ يَنْكَسِفَانِ لِمَوْتِ أَحَدٍ وَلاَ لِحَيَاتِهِ، فَإِذَا رَأَيْتُمُوهُمَا فَادْعُوا اللَّهَ وَصَلُّوا حَتَّى يَنْجَلِيَ "

Narrated 'Abdullah bin Abbas :Once solar eclipse occurred during the lifetime of Allah's Messenger ﷺ . He offered the eclipse prayer. His companions asked, "O Allah's Messenger ﷺ ! We saw you trying to take something while standing at your place and then we saw you retreating." The Prophet ﷺ said, "I was shown Paradise and wanted to have a bunch of fruit from it. Had I taken it, you would have eaten from it as long as the world remains". - Sahih al-Bukhari 748

حَدَّثَنَا إِسْمَاعِيلُ، قَالَ حَدَّثَنِي مَالِكٌ، عَنْ زَيْدِ بْنِ أَسْلَمَ، عَنْ عَطَاءِ بْنِ يَسَارٍ، عَنْ عَبْدِ اللَّهِ بْنِ عَبَّاسٍ، رضى الله عنهما قَالَ خَسَفَتِ الشَّمْسُ عَلَى عَهْدِ رَسُولِ اللَّهِ صلى الله عليه وسلم فَصَلَّى، قَالُوا يَا رَسُولَ اللَّهِ، رَأَيْنَاكَ تَنَاوَلُ شَيْئًا فِي مَقَامِكَ، ثُمَّ رَأَيْنَاكَ تَكَعْكَعْتَ. قَالَ " إِنِّي أُرِيتُ الْجَنَّةَ، فَتَنَاوَلْتُ مِنْهَا عُنْقُودًا، وَلَوْ أَخَذْتُهُ لأَكَلْتُمْ مِنْهُ مَا بَقِيَتِ الدُّنْيَا ".

Narrated `Abdullah bin `Abbas :During the lifetime of Allah's Messenger ﷺ, the sun eclipsed. Allah's Messenger ﷺ offered the prayer of (the) eclipse) and so did the people along with him. He performed a long Qiyam (standing posture) during which Surat-al-Baqara could have been recited; then he performed a pro-longed bowing, then raised his head and stood for a long time which was slightly less than that of the first Qiyam (and recited Qur'an). Then he performed a prolonged bowing again but the period was shorter than the period of the first bowing, then he stood up and then prostrated. Again he stood up, but this time the period of standing was less than the first standing. Then he performed a prolonged bowing but of a lesser duration than the first, then he stood up again for a long time but for a lesser duration than the first. Then he performed a prolonged bowing but of lesser duration than the first, and then he again stood up, and then prostrated and then finished his prayer. By then the sun eclipse had cleared. The Prophet ﷺ then said, "The sun and the moon are two signs among the signs of Allah, and they do not eclipse because of the death or birth of someone, so when you observe the eclipse, remember Allah (offer the eclipse prayer)." They (the people) said, "O Allah's Messenger ﷺ ! We saw you stretching your hand to take something at this place of yours, then we saw you stepping backward." He said, "I saw Paradise (or Paradise was shown to me), and I stretched my hand to pluck a bunch (of grapes), and had I plucked it, you would have eaten of it as long as this world exists. Then I saw the (Hell) Fire, and I have never before, seen such a horrible sight as that, and I saw that the majority of its dwellers were women." The people asked, "O Allah's Messenger ﷺ ! What is the reason for that?" He replied, "Because of their ungratefulness." It was said. "Do they disbelieve in Allah (are they ungrateful to Allah)?" He replied, "They are not thankful to their husbands and are ungrateful for the favors done to them. Even if you do good to one of them all your life, when she seems some harshness from you, she will say, "I have never seen any good from you.' " - Sahih al-Bukhari 5197

حَدَّثَنَا عَبْدُ اللَّهِ بْنُ يُوسُفَ، أَخْبَرَنَا مَالِكٌ، عَنْ زَيْدِ بْنِ أَسْلَمَ، عَنْ عَطَاءِ بْنِ يَسَارٍ، عَنْ عَبْدِ اللَّهِ بْنِ عَبَّاسٍ، أَنَّهُ قَالَ خَسَفَتِ الشَّمْسُ عَلَى عَهْدِ رَسُولِ اللَّهِ صلى الله عليه وسلم فَصَلَّى رَسُولُ اللَّهِ صلى الله عليه وسلم وَالنَّاسُ مَعَهُ، فَقَامَ قِيَامًا طَوِيلاً نَحْوًا مِنْ سُورَةِ الْبَقَرَةِ، ثُمَّ رَكَعَ رُكُوعًا طَوِيلاً، ثُمَّ رَفَعَ فَقَامَ قِيَامًا طَوِيلاً وَهُوَ دُونَ الْقِيَامِ الأَوَّلِ، ثُمَّ رَكَعَ رُكُوعًا طَوِيلاً وَهُوَ دُونَ الرُّكُوعِ الأَوَّلِ، ثُمَّ سَجَدَ، ثُمَّ قَامَ فَقَامَ قِيَامًا طَوِيلاً وَهُوَ دُونَ الْقِيَامِ الأَوَّلِ، ثُمَّ رَكَعَ رُكُوعًا طَوِيلاً وَهُوَ دُونَ الرُّكُوعِ الأَوَّلِ، ثُمَّ رَفَعَ فَقَامَ قِيَامًا طَوِيلاً وَهُوَ دُونَ الْقِيَامِ الأَوَّلِ، ثُمَّ رَكَعَ رُكُوعًا طَوِيلاً وَهُوَ دُونَ الرُّكُوعِ الأَوَّلِ، ثُمَّ رَفَعَ ثُمَّ سَجَدَ، ثُمَّ انْصَرَفَ، وَقَدْ تَجَلَّتِ الشَّمْسُ، فَقَالَ " إِنَّ الشَّمْسَ وَالْقَمَرَ آيَتَانِ مِنْ آيَاتِ اللَّهِ لاَ يَخْسِفَانِ لِمَوْتِ أَحَدٍ وَلاَ لِحَيَاتِهِ، فَإِذَا رَأَيْتُمْ ذَلِكَ فَاذْكُرُوا اللَّهَ ". قَالُوا يَا رَسُولَ اللَّهِ رَأَيْنَاكَ تَنَاوَلْتَ شَيْئًا فِي مَقَامِكَ هَذَا، ثُمَّ رَأَيْنَاكَ تَكَعْكَعْتَ. فَقَالَ " إِنِّي رَأَيْتُ الْجَنَّةَ ـ أَوْ أُرِيتُ الْجَنَّةَ ـ فَتَنَاوَلْتُ مِنْهَا عُنْقُودًا وَلَوْ أَخَذْتُهُ لأَكَلْتُمْ مِنْهُ مَا بَقِيَتِ الدُّنْيَا، وَرَأَيْتُ النَّارَ فَلَمْ أَرَ كَالْيَوْمِ مَنْظَرًا قَطُّ وَرَأَيْتُ أَكْثَرَ أَهْلِهَا النِّسَاءَ ". قَالُوا لِمَ يَا رَسُولَ اللَّهِ قَالَ " بِكُفْرِهِنَّ ". قِيلَ يَكْفُرْنَ بِاللَّهِ قَالَ " يَكْفُرْنَ الْعَشِيرَ، وَيَكْفُرْنَ الإِحْسَانَ، وَلَوْ أَحْسَنْتَ إِلَى إِحْدَاهُنَّ الدَّهْرَ، ثُمَّ رَأَتْ مِنْكَ شَيْئًا قَالَتْ مَا رَأَيْتُ مِنْكَ خَيْرًا قَطُّ ".

Narrated Al-Mughira bin Shu`ba: "The sun eclipsed in the lifetime of Allah's Messenger ﷺ on the day when (his son) Ibrahim died. So the people said that the sun had eclipsed because of the death of Ibrahim. Allah's Messenger ﷺ said, "The sun and the moon do not eclipse because of the death or life (i.e. birth) of someone. When you see the eclipse pray and invoke Allah.". – Sahih al-Bukhari 1043

حَدَّثَنَا عَبْدُ اللَّهِ بْنُ مُحَمَّدٍ، قَالَ حَدَّثَنَا هَاشِمُ بْنُ الْقَاسِمِ، قَالَ حَدَّثَنَا شَيْبَانُ أَبُو مُعَاوِيَةَ، عَنْ زِيَادِ بْنِ عِلاَقَةَ، عَنِ الْمُغِيرَةِ بْنِ شُعْبَةَ، قَالَ كَسَفَتِ الشَّمْسُ عَلَى عَهْدِ رَسُولِ اللَّهِ صلى الله عليه وسلم يَوْمَ مَاتَ إِبْرَاهِيمُ، فَقَالَ النَّاسُ كَسَفَتِ الشَّمْسُ لِمَوْتِ

إِبْرَاهِيمَ. فَقَالَ رَسُولُ اللَّهِ صلى الله عليه وسلم " إِنَّ الشَّمْسَ وَالْقَمَرَ لاَ يَنْكَسِفَانِ لِمَوْتِ أَحَدٍ وَلاَ لِحَيَاتِهِ، فَإِذَا رَأَيْتُمْ فَصَلُّوا وَادْعُوا اللَّهَ ".

Narrated `Aisha :In the lifetime of Allah's Messenger ﷺ the sun eclipsed, so he led the people in prayer, and stood up and performed a long Qiyam, then bowed for a long while. He stood up again and performed a long Qiyam but this time the period of standing was shorter than the first. He bowed again for a long time but shorter than the first one, then he prostrated and prolonged the prostration. He did the same in the second rak`a as he did in the first and then finished the prayer; by then the sun (eclipse) had cleared. He delivered the Khutba (sermon) and after praising and glorifying Allah he said, "The sun and the moon are two signs against the signs of Allah; they do not eclipse on the death or life of anyone. So when you see the eclipse, remember Allah and say Takbir, pray and give Sadaqa." The Prophet then said, "O followers of Muhammad! By Allah! There is none who has more ghaira (selfrespect) than Allah as He has forbidden that His slaves, male or female commit adultery (illegal sexual intercourse). O followers of Muhammad! By Allah! If you knew that which I know you would laugh little and weep much – .Sahih al-Bukhari 1044

حَدَّثَنَا عَبْدُ اللَّهِ بْنُ مَسْلَمَةَ، عَنْ مَالِكٍ، عَنْ هِشَامِ بْنِ عُرْوَةَ، عَنْ أَبِيهِ، عَنْ عَائِشَةَ، أَنَّهَا قَالَتْ خَسَفَتِ الشَّمْسُ فِي عَهْدِ رَسُولِ اللَّهِ صلى الله عليه وسلم فَصَلَّى رَسُولُ اللَّهِ صلى الله عليه وسلم بِالنَّاسِ، فَقَامَ فَأَطَالَ الْقِيَامَ، ثُمَّ رَكَعَ فَأَطَالَ الرُّكُوعَ، ثُمَّ قَامَ فَأَطَالَ الْقِيَامَ وَهْوَ دُونَ الْقِيَامِ الأَوَّلِ، ثُمَّ رَكَعَ فَأَطَالَ الرُّكُوعَ، وَهْوَ دُونَ الرُّكُوعِ الأَوَّلِ، ثُمَّ سَجَدَ فَأَطَالَ السُّجُودَ، ثُمَّ فَعَلَ فِي الرَّكْعَةِ الثَّانِيَةِ مِثْلَ مَا فَعَلَ فِي الأُولَى، ثُمَّ انْصَرَفَ وَقَدِ انْجَلَتِ الشَّمْسُ، فَخَطَبَ النَّاسَ، فَحَمِدَ اللَّهَ، وَأَثْنَى عَلَيْهِ ثُمَّ قَالَ " إِنَّ الشَّمْسَ وَالْقَمَرَ آيَتَانِ مِنْ آيَاتِ اللَّهِ، لاَ يَنْخَسِفَانِ لِمَوْتِ أَحَدٍ وَلاَ لِحَيَاتِهِ، فَإِذَا رَأَيْتُمْ ذَلِكَ فَادْعُوا اللَّهَ وَكَبِّرُوا، وَصَلُّوا وَتَصَدَّقُوا ". ثُمَّ قَالَ " يَا أُمَّةَ مُحَمَّدٍ، وَاللَّهِ مَا مِنْ أَحَدٍ أَغْيَرُ مِنَ اللَّهِ أَنْ يَزْنِيَ عَبْدُهُ أَوْ تَزْنِيَ أَمَتُهُ، يَا أُمَّةَ مُحَمَّدٍ، وَاللَّهِ لَوْ تَعْلَمُونَ مَا أَعْلَمُ لَضَحِكْتُمْ قَلِيلاً وَلَبَكَيْتُمْ كَثِيرًا ".

Narrated Asma' bint Abu Bakr: I came to `Aisha the wife of the Prophet ﷺ during the solar eclipse. The people were standing and offering the prayer and she was also praying. I asked her, "What is wrong with the people?" She beckoned with her hand towards the sky and said, "Subhan Allah." I asked her, "Is there a sign?" She pointed out, "Yes." So I, too, stood for the prayer till I fell unconscious and later on I poured water on my head. After the prayer, Allah's Messenger ﷺ praised and glorified Allah and said, "Just now I have seen something which I never saw before at this place of mine, including Paradise and Hell. I have been inspired (and have understood) that you will be put to trials in your graves and these trials will be like the trials of Ad-Dajjal, or nearly like it (the sub narrator is not sure of what Asma' said). Angels will come to every one of you and ask, 'What do you know about this man?' A believer will reply, 'He is Muhammad, Allah's Messenger ﷺ, and he came to us with self-evident truth and guidance. So we accepted his teaching, believed and followed him.' Then the angels will say to him to sleep in peace as they have come to know that he was a believer. On the other hand a hypocrite or a doubtful person will reply, 'I do not know but heard the people saying something and so I said the same.' ". – Sahih al-Bukhari 184

حَدَّثَنَا إِسْمَاعِيلُ، قَالَ حَدَّثَنِي مَالِكٌ، عَنْ هِشَامِ بْنِ عُرْوَةَ، عَنِ امْرَأَتِهِ، فَاطِمَةَ عَنْ جَدَّتِهَا، أَسْمَاءَ بِنْتِ أَبِي بَكْرٍ أَنَّهَا قَالَتْ أَتَيْتُ عَائِشَةَ زَوْجَ النَّبِيِّ صلى الله عليه وسلم حِينَ خَسَفَتِ الشَّمْسُ، فَإِذَا النَّاسُ قِيَامٌ يُصَلُّونَ، وَإِذَا هِيَ قَائِمَةٌ تُصَلِّي فَقُلْتُ مَا لِلنَّاسِ فَأَشَارَتْ بِيَدِهَا نَحْوَ السَّمَاءِ وَقَالَتْ سُبْحَانَ اللَّهِ. فَقُلْتُ آيَةٌ فَأَشَارَتْ أَىْ نَعَمْ. فَقُمْتُ حَتَّى تَجَلاَّنِي الْغَشْىُ، وجعلت أصب فَوْقَ رَأْسِي مَاءً، فَلَمَّا انْصَرَفَ رَسُولُ اللَّهِ صلى الله عليه وسلم حَمِدَ اللَّهَ وَأَثْنَى عَلَيْهِ، ثُمَّ قَالَ " مَا مِنْ شَىْءٍ كُنْتُ لَمْ أَرَهُ إِلاَّ قَدْ رَأَيْتُهُ فِي مَقَامِي هَذَا حَتَّى الْجَنَّةِ وَالنَّارِ، وَلَقَدْ أُوحِيَ إِلَىَّ أَنَّكُمْ تُفْتَنُونَ فِي الْقُبُورِ مِثْلَ أَوْ قَرِيبًا مِنْ فِتْنَةِ الدَّجَّالِ ـ لاَ أَدْرِي أَىَّ ذَلِكَ قَالَتْ أَسْمَاءُ ـ يُؤْتَى أَحَدُكُمْ فَيُقَالُ مَا عِلْمُكَ بِهَذَا الرَّجُلِ فَأَمَّا الْمُؤْمِنُ ـ أَوِ الْمُوقِنُ لاَ أَدْرِي أَىَّ ذَلِكَ قَالَتْ أَسْمَاءُ ـ فَيَقُولُ هُوَ مُحَمَّدٌ رَسُولُ اللَّهِ، جَاءَنَا بِالْبَيِّنَاتِ وَالْهُدَى، فَأَجَبْنَا وَآمَنَّا وَاتَّبَعْنَا، فَيُقَالُ نَمْ صَالِحًا، فَقَدْ عَلِمْنَا إِنْ كُنْتَ لَمُؤْمِنًا، وَأَمَّا الْمُنَافِقُ ـ أَوِ الْمُرْتَابُ لاَ أَدْرِي أَىَّ ذَلِكَ قَالَتْ أَسْمَاءُ ـ فَيَقُولُ لاَ أَدْرِي، سَمِعْتُ النَّاسَ يَقُولُونَ شَيْئًا فَقُلْتُهُ ".

The Book of **Mubahala** مُبَاهَلَة

And if anyone disputes with you about him, after the knowledge that has come to you, say, "Come, let us call our children and your children, and our women and your women, and ourselves and yourselves, and let us invoke Allah's curse on the liars." – Surah Al-Imran 3:61
فَمَنْ حَآجَّكَ فِيهِ مِنۢ بَعْدِ مَا جَآءَكَ مِنَ ٱلْعِلْمِ فَقُلْ تَعَالَوْا۟ نَدْعُ أَبْنَآءَنَا وَأَبْنَآءَكُمْ وَنِسَآءَنَا وَنِسَآءَكُمْ وَأَنفُسَنَا وَأَنفُسَكُمْ ثُمَّ نَبْتَهِلْ فَنَجْعَل لَّعْنَتَ ٱللَّهِ عَلَى ٱلْكَـٰذِبِينَ

Amir b. Sa'd b. Abi Waqqas reported on the authority of his father that Muawiya b. Abi Sufyan appointed Sa'd as the Governor and said: What prevents you from abusing Abu Turab (Hadrat 'Ali), whereupon be said: It is because of three things which I remember Allah's Messenger ﷺ having said about him that I would not abuse him and even if I find one of those three things for me, it would be more dear to me than the red camels. I heard Allah's Messenger ﷺ say about 'Ali as he left him behind in one of his campaigns (that was Tabuk). 'Ali said to him: Allah's Messenger, you leave me behind along with women and children. Thereupon Allah's Messenger ﷺ said to him: Aren't you satisfied with being unto me what Aaron was unto Moses but with this exception that there is no prophethood after me. And I (also) heard him say on the Day of Khaibar: I would certainly give this standard to a person who loves Allah and his Messenger, and Allah and his Messenger love him too. He (the narrator) said: We had been anxiously waiting for it, when he (the Holy Prophet) said: Call 'Ali. He was called and his eyes were inflamed. He applied saliva to his eyes and handed over the standard to him, and Allah gave him victory. (The third occasion is this) when the (following) verse was revealed: "Let us summon our children and your children." Allah's Messenger ﷺ called 'Ali, Fatima, Hasan and Husain and said: O Allah, they are my family. – Sahih Muslim 2404 d
حَدَّثَنَا قُتَيْبَةُ بْنُ سَعِيدٍ، وَمُحَمَّدُ بْنُ عَبَّادٍ، - وَتَقَارَبَا فِي اللَّفْظِ – قَالاَ حَدَّثَنَا حَاتِمٌ، - وَهُوَ ابْنُ إِسْمَاعِيلَ – عَنْ بُكَيْرِ بْنِ مِسْمَارٍ، عَنْ عَامِرِ بْنِ سَعْدِ بْنِ أَبِي وَقَّاصٍ، عَنْ أَبِيهِ، قَالَ أَمَرَ مُعَاوِيَةُ بْنُ أَبِي سُفْيَانَ سَعْدًا فَقَالَ مَا مَنَعَكَ أَنْ تَسُبَّ أَبَا التُّرَابِ فَقَالَ أَمَّا مَا ذَكَرْتُ ثَلاَثًا قَالَهُنَّ لَهُ رَسُولُ اللَّهِ صلى الله عليه وسلم فَلَنْ أَسُبَّهُ لأَنْ تَكُونَ لِي وَاحِدَةٌ مِنْهُنَّ أَحَبُّ إِلَىَّ مِنْ حُمْرِ النَّعَمِ سَمِعْتُ رَسُولَ اللَّهِ صلى الله عليه وسلم يَقُولُ لَهُ خَلَّفَهُ فِي بَعْضِ مَغَازِيهِ فَقَالَ لَهُ عَلِيٌّ يَا رَسُولَ اللَّهِ خَلَّفْتَنِي مَعَ النِّسَاءِ وَالصِّبْيَانِ فَقَالَ لَهُ رَسُولُ اللَّهِ صلى الله عليه وسلم " أَمَا تَرْضَى أَنْ تَكُونَ مِنِّي بِمَنْزِلَةِ هَارُونَ مِنْ مُوسَى إِلاَّ أَنَّهُ لاَ نُبُوَّةَ بَعْدِي " . وَسَمِعْتُهُ يَقُولُ يَوْمَ خَيْبَرَ " لأُعْطِيَنَّ الرَّايَةَ رَجُلاً يُحِبُّ اللَّهَ وَرَسُولَهُ وَيُحِبُّهُ اللَّهُ وَرَسُولُهُ " . قَالَ فَتَطَاوَلْنَا لَهَا فَقَالَ " ادْعُوا لِي عَلِيًّا " . فَأُتِيَ بِهِ أَرْمَدَ فَبَصَقَ فِي عَيْنِهِ وَدَفَعَ الرَّايَةَ إِلَيْهِ فَفَتَحَ اللَّهُ عَلَيْهِ وَلَمَّا نَزَلَتْ هَذِهِ الآيَةُ { فَقُلْ تَعَالَوْا نَدْعُ أَبْنَاءَنَا وَأَبْنَاءَكُمْ} دَعَا رَسُولُ اللَّهِ صلى الله عليه وسلم عَلِيًّا وَفَاطِمَةَ وَحَسَنًا وَحُسَيْنًا فَقَالَ " اللَّهُمَّ هَؤُلاَءِ أَهْلِي " .

Narrated Anas bin Malik: Allah sent down His Divine Inspiration to His Apostle continuously and abundantly during the period preceding his death till He took him unto Him. That was the period of the greatest part of revelation; and Allah's Messenger ﷺ died after that. – Al-Bukhari 4982
حَدَّثَنَا عَمْرُو بْنُ مُحَمَّدٍ، حَدَّثَنَا يَعْقُوبُ بْنُ إِبْرَاهِيمَ، حَدَّثَنَا أَبِي، عَنْ صَالِحِ بْنِ كَيْسَانَ، عَنِ ابْنِ شِهَابٍ، قَالَ أَخْبَرَنِي أَنَسُ بْنُ مَالِكٍ ـ رضى الله عنه ـ أَنَّ اللَّهَ، تَعَالَى تَابَعَ عَلَى رَسُولِهِ صلى الله عليه وسلم قَبْلَ وَفَاتِهِ حَتَّى تَوَفَّاهُ أَكْثَرَ مَا كَانَ الْوَحْىُ، ثُمَّ تُوُفِّيَ رَسُولُ اللَّهِ صلى الله عليه وسلم بَعْدُ.

The Book of
Al-Hajjat-ul-Wada
الحجة الوداع

Narrated `Urwa: `Aisha said, "We set out with the Prophet ﷺ in his last Hajj. Some of us intended to perform `Umra while others Hajj. When we reached Mecca, Allah's Messenger ﷺ said, 'Those who had assumed the Ihram for `Umra and had not brought the Hadi should finish his Ihram and whoever had assumed the Ihram for `Umra and brought the Hadi should not finish the Ihram till he has slaughtered his Hadi and whoever had assumed the Ihram for Hajj should complete his Hajj." `Aisha further said, "I got my periods (menses) and kept on menstruating till the day of `Arafat, and I had assumed the Ihram for `Umra only (Tamattu`). The Prophet ﷺ ordered me to undo and comb my head hair and assume the Ihram for Hajj only and leave the `Umra. I did the same till I completed the Hajj. Then the Prophet ﷺ sent `Abdur Rahman bin Abi Bakr with me and ordered me to perform `Umra from at-Tan`im in lieu of the missed `Umra." – Sahih al-Bukhari 319

حَدَّثَنَا يَحْيَى بْنُ بُكَيْرٍ، قَالَ حَدَّثَنَا اللَّيْثُ، عَنْ عُقَيْلٍ، عَنِ ابْنِ شِهَابٍ، عَنْ عُرْوَةَ، عَنْ عَائِشَةَ، قَالَتْ خَرَجْنَا مَعَ النَّبِيِّ صلى الله عليه وسلم فِي حَجَّةِ الْوَدَاعِ، فَمِنَّا مَنْ أَهَلَّ بِعُمْرَةٍ، وَمِنَّا مَنْ أَهَلَّ بِحَجٍّ، فَقَدِمْنَا مَكَّةَ فَقَالَ رَسُولُ اللَّهِ صلى الله عليه وسلم " مَنْ أَحْرَمَ بِعُمْرَةٍ وَلَمْ يُهْدِ فَلْيُحْلِلْ، وَمَنْ أَحْرَمَ بِعُمْرَةٍ وَأَهْدَى فَلاَ يَحِلُّ حَتَّى يَحِلَّ بِنَحْرِ هَدْيِهِ، وَمَنْ أَهَلَّ بِحَجٍّ فَلْيُتِمَّ حَجَّهُ ". قَالَتْ فَحِضْتُ فَلَمْ أَزَلْ حَائِضًا حَتَّى كَانَ يَوْمُ عَرَفَةَ، وَلَمْ أُهْلِلْ إِلاَّ بِعُمْرَةٍ، فَأَمَرَنِي النَّبِيُّ صلى الله عليه وسلم أَنْ أَنْقُضَ رَأْسِي وَأَمْتَشِطَ، وَأُهِلَّ بِحَجٍّ، وَأَتْرُكَ الْعُمْرَةَ، فَفَعَلْتُ ذَلِكَ حَتَّى قَضَيْتُ حَجِّي، فَبَعَثَ مَعِي عَبْدَ الرَّحْمَنِ بْنَ أَبِي بَكْرٍ، وَأَمَرَنِي أَنْ أَعْتَمِرَ مَكَانَ عُمْرَتِي مِنَ التَّنْعِيمِ.

Narrated Ibn `Umar: During the last Hajj (Hajj-al-Wada`) of Allah's Messenger ﷺ he performed `Umra and Hajj. He drove a Hadi along with him from Dhul-Hulaifa. Allah's Messenger ﷺ started by assuming Ihram for `Umra and Hajj. And the people, too, performed the `Umra and Hajj along with the Prophet. Some of them brought the Hadi and drove it along with them, while the others did not. So, when the Prophet ﷺ arrived at Mecca. He said to the people, "Whoever among you has driven the Hadi, should not finish his Ihram till he completes his Hajj. And whoever among you has not (driven) the Hadi with him, should perform Tawaf of the Ka`ba and the Tawaf between Safa and Marwa, then cut short his hair and finish his Ihram, and should later assume Ihram for Hajj; but he must offer a Hadi (sacrifice); and if anyone cannot afford a Hadi, he should fast for three days during the Hajj and seven days when he returns home. The Prophet ﷺ performed Tawaf of the Ka`ba on his arrival (at Mecca); he touched the (Black Stone) corner first of all and then did Ramal (fast walking with moving of the shoulders) during the first three rounds round the Ka`ba, and during the last four rounds he walked. After finishing Tawaf of the Ka`ba, he offered a two rak`at prayer at Maqam Ibrahim, and after finishing the prayer he went to Safa and Marwa and performed seven rounds of Tawaf between them and did not do any deed forbidden because of Ihram, till he finished all the ceremonies of his Hajj and sacrificed his Hadi on the day of Nahr (10th day of Dhul Hijja). He then hastened onwards (to Mecca) and performed Tawaf of the Ka`ba and then everything that was forbidden because of Ihram became permissible. Those who took and drove the Hadi with them did the same as Allah's Messenger ﷺ did. – Sahih al-Bukhari 1691

حَدَّثَنَا يَحْيَى بْنُ بُكَيْرٍ، حَدَّثَنَا اللَّيْثُ، عَنْ عُقَيْلٍ، عَنِ ابْنِ شِهَابٍ، عَنْ سَالِمِ بْنِ عَبْدِ اللَّهِ، أَنَّ ابْنَ عُمَرَ ـ رضى الله عنهما ـ قَالَ تَمَتَّعَ رَسُولُ اللَّهِ صلى الله عليه وسلم فِي حَجَّةِ الْوَدَاعِ بِالْعُمْرَةِ إِلَى الْحَجِّ، وَأَهْدَى فَسَاقَ مَعَهُ الْهَدْىَ مِنْ ذِي الْحُلَيْفَةِ، وَبَدَأَ رَسُولُ اللَّهِ صلى الله عليه وسلم فَأَهَلَّ بِالْعُمْرَةِ، ثُمَّ أَهَلَّ بِالْحَجِّ، فَتَمَتَّعَ النَّاسُ مَعَ النَّبِيِّ صلى الله عليه وسلم بِالْعُمْرَةِ إِلَى

الْحَجِّ، فَكَانَ مِنَ النَّاسِ مَنْ أَهْدَى فَسَاقَ الْهَدْىَ، وَمِنْهُمْ مَنْ لَمْ يُهْدِ، فَلَمَّا قَدِمَ النَّبِيُّ صلى الله عليه وسلم مَكَّةَ، قَالَ لِلنَّاسِ " مَنْ كَانَ مِنْكُمْ أَهْدَى فَإِنَّهُ لاَ يَحِلُّ لِشَىْءٍ حَرُمَ مِنْهُ حَتَّى يَقْضِيَ حَجَّهُ، وَمَنْ لَمْ يَكُنْ مِنْكُمْ أَهْدَى فَلْيَطُفْ بِالْبَيْتِ، وَبِالصَّفَا وَالْمَرْوَةِ، وَلْيُقَصِّرْ، وَلْيَحْلِلْ، ثُمَّ لِيُهِلَّ بِالْحَجِّ، فَمَنْ لَمْ يَجِدْ هَدْيًا فَلْيَصُمْ ثَلاَثَةَ أَيَّامٍ فِي الْحَجِّ وَسَبْعَةً إِذَا رَجَعَ إِلَى أَهْلِهِ ". فَطَافَ حِينَ قَدِمَ مَكَّةَ، وَاسْتَلَمَ الرُّكْنَ أَوَّلَ شَىْءٍ، ثُمَّ خَبَّ ثَلاَثَةَ أَطْوَافٍ، وَمَشَى أَرْبَعًا، فَرَكَعَ حِينَ قَضَى طَوَافَهُ بِالْبَيْتِ عِنْدَ الْمَقَامِ رَكْعَتَيْنِ، ثُمَّ سَلَّمَ، فَانْصَرَفَ فَأَتَى الصَّفَا فَطَافَ بِالصَّفَا وَالْمَرْوَةِ سَبْعَةَ أَطْوَافٍ، ثُمَّ لَمْ يَحْلِلْ مِنْ شَىْءٍ حَرُمَ مِنْهُ حَتَّى قَضَى حَجَّهُ وَنَحَرَ هَدْيَهُ يَوْمَ النَّحْرِ، وَأَفَاضَ فَطَافَ بِالْبَيْتِ، ثُمَّ حَلَّ مِنْ كُلِّ شَىْءٍ حَرُمَ مِنْهُ، وَفَعَلَ مِثْلَ مَا فَعَلَ رَسُولُ اللَّهِ صلى الله عليه وسلم مَنْ أَهْدَى وَسَاقَ الْهَدْىَ مِنَ النَّاسِ

Narrated Ibn `Abbas.: In his Last Hajj the Prophet ﷺ performed Tawaf of the Ka`ba riding a camel and pointed a bent-headed stick towards the Corner (Black Stone). – Al-Bukhari 1607

حَدَّثَنَا أَحْمَدُ بْنُ صَالِحٍ، وَيَحْيَى بْنُ سُلَيْمَانَ، قَالاَ حَدَّثَنَا ابْنُ وَهْبٍ، قَالَ أَخْبَرَنِي يُونُسُ، عَنِ ابْنِ شِهَابٍ، عَنْ عُبَيْدِ اللَّهِ بْنِ عَبْدِ اللَّهِ، عَنِ ابْنِ عَبَّاسٍ ـ رضى الله عنهما ـ قَالَ طَافَ النَّبِيُّ صلى الله عليه وسلم فِي حَجَّةِ الْوَدَاعِ عَلَى بَعِيرٍ، يَسْتَلِمُ الرُّكْنَ بِمِحْجَنٍ. تَابَعَهُ الدَّرَاوَرْدِيُّ عَنِ ابْنِ أَخِي الزُّهْرِيِّ عَنْ عَمِّهِ.

Narrated Ibn `Umar: We were talking about Hajjat-ul-Wada`, while the Prophet ﷺ was amongst us. We did not know what Hajjat-ul-Wada` signified. The Prophet ﷺ praised Allah and then mentioned Al-Masih Ad-Dajjal and described him extensively, saying, "Allah did not send any prophet but that prophet warned his nation of Al-Masih Ad-Dajjal. Noah and the prophets following him warned (their people) of him. He will appear amongst you (O Muhammad's followers), and if it happens that some of his qualities may be hidden from you, but your Lord's State is clear to you and not hidden from you. The Prophet ﷺ said it thrice. Verily, your Lord is not blind in one eye, while he (i.e. Ad-Dajjal) is blind in the right eye which looks like a grape bulging out (of its cluster). No doubt,! Allah has made your blood and your properties sacred to one another like the sanctity of this day of yours, in this town of yours, in this month of yours." The Prophet ﷺ added: No doubt! Haven't I conveyed Allah's Message to you? " They replied, "Yes," The Prophet ﷺ said thrice, "O Allah! Be witness for it." The Prophet ﷺ added, "Woe to you!" (or said), "May Allah be merciful to you! Do not become infidels after me (i.e. my death) by cutting the necks (throats) of one another.". – Sahih al-Bukhari 4402, 4403

حَدَّثَنَا يَحْيَى بْنُ سُلَيْمَانَ، قَالَ أَخْبَرَنِي ابْنُ وَهْبٍ، قَالَ حَدَّثَنِي عُمَرُ بْنُ مُحَمَّدٍ، أَنَّ أَبَاهُ، حَدَّثَهُ عَنِ ابْنِ عُمَرَ ـ رضى الله عنهما ـ قَالَ كُنَّا نَتَحَدَّثُ بِحَجَّةِ الْوَدَاعِ وَالنَّبِيُّ صلى الله عليه وسلم بَيْنَ أَظْهُرِنَا، وَلاَ نَدْرِي مَا حَجَّةُ الْوَدَاعِ، فَحَمِدَ اللَّهَ وَأَثْنَى عَلَيْهِ ثُمَّ ذَكَرَ الْمَسِيحَ الدَّجَّالَ فَأَطْنَبَ فِي ذِكْرِهِ وَقَالَ " مَا بَعَثَ اللَّهُ مِنْ نَبِيٍّ إِلاَّ أَنْذَرَ أُمَّتَهُ، أَنْذَرَهُ نُوحٌ وَالنَّبِيُّونَ مِنْ بَعْدِهِ، وَإِنَّهُ يَخْرُجُ فِيكُمْ، فَمَا خَفِيَ عَلَيْكُمْ مِنْ شَأْنِهِ فَلَيْسَ يَخْفَى عَلَيْكُمْ أَنَّ رَبَّكُمْ لَيْسَ عَلَى مَا يَخْفَى عَلَيْكُمْ ثَلاَثًا، إِنَّ رَبَّكُمْ لَيْسَ بِأَعْوَرَ، وَإِنَّهُ أَعْوَرُ عَيْنِ الْيُمْنَى، كَأَنَّ عَيْنَهُ عِنَبَةٌ طَافِيَةٌ ". " أَلاَ إِنَّ اللَّهَ حَرَّمَ عَلَيْكُمْ دِمَاءَكُمْ وَأَمْوَالَكُمْ، كَحُرْمَةِ يَوْمِكُمْ هَذَا، فِي بَلَدِكُمْ هَذَا، فِي شَهْرِكُمْ هَذَا، أَلاَ هَلْ بَلَّغْتُ ". قَالُوا نَعَمْ. قَالَ " اللَّهُمَّ اشْهَدْ، ثَلاَثًا، وَيْلَكُمْ، أَوْ وَيْحَكُمْ، انْظُرُوا لاَ تَرْجِعُوا بَعْدِي كُفَّارًا، يَضْرِبُ بَعْضُكُمْ رِقَابَ بَعْضٍ ".

Narrated `Abdullah bin `Amr bin Al `Aas: Allah's Messenger ﷺ stopped (for a while near the Jimar) at Mina during his last Hajj for the people and they were asking him questions. A man came and said, "I forgot and got my head shaved before slaughtering the Hadi (sacrificing animal)." The Prophet ﷺ said, "There is no harm, go and do the slaughtering now." Then another person came and said, "I forgot and slaughtered (the camel) before Rami (throwing of the pebbles) at the Jamra." The Prophet ﷺ said, "Do the Rami now and there is no harm." The narrator added: So on that day, when the Prophet ﷺ was asked about anything (as regards the ceremonies of Hajj) performed before or after its due time, his reply was: "Do it (now) and there is no harm.". - Sahih al-Bukhari 83

حَدَّثَنَا إِسْمَاعِيلُ، قَالَ حَدَّثَنِي مَالِكٌ، عَنِ ابْنِ شِهَابٍ، عَنْ عِيسَى بْنِ طَلْحَةَ بْنِ عُبَيْدِ اللَّهِ، عَنْ عَبْدِ اللَّهِ بْنِ عَمْرِو بْنِ الْعَاصِ، أَنَّ رَسُولَ اللَّهِ صلى الله عليه وسلم وَقَفَ فِي حَجَّةِ الْوَدَاعِ بِمِنًى لِلنَّاسِ يَسْأَلُونَهُ، فَجَاءَهُ رَجُلٌ فَقَالَ لَمْ أَشْعُرْ فَحَلَقْتُ قَبْلَ أَنْ أَذْبَحَ. فَقَالَ " اذْبَحْ وَلاَ حَرَجَ ". فَجَاءَ آخَرُ فَقَالَ لَمْ أَشْعُرْ، فَنَحَرْتُ قَبْلَ أَنْ أَرْمِيَ. قَالَ " ارْمِ وَلاَ حَرَجَ ". فَمَا سُئِلَ النَّبِيُّ صلى الله عليه وسلم عَنْ شَىْءٍ قُدِّمَ وَلاَ أُخِّرَ إِلاَّ قَالَ افْعَلْ وَلاَ حَرَجَ

Narrated `Aisha: During Hajjat-al-Wada`, I perfumed Allah's Messenger ﷺ with Dharira with my own hands, both on his assuming Ihram and on finishing it. – Sahih al-Bukhari 5930

حَدَّثَنَا عُثْمَانُ بْنُ الْهَيْثَمِ، أَوْ مُحَمَّدٌ عَنْهُ عَنِ ابْنِ جُرَيْجٍ، أَخْبَرَنِي عُمَرُ بْنُ عَبْدِ اللَّهِ بْنِ عُرْوَةَ، سَمِعَ عُرْوَةَ، وَالْقَاسِمَ، يُخْبِرَانِ عَنْ عَائِشَةَ، قَالَتْ طَيَّبْتُ رَسُولَ اللَّهِ صلى الله عليه وسلم بِيَدَىَّ بِذَرِيرَةٍ فِي حَجَّةِ الْوَدَاعِ، لِلْحِلِّ وَالإِحْرَامِ

Narrated `Abdullah bin Yazid Al-Khatmi: That Abu Aiyub informed him that he offered the Maghrib and `Isha' prayers together with the Prophet during Hajjat-ul-Wada`. – Sahih al-Bukhari 4414

حَدَّثَنَا عَبْدُ اللَّهِ بْنُ مَسْلَمَةَ، عَنْ مَالِكٍ، عَنْ يَحْيَى بْنِ سَعِيدٍ، عَنْ عَدِيِّ بْنِ ثَابِتٍ، عَنْ عَبْدِ اللَّهِ بْنِ يَزِيدَ الْخَطْمِيِّ، أَنَّ أَبَا أَيُّوبَ، أَخْبَرَهُ أَنَّهُ، صَلَّى مَعَ رَسُولِ اللَّهِ صلى الله عليه وسلم فِي حَجَّةِ الْوَدَاعِ الْمَغْرِبَ وَالْعِشَاءَ جَمِيعًا

Narrated `Abdullah bin `Abbas: That he came riding a donkey when Allah 's Apostle was standing at Mina during Hajjat-ul-Wada`, leading the people in prayer. The donkey passed in front of a part of the row (of the people offering the prayer). Then he dismounted from it and took his position in the row with the people. – Sahih al-Bukhari 4412

حَدَّثَنَا يَحْيَى بْنُ قَزَعَةَ، حَدَّثَنَا مَالِكٌ، عَنِ ابْنِ شِهَابٍ. وَقَالَ اللَّيْثُ حَدَّثَنِي يُونُسُ، عَنِ ابْنِ شِهَابٍ، حَدَّثَنِي عُبَيْدُ اللَّهِ بْنُ عَبْدِ اللَّهِ، أَنَّ عَبْدَ اللَّهِ بْنَ عَبَّاسٍ ـ رضى الله عنهما ـ أَخْبَرَهُ أَنَّهُ، أَقْبَلَ يَسِيرُ عَلَى حِمَارٍ، وَرَسُولُ اللَّهِ صلى الله عليه وسلم قَائِمٌ بِمِنًى فِي حَجَّةِ الْوَدَاعِ يُصَلِّي بِالنَّاسِ، فَسَارَ الْحِمَارُ بَيْنَ يَدَىْ بَعْضِ الصَّفِّ، ثُمَّ نَزَلَ عَنْهُ، فَصَفَّ مَعَ النَّاسِ.

Narrated `Abdullah bin `Abbas :Al-Fadl was riding behind the Prophet ﷺ and a woman from the tribe of Khath'am came up. Al-Fadl started looking at her and she looked at him. The Prophet ﷺ turned Al-Fadl's face to the other side. She said, "My father has come under Allah's obligation of performing Hajj but he is a very old man and cannot sit properly on his Mount. Shall I perform Hajj on his behalf? The Prophet ﷺ replied in the affirmative. That happened during Hajjat-al-Wada` of the Prophet ﷺ. - Sahih al-Bukhari 1854

حَدَّثَنَا مُوسَى بْنُ إِسْمَاعِيلَ، حَدَّثَنَا عَبْدُ الْعَزِيزِ بْنُ أَبِي سَلَمَةَ، حَدَّثَنَا ابْنُ شِهَابٍ، عَنْ سُلَيْمَانَ بْنِ يَسَارٍ، عَنِ ابْنِ عَبَّاسٍ ـ رضى الله عنهما ـ قَالَ جَاءَتِ امْرَأَةٌ مِنْ خَثْعَمَ، عَامَ حَجَّةِ الْوَدَاعِ، قَالَتْ يَا رَسُولَ اللَّهِ إِنَّ فَرِيضَةَ اللَّهِ عَلَى عِبَادِهِ فِي الْحَجِّ أَدْرَكَتْ أَبِي شَيْخًا كَبِيرًا، لاَ يَسْتَطِيعُ أَنْ يَسْتَوِيَ عَلَى الرَّاحِلَةِ فَهَلْ يَقْضِي عَنْهُ أَنْ أَحُجَّ عَنْهُ قَالَ " نَعَمْ ".

Narrated Subaia bint Al-Harith: That she was married to Sad bin Khaula who was from the tribe of Bani 'Amr bin Luai, and was one of those who fought the Badr battle. He died while she wa pregnant during Hajjat-ul-Wada.' Soon after his death, she gave birth to a child. When she completed the term of deliver (i.e. became clean), she prepared herself for suitors. Abu As-Sanabil bin Bu'kak, a man from the tribe of Bani Abd-ud-Dal called on her and said to her, "What! I see you dressed up for the people to ask you in marriage. Do you want to marry By Allah, you are not allowed to marry unless four months and ten days have elapsed (after your husband's death)." Subai'a in her narration said, "When he (i.e. Abu As-Sanabil) said this to me. I put on my dress in the evening and went to Allah's Messenger ﷺ and asked him about this problem. He gave the verdict that I was free to marry as I had already given birth to my child and ordered me to marry if I wished." – Sahih al-Bukhari 3991

وَقَالَ اللَّيْثُ حَدَّثَنِي يُونُسُ، عَنِ ابْنِ شِهَابٍ، قَالَ حَدَّثَنِي عُبَيْدُ اللَّهِ بْنُ عَبْدِ اللَّهِ بْنِ عُتْبَةَ، أَنَّ أَبَاهُ، كَتَبَ إِلَى عُمَرَ بْنِ عَبْدِ اللَّهِ بْنِ الأَرْقَمِ الزُّهْرِيِّ، يَأْمُرُهُ أَنْ يَدْخُلَ، عَلَى سُبَيْعَةَ بِنْتِ الْحَارِثِ الأَسْلَمِيَّةِ، فَيَسْأَلَهَا عَنْ حَدِيثِهَا وَعَنْ مَا قَالَ لَهَا رَسُولُ اللَّهِ صلى الله عليه وسلم حِينَ اسْتَفْتَتْهُ، فَكَتَبَ عُمَرُ بْنُ عَبْدِ اللَّهِ بْنِ الأَرْقَمِ إِلَى عَبْدِ اللَّهِ بْنِ عُتْبَةَ يُخْبِرُهُ أَنَّ سُبَيْعَةَ بِنْتَ الْحَارِثِ أَخْبَرَتْهُ أَنَّهَا كَانَتْ تَحْتَ سَعْدِ ابْنِ خَوْلَةَ، وَهُوَ مِنْ بَنِي عَامِرِ بْنِ لُؤَىٍّ، وَكَانَ مِمَّنْ شَهِدَ بَدْرًا، فَتُوُفِّيَ عَنْهَا فِي حَجَّةِ الْوَدَاعِ وَهْىَ حَامِلٌ، فَلَمْ تَنْشَبْ أَنْ وَضَعَتْ حَمْلَهَا بَعْدَ وَفَاتِهِ، فَلَمَّا تَعَلَّتْ مِنْ نِفَاسِهَا تَجَمَّلَتْ لِلْخُطَّابِ، فَدَخَلَ عَلَيْهَا أَبُو السَّنَابِلِ بْنُ بَعْكَكٍ ـ رَجُلٌ مِنْ بَنِي عَبْدِ الدَّارِ ـ فَقَالَ لَهَا مَا لِي أَرَاكِ تَجَمَّلْتِ لِلْخُطَّابِ تُرَجِّينَ النِّكَاحَ فَإِنَّكِ وَاللَّهِ مَا أَنْتِ بِنَاكِحٍ حَتَّى تَمُرَّ عَلَيْكِ أَرْبَعَةُ أَشْهُرٍ وَعَشْرٌ. قَالَتْ سُبَيْعَةُ فَلَمَّا قَالَ لِي ذَلِكَ جَمَعْتُ عَلَىَّ ثِيَابِي حِينَ أَمْسَيْتُ، وَأَتَيْتُ رَسُولَ اللَّهِ صلى الله عليه وسلم فَسَأَلْتُهُ عَنْ ذَلِكَ، فَأَفْتَانِي بِأَنِّي قَدْ حَلَلْتُ حِينَ وَضَعْتُ حَمْلِي، وَأَمَرَنِي بِالتَّزَوُّجِ إِنْ بَدَا لِي. تَابَعَهُ أَصْبَغُ عَنِ ابْنِ وَهْبٍ عَنْ يُونُسَ. وَقَالَ اللَّيْثُ حَدَّثَنِي يُونُسُ، عَنِ ابْنِ شِهَابٍ، وَسَأَلْنَاهُ، فَقَالَ أَخْبَرَنِي مُحَمَّدُ بْنُ عَبْدِ الرَّحْمَنِ بْنِ ثَوْبَانَ، مَوْلَى بَنِي عَامِرِ بْنِ لُؤَىٍّ أَنَّ مُحَمَّدَ بْنَ إِيَاسِ بْنِ الْبُكَيْرِ، وَكَانَ، أَبُوهُ شَهِدَ بَدْرًا أَخْبَرَهُ

The Book of
Muhammad'sﷺ fatal illness
مرض محمد القاتل

Narrated 'Ubaidullah Ibn `Abdullah bin `Utba: I went to `Aisha and asked her to describe to me the illness of Allah's Messengerﷺ. Aisha said, "Yes. The Prophet became seriously ill and asked whether the people had prayed. We replied, 'No. O Allah's Apostle! They are waiting for you.' He added, 'Put water for me in a trough." `Aisha added, "We did so. He took a bath and tried to get up but fainted. When he recovered, he again asked whether the people had prayed. We said, 'No, they are waiting for you. O Allah's Messengerﷺ', He again said, 'Put water in a trough for me.' He sat down and took a bath and tried to get up but fainted again. Then he recovered and said, 'Have the people prayed?' We replied, 'No, they are waiting for you. O Allah's Apostle.' He said, 'Put water for me in the trough.' Then he sat down and washed himself and tried to get up but he fainted. When he recovered, he asked, 'Have the people prayed?' We said, 'No, they are waiting for you. O Allah's Messengerﷺ ! The people were in the mosque waiting for the Prophetﷺ for the `Isha prayer. The Prophetﷺ sent for Abu Bakr to lead the people in the prayer. The messenger went to Abu Bakr and said, 'Allah's Messengerﷺ orders you to lead the people in the prayer.' Abu Bakr was a softhearted man, so he asked `Umar to lead the prayer but `Umar replied, 'You are more rightful.' So Abu Bakr led the prayer in those days. When the Prophetﷺ felt a bit better, he came out for the Zuhr prayer with the help of two persons one of whom was Al-`Abbas. While Abu Bakr was leading the people in the prayer. When Abu Bakr saw him he wanted to retreat but the Prophetﷺ beckoned him not to do so and asked them to make him sit beside Abu Bakr and they did so. Abu Bakr was following the Prophet (in the prayer) and the people were following Abu Bakr. The Prophet (prayed) sitting." 'Ubaidullah added "I went to `Abdullah bin `Abbas and asked him, Shall I tell you what Aisha has told me about the fatal illness of the Prophet?' Ibn `Abbas said, 'Go ahead. I told him her narration and he did not deny anything of it but asked whether `Aisha told me the name of the second person (who helped the Prophetﷺ) along with Al-Abbas. I said. 'No.' He said, 'He was `Ali (Ibn Abi Talib). – Sahih al-Bukhari 687

حَدَّثَنَا أَحْمَدُ بْنُ يُونُسَ، قَالَ حَدَّثَنَا زَائِدَةُ، عَنْ مُوسَى بْنِ أَبِي عَائِشَةَ، عَنْ عُبَيْدِ اللَّهِ بْنِ عَبْدِ اللَّهِ بْنِ عُتْبَةَ، قَالَ دَخَلْتُ عَلَى عَائِشَةَ فَقُلْتُ أَلاَ تُحَدِّثِينِي عَنْ مَرَضِ رَسُولِ اللَّهِ صلى الله عليه وسلم قَالَتْ بَلَى، ثَقُلَ النَّبِيُّ صلى الله عليه وسلم فَقَالَ " أَصَلَّى النَّاسُ ". قُلْنَا لاَ، هُمْ يَنْتَظِرُونَكَ. قَالَ " ضَعُوا لِي مَاءً فِي الْمِخْضَبِ ". قَالَتْ فَفَعَلْنَا فَاغْتَسَلَ فَذَهَبَ لِيَنُوءَ فَأُغْمِيَ عَلَيْهِ، ثُمَّ أَفَاقَ فَقَالَ صلى الله عليه وسلم " أَصَلَّى النَّاسُ ". قُلْنَا لاَ، هُمْ يَنْتَظِرُونَكَ يَا رَسُولَ اللَّهِ. قَالَ " ضَعُوا لِي مَاءً فِي الْمِخْضَبِ ". قَالَتْ فَقَعَدَ فَاغْتَسَلَ، ثُمَّ ذَهَبَ لِيَنُوءَ فَأُغْمِيَ عَلَيْهِ، ثُمَّ أَفَاقَ فَقَالَ " أَصَلَّى النَّاسُ ". قُلْنَا لاَ، هُمْ يَنْتَظِرُونَكَ يَا رَسُولَ اللَّهِ. فَقَالَ " ضَعُوا لِي مَاءً فِي الْمِخْضَبِ "، فَقَعَدَ فَاغْتَسَلَ، ثُمَّ ذَهَبَ لِيَنُوءَ فَأُغْمِيَ عَلَيْهِ، ثُمَّ أَفَاقَ فَقَالَ " أَصَلَّى النَّاسُ ". فَقُلْنَا لاَ، هُمْ يَنْتَظِرُونَكَ يَا رَسُولَ اللَّهِ ـ وَالنَّاسُ عُكُوفٌ فِي الْمَسْجِدِ يَنْتَظِرُونَ النَّبِيَّ عَلَيْهِ السَّلاَمُ لِصَلاَةِ الْعِشَاءِ الآخِرَةِ ـ فَأَرْسَلَ النَّبِيُّ صلى الله عليه وسلم إِلَى أَبِي بَكْرٍ بِأَنْ يُصَلِّيَ بِالنَّاسِ، فَأَتَاهُ الرَّسُولُ فَقَالَ إِنَّ رَسُولَ اللَّهِ صلى الله عليه وسلم يَأْمُرُكَ أَنْ تُصَلِّيَ بِالنَّاسِ. فَقَالَ أَبُو بَكْرٍ ـ وَكَانَ رَجُلاً رَقِيقًا ـ يَا عُمَرُ صَلِّ بِالنَّاسِ. فَقَالَ لَهُ عُمَرُ أَنْتَ أَحَقُّ بِذَلِكَ. فَصَلَّى أَبُو بَكْرٍ تِلْكَ الأَيَّامَ، ثُمَّ إِنَّ النَّبِيَّ صلى الله عليه وسلم وَجَدَ مِنْ نَفْسِهِ خِفَّةً فَخَرَجَ بَيْنَ رَجُلَيْنِ أَحَدُهُمَا الْعَبَّاسُ لِصَلاَةِ الظُّهْرِ، وَأَبُو بَكْرٍ يُصَلِّي بِالنَّاسِ، فَلَمَّا رَآهُ أَبُو بَكْرٍ ذَهَبَ لِيَتَأَخَّرَ فَأَوْمَأَ إِلَيْهِ النَّبِيُّ صلى الله عليه وسلم بِأَنْ لاَ يَتَأَخَّرَ. قَالَ " أَجْلِسَانِي إِلَى جَنْبِهِ ". فَأَجْلَسَاهُ إِلَى جَنْبِ أَبِي بَكْرٍ. قَالَ فَجَعَلَ أَبُو بَكْرٍ يُصَلِّي وَهْوَ يَأْتَمُّ بِصَلاَةِ النَّبِيِّ صلى الله عليه وسلم وَالنَّاسُ بِصَلاَةِ أَبِي بَكْرٍ، وَالنَّبِيُّ صلى الله عليه وسلم قَاعِدٌ. قَالَ عُبَيْدُ اللَّهِ فَدَخَلْتُ عَلَى عَبْدِ اللَّهِ بْنِ عَبَّاسٍ فَقُلْتُ لَهُ أَلاَ أَعْرِضُ عَلَيْكَ مَا حَدَّثَتْنِي عَائِشَةُ عَنْ مَرَضِ النَّبِيِّ صلى الله عليه وسلم قَالَ هَاتِ. فَعَرَضْتُ عَلَيْهِ حَدِيثَهَا، فَمَا أَنْكَرَ مِنْهُ شَيْئًا، غَيْرَ أَنَّهُ قَالَ أَسَمَّتْ لَكَ الرَّجُلَ الَّذِي كَانَ مَعَ الْعَبَّاسِ قُلْتُ لاَ. قَالَ هُوَ عَلِيٌّ.

Narrated `Aisha: The Prophetﷺ called Fatima during his fatal illness and told her something secretly and she wept. Then he called her again and told her something secretly, and she started laughing. When we asked her about that, she said, "The Prophet ﷺ first told me secretly that he would expire in that disease in which he died, so I wept; then he told me secretly that I would be the first of his family to follow him, so I laughed (at that time). – Sahih Al-Bukhari 4433, 4434

حَدَّثَنَا يَسَرَةُ بْنُ صَفْوَانَ بْنِ جَمِيلٍ اللَّخْمِيُّ، حَدَّثَنَا إِبْرَاهِيمُ بْنُ سَعْدٍ، عَنْ أَبِيهِ، عَنْ عُرْوَةَ، عَنْ عَائِشَةَ ـ رضى الله عنها ـ قَالَتْ دَعَا النَّبِيُّ صلى الله عليه وسلم فَاطِمَةَ ـ عَلَيْهَا السَّلاَمُ ـ فِي شَكْوَاهُ الَّذِي قُبِضَ فِيهِ، فَسَارَّهَا بِشَىْءٍ، فَبَكَتْ، ثُمَّ دَعَاهَا فَسَارَّهَا بِشَىْءٍ فَضَحِكَتْ فَسَأَلْنَا عَنْ ذَلِكَ. فَقَالَتْ سَارَّنِي النَّبِيُّ صلى الله عليه وسلم أَنَّهُ يُقْبَضُ فِي وَجَعِهِ الَّذِي تُوُفِّيَ فِيهِ فَبَكَيْتُ، ثُمَّ سَارَّنِي فَأَخْبَرَنِي أَنِّي أَوَّلُ أَهْلِهِ يَتْبَعُهُ فَضَحِكْتُ.

Narrated Anas: When the ailment of the Prophet ﷺ got aggravated, he became unconscious whereupon Fatima said, "Oh, how distressed my father is!" He said, "Your father will have no more distress after today." When he expired, she said, "O Father! Who has responded to the call of the Lord Who has invited him! O Father, whose dwelling place is the Garden of Paradise (i.e. Al-Firdaus)! O Father! We convey this news (of your death) to Gabriel." When he was buried, Fatima said, "O Anas! Do you feel pleased to throw earth over Allah's Messenger – Sahih Al-Bukhari 4462

حَدَّثَنَا سُلَيْمَانُ بْنُ حَرْبٍ، حَدَّثَنَا حَمَّادٌ، عَنْ ثَابِتٍ، عَنْ أَنَسٍ، قَالَ لَمَّا ثَقُلَ النَّبِيُّ صلى الله عليه وسلم جَعَلَ يَتَغَشَّاهُ، فَقَالَتْ فَاطِمَةُ ـ عَلَيْهَا السَّلاَمُ ـ وَاكَرْبَ أَبَاهُ. فَقَالَ لَهَا " لَيْسَ عَلَى أَبِيكِ كَرْبٌ بَعْدَ الْيَوْمِ ". فَلَمَّا مَاتَ قَالَتْ يَا أَبَتَاهْ، أَجَابَ رَبًّا دَعَاهُ، يَا أَبَتَاهْ مَنْ جَنَّةُ الْفِرْدَوْسِ مَأْوَاهُ، يَا أَبَتَاهْ إِلَى جِبْرِيلَ نَنْعَاهْ. فَلَمَّا دُفِنَ قَالَتْ فَاطِمَةُ ـ عَلَيْهَا السَّلاَمُ ـ يَا أَنَسُ، أَطَابَتْ أَنْفُسُكُمْ أَنْ تَحْثُوا عَلَى رَسُولِ اللَّهِ صلى الله عليه وسلم التُّرَابَ

Narrated Aisha: (the wife of the Prophet) "When the ailment of Allah's Messenger ﷺ became aggravated, he requested his wives to permit him to be (treated) nursed in my house, and they gave him permission. He came out (to my house), walking between two men with his feet dragging on the ground, between `Abbas bin `Abdul—Muttalib and another man" 'Ubaidullah said, "I told `Abdullah of what `Aisha had said, `Abdullah bin `Abbas said to me, 'Do you know who is the other man whom `Aisha did not name?' I said, 'No.' Ibn `Abbas said, 'It was `Ali bin Abu Talib." `Aisha, the wife of the Prophet ﷺ used to narrate saying, "When Allah's Messenger ﷺ entered my house and his disease became aggravated, he said, " Pour on me the water of seven water skins, the mouths of which have not been untied, so that I may give advice to the people.' So we let him sit in a big basin belonging to Hafsa, the wife of the Prophet ﷺ and then started to pour water on him from these water skins till he started pointing to us with his hands intending to say, 'You have done your job." `Aisha added, "Then he went out to the people and led them in prayer and preached to them.". – Al-Bukhari 4442

حَدَّثَنَا سَعِيدُ بْنُ عُفَيْرٍ، قَالَ حَدَّثَنِي اللَّيْثُ، قَالَ حَدَّثَنِي عُقَيْلٌ، عَنِ ابْنِ شِهَابٍ، قَالَ أَخْبَرَنِي عُبَيْدُ اللَّهِ بْنُ عَبْدِ اللَّهِ بْنِ عُتْبَةَ بْنِ مَسْعُودٍ، أَنَّ عَائِشَةَ، زَوْجَ النَّبِيِّ صلى الله عليه وسلم قَالَتْ لَمَّا ثَقُلَ رَسُولُ اللَّهِ صلى الله عليه وسلم وَاشْتَدَّ بِهِ وَجَعُهُ اسْتَأْذَنَ أَزْوَاجَهُ أَنْ يُمَرَّضَ فِي بَيْتِي، فَأَذِنَّ لَهُ، فَخَرَجَ وَهْوَ بَيْنَ الرَّجُلَيْنِ تَخُطُّ رِجْلاَهُ فِي الأَرْضِ، بَيْنَ عَبَّاسِ بْنِ عَبْدِ الْمُطَّلِبِ وَبَيْنَ رَجُلٍ آخَرَ. قَالَ عُبَيْدُ اللَّهِ فَأَخْبَرْتُ عَبْدَ اللَّهِ بِالَّذِي قَالَتْ عَائِشَةُ، فَقَالَ لِي عَبْدُ اللَّهِ بْنُ عَبَّاسٍ هَلْ تَدْرِي مَنِ الرَّجُلُ الآخَرُ الَّذِي لَمْ تُسَمِّ عَائِشَةُ قَالَ قُلْتُ لاَ. قَالَ ابْنُ عَبَّاسٍ هُوَ عَلِيٌّ. وَكَانَتْ عَائِشَةُ زَوْجُ النَّبِيِّ صلى الله عليه وسلم تُحَدِّثُ أَنَّ رَسُولَ اللَّهِ صلى الله عليه وسلم لَمَّا دَخَلَ بَيْتِي وَاشْتَدَّ بِهِ وَجَعُهُ قَالَ " هَرِيقُوا عَلَىَّ مِنْ سَبْعِ قِرَبٍ لَمْ تُحْلَلْ أَوْكِيَتُهُنَّ لَعَلِّي أَعْهَدُ إِلَى النَّاسِ ". فَأَجْلَسْنَاهُ فِي مِخْضَبٍ لِحَفْصَةَ زَوْجِ النَّبِيِّ صلى الله عليه وسلم، ثُمَّ طَفِقْنَا نَصُبُّ عَلَيْهِ مِنْ تِلْكَ الْقِرَبِ، حَتَّى طَفِقَ يُشِيرُ إِلَيْنَا بِيَدِهِ أَنْ قَدْ فَعَلْتُنَّ. قَالَتْ ثُمَّ خَرَجَ إِلَى النَّاسِ فَصَلَّى لَهُمْ وَخَطَبَهُمْ

Narrated Anas bin Malik: While the Muslims were offering the Fajr prayer on Monday and Abu Bakr was leading them in prayer, suddenly Allah's Messenger ﷺ lifted the curtain of `Aisha's dwelling and looked at them while they were in the rows of the prayers and smiled. Abu Bakr retreated to join the row, thinking that Allah's Apostle wanted to come out for the prayer. The Muslims were about to be put to trial in their prayer (i.e. were about to give up praying) because of being overjoyed at seeing Allah's Messenger ﷺ .But Allah's Apostle beckoned them with his hand to complete their prayer and then entered the dwelling and let fall the curtain. – Sahih Al-Bukhari 4448

حَدَّثَنَا سَعِيدُ بْنُ عُفَيْرٍ، قَالَ حَدَّثَنِي اللَّيْثُ، قَالَ حَدَّثَنِي عُقَيْلٌ، عَنِ ابْنِ شِهَابٍ، قَالَ حَدَّثَنِي أَنَسُ بْنُ مَالِكٍ ـ رضى الله عنه ـ أَنَّ الْمُسْلِمِينَ، بَيْنَا هُمْ فِي صَلاَةِ الْفَجْرِ مِنْ يَوْمِ الاِثْنَيْنِ وَأَبُو بَكْرٍ يُصَلِّي لَهُمْ لَمْ يَفْجَأْهُمْ إِلاَّ رَسُولُ اللَّهِ صلى الله عليه وسلم قَدْ كَشَفَ سِتْرَ حُجْرَةِ عَائِشَةَ، فَنَظَرَ إِلَيْهِمْ وَهُمْ فِي صُفُوفِ الصَّلاَةِ. ثُمَّ تَبَسَّمَ يَضْحَكُ، فَنَكَصَ أَبُو بَكْرٍ عَلَى عَقِبَيْهِ لِيَصِلَ الصَّفَّ، وَظَنَّ أَنَّ رَسُولَ اللَّهِ صلى الله عليه وسلم يُرِيدُ أَنْ يَخْرُجَ إِلَى الصَّلاَةِ فَقَالَ أَنَسٌ وَهَمَّ الْمُسْلِمُونَ أَنْ يَفْتَتِنُوا فِي صَلاَتِهِمْ فَرَحًا بِرَسُولِ اللَّهِ صلى الله عليه وسلم فَأَشَارَ إِلَيْهِمْ بِيَدِهِ رَسُولُ اللَّهِ صلى الله عليه وسلم أَنْ أَتِمُّوا صَلاَتَكُمْ، ثُمَّ دَخَلَ الْحُجْرَةَ وَأَرْخَى السِّتْرَ

Narrated `Aisha: The Prophet ﷺ in his ailment in which he died, used to say, "O `Aisha! I still feel the pain caused by the food I ate at Khaibar, and at this time, I feel as if my aorta is being cut from that poison.". – Sahih Al-Bukhari 4428

وَقَالَ يُونُسُ عَنِ الزُّهْرِيِّ، قَالَ عُرْوَةُ قَالَتْ عَائِشَةُ ـ رضى الله عنها ـ كَانَ النَّبِيُّ صلى الله عليه وسلم يَقُولُ فِي مَرَضِهِ الَّذِي مَاتَ فِيهِ " يَا عَائِشَةُ مَا أَزَالُ أَجِدُ أَلَمَ الطَّعَامِ الَّذِي أَكَلْتُ بِخَيْبَرَ، فَهَذَا أَوَانُ وَجَدْتُ انْقِطَاعَ أَبْهَرِي مِنْ ذَلِكَ السَّمِّ "

Narrated `Aisha: Used to hear (from the Prophet) that no Prophet dies till he is given the option to select either the worldly life or the life of the Hereafter. I heard the Prophet ﷺ in his fatal disease, with his voice becoming hoarse, saying, "In the company of those on whom is the grace of Allah ..(to the end of the Verse)." (4.69) Thereupon I thought that the Prophet ﷺ had been given the option. – Sahih Al-Bukhari 4435

حَدَّثَنِي مُحَمَّدُ بْنُ بَشَّارٍ، حَدَّثَنَا غُنْدَرٌ، حَدَّثَنَا شُعْبَةُ، عَنْ سَعْدٍ، عَنْ عُرْوَةَ، عَنْ عَائِشَةَ، قَالَتْ كُنْتُ أَسْمَعُ أَنَّهُ لاَ يَمُوتُ نَبِيٌّ حَتَّى يُخَيَّرَ بَيْنَ الدُّنْيَا وَالآخِرَةِ، فَسَمِعْتُ النَّبِيَّ صلى الله عليه وسلم يَقُولُ فِي مَرَضِهِ الَّذِي مَاتَ فِيهِ وَأَخَذَتْهُ بُحَّةٌ يَقُولُ {مَعَ الَّذِينَ أَنْعَمَ اللَّهُ عَلَيْهِمْ} الآيَةَ، فَظَنَنْتُ أَنَّهُ خُيِّرَ

Narrated `Abdullah bin `Abbas: `Ali bin Abu Talib came out of the house of Allah's Messenger ﷺ during his fatal illness. The people asked, "O Abu Hasan (i.e. `Ali)! How is the health of Allah's Messenger ﷺ this morning?" `Ali replied, "He has recovered with the Grace of Allah." `Abbas bin `Abdul Muttalib held him by the hand and said to him, "In three days you, by Allah, will be ruled (by somebody else ), And by Allah, I feel that Allah's Apostle will die from this ailment of his, for I know how the faces of the offspring of `Abdul Muttalib look at the time of their death. So let us go to Allah's Messenger ﷺ and ask him who will take over the Caliphate. If it is given to us we will know as to it, and if it is given to somebody else, we will inform him so that he may tell the new ruler to take care of us." `Ali said, "By Allah, if we asked Allah's Apostle for it (i.e. the Caliphate) and he denied it us, the people will never give it to us after that. And by Allah, I will not ask Allah's Messenger ﷺ for it." - Sahih Al-Bukhari 4447

حَدَّثَنِي إِسْحَاقُ، أَخْبَرَنَا بِشْرُ بْنُ شُعَيْبِ بْنِ أَبِي حَمْزَةَ، قَالَ حَدَّثَنِي أَبِي، عَنِ الزُّهْرِيِّ، قَالَ أَخْبَرَنِي عَبْدُ اللَّهِ بْنُ كَعْبِ بْنِ مَالِكٍ الأَنْصَارِيُّ ـ وَكَانَ كَعْبُ بْنُ مَالِكٍ أَحَدَ الثَّلاَثَةِ الَّذِينَ تِيبَ عَلَيْهِمْ أَنَّ عَبْدَ اللَّهِ بْنَ عَبَّاسٍ أَخْبَرَهُ أَنَّ عَلِيَّ بْنَ أَبِي طَالِبٍ ـ رضى الله عنه ـ خَرَجَ مِنْ عِنْدِ رَسُولِ اللَّهِ صلى الله عليه وسلم فِي وَجَعِهِ الَّذِي تُوُفِّيَ فِيهِ، فَقَالَ النَّاسُ يَا أَبَا حَسَنٍ، كَيْفَ أَصْبَحَ رَسُولُ اللَّهِ صلى الله عليه وسلم فَقَالَ أَصْبَحَ بِحَمْدِ اللَّهِ بَارِئًا، فَأَخَذَ بِيَدِهِ عَبَّاسُ بْنُ عَبْدِ الْمُطَّلِبِ، فَقَالَ لَهُ أَنْتَ وَاللَّهِ بَعْدَ ثَلاَثٍ عَبْدُ الْعَصَا، وَإِنِّي وَاللَّهِ لأُرَى رَسُولَ اللَّهِ صلى الله عليه وسلم سَوْفَ يُتَوَفَّى مِنْ وَجَعِهِ هَذَا، إِنِّي لأَعْرِفُ وُجُوهَ بَنِي عَبْدِ الْمُطَّلِبِ عِنْدَ الْمَوْتِ، اذْهَبْ بِنَا إِلَى رَسُولِ اللَّهِ صلى الله عليه وسلم فَلْنَسْأَلْهُ فِيمَنْ هَذَا الأَمْرُ، إِنْ كَانَ فِينَا عَلِمْنَا ذَلِكَ، وَإِنْ كَانَ فِي غَيْرِنَا عَلِمْنَاهُ فَأَوْصَى بِنَا. فَقَالَ عَلِيٌّ إِنَّا وَاللَّهِ لَئِنْ سَأَلْنَاهَا رَسُولَ اللَّهِ صلى الله عليه وسلم فَمَنَعَنَاهَا لاَ يُعْطِينَاهَا النَّاسُ بَعْدَهُ، وَإِنِّي وَاللَّهِ لاَ أَسْأَلُهَا رَسُولَ اللَّهِ صلى الله عليه وسلم

Narrated Ubaidullah bin `Abdullah: Ibn `Abbas said, "When Allah's Messenger ﷺ was on his deathbed and there were some men in the house, he said, 'Come near, I will write for you something after which you will not go astray.' Some of them (i.e. his companions) said, 'Allah's Messenger ﷺ is seriously ill and you have the (Holy) Qur'an. Allah's Book is sufficient for us.' So the people in the house differed and started disputing. Some of them said, 'Give him writing material so that he may write for you something after which you will not go astray.' While the others said the other way round. So when their talk and differences increased, Allah's Apostle said, "Get up." Ibn `Abbas used to say, "No doubt, it was very unfortunate (a great disaster) that Allah's Messenger ﷺ was prevented from writing for them that writing because of their differences and noise.". – Sahih Al-Bukhari 4432

حَدَّثَنَا عَلِيُّ بْنُ عَبْدِ اللَّهِ، حَدَّثَنَا عَبْدُ الرَّزَّاقِ، أَخْبَرَنَا مَعْمَرٌ، عَنِ الزُّهْرِيِّ، عَنْ عُبَيْدِ اللَّهِ بْنِ عَبْدِ اللَّهِ بْنِ عُتْبَةَ، عَنِ ابْنِ عَبَّاسٍ ـ رضى الله عنهما ـ قَالَ لَمَّا حُضِرَ رَسُولُ اللَّهِ صلى الله عليه وسلم وَفِي الْبَيْتِ رِجَالٌ، فَقَالَ النَّبِيُّ صلى الله عليه وسلم " هَلُمُّوا أَكْتُبْ لَكُمْ كِتَابًا لاَ تَضِلُّوا بَعْدَهُ ". فَقَالَ بَعْضُهُمْ إِنَّ رَسُولَ اللَّهِ صلى الله عليه وسلم قَدْ غَلَبَهُ الْوَجَعُ وَعِنْدَكُمُ الْقُرْآنُ، حَسْبُنَا كِتَابُ اللَّهِ. فَاخْتَلَفَ أَهْلُ الْبَيْتِ وَاخْتَصَمُوا، فَمِنْهُمْ مَنْ يَقُولُ قَرِّبُوا يَكْتُبُ لَكُمْ كِتَابًا لاَ تَضِلُّوا بَعْدَهُ. وَمِنْهُمْ مَنْ يَقُولُ غَيْرَ ذَلِكَ، فَلَمَّا أَكْثَرُوا اللَّغْوَ وَالاِخْتِلاَفَ قَالَ رَسُولُ اللَّهِ صلى الله عليه وسلم " قُومُوا ". قَالَ عُبَيْدُ اللَّهِ فَكَانَ يَقُولُ ابْنُ عَبَّاسٍ إِنَّ الرَّزِيَّةَ كُلَّ الرَّزِيَّةِ مَا حَالَ بَيْنَ رَسُولِ اللَّهِ صلى الله عليه وسلم وَبَيْنَ أَنْ يَكْتُبَ لَهُمْ ذَلِكَ الْكِتَابَ لاِخْتِلاَفِهِمْ وَلَغَطِهِمْ.

Narrated Ibn Abu Mulaika: Ibn `Abbas recited: "(Respite will be granted) until when the Apostles gave up hope (of their people) and thought that they were denied (by their people). There came to them Our Help ...." (12.110) reading Kudhibu without doubling the sound 'dh', and that was what he understood of the Verse. Then he went on reciting: "..even the Apostle and those who believed along with him said: When (will come) Allah's Help? Yes, verily, Allah's Help is near." (2.214) Then I met `Urwa bin Az-Zubair and I mentioned that to him. He said, "Aisha said, 'Allah forbid! By Allah, Allah never promised His Apostle anything but he knew that it would certainly happen before he died. But trials were continuously presented before the Apostles till they were afraid that their followers would accuse them of telling lies. So I used to recite:-- "Till they (come to) think that they were treated as liars." Reading 'Kudh-dhibu with double 'dh.'. – Sahih al-Bukhari 4524, 4525

حَدَّثَنَا إِبْرَاهِيمُ بْنُ مُوسَى، أَخْبَرَنَا هِشَامٌ، عَنِ ابْنِ جُرَيْجٍ، قَالَ سَمِعْتُ ابْنَ أَبِي مُلَيْكَةَ، يَقُولُ قَالَ ابْنُ عَبَّاسٍ ـ رضى الله عنهما ـ {حَتَّى إِذَا اسْتَيْأَسَ الرُّسُلُ وَظَنُّوا أَنَّهُمْ قَدْ كُذِبُوا} خَفِيفَةً، ذَهَبَ بِهَا هُنَاكَ، وَتَلاَ {حَتَّى يَقُولَ الرَّسُولُ وَالَّذِينَ آمَنُوا مَعَهُ مَتَى نَصْرُ اللَّهِ أَلاَ إِنَّ نَصْرَ اللَّهِ قَرِيبٌ} فَلَقِيتُ عُرْوَةَ بْنَ الزُّبَيْرِ فَذَكَرْتُ لَهُ ذَلِكَ فَقَالَ قَالَتْ عَائِشَةُ مَعَاذَ اللَّهِ، وَاللَّهِ مَا وَعَدَ اللَّهُ رَسُولَهُ مِنْ شَىْءٍ قَطُّ إِلاَّ عَلِمَ أَنَّهُ كَائِنٌ قَبْلَ أَنْ يَمُوتَ، وَلَكِنْ لَمْ يَزَلِ الْبَلاَءُ بِالرُّسُلِ حَتَّى خَافُوا أَنْ يَكُونَ مَنْ مَعَهُمْ يُكَذِّبُونَهُمْ، فَكَانَتْ تَقْرَؤُهَا {وَظَنُّوا أَنَّهُمْ قَدْ كُذِّبُوا} مُثَقَّلَةً.

Narrated Ibn `Abbas: `Umar used to make me sit with the elderly men who had fought in the Battle of Badr. Some of them felt it (did not like that) and said to `Umar "Why do you bring in this boy to sit with us while we have sons like him?" `Umar replied, "Because of what you know of his position (i.e. his religious knowledge.)" One day `Umar called me and made me sit in the gathering of those people; and I think that he called me just to show them. (my religious knowledge). `Umar then asked them (in my presence). "What do you say about the interpretation of the Statement of Allah: 'When comes Help of Allah (to you O, Muhammad against your enemies) and the conquest (of Mecca).' (110.1) Some of them said, "We are ordered to praise Allah and ask for His forgiveness when Allah's Help and the conquest (of Mecca) comes to us." Some others kept quiet and did not say anything. On that, `Umar asked me, "Do you say the same, O Ibn `Abbas?" I replied, "No." He said, 'What do you say then?" I replied, "That is the sign of the death of Allah's Messenger ﷺ which Allah informed him of. Allah said:-- '(O Muhammad) When comes the Help of Allah (to you against your enemies) and the conquest (of Mecca) (which is the sign of your death). You should celebrate the praises of your Lord and ask for His Forgiveness, and He is the One Who accepts the repentance and forgives.' (110.3) On that `Umar said, "I do not know anything about it other than what you have said." – Sahih al-Bukhari 4970

حَدَّثَنَا مُوسَى بْنُ إِسْمَاعِيلَ، حَدَّثَنَا أَبُو عَوَانَةَ، عَنْ أَبِي بِشْرٍ، عَنْ سَعِيدِ بْنِ جُبَيْرٍ، عَنِ ابْنِ عَبَّاسٍ، قَالَ كَانَ عُمَرُ يُدْخِلُنِي مَعَ أَشْيَاخِ بَدْرٍ، فَكَأَنَّ بَعْضَهُمْ وَجَدَ فِي نَفْسِهِ فَقَالَ لِمَ تُدْخِلُ هَذَا مَعَنَا وَلَنَا أَبْنَاءٌ مِثْلُهُ فَقَالَ عُمَرُ إِنَّهُ مِنْ حَيْثُ عَلِمْتُمْ. فَدَعَا ذَاتَ يَوْمٍ ـ فَأَدْخَلَهُ مَعَهُمْ ـ فَمَا رُئِيتُ أَنَّهُ دَعَانِي يَوْمَئِذٍ إِلاَّ لِيُرِيَهُمْ. قَالَ مَا تَقُولُونَ فِي قَوْلِ اللَّهِ تَعَالَى {إِذَا جَاءَ نَصْرُ اللَّهِ وَالْفَتْحُ} فَقَالَ بَعْضُهُمْ أُمِرْنَا نَحْمَدُ اللَّهَ وَنَسْتَغْفِرُهُ، إِذَا نُصِرْنَا وَفُتِحَ عَلَيْنَا. وَسَكَتَ بَعْضُهُمْ فَلَمْ يَقُلْ شَيْئًا فَقَالَ لِي أَكَذَاكَ تَقُولُ يَا ابْنَ عَبَّاسٍ فَقُلْتُ لاَ. قَالَ فَمَا تَقُولُ قُلْتُ هُوَ أَجَلُ رَسُولِ اللَّهِ صلى الله عليه وسلم أَعْلَمَهُ لَهُ، قَالَ {إِذَا جَاءَ نَصْرُ اللَّهِ وَالْفَتْحُ} وَذَلِكَ عَلاَمَةُ أَجَلِكَ {فَسَبِّحْ بِحَمْدِ رَبِّكَ وَاسْتَغْفِرْهُ إِنَّهُ كَانَ تَوَّابًا}. فَقَالَ عُمَرُ مَا أَعْلَمُ مِنْهَا إِلاَّ مَا تَقُولُ

Narrated `Aisha: Allah's Messenger ﷺ was shrouded in three Yemenite white Suhuliya of cotton, and in them there was neither a shirt nor a turban." – Sahih al-Bukhari 1264
حَدَّثَنَا مُحَمَّدُ بْنُ مُقَاتِلٍ، أَخْبَرَنَا عَبْدُ اللَّهِ، أَخْبَرَنَا هِشَامُ بْنُ عُرْوَةَ، عَنْ أَبِيهِ، عَنْ عَائِشَةَ ـ رضى الله عنها ـ أَنَّ رَسُولَ اللَّهِ صلى الله عليه وسلم كُفِّنَ فِي ثَلاَثَةِ أَثْوَابٍ يَمَانِيَةٍ بِيضٍ سَحُولِيَّةٍ مِنْ كُرْسُفٍ، لَيْسَ فِيهِنَّ قَمِيصٌ وَلاَ عِمَامَةٌ.

Surah An-Nasr
سورة النصر

When comes the victory of Allah, and the Conquest And you see mankind entering the Religion of Allah in troops So extol with the praise of your Lord, and ask Him forgiveness; surely He has (always) been Superbly Relenting – Surah An-Nasr
إِذَا جَاءَ نَصْرُ اللَّهِ وَالْفَتْحُ وَرَأَيْتَ النَّاسَ يَدْخُلُونَ فِي دِينِ اللَّهِ أَفْوَاجًا فَسَبِّحْ بِحَمْدِ رَبِّكَ وَاسْتَغْفِرْهُ إِنَّهُ كَانَ تَوَّابًا

Narrated Ibn `Abbas: Allah's Messenger ﷺ stayed in Mecca for thirteen years (after receiving the first Divine Inspiration) and died at the age of sixty-three. – Sahih al-Bukhari 3903
حَدَّثَنِي مَطَرُ بْنُ الْفَضْلِ، حَدَّثَنَا رَوْحُ بْنُ عُبَادَةَ، حَدَّثَنَا زَكَرِيَّاءُ بْنُ إِسْحَاقَ، حَدَّثَنَا عَمْرُو بْنُ دِينَارٍ، عَنِ ابْنِ عَبَّاسٍ، قَالَ مَكَثَ رَسُولُ اللَّهِ صلى الله عليه وسلم بِمَكَّةَ ثَلاَثَ عَشْرَةَ، وَتُوُفِّيَ وَهُوَ ابْنُ ثَلاَثٍ وَسِتِّينَ

Narrated `Aisha: Abu Bakr came from his house at As-Sunh on a horse. He dismounted and entered the Mosque, but did not speak to the people till he entered upon `Aisha and went straight to Allah's Messenger ﷺ who was covered with Hibra cloth (i.e. a kind of Yemenite cloth). He then uncovered the Prophet's face and bowed over him and kissed him and wept, saying, "Let my father and mother be sacrificed for you. By Allah, Allah will never cause you to die twice. As for the death which was written for you, has come upon you." Narrated Ibn `Abbas: Abu Bakr went out while `Umar bin Al-Khattab was talking to the people. Abu Bakr said, "Sit down, O `Umar!" But `Umar refused to sit down. So the people came to Abu Bakr and left `Umar. Abu Bakr said, "To proceed, if anyone amongst you used to worship Muhammad , then Muhammad is dead, but if (anyone of) you used to worship Allah, then Allah is Alive and shall never die. Allah said:--"Muhammad is no more than an Apostle, and Indeed (many) apostles have passed away before him..(till the end of the Verse)......Allah will reward to those who are thankful." (3.144) By Allah, it was as if the people never knew that Allah had revealed this Verse before till Abu Bakr recited it and all the people received it from him, and I heard everybody reciting it (then). Narrated Az-Zuhri: Sa`id bin Al-Musaiyab told me that `Umar said, "By Allah, when I heard Abu Bakr reciting it, my legs could not support me and I fell down at the very moment of hearing him reciting it, declaring that the Prophet ﷺ had died.". – Sahih Al-Bukhari 4452, 4453, 4454
حَدَّثَنَا يَحْيَى بْنُ بُكَيْرٍ، حَدَّثَنَا اللَّيْثُ، عَنْ عُقَيْلٍ، عَنِ ابْنِ شِهَابٍ، قَالَ أَخْبَرَنِي أَبُو سَلَمَةَ، أَنَّ عَائِشَةَ، أَخْبَرَتْهُ أَنَّ أَبَا بَكْرٍ ـ رضى الله عنه ـ أَقْبَلَ عَلَى فَرَسٍ مِنْ مَسْكَنِهِ بِالسُّنْحِ حَتَّى نَزَلَ، فَدَخَلَ الْمَسْجِدَ فَلَمْ يُكَلِّمِ النَّاسَ حَتَّى دَخَلَ عَلَى عَائِشَةَ، فَتَيَمَّمَ رَسُولَ اللَّهِ صلى الله عليه وسلم وَهْوَ مُغَشًّى بِثَوْبِ حِبَرَةٍ، فَكَشَفَ عَنْ وَجْهِهِ ثُمَّ أَكَبَّ عَلَيْهِ فَقَبَّلَهُ وَبَكَى. ثُمَّ قَالَ بِأَبِي أَنْتَ وَأُمِّي، وَاللَّهِ لاَ يَجْمَعُ اللَّهُ عَلَيْكَ مَوْتَتَيْنِ، أَمَّا الْمَوْتَةُ الَّتِي كُتِبَتْ عَلَيْكَ فَقَدْ مُتَّهَا. قَالَ الزُّهْرِيُّ وَحَدَّثَنِي أَبُو سَلَمَةَ، عَنْ عَبْدِ اللَّهِ بْنِ عَبَّاسٍ، أَنَّ أَبَا بَكْرٍ، خَرَجَ وَعُمَرُ يُكَلِّمُ النَّاسَ فَقَالَ اجْلِسْ يَا عُمَرُ، فَأَبَى عُمَرُ أَنْ يَجْلِسَ. فَأَقْبَلَ النَّاسُ إِلَيْهِ وَتَرَكُوا عُمَرَ، فَقَالَ أَبُو بَكْرٍ أَمَّا بَعْدُ مَنْ كَانَ مِنْكُمْ يَعْبُدُ مُحَمَّدًا صلى الله عليه وسلم فَإِنَّ مُحَمَّدًا قَدْ مَاتَ، وَمَنْ كَانَ مِنْكُمْ يَعْبُدُ اللَّهَ فَإِنَّ اللَّهَ حَىٌّ لاَ يَمُوتُ، قَالَ اللَّهُ {وَمَا مُحَمَّدٌ إِلاَّ رَسُولٌ قَدْ خَلَتْ مِنْ قَبْلِهِ الرُّسُلُ} إِلَى قَوْلِهِ {الشَّاكِرِينَ} وَقَالَ وَاللَّهِ لَكَأَنَّ النَّاسَ لَمْ يَعْلَمُوا أَنَّ اللَّهَ أَنْزَلَ هَذِهِ الآيَةَ حَتَّى تَلاَهَا أَبُو بَكْرٍ، فَتَلَقَّاهَا مِنْهُ النَّاسُ كُلُّهُمْ فَمَا أَسْمَعُ بَشَرًا مِنَ النَّاسِ إِلاَّ يَتْلُوهَا. فَأَخْبَرَنِي سَعِيدُ بْنُ الْمُسَيَّبِ أَنَّ عُمَرَ قَالَ وَاللَّهِ مَا هُوَ إِلاَّ أَنْ سَمِعْتُ أَبَا بَكْرٍ تَلاَهَا فَعَقِرْتُ حَتَّى مَا تُقِلُّنِي رِجْلاَىَ، وَحَتَّى أَهْوَيْتُ إِلَى الأَرْضِ حِينَ سَمِعْتُهُ تَلاَهَا أَنَّ النَّبِيَّ صلى الله عليه وسلم قَدْ مَاتَ

Narrated Anas :While the Muslims were offering the Fajr prayer, Allah's Messenger ﷺ suddenly appeared before them by living the curtain of the dwelling place of `Aisha, looked towards the Muslims who were standing in rows. He smiled with pleasure. Abu Bakr started retreating to join the row on the assumption that the Prophet wanted to come out for the prayer. The Muslims intended to leave the prayer (and were on the verge of being put to trial), but the Prophetﷺ beckoned them to complete their prayer and then he let the curtain fall. He died in the last hours of that day. - Sahih al-Bukhari 754

حَدَّثَنَا يَحْيَى بْنُ بُكَيْرٍ، قَالَ حَدَّثَنَا لَيْثُ بْنُ سَعْدٍ، عَنْ عُقَيْلٍ، عَنِ ابْنِ شِهَابٍ، قَالَ أَخْبَرَنِي أَنَسٌ، قَالَ بَيْنَمَا الْمُسْلِمُونَ فِي صَلاَةِ الْفَجْرِ لَمْ يَفْجَأْهُمْ إِلاَّ رَسُولُ اللَّهِ صلى الله عليه وسلم كَشَفَ سِتْرَ حُجْرَةِ عَائِشَةَ فَنَظَرَ إِلَيْهِمْ وَهُمْ صُفُوفٌ، فَتَبَسَّمَ يَضْحَكُ، وَنَكَصَ أَبُو بَكْرٍ رضى الله عنه عَلَى عَقِبَيْهِ لِيَصِلَ لَهُ الصَّفَّ فَظَنَّ أَنَّهُ يُرِيدُ الْخُرُوجَ، وَهَمَّ الْمُسْلِمُونَ أَنْ يَفْتَتِنُوا فِي صَلاَتِهِمْ، فَأَشَارَ إِلَيْهِمْ أَتِمُّوا صَلاَتَكُمْ، فَأَرْخَى السِّتْرَ، وَتُوُفِّيَ مِنْ آخِرِ ذَلِكَ الْيَوْمِ.

Narrated `Amr bin Al-Harith: The Prophetﷺ did not leave behind him after his death, anything except his arms, his white mule, and a piece of land at Khaibar which he left to be given in charity . – Sahih Al-Bukhari 2912

حَدَّثَنَا عَمْرُو بْنُ عَبَّاسٍ، حَدَّثَنَا عَبْدُ الرَّحْمَنِ، عَنْ سُفْيَانَ، عَنْ أَبِي إِسْحَاقَ، عَنْ عَمْرِو بْنِ الْحَارِثِ، قَالَ مَا تَرَكَ النَّبِيُّ صلى الله عليه وسلم إِلاَّ سِلاَحَهُ وَبَغْلَةً بَيْضَاءَ وَأَرْضًا جَعَلَهَا صَدَقَةً

Narrated `Umar: When Allah took away the soul of His Prophet at his death, the Ansar assembled In the shed of Bani Sa`ida. I said to Abu Bakr, "Let us go." So, we come to them (i.e. to Ansar) at the shed of Bani Sa`ida. (See Hadith No. 19, Vol. 5 for details). – Sahih Al-Bukhari 2462

حَدَّثَنَا يَحْيَى بْنُ سُلَيْمَانَ، قَالَ حَدَّثَنِي ابْنُ وَهْبٍ، قَالَ حَدَّثَنِي مَالِكٌ. وَأَخْبَرَنِي يُونُسُ، عَنِ ابْنِ شِهَابٍ، أَخْبَرَنِي عُبَيْدُ اللَّهِ بْنُ عَبْدِ اللَّهِ بْنِ عُتْبَةَ، أَنَّ ابْنَ عَبَّاسٍ، أَخْبَرَهُ عَنْ عُمَرَ ـ رضى الله عنهم ـ قَالَ حِينَ تَوَفَّى اللَّهُ نَبِيَّهُ صلى الله عليه وسلم إِنَّ الأَنْصَارَ اجْتَمَعُوا فِي سَقِيفَةِ بَنِي سَاعِدَةَ، فَقُلْتُ لأَبِي بَكْرٍ انْطَلِقْ بِنَا. فَجِئْنَاهُمْ فِي سَقِيفَةِ بَنِي سَاعِدَةَ

Narrated 'Aisha: (the wife of the Prophet) Allah's Messengerﷺ died while Abu Bakr was at a place called As-Sunah (Al-'Aliya) 'Umar stood up and said, "By Allah! Allah's Messengerﷺ is not dead!" 'Umar (later on) said, "By Allah! Nothing occurred to my mind except that." He said, "Verily! Allah will resurrect him and he will cut the hands and legs of some men." Then Abu Bakr came and uncovered the face of Allah's Messengerﷺ, kissed him and said, "Let my mother and father be sacrificed for you, (O Allah's Messenger ﷺ, (you are good in life and in death. By Allah in Whose Hands my life is, Allah will never make you taste death twice." Then he went out and said, "O oath-taker! Don't be hasty." When Abu Bakr spoke, 'Umar sat down. Abu Bakr praised and glorified Allah and said, No doubt! Whoever worshipped Muhammad, then Muhammad is dead, but whoever worshipped Allah, then Allah is Alive and shall never die." Then he recited Allah's Statement.:-- "(O Muhammad) Verily you will die, and they also will die." (39.30) He also recited:-- "Muhammad is no more than an Apostle; and indeed many Apostles have passed away, before him, If he dies Or is killed, will you then Turn back on your heels? And he who turns back On his heels, not the least Harm will he do to Allah And Allah will give reward to those Who are grateful." (3.144) The people wept loudly, and the Ansar were assembled with Sad bin 'Ubada in the shed of Bani Saida. They said (to the emigrants). "There should be one 'Amir from us and one from you." Then Abu Bakr, Umar bin Al-Khattab and Abu 'baida bin Al-Jarrah went to them. 'Umar wanted to speak but Abu Bakr stopped him. 'Umar later on used to say, "By Allah, I intended only to say something that appealed to me and I was afraid that Abu Bakr would not speak so well. Then Abu Bakr spoke and his speech was very eloquent. He said in his statement, "We are the rulers and you (Ansars) are the ministers (i.e. advisers)," Hubab bin Al-Mundhir said, "No, by Allah we won't accept this. But there must be a ruler from us and a ruler from you." Abu Bakr said, "No, we will be the rulers and you will be the ministers, for they (i.e. Quarish) are the best family amongst the 'Arabs and of best origin. So you should elect either 'Umar or Abu 'Ubaida bin Al-Jarrah as your ruler." 'Umar said (to Abu Bakr), "No but we elect you, for you are our chief and the best amongst us and the most beloved of all of us to Allah's Messenger ﷺ," So 'Umar took Abu Bakr's hand and gave the pledge of allegiance and the people too gave the pledge of allegiance to Abu Bakr. Someone said, "You have killed Sad bin Ubada." 'Umar said, "Allah has killed him.". – Sahih Al-Bukhari 3667, 3668

حَدَّثَنَا إِسْمَاعِيلُ بْنُ عَبْدِ اللَّهِ، حَدَّثَنَا سُلَيْمَانُ بْنُ بِلاَلٍ، عَنْ هِشَامِ بْنِ عُرْوَةَ، عَنْ عُرْوَةَ بْنِ الزُّبَيْرِ، عَنْ عَائِشَةَ ـ رضى الله عنها ـ زَوْجِ النَّبِيِّ صلى الله عليه وسلم أَنَّ رَسُولَ اللَّهِ صلى الله عليه وسلم مَاتَ وَأَبُو بَكْرٍ بِالسُّنْحِ ـ قَالَ إِسْمَاعِيلُ يَعْنِي بِالْعَالِيَةِ ـ فَقَامَ عُمَرُ يَقُولُ وَاللَّهِ مَا مَاتَ رَسُولُ اللَّهِ صلى الله عليه وسلم. قَالَتْ وَقَالَ عُمَرُ وَاللَّهِ مَا كَانَ يَقَعُ فِي نَفْسِي إِلاَّ ذَاكَ وَلَيَبْعَثَنَّهُ اللَّهُ فَلَيَقْطَعَنَّ أَيْدِيَ رِجَالٍ وَأَرْجُلَهُمْ. فَجَاءَ أَبُو بَكْرٍ فَكَشَفَ عَنْ رَسُولِ اللَّهِ صلى الله عليه وسلم فَقَبَّلَهُ قَالَ بِأَبِي أَنْتَ وَأُمِّي طِبْتَ حَيًّا وَمَيِّتًا، وَالَّذِي نَفْسِي بِيَدِهِ لاَ يُذِيقُكَ اللَّهُ الْمَوْتَتَيْنِ أَبَدًا. ثُمَّ خَرَجَ فَقَالَ أَيُّهَا الْحَالِفُ عَلَى رِسْلِكَ. فَلَمَّا تَكَلَّمَ أَبُو بَكْرٍ جَلَسَ عُمَرُ. فَحَمِدَ اللَّهَ أَبُو بَكْرٍ وَأَثْنَى عَلَيْهِ وَقَالَ أَلاَ مَنْ كَانَ يَعْبُدُ مُحَمَّدًا صلى الله عليه وسلم فَإِنَّ مُحَمَّدًا قَدْ مَاتَ، وَمَنْ كَانَ يَعْبُدُ اللَّهَ فَإِنَّ اللَّهَ حَيٌّ لاَ يَمُوتُ. وَقَالَ {إِنَّكَ مَيِّتٌ وَإِنَّهُمْ مَيِّتُونَ} وَقَالَ {وَمَا مُحَمَّدٌ إِلاَّ رَسُولٌ قَدْ خَلَتْ مِنْ قَبْلِهِ الرُّسُلُ أَفَإِنْ مَاتَ أَوْ قُتِلَ انْقَلَبْتُمْ عَلَى أَعْقَابِكُمْ وَمَنْ يَنْقَلِبْ عَلَى عَقِبَيْهِ فَلَنْ يَضُرَّ اللَّهَ شَيْئًا وَسَيَجْزِي اللَّهُ الشَّاكِرِينَ} قَالَ فَنَشَجَ النَّاسُ يَبْكُونَ ـ قَالَ ـ وَاجْتَمَعَتِ الأَنْصَارُ إِلَى سَعْدِ بْنِ عُبَادَةَ فِي سَقِيفَةِ بَنِي سَاعِدَةَ فَقَالُوا مِنَّا أَمِيرٌ وَمِنْكُمْ أَمِيرٌ، فَذَهَبَ إِلَيْهِمْ أَبُو بَكْرٍ وَعُمَرُ بْنُ الْخَطَّابِ وَأَبُو عُبَيْدَةَ بْنُ الْجَرَّاحِ، فَذَهَبَ عُمَرُ يَتَكَلَّمُ فَأَسْكَتَهُ أَبُو بَكْرٍ، وَكَانَ عُمَرُ يَقُولُ وَاللَّهِ مَا أَرَدْتُ بِذَلِكَ إِلاَّ أَنِّي قَدْ هَيَّأْتُ كَلاَمًا قَدْ أَعْجَبَنِي خَشِيتُ أَنْ لاَ يَبْلُغَهُ أَبُو بَكْرٍ، ثُمَّ تَكَلَّمَ أَبُو بَكْرٍ فَتَكَلَّمَ أَبْلَغَ النَّاسِ فَقَالَ فِي كَلاَمِهِ نَحْنُ الأُمَرَاءُ وَأَنْتُمُ الْوُزَرَاءُ. فَقَالَ حُبَابُ بْنُ الْمُنْذِرِ لاَ وَاللَّهِ لاَ نَفْعَلُ، مِنَّا أَمِيرٌ وَمِنْكُمْ أَمِيرٌ. فَقَالَ أَبُو بَكْرٍ لاَ، وَلَكِنَّا الأُمَرَاءُ وَأَنْتُمُ الْوُزَرَاءُ هُمْ أَوْسَطُ الْعَرَبِ دَارًا، وَأَعْرَبُهُمْ أَحْسَابًا فَبَايِعُوا عُمَرَ أَوْ أَبَا عُبَيْدَةَ. فَقَالَ عُمَرُ بَلْ نُبَايِعُكَ أَنْتَ، فَأَنْتَ سَيِّدُنَا وَخَيْرُنَا وَأَحَبُّنَا إِلَى رَسُولِ اللَّهِ صلى الله عليه وسلم. فَأَخَذَ عُمَرُ بِيَدِهِ فَبَايَعَهُ، وَبَايَعَهُ النَّاسُ، فَقَالَ قَائِلٌ قَتَلْتُمْ سَعْدَ بْنَ عُبَادَةَ. فَقَالَ عُمَرُ قَتَلَهُ اللَّهُ

Narrated Anas bin Malik: That he heard `Umar's second speech he delivered when he sat on the pulpit on the day following the death of the Prophet ﷺ Umar recited the Tashahhud while Abu Bakr was silent. `Umar said, "I wish that Allah's Messenger ﷺ had outlived all of us, i.e., had been the last (to die). But if Muhammad is dead, Allah nevertheless has kept the light amongst you from which you can receive the same guidance as Allah guided Muhammad with that. And Abu Bakr is the companion of Allah's Messenger ﷺ He is the second of the two in the cave. He is the most entitled person among the Muslims to manage your affairs. Therefore get up and swear allegiance to him." Some people had already taken the oath of allegiance to him in the shed of Bani Sa`ida but the oath of allegiance taken by the public was taken at the pulpit. I heard `Umar saying to Abu Bakr on that day. "Please ascend the pulpit," and kept on urging him till he ascended the pulpit whereupon, all the people swore allegiance to him. – Sahih Al-Bukhari 7219

حَدَّثَنَا إِبْرَاهِيمُ بْنُ مُوسَى، أَخْبَرَنَا هِشَامٌ، عَنْ مَعْمَرٍ، عَنِ الزُّهْرِيِّ، أَخْبَرَنِي أَنَسُ بْنُ مَالِكٍ ـ رضى الله عنه ـ أَنَّهُ سَمِعَ خُطْبَةَ، عُمَرَ الآخِرَةَ حِينَ جَلَسَ عَلَى الْمِنْبَرِ، وَذَلِكَ الْغَدُ مِنْ يَوْمِ تُوُفِّيَ النَّبِيُّ صلى الله عليه وسلم فَتَشَهَّدَ وَأَبُو بَكْرٍ صَامِتٌ لاَ يَتَكَلَّمُ قَالَ كُنْتُ أَرْجُو أَنْ يَعِيشَ رَسُولُ اللَّهِ صلى الله عليه وسلم حَتَّى يَدْبُرَنَا ـ يُرِيدُ بِذَلِكَ أَنْ يَكُونَ آخِرَهُمْ ـ فَإِنْ يَكُ مُحَمَّدٌ صلى الله عليه وسلم قَدْ مَاتَ، فَإِنَّ اللَّهَ تَعَالَى قَدْ جَعَلَ بَيْنَ أَظْهُرِكُمْ نُورًا تَهْتَدُونَ بِهِ بِمَا هَدَى اللَّهُ مُحَمَّدًا صلى الله عليه وسلم وَإِنَّ أَبَا بَكْرٍ صَاحِبُ رَسُولِ اللَّهِ صلى الله عليه وسلم ثَانِي اثْنَيْنِ، فَإِنَّهُ أَوْلَى الْمُسْلِمِينَ بِأُمُورِكُمْ، فَقُومُوا فَبَايِعُوهُ. وَكَانَتْ طَائِفَةٌ مِنْهُمْ قَدْ بَايَعُوهُ قَبْلَ ذَلِكَ فِي سَقِيفَةِ بَنِي سَاعِدَةَ، وَكَانَتْ بَيْعَةُ الْعَامَّةِ عَلَى الْمِنْبَرِ. قَالَ الزُّهْرِيُّ عَنْ أَنَسِ بْنِ مَالِكٍ سَمِعْتُ عُمَرَ يَقُولُ لأَبِي بَكْرٍ يَوْمَئِذٍ اصْعَدِ الْمِنْبَرَ. فَلَمْ يَزَلْ بِهِ حَتَّى صَعِدَ الْمِنْبَرَ، فَبَايَعَهُ النَّاسُ عَامَّةً

Narrated Al-Aswad: In the presence of `Aisha some people mentioned that the Prophet ﷺ had appointed `Ali by will as his successor. `Aisha said, "When did he appoint him by will? Verily when he died he was resting against my chest (or said: in my lap) and he asked for a wash-basin and then collapsed while in that state, and I could not even perceive that he had died, so when did he appoint him by will?". – Sahih Al-Bukhari 2741

حَدَّثَنَا عَمْرُو بْنُ زُرَارَةَ، أَخْبَرَنَا إِسْمَاعِيلُ، عَنِ ابْنِ عَوْنٍ، عَنْ إِبْرَاهِيمَ، عَنِ الأَسْوَدِ، قَالَ ذَكَرُوا عِنْدَ عَائِشَةَ أَنَّ عَلِيًّا ـ رضى الله عنهما ـ كَانَ وَصِيًّا. فَقَالَتْ مَتَى أَوْصَى إِلَيْهِ وَقَدْ كُنْتُ مُسْنِدَتَهُ إِلَى صَدْرِي ـ أَوْ قَالَتْ حَجْرِي ـ فَدَعَا بِالطَّسْتِ، فَلَقَدِ انْخَنَثَ فِي حَجْرِي، فَمَا شَعَرْتُ أَنَّهُ قَدْ مَاتَ، فَمَتَى أَوْصَى إِلَيْهِ

The Book of
Quraish
قريش

The nephew of Suraqa bin Ju'sham said that his father informed him that he heard Suraqa bin Ju'sham saying, "The messengers of the heathens of Quraish came to us declaring that they had assigned for the persons why would kill or arrest Allah's Messenger ﷺ and Abu Bakr, a reward equal to their bloodmoney. While I was sitting in one of the gatherings of my tribe. Bani Mudlij, a man from them came to us and stood up while we were sitting, and said, "O Suraqa! No doubt, I have just seen some people far away on the seashore, and I think they are Muhammad and his companions." Suraqa added, "I too realized that it must have been they. But I said 'No, it is not they, but you have seen so-and-so, and so-and-so whom we saw set out.' I stayed in the gathering for a while and then got up and left for my home. And ordered my slave-girl to get my horse which was behind a hillock, and keep it ready for me. Then I took my spear and left by the back door of my house dragging the lower end of the spear on the ground and keeping it low. Then I reached my horse, mounted it and made it gallop. When I approached them (i.e. Muhammad and Abu Bakr), my horse stumbled and I fell down from it, Then I stood up, got hold of my quiver and took out the divining arrows and drew lots as to whether I should harm them (i.e. the Prophet ﷺ and Abu Bakr) or not, and the lot which I disliked came out. But I remounted my horse and let it gallop, giving no importance to the divining arrows. When I heard the recitation of the Quran by Allah's Messenger ﷺ who did not look hither and thither while Abu Bakr was doing it often, suddenly the forelegs of my horse sank into the ground up to the knees, and I fell down from it. Then I rebuked it and it got up but could hardly take out its forelegs from the ground, and when it stood up straight again, its fore-legs caused dust to rise up in the sky like smoke. Then again I drew lots with the divining arrows, and the lot which I disliked, came out. So I called upon them to feel secure. They stopped, and I remounted my horse and went to them. When I saw how I had been hampered from harming them, it came to my mind that the cause of Allah's Messenger ﷺ (i.e. Islam) will become victorious. So I said to him, "Your people have assigned a reward equal to the bloodmoney for your head." Then I told them all the plans the people of Mecca had made concerning them. Then I offered them some journey food and goods but they refused to take anything and did not ask for anything, but the Prophet ﷺ said, "Do not tell others about us." Then I requested him to write for me a statement of security and peace. He ordered 'Amr bin Fuhaira who wrote it for me on a parchment, and then Allah's Messenger ﷺ proceeded on his way. Narrated 'Urwa bin Az-Zubair: Allah's Messenger ﷺ met Az-Zubair in a caravan of Muslim merchants who were returning from Sham. Az-Zubair provided Allah's Messenger ﷺ and Abu Bakr with white clothes to wear. When the Muslims of Medina heard the news of the departure of Allah's Messenger ﷺ from Mecca (towards Medina), they started going to the Harra every morning . They would wait for him till the heat of the noon forced them to return. One day, after waiting for a long while, they returned home, and when they went into their houses, a Jew climbed up the roof of one of the forts of his people to look for some thing, and he saw Allah's Messenger ﷺ and his companions dressed in white clothes, emerging out of the desert mirage. The Jew could not help shouting at the top of his voice, "O you 'Arabs! Here is your great man whom you have been waiting for!" So all the Muslims rushed to their arms and received Allah's Messenger ﷺ on the summit of Harra. The Prophet ﷺ turned with them to the right and alighted at the quarters of Bani

‘Amr bin ‘Auf, and this was on Monday in the month of Rabi-ul-Awal. Abu Bakr stood up, receiving the people while Allah’s Messenger ﷺ sat down and kept silent. Some of the Ansar who came and had not seen Allah’s Messenger ﷺ before, began greeting Abu Bakr, but when the sunshine fell on Allah’s Messenger ﷺ and Abu Bakr came forward and shaded him with his sheet only then the people came to know Allah’s Messenger ﷺ. Allah’s Messenger ﷺ stayed with Bani ‘Amr bin ‘Auf for ten nights and established the mosque (mosque of Quba) which was founded on piety. Allah’s Messenger ﷺ prayed in it and then mounted his she-camel and proceeded on, accompanied by the people till his she-camel knelt down at (the place of) the Mosque of Allah’s Messenger ﷺ at Medina. Some Muslims used to pray there in those days, and that place was a yard for drying dates belonging to Suhail and Sahl, the orphan boys who were under the guardianship of ‘Asad bin Zurara. When his she-camel knelt down, Allah’s Messenger ﷺ said, “This place, Allah willing, will be our abiding place.” Allah’s Messenger ﷺ then called the two boys and told them to suggest a price for that yard so that he might take it as a mosque. The two boys said, “No, but we will give it as a gift, O Allah’s Messenger ﷺ !” Allah’s Messenger ﷺ then built a mosque there. The Prophet ﷺ himself started carrying unburnt bricks for its building and while doing so, he was saying “This load is better than the load of Khaibar, for it is more pious in the Sight of Allah and purer and better rewardable.” He was also saying, “O Allah! The actual reward is the reward in the Hereafter, so bestow Your Mercy on the Ansar and the Emigrants.” Thus the Prophet ﷺ recited (by way of proverb) the poem of some Muslim poet whose name is unknown to me. (Ibn Shibab said, “In the Hadiths it does not occur that Allah’s Apostle Recited a complete poetic verse other than this one.”). – Sahih Al-Bukhari 3906

قَالَ ابْنُ شِهَابٍ وَأَخْبَرَنِي عَبْدُ الرَّحْمَنِ بْنُ مَالِكٍ الْمُدْلِجِيُّ ـ وَهْوَ ابْنُ أَخِي سُرَاقَةَ بْنِ مَالِكِ بْنِ جُعْشُمٍ ـ أَنَّ أَبَاهُ، أَخْبَرَهُ أَنَّهُ، سَمِعَ سُرَاقَةَ بْنَ جُعْشُمٍ، يَقُولُ جَاءَنَا رُسُلُ كُفَّارِ قُرَيْشٍ يَجْعَلُونَ فِي رَسُولِ اللَّهِ صلى الله عليه وسلم وَأَبِي بَكْرٍ دِيَةَ كُلِّ وَاحِدٍ مِنْهُمَا، مَنْ قَتَلَهُ أَوْ أَسَرَهُ، فَبَيْنَمَا أَنَا جَالِسٌ فِي مَجْلِسٍ مِنْ مَجَالِسِ قَوْمِي بَنِي مُدْلِجٍ أَقْبَلَ رَجُلٌ مِنْهُمْ حَتَّى قَامَ عَلَيْنَا وَنَحْنُ جُلُوسٌ، فَقَالَ يَا سُرَاقَةُ، إِنِّي قَدْ رَأَيْتُ آنِفًا أَسْوِدَةً بِالسَّاحِلِ ـ أُرَاهَا مُحَمَّدًا وَأَصْحَابَهُ. قَالَ سُرَاقَةُ فَعَرَفْتُ أَنَّهُمْ هُمْ، فَقُلْتُ لَهُ إِنَّهُمْ لَيْسُوا بِهِمْ، وَلَكِنَّكَ رَأَيْتَ فُلاَنًا وَفُلاَنًا انْطَلَقُوا بِأَعْيُنِنَا. ثُمَّ لَبِثْتُ فِي الْمَجْلِسِ سَاعَةً، ثُمَّ قُمْتُ فَدَخَلْتُ فَأَمَرْتُ جَارِيَتِي أَنْ تَخْرُجَ بِفَرَسِي وَهْىَ مِنْ وَرَاءِ أَكَمَةٍ فَتَحْبِسَهَا عَلَىَّ، وَأَخَذْتُ رُمْحِي، فَخَرَجْتُ بِهِ مِنْ ظَهْرِ الْبَيْتِ، فَحَطَطْتُ بِزُجِّهِ الأَرْضَ، وَخَفَضْتُ عَالِيَهُ حَتَّى أَتَيْتُ فَرَسِي فَرَكِبْتُهَا، فَرَفَعْتُهَا تُقَرِّبُ بِي حَتَّى دَنَوْتُ مِنْهُمْ، فَعَثَرَتْ بِي فَرَسِي، فَخَرَرْتُ عَنْهَا فَقُمْتُ، فَأَهْوَيْتُ يَدِي إِلَى كِنَانَتِي فَاسْتَخْرَجْتُ مِنْهَا الأَزْلاَمَ، فَاسْتَقْسَمْتُ بِهَا أَضُرُّهُمْ أَمْ لاَ فَخَرَجَ الَّذِي أَكْرَهُ، فَرَكِبْتُ فَرَسِي، وَعَصَيْتُ الأَزْلاَمَ، تُقَرِّبُ بِي حَتَّى إِذَا سَمِعْتُ قِرَاءَةَ رَسُولِ اللَّهِ صلى الله عليه وسلم وَهْوَ لاَ يَلْتَفِتُ، وَأَبُو بَكْرٍ يُكْثِرُ الاِلْتِفَاتَ سَاخَتْ يَدَا فَرَسِي فِي الأَرْضِ حَتَّى بَلَغَتَا الرُّكْبَتَيْنِ، فَخَرَرْتُ عَنْهَا ثُمَّ زَجَرْتُهَا فَنَهَضَتْ، فَلَمْ تَكَدْ تُخْرِجُ يَدَيْهَا، فَلَمَّا اسْتَوَتْ قَائِمَةً، إِذَا لأَثَرِ يَدَيْهَا عُثَانٌ سَاطِعٌ فِي السَّمَاءِ مِثْلُ الدُّخَانِ، فَاسْتَقْسَمْتُ بِالأَزْلاَمِ، فَخَرَجَ الَّذِي أَكْرَهُ، فَنَادَيْتُهُمْ بِالأَمَانِ فَوَقَفُوا، فَرَكِبْتُ فَرَسِي حَتَّى جِئْتُهُمْ، وَوَقَعَ فِي نَفْسِي حِينَ لَقِيتُ مَا لَقِيتُ مِنَ الْحَبْسِ عَنْهُمْ أَنْ سَيَظْهَرُ أَمْرُ رَسُولِ اللَّهِ صلى الله عليه وسلم فَقُلْتُ لَهُ إِنَّ قَوْمَكَ قَدْ جَعَلُوا فِيكَ الدِّيَةَ. وَأَخْبَرْتُهُمْ أَخْبَارَ مَا يُرِيدُ النَّاسُ بِهِمْ، وَعَرَضْتُ عَلَيْهِمِ الزَّادَ وَالْمَتَاعَ، فَلَمْ يَرْزَآنِي وَلَمْ يَسْأَلاَنِي إِلاَّ أَنْ قَالَ أَخْفِ عَنَّا. فَسَأَلْتُهُ أَنْ يَكْتُبَ لِي كِتَابَ أَمْنٍ، فَأَمَرَ عَامِرَ بْنَ فُهَيْرَةَ، فَكَتَبَ فِي رُقْعَةٍ مِنْ أَدِيمٍ، ثُمَّ مَضَى رَسُولُ اللَّهِ صلى الله عليه وسلم. قَالَ ابْنُ شِهَابٍ فَأَخْبَرَنِي عُرْوَةُ بْنُ الزُّبَيْرِ أَنَّ رَسُولَ اللَّهِ صلى الله عليه وسلم لَقِيَ الزُّبَيْرَ فِي رَكْبٍ مِنَ الْمُسْلِمِينَ كَانُوا تِجَارًا قَافِلِينَ مِنَ الشَّأْمِ، فَكَسَا الزُّبَيْرُ رَسُولَ اللَّهِ صلى الله عليه وسلم وَأَبَا بَكْرٍ ثِيَابَ بَيَاضٍ، وَسَمِعَ الْمُسْلِمُونَ بِالْمَدِينَةِ مَخْرَجَ رَسُولِ اللَّهِ صلى الله عليه وسلم مِنْ مَكَّةَ، فَكَانُوا يَغْدُونَ كُلَّ غَدَاةٍ إِلَى الْحَرَّةِ فَيَنْتَظِرُونَهُ، حَتَّى يَرُدَّهُمْ حَرُّ الظَّهِيرَةِ، فَانْقَلَبُوا يَوْمًا بَعْدَ مَا أَطَالُوا انْتِظَارَهُمْ، فَلَمَّا أَوَوْا إِلَى بُيُوتِهِمْ، أَوْفَى رَجُلٌ مِنْ يَهُودَ عَلَى أُطُمٍ مِنْ آطَامِهِمْ لأَمْرٍ يَنْظُرُ إِلَيْهِ، فَبَصُرَ بِرَسُولِ اللَّهِ صلى الله عليه وسلم وَأَصْحَابِهِ مُبَيَّضِينَ يَزُولُ بِهِمُ السَّرَابُ، فَلَمْ يَمْلِكِ الْيَهُودِيُّ أَنْ قَالَ بِأَعْلَى صَوْتِهِ يَا مَعَاشِرَ الْعَرَبِ هَذَا جَدُّكُمُ الَّذِي تَنْتَظِرُونَ. فَثَارَ الْمُسْلِمُونَ إِلَى السِّلاَحِ، فَتَلَقَّوْا رَسُولَ اللَّهِ صلى الله عليه وسلم بِظَهْرِ الْحَرَّةِ، فَعَدَلَ بِهِمْ ذَاتَ الْيَمِينِ حَتَّى نَزَلَ بِهِمْ فِي بَنِي عَمْرِو بْنِ عَوْفٍ، وَذَلِكَ يَوْمَ الاِثْنَيْنِ مِنْ شَهْرِ رَبِيعٍ الأَوَّلِ، فَقَامَ أَبُو بَكْرٍ لِلنَّاسِ، وَجَلَسَ رَسُولُ اللَّهِ صلى الله عليه وسلم صَامِتًا، فَطَفِقَ مَنْ جَاءَ مِنَ الأَنْصَارِ مِمَّنْ لَمْ يَرَ رَسُولَ اللَّهِ صلى الله عليه وسلم يُحَيِّي أَبَا بَكْرٍ، حَتَّى أَصَابَتِ الشَّمْسُ رَسُولَ اللَّهِ صلى الله عليه وسلم فَأَقْبَلَ أَبُو بَكْرٍ حَتَّى ظَلَّلَ عَلَيْهِ بِرِدَائِهِ، فَعَرَفَ النَّاسُ رَسُولَ اللَّهِ صلى الله عليه وسلم عِنْدَ ذَلِكَ، فَلَبِثَ رَسُولُ اللَّهِ صلى الله عليه وسلم فِي بَنِي عَمْرِو بْنِ عَوْفٍ بِضْعَ عَشْرَةَ لَيْلَةً وَأُسِّسَ الْمَسْجِدُ الَّذِي أُسِّسَ عَلَى التَّقْوَى، وَصَلَّى فِيهِ رَسُولُ اللَّهِ صلى الله عليه وسلم، ثُمَّ رَكِبَ رَاحِلَتَهُ فَسَارَ يَمْشِي مَعَهُ النَّاسُ حَتَّى بَرَكَتْ عِنْدَ مَسْجِدِ الرَّسُولِ صلى الله عليه وسلم بِالْمَدِينَةِ، وَهْوَ يُصَلِّي فِيهِ يَوْمَئِذٍ رِجَالٌ مِنَ الْمُسْلِمِينَ، وَكَانَ مِرْبَدًا لِلتَّمْرِ لِسُهَيْلٍ وَسَهْلٍ غُلاَمَيْنِ يَتِيمَيْنِ فِي حَجْرِ أَسْعَدَ بْنِ

زُرَارَةَ، فَقَالَ رَسُولُ اللَّهِ صلى الله عليه وسلم حِينَ بَرَكَتْ بِهِ رَاحِلَتُهُ " هَذَا إِنْ شَاءَ اللَّهُ الْمَنْزِلُ ". ثُمَّ دَعَا رَسُولُ اللَّهِ صلى الله عليه وسلم الْغُلاَمَيْنِ، فَسَاوَمَهُمَا بِالْمِرْبَدِ لِيَتَّخِذَهُ مَسْجِدًا، فَقَالاَ لاَ بَلْ نَهَبُهُ لَكَ يَا رَسُولَ اللَّهِ، ثُمَّ بَنَاهُ مَسْجِدًا، وَطَفِقَ رَسُولُ اللَّهِ صلى الله عليه وسلم يَنْقُلُ مَعَهُمُ اللَّبِنَ فِي بُنْيَانِهِ، وَيَقُولُ وَهُوَ يَنْقُلُ اللَّبِنَ " هَذَا الْحِمَالُ لاَ حِمَالَ خَيْبَرْ هَذَا أَبَرُّ رَبَّنَا وَأَطْهَرْ ". وَيَقُولُ " اللَّهُمَّ إِنَّ الأَجْرَ أَجْرُ الآخِرَهْ فَارْحَمِ الأَنْصَارَ وَالْمُهَاجِرَهْ ". فَتَمَثَّلَ بِشِعْرِ رَجُلٍ مِنَ الْمُسْلِمِينَ لَمْ يُسَمَّ لِي. قَالَ ابْنُ شِهَابٍ وَلَمْ يَبْلُغْنَا فِي الأَحَادِيثِ أَنَّ رَسُولَ اللَّهِ صلى الله عليه وسلم تَمَثَّلَ بِبَيْتِ شِعْرٍ تَامٍّ غَيْرَ هذه الآيات

Narrated `Amr bin Maimun: `Abdullah bin Mas`ud said, “While Allah’s Messenger ﷺ was praying beside the Ka`ba, there were some Quraish people sitting in a gathering. One of them said, ‘Don’t you see this (who does deeds just to show off)? Who amongst you can go and bring the dung, blood and the Abdominal contents (intestines, etc.) of the slaughtered camels of the family of so and so and then wait till he prostrates and put that in between his shoulders?’ The most unfortunate amongst them (`Uqba bin Abi Mu’ait) went (and brought them) and when Allah’s Messenger ﷺ prostrated, he put them between his shoulders. The Prophet remained in prostration and they laughed so much so that they fell on each other. A passerby went to Fatima, who was a young girl in those days. She came running and the Prophet ﷺ was still in prostration. She removed them and cursed upon the Quraish on their faces. When Allah’s Messenger ﷺ completed his prayer, he said, ‘O Allah! Take revenge on Quraish.’ He said so thrice and added, ‘O Allah! Take revenge on `Amr bin Hisham, `Utba bin Rabi`a, Shaiba bin Rabi`a, Al-Walid bin `Utba, Umaiya bin Khalaf, `Uqba bin Abi Mu’ait and `Umar a bin Al-Walid.” `Abdullah added, “By Allah! I saw all of them dead in the battle field on the day of Badr and they were dragged and thrown in the Qalib (a well) at Badr: Allah’s Messenger ﷺ then said, ‘Allah’s curse has descended upon the people of the Qalib (well). – Sahih Al-Bukhari 520

حَدَّثَنَا أَحْمَدُ بْنُ إِسْحَاقَ السُّرْمَارِيُّ، قَالَ حَدَّثَنَا عُبَيْدُ اللَّهِ بْنُ مُوسَى، قَالَ حَدَّثَنَا إِسْرَائِيلُ، عَنْ أَبِي إِسْحَاقَ، عَنْ عَمْرِو بْنِ مَيْمُونٍ، عَنْ عَبْدِ اللَّهِ، قَالَ بَيْنَمَا رَسُولُ اللَّهِ صلى الله عليه وسلم قَائِمٌ يُصَلِّي عِنْدَ الْكَعْبَةِ، وَجَمْعُ قُرَيْشٍ فِي مَجَالِسِهِمْ إِذْ قَالَ قَائِلٌ مِنْهُمْ أَلاَ تَنْظُرُونَ إِلَى هَذَا الْمُرَائِي أَيُّكُمْ يَقُومُ إِلَى جَزُورِ آلِ فُلاَنٍ، فَيَعْمِدُ إِلَى فَرْثِهَا وَدَمِهَا وَسَلاَهَا فَيَجِيءُ بِهِ، ثُمَّ يُمْهِلُهُ حَتَّى إِذَا سَجَدَ وَضَعَهُ بَيْنَ كَتِفَيْهِ فَانْبَعَثَ أَشْقَاهُمْ، فَلَمَّا سَجَدَ رَسُولُ اللَّهِ صلى الله عليه وسلم وَضَعَهُ بَيْنَ كَتِفَيْهِ، وَثَبَتَ النَّبِيُّ صلى الله عليه وسلم سَاجِدًا، فَضَحِكُوا حَتَّى مَالَ بَعْضُهُمْ إِلَى بَعْضٍ مِنَ الضَّحِكِ، فَانْطَلَقَ مُنْطَلِقٌ إِلَى فَاطِمَةَ ـ عَلَيْهَا السَّلاَمُ ـ وَهْىَ جُوَيْرِيَةٌ، فَأَقْبَلَتْ تَسْعَى وَثَبَتَ النَّبِيُّ صلى الله عليه وسلم سَاجِدًا حَتَّى أَلْقَتْهُ عَنْهُ، وَأَقْبَلَتْ عَلَيْهِمْ تَسُبُّهُمْ، فَلَمَّا قَضَى رَسُولُ اللَّهِ صلى الله عليه وسلم الصَّلاَةَ قَالَ " اللَّهُمَّ عَلَيْكَ بِقُرَيْشٍ، اللَّهُمَّ عَلَيْكَ بِقُرَيْشٍ، اللَّهُمَّ عَلَيْكَ بِقُرَيْشٍ ـ ثُمَّ سَمَّى ـ اللَّهُمَّ عَلَيْكَ بِعَمْرِو بْنِ هِشَامٍ، وَعُتْبَةَ بْنِ رَبِيعَةَ، وَشَيْبَةَ بْنِ رَبِيعَةَ، وَالْوَلِيدِ بْنِ عُتْبَةَ، وَأُمَيَّةَ بْنِ خَلَفٍ، وَعُقْبَةَ بْنِ أَبِي مُعَيْطٍ، وَعُمَارَةَ بْنِ الْوَلِيدِ ". قَالَ عَبْدُ اللَّهِ فَوَاللَّهِ لَقَدْ رَأَيْتُهُمْ صَرْعَى يَوْمَ بَدْرٍ، ثُمَّ سُحِبُوا إِلَى الْقَلِيبِ قَلِيبِ بَدْرٍ، ثُمَّ قَالَ رَسُولُ اللَّهِ صلى الله عليه وسلم " وَأُتْبِعَ أَصْحَابُ الْقَلِيبِ لَعْنَةً ".

Narrated `Abdullah: While Allah’s Messenger ﷺ was prostrating (as stated below). Narrated `Abdullah bin Mas`ud: Once the Prophet ﷺ was offering prayers at the Ka`ba. Abu Jahl was sitting with some of his companions. One of them said to the others, “Who amongst you will bring the Abdominal contents (intestines, etc.) of a camel of Bani so and so and put it on the back of Muhammad, when he prostrates?” The most unfortunate of them got up and brought it. He waited till the Prophet ﷺ prostrated and then placed it on his back between his shoulders. I was watching but could not do any thing. I wish I had some people with me to hold out against them. They started laughing and falling on one another. Allah’s Messenger ﷺ was in prostration and he did not lift his head up till Fatima (Prophet's daughter) came and threw that (camel's Abdominal contents) away from his back. He raised his head and said thrice, “O Allah! Punish Quraish.” So it was hard for Abu Jahl and his companions when the Prophet invoked Allah against them as they had a conviction that the prayers and invocations were accepted in this city (Mecca). The Prophet ﷺ said, “O Allah! Punish Abu Jahl, `Utba bin Rabi`a, Shaiba bin Rabi`a, Al-Walid bin `Utba, Umaiya bin Khalaf, and `Uqba bin Al Mu’it (and he mentioned the seventh whose name I cannot recall). By Allah in Whose Hands my life is, I saw the dead bodies of those persons who were counted by Allah's Messengerﷺ in the Qalib (one of the wells) of Badr. – Al-Bukhari 240

حَدَّثَنَا عَبْدَانُ، قَالَ أَخْبَرَنِي أَبِي، عَنْ شُعْبَةَ، عَنْ أَبِي إِسْحَاقَ، عَنْ عَمْرِو بْنِ مَيْمُونٍ، عَنْ عَبْدِ اللَّهِ، قَالَ بَيْنَا رَسُولُ اللَّهِ صلى الله عليه وسلم سَاجِدٌ ح قَالَ وَحَدَّثَنِي أَحْمَدُ بْنُ عُثْمَانَ قَالَ حَدَّثَنَا شُرَيْحُ بْنُ مَسْلَمَةَ قَالَ حَدَّثَنَا إِبْرَاهِيمُ بْنُ يُوسُفَ عَنْ أَبِيهِ عَنْ أَبِي إِسْحَاقَ قَالَ حَدَّثَنِي عَمْرُو بْنُ مَيْمُونٍ أَنَّ عَبْدَ اللَّهِ بْنَ مَسْعُودٍ حَدَّثَهُ أَنَّ النَّبِيَّ صلى الله عليه وسلم كَانَ يُصَلِّي عِنْدَ الْبَيْتِ، وَأَبُو جَهْلٍ وَأَصْحَابٌ لَهُ جُلُوسٌ، إِذْ قَالَ بَعْضُهُمْ لِبَعْضٍ أَيُّكُمْ يَجِيءُ بِسَلَى جَزُورِ بَنِي فُلاَنٍ فَيَضَعُهُ عَلَى ظَهْرِ مُحَمَّدٍ إِذَا سَجَدَ فَانْبَعَثَ أَشْقَى الْقَوْمِ فَجَاءَ بِهِ، فَنَظَرَ حَتَّى إِذَا سَجَدَ النَّبِيُّ صلى الله عليه وسلم وَضَعَهُ عَلَى ظَهْرِهِ بَيْنَ كَتِفَيْهِ وَأَنَا أَنْظُرُ، لاَ أُغَيِّرُ شَيْئًا، لَوْ كَانَ لِي مَنْعَةٌ. قَالَ فَجَعَلُوا يَضْحَكُونَ وَيُحِيلُ بَعْضُهُمْ عَلَى بَعْضٍ، وَرَسُولُ اللَّهِ صلى الله عليه وسلم سَاجِدٌ لاَ يَرْفَعُ رَأْسَهُ، حَتَّى جَاءَتْهُ فَاطِمَةُ، فَطَرَحَتْ عَنْ ظَهْرِهِ، فَرَفَعَ رَأْسَهُ ثُمَّ قَالَ " اللَّهُمَّ عَلَيْكَ بِقُرَيْشٍ ". ثَلاَثَ مَرَّاتٍ، فَشَقَّ عَلَيْهِمْ إِذْ دَعَا عَلَيْهِمْ ـ قَالَ وَكَانُوا يُرَوْنَ أَنَّ الدَّعْوَةَ فِي ذَلِكَ الْبَلَدِ مُسْتَجَابَةٌ ـ ثُمَّ سَمَّى " اللَّهُمَّ عَلَيْكَ بِأَبِي جَهْلٍ، وَعَلَيْكَ بِعُتْبَةَ بْنِ رَبِيعَةَ، وَشَيْبَةَ بْنِ رَبِيعَةَ، وَالْوَلِيدِ بْنِ عُتْبَةَ، وَأُمَيَّةَ بْنِ خَلَفٍ، وَعُقْبَةَ بْنِ أَبِي مُعَيْطٍ ". وَعَدَّ السَّابِعَ فَلَمْ يَحْفَظْهُ قَالَ فَوَالَّذِي نَفْسِي بِيَدِهِ، لَقَدْ رَأَيْتُ الَّذِينَ عَدَّ رَسُولُ اللَّهِ صلى الله عليه وسلم صَرْعَى فِي الْقَلِيبِ قَلِيبِ بَدْرٍ.

Narrated Jundab bin `Abdullah: Gabriel did not come to the Prophet (for some time) and so one of the Quraish women said, "His Satan has deserted him." So came the Divine Revelation: "By the forenoon And by the night When it is still! Your Lord (O Muhammad) has neither Forsaken you Nor hated you." (93.1-3). – Sahih Al-Bukhari 1125

حَدَّثَنَا مُحَمَّدُ بْنُ كَثِيرٍ، قَالَ أَخْبَرَنَا سُفْيَانُ، عَنِ الأَسْوَدِ بْنِ قَيْسٍ، عَنْ جُنْدَبِ بْنِ عَبْدِ اللَّهِ ـ رضى الله عنه ـ قَالَ احْتَبَسَ جِبْرِيلُ صلى الله عليه وسلم عَلَى النَّبِيِّ صلى الله عليه وسلم فَقَالَتِ امْرَأَةٌ مِنْ قُرَيْشٍ أَبْطَأَ عَلَيْهِ شَيْطَانُهُ. فَنَزَلَتْ {وَالضُّحَى * وَاللَّيْلِ إِذَا سَجَى * مَا وَدَّعَكَ رَبُّكَ وَمَا قَلَى}

Narrated Masruq: One day I went to Ibn Mas`ud who said, "When Quraish delayed in embracing Islam, the Prophetﷺ I invoked Allah to curse them, so they were afflicted with a (famine) year because of which many of them died and they ate the carcasses and Abu Sufyan came to the Prophetﷺ and said, 'O Muhammad! You came to order people to keep good relation with kith and kin and your nation is being destroyed, so invoke Allah I ? So the Prophetﷺ I recited the Holy verses of Sirat-Ad-Dukhan: 'Then watch you For the day that The sky will Bring forth a kind Of smoke Plainly visible.' (44.10) When the famine was taken off, the people renegade once again as nonbelievers. The statement of Allah, (in Sura "Ad-Dukhan"-44) refers to that: 'On the day when We shall seize You with a mighty grasp.' (44.16) And that was what happened on the day of the battle of Badr." Asbath added on the authority of Mansur, "Allah's Messengerﷺ prayed for them and it rained heavily for seven days. So the people complained of the excessive rain. The Prophetﷺ said, 'O Allah! (Let it rain) around us and not on us.' So the clouds dispersed over his head and it rained over the surroundings.". – Sahih Al-Bukhari 1020

حَدَّثَنَا مُحَمَّدُ بْنُ كَثِيرٍ، عَنْ سُفْيَانَ، حَدَّثَنَا مَنْصُورٌ، وَالأَعْمَشُ، عَنْ أَبِي الضُّحَى، عَنْ مَسْرُوقٍ، قَالَ أَتَيْتُ ابْنَ مَسْعُودٍ فَقَالَ إِنَّ قُرَيْشًا أَبْطَئُوا عَنِ الإِسْلاَمِ، فَدَعَا عَلَيْهِمُ النَّبِيُّ صلى الله عليه وسلم فَأَخَذَتْهُمْ سَنَةٌ حَتَّى هَلَكُوا فِيهَا وَأَكَلُوا الْمَيْتَةَ وَالْعِظَامَ، فَجَاءَهُ أَبُو سُفْيَانَ فَقَالَ يَا مُحَمَّدُ، جِئْتَ تَأْمُرُ بِصِلَةِ الرَّحِمِ، وَإِنَّ قَوْمَكَ هَلَكُوا، فَادْعُ اللَّهَ. فَقَرَأَ {فَارْتَقِبْ يَوْمَ تَأْتِي السَّمَاءُ بِدُخَانٍ مُبِينٍ} ثُمَّ عَادُوا إِلَى كُفْرِهِمْ فَذَلِكَ قَوْلُهُ تَعَالَى {يَوْمَ نَبْطِشُ الْبَطْشَةَ الْكُبْرَى} يَوْمَ بَدْرٍ. قَالَ وَزَادَ أَسْبَاطٌ عَنْ مَنْصُورٍ فَدَعَا رَسُولُ اللَّهِ صلى الله عليه وسلم، فَسُقُوا الْغَيْثَ، فَأَطْبَقَتْ عَلَيْهِمْ سَبْعًا، وَشَكَا النَّاسُ كَثْرَةَ الْمَطَرِ فَقَالَ " اللَّهُمَّ حَوَالَيْنَا وَلاَ عَلَيْنَا ". فَانْحَدَرَتِ السَّحَابَةُ عَنْ رَأْسِهِ، فَسُقُوا النَّاسُ حَوْلَهُمْ

Narrated Anas: That the Meccan people requested Allah's Messengerﷺ to show them a miracle, and so he showed them the splitting of the moon. – Sahih Al-Bukhari 3637

حَدَّثَنِي عَبْدُ اللَّهِ بْنُ مُحَمَّدٍ، حَدَّثَنَا يُونُسُ، حَدَّثَنَا شَيْبَانُ، عَنْ قَتَادَةَ، عَنْ أَنَسِ بْنِ مَالِكٍ. وَقَالَ لِي خَلِيفَةُ حَدَّثَنَا يَزِيدُ بْنُ زُرَيْعٍ، حَدَّثَنَا سَعِيدٌ، عَنْ قَتَادَةَ، عَنْ أَنَسِ بْنِ مَالِكٍ ـ رضى الله عنه ـ أَنَّهُ حَدَّثَهُمْ أَنَّ أَهْلَ مَكَّةَ سَأَلُوا رَسُولَ اللَّهِ صلى الله عليه وسلم أَنْ يُرِيَهُمْ آيَةً، فَأَرَاهُمُ انْشِقَاقَ الْقَمَرِ

Narrated `Aisha: I asked the Prophetﷺ about the wall (outside the Ka`ba). "Is it regarded as part of the Ka`ba?" He replied, "Yes." I said, "Then why didn't the people include it in the Ka`ba?" He said, "(Because) your people ran short of money." I asked, "Then why is its gate so high?" He replied, "Your people did so in order to admit to it whom they would and forbid whom they would. Were your people not still close to the period of ignorance, and were I not afraid that their hearts might deny my action, then surely I would include the wall in the Ka`ba and make its gate touch the ground." - Sahih Al-Bukhari 7243
حَدَّثَنَا مُسَدَّدٌ، حَدَّثَنَا أَبُو الأَحْوَصِ، حَدَّثَنَا أَشْعَثُ، عَنِ الأَسْوَدِ بْنِ يَزِيدَ، عَنْ عَائِشَةَ، قَالَتْ سَأَلْتُ النَّبِيَّ صلى الله عليه وسلم عَنِ الْجَدْرِ أَمِنَ الْبَيْتِ هُوَ قَالَ " نَعَمْ ". قُلْتُ فَمَا لَهُمْ لَمْ يُدْخِلُوهُ فِي الْبَيْتِ قَالَ " إِنَّ قَوْمَكِ قَصَّرَتْ بِهِمُ النَّفَقَةُ ". قُلْتُ فَمَا شَأْنُ بَابِهِ مُرْتَفِعًا قَالَ " فَعَلَ ذَاكِ قَوْمُكِ، لِيُدْخِلُوا مَنْ شَاءُوا، وَيَمْنَعُوا مَنْ شَاءُوا، لَوْلاَ أَنَّ قَوْمَكِ حَدِيثٌ عَهْدُهُمْ بِالْجَاهِلِيَّةِ، فَأَخَافُ أَنْ تُنْكِرَ قُلُوبُهُمْ أَنْ أُدْخِلَ الْجَدْرَ فِي الْبَيْتِ، وَأَنْ أُلْصِقَ بَابَهُ فِي الأَرْضِ "

Narrated `Amr bin Dinar and 'Ubaidullah bin Abi Yazid: In the lifetime of the Prophet (ﷺ) there was no wall around the Ka`ba and the people used to pray around the Ka`ba till `Umar became the Caliph and he built the wall around it. 'Ubaidullah further said, "Its wall was low, so Ibn Az-Zubair built it – ".Sahih al-Bukhari 3830
حَدَّثَنَا أَبُو النُّعْمَانِ، حَدَّثَنَا حَمَّادُ بْنُ زَيْدٍ، عَنْ عَمْرِو بْنِ دِينَارٍ، وَعُبَيْدِ اللَّهِ بْنِ أَبِي يَزِيدَ، قَالاَ لَمْ يَكُنْ عَلَى عَهْدِ النَّبِيِّ صلى الله عليه وسلم حَوْلَ الْبَيْتِ حَائِطٌ، كَانُوا يُصَلُّونَ حَوْلَ الْبَيْتِ، حَتَّى كَانَ عُمَرُ، فَبَنَى حَوْلَهُ حَائِطًا ـ قَالَ عُبَيْدُ اللَّهِ ـ جَدْرُهُ قَصِيرٌ، فَبَنَاهُ ابْنُ الزُّبَيْرِ.

Narrated Aswad: Ibn Az-Zubair said to me, "Aisha used to tell you secretly a number of things. What did she tell you about the Ka`ba?" I replied, "She told me that once the Prophetﷺ said, 'O `Aisha! Had not your people been still close to the pre-Islamic period of ignorance (infidelity)! I would have dismantled the Ka`ba and would have made two doors in it; one for entrance and the other for exit." Later on Ibn Az-Zubair did the same. – Sahih Al-Bukhari 126
حَدَّثَنَا عُبَيْدُ اللَّهِ بْنُ مُوسَى، عَنْ إِسْرَائِيلَ، عَنْ أَبِي إِسْحَاقَ، عَنِ الأَسْوَدِ، قَالَ قَالَ لِي ابْنُ الزُّبَيْرِ كَانَتْ عَائِشَةُ تُسِرُّ إِلَيْكَ كَثِيرًا فَمَا حَدَّثَتْكَ فِي الْكَعْبَةِ قُلْتُ قَالَتْ لِي قَالَ النَّبِيُّ صلى الله عليه وسلم " يَا عَائِشَةُ، لَوْلاَ قَوْمُكِ حَدِيثٌ عَهْدُهُمْ ـ قَالَ ابْنُ الزُّبَيْرِ بِكُفْرٍ ـ لَنَقَضْتُ الْكَعْبَةَ فَجَعَلْتُ لَهَا بَابَيْنِ باب يَدْخُلُ النَّاسُ، وَبَابٌ يَخْرُجُونَ ". فَفَعَلَهُ ابْنُ الزُّبَيْرِ.

Narrated `Abdullah bin `Umar: While `Umar was at home in a state of fear, there came Al-`As bin Wail As-Sahmi Abu `Amr, wearing an embroidered cloak and a shirt having silk hems. He was from the tribe of Bani Sahm who were our allies during the pre-Islamic period of ignorance. Al-`As said to `Umar "What is wrong with you?" He said, "Your people claim that they would kill me if I become a Muslim." Al-`As said, "Nobody will harm you after I have given protection to you." So Al-`As went out and met the people streaming in the whole valley. He said, "Where are you going?" They said, "We want Ibn Al-Khattab who has embraced Islam." Al-`As said, "There is no way for anybody to touch him." So the people retreated. – Sahih Al-Bukhari 3864
حَدَّثَنَا يَحْيَى بْنُ سُلَيْمَانَ، قَالَ حَدَّثَنِي ابْنُ وَهْبٍ، قَالَ حَدَّثَنِي عُمَرُ بْنُ مُحَمَّدٍ، قَالَ فَأَخْبَرَنِي جَدِّي، زَيْدُ بْنُ عَبْدِ اللَّهِ بْنِ عُمَرَ عَنْ أَبِيهِ، قَالَ بَيْنَمَا هُوَ فِي الدَّارِ خَائِفًا، إِذْ جَاءَهُ الْعَاصِ بْنُ وَائِلٍ السَّهْمِيُّ أَبُو عَمْرٍو، عَلَيْهِ حُلَّةُ حِبَرَةٍ، وَقَمِيصٌ مَكْفُوفٌ بِحَرِيرٍ، وَهُوَ مِنْ بَنِي سَهْمٍ، وَهُمْ حُلَفَاؤُنَا فِي الْجَاهِلِيَّةِ فَقَالَ لَهُ مَا بَالُكَ قَالَ زَعَمَ قَوْمُكَ أَنَّهُمْ سَيَقْتُلُونِي إِنْ أَسْلَمْتُ. قَالَ لاَ سَبِيلَ إِلَيْكَ. بَعْدَ أَنْ قَالَهَا أَمِنْتُ، فَخَرَجَ الْعَاصِ، فَلَقِيَ النَّاسَ قَدْ سَالَ بِهِمُ الْوَادِي فَقَالَ أَيْنَ تُرِيدُونَ فَقَالُوا نُرِيدُ هَذَا ابْنَ الْخَطَّابِ الَّذِي صَبَا. قَالَ لاَ سَبِيلَ إِلَيْهِ. فَكَرَّ النَّاسُ.

Narrated `Abdullah bin `Umar: `Umar bin Al-Khattab saw a silken cloak (being sold) at the gate of the Mosque and said to Allah's Apostle, "I wish you would buy this to wear on Fridays and also on occasions of the arrivals of the delegations." Allah's Messengerﷺ replied, "This will be worn by a person who will have no share (reward) in the Hereafter." Later on similar cloaks were given to Allah's Messenger ﷺ and he gave one of them to `Umar bin Al-Khattab. On that `Umar said, "O Allah's Messenger ﷺ ! You have given me this cloak although on the cloak of Atarid (a cloak merchant who was selling that silken cloak at the gate of the mosque) you passed such and such a remark." Allah's Messenger ﷺ replied, "I have not given you this to wear". And so `Umar bin Al-Khattab gave it to his pagan brother in Mecca to wear. – Sahih Al-Bukhari 886

حَدَّثَنَا عَبْدُ اللَّهِ بْنُ يُوسُفَ، قَالَ أَخْبَرَنَا مَالِكٌ، عَنْ نَافِعٍ، عَنْ عَبْدِ اللَّهِ بْنِ عُمَرَ، أَنَّ عُمَرَ بْنَ الْخَطَّابِ، رَأَى حُلَّةَ سِيَرَاءَ عِنْدَ بَابِ الْمَسْجِدِ فَقَالَ يَا رَسُولَ اللَّهِ، لَوِ اشْتَرَيْتَ هَذِهِ فَلَبِسْتَهَا يَوْمَ الْجُمُعَةِ وَلِلْوَفْدِ إِذَا قَدِمُوا عَلَيْكَ. فَقَالَ رَسُولُ اللَّهِ صلى الله عليه وسلم " إِنَّمَا يَلْبَسُ هَذِهِ مَنْ لاَ خَلاَقَ لَهُ فِي الآخِرَةِ ". ثُمَّ جَاءَتْ رَسُولَ اللَّهِ صلى الله عليه وسلم مِنْهَا حُلَلٌ، فَأَعْطَى عُمَرَ بْنَ الْخَطَّابِ ـ رضى الله عنه ـ مِنْهَا حُلَّةً فَقَالَ عُمَرُ يَا رَسُولَ اللَّهِ، كَسَوْتَنِيهَا وَقَدْ قُلْتَ فِي حُلَّةِ عُطَارِدٍ مَا قُلْتَ قَالَ رَسُولُ اللَّهِ صلى الله عليه وسلم " إِنِّي لَمْ أَكْسُكَهَا لِتَلْبَسَهَا ". فَكَسَاهَا عُمَرُ بْنُ الْخَطَّابِ ـ رضى الله عنه ـ أَخًا لَهُ بِمَكَّةَ مُشْرِكًا

Narrated `Amr bin Taghlib: Some property or something was brought to Allah's Messenger ﷺ and he distributed it. He gave to some men and ignored the others. Later he got the news of his being admonished by those whom he had ignored. So he glorified and praised Allah and said, "Amma ba'du. By Allah, I may give to a man and ignore another, although the one whom I ignore is more beloved to me than the one whom I give. But I give to some people as I feel that they have no patience and no contentment in their hearts and I leave those who are patient and self-content with the goodness and wealth which Allah has put into their hearts and `Amr bin Taghlib is one of them." `Amr added, By Allah! Those words of Allah's Apostle are more beloved to me than the best red camels. – Sahih Al-Bukhari 923. [14]

حَدَّثَنَا مُحَمَّدُ بْنُ مَعْمَرٍ، قَالَ حَدَّثَنَا أَبُو عَاصِمٍ، عَنْ جَرِيرِ بْنِ حَازِمٍ، قَالَ سَمِعْتُ الْحَسَنَ، يَقُولُ حَدَّثَنَا عَمْرُو بْنُ تَغْلِبَ، أَنَّ رَسُولَ اللَّهِ صلى الله عليه وسلم أُتِيَ بِمَالٍ أَوْ سَبْىٍ فَقَسَمَهُ، فَأَعْطَى رِجَالاً وَتَرَكَ رِجَالاً فَبَلَغَهُ أَنَّ الَّذِينَ تَرَكَ عَتَبُوا، فَحَمِدَ اللَّهَ ثُمَّ أَثْنَى عَلَيْهِ، ثُمَّ قَالَ " أَمَّا بَعْدُ، فَوَاللَّهِ إِنِّي لأُعْطِي الرَّجُلَ، وَأَدَعُ الرَّجُلَ، وَالَّذِي أَدَعُ أَحَبُّ إِلَىَّ مِنَ الَّذِي أُعْطِي وَلَكِنْ أُعْطِي أَقْوَامًا لِمَا أَرَى فِي قُلُوبِهِمْ مِنَ الْجَزَعِ وَالْهَلَعِ، وَأَكِلُ أَقْوَامًا إِلَى مَا جَعَلَ اللَّهُ فِي قُلُوبِهِمْ مِنَ الْغِنَى وَالْخَيْرِ، فِيهِمْ عَمْرُو بْنُ تَغْلِبَ ". فَوَاللَّهِ مَا أُحِبُّ أَنَّ لِي بِكَلِمَةِ رَسُولِ اللَّهِ صلى الله عليه وسلم حُمْرَ النَّعَمِ. تَابَعَهُ يُونُسُ

Narrated `Aisha: The Quraish people became very worried about the Makhzumiya lady who had committed theft. They said, "Nobody can speak (in favor of the lady) to Allah's Messenger ﷺ and nobody dares do that except Usama who is the favorite of Allah's Messenger ﷺ". When Usama spoke to Allah's Messenger ﷺ about that matter, Allah's Messenger ﷺ said, "Do you intercede (with me) to violate one of the legal punishment of Allah?" Then he got up and addressed the people, saying, "O people! The nations before you went astray because if a noble person committed theft, they used to leave him, but if a weak person among them committed theft, they used to inflict the legal punishment on him. By Allah, if Fatima, the daughter of Muhammad committed theft, Muhammad will cut off her hand.!". – Sahih Al-Bukhari 6788

حَدَّثَنَا سَعِيدُ بْنُ سُلَيْمَانَ، حَدَّثَنَا اللَّيْثُ، عَنِ ابْنِ شِهَابٍ، عَنْ عُرْوَةَ، عَنْ عَائِشَةَ ـ رضى الله عنها أَنَّ قُرَيْشًا، أَهَمَّتْهُمُ الْمَرْأَةُ الْمَخْزُومِيَّةُ الَّتِي سَرَقَتْ فَقَالُوا مَنْ يُكَلِّمُ رَسُولَ اللَّهِ صلى الله عليه وسلم وَمَنْ يَجْتَرِئُ عَلَيْهِ إِلاَّ أُسَامَةُ حِبُّ رَسُولِ اللَّهِ صلى الله عليه وسلم. فَكَلَّمَ رَسُولَ اللَّهِ صلى الله عليه وسلم فَقَالَ " أَتَشْفَعُ فِي حَدٍّ مِنْ حُدُودِ اللَّهِ ". ثُمَّ قَامَ فَخَطَبَ قَالَ " يَا أَيُّهَا النَّاسُ إِنَّمَا ضَلَّ مَنْ قَبْلَكُمْ أَنَّهُمْ كَانُوا إِذَا سَرَقَ الشَّرِيفُ تَرَكُوهُ، وَإِذَا سَرَقَ الضَّعِيفُ فِيهِمْ أَقَامُوا عَلَيْهِ الْحَدَّ، وَايْمُ اللَّهِ لَوْ أَنَّ فَاطِمَةَ بِنْتَ مُحَمَّدٍ سَرَقَتْ لَقَطَعَ مُحَمَّدٌ يَدَهَا "

Narrated Al-Miswar bin Makhrama: `Ali demanded the hand of the daughter of Abu Jahl. Fatima heard of this and went to Allah's Messenger ﷺ saying, "Your people think that you do

---

[14] Refers to the distribution of battle Hunain with the Quraish and Ansar

not become angry for the sake of your daughters as `Ali is now going to marry the daughter of Abu Jahl. "On that Allah's Messenger ﷺ got up and after his recitation of Tashah-hud. I heard him saying, "Then after! I married one of my daughters to Abu Al-`As bin Al- Rabi` (the husband of Zainab, the daughter of the Prophet ﷺ) before Islam and he proved truthful in whatever he said to me. No doubt, Fatima is a part of me, I hate to see her being troubled. By Allah, the daughter of Allah's Messenger ﷺ and the daughter of Allah's Enemy cannot be the wives of one man." So `Ali gave up that engagement. 'Al-Miswar further said: I heard the Prophet ﷺ talking and he mentioned a son-in-law of his belonging to the tribe of Bani `Abd-Shams. He highly praised him concerning that relationship and said (whenever) he spoke to me, he spoke the truth, and whenever he promised me, he fulfilled his promise.". – Sahih Al-Bukhari 3729

حَدَّثَنَا أَبُو الْيَمَانِ، أَخْبَرَنَا شُعَيْبٌ، عَنِ الزُّهْرِيِّ، قَالَ حَدَّثَنِي عَلِيُّ بْنُ حُسَيْنٍ، أَنَّ الْمِسْوَرَ بْنَ مَخْرَمَةَ، قَالَ إِنَّ عَلِيًّا خَطَبَ بِنْتَ أَبِي جَهْلٍ، فَسَمِعَتْ بِذَلِكَ، فَاطِمَةُ، فَأَتَتْ رَسُولَ اللَّهِ صلى الله عليه وسلم فَقَالَتْ يَزْعُمُ قَوْمُكَ أَنَّكَ لاَ تَغْضَبُ لِبَنَاتِكَ، هَذَا عَلِيٌّ نَاكِحٌ بِنْتَ أَبِي جَهْلٍ، فَقَامَ رَسُولُ اللَّهِ صلى الله عليه وسلم فَسَمِعْتُهُ حِينَ تَشَهَّدَ يَقُولُ " أَمَّا بَعْدُ أَنْكَحْتُ أَبَا الْعَاصِ بْنَ الرَّبِيعِ، فَحَدَّثَنِي وَصَدَقَنِي، وَإِنَّ فَاطِمَةَ بَضْعَةٌ مِنِّي، وَإِنِّي أَكْرَهُ أَنْ يَسُوءَهَا، وَاللَّهِ لاَ تَجْتَمِعُ بِنْتُ رَسُولِ اللَّهِ صلى الله عليه وسلم وَبِنْتُ عَدُوِّ اللَّهِ عِنْدَ رَجُلٍ وَاحِدٍ ". فَتَرَكَ عَلِيٌّ الْخِطْبَةَ. وَزَادَ مُحَمَّدُ بْنُ عَمْرِو بْنِ حَلْحَلَةَ عَنِ ابْنِ شِهَابٍ عَنْ عَلِيٍّ عَنْ مِسْوَرٍ، سَمِعْتُ النَّبِيَّ صلى الله عليه وسلم وَذَكَرَ صِهْرًا لَهُ مِنْ بَنِي عَبْدِ شَمْسٍ فَأَثْنَى عَلَيْهِ فِي مُصَاهَرَتِهِ إِيَّاهُ فَأَحْسَنَ قَالَ " حَدَّثَنِي فَصَدَقَنِي، وَوَعَدَنِي فَوَفَى لِي ".

Narrated Al-Ahnaf bin Qais: While I was sitting with some people from Quraish, a man with very rough hair, clothes, and appearance came and stood in front of us, greeted us and said, "Inform those who hoard wealth, that a stone will be heated in the Hell-fire and will be put on the nipples of their breasts till it comes out from the bones of their shoulders and then put on the bones of their shoulders till it comes through the nipples of their breasts the stone will be moving and hitting." After saying that, the person retreated and sat by the side of the pillar, I followed him and sat beside him, and I did not know who he was. I said to him, "I think the people disliked what you had said." He said, "These people do not understand anything, although my friend told me." I asked, "Who is your friend?" He said, "The Prophet ﷺ said (to me), 'O Abu Dhar! Do you see the mountain of Uhud?' And on that I (Abu Dhar) started looking towards the sun to judge how much remained of the day as I thought that Allah's Messenger ﷺ wanted to send me to do something for him and I said, 'Yes!' He said, 'I do not love to have gold equal to the mountain of Uhud unless I spend it all (in Allah's cause) except three Dinars (pounds). These people do not understand and collect worldly wealth. No, by Allah, Neither I ask them for worldly benefits nor am I in need of their religious advice till I meet Allah, The Honorable, The Majestic.' " – Sahih Al-Bukhari 1407, 1408

حَدَّثَنَا عَيَّاشٌ، حَدَّثَنَا عَبْدُ الأَعْلَى، حَدَّثَنَا الْجُرَيْرِيُّ، عَنْ أَبِي الْعَلاَءِ، عَنِ الأَحْنَفِ بْنِ قَيْسٍ، قَالَ جَلَسْتُ. وَحَدَّثَنِي إِسْحَاقُ بْنُ مَنْصُورٍ، أَخْبَرَنَا عَبْدُ الصَّمَدِ، قَالَ حَدَّثَنِي أَبِي، حَدَّثَنَا الْجُرَيْرِيُّ، حَدَّثَنَا أَبُو الْعَلاَءِ بْنُ الشِّخِّيرِ، أَنَّ الأَحْنَفَ بْنَ قَيْسٍ، حَدَّثَهُمْ قَالَ جَلَسْتُ إِلَى مَلإٍ مِنْ قُرَيْشٍ، فَجَاءَ رَجُلٌ خَشِنُ الشَّعَرِ وَالثِّيَابِ وَالْهَيْئَةِ حَتَّى قَامَ عَلَيْهِمْ فَسَلَّمَ ثُمَّ قَالَ بَشِّرِ الْكَانِزِينَ بِرَضْفٍ يُحْمَى عَلَيْهِ فِي نَارِ جَهَنَّمَ، ثُمَّ يُوضَعُ عَلَى حَلَمَةِ ثَدْىِ أَحَدِهِمْ حَتَّى يَخْرُجَ مِنْ نُغْضِ كَتِفِهِ، وَيُوضَعُ عَلَى نُغْضِ كَتِفِهِ حَتَّى يَخْرُجَ مِنْ حَلَمَةِ ثَدْيِهِ يَتَزَلْزَلُ، ثُمَّ وَلَّى فَجَلَسَ إِلَى سَارِيَةٍ، وَتَبِعْتُهُ وَجَلَسْتُ إِلَيْهِ، وَأَنَا لاَ أَدْرِي مَنْ هُوَ فَقُلْتُ لَهُ لاَ أُرَى الْقَوْمَ إِلاَّ قَدْ كَرِهُوا الَّذِي قُلْتَ. قَالَ إِنَّهُمْ لاَ يَعْقِلُونَ شَيْئًا. قَالَ لِي خَلِيلِي ـ قَالَ قُلْتُ مَنْ خَلِيلُكَ قَالَ النَّبِيُّ صلى الله عليه وسلم ـ " يَا أَبَا ذَرٍّ أَتُبْصِرُ أُحُدًا ". قَالَ فَنَظَرْتُ إِلَى الشَّمْسِ مَا بَقِيَ مِنَ النَّهَارِ وَأَنَا أُرَى أَنَّ رَسُولَ اللَّهِ صلى الله عليه وسلم يُرْسِلُنِي فِي حَاجَةٍ لَهُ، قُلْتُ نَعَمْ. قَالَ " مَا أُحِبُّ أَنَّ لِي مِثْلَ أُحُدٍ ذَهَبًا أُنْفِقُهُ كُلَّهُ إِلاَّ ثَلاَثَةَ دَنَانِيرَ ". وَإِنَّ هَؤُلاَءِ لاَ يَعْقِلُونَ، إِنَّمَا يَجْمَعُونَ الدُّنْيَا. لاَ وَاللَّهِ لاَ أَسْأَلُهُمْ دُنْيَا، وَلاَ أَسْتَفْتِيهِمْ عَنْ دِينٍ حَتَّى أَلْقَى اللَّهَ.

Narrated Sa`d: I was one of (the first) seven (who had embraced Islam) with Allah's Messenger ﷺ and we had nothing to eat then, except the leaves of the Habala or Hubula tree, so that our stool used to be similar to that of sheep. Now the tribe of Bani Asad wants to teach me Islam; I would be a loser and all my efforts would be in vain (if I learn Islam anew from them). – Sahih Al-Bukhari 5412

حَدَّثَنَا عَبْدُ اللَّهِ بْنُ مُحَمَّدٍ، حَدَّثَنَا وَهْبُ بْنُ جَرِيرٍ، حَدَّثَنَا شُعْبَةُ، عَنْ إِسْمَاعِيلَ، عَنْ قَيْسٍ، عَنْ سَعْدٍ، قَالَ رَأَيْتُنِي سَابِعَ سَبْعَةٍ مَعَ النَّبِيِّ صلى الله عليه وسلم مَا لَنَا طَعَامٌ إِلاَّ وَرَقُ الْحُبْلَةِ ـ أَوِ الْحَبَلَةِ ـ حَتَّى يَضَعَ أَحَدُنَا مَا تَضَعُ الشَّاةُ، ثُمَّ أَصْبَحَتْ بَنُو أَسَدٍ تُعَزِّرُنِي عَلَى الإِسْلاَمِ، خَسِرْتُ إِذًا وَضَلَّ سَعْيِي

Narrated `Abdullah: Two person of Bani Thaqif and one from Quarish (or two persons from Quraish and one from Bani Thaqif) who had fat bellies but little wisdom, met near the Ka`ba. One of them said, "Did you see that Allah hears what we say?" The other said, "He hears us if we speak aloud, but He does not hear if we speak in stealthy quietness (softly)." The third fellow said, "If He hears when we speak aloud, then He surely hears us if we speak in stealthy quietness (softly)." So Allah revealed the Verse:-- 'And you have not been screening against yourselves, lest your ears, and your eyes and your skins should testify against you..." (41.22). – Al-Bukhari 7521

حَدَّثَنَا الْحُمَيْدِيُّ، حَدَّثَنَا سُفْيَانُ، حَدَّثَنَا مَنْصُورٌ، عَنْ مُجَاهِدٍ، عَنْ أَبِي مَعْمَرٍ، عَنْ عَبْدِ اللَّهِ ـ رضى الله عنه ـ قَالَ اجْتَمَعَ عِنْدَ الْبَيْتِ ثَقَفِيَّانِ وَقُرَشِيٌّ، أَوْ قُرَشِيَّانِ وَثَقَفِيٌّ، كَثِيرَةٌ شَحْمُ بُطُونِهِمْ قَلِيلَةٌ فِقْهُ قُلُوبِهِمْ فَقَالَ أَحَدُهُمْ أَتَرَوْنَ أَنَّ اللَّهَ يَسْمَعُ مَا نَقُولُ قَالَ الآخَرُ يَسْمَعُ إِنْ جَهَرْنَا وَلاَ يَسْمَعُ إِنْ أَخْفَيْنَا وَقَالَ الآخَرُ إِنْ كَانَ يَسْمَعُ إِذَا جَهَرْنَا فَإِنَّهُ يَسْمَعُ إِذَا أَخْفَيْنَا. فَأَنْزَلَ اللَّهُ تَعَالَى {وَمَا كُنْتُمْ تَسْتَتِرُونَ أَنْ يَشْهَدَ عَلَيْكُمْ سَمْعُكُمْ وَلاَ أَبْصَارُكُمْ وَلاَ جُلُودُكُمْ} الآيَةَ

Narrated Ibn `Abbas: The first event of Qasama in the pre-Islamic period of ignorance was practiced by us (i.e. Banu Hashim). A man from Banu Hashim was employed by a Quraishi man from another branch-family. The (Hashimi) laborer set out with the Quraishi driving his camels. There passed by him another man from Banu Hashim. The leather rope of the latter's bag had broken so he said to the laborer, "Will you help me by giving me a rope in order to tie the handle of my bag lest the camels should run away from me?" The laborer gave him a rope and the latter tied his bag with it. When the caravan halted, all the camels' legs were tied with their fetters except one camel. The employer asked the laborer, "Why, from among all the camels has this camel not been fettered?" He replied, "There is no fetter for it." The Quraishi asked, "Where is its fetter?" and hit the laborer with a stick that caused his death (later on Just before his death) a man from Yemen passed by him. The laborer asked (him), "Will you go for the pilgrimage?" He replied, "I do not think I will attend it, but perhaps I will attend it." The (Hashimi) laborer said, "Will you please convey a message for me once in your life?" The other man said, "yes." The laborer wrote: 'When you attend the pilgrimage, call the family of Quraish, and if they respond to you, call the family of Banu Hashim, and if they respond to you, ask about Abu Talib and tell him that so-and-so has killed me for a fetter." Then the laborer expired. When the employer reached (Mecca), Abu Talib visited him and asked, "What has happened to our companion?" He said, "He became ill and I looked after him nicely (but he died) and I buried him." Then Abu Talib said, "The deceased deserved this from you." After some time, the messenger whom the laborer has asked to convey the message, reached during the pilgrimage season. He called, "O the family of Quraish!" The people replied, "This is Quraish." Then he called, "O the family of Banu Hashim!" Again the people replied, "This is Banu Hashim." He asked, "Who is Abu Talib?" The people replied, "This is Abu Talib." He said, "'So-and-so has asked me to convey a message to you that so-and-so has killed him for a fetter (of a camel)." Then Abu Talib went to the (Quraishi) killer and said to him, "Choose one of three alternatives: (i) If you wish, give us one-hundred camels because you have murdered our companion, (ii) or if you wish, fifty of your men should take an oath that you have not murdered our companion, and if you do not accept this, (iii) we will kill you in Qisas." The killer went to his people and they said, "We will take an oath." Then a woman from Banu Hashim who was married to one of them (i.e.the Quraishis) and had given birth to a child from him, came to Abu Talib and said, "O Abu Talib! I wish that my son from among the fifty men, should be excused from this oath, and that he should not take the oath where the oathtaking is carried on." Abu Talib excused him. Then another man from them came (to Abu Talib) and said, "O Abu Talib! You want fifty persons to take an oath instead of giving a hundred camels, and that means each man has to give two camels (in case he does not take an oath). So there are two camels I would like you to accept from me and excuse me from taking an oath where the oaths are taken. Abu Talib accepted them from him. Then 48 men came and took the oath. Ibn `Abbas further said By Him in Whose Hand my life is, before the end of that year, none of those 48 persons remained alive. – Sahih Al-Bukhari 3845

حَدَّثَنَا أَبُو مَعْمَرٍ، حَدَّثَنَا عَبْدُ الْوَارِثِ، حَدَّثَنَا قَطَنٌ أَبُو الْهَيْثَمِ، حَدَّثَنَا أَبُو يَزِيدَ الْمَدَنِيُّ، عَنْ عِكْرِمَةَ، عَنِ ابْنِ عَبَّاسٍ ـ رضى الله عنهما ـ قَالَ إِنَّ أَوَّلَ قَسَامَةٍ كَانَتْ فِي الْجَاهِلِيَّةِ لَفِينَا بَنِي هَاشِمٍ، كَانَ رَجُلٌ مِنْ بَنِي هَاشِمٍ اسْتَأْجَرَهُ رَجُلٌ مِنْ قُرَيْشٍ مِنْ فَخِذٍ أُخْرَى، فَانْطَلَقَ مَعَهُ فِي إِبِلِهِ، فَمَرَّ رَجُلٌ بِهِ مِنْ بَنِي هَاشِمٍ قَدِ انْقَطَعَتْ عُرْوَةُ جُوَالِقِهِ فَقَالَ أَغِثْنِي بِعِقَالٍ أَشُدُّ بِهِ عُرْوَةَ جُوَالِقِي، لاَ تَنْفِرُ الإِبِلُ. فَأَعْطَاهُ عِقَالاً، فَشَدَّ بِهِ عُرْوَةَ جُوَالِقِهِ، فَلَمَّا نَزَلُوا عُقِلَتِ الإِبِلُ إِلاَّ بَعِيرًا وَاحِدًا، فَقَالَ الَّذِي اسْتَأْجَرَهُ مَا شَأْنُ هَذَا الْبَعِيرِ لَمْ يُعْقَلْ مِنْ بَيْنِ الإِبِلِ قَالَ لَيْسَ لَهُ عِقَالٌ. قَالَ فَأَيْنَ عِقَالُهُ قَالَ فَحَذَفَهُ بِعَصًا كَانَ فِيهَا أَجَلُهُ، فَمَرَّ بِهِ رَجُلٌ مِنْ أَهْلِ الْيَمَنِ، فَقَالَ أَتَشْهَدُ الْمَوْسِمَ قَالَ مَا أَشْهَدُ، وَرُبَّمَا شَهِدْتُهُ. قَالَ هَلْ أَنْتَ مُبْلِغٌ عَنِّي رِسَالَةً مَرَّةً مِنَ الدَّهْرِ قَالَ نَعَمْ. قَالَ فَكُنْتَ إِذَا أَنْتَ شَهِدْتَ الْمَوْسِمَ فَنَادِ يَا آلَ قُرَيْشٍ. فَإِذَا أَجَابُوكَ، فَنَادِ يَا آلَ بَنِي هَاشِمٍ. فَإِنْ أَجَابُوكَ فَسَلْ عَنْ أَبِي طَالِبٍ، فَأَخْبِرْهُ أَنَّ فُلاَنًا قَتَلَنِي فِي عِقَالٍ، وَمَاتَ الْمُسْتَأْجَرُ، فَلَمَّا قَدِمَ الَّذِي اسْتَأْجَرَهُ أَتَاهُ أَبُو طَالِبٍ فَقَالَ مَا فَعَلَ صَاحِبُنَا قَالَ مَرِضَ، فَأَحْسَنْتُ الْقِيَامَ عَلَيْهِ، فَوَلِيتُ دَفْنَهُ. قَالَ قَدْ كَانَ أَهْلَ ذَاكَ مِنْكَ. فَمَكُثَ حِينًا، ثُمَّ إِنَّ الرَّجُلَ الَّذِي أَوْصَى إِلَيْهِ أَنْ يُبْلِغَ عَنْهُ وَافَى الْمَوْسِمَ فَقَالَ يَا آلَ قُرَيْشٍ. قَالُوا هَذِهِ قُرَيْشٌ. قَالَ يَا آلَ بَنِي هَاشِمٍ. قَالُوا هَذِهِ بَنُو هَاشِمٍ. قَالَ أَيْنَ أَبُو طَالِبٍ قَالُوا هَذَا أَبُو طَالِبٍ. قَالَ أَمَرَنِي فُلاَنٌ أَنْ أُبْلِغَكَ رِسَالَةً أَنَّ فُلاَنًا قَتَلَهُ فِي عِقَالٍ. فَأَتَاهُ أَبُو طَالِبٍ فَقَالَ لَهُ اخْتَرْ مِنَّا إِحْدَى ثَلاَثٍ، إِنْ شِئْتَ أَنْ تُؤَدِّيَ مِائَةً مِنَ الإِبِلِ، فَإِنَّكَ قَتَلْتَ صَاحِبَنَا، وَإِنْ شِئْتَ حَلَفَ خَمْسُونَ مِنْ قَوْمِكَ أَنَّكَ لَمْ تَقْتُلْهُ، فَإِنْ أَبَيْتَ قَتَلْنَاكَ بِهِ فَأَتَى قَوْمَهُ، فَقَالُوا نَحْلِفُ. فَأَتَتْهُ امْرَأَةٌ مِنْ بَنِي هَاشِمٍ كَانَتْ تَحْتَ رَجُلٍ مِنْهُمْ قَدْ وَلَدَتْ لَهُ. فَقَالَتْ يَا أَبَا طَالِبٍ أُحِبُّ أَنْ تُجِيزَ ابْنِي هَذَا بِرَجُلٍ مِنَ الْخَمْسِينَ وَلاَ تَصْبُرْ يَمِينَهُ حَيْثُ تُصْبَرُ الأَيْمَانُ. فَفَعَلَ فَأَتَاهُ رَجُلٌ مِنْهُمْ فَقَالَ يَا أَبَا طَالِبٍ، أَرَدْتَ خَمْسِينَ رَجُلاً أَنْ يَحْلِفُوا مَكَانَ مِائَةٍ مِنَ الإِبِلِ، يُصِيبُ كُلَّ رَجُلٍ بَعِيرَانِ، هَذَانِ بَعِيرَانِ فَاقْبَلْهُمَا عَنِّي وَلاَ تَصْبُرْ يَمِينِي حَيْثُ تُصْبَرُ الأَيْمَانُ. فَقَبِلَهُمَا، وَجَاءَ ثَمَانِيَةٌ وَأَرْبَعُونَ فَحَلَفُوا. قَالَ ابْنُ عَبَّاسٍ فَوَالَّذِي نَفْسِي بِيَدِهِ، مَا حَالَ الْحَوْلُ وَمِنَ الثَّمَانِيَةِ وَأَرْبَعِينَ عَيْنٌ تَطْرِفُ.

And they exclaimed, "If only this Quran was revealed to a great man from ⌜one of⌝ the two cities!" – Surah Az-Zukhruf 43:31 [15]

وَقَالُوا۟ لَوْلَا نُزِّلَ هَـٰذَا ٱلْقُرْءَانُ عَلَىٰ رَجُلٍ مِّنَ ٱلْقَرْيَتَيْنِ عَظِيمٍ

Narrated Al-Bara bin Azib: The Prophet ﷺ appointed `Abdullah bin Jubair as the commander of the infantry men (archers) who were fifty on the day (of the battle) of Uhud. He instructed them, "Stick to your place, and don't leave it even if you see birds snatching us, till I send for you; and if you see that we have defeated the infidels and made them flee, even then you should not leave your place till I send for you." Then the infidels were defeated. By Allah, I saw the women fleeing lifting up their clothes revealing their leg-bangles and their legs. So, the companions of `Abdullah bin Jubair said, "The booty! O people, the booty ! Your companions have become victorious, what are you waiting for now?" `Abdullah bin Jubair said, "Have you forgotten what Allah's Messenger ﷺ said to you?" They replied, "By Allah! We will go to the people (i.e. the enemy) and collect our share from the war booty." But when

---

[15] The arrogant desires of pagan Quraish. Many of our best scholars are from other lands. Tabari from Iran , Muslim from Iran , Bukhari from Uzbekistan. Hanafi from Iraq, Ahmad ibn hanbal from Iraq. Focus and do your best.

they went to them, they were forced to turn back defeated. At that time Allah's Messenger ﷺ in their rear was calling them back. Only twelve men remained with the Prophet ﷺ and the infidels martyred seventy men from us. On the day (of the battle) of Badr, the Prophet ﷺ and his companions had caused the 'Pagans to lose 140 men, seventy of whom were captured and seventy were killed. Then Abu Sufyan asked thrice, "Is Muhammad present amongst these people?" The Prophet ﷺ ordered his companions not to answer him. Then he asked thrice, "Is the son of Abu Quhafa present amongst these people?" He asked again thrice, "Is the son of Al-Khattab present amongst these people?" He then returned to his companions and said, "As for these (men), they have been killed." `Umar could not control himself and said (to Abu Sufyan), "You told a lie, by Allah! O enemy of Allah! All those you have mentioned are alive, and the thing which will make you unhappy is still there." Abu Sufyan said, "Our victory today is a counterbalance to yours in the battle of Badr, and in war (the victory) is always undecided and is shared in turns by the belligerents, and you will find some of your (killed) men mutilated, but I did not urge my men to do so, yet I do not feel sorry for their deed" After that he started reciting cheerfully, "O Hubal, be high! (1) On that the Prophet ﷺ said (to his companions), "Why don't you answer him back?" They said, "O Allah's Messenger ﷺ What shall we say?" He said, "Say, Allah is Higher and more Sublime." (Then) Abu Sufyan said, "We have the (idol) Al `Uzza, and you have no `Uzza." The Prophet said (to his companions), "Why don't you answer him back?" They asked, "O Allah's Messenger ﷺ! What shall we say?" He said, "Says Allah is our Helper and you have no helper.". – Sahih Al-Bukhari 3039

حَدَّثَنَا عَمْرُو بْنُ خَالِدٍ، حَدَّثَنَا زُهَيْرٌ، حَدَّثَنَا أَبُو إِسْحَاقَ، قَالَ سَمِعْتُ الْبَرَاءَ بْنَ عَازِبٍ ـ رضى الله عنهما ـ يُحَدِّثُ قَالَ جَعَلَ النَّبِيُّ صلى الله عليه وسلم عَلَى الرَّجَّالَةِ يَوْمَ أُحُدٍ ـ وَكَانُوا خَمْسِينَ رَجُلاً ـ عَبْدَ اللَّهِ بْنَ جُبَيْرٍ فَقَالَ " إِنْ رَأَيْتُمُونَا تَخْطَفُنَا الطَّيْرُ، فَلاَ تَبْرَحُوا مَكَانَكُمْ هَذَا حَتَّى أُرْسِلَ إِلَيْكُمْ، وَإِنْ رَأَيْتُمُونَا هَزَمْنَا الْقَوْمَ وَأَوْطَأْنَاهُمْ فَلاَ تَبْرَحُوا حَتَّى أُرْسِلَ إِلَيْكُمْ " فَهَزَمُوهُمْ. قَالَ فَأَنَا وَاللَّهِ رَأَيْتُ النِّسَاءَ يَشْتَدِدْنَ قَدْ بَدَتْ خَلاَخِلُهُنَّ وَأَسْوُقُهُنَّ رَافِعَاتٍ ثِيَابَهُنَّ، فَقَالَ أَصْحَابُ عَبْدِ اللَّهِ بْنِ جُبَيْرٍ الْغَنِيمَةَ ـ أَىْ قَوْمِ ـ الْغَنِيمَةَ، ظَهَرَ أَصْحَابُكُمْ فَمَا تَنْتَظِرُونَ فَقَالَ عَبْدُ اللَّهِ بْنُ جُبَيْرٍ أَنَسِيتُمْ مَا قَالَ لَكُمْ رَسُولُ اللَّهِ صلى الله عليه وسلم قَالُوا وَاللَّهِ لَنَأْتِيَنَّ النَّاسَ فَلَنُصِيبَنَّ مِنَ الْغَنِيمَةِ. فَلَمَّا أَتَوْهُمْ صُرِفَتْ وُجُوهُهُمْ فَأَقْبَلُوا مُنْهَزِمِينَ، فَذَاكَ إِذْ يَدْعُوهُمُ الرَّسُولُ فِي أُخْرَاهُمْ، فَلَمْ يَبْقَ مَعَ النَّبِيِّ صلى الله عليه وسلم غَيْرُ اثْنَىْ عَشَرَ رَجُلاً، فَأَصَابُوا مِنَّا سَبْعِينَ، وَكَانَ النَّبِيُّ صلى الله عليه وسلم وَأَصْحَابُهُ أَصَابَ مِنَ الْمُشْرِكِينَ يَوْمَ بَدْرٍ أَرْبَعِينَ وَمِائَةً سَبْعِينَ أَسِيرًا وَسَبْعِينَ قَتِيلاً، فَقَالَ أَبُو سُفْيَانَ أَفِي الْقَوْمِ مُحَمَّدٌ ثَلاَثَ مَرَّاتٍ، فَنَهَاهُمُ النَّبِيُّ صلى الله عليه وسلم أَنْ يُجِيبُوهُ ثُمَّ قَالَ أَفِي الْقَوْمِ ابْنُ أَبِي قُحَافَةَ ثَلاَثَ مَرَّاتٍ، ثُمَّ قَالَ أَفِي الْقَوْمِ ابْنُ الْخَطَّابِ ثَلاَثَ مَرَّاتٍ، ثُمَّ رَجَعَ إِلَى أَصْحَابِهِ فَقَالَ أَمَّا هَؤُلاَءِ فَقَدْ قُتِلُوا. فَمَا مَلَكَ عُمَرُ نَفْسَهُ فَقَالَ كَذَبْتَ وَاللَّهِ يَا عَدُوَّ اللَّهِ، إِنَّ الَّذِينَ عَدَدْتَ لأَحْيَاءٌ كُلُّهُمْ، وَقَدْ بَقِيَ لَكَ مَا يَسُوؤُكَ. قَالَ يَوْمٌ بِيَوْمِ بَدْرٍ، وَالْحَرْبُ سِجَالٌ، إِنَّكُمْ سَتَجِدُونَ فِي الْقَوْمِ مُثْلَةً لَمْ آمُرْ بِهَا وَلَمْ تَسُؤْنِي، ثُمَّ أَخَذَ يَرْتَجِزُ أُعْلُ هُبَلْ، أُعْلُ هُبَلْ. قَالَ النَّبِيُّ صلى الله عليه وسلم " أَلاَ تُجِيبُوا لَهُ ". قَالُوا يَا رَسُولَ اللَّهِ، مَا نَقُولُ قَالَ " قُولُوا اللَّهُ أَعْلَى وَأَجَلُّ ". قَالَ إِنَّ لَنَا الْعُزَّى وَلاَ عُزَّى لَكُمْ. فَقَالَ النَّبِيُّ صلى الله عليه وسلم " أَلاَ تُجِيبُوا لَهُ ". قَالَ قَالُوا يَا رَسُولَ اللَّهِ، مَا نَقُولُ قَالَ " قُولُوا اللَّهُ مَوْلاَنَا وَلاَ مَوْلَى لَكُمْ ".

Narrated Usama bin Zaid: I asked the Prophet ﷺ during his Hajj, "O Allah's Messenger ﷺ! Where will you stay tomorrow?" He said, "Has `Aqil left for us any house?" He then added, "Tomorrow we will stay at Khaif Bani Kinana, i.e. Al-Muhassab, where (the Pagans of) Quraish took an oath of Kufr (i.e. to be loyal to heathenism) in that Bani Kinana got allied with Quraish against Bani Hashim on the terms that they would not deal with the members of the is tribe or give them shelter." (Az-Zuhri said, "Khaif means valley.") (See Hadith No. 659, Vol. 2) ,- Sahih Al-Bukhari 3058

حَدَّثَنَا مَحْمُودٌ، أَخْبَرَنَا عَبْدُ الرَّزَّاقِ، أَخْبَرَنَا مَعْمَرٌ، عَنِ الزُّهْرِيِّ، عَنْ عَلِيِّ بْنِ حُسَيْنٍ، عَنْ عَمْرِو بْنِ عُثْمَانَ بْنِ عَفَّانَ، عَنْ أُسَامَةَ بْنِ زَيْدٍ، قَالَ قُلْتُ يَا رَسُولَ اللَّهِ، أَيْنَ تَنْزِلُ غَدًا فِي حَجَّتِهِ. قَالَ " وَهَلْ تَرَكَ لَنَا عَقِيلٌ مَنْزِلاً ". ثُمَّ قَالَ "نَحْنُ نَازِلُونَ غَدًا بِخَيْفِ بَنِي كِنَانَةَ الْمُحَصَّبِ، حَيْثُ قَاسَمَتْ قُرَيْشٌ عَلَى الْكُفْرِ ". وَذَلِكَ أَنَّ بَنِي كِنَانَةَ حَالَفَتْ قُرَيْشًا عَلَى بَنِي هَاشِمٍ أَنْ لاَ يُبَايِعُوهُمْ وَلاَ يُئْوُوهُمْ. قَالَ الزُّهْرِيُّ وَالْخَيْفُ الْوَادِي

If you fear treachery on the part of a people, break off with them in a like manner. Allah does not like the treacherous. – Surah Al-Anfal 8:58

وَإِمَّا تَخَافَنَّ مِن قَوْمٍ خِيَانَةً فَٱنۢبِذْ إِلَيْهِمْ عَلَىٰ سَوَآءٍ إِنَّ ٱللَّهَ لَا يُحِبُّ ٱلْخَآئِنِينَ

And as for those who put up a mosque by way of harming and disbelief, and to disunite the believers, and as an outpost for those who warred against Allah and His Messenger aforetime, they will indeed swear that their intention is nothing but good. Allah bears witness that they are certainly liars. Never stand you therein. Verily, the mosque whose foundation was laid from the first day on piety is more worthy that you stand therein (to pray). In it are men who love to clean and to purify themselves. And Allah loves those who make themselves clean and pure (i.e. who clean their private parts with dust [i.e. to be considered as soap) and water from urine and stools, after answering the call of nature]. – Surah At-Taubah 9:107&108[16]

وَٱلَّذِينَ ٱتَّخَذُوا۟ مَسْجِدًا ضِرَارًا وَكُفْرًا وَتَفْرِيقًۢا بَيْنَ ٱلْمُؤْمِنِينَ وَإِرْصَادًا لِّمَنْ حَارَبَ ٱللَّهَ وَرَسُولَهُۥ مِن قَبْلُ ۚ وَلَيَحْلِفُنَّ إِنْ أَرَدْنَآ إِلَّا ٱلْحُسْنَىٰ ۖ وَٱللَّهُ يَشْهَدُ إِنَّهُمْ لَكَٰذِبُونَ لَا تَقُمْ فِيهِ أَبَدًا ۚ لَّمَسْجِدٌ أُسِّسَ عَلَى ٱلتَّقْوَىٰ مِنْ أَوَّلِ يَوْمٍ أَحَقُّ أَن تَقُومَ فِيهِ ۚ فِيهِ رِجَالٌ يُحِبُّونَ أَن يَتَطَهَّرُوا۟ ۚ وَٱللَّهُ يُحِبُّ ٱلْمُطَّهِّرِينَ

The Arabs say: "We believe." Say: "You believe not but you only say, 'We have surrendered (in Islam),' for Faith has not yet entered your hearts. But if you obey Allah and His Messenger , He will not decrease anything in reward for your deeds. Verily, Allah is Oft-Forgiving, Most Merciful.". – Surah Al-Hujurat 49:14

قَالَتِ ٱلْأَعْرَابُ ءَامَنَّا ۖ قُل لَّمْ تُؤْمِنُوا۟ وَلَٰكِن قُولُوٓا۟ أَسْلَمْنَا وَلَمَّا يَدْخُلِ ٱلْإِيمَٰنُ فِى قُلُوبِكُمْ ۖ وَإِن تُطِيعُوا۟ ٱللَّهَ وَرَسُولَهُۥ لَا يَلِتْكُم مِّنْ أَعْمَٰلِكُمْ شَيْـًٔا ۚ إِنَّ ٱللَّهَ غَفُورٌ رَّحِيمٌ

Those who disbelieve say, "This is nothing but a lie that he made up, and others have helped him at it." They have committed an injustice and a perjury. And they say, "Tales of the ancients; he wrote them down; they are dictated to him morning and evening." Say, "It was revealed by He who knows the Secret in the heavens and the earth. He is always Forgiving and Merciful." And they say, "What sort of messenger is this, who eats food, and walks in the marketplaces? If only an angel was sent down with him, to be alongside him a warner." Or, "If only a treasure was dropped on him." Or, "If only he had a garden from which he eats." The evildoers also say, "You are following but a man under spell." Look how they invent examples for you. They have gone astray, and cannot find a way. - Surah Al-Furqan 25:4-9

وَقَالَ ٱلَّذِينَ كَفَرُوٓا۟ إِنْ هَٰذَآ إِلَّآ إِفْكٌ ٱفْتَرَىٰهُ وَأَعَانَهُۥ عَلَيْهِ قَوْمٌ ءَاخَرُونَ ۖ فَقَدْ جَآءُو ظُلْمًا وَزُورًا وَقَالُوٓا۟ أَسَٰطِيرُ ٱلْأَوَّلِينَ ٱكْتَتَبَهَا فَهِىَ تُمْلَىٰ عَلَيْهِ بُكْرَةً وَأَصِيلًا قُلْ أَنزَلَهُ ٱلَّذِى يَعْلَمُ ٱلسِّرَّ فِى ٱلسَّمَٰوَٰتِ وَٱلْأَرْضِ ۚ إِنَّهُۥ كَانَ غَفُورًا رَّحِيمًا وَقَالُوا۟ مَالِ هَٰذَا

---

[16] The majority of English translators will use the word "bedouins" whenever the "Arabs" are referred to in a negative sense in both Quran and Hadith . However when Allah and His Messenger said Arab it should be understood as Arab. As Allah use's the word bedouins in ayat .....that We have made equal to mankind- (alike are) him who consecrates himself therein and the nomad..... – Surah Al-Hajj 22:25

ٱلَّذِى جَعَلْنَٰهُ لِلنَّاسِ سَوَآءً ٱلْعَٰكِفُ فِيهِ وَٱلْبَادِ ۚ.....

And .....and [when] He brought you [all to me] from the desert..... – Surah Yusuf 12:100

وَجَآءَ بِكُم مِّنَ ٱلْبَدْوِ..........that We have made equal to mankind- (alike are) him who consecrates himself therein and the nomad..... – Surah Al-Hajj 22:25

ٱلَّذِى جَعَلْنَٰهُ لِلنَّاسِ سَوَآءً ٱلْعَٰكِفُ فِيهِ وَٱلْبَادِ ۚ.....

If Allah or His Messenger meant bedouins they would have said so.

ٱلرَّسُولِ يَأْكُلُ ٱلطَّعَامَ وَيَمْشِى فِى ٱلْأَسْوَاقِ لَوْلَآ أُنزِلَ إِلَيْهِ مَلَكٌ فَيَكُونَ مَعَهُۥ نَذِيرًا أَوْ يُلْقَىٰٓ إِلَيْهِ كَنزٌ أَوْ تَكُونُ لَهُۥ جَنَّةٌ يَأْكُلُ
مِنْهَا ۚ وَقَالَ ٱلظَّٰلِمُونَ إِن تَتَّبِعُونَ إِلَّا رَجُلًا مَّسْحُورًا ٱنظُرْ كَيْفَ ضَرَبُوا۟ لَكَ ٱلْأَمْثَٰلَ فَضَلُّوا۟ فَلَا يَسْتَطِيعُونَ سَبِيلًا

Otherwise, if a calamity befell them as a result of what their hands have perpetrated, they would say, "Our Lord, if only You had sent us a messenger, we would have followed Your revelations, and been among the believers." But when the truth came to them from Us, they said, "If only he was given the like of what was given to Moses." Did they not disbelieve in what was given to Moses in the past? They said, "Two works of magic backing one another." And they said, "We are disbelieving in both." Say, "Then bring a scripture from Allah, more conductive to guidance than both, and I will follow it, if you are truthful." But if they fail to respond to you, know that they follow their fancies. And who is more lost than him who follows his fancy without guidance from Allah? Allah does not guide the unjust people. We have delivered the Word to them, that they may remember. Those to whom We gave the Scripture before it believe in it. When it is recited to them, they say, "We have believed in it; it is the truth from our Lord; we were Muslims prior to it." These will be given their reward twice, because they persevered; and they counter evil with good; and from Our provisions to them, they give. And when they hear vain talk, they avoid it, and say, "We have our deeds, and you have your deeds; peace be upon you; we do not desire the ignorant." You cannot guide whom you love, but Allah guides whom He wills, and He knows best those who are guided. And they say, "If we follow the guidance with you, we will be snatched from our land." Did We not establish for them a Safe Sanctuary, to which are brought all kinds of fruits, as provision from Ourselves? But most of them do not know. And how many a city did We destroy for turning unappreciative of its livelihood? Here are their homes, uninhabited after them, except for a few. And We became the Inheritors. Your Lord never destroys cities without first sending a messenger in their midst, reciting to them Our revelations. And We never destroy the cities, unless their people are wrongdoers. Whatever thing you are given is but the material of this world, and its glitter. But what Is with Allah is better, and longer lasting. Do you not comprehend? Can someone to whom We have made a fine promise—which he will attain—be equal to someone to whom We have given enjoyments in this world, but who will be on Resurrection Day, among the arraigned? On the Day when He will call to them, and say, "Where are My associates whom you used to claim?" Those against whom the sentence is justified will say, "Our Lord, these are they whom we misled. We misled them, as we were misled. We beg Your forgiveness; it was not us they used to worship." And it will be said, "Call on your partners." And they will call on them, but they will not respond to them. And they will see the suffering. If only they were guided. On the Day when He will call to them, and say, "What did you answer the Messengers?"They will be blinded by the facts on that Day, and they will not question each other. But he who repents, and believes, and does righteous deeds, may well be among the winners. – Surah Al-Qasas 28:47-63

وَلَوْلَآ أَن تُصِيبَهُم مُّصِيبَةٌۢ بِمَا قَدَّمَتْ أَيْدِيهِمْ فَيَقُولُوا۟ رَبَّنَا لَوْلَآ أَرْسَلْتَ إِلَيْنَا رَسُولًا فَنَتَّبِعَ ءَايَٰتِكَ وَنَكُونَ مِنَ ٱلْمُؤْمِنِينَ فَلَمَّا
جَآءَهُمُ ٱلْحَقُّ مِنْ عِندِنَا قَالُوا۟ لَوْلَآ أُوتِىَ مِثْلَ مَآ أُوتِىَ مُوسَىٰٓ ۚ أَوَلَمْ يَكْفُرُوا۟ بِمَآ أُوتِىَ مُوسَىٰ مِن قَبْلُ ۖ قَالُوا۟ سِحْرَانِ تَظَٰهَرَا
وَقَالُوٓا۟ إِنَّا بِكُلٍّ كَٰفِرُونَ قُلْ فَأْتُوا۟ بِكِتَٰبٍ مِّنْ عِندِ ٱللَّهِ هُوَ أَهْدَىٰ مِنْهُمَآ أَتَّبِعْهُ إِن كُنتُمْ صَٰدِقِينَ فَإِن لَّمْ يَسْتَجِيبُوا۟ لَكَ فَٱعْلَمْ أَنَّمَا
يَتَّبِعُونَ أَهْوَآءَهُمْ ۚ وَمَنْ أَضَلُّ مِمَّنِ ٱتَّبَعَ هَوَىٰهُ بِغَيْرِ هُدًى مِّنَ ٱللَّهِ ۚ إِنَّ ٱللَّهَ لَا يَهْدِى ٱلْقَوْمَ ٱلظَّٰلِمِينَ وَلَقَدْ وَصَّلْنَا لَهُمُ ٱلْقَوْلَ لَعَلَّهُمْ
يَتَذَكَّرُونَ ٱلَّذِينَ ءَاتَيْنَٰهُمُ ٱلْكِتَٰبَ مِن قَبْلِهِۦ هُم بِهِۦ يُؤْمِنُونَ وَإِذَا يُتْلَىٰ عَلَيْهِمْ قَالُوٓا۟ ءَامَنَّا بِهِۦٓ إِنَّهُ ٱلْحَقُّ مِن رَّبِّنَآ إِنَّا كُنَّا مِن
قَبْلِهِۦ مُسْلِمِينَ أُو۟لَٰٓئِكَ يُؤْتَوْنَ أَجْرَهُم مَّرَّتَيْنِ بِمَا صَبَرُوا۟ وَيَدْرَءُونَ بِٱلْحَسَنَةِ ٱلسَّيِّئَةَ وَمِمَّا رَزَقْنَٰهُمْ يُنفِقُونَ وَإِذَا سَمِعُوا۟ ٱللَّغْوَ
أَعْرَضُوا۟ عَنْهُ وَقَالُوا۟ لَنَآ أَعْمَٰلُنَا وَلَكُمْ أَعْمَٰلُكُمْ سَلَٰمٌ عَلَيْكُمْ لَا نَبْتَغِى ٱلْجَٰهِلِينَ إِنَّكَ لَا تَهْدِى مَنْ أَحْبَبْتَ وَلَٰكِنَّ ٱللَّهَ يَهْدِى مَن
يَشَآءُ ۚ وَهُوَ أَعْلَمُ بِٱلْمُهْتَدِينَ وَقَالُوٓا۟ إِن نَّتَّبِعِ ٱلْهُدَىٰ مَعَكَ نُتَخَطَّفْ مِنْ أَرْضِنَآ ۚ أَوَلَمْ نُمَكِّن لَّهُمْ حَرَمًا ءَامِنًا يُجْبَىٰٓ إِلَيْهِ ثَمَرَٰتُ
كُلِّ شَىْءٍ رِّزْقًا مِّن لَّدُنَّا وَلَٰكِنَّ أَكْثَرَهُمْ لَا يَعْلَمُونَ وَكَمْ أَهْلَكْنَا مِن قَرْيَةٍۭ بَطِرَتْ مَعِيشَتَهَا ۖ فَتِلْكَ مَسَٰكِنُهُمْ لَمْ تُسْكَن مِّنۢ
بَعْدِهِمْ إِلَّا قَلِيلًا ۖ وَكُنَّا نَحْنُ ٱلْوَٰرِثِينَ وَمَا كَانَ رَبُّكَ مُهْلِكَ ٱلْقُرَىٰ حَتَّىٰ يَبْعَثَ فِىٓ أُمِّهَا رَسُولًا يَتْلُوا۟ عَلَيْهِمْ ءَايَٰتِنَا ۚ وَمَا كُنَّا

مُهْلِكِى ٱلْقُرَىٰٓ إِلَّا وَأَهْلُهَا ظَـٰلِمُونَ وَمَآ أُوتِيتُم مِّن شَىْءٍ فَمَتَـٰعُ ٱلْحَيَوٰةِ ٱلدُّنْيَا وَزِينَتُهَا ۚ وَمَا عِندَ ٱللَّهِ خَيْرٌ وَأَبْقَىٰٓ ۚ أَفَلَا تَعْقِلُونَ أَفَمَن وَعَدْنَـٰهُ وَعْدًا حَسَنًا فَهُوَ لَـٰقِيهِ كَمَن مَّتَّعْنَـٰهُ مَتَـٰعَ ٱلْحَيَوٰةِ ٱلدُّنْيَا ثُمَّ هُوَ يَوْمَ ٱلْقِيَـٰمَةِ مِنَ ٱلْمُحْضَرِينَ وَيَوْمَ يُنَادِيهِمْ فَيَقُولُ أَيْنَ شُرَكَآءِىَ ٱلَّذِينَ كُنتُمْ تَزْعُمُونَ قَالَ ٱلَّذِينَ حَقَّ عَلَيْهِمُ ٱلْقَوْلُ رَبَّنَا هَـٰٓؤُلَآءِ ٱلَّذِينَ أَغْوَيْنَآ أَغْوَيْنَـٰهُمْ كَمَا غَوَيْنَا ۖ تَبَرَّأْنَآ إِلَيْكَ ۖ مَا كَانُوٓا۟ إِيَّانَا يَعْبُدُونَ

And why is it that you do not spend in the cause of Allah, when to Allah belongs the inheritance of the heavens and the earth? Not equal among you are those who contributed before the conquest, and fought. Those are higher in rank than those who contributed afterwards, and fought. But Allah promises both a good reward. Allah is Well Experienced in what you do. - Surah Al-Hadid 57:10
وَمَا لَكُمْ أَلَّا تُنفِقُوا۟ فِى سَبِيلِ ٱللَّهِ وَلِلَّهِ مِيرَٰثُ ٱلسَّمَـٰوَٰتِ وَٱلْأَرْضِ ۚ لَا يَسْتَوِى مِنكُم مَّنْ أَنفَقَ مِن قَبْلِ ٱلْفَتْحِ وَقَـٰتَلَ ۚ أُو۟لَـٰٓئِكَ أَعْظَمُ دَرَجَةً مِّنَ ٱلَّذِينَ أَنفَقُوا۟ مِنۢ بَعْدُ وَقَـٰتَلُوا۟ ۚ وَكُلًّا وَعَدَ ٱللَّهُ ٱلْحُسْنَىٰ ۚ وَٱللَّهُ بِمَا تَعْمَلُونَ خَبِيرٌ

Narrated `Abdullah bin `Umar: Allah's Messenger ﷺ said. "While I was sleeping, I saw myself (in a dream) performing Tawaf around the Ka`ba. Behold, I saw a reddish-white man with lank hair, and water was dropping from his head. I asked, "Who is this?' They replied, 'The son of Mary.' Then I turned my face to see another man with a huge body, red complexion and curly hair and blind in one eye. His eye looked like a protruding out grape. They said (to me), He is Ad-Dajjal." The Prophet ﷺ added, "The man he resembled most is Ibn Qatan, a man from the tribe of Khuza`a. ". – Sahih Al-Bukhari 7128
حَدَّثَنَا يَحْيَى بْنُ بُكَيْرٍ، حَدَّثَنَا اللَّيْثُ، عَنْ عُقَيْلٍ، عَنِ ابْنِ شِهَابٍ، عَنْ سَالِمٍ، عَنْ عَبْدِ اللَّهِ بْنِ عُمَرَ، أَنَّ رَسُولَ اللَّهِ صلى الله عليه وسلم قَالَ " بَيْنَا أَنَا نَائِمٌ أَطُوفُ بِالْكَعْبَةِ، فَإِذَا رَجُلٌ آدَمُ سَبْطُ الشَّعَرِ يَنْطُفُ ـ أَوْ يُهَرَاقُ ـ رَأْسُهُ مَاءً قُلْتُ مَنْ هَذَا قَالُوا ابْنُ مَرْيَمَ. ثُمَّ ذَهَبْتُ أَلْتَفِتُ، فَإِذَا رَجُلٌ جَسِيمٌ أَحْمَرُ جَعْدُ الرَّأْسِ أَعْوَرُ الْعَيْنِ، كَأَنَّ عَيْنَهُ عِنَبَةٌ طَافِيَةٌ قَالُوا هَذَا الدَّجَّالُ. أَقْرَبُ النَّاسِ بِهِ شَبَهًا ابْنُ قَطَنٍ ". رَجُلٌ مِنْ خُزَاعَةَ

Narrated Zainab bint Jahsh: That one day Allah's Messenger ﷺ entered upon her in a state of fear and said, "None has the right to be worshipped but Allah! Woe to the Arabs from the Great evil that has approached (them). Today a hole has been opened in the dam of Gog and Magog like this." The Prophet ﷺ made a circle with his index finger and thumb. Zainab bint Jahsh added: I said, "O Alllah's Apostle! Shall we be destroyed though there will be righteous people among us?" The Prophet ﷺ said, "Yes, if the (number) of evil (persons) increased.". – Al-Bukhari 7135
حَدَّثَنَا أَبُو الْيَمَانِ، أَخْبَرَنَا شُعَيْبٌ، عَنِ الزُّهْرِيِّ، ح وَحَدَّثَنَا إِسْمَاعِيلُ، حَدَّثَنِي أَخِي، عَنْ سُلَيْمَانَ، عَنْ مُحَمَّدِ بْنِ أَبِي عَتِيقٍ، عَنِ ابْنِ شِهَابٍ، عَنْ عُرْوَةَ بْنِ الزُّبَيْرِ، أَنَّ زَيْنَبَ ابْنَةَ أَبِي سَلَمَةَ، حَدَّثَتْهُ عَنْ أُمِّ حَبِيبَةَ بِنْتِ أَبِي سُفْيَانَ، عَنْ زَيْنَبَ ابْنَةِ جَحْشٍ، أَنَّ رَسُولَ اللَّهِ صلى الله عليه وسلم دَخَلَ عَلَيْهَا يَوْمًا فَزِعًا يَقُولُ " لاَ إِلَهَ إِلاَّ اللَّهُ، وَيْلٌ لِلْعَرَبِ مِنْ شَرٍّ قَدِ اقْتَرَبَ، فُتِحَ الْيَوْمَ مِنْ رَدْمِ يَأْجُوجَ وَمَأْجُوجَ مِثْلُ هَذِهِ ". وَحَلَّقَ بِإِصْبَعَيْهِ الإِبْهَامِ وَالَّتِي تَلِيهَا. قَالَتْ زَيْنَبُ ابْنَةُ جَحْشٍ فَقُلْتُ يَا رَسُولَ اللَّهِ أَفَنَهْلِكُ وَفِينَا الصَّالِحُونَ قَالَ " نَعَمْ إِذَا كَثُرَ الْخُبْثُ ".

Narrated Ibn `Abbas: Regarding the Statement of Allah:--"Those who have changed Allah's Blessings for disbelief..." (14.28) The people meant here by Allah, are the infidels of Quraish. (`Amr, a sub-narrator said, "Those are (the infidels of) Quraish and Muhammad is Allah's Blessing. Regarding Allah's Statement:" and have led their people Into the house of destruction? (14.29) Ibn `Abbas said, "It means the Fire they will suffer from (after their death) on the day of Badr.". – Sahih Al-Bukhari 3977
حَدَّثَنَا الْحُمَيْدِيُّ، حَدَّثَنَا سُفْيَانُ، حَدَّثَنَا عَمْرٌو، عَنْ عَطَاءٍ، عَنِ ابْنِ عَبَّاسٍ ـ رضى الله عنهما {الَّذِينَ بَدَّلُوا نِعْمَةَ اللَّهِ كُفْرًا} قَالَ هُمْ وَاللَّهِ كُفَّارُ قُرَيْشٍ. قَالَ عَمْرٌو هُمْ قُرَيْشٌ وَمُحَمَّدٌ صلى الله عليه وسلم نِعْمَةُ اللَّهِ {وَأَحَلُّوا قَوْمَهُمْ دَارَ الْبَوَارِ } قَالَ النَّارَ يَوْمَ بَدْرٍ.

Narrated Abu Huraira: I heard the truthful and trusted by Allah (i.e., the Prophetﷺ) saying, “The destruction of my followers will be through the hands of young men from Quraish.”. – Sahih al-Bukhari 7058

حَدَّثَنَا مُوسَى بْنُ إِسْمَاعِيلَ، حَدَّثَنَا عَمْرُو بْنُ يَحْيَى بْنِ سَعِيدِ بْنِ عَمْرِو بْنِ سَعِيدٍ، قَالَ أَخْبَرَنِي جَدِّي، قَالَ كُنْتُ جَالِسًا مَعَ أَبِي هُرَيْرَةَ فِي مَسْجِدِ النَّبِيِّ صلى الله عليه وسلم بِالْمَدِينَةِ وَمَعَنَا مَرْوَانُ قَالَ أَبُو هُرَيْرَةَ سَمِعْتُ الصَّادِقَ الْمَصْدُوقَ يَقُولُ " هَلَكَةُ أُمَّتِي عَلَى يَدَىْ غِلْمَةٍ مِنْ قُرَيْشٍ ". فَقَالَ مَرْوَانُ لَعْنَةُ اللَّهِ عَلَيْهِمْ غِلْمَةً. فَقَالَ أَبُو هُرَيْرَةَ لَوْ شِئْتُ أَنْ أَقُولَ بَنِي فُلاَنٍ وَبَنِي فُلاَنٍ لَفَعَلْتُ. فَكُنْتُ أَخْرُجُ مَعَ جَدِّي إِلَى بَنِي مَرْوَانَ حِينَ مَلَكُوا بِالشَّأْمِ، فَإِذَا رَآهُمْ غِلْمَانًا أَحْدَاثًا قَالَ لَنَا عَسَى هَؤُلاَءِ أَنْ يَكُونُوا مِنْهُمْ قُلْنَا أَنْتَ أَعْلَمُ

The Book of
Al-Hums
الْحُمْسَ

Narrated `Urwa: During the Pre-Islamic period of Ignorance, the people used to perform Tawaf of the Ka`ba naked except the Hums; and the Hums were Quraish and their offspring. The Hums used to give clothes to the men who would perform the Tawaf wearing them; and women (of the Hums) used to give clothes to the women who would perform the Tawaf wearing them. Those to whom the Hums did not give clothes would perform Tawaf round the Ka`ba naked. Most of the people used to go away (disperse) directly from `Arafat but they (Hums) used to depart after staying at Al-Muzdalifa. `Urwa added, “My father narrated that `Aisha had said, ‘The following verses were revealed about the Hums: Then depart from the place whence all the people depart—(2.199) `Urwa added, “They (the Hums) used to stay at Al-Muzdalifa and used to depart from there (to Mina) and so they were sent to `Arafat (by Allah’s order).”. – Sahih Al-Bukhari 1665

حَدَّثَنَا فَرْوَةُ بْنُ أَبِي الْمَغْرَاءِ، حَدَّثَنَا عَلِيُّ بْنُ مُسْهِرٍ، عَنْ هِشَامِ بْنِ عُرْوَةَ، قَالَ عُرْوَةُ كَانَ النَّاسُ يَطُوفُونَ فِي الْجَاهِلِيَّةِ عُرَاةً إِلاَّ الْحُمْسَ، وَالْحُمْسُ قُرَيْشٌ وَمَا وَلَدَتْ، وَكَانَتِ الْحُمْسُ يَحْتَسِبُونَ عَلَى النَّاسِ يُعْطِي الرَّجُلُ الرَّجُلَ الثِّيَابَ يَطُوفُ فِيهَا، وَتُعْطِي الْمَرْأَةُ الْمَرْأَةَ الثِّيَابَ تَطُوفُ فِيهَا، فَمَنْ لَمْ يُعْطِهِ الْحُمْسُ طَافَ بِالْبَيْتِ عُرْيَانًا، وَكَانَ يُفِيضُ جَمَاعَةُ النَّاسِ مِنْ عَرَفَاتٍ، وَيُفِيضُ الْحُمْسُ مِنْ جَمْعٍ. قَالَ وَأَخْبَرَنِي أَبِي عَنْ عَائِشَةَ ـ رضى الله عنها ـ أَنَّ هَذِهِ الآيَةَ نَزَلَتْ فِي الْحُمْسِ {ثُمَّ أَفِيضُوا مِنْ حَيْثُ أَفَاضَ النَّاسُ} قَالَ كَانُوا يُفِيضُونَ مِنْ جَمْعٍ فَدُفِعُوا إِلَى عَرَفَاتٍ

Narrated `Aisha: The Quraish people and those who embraced their religion, used to stay at Muzdalifa and used to call themselves Al-Hums, while the rest of the Arabs used to stay at `Arafat. When Islam came, Allah ordered His Prophet to go to `Arafat and stay at it, and then pass on from there, and that is what is meant by the Statement of Allah:--“Then depart from the place whence all the people depart......” (2.199). – Sahih Al-Bukhari 4520

حَدَّثَنَا عَلِيُّ بْنُ عَبْدِ اللَّهِ، حَدَّثَنَا مُحَمَّدُ بْنُ خَازِمٍ، حَدَّثَنَا هِشَامٌ، عَنْ أَبِيهِ، عَنْ عَائِشَةَ ـ رضى الله عنها ـ كَانَتْ قُرَيْشٌ وَمَنْ دَانَ دِينَهَا يَقِفُونَ بِالْمُزْدَلِفَةِ، وَكَانُوا يُسَمَّوْنَ الْحُمْسَ، وَكَانَ سَائِرُ الْعَرَبِ يَقِفُونَ بِعَرَفَاتٍ، فَلَمَّا جَاءَ الإِسْلاَمُ أَمَرَ اللَّهُ نَبِيَّهُ صلى الله عليه وسلم أَنْ يَأْتِيَ عَرَفَاتٍ، ثُمَّ يَقِفَ بِهَا ثُمَّ يُفِيضَ مِنْهَا، فَذَلِكَ قَوْلُهُ تَعَالَى {ثُمَّ أَفِيضُوا مِنْ حَيْثُ أَفَاضَ النَّاسُ}

Narrated Muhammad bin Jubair bin Mut`im: My father said, “(Before Islam) I was looking for my camel ..” The same narration is told by a different sub-narrator. Jubair bin Mut`im said, “My camel was lost and I went out in search of it on the day of `Arafat, and I saw the Prophet ﷺ standing in `Arafat. I said to myself: By Allah he is from the Hums (literally: strictly religious, Quraish were called so, as they used to say, ‘We are the people of Allah we shall not go out of the sanctuary). What has brought him here?”. – Sahih Al-Bukhari 1664

حَدَّثَنَا عَلِيُّ بْنُ عَبْدِ اللَّهِ، حَدَّثَنَا سُفْيَانُ، حَدَّثَنَا عَمْرٌو، حَدَّثَنَا مُحَمَّدُ بْنُ جُبَيْرِ بْنِ مُطْعِمٍ، عَنْ أَبِيهِ، كُنْتُ أَطْلُبُ بَعِيرًا لِي.
وَحَدَّثَنَا مُسَدَّدٌ، حَدَّثَنَا سُفْيَانُ، عَنْ عَمْرٍو، سَمِعَ مُحَمَّدَ بْنَ جُبَيْرٍ، عَنْ أَبِيهِ، جُبَيْرِ بْنِ مُطْعِمٍ قَالَ أَضْلَلْتُ بَعِيرًا لِي، فَذَهَبْتُ أَطْلُبُهُ يَوْمَ عَرَفَةَ، فَرَأَيْتُ النَّبِيَّ صلى الله عليه وسلم وَاقِفًا بِعَرَفَةَ، فَقُلْتُ هَذَا وَاللَّهِ مِنَ الْحُمْسِ فَمَا شَأْنُهُ هَا هُنَا

And they exclaimed, "If only this Quran was revealed to a great man from ˹one of˺ the two cities!" Is it they who distribute your Lord's mercy? We ˹alone˺ have distributed their ˹very˺ livelihood among them in this worldly life and raised some of them in rank above others so that some may employ others in service. ˹But˺ your Lord's mercy is far better than whatever ˹wealth˺ they amass. – Surah Az-Zukhruf 43:31&32

وَقَالُوا۟ لَوْلَا نُزِّلَ هَـٰذَا ٱلْقُرْءَانُ عَلَىٰ رَجُلٍ مِّنَ ٱلْقَرْيَتَيْنِ عَظِيمٍ أَهُمْ يَقْسِمُونَ رَحْمَتَ رَبِّكَ ۚ نَحْنُ قَسَمْنَا بَيْنَهُم مَّعِيشَتَهُمْ فِى ٱلْحَيَوٰةِ ٱلدُّنْيَا ۚ وَرَفَعْنَا بَعْضَهُمْ فَوْقَ بَعْضٍ دَرَجَـٰتٍ لِّيَتَّخِذَ بَعْضُهُم بَعْضًا سُخْرِيًّا ۗ وَرَحْمَتُ رَبِّكَ خَيْرٌ مِّمَّا يَجْمَعُونَ

Narrated Abu Qilaba: Once `Umar bin `Abdul `Aziz sat on his throne in the courtyard of his house so that the people might gather before him. Then he admitted them and (when they came in), he said, "What do you think of Al-Qasama?" They said, "We say that it is lawful to depend on Al-Qasama in Qisas, as the previous Muslim Caliphs carried out Qisas depending on it." Then he said to me, "O Abu Qilaba! What do you say about it?" He let me appear before the people and I said, "O Chief of the Believers! You have the chiefs of the army staff and the nobles of the Arabs. If fifty of them testified that a married man had committed illegal sexual intercourse in Damascus but they had not seen him (doing so), would you stone him?" He said, "No." I said, "If fifty of them testified that a man had committed theft in Hums, would you cut off his hand though they did not see him?" He replied, "No." I said, "By Allah, Allah's Messenger ﷺ never killed anyone except in one of the following three situations: (1) A person who killed somebody unjustly, was killed (in Qisas,) (2) a married person who committed illegal sexual intercourse and (3) a man who fought against Allah and His Apostle and deserted Islam and became an apostate." Then the people said, "Didn't Anas bin Malik narrate that Allah's Messenger ﷺ cut off the hands of the thieves, branded their eyes and then, threw them in the sun?" I said, "I shall tell you the narration of Anas. Anas said: "Eight persons from the tribe of `Ukl came to Allah's Messenger ﷺ and gave the Pledge of allegiance for Islam (became Muslim). The climate of the place (Medina) did not suit them, so they became sick and complained about that to Allah's Messenger ﷺ. He said (to them), "Won't you go out with the shepherd of our camels and drink of the camels' milk and urine (as medicine)?" They said, "Yes." So they went out and drank the camels' milk and urine, and after they became healthy, they killed the shepherd of Allah's Messenger ﷺ and took away all the camels. This news reached Allah's Messenger ﷺ , so he sent (men) to follow their traces and they were captured and brought (to the Prophet). He then ordered to cut their hands and feet, and their eyes were branded with heated pieces of iron, and then he threw them in the sun till they died." I said, "What can be worse than what those people did? They deserted Islam, committed murder and theft." Then 'Anbasa bin Sa`id said, "By Allah, I never heard a narration like this of today." I said, "O 'Anbasa! You deny my narration?" 'Anbasa said, "No, but you have related the narration in the way it should be related. By Allah, these people are in welfare as long as this Sheikh (Abu Qilaba) is among them." I added, "Indeed in this event there has been a tradition set by Allah's Messenger ﷺ. The narrator added: Some Ansari people came to the Prophet ﷺ and discussed some matters with him, a man from amongst them went out and was murdered. Those people went out after him, and behold, their companion was swimming in blood. They returned to Allah's Messenger ﷺ and said to him, "O Allah's Apostle, we have found our companion who had talked with us and gone out before us, swimming in blood (killed)." Allah's Messenger ﷺ went out and asked them,

"Whom do you suspect or whom do you think has killed him?" They said, "We think that the Jews have killed him." The Prophet ﷺ sent for the Jews and asked them, "Did you kill this (person)?" They replied, "No." He asked the Al-Ansars, "Do you agree that I let fifty Jews take an oath that they have not killed him?" They said, "It matters little for the Jews to kill us all and then take false oaths." He said, "Then would you like to receive the Diya after fifty of you have taken an oath (that the Jews have killed your man)?" They said, "We will not take the oath." Then the Prophet ﷺ himself paid them the Diya (Blood-money)." The narrator added, "The tribe of Hudhail repudiated one of their men (for his evil conduct) in the Pre-Islamic period of Ignorance. Then, at a place called Al-Batha' (near Mecca), the man attacked a Yemenite family at night to steal from them, but a man from the family noticed him and struck him with his sword and killed him. The tribe of Hudhail came and captured the Yemenite and brought him to `Umar during the Hajj season and said, "He has killed our companion." The Yemenite said, "But these people had repudiated him (i.e., their companion)." `Umar said, "Let fifty persons of Hudhail swear that they had not repudiated him." So forty-nine of them took the oath and then a person belonging to them, came from Sham and they requested him to swear similarly, but he paid one-thousand Dirhams instead of taking the oath. They called another man instead of him and the new man shook hands with the brother of the deceased. Some people said, "We and those fifty men who had taken false oaths (Al-Qasama) set out, and when they reached a place called Nakhlah, it started raining so they entered a cave in the mountain, and the cave collapsed on those fifty men who took the false oath, and all of them died except the two persons who had shaken hands with each other. They escaped death but a stone fell on the leg of the brother of the deceased and broke it, whereupon he survived for one year and then died." I further said, "`Abdul Malik bin Marwan sentenced a man to death in Qisas (equality in punishment) for murder, basing his judgment on Al-Qasama, but later on he regretted that judgment and ordered that the names of the fifty persons who had taken the oath (Al-Qasama), be erased from the register, and he exiled them in Sham." – Sahih Al-Bukhari 6899

حَدَّثَنَا قُتَيْبَةُ بْنُ سَعِيدٍ، حَدَّثَنَا أَبُو بِشْرٍ، إِسْمَاعِيلُ بْنُ إِبْرَاهِيمَ الأَسَدِيُّ حَدَّثَنَا الْحَجَّاجُ بْنُ أَبِي عُثْمَانَ، حَدَّثَنِي أَبُو رَجَاءٍ، مِنْ آلِ أَبِي قِلاَبَةَ حَدَّثَنِي أَبُو قِلاَبَةَ، أَنَّ عُمَرَ بْنَ عَبْدِ الْعَزِيزِ، أَبْرَزَ سَرِيرَهُ يَوْمًا لِلنَّاسِ، ثُمَّ أَذِنَ لَهُمْ فَدَخَلُوا فَقَالَ مَا تَقُولُونَ فِي الْقَسَامَةِ قَالَ نَقُولُ الْقَسَامَةُ الْقَوَدُ بِهَا حَقٌّ، وَقَدْ أَقَادَتْ بِهَا الْخُلَفَاءُ. قَالَ لِي مَا تَقُولُ يَا أَبَا قِلاَبَةَ وَنَصَبَنِي لِلنَّاسِ. فَقُلْتُ يَا أَمِيرَ الْمُؤْمِنِينَ عِنْدَكَ رُءُوسُ الأَجْنَادِ وَأَشْرَافُ الْعَرَبِ، أَرَأَيْتَ لَوْ أَنَّ خَمْسِينَ مِنْهُمْ شَهِدُوا عَلَى رَجُلٍ مُحْصَنٍ بِدِمَشْقَ أَنَّهُ قَدْ زَنَى، لَمْ يَرَوْهُ أَكُنْتَ تَرْجُمُهُ قَالَ لاَ. قُلْتُ أَرَأَيْتَ لَوْ أَنَّ خَمْسِينَ مِنْهُمْ شَهِدُوا عَلَى رَجُلٍ بِحِمْصَ أَنَّهُ سَرَقَ أَكُنْتَ تَقْطَعُهُ وَلَمْ يَرَوْهُ قَالَ لاَ. قُلْتُ فَوَاللَّهِ مَا قَتَلَ رَسُولُ اللَّهِ صلى الله عليه وسلم قَطُّ، إِلاَّ فِي إِحْدَى ثَلاَثِ خِصَالٍ رَجُلٌ قَتَلَ بِجَرِيرَةِ نَفْسِهِ فَقُتِلَ، أَوْ رَجُلٌ زَنَى بَعْدَ إِحْصَانٍ، أَوْ رَجُلٌ حَارَبَ اللَّهَ وَرَسُولَهُ وَارْتَدَّ عَنِ الإِسْلاَمِ. فَقَالَ الْقَوْمُ أَوَلَيْسَ قَدْ حَدَّثَ أَنَسُ بْنُ مَالِكٍ أَنَّ رَسُولَ اللَّهِ صلى الله عليه وسلم قَطَعَ فِي السَّرَقِ وَسَمَرَ الأَعْيُنَ، ثُمَّ نَبَذَهُمْ فِي الشَّمْسِ. فَقُلْتُ أَنَا أُحَدِّثُكُمْ حَدِيثَ أَنَسٍ، حَدَّثَنِي أَنَسٌ أَنَّ نَفَرًا مِنْ عُكْلٍ ثَمَانِيَةً قَدِمُوا عَلَى رَسُولِ اللَّهِ صلى الله عليه وسلم فَبَايَعُوهُ عَلَى الإِسْلاَمِ، فَاسْتَوْخَمُوا الأَرْضَ فَسَقِمَتْ أَجْسَامُهُمْ، فَشَكَوْا ذَلِكَ إِلَى رَسُولِ اللَّهِ صلى الله عليه وسلم قَالَ " أَفَلاَ تَخْرُجُونَ مَعَ رَاعِينَا فِي إِبِلِهِ، فَتُصِيبُونَ مِنْ أَلْبَانِهَا وَأَبْوَالِهَا ". قَالُوا بَلَى، فَخَرَجُوا فَشَرِبُوا مِنْ أَلْبَانِهَا وَأَبْوَالِهَا فَصَحُّوا، فَقَتَلُوا رَاعِيَ رَسُولِ اللَّهِ صلى الله عليه وسلم وَأَطْرَدُوا النَّعَمَ، فَبَلَغَ ذَلِكَ رَسُولَ اللَّهِ صلى الله عليه وسلم فَأَرْسَلَ فِي آثَارِهِمْ، فَأُدْرِكُوا فَجِيءَ بِهِمْ، فَأَمَرَ بِهِمْ فَقُطِّعَتْ أَيْدِيهِمْ وَأَرْجُلُهُمْ، وَسَمَرَ أَعْيُنَهُمْ، ثُمَّ نَبَذَهُمْ فِي الشَّمْسِ حَتَّى مَاتُوا. قُلْتُ وَأَىُّ شَىْءٍ أَشَدُّ مِمَّا صَنَعَ هَؤُلاَءِ ارْتَدُّوا عَنِ الإِسْلاَمِ وَقَتَلُوا وَسَرَقُوا. فَقَالَ عَنْبَسَةُ بْنُ سَعِيدٍ وَاللَّهِ إِنْ سَمِعْتُ كَالْيَوْمِ قَطُّ. فَقُلْتُ أَتَرُدُّ عَلَىَّ حَدِيثِي يَا عَنْبَسَةُ قَالَ لاَ، وَلَكِنْ جِئْتَ بِالْحَدِيثِ عَلَى وَجْهِهِ، وَاللَّهِ لاَ يَزَالُ هَذَا الْجُنْدُ بِخَيْرٍ مَا عَاشَ هَذَا الشَّيْخُ بَيْنَ أَظْهُرِهِمْ. قُلْتُ وَقَدْ كَانَ فِي هَذَا سُنَّةٌ مِنْ رَسُولِ اللَّهِ صلى الله عليه وسلم دَخَلَ عَلَيْهِ نَفَرٌ مِنَ الأَنْصَارِ فَتَحَدَّثُوا عِنْدَهُ، فَخَرَجَ رَجُلٌ مِنْهُمْ بَيْنَ أَيْدِيهِمْ فَقُتِلَ، فَخَرَجُوا بَعْدَهُ، فَإِذَا هُمْ بِصَاحِبِهِمْ يَتَشَحَّطُ فِي الدَّمِ، فَرَجَعُوا إِلَى رَسُولِ اللَّهِ صلى الله عليه وسلم فَقَالُوا يَا رَسُولَ اللَّهِ صَاحِبُنَا كَانَ تَحَدَّثَ مَعَنَا، فَخَرَجَ بَيْنَ أَيْدِينَا، فَإِذَا نَحْنُ بِهِ يَتَشَحَّطُ فِي الدَّمِ. فَخَرَجَ رَسُولُ اللَّهِ صلى الله عليه وسلم فَقَالَ " بِمَنْ تَظُنُّونَ أَوْ تَرَوْنَ قَتَلَهُ ". قَالُوا نَرَى أَنَّ الْيَهُودَ قَتَلَتْهُ. فَأَرْسَلَ إِلَى الْيَهُودِ فَدَعَاهُمْ. فَقَالَ " آنْتُمْ قَتَلْتُمْ هَذَا ". قَالُوا لاَ. قَالَ " أَتَرْضَوْنَ نَفَلَ خَمْسِينَ مِنَ الْيَهُودِ مَا قَتَلُوهُ ". فَقَالُوا مَا يُبَالُونَ أَنْ يَقْتُلُونَا أَجْمَعِينَ ثُمَّ يَنْتَفِلُونَ. قَالَ " أَفَتَسْتَحِقُّونَ الدِّيَةَ بِأَيْمَانِ خَمْسِينَ مِنْكُمْ ". قَالُوا مَا كُنَّا لِنَحْلِفَ، فَوَدَاهُ مِنْ عِنْدِهِ. قُلْتُ وَقَدْ كَانَتْ هُذَيْلٌ خَلَعُوا خَلِيعًا لَهُمْ فِي الْجَاهِلِيَّةِ فَطَرَقَ أَهْلَ بَيْتٍ مِنَ الْيَمَنِ بِالْبَطْحَاءِ فَانْتَبَهَ لَهُ رَجُلٌ مِنْهُمْ فَحَذَفَهُ بِالسَّيْفِ فَقَتَلَهُ، فَجَاءَتْ هُذَيْلٌ فَأَخَذُوا الْيَمَانِيَ فَرَفَعُوهُ إِلَى عُمَرَ بِالْمَوْسِمِ وَقَالُوا قَتَلَ

صَاحِبَنَا. فَقَالَ إِنَّهُمْ قَدْ خَلَعُوهُ. فَقَالَ يُقْسِمُ خَمْسُونَ مِنْ هُذَيْلٍ مَا خَلَعُوهُ. قَالَ فَأَقْسَمَ مِنْهُمْ تِسْعَةٌ وَأَرْبَعُونَ رَجُلاً، وَقَدِمَ رَجُلٌ مِنْهُمْ مِنَ الشَّأْمِ فَسَأَلُوهُ أَنْ يُقْسِمَ فَافْتَدَى يَمِينَهُ مِنْهُمْ بِأَلْفِ دِرْهَمٍ، فَأَدْخَلُوا مَكَانَهُ رَجُلاً آخَرَ، فَدَفَعَهُ إِلَى أَخِي الْمَقْتُولِ فَقُرِنَتْ يَدُهُ بِيَدِهِ، قَالُوا فَانْطَلَقَا وَالْخَمْسُونَ الَّذِينَ أَقْسَمُوا حَتَّى إِذَا كَانُوا بِنَخْلَةَ، أَخَذَتْهُمُ السَّمَاءُ فَدَخَلُوا فِي غَارٍ فِي الْجَبَلِ، فَانْهَجَمَ الْغَارُ عَلَى الْخَمْسِينَ الَّذِينَ أَقْسَمُوا فَمَاتُوا جَمِيعًا، وَأَفْلَتَ الْقَرِينَانِ وَاتَّبَعَهُمَا حَجَرٌ فَكَسَرَ رِجْلَ أَخِي الْمَقْتُولِ، فَعَاشَ حَوْلاً ثُمَّ مَاتَ. قُلْتُ وَقَدْ كَانَ عَبْدُ الْمَلِكِ بْنُ مَرْوَانَ أَقَادَ رَجُلاً بِالْقَسَامَةِ ثُمَّ نَدِمَ بَعْدَ مَا صَنَعَ، فَأَمَرَ بِالْخَمْسِينَ الَّذِينَ أَقْسَمُوا فَمُحُوا مِنَ الدِّيوَانِ وَسَيَّرَهُمْ إِلَى الشَّأْمِ

Narrated Jafar bin `Amr bin Umaiya: I went out with 'Ubaidullah bin `Adi Al-Khaiyar. When we reached Hims (i.e. a town in Syria), 'Ubaidullah bin `Adi said (to me), "Would you like to see Wahshi so that we may ask him about the killing of Hamza?" I replied, "Yes." Wahshi used to live in Hims. We enquired about him and somebody said to us, "He is that in the shade of his palace, as if he were a full water skin." So we went up to him, and when we were at a short distance from him, we greeted him and he greeted us in return. 'Ubaidullah was wearing his turban and Wahshi could not see except his eyes and feet. 'Ubaidullah said, "O Wahshi! Do you know me?" Wahshi looked at him and then said, "No, by Allah! But I know that `Adi bin Al-Khiyar married a woman called Um Qital, the daughter of Abu Al-Is, and she delivered a boy for him at Mecca, and I looked for a wet nurse for that child. (Once) I carried that child along with his mother and then I handed him over to her, and your feet resemble that child's feet." Then 'Ubaidullah uncovered his face and said (to Wahshi), "Will you tell us (the story of) the killing of Hamza?" Wahshi replied "Yes, Hamza killed Tuaima bin `Adi bin Al-Khaiyar at Badr (battle) so my master, Jubair bin Mut`im said to me, 'If you kill Hamza in revenge for my uncle, then you will be set free." When the people set out (for the battle of Uhud) in the year of 'Ainain ..'Ainain is a mountain near the mountain of Uhud, and between it and Uhud there is a valley.. I went out with the people for the battle. When the army aligned for the fight, Siba' came out and said, 'Is there any (Muslim) to accept my challenge to a duel?' Hamza bin `Abdul Muttalib came out and said, 'O Siba'. O Ibn Um Anmar, the one who circumcises other ladies! Do you challenge Allah and His Apostle?' Then Hamza attacked and killed him, causing him to be non-extant like the bygone yesterday. I hid myself under a rock, and when he (i.e. Hamza) came near me, I threw my spear at him, driving it into his umbilicus so that it came out through his buttocks, causing him to die. When all the people returned to Mecca, I too returned with them. I stayed in (Mecca) till Islam spread in it (i.e. Mecca). Then I left for Taif, and when the people (of Taif) sent their messengers to Allah's Messenger ﷺ ,I was told that the Prophet ﷺ did not harm the messengers; So I too went out with them till I reached Allah's Messenger ﷺ .When he saw me, he said, 'Are you Wahshi?' I said, 'Yes.' He said, 'Was it you who killed Hamza?' I replied, 'What happened is what you have been told of.' He said, 'Can you hide your face from me?' So I went out when Allah's Messenger ﷺ died, and Musailamah Al-Kadhdhab appeared (claiming to be a prophet). I said, 'I will go out to Musailamah so that I may kill him, and make amends for killing Hamza. So I went out with the people (to fight Musailamah and his followers) and then famous events took place concerning that battle. Suddenly I saw a man (i.e. Musailamah) standing near a gap in a wall. He looked like an ash-colored camel and his hair was dishevelled. So I threw my spear at him, driving it into his chest in between his breasts till it passed out through his shoulders, and then an Ansari man attacked him and struck him on the head with a sword. `Abdullah bin `Umar said, 'A slave girl on the roof of a house said: Alas! The chief of the believers (i.e. Musailamah) has been killed by a black slave.". – Sahih Al-Bukhari 4072

حَدَّثَنِي أَبُو جَعْفَرٍ، مُحَمَّدُ بْنُ عَبْدِ اللَّهِ حَدَّثَنَا حُجَيْنُ بْنُ الْمُثَنَّى، حَدَّثَنَا عَبْدُ الْعَزِيزِ بْنُ عَبْدِ اللَّهِ بْنِ أَبِي سَلَمَةَ، عَنْ عَبْدِ اللَّهِ بْنِ الْفَضْلِ، عَنْ سُلَيْمَانَ بْنِ يَسَارٍ، عَنْ جَعْفَرِ بْنِ عَمْرِو بْنِ أُمَيَّةَ الضَّمْرِيِّ، قَالَ خَرَجْتُ مَعَ عُبَيْدِ اللَّهِ بْنِ عَدِيِّ بْنِ الْخِيَارِ، فَلَمَّا قَدِمْنَا حِمْصَ قَالَ لِي عُبَيْدُ اللَّهِ هَلْ لَكَ فِي وَحْشِيٍّ نَسْأَلُهُ عَنْ قَتْلِ حَمْزَةَ قُلْتُ نَعَمْ. وَكَانَ وَحْشِيٌّ يَسْكُنُ حِمْصَ فَسَأَلْنَا عَنْهُ

فَقِيلَ لَنَا هُوَ ذَاكَ فِي ظِلِّ قَصْرِهِ، كَأَنَّهُ حَمِيتٌ. قَالَ فَجِئْنَا حَتَّى وَقَفْنَا عَلَيْهِ بِيَسِيرٍ، فَسَلَّمْنَا، فَرَدَّ السَّلاَمَ، قَالَ وَعُبَيْدُ اللَّهِ مُعْتَجِرٌ بِعِمَامَتِهِ، مَا يَرَى وَحْشِيٌّ إِلاَّ عَيْنَيْهِ وَرِجْلَيْهِ، فَقَالَ عُبَيْدُ اللَّهِ يَا وَحْشِيُّ أَتَعْرِفُنِي قَالَ فَنَظَرَ إِلَيْهِ ثُمَّ قَالَ لاَ وَاللَّهِ إِلاَّ أَنِّي أَعْلَمُ أَنَّ عَدِيَّ بْنَ الْخِيَارِ تَزَوَّجَ امْرَأَةً يُقَالُ لَهَا أُمُّ قِتَالٍ بِنْتُ أَبِي الْعِيصِ، فَوَلَدَتْ لَهُ غُلاَمًا بِمَكَّةَ، فَكُنْتُ أَسْتَرْضِعُ لَهُ، فَحَمَلْتُ ذَلِكَ الْغُلاَمَ مَعَ أُمِّهِ، فَنَاوَلْتُهَا إِيَّاهُ، فَلَكَأَنِّي نَظَرْتُ إِلَى قَدَمَيْكَ. قَالَ فَكَشَفَ عُبَيْدُ اللَّهِ عَنْ وَجْهِهِ ثُمَّ قَالَ أَلاَ تُخْبِرُنَا بِقَتْلِ حَمْزَةَ قَالَ نَعَمْ، إِنَّ حَمْزَةَ قَتَلَ طُعَيْمَةَ بْنَ عَدِيِّ بْنِ الْخِيَارِ بِبَدْرٍ، فَقَالَ لِي مَوْلاَىَ جُبَيْرُ بْنُ مُطْعِمٍ إِنْ قَتَلْتَ حَمْزَةَ بِعَمِّي فَأَنْتَ حُرٌّ، قَالَ فَلَمَّا أَنْ خَرَجَ النَّاسُ عَامَ عَيْنَيْنِ ـ وَعَيْنَيْنِ جَبَلٌ بِحِيَالِ أُحُدٍ، بَيْنَهُ وَبَيْنَهُ وَادٍ ـ خَرَجْتُ مَعَ النَّاسِ إِلَى الْقِتَالِ، فَلَمَّا اصْطَفُّوا لِلْقِتَالِ خَرَجَ سِبَاعٌ فَقَالَ هَلْ مِنْ مُبَارِزٍ قَالَ فَخَرَجَ إِلَيْهِ حَمْزَةُ بْنُ عَبْدِ الْمُطَّلِبِ فَقَالَ يَا سِبَاعُ يَا ابْنَ أُمِّ أَنْمَارٍ مُقَطِّعَةِ الْبُظُورِ، أَتُحَادُّ اللَّهَ وَرَسُولَهُ صلى الله عليه وسلم قَالَ ثُمَّ شَدَّ عَلَيْهِ فَكَانَ كَأَمْسِ الذَّاهِبِ ـ قَالَ ـ وَكَمَنْتُ لِحَمْزَةَ تَحْتَ صَخْرَةٍ فَلَمَّا دَنَا مِنِّي رَمَيْتُهُ بِحَرْبَتِي، فَأَضَعُهَا فِي ثُنَّتِهِ حَتَّى خَرَجَتْ مِنْ بَيْنِ وَرِكَيْهِ ـ قَالَ ـ فَكَانَ ذَاكَ الْعَهْدَ بِهِ، فَلَمَّا رَجَعَ النَّاسُ رَجَعْتُ مَعَهُمْ فَأَقَمْتُ بِمَكَّةَ، حَتَّى فَشَا فِيهَا الإِسْلاَمُ، ثُمَّ خَرَجْتُ إِلَى الطَّائِفِ، فَأَرْسَلُوا إِلَى رَسُولِ اللَّهِ صلى الله عليه وسلم رَسُولاً، فَقِيلَ لِي إِنَّهُ لاَ يَهِيجُ الرُّسُلَ ـ قَالَ ـ فَخَرَجْتُ مَعَهُمْ حَتَّى قَدِمْتُ عَلَى رَسُولِ اللَّهِ صلى الله عليه وسلم فَلَمَّا رَآنِي قَالَ " آنْتَ وَحْشِيٌّ ". قُلْتُ نَعَمْ. قَالَ " أَنْتَ قَتَلْتَ حَمْزَةَ ". قُلْتُ قَدْ كَانَ مِنَ الأَمْرِ مَا بَلَغَكَ. قَالَ " فَهَلْ تَسْتَطِيعُ أَنْ تُغَيِّبَ وَجْهَكَ عَنِّي ". قَالَ فَخَرَجْتُ، فَلَمَّا قُبِضَ رَسُولُ اللَّهِ صلى الله عليه وسلم فَخَرَجَ مُسَيْلِمَةُ الْكَذَّابُ قُلْتُ لأَخْرُجَنَّ إِلَى مُسَيْلِمَةَ لَعَلِّي أَقْتُلُهُ فَأُكَافِئَ بِهِ حَمْزَةَ ـ قَالَ ـ فَخَرَجْتُ مَعَ النَّاسِ، فَكَانَ مِنْ أَمْرِهِ مَا كَانَ ـ قَالَ ـ فَإِذَا رَجُلٌ قَائِمٌ فِي ثَلْمَةِ جِدَارٍ، كَأَنَّهُ جَمَلٌ أَوْرَقُ ثَائِرُ الرَّأْسِ ـ قَالَ ـ فَرَمَيْتُهُ بِحَرْبَتِي، فَأَضَعُهَا بَيْنَ ثَدْيَيْهِ حَتَّى خَرَجَتْ مِنْ بَيْنِ كَتِفَيْهِ ـ قَالَ ـ وَوَثَبَ إِلَيْهِ رَجُلٌ مِنَ الأَنْصَارِ، فَضَرَبَهُ بِالسَّيْفِ عَلَى هَامَتِهِ. قَالَ قَالَ عَبْدُ اللَّهِ بْنُ الْفَضْلِ فَأَخْبَرَنِي سُلَيْمَانُ بْنُ يَسَارٍ أَنَّهُ سَمِعَ عَبْدَ اللَّهِ بْنَ عُمَرَ يَقُولُ فَقَالَتْ جَارِيَةٌ عَلَى ظَهْرِ بَيْتٍ وَا أَمِيرَ الْمُؤْمِنِينَ، قَتَلَهُ الْعَبْدُ الأَسْوَدُ

Narrated Khalid bin Madan: That ‘Umair bin Al-Aswad Al-Anasi told him that he went to ‘Ubada bin As-Samit while he was staying in his house at the sea-shore of Hims with (his wife) Um Haram. ‘Umair said. Um Haram informed us that she heard the Prophet ﷺ saying, “Paradise is granted to the first batch of my followers who will undertake a naval expedition.” Um Haram added, I said, ‘O Allah’s Messenger ﷺ ! Will I be amongst them?’ He replied, ‘You are amongst them.’ The Prophet ﷺ then said, ‘The first army amongst’ my followers who will invade Caesar’s City will be forgiven their sins.’ I asked, ‘Will I be one of them, O Allah’s Messenger ﷺ?’ He replied in the negative.” – Sahih Al-Bukhari 2924

حَدَّثَنِي إِسْحَاقُ بْنُ يَزِيدَ الدِّمَشْقِيُّ، حَدَّثَنَا يَحْيَى بْنُ حَمْزَةَ، قَالَ حَدَّثَنِي ثَوْرُ بْنُ يَزِيدَ، عَنْ خَالِدِ بْنِ مَعْدَانَ، أَنَّ عُمَيْرَ بْنَ الأَسْوَدِ الْعَنْسِيَّ، حَدَّثَهُ أَنَّهُ، أَتَى عُبَادَةَ بْنَ الصَّامِتِ وَهْوَ نَازِلٌ فِي سَاحِلِ حِمْصَ، وَهْوَ فِي بِنَاءٍ لَهُ وَمَعَهُ أُمُّ حَرَامٍ، قَالَ عُمَيْرٌ فَحَدَّثَتْنَا أُمُّ حَرَامٍ أَنَّهَا سَمِعَتِ النَّبِيَّ صلى الله عليه وسلم يَقُولُ " أَوَّلُ جَيْشٍ مِنْ أُمَّتِي يَغْزُونَ الْبَحْرَ قَدْ أَوْجَبُوا ". قَالَتْ أُمُّ حَرَامٍ قُلْتُ يَا رَسُولَ اللَّهِ أَنَا فِيهِمْ. قَالَ " أَنْتِ فِيهِمْ ". ثُمَّ قَالَ النَّبِيُّ صلى الله عليه وسلم " أَوَّلُ جَيْشٍ مِنْ أُمَّتِي يَغْزُونَ مَدِينَةَ قَيْصَرَ مَغْفُورٌ لَهُمْ ". فَقُلْتُ أَنَا فِيهِمْ يَا رَسُولَ اللَّهِ. قَالَ " لاَ ".

Narrated ‘Alqama: While we were in the city of Hims (in Syria), Ibn Mas`ud recited Surat Yusuf. A man said to him), “It was not revealed in this way.” Then Ibn Mas`ud said, “I recited it in this way before Allah’s Messenger ﷺ and he confirmed my recitation by saying, ‘Well done!’ ” Ibn Mas`ud detected the smell of wine from the man’s mouth, so he said to him, “Aren’t you ashamed of telling a lie about Allah’s Book and (along with this) you drink alcoholic liquors too?” Then he lashed him according to the law. – Sahih Al-Bukhari 5001

حَدَّثَنِي مُحَمَّدُ بْنُ كَثِيرٍ، أَخْبَرَنَا سُفْيَانُ، عَنِ الأَعْمَشِ، عَنْ إِبْرَاهِيمَ، عَنْ عَلْقَمَةَ، قَالَ كُنَّا بِحِمْصَ فَقَرَأَ ابْنُ مَسْعُودٍ سُورَةَ يُوسُفَ، فَقَالَ رَجُلٌ مَا هَكَذَا أُنْزِلَتْ قَالَ قَرَأْتُ عَلَى رَسُولِ اللَّهِ صلى الله عليه وسلم فَقَالَ أَحْسَنْتَ. وَوَجَدَ مِنْهُ رِيحَ الْخَمْرِ فَقَالَ أَتَجْمَعُ أَنْ تُكَذِّبَ بِكِتَابِ اللَّهِ وَتَشْرَبَ الْخَمْرَ. فَضَرَبَهُ الْحَدَّ

.....Heraclius wrote to a friend of his in Rome, who was his equal in knowledge, and Heraclius went to Homs. He did not reach Homs until a letter came to him from his friend agreeing with Heraclius’s opinion that the Prophet ﷺ, had come out and that he was a prophet. So Heraclius gave permission to the nobles of Rome to a gathering of his in Homs, then he ordered its gates to be closed..... – Sahih Al-Bukhari 7

كَتَبَ هِرَقْلُ إِلَى صَاحِبٍ لَهُ بِرُومِيَةَ، وَكَانَ نَظِيرَهُ فِي الْعِلْمِ، وَسَارَ هِرَقْلُ إِلَى حِمْصَ، فَلَمْ يَرِمْ حِمْصَ حَتَّى أَتَاهُ كِتَابٌ مِنْ صَاحِبِهِ يُوَافِقُ رَأْىَ هِرَقْلَ عَلَى خُرُوجِ النَّبِيِّ صلى الله عليه وسلم وَأَنَّهُ نَبِيٌّ، فَأَذِنَ هِرَقْلُ لِعُظَمَاءِ الرُّومِ فِي دَسْكَرَةٍ لَهُ بِحِمْصَ ثُمَّ أَمَرَ بِأَبْوَابِهَا فَغُلِّقَتْ،

The Book of
Nejd
نجد

Narrated Ibn `Umar: (The Prophet) said, "O Allah! Bless our Sham and our Yemen." People said, "Our Najd as well." The Prophet again said, "O Allah! Bless our Sham and Yemen." They said again, "Our Najd as well." On that the Prophet ﷺ said, "There will appear earthquakes and afflictions, and from there will come out the side of the head of Satan." – Sahih Al-Bukhari 1037

حَدَّثَنَا مُحَمَّدُ بْنُ الْمُثَنَّى، قَالَ حَدَّثَنَا حُسَيْنُ بْنُ الْحَسَنِ، قَالَ حَدَّثَنَا ابْنُ عَوْنٍ، عَنْ نَافِعٍ، عَنِ ابْنِ عُمَرَ، قَالَ اللَّهُمَّ بَارِكْ لَنَا فِي شَامِنَا وَفِي يَمَنِنَا. قَالَ قَالُوا وَفِي نَجْدِنَا قَالَ قَالَ اللَّهُمَّ بَارِكْ لَنَا فِي شَامِنَا وَفِي يَمَنِنَا. قَالَ قَالُوا وَفِي نَجْدِنَا قَالَ قَالَ هُنَاكَ الزَّلاَزِلُ وَالْفِتَنُ، وَبِهَا يَطْلُعُ قَرْنُ الشَّيْطَانِ.

Narrated Salim's father: The Prophet ﷺ stood up beside the pulpit (and pointed with his finger towards the East) and said, "Afflictions are there! Afflictions are there, from where the side of the head of Satan comes out," or said, "..the side of the sun..". – Sahih Al-Bukhari 7092

حَدَّثَنِي عَبْدُ اللَّهِ بْنُ مُحَمَّدٍ، حَدَّثَنَا هِشَامُ بْنُ يُوسُفَ، عَنْ مَعْمَرٍ، عَنِ الزُّهْرِيِّ، عَنْ سَالِمٍ، عَنْ أَبِيهِ، عَنِ النَّبِيِّ صلى الله عليه وسلم أَنَّهُ قَامَ إِلَى جَنْبِ الْمِنْبَرِ فَقَالَ " الْفِتْنَةُ هَا هُنَا الْفِتْنَةُ هَا هُنَا مِنْ حَيْثُ يَطْلُعُ قَرْنُ الشَّيْطَانِ ". أَوْ قَالَ " قَرْنُ الشَّمْسِ ".

Narrated `Abdullah: The Prophet ﷺ stood up and delivered a sermon, and pointing to `Aisha's house (i.e. eastwards), he said thrice, "Affliction (will appear from) here," and, "from where the side of the Satan's head comes out (i.e. from the East). – Sahih Al-Bukhari 3104

حَدَّثَنَا مُوسَى بْنُ إِسْمَاعِيلَ، حَدَّثَنَا جُوَيْرِيَةُ، عَنْ نَافِعٍ، عَنْ عَبْدِ اللَّهِ ـ رضى الله عنه ـ قَالَ قَامَ النَّبِيُّ صلى الله عليه وسلم خَطِيبًا فَأَشَارَ نَحْوَ مَسْكَنِ عَائِشَةَ فَقَالَ " هُنَا الْفِتْنَةُ ـ ثَلاَثًا ـ مِنْ حَيْثُ يَطْلُعُ قَرْنُ الشَّيْطَانِ ".

Narrated Jabir bin `Abdullah: That he proceeded in the company of Allah's Messenger ﷺ towards Najd to participate in a Ghazwa. (Holybattle) When Allah's Messenger ﷺ returned, he too returned with him. Midday came upon them while they were in a valley having many thorny trees. Allah's Messenger ﷺ and the people dismounted and dispersed to rest in the shade of the trees. Allah's Messenger ﷺ rested under a tree and hung his sword on it. We all took a nap and suddenly we heard Allah's Messenger ﷺ calling us. (We woke up) to see a bedouin with him. The Prophet ﷺ said, "This bedouin took out my sword while I was sleeping and when I woke up, I found the unsheathed sword in his hand and he challenged me saying, 'Who will save you from me?' I said thrice, 'Allah.' The Prophet ﷺ did not punish him but sat down. – Al-Bukhari 2910. [17]

حَدَّثَنَا أَبُو الْيَمَانِ، أَخْبَرَنَا شُعَيْبٌ، عَنِ الزُّهْرِيِّ، قَالَ حَدَّثَنِي سِنَانُ بْنُ أَبِي سِنَانٍ الدُّؤَلِيُّ، وَأَبُو سَلَمَةَ بْنُ عَبْدِ الرَّحْمَنِ أَنَّ جَابِرَ بْنَ عَبْدِ اللَّهِ ـ رضى الله عنهما ـ أَخْبَرَ أَنَّهُ، غَزَا مَعَ رَسُولِ اللَّهِ صلى الله عليه وسلم قِبَلَ نَجْدٍ، فَلَمَّا قَفَلَ رَسُولُ اللَّهِ صلى الله عليه وسلم قَفَلَ مَعَهُ، فَأَدْرَكَتْهُمُ الْقَائِلَةُ فِي وَادٍ كَثِيرِ الْعِضَاهِ، فَنَزَلَ رَسُولُ اللَّهِ صلى الله عليه وسلم وَتَفَرَّقَ النَّاسُ يَسْتَظِلُّونَ بِالشَّجَرِ، فَنَزَلَ رَسُولُ اللَّهِ صلى الله عليه وسلم تَحْتَ سَمُرَةٍ وَعَلَّقَ بِهَا سَيْفَهُ وَنِمْنَا نَوْمَةً، فَإِذَا رَسُولُ اللَّهِ صلى الله

---

[17] This event occurred during the battle of Riqa , Sahih Al-Bukhari 4136

عليه وسلم يَدْعُونَا وَإِذَا عِنْدَهُ أَعْرَابِيٌّ فَقَالَ " إِنَّ هَذَا اخْتَرَطَ عَلَىَّ سَيْفِي وَأَنَا نَائِمٌ، فَاسْتَيْقَظْتُ وَهْوَ فِي يَدِهِ صَلْتًا ". فَقَالَ مَنْ يَمْنَعُكَ مِنِّي فَقُلْتُ " اللَّهُ ". ثَلاَثًا وَلَمْ يُعَاقِبْهُ وَجَلَسَ.

Narrated Abu Sa`id: `Ali sent a piece of gold to the Prophet ﷺ who distributed it among four persons: Al-Aqra' bin H`Abis Al-Hanzali from the tribe of Mujashi, 'Uyaina bin Badr Al-Fazari, Zaid at-Ta'I who belonged to (the tribe of) Bani Nahban, and 'Alqama bin Ulatha Al-`Amir who belonged to (the tribe of) Bani Kilab. So the Quraish and the Ansar became angry and said, "He (i.e. the Prophet,) gives the chief of Najd and does not give us." The Prophet ﷺ said, "I give them) so as to attract their hearts (to Islam)." Then a man with sunken eyes, prominent checks, a raised forehead, a thick beard and a shaven head, came (in front of the Prophet ﷺ (and said, "Be afraid of Allah, O Muhammad!" The Prophet ﷺ said "Who would obey Allah if I disobeyed Him? (Is it fair that) Allah has trusted all the people of the earth to me while, you do not trust me?" Somebody who, I think was Khalid bin Al-Walid, requested the Prophet ﷺ to let him chop that man's head off, but he prevented him. When the man left, the Prophet ﷺ said, "Among the off-spring of this man will be some who will recite the Qur'an but the Qur'an will not reach beyond their throats (i.e. they will recite like parrots and will not understand it nor act on it), and they will renegade from the religion as an arrow goes through the game's body. They will kill the Muslims but will not disturb the idolaters. If I should live up to their time' I will kill them as the people of 'Ad were killed (i.e. I will kill all of them).". – Sahih Al-Bukhari 3344

قَالَ وَقَالَ ابْنُ كَثِيرٍ عَنْ سُفْيَانَ، عَنْ أَبِيهِ، عَنِ ابْنِ أَبِي نُعْمٍ، عَنْ أَبِي سَعِيدٍ ـ رضى الله عنه ـ قَالَ بَعَثَ عَلِيٌّ ـ رضى الله عنه ـ إِلَى النَّبِيِّ صلى الله عليه وسلم بِذُهَيْبَةٍ فَقَسَمَهَا بَيْنَ الأَرْبَعَةِ الأَقْرَعِ بْنِ حَابِسٍ الْحَنْظَلِيِّ ثُمَّ الْمُجَاشِعِيِّ، وَعُيَيْنَةَ بْنِ بَدْرٍ الْفَزَارِيِّ، وَزَيْدٍ الطَّائِيِّ ثُمَّ أَحَدِ بَنِي نَبْهَانَ، وَعَلْقَمَةَ بْنِ عُلاَثَةَ الْعَامِرِيِّ ثُمَّ أَحَدِ بَنِي كِلاَبٍ، فَغَضِبَتْ قُرَيْشٌ وَالأَنْصَارُ، قَالُوا يُعْطِي صَنَادِيدَ أَهْلِ نَجْدٍ وَيَدَعُنَا. قَالَ " إِنَّمَا أَتَأَلَّفُهُمْ ". فَأَقْبَلَ رَجُلٌ غَائِرُ الْعَيْنَيْنِ مُشْرِفُ الْوَجْنَتَيْنِ، نَاتِئُ الْجَبِينِ، كَثُّ اللِّحْيَةِ، مَحْلُوقٌ فَقَالَ اتَّقِ اللَّهَ يَا مُحَمَّدُ. فَقَالَ " مَنْ يُطِعِ اللَّهَ إِذَا عَصَيْتُ، أَيَأْمَنُنِي اللَّهُ عَلَى أَهْلِ الأَرْضِ فَلاَ تَأْمَنُونِي ". فَسَأَلَهُ رَجُلٌ قَتْلَهُ ـ أَحْسِبُهُ خَالِدَ بْنَ الْوَلِيدِ ـ فَمَنَعَهُ، فَلَمَّا وَلَّى قَالَ " إِنَّ مِنْ ضِئْضِئِ هَذَا ـ أَوْ فِي عَقِبِ هَذَا ـ قَوْمٌ يَقْرَءُونَ الْقُرْآنَ، لاَ يُجَاوِزُ حَنَاجِرَهُمْ، يَمْرُقُونَ مِنَ الدِّينِ مُرُوقَ السَّهْمِ مِنَ الرَّمِيَّةِ، يَقْتُلُونَ أَهْلَ الإِسْلاَمِ، وَيَدَعُونَ أَهْلَ الأَوْثَانِ، لَئِنْ أَنَا أَدْرَكْتُهُمْ لأَقْتُلَنَّهُمْ قَتْلَ عَادٍ "

Narrated Nafi` from Ibn `Umar: Allah's Messenger ﷺ sent a Sariya towards Najd, and `Abdullah bin `Umar was in the Sariya. They gained a great number of camels as war booty. The share of each one of them was twelve or eleven camels, and they were given an extra camel each. – Sahih Al-Bukhari 3134

حَدَّثَنَا عَبْدُ اللَّهِ بْنُ يُوسُفَ، أَخْبَرَنَا مَالِكٌ، عَنْ نَافِعٍ، عَنِ ابْنِ عُمَرَ ـ رضى الله عنهما أَنَّ رَسُولَ اللَّهِ صلى الله عليه وسلم بَعَثَ سَرِيَّةً فِيهَا عَبْدُ اللَّهِ قِبَلَ نَجْدٍ، فَغَنِمُوا إِبِلاً كَثِيرًا، فَكَانَتْ سِهَامُهُمُ اثْنَىْ عَشَرَ بَعِيرًا أَوْ أَحَدَ عَشَرَ بَعِيرًا، وَنُفِّلُوا بَعِيرًا بَعِيرًا

Narrated `Abdullah bin `Abbas: Allah's Messenger ﷺ said, "While I was sleeping, two golden bangles were put in my two hands, so I got scared (frightened) and disliked it, but I was given permission to blow them off, and they flew away. I interpret it as a symbol of two liars who will appear." 'Ubaidullah said, "One of them was Al-`Ansi who was killed by Fairuz at Yemen and the other was Musailama (at Najd) . – Sahih Al-Bukhari 7034

فَقَالَ ابْنُ عَبَّاسٍ ذُكِرَ لِي أَنَّ رَسُولَ اللَّهِ صلى الله عليه وسلم قَالَ " بَيْنَا أَنَا نَائِمٌ رَأَيْتُ أَنَّهُ وُضِعَ فِي يَدَىَّ سِوَارَانِ مِنْ ذَهَبٍ، فَفُظِعْتُهُمَا وَكَرِهْتُهُمَا، فَأُذِنَ لِي، فَنَفَخْتُهُمَا فَطَارَا، فَأَوَّلْتُهُمَا كَذَّابَيْنِ يَخْرُجَانِ ". فَقَالَ عُبَيْدُ اللَّهِ أَحَدُهُمَا الْعَنْسِيُّ الَّذِي قَتَلَهُ فَيْرُوزُ بِالْيَمَنِ، وَالآخَرُ مُسَيْلِمَةُ

Narrated Abu Bakra: The Prophet ﷺ said, "Do you think that the tribes of Juhaina, Muzaina, Aslam and Ghifar are better than the tribes of Bani Tamim, Bani Asad, Bani `Abdullah bin

Ghatafan and Bani Amir bin Sasaa?" A man said, "They were unsuccessful and losers." The Prophet ﷺ added, "(Yes), they are better than the tribes of Bani Tamim, Bani Asad, Bani `Abdullah bin Ghatafan and Bani Amir bin Sasaa." – Sahih Al-Bukhari 3515

حَدَّثَنَا قَبِيصَةُ، حَدَّثَنَا سُفْيَانُ. حَدَّثَنِي مُحَمَّدُ بْنُ بَشَّارٍ، حَدَّثَنَا ابْنُ مَهْدِيٍّ، عَنْ سُفْيَانَ، عَنْ عَبْدِ الْمَلِكِ بْنِ عُمَيْرٍ، عَنْ عَبْدِ الرَّحْمَنِ بْنِ أَبِي بَكْرَةَ، عَنْ أَبِيهِ، قَالَ النَّبِيُّ صلى الله عليه وسلم " أَرَأَيْتُمْ إِنْ كَانَ جُهَيْنَةُ وَمُزَيْنَةُ وَأَسْلَمُ وَغِفَارُ خَيْرًا مِنْ بَنِي تَمِيمٍ وَبَنِي أَسَدٍ، وَمِنْ بَنِي عَبْدِ اللَّهِ بْنِ غَطَفَانَ وَمِنْ بَنِي عَامِرِ بْنِ صَعْصَعَةَ ". فَقَالَ رَجُلٌ خَابُوا وَخَسِرُوا. فَقَالَ " هُمْ خَيْرٌ مِنْ بَنِي تَمِيمٍ وَمِنْ بَنِي أَسَدٍ، وَمِنْ بَنِي عَبْدِ اللَّهِ بْنِ غَطَفَانَ، وَمِنْ بَنِي عَامِرِ بْنِ صَعْصَعَةَ ".

Narrated Hudhaifa bin Al-Yaman: The people used to ask Allah's Messenger ﷺ about the good but I used to ask him about the evil lest I should be overtaken by them. So I said, "O Allah's Messenger ﷺ ! We were living in ignorance and in an (extremely) worst atmosphere, then Allah brought to us this good (i.e., Islam); will there be any evil after this good?" He said, "Yes." I said, 'Will there be any good after that evil?" He replied, "Yes, but it will be tainted (not pure.)'' I asked, "What will be its taint?" He replied, "(There will be) some people who will guide others not according to my tradition? You will approve of some of their deeds and disapprove of some others." I asked, "Will there be any evil after that good?" He replied, "Yes, (there will be) some people calling at the gates of the (Hell) Fire, and whoever will respond to their call, will be thrown by them into the (Hell) Fire." I said, "O Allah s Apostle! Will you describe them to us?" He said, "They will be from our own people and will speak our language." I said, "What do you order me to do if such a state should take place in my life?" He said, "Stick to the group of Muslims and their Imam (ruler)." I said, "If there is neither a group of Muslims nor an Imam (ruler)?" He said, "Then turn away from all those sects even if you were to bite (eat) the roots of a tree till death overtakes you while you are in that state.". – Sahih Al-Bukhari 7084

حَدَّثَنَا مُحَمَّدُ بْنُ الْمُثَنَّى، حَدَّثَنَا الْوَلِيدُ بْنُ مُسْلِمٍ، حَدَّثَنَا ابْنُ جَابِرٍ، حَدَّثَنِي بُسْرُ بْنُ عُبَيْدِ اللَّهِ الْحَضْرَمِيُّ، أَنَّهُ سَمِعَ أَبَا إِدْرِيسَ الْخَوْلاَنِيَّ، أَنَّهُ سَمِعَ حُذَيْفَةَ بْنَ الْيَمَانِ، يَقُولُ كَانَ النَّاسُ يَسْأَلُونَ رَسُولَ اللَّهِ صلى الله عليه وسلم عَنِ الْخَيْرِ، وَكُنْتُ أَسْأَلُهُ عَنِ الشَّرِّ، مَخَافَةَ أَنْ يُدْرِكَنِي فَقُلْتُ يَا رَسُولَ اللَّهِ إِنَّا كُنَّا فِي جَاهِلِيَّةٍ وَشَرٍّ فَجَاءَنَا اللَّهُ بِهَذَا الْخَيْرِ، فَهَلْ بَعْدَ هَذَا الْخَيْرِ مِنْ شَرٍّ قَالَ " نَعَمْ ". قُلْتُ وَهَلْ بَعْدَ ذَلِكَ الشَّرِّ مِنْ خَيْرٍ قَالَ " نَعَمْ، وَفِيهِ دَخَنٌ ". قُلْتُ وَمَا دَخَنُهُ قَالَ " قَوْمٌ يَهْدُونَ بِغَيْرِ هَدْيِي، تَعْرِفُ مِنْهُمْ وَتُنْكِرُ ". قُلْتُ فَهَلْ بَعْدَ ذَلِكَ الْخَيْرِ مِنْ شَرٍّ قَالَ " نَعَمْ، دُعَاةٌ عَلَى أَبْوَابِ جَهَنَّمَ، مَنْ أَجَابَهُمْ إِلَيْهَا قَذَفُوهُ فِيهَا ". قُلْتُ يَا رَسُولَ اللَّهِ صِفْهُمْ لَنَا. قَالَ " هُمْ مِنْ جِلْدَتِنَا، وَيَتَكَلَّمُونَ بِأَلْسِنَتِنَا ". قُلْتُ فَمَا تَأْمُرُنِي إِنْ أَدْرَكَنِي ذَلِكَ قَالَ " تَلْزَمُ جَمَاعَةَ الْمُسْلِمِينَ وَإِمَامَهُمْ ". قُلْتُ فَإِنْ لَمْ يَكُنْ لَهُمْ جَمَاعَةٌ وَلاَ إِمَامٌ قَالَ " فَاعْتَزِلْ تِلْكَ الْفِرَقَ كُلَّهَا، وَلَوْ أَنْ تَعَضَّ بِأَصْلِ شَجَرَةٍ، حَتَّى يُدْرِكَكَ الْمَوْتُ، وَأَنْتَ عَلَى ذَلِكَ "

Narrated `Abdullah bin `Umar: Allah's Messenger ﷺ said. "While I was sleeping, I saw myself (in a dream) performing Tawaf around the Ka`ba. Behold, I saw a reddish-white man with lank hair, and water was dropping from his head. I asked, "Who is this?' They replied, 'The son of Mary.' Then I turned my face to see another man with a huge body, red complexion and curly hair and blind in one eye. His eye looked like a protruding out grape. They said (to me), He is Ad-Dajjal." The Prophet ﷺ added, "The man he resembled most is Ibn Qatan, a man from the tribe of Khuza`a. ". – Sahih Al-Bukhari 7128

حَدَّثَنَا أَبُو الْيَمَانِ، أَخْبَرَنَا شُعَيْبٌ، عَنِ الزُّهْرِيِّ، ح وَحَدَّثَنَا إِسْمَاعِيلُ، حَدَّثَنِي أَخِي، عَنْ سُلَيْمَانَ، عَنْ مُحَمَّدِ بْنِ أَبِي عَتِيقٍ، عَنِ ابْنِ شِهَابٍ، عَنْ عُرْوَةَ بْنِ الزُّبَيْرِ، أَنَّ زَيْنَبَ ابْنَةَ أَبِي سَلَمَةَ، حَدَّثَتْهُ عَنْ أُمِّ حَبِيبَةَ بِنْتِ أَبِي سُفْيَانَ، عَنْ زَيْنَبَ ابْنَةِ جَحْشٍ، أَنَّ رَسُولَ اللَّهِ صلى الله عليه وسلم دَخَلَ عَلَيْهَا يَوْمًا فَزِعًا يَقُولُ " لاَ إِلَهَ إِلاَّ اللَّهُ، وَيْلٌ لِلْعَرَبِ مِنْ شَرٍّ قَدِ اقْتَرَبَ، فُتِحَ الْيَوْمَ مِنْ رَدْمِ يَأْجُوجَ وَمَأْجُوجَ مِثْلُ هَذِهِ ". وَحَلَّقَ بِإِصْبَعَيْهِ الإِبْهَامِ وَالَّتِي تَلِيهَا. قَالَتْ زَيْنَبُ ابْنَةُ جَحْشٍ فَقُلْتُ يَا رَسُولَ اللَّهِ أَفَنَهْلِكُ وَفِينَا الصَّالِحُونَ قَالَ " نَعَمْ إِذَا كَثُرَ الْخُبْثُ "..

Narrated Ibn `Umar: The Prophet ﷺ sent a Sariya towards Najd and I was in it, and our share from the booty amounted to twelve camels each, and we were given an additional camel each. So we returned with thirteen camels each. – Sahih al-Bukhari 4338

حَدَّثَنَا أَبُو النُّعْمَانِ، حَدَّثَنَا حَمَّادٌ، حَدَّثَنَا أَيُّوبُ، عَنْ نَافِعٍ، عَنِ ابْنِ عُمَرَ ـ رضى الله عنهما ـ قَالَ بَعَثَ النَّبِيُّ صلى الله عليه وسلم سَرِيَّةً قِبَلَ نَجْدٍ، فَكُنْتُ فِيهَا، فَبَلَغَتْ سِهَامُنَا اثْنَىْ عَشَرَ بَعِيرًا، وَنُفِّلْنَا بَعِيرًا بَعِيرًا، فَرَجَعْنَا بِثَلاَثَةَ عَشَرَ بَعِيرًا.

Narrated Abu Huraira: The Prophet ﷺ sent some horsemen to Najd and they arrested and brought a man called Thumama bin Uthal from the tribe of Bani Hanifa, and they fastened him to one of the pillars of the Mosque. – Sahih al-Bukhari 2423

حَدَّثَنَا عَبْدُ اللَّهِ بْنُ يُوسُفَ، حَدَّثَنَا اللَّيْثُ، قَالَ حَدَّثَنِي سَعِيدُ بْنُ أَبِي سَعِيدٍ، سَمِعَ أَبَا هُرَيْرَةَ ـ رضى الله عنه ـ قَالَ بَعَثَ النَّبِيُّ صلى الله عليه وسلم خَيْلاً قِبَلَ نَجْدٍ، فَجَاءَتْ بِرَجُلٍ مِنْ بَنِي حَنِيفَةَ يُقَالُ لَهُ ثُمَامَةُ بْنُ أُثَالٍ فَرَبَطُوهُ بِسَارِيَةٍ مِنْ سَوَارِي الْمَسْجِدِ.

Narrated Sinan and Abu Salama: Jabir mentioned that he had participated in a Ghazwa towards Najd in the company of Allah's Messenger ﷺ . – Sahih al-Bukhari 4134

حَدَّثَنَا أَبُو الْيَمَانِ، حَدَّثَنَا شُعَيْبٌ، عَنِ الزُّهْرِيِّ، قَالَ حَدَّثَنِي سِنَانٌ، وَأَبُو سَلَمَةَ أَنَّ جَابِرًا، أَخْبَرَ أَنَّهُ، غَزَا مَعَ رَسُولِ اللَّهِ صلى الله عليه وسلم قِبَلَ نَجْدٍ.

Narrated Anas: On the day of the Conquest of Mecca, when the Prophet ﷺ had given (from the booty) the Quraish, the Ansar said, "By Allah, this is indeed very strange: While our swords are still dribbling with the blood of Quraish, our war booty are distributed amongst them." When this news reached the Prophet ﷺ he called the Ansar and said, "What is this news that has reached me from you?" They used not to tell lies, so they replied, "What has reached you is true." He said, "Doesn't it please you that the people take the booty to their homes and you take Allah's Messenger ﷺ to your homes? If the Ansar took their way through a valley or a mountain pass, I would take the Ansar's valley or a mountain pass." - Sahih al-Bukhari 3778

حَدَّثَنَا أَبُو الْوَلِيدِ، حَدَّثَنَا شُعْبَةُ، عَنْ أَبِي التَّيَّاحِ، قَالَ سَمِعْتُ أَنَسًا ـ رضى الله عنه ـ يَقُولُ قَالَتِ الأَنْصَارُ يَوْمَ فَتْحِ مَكَّةَ ـ وَأَعْطَى قُرَيْشًا ـ وَاللَّهِ إِنَّ هَذَا لَهُوَ الْعَجَبُ، إِنَّ سُيُوفَنَا تَقْطُرُ مِنْ دِمَاءِ قُرَيْشٍ، وَغَنَائِمُنَا تُرَدُّ عَلَيْهِمْ. فَبَلَغَ ذَلِكَ النَّبِيَّ صلى الله عليه وسلم فَدَعَا الأَنْصَارَ قَالَ فَقَالَ " مَا الَّذِي بَلَغَنِي عَنْكُمْ ". وَكَانُوا لاَ يَكْذِبُونَ. فَقَالُوا هُوَ الَّذِي بَلَغَكَ. قَالَ " أَوَلاَ تَرْضَوْنَ أَنْ يَرْجِعَ النَّاسُ بِالْغَنَائِمِ إِلَى بُيُوتِهِمْ، وَتَرْجِعُونَ بِرَسُولِ اللَّهِ صلى الله عليه وسلم إِلَى بُيُوتِكُمْ لَوْ سَلَكَتِ الأَنْصَارُ وَادِيًا أَوْ شِعْبًا، لَسَلَكْتُ وَادِيَ الأَنْصَارِ أَوْ شِعْبَهُمْ

The Book of
Shams
شمس

Narrated Ibn `Umar: (The Prophet) said, “O Allah! Bless our Sham and our Yemen.” People said, “Our Najd as well.” The Prophet again said, “O Allah! Bless our Sham and Yemen.” They said again, “Our Najd as well." On that the Prophet ﷺ said, "There will appear earthquakes and afflictions, and from there will come out the side of the head of Satan." – Sahih al-Bukhari 1037

حَدَّثَنَا مُحَمَّدُ بْنُ الْمُثَنَّى، قَالَ حَدَّثَنَا حُسَيْنُ بْنُ الْحَسَنِ، قَالَ حَدَّثَنَا ابْنُ عَوْنٍ، عَنْ نَافِعٍ، عَنِ ابْنِ عُمَرَ، قَالَ اللَّهُمَّ بَارِكْ لَنَا فِي شَامِنَا وَفِي يَمَنِنَا. قَالَ قَالُوا وَفِي نَجْدِنَا قَالَ قَالَ اللَّهُمَّ بَارِكْ لَنَا فِي شَامِنَا وَفِي يَمَنِنَا. قَالَ قَالُوا وَفِي نَجْدِنَا قَالَ قَالَ هُنَاكَ الزَّلاَزِلُ وَالْفِتَنُ، وَبِهَا يَطْلُعُ قَرْنُ الشَّيْطَانِ.

Narrated Jubair bin Mut`im: I and `Uthman bin `Affan went to Allah’s Messenger ﷺ and said, “O Allah’s Messenger ﷺ ! You have given to Bani Al-Muttalib and left us although they and we are of the same kinship to you.” Allah’s Messenger ﷺ said, “Bani Muttalib and Bani Hashim are one and the same.” The Prophet ﷺ did not give a share to Bani `Abd Shams and Bani Naufai. (Ibn ‘Is-haq said, “Abd Shams and Hashim and Al-Muttalib were maternal brothers and their mother was ‘Atika bint Murra and Naufal was their paternal brother.) – Sahih al-Bukhari 3140

حَدَّثَنَا عَبْدُ اللَّهِ بْنُ يُوسُفَ، حَدَّثَنَا اللَّيْثُ، عَنْ عُقَيْلٍ، عَنِ ابْنِ شِهَابٍ، عَنِ ابْنِ الْمُسَيَّبِ، عَنْ جُبَيْرِ بْنِ مُطْعِمٍ، قَالَ مَشَيْتُ أَنَا وَعُثْمَانُ بْنُ عَفَّانَ، إِلَى رَسُولِ اللَّهِ صلى الله عليه وسلم فَقُلْنَا يَا رَسُولَ اللَّهِ، أَعْطَيْتَ بَنِي الْمُطَّلِبِ وَتَرَكْتَنَا، وَنَحْنُ وَهُمْ مِنْكَ بِمَنْزِلَةٍ وَاحِدَةٍ. فَقَالَ رَسُولُ اللَّهِ صلى الله عليه وسلم " إِنَّمَا بَنُو الْمُطَّلِبِ وَبَنُو هَاشِمٍ شَىْءٌ وَاحِدٌ ". قَالَ اللَّيْثُ حَدَّثَنِي يُونُسُ وَزَادَ قَالَ جُبَيْرٌ وَلَمْ يَقْسِمِ النَّبِيُّ صلى الله عليه وسلم لِبَنِي عَبْدِ شَمْسٍ وَلاَ لِبَنِي نَوْفَلٍ. وَقَالَ ابْنُ إِسْحَاقَ عَبْدُ شَمْسٍ وَهَاشِمٌ وَالْمُطَّلِبُ إِخْوَةٌ لأُمٍّ، وَأُمُّهُمْ عَاتِكَةُ بِنْتُ مُرَّةَ، وَكَانَ نَوْفَلٌ أَخَاهُمْ لأَبِيهِمْ

Narrated Sufyan b. Abu Zuhair: I heard Allah’s Messenger ﷺ saying, “Yemen will be conquered and some people will migrate (from Medina) and will urge their families, and those who will obey them to migrate (to Yemen) although Medina will be better for them; if they but knew. Sham will also be conquered and some people will migrate (from Medina) and will urge their families and those who will obey them, to migrate (to Sham) although Medina will be better for them; if they but knew. ‘Iraq will be conquered and some people will migrate (from Medina) and will urge their families and those who will obey them to migrate (to 'Iraq) although Medina will be better for them; if they but knew.”. – Sahih al-Bukhari 1875

حَدَّثَنَا عَبْدُ اللَّهِ بْنُ يُوسُفَ، أَخْبَرَنَا مَالِكٌ، عَنْ هِشَامِ بْنِ عُرْوَةَ، عَنْ أَبِيهِ، عَنْ عَبْدِ اللَّهِ بْنِ الزُّبَيْرِ، عَنْ سُفْيَانَ بْنِ أَبِي زُهَيْرٍ ـ رضى الله عنه ـ أَنَّهُ قَالَ سَمِعْتُ رَسُولَ اللَّهِ صلى الله عليه وسلم يَقُولُ " تُفْتَحُ الْيَمَنُ فَيَأْتِي قَوْمٌ يُبِسُّونَ، فَيَتَحَمَّلُونَ بِأَهْلِيهِمْ وَمَنْ أَطَاعَهُمْ، وَالْمَدِينَةُ خَيْرٌ لَهُمْ لَوْ كَانُوا يَعْلَمُونَ، وَتُفْتَحُ الشَّأْمُ، فَيَأْتِي قَوْمٌ يُبِسُّونَ فَيَتَحَمَّلُونَ بِأَهْلِيهِمْ وَمَنْ أَطَاعَهُمْ، وَالْمَدِينَةُ خَيْرٌ لَهُمْ لَوْ كَانُوا يَعْلَمُونَ، وَتُفْتَحُ الْعِرَاقُ، فَيَأْتِي قَوْمٌ يُبِسُّونَ فَيَتَحَمَّلُونَ بِأَهْلِيهِمْ وَمَنْ أَطَاعَهُمْ. وَالْمَدِينَةُ خَيْرٌ لَهُمْ لَوْ كَانُوا يَعْلَمُونَ "

Narrated ‘ `Abdullah bin `Abbas: That Abu Sufyan bin Harb Informed him that Heraclius called him and the members of a caravan from Quraish who had gone to Sham as traders, during the truce which Allah’s Messenger ﷺ had concluded with Abu Sufyan and the Quraish infidels. – Sahih al-Bukhari 3174

حَدَّثَنَا يَحْيَى بْنُ بُكَيْرٍ، حَدَّثَنَا اللَّيْثُ، عَنْ يُونُسَ، عَنِ ابْنِ شِهَابٍ، عَنْ عُبَيْدِ اللَّهِ بْنِ عَبْدِ اللَّهِ بْنِ عُتْبَةَ، أَخْبَرَهُ أَنَّ عَبْدَ اللَّهِ بْنَ عَبَّاسٍ أَخْبَرَهُ أَنَّ أَبَا سُفْيَانَ بْنَ حَرْبٍ أَخْبَرَهُ أَنَّ هِرَقْلَ أَرْسَلَ إِلَيْهِ فِي رَكْبٍ مِنْ قُرَيْشٍ كَانُوا تِجَارًا بِالشَّأْمِ فِي الْمُدَّةِ الَّتِي مَادَّ فِيهَا رَسُولُ اللَّهِ صلى الله عليه وسلم أَبَا سُفْيَانَ فِي كُفَّارِ قُرَيْشٍ.

Narrated `Abdullah bin 'Amir bin Rabi`a: Umar bin Al-Khattab left for Sham, and when he reached a placed called Sargh, he came to know that there was an outbreak of an epidemic (of plague) in Sham. Then `AbdurRahman bin `Auf told him that Allah's Messenger ﷺ said, "If you hear the news of an outbreak of an epidemic (plague) in a certain place, do not enter that place: and if the epidemic falls in a place while you are present in it, do not leave that place to escape from the epidemic." So `Umar returned from Sargh. - Sahih al-Bukhari 6973

حَدَّثَنَا عَبْدُ اللَّهِ بْنُ مَسْلَمَةَ، عَنْ مَالِكٍ، عَنِ ابْنِ شِهَابٍ، عَنْ عَبْدِ اللَّهِ بْنِ عَامِرِ بْنِ رَبِيعَةَ، أَنَّ عُمَرَ بْنَ الْخَطَّابِ ـ رضى الله عنه ـ خَرَجَ إِلَى الشَّأْمِ، فَلَمَّا جَاءَ بِسَرْغَ بَلَغَهُ أَنَّ الْوَبَاءَ وَقَعَ بِالشَّأْمِ فَأَخْبَرَهُ عَبْدُ الرَّحْمَنِ بْنُ عَوْفٍ أَنَّ رَسُولَ اللَّهِ صلى الله عليه وسلم قَالَ " إِذَا سَمِعْتُمْ بِأَرْضٍ فَلاَ تَقْدَمُوا عَلَيْهِ، وَإِذَا وَقَعَ بِأَرْضٍ وَأَنْتُمْ بِهَا فَلاَ تَخْرُجُوا فِرَارًا مِنْهُ ". فَرَجَعَ عُمَرُ مِنْ سَرْغَ. وَعَنِ ابْنِ شِهَابٍ عَنْ سَالِمِ بْنِ عَبْدِ اللَّهِ أَنَّ عُمَرَ إِنَّمَا انْصَرَفَ مِنْ حَدِيثِ عَبْدِ الرَّحْمَنِ.

Narrated `Abdullah bin `Umar: I went up to the roof of Hafsa's house for some job and I saw Allah's Messenger ﷺ answering the call of nature facing Sham (Syria, Jordan, Palestine and Lebanon regarded as one country) with his back towards the Qibla. (See Hadith No. 147). – Sahih al-Bukhari 148

حَدَّثَنَا إِبْرَاهِيمُ بْنُ الْمُنْذِرِ، قَالَ حَدَّثَنَا أَنَسُ بْنُ عِيَاضٍ، عَنْ عُبَيْدِ اللَّهِ، عَنْ مُحَمَّدِ بْنِ يَحْيَى بْنِ حَبَّانَ، عَنْ وَاسِعِ بْنِ حَبَّانَ، عَنْ عَبْدِ اللَّهِ بْنِ عُمَرَ، قَالَ ارْتَقَيْتُ فَوْقَ ظَهْرِ بَيْتِ حَفْصَةَ لِبَعْضِ حَاجَتِي، فَرَأَيْتُ رَسُولَ اللَّهِ صلى الله عليه وسلم يَقْضِي حَاجَتَهُ مُسْتَدْبِرَ الْقِبْلَةِ مُسْتَقْبِلَ الشَّأْمِ.

Narrated Jabir bin `Abdullah: I sold a camel to the Prophet ﷺ on one of the journeys. When we reached Medina, he ordered me to go to the Mosque and offer two rak`at. Then he weighed for me (the price of the camel in gold) and gave an extra amount over it. A part of it remained with me till it was taken by the army of Sham on the day of Harra.". – Sahih al-Bukhari 2604

حَدَّثَنَا مُحَمَّدُ بْنُ بَشَّارٍ، حَدَّثَنَا غُنْدَرٌ، حَدَّثَنَا شُعْبَةُ، عَنْ مُحَارِبٍ، سَمِعْتُ جَابِرَ بْنَ عَبْدِ اللَّهِ ـ رضى الله عنهما ـ يَقُولُ بِعْتُ مِنَ النَّبِيِّ صلى الله عليه وسلم بَعِيرًا فِي سَفَرٍ، فَلَمَّا أَتَيْنَا الْمَدِينَةَ قَالَ " ائْتِ الْمَسْجِدَ فَصَلِّ رَكْعَتَيْنِ ". فَوَزَنَ ـ قَالَ شُعْبَةُ أُرَاهُ فَوَزَنَ لِي فَأَرْجَحَ، فَمَا زَالَ مِنْهَا شَىْءٌ حَتَّى أَصَابَهَا أَهْلُ الشَّأْمِ يَوْمَ الْحَرَّةِ

Narrated Alqama: I went to Sham (and asked. "Who is here?"), The people said, "Abu Ad-Darda." Abu Darda said, "Is the person whom Allah has protected against Satan, (as Allah's Messenger ﷺ said) amongst you". The subnarrator, Mughira said that the person who was given Allah's Refuge through the tongue of the Prophet was `Ammar (bin Yasir). – Sahih al-Bukhari 3287

حَدَّثَنَا مَالِكُ بْنُ إِسْمَاعِيلَ، حَدَّثَنَا إِسْرَائِيلُ، عَنِ الْمُغِيرَةِ، عَنْ إِبْرَاهِيمَ، عَنْ عَلْقَمَةَ، قَالَ قَدِمْتُ الشَّأْمَ {فَقُلْتُ مَنْ هَا هُنَا} قَالُوا أَبُو الدَّرْدَاءِ قَالَ أَفِيكُمُ الَّذِي أَجَارَهُ اللَّهُ مِنَ الشَّيْطَانِ عَلَى لِسَانِ نَبِيِّهِ صلى الله عليه وسلم حَدَّثَنَا سُلَيْمَانُ بْنُ حَرْبٍ حَدَّثَنَا شُعْبَةُ عَنْ مُغِيرَةَ وَقَالَ الَّذِي أَجَارَهُ اللَّهُ عَلَى لِسَانِ نَبِيِّهِ صلى الله عليه وسلم يَعْنِي عَمَّارًا

Narrated `Abdullah bin `Umar: While the people were at Quba offering the morning prayer, suddenly a person came to them saying, "Tonight Divine Inspiration has been revealed to Allah's Messenger ﷺ and he has been ordered to face the Ka`ba (in prayers): therefore you people should face it." There faces were towards Sham, so they turned their faces towards the Ka`ba (at Mecca). – Sahih al-Bukhari 7251

حَدَّثَنَا إِسْمَاعِيلُ، حَدَّثَنِي مَالِكٌ، عَنْ عَبْدِ اللَّهِ بْنِ دِينَارٍ، عَنْ عَبْدِ اللَّهِ بْنِ عُمَرَ، قَالَ بَيْنَا النَّاسُ بِقُبَاءٍ فِي صَلاَةِ الصُّبْحِ إِذْ جَاءَهُمْ آتٍ فَقَالَ إِنَّ رَسُولَ اللَّهِ صلى الله عليه وسلم قَدْ أُنْزِلَ عَلَيْهِ اللَّيْلَةَ قُرْآنٌ، وَقَدْ أُمِرَ أَنْ يَسْتَقْبِلَ الْكَعْبَةَ فَاسْتَقْبِلُوهَا. وَكَانَتْ وُجُوهُهُمْ إِلَى الشَّأْمِ فَاسْتَدَارُوا إِلَى الْكَعْبَةِ

Narrated Abu Huraira: I heard Allah's Messenger ﷺ saying, "Pride and arrogance are characteristics of the rural bedouins while calmness is found among the owners of sheep. Belief is Yemenite, and wisdom is also Yemenite i.e. the Yemenites are well-known for their true belief and wisdom)." Abu `Abdullah (Al-Bukhari) said, "Yemen was called so because it is situated to the right of the Ka`ba, and Sham was called so because it is situated to the left of the Ka`ba." – Sahih al-Bukhari 3499

حَدَّثَنَا أَبُو الْيَمَانِ، أَخْبَرَنَا شُعَيْبٌ، عَنِ الزُّهْرِيِّ، قَالَ أَخْبَرَنِي أَبُو سَلَمَةَ بْنُ عَبْدِ الرَّحْمَنِ، أَنَّ أَبَا هُرَيْرَةَ ـ رضى الله عنه ـ قَالَ سَمِعْتُ رَسُولَ اللَّهِ صلى الله عليه وسلم يَقُولُ " الْفَخْرُ وَالْخُيَلاَءُ فِي الْفَدَّادِينَ أَهْلِ الْوَبَرِ، وَالسَّكِينَةُ فِي أَهْلِ الْغَنَمِ، وَالإِيمَانُ يَمَانٍ، وَالْحِكْمَةُ يَمَانِيَةٌ ". سُمِّيَتِ الْيَمَنَ لأَنَّهَا عَنْ يَمِينِ الْكَعْبَةِ، وَالشَّأْمَ عَنْ يَسَارِ الْكَعْبَةِ، وَالْمَشْأَمَةُ الْمَيْسَرَةُ، وَالْيَدُ الْيُسْرَى الشُّؤْمَى، وَالْجَانِبُ الأَيْسَرُ الأَشْأَمُ.

The Book of
Al-Hijr
الْحِجْرِ

Narrated Ibn `Umar: When Allah's Messenger ﷺ landed at Al-Hijr during the Ghazwa of Tabuk, he ordered his companions not to drink water from its well or reserve water from it. They said, "We have already kneaded the dough with its water. And also filled our bags with its water." On that, the Prophet ﷺ ordered them to throw away the dough and pour out the water. – Sahih al-Bukhari 3378

حَدَّثَنَا مُحَمَّدُ بْنُ مِسْكِينٍ أَبُو الْحَسَنِ، حَدَّثَنَا يَحْيَى بْنُ حَسَّانَ بْنِ حَيَّانَ أَبُو زَكَرِيَّاءَ، حَدَّثَنَا سُلَيْمَانُ، عَنْ عَبْدِ اللَّهِ بْنِ دِينَارٍ، عَنِ ابْنِ عُمَرَ ـ رضى الله عنهما أَنَّ رَسُولَ اللَّهِ صلى الله عليه وسلم لَمَّا نَزَلَ الْحِجْرَ فِي غَزْوَةِ تَبُوكَ أَمَرَهُمْ أَنْ لاَ يَشْرَبُوا مِنْ بِئْرِهَا، وَلاَ يَسْتَقُوا مِنْهَا فَقَالُوا قَدْ عَجَنَّا مِنْهَا، وَاسْتَقَيْنَا. فَأَمَرَهُمْ أَنْ يَطْرَحُوا ذَلِكَ الْعَجِينَ وَيُهَرِيقُوا ذَلِكَ الْمَاءَ. وَيُرْوَى عَنْ سَبْرَةَ بْنِ مَعْبَدٍ وَأَبِي الشُّمُوسِ أَنَّ النَّبِيَّ صلى الله عليه وسلم أَمَرَ بِإِلْقَاءِ الطَّعَامِ. وَقَالَ أَبُو ذَرٍّ عَنِ النَّبِيِّ صلى الله عليه وسلم " مَنِ اعْتَجَنَ بِمَائِهِ ".

Narrated `Abdullah bin `Umar: (While we were going for the Battle of Tabuk and when we reached the places of the dwellers of Al- Hijr), Allah's Messenger ﷺ said about the dwellers of Al-Hijr (to us). "Do not enter (the dwelling places) of these people unless you enter weeping, but if you weep not, then do not enter upon them, lest you be afflicted with what they were afflicted with.". – Sahih al-Bukhari 4702

حَدَّثَنَا إِبْرَاهِيمُ بْنُ الْمُنْذِرِ، حَدَّثَنَا مَعْنٌ، قَالَ حَدَّثَنِي مَالِكٌ، عَنْ عَبْدِ اللَّهِ بْنِ دِينَارٍ، عَنْ عَبْدِ اللَّهِ بْنِ عُمَرَ ـ رضى الله عنهما ـ أَنَّ رَسُولَ اللَّهِ صلى الله عليه وسلم قَالَ لأَصْحَابِ الْحِجْرِ " لاَ تَدْخُلُوا عَلَى هَؤُلاَءِ الْقَوْمِ إِلاَّ أَنْ تَكُونُوا بَاكِينَ فَإِنْ لَمْ تَكُونُوا بَاكِينَ فَلاَ تَدْخُلُوا عَلَيْهِمْ أَنْ يُصِيبَكُمْ مِثْلُ مَا أَصَابَهُمْ "

Narrated Ibn `Umar: Allah's Messenger ﷺ said to his companions who were at Al-Hijr, "Do not enter upon these people who are being punished, except in a weeping state, lest the same calamity as of theirs should befall you...". – Sahih al-Bukhari 4420

حَدَّثَنَا يَحْيَى بْنُ بُكَيْرٍ، حَدَّثَنَا مَالِكٌ، عَنْ عَبْدِ اللَّهِ بْنِ دِينَارٍ، عَنِ ابْنِ عُمَرَ ـ رضى الله عنهما ـ قَالَ قَالَ رَسُولُ اللَّهِ صلى الله عليه وسلم لأَصْحَابِ الْحِجْرِ " لاَ تَدْخُلُوا عَلَى هَؤُلاَءِ الْمُعَذَّبِينَ إِلاَّ أَنْ تَكُونُوا بَاكِينَ، أَنْ يُصِيبَكُمْ مِثْلُ مَا أَصَابَهُمْ "

Abu Ash-Sha'tha said, "Who keeps away from some portion of the Ka'bah?" Mu'awiya used to touch the four corners of the Ka'bah, Ibn 'Abbas said to him, "These two corners (the one facing the Hijr) are not to be touched." Mu'awiya said, "Nothing is untouchable in the Ka'bah." And Ibn Az-Zubair used to touch all the corners of the Ka'bah. – Sahih al-Bukhari 1608

وَقَالَ مُحَمَّدُ بْنُ بَكْرٍ أَخْبَرَنَا ابْنُ جُرَيْجٍ، أَخْبَرَنِي عَمْرُو بْنُ دِينَارٍ، عَنْ أَبِي الشَّعْثَاءِ، أَنَّهُ قَالَ وَمَنْ يَتَّقِي شَيْئًا مِنَ الْبَيْتِ، وَكَانَ مُعَاوِيَةُ يَسْتَلِمُ الأَرْكَانَ، فَقَالَ لَهُ ابْنُ عَبَّاسٍ ـ رضى الله عنهما ـ إِنَّهُ لاَ يُسْتَلَمُ هَذَانِ الرُّكْنَانِ. فَقَالَ لَيْسَ شَىْءٌ مِنَ الْبَيْتِ مَهْجُورًا، وَكَانَ ابْنُ الزُّبَيْرِ ـ رضى الله عنهما ـ يَسْتَلِمُهُنَّ كُلَّهُنَّ

Narrated Yazid bin Ruman from `Urwa: `Aisha said that the Prophet ﷺ said to her, "O Aisha! Were your nation not close to the Pre-Islamic Period of Ignorance, I would have had the Ka`ba demolished and would have included in it the portion which had been left, and would have made it at a level with the ground and would have made two doors for it, one towards the east and the other towards the west, and then by doing this it would have been built on the foundations laid by Abraham." That was what urged Ibn-Az-Zubair to demolish the Ka`ba. Jazz said, "I saw Ibn-Az-Zubair when he demolished and rebuilt the Ka`ba and included in it a portion of Al-Hijr (the unroofed portion of Ka`ba which is at present in the form of a compound towards the northwest of the Ka`ba). I saw the original foundations of Abraham which were of stones resembling the humps of camels." So Jarir asked Yazid, "Where was the place of those stones?" Jazz said, "I will just now show it to you." So Jarir accompanied Yazid and entered Al-Hijr, and Jazz pointed to a place and said, "Here it is." Jarir said, "It appeared to me about six cubits from Al-Hijr or so.". – Sahih al-Bukhari 1586

حَدَّثَنَا بَيَانُ بْنُ عَمْرٍو، حَدَّثَنَا يَزِيدُ، حَدَّثَنَا جَرِيرُ بْنُ حَازِمٍ، حَدَّثَنَا يَزِيدُ بْنُ رُومَانَ، عَنْ عُرْوَةَ، عَنْ عَائِشَةَ ـ رضى الله عنها ـ أَنَّ النَّبِيَّ صلى الله عليه وسلم قَالَ لَهَا " يَا عَائِشَةُ لَوْلاَ أَنَّ قَوْمَكِ حَدِيثُ عَهْدٍ بِجَاهِلِيَّةٍ لأَمَرْتُ بِالْبَيْتِ فَهُدِمَ، فَأَدْخَلْتُ فِيهِ مَا أُخْرِجَ مِنْهُ وَأَلْزَقْتُهُ بِالأَرْضِ، وَجَعَلْتُ لَهُ بَابَيْنِ بَابًا شَرْقِيًّا وَبَابًا غَرْبِيًّا، فَبَلَغْتُ بِهِ أَسَاسَ إِبْرَاهِيمَ ". فَذَلِكَ الَّذِي حَمَلَ ابْنَ الزُّبَيْرِ ـ رضى الله عنهما ـ عَلَى هَدْمِهِ. قَالَ يَزِيدُ وَشَهِدْتُ ابْنَ الزُّبَيْرِ حِينَ هَدَمَهُ وَبَنَاهُ وَأَدْخَلَ فِيهِ مِنَ الْحِجْرِ، وَقَدْ رَأَيْتُ أَسَاسَ إِبْرَاهِيمَ حِجَارَةً كَأَسْنِمَةِ الإِبِلِ. قَالَ جَرِيرٌ فَقُلْتُ لَهُ أَيْنَ مَوْضِعُهُ قَالَ أُرِيكَهُ الآنَ. فَدَخَلْتُ مَعَهُ الْحِجْرَ فَأَشَارَ إِلَى مَكَانٍ فَقَالَ هَا هُنَا. قَالَ جَرِيرٌ فَحَزَرْتُ مِنَ الْحِجْرِ سِتَّةَ أَذْرُعٍ أَوْ نَحْوَهَا

Narrated `Abdullah bin `Umar: (While we were going for the Battle of Tabuk and when we reached the places of the dwellers of Al- Hijr), Allah's Messenger ﷺ said about the dwellers of Al-Hijr (to us). "Do not enter (the dwelling places) of these people unless you enter weeping, but if you weep not, then do not enter upon them, lest you be afflicted with what they were afflicted with.". – Sahih al-Bukhari 4702

حَدَّثَنَا إِبْرَاهِيمُ بْنُ الْمُنْذِرِ، حَدَّثَنَا مَعْنٌ، قَالَ حَدَّثَنِي مَالِكٌ، عَنْ عَبْدِ اللَّهِ بْنِ دِينَارٍ، عَنْ عَبْدِ اللَّهِ بْنِ عُمَرَ ـ رضى الله عنهما ـ أَنَّ رَسُولَ اللَّهِ صلى الله عليه وسلم قَالَ لأَصْحَابِ الْحِجْرِ " لاَ تَدْخُلُوا عَلَى هَؤُلاَءِ الْقَوْمِ إِلاَّ أَنْ تَكُونُوا بَاكِينَ فَإِنْ لَمْ تَكُونُوا بَاكِينَ فَلاَ تَدْخُلُوا عَلَيْهِمْ أَنْ يُصِيبَكُمْ مِثْلُ مَا أَصَابَهُمْ "

Narrated Jabir bin `Abdullah: The Prophet ﷺ said, "When the Quraish disbelieved me (concerning my night journey), I stood up in Al- Hijr (the unroofed portion of the Ka`ba) and Allah displayed Bait-ul-Maqdis before me, and I started to inform them (Quraish) about its signs while looking at it.". – Sahih al-Bukhari 4710

حَدَّثَنَا أَحْمَدُ بْنُ صَالِحٍ، حَدَّثَنَا ابْنُ وَهْبٍ، قَالَ أَخْبَرَنِي يُونُسُ، عَنِ ابْنِ شِهَابٍ، قَالَ أَبُو سَلَمَةَ سَمِعْتُ جَابِرَ بْنَ عَبْدِ اللَّهِ ـ رضى الله عنهما ـ قَالَ سَمِعْتُ النَّبِيَّ صلى الله عليه وسلم يَقُولُ " لَمَّا كَذَّبَنِي قُرَيْشٌ قُمْتُ فِي الْحِجْرِ، فَجَلَّى اللَّهُ لِي بَيْتَ الْمَقْدِسِ فَطَفِقْتُ أُخْبِرُهُمْ عَنْ آيَاتِهِ وَأَنَا أَنْظُرُ إِلَيْهِ ". زَادَ يَعْقُوبُ بْنُ إِبْرَاهِيمَ حَدَّثَنَا ابْنُ أَخِي ابْنِ شِهَابٍ عَنْ عَمِّهِ " لَمَّا كَذَّبَنِي قُرَيْشٌ حِينَ أُسْرِيَ بِي إِلَى بَيْتِ الْمَقْدِسِ ". نَحْوَهُ. {قَاصِفًا} رِيحٌ تَقْصِفُ كُلَّ شَىْءٍ.

Narrated `Aisha: (The wife of the Prophet) Allah's Messenger ﷺ said (to her). "Don't you see that when your folk built the Ka`ba, they did not build it on all the foundations built by Abraham?" I said, "O Allah's Messenger ﷺ ! Why don't we rebuild it on the foundations of Abraham?" He said. "But for the fact that your folk have recently given up infidelity (I would have done so). Narrated Ibn `Umar: Aisha must have heard this from Allah's Messenger ﷺ for I see that Allah's Messenger ﷺ used not to touch the two corners facing Al-Hijr only because the House had not been built on the foundations of Abraham.''. – Sahih al-Bukhari 3368

حَدَّثَنَا عَبْدُ اللَّهِ بْنُ يُوسُفَ، أَخْبَرَنَا مَالِكٌ، عَنِ ابْنِ شِهَابٍ، عَنْ سَالِمِ بْنِ عَبْدِ اللَّهِ، أَنَّ ابْنَ أَبِي بَكْرٍ، أَخْبَرَ عَبْدَ اللَّهِ بْنَ عُمَرَ، عَنْ عَائِشَةَ ـ رضى الله عنهم ـ زَوْجِ النَّبِيِّ صلى الله عليه وسلم أَنَّ رَسُولَ اللَّهِ صلى الله عليه وسلم قَالَ " أَلَمْ تَرَىْ أَنَّ قَوْمَكِ بَنَوُا الْكَعْبَةَ اقْتَصَرُوا عَنْ قَوَاعِدِ إِبْرَاهِيمَ ". فَقُلْتُ يَا رَسُولَ اللَّهِ، أَلاَ تَرُدُّهَا عَلَى قَوَاعِدِ إِبْرَاهِيمَ. فَقَالَ " لَوْلاَ حِدْثَانُ قَوْمِكِ بِالْكُفْرِ ". فَقَالَ عَبْدُ اللَّهِ بْنُ عُمَرَ لَئِنْ كَانَتْ عَائِشَةُ سَمِعَتْ هَذَا مِنْ رَسُولِ اللَّهِ صلى الله عليه وسلم مَا أُرَى أَنَّ رَسُولَ اللَّهِ صلى الله عليه وسلم تَرَكَ اسْتِلاَمَ الرُّكْنَيْنِ اللَّذَيْنِ يَلِيَانِ الْحِجْرَ إِلاَّ أَنَّ الْبَيْتَ لَمْ يُتَمَّمْ عَلَى قَوَاعِدِ إِبْرَاهِيمَ. وَقَالَ إِسْمَاعِيلُ عَبْدُ اللَّهِ بْنُ مُحَمَّدِ بْنِ أَبِي بَكْرٍ

The Book of
Muhajirun
مهاجرون

As for the foremost—the first of the Emigrants and the Helpers—and those who follow them in goodness, Allah is pleased with them and they are pleased with Him. And He has prepared for them Gardens under which rivers flow, to stay there for ever and ever. That is the ultimate triumph. – Surah At-Tawbah 9:100

وَٱلسَّٰبِقُونَ ٱلْأَوَّلُونَ مِنَ ٱلْمُهَٰجِرِينَ وَٱلْأَنصَارِ وَٱلَّذِينَ ٱتَّبَعُوهُم بِإِحْسَٰنٍ رَّضِىَ ٱللَّهُ عَنْهُمْ وَرَضُوا۟ عَنْهُ وَأَعَدَّ لَهُمْ جَنَّٰتٍ تَجْرِى تَحْتَهَا ٱلْأَنْهَٰرُ خَٰلِدِينَ فِيهَآ أَبَدًا ذَٰلِكَ ٱلْفَوْزُ ٱلْعَظِيمُ

Allah has certainly turned in mercy to the Prophet as well as the Emigrants and the Helpers who stood by him in the time of hardship, after the hearts of a group of them had almost faltered. He then accepted their repentance. Surely He is Ever Gracious and Most Merciful to them. – Surah At-Tawbah 9:117

لَّقَد تَّابَ ٱللَّهُ عَلَى ٱلنَّبِىِّ وَٱلْمُهَٰجِرِينَ وَٱلْأَنصَارِ ٱلَّذِينَ ٱتَّبَعُوهُ فِى سَاعَةِ ٱلْعُسْرَةِ مِنۢ بَعْدِ مَا كَادَ يَزِيغُ قُلُوبُ فَرِيقٍ مِّنْهُمْ ثُمَّ تَابَ عَلَيْهِمْ إِنَّهُۥ بِهِمْ رَءُوفٌ رَّحِيمٌ

`Abdullah bin Abi `Aufa said, "The people (who gave the Pledge of allegiance) under the Tree numbered 1300 and the number of Bani Aslam was 1/8 of the Emigrants.". – Al-Bukhari 4155

وَقَالَ عُبَيْدُ اللَّهِ بْنُ مُعَاذٍ حَدَّثَنَا أَبِي، حَدَّثَنَا شُعْبَةُ، عَنْ عَمْرِو بْنِ مُرَّةَ، حَدَّثَنِي عَبْدُ اللَّهِ بْنُ أَبِي أَوْفَى ـ رضى الله عنهما ـ كَانَ أَصْحَابُ الشَّجَرَةِ أَلْفًا وَثَلاَثَمِائَةٍ، وَكَانَتْ أَسْلَمُ ثُمُنَ الْمُهَاجِرِينَ. تَابَعَهُ مُحَمَّدُ بْنُ بَشَّارٍ حَدَّثَنَا أَبُو دَاوُدَ حَدَّثَنَا شُعْبَةُ.

Narrated Anas: When `Abdur-Rahman bin `Auf married an Ansari woman, the Prophet ﷺ asked him, "How much Mahr did you give her?" `Abdur-Rahman said, "Gold equal to the weight of a date stone." Anas added: When they (i.e. the Prophet ﷺ and his companions) arrived at Medina, the emigrants stayed at the Ansar's houses. `Abdur-Rahman bin `Auf stayed at Sa`d bin Ar-Rabi's house. Sa`d said to `Abdur- Rahman, "I will divide and share my property with you and will give one of my two wives to you." `Abdur-Rahman said, "May Allah bless you, your wives and property (I am not in need of that; but kindly show me the way to the market)." So `Abdur-Rahman went to the market and traded there gaining a profit of some dried yoghurt and butter, and married (an Ansari woman). The Prophet ﷺ said to him, "Give a banquet, even if with one sheep.". – Sahih Al-Bukhari 5167

حَدَّثَنَا عَلِيٌّ، حَدَّثَنَا سُفْيَانُ، قَالَ حَدَّثَنِي حُمَيْدٌ، أَنَّهُ سَمِعَ أَنَسًا ـ رضى الله عنه ـ قَالَ سَأَلَ النَّبِيُّ صلى الله عليه وسلم عَبْدَ الرَّحْمَنِ بْنَ عَوْفٍ وَتَزَوَّجَ امْرَأَةً مِنَ الأَنْصَارِ " كَمْ أَصْدَقْتَهَا ". قَالَ وَزْنَ نَوَاةٍ مِنْ ذَهَبٍ. وَعَنْ حُمَيْدٍ سَمِعْتُ أَنَسًا قَالَ لَمَّا قَدِمُوا الْمَدِينَةَ نَزَلَ الْمُهَاجِرُونَ عَلَى الأَنْصَارِ فَنَزَلَ عَبْدُ الرَّحْمَنِ بْنُ عَوْفٍ عَلَى سَعْدِ بْنِ الرَّبِيعِ فَقَالَ أُقَاسِمُكَ مَالِي وَأَنْزِلُ لَكَ عَنْ إِحْدَى امْرَأَتَىَّ. قَالَ بَارَكَ اللَّهُ لَكَ فِي أَهْلِكَ وَمَالِكَ. فَخَرَجَ إِلَى السُّوقِ فَبَاعَ وَاشْتَرَى فَأَصَابَ شَيْئًا مِنْ أَقِطٍ وَسَمْنٍ فَتَزَوَّجَ فَقَالَ النَّبِيُّ صلى الله عليه وسلم " أَوْلِمْ وَلَوْ بِشَاةٍ "

Narrated `Aishah: May Allah bestow His Mercy on the early emigrant women. When Allah revealed: "... and to draw their veils all over their Juyubihinna (i.e., their bodies, faces, necks and bosoms)..." (V.24:31) they tore their Murat (woolen dresses or waist-binding clothes or aprons etc.) and covered their heads and faces with those torn Muruts. – Sahih Al-Bukhari 4758

وَقَالَ أَحْمَدُ بْنُ شَبِيبٍ حَدَّثَنَا أَبِي، عَنْ يُونُسَ، قَالَ ابْنُ شِهَابٍ عَنْ عُرْوَةَ، عَنْ عَائِشَةَ ـ رضى الله عنها ـ قَالَتْ يَرْحَمُ اللَّهُ نِسَاءَ الْمُهَاجِرَاتِ الأُوَلَ، لَمَّا أَنْزَلَ اللَّهُ {وَلْيَضْرِبْنَ بِخُمُرِهِنَّ عَلَى جُيُوبِهِنَّ} شَقَّقْنَ مُرُوطَهُنَّ فَاخْتَمَرْنَ بِهَا.

Narrated Asma: I prepared the journey-food for Allah's Messenger ﷺ in Abu Bakr's house when he intended to emigrate to Medina. I could not find anything to tie the food-container and the water skin with. So, I said to Abu Bakr, "By Allah, I do not find anything to tie (these things) with except my waist belt." He said, "Cut it into two pieces and tie the water-skin with one piece and the food-container with the other (the subnarrator added, "She did accordingly and that was the reason for calling her Dhatun-Nitaqain (i.e. twobelted woman). – Sahih Al-Bukhari 2979

حَدَّثَنَا عُبَيْدُ بْنُ إِسْمَاعِيلَ، حَدَّثَنَا أَبُو أُسَامَةَ، عَنْ هِشَامٍ، قَالَ أَخْبَرَنِي أَبِي وَ، حَدَّثَتْنِي أَيْضًا، فَاطِمَةُ عَنْ أَسْمَاءَ ـ رضى الله عنها ـ قَالَتْ صَنَعْتُ سُفْرَةَ رَسُولِ اللَّهِ صلى الله عليه وسلم فِي بَيْتِ أَبِي بَكْرٍ حِينَ أَرَادَ أَنْ يُهَاجِرَ إِلَى الْمَدِينَةِ، قَالَتْ فَلَمْ نَجِدْ لِسُفْرَتِهِ وَلاَ لِسِقَائِهِ مَا نَرْبِطُهُمَا بِهِ، فَقُلْتُ لأَبِي بَكْرٍ وَاللَّهِ مَا أَجِدُ شَيْئًا أَرْبِطُ بِهِ إِلاَّ نِطَاقِي. قَالَ فَشُقِّيهِ بِاثْنَيْنِ، فَارْبِطِيهِ بِوَاحِدٍ السِّقَاءَ وَبِالآخَرِ السُّفْرَةَ. فَفَعَلْتُ، فَلِذَلِكَ سُمِّيَتْ ذَاتَ النِّطَاقَيْنِ.

Narrated Asma: That she conceived `Abdullah bin Az-Zubair. She added, "I migrated to Medina while I was at full term of pregnancy and alighted at Quba where I gave birth to him. Then I brought him to the Prophet ﷺ and put him in his lap. The Prophet ﷺ asked for a date, chewed it, and put some of its juice in the child's mouth. So, the first thing that entered the child's stomach was the saliva of Allah's Messenger ﷺ. Then the Prophet rubbed the child's palate with a date and invoked for Allah's Blessings on him, and he was the first child born amongst the Emigrants in the Islamic Land (i.e. Medina). – Sahih Al-Bukhari 3909

حَدَّثَنِي زَكَرِيَّاءُ بْنُ يَحْيَى، عَنْ أَبِي أُسَامَةَ، عَنْ هِشَامِ بْنِ عُرْوَةَ، عَنْ أَبِيهِ، عَنْ أَسْمَاءَ ـ رضى الله عنها ـ أَنَّهَا حَمَلَتْ بِعَبْدِ اللَّهِ بْنِ الزُّبَيْرِ، قَالَتْ فَخَرَجْتُ وَأَنَا مُتِمٌّ، فَأَتَيْتُ الْمَدِينَةَ، فَنَزَلْتُ بِقُبَاءٍ، فَوَلَدْتُهُ بِقُبَاءٍ، ثُمَّ أَتَيْتُ بِهِ النَّبِيَّ صلى الله عليه وسلم فَوَضَعْتُهُ فِي حَجْرِهِ، ثُمَّ دَعَا بِتَمْرَةٍ، فَمَضَغَهَا، ثُمَّ تَفَلَ فِي فِيهِ، فَكَانَ أَوَّلَ شَىْءٍ دَخَلَ جَوْفَهُ رِيقُ رَسُولِ اللَّهِ صلى الله عليه وسلم، ثُمَّ حَنَّكَهُ بِتَمْرَةٍ ثُمَّ دَعَا لَهُ وَبَرَّكَ عَلَيْهِ، وَكَانَ أَوَّلَ مَوْلُودٍ وُلِدَ فِي الإِسْلاَمِ. تَابَعَهُ خَالِدُ بْنُ مَخْلَدٍ عَنْ عَلِيِّ بْنِ مُسْهِرٍ عَنْ هِشَامٍ عَنْ أَبِيهِ عَنْ أَسْمَاءَ ـ رضى الله عنها ـ أَنَّهَا هَاجَرَتْ إِلَى النَّبِيِّ صلى الله عليه وسلم وَهْىَ حُبْلَى.

Narrated Ibn `Umar: `Umar bin Al-Khattab fixed a grant of 4000 (Dirhams) for every Early Emigrant (i.e. Muhajir) and fixed a grant of 3500 (Dirhams) only for Ibn `Umar. Somebody said to `Umar, "Ibn `Umar is also one of the Early Emigrants; why do you give him less than four-thousand?" `Umar replied, "His parents took him with them when they migrated, so he was not like the one who had migrated by himself. – Sahih Al-Bukhari 3912

حَدَّثَنَا إِبْرَاهِيمُ بْنُ مُوسَى، أَخْبَرَنَا هِشَامٌ، عَنِ ابْنِ جُرَيْجٍ، قَالَ أَخْبَرَنِي عُبَيْدُ اللَّهِ بْنُ عُمَرَ، عَنْ نَافِعٍ يَعْنِي، عَنِ ابْنِ عُمَرَ، عَنْ عُمَرَ بْنِ الْخَطَّابِ، رضى الله عنه قَالَ كَانَ فَرَضَ لِلْمُهَاجِرِينَ الأَوَّلِينَ أَرْبَعَةَ آلاَفٍ فِي أَرْبَعَةٍ، وَفَرَضَ لاِبْنِ عُمَرَ ثَلاَثَةَ آلاَفٍ وَخَمْسَمِائَةٍ فَقِيلَ لَهُ هُوَ مِنَ الْمُهَاجِرِينَ، فَلِمَ نَقَصْتَهُ مِنْ أَرْبَعَةِ آلاَفٍ فَقَالَ إِنَّمَا هَاجَرَ بِهِ أَبَوَاهُ. يَقُولُ لَيْسَ هُوَ كَمَنْ هَاجَرَ بِنَفْسِهِ

Those who believed, and emigrated, and struggled for Allah's cause, and those who gave shelter and support—these are the true believers. They will have forgiveness, and a bountiful provision. As for those who believed afterwards, and emigrated and struggled with you—these belong with you. But family members are nearer to one another in the Book of Allah. Allah is Cognizant of everything. – Surah Al-Anfal 8:74&75

وَٱلَّذِينَ ءَامَنُوا۟ وَهَاجَرُوا۟ وَجَـٰهَدُوا۟ فِى سَبِيلِ ٱللَّهِ وَٱلَّذِينَ ءَاوَوا۟ وَّنَصَرُوٓا۟ أُو۟لَـٰٓئِكَ هُمُ ٱلْمُؤْمِنُونَ حَقًّا ۚ لَّهُم مَّغْفِرَةٌ وَرِزْقٌ كَرِيمٌ وَٱلَّذِينَ ءَامَنُوا۟ مِنۢ بَعْدُ وَهَاجَرُوا۟ وَجَـٰهَدُوا۟ مَعَكُمْ فَأُو۟لَـٰٓئِكَ مِنكُمْ ۚ وَأُو۟لُوا۟ ٱلْأَرْحَامِ بَعْضُهُمْ أَوْلَىٰ بِبَعْضٍ فِى كِتَـٰبِ ٱللَّهِ ۗ إِنَّ ٱللَّهَ بِكُلِّ شَىْءٍ عَلِيمٌۢ

Those who believed, and those who migrated and fought for the sake of Allah—those look forward to Allah's mercy. Allah is Forgiving and Merciful. . – Surah Al-Baqarah 2:218

إِنَّ ٱلَّذِينَ ءَامَنُوا۟ وَٱلَّذِينَ هَاجَرُوا۟ وَجَـٰهَدُوا۟ فِى سَبِيلِ ٱللَّهِ أُو۟لَـٰٓئِكَ يَرْجُونَ رَحْمَتَ ٱللَّهِ ۚ وَٱللَّهُ غَفُورٌ رَّحِيمٌ

The Book of
Medina
المدينة المنورة

Narrated Anas: The Prophetﷺ said, “O Allah! Bestow on Medina twice the blessings You bestowed on Mecca.”. – Sahih Al-Bukhari 1885 [18]

حَدَّثَنَا عَبْدُ اللَّهِ بْنُ مُحَمَّدٍ، حَدَّثَنَا وَهْبُ بْنُ جَرِيرٍ، حَدَّثَنَا أَبِي، سَمِعْتُ يُونُسَ، عَنِ ابْنِ شِهَابٍ، عَنْ أَنَسٍ ـ رضى الله عنه ـ عَنِ النَّبِيِّ صلى الله عليه وسلم قَالَ " اللَّهُمَّ اجْعَلْ بِالْمَدِينَةِ ضِعْفَىْ مَا جَعَلْتَ بِمَكَّةَ مِنَ الْبَرَكَةِ ". تَابَعَهُ عُثْمَانُ بْنُ عُمَرَ عَنْ يُونُسَ

Narrated Sahl bin Sa`d: The Prophet’s companions did not take as a starting date for the Muslim calendar, the day, the Prophetﷺ had been sent as an Apostle or the day of his death, but the day of his arrival at Medina. – Sahih Al-Bukhari 3934

حَدَّثَنَا عَبْدُ اللَّهِ بْنُ مَسْلَمَةَ، حَدَّثَنَا عَبْدُ الْعَزِيزِ، عَنْ أَبِيهِ، عَنْ سَهْلِ بْنِ سَعْدٍ، قَالَ مَا عَدُّوا مِنْ مَبْعَثِ النَّبِيِّ صلى الله عليه وسلم وَلاَ مِنْ وَفَاتِهِ، مَا عَدُّوا إِلاَّ مِنْ مَقْدَمِهِ الْمَدِينَةَ.

Narrated Anas bin Malik: The Prophetﷺ said to Abu Talha, “Choose one of your boys to serve me.” So Abu Talha took me (to serve the Prophetﷺ) by giving me a ride behind him (on his camel). So I used to serve Allah’s Messengerﷺ whenever he stayed somewhere. I used to hear him saying, “O Allah! I seek refuge with you (Allah) from (worries) care and grief, from incapacity and laziness, from miserliness and cowardice, from being heavily in debt and from being overpowered by other men.” I kept on serving him till he returned from (the battle of) Khaibar. He then brought Safiya, the daughter of Huyay whom he had got (from the booty). I saw him making a kind of cushion with a cloak or a garment for her. He then let her ride behind him. When we reached a place called As-Sahba’, he prepared (a special meal called) Hais, and asked me to invite the men who (came and) ate, and that was the marriage banquet given on the consummation of his marriage to her. Then he proceeded till the mountain of Uhud appeared, whereupon he said, “This mountain loves us and we love it.” When he approached Medina, he said, “O Allah! I make the land between its (i.e., Medina’s) two mountains a sanctuary, as the prophet Abraham made Mecca a sanctuary. O Allah! Bless them (the people of Medina) in their Mudd and the Sa’ (units of measuring). – Sahih Al-Bukhari 6363

حَدَّثَنَا قُتَيْبَةُ بْنُ سَعِيدٍ، حَدَّثَنَا إِسْمَاعِيلُ بْنُ جَعْفَرٍ، عَنْ عَمْرِو بْنِ أَبِي عَمْرٍو، مَوْلَى الْمُطَّلِبِ بْنِ عَبْدِ اللَّهِ بْنِ حَنْطَبٍ أَنَّهُ سَمِعَ أَنَسَ بْنَ مَالِكٍ، يَقُولُ قَالَ رَسُولُ اللَّهِ صلى الله عليه وسلم لأَبِي طَلْحَةَ " الْتَمِسْ لَنَا غُلاَمًا مِنْ غِلْمَانِكُمْ يَخْدُمُنِي ". فَخَرَجَ بِي أَبُو طَلْحَةَ يُرْدِفُنِي وَرَاءَهُ، فَكُنْتُ أَخْدُمُ رَسُولَ اللَّهِ صلى الله عليه وسلم كُلَّمَا نَزَلَ، فَكُنْتُ أَسْمَعُهُ يُكْثِرُ أَنْ يَقُولَ " اللَّهُمَّ إِنِّي أَعُوذُ بِكَ مِنَ الْهَمِّ وَالْحَزَنِ، وَالْعَجْزِ وَالْكَسَلِ، وَالْبُخْلِ وَالْجُبْنِ، وَضَلَعِ الدَّيْنِ، وَغَلَبَةِ الرِّجَالِ ". فَلَمْ أَزَلْ أَخْدُمُهُ حَتَّى أَقْبَلْنَا مِنْ خَيْبَرَ، وَأَقْبَلَ بِصَفِيَّةَ بِنْتِ حُيَىٍّ قَدْ حَازَهَا، فَكُنْتُ أَرَاهُ يُحَوِّي وَرَاءَهُ بِعَبَاءَةٍ أَوْ كِسَاءٍ ثُمَّ يُرْدِفُهَا وَرَاءَهُ حَتَّى إِذَا كُنَّا بِالصَّهْبَاءِ صَنَعَ حَيْسًا فِي نِطَعٍ، ثُمَّ أَرْسَلَنِي فَدَعَوْتُ رِجَالاً فَأَكَلُوا، وَكَانَ ذَلِكَ بِنَاءَهُ بِهَا، ثُمَّ أَقْبَلَ حَتَّى بَدَا لَهُ أُحُدٌ قَالَ " هَذَا جُبَيْلٌ يُحِبُّنَا وَنُحِبُّهُ ". فَلَمَّا أَشْرَفَ عَلَى الْمَدِينَةِ قَالَ " اللَّهُمَّ إِنِّي أُحَرِّمُ مَا بَيْنَ جَبَلَيْهَا مِثْلَ مَا حَرَّمَ بِهِ إِبْرَاهِيمُ مَكَّةَ، اللَّهُمَّ بَارِكْ لَهُمْ فِي مُدِّهِمْ وَصَاعِهِمْ "

Narrated `Aisha: When Allah’s Messengerﷺ came to Medina, Abu Bakr and Bilal got fever, and I went to both of them and said, “O my father, how do you feel? O Bilal, how do you feel?” Whenever Abu Bakr’s fever got worse, he would say, “Every man will meet his death

---

[18] Banu Nadir, Banu Qainuqa, and Banu Qurayza migrated to yathrib after the Jewish–Roman War’s (66–73 CE), Diaspora Revolt (115–117 CE), Bar Kokhba Revolt (132–136 CE)

once in one morning while he will be among his family, for death is really nearer to him than his leather shoe laces (to his feet)." And whenever fever deserted Bilal, he would say aloud, "Would that I know whether I shall spend a night in the valley (of Mecca) with Idhkhir and Jalil (i.e. kinds of grass) around me, and whether I shall drink one day the water of Mijannah, and whether I shall see once again the hills of Shamah and Tafil?" Then I went to Allah's Messenger ﷺ and told him of that. He said, "O Allah, make us love Medina as much as or more than we used to love Mecca, O Allah, make it healthy and bless its Sa' and Mud (i.e. measures), and take away its fever to Al-Juhfa.". – Sahih Al-Bukhari 3926

حَدَّثَنَا عَبْدُ اللَّهِ بْنُ يُوسُفَ، أَخْبَرَنَا مَالِكٌ، عَنْ هِشَامِ بْنِ عُرْوَةَ، عَنْ أَبِيهِ، عَنْ عَائِشَةَ ـ رضى الله عنها ـ أَنَّهَا قَالَتْ لَمَّا قَدِمَ رَسُولُ اللَّهِ صلى الله عليه وسلم الْمَدِينَةَ وُعِكَ أَبُو بَكْرٍ وَبِلاَلٌ ـ قَالَتْ ـ فَدَخَلْتُ عَلَيْهِمَا فَقُلْتُ يَا أَبَتِ كَيْفَ تَجِدُكَ وَيَا بِلاَلُ، كَيْفَ تَجِدُكَ قَالَتْ فَكَانَ أَبُو بَكْرٍ إِذَا أَخَذَتْهُ الْحُمَّى يَقُولُ كُلُّ امْرِئٍ مُصَبَّحٌ فِي أَهْلِهِ وَالْمَوْتُ أَدْنَى مِنْ شِرَاكِ نَعْلِهِ وَكَانَ بِلاَلٌ إِذَا أَقْلَعَ عَنْهُ الْحُمَّى يَرْفَعُ عَقِيرَتَهُ وَيَقُولُ أَلاَ لَيْتَ شِعْرِي هَلْ أَبِيتَنَّ لَيْلَةً بِوَادٍ وَحَوْلِي إِذْخِرٌ وَجَلِيلُ وَهَلْ أَرِدَنْ يَوْمًا مِيَاهَ مَجَنَّةٍ وَهَلْ يَبْدُوَنْ لِي شَامَةٌ وَطَفِيلُ قَالَتْ عَائِشَةُ فَجِئْتُ رَسُولَ اللَّهِ صلى الله عليه وسلم فَأَخْبَرْتُهُ فَقَالَ " اللَّهُمَّ حَبِّبْ إِلَيْنَا الْمَدِينَةَ كَحُبِّنَا مَكَّةَ أَوْ أَشَدَّ، وَصَحِّحْهَا وَبَارِكْ لَنَا فِي صَاعِهَا وَمُدِّهَا، وَانْقُلْ حُمَّاهَا فَاجْعَلْهَا بِالْجُحْفَةِ "

Narrated `Abdullah bin Zaid: The Prophet ﷺ said, "The Prophet ﷺ Abraham made Mecca a sanctuary, and asked for Allah's blessing in it. I made Medina a sanctuary as Abraham made Mecca a sanctuary and I asked for Allah's Blessing in its measures the Mudd and the Sa as Abraham did for Mecca. – Sahih Al-Bukhari 2129

حَدَّثَنَا مُوسَى، حَدَّثَنَا وُهَيْبٌ، حَدَّثَنَا عَمْرُو بْنُ يَحْيَى، عَنْ عَبَّادِ بْنِ تَمِيمٍ الأَنْصَارِيِّ، عَنْ عَبْدِ اللَّهِ بْنِ زَيْدٍ ـ رضى الله عنه ـ عَنِ النَّبِيِّ صلى الله عليه وسلم " أَنَّ إِبْرَاهِيمَ حَرَّمَ مَكَّةَ، وَدَعَا لَهَا، وَحَرَّمْتُ الْمَدِينَةَ كَمَا حَرَّمَ إِبْرَاهِيمُ مَكَّةَ، وَدَعَوْتُ لَهَا فِي مُدِّهَا وَصَاعِهَا، مِثْلَ مَا دَعَا إِبْرَاهِيمُ ـ عَلَيْهِ السَّلاَمُ ـ لِمَكَّةَ ".

Narrated Anas bin Malik: Allah's Messenger ﷺ said, "O Allah! Bestow Your Blessings on their measures, and bestow Your Blessings on their Sa' and Mudd." He meant those of the people of Medina. – Sahih Al-Bukhari 7331

حَدَّثَنَا عَبْدُ اللَّهِ بْنُ مَسْلَمَةَ، عَنْ مَالِكٍ، عَنْ إِسْحَاقَ بْنِ عَبْدِ اللَّهِ بْنِ أَبِي طَلْحَةَ، عَنْ أَنَسِ بْنِ مَالِكٍ، أَنَّ رَسُولَ اللَّهِ صلى الله عليه وسلم قَالَ " اللَّهُمَّ بَارِكْ لَهُمْ فِي مِكْيَالِهِمْ، وَبَارِكْ لَهُمْ فِي صَاعِهِمْ وَمُدِّهِمْ " يَعْنِي أَهْلَ الْمَدِينَةِ.

Narrated Humaid: Anas said, "Whenever Allah's Messenger ﷺ returned from a journey, he, on seeing the high places of Medina, would make his she-camel proceed faster; and if it were another animal, even then he used to make it proceed faster." Narrated Humaid that the Prophet ﷺ used to make it proceed faster out of his love for Medina. Narrated Anas: As above, but mentioned "the walls of Medina" instead of "the high places of Medina." Al-Harith bin `Umar agrees with Anas. – Sahih Al-Bukhari 1802

حَدَّثَنَا سَعِيدُ بْنُ أَبِي مَرْيَمَ، أَخْبَرَنَا مُحَمَّدُ بْنُ جَعْفَرٍ، قَالَ أَخْبَرَنِي حُمَيْدٌ، أَنَّهُ سَمِعَ أَنَسًا ـ رضى الله عنه ـ يَقُولُ كَانَ رَسُولُ اللَّهِ صلى الله عليه وسلم إِذَا قَدِمَ مِنْ سَفَرٍ، فَأَبْصَرَ دَرَجَاتِ الْمَدِينَةِ أَوْضَعَ نَاقَتَهُ، وَإِنْ كَانَتْ دَابَّةً حَرَّكَهَا. قَالَ أَبُو عَبْدِ اللَّهِ زَادَ الْحَارِثُ بْنُ عُمَيْرٍ عَنْ حُمَيْدٍ حَرَّكَهَا مِنْ حُبِّهَا.

حَدَّثَنَا قُتَيْبَةُ، حَدَّثَنَا إِسْمَاعِيلُ، عَنْ حُمَيْدٍ، عَنْ أَنَسٍ، قَالَ جُدُرَاتِ. تَابَعَهُ الْحَارِثُ بْنُ عُمَيْرٍ.

Narrated Muharib bin Dithar: Jabir bin `Abdullah said, "When Allah's Messenger ﷺ arrived at Medina, he slaughtered a camel or a cow." Jabir added, "The Prophet ﷺ bought a camel from me for two Uqiyas (of gold) and one or two Dirhams. When he reached Sirar, he ordered that a cow be slaughtered and they ate its meat. When he arrived at Medina, he ordered me to go to the Mosque and offer two rak`at, and weighed (and gave) me the price of the camel.". – Sahih Al-Bukhari 3089

حَدَّثَنِي مُحَمَّدٌ، أَخْبَرَنَا وَكِيعٌ، عَنْ شُعْبَةَ، عَنْ مُحَارِبِ بْنِ دِثَارٍ، عَنْ جَابِرِ بْنِ عَبْدِ اللَّهِ ـ رضى الله عنهما أَنَّ رَسُولَ اللَّهِ صلى الله عليه وسلم لَمَّا قَدِمَ الْمَدِينَةَ نَحَرَ جَزُورًا أَوْ بَقَرَةً. زَادَ مُعَاذٌ عَنْ شُعْبَةَ عَنْ مُحَارِبٍ سَمِعَ جَابِرَ بْنَ عَبْدِ اللَّهِ اشْتَرَى

مِنِى النَّبِيُّ صلى الله عليه وسلم بَعِيرًا بِوَقِيَّتَيْنِ وَدِرْهَمٍ أَوْ دِرْهَمَيْنِ، فَلَمَّا قَدِمَ صِرَارًا أَمَرَ بِبَقَرَةٍ فَذُبِحَتْ فَأَكَلُوا مِنْهَا، فَلَمَّا قَدِمَ الْمَدِينَةَ أَمَرَنِي أَنْ آتِيَ الْمَسْجِدَ فَأُصَلِّيَ رَكْعَتَيْنِ، وَوَزَنَ لِي ثَمَنَ الْبَعِيرِ

Narrated Abu Bakra: The Prophet ﷺ said, "The terror caused by Al-Masih Ad-Dajjal will not enter Medina and at that time Medina will have seven gates and there will be two angels at each gate (guarding them). – Sahih Al-Bukhari 7125

حَدَّثَنَا عَبْدُ الْعَزِيزِ بْنُ عَبْدِ اللَّهِ، حَدَّثَنَا إِبْرَاهِيمُ بْنُ سَعْدٍ، عَنْ أَبِيهِ، عَنْ جَدِّهِ، عَنْ أَبِي بَكْرَةَ، عَنِ النَّبِيِّ صلى الله عليه وسلم قَالَ " لاَ يَدْخُلُ الْمَدِينَةَ رُعْبُ الْمَسِيحِ الدَّجَّالِ، وَلَهَا يَوْمَئِذٍ سَبْعَةُ أَبْوَابٍ، عَلَى كُلِّ بَابٍ مَلَكَانِ "

Narrated Ibn 'Abbas: I used to teach Qur'an to 'Abdur-Rahman bin Auf. When Umar performed his last Hajj, 'Abdur-Rahman said (to me) at Mina, "Would that you had seen Chief of the believers today! A man came to him and said, "So-and-so has said, "If Chief of the Believers died, we will give the oath of allegiance to such-and-such person,' 'Umar said, 'I will get up tonight and warn those who want to usurp the people's rights.' I said, 'Do not do so, for the season (of Hajj) gathers the riffraff mob who will form the majority of your audience, and I am afraid that they will not understand (the meaning of) your saying properly and may spread (an incorrect statement) everywhere. You should wait till we reach Medina, the place of migration and the place of the Sunna (the Prophet's Traditions). There you will meet the companions of Allah's Messenger ﷺ from the Muhajirin and the Ansar who will understand your statement and place it in its proper position' 'Umar said, 'By Allah, I shall do so the first time I stand (to address the people) in Medina.' When we reached Medina, 'Umar (in a Friday Khutba-sermon) said, "No doubt, Allah sent Muhammad with the Truth and revealed to him the Book (Quran), and among what was revealed, was the Verse of Ar-Rajm (stoning adulterers to death).'" – Sahih Al-Bukhari 7323

حَدَّثَنَا مُوسَى بْنُ إِسْمَاعِيلَ، حَدَّثَنَا عَبْدُ الْوَاحِدِ، حَدَّثَنَا مَعْمَرٌ، عَنِ الزُّهْرِيِّ، عَنْ عُبَيْدِ اللَّهِ بْنِ عَبْدِ اللَّهِ، قَالَ حَدَّثَنِي ابْنُ عَبَّاسٍ ـ رضى الله عنهما ـ قَالَ كُنْتُ أُقْرِئُ عَبْدَ الرَّحْمَنِ بْنَ عَوْفٍ، فَلَمَّا كَانَ آخِرَ حَجَّةٍ حَجَّهَا عُمَرُ فَقَالَ عَبْدُ الرَّحْمَنِ بِمِنًى، لَوْ شَهِدْتَ أَمِيرَ الْمُؤْمِنِينَ أَتَاهُ رَجُلٌ قَالَ إِنَّ فُلاَنًا يَقُولُ لَوْ مَاتَ أَمِيرُ الْمُؤْمِنِينَ لَبَايَعْنَا فُلاَنًا. فَقَالَ عُمَرُ لأَقُومَنَّ الْعَشِيَّةَ فَأُحَذِّرَ هَؤُلاَءِ الرَّهْطَ الَّذِينَ يُرِيدُونَ أَنْ يَغْصِبُوهُمْ. قُلْتُ لاَ تَفْعَلْ فَإِنَّ الْمَوْسِمَ يَجْمَعُ رَعَاعَ النَّاسِ يَغْلِبُونَ عَلَى مَجْلِسِكَ، فَأَخَافُ أَنْ لاَ يُنْزِلُوهَا عَلَى وَجْهِهَا فَيُطِيرُ بِهَا كُلُّ مُطِيرٍ، فَأَمْهِلْ حَتَّى تَقْدَمَ الْمَدِينَةَ دَارَ الْهِجْرَةِ وَدَارَ السُّنَّةِ، فَتَخْلُصَ بِأَصْحَابِ رَسُولِ اللَّهِ صلى الله عليه وسلم مِنَ الْمُهَاجِرِينَ وَالأَنْصَارِ فَيَحْفَظُوا مَقَالَتَكَ، وَيُنَزِّلُوهَا عَلَى وَجْهِهَا. فَقَالَ وَاللَّهِ لأَقُومَنَّ بِهِ فِي أَوَّلِ مَقَامٍ أَقُومُهُ بِالْمَدِينَةِ. قَالَ ابْنُ عَبَّاسٍ فَقَدِمْنَا الْمَدِينَةَ فَقَالَ إِنَّ اللَّهَ بَعَثَ مُحَمَّدًا صلى الله عليه وسلم بِالْحَقِّ وَأَنْزَلَ عَلَيْهِ الْكِتَابَ، فَكَانَ فِيمَا أُنْزِلَ آيَةُ الرَّجْمِ

Narrated Al-Sa'ib bin Yazid: I was standing in the mosque and somebody threw a gravel at me. I looked and found that he was `Umar bin Al-Khattab. He said to me, "Fetch those two men to me." When I did, he said to them, "Who are you? (Or) where do you come from?" They replied, "We are from Ta'if." `Umar said, "Were you from this city (Medina) I would have punished you for raising your voices in the mosque of Allah's Messenger ﷺ. – Sahih Al-Bukhari 470

حَدَّثَنَا عَلِيُّ بْنُ عَبْدِ اللَّهِ، قَالَ حَدَّثَنَا يَحْيَى بْنُ سَعِيدٍ، قَالَ حَدَّثَنَا الْجُعَيْدُ بْنُ عَبْدِ الرَّحْمَنِ، قَالَ حَدَّثَنِي يَزِيدُ بْنُ خُصَيْفَةَ، عَنِ السَّائِبِ بْنِ يَزِيدَ، قَالَ كُنْتُ قَائِمًا فِي الْمَسْجِدِ فَحَصَبَنِي رَجُلٌ، فَنَظَرْتُ فَإِذَا عُمَرُ بْنُ الْخَطَّابِ فَقَالَ اذْهَبْ فَأْتِنِي بِهَذَيْنِ. فَجِئْتُهُ بِهِمَا. قَالَ مَنْ أَنْتُمَا ـ أَوْ مِنْ أَيْنَ أَنْتُمَا قَالاَ مِنْ أَهْلِ الطَّائِفِ. قَالَ لَوْ كُنْتُمَا مِنْ أَهْلِ الْبَلَدِ لأَوْجَعْتُكُمَا، تَرْفَعَانِ أَصْوَاتَكُمَا فِي مَسْجِدِ رَسُولِ اللَّهِ صلى الله عليه وسلم

Narrated Al-Qasim: A woman from the offspring of Ja`far was afraid lest her guardian marry her (to somebody) against her will. So she sent for two elderly men from the Ansar, `AbdurRahman and Mujammi', the two sons of Jariya, and they said to her, "Don't be afraid, for Khansa' bint Khidam was given by her father in marriage against her will, then the Prophet ﷺ cancelled that marriage." (See Hadith No. 78). – Sahih Al-Bukhari 6969

حَدَّثَنَا عَلِيُّ بْنُ عَبْدِ اللَّهِ، حَدَّثَنَا سُفْيَانُ، حَدَّثَنَا يَحْيَى بْنُ سَعِيدٍ، عَنِ الْقَاسِمِ، أَنَّ امْرَأَةً، مِنْ وَلَدِ جَعْفَرٍ تَخَوَّفَتْ أَنْ يُزَوِّجَهَا وَلِيُّهَا وَهْىَ كَارِهَةٌ فَأَرْسَلَتْ إِلَى شَيْخَيْنِ مِنَ الأَنْصَارِ عَبْدِ الرَّحْمَنِ وَمُجَمِّعٍ ابْنَىْ جَارِيَةَ قَالاَ فَلاَ تَخْشَيْنَ، فَإِنَّ خَنْسَاءَ بِنْتَ خِذَامٍ أَنْكَحَهَا أَبُوهَا وَهْىَ كَارِهَةٌ، فَرَدَّ النَّبِيُّ صلى الله عليه وسلم ذَلِكَ. قَالَ سُفْيَانُ وَأَمَّا عَبْدُ الرَّحْمَنِ فَسَمِعْتُهُ يَقُولُ عَنْ أَبِيهِ إِنَّ خَنْسَاءَ

Narrated Humaid: Anas said, "The Prophet ﷺ said, 'O Bani Salima! Don't you think that for every step of yours (that you take towards the mosque) there is a reward (while coming for prayer)?" Mujahid said: "Regarding Allah's Statement: "We record that which they have sent before (them), and their traces" (36.12). 'Their traces' means 'their steps.' " And Anas said that the people of Bani Salima wanted to shift to a place near the Prophet ﷺ but Allah's Messenger ﷺ disliked the idea of leaving their houses uninhabited and said, "Don't you think that you will get the reward for your footprints." Mujahid said, "Their foot prints mean their foot steps and their going on foot.". – Sahih Al-Bukhari 655, 656

حَدَّثَنَا مُحَمَّدُ بْنُ عَبْدِ اللَّهِ بْنِ حَوْشَبٍ، قَالَ حَدَّثَنَا عَبْدُ الْوَهَّابِ، قَالَ حَدَّثَنَا حُمَيْدٌ، عَنْ أَنَسٍ، قَالَ قَالَ النَّبِيُّ صلى الله عليه وسلم " يَا بَنِي سَلِمَةَ أَلاَ تَحْتَسِبُونَ آثَارَكُمْ ". وَقَالَ مُجَاهِدٌ فِي قَوْلِهِ {وَنَكْتُبُ مَا قَدَّمُوا وَآثَارَهُمْ} قَالَ خُطَاهُمْ. وَقَالَ ابْنُ أَبِي مَرْيَمَ أَخْبَرَنَا يَحْيَى بْنُ أَيُّوبَ، حَدَّثَنِي حُمَيْدٌ، حَدَّثَنِي أَنَسٌ، أَنَّ بَنِي سَلِمَةَ، أَرَادُوا أَنْ يَتَحَوَّلُوا، عَنْ مَنَازِلِهِمْ، فَيَنْزِلُوا قَرِيبًا مِنَ النَّبِيِّ صلى الله عليه وسلم قَالَ فَكَرِهَ رَسُولُ اللَّهِ صلى الله عليه وسلم أَنْ يُعْرُوا {الْمَدِينَةَ} فَقَالَ " أَلاَ تَحْتَسِبُونَ آثَارَكُمْ ". قَالَ مُجَاهِدٌ خُطَاهُمْ آثَارُهُمْ أَنْ يُمْشَى فِي الأَرْضِ بِأَرْجُلِهِمْ.

Narrated Ibrahim At Taimi's father: `Ali addressed us while he was standing on a brick pulpit and carrying a sword from which was hanging a scroll He said "By Allah, we have no book to read except Allah's Book and whatever is on this scroll," And then he unrolled it, and behold, in it was written what sort of camels were to be given as blood money, and there was also written in it: 'Medina is a sanctuary form 'Air (mountain) to such and such place so whoever innovates in it an heresy or commits a sin therein, he will incur the curse of Allah, the angels, and all the people and Allah will not accept his compulsory or optional good deeds.' There was also written in it: 'The asylum (pledge of protection) granted by any Muslims is one and the same, (even a Muslim of the lowest status is to be secured and respected by all the other Muslims, and whoever betrays a Muslim in this respect (by violating the pledge) will incur the curse of Allah, the angels, and all the people, and Allah will not accept his compulsory or optional good deeds.' There was also written in it: 'Whoever (freed slave) befriends (takes as masters) other than his real masters (manumitters) without their permission will incur the curse of Allah, the angels, and all the people, and Allah will not accept his compulsory or optional good deeds. ' (See Hadith No. 94, Vol. 3). – Sahih Al-Bukhari 7300

حَدَّثَنَا عُمَرُ بْنُ حَفْصِ بْنِ غِيَاثٍ، حَدَّثَنَا أَبِي، حَدَّثَنَا الأَعْمَشُ، حَدَّثَنِي إِبْرَاهِيمُ التَّيْمِيُّ، حَدَّثَنِي أَبِي قَالَ، خَطَبَنَا عَلِيٌّ ـ رضى الله عنه ـ عَلَى مِنْبَرٍ مِنْ آجُرٍّ، وَعَلَيْهِ سَيْفٌ فِيهِ صَحِيفَةٌ مُعَلَّقَةٌ فَقَالَ وَاللَّهِ مَا عِنْدَنَا مِنْ كِتَابٍ يُقْرَأُ إِلاَّ كِتَابُ اللَّهِ وَمَا فِي هَذِهِ الصَّحِيفَةِ. فَنَشَرَهَا فَإِذَا فِيهَا أَسْنَانُ الإِبِلِ وَإِذَا فِيهَا " الْمَدِينَةُ حَرَمٌ مِنْ عَيْرٍ إِلَى كَذَا، فَمَنْ أَحْدَثَ فِيهَا حَدَثًا فَعَلَيْهِ لَعْنَةُ اللَّهِ وَالْمَلاَئِكَةِ وَالنَّاسِ أَجْمَعِينَ، لاَ يَقْبَلُ اللَّهُ مِنْهُ صَرْفًا وَلاَ عَدْلاً ". وَإِذَا فِيهِ " ذِمَّةُ الْمُسْلِمِينَ وَاحِدَةٌ يَسْعَى بِهَا أَدْنَاهُمْ، فَمَنْ أَخْفَرَ مُسْلِمًا فَعَلَيْهِ لَعْنَةُ اللَّهِ وَالْمَلاَئِكَةِ وَالنَّاسِ أَجْمَعِينَ، لاَ يَقْبَلُ اللَّهُ مِنْهُ صَرْفًا وَلاَ عَدْلاً ". وَإِذَا فِيهَا " مَنْ وَالَى قَوْمًا بِغَيْرِ إِذْنِ مَوَالِيهِ فَعَلَيْهِ لَعْنَةُ اللَّهِ وَالْمَلاَئِكَةِ وَالنَّاسِ أَجْمَعِينَ لاَ يَقْبَلُ اللَّهُ مِنْهُ صَرْفًا وَلاَ عَدْلاً "

Narrated Ibn Shihab from `Urwa: `Aisha said, "Once Allah's Messenger ﷺ delayed the `Isha' prayer till `Umar reminded him by saying, "The prayer!" The women and children have slept. Then the Prophet ﷺ came out and said, 'None amongst the dwellers of the earth has been waiting for it (the prayer) except you." `Urwa said, "Nowhere except in Medina the prayer used to be offered (in those days)." He further said, "The Prophet ﷺ used to offer the `Isha' prayer in the period between the disappearance of the twilight and the end of the first third of the night.". – Sahih al-Bukhari 569

حَدَّثَنَا أَيُّوبُ بْنُ سُلَيْمَانَ، قَالَ حَدَّثَنِي أَبُو بَكْرٍ، عَنْ سُلَيْمَانَ، قَالَ صَالِحُ بْنُ كَيْسَانَ أَخْبَرَنِي ابْنُ شِهَابٍ، عَنْ عُرْوَةَ، أَنَّ عَائِشَةَ، قَالَتْ أَعْتَمَ رَسُولُ اللَّهِ صلى الله عليه وسلم بِالْعِشَاءِ حَتَّى نَادَاهُ عُمَرُ الصَّلاَةَ، نَامَ النِّسَاءُ وَالصِّبْيَانُ. فَخَرَجَ فَقَالَ " مَا يَنْتَظِرُهَا أَحَدٌ مِنْ أَهْلِ الأَرْضِ غَيْرُكُمْ ". قَالَ وَلاَ يُصَلَّى يَوْمَئِذٍ إِلاَّ بِالْمَدِينَةِ، وَكَانُوا يُصَلُّونَ فِيمَا بَيْنَ أَنْ يَغِيبَ الشَّفَقُ إِلَى ثُلُثِ اللَّيْلِ الأَوَّلِ.

Narrated Ibn `Umar: I'm When the Muslims arrived at Medina, they used to assemble for the prayer, and used to guess the time for it. During those days, the practice of Adhan for the prayers had not been introduced yet. Once they discussed this problem regarding the call for prayer. Some people suggested the use of a bell like the Christians, others proposed a trumpet like the horn used by the Jews, but `Umar was the first to suggest that a man should call (the people) for the prayer; so Allah's Messenger ﷺ ordered Bilal to get up and pronounce the Adhan for prayers. – Sahih al-Bukhari 604

حَدَّثَنَا مَحْمُودُ بْنُ غَيْلاَنَ، قَالَ حَدَّثَنَا عَبْدُ الرَّزَّاقِ، قَالَ أَخْبَرَنَا ابْنُ جُرَيْجٍ، قَالَ أَخْبَرَنِي نَافِعٌ، أَنَّ ابْنَ عُمَرَ، كَانَ يَقُولُ كَانَ الْمُسْلِمُونَ حِينَ قَدِمُوا الْمَدِينَةَ يَجْتَمِعُونَ فَيَتَحَيَّنُونَ الصَّلاَةَ، لَيْسَ يُنَادَى لَهَا، فَتَكَلَّمُوا يَوْمًا فِي ذَلِكَ، فَقَالَ بَعْضُهُمُ اتَّخِذُوا نَاقُوسًا مِثْلَ نَاقُوسِ النَّصَارَى. وَقَالَ بَعْضُهُمْ بَلْ بُوقًا مِثْلَ قَرْنِ الْيَهُودِ. فَقَالَ عُمَرُ أَوَلاَ تَبْعَثُونَ رَجُلاً يُنَادِي بِالصَّلاَةِ. فَقَالَ رَسُولُ اللَّهِ صلى الله عليه وسلم " يَا بِلاَلُ قُمْ فَنَادِ بِالصَّلاَةِ "

Narrated `Aisha: Once Allah's Messenger ﷺ delayed the `Isha' prayer till `Umar informed him that the women and children had slept. The Prophet ﷺ came out and said, "None except you from amongst the dwellers of earth is waiting for this prayer." In those days, there was no prayer except in Medina and they used to pray the `Isha' prayer between the disappearance of the twilight and the first third of the night. – Sahih al-Bukhari 864

حَدَّثَنَا أَبُو الْيَمَانِ، قَالَ أَخْبَرَنَا شُعَيْبٌ، عَنِ الزُّهْرِيِّ، قَالَ أَخْبَرَنِي عُرْوَةُ بْنُ الزُّبَيْرِ، عَنْ عَائِشَةَ ـ رضى الله عنها ـ قَالَتْ أَعْتَمَ رَسُولُ اللَّهِ صلى الله عليه وسلم بِالْعَتَمَةِ حَتَّى نَادَاهُ عُمَرُ نَامَ النِّسَاءُ وَالصِّبْيَانُ. فَخَرَجَ النَّبِيُّ صلى الله عليه وسلم فَقَالَ " مَا يَنْتَظِرُهَا أَحَدٌ غَيْرُكُمْ مِنْ أَهْلِ الأَرْضِ ". وَلاَ يُصَلَّى يَوْمَئِذٍ إِلاَّ بِالْمَدِينَةِ، وَكَانُوا يُصَلُّونَ الْعَتَمَةَ فِيمَا بَيْنَ أَنْ يَغِيبَ الشَّفَقُ إِلَى ثُلُثِ اللَّيْلِ الأَوَّلِ.

The Book of
Ansar
أنصار

Narrated Ibn `Abbas: Once the Prophetﷺ ascended the pulpit and it was the last gathering in which he took part. He was covering his shoulder with a big cloak and binding his head with an oily bandage. He glorified and praised Allah and said, "O people! Come to me." So the people came and gathered around him and he then said, "Amma ba'du." "From now onward the Ansar will decrease and other people will increase. So anybody who becomes a ruler of the followers of Muhammad and has the power to harm or benefit people then he should accept the good from the benevolent amongst them (Ansar) and overlook the faults of their wrong-doers.". – Sahih Al-Bukhari 927

حَدَّثَنَا إِسْمَاعِيلُ بْنُ أَبَانَ، قَالَ حَدَّثَنَا ابْنُ الْغَسِيلِ، قَالَ حَدَّثَنَا عِكْرِمَةُ، عَنِ ابْنِ عَبَّاسٍ ـ رضى الله عنهما ـ قَالَ صَعِدَ النَّبِيُّ صلى الله عليه وسلم الْمِنْبَرَ وَكَانَ آخِرَ مَجْلِسٍ جَلَسَهُ مُتَعَطِّفًا مِلْحَفَةً عَلَى مَنْكِبَيْهِ، قَدْ عَصَبَ رَأْسَهُ بِعِصَابَةٍ دَسِمَةٍ، فَحَمِدَ اللَّهَ وَأَثْنَى عَلَيْهِ ثُمَّ قَالَ " أَيُّهَا النَّاسُ إِلَىَّ ". فَثَابُوا إِلَيْهِ ثُمَّ قَالَ " أَمَّا بَعْدُ، فَإِنَّ هَذَا الْحَىَّ مِنَ الأَنْصَارِ يَقِلُّونَ، وَيَكْثُرُ النَّاسُ، فَمَنْ وَلِيَ شَيْئًا مِنْ أُمَّةِ مُحَمَّدٍ صلى الله عليه وسلم فَاسْتَطَاعَ أَنْ يَضُرَّ فِيهِ أَحَدًا أَوْ يَنْفَعَ فِيهِ أَحَدًا، فَلْيَقْبَلْ مِنْ مُحْسِنِهِمْ، وَيَتَجَاوَزْ عَنْ مُسِيِّهِمْ ".

Narrated Anas: The Prophetﷺ decided to grant a portion of (the uncultivated land of) Bahrain to the Ansar. The Ansar said, "(We will not accept it) till you give a similar portion to our emigrant brothers (from Quraish)." He said, "(O Ansar!) You will soon see people giving preference to others, so remain patient till you meet me (on the Day of Resurrection). – Sahih Al-Bukhari 2376

حَدَّثَنَا سُلَيْمَانُ بْنُ حَرْبٍ، حَدَّثَنَا حَمَّادٌ، عَنْ يَحْيَى بْنِ سَعِيدٍ، قَالَ سَمِعْتُ أَنَسًا ـ رضى الله عنه ـ قَالَ أَرَادَ النَّبِيُّ صلى الله عليه وسلم أَنْ يُقْطِعَ مِنَ الْبَحْرَيْنِ، فَقَالَتِ الأَنْصَارُ حَتَّى تُقْطِعَ لإِخْوَانِنَا مِنَ الْمُهَاجِرِينَ مِثْلَ الَّذِي تُقْطِعُ لَنَا قَالَ " سَتَرَوْنَ بَعْدِي أَثَرَةً فَاصْبِرُوا حَتَّى تَلْقَوْنِي ".

Narrated Al-Bara: I heard the Prophetﷺ saying (or the Prophetﷺ said), "None loves the Ansar but a believer, and none hates them but a hypocrite. So Allah will love him who loves them, and He will hate him who hates them.". - Sahih Al-Bukhari 3783

حَدَّثَنَا حَجَّاجُ بْنُ مِنْهَالٍ، حَدَّثَنَا شُعْبَةُ، قَالَ أَخْبَرَنِي عَدِيُّ بْنُ ثَابِتٍ، قَالَ سَمِعْتُ الْبَرَاءَ ـ رضى الله عنه ـ قَالَ سَمِعْتُ النَّبِيَّ صلى الله عليه وسلم أَوْ قَالَ قَالَ النَّبِيُّ صلى الله عليه وسلم " الأَنْصَارُ لاَ يُحِبُّهُمْ إِلاَّ مُؤْمِنٌ، وَلاَ يُبْغِضُهُمْ إِلاَّ مُنَافِقٌ، فَمَنْ أَحَبَّهُمْ أَحَبَّهُ اللَّهُ، وَمَنْ أَبْغَضَهُمْ أَبْغَضَهُ اللَّهُ "

Narrated Anas bin Malik: The Prophetﷺ said, "The sign of Belief is to love the Ansar, and the sign of hypocrisy is to hate the Ansar." – Sahih Al-Bukhari 3784

حَدَّثَنَا مُسْلِمُ بْنُ إِبْرَاهِيمَ، حَدَّثَنَا شُعْبَةُ، عَنْ عَبْدِ اللَّهِ بْنِ عَبْدِ اللَّهِ بْنِ جَبْرٍ، عَنْ أَنَسِ بْنِ مَالِكٍ ـ رضى الله عنه ـ عَنِ النَّبِيِّ صلى الله عليه وسلم قَالَ " آيَةُ الإِيمَانِ حُبُّ الأَنْصَارِ، وَآيَةُ النِّفَاقِ بُغْضُ الأَنْصَارِ "

Narrated Anas: The Prophetﷺ saw the women and children (of the Ansar) coming forward. (The sub-narrator said, "I think that Anas said, 'They were returning from a wedding party.") The Prophetﷺ stood up and said thrice, "By Allah! You are from the most beloved people to me." – Sahih al-Bukhari 3785

حَدَّثَنَا أَبُو مَعْمَرٍ، حَدَّثَنَا عَبْدُ الْوَارِثِ، حَدَّثَنَا عَبْدُ الْعَزِيزِ، عَنْ أَنَسٍ ـ رضى الله عنه ـ قَالَ رَأَى النَّبِيُّ صلى الله عليه وسلم النِّسَاءَ وَالصِّبْيَانَ مُقْبِلِينَ ـ قَالَ حَسِبْتُ أَنَّهُ قَالَ مِنْ عُرُسٍ ـ فَقَامَ النَّبِيُّ صلى الله عليه وسلم مُمْثِلاً، فَقَالَ " اللَّهُمَّ أَنْتُمْ مِنْ أَحَبِّ النَّاسِ إِلَىَّ ". قَالَهَا ثَلاَثَ مِرَارٍ

Narrated Abu Humaid: The Prophet ﷺ said, "The best of the Ansar families (homes) are the families (homes) of Banu An- Najjar, and then that of Banu `Abdul Ash-hal, and then that of Banu Al-Harith, and then that of Banu Saida; and there is good in all the families (homes) of the Ansar." Sa`d bin 'Ubada followed us and said, "O Abu Usaid ! Don't you see that the Prophet ﷺ compared the Ansar and made us the last of them in superiority? Then Sa`d met the Prophet ﷺ and said, "O Allah's Messenger ﷺ ! In comparing the Ansar's families (homes) as to the degree of superiority, you have made us the last of them." Allah's Messenger ﷺ replied, "Isn't it sufficient that you are regarded amongst the best?". – Sahih Al-Bukhari 3791
حَدَّثَنَا خَالِدُ بْنُ مَخْلَدٍ، حَدَّثَنَا سُلَيْمَانُ، قَالَ حَدَّثَنِي عَمْرُو بْنُ يَحْيَى، عَنْ عَبَّاسِ بْنِ سَهْلٍ، عَنْ أَبِي حُمَيْدٍ، عَنِ النَّبِيِّ صلى الله عليه وسلم قَالَ " إِنَّ خَيْرَ دُورِ الأَنْصَارِ دَارُ بَنِي النَّجَّارِ، ثُمَّ عَبْدِ الأَشْهَلِ، ثُمَّ دَارُ بَنِي الْحَارِثِ، ثُمَّ بَنِي سَاعِدَةَ، وَفِي كُلِّ دُورِ الأَنْصَارِ خَيْرٌ ". فَلَحِقْنَا سَعْدَ بْنَ عُبَادَةَ فَقَالَ أَبَا أُسَيْدٍ أَلَمْ تَرَ أَنَّ نَبِيَّ اللَّهِ صلى الله عليه وسلم خَيَّرَ الأَنْصَارَ فَجَعَلَنَا أَخِيرًا فَأَدْرَكَ سَعْدٌ النَّبِيَّ صلى الله عليه وسلم فَقَالَ يَا رَسُولَ اللَّهِ، خُيِّرَ دُورُ الأَنْصَارِ فَجُعِلْنَا آخِرًا. فَقَالَ " أَوَلَيْسَ بِحَسْبِكُمْ أَنْ تَكُونُوا مِنَ الْخِيَارِ "

Narrated Sahl: Allah's Messenger ﷺ came to us while we were digging the trench and carrying out the earth on our backs. Allah's Messenger ﷺ then said, "O Allah ! There is no life except the life of the Hereafter, so please forgive the Emigrants and the Ansar.". – Sahih Al-Bukhari 3797
حَدَّثَنِي مُحَمَّدُ بْنُ عُبَيْدِ اللَّهِ، حَدَّثَنَا ابْنُ أَبِي حَازِمٍ، عَنْ أَبِيهِ، عَنْ سَهْلٍ، قَالَ جَاءَنَا رَسُولُ اللَّهِ صلى الله عليه وسلم وَنَحْنُ نَحْفِرُ الْخَنْدَقَ وَنَنْقُلُ التُّرَابَ عَلَى أَكْتَادِنَا، فَقَالَ رَسُولُ اللَّهِ صلى الله عليه وسلم " اللَّهُمَّ لاَ عَيْشَ إِلاَّ عَيْشُ الآخِرَهْ فَاغْفِرْ لِلْمُهَاجِرِينَ وَالأَنْصَارِ ".

Narrated Sahl bin Sa`d: The Prophet's companions did not take as a starting date for the Muslim calendar, the day, the Prophet ﷺ had been sent as an Apostle or the day of his death, but the day of his arrival at Medina. – Sahih Al-Bukhari 3934
حَدَّثَنَا عَبْدُ اللَّهِ بْنُ مَسْلَمَةَ، حَدَّثَنَا عَبْدُ الْعَزِيزِ، عَنْ أَبِيهِ، عَنْ سَهْلِ بْنِ سَعْدٍ، قَالَ مَا عَدُّوا مِنْ مَبْعَثِ النَّبِيِّ صلى الله عليه وسلم وَلاَ مِنْ وَفَاتِهِ، مَا عَدُّوا إِلاَّ مِنْ مَقْدَمِهِ الْمَدِينَةَ.

Narrated Al-Bara: I and Ibn `Umar were considered too young (to take part) in the battle of Badr, and the number of the Emigrant warriors were over sixty (men) and the Ansar were over 249.. – Sahih Al-Bukhari 3956
حَدَّثَنِي مَحْمُودٌ، حَدَّثَنَا وَهْبٌ، عَنْ شُعْبَةَ، عَنْ أَبِي إِسْحَاقَ، عَنِ الْبَرَاءِ، قَالَ اسْتُصْغِرْتُ أَنَا وَابْنُ عُمَرَ يَوْمَ بَدْرٍ، وَكَانَ الْمُهَاجِرُونَ يَوْمَ بَدْرٍ نَيِّفًا عَلَى سِتِّينَ، وَالأَنْصَارُ نَيِّفًا وَأَرْبَعِينَ وَمِائَتَيْنِ.

Narrated Anas bin Malik: Once the Prophet ﷺ saw some women and children coming from a wedding party. He got up energetically and happily and said, "By Allah! You (i.e., the Ansar) are the most beloved of all people to me.". – Sahih Al-Bukhari 5180
حَدَّثَنَا عَبْدُ الرَّحْمَنِ بْنُ الْمُبَارَكِ، حَدَّثَنَا عَبْدُ الْوَارِثِ، حَدَّثَنَا عَبْدُ الْعَزِيزِ بْنُ صُهَيْبٍ، عَنْ أَنَسِ بْنِ مَالِكٍ ـ رضى الله عنه ـ قَالَ أَبْصَرَ النَّبِيُّ صلى الله عليه وسلم نِسَاءً وَصِبْيَانًا مُقْبِلِينَ مِنْ عُرْسٍ، فَقَامَ مُمْتَنًّا فَقَالَ " اللَّهُمَّ أَنْتُمْ مِنْ أَحَبِّ النَّاسِ إِلَىَّ "

Narrated `Abdullah: The Prophet ﷺ said, "I saw (in a dream) a black woman with unkempt hair going out of Medina and settling at Mahai'a, i.e., Al-Juhfa. I interpreted that as a symbol of epidemic of Medina being transferred to that place (Al-Juhfa). – Sahih Al-Bukhari 7038. [19]

[19] Al-Juhfa is the Miqat of Sham . Damascus; Ash-Sham.

حَدَّثَنَا إِسْمَاعِيلُ بْنُ عَبْدِ اللَّهِ، حَدَّثَنِي أَخِي عَبْدُ الْحَمِيدِ، عَنْ سُلَيْمَانَ بْنِ بِلاَلٍ، عَنْ مُوسَى بْنِ عُقْبَةَ، عَنْ سَالِمِ بْنِ عَبْدِ اللَّهِ، عَنْ أَبِيهِ، أَنَّ النَّبِيَّ صلى الله عليه وسلم قَالَ " رَأَيْتُ كَأَنَّ امْرَأَةً سَوْدَاءَ ثَائِرَةَ الرَّأْسِ، خَرَجَتْ مِنَ الْمَدِينَةِ، حَتَّى قَامَتْ بِمَهْيَعَةَ ـ وَهْىَ الْجُحْفَةُ ـ فَأَوَّلْتُ أَنَّ وَبَاءَ الْمَدِينَةِ نُقِلَ إِلَيْهَا ".

Narrated Salim bin `Abdullah from his father: I heard Allah's Messenger ﷺ saying, "The Miqat for the people of Medina is Dhul-Hulaifa; for the people of Sham is Mahita; (i.e. Al-Juhfa); and for the people of Najd is Qarn. And said Ibn `Umar, "They claim, but I did not hear personally, that the Prophet ﷺ said, "The Miqat for the people of Yemen is Yalamlam.". – Sahih Al-Bukhari 1528

حَدَّثَنَا أَحْمَدُ، حَدَّثَنَا ابْنُ وَهْبٍ، قَالَ أَخْبَرَنِي يُونُسُ، عَنِ ابْنِ شِهَابٍ، عَنْ سَالِمِ بْنِ عَبْدِ اللَّهِ، عَنْ أَبِيهِ ـ رضى الله عنه ـ سَمِعْتُ رَسُولَ اللَّهِ صلى الله عليه وسلم يَقُولُ " مُهَلُّ أَهْلِ الْمَدِينَةِ ذُو الْحُلَيْفَةِ، وَمُهَلُّ أَهْلِ الشَّأْمِ مَهْيَعَةُ وَهِيَ الْجُحْفَةُ، وَأَهْلِ نَجْدٍ قَرْنٌ ". قَالَ ابْنُ عُمَرَ ـ رضى الله عنهما ـ زَعَمُوا أَنَّ النَّبِيَّ صلى الله عليه وسلم قَالَ وَلَمْ أَسْمَعْهُ " وَمُهَلُّ أَهْلِ الْيَمَنِ يَلَمْلَمُ ".

Narrated Anas: The Prophet ﷺ said, "Love for the Ansar is a sign of faith and hatred for the Ansar is a sign of hypocrisy.". – Sahih Al-Bukhari 17

حَدَّثَنَا أَبُو الْوَلِيدِ، قَالَ حَدَّثَنَا شُعْبَةُ، قَالَ أَخْبَرَنِي عَبْدُ اللَّهِ بْنُ عَبْدِ اللَّهِ بْنِ جَبْرٍ، قَالَ سَمِعْتُ أَنَسًا، عَنِ النَّبِيِّ صلى الله عليه وسلم قَالَ " آيَةُ الإِيمَانِ حُبُّ الأَنْصَارِ، وَآيَةُ النِّفَاقِ بُغْضُ الأَنْصَارِ ".

Narrated `Abdullah bin Zaid: The Prophet ﷺ said, "But for the emigration, I would have been one of the Ansar; and if the people took their way in a valley (or a mountain pass), I would take Ansar's valley or their mountain pass.". – Sahih Al-Bukhari 7245

حَدَّثَنَا مُوسَى، حَدَّثَنَا وُهَيْبٌ، عَنْ عَمْرِو بْنِ يَحْيَى، عَنْ عَبَّادِ بْنِ تَمِيمٍ، عَنْ عَبْدِ اللَّهِ بْنِ زَيْدٍ، عَنِ النَّبِيِّ صلى الله عليه وسلم قَالَ " لَوْلاَ الْهِجْرَةُ لَكُنْتُ امْرَأً مِنَ الأَنْصَارِ، وَلَوْ سَلَكَ النَّاسُ وَادِيًا أَوْ شِعْبًا، لَسَلَكْتُ وَادِيَ الأَنْصَارِ وَشِعْبَهَا ". تَابَعَهُ أَبُو التَّيَّاحِ عَنْ أَنَسٍ عَنِ النَّبِيِّ صلى الله عليه وسلم فِي الشِّعْبِ.

Narrated Qatada: We do not know of any tribe amongst the 'Arab tribes who lost more martyrs than Al-Ansar, and they will have superiority on the Day of Resurrection. Anas bin Malik told us that seventy from the Ansar were martyred on the day of Uhud, and seventy on the day (of the battle of) Bir Ma'una, and seventy on the day of Al-Yamama. Anas added, "The battle of Bir Ma'una took place during the lifetime of Allah's Messenger ﷺ and the battle of Al-Yamama, during the caliphate of Abu Bakr, and it was the day when Musailamah Al-Kadhdhab was killed.". – Sahih Al-Bukhari 4078

حَدَّثَنِي عَمْرُو بْنُ عَلِيٍّ، حَدَّثَنَا مُعَاذُ بْنُ هِشَامٍ، قَالَ حَدَّثَنِي أَبِي، عَنْ قَتَادَةَ، قَالَ مَا نَعْلَمُ حَيًّا مِنْ أَحْيَاءِ الْعَرَبِ أَكْثَرَ شَهِيدًا أَعَزَّ يَوْمَ الْقِيَامَةِ مِنَ الأَنْصَارِ. قَالَ قَتَادَةُ وَحَدَّثَنَا أَنَسُ بْنُ مَالِكٍ أَنَّهُ قُتِلَ مِنْهُمْ يَوْمَ أُحُدٍ سَبْعُونَ، وَيَوْمَ بِئْرِ مَعُونَةَ سَبْعُونَ، وَيَوْمَ الْيَمَامَةِ سَبْعُونَ، قَالَ وَكَانَ بِئْرُ مَعُونَةَ عَلَى عَهْدِ رَسُولِ اللَّهِ صلى الله عليه وسلم، وَيَوْمُ الْيَمَامَةِ عَلَى عَهْدِ أَبِي بَكْرٍ يَوْمَ مُسَيْلِمَةَ الْكَذَّابِ.

The Book of

Accuse your opinion over your religion

اتَّهِمُوا رَأْيَكُمْ عَلَى دِينِكُ

Narrated Ibn Shihab: Once `Umar bin `Abdul `Aziz delayed the prayer and `Urwa bin Az-Zubair went to him and said, "Once in 'Iraq, Al-Mughira bin Shu`ba delayed his prayers and Abi Mas`ud Al-Ansari went to him and said, 'O Mughira! What is this? Don't you know that once Gabriel came and offered the prayer (Fajr prayer) and Allah's Messenger ﷺ prayed too, then he prayed again (Zuhr prayer) and so did Allah's Apostle and again he prayed (`Asr prayers and Allah's Messenger ﷺ did the same; again he prayed (Maghrib-prayer) and so did Allah's Messenger ﷺ and again prayed (`Isha prayer) and so did Allah's Apostle and (Gabriel) said, 'I was ordered to do so (to demonstrate the prayers prescribed to you)?'" `Umar (bin `Abdul `Aziz) said to `Urwa, "Be sure of what you Say. Did Gabriel lead Allah's Messenger ﷺ at the stated times of the prayers?" `Urwa replied, "Bashir bin Abi Mas`ud narrated like this on the authority of his father." `Urwa added, "Aisha told me that Allah's Messenger ﷺ used to pray `Asr prayer when the sunshine was still inside her residence (during the early time of `Asr). – Sahih Al-Bukhari 521, 522

حَدَّثَنَا عَبْدُ اللَّهِ بْنُ مَسْلَمَةَ، قَالَ قَرَأْتُ عَلَى مَالِكٍ عَنِ ابْنِ شِهَابٍ، أَنَّ عُمَرَ بْنَ عَبْدِ الْعَزِيزِ، أَخَّرَ الصَّلاَةَ يَوْمًا، فَدَخَلَ عَلَيْهِ عُرْوَةُ بْنُ الزُّبَيْرِ، فَأَخْبَرَهُ أَنَّ الْمُغِيرَةَ بْنَ شُعْبَةَ أَخَّرَ الصَّلاَةَ يَوْمًا وَهُوَ بِالْعِرَاقِ، فَدَخَلَ عَلَيْهِ أَبُو مَسْعُودٍ الأَنْصَارِيُّ فَقَالَ مَا هَذَا يَا مُغِيرَةُ أَلَيْسَ قَدْ عَلِمْتَ أَنَّ جِبْرِيلَ نَزَلَ فَصَلَّى، فَصَلَّى رَسُولُ اللَّهِ صلى الله عليه وسلم ثُمَّ صَلَّى فَصَلَّى رَسُولُ اللَّهِ صلى الله عليه وسلم ثُمَّ صَلَّى فَصَلَّى رَسُولُ اللَّهِ صلى الله عليه وسلم ثُمَّ صَلَّى فَصَلَّى رَسُولُ اللَّهِ صلى الله عليه وسلم ثُمَّ صَلَّى فَصَلَّى رَسُولُ اللَّهِ صلى الله عليه وسلم ثُمَّ قَالَ " بِهَذَا أُمِرْتُ ". فَقَالَ عُمَرُ لِعُرْوَةَ اعْلَمْ مَا تُحَدِّثُ أَوَإِنَّ جِبْرِيلَ هُوَ أَقَامَ لِرَسُولِ اللَّهِ صلى الله عليه وسلم وَقْتَ الصَّلاَةِ. قَالَ عُرْوَةُ كَذَلِكَ كَانَ بَشِيرُ بْنُ أَبِي مَسْعُودٍ يُحَدِّثُ عَنْ أَبِيهِ. قَالَ عُرْوَةُ وَلَقَدْ حَدَّثَتْنِي عَائِشَةُ، أَنَّ رَسُولَ اللَّهِ صلى الله عليه وسلم كَانَ يُصَلِّي الْعَصْرَ، وَالشَّمْسُ فِي حُجْرَتِهَا قَبْلَ أَنْ تَظْهَرَ.

Narrated Muawiya: You offer a prayer which I did not see being offered by Allah's Messenger ﷺ when we were in his company and he certainly had forbidden it (i.e. two rak`at after the `Asr prayer). – Sahih Al-Bukhari 587

حَدَّثَنَا مُحَمَّدُ بْنُ أَبَانَ، قَالَ حَدَّثَنَا غُنْدَرٌ، قَالَ حَدَّثَنَا شُعْبَةُ، عَنْ أَبِي التَّيَّاحِ، قَالَ سَمِعْتُ حُمْرَانَ بْنَ أَبَانَ، يُحَدِّثُ عَنْ مُعَاوِيَةَ، قَالَ إِنَّكُمْ لَتُصَلُّونَ صَلاَةً، لَقَدْ صَحِبْنَا رَسُولَ اللَّهِ صلى الله عليه وسلم فَمَا رَأَيْنَاهُ يُصَلِّيهَا، وَلَقَدْ نَهَى عَنْهُمَا، يَعْنِي الرَّكْعَتَيْنِ بَعْدَ الْعَصْرِ.

Narrated `Aisha: By Allah, Who took away the Prophet. The Prophet ﷺ never missed them (two rak`at) after the `Asr prayer till he met Allah and he did not meet Allah till it became heavy for him to pray while standing so he used to offer most of the prayers while sitting. (She meant the two rak`at after `Asr) He used to pray them in the house and never prayed them in the mosque lest it might be hard for his followers and he loved what was easy for them . – Sahih Al-Bukhari 590

حَدَّثَنَا أَبُو نُعَيْمٍ، قَالَ حَدَّثَنَا عَبْدُ الْوَاحِدِ بْنُ أَيْمَنَ، قَالَ حَدَّثَنِي أَبِي أَنَّهُ، سَمِعَ عَائِشَةَ، قَالَتْ وَالَّذِي ذَهَبَ بِهِ مَا تَرَكَهُمَا حَتَّى لَقِيَ اللَّهَ، وَمَا لَقِيَ اللَّهَ تَعَالَى حَتَّى ثَقُلَ عَنِ الصَّلاَةِ، وَكَانَ يُصَلِّي كَثِيرًا مِنْ صَلاَتِهِ قَاعِدًا ـ تَعْنِي الرَّكْعَتَيْنِ بَعْدَ الْعَصْرِ ـ وَكَانَ النَّبِيُّ صلى الله عليه وسلم يُصَلِّيهِمَا، وَلاَ يُصَلِّيهِمَا فِي الْمَسْجِدِ مَخَافَةَ أَنْ يُثَقِّلَ عَلَى أُمَّتِهِ، وَكَانَ يُحِبُّ مَا يُخَفِّفُ عَنْهُمْ

Narrated Aisha: (the wife of the Prophet) "Whenever Allah's Messenger ﷺ intended to go on a journey, he would draw lots amongst his wives and would take with him the one upon whom the lot fell. During a Ghazwa of his, he drew lots amongst us and the lot fell upon me, and I proceeded with him after Allah had decreed the use of the veil by women. I was carried in a Howdah (on the camel) and dismounted while still in it. When Allah's Messenger ﷺ was through with his Ghazwa and returned home, and we approached the city of Medina, Allah's Messenger ordered us to proceed at night. When the order of setting off was given, I walked till I was past the army to answer the call of nature. After finishing I returned (to the camp) to depart (with the others) and suddenly realized that my necklace over my chest was missing. So, I returned to look for it and was delayed because of that. The people who used to carry me on the camel, came to my Howdah and put it on the back of the camel, thinking that I was in it, as, at that time, women were light in weight, and thin and lean, and did not use to eat much. So, those people did not feel the difference in the heaviness of the Howdah while lifting it, and they put it over the camel. At that time I was a young lady. They set the camel moving and proceeded on. I found my necklace after the army had gone, and came to their camp to find nobody. So, I went to the place where I used to stay, thinking that they would discover my absence and come back in my search. While in that state, I felt sleepy and slept. Safwan bin Mu'attal As-Sulami Adh-Dhakwani was behind the army and reached my abode in the morning. When he saw a sleeping person, he came to me, and he used to see me before veiling. So, I got up when I heard him saying, "Inna lil-lah-wa inn a ilaihi rajiun (We are for Allah, and we will return to Him)." He made his camel knell down. He got down from his camel, and put his leg on the front legs of the camel and then I rode and sat over it. Safwan set out walking, leading the camel by the rope till we reached the army who had halted to take rest at midday. Then whoever was meant for destruction, fell into destruction, (some people accused me falsely) and the leader of the false accusers was `Abdullah bin Ubai bin Salul. After that we returned to Medina, and I became ill for one month while the people were spreading the forged statements of the false accusers. I was feeling during my ailment as if I were not receiving the usual kindness from the Prophet which I used to receive from him when I got sick. But he would come, greet and say, 'How is that (girl)?' I did not know anything of what was going on till I recovered from my ailment and went out with Um Mistah to the Manasi where we used to answer the call of nature, and we used not to go to answer the call of nature except from night to night and that was before we had lavatories near to our houses. And this habit of ours was similar to the habit of the old 'Arabs in the open country (or away from houses). So. I and Um Mistah bint Ruhm went out walking. Um Mistah stumbled because of her long dress and on that she said, 'Let Mistah be ruined.' I said, 'You are saying a bad word. Why are you abusing a man who took part in (the battle of) Badr?' She said, 'O Hanata (you there) didn't you hear what they said?' Then she told me the rumors of the false accusers. My sickness was aggravated, and when I returned home, Allah's Messenger came to me, and after greeting he said, 'How is that (girl)?' I requested him to allow me to go to my parents. I wanted then to be sure of the news through them I Allah's Messenger allowed me, and I went to my parents and asked my mother, 'What are the people talking about?' She said, 'O my daughter! Don't worry much about this matter. By Allah, never is there a charming woman loved by her husband who has other wives, but the women would forge false news about her.' I said, 'Glorified be Allah! Are the people really taking of this matter?' That night I kept on weeping and could not sleep till morning. In the morning Allah's Messenger called `Ali bin Abu Talib and Usama bin Zaid when he saw the Divine Inspiration delayed, to consul them about divorcing his wife (i.e. 'Aisha). Usama bin Zaid said what he knew of the good reputation of his wives and added, 'O Allah's Messenger ! Keep you wife, for, by Allah, we know nothing about her but good.' `Ali bin Abu Talib said, 'O Allah's Messenger ! Allah has no imposed restrictions on you, and there are many women other than she, yet you may ask the woman-servant who will tell you the truth.' On that Allah's Messenger called Barirah and said, 'O Barirah. Did you ever see anything which roused your suspicions about her?' Barirah said, 'No, by Allah Who has sent you with the Truth, I have never seen in her anything faulty except that she is a girl of immature age, who sometimes sleeps and leaves the dough for the goats to eat.' On that day Allah's Messenger ascended the pulpit and requested that somebody support him in punishing `Abdullah bin Ubai bin Salul. Allah's Apostle said, 'Who will support me to punish that person (`Abdullah bin Ubai bin Salul) who has hurt me by slandering the reputation of my family? By Allah, I know nothing about my family but good, and they have accused a person about whom I know nothing except good, and he never entered my house except in my company.' Sa`d bin Mu`adh got up and said, 'O Allah's Messenger! By Allah, I will relieve you from him. If that man is from the tribe of the Aus, then we will chop his head off, and if he is from our brothers, the Khazraj, then order us, and we will fulfill your order.' On that Sa`d bin 'Ubada, the chief of the Khazraj and before this incident, he had been a pious man, got up, motivated by his zeal for his tribe and said, 'By Allah, you have told a lie; you cannot kill him, and you will never be able to kill him.' On that Usaid bin Al-Hadir got up and said (to Sa`d bin 'Ubada), 'By Allah! You are a liar. By Allah, we will kill him; and you are a hypocrite, defending the hypocrites.' On this the two tribes of Aus and Khazraj got excited and were about to fight each other, while Allah's Messenger was standing on the pulpit. He got down and quieted them till they became silent and he kept quiet. On that day I kept on weeping so much so that neither did my tears stop, nor could I sleep. In the morning my parents were with me and I had wept for two nights and a day, till I thought my liver would burst from weeping. While they were sitting with me and I was weeping, an Ansari woman asked my permission to enter, and I allowed her to come in. She sat down and started weeping with me. While we were in this state, Allah's Messenger came and sat down and he had never sat with me since the day they forged the accusation. No revelation regarding my case came to him for a month. He recited Tashah-hud (i.e. None has the right to be worshipped but Allah and Muhammad is His Apostle) and then said, 'O `Aisha! I have been informed such-and-such about you; if you are innocent, then Allah will soon reveal your Innocence, and if you have committed a sin, then repent to Allah and ask Him to forgive you, for when a person confesses his sin and asks Allah for forgiveness, Allah accepts his repentance.' When Allah's Messenger finished his speech my tears ceased completely and there remained not even a single drop of it. I requested my father to reply to Allah's Messenger on my behalf. My father said, By Allah, I do not know what to say to Allah's Messenger. I said to my mother, 'Talk to Allah's Messenger on my behalf.' She said, 'By Allah, I do not know what to say to Allah's Apostle. I was a young girl and did not have much knowledge of the Qur'an. I said. 'I know, by Allah, that you have listened to what people are saying and that has been planted in your minds and you have taken it as a truth. Now, if I told you that I am innocent and Allah knows that I am innocent, you would not believe me and if I confessed to you falsely that I am guilty, and Allah knows that I am innocent you would believe me. By Allah, I don't compare my situation with you except to the situation of Joseph's father (i.e. Jacob) who said, 'So (for me) patience is most fitting against that which you assert and it is Allah (Alone) whose help can be sought.' Then I turned to the other side of my bed hoping that Allah would prove my innocence. By Allah I never thought that Allah would reveal Divine Inspiration in my case, as I considered myself too inferior to be talked of in the Holy Qur'an. I had hoped that Allah's Messenger might have a dream in which Allah would prove my innocence. By Allah, Allah's Apostle had not got up and nobody had left the house before the Divine Inspiration came to Allah's Apostle. So, there overtook him the same state which used to overtake him, (when he used to have, on being inspired divinely). He was sweating so much so that the drops of the sweat were dropping like pearls though it was a (cold) wintry day. When that state of Allah's Messenger ﷺ was over, he was smiling and the first word he said, `Aisha! Thank Allah, for Allah has declared your innocence.' My mother told me to go to Allah's Messenger ﷺ. I replied, 'By Allah I will not go to him and will not thank but Allah.' So Allah revealed: "Verily! They who spread the slander are a gang among you . . ." (24.11) When Allah gave the declaration of my Innocence, Abu Bakr, who used to provide for Mistah bin Uthatha for he was his relative, said, 'By Allah, I will never provide Mistah with anything because of what he said about Aisha.' But Allah later revealed: -- "And let not those who are good and wealthy among you swear not to help their kinsmen, those in need and those who left their homes in Allah's Cause. Let them forgive and overlook. Do you not wish that Allah should forgive you? Verily! Allah is Oft-forgiving, Most Merciful." (24.22) After that Abu Bakr said, 'Yes ! By Allah! I like that Allah should forgive me,' and resumed helping Mistah whom he used to help before. Allah's Messenger ﷺ also asked Zainab bint Jahsh (i.e. the Prophet's wife about me saying, 'What do you know and what did you see?' She replied, 'O Allah's Messenger ﷺ! I refrain to claim hearing or seeing what I have not heard or seen. By Allah, I know nothing except goodness about Aisha." Aisha further added "Zainab was competing with me (in her beauty and the Prophet's love), yet Allah protected her (from being malicious), for she had piety.". – Sahih Al-Bukhari 2661

حَدَّثَنَا أَبُو الرَّبِيعِ، سُلَيْمَانُ بْنُ دَاوُدَ وَأَفْهَمَنِي بَعْضَهُ أَحْمَدُ حَدَّثَنَا فُلَيْحُ بْنُ سُلَيْمَانَ، عَنِ ابْنِ شِهَابٍ الزُّهْرِيِّ، عَنْ عُرْوَةَ بْنِ الزُّبَيْرِ، وَسَعِيدِ بْنِ الْمُسَيَّبِ، وَعَلْقَمَةَ بْنِ وَقَّاصٍ اللَّيْثِيِّ، وَعُبَيْدِ اللَّهِ بْنِ عَبْدِ اللَّهِ بْنِ عُتْبَةَ، عَنْ عَائِشَةَ ـ رضى الله عنها ـ زَوْجِ النَّبِيِّ صلى الله عليه وسلم حِينَ قَالَ لَهَا أَهْلُ الإِفْكِ مَا قَالُوا، فَبَرَّأَهَا اللَّهُ مِنْهُ، قَالَ الزُّهْرِيُّ، وَكُلُّهُمْ حَدَّثَنِي طَائِفَةً مِنْ حَدِيثِهَا وَبَعْضُهُمْ أَوْعَى مِنْ بَعْضٍ، وَأَثْبَتُ لَهُ اقْتِصَاصًا، وَقَدْ وَعَيْتُ عَنْ كُلِّ وَاحِدٍ مِنْهُمُ الْحَدِيثَ الَّذِي حَدَّثَنِي عَنْ عَائِشَةَ، وَبَعْضُ حَدِيثِهِمْ يُصَدِّقُ بَعْضًا. زَعَمُوا أَنَّ عَائِشَةَ قَالَتْ كَانَ رَسُولُ اللَّهِ صلى الله عليه وسلم إِذَا أَرَادَ أَنْ يَخْرُجَ سَفَرًا أَقْرَعَ بَيْنَ أَزْوَاجِهِ، فَأَيَّتُهُنَّ خَرَجَ سَهْمُهَا خَرَجَ بِهَا مَعَهُ، فَأَقْرَعَ بَيْنَنَا فِي غَزَاةٍ غَزَاهَا فَخَرَجَ سَهْمِي، فَخَرَجْتُ مَعَهُ بَعْدَ مَا أُنْزِلَ الْحِجَابُ، فَأَنَا أُحْمَلُ فِي هَوْدَجٍ وَأُنْزَلُ فِيهِ، فَسِرْنَا حَتَّى إِذَا فَرَغَ رَسُولُ اللَّهِ صلى الله عليه وسلم مِنْ غَزْوَتِهِ تِلْكَ، وَقَفَلَ وَدَنَوْنَا مِنَ الْمَدِينَةِ، آذَنَ لَيْلَةً بِالرَّحِيلِ، فَقُمْتُ حِينَ آذَنُوا بِالرَّحِيلِ، فَمَشَيْتُ حَتَّى جَاوَزْتُ الْجَيْشَ، فَلَمَّا قَضَيْتُ شَأْنِي أَقْبَلْتُ إِلَى الرَّحْلِ، فَلَمَسْتُ صَدْرِي، فَإِذَا عِقْدٌ لِي مِنْ جَزْعِ أَظْفَارٍ قَدِ انْقَطَعَ، فَرَجَعْتُ فَالْتَمَسْتُ عِقْدِي، فَحَبَسَنِي ابْتِغَاؤُهُ، فَأَقْبَلَ الَّذِينَ يَرْحَلُونَ لِي، فَاحْتَمَلُوا هَوْدَجِي فَرَحَلُوهُ عَلَى بَعِيرِي الَّذِي كُنْتُ أَرْكَبُ، وَهُمْ يَحْسِبُونَ أَنِّي فِيهِ، وَكَانَ النِّسَاءُ إِذْ ذَاكَ خِفَافًا لَمْ يَثْقُلْنَ وَلَمْ يَغْشَهُنَّ اللَّحْمُ، وَإِنَّمَا يَأْكُلْنَ الْعُلْقَةَ مِنَ الطَّعَامِ، فَلَمْ يَسْتَنْكِرِ الْقَوْمُ حِينَ رَفَعُوهُ ثِقَلَ الْهَوْدَجِ فَاحْتَمَلُوهُ وَكُنْتُ جَارِيَةً حَدِيثَةَ السِّنِّ، فَبَعَثُوا الْجَمَلَ وَسَارُوا، فَوَجَدْتُ عِقْدِي بَعْدَ مَا اسْتَمَرَّ الْجَيْشُ، فَجِئْتُ مَنْزِلَهُمْ وَلَيْسَ فِيهِ أَحَدٌ، فَأَمَمْتُ مَنْزِلِي الَّذِي كُنْتُ بِهِ فَظَنَنْتُ أَنَّهُمْ سَيَفْقِدُونِي فَيَرْجِعُونَ إِلَيَّ، فَبَيْنَا أَنَا جَالِسَةٌ غَلَبَتْنِي عَيْنَاىَ فَنِمْتُ، وَكَانَ صَفْوَانُ بْنُ الْمُعَطَّلِ السُّلَمِيُّ ثُمَّ الذَّكْوَانِيُّ مِنْ وَرَاءِ الْجَيْشِ، فَأَصْبَحَ عِنْدَ مَنْزِلِي فَرَأَى سَوَادَ إِنْسَانٍ نَائِمٍ فَأَتَانِي، وَكَانَ يَرَانِي قَبْلَ الْحِجَابِ فَاسْتَيْقَظْتُ بِاسْتِرْجَاعِهِ حِينَ أَنَاخَ رَاحِلَتَهُ، فَوَطِئَ يَدَهَا فَرَكِبْتُهَا فَانْطَلَقَ يَقُودُ بِي الرَّاحِلَةَ، حَتَّى أَتَيْنَا الْجَيْشَ بَعْدَ مَا نَزَلُوا مُعَرِّسِينَ فِي نَحْرِ الظَّهِيرَةِ، فَهَلَكَ مَنْ هَلَكَ، وَكَانَ الَّذِي تَوَلَّى الإِفْكَ عَبْدُ اللَّهِ بْنُ أُبَىٍّ ابْنُ سَلُولَ، فَقَدِمْنَا الْمَدِينَةَ فَاشْتَكَيْتُ بِهَا شَهْرًا، يُفِيضُونَ مِنْ قَوْلِ أَصْحَابِ الإِفْكِ، وَيَرِيبُنِي فِي وَجَعِي أَنِّي لاَ أَرَى مِنَ النَّبِيِّ صلى الله عليه وسلم اللُّطْفَ الَّذِي كُنْتُ أَرَى مِنْهُ حِينَ أَمْرَضُ، إِنَّمَا يَدْخُلُ فَيُسَلِّمُ ثُمَّ يَقُولُ " كَيْفَ تِيكُمْ ". لاَ أَشْعُرُ بِشَىْءٍ مِنْ ذَلِكَ حَتَّى نَقَهْتُ، فَخَرَجْتُ أَنَا وَأُمُّ مِسْطَحٍ قِبَلَ الْمَنَاصِعِ مُتَبَرَّزُنَا، لاَ نَخْرُجُ إِلاَّ لَيْلاً إِلَى لَيْلٍ، وَذَلِكَ قَبْلَ أَنْ نَتَّخِذَ الْكُنُفَ قَرِيبًا مِنْ بُيُوتِنَا، وَأَمْرُنَا أَمْرُ الْعَرَبِ الأُوَلِ فِي الْبَرِّيَّةِ أَوْ فِي التَّنَزُّهِ، فَأَقْبَلْتُ أَنَا وَأُمُّ مِسْطَحٍ بِنْتُ أَبِي رُهْمٍ نَمْشِي، فَعَثَرَتْ فِي مِرْطِهَا فَقَالَتْ تَعِسَ مِسْطَحٌ، فَقُلْتُ لَهَا بِئْسَ مَا قُلْتِ، أَتَسُبِّينَ رَجُلاً شَهِدَ بَدْرًا فَقَالَتْ يَا هَنْتَاهْ أَلَمْ تَسْمَعِي مَا قَالُوا فَأَخْبَرَتْنِي بِقَوْلِ أَهْلِ الإِفْكِ، فَازْدَدْتُ مَرَضًا إِلَى مَرَضِي، فَلَمَّا رَجَعْتُ إِلَى بَيْتِي دَخَلَ عَلَىَّ رَسُولُ اللَّهِ صلى الله عليه وسلم فَسَلَّمَ فَقَالَ " كَيْفَ تِيكُمْ ". فَقُلْتُ ائْذَنْ لِي إِلَى أَبَوَىَّ. قَالَتْ وَأَنَا حِينَئِذٍ أُرِيدُ أَنْ أَسْتَيْقِنَ الْخَبَرَ مِنْ قِبَلِهِمَا، فَأَذِنَ لِي رَسُولُ اللَّهِ صلى الله عليه وسلم فَأَتَيْتُ أَبَوَىَّ فَقُلْتُ لأُمِّي مَا يَتَحَدَّثُ بِهِ النَّاسُ فَقَالَتْ يَا بُنَيَّةُ هَوِّنِي عَلَى نَفْسِكِ الشَّأْنَ، فَوَاللَّهِ لَقَلَّمَا كَانَتِ امْرَأَةٌ قَطُّ وَضِيئَةٌ عِنْدَ رَجُلٍ يُحِبُّهَا وَلَهَا ضَرَائِرُ إِلاَّ أَكْثَرْنَ عَلَيْهَا. فَقُلْتُ سُبْحَانَ اللَّهِ وَلَقَدْ يَتَحَدَّثُ النَّاسُ بِهَذَا قَالَتْ فَبِتُّ تِلْكَ اللَّيْلَةَ حَتَّى أَصْبَحْتُ لاَ يَرْقَأُ لِي دَمْعٌ وَلاَ أَكْتَحِلُ بِنَوْمٍ، ثُمَّ أَصْبَحْتُ فَدَعَا رَسُولُ اللَّهِ صلى الله عليه وسلم عَلِيَّ بْنَ أَبِي طَالِبٍ وَأُسَامَةَ بْنَ زَيْدٍ حِينَ اسْتَلْبَثَ الْوَحْىُ، يَسْتَشِيرُهُمَا فِي فِرَاقِ أَهْلِهِ، فَأَمَّا أُسَامَةُ فَأَشَارَ عَلَيْهِ بِالَّذِي يَعْلَمُ فِي نَفْسِهِ مِنَ الْوُدِّ لَهُمْ، فَقَالَ أُسَامَةُ أَهْلُكَ يَا رَسُولَ اللَّهِ وَلاَ نَعْلَمُ وَاللَّهِ إِلاَّ خَيْرًا، وَأَمَّا عَلِيُّ بْنُ أَبِي طَالِبٍ فَقَالَ يَا رَسُولَ اللَّهِ لَمْ يُضَيِّقِ اللَّهُ عَلَيْكَ وَالنِّسَاءُ سِوَاهَا كَثِيرٌ، وَسَلِ الْجَارِيَةَ تَصْدُقْكَ. فَدَعَا رَسُولُ اللَّهِ صلى الله عليه وسلم بَرِيرَةَ فَقَالَ " يَا بَرِيرَةُ هَلْ رَأَيْتِ فِيهَا شَيْئًا يَرِيبُكِ ". فَقَالَتْ بَرِيرَةُ لاَ وَالَّذِي بَعَثَكَ بِالْحَقِّ، إِنْ رَأَيْتُ مِنْهَا أَمْرًا أَغْمِصُهُ عَلَيْهَا أَكْثَرَ مِنْ أَنَّهَا جَارِيَةٌ حَدِيثَةُ السِّنِّ تَنَامُ عَنِ الْعَجِينِ فَتَأْتِي الدَّاجِنُ فَتَأْكُلُهُ. فَقَامَ رَسُولُ اللَّهِ صلى الله عليه وسلم مِنْ يَوْمِهِ، فَاسْتَعْذَرَ مِنْ عَبْدِ اللَّهِ بْنِ أُبَىٍّ ابْنِ سَلُولَ فَقَالَ رَسُولُ

اللَّهِ صلى الله عليه وسلم " مَنْ يَعْذِرُنِي مِنْ رَجُلٍ بَلَغَنِي أَذَاهُ فِي أَهْلِي، فَوَاللَّهِ مَا عَلِمْتُ عَلَى أَهْلِي إِلاَّ خَيْرًا، وَقَدْ ذَكَرُوا رَجُلاً مَا عَلِمْتُ عَلَيْهِ إِلاَّ خَيْرًا، وَمَا كَانَ يَدْخُلُ عَلَى أَهْلِي إِلاَّ مَعِي ". فَقَامَ سَعْدُ بْنُ مُعَاذٍ فَقَالَ يَا رَسُولَ اللَّهِ أَنَا وَاللَّهِ أَعْذِرُكَ مِنْهُ، إِنْ كَانَ مِنَ الأَوْسِ ضَرَبْنَا عُنُقَهُ، وَإِنْ كَانَ مِنْ إِخْوَانِنَا مِنَ الْخَزْرَجِ أَمَرْتَنَا فَفَعَلْنَا فِيهِ أَمْرَكَ. فَقَامَ سَعْدُ بْنُ عُبَادَةَ وَهُوَ سَيِّدُ الْخَزْرَجِ، وَكَانَ قَبْلَ ذَلِكَ رَجُلاً صَالِحًا وَلَكِنِ احْتَمَلَتْهُ الْحَمِيَّةُ فَقَالَ كَذَبْتَ لَعَمْرُ اللَّهِ، لاَ تَقْتُلُهُ وَلاَ تَقْدِرُ عَلَى ذَلِكَ، فَقَامَ أُسَيْدُ بْنُ الْحُضَيْرِ فَقَالَ كَذَبْتَ لَعَمْرُ اللَّهِ، وَاللَّهِ لَنَقْتُلَنَّهُ، فَإِنَّكَ مُنَافِقٌ تُجَادِلُ عَنِ الْمُنَافِقِينَ. فَثَارَ الْحَيَّانِ الأَوْسُ وَالْخَزْرَجُ حَتَّى هَمُّوا، وَرَسُولُ اللَّهِ صلى الله عليه وسلم عَلَى الْمِنْبَرِ فَنَزَلَ فَخَفَّضَهُمْ حَتَّى سَكَتُوا وَسَكَتَ، وَبَكَيْتُ يَوْمِي لاَ يَرْقَأُ لِي دَمْعٌ وَلاَ أَكْتَحِلُ بِنَوْمٍ، فَأَصْبَحَ عِنْدِي أَبَوَاىَ، قَدْ بَكَيْتُ لَيْلَتَيْنِ وَيَوْمًا حَتَّى أَظُنُّ أَنَّ الْبُكَاءَ فَالِقٌ كَبِدِي ـ قَالَتْ ـ فَبَيْنَا هُمَا جَالِسَانِ عِنْدِي وَأَنَا أَبْكِي إِذِ اسْتَأْذَنَتِ امْرَأَةٌ مِنَ الأَنْصَارِ فَأَذِنْتُ لَهَا، فَجَلَسَتْ تَبْكِي مَعِي، فَبَيْنَا نَحْنُ كَذَلِكَ إِذْ دَخَلَ رَسُولُ اللَّهِ صلى الله عليه وسلم فَجَلَسَ، وَلَمْ يَجْلِسْ عِنْدِي مِنْ يَوْمِ قِيلَ فِيَّ مَا قِيلَ قَبْلَهَا، وَقَدْ مَكُثَ شَهْرًا لاَ يُوحَى إِلَيْهِ فِي شَأْنِي شَىْءٌ ـ قَالَتْ ـ فَتَشَهَّدَ ثُمَّ قَالَ " يَا عَائِشَةُ فَإِنَّهُ بَلَغَنِي عَنْكِ كَذَا وَكَذَا، فَإِنْ كُنْتِ بَرِيئَةً فَسَيُبَرِّئُكِ اللَّهُ، وَإِنْ كُنْتِ أَلْمَمْتِ فَاسْتَغْفِرِي اللَّهَ وَتُوبِي إِلَيْهِ، فَإِنَّ الْعَبْدَ إِذَا اعْتَرَفَ بِذَنْبِهِ ثُمَّ تَابَ تَابَ اللَّهُ عَلَيْهِ ". فَلَمَّا قَضَى رَسُولُ اللَّهِ صلى الله عليه وسلم مَقَالَتَهُ قَلَصَ دَمْعِي حَتَّى مَا أُحِسُّ مِنْهُ قَطْرَةً وَقُلْتُ لأَبِي أَجِبْ عَنِّي رَسُولَ اللَّهِ صلى الله عليه وسلم. قَالَ وَاللَّهِ مَا أَدْرِي مَا أَقُولُ لِرَسُولِ اللَّهِ صلى الله عليه وسلم. فَقُلْتُ لأُمِّي أَجِيبِي عَنِّي رَسُولَ اللَّهِ صلى الله عليه وسلم فِيمَا قَالَ. قَالَتْ وَاللَّهِ مَا أَدْرِي مَا أَقُولُ لِرَسُولِ اللَّهِ صلى الله عليه وسلم. قَالَتْ وَأَنَا جَارِيَةٌ حَدِيثَةُ السِّنِّ لاَ أَقْرَأُ كَثِيرًا مِنَ الْقُرْآنِ فَقُلْتُ إِنِّي وَاللَّهِ لَقَدْ عَلِمْتُ أَنَّكُمْ سَمِعْتُمْ مَا يَتَحَدَّثُ بِهِ النَّاسُ، وَوَقَرَ فِي أَنْفُسِكُمْ وَصَدَّقْتُمْ بِهِ، وَلَئِنْ قُلْتُ لَكُمْ إِنِّي بَرِيئَةٌ. وَاللَّهُ يَعْلَمُ إِنِّي لَبَرِيئَةٌ لاَ تُصَدِّقُونِي بِذَلِكَ، وَلَئِنِ اعْتَرَفْتُ لَكُمْ بِأَمْرٍ، وَاللَّهُ يَعْلَمُ أَنِّي بَرِيئَةٌ لَتُصَدِّقُنِّي وَاللَّهِ مَا أَجِدُ لِي وَلَكُمْ مَثَلاً إِلاَّ أَبَا يُوسُفَ إِذْ قَالَ {فَصَبْرٌ جَمِيلٌ وَاللَّهُ الْمُسْتَعَانُ عَلَى مَا تَصِفُونَ} ثُمَّ تَحَوَّلْتُ عَلَى فِرَاشِي، وَأَنَا أَرْجُو أَنْ يُبَرِّئَنِي اللَّهُ، وَلَكِنْ وَاللَّهِ مَا ظَنَنْتُ أَنْ يُنْزِلَ فِي شَأْنِي وَحْيًا، وَلأَنَا أَحْقَرُ فِي نَفْسِي مِنْ أَنْ يُتَكَلَّمَ بِالْقُرْآنِ فِي أَمْرِي، وَلَكِنِّي كُنْتُ أَرْجُو أَنْ يَرَى رَسُولُ اللَّهِ صلى الله عليه وسلم فِي النَّوْمِ رُؤْيَا يُبَرِّئُنِي اللَّهُ، فَوَاللَّهِ مَا رَامَ مَجْلِسَهُ وَلاَ خَرَجَ أَحَدٌ مِنْ أَهْلِ الْبَيْتِ حَتَّى أُنْزِلَ عَلَيْهِ، فَأَخَذَهُ مَا كَانَ يَأْخُذُهُ مِنَ الْبُرَحَاءِ، حَتَّى إِنَّهُ لَيَتَحَدَّرُ مِنْهُ مِثْلُ الْجُمَانِ مِنَ الْعَرَقِ فِي يَوْمٍ شَاتٍ، فَلَمَّا سُرِّيَ عَنْ رَسُولِ اللَّهِ صلى الله عليه وسلم وَهُوَ يَضْحَكُ، فَكَانَ أَوَّلَ كَلِمَةٍ تَكَلَّمَ بِهَا أَنْ قَالَ لِي " يَا عَائِشَةُ، احْمَدِي اللَّهَ فَقَدْ بَرَّأَكِ اللَّهُ ". فَقَالَتْ لِي أُمِّي قُومِي إِلَى رَسُولِ اللَّهِ صلى الله عليه وسلم. فَقُلْتُ لاَ وَاللَّهِ، لاَ أَقُومُ إِلَيْهِ، وَلاَ أَحْمَدُ إِلاَّ اللَّهَ فَأَنْزَلَ اللَّهُ تَعَالَى {إِنَّ الَّذِينَ جَاءُوا بِالإِفْكِ عُصْبَةٌ مِنْكُمْ} الآيَاتِ، فَلَمَّا أَنْزَلَ اللَّهُ هَذَا فِي بَرَاءَتِي قَالَ أَبُو بَكْرٍ الصِّدِّيقُ ـ رضى الله عنه ـ وَكَانَ يُنْفِقُ عَلَى مِسْطَحِ بْنِ أُثَاثَةَ لِقَرَابَتِهِ مِنْهُ وَاللَّهِ لاَ أُنْفِقُ عَلَى مِسْطَحٍ شَيْئًا أَبَدًا بَعْدَ مَا قَالَ لِعَائِشَةَ. فَأَنْزَلَ اللَّهُ تَعَالَى {وَلاَ يَأْتَلِ أُولُو الْفَضْلِ مِنْكُمْ وَالسَّعَةِ} إِلَى قَوْلِهِ {غَفُورٌ رَحِيمٌ} فَقَالَ أَبُو بَكْرٍ بَلَى، وَاللَّهِ إِنِّي لأُحِبُّ أَنْ يَغْفِرَ اللَّهُ لِي، فَرَجَعَ إِلَى مِسْطَحٍ الَّذِي كَانَ يُجْرِي عَلَيْهِ. وَكَانَ رَسُولُ اللَّهِ صلى الله عليه وسلم يَسْأَلُ زَيْنَبَ بِنْتَ جَحْشٍ عَنْ أَمْرِي، فَقَالَ " يَا زَيْنَبُ، مَا عَلِمْتِ مَا رَأَيْتِ ". فَقَالَتْ يَا رَسُولَ اللَّهِ، أَحْمِي سَمْعِي وَبَصَرِي، وَاللَّهِ مَا عَلِمْتُ عَلَيْهَا إِلاَّ خَيْرًا، قَالَتْ وَهْىَ الَّتِي كَانَتْ تُسَامِينِي، فَعَصَمَهَا اللَّهُ بِالْوَرَعِ. قَالَ وَحَدَّثَنَا فُلَيْحٌ، عَنْ هِشَامِ بْنِ عُرْوَةَ، عَنْ عُرْوَةَ، عَنْ عَائِشَةَ، وَعَبْدِ اللَّهِ بْنِ الزُّبَيْرِ، مِثْلَهُ. قَالَ وَحَدَّثَنَا فُلَيْحٌ، عَنْ رَبِيعَةَ بْنِ أَبِي عَبْدِ الرَّحْمَنِ، وَيَحْيَى بْنِ سَعِيدٍ، عَنِ الْقَاسِمِ بْنِ مُحَمَّدِ بْنِ أَبِي بَكْرٍ، مِثْلَهُ.

Narrated `Abdullah bin Ka`b:That Ka`b bin Malik told him that in the lifetime of Allah's Messenger ﷺ he demanded his debt from Ibn Abu Hadrad in the Mosque. Their voices grew louder till Allah's Messenger ﷺ heard them while he was in his house. So he lifted the curtain of his room and called Ka`b bin Malik saying, "O Ka`b!" He replied, "Labbaik! O Allah's Messenger ﷺ!" He beckoned to him with his hand suggesting that he deduct half the debt. Ka`b said, "I agree, O Allah's Messenger ﷺ!" Allah's Messenger ﷺ then said (to Ibn Abu Hadrad), "Get up and pay him the rest.". – Sahih Al-Bukhari 2710

حَدَّثَنَا عَبْدُ اللَّهِ بْنُ مُحَمَّدٍ، حَدَّثَنَا عُثْمَانُ بْنُ عُمَرَ، أَخْبَرَنَا يُونُسُ، وَقَالَ اللَّيْثُ حَدَّثَنِي يُونُسُ، عَنِ ابْنِ شِهَابٍ، أَخْبَرَنِي عَبْدُ اللَّهِ بْنُ كَعْبٍ، أَنَّ كَعْبَ بْنَ مَالِكٍ، أَخْبَرَهُ أَنَّهُ، تَقَاضَى ابْنَ أَبِي حَدْرَدٍ دَيْنًا كَانَ لَهُ عَلَيْهِ فِي عَهْدِ رَسُولِ اللَّهِ صلى الله عليه وسلم فِي الْمَسْجِدِ، فَارْتَفَعَتْ أَصْوَاتُهُمَا حَتَّى سَمِعَهَا رَسُولُ اللَّهِ صلى الله عليه وسلم وَهْوَ فِي بَيْتٍ، فَخَرَجَ رَسُولُ اللَّهِ صلى الله عليه وسلم إِلَيْهِمَا حَتَّى كَشَفَ سِجْفَ حُجْرَتِهِ، فَنَادَى كَعْبَ بْنَ مَالِكٍ فَقَالَ " يَا كَعْبُ ". فَقَالَ لَبَّيْكَ يَا رَسُولَ اللَّهِ. فَأَشَارَ بِيَدِهِ أَنْ ضَعِ الشَّطْرَ. فَقَالَ كَعْبٌ قَدْ فَعَلْتُ يَا رَسُولَ اللَّهِ. فَقَالَ رَسُولُ اللَّهِ صلى الله عليه وسلم " قُمْ فَاقْضِهِ "

Narrated Az-Zuhri: Salim bin `Abdullah told me that Rafi` bin Khadij told `Abdullah bin `Umar that his two paternal uncles who had fought in the battle of Badr informed him that Allah's Messenger ﷺ forbade the renting of fields. I said to Salim, "Do you rent your land?" He said, "Yes, for Rafi` is mistaken.". – Sahih Al-Bukhari 4012, 4013

حَدَّثَنَا عَبْدُ اللَّهِ بْنُ مُحَمَّدِ بْنِ أَسْمَاءَ، حَدَّثَنَا جُوَيْرِيَةُ، عَنْ مَالِكٍ، عَنِ الزُّهْرِيِّ، أَنَّ سَالِمَ بْنَ عَبْدِ اللَّهِ، أَخْبَرَهُ قَالَ أَخْبَرَ رَافِعُ بْنُ خَدِيجٍ عَبْدَ اللَّهِ بْنَ عُمَرَ، أَنَّ عَمَّيْهِ، وَكَانَا، شَهِدَا بَدْرًا أَخْبَرَاهُ أَنَّ رَسُولَ اللَّهِ صلى الله عليه وسلم نَهَى عَنْ كِرَاءِ الْمَزَارِعِ. قُلْتُ لِسَالِمٍ فَتُكْرِيهَا أَنْتَ قَالَ نَعَمْ، إِنَّ رَافِعًا أَكْثَرَ عَلَى نَفْسِهِ.

Narrated Sa`id bin Jubair: I said to Ibn `Abbas, "Nauf-al-Bakali " claims that Moses of Bani Israel was not Moses, the companion of Al-Khadir." Ibn `Abbas said, "Allah's enemy tells a lie! Ubai bin Ka`b narrated to us that Allah's Messenger ﷺ said, 'Moses got up to deliver a sermon before Bani Israel and he was asked, 'Who is the most learned person among the people?' Moses replied, 'I (am the most learned).' Allah then admonished Moses for he did not ascribe all knowledge to Allah only (Then) came the Divine Inspiration:-- 'Yes, one of Our slaves at the junction of the two seas is more learned than you.' Moses said, 'O my Lord ! How can meet him?' Allah said, 'Take a fish in a basket and wherever the fish is lost, follow it (you will find him at that place). So Moses set out along with his attendant Yusha` bin Noon, and they carried with them a fish till they reached a rock and rested there. Moses put his head down and slept. (Sufyan, a sub-narrator said that somebody other than `Amr said) 'At the rock there was a water spring called 'Al-Hayat' and none came in touch with its water but became alive. So some of the water of that spring fell over that fish, so it moved and slipped out of the basket and entered the sea. When Moses woke up, he asked his attendant, 'Bring our early meal' (18.62). The narrator added: Moses did not suffer from fatigue except after he had passed the place he had been ordered to observe. His attendant Yusha` bin Noon said to him, 'Do you remember (what happened) when we betook ourselves to the rock? I did indeed forget (about) the fish ...' (18.63) The narrator added: So they came back, retracing their steps and then they found in the sea, the way of the fish looking like a tunnel. So there was an astonishing event for his attendant, and there was tunnel for the fish. When they reached the rock, they found a man covered with a garment. Moses greeted him. The man said astonishingly, 'Is there any such greeting in your land?' Moses said, 'I am Moses.' The man said, 'Moses of Bani Israel?' Moses said, 'Yes,' and added, 'may I follow you so that you teach me something of the Knowledge which you have been taught?' (18.66). Al-Khadir said to him, 'O Moses! You have something of Allah's knowledge which Allah has taught you and which I do not know; and I have something of Allah's knowledge which Allah has taught me and which you do not know.' Moses said, 'But I will follow you.' Al-Khadir said, 'Then if you follow me, ask me no question about anything until I myself speak to you concerning it.' (18.70). After that both of them proceeded along the seashore. There passed by them a boat whose crew recognized Al-Khadir and received them on board free of charge. So they both got on board. A sparrow came and sat on the edge of the boat and dipped its beak unto the sea. Al-Khadir said to Moses. 'My knowledge and your knowledge and all the creation's knowledge compared to Allah's knowledge is not more than the water taken by this sparrow's beak.' Then Moses was startled by Al-Khadir's action of taking an adze and scuttling the boat with it. Moses said to him, 'These people gave us a free lift, but you intentionally scuttled their boat so as to drown them. Surely you have...' (18.71) Then they both proceeded and found a boy playing with other boys. Al-Khadir took hold of him by the head and cut it off. Moses said to him, 'Have you killed an innocent soul who has killed nobody? Surely you have done an illegal thing! ' (18.74) He said, "Didn't I tell you that you will not be able to have patient with me up to but they refused to entertain them as their guests. There they found a wall therein at the point of collapsing.' (18.75-77) Al-Khadir moved his hand thus and set it upright (repaired it). Moses said to him, 'When we entered this town, they neither gave us hospitality nor fed us; if you had wished, you could have taken wages for it,' Al- Khadir said, 'This is the parting between you and me I will tell you the interpretation of (those things) about which you were unable to hold patience.'...(18.78) Allah's Messenger ﷺ said, 'We wished that Moses could have been more patient so that He (Allah) could have described to us more about their

story.' Ibn `Abbas used to recite:-- 'And in front (ahead) of them there was a king who used to seize every (serviceable) boat by force. (18.79) ...and as for the boy he was a disbeliever. ".
– Sahih Al-Bukhari 4727

حَدَّثَنِي قُتَيْبَةُ بْنُ سَعِيدٍ، قَالَ حَدَّثَنِي سُفْيَانُ بْنُ عُيَيْنَةَ، عَنْ عَمْرِو بْنِ دِينَارٍ، عَنْ سَعِيدِ بْنِ جُبَيْرٍ، قَالَ قُلْتُ لاِبْنِ عَبَّاسٍ إِنَّ نَوْفًا الْبَكَالِيَّ يَزْعُمُ أَنَّ مُوسَى بَنِي إِسْرَائِيلَ لَيْسَ بِمُوسَى الْخَضِرِ. فَقَالَ كَذَبَ عَدُوُّ اللَّهِ حَدَّثَنَا أُبَىُّ بْنُ كَعْبٍ عَنْ رَسُولِ اللَّهِ صلى الله عليه وسلم قَالَ " قَامَ مُوسَى خَطِيبًا فِي بَنِي إِسْرَائِيلَ فَقِيلَ لَهُ أَىُّ النَّاسِ أَعْلَمُ قَالَ أَنَا، فَعَتَبَ اللَّهُ عَلَيْهِ، إِذْ لَمْ يَرُدَّ الْعِلْمَ إِلَيْهِ، وَأَوْحَى إِلَيْهِ بَلَى عَبْدٌ مِنْ عِبَادِي بِمَجْمَعِ الْبَحْرَيْنِ، هُوَ أَعْلَمُ مِنْكَ قَالَ أَىْ رَبِّ كَيْفَ السَّبِيلُ إِلَيْهِ قَالَ تَأْخُذُ حُوتًا فِي مِكْتَلٍ فَحَيْثُمَا فَقَدْتَ الْحُوتَ فَاتَّبِعْهُ قَالَ فَخَرَجَ مُوسَى، وَمَعَهُ فَتَاهُ يُوشَعُ بْنُ نُونٍ، وَمَعَهُمَا الْحُوتُ حَتَّى انْتَهَيَا إِلَى الصَّخْرَةِ، فَنَزَلاَ عِنْدَهَا قَالَ فَوَضَعَ مُوسَى رَأْسَهُ فَنَامَ ـ قَالَ سُفْيَانُ وَفِي حَدِيثِ غَيْرِ عَمْرٍو قَالَ ـ وَفِي أَصْلِ الصَّخْرَةِ عَيْنٌ يُقَالُ لَهَا الْحَيَاةُ لاَ يُصِيبُ مِنْ مَائِهَا شَىْءٌ إِلاَّ حَيِيَ، فَأَصَابَ الْحُوتَ مِنْ مَاءِ تِلْكَ الْعَيْنِ، قَالَ فَتَحَرَّكَ، وَانْسَلَّ مِنَ الْمِكْتَلِ، فَدَخَلَ الْبَحْرَ فَلَمَّا اسْتَيْقَظَ مُوسَى {قَالَ لِفَتَاهُ آتِنَا غَدَاءَنَا} الآيَةَ قَالَ وَلَمْ يَجِدِ النَّصَبَ حَتَّى جَاوَزَ مَا أُمِرَ بِهِ، قَالَ لَهُ فَتَاهُ يُوشَعُ بْنُ نُونٍ {أَرَأَيْتَ إِذْ أَوَيْنَا إِلَى الصَّخْرَةِ فَإِنِّي نَسِيتُ الْحُوتَ} الآيَةَ قَالَ فَرَجَعَا يَقُصَّانِ فِي آثَارِهِمَا، فَوَجَدَا فِي الْبَحْرِ كَالطَّاقِ مَمَرَّ الْحُوتِ، فَكَانَ لِفَتَاهُ عَجَبًا، وَلِلْحُوتِ سَرَبًا قَالَ فَلَمَّا انْتَهَيَا إِلَى الصَّخْرَةِ، إِذْ هُمَا بِرَجُلٍ مُسَجًّى بِثَوْبٍ، فَسَلَّمَ عَلَيْهِ مُوسَى قَالَ وَأَنَّى بِأَرْضِكَ السَّلاَمُ فَقَالَ أَنَا مُوسَى. قَالَ مُوسَى بَنِي إِسْرَائِيلَ قَالَ نَعَمْ هَلْ أَتَّبِعُكَ عَلَى أَنْ تُعَلِّمَنِي مِمَّا عُلِّمْتَ رَشَدًا. قَالَ لَهُ الْخَضِرُ يَا مُوسَى إِنَّكَ عَلَى عِلْمٍ مِنْ عِلْمِ اللَّهِ عَلَّمَكَهُ اللَّهُ لاَ أَعْلَمُهُ، وَأَنَا عَلَى عِلْمٍ مِنْ عِلْمِ اللَّهِ عَلَّمَنِيهِ اللَّهُ لاَ تَعْلَمُهُ. قَالَ بَلْ أَتَّبِعُكَ. قَالَ فَإِنِ اتَّبَعْتَنِي فَلاَ تَسْأَلْنِي عَنْ شَىْءٍ حَتَّى أُحْدِثَ لَكَ مِنْهُ ذِكْرًا، فَانْطَلَقَا يَمْشِيَانِ عَلَى السَّاحِلِ فَمَرَّتْ بِهِمَا سَفِينَةٌ فَعُرِفَ الْخَضِرُ فَحَمَلُوهُمْ فِي سَفِينَتِهِمْ بِغَيْرِ نَوْلٍ ـ يَقُولُ بِغَيْرِ أَجْرٍ ـ فَرَكِبَا السَّفِينَةَ قَالَ وَوَقَعَ عُصْفُورٌ عَلَى حَرْفِ السَّفِينَةِ، فَغَمَسَ مِنْقَارَهُ الْبَحْرَ فَقَالَ الْخَضِرُ لِمُوسَى مَا عِلْمُكَ وَعِلْمِي وَعِلْمُ الْخَلاَئِقِ فِي عِلْمِ اللَّهِ إِلاَّ مِقْدَارُ مَا غَمَسَ هَذَا الْعُصْفُورُ مِنْقَارَهُ قَالَ فَلَمْ يَفْجَأْ مُوسَى، إِذْ عَمَدَ الْخَضِرُ إِلَى قَدُومٍ فَخَرَقَ السَّفِينَةَ، فَقَالَ لَهُ مُوسَى قَوْمٌ حَمَلُونَا بِغَيْرِ نَوْلٍ، عَمَدْتَ إِلَى سَفِينَتِهِمْ فَخَرَقْتَهَا {لِتُغْرِقَ أَهْلَهَا لَقَدْ جِئْتَ} الآيَةَ فَانْطَلَقَا إِذَا هُمَا بِغُلاَمٍ يَلْعَبُ مَعَ الْغِلْمَانِ، فَأَخَذَ الْخَضِرُ بِرَأْسِهِ فَقَطَعَهُ. قَالَ لَهُ مُوسَى {أَقَتَلْتَ نَفْسًا زَكِيَّةً بِغَيْرِ نَفْسٍ لَقَدْ جِئْتَ شَيْئًا نُكْرًا * قَالَ أَلَمْ أَقُلْ لَكَ إِنَّكَ لَنْ تَسْتَطِيعَ مَعِيَ صَبْرًا} إِلَى قَوْلِهِ {فَأَبَوْا أَنْ يُضَيِّفُوهُمَا فَوَجَدَا فِيهَا جِدَارًا يُرِيدُ أَنْ يَنْقَضَّ} فَقَالَ بِيَدِهِ هَكَذَا فَأَقَامَهُ، فَقَالَ لَهُ مُوسَى إِنَّا دَخَلْنَا هَذِهِ الْقَرْيَةَ، فَلَمْ يُضَيِّفُونَا وَلَمْ يُطْعِمُونَا، لَوْ شِئْتَ لاَتَّخَذْتَ عَلَيْهِ أَجْرًا. قَالَ هَذَا فِرَاقُ بَيْنِي وَبَيْنِكَ سَأُنَبِّئُكَ بِتَأْوِيلِ مَا لَمْ تَسْتَطِعْ عَلَيْهِ صَبْرًا. فَقَالَ رَسُولُ اللَّهِ صلى الله عليه وسلم " وَدِدْنَا أَنَّ مُوسَى صَبَرَ حَتَّى يُقَصَّ عَلَيْنَا مِنْ أَمْرِهِمَا ". قَالَ وَكَانَ ابْنُ عَبَّاسٍ يَقْرَأُ وَكَانَ أَمَامَهُمْ مَلِكٌ يَأْخُذُ كُلَّ سَفِينَةٍ صَالِحَةٍ غَصْبًا، وَأَمَّا الْغُلاَمُ فَكَانَ كَافِرًا.

Narrated Sa`id bin Jubair: The people of Kufa differed as regards the killing of a believer so I entered upon Ibn `Abbas (and asked him) about that. Ibn `Abbas said, "The Verse (in Surat-An-Nisa', 4:93) was the last thing revealed in this respect and nothing cancelled its validity.".
– Sahih Al-Bukhari 4763

حَدَّثَنِي مُحَمَّدُ بْنُ بَشَّارٍ، حَدَّثَنَا غُنْدَرٌ، حَدَّثَنَا شُعْبَةُ، عَنِ الْمُغِيرَةِ بْنِ النُّعْمَانِ، عَنْ سَعِيدِ بْنِ جُبَيْرٍ، قَالَ اخْتَلَفَ أَهْلُ الْكُوفَةِ فِي قَتْلِ الْمُؤْمِنِ، فَرَحَلْتُ فِيهِ إِلَى ابْنِ عَبَّاسٍ، فَقَالَ نَزَلَتْ فِي آخِرِ مَا نَزَلَ وَلَمْ يَنْسَخْهَا شَىْءٌ.

Narrated Masruq: While a man was delivering a speech in the tribe of Kinda, he said, "Smoke will prevail on the Day of Resurrection and will deprive the hypocrites their faculties of hearing and seeing. The believers will be afflicted with something like cold only thereof." That news scared us, so I went to (Abdullah) Ibn Mas`ud while he was reclining (and told him the story) whereupon he became angry, sat up and said, "He who knows a thing can say, it, but if he does not know, he should say, 'Allah knows best,' for it is an aspect of knowledge to say, 'I do not know,' if you do not know a certain thing. Allah said to His prophet. 'Say (O Muhammad): No wage do I ask of you for this (Qur'an), nor I am one of the pretenders (a person who pretends things which do not exist.)' (38.86) The Qur'aish delayed in embracing Islam for a period, so the Prophet ﷺ invoked evil on them, saying, 'O Allah! Help me against them by sending seven years of (famine) like those of Joseph.' So they were afflicted with such a severe year of famine that they were destroyed therein and ate dead animals and bones. They started seeing something like smoke between the sky and the earth (because of severe hunger). Abu Sufyan then came (to the Prophet) and said, "O Muhammad! You came to order us for to keep good relations with Kith and kin, and your kinsmen have now perished, so please invoke Allah (to relieve them).' Then Ibn Mas`ud recited:-- 'Then watch you for the day that the sky will bring forth a kind of smoke plainly visible....but truly you will return! (to disbelief) (44.10-15) Ibn Mas`ud added, Then the punishment was stopped, but truly, they reverted to heathenism (their old way). So Allah (threatened them thus): 'On the day when we shall seize you with a mighty grasp.' (44.16) And that was the day of the Battle of Badr. Allah's saying- "Lizama" (the punishment) refers to the day of Badr Allah's Statement: Alif-Lam-Mim, the Romans have been defeated, and they, after their defeat, will be victorious,' (30.1- 3) (This verse): Indicates that the defeat of Byzantine has already passed. – Sahih Al-Bukhari 4774

حَدَّثَنَا مُحَمَّدُ بْنُ كَثِيرٍ، حَدَّثَنَا سُفْيَانُ، حَدَّثَنَا مَنْصُورٌ، وَالأَعْمَشُ، عَنْ أَبِي الضُّحَى، عَنْ مَسْرُوقٍ، قَالَ بَيْنَمَا رَجُلٌ يُحَدِّثُ فِي كِنْدَةَ فَقَالَ يَجِيءُ دُخَانٌ يَوْمَ الْقِيَامَةِ فَيَأْخُذُ بِأَسْمَاعِ الْمُنَافِقِينَ وَأَبْصَارِهِمْ، يَأْخُذُ الْمُؤْمِنَ كَهَيْئَةِ الزُّكَامِ. فَفَزِعْنَا، فَأَتَيْتُ ابْنَ مَسْعُودٍ، وَكَانَ مُتَّكِئًا، فَغَضِبَ فَجَلَسَ فَقَالَ مَنْ عَلِمَ فَلْيَقُلْ، وَمَنْ لَمْ يَعْلَمْ فَلْيَقُلِ اللَّهُ أَعْلَمُ. فَإِنَّ مِنَ الْعِلْمِ أَنْ يَقُولَ لِمَا لاَ يَعْلَمُ لاَ أَعْلَمُ. فَإِنَّ اللَّهَ قَالَ لِنَبِيِّهِ صلى الله عليه وسلم {قُلْ مَا أَسْأَلُكُمْ عَلَيْهِ مِنْ أَجْرٍ وَمَا أَنَا مِنَ الْمُتَكَلِّفِينَ} وَإِنَّ قُرَيْشًا أَبْطَئُوا عَنِ الإِسْلاَمِ فَدَعَا عَلَيْهِمِ النَّبِيُّ صلى الله عليه وسلم فَقَالَ " اللَّهُمَّ أَعِنِّي عَلَيْهِمْ بِسَبْعٍ كَسَبْعِ يُوسُفَ، فَأَخَذَتْهُمْ سَنَةٌ حَتَّى هَلَكُوا فِيهَا، وَأَكَلُوا الْمَيْتَةَ وَالْعِظَامَ وَيَرَى الرَّجُلُ مَا بَيْنَ السَّمَاءِ وَالأَرْضِ كَهَيْئَةِ الدُّخَانِ "، فَجَاءَهُ أَبُو سُفْيَانَ فَقَالَ يَا مُحَمَّدُ جِئْتَ تَأْمُرُنَا بِصِلَةِ الرَّحِمِ، وَإِنَّ قَوْمَكَ قَدْ هَلَكُوا فَادْعُ اللَّهَ، فَقَرَأَ {فَارْتَقِبْ يَوْمَ تَأْتِي السَّمَاءُ بِدُخَانٍ مُبِينٍ} إِلَى قَوْلِهِ {عَائِدُونَ} أَفَيُكْشَفُ عَنْهُمْ عَذَابُ الآخِرَةِ إِذَا جَاءَ ثُمَّ عَادُوا إِلَى كُفْرِهِمْ فَذَلِكَ قَوْلُهُ تَعَالَى {يَوْمَ نَبْطِشُ الْبَطْشَةَ الْكُبْرَى} يَوْمَ بَدْرٍ وَلِزَامًا يَوْمَ بَدْرٍ {الم * غُلِبَتِ الرُّومُ} إِلَى {سَيَغْلِبُونَ} وَالرُّومُ قَدْ مَضَى.

Narrated: Abu `Abdur-Rahman and Hibban bin 'Atiyya had a dispute. Abu `Abdur-Rahman said to Hibban, "You know what made your companions (i.e. `Ali) dare to shed blood." Hibban said, "Come on! What is that?" `Abdur-Rahman said, "Something I heard him saying." The other said, "What was it?" `AbdurRahman said, "`Ali said, Allah's Messenger ﷺ sent for me, Az-Zubair and Abu Marthad, and all of us were cavalry men, and said, 'Proceed to Raudat-Hajj (Abu Salama said that Abu 'Awana called it like this, i.e., Hajj where there is a woman carrying a letter from Hatib bin Abi Balta'a to the pagans (of Mecca). So bring that letter to me.' So we proceeded riding on our horses till we overtook her at the same place of which Allah's Messenger ﷺ had told us. She was traveling on her camel. In that letter Hatib had written to the Meccans about the proposed attached of Allah's Messenger ﷺ against them. We asked her, "Where is the letter which is with you?' She replied, 'I haven't got any letter.' So we made her camel kneel down and searched her luggage, but we did not find anything. My two companions said, 'We do not think that she has got a letter.' I said, 'We know that Allah's Messenger ﷺ has not told a lie.'" Then `Ali took an oath saying, "By Him by Whom one should swear! You shall either bring out the letter or we shall strip off your clothes." She then stretched out her hand for her girdle (round her waist) and brought out the paper (letter). They took the letter to Allah's Messenger ﷺ. Umar said, "O Allah's Messenger ﷺ! (Hatib) has betrayed Allah, His Apostle and the believers; let me chop off his neck!" Allah's Messenger ﷺ said, "O Hatib! What obliged you to do what you have done?" Hatib replied, "O Allah's Messenger ﷺ! Why (for what reason) should I not believe in Allah and His Apostle? But I intended to do the (Mecca) people a favor by virtue of which my family and property may be protected as there is none of your companions but has some of his people (relatives) whom Allah urges to protect his family and property." The Prophet ﷺ said, "He has said the truth; therefore, do not say anything to him except good." `Umar again said, "O Allah's Messenger ﷺ ! He has betrayed Allah, His Apostle and the believers; let me chop his neck off!" The Prophet ﷺ said, "Isn't he from those who fought the battle of Badr? And what do you know, Allah might have looked at them (Badr warriors) and said (to them), 'Do what you like, for I have granted you Paradise?' " On that, `Umar's eyes became flooded with tears and he said, "Allah and His Apostle know best.". – Sahih Al-Bukhari 6939

حَدَّثَنَا مُوسَى بْنُ إِسْمَاعِيلَ، حَدَّثَنَا أَبُو عَوَانَةَ، عَنْ حُصَيْنٍ، عَنْ فُلاَنٍ، قَالَ تَنَازَعَ أَبُو عَبْدِ الرَّحْمَنِ وَحِبَّانُ بْنُ عَطِيَّةَ فَقَالَ أَبُو عَبْدِ الرَّحْمَنِ لِحِبَّانَ لَقَدْ عَلِمْتُ الَّذِي جَرَّأَ صَاحِبَكَ عَلَى الدِّمَاءِ يَعْنِي عَلِيًّا. قَالَ مَا هُوَ لاَ أَبَا لَكَ قَالَ شَىْءٌ سَمِعْتُهُ يَقُولُهُ. قَالَ مَا هُوَ قَالَ بَعَثَنِي رَسُولُ اللَّهِ صلى الله عليه وسلم وَالزُّبَيْرَ وَأَبَا مَرْثَدٍ وَكُلُّنَا فَارِسٌ قَالَ " انْطَلِقُوا حَتَّى تَأْتُوا رَوْضَةَ حَاجٍ - قَالَ أَبُو سَلَمَةَ هَكَذَا قَالَ أَبُو عَوَانَةَ حَاجٍ - فَإِنَّ فِيهَا امْرَأَةً مَعَهَا صَحِيفَةٌ مِنْ حَاطِبِ بْنِ أَبِي بَلْتَعَةَ إِلَى الْمُشْرِكِينَ فَأْتُونِي بِهَا ". فَانْطَلَقْنَا عَلَى أَفْرَاسِنَا حَتَّى أَدْرَكْنَاهَا حَيْثُ قَالَ لَنَا رَسُولُ اللَّهِ صلى الله عليه وسلم تَسِيرُ عَلَى بَعِيرٍ لَهَا، وَكَانَ كَتَبَ إِلَى أَهْلِ مَكَّةَ بِمَسِيرِ رَسُولِ اللَّهِ صلى الله عليه وسلم إِلَيْهِمْ. فَقُلْنَا أَيْنَ الْكِتَابُ الَّذِي مَعَكِ قَالَتْ مَا مَعِي كِتَابٌ. فَأَنَخْنَا بِهَا بَعِيرَهَا، فَابْتَغَيْنَا فِي رَحْلِهَا فَمَا وَجَدْنَا شَيْئًا. فَقَالَ صَاحِبِي مَا نَرَى مَعَهَا كِتَابًا. قَالَ فَقُلْتُ لَقَدْ عَلِمْنَا مَا كَذَبَ رَسُولُ اللَّهِ صلى الله عليه وسلم ثُمَّ حَلَفَ عَلِيٌّ وَالَّذِي يُحْلَفُ بِهِ لَتُخْرِجِنَّ الْكِتَابَ أَوْ لأُجَرِّدَنَّكِ. فَأَهْوَتْ إِلَى حُجْزَتِهَا وَهْىَ مُحْتَجِزَةٌ بِكِسَاءٍ فَأَخْرَجَتِ الصَّحِيفَةَ، فَأَتَوْا بِهَا رَسُولَ اللَّهِ صلى الله عليه وسلم فَقَالَ عُمَرُ يَا رَسُولَ اللَّهِ قَدْ خَانَ اللَّهَ وَرَسُولَهُ وَالْمُؤْمِنِينَ. دَعْنِي فَأَضْرِبَ عُنُقَهُ. فَقَالَ رَسُولُ اللَّهِ صلى الله عليه وسلم " يَا حَاطِبُ مَا حَمَلَكَ عَلَى مَا صَنَعْتَ ". قَالَ يَا رَسُولَ اللَّهِ مَالِي أَنْ لاَ أَكُونَ مُؤْمِنًا بِاللَّهِ وَرَسُولِهِ، وَلَكِنِّي أَرَدْتُ أَنْ يَكُونَ لِي عِنْدَ الْقَوْمِ يَدٌ، يُدْفَعُ بِهَا عَنْ أَهْلِي وَمَالِي، وَلَيْسَ مِنْ أَصْحَابِكَ أَحَدٌ إِلاَّ لَهُ هُنَالِكَ مِنْ قَوْمِهِ مَنْ يَدْفَعُ اللَّهُ بِهِ عَنْ أَهْلِهِ وَمَالِهِ. قَالَ " صَدَقَ، لاَ تَقُولُوا لَهُ إِلاَّ خَيْرًا ". قَالَ فَعَادَ عُمَرُ فَقَالَ يَا رَسُولَ اللَّهِ قَدْ خَانَ اللَّهَ وَرَسُولَهُ وَالْمُؤْمِنِينَ، دَعْنِي فَلأَضْرِبَ عُنُقَهُ. قَالَ " أَوَلَيْسَ مِنْ أَهْلِ بَدْرٍ، وَمَا يُدْرِيكَ لَعَلَّ اللَّهَ اطَّلَعَ عَلَيْهِمْ فَقَالَ اعْمَلُوا مَا شِئْتُمْ فَقَدْ أَوْجَبْتُ لَكُمُ الْجَنَّةَ ". فَاغْرَوْرَقَتْ عَيْنَاهُ فَقَالَ اللَّهُ وَرَسُولُهُ أَعْلَمُ

Narrated `Abdullah: The Prophetﷺ said, "If somebody on the demand of a judge takes an oath to grab (a Muslim's) property and he is liar in it, he will meet Allah Who will be angry with him". So Allah revealed,:-- 'Verily! Those who purchase a small gain at the cost of Allah's Covenant and their oaths..' (3.77) 'Al- Ashath came while `Abdullah was narrating (this) to the people. Al-Ashath said, "This verse was revealed regarding me and another man with whom I had a quarrel about a well. The Prophetﷺ said (to me), "Do you have any evidence?' I replied, 'No.' He said, 'Let your opponent take an oath.' I said: I am sure he would take a (false) oath." Thereupon it was revealed: 'Verily! Those who purchase a small gain at the cost of Allah's Covenant....' (3.77) (See Hadith No. 72, Vol 6). – Sahih Al-Bukhari 7183, 7184
حَدَّثَنَا إِسْحَاقُ بْنُ نَصْرٍ، حَدَّثَنَا عَبْدُ الرَّزَّاقِ، أَخْبَرَنَا سُفْيَانُ، عَنْ مَنْصُورٍ، وَالأَعْمَشِ، عَنْ أَبِي وَائِلٍ، قَالَ قَالَ عَبْدُ اللَّهِ قَالَ النَّبِيُّ صلى الله عليه وسلم " لاَ يَحْلِفُ عَلَى يَمِينِ صَبْرٍ، يَقْتَطِعُ مَالاً وَهْوَ فِيهَا فَاجِرٌ، إِلاَّ لَقِيَ اللَّهَ وَهْوَ عَلَيْهِ غَضْبَانُ ". فَأَنْزَلَ اللَّهُ {إِنَّ الَّذِينَ يَشْتَرُونَ بِعَهْدِ اللَّهِ} الآيَةَ. فَجَاءَ الأَشْعَثُ وَعَبْدُ اللَّهِ يُحَدِّثُهُمْ فَقَالَ فِيَّ نَزَلَتْ وَفِي رَجُلٍ خَاصَمْتُهُ فِي بِئْرٍ فَقَالَ النَّبِيُّ صلى الله عليه وسلم " أَلَكَ بَيِّنَةٌ ". قُلْتُ لاَ. قَالَ " فَلْيَحْلِفْ ". قُلْتُ إِذًا يَحْلِفُ. فَنَزَلَتْ {إِنَّ الَّذِينَ يَشْتَرُونَ بِعَهْدِ اللَّهِ} الآيَةَ

Narrated Qasim bin Muhammad and Sulaiman bin Yasar: That Yahya bin Sa`id bin Al-`As divorced the daughter of `Abdur-Rahman bin Al-Hakarn. `Abdur- Rahman took her to his house. On that `Aisha sent a message to Marwan bin Al-Hakam who was the ruler of Medina, saying, "Fear Allah, and urge your brother) to return her to her house." Marwan (in Sulaiman's version) said, "Abdur-Rahman bin Al-Hakam did not obey me (or had a convincing argument)." (In Al-Qasim's versions Marwan said, "Have you not heard of the case of Fatima bint Qais?" Aisha said, "The case of Fatima bint Qais is not in your favor.' Marwan bin Al-Hakam said to `Aisha, "The reason that made Fatima bint Qais go to her father's house is just applicable to the daughter of `Abdur-Rahman.". – Sahih Al-Bukhari 5321, 5322
حَدَّثَنَا إِسْمَاعِيلُ، حَدَّثَنَا مَالِكٌ، عَنْ يَحْيَى بْنِ سَعِيدٍ، عَنِ الْقَاسِمِ بْنِ مُحَمَّدٍ، أَنَّهُ سَمِعَهُ يَذْكُرُ، أَنَّ يَحْيَى بْنَ سَعِيدِ بْنِ الْعَاصِ، طَلَّقَ بِنْتَ عَبْدِ الرَّحْمَنِ بْنِ الْحَكَمِ، فَانْتَقَلَهَا عَبْدُ الرَّحْمَنِ، فَأَرْسَلَتْ عَائِشَةُ أُمُّ الْمُؤْمِنِينَ إِلَى مَرْوَانَ وَهْوَ أَمِيرُ الْمَدِينَةِ اتَّقِ اللَّهَ وَارْدُدْهَا إِلَى بَيْتِهَا. قَالَ مَرْوَانُ فِي حَدِيثِ سُلَيْمَانَ إِنَّ عَبْدَ الرَّحْمَنِ بْنَ الْحَكَمِ غَلَبَنِي. وَقَالَ الْقَاسِمُ بْنُ مُحَمَّدٍ أَوَمَا بَلَغَكِ شَأْنُ فَاطِمَةَ بِنْتِ قَيْسٍ قَالَتْ لاَ يَضُرُّكَ أَنْ لاَ تَذْكُرَ حَدِيثَ فَاطِمَةَ. فَقَالَ مَرْوَانُ بْنُ الْحَكَمِ إِنْ كَانَ بِكِ شَرٌّ فَحَسْبُكِ مَا بَيْنَ هَذَيْنِ مِنَ الشَّرِّ.

Narrated Mahmud bin Ar-rabi' Al-Ansari: That he remembered Allah's Messengerﷺ and he also remembered a mouthful of water which he had thrown on his face, after taking it from a well that was in their house. Mahmud said that he had heard `Itban bin Malik, who was present with Allah's Messengerﷺ in the battle of Badr saying, "I used to lead my people at

Bani Salim in the prayer and there was a valley between me and those people. Whenever it rained it used to be difficult for me to cross it to go to their mosque. So I went to Allah's Messenger ﷺ and said, 'I have weak eyesight and the valley between me and my people flows during the rainy season and it becomes difficult for me to cross it; I wish you would come to my house and pray at a place so that I could take that place as a praying place.' Allah's Messenger ﷺ said, 'I will do so.' So Allah's Messenger ﷺ and Abu Bakr came to my house in the (next) morning after the sun had risen high. Allah's Messenger ﷺ asked my permission to let him in and I admitted him. He did not sit before saying, 'Where do you want us to offer the prayer in your house?' I pointed to the place where I wanted him to pray. So Allah's Messenger ﷺ stood up for the prayer and started the prayer with Takbir and we aligned in rows behind him; and he offered two rak`at, and finished them with Taslim, and we also performed Taslim with him. I detained him for a meal called "Khazir" which I had prepared for him.—("Khazir" is a special type of dish prepared from barley flour and meat soup)—When the neighbors got the news that Allah's Messenger ﷺ was in my house, they poured it till there were a great number of men in the house. One of them said, 'What is wrong with Malik, for I do not see him?' One of them replied, 'He is a hypocrite and does not love Allah and His Apostle.' On that Allah's Apostle said, 'Don't say this. Haven't you seen that he said, 'None has the right to be worshipped but Allah for Allah's sake only.' The man replied, 'Allah and His Apostle know better; but by Allah, we never saw him but helping and talking with the hypocrites.' Allah's Messenger ﷺ replied, 'No doubt, whoever says. None has the right to be worshipped but Allah, and by that he wants the pleasures of Allah, then Allah will save him from Hell." Mahmud added, "I told the above narration to some people, one of whom was Abu Aiyub, the companion of Allah's Messenger ﷺ in the battle in which he (Abu Aiyub) died and Yazid bin Mu'awiya was their leader in Roman Territory. Abu Aiyub denounced the narration and said, 'I doubt that Allah's Messenger ﷺ ever said what you have said.' I felt that too much, and I vowed to Allah that if I remained alive in that holy battle, I would (go to Medina and) ask `Itban bin Malik if he was still living in the mosque of his people. So when he returned, I assumed Ihram for Hajj or `Umra and then I proceeded on till I reached Medina. I went to Bani Salim and `Itban bin Malik, who was by then an old blind man, was leading his people in the prayer. When he finished the prayer, I greeted him and introduced myself to him and then asked him about that narration. He told that narration again in the same manner as he had narrated it the first time.". – Sahih Al-Bukhari 1185, 1186

حَدَّثَنِي إِسْحَاقُ، حَدَّثَنَا يَعْقُوبُ بْنُ إِبْرَاهِيمَ، حَدَّثَنَا أَبِي، عَنِ ابْنِ شِهَابٍ، قَالَ أَخْبَرَنِي مَحْمُودُ بْنُ الرَّبِيعِ الأَنْصَارِيُّ، أَنَّهُ عَقَلَ رَسُولَ اللَّهِ صلى الله عليه وسلم، وَعَقَلَ مَجَّةً مَجَّهَا فِي وَجْهِهِ مِنْ بِئْرٍ كَانَتْ فِي دَارِهِمْ. فَزَعَمَ مَحْمُودٌ أَنَّهُ سَمِعَ عِتْبَانَ بْنَ مَالِكٍ الأَنْصَارِيَّ ـ رضى الله عنه ـ وَكَانَ مِمَّنْ شَهِدَ بَدْرًا مَعَ رَسُولِ اللَّهِ صلى الله عليه وسلم يَقُولُ كُنْتُ أُصَلِّي لِقَوْمِي بِبَنِي سَالِمٍ، وَكَانَ يَحُولُ بَيْنِي وَبَيْنَهُمْ وَادٍ إِذَا جَاءَتِ الأَمْطَارُ فَيَشُقُّ عَلَىَّ اجْتِيَازُهُ قِبَلَ مَسْجِدِهِمْ، فَجِئْتُ رَسُولَ اللَّهِ صلى الله عليه وسلم فَقُلْتُ لَهُ إِنِّي أَنْكَرْتُ بَصَرِي، وَإِنَّ الْوَادِيَ الَّذِي بَيْنِي وَبَيْنَ قَوْمِي يَسِيلُ إِذَا جَاءَتِ الأَمْطَارُ فَيَشُقُّ عَلَىَّ اجْتِيَازُهُ، فَوَدِدْتُ أَنَّكَ تَأْتِي فَتُصَلِّي مِنْ بَيْتِي مَكَانًا أَتَّخِذُهُ مُصَلًّى. فَقَالَ رَسُولُ اللَّهِ صلى الله عليه وسلم " سَأَفْعَلُ ". فَغَدَا عَلَىَّ رَسُولُ اللَّهِ صلى الله عليه وسلم وَأَبُو بَكْرٍ ـ رضى الله عنه ـ بَعْدَ مَا اشْتَدَّ النَّهَارُ فَاسْتَأْذَنَ رَسُولُ اللَّهِ صلى الله عليه وسلم فَأَذِنْتُ لَهُ فَلَمْ يَجْلِسْ حَتَّى قَالَ " أَيْنَ تُحِبُّ أَنْ أُصَلِّيَ مِنْ بَيْتِكَ ". فَأَشَرْتُ لَهُ إِلَى الْمَكَانِ الَّذِي أُحِبُّ أَنْ أُصَلِّيَ فِيهِ، فَقَامَ رَسُولُ اللَّهِ صلى الله عليه وسلم فَكَبَّرَ وَصَفَفْنَا وَرَاءَهُ، فَصَلَّى رَكْعَتَيْنِ، ثُمَّ سَلَّمَ وَسَلَّمْنَا حِينَ سَلَّمَ، فَحَبَسْتُهُ عَلَى خَزِيرٍ يُصْنَعُ لَهُ فَسَمِعَ أَهْلُ الدَّارِ رَسُولَ اللَّهِ صلى الله عليه وسلم فِي بَيْتِي فَثَابَ رِجَالٌ مِنْهُمْ حَتَّى كَثُرَ الرِّجَالُ فِي الْبَيْتِ. فَقَالَ رَجُلٌ مِنْهُمْ مَا فَعَلَ مَالِكٌ لاَ أَرَاهُ. فَقَالَ رَجُلٌ مِنْهُمْ ذَاكَ مُنَافِقٌ لاَ يُحِبُّ اللَّهَ وَرَسُولَهُ. فَقَالَ رَسُولُ اللَّهِ صلى الله عليه وسلم " لاَ تَقُلْ ذَاكَ أَلاَ تَرَاهُ قَالَ لاَ إِلَهَ إِلاَّ اللَّهُ. يَبْتَغِي بِذَلِكَ وَجْهَ اللَّهِ ". فَقَالَ اللَّهُ وَرَسُولُهُ أَعْلَمُ. أَمَّا نَحْنُ فَوَاللَّهِ لاَ نَرَى وُدَّهُ وَلاَ حَدِيثَهُ إِلاَّ إِلَى الْمُنَافِقِينَ. قَالَ رَسُولُ اللَّهِ صلى الله عليه وسلم " فَإِنَّ اللَّهَ قَدْ حَرَّمَ عَلَى النَّارِ مَنْ قَالَ لاَ إِلَهَ إِلاَّ اللَّهُ. يَبْتَغِي بِذَلِكَ وَجْهَ اللَّهِ ". قَالَ مَحْمُودٌ فَحَدَّثْتُهَا قَوْمًا فِيهِمْ أَبُو أَيُّوبَ صَاحِبُ رَسُولِ اللَّهِ صلى الله عليه وسلم فِي غَزْوَتِهِ الَّتِي تُوُفِّيَ فِيهَا وَيَزِيدُ بْنُ مُعَاوِيَةَ عَلَيْهِمْ بِأَرْضِ الرُّومِ، فَأَنْكَرَهَا عَلَىَّ أَبُو أَيُّوبَ قَالَ وَاللَّهِ مَا أَظُنُّ رَسُولَ اللَّهِ صلى الله عليه وسلم قَالَ مَا قُلْتَ قَطُّ. فَكَبُرَ ذَلِكَ عَلَىَّ فَجَعَلْتُ لِلَّهِ عَلَىَّ إِنْ سَلَّمَنِي حَتَّى أَقْفُلَ مِنْ غَزْوَتِي أَنْ أَسْأَلَ عَنْهَا عِتْبَانَ بْنَ مَالِكٍ ـ رضى الله عنه ـ إِنْ وَجَدْتُهُ حَيًّا فِي

مَسْجِدِ قَوْمِهِ، فَقَفَلْتُ فَأَهْلَلْتُ بِحَجَّةٍ أَوْ بِعُمْرَةٍ، ثُمَّ سِرْتُ حَتَّى قَدِمْتُ الْمَدِينَةَ فَأَتَيْتُ بَنِي سَالِمٍ، فَإِذَا عِتْبَانُ شَيْخٌ أَعْمَى يُصَلِّي لِقَوْمِهِ فَلَمَّا سَلَّمَ مِنَ الصَّلاَةِ سَلَّمْتُ عَلَيْهِ وَأَخْبَرْتُهُ مَنْ أَنَا، ثُمَّ سَأَلْتُهُ عَنْ ذَلِكَ الْحَدِيثِ فَحَدَّثَنِيهِ كَمَا حَدَّثَنِيهِ أَوَّلَ مَرَّةٍ.

Narrated Mujahid: I was in the company of Ibn `Abbas and the people talked about Ad-Dajjal and said, "Ad-Dajjal will come with the word Kafir (non-believer) written in between his eyes." On that Ibn `Abbas said, "I have not heard this from the Prophet ﷺ but I heard him saying, 'As if I saw Moses just now entering the valley reciting Talbyia. ' ". – Sahih Al-Bukhari 1555

حَدَّثَنَا مُحَمَّدُ بْنُ الْمُثَنَّى، قَالَ حَدَّثَنِي ابْنُ أَبِي عَدِيٍّ، عَنِ ابْنِ عَوْنٍ، عَنْ مُجَاهِدٍ، قَالَ كُنَّا عِنْدَ ابْنِ عَبَّاسٍ ـ رضى الله عنهما ـ فَذَكَرُوا الدَّجَّالَ أَنَّهُ قَالَ " مَكْتُوبٌ بَيْنَ عَيْنَيْهِ كَافِرٌ ". فَقَالَ ابْنُ عَبَّاسٍ لَمْ أَسْمَعْهُ وَلَكِنَّهُ قَالَ " أَمَّا مُوسَى كَأَنِّي أَنْظُرُ إِلَيْهِ إِذِ انْحَدَرَ فِي الْوَادِي يُلَبِّي "

Narrated Mujahid: Urwa bin Az-Zubair and I entered the Mosque (of the Prophet) and saw `Abdullah bin `Umar sitting near the dwelling place of Aisha and some people were offering the Duha prayer. We asked him about their prayer and he replied that it was a heresy. He (Urwa) then asked him how many times the Prophet ﷺ had performed `Umra. He replied, 'Four times; one of them was in the month of Rajab." We disliked to contradict him. Then we heard `Aisha, the Mother of faithful believers cleaning her teeth with Siwak in the dwelling place. 'Urwa said, "O Mother! O Mother of the believers! Don't you hear what Abu `Abdur Rahman is saying?" She said, "What does he say?" 'Urwa said, "He says that Allah's Messenger ﷺ performed four `Umra and one of them was in the month of Rajab." `Aisha said, "May Allah be merciful to Abu `Abdur Rahman! The Prophet ﷺ did not perform any `Umra except that he was with him, and he never performed any `Umra in Rajab.". – Sahih Al-Bukhari 1775, 1776

حَدَّثَنَا قُتَيْبَةُ، حَدَّثَنَا جَرِيرٌ، عَنْ مَنْصُورٍ، عَنْ مُجَاهِدٍ، قَالَ دَخَلْتُ أَنَا وَعُرْوَةُ بْنُ الزُّبَيْرِ الْمَسْجِدَ،، فَإِذَا عَبْدُ اللَّهِ بْنُ عُمَرَ ـ رضى الله عنهما ـ جَالِسٌ إِلَى حُجْرَةِ عَائِشَةَ، وَإِذَا نَاسٌ يُصَلُّونَ فِي الْمَسْجِدِ صَلاَةَ الضُّحَى. قَالَ فَسَأَلْنَاهُ عَنْ صَلاَتِهِمْ. فَقَالَ بِدْعَةٌ. ثُمَّ قَالَ لَهُ كَمِ اعْتَمَرَ رَسُولُ اللَّهِ صلى الله عليه وسلم قَالَ أَرْبَعٌ إِحْدَاهُنَّ فِي رَجَبٍ، فَكَرِهْنَا أَنْ نَرُدَّ عَلَيْهِ. قَالَ وَسَمِعْنَا اسْتِنَانَ، عَائِشَةَ أُمِّ الْمُؤْمِنِينَ فِي الْحُجْرَةِ، فَقَالَ عُرْوَةُ يَا أُمَّاهُ، يَا أُمَّ الْمُؤْمِنِينَ. أَلاَ تَسْمَعِينَ مَا يَقُولُ أَبُو عَبْدِ الرَّحْمَنِ. قَالَتْ مَا يَقُولُ قَالَ يَقُولُ إِنَّ رَسُولَ اللَّهِ صلى الله عليه وسلم اعْتَمَرَ أَرْبَعَ عُمَرَاتٍ إِحْدَاهُنَّ فِي رَجَبٍ. قَالَتْ يَرْحَمُ اللَّهُ أَبَا عَبْدِ الرَّحْمَنِ، مَا اعْتَمَرَ عُمْرَةً إِلاَّ وَهُوَ شَاهِدُهُ، وَمَا اعْتَمَرَ فِي رَجَبٍ قَطُّ

Narrated `Abdullah bin `Abbas: `Umar bin Al-Khattab departed for Sham and when he reached Sargh, the commanders of the (Muslim) army, Abu 'Ubaida bin Al-Jarrah and his companions met him and told him that an epidemic had broken out in Sham. `Umar said, "Call for me the early emigrants." So `Umar called them, consulted them and informed them that an epidemic had broken out in Sham. Those people differed in their opinions. Some of them said, "We have come out for a purpose and we do not think that it is proper to give it up," while others said (to `Umar), "You have along with you. Other people and the companions of Allah's Messenger ﷺ so do not advise that we take them to this epidemic." `Umar said to them, "Leave me now." Then he said, "Call the Ansar for me." I called them and he consulted them and they followed the way of the emigrants and differed as they did. He then said to them, Leave me now," and added, "Call for me the old people of Quraish who emigrated in the year of the Conquest of Mecca." I called them and they gave a unanimous opinion saying, "We advise that you should return with the people and do not take them to that (place) of epidemic." So `Umar made an announcement, "I will ride back to Medina in the morning, so you should do the same." Abu 'Ubaida bin Al-Jarrah said (to `Umar), "Are you running away from what Allah had ordained?" `Umar said, "Would that someone else had said such a thing, O Abu 'Ubaida! Yes, we are running from what Allah had ordained to what Allah has ordained. Don't you agree that if you had camels that went down a valley having two places, one green and the other dry, you would graze them on the green one only if Allah had ordained that, and you would graze them on the dry one only if Allah had ordained that?" At that time `Abdur-Rahman bin `Auf, who had been absent because of some job, came and said, "I have some knowledge about this. I have heard Allah's Messenger ﷺ saying, 'If you hear about it (an outbreak of plague) in a land, do not go to it; but if plague breaks out in a country where you are staying, do not run away from it.' " `Umar thanked Allah and returned to Medina. – Sahih Al-Bukhari 5729

حَدَّثَنَا عَبْدُ اللَّهِ بْنُ يُوسُفَ، أَخْبَرَنَا مَالِكٌ، عَنِ ابْنِ شِهَابٍ، عَنْ عَبْدِ الْحَمِيدِ بْنِ عَبْدِ الرَّحْمَنِ بْنِ زَيْدِ بْنِ الْخَطَّابِ، عَنْ عَبْدِ اللَّهِ بْنِ عَبْدِ اللَّهِ بْنِ الْحَارِثِ بْنِ نَوْفَلٍ، عَنْ عَبْدِ اللَّهِ بْنِ عَبَّاسٍ، أَنَّ عُمَرَ بْنَ الْخَطَّابِ ـ رضى الله عنه ـ خَرَجَ إِلَى الشَّأْمِ حَتَّى إِذَا كَانَ بِسَرْغَ لَقِيَهُ أُمَرَاءُ الأَجْنَادِ أَبُو عُبَيْدَةَ بْنُ الْجَرَّاحِ وَأَصْحَابُهُ، فَأَخْبَرُوهُ أَنَّ الْوَبَاءَ قَدْ وَقَعَ بِأَرْضِ الشَّأْمِ. قَالَ ابْنُ عَبَّاسٍ فَقَالَ عُمَرُ ادْعُ لِي الْمُهَاجِرِينَ الأَوَّلِينَ. فَدَعَاهُمْ فَاسْتَشَارَهُمْ وَأَخْبَرَهُمْ أَنَّ الْوَبَاءَ قَدْ وَقَعَ بِالشَّأْمِ فَاخْتَلَفُوا. فَقَالَ بَعْضُهُمْ قَدْ خَرَجْتَ لأَمْرٍ، وَلاَ نَرَى أَنْ تَرْجِعَ عَنْهُ. وَقَالَ بَعْضُهُمْ مَعَكَ بَقِيَّةُ النَّاسِ وَأَصْحَابُ رَسُولِ اللَّهِ صلى الله عليه وسلم وَلاَ نَرَى أَنْ تُقْدِمَهُمْ عَلَى هَذَا الْوَبَاءِ. فَقَالَ ارْتَفِعُوا عَنِّي. ثُمَّ قَالَ ادْعُوا لِي الأَنْصَارَ. فَدَعَوْتُهُمْ فَاسْتَشَارَهُمْ، فَسَلَكُوا سَبِيلَ الْمُهَاجِرِينَ، وَاخْتَلَفُوا كَاخْتِلاَفِهِمْ، فَقَالَ ارْتَفِعُوا عَنِّي. ثُمَّ قَالَ ادْعُ لِي مَنْ كَانَ هَا هُنَا مِنْ مَشْيَخَةِ قُرَيْشٍ مِنْ مُهَاجِرَةِ الْفَتْحِ. فَدَعَوْتُهُمْ، فَلَمْ يَخْتَلِفْ مِنْهُمْ عَلَيْهِ رَجُلاَنِ، فَقَالُوا نَرَى أَنْ تَرْجِعَ بِالنَّاسِ، وَلاَ تُقْدِمَهُمْ عَلَى هَذَا الْوَبَاءِ، فَنَادَى عُمَرُ فِي النَّاسِ، إِنِّي مُصَبِّحٌ عَلَى ظَهْرٍ، فَأَصْبِحُوا عَلَيْهِ. قَالَ أَبُو عُبَيْدَةَ بْنُ الْجَرَّاحِ أَفِرَارًا مِنْ قَدَرِ اللَّهِ فَقَالَ عُمَرُ لَوْ غَيْرُكَ قَالَهَا يَا أَبَا عُبَيْدَةَ، نَعَمْ نَفِرُّ مِنْ قَدَرِ اللَّهِ إِلَى قَدَرِ اللَّهِ، أَرَأَيْتَ لَوْ كَانَ لَكَ إِبِلٌ هَبَطَتْ وَادِيًا لَهُ عُدْوَتَانِ، إِحْدَاهُمَا خَصِبَةٌ، وَالأُخْرَى جَدْبَةٌ، أَلَيْسَ إِنْ رَعَيْتَ الْخَصْبَةَ رَعَيْتَهَا بِقَدَرِ اللَّهِ، وَإِنْ رَعَيْتَ الْجَدْبَةَ رَعَيْتَهَا بِقَدَرِ اللَّهِ قَالَ فَجَاءَ عَبْدُ الرَّحْمَنِ بْنُ عَوْفٍ، وَكَانَ مُتَغَيِّبًا فِي بَعْضِ حَاجَتِهِ فَقَالَ إِنَّ عِنْدِي فِي هَذَا عِلْمًا سَمِعْتُ رَسُولَ اللَّهِ صلى الله عليه وسلم يَقُولُ " إِذَا سَمِعْتُمْ بِهِ بِأَرْضٍ فَلاَ تَقْدَمُوا عَلَيْهِ، وَإِذَا وَقَعَ بِأَرْضٍ وَأَنْتُمْ بِهَا فَلاَ تَخْرُجُوا فِرَارًا مِنْهُ ". قَالَ فَحَمِدَ اللَّهَ عُمَرُ ثُمَّ انْصَرَفَ

Narrated Nafi`: Ibn `Umar used to rent his farms in the time of Abu Bakr, `Umar, `Uthman, and in the early days of Muawiya. Then he was told the narration of Rafi` 'bin Khadij that the Prophet ﷺ had forbidden the renting of farms. Ibn `Umar went to Rafi` and I accompanied him. He asked Rafi` who replied that the Prophet had forbidden the renting of farms. Ibn `Umar said, "You know that we used to rent our farms in the lifetime of Allah's Messenger ﷺ for the yield of the banks of the water streams (rivers) and for certain amount of figs. – Sahih Al-Bukhari 2343, 2344

حَدَّثَنَا سُلَيْمَانُ بْنُ حَرْبٍ، حَدَّثَنَا حَمَّادٌ، عَنْ أَيُّوبَ، عَنْ نَافِعٍ، أَنَّ ابْنَ عُمَرَ ـ رضى الله عنهما ـ كَانَ يُكْرِي مَزَارِعَهُ عَلَى عَهْدِ النَّبِيِّ صلى الله عليه وسلم وَأَبِي بَكْرٍ وَعُمَرَ وَعُثْمَانَ وَصَدْرًا مِنْ إِمَارَةِ مُعَاوِيَةَ. ثُمَّ حُدِّثَ عَنْ رَافِعِ بْنِ خَدِيجٍ، أَنَّ النَّبِيَّ صلى الله عليه وسلم نَهَى عَنْ كِرَاءِ الْمَزَارِعِ، فَذَهَبَ ابْنُ عُمَرَ إِلَى رَافِعٍ فَذَهَبْتُ مَعَهُ، فَسَأَلَهُ فَقَالَ نَهَى النَّبِيُّ صلى الله عليه وسلم عَنْ كِرَاءِ الْمَزَارِعِ. فَقَالَ ابْنُ عُمَرَ قَدْ عَلِمْتَ أَنَّا كُنَّا نُكْرِي مَزَارِعَنَا عَلَى عَهْدِ رَسُولِ اللَّهِ صلى الله عليه وسلم بِمَا عَلَى الأَرْبِعَاءِ وَبِشَىْءٍ مِنَ التِّبْنِ

Ibn 'Abbas further said, "Seven types of marriages are unlawful because of blood relations, and seven because of marriage relations." Then Ibn 'Abbas recited the Verse: "Forbidden for you (for marriages) are your mothers..." (4:23). 'Abdullah bin Ja'far married the daughter and wife of 'Ali at the same time (they were step-daughter and mother). Ibn Sirin said, "There is no harm in that." But Al-Hasan Al-Basri disapproved of it at first, but then said that there was no harm in it. Al-Hasan bin Al-Hasan bin 'Ali married two of his cousins in one night. Ja'far bin Zaid disapproved of that because of it would bring hatred (between the two cousins), but it is not unlawful, as Allah said, "Lawful to you are all others [beyond those (mentioned)]. (4:24). Ibn 'Abbas said: "If somebody commits illegal sexual intercourse with his wife's sister, his wife does not become unlawful for him." And narrated Abu Ja'far, "If a person commits homosexuality with a boy, then the mother of that boy is unlawful for him to marry." Narrated Ibn 'Abbas, "If one commits illegal sexual intercourse with his mother in law, then his married relation to his wife does not become unlawful." Abu Nasr reported to have said that Ibn 'Abbas in the above case, regarded his marital relation to his wife unlawful, but Abu Nasr is not known well for hearing Hadith from Ibn 'Abbas. Imran bin Hussain, Jabir b. Zaid, Al-Hasan and some other Iraqi's, are reported to have judged that his marital relations to his wife would be unlawful. In the above case Abu Hurairah said, "The marital relation to one's wife does not become unlawful except if one as had sexual intercourse (with her mother)." Ibn Al-Musaiyab, 'Urwa, and Az-Zuhri allows such person to keep his wife. 'Ali said, "His marital relations to his wife does not become unlawful.". – Sahih Al-Bukhari 5105

وَقَالَ لَنَا أَحْمَدُ بْنُ حَنْبَلٍ حَدَّثَنَا يَحْيَى بْنُ سَعِيدٍ، عَنْ سُفْيَانَ، حَدَّثَنِي حَبِيبٌ، عَنْ سَعِيدٍ، عَنِ ابْنِ عَبَّاسٍ، حَرُمَ مِنَ النَّسَبِ سَبْعٌ، وَمِنَ الصِّهْرِ سَبْعٌ. ثُمَّ قَرَأَ {حُرِّمَتْ عَلَيْكُمْ أُمَّهَاتُكُمْ} الآيَةَ. وَجَمَعَ عَبْدُ اللَّهِ بْنُ جَعْفَرٍ بَيْنَ ابْنَةِ عَلِيٍّ وَامْرَأَةِ عَلِيٍّ. وَقَالَ ابْنُ سِيرِينَ لاَ بَأْسَ بِهِ. وَكَرِهَهُ الْحَسَنُ مَرَّةً ثُمَّ قَالَ لاَ بَأْسَ بِهِ. وَجَمَعَ الْحَسَنُ بْنُ الْحَسَنِ بْنِ عَلِيٍّ بَيْنَ ابْنَتَىْ عَمٍّ فِي لَيْلَةٍ، وَكَرِهَهُ جَابِرُ بْنُ زَيْدٍ لِلْقَطِيعَةِ، وَلَيْسَ فِيهِ تَحْرِيمٌ لِقَوْلِهِ تَعَالَى {وَأُحِلَّ لَكُمْ مَا وَرَاءَ ذَلِكُمْ} وَقَالَ عِكْرِمَةُ عَنِ ابْنِ عَبَّاسٍ إِذَا زَنَى بِأُخْتِ امْرَأَتِهِ لَمْ تَحْرُمْ عَلَيْهِ امْرَأَتُهُ. وَيُرْوَى عَنْ يَحْيَى الْكِنْدِيِّ عَنِ الشَّعْبِيِّ وَأَبِي جَعْفَرٍ، فِيمَنْ يَلْعَبُ بِالصَّبِيِّ إِنْ أَدْخَلَهُ فِيهِ، فَلاَ يَتَزَوَّجَنَّ أُمَّهُ، وَيَحْيَى هَذَا غَيْرُ مَعْرُوفٍ، لَمْ يُتَابَعْ عَلَيْهِ. وَقَالَ عِكْرِمَةُ عَنِ ابْنِ عَبَّاسٍ إِذَا زَنَى بِهَا لَمْ تَحْرُمْ عَلَيْهِ امْرَأَتُهُ. وَيُذْكَرُ عَنْ أَبِي نَصْرٍ أَنَّ ابْنَ عَبَّاسٍ حَرَّمَهُ. وَأَبُو نَصْرٍ هَذَا لَمْ يُعْرَفْ بِسَمَاعِهِ مِنِ ابْنِ عَبَّاسٍ. وَيُرْوَى عَنْ عِمْرَانَ بْنِ حُصَيْنٍ وَجَابِرِ بْنِ زَيْدٍ وَالْحَسَنِ وَبَعْضِ أَهْلِ الْعِرَاقِ تَحْرُمُ عَلَيْهِ. وَقَالَ أَبُو هُرَيْرَةَ لاَ تَحْرُمُ حَتَّى يُلْزِقَ بِالأَرْضِ يَعْنِي يُجَامِعَ. وَجَوَّزَهُ ابْنُ الْمُسَيَّبِ وَعُرْوَةُ وَالزُّهْرِيُّ. وَقَالَ الزُّهْرِيُّ قَالَ عَلِيٌّ لاَ تَحْرُمُ. وَهَذَا مُرْسَلٌ

Narrated 'Abdullah: Nafi narrated to me that 'Abdullah said that Allah's Messenger ﷺ forbade the Shighar. I asked Nafi', "What is the Shighar?" He said, "It is to marry the daughter of a man and marry one's daughter to that man (at the same time) without Mahr (in both cases); or to marry the sister of a man and marry one's own sister to that man without Mahr." Some people said, "If one, by a trick, marries on the basis of Shighar, the marriage is valid but its condition is illegal." The same scholar said regarding Al-Mut'a, "The marriage is invalid and its condition is illegal." Some others said, "The Mut'a and the Shighar are permissible but the condition is illegal.". – Sahih Al-Bukhari 6960

حَدَّثَنَا مُسَدَّدٌ، حَدَّثَنَا يَحْيَى بْنُ سَعِيدٍ، عَنْ عُبَيْدِ اللَّهِ، قَالَ حَدَّثَنِي نَافِعٌ، عَنْ عَبْدِ اللَّهِ ـ رضى الله عنه ـ أَنَّ رَسُولَ اللَّهِ صلى الله عليه وسلم نَهَى عَنِ الشِّغَارِ. قُلْتُ لِنَافِعٍ مَا الشِّغَارُ قَالَ يَنْكِحُ ابْنَةَ الرَّجُلِ وَيُنْكِحُهُ ابْنَتَهُ بِغَيْرِ صَدَاقٍ، وَيَنْكِحُ أُخْتَ الرَّجُلِ وَيُنْكِحُهُ أُخْتَهُ بِغَيْرِ صَدَاقٍ. وَقَالَ بَعْضُ النَّاسِ إِنِ احْتَالَ حَتَّى تَزَوَّجَ عَلَى الشِّغَارِ، فَهْوَ جَائِزٌ، وَالشَّرْطُ بَاطِلٌ. وَقَالَ فِي الْمُتْعَةِ النِّكَاحُ فَاسِدٌ، وَالشَّرْطُ بَاطِلٌ. وَقَالَ بَعْضُهُمُ الْمُتْعَةُ وَالشِّغَارُ جَائِزٌ، وَالشَّرْطُ بَاطِلٌ.

Narrated Muhammad bin `Ali: `Ali was told that Ibn `Abbas did not see any harm in the Mut'a marriage. `Ali said, "Allah's Messenger ﷺ forbade the Mut'a marriage on the Day of the battle of Khaibar and he forbade the eating of donkey's meat." Some people said, "If one, by a tricky way, marries temporarily, his marriage is illegal." Others said, "The marriage is valid but its condition is illegal." - Sahih Al-Bukhari 6961

حَدَّثَنَا مُسَدَّدٌ، حَدَّثَنَا يَحْيَى، عَنْ عُبَيْدِ اللَّهِ بْنِ عُمَرَ، حَدَّثَنَا الزُّهْرِيُّ، عَنِ الْحَسَنِ، وَعَبْدِ اللَّهِ، ابْنَىْ مُحَمَّدِ بْنِ عَلِيٍّ عَنْ أَبِيهِمَا، أَنَّ عَلِيًّا ـ رضى الله عنه ـ قِيلَ لَهُ إِنَّ ابْنَ عَبَّاسٍ لاَ يَرَى بِمُتْعَةِ النِّسَاءِ بَأْسًا. فَقَالَ إِنَّ رَسُولَ اللَّهِ صلى الله عليه وسلم نَهَى عَنْهَا يَوْمَ خَيْبَرَ، وَعَنْ لُحُومِ الْحُمُرِ الإِنْسِيَّةِ. وَقَالَ بَعْضُ النَّاسِ إِنِ احْتَالَ حَتَّى تَمَتَّعَ، فَالنِّكَاحُ فَاسِدٌ. وَقَالَ بَعْضُهُمُ النِّكَاحُ جَائِزٌ وَالشَّرْطُ بَاطِلٌ.

Narrated Al-Ahnaf bin Qais: While I was sitting with some people from Quraish, a man with very rough hair, clothes, and appearance came and stood in front of us, greeted us and said, "Inform those who hoard wealth, that a stone will be heated in the Hell-fire and will be put on the nipples of their breasts till it comes out from the bones of their shoulders and then put on the bones of their shoulders till it comes through the nipples of their breasts the stone will be moving and hitting." After saying that, the person retreated and sat by the side of the pillar, I followed him and sat beside him, and I did not know who he was. I said to him, "I think the people disliked what you had said." He said, "These people do not understand anything, although my friend told me." I asked, "Who is your friend?" He said, "The Prophet ﷺ

said (to me), 'O Abu Dhar! Do you see the mountain of Uhud?' And on that I (Abu Dhar) started looking towards the sun to judge how much remained of the day as I thought that Allah's Messenger ﷺ wanted to send me to do something for him and I said, 'Yes!' He said, 'I do not love to have gold equal to the mountain of Uhud unless I spend it all (in Allah's cause) except three Dinars (pounds). These people do not understand and collect worldly wealth. No, by Allah, Neither I ask them for worldly benefits nor am I in need of their religious advice till I meet Allah, The Honorable, The Majestic." '. – Sahih Al-Bukhari 1407, 1408

حَدَّثَنَا عَيَّاشٌ، حَدَّثَنَا عَبْدُ الأَعْلَى، حَدَّثَنَا الْجُرَيْرِيُّ، عَنْ أَبِي الْعَلاَءِ، عَنِ الأَحْنَفِ بْنِ قَيْسٍ، قَالَ جَلَسْتُ. وَحَدَّثَنِي إِسْحَاقُ بْنُ مَنْصُورٍ، أَخْبَرَنَا عَبْدُ الصَّمَدِ، قَالَ حَدَّثَنِي أَبِي، حَدَّثَنَا الْجُرَيْرِيُّ، حَدَّثَنَا أَبُو الْعَلاَءِ بْنُ الشِّخِّيرِ، أَنَّ الأَحْنَفَ بْنَ قَيْسٍ، حَدَّثَهُمْ قَالَ جَلَسْتُ إِلَى مَلإٍ مِنْ قُرَيْشٍ، فَجَاءَ رَجُلٌ خَشِنُ الشَّعَرِ وَالثِّيَابِ وَالْهَيْئَةِ حَتَّى قَامَ عَلَيْهِمْ فَسَلَّمَ ثُمَّ قَالَ بَشِّرِ الْكَانِزِينَ بِرَضْفٍ يُحْمَى عَلَيْهِ فِي نَارِ جَهَنَّمَ، ثُمَّ يُوضَعُ عَلَى حَلَمَةِ ثَدْىِ أَحَدِهِمْ حَتَّى يَخْرُجَ مِنْ نُغْضِ كَتِفِهِ، وَيُوضَعُ عَلَى نُغْضِ كَتِفِهِ حَتَّى يَخْرُجَ مِنْ حَلَمَةِ ثَدْيِهِ يَتَزَلْزَلُ، ثُمَّ وَلَّى فَجَلَسَ إِلَى سَارِيَةٍ، وَتَبِعْتُهُ وَجَلَسْتُ إِلَيْهِ، وَأَنَا لاَ أَدْرِي مَنْ هُوَ فَقُلْتُ لَهُ لاَ أُرَى الْقَوْمَ إِلاَّ قَدْ كَرِهُوا الَّذِي قُلْتَ. قَالَ إِنَّهُمْ لاَ يَعْقِلُونَ شَيْئًا. قَالَ لِي خَلِيلِي ـ قَالَ قُلْتُ مَنْ خَلِيلُكَ قَالَ النَّبِيُّ صلى الله عليه وسلم ـ " يَا أَبَا ذَرٍّ أَتُبْصِرُ أُحُدًا ". قَالَ فَنَظَرْتُ إِلَى الشَّمْسِ مَا بَقِيَ مِنَ النَّهَارِ وَأَنَا أُرَى أَنَّ رَسُولَ اللَّهِ صلى الله عليه وسلم يُرْسِلُنِي فِي حَاجَةٍ لَهُ، قُلْتُ نَعَمْ. قَالَ " مَا أُحِبُّ أَنَّ لِي مِثْلَ أُحُدٍ ذَهَبًا أُنْفِقُهُ كُلَّهُ إِلاَّ ثَلاَثَةَ دَنَانِيرَ ". وَإِنَّ هَؤُلاَءِ لاَ يَعْقِلُونَ، إِنَّمَا يَجْمَعُونَ الدُّنْيَا. لاَ وَاللَّهِ لاَ أَسْأَلُهُمْ دُنْيَا، وَلاَ أَسْتَفْتِيهِمْ عَنْ دِينٍ حَتَّى أَلْقَى اللَّهَ.

Narrated Sa`d: I was one of (the first) seven (who had embraced Islam) with Allah's Messenger ﷺ and we had nothing to eat then, except the leaves of the Habala or Hubula tree, so that our stool used to be similar to that of sheep. Now the tribe of Bani Asad wants to teach me Islam; I would be a loser and all my efforts would be in vain (if I learn Islam anew from them). – Sahih Al-Bukhari 5412

حَدَّثَنَا عَبْدُ اللَّهِ بْنُ مُحَمَّدٍ، حَدَّثَنَا وَهْبُ بْنُ جَرِيرٍ، حَدَّثَنَا شُعْبَةُ، عَنْ إِسْمَاعِيلَ، عَنْ قَيْسٍ، عَنْ سَعْدٍ، قَالَ رَأَيْتُنِي سَابِعَ سَبْعَةٍ مَعَ النَّبِيِّ صلى الله عليه وسلم مَا لَنَا طَعَامٌ إِلاَّ وَرَقُ الْحُبْلَةِ ـ أَوِ الْحَبَلَةِ ـ حَتَّى يَضَعَ أَحَدُنَا مَا تَضَعُ الشَّاةُ، ثُمَّ أَصْبَحَتْ بَنُو أَسَدٍ تُعَزِّرُنِي عَلَى الإِسْلاَمِ، خَسِرْتُ إِذًا وَضَلَّ سَعْيِي.

Narrated `Abdullah: Two person of Bani Thaqif and one from Quarish (or two persons from Quraish and one from Bani Thaqif) who had fat bellies but little wisdom, met near the Ka`ba. One of them said, "Did you see that Allah hears what we say? " The other said, "He hears us if we speak aloud, but He does not hear if we speak in stealthy quietness (softly)." The third fellow said, "If He hears when we speak aloud, then He surely hears us if we speak in stealthy quietness (softly)." So Allah revealed the Verse:-- 'And you have not been screening against yourselves, lest your ears, and your eyes and your skins should testify against you..." (41.22). – Al-Bukhari 7521

حَدَّثَنَا الْحُمَيْدِيُّ، حَدَّثَنَا سُفْيَانُ، حَدَّثَنَا مَنْصُورٌ، عَنْ مُجَاهِدٍ، عَنْ أَبِي مَعْمَرٍ، عَنْ عَبْدِ اللَّهِ ـ رضى الله عنه ـ قَالَ اجْتَمَعَ عِنْدَ الْبَيْتِ ثَقَفِيَّانِ وَقُرَشِيٌّ، أَوْ قُرَشِيَّانِ وَثَقَفِيٌّ، كَثِيرَةٌ شَحْمُ بُطُونِهِمْ قَلِيلَةٌ فِقْهُ قُلُوبِهِمْ فَقَالَ أَحَدُهُمْ أَتُرَوْنَ أَنَّ اللَّهَ يَسْمَعُ مَا نَقُولُ قَالَ الآخَرُ يَسْمَعُ إِنْ جَهَرْنَا وَلاَ يَسْمَعُ إِنْ أَخْفَيْنَا وَقَالَ الآخَرُ إِنْ كَانَ يَسْمَعُ إِذَا جَهَرْنَا فَإِنَّهُ يَسْمَعُ إِذَا أَخْفَيْنَا. فَأَنْزَلَ اللَّهُ تَعَالَى {وَمَا كُنْتُمْ تَسْتَتِرُونَ أَنْ يَشْهَدَ عَلَيْكُمْ سَمْعُكُمْ وَلاَ أَبْصَارُكُمْ وَلاَ جُلُودُكُمْ} الآيَةَ.

Narrated Huzail bin Shirahbil: Abu Musa was asked regarding (the inheritance of) a daughter, a son's daughter, and a sister. He said, "The daughter will take one-half and the sister will take one-half. If you go to Ibn Mas`ud, he will tell you the same." Ibn Mas`ud was asked and was told of Abu Musa's verdict. Ibn Mas`ud then said, "If I give the same verdict, I would stray and would not be of the rightly-guided. The verdict I will give in this case, will be the same as the Prophet ﷺ did, i.e. one-half is for daughter, and one-sixth for the son's daughter, i.e. both shares make two-thirds of the total property; and the rest is for the sister." Afterwards we cams to Abu Musa and informed him of Ibn Mas`ud's verdict, whereupon he said, "So, do not ask me for verdicts, as long as this learned man is among you.". – Sahih Al-Bukhari 6736

حَدَّثَنَا آدَمُ، حَدَّثَنَا شُعْبَةُ، حَدَّثَنَا أَبُو قَيْسٍ، سَمِعْتُ هُزَيْلَ بْنَ شُرَحْبِيلَ، قَالَ سُئِلَ أَبُو مُوسَى عَنِ ابْنَةٍ وَابْنَةِ ابْنٍ وَأُخْتٍ، فَقَالَ لِلاِبْنَةِ النِّصْفُ وَلِلأُخْتِ النِّصْفُ، وَأْتِ ابْنَ مَسْعُودٍ فَسَيُتَابِعُنِي. فَسُئِلَ ابْنُ مَسْعُودٍ وَأُخْبِرَ بِقَوْلِ أَبِي مُوسَى، فَقَالَ لَقَدْ ضَلَلْتُ إِذًا وَمَا أَنَا مِنَ الْمُهْتَدِينَ،، أَقْضِي فِيهَا بِمَا قَضَى النَّبِيُّ صلى الله عليه وسلم " لِلاِبْنَةِ النِّصْفُ، وَلاِبْنَةِ ابْنٍ السُّدُسُ تَكْمِلَةَ الثُّلُثَيْنِ، وَمَا بَقِيَ فَلِلأُخْتِ ". فَأَتَيْنَا أَبَا مُوسَى فَأَخْبَرْنَاهُ بِقَوْلِ ابْنِ مَسْعُودٍ، فَقَالَ لاَ تَسْأَلُونِي مَا دَامَ هَذَا الْحَبْرُ فِيكُمْ.

Narrated `Aisha: I bought Barira (a female slave). The Prophetﷺ said (to me), "Buy her as the Wala' is for the manumitted." Once she was given a sheep (in charity). The Prophetﷺ said, "It (the sheep) is a charitable gift for her (Barira) and a gift for us." Al-Hakam said, "Barira's husband was a free man." Ibn `Abbas said, 'When I saw him, he was a slave.". – Sahih Al-Bukhari 6751

حَدَّثَنَا حَفْصُ بْنُ عُمَرَ، حَدَّثَنَا شُعْبَةُ، عَنِ الْحَكَمِ، عَنْ إِبْرَاهِيمَ، عَنِ الأَسْوَدِ، عَنْ عَائِشَةَ، قَالَتِ اشْتَرَيْتُ بَرِيرَةَ فَقَالَ النَّبِيُّ صلى الله عليه وسلم " اشْتَرِيهَا، فَإِنَّ الْوَلاَءَ لِمَنْ أَعْتَقَ ". وَأُهْدِيَ لَهَا شَاةٌ فَقَالَ " هُوَ لَهَا صَدَقَةٌ، وَلَنَا هَدِيَّةٌ ". قَالَ الْحَكَمُ وَكَانَ زَوْجُهَا حُرًّا، وَقَوْلُ الْحَكَمِ مُرْسَلٌ. وَقَالَ ابْنُ عَبَّاسٍ رَأَيْتُهُ عَبْدًا.

Narrated Al-Aswad: `Aisha bought Barira in order to manumit her, but her masters stipulated that her Wala' (after her death) would be for them. `Aisha said, "O Allah's Messengerﷺ! I have bought Barira in order to manumit her, but her masters stipulated that her Wala' will be for them." The Prophetﷺ said, "Manumit her as the Wala is for the one who manumits (the slave)," or said, "The one who pays her price." Then `Aisha bought and manumitted her. After that, Barira was given the choice (by the Prophet) (to stay with her husband or leave him). She said, "If he gave me so much and so much (money) I would not stay with him." (Al-Aswad added: Her husband was a free man.) The sub-narrator added: The series of the narrators of Al-Aswad's statement is incomplete. The statement of Ibn `Abbas, i.e., when I saw him he was a slave, is more authentic. – Sahih Al-Bukhari 6754

حَدَّثَنَا مُوسَى، حَدَّثَنَا أَبُو عَوَانَةَ، عَنْ مَنْصُورٍ، عَنْ إِبْرَاهِيمَ، عَنِ الأَسْوَدِ، أَنَّ عَائِشَةَ ـ رضى الله عنها ـ اشْتَرَتْ بَرِيرَةَ، لِتُعْتِقَهَا، وَاشْتَرَطَ أَهْلُهَا وَلاَءَهَا فَقَالَتْ يَا رَسُولَ اللَّهِ إِنِّي اشْتَرَيْتُ بَرِيرَةَ لأُعْتِقَهَا، وَإِنَّ أَهْلَهَا يَشْتَرِطُونَ وَلاَءَهَا. فَقَالَ " أَعْتِقِيهَا فَإِنَّمَا الْوَلاَءُ لِمَنْ أَعْتَقَ ". أَوْ قَالَ " أَعْطَى الثَّمَنَ ". قَالَ فَاشْتَرَتْهَا فَأَعْتَقَتْهَا. قَالَ وَخُيِّرَتْ فَاخْتَارَتْ نَفْسَهَا وَقَالَتْ لَوْ أُعْطِيتُ كَذَا وَكَذَا مَا كُنْتُ مَعَهُ. قَالَ الأَسْوَدُ وَكَانَ زَوْجُهَا حُرًّا. قَوْلُ الأَسْوَدِ مُنْقَطِعٌ، وَقَوْلُ ابْنِ عَبَّاسٍ رَأَيْتُهُ عَبْدًا. أَصَحُّ

Narrated Shaqiq bin Salama :I was with `Abdullah and Abu Musa; the latter asked the former, "O Abu `Abdur-Rahman! What is your opinion if somebody becomes Junub and no water is available?" `Abdullah replied, "Do not pray till water is found." Abu Musa said, "What do you say about the statement of `Ammar) who was ordered by the Prophet (ﷺ) to perform Tayammum .(The Prophet (ﷺ) said to him: "Perform Tayammum and that would be sufficient." `Abdullah replied, "Don't you see that `Umar was not satisfied by `Ammar's statement?" Abu- Musa said, "All right, leave `Ammar's statement, but what will you say about this verse (of Tayammum)?" `Abdullah kept quiet and then said, "If we allowed it, then they would probably perform Tayammum even if water was available, if one of them found it (water) cold." The narrator added, "I said to Shaqiq, "Then did `Abdullah dislike to perform Tayammum because of this?" He replied, "Yes – ".Sahih al-Bukhari 346

حَدَّثَنَا عُمَرُ بْنُ حَفْصٍ، قَالَ حَدَّثَنَا أَبِي قَالَ، حَدَّثَنَا الأَعْمَشُ، قَالَ سَمِعْتُ شَقِيقَ بْنَ سَلَمَةَ، قَالَ كُنْتُ عِنْدَ عَبْدِ اللَّهِ وَأَبِي مُوسَى فَقَالَ لَهُ أَبُو مُوسَى أَرَأَيْتَ يَا أَبَا عَبْدِ الرَّحْمَنِ إِذَا أَجْنَبَ فَلَمْ يَجِدْ، مَاءً كَيْفَ يَصْنَعُ فَقَالَ عَبْدُ اللَّهِ لاَ يُصَلِّي حَتَّى يَجِدَ الْمَاءَ. فَقَالَ أَبُو مُوسَى فَكَيْفَ تَصْنَعُ بِقَوْلِ عَمَّارٍ حِينَ قَالَ لَهُ النَّبِيُّ صلى الله عليه وسلم " كَانَ يَكْفِيكَ " قَالَ أَلَمْ تَرَ عُمَرَ لَمْ يَقْنَعْ بِذَلِكَ. فَقَالَ أَبُو مُوسَى فَدَعْنَا مِنْ قَوْلِ عَمَّارٍ، كَيْفَ تَصْنَعُ بِهَذِهِ الآيَةِ فَمَا دَرَى عَبْدُ اللَّهِ مَا يَقُولُ فَقَالَ إِنَّا لَوْ رَخَّصْنَا لَهُمْ فِي هَذَا لأَوْشَكَ إِذَا بَرَدَ عَلَى أَحَدِهِمُ الْمَاءُ أَنْ يَدَعَهُ وَيَتَيَمَّمَ. فَقُلْتُ لِشَقِيقٍ فَإِنَّمَا كَرِهَ عَبْدُ اللَّهِ لِهَذَا قَالَ نَعَمْ.

Narrated `Aisha: The Prophetﷺ recited (the Qur'an) aloud during the eclipse prayer and when he had finished the eclipse prayer he said the Takbir and bowed. When he stood straight from bowing he would say "Sami 'allahu liman hamidah Rabbana wa laka l-hamd." And he would again start reciting. In the eclipse prayer there are four bowing and four prostrations in two rak`at. Al-Auza'I and others said that they had heard Az-Zuhri from 'Urwa from `Aisha saying, "In the lifetime of Allah's Messenger ﷺ the sun eclipsed, and he made a person to announce: 'Prayer in congregation.' He led the prayer and performed four bowing and four prostrations in two rak`at." Narrated Al-Walid that `Abdur-Rahman bin Namir had informed him that he had heard the same. Ibn Shihab heard the same. Az-Zuhri said, "I asked ('Urwa), 'What did your brother `Abdullah bin Az-Zubair do? He prayed two rak`at (of the eclipse prayer) like the morning prayer, when he offered the (eclipse) prayer in Medina.' 'Urwa replied that he had missed (i.e. did not pray according to) the Prophet's tradition." Sulaiman bin Kathir and Sufyan bin Husain narrated from Az-Zuhri that the prayer for the eclipse used to be offered with loud recitation. – Sahih al-Bukhari 1065, 1066

حَدَّثَنَا مُحَمَّدُ بْنُ مِهْرَانَ، قَالَ حَدَّثَنَا الْوَلِيدُ، قَالَ أَخْبَرَنَا ابْنُ نَمِرٍ، سَمِعَ ابْنَ شِهَابٍ، عَنْ عُرْوَةَ، عَنْ عَائِشَةَ ـ رضى الله عنها ـ جَهَرَ النَّبِيُّ صلى الله عليه وسلم فِي صَلاَةِ الْخُسُوفِ بِقِرَاءَتِهِ، فَإِذَا فَرَغَ مِنْ قِرَاءَتِهِ كَبَّرَ فَرَكَعَ، وَإِذَا رَفَعَ مِنَ الرَّكْعَةِ قَالَ سَمِعَ اللَّهُ لِمَنْ حَمِدَهُ، رَبَّنَا وَلَكَ الْحَمْدُ. ثُمَّ يُعَاوِدُ الْقِرَاءَةَ فِي صَلاَةِ الْكُسُوفِ، أَرْبَعَ رَكَعَاتٍ فِي رَكْعَتَيْنِ وَأَرْبَعَ سَجَدَاتٍ.
وَقَالَ الأَوْزَاعِيُّ وَغَيْرُهُ سَمِعْتُ الزُّهْرِيَّ، عَنْ عُرْوَةَ، عَنْ عَائِشَةَ ـ رضى الله عنها ـ أَنَّ الشَّمْسَ، خَسَفَتْ عَلَى عَهْدِ رَسُولِ اللَّهِ صلى الله عليه وسلم فَبَعَثَ مُنَادِيًا بِالصَّلاَةُ جَامِعَةٌ، فَتَقَدَّمَ فَصَلَّى أَرْبَعَ رَكَعَاتٍ فِي رَكْعَتَيْنِ وَأَرْبَعَ سَجَدَاتٍ. وَأَخْبَرَنِي عَبْدُ الرَّحْمَنِ بْنُ نَمِرٍ سَمِعَ ابْنَ شِهَابٍ مِثْلَهُ. قَالَ الزُّهْرِيُّ فَقُلْتُ مَا صَنَعَ أَخُوكَ ذَلِكَ، عَبْدُ اللَّهِ بْنُ الزُّبَيْرِ مَا صَلَّى إِلاَّ رَكْعَتَيْنِ مِثْلَ الصُّبْحِ إِذْ صَلَّى بِالْمَدِينَةِ. قَالَ أَجَلْ، إِنَّهُ أَخْطَأَ السُّنَّةَ. تَابَعَهُ سُفْيَانُ بْنُ حُسَيْنٍ وَسُلَيْمَانُ بْنُ كَثِيرٍ عَنِ الزُّهْرِيِّ فِي الْجَهْرِ.

Yahya related to me from Malik from Yahya ibn Said that Abdullah ibn Masud said to a certain man, "You are in a time when men of understanding (fuqaha) are many and Qur'an reciters are few, when the limits of behaviour defined in the Qur'an are guarded and its letters are lost, when few people ask and many give, when they make the prayer long and the khutba short, and put their actions before their desires. A time will come upon men when their fuqaha are few but their Qur'an reciters are many, when the letters of the Qur'an are guarded carefully but its limits are lost, when many ask but few give, when they make the khutba long but the prayer short, and put their desires before their actions." – Muwatta Malik - Shortening the Prayer

وَحَدَّثَنِي عَنْ مَالِكٍ، عَنْ يَحْيَى بْنِ سَعِيدٍ، أَنَّ عَبْدَ اللَّهِ بْنَ مَسْعُودٍ، قَالَ لإِنْسَانٍ إِنَّكَ فِي زَمَانٍ كَثِيرٌ فُقَهَاؤُهُ قَلِيلٌ قُرَّاؤُهُ تُحْفَظُ فِيهِ حُدُودُ الْقُرْآنِ وَتُضَيَّعُ حُرُوفُهُ قَلِيلٌ مَنْ يَسْأَلُ كَثِيرٌ مَنْ يُعْطِي يُطِيلُونَ فِيهِ الصَّلاَةَ وَيَقْصُرُونَ الْخُطْبَةَ يُبَدُّونَ أَعْمَالَهُمْ قَبْلَ أَهْوَائِهِمْ وَسَيَأْتِي عَلَى النَّاسِ زَمَانٌ قَلِيلٌ فُقَهَاؤُهُ كَثِيرٌ قُرَّاؤُهُ يُحْفَظُ فِيهِ حُرُوفُ الْقُرْآنِ وَتُضَيَّعُ حُدُودُهُ كَثِيرٌ مَنْ يَسْأَلُ قَلِيلٌ مَنْ يُعْطِي يُطِيلُونَ فِيهِ الْخُطْبَةَ وَيَقْصُرُونَ الصَّلاَةَ يُبَدُّونَ فِيهِ أَهْوَاءَهُمْ قَبْلَ أَعْمَالِهِمْ

The Book of
Warning of changes to the Sunnah
التحذير من تغيير السنة

Narrated `Abdullah: The Prophetﷺ said, "I am your predecessor at the Lake-Fount (Kauthar) and some men amongst you will be brought to me, and when I will try to hand them some water, they will be pulled away from me by force whereupon I will say, 'O Lord, my companions!' Then the Almighty will say, 'You do not know what they did after you left, they introduced new things into the religion after you.'". – Sahih Al-Bukhari 7049

حَدَّثَنَا مُوسَى بْنُ إِسْمَاعِيلَ، حَدَّثَنَا أَبُو عَوَانَةَ، عَنْ مُغِيرَةَ، عَنْ أَبِي وَائِلٍ، قَالَ قَالَ عَبْدُ اللَّهِ قَالَ النَّبِيُّ صلى الله عليه وسلم " أَنَا فَرَطُكُمْ عَلَى الْحَوْضِ، لَيُرْفَعَنَّ إِلَىَّ رِجَالٌ مِنْكُمْ حَتَّى إِذَا أَهْوَيْتُ لأُنَاوِلَهُمُ اخْتُلِجُوا دُونِي فَأَقُولُ أَىْ رَبِّ أَصْحَابِي. يَقُولُ لاَ تَدْرِي مَا أَحْدَثُوا بَعْدَكَ ".

Narrated Hudhaifa bin Al-Yaman: The people used to ask Allah's Messengerﷺ about the good but I used to ask him about the evil lest I should be overtaken by them. So I said, "O Allah's Messengerﷺ! We were living in ignorance and in an (extremely) worst atmosphere, then Allah brought to us this good (i.e., Islam); will there be any evil after this good?" He said, "Yes." I said, 'Will there be any good after that evil?" He replied, "Yes, but it will be tainted (not pure.)'' I asked, "What will be its taint?" He replied, "(There will be) some people who will guide others not according to my tradition? You will approve of some of their deeds and disapprove of some others." I asked, "Will there be any evil after that good?" He replied, "Yes, (there will be) some people calling at the gates of the (Hell) Fire, and whoever will respond to their call, will be thrown by them into the (Hell) Fire." I said, "O Allah s Apostle! Will you describe them to us?" He said, "They will be from our own people and will speak our language." I said, "What do you order me to do if such a state should take place in my life?" He said, "Stick to the group of Muslims and their Imam (ruler)." I said, "If there is neither a group of Muslims nor an Imam (ruler)?" He said, "Then turn away from all those sects even if you were to bite (eat) the roots of a tree till death overtakes you while you are in that state.". – Sahih Al-Bukhari 7084

حَدَّثَنَا مُحَمَّدُ بْنُ الْمُثَنَّى، حَدَّثَنَا الْوَلِيدُ بْنُ مُسْلِمٍ، حَدَّثَنَا ابْنُ جَابِرٍ، حَدَّثَنِي بُسْرُ بْنُ عُبَيْدِ اللَّهِ الْحَضْرَمِيُّ، أَنَّهُ سَمِعَ أَبَا إِدْرِيسَ الْخَوْلاَنِيَّ، أَنَّهُ سَمِعَ حُذَيْفَةَ بْنَ الْيَمَانِ، يَقُولُ كَانَ النَّاسُ يَسْأَلُونَ رَسُولَ اللَّهِ صلى الله عليه وسلم عَنِ الْخَيْرِ، وَكُنْتُ أَسْأَلُهُ عَنِ الشَّرِّ، مَخَافَةَ أَنْ يُدْرِكَنِي فَقُلْتُ يَا رَسُولَ اللَّهِ إِنَّا كُنَّا فِي جَاهِلِيَّةٍ وَشَرٍّ فَجَاءَنَا اللَّهُ بِهَذَا الْخَيْرِ، فَهَلْ بَعْدَ هَذَا الْخَيْرِ مِنْ شَرٍّ قَالَ " نَعَمْ ". قُلْتُ وَهَلْ بَعْدَ ذَلِكَ الشَّرِّ مِنْ خَيْرٍ قَالَ " نَعَمْ، وَفِيهِ دَخَنٌ ". قُلْتُ وَمَا دَخَنُهُ قَالَ " قَوْمٌ يَهْدُونَ بِغَيْرِ هَدْيِي، تَعْرِفُ مِنْهُمْ وَتُنْكِرُ ". قُلْتُ فَهَلْ بَعْدَ ذَلِكَ الْخَيْرِ مِنْ شَرٍّ قَالَ " نَعَمْ، دُعَاةٌ عَلَى أَبْوَابِ جَهَنَّمَ، مَنْ أَجَابَهُمْ إِلَيْهَا قَذَفُوهُ فِيهَا ". قُلْتُ يَا رَسُولَ اللَّهِ صِفْهُمْ لَنَا. قَالَ " هُمْ مِنْ جِلْدَتِنَا، وَيَتَكَلَّمُونَ بِأَلْسِنَتِنَا ". قُلْتُ فَمَا تَأْمُرُنِي إِنْ أَدْرَكَنِي ذَلِكَ قَالَ " تَلْزَمُ جَمَاعَةَ الْمُسْلِمِينَ وَإِمَامَهُمْ ". قُلْتُ فَإِنْ لَمْ يَكُنْ لَهُمْ جَمَاعَةٌ وَلاَ إِمَامٌ قَالَ " فَاعْتَزِلْ تِلْكَ الْفِرَقَ كُلَّهَا، وَلَوْ أَنْ تَعَضَّ بِأَصْلِ شَجَرَةٍ، حَتَّى يُدْرِكَكَ الْمَوْتُ، وَأَنْتَ عَلَى ذَلِكَ "

Narrated Qais bin Abi Hazim: Abu Bakr went to a lady from the Ahmas tribe called Zainab bint Al-Muhajir and found that she refused to speak. He asked, "Why does she not speak." The people said, "She has intended to perform Hajj without speaking." He said to her, "Speak, for it is illegal not to speak, as it is an action of the pre-islamic period of ignorance. So she spoke and said, "Who are you?" He said, "A man from the Emigrants." She asked, "Which Emigrants?" He replied, "From Quraish." She asked, "From what branch of Quraish are you?" He said, "You ask too many questions; I am Abu Bakr." She said, "How long shall we enjoy this good order (i.e. Islamic religion) which Allah has brought after the period of ignorance?" He said, "You will enjoy it as long as your Imams keep on abiding by its rules and regulations."

She asked, "What are the Imams?" He said, "Were there not heads and chiefs of your nation who used to order the people and they used to obey them?" She said, "Yes." He said, "So they (i.e. the Imams) are those whom I meant.". – Sahih Al-Bukhari 3834

حَدَّثَنَا أَبُو النُّعْمَانِ، حَدَّثَنَا أَبُو عَوَانَةَ، عَنْ بَيَانٍ أَبِي بِشْرٍ، عَنْ قَيْسِ بْنِ أَبِي حَازِمٍ، قَالَ دَخَلَ أَبُو بَكْرٍ عَلَى امْرَأَةٍ مِنْ أَحْمَسَ يُقَالُ لَهَا زَيْنَبُ، فَرَآهَا لاَ تَكَلَّمُ، فَقَالَ مَا لَهَا لاَ تَكَلَّمُ قَالُوا حَجَّتْ مُصْمِتَةً. قَالَ لَهَا تَكَلَّمِي، فَإِنَّ هَذَا لاَ يَحِلُّ، هَذَا مِنْ عَمَلِ الْجَاهِلِيَّةِ. فَتَكَلَّمَتْ، فَقَالَتْ مَنْ أَنْتَ قَالَ امْرُؤٌ مِنَ الْمُهَاجِرِينَ. قَالَتْ أَيُّ الْمُهَاجِرِينَ قَالَ مِنْ قُرَيْشٍ. قَالَتْ مِنْ أَىِّ قُرَيْشٍ أَنْتَ قَالَ إِنَّكِ لَسَئُولٌ أَنَا أَبُو بَكْرٍ. قَالَتْ مَا بَقَاؤُنَا عَلَى هَذَا الأَمْرِ الصَّالِحِ الَّذِي جَاءَ اللَّهُ بِهِ بَعْدَ الْجَاهِلِيَّةِ قَالَ بَقَاؤُكُمْ عَلَيْهِ مَا اسْتَقَامَتْ بِكُمْ أَئِمَّتُكُمْ. قَالَتْ وَمَا الأَئِمَّةُ قَالَ أَمَا كَانَ لِقَوْمِكِ رُءُوسٌ وَأَشْرَافٌ يَأْمُرُونَهُمْ فَيُطِيعُونَهُمْ قَالَتْ بَلَى. قَالَ فَهُمْ أُولَئِكِ عَلَى النَّاسِ

Narrated Mirdas Al-Aslami: The Prophet ﷺ said, "The righteous (pious people will depart (die) in succession one after the other, and there will remain (on the earth) useless people like the useless husk of barley seeds or bad dates. – Sahih Al-Bukhari 6434

حَدَّثَنِي يَحْيَى بْنُ حَمَّادٍ، حَدَّثَنَا أَبُو عَوَانَةَ، عَنْ بَيَانٍ، عَنْ قَيْسِ بْنِ أَبِي حَازِمٍ، عَنْ مِرْدَاسٍ الأَسْلَمِيِّ، قَالَ قَالَ النَّبِيُّ صلى الله عليه وسلم " يَذْهَبُ الصَّالِحُونَ الأَوَّلُ فَالأَوَّلُ، وَيَبْقَى حُفَالَةٌ كَحُفَالَةِ الشَّعِيرِ أَوِ التَّمْرِ، لاَ يُبَالِيهِمُ اللَّهُ بَالَةً ". قَالَ أَبُو عَبْدِ اللَّهِ يُقَالُ حُفَالَةٌ وَحُثَالَةٌ.

Narrated Al-Musaiyab: I met Al-Bara bin `Azib and said (to him). "May you live prosperously! You enjoyed the company of the Prophet ﷺ and gave him the Pledge of allegiance (of Al-Hudaibiya) under the Tree." On that, Al- Bara' said, "O my nephew! You do not know what we have done after him (i.e. his death). – Sahih Al-Bukhari 4170

حَدَّثَنِي أَحْمَدُ بْنُ إِشْكَابٍ، حَدَّثَنَا مُحَمَّدُ بْنُ فُضَيْلٍ، عَنِ الْعَلاَءِ بْنِ الْمُسَيَّبِ، عَنْ أَبِيهِ، قَالَ لَقِيتُ الْبَرَاءَ بْنَ عَازِبٍ ـ رضى الله عنهما ـ فَقُلْتُ طُوبَى لَكَ صَحِبْتَ النَّبِيَّ صلى الله عليه وسلم وَبَايَعْتَهُ تَحْتَ الشَّجَرَةِ. فَقَالَ يَا ابْنَ أَخِي إِنَّكَ لاَ تَدْرِي مَا أَحْدَثْنَا بَعْدَهُ.

Narrated Sa`d: I was one of (the first) seven (who had embraced Islam) with Allah's Messenger ﷺ and we had nothing to eat then, except the leaves of the Habala or Hubula tree, so that our stool used to be similar to that of sheep. Now the tribe of Bani Asad wants to teach me Islam; I would be a loser and all my efforts would be in vain (if I learn Islam anew from them). – Sahih Al-Bukhari 5412

حَدَّثَنَا عَبْدُ اللَّهِ بْنُ مُحَمَّدٍ، حَدَّثَنَا وَهْبُ بْنُ جَرِيرٍ، حَدَّثَنَا شُعْبَةُ، عَنْ إِسْمَاعِيلَ، عَنْ قَيْسٍ، عَنْ سَعْدٍ، قَالَ رَأَيْتُنِي سَابِعَ سَبْعَةٍ مَعَ النَّبِيِّ صلى الله عليه وسلم مَا لَنَا طَعَامٌ إِلاَّ وَرَقُ الْحُبْلَةِ ـ أَوِ الْحَبَلَةِ ـ حَتَّى يَضَعَ أَحَدُنَا مَا تَضَعُ الشَّاةُ، ثُمَّ أَصْبَحَتْ بَنُو أَسَدٍ تُعَزِّرُنِي عَلَى الإِسْلاَمِ، خَسِرْتُ إِذًا وَضَلَّ سَعْيِي

Narrated Sa`id Al-Maqburi: That his father said, "While we were accompanying a funeral procession, Abu Huraira got hold of the hand of Marwan and they sat down before the coffin was put down. Then Abu Sa`id came and took hold of Marwan's hand and said, "Get up. By Allah, no doubt this (i.e. Abu Huraira) knows that the Prophet forbade us to do that." Abu Huraira said, "He (Abu Sa`id) has spoken the truth.". – Sahih Al-Bukhari 1309

حَدَّثَنَا أَحْمَدُ بْنُ يُونُسَ، حَدَّثَنَا ابْنُ أَبِي ذِئْبٍ، عَنْ سَعِيدٍ الْمَقْبُرِيِّ، عَنْ أَبِيهِ، قَالَ كُنَّا فِي جَنَازَةٍ فَأَخَذَ أَبُو هُرَيْرَةَ ـ رضى الله عنه ـ بِيَدِ مَرْوَانَ فَجَلَسَا قَبْلَ أَنْ تُوضَعَ، فَجَاءَ أَبُو سَعِيدٍ ـ رضى الله عنه ـ فَأَخَذَ بِيَدِ مَرْوَانَ فَقَالَ قُمْ فَوَاللَّهِ لَقَدْ عَلِمَ هَذَا أَنَّ النَّبِيَّ صلى الله عليه وسلم نَهَانَا عَنْ ذَلِكَ. فَقَالَ أَبُو هُرَيْرَةَ صَدَقَ.

Narrated Abu Sa`id Al-Khudri: In the lifetime of the Prophet ﷺ we used to give one Sa' of food or one Sa' of dates or one Sa' of barley or one Sa' of Raisins (dried grapes) as Sadaqat-ul-Fitr. And when Muawiya became the Caliph and the wheat was (available in abundance) he said, "I think (observe) that one Mudd (of wheat) equals two Mudds (of any of the above mentioned things). – Sahih Al-Bukhari 1508

حَدَّثَنَا عَبْدُ اللَّهِ بْنُ مُنِيرٍ، سَمِعَ يَزِيدَ الْعَدَنِيَّ، حَدَّثَنَا سُفْيَانُ، عَنْ زَيْدِ بْنِ أَسْلَمَ، قَالَ حَدَّثَنِي عِيَاضُ بْنُ عَبْدِ اللَّهِ بْنِ أَبِي سَرْحٍ، عَنْ أَبِي سَعِيدٍ الْخُدْرِيِّ ـ رضى الله عنه ـ قَالَ كُنَّا نُعْطِيهَا فِي زَمَانِ النَّبِيِّ صلى الله عليه وسلم صَاعًا مِنْ طَعَامٍ، أَوْ صَاعًا مِنْ تَمْرٍ، أَوْ صَاعًا مِنْ شَعِيرٍ، أَوْ صَاعًا مِنْ زَبِيبٍ، فَلَمَّا جَاءَ مُعَاوِيَةُ وَجَاءَتِ السَّمْرَاءُ قَالَ أُرَى مُدًّا مِنْ هَذَا يَعْدِلُ مُدَّيْنِ

Narrated Zaid bin Wahab: I passed by a place called Ar-Rabadha and by chance I met Abu Dhar and asked him, "What has brought you to this place?" He said, "I was in Sham and differed with Muawiya on the meaning of (the following verses of the Qur'an): 'They who hoard up gold and silver and spend them not in the way of Allah.' (9.34). Muawiya said, 'This verse is revealed regarding the people of the scriptures." I said, It was revealed regarding us and also the people of the scriptures." So we had a quarrel and Mu'awiya sent a complaint against me to `Uthman. `Uthman wrote to me to come to Medina, and I came to Medina. Many people came to me as if they had not seen me before. So I told this to `Uthman who said to me, "You may depart and live nearby if you wish." That was the reason for my being here for even if an Ethiopian had been nominated as my ruler, I would have obeyed him . – Sahih Al-Bukhari 1406

حَدَّثَنَا عَلِيٌّ، سَمِعَ هُشَيْمًا، أَخْبَرَنَا حُصَيْنٌ، عَنْ زَيْدِ بْنِ وَهْبٍ، قَالَ مَرَرْتُ بِالرَّبَذَةِ فَإِذَا أَنَا بِأَبِي، ذَرٍّ ـ رضى الله عنه ـ فَقُلْتُ لَهُ مَا أَنْزَلَكَ مَنْزِلَكَ هَذَا قَالَ كُنْتُ بِالشَّأْمِ، فَاخْتَلَفْتُ أَنَا وَمُعَاوِيَةُ فِي الَّذِينَ يَكْنِزُونَ الذَّهَبَ وَالْفِضَّةَ وَلاَ يُنْفِقُونَهَا فِي سَبِيلِ اللَّهِ. قَالَ مُعَاوِيَةُ نَزَلَتْ فِي أَهْلِ الْكِتَابِ. فَقُلْتُ نَزَلَتْ فِينَا وَفِيهِمْ. فَكَانَ بَيْنِي وَبَيْنَهُ فِي ذَاكَ، وَكَتَبَ إِلَى عُثْمَانَ ـ رضى الله عنه ـ يَشْكُونِي، فَكَتَبَ إِلَىَّ عُثْمَانُ أَنِ اقْدَمِ الْمَدِينَةَ. فَقَدِمْتُهَا فَكَثُرَ عَلَىَّ النَّاسُ حَتَّى كَأَنَّهُمْ لَمْ يَرَوْنِي قَبْلَ ذَلِكَ، فَذَكَرْتُ ذَاكَ لِعُثْمَانَ فَقَالَ لِي إِنْ شِئْتَ تَنَحَّيْتَ فَكُنْتَ قَرِيبًا. فَذَاكَ الَّذِي أَنْزَلَنِي هَذَا الْمَنْزِلَ، وَلَوْ أَمَّرُوا عَلَىَّ حَبَشِيًّا لَسَمِعْتُ وَأَطَعْتُ.

The Book of
Bid'ah
الْبِدْعَةُ

Narrated Tariq bin `Abdur-Rahman: When I set out for Hajj, I passed by some people offering a prayer, I asked, "What is this mosque?" They said, "This is the Tree where Allah's Messengerﷺ took the Ar-Ridwan Pledge of allegiance. Then I went to Sa`id bin Musaiyab and informed him about it. Sa`id said, "My father said that he was amongst those who had given the Pledge of allegiance to Allah's Messengerﷺ beneath the Tree. He (i.e. my father) said, "When we set out the following year, we forgot the Tree and were unable to recognize it. "Then Sa`id said (perhaps ironically) "The companions of the Prophetﷺ could not recognize it; nevertheless, you do recognize it; therefore you have a better knowledge." – Sahih Al-Bukhari 4163

حَدَّثَنَا مَحْمُودٌ، حَدَّثَنَا عُبَيْدُ اللَّهِ، عَنْ إِسْرَائِيلَ، عَنْ طَارِقِ بْنِ عَبْدِ الرَّحْمَنِ، قَالَ انْطَلَقْتُ حَاجًّا فَمَرَرْتُ بِقَوْمٍ يُصَلُّونَ قُلْتُ مَا هَذَا الْمَسْجِدُ قَالُوا هَذِهِ الشَّجَرَةُ، حَيْثُ بَايَعَ رَسُولُ اللَّهِ صلى الله عليه وسلم بَيْعَةَ الرُّضْوَانِ. فَأَتَيْتُ سَعِيدَ بْنَ الْمُسَيَّبِ فَأَخْبَرْتُهُ فَقَالَ سَعِيدٌ حَدَّثَنِي أَبِي أَنَّهُ كَانَ فِيمَنْ بَايَعَ رَسُولَ اللَّهِ صلى الله عليه وسلم تَحْتَ الشَّجَرَةِ، قَالَ فَلَمَّا خَرَجْنَا مِنَ الْعَامِ الْمُقْبِلِ نَسِينَاهَا، فَلَمْ نَقْدِرْ عَلَيْهَا. فَقَالَ سَعِيدٌ إِنَّ أَصْحَابَ مُحَمَّدٍ صلى الله عليه وسلم لَمْ يَعْلَمُوهَا وَعَلِمْتُمُوهَا أَنْتُمْ، فَأَنْتُمْ أَعْلَمُ

Narrated Abu Sa`id Al-Khudri: The Prophetﷺ used to proceed to the Musalla on the days of Id-ul-Fitr and Id-ul-Adha; the first thing to begin with was the prayer and after that he would stand in front of the people and the people would keep sitting in their rows. Then he would preach to them, advise them and give them orders, (i.e. Khutba). And after that if he wished to send an army for an expedition, he would do so; or if he wanted to give and order, he would do so, and then depart. The people followed this tradition till I went out with Marwan, the Governor of Medina, for the prayer of Id-ul-Adha or Id-ul-Fitr. When we reached the Musalla, there was a pulpit made by Kathir bin As-Salt. Marwan wanted to get up on that pulpit before the prayer. I got hold of his clothes but he pulled them and ascended the pulpit and delivered the Khutba before the prayer. I said to him, "By Allah, you have changed (the Prophet's tradition)." He replied, "O Abu Sa`id! Gone is that which you know." I said, "By Allah! What I know is better than what I do not know." Marwan said, "People do not sit to listen to our Khutba after the prayer, so I delivered the Khutba before the prayer." – Sahih Al-Bukhari 956

حَدَّثَنَا سَعِيدُ بْنُ أَبِي مَرْيَمَ، قَالَ حَدَّثَنَا مُحَمَّدُ بْنُ جَعْفَرٍ، قَالَ أَخْبَرَنِي زَيْدٌ، عَنْ عِيَاضِ بْنِ عَبْدِ اللَّهِ بْنِ أَبِي سَرْحٍ، عَنْ أَبِي سَعِيدٍ الْخُدْرِيِّ، قَالَ كَانَ رَسُولُ اللَّهِ صلى الله عليه وسلم يَخْرُجُ يَوْمَ الْفِطْرِ وَالأَضْحَى إِلَى الْمُصَلَّى، فَأَوَّلُ شَىْءٍ يَبْدَأُ بِهِ الصَّلاَةُ ثُمَّ يَنْصَرِفُ، فَيَقُومُ مُقَابِلَ النَّاسِ، وَالنَّاسُ جُلُوسٌ عَلَى صُفُوفِهِمْ، فَيَعِظُهُمْ وَيُوصِيهِمْ وَيَأْمُرُهُمْ، فَإِنْ كَانَ يُرِيدُ أَنْ يَقْطَعَ بَعْثًا قَطَعَهُ، أَوْ يَأْمُرَ بِشَىْءٍ أَمَرَ بِهِ، ثُمَّ يَنْصَرِفُ. قَالَ أَبُو سَعِيدٍ فَلَمْ يَزَلِ النَّاسُ عَلَى ذَلِكَ حَتَّى خَرَجْتُ مَعَ مَرْوَانَ وَهْوَ أَمِيرُ الْمَدِينَةِ فِي أَضْحًى أَوْ فِطْرٍ، فَلَمَّا أَتَيْنَا الْمُصَلَّى إِذَا مِنْبَرٌ بَنَاهُ كَثِيرُ بْنُ الصَّلْتِ، فَإِذَا مَرْوَانُ يُرِيدُ أَنْ يَرْتَقِيَهُ قَبْلَ أَنْ يُصَلِّيَ، فَجَبَذْتُ بِثَوْبِهِ فَجَبَذَنِي فَارْتَفَعَ، فَخَطَبَ قَبْلَ الصَّلاَةِ، فَقُلْتُ لَهُ غَيَّرْتُمْ وَاللَّهِ. فَقَالَ أَبَا سَعِيدٍ، قَدْ ذَهَبَ مَا تَعْلَمُ. فَقُلْتُ مَا أَعْلَمُ وَاللَّهِ خَيْرٌ مِمَّا لاَ أَعْلَمُ. فَقَالَ إِنَّ النَّاسَ لَمْ يَكُونُوا يَجْلِسُونَ لَنَا بَعْدَ الصَّلاَةِ فَجَعَلْتُهَا قَبْلَ الصَّلاَةِ.

Narrated Abu Sa'id Al-Khudri: In the lifetime of the Prophetﷺ we used to give one Sa' of food or one Sa' of dates or one Sa' of barley or one Sa' of Raisins (dried grapes) as Sadaqat-ul-Fitr. And when Muawiya became the Caliph and the wheat was (available in abundance) he said, "I think (observe) that one Mudd (of wheat) equals two Mudds (of any of the above mentioned things). – Sahih Al-Bukhari 1508

حَدَّثَنَا عَبْدُ اللَّهِ بْنُ مُنِيرٍ، سَمِعَ يَزِيدَ الْعَدَنِيَّ، حَدَّثَنَا سُفْيَانُ، عَنْ زَيْدِ بْنِ أَسْلَمَ، قَالَ حَدَّثَنِي عِيَاضُ بْنُ عَبْدِ اللَّهِ بْنِ أَبِي سَرْحٍ، عَنْ أَبِي سَعِيدٍ الْخُدْرِيِّ ـ رضى الله عنه ـ قَالَ كُنَّا نُعْطِيهَا فِي زَمَانِ النَّبِيِّ صلى الله عليه وسلم صَاعًا مِنْ طَعَامٍ، أَوْ صَاعًا مِنْ تَمْرٍ، أَوْ صَاعًا مِنْ شَعِيرٍ، أَوْ صَاعًا مِنْ زَبِيبٍ، فَلَمَّا جَاءَ مُعَاوِيَةُ وَجَاءَتِ السَّمْرَاءُ قَالَ أُرَى مُدًّا مِنْ هَذَا يَعْدِلُ مُدَّيْنِ

Narrated Marwan bin Al-Hakam: I saw `Uthman and `Ali. `Uthman used to forbid people to perform Hajj-at-Tamattu` and Hajj-al- Qiran (Hajj and `Umra together), and when `Ali saw (this act of `Uthman), he assumed Ihram for Hajj and `Umra together saying, "Lubbaik for `Umra and Hajj," and said, "I will not leave the tradition of the Prophet ﷺ on the saying of somebody.". – Sahih Al-Bukhari 1563

حَدَّثَنَا مُحَمَّدُ بْنُ بَشَّارٍ، حَدَّثَنَا غُنْدَرٌ، حَدَّثَنَا شُعْبَةُ، عَنِ الْحَكَمِ، عَنْ عَلِيِّ بْنِ حُسَيْنٍ، عَنْ مَرْوَانَ بْنِ الْحَكَمِ، قَالَ شَهِدْتُ عُثْمَانَ وَعَلِيًّا ـ رضى الله عنهما ـ وَعُثْمَانُ يَنْهَى عَنِ الْمُتْعَةِ وَأَنْ يُجْمَعَ بَيْنَهُمَا‏.‏ فَلَمَّا رَأَى عَلِيٌّ، أَهَلَّ بِهِمَا لَبَّيْكَ بِعُمْرَةٍ وَحَجَّةٍ قَالَ مَا كُنْتُ لأَدَعَ سُنَّةَ النَّبِيِّ صلى الله عليه وسلم لِقَوْلِ أَحَدٍ

Abu Ash-Sha'tha said, "Who keeps away from some portion of the Ka'bah?" Mu'awiya used to touch the four corners of the Ka'bah, Ibn 'Abbas said to him, "These two corners (the one facing the Hijr) are not to be touched." Mu'awiya said, "Nothing is untouchable in the Ka'bah." And Ibn Az-Zubair used to touch all the corners of the Ka'bah. – Sahih Al-Bukhari 1608

وَقَالَ مُحَمَّدُ بْنُ بَكْرٍ أَخْبَرَنَا ابْنُ جُرَيْجٍ، أَخْبَرَنِي عَمْرُو بْنُ دِينَارٍ، عَنْ أَبِي الشَّعْثَاءِ، أَنَّهُ قَالَ وَمَنْ يَتَّقِي شَيْئًا مِنَ الْبَيْتِ، وَكَانَ مُعَاوِيَةُ يَسْتَلِمُ الأَرْكَانَ، فَقَالَ لَهُ ابْنُ عَبَّاسٍ ـ رضى الله عنهما ـ إِنَّهُ لاَ يُسْتَلَمُ هَذَانِ الرُّكْنَانِ‏.‏ فَقَالَ لَيْسَ شَىْءٌ مِنَ الْبَيْتِ مَهْجُورًا، وَكَانَ ابْنُ الزُّبَيْرِ ـ رضى الله عنهما ـ يَسْتَلِمُهُنَّ كُلَّهُنَّ‏.‏

Narrated Sa`id bin Zaid bin `Amr bin Nufail: That Arwa sued him before Marwan for a right, which she claimed, he had deprived her of. On that Sa`id said, "How should I deprive her of her right? I testify that I heard Allah's Messenger ﷺ saying, 'If anyone takes a span of land unjustly, his neck will be encircled with it down seven earths on the Day of Resurrection.". – Sahih Al-Bukhari 3198

حَدَّثَنِي عُبَيْدُ بْنُ إِسْمَاعِيلَ، حَدَّثَنَا أَبُو أُسَامَةَ، عَنْ هِشَامٍ، عَنْ أَبِيهِ، عَنْ سَعِيدِ بْنِ زَيْدِ بْنِ عَمْرِو بْنِ نُفَيْلٍ، أَنَّهُ خَاصَمَتْهُ أَرْوَى فِي حَقٍّ زَعَمَتْ أَنَّهُ انْتَقَصَهُ لَهَا إِلَى مَرْوَانَ، فَقَالَ سَعِيدٌ أَنَا أَنْتَقِصُ مِنْ حَقِّهَا شَيْئًا، أَشْهَدُ لَسَمِعْتُ رَسُولَ اللَّهِ صلى الله عليه وسلم يَقُولُ ‏"‏ مَنْ أَخَذَ شِبْرًا مِنَ الأَرْضِ ظُلْمًا، فَإِنَّهُ يُطَوَّقُهُ يَوْمَ الْقِيَامَةِ مِنْ سَبْعِ أَرَضِينَ ‏"‏‏.‏ قَالَ ابْنُ أَبِي الزِّنَادِ عَنْ هِشَامٍ عَنْ أَبِيهِ قَالَ قَالَ لِي سَعِيدُ بْنُ زَيْدٍ دَخَلْتُ عَلَى النَّبِيِّ صلى الله عليه وسلم‏.‏

Narrated Tariq bin `Abdur-Rahman: When I set out for Hajj, I passed by some people offering a prayer, I asked, "What is this mosque?" They said, "This is the Tree where Allah's Messenger ﷺ took the Ar-Ridwan Pledge of allegiance. Then I went to Sa`id bin Musaiyab and informed him about it. Sa`id said, "My father said that he was amongst those who had given the Pledge of allegiance to Allah's Messenger ﷺ beneath the Tree. He (i.e. my father) said, "When we set out the following year, we forgot the Tree and were unable to recognize it. "Then Sa`id said (perhaps ironically) "The companions of the Prophet ﷺ could not recognize it; nevertheless, you do recognize it; therefore you have a better knowledge.". – Sahih Al-Bukhari 4163

حَدَّثَنَا مَحْمُودٌ، حَدَّثَنَا عُبَيْدُ اللَّهِ، عَنْ إِسْرَائِيلَ، عَنْ طَارِقِ بْنِ عَبْدِ الرَّحْمَنِ، قَالَ انْطَلَقْتُ حَاجًّا فَمَرَرْتُ بِقَوْمٍ يُصَلُّونَ قُلْتُ مَا هَذَا الْمَسْجِدُ قَالُوا هَذِهِ الشَّجَرَةُ، حَيْثُ بَايَعَ رَسُولُ اللَّهِ صلى الله عليه وسلم بَيْعَةَ الرُّضْوَانِ‏.‏ فَأَتَيْتُ سَعِيدَ بْنَ الْمُسَيَّبِ فَأَخْبَرْتُهُ فَقَالَ سَعِيدٌ حَدَّثَنِي أَبِي أَنَّهُ كَانَ فِيمَنْ بَايَعَ رَسُولَ اللَّهِ صلى الله عليه وسلم تَحْتَ الشَّجَرَةِ، قَالَ فَلَمَّا خَرَجْنَا مِنَ الْعَامِ الْمُقْبِلِ نَسِينَاهَا، فَلَمْ نَقْدِرْ عَلَيْهَا‏.‏ فَقَالَ سَعِيدٌ إِنَّ أَصْحَابَ مُحَمَّدٍ صلى الله عليه وسلم لَمْ يَعْلَمُوهَا وَعَلِمْتُمُوهَا أَنْتُمْ، فَأَنْتُمْ أَعْلَمُ

Narrated Jarir: While I was at Yemen, I met two men from Yemen called Dhu Kala and Dhu `Amr, and I started telling them about Allah's Messenger ﷺ. Dhu `Amr said to me, "If what you are saying about your friend (i.e. the Prophet) is true, then he has died three days ago." Then both of them accompanied me to Medina, and when we had covered some distance on the way to Medina, we saw some riders coming from Medina. We asked them and they said, "Allah's Messenger ﷺ has died and Abu Bakr has been appointed as the Caliph and the people are in a good state.' Then they said, "Tell your friend (Abu Bakr) that we have come (to visit him), and if Allah will, we will come again." So they both returned to Yemen. When I told Abu Bakr their statement, he said to me, "I wish you had brought them (to me)." Afterwards I met Dhu `Amr, and he said to me, "O Jarir! You have done a favor to me and I am going to tell you something, i.e. you, the nation of 'Arabs, will remain prosperous as long as you choose and appoint another chief whenever a former one is dead. But if authority is obtained by the power of the sword, then the rulers will become kings who will get angry, as kings get angry, and will be delighted as kings get delighted.". – Sahih Al-Bukhari 4359

حَدَّثَنِي عَبْدُ اللَّهِ بْنُ أَبِي شَيْبَةَ الْعَبْسِيُّ، حَدَّثَنَا ابْنُ إِدْرِيسَ، عَنْ إِسْمَاعِيلَ بْنِ أَبِي خَالِدٍ، عَنْ قَيْسٍ، عَنْ جَرِيرٍ، قَالَ كُنْتُ بِالْبَحْرِ فَلَقِيتُ رَجُلَيْنِ مِنْ أَهْلِ الْيَمَنِ ذَا كَلاَعٍ وَذَا عَمْرٍو، فَجَعَلْتُ أُحَدِّثُهُمْ عَنْ رَسُولِ اللَّهِ صلى الله عليه وسلم فَقَالَ لَهُ ذُو عَمْرٍو لَئِنْ كَانَ الَّذِي تَذْكُرُ مِنْ أَمْرِ صَاحِبِكَ، لَقَدْ مَرَّ عَلَى أَجَلِهِ مُنْذُ ثَلاَثٍ. وَأَقْبَلاَ مَعِي حَتَّى إِذَا كُنَّا فِي بَعْضِ الطَّرِيقِ رُفِعَ لَنَا رَكْبٌ مِنْ قِبَلِ الْمَدِينَةِ فَسَأَلْنَاهُمْ فَقَالُوا قُبِضَ رَسُولُ اللَّهِ صلى الله عليه وسلم وَاسْتُخْلِفَ أَبُو بَكْرٍ وَالنَّاسُ صَالِحُونَ. فَقَالاَ أَخْبِرْ صَاحِبَكَ أَنَّا قَدْ جِئْنَا وَلَعَلَّنَا سَنَعُودُ إِنْ شَاءَ اللَّهُ، وَرَجَعَا إِلَى الْيَمَنِ فَأَخْبَرْتُ أَبَا بَكْرٍ بِحَدِيثِهِمْ قَالَ أَفَلاَ جِئْتَ بِهِمْ. فَلَمَّا كَانَ بَعْدُ قَالَ لِي ذُو عَمْرٍو يَا جَرِيرُ إِنَّ بِكَ عَلَىَّ كَرَامَةً، وَإِنِّي مُخْبِرُكَ خَبَرًا، إِنَّكُمْ مَعْشَرَ الْعَرَبِ لَنْ تَزَالُوا بِخَيْرٍ مَا كُنْتُمْ إِذَا هَلَكَ أَمِيرٌ تَأَمَّرْتُمْ فِي آخَرَ، فَإِذَا كَانَتْ بِالسَّيْفِ كَانُوا مُلُوكًا يَغْضَبُونَ غَضَبَ الْمُلُوكِ وَيَرْضَوْنَ رِضَا الْمُلُوكِ

Narrated `Abdullah bin Mas`ud: The Prophet ﷺ recited Surat-an-Najm (53) and prostrated while reciting it and all the people prostrated and a man amongst the people took a handful of stones or earth and raised it to his face and said, "This is sufficient for me. Later on I saw him killed as a non-believer.". – Sahih Al-Bukhari 1070

حَدَّثَنَا حَفْصُ بْنُ عُمَرَ، قَالَ حَدَّثَنَا شُعْبَةُ، عَنْ أَبِي إِسْحَاقَ، عَنِ الأَسْوَدِ، عَنْ عَبْدِ اللَّهِ ـ رضى الله عنه ـ أَنَّ النَّبِيَّ صلى الله عليه وسلم قَرَأَ سُورَةَ النَّجْمِ فَسَجَدَ بِهَا، فَمَا بَقِيَ أَحَدٌ مِنَ الْقَوْمِ إِلاَّ سَجَدَ، فَأَخَذَ رَجُلٌ مِنَ الْقَوْمِ كَفًّا مِنْ حَصًى أَوْ تُرَابٍ، فَرَفَعَهُ إِلَى وَجْهِهِ وَقَالَ يَكْفِينِي هَذَا، فَلَقَدْ رَأَيْتُهُ بَعْدُ قُتِلَ كَافِرًا.

Narrated `Abbas bin Tamim: When it was the day (of the battle) of Al-Harra the people were giving Pledge of allegiance to `Abdullah bin Hanzala. Ibn Zaid said, "For what are the people giving Pledge of allegiance to `Abdullah bin Hanzala?" It was said to him, "For death." Ibn Zaid said, "I will never give the Pledge of allegiance for that to anybody else after Allah's Messenger ﷺ." Ibn Zaid was one of those who had witnessed the day of Al-Hudaibiya with the Prophet. – Sahih Al-Bukhari 4167

حَدَّثَنَا إِسْمَاعِيلُ، عَنْ أَخِيهِ، عَنْ سُلَيْمَانَ، عَنْ عَمْرِو بْنِ يَحْيَى، عَنْ عَبَّادِ بْنِ تَمِيمٍ، قَالَ لَمَّا كَانَ يَوْمُ الْحَرَّةِ وَالنَّاسُ يُبَايِعُونَ لِعَبْدِ اللَّهِ بْنِ حَنْظَلَةَ فَقَالَ ابْنُ زَيْدٍ عَلَى مَا يُبَايِعُ ابْنُ حَنْظَلَةَ النَّاسَ قِيلَ لَهُ عَلَى الْمَوْتِ. قَالَ لاَ أُبَايِعُ عَلَى ذَلِكَ أَحَدًا بَعْدَ رَسُولِ اللَّهِ صلى الله عليه وسلم. وَكَانَ شَهِدَ مَعَهُ الْحُدَيْبِيَةَ.

'Abdur Rahman bin 'Abdul Qari said, "I went out in the company of 'Umar bin Al-Khattab one night in Ramadan to the mosque and found the people praying in different groups. A man praying alone or a man praying with a little group behind him. So, 'Umar said, 'In my opinion I would better collect these (people) under the leadership of one Qari (Reciter) (i.e. let them pray in congregation!)'. So, he made up his mind to congregate them behind Ubai bin Ka'b. Then on another night I went again in his company and the people were praying behind their reciter. On that, 'Umar remarked, 'What an excellent Bid'a (i.e. innovation in religion) this is; but the prayer which they do not perform, but sleep at its time is better than the one they are offering.' He meant the prayer in the last part of the night. (In those days) people used to pray in the early part of the night.". – Sahih Al-Bukhari 2010

وَعَنِ ابْنِ شِهَابٍ، عَنْ عُرْوَةَ بْنِ الزُّبَيْرِ، عَنْ عَبْدِ الرَّحْمَنِ بْنِ عَبْدٍ الْقَارِيِّ، أَنَّهُ قَالَ خَرَجْتُ مَعَ عُمَرَ بْنِ الْخَطَّابِ - رضى الله عنه - لَيْلَةً فِي رَمَضَانَ، إِلَى الْمَسْجِدِ، فَإِذَا النَّاسُ أَوْزَاعٌ مُتَفَرِّقُونَ يُصَلِّي الرَّجُلُ لِنَفْسِهِ، وَيُصَلِّي الرَّجُلُ فَيُصَلِّي بِصَلاَتِهِ الرَّهْطُ فَقَالَ عُمَرُ إِنِّي أَرَى لَوْ جَمَعْتُ هَؤُلاَءِ عَلَى قَارِئٍ وَاحِدٍ لَكَانَ أَمْثَلَ. ثُمَّ عَزَمَ فَجَمَعَهُمْ عَلَى أُبَىِّ بْنِ كَعْبٍ، ثُمَّ خَرَجْتُ مَعَهُ لَيْلَةً أُخْرَى، وَالنَّاسُ يُصَلُّونَ بِصَلاَةِ قَارِئِهِمْ، قَالَ عُمَرُ نِعْمَ الْبِدْعَةُ هَذِهِ، وَالَّتِي يَنَامُونَ عَنْهَا أَفْضَلُ مِنَ الَّتِي يَقُومُونَ. يُرِيدُ آخِرَ اللَّيْلِ، وَكَانَ النَّاسُ يَقُومُونَ أَوَّلَهُ

It was narrated that Saeed bin Jubair said: "I was with Ibn Abbas in Arafat and he said: 'Why do I not hear the people reciting Talbiyah?' I said: They are afraid of Muawiyah.' So Ibn Abbas went out of his tent and said: "Labbaik Allahumma Labbaik, Labbaik! They are only forsaking the Sunnah out of hatred for Ali.'" - Sunan an-Nasa'I 3006

أَخْبَرَنَا أَحْمَدُ بْنُ عُثْمَانَ بْنِ حَكِيمٍ الأَوْدِيُّ، قَالَ حَدَّثَنَا خَالِدُ بْنُ مَخْلَدٍ، قَالَ حَدَّثَنَا عَلِيُّ بْنُ صَالِحٍ، عَنْ مَيْسَرَةَ بْنِ حَبِيبٍ، عَنِ الْمِنْهَالِ بْنِ عَمْرٍو، عَنْ سَعِيدِ بْنِ جُبَيْرٍ، قَالَ كُنْتُ مَعَ ابْنِ عَبَّاسٍ بِعَرَفَاتٍ فَقَالَ مَا لِي لاَ أَسْمَعُ النَّاسَ يُلَبُّونَ قُلْتُ يَخَافُونَ مِنْ مُعَاوِيَةَ . فَخَرَجَ ابْنُ عَبَّاسٍ مِنْ فُسْطَاطِهِ فَقَالَ لَبَّيْكَ اللَّهُمَّ لَبَّيْكَ لَبَّيْكَ فَإِنَّهُمْ قَدْ تَرَكُوا السُّنَّةَ مِنْ بُغْضِ عَلِيٍّ

Narrated Az-Zuhri: I said to 'Urwa, "When the sun eclipsed at Medina your brother (`Abdullah bin Az-Zubair) offered only a two-rak`at prayer like that of the morning (Fajr) prayer." 'Urwa replied, "Yes, for he missed the Prophet's tradition (concerning this matter)".. – Sahih al-Bukhari 1046

سَمِعْتُ الزُّهْرِيَّ، قَالَ سَأَلْتُ عُرْوَةَ مَا صَنَعَ أَخُوكَ عَبْدُ اللَّهِ بْنُ الزُّبَيْرِ حِينَ صَلَّى بِالْمَدِينَةِ رَكْعَتَيْنِ مِثْلَ صَلاَةِ الصُّبْحِ حِينَ كَسَفَتِ الشَّمْسُ. فَقَالَ قَدْ أَخْطَأَ السُّنَّةَ

The Book of
Except a group of true believers
إِلَّا فَرِيقًا مِّنَ ٱلْمُؤْمِنِينَ

In no way indeed will Allah leave out the believers in whatever (state) you are till He discriminates the wicked from good, and in no way indeed will Allah (allow you) to view the Unseen; but Allah selects out of His Messengers whom He decides. So believe in Allah and His Messengers, and in case you believe and are pious, then there will be for you a magnificent reward. – Surah Al-Imran 3:179

مَّا كَانَ ٱللَّهُ لِيَذَرَ ٱلْمُؤْمِنِينَ عَلَىٰ مَآ أَنتُمْ عَلَيْهِ حَتَّىٰ يَمِيزَ ٱلْخَبِيثَ مِنَ ٱلطَّيِّبِ ۗ وَمَا كَانَ ٱللَّهُ لِيُطْلِعَكُمْ عَلَى ٱلْغَيْبِ وَلَٰكِنَّ ٱللَّهَ يَجْتَبِى مِن رُّسُلِهِۦ مَن يَشَآءُ ۖ فَـَٔامِنُوا۟ بِٱللَّهِ وَرُسُلِهِۦ ۚ وَإِن تُؤْمِنُوا۟ وَتَتَّقُوا۟ فَلَكُمْ أَجْرٌ عَظِيمٌ

And the forerunners, the forerunners. Those are the nearest. In the Gardens of Bliss. A throng from the ancients. And a small band from the latecomers. – Surah Al-Waqi'ah 56:10-14

وَٱلسَّٰبِقُونَ ٱلسَّٰبِقُونَ أُو۟لَٰٓئِكَ ٱلْمُقَرَّبُونَ فِى جَنَّٰتِ ٱلنَّعِيمِ ثُلَّةٌ مِّنَ ٱلْأَوَّلِينَ وَقَلِيلٌ مِّنَ ٱلْـَٔاخِرِينَ

You will not find a people who believe in Allah and the Last Day, loving those who oppose Allah and His Messenger, even if they were their parents, or their children, or their siblings, or their close relatives. These—He has inscribed faith in their hearts, and has supported them with a spirit from Him. And He will admit them into Gardens beneath which rivers flow, wherein they will dwell forever. Allah is pleased with them, and they are pleased with Him. These are the partisans of Allah. Indeed, it is Allah's partisans who are the successful. – Surah Al-Mujadilah 58:22

لَّا تَجِدُ قَوْمًا يُؤْمِنُونَ بِٱللَّهِ وَٱلْيَوْمِ ٱلْـَٔاخِرِ يُوَآدُّونَ مَنْ حَآدَّ ٱللَّهَ وَرَسُولَهُۥ وَلَوْ كَانُوٓا۟ ءَابَآءَهُمْ أَوْ أَبْنَآءَهُمْ أَوْ إِخْوَٰنَهُمْ أَوْ عَشِيرَتَهُمْ ۚ أُو۟لَٰٓئِكَ كَتَبَ فِى قُلُوبِهِمُ ٱلْإِيمَٰنَ وَأَيَّدَهُم بِرُوحٍ مِّنْهُ ۖ وَيُدْخِلُهُمْ جَنَّٰتٍ تَجْرِى مِن تَحْتِهَا ٱلْأَنْهَٰرُ خَٰلِدِينَ فِيهَا ۚ رَضِىَ ٱللَّهُ عَنْهُمْ وَرَضُوا۟ عَنْهُ ۚ أُو۟لَٰٓئِكَ حِزْبُ ٱللَّهِ ۚ أَلَآ إِنَّ حِزْبَ ٱللَّهِ هُمُ ٱلْمُفْلِحُونَ

Satan was correct in his assessment of them. They followed him, except for a group of believers. – Surah Saba 34:20

وَلَقَدْ صَدَّقَ عَلَيْهِمْ إِبْلِيسُ ظَنَّهُۥ فَٱتَّبَعُوهُ إِلَّا فَرِيقًا مِّنَ ٱلْمُؤْمِنِينَ

Narrated Ibn `Abbas: A man came to Allah's Messenger ﷺ and said, "I saw in a dream, a cloud having shade. Butter and honey were dropping from it and I saw the people gathering it in their hands, some gathering much and some a little. And behold, there was a rope extending from the earth to the sky, and I saw that you (the Prophet) held it and went up, and then another man held it and went up and (after that) another (third) held it and went up, and then after another (fourth) man held it, but it broke and then got connected again." Abu Bakr said, "O Allah's Messenger ﷺ! Let my father be sacrificed for you! Allow me to interpret this dream." The Prophet ﷺ said to him, "Interpret it." Abu Bakr said, "The cloud with shade symbolizes Islam, and the butter and honey dropping from it, symbolizes the Qur'an, its sweetness dropping and some people learning much of the Qur'an and some a little. The rope which is extended from the sky to the earth is the Truth which you (the Prophet) are following. You follow it and Allah will raise you high with it, and then another man will follow it and will rise up with it and another person will follow it and then another man will follow it but it will break and then it will be connected for him and he will rise up with it. O Allah's Messenger ﷺ! Let my father be sacrificed for you! Am I right or wrong?" The Prophet replied, "You are right in some of it and wrong in some." Abu Bakr said, "O Allah's Prophet! By Allah, you must tell me in what I was wrong." The Prophet ﷺ said, "Do not swear.". – Sahih Al-Bukhari 7046

حَدَّثَنِي يَحْيَى بْنُ بُكَيْرٍ، حَدَّثَنَا اللَّيْثُ، عَنْ يُونُسَ، عَنِ ابْنِ شِهَابٍ، عَنْ عُبَيْدِ اللَّهِ بْنِ عَبْدِ اللَّهِ بْنِ عُتْبَةَ، أَنَّ ابْنَ عَبَّاسٍ ـ رضى الله عنهما ـ كَانَ يُحَدِّثُ أَنَّ رَجُلاً أَتَى رَسُولَ اللَّهِ صلى الله عليه وسلم فَقَالَ إِنِّي رَأَيْتُ اللَّيْلَةَ فِي الْمَنَامِ ظُلَّةً تَنْطُفُ السَّمْنَ وَالْعَسَلَ، فَأَرَى النَّاسَ يَتَكَفَّفُونَ مِنْهَا فَالْمُسْتَكْثِرُ وَالْمُسْتَقِلُّ، وَإِذَا سَبَبٌ وَاصِلٌ مِنَ الأَرْضِ إِلَى السَّمَاءِ، فَأَرَاكَ أَخَذْتَ بِهِ فَعَلَوْتَ، ثُمَّ أَخَذَ بِهِ رَجُلٌ آخَرُ فَعَلاَ بِهِ، ثُمَّ أَخَذَ بِهِ رَجُلٌ آخَرُ فَعَلاَ بِهِ ثُمَّ أَخَذَ بِهِ رَجُلٌ آخَرُ فَانْقَطَعَ ثُمَّ وُصِلَ. فَقَالَ أَبُو بَكْرٍ يَا رَسُولَ اللَّهِ بِأَبِي أَنْتَ وَاللَّهِ لَتَدَعَنِّي فَأَعْبُرَهَا. فَقَالَ النَّبِيُّ صلى الله عليه وسلم " اعْبُرْ ". قَالَ أَمَّا الظُّلَّةُ فَالإِسْلاَمُ، وَأَمَّا الَّذِي يَنْطِفُ مِنَ الْعَسَلِ وَالسَّمْنِ فَالْقُرْآنُ حَلاَوَتُهُ تَنْطُفُ، فَالْمُسْتَكْثِرُ مِنَ الْقُرْآنِ وَالْمُسْتَقِلُّ، وَأَمَّا السَّبَبُ الْوَاصِلُ مِنَ السَّمَاءِ إِلَى الأَرْضِ فَالْحَقُّ الَّذِي أَنْتَ عَلَيْهِ تَأْخُذُ بِهِ فَيُعْلِيكَ اللَّهُ، ثُمَّ يَأْخُذُ بِهِ رَجُلٌ مِنْ بَعْدِكَ فَيَعْلُو بِهِ، ثُمَّ يَأْخُذُ رَجُلٌ آخَرُ فَيَعْلُو بِهِ، ثُمَّ يَأْخُذُهُ رَجُلٌ آخَرُ فَيَنْقَطِعُ بِهِ ثُمَّ يُوَصَّلُ لَهُ فَيَعْلُو بِهِ، فَأَخْبِرْنِي يَا رَسُولَ اللَّهِ بِأَبِي أَنْتَ أَصَبْتُ أَمْ أَخْطَأْتُ. قَالَ النَّبِيُّ صلى الله عليه وسلم " أَصَبْتَ بَعْضًا وَأَخْطَأْتَ بَعْضًا ". قَالَ فَوَاللَّهِ لَتُحَدِّثَنِّي بِالَّذِي أَخْطَأْتُ. قَالَ " لاَ تُقْسِمْ ".

Narrated `Abdullah: The Prophet ﷺ said, "The people of my generation are the best, then those who follow them, and then whose who follow the latter. After that there will come some people whose witness will go ahead of their oaths, and their oaths will go ahead of their witness." Ibrahim (a sub-narrator) said, "We used to be beaten for taking oaths by saying, 'I bear witness by the Name of Allah or by the Covenant of Allah.". – Sahih Al-Bukhari 2652

حَدَّثَنَا مُحَمَّدُ بْنُ كَثِيرٍ، أَخْبَرَنَا سُفْيَانُ، عَنْ مَنْصُورٍ، عَنْ إِبْرَاهِيمَ، عَنْ عَبِيدَةَ، عَنْ عَبْدِ اللَّهِ ـ رضى الله عنه ـ عَنِ النَّبِيِّ صلى الله عليه وسلم قَالَ " خَيْرُ النَّاسِ قَرْنِي، ثُمَّ الَّذِينَ يَلُونَهُمْ، ثُمَّ الَّذِينَ يَلُونَهُمْ، ثُمَّ يَجِيءُ أَقْوَامٌ تَسْبِقُ شَهَادَةُ أَحَدِهِمْ يَمِينَهُ، وَيَمِينُهُ شَهَادَتَهُ ". قَالَ إِبْرَاهِيمُ وَكَانُوا يَضْرِبُونَنَا عَلَى الشَّهَادَةِ وَالْعَهْدِ.

Narrated Abu Sa`id Al-Khudri: The Prophet ﷺ said, "A time will come when groups of people will go for battle and it will be asked, 'Is there anyone amongst you who has enjoyed the company of the Prophet?' The answer will be, 'Yes.' Then they will be given victory (by Allah) (because of him). Then a time will come when it will be asked. 'Is there anyone amongst you who has enjoyed the company of the companions of the Prophet?' It will be said, 'Yes,' and they will be given victory (by Allah). Then a time will come when it will be said. 'Is there anyone amongst you who has enjoyed the company of the companions of the companions of the Prophet?' It will be said, 'Yes,' and they will be given victory (by Allah). – Sahih Al-Bukhari 2897

حَدَّثَنَا عَبْدُ اللَّهِ بْنُ مُحَمَّدٍ، حَدَّثَنَا سُفْيَانُ، عَنْ عَمْرٍو، سَمِعَ جَابِرًا، عَنْ أَبِي سَعِيدٍ الْخُدْرِيِّ ـ رضى الله عنهم ـ عَنِ النَّبِيِّ صلى الله عليه وسلم قَالَ " يَأْتِي زَمَانٌ يَغْزُو فِئَامٌ مِنَ النَّاسِ، فَيُقَالُ فِيكُمْ مَنْ صَحِبَ النَّبِيَّ صلى الله عليه وسلم فَيُقَالُ نَعَمْ. فَيُفْتَحُ عَلَيْهِ، ثُمَّ يَأْتِي زَمَانٌ فَيُقَالُ فِيكُمْ مَنْ صَحِبَ أَصْحَابَ النَّبِيِّ صلى الله عليه وسلم فَيُقَالُ نَعَمْ. فَيُفْتَحُ، ثُمَّ يَأْتِي زَمَانٌ فَيُقَالُ فِيكُمْ مَنْ صَحِبَ صَاحِبَ أَصْحَابِ النَّبِيِّ صلى الله عليه وسلم فَيُقَالُ نَعَمْ. فَيُفْتَحُ "

Narrated Zahdam bin Mudarrib: `Imran bin Husain said: The Prophet ﷺ said, "The best people are my contemporaries (i.e., the present (my) generation) and then those who come after them (i.e., the next generation)." `Imran added: I am not sure whether the Prophet ﷺ repeated the statement twice after his first saying. The Prophet ﷺ added, "And after them there will come people who will bear witness, though they will not be asked to give their witness; and they will be treacherous and nobody will trust them, and they will make vows, but will not fulfill them, and fatness will appear among them.". – Sahih Al-Bukhari 6428

حَدَّثَنِي مُحَمَّدُ بْنُ بَشَّارٍ، حَدَّثَنَا غُنْدَرٌ، حَدَّثَنَا شُعْبَةُ، قَالَ سَمِعْتُ أَبَا جَمْرَةَ، قَالَ حَدَّثَنِي زَهْدَمُ بْنُ مُضَرِّبٍ، قَالَ سَمِعْتُ عِمْرَانَ بْنَ حُصَيْنٍ ـ رضى الله عنهما ـ عَنِ النَّبِيِّ صلى الله عليه وسلم قَالَ " خَيْرُكُمْ قَرْنِي، ثُمَّ الَّذِينَ يَلُونَهُمْ، ثُمَّ الَّذِينَ يَلُونَهُمْ ". قَالَ عِمْرَانُ فَمَا أَدْرِي قَالَ النَّبِيُّ صلى الله عليه وسلم بَعْدَ قَوْلِهِ مَرَّتَيْنِ أَوْ ثَلاَثًا " ثُمَّ يَكُونُ بَعْدَهُمْ قَوْمٌ يَشْهَدُونَ وَلاَ يُسْتَشْهَدُونَ، وَيَخُونُونَ وَلاَ يُؤْتَمَنُونَ، وَيَنْذِرُونَ وَلاَ يَفُونَ وَيَظْهَرُ فِيهِمُ السِّمَنُ ".

Narrated `Abdullah: The Prophet ﷺ was asked, "Who are the best people?" He replied: The people of my generation, and then those who will follow (come after) them, and then those who will come after the later; after that there will come some people whose witness will precede their oaths and their oaths will go ahead of their witness." Ibrahim (a sub-narrator) said, "When we were young, our elder friends used to prohibit us from taking oaths by saying, 'I bear witness swearing by Allah, or by Allah's Covenant."'. – Sahih Al-Bukhari 6658
حَدَّثَنَا سَعْدُ بْنُ حَفْصٍ، حَدَّثَنَا شَيْبَانُ، عَنْ مَنْصُورٍ، عَنْ إِبْرَاهِيمَ، عَنْ عَبِيدَةَ، عَنْ عَبْدِ اللَّهِ، قَالَ سُئِلَ النَّبِيُّ صلى الله عليه وسلم أَىُّ النَّاسِ خَيْرٌ قَالَ " قَرْنِي، ثُمَّ الَّذِينَ يَلُونَهُمْ، ثُمَّ الَّذِينَ يَلُونَهُمْ، ثُمَّ يَجِيءُ قَوْمٌ تَسْبِقُ شَهَادَةُ أَحَدِهِمْ يَمِينَهُ، وَيَمِينُهُ شَهَادَتَهُ ". قَالَ إِبْرَاهِيمُ وَكَانَ أَصْحَابُنَا يَنْهَوْنَا وَنَحْنُ غِلْمَانٌ أَنْ نَحْلِفَ بِالشَّهَادَةِ وَالْعَهْدِ.

Narrated Ibn `Abbas: Allah's Messenger ﷺ (in his fatal illness) came out wrapped in a sheet covering his shoulders and his head was tied with an oily tape of cloth till he sat on the pulpit, and after praising and glorifying Allah, he said, "Then-after, O people! The people will go on increasing, but the Ansar will go on decreasing till they become just like salt in a meal. So whoever amongst you will be the ruler and have the power to harm or benefit others, should accept the good of the good-doers amongst them and excuse the wrongdoers amongst them." – Sahih al-Bukhari 3800
حَدَّثَنَا أَحْمَدُ بْنُ يَعْقُوبَ، حَدَّثَنَا ابْنُ الْغَسِيلِ، سَمِعْتُ عِكْرِمَةَ، يَقُولُ سَمِعْتُ ابْنَ عَبَّاسٍ ـ رضى الله عنهما ـ يَقُولُ خَرَجَ رَسُولُ اللَّهِ صلى الله عليه وسلم وَعَلَيْهِ مِلْحَفَةٌ، مُتَعَطِّفًا بِهَا عَلَى مَنْكِبَيْهِ، وَعَلَيْهِ عِصَابَةٌ دَسْمَاءُ حَتَّى جَلَسَ عَلَى الْمِنْبَرِ، فَحَمِدَ اللَّهَ وَأَثْنَى عَلَيْهِ، ثُمَّ قَالَ " أَمَّا بَعْدُ، أَيُّهَا النَّاسُ، فَإِنَّ النَّاسَ يَكْثُرُونَ وَتَقِلُّ الأَنْصَارُ، حَتَّى يَكُونُوا كَالْمِلْحِ فِي الطَّعَامِ، فَمَنْ وَلِيَ مِنْكُمْ أَمْرًا يَضُرُّ فِيهِ أَحَدًا أَوْ يَنْفَعُهُ، فَلْيَقْبَلْ مِنْ مُحْسِنِهِمْ، وَيَتَجَاوَزْ عَنْ مُسِيئِهِمْ

Except for the most faithful bondmen of Allah – Surah As-Saffat 37:40
إِلَّا عِبَادَ ٱللَّهِ ٱلْمُخْلَصِينَ

Except for the most faithful bondmen of Allah – Surah As-Saffat 37:74
إِلَّا عِبَادَ ٱللَّهِ ٱلْمُخْلَصِينَ

Except for the most faithful bondmen of Allah – Surah As-Saffat 37:128
إِلَّا عِبَادَ ٱللَّهِ ٱلْمُخْلَصِينَ

Except (for) the most faithful bondmen of Allah – Surah As-Saffat 37:160
إِلَّا عِبَادَ ٱللَّهِ ٱلْمُخْلَصِينَ

Excepting Your bondmen among them that are most faithful (to You)." – Surah Sad 38:83
إِلَّا عِبَادَكَ مِنْهُمُ ٱلْمُخْلَصِينَ

The Book of
Brief Musnad of influential Sahabah
مسند مختصر للصحابة المؤثرين

Abu Bakr
أَبِي بَكْرٍ

Narrated Abu Qatada: We set out in the company of Allah's Messenger ﷺ on the day (of the battle) of Hunain. When we faced the enemy, the Muslims retreated and I saw a pagan throwing himself over a Muslim. I turned around and came upon him from behind and hit him on the shoulder with the sword He (i.e. the pagan) came towards me and seized me so violently that I felt as if it were death itself, but death overtook him and he released me. I followed `Umar bin Al Khattab and asked (him), "What is wrong with the people (fleeing)?" He replied, "This is the Will of Allah," After the people returned, the Prophet ﷺ sat and said, "Anyone who has killed an enemy and has a proof of that, will posses his spoils." I got up and said, "Who will be a witness for me?" and then sat down. The Prophet ﷺ again said, "Anyone who has killed an enemy and has proof of that, will possess his spoils." I (again) got up and said, "Who will be a witness for me?" and sat down. Then the Prophet ﷺ said the same for the third time. I again got up, and Allah's Messenger ﷺ said, "O Abu Qatada! What is your story?" Then I narrated the whole story to him. A man (got up and) said, "O Allah's Messenger ﷺ! He is speaking the truth, and the spoils of the killed man are with me. So please compensate him on my behalf." On that Abu Bakr As-Siddiq said, "No, by Allah, he (i.e. Allah's Messenger ﷺ) will not agree to give you the spoils gained by one of Allah's Lions who fights on the behalf of Allah and His Apostle." The Prophet ﷺ said, "Abu Bakr has spoken the truth." So, Allah's Messenger ﷺ gave the spoils to me. I sold that armor (i.e. the spoils) and with its price I bought a garden at Bani Salima, and this was my first property which I gained after my conversion to Islam. – Sahih Al-Bukhari 3142

حَدَّثَنَا عَبْدُ اللَّهِ بْنُ مَسْلَمَةَ، عَنْ مَالِكٍ، عَنْ يَحْيَى بْنِ سَعِيدٍ، عَنِ ابْنِ أَفْلَحَ، عَنْ أَبِي مُحَمَّدٍ، مَوْلَى أَبِي قَتَادَةَ عَنْ أَبِي قَتَادَةَ ـ رضى الله عنه ـ قَالَ خَرَجْنَا مَعَ رَسُولِ اللَّهِ صلى الله عليه وسلم عَامَ حُنَيْنٍ، فَلَمَّا الْتَقَيْنَا كَانَتْ لِلْمُسْلِمِينَ جَوْلَةٌ، فَرَأَيْتُ رَجُلاً مِنَ الْمُشْرِكِينَ عَلاَ رَجُلاً مِنَ الْمُسْلِمِينَ، فَاسْتَدَرْتُ حَتَّى أَتَيْتُهُ مِنْ وَرَائِهِ حَتَّى ضَرَبْتُهُ بِالسَّيْفِ عَلَى حَبْلِ عَاتِقِهِ، فَأَقْبَلَ عَلَىَّ فَضَمَّنِي ضَمَّةً وَجَدْتُ مِنْهَا رِيحَ الْمَوْتِ، ثُمَّ أَدْرَكَهُ الْمَوْتُ فَأَرْسَلَنِي، فَلَحِقْتُ عُمَرَ بْنَ الْخَطَّابِ فَقُلْتُ مَا بَالُ النَّاسِ قَالَ أَمْرُ اللَّهِ، ثُمَّ إِنَّ النَّاسَ رَجَعُوا، وَجَلَسَ النَّبِيُّ صلى الله عليه وسلم فَقَالَ " مَنْ قَتَلَ قَتِيلاً لَهُ عَلَيْهِ بَيِّنَةٌ فَلَهُ سَلَبُهُ ". فَقُمْتُ فَقُلْتُ مَنْ يَشْهَدُ لِي ثُمَّ جَلَسْتُ ثُمَّ قَالَ " مَنْ قَتَلَ قَتِيلاً لَهُ عَلَيْهِ بَيِّنَةٌ فَلَهُ سَلَبُهُ " فَقُمْتُ فَقُلْتُ مَنْ يَشْهَدُ لِي ثُمَّ جَلَسْتُ، ثُمَّ قَالَ الثَّالِثَةَ مِثْلَهُ فَقَالَ رَجُلٌ صَدَقَ يَا رَسُولَ اللَّهِ، وَسَلَبُهُ عِنْدِي فَأَرْضِهِ عَنِّي. فَقَالَ أَبُو بَكْرٍ الصِّدِّيقُ ـ رضى الله عنه لاَهَا اللَّهِ إِذًا يَعْمِدُ إِلَى أَسَدٍ مِنْ أُسْدِ اللَّهِ يُقَاتِلُ عَنِ اللَّهِ وَرَسُولِهِ صلى الله عليه وسلم يُعْطِيكَ سَلَبَهُ. فَقَالَ النَّبِيُّ صلى الله عليه وسلم " صَدَقَ ". فَأَعْطَاهُ فَبِعْتُ الدِّرْعَ، فَابْتَعْتُ بِهِ مَخْرِفًا فِي بَنِي سَلِمَةَ، فَإِنَّهُ لأَوَّلُ مَالٍ تَأَثَّلْتُهُ فِي الإِسْلاَمِ

Narrated `Aisha: That during the Mina days, Abu Bakr came to her, while there where two girls with her, beating drums, and the Prophet ﷺ was (lying) covering himself with his garment. Abu Bakr rebuked the two girls, but the Prophet ﷺ uncovered his face and said, "O Abu Bakr! Leave them, for these are the days of Id (festival)." Those days were the days of Mina-. `Aisha added, "I was being screened by the Prophet ﷺ while I was watching the Ethiopians playing in the Mosque. `Umar rebuked them, but the Prophet ﷺ said, "Leave them, O Bani Arfida! Play. (for) you are safe.". – Sahih Al-Bukhari 3529, 3530

حَدَّثَنَا يَحْيَى بْنُ بُكَيْرٍ، حَدَّثَنَا اللَّيْثُ، عَنْ عُقَيْلٍ، عَنِ ابْنِ شِهَابٍ، عَنْ عُرْوَةَ، عَنْ عَائِشَةَ، أَنَّ أَبَا بَكْرٍ ـ رضى الله عنه ـ دَخَلَ عَلَيْهَا وَعِنْدَهَا جَارِيَتَانِ فِي أَيَّامِ مِنًى تُدَفِّفَانِ وَتَضْرِبَانِ، وَالنَّبِيُّ صلى الله عليه وسلم مُتَغَشٍّ بِثَوْبِهِ، فَانْتَهَرَهُمَا أَبُو بَكْرٍ،

فَكَشَفَ النَّبِيُّ صلى الله عليه وسلم عَنْ وَجْهِهِ، فَقَالَ " دَعْهُمَا يَا أَبَا بَكْرٍ، فَإِنَّهَا أَيَّامُ عِيدٍ، وَتِلْكَ الأَيَّامُ أَيَّامُ مِنًى ". وَقَالَتْ عَائِشَةُ رَأَيْتُ النَّبِيَّ صلى الله عليه وسلم يَسْتُرُنِي، وَأَنَا أَنْظُرُ إِلَى الْحَبَشَةِ، وَهُمْ يَلْعَبُونَ فِي الْمَسْجِدِ فَزَجَرَهُمْ {عُمَرُ} فَقَالَ النَّبِيُّ صلى الله عليه وسلم " دَعْهُمْ أَمْنًا بَنِي أَرْفَدَةَ ". يَعْنِي مِنَ الأَمْنِ

Narrated Abu `Uthman: `Abdur Rahman bin Abi Bakr said, "The Suffa Companions were poor people and the Prophet ﷺ said, 'Whoever has food for two persons should take a third one from them (Suffa companions). And whosoever has food for four persons he should take one or two from them' Abu Bakr took three men and the Prophet ﷺ took ten of them." `Abdur Rahman added, my father my mother and I were there (in the house). (The sub-narrator is in doubt whether `Abdur Rahman also said, 'My wife and our servant who was common for both my house and Abu Bakr's house). Abu Bakr took his supper with the Prophet ﷺ and remained there till the `Isha' prayer was offered. Abu Bakr went back and stayed with the Prophet ﷺ till the Prophet ﷺ took his meal and then Abu Bakr returned to his house after a long portion of the night had passed. Abu Bakr's wife said, 'What detained you from your guests (or guest)?' He said, 'Have you not served them yet?' She said, 'They refused to eat until you come. The food was served for them but they refused." `Abdur Rahman added, "I went away and hid myself (being afraid of Abu Bakr) and in the meantime he (Abu Bakr) called me, 'O Ghunthar (a harsh word)!' and also called me bad names and abused me and then said (to his family), 'Eat. No welcome for you.' Then (the supper was served). Abu Bakr took an oath that he would not eat that food. The narrator added: By Allah, whenever any one of us (myself and the guests of Suffa companions) took anything from the food, it increased from underneath. We all ate to our fill and the food was more than it was before its serving. Abu Bakr looked at it (the food) and found it as it was before serving or even more than that. He addressed his wife (saying) 'O the sister of Bani Firas! What is this?' She said, 'O the pleasure of my eyes! The food is now three times more than it was before.' Abu Bakr ate from it, and said, 'That (oath) was from Satan' meaning his oath (not to eat). Then he again took a morsel (mouthful) from it and then took the rest of it to the Prophet. So that meal was with the Prophet. There was a treaty between us and some people, and when the period of that treaty had elapsed the Prophet ﷺ divided us into twelve (groups) (the Prophet's companions) each being headed by a man. Allah knows how many men were under the command of each (leader). So all of them (12 groups of men) ate of that meal.". – Sahih Al-Bukhari 602

حَدَّثَنَا أَبُو النُّعْمَانِ، قَالَ حَدَّثَنَا مُعْتَمِرُ بْنُ سُلَيْمَانَ، قَالَ حَدَّثَنَا أَبِي، حَدَّثَنَا أَبُو عُثْمَانَ، عَنْ عَبْدِ الرَّحْمَنِ بْنِ أَبِي بَكْرٍ، أَنَّ أَصْحَابَ الصُّفَّةِ، كَانُوا أُنَاسًا فُقَرَاءَ، وَأَنَّ النَّبِيَّ صلى الله عليه وسلم قَالَ " مَنْ كَانَ عِنْدَهُ طَعَامُ اثْنَيْنِ فَلْيَذْهَبْ بِثَالِثٍ، وَإِنْ أَرْبَعٌ فَخَامِسٌ أَوْ سَادِسٌ ". وَأَنَّ أَبَا بَكْرٍ جَاءَ بِثَلاَثَةٍ فَانْطَلَقَ النَّبِيُّ صلى الله عليه وسلم بِعَشَرَةٍ، قَالَ فَهْوَ أَنَا وَأَبِي وَأُمِّي، فَلاَ أَدْرِي قَالَ وَامْرَأَتِي وَخَادِمٌ بَيْنَنَا وَبَيْنَ بَيْتِ أَبِي بَكْرٍ. وَإِنَّ أَبَا بَكْرٍ تَعَشَّى عِنْدَ النَّبِيِّ صلى الله عليه وسلم ثُمَّ لَبِثَ حَيْثُ صُلِّيَتِ الْعِشَاءُ، ثُمَّ رَجَعَ فَلَبِثَ حَتَّى تَعَشَّى النَّبِيُّ صلى الله عليه وسلم فَجَاءَ بَعْدَ مَا مَضَى مِنَ اللَّيْلِ مَا شَاءَ اللَّهُ، قَالَتْ لَهُ امْرَأَتُهُ وَمَا حَبَسَكَ عَنْ أَضْيَافِكَ ـ أَوْ قَالَتْ ضَيْفِكَ ـ قَالَ أَوَمَا عَشَّيْتِيهِمْ قَالَتْ أَبَوْا حَتَّى تَجِيءَ، قَدْ عُرِضُوا فَأَبَوْا. قَالَ فَذَهَبْتُ أَنَا فَاخْتَبَأْتُ فَقَالَ يَا غُنْثَرُ، فَجَدَّعَ وَسَبَّ، وَقَالَ كُلُوا لاَ هَنِيئًا. فَقَالَ وَاللَّهِ لاَ أَطْعَمُهُ أَبَدًا، وَايْمُ اللَّهِ مَا كُنَّا نَأْخُذُ مِنْ لُقْمَةٍ إِلاَّ رَبَا مِنْ أَسْفَلِهَا أَكْثَرُ مِنْهَا. قَالَ يَعْنِي حَتَّى شَبِعُوا وَصَارَتْ أَكْثَرَ مِمَّا كَانَتْ قَبْلَ ذَلِكَ، فَنَظَرَ إِلَيْهَا أَبُو بَكْرٍ فَإِذَا هِيَ كَمَا هِيَ أَوْ أَكْثَرُ مِنْهَا. فَقَالَ لاِمْرَأَتِهِ يَا أُخْتَ بَنِي فِرَاسٍ مَا هَذَا قَالَتْ لاَ وَقُرَّةِ عَيْنِي لَهِيَ الآنَ أَكْثَرُ مِنْهَا قَبْلَ ذَلِكَ بِثَلاَثِ مَرَّاتٍ. فَأَكَلَ مِنْهَا أَبُو بَكْرٍ وَقَالَ إِنَّمَا كَانَ ذَلِكَ مِنَ الشَّيْطَانِ ـ يَعْنِي يَمِينَهُ ـ ثُمَّ أَكَلَ مِنْهَا لُقْمَةً، ثُمَّ حَمَلَهَا إِلَى النَّبِيِّ صلى الله عليه وسلم فَأَصْبَحَتْ عِنْدَهُ، وَكَانَ بَيْنَنَا وَبَيْنَ قَوْمٍ عَقْدٌ، فَمَضَى الأَجَلُ، فَفَرَّقَنَا اثْنَا عَشَرَ رَجُلاً، مَعَ كُلِّ رَجُلٍ مِنْهُمْ أُنَاسٌ، اللَّهُ أَعْلَمُ كَمْ مَعَ كُلِّ رَجُلٍ فَأَكَلُوا مِنْهَا أَجْمَعُونَ، أَوْ كَمَا قَالَ.

Narrated Qais bin Abi Hazim: Abu Bakr went to a lady from the Ahmas tribe called Zainab bint Al-Muhajir and found that she refused to speak. He asked, "Why does she not speak." The people said, "She has intended to perform Hajj without speaking." He said to her, "Speak, for it is illegal not to speak, as it is an action of the pre-islamic period of ignorance. So she spoke and said, "Who are you?" He said, "A man from the Emigrants." She asked, "Which Emigrants?" He replied, "From Quraish." She asked, "From what branch of Quraish are you?" He said, "You ask too many questions; I am Abu Bakr." She said, "How long shall we enjoy this good order (i.e. Islamic religion) which Allah has brought after the period of ignorance?" He said, "You will enjoy it as long as your Imams keep on abiding by its rules and regulations." She asked, "What are the Imams?" He said, "Were there not heads and chiefs of your nation who used to order the people and they used to obey them?" She said, "Yes." He said, "So they (i.e. the Imams) are those whom I meant.". – Sahih Al-Bukhari 3834

حَدَّثَنَا أَبُو النُّعْمَانِ، حَدَّثَنَا أَبُو عَوَانَةَ، عَنْ بَيَانٍ أَبِي بِشْرٍ، عَنْ قَيْسِ بْنِ أَبِي حَازِمٍ، قَالَ دَخَلَ أَبُو بَكْرٍ عَلَى امْرَأَةٍ مِنْ أَحْمَسَ يُقَالُ لَهَا زَيْنَبُ، فَرَآهَا لاَ تَكَلَّمُ، فَقَالَ مَا لَهَا لاَ تَكَلَّمُ قَالُوا حَجَّتْ مُصْمِتَةً. قَالَ لَهَا تَكَلَّمِي، فَإِنَّ هَذَا لاَ يَحِلُّ، هَذَا مِنْ عَمَلِ الْجَاهِلِيَّةِ. فَتَكَلَّمَتْ، فَقَالَتْ مَنْ أَنْتَ قَالَ امْرُؤٌ مِنَ الْمُهَاجِرِينَ. قَالَتْ أَىُّ الْمُهَاجِرِينَ قَالَ مِنْ قُرَيْشٍ. قَالَتْ مِنْ أَىِّ قُرَيْشٍ أَنْتَ قَالَ إِنَّكِ لَسَئُولٌ أَنَا أَبُو بَكْرٍ. قَالَتْ مَا بَقَاؤُنَا عَلَى هَذَا الأَمْرِ الصَّالِحِ الَّذِي جَاءَ اللَّهُ بِهِ بَعْدَ الْجَاهِلِيَّةِ قَالَ بَقَاؤُكُمْ عَلَيْهِ مَا اسْتَقَامَتْ بِكُمْ أَئِمَّتُكُمْ. قَالَتْ وَمَا الأَئِمَّةُ قَالَ أَمَا كَانَ لِقَوْمِكِ رُءُوسٌ وَأَشْرَافٌ يَأْمُرُونَهُمْ فَيُطِيعُونَهُمْ قَالَتْ بَلَى. قَالَ فَهُمْ أُولَئِكَ عَلَى النَّاسِ

Narrated `Aisha: Abu Bakr had a slave who used to give him some of his earnings. Abu Bakr used to eat from it. One day he brought something and Abu Bakr ate from it. The slave said to him, "Do you know what this is?" Abu Bakr then enquired, "What is it?" The slave said, "Once, in the pre-Islamic period of ignorance I foretold somebody's future though I did not know this knowledge of foretelling but I, cheated him, and when he met me, he gave me something for that service, and that is what you have eaten from." Then Abu Bakr put his hand in his mouth and vomited whatever was present in his stomach. – Sahih Al-Bukhari 3842

حَدَّثَنَا إِسْمَاعِيلُ، حَدَّثَنِي أَخِي، عَنْ سُلَيْمَانَ، عَنْ يَحْيَى بْنِ سَعِيدٍ، عَنْ عَبْدِ الرَّحْمَنِ بْنِ الْقَاسِمِ، عَنِ الْقَاسِمِ بْنِ مُحَمَّدٍ، عَنْ عَائِشَةَ ـ رضى الله عنها ـ قَالَتْ كَانَ لأَبِي بَكْرٍ غُلاَمٌ يُخْرِجُ لَهُ الْخَرَاجَ، وَكَانَ أَبُو بَكْرٍ يَأْكُلُ مِنْ خَرَاجِهِ، فَجَاءَ يَوْمًا بِشَىْءٍ فَأَكَلَ مِنْهُ أَبُو بَكْرٍ فَقَالَ لَهُ الْغُلاَمُ تَدْرِي مَا هَذَا فَقَالَ أَبُو بَكْرٍ وَمَا هُوَ قَالَ كُنْتُ تَكَهَّنْتُ لإِنْسَانٍ فِي الْجَاهِلِيَّةِ وَمَا أُحْسِنُ الْكِهَانَةَ، إِلاَّ أَنِّي خَدَعْتُهُ، فَلَقِيَنِي فَأَعْطَانِي بِذَلِكَ، فَهَذَا الَّذِي أَكَلْتَ مِنْهُ. فَأَدْخَلَ أَبُو بَكْرٍ يَدَهُ فَقَاءَ كُلَّ شَىْءٍ فِي بَطْنِهِ

Narrated Abu Sa`id Al-Khudri: Allah's Messenger ﷺ sat on the pulpit and said, "Allah has given one of His Slaves the choice of receiving the splendor and luxury of the worldly life whatever he likes or to accept the good (of the Hereafter) which is with Allah. So he has chosen that good which is with Allah." On that Abu Bakr wept and said, "Our fathers and mothers be sacrificed for you." We became astonished at this. The people said, "Look at this old man! Allah's Messenger ﷺ talks about a Slave of Allah to whom He has given the option to choose either the splendor of this worldly life or the good which is with Him, while he says. 'our fathers and mothers be sacrifice(I for you." But it was Allah's Messenger ﷺ who had been given option, and Abu Bakr knew it better than we. Allah's Messenger ﷺ added, "No doubt, I am indebted to Abu Bakr more than to anybody else regarding both his companionship and his wealth. And if I had to take a Khalil from my followers, I would certainly have taken Abu Bakr, but the fraternity of Islam is. Sufficient. Let no door (i.e. Khoukha) of the Mosque remain open, except the door of Abu Bakr.". – Sahih Al-Bukhari 3904

حَدَّثَنَا إِسْمَاعِيلُ بْنُ عَبْدِ اللَّهِ، قَالَ حَدَّثَنِي مَالِكٌ، عَنْ أَبِي النَّضْرِ، مَوْلَى عُمَرَ بْنِ عُبَيْدِ اللَّهِ عَنْ عُبَيْدٍ ـ يَعْنِي ابْنَ حُنَيْنٍ ـ عَنْ أَبِي سَعِيدٍ الْخُدْرِيِّ، رضى الله عنه أَنَّ رَسُولَ اللَّهِ صلى الله عليه وسلم جَلَسَ عَلَى الْمِنْبَرِ فَقَالَ " إِنَّ عَبْدًا خَيَّرَهُ اللَّهُ بَيْنَ أَنْ يُؤْتِيَهُ مِنْ زَهْرَةِ الدُّنْيَا مَا شَاءَ، وَبَيْنَ مَا عِنْدَهُ، فَاخْتَارَ مَا عِنْدَهُ ". فَبَكَى أَبُو بَكْرٍ وَقَالَ فَدَيْنَاكَ بِآبَائِنَا وَأُمَّهَاتِنَا. فَعَجِبْنَا لَهُ، وَقَالَ النَّاسُ انْظُرُوا إِلَى هَذَا الشَّيْخِ، يُخْبِرُ رَسُولُ اللَّهِ صلى الله عليه وسلم عَنْ عَبْدٍ خَيَّرَهُ اللَّهُ بَيْنَ أَنْ يُؤْتِيَهُ مِنْ زَهْرَةِ الدُّنْيَا وَبَيْنَ مَا عِنْدَهُ وَهْوَ يَقُولُ فَدَيْنَاكَ بِآبَائِنَا وَأُمَّهَاتِنَا. فَكَانَ رَسُولُ اللَّهِ صلى الله عليه وسلم هُوَ الْمُخَيَّرَ، وَكَانَ أَبُو بَكْرٍ هُوَ

أَعْلَمَنَا بِهِ. وَقَالَ رَسُولُ اللَّهِ صلى الله عليه وسلم " إِنَّ مِنْ أَمَنِّ النَّاسِ عَلَىَّ فِي صُحْبَتِهِ وَمَالِهِ أَبَا بَكْرٍ، وَلَوْ كُنْتُ مُتَّخِذًا خَلِيلاً مِنْ أُمَّتِي لاَتَّخَذْتُ أَبَا بَكْرٍ، إِلاَّ خُلَّةَ الإِسْلاَمِ، لاَ يَبْقَيَنَّ فِي الْمَسْجِدِ خَوْخَةٌ إِلاَّ خَوْخَةُ أَبِي بَكْرٍ "

Narrated 'Aisha: (the wife of the Prophet) I never remembered my parents believing in any religion other than the true religion (i.e. Islam), and (I don't remember) a single day passing without our being visited by Allah's Messenger ﷺ in the morning and in the evening. When the Muslims were put to test (i.e. troubled by the pagans), Abu Bakr set out migrating to the land of Ethiopia, and when he reached Bark-al-Ghimad, Ibn Ad-Daghina, the chief of the tribe of Qara, met him and said, "O Abu Bakr! Where are you going?" Abu Bakr replied, "My people have turned me out (of my country), so I want to wander on the earth and worship my Lord." Ibn Ad-Daghina said, "O Abu Bakr! A man like you should not leave his home-land, nor should he be driven out, because you help the destitute, earn their livings, and you keep good relations with your Kith and kin, help the weak and poor, entertain guests generously, and help the calamity-stricken persons. Therefore I am your protector. Go back and worship your Lord in your town." So Abu Bakr returned and Ibn Ad-Daghina accompanied him. In the evening Ibn Ad-Daghina visited the nobles of Quraish and said to them. "A man like Abu Bakr should not leave his homeland, nor should he be driven out. Do you (i.e. Quraish) drive out a man who helps the destitute, earns their living, keeps good relations with his Kith and kin, helps the weak and poor, entertains guests generously and helps the calamity-stricken persons?" So the people of Quraish could not refuse Ibn Ad-Daghina's protection, and they said to Ibn Ad-Daghina, "Let Abu Bakr worship his Lord in his house. He can pray and recite there whatever he likes, but he should not hurt us with it, and should not do it publicly, because we are afraid that he may affect our women and children." Ibn Ad-Daghina told Abu Bakr of all that. Abu Bakr stayed in that state, worshipping his Lord in his house. He did not pray publicly, nor did he recite Quran outside his house. Then a thought occurred to Abu Bakr to build a mosque in front of his house, and there he used to pray and recite the Quran. The women and children of the pagans began to gather around him in great number. They used to wonder at him and look at him. Abu Bakr was a man who used to weep too much, and he could not help weeping on reciting the Quran. That situation scared the nobles of the pagans of Quraish, so they sent for Ibn Ad-Daghina. When he came to them, they said, "We accepted your protection of Abu Bakr on condition that he should worship his Lord in his house, but he has violated the conditions and he has built a mosque in front of his house where he prays and recites the Quran publicly. We are now afraid that he may affect our women and children unfavorably. So, prevent him from that. If he likes to confine the worship of his Lord to his house, he may do so, but if he insists on doing that openly, ask him to release you from your obligation to protect him, for we dislike to break our pact with you, but we deny Abu Bakr the right to announce his act publicly." Ibn Ad-Daghina went to Abu- Bakr and said, ("O Abu Bakr!) You know well what contract I have made on your behalf; now, you are either to abide by it, or else release me from my obligation of protecting you, because I do not want the 'Arabs hear that my people have dishonored a contract I have made on behalf of another man." Abu Bakr replied, "I release you from your pact to protect me, and am pleased with the protection from Allah." At that time the Prophet ﷺ was in Mecca, and he said to the Muslims, "In a dream I have been shown your migration place, a land of date palm trees, between two mountains, the two stony tracts." So, some people migrated to Medina, and most of those people who had previously migrated to the land of Ethiopia, returned to Medina. Abu Bakr also prepared to leave for Medina, but Allah's Messenger ﷺ said to him, "Wait for a while, because I hope that I will be allowed to migrate also." Abu Bakr said, "Do you indeed expect this? Let my father be sacrificed for you!" The Prophet ﷺ said, "Yes." So Abu Bakr did not migrate for the sake of Allah's Messenger ﷺ in order to accompany him. He fed two she-camels he possessed with the leaves of As-Samur tree that fell on being struck by a stick for four months. One day, while we were sitting in Abu Bakr's house at noon, someone said to Abu Bakr, "This is Allah's Messenger ﷺ with his head covered coming at a time at which he never used to visit us before." Abu Bakr said, "May my parents be sacrificed for him. By Allah, he has not come at this hour except for a great necessity." So Allah's Messenger ﷺ came and asked permission to enter, and he was allowed to enter. When he entered, he said to Abu Bakr. "Tell everyone who is present with you to go away." Abu Bakr replied, "There are none but your family. May my father be sacrificed for you, O Allah's Messenger ﷺ!" The Prophet ﷺ said, "I have been given permission to migrate." Abu Bakr said, "Shall I accompany you? May my father be sacrificed for you, O Allah's Messenger ﷺ!" Allah's Messenger ﷺ said, "Yes." Abu Bakr said, "O Allah's Messenger ﷺ! May my father be sacrificed for you, take one of these two she-camels of mine." Allah's Messenger ﷺ replied, "(I will accept it) with payment." So we prepared the baggage quickly and put some journey food in a leather bag for them. Asma, Abu Bakr's daughter, cut a piece from her waist belt and tied the mouth of the leather bag with it, and for that reason she was named Dhat-un-Nitaqain (i.e. the owner of two belts). Then Allah's Messenger ﷺ and Abu Bakr reached a cave on the mountain of Thaur and stayed there for three nights. 'Abdullah bin Abi Bakr who was intelligent and a sagacious youth, used to stay (with them) aver night. He used to leave them before day break so that in the morning he would be with Quraish as if he had spent the night in Mecca. He would keep in mind any plot made against them, and when it became dark he would (go and) inform them of it. 'Amir bin Fuhaira, the freed slave of Abu Bakr, used to bring the milch sheep (of his master, Abu Bakr) to them a little while after nightfall in order to rest the sheep there. So they always had fresh milk at night, the milk of their sheep, and the milk which they warmed by throwing heated stones in it. 'Amir bin Fuhaira would then call the herd away when it was still dark (before daybreak). He did the same in each of those three nights. Allah's Messenger ﷺ and Abu Bakr had hired a man from the tribe of Bani Ad-Dail from the family of Bani Abd bin Adi as an expert guide, and he was in alliance with the family of Al-'As bin Wail As-Sahmi and he was on the religion of the infidels of Quraish. The Prophet ﷺ and Abu Bakr trusted him and gave him their two she-camels and took his promise to bring their two she camels to the cave of the mountain of Thaur in the morning after three nights later. And (when they set out), 'Amir bin Fuhaira and the guide went along with them and the guide led them along the sea-shore. – Sahih Al-Bukhari 3905

حَدَّثَنَا يَحْيَى بْنُ بُكَيْرٍ، حَدَّثَنَا اللَّيْثُ، عَنْ عُقَيْلٍ، قَالَ ابْنُ شِهَابٍ فَأَخْبَرَنِي عُرْوَةُ بْنُ الزُّبَيْرِ، أَنَّ عَائِشَةَ ـ رضى الله عنها ـ زَوْجَ النَّبِيِّ صلى الله عليه وسلم قَالَتْ لَمْ أَعْقِلْ أَبَوَىَّ قَطُّ إِلاَّ وَهُمَا يَدِينَانِ الدِّينَ، وَلَمْ يَمُرَّ عَلَيْنَا يَوْمٌ إِلاَّ يَأْتِينَا فِيهِ رَسُولُ اللَّهِ صلى الله عليه وسلم طَرَفَىِ النَّهَارِ بُكْرَةً وَعَشِيَّةً، فَلَمَّا ابْتُلِيَ الْمُسْلِمُونَ خَرَجَ أَبُو بَكْرٍ مُهَاجِرًا نَحْوَ أَرْضِ الْحَبَشَةِ، حَتَّى بَلَغَ بَرْكَ الْغِمَادِ لَقِيَهُ ابْنُ الدَّغِنَةِ وَهْوَ سَيِّدُ الْقَارَةِ. فَقَالَ أَيْنَ تُرِيدُ يَا أَبَا بَكْرٍ فَقَالَ أَبُو بَكْرٍ أَخْرَجَنِي قَوْمِي، فَأُرِيدُ أَنْ أَسِيحَ فِي الأَرْضِ وَأَعْبُدَ رَبِّي. قَالَ ابْنُ الدَّغِنَةِ فَإِنَّ مِثْلَكَ يَا أَبَا بَكْرٍ لاَ يَخْرُجُ وَلاَ يُخْرَجُ، إِنَّكَ تَكْسِبُ الْمَعْدُومَ، وَتَصِلُ الرَّحِمَ وَتَحْمِلُ الْكَلَّ، وَتَقْرِي الضَّيْفَ، وَتُعِينُ عَلَى نَوَائِبِ الْحَقِّ، فَأَنَا لَكَ جَارٌ، ارْجِعْ وَاعْبُدْ رَبَّكَ بِبَلَدِكَ. فَرَجَعَ وَارْتَحَلَ مَعَهُ ابْنُ الدَّغِنَةِ، فَطَافَ ابْنُ الدَّغِنَةِ عَشِيَّةً فِي أَشْرَافِ قُرَيْشٍ، فَقَالَ لَهُمْ إِنَّ أَبَا بَكْرٍ لاَ يَخْرُجُ مِثْلُهُ وَلاَ يُخْرَجُ، أَتُخْرِجُونَ رَجُلاً يَكْسِبُ الْمَعْدُومَ، وَيَصِلُ الرَّحِمَ، وَيَحْمِلُ الْكَلَّ، وَيَقْرِي الضَّيْفَ، وَيُعِينُ عَلَى نَوَائِبِ الْحَقِّ فَلَمْ تُكَذِّبْ قُرَيْشٌ بِجِوَارِ ابْنِ الدَّغِنَةِ، وَقَالُوا لاِبْنِ الدَّغِنَةِ مُرْ أَبَا بَكْرٍ فَلْيَعْبُدْ رَبَّهُ فِي دَارِهِ، فَلْيُصَلِّ فِيهَا وَلْيَقْرَأْ مَا شَاءَ، وَلاَ يُؤْذِينَا بِذَلِكَ، وَلاَ يَسْتَعْلِنْ بِهِ، فَإِنَّا نَخْشَى أَنْ يَفْتِنَ نِسَاءَنَا وَأَبْنَاءَنَا. فَقَالَ ذَلِكَ ابْنُ الدَّغِنَةِ لأَبِي بَكْرٍ، فَلَبِثَ أَبُو بَكْرٍ بِذَلِكَ يَعْبُدُ رَبَّهُ فِي دَارِهِ، وَلاَ يَسْتَعْلِنُ بِصَلاَتِهِ، وَلاَ يَقْرَأُ فِي غَيْرِ دَارِهِ، ثُمَّ بَدَا لأَبِي بَكْرٍ فَابْتَنَى مَسْجِدًا بِفِنَاءِ دَارِهِ وَكَانَ يُصَلِّي فِيهِ وَيَقْرَأُ الْقُرْآنَ، فَيَنْقَذِفُ عَلَيْهِ نِسَاءُ الْمُشْرِكِينَ وَأَبْنَاؤُهُمْ، وَهُمْ يَعْجَبُونَ مِنْهُ، وَيَنْظُرُونَ إِلَيْهِ، وَكَانَ أَبُو بَكْرٍ رَجُلاً بَكَّاءً، لاَ يَمْلِكُ عَيْنَيْهِ إِذَا قَرَأَ الْقُرْآنَ، وَأَفْزَعَ ذَلِكَ أَشْرَافَ قُرَيْشٍ مِنَ الْمُشْرِكِينَ، فَأَرْسَلُوا إِلَى ابْنِ الدَّغِنَةِ، فَقَدِمَ عَلَيْهِمْ. فَقَالُوا إِنَّا كُنَّا أَجَرْنَا أَبَا بَكْرٍ بِجِوَارِكَ، عَلَى أَنْ يَعْبُدَ رَبَّهُ فِي دَارِهِ، فَقَدْ جَاوَزَ ذَلِكَ، فَابْتَنَى مَسْجِدًا بِفِنَاءِ دَارِهِ، فَأَعْلَنَ بِالصَّلاَةِ وَالْقِرَاءَةِ فِيهِ، وَإِنَّا قَدْ خَشِينَا أَنْ يَفْتِنَ نِسَاءَنَا وَأَبْنَاءَنَا فَانْهَهُ، فَإِنْ أَحَبَّ أَنْ يَقْتَصِرَ عَلَى أَنْ يَعْبُدَ رَبَّهُ فِي دَارِهِ فَعَلَ، وَإِنْ أَبَى إِلاَّ أَنْ يُعْلِنَ بِذَلِكَ فَسَلْهُ أَنْ يَرُدَّ إِلَيْكَ ذِمَّتَكَ، فَإِنَّا قَدْ كَرِهْنَا أَنْ نُخْفِرَكَ، وَلَسْنَا مُقِرِّينَ لأَبِي بَكْرٍ الاِسْتِعْلاَنَ. قَالَتْ عَائِشَةُ فَأَتَى ابْنُ الدَّغِنَةِ إِلَى أَبِي بَكْرٍ فَقَالَ قَدْ عَلِمْتَ الَّذِي عَاقَدْتُ لَكَ عَلَيْهِ، فَإِمَّا أَنْ تَقْتَصِرَ عَلَى ذَلِكَ، وَإِمَّا أَنْ تَرْجِعَ إِلَىَّ ذِمَّتِي، فَإِنِّي لاَ أُحِبُّ أَنْ تَسْمَعَ الْعَرَبُ أَنِّي أُخْفِرْتُ فِي رَجُلٍ عَقَدْتُ لَهُ. فَقَالَ أَبُو بَكْرٍ فَإِنِّي أَرُدُّ إِلَيْكَ جِوَارَكَ وَأَرْضَى بِجِوَارِ اللَّهِ عَزَّ وَجَلَّ.

وَالنَّبِيُّ صلى الله عليه وسلم يَوْمَئِذٍ بِمَكَّةَ، فَقَالَ النَّبِيُّ صلى الله عليه وسلم لِلْمُسْلِمِينَ " إِنِّي أُرِيتُ دَارَ هِجْرَتِكُمْ ذَاتَ نَخْلٍ بَيْنَ لاَبَتَيْنِ ". وَهُمَا الْحَرَّتَانِ، فَهَاجَرَ مَنْ هَاجَرَ قِبَلَ الْمَدِينَةِ، وَرَجَعَ عَامَّةُ مَنْ كَانَ هَاجَرَ بِأَرْضِ الْحَبَشَةِ إِلَى الْمَدِينَةِ، وَتَجَهَّزَ أَبُو بَكْرٍ قِبَلَ الْمَدِينَةِ، فَقَالَ لَهُ رَسُولُ اللَّهِ صلى الله عليه وسلم " عَلَى رِسْلِكَ، فَإِنِّي أَرْجُو أَنْ يُؤْذَنَ لِي ". فَقَالَ أَبُو بَكْرٍ وَهَلْ تَرْجُو ذَلِكَ بِأَبِي أَنْتَ قَالَ " نَعَمْ ". فَحَبَسَ أَبُو بَكْرٍ نَفْسَهُ عَلَى رَسُولِ اللَّهِ صلى الله عليه وسلم لِيَصْحَبَهُ، وَعَلَفَ رَاحِلَتَيْنِ كَانَتَا عِنْدَهُ وَرَقَ السَّمُرِ وَهْوَ الْخَبَطُ أَرْبَعَةَ أَشْهُرٍ. قَالَ ابْنُ شِهَابٍ قَالَ عُرْوَةُ قَالَتْ عَائِشَةُ فَبَيْنَمَا نَحْنُ يَوْمًا جُلُوسٌ فِي بَيْتِ أَبِي بَكْرٍ فِي نَحْرِ الظَّهِيرَةِ قَالَ قَائِلٌ لأَبِي بَكْرٍ هَذَا رَسُولُ اللَّهِ صلى الله عليه وسلم مُتَقَنِّعًا ـ فِي سَاعَةٍ لَمْ يَكُنْ يَأْتِينَا فِيهَا ـ فَقَالَ أَبُو بَكْرٍ فِدَاءٌ لَهُ أَبِي وَأُمِّي، وَاللَّهِ مَا جَاءَ بِهِ فِي هَذِهِ السَّاعَةِ إِلاَّ أَمْرٌ. قَالَتْ فَجَاءَ رَسُولُ اللَّهِ صلى الله عليه وسلم فَاسْتَأْذَنَ، فَأُذِنَ لَهُ فَدَخَلَ، فَقَالَ النَّبِيُّ صلى الله عليه وسلم لأَبِي بَكْرٍ " أَخْرِجْ مَنْ عِنْدَكَ ". فَقَالَ أَبُو بَكْرٍ إِنَّمَا هُمْ أَهْلُكَ بِأَبِي أَنْتَ يَا رَسُولَ اللَّهِ. قَالَ " فَإِنِّي قَدْ أُذِنَ لِي فِي الْخُرُوجِ ". فَقَالَ أَبُو بَكْرٍ الصَّحَابَةُ بِأَبِي أَنْتَ يَا رَسُولَ اللَّهِ. قَالَ رَسُولُ اللَّهِ صلى الله عليه وسلم " نَعَمْ ". قَالَ أَبُو بَكْرٍ فَخُذْ بِأَبِي أَنْتَ يَا رَسُولَ اللَّهِ إِحْدَى رَاحِلَتَىَّ هَاتَيْنِ. قَالَ رَسُولُ اللَّهِ صلى الله عليه وسلم " بِالثَّمَنِ ". قَالَتْ عَائِشَةُ فَجَهَّزْنَاهُمَا أَحَثَّ الْجِهَازِ، وَصَنَعْنَا لَهُمَا سُفْرَةً فِي جِرَابٍ، فَقَطَعَتْ أَسْمَاءُ بِنْتُ أَبِي بَكْرٍ قِطْعَةً مِنْ نِطَاقِهَا فَرَبَطَتْ بِهِ عَلَى فَمِ الْجِرَابِ، فَبِذَلِكَ سُمِّيَتْ ذَاتَ النِّطَاقِ ـ قَالَتْ ـ ثُمَّ لَحِقَ رَسُولُ اللَّهِ صلى الله عليه وسلم وَأَبُو بَكْرٍ بِغَارٍ فِي جَبَلِ ثَوْرٍ فَكَمَنَا فِيهِ ثَلاَثَ لَيَالٍ، يَبِيتُ عِنْدَهُمَا عَبْدُ اللَّهِ بْنُ أَبِي بَكْرٍ وَهْوَ غُلاَمٌ شَابٌّ ثَقِفٌ لَقِنٌ، فَيُدْلِجُ مِنْ عِنْدِهِمَا بِسَحَرٍ، فَيُصْبِحُ مَعَ قُرَيْشٍ بِمَكَّةَ كَبَائِتٍ، فَلاَ يَسْمَعُ أَمْرًا يُكْتَادَانِ بِهِ إِلاَّ وَعَاهُ، حَتَّى يَأْتِيَهُمَا بِخَبَرِ ذَلِكَ حِينَ يَخْتَلِطُ الظَّلاَمُ، وَيَرْعَى عَلَيْهِمَا عَامِرُ بْنُ فُهَيْرَةَ مَوْلَى أَبِي بَكْرٍ مِنْحَةً مِنْ غَنَمٍ، فَيُرِيحُهَا عَلَيْهِمَا حِينَ يَذْهَبُ سَاعَةٌ مِنَ الْعِشَاءِ، فَيَبِيتَانِ فِي رِسْلٍ وَهْوَ لَبَنُ مِنْحَتِهِمَا وَرَضِيفِهِمَا، حَتَّى يَنْعِقَ بِهَا عَامِرُ بْنُ فُهَيْرَةَ بِغَلَسٍ، يَفْعَلُ ذَلِكَ فِي كُلِّ لَيْلَةٍ مِنْ تِلْكَ اللَّيَالِي الثَّلاَثِ، وَاسْتَأْجَرَ رَسُولُ اللَّهِ صلى الله عليه وسلم وَأَبُو بَكْرٍ رَجُلاً مِنْ بَنِي الدِّيلِ، وَهْوَ مِنْ بَنِي عَبْدِ بْنِ عَدِيٍّ هَادِيًا خِرِّيتًا ـ وَالْخِرِّيتُ الْمَاهِرُ بِالْهِدَايَةِ ـ قَدْ غَمَسَ حِلْفًا فِي آلِ الْعَاصِ بْنِ وَائِلٍ السَّهْمِيِّ، وَهْوَ عَلَى دِينِ كُفَّارِ قُرَيْشٍ فَأَمِنَاهُ، فَدَفَعَا إِلَيْهِ رَاحِلَتَيْهِمَا، وَوَاعَدَاهُ غَارَ ثَوْرٍ بَعْدَ ثَلاَثِ لَيَالٍ بِرَاحِلَتَيْهِمَا صُبْحَ ثَلاَثٍ، وَانْطَلَقَ مَعَهُمَا عَامِرُ بْنُ فُهَيْرَةَ وَالدَّلِيلُ فَأَخَذَ بِهِمْ طَرِيقَ السَّوَاحِلِ

Al-Bara added: I then went with Abu Bakr into his home (carrying that saddle) and there I saw his daughter `Aisha Lying in a bed because of heavy fever and I saw her father Abu Bakr kissing her cheek and saying, “How are you, little daughter?”. – Sahih Al-Bukhari 3918

قَالَ الْبَرَاءُ فَدَخَلْتُ مَعَ أَبِي بَكْرٍ عَلَى أَهْلِهِ، فَإِذَا عَائِشَةُ ابْنَتُهُ مُضْطَجِعَةٌ، قَدْ أَصَابَتْهَا حُمَّى، فَرَأَيْتُ أَبَاهَا فَقَبَّلَ خَدَّهَا، وَقَالَ كَيْفَ أَنْتِ يَا بُنَيَّةُ

Narrated `Aisha: Fatima and Al-`Abbas came to Abu Bakr, claiming their inheritance of the Prophet’s land of Fadak and his share from Khaibar. Abu Bakr said, “I heard the Prophet ﷺ saying, ‘Our property is not inherited, and whatever we leave is to be given in charity. But the family of Muhammad can take their sustenance from this property.’ By Allah, I would love to do good to the Kith and kin of Allah’s Apostle rather than to my own Kith and kin.”. – Sahih Al-Bukhari 4035, 4036

حَدَّثَنَا إِبْرَاهِيمُ بْنُ مُوسَى، أَخْبَرَنَا هِشَامٌ، أَخْبَرَنَا مَعْمَرٌ، عَنِ الزُّهْرِيِّ، عَنْ عُرْوَةَ، عَنْ عَائِشَةَ، أَنَّ فَاطِمَةَ ـ عَلَيْهَا السَّلاَمُ ـ وَالْعَبَّاسَ أَتَيَا أَبَا بَكْرٍ يَلْتَمِسَانِ مِيرَاثَهُمَا، أَرْضَهُ مِنْ فَدَكٍ، وَسَهْمَهُ مِنْ خَيْبَرَ. فَقَالَ أَبُو بَكْرٍ سَمِعْتُ النَّبِيَّ صلى الله عليه وسلم يَقُولُ " لاَ نُورَثُ، مَا تَرَكْنَا صَدَقَةٌ، إِنَّمَا يَأْكُلُ آلُ مُحَمَّدٍ فِي هَذَا الْمَالِ ". وَاللَّهِ لَقَرَابَةُ رَسُولِ اللَّهِ صلى الله عليه وسلم أَحَبُّ إِلَىَّ أَنْ أَصِلَ مِنْ قَرَابَتِي

Narrated `Aisha: Regarding the Holy Verse: “Those who responded (To the call) of Allah And the Apostle (Muhammad), After being wounded, For those of them Who did good deeds And refrained from wrong, there is a great reward.” (3.172) She said to `Urwa, “O my nephew! Your father, Az-Zubair and Abu Bakr were amongst them (i.e. those who responded to the call of Allah and the Apostle on the day (of the battle of Uhud). When Allah’s Messenger ﷺ, suffered what he suffered on the day of Uhud and the pagans left, the Prophet ﷺ was afraid that they might return. So he said, ‘Who will go on their (i.e. pagans’) track?’ He then selected seventy men from amongst them (for this purpose).” (The sub-narrator added, “Abu Bakr and Az- Zubair were amongst them.”). – Sahih Al-Bukhari 4077

حَدَّثَنَا مُحَمَّدٌ، حَدَّثَنَا أَبُو مُعَاوِيَةَ، عَنْ هِشَامٍ، عَنْ أَبِيهِ، عَنْ عَائِشَةَ ـ رضى الله عنها {الَّذِينَ اسْتَجَابُوا لله وَالرَّسُولِ مِنْ بَعْدِ مَا أَصَابَهُمُ الْقَرْحُ لِلَّذِينَ أَحْسَنُوا مِنْهُمْ وَاتَّقَوْا أَجْرٌ عَظِيمٌ} قَالَتْ لِعُرْوَةَ يَا ابْنَ أُخْتِي كَانَ أَبُوكَ مِنْهُمُ الزُّبَيْرُ وَأَبُو بَكْرٍ، لَمَّا أَصَابَ رَسُولَ اللَّهِ صلى الله عليه وسلم مَا أَصَابَ يَوْمَ أُحُدٍ، وَانْصَرَفَ عَنْهُ الْمُشْرِكُونَ خَافَ أَنْ يَرْجِعُوا قَالَ " مَنْ يَذْهَبُ فِي إِثْرِهِمْ ". فَانْتَدَبَ مِنْهُمْ سَبْعُونَ رَجُلاً، قَالَ كَانَ فِيهِمْ أَبُو بَكْرٍ وَالزُّبَيْرُ.

Narrated Salama bin Al-Akwa`: I fought in seven Ghazwat (i.e. battles) along with the Prophet ﷺ and fought in nine battles, fought by armies dispatched by the Prophet. Once Abu

Bakr was our commander and at another time, Usama was our commander. – Sahih Al-Bukhari 4270

حَدَّثَنَا قُتَيْبَةُ بْنُ سَعِيدٍ، حَدَّثَنَا حَاتِمٌ، عَنْ يَزِيدَ بْنِ أَبِي عُبَيْدٍ، قَالَ سَمِعْتُ سَلَمَةَ بْنَ الأَكْوَعِ، يَقُولُ غَزَوْتُ مَعَ النَّبِيِّ صلى الله عليه وسلم سَبْعَ غَزَوَاتٍ، وَخَرَجْتُ فِيمَا يَبْعَثُ مِنَ الْبُعُوثِ تِسْعَ غَزَوَاتٍ، مَرَّةً عَلَيْنَا أَبُو بَكْرٍ، وَمَرَّةً عَلَيْنَا أُسَامَةُ.

Narrated Abu Huraira: That during the Hajj in which the Prophetﷺ had made Abu Bakr As Siddiq as chief of the, Hajj before the Hajj-ul-Wida,' on the day of Nahr, Abu Bakr sent him along with a group of persons to announce to the people. "No pagan is permitted to perform Hajj after this year, and nobody is permitted to perform the Tawaf of the Ka`ba naked.". – Sahih Al-Bukhari 4363

حَدَّثَنَا سُلَيْمَانُ بْنُ دَاوُدَ أَبُو الرَّبِيعِ، حَدَّثَنَا فُلَيْحٌ، عَنِ الزُّهْرِيِّ، عَنْ حُمَيْدِ بْنِ عَبْدِ الرَّحْمَنِ، عَنْ أَبِي هُرَيْرَةَ، أَنَّ أَبَا بَكْرٍ الصِّدِّيقَ ـ رضى الله عنه ـ بَعَثَهُ فِي الْحَجَّةِ الَّتِي أَمَّرَهُ النَّبِيُّ صلى الله عليه وسلم قَبْلَ حَجَّةِ الْوَدَاعِ يَوْمَ النَّحْرِ فِي رَهْطٍ يُؤَذِّنُ فِي النَّاسِ لاَ يَحُجُّ بَعْدَ الْعَامِ مُشْرِكٌ وَلاَ يَطُوفُ بِالْبَيْتِ عُرْيَانٌ

Narrated 'Urwa: The Prophetﷺ asked Abu Bakr for `Aisha's hand in marriage. Abu Bakr said "But I am your brother." The Prophetﷺ said, "You are my brother in Allah's religion and His Book, but she (Aisha) is lawful for me to marry.". – Sahih Al-Bukhari 5081

حَدَّثَنَا عَبْدُ اللَّهِ بْنُ يُوسُفَ، حَدَّثَنَا اللَّيْثُ، عَنْ يَزِيدَ، عَنْ عِرَاكٍ، عَنْ عُرْوَةَ، أَنَّ النَّبِيَّ صلى الله عليه وسلم خَطَبَ عَائِشَةَ إِلَى أَبِي بَكْرٍ فَقَالَ لَهُ أَبُو بَكْرٍ إِنَّمَا أَنَا أَخُوكَ، فَقَالَ " أَنْتَ أَخِي فِي دِينِ اللَّهِ وَكِتَابِهِ وَهْىَ لِي حَلاَلٌ ".

Narrated Ibn Abi Mulaika: The two righteous persons were about to be ruined. They were Abu Bakr and `Umar who raised their voices in the presence of the Prophetﷺ when a mission from Bani Tamim came to him. One of the two recommended Al-Aqra' bin Habeas, the brother of Bani Mujashi (to be their governor) while the other recommended somebody else. (Nafi`, the sub-narrator said, I do not remember his name). Abu Bakr said to `Umar, "You wanted nothing but to oppose me!" `Umar said, "I did not intend to oppose you." Their voices grew loud in that argument, so Allah revealed: 'O you who believe! Raise not your voices above the voice of the Prophet.' (49.2) Ibn Az-Zubair said, "Since the revelation of this Verse, `Umar used to speak in such a low tone that the Prophetﷺ had to ask him to repeat his statements." But Ibn Az-Zubair did not mention the same about his (maternal) grandfather (i.e. Abu Bakr). – Sahih Al-Bukhari 4845

حَدَّثَنَا يَسَرَةُ بْنُ صَفْوَانَ بْنِ جَمِيلٍ اللَّخْمِيُّ، حَدَّثَنَا نَافِعُ بْنُ عُمَرَ، عَنِ ابْنِ أَبِي مُلَيْكَةَ، قَالَ كَادَ الْخَيِّرَانِ أَنْ يَهْلِكَا ـ أَبَا بَكْرٍ وَعُمَرَ ـ رضى الله عنهما ـ رَفَعَا أَصْوَاتَهُمَا عِنْدَ النَّبِيِّ صلى الله عليه وسلم حِينَ قَدِمَ عَلَيْهِ رَكْبُ بَنِي تَمِيمٍ، فَأَشَارَ أَحَدُهُمَا بِالأَقْرَعِ بْنِ حَابِسٍ أَخِي بَنِي مُجَاشِعٍ، وَأَشَارَ الآخَرُ بِرَجُلٍ آخَرَ ـ قَالَ نَافِعٌ لاَ أَحْفَظُ اسْمَهُ ـ فَقَالَ أَبُو بَكْرٍ لِعُمَرَ مَا أَرَدْتَ إِلاَّ خِلاَفِي‏.‏ قَالَ مَا أَرَدْتُ خِلاَفَكَ‏.‏ فَارْتَفَعَتْ أَصْوَاتُهُمَا فِي ذَلِكَ، فَأَنْزَلَ اللَّهُ ‏{‏يَا أَيُّهَا الَّذِينَ آمَنُوا لاَ تَرْفَعُوا أَصْوَاتَكُمْ‏}‏ الآيَةَ‏.‏ قَالَ ابْنُ الزُّبَيْرِ فَمَا كَانَ عُمَرُ يُسْمِعُ رَسُولَ اللَّهِ صلى الله عليه وسلم بَعْدَ هَذِهِ الآيَةِ حَتَّى يَسْتَفْهِمَهُ‏.‏ وَلَمْ يَذْكُرْ ذَلِكَ عَنْ أَبِيهِ، يَعْنِي أَبَا بَكْرٍ

Narrated `Abbas: Allah's Messengerﷺ while in a tent on the day of the Battle of Badr, said, "O Allah! I request you (to fulfill) Your promise and contract! O Allah! If You wish that you will not be worshipped henceforth.." On that Abu Bakr held the Prophetﷺ by the hand and said, "That is enough, O Allah's Messengerﷺ You have appealed to your Lord too pressingly," while the Prophetﷺ was putting on his armor. So Allah's Messengerﷺ went out, reciting Their multitude will be put to flight, and they will show their backs.' (54.45). – Sahih Al-Bukhari 4875

حَدَّثَنَا مُحَمَّدُ بْنُ عَبْدِ اللَّهِ بْنِ حَوْشَبٍ، حَدَّثَنَا عَبْدُ الْوَهَّابِ، حَدَّثَنَا خَالِدٌ، عَنْ عِكْرِمَةَ، عَنِ ابْنِ عَبَّاسٍ، وَحَدَّثَنِي مُحَمَّدٌ، حَدَّثَنَا عَفَّانُ بْنُ مُسْلِمٍ، عَنْ وُهَيْبٍ، حَدَّثَنَا خَالِدٌ، عَنْ عِكْرِمَةَ، عَنِ ابْنِ عَبَّاسٍ ـ رضى الله عنهما ـ أَنَّ رَسُولَ اللَّهِ صلى الله عليه وسلم قَالَ وَهْوَ فِي قُبَّةٍ يَوْمَ بَدْرٍ " اللَّهُمَّ إِنِّي أَنْشُدُكَ عَهْدَكَ وَوَعْدَكَ، اللَّهُمَّ إِنْ تَشَأْ لاَ تُعْبَدْ بَعْدَ الْيَوْمِ ". فَأَخَذَ أَبُو بَكْرٍ بِيَدِهِ فَقَالَ حَسْبُكَ يَا رَسُولَ اللَّهِ، أَلْحَحْتَ عَلَى رَبِّكَ. وَهْوَ يَثِبُ فِي الدِّرْعِ، فَخَرَجَ وَهْوَ يَقُولُ " {سَيُهْزَمُ الْجَمْعُ وَيُوَلُّونَ الدُّبُرَ}.

Narrated Az-Zuhri: I heard `Urwa bin Az-Zubair, Sa`id bin Al-Musaiyab, 'Alqama bin Waqqas and 'Ubaidullah bin `Abdullah bin `Uqba relating from `Aisha, the wife of the Prophet ﷺ the narration of the people (i.e. the liars) who spread the slander against her and they said what they said, and how Allah revealed her innocence. Each of them related to me a portion of that narration. (They said that `Aisha said), "Then Allah revealed the ten Verses starting with:--'Verily! Those who spread the slander..' (24.11-21) All these verses were in proof of my innocence. Abu Bakr As-Siddiq who used to provide for Mistah some financial aid because of his relation to him, said, "By Allah, I will never give anything (in charity) to Mistah, after what he has said about `Aisha" Then Allah revealed:-- 'And let not those among you who are good and are wealthy swear not to give (any sort of help) to their kins men....' (24.22) On that, Abu Bakr said, "Yes, by Allah, I like that Allah should forgive me." And then resumed giving Mistah the aid he used to give him and said, "By Allah! I will never withhold it from him.". – Sahih Al-Bukhari 6679

حَدَّثَنَا عَبْدُ الْعَزِيزِ، حَدَّثَنَا إِبْرَاهِيمُ، عَنْ صَالِحٍ، عَنِ ابْنِ شِهَابٍ، ح وَحَدَّثَنَا الْحَجَّاجُ، حَدَّثَنَا عَبْدُ اللَّهِ بْنُ عُمَرَ النُّمَيْرِيُّ، حَدَّثَنَا يُونُسُ بْنُ يَزِيدَ الأَيْلِيُّ، قَالَ سَمِعْتُ الزُّهْرِيَّ، قَالَ سَمِعْتُ عُرْوَةَ بْنَ الزُّبَيْرِ، وَسَعِيدَ بْنَ الْمُسَيَّبِ، وَعَلْقَمَةَ بْنَ وَقَّاصٍ، وَعُبَيْدَ اللَّهِ بْنَ عَبْدِ اللَّهِ بْنِ عُتْبَةَ، عَنْ حَدِيثِ، عَائِشَةَ زَوْجِ النَّبِيِّ صلى الله عليه وسلم حِينَ قَالَ لَهَا أَهْلُ الإِفْكِ مَا قَالُوا، فَبَرَّأَهَا اللَّهُ مِمَّا قَالُوا ـ كُلٌّ حَدَّثَنِي طَائِفَةً مِنَ الْحَدِيثِ ـ فَأَنْزَلَ اللَّهُ {إِنَّ الَّذِينَ جَاءُوا بِالإِفْكِ} الْعَشْرَ الآيَاتِ كُلَّهَا فِي بَرَاءَتِي. فَقَالَ أَبُو بَكْرٍ الصِّدِّيقُ ـ وَكَانَ يُنْفِقُ عَلَى مِسْطَحٍ لِقَرَابَتِهِ مِنْهُ ـ وَاللَّهِ لاَ أُنْفِقُ عَلَى مِسْطَحٍ شَيْئًا أَبَدًا، بَعْدَ الَّذِي قَالَ لِعَائِشَةَ. فَأَنْزَلَ اللَّهُ {وَلاَ يَأْتَلِ أُولُو الْفَضْلِ مِنْكُمْ وَالسَّعَةِ أَنْ يُؤْتُوا أُولِي الْقُرْبَى} الآيَةَ. قَالَ أَبُو بَكْرٍ بَلَى وَاللَّهِ إِنِّي لأُحِبُّ أَنْ يَغْفِرَ اللَّهُ لِي. فَرَجَعَ إِلَى مِسْطَحٍ النَّفَقَةَ الَّتِي كَانَ يُنْفِقُ عَلَيْهِ وَقَالَ وَاللَّهِ لاَ أَنْزِعُهَا عَنْهُ أَبَدًا

Narrated Abu Huraira: When the Prophet ﷺ died and Abu Bakr became his successor and some of the Arabs reverted to disbelief, `Umar said, "O Abu Bakr! How can you fight these people although Allah's Messenger ﷺ said, 'I have been ordered to fight the people till they say: 'None has the right to be worshipped but Allah, 'and whoever said, 'None has the right to be worshipped but Allah', Allah will save his property and his life from me, unless (he does something for which he receives legal punishment) justly, and his account will be with Allah?' "Abu Bakr said, "By Allah! I will fight whoever differentiates between prayers and Zakat as Zakat is the right to be taken from property (according to Allah's Orders). By Allah! If they refused to pay me even a kid they used to pay to Allah's Messenger ﷺ, I would fight with them for withholding it." `Umar said, "By Allah: It was nothing, but I noticed that Allah opened Abu Bakr's chest towards the decision to fight, therefore I realized that his decision was right.". – Sahih Al-Bukhari 6924, 6925

حَدَّثَنَا يَحْيَى بْنُ بُكَيْرٍ، حَدَّثَنَا اللَّيْثُ، عَنْ عُقَيْلٍ، عَنِ ابْنِ شِهَابٍ، أَخْبَرَنِي عُبَيْدُ اللَّهِ بْنُ عَبْدِ اللَّهِ بْنِ عُتْبَةَ، أَنَّ أَبَا هُرَيْرَةَ، قَالَ لَمَّا تُوُفِّيَ النَّبِيُّ صلى الله عليه وسلم وَاسْتُخْلِفَ أَبُو بَكْرٍ، وَكَفَرَ مَنْ كَفَرَ مِنَ الْعَرَبِ، قَالَ عُمَرُ يَا أَبَا بَكْرٍ، كَيْفَ تُقَاتِلُ النَّاسَ، وَقَدْ قَالَ رَسُولُ اللَّهِ صلى الله عليه وسلم " أُمِرْتُ أَنْ أُقَاتِلَ النَّاسَ حَتَّى يَقُولُوا لاَ إِلَهَ إِلاَّ اللَّهُ. فَمَنْ قَالَ لاَ إِلَهَ إِلاَّ اللَّهُ. عَصَمَ مِنِّي مَالَهُ وَنَفْسَهُ، إِلاَّ بِحَقِّهِ، وَحِسَابُهُ عَلَى اللَّهِ ". قَالَ أَبُو بَكْرٍ وَاللَّهِ لأُقَاتِلَنَّ مَنْ فَرَّقَ بَيْنَ الصَّلاَةِ وَالزَّكَاةِ، فَإِنَّ الزَّكَاةَ حَقُّ الْمَالِ، وَاللَّهِ لَوْ مَنَعُونِي عَنَاقًا كَانُوا يُؤَدُّونَهَا إِلَى رَسُولِ اللَّهِ صلى الله عليه وسلم لَقَاتَلْتُهُمْ عَلَى مَنْعِهَا. قَالَ عُمَرُ فَوَاللَّهِ مَا هُوَ إِلاَّ أَنْ رَأَيْتُ أَنْ قَدْ شَرَحَ اللَّهُ صَدْرَ أَبِي بَكْرٍ لِلْقِتَالِ فَعَرَفْتُ أَنَّهُ الْحَقُّ.

Narrate Aisha: Abu Bakr married a woman from the tribe of Bani Kalb, called Um Bakr. When Abu Bakr migrated to Medina, he divorced her and she was married by her cousin, the poet who said the following poem lamenting the infidels of Quraish: "What is there kept in the well, The well of Badr, (The owners of) the trays of Roasted camel humps? What is there kept in the well, The well of Badr, (The owners of) lady singers And friends of the honorable companions; who used to drink (wine) together, Um Bakr greets us With the greeting of peace, But can I find peace After my people have gone? The Apostle tells us that We shall live again, But what sort of life will owls and skulls live?: - Sahih Al-Bukhari 3921

حَدَّثَنَا أَصْبَغُ، حَدَّثَنَا ابْنُ وَهْبٍ، عَنْ يُونُسَ، عَنِ ابْنِ شِهَابٍ، عَنْ عُرْوَةَ بْنِ الزُّبَيْرِ، عَنْ عَائِشَةَ، أَنَّ أَبَا بَكْرٍ ـ رضى الله عنه ـ تَزَوَّجَ امْرَأَةً مِنْ كَلْبٍ يُقَالُ لَهَا أُمُّ بَكْرٍ، فَلَمَّا هَاجَرَ أَبُو بَكْرٍ طَلَّقَهَا، فَتَزَوَّجَهَا ابْنُ عَمِّهَا، هَذَا الشَّاعِرُ الَّذِي قَالَ هَذِهِ الْقَصِيدَةَ، رَثَى كُفَّارَ قُرَيْشٍ

وَمَاذَا بِالْقَلِيبِ قَلِيبِ بَدْرٍ مِنَ الشِّيزَى تُزَيَّنُ بِالسَّنَامِ وَمَاذَا بِالْقَلِيبِ، قَلِيبِ بَدْرٍ مِنَ الْقَيْنَاتِ وَالشَّرْبِ الْكِرَامِ تُحَيِّي بِالسَّلاَمَةِ أُمُّ بَكْرٍ وَهَلْ لِي بَعْدَ قَوْمِي مِنْ سَلاَمِ يُحَدِّثُنَا الرَّسُولُ بِأَنْ سَنَحْيَا وَكَيْفَ حَيَاةُ أَصْدَاءٍ وَهَامِ

Narrated `Aisha: We went out with Allah's Messenger ﷺ on one of his journeys till we reached Al-Baida or Dhatul-Jaish where my necklace got broken (and lost). Allah's Messenger ﷺ stopped to search for it and the people too stopped with him. There was no water at that place and they had no water with them. So they went to Abu Bakr and said, "Don't you see what `Aisha has done? She has made Allah's Messenger ﷺ and the people stop where there is no water and they have no water with them. Abu Bakr came while Allah's Apostle was sleeping with his head on my thigh and said, "You detained Allah Apostle and the people where there is no water and they have no water." He then admonished me and said what Allah wished and pinched me at my flanks with his hands, but I did not move because the head of Allah's Messenger ﷺ was on my thigh . Allah's Messenger ﷺ kept on sleeping till be got up in the morning and found no water. Then Allah revealed the Divine Verse of Tayammum, and the people performed Tayammum. Usaid bin AlHudair said. "O family of Abu Bakr! This is not the first blessings of yours." We urged the camel on which I was sitting to get up from its place and the necklace was found under it. – Sahih Al-Bukhari 3672

حَدَّثَنَا قُتَيْبَةُ بْنُ سَعِيدٍ، عَنْ مَالِكٍ، عَنْ عَبْدِ الرَّحْمَنِ بْنِ الْقَاسِمِ، عَنْ أَبِيهِ، عَنْ عَائِشَةَ ـ رضى الله عنها ـ أَنَّهَا قَالَتْ خَرَجْنَا مَعَ رَسُولِ اللَّهِ صلى الله عليه وسلم فِي بَعْضِ أَسْفَارِهِ، حَتَّى إِذَا كُنَّا بِالْبَيْدَاءِ أَوْ بِذَاتِ الْجَيْشِ انْقَطَعَ عِقْدٌ لِي، فَأَقَامَ رَسُولُ اللَّهِ صلى الله عليه وسلم عَلَى الْتِمَاسِهِ، وَأَقَامَ النَّاسُ مَعَهُ، وَلَيْسُوا عَلَى مَاءٍ وَلَيْسَ مَعَهُمْ مَاءٌ، فَأَتَى النَّاسُ أَبَا بَكْرٍ، فَقَالُوا أَلاَ تَرَى مَا صَنَعَتْ عَائِشَةُ أَقَامَتْ بِرَسُولِ اللَّهِ صلى الله عليه وسلم وَبِالنَّاسِ مَعَهُ، وَلَيْسُوا عَلَى مَاءٍ وَلَيْسَ مَعَهُمْ مَاءٌ، فَجَاءَ أَبُو بَكْرٍ وَرَسُولُ اللَّهِ صلى الله عليه وسلم وَاضِعٌ رَأْسَهُ عَلَى فَخِذِي قَدْ نَامَ، فَقَالَ حَبَسْتِ رَسُولَ اللَّهِ صلى الله عليه وسلم وَالنَّاسَ، وَلَيْسُوا عَلَى مَاءٍ وَلَيْسَ مَعَهُمْ مَاءٌ قَالَتْ فَعَاتَبَنِي، وَقَالَ مَا شَاءَ اللَّهُ أَنْ يَقُولَ، وَجَعَلَ يَطْعُنُنِي بِيَدِهِ فِي خَاصِرَتِي، فَلاَ يَمْنَعُنِي مِنَ التَّحَرُّكِ إِلاَّ مَكَانُ رَسُولِ اللَّهِ صلى الله عليه وسلم عَلَى فَخِذِي، فَنَامَ رَسُولُ اللَّهِ صلى الله عليه وسلم حَتَّى أَصْبَحَ عَلَى غَيْرِ مَاءٍ فَأَنْزَلَ اللَّهُ آيَةَ التَّيَمُّمِ، فَتَيَمَّمُوا، فَقَالَ أُسَيْدُ بْنُ الْحُضَيْرِ مَا هِيَ بِأَوَّلِ بَرَكَتِكُمْ يَا آلَ أَبِي بَكْرٍ. فَقَالَتْ عَائِشَةُ فَبَعَثْنَا الْبَعِيرَ الَّذِي كُنْتُ عَلَيْهِ فَوَجَدْنَا الْعِقْدَ تَحْتَهُ

Narrated Zaid bin Thabit Al-Ansari: Who was one of those who used to write the Divine Revelation: Abu Bakr sent for me after the (heavy) casualties among the warriors (of the battle) of Yamama (where a great number of Qurra' were killed). `Umar was present with Abu Bakr who said, `Umar has come to me and said, The people have suffered heavy casualties on the day of (the battle of) Yamama, and I am afraid that there will be more casualties among the Qurra' (those who know the Qur'an by heart) at other battle-fields, whereby a large part of the Qur'an may be lost, unless you collect it. And I am of the opinion that you should collect the Qur'an." Abu Bakr added, "I said to `Umar, 'How can I do something which Allah's Apostle has not done?' `Umar said (to me), 'By Allah, it is (really) a good thing.' So `Umar kept on pressing, trying to persuade me to accept his proposal, till Allah opened my bosom for it and I had the same opinion as `Umar." (Zaid bin Thabit added:) `Umar was sitting with him (Abu Bakr) and was not speaking. Me). "You are a wise young man and we do not suspect you (of telling lies or of forgetfulness): and you used to write the Divine Inspiration for Allah's Messenger ﷺ. Therefore, look for the Qur'an and collect it (in one manuscript). " By Allah, if he (Abu Bakr) had ordered me to shift one of the mountains (from its place) it would not have been harder for me than what he had ordered me concerning the collection of the Qur'an. I said to both of them, "How dare you do a thing which the Prophet has not done?" Abu Bakr said, "By Allah, it is (really) a good thing. So I kept on arguing with him about it till Allah opened my bosom for that which He had opened the bosoms of Abu Bakr and `Umar. So I started locating Qur'anic material and collecting it from parchments, scapula, leaf-stalks of date palms and from the memories of men (who knew it by heart). I found with Khuza`ima two Verses of Surat-at-Tauba which I had not found with anybody else, (and they were):-- "Verily there has come to you an Apostle (Muhammad) from amongst yourselves. It grieves him that you should receive any injury or difficulty He (Muhammad) is ardently anxious over you (to be rightly guided)" (9.128) The manuscript on which the Qur'an was collected, remained with Abu Bakr till Allah took him unto Him, and then with `Umar till Allah took him unto Him, and finally it remained with Hafsa, `Umar's daughter. – Sahih Al-Bukhari 4679

حَدَّثَنَا أَبُو الْيَمَانِ، أَخْبَرَنَا شُعَيْبٌ، عَنِ الزُّهْرِيِّ، قَالَ أَخْبَرَنِي ابْنُ السَّبَّاقِ، أَنَّ زَيْدَ بْنَ ثَابِتٍ الأَنْصَارِيَّ ـ رضى الله عنه ـ وَكَانَ مِمَّنْ يَكْتُبُ الْوَحْىَ قَالَ أَرْسَلَ إِلَىَّ أَبُو بَكْرٍ مَقْتَلَ أَهْلِ الْيَمَامَةِ وَعِنْدَهُ عُمَرُ، فَقَالَ أَبُو بَكْرٍ إِنَّ عُمَرَ أَتَانِي فَقَالَ إِنَّ الْقَتْلَ قَدِ اسْتَحَرَّ يَوْمَ الْيَمَامَةِ بِالنَّاسِ، وَإِنِّي أَخْشَى أَنْ يَسْتَحِرَّ الْقَتْلُ بِالْقُرَّاءِ فِي الْمَوَاطِنِ فَيَذْهَبَ كَثِيرٌ مِنَ الْقُرْآنِ، إِلاَّ أَنْ تَجْمَعُوهُ، وَإِنِّي لأَرَى أَنْ تَجْمَعَ الْقُرْآنَ. قَالَ أَبُو بَكْرٍ قُلْتُ لِعُمَرَ كَيْفَ أَفْعَلُ شَيْئًا لَمْ يَفْعَلْهُ رَسُولُ اللَّهِ صلى الله عليه وسلم فَقَالَ عُمَرُ هُوَ وَاللَّهِ خَيْرٌ. فَلَمْ يَزَلْ عُمَرُ يُرَاجِعُنِي فِيهِ حَتَّى شَرَحَ اللَّهُ لِذَلِكَ صَدْرِي، وَرَأَيْتُ الَّذِي رَأَى عُمَرُ. قَالَ زَيْدُ بْنُ ثَابِتٍ وَعُمَرُ عِنْدَهُ جَالِسٌ لاَ يَتَكَلَّمُ. فَقَالَ أَبُو بَكْرٍ إِنَّكَ رَجُلٌ شَابٌّ عَاقِلٌ وَلاَ نَتَّهِمُكَ، كُنْتَ تَكْتُبُ الْوَحْىَ لِرَسُولِ اللَّهِ صلى الله عليه وسلم فَتَتَبَّعِ الْقُرْآنَ فَاجْمَعْهُ. فَوَاللَّهِ لَوْ كَلَّفَنِي نَقْلَ جَبَلٍ مِنَ الْجِبَالِ مَا كَانَ أَثْقَلَ عَلَىَّ مِمَّا أَمَرَنِي بِهِ مِنْ جَمْعِ الْقُرْآنِ قُلْتُ كَيْفَ تَفْعَلاَنِ شَيْئًا لَمْ يَفْعَلْهُ النَّبِيُّ صلى الله عليه وسلم فَقَالَ أَبُو بَكْرٍ هُوَ وَاللَّهِ خَيْرٌ، فَلَمْ أَزَلْ أُرَاجِعُهُ حَتَّى شَرَحَ اللَّهُ صَدْرِي لِلَّذِي شَرَحَ اللَّهُ لَهُ صَدْرَ أَبِي بَكْرٍ وَعُمَرَ، فَقُمْتُ فَتَتَبَّعْتُ الْقُرْآنَ أَجْمَعُهُ مِنَ الرِّقَاعِ وَالأَكْتَافِ وَالْعُسُبِ وَصُدُورِ الرِّجَالِ، حَتَّى وَجَدْتُ مِنْ سُورَةِ التَّوْبَةِ آيَتَيْنِ مَعَ خُزَيْمَةَ الأَنْصَارِيِّ، لَمْ أَجِدْهُمَا مَعَ أَحَدٍ غَيْرِهِ {لَقَدْ جَاءَكُمْ رَسُولٌ مِنْ أَنْفُسِكُمْ عَزِيزٌ عَلَيْهِ مَا عَنِتُّمْ حَرِيصٌ عَلَيْكُمْ} إِلَى آخِرِهِمَا، وَكَانَتِ الصُّحُفُ الَّتِي جُمِعَ فِيهَا الْقُرْآنُ عِنْدَ أَبِي بَكْرٍ حَتَّى تَوَفَّاهُ اللَّهُ، ثُمَّ عِنْدَ عُمَرَ حَتَّى تَوَفَّاهُ اللَّهُ، ثُمَّ عِنْدَ حَفْصَةَ بِنْتِ عُمَرَ. تَابَعَهُ عُثْمَانُ بْنُ عُمَرَ وَاللَّيْثُ عَنْ يُونُسَ عَنِ ابْنِ شِهَابٍ. وَقَالَ اللَّيْثُ حَدَّثَنِي عَبْدُ الرَّحْمَنِ بْنُ خَالِدٍ عَنِ ابْنِ شِهَابٍ وَقَالَ مَعَ أَبِي خُزَيْمَةَ الأَنْصَارِيِّ. وَقَالَ مُوسَى عَنْ إِبْرَاهِيمَ حَدَّثَنَا ابْنُ شِهَابٍ مَعَ أَبِي خُزَيْمَةَ. وَتَابَعَهُ يَعْقُوبُ بْنُ إِبْرَاهِيمَ عَنْ أَبِيهِ. وَقَالَ أَبُو ثَابِتٍ حَدَّثَنَا إِبْرَاهِيمُ وَقَالَ مَعَ خُزَيْمَةَ، أَوْ أَبِي خُزَيْمَةَ.

Narrated Hisham's father: Aisha said, "I went to Abu Bakr (during his fatal illness) and he asked me, 'In how many garments was the Prophet ﷺ shrouded?' She replied, 'In three Suhuliya pieces of white cloth of cotton, and there was neither a shirt nor a turban among them.' Abu Bakr further asked her, 'On which day did the Prophet die?' She replied, 'He died on Monday.' He asked, 'What is today?' She replied, 'Today is Monday.' He added, 'I hope I shall die sometime between this morning and tonight.' Then he looked at a garment that he was wearing during his illness and it had some stains of saffron. Then he said, 'Wash this garment of mine and add two more garments and shroud me in them.' I said, 'This is worn out.' He said, 'A living person has more right to wear new clothes than a dead one; the shroud is only for the body's pus.' He did not die till it was the night of Tuesday and was buried before the morning.". – Sahih Al-Bukhari 1387

حَدَّثَنَا مُعَلَّى بْنُ أَسَدٍ، حَدَّثَنَا وُهَيْبٌ، عَنْ هِشَامٍ، عَنْ أَبِيهِ، عَنْ عَائِشَةَ ـ رضى الله عنها ـ قَالَتْ دَخَلْتُ عَلَى أَبِي بَكْرٍ ـ رضى الله عنه ـ فَقَالَ فِي كَمْ كَفَّنْتُمُ النَّبِيَّ صلى الله عليه وسلم قَالَتْ فِي ثَلاَثَةِ أَثْوَابٍ بِيضٍ سَحُولِيَّةٍ، لَيْسَ فِيهَا قَمِيصٌ وَلاَ عِمَامَةٌ. وَقَالَ لَهَا فِي أَىِّ يَوْمٍ تُوُفِّيَ رَسُولُ اللَّهِ صلى الله عليه وسلم قَالَتْ يَوْمَ الاِثْنَيْنِ. قَالَ فَأَىُّ يَوْمٍ هَذَا قَالَتْ يَوْمُ الاِثْنَيْنِ. قَالَ أَرْجُو فِيمَا بَيْنِي وَبَيْنَ اللَّيْلِ. فَنَظَرَ إِلَى ثَوْبٍ عَلَيْهِ كَانَ يُمَرَّضُ فِيهِ، بِهِ رَدْعٌ مِنْ زَعْفَرَانٍ فَقَالَ اغْسِلُوا ثَوْبِي هَذَا، وَزِيدُوا عَلَيْهِ ثَوْبَيْنِ فَكَفِّنُونِي فِيهَا. قُلْتُ إِنَّ هَذَا خَلَقٌ. قَالَ إِنَّ الْحَىَّ أَحَقُّ بِالْجَدِيدِ مِنَ الْمَيِّتِ، إِنَّمَا هُوَ لِلْمُهْلَةِ. فَلَمْ يُتَوَفَّ حَتَّى أَمْسَى مِنْ لَيْلَةِ الثُّلاَثَاءِ وَدُفِنَ قَبْلَ أَنْ يُصْبِحَ.

If you do not help him, Allah has already helped him, when those who disbelieved expelled him, and he was the second of two in the cave. He said to his friend, "Do not worry, Allah is with us." And Allah made His tranquility descend upon him, and supported him with forces you did not see, and made the word of those who disbelieved the lowest, while the Word of Allah is the Highest. Allah is Mighty and Wise. – Surah At-Taubah 9:40

إِلَّا تَنصُرُوهُ فَقَدْ نَصَرَهُ ٱللَّهُ إِذْ أَخْرَجَهُ ٱلَّذِينَ كَفَرُوا۟ ثَانِىَ ٱثْنَيْنِ إِذْ هُمَا فِى ٱلْغَارِ إِذْ يَقُولُ لِصَـٰحِبِهِۦ لَا تَحْزَنْ إِنَّ ٱللَّهَ مَعَنَا ۖ فَأَنزَلَ ٱللَّهُ سَكِينَتَهُۥ عَلَيْهِ وَأَيَّدَهُۥ بِجُنُودٍ لَّمْ تَرَوْهَا وَجَعَلَ كَلِمَةَ ٱلَّذِينَ كَفَرُوا۟ ٱلسُّفْلَىٰ ۗ وَكَلِمَةُ ٱللَّهِ هِىَ ٱلْعُلْيَا ۗ وَٱللَّهُ عَزِيزٌ حَكِيمٌ

Umar bin Al-Khattab

عُمَرَ بْنِ الْخَطَّاب

Narrated `Abdur Rahman bin Abza: A man came to `Umar bin Al-Khattab and said, "I became Junub but no water was available." `Ammar bin Yasir said to `Umar, "Do you remember that you and I (became Junub while both of us) were together on a journey and you didn't pray but I rolled myself on the ground and prayed? I informed the Prophetﷺ about it and he said, 'It would have been sufficient for you to do like this.' The Prophet then stroked lightly the earth with his hands and then blew off the dust and passed his hands over his face and hands.". – Sahih Al-Bukhari 338

حَدَّثَنَا آدَمُ، قَالَ حَدَّثَنَا شُعْبَةُ، حَدَّثَنَا الْحَكَمُ، عَنْ ذَرٍّ، عَنْ سَعِيدِ بْنِ عَبْدِ الرَّحْمَنِ بْنِ أَبْزَى، عَنْ أَبِيهِ، قَالَ جَاءَ رَجُلٌ إِلَى عُمَرَ بْنِ الْخَطَّابِ فَقَالَ إِنِّي أَجْنَبْتُ فَلَمْ أُصِبِ الْمَاءَ. فَقَالَ عَمَّارُ بْنُ يَاسِرٍ لِعُمَرَ بْنِ الْخَطَّابِ أَمَا تَذْكُرُ أَنَّا كُنَّا فِي سَفَرٍ أَنَا وَأَنْتَ فَأَمَّا أَنْتَ فَلَمْ تُصَلِّ، وَأَمَّا أَنَا فَتَمَعَّكْتُ فَصَلَّيْتُ، فَذَكَرْتُ لِلنَّبِيِّ صلى الله عليه وسلم فَقَالَ النَّبِيُّ صلى الله عليه وسلم " إِنَّمَا كَانَ يَكْفِيكَ هَكَذَا ". فَضَرَبَ النَّبِيُّ صلى الله عليه وسلم بِكَفَّيْهِ الأَرْضَ، وَنَفَخَ فِيهِمَا ثُمَّ مَسَحَ بِهِمَا وَجْهَهُ وَكَفَّيْهِ.

Narrated Ibn `Umar: When the people of Khaibar dislocated `Abdullah bin `Umar's hands and feet, `Umar got up delivering a sermon saying, "No doubt, Allah's Messengerﷺ made a contract with the Jews concerning their properties, and said to them, 'We allow you (to stand in your land) as long as Allah allows you.' Now `Abdullah bin `Umar went to his land and was attacked at night, and his hands and feet were dislocated, and as we have no enemies there except those Jews, they are our enemies and the only people whom we suspect, I have made up my mind to exile them." When `Umar decided to carry out his decision, a son of Abu Al-Haqiq's came and addressed `Umar, "O chief of the believers, will you exile us although Muhammad allowed us to stay at our places, and made a contract with us about our properties, and accepted the condition of our residence in our land?" `Umar said, "Do you think that I have forgotten the statement of Allah's Messengerﷺ, i.e. What will your condition be when you are expelled from Khaibar and your camel will be carrying you night after night?" The Jew replied, "That was joke from Abul-Qasim." `Umar said, "O the enemy of Allah! You are telling a lie." `Umar then drove them out and paid them the price of their properties in the form of fruits, money, camel saddles and ropes, etc.". – Sahih Al-Bukhari 2730

حَدَّثَنَا أَبُو أَحْمَدَ، حَدَّثَنَا مُحَمَّدُ بْنُ يَحْيَى أَبُو غَسَّانَ الْكِنَانِيُّ، أَخْبَرَنَا مَالِكٌ، عَنْ نَافِعٍ، عَنِ ابْنِ عُمَرَ ـ رضى الله عنهما ـ قَالَ لَمَّا فَدَعَ أَهْلُ خَيْبَرَ عَبْدَ اللَّهِ بْنَ عُمَرَ، قَامَ عُمَرُ خَطِيبًا فَقَالَ إِنَّ رَسُولَ اللَّهِ صلى الله عليه وسلم كَانَ عَامَلَ يَهُودَ خَيْبَرَ عَلَى أَمْوَالِهِمْ، وَقَالَ " نُقِرُّكُمْ مَا أَقَرَّكُمُ اللَّهُ ". وَإِنَّ عَبْدَ اللَّهِ بْنَ عُمَرَ خَرَجَ إِلَى مَالِهِ هُنَاكَ فَعُدِيَ عَلَيْهِ مِنَ اللَّيْلِ، فَفُدِعَتْ يَدَاهُ وَرِجْلاَهُ، وَلَيْسَ لَنَا هُنَاكَ عَدُوٌّ غَيْرُهُمْ، هُمْ عَدُوُّنَا وَتُهَمَتُنَا، وَقَدْ رَأَيْتُ إِجْلاَءَهُمْ، فَلَمَّا أَجْمَعَ عُمَرُ عَلَى ذَلِكَ أَتَاهُ أَحَدُ بَنِي أَبِي الْحُقَيْقِ، فَقَالَ يَا أَمِيرَ الْمُؤْمِنِينَ، أَتُخْرِجُنَا وَقَدْ أَقَرَّنَا مُحَمَّدٌ صلى الله عليه وسلم وَعَامَلَنَا عَلَى الأَمْوَالِ، وَشَرَطَ ذَلِكَ لَنَا فَقَالَ عُمَرُ أَظَنَنْتَ أَنِّي نَسِيتُ قَوْلَ رَسُولِ اللَّهِ صلى الله عليه وسلم " كَيْفَ بِكَ إِذَا أُخْرِجْتَ مِنْ خَيْبَرَ تَعْدُو بِكَ قَلُوصُكَ، لَيْلَةً بَعْدَ لَيْلَةٍ ". فَقَالَ كَانَتْ هَذِهِ هُزَيْلَةً مِنْ أَبِي الْقَاسِمِ. قَالَ كَذَبْتَ يَا عَدُوَّ اللَّهِ. فَأَجْلاَهُمْ عُمَرُ وَأَعْطَاهُمْ قِيمَةَ مَا كَانَ لَهُمْ مِنَ الثَّمَرِ مَالاً وَإِبِلاً وَعُرُوضًا، مِنْ أَقْتَابٍ وَحِبَالٍ وَغَيْرِ ذَلِكَ. رَوَاهُ حَمَّادُ بْنُ سَلَمَةَ عَنْ عُبَيْدِ اللَّهِ، أَحْسِبُهُ عَنْ نَافِعٍ، عَنِ ابْنِ عُمَرَ، عَنْ عُمَرَ، عَنِ النَّبِيِّ صلى الله عليه وسلم، اخْتَصَرَهُ.

Narrated Tha`laba bin Abi Malik: `Umar bin Al-Khattab distributed some garments amongst the women of Medina. One good garment remained, and one of those present with him said, "O chief of the believers! Give this garment to your wife, the (grand) daughter of Allah's Messengerﷺ." They meant Um Kulthum, the daughter of `Ali. `Umar said, Um Salit has more right (to have it)." Um Salit was amongst those Ansari women who had given the pledge of allegiance to Allah's Messengerﷺ'. Umar said, "She (i.e. Um Salit) used to carry the water skins for us on the day of Uhud.". – Sahih Al-Bukhari 2881

حَدَّثَنَا عَبْدَانُ، أَخْبَرَنَا عَبْدُ اللَّهِ، أَخْبَرَنَا يُونُسُ، عَنِ ابْنِ شِهَابٍ، قَالَ ثَعْلَبَةُ بْنُ أَبِي مَالِكٍ إِنَّ عُمَرَ بْنَ الْخَطَّابِ ـ رضى الله عنه ـ قَسَمَ مُرُوطًا بَيْنَ نِسَاءٍ مِنْ نِسَاءِ الْمَدِينَةِ، فَبَقِيَ مِرْطٌ جَيِّدٌ فَقَالَ لَهُ بَعْضُ مَنْ عِنْدَهُ يَا أَمِيرَ الْمُؤْمِنِينَ أَعْطِ هَذَا ابْنَةَ رَسُولِ اللَّهِ صلى الله عليه وسلم الَّتِي عِنْدَكَ. يُرِيدُونَ أُمَّ كُلْثُومٍ بِنْتَ عَلِيٍّ. فَقَالَ عُمَرُ أُمُّ سَلِيطٍ أَحَقُّ. وَأُمُّ سَلِيطٍ مِنْ نِسَاءِ الأَنْصَارِ، مِمَّنْ بَايَعَ رَسُولَ اللَّهِ صلى الله عليه وسلم. قَالَ عُمَرُ فَإِنَّهَا كَانَتْ تَزْفِرُ لَنَا الْقِرَبَ يَوْمَ أُحُدٍ. قَالَ أَبُو عَبْدِ اللَّهِ تَزْفِرُ تَخِيطُ

Narrated Nafi`: `Umar bin Al-Khattab said, "O Allah's Messenger ﷺ! I vowed to observe I`tikaf for one day during the PreIslamic period." The Prophet ﷺ ordered him to fulfill his vow. `Umar gained two lady captives from the war prisoners of Hunain and he left them in some of the houses at Mecca. When Allah's Messenger ﷺ freed the captives of Hunain without ransom, they came out walking in the streets. `Umar said (to his son), "O `Abdullah! See what is the matter." `Abdullah replied, "Allah's Messenger ﷺ has freed the captives without ransom." He said (to him), "Go and set free those two slave girls." (Nafi` added:) Allah's Apostle did not perform the `Umra from Al-Jarana, and if he had performed the `Umra, it would not have been hidden from `Abdullah. – Sahih Al-Bukhari 3144

حَدَّثَنَا أَبُو النُّعْمَانِ، حَدَّثَنَا حَمَّادُ بْنُ زَيْدٍ، عَنْ أَيُّوبَ، عَنْ نَافِعٍ، أَنَّ عُمَرَ بْنَ الْخَطَّابِ ـ رضى الله عنه ـ قَالَ يَا رَسُولَ اللَّهِ إِنَّهُ كَانَ عَلَيَّ اعْتِكَافُ يَوْمٍ فِي الْجَاهِلِيَّةِ، فَأَمَرَهُ أَنْ يَفِيَ بِهِ. قَالَ وَأَصَابَ عُمَرُ جَارِيَتَيْنِ مِنْ سَبْىِ حُنَيْنٍ، فَوَضَعَهُمَا فِي بَعْضِ بُيُوتِ مَكَّةَ ـ قَالَ ـ فَمَنَّ رَسُولُ اللَّهِ صلى الله عليه وسلم عَلَى سَبْىِ حُنَيْنٍ، فَجَعَلُوا يَسْعَوْنَ فِي السِّكَكِ فَقَالَ عُمَرُ يَا عَبْدَ اللَّهِ، انْظُرْ مَا هَذَا فَقَالَ مَنَّ رَسُولُ اللَّهِ صلى الله عليه وسلم عَلَى السَّبْىِ. قَالَ اذْهَبْ فَأَرْسِلِ الْجَارِيَتَيْنِ. قَالَ نَافِعٌ وَلَمْ يَعْتَمِرْ رَسُولُ اللَّهِ صلى الله عليه وسلم مِنَ الْجِعْرَانَةِ وَلَوِ اعْتَمَرَ لَمْ يَخْفَ عَلَى عَبْدِ اللَّهِ. وَزَادَ جَرِيرُ بْنُ حَازِمٍ عَنْ أَيُّوبَ عَنْ نَافِعٍ عَنِ ابْنِ عُمَرَ قَالَ مِنَ الْخُمُسِ. وَرَوَاهُ مَعْمَرٌ عَنْ أَيُّوبَ عَنْ نَافِعٍ عَنِ ابْنِ عُمَرَ فِي النَّذْرِ وَلَمْ يَقُلْ يَوْمَ.

Narrated Sa`id bin Al-Musaiyab: `Umar came to the Mosque while Hassan was reciting a poem. (`Umar disapproved of that). On that Hassan said, "I used to recite poetry in this very Mosque in the presence of one (i.e. the Prophet ﷺ) who was better than you." Then he turned towards Abu Huraira and said (to him), "I ask you by Allah, did you hear Allah's Messenger ﷺ saying (to me), "Retort on my behalf. O Allah! Support him (i.e. Hassan) with the Holy Spirit?" Abu Huraira said, "Yes.". – Sahih Al-Bukhari 3212

حَدَّثَنَا عَلِيُّ بْنُ عَبْدِ اللَّهِ، حَدَّثَنَا سُفْيَانُ، حَدَّثَنَا الزُّهْرِيُّ، عَنْ سَعِيدِ بْنِ الْمُسَيَّبِ، قَالَ مَرَّ عُمَرُ فِي الْمَسْجِدِ وَحَسَّانُ يُنْشِدُ، فَقَالَ كُنْتُ أُنْشِدُ فِيهِ، وَفِيهِ مَنْ هُوَ خَيْرٌ مِنْكَ، ثُمَّ الْتَفَتَ إِلَى أَبِي هُرَيْرَةَ، فَقَالَ أَنْشُدُكَ بِاللَّهِ، أَسَمِعْتَ رَسُولَ اللَّهِ صلى الله عليه وسلم يَقُولُ " أَجِبْ عَنِّي، اللَّهُمَّ أَيِّدْهُ بِرُوحِ الْقُدُسِ ". قَالَ نَعَمْ

Narrated `Amr bin Maimun: I saw `Umar bin Al-Khattab a few days before he was stabbed in Medina. He was standing with Hudhaifa bin Al-Yaman and `Uthman bin Hunaif to whom he said, "What have you done? Do you think that you have imposed more taxation on the land (of As-Swad i.e. 'Iraq) than it can bear?" They replied, "We have imposed on it what it can bear because of its great yield." `Umar again said, "Check whether you have imposed on the land what it can not bear." They said, "No, (we haven't)." `Umar added, "If Allah should keep me alive I will let the widows of Iraq need no men to support them after me." But only four days had elapsed when he was stabbed (to death ). The day he was stabbed, I was standing and there was nobody between me and him (i.e. `Umar) except `Abdullah bin `Abbas. Whenever `Umar passed between the two rows, he would say, "Stand in straight lines." When he saw no defect (in the rows), he would go forward and start the prayer with Takbir. He would recite Surat Yusuf or An-Nahl or the like in the first rak`a so that the people may have the time to Join the prayer. As soon as he said Takbir, I heard him saying, "The dog has killed or eaten me," at the time he (i.e. the murderer) stabbed him. A non-Arab infidel proceeded on carrying a double-edged knife and stabbing all the persons he passed by on the right and left (till) he stabbed thirteen persons out of whom seven died. When one of the Muslims saw that, he threw a cloak on him. Realizing that he had been captured, the non-Arab infidel killed himself, `Umar held the hand of `Abdur-Rahman bin `Auf and let him lead the prayer. Those who were standing by the side of `Umar saw what I saw, but the people who were in the other parts of the Mosque did not see anything, but they lost the voice of `Umar and they were saying, "Subhan Allah! Subhan Allah! (i.e. Glorified be Allah)." `Abdur-Rahman bin `Auf led the people a short prayer. When they finished the prayer, `Umar said, "O Ibn `Abbas! Find out who attacked me." Ibn `Abbas kept on looking here and there for a short time and came to say. "The slave of Al Mughira." On that `Umar said, "The craftsman?" Ibn `Abbas said, "Yes." `Umar said, "May Allah curse him. I did not treat him unjustly. All the Praises are for Allah Who has not caused me to die at the hand of a man who claims himself to be a Muslim. No doubt, you and your father (Abbas) used to love to have more non-Arab infidels in Medina." Al-Abbas had the greatest number of slaves. Ibn `Abbas said to `Umar. "If you wish, we will do." He meant, "If you wish we will kill them." `Umar said, "You are mistaken (for you can't kill them) after they have spoken your language, prayed towards your Qibla, and performed Hajj like yours." Then `Umar was carried to his house, and we went along with him, and the people were as if they had never suffered a calamity before. Some said, "Do not worry (he will be Alright soon)." Some said, "We are afraid (that he will die)." Then an infusion of dates was brought to him and he drank it but it came out (of the wound) of his belly. Then milk was brought to him and he drank it, and it also came out of his belly. The people realized that he would die. We went to him, and the people came, praising him. A young man came saying, "O chief of the believers! Receive the glad tidings from Allah to you due to your company with Allah's Messenger ﷺ and your superiority in Islam which you know. Then you became the ruler (i.e. Caliph) and you ruled with justice and finally you have been martyred." `Umar said, "I wish that all these privileges will counterbalance (my shortcomings) so that I will neither lose nor gain anything." When the young man turned back to leave, his clothes seemed to be touching the ground. `Umar said, "Call the young man back to me." (When he came back) `Umar said, "O son of my brother! Lift your clothes, for this will keep your clothes clean and save you from the Punishment of your Lord." `Umar further said, "O `Abdullah bin `Umar! See how much I am in debt to others." When the debt was checked, it amounted to approximately eighty-six thousand. `Umar said, "If the property of `Umar's family covers the debt, then pay the debt thereof; otherwise request it from Bani `Adi bin Ka`b, and if that too is not sufficient, ask for it from Quraish tribe, and do not ask for it from any one else, and pay this debt on my behalf." `Umar then said (to `Abdullah), "Go to `Aisha (the mother of the believers) and say: "`Umar is paying his salutation to you. But don't say: 'The chief of the believers,' because today I am not the chief of the believers. And say: "`Umar bin Al-Khattab asks the permission to be buried with his two companions (i.e. the Prophet, and Abu Bakr)." `Abdullah greeted `Aisha and asked for the permission for entering, and then entered to her and found her sitting and weeping. He said to her, "`Umar bin Al-Khattab is paying his salutations to you, and asks the permission to be buried with his two companions." She said, "I had the idea of having this place for myself, but today I prefer `Umar to myself." When he returned it was said (to `Umar), "`Abdullah bin `Umar has come." `Umar said, "Make me sit up." Somebody supported him against his body and `Umar asked (`Abdullah), "What news do you have?" He said, "O chief of the believers! It is as you wish. She has given the permission." `Umar said, "Praise be to Allah, there was nothing more important to me than this. So when I die, take me, and greet `Aisha and say: "`Umar bin Al-Khattab asks the permission (to be buried with the Prophet ﷺ),and if she gives the permission, bury me there, and if she refuses, then take me to the grave-yard of the Muslims." Then Hafsa (the mother of the believers) came with many other women walking with her. When we saw her, we went away. She went in (to `Umar) and wept there for sometime. When the men asked for permission to enter, she went into another place, and we heard her weeping inside. The people said (to `Umar), "O chief of the believers! Appoint a successor." `Umar said, "I do not find anyone more suitable for the job than the following persons or group whom Allah's Messenger ﷺ had been pleased with before he died." Then `Umar mentioned `Ali, `Uthman, AzZubair, Talha, Sa`d and `Abdur-Rahman (bin `Auf) and said, "Abdullah bin `Umar will be a witness to you, but he will have no share in the rule. His being a witness will compensate him for not sharing the right of ruling. If Sa`d becomes the ruler, it will be alright: otherwise, whoever becomes the ruler should seek his help, as I have not dismissed him because of disability or dishonesty." `Umar added, "I recommend that my successor takes care of the early emigrants; to know their rights and protect their honor and sacred things. I also recommend that he be kind to the Ansar who had lived in Medina before the emigrants and Belief had entered their hearts before them. I recommend that the (ruler) should accept the good of the righteous among them and excuse their wrong-doers, and I recommend that he should do good to all the people of the towns (Al-Ansar), as they are the protectors of Islam and the source of wealth and the source of annoyance to the enemy. I also recommend that nothing be taken from them except from their surplus with their consent. I also recommend that he do good to the 'Arab bedouin, as they are the origin of the 'Arabs and the material of Islam. He should take from what is inferior, amongst their properties and distribute that to the poor amongst them. I also recommend him concerning Allah's and His Apostle's protectees (i.e. Dhimmis) to fulfill their contracts and to fight for them and not to overburden them with what is beyond their ability." So when `Umar expired, we carried him out and set out walking. `Abdullah bin `Umar greeted (`Aisha) and said, "`Umar bin Al-Khattab asks for the permission." `Aisha said, "Bring him in." He was brought in and buried beside his two companions. When he was buried, the group (recommended by `Umar) held a meeting. Then `Abdur-Rahman said, " Reduce the candidates for rulership to three of you." Az-Zubair said, "I give up my right to `Ali." Talha said, "I give up my right to `Uthman," Sa`d, 'I give up my right to `Abdur-Rahman bin `Auf." `Abdur-Rahman then said (to `Uthman and `Ali), "Now which of you is willing to give up his right of candidacy to that he may choose the better of the (remaining) two, bearing in mind that Allah and Islam will be his witnesses." So both the sheiks (i.e. `Uthman and `Ali) kept silent. `Abdur-Rahman said, "Will you both leave this matter to me, and I take Allah as my Witness that I will not choose but the better of you?" They said, "Yes." So `Abdur-Rahman took the hand of one of them (i.e. `Ali) and said, "You are related to Allah's Messenger ﷺ and one of the earliest Muslims as you know well. So I ask you by Allah to promise that if I select you as a ruler you will do justice, and if I select `Uthman as a ruler you will listen to him and obey him." Then he took the other (i.e. `Uthman) aside and said the same to him. When `Abdur-Rahman secured (their agreement to) this covenant, he said, "O `Uthman! Raise your hand." So he (i.e. `Abdur-Rahman) gave him (i.e. `Uthman) the solemn pledge, and then `Ali gave him the pledge of allegiance and then all the (Medina) people gave him the pledge of allegiance. – Sahih Al-Bukhari 3700

حَدَّثَنَا مُوسَى بْنُ إِسْمَاعِيلَ، حَدَّثَنَا أَبُو عَوَانَةَ، عَنْ حُصَيْنٍ، عَنْ عَمْرِو بْنِ مَيْمُونٍ، قَالَ رَأَيْتُ عُمَرَ بْنَ الْخَطَّابِ ـ رضى الله عنه ـ قَبْلَ أَنْ يُصَابَ بِأَيَّامٍ بِالْمَدِينَةِ وَقَفَ عَلَى حُذَيْفَةَ بْنِ الْيَمَانِ وَعُثْمَانَ بْنِ حُنَيْفٍ، قَالَ كَيْفَ فَعَلْتُمَا أَتَخَافَانِ أَنْ تَكُونَا قَدْ حَمَّلْتُمَا الأَرْضَ مَا لاَ تُطِيقُ قَالاَ حَمَّلْنَاهَا أَمْرًا هِيَ لَهُ مُطِيقَةٌ، مَا فِيهَا كَبِيرُ فَضْلٍ. قَالَ انْظُرَا أَنْ تَكُونَا حَمَّلْتُمَا الأَرْضَ مَا لاَ تُطِيقُ، قَالَ قَالاَ لاَ. فَقَالَ عُمَرُ لَئِنْ سَلَّمَنِي اللَّهُ لأَدَعَنَّ أَرَامِلَ أَهْلِ الْعِرَاقِ لاَ يَحْتَجْنَ إِلَى رَجُلٍ بَعْدِي أَبَدًا. قَالَ فَمَا أَتَتْ عَلَيْهِ إِلاَّ رَابِعَةٌ حَتَّى أُصِيبَ. قَالَ إِنِّي لَقَائِمٌ مَا بَيْنِي وَبَيْنَهُ إِلاَّ عَبْدُ اللَّهِ بْنُ عَبَّاسٍ غَدَاةَ أُصِيبَ، وَكَانَ إِذَا مَرَّ بَيْنَ الصَّفَّيْنِ قَالَ اسْتَوُوا. حَتَّى إِذَا لَمْ يَرَ فِيهِنَّ خَلَلاً تَقَدَّمَ فَكَبَّرَ، وَرُبَّمَا قَرَأَ سُورَةَ يُوسُفَ، أَوِ النَّحْلَ، أَوْ نَحْوَ ذَلِكَ، فِي الرَّكْعَةِ الأُولَى حَتَّى يَجْتَمِعَ النَّاسُ، فَمَا هُوَ إِلاَّ أَنْ كَبَّرَ فَسَمِعْتُهُ يَقُولُ قَتَلَنِي ـ أَوْ أَكَلَنِي ـ الْكَلْبُ. حِينَ طَعَنَهُ، فَطَارَ الْعِلْجُ بِسِكِّينٍ ذَاتِ طَرَفَيْنِ لاَ

يَمُرُّ عَلَى أَحَدٍ يَمِينًا وَلاَ شِمَالاً إِلاَّ طَعَنَهُ حَتَّى طَعَنَ ثَلاَثَةَ عَشَرَ رَجُلاً، مَاتَ مِنْهُمْ سَبْعَةٌ، فَلَمَّا رَأَى ذَلِكَ رَجُلٌ مِنَ الْمُسْلِمِينَ، طَرَحَ عَلَيْهِ بُرْنُسًا، فَلَمَّا ظَنَّ الْعِلْجُ أَنَّهُ مَأْخُوذٌ نَحَرَ نَفْسَهُ، وَتَنَاوَلَ عُمَرُ يَدَ عَبْدِ الرَّحْمَنِ بْنِ عَوْفٍ فَقَدَّمَهُ، فَمَنْ يَلِي عُمَرَ فَقَدْ رَأَى الَّذِي أَرَى، وَأَمَّا نَوَاحِي الْمَسْجِدِ فَإِنَّهُمْ لاَ يَدْرُونَ غَيْرَ أَنَّهُمْ قَدْ فَقَدُوا صَوْتَ عُمَرَ وَهُمْ يَقُولُونَ سُبْحَانَ اللَّهِ سُبْحَانَ اللَّهِ. فَصَلَّى بِهِمْ عَبْدُ الرَّحْمَنِ صَلاَةً خَفِيفَةً، فَلَمَّا انْصَرَفُوا. قَالَ يَا ابْنَ عَبَّاسٍ، انْظُرْ مَنْ قَتَلَنِي. فَجَالَ سَاعَةً، ثُمَّ جَاءَ، فَقَالَ غُلاَمُ الْمُغِيرَةِ. قَالَ الصَّنَعُ قَالَ نَعَمْ. قَالَ قَاتَلَهُ اللَّهُ لَقَدْ أَمَرْتُ بِهِ مَعْرُوفًا، الْحَمْدُ لِلَّهِ الَّذِي لَمْ يَجْعَلْ مَنِيَّتِي بِيَدِ رَجُلٍ يَدَّعِي الإِسْلاَمَ، قَدْ كُنْتَ أَنْتَ وَأَبُوكَ تُحِبَّانِ أَنْ تَكْثُرَ الْعُلُوجُ بِالْمَدِينَةِ وَكَانَ {الْعَبَّاسُ} أَكْثَرَهُمْ رَقِيقًا. فَقَالَ إِنْ شِئْتَ فَعَلْتُ. أَىْ إِنْ شِئْتَ قَتَلْنَا. قَالَ كَذَبْتَ، بَعْدَ مَا تَكَلَّمُوا بِلِسَانِكُمْ، وَصَلَّوْا قِبْلَتَكُمْ وَحَجُّوا حَجَّكُمْ فَاحْتُمِلَ إِلَى بَيْتِهِ فَانْطَلَقْنَا مَعَهُ، وَكَأَنَّ النَّاسَ لَمْ تُصِبْهُمْ مُصِيبَةٌ قَبْلَ يَوْمَئِذٍ، فَقَائِلٌ يَقُولُ لاَ بَأْسَ. وَقَائِلٌ يَقُولُ أَخَافُ عَلَيْهِ، فَأُتِيَ بِنَبِيذٍ فَشَرِبَهُ فَخَرَجَ مِنْ جَوْفِهِ، ثُمَّ أُتِيَ بِلَبَنٍ فَشَرِبَهُ فَخَرَجَ مِنْ جُرْحِهِ، فَعَلِمُوا أَنَّهُ مَيِّتٌ، فَدَخَلْنَا عَلَيْهِ، وَجَاءَ النَّاسُ يُثْنُونَ عَلَيْهِ، وَجَاءَ رَجُلٌ شَابٌّ، فَقَالَ أَبْشِرْ يَا أَمِيرَ الْمُؤْمِنِينَ بِبُشْرَى اللَّهِ لَكَ مِنْ صُحْبَةِ رَسُولِ اللَّهِ صلى الله عليه وسلم وَقَدَمٍ فِي الإِسْلاَمِ مَا قَدْ عَلِمْتَ، ثُمَّ وَلِيتَ فَعَدَلْتَ، ثُمَّ شَهَادَةٌ. قَالَ وَدِدْتُ أَنَّ ذَلِكَ كَفَافٌ لاَ عَلَيَّ وَلاَ لِي. فَلَمَّا أَدْبَرَ، إِذَا إِزَارُهُ يَمَسُّ الأَرْضَ. قَالَ رُدُّوا عَلَيَّ الْغُلاَمَ قَالَ ابْنَ أَخِي ارْفَعْ ثَوْبَكَ، فَإِنَّهُ أَبْقَى لِثَوْبِكَ وَأَتْقَى لِرَبِّكَ، يَا عَبْدَ اللَّهِ بْنَ عُمَرَ انْظُرْ مَا عَلَيَّ مِنَ الدَّيْنِ. فَحَسَبُوهُ فَوَجَدُوهُ سِتَّةً وَثَمَانِينَ أَلْفًا أَوْ نَحْوَهُ، قَالَ إِنْ وَفَى لَهُ مَالُ آلِ عُمَرَ، فَأَدِّهِ مِنْ أَمْوَالِهِمْ، وَإِلاَّ فَسَلْ فِي بَنِي عَدِيِّ بْنِ كَعْبٍ، فَإِنْ لَمْ تَفِ أَمْوَالُهُمْ فَسَلْ فِي قُرَيْشٍ، وَلاَ تَعْدُهُمْ إِلَى غَيْرِهِمْ، فَأَدِّ عَنِّي هَذَا الْمَالَ، انْطَلِقْ إِلَى عَائِشَةَ أُمِّ الْمُؤْمِنِينَ فَقُلْ يَقْرَأُ عَلَيْكِ عُمَرُ السَّلاَمَ. وَلاَ تَقُلْ أَمِيرُ الْمُؤْمِنِينَ. فَإِنِّي لَسْتُ الْيَوْمَ لِلْمُؤْمِنِينَ أَمِيرًا، وَقُلْ يَسْتَأْذِنُ عُمَرُ بْنُ الْخَطَّابِ أَنْ يُدْفَنَ مَعَ صَاحِبَيْهِ. فَسَلَّمَ وَاسْتَأْذَنَ، ثُمَّ دَخَلَ عَلَيْهَا، فَوَجَدَهَا قَاعِدَةً تَبْكِي فَقَالَ يَقْرَأُ عَلَيْكِ عُمَرُ بْنُ الْخَطَّابِ السَّلاَمَ وَيَسْتَأْذِنُ أَنْ يُدْفَنَ مَعَ صَاحِبَيْهِ. فَقَالَتْ كُنْتُ أُرِيدُهُ لِنَفْسِي، وَلأُوثِرَنَّ بِهِ الْيَوْمَ عَلَى نَفْسِي. فَلَمَّا أَقْبَلَ قِيلَ هَذَا عَبْدُ اللَّهِ بْنُ عُمَرَ قَدْ جَاءَ. قَالَ ارْفَعُونِي، فَأَسْنَدَهُ رَجُلٌ إِلَيْهِ، فَقَالَ مَا لَدَيْكَ قَالَ الَّذِي تُحِبُّ يَا أَمِيرَ الْمُؤْمِنِينَ أَذِنَتْ. قَالَ الْحَمْدُ لِلَّهِ، مَا كَانَ مِنْ شَىْءٍ أَهَمُّ إِلَيَّ مِنْ ذَلِكَ، فَإِذَا أَنَا قَضَيْتُ فَاحْمِلُونِي ثُمَّ سَلِّمْ فَقُلْ يَسْتَأْذِنُ عُمَرُ بْنُ الْخَطَّابِ، فَإِنْ أَذِنَتْ لِي فَأَدْخِلُونِي، وَإِنْ رَدَّتْنِي رُدُّونِي إِلَى مَقَابِرِ الْمُسْلِمِينَ. وَجَاءَتْ أُمُّ الْمُؤْمِنِينَ حَفْصَةُ وَالنِّسَاءُ تَسِيرُ مَعَهَا، فَلَمَّا رَأَيْنَاهَا قُمْنَا، فَوَلَجَتْ عَلَيْهِ فَبَكَتْ عِنْدَهُ سَاعَةً، وَاسْتَأْذَنَ الرِّجَالُ، فَوَلَجَتْ دَاخِلاً لَهُمْ، فَسَمِعْنَا بُكَاءَهَا مِنَ الدَّاخِلِ. فَقَالُوا أَوْصِ يَا أَمِيرَ الْمُؤْمِنِينَ اسْتَخْلِفْ. قَالَ مَا أَجِدُ أَحَقَّ بِهَذَا الأَمْرِ مِنْ هَؤُلاَءِ النَّفَرِ أَوِ الرَّهْطِ الَّذِينَ تُوُفِّيَ رَسُولُ اللَّهِ صلى الله عليه وسلم وَهْوَ عَنْهُمْ رَاضٍ. فَسَمَّى عَلِيًّا وَعُثْمَانَ وَالزُّبَيْرَ وَطَلْحَةَ وَسَعْدًا وَعَبْدَ الرَّحْمَنِ وَقَالَ يَشْهَدُكُمْ عَبْدُ اللَّهِ بْنُ عُمَرَ وَلَيْسَ لَهُ مِنَ الأَمْرِ شَىْءٌ ـ كَهَيْئَةِ التَّعْزِيَةِ لَهُ ـ فَإِنْ أَصَابَتِ الإِمْرَةُ سَعْدًا فَهْوَ ذَاكَ، وَإِلاَّ فَلْيَسْتَعِنْ بِهِ أَيُّكُمْ مَا أُمِّرَ، فَإِنِّي لَمْ أَعْزِلْهُ عَنْ عَجْزٍ وَلاَ خِيَانَةٍ وَقَالَ أُوصِي الْخَلِيفَةَ مِنْ بَعْدِي بِالْمُهَاجِرِينَ الأَوَّلِينَ أَنْ يَعْرِفَ لَهُمْ حَقَّهُمْ، وَيَحْفَظَ لَهُمْ حُرْمَتَهُمْ، وَأُوصِيهِ بِالأَنْصَارِ خَيْرًا، الَّذِينَ تَبَوَّءُوا الدَّارَ وَالإِيمَانَ مِنْ قَبْلِهِمْ، أَنْ يُقْبَلَ مِنْ مُحْسِنِهِمْ، وَأَنْ يُعْفَى عَنْ مُسِيئِهِمْ، وَأُوصِيهِ بِأَهْلِ الأَمْصَارِ خَيْرًا فَإِنَّهُمْ رِدْءُ الإِسْلاَمِ، وَجُبَاةُ الْمَالِ، وَغَيْظُ الْعَدُوِّ، وَأَنْ لاَ يُؤْخَذَ مِنْهُمْ إِلاَّ فَضْلُهُمْ عَنْ رِضَاهُمْ، وَأُوصِيهِ بِالأَعْرَابِ خَيْرًا، فَإِنَّهُمْ أَصْلُ الْعَرَبِ وَمَادَّةُ الإِسْلاَمِ أَنْ يُؤْخَذَ مِنْ حَوَاشِي أَمْوَالِهِمْ وَتُرَدَّ عَلَى فُقَرَائِهِمْ، وَأُوصِيهِ بِذِمَّةِ اللَّهِ وَذِمَّةِ رَسُولِهِ صلى الله عليه وسلم أَنْ يُوفَى لَهُمْ بِعَهْدِهِمْ، وَأَنْ يُقَاتَلَ مِنْ وَرَائِهِمْ، وَلاَ يُكَلَّفُوا إِلاَّ طَاقَتَهُمْ. فَلَمَّا قُبِضَ خَرَجْنَا بِهِ فَانْطَلَقْنَا نَمْشِي فَسَلَّمَ عَبْدُ اللَّهِ بْنُ عُمَرَ قَالَ يَسْتَأْذِنُ عُمَرُ بْنُ الْخَطَّابِ. قَالَتْ أَدْخِلُوهُ. فَأُدْخِلَ، فَوُضِعَ هُنَالِكَ مَعَ صَاحِبَيْهِ، فَلَمَّا فُرِغَ مِنْ دَفْنِهِ اجْتَمَعَ هَؤُلاَءِ الرَّهْطُ، فَقَالَ عَبْدُ الرَّحْمَنِ اجْعَلُوا أَمْرَكُمْ إِلَى ثَلاَثَةٍ مِنْكُمْ. فَقَالَ الزُّبَيْرُ قَدْ جَعَلْتُ أَمْرِي إِلَى عَلِيٍّ. فَقَالَ طَلْحَةُ قَدْ جَعَلْتُ أَمْرِي إِلَى عُثْمَانَ. وَقَالَ سَعْدٌ قَدْ جَعَلْتُ أَمْرِي إِلَى عَبْدِ الرَّحْمَنِ بْنِ عَوْفٍ. فَقَالَ عَبْدُ الرَّحْمَنِ أَيُّكُمَا تَبَرَّأَ مِنْ هَذَا الأَمْرِ فَنَجْعَلُهُ إِلَيْهِ، وَاللَّهُ عَلَيْهِ وَالإِسْلاَمُ لَيَنْظُرَنَّ أَفْضَلَهُمْ فِي نَفْسِهِ. فَأُسْكِتَ الشَّيْخَانِ، فَقَالَ عَبْدُ الرَّحْمَنِ أَفَتَجْعَلُونَهُ إِلَيَّ، وَاللَّهُ عَلَيَّ أَنْ لاَ آلُوَ عَنْ أَفْضَلِكُمْ قَالاَ نَعَمْ، فَأَخَذَ بِيَدِ أَحَدِهِمَا فَقَالَ لَكَ قَرَابَةٌ مِنْ رَسُولِ اللَّهِ صلى الله عليه وسلم وَالْقَدَمُ فِي الإِسْلاَمِ مَا قَدْ عَلِمْتَ، فَاللَّهُ عَلَيْكَ لَئِنْ أَمَّرْتُكَ لَتَعْدِلَنَّ، وَلَئِنْ أَمَّرْتُ عُثْمَانَ لَتَسْمَعَنَّ وَلَتُطِيعَنَّ. ثُمَّ خَلاَ بِالآخَرِ فَقَالَ لَهُ مِثْلَ ذَلِكَ، فَلَمَّا أَخَذَ الْمِيثَاقَ قَالَ ارْفَعْ يَدَكَ يَا عُثْمَانُ. فَبَايَعَهُ، فَبَايَعَ لَهُ عَلِيٌّ، وَوَلَجَ أَهْلُ الدَّارِ فَبَايَعُوهُ.

Narrated ‘Ubaid bin `Umair: Abu Musa asked `Umar to admit him but he was not admitted as `Umar was busy, so Abu Musa went back. When `Umar finished his job he said, “Didn’t I hear the voice of `Abdullah bin Qais? Let him come in.” `Umar was told that he had left. So, he sent for him and on his arrival, he (Abu Musa) said, “We were ordered to do so (i.e. to leave if not admitted after asking permission thrice). `Umar told him, “Bring witness in proof of your statement.” Abu Musa went to the Ansar’s meeting places and asked them. They said, “None amongst us will give this witness except the youngest of us, Abu Sa`id Al-Khudri. Abu Musa then took Abu Sa`id Al-Khudri (to `Umar) and `Umar said, surprisingly, “Has this order of Allah’s Messenger ﷺ been hidden from me?” (Then he’added), “I used to be busy trading in markets.”. – Sahih Al-Bukhari 2062

حَدَّثَنَا مُحَمَّدُ بْنُ سَلاَمٍ، أَخْبَرَنَا مَخْلَدُ بْنُ يَزِيدَ، أَخْبَرَنَا ابْنُ جُرَيْجٍ، قَالَ أَخْبَرَنِي عَطَاءٌ، عَنْ عُبَيْدِ بْنِ عُمَيْرٍ، أَنَّ أَبَا مُوسَى الأَشْعَرِيَّ، اسْتَأْذَنَ عَلَى عُمَرَ بْنِ الْخَطَّابِ ـ رضى الله عنه ـ فَلَمْ يُؤْذَنْ لَهُ، وَكَأَنَّهُ كَانَ مَشْغُولاً فَرَجَعَ أَبُو مُوسَى، فَفَرَغَ عُمَرُ فَقَالَ أَلَمْ أَسْمَعْ صَوْتَ عَبْدِ اللَّهِ بْنِ قَيْسٍ ائْذَنُوا لَهُ قِيلَ قَدْ رَجَعَ. فَدَعَاهُ. فَقَالَ كُنَّا نُؤْمَرُ بِذَلِكَ. فَقَالَ تَأْتِينِي عَلَى ذَلِكَ

بِالْبَيِّنَةِ. فَانْطَلَقَ إِلَى مَجْلِسِ الأَنْصَارِ، فَسَأَلَهُمْ. فَقَالُوا لاَ يَشْهَدُ لَكَ عَلَى هَذَا إِلاَّ أَصْغَرُنَا أَبُو سَعِيدٍ الْخُدْرِيُّ. فَذَهَبَ بِأَبِي سَعِيدٍ الْخُدْرِيِّ. فَقَالَ عُمَرُ أَخَفِيَ عَلَىَّ مِنْ أَمْرِ رَسُولِ اللَّهِ صلى الله عليه وسلم أَلْهَانِي الصَّفْقُ بِالأَسْوَاقِ. يَعْنِي الْخُرُوجَ إِلَى تِجَارَةٍ

Narrated Sa`id bin Jubair: About Ibn `Abbas: `Umar bin Al-Khattab used to treat Ibn `Abbas very favorably `Abdur Rahman bin `Auf said to him. "We also have sons that are equal to him (but you are partial to him.)" `Umar said, "It is because of his knowledge." Then `Umar asked Ibn `Abbas about the interpretation of the Verse:- 'When come the Help of Allah and the conquest (of Mecca) (110.1) Ibn `Abbas said. "It portended the death of Allah's Messenger ﷺ, which Allah had informed him of." `Umar said, "I do not know from this Verse but what you know.". – Sahih Al-Bukhari 3627

حَدَّثَنَا مُحَمَّدُ بْنُ عَرْعَرَةَ، حَدَّثَنَا شُعْبَةُ، عَنْ أَبِي بِشْرٍ، عَنْ سَعِيدِ بْنِ جُبَيْرٍ، عَنِ ابْنِ عَبَّاسٍ، قَالَ كَانَ عُمَرُ بْنُ الْخَطَّابِ ـ رضى الله عنه ـ يُدْنِي ابْنَ عَبَّاسٍ، فَقَالَ لَهُ عَبْدُ الرَّحْمَنِ بْنُ عَوْفٍ إِنَّ لَنَا أَبْنَاءً مِثْلَهُ. فَقَالَ إِنَّهُ مِنْ حَيْثُ تَعْلَمُ. فَسَأَلَ عُمَرُ ابْنَ عَبَّاسٍ عَنْ هَذِهِ الآيَةِ {إِذَا جَاءَ نَصْرُ اللَّهِ وَالْفَتْحُ}. فَقَالَ أَجَلُ رَسُولِ اللَّهِ صلى الله عليه وسلم أَعْلَمَهُ إِيَّاهُ. قَالَ مَا أَعْلَمُ مِنْهَا إِلاَّ مَا تَعْلَمُ

Narrated Qais: I heard Sa`id bin Zaid bin `Amr bin Nufail saying in the mosque of Al-Kufa. "By Allah, I have seen myself tied and forced by `Umar to leave Islam before `Umar himself embraced Islam. And if the mountain of Uhud could move from its place for the evil which you people have done to `Uthman, then it would have the right to move from its place.". – Sahih Al-Bukhari 3862

حَدَّثَنَا قُتَيْبَةُ بْنُ سَعِيدٍ، حَدَّثَنَا سُفْيَانُ، عَنْ إِسْمَاعِيلَ، عَنْ قَيْسٍ، قَالَ سَمِعْتُ سَعِيدَ بْنَ زَيْدِ بْنِ عَمْرِو بْنِ نُفَيْلٍ، فِي مَسْجِدِ الْكُوفَةِ يَقُولُ وَاللَّهِ لَقَدْ رَأَيْتُنِي وَإِنَّ عُمَرَ لَمُوثِقِي عَلَى الإِسْلاَمِ قَبْلَ أَنْ يُسْلِمَ عُمَرُ، وَلَوْ أَنَّ أُحُدًا ارْفَضَّ لِلَّذِي صَنَعْتُمْ بِعُثْمَانَ لَكَانَ مَحْقُوقًا أَنْ يَرْفَضَّ.

Narrated `Abdullah bin `Amr bin Rabi`a: Who was one of the leaders of Bani `Adi and his father participated in the battle of Badr in the company of the Prophet. `Umar appointed Qudama bin Maz'un as ruler of Bahrain, Qudama was one of the warriors of the battle of Badr and was the maternal uncle of `Abdullah bin `Umar and Hafsa. – Sahih Al-Bukhari 4011

حَدَّثَنَا أَبُو الْيَمَانِ، أَخْبَرَنَا شُعَيْبٌ، عَنِ الزُّهْرِيِّ، قَالَ أَخْبَرَنِي عَبْدُ اللَّهِ بْنُ عَامِرِ بْنِ رَبِيعَةَ، وَكَانَ، مِنْ أَكْبَرِ بَنِي عَدِيٍّ وَكَانَ أَبُوهُ شَهِدَ بَدْرًا مَعَ النَّبِيِّ صلى الله عليه وسلم أَنَّ عُمَرَ اسْتَعْمَلَ قُدَامَةَ بْنَ مَظْعُونٍ عَلَى الْبَحْرَيْنِ، وَكَانَ شَهِدَ بَدْرًا، وَهُوَ خَالُ عَبْدِ اللَّهِ بْنِ عُمَرَ وَحَفْصَةَ رضى الله عنهم

Narrated Tha`laba bin Abi Malik: `Umar bin Al-Khattab distributed woolen clothes amongst some women of Medina, and a nice woolen garment remained. Some of those who were sitting with him, said, "O chief of the believers! Give it to the daughter of Allah's Messenger ﷺ who is with you," and by that, they meant Um Kulthum, the daughter of `Ali. `Umar said, "Um Salit has got more right than she." Um Salit was amongst those Ansari women who had given the pledge of allegiance to Allah's Messenger ﷺ. Umar added, "She (i.e. Um Salit) used to carry the filled water skins for us on the day of the battle of Uhud.". – Sahih Al-Bukhari 4071

حَدَّثَنَا يَحْيَى بْنُ بُكَيْرٍ، حَدَّثَنَا اللَّيْثُ، عَنْ يُونُسَ، عَنِ ابْنِ شِهَابٍ، وَقَالَ ثَعْلَبَةُ بْنُ أَبِي مَالِكٍ إِنَّ عُمَرَ بْنَ الْخَطَّابِ ـ رضى الله عنه ـ قَسَمَ مُرُوطًا بَيْنَ نِسَاءٍ مِنْ نِسَاءِ أَهْلِ الْمَدِينَةِ، فَبَقِيَ مِنْهَا مِرْطٌ جَيِّدٌ، فَقَالَ لَهُ بَعْضُ مَنْ عِنْدَهُ يَا أَمِيرَ الْمُؤْمِنِينَ أَعْطِ هَذَا بِنْتَ رَسُولِ اللَّهِ صلى الله عليه وسلم الَّتِي عِنْدَكَ. يُرِيدُونَ أُمَّ كُلْثُومٍ بِنْتَ عَلِيٍّ. فَقَالَ عُمَرُ أُمُّ سَلِيطٍ أَحَقُّ بِهِ. وَأُمُّ سَلِيطٍ مِنْ نِسَاءِ الأَنْصَارِ مِمَّنْ بَايَعَ رَسُولَ اللَّهِ صلى الله عليه وسلم، قَالَ عُمَرُ فَإِنَّهَا كَانَتْ تُزْفِرُ لَنَا الْقِرَبَ يَوْمَ أُحُدٍ

Narrated Aslam: Once I went with `Umar bin Al-Khattab to the market. A young woman followed `Umar and said, "O chief of the believers! My husband has died, leaving little children. By Allah, they have not even a sheep's trotter to cook; they have no farms or animals. I am afraid that they may die because of hunger, and I am the daughter of Khufaf bin Ima Al-Ghafari, and my father witnessed the Pledge of allegiance) of Al-Hudaibiya with the Prophet.' `Umar stopped and did not proceed, and said, "I welcome my near relative." Then he went towards a strong camel which was tied in the house, and carried on to it, two sacks he had loaded with food grains and put between them money and clothes and gave her its rope to hold and said, "Lead it, and this provision will not finish till Allah gives you a good supply." A man said, "O chief of the believers! You have given her too much." "`Umar said disapprovingly. "May your mother be bereaved of you! By Allah, I have seen her father and brother besieging a fort for a long time and conquering it, and then we were discussing what their shares they would have from that war booty.". – Sahih Al-Bukhari 4160, 4161

حَدَّثَنَا إِسْمَاعِيلُ بْنُ عَبْدِ اللَّهِ، قَالَ حَدَّثَنِي مَالِكٌ، عَنْ زَيْدِ بْنِ أَسْلَمَ، عَنْ أَبِيهِ، قَالَ خَرَجْتُ مَعَ عُمَرَ بْنِ الْخَطَّابِ ـ رضى الله عنه ـ إِلَى السُّوقِ، فَلَحِقَتْ عُمَرَ امْرَأَةٌ شَابَّةٌ فَقَالَتْ يَا أَمِيرَ الْمُؤْمِنِينَ هَلَكَ زَوْجِي وَتَرَكَ صِبْيَةً صِغَارًا، وَاللَّهِ مَا يُنْضِجُونَ كُرَاعًا، وَلاَ لَهُمْ زَرْعٌ وَلاَ ضَرْعٌ، وَخَشِيتُ أَنْ تَأْكُلَهُمُ الضَّبُعُ، وَأَنَا بِنْتُ خُفَافِ بْنِ إِيمَاءَ الْغِفَارِيِّ، وَقَدْ شَهِدَ أَبِي الْحُدَيْبِيَةَ مَعَ النَّبِيِّ صلى الله عليه وسلم، فَوَقَفَ مَعَهَا عُمَرُ، وَلَمْ يَمْضِ، ثُمَّ قَالَ مَرْحَبًا بِنَسَبٍ قَرِيبٍ. ثُمَّ انْصَرَفَ إِلَى بَعِيرٍ ظَهِيرٍ كَانَ مَرْبُوطًا فِي الدَّارِ، فَحَمَلَ عَلَيْهِ غِرَارَتَيْنِ مَلأَهُمَا طَعَامًا، وَحَمَلَ بَيْنَهُمَا نَفَقَةً وَثِيَابًا، ثُمَّ نَاوَلَهَا بِخِطَامِهِ ثُمَّ قَالَ اقْتَادِيهِ فَلَنْ يَفْنَى حَتَّى يَأْتِيَكُمُ اللَّهُ بِخَيْرٍ. فَقَالَ رَجُلٌ يَا أَمِيرَ الْمُؤْمِنِينَ أَكْثَرْتَ لَهَا. قَالَ عُمَرُ ثَكِلَتْكَ أُمُّكَ، وَاللَّهِ إِنِّي لأَرَى أَبَا هَذِهِ وَأَخَاهَا قَدْ حَاصَرَا حِصْنًا زَمَانًا، فَافْتَتَحَاهُ، ثُمَّ أَصْبَحْنَا نَسْتَفِيءُ سُهْمَانَهُمَا فِيهِ.

Narrated Zaid bin Aslam: My father said, "Allah's Messenger ﷺ was proceeding at night on one of his journeys and `Umar bin Al- Khattab was going along with him. `Umar bin Al-Khattab asked him (about something) but Allah's Apostle did not answer him. `Umar asked him again, but he did not answer him. He asked him again (for the third time) but he did not answer him. On that `Umar bin Al-Khattab addressed himself saying, "May your mother be bereaved of you, O `Umar, for you have asked Allah's Messenger ﷺ thrice, yet he has not answered you." `Umar said, "Then I made my camel run fast and took it in front of the other Muslims, and I was afraid that something might be revealed in my connection. I had hardly waited for a moment when I heard somebody calling me. I said, 'I was afraid that something might have been revealed about me.' Then I came to Allah's Messenger ﷺ and greeted him. He (i.e. the Prophet) said, 'Tonight there has been revealed to me, a Sura which is dearer to me than (all the world) on which the sun rises,' and then he recited: 'Verily! We have granted you (O Muhammad) A manifest victory." (48.1). – Sahih Al-Bukhari 4177

حَدَّثَنِي عَبْدُ اللَّهِ بْنُ يُوسُفَ، أَخْبَرَنَا مَالِكٌ، عَنْ زَيْدِ بْنِ أَسْلَمَ، عَنْ أَبِيهِ، أَنَّ رَسُولَ اللَّهِ صلى الله عليه وسلم كَانَ يَسِيرُ فِي بَعْضِ أَسْفَارِهِ، وَعُمَرُ بْنُ الْخَطَّابِ يَسِيرُ مَعَهُ لَيْلاً، فَسَأَلَهُ عُمَرُ بْنُ الْخَطَّابِ عَنْ شَىْءٍ فَلَمْ يُجِبْهُ رَسُولُ اللَّهِ صلى الله عليه وسلم ثُمَّ سَأَلَهُ فَلَمْ يُجِبْهُ، ثُمَّ سَأَلَهُ فَلَمْ يُجِبْهُ وَقَالَ عُمَرُ بْنُ الْخَطَّابِ ثَكِلَتْكَ أُمُّكَ يَا عُمَرُ، نَزَرْتَ رَسُولَ اللَّهِ صلى الله عليه وسلم ثَلاَثَ مَرَّاتٍ، كُلُّ ذَلِكَ لاَ يُجِيبُكَ. قَالَ عُمَرُ فَحَرَّكْتُ بَعِيرِي ثُمَّ تَقَدَّمْتُ أَمَامَ الْمُسْلِمِينَ، وَخَشِيتُ أَنْ يَنْزِلَ فِيَّ قُرْآنٌ، فَمَا نَشِبْتُ أَنْ سَمِعْتُ صَارِخًا يَصْرُخُ بِي ـ قَالَ ـ فَقُلْتُ لَقَدْ خَشِيتُ أَنْ يَكُونَ نَزَلَ فِيَّ قُرْآنٌ. وَجِئْتُ رَسُولَ اللَّهِ صلى الله عليه وسلم فَسَلَّمْتُ عَلَيْهِ فَقَالَ " لَقَدْ أُنْزِلَتْ عَلَىَّ اللَّيْلَةَ سُورَةٌ لَهِيَ أَحَبُّ إِلَىَّ مِمَّا طَلَعَتْ عَلَيْهِ الشَّمْسُ، ثُمَّ قَرَأَ {إِنَّا فَتَحْنَا لَكَ فَتْحًا مُبِينًا}."

Narrated Nafi`: The people used to say that Ibn `Umar had embraced Islam before `Umar. This is not true. What happened is that `Umar sent `Abdullah to bring his horse from an Ansari man so as to fight on it. At that time the people were giving the Pledge of allegiance to Allah's Messenger ﷺ near the Tree, and `Umar was not aware of that. So `Abdullah (bin `Umar) gave the Pledge of Allegiance (to the Prophet) and went to take the horse and brought it to `Umar. While `Umar was putting on the armor to get ready for fighting, `Abdullah informed him that the people were giving the Pledge of allegiance to Allah's Apostle beneath the Tree. So `Umar set out and `Abdullah accompanied him till he gave the Pledge of allegiance to Allah's

Messenger ﷺ, and it was this event that made people say that Ibn `Umar had embraced Islam before `Umar. – Sahih Al-Bukhari 4186

حَدَّثَنِي شُجَاعُ بْنُ الْوَلِيدِ، سَمِعَ النَّضْرَ بْنَ مُحَمَّدٍ، حَدَّثَنَا صَخْرٌ، عَنْ نَافِعٍ، قَالَ إِنَّ النَّاسَ يَتَحَدَّثُونَ أَنَّ ابْنَ عُمَرَ، أَسْلَمَ قَبْلَ عُمَرَ، وَلَيْسَ كَذَلِكَ، وَلَكِنْ عُمَرُ يَوْمَ الْحُدَيْبِيَةِ أَرْسَلَ عَبْدَ اللَّهِ إِلَى فَرَسٍ لَهُ عِنْدَ رَجُلٍ مِنَ الأَنْصَارِ يَأْتِي بِهِ لِيُقَاتِلَ عَلَيْهِ، وَرَسُولُ اللَّهِ صلى الله عليه وسلم يُبَايِعُ عِنْدَ الشَّجَرَةِ، وَعُمَرُ لاَ يَدْرِي بِذَلِكَ، فَبَايَعَهُ عَبْدُ اللَّهِ، ثُمَّ ذَهَبَ إِلَى الْفَرَسِ، فَجَاءَ بِهِ إِلَى عُمَرَ، وَعُمَرُ يَسْتَلْئِمُ لِلْقِتَالِ، فَأَخْبَرَهُ أَنَّ رَسُولَ اللَّهِ صلى الله عليه وسلم يُبَايِعُ تَحْتَ الشَّجَرَةِ ـ قَالَ ـ فَانْطَلَقَ فَذَهَبَ مَعَهُ حَتَّى بَايَعَ رَسُولَ اللَّهِ صلى الله عليه وسلم، فَهِيَ الَّتِي يَتَحَدَّثُ النَّاسُ أَنَّ ابْنَ عُمَرَ أَسْلَمَ قَبْلَ عُمَرَ

Narrated Abu Musa: The news of the migration of the Prophet (from Mecca to Medina) reached us while we were in Yemen. So we set out as emigrants towards him. We were (three) I and my two brothers. I was the youngest of them, and one of the two was Abu Burda, and the other, Abu Ruhm, and our total number was either 53 or 52 men from my people. We got on board a boat and our boat took us to Negus in Ethiopia. There we met Ja`far bin Abi Talib and stayed with him. Then we all came (to Medina) and met the Prophet ﷺ at the time of the conquest of Khaibar. Some of the people used to say to us, namely the people of the ship, "We have migrated before you." Asma' bint 'Umais who was one of those who had come with us, came as a visitor to Hafsa, the wife the Prophet ﷺ. She had migrated along with those other Muslims who migrated to Negus. `Umar came to Hafsa while Asma' bint 'Umais was with her. `Umar, on seeing Asma,' said, "Who is this?" She said, "Asma' bint 'Umais," `Umar said, "Is she the Ethiopian? Is she the sea-faring lady?" Asma' replied, "Yes." `Umar said, "We have migrated before you (people of the boat), so we have got more right than you over Allah's Messenger ﷺ" On that Asma' became angry and said, "No, by Allah, while you were with Allah's Messenger ﷺ who was feeding the hungry ones amongst you, and advised the ignorant ones amongst you, we were in the far-off hated land of Ethiopia, and all that was for the sake of Allah's Messenger ﷺ. By Allah, I will neither eat any food nor drink anything till I inform Allah's Messenger ﷺ of all that you have said. There we were harmed and frightened. I will mention this to the Prophet ﷺ and will not tell a lie or curtail your saying or add something to it.". – Sahih Al-Bukhari 4230

حَدَّثَنِي مُحَمَّدُ بْنُ الْعَلاَءِ، حَدَّثَنَا أَبُو أُسَامَةَ، حَدَّثَنَا بُرَيْدُ بْنُ عَبْدِ اللَّهِ، عَنْ أَبِي بُرْدَةَ، عَنْ أَبِي مُوسَى ـ رضى الله عنه ـ قَالَ بَلَغَنَا مَخْرَجُ النَّبِيِّ صلى الله عليه وسلم وَنَحْنُ بِالْيَمَنِ، فَخَرَجْنَا مُهَاجِرِينَ إِلَيْهِ أَنَا، وَأَخَوَانِ لِي أَنَا أَصْغَرُهُمْ، أَحَدُهُمَا أَبُو بُرْدَةَ، وَالآخَرُ أَبُو رُهْمٍ ـ إِمَّا قَالَ بِضْعٌ وَإِمَّا قَالَ ـ فِي ثَلاَثَةٍ وَخَمْسِينَ أَوِ اثْنَيْنِ وَخَمْسِينَ رَجُلاً مِنْ قَوْمِي، فَرَكِبْنَا سَفِينَةً، فَأَلْقَتْنَا سَفِينَتُنَا إِلَى النَّجَاشِيِّ بِالْحَبَشَةِ، فَوَافَقْنَا جَعْفَرَ بْنَ أَبِي طَالِبٍ فَأَقَمْنَا مَعَهُ حَتَّى قَدِمْنَا جَمِيعًا، فَوَافَقْنَا النَّبِيَّ صلى الله عليه وسلم حِينَ افْتَتَحَ خَيْبَرَ، وَكَانَ أُنَاسٌ مِنَ النَّاسِ يَقُولُونَ لَنَا ـ يَعْنِي لأَهْلِ السَّفِينَةِ ـ سَبَقْنَاكُمْ بِالْهِجْرَةِ، وَدَخَلَتْ أَسْمَاءُ بِنْتُ عُمَيْسٍ، وَهْىَ مِمَّنْ قَدِمَ مَعَنَا، عَلَى حَفْصَةَ زَوْجِ النَّبِيِّ صلى الله عليه وسلم زَائِرَةً، وَقَدْ كَانَتْ هَاجَرَتْ إِلَى النَّجَاشِيِّ فِيمَنْ هَاجَرَ، فَدَخَلَ عُمَرُ عَلَى حَفْصَةَ وَأَسْمَاءُ عِنْدَهَا، فَقَالَ عُمَرُ حِينَ رَأَى أَسْمَاءَ مَنْ هَذِهِ قَالَتْ أَسْمَاءُ بِنْتُ عُمَيْسٍ. قَالَ عُمَرُ الْحَبَشِيَّةُ هَذِهِ الْبَحْرِيَّةُ هَذِهِ قَالَتْ أَسْمَاءُ نَعَمْ. قَالَ سَبَقْنَاكُمْ بِالْهِجْرَةِ، فَنَحْنُ أَحَقُّ بِرَسُولِ اللَّهِ صلى الله عليه وسلم مِنْكُمْ. فَغَضِبَتْ وَقَالَتْ كَلاَّ وَاللَّهِ، كُنْتُمْ مَعَ رَسُولِ اللَّهِ صلى الله عليه وسلم يُطْعِمُ جَائِعَكُمْ، وَيَعِظُ جَاهِلَكُمْ، وَكُنَّا فِي دَارِ أَوْ فِي أَرْضِ الْبُعَدَاءِ الْبُغَضَاءِ بِالْحَبَشَةِ، وَذَلِكَ فِي اللَّهِ وَفِي رَسُولِهِ صلى الله عليه وسلم وَايْمُ اللَّهِ، لاَ أَطْعَمُ طَعَامًا، وَلاَ أَشْرَبُ شَرَابًا حَتَّى أَذْكُرَ مَا قُلْتَ لِرَسُولِ اللَّهِ صلى الله عليه وسلم وَنَحْنُ كُنَّا نُؤْذَى وَنُخَافُ، وَسَأَذْكُرُ ذَلِكَ لِلنَّبِيِّ صلى الله عليه وسلم وَأَسْأَلُهُ، وَاللَّهِ لاَ أَكْذِبُ وَلاَ أَزِيغُ وَلاَ أَزِيدُ عَلَيْهِ.

So when the Prophet ﷺ came, she said, "O Allah's Prophet `Umar has said so-and-so." He said (to Asma'), "What did you say to him?" Asma's aid, "I told him so-and-so." The Prophet ﷺ said, "He (i.e. `Umar) has not got more right than you people over me, as he and his companions have (the reward of) only one migration, and you, the people of the boat, have (the reward of) two migrations." Asma' later on said, "I saw Abu Musa and the other people of the boat coming to me in successive groups, asking me about this narration,, and to them nothing in the world was more cheerful and greater than what the Prophet ﷺ had said about them."

Narrated Abu Burda: Asma' said, "I saw Abu Musa requesting me to repeat this narration again and again.". – Sahih Al-Bukhari 4231

فَلَمَّا جَاءَ النَّبِيُّ صلى الله عليه وسلم قَالَتْ يَا نَبِيَّ اللَّهِ إِنَّ عُمَرَ قَالَ كَذَا وَكَذَا. قَالَ " فَمَا قُلْتِ لَهُ ". قَالَتْ قُلْتُ لَهُ كَذَا وَكَذَا. قَالَ " لَيْسَ بِأَحَقَّ بِي مِنْكُمْ، وَلَهُ وَلأَصْحَابِهِ هِجْرَةٌ وَاحِدَةٌ، وَلَكُمْ أَنْتُمْ أَهْلَ السَّفِينَةِ هِجْرَتَانِ ". قَالَتْ فَلَقَدْ رَأَيْتُ أَبَا مُوسَى وَأَصْحَابَ السَّفِينَةِ يَأْتُونِي أَرْسَالاً، يَسْأَلُونِي عَنْ هَذَا الْحَدِيثِ، مَا مِنَ الدُّنْيَا شَىْءٌ هُمْ بِهِ أَفْرَحُ وَلاَ أَعْظَمُ فِي أَنْفُسِهِمْ مِمَّا قَالَ لَهُمُ النَّبِيُّ صلى الله عليه وسلم. قَالَ أَبُو بُرْدَةَ قَالَتْ أَسْمَاءُ فَلَقَدْ رَأَيْتُ أَبَا مُوسَى وَإِنَّهُ لَيَسْتَعِيدُ هَذَا الْحَدِيثَ مِنِّي

Narrated Abu Musa Al-Ash`ari: Allah's Messenger ﷺ sent me (as a governor) to the land of my people, and I came while Allah's Messenger ﷺ was encamping at a place called Al-Abtah. The Prophet ﷺ said, "Have you made the intention to perform the Hajj, O `Abdullah bin Qais?" I replied, "Yes, O Allah's Messenger ﷺ!" He said, "What did you say?" I replied, "I said, 'Labbaik' and expressed the same intention as yours." He said, "Have you driven the Hadi along with you?" I replied, "No, I did not drive the Hadi." He said, "So perform the Tawaf of the Ka`ba and then the Sai, between Safa and Marwa and then finish the state of Ihram." So I did the same, and one of the women of (the tribe of) Banu-Qais combed my hair. We continued follow in that tradition till the caliphate of `Umar. – Sahih Al-Bukhari 4346

حَدَّثَنِي عَبَّاسُ بْنُ الْوَلِيدِ، حَدَّثَنَا عَبْدُ الْوَاحِدِ، عَنْ أَيُّوبَ بْنِ عَائِذٍ، حَدَّثَنَا قَيْسُ بْنُ مُسْلِمٍ، قَالَ سَمِعْتُ طَارِقَ بْنَ شِهَابٍ، يَقُولُ حَدَّثَنِي أَبُو مُوسَى الأَشْعَرِيُّ ـ رضى الله عنه ـ قَالَ بَعَثَنِي رَسُولُ اللَّهِ صلى الله عليه وسلم إِلَى أَرْضِ قَوْمِي، فَجِئْتُ وَرَسُولُ اللَّهِ صلى الله عليه وسلم مُنِيخٌ بِالأَبْطَحِ فَقَالَ " أَحَجَجْتَ يَا عَبْدَ اللَّهِ بْنَ قَيْسٍ ". قُلْتُ نَعَمْ يَا رَسُولَ اللَّهِ. قَالَ " كَيْفَ قُلْتَ ". قَالَ قُلْتُ لَبَّيْكَ إِهْلاَلاً كَإِهْلاَلِكَ. قَالَ " فَهَلْ سُقْتَ مَعَكَ هَدْيًا ". قُلْتُ لَمْ أَسُقْ. قَالَ " فَطُفْ بِالْبَيْتِ وَاسْعَ بَيْنَ الصَّفَا وَالْمَرْوَةِ ثُمَّ حِلَّ ". فَفَعَلْتُ حَتَّى مَشَطَتْ لِي امْرَأَةٌ مِنْ نِسَاءِ بَنِي قَيْسٍ، وَمَكُثْنَا بِذَلِكَ حَتَّى اسْتُخْلِفَ عُمَرُ

Narrated Ibn `Abbas: 'Uyaina bin Hisn bin Hudhaifa came and stayed with his nephew Al-Hurr bin Qais who was one of those whom `Umar used to keep near him, as the Qurra' (learned men knowing Qur'an by heart) were the people of `Umar's meetings and his advisors whether they were old or young. 'Uyaina said to his nephew, "O son of my brother! You have an approach to this chief, so get for me the permission to see him." Al-Hurr said, "I will get the permission for you to see him." So Al-Hurr asked the permission for 'Uyaina and `Umar admitted him. When 'Uyaina entered upon him, he said, "Beware! O the son of Al-Khattab! By Allah, you neither give us sufficient provision nor judge among us with justice." Thereupon `Umar became so furious that he intended to harm him, but Al-Hurr said, "O chief of the Believers! Allah said to His Prophet: "Hold to forgiveness; command what is right; and leave (don't punish) the foolish." (7.199) and this (i.e. 'Uyaina) is one of the foolish." By Allah, `Umar did not overlook that Verse when Al-Hurr recited it before him; he observed (the orders of) Allah's Book strictly. – Sahih Al-Bukhari 4642

حَدَّثَنَا أَبُو الْيَمَانِ، أَخْبَرَنَا شُعَيْبٌ، عَنِ الزُّهْرِيِّ، قَالَ أَخْبَرَنِي عُبَيْدُ اللَّهِ بْنُ عَبْدِ اللَّهِ بْنِ عُتْبَةَ، أَنَّ ابْنَ عَبَّاسٍ ـ رضى الله عنهما ـ قَالَ قَدِمَ عُيَيْنَةُ بْنُ حِصْنِ بْنِ حُذَيْفَةَ فَنَزَلَ عَلَى ابْنِ أَخِيهِ الْحُرِّ بْنِ قَيْسٍ، وَكَانَ مِنَ النَّفَرِ الَّذِينَ يُدْنِيهِمْ عُمَرُ، وَكَانَ الْقُرَّاءُ أَصْحَابَ مَجَالِسِ عُمَرَ وَمُشَاوَرَتِهِ كُهُولاً كَانُوا أَوْ شُبَّانًا. فَقَالَ عُيَيْنَةُ لاِبْنِ أَخِيهِ يَا ابْنَ أَخِي، لَكَ وَجْهٌ عِنْدَ هَذَا الأَمِيرِ فَاسْتَأْذِنْ لِي عَلَيْهِ. قَالَ سَأَسْتَأْذِنُ لَكَ عَلَيْهِ. قَالَ ابْنُ عَبَّاسٍ فَاسْتَأْذَنَ الْحُرُّ لِعُيَيْنَةَ فَأَذِنَ لَهُ عُمَرُ، فَلَمَّا دَخَلَ عَلَيْهِ قَالَ هِيْ يَا ابْنَ الْخَطَّابِ، فَوَاللَّهِ مَا تُعْطِينَا الْجَزْلَ، وَلاَ تَحْكُمُ بَيْنَنَا بِالْعَدْلِ. فَغَضِبَ عُمَرُ حَتَّى هَمَّ بِهِ، فَقَالَ لَهُ الْحُرُّ يَا أَمِيرَ الْمُؤْمِنِينَ إِنَّ اللَّهَ تَعَالَى قَالَ لِنَبِيِّهِ صلى الله عليه وسلم {خُذِ الْعَفْوَ وَأْمُرْ بِالْعُرْفِ وَأَعْرِضْ عَنِ الْجَاهِلِينَ} وَإِنَّ هَذَا مِنَ الْجَاهِلِينَ. وَاللَّهِ مَا جَاوَزَهَا عُمَرُ حِينَ تَلاَهَا عَلَيْهِ، وَكَانَ وَقَّافًا عِنْدَ كِتَابِ اللَّهِ.

Narrated Ibn `Abbas: I had been eager to ask `Umar bin Al-Khattab about the two ladies from among the wives of the Prophet regarding whom Allah said 'If you two (wives of the Prophet ﷺ namely Aisha and Hafsa) turn in repentance to Allah, your hearts are indeed so inclined (to oppose what the Prophet ﷺ likes). (66.4) till `Umar performed the Hajj and I too, performed the Hajj along with him. (On the way) `Umar went aside to answer the call of nature, and I also went aside along with him carrying a tumbler full of water, and when `Umar had finished answering the call of nature, I poured water over his hands and he performed the ablution. Then I said to him, "O chief of the Believers! Who were the two ladies from among the wives of the Prophetﷺ regarding whom Allah said: 'If you two (wives of the Prophet) turn in repentance to Allah your hearts are indeed so inclined (to oppose what the Prophetﷺ likes)?" (66.4) He said, "I am astonished at your question, O Ibn `Abbas. They were `Aisha and Hafsa." Then `Umar went on narrating the Hadith and said, "I and an Ansari neighbor of mine from Bani Umaiyya bin Zaid who used to live in `Awali-al-Medina, used to visit the Prophetﷺ in turn. He used to go one day and I another day. When I went, I would bring him the news of what had happened that day regarding the Divine Inspiration and other things, and when he went, he used to do the same for me. We, the people of Quraish used to have the upper hand over our wives, but when we came to the Ansar, we found that their women had the upper hand over their men, so our women also started learning the ways of the Ansari women. I shouted at my wife and she retorted against me and I disliked that she should answer me back. She said to me, 'Why are you so surprised at my answering you back? By Allah, the wives of the Prophet answer him back and some of them may leave (does not speak to) him throughout the day till the night.' The (talk) scared me and I said to her, 'Whoever has done so will be ruined!' Then I proceeded after dressing myself, and entered upon Hafsa and said to her, 'Does anyone of you keep the Prophetﷺ angry till night?' She said, 'Yes.' I said, 'You are a ruined losing person! Don't you fear that Allah may get angry for the anger of Allah's Messengerﷺ and thus you will be ruined? So do not ask more from the Prophetﷺ and do not answer him back and do not give up talking to him. Ask me whatever you need and do not be tempted to imitate your'neighbor (i.e., `Aisha) in her manners for she is more charming than you and more beloved to the Prophetﷺ." Umar added, "At that time a talk was circulating among us that (the tribe of) Ghassan were preparing their horses to invade us. My Ansari companion, on the day of his turn, went (to the town) and returned to us at night and knocked at my door violently and asked if I was there. I became horrified and came out to him. He said, 'Today a great thing has happened.' I asked, 'What is it? Have (the people of) Ghassan come?' He said, 'No, but (What has happened) is greater and more horrifying than that: Allah's Messengerﷺ has divorced his wives. `Umar added, "The Prophet kept away from his wives and I said "Hafsa is a ruined loser.' I had already thought that most probably this (divorce) would happen in the near future. So I dressed myself and offered the morning prayer with the Prophetﷺ and then the Prophet; entered an upper room and stayed there in seclusion. I entered upon Hafsa and saw her weeping. I asked, 'What makes you weep? Did I not warn you about that? Did the Prophetﷺ divorce you all?' She said, 'I do not know. There he is retired alone in the upper room.' I came out and sat near the pulpit and saw a group of people sitting around it and some of them were weeping. I sat with them for a while but could not endure the situation, so I went to the upper room where the Prophet; was and said to a black slave of his, 'Will you get the permission (of the Prophetﷺ) for `Umar (to enter)?' The slave went in, talked to the Prophetﷺ about it and then returned saying, 'I have spoken to the Prophetﷺ and mentioned you but he kept quiet.' Then I returned and sat with the group of people sitting near the pulpit. But I could not bear the situation and once again I said to the slave, 'Will you get the permission for `Umar?' He went in and returned saying, 'I mentioned you to him but he kept quiet.' So I returned again and sat with the group of people sitting near the pulpit, but I could not bear the situation, and so I went to the slave and said, 'Will you get the permission for `Umar?' He went in and returned to me saying, 'I mentioned you to him but he kept quiet.' When I was leaving, behold! The slave called me, saying, 'The Prophet ﷺ has given you permission.' Then I entered upon Allah's Messenger ﷺ and saw him Lying on a bed made of stalks of date palm leaves and there was no bedding between it and him. The stalks left marks on his side and he was leaning on a leather pillow stuffed with date-palm fires. I greeted him and while still standing I said, 'O Allah's Apostle! Have you divorced your wives?' He looked at me and said, 'No.' I said, 'Allah Akbar!' And then, while still standing, I said chatting, 'Will you heed what I say, O Allah's Messenger ﷺ? We, the people of Quraish used to have power over our women, but when we arrived at Medina we found that the men (here) were overpowered by their women.' The Prophet ﷺ smiled and then I said to him, 'Will you heed what I say, O Allah's Messenger ﷺ? I entered upon Hafsa and said to her, "Do not be tempted to imitate your companion (`Aisha), for she is more charming than you and more beloved to the Prophet.' " The Prophet ﷺ smiled for a second time. When I saw him smiling, I sat down. Then I looked around his house, and by Allah, I could not see anything of importance in his house except three hides, so I said, 'O Allah's Messenger ﷺ! Invoke Allah to make your followers rich, for the Persians and the Romans have been made prosperous and they have been given (the pleasures of the world), although they do not worship Allah.' Thereupon the Prophet ﷺ sat up as he was reclining. And said, 'Are you of such an opinion, O the son of Al-Khattab? These are the people who have received the rewards for their good deeds in this world.' I said, 'O Allah's Messenger ﷺ! Ask Allah to forgive me.' Then the Prophet ﷺ kept away from his wives for twenty-nine days because of the story which Hafsa had disclosed to `Aisha. The Prophet ﷺ had said, 'I will not enter upon them (my wives) for one month,' because of his anger towards them, when Allah had admonished him. So, when twenty nine days had passed, the Prophet ﷺ first entered upon `Aisha. `Aisha said to him, 'O Allah's Messenger ﷺ! You had sworn that you would not enter upon us for one month, but now only twenty-nine days have passed, for I have been counting them one by one.' The Prophet ﷺ said, 'The (present) month is of twenty nine days.' `Aisha added, 'Then Allah revealed the Verses of the option. (2) And out of all his-wives he asked me first, and I chose him.' Then he gave option to his other wives and they said what `Aisha had said . " (1) The Prophet, ' had decided to abstain from eating a certain kind of food becausee of a certain event, so Allah blamed him for doing so. Some of his wives were the cause of him taking that decision, therefore he deserted them for one month. See Qur'an: (66.4). – Sahih Al-Bukhari 5191

حَدَّثَنَا أَبُو الْيَمَانِ، أَخْبَرَنَا شُعَيْبٌ، عَنِ الزُّهْرِيِّ، قَالَ أَخْبَرَنِي عُبَيْدُ اللَّهِ بْنُ عَبْدِ اللَّهِ بْنِ أَبِي ثَوْرٍ، عَنْ عَبْدِ اللَّهِ بْنِ عَبَّاسٍ ـ رضى الله عنهما ـ قَالَ لَمْ أَزَلْ حَرِيصًا أَنْ أَسْأَلَ عُمَرَ بْنَ الْخَطَّابِ عَنِ الْمَرْأَتَيْنِ مِنْ أَزْوَاجِ النَّبِيِّ صلى الله عليه وسلم اللَّتَيْنِ قَالَ اللَّهُ تَعَالَى {إِنْ تَتُوبَا إِلَى اللَّهِ فَقَدْ صَغَتْ قُلُوبُكُمَا} حَتَّى حَجَّ وَحَجَجْتُ مَعَهُ، وَعَدَلَ وَعَدَلْتُ مَعَهُ بِإِدَاوَةٍ، فَتَبَرَّزَ، ثُمَّ جَاءَ فَسَكَبْتُ عَلَى يَدَيْهِ مِنْهَا فَتَوَضَّأَ فَقُلْتُ لَهُ يَا أَمِيرَ الْمُؤْمِنِينَ مَنِ الْمَرْأَتَانِ مِنْ أَزْوَاجِ النَّبِيِّ صلى الله عليه وسلم اللَّتَانِ قَالَ اللَّهُ تَعَالَى {إِنْ تَتُوبَا إِلَى اللَّهِ فَقَدْ صَغَتْ قُلُوبُكُمَا} قَالَ وَاعَجَبًا لَكَ يَا ابْنَ عَبَّاسٍ، هُمَا عَائِشَةُ وَحَفْصَةُ. ثُمَّ اسْتَقْبَلَ عُمَرُ الْحَدِيثَ يَسُوقُهُ قَالَ كُنْتُ أَنَا وَجَارٌ لِي مِنَ الأَنْصَارِ فِي بَنِي أُمَيَّةَ بْنِ زَيْدٍ، وَهُمْ مِنْ عَوَالِي الْمَدِينَةِ، وَكُنَّا نَتَنَاوَبُ النُّزُولَ عَلَى النَّبِيِّ صلى الله عليه وسلم فَيَنْزِلُ يَوْمًا وَأَنْزِلُ يَوْمًا، فَإِذَا نَزَلْتُ جِئْتُهُ بِمَا حَدَثَ مِنْ خَبَرِ ذَلِكَ الْيَوْمِ مِنَ الْوَحْىِ أَوْ غَيْرِهِ، وَإِذَا نَزَلَ فَعَلَ مِثْلَ ذَلِكَ، وَكُنَّا مَعْشَرَ قُرَيْشٍ نَغْلِبُ النِّسَاءَ، فَلَمَّا قَدِمْنَا عَلَى الأَنْصَارِ إِذَا قَوْمٌ تَغْلِبُهُمْ نِسَاؤُهُمْ، فَطَفِقَ نِسَاؤُنَا يَأْخُذْنَ مِنْ أَدَبِ نِسَاءِ الأَنْصَارِ، فَصَخِبْتُ عَلَى امْرَأَتِي فَرَاجَعَتْنِي فَأَنْكَرْتُ أَنْ تُرَاجِعَنِي قَالَتْ وَلِمَ تُنْكِرُ أَنْ أُرَاجِعَكَ فَوَاللَّهِ إِنَّ أَزْوَاجَ النَّبِيِّ صلى الله عليه وسلم لَيُرَاجِعْنَهُ، وَإِنَّ إِحْدَاهُنَّ لَتَهْجُرُهُ الْيَوْمَ حَتَّى اللَّيْلِ. فَأَفْزَعَنِي ذَلِكَ وَقُلْتُ لَهَا وَقَدْ خَابَ مَنْ فَعَلَ ذَلِكَ مِنْهُنَّ. ثُمَّ جَمَعْتُ عَلَىَّ ثِيَابِي فَنَزَلْتُ فَدَخَلْتُ عَلَى حَفْصَةَ فَقُلْتُ لَهَا أَىْ حَفْصَةُ أَتُغَاضِبُ إِحْدَاكُنَّ النَّبِيَّ صلى الله عليه وسلم الْيَوْمَ حَتَّى اللَّيْلِ قَالَتْ نَعَمْ. فَقُلْتُ قَدْ خِبْتِ وَخَسِرْتِ، أَفَتَأْمَنِينَ أَنْ يَغْضَبَ اللَّهُ لِغَضَبِ رَسُولِهِ صلى الله عليه وسلم فَتَهْلِكِي لاَ تَسْتَكْثِرِي النَّبِيَّ صلى الله عليه وسلم وَلاَ تُرَاجِعِيهِ فِي شَىْءٍ، وَلاَ تَهْجُرِيهِ، وَسَلِينِي مَا بَدَا لَكِ، وَلاَ يَغُرَّنَّكِ أَنْ كَانَتْ جَارَتُكِ أَوْضَأَ مِنْكِ، وَأَحَبَّ إِلَى النَّبِيِّ صلى الله عليه وسلم ـ يُرِيدُ عَائِشَةَ ـ قَالَ عُمَرُ وَكُنَّا قَدْ تَحَدَّثْنَا أَنَّ غَسَّانَ تُنْعِلُ الْخَيْلَ لِغَزْوِنَا، فَنَزَلَ صَاحِبِي الأَنْصَارِيُّ يَوْمَ نَوْبَتِهِ، فَرَجَعَ إِلَيْنَا عِشَاءً فَضَرَبَ بَابِي ضَرْبًا شَدِيدًا وَقَالَ أَثَمَّ هُوَ فَفَزِعْتُ فَخَرَجْتُ إِلَيْهِ، فَقَالَ قَدْ حَدَثَ الْيَوْمَ أَمْرٌ عَظِيمٌ. قُلْتُ مَا هُوَ، أَجَاءَ غَسَّانُ قَالَ لاَ بَلْ أَعْظَمُ مِنْ ذَلِكَ وَأَهْوَلُ، طَلَّقَ النَّبِيُّ صلى الله عليه وسلم نِسَاءَهُ. فَقُلْتُ خَابَتْ حَفْصَةُ وَخَسِرَتْ، قَدْ كُنْتُ أَظُنُّ هَذَا يُوشِكُ أَنْ يَكُونَ، فَجَمَعْتُ عَلَىَّ ثِيَابِي فَصَلَّيْتُ صَلاَةَ الْفَجْرِ مَعَ النَّبِيِّ صلى الله عليه وسلم فَدَخَلَ النَّبِيُّ صلى الله عليه وسلم مَشْرُبَةً لَهُ، فَاعْتَزَلَ فِيهَا، وَدَخَلْتُ عَلَى حَفْصَةَ فَإِذَا هِيَ تَبْكِي فَقُلْتُ مَا يُبْكِيكِ أَلَمْ أَكُنْ حَذَّرْتُكِ هَذَا أَطَلَّقَكُنَّ النَّبِيُّ صلى الله عليه وسلم قَالَتْ لاَ أَدْرِي هَا هُوَ ذَا مُعْتَزِلٌ فِي الْمَشْرُبَةِ. فَخَرَجْتُ فَجِئْتُ إِلَى الْمِنْبَرِ فَإِذَا حَوْلَهُ رَهْطٌ يَبْكِي بَعْضُهُمْ، فَجَلَسْتُ مَعَهُمْ قَلِيلاً ثُمَّ غَلَبَنِي مَا أَجِدُ، فَجِئْتُ الْمَشْرُبَةَ الَّتِي فِيهَا النَّبِيُّ صلى الله عليه وسلم فَقُلْتُ لِغُلاَمٍ لَهُ أَسْوَدَ اسْتَأْذِنْ لِعُمَرَ. فَدَخَلَ الْغُلاَمُ فَكَلَّمَ النَّبِيَّ صلى الله عليه وسلم ثُمَّ رَجَعَ فَقَالَ كَلَّمْتُ

النَّبِيَّ صلى الله عليه وسلم وَذَكَرْتُكَ لَهُ، فَصَمَتَ. فَانْصَرَفْتُ حَتَّى جَلَسْتُ مَعَ الرَّهْطِ الَّذِينَ عِنْدَ الْمِنْبَرِ، ثُمَّ غَلَبَنِي مَا أَجِدُ فَجِئْتُ فَقُلْتُ لِلْغُلاَمِ اسْتَأْذِنْ لِعُمَرَ. فَدَخَلَ ثُمَّ رَجَعَ فَقَالَ قَدْ ذَكَرْتُكَ لَهُ فَصَمَتَ. فَرَجَعْتُ فَجَلَسْتُ مَعَ الرَّهْطِ الَّذِينَ عِنْدَ الْمِنْبَرِ، ثُمَّ غَلَبَنِي مَا أَجِدُ فَجِئْتُ الْغُلاَمَ فَقُلْتُ اسْتَأْذِنْ لِعُمَرَ. فَدَخَلَ ثُمَّ رَجَعَ إِلَيَّ فَقَالَ قَدْ ذَكَرْتُكَ لَهُ فَصَمَتَ. فَلَمَّا وَلَّيْتُ مُنْصَرِفًا - قَالَ - إِذَا الْغُلاَمُ يَدْعُونِي فَقَالَ قَدْ أَذِنَ لَكَ النَّبِيُّ صلى الله عليه وسلم فَدَخَلْتُ عَلَى رَسُولِ اللَّهِ صلى الله عليه وسلم فَإِذَا هُوَ مُضْطَجِعٌ عَلَى رِمَالِ حَصِيرٍ، لَيْسَ بَيْنَهُ وَبَيْنَهُ فِرَاشٌ، قَدْ أَثَّرَ الرِّمَالُ بِجَنْبِهِ مُتَّكِئًا عَلَى وِسَادَةٍ مِنْ أَدَمٍ حَشْوُهَا لِيفٌ، فَسَلَّمْتُ عَلَيْهِ ثُمَّ قُلْتُ وَأَنَا قَائِمٌ يَا رَسُولَ اللَّهِ أَطَلَّقْتَ نِسَاءَكَ. فَرَفَعَ إِلَيَّ بَصَرَهُ فَقَالَ " لاَ ". فَقُلْتُ اللَّهُ أَكْبَرُ. ثُمَّ قُلْتُ وَأَنَا قَائِمٌ أَسْتَأْنِسُ يَا رَسُولَ اللَّهِ لَوْ رَأَيْتَنِي، وَكُنَّا مَعْشَرَ قُرَيْشٍ نَغْلِبُ النِّسَاءَ فَلَمَّا قَدِمْنَا الْمَدِينَةَ إِذَا قَوْمٌ تَغْلِبُهُمْ نِسَاؤُهُمْ، فَتَبَسَّمَ النَّبِيُّ صلى الله عليه وسلم ثُمَّ قُلْتُ يَا رَسُولَ اللَّهِ لَوْ رَأَيْتَنِي وَدَخَلْتُ عَلَى حَفْصَةَ فَقُلْتُ لَهَا لاَ يَغُرَّنَّكِ أَنْ كَانَتْ جَارَتُكِ أَوْضَأَ مِنْكِ وَأَحَبَّ إِلَى النَّبِيِّ صلى الله عليه وسلم يُرِيدُ عَائِشَةَ فَتَبَسَّمَ النَّبِيُّ صلى الله عليه وسلم تَبَسُّمَةً أُخْرَى، فَجَلَسْتُ حِينَ رَأَيْتُهُ تَبَسَّمَ، فَرَفَعْتُ بَصَرِي فِي بَيْتِهِ، فَوَاللَّهِ مَا رَأَيْتُ فِي بَيْتِهِ شَيْئًا يَرُدُّ الْبَصَرَ غَيْرَ أَهَبَةٍ ثَلاَثَةٍ، فَقُلْتُ يَا رَسُولَ اللَّهِ ادْعُ اللَّهَ فَلْيُوَسِّعْ عَلَى أُمَّتِكَ، فَإِنَّ فَارِسًا وَالرُّومَ قَدْ وُسِّعَ عَلَيْهِمْ، وَأُعْطُوا الدُّنْيَا وَهُمْ لاَ يَعْبُدُونَ اللَّهَ. فَجَلَسَ النَّبِيُّ صلى الله عليه وسلم وَكَانَ مُتَّكِئًا. فَقَالَ " أَوَفِي هَذَا أَنْتَ يَا ابْنَ الْخَطَّابِ، إِنَّ أُولَئِكَ قَوْمٌ عُجِّلُوا طَيِّبَاتِهِمْ فِي الْحَيَاةِ الدُّنْيَا ". فَقُلْتُ يَا رَسُولَ اللَّهِ اسْتَغْفِرْ لِي. فَاعْتَزَلَ النَّبِيُّ صلى الله عليه وسلم نِسَاءَهُ مِنْ أَجْلِ ذَلِكَ الْحَدِيثِ حِينَ أَفْشَتْهُ حَفْصَةُ إِلَى عَائِشَةَ تِسْعًا وَعِشْرِينَ لَيْلَةً وَكَانَ قَالَ " مَا أَنَا بِدَاخِلٍ عَلَيْهِنَّ شَهْرًا ". مِنْ شِدَّةِ مَوْجِدَتِهِ عَلَيْهِنَّ حِينَ عَاتَبَهُ اللَّهُ، فَلَمَّا مَضَتْ تِسْعٌ وَعِشْرُونَ لَيْلَةً دَخَلَ عَلَى عَائِشَةَ فَبَدَأَ بِهَا فَقَالَتْ لَهُ عَائِشَةُ يَا رَسُولَ اللَّهِ إِنَّكَ كُنْتَ قَدْ أَقْسَمْتَ أَنْ لاَ تَدْخُلَ عَلَيْنَا شَهْرًا، وَإِنَّمَا أَصْبَحْتَ مِنْ تِسْعٍ وَعِشْرِينَ لَيْلَةً أَعُدُّهَا عَدًّا. فَقَالَ " الشَّهْرُ تِسْعٌ وَعِشْرُونَ ". فَكَانَ ذَلِكَ الشَّهْرُ تِسْعًا وَعِشْرِينَ لَيْلَةً. قَالَتْ عَائِشَةُ ثُمَّ أَنْزَلَ اللَّهُ تَعَالَى آيَةَ التَّخَيُّرِ فَبَدَأَ بِي أَوَّلَ امْرَأَةٍ مِنْ نِسَائِهِ فَاخْتَرْتُهُ، ثُمَّ خَيَّرَ نِسَاءَهُ كُلَّهُنَّ فَقُلْنَ مِثْلَ مَا قَالَتْ عَائِشَةُ.

Narrated `Umar: I recommend that my successor should take care of and secure the rights of the early emigrants; and I also advise my successor to be kind to the Ansar who had homes (in Medina) and had adopted the Faith, before the Prophetﷺ migrated to them, and to accept the good from their good ones and excuse their wrong doers. – Sahih Al-Bukhari 4888

حَدَّثَنَا أَحْمَدُ بْنُ يُونُسَ، حَدَّثَنَا أَبُو بَكْرٍ، عَنْ حُصَيْنٍ، عَنْ عَمْرِو بْنِ مَيْمُونٍ، قَالَ قَالَ عُمَرُ رضى الله عنه أُوصِي الْخَلِيفَةَ بِالْمُهَاجِرِينَ الأَوَّلِينَ أَنْ يَعْرِفَ لَهُمْ حَقَّهُمْ، وَأُوصِي الْخَلِيفَةَ بِالأَنْصَارِ الَّذِينَ تَبَوَّءُوا الدَّارَ وَالإِيمَانَ مِنْ قَبْلِ أَنْ يُهَاجِرَ النَّبِيُّ صلى الله عليه وسلم أَنْ يَقْبَلَ مِنْ مُحْسِنِهِمْ وَيَعْفُوَ عَنْ مُسِيئِهِمْ.

Narrated Ibn `Abbas: When Allah's Messengerﷺ was on his death-bed and in the house there were some people among whom was `Umar bin Al-Khattab, the Prophetﷺ said, "Come, let me write for you a statement after which you will not go astray." `Umar said, "The Prophetﷺ is seriously ill and you have the Qur'an; so the Book of Allah is enough for us." The people present in the house differed and quarrelled. Some said "Go near so that the Prophetﷺ may write for you a statement after which you will not go astray," while the others said as `Umar said. When they caused a hue and cry before the Prophet, Allah's Messengerﷺ said, "Go away!" Narrated 'Ubaidullah: Ibn `Abbas used to say, "It was very unfortunate that Allah's Messengerﷺ was prevented from writing that statement for them because of their disagreement and noise.". – Sahih Al-Bukhari 5669

حَدَّثَنَا إِبْرَاهِيمُ بْنُ مُوسَى، حَدَّثَنَا هِشَامٌ، عَنْ مَعْمَرٍ، وَحَدَّثَنِي عَبْدُ اللَّهِ بْنُ مُحَمَّدٍ، حَدَّثَنَا عَبْدُ الرَّزَّاقِ، أَخْبَرَنَا مَعْمَرٌ، عَنِ الزُّهْرِيِّ، عَنْ عُبَيْدِ اللَّهِ بْنِ عَبْدِ اللَّهِ، عَنِ ابْنِ عَبَّاسٍ - رضى الله عنهما - قَالَ لَمَّا حُضِرَ رَسُولُ اللَّهِ صلى الله عليه وسلم وَفِي الْبَيْتِ رِجَالٌ فِيهِمْ عُمَرُ بْنُ الْخَطَّابِ قَالَ النَّبِيُّ صلى الله عليه وسلم " هَلُمَّ أَكْتُبْ لَكُمْ كِتَابًا لاَ تَضِلُّوا بَعْدَهُ ". فَقَالَ عُمَرُ إِنَّ النَّبِيَّ صلى الله عليه وسلم قَدْ غَلَبَ عَلَيْهِ الْوَجَعُ وَعِنْدَكُمُ الْقُرْآنُ، حَسْبُنَا كِتَابُ اللَّهِ فَاخْتَلَفَ أَهْلُ الْبَيْتِ فَاخْتَصَمُوا، مِنْهُمْ مَنْ يَقُولُ قَرِّبُوا يَكْتُبْ لَكُمُ النَّبِيُّ صلى الله عليه وسلم كِتَابًا لَنْ تَضِلُّوا بَعْدَهُ، وَمِنْهُمْ مَنْ يَقُولُ مَا قَالَ عُمَرُ فَلَمَّا أَكْثَرُوا اللَّغْوَ وَالاِخْتِلاَفَ عِنْدَ النَّبِيِّ صلى الله عليه وسلم قَالَ رَسُولُ اللَّهِ صلى الله عليه وسلم " قُومُوا ". قَالَ عُبَيْدُ اللَّهِ فَكَانَ ابْنُ عَبَّاسٍ يَقُولُ إِنَّ الرَّزِيَّةَ كُلَّ الرَّزِيَّةِ مَا حَالَ بَيْنَ رَسُولِ اللَّهِ صلى الله عليه وسلم وَبَيْنَ أَنْ يَكْتُبَ لَهُمْ ذَلِكَ الْكِتَابَ مِنِ اخْتِلاَفِهِمْ وَلَغَطِهِمْ

Narrated `Abdullah bin `Umar: It was said to 'Umar, "Will you appoint your successor?" `Umar said, "If I appoint a Caliph (as my successor) it is true that somebody who was better than I (i.e., Abu Bakr) did so, and if I leave the matter undecided, it is true that somebody who was better than I (i.e., Allah's Messengerﷺ) did so." On this, the people praised him. `Umar said, "People are of two kinds: Either one who is keen to take over the Caliphate or one who is afraid of assuming such a responsibility. I wish I could be free from its responsibility in that I would receive neither reward nor retribution I won't bear the burden of the caliphate in my death as I do in my life.". – Sahih Al-Bukhari 7218

حَدَّثَنَا مُحَمَّدُ بْنُ يُوسُفَ، أَخْبَرَنَا سُفْيَانُ، عَنْ هِشَامِ بْنِ عُرْوَةَ، عَنْ أَبِيهِ، عَنْ عَبْدِ اللَّهِ بْنِ عُمَرَ ـ رضى الله عنهما ـ قَالَ قِيلَ لِعُمَرَ أَلاَ تَسْتَخْلِفُ قَالَ إِنْ أَسْتَخْلِفْ فَقَدِ اسْتَخْلَفَ مَنْ هُوَ خَيْرٌ مِنِّي أَبُو بَكْرٍ، وَإِنْ أَتْرُكْ فَقَدْ تَرَكَ مَنْ هُوَ خَيْرٌ مِنِّي رَسُولُ اللَّهِ صلى الله عليه وسلم فَأَثْنَوْا عَلَيْهِ فَقَالَ رَاغِبٌ رَاهِبٌ، وَدِدْتُ أَنِّي نَجَوْتُ مِنْهَا كَفَافًا لاَ لِي وَلاَ عَلَىَّ لاَ أَتَحَمَّلُهَا حَيًّا وَمَيِّتًا.

Narrated Ibn `Abbas: For the whole year I had the desire to ask `Umar bin Al-Khattab regarding the explanation of a Verse (in Surat Al-Tahrim) but I could not ask him because I respected him very much. When he went to perform the Hajj, I too went along with him. On our return, while we were still on the way home. `Umar went aside to answer the call of nature by the Arak trees. I waited till he finished and then I proceeded with him and asked him. "O chief of the Believers! Who were the two wives of the Prophet ﷺ who aided one another against him?" He said, "They were Hafsa and `Aisha." Then I said to him, "By Allah, I wanted to ask you about this a year ago, but I could not do so owing to my respect for you." `Umar said, "Do not refrain from asking me. If you think that I have knowledge (about a certain matter), ask me; and if I know (something about it), I will tell you." Then `Umar added, "By Allah, in the Pre-Islamic Period of Ignorance we did not pay attention to women until Allah revealed regarding them what He revealed regarding them and assigned for them what He has assigned. Once while I was thinking over a certain matter, my wife said, "I recommend that you do so-and-so." I said to her, "What have you got to do with the is matter? Why do you poke your nose in a matter which I want to see fulfilled.?" She said, How strange you are, O son of Al-Khattab! You don't want to be argued with whereas your daughter, Hafsa surely, argues with Allah's Messenger ﷺ so much that he remains angry for a full day!" `Umar then reported; how he at once put on his outer garment and went to Hafsa and said to her, "O my daughter! Do you argue with Allah's Messenger ﷺ so that he remains angry the whole day?" H. afsa said, "By Allah, we argue with him." `Umar said, "Know that I warn you of Allah's punishment and the anger of Allah's Messenger ﷺ. O my daughter! Don't be betrayed by the one who is proud of her beauty because of the love of Allah's Messenger ﷺ for her (i.e. `Aisha)." `Umar addled, "Then I went out to Um Salama's house who was one of my relatives, and I talked to her. She said, O son of Al-Khattab! It is rather astonishing that you interfere in everything; you even want to interfere between Allah's Apostle and his wives!' By Allah, by her talk she influenced me so much that I lost some of my anger. I left her (and went home). At that time I had a friend from the Ansar who used to bring news (from the Prophet) in case of my absence, and I used to bring him the news if he was absent. In those days we were afraid of one of the kings of Ghassan tribe. We heard that he intended to move and attack us, so fear filled our hearts because of that. (One day) my Ansari friend unexpectedly knocked at my door, and said, "Open Open!' I said, 'Has the king of Ghassan come?' He said, 'No, but something worse; Allah's Messenger ﷺ has isolated himself from his wives.' I said, 'Let the nose of `Aisha and Hafsa be stuck to dust (i.e. humiliated)!' Then I put on my clothes and went to Allah's Messenger's ﷺ residence, and behold, he was staying in an upper room of his to which he ascended by a ladder, and a black slave of Allah's Messenger ﷺ was (sitting) on the first step. I said to him, 'Say (to the Prophet ﷺ) Umar bin Al-Khattab is here.' Then the Prophet ﷺ admitted me and I narrated the story to Allah's Messenger ﷺ. When I reached the story of Um Salama, Allah's Messenger ﷺ smiled while he was lying on a mat made of palm tree leaves with nothing between him and the mat. Underneath his head there was a leather pillow stuffed with palm fibres, and leaves of a saut tree were piled at his feet, and above his head hung a few water skins. On seeing the marks of the mat imprinted on his side, I wept.

He said.' 'Why are you weeping?' I replied, "O Allah's Messenger ﷺ! Caesar and Khosrau are leading the life (i.e. Luxurious life) while you, Allah's Messenger ﷺ though you are, is living in destitute". The Prophet ﷺ then replied. 'Won't you be satisfied that they enjoy this world and we the Hereafter?' ". – Sahih Al-Bukhari 4913

حَدَّثَنَا عَبْدُ الْعَزِيزِ بْنُ عَبْدِ اللَّهِ، حَدَّثَنَا سُلَيْمَانُ بْنُ بِلاَلٍ، عَنْ يَحْيَى، عَنْ عُبَيْدِ بْنِ حُنَيْنٍ، أَنَّهُ سَمِعَ ابْنَ عَبَّاسٍ ـ رضى الله عنهما ـ يُحَدِّثُ أَنَّهُ قَالَ مَكَثْتُ سَنَةً أُرِيدُ أَنْ أَسْأَلَ عُمَرَ بْنَ الْخَطَّابِ عَنْ آيَةٍ، فَمَا أَسْتَطِيعُ أَنْ أَسْأَلَهُ هَيْبَةً لَهُ، حَتَّى خَرَجَ حَاجًّا فَخَرَجْتُ مَعَهُ فَلَمَّا رَجَعْتُ وَكُنَّا بِبَعْضِ الطَّرِيقِ عَدَلَ إِلَى الأَرَاكِ لِحَاجَةٍ لَهُ ـ قَالَ ـ فَوَقَفْتُ لَهُ حَتَّى فَرَغَ سِرْتُ مَعَهُ فَقُلْتُ يَا أَمِيرَ الْمُؤْمِنِينَ مَنِ اللَّتَانِ تَظَاهَرَتَا عَلَى النَّبِيِّ صلى الله عليه وسلم مِنْ أَزْوَاجِهِ فَقَالَ تِلْكَ حَفْصَةُ وَعَائِشَةُ. قَالَ فَقُلْتُ وَاللَّهِ إِنْ كُنْتُ لأُرِيدُ أَنْ أَسْأَلَكَ عَنْ هَذَا مُنْذُ سَنَةٍ، فَمَا أَسْتَطِيعُ هَيْبَةً لَكَ. قَالَ فَلاَ تَفْعَلْ مَا ظَنَنْتَ أَنَّ عِنْدِي مِنْ عِلْمٍ فَاسْأَلْنِي، فَإِنْ كَانَ لِي عِلْمٌ خَبَّرْتُكَ بِهِ ـ قَالَ ـ ثُمَّ قَالَ عُمَرُ وَاللَّهِ إِنْ كُنَّا فِي الْجَاهِلِيَّةِ مَا نَعُدُّ لِلنِّسَاءِ أَمْرًا، حَتَّى أَنْزَلَ اللَّهُ فِيهِنَّ مَا أَنْزَلَ وَقَسَمَ لَهُنَّ مَا قَسَمَ ـ قَالَ ـ فَبَيْنَا أَنَا فِي أَمْرٍ أَتَأَمَّرُهُ إِذْ قَالَتِ امْرَأَتِي لَوْ صَنَعْتَ كَذَا وَكَذَا ـ قَالَ ـ فَقُلْتُ لَهَا مَا لَكِ وَلِمَا هَا هُنَا فِيمَا تَكَلُّفُكِ فِي أَمْرٍ أُرِيدُهُ. فَقَالَتْ لِي عَجَبًا لَكَ يَا ابْنَ الْخَطَّابِ مَا تُرِيدُ أَنْ تُرَاجَعَ أَنْتَ، وَإِنَّ ابْنَتَكَ لَتُرَاجِعُ رَسُولَ اللَّهِ صلى الله عليه وسلم حَتَّى يَظَلَّ يَوْمَهُ غَضْبَانَ. فَقَامَ عُمَرُ فَأَخَذَ رِدَاءَهُ مَكَانَهُ حَتَّى دَخَلَ عَلَى حَفْصَةَ فَقَالَ لَهَا يَا بُنَيَّةُ إِنَّكِ لَتُرَاجِعِينَ رَسُولَ اللَّهِ صلى الله عليه وسلم حَتَّى يَظَلَّ يَوْمَهُ غَضْبَانَ. فَقَالَتْ حَفْصَةُ وَاللَّهِ إِنَّا لَنُرَاجِعُهُ. فَقُلْتُ تَعْلَمِينَ أَنِّي أُحَذِّرُكِ عُقُوبَةَ اللَّهِ وَغَضَبَ رَسُولِهِ صلى الله عليه وسلم يَا بُنَيَّةُ لاَ يَغُرَّنَّكِ هَذِهِ الَّتِي أَعْجَبَهَا حُسْنُهَا حُبُّ رَسُولِ اللَّهِ صلى الله عليه وسلم إِيَّاهَا ـ يُرِيدُ عَائِشَةَ ـ قَالَ ثُمَّ خَرَجْتُ حَتَّى دَخَلْتُ عَلَى أُمِّ سَلَمَةَ لِقَرَابَتِي مِنْهَا فَكَلَّمْتُهَا. فَقَالَتْ أُمُّ سَلَمَةَ عَجَبًا لَكَ يَا ابْنَ الْخَطَّابِ دَخَلْتَ فِي كُلِّ شَىْءٍ، حَتَّى تَبْتَغِي أَنْ تَدْخُلَ بَيْنَ رَسُولِ اللَّهِ صلى الله عليه وسلم وَأَزْوَاجِهِ. فَأَخَذَتْنِي وَاللَّهِ أَخْذًا كَسَرَتْنِي عَنْ بَعْضِ مَا كُنْتُ أَجِدُ، فَخَرَجْتُ مِنْ عِنْدِهَا، وَكَانَ لِي صَاحِبٌ مِنَ الأَنْصَارِ إِذَا غِبْتُ أَتَانِي بِالْخَبَرِ، وَإِذَا غَابَ كُنْتُ أَنَا آتِيهِ بِالْخَبَرِ، وَنَحْنُ نَتَخَوَّفُ مَلِكًا مِنْ مُلُوكِ غَسَّانَ، ذُكِرَ لَنَا أَنَّهُ يُرِيدُ أَنْ يَسِيرَ إِلَيْنَا، فَقَدِ امْتَلأَتْ صُدُورُنَا مِنْهُ، فَإِذَا صَاحِبِي الأَنْصَارِيُّ يَدُقُّ الْبَابَ فَقَالَ افْتَحِ افْتَحْ. فَقُلْتُ جَاءَ الْغَسَّانِيُّ فَقَالَ بَلْ أَشَدُّ مِنْ ذَلِكَ. اعْتَزَلَ رَسُولُ اللَّهِ صلى الله عليه وسلم أَزْوَاجَهُ. فَقُلْتُ رَغَمَ أَنْفُ حَفْصَةَ وَعَائِشَةَ. فَأَخَذْتُ ثَوْبِي فَأَخْرُجُ حَتَّى جِئْتُ فَإِذَا رَسُولُ اللَّهِ صلى الله عليه وسلم فِي مَشْرُبَةٍ لَهُ يَرْقَى عَلَيْهَا بِعَجَلَةٍ، وَغُلاَمٌ لِرَسُولِ اللَّهِ صلى الله عليه وسلم أَسْوَدُ عَلَى رَأْسِ الدَّرَجَةِ فَقُلْتُ لَهُ قُلْ هَذَا عُمَرُ بْنُ الْخَطَّابِ. فَأَذِنَ لِي ـ قَالَ عُمَرُ ـ فَقَصَصْتُ عَلَى رَسُولِ اللَّهِ صلى الله عليه وسلم هَذَا الْحَدِيثَ، فَلَمَّا بَلَغْتُ حَدِيثَ أُمِّ سَلَمَةَ تَبَسَّمَ رَسُولُ اللَّهِ صلى الله عليه وسلم وَإِنَّهُ لَعَلَى حَصِيرٍ مَا بَيْنَهُ وَبَيْنَهُ شَىْءٌ، وَتَحْتَ رَأْسِهِ وِسَادَةٌ مِنْ أَدَمٍ حَشْوُهَا لِيفٌ، وَإِنَّ عِنْدَ رِجْلَيْهِ قَرَظًا مَصْبُوبًا، وَعِنْدَ رَأْسِهِ أَهَبٌ مُعَلَّقَةٌ فَرَأَيْتُ أَثَرَ الْحَصِيرِ فِي جَنْبِهِ فَبَكَيْتُ فَقَالَ " مَا يُبْكِيكَ ". فَقُلْتُ يَا رَسُولَ اللَّهِ إِنَّ كِسْرَى وَقَيْصَرَ فِيمَا هُمَا فِيهِ وَأَنْتَ رَسُولُ اللَّهِ. فَقَالَ " أَمَا تَرْضَى أَنْ تَكُونَ لَهُمُ الدُّنْيَا وَلَنَا الآخِرَةُ ".

Narrated `Abdullah bin Hisham: We were with the Prophet ﷺ and he was holding the hand of `Umar bin Al-Khattab. `Umar said to Him, "O Allah's Messenger ﷺ! You are dearer to me than everything except my own self." The Prophet ﷺ said, "No, by Him in Whose Hand my soul is, (you will not have complete faith) till I am dearer to you than your own self." Then `Umar said to him, "However, now, by Allah, you are dearer to me than my own self." The Prophet ﷺ said, "Now, O `Umar, (now you are a believer). – Sahih Al-Bukhari 6632

حَدَّثَنَا يَحْيَى بْنُ سُلَيْمَانَ، قَالَ حَدَّثَنِي ابْنُ وَهْبٍ، قَالَ أَخْبَرَنِي حَيْوَةُ، قَالَ حَدَّثَنِي أَبُو عَقِيلٍ، زُهْرَةُ بْنُ مَعْبَدٍ أَنَّهُ سَمِعَ جَدَّهُ عَبْدَ اللَّهِ بْنَ هِشَامٍ، قَالَ كُنَّا مَعَ النَّبِيِّ صلى الله عليه وسلم وَهْوَ آخِذٌ بِيَدِ عُمَرَ بْنِ الْخَطَّابِ فَقَالَ لَهُ عُمَرُ يَا رَسُولَ اللَّهِ لأَنْتَ أَحَبُّ إِلَىَّ مِنْ كُلِّ شَىْءٍ إِلاَّ مِنْ نَفْسِي. فَقَالَ النَّبِيُّ صلى الله عليه وسلم " لاَ وَالَّذِي نَفْسِي بِيَدِهِ حَتَّى أَكُونَ أَحَبَّ إِلَيْكَ مِنْ نَفْسِكَ ". فَقَالَ لَهُ عُمَرُ فَإِنَّهُ الآنَ وَاللَّهِ لأَنْتَ أَحَبُّ إِلَىَّ مِنْ نَفْسِي. فَقَالَ النَّبِيُّ صلى الله عليه وسلم " الآنَ يَا عُمَرُ ".

Narrated Ibn `Umar: That `Umar had vowed in the Pre-Islamic period to perform I`tikaf in Al-Masjid-al-Haram. (A subnarrator thinks that `Umar vowed to perform I`tikaf for one night.) Allah's Messenger ﷺ said to `Umar, "Fulfill your vow.". – Sahih Al-Bukhari 2043

حَدَّثَنَا عُبَيْدُ بْنُ إِسْمَاعِيلَ، حَدَّثَنَا أَبُو أُسَامَةَ، عَنْ عُبَيْدِ اللَّهِ، عَنْ نَافِعٍ، عَنِ ابْنِ عُمَرَ، أَنَّ عُمَرَ ـ رضى الله عنه ـ نَذَرَ فِي الْجَاهِلِيَّةِ أَنْ يَعْتَكِفَ فِي الْمَسْجِدِ الْحَرَامِ ـ قَالَ أُرَاهُ قَالَ ـ لَيْلَةً قَالَ لَهُ رَسُولُ اللَّهِ صلى الله عليه وسلم " أَوْفِ بِنَذْرِكَ ".

Narrated Abu Wail: I sat with Shaiba in this Mosque (Al-Masjid-Al-Haram), and he said, "`Umar once sat beside me here as you are now sitting, and said, 'I feel like distributing all the gold and silver that are in it (i.e., the Ka`ba) among the Muslims'. I said, 'You cannot do that.' `Umar said, 'Why?' I said, 'Your two (previous) companions (the Prophet ﷺ and Abu

Bakr) did not do it. `Umar said, 'They are the two persons whom one must follow.'" (See Hadith No. 664, Vol. 2). – Sahih Al-Bukhari 7275

حَدَّثَنَا عَمْرُو بْنُ عَبَّاسٍ، حَدَّثَنَا عَبْدُ الرَّحْمَنِ، حَدَّثَنَا سُفْيَانُ، عَنْ وَاصِلٍ، عَنْ أَبِي وَائِلٍ، قَالَ جَلَسْتُ إِلَى شَيْبَةَ فِي هَذَا الْمَسْجِدِ قَالَ جَلَسَ إِلَىَّ عُمَرُ فِي مَجْلِسِكَ هَذَا فَقَالَ هَمَمْتُ أَنْ لاَ أَدَعَ فِيهَا صَفْرَاءَ وَلاَ بَيْضَاءَ إِلاَّ قَسَمْتُهَا بَيْنَ الْمُسْلِمِينَ. قُلْتُ مَا أَنْتَ بِفَاعِلٍ. قَالَ لِمَ. قُلْتُ لَمْ يَفْعَلْهُ صَاحِبَاكَ قَالَ هُمَا الْمَرْآنِ يُقْتَدَى بِهِمَا

Narrated `Abdullah bin `Abbas: Uyaina bin Hisn bin Hudhaifa bin Badr came and stayed (at Medina) with his nephew Al-Hurr bin Qais bin Hisn who was one of those whom `Umar used to keep near him, as the Qurra' (learned men knowing Qur'an by heart) were the people of `Umar's meetings and his advisors whether they were old or young. 'Uyaina said to his nephew, "O my nephew! Have you an approach to this chief so as to get for me the permission to see him?" His nephew said, "I will get the permission for you to see him." (Ibn `Abbas added: ) So he took the permission for 'Uyaina, and when the latter entered, he said, "O the son of Al-Khattab! By Allah, you neither give us sufficient provision nor judge among us with justice." On that `Umar became so furious that he intended to harm him. Al-Hurr, said, "O Chief of the Believers!" Allah said to His Apostle 'Hold to forgiveness, command what is good (right), and leave the foolish (i.e. do not punish them).' (7.199) and this person is among the foolish." By Allah, `Umar did not overlook that Verse when Al-Hurr recited it before him, and `Umar said to observe (the orders of) Allah's Book strictly." (See Hadith No. 166, Vol. 6). – Sahih Al-Bukhari 7286

حَدَّثَنِي إِسْمَاعِيلُ، حَدَّثَنِي ابْنُ وَهْبٍ، عَنْ يُونُسَ، عَنِ ابْنِ شِهَابٍ، حَدَّثَنِي عُبَيْدُ اللَّهِ بْنُ عَبْدِ اللَّهِ بْنِ عُتْبَةَ، أَنَّ عَبْدَ اللَّهِ بْنَ عَبَّاسٍ ـ رضى الله عنهما ـ قَالَ قَدِمَ عُيَيْنَةُ بْنُ حِصْنِ بْنِ حُذَيْفَةَ بْنِ بَدْرٍ فَنَزَلَ عَلَى ابْنِ أَخِيهِ الْحُرِّ بْنِ قَيْسِ بْنِ حِصْنٍ، وَكَانَ مِنَ النَّفَرِ الَّذِينَ يُدْنِيهِمْ عُمَرُ، وَكَانَ الْقُرَّاءُ أَصْحَابَ مَجْلِسِ عُمَرَ وَمُشَاوَرَتِهِ كُهُولاً كَانُوا أَوْ شُبَّانًا فَقَالَ عُيَيْنَةُ لاِبْنِ أَخِيهِ يَا ابْنَ أَخِي هَلْ لَكَ وَجْهٌ عِنْدَ هَذَا الأَمِيرِ فَتَسْتَأْذِنَ لِي عَلَيْهِ قَالَ سَأَسْتَأْذِنُ لَكَ عَلَيْهِ. قَالَ ابْنُ عَبَّاسٍ فَاسْتَأْذَنَ لِعُيَيْنَةَ فَلَمَّا دَخَلَ قَالَ يَا ابْنَ الْخَطَّابِ وَاللَّهِ مَا تُعْطِينَا الْجَزْلَ، وَمَا تَحْكُمُ بَيْنَنَا بِالْعَدْلِ. فَغَضِبَ عُمَرُ حَتَّى هَمَّ بِأَنْ يَقَعَ بِهِ فَقَالَ الْحُرُّ يَا أَمِيرَ الْمُؤْمِنِينَ إِنَّ اللَّهَ تَعَالَى قَالَ لِنَبِيِّهِ صلى الله عليه وسلم {خُذِ الْعَفْوَ وَأْمُرْ بِالْعُرْفِ وَأَعْرِضْ عَنِ الْجَاهِلِينَ} وَإِنَّ هَذَا مِنَ الْجَاهِلِينَ. فَوَاللَّهِ مَا جَاوَزَهَا عُمَرُ حِينَ تَلاَهَا عَلَيْهِ، وَكَانَ وَقَّافًا عِنْدَ كِتَابِ اللَّهِ

Narrated Abu Musa Al-Ash`ari: I came to the Prophet ﷺ at Al-Batha' while his camel was kneeling down and he asked me, "Have you intended to perform the Hajj?" I replied in the affirmative. He asked me, 'With what intention have you assumed Ihram?" I replied, "I have assumed Ihram with the same intention as that of the Prophet. He said, "You have done well. Perform the Tawaf of the Ka`ba and (the Sai) between As-Safa and Al- Marwa and then finish the Ihram." So, I performed the Tawaf around the Ka`ba and the Sai) between As-Safa and Al-Marwa and then went to a woman of the tribe of Qais who cleaned my head from lice. Later I assumed the Ihram for Hajj. I used to give the verdict of doing the same till the caliphate of `Umar who said, "If you follow the Holy Book then it orders you to remain in the state of Ihram till you finish from Hajj, if you follow the Prophet ﷺ then he did not finish his Ihram till the Hadi (sacrifice) had reached its place of slaughtering (Hajj-al-Qiran). – Sahih Al-Bukhari 1795

حَدَّثَنَا مُحَمَّدُ بْنُ بَشَّارٍ، حَدَّثَنَا غُنْدَرٌ، حَدَّثَنَا شُعْبَةُ، عَنْ قَيْسِ بْنِ مُسْلِمٍ، عَنْ طَارِقِ بْنِ شِهَابٍ، عَنْ أَبِي مُوسَى الأَشْعَرِيِّ ـ رضى الله عنه ـ قَالَ قَدِمْتُ عَلَى النَّبِيِّ صلى الله عليه وسلم بِالْبَطْحَاءِ وَهُوَ مُنِيخٌ فَقَالَ " أَحَجَجْتَ ". قُلْتُ نَعَمْ. قَالَ " بِمَا أَهْلَلْتَ ". قُلْتُ لَبَّيْكَ بِإِهْلاَلٍ كَإِهْلاَلِ النَّبِيِّ صلى الله عليه وسلم قَالَ " أَحْسَنْتَ. طُفْ بِالْبَيْتِ وَبِالصَّفَا وَالْمَرْوَةِ ثُمَّ أَحِلَّ ". فَطُفْتُ بِالْبَيْتِ، وَبِالصَّفَا وَالْمَرْوَةِ، ثُمَّ أَتَيْتُ امْرَأَةً مِنْ قَيْسٍ، فَفَلَتْ رَأْسِي، ثُمَّ أَهْلَلْتُ بِالْحَجِّ. فَكُنْتُ أُفْتِي بِهِ، حَتَّى كَانَ فِي خِلاَفَةِ عُمَرَ فَقَالَ إِنْ أَخَذْنَا بِكِتَابِ اللَّهِ فَإِنَّهُ يَأْمُرُنَا بِالتَّمَامِ، وَإِنْ أَخَذْنَا بِقَوْلِ النَّبِيِّ صلى الله عليه وسلم فَإِنَّهُ لَمْ يَحِلَّ حَتَّى يَبْلُغَ الْهَدْىُ مَحِلَّهُ

Narrated ‘Ubai bin `Umar: Abu Musa asked permission to enter upon `Umar, but seeing that he was busy, he went away. `Umar then said, “Didn’t I hear the voice of `Abdullah bin Qais? Allow him to come in.” He was called in and `Umar said to him, “What made you do what you did.” He replied, “We have been instructed thus by the Prophet” `Umar said, “Bring proof (witness) for this, other wise I will do so-and-so to you.” Then `Abdullah bin Qais went to a gathering of the Ansar who then said, “None but the youngest of us will give the witness for it.” So Abu Sa`id Al-Khudri got up and said, “We used to be instructed thus (by the Prophet).” `Umar said, “This tradition of the Prophetﷺ remained hidden from me. Business in the market kept me busy.”. – Sahih Al-Bukhari 7353

حَدَّثَنَا مُسَدَّدٌ، حَدَّثَنَا يَحْيَى، عَنِ ابْنِ جُرَيْجٍ، حَدَّثَنِي عَطَاءٌ، عَنْ عُبَيْدِ بْنِ عُمَيْرٍ، قَالَ اسْتَأْذَنَ أَبُو مُوسَى عَلَى عُمَرَ فَكَأَنَّهُ وَجَدَهُ مَشْغُولاً فَرَجَعَ، فَقَالَ عُمَرُ أَلَمْ أَسْمَعْ صَوْتَ عَبْدِ اللَّهِ بْنِ قَيْسٍ، ائْذَنُوا لَهُ. فَدُعِيَ لَهُ فَقَالَ مَا حَمَلَكَ عَلَى مَا صَنَعْتَ فَقَالَ إِنَّا كُنَّا نُؤْمَرُ بِهَذَا. قَالَ فَأْتِنِي عَلَى هَذَا بِبَيِّنَةٍ أَوْ لأَفْعَلَنَّ بِكَ. فَانْطَلَقَ إِلَى مَجْلِسٍ مِنَ الأَنْصَارِ فَقَالُوا لاَ يَشْهَدُ إِلاَّ أَصَاغِرُنَا. فَقَامَ أَبُو سَعِيدٍ الْخُدْرِيُّ فَقَالَ قَدْ كُنَّا نُؤْمَرُ بِهَذَا. فَقَالَ عُمَرُ خَفِيَ عَلَىَّ هَذَا مِنْ أَمْرِ النَّبِيِّ صلى الله عليه وسلم، أَلْهَانِي الصَّفْقُ بِالأَسْوَاقِ

Narrated `Abdullah bin `Umar: Sa`d bin ‘Ubada became sick and the Prophetﷺ along with `Abdur Rahman bin `Auf, Sa`d bin Abi Waqqas and `Abdullah bin Mas`ud visited him to inquire about his health. When he came to him, he found him surrounded by his household and he asked, “Has he died?” They said, “No, O Allah’s Apostle.” The Prophetﷺ wept and when the people saw the weeping of Allah’s Messengerﷺ they all wept. He said, “Will you listen? Allah does not punish for shedding tears, nor for the grief of the heart but he punishes or bestows His Mercy because of this.” He pointed to his tongue and added, “The deceased is punished for the wailing of his relatives over him.” `Umar used to beat with a stick and throw stones and put dust over the faces (of those who used to wail over the dead). – Sahih Al-Bukhari 1304

حَدَّثَنَا أَصْبَغُ، عَنِ ابْنِ وَهْبٍ، قَالَ أَخْبَرَنِي عَمْرٌو، عَنْ سَعِيدِ بْنِ الْحَارِثِ الأَنْصَارِيِّ، عَنْ عَبْدِ اللَّهِ بْنِ عُمَرَ ـ رضى الله عنهما ـ قَالَ اشْتَكَى سَعْدُ بْنُ عُبَادَةَ شَكْوَى لَهُ فَأَتَاهُ النَّبِيُّ صلى الله عليه وسلم يَعُودُهُ مَعَ عَبْدِ الرَّحْمَنِ بْنِ عَوْفٍ وَسَعْدِ بْنِ أَبِي وَقَّاصٍ وَعَبْدِ اللَّهِ بْنِ مَسْعُودٍ ـ رضى الله عنهم ـ فَلَمَّا دَخَلَ عَلَيْهِ فَوَجَدَهُ فِي غَاشِيَةِ أَهْلِهِ فَقَالَ " قَدْ قَضَى ". قَالُوا لاَ يَا رَسُولَ اللَّهِ. فَبَكَى النَّبِيُّ صلى الله عليه وسلم فَلَمَّا رَأَى الْقَوْمُ بُكَاءَ النَّبِيِّ صلى الله عليه وسلم بَكَوْا فَقَالَ " أَلاَ تَسْمَعُونَ إِنَّ اللَّهَ لاَ يُعَذِّبُ بِدَمْعِ الْعَيْنِ، وَلاَ بِحُزْنِ الْقَلْبِ، وَلَكِنْ يُعَذِّبُ بِهَذَا ـ وَأَشَارَ إِلَى لِسَانِهِ ـ أَوْ يَرْحَمُ وَإِنَّ الْمَيِّتَ يُعَذَّبُ بِبُكَاءِ أَهْلِهِ عَلَيْهِ ". وَكَانَ عُمَرُ ـ رضى الله عنه ـ يَضْرِبُ فِيهِ بِالْعَصَا، وَيَرْمِي بِالْحِجَارَةِ وَيَحْثِي بِالتُّرَابِ

‘Abdur Rahman bin ‘Abdul Qari said, “I went out in the company of ‘Umar bin Al-Khattab one night in Ramadan to the mosque and found the people praying in different groups. A man praying alone or a man praying with a little group behind him. So, ‘Umar said, ‘In my opinion I would better collect these (people) under the leadership of one Qari (Reciter) (i.e. let them pray in congregation!)’. So, he made up his mind to congregate them behind Ubai bin Ka’b. Then on another night I went again in his company and the people were praying behind their reciter. On that, ‘Umar remarked, ‘What an excellent Bid’a (i.e. innovation in religion) this is; but the prayer which they do not perform, but sleep at its time is better than the one they are offering.' He meant the prayer In the last part of the night. (In those days) people used to pray in the early part of the night.”. – Sahih Al-Bukhari 2010

وَعَنِ ابْنِ شِهَابٍ، عَنْ عُرْوَةَ بْنِ الزُّبَيْرِ، عَنْ عَبْدِ الرَّحْمَنِ بْنِ عَبْدٍ الْقَارِيِّ، أَنَّهُ قَالَ خَرَجْتُ مَعَ عُمَرَ بْنِ الْخَطَّابِ ـ رضى الله عنه ـ لَيْلَةً فِي رَمَضَانَ، إِلَى الْمَسْجِدِ، فَإِذَا النَّاسُ أَوْزَاعٌ مُتَفَرِّقُونَ يُصَلِّي الرَّجُلُ لِنَفْسِهِ، وَيُصَلِّي الرَّجُلُ فَيُصَلِّي بِصَلاَتِهِ الرَّهْطُ فَقَالَ عُمَرُ إِنِّي أَرَى لَوْ جَمَعْتُ هَؤُلاَءِ عَلَى قَارِئٍ وَاحِدٍ لَكَانَ أَمْثَلَ. ثُمَّ عَزَمَ فَجَمَعَهُمْ عَلَى أُبَىِّ بْنِ كَعْبٍ، ثُمَّ خَرَجْتُ مَعَهُ لَيْلَةً أُخْرَى، وَالنَّاسُ يُصَلُّونَ بِصَلاَةِ قَارِئِهِمْ، قَالَ عُمَرُ نِعْمَ الْبِدْعَةُ هَذِهِ، وَالَّتِي يَنَامُونَ عَنْهَا أَفْضَلُ مِنَ الَّتِي يَقُومُونَ. يُرِيدُ آخِرَ اللَّيْلِ، وَكَانَ النَّاسُ يَقُومُونَ أَوَّلَهُ

Narrated Aba `Uthman An-Nahdi: While we were with `Utba bin Farqad at Adharbijan, there came `Umar's letter indicating that Allah's Apostle had forbidden the use of silk except this much, then he pointed with his index and middle fingers. To our knowledge, by that he meant embroidery. – Sahih Al-Bukhari 5828

حَدَّثَنَا آدَمُ، حَدَّثَنَا شُعْبَةُ، حَدَّثَنَا قَتَادَةُ، قَالَ سَمِعْتُ أَبَا عُثْمَانَ النَّهْدِيَّ، أَتَانَا كِتَابُ عُمَرَ وَنَحْنُ مَعَ عُتْبَةَ بْنِ فَرْقَدٍ بِأَذْرَبِيجَانَ أَنَّ رَسُولَ اللَّهِ صلى الله عليه وسلم نَهَى عَنِ الْحَرِيرِ، إِلاَّ هَكَذَا، وَأَشَارَ بِإِصْبَعَيْهِ اللَّتَيْنِ تَلِيَانِ الإِبْهَامَ قَالَ فِيمَا عَلِمْنَا أَنَّهُ يَعْنِي الأَعْلاَمَ

Narrated Abu `Uthman: While we were at Adharbijan, `Umar wrote to us: 'Allah's Messenger ﷺforbade wearing silk except this much. Then the Prophetﷺ approximated his two fingers (index and middle fingers) (to illustrate that) to us.' Zuhair (the sub-narrator) raised up his middle and index fingers. – Sahih Al-Bukhari 5829

حَدَّثَنَا أَحْمَدُ بْنُ يُونُسَ، حَدَّثَنَا زُهَيْرٌ، حَدَّثَنَا عَاصِمٌ، عَنْ أَبِي عُثْمَانَ، قَالَ كَتَبَ إِلَيْنَا عُمَرُ وَنَحْنُ بِأَذْرَبِيجَانَ أَنَّ النَّبِيَّ صلى الله عليه وسلم نَهَى عَنْ لُبْسِ الْحَرِيرِ إِلاَّ هَكَذَا، وَصَفَّ لَنَا النَّبِيُّ صلى الله عليه وسلم إِصْبَعَيْهِ. وَرَفَعَ زُهَيْرٌ الْوُسْطَى وَالسَّبَّابَةَ.

Narrated `Ali: Allah's Messengerﷺ sent me, Az-Zubair bin Al-Awwam and Abu Marthad Al-Ghanawi, and all of us were horsemen, and he said, "Proceed till you reach Rawdat Khakh, where there is a woman from the pagans carrying a letter sent by Hatib bin Abi Balta'a to the pagans (of Mecca)." So we overtook her while she was proceeding on her camel at the same place as Allah's Messengerﷺ told us. We said (to her) "Where is the letter which is with you?" She said, "I have no letter with me." So we made her camel kneel down and searched her mount (baggage etc) but could not find anything. My two companions said, "We do not see any letter." I said, "I know that Allah's Messengerﷺ did not tell a lie. By Allah, if you (the lady) do not bring out the letter, I will strip you of your clothes' When she noticed that I was serious, she put her hand into the knot of her waist sheet, for she was tying a sheet round herself, and brought out the letter. So we proceeded to Allah's Messengerﷺ with the letter. The Prophetﷺ said (to Habib), "What made you o what you have done, O Hatib?" Hatib replied, "I have done nothing except that I believe in Allah and His Apostle, and I have not changed or altered (my religion). But I wanted to do the favor to the people (pagans of Mecca) through which Allah might protect my family and my property, as there is none among your companions but has someone in Mecca through whom Allah protects his property (against harm). The Prophetﷺ said, "Habib has told you the truth, so do not say to him (anything) but good." `Umar bin Al-Khattab said, "Verily he has betrayed Allah, His Apostle, and the believers! Allow me to chop his neck off!" The Prophetﷺ said, "O `Umar! What do you know; perhaps Allah looked upon the Badr warriors and said, 'Do whatever you like, for I have ordained that you will be in Paradise.'" On that `Umar wept and said, "Allah and His Apostle know best.". – Sahih Al-Bukhari 6259

حَدَّثَنَا يُوسُفُ بْنُ بُهْلُولٍ، حَدَّثَنَا ابْنُ إِدْرِيسَ، قَالَ حَدَّثَنِي حُصَيْنُ بْنُ عَبْدِ الرَّحْمَنِ، عَنْ سَعْدِ بْنِ عُبَيْدَةَ، عَنْ أَبِي عَبْدِ الرَّحْمَنِ السُّلَمِيِّ، عَنْ عَلِيٍّ ـ رضى الله عنه ـ قَالَ بَعَثَنِي رَسُولُ اللَّهِ صلى الله عليه وسلم وَالزُّبَيْرَ بْنَ الْعَوَّامِ وَأَبَا مَرْثَدٍ الْغَنَوِيَّ وَكُلُّنَا فَارِسٌ فَقَالَ " انْطَلِقُوا حَتَّى تَأْتُوا رَوْضَةَ خَاخٍ، فَإِنَّ بِهَا امْرَأَةً مِنَ الْمُشْرِكِينَ مَعَهَا صَحِيفَةٌ مِنْ حَاطِبِ بْنِ أَبِي بَلْتَعَةَ إِلَى الْمُشْرِكِينَ ". قَالَ فَأَدْرَكْنَاهَا تَسِيرُ عَلَى جَمَلٍ لَهَا حَيْثُ قَالَ لَنَا رَسُولُ اللَّهِ صلى الله عليه وسلم قَالَ قُلْنَا أَيْنَ الْكِتَابُ الَّذِي مَعَكِ قَالَتْ مَا مَعِي كِتَابٌ. فَأَنَخْنَا بِهَا، فَابْتَغَيْنَا فِي رَحْلِهَا فَمَا وَجَدْنَا شَيْئًا، قَالَ صَاحِبَاىَ مَا نَرَى كِتَابًا. قَالَ قُلْتُ لَقَدْ عَلِمْتُ مَا كَذَبَ رَسُولُ اللَّهِ صلى الله عليه وسلم وَالَّذِي يُحْلَفُ بِهِ لَتُخْرِجِنَّ الْكِتَابَ أَوْ لأُجَرِّدَنَّكِ. قَالَ فَلَمَّا رَأَتِ الْجِدَّ مِنِّي أَهْوَتْ بِيَدِهَا إِلَى حُجْزَتِهَا وَهْىَ مُحْتَجِزَةٌ بِكِسَاءٍ فَأَخْرَجَتِ الْكِتَابَ ـ قَالَ ـ فَانْطَلَقْنَا بِهِ إِلَى رَسُولِ اللَّهِ صلى الله عليه وسلم فَقَالَ " مَا حَمَلَكَ يَا حَاطِبُ عَلَى مَا صَنَعْتَ ". قَالَ مَا بِي إِلاَّ أَنْ أَكُونَ مُؤْمِنًا بِاللَّهِ وَرَسُولِهِ، وَمَا غَيَّرْتُ وَلاَ بَدَّلْتُ، أَرَدْتُ أَنْ تَكُونَ لِي عِنْدَ الْقَوْمِ يَدٌ يَدْفَعُ اللَّهُ بِهَا عَنْ أَهْلِي وَمَالِي، وَلَيْسَ مِنْ أَصْحَابِكَ هُنَاكَ إِلاَّ وَلَهُ مَنْ يَدْفَعُ اللَّهُ بِهِ عَنْ أَهْلِهِ وَمَالِهِ. قَالَ " صَدَقَ فَلاَ تَقُولُوا لَهُ إِلاَّ خَيْرًا ". قَالَ فَقَالَ عُمَرُ بْنُ الْخَطَّابِ إِنَّهُ قَدْ خَانَ اللَّهَ وَرَسُولَهُ وَالْمُؤْمِنِينَ، فَدَعْنِي

فَأَضْرِبَ عُنُقَهُ. قَالَ فَقَالَ " يَا عُمَرُ وَمَا يُدْرِيكَ لَعَلَّ اللَّهَ قَدِ اطَّلَعَ عَلَى أَهْلِ بَدْرٍ فَقَالَ اعْمَلُوا مَا شِئْتُمْ فَقَدْ وَجَبَتْ لَكُمُ الْجَنَّةُ ".
قَالَ فَدَمَعَتْ عَيْنَا عُمَرَ وَقَالَ اللَّهُ وَرَسُولُهُ أَعْلَمُ.

Narrated `Aisha: (mother of the believers) After the death of Allah 's Apostle Fatima the daughter of Allah's Messenger ﷺ asked Abu Bakr As-Siddiq to give her, her share of inheritance from what Allah's Messenger ﷺ had left of the Fai (i.e. booty gained without fighting) which Allah had given him. Abu Bakr said to her, "Allah's Apostle said, 'Our property will not be inherited, whatever we (i.e. prophets) leave is Sadaqa (to be used for charity)." Fatima, the daughter of Allah's Messenger ﷺ got angry and stopped speaking to Abu Bakr, and continued assuming that attitude till she died. Fatima remained alive for six months after the death of Allah's Messenger ﷺ. She used to ask Abu Bakr for her share from the property of Allah's Messenger ﷺ which he left at Khaibar, and Fadak, and his property at Medina (devoted for charity). Abu Bakr refused to give her that property and said, "I will not leave anything Allah's Messenger ﷺ used to do, because I am afraid that if I left something from the Prophet's tradition, then I would go astray." (Later on) `Umar gave the Prophet's property (of Sadaqa) at Medina to `Ali and `Abbas, but he withheld the properties of Khaibar and Fadak in his custody and said, "These two properties are the Sadaqa which Allah's Apostle used to use for his expenditures and urgent needs. Now their management is to be entrusted to the ruler." (Az-Zuhri said, "They have been managed in this way till today."). – Sahih Al-Bukhari 3092, 3093

حَدَّثَنَا عَبْدُ الْعَزِيزِ بْنُ عَبْدِ اللَّهِ، حَدَّثَنَا إِبْرَاهِيمُ بْنُ سَعْدٍ، عَنْ صَالِحٍ، عَنِ ابْنِ شِهَابٍ، قَالَ أَخْبَرَنِي عُرْوَةُ بْنُ الزُّبَيْرِ، أَنَّ عَائِشَةَ أُمَّ الْمُؤْمِنِينَ ـ رضى الله عنها ـ أَخْبَرَتْهُ أَنَّ فَاطِمَةَ ـ عَلَيْهَا السَّلاَمُ ـ ابْنَةَ رَسُولِ اللَّهِ صلى الله عليه وسلم سَأَلَتْ أَبَا بَكْرٍ الصِّدِّيقَ بَعْدَ وَفَاةِ رَسُولِ اللَّهِ صلى الله عليه وسلم أَنْ يَقْسِمَ لَهَا مِيرَاثَهَا، مَا تَرَكَ رَسُولُ اللَّهِ صلى الله عليه وسلم مِمَّا أَفَاءَ اللَّهُ عَلَيْهِ. فَقَالَ لَهَا أَبُو بَكْرٍ إِنَّ رَسُولَ اللَّهِ صلى الله عليه وسلم قَالَ " لاَ نُورَثُ مَا تَرَكْنَا صَدَقَةٌ ". فَغَضِبَتْ فَاطِمَةُ بِنْتُ رَسُولِ اللَّهِ صلى الله عليه وسلم فَهَجَرَتْ أَبَا بَكْرٍ، فَلَمْ تَزَلْ مُهَاجِرَتَهُ حَتَّى تُوُفِّيَتْ وَعَاشَتْ بَعْدَ رَسُولِ اللَّهِ صلى الله عليه وسلم سِتَّةَ أَشْهُرٍ. قَالَتْ وَكَانَتْ فَاطِمَةُ تَسْأَلُ أَبَا بَكْرٍ نَصِيبَهَا مِمَّا تَرَكَ رَسُولُ اللَّهِ صلى الله عليه وسلم مِنْ خَيْبَرَ وَفَدَكٍ وَصَدَقَتِهِ بِالْمَدِينَةِ، فَأَبَى أَبُو بَكْرٍ عَلَيْهَا ذَلِكَ، وَقَالَ لَسْتُ تَارِكًا شَيْئًا كَانَ رَسُولُ اللَّهِ صلى الله عليه وسلم يَعْمَلُ بِهِ إِلاَّ عَمِلْتُ بِهِ، فَإِنِّي أَخْشَى إِنْ تَرَكْتُ شَيْئًا مِنْ أَمْرِهِ أَنْ أَزِيغَ. فَأَمَّا صَدَقَتُهُ بِالْمَدِينَةِ فَدَفَعَهَا عُمَرُ إِلَى عَلِيٍّ وَعَبَّاسٍ، فَأَمَّا خَيْبَرُ وَفَدَكُ فَأَمْسَكَهَا عُمَرُ وَقَالَ هُمَا صَدَقَةُ رَسُولِ اللَّهِ صلى الله عليه وسلم كَانَتَا لِحُقُوقِهِ الَّتِي تَعْرُوهُ وَنَوَائِبِهِ، وَأَمْرُهُمَا إِلَى مَنْ وَلِيَ الأَمْرَ. قَالَ فَهُمَا عَلَى ذَلِكَ إِلَى الْيَوْمِ.
قَالَ أَبُو عَبْد اللَّهِ اعْتَرَاكَ افْتَعَلْتَ مِنْ عَرَوْتُهُ فَأَصَبْتُهُ وَمِنْهُ يَعْرُوهُ وَاعْتَرَانِي

Narrated `Umar bin Al-Khattab: By Him in Whose Hand my soul is, were I not afraid that the other Muslims might be left in poverty, I would divide (the land of) whatever village I may conquer (among the fighters), as the Prophet ﷺ divided the land of Khaibar. But I prefer to leave it as a (source of) a common treasury for them to distribute it revenue amongst themselves. – Sahih Al-Bukhari 4235

حَدَّثَنَا سَعِيدُ بْنُ أَبِي مَرْيَمَ، أَخْبَرَنَا مُحَمَّدُ بْنُ جَعْفَرٍ، قَالَ أَخْبَرَنِي زَيْدٌ، عَنْ أَبِيهِ، أَنَّهُ سَمِعَ عُمَرَ بْنَ الْخَطَّابِ ـ رضى الله عنه ـ يَقُولُ أَمَا وَالَّذِي نَفْسِي بِيَدِهِ، لَوْلاَ أَنْ أَتْرُكَ آخِرَ النَّاسِ بَبَّانًا لَيْسَ لَهُمْ شَىْءٌ، مَا فُتِحَتْ عَلَىَّ قَرْيَةٌ إِلاَّ قَسَمْتُهَا كَمَا قَسَمَ النَّبِيُّ صلى الله عليه وسلم خَيْبَرَ، وَلَكِنِّي أَتْرُكُهَا خِزَانَةً لَهُمْ يَقْتَسِمُونَهَا

Narrated Bukair: That Kuraib, the freed slave of Ibn `Abbas told him that Ibn `Abbas, `Abdur-Rahman bin Azhar and Al-Miswar bin Makhrama sent him to `Aisha saying, "Pay her our greetings and ask her about our offering of the two-rak`at after `Asr Prayer, and tell her that we have been informed that you offer these two rak`at while we have heard that the Prophet ﷺ had forbidden their offering." Ibn `Abbas said, "I and `Umar used to beat the people for their offering them." Kuraib added, "I entered upon her and delivered their message to her.' She said, 'Ask Um Salama.' So, I informed them (of `Aisha's answer) and they sent me to Um

Salama for the same purpose as they sent me to `Aisha. Um Salama replied, 'I heard the Prophet ﷺ forbidding the offering of these two rak`at. Once the Prophet ﷺ offered the `Asr prayer, and then came to me. And at that time some Ansari women from the Tribe of Banu Haram were with me. Then (the Prophet ﷺ) offered those two rak`at, and I sent my (lady) servant to him, saying, 'Stand beside him and say (to him): Um Salama says, 'O Allah's Messenger ﷺ! Didn't I hear you forbidding the offering of these two rak`at (after the `Asr prayer yet I see you offering them?' And if he beckons to you with his hand, then wait behind.' So the lady slave did that and the Prophet ﷺ beckoned her with his hand, and she stayed behind, and when the Prophet ﷺ finished his prayer, he said, 'O the daughter of Abu Umaiya (i.e. Um Salama), You were asking me about these two rak`at after the `Asr prayer. In fact, some people from the tribe of `Abdul Qais came to me to embrace Islam and busied me so much that I did not offer the two rak`at which were offered after Zuhr compulsory prayer, and these two rak`at (you have seen me offering) make up for those.". – Sahih Al-Bukhari 4370

حَدَّثَنَا يَحْيَى بْنُ سُلَيْمَانَ، حَدَّثَنِي ابْنُ وَهْبٍ، أَخْبَرَنِي عَمْرٌو، وَقَالَ بَكْرُ بْنُ مُضَرَ عَنْ عَمْرِو بْنِ الْحَارِثِ، عَنْ بُكَيْرٍ، أَنَّ كُرَيْبًا، مَوْلَى ابْنِ عَبَّاسٍ حَدَّثَهُ أَنَّ ابْنَ عَبَّاسٍ وَعَبْدَ الرَّحْمَنِ بْنَ أَزْهَرَ وَالْمِسْوَرَ بْنَ مَخْرَمَةَ أَرْسَلُوا إِلَى عَائِشَةَ ـ رضى الله عنها ـ فَقَالُوا اقْرَأْ عَلَيْهَا السَّلاَمَ مِنَّا جَمِيعًا، وَسَلْهَا عَنِ الرَّكْعَتَيْنِ بَعْدَ الْعَصْرِ، وَإِنَّا أُخْبِرْنَا أَنَّكِ تُصَلِّيهَا، وَقَدْ بَلَغَنَا أَنَّ النَّبِيَّ صلى الله عليه وسلم نَهَى عَنْهَا، قَالَ ابْنُ عَبَّاسٍ وَكُنْتُ أَضْرِبُ مَعَ عُمَرَ النَّاسَ عَنْهُمَا. قَالَ كُرَيْبٌ فَدَخَلْتُ عَلَيْهَا، وَبَلَّغْتُهَا مَا أَرْسَلُونِي، فَقَالَتْ سَلْ أُمَّ سَلَمَةَ. فَأَخْبَرْتُهُمْ، فَرَدُّونِي إِلَى أُمِّ سَلَمَةَ بِمِثْلِ مَا أَرْسَلُونِي إِلَى عَائِشَةَ، فَقَالَتْ أُمُّ سَلَمَةَ سَمِعْتُ النَّبِيَّ صلى الله عليه وسلم يَنْهَى عَنْهُمَا، وَإِنَّهُ صَلَّى الْعَصْرَ ثُمَّ دَخَلَ عَلَيَّ وَعِنْدِي نِسْوَةٌ مِنْ بَنِي حَرَامٍ مِنَ الأَنْصَارِ، فَصَلاَّهُمَا، فَأَرْسَلْتُ إِلَيْهِ الْخَادِمَ فَقُلْتُ قُومِي إِلَى جَنْبِهِ فَقُولِي تَقُولُ أُمُّ سَلَمَةَ يَا رَسُولَ اللَّهِ أَلَمْ أَسْمَعْكَ تَنْهَى عَنْ هَاتَيْنِ الرَّكْعَتَيْنِ فَأَرَاكَ تُصَلِّيهِمَا. فَإِنْ أَشَارَ بِيَدِهِ فَاسْتَأْخِرِي. فَفَعَلَتِ الْجَارِيَةُ، فَأَشَارَ بِيَدِهِ، فَاسْتَأْخَرَتْ عَنْهُ، فَلَمَّا انْصَرَفَ قَالَ " يَا بِنْتَ أَبِي أُمَيَّةَ، سَأَلْتِ عَنِ الرَّكْعَتَيْنِ بَعْدَ الْعَصْرِ، إِنَّهُ أَتَانِي أُنَاسٌ مِنْ عَبْدِ الْقَيْسِ بِالإِسْلاَمِ مِنْ قَوْمِهِمْ، فَشَغَلُونِي عَنِ الرَّكْعَتَيْنِ اللَّتَيْنِ بَعْدَ الظُّهْرِ، فَهُمَا هَاتَانِ ".

Narrated Abu Ad-Darda: There was a dispute between Abu Bakr and `Umar, and Abu Bakr made `Umar angry. So `Umar left angrily. Abu Bakr followed him, requesting him to ask forgiveness (of Allah) for him, but `Umar refused to do so and closed his door in Abu Bakr's face. So Abu Bakr went to Allah's Messenger ﷺ while we were with him. Allah's Messenger ﷺ said, "This friend of yours must have quarrelled (with somebody)." In the meantime `Umar repented and felt sorry for what he had done, so he came, greeted (those who were present) and sat with the Prophet ﷺ and related the story to him. Allah's Messenger ﷺ became angry and Abu Bakr started saying, "O Allah's Messenger ﷺ! By Allah, I was more at fault (than `Umar)." Allah's Apostle said, "Are you (people) leaving for me my companion? (Abu Bakr), Are you (people) leaving for me my companion? When I said, 'O people I am sent to you all as the Messenger of Allah,' you said, 'You tell a lie.' While Abu Bakr said, 'You have spoken the truth .". – Sahih Al-Bukhari 4640

حَدَّثَنَا عَبْدُ اللَّهِ، حَدَّثَنَا سُلَيْمَانُ بْنُ عَبْدِ الرَّحْمَنِ، وَمُوسَى بْنُ هَارُونَ، قَالاَ حَدَّثَنَا الْوَلِيدُ بْنُ مُسْلِمٍ، حَدَّثَنَا عَبْدُ اللَّهِ بْنُ الْعَلاَءِ بْنِ زَبْرٍ، قَالَ حَدَّثَنِي بُسْرُ بْنُ عُبَيْدِ اللَّهِ، قَالَ حَدَّثَنِي أَبُو إِدْرِيسَ الْخَوْلاَنِيُّ، قَالَ سَمِعْتُ أَبَا الدَّرْدَاءِ، يَقُولُ كَانَتْ بَيْنَ أَبِي بَكْرٍ وَعُمَرَ مُحَاوَرَةٌ، فَأَغْضَبَ أَبُو بَكْرٍ عُمَرَ، فَانْصَرَفَ عَنْهُ عُمَرُ مُغْضَبًا، فَاتَّبَعَهُ أَبُو بَكْرٍ يَسْأَلُهُ أَنْ يَسْتَغْفِرَ لَهُ، فَلَمْ يَفْعَلْ حَتَّى أَغْلَقَ بَابَهُ فِي وَجْهِهِ، فَأَقْبَلَ أَبُو بَكْرٍ إِلَى رَسُولِ اللَّهِ صلى الله عليه وسلم فَقَالَ أَبُو الدَّرْدَاءِ وَنَحْنُ عِنْدَهُ فَقَالَ رَسُولُ اللَّهِ صلى الله عليه وسلم " أَمَّا صَاحِبُكُمْ هَذَا فَقَدْ غَامَرَ ". قَالَ وَنَدِمَ عُمَرُ عَلَى مَا كَانَ مِنْهُ فَأَقْبَلَ حَتَّى سَلَّمَ وَجَلَسَ إِلَى النَّبِيِّ صلى الله عليه وسلم وَقَصَّ عَلَى رَسُولِ اللَّهِ صلى الله عليه وسلم الْخَبَرَ. قَالَ أَبُو الدَّرْدَاءِ وَغَضِبَ رَسُولُ اللَّهِ صلى الله عليه وسلم وَجَعَلَ أَبُو بَكْرٍ يَقُولُ وَاللَّهِ يَا رَسُولَ اللَّهِ لأَنَا كُنْتُ أَظْلَمَ فَقَالَ رَسُولُ اللَّهِ صلى الله عليه وسلم " هَلْ أَنْتُمْ تَارِكُو لِي صَاحِبِي هَلْ أَنْتُمْ تَارِكُو لِي صَاحِبِي إِنِّي قُلْتُ يَا أَيُّهَا النَّاسُ إِنِّي رَسُولُ اللَّهِ إِلَيْكُمْ جَمِيعًا فَقُلْتُمْ كَذَبْتَ. وَقَالَ أَبُو بَكْرٍ صَدَقْتَ قَالَ أَبُو عَبْد اللَّهِ غَامَرَ سَبَقَ بِالْخَيْرِ".

Narrated `Abdullah bin Az-Zubair: A group of Bani Tamim came to the Prophet (and requested him to appoint a governor for them). Abu Bakr said, "Appoint Al-Qaqa bin Mabad." `Umar said, "Appoint Al-Aqra' bin Habeas." On that Abu Bakr said (to `Umar). "You did not want but to oppose me!" `Umar replied "I did not intend to oppose you!" So both of them argued till their voices grew loud. So the following Verse was revealed: ‘O you who believe! Be not forward……’ (49.1). – Sahih Al-Bukhari 4847

حَدَّثَنَا الْحَسَنُ بْنُ مُحَمَّدٍ، حَدَّثَنَا حَجَّاجٌ، عَنِ ابْنِ جُرَيْجٍ، قَالَ أَخْبَرَنِي ابْنُ أَبِي مُلَيْكَةَ، أَنَّ عَبْدَ اللَّهِ بْنَ الزُّبَيْرِ، أَخْبَرَهُمْ أَنَّهُ، قَدِمَ رَكْبٌ مِنْ بَنِي تَمِيمٍ عَلَى النَّبِيِّ صلى الله عليه وسلم فَقَالَ أَبُو بَكْرٍ أَمِّرِ الْقَعْقَاعَ بْنَ مَعْبَدٍ. وَقَالَ عُمَرُ بَلْ أَمِّرِ الأَقْرَعَ بْنَ حَابِسٍ. فَقَالَ أَبُو بَكْرٍ مَا أَرَدْتَ إِلَى - أَوْ إِلاَّ - خِلاَفِي. فَقَالَ عُمَرُ مَا أَرَدْتُ خِلاَفَكَ. فَتَمَارَيَا حَتَّى ارْتَفَعَتْ أَصْوَاتُهُمَا، فَنَزَلَ فِي ذَلِكَ {يَا أَيُّهَا الَّذِينَ آمَنُوا لاَ تُقَدِّمُوا بَيْنَ يَدَىِ اللَّهِ وَرَسُولِهِ} حَتَّى انْقَضَتِ الآيَةُ.

Narrated Ibn ‘Abbas: Qariba, The daughter of Abi Umaiyya, was the wife of ‘Umar bin Al-Khattab. ‘Umar divorced her and then Mu’awiyya bin Abi Sufyan married her. Similarly, Um Al-Hakam, the daughter of Abi Sufyan was the wife of ‘Iyad bin Ghanm Al-Fihri. He divorced her and then ‘Abdullah bin ‘Uthman Al-Thaqafi married her. – Sahih Al-Bukhari 5287

وَقَالَ عَطَاءٌ عَنِ ابْنِ عَبَّاسٍ، كَانَتْ قَرِيبَةُ بِنْتُ أَبِي أُمَيَّةَ عِنْدَ عُمَرَ بْنِ الْخَطَّابِ فَطَلَّقَهَا، فَتَزَوَّجَهَا مُعَاوِيَةُ بْنُ أَبِي سُفْيَانَ، وَكَانَتْ أُمُّ الْحَكَمِ ابْنَةُ أَبِي سُفْيَانَ تَحْتَ عِيَاضِ بْنِ غَنْمٍ الْفِهْرِيِّ فَطَلَّقَهَا، فَتَزَوَّجَهَا عَبْدُ اللَّهِ بْنُ عُثْمَانَ الثَّقَفِيُّ.

Narrated \`Abdur Rahman bin Abza: A man came to \`Umar bin Al-Khattab and said, “I became Junub but no water was available.” \`Ammar bin Yasir said to \`Umar, “Do you remember that you and I (became Junub while both of us) were together on a journey and you didn’t pray but I rolled myself on the ground and prayed? I informed the Prophetﷺ about it and he said, ‘It would have been sufficient for you to do like this.’ The Prophet then stroked lightly the earth with his hands and then blew off the dust and passed his hands over his face and hands.”. – Sahih Al-Bukhari 338

حَدَّثَنَا آدَمُ، قَالَ حَدَّثَنَا شُعْبَةُ، حَدَّثَنَا الْحَكَمُ، عَنْ ذَرٍّ، عَنْ سَعِيدِ بْنِ عَبْدِ الرَّحْمَنِ بْنِ أَبْزَى، عَنْ أَبِيهِ، قَالَ جَاءَ رَجُلٌ إِلَى عُمَرَ بْنِ الْخَطَّابِ فَقَالَ إِنِّي أَجْنَبْتُ فَلَمْ أُصِبِ الْمَاءَ. فَقَالَ عَمَّارُ بْنُ يَاسِرٍ لِعُمَرَ بْنِ الْخَطَّابِ أَمَا تَذْكُرُ أَنَّا كُنَّا فِي سَفَرٍ أَنَا وَأَنْتَ فَأَمَّا أَنْتَ فَلَمْ تُصَلِّ، وَأَمَّا أَنَا فَتَمَعَّكْتُ فَصَلَّيْتُ، فَذَكَرْتُ لِلنَّبِيِّ صلى الله عليه وسلم فَقَالَ النَّبِيُّ صلى الله عليه وسلم " إِنَّمَا كَانَ يَكْفِيكَ هَكَذَا ". فَضَرَبَ النَّبِيُّ صلى الله عليه وسلم بِكَفَّيْهِ الأَرْضَ، وَنَفَخَ فِيهِمَا ثُمَّ مَسَحَ بِهِمَا وَجْهَهُ وَكَفَّيْهِ.

Umar said’ “I think of organizing my troops while I am in Şalat (prayer).” Sahih Al-Bukhari vol. 2 pg. 185

و قال عمر رضي الله عنه : اني لاجهز جيشي و انا في الصلاة.

Narrated \`Abdullah bin \`Umar: While \`Umar was at home in a state of fear, there came Al-\`As bin Wail As-Sahmi Abu \`Amr, wearing an embroidered cloak and a shirt having silk hems. He was from the tribe of Bani Sahm who were our allies during the pre-Islamic period of ignorance. Al-\`As said to \`Umar “What is wrong with you?” He said, “Your people claim that they would kill me if I become a Muslim.” Al-\`As said, “Nobody will harm you after I have given protection to you.” So Al-\`As went out and met the people streaming in the whole valley. He said, “Where are you going?” They said, “We want Ibn Al-Khattab who has embraced Islam.” Al-\`As said, “There is no way for anybody to touch him.” So the people retreated. – Sahih al-Bukhari 3864

حَدَّثَنَا يَحْيَى بْنُ سُلَيْمَانَ، قَالَ حَدَّثَنِي ابْنُ وَهْبٍ، قَالَ حَدَّثَنِي عُمَرُ بْنُ مُحَمَّدٍ، قَالَ فَأَخْبَرَنِي جَدِّي، زَيْدُ بْنُ عَبْدِ اللَّهِ بْنِ عُمَرَ عَنْ أَبِيهِ، قَالَ بَيْنَمَا هُوَ فِي الدَّارِ خَائِفًا، إِذْ جَاءَهُ الْعَاصِ بْنُ وَائِلٍ السَّهْمِيُّ أَبُو عَمْرٍو، عَلَيْهِ حُلَّةُ حِبَرَةٍ، وَقَمِيصٌ مَكْفُوفٌ بِحَرِيرٍ، وَهُوَ مِنْ بَنِي سَهْمٍ، وَهُمْ حُلَفَاؤُنَا فِي الْجَاهِلِيَّةِ فَقَالَ لَهُ مَا بَالُكَ قَالَ زَعَمَ قَوْمُكَ أَنَّهُمْ سَيَقْتُلُونِي إِنْ أَسْلَمْتُ. قَالَ لاَ سَبِيلَ إِلَيْكَ. بَعْدَ أَنْ قَالَهَا أَمِنْتُ، فَخَرَجَ الْعَاصِ، فَلَقِيَ النَّاسَ قَدْ سَالَ بِهِمُ الْوَادِي فَقَالَ أَيْنَ تُرِيدُونَ فَقَالُوا نُرِيدُ هَذَا ابْنَ الْخَطَّابِ الَّذِي صَبَا. قَالَ لاَ سَبِيلَ إِلَيْهِ. فَكَرَّ النَّاسُ

Uthman ibn Affan ibn Abi al-As

عُثْمَان بْن عَفَّان بْن أَبِي الْعَاص

Narrated `Abdullah bin `Umar: In the lifetime of Allah's Messenger ﷺ the mosque was built of adobes, its roof of the leaves of date-palms and its pillars of the stems of date-palms. Abu Bakr did not alter it. `Umar expanded it on the same pattern as it was in the lifetime of Allah's Messenger ﷺ by using adobes, leaves of date-palms and changing the pillars into wooden ones. `Uthman changed it by expanding it to a great extent and built its walls with engraved stones and lime and made its pillars of engraved stones and its roof of teak wood. – Sahih Al-Bukhari 446

حَدَّثَنَا عَلِيُّ بْنُ عَبْدِ اللَّهِ، قَالَ حَدَّثَنَا يَعْقُوبُ بْنُ إِبْرَاهِيمَ بْنِ سَعْدٍ، قَالَ حَدَّثَنِي أَبِي، عَنْ صَالِحِ بْنِ كَيْسَانَ، قَالَ حَدَّثَنَا نَافِعٌ، أَنَّ عَبْدَ اللَّهِ، أَخْبَرَهُ أَنَّ الْمَسْجِدَ كَانَ عَلَى عَهْدِ رَسُولِ اللَّهِ صلى الله عليه وسلم مَبْنِيًّا بِاللَّبِنِ، وَسَقْفُهُ الْجَرِيدُ، وَعُمُدُهُ خَشَبُ النَّخْلِ، فَلَمْ يَزِدْ فِيهِ أَبُو بَكْرٍ شَيْئًا، وَزَادَ فِيهِ عُمَرُ وَبَنَاهُ عَلَى بُنْيَانِهِ فِي عَهْدِ رَسُولِ اللَّهِ صلى الله عليه وسلم بِاللَّبِنِ وَالْجَرِيدِ، وَأَعَادَ عُمُدَهُ خَشَبًا، ثُمَّ غَيَّرَهُ عُثْمَانُ، فَزَادَ فِيهِ زِيَادَةً كَثِيرَةً، وَبَنَى جِدَارَهُ بِالْحِجَارَةِ الْمَنْقُوشَةِ وَالْقَصَّةِ، وَجَعَلَ عُمُدَهُ مِنْ حِجَارَةٍ مَنْقُوشَةٍ، وَسَقَفَهُ بِالسَّاجِ

Narrated 'Ubaidullah Al-Khaulani: I heard `Uthman bin `Affan saying, when people argued too much about his intention to reconstruct the mosque of Allah's Messenge ﷺ, "You have talked too much. I heard the Prophet ﷺ saying, 'Whoever built a mosque, (Bukair thought that `Asim, another sub-narrator, added, "Intending Allah's Pleasure"), Allah would build for him a similar place in Paradise.' ". – Sahih Al-Bukhari 450

حَدَّثَنَا يَحْيَى بْنُ سُلَيْمَانَ، حَدَّثَنِي ابْنُ وَهْبٍ، أَخْبَرَنِي عَمْرٌو، أَنَّ بُكَيْرًا، حَدَّثَهُ أَنَّ عَاصِمَ بْنَ عُمَرَ بْنِ قَتَادَةَ حَدَّثَهُ أَنَّهُ، سَمِعَ عُبَيْدَ اللَّهِ الْخَوْلاَنِيَّ، أَنَّهُ سَمِعَ عُثْمَانَ بْنَ عَفَّانَ، يَقُولُ عِنْدَ قَوْلِ النَّاسِ فِيهِ حِينَ بَنَى مَسْجِدَ الرَّسُولِ صلى الله عليه وسلم إِنَّكُمْ أَكْثَرْتُمْ، وَإِنِّي سَمِعْتُ النَّبِيَّ صلى الله عليه وسلم يَقُولُ " مَنْ بَنَى مَسْجِدًا ـ قَالَ بُكَيْرٌ حَسِبْتُ أَنَّهُ قَالَ ـ يَبْتَغِي بِهِ وَجْهَ اللَّهِ، بَنَى اللَّهُ لَهُ مِثْلَهُ فِي الْجَنَّةِ "

Narrated Ibn Al-Hanafiya: If `Ali had spoken anything bad about `Uthman then he would have mentioned the day when some persons came to him and complained about the Zakat officials of `Uthman. `Ali then said to me, "Go to `Uthman and say to him, 'This document contains the regulations of spending the Sadaqa of Allah's Apostle so order your Zakat officials to act accordingly." I took the document to `Uthman. `Uthman said, "Take it away, for we are not in need of it." I returned to `Ali with it and informed him of that. He said, "Put it whence you took it.". – Sahih Al-Bukhari 3111

حَدَّثَنَا قُتَيْبَةُ بْنُ سَعِيدٍ، حَدَّثَنَا سُفْيَانُ، عَنْ مُحَمَّدِ بْنِ سُوقَةَ، عَنْ مُنْذِرٍ، عَنِ ابْنِ الْحَنَفِيَّةِ، قَالَ لَوْ كَانَ عَلِيٌّ ـ رضى الله عنه ـ ذَاكِرًا عُثْمَانَ ـ رضى الله عنه ـ ذَكَرَهُ يَوْمَ جَاءَهُ نَاسٌ فَشَكَوْا سُعَاةَ عُثْمَانَ، فَقَالَ لِي عَلِيٌّ اذْهَبْ إِلَى عُثْمَانَ فَأَخْبِرْهُ أَنَّهَا صَدَقَةُ رَسُولِ اللَّهِ صلى الله عليه وسلم، فَمُرْ سُعَاتَكَ يَعْمَلُونَ فِيهَا. فَأَتَيْتُهُ بِهَا فَقَالَ أَغْنِهَا عَنَّا. فَأَتَيْتُ بِهَا عَلِيًّا فَأَخْبَرْتُهُ فَقَالَ ضَعْهَا حَيْثُ أَخَذْتَهَا

Narrated Jubair bin Mut`im: `Uthman bin `Affan went (to the Prophet) and said, "O Allah's Messenger ﷺ !You gave property to Bani Al-Muttalib and did not give us, although we and they are of the same degree of relationship to you." The Prophet ﷺ said, "Only Bani Hashim and Bani Al Muttalib are one thing (as regards family status). – Sahih Al-Bukhari 3502

حَدَّثَنَا يَحْيَى بْنُ بُكَيْرٍ، حَدَّثَنَا اللَّيْثُ، عَنْ عُقَيْلٍ، عَنِ ابْنِ شِهَابٍ، عَنِ ابْنِ الْمُسَيَّبِ، عَنْ جُبَيْرِ بْنِ مُطْعِمٍ، قَالَ مَشَيْتُ أَنَا وَعُثْمَانُ بْنُ عَفَّانَ،، فَقَالَ يَا رَسُولَ اللَّهِ أَعْطَيْتَ بَنِي الْمُطَّلِبِ وَتَرَكْتَنَا، وَإِنَّمَا نَحْنُ وَهُمْ مِنْكَ بِمَنْزِلَةٍ وَاحِدَةٍ. فَقَالَ النَّبِيُّ صلى الله عليه وسلم " إِنَّمَا بَنُو هَاشِمٍ وَبَنُو الْمُطَّلِبِ شَىْءٌ وَاحِدٌ "

Narrated 'Ubaidullah bin `Adi bin Al-Khiyar: That Al-Miswar bin Makhrama and `Abdur-Rahman bin Al-Aswad bin 'Abu Yaghuth had said to him, "What prevents you from speaking to your uncle `Uthman regarding his brother Al-Walid bin `Uqba?" The people were speaking against the latter for what he had done. 'Ubaidullah said, "So I kept waiting for `Uthman, and when he went out for the prayer, I said to him, 'I have got something to say to you as a piece of advice.' `Uthman said, 'O man! I seek Refuge with Allah from you. So I went away. When I finished my prayer, I sat with Al-Miswar and Ibn 'Abu Yaghutb and talked to both of them of what I had said to `Uthman and what he had said to me. They said, 'You have done your duty.' So while I was sitting with them. `Uthman's Messenger came to me. They said, 'Allah has put you to trial." I set out and when I reached `Uthman, he said, 'What is your advice which you mentioned a while ago?' I recited Tashahhud and added, 'Allah has sent Muhammad and has revealed the Holy Book (i.e. Qur'an) to him. You (O `Uthman!) were amongst those who responded to the call of Allah and His Apostle and had faith in him. And you took part in the first two migrations (to Ethiopia and to Medina), and you enjoyed the company of Allah's Messenger ﷺ and learned his traditions and advice. Now the people are talking much about Al-Walid bin `Uqba and so it is your duty to impose on him the legal punishment.' `Uthman then said to me, 'O my nephew! Did you ever meet Allah's Messenger ﷺ?' I said, 'No, but his knowledge has reached me as it has reached the virgin in her seclusion.' `Uthman then recited Tashahhud and said, 'No doubt, Allah has sent Muhammad with the Truth and has revealed to him His Holy Book (i.e. Qur'an) and I was amongst those who responded to the call of Allah and His Apostle and I had faith in Muhammad's Mission, and I had performed the first two migrations as you have said, and I enjoyed the company of Allah's Messenger ﷺ and gave the pledge of allegiance to him. By Allah, I never disobeyed him and never cheated him till Allah caused him to die. Then Allah made Abu Bakr Caliph, and by Allah, I was never disobedient to him, nor did I cheat him. Then `Umar became Caliph, and by Allah, I was never disobedient to him, nor did I cheat him. Then I became Caliph. Have I not then the same rights over you as they had over me?' I replied in the affirmative. `Uthman further said, 'The what are these talks which are reaching me from you? As for what you ha mentioned about Al-Walid bin 'Uqb; Allah willing, I shall give him the leg; punishment justly. Then `Uthman ordered that Al-Walid be flogged fort lashes. He ordered `Ali to flog him an he himself flogged him as well.". – Sahih Al-Bukhari 3872

حَدَّثَنَا عَبْدُ اللَّهِ بْنُ مُحَمَّدٍ الْجُعْفِيُّ، حَدَّثَنَا هِشَامٌ، أَخْبَرَنَا مَعْمَرٌ، عَنِ الزُّهْرِيِّ، حَدَّثَنَا عُرْوَةُ بْنُ الزُّبَيْرِ، أَنَّ عُبَيْدَ اللَّهِ بْنَ عَدِيِّ بْنِ الْخِيَارِ، أَخْبَرَهُ أَنَّ الْمِسْوَرَ بْنَ مَخْرَمَةَ وَعَبْدَ الرَّحْمَنِ بْنَ الأَسْوَدِ بْنِ عَبْدِ يَغُوثَ قَالاَ لَهُ مَا يَمْنَعُكَ أَنْ تُكَلِّمَ خَالَكَ عُثْمَانَ فِي أَخِيهِ الْوَلِيدِ بْنِ عُقْبَةَ وَكَانَ أَكْثَرَ النَّاسُ فِيمَا فَعَلَ بِهِ. قَالَ عُبَيْدُ اللَّهِ فَانْتَصَبْتُ لِعُثْمَانَ حِينَ خَرَجَ إِلَى الصَّلاَةِ فَقُلْتُ لَهُ إِنَّ لِي إِلَيْكَ حَاجَةً وَهْىَ نَصِيحَةٌ. فَقَالَ أَيُّهَا الْمَرْءُ، أَعُوذُ بِاللَّهِ مِنْكَ، فَانْصَرَفْتُ، فَلَمَّا قَضَيْتُ الصَّلاَةَ جَلَسْتُ إِلَى الْمِسْوَرِ وَإِلَى ابْنِ عَبْدِ يَغُوثَ، فَحَدَّثْتُهُمَا بِالَّذِي قُلْتُ لِعُثْمَانَ وَقَالَ لِي. فَقَالاَ قَدْ قَضَيْتَ الَّذِي كَانَ عَلَيْكَ. فَبَيْنَمَا أَنَا جَالِسٌ مَعَهُمَا، إِذْ جَاءَنِي رَسُولُ عُثْمَانَ، فَقَالاَ لِي قَدِ ابْتَلاَكَ اللَّهُ. فَانْطَلَقْتُ حَتَّى دَخَلْتُ عَلَيْهِ، فَقَالَ مَا نَصِيحَتُكَ الَّتِي ذَكَرْتَ آنِفًا قَالَ فَتَشَهَّدْتُ ثُمَّ قُلْتُ إِنَّ اللَّهَ بَعَثَ مُحَمَّدًا صلى الله عليه وسلم وَأَنْزَلَ عَلَيْهِ الْكِتَابَ، وَكُنْتَ مِمَّنِ اسْتَجَابَ لِلَّهِ وَرَسُولِهِ صلى الله عليه وسلم وَآمَنْتَ بِهِ، وَهَاجَرْتَ الْهِجْرَتَيْنِ الأُولَيَيْنِ، وَصَحِبْتَ رَسُولَ اللَّهِ صلى الله عليه وسلم وَرَأَيْتَ هَدْيَهُ، وَقَدْ أَكْثَرَ النَّاسُ فِي شَأْنِ الْوَلِيدِ بْنِ عُقْبَةَ، فَحَقٌّ عَلَيْكَ أَنْ تُقِيمَ عَلَيْهِ الْحَدَّ. فَقَالَ لِي يَا ابْنَ أَخِي أَدْرَكْتَ رَسُولَ اللَّهِ صلى الله عليه وسلم قَالَ قُلْتُ لاَ، وَلَكِنْ قَدْ خَلَصَ إِلَىَّ مِنْ عِلْمِهِ مَا خَلَصَ إِلَى الْعَذْرَاءِ فِي سِتْرِهَا. قَالَ فَتَشَهَّدَ عُثْمَانُ فَقَالَ إِنَّ اللَّهَ قَدْ بَعَثَ مُحَمَّدًا صلى الله عليه وسلم بِالْحَقِّ وَأَنْزَلَ عَلَيْهِ الْكِتَابَ، وَكُنْتُ مِمَّنِ اسْتَجَابَ لِلَّهِ وَرَسُولِهِ صلى الله عليه وسلم وَآمَنْتُ بِمَا بُعِثَ بِهِ مُحَمَّدٌ صلى الله عليه وسلم. وَهَاجَرْتُ الْهِجْرَتَيْنِ الأُولَيَيْنِ كَمَا قُلْتَ، وَصَحِبْتُ رَسُولَ اللَّهِ صلى الله عليه وسلم وَبَايَعْتُهُ، وَاللَّهِ مَا عَصَيْتُهُ وَلاَ غَشَشْتُهُ حَتَّى تَوَفَّاهُ اللَّهُ، ثُمَّ اسْتَخْلَفَ اللَّهُ أَبَا بَكْرٍ فَوَاللَّهِ مَا عَصَيْتُهُ وَلاَ غَشَشْتُهُ، ثُمَّ اسْتُخْلِفَ عُمَرُ، فَوَاللَّهِ مَا عَصَيْتُهُ وَلاَ غَشَشْتُهُ، ثُمَّ اسْتُخْلِفْتُ، أَفَلَيْسَ لِي عَلَيْكُمْ مِثْلُ الَّذِي كَانَ لَهُمْ عَلَىَّ قَالَ بَلَى. قَالَ فَمَا هَذِهِ الأَحَادِيثُ الَّتِي تَبْلُغُنِي عَنْكُمْ فَأَمَّا مَا ذَكَرْتَ مِنْ شَأْنِ الْوَلِيدِ بْنِ عُقْبَةَ، فَسَنَأْخُذُ فِيهِ إِنْ شَاءَ اللَّهُ بِالْحَقِّ قَالَ فَجَلَدَ الْوَلِيدَ أَرْبَعِينَ جَلْدَةً، وَأَمَرَ عَلِيًّا أَنْ يَجْلِدَهُ، وَكَانَ هُوَ يَجْلِدُهُ. وَقَالَ يُونُسُ وَابْنُ أَخِي الزُّهْرِيِّ عَنِ الزُّهْرِيِّ أَفَلَيْسَ لِي عَلَيْكُمْ مِنَ الْحَقِّ مِثْلُ الَّذِي كَانَ لَهُمْ.

قَالَ أَبُو عَبْد اللَّهِ بَلاَءٌ مِنْ رَبِّكُمْ مَا ابْتُلِيتُمْ بِهِ مِنْ شِدَّةٍ وَفِي مَوْضِعِ الْبَلاَءُ الِابْتِلَاءُ وَالتَّمْحِيصُ مَنْ بَلَوْتُهُ وَمَحَّصْتُهُ أَيْ اسْتَخْرَجْتُ مَا عِنْدَهُ يَبْلُو يَخْتَبِرُ مُبْتَلِيكُمْ مُخْتَبِرُكُمْ وَأَمَّا قَوْلُهُ بَلَاءٌ عَظِيمٌ النِّعَمُ وَهِيَ مِنْ أَبْلَيْتُهُ وَتِلْكَ مِنْ ابْتَلَيْتُهُ

Narrated Ibn Az-Zubair: I said to `Uthman bin `Affan (while he was collecting the Qur'an) regarding the Verse:-- "Those of you who die and leave wives ..." (2.240) "This Verse was abrogated by an other Verse. So why should you write it? (Or leave it in the Qur'an)?" `Uthman said. "O son of my brother! I will not shift anything of it from its place.". – Sahih Al-Bukhari 4530

حَدَّثَنِي أُمَيَّةُ بْنُ بِسْطَامٍ، حَدَّثَنَا يَزِيدُ بْنُ زُرَيْعٍ، عَنْ حَبِيبٍ، عَنِ ابْنِ أَبِي مُلَيْكَةَ، قَالَ ابْنُ الزُّبَيْرِ قُلْتُ لِعُثْمَانَ بْنِ عَفَّانَ {وَالَّذِينَ يُتَوَفَّوْنَ مِنْكُمْ وَيَذَرُونَ أَزْوَاجًا} قَالَ قَدْ نَسَخَتْهَا الآيَةُ الأُخْرَى فَلِمَ تَكْتُبُهَا أَوْ تَدَعُهَا قَالَ يَا ابْنَ أَخِي، لاَ أُغَيِّرُ شَيْئًا مِنْهُ مِنْ مَكَانِهِ

Narrated Anas bin Malik: Hudhaifa bin Al-Yaman came to `Uthman at the time when the people of Sham and the people of Iraq were Waging war to conquer Arminya and Adharbijan. Hudhaifa was afraid of their (the people of Sham and Iraq) differences in the recitation of the Qur'an, so he said to `Uthman, "O chief of the Believers! Save this nation before they differ about the Book (Qur'an) as Jews and the Christians did before." So `Uthman sent a message to Hafsa saying, "Send us the manuscripts of the Qur'an so that we may compile the Qur'anic materials in perfect copies and return the manuscripts to you." Hafsa sent it to `Uthman. `Uthman then ordered Zaid bin Thabit, `Abdullah bin AzZubair, Sa`id bin Al-As and `AbdurRahman bin Harith bin Hisham to rewrite the manuscripts in perfect copies. `Uthman said to the three Quraishi men, "In case you disagree with Zaid bin Thabit on any point in the Qur'an, then write it in the dialect of Quraish, the Qur'an was revealed in their tongue." They did so, and when they had written many copies, `Uthman returned the original manuscripts to Hafsa. `Uthman sent to every Muslim province one copy of what they had copied, and ordered that all the other Qur'anic materials, whether written in fragmentary manuscripts or whole copies, be burnt. – Sahih Al-Bukhari 4987

حَدَّثَنَا مُوسَى، حَدَّثَنَا إِبْرَاهِيمُ، حَدَّثَنَا ابْنُ شِهَابٍ، أَنَّ أَنَسَ بْنَ مَالِكٍ، حَدَّثَهُ أَنَّ حُذَيْفَةَ بْنَ الْيَمَانِ قَدِمَ عَلَى عُثْمَانَ وَكَانَ يُغَازِي أَهْلَ الشَّأْمِ فِي فَتْحِ إِرْمِينِيَةَ وَأَذْرَبِيجَانَ مَعَ أَهْلِ الْعِرَاقِ فَأَفْزَعَ حُذَيْفَةَ اخْتِلاَفُهُمْ فِي الْقِرَاءَةِ فَقَالَ حُذَيْفَةُ لِعُثْمَانَ يَا أَمِيرَ الْمُؤْمِنِينَ أَدْرِكْ هَذِهِ الأُمَّةَ قَبْلَ أَنْ يَخْتَلِفُوا فِي الْكِتَابِ اخْتِلاَفَ الْيَهُودِ وَالنَّصَارَى فَأَرْسَلَ عُثْمَانُ إِلَى حَفْصَةَ أَنْ أَرْسِلِي إِلَيْنَا بِالصُّحُفِ نَنْسَخُهَا فِي الْمَصَاحِفِ ثُمَّ نَرُدُّهَا إِلَيْكِ فَأَرْسَلَتْ بِهَا حَفْصَةُ إِلَى عُثْمَانَ فَأَمَرَ زَيْدَ بْنَ ثَابِتٍ وَعَبْدَ اللَّهِ بْنَ الزُّبَيْرِ وَسَعِيدَ بْنَ الْعَاصِ وَعَبْدَ الرَّحْمَنِ بْنَ الْحَارِثِ بْنِ هِشَامٍ فَنَسَخُوهَا فِي الْمَصَاحِفِ وَقَالَ عُثْمَانُ لِلرَّهْطِ الْقُرَشِيِّينَ الثَّلاَثَةِ إِذَا اخْتَلَفْتُمْ أَنْتُمْ وَزَيْدُ بْنُ ثَابِتٍ فِي شَىْءٍ مِنَ الْقُرْآنِ فَاكْتُبُوهُ بِلِسَانِ قُرَيْشٍ فَإِنَّمَا نَزَلَ بِلِسَانِهِمْ فَفَعَلُوا حَتَّى إِذَا نَسَخُوا الصُّحُفَ فِي الْمَصَاحِفِ رَدَّ عُثْمَانُ الصُّحُفَ إِلَى حَفْصَةَ وَأَرْسَلَ إِلَى كُلِّ أُفُقٍ بِمُصْحَفٍ مِمَّا نَسَخُوا وَأَمَرَ بِمَا سِوَاهُ مِنَ الْقُرْآنِ فِي كُلِّ صَحِيفَةٍ أَوْ مُصْحَفٍ أَنْ يُحْرَقَ

Anas added: The ring of the Prophetﷺ was in his hand, and after him, in Abu Bakr's hand, and then in `Umar's hand after Abu Bakr. When `Uthman was the Caliph, once he was sitting at the well of Aris. He removed the ring from his hand and while he was trifling with it, dropped into the well. We kept on going to the well with `Uthman for three days looking for the ring, and finally the well was drained, but the ring was not found. – Sahih Al-Bukhari 5879

وَزَادَنِي أَحْمَدُ حَدَّثَنَا الأَنْصَارِيُّ، قَالَ حَدَّثَنِي أَبِي، عَنْ ثُمَامَةَ، عَنْ أَنَسٍ، قَالَ كَانَ خَاتَمُ النَّبِيِّ صلى الله عليه وسلم فِي يَدِهِ، وَفِي يَدِ أَبِي بَكْرٍ بَعْدَهُ، وَفِي يَدِ عُمَرَ بَعْدَ أَبِي بَكْرٍ، فَلَمَّا كَانَ عُثْمَانُ جَلَسَ عَلَى بِئْرِ أَرِيسَ ـ قَالَ ـ فَأَخْرَجَ الْخَاتَمَ، فَجَعَلَ يَعْبَثُ بِهِ فَسَقَطَ قَالَ فَاخْتَلَفْنَا ثَلاَثَةَ أَيَّامٍ مَعَ عُثْمَانَ فَنَنْزَحُ الْبِئْرَ فَلَمْ نَجِدْهُ

Narrated Abu Wail: Someone said to Usama, "Will you not talk to this (Uthman)?" Usama said, "I talked to him (secretly) without being the first man to open an evil door. I will never tell a ruler who rules over two men or more that he is good after I heard Allah's Messengerﷺ saying, 'A man will be brought and put in Hell (Fire) and he will circumambulate (go around and round) in Hell (Fire) like a donkey of a (flour) grinding mill, and all the people of Hell (Fire)

will gather around him and will say to him, O so-and-so! Didn't you use to order others for good and forbid them from evil?' That man will say, 'I used to order others to do good but I myself never used to do it, and I used to forbid others from evil while I myself used to do evil.' ". – Sahih Al-Bukhari 7098
حَدَّثَنِي بِشْرُ بْنُ خَالِدٍ، أَخْبَرَنَا مُحَمَّدُ بْنُ جَعْفَرٍ، عَنْ شُعْبَةَ، عَنْ سُلَيْمَانَ، سَمِعْتُ أَبَا وَائِلٍ، قَالَ قِيلَ لأُسَامَةَ أَلاَ تُكَلِّمُ هَذَا. قَالَ قَدْ كَلَّمْتُهُ مَا دُونَ أَنْ أَفْتَحَ بَابًا، أَكُونُ أَوَّلَ مَنْ يَفْتَحُهُ، وَمَا أَنَا بِالَّذِي أَقُولُ لِرَجُلٍ بَعْدَ أَنْ يَكُونَ أَمِيرًا عَلَى رَجُلَيْنِ أَنْتَ خَيْرٌ. بَعْدَ مَا سَمِعْتُ مِنْ رَسُولِ اللَّهِ صلى الله عليه وسلم يَقُولُ " يُجَاءُ بِرَجُلٍ فَيُطْرَحُ فِي النَّارِ، فَيَطْحَنُ فِيهَا كَطَحْنِ الْحِمَارِ بِرَحَاهُ، فَيُطِيفُ بِهِ أَهْلُ النَّارِ فَيَقُولُونَ أَىْ فُلاَنُ أَلَسْتَ كُنْتَ تَأْمُرُ بِالْمَعْرُوفِ، وَتَنْهَى عَنِ الْمُنْكَرِ فَيَقُولُ إِنِّي كُنْتُ آمُرُ بِالْمَعْرُوفِ وَلاَ أَفْعَلُهُ، وَأَنْهَى عَنِ الْمُنْكَرِ وَأَفْعَلُهُ ".

Narrated `Abdullah bin `Umar: I offered the prayer with the Prophet, Abu Bakr and `Umar at Mina and it was of two rak`at. `Uthman in the early days of his caliphate did the same, but later on he started praying the full prayer. – Sahih al-Bukhari 1082
حَدَّثَنَا مُسَدَّدٌ، قَالَ حَدَّثَنَا يَحْيَى، عَنْ عُبَيْدِ اللَّهِ، قَالَ أَخْبَرَنِي نَافِعٌ، عَنْ عَبْدِ اللَّهِ ـ رضى الله عنه ـ قَالَ صَلَّيْتُ مَعَ النَّبِيِّ صلى الله عليه وسلم بِمِنًى رَكْعَتَيْنِ، وَأَبِي بَكْرٍ وَعُمَرَ، وَمَعَ عُثْمَانَ صَدْرًا مِنْ إِمَارَتِهِ ثُمَّ أَتَمَّهَا

Narrated `Abdur Rahman bin Yazid: We offered a four rak`at prayer at Mina behind Ibn `Affan . `Abdullah bin Mas`ud was informed about it. He said sadly, "Truly to Allah we belong and truly to Him we shall return." And added, "I prayed two rak`at with Allah's Messenger ﷺ at Mina and similarly with Abu Bakr and with `Umar (during their caliphates)." He further said, "May I be lucky enough to have two of the four rak`at accepted (by Allah).". – Sahih Al-Bukhari 1084
حَدَّثَنَا قُتَيْبَةُ، قَالَ حَدَّثَنَا عَبْدُ الْوَاحِدِ، عَنِ الأَعْمَشِ، قَالَ حَدَّثَنَا إِبْرَاهِيمُ، قَالَ سَمِعْتُ عَبْدَ الرَّحْمَنِ بْنَ يَزِيدَ، يَقُولُ صَلَّى بِنَا عُثْمَانُ بْنُ عَفَّانَ ـ رضى الله عنه ـ بِمِنًى أَرْبَعَ رَكَعَاتٍ، فَقِيلَ ذَلِكَ لِعَبْدِ اللَّهِ بْنِ مَسْعُودٍ ـ رضى الله عنه ـ فَاسْتَرْجَعَ ثُمَّ قَالَ صَلَّيْتُ مَعَ رَسُولِ اللَّهِ صلى الله عليه وسلم بِمِنًى رَكْعَتَيْنِ، وَصَلَّيْتُ مَعَ أَبِي بَكْرٍ ـ رضى الله عنه ـ بِمِنًى رَكْعَتَيْنِ، وَصَلَّيْتُ مَعَ عُمَرَ بْنِ الْخَطَّابِ ـ رضى الله عنه ـ بِمِنًى رَكْعَتَيْنِ، فَلَيْتَ حَظِّي مِنْ أَرْبَعِ رَكَعَاتٍ رَكْعَتَانِ مُتَقَبَّلَتَانِ

Narrated `Aisha: "When the prayers were first enjoined they were of two rak`at each. Later the prayer in a journey was kept as it was but the prayers for non-travelers were completed." Az-Zuhri said, "I asked `Urwa what made Aisha pray the full prayers (in journey)." He replied, "She did the same as `Uthman did.". – Sahih al-Bukhari 1090
حَدَّثَنَا عَبْدُ اللَّهِ بْنُ مُحَمَّدٍ، قَالَ حَدَّثَنَا سُفْيَانُ، عَنِ الزُّهْرِيِّ، عَنْ عُرْوَةَ، عَنْ عَائِشَةَ ـ رضى الله عنها ـ قَالَتِ الصَّلاَةُ أَوَّلُ مَا فُرِضَتْ رَكْعَتَيْنِ فَأُقِرَّتْ صَلاَةُ السَّفَرِ، وَأُتِمَّتْ صَلاَةُ الْحَضَرِ. قَالَ الزُّهْرِيُّ فَقُلْتُ لِعُرْوَةَ مَا بَالُ عَائِشَةَ تُتِمُّ قَالَ تَأَوَّلَتْ مَا تَأَوَّلَ عُثْمَانُ

Narrated Marwan bin Al-Hakam: I saw `Uthman and `Ali. `Uthman used to forbid people to perform Hajj-at-Tamattu` and Hajj-al- Qiran (Hajj and `Umra together), and when `Ali saw (this act of `Uthman), he assumed Ihram for Hajj and `Umra together saying, "Lubbaik for `Umra and Hajj," and said, "I will not leave the tradition of the Prophet ﷺ on the saying of somebody.". – Sahih Al-Bukhari 1563
حَدَّثَنَا مُحَمَّدُ بْنُ بَشَّارٍ، حَدَّثَنَا غُنْدَرٌ، حَدَّثَنَا شُعْبَةُ، عَنِ الْحَكَمِ، عَنْ عَلِيِّ بْنِ حُسَيْنٍ، عَنْ مَرْوَانَ بْنِ الْحَكَمِ، قَالَ شَهِدْتُ عُثْمَانَ وَعَلِيًّا ـ رضى الله عنهما ـ وَعُثْمَانُ يَنْهَى عَنِ الْمُتْعَةِ وَأَنْ يُجْمَعَ بَيْنَهُمَا فَلَمَّا رَأَى عَلِيٌّ، أَهَلَّ بِهِمَا لَبَّيْكَ بِعُمْرَةٍ وَحَجَّةٍ قَالَ مَا كُنْتُ لأَدَعَ سُنَّةَ النَّبِيِّ صلى الله عليه وسلم لِقَوْلِ أَحَدٍ

Narrated Ibrahim's grand-father that 'Umar(ra) in his last Hajj allowed the wives of the Prophet ﷺ to perform Hajj and he sent with them 'Uthman bin 'Affan(ra) and 'Abdur-Rahman bin 'Auf(ra) as escorts. – Sahih Al-Bukhari 1860

وَقَالَ لِي أَحْمَدُ بْنُ مُحَمَّدٍ حَدَّثَنَا إِبْرَاهِيمُ، عَنْ أَبِيهِ، عَنْ جَدِّهِ، أَذِنَ عُمَرُ ـ رضى الله عنه ـ لأَزْوَاجِ النَّبِيِّ صلى الله عليه وسلم فِي آخِرِ حَجَّةٍ حَجَّهَا، فَبَعَثَ مَعَهُنَّ عُثْمَانَ بْنَ عَفَّانَ وَعَبْدَ الرَّحْمَنِ بْنَ عَوْفٍ.

Narrated Aslam: `Umar bin Al-Khattab appointed a freed slave of his, called Hunai, manager of the Hima (i.e. a pasture devoted for grazing the animals of the Zakat or other specified animals). He said to him, "O Hunai! Don't oppress the Muslims and ward off their curse (invocations against you) for the invocation of the oppressed is responded to (by Allah); and allow the shepherd having a few camels and those having a few sheep (to graze their animals), and take care not to allow the livestock of `Abdur-Rahman bin `Auf and the livestock of (`Uthman) bin `Affan, for if their livestock should perish, then they have their farms and gardens, while those who own a few camels and those who own a few sheep, if their livestock should perish, would bring their dependents to me and appeal for help saying, 'O chief of the believers! O chief of the believers!' Would I then neglect them? (No, of course). So, I find it easier to let them have water and grass rather than to give them gold and silver (from the Muslims' treasury). By Allah, these people think that I have been unjust to them. This is their land, and during the preIslamic period, they fought for it and they embraced Islam (willingly) while it was in their possession. By Him in Whose Hand my life is! Were it not for the animals (in my custody) which I give to be ridden for striving in Allah's Cause, I would not have turned even a span of their land into a Hima.". – Sahih Al-Bukhari 3059

حَدَّثَنَا إِسْمَاعِيلُ، قَالَ حَدَّثَنِي مَالِكٌ، عَنْ زَيْدِ بْنِ أَسْلَمَ، عَنْ أَبِيهِ، أَنَّ عُمَرَ بْنَ الْخَطَّابِ ـ رضى الله عنه ـ اسْتَعْمَلَ مَوْلًى لَهُ يُدْعَى هُنَيًّا عَلَى الْحِمَى فَقَالَ يَا هُنَىُّ، اضْمُمْ جَنَاحَكَ عَنِ الْمُسْلِمِينَ، وَاتَّقِ دَعْوَةَ الْمَظْلُومِ، فَإِنَّ دَعْوَةَ الْمَظْلُومِ مُسْتَجَابَةٌ، وَأَدْخِلْ رَبَّ الصُّرَيْمَةِ وَرَبَّ الْغُنَيْمَةِ، وَإِيَّاىَ وَنَعَمَ ابْنِ عَوْفٍ، وَنَعَمَ ابْنِ عَفَّانَ، فَإِنَّهُمَا إِنْ تَهْلِكْ مَاشِيَتُهُمَا يَرْجِعَا إِلَى نَخْلٍ وَزَرْعٍ، وَإِنَّ رَبَّ الصُّرَيْمَةِ وَرَبَّ الْغُنَيْمَةِ إِنْ تَهْلِكْ مَاشِيَتُهُمَا يَأْتِنِي بِبَنِيهِ فَيَقُولُ يَا أَمِيرَ الْمُؤْمِنِينَ. أَفَتَارِكُهُمْ أَنَا لاَ أَبَا لَكَ فَالْمَاءُ وَالْكَلأُ أَيْسَرُ عَلَىَّ مِنَ الذَّهَبِ وَالْوَرِقِ، وَايْمُ اللَّهِ، إِنَّهُمْ لَيَرَوْنَ أَنِّي قَدْ ظَلَمْتُهُمْ، إِنَّهَا لَبِلاَدُهُمْ فَقَاتَلُوا عَلَيْهَا فِي الْجَاهِلِيَّةِ، وَأَسْلَمُوا عَلَيْهَا فِي الإِسْلاَمِ، وَالَّذِي نَفْسِي بِيَدِهِ لَوْلاَ الْمَالُ الَّذِي أَحْمِلُ عَلَيْهِ فِي سَبِيلِ اللَّهِ مَا حَمَيْتُ عَلَيْهِمْ مِنْ بِلاَدِهِمْ شِبْرًا

Narrated `Uthman: (the son of Muhib) An Egyptian who came and performed the Hajj to the Ka`ba saw some people sitting. He enquire, "Who are these people?" Somebody said, "They are the tribe of Quraish." He said, "Who is the old man sitting amongst them?" The people replied, "He is `Abdullah bin `Umar." He said, "O Ibn `Umar! I want to ask you about something; please tell me about it. Do you know that `Uthman fled away on the day (of the battle) of Uhud?" Ibn `Umar said, "Yes." The (Egyptian) man said, "Do you know that `Uthman was absent on the day (of the battle) of Badr and did not join it?" Ibn `Umar said, "Yes." The man said, "Do you know that he failed to attend the Ar Ridwan pledge and did not witness it (i.e. Hudaibiya pledge of allegiance)?" Ibn `Umar said, "Yes." The man said, "Allahu Akbar!" Ibn `Umar said, "Let me explain to you (all these three things). As for his flight on the day of Uhud, I testify that Allah has excused him and forgiven him; and as for his absence from the battle of Badr, it was due to the fact that the daughter of Allah's Messenger ﷺ was his wife and she was sick then. Allah's Messenger ﷺ said to him, "You will receive the same reward and share (of the booty) as anyone of those who participated in the battle of Badr (if you stay with her).' As for his absence from the Ar-Ridwan pledge of allegiance, had there been any person in Mecca more respectable than `Uthman (to be sent as a representative). Allah's Messenger ﷺ would have sent him instead of him. No doubt, Allah's Messenger ﷺ had sent him, and the incident of the Ar-Ridwan pledge of Allegiance happened after `Uthman had gone to Mecca. Allah's Messenger ﷺ held out his right hand saying, 'This is `Uthman's hand.' He stroke his (other) hand with it saying, 'This (pledge of allegiance) is on the behalf of `Uthman.' Then Ibn `Umar said to the man, 'Bear (these) excuses in mind with you.'. – Sahih Al-Bukhari 3698

حَدَّثَنَا مُوسَى بْنُ إِسْمَاعِيلَ، حَدَّثَنَا أَبُو عَوَانَةَ، حَدَّثَنَا عُثْمَانُ ـ هُوَ ابْنُ مَوْهَبٍ ـ قَالَ جَاءَ رَجُلٌ مَنْ أَهْلِ مِصْرَ حَجَّ الْبَيْتَ فَرَأَى قَوْمًا جُلُوسًا، فَقَالَ مَنْ هَؤُلاَءِ الْقَوْمُ قَالَ هَؤُلاَءِ قُرَيْشٌ. قَالَ فَمَنِ الشَّيْخُ فِيهِمْ قَالُوا عَبْدُ اللَّهِ بْنُ عُمَرَ. قَالَ يَا ابْنَ عُمَرَ إِنِّي سَائِلُكَ عَنْ شَىْءٍ فَحَدِّثْنِي هَلْ تَعْلَمُ أَنَّ عُثْمَانَ فَرَّ يَوْمَ أُحُدٍ قَالَ نَعَمْ. قَالَ تَعْلَمُ أَنَّهُ تَغَيَّبَ عَنْ بَدْرٍ وَلَمْ يَشْهَدْ قَالَ نَعَمْ. قَالَ تَعْلَمُ أَنَّهُ تَغَيَّبَ عَنْ بَيْعَةِ الرِّضْوَانِ فَلَمْ يَشْهَدْهَا قَالَ نَعَمْ. قَالَ اللَّهُ أَكْبَرُ. قَالَ ابْنُ عُمَرَ تَعَالَ أُبَيِّنْ لَكَ أَمَّا فِرَارُهُ يَوْمَ أُحُدٍ فَأَشْهَدُ أَنَّ اللَّهَ عَفَا عَنْهُ وَغَفَرَ لَهُ، وَأَمَّا تَغَيُّبُهُ عَنْ بَدْرٍ، فَإِنَّهُ كَانَتْ تَحْتَهُ بِنْتُ رَسُولِ اللَّهِ صلى الله عليه وسلم وَكَانَتْ مَرِيضَةً، فَقَالَ لَهُ رَسُولُ اللَّهِ صلى الله عليه وسلم " إِنَّ لَكَ أَجْرَ رَجُلٍ مِمَّنْ شَهِدَ بَدْرًا وَسَهْمَهُ ". وَأَمَّا تَغَيُّبُهُ عَنْ بَيْعَةِ الرِّضْوَانِ فَلَوْ كَانَ أَحَدٌ أَعَزَّ بِبَطْنِ مَكَّةَ مِنْ عُثْمَانَ لَبَعَثَهُ مَكَانَهُ فَبَعَثَ رَسُولُ اللَّهِ صلى الله عليه وسلم عُثْمَانَ وَكَانَتْ بَيْعَةُ الرِّضْوَانِ بَعْدَ مَا ذَهَبَ عُثْمَانُ إِلَى مَكَّةَ، فَقَالَ رَسُولُ اللَّهِ صلى الله عليه وسلم بِيَدِهِ الْيُمْنَى " هَذِهِ يَدُ عُثْمَانَ ". فَضَرَبَ بِهَا عَلَى يَدِهِ، فَقَالَ " هَذِهِ لِعُثْمَانَ ". فَقَالَ لَهُ ابْنُ عُمَرَ اذْهَبْ بِهَا الآنَ مَعَكَ

Narrated Sa`d bin 'Ubaida: Abu `Abdur-Rahman who was one of the supporters of `Uthman said to Abu Talha who was one of the supporters of `Ali, "I perfectly know what encouraged your leader (i.e. `Ali) to shed blood. I heard him saying: Once the Prophet ﷺ sent me and Az-Zubair saying, 'Proceed to such-and-such Ar-Roudah (place) where you will find a lady whom Hatib has given a letter. So when we arrived at Ar-Roudah, we requested the lady to hand over the letter to us. She said, 'Hatib has not given me any letter.' We said to her. 'Take out the letter or else we will strip off your clothes.' So she took it out of her braid. So the Prophet ﷺ sent for Hatib, (who came) and said, 'Don't hurry in judging me, for, by Allah, I have not become a disbeliever, and my love to Islam is increasing. (The reason for writing this letter was) that there is none of your companions but has relatives in Mecca who look after their families and property, while I have nobody there, so I wanted to do them some favor (so that they might look after my family and property).' The Prophet ﷺ believed him. `Umar said, 'Allow me to chop off his (i.e. Hatib's) neck as he has done hypocrisy.' The Prophet ﷺ said, (to `Umar), 'Who knows, perhaps Allah has looked at the warriors of Badr and said (to them), 'Do whatever you like, for I have forgiven you.' " `Abdur-Rahman added, "So this is what encouraged him (i.e. `Ali). – Sahih Al-Bukhari 3081

حَدَّثَنِي مُحَمَّدُ بْنُ عَبْدِ اللَّهِ بْنِ حَوْشَبٍ الطَّائِفِيُّ، حَدَّثَنَا هُشَيْمٌ، أَخْبَرَنَا حُصَيْنٌ، عَنْ سَعْدِ بْنِ عُبَيْدَةَ، عَنْ أَبِي عَبْدِ الرَّحْمَنِ، وَكَانَ، عُثْمَانِيًّا فَقَالَ لاِبْنِ عَطِيَّةَ وَكَانَ عَلَوِيًّا إِنِّي لأَعْلَمُ مَا الَّذِي جَرَّأَ صَاحِبَكَ عَلَى الدِّمَاءِ سَمِعْتُهُ يَقُولُ بَعَثَنِي النَّبِيُّ صلى الله عليه وسلم وَالزُّبَيْرَ، فَقَالَ " ائْتُوا رَوْضَةَ كَذَا، وَتَجِدُونَ بِهَا امْرَأَةً أَعْطَاهَا حَاطِبٌ كِتَابًا ". فَأَتَيْنَا الرَّوْضَةَ فَقُلْنَا الْكِتَابَ. قَالَتْ لَمْ يُعْطِنِي. فَقُلْنَا لَتُخْرِجِنَّ أَوْ لأُجَرِّدَنَّكِ. فَأَخْرَجَتْ مِنْ حُجْزَتِهَا، فَأَرْسَلَ إِلَى حَاطِبٍ فَقَالَ لاَ تَعْجَلْ، وَاللَّهِ مَا كَفَرْتُ وَلاَ ازْدَدْتُ لِلإِسْلاَمِ إِلاَّ حُبًّا، وَلَمْ يَكُنْ أَحَدٌ مِنْ أَصْحَابِكَ إِلاَّ وَلَهُ بِمَكَّةَ مَنْ يَدْفَعُ اللَّهُ بِهِ عَنْ أَهْلِهِ وَمَالِهِ، وَلَمْ يَكُنْ لِي أَحَدٌ، فَأَحْبَبْتُ أَنْ أَتَّخِذَ عِنْدَهُمْ يَدًا. فَصَدَّقَهُ النَّبِيُّ صلى الله عليه وسلم. قَالَ عُمَرُ دَعْنِي أَضْرِبْ عُنُقَهُ، فَإِنَّهُ قَدْ نَافَقَ. فَقَالَ " مَا يُدْرِيكَ لَعَلَّ اللَّهَ اطَّلَعَ عَلَى أَهْلِ بَدْرٍ، فَقَالَ اعْمَلُوا مَا شِئْتُمْ ". فَهَذَا الَّذِي جَرَّأَهُ

Narrated Abu Wail: Somebody said to Usama, "Will you go to so-and-so (i.e. `Uthman) and talk to him (i.e. advise him regarding ruling the country)?" He said, "You see that I don't talk to him. Really I talk to (advise) him secretly without opening a gate (of affliction), for neither do I want to be the first to open it (i.e. rebellion), nor will I say to a man who is my ruler that he is the best of all the people after I have heard something from Allah s Apostle ." They said, What have you heard him saying? He said, "I have heard him saying, "A man will be brought on the Day of Resurrection and thrown in the (Hell) Fire, so that his intestines will come out, and he will go around like a donkey goes around a millstone. The people of (Hell) Fire will gather around him and say: O so-and-so! What is wrong with you? Didn't you use to order us to do good deeds and forbid us to do bad deeds? He will reply: Yes, I used to order you to do good deeds, but I did not do them myself, and I used to forbid you to do bad deeds, yet I used to do them myself.". – Sahih Al-Bukhari 3267

حَدَّثَنَا عَلِيٌّ، حَدَّثَنَا سُفْيَانُ، عَنِ الأَعْمَشِ، عَنْ أَبِي وَائِلٍ،، قَالَ قِيلَ لأُسَامَةَ لَوْ أَتَيْتَ فُلاَنًا فَكَلَّمْتَهُ. قَالَ إِنَّكُمْ لَتُرَوْنَ أَنِّي لاَ أُكَلِّمُهُ إِلاَّ أُسْمِعُكُمْ، إِنِّي أُكَلِّمُهُ فِي السِّرِّ دُونَ أَنْ أَفْتَحَ بَابًا لاَ أَكُونُ أَوَّلَ مَنْ فَتَحَهُ، وَلاَ أَقُولُ لِرَجُلٍ أَنْ كَانَ عَلَىَّ أَمِيرًا إِنَّهُ

خَيْرُ النَّاسِ بَعْدَ شَىْءٍ سَمِعْتُهُ مِنْ رَسُولِ اللَّهِ صلى الله عليه وسلم. قَالُوا وَمَا سَمِعْتَهُ يَقُولُ قَالَ سَمِعْتُهُ يَقُولُ " يُجَاءُ بِالرَّجُلِ يَوْمَ الْقِيَامَةِ فَيُلْقَى فِي النَّارِ، فَتَنْدَلِقُ أَقْتَابُهُ فِي النَّارِ، فَيَدُورُ كَمَا يَدُورُ الْحِمَارُ بِرَحَاهُ، فَيَجْتَمِعُ أَهْلُ النَّارِ عَلَيْهِ، فَيَقُولُونَ أَىْ فُلاَنُ، مَا شَأْنُكَ أَلَيْسَ كُنْتَ تَأْمُرُنَا بِالْمَعْرُوفِ وَتَنْهَى عَنِ الْمُنْكَرِ قَالَ كُنْتُ آمُرُكُمْ بِالْمَعْرُوفِ وَلاَ آتِيهِ، وَأَنْهَاكُمْ عَنِ الْمُنْكَرِ وَآتِيهِ ". رَوَاهُ غُنْدَرٌ عَنْ شُعْبَةَ عَنِ الأَعْمَشِ.

Narrated ‘Ubaid-Ullah bin Adi bin Khiyar: I went to ‘Uthman bin Affan while he was besieged, and said to him, “You are the chief of all Muslims in general and you see what has befallen you. We are led in the Salat (prayer) by a leader of Al-Fitan (trials and afflictions etc.) and we are afraid of being sinful in following him.” ‘Uthman said. “As-Salat (the prayers) is the best of all deeds so when the people do good deeds do the same with them and when they do bad deeds, avoid those bad deeds.” Az-Zuhri said, “In our opinion one should not offer Salat behind an effeminate person unless there is no alternative.”. – Sahih Al-Bukhari 695

قَالَ أَبُو عَبْدِ اللَّهِ وَقَالَ لَنَا مُحَمَّدُ بْنُ يُوسُفَ حَدَّثَنَا الأَوْزَاعِيُّ، حَدَّثَنَا الزُّهْرِيُّ، عَنْ حُمَيْدِ بْنِ عَبْدِ الرَّحْمَنِ، عَنْ عُبَيْدِ اللَّهِ بْنِ عَدِيِّ بْنِ خِيَارٍ، أَنَّهُ دَخَلَ عَلَى عُثْمَانَ بْنِ عَفَّانَ ـ رضى الله عنه ـ وَهْوَ مَحْصُورٌ فَقَالَ إِنَّكَ إِمَامُ عَامَّةٍ، وَنَزَلَ بِكَ مَا تَرَى وَيُصَلِّي لَنَا إِمَامُ فِتْنَةٍ وَنَتَحَرَّجُ. فَقَالَ الصَّلاَةُ أَحْسَنُ مَا يَعْمَلُ النَّاسُ، فَإِذَا أَحْسَنَ النَّاسُ فَأَحْسِنْ مَعَهُمْ، وَإِذَا أَسَاءُوا فَاجْتَنِبْ إِسَاءَتَهُمْ. وَقَالَ الزُّبَيْدِيُّ قَالَ الزُّهْرِيُّ لاَ نَرَى أَنْ يُصَلَّى خَلْفَ الْمُخَنَّثِ إِلاَّ مِنْ ضَرُورَةٍ لاَ بُدَّ مِنْهَا.

Narrated ‘Ubaidullah bin `Adi bin Al-Khiyar: Al-Miswar bin Makhrama and `Abdur-Rahman bin Al-Aswad bin ‘Abu Yaghuth said (to me), “What forbids you to talk to `Uthman about his brother Al-Walid because people have talked much about him?” So I went to `Uthman and when he went out for prayer I said (to him), “I have something to say to you and it is a piece of advice for you “ `Uthman said, “O man, from you.” (`Umar said: I see that he said, “I seek Refuge with Allah from you.”) So I left him and went to them. Then the messenger of `Uthman came and I went to him (i.e. `Uthman), `Uthman asked, “What is your advice?” I replied, “Allah sent Muhammad with the Truth, and revealed the Divine Book (i.e. Qur’an) to him; and you were amongst those who followed Allah and His Apostle, and you participated in the two migrations (to Ethiopia and to Medina) and enjoyed the company of Allah’s Messenger ﷺ and saw his way. No doubt, the people are talking much about Al-Walid.” `Uthman said, “Did you receive your knowledge directly from Allah’s Messenger ﷺ?” I said, “No, but his knowledge did reach me and it reached (even) to a virgin in her seclusion.” `Uthman said, “And then Allah sent Muhammad with the Truth and I was amongst those who followed Allah and His Apostle and I believed in what ever he (i.e. the Prophet) was sent with, and participated in two migrations, as you have said, and I enjoyed the company of Allah’s Messenger ﷺ and gave the pledge of allegiance him. By Allah! I never disobeyed him, nor did I cheat him till Allah took him unto Him. Then I treated Abu Bakr and then `Umar similarly and then I was made Caliph. So, don’t I have rights similar to theirs?” I said, “Yes.” He said, “Then what are these talks reaching me from you people? Now, concerning what you mentioned about the question of Al-Walid, Allah willing, I shall deal with him according to what is right.” Then he called `Ali and ordered him to flog him, and `Ali flogged him (i.e. Al-Walid) eighty lashes. – Sahih Al-Bukhari 3696

حَدَّثَنِي أَحْمَدُ بْنُ شَبِيبِ بْنِ سَعِيدٍ، قَالَ حَدَّثَنِي أَبِي، عَنْ يُونُسَ، قَالَ ابْنُ شِهَابٍ أَخْبَرَنِي عُرْوَةُ، أَنَّ عُبَيْدَ اللَّهِ بْنَ عَدِيِّ بْنِ الْخِيَارِ، أَخْبَرَهُ أَنَّ الْمِسْوَرَ بْنَ مَخْرَمَةَ وَعَبْدَ الرَّحْمَنِ بْنَ الأَسْوَدِ بْنِ عَبْدِ يَغُوثَ قَالاَ مَا يَمْنَعُكَ أَنْ تُكَلِّمَ عُثْمَانَ لأَخِيهِ الْوَلِيدِ فَقَدْ أَكْثَرَ النَّاسُ فِيهِ. فَقَصَدْتُ لِعُثْمَانَ حَتَّى خَرَجَ إِلَى الصَّلاَةِ، قُلْتُ إِنَّ لِي إِلَيْكَ حَاجَةً، وَهِيَ نَصِيحَةٌ لَكَ. قَالَ يَا أَيُّهَا الْمَرْءُ ـ قَالَ مَعْمَرٌ أُرَاهُ قَالَ ـ أَعُوذُ بِاللَّهِ مِنْكَ. فَانْصَرَفْتُ، فَرَجَعْتُ إِلَيْهِمْ إِذْ جَاءَ رَسُولُ عُثْمَانَ فَأَتَيْتُهُ، فَقَالَ مَا نَصِيحَتُكَ فَقُلْتُ إِنَّ اللَّهَ سُبْحَانَهُ بَعَثَ مُحَمَّدًا صلى الله عليه وسلم بِالْحَقِّ، وَأَنْزَلَ عَلَيْهِ الْكِتَابَ، وَكُنْتَ مِمَّنِ اسْتَجَابَ لِلَّهِ وَلِرَسُولِهِ، فَهَاجَرْتَ الْهِجْرَتَيْنِ، وَصَحِبْتَ رَسُولَ اللَّهِ صلى الله عليه وسلم وَرَأَيْتَ هَدْيَهُ، وَقَدْ أَكْثَرَ النَّاسُ فِي شَأْنِ الْوَلِيدِ. قَالَ أَدْرَكْتَ رَسُولَ اللَّهِ صلى الله عليه وسلم قُلْتُ لاَ وَلَكِنْ خَلَصَ إِلَىَّ مِنْ عِلْمِهِ مَا يَخْلُصُ إِلَى الْعَذْرَاءِ فِي سِتْرِهَا. قَالَ أَمَّا بَعْدُ فَإِنَّ اللَّهَ بَعَثَ مُحَمَّدًا صلى الله عليه وسلم بِالْحَقِّ، فَكُنْتُ مِمَّنِ اسْتَجَابَ لِلَّهِ وَلِرَسُولِهِ وَآمَنْتُ بِمَا بُعِثَ بِهِ، وَهَاجَرْتُ الْهِجْرَتَيْنِ كَمَا قُلْتَ،

وَصَحِبْتُ رَسُولَ اللَّهِ صلى الله عليه وسلم وَبَايَعْتُهُ، فَوَاللَّهِ مَا عَصَيْتُهُ وَلاَ غَشَشْتُهُ حَتَّى تَوَفَّاهُ اللَّهُ، ثُمَّ أَبُو بَكْرٍ مِثْلُهُ، ثُمَّ عُمَرُ مِثْلُهُ، ثُمَّ اسْتُخْلِفْتُ، أَفَلَيْسَ لِي مِنَ الْحَقِّ مِثْلُ الَّذِي لَهُمْ قُلْتُ بَلَى. قَالَ فَمَا هَذِهِ الأَحَادِيثُ الَّتِي تَبْلُغُنِي عَنْكُمْ أَمَّا مَا ذَكَرْتَ مِنْ شَأْنِ الْوَلِيدِ، فَسَنَأْخُذُ فِيهِ بِالْحَقِّ إِنْ شَاءَ اللَّهُ، ثُمَّ دَعَا عَلِيًّا فَأَمَرَهُ أَنْ يَجْلِدَهُ فَجَلَدَهُ ثَمَانِينَ

Narrated Anas: The Prophetﷺ ascended the mountain of Uhud and Abu Bakr, `Umar and `Uthman were accompanying him. The mountain gave a shake (i.e. trembled underneath them) . The Prophetﷺ said, "O Uhud ! Be calm." I think that the Prophetﷺ hit it with his foot, adding, "For upon you there are none but a Prophet, a Siddiq and two martyrs.". – Sahih Al-Bukhari 3699

حَدَّثَنَا مُسَدَّدٌ، حَدَّثَنَا يَحْيَى، عَنْ سَعِيدٍ، عَنْ قَتَادَةَ، أَنَّ أَنَسًا ـ رضى الله عنه ـ حَدَّثَهُمْ قَالَ صَعِدَ النَّبِيُّ صلى الله عليه وسلم أُحُدًا، وَمَعَهُ أَبُو بَكْرٍ وَعُمَرُ وَعُثْمَانُ، فَرَجَفَ وَقَالَ " اسْكُنْ أُحُدُ ـ أَظُنُّهُ ضَرَبَهُ بِرِجْلِهِ ـ فَلَيْسَ عَلَيْكَ إِلاَّ نَبِيٌّ وَصِدِّيقٌ وَشَهِيدَانِ "

Anas added: The ring of the Prophetﷺ was in his hand, and after him, in Abu Bakr's hand, and then in `Umar's hand after Abu Bakr. When `Uthman was the Caliph, once he was sitting at the well of Aris. He removed the ring from his hand and while he was trifling with it, dropped into the well. We kept on going to the well with `Uthman for three days looking for the ring, and finally the well was drained, but the ring was not found. – Sahih Al-Bukhari 5879

وَزَادَنِي أَحْمَدُ حَدَّثَنَا الأَنْصَارِيُّ، قَالَ حَدَّثَنِي أَبِي، عَنْ ثُمَامَةَ، عَنْ أَنَسٍ، قَالَ كَانَ خَاتَمُ النَّبِيِّ صلى الله عليه وسلم فِي يَدِهِ، وَفِي يَدِ أَبِي بَكْرٍ بَعْدَهُ، وَفِي يَدِ عُمَرَ بَعْدَ أَبِي بَكْرٍ، فَلَمَّا كَانَ عُثْمَانُ جَلَسَ عَلَى بِئْرِ أَرِيسَ ـ قَالَ ـ فَأَخْرَجَ الْخَاتَمَ، فَجَعَلَ يَعْبَثُ بِهِ فَسَقَطَ قَالَ فَاخْتَلَفْنَا ثَلاَثَةَ أَيَّامٍ مَعَ عُثْمَانَ فَنَنْزَحُ الْبِئْرَ فَلَمْ نَجِدْهُ

Narrated Az-Zuhri: I heard As-Saib bin Yazid, saying, "In the lifetime of Allah's Messengerﷺ and Abu Bakr and `Umar, the Adhan for the Jumua prayer used to be pronounced after the Imam had taken his seat on the pulpit. But when the people increased in number during the caliphate of `Uthman, he introduced a third Adhan (on Friday for the Jumua prayer) and it was pronounced at Az-Zaura' and that new state of affairs remained so in the succeeding years. – Sahih al-Bukhari 916

حَدَّثَنَا مُحَمَّدُ بْنُ مُقَاتِلٍ، قَالَ أَخْبَرَنَا عَبْدُ اللَّهِ، قَالَ أَخْبَرَنَا يُونُسُ، عَنِ الزُّهْرِيِّ، قَالَ سَمِعْتُ السَّائِبَ بْنَ يَزِيدَ، يَقُولُ إِنَّ الأَذَانَ يَوْمَ الْجُمُعَةِ كَانَ أَوَّلُهُ حِينَ يَجْلِسُ الإِمَامُ يَوْمَ الْجُمُعَةِ عَلَى الْمِنْبَرِ فِي عَهْدِ رَسُولِ اللَّهِ صلى الله عليه وسلم وَأَبِي بَكْرٍ وَعُمَرَ ـ رضى الله عنهما ـ فَلَمَّا كَانَ فِي خِلاَفَةِ عُثْمَانَ ـ رضى الله عنه ـ وَكَثُرُوا، أَمَرَ عُثْمَانُ يَوْمَ الْجُمُعَةِ بِالأَذَانِ الثَّالِثِ، فَأُذِّنَ بِهِ عَلَى الزَّوْرَاءِ، فَثَبَتَ الأَمْرُ عَلَى ذَلِكَ

Narrated `Abdur Rahman bin Yazid: We offered a four rak`at prayer at Mina behind Ibn `Affan . `Abdullah bin Mas`ud was informed about it. He said sadly, "Truly to Allah we belong and truly to Him we shall return." And added, "I prayed two rak`at with Allah's Messengerﷺ at Mina and similarly with Abu Bakr and with `Umar (during their caliphates)." He further said, "May I be lucky enough to have two of the four rak`at accepted (by Allah) – ".Sahih al-Bukhari 1084

حَدَّثَنَا قُتَيْبَةُ، قَالَ حَدَّثَنَا عَبْدُ الْوَاحِدِ، عَنِ الأَعْمَشِ، قَالَ حَدَّثَنَا إِبْرَاهِيمُ، قَالَ سَمِعْتُ عَبْدَ الرَّحْمَنِ بْنَ يَزِيدَ، يَقُولُ صَلَّى بِنَا عُثْمَانُ بْنُ عَفَّانَ ـ رضى الله عنه ـ بِمِنًى أَرْبَعَ رَكَعَاتٍ، فَقِيلَ ذَلِكَ لِعَبْدِ اللَّهِ بْنِ مَسْعُودٍ ـ رضى الله عنه ـ فَاسْتَرْجَعَ ثُمَّ قَالَ صَلَّيْتُ مَعَ رَسُولِ اللَّهِ صلى الله عليه وسلم بِمِنًى رَكْعَتَيْنِ، وَصَلَّيْتُ مَعَ أَبِي بَكْرٍ ـ رضى الله عنه ـ بِمِنًى رَكْعَتَيْنِ، وَصَلَّيْتُ مَعَ عُمَرَ بْنِ الْخَطَّابِ ـ رضى الله عنه ـ بِمِنًى رَكْعَتَيْنِ، فَلَيْتَ حَظِّي مِنْ أَرْبَعِ رَكَعَاتٍ رَكْعَتَانِ مُتَقَبَّلَتَانِ.

ʿAbd al-Raḥmān ibn ʿAwf

عبد الرحمن بن عوف

Narrated Al-Miswar bin Makhrama: The group of people whom `Umar had selected as candidates for the Caliphate gathered and consulted each other. `Abdur-Rahman said to them, “I am not going to compete with you in this matter, but if you wish, I would select for you a caliph from among you.” So all of them agreed to let `Abdur-Rahman decide the case. So when the candidates placed the case in the hands of `Abdur-Rahman, the people went towards him and nobody followed the rest of the group nor obeyed any after him. So the people followed `Abdur-Rahman and consulted him all those nights till there came the night we gave the oath of allegiance to `Uthman. Al-Miswar (bin Makhrama) added: `Abdur-Rahman called on me after a portion of the night had passed and knocked on my door till I got up, and he said to me, “I see you have been sleeping! By Allah, during the last three nights I have not slept enough. Go and call Az-Zubair and Sa`d.' So I called them for him and he consulted them and then called me saying, 'Call `Ali for me.” I called `Ali and he held a private talk with him till very late at night, and then 'Al, got up to leave having had much hope (to be chosen as a Caliph) but `Abdur-Rahman was afraid of something concerning `Ali. `Abdur-Rahman then said to me, “Call `Uthman for me.” I called him and he kept on speaking to him privately till the Mu'adh-dhin put an end to their talk by announcing the Adhan for the Fajr prayer. When the people finished their morning prayer and that (six men) group gathered near the pulpit, `Abdur-Rahman sent for all the Muhajirin (emigrants) and the Ansar present there and sent for the army chief who had performed the Hajj with `Umar that year. When all of them had gathered, `Abdur- Rahman said, “None has the right to be worshipped but Allah,” and added, “Now then, O `Ali, I have looked at the people's tendencies and noticed that they do not consider anybody equal to `Uthman, so you should not incur blame (by disagreeing).” Then `Abdur-Rahman said (to `Uthman), “I gave the oath of allegiance to you on condition that you will follow Allah's Laws and the traditions of Allah's Apostle and the traditions of the two Caliphs after him.” So `Abdur-Rahman gave the oath of allegiance to him, and so did the people including the Muhajirin (emigrants) and the Ansar and the chiefs of the army staff and all the Muslims. – Sahih Al-Bukhari 7207

حَدَّثَنَا عَبْدُ اللَّهِ بْنُ مُحَمَّدِ بْنِ أَسْمَاءَ، حَدَّثَنَا جُوَيْرِيَةُ، عَنْ مَالِكٍ، عَنِ الزُّهْرِيِّ، أَنَّ حُمَيْدَ بْنَ عَبْدِ الرَّحْمَنِ، أَخْبَرَهُ أَنَّ الْمِسْوَرَ بْنَ مَخْرَمَةَ أَخْبَرَهُ. أَنَّ الرَّهْطَ الَّذِينَ وَلاَّهُمْ عُمَرُ اجْتَمَعُوا فَتَشَاوَرُوا، قَالَ لَهُمْ عَبْدُ الرَّحْمَنِ لَسْتُ بِالَّذِي أُنَافِسُكُمْ عَلَى هَذَا الأَمْرِ، وَلَكِنَّكُمْ إِنْ شِئْتُمُ اخْتَرْتُ لَكُمْ مِنْكُمْ. فَجَعَلُوا ذَلِكَ إِلَى عَبْدِ الرَّحْمَنِ، فَلَمَّا وَلَّوْا عَبْدَ الرَّحْمَنِ أَمْرَهُمْ فَمَالَ النَّاسُ عَلَى عَبْدِ الرَّحْمَنِ، حَتَّى مَا أَرَى أَحَدًا مِنَ النَّاسِ يَتْبَعُ أُولَئِكَ الرَّهْطَ وَلاَ يَطَأُ عَقِبَهُ، وَمَالَ النَّاسُ عَلَى عَبْدِ الرَّحْمَنِ يُشَاوِرُونَهُ تِلْكَ اللَّيَالِيَ حَتَّى إِذَا كَانَتِ اللَّيْلَةُ الَّتِي أَصْبَحْنَا مِنْهَا، فَبَايَعْنَا عُثْمَانَ قَالَ الْمِسْوَرُ طَرَقَنِي عَبْدُ الرَّحْمَنِ بَعْدَ هَجْعٍ مِنَ اللَّيْلِ فَضَرَبَ الْبَابَ حَتَّى اسْتَيْقَظْتُ فَقَالَ أَرَاكَ نَائِمًا، فَوَاللَّهِ مَا اكْتَحَلْتُ هَذِهِ اللَّيْلَةَ بِكَبِيرِ نَوْمٍ، انْطَلِقْ فَادْعُ الزُّبَيْرَ وَسَعْدًا، فَدَعَوْتُهُمَا لَهُ فَشَاوَرَهُمَا ثُمَّ دَعَانِي فَقَالَ ادْعُ لِي عَلِيًّا. فَدَعَوْتُهُ فَنَاجَاهُ حَتَّى ابْهَارَّ اللَّيْلُ، ثُمَّ قَامَ عَلِيٌّ مِنْ عِنْدِهِ، وَهُوَ عَلَى طَمَعٍ، وَقَدْ كَانَ عَبْدُ الرَّحْمَنِ يَخْشَى مِنْ عَلِيٍّ شَيْئًا، ثُمَّ قَالَ ادْعُ لِي عُثْمَانَ، فَدَعَوْتُهُ فَنَاجَاهُ حَتَّى فَرَّقَ بَيْنَهُمَا الْمُؤَذِّنُ بِالصُّبْحِ، فَلَمَّا صَلَّى لِلنَّاسِ الصُّبْحَ وَاجْتَمَعَ أُولَئِكَ الرَّهْطُ عِنْدَ الْمِنْبَرِ، فَأَرْسَلَ إِلَى مَنْ كَانَ حَاضِرًا مِنَ الْمُهَاجِرِينَ وَالأَنْصَارِ، وَأَرْسَلَ إِلَى أُمَرَاءِ الأَجْنَادِ وَكَانُوا وَافَوْا تِلْكَ الْحَجَّةَ مَعَ عُمَرَ، فَلَمَّا اجْتَمَعُوا تَشَهَّدَ عَبْدُ الرَّحْمَنِ ثُمَّ قَالَ أَمَّا بَعْدُ يَا عَلِيُّ، إِنِّي قَدْ نَظَرْتُ فِي أَمْرِ النَّاسِ فَلَمْ أَرَهُمْ يَعْدِلُونَ بِعُثْمَانَ، فَلاَ تَجْعَلَنَّ عَلَى نَفْسِكَ سَبِيلاً. فَقَالَ أُبَايِعُكَ عَلَى سُنَّةِ اللَّهِ وَرَسُولِهِ وَالْخَلِيفَتَيْنِ مِنْ بَعْدِهِ. فَبَايَعَهُ عَبْدُ الرَّحْمَنِ، وَبَايَعَهُ النَّاسُ الْمُهَاجِرُونَ وَالأَنْصَارُ وَأُمَرَاءُ الأَجْنَادِ وَالْمُسْلِمُونَ

Narrated Sa`d bin 'Ubaida: Abu `Abdur-Rahman who was one of the supporters of `Uthman said to Abu Talha who was one of the supporters of `Ali, “I perfectly know what encouraged your leader (i.e. `Ali) to shed blood. I heard him saying: Once the Prophet ﷺ sent me and Az-Zubair saying, 'Proceed to such-and-such Ar-Roudah (place) where you will find a lady whom Hatib has given a letter. So when we arrived at Ar-Roudah, we requested the lady to hand over the letter to us. She said, 'Hatib has not given me any letter.' We said to her. 'Take out the letter or else we will strip off your clothes.' So she took it out of her braid. So the Prophet ﷺ sent for Hatib, (who came) and said, 'Don't hurry in judging me, for, by Allah, I have not become a disbeliever, and my love to Islam is increasing. (The reason for writing this letter was) that there is none of your companions but has relatives in Mecca who look after their families and property, while I have nobody there, so I wanted to do them some favor (so that they might look after my family and property).' The Prophet ﷺ believed him. `Umar said, 'Allow me to chop off his (i.e. Hatib's) neck as he has done hypocrisy.' The Prophet ﷺ said, (to `Umar), 'Who knows, perhaps Allah has looked at the warriors of Badr and said (to them), 'Do whatever you like, for I have forgiven you.' " `Abdur-Rahman added, "So this is what encouraged him (i.e. `Ali). – Sahih Al-Bukhari 3081.

حَدَّثَنِي مُحَمَّدُ بْنُ عَبْدِ اللَّهِ بْنِ حَوْشَبٍ الطَّائِفِيُّ، حَدَّثَنَا هُشَيْمٌ، أَخْبَرَنَا حُصَيْنٌ، عَنْ سَعْدِ بْنِ عُبَيْدَةَ، عَنْ أَبِي عَبْدِ الرَّحْمَنِ، وَكَانَ، عُثْمَانِيًّا فَقَالَ لاِبْنِ عَطِيَّةَ وَكَانَ عَلَوِيًّا إِنِّي لأَعْلَمُ مَا الَّذِي جَرَّأَ صَاحِبَكَ عَلَى الدِّمَاءِ سَمِعْتُهُ يَقُولُ بَعَثَنِي النَّبِيُّ صلى الله عليه وسلم وَالزُّبَيْرَ، فَقَالَ " ائْتُوا رَوْضَةَ كَذَا، وَتَجِدُونَ بِهَا امْرَأَةً أَعْطَاهَا حَاطِبٌ كِتَابًا ". فَأَتَيْنَا الرَّوْضَةَ فَقُلْنَا الْكِتَابَ. قَالَتْ لَمْ يُعْطِنِي. فَقُلْنَا لَتُخْرِجِنَّ أَوْ لأُجَرِّدَنَّكِ. فَأَخْرَجَتْ مِنْ حُجْزَتِهَا، فَأَرْسَلَ إِلَى حَاطِبٍ فَقَالَ لاَ تَعْجَلْ، وَاللَّهِ مَا كَفَرْتُ وَلاَ ازْدَدْتُ لِلإِسْلاَمِ إِلاَّ حُبًّا، وَلَمْ يَكُنْ أَحَدٌ مِنْ أَصْحَابِكَ إِلاَّ وَلَهُ بِمَكَّةَ مَنْ يَدْفَعُ اللَّهُ بِهِ عَنْ أَهْلِهِ وَمَالِهِ، وَلَمْ يَكُنْ لِي أَحَدٌ، فَأَحْبَبْتُ أَنْ أَتَّخِذَ عِنْدَهُمْ يَدًا. فَصَدَّقَهُ النَّبِيُّ صلى الله عليه وسلم. قَالَ عُمَرُ دَعْنِي أَضْرِبْ عُنُقَهُ، فَإِنَّهُ قَدْ نَافَقَ. فَقَالَ " مَا يُدْرِيكَ لَعَلَّ اللَّهَ اطَّلَعَ عَلَى أَهْلِ بَدْرٍ، فَقَالَ اعْمَلُوا مَا شِئْتُمْ ". فَهَذَا الَّذِي جَرَّأَهُ

Narrated Malik bin Aus: While I was at home, the sun rose high and it got hot. Suddenly the messenger of `Umar bin Al- Khattab came to me and said, "The chief of the believers has sent for you." So, I went along with him till I entered the place where `Umar was sitting on a bedstead made of date-palm leaves and covered with no mattress, and he was leaning over a leather pillow. I greeted him and sat down. He said, "O Mali! Some persons of your people who have families came to me and I have ordered that a gift should be given to them, so take it and distribute it among them." I said, "O chief of the believers! I wish that you order someone else to do it." He said, "O man! Take it." While I was sitting there with him, his doorman Yarfa' came saying, "`Uthman, `Abdur-Rahman bin `Auf, Az-Zubair and Sa`d bin Abi Waqqas are asking your permission (to see you); may I admit them?" `Umar said, "Yes", So they were admitted and they came in, greeted him, and sat down. After a while Yarfa' came again and said, "May I admit `Ali and `Abbas?" `Umar said, "yes." So, they were admitted and they came in and greeted (him) and sat down. Then `Abbas said, "O chief of the believers! Judge between me and this (i.e. `Ali)." They had a dispute regarding the property of Bani An-Nadir which Allah had given to His Apostle as Fai. The group (i.e. `Uthman and his companions) said, "O chief of the believers! Judge between them and relieve both of them front each other." `Umar said, "Be patient! I beseech you by Allah by Whose Permission the Heaven and the Earth exist, do you know that Allah's Messenger ﷺ said, 'Our (i.e. prophets') property will not be inherited, and whatever we leave, is Sadaqa (to be used for charity),' and Allah's Messenger ﷺ meant himself (by saying "we")?" The group said, "He said so." `Umar then turned to `Ali and `Abbas and said, "I beseech you by Allah, do you know that Allah's Messenger ﷺ said so?" They replied, " He said so." `Umar then said, "So, I will talk to you about this matter. Allah bestowed on His Apostle with a special favor of something of this Fai (booty) which he gave to nobody else." `Umar then recited the Holy Verses: "What Allah bestowed as (Fai) Booty on his Apostle (Muhammad) from them --- for this you made no expedition with either cavalry or camelry: But Allah gives power to His Apostles over whomever He will 'And Allah is able to do all things." 9:6) `Umar added "So this property was especially given to Allah's Messenger ﷺ, but, by Allah, neither did he take possession of it and leave your, nor did he favor himself with it to your exclusion, but he gave It to all of you and distributed it amongst you till this property remained out of it. Allah's Messenger ﷺ used to spend the yearly expenses of his family out of this property and used to keep the rest of its revenue to be spent on Allah 's Cause. Allah 's Apostle kept on doing this during all his lifetime. I ask you by Allah do you know this?" They replies in the affirmative. `Umar then said to `Ali and `Abbas. "I ask you by Allah, do you know this?" `Umar added, "When Allah had taken His Prophet unto Him, 'Abu Bakr said, 'I am the successor of Allah's Messenger ﷺ so, Abu Bakr took over that property and managed it in the same way as Allah's Messenger ﷺ used to do, and Allah knows that he was true, pious and rightly guided, and he was a follower of what was right. Then Allah took Abu Bakr unto Him and I became Abu Bakr's successor, and I kept that property in my possession for the first two years of my Caliphate, managing it in the same way as Allah's Messenger ﷺ used to do and as Abu Bakr used to do, and Allah knows that I have been true, pious, rightly guided, and a follower of what is right. Now you both (i.e. 'Ah and `Abbas) came to talk to me, bearing the same claim and presenting the same case; you, `Abbas, came to me asking for your share from your nephew's property, and this man, i.e. `Ali, came to me asking for his wife's share from her father's property. I told you both that Allah's Messenger ﷺ said, 'Our (prophets') properties are not to be inherited, but what we leave is Sadaqa (to be used for charity).' When I thought it right that I should hand over this property to you, I said to you, 'I am ready to hand over this property to you if you wish, on the condition that you would take Allah's Pledge and Convention that you would manage it in the same way as Allah's Messenger ﷺ used to, and as Abu Bakr used to do, and as I have done since I was in charge of it.' So, both of you said (to me), 'Hand it over to us,' and on that condition I handed it over to you. So, I ask you by Allah, did I hand it over to them on this condition?" The group aid, "Yes." Then `Umar faced `Ali and `Abbas saying, "I ask you by Allah, did I hand it over to you on this condition?" They said, "Yes. " He said, " Do you want now to give a different decision? By Allah, by Whose Leave both the Heaven and the Earth exist, I will never give any decision other than that (I have already given). And if you are unable to manage it, then return it to me, and I will do the job on your behalf.". – Sahih Al-Bukhari 3094

حَدَّثَنَا إِسْحَاقُ بْنُ مُحَمَّدٍ الْفَرْوِيُّ، حَدَّثَنَا مَالِكُ بْنُ أَنَسٍ، عَنِ ابْنِ شِهَابٍ، عَنْ مَالِكِ بْنِ أَوْسِ بْنِ الْحَدَثَانِ،، وَكَانَ، مُحَمَّدُ بْنُ جُبَيْرٍ ذَكَرَ لِي ذِكْرًا مِنْ حَدِيثِهِ ذَلِكَ، فَانْطَلَقْتُ حَتَّى أَدْخُلَ عَلَى مَالِكِ بْنِ أَوْسٍ، فَسَأَلْتُهُ عَنْ ذَلِكَ الْحَدِيثِ فَقَالَ مَالِكٌ بَيْنَا أَنَا جَالِسٌ فِي أَهْلِي حِينَ مَتَعَ النَّهَارُ، إِذَا رَسُولُ عُمَرَ بْنِ الْخَطَّابِ يَأْتِينِي فَقَالَ أَجِبْ أَمِيرَ الْمُؤْمِنِينَ. فَانْطَلَقْتُ مَعَهُ حَتَّى أَدْخُلَ عَلَى عُمَرَ، فَإِذَا هُوَ جَالِسٌ عَلَى رِمَالِ سَرِيرٍ، لَيْسَ بَيْنَهُ وَبَيْنَهُ فِرَاشٌ مُتَّكِئٌ عَلَى وِسَادَةٍ مِنْ أَدَمٍ، فَسَلَّمْتُ عَلَيْهِ ثُمَّ جَلَسْتُ فَقَالَ يَا مَالِ، إِنَّهُ قَدِمَ عَلَيْنَا مِنْ قَوْمِكَ أَهْلُ أَبْيَاتٍ، وَقَدْ أَمَرْتُ فِيهِمْ بِرَضْخٍ فَاقْبِضْهُ فَاقْسِمْهُ بَيْنَهُمْ. فَقُلْتُ يَا أَمِيرَ الْمُؤْمِنِينَ، لَوْ أَمَرْتَ بِهِ غَيْرِي. قَالَ اقْبِضْهُ أَيُّهَا الْمَرْءُ. فَبَيْنَا أَنَا جَالِسٌ عِنْدَهُ أَتَاهُ حَاجِبُهُ يَرْفَا فَقَالَ هَلْ لَكَ فِي عُثْمَانَ وَعَبْدِ الرَّحْمَنِ بْنِ عَوْفٍ وَالزُّبَيْرِ وَسَعْدِ بْنِ أَبِي وَقَّاصٍ يَسْتَأْذِنُونَ قَالَ نَعَمْ. فَأَذِنَ لَهُمْ فَدَخَلُوا فَسَلَّمُوا وَجَلَسُوا، ثُمَّ جَلَسَ يَرْفَا يَسِيرًا ثُمَّ قَالَ هَلْ لَكَ فِي عَلِيٍّ وَعَبَّاسٍ قَالَ نَعَمْ. فَأَذِنَ لَهُمَا، فَدَخَلاَ فَسَلَّمَا فَجَلَسَا، فَقَالَ عَبَّاسٌ يَا أَمِيرَ الْمُؤْمِنِينَ، اقْضِ بَيْنِي وَبَيْنَ هَذَا. وَهُمَا يَخْتَصِمَانِ فِيمَا أَفَاءَ اللَّهُ عَلَى رَسُولِهِ صلى الله عليه وسلم مِنْ بَنِي النَّضِيرِ. فَقَالَ الرَّهْطُ عُثْمَانُ وَأَصْحَابُهُ يَا أَمِيرَ الْمُؤْمِنِينَ، اقْضِ بَيْنَهُمَا وَأَرِحْ أَحَدَهُمَا مِنَ الآخَرِ. قَالَ عُمَرُ تَيْدَكُمْ، أَنْشُدُكُمْ بِاللَّهِ الَّذِي بِإِذْنِهِ تَقُومُ السَّمَاءُ وَالأَرْضُ، هَلْ تَعْلَمُونَ أَنَّ رَسُولَ اللَّهِ صلى الله عليه وسلم قَالَ " لاَ نُورَثُ مَا تَرَكْنَا صَدَقَةٌ ". يُرِيدُ رَسُولُ اللَّهِ صلى الله عليه وسلم نَفْسَهُ. قَالَ الرَّهْطُ قَدْ قَالَ ذَلِكَ. فَأَقْبَلَ عُمَرُ عَلَى عَلِيٍّ وَعَبَّاسٍ فَقَالَ أَنْشُدُكُمَا اللَّهَ، أَتَعْلَمَانِ أَنَّ رَسُولَ اللَّهِ صلى الله عليه وسلم قَدْ قَالَ ذَلِكَ قَالاَ قَدْ قَالَ ذَلِكَ. قَالَ عُمَرُ فَإِنِّي أُحَدِّثُكُمْ عَنْ هَذَا الأَمْرِ، إِنَّ اللَّهَ قَدْ خَصَّ رَسُولَهُ صلى الله عليه وسلم فِي هَذَا الْفَىْءِ بِشَىْءٍ لَمْ يُعْطِهِ أَحَدًا غَيْرَهُ ـ ثُمَّ قَرَأَ {وَمَا أَفَاءَ اللَّهُ عَلَى رَسُولِهِ مِنْهُمْ} إِلَى قَوْلِهِ {قَدِيرٌ} ـ فَكَانَتْ هَذِهِ خَالِصَةً لِرَسُولِ اللَّهِ صلى الله عليه وسلم. وَاللَّهِ مَا احْتَازَهَا دُونَكُمْ، وَلاَ اسْتَأْثَرَ بِهَا عَلَيْكُمْ قَدْ أَعْطَاكُمُوهُ، وَبَثَّهَا فِيكُمْ حَتَّى بَقِيَ مِنْهَا هَذَا الْمَالُ، فَكَانَ رَسُولُ اللَّهِ صلى الله عليه وسلم يُنْفِقُ عَلَى أَهْلِهِ نَفَقَةَ سَنَتِهِمْ مِنْ هَذَا الْمَالِ، ثُمَّ يَأْخُذُ مَا بَقِيَ فَيَجْعَلُهُ مَجْعَلَ مَالِ اللَّهِ، فَعَمِلَ رَسُولُ اللَّهِ صلى الله عليه وسلم بِذَلِكَ حَيَاتَهُ، أَنْشُدُكُمْ بِاللَّهِ هَلْ تَعْلَمُونَ ذَلِكَ قَالُوا نَعَمْ. ثُمَّ قَالَ لِعَلِيٍّ وَعَبَّاسٍ أَنْشُدُكُمَا بِاللَّهِ هَلْ تَعْلَمَانِ ذَلِكَ قَالَ عُمَرُ ثُمَّ تَوَفَّى اللَّهُ نَبِيَّهُ صلى الله عليه وسلم فَقَالَ أَبُو بَكْرٍ أَنَا وَلِيُّ رَسُولِ اللَّهِ صلى الله عليه وسلم. فَقَبَضَهَا أَبُو بَكْرٍ، فَعَمِلَ فِيهَا بِمَا عَمِلَ رَسُولُ اللَّهِ صلى الله عليه وسلم، وَاللَّهُ يَعْلَمُ إِنَّهُ فِيهَا لَصَادِقٌ بَارٌّ رَاشِدٌ تَابِعٌ لِلْحَقِّ، ثُمَّ تَوَفَّى اللَّهُ أَبَا بَكْرٍ، فَكُنْتُ أَنَا وَلِيَّ أَبِي بَكْرٍ، فَقَبَضْتُهَا سَنَتَيْنِ مِنْ إِمَارَتِي، أَعْمَلُ فِيهَا بِمَا عَمِلَ رَسُولُ اللَّهِ صلى الله عليه وسلم وَمَا عَمِلَ فِيهَا أَبُو بَكْرٍ، وَاللَّهُ يَعْلَمُ إِنِّي فِيهَا لَصَادِقٌ بَارٌّ رَاشِدٌ تَابِعٌ لِلْحَقِّ، ثُمَّ جِئْتُمَانِي تُكَلِّمَانِي

وَكَلِمَتُكُمَا وَاحِدَةٌ، وَأَمْرُكُمَا وَاحِدٌ، جِئْتَنِي يَا عَبَّاسُ تَسْأَلُنِي نَصِيبَكَ مِنِ ابْنِ أَخِيكَ، وَجَاءَنِي هَذَا ـ يُرِيدُ عَلِيًّا ـ يُرِيدُ نَصِيبَ امْرَأَتِهِ مِنْ أَبِيهَا، فَقُلْتُ لَكُمَا إِنَّ رَسُولَ اللَّهِ صلى الله عليه وسلم قَالَ " لاَ نُورَثُ مَا تَرَكْنَا صَدَقَةٌ ". فَلَمَّا بَدَا لِي أَنْ أَدْفَعَهُ إِلَيْكُمَا قُلْتُ إِنْ شِئْتُمَا دَفَعْتُهَا إِلَيْكُمَا عَلَى أَنَّ عَلَيْكُمَا عَهْدَ اللَّهِ وَمِيثَاقَهُ لَتَعْمَلاَنِ فِيهَا بِمَا عَمِلَ فِيهَا رَسُولُ اللَّهِ صلى الله عليه وسلم، وَبِمَا عَمِلَ فِيهَا أَبُو بَكْرٍ، وَبِمَا عَمِلْتُ فِيهَا مُنْذُ وَلِيتُهَا، فَقُلْتُمَا ادْفَعْهَا إِلَيْنَا. فَبِذَلِكَ دَفَعْتُهَا إِلَيْكُمَا، فَأَنْشُدُكُمْ بِاللَّهِ، هَلْ دَفَعْتُهَا إِلَيْهِمَا بِذَلِكَ قَالَ الرَّهْطُ نَعَمْ. ثُمَّ أَقْبَلَ عَلَى عَلِيٍّ وَعَبَّاسٍ فَقَالَ أَنْشُدُكُمَا بِاللَّهِ هَلْ دَفَعْتُهَا إِلَيْكُمَا بِذَلِكَ قَالاَ نَعَمْ. قَالَ فَتَلْتَمِسَانِ مِنِّي قَضَاءً غَيْرَ ذَلِكَ فَوَاللَّهِ الَّذِي بِإِذْنِهِ تَقُومُ السَّمَاءُ وَالأَرْضُ، لاَ أَقْضِي فِيهَا قَضَاءً غَيْرَ ذَلِكَ، فَإِنْ عَجَزْتُمَا عَنْهَا فَادْفَعَاهَا إِلَىَّ، فَإِنِّي أَكْفِيكُمَاهَا.

Narrated `Abdur-Rahman bin `Auf: While I was standing in the row on the day (of the battle) of Badr, I looked to my right and my left and saw two young Ansari boys, and I wished I had been stronger than they. One of them called my attention saying, "O Uncle! Do you know Abu Jahl?" I said, "Yes, What do you want from him, O my nephew?" He said, "I have been informed that he abuses Allah's Messenger ﷺ. By Him in Whose Hands my life is, if I should see him, then my body will not leave his body till either of us meet his fate." I was astonished at that talk. Then the other boy called my attention saying the same as the other had said. After a while I saw Abu Jahl walking amongst the people. I said (to the boys), "Look! This Is the man you asked me about." So, both of them attacked him with their swords and struck him to death and returned to Allah's Apostle to inform him of that. Allah's Messenger asked, "Which of you has killed him?" Each of them said, "I Have killed him." Allah's Messenger ﷺ asked, "Have you cleaned your swords?" They said, "No. " He then looked at their swords and said, "No doubt, you both have killed him and the spoils of the deceased will be given to Mu`adh bin `Amr bin Al-Jamuh." The two boys were Mu`adh bin 'Afra and Mu`adh bin `Amr bin Al-Jamuh. – Sahih Al-Bukhari 3141

حَدَّثَنَا مُسَدَّدٌ، حَدَّثَنَا يُوسُفُ بْنُ الْمَاجِشُونِ، عَنْ صَالِحِ بْنِ إِبْرَاهِيمَ بْنِ عَبْدِ الرَّحْمَنِ بْنِ عَوْفٍ، عَنْ أَبِيهِ، عَنْ جَدِّهِ، قَالَ بَيْنَا أَنَا وَاقِفٌ، فِي الصَّفِّ يَوْمَ بَدْرٍ فَنَظَرْتُ عَنْ يَمِينِي، وَشِمَالِي، فَإِذَا أَنَا بِغُلاَمَيْنِ، مِنَ الأَنْصَارِ حَدِيثَةٍ أَسْنَانُهُمَا، تَمَنَّيْتُ أَنْ أَكُونَ بَيْنَ أَضْلَعَ مِنْهُمَا، فَغَمَزَنِي أَحَدُهُمَا فَقَالَ يَا عَمِّ، هَلْ تَعْرِفُ أَبَا جَهْلٍ قُلْتُ نَعَمْ، مَا حَاجَتُكَ إِلَيْهِ يَا ابْنَ أَخِي قَالَ أُخْبِرْتُ أَنَّهُ يَسُبُّ رَسُولَ اللَّهِ صلى الله عليه وسلم، وَالَّذِي نَفْسِي بِيَدِهِ لَئِنْ رَأَيْتُهُ لاَ يُفَارِقُ سَوَادِي سَوَادَهُ حَتَّى يَمُوتَ الأَعْجَلُ مِنَّا. فَتَعَجَّبْتُ لِذَلِكَ، فَغَمَزَنِي الآخَرُ فَقَالَ لِي مِثْلَهَا، فَلَمْ أَنْشَبْ أَنْ نَظَرْتُ إِلَى أَبِي جَهْلٍ يَجُولُ فِي النَّاسِ، قُلْتُ أَلاَ إِنَّ هَذَا صَاحِبُكُمَا الَّذِي سَأَلْتُمَانِي. فَابْتَدَرَاهُ بِسَيْفَيْهِمَا فَضَرَبَاهُ حَتَّى قَتَلاَهُ، ثُمَّ انْصَرَفَا إِلَى رَسُولِ اللَّهُ صلى الله عليه وسلم فَأَخْبَرَاهُ فَقَالَ " أَيُّكُمَا قَتَلَهُ ". قَالَ كُلُّ وَاحِدٍ مِنْهُمَا أَنَا قَتَلْتُهُ. فَقَالَ " هَلْ مَسَحْتُمَا سَيْفَيْكُمَا ". قَالاَ لاَ. فَنَظَرَ فِي السَّيْفَيْنِ فَقَالَ " كِلاَكُمَا قَتَلَهُ ". سَلَبُهُ لِمُعَاذِ بْنِ عَمْرِو بْنِ الْجَمُوحِ. وَكَانَا مُعَاذَ ابْنَ عَفْرَاءَ وَمُعَاذَ بْنَ عَمْرِو بْنِ الْجَمُوحِ.
قَالَ مُحَمَّدٌ سَمِعَ يُوسُفُ صَالِحًا وَإِبْرَاهِيمَ أَبَاهُ (عَبْدِ الرَّحْمَنِ بْنِ عَوْفٍ)

Narrated Ibn `Abbas: During the last Hajj led by `Umar, `Abdur-Rahman bin `Auf returned to his family at Mina and met me there. `AbdurRahman said (to `Umar), "O chief of the believers! The season of Hajj is the season when there comes the scum of the people (besides the good amongst them), so I recommend that you should wait till you go back to Medina, for it is the place of Migration and Sunna (i.e. the Prophet's tradition), and there you will be able to refer the matter to the religious scholars and the nobles and the people of wise opinions." `Umar said, "I will speak of it in Medina on my very first sermon I will deliver there.". – Sahih Al-Bukhari 3928

حَدَّثَنَا يَحْيَى بْنُ سُلَيْمَانَ، حَدَّثَنِي ابْنُ وَهْبٍ، حَدَّثَنَا مَالِكٌ. وَأَخْبَرَنِي يُونُسُ، عَنِ ابْنِ شِهَابٍ، قَالَ أَخْبَرَنِي عُبَيْدُ اللَّهِ بْنُ عَبْدِ اللَّهِ، أَنَّ ابْنَ عَبَّاسٍ، أَخْبَرَهُ أَنَّ عبد الرَّحْمَنِ بْنَ عَوْفٍ رَجَعَ إِلَى أَهْلِهِ وَهْوَ بِمِنًى، فِي آخِرِ حَجَّةٍ حَجَّهَا عُمَرُ، فَوَجَدَنِي، فَقَالَ عَبْدُ الرَّحْمَنِ فَقُلْتُ يَا أَمِيرَ الْمُؤْمِنِينَ إِنَّ الْمَوْسِمَ يَجْمَعُ رَعَاعَ النَّاسِ، وَإِنِّي أَرَى أَنْ تُمْهِلَ حَتَّى تَقْدَمَ الْمَدِينَةَ، فَإِنَّهَا دَارُ الْهِجْرَةِ وَالسُّنَّةِ، وَتَخْلُصَ لأَهْلِ الْفِقْهِ وَأَشْرَافِ النَّاسِ وَذَوِي رَأْيِهِمْ. قَالَ عُمَرُ لأَقُومَنَّ فِي أَوَّلِ مَقَامٍ أَقُومُهُ بِالْمَدِينَةِ

Narrated Sa`d bin Ibrahim: A meal was brought to `Abdur-Rahman bin `Auf while he was fasting. He said, "Mus`ab bin `Umar was martyred, and he was better than I, yet he was shrouded in a Burda (i.e. a sheet) so that, if his head was covered, his feet became naked, and if his feet were covered, his head became naked." `Abdur-Rahman added, "Hamza was martyred and he was better than 1. Then worldly wealth was bestowed upon us and we were given thereof too much. We are afraid that the reward of our deeds have been given to us in this life." `Abdur-Rahman then started weeping so much that he left the food. – Sahih Al-Bukhari 4045

حَدَّثَنَا عَبْدَانُ، حَدَّثَنَا عَبْدُ اللَّهِ، أَخْبَرَنَا شُعْبَةُ، عَنْ سَعْدِ بْنِ إِبْرَاهِيمَ، عَنْ أَبِيهِ، إِبْرَاهِيمَ أَنَّ عَبْدَ الرَّحْمَنِ بْنَ عَوْفٍ، أُتِيَ بِطَعَامٍ، وَكَانَ صَائِمًا فَقَالَ قُتِلَ مُصْعَبُ بْنُ عُمَيْرٍ، وَهْوَ خَيْرٌ مِنِّي، كُفِّنَ فِي بُرْدَةٍ، إِنْ غُطِّيَ رَأْسُهُ بَدَتْ رِجْلاَهُ، وَإِنْ غُطِّيَ رِجْلاَهُ بَدَا رَأْسُهُ ـ وَأُرَاهُ قَالَ ـ وَقُتِلَ حَمْزَةُ وَهْوَ خَيْرٌ مِنِّي، ثُمَّ بُسِطَ لَنَا مِنَ الدُّنْيَا مَا بُسِطَ، أَوْ قَالَ أُعْطِينَا مِنَ الدُّنْيَا مَا أُعْطِينَا، وَقَدْ خَشِينَا أَنْ تَكُونَ حَسَنَاتُنَا عُجِّلَتْ لَنَا. ثُمَّ جَعَلَ يَبْكِي حَتَّى تَرَكَ الطَّعَامَ.

Narrated Salama bin Al-Akwa`: Once I went (from Medina) towards (Al-Ghaba) before the first Adhan of the Fajr Prayer. The shecamels of Allah's Messenger ﷺ used to graze at a place called Dhi-Qarad. A slave of `Abdur-Rahman bin `Auf met me (on the way) and said, "The she-camels of Allah's Messenger ﷺ had been taken away by force." I asked, "Who had taken them?" He replied "(The people of) Ghatafan." I made three loud cries (to the people of Medina) saying, "O Sabahah!" I made the people between the two mountains of Medina hear me. Then I rushed onward and caught up with the robbers while they were watering the camels. I started throwing arrows at them as I was a good archer and I was saying, "I am the son of Al-Akwa`, and today will perish the wicked people." I kept on saying like that till I restored the shecamels (of the Prophet), I also snatched thirty Burda (i.e. garments) from them. Then the Prophet ﷺ and the other people came there, and I said, "O Allah's Prophet! I have stopped the people (of Ghatafan) from taking water and they are thirsty now. So send (some people) after them now." On that the Prophet said, "O the son of Al-Akwa`! You have over-powered them, so forgive them." Then we all came back and Allah's Messenger ﷺ seated me behind him on his she-camel till we entered Medina. – Sahih Al-Bukhari 4194

حَدَّثَنَا قُتَيْبَةُ بْنُ سَعِيدٍ، حَدَّثَنَا حَاتِمٌ، عَنْ يَزِيدَ بْنِ أَبِي عُبَيْدٍ، قَالَ سَمِعْتُ سَلَمَةَ بْنَ الأَكْوَعِ، يَقُولُ خَرَجْتُ قَبْلَ أَنْ يُؤَذَّنَ، بِالأُولَى، وَكَانَتْ لِقَاحُ رَسُولِ اللَّهِ صلى الله عليه وسلم تَرْعَى بِذِي قَرَدٍ ـ قَالَ ـ فَلَقِيَنِي غُلاَمٌ لِعَبْدِ الرَّحْمَنِ بْنِ عَوْفٍ فَقَالَ أُخِذَتْ لِقَاحُ رَسُولِ اللَّهِ صلى الله عليه وسلم قُلْتُ مَنْ أَخَذَهَا قَالَ غَطَفَانُ. قَالَ فَصَرَخْتُ ثَلاَثَ صَرَخَاتٍ ـ يَا صَبَاحَاهْ ـ قَالَ فَأَسْمَعْتُ مَا بَيْنَ لاَبَتَىِ الْمَدِينَةِ، ثُمَّ انْدَفَعْتُ عَلَى وَجْهِي حَتَّى أَدْرَكْتُهُمْ وَقَدْ أَخَذُوا يَسْتَقُونَ مِنَ الْمَاءِ، فَجَعَلْتُ أَرْمِيهِمْ بِنَبْلِي، وَكُنْتُ رَامِيًا، وَأَقُولُ أَنَا ابْنُ الأَكْوَعِ، الْيَوْمُ يَوْمُ الرُّضَّعْ. وَأَرْتَجِزُ حَتَّى اسْتَنْقَذْتُ اللِّقَاحَ مِنْهُمْ، وَاسْتَلَبْتُ مِنْهُمْ ثَلاَثِينَ بُرْدَةً، قَالَ وَجَاءَ النَّبِيُّ صلى الله عليه وسلم وَالنَّاسُ فَقُلْتُ يَا نَبِيَّ اللَّهِ قَدْ حَمَيْتُ الْقَوْمَ الْمَاءَ وَهُمْ عِطَاشٌ، فَابْعَثْ إِلَيْهِمُ السَّاعَةَ. فَقَالَ " يَا ابْنَ الأَكْوَعِ، مَلَكْتَ فَأَسْجِحْ ". قَالَ ثُمَّ رَجَعْنَا وَيُرْدِفُنِي رَسُولُ اللَّهِ صلى الله عليه وسلم عَلَى نَاقَتِهِ حَتَّى دَخَلْنَا الْمَدِينَةَ

Narrated Ibn `Abbas: `Umar bin Al-Khattab used to let Ibn `Abbas sit beside him, so `AbdurRahman bin `Auf said to `Umar, "We have sons similar to him." `Umar replied, "(I respect him) because of his status that you know." `Umar then asked Ibn `Abbas about the meaning of this Holy Verse:-- "When comes the help of Allah and the conquest of Mecca . . ." (110.1) Ibn `Abbas replied, "That indicated the death of Allah's Messenger ﷺ which Allah informed him of." `Umar said, "I do not understand of it except what you understand.". – Sahih Al-Bukhari 4430

حَدَّثَنَا مُحَمَّدُ بْنُ عَرْعَرَةَ، حَدَّثَنَا شُعْبَةُ، عَنْ أَبِي بِشْرٍ، عَنْ سَعِيدِ بْنِ جُبَيْرٍ، عَنِ ابْنِ عَبَّاسٍ، قَالَ كَانَ عُمَرُ بْنُ الْخَطَّابِ ـ رضى الله عنه ـ يُدْنِي ابْنَ عَبَّاسٍ فَقَالَ لَهُ عَبْدُ الرَّحْمَنِ بْنُ عَوْفٍ إِنَّ لَنَا أَبْنَاءً مِثْلَهُ. فَقَالَ إِنَّهُ مِنْ حَيْثُ تَعْلَمُ. فَسَأَلَ عُمَرُ ابْنَ عَبَّاسٍ عَنْ هَذِهِ الآيَةِ {إِذَا جَاءَ نَصْرُ اللَّهِ وَالْفَتْحُ} فَقَالَ أَجَلُ رَسُولِ اللَّهِ صلى الله عليه وسلم أَعْلَمَهُ إِيَّاهُ، فَقَالَ مَا أَعْلَمُ مِنْهَا إِلاَّ مَا تَعْلَمُ

Narrated Ibn `Abbas: Regarding the Verse: "Because of the inconvenience of rain or because you are ill." (4.102) (It was revealed in connection with) `Abdur-Rahman bin `Auf who was wounded. – Sahih Al-Bukhari 4599

حَدَّثَنَا مُحَمَّدُ بْنُ مُقَاتِلٍ أَبُو الْحَسَنِ، أَخْبَرَنَا حَجَّاجٌ، عَنِ ابْنِ جُرَيْجٍ، قَالَ أَخْبَرَنِي يَعْلَى، عَنْ سَعِيدِ بْنِ جُبَيْرٍ، عَنِ ابْنِ عَبَّاسٍ ـ رضى الله عنهما ـ {إِنْ كَانَ بِكُمْ أَذًى مِنْ مَطَرٍ أَوْ كُنْتُمْ مَرْضَى} قَالَ عَبْدُ الرَّحْمَنِ بْنُ عَوْفٍ كَانَ جَرِيحًا

When you are among them, and you stand to lead them in prayer, let a group of them stand with you, and let them hold their weapons. Then, when they have done their prostrations, let them withdraw to the rear, and let another group, that have not prayed yet, come forward and pray with you; and let them take their precautions and their weapons. Those who disbelieve would like you to neglect your weapons and your equipment, so they can attack you in a single assault. You commit no error, if you are hampered by rain or are sick, by putting down your weapons; but take precautions. Indeed, Allah has prepared for the disbelievers a demeaning punishment. – Surah An-Nisa 4:102
وَإِذَا كُنتَ فِيهِمْ فَأَقَمْتَ لَهُمُ ٱلصَّلَوٰةَ فَلْتَقُمْ طَآئِفَةٌ مِّنْهُم مَّعَكَ وَلْيَأْخُذُوٓا۟ أَسْلِحَتَهُمْ ۖ فَإِذَا سَجَدُوا۟ فَلْيَكُونُوا۟ مِن وَرَآئِكُمْ وَلْتَأْتِ طَآئِفَةٌ أُخْرَىٰ لَمْ يُصَلُّوا۟ فَلْيُصَلُّوا۟ مَعَكَ وَلْيَأْخُذُوا۟ حِذْرَهُمْ وَأَسْلِحَتَهُمْ ۗ وَدَّ ٱلَّذِينَ كَفَرُوا۟ لَوْ تَغْفُلُونَ عَنْ أَسْلِحَتِكُمْ وَأَمْتِعَتِكُمْ فَيَمِيلُونَ عَلَيْكُم مَّيْلَةً وَٰحِدَةً ۚ وَلَا جُنَاحَ عَلَيْكُمْ إِن كَانَ بِكُمْ أَذًى مِّن مَّطَرٍ أَوْ كُنتُم مَّرْضَىٰٓ أَن تَضَعُوٓا۟ أَسْلِحَتَكُمْ ۖ وَخُذُوا۟ حِذْرَكُمْ ۗ إِنَّ ٱللَّهَ أَعَدَّ لِلْكَٰفِرِينَ عَذَابًا مُّهِينًا

Narrated Sa`d from his father: Once the meal of `Abdur-Rahman bin `Auf was brought in front of him, and he said, "Mus`ab bin `Umair was martyred and he was better than I, and he had nothing except his Burd (a black square narrow dress) to be shrouded in. Hamza or another person was martyred and he was also better than I and he had nothing to be shrouded in except his Burd. No doubt, I fear that the rewards of my deeds might have been given early in this world." Then he started weeping. – Sahih Al-Bukhari 1274
حَدَّثَنَا أَحْمَدُ بْنُ مُحَمَّدٍ الْمَكِّيُّ، حَدَّثَنَا إِبْرَاهِيمُ بْنُ سَعْدٍ، عَنْ سَعْدٍ، عَنْ أَبِيهِ، قَالَ أُتِيَ عَبْدُ الرَّحْمَنِ بْنُ عَوْفٍ ـ رضى الله عنه ـ يَوْمًا بِطَعَامِهِ فَقَالَ قُتِلَ مُصْعَبُ بْنُ عُمَيْرٍ ـ وَكَانَ خَيْرًا مِنِّي ـ فَلَمْ يُوجَدْ لَهُ مَا يُكَفَّنُ فِيهِ إِلاَّ بُرْدَةٌ، وَقُتِلَ حَمْزَةُ أَوْ رَجُلٌ آخَرُ خَيْرٌ مِنِّي فَلَمْ يُوجَدْ لَهُ مَا يُكَفَّنُ فِيهِ إِلاَّ بُرْدَةٌ، لَقَدْ خَشِيتُ أَنْ يَكُونَ قَدْ عُجِّلَتْ لَنَا طَيِّبَاتُنَا فِي حَيَاتِنَا الدُّنْيَا، ثُمَّ جَعَلَ يَبْكِي

Narrated `Abdur-Rahman bin `Auf: I got an agreement written between me and Umaiya bin Khalaf that Umaiya would look after my property (or family) in Mecca and I would look after his in Medina. When I mentioned the word 'Abdur Rahman' in the documents, Umaiya said, "I do not know 'Ar-Rahman.' Write down to me your name, (with which you called yourself) in the Pre-Islamic Period of Ignorance." So, I wrote my name ' `Abdu `Amr'. On the day (of the battle) of Badr, when all the people went to sleep, I went up the hill to protect him. Bilal(1) saw him (i.e. Umaiya) and went to a gathering of Ansar and said, "(Here is) Umaiya bin Khalaf! Woe to me if he escapes!" So, a group of Ansar went out with Bilal to follow us (`Abdur-Rahman and Umaiya). Being afraid that they would catch us, I left Umaiya's son for them to keep them busy but the Ansar killed the son and insisted on following us. Umaiya was a fat man, and when they approached us, I told him to kneel down, and he knelt, and I laid myself on him to protect him, but the Ansar killed him by passing their swords underneath me, and one of them injured my foot with his sword. (The sub narrator said, " `Abdur-Rahman used to show us the trace of the wound on the back of his foot."). – Sahih Al-Bukhari 2301
حَدَّثَنَا عَبْدُ الْعَزِيزِ بْنُ عَبْدِ اللَّهِ، قَالَ حَدَّثَنِي يُوسُفُ بْنُ الْمَاجِشُونِ، عَنْ صَالِحِ بْنِ إِبْرَاهِيمَ بْنِ عَبْدِ الرَّحْمَنِ بْنِ عَوْفٍ، عَنْ أَبِيهِ، عَنْ جَدِّهِ عَبْدِ الرَّحْمَنِ بْنِ عَوْفٍ ـ رضى الله عنه ـ قَالَ كَاتَبْتُ أُمَيَّةَ بْنَ خَلَفٍ كِتَابًا بِأَنْ يَحْفَظَنِي فِي صَاغِيَتِي بِمَكَّةَ، وَأَحْفَظَهُ فِي صَاغِيَتِهِ بِالْمَدِينَةِ، فَلَمَّا ذَكَرْتُ الرَّحْمَنَ قَالَ لاَ أَعْرِفُ الرَّحْمَنَ، كَاتِبْنِي بِاسْمِكَ الَّذِي كَانَ فِي الْجَاهِلِيَّةِ.
فَكَاتَبْتُهُ عَبْدُ عَمْرٍو فَلَمَّا كَانَ فِي يَوْمِ بَدْرٍ خَرَجْتُ إِلَى جَبَلٍ لأُحْرِزَهُ حِينَ نَامَ النَّاسُ فَأَبْصَرَهُ بِلاَلٌ فَخَرَجَ حَتَّى وَقَفَ عَلَى مَجْلِسٍ مِنَ الأَنْصَارِ فَقَالَ أُمَيَّةُ بْنُ خَلَفٍ، لاَ نَجَوْتُ إِنْ نَجَا أُمَيَّةُ. فَخَرَجَ مَعَهُ فَرِيقٌ مِنَ الأَنْصَارِ فِي آثَارِنَا، فَلَمَّا خَشِيتُ أَنْ يَلْحَقُونَا خَلَّفْتُ لَهُمُ ابْنَهُ، لأَشْغَلَهُمْ فَقَتَلُوهُ ثُمَّ أَبَوْا حَتَّى يَتْبَعُونَا، وَكَانَ رَجُلاً ثَقِيلاً، فَلَمَّا أَدْرَكُونَا قُلْتُ لَهُ ابْرُكْ. فَبَرَكَ، فَأَلْقَيْتُ عَلَيْهِ نَفْسِي لأَمْنَعَهُ، فَتَخَلَّلُوهُ بِالسُّيُوفِ مِنْ تَحْتِي، حَتَّى قَتَلُوهُ، وَأَصَابَ أَحَدُهُمْ رِجْلِي بِسَيْفِهِ، وَكَانَ عَبْدُ الرَّحْمَنِ بْنُ عَوْفٍ يُرِينَا ذَلِكَ الأَثَرَ فِي ظَهْرِ قَدَمِهِ. قَالَ أَبُو عَبْد اللَّهِ سَمِعَ يُوسُفُ صَالِحًا وَإِبْرَاهِيمُ أَبَاهُ

Narrated `Abdullah bin 'Amir bin Rabi`a: `Umar bin Al-Khattab left for Sham, and when he reached a placed called Sargh, he came to know that there was an outbreak of an epidemic (of plague) in Sham. Then `AbdurRahman bin `Auf told him that Allah's Messenger ﷺ said, "If you hear the news of an outbreak of an epidemic (plague) in a certain place, do not enter that place: and if the epidemic falls in a place while you are present in it, do not leave that place to escape from the epidemic." So `Umar returned from Sargh. – Sahih Al-Bukhari 6973
حَدَّثَنَا عَبْدُ اللَّهِ بْنُ مَسْلَمَةَ، عَنْ مَالِكٍ، عَنِ ابْنِ شِهَابٍ، عَنْ عَبْدِ اللَّهِ بْنِ عَامِرِ بْنِ رَبِيعَةَ، أَنَّ عُمَرَ بْنَ الْخَطَّابِ ـ رضى الله عنه ـ خَرَجَ إِلَى الشَّأْمِ، فَلَمَّا جَاءَ بِسَرْغَ بَلَغَهُ أَنَّ الْوَبَاءَ وَقَعَ بِالشَّأْمِ فَأَخْبَرَهُ عَبْدُ الرَّحْمَنِ بْنُ عَوْفٍ أَنَّ رَسُولَ اللَّهِ صلى الله عليه وسلم قَالَ " إِذَا سَمِعْتُمْ بِأَرْضٍ فَلاَ تَقْدَمُوا عَلَيْهِ، وَإِذَا وَقَعَ بِأَرْضٍ وَأَنْتُمْ بِهَا فَلاَ تَخْرُجُوا فِرَارًا مِنْهُ ". فَرَجَعَ عُمَرُ مِنْ سَرْغَ. وَعَنِ ابْنِ شِهَابٍ عَنْ سَالِمِ بْنِ عَبْدِ اللَّهِ أَنَّ عُمَرَ إِنَّمَا انْصَرَفَ مِنْ حَدِيثِ عَبْدِ الرَّحْمَنِ

Narrated Anas: `Abdur Rahman bin `Auf and Az-Zubair complained to the Prophet, i.e. about the lice (that caused itching) so he allowed them to wear silken clothes. I saw them wearing such clothes in a holy battle. – Sahih Al-Bukhari 2920
حَدَّثَنَا أَبُو الْوَلِيدِ، حَدَّثَنَا هَمَّامٌ، عَنْ قَتَادَةَ، عَنْ أَنَسٍ، حَدَّثَنَا مُحَمَّدُ بْنُ سِنَانٍ، حَدَّثَنَا هَمَّامٌ، عَنْ قَتَادَةَ، عَنْ أَنَسٍ ـ رضى الله عنه ـ أَنَّ عَبْدَ، الرَّحْمَنِ بْنَ عَوْفٍ وَالزُّبَيْرَ شَكَوَا إِلَى النَّبِيِّ صلى الله عليه وسلم ـ يَعْنِي الْقَمْلَ ـ فَأَرْخَصَ لَهُمَا فِي الْحَرِيرِ، فَرَأَيْتُهُ عَلَيْهِمَا فِي غَزَاةٍ

Narrated Anas: When `Abdur-Rahman bin `Auf came to Medina and the Prophet ﷺ established the bond of brotherhood between him and Sa`d bin Ar-Rabi-al-Ansari, Saud suggested that `Abdur-Rahman should accept half of his property and family. `Abdur Rahman said, "May Allah bless you in your family and property; guide me to the market." So `Abdur-Rahman (while doing business in the market) made some profit of some condensed dry yoghurt and butter. After a few days the Prophet ﷺ saw him wearing clothes stained with yellow perfume. The Prophet ﷺ asked, "What is this, O `Abdur-Rahman?" He said, "O Allah's Messenger ﷺ! I have married an Ansar' woman." The Prophet ﷺ asked, "What have you given her as Mahr?" He (i.e. `Abdur-Rahman) said, "A piece of gold, about the weight of a date stone." Then the Prophet said, Give a banquet, even though of a sheep." – Sahih Al-Bukhari 3937
حَدَّثَنَا مُحَمَّدُ بْنُ يُوسُفَ، حَدَّثَنَا سُفْيَانُ، عَنْ حُمَيْدٍ، عَنْ أَنَسٍ ـ رضى الله عنه ـ قَالَ قَدِمَ عَبْدُ الرَّحْمَنِ بْنُ عَوْفٍ، فَآخَى النَّبِيُّ صلى الله عليه وسلم بَيْنَهُ وَبَيْنَ سَعْدِ بْنِ الرَّبِيعِ الأَنْصَارِيِّ، فَعَرَضَ عَلَيْهِ أَنْ يُنَاصِفَهُ أَهْلَهُ وَمَالَهُ، فَقَالَ عَبْدُ الرَّحْمَنِ بَارَكَ اللَّهُ لَكَ فِي أَهْلِكَ وَمَالِكَ، دُلَّنِي عَلَى السُّوقِ. فَرَبِحَ شَيْئًا مِنْ أَقِطٍ وَسَمْنٍ، فَرَآهُ النَّبِيُّ صلى الله عليه وسلم بَعْدَ أَيَّامٍ وَعَلَيْهِ وَضَرٌ مِنْ صُفْرَةٍ، فَقَالَ النَّبِيُّ صلى الله عليه وسلم " مَهْيَمْ يَا عَبْدَ الرَّحْمَنِ ". قَالَ يَا رَسُولَ اللَّهِ، تَزَوَّجْتُ امْرَأَةً مِنَ الأَنْصَارِ. قَالَ " فَمَا سُقْتَ فِيهَا ". فَقَالَ وَزْنَ نَوَاةٍ مِنْ ذَهَبٍ. فَقَالَ النَّبِيُّ صلى الله عليه وسلم " أَوْلِمْ وَلَوْ بِشَاةٍ ".

Abu- Talha

أبو طلحة

Narrated Anas: When Allah's Messenger ﷺ got his head shaved, Abu- Talha was the first to take some of his hair. – Sahih Al-Bukhari 171

حَدَّثَنَا مُحَمَّدُ بْنُ عَبْدِ الرَّحِيمِ، قَالَ أَخْبَرَنَا سَعِيدُ بْنُ سُلَيْمَانَ، قَالَ حَدَّثَنَا عَبَّادٌ، عَنِ ابْنِ عَوْنٍ، عَنِ ابْنِ سِيرِينَ، عَنْ أَنَسٍ، أَنَّ رَسُولَ اللَّهِ صلى الله عليه وسلم لَمَّا حَلَقَ رَأْسَهُ كَانَ أَبُو طَلْحَةَ أَوَّلَ مَنْ أَخَذَ مِنْ شَعَرِهِ.

Narrated Anas bin Malik: Abu Talha and the Prophet ﷺ used to shield themselves with one shield. Abu Talha was a good archer, and when he threw (his arrows) the Prophet ﷺ would look at the target of his arrows. – Sahih Al-Bukhari 2902

حَدَّثَنَا أَحْمَدُ بْنُ مُحَمَّدٍ، أَخْبَرَنَا عَبْدُ اللَّهِ، أَخْبَرَنَا الأَوْزَاعِيُّ، عَنْ إِسْحَاقَ بْنِ عَبْدِ اللَّهِ بْنِ أَبِي طَلْحَةَ، عَنْ أَنَسِ بْنِ مَالِكٍ ـ رضى الله عنه ـ قَالَ كَانَ أَبُو طَلْحَةَ يَتَتَرَّسُ مَعَ النَّبِيِّ صلى الله عليه وسلم بِتُرْسٍ وَاحِدٍ، وَكَانَ أَبُو طَلْحَةَ حَسَنَ الرَّمْىِ، فَكَانَ إِذَا رَمَى تَشَرَّفَ النَّبِيُّ صلى الله عليه وسلم فَيَنْظُرُ إِلَى مَوْضِعِ نَبْلِهِ

Narrated As-Sa'-ib bin Yazid: I was in the company of Talha bin 'Ubaidullah, Sa`d, Al-Miqdad bin Al-Aswad and `Abdur Rahman bin `Auf and I heard none of them narrating anything from Allah's Messenger ﷺ but Talha was talking about the day (of the battle) of Uhud. – Sahih Al-Bukhari 2824

حَدَّثَنَا قُتَيْبَةُ بْنُ سَعِيدٍ، حَدَّثَنَا حَاتِمٌ، عَنْ مُحَمَّدِ بْنِ يُوسُفَ، عَنِ السَّائِبِ بْنِ يَزِيدَ، قَالَ صَحِبْتُ طَلْحَةَ بْنَ عُبَيْدِ اللَّهِ وَسَعْدًا وَالْمِقْدَادَ بْنَ الأَسْوَدِ وَعَبْدَ الرَّحْمَنِ بْنَ عَوْفٍ ـ رضى الله عنهم ـ فَمَا سَمِعْتُ أَحَدًا، مِنْهُمْ يُحَدِّثُ عَنْ رَسُولِ اللَّهِ صلى الله عليه وسلم، إِلاَّ أَنِّي سَمِعْتُ طَلْحَةَ يُحَدِّثُ عَنْ يَوْمِ أُحُدٍ

Narrated Anas bin Malik: Once the people of Medina were frightened, so the Prophet ﷺ rode a horse belonging to Abu Talha and it ran slowly, or was of narrow paces. When he returned, he said, "I found your (i.e. Abu Talha's) horse very fast. After that the horse could not be surpassed in running..' - Sahih Al-Bukhari 2867

حَدَّثَنَا عَبْدُ الأَعْلَى بْنُ حَمَّادٍ، حَدَّثَنَا يَزِيدُ بْنُ زُرَيْعٍ، حَدَّثَنَا سَعِيدٌ، عَنْ قَتَادَةَ، عَنْ أَنَسِ بْنِ مَالِكٍ ـ رضى الله عنه أَنَّ أَهْلَ الْمَدِينَةِ فَزِعُوا مَرَّةً، فَرَكِبَ النَّبِيُّ صلى الله عليه وسلم فَرَسًا لأَبِي طَلْحَةَ كَانَ يَقْطِفُ ـ أَوْ كَانَ فِيهِ قِطَافٌ ـ فَلَمَّا رَجَعَ قَالَ " وَجَدْنَا فَرَسَكُمْ هَذَا بَحْرًا ". فَكَانَ بَعْدَ ذَلِكَ لاَ يُجَارَى

Narrated Sa`d bin 'Ubaida: Abu `Abdur-Rahman who was one of the supporters of `Uthman said to Abu Talha who was one of the supporters of `Ali, "I perfectly know what encouraged your leader (i.e. `Ali) to shed blood. I heard him saying: Once the Prophet ﷺ sent me and Az-Zubair saying, 'Proceed to such-and-such Ar-Roudah (place) where you will find a lady whom Hatib has given a letter. So when we arrived at Ar-Roudah, we requested the lady to hand over the letter to us. She said, 'Hatib has not given me any letter.' We said to her. 'Take out the letter or else we will strip off your clothes.' So she took it out of her braid. So the Prophet ﷺ sent for Hatib, (who came) and said, 'Don't hurry in judging me, for, by Allah, I have not become a disbeliever, and my love to Islam is increasing. (The reason for writing this letter was) that there is none of your companions but has relatives in Mecca who look after their families and property, while I have nobody there, so I wanted to do them some favor (so that they might look after my family and property).' The Prophet ﷺ believed him. `Umar said, 'Allow me to chop off his (i.e. Hatib's) neck as he has done hypocrisy.' The Prophet ﷺ said, (to `Umar), 'Who knows, perhaps Allah has looked at the warriors of Badr and said (to them), 'Do whatever you like, for I have forgiven you.' " `Abdur-Rahman added, "So this is what encouraged him (i.e. `Ali). – Sahih Al-Bukhari 3081

حَدَّثَنِي مُحَمَّدُ بْنُ عَبْدِ اللَّهِ بْنِ حَوْشَبٍ الطَّائِفِيُّ، حَدَّثَنَا هُشَيْمٌ، أَخْبَرَنَا حُصَيْنٌ، عَنْ سَعْدِ بْنِ عُبَيْدَةَ، عَنْ أَبِي عَبْدِ الرَّحْمَنِ، وَكَانَ، عُثْمَانِيًّا فَقَالَ لاِبْنِ عَطِيَّةَ وَكَانَ عَلَوِيًّا إِنِّي لأَعْلَمُ مَا الَّذِي جَرَّأَ صَاحِبَكَ عَلَى الدِّمَاءِ سَمِعْتُهُ يَقُولُ بَعَثَنِي النَّبِيُّ صلى الله عليه وسلم وَالزُّبَيْرَ، فَقَالَ " ائْتُوا رَوْضَةَ كَذَا، وَتَجِدُونَ بِهَا امْرَأَةً أَعْطَاهَا حَاطِبٌ كِتَابًا ". فَأَتَيْنَا الرَّوْضَةَ فَقُلْنَا الْكِتَابَ. قَالَتْ لَمْ يُعْطِنِي. فَقُلْنَا لَتُخْرِجِنَّ أَوْ لأُجَرِّدَنَّكِ. فَأَخْرَجَتْ مِنْ حُجْزَتِهَا، فَأَرْسَلَ إِلَى حَاطِبٍ فَقَالَ لاَ تَعْجَلْ، وَاللَّهِ مَا كَفَرْتُ وَلاَ ازْدَدْتُ لِلإِسْلاَمِ إِلاَّ حُبًّا، وَلَمْ يَكُنْ أَحَدٌ مِنْ أَصْحَابِكَ إِلاَّ وَلَهُ بِمَكَّةَ مَنْ يَدْفَعُ اللَّهُ بِهِ عَنْ أَهْلِهِ وَمَالِهِ، وَلَمْ يَكُنْ لِي أَحَدٌ، فَأَحْبَبْتُ أَنْ أَتَّخِذَ عِنْدَهُمْ يَدًا. فَصَدَّقَهُ النَّبِيُّ صلى الله عليه وسلم. قَالَ عُمَرُ دَعْنِي أَضْرِبْ عُنُقَهُ، فَإِنَّهُ قَدْ نَافَقَ. فَقَالَ " مَا يُدْرِيكَ لَعَلَّ اللَّهَ اطَّلَعَ عَلَى أَهْلِ بَدْرٍ، فَقَالَ اعْمَلُوا مَا شِئْتُمْ ". فَهَذَا الَّذِي جَرَّأَهُ

Narrated `Abdul `Aziz: Anas said, 'When Allah's Messenger ﷺ invaded Khaibar, we offered the Fajr prayer there (early in the morning) when it was still dark. The Prophet ﷺ rode and Abu Talha rode too and I was riding behind Abu Talha. The Prophet ﷺ passed through the lane of Khaibar quickly and my knee was touching the thigh of the Prophet ﷺ. He uncovered his thigh and I saw the whiteness of the thigh of the Prophet. When he entered the town, he said, 'Allahu Akbar! Khaibar is ruined. Whenever we approach near a (hostile) nation (to fight) then evil will be the morning of those who have been warned.' He repeated this thrice. The people came out for their jobs and some of them said, 'Muhammad (has come).' (Some of our companions added, "With his army.") We conquered Khaibar, took the captives, and the booty was collected. Dihya came and said, 'O Allah's Prophet! Give me a slave girl from the captives.' The Prophet said, 'Go and take any slave girl.' He took Safiya bint Huyai. A man came to the Prophet ﷺ and said, 'O Allah's Messenger ﷺ! You gave Safiya bint Huyai to Dihya and she is the chief mistress of the tribes of Quraidha and An-Nadir and she befits none but you.' So the Prophet ﷺ said, 'Bring him along with her.' So Dihya came with her and when the Prophet ﷺ saw her, he said to Dihya, 'Take any slave girl other than her from the captives.' Anas added: The Prophet ﷺ then manumitted her and married her." Thabit asked Anas, "O Abu Hamza! What did the Prophet ﷺ pay her (as Mahr)?" He said, "Her self was her Mahr for he manumitted her and then married her." Anas added, "While on the way, Um Sulaim dressed her for marriage (ceremony) and at night she sent her as a bride to the Prophet ﷺ. So the Prophet was a bridegroom and he said, 'Whoever has anything (food) should bring it.' He spread out a leather sheet (for the food) and some brought dates and others cooking butter. (I think he (Anas) mentioned As-Sawaq). So they prepared a dish of Hais (a kind of meal). And that was Walima (the marriage banquet) of Allah's Messenger ﷺ." - Sahih Al-Bukhari 371

حَدَّثَنَا يَعْقُوبُ بْنُ إِبْرَاهِيمَ، قَالَ حَدَّثَنَا إِسْمَاعِيلُ ابْنُ عُلَيَّةَ، قَالَ حَدَّثَنَا عَبْدُ الْعَزِيزِ بْنُ صُهَيْبٍ، عَنْ أَنَسٍ، أَنَّ رَسُولَ اللَّهِ صلى الله عليه وسلم غَزَا خَيْبَرَ، فَصَلَّيْنَا عِنْدَهَا صَلاَةَ الْغَدَاةِ بِغَلَسٍ، فَرَكِبَ نَبِيُّ اللَّهِ صلى الله عليه وسلم وَرَكِبَ أَبُو طَلْحَةَ، وَأَنَا رَدِيفُ أَبِي طَلْحَةَ، فَأَجْرَى نَبِيُّ اللَّهِ صلى الله عليه وسلم فِي زُقَاقِ خَيْبَرَ، وَإِنَّ رُكْبَتِي لَتَمَسُّ فَخِذَ نَبِيِّ اللَّهِ صلى الله عليه وسلم، ثُمَّ حَسَرَ الإِزَارَ عَنْ فَخِذِهِ حَتَّى إِنِّي أَنْظُرُ إِلَى بَيَاضِ فَخِذِ نَبِيِّ اللَّهِ صلى الله عليه وسلم، فَلَمَّا دَخَلَ الْقَرْيَةَ قَالَ " اللَّهُ أَكْبَرُ، خَرِبَتْ خَيْبَرُ، إِنَّا إِذَا نَزَلْنَا بِسَاحَةِ قَوْمٍ فَسَاءَ صَبَاحُ الْمُنْذَرِينَ ". قَالَهَا ثَلاَثًا. قَالَ وَخَرَجَ الْقَوْمُ إِلَى أَعْمَالِهِمْ فَقَالُوا مُحَمَّدٌ ـ قَالَ عَبْدُ الْعَزِيزِ وَقَالَ بَعْضُ أَصْحَابِنَا ـ وَالْخَمِيسُ. يَعْنِي الْجَيْشَ، قَالَ فَأَصَبْنَاهَا عَنْوَةً، فَجُمِعَ السَّبْىُ، فَجَاءَ دِحْيَةُ فَقَالَ يَا نَبِيَّ اللَّهِ، أَعْطِنِي جَارِيَةً مِنَ السَّبْىِ. قَالَ " اذْهَبْ فَخُذْ جَارِيَةً ". فَأَخَذَ صَفِيَّةَ بِنْتَ حُيَىٍّ، فَجَاءَ رَجُلٌ إِلَى النَّبِيِّ صلى الله عليه وسلم فَقَالَ يَا نَبِيَّ اللَّهِ، أَعْطَيْتَ دِحْيَةَ صَفِيَّةَ بِنْتَ حُيَىٍّ سَيِّدَةَ قُرَيْظَةَ وَالنَّضِيرِ، لاَ تَصْلُحُ إِلاَّ لَكَ. قَالَ " ادْعُوهُ بِهَا ". فَجَاءَ بِهَا، فَلَمَّا نَظَرَ إِلَيْهَا النَّبِيُّ صلى الله عليه وسلم قَالَ " خُذْ جَارِيَةً مِنَ السَّبْىِ غَيْرَهَا ". قَالَ فَأَعْتَقَهَا النَّبِيُّ صلى الله عليه وسلم وَتَزَوَّجَهَا. فَقَالَ لَهُ ثَابِتٌ يَا أَبَا حَمْزَةَ، مَا أَصْدَقَهَا قَالَ نَفْسَهَا، أَعْتَقَهَا وَتَزَوَّجَهَا، حَتَّى إِذَا كَانَ بِالطَّرِيقِ جَهَّزَتْهَا لَهُ أُمُّ سُلَيْمٍ فَأَهْدَتْهَا لَهُ مِنَ اللَّيْلِ، فَأَصْبَحَ النَّبِيُّ صلى الله عليه وسلم عَرُوسًا فَقَالَ " مَنْ كَانَ عِنْدَهُ شَىْءٌ فَلْيَجِئْ بِهِ ". وَبَسَطَ نِطَعًا، فَجَعَلَ الرَّجُلُ يَجِيءُ بِالتَّمْرِ، وَجَعَلَ الرَّجُلُ يَجِيءُ بِالسَّمْنِ ـ قَالَ وَأَحْسِبُهُ قَدْ ذَكَرَ السَّوِيقَ ـ قَالَ فَحَاسُوا حَيْسًا، فَكَانَتْ وَلِيمَةَ رَسُولِ اللَّهِ صلى الله عليه وسلم.

Narrated Anas bin Malik: The Prophet ﷺ said to Abu Talha, "Choose one of your boys to serve me." So Abu Talha took me (to serve the Prophet ﷺ) by giving me a ride behind him (on his camel). So I used to serve Allah's Messenger ﷺ whenever he stayed somewhere. I used to hear him saying, "O Allah! I seek refuge with you (Allah) from (worries) care and grief, from incapacity and laziness, from miserliness and cowardice, from being heavily in debt and from being overpowered by other men." I kept on serving him till he returned from (the battle of) Khaibar. He then brought Safiya, the daughter of Huyay whom he had got (from the booty). I saw him making a kind of cushion with a cloak or a garment for her. He then let her ride behind him. When we reached a place called As-Sahba', he prepared (a special meal called) Hais, and asked me to invite the men who (came and) ate, and that was the marriage banquet given on the consummation of his marriage to her. Then he proceeded till the mountain of Uhud appeared, whereupon he said, "This mountain loves us and we love it." When he approached Medina, he said, "O Allah! I make the land between its (i.e., Medina's) two mountains a sanctuary, as the prophet Abraham made Mecca a sanctuary. O Allah! Bless them (the people of Medina) in their Mudd and the Sa' (units of measuring). – Sahih Al-Bukhari 6363

حَدَّثَنَا قُتَيْبَةُ بْنُ سَعِيدٍ، حَدَّثَنَا إِسْمَاعِيلُ بْنُ جَعْفَرٍ، عَنْ عَمْرِو بْنِ أَبِي عَمْرٍو، مَوْلَى الْمُطَّلِبِ بْنِ عَبْدِ اللَّهِ بْنِ حَنْطَبٍ أَنَّهُ سَمِعَ أَنَسَ بْنَ مَالِكٍ، يَقُولُ قَالَ رَسُولُ اللَّهِ صلى الله عليه وسلم لأَبِي طَلْحَةَ " الْتَمِسْ لَنَا غُلاَمًا مِنْ غِلْمَانِكُمْ يَخْدُمُنِي ". فَخَرَجَ بِي أَبُو طَلْحَةَ يُرْدِفُنِي وَرَاءَهُ، فَكُنْتُ أَخْدُمُ رَسُولَ اللَّهِ صلى الله عليه وسلم كُلَّمَا نَزَلَ، فَكُنْتُ أَسْمَعُهُ يُكْثِرُ أَنْ يَقُولَ " اللَّهُمَّ إِنِّي أَعُوذُ بِكَ مِنَ الْهَمِّ وَالْحَزَنِ، وَالْعَجْزِ وَالْكَسَلِ، وَالْبُخْلِ وَالْجُبْنِ، وَضَلَعِ الدَّيْنِ، وَغَلَبَةِ الرِّجَالِ ". فَلَمْ أَزَلْ أَخْدُمُهُ حَتَّى أَقْبَلْنَا مِنْ خَيْبَرَ، وَأَقْبَلَ بِصَفِيَّةَ بِنْتِ حُيَيٍّ قَدْ حَازَهَا، فَكُنْتُ أَرَاهُ يُحَوِّي وَرَاءَهُ بِعَبَاءَةٍ أَوْ كِسَاءٍ ثُمَّ يُرْدِفُهَا وَرَاءَهُ حَتَّى إِذَا كُنَّا بِالصَّهْبَاءِ صَنَعَ حَيْسًا فِي نِطَعٍ، ثُمَّ أَرْسَلَنِي فَدَعَوْتُ رِجَالاً فَأَكَلُوا، وَكَانَ ذَلِكَ بِنَاءَهُ بِهَا، ثُمَّ أَقْبَلَ حَتَّى بَدَا لَهُ أُحُدٌ قَالَ " هَذَا جُبَيْلٌ يُحِبُّنَا وَنُحِبُّهُ ". فَلَمَّا أَشْرَفَ عَلَى الْمَدِينَةِ قَالَ " اللَّهُمَّ إِنِّي أُحَرِّمُ مَا بَيْنَ جَبَلَيْهَا مِثْلَ مَا حَرَّمَ بِهِ إِبْرَاهِيمُ مَكَّةَ، اللَّهُمَّ بَارِكْ لَهُمْ فِي مُدِّهِمْ وَصَاعِهِمْ "

Narrated Anas: I was the butler of the people in the house of Abu Talha, and in those days drinks were prepared from dates. Allah's Messenger ﷺ ordered somebody to announce that alcoholic drinks had been prohibited. Abu Talha ordered me to go out and spill the wine. I went out and spilled it, and it flowed in the streets of Medina. Some people said, "Some people were killed and wine was still in their stomachs." On that the Divine revelation came:-- "On those who believe And do good deeds There is no blame For what they ate (in the past)." (5.93). – Sahih Al-Bukhari 2464

حَدَّثَنَا مُحَمَّدُ بْنُ عَبْدِ الرَّحِيمِ أَبُو يَحْيَى، أَخْبَرَنَا عَفَّانُ، حَدَّثَنَا حَمَّادُ بْنُ زَيْدٍ، حَدَّثَنَا ثَابِتٌ، عَنْ أَنَسٍ ـ رضى الله عنه ـ كُنْتُ سَاقِيَ الْقَوْمِ فِي مَنْزِلِ أَبِي طَلْحَةَ، وَكَانَ خَمْرُهُمْ يَوْمَئِذٍ الْفَضِيخَ، فَأَمَرَ رَسُولُ اللَّهِ صلى الله عليه وسلم مُنَادِيًا يُنَادِي " أَلاَ إِنَّ الْخَمْرَ قَدْ حُرِّمَتْ ". قَالَ فَقَالَ لِي أَبُو طَلْحَةَ اخْرُجْ فَأَهْرِقْهَا، فَخَرَجْتُ فَهَرَقْتُهَا، فَجَرَتْ فِي سِكَكِ الْمَدِينَةِ فَقَالَ بَعْضُ الْقَوْمِ قَدْ قُتِلَ قَوْمٌ وَهْىَ فِي بُطُونِهِمْ. فَأَنْزَلَ اللَّهُ {لَيْسَ عَلَى الَّذِينَ آمَنُوا وَعَمِلُوا الصَّالِحَاتِ جُنَاحٌ فِيمَا طَعِمُوا} الآيَةَ

Narrated 'Is-haq bin `Abdullah bin Al Talha: I heard Anas bin Malik saying, "Abu Talha had more property of date-palm trees gardens than any other amongst the Ansar in Medina and the most beloved of them to him was Bairuha garden, and it was in front of the Mosque of the Prophet ﷺ. Allah's Messenger ﷺ used to go there and used to drink its nice water." Anas added, "When these verses were revealed:--'By no means shall you Attain righteousness unless You spend (in charity) of that Which you love. ' (3.92) Abu Talha said to Allah's Messenger' ﷺ O Allah's Messenger ﷺ! Allah, the Blessed, the Superior says: By no means shall you attain righteousness, unless you spend (in charity) of that which you love. And no doubt, Bairuha' garden is the most beloved of all my property to me. So I want to give it in charity in Allah's Cause. I expect its reward from Allah. O Allah's Messenger ﷺ! Spend it where Allah makes you think it feasible.' On that Allah's Apostle said, 'Bravo! It is useful property. I have heard what you have said (O Abu Talha), and I think it would be proper if you gave it to your Kith and kin.' Abu Talha said, I will do so, O Allah's Apostle.' Then Abu Talha distributed that garden amongst his relatives and his cousins.". – Sahih Al-Bukhari 1461

حَدَّثَنَا عَبْدُ اللَّهِ بْنُ يُوسُفَ، أَخْبَرَنَا مَالِكٌ، عَنْ إِسْحَاقَ بْنِ عَبْدِ اللَّهِ بْنِ أَبِي طَلْحَةَ، أَنَّهُ سَمِعَ أَنَسَ بْنَ مَالِكٍ ـ رضى الله عنه ـ يَقُولُ كَانَ أَبُو طَلْحَةَ أَكْثَرَ الأَنْصَارِ بِالْمَدِينَةِ مَالاً مِنْ نَخْلٍ، وَكَانَ أَحَبَّ أَمْوَالِهِ إِلَيْهِ بَيْرُحَاءَ وَكَانَتْ مُسْتَقْبِلَةَ الْمَسْجِدِ، وَكَانَ رَسُولُ اللَّهِ صلى الله عليه وسلم يَدْخُلُهَا وَيَشْرَبُ مِنْ مَاءٍ فِيهَا طَيِّبٍ قَالَ أَنَسٌ فَلَمَّا أُنْزِلَتْ هَذِهِ الآيَةُ {لَنْ تَنَالُوا الْبِرَّ حَتَّى تُنْفِقُوا مِمَّا تُحِبُّونَ} قَامَ أَبُو طَلْحَةَ إِلَى رَسُولِ اللَّهِ صلى الله عليه وسلم فَقَالَ يَا رَسُولَ اللَّهِ. إِنَّ اللَّهَ تَبَارَكَ وَتَعَالَى يَقُولُ {لَنْ تَنَالُوا الْبِرَّ حَتَّى تُنْفِقُوا مِمَّا تُحِبُّونَ} وَإِنَّ أَحَبَّ أَمْوَالِي إِلَىَّ بَيْرُحَاءَ، وَإِنَّهَا صَدَقَةٌ لِلَّهِ أَرْجُو بِرَّهَا وَذُخْرَهَا عِنْدَ اللَّهِ، فَضَعْهَا يَا رَسُولَ اللَّهِ حَيْثُ أَرَاكَ اللَّهُ. قَالَ فَقَالَ رَسُولُ اللَّهِ صلى الله عليه وسلم " بَخْ، ذَلِكَ مَالٌ رَابِحٌ، ذَلِكَ مَالٌ رَابِحٌ، وَقَدْ سَمِعْتُ مَا قُلْتَ وَإِنِّي أَرَى أَنْ تَجْعَلَهَا فِي الأَقْرَبِينَ ". فَقَالَ أَبُو طَلْحَةَ أَفْعَلُ يَا رَسُولَ اللَّهِ. فَقَسَمَهَا أَبُو طَلْحَةَ فِي أَقَارِبِهِ وَبَنِي عَمِّهِ. تَابَعَهُ رَوْحٌ. وَقَالَ يَحْيَى بْنُ يَحْيَى وَإِسْمَاعِيلُ عَنْ مَالِكٍ رَايِحٌ

Narrated Anas bin Malik: Abu Talha said to Um Sulaim, "I have heard the voice of Allah's Messenger ﷺ which was feeble, and I think that he is hungry. Have you got something (to eat)?" She took out some loaves of barley bread, then took her face-covering sheet and wrapped the bread in part of it, and pushed it under my garment and turned the rest of it around my body and sent me to Allah's Messenger ﷺ. I went with that, and found Allah's Messenger ﷺ in the mosque with some people. I stood up near them, and Allah's Messenger ﷺ asked me, "Have you been sent by Abu Talha?" I said, "Yes." He asked, "With some food (for us)?" I said, "Yes." Then Allah's Messenger ﷺ said to all those who were with him, "Get up!" He set out (and all the people accompanied him) and I proceeded ahead of them till I came to Abu Talha. Abu Talha then said, "O Um Sulaim! Allah's Messenger ﷺ has arrived along with the people, and we do not have food enough to feed them all." She said, "Allah and His Apostle know better." So Abu Talha went out till he met Allah's Messenger ﷺ. Then Abu Talha and Allah's Messenger ﷺ came and entered the house. Allah's Apostle said, "Um Sulaim ! Bring whatever you have." She brought that very bread. The Prophet ﷺ ordered that it be crushed into small pieces, and Um Sulaim pressed a skin of butter on it. Then Allah's Apostle said whatever Allah wished him to say (to bless the food) and then added, "Admit ten (men)." So they were admitted, ate their fill and went out. The Prophet ﷺ then said, "Admit ten (more)." They were admitted, ate their full, and went out. He then again said, "Admit ten more!" They were admitted, ate their fill, and went out. He admitted ten more, and so all those people ate their fill, and they were eighty men. – Sahih Al-Bukhari 5381

حَدَّثَنَا إِسْمَاعِيلُ، قَالَ حَدَّثَنِي مَالِكٌ، عَنْ إِسْحَاقَ بْنِ عَبْدِ اللَّهِ بْنِ أَبِي طَلْحَةَ، أَنَّهُ سَمِعَ أَنَسَ بْنَ مَالِكٍ، يَقُولُ قَالَ أَبُو طَلْحَةَ لأُمِّ سُلَيْمٍ لَقَدْ سَمِعْتُ صَوْتَ، رَسُولِ اللَّهِ صلى الله عليه وسلم ضَعِيفًا أَعْرِفُ فِيهِ الْجُوعَ، فَهَلْ عِنْدَكِ مِنْ شَىْءٍ فَأَخْرَجَتْ أَقْرَاصًا مِنْ شَعِيرٍ، ثُمَّ أَخْرَجَتْ خِمَارًا لَهَا فَلَفَّتِ الْخُبْزَ بِبَعْضِهِ، ثُمَّ دَسَّتْهُ تَحْتَ ثَوْبِي وَرَدَّتْنِي بِبَعْضِهِ، ثُمَّ أَرْسَلَتْنِي إِلَى رَسُولِ اللَّهِ صلى الله عليه وسلم قَالَ فَذَهَبْتُ بِهِ فَوَجَدْتُ رَسُولَ اللَّهِ صلى الله عليه وسلم فِي الْمَسْجِدِ وَمَعَهُ النَّاسُ، فَقُمْتُ عَلَيْهِمْ فَقَالَ لِي رَسُولُ اللَّهِ صلى الله عليه وسلم " أَرْسَلَكَ أَبُو طَلْحَةَ ". فَقُلْتُ نَعَمْ. قَالَ " بِطَعَامٍ ". قَالَ فَقُلْتُ نَعَمْ. فَقَالَ رَسُولُ اللَّهِ صلى الله عليه وسلم لِمَنْ مَعَهُ " قُومُوا ". فَانْطَلَقَ وَانْطَلَقْتُ بَيْنَ أَيْدِيهِمْ حَتَّى جِئْتُ أَبَا طَلْحَةَ، فَقَالَ أَبُو طَلْحَةَ يَا أُمَّ سُلَيْمٍ قَدْ جَاءَ رَسُولُ اللَّهِ صلى الله عليه وسلم بِالنَّاسِ، وَلَيْسَ عِنْدَنَا مِنَ الطَّعَامِ مَا نُطْعِمُهُمْ. فَقَالَتِ اللَّهُ وَرَسُولُهُ أَعْلَمُ. قَالَ فَانْطَلَقَ أَبُو طَلْحَةَ حَتَّى لَقِيَ رَسُولَ اللَّهِ صلى الله عليه وسلم فَأَقْبَلَ أَبُو طَلْحَةَ وَرَسُولُ اللَّهِ صلى الله عليه وسلم حَتَّى دَخَلاَ، فَقَالَ رَسُولُ اللَّهِ صلى الله عليه وسلم " هَلُمِّي يَا أُمَّ سُلَيْمٍ مَا عِنْدَكِ ". فَأَتَتْ بِذَلِكَ الْخُبْزِ فَأَمَرَ بِهِ فَفُتَّ وَعَصَرَتْ أُمُّ سُلَيْمٍ عُكَّةً لَهَا فَأَدَمَتْهُ، ثُمَّ قَالَ فِيهِ رَسُولُ اللَّهِ صلى الله عليه وسلم مَا شَاءَ اللَّهُ أَنْ يَقُولَ ثُمَّ قَالَ " ائْذَنْ لِعَشَرَةٍ ". فَأَذِنَ لَهُمْ، فَأَكَلُوا حَتَّى شَبِعُوا، ثُمَّ خَرَجُوا، ثُمَّ قَالَ " ائْذَنْ لِعَشَرَةٍ ". فَأَذِنَ لَهُمْ فَأَكَلُوا حَتَّى شَبِعُوا، ثُمَّ خَرَجُوا، ثُمَّ قَالَ " ائْذَنْ لِعَشَرَةٍ ". فَأَذِنَ لَهُمْ فَأَكَلُوا حَتَّى شَبِعُوا ثُمَّ خَرَجُوا، ثُمَّ أَذِنَ لِعَشَرَةٍ، فَأَكَلَ الْقَوْمُ كُلُّهُمْ وَشَبِعُوا، وَالْقَوْمُ ثَمَانُونَ رَجُلاً.

Narrated Anas bin Malik: That he and Abu Talha were coming in the company of the Prophet (towards Medina), while Safiya (the Prophet's wife) was riding behind him on his she-camel. After they had covered a portion of the way suddenly the foot of the she-camel slipped and both the Prophet ﷺ and the woman (i.e., his wife, Safiya) fell down. Abu Talha jumped quickly off his camel and came to the Prophet (saying.) "O Allah's Messenger ﷺ! Let Allah sacrifice me for you! Have you received any injury?" The prophet ﷺ said, "No, but take care of the woman (my wife)." Abu Talha covered his face with his garment and went towards her and threw his garment over her. Then the woman got up and Abu Talha prepared their she-camel (by tightening its saddle, etc.) and both of them (the Prophet ﷺ and Safiya) mounted it. Then all of them proceeded and when they approached near Medina, or saw Medina, the Prophet ﷺ said, "Ayibun, taibun, `abidun, liRabbina hamidun (We are coming back (to Medina) with repentance, worshiping (our Lord) and celebrating His (our Lord's) praises". The Prophet ﷺ continued repeating these words till he entered the city of Medina. – Sahih Al-Bukhari 6185

حَدَّثَنَا عَلِيُّ بْنُ عَبْدِ اللَّهِ، حَدَّثَنَا بِشْرُ بْنُ الْمُفَضَّلِ، حَدَّثَنَا يَحْيَى بْنُ أَبِي إِسْحَاقَ، عَنْ أَنَسِ بْنِ مَالِكٍ، أَنَّهُ أَقْبَلَ هُوَ وَأَبُو طَلْحَةَ مَعَ النَّبِيِّ صلى الله عليه وسلم وَمَعَ النَّبِيِّ صلى الله عليه وسلم صَفِيَّةُ، مُرْدِفُهَا عَلَى رَاحِلَتِهِ، فَلَمَّا كَانُوا بِبَعْضِ الطَّرِيقِ عَثَرَتِ النَّاقَةُ، فَصُرِعَ النَّبِيُّ صلى الله عليه وسلم وَالْمَرْأَةُ، وَأَنَّ أَبَا طَلْحَةَ ـ قَالَ أَحْسِبُ ـ اقْتَحَمَ عَنْ بَعِيرِهِ، فَأَتَى رَسُولَ اللَّهِ صلى الله عليه وسلم فَقَالَ يَا نَبِيَّ اللَّهِ جَعَلَنِي اللَّهُ فِدَاكَ، هَلْ أَصَابَكَ مِنْ شَىْءٍ. قَالَ " لاَ وَلَكِنْ عَلَيْكَ بِالْمَرْأَةِ ". فَأَلْقَى أَبُو طَلْحَةَ ثَوْبَهُ عَلَى وَجْهِهِ فَقَصَدَ قَصْدَهَا، فَأَلْقَى ثَوْبَهُ عَلَيْهَا فَقَامَتِ الْمَرْأَةُ، فَشَدَّ لَهُمَا عَلَى رَاحِلَتِهِمَا فَرَكِبَا، فَسَارُوا حَتَّى إِذَا كَانُوا بِظَهْرِ الْمَدِينَةِ ـ أَوْ قَالَ أَشْرَفُوا عَلَى الْمَدِينَةِ ـ قَالَ النَّبِيُّ صلى الله عليه وسلم " آيِبُونَ تَائِبُونَ، عَابِدُونَ لِرَبِّنَا حَامِدُونَ ". فَلَمْ يَزَلْ يَقُولُهَا حَتَّى دَخَلَ الْمَدِينَةَ.

Narrated Qais bin Abi Hazim: I saw Talha's paralyzed hand with which he had protected the Prophet (from an arrow) . – Sahih Al-Bukhari 3724

حَدَّثَنَا مُسَدَّدٌ، حَدَّثَنَا خَالِدٌ، حَدَّثَنَا ابْنُ أَبِي خَالِدٍ، عَنْ قَيْسِ بْنِ أَبِي حَازِمٍ،، قَالَ رَأَيْتُ يَدَ طَلْحَةَ الَّتِي وَقَى بِهَا النَّبِيَّ صلى الله عليه وسلم قَدْ شَلَّتْ

Aishah bint Abu Bakr
عائشة بنت أبي بكر

Narrated Al-Qasim: Aisha said that she hung a curtain decorated with pictures (of animals) on a cupboard. The Prophet ﷺ tore that curtain and she turned it into two cushions which remained in the house for the Prophet ﷺ to sit on. – Sahih Al-Bukhari 2479

حَدَّثَنَا إِبْرَاهِيمُ بْنُ الْمُنْذِرِ، حَدَّثَنَا أَنَسُ بْنُ عِيَاضٍ، عَنْ عُبَيْدِ اللَّهِ، عَنْ عَبْدِ الرَّحْمَنِ بْنِ الْقَاسِمِ، عَنْ أَبِيهِ الْقَاسِمِ، عَنْ عَائِشَةَ ـ رضى الله عنها ـ أَنَّهَا كَانَتِ اتَّخَذَتْ عَلَى سَهْوَةٍ لَهَا سِتْرًا فِيهِ تَمَاثِيلُ، فَهَتَكَهُ النَّبِيُّ صلى الله عليه وسلم، فَاتَّخَذَتْ مِنْهُ نُمْرُقَتَيْنِ، فَكَانَتَا فِي الْبَيْتِ يَجْلِسُ عَلَيْهِمَا.

Narrated Aisha: Once the Prophet ﷺ came to me while a man was in my house. He said, "O `Aisha! Who is this (man)?" I replied, "My foster brothers" He said, "O `Aisha! Be sure about your foster brothers, as fostership is only valid if it takes place in the suckling period (before two years of age). – Sahih Al-Bukhari 2647

حَدَّثَنَا مُحَمَّدُ بْنُ كَثِيرٍ، أَخْبَرَنَا سُفْيَانُ، عَنْ أَشْعَثَ بْنِ أَبِي الشَّعْثَاءِ، عَنْ أَبِيهِ، عَنْ مَسْرُوقٍ، أَنَّ عَائِشَةَ ـ رضى الله عنها ـ قَالَتْ دَخَلَ عَلَىَّ النَّبِيُّ صلى الله عليه وسلم وَعِنْدِي رَجُلٌ، قَالَ " يَا عَائِشَةُ مَنْ هَذَا ". قُلْتُ أَخِي مِنَ الرَّضَاعَةِ. قَالَ " يَا عَائِشَةُ، انْظُرْنَ مَنْ إِخْوَانُكُنَّ، فَإِنَّمَا الرَّضَاعَةُ مِنَ الْمَجَاعَةِ ". تَابَعَهُ ابْنُ مَهْدِيٍّ عَنْ سُفْيَانَ

Narrated Al-Aswad: In the presence of `Aisha some people mentioned that the Prophet ﷺ had appointed `Ali by will as his successor. `Aisha said, "When did he appoint him by will? Verily when he died he was resting against my chest (or said: in my lap) and he asked for a wash-basin and then collapsed while in that state, and I could not even perceive that he had died, so when did he appoint him by will?". – Sahih Al-Bukhari 2741

حَدَّثَنَا عَمْرُو بْنُ زُرَارَةَ، أَخْبَرَنَا إِسْمَاعِيلُ، عَنِ ابْنِ عَوْنٍ، عَنْ إِبْرَاهِيمَ، عَنِ الأَسْوَدِ، قَالَ ذَكَرُوا عِنْدَ عَائِشَةَ أَنَّ عَلِيًّا ـ رضى الله عنهما ـ كَانَ وَصِيًّا. فَقَالَتْ مَتَى أَوْصَى إِلَيْهِ وَقَدْ كُنْتُ مُسْنِدَتَهُ إِلَى صَدْرِي ـ أَوْ قَالَتْ حَجْرِي ـ فَدَعَا بِالطَّسْتِ، فَلَقَدِ انْخَنَثَ فِي حَجْرِي، فَمَا شَعَرْتُ أَنَّهُ قَدْ مَاتَ، فَمَتَى أَوْصَى إِلَيْهِ

Al-Bara added: I then went with Abu Bakr into his home (carrying that saddle) and there I saw his daughter `Aisha Lying in a bed because of heavy fever and I saw her father Abu Bakr kissing her cheek and saying, "How are you, little daughter?" -Sahih al-Bukhari 3918

قَالَ الْبَرَاءُ فَدَخَلْتُ مَعَ أَبِي بَكْرٍ عَلَى أَهْلِهِ، فَإِذَا عَائِشَةُ ابْنَتُهُ مُضْطَجِعَةٌ، قَدْ أَصَابَتْهَا حُمَّى، فَرَأَيْتُ أَبَاهَا فَقَبَّلَ خَدَّهَا، وَقَالَ كَيْفَ أَنْتِ يَا بُنَيَّةُ

Narrated `Aisha: I stuffed for the Prophetﷺ a pillow decorated with pictures (of animals) which looked like a Namruqa (i.e. a small cushion). He came and stood between the two doors and his face began to change. I said, "O Allah's Messengerﷺ! What did we do wrong?" He said, "What is this pillow?" I said, "I have prepared this pillow for you, so that you may recline on it." He said, "Don't you know that angels do not enter a house wherein there are pictures; and whoever makes a picture will be punished on the Day of Resurrection and will be asked to give life to (what he has created)?". – Sahih Al-Bukhari 3224

حَدَّثَنَا مُحَمَّدٌ، أَخْبَرَنَا مَخْلَدٌ، أَخْبَرَنَا ابْنُ جُرَيْجٍ، عَنْ إِسْمَاعِيلَ بْنِ أُمَيَّةَ، أَنَّ نَافِعًا، حَدَّثَهُ أَنَّ الْقَاسِمَ بْنَ مُحَمَّدٍ حَدَّثَهُ عَنْ عَائِشَةَ ـ رضى الله عنها ـ قَالَتْ حَشَوْتُ لِلنَّبِيِّ صلى الله عليه وسلم وِسَادَةً فِيهَا تَمَاثِيلُ كَأَنَّهَا نُمْرُقَةٌ، فَجَاءَ فَقَامَ بَيْنَ الْبَابَيْنِ وَجَعَلَ يَتَغَيَّرُ وَجْهُهُ، فَقُلْتُ مَا لَنَا يَا رَسُولَ اللَّهِ. قَالَ " مَا بَالُ هَذِهِ الْوِسَادَةِ ". قَالَتْ وِسَادَةٌ جَعَلْتُهَا لَكَ لِتَضْطَجِعَ عَلَيْهَا. قَالَ " أَمَا عَلِمْتِ أَنَّ الْمَلاَئِكَةَ لاَ تَدْخُلُ بَيْتًا فِيهِ صُورَةٌ، وَأَنَّ مَنْ صَنَعَ الصُّورَةَ يُعَذَّبُ يَوْمَ الْقِيَامَةِ يَقُولُ أَحْيُوا مَا خَلَقْتُمْ "

Narrated 'Aisha: Once Hala bint Khuwailid, Khadija's sister, asked the permission of the Prophetﷺ to enter. On that, the Prophetﷺ remembered the way Khadija used to ask permission, and that upset him. He said, "O Allah! Hala!" So I became jealous and said, "What makes you remember an old woman amongst the old women of Quraish an old woman (with a teethless mouth) of red gums who died long ago, and in whose place Allah has given you somebody better than her?". – Sahih Al-Bukhari 3821

وَقَالَ إِسْمَاعِيلُ بْنُ خَلِيلٍ أَخْبَرَنَا عَلِيُّ بْنُ مُسْهِرٍ، عَنْ هِشَامٍ، عَنْ أَبِيهِ، عَنْ عَائِشَةَ ـ رضى الله عنها ـ قَالَتِ اسْتَأْذَنَتْ هَالَةُ بِنْتُ خُوَيْلِدٍ أُخْتُ خَدِيجَةَ عَلَى رَسُولِ اللَّهِ صلى الله عليه وسلم، فَعَرَفَ اسْتِئْذَانَ خَدِيجَةَ فَارْتَاعَ لِذَلِكَ، فَقَالَ " اللَّهُمَّ هَالَةَ ". قَالَتْ فَغِرْتُ فَقُلْتُ مَا تَذْكُرُ مِنْ عَجُوزٍ مِنْ عَجَائِزِ قُرَيْشٍ، حَمْرَاءِ الشِّدْقَيْنِ، هَلَكَتْ فِي الدَّهْرِ، قَدْ أَبْدَلَكَ اللَّهُ خَيْرًا مِنْهَا

Narrated Aisha: The Prophetﷺ engaged me when I was a girl of six (years). We went to Medina and stayed at the home of Bani-al-Harith bin Khazraj. Then I got ill and my hair fell down. Later on my hair grew (again) and my mother, Um Ruman, came to me while I was playing in a swing with some of my girl friends. She called me, and I went to her, not knowing what she wanted to do to me. She caught me by the hand and made me stand at the door of the house. I was breathless then, and when my breathing became All right, she took some water and rubbed my face and head with it. Then she took me into the house. There in the house I saw some Ansari women who said, "Best wishes and Allah's Blessing and a good luck." Then she entrusted me to them and they prepared me (for the marriage). Unexpectedly Allah's Apostle came to me in the forenoon and my mother handed me over to him, and at that time I was a girl of nine years of age. – Sahih Al-Bukhari 3894

حَدَّثَنِي فَرْوَةُ بْنُ أَبِي الْمَغْرَاءِ، حَدَّثَنَا عَلِيُّ بْنُ مُسْهِرٍ، عَنْ هِشَامٍ، عَنْ أَبِيهِ، عَنْ عَائِشَةَ ـ رضى الله عنها ـ قَالَتْ تَزَوَّجَنِي النَّبِيُّ صلى الله عليه وسلم وَأَنَا بِنْتُ سِتِّ سِنِينَ، فَقَدِمْنَا الْمَدِينَةَ فَنَزَلْنَا فِي بَنِي الْحَارِثِ بْنِ خَزْرَجٍ، فَوُعِكْتُ فَتَمَرَّقَ شَعَرِي فَوَفَى جُمَيْمَةً، فَأَتَتْنِي أُمِّي أُمُّ رُومَانَ وَإِنِّي لَفِي أُرْجُوحَةٍ وَمَعِي صَوَاحِبُ لِي، فَصَرَخَتْ بِي فَأَتَيْتُهَا لاَ أَدْرِي مَا تُرِيدُ بِي فَأَخَذَتْ بِيَدِي حَتَّى أَوْقَفَتْنِي عَلَى بَابِ الدَّارِ، وَإِنِّي لأُنْهِجُ، حَتَّى سَكَنَ بَعْضُ نَفَسِي، ثُمَّ أَخَذَتْ شَيْئًا مِنْ مَاءٍ فَمَسَحَتْ بِهِ وَجْهِي وَرَأْسِي ثُمَّ أَدْخَلَتْنِي الدَّارَ فَإِذَا نِسْوَةٌ مِنَ الأَنْصَارِ فِي الْبَيْتِ فَقُلْنَ عَلَى الْخَيْرِ وَالْبَرَكَةِ، وَعَلَى خَيْرِ طَائِرٍ. فَأَسْلَمَتْنِي

إِلَيْهِنَّ فَأَصْلَحْنَ مِنْ شَأْنِي، فَلَمْ يَرُعْنِي إِلاَّ رَسُولُ اللَّهِ صلى الله عليه وسلم ضُحًى، فَأَسْلَمَتْنِي إِلَيْهِ، وَأَنَا يَوْمَئِذٍ بِنْتُ تِسْعِ سِنِينَ.

Narrated `Aisha: Whenever Allah's Messenger ﷺ intended to go on a journey, he used to draw lots amongst his wives, and Allah's Messenger ﷺ used to take with him the one on whom lot fell. He drew lots amongst us during one of the Ghazwat which he fought. The lot fell on me and so I proceeded with Allah's Messenger ﷺ after Allah's order of veiling (the women) had been revealed. I was carried (on the back of a camel) in my howdah and carried down while still in it (when we came to a halt). So we went on till Allah's Messenger ﷺ had finished from that Ghazwa of his and returned. When we approached the city of Medina he announced at night that it was time for departure. So when they announced the news of departure, I got up and went away from the army camps, and after finishing from the call of nature, I came back to my riding animal. I touched my chest to find that my necklace which was made of Zifar beads (i.e. Yemenite beads partly black and partly white) was missing. So I returned to look for my necklace and my search for it detained me. (In the meanwhile) the people who used to carry me on my camel, came and took my howdah and put it on the back of my camel on which I used to ride, as they considered that I was in it. In those days women were light in weight for they did not get fat, and flesh did not cover their bodies in abundance as they used to eat only a little food. Those people therefore, disregarded the lightness of the howdah while lifting and carrying it; and at that time I was still a young girl. They made the camel rise and all of them left (along with it). I found my necklace after the army had gone. Then I came to their camping place to find no call maker of them, nor one who would respond to the call. So I intended to go to the place where I used to stay, thinking that they would miss me and come back to me (in my search). While I was sitting in my resting place, I was overwhelmed by sleep and slept. Safwan bin Al-Muattal As-Sulami Adh-Dhakwani was behind the army. When he reached my place in the morning, he saw the figure of a sleeping person and he recognized me on seeing me as he had seen me before the order of compulsory veiling (was prescribed). So I woke up when he recited Istirja' (i.e. "Inna li l-lahi wa inna llaihi raji'un") as soon as he recognized me. I veiled my face with my head cover at once, and by Allah, we did not speak a single word, and I did not hear him saying any word besides his Istirja'. He dismounted from his camel and made it kneel down, putting his leg on its front legs and then I got up and rode on it. Then he set out leading the camel that was carrying me till we overtook the army in the extreme heat of midday while they were at a halt (taking a rest). (Because of the event) some people brought destruction upon themselves and the one who spread the Ifk (i.e. slander) more, was `Abdullah bin Ubai Ibn Salul." (Urwa said, "The people propagated the slander and talked about it in his (i.e. `Abdullah's) presence and he confirmed it and listened to it and asked about it to let it prevail." `Urwa also added, "None was mentioned as members of the slanderous group besides (`Abdullah) except Hassan bin Thabit and Mistah bin Uthatha and Hamna bint Jahsh along with others about whom I have no knowledge, but they were a group as Allah said. It is said that the one who carried most of the slander was `Abdullah bin Ubai bin Salul." `Urwa added, "`Aisha disliked to have Hassan abused in her presence and she used to say, 'It was he who said: My father and his (i.e. my father's) father and my honor are all for the protection of Muhammad's honor from you."). `Aisha added, "After we returned to Medina, I became ill for a month. The people were propagating the forged statements of the slanderers while I was unaware of anything of all that, but I felt that in my present ailment, I was not receiving the same kindness from Allah's Messenger ﷺ as I used to receive when I got sick. (But now) Allah's Messenger ﷺ would only come, greet me and say,' How is that (lady)?' and leave. That roused my doubts, but I did not discover the evil (i.e. slander) till I went out after my convalescence, I went out with Um Mistah to Al-Manasi' where we used to answer the call of nature and we used not to go out (to answer the call of nature) except at night, and that was before we had latrines near our houses. And this habit of our concerning evacuating the bowels, was similar to the habits of the old 'Arabs living in the deserts, for it would be troublesome for us to take latrines near our houses. So I and Um Mistah who was the daughter of Abu Ruhm bin Al-Muttalib bin `Abd Manaf, whose mother was the daughter of Sakhr bin 'Amir and the aunt of Abu Bakr As-Siddiq and whose son was Mistah bin Uthatha bin `Abbas bin Al-Muttalib, went out. I and Um Mistah returned to my house after we finished answering the call of nature. Um Mistah stumbled by getting her foot entangled in her covering sheet and on that she said, 'Let Mistah be ruined!' I said, 'What a hard word you have said. Do you abuse a man who took part in the battle of Badr?' On that she said, 'O you Hantah! Didn't you hear what he (i.e. Mistah) said? 'I said, 'What did he say?' Then she told me the slander of the people of Ifk. So my ailment was aggravated, and when I reached my home, Allah's Messenger ﷺ came to me, and after greeting me, said, 'How is that (lady)?' I said, 'Will you allow me to go to my parents?' as I wanted to be sure about the news through them. Allah's Apostle allowed me (and I went to my parents) and asked my mother, 'O mother! What are the people talking about?' She said, 'O my daughter! Don't worry, for scarcely is there a charming woman who is loved by her husband and whose husband has other wives besides herself that they (i.e. women) would find faults with her.' I said, 'Subhan-Allah! (I testify the uniqueness of Allah). Are the people really talking in this way?' I kept on weeping that night till dawn I could neither stop weeping nor sleep then in the morning again, I kept on weeping. When the Divine Inspiration was delayed. Allah's Messenger ﷺ called `Ali bin Abi Talib and Usama bin Zaid to ask and consult them about divorcing me. Usama bin Zaid said what he knew of my innocence, and the respect he preserved in himself for me. Usama said, '(O Allah's Messenger!) She is your wife and we do not know anything except good about her.' `Ali bin Abi Talib said, 'O Allah's Messenger ﷺ! Allah does not put you in difficulty and there are plenty of women other than she, yet, ask the maid-servant who will tell you the truth.' On that Allah's Messenger ﷺ called Barira (i.e. the maid-servant) and said, 'O Barira! Did you ever see anything which aroused your suspicion?' Barira said to him, 'By Him Who has sent you with the Truth. I have never seen anything in her (i.e. Aisha) which I would conceal, except that she is a young girl who sleeps leaving the dough of her family exposed so that the domestic goats come and eat it.' So, on that day, Allah's Messenger ﷺ got up on the pulpit and complained about `Abdullah bin Ubai (bin Salul) before his companions, saying, 'O you Muslims! Who will relieve me from that man who has hurt me with his evil statement about my family? By Allah, I know nothing except good about my family and they have blamed a man about whom I know nothing except good and he used never to enter my home except with me.' Sa`d bin Mu`adh the brother of Banu `Abd Al-Ashhal got up and said, 'O Allah's Messenger ﷺ! I will relieve you from him; if he is from the tribe of Al-Aus, then I will chop his head off, and if he is from our brothers, i.e. Al-Khazraj, then order us, and we will fulfill your order.' On that, a man from Al-Khazraj got up. Um Hassan, his cousin, was from his branch tribe, and he was Sa`d bin Ubada, chief of Al-Khazraj. Before this incident, he was a pious man, but his love for his tribe goaded him into saying to Sa`d (bin Mu`adh). 'By Allah, you have told a lie; you shall not and cannot kill him. If he belonged to your people, you would not wish him to be killed.' On that, Usaid bin Hudair who was the cousin of Sa`d (bin Mu`adh) got up and said to Sa`d bin 'Ubada, 'By Allah! You are a liar! We will surely kill him, and you are a hypocrite arguing on the behalf of hypocrites.' On this, the two tribes of Al-Aus and Al Khazraj got so much excited that they were about to fight while Allah's Messengerﷺ was standing on the pulpit. Allah's Messenger ﷺkept on quietening them till they became silent and so did he. All that day I kept on weeping with my tears never ceasing, and I could never sleep. In the morning my parents were with me and I wept for two nights and a day with my tears never ceasing and I could never sleep till I thought that my liver would burst from weeping. So, while my parents were sitting with me and I was weeping, an Ansari woman asked me to grant her admittance. I allowed her to come in, and when she came in, she sat down and started weeping with me. While we were in this state, Allah's Messengerﷺ came, greeted us and sat down. He had never sat with me since that day of the slander. A month had elapsed and no Divine Inspiration came to him about my case. Allah's Apostle then recited Tashah-hud and then said, 'Amma Badu, O `Aisha! I have been informed so-andso about you; if you are innocent, then soon Allah will reveal your innocence, and if you have committed a sin, then repent to Allah and ask Him for forgiveness for when a slave confesses his sins and asks Allah for forgiveness, Allah accepts his repentance.' : -5.462:... ... When Allah's Messengerﷺ finished his speech, my tears ceased flowing completely that I no longer felt a single drop of tear flowing. I said to my father, 'Reply to Allah's Messengerﷺ on my behalf concerning what he has said.' My father said, 'By Allah, I do not know what to say to Allah's Messengerﷺ. Then I said to my mother, 'Reply to Allah's Messengerﷺ on my behalf concerning what he has said.' She said, 'By Allah, I do not know what to say to Allah's Messengerﷺ. In spite of the fact that I was a young girl and had a little knowledge of Qur'an, I said, 'By Allah, no doubt I know that you heard this (slanderous) speech so that it has been planted in your hearts (i.e. minds) and you have taken it as a truth. Now if I tell you that I am innocent, you will not believe me, and if confess to you about it, and Allah knows that I am innocent, you will surely believe me. By Allah, I find no similitude for me and you except that of Joseph's father when he said, '(For me) patience in the most fitting against that which you assert; it is Allah (Alone) Whose Help can be sought.' Then I turned to the other side and lay on my bed; and Allah knew then that I was innocent and hoped that Allah would reveal my innocence. But, by Allah, I never thought that Allah would reveal about my case, Divine Inspiration, that would be recited (forever) as I considered myself too unworthy to be talked of by Allah with something of my concern, but I hoped that Allah's Messengerﷺ might have a dream in which Allah would prove my innocence. But, by Allah, before Allah's Messengerﷺ left his seat and before any of the household left, the Divine inspiration came to Allah's Messengerﷺ. So there overtook him the same hard condition which used to overtake him, (when he used to be inspired Divinely). The sweat was dropping from his body like pearls though it was a wintry day and that was because of the weighty statement which was being revealed to him. When that state of Allah's Messengerﷺ was over, he got up smiling, and the first word he said was, 'O `Aisha! Allah has declared your innocence!' Then my Mother said to me, 'Get up and go to him (i.e. Allah's Messengerﷺ). I replied, 'By Allah, I will not go to him, and I praise none but Allah. So Allah revealed the ten Verses:- - "Verily! They who spread the slander Are a gang, among you............." (24.11-20) Allah revealed those Qur'anic Verses to declare my innocence. Abu Bakr As-Siddiq who used to disburse money for Mistah bin Uthatha because of his relationship to him and his poverty, said, 'By Allah, I will never give to Mistah bin Uthatha anything after what he has said about Aisha.' Then Allah revealed:-- "And let not those among you who are good and wealthy swear not to give (any sort of help) to their kinsmen, those in need, and those who have left their homes for Allah's cause, let them pardon and forgive. Do you not love that Allah should forgive you? And Allah is oft-Forgiving Most Merciful." (24.22) Abu Bakr As-Siddiq said, 'Yes, by Allah, I would like that Allah forgive me.' And went on giving Mistah the money he used to give him before. He also added, 'By Allah, I will never deprive him of it at all.' Aisha further said:." Allah's Messenger ﷺ also asked Zainab bint Jahsh (i.e. his wife) about my case. He said to Zainab, 'What do you know and what did you see?" She replied, "O Allah's Messenger ﷺ! I refrain from claiming falsely that I have heard or seen anything. By Allah, I know nothing except good (about `Aisha).' From amongst the wives of the Prophet ﷺ Zainab was my peer (in beauty and in the love she received from the Prophet) but Allah saved her from that evil because of her piety. Her sister Hamna, started struggling on her behalf and she was destroyed along with those who were destroyed. The man who was blamed said, 'Subhan-Allah! By Him in Whose Hand my soul is, I have never uncovered the cover (i.e. veil) of any female.' Later on the man was martyred in Allah's Cause." - Sahih Al-Bukhari 4141

حَدَّثَنَا عَبْدُ الْعَزِيزِ بْنُ عَبْدِ اللَّهِ، حَدَّثَنَا إِبْرَاهِيمُ بْنُ سَعْدٍ، عَنْ صَالِحٍ، عَنِ ابْنِ شِهَابٍ، قَالَ حَدَّثَنِي عُرْوَةُ بْنُ الزُّبَيْرِ، وَسَعِيدُ بْنُ الْمُسَيَّبِ، وَعَلْقَمَةُ بْنُ وَقَّاصٍ، وَعُبَيْدُ اللَّهِ بْنُ عَبْدِ اللَّهِ بْنِ عُتْبَةَ بْنِ مَسْعُودٍ، عَنْ عَائِشَةَ، رضى الله عنها زَوْجِ النَّبِيِّ صلى الله عليه وسلم حِينَ قَالَ لَهَا أَهْلُ الإِفْكِ مَا قَالُوا، وَكُلُّهُمْ حَدَّثَنِي طَائِفَةً مِنْ حَدِيثِهَا، وَبَعْضُهُمْ كَانَ أَوْعَى لِحَدِيثِهَا مِنْ بَعْضٍ وَأَثْبَتَ لَهُ اقْتِصَاصًا، وَقَدْ وَعَيْتُ عَنْ كُلِّ رَجُلٍ مِنْهُمُ الْحَدِيثَ الَّذِي حَدَّثَنِي عَنْ عَائِشَةَ، وَبَعْضُ حَدِيثِهِمْ يُصَدِّقُ بَعْضًا، وَإِنْ كَانَ بَعْضُهُمْ أَوْعَى لَهُ مِنْ بَعْضٍ، قَالُوا قَالَتْ عَائِشَةُ كَانَ رَسُولُ اللَّهِ صلى الله عليه وسلم إِذَا أَرَادَ سَفَرًا أَقْرَعَ بَيْنَ أَزْوَاجِهِ، فَأَيُّهُنَّ خَرَجَ سَهْمُهَا، خَرَجَ بِهَا رَسُولُ اللَّهِ صلى الله عليه وسلم مَعَهُ، قَالَتْ عَائِشَةُ فَأَقْرَعَ بَيْنَنَا فِي غَزْوَةٍ غَزَاهَا فَخَرَجَ فِيهَا سَهْمِي، فَخَرَجْتُ مَعَ رَسُولِ اللَّهِ صلى الله عليه وسلم بَعْدَ مَا أُنْزِلَ الْحِجَابُ، فَكُنْتُ أُحْمَلُ فِي هَوْدَجِي وَأُنْزَلُ فِيهِ، فَسِرْنَا حَتَّى إِذَا فَرَغَ رَسُولُ اللَّهِ صلى الله عليه وسلم مِنْ غَزْوَتِهِ تِلْكَ وَقَفَلَ، دَنَوْنَا مِنَ الْمَدِينَةِ قَافِلِينَ، آذَنَ لَيْلَةً بِالرَّحِيلِ، فَقُمْتُ حِينَ آذَنُوا بِالرَّحِيلِ فَمَشَيْتُ حَتَّى جَاوَزْتُ الْجَيْشَ، فَلَمَّا قَضَيْتُ شَأْنِي أَقْبَلْتُ إِلَى رَحْلِي، فَلَمَسْتُ صَدْرِي، فَإِذَا عِقْدٌ لِي مِنْ جَزْعِ ظَفَارِ قَدِ انْقَطَعَ، فَرَجَعْتُ فَالْتَمَسْتُ عِقْدِي، فَحَبَسَنِي ابْتِغَاؤُهُ، قَالَتْ وَأَقْبَلَ الرَّهْطُ الَّذِينَ كَانُوا يُرَحِّلُونِي فَاحْتَمَلُوا هَوْدَجِي، فَرَحَلُوهُ عَلَى بَعِيرِي الَّذِي كُنْتُ أَرْكَبُ عَلَيْهِ، وَهُمْ يَحْسِبُونَ أَنِّي فِيهِ، وَكَانَ النِّسَاءُ إِذْ ذَاكَ خِفَافًا لَمْ يَهْبُلْنَ وَلَمْ يَغْشَهُنَّ اللَّحْمُ، إِنَّمَا يَأْكُلْنَ الْعُلْقَةَ مِنَ الطَّعَامِ، فَلَمْ يَسْتَنْكِرِ الْقَوْمُ خِفَّةَ الْهَوْدَجِ حِينَ رَفَعُوهُ وَحَمَلُوهُ، وَكُنْتُ جَارِيَةً حَدِيثَةَ السِّنِّ، فَبَعَثُوا الْجَمَلَ فَسَارُوا، وَوَجَدْتُ عِقْدِي بَعْدَ مَا اسْتَمَرَّ الْجَيْشُ، فَجِئْتُ مَنَازِلَهُمْ وَلَيْسَ بِهَا مِنْهُمْ دَاعٍ وَلاَ مُجِيبٌ، فَتَيَمَّمْتُ مَنْزِلِي الَّذِي كُنْتُ بِهِ، وَظَنَنْتُ أَنَّهُمْ سَيَفْقِدُونِي فَيَرْجِعُونَ إِلَىَّ، فَبَيْنَا أَنَا جَالِسَةٌ فِي مَنْزِلِي غَلَبَتْنِي عَيْنِي فَنِمْتُ، وَكَانَ صَفْوَانُ بْنُ الْمُعَطَّلِ السُّلَمِيُّ ثُمَّ الذَّكْوَانِيُّ مِنْ وَرَاءِ الْجَيْشِ، فَأَصْبَحَ عِنْدَ مَنْزِلِي فَرَأَى سَوَادَ إِنْسَانٍ نَائِمٍ، فَعَرَفَنِي حِينَ رَآنِي، وَكَانَ رَآنِي قَبْلَ الْحِجَابِ، فَاسْتَيْقَظْتُ بِاسْتِرْجَاعِهِ حِينَ عَرَفَنِي، فَخَمَّرْتُ وَجْهِي بِجِلْبَابِي، وَاللَّهِ مَا تَكَلَّمْنَا بِكَلِمَةٍ وَلاَ سَمِعْتُ مِنْهُ كَلِمَةً غَيْرَ اسْتِرْجَاعِهِ، وَهَوَى حَتَّى أَنَاخَ رَاحِلَتَهُ، فَوَطِئَ عَلَى يَدِهَا، فَقُمْتُ إِلَيْهَا فَرَكِبْتُهَا، فَانْطَلَقَ يَقُودُ بِي الرَّاحِلَةَ حَتَّى أَتَيْنَا الْجَيْشَ مُوغِرِينَ فِي نَحْرِ الظَّهِيرَةِ، وَهُمْ نُزُولٌ ـ قَالَتْ ـ فَهَلَكَ {فِيَّ} مَنْ هَلَكَ، وَكَانَ الَّذِي تَوَلَّى كِبْرَ الإِفْكِ عَبْدَ اللَّهِ بْنَ أُبَىٍّ ابْنَ سَلُولَ. قَالَ عُرْوَةُ أُخْبِرْتُ أَنَّهُ كَانَ يُشَاعُ وَيُتَحَدَّثُ بِهِ عِنْدَهُ، فَيُقِرُّهُ وَيَسْتَمِعُهُ وَيَسْتَوْشِيهِ. وَقَالَ عُرْوَةُ أَيْضًا لَمْ يُسَمَّ مِنْ أَهْلِ الإِفْكِ أَيْضًا إِلاَّ حَسَّانُ بْنُ ثَابِتٍ، وَمِسْطَحُ بْنُ أُثَاثَةَ، وَحَمْنَةُ بِنْتُ جَحْشٍ فِي نَاسٍ آخَرِينَ، لاَ عِلْمَ لِي بِهِمْ، غَيْرَ أَنَّهُمْ عُصْبَةٌ ـ كَمَا قَالَ اللَّهُ تَعَالَى ـ وَإِنَّ كِبْرَ ذَلِكَ يُقَالُ عَبْدُ اللَّهِ بْنُ أُبَىٍّ ابْنُ سَلُولَ. قَالَ عُرْوَةُ كَانَتْ عَائِشَةُ تَكْرَهُ أَنْ يُسَبَّ عِنْدَهَا حَسَّانُ، وَتَقُولُ إِنَّهُ الَّذِي قَالَ:

فَإِنَّ أَبِي وَوَالِدَهُ وَعِرْضِي لِعِرْضِ مُحَمَّدٍ مِنْكُمْ وِقَاءُ

قَالَتْ عَائِشَةُ فَقَدِمْنَا الْمَدِينَةَ فَاشْتَكَيْتُ حِينَ قَدِمْتُ شَهْرًا، وَالنَّاسُ يُفِيضُونَ فِي قَوْلِ أَصْحَابِ الإِفْكِ، لاَ أَشْعُرُ بِشَىْءٍ مِنْ ذَلِكَ، وَهْوَ يَرِيبُنِي فِي وَجَعِي أَنِّي لاَ أَعْرِفُ مِنْ رَسُولِ اللَّهِ صلى الله عليه وسلم اللُّطْفَ الَّذِي كُنْتُ أَرَى مِنْهُ حِينَ أَشْتَكِي، إِنَّمَا يَدْخُلُ عَلَىَّ رَسُولُ اللَّهِ صلى الله عليه وسلم فَيُسَلِّمُ ثُمَّ يَقُولُ " كَيْفَ تِيكُمْ " ثُمَّ يَنْصَرِفُ، فَذَلِكَ يَرِيبُنِي وَلاَ أَشْعُرُ بِالشَّرِّ، حَتَّى خَرَجْتُ حِينَ نَقَهْتُ، فَخَرَجْتُ مَعَ أُمِّ مِسْطَحٍ قِبَلَ الْمَنَاصِعِ، وَكَانَ مُتَبَرَّزَنَا، وَكُنَّا لاَ نَخْرُجُ إِلاَّ لَيْلاً إِلَى لَيْلٍ، وَذَلِكَ قَبْلَ أَنْ نَتَّخِذَ الْكُنُفَ قَرِيبًا مِنْ بُيُوتِنَا. قَالَتْ وَأَمْرُنَا أَمْرُ الْعَرَبِ الأُوَلِ فِي الْبَرِّيَّةِ قِبَلَ الْغَائِطِ، وَكُنَّا نَتَأَذَّى بِالْكُنُفِ أَنْ نَتَّخِذَهَا عِنْدَ بُيُوتِنَا، قَالَتْ فَانْطَلَقْتُ أَنَا وَأُمُّ مِسْطَحٍ وَهْىَ ابْنَةُ أَبِي رُهْمِ بْنِ الْمُطَّلِبِ بْنِ عَبْدِ مَنَافٍ، وَأُمُّهَا بِنْتُ صَخْرِ بْنِ عَامِرٍ خَالَةُ أَبِي بَكْرٍ الصِّدِّيقِ، وَابْنُهَا مِسْطَحُ بْنُ أُثَاثَةَ بْنِ عَبَّادِ بْنِ الْمُطَّلِبِ، فَأَقْبَلْتُ أَنَا وَأُمُّ مِسْطَحٍ قِبَلَ بَيْتِي، حِينَ فَرَغْنَا مِنْ شَأْنِنَا، فَعَثَرَتْ أُمُّ مِسْطَحٍ فِي مِرْطِهَا فَقَالَتْ تَعِسَ مِسْطَحٌ. فَقُلْتُ لَهَا بِئْسَ مَا قُلْتِ، أَتَسُبِّينَ رَجُلاً شَهِدَ بَدْرًا فَقَالَتْ أَىْ هَنْتَاهْ وَلَمْ تَسْمَعِي مَا قَالَ قَالَتْ وَقُلْتُ مَا قَالَ فَأَخْبَرَتْنِي بِقَوْلِ أَهْلِ الإِفْكِ ـ قَالَتْ ـ فَازْدَدْتُ مَرَضًا عَلَى مَرَضِي، فَلَمَّا رَجَعْتُ إِلَى بَيْتِي دَخَلَ عَلَىَّ رَسُولُ اللَّهِ صلى الله عليه وسلم فَسَلَّمَ ثُمَّ قَالَ " كَيْفَ تِيكُمْ ". فَقُلْتُ لَهُ أَتَأْذَنُ لِي أَنْ آتِيَ أَبَوَىَّ قَالَتْ وَأُرِيدُ أَنْ أَسْتَيْقِنَ الْخَبَرَ مِنْ قِبَلِهِمَا، قَالَتْ فَأَذِنَ لِي رَسُولُ اللَّهِ صلى الله عليه وسلم، فَقُلْتُ لأُمِّي يَا أُمَّتَاهُ مَاذَا يَتَحَدَّثُ النَّاسُ قَالَتْ يَا بُنَيَّةُ هَوِّنِي عَلَيْكِ، فَوَاللَّهِ لَقَلَّمَا كَانَتِ امْرَأَةٌ قَطُّ وَضِيئَةً عِنْدَ رَجُلٍ يُحِبُّهَا لَهَا ضَرَائِرُ إِلاَّ كَثَّرْنَ عَلَيْهَا. قَالَتْ فَقُلْتُ سُبْحَانَ اللَّهِ أَوَلَقَدْ تَحَدَّثَ النَّاسُ بِهَذَا قَالَتْ فَبَكَيْتُ تِلْكَ اللَّيْلَةَ، حَتَّى أَصْبَحْتُ لاَ يَرْقَأُ لِي دَمْعٌ، وَلاَ أَكْتَحِلُ بِنَوْمٍ، ثُمَّ أَصْبَحْتُ أَبْكِي ـ قَالَتْ ـ وَدَعَا رَسُولُ اللَّهِ صلى الله عليه وسلم عَلِيَّ بْنَ أَبِي طَالِبٍ وَأُسَامَةَ بْنَ زَيْدٍ حِينَ اسْتَلْبَثَ الْوَحْىُ يَسْأَلُهُمَا وَيَسْتَشِيرُهُمَا فِي فِرَاقِ أَهْلِهِ ـ قَالَتْ ـ فَأَمَّا أُسَامَةُ فَأَشَارَ عَلَى رَسُولِ اللَّهِ صلى الله عليه وسلم بِالَّذِي يَعْلَمُ مِنْ بَرَاءَةِ أَهْلِهِ، وَبِالَّذِي يَعْلَمُ لَهُمْ فِي نَفْسِهِ، فَقَالَ أُسَامَةُ أَهْلَكَ وَلاَ نَعْلَمُ إِلاَّ خَيْرًا. وَأَمَّا عَلِيٌّ فَقَالَ يَا رَسُولَ اللَّهِ لَمْ يُضَيِّقِ اللَّهُ عَلَيْكَ، وَالنِّسَاءُ سِوَاهَا كَثِيرٌ، وَسَلِ الْجَارِيَةَ

تَصْدُقْكَ. قَالَتْ فَدَعَا رَسُولُ اللَّهِ صلى الله عليه وسلم بَرِيرَةَ فَقَالَ " أَىْ بَرِيرَةُ هَلْ رَأَيْتِ مِنْ شَىْءٍ يَرِيبُكِ ". قَالَتْ لَهُ بَرِيرَةُ وَالَّذِي بَعَثَكَ بِالْحَقِّ مَا رَأَيْتُ عَلَيْهَا أَمْرًا قَطُّ أَغْمِصُهُ، غَيْرَ أَنَّهَا جَارِيَةٌ حَدِيثَةُ السِّنِّ تَنَامُ عَنْ عَجِينِ أَهْلِهَا، فَتَأْتِي الدَّاجِنُ فَتَأْكُلُهُ ـ قَالَتْ ـ فَقَامَ رَسُولُ اللَّهِ صلى الله عليه وسلم مِنْ يَوْمِهِ، فَاسْتَعْذَرَ مِنْ عَبْدِ اللَّهِ بْنِ أُبَىٍّ وَهْوَ عَلَى الْمِنْبَرِ فَقَالَ " يَا مَعْشَرَ الْمُسْلِمِينَ مَنْ يَعْذِرُنِي مِنْ رَجُلٍ قَدْ بَلَغَنِي عَنْهُ أَذَاهُ فِي أَهْلِي، وَاللَّهِ مَا عَلِمْتُ عَلَى أَهْلِي إِلاَّ خَيْرًا، وَلَقَدْ ذَكَرُوا رَجُلاً مَا عَلِمْتُ عَلَيْهِ إِلاَّ خَيْرًا، وَمَا يَدْخُلُ عَلَى أَهْلِي إِلاَّ مَعِي ". قَالَتْ فَقَامَ سَعْدُ بْنُ مُعَاذٍ أَخُو بَنِي عَبْدِ الأَشْهَلِ فَقَالَ أَنَا يَا رَسُولَ اللَّهِ أَعْذِرُكَ، فَإِنْ كَانَ مِنَ الأَوْسِ ضَرَبْتُ عُنُقَهُ، وَإِنْ كَانَ مِنْ إِخْوَانِنَا مِنَ الْخَزْرَجِ أَمَرْتَنَا فَفَعَلْنَا أَمْرَكَ. قَالَتْ فَقَامَ رَجُلٌ مِنَ الْخَزْرَجِ، وَكَانَتْ أُمُّ حَسَّانَ بِنْتَ عَمِّهِ مِنْ فَخِذِهِ، وَهْوَ سَعْدُ بْنُ عُبَادَةَ، وَهْوَ سَيِّدُ الْخَزْرَجِ ـ قَالَتْ ـ وَكَانَ قَبْلَ ذَلِكَ رَجُلاً صَالِحًا، وَلَكِنِ احْتَمَلَتْهُ الْحَمِيَّةُ فَقَالَ لِسَعْدٍ كَذَبْتَ لَعَمْرُ اللَّهِ لاَ تَقْتُلُهُ، وَلاَ تَقْدِرُ عَلَى قَتْلِهِ، وَلَوْ كَانَ مِنْ رَهْطِكَ مَا أَحْبَبْتَ أَنْ يُقْتَلَ. فَقَامَ أُسَيْدُ بْنُ حُضَيْرٍ ـ وَهْوَ ابْنُ عَمِّ سَعْدٍ ـ فَقَالَ لِسَعْدِ بْنِ عُبَادَةَ كَذَبْتَ لَعَمْرُ اللَّهِ لَنَقْتُلَنَّهُ، فَإِنَّكَ مُنَافِقٌ تُجَادِلُ عَنِ الْمُنَافِقِينَ. قَالَتْ فَثَارَ الْحَيَّانِ الأَوْسُ وَالْخَزْرَجُ حَتَّى هَمُّوا أَنْ يَقْتَتِلُوا، وَرَسُولُ اللَّهِ صلى الله عليه وسلم قَائِمٌ عَلَى الْمِنْبَرِ ـ قَالَتْ ـ فَلَمْ يَزَلْ رَسُولُ اللَّهِ صلى الله عليه وسلم يُخَفِّضُهُمْ حَتَّى سَكَتُوا وَسَكَتَ ـ قَالَتْ ـ فَبَكَيْتُ يَوْمِي ذَلِكَ كُلَّهُ، لاَ يَرْقَأُ لِي دَمْعٌ، وَلاَ أَكْتَحِلُ بِنَوْمٍ ـ قَالَتْ ـ وَأَصْبَحَ أَبَوَاىَ عِنْدِي، وَقَدْ بَكَيْتُ لَيْلَتَيْنِ وَيَوْمًا، لاَ يَرْقَأُ لِي دَمْعٌ، وَلاَ أَكْتَحِلُ بِنَوْمٍ، حَتَّى إِنِّي لأَظُنُّ أَنَّ الْبُكَاءَ فَالِقٌ كَبِدِي، فَبَيْنَا أَبَوَاىَ جَالِسَانِ عِنْدِي وَأَنَا أَبْكِي فَاسْتَأْذَنَتْ عَلَىَّ امْرَأَةٌ مِنَ الأَنْصَارِ، فَأَذِنْتُ لَهَا، فَجَلَسَتْ تَبْكِي مَعِي ـ قَالَتْ ـ فَبَيْنَا نَحْنُ عَلَى ذَلِكَ دَخَلَ رَسُولُ اللَّهِ صلى الله عليه وسلم عَلَيْنَا، فَسَلَّمَ ثُمَّ جَلَسَ ـ قَالَتْ ـ وَلَمْ يَجْلِسْ عِنْدِي مُنْذُ قِيلَ مَا قِيلَ قَبْلَهَا، وَقَدْ لَبِثَ شَهْرًا لاَ يُوحَى إِلَيْهِ فِي شَأْنِي بِشَىْءٍ ـ قَالَتْ ـ فَتَشَهَّدَ رَسُولُ اللَّهِ صلى الله عليه وسلم حِينَ جَلَسَ ثُمَّ قَالَ " أَمَّا بَعْدُ، يَا عَائِشَةُ إِنَّهُ بَلَغَنِي عَنْكِ كَذَا وَكَذَا، فَإِنْ كُنْتِ بَرِيئَةً، فَسَيُبَرِّئُكِ اللَّهُ، وَإِنْ كُنْتِ أَلْمَمْتِ بِذَنْبٍ، فَاسْتَغْفِرِي اللَّهَ وَتُوبِي إِلَيْهِ، فَإِنَّ الْعَبْدَ إِذَا اعْتَرَفَ ثُمَّ تَابَ تَابَ اللَّهُ عَلَيْهِ ". قَالَتْ فَلَمَّا قَضَى رَسُولُ اللَّهِ صلى الله عليه وسلم مَقَالَتَهُ قَلَصَ دَمْعِي حَتَّى مَا أُحِسُّ مِنْهُ قَطْرَةً، فَقُلْتُ لأَبِي أَجِبْ رَسُولَ اللَّهِ صلى الله عليه وسلم عَنِّي فِيمَا قَالَ. فَقَالَ أَبِي وَاللَّهِ مَا أَدْرِي مَا أَقُولُ لِرَسُولِ اللَّهِ صلى الله عليه وسلم. فَقُلْتُ لأُمِّي أَجِيبِي رَسُولَ اللَّهِ صلى الله عليه وسلم فِيمَا قَالَ. قَالَتْ أُمِّي وَاللَّهِ مَا أَدْرِي مَا أَقُولُ لِرَسُولِ اللَّهِ صلى الله عليه وسلم. فَقُلْتُ وَأَنَا جَارِيَةٌ حَدِيثَةُ السِّنِّ لاَ أَقْرَأُ مِنَ الْقُرْآنِ كَثِيرًا إِنِّي وَاللَّهِ لَقَدْ عَلِمْتُ لَقَدْ سَمِعْتُمْ هَذَا الْحَدِيثَ حَتَّى اسْتَقَرَّ فِي أَنْفُسِكُمْ وَصَدَّقْتُمْ بِهِ، فَلَئِنْ قُلْتُ لَكُمْ إِنِّي بَرِيئَةٌ لاَ تُصَدِّقُونِي، وَلَئِنِ اعْتَرَفْتُ لَكُمْ بِأَمْرٍ، وَاللَّهُ يَعْلَمُ أَنِّي مِنْهُ بَرِيئَةٌ لَتُصَدِّقُنِّي، فَوَاللَّهِ لاَ أَجِدُ لِي وَلَكُمْ مَثَلاً إِلاَّ أَبَا يُوسُفَ حِينَ قَالَ {فَصَبْرٌ جَمِيلٌ وَاللَّهُ الْمُسْتَعَانُ عَلَى مَا تَصِفُونَ} ثُمَّ تَحَوَّلْتُ وَاضْطَجَعْتُ عَلَى فِرَاشِي، وَاللَّهُ يَعْلَمُ أَنِّي حِينَئِذٍ بَرِيئَةٌ، وَأَنَّ اللَّهَ مُبَرِّئِي بِبَرَاءَتِي وَلَكِنْ وَاللَّهِ مَا كُنْتُ أَظُنُّ أَنَّ اللَّهَ مُنْزِلٌ فِي شَأْنِي وَحْيًا يُتْلَى، لَشَأْنِي فِي نَفْسِي كَانَ أَحْقَرَ مِنْ أَنْ يَتَكَلَّمَ اللَّهُ فِيَّ بِأَمْرٍ، وَلَكِنْ كُنْتُ أَرْجُو أَنْ يَرَى رَسُولُ اللَّهِ صلى الله عليه وسلم فِي النَّوْمِ رُؤْيَا يُبَرِّئُنِي اللَّهُ بِهَا، فَوَاللَّهِ مَا رَامَ رَسُولُ اللَّهِ صلى الله عليه وسلم مَجْلِسَهُ، وَلاَ خَرَجَ أَحَدٌ مِنْ أَهْلِ الْبَيْتِ، حَتَّى أُنْزِلَ عَلَيْهِ، فَأَخَذَهُ مَا كَانَ يَأْخُذُهُ مِنَ الْبُرَحَاءِ، حَتَّى إِنَّهُ لَيَتَحَدَّرُ مِنْهُ مِنَ الْعَرَقِ مِثْلُ الْجُمَانِ وَهْوَ فِي يَوْمٍ شَاتٍ، مِنْ ثِقَلِ الْقَوْلِ الَّذِي أُنْزِلَ عَلَيْهِ ـ قَالَتْ ـ فَسُرِّيَ عَنْ رَسُولِ اللَّهِ صلى الله عليه وسلم وَهْوَ يَضْحَكُ، فَكَانَتْ أَوَّلَ كَلِمَةٍ تَكَلَّمَ بِهَا أَنْ قَالَ " يَا عَائِشَةُ أَمَّا اللَّهُ فَقَدْ بَرَّأَكِ ". قَالَتْ فَقَالَتْ لِي أُمِّي قُومِي إِلَيْهِ. فَقُلْتُ وَاللَّهِ لاَ أَقُومُ إِلَيْهِ، فَإِنِّي لاَ أَحْمَدُ إِلاَّ اللَّهَ عَزَّ وَجَلَّ ـ قَالَتْ ـ وَأَنْزَلَ اللَّهُ تَعَالَى {إِنَّ الَّذِينَ جَاءُوا بِالإِفْكِ} الْعَشْرَ الآيَاتِ، ثُمَّ أَنْزَلَ اللَّهُ هَذَا فِي بَرَاءَتِي. قَالَ أَبُو بَكْرٍ الصِّدِّيقُ ـ وَكَانَ يُنْفِقُ عَلَى مِسْطَحِ بْنِ أُثَاثَةَ لِقَرَابَتِهِ مِنْهُ وَفَقْرِهِ ـ وَاللَّهِ لاَ أُنْفِقُ عَلَى مِسْطَحٍ شَيْئًا أَبَدًا بَعْدَ الَّذِي قَالَ لِعَائِشَةَ مَا قَالَ. فَأَنْزَلَ اللَّهُ { وَلاَ يَأْتَلِ أُولُو الْفَضْلِ مِنْكُمْ} إِلَى قَوْلِهِ {غَفُورٌ رَحِيمٌ} قَالَ أَبُو بَكْرٍ الصِّدِّيقُ بَلَى وَاللَّهِ إِنِّي لأُحِبُّ أَنْ يَغْفِرَ اللَّهُ لِي فَرَجَعَ إِلَى مِسْطَحٍ النَّفَقَةَ الَّتِي كَانَ يُنْفِقُ عَلَيْهِ وَقَالَ وَاللَّهِ لَا أَنْزِعُهَا مِنْهُ أَبَدًا قَالَتْ عَائِشَةُ وَكَانَ رَسُولُ اللَّهِ صَلَّى اللَّهُ عَلَيْهِ وَسَلَّمَ سَأَلَ زَيْنَبَ بِنْتَ جَحْشٍ عَنْ أَمْرِي فَقَالَ لِزَيْنَبَ مَاذَا عَلِمْتِ أَوْ رَأَيْتِ فَقَالَتْ يَا رَسُولَ اللَّهِ أَحْمِي سَمْعِي وَبَصَرِي وَاللَّهِ مَا عَلِمْتُ إِلَّا خَيْرًا قَالَتْ عَائِشَةُ وَهِيَ الَّتِي كَانَتْ تُسَامِينِي مِنْ أَزْوَاجِ النَّبِيِّ صَلَّى اللَّهُ عَلَيْهِ وَسَلَّمَ فَعَصَمَهَا اللَّهُ بِالْوَرَعِ قَالَتْ وَطَفِقَتْ أُخْتُهَا حَمْنَةُ تُحَارِبُ لَهَا فَهَلَكَتْ فِيمَنْ هَلَكَ قَالَ ابْنُ شِهَابٍ فَهَذَا الَّذِي بَلَغَنِي مِنْ حَدِيثِ هَؤُلَاءِ الرَّهْطِ ثُمَّ قَالَ عُرْوَةُ قَالَتْ عَائِشَةُ وَاللَّهِ إِنَّ الرَّجُلَ الَّذِي قِيلَ لَهُ مَا قِيلَ لَيَقُولُ سُبْحَانَ اللَّهِ فَوَالَّذِي نَفْسِي بِيَدِهِ مَا كَشَفْتُ مِنْ كَنَفِ أُنْثَى قَطُّ قَالَتْ ثُمَّ قُتِلَ بَعْدَ ذَلِكَ فِي سَبِيلِ اللَّهِ

Narrated `Aisha: Mother of the Believers: We, the wives of the Prophetﷺ were all sitting with the Prophetﷺ and none of us had left when Fatima came walking, and by Allah, her gait was very similar to that of Allah's Messengerﷺ. When he saw her, he welcomed her, saying, "Welcome, O my daughter!" Then he made her sit on his right or his left, confided something to her, whereupon she wept bitterly. When he noticed her sorrow, he confided something else to her for the second time, and she started laughing. Only I from among the Prophet's wives said to her, "(O Fatima), Allah's Messengerﷺ selected you from among us for the secret talk and still you weep?" When Allah's Messengerﷺ got up (and went away), I asked her, "What did he confide to you?" She said, "I wouldn't disclose the secrets of Allah's Messengerﷺ." But when he died I asked her, "I beseech you earnestly by what right I have on you, to tell me (that secret talk which the Prophet had with you)" She said, "As you ask me now, yes, (I will tell you)." She informed me, saying, "When he talked to me secretly the first time, he said that Gabriel used to review the Qur'an with him once every year. He added, 'But this year he reviewed it with me twice, and therefore I think that my time of death has approached. So, be afraid of Allah, and be patient, for I am the best predecessor for you (in the Hereafter).' " Fatima added, "So I wept as you (`Aisha) witnessed. And when the Prophet ﷺsaw me in this sorrowful state, he confided the second secret to me saying, 'O Fatima! Will you not be pleased that you will be chief of all the believing women (or chief of the women of this nation i.e. my followers?"). – Sahih Al-Bukhari 6285, 6286

حَدَّثَنَا مُوسَى، عَنْ أَبِي عَوَانَةَ، حَدَّثَنَا فِرَاسٌ، عَنْ عَامِرٍ، عَنْ مَسْرُوقٍ، حَدَّثَتْنِي عَائِشَةُ أُمُّ الْمُؤْمِنِينَ، قَالَتْ إِنَّا كُنَّا أَزْوَاجَ النَّبِيِّ صلى الله عليه وسلم عِنْدَهُ جَمِيعًا، لَمْ تُغَادَرْ مِنَّا وَاحِدَةٌ، فَأَقْبَلَتْ فَاطِمَةُ ـ عَلَيْهَا السَّلاَمُ ـ تَمْشِي، لاَ وَاللَّهِ مَا تَخْفَى مِشْيَتُهَا مِنْ مِشْيَةِ رَسُولِ اللَّهِ صلى الله عليه وسلم فَلَمَّا رَآهَا رَحَّبَ قَالَ " مَرْحَبًا بِابْنَتِي ". ثُمَّ أَجْلَسَهَا عَنْ يَمِينِهِ أَوْ عَنْ شِمَالِهِ، ثُمَّ سَارَّهَا فَبَكَتْ بُكَاءً شَدِيدًا، فَلَمَّا رَأَى حُزْنَهَا سَارَّهَا الثَّانِيَةَ إِذَا هِيَ تَضْحَكُ. فَقُلْتُ لَهَا أَنَا مِنْ بَيْنِ نِسَائِهِ خَصَّكِ رَسُولُ اللَّهِ صلى الله عليه وسلم بِالسِّرِّ مِنْ بَيْنِنَا، ثُمَّ أَنْتِ تَبْكِينَ، فَلَمَّا قَامَ رَسُولُ اللَّهِ صلى الله عليه وسلم سَأَلْتُهَا عَمَّا سَارَّكِ قَالَتْ مَا كُنْتُ لأُفْشِيَ عَلَى رَسُولِ اللَّهِ صلى الله عليه وسلم سِرَّهُ. فَلَمَّا تُوُفِّيَ قُلْتُ لَهَا عَزَمْتُ عَلَيْكِ بِمَا لِي عَلَيْكِ مِنَ الْحَقِّ لَمَّا أَخْبَرْتِنِي. قَالَتْ أَمَّا الآنَ فَنَعَمْ. فَأَخْبَرَتْنِي قَالَتْ أَمَّا حِينَ سَارَّنِي فِي الأَمْرِ الأَوَّلِ، فَإِنَّهُ أَخْبَرَنِي أَنَّ جِبْرِيلَ كَانَ يُعَارِضُهُ بِالْقُرْآنِ كُلَّ سَنَةٍ مَرَّةً " وَإِنَّهُ قَدْ عَارَضَنِي بِهِ الْعَامَ مَرَّتَيْنِ، وَلاَ أَرَى الأَجَلَ إِلاَّ قَدِ اقْتَرَبَ، فَاتَّقِي اللَّهَ وَاصْبِرِي، فَإِنِّي نِعْمَ السَّلَفُ أَنَا لَكِ ". قَالَتْ فَبَكَيْتُ بُكَائِي الَّذِي رَأَيْتِ، فَلَمَّا رَأَى جَزَعِي سَارَّنِي الثَّانِيَةَ قَالَ " يَا فَاطِمَةُ أَلاَ تَرْضَيْنَ أَنْ تَكُونِي سَيِّدَةَ نِسَاءِ الْمُؤْمِنِينَ ـ أَوْ ـ سَيِّدَةَ نِسَاءِ هَذِهِ الأُمَّةِ "

Narrated `Aisha: When the ailment of the Prophetﷺ became aggravated and his disease became severe, he asked his wives to permit him to be nursed (treated) in my house. So they gave him the permission. Then the Prophet came (to my house) with the support of two men, and his legs were dragging on the ground, between `Abbas, and another man." 'Ubaidullah (the sub narrator) said, "I informed `Abdullah bin `Abbas of what `Aisha said. Ibn `Abbas said: 'Do you know who was the other man?' I replied in the negative. Ibn `Abbas said, 'He was `Ali (bin Abi Talib)." `Aisha further said, "When the Prophetﷺ came to my house and his sickness became aggravated he ordered us to pour seven skins full of water on him, so that he might give some advice to the people. So he was seated in a Mikhdab (brass tub) belonging to Hafsa, the wife of the Prophet. Then, all of us started pouring water on him from the water skins till he beckoned to us to stop and that we have done (what he wanted us to do). After that he went out to the people.". – Sahih Al-Bukhari 198

حَدَّثَنَا أَبُو الْيَمَانِ، قَالَ أَخْبَرَنَا شُعَيْبٌ، عَنِ الزُّهْرِيِّ، قَالَ أَخْبَرَنِي عُبَيْدُ اللَّهِ بْنُ عَبْدِ اللَّهِ بْنِ عُتْبَةَ، أَنَّ عَائِشَةَ، قَالَتْ لَمَّا ثَقُلَ النَّبِيُّ صلى الله عليه وسلم وَاشْتَدَّ بِهِ وَجَعُهُ، اسْتَأْذَنَ أَزْوَاجَهُ فِي أَنْ يُمَرَّضَ فِي بَيْتِي، فَأَذِنَّ لَهُ، فَخَرَجَ النَّبِيُّ صلى الله عليه وسلم بَيْنَ رَجُلَيْنِ تَخُطُّ رِجْلاَهُ فِي الأَرْضِ بَيْنَ عَبَّاسٍ وَرَجُلٍ آخَرَ. قَالَ عُبَيْدُ اللَّهِ فَأَخْبَرْتُ عَبْدَ اللَّهِ بْنَ عَبَّاسٍ فَقَالَ أَتَدْرِي مَنِ الرَّجُلُ الآخَرُ قُلْتُ لاَ. قَالَ هُوَ عَلِيٌّ. وَكَانَتْ عَائِشَةُ ـ رضى الله عنها ـ تُحَدِّثُ أَنَّ النَّبِيَّ صلى الله عليه وسلم قَالَ بَعْدَ مَا دَخَلَ بَيْتَهُ وَاشْتَدَّ وَجَعُهُ " هَرِيقُوا عَلَىَّ مِنْ سَبْعِ قِرَبٍ، لَمْ تُحْلَلْ أَوْكِيَتُهُنَّ، لَعَلِّي أَعْهَدُ إِلَى النَّاسِ ". وَأُجْلِسَ فِي مِخْضَبٍ لِحَفْصَةَ زَوْجِ النَّبِيِّ صلى الله عليه وسلم، ثُمَّ طَفِقْنَا نَصُبُّ عَلَيْهِ تِلْكَ حَتَّى طَفِقَ يُشِيرُ إِلَيْنَا أَنْ قَدْ فَعَلْتُنَّ، ثُمَّ خَرَجَ إِلَى النَّاسِ

Narrated Yusuf bin Mahk: While I was with Aisha, the mother of the Believers, a person from Iraq came and asked, "What type of shroud is the best?" `Aisha said, "May Allah be merciful to you! What does it matter?" He said, "O mother of the Believers! Show me (the copy of) your Qur'an," She said, "Why?" He said, "In order to compile and arrange the Qur'an according to it, for people recite it with its Suras not in proper order." `Aisha said, "What does it matter which part of it you read first? (Be informed) that the first thing that was revealed thereof was a Sura from Al-Mufassal, and in it was mentioned Paradise and the Fire. When the people embraced Islam, the Verses regarding legal and illegal things were revealed. If the first thing to be revealed was: 'Do not drink alcoholic drinks.' People would have said, 'We will never leave alcoholic drinks,' and if there had been revealed, 'Do not commit illegal sexual intercourse, 'they would have said, 'We will never give up illegal sexual intercourse.'

While I was a young girl of playing age, the following Verse was revealed in Mecca to Muhammad: 'Nay! But the Hour is their appointed time (for their full recompense), and the Hour will be more grievous and more bitter.' (54.46) Sura Al-Baqara (The Cow) and Surat An-Nisa (The Women) were revealed while I was with him." Then `Aisha took out the copy of the Qur'an for the man and dictated to him the Verses of the Suras (in their proper order) . – Sahih Al-Bukhari 4993

حَدَّثَنَا إِبْرَاهِيمُ بْنُ مُوسَى، أَخْبَرَنَا هِشَامُ بْنُ يُوسُفَ، أَنَّ ابْنَ جُرَيْجٍ، أَخْبَرَهُمْ قَالَ وَأَخْبَرَنِي يُوسُفُ بْنُ مَاهَكَ، قَالَ إِنِّي عِنْدَ عَائِشَةَ أُمِّ الْمُؤْمِنِينَ ـ رضى الله عنها ـ إِذْ جَاءَهَا عِرَاقِيٌّ فَقَالَ أَىُّ الْكَفَنِ خَيْرٌ قَالَتْ وَيْحَكَ وَمَا يَضُرُّكَ قَالَ يَا أُمَّ الْمُؤْمِنِينَ أَرِينِي مُصْحَفَكِ. قَالَتْ لِمَ قَالَ لَعَلِّي أُوَلِّفُ الْقُرْآنَ عَلَيْهِ فَإِنَّهُ يُقْرَأُ غَيْرَ مُؤَلَّفٍ. قَالَتْ وَمَا يَضُرُّكَ أَيَّهُ قَرَأْتَ قَبْلُ، إِنَّمَا نَزَلَ أَوَّلَ مَا نَزَلَ مِنْهُ سُورَةٌ مِنَ الْمُفَصَّلِ فِيهَا ذِكْرُ الْجَنَّةِ وَالنَّارِ حَتَّى إِذَا ثَابَ النَّاسُ إِلَى الإِسْلاَمِ نَزَلَ الْحَلاَلُ وَالْحَرَامُ، وَلَوْ نَزَلَ أَوَّلَ شَىْءٍ لاَ تَشْرَبُوا الْخَمْرَ. لَقَالُوا لاَ نَدَعُ الْخَمْرَ أَبَدًا. وَلَوْ نَزَلَ. لاَ تَزْنُوا. لَقَالُوا لاَ نَدَعُ الزِّنَا أَبَدًا. لَقَدْ نَزَلَ بِمَكَّةَ عَلَى مُحَمَّدٍ صلى الله عليه وسلم وَإِنِّي لَجَارِيَةٌ أَلْعَبُ {بَلِ السَّاعَةُ مَوْعِدُهُمْ وَالسَّاعَةُ أَدْهَى وَأَمَرُّ} وَمَا نَزَلَتْ سُورَةُ الْبَقَرَةِ وَالنِّسَاءِ إِلاَّ وَأَنَا عِنْدَهُ. قَالَ فَأَخْرَجَتْ لَهُ الْمُصْحَفَ فَأَمْلَتْ عَلَيْهِ آىَ السُّوَرِ

Narrated `Aisha: I said, "O Allah's Messenger ﷺ! Suppose you landed in a valley where there is a tree of which something has been eaten and then you found trees of which nothing has been eaten, of which tree would you let your camel graze?" He said, "(I will let my camel graze) of the one of which nothing has been eaten before." (The sub-narrator added: `Aisha meant that Allah's Messenger ﷺ had not married a virgin besides herself .). – Sahih Al-Bukhari 5077

حَدَّثَنَا إِسْمَاعِيلُ بْنُ عَبْدِ اللَّهِ، قَالَ حَدَّثَنِي أَخِي، عَنْ سُلَيْمَانَ، عَنْ هِشَامِ بْنِ عُرْوَةَ، عَنْ أَبِيهِ، عَنْ عَائِشَةَ ـ رضى الله عنها ـ قَالَتْ قُلْتُ يَا رَسُولَ اللَّهِ أَرَأَيْتَ لَوْ نَزَلْتَ وَادِيًا وَفِيهِ شَجَرَةٌ قَدْ أُكِلَ مِنْهَا، وَوَجَدْتَ شَجَرًا لَمْ يُؤْكَلْ مِنْهَا، فِي أَيِّهَا كُنْتَ تُرْتِعُ بَعِيرَكَ قَالَ " فِي الَّذِي لَمْ يُرْتَعْ مِنْهَا ". تَعْنِي أَنَّ رَسُولَ اللَّهِ صلى الله عليه وسلم لَمْ يَتَزَوَّجْ بِكْرًا غَيْرَهَا.

Narrated `Aisha: That the Prophet ﷺ entered upon her while a man was sitting with her. Signs of answer seemed to appear on his face as if he disliked that. She said, "Here is my (foster) brother." He said, "Be sure as to who is your foster brother, for foster suckling relationship is established only when milk is the only food of the child." - Sahih Al-Bukhari 5102

حَدَّثَنَا أَبُو الْوَلِيدِ، حَدَّثَنَا شُعْبَةُ، عَنِ الأَشْعَثِ، عَنْ أَبِيهِ، عَنْ مَسْرُوقٍ، عَنْ عَائِشَةَ ـ رضى الله عنها ـ أَنَّ النَّبِيَّ صلى الله عليه وسلم دَخَلَ عَلَيْهَا وَعِنْدَهَا رَجُلٌ، فَكَأَنَّهُ تَغَيَّرَ وَجْهُهُ، كَأَنَّهُ كَرِهَ ذَلِكَ فَقَالَتْ إِنَّهُ أَخِي. فَقَالَ " انْظُرْنَ مَا إِخْوَانُكُنَّ، فَإِنَّمَا الرَّضَاعَةُ مِنَ الْمَجَاعَةِ "

Narrated Ibn `Abbas and `Aisha: Abu Bakr kissed (the forehead of) the Prophet ﷺ when he was dead. `Aisha added: We put medicine in one side of his mouth but he started waving us not to insert the medicine into his mouth. We said, "He dislikes the medicine as a patient usually does." But when he came to his senses he said, "Did I not forbid you to put medicine (by force) in the side of my mouth?" We said, "We thought it was just because a patient usually dislikes medicine." He said, "None of those who are in the house but will be forced to take medicine in the side of his mouth while I am watching, except Al-`Abbas, for he had not witnessed your deed.". – Sahih Al-Bukhari 5709-5712

حَدَّثَنَا عَلِيُّ بْنُ عَبْدِ اللَّهِ، حَدَّثَنَا يَحْيَى بْنُ سَعِيدٍ، حَدَّثَنَا سُفْيَانُ، قَالَ حَدَّثَنِي مُوسَى بْنُ أَبِي عَائِشَةَ، عَنْ عُبَيْدِ اللَّهِ بْنِ عَبْدِ اللَّهِ، عَنِ ابْنِ عَبَّاسٍ، وَعَائِشَةَ، أَنَّ أَبَا بَكْرٍ ـ رضى الله عنه ـ قَبَّلَ النَّبِيَّ صلى الله عليه وسلم وَهْوَ مَيِّتٌ، قَالَ وَقَالَتْ عَائِشَةُ لَدَدْنَاهُ فِي مَرَضِهِ، فَجَعَلَ يُشِيرُ إِلَيْنَا، أَنْ لاَ تَلُدُّونِي. فَقُلْنَا كَرَاهِيَةُ الْمَرِيضِ لِلدَّوَاءِ. فَلَمَّا أَفَاقَ قَالَ " أَلَمْ أَنْهَكُمْ أَنْ تَلُدُّونِي ". قُلْنَا كَرَاهِيَةَ الْمَرِيضِ لِلدَّوَاءِ. فَقَالَ " لاَ يَبْقَى فِي الْبَيْتِ أَحَدٌ إِلاَّ لُدَّ ـ وَأَنَا أَنْظُرُ ـ إِلاَّ الْعَبَّاسَ فَإِنَّهُ لَمْ يَشْهَدْكُمْ ".

Narrated Aisha: Magic was worked on Allah's Messenger ﷺ so that he used to think that he had sexual relations with his wives while he actually had not (Sufyan said: That is the hardest kind of magic as it has such an effect). Then one day he said, "O `Aisha do you know that

Allah has instructed me concerning the matter I asked Him about? Two men came to me and one of them sat near my head and the other sat near my feet. The one near my head asked the other. What is wrong with this man?' The latter replied the is under the effect of magic The first one asked, Who has worked magic on him?' The other replied Labid bin Al-A'sam, a man from Bani Zuraiq who was an ally of the Jews and was a hypocrite.' The first one asked, What material did he use)?' The other replied, 'A comb and the hair stuck to it.' The first one asked, 'Where (is that)?' The other replied. 'In a skin of pollen of a male date palm tree kept under a stone in the well of Dharwan' " So the Prophet ﷺ went to that well and took out those things and said "That was the well which was shown to me (in a dream) Its water looked like the infusion of Henna leaves and its date-palm trees looked like the heads of devils." The Prophet ﷺ added, "Then that thing was taken out' I said (to the Prophet ﷺ) "Why do you not treat yourself with Nashra?" He said, "Allah has cured me; I dislike to let evil spread among my people.". – Sahih Al-Bukhari 5765

حَدَّثَنِي عَبْدُ اللَّهِ بْنُ مُحَمَّدٍ، قَالَ سَمِعْتُ ابْنَ عُيَيْنَةَ، يَقُولُ أَوَّلُ مَنْ حَدَّثَنَا بِهِ ابْنُ جُرَيْجٍ، يَقُولُ حَدَّثَنِي آلُ، عُرْوَةَ عَنْ عُرْوَةَ، فَسَأَلْتُ هِشَامًا عَنْهُ فَحَدَّثَنَا عَنْ أَبِيهِ، عَنْ عَائِشَةَ ـ رضى الله عنها ـ قَالَتْ كَانَ رَسُولُ اللَّهِ صلى الله عليه وسلم سُحِرَ حَتَّى كَانَ يَرَى أَنَّهُ يَأْتِي النِّسَاءَ وَلاَ يَأْتِيهِنَّ. قَالَ سُفْيَانُ وَهَذَا أَشَدُّ مَا يَكُونُ مِنَ السِّحْرِ إِذَا كَانَ كَذَا. فَقَالَ " يَا عَائِشَةُ أَعَلِمْتِ أَنَّ اللَّهَ قَدْ أَفْتَانِي فِيمَا اسْتَفْتَيْتُهُ فِيهِ، أَتَانِي رَجُلاَنِ فَقَعَدَ أَحَدُهُمَا عِنْدَ رَأْسِي، وَالآخَرُ عِنْدَ رِجْلَىَّ، فَقَالَ الَّذِي عِنْدَ رَأْسِي لِلآخَرِ مَا بَالُ الرَّجُلِ قَالَ مَطْبُوبٌ. قَالَ وَمَنْ طَبَّهُ قَالَ لَبِيدُ بْنُ أَعْصَمَ، رَجُلٌ مِنْ بَنِي زُرَيْقٍ حَلِيفٌ لِيَهُودَ، كَانَ مُنَافِقًا. قَالَ وَفِيمَ قَالَ فِي مُشْطٍ وَمُشَاقَةٍ. قَالَ وَأَيْنَ قَالَ فِي جُفِّ طَلْعَةٍ ذَكَرٍ، تَحْتَ رَعُوفَةٍ، فِي بِئْرِ ذَرْوَانَ ". قَالَتْ فَأَتَى النَّبِيُّ صلى الله عليه وسلم الْبِئْرَ حَتَّى اسْتَخْرَجَهُ فَقَالَ " هَذِهِ الْبِئْرُ الَّتِي أُرِيتُهَا، وَكَأَنَّ مَاءَهَا نُقَاعَةُ الْحِنَّاءِ، وَكَأَنَّ نَخْلَهَا رُءُوسُ الشَّيَاطِينِ ". قَالَ فَاسْتُخْرِجَ، قَالَتْ فَقُلْتُ أَفَلاَ أَىْ تَنَشَّرْتَ. فَقَالَ " أَمَا وَاللَّهِ فَقَدْ شَفَانِي، وَأَكْرَهُ أَنْ أُثِيرَ عَلَى أَحَدٍ مِنَ النَّاسِ شَرًّا ".

Narrated `Aisha: (the wife of the Prophet) The wife of Rifa`a Al-Qurazi came to Allah's Messenger ﷺ while I was sitting, and Abu Bakr was also there. She said, 'O Allah s Apostle! I was the wife of Rifa`a and he divorced me irrevocably. Then I married `AbdurRahman bin Az-Zubair who, by Allah, O Allah's Messenger ﷺ, has only something like a fringe of a garment, Showing the fringe of her veil. Khalid bin Sa`id, who was standing at the door, for he had not been admitted, heard her statement and said, "O Abu Bakr! Why do you not stop this lady from saying such things openly before Allah's Messenger ﷺ?" No, by Allah, Allah's Messenger did nothing but smiled. Then he said to the lady, "Perhaps you want to return to Rifa`a? That is impossible unless `Abdur-Rahman consummates his marriage with you." That became the tradition after him. – Sahih Al-Bukhari 5792

حَدَّثَنَا أَبُو الْيَمَانِ، أَخْبَرَنَا شُعَيْبٌ، عَنِ الزُّهْرِيِّ، أَخْبَرَنِي عُرْوَةُ بْنُ الزُّبَيْرِ، أَنَّ عَائِشَةَ ـ رضى الله عنها ـ زَوْجَ النَّبِيِّ صلى الله عليه وسلم قَالَتْ جَاءَتِ امْرَأَةُ رِفَاعَةَ الْقُرَظِيِّ رَسُولَ اللَّهِ صلى الله عليه وسلم وَأَنَا جَالِسَةٌ وَعِنْدَهُ أَبُو بَكْرٍ فَقَالَتْ يَا رَسُولَ اللَّهِ إِنِّي كُنْتُ تَحْتَ رِفَاعَةَ فَطَلَّقَنِي فَبَتَّ طَلاَقِي، فَتَزَوَّجْتُ بَعْدَهُ عَبْدَ الرَّحْمَنِ بْنَ الزَّبِيرِ، وَإِنَّهُ وَاللَّهِ مَا مَعَهُ يَا رَسُولَ اللَّهِ إِلاَّ مِثْلُ هَذِهِ الْهُدْبَةِ. وَأَخَذَتْ هُدْبَةً مِنْ جِلْبَابِهَا، فَسَمِعَ خَالِدُ بْنُ سَعِيدٍ قَوْلَهَا وَهْوَ بِالْبَابِ لَمْ يُؤْذَنْ لَهُ، قَالَتْ فَقَالَ خَالِدٌ يَا أَبَا بَكْرٍ أَلاَ تَنْهَى هَذِهِ عَمَّا تَجْهَرُ بِهِ عِنْدَ رَسُولِ اللَّهِ صلى الله عليه وسلم فَلاَ وَاللَّهِ مَا يَزِيدُ رَسُولُ اللَّهِ صلى الله عليه وسلم عَلَى التَّبَسُّمِ، فَقَالَ لَهَا رَسُولُ اللَّهِ صلى الله عليه وسلم " لَعَلَّكِ تُرِيدِينَ أَنْ تَرْجِعِي إِلَى رِفَاعَةَ، لاَ، حَتَّى يَذُوقَ عُسَيْلَتَكِ وَتَذُوقِي عُسَيْلَتَهُ ". فَصَارَ سُنَّةً بَعْدُ

Narrated Abu Maryam `Abdullah bin Ziyad Al-Aasadi: When Talha, AzZubair and `Aisha moved to Basra, `Ali sent `Ammar bin Yasir and Hasan bin `Ali who came to us at Kufa and ascended the pulpit. Al-Hasan bin `Ali was at the top of the pulpit and `Ammar was below Al-Hasan. We all gathered before him. I heard `Ammar saying, "`Aisha has moved to Al-Busra. By Allah! She is the wife of your Prophet in this world and in the Hereafter. But Allah has put you to test whether you obey Him (Allah) or her (`Aisha). – Sahih Al-Bukhari 7100

حَدَّثَنَا عَبْدُ اللَّهِ بْنُ مُحَمَّدٍ، حَدَّثَنَا يَحْيَى بْنُ آدَمَ، حَدَّثَنَا أَبُو بَكْرِ بْنُ عَيَّاشٍ، حَدَّثَنَا أَبُو حَصِينٍ، حَدَّثَنَا أَبُو مَرْيَمَ عَبْدُ اللَّهِ بْنُ زِيَادٍ الأَسَدِيُّ، قَالَ لَمَّا سَارَ طَلْحَةُ وَالزُّبَيْرُ وَعَائِشَةُ إِلَى الْبَصْرَةِ بَعَثَ عَلِيٌّ عَمَّارَ بْنَ يَاسِرٍ وَحَسَنَ بْنَ عَلِيٍّ، فَقَدِمَا عَلَيْنَا الْكُوفَةَ

فَصَعِدَا الْمِنْبَرَ، فَكَانَ الْحَسَنُ بْنُ عَلِيٍّ فَوْقَ الْمِنْبَرِ فِي أَعْلاَهُ، وَقَامَ عَمَّارٌ أَسْفَلَ مِنَ الْحَسَنِ، فَاجْتَمَعْنَا إِلَيْهِ فَسَمِعْتُ عَمَّارًا يَقُولُ إِنَّ عَائِشَةَ قَدْ سَارَتْ إِلَى الْبَصْرَةِ، وَوَاللَّهِ إِنَّهَا لَزَوْجَةُ نَبِيِّكُمْ صلى الله عليه وسلم فِي الدُّنْيَا وَالآخِرَةِ، وَلَكِنَّ اللَّهَ تَبَارَكَ وَتَعَالَى ابْتَلاَكُمْ، لِيَعْلَمَ إِيَّاهُ تُطِيعُونَ أَمْ هِيَ

Narrated Masruq: We went to `Aisha while Hassan bin Thabit was with her reciting poetry to her from some of his poetic verses, saying "A chaste wise lady about whom nobody can have suspicion. She gets up with an empty stomach because she never eats the flesh of indiscreet (ladies)." `Aisha said to him, "But you are not like that." I said to her, "Why do you grant him admittance, though Allah said:-- "and as for him among them, who had the greater share therein, his will be a severe torment." (24.11) On that, `Aisha said, "And what punishment is more than blinding?" She, added, "Hassan used to defend or say poetry on behalf of Allah's Messenger ﷺ (against the infidels). – Sahih Al-Bukhari 4146

حَدَّثَنِي بِشْرُ بْنُ خَالِدٍ، أَخْبَرَنَا مُحَمَّدُ بْنُ جَعْفَرٍ، عَنْ شُعْبَةَ، عَنْ سُلَيْمَانَ، عَنْ أَبِي الضُّحَى، عَنْ مَسْرُوقٍ، قَالَ دَخَلْنَا عَلَى عَائِشَةَ ـ رضى الله عنها ـ وَعِنْدَهَا حَسَّانُ بْنُ ثَابِتٍ يُنْشِدُهَا شِعْرًا، يُشَبِّبُ بِأَبْيَاتٍ لَهُ وَقَالَ:
حَصَانٌ رَزَانٌ مَا تُزَنُّ بِرِيبَةٍ وَتُصْبِحُ غَرْثَى مِنْ لُحُومِ الْغَوَافِلِ
فَقَالَتْ لَهُ عَائِشَةُ لَكِنَّكَ لَسْتَ كَذَلِكَ. قَالَ مَسْرُوقٌ فَقُلْتُ لَهَا لِمَ تَأْذَنِينَ لَهُ أَنْ يَدْخُلَ عَلَيْكِ. وَقَدْ قَالَ اللَّهُ تَعَالَى {وَالَّذِي تَوَلَّى كِبْرَهُ مِنْهُمْ لَهُ عَذَابٌ عَظِيمٌ}. فَقَالَتْ وَأَىُّ عَذَابٍ أَشَدُّ مِنَ الْعَمَى. قَالَتْ لَهُ إِنَّهُ كَانَ يُنَافِحُ ـ أَوْ يُهَاجِي ـ عَنْ رَسُولِ اللَّهِ صلى الله عليه وسلم

Narrated Hisham's father: Khaula bint Hakim was one of those ladies who presented themselves to the Prophet ﷺ for marriage. `Aisha said, "Doesn't a lady feel ashamed for presenting herself to a man?" But when the Verse: "(O Muhammad) You may postpone (the turn of) any of them (your wives) that you please,' (33.51) was revealed, " `Aisha said, 'O Allah's Messenger ﷺ! I do not see, but, that your Lord hurries in pleasing you.' ". – Sahih Al-Bukhari 5113

حَدَّثَنَا مُحَمَّدُ بْنُ سَلاَمٍ، حَدَّثَنَا ابْنُ فُضَيْلٍ، حَدَّثَنَا هِشَامٌ، عَنْ أَبِيهِ، قَالَ كَانَتْ خَوْلَةُ بِنْتُ حَكِيمٍ مِنَ اللاَّئِي وَهَبْنَ أَنْفُسَهُنَّ لِلنَّبِيِّ صلى الله عليه وسلم فَقَالَتْ عَائِشَةُ أَمَا تَسْتَحِي الْمَرْأَةُ أَنْ تَهَبَ نَفْسَهَا لِلرَّجُلِ فَلَمَّا نَزَلَتْ {تُرْجِئُ مَنْ تَشَاءُ مِنْهُنَّ} قُلْتُ يَا رَسُولَ اللَّهِ مَا أَرَى رَبَّكَ إِلاَّ يُسَارِعُ فِي هَوَاكَ. رَوَاهُ أَبُو سَعِيدٍ الْمُؤَدِّبُ وَمُحَمَّدُ بْنُ بِشْرٍ وَعَبْدَةُ عَنْ هِشَامٍ عَنْ أَبِيهِ عَنْ عَائِشَةَ يَزِيدُ بَعْضُهُمْ عَلَى بَعْضٍ.

Narrated Abu Musa Al-Ash`ari: The Prophet ﷺ said, "Many men reached perfection but none among the women reached perfection except Mary, the daughter of 'Imran, and Asia, Pharoah's wife. And the superiority of `Aisha to other women is like the superiority of Tharid to other kinds of food. – Sahih Al-Bukhari 5418

حَدَّثَنَا مُحَمَّدُ بْنُ بَشَّارٍ، حَدَّثَنَا غُنْدَرٌ، حَدَّثَنَا شُعْبَةُ، عَنْ عَمْرِو بْنِ مُرَّةَ الْجَمَلِيِّ، عَنْ مُرَّةَ الْهَمْدَانِيِّ، عَنْ أَبِي مُوسَى الأَشْعَرِيِّ، عَنِ النَّبِيِّ صلى الله عليه وسلم قَالَ كَمَلَ مِنَ الرِّجَالِ كَثِيرٌ، وَلَمْ يَكْمُلْ مِنَ النِّسَاءِ إِلاَّ مَرْيَمُ بِنْتُ عِمْرَانَ وَآسِيَةُ امْرَأَةُ فِرْعَوْنَ، وَفَضْلُ عَائِشَةَ عَلَى النِّسَاءِ كَفَضْلِ الثَّرِيدِ عَلَى سَائِرِ الطَّعَامِ "

Narrated `Abis: I asked `Aisha "Did the Prophet ﷺ forbid eating the meat of sacrifices offered on `Id-ul-Adha for more than three days" She said, "The Prophet ﷺ did not do this except in the year when the people were hungry, so he wanted the rich to feed the poor. But later we used to store even a trotter of a sheep to eat it fifteen days later." She was asked, "What compelled you to do so?" She smiled and said, "The family of Muhammad did not eat to their satisfaction white bread with meat soup for three successive days till he met Allah.". – Sahih Al-Bukhari 5423

حَدَّثَنَا خَلاَّدُ بْنُ يَحْيَى، حَدَّثَنَا سُفْيَانُ، عَنْ عَبْدِ الرَّحْمَنِ بْنِ عَابِسٍ، عَنْ أَبِيهِ، قَالَ قُلْتُ لِعَائِشَةَ أَنَهَى النَّبِيُّ صلى الله عليه وسلم أَنْ تُؤْكَلَ لُحُومُ الأَضَاحِيِّ فَوْقَ ثَلاَثٍ قَالَتْ مَا فَعَلَهُ إِلاَّ فِي عَامٍ جَاعَ النَّاسُ فِيهِ، فَأَرَادَ أَنْ يُطْعِمَ الْغَنِيُّ الْفَقِيرَ، وَإِنْ كُنَّا لَنَرْفَعُ الْكُرَاعَ فَنَأْكُلُهُ بَعْدَ خَمْسَ عَشْرَةَ. قِيلَ مَا اضْطَرَّكُمْ إِلَيْهِ فَضَحِكَتْ قَالَتْ مَا شَبِعَ آلُ مُحَمَّدٍ صلى الله عليه وسلم مِنْ خُبْزِ بُرٍّ مَأْدُومٍ ثَلاَثَةَ أَيَّامٍ حَتَّى لَحِقَ بِاللَّهِ. وَقَالَ ابْنُ كَثِيرٍ أَخْبَرَنَا سُفْيَانُ حَدَّثَنَا عَبْدُ الرَّحْمَنِ بْنُ عَابِسٍ بِهَذَا

Narrated Al-Qasim bin Muhammad: `Aisha, (complaining of headache) said, "Oh, my head"! Allah's Messenger ﷺ said, "I wish that had happened while I was still living, for then I would ask Allah's Forgiveness for you and invoke Allah for you." Aisha said, "Wa thuklayah! By Allah, I think you want me to die; and If this should happen, you would spend the last part of the day sleeping with one of your wives!" The Prophet ﷺ said, "Nay, I should say, 'Oh my head!' I felt like sending for Abu Bakr and his son, and appoint him as my successor lest some people claimed something or some others wished something, but then I said (to myself), 'Allah would not allow it to be otherwise, and the Muslims would prevent it to be otherwise". – Sahih Al-Bukhari 5666

حَدَّثَنَا يَحْيَى بْنُ يَحْيَى أَبُو زَكَرِيَّاءَ، أَخْبَرَنَا سُلَيْمَانُ بْنُ بِلاَلٍ، عَنْ يَحْيَى بْنِ سَعِيدٍ، قَالَ سَمِعْتُ الْقَاسِمَ بْنَ مُحَمَّدٍ، قَالَ قَالَتْ عَائِشَةُ وَارَأْسَاهْ. فَقَالَ رَسُولُ اللَّهِ صلى الله عليه وسلم " ذَاكِ لَوْ كَانَ وَأَنَا حَىٌّ، فَأَسْتَغْفِرُ لَكِ وَأَدْعُو لَكِ ". فَقَالَتْ عَائِشَةُ وَاثُكْلِيَاهْ، وَاللَّهِ إِنِّي لأَظُنُّكَ تُحِبُّ مَوْتِي، وَلَوْ كَانَ ذَاكَ لَظَلِلْتَ آخِرَ يَوْمِكَ مُعَرِّسًا بِبَعْضِ أَزْوَاجِكَ. فَقَالَ النَّبِيُّ صلى الله عليه وسلم " بَلْ أَنَا وَارَأْسَاهْ لَقَدْ هَمَمْتُ أَوْ أَرَدْتُ أَنْ أُرْسِلَ إِلَى أَبِي بَكْرٍ وَابْنِهِ، وَأَعْهَدَ أَنْ يَقُولَ الْقَائِلُونَ أَوْ يَتَمَنَّى الْمُتَمَنُّونَ، ثُمَّ قُلْتُ يَأْبَى اللَّهُ وَيَدْفَعُ الْمُؤْمِنُونَ، أَوْ يَدْفَعُ اللَّهُ وَيَأْبَى الْمُؤْمِنُونَ ".

Narrated Anas: Aisha had a thick curtain (having pictures on it) and she screened the side of her I house with it. The Prophet ﷺ said to her, "Remove it from my sight, for its pictures are still coming to my mind in my prayers.". – Sahih Al-Bukhari 5959

حَدَّثَنَا عِمْرَانُ بْنُ مَيْسَرَةَ، حَدَّثَنَا عَبْدُ الْوَارِثِ، حَدَّثَنَا عَبْدُ الْعَزِيزِ بْنُ صُهَيْبٍ، عَنْ أَنَسٍ ـ رضى الله عنه ـ قَالَ كَانَ قِرَامٌ لِعَائِشَةَ سَتَرَتْ بِهِ جَانِبَ بَيْتِهَا، فَقَالَ لَهَا النَّبِيُّ صلى الله عليه وسلم " أَمِيطِي عَنِّي، فَإِنَّهُ لاَ تَزَالُ تَصَاوِيرُهُ تَعْرِضُ لِي فِي صَلاَتِي ".

Narrated `Aisha: (the wife of the Prophet) I bought a cushion having pictures on it. When Allah's Messenger ﷺ saw it, he stopped at the gate and did not enter. I noticed the signs of hatred (for that) on his face! I said, "O Allah's Messenger ﷺ! I turn to Allah and His Apostle in repentance! What sin have I committed?" He said, "What about this cushion?" I said, 'I bought it for you to sit on and recline on." Allah's Messenger ﷺ said, "The makers of these pictures will be punished (severely) on the Day of Resurrection and it will be said to them, 'Make alive what you have created.'" He added, "Angels do not enter a house in which there are pictures.". – Sahih Al-Bukhari 5961

حَدَّثَنَا عَبْدُ اللَّهِ بْنُ مَسْلَمَةَ، عَنْ مَالِكٍ، عَنْ نَافِعٍ، عَنِ الْقَاسِمِ بْنِ مُحَمَّدٍ، عَنْ عَائِشَةَ ـ رضى الله عنها ـ زَوْجِ النَّبِيِّ صلى الله عليه وسلم أَنَّهَا أَخْبَرَتْهُ أَنَّهَا اشْتَرَتْ نُمْرُقَةً فِيهَا تَصَاوِيرُ، فَلَمَّا رَآهَا رَسُولُ اللَّهِ صلى الله عليه وسلم قَامَ عَلَى الْبَابِ فَلَمْ يَدْخُلْ، فَعَرَفْتُ فِي وَجْهِهِ الْكَرَاهِيَةَ قَالَتْ يَا رَسُولَ اللَّهِ أَتُوبُ إِلَى اللَّهِ وَإِلَى رَسُولِهِ، مَاذَا أَذْنَبْتُ قَالَ " مَا بَالُ هَذِهِ النُّمْرُقَةِ ". فَقَالَتِ اشْتَرَيْتُهَا لِتَقْعُدَ عَلَيْهَا وَتَوَسَّدَهَا. فَقَالَ رَسُولُ اللَّهِ صلى الله عليه وسلم " إِنَّ أَصْحَابَ هَذِهِ الصُّوَرِ يُعَذَّبُونَ يَوْمَ الْقِيَامَةِ، وَيُقَالُ لَهُمْ أَحْيُوا مَا خَلَقْتُمْ ـ وَقَالَ ـ إِنَّ الْبَيْتَ الَّذِي فِيهِ الصُّوَرُ لاَ تَدْخُلُهُ الْمَلاَئِكَةُ ".

Narrated `Aisha: Allah's Messenger ﷺ said, "The people will be gathered barefooted, naked, and uncircumcised." I said, "O Allah's Messenger ﷺ! Will the men and the women look at each other?" He said, "The situation will be too hard for them to pay attention to that.". – Sahih Al-Bukhari 6527

حَدَّثَنَا قَيْسُ بْنُ حَفْصٍ، حَدَّثَنَا خَالِدُ بْنُ الْحَارِثِ، حَدَّثَنَا حَاتِمُ بْنُ أَبِي صَغِيرَةَ، عَنْ عَبْدِ اللَّهِ بْنِ أَبِي مُلَيْكَةَ، قَالَ حَدَّثَنِي الْقَاسِمُ بْنُ مُحَمَّدِ بْنِ أَبِي بَكْرٍ، أَنَّ عَائِشَةَ ـ رضى الله عنها ـ قَالَتْ قَالَ رَسُولُ اللَّهِ صلى الله عليه وسلم " تُحْشَرُونَ حُفَاةً عُرَاةً غُرْلاً " قَالَتْ عَائِشَةُ فَقُلْتُ يَا رَسُولَ اللَّهِ الرِّجَالُ وَالنِّسَاءُ يَنْظُرُ بَعْضُهُمْ إِلَى بَعْضٍ. فَقَالَ " الأَمْرُ أَشَدُّ مِنْ أَنْ يُهِمَّهُمْ ذَاكِ "

Narrated `Aisha: (the mother of believers) Allah's Messenger ﷺ during his fatal ailment said, "Order Abu Bakr to lead the people in prayer." I said, "If Abu Bakr stood at your place (in prayers, the people will not be able to hear him because of his weeping, so order `Umar to

lead the people in prayer." He again said, "Order Abu Bakr to lead the people in prayer " Then I said to Hafsa, "Will you say (to the Prophet), 'If Abu Bakr stood at your place, the people will not be able to hear him be cause of his weeping, so order `Umar to lead the people in prayer?" Hafsa did so, whereupon Allah's Messengerﷺ said, "You are like the companions of Joseph (See Qur'an, 12:30-32). Order Abu Bakr to lead the people in prayer." Hafsa then said to me, "I have never received any good from you!". – Sahih Al-Bukhari 7303
حَدَّثَنَا إِسْمَاعِيلُ، حَدَّثَنِي مَالِكٌ، عَنْ هِشَامِ بْنِ عُرْوَةَ، عَنْ أَبِيهِ، عَنْ عَائِشَةَ أُمِّ الْمُؤْمِنِينَ، أَنَّ رَسُولَ اللَّهِ صلى الله عليه وسلم قَالَ فِي مَرَضِهِ " مُرُوا أَبَا بَكْرٍ يُصَلِّي بِالنَّاسِ ". قَالَتْ عَائِشَةُ قُلْتُ إِنَّ أَبَا بَكْرٍ إِذَا قَامَ فِي مَقَامِكَ لَمْ يُسْمِعِ النَّاسَ مِنَ الْبُكَاءِ، فَمُرْ عُمَرَ فَلْيُصَلِّ. فَقَالَ " مُرُوا أَبَا بَكْرٍ فَلْيُصَلِّ بِالنَّاسِ ". فَقَالَتْ عَائِشَةُ فَقُلْتُ لِحَفْصَةَ قُولِي إِنَّ أَبَا بَكْرٍ إِذَا قَامَ فِي مَقَامِكَ لَمْ يُسْمِعِ النَّاسَ مِنَ الْبُكَاءِ، فَمُرْ عُمَرَ فَلْيُصَلِّ بِالنَّاسِ، فَفَعَلَتْ حَفْصَةُ. فَقَالَ رَسُولُ اللَّهِ صلى الله عليه وسلم " إِنَّكُنَّ لأَنْتُنَّ صَوَاحِبُ يُوسُفَ، مُرُوا أَبَا بَكْرٍ فَلْيُصَلِّ لِلنَّاسِ ". قَالَتْ حَفْصَةُ لِعَائِشَةَ مَا كُنْتُ لأُصِيبَ مِنْكِ خَيْرًا.

Narrated `Aisha: A woman asked the Prophetﷺ about the periods: How to take a bath after the periods. He said, "Take a perfumed piece of cloth and clean yourself with it." She said,' "How shall I clean myself with it, O Allah's Messenger?" The Prophetﷺ said, "Clean yourself" She said again, "How shall I clean myself, O Allah's Messengerﷺ?" The Prophetﷺ said, "Clean yourself with it." Then I knew what Allah's Messengerﷺ meant. So I pulled her aside and explained it to her. – Sahih Al-Bukhari 7357
حَدَّثَنَا يَحْيَى، حَدَّثَنَا ابْنُ عُيَيْنَةَ، عَنْ مَنْصُورِ بْنِ صَفِيَّةَ، عَنْ أُمِّهِ، عَنْ عَائِشَةَ، أَنَّ امْرَأَةً، سَأَلَتِ النَّبِيَّ صلى الله عليه وسلم. حَدَّثَنَا مُحَمَّدٌ ـ هُوَ ابْنُ عُقْبَةَ ـ حَدَّثَنَا الْفُضَيْلُ بْنُ سُلَيْمَانَ النُّمَيْرِيُّ الْبَصْرِيُّ حَدَّثَنَا مَنْصُورُ بْنُ عَبْدِ الرَّحْمَنِ ابْنُ شَيْبَةَ حَدَّثَتْنِي أُمِّي عَنْ عَائِشَةَ ـ رضى الله عنها ـ أَنَّ امْرَأَةً سَأَلَتِ النَّبِيَّ صلى الله عليه وسلم عَنِ الْحَيْضِ كَيْفَ تَغْتَسِلُ مِنْهُ قَالَ " تَأْخُذِينَ فِرْصَةً مُمَسَّكَةً فَتَوَضَّئِينَ بِهَا ". قَالَتْ كَيْفَ أَتَوَضَّأُ بِهَا يَا رَسُولَ اللَّهِ قَالَ النَّبِيُّ صلى الله عليه وسلم " تَوَضَّئِي ". قَالَتْ كَيْفَ أَتَوَضَّأُ بِهَا يَا رَسُولَ اللَّهِ قَالَ النَّبِيُّ صلى الله عليه وسلم " تَوَضَّئِينَ بِهَا ". قَالَتْ عَائِشَةُ فَعَرَفْتُ الَّذِي يُرِيدُ رَسُولُ اللَّهِ صلى الله عليه وسلم فَجَذَبْتُهَا إِلَيَّ فَعَلَّمْتُهَا

Narrated `Aisha: We performed Hajj with the Prophetﷺ and performed Tawaf-al-ifada on the Day of Nahr (slaughtering). Safiya got her menses and the Prophets desired from her what a husband desires from his wife. I said to him, "O Allah's Messenger! She is having her menses." He said, "Is she going to detain us?" We informed him that she had performed Tawaf-al-Ifada on the Day of Nahr. He said, "(Then you can) depart.". – Sahih Al-Bukhari 1733
حَدَّثَنَا يَحْيَى بْنُ بُكَيْرٍ، حَدَّثَنَا اللَّيْثُ، عَنْ جَعْفَرِ بْنِ رَبِيعَةَ، عَنِ الأَعْرَجِ، قَالَ حَدَّثَنِي أَبُو سَلَمَةَ بْنُ عَبْدِ الرَّحْمَنِ، أَنَّ عَائِشَةَ ـ رضى الله عنها ـ قَالَتْ حَجَجْنَا مَعَ النَّبِيِّ صلى الله عليه وسلم فَأَفَضْنَا يَوْمَ النَّحْرِ، فَحَاضَتْ صَفِيَّةُ، فَأَرَادَ النَّبِيُّ صلى الله عليه وسلم مِنْهَا مَا يُرِيدُ الرَّجُلُ مِنْ أَهْلِهِ. فَقُلْتُ يَا رَسُولَ اللَّهِ إِنَّهَا حَائِضٌ. قَالَ " حَابِسَتُنَا هِيَ ". قَالُوا يَا رَسُولَ اللَّهِ، أَفَاضَتْ يَوْمَ النَّحْرِ. قَالَ " اخْرُجُوا ". وَيُذْكَرُ عَنِ الْقَاسِمِ وَعُرْوَةَ وَالأَسْوَدِ عَنْ عَائِشَةَ ـ رضى الله عنها ـ أَفَاضَتْ صَفِيَّةُ يَوْمَ النَّحْرِ

Narrated `Aisha: Allah's Messengerﷺ used to send the Hadi from Medina and I used to twist the garlands for his Hadi and he did not keep away from any of these things which a Muhrim keeps away from. – Sahih Al-Bukhari 1698
حَدَّثَنَا عَبْدُ اللَّهِ بْنُ يُوسُفَ، حَدَّثَنَا اللَّيْثُ، حَدَّثَنَا ابْنُ شِهَابٍ، عَنْ عُرْوَةَ، وَعَنْ عَمْرَةَ بِنْتِ عَبْدِ الرَّحْمَنِ، أَنَّ عَائِشَةَ ـ رضى الله عنها ـ قَالَتْ كَانَ رَسُولُ اللَّهِ صلى الله عليه وسلم يُهْدِي مِنَ الْمَدِينَةِ، فَأَفْتِلُ قَلاَئِدَ هَدْيِهِ، ثُمَّ لاَ يَجْتَنِبُ شَيْئًا مِمَّا يَجْتَنِبُهُ الْمُحْرِمُ.

Narrated `Aisha: (At times) in Ramadan the Prophetﷺ used to take a bath in the morning not because of a wet dream and would continue his fast. – Sahih Al-Bukhari 1930
حَدَّثَنَا أَحْمَدُ بْنُ صَالِحٍ، حَدَّثَنَا ابْنُ وَهْبٍ، حَدَّثَنَا يُونُسُ، عَنِ ابْنِ شِهَابٍ، عَنْ عُرْوَةَ، وَأَبِي، بَكْرٍ قَالَتْ عَائِشَةُ ـ رضى الله عنها ـ كَانَ النَّبِيُّ صلى الله عليه وسلم يُدْرِكُهُ الْفَجْرُ {جُنُبًا} فِي رَمَضَانَ، مِنْ غَيْرِ حُلُمٍ فَيَغْتَسِلُ وَيَصُومُ

Narrated Abu Bakr bin `Abdur-Rahman: My father and I went to `Aisha and she said, "I testify that Allah's Messengerﷺ at times used to get up in the morning in a state of Janaba from sexual intercourse, not from a wet dream and then he would fast that day." Then he went to Um Salama and she also narrated a similar thing. – Sahih Al-Bukhari 1931, 1932

حَدَّثَنَا إِسْمَاعِيلُ، قَالَ حَدَّثَنِي مَالِكٌ، عَنْ سُمَىٍّ، مَوْلَى أَبِي بَكْرِ بْنِ عَبْدِ الرَّحْمَنِ بْنِ الْحَارِثِ بْنِ هِشَامِ بْنِ الْمُغِيرَةِ أَنَّهُ سَمِعَ أَبَا بَكْرِ بْنَ عَبْدِ الرَّحْمَنِ، كُنْتُ أَنَا وَأَبِي،، فَذَهَبْتُ مَعَهُ، حَتَّى دَخَلْنَا عَلَى عَائِشَةَ ـ رضى الله عنها ـ قَالَتْ أَشْهَدُ عَلَى رَسُولِ اللَّهِ صلى الله عليه وسلم إِنْ كَانَ لَيُصْبِحُ جُنُبًا مِنْ جِمَاعٍ غَيْرِ احْتِلاَمٍ، ثُمَّ يَصُومُهُ.
ثُمَّ دَخَلْنَا عَلَى أُمِّ سَلَمَةَ، فَقَالَتْ مِثْلَ ذَلِكَ.

Narrated `Aishah: I used to wash the semen off the clothes of the Prophet ﷺ and even then I used to notice one or more spots on them. – Sahih Al-Bukhari 232

حَدَّثَنَا عَمْرُو بْنُ خَالِدٍ، قَالَ حَدَّثَنَا زُهَيْرٌ، قَالَ حَدَّثَنَا عَمْرُو بْنُ مَيْمُونِ بْنِ مِهْرَانَ، عَنْ سُلَيْمَانَ بْنِ يَسَارٍ، عَنْ عَائِشَةَ، أَنَّهَا كَانَتْ تَغْسِلُ الْمَنِيَّ مِنْ ثَوْبِ النَّبِيِّ صلى الله عليه وسلم، ثُمَّ أَرَاهُ فِيهِ بُقْعَةً أَوْ بُقَعًا.

Narrated 'Aisha: (the wife of the Prophet) I never remembered my parents believing in any religion other than the true religion (i.e. Islam), and (I don't remember) a single day passing without our being visited by Allah's Messenger ﷺ in the morning and in the evening. When the Muslims were put to test (i.e. troubled by the pagans), Abu Bakr set out migrating to the land of Ethiopia, and when he reached Bark-al-Ghimad, Ibn Ad-Daghina, the chief of the tribe of Qara, met him and said, "O Abu Bakr! Where are you going?" Abu Bakr replied, "My people have turned me out (of my country), so I want to wander on the earth and worship my Lord." Ibn Ad-Daghina said, "O Abu Bakr! A man like you should not leave his home-land, nor should he be driven out, because you help the destitute, earn their livings, and you keep good relations with your Kith and kin, help the weak and poor, entertain guests generously, and help the calamity-stricken persons. Therefore I am your protector. Go back and worship your Lord in your town." So Abu Bakr returned and Ibn Ad-Daghina accompanied him. In the evening Ibn Ad-Daghina visited the nobles of Quraish and said to them. "A man like Abu Bakr should not leave his homeland, nor should he be driven out. Do you (i.e. Quraish) drive out a man who helps the destitute, earns their living, keeps good relations with his Kith and kin, helps the weak and poor, entertains guests generously and helps the calamity-stricken persons?" So the people of Quraish could not refuse Ibn Ad-Daghina's protection, and they said to Ibn Ad-Daghina, "Let Abu Bakr worship his Lord in his house. He can pray and recite there whatever he likes, but he should not hurt us with it, and should not do it publicly, because we are afraid that he may affect our women and children." Ibn Ad-Daghina told Abu Bakr of all that. Abu Bakr stayed in that state, worshipping his Lord in his house. He did not pray publicly, nor did he recite Quran outside his house. Then a thought occurred to Abu Bakr to build a mosque in front of his house, and there he used to pray and recite the Quran. The women and children of the pagans began to gather around him in great number. They used to wonder at him and look at him. Abu Bakr was a man who used to weep too much, and he could not help weeping on reciting the Quran. That situation scared the nobles of the pagans of Quraish, so they sent for Ibn Ad-Daghina. When he came to them, they said, "We accepted your protection of Abu Bakr on condition that he should worship his Lord in his house, but he has violated the conditions and he has built a mosque in front of his house where he prays and recites the Quran publicly. We are now afraid that he may affect our women and children unfavorably. So, prevent him from that. If he likes to confine the worship of his Lord to his house, he may do so, but if he insists on doing that openly, ask him to release you from your obligation to protect him, for we dislike to break our pact with you, but we deny Abu Bakr the right to announce his act publicly." Ibn Ad-Daghina went to Abu- Bakr and said, ("O Abu Bakr!) You know well what contract I have made on your behalf; now, you are either to abide by it, or else release me from my obligation of protecting you, because I do not want the

'Arabs hear that my people have dishonored a contract I have made on behalf of another man." Abu Bakr replied, "I release you from your pact to protect me, and am pleased with the protection from Allah." At that time the Prophetﷺ was in Mecca, and he said to the Muslims, "In a dream I have been shown your migration place, a land of date palm trees, between two mountains, the two stony tracts." So, some people migrated to Medina, and most of those people who had previously migrated to the land of Ethiopia, returned to Medina. Abu Bakr also prepared to leave for Medina, but Allah's Messengerﷺ said to him, "Wait for a while, because I hope that I will be allowed to migrate also." Abu Bakr said, "Do you indeed expect this? Let my father be sacrificed for you!" The Prophetﷺ said, "Yes." So Abu Bakr did not migrate for the sake of Allah's Messengerﷺ in order to accompany him. He fed two she-camels he possessed with the leaves of As-Samur tree that fell on being struck by a stick for four months. One day, while we were sitting in Abu Bakr's house at noon, someone said to Abu Bakr, "This is Allah's Messengerﷺ with his head covered coming at a time at which he never used to visit us before." Abu Bakr said, "May my parents be sacrificed for him. By Allah, he has not come at this hour except for a great necessity." So Allah's Messengerﷺ came and asked permission to enter, and he was allowed to enter. When he entered, he said to Abu Bakr. "Tell everyone who is present with you to go away." Abu Bakr replied, "There are none but your family. May my father be sacrificed for you, O Allah's Messengerﷺ!" The Prophetﷺ said, "I have been given permission to migrate." Abu Bakr said, "Shall I accompany you? May my father be sacrificed for you, O Allah's Messengerﷺ!" Allah's Messengerﷺ said, "Yes." Abu Bakr said, "O Allah's Messengerﷺ! May my father be sacrificed for you, take one of these two she-camels of mine." Allah's Messengerﷺ replied, "(I will accept it) with payment." So we prepared the baggage quickly and put some journey food in a leather bag for them. Asma, Abu Bakr's daughter, cut a piece from her waist belt and tied the mouth of the leather bag with it, and for that reason she was named Dhat-un-Nitaqain (i.e. the owner of two belts). Then Allah's Messengerﷺ and Abu Bakr reached a cave on the mountain of Thaur and stayed there for three nights. 'Abdullah bin Abi Bakr who was intelligent and a sagacious youth, used to stay (with them) aver night. He used to leave them before day break so that in the morning he would be with Quraish as if he had spent the night in Mecca. He would keep in mind any plot made against them, and when it became dark he would (go and) inform them of it. 'Amir bin Fuhaira, the freed slave of Abu Bakr, used to bring the milch sheep (of his master, Abu Bakr) to them a little while after nightfall in order to rest the sheep there. So they always had fresh milk at night, the milk of their sheep, and the milk which they warmed by throwing heated stones in it. 'Amir bin Fuhaira would then call the herd away when it was still dark (before daybreak). He did the same in each of those three nights. Allah's Messengerﷺ and Abu Bakr had hired a man from the tribe of Bani Ad-Dail from the family of Bani Abd bin Adi as an expert guide, and he was in alliance with the family of Al-'As bin Wail As-Sahmi and he was on the religion of the infidels of Quraish. The Prophetﷺ and Abu Bakr trusted him and gave him their two she-camels and took his promise to bring their two she camels to the cave of the mountain of Thaur in the morning after three nights later. And (when they set out), 'Amir bin Fuhaira and the guide went along with them and the guide led them along the sea-shore. – Sahih Al-Bukhari 3905

حَدَّثَنَا يَحْيَى بْنُ بُكَيْرٍ، حَدَّثَنَا اللَّيْثُ، عَنْ عُقَيْلٍ، قَالَ ابْنُ شِهَابٍ فَأَخْبَرَنِي عُرْوَةُ بْنُ الزُّبَيْرِ، أَنَّ عَائِشَةَ ـ رضى الله عنها ـ زَوْجَ النَّبِيِّ صلى الله عليه وسلم قَالَتْ لَمْ أَعْقِلْ أَبَوَىَّ قَطُّ إِلاَّ وَهُمَا يَدِينَانِ الدِّينَ، وَلَمْ يَمُرَّ عَلَيْنَا يَوْمٌ إِلاَّ يَأْتِينَا فِيهِ رَسُولُ اللَّهِ صلى الله عليه وسلم طَرَفَىِ النَّهَارِ بُكْرَةً وَعَشِيَّةً، فَلَمَّا ابْتُلِيَ الْمُسْلِمُونَ خَرَجَ أَبُو بَكْرٍ مُهَاجِرًا نَحْوَ أَرْضِ الْحَبَشَةِ، حَتَّى بَلَغَ بَرْكَ الْغِمَادِ لَقِيَهُ ابْنُ الدَّغِنَةِ وَهْوَ سَيِّدُ الْقَارَةِ. فَقَالَ أَيْنَ تُرِيدُ يَا أَبَا بَكْرٍ فَقَالَ أَبُو بَكْرٍ أَخْرَجَنِي قَوْمِي، فَأُرِيدُ أَنْ أَسِيحَ فِي الأَرْضِ وَأَعْبُدَ رَبِّي. قَالَ ابْنُ الدَّغِنَةِ فَإِنَّ مِثْلَكَ يَا أَبَا بَكْرٍ لاَ يَخْرُجُ وَلاَ يُخْرَجُ، إِنَّكَ تَكْسِبُ الْمَعْدُومَ، وَتَصِلُ الرَّحِمَ وَتَحْمِلُ الْكَلَّ، وَتَقْرِي الضَّيْفَ، وَتُعِينُ عَلَى نَوَائِبِ الْحَقِّ، فَأَنَا لَكَ جَارٌ، ارْجِعْ وَاعْبُدْ رَبَّكَ بِبَلَدِكَ. فَرَجَعَ وَارْتَحَلَ مَعَهُ ابْنُ الدَّغِنَةِ، فَطَافَ ابْنُ الدَّغِنَةِ عَشِيَّةً فِي أَشْرَافِ قُرَيْشٍ، فَقَالَ لَهُمْ إِنَّ أَبَا بَكْرٍ لاَ يَخْرُجُ

مِثْلُهُ وَلاَ يُخْرَجُ، أَتُخْرِجُونَ رَجُلاً يَكْسِبُ الْمَعْدُومَ، وَيَصِلُ الرَّحِمَ، وَيَحْمِلُ الْكَلَّ، وَيَقْرِي الضَّيْفَ، وَيُعِينُ عَلَى نَوَائِبِ الْحَقِّ فَلَمْ تُكَذِّبْ قُرَيْشٌ بِجِوَارِ ابْنِ الدَّغِنَةِ، وَقَالُوا لاِبْنِ الدَّغِنَةِ مُرْ أَبَا بَكْرٍ فَلْيَعْبُدْ رَبَّهُ فِي دَارِهِ، فَلْيُصَلِّ فِيهَا وَلْيَقْرَأْ مَا شَاءَ، وَلاَ يُؤْذِينَا بِذَلِكَ، وَلاَ يَسْتَعْلِنْ بِهِ، فَإِنَّا نَخْشَى أَنْ يَفْتِنَ نِسَاءَنَا وَأَبْنَاءَنَا. فَقَالَ ذَلِكَ ابْنُ الدَّغِنَةِ لأَبِي بَكْرٍ، فَلَبِثَ أَبُو بَكْرٍ بِذَلِكَ يَعْبُدُ رَبَّهُ فِي دَارِهِ، وَلاَ يَسْتَعْلِنُ بِصَلاَتِهِ، وَلاَ يَقْرَأُ فِي غَيْرِ دَارِهِ، ثُمَّ بَدَا لأَبِي بَكْرٍ فَابْتَنَى مَسْجِدًا بِفِنَاءِ دَارِهِ وَكَانَ يُصَلِّي فِيهِ وَيَقْرَأُ الْقُرْآنَ، فَيَنْقَذِفُ عَلَيْهِ نِسَاءُ الْمُشْرِكِينَ وَأَبْنَاؤُهُمْ، وَهُمْ يَعْجَبُونَ مِنْهُ، وَيَنْظُرُونَ إِلَيْهِ، وَكَانَ أَبُو بَكْرٍ رَجُلاً بَكَّاءً، لاَ يَمْلِكُ عَيْنَيْهِ إِذَا قَرَأَ الْقُرْآنَ، وَأَفْزَعَ ذَلِكَ أَشْرَافَ قُرَيْشٍ مِنَ الْمُشْرِكِينَ، فَأَرْسَلُوا إِلَى ابْنِ الدَّغِنَةِ، فَقَدِمَ عَلَيْهِمْ. فَقَالُوا إِنَّا كُنَّا أَجَرْنَا أَبَا بَكْرٍ بِجِوَارِكَ، عَلَى أَنْ يَعْبُدَ رَبَّهُ فِي دَارِهِ، فَقَدْ جَاوَزَ ذَلِكَ، فَابْتَنَى مَسْجِدًا بِفِنَاءِ دَارِهِ، فَأَعْلَنَ بِالصَّلاَةِ وَالْقِرَاءَةِ فِيهِ، وَإِنَّا قَدْ خَشِينَا أَنْ يَفْتِنَ نِسَاءَنَا وَأَبْنَاءَنَا فَانْهَهُ، فَإِنْ أَحَبَّ أَنْ يَقْتَصِرَ عَلَى أَنْ يَعْبُدَ رَبَّهُ فِي دَارِهِ فَعَلَ، وَإِنْ أَبَى إِلاَّ أَنْ يُعْلِنَ بِذَلِكَ فَسَلْهُ أَنْ يَرُدَّ إِلَيْكَ ذِمَّتَكَ، فَإِنَّا قَدْ كَرِهْنَا أَنْ نُخْفِرَكَ، وَلَسْنَا مُقِرِّينَ لأَبِي بَكْرٍ الاِسْتِعْلاَنَ. قَالَتْ عَائِشَةُ فَأَتَى ابْنُ الدَّغِنَةِ إِلَى أَبِي بَكْرٍ فَقَالَ قَدْ عَلِمْتَ الَّذِي عَاقَدْتُ لَكَ عَلَيْهِ، فَإِمَّا أَنْ تَقْتَصِرَ عَلَى ذَلِكَ، وَإِمَّا أَنْ تَرْجِعَ إِلَىَّ ذِمَّتِي، فَإِنِّي لاَ أُحِبُّ أَنْ تَسْمَعَ الْعَرَبُ أَنِّي أُخْفِرْتُ فِي رَجُلٍ عَقَدْتُ لَهُ. فَقَالَ أَبُو بَكْرٍ فَإِنِّي أَرُدُّ إِلَيْكَ جِوَارَكَ وَأَرْضَى بِجِوَارِ اللَّهِ عَزَّ وَجَلَّ. وَالنَّبِيُّ صلى الله عليه وسلم يَوْمَئِذٍ بِمَكَّةَ، فَقَالَ النَّبِيُّ صلى الله عليه وسلم لِلْمُسْلِمِينَ " إِنِّي أُرِيتُ دَارَ هِجْرَتِكُمْ ذَاتَ نَخْلٍ بَيْنَ لاَبَتَيْنِ ". وَهُمَا الْحَرَّتَانِ، فَهَاجَرَ مَنْ هَاجَرَ قِبَلَ الْمَدِينَةِ، وَرَجَعَ عَامَّةُ مَنْ كَانَ هَاجَرَ بِأَرْضِ الْحَبَشَةِ إِلَى الْمَدِينَةِ، وَتَجَهَّزَ أَبُو بَكْرٍ قِبَلَ الْمَدِينَةِ، فَقَالَ لَهُ رَسُولُ اللَّهِ صلى الله عليه وسلم " عَلَى رِسْلِكَ، فَإِنِّي أَرْجُو أَنْ يُؤْذَنَ لِي ". فَقَالَ أَبُو بَكْرٍ وَهَلْ تَرْجُو ذَلِكَ بِأَبِي أَنْتَ قَالَ " نَعَمْ ". فَحَبَسَ أَبُو بَكْرٍ نَفْسَهُ عَلَى رَسُولِ اللَّهِ صلى الله عليه وسلم لِيَصْحَبَهُ، وَعَلَفَ رَاحِلَتَيْنِ كَانَتَا عِنْدَهُ وَرَقَ السَّمُرِ وَهْوَ الْخَبَطُ أَرْبَعَةَ أَشْهُرٍ. قَالَ ابْنُ شِهَابٍ قَالَ عُرْوَةُ قَالَتْ عَائِشَةُ فَبَيْنَمَا نَحْنُ يَوْمًا جُلُوسٌ فِي بَيْتِ أَبِي بَكْرٍ فِي نَحْرِ الظَّهِيرَةِ قَالَ قَائِلٌ لأَبِي بَكْرٍ هَذَا رَسُولُ اللَّهِ صلى الله عليه وسلم مُتَقَنِّعًا ـ فِي سَاعَةٍ لَمْ يَكُنْ يَأْتِينَا فِيهَا ـ فَقَالَ أَبُو بَكْرٍ فِدَاءٌ لَهُ أَبِي وَأُمِّي، وَاللَّهِ مَا جَاءَ بِهِ فِي هَذِهِ السَّاعَةِ إِلاَّ أَمْرٌ. قَالَتْ فَجَاءَ رَسُولُ اللَّهِ صلى الله عليه وسلم فَاسْتَأْذَنَ، فَأُذِنَ لَهُ فَدَخَلَ، فَقَالَ النَّبِيُّ صلى الله عليه وسلم لأَبِي بَكْرٍ " أَخْرِجْ مَنْ عِنْدَكَ ". فَقَالَ أَبُو بَكْرٍ إِنَّمَا هُمْ أَهْلُكَ بِأَبِي أَنْتَ يَا رَسُولَ اللَّهِ. قَالَ " فَإِنِّي قَدْ أُذِنَ لِي فِي الْخُرُوجِ ". فَقَالَ أَبُو بَكْرٍ الصَّحَابَةُ بِأَبِي أَنْتَ يَا رَسُولَ اللَّهِ. قَالَ رَسُولُ اللَّهِ صلى الله عليه وسلم " نَعَمْ ". قَالَ أَبُو بَكْرٍ فَخُذْ بِأَبِي أَنْتَ يَا رَسُولَ اللَّهِ إِحْدَى رَاحِلَتَىَّ هَاتَيْنِ. قَالَ رَسُولُ اللَّهِ صلى الله عليه وسلم " بِالثَّمَنِ ". قَالَتْ عَائِشَةُ فَجَهَّزْنَاهُمَا أَحَثَّ الْجِهَازِ، وَصَنَعْنَا لَهُمَا سُفْرَةً فِي جِرَابٍ، فَقَطَعَتْ أَسْمَاءُ بِنْتُ أَبِي بَكْرٍ قِطْعَةً مِنْ نِطَاقِهَا فَرَبَطَتْ بِهِ عَلَى فَمِ الْجِرَابِ، فَبِذَلِكَ سُمِّيَتْ ذَاتَ النِّطَاقِ ـ قَالَتْ ـ ثُمَّ لَحِقَ رَسُولُ اللَّهِ صلى الله عليه وسلم وَأَبُو بَكْرٍ بِغَارٍ فِي جَبَلِ ثَوْرٍ فَكَمَنَا فِيهِ ثَلاَثَ لَيَالٍ، يَبِيتُ عِنْدَهُمَا عَبْدُ اللَّهِ بْنُ أَبِي بَكْرٍ وَهْوَ غُلاَمٌ شَابٌّ ثَقِفٌ لَقِنٌ، فَيُدْلِجُ مِنْ عِنْدِهِمَا بِسَحَرٍ، فَيُصْبِحُ مَعَ قُرَيْشٍ بِمَكَّةَ كَبَائِتٍ، فَلاَ يَسْمَعُ أَمْرًا يُكْتَادَانِ بِهِ إِلاَّ وَعَاهُ، حَتَّى يَأْتِيَهُمَا بِخَبَرِ ذَلِكَ حِينَ يَخْتَلِطُ الظَّلاَمُ، وَيَرْعَى عَلَيْهِمَا عَامِرُ بْنُ فُهَيْرَةَ مَوْلَى أَبِي بَكْرٍ مِنْحَةً مِنْ غَنَمٍ، فَيُرِيحُهَا عَلَيْهِمَا حِينَ يَذْهَبُ سَاعَةٌ مِنَ الْعِشَاءِ، فَيَبِيتَانِ فِي رِسْلٍ وَهْوَ لَبَنُ مِنْحَتِهِمَا وَرَضِيفِهِمَا، حَتَّى يَنْعِقَ بِهَا عَامِرُ بْنُ فُهَيْرَةَ بِغَلَسٍ، يَفْعَلُ ذَلِكَ فِي كُلِّ لَيْلَةٍ مِنْ تِلْكَ اللَّيَالِي الثَّلاَثِ، وَاسْتَأْجَرَ رَسُولُ اللَّهِ صلى الله عليه وسلم وَأَبُو بَكْرٍ رَجُلاً مِنْ بَنِي الدِّيلِ، وَهْوَ مِنْ بَنِي عَبْدِ بْنِ عَدِيٍّ هَادِيًا خِرِّيتًا ـ وَالْخِرِّيتُ الْمَاهِرُ بِالْهِدَايَةِ ـ قَدْ غَمَسَ حِلْفًا فِي آلِ الْعَاصِ بْنِ وَائِلٍ السَّهْمِيِّ، وَهْوَ عَلَى دِينِ كُفَّارِ قُرَيْشٍ فَأَمِنَاهُ، فَدَفَعَا إِلَيْهِ رَاحِلَتَيْهِمَا، وَوَاعَدَاهُ غَارَ ثَوْرٍ بَعْدَ ثَلاَثِ لَيَالٍ بِرَاحِلَتَيْهِمَا صُبْحَ ثَلاَثٍ، وَانْطَلَقَ مَعَهُمَا عَامِرُ بْنُ فُهَيْرَةَ وَالدَّلِيلُ فَأَخَذَ بِهِمْ طَرِيقَ السَّوَاحِلِ

Narrated Abu Wail: When `Ali sent `Ammar and Al-Hasan to (the people of) Kufa to urge them to fight, `Ammar addressed them saying, “I know that she (i.e. `Aisha) is the wife of the Prophetﷺ in this world and in the Hereafter (world to come), but Allah has put you to test, whether you will follow Him (i.e. Allah) or her.”. – Sahih Al-Bukhari 3772

حَدَّثَنَا مُحَمَّدُ بْنُ بَشَّارٍ، حَدَّثَنَا غُنْدَرٌ، حَدَّثَنَا شُعْبَةُ، عَنِ الْحَكَمِ، سَمِعْتُ أَبَا وَائِلٍ، قَالَ لَمَّا بَعَثَ عَلِيٌّ عَمَّارًا وَالْحَسَنَ إِلَى الْكُوفَةِ لِيَسْتَنْفِرَهُمْ خَطَبَ عَمَّارٌ فَقَالَ إِنِّي لأَعْلَمُ أَنَّهَا زَوْجَتُهُ فِي الدُّنْيَا وَالآخِرَةِ، وَلَكِنَّ اللَّهَ ابْتَلاَكُمْ لِتَتَّبِعُوهُ أَوْ إِيَّاهَا

Narrated `Aisha: I did not feel jealous of any of the wives of the Prophetﷺ as much as I did of Khadija though I did not see her, but the Prophetﷺ used to mention her very often, and when ever he slaughtered a sheep, he would cut its parts and send them to the women friends of Khadija. When I sometimes said to him, “(You treat Khadija in such a way) as if there is no woman on earth except Khadija,” he would say, “Khadija was such-and-such, and from her I had children.”. – Sahih Al-Bukhari 3818

حَدَّثَنِي عُمَرُ بْنُ مُحَمَّدِ بْنِ حَسَنٍ، حَدَّثَنَا أَبِي، حَدَّثَنَا حَفْصٌ، عَنْ هِشَامٍ، عَنْ أَبِيهِ، عَنْ عَائِشَةَ ـ رضى الله عنها ـ قَالَتْ مَا غِرْتُ عَلَى أَحَدٍ مِنْ نِسَاءِ النَّبِيِّ صلى الله عليه وسلم مَا غِرْتُ عَلَى خَدِيجَةَ، وَمَا رَأَيْتُهَا، وَلَكِنْ كَانَ النَّبِيُّ صلى الله عليه وسلم يُكْثِرُ ذِكْرَهَا، وَرُبَّمَا ذَبَحَ الشَّاةَ، ثُمَّ يُقَطِّعُهَا أَعْضَاءً، ثُمَّ يَبْعَثُهَا فِي صَدَائِقِ خَدِيجَةَ، فَرُبَّمَا قُلْتُ لَهُ كَأَنَّهُ لَمْ يَكُنْ فِي الدُّنْيَا امْرَأَةٌ إِلاَّ خَدِيجَةُ. فَيَقُولُ إِنَّهَا كَانَتْ وَكَانَتْ، وَكَانَ لِي مِنْهَا وَلَدٌ.

Narrated `Aisha: That the Prophetﷺ married her when she was six years old and he consummated his marriage when she was nine years old. Hisham said: I have been informed that `Aisha remained with the Prophetﷺ for nine years (i.e. till his death). – Al-Bukhari 5134

حَدَّثَنَا مُعَلَّى بْنُ أَسَدٍ، حَدَّثَنَا وُهَيْبٌ، عَنْ هِشَامِ بْنِ عُرْوَةَ، عَنْ أَبِيهِ، عَنْ عَائِشَةَ، أَنَّ النَّبِيَّ صلى الله عليه وسلم تَزَوَّجَهَا وَهْىَ بِنْتُ سِتِّ سِنِينَ، وَبَنَى بِهَا وَهْىَ بِنْتُ تِسْعِ سِنِينَ. قَالَ هِشَامٌ وَأُنْبِئْتُ أَنَّهَا كَانَتْ عِنْدَهُ تِسْعَ سِنِينَ.

Narrated al-Qasim: Aisha said that whenever the Prophetﷺ intended to go on a journey, he drew lots among his wives (so as to take one of them along with him). During one of his journeys the lot fell on `Aisha and Hafsa. When night fell the Prophetﷺ would ride beside `Aisha and talk with her. One night Hafsa said to `Aisha, "Won't you ride my camel tonight and I ride yours, so that you may see (me) and I see (you) (in new situation)?" `Aisha said, "Yes, (I agree.)" So `Aisha rode, and then the Prophetﷺ came towards `Aisha's camel on which Hafsa was riding. He greeted Hafsa and then proceeded (beside her) till they dismounted (on the way). `Aisha missed him, and so, when they dismounted, she put her legs in the Idhkhir and said, "O Lord (Allah)! Send a scorpion or a snake to bite me for I am not to blame him (the Prophet. – Sahih Al-Bukhari 5211

حَدَّثَنَا أَبُو نُعَيْمٍ، حَدَّثَنَا عَبْدُ الْوَاحِدِ بْنُ أَيْمَنَ، قَالَ حَدَّثَنِي ابْنُ أَبِي مُلَيْكَةَ، عَنِ الْقَاسِمِ، عَنْ عَائِشَةَ، أَنَّ النَّبِيَّ صلى الله عليه وسلم كَانَ إِذَا خَرَجَ أَقْرَعَ بَيْنَ نِسَائِهِ، فَطَارَتِ الْقُرْعَةُ لِعَائِشَةَ وَحَفْصَةَ، وَكَانَ النَّبِيُّ صلى الله عليه وسلم إِذَا كَانَ بِاللَّيْلِ سَارَ مَعَ عَائِشَةَ يَتَحَدَّثُ، فَقَالَتْ حَفْصَةُ أَلاَ تَرْكَبِينَ اللَّيْلَةَ بَعِيرِي وَأَرْكَبُ بَعِيرَكِ تَنْظُرِينَ وَأَنْظُرُ، فَقَالَتْ بَلَى فَرَكِبَتْ فَجَاءَ النَّبِيُّ صلى الله عليه وسلم إِلَى جَمَلِ عَائِشَةَ وَعَلَيْهِ حَفْصَةُ فَسَلَّمَ عَلَيْهَا ثُمَّ سَارَ حَتَّى نَزَلُوا وَافْتَقَدَتْهُ عَائِشَةُ، فَلَمَّا نَزَلُوا جَعَلَتْ رِجْلَيْهَا بَيْنَ الإِذْخِرِ وَتَقُولُ يَا رَبِّ سَلِّطْ عَلَىَّ عَقْرَبًا أَوْ حَيَّةً تَلْدَغُنِي، وَلاَ أَسْتَطِيعُ أَنْ أَقُولَ لَهُ شَيْئًا

('Aishah, was led in the Salāt (prayer) by her slave Dhakwan who used to recite from the Mushaf [the written Qur'an (not from memory)]. Can an illegitimate boy A bedouin or a boy who has not reached the age of puberty lead the Şalāt? (It is Permissible according to) the statement of The Prophet , that the Imắm should be a Person who knows the Qur`an more than the Others. – Al-Bukhari Vol.1 Pg 395

و كانت عائشة يومها عبدها ذكوان من المصحف ، وولد البغي والاعرابي والغلام الذي لم يحتلم لقول النبي : "يومهم اقروهم لكتاب الله" ، و لا يمنع العبر من الجماعة بغير علة .

Narrated `Amra bint `Abdur-Rahman from `Aisha: Allah's Messengerﷺ mentioned that he would practice I`tikaf in the last ten days of Ramadan. `Aisha asked his permission to perform I`tikaf and he permitted her. Hafsa asked `Aisha to take his permission for her, and she did so. When Zainab bint Jahsh saw that, she ordered a tent to be pitched for her and it was pitched for her. Allah's Messengerﷺ used to proceed to his tent after the prayer. So, he saw the tents ans asked, "What is this?" He was told that those were the tents of Aisha, Hafsa, and Zainab. Allah's Apostle said, "Is it righteousness which they intended by doing so? I am not going to perform I`tikaf." So he returned home. When the fasting month was over, he performed Itikar for ten days in the month of Shawwal. – Sahih al-Bukhari 2045

حَدَّثَنَا مُحَمَّدُ بْنُ مُقَاتِلٍ أَبُو الْحَسَنِ، أَخْبَرَنَا عَبْدُ اللَّهِ، أَخْبَرَنَا الأَوْزَاعِيُّ، قَالَ حَدَّثَنِي يَحْيَى بْنُ سَعِيدٍ، قَالَ حَدَّثَتْنِي عَمْرَةُ بِنْتُ عَبْدِ الرَّحْمَنِ، عَنْ عَائِشَةَ ـ رضى الله عنها ـ أَنَّ رَسُولَ اللَّهِ صلى الله عليه وسلم ذَكَرَ أَنْ يَعْتَكِفَ الْعَشْرَ الأَوَاخِرَ مِنْ رَمَضَانَ، فَاسْتَأْذَنَتْهُ عَائِشَةُ فَأَذِنَ لَهَا، وَسَأَلَتْ حَفْصَةُ عَائِشَةَ أَنْ تَسْتَأْذِنَ لَهَا فَفَعَلَتْ فَلَمَّا رَأَتْ ذَلِكَ زَيْنَبُ ابْنَةُ جَحْشٍ أَمَرَتْ بِبِنَاءٍ فَبُنِيَ لَهَا قَالَتْ وَكَانَ رَسُولُ اللَّهِ صلى الله عليه وسلم إِذَا صَلَّى انْصَرَفَ إِلَى بِنَائِهِ فَبَصُرَ بِالأَبْنِيَةِ فَقَالَ " مَا هَذَا ". قَالُوا بِنَاءُ عَائِشَةَ وَحَفْصَةَ وَزَيْنَبَ. فَقَالَ رَسُولُ اللَّهِ صلى الله عليه وسلم " آلْبِرَّ أَرَدْنَ بِهَذَا مَا أَنَا بِمُعْتَكِفٍ ". فَرَجَعَ، فَلَمَّا أَفْطَرَ اعْتَكَفَ عَشْرًا مِنْ شَوَّالٍ

Narrated 'Aishia .

on one of his journeys (ﷺ) (the wife of the Prophet) We set out with Allah's Messenger .till we reached Al- Baida' or Dhatul-Jaish, a necklace of mine was broken (and lost) stayed there to search for it, and so did the people along with (ﷺ) Allah's Messenger him. There was no water at that place, so the people went to Abu- Bakr As-Siddiq and said, "Don't you see what `Aisha has done? She has made Allah's Apostle and the people stay where there is no water and they have no water with them." Abu Bakr ,was sleeping with his head on my thigh, He said (ﷺ) came while Allah's Messenger to me: "You have detained Allah's Messenger(ﷺ) and the people where there is no water and they have no water with them. So he admonished me and said what Allah wished him to say and hit me on my flank with his hand. Nothing prevented me from .on my thigh (ﷺ) moving (because of pain) but the position of Allah's Messenger got up when dawn broke and there was no water. So Allah (ﷺ) Allah's Messenger revealed the Divine Verses of Tayammum. So they all performed Tayammum. Usaid ".bin Hudair said, "O the family of Abu Bakr! This is not the first blessing of yours Then the camel on which I was riding was caused to move from its place and the necklace was found beneath

Sahih al-Bukhari 334

حَدَّثَنَا عَبْدُ اللَّهِ بْنُ يُوسُفَ، قَالَ أَخْبَرَنَا مَالِكٌ، عَنْ عَبْدِ الرَّحْمَنِ بْنِ الْقَاسِمِ، عَنْ أَبِيهِ، عَنْ عَائِشَةَ، زَوْجِ النَّبِيِّ صلى الله عليه وسلم قَالَتْ خَرَجْنَا مَعَ رَسُولِ اللَّهِ صلى الله عليه وسلم فِي بَعْضِ أَسْفَارِهِ، حَتَّى إِذَا كُنَّا بِالْبَيْدَاءِ ـ أَوْ بِذَاتِ الْجَيْشِ ـ انْقَطَعَ عِقْدٌ لِي، فَأَقَامَ رَسُولُ اللَّهِ صلى الله عليه وسلم عَلَى الْتِمَاسِهِ، وَأَقَامَ النَّاسُ مَعَهُ، وَلَيْسُوا عَلَى مَاءٍ، فَأَتَى النَّاسُ إِلَى أَبِي بَكْرٍ الصِّدِّيقِ فَقَالُوا أَلاَ تَرَى مَا صَنَعَتْ عَائِشَةُ أَقَامَتْ بِرَسُولِ اللَّهِ صلى الله عليه وسلم وَالنَّاسِ، وَلَيْسُوا عَلَى مَاءٍ، وَلَيْسَ مَعَهُمْ مَاءٌ. فَجَاءَ أَبُو بَكْرٍ وَرَسُولُ اللَّهِ صلى الله عليه وسلم وَاضِعٌ رَأْسَهُ عَلَى فَخِذِي قَدْ نَامَ فَقَالَ حَبَسْتِ رَسُولَ اللَّهِ صلى الله عليه وسلم وَالنَّاسَ، وَلَيْسُوا عَلَى مَاءٍ، وَلَيْسَ مَعَهُمْ مَاءٌ. فَقَالَتْ عَائِشَةُ فَعَاتَبَنِي أَبُو بَكْرٍ، وَقَالَ مَا شَاءَ اللَّهُ أَنْ يَقُولَ، وَجَعَلَ يَطْعُنُنِي بِيَدِهِ فِي خَاصِرَتِي، فَلاَ يَمْنَعُنِي مِنَ التَّحَرُّكِ إِلاَّ مَكَانُ رَسُولِ اللَّهِ صلى الله عليه وسلم عَلَى فَخِذِي، فَقَامَ رَسُولُ اللَّهِ صلى الله عليه وسلم حِينَ أَصْبَحَ عَلَى غَيْرِ مَاءٍ، فَأَنْزَلَ اللَّهُ آيَةَ التَّيَمُّمِ فَتَيَمَّمُوا. فَقَالَ أُسَيْدُ بْنُ الْحُضَيْرِ مَا هِيَ بِأَوَّلِ بَرَكَتِكُمْ يَا آلَ أَبِي بَكْرٍ. قَالَتْ فَبَعَثْنَا الْبَعِيرَ الَّذِي كُنْتُ عَلَيْهِ، فَأَصَبْنَا الْعِقْدَ تَحْتَهُ.

Narrated `Aisha was ordered (ﷺ) (the wife of the Prophet) when Allah's Messenger to give option to his wives, he started with me, saying, "I am going to mention to you something, but you shall not hasten (to give your reply) unless you consult your .knew that my parents would not order me to leave him (ﷺ) parents." The Prophet Then he said, "Allah says: 'O Prophet (Muhammad)! Say to your wives: If you desire the life of this world and its glitter........a great reward." (33.28-29) I said, "Then why I ".consult my parents? Verily, I seek Allah, His Apostle and the Home of the Hereafter Then all the other wives of the Prophet. – Sahih al-Bukhari 4786

وَقَالَ اللَّيْثُ حَدَّثَنِي يُونُسُ، عَنِ ابْنِ شِهَابٍ، قَالَ أَخْبَرَنِي أَبُو سَلَمَةَ بْنُ عَبْدِ الرَّحْمَنِ، أَنَّ عَائِشَةَ، زَوْجَ النَّبِيِّ صلى الله عليه وسلم قَالَتْ لَمَّا أُمِرَ رَسُولُ اللَّهِ صلى الله عليه وسلم بِتَخْيِيرِ أَزْوَاجِهِ بَدَأَ بِي فَقَالَ " إِنِّي ذَاكِرٌ لَكِ أَمْرًا فَلاَ عَلَيْكِ أَنْ لاَ تَعْجَلِي حَتَّى تَسْتَأْمِرِي أَبَوَيْكِ ". قَالَتْ وَقَدْ عَلِمَ أَنَّ أَبَوَىَّ لَمْ يَكُونَا يَأْمُرَانِي بِفِرَاقِهِ، قَالَتْ ثُمَّ قَالَ " إِنَّ اللَّهَ جَلَّ ثَنَاؤُهُ قَالَ {يَا أَيُّهَا النَّبِيُّ قُلْ لأَزْوَاجِكَ إِنْ كُنْتُنَّ تُرِدْنَ الْحَيَاةَ الدُّنْيَا وَزِينَتَهَا} إِلَى {أَجْرًا عَظِيمًا} ". قَالَتْ فَقُلْتُ فَفِي أَىِّ هَذَا أَسْتَأْمِرُ أَبَوَىَّ فَإِنِّي أُرِيدُ اللَّهَ وَرَسُولَهُ وَالدَّارَ الآخِرَةَ، قَالَتْ ثُمَّ فَعَلَ أَزْوَاجُ النَّبِيِّ صلى الله عليه وسلم مِثْلَ مَا فَعَلْتُ. تَابَعَهُ مُوسَى بْنُ أَعْيَنَ عَنْ مَعْمَرٍ عَنِ الزُّهْرِيِّ قَالَ أَخْبَرَنِي أَبُو سَلَمَةَ. وَقَالَ عَبْدُ الرَّزَّاقِ وَأَبُو سُفْيَانَ الْمَعْمَرِيُّ عَنْ مَعْمَرٍ عَنِ الزُّهْرِيِّ عَنْ عُرْوَةَ عَنْ عَائِشَةَ.

And as the Prophet (entrusted) a secret discourse to some of his spouses, then as soon as one of (them) (fully) informed (another) of it, and Allah disclosed it to him, he acquainted (her) of some part of it, and passed over (Literally: veered away from) (some) part. Then, as soon as he (fully) informed her of it, she said, "Who has informed you of this?" He said, "The Ever-Knowing, The Ever-Cognizant has (fully) informed me."

In case you two repent to Allah, then your hearts are readily attentive; and in 66:4
case you two back one another against him, then surely Allah, Ever He, is his ,Patronizer, and Jibril, (Angle Gabriel) and the righteous (among) the believers, and after that, the Angels are (his) backers

,It may be that, in case he divorces you, his Lord will give him, in exchange 66:5
spouses more charitable (i.e., better) than you, Muslim (i.e., who have surrendered to Allah) women, believing, devout, repentant, worshiping Allah), (and) wandering (Sometimes understood to mean "fasting") (in His way), who were married before and virgins (too) – Surah At-Tahrim 66:3-5

وَإِذْ أَسَرَّ ٱلنَّبِيُّ إِلَىٰ بَعْضِ أَزْوَٰجِهِۦ حَدِيثًا فَلَمَّا نَبَّأَتْ بِهِۦ وَأَظْهَرَهُ ٱللَّهُ عَلَيْهِ عَرَّفَ بَعْضَهُۥ وَأَعْرَضَ عَنۢ بَعْضٍ ۖ فَلَمَّا نَبَّأَهَا بِهِۦ قَالَتْ مَنْ أَنۢبَأَكَ هَٰذَا ۖ قَالَ نَبَّأَنِىَ ٱلْعَلِيمُ ٱلْخَبِيرُ إِن تَتُوبَآ إِلَى ٱللَّهِ فَقَدْ صَغَتْ قُلُوبُكُمَا ۖ وَإِن تَظَٰهَرَا عَلَيْهِ فَإِنَّ ٱللَّهَ هُوَ مَوْلَىٰهُ وَجِبْرِيلُ وَصَٰلِحُ ٱلْمُؤْمِنِينَ ۖ وَٱلْمَلَٰٓئِكَةُ بَعْدَ ذَٰلِكَ ظَهِيرٌ عَسَىٰ رَبُّهُۥٓ إِن طَلَّقَكُنَّ أَن يُبْدِلَهُۥٓ أَزْوَٰجًا خَيْرًا مِّنكُنَّ مُسْلِمَٰتٍ مُّؤْمِنَٰتٍ قَٰنِتَٰتٍ تَٰٓئِبَٰتٍ عَٰبِدَٰتٍ سَٰٓئِحَٰتٍ ثَيِّبَٰتٍ وَأَبْكَارًا

It was narrated from Anas, that the Messenger of Allah had a female slave with whom he had intercourse, but 'Aishah and Hafsah would not leave him alone until he said :that she was forbidden for him. Then Allah, the Mighty and Sublime, revealed '.O Prophet! Why do you forbid (for yourself) that which Allah has allowed to you" until the end of the Verse. – Sunan an-Nasa'i 3959

أَخْبَرَنِي إِبْرَاهِيمُ بْنُ يُونُسَ بْنِ مُحَمَّدٍ، حَرَمِيٌّ – هُوَ لَقَبُهُ – قَالَ حَدَّثَنَا أَبِي قَالَ، حَدَّثَنَا حَمَّادُ بْنُ سَلَمَةَ، عَنْ ثَابِتٍ، عَنْ أَنَسٍ، أَنَّ رَسُولَ اللَّهِ صلى الله عليه وسلم كَانَتْ لَهُ أَمَةٌ يَطَؤُهَا فَلَمْ تَزَلْ بِهِ عَائِشَةُ وَحَفْصَةُ حَتَّى حَرَّمَهَا عَلَى نَفْسِهِ فَأَنْزَلَ اللَّهُ عَزَّ وَجَلَّ { يَا أَيُّهَا النَّبِيُّ لِمَ تُحَرِّمُ مَا أَحَلَّ اللَّهُ لَكَ } إِلَى آخِرِ الآيَةِ .

Asma bint Abi Bakr

أسماء بنت أبي بكر

Narrated `Aisha: Some Muslim men emigrated to Ethiopia whereupon Abu Bakr also prepared himself for the emigration, but the Prophetﷺ said (to him), "Wait, for I hope that Allah will allow me also to emigrate." Abu Bakr said, "Let my father and mother be sacrificed for you. Do you hope that (emigration)?" The Prophet said, 'Yes." So Abu Bakr waited to accompany the Prophetﷺ and fed two she-camels he had on the leaves of As-Samur tree regularly for four months One day while we were sitting in our house at midday, someone said to Abu Bakr, "Here is Allah's Messengerﷺ, coming with his head and a part of his face covered with a cloth-covering at an hour he never used to come to us." Abu Bakr said, "Let my father and mother be sacrificed for you, (O Prophet)! An urgent matter must have brought you here at this hour." The Prophetﷺ came and asked the permission to enter, and he was allowed. The Prophetﷺ entered and said to Abu Bakr, "Let those who are with you, go out." Abu Bakr replied, "(There is no stranger); they are your family. Let my father be sacrificed for you, O Allah's Apostle!" The Prophetﷺ said, "I have been allowed to leave (Mecca)." Abu Bakr said, " I shall accompany you, O Allah's Messengerﷺ, Let my father be sacrificed for you!" The Prophetﷺ said, "Yes," Abu Bakr said, 'O Allah's Messengerﷺ! Let my father be sacrificed for you. Take one of these two shecamels of mine" The Prophetﷺ said. I will take it only after paying its price." So we prepared their baggage and put their journey food In a leather bag. And Asma' bint Abu Bakr cut a piece of her girdle and tied the mouth of the leather bag with it. That is why she was called Dhatan- Nitaqaln. Then the Prophetﷺ and Abu Bakr went to a cave in a mountain called Thour and remained there for three nights. `Abdullah bin Abu Bakr. Who was a young intelligent man. Used to stay with them at night and leave before dawn so that in the morning, he would he with the Quraish at Mecca as if he had spent the night among them. If he heard of any plot contrived by the Quraish against the Prophet and Abu Bakr, he would understand it and (return to) inform them of it when it became dark. 'Amir bin Fuhaira, the freed slave of Abu Bakr used to graze a flock of milch sheep for them and he used to take those sheep to them when an hour had passed after the `Isha prayer. They would sleep soundly till 'Amir bin Fuhaira awakened them when it was still dark. He used to do that in each of those three nights. – Sahih Al-Bukhari 5807

حَدَّثَنَا إِبْرَاهِيمُ بْنُ مُوسَى، أَخْبَرَنَا هِشَامٌ، عَنْ مَعْمَرٍ، عَنِ الزُّهْرِيِّ، عَنْ عُرْوَةَ، عَنْ عَائِشَةَ ـ رضى الله عنها ـ قَالَتْ هَاجَرَ إِلَى الْحَبَشَةِ نَاسٌ مِنَ الْمُسْلِمِينَ، وَتَجَهَّزَ أَبُو بَكْرٍ مُهَاجِرًا، فَقَالَ النَّبِيُّ صلى الله عليه وسلم " عَلَى رِسْلِكَ، فَإِنِّي أَرْجُو أَنْ يُؤْذَنَ لِي ". فَقَالَ أَبُو بَكْرٍ أَوَ تَرْجُوهُ بِأَبِي أَنْتَ قَالَ " نَعَمْ ". فَحَبَسَ أَبُو بَكْرٍ نَفْسَهُ عَلَى النَّبِيِّ صلى الله عليه وسلم لِصُحْبَتِهِ، وَعَلَفَ رَاحِلَتَيْنِ كَانَتَا عِنْدَهُ وَرَقَ السَّمُرِ أَرْبَعَةَ أَشْهُرٍ. قَالَ عُرْوَةُ قَالَتْ عَائِشَةُ فَبَيْنَا نَحْنُ يَوْمًا جُلُوسٌ فِي بَيْتِنَا فِي نَحْرِ الظَّهِيرَةِ فَقَالَ قَائِلٌ لأَبِي بَكْرٍ هَذَا رَسُولُ اللَّهِ صلى الله عليه وسلم مُقْبِلاً مُتَقَنِّعًا، فِي سَاعَةٍ لَمْ يَكُنْ يَأْتِينَا فِيهَا. قَالَ أَبُو بَكْرٍ فِدًا لَهُ بِأَبِي وَأُمِّي، وَاللَّهِ إِنْ جَاءَ بِهِ فِي هَذِهِ السَّاعَةِ إِلاَّ لأَمْرٍ. فَجَاءَ النَّبِيُّ صلى الله عليه وسلم فَاسْتَأْذَنَ، فَأَذِنَ لَهُ فَدَخَلَ، فَقَالَ حِينَ دَخَلَ لأَبِي بَكْرٍ " أَخْرِجْ مَنْ عِنْدَكَ ". قَالَ إِنَّمَا هُمْ أَهْلُكَ بِأَبِي أَنْتَ يَا رَسُولَ اللَّهِ. قَالَ " فَإِنِّي قَدْ أُذِنَ لِي فِي الْخُرُوجِ ". قَالَ فَالصُّحْبَةُ بِأَبِي أَنْتَ يَا رَسُولَ اللَّهِ. قَالَ " نَعَمْ ". قَالَ فَخُذْ بِأَبِي أَنْتَ يَا رَسُولَ اللَّهِ إِحْدَى رَاحِلَتَيَّ هَاتَيْنِ. قَالَ النَّبِيُّ صلى الله عليه وسلم " بِالثَّمَنِ ". قَالَتْ فَجَهَّزْنَاهُمَا أَحَثَّ الْجِهَازِ، وَضَعْنَا لَهُمَا سُفْرَةً فِي جِرَابٍ، فَقَطَعَتْ أَسْمَاءُ بِنْتُ أَبِي بَكْرٍ قِطْعَةً مِنْ نِطَاقِهَا، فَأَوْكَتْ بِهِ الْجِرَابَ، وَلِذَلِكَ كَانَتْ تُسَمَّى ذَاتَ النِّطَاقِ، ثُمَّ لَحِقَ النَّبِيُّ صلى الله عليه وسلم وَأَبُو بَكْرٍ بِغَارٍ فِي جَبَلٍ يُقَالُ لَهُ ثَوْرٌ، فَمَكُثَ فِيهِ ثَلاَثَ لَيَالٍ يَبِيتُ عِنْدَهُمَا عَبْدُ اللَّهِ بْنُ أَبِي بَكْرٍ، وَهْوَ غُلاَمٌ شَابٌّ لَقِنٌ ثَقِفٌ، فَيَرْحَلُ مِنْ عِنْدِهِمَا سَحَرًا، فَيُصْبِحُ مَعَ قُرَيْشٍ بِمَكَّةَ كَبَائِتٍ، فَلاَ يَسْمَعُ أَمْرًا يُكَادَانِ بِهِ إِلاَّ وَعَاهُ، حَتَّى يَأْتِيَهُمَا بِخَبَرِ ذَلِكَ حِينَ يَخْتَلِطُ الظَّلاَمُ، وَيَرْعَى عَلَيْهِمَا عَامِرُ بْنُ فُهَيْرَةَ مَوْلَى أَبِي بَكْرٍ مِنْحَةً مِنْ غَنَمٍ، فَيُرِيحُهَا عَلَيْهِمَا حِينَ تَذْهَبُ سَاعَةٌ مِنَ الْعِشَاءِ، فَيَبِيتَانِ فِي رِسْلِهَا حَتَّى يَنْعِقَ بِهَا عَامِرُ بْنُ فُهَيْرَةَ بِغَلَسٍ، يَفْعَلُ ذَلِكَ كُلَّ لَيْلَةٍ مِنْ تِلْكَ اللَّيَالِي الثَّلاَثِ.

Narrated Ibn Abi Mulaika: There was a disagreement between them (i.e. Ibn `Abbas and Ibn Az-Zubair) so I went to Ibn `Abbas in the morning and said (to him), "Do you want to fight against Ibn Zubair and thus make lawful what Allah has made unlawful (i.e. fighting in Meccas?" Ibn `Abbas said, "Allah forbid! Allah ordained that Ibn Zubair and Bani Umaiya would permit (fighting in Mecca), but by Allah, I will never regard it as permissible." Ibn `Abbas added. "The people asked me to take the oath of allegiance to Ibn AzZubair. I said, 'He is really entitled to assume authority for his father, Az-Zubair was the helper of the Prophet, his (maternal) grandfather, Abu Bakr was (the Prophet's) companion in the cave, his mother, Asma' was 'Dhatun-Nitaq', his aunt, `Aisha was the mother of the Believers, his paternal aunt, Khadija was the wife of the Prophetﷺ, and the paternal aunt of the Prophetﷺ was his grandmother. He himself is pious and chaste in Islam, well versed in the Knowledge of the Qur'an. By Allah! (Really, I left my relatives, Bani Umaiya for his sake though) they are my close relatives, and if they should be my rulers, they are equally apt to be so and are descended from a noble family. – Sahih Al-Bukhari 4665

حَدَّثَنِي عَبْدُ اللَّهِ بْنُ مُحَمَّدٍ، قَالَ حَدَّثَنِي يَحْيَى بْنُ مَعِينٍ، حَدَّثَنَا حَجَّاجٌ، قَالَ ابْنُ جُرَيْجٍ قَالَ ابْنُ أَبِي مُلَيْكَةَ وَكَانَ بَيْنَهُمَا شَىْءٌ فَغَدَوْتُ عَلَى ابْنِ عَبَّاسٍ فَقُلْتُ أَتُرِيدُ أَنْ تُقَاتِلَ ابْنَ الزُّبَيْرِ، فَتُحِلُّ حَرَمَ اللَّهِ. فَقَالَ مَعَاذَ اللَّهِ، إِنَّ اللَّهَ كَتَبَ ابْنَ الزُّبَيْرِ وَبَنِي أُمَيَّةَ مُحِلِّينَ، وَإِنِّي وَاللَّهِ لاَ أُحِلُّهُ أَبَدًا. قَالَ قَالَ النَّاسُ بَايِعْ لاِبْنِ الزُّبَيْرِ. فَقُلْتُ وَأَيْنَ بِهَذَا الأَمْرِ عَنْهُ أَمَّا أَبُوهُ فَحَوَارِيُّ النَّبِيِّ صلى الله عليه وسلم، يُرِيدُ الزُّبَيْرَ، وَأَمَّا جَدُّهُ فَصَاحِبُ الْغَارِ، يُرِيدُ أَبَا بَكْرٍ، وَأُمُّهُ فَذَاتُ النِّطَاقِ، يُرِيدُ أَسْمَاءَ، وَأَمَّا خَالَتُهُ فَأُمُّ الْمُؤْمِنِينَ، يُرِيدُ عَائِشَةَ، وَأَمَّا عَمَّتُهُ فَزَوْجُ النَّبِيِّ صلى الله عليه وسلم، يُرِيدُ خَدِيجَةَ، وَأَمَّا عَمَّةُ النَّبِيِّ صلى الله عليه وسلم فَجَدَّتُهُ، يُرِيدُ صَفِيَّةَ، ثُمَّ عَفِيفٌ فِي الإِسْلاَمِ، قَارِئٌ لِلْقُرْآنِ. وَاللَّهِ إِنْ وَصَلُونِي وَصَلُونِي مِنْ قَرِيبٍ، وَإِنْ رَبُّونِي رَبَّنِي أَكْفَاءٌ كِرَامٌ، فَآثَرَ التُّوَيْتَاتِ وَالأُسَامَاتِ وَالْحُمَيْدَاتِ، يُرِيدُ أَبْطُنًا مِنْ بَنِي أَسَدٍ بَنِي تُوَيْتٍ وَبَنِي أُسَامَةَ وَبَنِي أَسَدٍ، إِنَّ ابْنَ أَبِي الْعَاصِ بَرَزَ يَمْشِي الْقُدَمِيَّةَ، يَعْنِي عَبْدَ الْمَلِكِ بْنَ مَرْوَانَ، وَإِنَّهُ لَوَّى ذَنَبَهُ، يَعْنِي ابْنَ الزُّبَيْرِ.

Narrated Asma' bint Abu Bakr: When Az-Zubair married me, he had no real property or any slave or anything else except a camel which drew water from the well, and his horse. I used to feed his horse with fodder and drew water and sew the bucket for drawing it, and prepare the dough, but I did not know how to bake bread. So our Ansari neighbors used to bake bread for me, and they were honorable ladies. I used to carry the date stones on my head from Zubair's land given to him by Allah's Messengerﷺ and this land was two third Farsakh (about two miles) from my house. One day, while I was coming with the date stones on my head, I met Allah's Messengerﷺ along with some Ansari people. He called me and then, (directing his camel to kneel down) said, "Ikh! Ikh!" so as to make me ride behind him (on his camel). I felt shy to travel with the men and remembered Az-Zubair and his sense of Ghira, as he was one of those people who had the greatest sense of Ghira. Allah's Messengerﷺ noticed that I felt shy, so he proceeded. I came to Az-Zubair and said, "I met Allah's Messengerﷺ while I was carrying a load of date stones on my head, and he had some companions with him. He made his camel kneel down so that I might ride, but I felt shy in his presence and remembered your sense of Ghira (See the glossary). On that Az-Zubair said, "By Allah, your carrying the date stones (and you being seen by the Prophetﷺ in such a state) is more shameful to me than your riding with him." (I continued serving in this way) till Abu Bakr sent me a servant to look after the horse, whereupon I felt as if he had set me free. – Sahih Al-Bukhari 5224

حَدَّثَنَا مَحْمُودٌ، حَدَّثَنَا أَبُو أُسَامَةَ، حَدَّثَنَا هِشَامٌ، قَالَ أَخْبَرَنِي أَبِي، عَنْ أَسْمَاءَ بِنْتِ أَبِي بَكْرٍ ـ رضى الله عنهما ـ قَالَتْ تَزَوَّجَنِي الزُّبَيْرُ، وَمَا لَهُ فِي الأَرْضِ مِنْ مَالٍ، وَلاَ مَمْلُوكٍ، وَلاَ شَىْءٍ غَيْرَ نَاضِحٍ، وَغَيْرَ فَرَسِهِ، فَكُنْتُ أَعْلِفُ فَرَسَهُ، وَأَسْتَقِي الْمَاءَ، وَأَخْرِزُ غَرْبَهُ وَأَعْجِنُ، وَلَمْ أَكُنْ أُحْسِنُ أَخْبِزُ، وَكَانَ يَخْبِزُ جَارَاتٌ لِي مِنَ الأَنْصَارِ وَكُنَّ نِسْوَةَ صِدْقٍ، وَكُنْتُ أَنْقُلُ النَّوَى مِنْ أَرْضِ الزُّبَيْرِ الَّتِي أَقْطَعَهُ رَسُولُ اللَّهِ صلى الله عليه وسلم عَلَى رَأْسِي، وَهْىَ مِنِّي عَلَى ثُلُثَىْ فَرْسَخٍ، فَجِئْتُ يَوْمًا وَالنَّوَى عَلَى رَأْسِي فَلَقِيتُ رَسُولَ اللَّهِ صلى الله عليه وسلم وَمَعَهُ نَفَرٌ مِنَ الأَنْصَارِ فَدَعَانِي ثُمَّ قَالَ " إِخْ إِخْ ". لِيَحْمِلَنِي خَلْفَهُ، فَاسْتَحْيَيْتُ أَنْ أَسِيرَ مَعَ الرِّجَالِ، وَذَكَرْتُ الزُّبَيْرَ وَغَيْرَتَهُ، وَكَانَ أَغْيَرَ النَّاسِ، فَعَرَفَ رَسُولُ اللَّهِ صلى الله عليه وسلم أَنِّي قَدِ اسْتَحْيَيْتُ فَمَضَى، فَجِئْتُ الزُّبَيْرَ فَقُلْتُ لَقِيَنِي رَسُولُ اللَّهِ صلى الله عليه وسلم وَعَلَى رَأْسِي النَّوَى، وَمَعَهُ

نَفَرٌ مِنْ أَصْحَابِهِ، فَأَنَاخَ لأَرْكَبَ، فَاسْتَحْيَيْتُ مِنْهُ وَعَرَفْتُ غَيْرَتَكَ. فَقَالَ وَاللَّهِ لَحَمْلُكِ النَّوَى كَانَ أَشَدَّ عَلَيَّ مِنْ رُكُوبِكِ مَعَهُ. قَالَتْ حَتَّى أَرْسَلَ إِلَيَّ أَبُو بَكْرٍ بَعْدَ ذَلِكَ بِخَادِمٍ يَكْفِينِي سِيَاسَةَ الْفَرَسِ، فَكَأَنَّمَا أَعْتَقَنِي.

Narrated Asma': I came to `Aisha while she was praying, and said to her, "What has happened to the people?" She pointed out towards the sky. (I looked towards the mosque), and saw the people offering the prayer. Aisha said, "Subhan Allah." I said to her, "Is there a sign?" She nodded with her head meaning, "Yes." I, too, then stood (for the prayer of eclipse) till I became (nearly) unconscious and later on I poured water on my head. After the prayer, the Prophet ﷺ praised and glorified Allah and then said, "Just now at this place I have seen what I have never seen before, including Paradise and Hell. No doubt it has been inspired to me that you will be put to trials in your graves and these trials will be like the trials of Masih-ad-Dajjal or nearly like it (the sub narrator is not sure which expression Asma' used). You will be asked, 'What do you know about this man (the Prophet ﷺ Muhammad)?' Then the faithful believer (or Asma' said a similar word) will reply, 'He is Muhammad Allah's Messenger ﷺ who had come to us with clear evidences and guidance and so we accepted his teachings and followed him. And he is Muhammad.' And he will repeat it thrice. Then the angels will say to him, 'Sleep in peace as we have come to know that you were a faithful believer.' On the other hand, a hypocrite or a doubtful person will reply, 'I do not know, but I heard the people saying something and so I said it.' (the same). ". – Sahih Al-Bukhari 86

حَدَّثَنَا مُوسَى بْنُ إِسْمَاعِيلَ، قَالَ حَدَّثَنَا وُهَيْبٌ، قَالَ حَدَّثَنَا هِشَامٌ، عَنْ فَاطِمَةَ، عَنْ أَسْمَاءَ، قَالَتْ أَتَيْتُ عَائِشَةَ وَهِيَ تُصَلِّي فَقُلْتُ مَا شَأْنُ النَّاسِ فَأَشَارَتْ إِلَى السَّمَاءِ، فَإِذَا النَّاسُ قِيَامٌ، فَقَالَتْ سُبْحَانَ اللَّهِ. قُلْتُ آيَةٌ فَأَشَارَتْ بِرَأْسِهَا، أَىْ نَعَمْ، فَقُمْتُ حَتَّى تَجَلاَّنِي الْغَشْىُ، فَجَعَلْتُ أَصُبُّ عَلَى رَأْسِي الْمَاءَ، فَحَمِدَ اللَّهَ عَزَّ وَجَلَّ النَّبِيُّ صلى الله عليه وسلم وَأَثْنَى عَلَيْهِ، ثُمَّ قَالَ " مَا مِنْ شَىْءٍ لَمْ أَكُنْ أُرِيتُهُ إِلاَّ رَأَيْتُهُ فِي مَقَامِي حَتَّى الْجَنَّةَ وَالنَّارَ، فَأُوحِيَ إِلَيَّ أَنَّكُمْ تُفْتَنُونَ فِي قُبُورِكُمْ، مِثْلَ ـ أَوْ قَرِيبًا لاَ أَدْرِي أَىَّ ذَلِكَ قَالَتْ أَسْمَاءُ ـ مِنْ فِتْنَةِ الْمَسِيحِ الدَّجَّالِ، يُقَالُ مَا عِلْمُكَ بِهَذَا الرَّجُلِ فَأَمَّا الْمُؤْمِنُ ـ أَوِ الْمُوقِنُ لاَ أَدْرِي بِأَيِّهِمَا قَالَتْ أَسْمَاءُ ـ فَيَقُولُ هُوَ مُحَمَّدٌ رَسُولُ اللَّهِ جَاءَنَا بِالْبَيِّنَاتِ وَالْهُدَى، فَأَجَبْنَا وَاتَّبَعْنَا، هُوَ مُحَمَّدٌ. ثَلاَثًا، فَيُقَالُ نَمْ صَالِحًا، قَدْ عَلِمْنَا إِنْ كُنْتَ لَمُوقِنًا بِهِ، وَأَمَّا الْمُنَافِقُ ـ أَوِ الْمُرْتَابُ لاَ أَدْرِي أَىَّ ذَلِكَ قَالَتْ أَسْمَاءُ ـ فَيَقُولُ لاَ أَدْرِي، سَمِعْتُ النَّاسَ يَقُولُونَ شَيْئًا فَقُلْتُهُ ".

Narrated `Urwa: `Aisha said, "The first thing the Prophet ﷺ did on reaching Mecca, was the ablution and then he performed Tawaf of the Ka`ba and that was not `Umra (alone), (but Hajj-al-Qiran). `Urwa added: Later Abu Bakr and `Umar did the same in their Hajj." And I performed the Hajj with my father Az- Zubair, and the first thing he did was Tawaf of the Ka`ba. Later I saw the Muhajirin (Emigrants) and the Ansar doing the same. My mother (Asma') told me that she, her sister (`Aisha), Az-Zubair and such and such persons assumed Ihram for `Umra, and after they passed their hands over the Black Stone Corner (of the Ka`ba) they finished the Ihram. (i.e. After doing Tawaf of the Ka`ba and Sa`I between Safa-Marwa. – Sahih Al-Bukhari 1614, 1615

حَدَّثَنَا أَصْبَغُ، عَنِ ابْنِ وَهْبٍ، أَخْبَرَنِي عَمْرٌو، عَنْ مُحَمَّدِ بْنِ عَبْدِ الرَّحْمَنِ،، ذَكَرْتُ لِعُرْوَةَ، قَالَ فَأَخْبَرَتْنِي عَائِشَةُ ـ رضى الله عنها ـ أَنَّ أَوَّلَ، شَىْءٍ بَدَأَ بِهِ حِينَ قَدِمَ النَّبِيُّ صلى الله عليه وسلم أَنَّهُ تَوَضَّأَ، ثُمَّ طَافَ، ثُمَّ لَمْ تَكُنْ عُمْرَةً، ثُمَّ حَجَّ أَبُو بَكْرٍ وَعُمَرُ ـ رضى الله عنهما ـ مِثْلَهُ، ثُمَّ حَجَجْتُ مَعَ أَبِي الزُّبَيْرِ ـ رضى الله عنه ـ فَأَوَّلُ شَىْءٍ بَدَأَ بِهِ الطَّوَافُ، ثُمَّ رَأَيْتُ الْمُهَاجِرِينَ وَالأَنْصَارَ يَفْعَلُونَهُ، وَقَدْ أَخْبَرَتْنِي أُمِّي أَنَّهَا أَهَلَّتْ هِيَ وَأُخْتُهَا وَالزُّبَيْرُ وَفُلاَنٌ وَفُلاَنٌ بِعُمْرَةٍ، فَلَمَّا مَسَحُوا الرُّكْنَ حَلُّوا

Narrated Asma bint Abi Bakr: I saw Zaid bin Amr bin Nufail standing with his back against the Ka'ba and saying, "O people of Quraish! By Allah, none amongst you is on the religion of Abraham except me." He used to preserve the lives of little girls: If somebody wanted to kill his daughter he would say to him, "Do not kill her for I will feed her on your behalf." So he would take her, and when she grew up nicely, he would say to her father, "Now if you want her, I will give her to you, and if you wish, I will feed her on your behalf.". – Sahih Al-Bukhari 3828

وَقَالَ اللَّيْثُ كَتَبَ إِلَيَّ هِشَامٌ عَنْ أَبِيهِ، عَنْ أَسْمَاءَ بِنْتِ أَبِي بَكْرٍ ـ رضى الله عنهما ـ قَالَتْ رَأَيْتُ زَيْدَ بْنَ عَمْرِو بْنِ نُفَيْلٍ قَائِمًا مُسْنِدًا ظَهْرَهُ إِلَى الْكَعْبَةِ يَقُولُ يَا مَعَاشِرَ قُرَيْشٍ، وَاللَّهِ مَا مِنْكُمْ عَلَى دِينِ إِبْرَاهِيمَ غَيْرِي، وَكَانَ يُحْيِي الْمَوْءُودَةَ، يَقُولُ لِلرَّجُلِ إِذَا أَرَادَ أَنْ يَقْتُلَ ابْنَتَهُ لاَ تَقْتُلْهَا، أَنَا أَكْفِيكَهَا مَئُونَتَهَا. فَيَأْخُذُهَا فَإِذَا تَرَعْرَعَتْ قَالَ لأَبِيهَا إِنْ شِئْتَ دَفَعْتُهَا إِلَيْكَ، وَإِنْ شِئْتَ كَفَيْتُكَ مَئُونَتَهَا

Narrated Asma 'bint Abu Bakr: The Prophet ﷺ said, "I will be standing at the Lake-Fount so that I will see whom among you will come to me; and some people will be taken away from me, and I will say, 'O Lord, (they are) from me and from my followers.' Then it will be said, 'Did you notice what they did after you? By Allah, they kept on turning on their heels (turned as renegades).' " The sub-narrator, Ibn Abi Mulaika said, "O Allah, we seek refuge with You from turning on our heels, or being put to trial in our religion.". – Sahih Al-Bukhari 6593

حَدَّثَنَا سَعِيدُ بْنُ أَبِي مَرْيَمَ، عَنْ نَافِعِ بْنِ عُمَرَ، قَالَ حَدَّثَنِي ابْنُ أَبِي مُلَيْكَةَ، عَنْ أَسْمَاءَ بِنْتِ أَبِي بَكْرٍ ـ رضى الله عنهما ـ قَالَتْ قَالَ النَّبِيُّ صلى الله عليه وسلم " إِنِّي عَلَى الْحَوْضِ حَتَّى أَنْظُرَ مَنْ يَرِدُ عَلَيَّ مِنْكُمْ، وَسَيُؤْخَذُ نَاسٌ دُونِي فَأَقُولُ يَا رَبِّ مِنِّي وَمِنْ أُمَّتِي. فَيُقَالُ هَلْ شَعَرْتَ مَا عَمِلُوا بَعْدَكَ وَاللَّهِ مَا بَرِحُوا يَرْجِعُونَ عَلَى أَعْقَابِهِمْ ". فَكَانَ ابْنُ أَبِي مُلَيْكَةَ يَقُولُ اللَّهُمَّ إِنَّا نَعُوذُ بِكَ أَنْ نَرْجِعَ عَلَى أَعْقَابِنَا أَوْ نُفْتَنَ عَنْ دِينِنَا. {أَعْقَابِكُمْ تَنْكِصُونَ} تَرْجِعُونَ عَلَى الْعَقِبِ.

Narrated Asma: That she conceived `Abdullah bin Az-Zubair. She added, "I migrated to Medina while I was at full term of pregnancy and alighted at Quba where I gave birth to him. Then I brought him to the Prophet ﷺ and put him in his lap. The Prophet ﷺ asked for a date, chewed it, and put some of its juice in the child's mouth. So, the first thing that entered the child's stomach was the saliva of Allah's Messenger ﷺ. Then the Prophet rubbed the child's palate with a date and invoked for Allah's Blessings on him, and he was the first child born amongst the Emigrants in the Islamic Land (i.e. Medina). – Sahih Al-Bukhari 3909

حَدَّثَنِي زَكَرِيَّاءُ بْنُ يَحْيَى، عَنْ أَبِي أُسَامَةَ، عَنْ هِشَامِ بْنِ عُرْوَةَ، عَنْ أَبِيهِ، عَنْ أَسْمَاءَ ـ رضى الله عنها ـ أَنَّهَا حَمَلَتْ بِعَبْدِ اللَّهِ بْنِ الزُّبَيْرِ، قَالَتْ فَخَرَجْتُ وَأَنَا مُتِمٌّ، فَأَتَيْتُ الْمَدِينَةَ، فَنَزَلْتُ بِقُبَاءٍ، فَوَلَدْتُهُ بِقُبَاءٍ، ثُمَّ أَتَيْتُ بِهِ النَّبِيَّ صلى الله عليه وسلم فَوَضَعْتُهُ فِي حَجْرِهِ، ثُمَّ دَعَا بِتَمْرَةٍ، فَمَضَغَهَا، ثُمَّ تَفَلَ فِي فِيهِ، فَكَانَ أَوَّلَ شَىْءٍ دَخَلَ جَوْفَهُ رِيقُ رَسُولِ اللَّهِ صلى الله عليه وسلم، ثُمَّ حَنَّكَهُ بِتَمْرَةٍ ثُمَّ دَعَا لَهُ وَبَرَّكَ عَلَيْهِ، وَكَانَ أَوَّلَ مَوْلُودٍ وُلِدَ فِي الإِسْلاَمِ. تَابَعَهُ خَالِدُ بْنُ مَخْلَدٍ عَنْ عَلِيِّ بْنِ مُسْهِرٍ عَنْ هِشَامٍ عَنْ أَبِيهِ عَنْ أَسْمَاءَ ـ رضى الله عنها ـ أَنَّهَا هَاجَرَتْ إِلَى النَّبِيِّ صلى الله عليه وسلم وَهْىَ حُبْلَى.

Narrated `Abdullah: (the slave of Asma') During the night of Jam', Asma' got down at Al-Muzdalifa and stood up for (offering) the prayer and offered the prayer for some time and then asked, "O my son! Has the moon set?" I replied in the negative and she again prayed for another period and then asked, "Has the moon set?" I replied, "Yes." So she said that we should set out (for Mina), and we departed and went on till she threw pebbles at the Jamra (Jamrat-Al-`Aqaba) and then she returned to her dwelling place and offered the morning prayer. I asked her, "O you! I think we have come (to Mina) early in the night." She replied, "O my son! Allah's Messenger ﷺ gave permission to the women to do so.". – Sahih Al-Bukhari 1679

حَدَّثَنَا مُسَدَّدٌ، عَنْ يَحْيَى، عَنِ ابْنِ جُرَيْجٍ، قَالَ حَدَّثَنِي عَبْدُ اللَّهِ، مَوْلَى أَسْمَاءَ عَنْ أَسْمَاءَ، أَنَّهَا نَزَلَتْ لَيْلَةَ جَمْعٍ عِنْدَ الْمُزْدَلِفَةِ، فَقَامَتْ تُصَلِّي، فَصَلَّتْ سَاعَةً، ثُمَّ قَالَتْ يَا بُنَىَّ هَلْ غَابَ الْقَمَرُ قُلْتُ لاَ. فَصَلَّتْ سَاعَةً، ثُمَّ قَالَتْ هَلْ غَابَ الْقَمَرُ قُلْتُ نَعَمْ. قَالَتْ فَارْتَحِلُوا. فَارْتَحَلْنَا، وَمَضَيْنَا حَتَّى رَمَتِ الْجَمْرَةَ، ثُمَّ رَجَعَتْ فَصَلَّتِ الصُّبْحَ فِي مَنْزِلِهَا. فَقُلْتُ لَهَا يَا هَنْتَاهْ مَا أُرَانَا إِلاَّ قَدْ غَلَّسْنَا. قَالَتْ يَا بُنَىَّ، إِنَّ رَسُولَ اللَّهِ صلى الله عليه وسلم أَذِنَ لِلظُّعُنِ

Narrated Al-Aswad: `Abdullah the slave of Asma bint Abu Bakr, told me that he used to hear Asma', whenever she passed by Al-Hajun, saying, "May Allah bless His Apostle Muhammad. Once we dismounted here with him, and at that time we were traveling with light luggage;

we had a few riding animals and a little food ration. I, my sister, `Aisha, Az-Zubair and such and such persons performed `Umra, and when we had passed our hands over the Ka`ba (i.e. performed Tawaf round the Ka`ba and between As-Safa and Al- Marwa) we finished our Ihram. Later on we assumed Ihram for Hajj the same evening." – Sahih Al-Bukhari 1796

حَدَّثَنَا أَحْمَدُ بْنُ عِيسَى، حَدَّثَنَا ابْنُ وَهْبٍ، أَخْبَرَنَا عَمْرٌو، عَنْ أَبِي الأَسْوَدِ، أَنَّ عَبْدَ اللهِ، مَوْلَى أَسْمَاءَ بِنْتِ أَبِي بَكْرٍ حَدَّثَهُ أَنَّهُ، كَانَ يَسْمَعُ أَسْمَاءَ تَقُولُ كُلَّمَا مَرَّتْ بِالْحَجُونِ صَلَّى اللهُ عَلَى مُحَمَّدٍ لَقَدْ نَزَلْنَا مَعَهُ هَا هُنَا، وَنَحْنُ يَوْمَئِذٍ خِفَافٌ، قَلِيلٌ ظَهْرُنَا، قَلِيلَةٌ أَزْوَادُنَا، فَاعْتَمَرْتُ أَنَا وَأُخْتِي عَائِشَةُ وَالزُّبَيْرُ وَفُلاَنٌ وَفُلاَنٌ، فَلَمَّا مَسَحْنَا الْبَيْتَ أَحْلَلْنَا، ثُمَّ أَهْلَلْنَا مِنَ الْعَشِيِّ بِالْحَجِّ

Narrated Asma: Some lady said, "O Allah's Messenger ﷺ! My husband has another wife, so it is sinful of me to claim that he has given me what he has not given me (in order to tease her)?" Allah's Messenger ﷺ said, The one who pretends that he has been given what he has not been given, is just like the (false) one who wears two garments of falsehood.". – Sahih Al-Bukhari 5219

حَدَّثَنَا سُلَيْمَانُ بْنُ حَرْبٍ، حَدَّثَنَا حَمَّادُ بْنُ زَيْدٍ، عَنْ هِشَامٍ، عَنْ فَاطِمَةَ، عَنْ أَسْمَاءَ، عَنِ النَّبِيِّ صلى الله عليه وسلم. حَدَّثَنِي مُحَمَّدُ بْنُ الْمُثَنَّى، حَدَّثَنَا يَحْيَى، عَنْ هِشَامٍ، حَدَّثَتْنِي فَاطِمَةُ، عَنْ أَسْمَاءَ، أَنَّ امْرَأَةً، قَالَتْ يَا رَسُولَ اللهِ إِنَّ لِي ضَرَّةً، فَهَلْ عَلَىَّ جُنَاحٌ إِنْ تَشَبَّعْتُ مِنْ زَوْجِي غَيْرَ الَّذِي يُعْطِينِي فَقَالَ رَسُولُ اللهِ صلى الله عليه وسلم " الْمُتَشَبِّعُ بِمَا لَمْ يُعْطَ كَلاَبِسِ ثَوْبَىْ زُورٍ "

Narrated Asma 'bint Abi Bakr: During the period of the peace treaty of Quraish with Allah's Messenger ﷺ, my mother, accompanied by her father, came to visit me, and she was a pagan. I consulted Allah's Messenger ﷺ, "O Allah's Messenger ﷺ! My mother has come to me and she desires to receive a reward from me, shall I keep good relation with her?" He said, "Yes, keep good relation with her.". – Sahih Al-Bukhari 3183

حَدَّثَنَا قُتَيْبَةُ بْنُ سَعِيدٍ، حَدَّثَنَا حَاتِمٌ، عَنْ هِشَامِ بْنِ عُرْوَةَ، عَنْ أَبِيهِ، عَنْ أَسْمَاءَ ابْنَةِ أَبِي بَكْرٍ ـ رضى الله عنهما ـ قَالَتْ قَدِمَتْ عَلَىَّ أُمِّي وَهْىَ مُشْرِكَةٌ فِي عَهْدِ قُرَيْشٍ، إِذْ عَاهَدُوا رَسُولَ اللهِ صلى الله عليه وسلم وَمُدَّتِهِمْ، مَعَ أَبِيهَا، فَاسْتَفْتَتْ رَسُولَ اللهِ صلى الله عليه وسلم فَقَالَتْ يَا رَسُولَ اللهِ، إِنَّ أُمِّي قَدِمَتْ عَلَىَّ، وَهْىَ رَاغِبَةٌ، أَفَأَصِلُهَا قَالَ " نَعَمْ، صِلِيهَا "

Narrated Asma bint Abu Bakr: I used to carry the date stones on my head from the land of Az-Zubair which Allah's Messenger ﷺ had given to him, and it was at a distance of 2/3 of a Farsakh from my house. Narrated Hisham's father: The Prophet ﷺ gave Az-Zubair a piece of land from the property of Bani An- Nadir (gained as war booty). – Sahih Al-Bukhari 3151

حَدَّثَنَا مَحْمُودُ بْنُ غَيْلاَنَ، حَدَّثَنَا أَبُو أُسَامَةَ، حَدَّثَنَا هِشَامٌ، قَالَ أَخْبَرَنِي أَبِي، عَنْ أَسْمَاءَ ابْنَةِ أَبِي بَكْرٍ ـ رضى الله عنهما ـ قَالَتْ كُنْتُ أَنْقُلُ النَّوَى مِنْ أَرْضِ الزُّبَيْرِ الَّتِي أَقْطَعَهُ رَسُولُ اللهِ صلى الله عليه وسلم عَلَى رَأْسِي، وَهْىَ مِنِّي عَلَى ثُلُثَىْ فَرْسَخٍ. وَقَالَ أَبُو ضَمْرَةَ عَنْ هِشَامٍ عَنْ أَبِيهِ أَنَّ النَّبِيَّ صلى الله عليه وسلم أَقْطَعَ الزُّبَيْرَ أَرْضًا مِنْ أَمْوَالِ بَنِي النَّضِيرِ

Narrated Asma' bint Abi Bakr: Allah's Messenger ﷺ once stood up delivering a sermon and mentioned the trial which people will face in the grave. When he mentioned that, the Muslims started shouting loudly. – Sahih Al-Bukhari 1373

حَدَّثَنَا يَحْيَى بْنُ سُلَيْمَانَ، حَدَّثَنَا ابْنُ وَهْبٍ، قَالَ أَخْبَرَنِي يُونُسُ، عَنِ ابْنِ شِهَابٍ، أَخْبَرَنِي عُرْوَةُ بْنُ الزُّبَيْرِ، أَنَّهُ سَمِعَ أَسْمَاءَ بِنْتَ أَبِي بَكْرٍ ـ رضى الله عنهما ـ تَقُولُ قَامَ رَسُولُ اللهِ صلى الله عليه وسلم خَطِيبًا فَذَكَرَ فِتْنَةَ الْقَبْرِ الَّتِي يَفْتَتِنُ فِيهَا الْمَرْءُ، فَلَمَّا ذَكَرَ ذَلِكَ ضَجَّ الْمُسْلِمُونَ ضَجَّةً.

Narrated Asma: Allah's Messenger ﷺ said, "Give (in charity) and do not give reluctantly lest Allah should give you in a limited amount; and do not withhold your money lest Allah should withhold it from you.". – Sahih Al-Bukhari 2591

حَدَّثَنَا عُبَيْدُ اللهِ بْنُ سَعِيدٍ، حَدَّثَنَا عَبْدُ اللهِ بْنُ نُمَيْرٍ، حَدَّثَنَا هِشَامُ بْنُ عُرْوَةَ، عَنْ فَاطِمَةَ، عَنْ أَسْمَاءَ، أَنَّ رَسُولَ اللهِ صلى الله عليه وسلم قَالَ " أَنْفِقِي وَلاَ تُحْصِي فَيُحْصِيَ اللهُ عَلَيْكِ، وَلاَ تُوعِي فَيُوعِيَ اللهُ عَلَيْكِ ".

ʿAbd al-Raḥmān ibn Abu Bakr

عبد الرحمن بن أبي بكر

Narrated Abu `Uthman: `Abdur Rahman bin Abi Bakr said, "The Suffa Companions were poor people and the Prophetﷺ said, 'Whoever has food for two persons should take a third one from them (Suffa companions). And whosoever has food for four persons he should take one or two from them' Abu Bakr took three men and the Prophetﷺ took ten of them." `Abdur Rahman added, my father my mother and I were there (in the house). (The sub-narrator is in doubt whether `Abdur Rahman also said, 'My wife and our servant who was common for both my house and Abu Bakr's house). Abu Bakr took his supper with the Prophetﷺ and remained there till the `Isha' prayer was offered. Abu Bakr went back and stayed with the Prophetﷺ till the Prophetﷺ took his meal and then Abu Bakr returned to his house after a long portion of the night had passed. Abu Bakr's wife said, 'What detained you from your guests (or guest)?' He said, 'Have you not served them yet?' She said, 'They refused to eat until you come. The food was served for them but they refused." `Abdur Rahman added, "I went away and hid myself (being afraid of Abu Bakr) and in the meantime he (Abu Bakr) called me, 'O Ghunthar (a harsh word)!' and also called me bad names and abused me and then said (to his family), 'Eat. No welcome for you.' Then (the supper was served). Abu Bakr took an oath that he would not eat that food. The narrator added: By Allah, whenever any one of us (myself and the guests of Suffa companions) took anything from the food, it increased from underneath. We all ate to our fill and the food was more than it was before its serving. Abu Bakr looked at it (the food) and found it as it was before serving or even more than that. He addressed his wife (saying) 'O the sister of Bani Firas! What is this?' She said, 'O the pleasure of my eyes! The food is now three times more than it was before.' Abu Bakr ate from it, and said, 'That (oath) was from Satan' meaning his oath (not to eat). Then he again took a morsel (mouthful) from it and then took the rest of it to the Prophet. So that meal was with the Prophet. There was a treaty between us and some people, and when the period of that treaty had elapsed the Prophetﷺ divided us into twelve (groups) (the Prophet's companions) each being headed by a man. Allah knows how many men were under the command of each (leader). So all of them (12 groups of men) ate of that meal.". – Sahih Al-Bukhari 602

حَدَّثَنَا أَبُو النُّعْمَانِ، قَالَ حَدَّثَنَا مُعْتَمِرُ بْنُ سُلَيْمَانَ، قَالَ حَدَّثَنَا أَبِي، حَدَّثَنَا أَبُو عُثْمَانَ، عَنْ عَبْدِ الرَّحْمَنِ بْنِ أَبِي بَكْرٍ، أَنَّ أَصْحَابَ الصُّفَّةِ، كَانُوا أُنَاسًا فُقَرَاءَ، وَأَنَّ النَّبِيَّ صلى الله عليه وسلم قَالَ " مَنْ كَانَ عِنْدَهُ طَعَامُ اثْنَيْنِ فَلْيَذْهَبْ بِثَالِثٍ، وَإِنْ أَرْبَعٌ فَخَامِسٌ أَوْ سَادِسٌ ". وَأَنَّ أَبَا بَكْرٍ جَاءَ بِثَلاَثَةٍ فَانْطَلَقَ النَّبِيُّ صلى الله عليه وسلم بِعَشَرَةٍ، قَالَ فَهْوَ أَنَا وَأَبِي وَأُمِّي، فَلاَ أَدْرِي قَالَ وَامْرَأَتِي وَخَادِمٌ بَيْنَنَا وَبَيْنَ بَيْتِ أَبِي بَكْرٍ. وَإِنَّ أَبَا بَكْرٍ تَعَشَّى عِنْدَ النَّبِيِّ صلى الله عليه وسلم ثُمَّ لَبِثَ حَيْثُ صُلِّيَتِ الْعِشَاءُ، ثُمَّ رَجَعَ فَلَبِثَ حَتَّى تَعَشَّى النَّبِيُّ صلى الله عليه وسلم فَجَاءَ بَعْدَ مَا مَضَى مِنَ اللَّيْلِ مَا شَاءَ اللَّهُ، قَالَتْ لَهُ امْرَأَتُهُ وَمَا حَبَسَكَ عَنْ أَضْيَافِكَ ـ أَوْ قَالَتْ ضَيْفِكَ ـ قَالَ أَوَمَا عَشَّيْتِيهِمْ قَالَتْ أَبَوْا حَتَّى تَجِيءَ، قَدْ عُرِضُوا فَأَبَوْا. قَالَ فَذَهَبْتُ أَنَا فَاخْتَبَأْتُ فَقَالَ يَا غُنْثَرُ، فَجَدَّعَ وَسَبَّ، وَقَالَ كُلُوا لاَ هَنِيئًا. فَقَالَ وَاللَّهِ لاَ أَطْعَمُهُ أَبَدًا، وَايْمُ اللَّهِ مَا كُنَّا نَأْخُذُ مِنْ لُقْمَةٍ إِلاَّ رَبَا مِنْ أَسْفَلِهَا أَكْثَرُ مِنْهَا. قَالَ يَعْنِي حَتَّى شَبِعُوا وَصَارَتْ أَكْثَرَ مِمَّا كَانَتْ قَبْلَ ذَلِكَ، فَنَظَرَ إِلَيْهَا أَبُو بَكْرٍ فَإِذَا هِيَ كَمَا هِيَ أَوْ أَكْثَرُ مِنْهَا. فَقَالَ لاِمْرَأَتِهِ يَا أُخْتَ بَنِي فِرَاسٍ مَا هَذَا قَالَتْ لاَ وَقُرَّةِ عَيْنِي لَهِيَ الآنَ أَكْثَرُ مِنْهَا قَبْلَ ذَلِكَ بِثَلاَثِ مَرَّاتٍ. فَأَكَلَ مِنْهَا أَبُو بَكْرٍ وَقَالَ إِنَّمَا كَانَ ذَلِكَ مِنَ الشَّيْطَانِ ـ يَعْنِي يَمِينَهُ ـ ثُمَّ أَكَلَ مِنْهَا لُقْمَةً، ثُمَّ حَمَلَهَا إِلَى النَّبِيِّ صلى الله عليه وسلم فَأَصْبَحَتْ عِنْدَهُ، وَكَانَ بَيْنَنَا وَبَيْنَ قَوْمٍ عَقْدٌ، فَمَضَى الأَجَلُ، فَفَرَّقَنَا اثْنَا عَشَرَ رَجُلاً، مَعَ كُلِّ رَجُلٍ مِنْهُمْ أُنَاسٌ، اللَّهُ أَعْلَمُ كَمْ مَعَ كُلِّ رَجُلٍ فَأَكَلُوا مِنْهَا أَجْمَعُونَ، أَوْ كَمَا قَالَ.

Narrated `Abdur-Rahman bin Abi Bakr As-Siddiq: The Prophetﷺ ordered me to let `Aisha sit behind me (on the animal) and to let her perform `Umra from at-Tan`im. – Sahih Al-Bukhari 2985

حَدَّثَنِي عَبْدُ اللَّهِ، حَدَّثَنَا ابْنُ عُيَيْنَةَ، عَنْ عَمْرِو بْنِ دِينَارٍ، عَنْ عَمْرِو بْنِ أَوْسٍ، عَنْ عَبْدِ الرَّحْمَنِ بْنِ أَبِي بَكْرٍ الصِّدِّيقِ - رضى الله عنهما - قَالَ أَمَرَنِي النَّبِيُّ صلى الله عليه وسلم أَنْ أُرْدِفَ عَائِشَةَ وَأُعْمِرَهَا مِنَ التَّنْعِيمِ.

Narrated Yusuf bin Mahak: Marwan had been appointed as the governor of Hijaz by Muawiya. He delivered a sermon and mentioned Yazid bin Muawiya so that the people might take the oath of allegiance to him as the successor of his father (Muawiya). Then `Abdur Rahman bin Abu Bakr told him something whereupon Marwan ordered that he be arrested. But `Abdur-Rahman entered `Aisha's house and they could not arrest him. Marwan said, "It is he (`AbdurRahman) about whom Allah revealed this Verse:-- 'And the one who says to his parents: 'Fie on you! Do you hold out the promise to me..?'" On that, `Aisha said from behind a screen, "Allah did not reveal anything from the Qur'an about us except what was connected with the declaration of my innocence (of the slander). – Sahih Al-Bukhari 4827

حَدَّثَنَا مُوسَى بْنُ إِسْمَاعِيلَ، حَدَّثَنَا أَبُو عَوَانَةَ، عَنْ أَبِي بِشْرٍ، عَنْ يُوسُفَ بْنِ مَاهَكَ، قَالَ كَانَ مَرْوَانُ عَلَى الْحِجَازِ اسْتَعْمَلَهُ مُعَاوِيَةُ، فَخَطَبَ فَجَعَلَ يَذْكُرُ يَزِيدَ بْنَ مُعَاوِيَةَ، لِكَىْ يُبَايَعَ لَهُ بَعْدَ أَبِيهِ، فَقَالَ لَهُ عَبْدُ الرَّحْمَنِ بْنُ أَبِي بَكْرٍ شَيْئًا، فَقَالَ خُذُوهُ. فَدَخَلَ بَيْتَ عَائِشَةَ فَلَمْ يَقْدِرُوا {عَلَيْهِ} فَقَالَ مَرْوَانُ إِنَّ هَذَا الَّذِي أَنْزَلَ اللَّهُ فِيهِ {وَالَّذِي قَالَ لِوَالِدَيْهِ أُفٍّ لَكُمَا أَتَعِدَانِنِي}. فَقَالَتْ عَائِشَةُ مِنْ وَرَاءِ الْحِجَابِ مَا أَنْزَلَ اللَّهُ فِينَا شَيْئًا مِنَ الْقُرْآنِ إِلاَّ أَنَّ اللَّهَ أَنْزَلَ عُذْرِي.

Narrated Salim: `Abdul Malik wrote to Al-Hajjaj that he should not differ from Ibn `Umar during Hajj. On the Day of `Arafat, when the sun declined at midday, Ibn `Umar came along with me and shouted near Al- Hajjaj's cotton (cloth) tent. Al-Hajjaj came Out, wrapping himself with a waist-sheet dyed with safflower, and said, "O Abu `Abdur-Rahman! What is the matter?" He said, If you want to follow the Sunna (the tradition of the Prophet ﷺ) then proceed (to `Arafat)." Al-Hajjaj asked, "At this very hour?" Ibn `Umar said, "Yes." He replied, "Please wait for me till I pour some water over my head (i.e. take a bath) and come out." Then Ibn `Umar dismounted and waited till Al-Hajjaj came out. So, he (Al-Hajjaj) walked in between me and my father (Ibn `Umar). I said to him, "If you want to follow the Sunna then deliver a brief sermon and hurry up for the stay at `Arafat." He started looking at `Abdullah (Ibn `Umar) (inquiringly), and when `Abdullah noticed that, he said that he had told the truth. – Sahih Al-Bukhari 1660

حَدَّثَنَا عَبْدُ اللَّهِ بْنُ يُوسُفَ، أَخْبَرَنَا مَالِكٌ، عَنِ ابْنِ شِهَابٍ، عَنْ سَالِمٍ، قَالَ كَتَبَ عَبْدُ الْمَلِكِ إِلَى الْحَجَّاجِ أَنْ لاَ يُخَالِفَ ابْنَ عُمَرَ فِي الْحَجِّ، فَجَاءَ ابْنُ عُمَرَ - رضى الله عنه - وَأَنَا مَعَهُ يَوْمَ عَرَفَةَ حِينَ زَالَتِ الشَّمْسُ، فَصَاحَ عِنْدَ سُرَادِقِ الْحَجَّاجِ، فَخَرَجَ وَعَلَيْهِ مِلْحَفَةٌ مُعَصْفَرَةٌ فَقَالَ مَا لَكَ يَا أَبَا عَبْدِ الرَّحْمَنِ فَقَالَ الرَّوَاحَ إِنْ كُنْتَ تُرِيدُ السُّنَّةَ. قَالَ هَذِهِ السَّاعَةَ قَالَ نَعَمْ. قَالَ فَأَنْظِرْنِي حَتَّى أُفِيضَ عَلَى رَأْسِي ثُمَّ أَخْرُجَ. فَنَزَلَ حَتَّى خَرَجَ الْحَجَّاجُ، فَسَارَ بَيْنِي وَبَيْنَ أَبِي، فَقُلْتُ إِنْ كُنْتَ تُرِيدُ السُّنَّةَ فَاقْصُرِ الْخُطْبَةَ وَعَجِّلِ الْوُقُوفَ. فَجَعَلَ يَنْظُرُ إِلَى عَبْدِ اللَّهِ، فَلَمَّا رَأَى ذَلِكَ عَبْدُ اللَّهِ قَالَ صَدَقَ

Narrated Ibn `Umar: The Prophet ﷺ said, "The buyer and the seller have the option to cancel or confirm the bargain before they separate from each other or if the sale is optional." Nafi` said, "Ibn `Umar used to separate quickly from the seller if he had bought a thing which he liked.". – Sahih Al-Bukhari 2107

حَدَّثَنَا صَدَقَةُ، أَخْبَرَنَا عَبْدُ الْوَهَّابِ، قَالَ سَمِعْتُ يَحْيَى، قَالَ سَمِعْتُ نَافِعًا، عَنِ ابْنِ عُمَرَ، رضى الله عنهما عَنِ النَّبِيِّ صلى الله عليه وسلم قَالَ " إِنَّ الْمُتَبَايِعَيْنِ بِالْخِيَارِ فِي بَيْعِهِمَا، مَا لَمْ يَتَفَرَّقَا، أَوْ يَكُونُ الْبَيْعُ خِيَارًا ". قَالَ نَافِعٌ وَكَانَ ابْنُ عُمَرَ إِذَا اشْتَرَى شَيْئًا يُعْجِبُهُ فَارَقَ صَاحِبَهُ

Narrated `Uthman: (the son of Muhib) An Egyptian who came and performed the Hajj to the Ka`ba saw some people sitting. He enquire, "Who are these people?" Somebody said, "They are the tribe of Quraish." He said, "Who is the old man sitting amongst them?" The people replied, "He is `Abdullah bin `Umar." He said, "O Ibn `Umar! I want to ask you about something; please tell me about it. Do you know that `Uthman fled away on the day (of the battle) of Uhud?" Ibn `Umar said, "Yes." The (Egyptian) man said, "Do you know that `Uthman was absent on the day (of the battle) of Badr and did not join it?" Ibn `Umar said, "Yes." The man said, "Do you know that he failed to attend the Ar Ridwan pledge and did not witness it (i.e. Hudaibiya pledge of allegiance)?" Ibn `Umar said, "Yes." The man said, "Allahu Akbar!" Ibn `Umar said, "Let me explain to you (all these three things). As for his flight on the day of Uhud, I testify that Allah has excused him and forgiven him; and as for his absence from the battle of Badr, it was due to the fact that the daughter of Allah's Messenger ﷺ was his wife and she was sick then. Allah's Messenger ﷺ said to him, "You will receive the same reward and share (of the booty) as anyone of those who participated in the battle of Badr (if you stay with her).' As for his absence from the Ar-Ridwan pledge of allegiance, had there been any person in Mecca more respectable than `Uthman (to be sent as a representative). Allah's Messenger ﷺ would have sent him instead of him. No doubt, Allah's Messenger ﷺ had sent him, and the incident of the Ar-Ridwan pledge of Allegiance happened after `Uthman had gone to Mecca. Allah's Messenger ﷺ held out his right hand saying, 'This is `Uthman's hand.' He stroke his (other) hand with it saying, 'This (pledge of allegiance) is on the behalf of `Uthman.' Then Ibn `Umar said to the man, 'Bear (these) excuses in mind with you.'. – Sahih Al-Bukhari 3698

حَدَّثَنَا مُوسَى بْنُ إِسْمَاعِيلَ، حَدَّثَنَا أَبُو عَوَانَةَ، حَدَّثَنَا عُثْمَانُ ـ هُوَ ابْنُ مَوْهَبٍ ـ قَالَ جَاءَ رَجُلٌ مَنْ أَهْلِ مِصْرَ حَجَّ الْبَيْتَ فَرَأَى قَوْمًا جُلُوسًا، فَقَالَ مَنْ هَؤُلاَءِ الْقَوْمُ قَالَ هَؤُلاَءِ قُرَيْشٌ. قَالَ فَمَنِ الشَّيْخُ فِيهِمْ قَالُوا عَبْدُ اللَّهِ بْنُ عُمَرَ. قَالَ يَا ابْنَ عُمَرَ إِنِّي سَائِلُكَ عَنْ شَىْءٍ فَحَدِّثْنِي هَلْ تَعْلَمُ أَنَّ عُثْمَانَ فَرَّ يَوْمَ أُحُدٍ قَالَ نَعَمْ. قَالَ تَعْلَمُ أَنَّهُ تَغَيَّبَ عَنْ بَدْرٍ وَلَمْ يَشْهَدْ قَالَ نَعَمْ. قَالَ تَعْلَمُ أَنَّهُ تَغَيَّبَ عَنْ بَيْعَةِ الرُّضْوَانِ فَلَمْ يَشْهَدْهَا قَالَ نَعَمْ. قَالَ اللَّهُ أَكْبَرُ. قَالَ ابْنُ عُمَرَ تَعَالَ أُبَيِّنْ لَكَ أَمَّا فِرَارُهُ يَوْمَ أُحُدٍ فَأَشْهَدُ أَنَّ اللَّهَ عَفَا عَنْهُ وَغَفَرَ لَهُ، وَأَمَّا تَغَيُّبُهُ عَنْ بَدْرٍ، فَإِنَّهُ كَانَتْ تَحْتَهُ بِنْتُ رَسُولِ اللَّهِ صلى الله عليه وسلم وَكَانَتْ مَرِيضَةً، فَقَالَ لَهُ رَسُولُ اللَّهِ صلى الله عليه وسلم " إِنَّ لَكَ أَجْرَ رَجُلٍ مِمَّنْ شَهِدَ بَدْرًا وَسَهْمَهُ ". وَأَمَّا تَغَيُّبُهُ عَنْ بَيْعَةِ الرُّضْوَانِ فَلَوْ كَانَ أَحَدٌ أَعَزَّ بِبَطْنِ مَكَّةَ مِنْ عُثْمَانَ لَبَعَثَهُ مَكَانَهُ فَبَعَثَ رَسُولُ اللَّهِ صلى الله عليه وسلم عُثْمَانَ وَكَانَتْ بَيْعَةُ الرُّضْوَانِ بَعْدَ مَا ذَهَبَ عُثْمَانُ إِلَى مَكَّةَ، فَقَالَ رَسُولُ اللَّهِ صلى الله عليه وسلم بِيَدِهِ الْيُمْنَى " هَذِهِ يَدُ عُثْمَانَ ". فَضَرَبَ بِهَا عَلَى يَدِهِ، فَقَالَ " هَذِهِ لِعُثْمَانَ ". فَقَالَ لَهُ ابْنُ عُمَرَ اذْهَبْ بِهَا الآنَ مَعَكَ

Abd Allāh ibn ʿUmar ibn al-Khaṭṭāb

عبد الله بن عمر ابن الخطاب

Narrated `Ubaid Ibn Juraij: I asked `Abdullah bin `Umar, "O Abu `Abdur-Rahman! I saw you doing four things which I never saw being done by anyone of you companions?" `Abdullah bin `Umar said, "What are those, O Ibn Juraij?" I said, "I never saw you touching any corner of the Ka`ba except these (two) facing south (Yemen) and I saw you wearing shoes made of tanned leather and dyeing your hair with Hinna (a kind of red dye). I also noticed that whenever you were in Mecca, the people assume Ihram on seeing the new moon crescent (1st of Dhul-Hijja) while you did not assume the Ihlal (Ihram) –(Ihram is also called Ihlal which means 'Loud calling' because a Muhrim has to recite Talbiya aloud when assuming the state of Ihram) – till the 8th of Dhul-Hijja (Day of Tarwiya). `Abdullah replied, "Regarding the corners of Ka`ba, I never saw Allah's Messenger ﷺ touching except those facing south (Yemen) and regarding the tanned leather shoes, no doubt I saw Allah's Messenger ﷺ wearing non-hairy shoes and he used to perform ablution while wearing the shoes (i.e. wash his feet and then put on the shoes). So I love to wear similar shoes. And about the dyeing of hair with Hinna; no doubt I saw Allah's Messenger ﷺ dyeing his hair with it and that is why I like to dye (my hair with it). Regarding Ihlal, I did not see Allah's Messenger ﷺ assuming Ihlal till he set out for Hajj (on the 8th of Dhul-Hijja). – Sahih Al-Bukhari 166

حَدَّثَنَا عَبْدُ اللَّهِ بْنُ يُوسُفَ، قَالَ أَخْبَرَنَا مَالِكٌ، عَنْ سَعِيدٍ الْمَقْبُرِيِّ، عَنْ عُبَيْدِ بْنِ جُرَيْجٍ، أَنَّهُ قَالَ لِعَبْدِ اللَّهِ بْنِ عُمَرَ يَا أَبَا عَبْدِ الرَّحْمَنِ، رَأَيْتُكَ تَصْنَعُ أَرْبَعًا لَمْ أَرَ أَحَدًا مِنْ أَصْحَابِكَ يَصْنَعُهَا. قَالَ وَمَا هِيَ يَا ابْنَ جُرَيْجٍ قَالَ رَأَيْتُكَ لاَ تَمَسُّ مِنَ الأَرْكَانِ إِلاَّ الْيَمَانِيَيْنِ، وَرَأَيْتُكَ تَلْبَسُ النِّعَالَ السِّبْتِيَّةَ، وَرَأَيْتُكَ تَصْبُغُ بِالصُّفْرَةِ، وَرَأَيْتُكَ إِذَا كُنْتَ بِمَكَّةَ أَهَلَّ النَّاسُ إِذَا رَأَوُا الْهِلاَلَ وَلَمْ تُهِلَّ أَنْتَ حَتَّى كَانَ يَوْمُ التَّرْوِيَةِ. قَالَ عَبْدُ اللَّهِ أَمَّا الأَرْكَانُ فَإِنِّي لَمْ أَرَ رَسُولَ اللَّهِ صلى الله عليه وسلم يَمَسُّ إِلاَّ الْيَمَانِيَيْنِ، وَأَمَّا النِّعَالُ السِّبْتِيَّةُ فَإِنِّي رَأَيْتُ رَسُولَ اللَّهِ صلى الله عليه وسلم يَلْبَسُ النَّعْلَ الَّتِي لَيْسَ فِيهَا شَعَرٌ وَيَتَوَضَّأُ فِيهَا، فَأَنَا أُحِبُّ أَنْ أَلْبَسَهَا، وَأَمَّا الصُّفْرَةُ فَإِنِّي رَأَيْتُ رَسُولَ اللَّهِ صلى الله عليه وسلم يَصْبُغُ بِهَا، فَأَنَا أُحِبُّ أَنْ أَصْبُغَ بِهَا، وَأَمَّا الإِهْلاَلُ فَإِنِّي لَمْ أَرَ رَسُولَ اللَّهِ صلى الله عليه وسلم يُهِلُّ حَتَّى تَنْبَعِثَ بِهِ رَاحِلَتُهُ.

Narrated Muhammad bin Al-Muntathir:On the authority of his father that he had asked `Aisha about the saying of Ibn `Umar (i.e. he did not like to be a Muhrim while the smell of scent was still coming from his body). `Aisha said, "I scented Allah's Messenger ﷺ and he went round (had sexual intercourse with) all his wives, and in the morning he was Muhrim (after taking a bath).". – Sahih Al-Bukhari 270

حَدَّثَنَا أَبُو النُّعْمَانِ، قَالَ حَدَّثَنَا أَبُو عَوَانَةَ، عَنْ إِبْرَاهِيمَ بْنِ مُحَمَّدِ بْنِ الْمُنْتَشِرِ، عَنْ أَبِيهِ، قَالَ سَأَلْتُ عَائِشَةَ فَذَكَرْتُ لَهَا قَوْلَ ابْنِ عُمَرَ مَا أُحِبُّ أَنْ أُصْبِحَ، مُحْرِمًا أَنْضَخُ طِيبًا. فَقَالَتْ عَائِشَةُ أَنَا طَيَّبْتُ رَسُولَ اللَّهِ صلى الله عليه وسلم ثُمَّ طَافَ فِي نِسَائِهِ ثُمَّ أَصْبَحَ مُحْرِمًا

Narrated Salim: `Abdullah bin `Umar said, "I knew that the land was rented for cultivation in the lifetime of Allah's Apostle ." Later on Ibn `Umar was afraid that the Prophet ﷺ had forbidden it, and he had no knowledge of it, so he gave up renting his land. – Sahih Al-Bukhari 2345

حَدَّثَنَا يَحْيَى بْنُ بُكَيْرٍ، حَدَّثَنَا اللَّيْثُ، عَنْ عُقَيْلٍ، عَنِ ابْنِ شِهَابٍ، أَخْبَرَنِي سَالِمٌ، أَنَّ عَبْدَ اللَّهِ بْنَ عُمَرَ ـ رضى الله عنهما ـ قَالَ كُنْتُ أَعْلَمُ فِي عَهْدِ رَسُولِ اللَّهِ صلى الله عليه وسلم أَنَّ الأَرْضَ تُكْرَى. ثُمَّ خَشِيَ عَبْدُ اللَّهِ أَنْ يَكُونَ النَّبِيُّ صلى الله عليه وسلم قَدْ أَحْدَثَ فِي ذَلِكَ شَيْئًا لَمْ يَكُنْ يَعْلَمُهُ، فَتَرَكَ كِرَاءَ الأَرْضِ

Mujahid said , "Once I said to Ibn 'Umar let us proceed for Jihad," Ibn_'Umar replied, 'I would like to support you with some of my money.' I replied, Allah has given me enough.' He said, Your wealth is for you, but I like that some of my money be spent in this cause."" – Sahih Al-Bukhari Vol 4 page 137

و قال مجاهد : قلت لا بن عمر : الغزو ، قال : اني احب ان أعينكم بطاءفة من مالي، قلت : أوسع الله علي ، قال : ان غناك لك، و اني احب ان يكون من مالي في هذا الوجه.

Narrated `Abdullah bin Dinar: One day Ibn `Umar, while in the Mosque, looked at a man who was dragging his clothes while walking in one of the corners of the Mosque He said, "See who is that. I wish he was near to me." Somebody then said (to Ibn `Umar), "Don't you know him, O Abu `Abdur-Rahman? He is Muhammad bin Usama." On that Ibn `Umar bowed his head and dug the earth with his hands and then, said, "If Allah's Messenger ﷺ saw him, he would have loved him.". – Sahih Al-Bukhari 3734

حَدَّثَنِي الْحَسَنُ بْنُ مُحَمَّدٍ، حَدَّثَنَا أَبُو عَبَّادٍ، يَحْيَى بْنُ عَبَّادٍ حَدَّثَنَا الْمَاجِشُونُ، أَخْبَرَنَا عَبْدُ اللَّهِ بْنُ دِينَارٍ، قَالَ نَظَرَ ابْنُ عُمَرَ يَوْمًا وَهْوَ فِي الْمَسْجِدِ إِلَى رَجُلٍ يَسْحَبُ ثِيَابَهُ فِي نَاحِيَةٍ مِنَ الْمَسْجِدِ فَقَالَ انْظُرْ مَنْ هَذَا لَيْتَ هَذَا عِنْدِي. قَالَ لَهُ إِنْسَانٌ أَمَا تَعْرِفُ هَذَا يَا أَبَا عَبْدِ الرَّحْمَنِ هَذَا مُحَمَّدُ بْنُ أُسَامَةَ، قَالَ فَطَأْطَأَ ابْنُ عُمَرَ رَأْسَهُ، وَنَقَرَ بِيَدَيْهِ فِي الأَرْضِ، ثُمَّ قَالَ لَوْ رَآهُ رَسُولُ اللَّهِ صلى الله عليه وسلم لأَحَبَّهُ.

Narrated Hisham's father: It was mentioned before `Aisha that Ibn `Umar attributed the following statement to the Prophet ﷺ "The dead person is punished in the grave because of the crying and lamentation Of his family." On that, `Aisha said, "But Allah's Messenger ﷺ said, 'The dead person is punished for his crimes and sins while his family cry over him then." She added, "And this is similar to the statement of Allah's Messenger ﷺ when he stood by the (edge of the) well which contained the corpses of the pagans killed at Badr, 'They hear what I say.' She added, "But he said now they know very well what I used to tell them was the truth." `Aisha then recited: 'You cannot make the dead hear.' (30.52) and 'You cannot make those who are in their Graves, hear you.' (35.22) that is, when they had taken their places in the (Hell) Fire. – Sahih Al-Bukhari 3978, 3979

حَدَّثَنِي عُبَيْدُ بْنُ إِسْمَاعِيلَ، حَدَّثَنَا أَبُو أُسَامَةَ، عَنْ هِشَامٍ، عَنْ أَبِيهِ، قَالَ ذُكِرَ عِنْدَ عَائِشَةَ ـ رضى الله عنها ـ أَنَّ ابْنَ عُمَرَ رَفَعَ إِلَى النَّبِيِّ صلى الله عليه وسلم " إِنَّ الْمَيِّتَ يُعَذَّبُ فِي قَبْرِهِ بِبُكَاءِ أَهْلِهِ ". فَقَالَتْ إِنَّمَا قَالَ رَسُولُ اللَّهِ صلى الله عليه وسلم " إِنَّهُ لَيُعَذَّبُ بِخَطِيئَتِهِ وَذَنْبِهِ، وَإِنَّ أَهْلَهُ لَيَبْكُونَ عَلَيْهِ الآنَ ". قَالَتْ وَذَاكَ مِثْلُ قَوْلِهِ إِنَّ رَسُولَ اللَّهِ صلى الله عليه وسلم قَامَ عَلَى الْقَلِيبِ وَفِيهِ قَتْلَى بَدْرٍ مِنَ الْمُشْرِكِينَ، فَقَالَ لَهُمْ مَا قَالَ إِنَّهُمْ لَيَسْمَعُونَ مَا أَقُولُ. إِنَّمَا قَالَ " إِنَّهُمُ الآنَ لَيَعْلَمُونَ أَنَّ مَا كُنْتُ أَقُولُ لَهُمْ حَقٌّ ". ثُمَّ قَرَأَتْ {إِنَّكَ لاَ تُسْمِعُ الْمَوْتَى} {وَمَا أَنْتَ بِمُسْمِعٍ مَنْ فِي الْقُبُورِ} تَقُولُ حِينَ تَبَوَّءُوا مَقَاعِدَهُمْ مِنَ النَّارِ

Narrated `Uthman bin Mauhab: A man came to perform the Hajj to (Allah's) House. Seeing some people sitting, he said, "Who are these sitting people?" Somebody said, "They are the people of Quraish." He said, "Who is the old man?" They said, "Ibn `Umar." He went to him and said, "I want to ask you about something; will you tell me about it? I ask you with the respect due to the sanctity of this (Sacred) House, do you know that `Uthman bin `Affan fled on the day of Uhud?" Ibn `Umar said, "Yes." He said, "Do you know that he (i.e. `Uthman) was absent from the Badr (battle) and did not join it?" Ibn `Umar said, "Yes." He said, "Do you know that he failed to be present at the Ridwan Pledge of allegiance (i.e. Pledge of allegiance at Hudaibiya) and did not witness it?" Ibn `Umar replied, "Yes," He then said, "Allahu- Akbar!" Ibn `Umar said, "Come along; I will inform you and explain to you what you have asked. As for the flight (of `Uthman) on the day of Uhud, I testify that Allah forgave him. As regards his absence from the Badr (battle), he was married to the daughter of Allah's Messenger ﷺ and she was ill, so the Prophet ﷺ said to him, 'You will have such reward as a man who has fought the Badr battle will get, and will also have the same share of the booty.' As for his absence from the Ridwan Pledge of allegiance if there had been anybody more respected by the Meccans than `Uthman bin `Affan, the Prophet would surely have sent that man instead of `Uthman. So the Prophet ﷺ sent him (i.e. `Uthman to Mecca) and the Ridwan Pledge of allegiance took place after `Uthman had gone to Mecca. The Prophet raised his right hand saying. 'This is the hand of `Uthman,' and clapped it over his other hand and said, "This is for `Uthman.'" Ibn `Umar then said (to the man), "Go now, after taking this information.". – Sahih Al-Bukhari 4066

حَدَّثَنَا عَبْدَانُ، أَخْبَرَنَا أَبُو حَمْزَةَ، عَنْ عُثْمَانَ بْنِ مَوْهَبٍ، قَالَ جَاءَ رَجُلٌ حَجَّ الْبَيْتَ فَرَأَى قَوْمًا جُلُوسًا فَقَالَ مَنْ هَؤُلاَءِ الْقُعُودُ قَالُوا هَؤُلاَءِ قُرَيْشٌ. قَالَ مَنِ الشَّيْخُ قَالُوا ابْنُ عُمَرَ. فَأَتَاهُ فَقَالَ إِنِّي سَائِلُكَ عَنْ شَىْءٍ أَتُحَدِّثُنِي، قَالَ أَنْشُدُكَ بِحُرْمَةِ هَذَا الْبَيْتِ أَتَعْلَمُ أَنَّ عُثْمَانَ بْنَ عَفَّانَ فَرَّ يَوْمَ أُحُدٍ قَالَ نَعَمْ. قَالَ فَتَعْلَمُهُ تَغَيَّبَ عَنْ بَدْرٍ فَلَمْ يَشْهَدْهَا قَالَ نَعَمْ. قَالَ فَتَعْلَمُ أَنَّهُ تَخَلَّفَ عَنْ بَيْعَةِ الرُّضْوَانِ فَلَمْ يَشْهَدْهَا قَالَ نَعَمْ. قَالَ فَكَبَّرَ. قَالَ ابْنُ عُمَرَ تَعَالَ لأُخْبِرَكَ وَلأُبَيِّنَ لَكَ عَمَّا سَأَلْتَنِي عَنْهُ، أَمَّا فِرَارُهُ يَوْمَ أُحُدٍ فَأَشْهَدُ أَنَّ اللَّهَ عَفَا عَنْهُ، وَأَمَّا تَغَيُّبُهُ عَنْ بَدْرٍ فَإِنَّهُ كَانَ تَحْتَهُ بِنْتُ رَسُولِ اللَّهِ صلى الله عليه وسلم وَكَانَتْ مَرِيضَةً، فَقَالَ لَهُ النَّبِيُّ صلى الله عليه وسلم " إِنَّ لَكَ أَجْرَ رَجُلٍ مِمَّنْ شَهِدَ بَدْرًا وَسَهْمَهُ ". وَأَمَّا تَغَيُّبُهُ عَنْ بَيْعَةِ الرُّضْوَانِ فَإِنَّهُ لَوْ كَانَ أَحَدٌ أَعَزَّ بِبَطْنِ مَكَّةَ مِنْ عُثْمَانَ بْنِ عَفَّانَ لَبَعَثَهُ مَكَانَهُ، فَبَعَثَ عُثْمَانَ، وَكَانَ بَيْعَةُ الرُّضْوَانِ بَعْدَ مَا ذَهَبَ عُثْمَانُ إِلَى مَكَّةَ فَقَالَ النَّبِيُّ صلى الله عليه وسلم بِيَدِهِ الْيُمْنَى " هَذِهِ يَدُ عُثْمَانَ ". فَضَرَبَ بِهَا عَلَى يَدِهِ فَقَالَ " هَذِهِ لِعُثْمَانَ ". اذْهَبْ بِهَذَا الآنَ مَعَكَ

Narrated Mujahid: `Urwa and I entered the Mosque and found `Abdullah bin `Umar sitting beside the dwelling place of `Aisha. `Urwa asked (Ibn `Umar), "How many `Umras did the Prophet ﷺ perform?" Ibn `Umar replied, "Four, one of which was in Rajab." Then we heard `Aisha brushing her teeth whereupon `Urwa said, "O mother of the believers! Don't you hear what Abu `Abdur-Rahman is saying? He is saying that the Prophet performed four `Umra, one of which was in Rajab." `Aisha said, "The Prophet ﷺ did not perform any `Umra but he (i.e. Ibn `Umar) witnessed it. And he (the Prophet ﷺ) never did any `Umra in (the month of) Rajab.". – Sahih Al-Bukhari 4253, 4254

حَدَّثَنِي عُثْمَانُ بْنُ أَبِي شَيْبَةَ، حَدَّثَنَا جَرِيرٌ، عَنْ مَنْصُورٍ، عَنْ مُجَاهِدٍ، قَالَ دَخَلْتُ أَنَا وَعُرْوَةُ بْنُ الزُّبَيْرِ الْمَسْجِدَ، فَإِذَا عَبْدُ اللَّهِ بْنُ عُمَرَ ـ رضى الله عنهما ـ جَالِسٌ إِلَى حُجْرَةِ عَائِشَةَ ثُمَّ قَالَ كَمِ اعْتَمَرَ النَّبِيُّ صلى الله عليه وسلم قَالَ أَرْبَعًا {إِحْدَاهُنَّ فِي رَجَبٍ} ثُمَّ سَمِعْنَا اسْتِنَانَ، عَائِشَةَ قَالَ عُرْوَةُ يَا أُمَّ الْمُؤْمِنِينَ أَلاَ تَسْمَعِينَ مَا يَقُولُ أَبُو عَبْدِ الرَّحْمَنِ إِنَّ النَّبِيَّ صلى الله عليه وسلم اعْتَمَرَ أَرْبَعَ عُمَرٍ. فَقَالَتْ مَا اعْتَمَرَ النَّبِيُّ صلى الله عليه وسلم عُمْرَةً إِلاَّ وَهْوَ شَاهِدُهُ، وَمَا اعْتَمَرَ فِي رَجَبٍ قَطُّ

Narrated Nafi`: During the affliction of Ibn Az-Zubair, two men came to Ibn `Umar and said, "The people are lost, and you are the son of `Umar, and the companion of the Prophet, so what forbids you from coming out?" He said, "What forbids me is that Allah has prohibited the shedding of my brother's blood." They both said, "Didn't Allah say, 'And fight then until there is no more affliction?" He said "We fought until there was no more affliction and the worship is for Allah (Alone while you want to fight until there is affliction and until the worship become for other than Allah." Narrated Nafi` (through another group of sub-narrators): A man came to Ibn `Umar and said, "O Abu `Abdur Rahman! What made you perform Hajj in one year and Umra in another year and leave the Jihad for Allah' Cause though you know how much Allah recommends it?" Ibn `Umar replied, "O son of my brother! Islam is founded on five principles, i.e. believe in Allah and His Apostle, the five compulsory prayers, the fasting of the month of Ramadan, the payment of Zakat, and the Hajj to the House (of Allah)." The man said, "O Abu `Abdur Rahman! Won't you listen to why Allah has mentioned in His Book: 'If two groups of believers fight each other, then make peace between them, but if one of then transgresses beyond bounds against the other, then you all fight against the one that transgresses. (49.9) and:--"And fight them till there is no more affliction (i.e. no more worshiping of others along with Allah)." Ibn `Umar said, "We did it, during the lifetime of Allah's Messenger ﷺ when Islam had only a few followers. A man would be put to trial because of his religion; he would either be killed or tortured. But when the Muslims increased, there was no more afflictions or oppressions." The man said, "What is your opinion about `Uthman and `Ali?" Ibn `Umar said, "As for `Uthman, it seems that Allah has forgiven him, but you people dislike that he should be forgiven. And as for `Ali, he is the cousin of Allah's Messenger ﷺ and his son-in-law." Then he pointed with his hand and said, "That is his house which you see.". – Sahih Al-Bukhari 4513, 4514, 4515

حَدَّثَنَا مُحَمَّدُ بْنُ بَشَّارٍ، حَدَّثَنَا عَبْدُ الْوَهَّابِ، حَدَّثَنَا عُبَيْدُ اللَّهِ، عَنْ نَافِعٍ، عَنِ ابْنِ عُمَرَ ـ رضى الله عنهما ـ أَتَاهُ رَجُلاَنِ فِي فِتْنَةِ ابْنِ الزُّبَيْرِ فَقَالاَ إِنَّ النَّاسَ قَدْ ضُيِّعُوا، وَأَنْتَ ابْنُ عُمَرَ وَصَاحِبُ النَّبِيِّ صلى الله عليه وسلم فَمَا يَمْنَعُكَ أَنْ تَخْرُجَ فَقَالَ يَمْنَعُنِي أَنَّ اللَّهَ حَرَّمَ دَمَ أَخِي. فَقَالاَ أَلَمْ يَقُلِ اللَّهُ {وَقَاتِلُوهُمْ حَتَّى لاَ تَكُونَ فِتْنَةٌ } فَقَالَ قَاتَلْنَا حَتَّى لَمْ تَكُنْ فِتْنَةٌ، وَكَانَ الدِّينُ لِلَّهِ، وَأَنْتُمْ تُرِيدُونَ أَنْ تُقَاتِلُوا حَتَّى تَكُونَ فِتْنَةٌ، وَيَكُونَ الدِّينُ لِغَيْرِ اللَّهِ. وَزَادَ عُثْمَانُ بْنُ صَالِحٍ عَنِ ابْنِ وَهْبٍ، قَالَ أَخْبَرَنِي فُلاَنٌ، وَحَيْوَةُ بْنُ شُرَيْحٍ، عَنْ بَكْرِ بْنِ عَمْرٍو الْمَعَافِرِيِّ، أَنَّ بُكَيْرَ بْنَ عَبْدِ اللَّهِ، حَدَّثَهُ عَنْ نَافِعٍ، أَنَّ رَجُلاً، أَتَى ابْنَ عُمَرَ فَقَالَ يَا أَبَا عَبْدِ الرَّحْمَنِ مَا حَمَلَكَ عَلَى أَنْ تَحُجَّ عَامًا وَتَعْتَمِرَ عَامًا، وَتَتْرُكَ الْجِهَادَ فِي سَبِيلِ اللَّهِ عَزَّ وَجَلَّ، وَقَدْ عَلِمْتَ مَا رَغَّبَ اللَّهُ فِيهِ قَالَ يَا ابْنَ أَخِي بُنِيَ الإِسْلاَمُ عَلَى خَمْسٍ إِيمَانٍ بِاللَّهِ وَرَسُولِهِ، وَالصَّلاَةِ الْخَمْسِ، وَصِيَامِ رَمَضَانَ، وَأَدَاءِ الزَّكَاةِ، وَحَجِّ الْبَيْتِ. قَالَ يَا أَبَا عَبْدِ الرَّحْمَنِ، أَلاَ تَسْمَعُ مَا ذَكَرَ اللَّهُ فِي كِتَابِهِ {وَإِنْ طَائِفَتَانِ مِنَ الْمُؤْمِنِينَ اقْتَتَلُوا فَأَصْلِحُوا بَيْنَهُمَا} {إِلَى أَمْرِ اللَّهِ} {قَاتِلُوهُمْ حَتَّى لاَ تَكُونَ فِتْنَةٌ} قَالَ فَعَلْنَا عَلَى عَهْدِ رَسُولِ اللَّهِ صلى الله عليه وسلم وَكَانَ الإِسْلاَمُ قَلِيلاً، فَكَانَ الرَّجُلُ يُفْتَنُ فِي دِينِهِ إِمَّا قَتَلُوهُ، وَإِمَّا يُعَذِّبُوهُ، حَتَّى كَثُرَ الإِسْلاَمُ فَلَمْ تَكُنْ فِتْنَةٌ. قَالَ فَمَا قَوْلُكَ فِي عَلِيٍّ وَعُثْمَانَ قَالَ أَمَّا عُثْمَانُ فَكَأَنَّ اللَّهَ عَفَا عَنْهُ، وَأَمَّا أَنْتُمْ فَكَرِهْتُمْ أَنْ تَعْفُوا عَنْهُ، وَأَمَّا عَلِيٌّ فَابْنُ عَمِّ رَسُولِ اللَّهِ صلى الله عليه وسلم وَخَتَنُهُ. وَأَشَارَ بِيَدِهِ فَقَالَ هَذَا بَيْتُهُ حَيْثُ تَرَوْنَ.

Narrated Safwan bin Muhriz: While Ibn `Umar was performing the Tawaf (around the Ka`ba), a man came up to him and said, "O Abu `AbdurRahman!" or said, "O Ibn `Umar! Did you hear anything from the Prophet ﷺ about An35 Najwa?" Ibn `Umar said, "I heard the Prophet

ﷺsaying, ‘The Believer will be brought near his Lord.” (Hisham, a sub-narrator said, reporting the Prophet’s words), “The believer will come near (his Lord) till his Lord covers him with His screen and makes him confess his sins. (Allah will ask him), ‘Do you know (that you did) ‘such-and-such sin?” He will say twice, ‘Yes, I do.’ Then Allah will say, ‘I concealed it in the world and I forgive it for you today.’ Then the record of his good deeds will be folded up. As for the others, or the disbelievers, it will be announced publicly before the witnesses: ‘These are ones who lied against their Lord.”. – Sahih Al-Bukhari 4685

حَدَّثَنَا مُسَدَّدٌ، حَدَّثَنَا يَزِيدُ بْنُ زُرَيْعٍ، حَدَّثَنَا سَعِيدٌ، وَهِشَامٌ، قَالاَ حَدَّثَنَا قَتَادَةُ، عَنْ صَفْوَانَ بْنِ مُحْرِزٍ، قَالَ بَيْنَا ابْنُ عُمَرَ يَطُوفُ إِذْ عَرَضَ رَجُلٌ فَقَالَ يَا أَبَا عَبْدِ الرَّحْمَنِ ـ أَوْ قَالَ يَا ابْنَ عُمَرَ ـ سَمِعْتَ النَّبِيَّ صلى الله عليه وسلم فِي النَّجْوَى فَقَالَ سَمِعْتُ النَّبِيَّ صلى الله عليه وسلم يَقُولُ " يُدْنَى الْمُؤْمِنُ مِنْ رَبِّهِ ـ وَقَالَ هِشَامٌ يَدْنُو الْمُؤْمِنُ ـ حَتَّى يَضَعَ عَلَيْهِ كَنَفَهُ، فَيُقَرِّرُهُ بِذُنُوبِهِ تَعْرِفُ ذَنْبَ كَذَا يَقُولُ أَعْرِفُ، يَقُولُ رَبِّ أَعْرِفُ مَرَّتَيْنِ، فَيَقُولُ سَتَرْتُهَا فِي الدُّنْيَا وَأَغْفِرُهَا لَكَ الْيَوْمَ ثُمَّ تُطْوَى صَحِيفَةُ حَسَنَاتِهِ، وَأَمَّا الآخَرُونَ أَوِ الْكُفَّارُ فَيُنَادَى عَلَى رُءُوسِ الأَشْهَادِ هَؤُلاَءِ الَّذِينَ كَذَبُوا عَلَى رَبِّهِمْ ". وَقَالَ شَيْبَانُ عَنْ قَتَادَةَ حَدَّثَنَا صَفْوَانُ.

Narrated Ibn Abi Na’m: I was present when a man asked Ibn `Umar about the blood of mosquitoes. Ibn `Umar said, “From where are you?” The man replied. “From Iraq.” Ibn `Umar said, “Look at that! He is asking me about the blood of Mosquitoes while they (the Iraqis) have killed the (grand) son of the Prophet. I have heard the Prophetﷺ saying, “They (Hasan and Husain) are my two sweet-smelling flowers in this world.”. – Sahih Al-Bukhari 5994

حَدَّثَنَا مُوسَى بْنُ إِسْمَاعِيلَ، حَدَّثَنَا مَهْدِيٌّ، حَدَّثَنَا ابْنُ أَبِي يَعْقُوبَ، عَنِ ابْنِ أَبِي نُعْمٍ، قَالَ كُنْتُ شَاهِدًا لاِبْنِ عُمَرَ وَسَأَلَهُ رَجُلٌ عَنْ دَمِ الْبَعُوضِ. فَقَالَ مِمَّنْ أَنْتَ فَقَالَ مِنْ أَهْلِ الْعِرَاقِ. قَالَ انْظُرُوا إِلَى هَذَا، يَسْأَلُنِي عَنْ دَمِ الْبَعُوضِ وَقَدْ قَتَلُوا ابْنَ النَّبِيِّ صلى الله عليه وسلم وَسَمِعْتُ النَّبِيَّ صلى الله عليه وسلم يَقُولُ " هُمَا رَيْحَانَتَاىَ مِنَ الدُّنْيَا "

Narrated Nafi`: Ibn `Umar used to give the Zakat of Ramadan (Zakat-al-Fitr) according to the Mudd of the Prophet, the first Mudd, and he also used to give things for expiation for oaths according to the Mudd of the Prophet. Abu Qutaiba said, “Malik said to us, ‘Our Mudd (i.e., of Medina) is better than yours and we do not see any superiority except in the Mudd of the Prophet!’ Malik further said, to me, ‘If a ruler came to you and fixed a Mudd smaller than the one of the Prophet, by what Mudd would you measure what you give (for expiation or Zakat-al-Fitr?’ I replied, ‘We would give it according to the Mudd of the Prophet’ On that, Malik said, ‘Then, don’t you see that we have to revert to the Mudd of the Prophet ultimately?’”. – Sahih Al-Bukhari 6713

حَدَّثَنَا مُنْذِرُ بْنُ الْوَلِيدِ الْجَارُودِيُّ، حَدَّثَنَا أَبُو قُتَيْبَةَ ـ وَهْوَ سَلْمٌ ـ حَدَّثَنَا مَالِكٌ، عَنْ نَافِعٍ، قَالَ كَانَ ابْنُ عُمَرَ يُعْطِي زَكَاةَ رَمَضَانَ بِمُدِّ النَّبِيِّ صلى الله عليه وسلم الْمُدِّ الأَوَّلِ، وَفِي كَفَّارَةِ الْيَمِينِ بِمُدِّ النَّبِيِّ صلى الله عليه وسلم. قَالَ أَبُو قُتَيْبَةَ قَالَ لَنَا مَالِكٌ مُدُّنَا أَعْظَمُ مِنْ مُدِّكُمْ وَلاَ نَرَى الْفَضْلَ إِلاَّ فِي مُدِّ النَّبِيِّ صلى الله عليه وسلم. وَقَالَ لِي مَالِكٌ لَوْ جَاءَكُمْ أَمِيرٌ فَضَرَبَ مُدًّا أَصْغَرَ مِنْ مُدِّ النَّبِيِّ صلى الله عليه وسلم بِأَىِّ شَىْءٍ كُنْتُمْ تُعْطُونَ قُلْتُ كُنَّا نُعْطِي بِمُدِّ النَّبِيِّ صلى الله عليه وسلم قَالَ أَفَلاَ تَرَى أَنَّ الأَمْرَ إِنَّمَا يَعُودُ إِلَى مُدِّ النَّبِيِّ صلى الله عليه وسلم.

Narrated Ibn `Umar: Men from the companions of Allah’s Messengerﷺ used to see dreams during the lifetime of Allah’s Messengerﷺ and they used to narrate those dreams to Allah’s Messenger ﷺ. Allah’s Messengerﷺ would interpret them as Allah wished. I was a young man and used to stay in the mosque before my wedlock. I said to myself, “If there were any good in myself, I too would see what these people see.” So when I went to bed one night, I said, “O Allah! If you see any good in me, show me a good dream.” So while I was in that state, there came to me (in a dream) two angels. In the hand of each of them, there was a mace of iron, and both of them were taking me to Hell, and I was between them, invoking Allah, “O Allah! I seek refuge with You from Hell.” Then I saw myself being confronted by another angel holding a mace of iron in his hand. He said to me, “Do not be afraid, you will be an excellent man if you only pray more often." So they took me till they stopped me at the edge of Hell, and behold, it was built inside like a well and it had side posts like those of a well, and beside each post there was an angel carrying an iron mace. I saw therein many people hanging upside down with iron chains, and I recognized therein some men from the Quraish. Then (the angels) took me to the right side. I narrated this dream to (my sister) Hafsa and she told it to Allah's Messenger ﷺ. Allah's Messenger ﷺ said, "No doubt, `Abdullah is a good man." (Nafi` said, "Since then `Abdullah bin `Umar used to pray much.). – Sahih Al-Bukhari 7028, 7029

حَدَّثَنِي عُبَيْدُ اللَّهِ بْنُ سَعِيدٍ، حَدَّثَنَا عَفَّانُ بْنُ مُسْلِمٍ، حَدَّثَنَا صَخْرُ بْنُ جُوَيْرِيَةَ، حَدَّثَنَا نَافِعٌ، أَنَّ ابْنَ عُمَرَ، قَالَ إِنَّ رِجَالاً مِنْ أَصْحَابِ رَسُولِ اللَّهِ صلى الله عليه وسلم كَانُوا يَرَوْنَ الرُّؤْيَا عَلَى عَهْدِ رَسُولِ اللَّهِ صلى الله عليه وسلم فَيَقُصُّونَهَا عَلَى رَسُولِ اللَّهِ صلى الله عليه وسلم فَيَقُولُ فِيهَا رَسُولُ اللَّهِ صلى الله عليه وسلم مَا شَاءَ اللَّهُ، وَأَنَا غُلاَمٌ حَدِيثُ السِّنِّ وَبَيْتِي الْمَسْجِدُ قَبْلَ أَنْ أَنْكِحَ، فَقُلْتُ فِي نَفْسِي لَوْ كَانَ فِيكَ خَيْرٌ لَرَأَيْتَ مِثْلَ مَا يَرَى هَؤُلاَءِ. فَلَمَّا اضْطَجَعْتُ لَيْلَةً قُلْتُ اللَّهُمَّ إِنْ كُنْتَ تَعْلَمُ فِيَّ خَيْرًا فَأَرِنِي رُؤْيَا. فَبَيْنَمَا أَنَا كَذَلِكَ إِذْ جَاءَنِي مَلَكَانِ فِي يَدِ كُلِّ وَاحِدٍ مِنْهُمَا مَقْمَعَةٌ مِنْ حَدِيدٍ، يُقْبِلاَ بِي إِلَى جَهَنَّمَ، وَأَنَا بَيْنَهُمَا أَدْعُو اللَّهَ اللَّهُمَّ أَعُوذُ بِكَ مِنْ جَهَنَّمَ. ثُمَّ أُرَانِي لَقِيَنِي مَلَكٌ فِي يَدِهِ مِقْمَعَةٌ مِنْ حَدِيدٍ فَقَالَ لَنْ تُرَاعَ، نِعْمَ الرَّجُلُ أَنْتَ لَوْ تُكْثِرُ الصَّلاَةَ. فَانْطَلَقُوا بِي حَتَّى وَقَفُوا بِي عَلَى شَفِيرِ جَهَنَّمَ فَإِذَا هِيَ مَطْوِيَّةٌ كَطَيِّ الْبِئْرِ، لَهُ قُرُونٌ كَقَرْنِ الْبِئْرِ، بَيْنَ كُلِّ قَرْنَيْنِ مَلَكٌ بِيَدِهِ مِقْمَعَةٌ مِنْ حَدِيدٍ، وَأَرَى فِيهَا رِجَالاً مُعَلَّقِينَ بِالسَّلاَسِلِ، رُءُوسُهُمْ أَسْفَلَهُمْ، عَرَفْتُ فِيهَا رِجَالاً مِنْ قُرَيْشٍ، فَانْصَرَفُوا بِي عَنْ ذَاتِ الْيَمِينِ. فَقَصَصْتُهَا عَلَى حَفْصَةَ فَقَصَّتْهَا حَفْصَةُ عَلَى رَسُولِ اللَّهِ صلى الله عليه وسلم فَقَالَ رَسُولُ اللَّهِ صلى الله عليه وسلم " إِنَّ عَبْدَ اللَّهِ رَجُلٌ صَالِحٌ ". فَقَالَ نَافِعٌ لَمْ يَزَلْ بَعْدَ ذَلِكَ يُكْثِرُ الصَّلاَةَ

Narrated `Ikrima bin Khalid: Ibn `Umar said, "I went to Hafsa while water was dribbling from her twined braids. I said, 'The condition of the people is as you see, and no authority has been given to me.' Hafsa said, (to me), 'Go to them, and as they (i.e. the people) are waiting for you, and I am afraid your absence from them will produce division amongst them.' " So Hafsa did not leave Ibn `Umar till we went to them. When the people differed. Muawiya addressed the people saying, "'If anybody wants to say anything in this matter of the Caliphate, he should show up and not conceal himself, for we are more rightful to be a Caliph than he and his father." On that, Habib bin Masalama said (to Ibn `Umar), "Why don't you reply to him (i.e. Muawiya)?" `Abdullah bin `Umar said, "I untied my garment that was going round my back and legs while I was sitting and was about to say, 'He who fought against you and against your father for the sake of Islam, is more rightful to be a Caliph,' but I was afraid that my statement might produce differences amongst the people and cause bloodshed, and my statement might be interpreted not as I intended. (So I kept quiet) remembering what Allah has prepared in the Gardens of Paradise (for those who are patient and prefer the Hereafter to this worldly life)." Habib said, "You did what kept you safe and secure (i.e. you were wise in doing so). – Sahih Al-Bukhari 4108

حَدَّثَنِي إِبْرَاهِيمُ بْنُ مُوسَى، أَخْبَرَنَا هِشَامٌ، عَنْ مَعْمَرٍ، عَنِ الزُّهْرِيِّ، عَنْ سَالِمٍ، عَنِ ابْنِ عُمَرَ، قَالَ وَأَخْبَرَنِي ابْنُ طَاوُسٍ، عَنْ عِكْرِمَةَ بْنِ خَالِدٍ، عَنِ ابْنِ عُمَرَ، قَالَ دَخَلْتُ عَلَى حَفْصَةَ وَنَسْوَاتُهَا تَنْطُفُ، قُلْتُ قَدْ كَانَ مِنْ أَمْرِ النَّاسِ مَا تَرَيْنَ، فَلَمْ يُجْعَلْ لِي مِنَ الأَمْرِ شَىْءٌ. فَقَالَتِ الْحَقْ فَإِنَّهُمْ يَنْتَظِرُونَكَ، وَأَخْشَى أَنْ يَكُونَ فِي احْتِبَاسِكَ عَنْهُمْ فُرْقَةٌ. فَلَمْ تَدَعْهُ حَتَّى ذَهَبَ، فَلَمَّا تَفَرَّقَ النَّاسُ خَطَبَ مُعَاوِيَةُ قَالَ مَنْ كَانَ يُرِيدُ أَنْ يَتَكَلَّمَ فِي هَذَا الأَمْرِ فَلْيُطْلِعْ لَنَا قَرْنَهُ، فَلَنَحْنُ أَحَقُّ بِهِ مِنْهُ وَمِنْ أَبِيهِ. قَالَ حَبِيبُ بْنُ مَسْلَمَةَ فَهَلاَّ أَجَبْتَهُ قَالَ عَبْدُ اللَّهِ فَحَلَلْتُ حُبْوَتِي وَهَمَمْتُ أَنْ أَقُولَ أَحَقُّ بِهَذَا الأَمْرِ مِنْكَ مَنْ قَاتَلَكَ وَأَبَاكَ عَلَى الإِسْلاَمِ. فَخَشِيتُ أَنْ أَقُولَ كَلِمَةً تُفَرِّقُ بَيْنَ الْجَمْعِ، وَتَسْفِكُ الدَّمَ، وَيُحْمَلُ عَنِّي غَيْرُ ذَلِكَ، فَذَكَرْتُ مَا أَعَدَّ اللَّهُ فِي الْجِنَانِ. قَالَ حَبِيبٌ حُفِظْتَ وَعُصِمْتَ. قَالَ مَحْمُودٌ عَنْ عَبْدِ الرَّزَّاقِ وَنَوْسَاتُهَا

Narrated 'Abdullah bin 'Ubaidullah bin Abi Mulaika: The sons of Suhaib, (Suhaib, who was the freed slave of Bani Jud'an) claimed that Allah's Messenger ﷺ had given two houses and one room to Suhaib. Marwan asked, "Who will testify to your claim?" They replied that Ibn 'Umar would do so. Marwan sent for Ibn 'Umar who testified that Allah's Messenger ﷺ had really given Suhaib two houses and a room. So, Marwan gave the verdict (in favour of Suhaib's sons), because of (Ibn 'Umar's) witness. – Sahih Al-Bukhari 2624

حَدَّثَنَا إِبْرَاهِيمُ بْنُ مُوسَى، أَخْبَرَنَا هِشَامُ بْنُ يُوسُفَ، أَنَّ ابْنَ جُرَيْجٍ، أَخْبَرَهُمْ قَالَ أَخْبَرَنِي عَبْدُ اللَّهِ بْنُ عُبَيْدِ اللَّهِ بْنِ أَبِي مُلَيْكَةَ، أَنَّ بَنِي صُهَيْبٍ، مَوْلَى ابْنِ جُدْعَانَ ادَّعَوْا بَيْتَيْنِ وَحُجْرَةً، أَنَّ رَسُولَ اللَّهِ صلى الله عليه وسلم أَعْطَى ذَلِكَ صُهَيْبًا، فَقَالَ مَرْوَانُ مَنْ يَشْهَدُ لَكُمَا عَلَى ذَلِكَ قَالُوا ابْنُ عُمَرَ. فَدَعَاهُ فَشَهِدَ لأَعْطَى رَسُولُ اللَّهِ صلى الله عليه وسلم صُهَيْبًا بَيْتَيْنِ وَحُجْرَةً. فَقَضَى مَرْوَانُ بِشَهَادَتِهِ لَهُمْ.

Narrated Qais bin 'Ubada: I was sitting in a gathering in which there was Sa`d bin Malik and Ibn `Umar. `Abdullah bin Salam passed in front of them and they said, "This man is from the people of Paradise." I said to `Abdullah bin Salam, "They said so-and-so." He replied, "Subhan Allah! They ought not to have said things of which they have no knowledge, but I saw (in a dream) that a post was fixed in a green garden. At the top of the post there was a handhold and below it there was a servant. I was asked to climb (the post). So I climbed it till I got hold of the handhold." Then I narrated this dream to Allah's Messenger ﷺ. Allah's Apostle said, "`Abdullah will die while still holding the firm reliable handhold (i.e., Islam). – Sahih Al-Bukhari 7010

حَدَّثَنَا عَبْدُ اللَّهِ بْنُ مُحَمَّدٍ الْجُعْفِيُّ، حَدَّثَنَا حَرَمِيُّ بْنُ عُمَارَةَ، حَدَّثَنَا قُرَّةُ بْنُ خَالِدٍ، عَنْ مُحَمَّدِ بْنِ سِيرِينَ، قَالَ قَالَ قَيْسُ بْنُ عُبَادٍ كُنْتُ فِي حَلْقَةٍ فِيهَا سَعْدُ بْنُ مَالِكٍ وَابْنُ عُمَرَ فَمَرَّ عَبْدُ اللَّهِ بْنُ سَلاَمٍ فَقَالُوا هَذَا رَجُلٌ مِنْ أَهْلِ الْجَنَّةِ. فَقُلْتُ لَهُ إِنَّهُمْ قَالُوا كَذَا وَكَذَا. قَالَ سُبْحَانَ اللَّهِ مَا كَانَ يَنْبَغِي لَهُمْ أَنْ يَقُولُوا مَا لَيْسَ لَهُمْ بِهِ عِلْمٌ، إِنَّمَا رَأَيْتُ كَأَنَّمَا عَمُودٌ وُضِعَ فِي رَوْضَةٍ خَضْرَاءَ، فَنُصِبَ فِيهَا وَفِي رَأْسِهَا عُرْوَةٌ وَفِي أَسْفَلِهَا مِنْصَفٌ ـ وَالْمِنْصَفُ الْوَصِيفُ ـ فَقِيلَ ارْقَهْ. فَرَقِيتُ حَتَّى أَخَذْتُ بِالْعُرْوَةِ. فَقَصَصْتُهَا عَلَى رَسُولِ اللَّهِ صلى الله عليه وسلم فَقَالَ رَسُولُ اللَّهِ صلى الله عليه وسلم " يَمُوتُ عَبْدُ اللَّهِ وَهْوَ آخِذٌ بِالْعُرْوَةِ الْوُثْقَى ".

Narrated Nafi`: When the people of Medina dethroned Yazid bin Muawiya, Ibn `Umar gathered his special friends and children and said, "I heard the Prophet ﷺ saying, 'A flag will be fixed for every betrayer on the Day of Resurrection,' and we have given the oath of allegiance to this person (Yazid) in accordance with the conditions enjoined by Allah and His Apostle and I do not know of anything more faithless than fighting a person who has been given the oath of allegiance in accordance with the conditions enjoined by Allah and His Apostle , and if ever I learn that any person among you has agreed to dethrone Yazid, by giving the oath of allegiance (to somebody else) then there will be separation between him and me.". – Sahih Al-Bukhari 7111

حَدَّثَنَا سُلَيْمَانُ بْنُ حَرْبٍ، حَدَّثَنَا حَمَّادُ بْنُ زَيْدٍ، عَنْ أَيُّوبَ، عَنْ نَافِعٍ، قَالَ لَمَّا خَلَعَ أَهْلُ الْمَدِينَةِ يَزِيدَ بْنَ مُعَاوِيَةَ جَمَعَ ابْنُ عُمَرَ حَشَمَهُ وَوَلَدَهُ فَقَالَ إِنِّي سَمِعْتُ النَّبِيَّ صلى الله عليه وسلم يَقُولُ " يُنْصَبُ لِكُلِّ غَادِرٍ لِوَاءٌ يَوْمَ الْقِيَامَةِ ". وَإِنَّا قَدْ بَايَعْنَا هَذَا الرَّجُلَ عَلَى بَيْعِ اللَّهِ وَرَسُولِهِ، وَإِنِّي لاَ أَعْلَمُ غَدْرًا أَعْظَمَ مِنْ أَنْ يُبَايَعَ رَجُلٌ عَلَى بَيْعِ اللَّهِ وَرَسُولِهِ، ثُمَّ يُنْصَبُ لَهُ الْقِتَالُ، وَإِنِّي لاَ أَعْلَمُ أَحَدًا مِنْكُمْ خَلَعَهُ، وَلاَ بَايَعَ فِي هَذَا الأَمْرِ، إِلاَّ كَانَتِ الْفَيْصَلَ بَيْنِي وَبَيْنَهُ

Narrated Ibn `Umar: Allah's Messenger ﷺ said, "This matter (caliphate) will remain with the Quraish even if only two of them were still existing.". – Sahih Al-Bukhari 7140

حَدَّثَنَا أَحْمَدُ بْنُ يُونُسَ، حَدَّثَنَا عَاصِمُ بْنُ مُحَمَّدٍ، سَمِعْتُ أَبِي يَقُولُ، قَالَ ابْنُ عُمَرَ قَالَ رَسُولُ اللَّهِ صلى الله عليه وسلم " لاَ يَزَالُ الأَمْرُ فِي قُرَيْشٍ مَا بَقِيَ مِنْهُمُ اثْنَانِ "

Narrated `Abdullah bin Dinar: `Abdullah Bin `Umar wrote to `Abdul Malik bin Marwan, swearing allegiance to him: 'I swear allegiance to you in that I will listen and obey what is in accordance with the Laws of Allah and the Tradition of His Apostle as much as I can.'. – Sahih Al-Bukhari 7272

حَدَّثَنَا إِسْمَاعِيلُ، حَدَّثَنِي مَالِكٌ، عَنْ عَبْدِ اللَّهِ بْنِ دِينَارٍ، أَنَّ عَبْدَ اللَّهِ بْنَ عُمَرَ، كَتَبَ إِلَى عَبْدِ الْمَلِكِ بْنِ مَرْوَانَ يُبَايِعُهُ، وَأُقِرُّ لَكَ بِالسَّمْعِ وَالطَّاعَةِ عَلَى سُنَّةِ اللَّهِ وَسُنَّةِ رَسُولِهِ، فِيمَا اسْتَطَعْتُ

Narrated `Abdullah bin `Umar: Regarding Al-Harauriyya: The Prophetﷺ said, “They will go out of Islam as an arrow darts out of the game’s body.’. – Sahih Al-Bukhari 6932
حَدَّثَنَا يَحْيَى بْنُ سُلَيْمَانُ، حَدَّثَنِي ابْنُ وَهْبٍ، قَالَ حَدَّثَنِي عُمَرُ، أَنَّ أَبَاهُ، حَدَّثَهُ عَنْ عَبْدِ اللَّهِ بْنِ عُمَرَ ـ وَذَكَرَ الْحَرُورِيَّةَ ـ فَقَالَ قَالَ النَّبِيُّ صلى الله عليه وسلم " يَمْرُقُونَ مِنَ الإِسْلاَمِ مُرُوقَ السَّهْمِ مِنَ الرَّمِيَّةِ "

Narrated `Abdullah bin ‘Ubaidullah bin Abi Mulaika: One of the daughters of `Uthman died at Mecca. We went to attend her funeral procession. Ibn `Umar and Ibn `Abbas were also present. I sat in between them (or said, I sat beside one of them. Then a man came and sat beside me.) `Abdullah bin `Umar said to `Amr bin `Uthman, “Will you not prohibit crying as Allah’s Messengerﷺ has said, ‘The dead person is tortured by the crying of his relatives.?” Ibn `Abbas said, “`Umar used to say so.” Then he added narrating, “I accompanied `Umar on a journey from Mecca till we reached Al-Baida. There he saw some travelers in the shade of a Samura (A kind of forest tree). He said (to me), “Go and see who those travelers are.” So I went and saw that one of them was Suhaib. I told this to `Umar who then asked me to call him. So I went back to Suhaib and said to him, “Depart and follow the chief of the faithful believers.” Later, when `Umar was stabbed, Suhaib came in weeping and saying, “O my brother, O my friend!” (on this `Umar said to him, “O Suhaib! Are you weeping for me while the Prophetﷺ said, “The dead person is punished by some of the weeping of his relatives?” Ibn `Abbas added, “When `Umar died I told all this to Aisha and she said, ‘May Allah be merciful to `Umar. By Allah, Allah’s Messengerﷺ did not say that a believer is punished by the weeping of his relatives. But he said, Allah increases the punishment of a non-believer because of the weeping of his relatives.” Aisha further added, “The Qur’an is sufficient for you (to clear up this point) as Allah has stated: ‘No burdened soul will bear another’s burden.’ “ (35.18). Ibn `Abbas then said, “Only Allah makes one laugh or cry.” Ibn `Umar did not say anything after that. – Sahih Al-Bukhari 1286, 1287, 1288
حَدَّثَنَا عَبْدَانُ، حَدَّثَنَا عَبْدُ اللَّهِ، أَخْبَرَنَا ابْنُ جُرَيْجٍ، قَالَ أَخْبَرَنِي عَبْدُ اللَّهِ بْنُ عُبَيْدِ اللَّهِ بْنِ أَبِي مُلَيْكَةَ، قَالَ تُوُفِّيَتِ ابْنَةٌ لِعُثْمَانَ ـ رضى الله عنه ـ بِمَكَّةَ وَجِئْنَا لِنَشْهَدَهَا، وَحَضَرَهَا ابْنُ عُمَرَ وَابْنُ عَبَّاسٍ ـ رضى الله عنهم ـ وَإِنِّي لَجَالِسٌ بَيْنَهُمَا ـ أَوْ قَالَ جَلَسْتُ إِلَى أَحَدِهِمَا. ثُمَّ جَاءَ الآخَرُ، فَجَلَسَ إِلَى جَنْبِي فَقَالَ عَبْدُ اللَّهِ بْنُ عُمَرَ ـ رضى الله عنهما ـ لِعَمْرِو بْنِ عُثْمَانَ أَلاَ تَنْهَى عَنِ الْبُكَاءِ، فَإِنَّ رَسُولَ اللَّهِ صلى الله عليه وسلم قَالَ " إِنَّ الْمَيِّتَ لَيُعَذَّبُ بِبُكَاءِ أَهْلِهِ عَلَيْهِ ". فَقَالَ ابْنُ عَبَّاسٍ ـ رضى الله عنهما ـ قَدْ كَانَ عُمَرُ ـ رضى الله عنه ـ يَقُولُ بَعْضَ ذَلِكَ، ثُمَّ حَدَّثَ قَالَ صَدَرْتُ مَعَ عُمَرَ ـ رضى الله عنه ـ مِنْ مَكَّةَ حَتَّى إِذَا كُنَّا بِالْبَيْدَاءِ، إِذَا هُوَ بِرَكْبٍ تَحْتَ ظِلِّ سَمُرَةٍ فَقَالَ اذْهَبْ، فَانْظُرْ مَنْ هَؤُلاَءِ الرَّكْبُ قَالَ فَنَظَرْتُ فَإِذَا صُهَيْبٌ، فَأَخْبَرْتُهُ فَقَالَ ادْعُهُ لِي. فَرَجَعْتُ إِلَى صُهَيْبٍ فَقُلْتُ ارْتَحِلْ فَالْحَقْ أَمِيرَ الْمُؤْمِنِينَ. فَلَمَّا أُصِيبَ عُمَرُ دَخَلَ صُهَيْبٌ يَبْكِي يَقُولُ وَاأَخَاهُ، وَاصَاحِبَاهُ. فَقَالَ عُمَرُ ـ رضى الله عنه ـ يَا صُهَيْبُ أَتَبْكِي عَلَىَّ وَقَدْ قَالَ رَسُولُ اللَّهِ صلى الله عليه وسلم " إِنَّ الْمَيِّتَ يُعَذَّبُ بِبَعْضِ بُكَاءِ أَهْلِهِ عَلَيْهِ ". قَالَ ابْنُ عَبَّاسٍ ـ رضى الله عنهما فَلَمَّا مَاتَ عُمَرُ ـ رضى الله عنه ـ ذَكَرْتُ ذَلِكَ لِعَائِشَةَ ـ رضى الله عنها ـ فَقَالَتْ رَحِمَ اللَّهُ عُمَرَ، وَاللَّهِ مَا حَدَّثَ رَسُولُ اللَّهِ صلى الله عليه وسلم إِنَّ اللَّهَ لَيُعَذِّبُ الْمُؤْمِنَ بِبُكَاءِ أَهْلِهِ عَلَيْهِ.
وَلَكِنَّ رَسُولَ اللَّهِ صلى الله عليه وسلم قَالَ " إِنَّ اللَّهَ لَيَزِيدُ الْكَافِرَ عَذَابًا بِبُكَاءِ أَهْلِهِ عَلَيْهِ ". وَقَالَتْ حَسْبُكُمُ الْقُرْآنُ {وَلاَ تَزِرُ وَازِرَةٌ وِزْرَ أُخْرَى}. قَالَ ابْنُ عَبَّاسٍ ـ رضى الله عنهما ـ عِنْدَ ذَلِكَ وَاللَّهُ هُوَ أَضْحَكَ وَأَبْكَى. قَالَ ابْنُ أَبِي مُلَيْكَةَ وَاللَّهِ مَا قَالَ ابْنُ عُمَرَ ـ رضى الله عنهما ـ شَيْئًا.

Narrated Nafi`: Once a slave of Ibn `Umar fled and joined the Byzantine. Khalid bin Al-Walid got him back and returned him to `Abdullah (bin `Umar). Once a horse of Ibn `Umar also ran away and followed the Byzantines, and he (i.e. Khalid) got it back and returned it to `Abdullah. – Sahih Al-Bukhari 3068
حَدَّثَنَا مُحَمَّدُ بْنُ بَشَّارٍ، حَدَّثَنَا يَحْيَى، عَنْ عُبَيْدِ اللَّهِ، قَالَ أَخْبَرَنِي نَافِعٌ، أَنَّ عَبْدًا، لاِبْنِ عُمَرَ أَبَقَ فَلَحِقَ بِالرُّومِ، فَظَهَرَ عَلَيْهِ خَالِدُ بْنُ الْوَلِيدِ، فَرَدَّهُ عَلَى عَبْدِ اللَّهِ، وَأَنَّ فَرَسًا لاِبْنِ عُمَرَ عَارَ فَلَحِقَ بِالرُّومِ، فَظَهَرَ عَلَيْهِ فَرَدُّوهُ عَلَى عَبْدِ اللَّهِ.
قَالَ أَبُو عَبْد اللَّهِ عَارَ مُشْتَقٌّ مِنَ الْعَيْرِ وَهُوَ حِمَارُ وَحْشٍ أَيْ هَرَبَ

Narrated Ibn `Umar: During the lifetime of the Prophetﷺ we used to avoid chatting leisurely and freely with our wives lest some Divine inspiration might be revealed concerning us. But when the Prophetﷺ had died, we started chatting leisurely and freely (with them). – Sahih Al-Bukhari 5187

حَدَّثَنَا أَبُو نُعَيْمٍ، حَدَّثَنَا سُفْيَانُ، عَنْ عَبْدِ اللَّهِ بْنِ دِينَارٍ، عَنِ ابْنِ عُمَرَ ـ رضى الله عنهما ـ قَالَ كُنَّا نَتَّقِي الْكَلاَمَ وَالاِنْبِسَاطَ إِلَى نِسَائِنَا عَلَى عَهْدِ النَّبِيِّ صلى الله عليه وسلم هَيْبَةَ أَنْ يُنْزَلَ فِينَا شَىْءٌ فَلَمَّا تُوُفِّيَ النَّبِيُّ صلى الله عليه وسلم تَكَلَّمْنَا وَانْبَسَطْنَا.

Narrated Ibn `Umar: The Prophetﷺ said, "It is better for a man to fill the inside of his body with pus than to fill it with poetry.". – Sahih Al-Bukhari 6154

حَدَّثَنَا عُبَيْدُ اللَّهِ بْنُ مُوسَى، أَخْبَرَنَا حَنْظَلَةُ، عَنْ سَالِمٍ، عَنِ ابْنِ عُمَرَ ـ رضى الله عنهما ـ عَنِ النَّبِيِّ صلى الله عليه وسلم قَالَ " لأَنْ يَمْتَلِئَ جَوْفُ أَحَدِكُمْ قَيْحًا خَيْرٌ لَهُ مِنْ أَنْ يَمْتَلِئَ شِعْرًا "

Narrated Sa`id bin Jubair: `Abdullah bin `Umar came to us and we hoped that he would narrate to us a good Hadith. But before we asked him, a man got up and said to him, "O Abu `Abdur-Rahman! Narrate to us about the battles during the time of the afflictions, as Allah says:-- 'And fight them until there is no more afflictions (i.e. no more worshipping of others besides Allah).'" (2.193) Ibn `Umar said (to the man), "Do you know what is meant by afflictions? Let your mother bereave you! Muhammad used to fight against the pagans, for a Muslim was put to trial in his religion (The pagans will either kill him or chain him as a captive). His fighting was not like your fighting which is carried on for the sake of ruling.". – Sahih Al-Bukhari 7095

حَدَّثَنَا إِسْحَاقُ الْوَاسِطِيُّ، حَدَّثَنَا خَالِدٌ، عَنْ بَيَانٍ، عَنْ وَبَرَةَ بْنِ عَبْدِ الرَّحْمَنِ، عَنْ سَعِيدِ بْنِ جُبَيْرٍ، قَالَ خَرَجَ عَلَيْنَا عَبْدُ اللَّهِ بْنُ عُمَرَ فَرَجَوْنَا أَنْ يُحَدِّثَنَا، حَدِيثًا حَسَنًا ـ قَالَ ـ فَبَادَرَنَا إِلَيْهِ رَجُلٌ فَقَالَ يَا أَبَا عَبْدِ الرَّحْمَنِ حَدِّثْنَا عَنِ الْقِتَالِ فِي الْفِتْنَةِ وَاللَّهُ يَقُولُ {وَقَاتِلُوهُمْ حَتَّى لاَ تَكُونَ فِتْنَةٌ} فَقَالَ هَلْ تَدْرِي مَا الْفِتْنَةُ ثَكِلَتْكَ أُمُّكَ، إِنَّمَا كَانَ مُحَمَّدٌ صلى الله عليه وسلم يُقَاتِلُ الْمُشْرِكِينَ، وَكَانَ الدُّخُولُ فِي دِينِهِمْ فِتْنَةً، وَلَيْسَ كَقِتَالِكُمْ عَلَى الْمُلْكِ

Narrated `Abdullah bin `Umar: That he had divorced his wife during her menses. `Umar mentioned that to the Prophet. Allah's Apostle became angry and said, "He must take her back (his wife) and keep her with him till she becomes clean from her menses and then to wait till she gets her next period and becomes clean again from it and only then, if he wants to divorce her, he may do so.". – Sahih Al-Bukhari 7160

حَدَّثَنَا مُحَمَّدُ بْنُ أَبِي يَعْقُوبَ الْكِرْمَانِيُّ، حَدَّثَنَا حَسَّانُ بْنُ إِبْرَاهِيمَ، حَدَّثَنَا يُونُسُ، قَالَ مُحَمَّدٌ أَخْبَرَنِي سَالِمٌ، أَنَّ عَبْدَ اللَّهِ بْنَ عُمَرَ، أَخْبَرَهُ أَنَّهُ، طَلَّقَ امْرَأَتَهُ وَهْىَ حَائِضٌ، فَذَكَرَ عُمَرُ لِلنَّبِيِّ صلى الله عليه وسلم، فَتَغَيَّظَ فِيهِ رَسُولُ اللَّهِ صلى الله عليه وسلم ثُمَّ قَالَ " لِيُرَاجِعْهَا، ثُمَّ لِيُمْسِكْهَا حَتَّى تَطْهُرَ، ثُمَّ تَحِيضَ فَتَطْهُرَ، فَإِنْ بَدَا لَهُ أَنْ يُطَلِّقَهَا فَلْيُطَلِّقْهَا "

And Ibn 'Umar used to consider them (Al-Khawārij and Al-Mulhidūn) the_worst of Allāh's creatures and said, These people took some Verses that had been revealed concerning the disbelievers and interpreted them as describing the believers." -Sahih Al-Bukhari vol.9 page 49

و كان ابن عمر يراهم شرار خلق الله، و قال : أنهم انطلقوا الى ايات نزلت في الكفار فجعلوها على المؤمنين .

Ibn 'Umar used to cut his moustache_so short that the whiteness of his skin (above the upper lip) was visible , and he used to cut (the hair) between his moustaches and his beard. – Sahih Al-Bukhari vol. 7 page 419

و كان ابن عمر يحفي شاربه حتى ينظر الى بياض الجلد ، و يأخذ هذين، يعني بين الشارب و اللحية.

Ibn Umar used to prostrate without ablution. – Sahih Al-Bukhari vol. 2 pg 118

و كان ابن عمر رضي الله عنهما يسجد على غير وضوء.

Narrated Ibn `Umar: `Umar bin Al-Khattab fixed a grant of 4000 (Dirhams) for every Early Emigrant (i.e. Muhajir) and fixed a grant of 3500 (Dirhams) only for Ibn `Umar. Somebody said to `Umar, "Ibn `Umar is also one of the Early Emigrants; why do you give him less than four-thousand?" `Umar replied, "His parents took him with them when they migrated, so he was not like the one who had migrated by himself. – Sahih al-Bukhari 3912
حَدَّثَنَا إِبْرَاهِيمُ بْنُ مُوسَى، أَخْبَرَنَا هِشَامٌ، عَنِ ابْنِ جُرَيْجٍ، قَالَ أَخْبَرَنِي عُبَيْدُ اللَّهِ بْنُ عُمَرَ، عَنْ نَافِعٍ يَعْنِي، عَنِ ابْنِ عُمَرَ، عَنْ عُمَرَ بْنِ الْخَطَّابِ، رضى الله عنه قَالَ كَانَ فَرَضَ لِلْمُهَاجِرِينَ الأَوَّلِينَ أَرْبَعَةَ آلاَفٍ فِي أَرْبَعَةٍ، وَفَرَضَ لاِبْنِ عُمَرَ ثَلاَثَةَ آلاَفٍ وَخَمْسَمِائَةٍ فَقِيلَ لَهُ هُوَ مِنَ الْمُهَاجِرِينَ، فَلِمَ نَقَصْتَهُ مِنْ أَرْبَعَةِ آلاَفٍ فَقَالَ إِنَّمَا هَاجَرَ بِهِ أَبَوَاهُ. يَقُولُ لَيْسَ هُوَ كَمَنْ هَاجَرَ بِنَفْسِهِ

Narrated Abu `Uthman: I heard that Ibn `Umar used to become angry if someone mentioned that he had migrated before his father (`Umar), and he used to say, " `Umar and I came to Allah's Messenger ﷺ and found him having his midday rest, so we returned home. Then `Umar sent me again (to the Prophet ﷺ ) and said, 'Go and see whether he is awake.' I went to him and entered his place and gave him the pledge of allegiance. Then I went back to `Umar and informed him that the Prophet ﷺ was awake. So we both went, running slowly, and when `Umar entered his place, he gave him the pledge of allegiance and thereafter I too gave him the pledge of allegiance." – Sahih al-Bukhari 3916
حَدَّثَنِي مُحَمَّدُ بْنُ صَبَّاحٍ ـ أَوْ بَلَغَنِي عَنْهُ ـ حَدَّثَنَا إِسْمَاعِيلُ، عَنْ عَاصِمٍ، عَنْ أَبِي عُثْمَانَ، قَالَ سَمِعْتُ ابْنَ عُمَرَ ـ رضى الله عنهما ـ إِذَا قِيلَ لَهُ هَاجَرَ قَبْلَ أَبِيهِ يَغْضَبُ، قَالَ وَقَدِمْتُ أَنَا وَعُمَرُ عَلَى رَسُولِ اللَّهِ صلى الله عليه وسلم فَوَجَدْنَاهُ قَائِلاً فَرَجَعْنَا إِلَى الْمَنْزِلِ، فَأَرْسَلَنِي عُمَرُ وَقَالَ اذْهَبْ فَانْظُرْ هَلِ اسْتَيْقَظَ فَأَتَيْتُهُ، فَدَخَلْتُ عَلَيْهِ فَبَايَعْتُهُ، ثُمَّ انْطَلَقْتُ إِلَى عُمَرَ، فَأَخْبَرْتُهُ أَنَّهُ قَدِ اسْتَيْقَظَ، فَانْطَلَقْنَا إِلَيْهِ نُهَرْوِلُ هَرْوَلَةً حَتَّى دَخَلَ عَلَيْهِ فَبَايَعَهُ ثُمَّ بَايَعْتُهُ

Anas ibn Mālik ibn Naḍr al-Khazrajī al-Anṣārī

أنس بن مالك الخزرجي الأنصاري

Narrated Anas bin Malik: The Prophetﷺ said to Abu Talha, "Choose one of your boys to serve me." So Abu Talha took me (to serve the Prophetﷺ) by giving me a ride behind him (on his camel). So I used to serve Allah's Messengerﷺ whenever he stayed somewhere. I used to hear him saying, "O Allah! I seek refuge with you (Allah) from (worries) care and grief, from incapacity and laziness, from miserliness and cowardice, from being heavily in debt and from being overpowered by other men." I kept on serving him till he returned from (the battle of) Khaibar. He then brought Safiya, the daughter of Huyay whom he had got (from the booty). I saw him making a kind of cushion with a cloak or a garment for her. He then let her ride behind him. When we reached a place called As-Sahba', he prepared (a special meal called) Hais, and asked me to invite the men who (came and) ate, and that was the marriage banquet given on the consummation of his marriage to her. Then he proceeded till the mountain of Uhud appeared, whereupon he said, "This mountain loves us and we love it." When he approached Medina, he said, "O Allah! I make the land between its (i.e., Medina's) two mountains a sanctuary, as the prophet Abraham made Mecca a sanctuary. O Allah! Bless them (the people of Medina) in their Mudd and the Sa' (units of measuring). – Sahih Al-Bukhari 6363

حَدَّثَنَا قُتَيْبَةُ بْنُ سَعِيدٍ، حَدَّثَنَا إِسْمَاعِيلُ بْنُ جَعْفَرٍ، عَنْ عَمْرِو بْنِ أَبِي عَمْرٍو، مَوْلَى الْمُطَّلِبِ بْنِ عَبْدِ اللَّهِ بْنِ حَنْطَبٍ أَنَّهُ سَمِعَ أَنَسَ بْنَ مَالِكٍ، يَقُولُ قَالَ رَسُولُ اللَّهِ صلى الله عليه وسلم لأَبِي طَلْحَةَ " الْتَمِسْ لَنَا غُلاَمًا مِنْ غِلْمَانِكُمْ يَخْدُمُنِي ". فَخَرَجَ بِي أَبُو طَلْحَةَ يُرْدِفُنِي وَرَاءَهُ، فَكُنْتُ أَخْدُمُ رَسُولَ اللَّهِ صلى الله عليه وسلم كُلَّمَا نَزَلَ، فَكُنْتُ أَسْمَعُهُ يُكْثِرُ أَنْ يَقُولَ " اللَّهُمَّ إِنِّي أَعُوذُ بِكَ مِنَ الْهَمِّ وَالْحَزَنِ، وَالْعَجْزِ وَالْكَسَلِ، وَالْبُخْلِ وَالْجُبْنِ، وَضَلَعِ الدَّيْنِ، وَغَلَبَةِ الرِّجَالِ ". فَلَمْ أَزَلْ أَخْدُمُهُ حَتَّى أَقْبَلْنَا مِنْ خَيْبَرَ، وَأَقْبَلَ بِصَفِيَّةَ بِنْتِ حُيَيٍّ قَدْ حَازَهَا، فَكُنْتُ أَرَاهُ يُحَوِّي وَرَاءَهُ بِعَبَاءَةٍ أَوْ كِسَاءٍ ثُمَّ يُرْدِفُهَا وَرَاءَهُ حَتَّى إِذَا كُنَّا بِالصَّهْبَاءِ صَنَعَ حَيْسًا فِي نِطَعٍ، ثُمَّ أَرْسَلَنِي فَدَعَوْتُ رِجَالاً فَأَكَلُوا، وَكَانَ ذَلِكَ بِنَاءَهُ بِهَا، ثُمَّ أَقْبَلَ حَتَّى بَدَا لَهُ أُحُدٌ قَالَ " هَذَا جُبَيْلٌ يُحِبُّنَا وَنُحِبُّهُ ". فَلَمَّا أَشْرَفَ عَلَى الْمَدِينَةِ قَالَ " اللَّهُمَّ إِنِّي أُحَرِّمُ مَا بَيْنَ جَبَلَيْهَا مِثْلَ مَا حَرَّمَ بِهِ إِبْرَاهِيمُ مَكَّةَ، اللَّهُمَّ بَارِكْ لَهُمْ فِي مُدِّهِمْ وَصَاعِهِمْ "

Narrated Anas: My mother, Um Sulaim, took a Mudd of barley grain, ground it and made porridge from it, and pressed (over it), a butter skin she had with her. Then she sent me to the Prophet, and I reached him while he was sitting with his companions. I invited him, whereupon he said, "And those who are with me?' I returned and said, "He says, 'And those who are with me?" Abu Talha went out to him and said, "O Allah's Messengerﷺ! It is just a meal prepared by Um Sulaim." The Prophetﷺ entered and the food was brought to him. He said, "Let ten persons enter upon me." Those ten entered and ate their fill. Again he said, 'Let ten (more) enter upon me." Those ten entered and ate their fill. Then he said, "Let ten (more) enter upon me." He called forty persons in all Then Allah's Messengerﷺ ate and got up. I started looking (at the food) to see if it decreased or not. – Sahih Al-Bukhari 5450

حَدَّثَنَا الصَّلْتُ بْنُ مُحَمَّدٍ، حَدَّثَنَا حَمَّادُ بْنُ زَيْدٍ، عَنِ الْجَعْدِ أَبِي عُثْمَانَ، عَنْ أَنَسٍ. وَعَنْ هِشَامٍ، عَنْ مُحَمَّدٍ، عَنْ أَنَسٍ. وَعَنْ سِنَانٍ أَبِي رَبِيعَةَ، عَنْ أَنَسٍ، أَنَّ أُمَّ سُلَيْمٍ، أُمَّهُ عَمَدَتْ إِلَى مُدٍّ مِنْ شَعِيرٍ، جَشَّتْهُ وَجَعَلَتْ مِنْهُ خَطِيفَةً، وَعَصَرَتْ عُكَّةً عِنْدَهَا، ثُمَّ بَعَثَتْنِي إِلَى النَّبِيِّ صلى الله عليه وسلم فَأَتَيْتُهُ وَهْوَ فِي أَصْحَابِهِ فَدَعَوْتُهُ قَالَ " وَمَنْ مَعِي ". فَجِئْتُ فَقُلْتُ إِنَّهُ يَقُولُ، وَمَنْ مَعِي. فَخَرَجَ إِلَيْهِ أَبُو طَلْحَةَ قَالَ يَا رَسُولَ اللَّهِ إِنَّمَا هُوَ شَىْءٌ صَنَعَتْهُ أُمُّ سُلَيْمٍ، فَدَخَلَ فَجِيءَ بِهِ وَقَالَ " أَدْخِلْ عَلَىَّ عَشَرَةً ". فَدَخَلُوا فَأَكَلُوا حَتَّى شَبِعُوا، ثُمَّ قَالَ " أَدْخِلْ عَلَىَّ عَشَرَةً ". فَدَخَلُوا فَأَكَلُوا حَتَّى شَبِعُوا، ثُمَّ قَالَ " أَدْخِلْ عَلَىَّ عَشَرَةً ". حَتَّى عَدَّ أَرْبَعِينَ، ثُمَّ أَكَلَ النَّبِيُّ صلى الله عليه وسلم ثُمَّ قَامَ، فَجَعَلْتُ أَنْظُرُ هَلْ نَقَصَ مِنْهَا شَىْءٌ.

Narrated Qatada: We used to go to Anas bin Malik and see his baker standing (preparing the bread). Anas said, "Eat. I have not known that the Prophetﷺ ever saw a thin well-baked loaf of bread till he died, and he never saw a roasted sheep with his eyes.". – Sahih Al-Bukhari 6457

حَدَّثَنَا هُدْبَةُ بْنُ خَالِدٍ، حَدَّثَنَا هَمَّامُ بْنُ يَحْيَى، حَدَّثَنَا قَتَادَةُ، قَالَ كُنَّا نَأْتِي أَنَسَ بْنَ مَالِكٍ وَخَبَّازُهُ قَائِمٌ وَقَالَ كُلُوا فَمَا أَعْلَمُ النَّبِيَّ صلى الله عليه وسلم رَأَى رَغِيفًا مُرَقَّقًا، حَتَّى لَحِقَ بِاللَّهِ، وَلاَ رَأَى شَاةً سَمِيطًا بِعَيْنِهِ قَطُّ

Narrated Anas: To the best of my knowledge, the Prophet ﷺ did not take his meals in a big tray at all, nor did he ever eat well-baked thin bread, nor did he ever eat at a dining table. – Sahih Al-Bukhari 5386

حَدَّثَنَا عَلِيُّ بْنُ عَبْدِ اللَّهِ، حَدَّثَنَا مُعَاذُ بْنُ هِشَامٍ، قَالَ حَدَّثَنِي أَبِي، عَنْ يُونُسَ ـ قَالَ عَلِيٌّ هُوَ الإِسْكَافُ ـ عَنْ قَتَادَةَ، عَنْ أَنَسٍ، رضى الله عنه قَالَ مَا عَلِمْتُ النَّبِيَّ صلى الله عليه وسلم أَكَلَ عَلَى سُكُرُّجَةٍ قَطُّ، وَلاَ خُبِزَ لَهُ مُرَقَّقٌ قَطُّ، وَلاَ أَكَلَ عَلَى خِوَانٍ. قِيلَ لِقَتَادَةَ فَعَلَى مَا كَانُوا يَأْكُلُونَ قَالَ عَلَى السُّفَرِ

Narrated Abu `Imran: Anas looked at the people wearing Tailsans (i.e. a special kind of head covering worn by Jews in old days). On that Anas said, "At this moment they (i.e. those people) look like the Jews of Khaibar.". – Sahih Al-Bukhari 4208

حَدَّثَنَا مُحَمَّدُ بْنُ سَعِيدٍ الْخُزَاعِيُّ، حَدَّثَنَا زِيَادُ بْنُ الرَّبِيعِ، عَنْ أَبِي عِمْرَانَ، قَالَ نَظَرَ أَنَسٌ إِلَى النَّاسِ يَوْمَ الْجُمُعَةِ، فَرَأَى طَيَالِسَةً فَقَالَ كَأَنَّهُمُ السَّاعَةَ يَهُودُ خَيْبَرَ.

Narrated Anas: None remains of those who prayed facing both Qiblas (that is, Jerusalem and Mecca) except myself. – Sahih Al-Bukhari 4489

حَدَّثَنَا عَلِيُّ بْنُ عَبْدِ اللَّهِ، حَدَّثَنَا مُعْتَمِرٌ، عَنْ أَبِيهِ، عَنْ أَنَسٍ ـ رضى الله عنه ـ قَالَ لَمْ يَبْقَ مِمَّنْ صَلَّى الْقِبْلَتَيْنِ غَيْرِي.

Narrated Anas bin Malik: When the Prophet ﷺ died, none had collected the Qur'an but four persons;: Abu Ad-Darda'. Mu`adh bin Jabal, Zaid bin Thabit and Abu Zaid. We were the inheritor (of Abu Zaid) as he had no offspring . – Sahih Al-Bukhari 5004

حَدَّثَنَا مُعَلَّى بْنُ أَسَدٍ، حَدَّثَنَا عَبْدُ اللَّهِ بْنُ الْمُثَنَّى، قَالَ حَدَّثَنِي ثَابِتٌ الْبُنَانِيُّ، وَثُمَامَةُ، عَنْ أَنَسٍ، قَالَ مَاتَ النَّبِيُّ صلى الله عليه وسلم وَلَمْ يَجْمَعِ الْقُرْآنَ غَيْرُ أَرْبَعَةٍ أَبُو الدَّرْدَاءِ وَمُعَاذُ بْنُ جَبَلٍ وَزَيْدُ بْنُ ثَابِتٍ وَأَبُو زَيْدٍ. قَالَ وَنَحْنُ وَرِثْنَاهُ.

Narrated Thabit Al-Banani: I was with Anas while his daughter was present with him. Anas said, "A woman came to Allah's Apostle and presented herself to him, saying, 'O Allah's Messenger ﷺ, have you any need for me (i.e. would you like to marry me)?' "Thereupon Anas's daughter said, "What a shameless lady she was ! Shame! Shame!" Anas said, "She was better than you; she had a liking for the Prophet ﷺ so she presented herself for marriage to him.". – Sahih Al-Bukhari 5120

حَدَّثَنَا عَلِيُّ بْنُ عَبْدِ اللَّهِ، حَدَّثَنَا مَرْحُومٌ، قَالَ سَمِعْتُ ثَابِتًا الْبُنَانِيَّ، قَالَ كُنْتُ عِنْدَ أَنَسٍ وَعِنْدَهُ ابْنَةٌ لَهُ، قَالَ أَنَسٌ جَاءَتِ امْرَأَةٌ إِلَى رَسُولِ اللَّهِ صلى الله عليه وسلم تَعْرِضُ عَلَيْهِ نَفْسَهَا قَالَتْ يَا رَسُولَ اللَّهِ أَلَكَ بِي حَاجَةٌ، فَقَالَتْ بِنْتُ أَنَسٍ مَا أَقَلَّ حَيَاءَهَا وَاسَوْأَتَاهْ وَاسَوْأَتَاهْ. قَالَ هِيَ خَيْرٌ مِنْكِ رَغِبَتْ فِي النَّبِيِّ صلى الله عليه وسلم فَعَرَضَتْ عَلَيْهِ نَفْسَهَا

Narrated Anas: When the ailment of the Prophet ﷺ got aggravated, he became unconscious whereupon Fatima said, "Oh, how distressed my father is!" He said, "Your father will have no more distress after today." When he expired, she said, "O Father! Who has responded to the call of the Lord Who has invited him! O Father, whose dwelling place is the Garden of Paradise (i.e. Al-Firdaus)! O Father! We convey this news (of your death) to Gabriel." When he was buried, Fatima said, "O Anas! Do you feel pleased to throw earth over Allah's Messenger?" - Sahih Al-Bukhari 4462

حَدَّثَنَا سُلَيْمَانُ بْنُ حَرْبٍ، حَدَّثَنَا حَمَّادٌ، عَنْ ثَابِتٍ، عَنْ أَنَسٍ، قَالَ لَمَّا ثَقُلَ النَّبِيُّ صلى الله عليه وسلم جَعَلَ يَتَغَشَّاهُ، فَقَالَتْ فَاطِمَةُ ـ عَلَيْهَا السَّلاَمُ ـ وَاكَرْبَ أَبَاهُ. فَقَالَ لَهَا " لَيْسَ عَلَى أَبِيكِ كَرْبٌ بَعْدَ الْيَوْمِ ". فَلَمَّا مَاتَ قَالَتْ يَا أَبَتَاهْ، أَجَابَ رَبًّا

دَعَاهُ، يَا أَبَتَاهْ مَنْ جَنَّةُ الْفِرْدَوْسِ مَأْوَاهُ، يَا أَبَتَاهْ إِلَى جِبْرِيلَ نَنْعَاهْ. فَلَمَّا دُفِنَ قَالَتْ فَاطِمَةُ ـ عَلَيْهَا السَّلاَمُ ـ يَا أَنَسُ، أَطَابَتْ أَنْفُسُكُمْ أَنْ تَحْثُوا عَلَى رَسُولِ اللَّهِ صلى الله عليه وسلم التُّرَابَ

Narrated Anas bin Malik: The Prophet ﷺ used to mix with us to the extent that he would say to a younger brother of mine, 'O Aba `Umair! What did the Nughair (a kind of bird) do?". – Sahih Al-Bukhari 6129

حَدَّثَنَا آدَمُ، حَدَّثَنَا شُعْبَةُ، حَدَّثَنَا أَبُو التَّيَّاحِ، قَالَ سَمِعْتُ أَنَسَ بْنَ مَالِكٍ ـ رضى الله عنه ـ يَقُولُ إِنْ كَانَ النَّبِيُّ صلى الله عليه وسلم لَيُخَالِطُنَا حَتَّى يَقُولَ لأَخٍ لِي صَغِيرٍ " يَا أَبَا عُمَيْرٍ مَا فَعَلَ النُّغَيْرُ ".

Narrated Rabi`a bin Abi `Abdur-Rahman: I heard Anas bin Malik describing the Prophet ﷺ saying, "He was of medium height amongst the people, neither tall nor short; he had a rosy color, neither absolutely white nor deep brown; his hair was neither completely curly nor quite lank. Divine Inspiration was revealed to him when he was forty years old. He stayed ten years in Mecca receiving the Divine Inspiration, and stayed in Medina for ten more years. When he expired, he had scarcely twenty white hairs in his head and beard." Rabi`a said, "I saw some of his hairs and it was red. When I asked about that, I was told that it turned red because of scent. ". – Sahih Al-Bukhari 3547

حَدَّثَنِي ابْنُ بُكَيْرٍ، قَالَ حَدَّثَنِي اللَّيْثُ، عَنْ خَالِدٍ، عَنْ سَعِيدِ بْنِ أَبِي هِلاَلٍ، عَنْ رَبِيعَةَ بْنِ أَبِي عَبْدِ الرَّحْمَنِ، قَالَ سَمِعْتُ أَنَسَ بْنَ مَالِكٍ، يَصِفُ النَّبِيَّ صلى الله عليه وسلم قَالَ كَانَ رَبْعَةً مِنَ الْقَوْمِ، لَيْسَ بِالطَّوِيلِ وَلاَ بِالْقَصِيرِ، أَزْهَرَ اللَّوْنِ لَيْسَ بِأَبْيَضَ أَمْهَقَ وَلاَ آدَمَ، لَيْسَ بِجَعْدٍ قَطَطٍ وَلاَ سَبْطٍ رَجِلٍ، أُنْزِلَ عَلَيْهِ وَهْوَ ابْنُ أَرْبَعِينَ، فَلَبِثَ بِمَكَّةَ عَشْرَ سِنِينَ يُنْزَلُ عَلَيْهِ وَبِالْمَدِينَةِ عَشْرَ سِنِينَ، وَلَيْسَ فِي رَأْسِهِ وَلِحْيَتِهِ عِشْرُونَ شَعَرَةً بَيْضَاءَ. قَالَ رَبِيعَةُ فَرَأَيْتُ شَعَرًا مِنْ شَعَرِهِ، فَإِذَا هُوَ أَحْمَرُ فَسَأَلْتُ فَقِيلَ احْمَرَّ مِنَ الطِّيبِ

Narrated Anas: The Prophet ﷺ paid a visit to Um-Sulaim and she placed before him dates and ghee. The Prophet ﷺ said, "Replace the ghee and dates in their respective containers for I am fasting." Then he stood somewhere in her house and offered an optional prayer and then he invoked good on Um-Sulaim and her family. Then Um-Sulaim said, "O Allah's Messenger ﷺ! I have a special request (today)." He said, "What is it?" She replied, "(Please invoke for) your servant Anas." So Allah's Messenger ﷺ did not leave anything good in the world or the Hereafter which he did not invoke (Allah to bestow) on me and said, "O Allah! Give him (i.e. Anas) property and children and bless him." Thus I am one of the richest among the Ansar and my daughter Umaina told me that when Al-Hajjaj came to Basra, more than 120 of my offspring had been buried. – Sahih Al-Bukhari 1982

حَدَّثَنَا مُحَمَّدُ بْنُ الْمُثَنَّى، قَالَ حَدَّثَنِي خَالِدٌ ـ هُوَ ابْنُ الْحَارِثِ ـ حَدَّثَنَا حُمَيْدٌ، عَنْ أَنَسٍ ـ رضى الله عنه ـ دَخَلَ النَّبِيُّ صلى الله عليه وسلم عَلَى أُمِّ سُلَيْمٍ، فَأَتَتْهُ بِتَمْرٍ وَسَمْنٍ، قَالَ " أَعِيدُوا سَمْنَكُمْ فِي سِقَائِهِ، وَتَمْرَكُمْ فِي وِعَائِهِ، فَإِنِّي صَائِمٌ ". ثُمَّ قَامَ إِلَى نَاحِيَةٍ مِنَ الْبَيْتِ، فَصَلَّى غَيْرَ الْمَكْتُوبَةِ، فَدَعَا لأُمِّ سُلَيْمٍ، وَأَهْلِ بَيْتِهَا، فَقَالَتْ أُمُّ سُلَيْمٍ يَا رَسُولَ اللَّهِ، إِنَّ لِي خُوَيْصَةً، قَالَ " مَا هِيَ ". قَالَتْ خَادِمُكَ أَنَسٌ. فَمَا تَرَكَ خَيْرَ آخِرَةٍ وَلاَ دُنْيَا إِلاَّ دَعَا لِي بِهِ قَالَ " اللَّهُمَّ ارْزُقْهُ مَالاً وَوَلَدًا وَبَارِكْ لَهُ ". فَإِنِّي لَمِنْ أَكْثَرِ الأَنْصَارِ مَالاً. وَحَدَّثَتْنِي ابْنَتِي أُمَيْنَةُ أَنَّهُ دُفِنَ لِصُلْبِي مَقْدَمَ حَجَّاجٍ الْبَصْرَةَ بِضْعٌ وَعِشْرُونَ وَمِائَةٌ. حَدَّثَنَا ابْنُ أَبِي مَرْيَمَ، أَخْبَرَنَا يَحْيَى، قَالَ حَدَّثَنِي حُمَيْدٌ، سَمِعَ أَنَسًا ـ رضى الله عنه ـ عَنِ النَّبِيِّ صلى الله عليه وسلم

Sa'd ibn 'Ubadah ibn Dulaym

سعد بن عبادة بن دليم

Narrated Hisham's father: When Allah's Messenger ﷺ set out (towards Mecca) during the year of the Conquest (of Mecca) and this news reached (the infidels of Quraish), Abu Sufyan, Hakim bin Hizam and Budail bin Warqa came out to gather information about Allah's Messenger ﷺ, They proceeded on their way till they reached a place called Marr-az-Zahran (which is near Mecca). Behold! There they saw many fires as if they were the fires of `Arafat. Abu Sufyan said, "What is this? It looked like the fires of `Arafat." Budail bin Warqa' said, "Banu `Amr are less in number than that." Some of the guards of Allah's Messenger ﷺ saw them and took them over, caught them and brought them to Allah's Messenger ﷺ. Abu Sufyan embraced Islam. When the Prophet ﷺ proceeded, he said to Al-Abbas, "Keep Abu Sufyan standing at the top of the mountain so that he would look at the Muslims. So Al-`Abbas kept him standing (at that place) and the tribes with the Prophet ﷺ started passing in front of Abu Sufyan in military batches. A batch passed and Abu Sufyan said, "O `Abbas Who are these?" `Abbas said, "They are (Banu) Ghifar." Abu Sufyan said, I have got nothing to do with Ghifar." Then (a batch of the tribe of) Juhaina passed by and he said similarly as above. Then (a batch of the tribe of) Sa`d bin Huzaim passed by and he said similarly as above. Then (Banu) Sulaim passed by and he said similarly as above. Then came a batch, the like of which Abu Sufyan had not seen. He said, "Who are these?" `Abbas said, "They are the Ansar headed by Sa`d bin Ubada, the one holding the flag." Sa`d bin Ubada said, "O Abu Sufyan! Today is the day of a great battle and today (what is prohibited in) the Ka`ba will be permissible." Abu Sufyan said., "O `Abbas! How excellent the day of destruction is! "Then came another batch (of warriors) which was the smallest of all the batches, and in it there was Allah's Messenger ﷺ and his companions and the flag of the Prophet ﷺ was carried by Az-Zubair bin Al Awwam. When Allah's Messenger ﷺ passed by Abu Sufyan, the latter said, (to the Prophet), "Do you know what Sa`d bin 'Ubada said?" The Prophet ﷺ said, "What did he say?" Abu Sufyan said, "He said so-and-so." The Prophet ﷺ said, "Sa`d told a lie, but today Allah will give superiority to the Ka`ba and today the Ka`ba will be covered with a (cloth) covering." Allah's Messenger ﷺ ordered that his flag be fixed at Al-Hajun. Narrated `Urwa: Nafi` bin Jubair bin Mut`im said, "I heard Al-Abbas saying to Az-Zubair bin Al- `Awwam, 'O Abu `Abdullah ! Did Allah's Messenger ﷺ order you to fix the flag here?' "Allah's Messenger ﷺ ordered Khalid bin Al-Walid to enter Mecca from its upper part from Ka'da while the Prophet ﷺ himself entered from Kuda. Two men from the cavalry of Khalid bin Al-Wahd named Hubaish bin Al-Ash'ar and Kurz bin Jabir Al-Fihri were martyred on that day. – Sahih Al-Bukhari 4280

حَدَّثَنَا عُبَيْدُ بْنُ إِسْمَاعِيلَ، حَدَّثَنَا أَبُو أُسَامَةَ، عَنْ هِشَامٍ، عَنْ أَبِيهِ، قَالَ لَمَّا سَارَ رَسُولُ اللَّهِ صلى الله عليه وسلم عَامَ الْفَتْحِ فَبَلَغَ ذَلِكَ قُرَيْشًا، خَرَجَ أَبُو سُفْيَانَ بْنُ حَرْبٍ وَحَكِيمُ بْنُ حِزَامٍ وَبُدَيْلُ بْنُ وَرْقَاءَ يَلْتَمِسُونَ الْخَبَرَ عَنْ رَسُولِ اللَّهِ صلى الله عليه وسلم فَأَقْبَلُوا يَسِيرُونَ حَتَّى أَتَوْا مَرَّ الظَّهْرَانِ، فَإِذَا هُمْ بِنِيرَانٍ كَأَنَّهَا نِيرَانُ عَرَفَةَ، فَقَالَ أَبُو سُفْيَانَ مَا هَذِهِ لَكَأَنَّهَا نِيرَانُ عَرَفَةَ. فَقَالَ بُدَيْلُ بْنُ وَرْقَاءَ نِيرَانُ بَنِي عَمْرٍو. فَقَالَ أَبُو سُفْيَانَ عَمْرٌو أَقَلُّ مِنْ ذَلِكَ. فَرَآهُمْ نَاسٌ مِنْ حَرَسِ رَسُولِ اللَّهِ صلى الله عليه وسلم فَأَدْرَكُوهُمْ فَأَخَذُوهُمْ، فَأَتَوْا بِهِمْ رَسُولَ اللَّهِ صلى الله عليه وسلم فَأَسْلَمَ أَبُو سُفْيَانَ، فَلَمَّا سَارَ قَالَ لِلْعَبَّاسِ " احْبِسْ أَبَا سُفْيَانَ عِنْدَ حَطْمِ الْخَيْلِ حَتَّى يَنْظُرَ إِلَى الْمُسْلِمِينَ ". فَحَبَسَهُ الْعَبَّاسُ، فَجَعَلَتِ الْقَبَائِلُ تَمُرُّ مَعَ النَّبِيِّ صلى الله عليه وسلم تَمُرُّ كَتِيبَةً كَتِيبَةً عَلَى أَبِي سُفْيَانَ، فَمَرَّتْ كَتِيبَةٌ قَالَ يَا عَبَّاسُ مَنْ هَذِهِ قَالَ هَذِهِ غِفَارُ. قَالَ مَا لِي وَلِغِفَارَ ثُمَّ مَرَّتْ جُهَيْنَةُ، قَالَ مِثْلَ ذَلِكَ، ثُمَّ مَرَّتْ سَعْدُ بْنُ هُذَيْمٍ، فَقَالَ مِثْلَ ذَلِكَ، وَمَرَّتْ سُلَيْمُ، فَقَالَ مِثْلَ ذَلِكَ، حَتَّى أَقْبَلَتْ كَتِيبَةٌ لَمْ يَرَ مِثْلَهَا، قَالَ مَنْ هَذِهِ قَالَ هَؤُلاَءِ الأَنْصَارُ عَلَيْهِمْ سَعْدُ بْنُ عُبَادَةَ مَعَهُ الرَّايَةُ. فَقَالَ سَعْدُ بْنُ عُبَادَةَ يَا أَبَا سُفْيَانَ الْيَوْمُ يَوْمُ الْمَلْحَمَةِ، الْيَوْمَ تُسْتَحَلُّ الْكَعْبَةُ. فَقَالَ أَبُو سُفْيَانَ يَا عَبَّاسُ حَبَّذَا يَوْمُ الذِّمَارِ. ثُمَّ جَاءَتْ كَتِيبَةٌ، وَهْىَ أَقَلُّ الْكَتَائِبِ، فِيهِمْ رَسُولُ اللَّهِ صلى الله عليه وسلم وَأَصْحَابُهُ، وَرَايَةُ النَّبِيِّ صلى الله عليه وسلم مَعَ الزُّبَيْرِ بْنِ الْعَوَّامِ، فَلَمَّا مَرَّ رَسُولُ اللَّهِ صلى الله عليه وسلم بِأَبِي سُفْيَانَ قَالَ أَلَمْ تَعْلَمْ مَا قَالَ سَعْدُ بْنُ عُبَادَةَ قَالَ " مَا قَالَ ". قَالَ كَذَا وَكَذَا. فَقَالَ " كَذَبَ سَعْدٌ، وَلَكِنْ هَذَا يَوْمٌ يُعَظِّمُ اللَّهُ فِيهِ الْكَعْبَةَ، وَيَوْمٌ تُكْسَى فِيهِ الْكَعْبَةُ ". قَالَ وَأَمَرَ رَسُولُ اللَّهِ صلى الله عليه وسلم أَنْ تُرْكَزَ رَايَتُهُ بِالْحَجُونِ. قَالَ عُرْوَةُ وَأَخْبَرَنِي نَافِعُ بْنُ جُبَيْرِ بْنِ مُطْعِمٍ قَالَ سَمِعْتُ الْعَبَّاسَ يَقُولُ لِلزُّبَيْرِ بْنِ الْعَوَّامِ يَا أَبَا عَبْدِ اللَّهِ، هَا هُنَا أَمَرَكَ رَسُولُ اللَّهِ صلى الله عليه وسلم أَنْ تَرْكُزَ الرَّايَةَ، قَالَ وَأَمَرَ رَسُولُ اللَّهِ صلى

الله عليه وسلم يَوْمَئِذٍ خَالِدَ بْنَ الْوَلِيدِ أَنْ يَدْخُلَ مِنْ أَعْلَى مَكَّةَ مِنْ كَدَاءٍ، وَدَخَلَ النَّبِيُّ صلى الله عليه وسلم مِنْ كُدَا، فَقُتِلَ مِنْ خَيْلِ خَالِدٍ يَوْمَئِذٍ رَجُلاَنِ حُبَيْشُ بْنُ الأَشْعَرِ وَكُرْزُ بْنُ جَابِرٍ الْفِهْرِيُّ

Narrated Al-Mughira: Sa`d bin Ubada said, "If I found a man with my wife, I would kill him with the sharp side of my sword." When the Prophetﷺ heard that he said, "Do you wonder at Sa`d's sense of ghira (self-respect)? Verily, I have more sense of ghira than Sa`d, and Allah has more sense of ghira than I.". – Sahih Al-Bukhari 6846

حَدَّثَنَا مُوسَى، حَدَّثَنَا أَبُو عَوَانَةَ، حَدَّثَنَا عَبْدُ الْمَلِكِ، عَنْ وَرَّادٍ، كَاتِبِ الْمُغِيرَةِ عَنِ الْمُغِيرَةِ، قَالَ قَالَ سَعْدُ بْنُ عُبَادَةَ لَوْ رَأَيْتُ رَجُلاً مَعَ امْرَأَتِي لَضَرَبْتُهُ بِالسَّيْفِ غَيْرَ مُصْفَحٍ. فَبَلَغَ ذَلِكَ النَّبِيَّ صلى الله عليه وسلم فَقَالَ " أَتَعْجَبُونَ مِنْ غَيْرَةِ سَعْدٍ، لأَنَا أَغْيَرُ مِنْهُ، وَاللَّهُ أَغْيَرُ مِنِّي "

Narrated Ibn `Abbas: The mother of Sa`d bin 'Ubada died in his absence. He said, "O Allah's Messengerﷺ! My mother died in my absence; will it be of any benefit for her if I give Sadaqa on her behalf?" The Prophetﷺ said, "Yes," Sa`d said, "I make you a witness that I gave my garden called Al Makhraf in charity on her behalf.". – Sahih Al-Bukhari 2756

حَدَّثَنَا مُحَمَّدٌ، أَخْبَرَنَا مَخْلَدُ بْنُ يَزِيدَ، أَخْبَرَنَا ابْنُ جُرَيْجٍ، قَالَ أَخْبَرَنِي يَعْلَى، أَنَّهُ سَمِعَ عِكْرِمَةَ، يَقُولُ أَنْبَأَنَا ابْنُ عَبَّاسٍ ـ رضى الله عنهما ـ أَنَّ سَعْدَ بْنَ عُبَادَةَ ـ رضى الله عنه ـ تُوُفِّيَتْ أُمُّهُ وَهْوَ غَائِبٌ عَنْهَا، فَقَالَ يَا رَسُولَ اللَّهِ إِنَّ أُمِّي تُوُفِّيَتْ وَأَنَا غَائِبٌ عَنْهَا، أَيَنْفَعُهَا شَىْءٌ إِنْ تَصَدَّقْتُ بِهِ عَنْهَا قَالَ " نَعَمْ ". قَالَ فَإِنِّي أُشْهِدُكَ أَنَّ حَائِطِي الْمِخْرَافَ صَدَقَةٌ عَلَيْهَا

Narrated Sa`d: On the day of the battle of Uhud the Prophetﷺ mentioned for me both his parents (i.e. saying, "Let my parents be sacrificed for you."). – Sahih Al-Bukhari 3725

حَدَّثَنِي مُحَمَّدُ بْنُ الْمُثَنَّى، حَدَّثَنَا عَبْدُ الْوَهَّابِ، قَالَ سَمِعْتُ يَحْيَى، قَالَ سَمِعْتُ سَعِيدَ بْنَ الْمُسَيَّبِ، قَالَ سَمِعْتُ سَعْدًا، يَقُولُ جَمَعَ لِي النَّبِيُّ صلى الله عليه وسلم أَبَوَيْهِ يَوْمَ أُحُدٍ.

Narrated Sa`d: No doubt, (for some time) I stood for one-third of the Muslims. – Sahih Al-Bukhari 3726

حَدَّثَنَا مَكِّيُّ بْنُ إِبْرَاهِيمَ، حَدَّثَنَا هَاشِمُ بْنُ هَاشِمٍ، عَنْ عَامِرِ بْنِ سَعْدٍ، عَنْ أَبِيهِ، قَالَ لَقَدْ رَأَيْتُنِي وَأَنَا ثُلُثُ الإِسْلاَمِ.

Narrated Qais: I heard Sa`d saying, "I was the first amongst the 'Arabs who shot an arrow for Allah's Cause. We used to fight along with the Prophets, while we had nothing to eat except the leaves of trees so that one's excrete would look like the excrete balls of camel or a sheep, containing nothing to mix them together. Today Banu Asad tribe blame me for not having understood Islam. I would be a loser if my deeds were in vain." Those people complained about Sa`d to `Umar, claiming that he did not offer his prayers perfectly. – Sahih Al-Bukhari 3728

حَدَّثَنَا عَمْرُو بْنُ عَوْنٍ، حَدَّثَنَا خَالِدُ بْنُ عَبْدِ اللَّهِ، عَنْ إِسْمَاعِيلَ، عَنْ قَيْسٍ، قَالَ سَمِعْتُ سَعْدًا ـ رضى الله عنه ـ يَقُولُ إِنِّي لأَوَّلُ الْعَرَبِ رَمَى بِسَهْمٍ فِي سَبِيلِ اللَّهِ، وَكُنَّا نَغْزُو مَعَ النَّبِيِّ صلى الله عليه وسلم وَمَا لَنَا طَعَامٌ إِلاَّ وَرَقُ الشَّجَرِ، حَتَّى إِنَّ أَحَدَنَا لَيَضَعُ كَمَا يَضَعُ الْبَعِيرُ أَوِ الشَّاةُ، مَا لَهُ خِلْطٌ، ثُمَّ أَصْبَحَتْ بَنُو أَسَدٍ تُعَزِّرُنِي عَلَى الإِسْلاَمِ، لَقَدْ خِبْتُ إِذًا وَضَلَّ عَمَلِي. وَكَانُوا وَشَوْا بِهِ إِلَى عُمَرَ، قَالُوا لاَ يُحْسِنُ يُصَلِّي

Narrated `Ali: I never saw the Prophetﷺ saying, "Let my parents sacrifice their lives for you," to any man after Sa`d. I heard him saying (to him), "Throw (the arrows)! Let my parents sacrifice their lives for you.". – Sahih Al-Bukhari 2905

حَدَّثَنَا مُسَدَّدٌ، حَدَّثَنَا يَحْيَى، عَنْ سُفْيَانَ، قَالَ حَدَّثَنِي سَعْدُ بْنُ إِبْرَاهِيمَ، عَنْ عَبْدِ اللَّهِ بْنِ شَدَّادٍ، عَنْ عَلِيٍّ، حَدَّثَنَا قَبِيصَةُ، حَدَّثَنَا سُفْيَانُ، عَنْ سَعْدِ بْنِ إِبْرَاهِيمَ، قَالَ حَدَّثَنِي عَبْدُ اللَّهِ بْنُ شَدَّادٍ، قَالَ سَمِعْتُ عَلِيًّا ـ رضى الله عنه ـ يَقُولُ مَا رَأَيْتُ النَّبِيَّ صلى الله عليه وسلم يُفَدِّي رَجُلاً بَعْدَ سَعْدٍ، سَمِعْتُهُ يَقُولُ " ارْمِ فِدَاكَ أَبِي وَأُمِّي "

Narrated Abu Humaid: The Prophetﷺ said, "The best of the Ansar families (homes) are the families (homes) of Banu An- Najjar, and then that of Banu `Abdul Ash-hal, and then that of Banu Al-Harith, and then that of Banu Saida; and there is good in all the families (homes) of the Ansar." Sa`d bin 'Ubada followed us and said, "O Abu Usaid ! Don't you see that the

Prophetﷺ compared the Ansar and made us the last of them in superiority? Then Sa`d met the Prophetﷺ and said, "O Allah's Messengerﷺ! In comparing the Ansar's families (homes) as to the degree of superiority, you have made us the last of them." Allah's Messenger ﷺreplied, "Isn't it sufficient that you are regarded amongst the best?". – Sahih Al-Bukhari 3791

حَدَّثَنَا خَالِدُ بْنُ مَخْلَدٍ، حَدَّثَنَا سُلَيْمَانُ، قَالَ حَدَّثَنِي عَمْرُو بْنُ يَحْيَى، عَنْ عَبَّاسِ بْنِ سَهْلٍ، عَنْ أَبِي حُمَيْدٍ، عَنِ النَّبِيِّ صلى الله عليه وسلم قَالَ " إِنَّ خَيْرَ دُورِ الأَنْصَارِ دَارُ بَنِي النَّجَّارِ، ثُمَّ عَبْدِ الأَشْهَلِ، ثُمَّ دَارُ بَنِي الْحَارِثِ، ثُمَّ بَنِي سَاعِدَةَ، وَفِي كُلِّ دُورِ الأَنْصَارِ خَيْرٌ ". فَلَحِقْنَا سَعْدَ بْنَ عُبَادَةَ فَقَالَ أَبَا أُسَيْدٍ أَلَمْ تَرَ أَنَّ نَبِيَّ اللَّهِ صلى الله عليه وسلم خَيَّرَ الأَنْصَارَ فَجَعَلَنَا أَخِيرًا فَأَدْرَكَ سَعْدٌ النَّبِيَّ صلى الله عليه وسلم فَقَالَ يَا رَسُولَ اللَّهِ، خُيِّرَ دُورُ الأَنْصَارِ فَجُعِلْنَا آخِرًا. فَقَالَ " أَوَلَيْسَ بِحَسْبِكُمْ أَنْ تَكُونُوا مِنَ الْخِيَارِ "

Narrated `Abdullah bin `Umar: Sa`d bin 'Ubada became sick and the Prophetﷺ along with `Abdur Rahman bin `Auf, Sa`d bin Abi Waqqas and `Abdullah bin Mas`ud visited him to inquire about his health. When he came to him, he found him surrounded by his household and he asked, "Has he died?" They said, "No, O Allah's Apostle." The Prophetﷺ wept and when the people saw the weeping of Allah's Messengerﷺ they all wept. He said, "Will you listen? Allah does not punish for shedding tears, nor for the grief of the heart but he punishes or bestows His Mercy because of this." He pointed to his tongue and added, "The deceased is punished for the wailing of his relatives over him." `Umar used to beat with a stick and throw stones and put dust over the faces (of those who used to wail over the dead). – Sahih Al-Bukhari 1304

حَدَّثَنَا أَصْبَغُ، عَنِ ابْنِ وَهْبٍ، قَالَ أَخْبَرَنِي عَمْرٌو، عَنْ سَعِيدِ بْنِ الْحَارِثِ الأَنْصَارِيِّ، عَنْ عَبْدِ اللَّهِ بْنِ عُمَرَ ـ رضى الله عنهما ـ قَالَ اشْتَكَى سَعْدُ بْنُ عُبَادَةَ شَكْوَى لَهُ فَأَتَاهُ النَّبِيُّ صلى الله عليه وسلم يَعُودُهُ مَعَ عَبْدِ الرَّحْمَنِ بْنِ عَوْفٍ وَسَعْدِ بْنِ أَبِي وَقَّاصٍ وَعَبْدِ اللَّهِ بْنِ مَسْعُودٍ ـ رضى الله عنهم ـ فَلَمَّا دَخَلَ عَلَيْهِ فَوَجَدَهُ فِي غَاشِيَةِ أَهْلِهِ فَقَالَ " قَدْ قَضَى ". قَالُوا لاَ يَا رَسُولَ اللَّهِ. فَبَكَى النَّبِيُّ صلى الله عليه وسلم فَلَمَّا رَأَى الْقَوْمُ بُكَاءَ النَّبِيِّ صلى الله عليه وسلم بَكَوْا فَقَالَ " أَلاَ تَسْمَعُونَ إِنَّ اللَّهَ لاَ يُعَذِّبُ بِدَمْعِ الْعَيْنِ، وَلاَ بِحُزْنِ الْقَلْبِ، وَلَكِنْ يُعَذِّبُ بِهَذَا ـ وَأَشَارَ إِلَى لِسَانِهِ ـ أَوْ يَرْحَمُ وَإِنَّ الْمَيِّتَ يُعَذَّبُ بِبُكَاءِ أَهْلِهِ عَلَيْهِ ". وَكَانَ عُمَرُ ـ رضى الله عنه ـ يَضْرِبُ فِيهِ بِالْعَصَا، وَيَرْمِي بِالْحِجَارَةِ وَيَحْثِي بِالتُّرَابِ

Narrated Usama bin Zaid: The daughter of the Prophetﷺ sent (a messenger) to the Prophetﷺ requesting him to come as her child was dying (or was gasping), but the Prophetﷺ returned the messenger and told him to convey his greeting to her and say: "Whatever Allah takes is for Him and whatever He gives, is for Him, and everything with Him has a limited fixed term (in this world) and so she should be patient and hope for Allah's reward." She again sent for him, swearing that he should come. The Prophetﷺ got up, and so did Sa`d bin 'Ubada, Mu`adh bin Jabal, Ubai bin Ka`b, Zaid bin Thabit and some other men. The child was brought to Allah's Messengerﷺ while his breath was disturbed in his chest (the sub-narrator thinks that Usama added: ) as if it was a leather water-skin. On that the eyes of the Prophet ﷺ started shedding tears. Sa`d said, "O Allah's Messengerﷺ! What is this?" He replied, "It is mercy which Allah has lodged in the hearts of His slaves, and Allah is merciful only to those of His slaves who are merciful (to others). – Sahih Al-Bukhari 1284

حَدَّثَنَا عَبْدَانُ، وَمُحَمَّدٌ، قَالاَ أَخْبَرَنَا عَبْدُ اللَّهِ، أَخْبَرَنَا عَاصِمُ بْنُ سُلَيْمَانَ، عَنْ أَبِي عُثْمَانَ، قَالَ حَدَّثَنِي أُسَامَةُ بْنُ زَيْدٍ ـ رضى الله عنهما ـ قَالَ أَرْسَلَتِ ابْنَةُ النَّبِيِّ صلى الله عليه وسلم إِلَيْهِ إِنَّ ابْنًا لِي قُبِضَ فَائْتِنَا. فَأَرْسَلَ يُقْرِئُ السَّلاَمَ وَيَقُولُ " إِنَّ لِلَّهِ مَا أَخَذَ وَلَهُ مَا أَعْطَى وَكُلٌّ عِنْدَهُ بِأَجَلٍ مُسَمًّى، فَلْتَصْبِرْ وَلْتَحْتَسِبْ ". فَأَرْسَلَتْ إِلَيْهِ تُقْسِمُ عَلَيْهِ لَيَأْتِيَنَّهَا، فَقَامَ وَمَعَهُ سَعْدُ بْنُ عُبَادَةَ وَمُعَاذُ بْنُ جَبَلٍ وَأُبَىُّ بْنُ كَعْبٍ وَزَيْدُ بْنُ ثَابِتٍ وَرِجَالٌ، فَرُفِعَ إِلَى رَسُولِ اللَّهِ صلى الله عليه وسلم الصَّبِيُّ وَنَفْسُهُ تَتَقَعْقَعُ ـ قَالَ حَسِبْتُهُ أَنَّهُ قَالَ ـ كَأَنَّهَا شَنٌّ. فَفَاضَتْ عَيْنَاهُ. فَقَالَ سَعْدٌ يَا رَسُولَ اللَّهِ مَا هَذَا فَقَالَ " هَذِهِ رَحْمَةٌ جَعَلَهَا اللَّهُ فِي قُلُوبِ عِبَادِهِ، وَإِنَّمَا يَرْحَمُ اللَّهُ مِنْ عِبَادِهِ الرُّحَمَاءَ "

Narrated Usama bin Zaid: The Prophetﷺ rode a donkey having a saddle with a Fadakiyya velvet covering. He mounted me behind him and went to visit Sa`d bin 'Ubada, and that had been before the battle of Badr. The Prophetﷺ proceeded till he passed by a gathering in which `Abdullah bin Ubai bin Salul was present, and that had been before `Abdullah embraced Islam. The gathering comprised of Muslims, polytheists, i.e., isolators and Jews. `Abdullah bin

Rawaha was also present in that gathering. When dust raised by the donkey covered the gathering, `Abdullah bin Ubai covered his nose with his upper garment and said, "Do not trouble us with dust." The Prophetﷺ greeted them, stopped and dismounted. Then he invited them to Allah (i.e., to embrace Islam) and recited to them some verses of the Holy Qur'an. On that, `Abdullah bin Ubai said, "O man ! There is nothing better than what you say if it is true. Do not trouble us with it in our gathering, but return to your house, and if somebody comes to you, teach him there." On that `Abdullah bin Rawaha said, Yes, O Allah's Messengerﷺ ! Bring your teachings to our gathering, for we love that." So the Muslims, the pagans and the Jews started abusing each other till they were about to fight. The Prophetﷺ kept on quietening them till they became calm. Thereupon the Prophet mounted his animal and proceeded till he entered upon Sa`d bin Ubada. He said to him "O Sa`d! Have you not heard what Abu Hubab (i.e., `Abdullah bin Ubai) said?" Sa`d said, 'O Allah's Apostle! Excuse and forgive him, for Allah has given you what He has given you. The people of this town (Medina decided unanimously to crown him and make him their chief by placing a turban on his head, but when that was prevented by the Truth which Allah had given you he (`Abdullah bin Ubai) was grieved out of jealously, and that was the reason which caused him to behave in the way you have seen." Narrated Usama bin Zaid: The Prophetﷺ rode a donkey having a saddle with a Fadakiyya velvet covering. He mounted me behind him and went to visit Sa`d bin 'Ubada, and that had been before the battle of Badr. The Prophetﷺ proceeded till he passed by a gathering in which `Abdullah bin Ubai bin Salul was present, and that had been before `Abdullah embraced Islam. The gathering comprised of Muslims, polytheists, i.e., isolators and Jews. `Abdullah bin Rawaha was also present in that gathering. When dust raised by the donkey covered the gathering, `Abdullah bin Ubai covered his nose with his upper garment and said, "Do not trouble us with dust." The Prophetﷺ greeted them, stopped and dismounted. Then he invited them to Allah (i.e., to embrace Islam) and recited to them some verses of the Holy Qur'an. On that, `Abdullah bin Ubai said, "O man ! There is nothing better than what you say if it is true. Do not trouble us with it in our gathering, but return to your house, and if somebody comes to you, teach him there." On that `Abdullah bin Rawaha said, Yes, O Allah's Messengerﷺ ! Bring your teachings to our gathering, for we love that." So the Muslims, the pagans and the Jews started abusing each other till they were about to fight. The Prophetﷺ kept on quietening them till they became calm. Thereupon the Prophet mounted his animal and proceeded till he entered upon Sa`d bin Ubada. He said to him "O Sa`d! Have you not heard what Abu Hubab (i.e., `Abdullah bin Ubai) said?" Sa`d said, 'O Allah's Apostle! Excuse and forgive him, for Allah has given you what He has given you. The people of this town (Medina decided unanimously to crown him and make him their chief by placing a turban on his head, but when that was prevented by the Truth which Allah had given you he (`Abdullah bin Ubai) was grieved out of jealously, and that was the reason which caused him to behave in the way you have seen.". – Sahih Al-Bukhari 5663

حَدَّثَنِي يَحْيَى بْنُ بُكَيْرٍ، حَدَّثَنَا اللَّيْثُ، عَنْ عُقَيْلٍ، عَنِ ابْنِ شِهَابٍ، عَنْ عُرْوَةَ، أَنَّ أُسَامَةَ بْنَ زَيْدٍ، أَخْبَرَهُ أَنَّ النَّبِيَّ صلى الله عليه وسلم رَكِبَ عَلَى حِمَارٍ عَلَى إِكَافٍ عَلَى قَطِيفَةٍ فَدَكِيَّةٍ، وَأَرْدَفَ أُسَامَةَ وَرَاءَهُ يَعُودُ سَعْدَ بْنَ عُبَادَةَ قَبْلَ وَقْعَةِ بَدْرٍ فَسَارَ حَتَّى مَرَّ بِمَجْلِسٍ فِيهِ عَبْدُ اللَّهِ بْنُ أُبَىٍّ ابْنُ سَلُولَ وَذَلِكَ قَبْلَ أَنْ يُسْلِمَ عَبْدُ اللَّهِ، وَفِي الْمَجْلِسِ أَخْلاَطٌ مِنَ الْمُسْلِمِينَ وَالْمُشْرِكِينَ عَبَدَةِ الأَوْثَانِ وَالْيَهُودِ، وَفِي الْمَجْلِسِ عَبْدُ اللَّهِ بْنُ رَوَاحَةَ، فَلَمَّا غَشِيَتِ الْمَجْلِسَ عَجَاجَةُ الدَّابَّةِ خَمَّرَ عَبْدُ اللَّهِ بْنُ أُبَىٍّ أَنْفَهُ بِرِدَائِهِ، قَالَ لاَ تُغَبِّرُوا عَلَيْنَا فَسَلَّمَ النَّبِيُّ صلى الله عليه وسلم وَوَقَفَ وَنَزَلَ فَدَعَاهُمْ إِلَى اللَّهِ فَقَرَأَ عَلَيْهِمُ الْقُرْآنَ، فَقَالَ لَهُ عَبْدُ اللَّهِ بْنُ أُبَىٍّ يَا أَيُّهَا الْمَرْءُ إِنَّهُ لاَ أَحْسَنَ مِمَّا تَقُولُ إِنْ كَانَ حَقًّا، فَلاَ تُؤْذِنَا بِهِ فِي مَجْلِسِنَا، وَارْجِعْ إِلَى رَحْلِكَ فَمَنْ جَاءَكَ فَاقْصُصْ عَلَيْهِ. قَالَ ابْنُ رَوَاحَةَ بَلَى يَا رَسُولَ اللَّهِ فَاغْشَنَا بِهِ فِي مَجَالِسِنَا فَإِنَّا نُحِبُّ ذَلِكَ فَاسْتَبَّ الْمُسْلِمُونَ وَالْمُشْرِكُونَ وَالْيَهُودُ حَتَّى كَادُوا يَتَثَاوَرُونَ فَلَمْ يَزَلِ النَّبِيُّ صلى الله عليه وسلم حَتَّى سَكَتُوا فَرَكِبَ النَّبِيُّ صلى الله عليه وسلم دَابَّتَهُ حَتَّى دَخَلَ عَلَى سَعْدِ بْنِ عُبَادَةَ فَقَالَ لَهُ " أَىْ سَعْدُ أَلَمْ تَسْمَعْ مَا قَالَ أَبُو حُبَابٍ ". يُرِيدُ عَبْدَ اللَّهِ بْنَ أُبَىٍّ. قَالَ سَعْدٌ يَا رَسُولَ اللَّهِ اعْفُ عَنْهُ وَاصْفَحْ فَلَقَدْ أَعْطَاكَ اللَّهُ مَا أَعْطَاكَ وَلَقَدِ اجْتَمَعَ أَهْلُ هَذِهِ الْبَحْرَةِ أَنْ يُتَوِّجُوهُ فَيُعَصِّبُوهُ فَلَمَّا رَدَّ ذَلِكَ بِالْحَقِّ الَّذِي أَعْطَاكَ شَرِقَ بِذَلِكَ، فَذَلِكَ الَّذِي فَعَلَ بِهِ مَا رَأَيْتَ.

Narrated Hisham's father: When Allah's Messenger ﷺ set out (towards Mecca) during the year of the Conquest (of Mecca) and this news reached (the infidels of Quraish), Abu Sufyan, Hakim bin Hizam and Budail bin Warqa came out to gather information about Allah's Messenger ﷺ, They proceeded on their way till they reached a place called Marr-az-Zahran (which is near Mecca). Behold! There they saw many fires as if they were the fires of `Arafat. Abu Sufyan said, "What is this? It looked like the fires of `Arafat." Budail bin Warqa' said, "Banu `Amr are less in number than that." Some of the guards of Allah's Messenger ﷺ saw them and took them over, caught them and brought them to Allah's Messenger ﷺ. Abu Sufyan embraced Islam. When the Prophet ﷺ proceeded, he said to Al-Abbas, "Keep Abu Sufyan standing at the top of the mountain so that he would look at the Muslims. So Al-`Abbas kept him standing (at that place) and the tribes with the Prophet ﷺ started passing in front of Abu Sufyan in military batches. A batch passed and Abu Sufyan said, "O `Abbas Who are these?" `Abbas said, "They are (Banu) Ghifar." Abu Sufyan said, I have got nothing to do with Ghifar." Then (a batch of the tribe of) Juhaina passed by and he said similarly as above. Then (a batch of the tribe of) Sa`d bin Huzaim passed by and he said similarly as above. Then (Banu) Sulaim passed by and he said similarly as above. Then came a batch, the like of which Abu Sufyan had not seen. He said, "Who are these?" `Abbas said, "They are the Ansar headed by Sa`d bin Ubada, the one holding the flag." Sa`d bin Ubada said, "O Abu Sufyan! Today is the day of a great battle and today (what is prohibited in) the Ka`ba will be permissible." Abu Sufyan said., "O `Abbas! How excellent the day of destruction is! "Then came another batch (of warriors) which was the smallest of all the batches, and in it there was Allah's Messenger ﷺ and his companions and the flag of the Prophet ﷺ was carried by Az-Zubair bin Al Awwam. When Allah's Messenger ﷺ passed by Abu Sufyan, the latter said, (to the Prophet), "Do you know what Sa`d bin 'Ubada said?" The Prophet ﷺ said, "What did he say?" Abu Sufyan said, "He said so-and-so." The Prophet ﷺ said, "Sa`d told a lie, but today Allah will give superiority to the Ka`ba and today the Ka`ba will be covered with a (cloth) covering." Allah's Messenger ﷺ ordered that his flag be fixed at Al-Hajun. Narrated `Urwa: Nafi` bin Jubair bin Mut`im said, "I heard Al-Abbas saying to Az-Zubair bin Al- `Awwam, 'O Abu `Abdullah ! Did Allah's Messenger ﷺ order you to fix the flag here?' " Allah's Messenger ﷺ ordered Khalid bin Al-Walid to enter Mecca from its upper part from Ka'da while the Prophet ﷺ himself entered from Kuda. Two men from the cavalry of Khalid bin Al-Wahd named Hubaish bin Al-Ash'ar and Kurz bin Jabir Al-Fihri were martyred on that day. – Sahih Al-Bukhari 4280

حَدَّثَنَا عُبَيْدُ بْنُ إِسْمَاعِيلَ، حَدَّثَنَا أَبُو أُسَامَةَ، عَنْ هِشَامٍ، عَنْ أَبِيهِ، قَالَ لَمَّا سَارَ رَسُولُ اللَّهِ صلى الله عليه وسلم عَامَ الْفَتْحِ فَبَلَغَ ذَلِكَ قُرَيْشًا، خَرَجَ أَبُو سُفْيَانَ بْنُ حَرْبٍ وَحَكِيمُ بْنُ حِزَامٍ وَبُدَيْلُ بْنُ وَرْقَاءَ يَلْتَمِسُونَ الْخَبَرَ عَنْ رَسُولِ اللَّهِ صلى الله عليه وسلم فَأَقْبَلُوا يَسِيرُونَ حَتَّى أَتَوْا مَرَّ الظَّهْرَانِ، فَإِذَا هُمْ بِنِيرَانٍ كَأَنَّهَا نِيرَانُ عَرَفَةَ، فَقَالَ أَبُو سُفْيَانَ مَا هَذِهِ لَكَأَنَّهَا نِيرَانُ عَرَفَةَ. فَقَالَ بُدَيْلُ بْنُ وَرْقَاءَ نِيرَانُ بَنِي عَمْرٍو. فَقَالَ أَبُو سُفْيَانَ عَمْرٌو أَقَلُّ مِنْ ذَلِكَ. فَرَآهُمْ نَاسٌ مِنْ حَرَسِ رَسُولِ اللَّهِ صلى الله عليه وسلم فَأَدْرَكُوهُمْ فَأَخَذُوهُمْ، فَأَتَوْا بِهِمْ رَسُولَ اللَّهِ صلى الله عليه وسلم فَأَسْلَمَ أَبُو سُفْيَانَ، فَلَمَّا سَارَ قَالَ لِلْعَبَّاسِ " احْبِسْ أَبَا سُفْيَانَ عِنْدَ حَطْمِ الْخَيْلِ حَتَّى يَنْظُرَ إِلَى الْمُسْلِمِينَ ". فَحَبَسَهُ الْعَبَّاسُ، فَجَعَلَتِ الْقَبَائِلُ تَمُرُّ مَعَ النَّبِيِّ صلى الله عليه وسلم تَمُرُّ كَتِيبَةً كَتِيبَةً عَلَى أَبِي سُفْيَانَ، فَمَرَّتْ كَتِيبَةٌ قَالَ يَا عَبَّاسُ مَنْ هَذِهِ قَالَ هَذِهِ غِفَارُ. قَالَ مَا لِي وَلِغِفَارَ ثُمَّ مَرَّتْ جُهَيْنَةُ، قَالَ مِثْلَ ذَلِكَ، ثُمَّ مَرَّتْ سَعْدُ بْنُ هُذَيْمٍ، فَقَالَ مِثْلَ ذَلِكَ، وَمَرَّتْ سُلَيْمُ، فَقَالَ مِثْلَ ذَلِكَ، حَتَّى أَقْبَلَتْ كَتِيبَةٌ لَمْ يَرَ مِثْلَهَا، قَالَ مَنْ هَذِهِ قَالَ هَؤُلاَءِ الأَنْصَارُ عَلَيْهِمْ سَعْدُ بْنُ عُبَادَةَ مَعَهُ الرَّايَةُ. فَقَالَ سَعْدُ بْنُ عُبَادَةَ يَا أَبَا سُفْيَانَ الْيَوْمُ يَوْمُ الْمَلْحَمَةِ، الْيَوْمَ تُسْتَحَلُّ الْكَعْبَةُ. فَقَالَ أَبُو سُفْيَانَ يَا عَبَّاسُ حَبَّذَا يَوْمُ الذِّمَارِ. ثُمَّ جَاءَتْ كَتِيبَةٌ، وَهْىَ أَقَلُّ الْكَتَائِبِ، فِيهِمْ رَسُولُ اللَّهِ صلى الله عليه وسلم وَأَصْحَابُهُ، وَرَايَةُ النَّبِيِّ صلى الله عليه وسلم مَعَ الزُّبَيْرِ بْنِ الْعَوَّامِ، فَلَمَّا مَرَّ رَسُولُ اللَّهِ صلى الله عليه وسلم بِأَبِي سُفْيَانَ قَالَ أَلَمْ تَعْلَمْ مَا قَالَ سَعْدُ بْنُ عُبَادَةَ قَالَ " مَا قَالَ ". قَالَ كَذَا وَكَذَا. فَقَالَ " كَذَبَ سَعْدٌ، وَلَكِنْ هَذَا يَوْمٌ يُعَظِّمُ اللَّهُ فِيهِ الْكَعْبَةَ، وَيَوْمٌ تُكْسَى فِيهِ الْكَعْبَةُ ". قَالَ وَأَمَرَ رَسُولُ اللَّهِ صلى الله عليه وسلم أَنْ تُرْكَزَ رَايَتُهُ بِالْحَجُونِ. قَالَ عُرْوَةُ وَأَخْبَرَنِي نَافِعُ بْنُ جُبَيْرِ بْنِ مُطْعِمٍ قَالَ سَمِعْتُ الْعَبَّاسَ يَقُولُ لِلزُّبَيْرِ بْنِ الْعَوَّامِ يَا أَبَا عَبْدِ اللَّهِ، هَا هُنَا أَمَرَكَ رَسُولُ اللَّهِ صلى الله عليه وسلم أَنْ تَرْكُزَ الرَّايَةَ، قَالَ وَأَمَرَ رَسُولُ اللَّهِ صلى الله عليه وسلم يَوْمَئِذٍ خَالِدَ بْنَ الْوَلِيدِ أَنْ يَدْخُلَ مِنْ أَعْلَى مَكَّةَ مِنْ كَدَاءٍ، وَدَخَلَ النَّبِيُّ صلى الله عليه وسلم مِنْ كُدَا، فَقُتِلَ مِنْ خَيْلِ خَالِدٍ يَوْمَئِذٍ رَجُلاَنِ حُبَيْشُ بْنُ الأَشْعَرِ وَكُرْزُ بْنُ جَابِرٍ الْفِهْرِيُّ

Narrated Aisha: (The wife of the Prophet) Whenever Allah's Messenger ﷺ intended to go on a journey, he used to draw lots among his wives and would take with him the one on whom the lot had fallen. Once he drew lots when he wanted to carry out a Ghazwa, and the lot came upon me. So I proceeded with Allah's Apostle after Allah's order of veiling (the women) had been revealed and thus I was carried in my howdah (on a camel) and dismounted while still in it. We carried on our journey, and when Allah's Apostle had finished his Ghazwa and returned and we approached Medina, Allah's Messenger ordered to proceed at night. When the army was ordered to resume the homeward journey, I got up and walked on till I left the army (camp) behind. When I had answered the call of nature, I went towards my howdah, but behold ! A necklace of mine made of Jaz Azfar (a kind of black bead) was broken and I looked for it and my search for it detained me. The group of people who used to carry me, came and carried my howdah on to the back of my camel on which I was riding, considering that I was therein. At that time women were light in weight and were not fleshy for they used to eat little (food), so those people did not feel the lightness of the howdah while raising it up, and I was still a young lady. They drove away the camel and proceeded. Then I found my necklace after the army had gone. I came to their camp but found nobody therein so I went to the place where I used to stay, thinking that they would miss me and come back in my search. While I was sitting at my place, I felt sleepy and slept. Safwan bin Al-Mu'attil As-Sulami Adh- Dhakw-ani was behind the army. He had started in the last part of the night and reached my stationing place in the morning and saw the figure of a sleeping person. He came to me and recognized me on seeing me for he used to see me before veiling. I got up because of his saying: "Inna Li l-lahi wa inna ilaihi rajiun," which he uttered on recognizing me. I covered my face with my garment, and by Allah, he did not say to me a single word except, "Inna Li l-lahi wa inna ilaihi rajiun," till he made his shecamel kneel down whereupon he trod on its forelegs and I mounted it. Then Safwan set out, leading the she-camel that was carrying me, till we met the army while they were resting during the hot midday. Then whoever was meant for destruction, fell in destruction, and the leader of the Ifk (forged statement) was `Abdullah bin Ubai bin Salul. After this we arrived at Medina and I became ill for one month while the people were spreading the forged statements of the people of the Ifk, and I was not aware of anything thereof. But what aroused my doubt while I was sick, was that I was no longer receiving from Allah's Messenger the same kindness as I used to receive when I fell sick. Allah's Messenger would enter upon me, say a greeting and add, "How is that (lady)?" and then depart. That aroused my suspicion but I was not aware of the propagated evil till I recovered from my ailment. I went out with Um Mistah to answer the call of nature towards Al-Manasi, the place where we used to relieve ourselves, and used not to go out for this purpose except from night to night, and that was before we had lavatories close to our houses. And this habit of ours was similar to the habit of the old 'Arabs (in the deserts or in the tents) concerning the evacuation of the bowels, for we considered it troublesome and harmful to take lavatories in the houses. So I went out with Um Mistah who was the daughter of Abi Ruhm bin `Abd Manaf, and her mother was daughter of Sakhr bin Amir who was the aunt of Abi Bakr As-Siddiq, and her son was Mistah bin Uthatha. When we had finished our affair, Um Mistah and I came back towards my house. Um Mistah stumbled over her robe whereupon she said, "Let Mistah be ruined ! " I said to her, "What a bad word you have said! Do you abuse a man who has taken part in the Battle of Badr?' She said, "O you there! Didn't you hear what he has said?" I said, "And what did he say?" She then told me the statement of the people of the Ifk (forged statement) which added to my ailment. When I returned home, Allah's Messenger came to me, and after greeting, he said, "How is that (lady)?" I said, "Will you allow me to go to my parents?" At that time I intended to be sure of the news through them. Allah's Messenger allowed me and I went to my parents and asked my mother, “O my mother! What are the people talking about?” My mother said, “O my daughter! Take it easy, for by Allah, there is no charming lady who is loved by her husband who has other wives as well, but that those wives would find fault with her.” I said, “Subhan Allah! Did the people really talk about that?” That night I kept on weeping the whole night till the morning. My tears never stopped, nor did I sleep, and morning broke while I was still weeping, Allah’s Messenger ﷺ called `Ali bin Abi Talib and Usama bin Zaid when the Divine Inspiration delayed, in order to consult them as to the idea of divorcing his wife. Usama bin Zaid told Allah’s Messenger ﷺ of what he knew about the innocence of his wife and of his affection he kept for her. He said, “O Allah’s Messenger! She is your wife, and we do not know anything about her except good." But `Ali bin Abi Talib said, "O Allah’s Messenger ﷺ! Allah does not impose restrictions on you; and there are plenty of women other than her. If you however, ask (her) slave girl, she will tell you the truth.” `Aisha added: So Allah’s Messenger ﷺ called for Barira and said, “O Barira! Did you ever see anything which might have aroused your suspicion? (as regards Aisha). Barira said, “By Allah Who has sent you with the truth, I have never seen anything regarding Aisha which I would blame her for except that she is a girl of immature age who sometimes sleeps and leaves the dough of her family unprotected so that the domestic goats come and eat it.” So Allah’s Messenger ﷺ got up (and addressed) the people an asked for somebody who would take revenge on `Abdullah bin Ubai bin Salul then. Allah’s Messenger ﷺ, while on the pulpit, said, “O Muslims! Who will help me against a man who has hurt me by slandering my family? By Allah, I know nothing except good about my family, and people have blamed a man of whom I know nothing except good, and he never used to visit my family except with me,” Sa`d bin Mu`adh Al-Ansari got up and said, “O Allah’s Messenger ﷺ! By Allah, I will relieve you from him. If he be from the tribe of (Bani) Al-Aus, then I will chop his head off; and if he be from our brethren, the Khazraj, then you give us your order and we will obey it.” On that, Sa`d bin ‘Ubada got up, and he was the chief of the Khazraj, and before this incident he had been a pious man but he was incited by his zeal for his tribe. He said to Sa`d (bin Mu`adh), “By Allah the Eternal, you have told a lie! You shall not kill him and you will never be able to kill him!” On that, Usaid bin Hudair, the cousin of Sa`d (bin Mu`adh) got up and said to Sa`d bin ‘Ubada, “You are a liar! By Allah the Eternal, we will surely kill him; and you are a hypocrite defending the hypocrites!” So the two tribes of Al-Aus and Al-Khazraj got excited till they were on the point of fighting with each other while Allah’s Messenger ﷺ was standing on the pulpit. Allah’s Messenger ﷺ continued quietening them till they became silent whereupon he’became silent too. On that day I kept on weeping so much that neither did my tears stop, nor could I sleep. In the morning my parents were with me, and I had wept for two nights and a day without sleeping and with incessant tears till they thought that my liver would burst with weeping. While they were with me and I was weeping, an Ansari woman asked permission to see me. I admitted her and she sat and started weeping with me. While I was in that state, Allah’s Apostle came to us, greeted, and sat down,. He had never sat with me since the day what was said, was said. He had stayed a month without receiving any Divine Inspiration concerning my case. Allah’s Messenger ﷺ recited the Tashahhud after he had sat down, and then said, “Thereafter, O `Aisha! I have been informed such and-such a thing about you; and if you are innocent, Allah will reveal your innocence, and if you have committed a sin, then ask for Allah’s forgiveness and repent to Him, for when a slave confesses his sin and then repents to Allah, Allah accepts his repentance.” When Allah’s Apostle had finished his speech, my tears ceased completely so that I no longer felt even a drop thereof. Then I said to my father, “Reply to Allah’s Messenger ﷺ on my behalf as to what he said.” He said, “By Allah, I do not know what to say to Allah's Messenger ﷺ." Then I said to my mother, "Reply to Allah's Apostle." She said, "I do not know what to say to Allah's Messenger ﷺ." Still a young girl as I was and though I had little knowledge of Qur'an, I said, "By Allah, I know that you heard this story (of the Ifk) so much so that it has been planted in your minds and you have believed it. So now, if I tell you that I am innocent, and Allah knows that I am innocent, you will not believe me; and if I confess something, and Allah knows that I am innocent of it, you will believe me. By Allah, I cannot find of you an example except that of Joseph's father: "So (for me) patience is most fitting against that which you assert and it is Allah (Alone) Whose help can be sought. Then I turned away and lay on my bed, and at that time I knew that I was innocent and that Allah would reveal my innocence. But by Allah, I never thought that Allah would sent down about my affair, Divine Inspiration that would be recited (forever), as I considered myself too unworthy to be talked of by Allah with something that was to be recited: but I hoped that Allah's Messenger ﷺ might have a vision in which Allah would prove my innocence. By Allah, Allah's Messenger ﷺ had not left his seat and nobody had left the house when the Divine Inspiration came to Allah's Messenger ﷺ. So there overtook him the same hard condition which used to overtake him (when he was Divinely Inspired) so that the drops of his sweat were running down, like pearls, though it was a (cold) winter day, and that was because of the heaviness of the Statement which was revealed to him. When that state of Allah's Messenger ﷺ was over, and he was smiling when he was relieved, the first word he said was, "Aisha, Allah has declared your innocence." My mother said to me, "Get up and go to him." I said, "By Allah, I will not go to him and I will not thank anybody but Allah." So Allah revealed: "Verily! They who spread the Slander are a gang among you. Think it not...." (24.11-20). When Allah revealed this to confirm my innocence, Abu Bakr As-Siddiq who used to provide for Mistah bin Uthatha because of the latter's kinship to him and his poverty, said, "By Allah, I will never provide for Mistah anything after what he has said about Aisha". So Allah revealed: (continued...) (continuing... 1): -6.274:... ... "Let not those among you who are good and are wealthy swear not to give (help) to their kinsmen, those in need, and those who have left their homes for Allah's Cause. Let them Pardon and forgive (i.e. do not punish them). Do you not love that should forgive you? Verily Allah is Oft-forgiving. Most Merciful." (24.22) Abu Bakr said, "Yes, by Allah, I wish that Allah should forgive me." So he resumed giving Mistah the aid he used to give him before and said, "By Allah, I will never withold it from him at all." Aisha further said: Allah's Messenger ﷺ also asked Zainab bint Jahsh about my case. He said, "O Zainab! What have you seen?" She replied, "O Allah's Messenger ﷺ! I protect my hearing and my sight (by refraining from telling lies). I know nothing but good (about Aisha)." Of all the wives of Allah's Messenger ﷺ, it was Zainab who aspired to receive from him the same favor as I used to receive, yet, Allah saved her (from telling lies) because of her piety. But her sister, Hamna, kept on fighting on her behalf so she was destroyed as were those who invented and spread the slander. – Sahih Al-Bukhari 4750

حَدَّثَنَا يَحْيَى بْنُ بُكَيْرٍ، حَدَّثَنَا اللَّيْثُ، عَنْ يُونُسَ، عَنِ ابْنِ شِهَابٍ، قَالَ أَخْبَرَنِي عُرْوَةُ بْنُ الزُّبَيْرِ، وَسَعِيدُ بْنُ الْمُسَيَّبِ، وَعَلْقَمَةُ بْنُ وَقَّاصٍ، وَعُبَيْدُ اللَّهِ بْنُ عَبْدِ اللَّهِ بْنِ عُتْبَةَ بْنِ مَسْعُودٍ، عَنْ حَدِيثِ، عَائِشَةَ ـ رضى الله عنها ـ زَوْجِ النَّبِيِّ صلى الله عليه وسلم حِينَ قَالَ لَهَا أَهْلُ الإِفْكِ مَا قَالُوا، فَبَرَّأَهَا اللَّهُ مِمَّا قَالُوا وَكُلٌّ حَدَّثَنِي طَائِفَةً مِنَ الْحَدِيثِ، وَبَعْضُ حَدِيثِهِمْ يُصَدِّقُ بَعْضًا، وَإِنْ كَانَ بَعْضُهُمْ أَوْعَى لَهُ مِنْ بَعْضٍ الَّذِي حَدَّثَنِي، عُرْوَةُ عَنْ عَائِشَةَ ـ رضى الله عنها ـ أَنَّ عَائِشَةَ ـ رضى الله عنها ـ زَوْجَ النَّبِيِّ صلى الله عليه وسلم قَالَتْ كَانَ رَسُولُ اللَّهِ صلى الله عليه وسلم إِذَا أَرَادَ أَنْ يَخْرُجَ أَقْرَعَ بَيْنَ أَزْوَاجِهِ، فَأَيَّتُهُنَّ خَرَجَ سَهْمُهَا خَرَجَ بِهَا رَسُولُ اللَّهِ صلى الله عليه وسلم مَعَهُ، قَالَتْ عَائِشَةُ فَأَقْرَعَ بَيْنَنَا فِي غَزْوَةٍ غَزَاهَا، فَخَرَجَ سَهْمِي، فَخَرَجْتُ مَعَ رَسُولِ اللَّهِ صلى الله عليه وسلم بَعْدَ مَا نَزَلَ الْحِجَابُ، فَأَنَا أُحْمَلُ فِي هَوْدَجِي وَأُنْزَلُ فِيهِ فَسِرْنَا حَتَّى إِذَا فَرَغَ رَسُولُ اللَّهِ صلى الله عليه وسلم مِنْ غَزْوَتِهِ تِلْكَ وَقَفَلَ، وَدَنَوْنَا مِنَ الْمَدِينَةِ قَافِلِينَ آذَنَ لَيْلَةً بِالرَّحِيلِ، فَقُمْتُ حِينَ آذَنُوا بِالرَّحِيلِ، فَمَشَيْتُ حَتَّى جَاوَزْتُ الْجَيْشَ، فَلَمَّا قَضَيْتُ شَأْنِي أَقْبَلْتُ إِلَى رَحْلِي، فَإِذَا عِقْدٌ لِي مِنْ جَزْعِ ظَفَارِ قَدِ انْقَطَعَ فَالْتَمَسْتُ عِقْدِي وَحَبَسَنِي ابْتِغَاؤُهُ وَأَقْبَلَ الرَّهْطُ الَّذِينَ كَانُوا يَرْحَلُونَ لِي، فَاحْتَمَلُوا هَوْدَجِي، فَرَحَلُوهُ عَلَى بَعِيرِي الَّذِي كُنْتُ رَكِبْتُ، وَهُمْ يَحْسِبُونَ أَنِّي فِيهِ، وَكَانَ النِّسَاءُ إِذْ ذَاكَ خِفَافًا لَمْ يُثْقِلْهُنَّ اللَّحْمُ، إِنَّمَا تَأْكُلُ الْعُلْقَةَ مِنَ الطَّعَامِ فَلَمْ يَسْتَنْكِرِ الْقَوْمُ خِفَّةَ الْهَوْدَجِ حِينَ رَفَعُوهُ، وَكُنْتُ جَارِيَةً حَدِيثَةَ السِّنِّ، فَبَعَثُوا الْجَمَلَ وَسَارُوا، فَوَجَدْتُ عِقْدِي بَعْدَ مَا اسْتَمَرَّ الْجَيْشُ، فَجِئْتُ مَنَازِلَهُمْ، وَلَيْسَ بِهَا

دَاعٍ وَلاَ مُجِيبٌ، فَأَمَمْتُ مَنْزِلِي الَّذِي كُنْتُ بِهِ وَظَنَنْتُ أَنَّهُمْ سَيَفْقِدُونِي فَيَرْجِعُونَ إِلَيَّ فَبَيْنَا أَنَا جَالِسَةٌ فِي مَنْزِلِي غَلَبَتْنِي عَيْنِي فَنِمْتُ، وَكَانَ صَفْوَانُ بْنُ الْمُعَطَّلِ السُّلَمِيُّ ثُمَّ الذَّكْوَانِيُّ مِنْ وَرَاءِ الْجَيْشِ، فَأَدْلَجَ فَأَصْبَحَ عِنْدَ مَنْزِلِي، فَرَأَى سَوَادَ إِنْسَانٍ نَائِمٍ، فَأَتَانِي فَعَرَفَنِي حِينَ رَآنِي، وَكَانَ يَرَانِي قَبْلَ الْحِجَابِ، فَاسْتَيْقَظْتُ بِاسْتِرْجَاعِهِ حِينَ عَرَفَنِي فَخَمَّرْتُ وَجْهِي بِجِلْبَابِي، وَاللَّهِ مَا كَلَّمَنِي كَلِمَةً وَلاَ سَمِعْتُ مِنْهُ كَلِمَةً غَيْرَ اسْتِرْجَاعِهِ، حَتَّى أَنَاخَ رَاحِلَتَهُ فَوَطِئَ عَلَى يَدَيْهَا فَرَكِبْتُهَا فَانْطَلَقَ يَقُودُ بِي الرَّاحِلَةَ حَتَّى أَتَيْنَا الْجَيْشَ، بَعْدَ مَا نَزَلُوا مُوغِرِينَ فِي نَحْرِ الظَّهِيرَةِ، فَهَلَكَ مَنْ هَلَكَ، وَكَانَ الَّذِي تَوَلَّى الإِفْكَ عَبْدَ اللَّهِ بْنَ أُبَىٍّ ابْنَ سَلُولَ فَقَدِمْنَا الْمَدِينَةَ، فَاشْتَكَيْتُ حِينَ قَدِمْتُ شَهْرًا، وَالنَّاسُ يُفِيضُونَ فِي قَوْلِ أَصْحَابِ الإِفْكِ، لاَ أَشْعُرُ بِشَىْءٍ مِنْ ذَلِكَ، وَهْوَ يَرِيبُنِي فِي وَجَعِي أَنِّي لاَ أَعْرِفُ مِنْ رَسُولِ اللَّهِ صلى الله عليه وسلم اللُّطْفَ الَّذِي كُنْتُ أَرَى مِنْهُ حِينَ أَشْتَكِي، إِنَّمَا يَدْخُلُ عَلَيَّ رَسُولُ اللَّهِ صلى الله عليه وسلم فَيُسَلِّمُ ثُمَّ يَقُولُ " كَيْفَ تِيكُمْ ". ثُمَّ يَنْصَرِفُ، فَذَاكَ الَّذِي يَرِيبُنِي، وَلاَ أَشْعُرُ حَتَّى خَرَجْتُ بَعْدَ مَا نَقَهْتُ، فَخَرَجَتْ مَعِي أُمُّ مِسْطَحٍ قِبَلَ الْمَنَاصِعِ، وَهْوَ مُتَبَرَّزُنَا، وَكُنَّا لاَ نَخْرُجُ إِلاَّ لَيْلاً إِلَى لَيْلٍ، وَذَلِكَ قَبْلَ أَنْ نَتَّخِذَ الْكُنُفَ قَرِيبًا مِنْ بُيُوتِنَا، وَأَمْرُنَا أَمْرُ الْعَرَبِ الأُوَلِ فِي التَّبَرُّزِ قِبَلَ الْغَائِطِ، فَكُنَّا نَتَأَذَّى بِالْكُنُفِ أَنْ نَتَّخِذَهَا عِنْدَ بُيُوتِنَا فَانْطَلَقْتُ أَنَا وَأُمُّ مِسْطَحٍ، وَهْىَ ابْنَةُ أَبِي رُهْمِ بْنِ عَبْدِ مَنَافٍ، وَأُمُّهَا بِنْتُ صَخْرِ بْنِ عَامِرٍ خَالَةُ أَبِي بَكْرٍ الصِّدِّيقِ، وَابْنُهَا مِسْطَحُ بْنُ أُثَاثَةَ، فَأَقْبَلْتُ أَنَا وَأُمُّ مِسْطَحٍ قِبَلَ بَيْتِي، قَدْ فَرَغْنَا مِنْ شَأْنِنَا، فَعَثَرَتْ أُمُّ مِسْطَحٍ فِي مِرْطِهَا فَقَالَتْ تَعِسَ مِسْطَحٌ. فَقُلْتُ لَهَا بِئْسَ مَا قُلْتِ أَتَسُبِّينَ رَجُلاً شَهِدَ بَدْرًا قَالَتْ أَىْ هَنْتَاهْ، أَوَلَمْ تَسْمَعِي مَا قَالَ قَالَتْ قُلْتُ وَمَا قَالَ فَأَخْبَرَتْنِي بِقَوْلِ أَهْلِ الإِفْكِ فَازْدَدْتُ مَرَضًا عَلَى مَرَضِي، فَلَمَّا رَجَعْتُ إِلَى بَيْتِي وَدَخَلَ عَلَيَّ رَسُولُ اللَّهِ صلى الله عليه وسلم تَعْنِي سَلَّمَ ثُمَّ قَالَ " كَيْفَ تِيكُمْ ". فَقُلْتُ أَتَأْذَنُ لِي أَنْ آتِيَ أَبَوَىَّ قَالَتْ وَأَنَا حِينَئِذٍ أُرِيدُ أَنْ أَسْتَيْقِنَ الْخَبَرَ مِنْ قِبَلِهِمَا، قَالَتْ فَأَذِنَ لِي رَسُولُ اللَّهِ صلى الله عليه وسلم فَجِئْتُ أَبَوَىَّ فَقُلْتُ لأُمِّي يَا أُمَّتَاهْ، مَا يَتَحَدَّثُ النَّاسُ قَالَتْ يَا بُنَيَّةُ، هَوِّنِي عَلَيْكِ فَوَاللَّهِ، لَقَلَّمَا كَانَتِ امْرَأَةٌ قَطُّ وَضِيئَةً عِنْدَ رَجُلٍ يُحِبُّهَا وَلَهَا ضَرَائِرُ إِلاَّ كَثَّرْنَ عَلَيْهَا. قَالَتْ فَقُلْتُ سُبْحَانَ اللَّهِ وَلَقَدْ تَحَدَّثَ النَّاسُ بِهَذَا قَالَتْ فَبَكَيْتُ تِلْكَ اللَّيْلَةَ حَتَّى أَصْبَحْتُ لاَ يَرْقَأُ لِي دَمْعٌ، وَلاَ أَكْتَحِلُ بِنَوْمٍ حَتَّى أَصْبَحْتُ أَبْكِي فَدَعَا رَسُولُ اللَّهِ صلى الله عليه وسلم عَلِيَّ بْنَ أَبِي طَالِبٍ، وَأُسَامَةَ بْنَ زَيْدٍ - رضي الله عنهما - حِينَ اسْتَلْبَثَ الْوَحْىُ، يَسْتَأْمِرُهُمَا فِي فِرَاقِ أَهْلِهِ، قَالَتْ فَأَمَّا أُسَامَةُ بْنُ زَيْدٍ فَأَشَارَ عَلَى رَسُولِ اللَّهِ صلى الله عليه وسلم بِالَّذِي يَعْلَمُ مِنْ بَرَاءَةِ أَهْلِهِ، وَبِالَّذِي يَعْلَمُ لَهُمْ فِي نَفْسِهِ مِنَ الْوُدِّ، فَقَالَ يَا رَسُولَ اللَّهِ، أَهْلَكَ، وَمَا نَعْلَمُ إِلاَّ خَيْرًا، وَأَمَّا عَلِيُّ بْنُ أَبِي طَالِبٍ فَقَالَ يَا رَسُولَ اللَّهِ، لَمْ يُضَيِّقِ اللَّهُ عَلَيْكَ وَالنِّسَاءُ سِوَاهَا كَثِيرٌ، وَإِنْ تَسْأَلِ الْجَارِيَةَ تَصْدُقْكَ، قَالَتْ فَدَعَا رَسُولُ اللَّهِ صلى الله عليه وسلم بَرِيرَةَ فَقَالَ " أَىْ بَرِيرَةُ، هَلْ رَأَيْتِ عَلَيْهَا مِنْ شَىْءٍ يَرِيبُكِ ". قَالَتْ بَرِيرَةُ لاَ وَالَّذِي بَعَثَكَ بِالْحَقِّ، إِنْ رَأَيْتُ عَلَيْهَا أَمْرًا أَغْمِصُهُ عَلَيْهَا أَكْثَرَ مِنْ أَنَّهَا جَارِيَةٌ حَدِيثَةُ السِّنِّ، تَنَامُ عَنْ عَجِينِ أَهْلِهَا، فَتَأْتِي الدَّاجِنُ فَتَأْكُلُهُ فَقَامَ رَسُولُ اللَّهِ صلى الله عليه وسلم فَاسْتَعْذَرَ يَوْمَئِذٍ مِنْ عَبْدِ اللَّهِ بْنِ أُبَىٍّ ابْنِ سَلُولَ، قَالَتْ، فَقَالَ رَسُولُ اللَّهِ صلى الله عليه وسلم وَهْوَ عَلَى الْمِنْبَرِ " يَا مَعْشَرَ الْمُسْلِمِينَ مَنْ يَعْذِرُنِي مِنْ رَجُلٍ، قَدْ بَلَغَنِي أَذَاهُ فِي أَهْلِ بَيْتِي، فَوَاللَّهِ مَا عَلِمْتُ عَلَى أَهْلِي إِلاَّ خَيْرًا، وَلَقَدْ ذَكَرُوا رَجُلاً، مَا عَلِمْتُ عَلَيْهِ إِلاَّ خَيْرًا، وَمَا كَانَ يَدْخُلُ عَلَى أَهْلِي إِلاَّ مَعِي ". فَقَامَ سَعْدُ بْنُ مُعَاذٍ الأَنْصَارِيُّ، فَقَالَ يَا رَسُولَ اللَّهِ أَنَا أَعْذِرُكَ مِنْهُ، إِنْ كَانَ مِنَ الأَوْسِ، ضَرَبْتُ عُنُقَهُ، وَإِنْ كَانَ مِنْ إِخْوَانِنَا مِنَ الْخَزْرَجِ، أَمَرْتَنَا، فَفَعَلْنَا أَمْرَكَ، قَالَتْ فَقَامَ سَعْدُ بْنُ عُبَادَةَ وَهْوَ سَيِّدُ الْخَزْرَجِ، وَكَانَ قَبْلَ ذَلِكَ رَجُلاً صَالِحًا، وَلَكِنِ احْتَمَلَتْهُ الْحَمِيَّةُ فَقَالَ لِسَعْدٍ كَذَبْتَ، لَعَمْرُ اللَّهِ لاَ تَقْتُلُهُ، وَلاَ تَقْدِرُ عَلَى قَتْلِهِ، فَقَامَ أُسَيْدُ بْنُ حُضَيْرٍ وَهْوَ ابْنُ عَمِّ سَعْدٍ، فَقَالَ لِسَعْدِ بْنِ عُبَادَةَ كَذَبْتَ، لَعَمْرُ اللَّهِ لَنَقْتُلَنَّهُ، فَإِنَّكَ مُنَافِقٌ تُجَادِلُ عَنِ الْمُنَافِقِينَ، فَتَثَاوَرَ الْحَيَّانِ الأَوْسُ وَالْخَزْرَجُ حَتَّى هَمُّوا أَنْ يَقْتَتِلُوا، وَرَسُولُ اللَّهِ صلى الله عليه وسلم قَائِمٌ عَلَى الْمِنْبَرِ، فَلَمْ يَزَلْ رَسُولُ اللَّهِ صلى الله عليه وسلم يُخَفِّضُهُمْ حَتَّى سَكَتُوا وَسَكَتَ، قَالَتْ فَمَكُثْتُ يَوْمِي ذَلِكَ لاَ يَرْقَأُ لِي دَمْعٌ وَلاَ أَكْتَحِلُ بِنَوْمٍ، قَالَتْ فَأَصْبَحَ أَبَوَاىَ عِنْدِي - وَقَدْ بَكَيْتُ لَيْلَتَيْنِ وَيَوْمًا لاَ أَكْتَحِلُ بِنَوْمٍ وَلاَ يَرْقَأُ لِي دَمْعٌ - يَظُنَّانِ أَنَّ الْبُكَاءَ فَالِقٌ كَبِدِي، قَالَتْ فَبَيْنَمَا هُمَا جَالِسَانِ عِنْدِي وَأَنَا أَبْكِي، فَاسْتَأْذَنَتْ عَلَيَّ امْرَأَةٌ مِنَ الأَنْصَارِ، فَأَذِنْتُ لَهَا، فَجَلَسَتْ تَبْكِي مَعِي، قَالَتْ فَبَيْنَا نَحْنُ عَلَى ذَلِكَ دَخَلَ عَلَيْنَا رَسُولُ اللَّهِ صلى الله عليه وسلم فَسَلَّمَ ثُمَّ جَلَسَ قَالَتْ وَلَمْ يَجْلِسْ عِنْدِي مُنْذُ قِيلَ مَا قِيلَ قَبْلَهَا، وَقَدْ لَبِثَ شَهْرًا، لاَ يُوحَى إِلَيْهِ فِي شَأْنِي، قَالَتْ فَتَشَهَّدَ رَسُولُ اللَّهِ صلى الله عليه وسلم حِينَ جَلَسَ ثُمَّ قَالَ " أَمَّا بَعْدُ يَا عَائِشَةُ، فَإِنَّهُ قَدْ بَلَغَنِي عَنْكِ كَذَا وَكَذَا، فَإِنْ كُنْتِ بَرِيئَةً فَسَيُبَرِّئُكِ اللَّهُ، وَإِنْ كُنْتِ أَلْمَمْتِ بِذَنْبٍ فَاسْتَغْفِرِي اللَّهَ وَتُوبِي إِلَيْهِ، فَإِنَّ الْعَبْدَ إِذَا اعْتَرَفَ بِذَنْبِهِ ثُمَّ تَابَ إِلَى اللَّهِ تَابَ اللَّهُ عَلَيْهِ ". قَالَتْ فَلَمَّا قَضَى رَسُولُ اللَّهِ صلى الله عليه وسلم مَقَالَتَهُ، قَلَصَ دَمْعِي حَتَّى مَا أُحِسُّ مِنْهُ قَطْرَةً، فَقُلْتُ لأَبِي أَجِبْ رَسُولَ اللَّهِ صلى الله عليه وسلم فِيمَا قَالَ. قَالَ وَاللَّهِ مَا أَدْرِي مَا أَقُولُ لِرَسُولِ اللَّهِ صلى الله عليه وسلم فَقُلْتُ لأُمِّي أَجِيبِي رَسُولَ اللَّهِ صلى الله عليه وسلم. قَالَتْ مَا أَدْرِي مَا أَقُولُ لِرَسُولِ اللَّهِ صلى الله عليه وسلم قَالَتْ فَقُلْتُ وَأَنَا جَارِيَةٌ حَدِيثَةُ السِّنِّ لاَ أَقْرَأُ كَثِيرًا مِنَ الْقُرْآنِ، إِنِّي وَاللَّهِ لَقَدْ عَلِمْتُ لَقَدْ سَمِعْتُمْ هَذَا الْحَدِيثَ حَتَّى اسْتَقَرَّ فِي أَنْفُسِكُمْ، وَصَدَّقْتُمْ بِهِ فَلَئِنْ قُلْتُ لَكُمْ إِنِّي بَرِيئَةٌ وَاللَّهُ يَعْلَمُ أَنِّي بَرِيئَةٌ لاَ تُصَدِّقُونِي بِذَلِكَ، وَلَئِنِ اعْتَرَفْتُ لَكُمْ بِأَمْرٍ، وَاللَّهُ يَعْلَمُ أَنِّي مِنْهُ بَرِيئَةٌ لَتُصَدِّقُنِّي، وَاللَّهِ مَا أَجِدُ لَكُمْ مَثَلاً إِلاَّ قَوْلَ أَبِي يُوسُفَ قَالَ {فَصَبْرٌ جَمِيلٌ وَاللَّهُ الْمُسْتَعَانُ عَلَى مَا تَصِفُونَ} قَالَتْ ثُمَّ تَحَوَّلْتُ فَاضْطَجَعْتُ عَلَى فِرَاشِي، قَالَتْ وَأَنَا حِينَئِذٍ أَعْلَمُ أَنِّي بَرِيئَةٌ، وَأَنَّ اللَّهَ مُبَرِّئِي بِبَرَاءَتِي، وَلَكِنْ وَاللَّهِ مَا كُنْتُ أَظُنُّ أَنَّ اللَّهَ مُنْزِلٌ فِي شَأْنِي وَحْيًا يُتْلَى، وَلَشَأْنِي فِي نَفْسِي كَانَ أَحْقَرَ مِنْ أَنْ يَتَكَلَّمَ اللَّهُ فِيَّ بِأَمْرٍ يُتْلَى، وَلَكِنْ كُنْتُ أَرْجُو أَنْ يَرَى رَسُولُ اللَّهِ صلى الله عليه وسلم فِي النَّوْمِ رُؤْيَا يُبَرِّئُنِي اللَّهُ بِهَا، قَالَتْ فَوَاللَّهِ مَا رَامَ رَسُولُ اللَّهِ صلى الله عليه وسلم وَلاَ خَرَجَ أَحَدٌ مِنْ أَهْلِ الْبَيْتِ حَتَّى أُنْزِلَ عَلَيْهِ، فَأَخَذَهُ مَا كَانَ يَأْخُذُهُ مِنَ الْبُرَحَاءِ حَتَّى إِنَّهُ لَيَتَحَدَّرُ مِنْهُ مِثْلُ الْجُمَانِ مِنَ الْعَرَقِ، وَهْوَ فِي يَوْمٍ شَاتٍ مِنْ ثِقَلِ الْقَوْلِ الَّذِي يُنْزَلُ عَلَيْهِ، قَالَتْ فَلَمَّا سُرِّيَ عَنْ رَسُولِ اللَّهِ صلى الله عليه وسلم سُرِّيَ عَنْهُ وَهْوَ يَضْحَكُ، فَكَانَتْ أَوَّلُ كَلِمَةٍ تَكَلَّمَ بِهَا " يَا عَائِشَةُ، أَمَّا اللَّهُ عَزَّ وَجَلَّ فَقَدْ بَرَّأَكِ ". فَقَالَتْ أُمِّي قُومِي إِلَيْهِ. قَالَتْ فَقُلْتُ وَاللَّهِ، لاَ أَقُومُ إِلَيْهِ، وَلاَ أَحْمَدُ إِلاَّ اللَّهَ عَزَّ وَجَلَّ. وَأَنْزَلَ اللَّهُ {إِنَّ الَّذِينَ جَاءُوا بِالإِفْكِ عُصْبَةٌ مِنْكُمْ لاَ تَحْسِبُوهُ} الْعَشْرَ الآيَاتِ كُلَّهَا، فَلَمَّا أَنْزَلَ اللَّهُ هَذَا فِي بَرَاءَتِي قَالَ أَبُو بَكْرٍ الصِّدِّيقُ - رضى الله عنه - وَكَانَ يُنْفِقُ عَلَى مِسْطَحِ بْنِ أُثَاثَةَ لِقَرَابَتِهِ مِنْهُ، وَفَقْرِهِ وَاللَّهِ لاَ أُنْفِقُ عَلَى مِسْطَحٍ شَيْئًا أَبَدًا بَعْدَ الَّذِي قَالَ لِعَائِشَةَ مَا قَالَ، فَأَنْزَلَ اللَّهُ {وَلاَ يَأْتَلِ أُولُو الْفَضْلِ مِنْكُمْ وَالسَّعَةِ أَنْ يُؤْتُوا أُولِي الْقُرْبَى وَالْمَسَاكِينَ وَالْمُهَاجِرِينَ فِي سَبِيلِ اللَّهِ وَلْيَعْفُوا وَلْيَصْفَحُوا أَلاَ تُحِبُّونَ أَنْ يَغْفِرَ اللَّهُ لَكُمْ وَاللَّهُ غَفُورٌ رَحِيمٌ} قَالَ أَبُو بَكْرٍ بَلَى، وَاللَّهِ إِنِّي أُحِبُّ أَنْ يَغْفِرَ اللَّهُ لِي، فَرَجَعَ إِلَى مِسْطَحٍ النَّفَقَةَ الَّتِي كَانَ يُنْفِقُ عَلَيْهِ، وَقَالَ وَاللَّهِ لاَ أَنْزِعُهَا مِنْهُ أَبَدًا. قَالَتْ عَائِشَةُ وَكَانَ رَسُولُ اللَّهِ صلى الله عليه وسلم يَسْأَلُ زَيْنَبَ ابْنَةَ جَحْشٍ عَنْ أَمْرِي، فَقَالَ " يَا زَيْنَبُ مَاذَا عَلِمْتِ أَوْ رَأَيْتِ ". فَقَالَتْ يَا رَسُولَ اللَّهِ، أَحْمِي سَمْعِي وَبَصَرِي، مَا عَلِمْتُ إِلاَّ خَيْرًا. قَالَتْ وَهْىَ الَّتِي كَانَتْ تُسَامِينِي مِنْ أَزْوَاجِ رَسُولِ اللَّهِ صلى الله عليه وسلم فَعَصَمَهَا اللَّهُ بِالْوَرَعِ، وَطَفِقَتْ أُخْتُهَا حَمْنَةُ تُحَارِبُ لَهَا فَهَلَكَتْ فِيمَنْ هَلَكَ مِنْ أَصْحَابِ الإِفْكِ

Sa`d bin Mu`adh

سَعْدِ بْنِ مُعَاذ

Narrated Al-Bara: The Prophetﷺ was given a silk garment as a gift and we started touching it with our hands and admiring it. On that the Prophetﷺ said, “Do you wonder at this?” We said, “Yes.” He said, “The handkerchiefs of Sa`d bin Mu`adh in Paradise are better than this.”. – Sahih Al-Bukhari 5836

حَدَّثَنَا عُبَيْدُ اللَّهِ بْنُ مُوسَى، عَنْ إِسْرَائِيلَ، عَنْ أَبِي إِسْحَاقَ، عَنِ الْبَرَاءِ ـ رضى الله عنه ـ قَالَ أُهْدِيَ لِلنَّبِيِّ صلى الله عليه وسلم ثَوْبُ حَرِيرٍ، فَجَعَلْنَا نَلْمُسُهُ، وَنَتَعَجَّبُ مِنْهُ، فَقَالَ النَّبِيُّ صلى الله عليه وسلم " أَتَعْجَبُونَ مِنْ هَذَا ". قُلْنَا نَعَمْ. قَالَ " مَنَادِيلُ سَعْدِ بْنِ مُعَاذٍ فِي الْجَنَّةِ خَيْرٌ مِنْ هَذَا

Abd Allah ibn Rawahah ibn Tha’laba

عَبْد ٱللَّه ٱبْن رَوَاحَة ٱبْن ثَعْلَبَة

Narrated Abu Ad-Darda: We set out with Allah’s Messengerﷺ on one of his journeys on a very hot day, and it was so hot that one had to put his hand over his head because of the severity of heat. None of us was fasting except the Prophet and Ibn Rawaha. – Sahih Al-Bukhari 1945

حَدَّثَنَا عَبْدُ اللَّهِ بْنُ يُوسُفَ، حَدَّثَنَا يَحْيَى بْنُ حَمْزَةَ، عَنْ عَبْدِ الرَّحْمَنِ بْنِ يَزِيدَ بْنِ جَابِرٍ، أَنَّ إِسْمَاعِيلَ بْنَ عُبَيْدِ اللَّهِ، حَدَّثَهُ عَنْ أُمِّ الدَّرْدَاءِ، عَنْ أَبِي الدَّرْدَاءِ ـ رضى الله عنه ـ قَالَ خَرَجْنَا مَعَ النَّبِيِّ صلى الله عليه وسلم فِي بَعْضِ أَسْفَارِهِ فِي يَوْمٍ حَارٍّ حَتَّى يَضَعَ الرَّجُلُ يَدَهُ عَلَى رَأْسِهِ مِنْ شِدَّةِ الْحَرِّ، وَمَا فِينَا صَائِمٌ إِلاَّ مَا كَانَ مِنَ النَّبِيِّ صلى الله عليه وسلم وَابْنِ رَوَاحَةَ.

Narrated Anas bin Malik: The Prophetﷺ delivered a sermon and said, “Zaid took the flag and was martyred, and then Ja`far took the flag and was martyred, and then `Abdullah bin Rawaha took the flag and was martyred too, and then Khalid bin Al-Walid took the flag though he was not appointed as a commander and Allah made him victorious.” The Prophetﷺ further added, “It would not please us to have them with us.” Aiyub, a sub-narrator, added, “Or the Prophet, shedding tears, said, ‘It would not please them to be with us.’”. – Sahih Al-Bukhari 2798

حَدَّثَنَا يُوسُفُ بْنُ يَعْقُوبَ الصَّفَّارُ، حَدَّثَنَا إِسْمَاعِيلُ ابْنُ عُلَيَّةَ، عَنْ أَيُّوبَ، عَنْ حُمَيْدِ بْنِ هِلاَلٍ، عَنْ أَنَسِ بْنِ مَالِكٍ ـ رضى الله عنه ـ قَالَ خَطَبَ النَّبِيُّ صلى الله عليه وسلم فَقَالَ " أَخَذَ الرَّايَةَ زَيْدٌ فَأُصِيبَ، ثُمَّ أَخَذَهَا جَعْفَرٌ فَأُصِيبَ، ثُمَّ أَخَذَهَا عَبْدُ اللَّهِ بْنُ رَوَاحَةَ فَأُصِيبَ، ثُمَّ أَخَذَهَا خَالِدُ بْنُ الْوَلِيدِ عَنْ غَيْرِ إِمْرَةٍ فَفُتِحَ لَهُ ـ وَقَالَ ـ مَا يَسُرُّنَا أَنَّهُمْ عِنْدَنَا ". قَالَ أَيُّوبُ أَوْ قَالَ " مَا يَسُرُّهُمْ أَنَّهُمْ عِنْدَنَا ". وَعَيْنَاهُ تَذْرِفَانِ.

Narrated Usama bin Zaid: Allah’s Messengerﷺ rode a donkey, equipped with a thick cloth-covering made in Fadak and was riding behind him. He was going to pay visit to Sa`d bin Ubada in Banu Al-Harith bin Al-Khazraj; and this incident happened before the battle of Badr. The Prophetﷺ passed by a gathering in which `Abdullah bin Ubai bin Salul was present, and that was before `Abdullah bin Ubai embraced Islam. Behold in that gathering there were people of different religions: there were Muslims, pagans, idol-worshippers and Jews, and in that gathering `Abdullah bin Rawaha was also present. When a cloud of dust raised by the donkey reached that gathering, `Abdullah bin Ubai covered his nose with his garment and then said, “Do not cover us with dust.” Then Allah’s Messengerﷺ greeted them and stopped and dismounted and invited them to Allah (i.e. to embrace Islam) and recited to them the Holy Qur’an. On that, `Abdullah bin Ubai bin Saluil said, “O man ! There is nothing better than that what you say. If it is the truth, then do not trouble us with it in our gatherings. Return to your mount (or residence) and if somebody comes to you, relate (your tales) to him." On that `Abdullah bin Rawaha said, "Yes, O Allah's Apostle! Bring it (i.e. what you want to say) to us in our gathering, for we love that." So the Muslims, the pagans and the Jews started abusing one another till they were on the point of fighting with one another. The Prophet ﷺ kept on quietening them till they became quiet, whereupon the Prophet rode his animal (mount) and proceeded till he entered upon Sa`d bin Ubada. The Prophet ﷺ said to Sa`d, "Did you not hear what 'Abu Hub-b said?" He meant `Abdullah bin Ubai. "He said so-andso." On that Sa`d bin Ubada said, "O Allah's Messenger ﷺ! Excuse and forgive him, for by Him Who revealed the Book to you, Allah brought the Truth which was sent to you at the time when the people of this town (i.e. Medina) had decided unanimously to crown him and tie a turban on his head (electing him as chief). But when Allah opposed that (decision) through the Truth which Allah gave to you, he (i.e. `Abdullah bin Ubai) was grieved with jealously. And that caused him to do what you have seen." So Allah's Messenger ﷺ excused him, for the Prophet ﷺ and his companions used to forgive the pagans and the people of Scripture as Allah had ordered them, and they used to put up with their mischief with patience. Allah said: "And you shall certainly hear much that will grieve you from those who received the Scripture before you and from the pagans.....'(3.186) And Allah also said:--"Many of the people of the Scripture wish if they could turn you away as disbelievers after you have believed, from selfish envy.." (2.109) So the Prophet ﷺ used to stick to the principle of forgiveness for them as long as Allah ordered him to do so till Allah permitted fighting them. So when Allah's Messenger ﷺ fought the battle of Badr and Allah killed the nobles of Quraish infidels through him, Ibn Ubai bin Salul and the pagans and idolaters who were with him, said, "This matter (i.e. Islam) has appeared (i.e. became victorious)." So they gave the pledge of allegiance (for embracing Islam) to Allah's Messenger ﷺ and became Muslims. – Sahih Al-Bukhari 4566

حَدَّثَنَا أَبُو الْيَمَانِ، أَخْبَرَنَا شُعَيْبٌ، عَنِ الزُّهْرِيِّ، قَالَ أَخْبَرَنِي عُرْوَةُ بْنُ الزُّبَيْرِ، أَنَّ أُسَامَةَ بْنَ زَيْدٍ ـ رضى الله عنهما ـ أَخْبَرَهُ أَنَّ رَسُولَ اللَّهِ صلى الله عليه وسلم رَكِبَ عَلَى حِمَارٍ عَلَى قَطِيفَةٍ فَدَكِيَّةٍ، وَأَرْدَفَ أُسَامَةَ بْنَ زَيْدٍ وَرَاءَهُ، يَعُودُ سَعْدَ بْنَ عُبَادَةَ فِي بَنِي الْحَارِثِ بْنِ الْخَزْرَجِ قَبْلَ وَقْعَةِ بَدْرٍ ـ قَالَ ـ حَتَّى مَرَّ بِمَجْلِسٍ فِيهِ عَبْدُ اللَّهِ بْنُ أُبَىٍّ ابْنُ سَلُولَ، وَذَلِكَ قَبْلَ أَنْ يُسْلِمَ عَبْدُ اللَّهِ بْنُ أُبَىٍّ فَإِذَا فِي الْمَجْلِسِ أَخْلاَطٌ مِنَ الْمُسْلِمِينَ وَالْمُشْرِكِينَ عَبَدَةِ الأَوْثَانِ وَالْيَهُودِ وَالْمُسْلِمِينَ، وَفِي الْمَجْلِسِ عَبْدُ اللَّهِ بْنُ رَوَاحَةَ، فَلَمَّا غَشِيَتِ الْمَجْلِسَ عَجَاجَةُ الدَّابَّةِ خَمَّرَ عَبْدُ اللَّهِ بْنُ أُبَىٍّ أَنْفَهُ بِرِدَائِهِ، ثُمَّ قَالَ لاَ تُغَبِّرُوا عَلَيْنَا. فَسَلَّمَ رَسُولُ اللَّهِ صلى الله عليه وسلم عَلَيْهِمْ ثُمَّ وَقَفَ فَنَزَلَ فَدَعَاهُمْ إِلَى اللَّهِ، وَقَرَأَ عَلَيْهِمُ الْقُرْآنَ، فَقَالَ عَبْدُ اللَّهِ بْنُ أُبَىٍّ ابْنُ سَلُولَ أَيُّهَا الْمَرْءُ، إِنَّهُ لاَ أَحْسَنَ مِمَّا تَقُولُ، إِنْ كَانَ حَقًّا، فَلاَ تُؤْذِينَا بِهِ فِي مَجْلِسِنَا، ارْجِعْ إِلَى رَحْلِكَ، فَمَنْ جَاءَكَ فَاقْصُصْ عَلَيْهِ. فَقَالَ عَبْدُ اللَّهِ بْنُ رَوَاحَةَ بَلَى يَا رَسُولَ اللَّهِ، فَاغْشَنَا بِهِ فِي مَجَالِسِنَا، فَإِنَّا نُحِبُّ ذَلِكَ. فَاسْتَبَّ الْمُسْلِمُونَ وَالْمُشْرِكُونَ وَالْيَهُودُ حَتَّى كَادُوا يَتَثَاوَرُونَ، فَلَمْ يَزَلِ النَّبِيُّ صلى الله عليه وسلم يُخَفِّضُهُمْ حَتَّى سَكَنُوا، ثُمَّ رَكِبَ النَّبِيُّ صلى الله عليه وسلم دَابَّتَهُ فَسَارَ حَتَّى دَخَلَ عَلَى سَعْدِ بْنِ عُبَادَةَ، فَقَالَ لَهُ النَّبِيُّ صلى الله عليه وسلم " يَا سَعْدُ أَلَمْ تَسْمَعْ مَا قَالَ أَبُو حُبَابٍ ". يُرِيدُ عَبْدَ اللَّهِ بْنَ أُبَىٍّ " قَالَ كَذَا وَكَذَا ". قَالَ سَعْدُ بْنُ عُبَادَةَ يَا رَسُولَ اللَّهِ، اعْفُ عَنْهُ وَاصْفَحْ عَنْهُ، فَوَالَّذِي أَنْزَلَ عَلَيْكَ الْكِتَابَ، لَقَدْ جَاءَ اللَّهُ بِالْحَقِّ الَّذِي أَنْزَلَ عَلَيْكَ، لَقَدِ اصْطَلَحَ أَهْلُ هَذِهِ الْبُحَيْرَةِ عَلَى أَنْ يُتَوِّجُوهُ فَيُعَصِّبُونَهُ بِالْعِصَابَةِ، فَلَمَّا أَبَى اللَّهُ ذَلِكَ بِالْحَقِّ الَّذِي أَعْطَاكَ اللَّهُ شَرِقَ بِذَلِكَ، فَذَلِكَ فَعَلَ بِهِ مَا رَأَيْتَ. فَعَفَا عَنْهُ رَسُولُ اللَّهِ صلى الله عليه وسلم وَكَانَ النَّبِيُّ صلى الله عليه وسلم وَأَصْحَابُهُ يَعْفُونَ عَنِ الْمُشْرِكِينَ وَأَهْلِ الْكِتَابِ كَمَا أَمَرَهُمُ اللَّهُ، وَيَصْبِرُونَ عَلَى الأَذَى قَالَ اللَّهُ عَزَّ وَجَلَّ {وَلَتَسْمَعُنَّ مِنَ الَّذِينَ أُوتُوا الْكِتَابَ مِنْ قَبْلِكُمْ وَمِنَ الَّذِينَ أَشْرَكُوا أَذًى كَثِيرًا } الآيَةَ، وَقَالَ اللَّهُ {وَدَّ كَثِيرٌ مِنْ أَهْلِ الْكِتَابِ لَوْ يَرُدُّونَكُمْ مِنْ بَعْدِ إِيمَانِكُمْ كُفَّارًا حَسَدًا مِنْ عِنْدِ أَنْفُسِهِمْ} إِلَى آخِرِ الآيَةِ، وَكَانَ النَّبِيُّ صلى الله عليه وسلم يَتَأَوَّلُ الْعَفْوَ مَا أَمَرَهُ اللَّهُ بِهِ، حَتَّى أَذِنَ اللَّهُ فِيهِمْ، فَلَمَّا غَزَا رَسُولُ اللَّهِ صلى الله عليه وسلم بَدْرًا، فَقَتَلَ اللَّهُ بِهِ صَنَادِيدَ كُفَّارِ قُرَيْشٍ قَالَ ابْنُ أُبَىٍّ ابْنُ سَلُولَ، وَمَنْ مَعَهُ مِنَ الْمُشْرِكِينَ، وَعَبَدَةِ الأَوْثَانِ هَذَا أَمْرٌ قَدْ تَوَجَّهَ. فَبَايَعُوا الرَّسُولَ صلى الله عليه وسلم عَلَى الإِسْلاَمِ فَأَسْلَمُوا.

Narrated `Aisha: When the Prophet ﷺ got the news of the death of Ibn Haritha, Ja`far and Ibn Rawaha he sat down and looked sad and I was looking at him through the chink of the door. A man came and told him about the crying of the women of Ja`far. The Prophet ﷺ ordered him to forbid them. The man went and came back saying that he had told them but they did not listen to him. The Prophet ﷺ said, "Forbid them." So again he went and came back for the third time and said, "O Allah's Messenger ﷺ! By Allah, they did not listen to us at all." (`Aisha added): Allah's Messenger ﷺ ordered him to go and put dust in their mouths. I said, (to that man) "May Allah stick your nose in the dust (i.e. humiliate you)! You could neither (persuade the women to) fulfill the order of Allah's Messenger ﷺ nor did you relieve Allah's Messenger ﷺ from fatigue. ". – Sahih Al-Bukhari 1299

حَدَّثَنَا مُحَمَّدُ بْنُ الْمُثَنَّى، حَدَّثَنَا عَبْدُ الْوَهَّابِ، قَالَ سَمِعْتُ يَحْيَى، قَالَ أَخْبَرَتْنِي عَمْرَةُ، قَالَتْ سَمِعْتُ عَائِشَةَ ـ رضى الله عنها ـ قَالَتْ لَمَّا جَاءَ النَّبِيَّ صلى الله عليه وسلم قَتْلُ ابْنِ حَارِثَةَ وَجَعْفَرٍ وَابْنِ رَوَاحَةَ جَلَسَ يُعْرَفُ فِيهِ الْحُزْنُ، وَأَنَا أَنْظُرُ مِنْ صَائِرِ الْبَابِ ـ شَقِّ الْبَابِ ـ فَأَتَاهُ رَجُلٌ، فَقَالَ إِنَّ نِسَاءَ جَعْفَرٍ، وَذَكَرَ بُكَاءَهُنَّ، فَأَمَرَهُ أَنْ يَنْهَاهُنَّ، فَذَهَبَ ثُمَّ أَتَاهُ الثَّانِيَةَ، لَمْ يُطِعْنَهُ فَقَالَ انْهَهُنَّ. فَأَتَاهُ الثَّالِثَةَ قَالَ وَاللَّهِ غَلَبْنَنَا يَا رَسُولَ اللَّهِ فَزَعَمَتْ أَنَّهُ قَالَ " فَاحْثُ فِي أَفْوَاهِهِنَّ التُّرَابَ ". فَقُلْتُ أَرْغَمَ اللَّهُ أَنْفَكَ، لَمْ تَفْعَلْ مَا أَمَرَكَ رَسُولُ اللَّهِ صلى الله عليه وسلم وَلَمْ تَتْرُكْ رَسُولَ اللَّهِ صلى الله عليه وسلم مِنَ الْعَنَاءِ.

Narrated Abu Huraira: That once Allah's Messenger ﷺ said, "Your brother, i.e. `Abdullah bin Rawaha does not say obscene (referring to his verses): Amongst us is Allah's Messenger ﷺ, who recites His Book when it dawns. He showed us the guidance, after we were blind. We believe that whatever he says will come true. And he spends his nights in such a way as his sides do not touch his bed. While the pagans were deeply asleep.". – Sahih Al-Bukhari 1155

حَدَّثَنَا يَحْيَى بْنُ بُكَيْرٍ، قَالَ حَدَّثَنَا اللَّيْثُ، عَنْ يُونُسَ، عَنِ ابْنِ شِهَابٍ، أَخْبَرَنِي الْهَيْثَمُ بْنُ أَبِي سِنَانٍ، أَنَّهُ سَمِعَ أَبَا هُرَيْرَةَ ـ رضى الله عنه ـ وَهُوَ يَقْصُصُ فِي قَصَصِهِ وَهُوَ يَذْكُرُ رَسُولَ اللَّهِ صلى الله عليه وسلم إِنَّ أَخًا لَكُمْ لاَ يَقُولُ الرَّفَثَ. يَعْنِي بِذَلِكَ عَبْدَ اللَّهِ بْنَ رَوَاحَةَ وَفِينَا رَسُولُ اللَّهِ يَتْلُو كِتَابَهُ إِذَا انْشَقَّ مَعْرُوفٌ مِنَ الْفَجْرِ سَاطِعُ أَرَانَا الْهُدَى بَعْدَ الْعَمَى فَقُلُوبُنَا بِهِ مُوقِنَاتٌ أَنَّ مَا قَالَ وَاقِعُ يَبِيتُ يُجَافِي جَنْبَهُ عَنْ فِرَاشِهِ إِذَا اسْتَثْقَلَتْ بِالْمُشْرِكِينَ الْمَضَاجِعُ تَابَعَهُ عُقَيْلٌ. وَقَالَ الزُّبَيْدِيُّ أَخْبَرَنِي الزُّهْرِيُّ عَنْ سَعِيدٍ وَالأَعْرَجِ عَنْ أَبِي هُرَيْرَةَ ـ رضى الله عنه

Narrated Anas bin Malik: Allah's Messenger ﷺ delivered a sermon and said, "Zaid received the flag and was martyred, then Ja`far took it and was martyred, then `Abdullah bin Rawaha took it and was martyred, and then Khalid bin Al-Walid took it without being appointed, and Allah gave him victory." The Prophet ﷺ added, "I am not pleased (or they will not be pleased) that they should remain (alive) with us," while his eyes were shedding tears. – Sahih Al-Bukhari 3063

حَدَّثَنَا يَعْقُوبُ بْنُ إِبْرَاهِيمَ، حَدَّثَنَا ابْنُ عُلَيَّةَ، عَنْ أَيُّوبَ، عَنْ حُمَيْدِ بْنِ هِلاَلٍ، عَنْ أَنَسِ بْنِ مَالِكٍ ـ رضى الله عنه ـ قَالَ خَطَبَ رَسُولُ اللَّهِ صلى الله عليه وسلم فَقَالَ " أَخَذَ الرَّايَةَ زَيْدٌ فَأُصِيبَ، ثُمَّ أَخَذَهَا جَعْفَرٌ فَأُصِيبَ، ثُمَّ أَخَذَهَا عَبْدُ اللَّهِ بْنُ رَوَاحَةَ فَأُصِيبَ، ثُمَّ أَخَذَهَا خَالِدُ بْنُ الْوَلِيدِ عَنْ غَيْرِ إِمْرَةٍ فَفُتِحَ عَلَيْهِ، وَمَا يَسُرُّنِي ـ أَوْ قَالَ مَا يَسُرُّهُمْ ـ أَنَّهُمْ عِنْدَنَا ". وَقَالَ وَإِنَّ عَيْنَيْهِ لَتَذْرِفَانِ.

Zayd ibn Amr ibn Nufayl

زيد بن عمرو بن نفيل

Narrated Ibn 'Umar: Zaid bin 'Amr bin Nufail went to Sham, inquiring about a true religion to follow. He met a Jewish religious scholar and asked him about their religion. He said, "I intend to embrace your religion, so tell me some thing about it." The Jew said, "You will not embrace our religion unless you receive your share of Allah's Anger." Zaid said, "'I do not run except from Allah's Anger, and I will never bear a bit of it if I have the power to avoid it. Can you tell me of some other religion?" He said, "I do not know any other religion except the Hanif." Zaid enquired, "What is Hanif?" He said, "Hanif is the religion of (the prophet) Abraham who was neither a Jew nor a Christian, and he used to worship None but Allah (Alone)" Then Zaid went

out and met a Christian religious scholar and told him the same as before. The Christian said, "You will not embrace our religion unless you get a share of Allah's Curse." Zaid replied, "I do not run except from Allah's Curse, and I will never bear any of Allah's Curse and His Anger if I have the power to avoid them. Will you tell me of some other religion?" He replied, "I do not know any other religion except Hanif." Zaid enquired, "What is Hanif?" He replied, Hanif is the religion of (the prophet) Abraham who was neither a Jew nor a Christian and he used to worship None but Allah (Alone)" When Zaid heard their Statement about (the religion of) Abraham, he left that place, and when he came out, he raised both his hands and said, "O Allah! I make You my Witness that I am on the religion of Abraham.". – Sahih Al-Bukhari 3827
قَالَ مُوسَى حَدَّثَنِي سَالِمُ بْنُ عَبْدِ اللَّهِ، وَلاَ أَعْلَمُهُ إِلاَّ تُحُدِّثَ بِهِ عَنِ ابْنِ عُمَرَ أَنَّ زَيْدَ بْنَ عَمْرِو بْنِ نُفَيْلٍ خَرَجَ إِلَى الشَّأْمِ، يَسْأَلُ عَنِ الدِّينِ وَيَتْبَعُهُ فَلَقِيَ عَالِمًا مِنَ الْيَهُودِ، فَسَأَلَهُ عَنْ دِينِهِمْ، فَقَالَ إِنِّي لَعَلِّي أَنْ أَدِينَ دِينَكُمْ، فَأَخْبِرْنِي. فَقَالَ لاَ تَكُونُ عَلَى دِينِنَا حَتَّى تَأْخُذَ بِنَصِيبِكَ مِنْ غَضَبِ اللَّهِ. قَالَ زَيْدٌ مَا أَفِرُّ إِلاَّ مِنْ غَضَبِ اللَّهِ، وَلاَ أَحْمِلُ مِنْ غَضَبِ اللَّهِ شَيْئًا أَبَدًا، وَأَنَّى أَسْتَطِيعُهُ فَهَلْ تَدُلُّنِي عَلَى غَيْرِهِ قَالَ مَا أَعْلَمُهُ إِلاَّ أَنْ يَكُونَ حَنِيفًا. قَالَ زَيْدٌ وَمَا الْحَنِيفُ قَالَ دِينُ إِبْرَاهِيمَ لَمْ يَكُنْ يَهُودِيًّا وَلاَ نَصْرَانِيًّا وَلاَ يَعْبُدُ إِلاَّ اللَّهَ. فَخَرَجَ زَيْدٌ فَلَقِيَ عَالِمًا مِنَ النَّصَارَى، فَذَكَرَ مِثْلَهُ، فَقَالَ لَنْ تَكُونَ عَلَى دِينِنَا حَتَّى تَأْخُذَ بِنَصِيبِكَ مِنْ لَعْنَةِ اللَّهِ. قَالَ مَا أَفِرُّ إِلاَّ مِنْ لَعْنَةِ اللَّهِ، وَلاَ أَحْمِلُ مِنْ لَعْنَةِ اللَّهِ وَلاَ مِنْ غَضَبِهِ شَيْئًا أَبَدًا، وَأَنَّى أَسْتَطِيعُ فَهَلْ تَدُلُّنِي عَلَى غَيْرِهِ قَالَ مَا أَعْلَمُهُ إِلاَّ أَنْ يَكُونَ حَنِيفًا. قَالَ وَمَا الْحَنِيفُ قَالَ دِينُ إِبْرَاهِيمَ لَمْ يَكُنْ يَهُودِيًّا وَلاَ نَصْرَانِيًّا وَلاَ يَعْبُدُ إِلاَّ اللَّهَ. فَلَمَّا رَأَى زَيْدٌ قَوْلَهُمْ فِي إِبْرَاهِيمَ ـ عَلَيْهِ السَّلاَمُ ـ خَرَجَ، فَلَمَّا بَرَزَ رَفَعَ يَدَيْهِ فَقَالَ اللَّهُمَّ إِنِّي أَشْهَدُ أَنِّي عَلَى دِينِ إِبْرَاهِيمَ

Narrated 'Abdullah bin 'Umar: The Prophet ﷺ met Zaid bin 'Amr bin Nufail in the bottom of (the valley of) Baldah before any Divine Inspiration came to the Prophet. A meal was presented to the Prophet ﷺ but he refused to eat from it. (Then it was presented to Zaid) who said, "I do not eat anything which you slaughter in the name of your stone idols. I eat none but those things on which Allah's Name has been mentioned at the time of slaughtering." Zaid bin 'Amr used to criticize the way Quraish used to slaughter their animals, and used to say, "Allah has created the sheep and He has sent the water for it from the sky, and He has grown the grass for it from the earth; yet you slaughter it in other than the Name of Allah. He used to say so, for he rejected that practice and considered it as something abominable. – Sahih Al-Bukhari 3826
حَدَّثَنِي مُحَمَّدُ بْنُ أَبِي بَكْرٍ، حَدَّثَنَا فُضَيْلُ بْنُ سُلَيْمَانَ، حَدَّثَنَا مُوسَى، حَدَّثَنَا سَالِمُ بْنُ عَبْدِ اللَّهِ، عَنْ عَبْدِ اللَّهِ بْنِ عُمَرَ، رضى الله عنهما أَنَّ النَّبِيَّ صلى الله عليه وسلم لَقِيَ زَيْدَ بْنَ عَمْرِو بْنِ نُفَيْلٍ بِأَسْفَلِ بَلْدَحَ، قَبْلَ أَنْ يَنْزِلَ عَلَى النَّبِيِّ صلى الله عليه وسلم الْوَحْىُ فَقُدِّمَتْ إِلَى النَّبِيِّ صلى الله عليه وسلم سُفْرَةٌ، فَأَبَى أَنْ يَأْكُلَ مِنْهَا ثُمَّ قَالَ زَيْدٌ إِنِّي لَسْتُ آكُلُ مِمَّا تَذْبَحُونَ عَلَى أَنْصَابِكُمْ، وَلاَ آكُلُ إِلاَّ مَا ذُكِرَ اسْمُ اللَّهِ عَلَيْهِ. وَأَنَّ زَيْدَ بْنَ عَمْرٍو كَانَ يَعِيبُ عَلَى قُرَيْشٍ ذَبَائِحَهُمْ، وَيَقُولُ الشَّاةُ خَلَقَهَا اللَّهُ، وَأَنْزَلَ لَهَا مِنَ السَّمَاءِ الْمَاءَ، وَأَنْبَتَ لَهَا مِنَ الأَرْضِ، ثُمَّ تَذْبَحُونَهَا عَلَى غَيْرِ اسْمِ اللَّهِ إِنْكَارًا لِذَلِكَ وَإِعْظَامًا لَهُ.

Narrated Asma bint Abi Bakr: I saw Zaid bin Amr bin Nufail standing with his back against the Ka'ba and saying, "O people of Quraish! By Allah, none amongst you is on the religion of Abraham except me." He used to preserve the lives of little girls: If somebody wanted to kill his daughter he would say to him, "Do not kill her for I will feed her on your behalf." So he would take her, and when she grew up nicely, he would say to her father, "Now if you want her, I will give her to you, and if you wish, I will feed her on your behalf.". – Sahih Al-Bukhari 3828
وَقَالَ اللَّيْثُ كَتَبَ إِلَيَّ هِشَامٌ عَنْ أَبِيهِ، عَنْ أَسْمَاءَ بِنْتِ أَبِي بَكْرٍ ـ رضى الله عنهما ـ قَالَتْ رَأَيْتُ زَيْدَ بْنَ عَمْرِو بْنِ نُفَيْلٍ قَائِمًا مُسْنِدًا ظَهْرَهُ إِلَى الْكَعْبَةِ يَقُولُ يَا مَعَاشِرَ قُرَيْشٍ، وَاللَّهِ مَا مِنْكُمْ عَلَى دِينِ إِبْرَاهِيمَ غَيْرِي، وَكَانَ يُحْيِي الْمَوْءُودَةَ، يَقُولُ لِلرَّجُلِ إِذَا أَرَادَ أَنْ يَقْتُلَ ابْنَتَهُ لاَ تَقْتُلْهَا، أَنَا أَكْفِيكَهَا مَئُونَتَهَا. فَيَأْخُذُهَا فَإِذَا تَرَعْرَعَتْ قَالَ لأَبِيهَا إِنْ شِئْتَ دَفَعْتُهَا إِلَيْكَ، وَإِنْ شِئْتَ كَفَيْتُكَ مَئُونَتَهَا

I heard Sa`id bin Zaid bin `Amr bin Nufail saying in the mosque of Al-Kufa. "By Allah, I have seen myself tied and forced by `Umar to leave Islam before `Umar himself embraced Islam.

And if the mountain of Uhud could move from its place for the evil which you people have done to `Uthman, then it would have the right to move from its place." Narrated Qais: I heard Sa`id bin Zaid bin `Amr bin Nufail saying in the mosque of Al-Kufa. "By Allah, I have seen myself tied and forced by `Umar to leave Islam before `Umar himself embraced Islam. And if the mountain of Uhud could move from its place for the evil which you people have done to `Uthman, then it would have the right to move from its place.". – Sahih Al-Bukhari 3862

حَدَّثَنَا قُتَيْبَةُ بْنُ سَعِيدٍ، حَدَّثَنَا سُفْيَانُ، عَنْ إِسْمَاعِيلَ، عَنْ قَيْسٍ، قَالَ سَمِعْتُ سَعِيدَ بْنَ زَيْدِ بْنِ عَمْرِو بْنِ نُفَيْلٍ، فِي مَسْجِدِ الْكُوفَةِ يَقُولُ وَاللَّهِ لَقَدْ رَأَيْتُنِي وَإِنَّ عُمَرَ لَمُوثِقِي عَلَى الإِسْلاَمِ قَبْلَ أَنْ يُسْلِمَ عُمَرُ، وَلَوْ أَنَّ أُحُدًا ارْفَضَّ لِلَّذِي صَنَعْتُمْ بِعُثْمَانَ لَكَانَ مَحْقُوقًا أَنْ يَرْفَضَّ.

Narrated Sa`id bin Zaid bin `Amr bin Nufail: That Arwa sued him before Marwan for a right, which she claimed, he had deprived her of. On that Sa`id said, "How should I deprive her of her right? I testify that I heard Allah's Messenger ﷺ saying, 'If anyone takes a span of land unjustly, his neck will be encircled with it down seven earths on the Day of Resurrection." – Sahih Al-Bukhari 3198

حَدَّثَنِي عُبَيْدُ بْنُ إِسْمَاعِيلَ، حَدَّثَنَا أَبُو أُسَامَةَ، عَنْ هِشَامٍ، عَنْ أَبِيهِ، عَنْ سَعِيدِ بْنِ زَيْدِ بْنِ عَمْرِو بْنِ نُفَيْلٍ، أَنَّهُ خَاصَمَتْهُ أَرْوَى فِي حَقٍّ زَعَمَتْ أَنَّهُ انْتَقَصَهُ لَهَا إِلَى مَرْوَانَ، فَقَالَ سَعِيدٌ أَنَا أَنْتَقِصُ مِنْ حَقِّهَا شَيْئًا، أَشْهَدُ لَسَمِعْتُ رَسُولَ اللَّهِ صلى الله عليه وسلم يَقُولُ " مَنْ أَخَذَ شِبْرًا مِنَ الأَرْضِ ظُلْمًا، فَإِنَّهُ يُطَوَّقُهُ يَوْمَ الْقِيَامَةِ مِنْ سَبْعِ أَرَضِينَ ". قَالَ ابْنُ أَبِي الزِّنَادِ عَنْ هِشَامٍ عَنْ أَبِيهِ قَالَ قَالَ لِي سَعِيدُ بْنُ زَيْدٍ دَخَلْتُ عَلَى النَّبِيِّ صلى الله عليه وسلم.

Sa'd ibn Abi Waqqas ibn Wuhayb al-Zuhri

سَعْد بْنِ أَبِي وَقَّاص بْنِ وهَيْب الزُّهري

Narrated `Abdullah bin `Umar: Sa`d bin 'Ubada became sick and the Prophet ﷺ along with `Abdur Rahman bin `Auf, Sa`d bin Abi Waqqas and `Abdullah bin Mas`ud visited him to inquire about his health. When he came to him, he found him surrounded by his household and he asked, "Has he died?" They said, "No, O Allah's Apostle." The Prophet ﷺ wept and when the people saw the weeping of Allah's Messenger ﷺ they all wept. He said, "Will you listen? Allah does not punish for shedding tears, nor for the grief of the heart but he punishes or bestows His Mercy because of this." He pointed to his tongue and added, "The deceased is punished for the wailing of his relatives over him." `Umar used to beat with a stick and throw stones and put dust over the faces (of those who used to wail over the dead). – Sahih Al-Bukhari 1304

حَدَّثَنَا أَصْبَغُ، عَنِ ابْنِ وَهْبٍ، قَالَ أَخْبَرَنِي عَمْرٌو، عَنْ سَعِيدِ بْنِ الْحَارِثِ الأَنْصَارِيِّ، عَنْ عَبْدِ اللَّهِ بْنِ عُمَرَ ـ رضى الله عنهما ـ قَالَ اشْتَكَى سَعْدُ بْنُ عُبَادَةَ شَكْوَى لَهُ فَأَتَاهُ النَّبِيُّ صلى الله عليه وسلم يَعُودُهُ مَعَ عَبْدِ الرَّحْمَنِ بْنِ عَوْفٍ وَسَعْدِ بْنِ أَبِي وَقَّاصٍ وَعَبْدِ اللَّهِ بْنِ مَسْعُودٍ ـ رضى الله عنهم ـ فَلَمَّا دَخَلَ عَلَيْهِ فَوَجَدَهُ فِي غَاشِيَةِ أَهْلِهِ فَقَالَ " قَدْ قَضَى ". قَالُوا لاَ يَا رَسُولَ اللَّهِ. فَبَكَى النَّبِيُّ صلى الله عليه وسلم فَلَمَّا رَأَى الْقَوْمُ بُكَاءَ النَّبِيِّ صلى الله عليه وسلم بَكَوْا فَقَالَ " أَلاَ تَسْمَعُونَ إِنَّ اللَّهَ لاَ يُعَذِّبُ بِدَمْعِ الْعَيْنِ، وَلاَ بِحُزْنِ الْقَلْبِ، وَلَكِنْ يُعَذِّبُ بِهَذَا ـ وَأَشَارَ إِلَى لِسَانِهِ ـ أَوْ يَرْحَمُ وَإِنَّ الْمَيِّتَ يُعَذَّبُ بِبُكَاءِ أَهْلِهِ عَلَيْهِ ". وَكَانَ عُمَرُ ـ رضى الله عنه ـ يَضْرِبُ فِيهِ بِالْعَصَا، وَيَرْمِي بِالْحِجَارَةِ وَيَحْثِي بِالتُّرَابِ

Narrated `Aisha: `Utba bin Abi Waqqas authorized his brother Sa`d to take the son of the slave-girl of Zam`a into his custody. `Utba said (to him). "He is my son." When Allah's Messenger ﷺ arrived in Mecca during the Conquest (of Mecca), Sa`d bin Abi Waqqas took the son of the slave-girl of Zam`a and took him to the Prophet ﷺ Abd bin Zam`a too came along with him. Sa`d said. "This is the son of my brother and the latter has informed me that he is his son." `Abd bin Zam`a said, "O Allah's Messenger ﷺ! This is my brother who is the son of the slave-girl of Zam`a and was born on his (i.e. Zam'as) bed.' Allah's Apostle looked at the son of the slave-girl of Zam`a and noticed that he, of all the people had the greatest resemblance to `Utba bin Abi Waqqas. Allah's Messenger ﷺ then said (to `Abd), " He is yours; he is your brother, O `Abd bin Zam`a, he was born on the bed (of your father)." (At the same time) Allah's Messenger ﷺ said (to his wife Sauda), "Veil yourself before him (i.e. the son of the slave-girl) O Sauda," because of the resemblance he noticed between him and `Utba bin Abi Waqqas. Allah's Apostle added, "The boy is for the bed (i.e. for the owner of the bed where he was born), and stone is for the adulterer." (Ibn Shihab said, "Abu Huraira used to say that (i.e. the last statement of the Prophet in the above Hadith 596, publicly."). – Sahih Al-Bukhari 4303

حَدَّثَنِي عَبْدُ اللَّهِ بْنُ مَسْلَمَةَ، عَنْ مَالِكٍ، عَنِ ابْنِ شِهَابٍ، عَنْ عُرْوَةَ بْنِ الزُّبَيْرِ، عَنْ عَائِشَةَ ـ رضى الله عنها ـ عَنِ النَّبِيِّ صلى الله عليه وسلم. وَقَالَ اللَّيْثُ حَدَّثَنِي يُونُسُ عَنِ ابْنِ شِهَابٍ أَخْبَرَنِي عُرْوَةُ بْنُ الزُّبَيْرِ أَنَّ عَائِشَةَ قَالَتْ كَانَ عُتْبَةُ بْنُ أَبِي وَقَّاصٍ عَهِدَ إِلَى أَخِيهِ سَعْدٍ أَنْ يَقْبِضَ ابْنَ وَلِيدَةِ زَمْعَةَ، وَقَالَ عُتْبَةُ إِنَّهُ ابْنِي. فَلَمَّا قَدِمَ رَسُولُ اللَّهِ صلى الله عليه وسلم مَكَّةَ فِي الْفَتْحِ أَخَذَ سَعْدُ بْنُ أَبِي وَقَّاصٍ ابْنَ وَلِيدَةِ زَمْعَةَ، فَأَقْبَلَ بِهِ إِلَى رَسُولِ اللَّهِ صلى الله عليه وسلم، وَأَقْبَلَ مَعَهُ عَبْدُ بْنُ زَمْعَةَ، فَقَالَ سَعْدُ بْنُ أَبِي وَقَّاصٍ هَذَا ابْنُ أَخِي، عَهِدَ إِلَىَّ أَنَّهُ ابْنُهُ. قَالَ عَبْدُ بْنُ زَمْعَةَ يَا رَسُولَ اللَّهِ، هَذَا أَخِي، هَذَا ابْنُ زَمْعَةَ، وُلِدَ عَلَى فِرَاشِهِ. فَنَظَرَ رَسُولُ اللَّهِ صلى الله عليه وسلم إِلَى ابْنِ وَلِيدَةِ زَمْعَةَ، فَإِذَا أَشْبَهُ النَّاسِ بِعُتْبَةَ بْنِ أَبِي وَقَّاصٍ، فَقَالَ رَسُولُ اللَّهِ صلى الله عليه وسلم " هُوَ لَكَ، هُوَ أَخُوكَ يَا عَبْدُ بْنَ زَمْعَةَ ". مِنْ أَجْلِ أَنَّهُ وُلِدَ عَلَى فِرَاشِهِ، وَقَالَ رَسُولُ اللَّهِ صلى الله عليه وسلم " احْتَجِبِي مِنْهُ يَا سَوْدَةُ ". لِمَا رَأَى مِنْ شَبَهِ عُتْبَةَ بْنِ أَبِي وَقَّاصٍ. قَالَ ابْنُ شِهَابٍ قَالَتْ عَائِشَةُ قَالَ رَسُولُ اللَّهِ صلى الله عليه وسلم " الْوَلَدُ لِلْفِرَاشِ وَلِلْعَاهِرِ الْحَجَرُ ". وَقَالَ ابْنُ شِهَابٍ وَكَانَ أَبُو هُرَيْرَةَ يَصِيحُ بِذَلِكَ

Narrated Sa`d (bin Abi Waqqas): Allah's Messenger ﷺ distributed something (from the resources of Zakat) amongst a group of people while I was sitting amongst them, but he left a man whom I considered the best of the lot. So, I went up to Allah's Messenger ﷺ and asked him secretly, "Why have you left that person? By Allah! I consider him a believer." The Prophet ﷺ said, "Or merely a Muslim (Who surrender to Allah)." I remained quiet for a while but could not help repeating my question because of what I knew about him. I said, "O Allah's Apostle! Why have you left that person? By Allah! I consider him a believer. " The Prophet ﷺ said, "Or merely a Muslim." I remained quiet for a while but could not help repeating my question because of what I knew about him. I said, "O Allah's Messenger ﷺ! Why have you left that person? By Allah! I consider him a believer." The Prophet ﷺ said, "Or merely a Muslim." Then Allah's Messenger ﷺ said, "I give to a person while another is dearer to me, for fear that he may be thrown in the Hell-fire on his face (by reneging from Islam).". – Sahih Al-Bukhari 1478

حَدَّثَنَا مُحَمَّدُ بْنُ غُرَيْرٍ الزُّهْرِيُّ، حَدَّثَنَا يَعْقُوبُ بْنُ إِبْرَاهِيمَ، عَنْ أَبِيهِ، عَنْ صَالِحِ بْنِ كَيْسَانَ، عَنِ ابْنِ شِهَابٍ، قَالَ أَخْبَرَنِي عَامِرُ بْنُ سَعْدٍ، عَنْ أَبِيهِ، قَالَ أَعْطَى رَسُولُ اللَّهِ صلى الله عليه وسلم رَهْطًا وَأَنَا جَالِسٌ فِيهِمْ قَالَ فَتَرَكَ رَسُولُ اللَّهِ صلى الله عليه وسلم مِنْهُمْ رَجُلاً لَمْ يُعْطِهِ، وَهُوَ أَعْجَبُهُمْ إِلَىَّ، فَقُمْتُ إِلَى رَسُولِ اللَّهِ صلى الله عليه وسلم فَسَارَرْتُهُ فَقُلْتُ مَا لَكَ عَنْ فُلاَنٍ وَاللَّهِ إِنِّي لأُرَاهُ مُؤْمِنًا. قَالَ " أَوْ مُسْلِمًا " قَالَ فَسَكَتُّ قَلِيلاً ثُمَّ غَلَبَنِي مَا أَعْلَمُ فِيهِ فَقُلْتُ يَا رَسُولَ اللَّهِ. مَا لَكَ عَنْ فُلاَنٍ وَاللَّهِ إِنِّي لأُرَاهُ مُؤْمِنًا. قَالَ " أَوْ مُسْلِمًا ". قَالَ فَسَكَتُّ قَلِيلاً ثُمَّ غَلَبَنِي مَا أَعْلَمُ فِيهِ فَقُلْتُ يَا رَسُولَ اللَّهِ مَا لَكَ عَنْ فُلاَنٍ وَاللَّهِ إِنِّي لأُرَاهُ مُؤْمِنًا. قَالَ " أَوْ مُسْلِمًا ـ يَعْنِي فَقَالَ ـ إِنِّي لأُعْطِي الرَّجُلَ وَغَيْرُهُ أَحَبُّ إِلَىَّ مِنْهُ، خَشْيَةَ أَنْ يُكَبَّ فِي النَّارِ عَلَى وَجْهِهِ ". وَعَنْ أَبِيهِ عَنْ صَالِحٍ عَنْ إِسْمَاعِيلَ بْنِ مُحَمَّدٍ أَنَّهُ قَالَ سَمِعْتُ أَبِي يُحَدِّثُ هَذَا فَقَالَ فِي حَدِيثِهِ فَضَرَبَ رَسُولُ اللَّهِ صلى الله عليه وسلم بِيَدِهِ فَجَمَعَ بَيْنَ عُنُقِي وَكَتِفِي ثُمَّ قَالَ " أَقْبِلْ أَىْ سَعْدُ إِنِّي لأُعْطِي الرَّجُلَ ". قَالَ أَبُو عَبْدِ اللَّهِ {فَكُبْكِبُوا} قُلِبُوا {مُكِبًّا} أَكَبَّ الرَّجُلُ إِذَا كَانَ فِعْلُهُ غَيْرَ وَاقِعٍ عَلَى أَحَدٍ، فَإِذَا وَقَعَ الْفِعْلُ قُلْتَ كَبَّهُ اللَّهُ لِوَجْهِهِ، وَكَبَبْتُهُ أَنَا

Narrated Malik bin Aus: While I was at home, the sun rose high and it got hot. Suddenly the messenger of `Umar bin Al- Khattab came to me and said, "The chief of the believers has sent for you." So, I went along with him till I entered the place where `Umar was sitting on a bedstead made of date-palm leaves and covered with no mattress, and he was leaning over a leather pillow. I greeted him and sat down. He said, "O Mali! Some persons of your people who have families came to me and I have ordered that a gift should be given to them, so take it and distribute it among them." I said, "O chief of the believers! I wish that you order someone else to do it." He said, "O man! Take it." While I was sitting there with him, his doorman Yarfa' came saying, "`Uthman, `Abdur-Rahman bin `Auf, Az-Zubair and Sa`d bin Abi Waqqas are asking your permission (to see you); may I admit them?" `Umar said, "Yes", So they were admitted and they came in, greeted him, and sat down. After a while Yarfa' came again and said, "May I admit `Ali and `Abbas?" `Umar said, "yes." So, they were admitted and they came in and greeted (him) and sat down. Then `Abbas said, "O chief of the believers! Judge between me and this (i.e. `Ali)." They had a dispute regarding the property of Bani An-Nadir which Allah had given to His Apostle as Fai. The group (i.e. `Uthman and his companions) said, "O chief of the believers! Judge between them and relieve both of them front each other." `Umar said, "Be patient! I beseech you by Allah by Whose Permission the Heaven and the Earth exist, do you know that Allah's Messenger said, 'Our (i.e. prophets') property will not be inherited, and whatever we leave, is Sadaqa (to be used for charity),' and Allah's Messenger meant himself (by saying "we")?" The group said, "He said so." `Umar then turned to `Ali and `Abbas and said, "I beseech you by Allah, do you know that Allah's Messenger said so?" They replied, " He said so." `Umar then said, "So, I will talk to you about this matter. Allah bestowed on His Apostle with a special favor of something of this Fai (booty) which he gave to nobody else." `Umar then recited the Holy Verses: "What Allah bestowed as (Fai) Booty on his Apostle (Muhammad) from them --- for this you made no expedition with either cavalry or camelry: But Allah gives power to His Apostles over whomever He will 'And Allah is able to do all things." 9:6) `Umar added "So this property was especially given to Allah's Messenger, but, by Allah, neither did he take possession of it and leave your, nor did he favor himself with it to your exclusion, but he gave It to all of you and distributed it amongst you till this property remained out of it. Allah's Messenger used to spend the yearly expenses of his family out of this property and used to keep the rest of its revenue to be spent on Allah 's Cause. Allah's Apostle kept on doing this during all his lifetime. I ask you by Allah do you know this?" They replies in the affirmative. `Umar then said to `Ali and `Abbas. "I ask you by Allah, do you know this?" `Umar added, "When Allah had taken His Prophet unto Him, 'Abu Bakr said, 'I am the successor of Allah's Messenger so, Abu Bakr took over that property and managed it in the same way as Allah's Messenger used to do, and Allah knows that he was true, pious and rightlyguided, and he was a follower of what was right. Then Allah took Abu Bakr unto Him and I became Abu Bakr's successor, and I kept that property in my possession for the first two years of my Caliphate, managing it in the same way as Allah's Messenger used to do and as Abu Bakr used to do, and Allah knows that I have been true, pious, rightly guided, and a follower of what is right. Now you both (i.e. 'Ah and `Abbas) came to talk to me, bearing the same claim and presenting the same case; you, `Abbas, came to me asking for your share from your nephew's property, and this man, i.e. `Ali, came to me asking for his wife's share from her father's property. I told you both that Allah's Messenger said, 'Our (prophets') properties are not to be inherited, but what we leave is Sadaqa (to be used for charity).' When I thought it right that I should hand over this property to you, I said to you, 'I am ready to hand over this property to you if you wish, on the condition that you would take Allah's Pledge and Convention that you would manage it in the same way as Allah's Messenger used to, and as Abu Bakr used to do, and as I have done since I was in charge of it.' So, both of you said (to me), 'Hand it over to us,' and on that condition I handed it over to you. So, I ask you by Allah, did I hand it over to them on this condition?" The group aid, "Yes." Then `Umar faced `Ali and `Abbas saying, "I ask you by Allah, did I hand it over to you on this condition?" They said, "Yes. " He said, " Do you want now to give a different decision? By Allah, by Whose Leave both the Heaven and the Earth exist, I will never give any decision other than that (I have already given). And if you are unable to manage it, then return it to me, and I will do the job on your behalf.". – Sahih Al-Bukhari 3094

حَدَّثَنَا إِسْحَاقُ بْنُ مُحَمَّدٍ الْفَرْوِيُّ، حَدَّثَنَا مَالِكُ بْنُ أَنَسٍ، عَنِ ابْنِ شِهَابٍ، عَنْ مَالِكِ بْنِ أَوْسِ بْنِ الْحَدَثَانِ،، وَكَانَ، مُحَمَّدُ بْنُ جُبَيْرٍ ذَكَرَ لِي ذِكْرًا مِنْ حَدِيثِهِ ذَلِكَ، فَانْطَلَقْتُ حَتَّى أَدْخُلَ عَلَى مَالِكِ بْنِ أَوْسٍ، فَسَأَلْتُهُ عَنْ ذَلِكَ الْحَدِيثِ فَقَالَ مَالِكٌ بَيْنَا أَنَا جَالِسٌ فِي أَهْلِي حِينَ مَتَعَ النَّهَارُ، إِذَا رَسُولُ عُمَرَ بْنِ الْخَطَّابِ يَأْتِينِي فَقَالَ أَجِبْ أَمِيرَ الْمُؤْمِنِينَ. فَانْطَلَقْتُ مَعَهُ حَتَّى أَدْخُلَ عَلَى عُمَرَ، فَإِذَا هُوَ جَالِسٌ عَلَى رِمَالِ سَرِيرٍ، لَيْسَ بَيْنَهُ وَبَيْنَهُ فِرَاشٌ مُتَّكِئٌ عَلَى وِسَادَةٍ مِنْ أَدَمٍ، فَسَلَّمْتُ عَلَيْهِ ثُمَّ جَلَسْتُ فَقَالَ يَا مَالِ، إِنَّهُ قَدِمَ عَلَيْنَا مِنْ قَوْمِكَ أَهْلُ أَبْيَاتٍ، وَقَدْ أَمَرْتُ فِيهِمْ بِرَضْخٍ فَاقْبِضْهُ فَاقْسِمْهُ بَيْنَهُمْ. فَقُلْتُ يَا أَمِيرَ الْمُؤْمِنِينَ، لَوْ أَمَرْتَ بِهِ غَيْرِي. قَالَ اقْبِضْهُ أَيُّهَا الْمَرْءُ. فَبَيْنَا أَنَا جَالِسٌ عِنْدَهُ أَتَاهُ حَاجِبُهُ يَرْفَا فَقَالَ هَلْ لَكَ فِي عُثْمَانَ وَعَبْدِ الرَّحْمَنِ بْنِ عَوْفٍ وَالزُّبَيْرِ وَسَعْدِ بْنِ أَبِي وَقَّاصٍ يَسْتَأْذِنُونَ قَالَ نَعَمْ. فَأَذِنَ لَهُمْ فَدَخَلُوا فَسَلَّمُوا وَجَلَسُوا، ثُمَّ جَلَسَ يَرْفَا يَسِيرًا ثُمَّ قَالَ هَلْ لَكَ فِي عَلِيٍّ وَعَبَّاسٍ قَالَ نَعَمْ. فَأَذِنَ لَهُمَا، فَدَخَلاَ فَسَلَّمَا فَجَلَسَا، فَقَالَ عَبَّاسٌ يَا أَمِيرَ الْمُؤْمِنِينَ، اقْضِ بَيْنِي وَبَيْنَ هَذَا. وَهُمَا يَخْتَصِمَانِ فِيمَا أَفَاءَ اللَّهُ عَلَى رَسُولِهِ صلى الله عليه وسلم مِنْ بَنِي النَّضِيرِ. فَقَالَ الرَّهْطُ عُثْمَانُ وَأَصْحَابُهُ يَا أَمِيرَ الْمُؤْمِنِينَ، اقْضِ بَيْنَهُمَا وَأَرِحْ أَحَدَهُمَا مِنَ الآخَرِ. قَالَ عُمَرُ تَيْدَكُمْ، أَنْشُدُكُمْ بِاللَّهِ الَّذِي بِإِذْنِهِ تَقُومُ السَّمَاءُ وَالأَرْضُ، هَلْ تَعْلَمُونَ أَنَّ رَسُولَ اللَّهِ صلى الله عليه وسلم قَالَ " لاَ نُورَثُ مَا تَرَكْنَا صَدَقَةٌ ". يُرِيدُ رَسُولُ اللَّهِ صلى الله عليه وسلم نَفْسَهُ. قَالَ الرَّهْطُ قَدْ قَالَ ذَلِكَ. فَأَقْبَلَ عُمَرُ عَلَى عَلِيٍّ وَعَبَّاسٍ فَقَالَ أَنْشُدُكُمَا اللَّهَ، أَتَعْلَمَانِ أَنَّ رَسُولَ اللَّهِ صلى الله عليه وسلم قَدْ قَالَ ذَلِكَ قَالاَ قَدْ قَالَ ذَلِكَ. قَالَ عُمَرُ فَإِنِّي أُحَدِّثُكُمْ عَنْ هَذَا الأَمْرِ، إِنَّ اللَّهَ قَدْ خَصَّ رَسُولَهُ صلى الله عليه وسلم فِي هَذَا الْفَىْءِ بِشَىْءٍ لَمْ يُعْطِهِ أَحَدًا غَيْرَهُ ـ ثُمَّ قَرَأَ {وَمَا أَفَاءَ اللَّهُ عَلَى رَسُولِهِ مِنْهُمْ} إِلَى قَوْلِهِ {قَدِيرٌ} ـ فَكَانَتْ هَذِهِ خَالِصَةً لِرَسُولِ اللَّهِ صلى الله عليه وسلم. وَاللَّهِ مَا احْتَازَهَا دُونَكُمْ، وَلاَ اسْتَأْثَرَ بِهَا عَلَيْكُمْ قَدْ أَعْطَاكُمُوهُ، وَبَثَّهَا فِيكُمْ حَتَّى بَقِيَ مِنْهَا هَذَا الْمَالُ، فَكَانَ رَسُولُ اللَّهِ صلى الله عليه وسلم يُنْفِقُ عَلَى أَهْلِهِ نَفَقَةَ سَنَتِهِمْ مِنْ هَذَا الْمَالِ، ثُمَّ يَأْخُذُ مَا بَقِيَ فَيَجْعَلُهُ مَجْعَلَ مَالِ اللَّهِ، فَعَمِلَ رَسُولُ اللَّهِ صلى الله عليه وسلم بِذَلِكَ حَيَاتَهُ، أَنْشُدُكُمْ بِاللَّهِ هَلْ تَعْلَمُونَ ذَلِكَ قَالُوا نَعَمْ. ثُمَّ قَالَ لِعَلِيٍّ وَعَبَّاسٍ أَنْشُدُكُمَا بِاللَّهِ هَلْ تَعْلَمَانِ ذَلِكَ قَالَ عُمَرُ ثُمَّ تَوَفَّى اللَّهُ نَبِيَّهُ صلى الله عليه وسلم فَقَالَ أَبُو بَكْرٍ أَنَا وَلِيُّ رَسُولِ اللَّهِ صلى الله عليه وسلم. فَقَبَضَهَا أَبُو بَكْرٍ، فَعَمِلَ فِيهَا بِمَا عَمِلَ رَسُولُ اللَّهِ صلى الله عليه وسلم، وَاللَّهُ يَعْلَمُ إِنَّهُ فِيهَا لَصَادِقٌ بَارٌّ رَاشِدٌ تَابِعٌ لِلْحَقِّ، ثُمَّ تَوَفَّى اللَّهُ أَبَا بَكْرٍ، فَكُنْتُ أَنَا وَلِيَّ أَبِي بَكْرٍ، فَقَبَضْتُهَا سَنَتَيْنِ مِنْ إِمَارَتِي، أَعْمَلُ فِيهَا بِمَا عَمِلَ رَسُولُ اللَّهِ صلى الله عليه وسلم وَمَا عَمِلَ فِيهَا أَبُو بَكْرٍ، وَاللَّهُ يَعْلَمُ إِنِّي فِيهَا لَصَادِقٌ بَارٌّ رَاشِدٌ تَابِعٌ لِلْحَقِّ، ثُمَّ جِئْتُمَانِي تُكَلِّمَانِي وَكَلِمَتُكُمَا وَاحِدَةٌ، وَأَمْرُكُمَا وَاحِدٌ، جِئْتَنِي يَا عَبَّاسُ تَسْأَلُنِي نَصِيبَكَ مِنِ ابْنِ أَخِيكَ، وَجَاءَنِي هَذَا ـ يُرِيدُ عَلِيًّا ـ يُرِيدُ نَصِيبَ امْرَأَتِهِ مِنْ أَبِيهَا، فَقُلْتُ لَكُمَا إِنَّ رَسُولَ اللَّهِ صلى الله عليه وسلم قَالَ " لاَ نُورَثُ مَا تَرَكْنَا صَدَقَةٌ ". فَلَمَّا بَدَا لِي أَنْ أَدْفَعَهُ إِلَيْكُمَا قُلْتُ إِنْ شِئْتُمَا دَفَعْتُهَا إِلَيْكُمَا عَلَى أَنَّ عَلَيْكُمَا عَهْدَ اللَّهِ وَمِيثَاقَهُ لَتَعْمَلاَنِ فِيهَا بِمَا عَمِلَ فِيهَا رَسُولُ اللَّهِ صلى الله عليه وسلم، وَبِمَا عَمِلَ فِيهَا أَبُو بَكْرٍ، وَبِمَا عَمِلْتُ فِيهَا مُنْذُ وَلِيتُهَا، فَقُلْتُمَا ادْفَعْهَا إِلَيْنَا. فَبِذَلِكَ دَفَعْتُهَا إِلَيْكُمَا، فَأَنْشُدُكُمْ بِاللَّهِ، هَلْ دَفَعْتُهَا إِلَيْهِمَا بِذَلِكَ قَالَ الرَّهْطُ نَعَمْ. ثُمَّ أَقْبَلَ عَلَى عَلِيٍّ وَعَبَّاسٍ فَقَالَ أَنْشُدُكُمَا بِاللَّهِ هَلْ دَفَعْتُهَا إِلَيْكُمَا بِذَلِكَ قَالاَ نَعَمْ. قَالَ فَتَلْتَمِسَانِ مِنِّي قَضَاءً غَيْرَ ذَلِكَ فَوَاللَّهِ الَّذِي بِإِذْنِهِ تَقُومُ السَّمَاءُ وَالأَرْضُ، لاَ أَقْضِي فِيهَا قَضَاءً غَيْرَ ذَلِكَ، فَإِنْ عَجَزْتُمَا عَنْهَا فَادْفَعَاهَا إِلَىَّ، فَإِنِّي أَكْفِيكُمَاهَا.

Narrated Sa`d bin Abi Waqqas: I was stricken by an ailment that led me to the verge of death. The Prophetﷺ came to pay me a visit. I said, "O Allah's Messengerﷺ! I have much property and no heir except my single daughter. Shall I give two-thirds of my property in charity?" He said, "No." I said, "Half of it?" He said, "No." I said, "Onethird of it?" He said, "You may do so) though one-third is also to a much, for it is better for you to leave your off-spring wealthy than to leave them poor, asking others for help. And whatever you spend (for Allah's sake) you will be rewarded for it, even for a morsel of food which you may put in the mouth of your wife." I said, "O Allah's Messenger! Will I remain behind and fail to complete my emigration?" The Prophetﷺ said, "If you are left behind after me, whatever good deeds you will do for Allah's sake, that will upgrade you and raise you high. May be you will have long life so that some people may benefit by you and others (the enemies) be harmed by you." But Allah's Messengerﷺ felt sorry for Sa`d bin Khaula as he died in Mecca. (Sufyan, a sub-narrator said that Sa`d bin Khaula was a man from the tribe of Bani 'Amir bin Lu'ai.). – Sahih Al-Bukhari 6733

حَدَّثَنَا الْحُمَيْدِيُّ، حَدَّثَنَا سُفْيَانُ، حَدَّثَنَا الزُّهْرِيُّ، قَالَ أَخْبَرَنِي عَامِرُ بْنُ سَعْدِ بْنِ أَبِي وَقَّاصٍ، عَنْ أَبِيهِ، قَالَ مَرِضْتُ بِمَكَّةَ مَرَضًا، فَأَشْفَيْتُ مِنْهُ عَلَى الْمَوْتِ، فَأَتَانِي النَّبِيُّ صلى الله عليه وسلم يَعُودُنِي فَقُلْتُ يَا رَسُولَ اللَّهِ إِنَّ لِي مَالاً كَثِيرًا، وَلَيْسَ يَرِثُنِي إِلاَّ ابْنَتِي، أَفَأَتَصَدَّقُ بِثُلُثَىْ مَالِي قَالَ " لاَ ". قَالَ قُلْتُ فَالشَّطْرُ قَالَ " لاَ ". قُلْتُ الثُّلُثُ قَالَ " الثُّلُثُ كَبِيرٌ إِنَّكَ إِنْ تَرَكْتَ وَلَدَكَ أَغْنِيَاءَ خَيْرٌ مِنْ أَنْ تَتْرُكَهُمْ عَالَةً يَتَكَفَّفُونَ النَّاسَ، وَإِنَّكَ لَنْ تُنْفِقَ نَفَقَةً إِلاَّ أُجِرْتَ عَلَيْهَا، حَتَّى اللُّقْمَةَ تَرْفَعُهَا إِلَى فِي امْرَأَتِكَ ". فَقُلْتُ يَا رَسُولَ اللَّهِ أَأُخَلَّفُ عَنْ هِجْرَتِي فَقَالَ " لَنْ تُخَلَّفَ بَعْدِي فَتَعْمَلَ عَمَلاً تُرِيدُ بِهِ وَجْهَ اللَّهِ، إِلاَّ ازْدَدْتَ بِهِ رِفْعَةً وَدَرَجَةً، وَلَعَلَّ أَنْ تُخَلَّفَ بَعْدِي حَتَّى يَنْتَفِعَ بِكَ أَقْوَامٌ وَيُضَرَّ بِكَ آخَرُونَ، لَكِنِ الْبَائِسُ سَعْدُ ابْنُ خَوْلَةَ يَرْثِي لَهُ رَسُولُ اللَّهِ صلى الله عليه وسلم أَنْ مَاتَ بِمَكَّةَ ". قَالَ سُفْيَانُ وَسَعْدُ بْنُ خَوْلَةَ رَجُلٌ مِنْ بَنِي عَامِرِ بْنِ لُؤَىٍّ.

Narrated `Abdullah bin `Umar: Sa`d bin Abi Waqqas said, "The Prophet ﷺ passed wet hands over his Khuffs (socks made from thick fabric or leather)." `Abdullah bin `Umar asked `Umar about it. `Umar replied in the affirmative and added, "Whenever Sa`d narrates a Hadith from the Prophet, there is no need to ask anyone else about it.". – Sahih Al-Bukhari 202

حَدَّثَنَا أَصْبَغُ بْنُ الْفَرَجِ الْمِصْرِيُّ، عَنِ ابْنِ وَهْبٍ، قَالَ حَدَّثَنِي عَمْرٌو، حَدَّثَنِي أَبُو النَّضْرِ، عَنْ أَبِي سَلَمَةَ بْنِ عَبْدِ الرَّحْمَنِ، عَنْ عَبْدِ اللَّهِ بْنِ عُمَرَ، عَنْ سَعْدِ بْنِ أَبِي وَقَّاصٍ، عَنِ النَّبِيِّ صلى الله عليه وسلم أَنَّهُ مَسَحَ عَلَى الْخُفَّيْنِ. وَأَنَّ عَبْدَ اللَّهِ بْنَ عُمَرَ سَأَلَ عُمَرَ عَنْ ذَلِكَ فَقَالَ نَعَمْ إِذَا حَدَّثَكَ شَيْئًا سَعْدٌ عَنِ النَّبِيِّ صلى الله عليه وسلم فَلاَ تَسْأَلْ عَنْهُ غَيْرَهُ. وَقَالَ مُوسَى بْنُ عُقْبَةَ أَخْبَرَنِي أَبُو النَّضْرِ أَنَّ أَبَا سَلَمَةَ أَخْبَرَهُ أَنَّ سَعْدًا حَدَّثَهُ فَقَالَ عُمَرُ لِعَبْدِ اللَّهِ. نَحْوَهُ.

Narrated Sa`d bin Abi Waqqas: The Prophet ﷺ used to teach us these words as he used to teach us the Book (Qur'an): "O Allah! Seek refuge with You from miserliness, and seek refuge with You from cowardice, and seek refuge with You from being brought back to (senile) geriatric old age, and seek refuge with You from the affliction of the world and from the punishment in the Hereafter.". – Sahih Al-Bukhari 6390

حَدَّثَنَا فَرْوَةُ بْنُ أَبِي الْمَغْرَاءِ، حَدَّثَنَا عَبِيدَةُ بْنُ حُمَيْدٍ، عَنْ عَبْدِ الْمَلِكِ بْنِ عُمَيْرٍ، عَنْ مُصْعَبِ بْنِ سَعْدِ بْنِ أَبِي وَقَّاصٍ، عَنْ أَبِيهِ ـ رضى الله عنه ـ قَالَ كَانَ النَّبِيُّ صلى الله عليه وسلم يُعَلِّمُنَا هَؤُلاَءِ الْكَلِمَاتِ كَمَا تُعَلَّمُ الْكِتَابَةُ " اللَّهُمَّ إِنِّي أَعُوذُ بِكَ مِنَ الْبُخْلِ، وَأَعُوذُ بِكَ مِنَ الْجُبْنِ، وَأَعُوذُ بِكَ مِنْ أَنْ نُرَدَّ إِلَى أَرْذَلِ الْعُمُرِ، وَأَعُوذُ بِكَ مِنْ فِتْنَةِ الدُّنْيَا، وَعَذَابِ الْقَبْرِ "

Narrated `Aisha: The Prophet ﷺ was vigilant one night and when he reached Medina, he said, "Would that a pious man from my companions guard me tonight!" Suddenly we heard the clatter of arms. He said, "Who is that? " He (The new comer) replied, " I am Sa`d bin Abi Waqqas and have come to guard you." So, the Prophet ﷺ slept (that night). – Sahih Al-Bukhari 2885

حَدَّثَنَا إِسْمَاعِيلُ بْنُ خَلِيلٍ، أَخْبَرَنَا عَلِيُّ بْنُ مُسْهِرٍ، أَخْبَرَنَا يَحْيَى بْنُ سَعِيدٍ، أَخْبَرَنَا عَبْدُ اللَّهِ بْنُ عَامِرِ بْنِ رَبِيعَةَ، قَالَ سَمِعْتُ عَائِشَةَ ـ رضى الله عنها ـ تَقُولُ كَانَ النَّبِيُّ صلى الله عليه وسلم سَهِرَ فَلَمَّا قَدِمَ الْمَدِينَةَ قَالَ " لَيْتَ رَجُلاً مِنْ أَصْحَابِي صَالِحًا يَحْرُسُنِي اللَّيْلَةَ ". إِذْ سَمِعْنَا صَوْتَ سِلاَحٍ فَقَالَ " مَنْ هَذَا ". فَقَالَ أَنَا سَعْدُ بْنُ أَبِي وَقَّاصٍ، جِئْتُ لأَحْرُسَكَ. وَنَامَ النَّبِيُّ صلى الله عليه وسلم

Narrated Sa`d bin Abi Waqqas: The Prophet ﷺ said, "The most sinful person among the Muslims is the one who asked about something which had not been prohibited, but was prohibited because of his asking.". – Sahih Al-Bukhari 7289

حَدَّثَنَا عَبْدُ اللَّهِ بْنُ يَزِيدَ الْمُقْرِئُ، حَدَّثَنَا سَعِيدٌ، حَدَّثَنِي عُقَيْلٌ، عَنِ ابْنِ شِهَابٍ، عَنْ عَامِرِ بْنِ سَعْدِ بْنِ أَبِي وَقَّاصٍ، عَنْ أَبِيهِ، أَنَّ النَّبِيَّ صلى الله عليه وسلم قَالَ " إِنَّ أَعْظَمَ الْمُسْلِمِينَ جُرْمًا مَنْ سَأَلَ عَنْ شَىْءٍ لَمْ يُحَرَّمْ، فَحُرِّمَ مِنْ أَجْلِ مَسْأَلَتِهِ "

Narrated Sa`d bin Abi Waqqas: I have never heard the Prophet ﷺ saying about anybody walking on the earth that he is from the people of Paradise except `Abdullah bin Salam. The following Verse was revealed concerning him: "And a witness from the children of Israel testifies that this Qur'an is true" (46.10). – Sahih Al-Bukhari 3812

حَدَّثَنَا عَبْدُ اللَّهِ بْنُ يُوسُفَ، قَالَ سَمِعْتُ مَالِكًا، يُحَدِّثُ عَنْ أَبِي النَّضْرِ، مَوْلَى عُمَرَ بْنِ عُبَيْدِ اللَّهِ عَنْ عَامِرِ بْنِ سَعْدِ بْنِ أَبِي وَقَّاصٍ، عَنْ أَبِيهِ، قَالَ مَا سَمِعْتُ النَّبِيَّ صلى الله عليه وسلم يَقُولُ لأَحَدٍ يَمْشِي عَلَى الأَرْضِ إِنَّهُ مِنْ أَهْلِ الْجَنَّةِ. إِلاَّ لِعَبْدِ اللَّهِ بْنِ سَلاَمٍ قَالَ وَفِيهِ نَزَلَتْ هَذِهِ الآيَةُ {وَشَهِدَ شَاهِدٌ مِنْ بَنِي إِسْرَائِيلَ} الآيَةَ. قَالَ لاَ أَدْرِي قَالَ مَالِكٌ الآيَةَ أَوْ فِي الْحَدِيثِ

Narrated Mus`ab bin Sa`d: Once Sa`d (bin Abi Waqqas) thought that he was superior to those who were below him in rank. On that the Prophet ﷺ said, "You gain no victory or livelihood except through (the blessings and invocations of) the poor amongst you.". – Sahih Al-Bukhari 2896

حَدَّثَنَا سُلَيْمَانُ بْنُ حَرْبٍ، حَدَّثَنَا مُحَمَّدُ بْنُ طَلْحَةَ، عَنْ طَلْحَةَ، عَنْ مُصْعَبِ بْنِ سَعْدٍ، قَالَ رَأَى سَعْدٌ ـ رضى الله عنه ـ أَنَّ لَهُ فَضْلاً عَلَى مَنْ دُونَهُ، فَقَالَ النَّبِيُّ صلى الله عليه وسلم " هَلْ تُنْصَرُونَ وَتُرْزَقُونَ إِلاَّ بِضُعَفَائِكُمْ ".

Uqba ibn Amir al-Juhani
عقبة بن عامر الجهني

Narrated `Uqba bin 'Amir: My sister vowed to go on foot to the Ka`ba, and she asked me to take the verdict of the Prophet ﷺ about it. So, I did and the Prophet ﷺ said, "She should walk and also should ride." Narrated Abul-Khair from `Uqba as above.- Sahih al-Bukhari 1866
حَدَّثَنَا إِبْرَاهِيمُ بْنُ مُوسَى، أَخْبَرَنَا هِشَامُ بْنُ يُوسُفَ، أَنَّ ابْنَ جُرَيْجٍ، أَخْبَرَهُمْ قَالَ أَخْبَرَنِي سَعِيدُ بْنُ أَبِي أَيُّوبَ، أَنَّ يَزِيدَ بْنَ أَبِي حَبِيبٍ، أَخْبَرَهُ أَنَّ أَبَا الْخَيْرِ حَدَّثَهُ عَنْ عُقْبَةَ بْنِ عَامِرٍ، قَالَ نَذَرَتْ أُخْتِي أَنْ تَمْشِيَ، إِلَى بَيْتِ اللَّهِ، وَأَمَرَتْنِي أَنْ أَسْتَفْتِيَ لَهَا النَّبِيَّ صلى الله عليه وسلم فَاسْتَفْتَيْتُهُ، فَقَالَ عَلَيْهِ السَّلاَمُ " لِتَمْشِ وَلْتَرْكَبْ ". قَالَ وَكَانَ أَبُو الْخَيْرِ لاَ يُفَارِقُ عُقْبَةَ. قَالَ أَبُو عَبْدِ اللَّهِ حَدَّثَنَا أَبُو عَاصِمٍ عَنِ ابْنِ جُرَيْجٍ عَنْ يَحْيَى بْنِ أَيُّوبَ عَنْ يَزِيدَ عَنْ أَبِي الْخَيْرِ عَنْ عُقْبَةَ فَذَكَرَ الْحَدِيثَ

Narrated Marthad bin `Abdullah Al-Yazani: I went to `Uqba bin 'Amir Al-Juhani and said, "Is it not surprising that Abi Tamim offers two rak`at before the Maghrib prayer?" `Uqba said, "We used to do so in the lifetime of Allah's Messenger ﷺ." I asked him, "What prevents you from offering it now?" He replied, "Business." – Sahih al-Bukhari 1184
حَدَّثَنَا عَبْدُ اللَّهِ بْنُ يَزِيدَ، قَالَ حَدَّثَنَا سَعِيدُ بْنُ أَبِي أَيُّوبَ، قَالَ حَدَّثَنِي يَزِيدُ بْنُ أَبِي حَبِيبٍ، قَالَ سَمِعْتُ مَرْثَدَ بْنَ عَبْدِ اللَّهِ الْيَزَنِيَّ، قَالَ أَتَيْتُ عُقْبَةَ بْنَ عَامِرٍ الْجُهَنِيَّ فَقُلْتُ أَلاَ أُعْجِبُكَ مِنْ أَبِي تَمِيمٍ يَرْكَعُ رَكْعَتَيْنِ قَبْلَ صَلاَةِ الْمَغْرِبِ. فَقَالَ عُقْبَةُ إِنَّا كُنَّا نَفْعَلُهُ عَلَى عَهْدِ رَسُولِ اللَّهِ صلى الله عليه وسلم. قُلْتُ فَمَا يَمْنَعُكَ الآنَ قَالَ الشُّغْلُ.

Narrated `Uqba bin 'Amir Al-Juhani: That the Prophet ﷺ distributed among his companions some animals for sacrifice (to be slaughtered on `Id-al-Adha). `Uqba's share was a Jadha'a (a six month old goat). `Uqba said, "O Allah's Messenger ﷺ ! I get in my share of Jadha'a (a six month old ram)." The Prophet ﷺ said, "Slaughter it as a sacrifice." – Sahih al-Bukhari 5547
حَدَّثَنَا مُعَاذُ بْنُ فَضَالَةَ، حَدَّثَنَا هِشَامٌ، عَنْ يَحْيَى، عَنْ بَعْجَةَ الْجُهَنِيِّ، عَنْ عُقْبَةَ بْنِ عَامِرٍ الْجُهَنِيِّ، قَالَ قَسَمَ النَّبِيُّ صلى الله عليه وسلم بَيْنَ أَصْحَابِهِ ضَحَايَا، فَصَارَتْ لِعُقْبَةَ جَذَعَةٌ. فَقُلْتُ يَا رَسُولَ اللَّهِ صَارَتْ جَذَعَةٌ. قَالَ " ضَحِّ بِهَا ".

Narrated Uqbah ibn Amir: When "Glorify the name of your mighty Lord" was revealed, the Messenger of Allah ﷺ said: Use it when bowing, and when "Glorify the name of your most high Lord" was revealed, he said: Use it when prostrating yourself. – Sunan Abi Dawud 869
حَدَّثَنَا الرَّبِيعُ بْنُ نَافِعٍ أَبُو تَوْبَةَ، وَمُوسَى بْنُ إِسْمَاعِيلَ، - الْمَعْنَى – قَالاَ حَدَّثَنَا ابْنُ الْمُبَارَكِ، عَنْ مُوسَى، - قَالَ أَبُو سَلَمَةَ مُوسَى بْنِ أَيُّوبَ – عَنْ عَمِّهِ، عَنْ عُقْبَةَ بْنِ عَامِرٍ، قَالَ لَمَّا نَزَلَتْ { فَسَبِّحْ بِاسْمِ رَبِّكَ الْعَظِيمِ } قَالَ رَسُولُ اللَّهِ صلى الله عليه وسلم " اجْعَلُوهَا فِي رُكُوعِكُمْ " . فَلَمَّا نَزَلَتْ { سَبِّحِ اسْمَ رَبِّكَ الأَعْلَى } قَالَ " اجْعَلُوهَا فِي سُجُودِكُمْ " .

Abdullah ibn Umm-Maktum
عبد الله بن أم مكتوم

Narrated Al-Bara: When the Verse:-- "Not equal are those of the believers who sit (at home)" (4.95) was revealed, Allah Apostle called for Zaid who wrote it. In the meantime Ibn Um

Maktum came and complained of his blindness, so Allah revealed: "Except those who are disabled (by injury or are blind or lame..." etc.) (4.95). – Sahih al-Bukhari 4593

حَدَّثَنَا حَفْصُ بْنُ عُمَرَ، حَدَّثَنَا شُعْبَةُ، عَنْ أَبِي إِسْحَاقَ، عَنِ الْبَرَاءِ ـ رضى الله عنه ـ قَالَ لَمَّا نَزَلَتْ {لاَ يَسْتَوِي الْقَاعِدُونَ مِنَ الْمُؤْمِنِينَ} دَعَا رَسُولُ اللَّهِ صلى الله عليه وسلم زَيْدًا فَكَتَبَهَا، فَجَاءَ ابْنُ أُمِّ مَكْتُومٍ فَشَكَا ضَرَارَتَهُ، فَأَنْزَلَ اللَّهُ {غَيْرَ أُولِي الضَّرَرِ}

Narrated Salim bin `Abdullah: My father said that Allah s Apostle said, "Bilal pronounces 'Adhan at night, so keep on eating and drinking (Suhur) till Ibn Um Maktum pronounces Adhan." Salim added, "He was a blind man who would not pronounce the Adhan unless he was told that the day had dawned." - Sahih al-Bukhari 617

حَدَّثَنَا عَبْدُ اللَّهِ بْنُ مَسْلَمَةَ، عَنْ مَالِكٍ، عَنِ ابْنِ شِهَابٍ، عَنْ سَالِمِ بْنِ عَبْدِ اللَّهِ، عَنْ أَبِيهِ، أَنَّ رَسُولَ اللَّهِ صلى الله عليه وسلم قَالَ " إِنَّ بِلاَلاً يُؤَذِّنُ بِلَيْلٍ، فَكُلُوا وَاشْرَبُوا حَتَّى يُنَادِيَ ابْنُ أُمِّ مَكْتُومٍ ". ثُمَّ قَالَ وَكَانَ رَجُلاً أَعْمَى لاَ يُنَادِي حَتَّى يُقَالَ لَهُ أَصْبَحْتَ أَصْبَحْتَ

Narrated Sahl bin Sa`d As-Sa`idi: I saw Marwan bin Al-Hakam sitting in the Mosque. So I came forward and sat by his side. He told us that Zaid bin Thabit had told him that Allah's Messenger ﷺ had dictated to him the Divine Verse: "Not equal are those believers who sit (at home) and those who strive hard and fight in the Cause of Allah with their wealth and lives.' (4.95) Zaid said, "Ibn-Maktum came to the Prophet ﷺ while he was dictating to me that very Verse. On that Ibn Um Maktum said, "O Allah's Messenger ﷺ ! If I had power, I would surely take part in Jihad." He was a blind man. So Allah sent down revelation to His Apostle while his thigh was on mine and it became so heavy for me that I feared that my thigh would be broken. Then that state of the Prophet ﷺ was over after Allah revealed "...except those who are disabled (by injury or are blind or lame etc.) (4.95) - Sahih al-Bukhari 2832

حَدَّثَنَا عَبْدُ الْعَزِيزِ بْنُ عَبْدِ اللَّهِ، حَدَّثَنَا إِبْرَاهِيمُ بْنُ سَعْدٍ الزُّهْرِيُّ، قَالَ حَدَّثَنِي صَالِحُ بْنُ كَيْسَانَ، عَنِ ابْنِ شِهَابٍ، عَنْ سَهْلِ بْنِ سَعْدٍ السَّاعِدِيِّ، أَنَّهُ قَالَ رَأَيْتُ مَرْوَانَ بْنَ الْحَكَمِ جَالِسًا فِي الْمَسْجِدِ، فَأَقْبَلْتُ حَتَّى جَلَسْتُ إِلَى جَنْبِهِ، فَأَخْبَرَنَا أَنَّ زَيْدَ بْنَ ثَابِتٍ أَخْبَرَهُ أَنَّ رَسُولَ اللَّهِ صلى الله عليه وسلم أَمْلَى عَلَيْهِ لاَ يَسْتَوِي الْقَاعِدُونَ مِنَ الْمُؤْمِنِينَ وَالْمُجَاهِدُونَ فِي سَبِيلِ اللَّهِ قَالَ فَجَاءَهُ ابْنُ أُمِّ مَكْتُومٍ وَهُوَ يُمِلُّهَا عَلَىَّ، فَقَالَ يَا رَسُولَ اللَّهِ، لَوْ أَسْتَطِيعُ الْجِهَادَ لَجَاهَدْتُ. وَكَانَ رَجُلاً أَعْمَى، فَأَنْزَلَ اللَّهُ تَبَارَكَ وَتَعَالَى عَلَى رَسُولِهِ صلى الله عليه وسلم وَفَخِذُهُ عَلَى فَخِذِي، فَثَقُلَتْ عَلَىَّ حَتَّى خِفْتُ أَنْ تَرُضَّ فَخِذِي، ثُمَّ سُرِّيَ عَنْهُ، فَأَنْزَلَ اللَّهُ عَزَّ وَجَلَّ {غَيْرُ أُولِي الضَّرَرِ}

Narrated Al-Bara: The first of the companions of the Prophet ﷺ who came to us (in Medina), were Mus`ab bin `Umar and Ibn Um Maktum, and they started teaching us the Qur'an. Then came `Ammar, Bilal and Sa`d. Afterwards `Umar bin Al-Kkattab came along with a batch of twenty (men): and after that the Prophet ﷺ came. I never saw the people of Medina so pleased with anything as they were with his arrival, so that even the little boys and girls were saying, "This is Allah's Messenger ﷺ who has come." He (the Prophet ﷺ) did not come (to Medina) till I had learnt Surat Al-Ala and also other similar Suras. – Sahih al-Bukhari 4941

حَدَّثَنَا عَبْدَانُ، قَالَ أَخْبَرَنِي أَبِي، عَنْ شُعْبَةَ، عَنْ أَبِي إِسْحَاقَ، عَنِ الْبَرَاءِ ـ رضى الله عنه ـ قَالَ أَوَّلُ مَنْ قَدِمَ عَلَيْنَا مِنْ أَصْحَابِ النَّبِيِّ صلى الله عليه وسلم مُصْعَبُ بْنُ عُمَيْرٍ وَابْنُ أُمِّ مَكْتُومٍ فَجَعَلاَ يُقْرِئَانِنَا الْقُرْآنَ، ثُمَّ جَاءَ عَمَّارٌ وَبِلاَلٌ وَسَعْدٌ ثُمَّ جَاءَ عُمَرُ بْنُ الْخَطَّابِ فِي عِشْرِينَ ثُمَّ جَاءَ النَّبِيُّ صلى الله عليه وسلم فَمَا رَأَيْتُ أَهْلَ الْمَدِينَةِ فَرِحُوا بِشَىْءٍ فَرَحَهُمْ بِهِ، حَتَّى رَأَيْتُ الْوَلاَئِدَ وَالصِّبْيَانَ يَقُولُونَ هَذَا رَسُولُ اللَّهِ قَدْ جَاءَ. فَمَا جَاءَ حَتَّى قَرَأْتُ {سَبِّحِ اسْمَ رَبِّكَ الأَعْلَى} فِي سُوَرٍ مِثْلِهَا

Āmir ibn ʿAbd Allāh ibn al-Jarrāḥ

عامر بن عبدالله بن الجراح

Narrated Jabir: The Prophet ﷺ sent us as an army unit of three hundred warriors under the command of Abu 'Ubaida to ambush a caravan of the Quraish. But we were struck with such severe hunger that we ate the Khabt (desert bushes), so our army was called the Army of the Khabt. Then the sea threw a huge fish called Al-`Anbar and we ate of it for half a month and rubbed our bodies with its fat till our bodies became healthy. Then Abu Ubaida took one of its ribs and fixed it over the ground and a rider passed underneath it. There was a man amongst us who slaughtered three camels when hunger became severe, and he slaughtered three more, but after that Abu 'Ubaida forbade him to do so. – Sahih Al-Bukhari 5494

حَدَّثَنَا عَبْدُ اللَّهِ بْنُ مُحَمَّدٍ، أَخْبَرَنَا سُفْيَانُ، عَنْ عَمْرٍو، قَالَ سَمِعْتُ جَابِرًا، يَقُولُ بَعَثَنَا النَّبِيُّ صلى الله عليه وسلم ثَلاَثَمِائَةِ رَاكِبٍ وَأَمِيرُنَا أَبُو عُبَيْدَةَ نَرْصُدُ عِيرًا لِقُرَيْشٍ فَأَصَابَنَا جُوعٌ شَدِيدٌ حَتَّى أَكَلْنَا الْخَبَطَ، فَسُمِّيَ جَيْشَ الْخَبَطِ وَأَلْقَى الْبَحْرُ حُوتًا يُقَالُ لَهُ الْعَنْبَرُ فَأَكَلْنَا نِصْفَ شَهْرٍ وَادَّهَنَّا بِوَدَكِهِ حَتَّى صَلَحَتْ أَجْسَامُنَا قَالَ فَأَخَذَ أَبُو عُبَيْدَةَ ضِلَعًا مِنْ أَضْلاَعِهِ فَنَصَبَهُ فَمَرَّ الرَّاكِبُ تَحْتَهُ، وَكَانَ فِينَا رَجُلٌ فَلَمَّا اشْتَدَّ الْجُوعُ نَحَرَ ثَلاَثَ جَزَائِرَ، ثُمَّ ثَلاَثَ جَزَائِرَ، ثُمَّ نَهَاهُ أَبُو عُبَيْدَةَ

Narrated Al-Miswar bin Makhrama: That `Amr bin `Auf, who was an ally of Bani 'Amir bin Luai and one of those who fought at Badr in the company of the Prophet ﷺ, said, "Allah's Messenger ﷺ sent Abu 'Ubaida bin Al-Jarrah to Bahrain to bring the Jizya taxation from its people, for Allah's Messenger ﷺ had made a peace treaty with the people of Bahrain and appointed Al-`Ala' bin Al-Hadrami as their ruler. So, Abu 'Ubaida arrived with the money from Bahrain. When the Ansar heard of the arrival of Abu 'Ubaida (on the next day) they offered the morning prayer with the Prophet ﷺ and when the morning prayer had finished, they presented themselves before him. On seeing the Ansar, Allah's Messenger ﷺ smiled and said, "I think you have heard that Abu 'Ubaida has brought something?" They replied, "Indeed, it is so, O Allah's Apostle!" He said, "Be happy, and hope for what will please you. By Allah, I am not afraid that you will be poor, but I fear that worldly wealth will be bestowed upon you as it was bestowed upon those who lived before you. So you will compete amongst yourselves for it, as they competed for it and it will destroy you as it did them.". – Sahih Al-Bukhari 4015

حَدَّثَنَا عَبْدَانُ، أَخْبَرَنَا عَبْدُ اللَّهِ، أَخْبَرَنَا مَعْمَرٌ، وَيُونُسُ، عَنِ الزُّهْرِيِّ، عَنْ عُرْوَةَ بْنِ الزُّبَيْرِ، أَنَّهُ أَخْبَرَهُ أَنَّ الْمِسْوَرَ بْنَ مَخْرَمَةَ أَخْبَرَهُ أَنَّ عَمْرَو بْنَ عَوْفٍ وَهْوَ حَلِيفٌ لِبَنِي عَامِرِ بْنِ لُؤَىٍّ، وَكَانَ شَهِدَ بَدْرًا مَعَ النَّبِيِّ صلى الله عليه وسلم أَنَّ رَسُولَ اللَّهِ صلى الله عليه وسلم بَعَثَ أَبَا عُبَيْدَةَ بْنَ الْجَرَّاحِ إِلَى الْبَحْرَيْنِ يَأْتِي بِجِزْيَتِهَا، وَكَانَ رَسُولُ اللَّهِ صلى الله عليه وسلم هُوَ صَالَحَ أَهْلَ الْبَحْرَيْنِ، وَأَمَّرَ عَلَيْهِمُ الْعَلاَءَ بْنَ الْحَضْرَمِيِّ، فَقَدِمَ أَبُو عُبَيْدَةَ بِمَالٍ مِنَ الْبَحْرَيْنِ فَسَمِعَتِ الأَنْصَارُ بِقُدُومِ أَبِي عُبَيْدَةَ، فَوَافَوْا صَلاَةَ الْفَجْرِ مَعَ النَّبِيِّ صلى الله عليه وسلم، فَلَمَّا انْصَرَفَ تَعَرَّضُوا لَهُ، فَتَبَسَّمَ رَسُولُ اللَّهِ صلى الله عليه وسلم حِينَ رَآهُمْ ثُمَّ قَالَ " أَظُنُّكُمْ سَمِعْتُمْ أَنَّ أَبَا عُبَيْدَةَ قَدِمَ بِشَىْءٍ ". قَالُوا أَجَلْ يَا رَسُولَ اللَّهِ. قَالَ " فَأَبْشِرُوا وَأَمِّلُوا مَا يَسُرُّكُمْ، فَوَاللَّهِ مَا الْفَقْرَ أَخْشَى عَلَيْكُمْ، وَلَكِنِّي أَخْشَى أَنْ تُبْسَطَ عَلَيْكُمُ الدُّنْيَا كَمَا بُسِطَتْ عَلَى مَنْ قَبْلَكُمْ، فَتَنَافَسُوهَا كَمَا تَنَافَسُوهَا، وَتُهْلِكَكُمْ كَمَا أَهْلَكَتْهُمْ ".

Narrated Wahab bin Kaisan: Jabir bin `Abdullah said, "Allah's Messenger ﷺ sent troops to the sea coast and appointed Abu 'Ubaida bin Al-Jarrah as their commander, and they were 300 (men). We set out, and we had covered some distance on the way, when our journey food ran short. So Abu 'Ubaida ordered that all the food present with the troops be collected, and it was collected. Our journey food was dates, and Abu Ubaida kept on giving us our daily ration from it little by little (piecemeal) till it decreased to such an extent that we did not receive except a date each." I asked (Jabir), "How could one date benefit you?" He said, "We came to know its value when even that finished." Jabir added, "Then we reached the sea (coast) where we found a fish like a small mountain. The people (i.e. troops) ate of it for 18 nights (i.e. days). Then Abu 'Ubaida ordered that two of its ribs be fixed on the ground (in the form of an arch) and that a she-camel be ridden and passed under them. So it passed under them without touching them.". – Sahih Al-Bukhari 4360

حَدَّثَنَا إِسْمَاعِيلُ، قَالَ حَدَّثَنِي مَالِكٌ، عَنْ وَهْبِ بْنِ كَيْسَانَ، عَنْ جَابِرِ بْنِ عَبْدِ اللَّهِ ـ رضى الله عنهما ـ أَنَّهُ قَالَ بَعَثَ رَسُولُ اللَّهِ صلى الله عليه وسلم بَعْثًا قِبَلَ السَّاحِلِ وَأَمَّرَ عَلَيْهِمْ أَبَا عُبَيْدَةَ بْنَ الْجَرَّاحِ وَهُمْ ثَلاَثُمِائَةٍ، فَخَرَجْنَا وَكُنَّا بِبَعْضِ الطَّرِيقِ فَنِيَ الزَّادُ فَأَمَرَ أَبُو عُبَيْدَةَ بِأَزْوَادِ الْجَيْشِ، فَجُمِعَ فَكَانَ مِزْوَدَىْ تَمْرٍ، فَكَانَ يَقُوتُنَا كُلَّ يَوْمٍ قَلِيلٌ قَلِيلٌ حَتَّى فَنِيَ، فَلَمْ يَكُنْ يُصِيبُنَا إِلاَّ تَمْرَةٌ تَمْرَةٌ فَقُلْتُ مَا تُغْنِي عَنْكُمْ تَمْرَةٌ فَقَالَ لَقَدْ وَجَدْنَا فَقْدَهَا حِينَ فَنِيَتْ. ثُمَّ انْتَهَيْنَا إِلَى الْبَحْرِ، فَإِذَا حُوتٌ مِثْلُ الظَّرِبِ فَأَكَلَ مِنْهَا الْقَوْمُ ثَمَانَ عَشْرَةَ لَيْلَةً، ثُمَّ أَمَرَ أَبُو عُبَيْدَةَ بِضِلَعَيْنِ مِنْ أَضْلاَعِهِ فَنُصِبَا، ثُمَّ أَمَرَ بِرَاحِلَةٍ فَرُحِلَتْ ثُمَّ مَرَّتْ تَحْتَهُمَا فَلَمْ تُصِبْهُمَا

Narrated Hudhaifa: Al-`Aqib and Saiyid, the rulers of Najran, came to Allah's Messenger ﷺ with the intention of doing Lian one of them said to the other, "Do not do (this Lian) for, by Allah, if he is a Prophet and we do this Lian, neither we, nor our offspring after us will be successful." Then both of them said (to the Prophet ﷺ), "We will give what you should ask but you should send a trustworthy man with us, and do not send any person with us but an honest one." The Prophet ﷺ said, "I will send an honest man who Is really trustworthy." Then every one of the companions of Allah's Messenger ﷺ wished to be that one. Then the Prophet said, "Get up, O Abu 'Ubaida bin Al-Jarrah." When he got up, Allah's Messenger ﷺ said, "This is the Trustworthy man of this (Muslim) nation.". – Sahih Al-Bukhari 4380

حَدَّثَنِي عَبَّاسُ بْنُ الْحُسَيْنِ، حَدَّثَنَا يَحْيَى بْنُ آدَمَ، عَنْ إِسْرَائِيلَ، عَنْ أَبِي إِسْحَاقَ، عَنْ صِلَةَ بْنِ زُفَرَ، عَنْ حُذَيْفَةَ، قَالَ جَاءَ الْعَاقِبُ وَالسَّيِّدُ صَاحِبَا نَجْرَانَ إِلَى رَسُولِ اللَّهِ صلى الله عليه وسلم يُرِيدَانِ أَنْ يُلاَعِنَاهُ، قَالَ فَقَالَ أَحَدُهُمَا لِصَاحِبِهِ لاَ تَفْعَلْ، فَوَاللَّهِ لَئِنْ كَانَ نَبِيًّا فَلاَعَنَّا، لاَ نُفْلِحُ نَحْنُ وَلاَ عَقِبُنَا مِنْ بَعْدِنَا. قَالاَ إِنَّا نُعْطِيكَ مَا سَأَلْتَنَا، وَابْعَثْ مَعَنَا رَجُلاً أَمِينًا، وَلاَ تَبْعَثْ مَعَنَا إِلاَّ أَمِينًا. فَقَالَ " لأَبْعَثَنَّ مَعَكُمْ رَجُلاً أَمِينًا حَقَّ أَمِينٍ ". فَاسْتَشْرَفَ لَهُ أَصْحَابُ رَسُولِ اللَّهِ صلى الله عليه وسلم فَقَالَ " قُمْ يَا أَبَا عُبَيْدَةَ بْنَ الْجَرَّاحِ ". فَلَمَّا قَامَ قَالَ رَسُولُ اللَّهِ صلى الله عليه وسلم " هَذَا أَمِينُ هَذِهِ الأُمَّةِ "

Narrated Al-Miswar bin Makhrama: That `Amr bin `Auf, who was an ally of Bani 'Amir bin Luai and one of those who fought at Badr in the company of the Prophet ﷺ, said, "Allah's Messenger ﷺ sent Abu 'Ubaida bin Al-Jarrah to Bahrain to bring the Jizya taxation from its people, for Allah's Messenger ﷺ had made a peace treaty with the people of Bahrain and appointed Al-`Ala' bin Al-Hadrami as their ruler. So, Abu 'Ubaida arrived with the money from Bahrain. When the Ansar heard of the arrival of Abu 'Ubaida (on the next day) they offered the morning prayer with the Prophet ﷺ and when the morning prayer had finished, they presented themselves before him. On seeing the Ansar, Allah's Messenger ﷺ smiled and said, "I think you have heard that Abu 'Ubaida has brought something?" They replied, "Indeed, it is so, O Allah's Apostle!" He said, "Be happy, and hope for what will please you. By Allah, I am not afraid that you will be poor, but I fear that worldly wealth will be bestowed upon you as it was bestowed upon those who lived before you. So you will compete amongst yourselves for it, as they competed for it and it will destroy you as it did them.". – Sahih Al-Bukhari 4015

حَدَّثَنَا عَبْدَانُ، أَخْبَرَنَا عَبْدُ اللَّهِ، أَخْبَرَنَا مَعْمَرٌ، وَيُونُسُ، عَنِ الزُّهْرِيِّ، عَنْ عُرْوَةَ بْنِ الزُّبَيْرِ، أَنَّهُ أَخْبَرَهُ أَنَّ الْمِسْوَرَ بْنَ مَخْرَمَةَ أَخْبَرَهُ أَنَّ عَمْرَو بْنَ عَوْفٍ وَهْوَ حَلِيفٌ لِبَنِي عَامِرِ بْنِ لُؤَىٍّ، وَكَانَ شَهِدَ بَدْرًا مَعَ النَّبِيِّ صلى الله عليه وسلم أَنَّ رَسُولَ اللَّهِ صلى الله عليه وسلم بَعَثَ أَبَا عُبَيْدَةَ بْنَ الْجَرَّاحِ إِلَى الْبَحْرَيْنِ يَأْتِي بِجِزْيَتِهَا، وَكَانَ رَسُولُ اللَّهِ صلى الله عليه وسلم هُوَ صَالَحَ أَهْلَ الْبَحْرَيْنِ، وَأَمَّرَ عَلَيْهِمِ الْعَلاَءَ بْنَ الْحَضْرَمِيِّ، فَقَدِمَ أَبُو عُبَيْدَةَ بِمَالٍ مِنَ الْبَحْرَيْنِ فَسَمِعَتِ الأَنْصَارُ بِقُدُومِ أَبِي عُبَيْدَةَ، فَوَافَوْا صَلاَةَ الْفَجْرِ مَعَ النَّبِيِّ صلى الله عليه وسلم، فَلَمَّا انْصَرَفَ تَعَرَّضُوا لَهُ، فَتَبَسَّمَ رَسُولُ اللَّهِ صلى الله عليه وسلم حِينَ رَآهُمْ ثُمَّ قَالَ " أَظُنُّكُمْ سَمِعْتُمْ أَنَّ أَبَا عُبَيْدَةَ قَدِمَ بِشَىْءٍ ". قَالُوا أَجَلْ يَا رَسُولَ اللَّهِ. قَالَ " فَأَبْشِرُوا وَأَمِّلُوا مَا يَسُرُّكُمْ، فَوَاللَّهِ مَا الْفَقْرَ أَخْشَى عَلَيْكُمْ، وَلَكِنِّي أَخْشَى أَنْ تُبْسَطَ عَلَيْكُمُ الدُّنْيَا كَمَا بُسِطَتْ عَلَى مَنْ قَبْلَكُمْ، فَتَنَافَسُوهَا كَمَا تَنَافَسُوهَا، وَتُهْلِكَكُمْ كَمَا أَهْلَكَتْهُمْ ".

Narrated `Abdullah bin `Abbas: `Umar bin Al-Khattab departed for Sham and when he reached Sargh, the commanders of the (Muslim) army, Abu 'Ubaida bin Al-Jarrah and his companions met him and told him that an epidemic had broken out in Sham. `Umar said, "Call for me the early emigrants." So `Umar called them, consulted them and informed them that an epidemic had broken out in Sham. Those people differed in their opinions. Some of them said, "We have come out for a purpose and we do not think that it is proper to give it up," while others said (to `Umar), "You have along with you. Other people and the companions of Allah's Messenger ﷺ so do not advise that we take them to this epidemic." `Umar said to them, "Leave me now." Then he said, "Call the Ansar for me." I called them and he consulted them and they followed the way of the emigrants and differed as they did. He then said to them, Leave me now," and added, "Call for me the old people of Quraish who emigrated in the year of the Conquest of Mecca." I called them and they gave a unanimous opinion saying, "We advise that you should return with the people and do not take them to that (place) of epidemic." So `Umar made an announcement, "I will ride back to Medina in the morning, so you should do the same." Abu 'Ubaida bin Al-Jarrah said (to `Umar), "Are you running away from what Allah had ordained?" `Umar said, "Would that someone else had said such a thing, O Abu 'Ubaida! Yes, we are running from what Allah had ordained to what Allah has ordained. Don't you agree that if you had camels that went down a valley having two places, one green and the other dry, you would graze them on the green one only if Allah had ordained that, and you would graze them on the dry one only if Allah had ordained that?" At that time `Abdur-Rahman bin `Auf, who had been absent because of some job, came and said, "I have some knowledge about this. I have heard Allah's Messenger ﷺ saying, 'If you hear about it (an outbreak of plague) in a land, do not go to it; but if plague breaks out in a country where you are staying, do not run away from it.' " `Umar thanked Allah and returned to Medina. – Sahih Al-Bukhari 5729

حَدَّثَنَا عَبْدُ اللَّهِ بْنُ يُوسُفَ، أَخْبَرَنَا مَالِكٌ، عَنِ ابْنِ شِهَابٍ، عَنْ عَبْدِ الْحَمِيدِ بْنِ عَبْدِ الرَّحْمَنِ بْنِ زَيْدِ بْنِ الْخَطَّابِ، عَنْ عَبْدِ اللَّهِ بْنِ عَبْدِ اللَّهِ بْنِ الْحَارِثِ بْنِ نَوْفَلٍ، عَنْ عَبْدِ اللَّهِ بْنِ عَبَّاسٍ، أَنَّ عُمَرَ بْنَ الْخَطَّابِ ـ رضى الله عنه ـ خَرَجَ إِلَى الشَّأْمِ حَتَّى إِذَا كَانَ بِسَرْغَ لَقِيَهُ أُمَرَاءُ الأَجْنَادِ أَبُو عُبَيْدَةَ بْنُ الْجَرَّاحِ وَأَصْحَابُهُ، فَأَخْبَرُوهُ أَنَّ الْوَبَاءَ قَدْ وَقَعَ بِأَرْضِ الشَّأْمِ. قَالَ ابْنُ عَبَّاسٍ فَقَالَ عُمَرُ ادْعُ لِي الْمُهَاجِرِينَ الأَوَّلِينَ. فَدَعَاهُمْ فَاسْتَشَارَهُمْ وَأَخْبَرَهُمْ أَنَّ الْوَبَاءَ قَدْ وَقَعَ بِالشَّأْمِ فَاخْتَلَفُوا. فَقَالَ بَعْضُهُمْ قَدْ خَرَجْتَ لأَمْرٍ، وَلاَ نَرَى أَنْ تَرْجِعَ عَنْهُ. وَقَالَ بَعْضُهُمْ مَعَكَ بَقِيَّةُ النَّاسِ وَأَصْحَابُ رَسُولِ اللَّهِ صلى الله عليه وسلم وَلاَ نَرَى أَنْ تُقْدِمَهُمْ عَلَى هَذَا الْوَبَاءِ. فَقَالَ ارْتَفِعُوا عَنِّي. ثُمَّ قَالَ ادْعُوا لِي الأَنْصَارَ. فَدَعَوْتُهُمْ فَاسْتَشَارَهُمْ، فَسَلَكُوا سَبِيلَ الْمُهَاجِرِينَ، وَاخْتَلَفُوا كَاخْتِلاَفِهِمْ، فَقَالَ ارْتَفِعُوا عَنِّي. ثُمَّ قَالَ ادْعُ لِي مَنْ كَانَ هَا هُنَا مِنْ مَشْيَخَةِ قُرَيْشٍ مِنْ مُهَاجِرَةِ الْفَتْحِ. فَدَعَوْتُهُمْ، فَلَمْ يَخْتَلِفْ مِنْهُمْ عَلَيْهِ رَجُلاَنِ، فَقَالُوا نَرَى أَنْ تَرْجِعَ بِالنَّاسِ، وَلاَ تُقْدِمَهُمْ عَلَى هَذَا الْوَبَاءِ، فَنَادَى عُمَرُ فِي النَّاسِ، إِنِّي مُصَبِّحٌ عَلَى ظَهْرٍ، فَأَصْبِحُوا عَلَيْهِ. قَالَ أَبُو عُبَيْدَةَ بْنُ الْجَرَّاحِ أَفِرَارًا مِنْ قَدَرِ اللَّهِ فَقَالَ عُمَرُ لَوْ غَيْرُكَ قَالَهَا يَا أَبَا عُبَيْدَةَ، نَعَمْ نَفِرُّ مِنْ قَدَرِ اللَّهِ إِلَى قَدَرِ اللَّهِ، أَرَأَيْتَ لَوْ كَانَ لَكَ إِبِلٌ هَبَطَتْ وَادِيًا لَهُ عُدْوَتَانِ، إِحْدَاهُمَا خَصِبَةٌ، وَالأُخْرَى جَدْبَةٌ، أَلَيْسَ إِنْ رَعَيْتَ الْخَصْبَةَ رَعَيْتَهَا بِقَدَرِ اللَّهِ، وَإِنْ رَعَيْتَ الْجَدْبَةَ رَعَيْتَهَا بِقَدَرِ اللَّهِ قَالَ فَجَاءَ عَبْدُ الرَّحْمَنِ بْنُ عَوْفٍ، وَكَانَ مُتَغَيِّبًا فِي بَعْضِ حَاجَتِهِ فَقَالَ إِنَّ عِنْدِي فِي هَذَا عِلْمًا سَمِعْتُ رَسُولَ اللَّهِ صلى الله عليه وسلم يَقُولُ " إِذَا سَمِعْتُمْ بِهِ بِأَرْضٍ فَلاَ تَقْدَمُوا عَلَيْهِ، وَإِذَا وَقَعَ بِأَرْضٍ وَأَنْتُمْ بِهَا فَلاَ تَخْرُجُوا فِرَارًا مِنْهُ ". قَالَ فَحَمِدَ اللَّهَ عُمَرُ ثُمَّ انْصَرَفَ

Narrated 'Aisha: (the wife of the Prophet) Allah's Messenger ﷺ died while Abu Bakr was at a place called As-Sunah (Al-'Aliya) 'Umar stood up and said, "By Allah! Allah's Messenger ﷺ is not dead!" 'Umar (later on) said, "By Allah! Nothing occurred to my mind except that." He said, "Verily! Allah will resurrect him and he will cut the hands and legs of some men." Then Abu Bakr came and uncovered the face of Allah's Messenger ﷺ, kissed him and said, "Let my mother and father be sacrificed for you, (O Allah's Messenger ﷺ), you are good in life and in death. By Allah in Whose Hands my life is, Allah will never make you taste death twice." Then he went out and said, "O oath-taker! Don't be hasty." When Abu Bakr spoke, 'Umar sat down. Abu Bakr praised and glorified Allah and said, No doubt! Whoever worshipped Muhammad, then Muhammad is dead, but whoever worshipped Allah, then Allah is Alive and shall never die." Then he recited Allah's Statement.:-- "(O Muhammad) Verily you will die, and they also will die." (39.30) He also recited:-- "Muhammad is no more than an Apostle; and indeed many Apostles have passed away, before him, If he dies Or is killed, will you then Turn back on your heels? And he who turns back On his heels, not the least Harm will he do to Allah And Allah will give reward to those Who are grateful." (3.144) The people wept loudly, and the Ansar were assembled with Sad bin 'Ubada in the shed of Bani Saida. They said (to the emigrants). "There should be one 'Amir from us and one from you." Then Abu Bakr, Umar bin Al-Khattab and Abu 'baida bin Al-Jarrah went to them. 'Umar wanted to speak but Abu Bakr stopped him. 'Umar later on used to say, "By Allah, I intended only to say something that appealed to me and I was afraid that Abu Bakr would not speak so well. Then Abu Bakr spoke and his speech was very eloquent. He said in his statement, "We are the rulers and you (Ansars) are the ministers (i.e. advisers)," Hubab bin Al-Mundhir said, "No, by Allah we won't accept this. But there must be a ruler from us and a ruler from you." Abu Bakr said, "No, we will be the rulers and you will be the ministers, for they (i.e. Quarish) are the best family amongst the 'Arabs and of best origin. So you should elect either 'Umar or Abu 'Ubaida bin Al-Jarrah as your ruler." 'Umar said (to Abu Bakr), "No but we elect you, for you are our chief and the best amongst us and the most beloved of all of us to Allah's Messenger ﷺ." So 'Umar took Abu Bakr's hand and gave the pledge of allegiance and the people too gave the pledge of allegiance to Abu Bakr. Someone said, "You have killed Sad bin Ubada." 'Umar said, "Allah has killed him.". – Sahih Al-Bukhari 3667, 3668

حَدَّثَنَا إِسْمَاعِيلُ بْنُ عَبْدِ اللَّهِ، حَدَّثَنَا سُلَيْمَانُ بْنُ بِلاَلٍ، عَنْ هِشَامِ بْنِ عُرْوَةَ، عَنْ عُرْوَةَ بْنِ الزُّبَيْرِ، عَنْ عَائِشَةَ ـ رضى الله عنها ـ زَوْجِ النَّبِيِّ صلى الله عليه وسلم أَنَّ رَسُولَ اللَّهِ صلى الله عليه وسلم مَاتَ وَأَبُو بَكْرٍ بِالسُّنْحِ ـ قَالَ إِسْمَاعِيلُ يَعْنِي بِالْعَالِيَةِ ـ فَقَامَ عُمَرُ يَقُولُ وَاللَّهِ مَا مَاتَ رَسُولُ اللَّهِ صلى الله عليه وسلم. قَالَتْ وَقَالَ عُمَرُ وَاللَّهِ مَا كَانَ يَقَعُ فِي نَفْسِي إِلاَّ ذَاكَ وَلَيَبْعَثَنَّهُ اللَّهُ فَلَيَقْطَعَنَّ أَيْدِيَ رِجَالٍ وَأَرْجُلَهُمْ. فَجَاءَ أَبُو بَكْرٍ فَكَشَفَ عَنْ رَسُولِ اللَّهِ صلى الله عليه وسلم فَقَبَّلَهُ قَالَ بِأَبِي أَنْتَ وَأُمِّي طِبْتَ حَيًّا وَمَيِّتًا، وَالَّذِي نَفْسِي بِيَدِهِ لاَ يُذِيقُكَ اللَّهُ الْمَوْتَتَيْنِ أَبَدًا. ثُمَّ خَرَجَ فَقَالَ أَيُّهَا الْحَالِفُ عَلَى رِسْلِكَ. فَلَمَّا تَكَلَّمَ أَبُو بَكْرٍ جَلَسَ عُمَرُ. فَحَمِدَ اللَّهَ أَبُو بَكْرٍ وَأَثْنَى عَلَيْهِ وَقَالَ أَلاَ مَنْ كَانَ يَعْبُدُ مُحَمَّدًا صلى الله عليه وسلم فَإِنَّ مُحَمَّدًا قَدْ مَاتَ، وَمَنْ كَانَ يَعْبُدُ اللَّهَ فَإِنَّ اللَّهَ حَيٌّ لاَ يَمُوتُ. وَقَالَ {إِنَّكَ مَيِّتٌ وَإِنَّهُمْ مَيِّتُونَ} وَقَالَ {وَمَا مُحَمَّدٌ إِلاَّ رَسُولٌ قَدْ خَلَتْ مِنْ قَبْلِهِ الرُّسُلُ أَفَإِنْ مَاتَ أَوْ قُتِلَ انْقَلَبْتُمْ عَلَى أَعْقَابِكُمْ وَمَنْ يَنْقَلِبْ عَلَى عَقِبَيْهِ فَلَنْ يَضُرَّ اللَّهَ شَيْئًا وَسَيَجْزِي اللَّهُ الشَّاكِرِينَ} قَالَ فَنَشَجَ النَّاسُ يَبْكُونَ ـ قَالَ ـ وَاجْتَمَعَتِ الأَنْصَارُ إِلَى سَعْدِ بْنِ عُبَادَةَ فِي سَقِيفَةِ بَنِي سَاعِدَةَ فَقَالُوا مِنَّا أَمِيرٌ وَمِنْكُمْ أَمِيرٌ، فَذَهَبَ إِلَيْهِمْ أَبُو بَكْرٍ وَعُمَرُ بْنُ الْخَطَّابِ وَأَبُو عُبَيْدَةَ بْنُ الْجَرَّاحِ، فَذَهَبَ عُمَرُ يَتَكَلَّمُ فَأَسْكَتَهُ أَبُو بَكْرٍ، وَكَانَ عُمَرُ يَقُولُ وَاللَّهِ مَا أَرَدْتُ بِذَلِكَ إِلاَّ أَنِّي قَدْ هَيَّأْتُ كَلاَمًا قَدْ أَعْجَبَنِي خَشِيتُ أَنْ لاَ يَبْلُغَهُ أَبُو بَكْرٍ، ثُمَّ تَكَلَّمَ أَبُو بَكْرٍ فَتَكَلَّمَ أَبْلَغَ النَّاسِ فَقَالَ فِي كَلاَمِهِ نَحْنُ الأُمَرَاءُ وَأَنْتُمُ الْوُزَرَاءُ. فَقَالَ حُبَابُ بْنُ الْمُنْذِرِ لاَ وَاللَّهِ لاَ نَفْعَلُ، مِنَّا أَمِيرٌ وَمِنْكُمْ أَمِيرٌ. فَقَالَ أَبُو بَكْرٍ لاَ، وَلَكِنَّا الأُمَرَاءُ وَأَنْتُمُ الْوُزَرَاءُ هُمْ أَوْسَطُ الْعَرَبِ دَارًا، وَأَعْرَبُهُمْ أَحْسَابًا فَبَايِعُوا عُمَرَ أَوْ أَبَا عُبَيْدَةَ. فَقَالَ عُمَرُ بَلْ نُبَايِعُكَ أَنْتَ، فَأَنْتَ سَيِّدُنَا وَخَيْرُنَا وَأَحَبُّنَا إِلَى رَسُولِ اللَّهِ صلى الله عليه وسلم. فَأَخَذَ عُمَرُ بِيَدِهِ فَبَايَعَهُ، وَبَايَعَهُ النَّاسُ، فَقَالَ قَائِلٌ قَتَلْتُمْ سَعْدَ بْنَ عُبَادَةَ. فَقَالَ عُمَرُ قَتَلَهُ اللَّهُ

Hudhaifa bin Al-Yaman
حُذَيْفَة بِن اَلْيَمَان

Narrated Hudhaifa: Allah's Messenger ﷺ related to us, two prophetic narrations one of which I have seen fulfilled and I am waiting for the fulfillment of the other. The Prophet ﷺ told us that the virtue of honesty descended in the roots of men's hearts (from Allah) and then they learned it from the Qur'an and then they learned it from the Sunna (the Prophet's traditions). The Prophet ﷺ further told us how that honesty will be taken away: He said: "Man will go to sleep during which honesty will be taken away from his heart and only its trace will remain in his heart like the trace of a dark spot; then man will go to sleep, during which honesty will decrease further still, so that its trace will resemble the trace of blister as when an ember is dropped on one's foot which would make it swell, and one would see it swollen but there would be nothing inside. People would be carrying out their trade but hardly will there be a trustworthy person. It will be said, 'in such-and-such tribe there is an honest man,' and later it will be said about some man, 'What a wise, polite and strong man he is!' Though he will not have faith equal even to a mustard seed in his heart." No doubt, there came upon me a time when I did not mind dealing (bargaining) with anyone of you, for if he was a Muslim his Islam would compel him to pay me what is due to me, and if he was a Christian, the Muslim official would compel him to pay me what is due to me, but today I do not deal except with such-and-such person. – Sahih Al-Bukhari 7086

حَدَّثَنَا مُحَمَّدُ بْنُ كَثِيرٍ، أَخْبَرَنَا سُفْيَانُ، حَدَّثَنَا الأَعْمَشُ، عَنْ زَيْدِ بْنِ وَهْبٍ، حَدَّثَنَا حُذَيْفَةُ، قَالَ حَدَّثَنَا رَسُولُ اللَّهِ صلى الله عليه وسلم حَدِيثَيْنِ رَأَيْتُ أَحَدَهُمَا وَأَنَا أَنْتَظِرُ الآخَرَ حَدَّثَنَا " أَنَّ الأَمَانَةَ نَزَلَتْ فِي جَذْرِ قُلُوبِ الرِّجَالِ، ثُمَّ عَلِمُوا مِنَ الْقُرْآنِ، ثُمَّ عَلِمُوا مِنَ السُّنَّةِ ". وَحَدَّثَنَا عَنْ رَفْعِهَا قَالَ " يَنَامُ الرَّجُلُ النَّوْمَةَ فَتُقْبَضُ الأَمَانَةُ مِنْ قَلْبِهِ، فَيَظَلُّ أَثَرُهَا مِثْلَ أَثَرِ الْوَكْتِ، ثُمَّ يَنَامُ النَّوْمَةَ فَتُقْبَضُ فَيَبْقَى فِيهَا أَثَرُهَا مِثْلَ أَثَرِ الْمَجْلِ، كَجَمْرٍ دَحْرَجْتَهُ عَلَى رِجْلِكَ فَنَفِطَ، فَتَرَاهُ مُنْتَبِرًا وَلَيْسَ فِيهِ شَىْءٌ، وَيُصْبِحُ النَّاسُ يَتَبَايَعُونَ فَلاَ يَكَادُ أَحَدٌ يُؤَدِّي الأَمَانَةَ فَيُقَالُ إِنَّ فِي بَنِي فُلاَنٍ رَجُلاً أَمِينًا. وَيُقَالُ لِلرَّجُلِ مَا أَعْقَلَهُ، وَمَا أَظْرَفَهُ، وَمَا أَجْلَدَهُ، وَمَا فِي قَلْبِهِ مِثْقَالُ حَبَّةِ خَرْدَلٍ مِنْ إِيمَانٍ، وَلَقَدْ أَتَى عَلَىَّ زَمَانٌ، وَلاَ أُبَالِي أَيُّكُمْ بَايَعْتُ، لَئِنْ كَانَ مُسْلِمًا رَدَّهُ عَلَىَّ الإِسْلاَمُ، وَإِنْ كَانَ نَصْرَانِيًّا رَدَّهُ عَلَىَّ سَاعِيهِ، وَأَمَّا الْيَوْمَ فَمَا كُنْتُ أُبَايِعُ إِلاَّ فُلاَنًا وَفُلاَنًا "

Narrated Ibn Abi Laila: While Hudhaita was at Mada'in, he asked for water. The chief of the village brought him a silver vessel. Hudhaifa threw it away and said, "I have thrown it away because I told him not to use it, but he has not stopped using it. The Prophet ﷺ forbade us to wear clothes of silk or Dibaj, and to drink in gold or silver utensils, and said, 'These things are for them (unbelievers) in this world and for you (Muslims) in the Hereafter.' ". – Sahih Al-Bukhari 5632

حَدَّثَنَا حَفْصُ بْنُ عُمَرَ، حَدَّثَنَا شُعْبَةُ، عَنِ الْحَكَمِ، عَنِ ابْنِ أَبِي لَيْلَى، قَالَ كَانَ حُذَيْفَةُ بِالْمَدَايِنِ فَاسْتَسْقَى، فَأَتَاهُ دِهْقَانٌ بِقَدَحِ فِضَّةٍ، فَرَمَاهُ بِهِ فَقَالَ إِنِّي لَمْ أَرْمِهِ إِلاَّ أَنِّي نَهَيْتُهُ فَلَمْ يَنْتَهِ، وَإِنَّ النَّبِيَّ صلى الله عليه وسلم نَهَانَا عَنِ الْحَرِيرِ وَالدِّيبَاجِ وَالشُّرْبِ فِي آنِيَةِ الذَّهَبِ وَالْفِضَّةِ وَقَالَ " هُنَّ لَهُمْ فِي الدُّنْيَا وَهْىَ لَكُمْ فِي الآخِرَةِ ".

Narrated Rabi bin Hirash: `Uqba bin `Amr said to Hudhaifa, "Won't you relate to us of what you have heard from Allah's Apostle ?" He said, "I heard him saying, "When Al-Dajjal appears, he will have fire and water along with him. What the people will consider as cold water, will be fire that will burn (things). So, if anyone of you comes across this, he should fall in the thing which will appear to him as fire, for in reality, it will be fresh cold water." Hudhaifa added, "I also heard him saying, 'From among the people preceding your generation, there was a man whom the angel of death visited to capture his soul. (So his soul was captured) and he was asked if he had done any good deed.' He replied, 'I don't remember any good deed.' He was asked to think it over. He said, 'I do not remember, except that I used to trade with the people in the world and I used to give a respite to the rich and forgive the poor (among my debtors). So Allah made him enter Paradise." Hudhaifa further said, "I also heard him saying, 'Once there was a man on his death-bed, who, losing every hope of surviving said to his family: When I die, gather for me a large heap of wood and make a fire (to burn me). When the fire eats my meat and reaches my bones, and when the bones burn, take and crush them into powder and wait for a windy day to throw it (i.e. the powder) over the sea. They did so, but Allah collected his particles and asked him: Why did you do so? He replied: For fear of You. So Allah forgave him." `Uqba bin `Amr said, "I heard him saying that the Israeli used to dig the grave of the dead (to steal their shrouds). – Sahih Al-Bukhari 3450, 3451, 3452

حَدَّثَنَا مُوسَى بْنُ إِسْمَاعِيلَ، حَدَّثَنَا أَبُو عَوَانَةَ، حَدَّثَنَا عَبْدُ الْمَلِكِ، عَنْ رِبْعِيِّ بْنِ حِرَاشٍ، قَالَ قَالَ عُقْبَةُ بْنُ عَمْرٍو لِحُذَيْفَةَ أَلاَ تُحَدِّثُنَا مَا سَمِعْتَ مِنْ رَسُولِ اللَّهِ صلى الله عليه وسلم قَالَ إِنِّي سَمِعْتُهُ يَقُولُ " إِنَّ مَعَ الدَّجَّالِ إِذَا خَرَجَ مَاءً وَنَارًا، فَأَمَّا الَّذِي يَرَى النَّاسُ أَنَّهَا النَّارُ فَمَاءٌ بَارِدٌ، وَأَمَّا الَّذِي يَرَى النَّاسُ أَنَّهُ مَاءٌ بَارِدٌ فَنَارٌ تُحْرِقُ، فَمَنْ أَدْرَكَ مِنْكُمْ فَلْيَقَعْ فِي الَّذِي يَرَى أَنَّهَا نَارٌ، فَإِنَّهُ عَذْبٌ بَارِدٌ ". قَالَ حُذَيْفَةُ وَسَمِعْتُهُ يَقُولُ " إِنَّ رَجُلاً كَانَ فِيمَنْ كَانَ قَبْلَكُمْ أَتَاهُ الْمَلَكُ لِيَقْبِضَ رُوحَهُ فَقِيلَ لَهُ هَلْ عَمِلْتَ مِنْ خَيْرٍ قَالَ مَا أَعْلَمُ، قِيلَ لَهُ انْظُرْ. قَالَ مَا أَعْلَمُ شَيْئًا غَيْرَ أَنِّي كُنْتُ أُبَايِعُ النَّاسَ فِي الدُّنْيَا وَأُجَازِيهِمْ، فَأُنْظِرُ الْمُوسِرَ، وَأَتَجَاوَزُ عَنِ الْمُعْسِرِ. فَأَدْخَلَهُ اللَّهُ الْجَنَّةَ ". فَقَالَ وَسَمِعْتُهُ يَقُولُ " إِنَّ رَجُلاً حَضَرَهُ الْمَوْتُ، فَلَمَّا يَئِسَ مِنَ الْحَيَاةِ أَوْصَى أَهْلَهُ إِذَا أَنَا مُتُّ فَاجْمَعُوا لِي حَطَبًا كَثِيرًا وَأَوْقِدُوا فِيهِ نَارًا حَتَّى إِذَا أَكَلَتْ لَحْمِي، وَخَلَصَتْ إِلَى عَظْمِي، فَامْتَحَشْتُ، فَخُذُوهَا فَاطْحَنُوهَا، ثُمَّ انْظُرُوا يَوْمًا رَاحًا فَاذْرُوهُ فِي الْيَمِّ. فَفَعَلُوا، فَجَمَعَهُ فَقَالَ لَهُ لِمَ فَعَلْتَ ذَلِكَ قَالَ مِنْ خَشْيَتِكَ. فَغَفَرَ اللَّهُ لَهُ ". قَالَ عُقْبَةُ بْنُ عَمْرٍو، وَأَنَا سَمِعْتُهُ يَقُولُ ذَاكَ، وَكَانَ نَبَّاشًا.

Narrated Ibrahim: 'Alaqama went to Sham and came to the mosque and offered a two-rak`at prayer, and invoked Allah: "O Allah! Bless me with a (pious) good companion." So he sat beside Abu Ad-Darda' who asked, "From where are you?" He said, "From the people of Kufa." Abu Darda' said, "Wasn't there among you the person who keeps the secrets (of the Prophet ﷺ) which nobody knew except him (i.e., Hudhaifa (bin Al-Yaman). And isn't there among you the person whom Allah gave refuge from Satan through the request (tongue) of Allah's Messenger ﷺ? (i.e., `Ammar). Isn't there among you the one who used to carry the Siwak and the cushion (or pillows (of the Prophets)? (i.e., Ibn Mas`ud). How did Ibn Mas`ud use to recite 'By the night as it conceals (the light)?" (Sura 92). 'Alqama said, "Wadhdhakari Wal Untha' (And by male and female.") Abu Ad-Darda added. 'These people continued to argue with me regarding it till they were about to cause me to have doubts although I heard it from Allah's Messenger. – Sahih Al-Bukhari 6278

حَدَّثَنَا يَحْيَى بْنُ جَعْفَرٍ، حَدَّثَنَا يَزِيدُ، عَنْ شُعْبَةَ، عَنْ مُغِيرَةَ، عَنْ إِبْرَاهِيمَ، عَنْ عَلْقَمَةَ، أَنَّهُ قَدِمَ الشَّأْمَ. وَحَدَّثَنَا أَبُو الْوَلِيدِ، حَدَّثَنَا شُعْبَةُ، عَنْ مُغِيرَةَ، عَنْ إِبْرَاهِيمَ، قَالَ ذَهَبَ عَلْقَمَةُ إِلَى الشَّأْمِ، فَأَتَى الْمَسْجِدَ فَصَلَّى رَكْعَتَيْنِ فَقَالَ اللَّهُمَّ ارْزُقْنِي جَلِيسًا. فَقَعَدَ إِلَى أَبِي الدَّرْدَاءِ فَقَالَ مِمَّنْ أَنْتَ قَالَ مِنْ أَهْلِ الْكُوفَةِ. قَالَ أَلَيْسَ فِيكُمْ صَاحِبُ السِّرِّ الَّذِي كَانَ لاَ يَعْلَمُهُ غَيْرُهُ - يَعْنِي حُذَيْفَةَ - أَلَيْسَ فِيكُمْ - أَوْ كَانَ فِيكُمُ - الَّذِي أَجَارَهُ اللَّهُ عَلَى لِسَانِ رَسُولِهِ صلى الله عليه وسلم مِنَ الشَّيْطَانِ - يَعْنِي عَمَّارًا - أَوَلَيْسَ فِيكُمْ صَاحِبُ السِّوَاكِ وَالْوِسَادِ - يَعْنِي ابْنَ مَسْعُودٍ - كَيْفَ كَانَ عَبْدُ اللَّهِ يَقْرَأُ {وَاللَّيْلِ إِذَا يَغْشَى}. قَالَ {وَالذَّكَرِ وَالأُنْثَى}. فَقَالَ مَا زَالَ هَؤُلاَءِ حَتَّى كَادُوا يُشَكِّكُونِي، وَقَدْ سَمِعْتُهَا مِنْ رَسُولِ اللَّهِ صلى الله عليه وسلم.

Narrated Hudhaifa bin Al-Yaman: The people used to ask Allah's Messenger ﷺ about the good but I used to ask him about the evil lest I should be overtaken by them. So I said, "O Allah's Messenger ﷺ! We were living in ignorance and in an (extremely) worst atmosphere, then Allah brought to us this good (i.e., Islam); will there be any evil after this good?" He said, "Yes." I said, 'Will there be any good after that evil?" He replied, "Yes, but it will be tainted (not pure.)'' I asked, "What will be its taint?" He replied, "(There will be) some people who will guide others not according to my tradition? You will approve of some of their deeds and disapprove of some others." I asked, "Will there be any evil after that good?" He replied, "Yes, (there will be) some people calling at the gates of the (Hell) Fire, and whoever will respond to their call, will be thrown by them into the (Hell) Fire." I said, "O Allah s Apostle! Will you describe them to us?" He said, "They will be from our own people and will speak our language." I said, "What do you order me to do if such a state should take place in my life?" He said, "Stick to the group of Muslims and their Imam (ruler)." I said, "If there is neither a group of Muslims nor an Imam (ruler)?" He said, "Then turn away from all those sects even if you were to bite (eat) the roots of a tree till death overtakes you while you are in that state.". – Sahih Al-Bukhari 7084

حَدَّثَنَا مُحَمَّدُ بْنُ الْمُثَنَّى، حَدَّثَنَا الْوَلِيدُ بْنُ مُسْلِمٍ، حَدَّثَنَا ابْنُ جَابِرٍ، حَدَّثَنِي بُسْرُ بْنُ عُبَيْدِ اللَّهِ الْحَضْرَمِيُّ، أَنَّهُ سَمِعَ أَبَا إِدْرِيسَ الْخَوْلاَنِيَّ، أَنَّهُ سَمِعَ حُذَيْفَةَ بْنَ الْيَمَانِ، يَقُولُ كَانَ النَّاسُ يَسْأَلُونَ رَسُولَ اللَّهِ صلى الله عليه وسلم عَنِ الْخَيْرِ، وَكُنْتُ أَسْأَلُهُ عَنِ الشَّرِّ، مَخَافَةَ أَنْ يُدْرِكَنِي فَقُلْتُ يَا رَسُولَ اللَّهِ إِنَّا كُنَّا فِي جَاهِلِيَّةٍ وَشَرٍّ فَجَاءَنَا اللَّهُ بِهَذَا الْخَيْرِ، فَهَلْ بَعْدَ هَذَا الْخَيْرِ مِنْ شَرٍّ قَالَ " نَعَمْ ". قُلْتُ وَهَلْ بَعْدَ ذَلِكَ الشَّرِّ مِنْ خَيْرٍ قَالَ " نَعَمْ، وَفِيهِ دَخَنٌ ". قُلْتُ وَمَا دَخَنُهُ قَالَ " قَوْمٌ يَهْدُونَ بِغَيْرِ هَدْيِي، تَعْرِفُ مِنْهُمْ وَتُنْكِرُ ". قُلْتُ فَهَلْ بَعْدَ ذَلِكَ الْخَيْرِ مِنْ شَرٍّ قَالَ " نَعَمْ، دُعَاةٌ عَلَى أَبْوَابِ جَهَنَّمَ، مَنْ أَجَابَهُمْ إِلَيْهَا قَذَفُوهُ فِيهَا ". قُلْتُ يَا رَسُولَ اللَّهِ صِفْهُمْ لَنَا. قَالَ " هُمْ مِنْ جِلْدَتِنَا، وَيَتَكَلَّمُونَ بِأَلْسِنَتِنَا ". قُلْتُ فَمَا تَأْمُرُنِي إِنْ أَدْرَكَنِي ذَلِكَ قَالَ " تَلْزَمُ جَمَاعَةَ الْمُسْلِمِينَ وَإِمَامَهُمْ ". قُلْتُ فَإِنْ لَمْ يَكُنْ لَهُمْ جَمَاعَةٌ وَلاَ إِمَامٌ قَالَ " فَاعْتَزِلْ تِلْكَ الْفِرَقَ كُلَّهَا وَلَوْ أَنْ تَعَضَّ بِأَصْلِ شَجَرَةٍ، حَتَّى يُدْرِكَكَ الْمَوْتُ، وَأَنْتَ عَلَى ذَلِكَ "

Narrated Hudhaifa: The Prophet ﷺ said (to us), " List the names of those people who have announced that they are Muslims." So, we listed one thousand and five hundred men. Then we wondered, "Should we be afraid (of infidels) although we are one thousand and five hundred in number?" No doubt, we witnessed ourselves being afflicted with such bad trials that one would have to offer the prayer alone in fear. Narrated Al-A`mash: “We (listed the Muslims and) found them five hundred.” And Abu Muawiya said, “Between six hundred to seven hundred.”. – Sahih Al-Bukhari 3060

حَدَّثَنَا مُحَمَّدُ بْنُ يُوسُفَ، حَدَّثَنَا سُفْيَانُ، عَنِ الأَعْمَشِ، عَنْ أَبِي وَائِلٍ، عَنْ حُذَيْفَةَ ـ رضى الله عنه ـ قَالَ قَالَ النَّبِيُّ صلى الله عليه وسلم " اكْتُبُوا لِي مَنْ تَلَفَّظَ بِالإِسْلاَمِ مِنَ النَّاسِ ". فَكَتَبْنَا لَهُ أَلْفًا وَخَمْسَمِائَةِ رَجُلٍ، فَقُلْنَا نَخَافُ وَنَحْنُ أَلْفٌ وَخَمْسُمِائَةٍ فَلَقَدْ رَأَيْتُنَا ابْتُلِينَا حَتَّى إِنَّ الرَّجُلَ لَيُصَلِّي وَحْدَهُ وَهْوَ خَائِفٌ. حَدَّثَنَا عَبْدَانُ، عَنْ أَبِي حَمْزَةَ، عَنِ الأَعْمَشِ، فَوَجَدْنَاهُمْ خَمْسَمِائَةٍ. قَالَ أَبُو مُعَاوِيَةَ مَا بَيْنَ سِتِّمِائَةٍ إِلَى سَبْعِمِائَةٍ

Narrated Hudhaifa: The Prophetﷺ said, “Before your time the angels received the soul of a man and asked him, ‘Did you do any good deeds (in your life)?’ He replied, ‘I used to order my employees to grant time to the rich person to pay his debts at his convenience.’ So Allah said to the angels; “Excuse him.” Rabi said that (the dead man said), ‘I used to be easy to the rich and grant time to the poor.’ Or, in another narration, ‘grant time to the well-off and forgive the needy,’ or, ‘accept from the well-off and forgive the needy.’. – Sahih Al-Bukhari 2077

حَدَّثَنَا أَحْمَدُ بْنُ يُونُسَ، حَدَّثَنَا زُهَيْرٌ، حَدَّثَنَا مَنْصُورٌ، أَنَّ رِبْعِيَّ بْنَ حِرَاشٍ، حَدَّثَهُ أَنَّ حُذَيْفَةَ ـ رضى الله عنه ـ حَدَّثَهُ قَالَ قَالَ النَّبِيُّ صلى الله عليه وسلم " تَلَقَّتِ الْمَلاَئِكَةُ رُوحَ رَجُلٍ مِمَّنْ كَانَ قَبْلَكُمْ قَالُوا أَعَمِلْتَ مِنَ الْخَيْرِ شَيْئًا قَالَ كُنْتُ آمُرُ فِتْيَانِي أَنْ يُنْظِرُوا وَيَتَجَاوَزُوا عَنِ الْمُوسِرِ قَالَ قَالَ فَتَجَاوَزُوا عَنْهُ ". وَقَالَ أَبُو مَالِكٍ عَنْ رِبْعِيٍّ " كُنْتُ أُيَسِّرُ عَلَى الْمُوسِرِ وَأُنْظِرُ الْمُعْسِرَ ". وَتَابَعَهُ شُعْبَةُ عَنْ عَبْدِ الْمَلِكِ عَنْ رِبْعِيٍّ. وَقَالَ أَبُو عَوَانَةَ عَنْ عَبْدِ الْمَلِكِ عَنْ رِبْعِيٍّ " أُنْظِرُ الْمُوسِرَ، وَأَتَجَاوَزُ عَنِ الْمُعْسِرِ ". وَقَالَ نُعَيْمُ بْنُ أَبِي هِنْدٍ عَنْ رِبْعِيٍّ " فَأَقْبَلُ مِنَ الْمُوسِرِ، وَأَتَجَاوَزُ عَنِ الْمُعْسِرِ ".

Narrated Anas bin Malik: Hudhaifa bin Al-Yaman came to `Uthman at the time when the people of Sham and the people of Iraq were Waging war to conquer Arminya and Adharbijan. Hudhaifa was afraid of their (the people of Sham and Iraq) differences in the recitation of the Qur’an, so he said to `Uthman, “O chief of the Believers! Save this nation before they differ about the Book (Qur’an) as Jews and the Christians did before.” So `Uthman sent a message to Hafsa saying, “Send us the manuscripts of the Qur’an so that we may compile the Qur’anic materials in perfect copies and return the manuscripts to you.” Hafsa sent it to `Uthman. `Uthman then ordered Zaid bin Thabit, `Abdullah bin AzZubair, Sa`id bin Al-As and `AbdurRahman bin Harith bin Hisham to rewrite the manuscripts in perfect copies. `Uthman said to the three Quraishi men, “In case you disagree with Zaid bin Thabit on any point in the Qur’an, then write it in the dialect of Quraish, the Qur’an was revealed in their tongue.” They did so, and when they had written many copies, `Uthman returned the original manuscripts to Hafsa. `Uthman sent to every Muslim province one copy of what they had copied, and ordered that all the other Qur’anic materials, whether written in fragmentary manuscripts or whole copies, be burnt. – Sahih Al-Bukhari 4987

حَدَّثَنَا مُوسَى، حَدَّثَنَا إِبْرَاهِيمُ، حَدَّثَنَا ابْنُ شِهَابٍ، أَنَّ أَنَسَ بْنَ مَالِكٍ، حَدَّثَهُ أَنَّ حُذَيْفَةَ بْنَ الْيَمَانِ قَدِمَ عَلَى عُثْمَانَ وَكَانَ يُغَازِي أَهْلَ الشَّأْمِ فِي فَتْحِ إِرْمِينِيَةَ وَأَذْرَبِيجَانَ مَعَ أَهْلِ الْعِرَاقِ فَأَفْزَعَ حُذَيْفَةَ اخْتِلاَفُهُمْ فِي الْقِرَاءَةِ فَقَالَ حُذَيْفَةُ لِعُثْمَانَ يَا أَمِيرَ الْمُؤْمِنِينَ أَدْرِكْ هَذِهِ الأُمَّةَ قَبْلَ أَنْ يَخْتَلِفُوا فِي الْكِتَابِ اخْتِلاَفَ الْيَهُودِ وَالنَّصَارَى فَأَرْسَلَ عُثْمَانُ إِلَى حَفْصَةَ أَنْ أَرْسِلِي إِلَيْنَا بِالصُّحُفِ نَنْسَخُهَا فِي الْمَصَاحِفِ ثُمَّ نَرُدُّهَا إِلَيْكِ فَأَرْسَلَتْ بِهَا حَفْصَةُ إِلَى عُثْمَانَ فَأَمَرَ زَيْدَ بْنَ ثَابِتٍ وَعَبْدَ اللَّهِ بْنَ الزُّبَيْرِ وَسَعِيدَ بْنَ الْعَاصِ وَعَبْدَ الرَّحْمَنِ بْنَ الْحَارِثِ بْنِ هِشَامٍ فَنَسَخُوهَا فِي الْمَصَاحِفِ وَقَالَ عُثْمَانُ لِلرَّهْطِ الْقُرَشِيِّينَ الثَّلاَثَةِ إِذَا اخْتَلَفْتُمْ أَنْتُمْ وَزَيْدُ بْنُ ثَابِتٍ فِي شَىْءٍ مِنَ الْقُرْآنِ فَاكْتُبُوهُ بِلِسَانِ قُرَيْشٍ فَإِنَّمَا نَزَلَ بِلِسَانِهِمْ فَفَعَلُوا حَتَّى إِذَا نَسَخُوا الصُّحُفَ فِي الْمَصَاحِفِ رَدَّ عُثْمَانُ الصُّحُفَ إِلَى حَفْصَةَ وَأَرْسَلَ إِلَى كُلِّ أُفُقٍ بِمُصْحَفٍ مِمَّا نَسَخُوا وَأَمَرَ بِمَا سِوَاهُ مِنَ الْقُرْآنِ فِي كُلِّ صَحِيفَةٍ أَوْ مُصْحَفٍ أَنْ يُحْرَقَ

Narrated Zaid bin Wahb: We were with Hudhaifa and he said, “None remains of the people described by this Verse (9.12), “Except three, and of the hypocrites except four.” A bedouin said, “You the companions of Muhammad! Tell us (things) and we do not know that about those who break open our houses and steal our precious things? ' He (Hudhaifa) replied, "Those are Al Fussaq (rebellious wrongdoers) (not disbelievers or hypocrites). Really, none remains of them (hypocrite) but four, one of whom is a very old man who, if he drinks water, does not feel its coldness.". – Sahih Al-Bukhari 4658

حَدَّثَنَا مُحَمَّدُ بْنُ الْمُثَنَّى، حَدَّثَنَا يَحْيَى، حَدَّثَنَا إِسْمَاعِيلُ، حَدَّثَنَا زَيْدُ بْنُ وَهْبٍ، قَالَ كُنَّا عِنْدَ حُذَيْفَةَ فَقَالَ مَا بَقِيَ مِنْ أَصْحَابِ هَذِهِ الآيَةِ إِلاَّ ثَلاَثَةٌ، وَلاَ مِنَ الْمُنَافِقِينَ إِلاَّ أَرْبَعَةٌ. فَقَالَ أَعْرَابِيٌّ إِنَّكُمْ أَصْحَابَ مُحَمَّدٍ صلى الله عليه وسلم تُخْبِرُونَا فَلاَ نَدْرِي فَمَا بَالُ هَؤُلاَءِ الَّذِينَ يَبْقُرُونَ بُيُوتَنَا وَيَسْرِقُونَ أَعْلاَقَنَا. قَالَ أُولَئِكَ الْفُسَّاقُ، أَجَلْ لَمْ يَبْقَ مِنْهُمْ إِلاَّ أَرْبَعَةٌ. أَحَدُهُمْ شَيْخٌ كَبِيرٌ لَوْ شَرِبَ الْمَاءَ الْبَارِدَ لَمَا وَجَدَ بَرْدَهُ

Narrated Hudhaifa: Whenever the Prophetﷺ intended to go to bed, he would recite: "Bismika Allahumma amutu wa ahya (With Your name, O Allah, I die and I live)." And when he woke up from his sleep, he would say: "Al-hamdu lil-lahil-ladhi ahyana ba'da ma amatana; wa ilaihi an-nushur (All the Praises are for Allah Who has made us alive after He made us die (sleep) and unto Him is the Resurrection). ". – Sahih Al-Bukhari 6324

حَدَّثَنَا أَبُو نُعَيْمٍ، حَدَّثَنَا سُفْيَانُ، عَنْ عَبْدِ الْمَلِكِ بْنِ عُمَيْرٍ، عَنْ رِبْعِيِّ بْنِ حِرَاشٍ، عَنْ حُذَيْفَةَ، قَالَ كَانَ النَّبِيُّ صلى الله عليه وسلم إِذَا أَرَادَ أَنْ يَنَامَ قَالَ " بِاسْمِكَ اللَّهُمَّ أَمُوتُ وَأَحْيَا ". وَإِذَا اسْتَيْقَظَ مِنْ مَنَامِهِ قَالَ " الْحَمْدُ لِلَّهِ الَّذِي أَحْيَانَا بَعْدَ مَا أَمَاتَنَا، وَإِلَيْهِ النُّشُورُ ".

Narrated Hudhaifa: The Prophetﷺ said, "There was a man amongst the people who had suspicion as to the righteousness of his deeds. Therefore he said to his family, 'If I die, take me and burn my corpse and throw my ashes into the sea on a hot (or windy) day.' They did so, but Allah, collected his particles and asked (him), What made you do what you did?' He replied, 'The only thing that made me do it, was that I was afraid of You.' So Allah forgave him.". – Sahih Al-Bukhari 6480

حَدَّثَنَا عُثْمَانُ بْنُ أَبِي شَيْبَةَ، حَدَّثَنَا جَرِيرٌ، عَنْ مَنْصُورٍ، عَنْ رِبْعِيٍّ، عَنْ حُذَيْفَةَ، عَنِ النَّبِيِّ صلى الله عليه وسلم قَالَ " كَانَ رَجُلٌ مِمَّنْ كَانَ قَبْلَكُمْ يُسِيءُ الظَّنَّ بِعَمَلِهِ، فَقَالَ لأَهْلِهِ إِذَا أَنَا مُتُّ فَخُذُونِي فَذَرُّونِي، فِي الْبَحْرِ فِي يَوْمٍ صَائِفٍ، فَفَعَلُوا بِهِ، فَجَمَعَهُ اللَّهُ ثُمَّ قَالَ مَا حَمَلَكَ عَلَى الَّذِي صَنَعْتَ قَالَ مَا حَمَلَنِي إِلاَّ مَخَافَتُكَ. فَغَفَرَ لَهُ "

Abu Dharr Al-Ghifari Al-Kinani

أَبُو ذَرّ ٱلْغِفَارِيّ ٱلْكِنَانِيّ

Narrated Abu Jamra: Ibn `Abbas said to us, "Shall I tell you the story of Abu Dhar's conversion to Islam?" We said, "Yes." He said, "Abu Dhar said: I was a man from the tribe of Ghifar. We heard that a man had appeared in Mecca, claiming to be a Prophet. ! said to my brother, 'Go to that man and talk to him and bring me his news.' He set out, met him and returned. I asked him, 'What is the news with you?' He said, 'By Allah, I saw a man enjoining what is good and forbidding what is evil.' I said to him, 'You have not satisfied me with this little information.' So, I took a waterskin and a stick and proceeded towards Mecca. Neither did I know him (i.e. the Prophetﷺ), nor did I like to ask anyone about him. I Kept on drinking Zam zam water and staying in the Mosque. Then `Ali passed by me and said, 'It seems you are a stranger?' I said, 'Yes.' He proceeded to his house and I accompanied him. Neither did he ask me anything, nor did I tell him anything. Next morning I went to the Mosque to ask about the Prophet but no-one told me anything about him. `Ali passed by me again and asked, 'Hasn't the man recognized his dwelling place yet' I said, 'No.' He said, 'Come along with me.' He asked me, 'What is your business? What has brought you to this town?' I said to him, 'If you keep my secret, I will tell you.' He said, 'I will do,' I said to him, 'We have heard that a person has appeared here, claiming to be a Prophet. I sent my brother to speak to him and when he returned, he did not bring a satisfactory report; so I thought of meeting him personally.' `Ali said (to Abu Dhar), 'You have reached your goal; I am going to him just now, so follow me, and wherever I enter, enter after me. If I should see someone who may cause you trouble, I will stand near a wall pretending to mend my shoes (as a warning), and you should go away then.' `Ali proceeded and I accompanied him till he entered a place, and I entered with him to the Prophet ﷺ to whom I said, 'Present (the principles of) Islam to me.' When he did, I embraced Islam 'immediately. He said to me, 'O Abu Dhar! Keep your conversion as a secret and return to your town; and when you hear of our victory, return to us. ' I said, 'By H him Who has sent you with the Truth, I will announce my conversion to Islam publicly amongst them (i.e. the infidels),' Abu Dhar went to the Mosque, where some people from Quraish were present, and said, 'O folk of Quraish ! I testify that None has the right to be worshipped except Allah, and I (also) testify that Muhammad is Allah's Slave and His Apostle.' (Hearing that) the Quraishi men said, 'Get at this Sabi (i.e. Muslim) !' They got up and beat me nearly to death. Al `Abbas saw me and threw himself over me to protect me. He then faced them and said, 'Woe to you! You want to kill a man from the tribe of Ghifar, although your trade and your communications are through the territory of Ghifar?' They therefore left me. The next morning I returned (to the Mosque) and said the same as I have said on the previous day. They again said, 'Get at this Sabi!' I was treated in the same way as on the previous day, and again Al-Abbas found me and threw himself over me to protect me and told them the same as he had said the day before.' So, that was the conversion of Abu Dhar (may Allah be Merciful to him) to Islam." . – Sahih Al-Bukhari 3522

حَدَّثَنَا زَيْدٌ ـ هُوَ ابْنُ أَخْزَمَ ـ قَالَ أَبُو قُتَيْبَةَ سَلْمُ بْنُ قُتَيْبَةَ حَدَّثَنِي مُثَنَّى بْنُ سَعِيدٍ الْقَصِيرُ، قَالَ حَدَّثَنِي أَبُو جَمْرَةَ، قَالَ لَنَا ابْنُ عَبَّاسٍ أَلاَ أُخْبِرُكُمْ بِإِسْلاَمِ أَبِي ذَرٍّ، قَالَ قُلْنَا بَلَى. قَالَ قَالَ أَبُو ذَرٍّ كُنْتُ رَجُلاً مِنْ غِفَارٍ، فَبَلَغَنَا أَنَّ رَجُلاً قَدْ خَرَجَ بِمَكَّةَ، يَزْعُمُ أَنَّهُ نَبِيٌّ، فَقُلْتُ لأَخِي انْطَلِقْ إِلَى هَذَا الرَّجُلِ كَلِّمْهُ وَأْتِنِي بِخَبَرِهِ. فَانْطَلَقَ فَلَقِيَهُ، ثُمَّ رَجَعَ فَقُلْتُ مَا عِنْدَكَ فَقَالَ وَاللَّهِ لَقَدْ رَأَيْتُ رَجُلاً يَأْمُرُ بِالْخَيْرِ وَيَنْهَى عَنِ الشَّرِّ. فَقُلْتُ لَهُ لَمْ تَشْفِنِي مِنَ الْخَبَرِ. فَأَخَذْتُ جِرَابًا وَعَصًا، ثُمَّ أَقْبَلْتُ إِلَى مَكَّةَ فَجَعَلْتُ لاَ أَعْرِفُهُ، وَأَكْرَهُ أَنْ أَسْأَلَ عَنْهُ، وَأَشْرَبُ مِنْ مَاءِ زَمْزَمَ وَأَكُونُ فِي الْمَسْجِدِ. قَالَ فَمَرَّ بِي عَلِيٌّ فَقَالَ كَأَنَّ الرَّجُلَ غَرِيبٌ. قَالَ قُلْتُ نَعَمْ. قَالَ فَانْطَلِقْ إِلَى الْمَنْزِلِ. قَالَ فَانْطَلَقْتُ مَعَهُ لاَ يَسْأَلُنِي عَنْ شَىْءٍ، وَلاَ أُخْبِرُهُ، فَلَمَّا أَصْبَحْتُ غَدَوْتُ إِلَى الْمَسْجِدِ لأَسْأَلَ عَنْهُ، وَلَيْسَ أَحَدٌ يُخْبِرُنِي عَنْهُ بِشَىْءٍ. قَالَ فَمَرَّ بِي عَلِيٌّ فَقَالَ أَمَا نَالَ لِلرَّجُلِ يَعْرِفُ مَنْزِلَهُ بَعْدُ قَالَ قُلْتُ لاَ. قَالَ انْطَلِقْ مَعِي. قَالَ فَقَالَ مَا أَمْرُكَ وَمَا أَقْدَمَكَ هَذِهِ الْبَلْدَةَ قَالَ قُلْتُ لَهُ إِنْ كَتَمْتَ عَلَىَّ أَخْبَرْتُكَ. قَالَ فَإِنِّي أَفْعَلُ. قَالَ قُلْتُ لَهُ بَلَغَنَا أَنَّهُ قَدْ خَرَجَ هَا هُنَا رَجُلٌ يَزْعُمُ أَنَّهُ نَبِيٌّ، فَأَرْسَلْتُ أَخِي لِيُكَلِّمَهُ فَرَجَعَ وَلَمْ يَشْفِنِي مِنَ الْخَبَرِ، فَأَرَدْتُ أَنْ أَلْقَاهُ. فَقَالَ لَهُ أَمَا إِنَّكَ قَدْ رَشَدْتَ، هَذَا وَجْهِي إِلَيْهِ، فَاتَّبِعْنِي، ادْخُلْ حَيْثُ أَدْخُلُ، فَإِنِّي إِنْ رَأَيْتُ أَحَدًا أَخَافُهُ عَلَيْكَ، قُمْتُ إِلَى الْحَائِطِ، كَأَنِّي أُصْلِحُ نَعْلِي، وَامْضِ أَنْتَ، فَمَضَى وَمَضَيْتُ مَعَهُ، حَتَّى دَخَلَ وَدَخَلْتُ مَعَهُ عَلَى النَّبِيِّ صلى الله عليه وسلم فَقُلْتُ لَهُ اعْرِضْ عَلَىَّ الإِسْلاَمَ. فَعَرَضَهُ فَأَسْلَمْتُ مَكَانِي، فَقَالَ لِي " يَا أَبَا ذَرٍّ اكْتُمْ هَذَا الأَمْرَ، وَارْجِعْ إِلَى بَلَدِكَ، فَإِذَا بَلَغَكَ ظُهُورُنَا فَأَقْبِلْ ". فَقُلْتُ وَالَّذِي بَعَثَكَ بِالْحَقِّ لأَصْرُخَنَّ بِهَا بَيْنَ أَظْهُرِهِمْ. فَجَاءَ إِلَى الْمَسْجِدِ، وَقُرَيْشٌ فِيهِ فَقَالَ يَا مَعْشَرَ قُرَيْشٍ، إِنِّي أَشْهَدُ أَنْ لاَ إِلَهَ إِلاَّ اللَّهُ، وَأَشْهَدُ أَنَّ مُحَمَّدًا عَبْدُهُ وَرَسُولُهُ. فَقَالُوا قُومُوا إِلَى هَذَا الصَّابِئِ. فَقَامُوا فَضُرِبْتُ لأَمُوتَ فَأَدْرَكَنِي الْعَبَّاسُ، فَأَكَبَّ عَلَىَّ ثُمَّ أَقْبَلَ عَلَيْهِمْ، فَقَالَ وَيْلَكُمْ تَقْتُلُونَ رَجُلاً مِنْ غِفَارَ، وَمَتْجَرُكُمْ وَمَمَرُّكُمْ عَلَى غِفَارَ. فَأَقْلَعُوا عَنِّي، فَلَمَّا أَنْ أَصْبَحْتُ الْغَدَ رَجَعْتُ فَقُلْتُ مِثْلَ مَا قُلْتُ بِالأَمْسِ، فَقَالُوا قُومُوا إِلَى هَذَا الصَّابِئِ. فَصُنِعَ {بِي} مِثْلَ مَا صُنِعَ بِالأَمْسِ وَأَدْرَكَنِي الْعَبَّاسُ فَأَكَبَّ عَلَىَّ، وَقَالَ مِثْلَ مَقَالَتِهِ بِالأَمْسِ. قَالَ فَكَانَ هَذَا أَوَّلَ إِسْلاَمِ أَبِي ذَرٍّ رَحِمَهُ اللَّهُ

Narrated Abu Dhar: I said, "O Allah's Messenger ﷺ! Which mosque was first built on the surface of the earth?" He said, "Al- Masjid-ul-,Haram (in Mecca)." I said, "Which was built next?" He replied "The mosque of Al-Aqsa (in Jerusalem) ." I said, "What was the period of construction between the two?" He said, "Forty years." He added, "Wherever (you may be, and) the prayer time becomes due, perform the prayer there, for the best thing is to do so (i.e. to offer the prayers in time). – Sahih Al-Bukhari 3366

حَدَّثَنَا مُوسَى بْنُ إِسْمَاعِيلَ، حَدَّثَنَا عَبْدُ الْوَاحِدِ، حَدَّثَنَا الأَعْمَشُ، حَدَّثَنَا إِبْرَاهِيمُ التَّيْمِيُّ، عَنْ أَبِيهِ، قَالَ سَمِعْتُ أَبَا ذَرٍّ ـ رضى الله عنه ـ قَالَ قُلْتُ يَا رَسُولَ اللَّهِ، أَىُّ مَسْجِدٍ وُضِعَ فِي الأَرْضِ أَوَّلُ قَالَ " الْمَسْجِدُ الْحَرَامُ ". قَالَ قُلْتُ ثُمَّ أَىٌّ قَالَ " الْمَسْجِدُ الأَقْصَى ". قُلْتُ كَمْ كَانَ بَيْنَهُمَا قَالَ " أَرْبَعُونَ سَنَةً، ثُمَّ أَيْنَمَا أَدْرَكَتْكَ الصَّلاَةُ بَعْدُ فَصَلِّهْ، فَإِنَّ الْفَضْلَ فِيهِ "

Narrated Anas (ra): Abu Dhar (ra) used to say that Allah's Messenger ﷺ said, "While I was at Makkah, the roof of my house was opened and Jibril descended, opened my chest, and washed it with Zamzam water. Then he brought a golden tray full of wisdom and faith, and having poured its contents into my chest, he closed it. Then he took my hand and ascended with me to the heaven. When Jibril reached the nearest heaven, he said to the gatekeeper of the heaven, 'Open (the gate).' The gatekeeper asked, 'who is it?' Jibril answered, 'Jibril'. He asked, 'Is there anyone with you?' Jibril replied, 'Muhammad ﷺ is with me.' He asked, 'Has he been called?', Jibril said, 'Yes'. So, the gate was opened and we went over the nearest heaven, and there we saw a man sitting with Aswida (a large number of people) of his right and Aswida on his left. When he looked towards his right, he laughed and when he looked towards his left he wept. He said (to me), 'Welcome, O pious Prophet and pious son'. I said, 'Who is this man O Jibril?' Jibril replied, 'He is Adam, and the people on his right and left are the souls of his offspring. Those on the right are the people of Paradise, and those on the left are the people of the (Hell) Fire. So, when he looks to the right, he laughs, and when he looks to the left he weeps.' Then Jibril ascended with me till he reached the second heaven and said to the gatekeeper, 'Open (the gate).' The gatekeeper said to him the same as the gatekeeper of the first heaven has said, and he opened the gate." Anas added: Abu Dhar mentioned that Prophet ﷺ met Idris, Musa (Moses), 'Isa (Jesus) and Ibrahim (Abraham) over the heavens, but he did not specify their places (i.e., on which heavens each of them was), but he mentioned that he (the Prophet (ﷺhad met Adam on the nearest heaven, and Ibrahim on the sixth. Anas said, "When Jibril and the Prophet ﷺ passed by Idris, the latter said, 'Welcome, O pious Prophet and pious brother!' the Prophet ﷺ asked, 'Who is he?' Jibril said, 'He is Idris.' " The Prophet ﷺ added, "Then I passed by Musa who said, 'Welcome, O pious Prophet and pious brother!' I said, 'Who is he?' Jibril said, 'He is Musa.' Then I passed by 'Isa who said, 'Welcome, O pious Prophet and pious brother!' I said, 'Who is he?' He replied, 'He is 'Isa.' Then I passed by the Prophet ﷺ Ibrahim who said, 'Welcome, O pious Prophet and pious son!' I said, 'Who is he?' Jibril replied, 'He is Ibrahim'." Narrated Ibn 'Abbas and Abu Haiyya Al-Ansari: The Prophet ﷺ said, "Then Jibril ascended with me to a place where I heard the creaking of pens." Ibn Hazm and Anas bin Malik state the Prophet ﷺ said, "Allah enjoined fifty Salat (prayers) on me. When I returned with this order of Allah, I passed by Musa who asked me, 'What has Allah enjoined on your followers?' I replied, 'He has enjoined fifty Salat (prayers) on them.' On the Musa said to me, 'Go back to your Lord (and appeal for reduction), for your followers will not be able to bear it.' So, I returned to my Lord and asked for some reduction, and He reduced it to half. When I passed by Musa again and informed him about it, he once more said to me, 'Go back to your Lord, for your followers will not be able to bear it.' So, I returned to my Lord similarly as before, and half of it was reduced. I again passed by Musa and he said to me, 'Go back to your Lord, for your followers will not be able to bear it.' I again returned to my Lord and He said, 'These are five (Salat-prayers) and they are all (equal to) fifty (in reward), for My Word does not change.' I returned to Musa, he again told me to return to my Lord (for further reduction) but I said to him 'I feel shy of asking my Lord now.' Then Jibril took me till we reached Sidrat-ul-Muntaha (i.e., lote tree of utmost boundary) which was shrouded in colors indescribable. Then I was admitted into Paradise where I found small tents (made) of pearls and its earth was musk (a kind of perfume).". – Sahih Al-Bukhari 3342

قَالَ عَبْدَانُ أَخْبَرَنَا عَبْدُ اللَّهِ، أَخْبَرَنَا يُونُسُ، عَنِ الزُّهْرِيِّ، ح حَدَّثَنَا أَحْمَدُ بْنُ صَالِحٍ، حَدَّثَنَا عَنْبَسَةُ، حَدَّثَنَا يُونُسُ، عَنِ ابْنِ شِهَابٍ، قَالَ قَالَ أَنَسٌ كَانَ أَبُو ذَرٍّ ـ رضى الله عنه ـ يُحَدِّثُ أَنَّ رَسُولَ اللَّهِ صلى الله عليه وسلم قَالَ " فُرِجَ سَقْفُ بَيْتِي وَأَنَا بِمَكَّةَ، فَنَزَلَ جِبْرِيلُ، فَفَرَجَ صَدْرِي، ثُمَّ غَسَلَهُ بِمَاءِ زَمْزَمَ، ثُمَّ جَاءَ بِطَسْتٍ مِنْ ذَهَبٍ مُمْتَلِئٍ حِكْمَةً وَإِيمَانًا فَأَفْرَغَهَا فِي صَدْرِي، ثُمَّ أَطْبَقَهُ ثُمَّ أَخَذَ بِيَدِي، فَعَرَجَ بِي إِلَى السَّمَاءِ، فَلَمَّا جَاءَ إِلَى السَّمَاءِ الدُّنْيَا، قَالَ جِبْرِيلُ لِخَازِنِ السَّمَاءِ افْتَحْ. قَالَ

مَنْ هَذَا قَالَ هَذَا جِبْرِيلُ. قَالَ مَعَكَ أَحَدٌ قَالَ مَعِي مُحَمَّدٌ. قَالَ أُرْسِلَ إِلَيْهِ قَالَ نَعَمْ، فَافْتَحْ. فَلَمَّا عَلَوْنَا السَّمَاءَ إِذَا رَجُلٌ عَنْ يَمِينِهِ أَسْوِدَةٌ، وَعَنْ يَسَارِهِ أَسْوِدَةٌ، فَإِذَا نَظَرَ قِبَلَ يَمِينِهِ ضَحِكَ، وَإِذَا نَظَرَ قِبَلَ شِمَالِهِ بَكَى فَقَالَ مَرْحَبًا بِالنَّبِيِّ الصَّالِحِ وَالاِبْنِ الصَّالِحِ. قُلْتُ مَنْ هَذَا يَا جِبْرِيلُ قَالَ هَذَا آدَمُ، وَهَذِهِ الأَسْوِدَةُ عَنْ يَمِينِهِ، وَعَنْ شِمَالِهِ نَسَمُ بَنِيهِ، فَأَهْلُ الْيَمِينِ مِنْهُمْ أَهْلُ الْجَنَّةِ، وَالأَسْوِدَةُ الَّتِي عَنْ شِمَالِهِ أَهْلُ النَّارِ، فَإِذَا نَظَرَ قِبَلَ يَمِينِهِ ضَحِكَ، وَإِذَا نَظَرَ قِبَلَ شِمَالِهِ بَكَى، ثُمَّ عَرَجَ بِي جِبْرِيلُ، حَتَّى أَتَى السَّمَاءَ الثَّانِيَةَ، فَقَالَ لِخَازِنِهَا افْتَحْ. فَقَالَ لَهُ خَازِنُهَا مِثْلَ مَا قَالَ الأَوَّلُ، فَفَتَحَ ". قَالَ أَنَسٌ فَذَكَرَ أَنَّهُ وَجَدَ فِي السَّمَوَاتِ إِدْرِيسَ وَمُوسَى وَعِيسَى وَإِبْرَاهِيمَ، وَلَمْ يُثْبِتْ لِي كَيْفَ مَنَازِلُهُمْ، غَيْرَ أَنَّهُ قَدْ ذَكَرَ أَنَّهُ وَجَدَ آدَمَ فِي السَّمَاءِ الدُّنْيَا، وَإِبْرَاهِيمَ فِي السَّادِسَةِ. وَقَالَ أَنَسٌ فَلَمَّا مَرَّ جِبْرِيلُ بِإِدْرِيسَ. قَالَ مَرْحَبًا بِالنَّبِيِّ الصَّالِحِ وَالأَخِ الصَّالِحِ. فَقُلْتُ مَنْ هَذَا قَالَ هَذَا إِدْرِيسُ، ثُمَّ مَرَرْتُ بِمُوسَى فَقَالَ مَرْحَبًا بِالنَّبِيِّ الصَّالِحِ وَالأَخِ الصَّالِحِ. قُلْتُ مَنْ هَذَا قَالَ هَذَا مُوسَى. ثُمَّ مَرَرْتُ بِعِيسَى، فَقَالَ مَرْحَبًا بِالنَّبِيِّ الصَّالِحِ وَالأَخِ الصَّالِحِ. قُلْتُ مَنْ هَذَا قَالَ عِيسَى. ثُمَّ مَرَرْتُ بِإِبْرَاهِيمَ، فَقَالَ مَرْحَبًا بِالنَّبِيِّ الصَّالِحِ وَالاِبْنِ الصَّالِحِ. قُلْتُ مَنْ هَذَا قَالَ هَذَا إِبْرَاهِيمُ. قَالَ وَأَخْبَرَنِي ابْنُ حَزْمٍ أَنَّ ابْنَ عَبَّاسٍ وَأَبَا حَبَّةَ الأَنْصَارِيَّ كَانَا يَقُولاَنِ قَالَ النَّبِيُّ صلى الله عليه وسلم " ثُمَّ عُرِجَ بِي حَتَّى ظَهَرْتُ لِمُسْتَوًى أَسْمَعُ صَرِيفَ الأَقْلاَمِ ". قَالَ ابْنُ حَزْمٍ وَأَنَسُ بْنُ مَالِكٍ ـ رضى الله عنهما ـ قَالَ النَّبِيُّ صلى الله عليه وسلم " فَفَرَضَ اللَّهُ عَلَىَّ خَمْسِينَ صَلاَةً، فَرَجَعْتُ بِذَلِكَ حَتَّى أَمُرَّ بِمُوسَى، فَقَالَ مُوسَى مَا الَّذِي فُرِضَ عَلَى أُمَّتِكَ قُلْتُ فَرَضَ عَلَيْهِمْ خَمْسِينَ صَلاَةً. قَالَ فَرَاجِعْ رَبَّكَ، فَإِنَّ أُمَّتَكَ لاَ تُطِيقُ ذَلِكَ. فَرَجَعْتُ فَرَاجَعْتُ رَبِّي فَوَضَعَ شَطْرَهَا، فَرَجَعْتُ إِلَى مُوسَى، فَقَالَ رَاجِعْ رَبَّكَ، فَذَكَرَ مِثْلَهُ، فَوَضَعَ شَطْرَهَا، فَرَجَعْتُ إِلَى مُوسَى، فَأَخْبَرْتُهُ فَقَالَ رَاجِعْ رَبَّكَ، فَإِنَّ أُمَّتَكَ لاَ تُطِيقُ ذَلِكَ، فَرَجَعْتُ فَرَاجَعْتُ رَبِّي فَقَالَ هِيَ خَمْسٌ، وَهْىَ خَمْسُونَ، لاَ يُبَدَّلُ الْقَوْلُ لَدَىَّ. فَرَجَعْتُ إِلَى مُوسَى، فَقَالَ رَاجِعْ رَبَّكَ. فَقُلْتُ قَدِ اسْتَحْيَيْتُ مِنْ رَبِّي، ثُمَّ انْطَلَقَ، حَتَّى أَتَى السِّدْرَةَ الْمُنْتَهَى، فَغَشِيَهَا أَلْوَانٌ لاَ أَدْرِي مَا هِيَ، ثُمَّ أُدْخِلْتُ {الْجَنَّةَ} فَإِذَا فِيهَا جَنَابِذُ اللُّؤْلُؤِ وَإِذَا تُرَابُهَا الْمِسْكُ "

Narrated Abu Dhar: Once, while I was in the company of the Prophet, he saw the mountain of Uhud and said, "I would not like to have this mountain turned into gold for me unless nothing of it, not even a single Dinar remains of it with me for more than three days (i.e. I will spend all of it in Allah's Cause), except that Dinar which I will keep for repaying debts." Then he said, "Those who are rich in this world would have little reward in the Hereafter except those who spend their money here and there (in Allah's Cause), and they are few in number." Then he ordered me to stay at my place and went not far away. I heard a voice and intended to go to him but I remembered his order, "Stay at your place till I return." On his return I said, "O Allah's Messenger ﷺ! (What was) that noise which I heard?" He said, "Did you hear anything?" I said, "Yes." He said, "Gabriel came and said to me, 'Whoever amongst your followers dies, worshipping none along with Allah, will enter Paradise.' " I said, "Even if he did such-and-such things (i.e. even if he stole or committed illegal sexual intercourse)" He said, "Yes.". – Sahih Al-Bukhari 2388

حَدَّثَنَا أَحْمَدُ بْنُ يُونُسَ، حَدَّثَنَا أَبُو شِهَابٍ، عَنِ الأَعْمَشِ، عَنْ زَيْدِ بْنِ وَهْبٍ، عَنْ أَبِي ذَرٍّ ـ رضى الله عنه ـ قَالَ كُنْتُ مَعَ النَّبِيِّ صلى الله عليه وسلم فَلَمَّا أَبْصَرَ ـ يَعْنِي أُحُدًا ـ قَالَ " مَا أُحِبُّ أَنَّهُ يُحَوَّلُ لِي ذَهَبًا يَمْكُثُ عِنْدِي مِنْهُ دِينَارٌ فَوْقَ ثَلاَثٍ، إِلاَّ دِينَارًا أُرْصِدُهُ لِدَيْنٍ ". ثُمَّ قَالَ " إِنَّ الأَكْثَرِينَ هُمُ الأَقَلُّونَ، إِلاَّ مَنْ قَالَ بِالْمَالِ هَكَذَا وَهَكَذَا ". وَأَشَارَ أَبُو شِهَابٍ بَيْنَ يَدَيْهِ وَعَنْ يَمِينِهِ وَعَنْ شِمَالِهِ ـ وَقَلِيلٌ مَا هُمْ ـ وَقَالَ مَكَانَكَ. وَتَقَدَّمَ غَيْرَ بَعِيدٍ، فَسَمِعْتُ صَوْتًا، فَأَرَدْتُ أَنْ آتِيَهُ، ثُمَّ ذَكَرْتُ قَوْلَهُ مَكَانَكَ حَتَّى آتِيَكَ، فَلَمَّا جَاءَ قُلْتُ يَا رَسُولَ اللَّهِ، الَّذِي سَمِعْتُ أَوْ قَالَ الصَّوْتُ الَّذِي سَمِعْتُ قَالَ " وَهَلْ سَمِعْتَ ". قُلْتُ نَعَمْ. قَالَ " أَتَانِي جِبْرِيلُ ـ عَلَيْهِ السَّلاَمُ ـ فَقَالَ مَنْ مَاتَ مِنْ أُمَّتِكَ لاَ يُشْرِكُ بِاللَّهِ شَيْئًا دَخَلَ الْجَنَّةَ ". قُلْتُ وَإِنْ فَعَلَ كَذَا وَكَذَا قَالَ " نَعَمْ "

Narrated Al-Ma'rur bin Suwaid: I saw Abu Dhar Al-Ghifari wearing a cloak, and his slave, too, was wearing a cloak. We asked him about that (i.e. how both were wearing similar cloaks). He replied, "Once I abused a man and he complained of me to the Prophet ﷺ. The Prophet ﷺ asked me, 'Did you abuse him by slighting his mother?' He added, 'Your slaves are your brethren upon whom Allah has given you authority. So, if one has one's brethren under one's control, one should feed them with the like of what one eats and clothe them with the like of what one wears. You should not overburden them with what they cannot bear, and if you do so, help them (in their hard job). – Sahih Al-Bukhari 2545

حَدَّثَنَا آدَمُ بْنُ أَبِي إِيَاسٍ، حَدَّثَنَا شُعْبَةُ، حَدَّثَنَا وَاصِلٌ الأَحْدَبُ، قَالَ سَمِعْتُ الْمَعْرُورَ بْنَ سُوَيْدٍ، قَالَ رَأَيْتُ أَبَا ذَرٍّ الْغِفَارِيَّ ـ رضى الله عنه ـ وَعَلَيْهِ حُلَّةٌ وَعَلَى غُلاَمِهِ حُلَّةٌ فَسَأَلْنَاهُ عَنْ ذَلِكَ فَقَالَ إِنِّي سَابَبْتُ رَجُلاً فَشَكَانِي إِلَى النَّبِيِّ صلى الله عليه

وسلم، فَقَالَ لِيَ النَّبِيُّ صلى الله عليه وسلم " أَعَيَّرْتَهُ بِأُمِّهِ ". ثُمَّ قَالَ " إِنَّ إِخْوَانَكُمْ خَوَلُكُمْ جَعَلَهُمُ اللَّهُ تَحْتَ أَيْدِيكُمْ، فَمَنْ كَانَ أَخُوهُ تَحْتَ يَدِهِ فَلْيُطْعِمْهُ مِمَّا يَأْكُلُ، وَلْيُلْبِسْهُ مِمَّا يَلْبَسُ، وَلاَ تُكَلِّفُوهُمْ مَا يَغْلِبُهُمْ، فَإِنْ كَلَّفْتُمُوهُمْ مَا يَغْلِبُهُمْ فَأَعِينُوهُمْ "

Narrated Abu Dhar: Once I went out at night and found Allah's Messenger ﷺ walking all alone accompanied by nobody, and I thought that perhaps he disliked that someone should accompany him. So I walked in the shade, away from the moonlight, but the Prophet ﷺ looked behind and saw me and said, "Who is that?" I replied, "Abu Dhar, let Allah get me sacrificed for you!" He said, "O Abu Dhar, come here!" So I accompanied him for a while and then he said, "The rich are in fact the poor (little rewarded) on the Day of Resurrection except him whom Allah gives wealth which he gives (in charity) to his right, left, front and back, and does good deeds with it. I walked with him a little longer. Then he said to me, "Sit down here." So he made me sit in an open space surrounded by rocks, and said to me, "Sit here till I come back to you." He went towards Al-Harra till I could not see him, and he stayed away for a long period, and then I heard him saying, while he was coming, "Even if he had committed theft, and even if he had committed illegal sexual intercourse?" When he came, I could not remain patient and asked him, "O Allah's Prophet! Let Allah get me sacrificed for you! Whom were you speaking to by the side of Al-Harra? I did not hear anybody responding to your talk." He said, "It was Gabriel who appeared to me beside Al-Harra and said, 'Give the good news to your followers that whoever dies without having worshipped anything besides Allah, will enter Paradise.' I said, 'O Gabriel! Even if he had committed theft or committed illegal sexual intercourse?' He said, 'Yes.' I said, 'Even if he has committed theft or committed illegal sexual intercourse?' He said, 'Yes.' I said, 'Even if he has committed theft or committed illegal sexual intercourse?' He said, 'Yes.' ". – Sahih Al-Bukhari 6443

حَدَّثَنَا قُتَيْبَةُ بْنُ سَعِيدٍ، حَدَّثَنَا جَرِيرٌ، عَنْ عَبْدِ الْعَزِيزِ بْنِ رُفَيْعٍ، عَنْ زَيْدِ بْنِ وَهْبٍ، عَنْ أَبِي ذَرٍّ ـ رضى الله عنه ـ قَالَ خَرَجْتُ لَيْلَةً مِنَ اللَّيَالِي فَإِذَا رَسُولُ اللَّهِ صلى الله عليه وسلم يَمْشِي وَحْدَهُ، وَلَيْسَ مَعَهُ إِنْسَانٌ ـ قَالَ ـ فَظَنَنْتُ أَنَّهُ يَكْرَهُ أَنْ يَمْشِيَ مَعَهُ أَحَدٌ ـ قَالَ ـ فَجَعَلْتُ أَمْشِي فِي ظِلِّ الْقَمَرِ فَالْتَفَتَ فَرَآنِي فَقَالَ " مَنْ هَذَا ". قُلْتُ أَبُو ذَرٍّ جَعَلَنِي اللَّهُ فِدَاءَكَ. قَالَ " يَا أَبَا ذَرٍّ تَعَالَهْ ". قَالَ فَمَشَيْتُ مَعَهُ سَاعَةً فَقَالَ " إِنَّ الْمُكْثِرِينَ هُمُ الْمُقِلُّونَ يَوْمَ الْقِيَامَةِ، إِلاَّ مَنْ أَعْطَاهُ اللَّهُ خَيْرًا، فَنَفَحَ فِيهِ يَمِينَهُ وَشِمَالَهُ وَبَيْنَ يَدَيْهِ وَوَرَاءَهُ، وَعَمِلَ فِيهِ خَيْرًا ". قَالَ فَمَشَيْتُ مَعَهُ سَاعَةً فَقَالَ لِي " اجْلِسْ هَا هُنَا ". قَالَ فَأَجْلَسَنِي فِي قَاعٍ حَوْلَهُ حِجَارَةٌ فَقَالَ لِي " اجْلِسْ هَا هُنَا حَتَّى أَرْجِعَ إِلَيْكَ ". قَالَ فَانْطَلَقَ فِي الْحَرَّةِ حَتَّى لاَ أَرَاهُ فَلَبِثَ عَنِّي فَأَطَالَ اللُّبْثَ، ثُمَّ إِنِّي سَمِعْتُهُ وَهْوَ مُقْبِلٌ وَهْوَ يَقُولُ " وَإِنْ سَرَقَ وَإِنْ زَنَى ". قَالَ فَلَمَّا جَاءَ لَمْ أَصْبِرْ حَتَّى قُلْتُ يَا نَبِيَّ اللَّهِ جَعَلَنِي اللَّهُ فِدَاءَكَ مَنْ تُكَلِّمُ فِي جَانِبِ الْحَرَّةِ مَا سَمِعْتُ أَحَدًا يَرْجِعُ إِلَيْكَ شَيْئًا. قَالَ " ذَلِكَ جِبْرِيلُ ـ عَلَيْهِ السَّلاَمُ ـ عَرَضَ لِي فِي جَانِبِ الْحَرَّةِ، قَالَ بَشِّرْ أُمَّتَكَ أَنَّهُ مَنْ مَاتَ لاَ يُشْرِكُ بِاللَّهِ شَيْئًا دَخَلَ الْجَنَّةَ، قُلْتُ يَا جِبْرِيلُ وَإِنْ سَرَقَ وَإِنْ زَنَى قَالَ نَعَمْ. قَالَ قُلْتُ وَإِنْ سَرَقَ وَإِنْ زَنَى قَالَ نَعَمْ، وَإِنْ شَرِبَ الْخَمْرَ. قَالَ النَّضْرُ أَخْبَرَنَا شُعْبَةُ، وَحَدَّثَنَا حَبِيبُ بْنُ أَبِي ثَابِتٍ، وَالأَعْمَشُ، وَعَبْدُ الْعَزِيزِ بْنُ رُفَيْعٍ، حَدَّثَنَا زَيْدُ بْنُ وَهْبٍ، بِهَذَا. قَالَ أَبُو عَبْدِ اللَّهِ حَدِيثُ أَبِي صَالِحٍ عَنْ أَبِي الدَّرْدَاءِ، مُرْسَلٌ، لاَ يَصِحُّ، إِنَّمَا أَرَدْنَا لِلْمَعْرِفَةِ، وَالصَّحِيحُ حَدِيثُ أَبِي ذَرٍّ. قِيلَ لأَبِي عَبْدِ اللَّهِ حَدِيثُ عَطَاءِ بْنِ يَسَارٍ عَنْ أَبِي الدَّرْدَاءِ قَالَ مُرْسَلٌ أَيْضًا لاَ يَصِحُّ، وَالصَّحِيحُ حَدِيثُ أَبِي ذَرٍّ. وَقَالَ اضْرِبُوا عَلَى حَدِيثِ أَبِي الدَّرْدَاءِ هَذَا. إِذَا مَاتَ قَالَ لاَ إِلَهَ إِلاَّ اللَّهُ. عِنْدَ الْمَوْتِ.

Narrated Zaid bin Wahab: I passed by a place called Ar-Rabadha and by chance I met Abu Dhar and asked him, "What has brought you to this place?" He said, "I was in Sham and differed with Muawiya on the meaning of (the following verses of the Qur'an): 'They who hoard up gold and silver and spend them not in the way of Allah.' (9.34). Muawiya said, 'This verse is revealed regarding the people of the scriptures." I said, It was revealed regarding us and also the people of the scriptures." So we had a quarrel and Mu'awiya sent a complaint against me to `Uthman. `Uthman wrote to me to come to Medina, and I came to Medina. Many people came to me as if they had not seen me before. So I told this to `Uthman who said to me, "You may depart and live nearby if you wish." That was the reason for my being here for even if an Ethiopian had been nominated as my ruler, I would have obeyed him . – Sahih Al-Bukhari 1406

حَدَّثَنَا عَلِيٌّ، سَمِعَ هُشَيْمًا، أَخْبَرَنَا حُصَيْنٌ، عَنْ زَيْدِ بْنِ وَهْبٍ، قَالَ مَرَرْتُ بِالرَّبَذَةِ فَإِذَا أَنَا بِأَبِي، ذَرٍّ ـ رضى الله عنه ـ فَقُلْتُ لَهُ مَا أَنْزَلَكَ مَنْزِلَكَ هَذَا قَالَ كُنْتُ بِالشَّأْمِ، فَاخْتَلَفْتُ أَنَا وَمُعَاوِيَةُ فِي الَّذِينَ يَكْنِزُونَ الذَّهَبَ وَالْفِضَّةَ وَلاَ يُنْفِقُونَهَا فِي سَبِيلِ اللَّهِ. قَالَ مُعَاوِيَةُ نَزَلَتْ فِي أَهْلِ الْكِتَابِ. فَقُلْتُ نَزَلَتْ فِينَا وَفِيهِمْ. فَكَانَ بَيْنِي وَبَيْنَهُ فِي ذَاكَ، وَكَتَبَ إِلَى عُثْمَانَ ـ رضى الله عنه ـ يَشْكُونِي، فَكَتَبَ إِلَىَّ عُثْمَانُ أَنِ اقْدَمِ الْمَدِينَةَ. فَقَدِمْتُهَا فَكَثُرَ عَلَىَّ النَّاسُ حَتَّى كَأَنَّهُمْ لَمْ يَرَوْنِي قَبْلَ ذَلِكَ، فَذَكَرْتُ ذَاكَ لِعُثْمَانَ فَقَالَ لِي إِنْ شِئْتَ تَنَحَّيْتَ فَكُنْتَ قَرِيبًا. فَذَاكَ الَّذِي أَنْزَلَنِي هَذَا الْمَنْزِلَ، وَلَوْ أَمَّرُوا عَلَىَّ حَبَشِيًّا لَسَمِعْتُ وَأَطَعْتُ.

Khalid ibn al-Walid ibn al-Mughira al-Makhzumi
خالد بن الوليد بن المغيرة المخزومي

Narrated Al-Miswar bin Makhrama and Marwan: (whose narrations attest each other) Allah's Messenger ﷺ set out at the time of Al-Hudaibiya (treaty), and when they proceeded for a distance, he said, "Khalid bin Al-Walid leading the cavalry of Quraish constituting the front of the army, is at a place called Al-Ghamim, so take the way on the right." By Allah, Khalid did not perceive the arrival of the Muslims till the dust arising from the march of the Muslim army reached him, and then he turned back hurriedly to inform Quraish. The Prophet ﷺ went on advancing till he reached the Thaniya (i.e. a mountainous way) through which one would go to them (i.e. people of Quraish). The she-camel of the Prophet ﷺ sat down. The people tried their best to cause the she-camel to get up but in vain, so they said, "Al-Qaswa' (i.e. the she-camel's name) has become stubborn! Al-Qaswa' has become stubborn!" The Prophet ﷺ said, "Al-Qaswa' has not become stubborn, for stubbornness is not her habit, but she was stopped by Him Who stopped the elephant." Then he said, "By the Name of Him in Whose Hands my soul is, if they (i.e. the Quraish infidels) ask me anything which will respect the ordinances of Allah, I will grant it to them." The Prophet ﷺ then rebuked the she-camel and she got up. The Prophet ﷺ changed his way till he dismounted at the farthest end of Al-Hudaibiya at a pit (i.e. well) containing a little water which the people used in small amounts, and in a short while the people used up all its water and complained to Allah's Messenger ﷺ of thirst. The Prophet ﷺ took an arrow out of his arrow-case and ordered them to put the arrow in that pit. By Allah, the water started and continued sprouting out till all the people quenched their thirst and returned with satisfaction. While they were still in that state, Budail bin Warqa-al- Khuza`I came with some persons from his tribe Khuza`a and they were the advisers of Allah's Messenger ﷺ who would keep no secret from him and were from the people of Tihama. Budail said, "I left Ka`b bin Luai and 'Amir bin Luai residing at the profuse water of Al-Hudaibiya and they had milch camels (or their women and children) with them, and will wage war against you, and will prevent you from visiting the Ka`ba." Allah's Messenger ﷺ said, "We have not come to fight anyone, but to perform the `Umra. No doubt, the war has weakened Quraish and they have suffered great losses, so if they wish, I will conclude a truce with them, during which they should refrain from interfering between me and the people (i.e. the 'Arab infidels other than Quraish), and if I have victory over those infidels, Quraish will have the option to embrace Islam as the other people do, if they wish; they will at least get strong enough to fight. But if they do not accept the truce, by Allah in Whose Hands my life is, I will fight with them defending my Cause till I get killed, but (I am sure) Allah will definitely make His Cause victorious." Budail said, "I will inform them of what you have said." So, he set off till he reached Quraish and said, "We have come from that man (i.e. Muhammad) whom we heard saying something which we will disclose to you if you should like." Some of the fools among Quraish shouted that they were not in need of this information, but the wiser among them said, "Relate what you heard him saying." Budail said, "I heard him saying so-and-so," relating what the Prophet ﷺ had told him. `Urwa bin Mas`ud got up and said, "O people! Aren't you the sons? They said, "Yes." He added, "Am I not the father?" They said, "Yes." He said, "Do you mistrust me?" They said, "No." He said, "Don't you know that I invited the people of `Ukaz for your help, and when they refused I brought my relatives and children and those who obeyed me (to help you)?" They said, "Yes." He said, "Well, this man (i.e. the Prophet) has offered you a reasonable proposal, you'd better accept it and allow me to meet him." They said, "You may meet him." So, he went to tht Prophet ﷺ and started talking to him. The Prophet ﷺ told him almost the same as he had told Budail. Then `Urwa said, "O Muhammad! Won't you feel any scruple in extirpating your relations? Have you ever heard of anyone amongst the Arabs extirpating his relatives before you? On the other hand, if the reverse should happen, (nobody will aid you, for) by Allah, I do not see (with you) dignified people, but people from various tribes who would run away leaving you alone." Hearing that, Abu Bakr abused him and said, "Do you say we would run and leave the Prophet ﷺ alone?" `Urwa said, "Who is that man?" They said, "He is Abu Bakr." `Urwa said to Abu Bakr, "By Him in Whose Hands my life is, were it not for the favor which you did to me and which I did not compensate, I would retort on you." `Urwa kept on talking to the Prophet ﷺ and seizing the Prophet's beard as he was talking while Al-Mughira bin Shu`ba was standing near the head of the Prophet, holding a sword and wearing a helmet. Whenever `Urwa stretched his hand towards the beard of the Prophet, Al-Mughira would hit his hand with the handle of the sword and say (to `Urwa), "Remove your hand from the beard of Allah's Messenger ﷺ." Urwa raised his head and asked, "Who is that?" The people said, "He is Al-Mughira bin Shu`ba." `Urwa said, "O treacherous! Am I not doing my best to prevent evil consequences of your treachery?" Before embracing Islam Al-Mughira was in the company of some people. He killed them and took their property and came (to Medina) to embrace Islam. The Prophet ﷺ said (to him, "As regards your Islam, I accept it, but as for the property I do not take anything of it. (As it was taken through treason). `Urwa then started looking at the Companions of the Prophet. By Allah, whenever Allah's Messenger ﷺ spat, the spittle would fall in the hand of one of them (i.e. the Prophet's companions) who would rub it on his face and skin; if he ordered them they would carry his orders immediately; if he performed ablution, they would struggle to take the remaining water; and when they spoke to him, they would lower their voices and would not look at his face constantly out of respect. `Urwa returned to his people and said, "O people! By Allah, I have been to the kings and to Caesar, Khosrau and An- Najashi, yet I have never seen any of them respected by his courtiers as much as Muhammad is respected by his companions. By Allah, if he spat, the spittle would fall in the hand of one of them (i.e. the Prophet's companions) who would rub it on his face and skin; if he ordered them, they would carry out his order immediately; if he performed ablution, they would struggle to take the remaining water; and when they spoke, they would lower their voices and would not look at his face constantly out of respect." `Urwa added, "No doubt, he has presented to you a good reasonable offer, so please accept it." A man from the tribe of Bani Kinana said, "Allow me to go to him," and they allowed him, and when he approached the Prophet and his companions, Allah's Messenger ﷺ said, "He is so-and-so who belongs to the tribe that respects the Budn (i.e. camels of the sacrifice). So, bring the Budn in front of him." So, the Budn were brought before him and the people received him while they were reciting Talbiya. When he saw that scene, he said, "Glorified be Allah! It is not fair to prevent these people from visiting the Ka`ba." When he returned to his people, he said, 'I saw the Budn garlanded (with colored knotted ropes) and marked (with stabs on their backs).

I do not think it is advisable to prevent them from visiting the Ka`ba." Another person called Mikraz bin Hafs got up and sought their permission to go to Muhammad, and they allowed him, too. When he approached the Muslims, the Prophet ﷺ said, "Here is Mikraz and he is a vicious man." Mikraz started talking to the Prophet and as he was talking, Suhail bin `Amr came. When Suhail bin `Amr came, the Prophet ﷺ said, "Now the matter has become easy." Suhail said to the Prophet "Please conclude a peace treaty with us." So, the Prophet ﷺ called the clerk and said to him, "Write: By the Name of Allah, the most Beneficent, the most Merciful." Suhail said, "As for 'Beneficent,' by Allah, I do not know what it means. So write: By Your Name O Allah, as you used to write previously." The Muslims said, "By Allah, we will not write except: By the Name of Allah, the most Beneficent, the most Merciful." The Prophet ﷺ said, "Write: By Your Name O Allah." Then he dictated, "This is the peace treaty which Muhammad, Allah's Messenger ﷺ has concluded." Suhail said, "By Allah, if we knew that you are Allah's Messenger ﷺ we would not prevent you from visiting the Ka`ba, and would not fight with you. So, write: "Muhammad bin `Abdullah." The Prophet ﷺ said, "By Allah! I am Apostle of Allah even if you people do not believe me. Write: Muhammad bin `Abdullah." (Az-Zuhri said, "The Prophet ﷺ accepted all those things, as he had already said that he would accept everything they would demand if it respects the ordinance of Allah, (i.e. by letting him and his companions perform `Umra.)" The Prophet ﷺ said to Suhail, "On the condition that you allow us to visit the House (i.e. Ka`ba) so that we may perform Tawaf around it." Suhail said, "By Allah, we will not (allow you this year) so as not to give chance to the 'Arabs to say that we have yielded to you, but we will allow you next year." So, the Prophet ﷺ got that written. Then Suhail said, "We also stipulate that you should return to us whoever comes to you from us, even if he embraced your religion." The Muslims said, "Glorified be Allah! How will such a person be returned to the pagans after he has become a Muslim? While they were in this state Abu- Jandal bin Suhail bin `Amr came from the valley of Mecca staggering with his fetters and fell down amongst the Muslims. Suhail said, "O Muhammad! This is the very first term with which we make peace with you, i.e. you shall return Abu Jandal to me." The Prophet ﷺ said, "The peace treaty has not been written yet." Suhail said, "I will never allow you to keep him." The Prophet ﷺ said, "Yes, do." He said, "I won't do.: Mikraz said, "We allow you (to keep him)." Abu Jandal said, "O Muslims! Will I be returned to the pagans though I have come as a Muslim? Don't you see how much I have suffered?" (continued...) (continuing... 1): -3.891:... ... Abu Jandal had been tortured severely for the Cause of Allah. `Umar bin Al-Khattab said, "I went to the Prophet ﷺ and said, 'Aren't you truly the Messenger of Allah?' The Prophet ﷺ said, 'Yes, indeed.' I said, 'Isn't our Cause just and the cause of the enemy unjust?' He said, 'Yes.' I said, 'Then why should we be humble in our religion?' He said, 'I am Allah's Messenger ﷺ and I do not disobey Him, and He will make me victorious.' I said, 'Didn't you tell us that we would go to the Ka`ba and perform Tawaf around it?' He said, 'Yes, but did I tell you that we would visit the Ka`ba this year?' I said, 'No.' He said, 'So you will visit it and perform Tawaf around it?' " `Umar further said, "I went to Abu Bakr and said, 'O Abu Bakr! Isn't he truly Allah's Prophet?' He replied, 'Yes.' I said, 'Then why should we be humble in our religion?' He said, 'Indeed, he is Allah's Messenger ﷺ and he does not disobey his Lord, and He will make him victorious. Adhere to him as, by Allah, he is on the right.' I said, 'Was he not telling us that we would go to the Ka`ba and perform Tawaf around it?' He said, 'Yes, but did he tell you that you would go to the Ka`ba this year?' I said, 'No.' He said, "You will go to Ka`ba and perform Tawaf around it." (Az-Zuhri said, " `Umar said, 'I performed many good deeds as expiation for the improper questions I asked them.' ") When the writing of the peace treaty was concluded, Allah's

Messenger ﷺ said to his companions, “Get up and' slaughter your sacrifices and get your head shaved.” By Allah none of them got up, and the Prophet repeated his order thrice. When none of them got up, he left them and went to Um Salama and told her of the people's attitudes towards him. Um Salama said, “O the Prophet ﷺ of Allah! Do you want your order to be carried out? Go out and don't say a word to anybody till you have slaughtered your sacrifice and call your barber to shave your head.” So, the Prophet ﷺ went out and did not talk to anyone of them till he did that, i.e. slaughtered the sacrifice and called his barber who shaved his head. Seeing that, the companions of the Prophet ﷺ got up, slaughtered their sacrifices, and started shaving the heads of one another, and there was so much rush that there was a danger of killing each other. Then some believing women came (to the Prophet ﷺ and Allah revealed the following Divine Verses:-- “O you who believe, when the believing women come to you as emigrants examine them . . .” (60.10) `Umar then divorced two wives of his who were infidels. Later on Muawiya bin Abu Sufyan married one of them, and Safwan bin Umaiya married the other. When the Prophet ﷺ returned to Medina, Abu Basir, a new Muslim convert from Quraish came to him. The Infidels sent in his pursuit two men who said (to the Prophet ﷺ), “Abide by the promise you gave us.” So, the Prophet ﷺ handed him over to them. They took him out (of the City) till they reached Dhul-Hulaifa where they dismounted to eat some dates they had with them. Abu Basir said to one of them, “By Allah, O so-and-so, I see you have a fine sword.” The other drew it out (of the scabbard) and said, “By Allah, it is very fine and I have tried it many times.” Abu Basir said, “Let me have a look at it.” When the other gave it to him, he hit him with it till he died, and his companion ran away till he came to Medina and entered the Mosque running. When Allah's Messenger ﷺ saw him he said, “This man appears to have been frightened.” When he reached the Prophet ﷺ he said, “My companion has been murdered and I would have been murdered too.” Abu Basir came and said, “O Allah's Messenger ﷺ, by Allah, Allah has made you fulfill your obligations by your returning me to them (i.e. the Infidels), but Allah has saved me from them.” The Prophet ﷺ said, “Woe to his mother! What excellent war kindler he would be, should he only have supporters.” When Abu Basir heard that he understood that the Prophet ﷺ would return him to them again, so he set off till he reached the seashore. Abu Jandal bin Suhail got himself released from them (i.e. infidels) and joined Abu Basir. So, whenever a man from Quraish embraced Islam he would follow Abu Basir till they formed a strong group. By Allah, whenever they heard about a caravan of Quraish heading towards Sham, they stopped it and attacked and killed them (i.e. infidels) and took their properties. The people of Quraish sent a message to the Prophet ﷺ requesting him for the Sake of Allah and Kith and kin to send for (i.e. Abu Basir and his companions) promising that whoever (amongst them) came to the Prophet ﷺ would be secure. So the Prophet ﷺ sent for them (i.e. Abu Basir's companions) and Allah I revealed the following Divine Verses: “And it is He Who Has withheld their hands from you and your hands From them in the midst of Mecca, After He made you the victorious over them. ... the unbelievers had pride and haughtiness, in their hearts ... the pride and haughtiness of the time of ignorance.” (48.24-26) And their pride and haughtiness was that they did not confess (write in the treaty) that he (i.e. Muhammad) was the Prophet of Allah and refused to write: “In the Name of Allah, the most Beneficent, the Most Merciful,” and they (the mushriks) prevented them (the Muslims) from visiting the House (the Ka`bah). – Sahih Al-Bukhari 2731, 2732

حَدَّثَنِي عَبْدُ اللَّهِ بْنُ مُحَمَّدٍ، حَدَّثَنَا عَبْدُ الرَّزَّاقِ، أَخْبَرَنَا مَعْمَرٌ، قَالَ أَخْبَرَنِي الزُّهْرِيُّ، قَالَ أَخْبَرَنِي عُرْوَةُ بْنُ الزُّبَيْرِ، عَنِ الْمِسْوَرِ بْنِ مَخْرَمَةَ، وَمَرْوَانَ، يُصَدِّقُ كُلُّ وَاحِدٍ مِنْهُمَا حَدِيثَ صَاحِبِهِ قَالَ خَرَجَ رَسُولُ اللَّهِ صلى الله عليه وسلم زَمَنَ الْحُدَيْبِيَةِ، حَتَّى كَانُوا بِبَعْضِ الطَّرِيقِ قَالَ النَّبِيُّ صلى الله عليه وسلم " إِنَّ خَالِدَ بْنَ الْوَلِيدِ بِالْغَمِيمِ فِي خَيْلٍ لِقُرَيْشٍ طَلِيعَةً فَخُذُوا ذَاتَ الْيَمِينِ ". فَوَاللَّهِ مَا شَعَرَ بِهِمْ خَالِدٌ حَتَّى إِذَا هُمْ بِقَتَرَةِ الْجَيْشِ، فَانْطَلَقَ يَرْكُضُ نَذِيرًا لِقُرَيْشٍ، وَسَارَ النَّبِيُّ صلى الله عليه وسلم حَتَّى إِذَا كَانَ بِالثَّنِيَّةِ الَّتِي يُهْبَطُ عَلَيْهِمْ مِنْهَا،

بَرَكَتْ بِهِ رَاحِلَتُهُ. فَقَالَ النَّاسُ حَلْ حَلْ. فَأَلَحَّتْ، فَقَالُوا خَلأَتِ الْقَصْوَاءُ، خَلأَتِ الْقَصْوَاءُ. فَقَالَ النَّبِيُّ صلى الله عليه وسلم " مَا خَلأَتِ الْقَصْوَاءُ، وَمَا ذَاكَ لَهَا بِخُلُقٍ، وَلَكِنْ حَبَسَهَا حَابِسُ الْفِيلِ، ثُمَّ قَالَ وَالَّذِي نَفْسِي بِيَدِهِ لاَ يَسْأَلُونِي خُطَّةً يُعَظِّمُونَ فِيهَا حُرُمَاتِ اللَّهِ إِلاَّ أَعْطَيْتُهُمْ إِيَّاهَا ". ثُمَّ زَجَرَهَا فَوَثَبَتْ، قَالَ فَعَدَلَ عَنْهُمْ حَتَّى نَزَلَ بِأَقْصَى الْحُدَيْبِيَةِ، عَلَى ثَمَدٍ قَلِيلِ الْمَاءِ يَتَبَرَّضُهُ النَّاسُ تَبَرُّضًا، فَلَمْ يُلَبِّثْهُ النَّاسُ حَتَّى نَزَحُوهُ، وَشُكِيَ إِلَى رَسُولِ اللَّهِ صلى الله عليه وسلم الْعَطَشُ، فَانْتَزَعَ سَهْمًا مِنْ كِنَانَتِهِ، ثُمَّ أَمَرَهُمْ أَنْ يَجْعَلُوهُ فِيهِ، فَوَاللَّهِ مَا زَالَ يَجِيشُ لَهُمْ بِالرِّيِّ حَتَّى صَدَرُوا عَنْهُ، فَبَيْنَمَا هُمْ كَذَلِكَ، إِذْ جَاءَ بُدَيْلُ بْنُ وَرْقَاءَ الْخُزَاعِيُّ فِي نَفَرٍ مِنْ قَوْمِهِ مِنْ خُزَاعَةَ، وَكَانُوا عَيْبَةَ نُصْحِ رَسُولِ اللَّهِ صلى الله عليه وسلم مِنْ أَهْلِ تِهَامَةَ، فَقَالَ إِنِّي تَرَكْتُ كَعْبَ بْنَ لُؤَىٍّ وَعَامِرَ بْنَ لُؤَىٍّ نَزَلُوا أَعْدَادَ مِيَاهِ الْحُدَيْبِيَةِ، وَمَعَهُمُ الْعُوذُ الْمَطَافِيلُ، وَهُمْ مُقَاتِلُوكَ وَصَادُّوكَ عَنِ الْبَيْتِ. فَقَالَ رَسُولُ اللَّهِ صلى الله عليه وسلم " إِنَّا لَمْ نَجِئْ لِقِتَالِ أَحَدٍ، وَلَكِنَّا جِئْنَا مُعْتَمِرِينَ، وَإِنَّ قُرَيْشًا قَدْ نَهِكَتْهُمُ الْحَرْبُ، وَأَضَرَّتْ بِهِمْ، فَإِنْ شَاءُوا مَادَدْتُهُمْ مُدَّةً، وَيُخَلُّوا بَيْنِي وَبَيْنَ النَّاسِ، فَإِنْ أَظْهَرْ فَإِنْ شَاءُوا أَنْ يَدْخُلُوا فِيمَا دَخَلَ فِيهِ النَّاسُ فَعَلُوا، وَإِلاَّ فَقَدْ جَمُّوا، وَإِنْ هُمْ أَبَوْا فَوَالَّذِي نَفْسِي بِيَدِهِ، لأُقَاتِلَنَّهُمْ عَلَى أَمْرِي هَذَا حَتَّى تَنْفَرِدَ سَالِفَتِي، وَلَيُنْفِذَنَّ اللَّهُ أَمْرَهُ ". فَقَالَ بُدَيْلٌ سَأُبَلِّغُهُمْ مَا تَقُولُ. قَالَ فَانْطَلَقَ حَتَّى أَتَى قُرَيْشًا قَالَ إِنَّا قَدْ جِئْنَاكُمْ مِنْ هَذَا الرَّجُلِ، وَسَمِعْنَاهُ يَقُولُ قَوْلاً، فَإِنْ شِئْتُمْ أَنْ نَعْرِضَهُ عَلَيْكُمْ فَعَلْنَا، فَقَالَ سُفَهَاؤُهُمْ لاَ حَاجَةَ لَنَا أَنْ تُخْبِرَنَا عَنْهُ بِشَىْءٍ. وَقَالَ ذَوُو الرَّأْىِ مِنْهُمْ هَاتِ مَا سَمِعْتَهُ يَقُولُ. قَالَ سَمِعْتُهُ يَقُولُ كَذَا وَكَذَا، فَحَدَّثَهُمْ بِمَا قَالَ النَّبِيُّ صلى الله عليه وسلم. فَقَامَ عُرْوَةُ بْنُ مَسْعُودٍ فَقَالَ أَىْ قَوْمِ أَلَسْتُمْ بِالْوَالِدِ قَالُوا بَلَى. قَالَ أَوَلَسْتُ بِالْوَلَدِ قَالُوا بَلَى. قَالَ فَهَلْ تَتَّهِمُونِي. قَالُوا لاَ. قَالَ أَلَسْتُمْ تَعْلَمُونَ أَنِّي اسْتَنْفَرْتُ أَهْلَ عُكَاظٍ، فَلَمَّا بَلَّحُوا عَلَىَّ جِئْتُكُمْ بِأَهْلِي وَوَلَدِي وَمَنْ أَطَاعَنِي قَالُوا بَلَى. قَالَ فَإِنَّ هَذَا قَدْ عَرَضَ لَكُمْ خُطَّةَ رُشْدٍ، اقْبَلُوهَا وَدَعُونِي آتِهِ. قَالُوا ائْتِهِ. فَأَتَاهُ فَجَعَلَ يُكَلِّمُ النَّبِيَّ صلى الله عليه وسلم فَقَالَ النَّبِيُّ صلى الله عليه وسلم نَحْوًا مِنْ قَوْلِهِ لِبُدَيْلٍ، فَقَالَ عُرْوَةُ عِنْدَ ذَلِكَ أَىْ مُحَمَّدُ، أَرَأَيْتَ إِنِ اسْتَأْصَلْتَ أَمْرَ قَوْمِكَ هَلْ سَمِعْتَ بِأَحَدٍ مِنَ الْعَرَبِ اجْتَاحَ أَهْلَهُ قَبْلَكَ وَإِنْ تَكُنِ الأُخْرَى، فَإِنِّي وَاللَّهِ لأَرَى وُجُوهًا، وَإِنِّي لأَرَى أَوْشَابًا مِنَ النَّاسِ خَلِيقًا أَنْ يَفِرُّوا وَيَدَعُوكَ. فَقَالَ لَهُ أَبُو بَكْرٍ امْصُصْ بَظْرَ اللاَّتِ، أَنَحْنُ نَفِرُّ عَنْهُ وَنَدَعُهُ فَقَالَ مَنْ ذَا قَالُوا أَبُو بَكْرٍ. قَالَ أَمَا وَالَّذِي نَفْسِي بِيَدِهِ لَوْلاَ يَدٌ كَانَتْ لَكَ عِنْدِي لَمْ أَجْزِكَ بِهَا لأَجَبْتُكَ. قَالَ وَجَعَلَ يُكَلِّمُ النَّبِيَّ صلى الله عليه وسلم فَكُلَّمَا تَكَلَّمَ أَخَذَ بِلِحْيَتِهِ، وَالْمُغِيرَةُ بْنُ شُعْبَةَ قَائِمٌ عَلَى رَأْسِ النَّبِيِّ صلى الله عليه وسلم وَمَعَهُ السَّيْفُ وَعَلَيْهِ الْمِغْفَرُ، فَكُلَّمَا أَهْوَى عُرْوَةُ بِيَدِهِ إِلَى لِحْيَةِ النَّبِيِّ صلى الله عليه وسلم ضَرَبَ يَدَهُ بِنَعْلِ السَّيْفِ، وَقَالَ لَهُ أَخِّرْ يَدَكَ عَنْ لِحْيَةِ رَسُولِ اللَّهِ صلى الله عليه وسلم. فَرَفَعَ عُرْوَةُ رَأْسَهُ فَقَالَ مَنْ هَذَا قَالُوا الْمُغِيرَةُ بْنُ شُعْبَةَ. فَقَالَ أَىْ غُدَرُ، أَلَسْتُ أَسْعَى فِي غَدْرَتِكَ وَكَانَ الْمُغِيرَةُ صَحِبَ قَوْمًا فِي الْجَاهِلِيَّةِ، فَقَتَلَهُمْ، وَأَخَذَ أَمْوَالَهُمْ، ثُمَّ جَاءَ فَأَسْلَمَ فَقَالَ النَّبِيُّ صلى الله عليه وسلم " أَمَّا الإِسْلاَمَ فَأَقْبَلُ، وَأَمَّا الْمَالَ فَلَسْتُ مِنْهُ فِي شَىْءٍ ". ثُمَّ إِنَّ عُرْوَةَ جَعَلَ يَرْمُقُ أَصْحَابَ النَّبِيِّ صلى الله عليه وسلم بِعَيْنَيْهِ. قَالَ فَوَاللَّهِ مَا تَنَخَّمَ رَسُولُ اللَّهِ صلى الله عليه وسلم نُخَامَةً إِلاَّ وَقَعَتْ فِي كَفِّ رَجُلٍ مِنْهُمْ فَدَلَكَ بِهَا وَجْهَهُ وَجِلْدَهُ، وَإِذَا أَمَرَهُمُ ابْتَدَرُوا أَمْرَهُ، وَإِذَا تَوَضَّأَ كَادُوا يَقْتَتِلُونَ عَلَى وَضُوئِهِ، وَإِذَا تَكَلَّمَ خَفَضُوا أَصْوَاتَهُمْ عِنْدَهُ، وَمَا يُحِدُّونَ إِلَيْهِ النَّظَرَ تَعْظِيمًا لَهُ، فَرَجَعَ عُرْوَةُ إِلَى أَصْحَابِهِ، فَقَالَ أَىْ قَوْمِ، وَاللَّهِ لَقَدْ وَفَدْتُ عَلَى الْمُلُوكِ، وَوَفَدْتُ عَلَى قَيْصَرَ وَكِسْرَى وَالنَّجَاشِيِّ وَاللَّهِ إِنْ رَأَيْتُ مَلِكًا قَطُّ، يُعَظِّمُهُ أَصْحَابُهُ مَا يُعَظِّمُ أَصْحَابُ مُحَمَّدٍ صلى الله عليه وسلم مُحَمَّدًا، وَاللَّهِ إِنْ تَنَخَّمَ نُخَامَةً إِلاَّ وَقَعَتْ فِي كَفِّ رَجُلٍ مِنْهُمْ، فَدَلَكَ بِهَا وَجْهَهُ وَجِلْدَهُ، وَإِذَا أَمَرَهُمُ ابْتَدَرُوا أَمْرَهُ وَإِذَا تَوَضَّأَ كَادُوا يَقْتَتِلُونَ عَلَى وَضُوئِهِ، وَإِذَا تَكَلَّمَ خَفَضُوا أَصْوَاتَهُمْ عِنْدَهُ، وَمَا يُحِدُّونَ إِلَيْهِ النَّظَرَ تَعْظِيمًا لَهُ، وَإِنَّهُ قَدْ عَرَضَ عَلَيْكُمْ خُطَّةَ رُشْدٍ، فَاقْبَلُوهَا. فَقَالَ رَجُلٌ مِنْ بَنِي كِنَانَةَ دَعُونِي آتِهِ. فَقَالُوا ائْتِهِ. فَلَمَّا أَشْرَفَ عَلَى النَّبِيِّ صلى الله عليه وسلم وَأَصْحَابِهِ، قَالَ رَسُولُ اللَّهِ صلى الله عليه وسلم " هَذَا فُلاَنٌ، وَهْوَ مِنْ قَوْمٍ يُعَظِّمُونَ الْبُدْنَ فَابْعَثُوهَا لَهُ ". فَبُعِثَتْ لَهُ وَاسْتَقْبَلَهُ النَّاسُ يُلَبُّونَ، فَلَمَّا رَأَى ذَلِكَ قَالَ سُبْحَانَ اللَّهِ مَا يَنْبَغِي لِهَؤُلاَءِ أَنْ يُصَدُّوا عَنِ الْبَيْتِ، فَلَمَّا رَجَعَ إِلَى أَصْحَابِهِ قَالَ رَأَيْتُ الْبُدْنَ قَدْ قُلِّدَتْ وَأُشْعِرَتْ، فَمَا أَرَى أَنْ يُصَدُّوا عَنِ الْبَيْتِ. فَقَامَ رَجُلٌ مِنْهُمْ يُقَالُ لَهُ مِكْرَزُ بْنُ حَفْصٍ. فَقَالَ دَعُونِي آتِهِ. فَقَالُوا ائْتِهِ. فَلَمَّا أَشْرَفَ عَلَيْهِمْ قَالَ النَّبِيُّ صلى الله عليه وسلم " هَذَا مِكْرَزٌ وَهْوَ رَجُلٌ فَاجِرٌ ". فَجَعَلَ يُكَلِّمُ النَّبِيَّ صلى الله عليه وسلم، فَبَيْنَمَا هُوَ يُكَلِّمُهُ إِذْ جَاءَ سُهَيْلُ بْنُ عَمْرٍو. قَالَ مَعْمَرٌ فَأَخْبَرَنِي أَيُّوبُ عَنْ عِكْرِمَةَ، أَنَّهُ لَمَّا جَاءَ سُهَيْلُ بْنُ عَمْرٍو قَالَ النَّبِيُّ صلى الله عليه وسلم " لَقَدْ سَهُلَ لَكُمْ مِنْ أَمْرِكُمْ ". قَالَ مَعْمَرٌ قَالَ الزُّهْرِيُّ فِي حَدِيثِهِ فَجَاءَ سُهَيْلُ بْنُ عَمْرٍو فَقَالَ هَاتِ، اكْتُبْ بَيْنَنَا وَبَيْنَكُمْ كِتَابًا، فَدَعَا النَّبِيُّ صلى الله عليه وسلم الْكَاتِبَ، فَقَالَ النَّبِيُّ صلى الله عليه وسلم " بِسْمِ اللَّهِ الرَّحْمَنِ الرَّحِيمِ ". قَالَ سُهَيْلٌ أَمَّا الرَّحْمَنُ فَوَاللَّهِ مَا أَدْرِي مَا هُوَ وَلَكِنِ اكْتُبْ بِاسْمِكَ اللَّهُمَّ. كَمَا كُنْتَ تَكْتُبُ. فَقَالَ الْمُسْلِمُونَ وَاللَّهِ لاَ نَكْتُبُهَا إِلاَّ بِسْمِ اللَّهِ الرَّحْمَنِ الرَّحِيمِ. فَقَالَ النَّبِيُّ صلى الله عليه وسلم " اكْتُبْ بِاسْمِكَ اللَّهُمَّ ". ثُمَّ قَالَ " هَذَا مَا قَاضَى عَلَيْهِ مُحَمَّدٌ رَسُولُ اللَّهِ ". فَقَالَ سُهَيْلٌ وَاللَّهِ لَوْ كُنَّا نَعْلَمُ أَنَّكَ رَسُولُ اللَّهِ مَا صَدَدْنَاكَ عَنِ الْبَيْتِ وَلاَ قَاتَلْنَاكَ، وَلَكِنِ اكْتُبْ مُحَمَّدُ بْنُ عَبْدِ اللَّهِ. فَقَالَ النَّبِيُّ صلى الله عليه وسلم " وَاللَّهِ إِنِّي لَرَسُولُ اللَّهِ وَإِنْ كَذَّبْتُمُونِي. اكْتُبْ مُحَمَّدُ بْنُ عَبْدِ اللَّهِ ". قَالَ الزُّهْرِيُّ وَذَلِكَ لِقَوْلِهِ " لاَ يَسْأَلُونِي خُطَّةً يُعَظِّمُونَ فِيهَا حُرُمَاتِ اللَّهِ إِلاَّ أَعْطَيْتُهُمْ إِيَّاهَا ". فَقَالَ لَهُ النَّبِيُّ صلى الله عليه وسلم " عَلَى أَنْ تُخَلُّوا بَيْنَنَا وَبَيْنَ الْبَيْتِ فَنَطُوفَ بِهِ ". فَقَالَ سُهَيْلٌ وَاللَّهِ لاَ تَتَحَدَّثُ الْعَرَبُ أَنَّا أُخِذْنَا ضُغْطَةً وَلَكِنْ ذَلِكَ مِنَ الْعَامِ الْمُقْبِلِ فَكَتَبَ. فَقَالَ سُهَيْلٌ وَعَلَى أَنَّهُ لاَ يَأْتِيكَ مِنَّا رَجُلٌ، وَإِنْ كَانَ عَلَى دِينِكَ، إِلاَّ رَدَدْتَهُ إِلَيْنَا. قَالَ الْمُسْلِمُونَ سُبْحَانَ اللَّهِ كَيْفَ يُرَدُّ إِلَى الْمُشْرِكِينَ وَقَدْ جَاءَ مُسْلِمًا فَبَيْنَمَا هُمْ كَذَلِكَ إِذْ دَخَلَ أَبُو جَنْدَلِ بْنُ سُهَيْلِ بْنِ عَمْرٍو يَرْسُفُ فِي قُيُودِهِ، وَقَدْ خَرَجَ مِنْ أَسْفَلِ مَكَّةَ، حَتَّى رَمَى بِنَفْسِهِ بَيْنَ أَظْهُرِ الْمُسْلِمِينَ. فَقَالَ سُهَيْلٌ هَذَا يَا مُحَمَّدُ أَوَّلُ مَا أُقَاضِيكَ عَلَيْهِ أَنْ تَرُدَّهُ إِلَىَّ. فَقَالَ النَّبِيُّ صلى الله عليه وسلم " إِنَّا لَمْ نَقْضِ الْكِتَابَ بَعْدُ ". قَالَ فَوَاللَّهِ إِذًا لَمْ أُصَالِحْكَ عَلَى شَىْءٍ أَبَدًا. قَالَ النَّبِيُّ صلى الله عليه وسلم " فَأَجِزْهُ لِي ". قَالَ مَا أَنَا بِمُجِيزِهِ لَكَ. قَالَ " بَلَى، فَافْعَلْ ". قَالَ مَا أَنَا بِفَاعِلٍ. قَالَ مِكْرَزٌ بَلْ قَدْ أَجَزْنَاهُ لَكَ. قَالَ أَبُو جَنْدَلٍ أَىْ مَعْشَرَ الْمُسْلِمِينَ، أُرَدُّ إِلَى الْمُشْرِكِينَ وَقَدْ جِئْتُ مُسْلِمًا أَلاَ تَرَوْنَ مَا قَدْ لَقِيتُ وَكَانَ قَدْ عُذِّبَ عَذَابًا شَدِيدًا فِي اللَّهِ. قَالَ فَقَالَ عُمَرُ بْنُ الْخَطَّابِ فَأَتَيْتُ نَبِيَّ اللَّهِ صلى الله عليه وسلم فَقُلْتُ أَلَسْتَ نَبِيَّ اللَّهِ حَقًّا قَالَ " بَلَى ". قُلْتُ أَلَسْنَا عَلَى الْحَقِّ وَعَدُوُّنَا عَلَى الْبَاطِلِ قَالَ " بَلَى ". قُلْتُ فَلِمَ نُعْطِي الدَّنِيَّةَ فِي دِينِنَا إِذًا قَالَ " إِنِّي رَسُولُ اللَّهِ، وَلَسْتُ أَعْصِيهِ وَهْوَ نَاصِرِي ". قُلْتُ أَوَلَيْسَ كُنْتَ تُحَدِّثُنَا أَنَّا سَنَأْتِي الْبَيْتَ فَنَطُوفُ بِهِ قَالَ " بَلَى، فَأَخْبَرْتُكَ أَنَّا نَأْتِيهِ الْعَامَ ". قَالَ قُلْتُ لاَ. قَالَ " فَإِنَّكَ آتِيهِ وَمُطَّوِّفٌ بِهِ ". قَالَ فَأَتَيْتُ أَبَا بَكْرٍ فَقُلْتُ يَا أَبَا بَكْرٍ، أَلَيْسَ هَذَا نَبِيَّ اللَّهِ حَقًّا قَالَ بَلَى. قُلْتُ أَلَسْنَا عَلَى الْحَقِّ وَعَدُوُّنَا عَلَى الْبَاطِلِ قَالَ بَلَى. قُلْتُ فَلِمَ نُعْطِي الدَّنِيَّةَ فِي دِينِنَا إِذًا قَالَ أَيُّهَا الرَّجُلُ، إِنَّهُ لَرَسُولُ اللَّهِ صلى الله عليه وسلم وَلَيْسَ يَعْصِي رَبَّهُ وَهْوَ نَاصِرُهُ، فَاسْتَمْسِكْ بِغَرْزِهِ، فَوَاللَّهِ إِنَّهُ عَلَى الْحَقِّ. قُلْتُ أَلَيْسَ كَانَ يُحَدِّثُنَا أَنَّا سَنَأْتِي الْبَيْتَ وَنَطُوفُ بِهِ قَالَ بَلَى، أَفَأَخْبَرَكَ أَنَّكَ تَأْتِيهِ الْعَامَ قُلْتُ لاَ. قَالَ فَإِنَّكَ آتِيهِ وَمُطَّوِّفٌ بِهِ. قَالَ الزُّهْرِيِّ قَالَ عُمَرُ فَعَمِلْتُ لِذَلِكَ أَعْمَالاً. قَالَ فَلَمَّا فَرَغَ مِنْ قَضِيَّةِ الْكِتَابِ قَالَ رَسُولُ اللَّهِ صلى الله عليه وسلم لأَصْحَابِهِ " قُومُوا فَانْحَرُوا، ثُمَّ احْلِقُوا ". قَالَ فَوَاللَّهِ مَا قَامَ مِنْهُمْ رَجُلٌ حَتَّى قَالَ ذَلِكَ ثَلاَثَ مَرَّاتٍ، فَلَمَّا لَمْ يَقُمْ مِنْهُمْ أَحَدٌ دَخَلَ عَلَى أُمِّ سَلَمَةَ، فَذَكَرَ لَهَا مَا لَقِيَ مِنَ النَّاسِ. فَقَالَتْ أُمُّ سَلَمَةَ يَا نَبِيَّ اللَّهِ، أَتُحِبُّ ذَلِكَ اخْرُجْ ثُمَّ لاَ تُكَلِّمْ أَحَدًا مِنْهُمْ كَلِمَةً حَتَّى تَنْحَرَ بُدْنَكَ، وَتَدْعُوَ حَالِقَكَ فَيَحْلِقَكَ. فَخَرَجَ فَلَمْ يُكَلِّمْ أَحَدًا مِنْهُمْ، حَتَّى فَعَلَ ذَلِكَ نَحَرَ بُدْنَهُ، وَدَعَا حَالِقَهُ فَحَلَقَهُ. فَلَمَّا رَأَوْا ذَلِكَ، قَامُوا فَنَحَرُوا، وَجَعَلَ بَعْضُهُمْ يَحْلِقُ بَعْضًا، حَتَّى كَادَ بَعْضُهُمْ يَقْتُلُ بَعْضًا غَمًّا، ثُمَّ جَاءَهُ نِسْوَةٌ مُؤْمِنَاتٌ فَأَنْزَلَ اللَّهُ تَعَالَى {يَا أَيُّهَا الَّذِينَ آمَنُوا إِذَا جَاءَكُمُ الْمُؤْمِنَاتُ مُهَاجِرَاتٍ فَامْتَحِنُوهُنَّ} حَتَّى بَلَغَ {بِعِصَمِ الْكَوَافِرِ} فَطَلَّقَ عُمَرُ يَوْمَئِذٍ امْرَأَتَيْنِ كَانَتَا لَهُ فِي

الشِّرْكِ، فَتَزَوَّجَ إِحْدَاهُمَا مُعَاوِيَةُ بْنُ أَبِي سُفْيَانَ، وَالأُخْرَى صَفْوَانُ بْنُ أُمَيَّةَ، ثُمَّ رَجَعَ النَّبِيُّ صلى الله عليه وسلم إِلَى الْمَدِينَةِ، فَجَاءَهُ أَبُو بَصِيرٍ - رَجُلٌ مِنْ قُرَيْشٍ - وَهْوَ مُسْلِمٌ فَأَرْسَلُوا فِي طَلَبِهِ رَجُلَيْنِ، فَقَالُوا الْعَهْدَ الَّذِي جَعَلْتَ لَنَا. فَدَفَعَهُ إِلَى الرَّجُلَيْنِ، فَخَرَجَا بِهِ حَتَّى بَلَغَا ذَا الْحُلَيْفَةِ، فَنَزَلُوا يَأْكُلُونَ مِنْ تَمْرٍ لَهُمْ، فَقَالَ أَبُو بَصِيرٍ لأَحَدِ الرَّجُلَيْنِ وَاللَّهِ إِنِّي لأَرَى سَيْفَكَ هَذَا يَا فُلاَنُ جَيِّدًا. فَاسْتَلَّهُ الآخَرُ فَقَالَ أَجَلْ، وَاللَّهِ إِنَّهُ لَجَيِّدٌ، لَقَدْ جَرَّبْتُ بِهِ ثُمَّ جَرَّبْتُ. فَقَالَ أَبُو بَصِيرٍ أَرِنِي أَنْظُرْ إِلَيْهِ، فَأَمْكَنَهُ مِنْهُ، فَضَرَبَهُ حَتَّى بَرَدَ، وَفَرَّ الآخَرُ، حَتَّى أَتَى الْمَدِينَةَ، فَدَخَلَ الْمَسْجِدَ يَعْدُو. فَقَالَ رَسُولُ اللَّهِ صلى الله عليه وسلم حِينَ رَآهُ " لَقَدْ رَأَى هَذَا ذُعْرًا ". فَلَمَّا انْتَهَى إِلَى النَّبِيِّ صلى الله عليه وسلم قَالَ قُتِلَ وَاللَّهِ صَاحِبِي وَإِنِّي لَمَقْتُولٌ، فَجَاءَ أَبُو بَصِيرٍ فَقَالَ يَا نَبِيَّ اللَّهِ، قَدْ وَاللَّهِ أَوْفَى اللَّهُ ذِمَّتَكَ، قَدْ رَدَدْتَنِي إِلَيْهِمْ ثُمَّ أَنْجَانِي اللَّهُ مِنْهُمْ. قَالَ النَّبِيُّ صلى الله عليه وسلم " وَيْلُ أُمِّهِ مِسْعَرَ حَرْبٍ، لَوْ كَانَ لَهُ أَحَدٌ ". فَلَمَّا سَمِعَ ذَلِكَ عَرَفَ أَنَّهُ سَيَرُدُّهُ إِلَيْهِمْ، فَخَرَجَ حَتَّى أَتَى سِيفَ الْبَحْرِ. قَالَ وَيَنْفَلِتُ مِنْهُمْ أَبُو جَنْدَلِ بْنُ سُهَيْلٍ، فَلَحِقَ بِأَبِي بَصِيرٍ، فَجَعَلَ لاَ يَخْرُجُ مِنْ قُرَيْشٍ رَجُلٌ قَدْ أَسْلَمَ إِلاَّ لَحِقَ بِأَبِي بَصِيرٍ، حَتَّى اجْتَمَعَتْ مِنْهُمْ عِصَابَةٌ، فَوَاللَّهِ مَا يَسْمَعُونَ بِعِيرٍ خَرَجَتْ لِقُرَيْشٍ إِلَى الشَّأْمِ إِلاَّ اعْتَرَضُوا لَهَا، فَقَتَلُوهُمْ، وَأَخَذُوا أَمْوَالَهُمْ، فَأَرْسَلَتْ قُرَيْشٌ إِلَى النَّبِيِّ صلى الله عليه وسلم تُنَاشِدُهُ بِاللَّهِ وَالرَّحِمِ لَمَّا أَرْسَلَ، فَمَنْ أَتَاهُ فَهْوَ آمِنٌ، فَأَرْسَلَ النَّبِيُّ صلى الله عليه وسلم إِلَيْهِمْ، فَأَنْزَلَ اللَّهُ تَعَالَى {وَهُوَ الَّذِي كَفَّ أَيْدِيَهُمْ عَنْكُمْ وَأَيْدِيَكُمْ عَنْهُمْ بِبَطْنِ مَكَّةَ مِنْ بَعْدِ أَنْ أَظْفَرَكُمْ عَلَيْهِمْ} حَتَّى بَلَغَ {الْحَمِيَّةَ حَمِيَّةَ الْجَاهِلِيَّةِ} وَكَانَتْ حَمِيَّتُهُمْ أَنَّهُمْ لَمْ يُقِرُّوا أَنَّهُ نَبِيُّ اللَّهِ، وَلَمْ يُقِرُّوا بِبِسْمِ اللَّهِ الرَّحْمَنِ الرَّحِيمِ، وَحَالُوا بَيْنَهُمْ وَبَيْنَ الْبَيْتِ

Narrated Hisham's father: When Allah's Messenger ﷺ set out (towards Mecca) during the year of the Conquest (of Mecca) and this news reached (the infidels of Quraish), Abu Sufyan, Hakim bin Hizam and Budail bin Warqa came out to gather information about Allah's Messenger ﷺ, They proceeded on their way till they reached a place called Marr-az-Zahran (which is near Mecca). Behold! There they saw many fires as if they were the fires of `Arafat. Abu Sufyan said, "What is this? It looked like the fires of `Arafat." Budail bin Warqa' said, "Banu `Amr are less in number than that." Some of the guards of Allah's Messenger ﷺ saw them and took them over, caught them and brought them to Allah's Messenger ﷺ. Abu Sufyan embraced Islam. When the Prophet ﷺ proceeded, he said to Al-Abbas, "Keep Abu Sufyan standing at the top of the mountain so that he would look at the Muslims. So Al-`Abbas kept him standing (at that place) and the tribes with the Prophet ﷺ started passing in front of Abu Sufyan in military batches. A batch passed and Abu Sufyan said, "O `Abbas Who are these?" `Abbas said, "They are (Banu) Ghifar." Abu Sufyan said, I have got nothing to do with Ghifar." Then (a batch of the tribe of) Juhaina passed by and he said similarly as above. Then (a batch of the tribe of) Sa`d bin Huzaim passed by and he said similarly as above. Then (Banu) Sulaim passed by and he said similarly as above. Then came a batch, the like of which Abu Sufyan had not seen. He said, "Who are these?" `Abbas said, "They are the Ansar headed by Sa`d bin Ubada, the one holding the flag." Sa`d bin Ubada said, "O Abu Sufyan! Today is the day of a great battle and today (what is prohibited in) the Ka`ba will be permissible." Abu Sufyan said., "O `Abbas! How excellent the day of destruction is! "Then came another batch (of warriors) which was the smallest of all the batches, and in it there was Allah's Messenger ﷺ and his companions and the flag of the Prophet ﷺ was carried by Az-Zubair bin Al Awwam. When Allah's Messenger ﷺ passed by Abu Sufyan, the latter said, (to the Prophet), "Do you know what Sa`d bin 'Ubada said?" The Prophet ﷺ said, "What did he say?" Abu Sufyan said, "He said so-and-so." The Prophet ﷺ said, "Sa`d told a lie, but today Allah will give superiority to the Ka`ba and today the Ka`ba will be covered with a (cloth) covering." Allah's Messenger ﷺ ordered that his flag be fixed at Al-Hajun. Narrated `Urwa: Nafi` bin Jubair bin Mut`im said, "I heard Al-Abbas saying to Az-Zubair bin Al- `Awwam, 'O Abu `Abdullah ! Did Allah's Messenger ﷺ order you to fix the flag here?' " Allah's Messenger ﷺ ordered Khalid bin Al-Walid to enter Mecca from its upper part from Ka'da while the Prophet ﷺ himself entered from Kuda. Two men from the cavalry of Khalid bin Al-Wahd named Hubaish bin Al-Ash'ar and Kurz bin Jabir Al-Fihri were martyred on that day. – Sahih Al-Bukhari 4280

حَدَّثَنَا عُبَيْدُ بْنُ إِسْمَاعِيلَ، حَدَّثَنَا أَبُو أُسَامَةَ، عَنْ هِشَامٍ، عَنْ أَبِيهِ، قَالَ لَمَّا سَارَ رَسُولُ اللَّهِ صلى الله عليه وسلم عَامَ الْفَتْحِ فَبَلَغَ ذَلِكَ قُرَيْشًا، خَرَجَ أَبُو سُفْيَانَ بْنُ حَرْبٍ وَحَكِيمُ بْنُ حِزَامٍ وَبُدَيْلُ بْنُ وَرْقَاءَ يَلْتَمِسُونَ الْخَبَرَ عَنْ رَسُولِ اللَّهِ صلى الله عليه وسلم فَأَقْبَلُوا يَسِيرُونَ حَتَّى أَتَوْا مَرَّ الظَّهْرَانِ، فَإِذَا هُمْ بِنِيرَانٍ كَأَنَّهَا نِيرَانُ عَرَفَةَ، فَقَالَ أَبُو سُفْيَانَ مَا هَذِهِ لَكَأَنَّهَا نِيرَانُ

عَرَفَةَ. فَقَالَ بُدَيْلُ بْنُ وَرْقَاءَ نِيرَانُ بَنِي عَمْرٍو. فَقَالَ أَبُو سُفْيَانَ عَمْرٌو أَقَلُّ مِنْ ذَلِكَ. فَرَآهُمْ نَاسٌ مِنْ حَرَسِ رَسُولِ اللَّهِ صلى الله عليه وسلم فَأَدْرَكُوهُمْ فَأَخَذُوهُمْ، فَأَتَوْا بِهِمْ رَسُولَ اللَّهِ صلى الله عليه وسلم فَأَسْلَمَ أَبُو سُفْيَانَ، فَلَمَّا سَارَ قَالَ لِلْعَبَّاسِ " احْبِسْ أَبَا سُفْيَانَ عِنْدَ حَطْمِ الْخَيْلِ حَتَّى يَنْظُرَ إِلَى الْمُسْلِمِينَ ". فَحَبَسَهُ الْعَبَّاسُ، فَجَعَلَتِ الْقَبَائِلُ تَمُرُّ مَعَ النَّبِيِّ صلى الله عليه وسلم تَمُرُّ كَتِيبَةً كَتِيبَةً عَلَى أَبِي سُفْيَانَ، فَمَرَّتْ كَتِيبَةٌ قَالَ يَا عَبَّاسُ مَنْ هَذِهِ قَالَ هَذِهِ غِفَارُ. قَالَ مَا لِي وَلِغِفَارَ ثُمَّ مَرَّتْ جُهَيْنَةُ، قَالَ مِثْلَ ذَلِكَ، ثُمَّ مَرَّتْ سَعْدُ بْنُ هُذَيْمٍ، فَقَالَ مِثْلَ ذَلِكَ، وَمَرَّتْ سُلَيْمُ، فَقَالَ مِثْلَ ذَلِكَ، حَتَّى أَقْبَلَتْ كَتِيبَةٌ لَمْ يَرَ مِثْلَهَا، قَالَ مَنْ هَذِهِ قَالَ هَؤُلاَءِ الأَنْصَارُ عَلَيْهِمْ سَعْدُ بْنُ عُبَادَةَ مَعَهُ الرَّايَةُ. فَقَالَ سَعْدُ بْنُ عُبَادَةَ يَا أَبَا سُفْيَانَ الْيَوْمُ يَوْمُ الْمَلْحَمَةِ، الْيَوْمَ تُسْتَحَلُّ الْكَعْبَةُ. فَقَالَ أَبُو سُفْيَانَ يَا عَبَّاسُ حَبَّذَا يَوْمُ الذِّمَارِ. ثُمَّ جَاءَتْ كَتِيبَةٌ، وَهْىَ أَقَلُّ الْكَتَائِبِ، فِيهِمْ رَسُولُ اللَّهِ صلى الله عليه وسلم وَأَصْحَابُهُ، وَرَايَةُ النَّبِيِّ صلى الله عليه وسلم مَعَ الزُّبَيْرِ بْنِ الْعَوَّامِ، فَلَمَّا مَرَّ رَسُولُ اللَّهِ صلى الله عليه وسلم بِأَبِي سُفْيَانَ قَالَ أَلَمْ تَعْلَمْ مَا قَالَ سَعْدُ بْنُ عُبَادَةَ قَالَ " مَا قَالَ ". قَالَ كَذَا وَكَذَا. فَقَالَ " كَذَبَ سَعْدٌ، وَلَكِنْ هَذَا يَوْمٌ يُعَظِّمُ اللَّهُ فِيهِ الْكَعْبَةَ، وَيَوْمٌ تُكْسَى فِيهِ الْكَعْبَةُ ". قَالَ وَأَمَرَ رَسُولُ اللَّهِ صلى الله عليه وسلم أَنْ تُرْكَزَ رَايَتُهُ بِالْحَجُونِ. قَالَ عُرْوَةُ وَأَخْبَرَنِي نَافِعُ بْنُ جُبَيْرِ بْنِ مُطْعِمٍ قَالَ سَمِعْتُ الْعَبَّاسَ يَقُولُ لِلزُّبَيْرِ بْنِ الْعَوَّامِ يَا أَبَا عَبْدِ اللَّهِ، هَا هُنَا أَمَرَكَ رَسُولُ اللَّهِ صلى الله عليه وسلم أَنْ تَرْكُزَ الرَّايَةَ، قَالَ وَأَمَرَ رَسُولُ اللَّهِ صلى الله عليه وسلم يَوْمَئِذٍ خَالِدَ بْنَ الْوَلِيدِ أَنْ يَدْخُلَ مِنْ أَعْلَى مَكَّةَ مِنْ كَدَاءٍ، وَدَخَلَ النَّبِيُّ صلى الله عليه وسلم مِنْ كُدَا، فَقُتِلَ مِنْ خَيْلِ خَالِدٍ يَوْمَئِذٍ رَجُلاَنِ حُبَيْشُ بْنُ الأَشْعَرِ وَكُرْزُ بْنُ جَابِرٍ الْفِهْرِيُّ

Narrated Khalid bin Al-Walid: That he went with Allah's Messenger ﷺ to the house of Maimuna, who was his and Ibn `Abbas' aunt. He found with her a roasted mastigure which her sister Hufaida bint Al-Harith had brought from Najd. Maimuna presented the mastigure before Allah's Messenger ﷺ who rarely started eating any (unfamiliar) food before it was described and named for him. (But that time) Allah's Messenger ﷺ stretched his hand towards the (meat of the) mastigure whereupon a lady from among those who were present, said, "You should inform Allah's Messenger ﷺ of what you have presented to him. O Allah's Messenger ﷺ! It is the meat of a mastigure." (On learning that) Allah's Messenger ﷺ withdrew his hand from the meat of the mastigure. Khalid bin Al-Walid said, "O Allah's Messenger ﷺ! Is this unlawful to eat?" Allah's Messenger ﷺ replied, "No, but it is not found in the land of my people, so I do not like it." Khalid said, "Then I pulled the mastigure (meat) towards me and ate it while Allah's Messenger ﷺ was looking at me. – Sahih Al-Bukhari 5391

حَدَّثَنَا مُحَمَّدُ بْنُ مُقَاتِلٍ أَبُو الْحَسَنِ، أَخْبَرَنَا عَبْدُ اللَّهِ، أَخْبَرَنَا يُونُسُ، عَنِ الزُّهْرِيِّ، قَالَ أَخْبَرَنِي أَبُو أُمَامَةَ بْنُ سَهْلِ بْنِ حُنَيْفٍ الأَنْصَارِيُّ، أَنَّ ابْنَ عَبَّاسٍ، أَخْبَرَهُ أَنَّ خَالِدَ بْنَ الْوَلِيدِ الَّذِي يُقَالُ لَهُ سَيْفُ اللَّهِ أَخْبَرَهُ أَنَّهُ، دَخَلَ مَعَ رَسُولِ اللَّهِ صلى الله عليه وسلم عَلَى مَيْمُونَةَ ـ وَهْىَ خَالَتُهُ وَخَالَةُ ابْنِ عَبَّاسٍ ـ فَوَجَدَ عِنْدَهَا ضَبًّا مَحْنُوذًا، قَدِمَتْ بِهِ أُخْتُهَا حُفَيْدَةُ بِنْتُ الْحَارِثِ مِنْ نَجْدٍ، فَقَدَّمَتِ الضَّبَّ لِرَسُولِ اللَّهِ صلى الله عليه وسلم وَكَانَ قَلَّمَا يُقَدِّمُ يَدَهُ لِطَعَامٍ حَتَّى يُحَدَّثَ بِهِ وَيُسَمَّى لَهُ، فَأَهْوَى رَسُولُ اللَّهِ صلى الله عليه وسلم يَدَهُ إِلَى الضَّبِّ، فَقَالَتِ امْرَأَةٌ مِنَ النِّسْوَةِ الْحُضُورِ أَخْبِرْنَ رَسُولَ اللَّهِ صلى الله عليه وسلم مَا قَدَّمْتُنَّ لَهُ، هُوَ الضَّبُّ يَا رَسُولَ اللَّهِ. فَرَفَعَ رَسُولُ اللَّهِ صلى الله عليه وسلم يَدَهُ عَنِ الضَّبِّ، فَقَالَ خَالِدُ بْنُ الْوَلِيدِ أَحَرَامٌ الضَّبُّ يَا رَسُولَ اللَّهِ قَالَ " لاَ وَلَكِنْ لَمْ يَكُنْ بِأَرْضِ قَوْمِي فَأَجِدُنِي أَعَافُهُ ". قَالَ خَالِدٌ فَاجْتَرَرْتُهُ فَأَكَلْتُهُ وَرَسُولُ اللَّهِ صلى الله عليه وسلم يَنْظُرُ إِلَىَّ

Narrated Al-Bara: Allah's Messenger ﷺ sent us to Yemen along with Khalid bin Al-Walid. Later on he sent `Ali bin Abi Talib in his place. The Prophet ﷺ said to `Ali, "Give Khalid's companions the choice of either staying with you (in Yemen) or returning to Medina." I was one of those who stayed with him (i.e. `Ali) and got several Awaq (of gold from the war booty. – Sahih Al-Bukhari 4349

حَدَّثَنِي أَحْمَدُ بْنُ عُثْمَانَ، حَدَّثَنَا شُرَيْحُ بْنُ مَسْلَمَةَ، حَدَّثَنَا إِبْرَاهِيمُ بْنُ يُوسُفَ بْنِ إِسْحَاقَ بْنِ أَبِي إِسْحَاقَ، حَدَّثَنِي أَبِي، عَنْ أَبِي إِسْحَاقَ، سَمِعْتُ الْبَرَاءَ ـ رضى الله عنه ـ بَعَثَنَا رَسُولُ اللَّهِ صلى الله عليه وسلم مَعَ خَالِدِ بْنِ الْوَلِيدِ إِلَى الْيَمَنِ، قَالَ ثُمَّ بَعَثَ عَلِيًّا بَعْدَ ذَلِكَ مَكَانَهُ فَقَالَ مُرْ أَصْحَابَ خَالِدٍ، مَنْ شَاءَ مِنْهُمْ أَنْ يُعَقِّبَ مَعَكَ فَلْيُعَقِّبْ، وَمَنْ شَاءَ فَلْيُقْبِلْ. فَكُنْتُ فِيمَنْ عَقَّبَ مَعَهُ، قَالَ فَغَنِمْتُ أَوَاقٍ ذَوَاتِ عَدَدٍ.

Narrated Salim's father: The Prophet ﷺ sent Khalid bin Al-Walid to the tribe of Jadhima and Khalid invited them to Islam but they could not express themselves by saying, "Aslamna (i.e. we have embraced Islam)," but they started saying "Saba'na! Saba'na (i.e. we have come out of one religion to another)." Khalid kept on killing (some of) them and taking (some of) them as captives and gave every one of us his Captive. When there came the day then Khalid ordered that each man (i.e. Muslim soldier) should kill his captive, I said, "By Allah, I will not kill my captive, and none of my companions will kill his captive." When we reached the Prophet, we mentioned to him the whole story. On that, the Prophet ﷺ raised both his hands and said twice, "O Allah! I am free from what Khalid has done." - Sahih Al-Bukhari 4339

حَدَّثَنِي مَحْمُودٌ، حَدَّثَنَا عَبْدُ الرَّزَّاقِ، أَخْبَرَنَا مَعْمَرٌ، وَحَدَّثَنِي نُعَيْمٌ، أَخْبَرَنَا عَبْدُ اللَّهِ، أَخْبَرَنَا مَعْمَرٌ، عَنِ الزُّهْرِيِّ، عَنْ سَالِمٍ، عَنْ أَبِيهِ، قَالَ بَعَثَ النَّبِيُّ صلى الله عليه وسلم خَالِدَ بْنَ الْوَلِيدِ إِلَى بَنِي جَذِيمَةَ، فَدَعَاهُمْ إِلَى الإِسْلاَمِ فَلَمْ يُحْسِنُوا أَنْ يَقُولُوا أَسْلَمْنَا. فَجَعَلُوا يَقُولُونَ صَبَأْنَا، صَبَأْنَا. فَجَعَلَ خَالِدٌ يَقْتُلُ مِنْهُمْ وَيَأْسِرُ، وَدَفَعَ إِلَى كُلِّ رَجُلٍ مِنَّا أَسِيرَهُ، حَتَّى إِذَا كَانَ يَوْمٌ أَمَرَ خَالِدٌ أَنْ يَقْتُلَ كُلُّ رَجُلٍ مِنَّا أَسِيرَهُ فَقُلْتُ وَاللَّهِ لاَ أَقْتُلُ أَسِيرِي، وَلاَ يَقْتُلُ رَجُلٌ مِنْ أَصْحَابِي أَسِيرَهُ، حَتَّى قَدِمْنَا عَلَى النَّبِيِّ صلى الله عليه وسلم فَذَكَرْنَاهُ، فَرَفَعَ النَّبِيُّ صلى الله عليه وسلم يَدَهُ فَقَالَ " اللَّهُمَّ إِنِّي أَبْرَأُ إِلَيْكَ مِمَّا صَنَعَ خَالِدٌ ". مَرَّتَيْنِ

Narrated Abu Huraira: Allah's Messenger ﷺ ordered (a person) to collect Zakat, and that person returned and told him that Ibn Jamil, Khalid bin Al-Walid, and `Abbas bin `Abdul Muttalib had refused to give Zakat." The Prophet said, "What made Ibn Jamil refuse to give Zakat though he was a poor man, and was made wealthy by Allah and His Apostle ? But you are unfair in asking Zakat from Khalid as he is keeping his armor for Allah's Cause (for Jihad). As for `Abbas bin `Abdul Muttalib, he is the uncle of Allah's Apostle ﷺ and Zakat is compulsory on him and he should pay it double.". – Sahih Al-Bukhari 1468

حَدَّثَنَا أَبُو الْيَمَانِ، أَخْبَرَنَا شُعَيْبٌ، حَدَّثَنَا أَبُو الزِّنَادِ، عَنِ الأَعْرَجِ، عَنْ أَبِي هُرَيْرَةَ ـ رضى الله عنه ـ قَالَ أَمَرَ رَسُولُ اللَّهِ صلى الله عليه وسلم بِالصَّدَقَةِ فَقِيلَ مَنَعَ ابْنُ جَمِيلٍ وَخَالِدُ بْنُ الْوَلِيدِ وَعَبَّاسُ بْنُ عَبْدِ الْمُطَّلِبِ. فَقَالَ النَّبِيُّ صلى الله عليه وسلم " مَا يَنْقِمُ ابْنُ جَمِيلٍ إِلاَّ أَنَّهُ كَانَ فَقِيرًا فَأَغْنَاهُ اللَّهُ وَرَسُولُهُ، وَأَمَّا خَالِدٌ فَإِنَّكُمْ تَظْلِمُونَ خَالِدًا، قَدِ احْتَبَسَ أَدْرَاعَهُ وَأَعْتُدَهُ فِي سَبِيلِ اللَّهِ، وَأَمَّا الْعَبَّاسُ بْنُ عَبْدِ الْمُطَّلِبِ فَعَمُّ رَسُولِ اللَّهِ صلى الله عليه وسلم فَهْىَ عَلَيْهِ صَدَقَةٌ وَمِثْلُهَا مَعَهَا ". تَابَعَهُ ابْنُ أَبِي الزِّنَادِ عَنْ أَبِيهِ. وَقَالَ ابْنُ إِسْحَاقَ عَنْ أَبِي الزِّنَادِ هِيَ عَلَيْهِ وَمِثْلُهَا مَعَهَا. وَقَالَ ابْنُ جُرَيْجٍ حُدِّثْتُ عَنِ الأَعْرَجِ بِمِثْلِهِ

Narrated Anas: The Prophet ﷺ had informed the people about the death of Zaid, Ja`far and Ibn Rawaha before the news of their death reached them. He said with his eyes flowing with tears, "Zaid took the flag and was martyred; then Ja`far took the flag and was martyred, and then Ibn Rawaha took the flag and was martyred. Finally the flag was taken by one of Allah's Swords (i.e. Khalid bin Al-Walid) and Allah gave them (i.e. the Muslims) victory.". – Sahih Al-Bukhari 3757

حَدَّثَنَا أَحْمَدُ بْنُ وَاقِدٍ، حَدَّثَنَا حَمَّادُ بْنُ زَيْدٍ، عَنْ أَيُّوبَ، عَنْ حُمَيْدِ بْنِ هِلاَلٍ، عَنْ أَنَسٍ ـ رضى الله عنه أَنَّ النَّبِيَّ صلى الله عليه وسلم نَعَى زَيْدًا وَجَعْفَرًا وَابْنَ رَوَاحَةَ لِلنَّاسِ قَبْلَ أَنْ يَأْتِيَهُمْ خَبَرُهُمْ، فَقَالَ " أَخَذَ الرَّايَةَ زَيْدٌ فَأُصِيبَ، ثُمَّ أَخَذَ جَعْفَرٌ فَأُصِيبَ، ثُمَّ أَخَذَ ابْنُ رَوَاحَةَ فَأُصِيبَ ـ وَعَيْنَاهُ تَذْرِفَانِ ـ حَتَّى أَخَذَ سَيْفٌ مِنْ سُيُوفِ اللَّهِ حَتَّى فَتَحَ اللَّهُ عَلَيْهِمْ "

Narrated Nafi' (ra): A horse of Ibn 'Umar fled and the enemy took it. Then the Muslims conquered the enemy and the horse was returned to him during the lifetime of Allah's Messenger ﷺ. And also, once a slave of Ibn 'Umar (ra) fled and joined the Byzantines, and when the Muslims conquered them, Khalid bin Al-Walid returned the slave to him after the death of the Prophet. – Sahih Al-Bukhari 3067

قَالَ ابْنُ نُمَيْرٍ حَدَّثَنَا عُبَيْدُ اللَّهِ، عَنْ نَافِعٍ، عَنِ ابْنِ عُمَرَ ـ رضى الله عنهما ـ قَالَ ذَهَبَ فَرَسٌ لَهُ فَأَخَذَهُ الْعَدُوُّ، فَظَهَرَ عَلَيْهِ الْمُسْلِمُونَ فَرُدَّ عَلَيْهِ فِي زَمَنِ رَسُولِ اللَّهِ صلى الله عليه وسلم، وَأَبَقَ عَبْدٌ لَهُ فَلَحِقَ بِالرُّومِ، فَظَهَرَ عَلَيْهِمُ الْمُسْلِمُونَ، فَرَدَّهُ عَلَيْهِ خَالِدُ بْنُ الْوَلِيدِ بَعْدَ النَّبِيِّ صلى الله عليه وسلم

Abū Hurayra ʿAbd al-Raḥmān ibn Ṣakhr al-Dawsī al-Zahrānī

أَبُو هُرَيْرَة عَبْد ٱلرَّحْمَٰن بْن صَخْر ٱلدَّوْسِيّ ٱلزَّهْرَانِيّ

Narrated Abu Huraira: On my way to the Prophet ﷺ I was reciting:-- 'What a long tedious tiresome night! Nevertheless, it has saved us From the land of Kufr (disbelief).' I had a slave who ran away from me on the way. When I went to the Prophet ﷺ and gave the pledge of allegiance for embracing Islam, the slave showed up while I was still with the Prophet ﷺ who remarked, "O Abu Huraira! Here is your slave!" I said, "I manumit him for Allah's Sake," and so I freed him. – Sahih Al-Bukhari 2531

حَدَّثَنَا عُبَيْدُ اللَّهِ بْنُ سَعِيدٍ، حَدَّثَنَا أَبُو أُسَامَةَ، حَدَّثَنَا إِسْمَاعِيلُ، عَنْ قَيْسٍ، عَنْ أَبِي هُرَيْرَةَ ـ رضى الله عنه ـ قَالَ لَمَّا قَدِمْتُ عَلَى النَّبِيِّ صلى الله عليه وسلم قُلْتُ فِي الطَّرِيقِ يَا لَيْلَةً مِنْ طُولِهَا وَعَنَائِهَا عَلَى أَنَّهَا مِنْ دَارَةِ الْكُفْرِ نَجَّتِ قَالَ وَأَبَقَ مِنِّي غُلاَمٌ لِي فِي الطَّرِيقِ ـ قَالَ ـ فَلَمَّا قَدِمْتُ عَلَى النَّبِيِّ صلى الله عليه وسلم بَايَعْتُهُ، فَبَيْنَا أَنَا عِنْدَهُ إِذْ طَلَعَ الْغُلاَمُ، فَقَالَ لِي رَسُولُ اللَّهِ صلى الله عليه وسلم " يَا أَبَا هُرَيْرَةَ، هَذَا غُلاَمُكَ ". فَقُلْتُ هُوَ حُرٌّ لِوَجْهِ اللَّهِ. فَأَعْتَقْتُهُ. لَمْ يَقُلْ أَبُو كُرَيْبٍ عَنْ أَبِي أُسَامَةَ حُرٌّ

Narrated Abu Huraira: Some poor people came to the Prophet ﷺ and said, "The wealthy people will get higher grades and will have permanent enjoyment and they pray like us and fast as we do. They have more money by which they perform the Hajj, and `Umra; fight and struggle in Allah's Cause and give in charity." The Prophet said, "Shall I not tell you a thing upon which if you acted you would catch up with those who have surpassed you? Nobody would overtake you and you would be better than the people amongst whom you live except those who would do the same. Say "Subhana l-lah", "Al hamdu li l-lah" and "Allahu Akbar" thirty three times each after every (compulsory) prayer." We differed and some of us said that we should say, "Subhan-al-lah" thirty three times and "Al hamdu li l-lah" thirty three times and "Allahu Akbar" thirty four times. I went to the Prophet ﷺ who said, "Say, "Subhan-al-lah" and "Al hamdu li l-lah" and "Allahu Akbar" all together, thirty three times.". – Sahih Al-Bukhari 843

حَدَّثَنَا مُحَمَّدُ بْنُ أَبِي بَكْرٍ، قَالَ حَدَّثَنَا مُعْتَمِرٌ، عَنْ عُبَيْدِ اللَّهِ، عَنْ سُمَىٍّ، عَنْ أَبِي صَالِحٍ، عَنْ أَبِي هُرَيْرَةَ ـ رضى الله عنه ـ قَالَ جَاءَ الْفُقَرَاءُ إِلَى النَّبِيِّ صلى الله عليه وسلم فَقَالُوا ذَهَبَ أَهْلُ الدُّثُورِ مِنَ الأَمْوَالِ بِالدَّرَجَاتِ الْعُلاَ وَالنَّعِيمِ الْمُقِيمِ، يُصَلُّونَ كَمَا نُصَلِّي، وَيَصُومُونَ كَمَا نَصُومُ، وَلَهُمْ فَضْلٌ مِنْ أَمْوَالٍ يَحُجُّونَ بِهَا، وَيَعْتَمِرُونَ، وَيُجَاهِدُونَ، وَيَتَصَدَّقُونَ قَالَ " أَلاَ أُحَدِّثُكُمْ بِأَمْرٍ إِنْ أَخَذْتُمْ بِهِ أَدْرَكْتُمْ مَنْ سَبَقَكُمْ وَلَمْ يُدْرِكْكُمْ أَحَدٌ بَعْدَكُمْ، وَكُنْتُمْ خَيْرَ مَنْ أَنْتُمْ بَيْنَ ظَهْرَانَيْهِ، إِلاَّ مَنْ عَمِلَ مِثْلَهُ تُسَبِّحُونَ وَتَحْمَدُونَ، وَتُكَبِّرُونَ خَلْفَ كُلِّ صَلاَةٍ ثَلاَثًا وَثَلاَثِينَ ". فَاخْتَلَفْنَا بَيْنَنَا فَقَالَ بَعْضُنَا نُسَبِّحُ ثَلاَثًا وَثَلاَثِينَ، وَنَحْمَدُ ثَلاَثًا وَثَلاَثِينَ، وَنُكَبِّرُ أَرْبَعًا وَثَلاَثِينَ. فَرَجَعْتُ إِلَيْهِ فَقَالَ " تَقُولُ سُبْحَانَ اللَّهِ، وَالْحَمْدُ لِلَّهِ، وَاللَّهُ أَكْبَرُ، حَتَّى يَكُونَ مِنْهُنَّ كُلِّهِنَّ ثَلاَثًا وَثَلاَثِينَ ".

Narrated Abu Huraira: The people said, "O Allah's Messenger ﷺ ! The rich people have got the highest degrees of prestige and the permanent pleasures (in this life and the life to come in the Hereafter)." He said, "How is that?" They said, "The rich pray as we pray, and strive in Allah's Cause as we do, and spend from their surplus wealth in charity, while we have no wealth (to spend likewise)." He said, "Shall I not tell you a thing, by doing which, you will catch up with those who are ahead of you and supersede those who will come after you; and nobody will be able to do such a good deed as you do except the one who does the same (deed as you do). That deed is to recite 'Subhan Allah ten times, and 'Al-Hamduli l-lah ten times, and 'AllahuAkbar' ten times after every prayer." – Sahih al-Bukhari 6329

حَدَّثَنِي إِسْحَاقُ، أَخْبَرَنَا يَزِيدُ، أَخْبَرَنَا وَرْقَاءُ، عَنْ سُمَىٍّ، عَنْ أَبِي صَالِحٍ، عَنْ أَبِي هُرَيْرَةَ. قَالُوا يَا رَسُولَ اللَّهِ ذَهَبَ أَهْلُ الدُّثُورِ بِالدَّرَجَاتِ وَالنَّعِيمِ الْمُقِيمِ. قَالَ " كَيْفَ ذَاكَ ". قَالَ صَلَّوْا كَمَا صَلَّيْنَا، وَجَاهَدُوا كَمَا جَاهَدْنَا، وَأَنْفَقُوا مِنْ فُضُولِ أَمْوَالِهِمْ، وَلَيْسَتْ لَنَا أَمْوَالٌ. قَالَ " أَفَلاَ أُخْبِرُكُمْ بِأَمْرٍ تُدْرِكُونَ مَنْ كَانَ قَبْلَكُمْ، وَتَسْبِقُونَ مَنْ جَاءَ بَعْدَكُمْ، وَلاَ يَأْتِي أَحَدٌ بِمِثْلِ مَا جِئْتُمْ، إِلاَّ مَنْ جَاءَ بِمِثْلِهِ، تُسَبِّحُونَ فِي دُبُرِ كُلِّ صَلاَةٍ عَشْرًا، وَتَحْمَدُونَ عَشْرًا، وَتُكَبِّرُونَ عَشْرًا ". تَابَعَهُ عُبَيْدُ اللَّهِ بْنُ

عُمَرَ عَنْ سُمَيٍّ وَرَوَاهُ ابْنُ عَجْلاَنَ عَنْ سُمَيٍّ وَرَجَاءِ بْنِ حَيْوَةَ. وَرَوَاهُ جَرِيرٌ عَنْ عَبْدِ الْعَزِيزِ بْنِ رُفَيْعٍ عَنْ أَبِي صَالِحٍ عَنْ أَبِي الدَّرْدَاءِ. وَرَوَاهُ سُهَيْلٌ عَنْ أَبِيهِ عَنْ أَبِي هُرَيْرَةَ عَنِ النَّبِيِّ صلى الله عليه وسلم

Narrated `Aisha and Umm Salama : At times, Allah's Messenger used to get up in the morning in the state of Janāba after having sexual relations with his wives. He would then take a bath and observe Saum (fast) Marwãn said to Abdur Rahmān, "I swear by Allah that you tell Abũ Hurairah_that_[the_Prophet used to be Junub (in state of Janaba) till the dawn, would then take a bath and observe saum (fast)],"". – Sahih Al-Bukhari 1925, 1926

حَدَّثَنَا عَبْدُ اللَّهِ بْنُ مَسْلَمَةَ، عَنْ مَالِكٍ، عَنْ سُمَيٍّ، مَوْلَى أَبِي بَكْرِ بْنِ عَبْدِ الرَّحْمَنِ بْنِ الْحَارِثِ بْنِ هِشَامِ بْنِ الْمُغِيرَةِ أَنَّهُ سَمِعَ أَبَا بَكْرِ بْنَ عَبْدِ الرَّحْمَنِ، قَالَ كُنْتُ أَنَا وَأَبِي، حِينَ دَخَلْنَا عَلَى عَائِشَةَ وَأُمِّ سَلَمَةَ ح. حَدَّثَنَا أَبُو الْيَمَانِ، أَخْبَرَنَا شُعَيْبٌ، عَنِ الزُّهْرِيِّ، قَالَ أَخْبَرَنِي أَبُو بَكْرِ بْنُ عَبْدِ الرَّحْمَنِ بْنِ الْحَارِثِ بْنِ هِشَامٍ، أَنَّ أَبَاهُ عَبْدَ الرَّحْمَنِ، أَخْبَرَ مَرْوَانَ، أَنَّ عَائِشَةَ، وَأُمَّ سَلَمَةَ أَخْبَرَتَاهُ أَنَّ رَسُولَ اللَّهِ صلى الله عليه وسلم كَانَ يُدْرِكُهُ الْفَجْرُ وَهُوَ جُنُبٌ مِنْ أَهْلِهِ، ثُمَّ يَغْتَسِلُ وَيَصُومُ. وَقَالَ مَرْوَانُ لِعَبْدِ الرَّحْمَنِ بْنِ الْحَارِثِ أُقْسِمُ بِاللَّهِ لَتُقَرِّعَنَّ بِهَا أَبَا هُرَيْرَةَ. وَمَرْوَانُ يَوْمَئِذٍ عَلَى الْمَدِينَةِ. فَقَالَ أَبُو بَكْرٍ فَكَرِهَ ذَلِكَ عَبْدُ الرَّحْمَنِ، ثُمَّ قُدِّرَ لَنَا أَنْ نَجْتَمِعَ بِذِي الْحُلَيْفَةِ، وَكَانَتْ لأَبِي هُرَيْرَةَ هُنَالِكَ أَرْضٌ، فَقَالَ عَبْدُ الرَّحْمَنِ لأَبِي هُرَيْرَةَ إِنِّي ذَاكِرٌ لَكَ أَمْرًا، وَلَوْلاَ مَرْوَانُ أَقْسَمَ عَلَىَّ فِيهِ لَمْ أَذْكُرْهُ لَكَ. فَذَكَرَ قَوْلَ عَائِشَةَ وَأُمِّ سَلَمَةَ. فَقَالَ كَذَلِكَ حَدَّثَنِي الْفَضْلُ بْنُ عَبَّاسٍ، وَهُنَّ أَعْلَمُ، وَقَالَ هَمَّامٌ وَابْنُ عَبْدِ اللَّهِ بْنِ عُمَرَ عَنْ أَبِي هُرَيْرَةَ كَانَ النَّبِيُّ صلى الله عليه وسلم يَأْمُرُ بِالْفِطْرِ. وَالأَوَّلُ أَسْنَدُ.

Narrated Abu Huraira: I went to Allah's Messenger ﷺ while he was at Khaibar after it had fallen in the Muslims' hands. I said, "O Allah's Messenger ﷺ ! Give me a share (from the land of Khaibar)." One of the sons of Sa'id bin Al-'As said, "O Allah's Messenger ﷺ! Do not give him a share." I said, "This is the murderer of Ibn Qauqal." The son of Said bin Al-As said, "Strange! A Wabr (i.e. guinea pig) who has come down to us from the mountain of Qaduim (i.e. grazing place of sheep) blames me for killing a Muslim who was given superiority by Allah because of me, and Allah did not disgrace me at his hands (i.e. was not killed as an infidel)." (The sub-narrator said "I do not know whether the Prophet ﷺ gave him a share or not."). – Sahih Al-Bukhari 2827

حَدَّثَنَا الْحُمَيْدِيُّ، حَدَّثَنَا سُفْيَانُ، حَدَّثَنَا الزُّهْرِيُّ، قَالَ أَخْبَرَنِي عَنْبَسَةُ بْنُ سَعِيدٍ، عَنْ أَبِي هُرَيْرَةَ ـ رضى الله عنه ـ قَالَ أَتَيْتُ رَسُولَ اللَّهِ صلى الله عليه وسلم وَهْوَ بِخَيْبَرَ بَعْدَ مَا افْتَتَحُوهَا، فَقُلْتُ يَا رَسُولَ اللَّهِ أَسْهِمْ لِي. فَقَالَ بَعْضُ بَنِي سَعِيدِ بْنِ الْعَاصِ لاَ تُسْهِمْ لَهُ يَا رَسُولَ اللَّهِ. فَقَالَ أَبُو هُرَيْرَةَ هَذَا قَاتِلُ ابْنِ قَوْقَلٍ. فَقَالَ ابْنُ سَعِيدِ بْنِ الْعَاصِ وَاعَجَبًا لِوَبْرٍ تَدَلَّى عَلَيْنَا مِنْ قَدُومِ ضَأْنٍ، يَنْعَى عَلَىَّ قَتْلَ رَجُلٍ مُسْلِمٍ أَكْرَمَهُ اللَّهُ عَلَى يَدَىَّ وَلَمْ يُهِنِّي عَلَى يَدَيْهِ. قَالَ فَلاَ أَدْرِي أَسْهَمَ لَهُ أَمْ لَمْ يُسْهِمْ لَهُ. قَالَ سُفْيَانُ وَحَدَّثَنِيهِ السَّعِيدِيُّ عَنْ جَدِّهِ عَنْ أَبِي هُرَيْرَةَ. قَالَ أَبُو عَبْدِ اللَّهِ السَّعِيدِيُّ عَمْرُو بْنُ يَحْيَى بْنِ سَعِيدِ بْنِ عَمْرِو بْنِ سَعِيدِ بْنِ الْعَاصِ

Narrated Abu Huraira: I said, "O Allah's Messenger ﷺ! I hear many narrations from you but I forget them." He said, "Spread your covering sheet." I spread my sheet and he moved both his hands as if scooping something and emptied them in the sheet and said, "Wrap it." I wrapped it round my body, and since then I have never forgotten. – Sahih Al-Bukhari 3648

حَدَّثَنِي إِبْرَاهِيمُ بْنُ الْمُنْذِرِ، حَدَّثَنَا ابْنُ أَبِي الْفُدَيْكِ، عَنِ ابْنِ أَبِي ذِئْبٍ، عَنِ الْمَقْبُرِيِّ، عَنْ أَبِي هُرَيْرَةَ ـ رضى الله عنه ـ قَالَ قُلْتُ يَا رَسُولَ اللَّهِ إِنِّي سَمِعْتُ مِنْكَ كَثِيرًا فَأَنْسَاهُ. قَالَ " ابْسُطْ رِدَاءَكَ ". فَبَسَطْتُ فَغَرَفَ بِيَدِهِ فِيهِ، ثُمَّ قَالَ " ضُمَّهُ " فَضَمَمْتُهُ، فَمَا نَسِيتُ حَدِيثًا بَعْدُ

Narrated Abu Huraira: I said, "O Allah's Messenger ﷺ! I am a young man and I am afraid that I may commit illegal sexual intercourse and I cannot afford to marry." He kept silent, and then repeated my question once again, but he kept silent. I said the same (for the third time) and he remained silent. Then repeated my question (for the fourth time), and only then the Prophet said, "O Abu Huraira! The pen has dried after writing what you are going to confront. So (it does not matter whether you) get yourself castrated or not.". – Sahih Al-Bukhari 5076

وَقَالَ أَصْبَغُ أَخْبَرَنِي ابْنُ وَهْبٍ، عَنْ يُونُسَ بْنِ يَزِيدَ، عَنِ ابْنِ شِهَابٍ، عَنْ أَبِي سَلَمَةَ، عَنْ أَبِي هُرَيْرَةَ ـ رضى الله عنه ـ قَالَ قُلْتُ يَا رَسُولَ اللَّهِ إِنِّي رَجُلٌ شَابٌّ وَأَنَا أَخَافُ عَلَى نَفْسِي الْعَنَتَ وَلاَ أَجِدُ مَا أَتَزَوَّجُ بِهِ النِّسَاءَ، فَسَكَتَ عَنِّي، ثُمَّ قُلْتُ

مِثْلَ ذَلِكَ، فَسَكَتَ عَنِّي ثُمَّ قُلْتُ مِثْلَ ذَلِكَ، فَسَكَتَ عَنِّي ثُمَّ قُلْتُ مِثْلَ ذَلِكَ، فَقَالَ النَّبِيُّ صلى الله عليه وسلم " يَا أَبَا هُرَيْرَةَ جَفَّ الْقَلَمُ بِمَا أَنْتَ لاَقٍ، فَاخْتَصِ عَلَى ذَلِكَ أَوْ ذَرْ "

Narrated Abu Huraira: The Prophet ﷺ said, "The best women are the riders of the camels and the righteous among the women of Quraish. They are the kindest women to their children in their childhood and the more careful women of the property of their husbands.". – Sahih Al-Bukhari 5082

حَدَّثَنَا أَبُو الْيَمَانِ، أَخْبَرَنَا شُعَيْبٌ، حَدَّثَنَا أَبُو الزِّنَادِ، عَنِ الأَعْرَجِ، عَنْ أَبِي هُرَيْرَةَ ـ رضى الله عنه ـ عَنِ النَّبِيِّ صلى الله عليه وسلم قَالَ " خَيْرُ نِسَاءٍ رَكِبْنَ الإِبِلَ صَالِحُو نِسَاءِ قُرَيْشٍ، أَحْنَاهُ عَلَى وَلَدٍ فِي صِغَرِهِ وَأَرْعَاهُ عَلَى زَوْجٍ فِي ذَاتِ يَدِهِ

Narrated Abu Zur'a: I entered a house in Medina with Abu Huraira, and he saw a man making pictures at the top of the house. Abu Huraira said, "I heard Allah's Messenger ﷺ saying that Allah said, 'Who would be more unjust than the one who tries to create the like of My creatures? Let them create a grain: let them create a gnat.' "Abu Huraira then asked for a water container and washed his arms up to his armpits. I said, "0 Abu I Huraira! Is this something you have heard I from Allah's Messenger ﷺ?" He said, "The limit for ablution is up to the place where the ornaments will reach on the Day of Resurrection.'. – Sahih Al-Bukhari 5953

حَدَّثَنَا مُوسَى، حَدَّثَنَا عَبْدُ الْوَاحِدِ، حَدَّثَنَا عُمَارَةُ، حَدَّثَنَا أَبُو زُرْعَةَ، قَالَ دَخَلْتُ مَعَ أَبِي هُرَيْرَةَ دَارًا بِالْمَدِينَةِ فَرَأَى أَعْلاَهَا مُصَوِّرًا يُصَوِّرُ، قَالَ سَمِعْتُ رَسُولَ اللَّهِ صلى الله عليه وسلم يَقُولُ " وَمَنْ أَظْلَمُ مِمَّنْ ذَهَبَ يَخْلُقُ كَخَلْقِي، فَلْيَخْلُقُوا حَبَّةً، وَلْيَخْلُقُوا ذَرَّةً ". ثُمَّ دَعَا بِتَوْرٍ مِنْ مَاءٍ فَغَسَلَ يَدَيْهِ حَتَّى بَلَغَ إِبْطَهُ فَقُلْتُ يَا أَبَا هُرَيْرَةَ أَشَىْءٌ سَمِعْتَهُ مِنْ رَسُولِ اللَّهِ صلى الله عليه وسلم قَالَ مُنْتَهَى الْحِلْيَةِ

Narrated Abu Sa`id Al-Khudri: Some women requested the Prophet ﷺ to fix a day for them as the men were taking all his time. On that he promised them one day for religious lessons and commandments. Once during such a lesson the Prophet said, "A woman whose three children die will be shielded by them from the Hell fire." On that a woman asked, "If only two die?" He replied, "Even two (will shield her from the Hell-fire). – Sahih al-Bukhari 101

حَدَّثَنَا آدَمُ، قَالَ حَدَّثَنَا شُعْبَةُ، قَالَ حَدَّثَنِي ابْنُ الأَصْبَهَانِيِّ، قَالَ سَمِعْتُ أَبَا صَالِحٍ، ذَكْوَانَ يُحَدِّثُ عَنْ أَبِي سَعِيدٍ الْخُدْرِيِّ، قَالَتِ النِّسَاءُ لِلنَّبِيِّ صلى الله عليه وسلم غَلَبَنَا عَلَيْكَ الرِّجَالُ، فَاجْعَلْ لَنَا يَوْمًا مِنْ نَفْسِكَ. فَوَعَدَهُنَّ يَوْمًا لَقِيَهُنَّ فِيهِ، فَوَعَظَهُنَّ وَأَمَرَهُنَّ، فَكَانَ فِيمَا قَالَ لَهُنَّ " مَا مِنْكُنَّ امْرَأَةٌ تُقَدِّمُ ثَلاَثَةً مِنْ وَلَدِهَا إِلاَّ كَانَ لَهَا حِجَابًا مِنَ النَّارِ ". فَقَالَتِ امْرَأَةٌ وَاثْنَيْنِ فَقَالَ " وَاثْنَيْنِ ".

Narrated Abu Sa`id Al-Khudri: As above (the sub narrators are different). Abu Huraira qualified the three children referred to in the above mentioned Hadith as not having reached the age of committing sins (i.e. age of puberty) . – Sahih Al-Bukhari 102

حَدَّثَنَا مُحَمَّدُ بْنُ بَشَّارٍ، قَالَ حَدَّثَنَا غُنْدَرٌ، قَالَ حَدَّثَنَا شُعْبَةُ، عَنْ عَبْدِ الرَّحْمَنِ بْنِ الأَصْبَهَانِيِّ، عَنْ ذَكْوَانَ، عَنْ أَبِي سَعِيدٍ الْخُدْرِيِّ، عَنِ النَّبِيِّ صلى الله عليه وسلم بِهَذَا. وَعَنْ عَبْدِ الرَّحْمَنِ بْنِ الأَصْبَهَانِيِّ، قَالَ سَمِعْتُ أَبَا حَازِمٍ، عَنْ أَبِي هُرَيْرَةَ، قَالَ " ثَلاَثَةً لَمْ يَبْلُغُوا الْحِنْثَ ".

Narrated Abu Huraira: Allah's Messenger ﷺ said, "The prayer of a person who does Hadath (passes urine, stool or wind) is not accepted till he performs the ablution." A person from Hadaramout asked Abu Huraira, "What is 'Hadath'?" Abu Huraira replied, " 'Hadath' means the passing of wind.". – Sahih Al-Bukhari 135

حَدَّثَنَا إِسْحَاقُ بْنُ إِبْرَاهِيمَ الْحَنْظَلِيُّ، قَالَ أَخْبَرَنَا عَبْدُ الرَّزَّاقِ، قَالَ أَخْبَرَنَا مَعْمَرٌ، عَنْ هَمَّامِ بْنِ مُنَبِّهٍ، أَنَّهُ سَمِعَ أَبَا هُرَيْرَةَ، يَقُولُ قَالَ رَسُولُ اللَّهِ صلى الله عليه وسلم " لاَ تُقْبَلُ صَلاَةُ مَنْ أَحْدَثَ حَتَّى يَتَوَضَّأَ ". قَالَ رَجُلٌ مِنْ حَضْرَمَوْتَ مَا الْحَدَثُ يَا أَبَا هُرَيْرَةَ قَالَ فُسَاءٌ أَوْ ضُرَاطٌ

Narrated `Abbad bin Tamim: My uncle said: The Prophet ﷺ said, "One should not leave his prayer unless he hears sound or smells something.". – Sahih Al-Bukhari 177

حَدَّثَنَا أَبُو الْوَلِيدِ، قَالَ حَدَّثَنَا ابْنُ عُيَيْنَةَ، عَنِ الزُّهْرِيِّ، عَنْ عَبَّادِ بْنِ تَمِيمٍ، عَنْ عَمِّهِ، عَنِ النَّبِيِّ صلى الله عليه وسلم قَالَ " لاَ يَنْصَرِفْ حَتَّى يَسْمَعَ صَوْتًا أَوْ يَجِدَ رِيحًا ".

Narrated Abu Huraira: The Prophet ﷺ said, "Solomon (the son of) David said, 'Tonight I will sleep with seventy ladies each of whom will conceive a child who will be a knight fighting for "Allah's Cause.' His companion said, 'If Allah will.' But Solomon did not say so; therefore none of those women got pregnant except one who gave birth to a half child." The Prophet ﷺ further said, "If the Prophet ﷺ Solomon had said it (i.e. 'If Allah will') he would have begotten children who would have fought in Allah's Cause." Shuaib and Ibn Abi Az-Zinad said, "Ninety (women) is more correct (than seventy). – Sahih Al-Bukhari 3424

حَدَّثَنَا خَالِدُ بْنُ مَخْلَدٍ، حَدَّثَنَا مُغِيرَةُ بْنُ عَبْدِ الرَّحْمَنِ، عَنْ أَبِي الزِّنَادِ، عَنِ الأَعْرَجِ، عَنْ أَبِي هُرَيْرَةَ، عَنِ النَّبِيِّ صلى الله عليه وسلم قَالَ " قَالَ سُلَيْمَانُ بْنُ دَاوُدَ لأَطُوفَنَّ اللَّيْلَةَ عَلَى سَبْعِينَ امْرَأَةً تَحْمِلُ كُلُّ امْرَأَةٍ فَارِسًا يُجَاهِدُ فِي سَبِيلِ اللَّهِ، فَقَالَ لَهُ صَاحِبُهُ إِنْ شَاءَ اللَّهُ. فَلَمْ يَقُلْ، وَلَمْ تَحْمِلْ شَيْئًا إِلاَّ وَاحِدًا سَاقِطًا إِحْدَى شِقَّيْهِ ". فَقَالَ النَّبِيُّ صلى الله عليه وسلم " لَوْ قَالَهَا لَجَاهَدُوا فِي سَبِيلِ اللَّهِ ". قَالَ شُعَيْبٌ وَابْنُ أَبِي الزِّنَادِ " تِسْعِينَ ". وَهْوَ أَصَحُّ

Narrated `Aisha: The Prophet ﷺ used to talk so clearly that if somebody wanted to count the number of his words, he could do so. Narrated `Urwa bin Az-Zubair: `Aisha said (to me), "Don't you wonder at Abu so-and-so who came and sat by my dwelling and started relating the traditions of Allah's Messenger ﷺ intending to let me hear that, while I was performing an optional prayer. He left before I finished my optional prayer. Had I found him still there. I would have said to him, 'Allah's Messenger ﷺ never talked so quickly and vaguely as you do.' ". – Sahih Al-Bukhari 3567, 3568

حَدَّثَنِي الْحَسَنُ بْنُ صَبَّاحٍ الْبَزَّارُ، حَدَّثَنَا سُفْيَانُ، عَنِ الزُّهْرِيِّ، عَنْ عُرْوَةَ، عَنْ عَائِشَةَ ـ رضى الله عنها أَنَّ النَّبِيَّ صلى الله عليه وسلم كَانَ يُحَدِّثُ حَدِيثًا لَوْ عَدَّهُ الْعَادُّ لأَحْصَاهُ. وَقَالَ اللَّيْثُ حَدَّثَنِي يُونُسُ، عَنِ ابْنِ شِهَابٍ، أَنَّهُ قَالَ أَخْبَرَنِي عُرْوَةُ بْنُ الزُّبَيْرِ، عَنْ عَائِشَةَ، أَنَّهَا قَالَتْ أَلاَ يُعْجِبُكَ أَبُو فُلاَنٍ جَاءَ فَجَلَسَ إِلَى جَانِبِ حُجْرَتِي يُحَدِّثُ عَنْ رَسُولِ اللَّهِ صلى الله عليه وسلم، يُسْمِعُنِي ذَلِكَ وَكُنْتُ أُسَبِّحُ فَقَامَ قَبْلَ أَنْ أَقْضِيَ سُبْحَتِي، وَلَوْ أَدْرَكْتُهُ لَرَدَدْتُ عَلَيْهِ، إِنَّ رَسُولَ اللَّهِ صلى الله عليه وسلم لَمْ يَكُنْ يَسْرُدُ الْحَدِيثَ كَسَرْدِكُمْ.

Narrated Abu Huraira: There is none among the companions of the Prophet ﷺ who has narrated more Hadiths than I except `Abdullah bin `Amr (bin Al-`As) who used to write them and I never did the same. – Sahih Al-Bukhari 113

حَدَّثَنَا عَلِيُّ بْنُ عَبْدِ اللَّهِ، قَالَ حَدَّثَنَا سُفْيَانُ، قَالَ حَدَّثَنَا عَمْرٌو، قَالَ أَخْبَرَنِي وَهْبُ بْنُ مُنَبِّهٍ، عَنْ أَخِيهِ، قَالَ سَمِعْتُ أَبَا هُرَيْرَةَ، يَقُولُ مَا مِنْ أَصْحَابِ النَّبِيِّ صلى الله عليه وسلم أَحَدٌ أَكْثَرَ حَدِيثًا عَنْهُ مِنِّي، إِلاَّ مَا كَانَ مِنْ عَبْدِ اللَّهِ بْنِ عَمْرٍو فَإِنَّهُ كَانَ يَكْتُبُ وَلاَ أَكْتُبُ. تَابَعَهُ مَعْمَرٌ عَنْ هَمَّامٍ عَنْ أَبِي هُرَيْرَةَ

Narrated Abu Huraira: I enjoyed the company of Allah's Messenger ﷺ for three years, and during the other years of my life, never was I so anxious to understand the (Prophet's) traditions as I was during those three years. I heard him saying, beckoning with his hand in this way, "Before the Hour you will fight with people who will have hairy shoes and live in Al-Bazir." (Sufyan, the sub-narrator once said, "And they are the people of Al-Bazir."). – Sahih Al-Bukhari 3591

حَدَّثَنَا عَلِيُّ بْنُ عَبْدِ اللَّهِ، حَدَّثَنَا سُفْيَانُ، قَالَ قَالَ إِسْمَاعِيلُ أَخْبَرَنِي قَيْسٌ، قَالَ أَتَيْنَا أَبَا هُرَيْرَةَ ـ رضى الله عنه ـ فَقَالَ صَحِبْتُ رَسُولَ اللَّهِ صلى الله عليه وسلم ثَلاَثَ سِنِينَ لَمْ أَكُنْ فِي سِنِيَّ أَحْرَصَ عَلَى أَنْ أَعِيَ الْحَدِيثَ مِنِّي فِيهِنَّ سَمِعْتُهُ يَقُولُ وَقَالَ هَكَذَا بِيَدِهِ " بَيْنَ يَدَىِ السَّاعَةِ تُقَاتِلُونَ قَوْمًا نِعَالُهُمُ الشَّعَرُ، وَهُوَ هَذَا الْبَارِزُ ". وَقَالَ سُفْيَانُ مَرَّةً وَهُمْ أَهْلُ الْبَارِزِ.

Jabir added, "We were with the Prophet ﷺ at Nakhl and he offered the Fear prayer." Abu Huraira said, "I offered the Fear prayer with the Prophet ﷺ during the Ghazwa (i.e. the battle) of Najd." Abu Huraira came to the Prophet ﷺ during the day of Khaibar. – Sahih Al-Bukhari 4137

وَقَالَ أَبُو الزُّبَيْرِ عَنْ جَابِرٍ، كُنَّا مَعَ النَّبِيِّ صلى الله عليه وسلم بِنَخْلٍ فَصَلَّى الْخَوْفَ. وَقَالَ أَبُو هُرَيْرَةَ صَلَّيْتُ مَعَ النَّبِيِّ صلى الله عليه وسلم غَزْوَةَ نَجْدٍ صَلاَةَ الْخَوْفِ. وَإِنَّمَا جَاءَ أَبُو هُرَيْرَةَ إِلَى النَّبِيِّ صلى الله عليه وسلم أَيَّامَ خَيْبَرَ

Narrated Abu Salama: A man came to Ibn `Abbas while Abu Huraira was sitting with him and said, "Give me your verdict regarding a lady who delivered a baby forty days after the death of her husband." Ibn `Abbas said, "This indicates the end of one of the two prescribed periods." I said "For those who are pregnant, their prescribed period is until they deliver their burdens." Abu Huraira said, I agree with my cousin (Abu Salama)." Then Ibn `Abbas sent his slave, Kuraib to Um Salama to ask her (regarding this matter). She replied. "The husband of Subai'a al Aslamiya was killed while she was pregnant, and she delivered a baby forty days after his death. Then her hand was asked in marriage and Allah's Messenger ﷺ married her (to somebody). Abu As-Sanabil was one of those who asked for her hand in marriage". – Sahih Al-Bukhari 4909

حَدَّثَنَا سَعْدُ بْنُ حَفْصٍ، حَدَّثَنَا شَيْبَانُ، عَنْ يَحْيَى، قَالَ أَخْبَرَنِي أَبُو سَلَمَةَ، قَالَ جَاءَ رَجُلٌ إِلَى ابْنِ عَبَّاسٍ وَأَبُو هُرَيْرَةَ جَالِسٌ عِنْدَهُ فَقَالَ أَفْتِنِي فِي امْرَأَةٍ وَلَدَتْ بَعْدَ زَوْجِهَا بِأَرْبَعِينَ لَيْلَةً. فَقَالَ ابْنُ عَبَّاسٍ آخِرُ الأَجَلَيْنِ. قُلْتُ أَنَا {وَأُولاَتُ الأَحْمَالِ أَجَلُهُنَّ أَنْ يَضَعْنَ حَمْلَهُنَّ} قَالَ أَبُو هُرَيْرَةَ أَنَا مَعَ ابْنِ أَخِي - يَعْنِي أَبَا سَلَمَةَ - فَأَرْسَلَ ابْنُ عَبَّاسٍ غُلاَمَهُ كُرَيْبًا إِلَى أُمِّ سَلَمَةَ يَسْأَلُهَا فَقَالَتْ قُتِلَ زَوْجُ سُبَيْعَةَ الأَسْلَمِيَّةِ وَهْىَ حُبْلَى، فَوَضَعَتْ بَعْدَ مَوْتِهِ بِأَرْبَعِينَ لَيْلَةً فَخُطِبَتْ فَأَنْكَحَهَا رَسُولُ اللَّهِ صلى الله عليه وسلم وَكَانَ أَبُو السَّنَابِلِ فِيمَنْ خَطَبَهَا.

Narrated Abu `Uthman: I was a guest of Abu Huraira for seven days. Abu Huraira, his wife and his slave used to get up and remain awake for one-third of the night by turns. Each would offer the night prayer and then awaken the other. I heard Abu Huraira saying, "Allah's Messenger ﷺ distributed dates among his companions and my share was seven dates, one of which was a Hashafa (a date which dried on the tree before it was fully ripe). Narrated Abu Huraira: The Prophet ﷺ distributed dates among us, and my share was five dates, four of which were good, and one was a ,Hashafa, and I found the Hashafa the hardest for my teeth. – Sahih Al-Bukhari 5441, 5441b

حَدَّثَنَا مُسَدَّدٌ، حَدَّثَنَا حَمَّادُ بْنُ زَيْدٍ، عَنْ عَبَّاسٍ الْجُرَيْرِيِّ، عَنْ أَبِي عُثْمَانَ، قَالَ تَضَيَّفْتُ أَبَا هُرَيْرَةَ سَبْعًا، فَكَانَ هُوَ وَامْرَأَتُهُ وَخَادِمُهُ يَعْتَقِبُونَ اللَّيْلَ أَثْلاَثًا، يُصَلِّي هَذَا، ثُمَّ يُوقِظُ هَذَا. وَسَمِعْتُهُ يَقُولُ قَسَمَ رَسُولُ اللَّهِ صلى الله عليه وسلم بَيْنَ أَصْحَابِهِ تَمْرًا، فَأَصَابَنِي سَبْعُ تَمَرَاتٍ إِحْدَاهُنَّ حَشَفَةٌ. حَدَّثَنَا مُحَمَّدُ بْنُ الصَّبَّاحِ، حَدَّثَنَا إِسْمَاعِيلُ بْنُ زَكَرِيَّاءَ، عَنْ عَاصِمٍ، عَنْ أَبِي عُثْمَانَ، عَنْ أَبِي هُرَيْرَةَ - رضى الله عنه - قَسَمَ النَّبِيُّ صلى الله عليه وسلم بَيْنَنَا تَمْرًا فَأَصَابَنِي مِنْهُ خَمْسٌ أَرْبَعُ تَمَرَاتٍ وَحَشَفَةٌ، ثُمَّ رَأَيْتُ الْحَشَفَةَ هِيَ أَشَدُّهُنَّ لِضِرْسِي.

Narrated Abu Huraira: By Allah except Whom none has the right to- be worshipped, (sometimes) I used to lay (sleep) on the ground on my liver (abdomen) because of hunger, and (sometimes) I used to bind a stone over my belly because of hunger. One day I sat by the way from where they (the Prophet ﷺ and his companions) used to come out. When Abu Bakr passed by, I asked him about a Verse from Allah's Book and I asked him only that he might satisfy my hunger, but he passed by and did not do so. Then `Umar passed by me and I asked him about a Verse from Allah's Book, and I asked him only that he might satisfy my hunger, but he passed by without doing so. Finally Abu-l-Qasim (the Prophet ﷺ) passed by me and he smiled when he saw me, for he knew what was in my heart and on my face. He said, "O Aba Hirr (Abu Huraira)!" I replied, "Labbaik, O Allah's Messenger ﷺ!" He said to me, "Follow me."

He left and I followed him. Then he entered the house and I asked permission to enter and was admitted. He found milk in a bowl and said, "From where is this milk?" They said, "It has been presented to you by such-and-such man (or by such and such woman)." He said, "O Aba Hirr!" I said, "Labbaik, O Allah's Messenger ﷺ!" He said, "Go and call the people of Suffa to me." These people of Suffa were the guests of Islam who had no families, nor money, nor anybody to depend upon, and whenever an object of charity was brought to the Prophet, he would send it to them and would not take anything from it, and whenever any present was given to him, he used to send some for them and take some of it for himself. The order of the Prophet upset me, and I said to myself, "How will this little milk be enough for the people of As- Suffa? Though I was more entitled to drink from that milk in order to strengthen myself", but behold! The Prophet ﷺ came to order me to give that milk to them. I wondered what will remain of that milk for me, but anyway, I could not but obey Allah and His Apostle so I went to the people of As-Suffa and called them, and they came and asked the Prophet's permission to enter. They were admitted and took their seats in the house. The Prophet ﷺ said, "O Aba-Hirr!" I said, "Labbaik, O Allah's Messenger ﷺ!" He said, "Take it and give it to them." So I took the bowl (of milk) and started giving it to one man who would drink his fill and return it to me, whereupon I would give it to another man who, in his turn, would drink his fill and return it to me, and I would then offer it to another man who would drink his fill and return it to me. Finally, after the whole group had drunk their fill, I reached the Prophet ﷺ who took the bowl and put it on his hand, looked at me and smiled and said. "O Aba Hirr!" I replied, "Labbaik, O Allah's Messenger ﷺ!" He said, "There remain you and I." I said, "You have said the truth, O Allah's Messenger ﷺ!" He said, "Sit down and drink." I sat down and drank. He said, "Drink," and I drank. He kept on telling me repeatedly to drink, till I said, "No. by Allah Who sent you with the Truth, I have no space for it (in my stomach)." He said, "Hand it over to me." When I gave him the bowl, he praised Allah and pronounced Allah's Name on it and drank the remaining milk. – Sahih Al-Bukhari 6452

حَدَّثَنِي أَبُو نُعَيْمٍ، بِنَحْوٍ مِنْ نِصْفِ هَذَا الْحَدِيثِ حَدَّثَنَا عُمَرُ بْنُ ذَرٍّ، حَدَّثَنَا مُجَاهِدٌ، أَنَّ أَبَا هُرَيْرَةَ، كَانَ يَقُولُ آللَّهِ الَّذِي لاَ إِلَهَ إِلاَّ هُوَ إِنْ كُنْتُ لأَعْتَمِدُ بِكَبِدِي عَلَى الأَرْضِ مِنَ الْجُوعِ، وَإِنْ كُنْتُ لأَشُدُّ الْحَجَرَ عَلَى بَطْنِي مِنَ الْجُوعِ، وَلَقَدْ قَعَدْتُ يَوْمًا عَلَى طَرِيقِهِمُ الَّذِي يَخْرُجُونَ مِنْهُ، فَمَرَّ أَبُو بَكْرٍ، فَسَأَلْتُهُ عَنْ آيَةٍ مِنْ كِتَابِ اللَّهِ، مَا سَأَلْتُهُ إِلاَّ لِيُشْبِعَنِي، فَمَرَّ وَلَمْ يَفْعَلْ، ثُمَّ مَرَّ بِي عُمَرُ فَسَأَلْتُهُ عَنْ آيَةٍ مِنْ كِتَابِ اللَّهِ، مَا سَأَلْتُهُ إِلاَّ لِيُشْبِعَنِي، فَمَرَّ فَلَمْ يَفْعَلْ، ثُمَّ مَرَّ بِي أَبُو الْقَاسِمِ صلى الله عليه وسلم فَتَبَسَّمَ حِينَ رَآنِي وَعَرَفَ، مَا فِي نَفْسِي وَمَا فِي وَجْهِي ثُمَّ قَالَ " أَبَا هِرٍّ ". قُلْتُ لَبَّيْكَ يَا رَسُولَ اللَّهِ. قَالَ " الْحَقْ ". وَمَضَى فَتَبِعْتُهُ، فَدَخَلَ فَاسْتَأْذَنَ، فَأَذِنَ لِي، فَدَخَلَ فَوَجَدَ لَبَنًا فِي قَدَحٍ فَقَالَ " مِنْ أَيْنَ هَذَا اللَّبَنُ ". قَالُوا أَهْدَاهُ لَكَ فُلاَنٌ أَوْ فُلاَنَةُ. قَالَ " أَبَا هِرٍّ ". قُلْتُ لَبَّيْكَ يَا رَسُولَ اللَّهِ. قَالَ " الْحَقْ إِلَى أَهْلِ الصُّفَّةِ فَادْعُهُمْ لِي ". قَالَ وَأَهْلُ الصُّفَّةِ أَضْيَافُ الإِسْلاَمِ، لاَ يَأْوُونَ إِلَى أَهْلٍ وَلاَ مَالٍ، وَلاَ عَلَى أَحَدٍ، إِذَا أَتَتْهُ صَدَقَةٌ بَعَثَ بِهَا إِلَيْهِمْ، وَلَمْ يَتَنَاوَلْ مِنْهَا شَيْئًا، وَإِذَا أَتَتْهُ هَدِيَّةٌ أَرْسَلَ إِلَيْهِمْ، وَأَصَابَ مِنْهَا وَأَشْرَكَهُمْ فِيهَا، فَسَاءَنِي ذَلِكَ فَقُلْتُ وَمَا هَذَا اللَّبَنُ فِي أَهْلِ الصُّفَّةِ كُنْتُ أَحَقُّ أَنَا أَنْ أُصِيبَ مِنْ هَذَا اللَّبَنِ شَرْبَةً أَتَقَوَّى بِهَا، فَإِذَا جَاءَ أَمَرَنِي فَكُنْتُ أَنَا أُعْطِيهِمْ، وَمَا عَسَى أَنْ يَبْلُغَنِي مِنْ هَذَا اللَّبَنِ، وَلَمْ يَكُنْ مِنْ طَاعَةِ اللَّهِ وَطَاعَةِ رَسُولِهِ صلى الله عليه وسلم بُدٌّ، فَأَتَيْتُهُمْ فَدَعَوْتُهُمْ فَأَقْبَلُوا، فَاسْتَأْذَنُوا فَأَذِنَ لَهُمْ، وَأَخَذُوا مَجَالِسَهُمْ مِنَ الْبَيْتِ قَالَ " يَا أَبَا هِرٍّ ". قُلْتُ لَبَّيْكَ يَا رَسُولَ اللَّهِ. قَالَ " خُذْ فَأَعْطِهِمْ ". قَالَ فَأَخَذْتُ الْقَدَحَ فَجَعَلْتُ أُعْطِيهِ الرَّجُلَ فَيَشْرَبُ حَتَّى يَرْوَى، ثُمَّ يَرُدُّ عَلَىَّ الْقَدَحَ، فَأُعْطِيهِ الرَّجُلَ فَيَشْرَبُ حَتَّى يَرْوَى، ثُمَّ يَرُدُّ عَلَىَّ الْقَدَحَ فَيَشْرَبُ حَتَّى يَرْوَى، ثُمَّ يَرُدُّ عَلَىَّ الْقَدَحَ، حَتَّى انْتَهَيْتُ إِلَى النَّبِيِّ صلى الله عليه وسلم وَقَدْ رَوِيَ الْقَوْمُ كُلُّهُمْ، فَأَخَذَ الْقَدَحَ فَوَضَعَهُ عَلَى يَدِهِ فَنَظَرَ إِلَىَّ فَتَبَسَّمَ فَقَالَ " أَبَا هِرٍّ ". قُلْتُ لَبَّيْكَ يَا رَسُولَ اللَّهِ. قَالَ " بَقِيتُ أَنَا وَأَنْتَ ". قُلْتُ صَدَقْتَ يَا رَسُولَ اللَّهِ. قَالَ " اقْعُدْ فَاشْرَبْ ". فَقَعَدْتُ فَشَرِبْتُ. فَقَالَ " اشْرَبْ ". فَشَرِبْتُ، فَمَا زَالَ يَقُولُ " اشْرَبْ ". حَتَّى قُلْتُ لاَ وَالَّذِي بَعَثَكَ بِالْحَقِّ، مَا أَجِدُ لَهُ مَسْلَكًا. قَالَ " فَأَرِنِي ". فَأَعْطَيْتُهُ الْقَدَحَ فَحَمِدَ اللَّهَ وَسَمَّى، وَشَرِبَ الْفَضْلَةَ

Narrated 'Ata (while Abu Huraira was narrating (see previous hadith): Abu Sa`id was sitting in the company of Abu Huraira and he did not deny anything of his narration till he reached his saying: "All this and as much again therewith are for you." Then Abu Sa`id said, "I heard Allah's

Messenger ﷺ saying, 'This is for you and ten times as much.' " Abu Huraira said, "In my memory it is 'as much again therewith.' ". – Sahih Al-Bukhari 6574

قَالَ عَطَاءٌ وَأَبُو سَعِيدٍ الْخُدْرِيُّ جَالِسٌ مَعَ أَبِي هُرَيْرَةَ، لاَ يُغَيِّرُ عَلَيْهِ شَيْئًا مِنْ حَدِيثِهِ حَتَّى انْتَهَى إِلَى قَوْلِهِ " هَذَا لَكَ وَمِثْلُهُ مَعَهُ ". قَالَ أَبُو سَعِيدٍ سَمِعْتُ رَسُولَ اللَّهِ صلى الله عليه وسلم يَقُولُ " هَذَا لَكَ وَعَشَرَةُ أَمْثَالِهِ ". قَالَ أَبُو هُرَيْرَةَ حَفِظْتُ " مِثْلُهُ مَعَهُ ".

Narrated Muhammad: We were with Abu Huraira while he was wearing two linen garments dyed with red clay. He cleaned his nose with his garment, saying, "Bravo! Bravo! Abu Huraira is cleaning his nose with linen! There came a time when I would fall senseless between the pulpit of Allah's Messenger ﷺ and `Aisha's dwelling whereupon a passerby would come and put his foot on my neck, considering me a mad man, but in fact, I had no madness, I suffered nothing but hunger.". – Sahih Al-Bukhari 7324

حَدَّثَنَا سُلَيْمَانُ بْنُ حَرْبٍ، حَدَّثَنَا حَمَّادٌ، عَنْ أَيُّوبَ، عَنْ مُحَمَّدٍ، قَالَ كُنَّا عِنْدَ أَبِي هُرَيْرَةَ وَعَلَيْهِ ثَوْبَانِ مُمَشَّقَانِ مِنْ كَتَّانٍ فَتَمَخَّطَ فَقَالَ بَخْ بَخْ أَبُو هُرَيْرَةَ يَتَمَخَّطُ فِي الْكَتَّانِ، لَقَدْ رَأَيْتُنِي وَإِنِّي لأَخِرُّ فِيمَا بَيْنَ مِنْبَرِ رَسُولِ اللَّهِ صلى الله عليه وسلم إِلَى حُجْرَةِ عَائِشَةَ مَغْشِيًّا عَلَيَّ، فَيَجِيءُ الْجَائِي فَيَضَعُ رِجْلَهُ عَلَى عُنُقِي، وَيُرَى أَنِّي مَجْنُونٌ، وَمَا بِي مِنْ جُنُونٍ، مَا بِي إِلاَّ الْجُوعُ

Narrated 'Ata' bin Yazid Al-Laithi: On the authority of Abu Huraira: The people said, "O Allah's Messenger ﷺ! Shall we see our Lord on the Day of Resurrection?" The Prophet ﷺ said, "Do you have any difficulty in seeing the moon on a full moon night?" They said, "No, O Allah's Messenger ﷺ." He said, "Do you have any difficulty in seeing the sun when there are no clouds?" They said, "No, O Allah's Messenger ﷺ." He said, "So you will see Him, like that. Allah will gather all the people on the Day of Resurrection, and say, 'Whoever worshipped something (in the world) should follow (that thing),' so, whoever worshipped the sun will follow the sun, and whoever worshiped the moon will follow the moon, and whoever used to worship certain (other false) deities, he will follow those deities. And there will remain only this nation with its good people (or its hypocrites). (The sub-narrator, Ibrahim is in doubt.) Allah will come to them and say, 'I am your Lord.' They will (deny Him and) say, 'We will stay here till our Lord comes, for when our Lord comes, we will recognize Him.' So Allah will come to them in His appearance which they know, and will say, 'I am your Lord.' They will say, 'You are our Lord,' so they will follow Him. Then a bridge will be laid across Hell (Fire)' I and my followers will be the first ones to go across it and none will speak on that Day except the Apostles. And the invocation of the Apostles on that Day will be, 'O Allah, save! Save!' In Hell (or over The Bridge) there will be hooks like the thorns of As-Sa'dan (thorny plant). Have you seen As-Sa'dan? " They replied, "Yes, O Allah's Messenger ﷺ!" He said, "So those hooks look like the thorns of As-Sa'dan, but none knows how big they are except Allah. Those hooks will snap the people away according to their deeds. Some of the people will stay in Hell (be destroyed) because of their (evil) deeds, and some will be cut or torn by the hooks (and fall into Hell) and some will be punished and then relieved. When Allah has finished His Judgments among the people, He will take whomever He will out of Hell through His Mercy. He will then order the angels to take out of the Fire all those who used to worship none but Allah from among those whom Allah wanted to be merciful to and those who testified (in the world) that none has the right to be worshipped but Allah. The angels will recognize them in the Fire by the marks of prostration (on their foreheads), for the Fire will eat up all the human body except the mark caused by prostration as Allah has forbidden the Fire to eat the mark of prostration. They will come out of the (Hell) Fire, completely burnt and then the water of life will be poured over them and they will grow under it as does a seed that comes in the mud of the torrent. Then Allah will finish the judgments among the people, and there will remain one man facing the (Hell) Fire and he will be the last person among the people of Hell to enter Paradise. He will say, 'O my Lord! Please turn my face away from the fire because its air has hurt me and its severe heat has burnt me.' So he will invoke Allah in the way Allah will wish him to invoke, and then Allah will say to him, 'If I grant you that, will you then ask for anything else?' He will reply, 'No, by Your Power, (Honor) I will not ask You for anything else.' He will give his Lord whatever promises and covenants Allah will demand. So Allah will turn his face away from Hell (Fire). When he will face Paradise and will see it, he will remain quiet for as long as Allah will wish him to remain quiet, then he will say, 'O my Lord! Bring me near to the gate of Paradise.' Allah will say to him, 'Didn't you give your promises and covenants that you would never ask for anything more than what you had been given? Woe on you, O Adam's son! How treacherous you are!' He will say, 'O my lord,' and will keep on invoking Allah till He says to him, 'If I give what you are asking, will you then ask for anything else?' He will reply, 'No, by Your (Honor) Power, I will not ask for anything else.' Then he will give covenants and promises to Allah and then Allah will bring him near to the gate of Paradise. When he stands at the gate of Paradise, Paradise will be opened and spread before him, and he will see its splendor and pleasures whereupon he will remain quiet as long as Allah will wish him to remain quiet, and then he will say, O my Lord! Admit me into Paradise.' Allah will say, 'Didn't you give your covenants and promises that you would not ask for anything more than what you had been given?' Allah will say, 'Woe on you, O Adam's son! How treacherous you are! ' The man will say, 'O my Lord! Do not make me the most miserable of Your creation,' and he will keep on invoking Allah till Allah will laugh because of his sayings, and when Allah will laugh because of him, He will say to him, 'Enter Paradise,' and when he will enter it, Allah will say to him, 'Wish for anything.' So he will ask his Lord, and he will wish for a great number of things, for Allah Himself will remind him to wish for certain things by saying, '(Wish for) so-and-so.' When there is nothing more to wish for, Allah will say, 'This is for you, and its equal (is for you) as well." 'Ata' bin Yazid added: Abu Sa'id Al-Khudri who was present with Abu Huraira, did not deny whatever the latter said, but when Abu Huraira said that Allah had said, "That is for you and its equal as well," Abu Sa'id Al-Khudri said, "And ten times as much, O Abu Huraira!" Abu Huraira said, "I do not remember, except his saying, 'That is for you and its equal as well.'" Abu Sa'id Al-Khudri then said, "I testify that I remember the Prophet ﷺ saying, 'That is for you, and ten times as much.' ' Abu Huraira then added, "That man will be the last person of the people of Paradise to enter Paradise.". – Sahih Al-Bukhari 7437, 7438

حَدَّثَنَا عَبْدُ الْعَزِيزِ بْنُ عَبْدِ اللَّهِ، حَدَّثَنَا إِبْرَاهِيمُ بْنُ سَعْدٍ، عَنِ ابْنِ شِهَابٍ، عَنْ عَطَاءِ بْنِ يَزِيدَ اللَّيْثِيِّ، عَنْ أَبِي هُرَيْرَةَ، أَنَّ النَّاسَ، قَالُوا يَا رَسُولَ اللَّهِ هَلْ نَرَى رَبَّنَا يَوْمَ الْقِيَامَةِ فَقَالَ رَسُولُ اللَّهِ صلى الله عليه وسلم " هَلْ تُضَارُّونَ فِي الْقَمَرِ لَيْلَةَ الْبَدْرِ ". قَالُوا لاَ يَا رَسُولَ اللَّهِ. قَالَ " فَهَلْ تُضَارُّونَ فِي الشَّمْسِ لَيْسَ دُونَهَا سَحَابٌ ". قَالُوا لاَ يَا رَسُولَ اللَّهِ. قَالَ " فَإِنَّكُمْ تَرَوْنَهُ كَذَلِكَ، يَجْمَعُ اللَّهُ النَّاسَ يَوْمَ الْقِيَامَةِ فَيَقُولُ مَنْ كَانَ يَعْبُدُ شَيْئًا فَلْيَتَّبِعْهُ. فَيَتْبَعُ مَنْ كَانَ يَعْبُدُ الشَّمْسَ الشَّمْسَ، وَيَتْبَعُ مَنْ كَانَ يَعْبُدُ الْقَمَرَ الْقَمَرَ، وَيَتْبَعُ مَنْ كَانَ يَعْبُدُ الطَّوَاغِيتَ الطَّوَاغِيتَ، وَتَبْقَى هَذِهِ الأُمَّةُ فِيهَا شَافِعُوهَا ـ أَوْ مُنَافِقُوهَا شَكَّ إِبْرَاهِيمُ ـ فَيَأْتِيهِمُ اللَّهُ فَيَقُولُ أَنَا رَبُّكُمْ. فَيَقُولُونَ هَذَا مَكَانُنَا حَتَّى يَأْتِيَنَا رَبُّنَا فَإِذَا جَاءَنَا رَبُّنَا عَرَفْنَاهُ فَيَأْتِيهِمُ اللَّهُ فِي صُورَتِهِ الَّتِي يَعْرِفُونَ فَيَقُولُ أَنَا رَبُّكُمْ. فَيَقُولُونَ أَنْتَ رَبُّنَا. فَيَتْبَعُونَهُ وَيُضْرَبُ الصِّرَاطُ بَيْنَ ظَهْرَىْ جَهَنَّمَ، فَأَكُونُ أَنَا وَأُمَّتِي أَوَّلَ مَنْ يُجِيزُهَا، وَلاَ يَتَكَلَّمُ يَوْمَئِذٍ إِلاَّ الرُّسُلُ، وَدَعْوَى الرُّسُلِ يَوْمَئِذٍ اللَّهُمَّ سَلِّمْ سَلِّمْ. وَفِي جَهَنَّمَ كَلاَلِيبُ مِثْلُ شَوْكِ السَّعْدَانِ، هَلْ رَأَيْتُمُ السَّعْدَانَ ". قَالُوا نَعَمْ يَا رَسُولَ اللَّهِ. قَالَ " فَإِنَّهَا مِثْلُ شَوْكِ السَّعْدَانِ، غَيْرَ أَنَّهُ لاَ يَعْلَمُ مَا قَدْرُ عِظَمِهَا إِلاَّ اللَّهُ، تَخْطَفُ النَّاسَ بِأَعْمَالِهِمْ، فَمِنْهُمُ الْمُوبَقُ بَقِيَ بِعَمَلِهِ، أَوِ الْمُوثَقُ بِعَمَلِهِ، وَمِنْهُمُ الْمُخَرْدَلُ أَوِ الْمُجَازَى أَوْ نَحْوُهُ، ثُمَّ يَتَجَلَّى حَتَّى إِذَا فَرَغَ اللَّهُ مِنَ الْقَضَاءِ بَيْنَ الْعِبَادِ وَأَرَادَ أَنْ يُخْرِجَ بِرَحْمَتِهِ مَنْ أَرَادَ مِنْ أَهْلِ النَّارِ أَمَرَ الْمَلاَئِكَةَ أَنْ يُخْرِجُوا مِنَ النَّارِ مَنْ كَانَ لاَ يُشْرِكُ بِاللَّهِ شَيْئًا، مِمَّنْ أَرَادَ اللَّهُ أَنْ يَرْحَمَهُ مِمَّنْ يَشْهَدُ أَنْ لاَ إِلَهَ إِلاَّ اللَّهُ، فَيَعْرِفُونَهُمْ فِي النَّارِ بِأَثَرِ السُّجُودِ، تَأْكُلُ النَّارُ ابْنَ آدَمَ إِلاَّ أَثَرَ السُّجُودِ، حَرَّمَ اللَّهُ عَلَى النَّارِ أَنْ تَأْكُلَ أَثَرَ السُّجُودِ، فَيَخْرُجُونَ مِنَ النَّارِ قَدِ امْتُحِشُوا، فَيُصَبُّ عَلَيْهِمْ مَاءُ الْحَيَاةِ فَيَنْبُتُونَ تَحْتَهُ كَمَا تَنْبُتُ الْحِبَّةُ فِي حَمِيلِ السَّيْلِ، ثُمَّ يَفْرُغُ اللَّهُ مِنَ الْقَضَاءِ بَيْنَ الْعِبَادِ، وَيَبْقَى رَجُلٌ مُقْبِلٌ بِوَجْهِهِ عَلَى النَّارِ هُوَ آخِرُ أَهْلِ النَّارِ دُخُولاً الْجَنَّةَ فَيَقُولُ أَىْ رَبِّ اصْرِفْ وَجْهِي عَنِ النَّارِ، فَإِنَّهُ قَدْ قَشَبَنِي رِيحُهَا وَأَحْرَقَنِي ذَكَاؤُهَا. فَيَدْعُو اللَّهَ بِمَا شَاءَ أَنْ يَدْعُوَهُ ثُمَّ يَقُولُ اللَّهُ هَلْ عَسَيْتَ إِنْ أُعْطِيتَ ذَلِكَ أَنْ تَسْأَلَنِي غَيْرَهُ. فَيَقُولُ لاَ وَعِزَّتِكَ لاَ أَسْأَلُكَ غَيْرَهُ، وَيُعْطِي

رَبَّهُ مِنْ عُهُودٍ وَمَوَاثِيقَ مَا شَاءَ، فَيَصْرِفُ اللَّهُ وَجْهَهُ عَنِ النَّارِ، فَإِذَا أَقْبَلَ عَلَى الْجَنَّةِ وَرَآهَا سَكَتَ مَا شَاءَ اللَّهُ أَنْ يَسْكُتَ ثُمَّ يَقُولُ أَىْ رَبِّ قَدِّمْنِي إِلَى بابِ الْجَنَّةِ. فَيَقُولُ اللَّهُ لَهُ أَلَسْتَ قَدْ أَعْطَيْتَ عُهُودَكَ وَمَوَاثِيقَكَ أَنْ لاَ تَسْأَلَنِي غَيْرَ الَّذِي أُعْطِيتَ أَبَدًا، وَيْلَكَ يَا ابْنَ آدَمَ مَا أَغْدَرَكَ. فَيَقُولُ أَىْ رَبِّ. وَيَدْعُو اللَّهَ حَتَّى يَقُولَ هَلْ عَسَيْتَ إِنْ أُعْطِيتَ ذَلِكَ أَنْ تَسْأَلَ غَيْرَهُ. فَيَقُولُ لاَ وَعِزَّتِكَ لاَ أَسْأَلُكَ غَيْرَهُ، وَيُعْطِي مَا شَاءَ مِنْ عُهُودٍ وَمَوَاثِيقَ، فَيُقَدِّمُهُ إِلَى بابِ الْجَنَّةِ، فَإِذَا قَامَ إِلَى بابِ الْجَنَّةِ انْفَهَقَتْ لَهُ الْجَنَّةُ فَرَأَى مَا فِيهَا مِنَ الْحَبْرَةِ وَالسُّرُورِ، فَيَسْكُتُ مَا شَاءَ اللَّهُ أَنْ يَسْكُتَ ثُمَّ يَقُولُ أَىْ رَبِّ أَدْخِلْنِي الْجَنَّةَ. فَيَقُولُ اللَّهُ أَلَسْتَ قَدْ أَعْطَيْتَ عُهُودَكَ وَمَوَاثِيقَكَ أَنْ لاَ تَسْأَلَ غَيْرَ مَا أُعْطِيتَ ـ فَيَقُولُ ـ وَيْلَكَ يَا ابْنَ آدَمَ مَا أَغْدَرَكَ. فَيَقُولُ أَىْ رَبِّ لاَ أَكُونَنَّ أَشْقَى خَلْقِكَ فَلاَ يَزَالُ يَدْعُو حَتَّى يَضْحَكَ اللَّهُ مِنْهُ فَإِذَا ضَحِكَ مِنْهُ قَالَ لَهُ ادْخُلِ الْجَنَّةَ. فَإِذَا دَخَلَهَا قَالَ اللَّهُ لَهُ تَمَنَّهْ. فَسَأَلَ رَبَّهُ وَتَمَنَّى حَتَّى إِنَّ اللَّهَ لَيُذَكِّرُهُ يَقُولُ كَذَا وَكَذَا، حَتَّى انْقَطَعَتْ بِهِ الأَمَانِيُّ قَالَ اللَّهُ ذَلِكَ لَكَ وَمِثْلُهُ مَعَهُ ". قَالَ عَطَاءُ بْنُ يَزِيدَ وَأَبُو سَعِيدٍ الْخُدْرِيُّ مَعَ أَبِي هُرَيْرَةَ لاَ يَرُدُّ عَلَيْهِ مِنْ حَدِيثِهِ شَيْئًا حَتَّى إِذَا حَدَّثَ أَبُو هُرَيْرَةَ أَنَّ اللَّهَ تَبَارَكَ وَتَعَالَى قَالَ " ذَلِكَ لَكَ وَمِثْلُهُ مَعَهُ ". قَالَ أَبُو سَعِيدٍ الْخُدْرِيُّ " وَعَشَرَةُ أَمْثَالِهِ مَعَهُ ". يَا أَبَا هُرَيْرَةَ. قَالَ أَبُو هُرَيْرَةَ مَا حَفِظْتُ إِلاَّ قَوْلَهُ " ذَلِكَ لَكَ وَمِثْلُهُ مَعَهُ ". قَالَ أَبُو سَعِيدٍ الْخُدْرِيُّ أَشْهَدُ أَنِّي حَفِظْتُ مِنْ رَسُولِ اللَّهِ صلى الله عليه وسلم قَوْلَهُ " ذَلِكَ لَكَ وَعَشَرَةُ أَمْثَالِهِ ". قَالَ أَبُو هُرَيْرَةَ فَذَلِكَ الرَّجُلُ آخِرُ أَهْلِ الْجَنَّةِ دُخُولاً الْجَنَّةَ.

Narrated Abu Huraira: The Prophet ﷺ said, "Allah said: "The son of Adam hurts Me by abusing Time, for I am Time; in My Hands are all things and I cause the revolution of night and day.' " (See Hadith No. 351, Vol. 6). – Sahih Al-Bukhari 7491

حَدَّثَنَا الْحُمَيْدِيُّ، حَدَّثَنَا سُفْيَانُ، حَدَّثَنَا الزُّهْرِيُّ، عَنْ سَعِيدِ بْنِ الْمُسَيَّبِ، عَنْ أَبِي هُرَيْرَةَ، قَالَ قَالَ النَّبِيُّ صلى الله عليه وسلم " قَالَ اللَّهُ تَعَالَى يُؤْذِينِي ابْنُ آدَمَ، يَسُبُّ الدَّهْرَ وَأَنَا الدَّهْرُ، بِيَدِي الأَمْرُ، أُقَلِّبُ اللَّيْلَ وَالنَّهَارَ "

Narrated Abu Huraira: Once the Prophet ﷺ was preaching while a bedouin was sitting there. The Prophet ﷺ said, "A man from among the people of Paradise will request Allah to allow him to cultivate the land Allah will say to him, 'Haven't you got whatever you desire?' He will reply, 'yes, but I like to cultivate the land (Allah will permit him and) he will sow the seeds, and within seconds the plants will grow and ripen and (the yield) will be harvested and piled in heaps like mountains. On that Allah will say (to him), "Take, here you are, O son of Adam, for nothing satisfies you.' "On that the bedouin said, "O Allah's Messenger ﷺ! Such man must be either from Quraish or from Ansar, for they are farmers while we are not." On that Allah's Messenger ﷺ smiled . – Sahih Al-Bukhari 7519

حَدَّثَنَا مُحَمَّدُ بْنُ سِنَانٍ، حَدَّثَنَا فُلَيْحٌ، حَدَّثَنَا هِلاَلٌ، عَنْ عَطَاءِ بْنِ يَسَارٍ، عَنْ أَبِي هُرَيْرَةَ، أَنَّ النَّبِيَّ صلى الله عليه وسلم كَانَ يَوْمًا يُحَدِّثُ وَعِنْدَهُ رَجُلٌ مِنْ أَهْلِ الْبَادِيَةِ " أَنَّ رَجُلاً مِنْ أَهْلِ الْجَنَّةِ اسْتَأْذَنَ رَبَّهُ فِي الزَّرْعِ فَقَالَ أَوَ لَسْتَ فِيمَا شِئْتَ. قَالَ بَلَى وَلَكِنِّي أُحِبُّ أَنْ أَزْرَعَ. فَأَسْرَعَ وَبَذَرَ فَتَبَادَرَ الطَّرْفَ نَبَاتُهُ وَاسْتِوَاؤُهُ وَاسْتِحْصَادُهُ وَتَكْوِيرُهُ أَمْثَالَ الْجِبَالِ فَيَقُولُ اللَّهُ تَعَالَى دُونَكَ يَا ابْنَ آدَمَ فَإِنَّهُ لاَ يُشْبِعُكَ شَىْءٌ ". فَقَالَ الأَعْرَابِيُّ يَا رَسُولَ اللَّهِ لاَ تَجِدُ هَذَا إِلاَّ قُرَشِيًّا أَوْ أَنْصَارِيًّا فَإِنَّهُمْ أَصْحَابُ زَرْعٍ، فَأَمَّا نَحْنُ فَلَسْنَا بِأَصْحَابِ زَرْعٍ. فَضَحِكَ رَسُولُ اللَّهِ صلى الله عليه وسلم.

Narrated Abu Huraira: The Prophet ﷺ said, "Jews and Christians do not dye their hair so you should do the opposite of what they do. – Sahih Al-Bukhari 5899

حَدَّثَنَا الْحُمَيْدِيُّ، حَدَّثَنَا سُفْيَانُ، حَدَّثَنَا الزُّهْرِيُّ، عَنْ أَبِي سَلَمَةَ، وَسُلَيْمَانَ بْنِ يَسَارٍ، عَنْ أَبِي هُرَيْرَةَ ـ رضى الله عنه ـ قَالَ النَّبِيُّ صلى الله عليه وسلم " إِنَّ الْيَهُودَ وَالنَّصَارَى لاَ يَصْبُغُونَ فَخَالِفُوهُمْ ".

Narrated Abu Huraira: "The Prophet ﷺ said, 'The best alms is that which is given when one is rich, and a giving hand is better than a taking one, and you should start first to support your dependents.' A wife says, 'You should either provide me with food or divorce me.' A slave says, 'Give me food and enjoy my service." A son says, "Give me food; to whom do you leave me?" The people said, "O Abu Huraira! Did you hear that from Allah's Messenger ﷺ?" He said, "No, it is from my own self.". – Sahih Al-Bukhari 5355

حَدَّثَنَا عُمَرُ بْنُ حَفْصٍ، حَدَّثَنَا أَبِي، حَدَّثَنَا الأَعْمَشُ، حَدَّثَنَا أَبُو صَالِحٍ، قَالَ حَدَّثَنِي أَبُو هُرَيْرَةَ ـ رضى الله عنه ـ قَالَ قَالَ النَّبِيُّ صلى الله عليه وسلم " أَفْضَلُ الصَّدَقَةِ مَا تَرَكَ غِنًى، وَالْيَدُ الْعُلْيَا خَيْرٌ مِنَ الْيَدِ السُّفْلَى، وَابْدَأْ بِمَنْ تَعُولُ ". تَقُولُ الْمَرْأَةُ إِمَّا أَنْ تُطْعِمَنِي وَإِمَّا أَنْ تُطَلِّقَنِي. وَيَقُولُ الْعَبْدُ أَطْعِمْنِي وَاسْتَعْمِلْنِي. وَيَقُولُ الاِبْنُ أَطْعِمْنِي، إِلَى مَنْ تَدَعُنِي فَقَالُوا يَا أَبَا هُرَيْرَةَ سَمِعْتَ هَذَا مِنْ رَسُولِ اللَّهِ صلى الله عليه وسلم. قَالَ لاَ هَذَا مِنْ كِيسِ أَبِي هُرَيْرَةَ

Narrated Sa`id Al-Maqburi: That his father said, “While we were accompanying a funeral procession, Abu Huraira got hold of the hand of Marwan and they sat down before the coffin was put down. Then Abu Sa`id came and took hold of Marwan’s hand and said, “Get up. By Allah, no doubt this (i.e. Abu Huraira) knows that the Prophet forbade us to do that.” Abu Huraira said, “He (Abu Sa`id) has spoken the truth.”. – Sahih Al-Bukhari 1309
حَدَّثَنَا أَحْمَدُ بْنُ يُونُسَ، حَدَّثَنَا ابْنُ أَبِي ذِئْبٍ، عَنْ سَعِيدٍ الْمَقْبُرِيِّ، عَنْ أَبِيهِ، قَالَ كُنَّا فِي جَنَازَةٍ فَأَخَذَ أَبُو هُرَيْرَةَ ـ رضى الله عنه ـ بِيَدِ مَرْوَانَ فَجَلَسَا قَبْلَ أَنْ تُوضَعَ، فَجَاءَ أَبُو سَعِيدٍ ـ رضى الله عنه ـ فَأَخَذَ بِيَدِ مَرْوَانَ فَقَالَ قُمْ فَوَاللَّهِ لَقَدْ عَلِمَ هَذَا أَنَّ النَّبِيَّ صلى الله عليه وسلم نَهَانَا عَنْ ذَلِكَ. فَقَالَ أَبُو هُرَيْرَةَ صَدَقَ.

Narrated Abu Huraira: When I came to the Prophetﷺ said on my way, “O what a long tedious tiresome night; nevertheless, it has rescued me from the place of Heathenism.” A slave of mine ran away on the way. When I reached the Prophetﷺ I gave him the oath of allegiance (for Islam), and while I was sitting with him, suddenly the slave appeared. The Prophetﷺ said to me. “O Abu Huraira! Here is your slave,” I said, “He (i.e. the slave) is (free) for Allah’s Sake,” and manumitted him. – Sahih Al-Bukhari 4393
حَدَّثَنِي مُحَمَّدُ بْنُ الْعَلاَءِ، حَدَّثَنَا أَبُو أُسَامَةَ، حَدَّثَنَا إِسْمَاعِيلُ، عَنْ قَيْسٍ، عَنْ أَبِي هُرَيْرَةَ، قَالَ لَمَّا قَدِمْتُ عَلَى النَّبِيِّ صلى الله عليه وسلم قُلْتُ فِي الطَّرِيقِ: يَا لَيْلَةً مِنْ طُولِهَا وَعَنَائِهَا عَلَى أَنَّهَا مِنْ دَارَةِ الْكُفْرِ نَجَّتِ وَأَبَقَ غُلاَمٌ لِي فِي الطَّرِيقِ، فَلَمَّا قَدِمْتُ عَلَى النَّبِيِّ صلى الله عليه وسلم فَبَايَعْتُهُ، فَبَيْنَا أَنَا عِنْدَهُ إِذْ طَلَعَ الْغُلاَمُ، فَقَالَ لِي النَّبِيُّ صلى الله عليه وسلم " يَا أَبَا هُرَيْرَةَ هَذَا غُلاَمُكَ ". فَقُلْتُ هُوَ لِوَجْهِ اللَّهِ تَعَالَى. فَأَعْتَقْتُهُ.

Narrated Nafi :Ibn Umar used to offer prayers (Nawafil) at the place where he had offered the compulsory prayer. Al-Qasim (bin Muhammad bin Abi Bakr) did the same. The narration coming from Abu Hurairah) from the Prophetﷺ forbidding the Imam from offering prayers (optional prayer) at the same place where he was offered the compulsory prayer is incorrect. Sahih al-Bukhari 848
وَقَالَ لَنَا آدَمُ حَدَّثَنَا شُعْبَةُ، عَنْ أَيُّوبَ، عَنْ نَافِعٍ، قَالَ كَانَ ابْنُ عُمَرَ يُصَلِّي فِي مَكَانِهِ الَّذِي صَلَّى فِيهِ الْفَرِيضَةَ. وَفَعَلَهُ الْقَاسِمُ. وَيُذْكَرُ عَنْ أَبِي هُرَيْرَةَ رَفَعَهُ لاَ يَتَطَوَّعُ الإِمَامُ فِي مَكَانِهِ. وَلَمْ يَصِحَّ.

Narrated Abu Salama: Abu Hurairah said, “No doubt, my Salat is similar to that of the Prophetﷺ.” Abu Hurairah used to recite Qunut after saying Sami’ Allahu liman hamida in the last Rak’a of the Zuhr, Isha and Fajr Prayers. He would ask Allah’s Forgiveness for the true believers and curse the disbelievers. – Sahih al-Bukhari 797
حَدَّثَنَا مُعَاذُ بْنُ فَضَالَةَ، قَالَ حَدَّثَنَا هِشَامٌ، عَنْ يَحْيَى، عَنْ أَبِي سَلَمَةَ، عَنْ أَبِي هُرَيْرَةَ، قَالَ لأُقَرِّبَنَّ صَلاَةَ النَّبِيِّ صلى الله عليه وسلم. فَكَانَ أَبُو هُرَيْرَةَ ـ رضى الله عنه ـ يَقْنُتُ فِي الرَّكْعَةِ الآخِرَةِ مِنْ صَلاَةِ الظُّهْرِ وَصَلاَةِ الْعِشَاءِ، وَصَلاَةِ الصُّبْحِ، بَعْدَ مَا يَقُولُ سَمِعَ اللَّهُ لِمَنْ حَمِدَهُ. فَيَدْعُو لِلْمُؤْمِنِينَ وَيَلْعَنُ الْكُفَّارَ.

Ubayy ibn Ka’b
أُبَيّ ٱبْن كَعْب

Narrated Zirr bin Hubaish: I asked Ubai bin Ka`b, “O Abu AlMundhir! Your brother, Ibn Mas`ud said so-and-so (i.e., the two Mu’awwidh-at do not belong to the Qur’an).” Ubai said, “I asked Allah’s Messengerﷺ about them, and he said, ‘They have been revealed to me, and I have recited them (as a part of the Qur’an),” So Ubai added, “So we say as Allah’s Messengerﷺ has said.”. – Sahih al-Bukhari 4977

حَدَّثَنَا عَلِيُّ بْنُ عَبْدِ اللَّهِ، حَدَّثَنَا سُفْيَانُ، حَدَّثَنَا عَبْدَةُ بْنُ أَبِي لُبَابَةَ، عَنْ زِرِّ بْنِ حُبَيْشٍ، وَحَدَّثَنَا عَاصِمٌ، عَنْ زِرٍّ، قَالَ سَأَلْتُ أُبَىَّ بْنَ كَعْبٍ قُلْتُ يَا أَبَا الْمُنْذِرِ إِنَّ أَخَاكَ ابْنَ مَسْعُودٍ يَقُولُ كَذَا وَكَذَا. فَقَالَ أُبَىٌّ سَأَلْتُ رَسُولَ اللَّهِ صلى الله عليه وسلم فَقَالَ لِي قِيلَ لِي. فَقُلْتُ، قَالَ فَنَحْنُ نَقُولُ كَمَا قَالَ رَسُولُ اللَّهِ صلى الله عليه وسلم

'Abdur Rahman bin 'Abdul Qari said, "I went out in the company of 'Umar bin Al-Khattab one night in Ramadan to the mosque and found the people praying in different groups. A man praying alone or a man praying with a little group behind him. So, 'Umar said, 'In my opinion I would better collect these (people) under the leadership of one Qari (Reciter) (i.e. let them pray in congregation!)'. So, he made up his mind to congregate them behind Ubai bin Ka'b. Then on another night I went again in his company and the people were praying behind their reciter. On that, 'Umar remarked, 'What an excellent Bid'a (i.e. innovation in religion) this is; but the prayer which they do not perform, but sleep at its time is better than the one they are offering.' He meant the prayer in the last part of the night. (In those days) people used to pray in the early part of the night." - Sahih al-Bukhari 2010

وَعَنِ ابْنِ شِهَابٍ، عَنْ عُرْوَةَ بْنِ الزُّبَيْرِ، عَنْ عَبْدِ الرَّحْمَنِ بْنِ عَبْدٍ الْقَارِيِّ، أَنَّهُ قَالَ خَرَجْتُ مَعَ عُمَرَ بْنِ الْخَطَّابِ ـ رضى الله عنه ـ لَيْلَةً فِي رَمَضَانَ، إِلَى الْمَسْجِدِ، فَإِذَا النَّاسُ أَوْزَاعٌ مُتَفَرِّقُونَ يُصَلِّي الرَّجُلُ لِنَفْسِهِ، وَيُصَلِّي الرَّجُلُ فَيُصَلِّي بِصَلاَتِهِ الرَّهْطُ فَقَالَ عُمَرُ إِنِّي أَرَى لَوْ جَمَعْتُ هَؤُلاَءِ عَلَى قَارِئٍ وَاحِدٍ لَكَانَ أَمْثَلَ. ثُمَّ عَزَمَ فَجَمَعَهُمْ عَلَى أُبَىِّ بْنِ كَعْبٍ، ثُمَّ خَرَجْتُ مَعَهُ لَيْلَةً أُخْرَى، وَالنَّاسُ يُصَلُّونَ بِصَلاَةِ قَارِئِهِمْ، قَالَ عُمَرُ نِعْمَ الْبِدْعَةُ هَذِهِ، وَالَّتِي يَنَامُونَ عَنْهَا أَفْضَلُ مِنَ الَّتِي يَقُومُونَ. يُرِيدُ آخِرَ اللَّيْلِ، وَكَانَ النَّاسُ يَقُومُونَ أَوَّلَهُ

Narrated Ubai bin Ka`b: Allah's Messenger ﷺ said, "Some poetry contains wisdom." – Sahih al-Bukhari 6145

حَدَّثَنَا أَبُو الْيَمَانِ، أَخْبَرَنَا شُعَيْبٌ، عَنِ الزُّهْرِيِّ، قَالَ أَخْبَرَنِي أَبُو بَكْرِ بْنُ عَبْدِ الرَّحْمَنِ، أَنَّ مَرْوَانَ بْنَ الْحَكَمِ، أَخْبَرَهُ أَنَّ عَبْدَ الرَّحْمَنِ بْنَ الأَسْوَدِ بْنِ عَبْدِ يَغُوثَ أَخْبَرَهُ أَنَّ أُبَىَّ بْنَ كَعْبٍ أَخْبَرَهُ أَنَّ رَسُولَ اللَّهِ صلى الله عليه وسلم قَالَ " إِنَّ مِنَ الشِّعْرِ حِكْمَةً ".

Narrated Masruq: `Abdullah (bin Mas`ud) was mentioned before `Abdullah bin `Amr. The latter said, "That is a man I continue to love because I heard Allah's Messenger ﷺ saying, ' Learn the recitation of the Qur'an from (any of these) four persons: `Abdullah bin Masud, Salim the freed slave of Abu Hudhaifa, Ubai bin Ka`b, and Mu`adh bin Jabal." I do not remember whether he mentioned Ubai first or Mu`adh. – Sahih al-Bukhari 3758

حَدَّثَنَا سُلَيْمَانُ بْنُ حَرْبٍ، حَدَّثَنَا شُعْبَةُ، عَنْ عَمْرِو بْنِ مُرَّةَ، عَنْ إِبْرَاهِيمَ، عَنْ مَسْرُوقٍ، قَالَ ذُكِرَ عَبْدُ اللَّهِ عِنْدَ عَبْدِ اللَّهِ بْنِ عَمْرٍو، فَقَالَ ذَاكَ رَجُلٌ لاَ أَزَالُ أُحِبُّهُ بَعْدَ مَا سَمِعْتُ رَسُولَ اللَّهِ صلى الله عليه وسلم يَقُولُ " اسْتَقْرِئُوا الْقُرْآنَ مِنْ أَرْبَعَةٍ مِنْ عَبْدِ اللَّهِ بْنِ مَسْعُودٍ، فَبَدَأَ بِهِ، وَسَالِمٍ مَوْلَى أَبِي حُذَيْفَةَ، وَأُبَىِّ بْنِ كَعْبٍ، وَمُعَاذِ بْنِ جَبَلٍ ". قَالَ لاَ أَدْرِي بَدَأَ بِأُبَىٍّ أَوْ بِمُعَاذٍ.

Narrated 'Abdullah bin Umar (ra): Once, Allah's Messenger ﷺ accompanied by Ubai bin Ka'b set out to Ibn Saiyyad. He was informed that Ibn Saiyyad was in a garden of date palms. When Allah's Messenger ﷺ entered the garden of date-palms, he started hiding himself behind the trunks of the palms while Ibn Saiyyad was covered with a velvet sheet with murmurs emanating from under it. Ibn Saiyyah's mother saw Allah's Messenger ﷺ and said, "O Saf! This is Muhammad." So Ibn Saiyyad got up. Allah's Messenger ﷺ said, "If she had left him (in his state), the truth would have been clear." - Sahih al-Bukhari 3033

قَالَ اللَّيْثُ حَدَّثَنِي عُقَيْلٌ، عَنِ ابْنِ شِهَابٍ، عَنْ سَالِمِ بْنِ عَبْدِ اللَّهِ، عَنْ عَبْدِ اللَّهِ بْنِ عُمَرَ ـ رضى الله عنهما ـ أَنَّهُ قَالَ انْطَلَقَ رَسُولُ اللَّهِ صلى الله عليه وسلم وَمَعَهُ أُبَىُّ بْنُ كَعْبٍ قِبَلَ ابْنِ صَيَّادٍ، فَحُدِّثَ بِهِ فِي نَخْلٍ، فَلَمَّا دَخَلَ عَلَيْهِ رَسُولُ اللَّهِ صلى الله عليه وسلم النَّخْلَ، طَفِقَ يَتَّقِي بِجُذُوعِ النَّخْلِ، وَابْنُ صَيَّادٍ فِي قَطِيفَةٍ لَهُ فِيهَا رَمْرَمَةٌ، فَرَأَتْ أُمُّ ابْنِ صَيَّادٍ رَسُولَ اللَّهِ صلى الله عليه وسلم فَقَالَتْ يَا صَافِ، هَذَا مُحَمَّدٌ، فَوَثَبَ ابْنُ صَيَّادٍ، فَقَالَ رَسُولُ اللَّهِ صلى الله عليه وسلم " لَوْ تَرَكَتْهُ بَيَّنَ

Opponents & Tulaqa (Emancipated prisoners of war)
المعارضون والطولاقة (أسرى الحرب المحررين)

When it was the day of (the battle of) Hunain, the Prophet ﷺ confronted the tribe of Hawazin while there were ten-thousand (men) besides the Tulaqa' (i.e. those who had embraced Islam on the day of the Conquest of Mecca) with the Prophet. When they (i.e. Muslims) fled, the Prophet ﷺ said, "O the group of Ansari" They replied, "Labbaik, O Allah's Messenger ﷺ and Sadaik! We are under your command." Then the Prophet ﷺ got down (from his mule) and said, "I am Allah's Slave and His Apostle." Then the pagans were defeated. The Prophet ﷺ distributed the war booty amongst the Tulaqa and Muhajirin (i.e. Emigrants) and did not give anything to the Ansar. So the Ansar spoke (i.e. were dissatisfied) and he called them and made them enter a leather tent and said, Won't you be pleased that the people take the sheep and camels, and you take Allah's Messenger ﷺ along with you?" The Prophet ﷺ added, "If the people took their way through a valley and the Ansar took their way through a mountain pass, then I would choose a mountain pass of the Ansar Narrated Anas: When it was the day of (the battle of) Hunain, the Prophet ﷺ confronted the tribe of Hawazin while there were ten-thousand (men) besides the Tulaqa' (i.e. those who had embraced Islam on the day of the Conquest of Mecca) with the Prophet. When they (i.e. Muslims) fled, the Prophet ﷺ said, "O the group of Ansari" They replied, "Labbaik, O Allah's Messenger ﷺ and Sadaik! We are under your command." Then the Prophet ﷺ got down (from his mule) and said, "I am Allah's Slave and His Apostle." Then the pagans were defeated. The Prophet ﷺ distributed the war booty amongst the Tulaqa and Muhajirin (i.e. Emigrants) and did not give anything to the Ansar. So the Ansar spoke (i.e. were dissatisfied) and he called them and made them enter a leather tent and said, Won't you be pleased that the people take the sheep and camels, and you take Allah's Messenger ﷺ along with you?" The Prophet ﷺ added, "If the people took their way through a valley and the Ansar took their way through a mountain pass, then I would choose a mountain pass of the Ansar." - Sahih Al-Bukhari 4333

حَدَّثَنَا عَلِيُّ بْنُ عَبْدِ اللَّهِ، حَدَّثَنَا أَزْهَرُ، عَنِ ابْنِ عَوْنٍ، أَنْبَأَنَا هِشَامُ بْنُ زَيْدِ بْنِ أَنَسٍ، عَنْ أَنَسٍ ـ رضى الله عنه ـ قَالَ لَمَّا كَانَ يَوْمَ حُنَيْنٍ الْتَقَى هَوَازِنُ وَمَعَ النَّبِيِّ صلى الله عليه وسلم عَشَرَةُ آلاَفٍ وَالطُّلَقَاءُ فَأَدْبَرُوا قَالَ " يَا مَعْشَرَ الأَنْصَارِ ". قَالُوا لَبَّيْكَ يَا رَسُولَ اللَّهِ وَسَعْدَيْكَ، لَبَّيْكَ نَحْنُ بَيْنَ يَدَيْكَ، فَنَزَلَ النَّبِيُّ صلى الله عليه وسلم فَقَالَ " أَنَا عَبْدُ اللَّهِ وَرَسُولُهُ ". فَانْهَزَمَ الْمُشْرِكُونَ، فَأَعْطَى الطُّلَقَاءَ وَالْمُهَاجِرِينَ وَلَمْ يُعْطِ الأَنْصَارَ شَيْئًا فَقَالُوا، فَدَعَاهُمْ فَأَدْخَلَهُمْ فِي قُبَّةٍ فَقَالَ " أَمَا تَرْضَوْنَ أَنْ يَذْهَبَ النَّاسُ بِالشَّاةِ وَالْبَعِيرِ، وَتَذْهَبُونَ بِرَسُولِ اللَّهِ صلى الله عليه وسلم "، فَقَالَ النَّبِيُّ صلى الله عليه وسلم "لَوْ سَلَكَ النَّاسُ وَادِيًا وَسَلَكَتِ الأَنْصَارُ شِعْبًا لاَخْتَرْتُ شِعْبَ الأَنْصَارِ

Narrated Anas Bin Malik: When it was the day (of the battle) of Hunain, the tributes of Hawazin and Ghatafan and others, along with their animals and offspring (and wives) came to fight against the Prophet ﷺ The Prophet ﷺ had with him, ten thousand men and some of the Tulaqa. The companions fled, leaving the Prophet ﷺ alone. The Prophet then made two calls which were clearly distinguished from each other. He turned right and said, "O the group of Ansar!" They said, "Labbaik, O Allah's Messenger ﷺ! Rejoice, for we are with you!" Then he turned left and said, "O the group of Ansar!" They said, "Labbaik! O Allah's Messenger ﷺ! Rejoice, for we are with you!" The Prophet ﷺ at that time, was riding on a white mule; then he dismounted and said, "I am Allah's Slave and His Apostle." The infidels then were defeated, and on that day the Prophet ﷺ gained a large amount of booty which he distributed amongst the Muhajirin and the Tulaqa and did not give anything to the Ansar. The Ansar said, “When there is a difficulty, we are called, but the booty is given to other than us.” The news reached the Prophetﷺ and he gathered them in a leather tent and said, “What is this news reaching me from you, O the group of Ansar?” They kept silent, He added,” O the group of Ansar! Won’t you be happy that the people take the worldly things and you take Allah’s Messengerﷺ to your homes reserving him for yourself?” They said, “Yes.” Then the Prophet said, “If the people took their way through a valley, and the Ansar took their way through a mountain pass, surely, I would take the Ansar’s mountain pass.” Hisham said, “O Abu Hamza (i.e. Anas)! Did you witness that? “ He replied, “And how could I be absent from him?” - Sahih Al-Bukhari 4337

حَدَّثَنَا مُحَمَّدُ بْنُ بَشَّارٍ، حَدَّثَنَا مُعَاذُ بْنُ مُعَاذٍ، حَدَّثَنَا ابْنُ عَوْنٍ، عَنْ هِشَامِ بْنِ زَيْدِ بْنِ أَنَسِ بْنِ مَالِكٍ، عَنْ أَنَسِ بْنِ مَالِكٍ ـ رضى الله عنه ـ قَالَ لَمَّا كَانَ يَوْمُ حُنَيْنٍ أَقْبَلَتْ هَوَازِنُ وَغَطَفَانُ وَغَيْرُهُمْ بِنَعَمِهِمْ وَذَرَارِيِّهِمْ، وَمَعَ النَّبِيِّ صلى الله عليه وسلم عَشَرَةُ آلاَفٍ وَمِنَ الطُّلَقَاءِ، فَأَدْبَرُوا عَنْهُ حَتَّى بَقِيَ وَحْدَهُ، فَنَادَى يَوْمَئِذٍ نِدَاءَيْنِ لَمْ يَخْلِطْ بَيْنَهُمَا، الْتَفَتَ عَنْ يَمِينِهِ، فَقَالَ " يَا مَعْشَرَ الأَنْصَارِ ". قَالُوا لَبَّيْكَ يَا رَسُولَ اللَّهِ، أَبْشِرْ نَحْنُ مَعَكَ. ثُمَّ الْتَفَتَ عَنْ يَسَارِهِ، فَقَالَ " يَا مَعْشَرَ الأَنْصَارِ ". قَالُوا لَبَّيْكَ يَا رَسُولَ اللَّهِ، أَبْشِرْ نَحْنُ مَعَكَ. وَهْوَ عَلَى بَغْلَةٍ بَيْضَاءَ، فَنَزَلَ فَقَالَ " أَنَا عَبْدُ اللَّهِ وَرَسُولُهُ "، فَانْهَزَمَ الْمُشْرِكُونَ، فَأَصَابَ يَوْمَئِذٍ غَنَائِمَ كَثِيرَةً، فَقَسَمَ فِي الْمُهَاجِرِينَ وَالطُّلَقَاءِ وَلَمْ يُعْطِ الأَنْصَارَ شَيْئًا، فَقَالَتِ الأَنْصَارُ إِذَا كَانَتْ شَدِيدَةٌ فَنَحْنُ نُدْعَى، وَيُعْطَى الْغَنِيمَةَ غَيْرُنَا. فَبَلَغَهُ ذَلِكَ، فَجَمَعَهُمْ فِي قُبَّةٍ، فَقَالَ " يَا مَعْشَرَ الأَنْصَارِ مَا حَدِيثٌ بَلَغَنِي عَنْكُمْ ". فَسَكَتُوا فَقَالَ " يَا مَعْشَرَ الأَنْصَارِ أَلاَ تَرْضَوْنَ أَنْ يَذْهَبَ النَّاسُ بِالدُّنْيَا، وَتَذْهَبُونَ بِرَسُولِ اللَّهِ صلى الله عليه وسلم تَحُوزُونَهُ إِلَى بُيُوتِكُمْ ". قَالُوا بَلَى. فَقَالَ رَسُولُ اللَّهِ صلى الله عليه وسلم " لَوْ سَلَكَ النَّاسُ وَادِيًا، وَسَلَكَتِ الأَنْصَارُ شِعْبًا لأَخَذْتُ شِعْبَ الأَنْصَارِ ". فَقَالَ هِشَامٌ يَا أَبَا حَمْزَةَ، وَأَنْتَ شَاهِدٌ ذَاكَ قَالَ وَأَيْنَ أَغِيبُ عَنْهُ

And what is the matter with you that you believe not in Allah! While the Messenger (Muhammad) invites you to believe in your Lord (Allah), and He (Allah) has indeed taken your covenant, if you are real believers. It is He Who sends down manifest Ayat (proofs, evidences, verses, lessons, signs, revelations, etc.) to His slave (Muhammad) that He may bring you out from darkness into light. And verily, Allah is to you full of kindness, Most Merciful. And what is the matter with you that you spend not in the Cause of Allah? And to Allah belongs the heritage of the heavens and the earth. Not equal among you are those who spent and fought before the conquering (of Makkah) (with those among you who did so later). Such are higher in degree than those who spent and fought afterwards. But to all, Allah has promised the best (reward). And Allah is All-Aware of what you do. Who is he that will lend to Allah a goodly loan, then (Allah) will increase it manifold to his credit (in repaying), and he will have (besides) a good reward (i.e. Paradise). On the Day you shall see the believing men and the believing women their light running forward before them and by their right hands. Glad tidings for you this Day! Gardens under which rivers flow (Paradise), to dwell therein forever! Truly, this is the great success! On the Day when the hypocrites men and women will say to the believers: “Wait for us! Let us get something from your light!” It will be said: “Go back to your rear! Then seek a light!” So a wall will be put up between them, with a gate therein. Inside it will be mercy, and outside it will be torment.” (The hypocrites) will call the believers: “Were we not with you?” The believers will reply: “Yes! But you led yourselves into temptations, you looked forward for our destruction; you doubted (in Faith); and you were deceived by false desires, till the Command of Allah came to pass. And the chief deceiver (Satan) deceived you in respect of Allah.” So this Day no ransom shall be taken from you (hypocrites), nor of those who disbelieved, (in the Oneness of Allah Islamic Monotheism). Your abode is the Fire, that is the proper place for you, and worst indeed is that destination.. – Surah Al-Hadid 57:8-15

وَمَا لَكُمْ لَا تُؤْمِنُونَ بِٱللَّهِ وَٱلرَّسُولُ يَدْعُوكُمْ لِتُؤْمِنُوا۟ بِرَبِّكُمْ وَقَدْ أَخَذَ مِيثَٰقَكُمْ إِن كُنتُم مُّؤْمِنِينَ هُوَ ٱلَّذِى يُنَزِّلُ عَلَىٰ عَبْدِهِۦٓ ءَايَٰتٍۭ بَيِّنَٰتٍ لِّيُخْرِجَكُم مِّنَ ٱلظُّلُمَٰتِ إِلَى ٱلنُّورِ ۚ وَإِنَّ ٱللَّهَ بِكُمْ لَرَءُوفٌ رَّحِيمٌ وَمَا لَكُمْ أَلَّا تُنفِقُوا۟ فِى سَبِيلِ ٱللَّهِ وَلِلَّهِ مِيرَٰثُ

ٱلسَّمَـٰوَٰتِ وَٱلْأَرْضِ ۚ لَا يَسْتَوِى مِنكُم مَّنْ أَنفَقَ مِن قَبْلِ ٱلْفَتْحِ وَقَـٰتَلَ ۚ أُو۟لَـٰٓئِكَ أَعْظَمُ دَرَجَةً مِّنَ ٱلَّذِينَ أَنفَقُوا۟ مِنۢ بَعْدُ وَقَـٰتَلُوا۟ ۚ
وَكُلًّا وَعَدَ ٱللَّهُ ٱلْحُسْنَىٰ ۚ وَٱللَّهُ بِمَا تَعْمَلُونَ خَبِيرٌ مَّن ذَا ٱلَّذِى يُقْرِضُ ٱللَّهَ قَرْضًا حَسَنًا فَيُضَـٰعِفَهُۥ لَهُۥ وَلَهُۥٓ أَجْرٌ كَرِيمٌ يَوْمَ تَرَى
ٱلْمُؤْمِنِينَ وَٱلْمُؤْمِنَـٰتِ يَسْعَىٰ نُورُهُم بَيْنَ أَيْدِيهِمْ وَبِأَيْمَـٰنِهِم بُشْرَىٰكُمُ ٱلْيَوْمَ جَنَّـٰتٌ تَجْرِى مِن تَحْتِهَا ٱلْأَنْهَـٰرُ خَـٰلِدِينَ فِيهَا ۚ ذَٰلِكَ هُوَ
ٱلْفَوْزُ ٱلْعَظِيمُ يَوْمَ يَقُولُ ٱلْمُنَـٰفِقُونَ وَٱلْمُنَـٰفِقَـٰتُ لِلَّذِينَ ءَامَنُوا۟ ٱنظُرُونَا نَقْتَبِسْ مِن نُّورِكُمْ قِيلَ ٱرْجِعُوا۟ وَرَآءَكُمْ فَٱلْتَمِسُوا۟ نُورًا
فَضُرِبَ بَيْنَهُم بِسُورٍ لَّهُۥ بَابٌۢ بَاطِنُهُۥ فِيهِ ٱلرَّحْمَةُ وَظَـٰهِرُهُۥ مِن قِبَلِهِ ٱلْعَذَابُ يُنَادُونَهُمْ أَلَمْ نَكُن مَّعَكُمْ ۖ قَالُوا۟ بَلَىٰ وَلَـٰكِنَّكُمْ فَتَنتُمْ
أَنفُسَكُمْ وَتَرَبَّصْتُمْ وَٱرْتَبْتُمْ وَغَرَّتْكُمُ ٱلْأَمَانِىُّ حَتَّىٰ جَآءَ أَمْرُ ٱللَّهِ وَغَرَّكُم بِٱللَّهِ ٱلْغَرُورُ فَٱلْيَوْمَ لَا يُؤْخَذُ مِنكُمْ فِدْيَةٌ وَلَا مِنَ ٱلَّذِينَ
كَفَرُوا۟ ۚ مَأْوَىٰكُمُ ٱلنَّارُ ۖ هِىَ مَوْلَىٰكُمْ ۖ وَبِئْسَ ٱلْمَصِيرُ

Amr ibn al-As ibn Wa'il al-Sahmi
عَمْرِو بْنِ الْعَاصِ بْنِ وَائِلِ السَّهْمِي

Narrated Al-Hasan Al-Basri: By Allah, Al-Hasan bin `Ali led large battalions like mountains against Muawiya. `Amr bin Al-As said (to Muawiya), "I surely see battalions which will not turn back before killing their opponents." Muawiya who was really the best of the two men said to him, "O `Amr! If these killed those and those killed these, who would be left with me for the jobs of the public, who would be left with me for their women, who would be left with me for their children?" Then Muawiya sent two Quraishi men from the tribe of `Abd-i-Shams called `Abdur Rahman bin Sumura and `Abdullah bin 'Amir bin Kuraiz to Al-Hasan saying to them, "Go to this man (i.e. Al-Hasan) and negotiate peace with him and talk and appeal to him." So, they went to Al-Hasan and talked and appealed to him to accept peace. Al-Hasan said, "We, the offspring of `Abdul Muttalib, have got wealth and people have indulged in killing and corruption (and money only will appease them)." They said to Al-Hasan, "Muawiya offers you so and so, and appeals to you and entreats you to accept peace." Al-Hasan said to them, "But who will be responsible for what you have said?" They said, "We will be responsible for it." So, whatever Al- Hasan asked they said, "We will be responsible for it for you." So, Al-Hasan concluded a peace treaty with Muawiya. Al-Hasan (Al-Basri) said: I heard Abu Bakr saying, "I saw Allah's Messenger ﷺ on the pulpit and Al-Hasan bin `Ali was by his side. The Prophet ﷺ was looking once at the people and once at Al-Hasan bin `Ali saying, 'This son of mine is a Saiyid (i.e. a noble) and may Allah make peace between two big groups of Muslims through him.". – Sahih Al-Bukhari 2704

حَدَّثَنَا عَبْدُ اللَّهِ بْنُ مُحَمَّدٍ، حَدَّثَنَا سُفْيَانُ، عَنْ أَبِي مُوسَى، قَالَ سَمِعْتُ الْحَسَنَ، يَقُولُ اسْتَقْبَلَ وَاللَّهِ الْحَسَنُ بْنُ عَلِيٍّ مُعَاوِيَةَ بِكَتَائِبَ أَمْثَالِ الْجِبَالِ فَقَالَ عَمْرُو بْنُ الْعَاصِ إِنِّي لأَرَى كَتَائِبَ لاَ تُوَلِّي حَتَّى تَقْتُلَ أَقْرَانَهَا. فَقَالَ لَهُ مُعَاوِيَةُ ـ وَكَانَ وَاللَّهِ خَيْرَ الرَّجُلَيْنِ ـ أَىْ عَمْرُو إِنْ قَتَلَ هَؤُلاَءِ هَؤُلاَءِ وَهَؤُلاَءِ هَؤُلاَءِ مَنْ لِي بِأُمُورِ النَّاسِ مَنْ لِي بِنِسَائِهِمْ، مَنْ لِي بِضَيْعَتِهِمْ فَبَعَثَ إِلَيْهِ رَجُلَيْنِ مِنْ قُرَيْشٍ مِنْ بَنِي عَبْدِ شَمْسٍ عَبْدَ الرَّحْمَنِ بْنَ سَمُرَةَ وَعَبْدَ اللَّهِ بْنَ عَامِرِ بْنِ كُرَيْزٍ، فَقَالَ اذْهَبَا إِلَى هَذَا الرَّجُلِ فَاعْرِضَا عَلَيْهِ، وَقُولاَ لَهُ، وَاطْلُبَا إِلَيْهِ. فَأَتَيَاهُ، فَدَخَلاَ عَلَيْهِ فَتَكَلَّمَا، وَقَالاَ لَهُ، فَطَلَبَا إِلَيْهِ، فَقَالَ لَهُمَا الْحَسَنُ بْنُ عَلِيٍّ إِنَّا بَنُو عَبْدِ الْمُطَّلِبِ، قَدْ أَصَبْنَا مِنْ هَذَا الْمَالِ، وَإِنَّ هَذِهِ الأُمَّةَ قَدْ عَاثَتْ فِي دِمَائِهَا. قَالاَ فَإِنَّهُ يَعْرِضُ عَلَيْكَ كَذَا وَكَذَا وَيَطْلُبُ إِلَيْكَ وَيَسْأَلُكَ. قَالَ فَمَنْ لِي بِهَذَا قَالاَ نَحْنُ لَكَ بِهِ. فَمَا سَأَلَهُمَا شَيْئًا إِلاَّ قَالاَ نَحْنُ لَكَ بِهِ. فَصَالَحَهُ، فَقَالَ الْحَسَنُ وَلَقَدْ سَمِعْتُ أَبَا بَكْرَةَ يَقُولُ رَأَيْتُ رَسُولَ اللَّهِ صلى الله عليه وسلم عَلَى الْمِنْبَرِ وَالْحَسَنُ بْنُ عَلِيٍّ إِلَى جَنْبِهِ، وَهْوَ يُقْبِلُ عَلَى النَّاسِ مَرَّةً وَعَلَيْهِ أُخْرَى وَيَقُولُ " إِنَّ ابْنِي هَذَا سَيِّدٌ، وَلَعَلَّ اللَّهَ أَنْ يُصْلِحَ بِهِ بَيْنَ فِئَتَيْنِ عَظِيمَتَيْنِ مِنَ الْمُسْلِمِينَ ". قَالَ لِي عَلِيُّ بْنُ عَبْدِ اللَّهِ إِنَّمَا ثَبَتَ لَنَا سَمَاعُ الْحَسَنِ مِنْ أَبِي بَكْرَةَ بِهَذَا الْحَدِيثِ.

Narrated `Amr bin Al-`As: I heard the Prophet ﷺ saying openly not secretly, "The family of Abu so-and-so (i.e. Talib) are not among my protectors." `Amr said that there was a blank space (1) in the Book of Muhammad bin Ja`far. He added, "My Protector is Allah and the righteous believing people." `Amr bin Al-`As added: I heard the Prophet ﷺ saying, 'But they (that family) have kinship (Rahm) with me and I will be good and dutiful to them. ". – Sahih Al-Bukhari 5990

حَدَّثَنَا عَمْرُو بْنُ عَبَّاسٍ، حَدَّثَنَا مُحَمَّدُ بْنُ جَعْفَرٍ، حَدَّثَنَا شُعْبَةُ، عَنْ إِسْمَاعِيلَ بْنِ أَبِي خَالِدٍ، عَنْ قَيْسِ بْنِ أَبِي حَازِمٍ، أَنَّ عَمْرَو بْنَ الْعَاصِ، قَالَ سَمِعْتُ النَّبِيَّ صلى الله عليه وسلم جِهَارًا غَيْرَ سِرٍّ يَقُولُ " إِنَّ آلَ أَبِي " ـ قَالَ عَمْرٌو فِي كِتَابِ مُحَمَّدِ بْنِ جَعْفَرٍ بَيَاضٌ ـ لَيْسُوا بِأَوْلِيَائِي، إِنَّمَا وَلِيِّيَ اللَّهُ وَصَالِحُ الْمُؤْمِنِينَ. زَادَ عَنْبَسَةُ بْنُ عَبْدِ الْوَاحِدِ عَنْ بَيَانٍ عَنْ قَيْسٍ عَنْ عَمْرِو بْنِ الْعَاصِ قَالَ سَمِعْتُ النَّبِيَّ صلى الله عليه وسلم " وَلَكِنْ لَهُمْ رَحِمٌ أَبُلُّهَا بِبَلاَلِهَا ". يَعْنِي أَصِلُهَا بِصِلَتِهَا.

Narrated `Urwa bin Az-Zubair: I asked Ibn `Amr bin Al-As, “Tell me of the worst thing which the pagans did to the Prophet.” He said, “While the Prophet ﷺ was praying in the Hijr of the Ka`ba; `Uqba bin Abi Mu’ait came and put his garment around the Prophet’s neck and throttled him violently. Abu Bakr came and caught him by his shoulder and pushed him away from the Prophet ﷺ and said, “Do you want to kill a man just because he says, ‘My Lord is Allah?’ ”. – Sahih Al-Bukhari 3856

حَدَّثَنَا عَيَّاشُ بْنُ الْوَلِيدِ، حَدَّثَنَا الْوَلِيدُ بْنُ مُسْلِمٍ، حَدَّثَنِي الأَوْزَاعِيُّ، حَدَّثَنِي يَحْيَى بْنُ أَبِي كَثِيرٍ، عَنْ مُحَمَّدِ بْنِ إِبْرَاهِيمَ التَّيْمِيِّ، قَالَ حَدَّثَنِي عُرْوَةُ بْنُ الزُّبَيْرِ، قَالَ سَأَلْتُ ابْنَ عَمْرِو بْنِ الْعَاصِ أَخْبِرْنِي بِأَشَدِّ، شَىْءٍ صَنَعَهُ الْمُشْرِكُونَ بِالنَّبِيِّ صلى الله عليه وسلم قَالَ بَيْنَا النَّبِيُّ صلى الله عليه وسلم يُصَلِّي فِي حِجْرِ الْكَعْبَةِ إِذْ أَقْبَلَ عُقْبَةُ بْنُ أَبِي مُعَيْطٍ، فَوَضَعَ ثَوْبَهُ فِي عُنُقِهِ فَخَنَقَهُ خَنْقًا شَدِيدًا، فَأَقْبَلَ أَبُو بَكْرٍ حَتَّى أَخَذَ بِمَنْكِبِهِ وَدَفَعَهُ عَنِ النَّبِيِّ صلى الله عليه وسلم قَالَ {أَتَقْتُلُونَ رَجُلاً أَنْ يَقُولَ رَبِّيَ اللَّهُ} الآيَةَ. تَابَعَهُ ابْنُ إِسْحَاقَ حَدَّثَنِي يَحْيَى بْنُ عُرْوَةَ عَنْ عُرْوَةَ، قُلْتُ لِعَبْدِ اللَّهِ بْنِ عَمْرٍو. وَقَالَ عَبْدَةُ عَنْ هِشَامٍ عَنْ أَبِيهِ قِيلَ لِعَمْرِو بْنِ الْعَاصِ. وَقَالَ مُحَمَّدُ بْنُ عَمْرٍو عَنْ أَبِي سَلَمَةَ حَدَّثَنِي عَمْرُو بْنُ الْعَاصِ.

Narrated `Abdullah bin `Amr bin Al-`As: Allah’s Messenger ﷺ said to me, “O `Abdullah! Do not be like so and so who used to pray at night and then stopped the night prayer.”. – Sahih Al-Bukhari 1152

حَدَّثَنَا عَبَّاسُ بْنُ الْحُسَيْنِ، حَدَّثَنَا مُبَشِّرٌ، عَنِ الأَوْزَاعِيِّ. وَحَدَّثَنِي مُحَمَّدُ بْنُ مُقَاتِلٍ أَبُو الْحَسَنِ، قَالَ أَخْبَرَنَا عَبْدُ اللَّهِ، أَخْبَرَنَا الأَوْزَاعِيُّ، قَالَ حَدَّثَنِي يَحْيَى بْنُ أَبِي كَثِيرٍ، قَالَ حَدَّثَنِي أَبُو سَلَمَةَ بْنُ عَبْدِ الرَّحْمَنِ، قَالَ حَدَّثَنِي عَبْدُ اللَّهِ بْنُ عَمْرِو بْنِ الْعَاصِ ـ رضى الله عنهما ـ قَالَ قَالَ لِي رَسُولُ اللَّهِ صلى الله عليه وسلم " يَا عَبْدَ اللَّهِ، لاَ تَكُنْ مِثْلَ فُلاَنٍ، كَانَ يَقُومُ اللَّيْلَ فَتَرَكَ قِيَامَ اللَّيْلِ ". وَقَالَ هِشَامٌ حَدَّثَنَا ابْنُ أَبِي الْعِشْرِينَ، حَدَّثَنَا الأَوْزَاعِيُّ، قَالَ حَدَّثَنِي يَحْيَى، عَنْ عُمَرَ بْنِ الْحَكَمِ بْنِ ثَوْبَانَ، قَالَ حَدَّثَنِي أَبُو سَلَمَةَ، مِثْلَهُ. وَتَابَعَهُ عَمْرُو بْنُ أَبِي سَلَمَةَ عَنِ الأَوْزَاعِيِّ.

Jubair bin Mutim
جبير بن مطعم

Narrated Muhammad bin Jubair bin Mut`im: My father said, “(Before Islam) I was looking for my camel ..” The same narration is told by a different sub-narrator. Jubair bin Mut`im said, “My camel was lost and I went out in search of it on the day of `Arafat, and I saw the Prophet ﷺ standing in `Arafat. I said to myself: By Allah he is from the Hums (literally: strictly religious, Quraish were called so, as they used to say, ‘We are the people of Allah we shall not go out of the sanctuary). What has brought him here?”. – Sahih Al-Bukhari 1664

حَدَّثَنَا عَلِيُّ بْنُ عَبْدِ اللَّهِ، حَدَّثَنَا سُفْيَانُ، حَدَّثَنَا عَمْرٌو، حَدَّثَنَا مُحَمَّدُ بْنُ جُبَيْرِ بْنِ مُطْعِمٍ، عَنْ أَبِيهِ، كُنْتُ أَطْلُبُ بَعِيرًا لِي. وَحَدَّثَنَا مُسَدَّدٌ، حَدَّثَنَا سُفْيَانُ، عَنْ عَمْرٍو، سَمِعَ مُحَمَّدَ بْنَ جُبَيْرٍ، عَنْ أَبِيهِ، جُبَيْرِ بْنِ مُطْعِمٍ قَالَ أَضْلَلْتُ بَعِيرًا لِي، فَذَهَبْتُ أَطْلُبُهُ يَوْمَ عَرَفَةَ، فَرَأَيْتُ النَّبِيَّ صلى الله عليه وسلم وَاقِفًا بِعَرَفَةَ، فَقُلْتُ هَذَا وَاللَّهِ مِنَ الْحُمْسِ فَمَا شَأْنُهُ هَا هُنَا

Narrated Jubair bin Mut`im: A lady came to Allah’s Messenger ﷺ and she talked to him about something, and he gave her some order. She said, “O Allah’s Messenger ﷺ! If I should not find you?” He said, “If you should not find me, then go to Abu Bakr.” Ibrahim bin Sa`d said, “As if she meant the death (of the Prophet). Sahih Al-Bukhari 7360

حَدَّثَنِي عُبَيْدُ اللَّهِ بْنُ سَعْدِ بْنِ إِبْرَاهِيمَ، حَدَّثَنَا أَبِي وَعَمِّي، قَالاَ حَدَّثَنَا أَبِي، عَنْ أَبِيهِ، أَخْبَرَنِي مُحَمَّدُ بْنُ جُبَيْرٍ، أَنَّ أَبَاهُ، جُبَيْرَ بْنَ مُطْعِمٍ أَخْبَرَهُ أَنَّ امْرَأَةً أَتَتْ رَسُولَ اللَّهِ صلى الله عليه وسلم فَكَلَّمَتْهُ فِي شَىْءٍ، فَأَمَرَهَا بِأَمْرٍ فَقَالَتْ أَرَأَيْتَ يَا رَسُولَ اللَّهِ إِنْ لَمْ أَجِدْكَ قَالَ " إِنْ لَمْ تَجِدِينِي فَأْتِي أَبَا بَكْرٍ ". زَادَ الْحُمَيْدِيُّ عَنْ إِبْرَاهِيمَ بْنِ سَعْدٍ كَأَنَّهَا تَعْنِي الْمَوْتَ.

Narrated Jafar bin `Amr bin Umaiya: I went out with 'Ubaidullah bin `Adi Al-Khaiyar. When we reached Hims (i.e. a town in Syria), 'Ubaidullah bin `Adi said (to me), "Would you like to see Wahshi so that we may ask him about the killing of Hamza?" I replied, "Yes." Wahshi used to live in Hims. We enquired about him and somebody said to us, "He is that in the shade of his palace, as if he were a full water skin." So we went up to him, and when we were at a short distance from him, we greeted him and he greeted us in return. 'Ubaidullah was wearing his turban and Wahshi could not see except his eyes and feet. 'Ubaidullah said, "O Wahshi! Do you know me?" Wahshi looked at him and then said, "No, by Allah! But I know that `Adi bin Al-Khiyar married a woman called Um Qital, the daughter of Abu Al-Is, and she delivered a boy for him at Mecca, and I looked for a wet nurse for that child. (Once) I carried that child along with his mother and then I handed him over to her, and your feet resemble that child's feet." Then 'Ubaidullah uncovered his face and said (to Wahshi), "Will you tell us (the story of) the killing of Hamza?" Wahshi replied "Yes, Hamza killed Tuaima bin `Adi bin Al-Khaiyar at Badr (battle) so my master, Jubair bin Mut`im said to me, 'If you kill Hamza in revenge for my uncle, then you will be set free." When the people set out (for the battle of Uhud) in the year of 'Ainain ..'Ainain is a mountain near the mountain of Uhud, and between it and Uhud there is a valley.. I went out with the people for the battle. When the army aligned for the fight, Siba' came out and said, 'Is there any (Muslim) to accept my challenge to a duel?' Hamza bin `Abdul Muttalib came out and said, 'O Siba'. O Ibn Um Anmar, the one who circumcises other ladies! Do you challenge Allah and His Apostle?' Then Hamza attacked and killed him, causing him to be non-extant like the bygone yesterday. I hid myself under a rock, and when he (i.e. Hamza) came near me, I threw my spear at him, driving it into his umbilicus so that it came out through his buttocks, causing him to die. When all the people returned to Mecca, I too returned with them. I stayed in (Mecca) till Islam spread in it (i.e. Mecca). Then I left for Taif, and when the people (of Taif) sent their messengers to Allah's Messenger, I was told that the Prophet ﷺ did not harm the messengers; So I too went out with them till I reached Allah's Messenger ﷺ. When he saw me, he said, 'Are you Wahshi?' I said, 'Yes.' He said, 'Was it you who killed Hamza?' I replied, 'What happened is what you have been told of.' He said, 'Can you hide your face from me?' So I went out when Allah's Messenger ﷺ died, and Musailamah Al-Kadhdhab appeared (claiming to be a prophet). I said, 'I will go out to Musailamah so that I may kill him, and make amends for killing Hamza. So I went out with the people (to fight Musailamah and his followers) and then famous events took place concerning that battle. Suddenly I saw a man (i.e. Musailamah) standing near a gap in a wall. He looked like an ash-colored camel and his hair was dishevelled. So I threw my spear at him, driving it into his chest in between his breasts till it passed out through his shoulders, and then an Ansari man attacked him and struck him on the head with a sword. `Abdullah bin `Umar said, 'A slave girl on the roof of a house said: Alas! The chief of the believers (i.e. Musailamah) has been killed by a black slave.". – Sahih Al-Bukhari 4072

حَدَّثَنِي أَبُو جَعْفَرٍ، مُحَمَّدُ بْنُ عَبْدِ اللَّهِ حَدَّثَنَا حُجَيْنُ بْنُ الْمُثَنَّى، حَدَّثَنَا عَبْدُ الْعَزِيزِ بْنُ عَبْدِ اللَّهِ بْنِ أَبِي سَلَمَةَ، عَنْ عَبْدِ اللَّهِ بْنِ الْفَضْلِ، عَنْ سُلَيْمَانَ بْنِ يَسَارٍ، عَنْ جَعْفَرِ بْنِ عَمْرِو بْنِ أُمَيَّةَ الضَّمْرِيِّ، قَالَ خَرَجْتُ مَعَ عُبَيْدِ اللَّهِ بْنِ عَدِيِّ بْنِ الْخِيَارِ، فَلَمَّا قَدِمْنَا حِمْصَ قَالَ لِي عُبَيْدُ اللَّهِ هَلْ لَكَ فِي وَحْشِيٍّ نَسْأَلُهُ عَنْ قَتْلِ حَمْزَةَ قُلْتُ نَعَمْ. وَكَانَ وَحْشِيٌّ يَسْكُنُ حِمْصَ فَسَأَلْنَا عَنْهُ فَقِيلَ لَنَا هُوَ ذَاكَ فِي ظِلِّ قَصْرِهِ، كَأَنَّهُ حَمِيتٌ. قَالَ فَجِئْنَا حَتَّى وَقَفْنَا عَلَيْهِ بِيَسِيرٍ، فَسَلَّمْنَا، فَرَدَّ السَّلاَمَ، قَالَ وَعُبَيْدُ اللَّهِ مُعْتَجِرٌ بِعِمَامَتِهِ، مَا يَرَى وَحْشِيٌّ إِلاَّ عَيْنَيْهِ وَرِجْلَيْهِ، فَقَالَ عُبَيْدُ اللَّهِ يَا وَحْشِيُّ أَتَعْرِفُنِي قَالَ فَنَظَرَ إِلَيْهِ ثُمَّ قَالَ لاَ وَاللَّهِ إِلاَّ أَنِّي أَعْلَمُ أَنَّ عَدِيَّ بْنَ الْخِيَارِ تَزَوَّجَ امْرَأَةً يُقَالُ لَهَا أُمُّ قِتَالٍ بِنْتُ أَبِي الْعِيصِ، فَوَلَدَتْ لَهُ غُلاَمًا بِمَكَّةَ، فَكُنْتُ أَسْتَرْضِعُ لَهُ،

فَحَمَلْتُ ذَلِكَ الْغُلاَمَ مَعَ أُمِّهِ، فَنَاوَلْتُهَا إِيَّاهُ، فَلَكَأَنِّي نَظَرْتُ إِلَى قَدَمَيْكَ. قَالَ فَكَشَفَ عُبَيْدُ اللَّهِ عَنْ وَجْهِهِ ثُمَّ قَالَ أَلاَ تُخْبِرُنَا بِقَتْلِ حَمْزَةَ قَالَ نَعَمْ، إِنَّ حَمْزَةَ قَتَلَ طُعَيْمَةَ بْنَ عَدِيِّ بْنِ الْخِيَارِ بِبَدْرٍ، فَقَالَ لِي مَوْلاَىَ جُبَيْرُ بْنُ مُطْعِمٍ إِنْ قَتَلْتَ حَمْزَةَ بِعَمِّي فَأَنْتَ حُرٌّ، قَالَ فَلَمَّا أَنْ خَرَجَ النَّاسُ عَامَ عَيْنَيْنِ ـ وَعَيْنَيْنِ جَبَلٌ بِحِيَالِ أُحُدٍ، بَيْنَهُ وَبَيْنَهُ وَادٍ ـ خَرَجْتُ مَعَ النَّاسِ إِلَى الْقِتَالِ، فَلَمَّا اصْطَفُّوا لِلْقِتَالِ خَرَجَ سِبَاعٌ فَقَالَ هَلْ مِنْ مُبَارِزٍ قَالَ فَخَرَجَ إِلَيْهِ حَمْزَةُ بْنُ عَبْدِ الْمُطَّلِبِ فَقَالَ يَا سِبَاعُ يَا ابْنَ أُمِّ أَنْمَارٍ مُقَطِّعَةِ الْبُظُورِ، أَتُحَادُّ اللَّهَ وَرَسُولَهُ صلى الله عليه وسلم قَالَ ثُمَّ شَدَّ عَلَيْهِ فَكَانَ كَأَمْسِ الذَّاهِبِ ـ قَالَ ـ وَكَمَنْتُ لِحَمْزَةَ تَحْتَ صَخْرَةٍ فَلَمَّا دَنَا مِنِّي رَمَيْتُهُ بِحَرْبَتِي، فَأَضَعُهَا فِي ثُنَّتِهِ حَتَّى خَرَجَتْ مِنْ بَيْنِ وَرِكَيْهِ ـ قَالَ ـ فَكَانَ ذَاكَ الْعَهْدَ بِهِ، فَلَمَّا رَجَعَ النَّاسُ رَجَعْتُ مَعَهُمْ فَأَقَمْتُ بِمَكَّةَ، حَتَّى فَشَا فِيهَا الإِسْلاَمُ، ثُمَّ خَرَجْتُ إِلَى الطَّائِفِ، فَأَرْسَلُوا إِلَى رَسُولِ اللَّهِ صلى الله عليه وسلم رَسُولاً، فَقِيلَ لِي إِنَّهُ لاَ يَهِيجُ الرُّسُلَ ـ قَالَ ـ فَخَرَجْتُ مَعَهُمْ حَتَّى قَدِمْتُ عَلَى رَسُولِ اللَّهِ صلى الله عليه وسلم فَلَمَّا رَآنِي قَالَ " آنْتَ وَحْشِيٌّ ". قُلْتُ نَعَمْ. قَالَ " أَنْتَ قَتَلْتَ حَمْزَةَ ". قُلْتُ قَدْ كَانَ مِنَ الأَمْرِ مَا بَلَغَكَ. قَالَ " فَهَلْ تَسْتَطِيعُ أَنْ تُغَيِّبَ وَجْهَكَ عَنِّي ". قَالَ فَخَرَجْتُ، فَلَمَّا قُبِضَ رَسُولُ اللَّهِ صلى الله عليه وسلم فَخَرَجَ مُسَيْلِمَةُ الْكَذَّابُ قُلْتُ لأَخْرُجَنَّ إِلَى مُسَيْلِمَةَ لَعَلِّي أَقْتُلُهُ فَأُكَافِئَ بِهِ حَمْزَةَ ـ قَالَ ـ فَخَرَجْتُ مَعَ النَّاسِ، فَكَانَ مِنْ أَمْرِهِ مَا كَانَ ـ قَالَ ـ فَإِذَا رَجُلٌ قَائِمٌ فِي ثَلْمَةِ جِدَارٍ، كَأَنَّهُ جَمَلٌ أَوْرَقُ ثَائِرُ الرَّأْسِ ـ قَالَ ـ فَرَمَيْتُهُ بِحَرْبَتِي، فَأَضَعُهَا بَيْنَ ثَدْيَيْهِ حَتَّى خَرَجَتْ مِنْ بَيْنِ كَتِفَيْهِ ـ قَالَ ـ وَوَثَبَ إِلَيْهِ رَجُلٌ مِنَ الأَنْصَارِ، فَضَرَبَهُ بِالسَّيْفِ عَلَى هَامَتِهِ. قَالَ قَالَ عَبْدُ اللَّهِ بْنُ الْفَضْلِ فَأَخْبَرَنِي سُلَيْمَانُ بْنُ يَسَارٍ أَنَّهُ سَمِعَ عَبْدَ اللَّهِ بْنَ عُمَرَ يَقُولُ فَقَالَتْ جَارِيَةٌ عَلَى ظَهْرِ بَيْتٍ وَا أَمِيرَ الْمُؤْمِنِينَ، قَتَلَهُ الْعَبْدُ الأَسْوَدُ

Narrated Jubair bin Mut`im: My father said, "I heard Allah's Messenger ﷺ reciting "at-Tur" (52) in the Maghrib prayer.". – Sahih Al-Bukhari 765

حَدَّثَنَا عَبْدُ اللَّهِ بْنُ يُوسُفَ، قَالَ أَخْبَرَنَا مَالِكٌ، عَنِ ابْنِ شِهَابٍ، عَنْ مُحَمَّدِ بْنِ جُبَيْرِ بْنِ مُطْعِمٍ، عَنْ أَبِيهِ، قَالَ سَمِعْتُ رَسُولَ اللَّهِ صلى الله عليه وسلم قَرَأَ فِي الْمَغْرِبِ بِالطُّورِ.

Narrated Jubair bin Mut`im: That while he was with Allah's Messenger ﷺ who was accompanied by the people on their way back from Hunain, the bedouins started begging things of Allah's Messenger ﷺ so much so that they forced him to go under a Samura tree where his loose outer garment was snatched away. On that, Allah's Messenger ﷺ stood up and said to them, "Return my garment to me. If I had as many camels as these trees, I would have distributed them amongst you; and you will not find me a miser or a liar or a coward." – Sahih Al-Bukhari 3148

حَدَّثَنَا عَبْدُ الْعَزِيزِ بْنُ عَبْدِ اللَّهِ الأُوَيْسِيُّ، حَدَّثَنَا إِبْرَاهِيمُ بْنُ سَعْدٍ، عَنْ صَالِحٍ، عَنِ ابْنِ شِهَابٍ، قَالَ أَخْبَرَنِي عُمَرُ بْنُ مُحَمَّدِ بْنِ جُبَيْرِ بْنِ مُطْعِمٍ، أَنَّ مُحَمَّدَ بْنَ جُبَيْرٍ، قَالَ أَخْبَرَنِي جُبَيْرُ بْنُ مُطْعِمٍ، أَنَّهُ بَيْنَا هُوَ مَعَ رَسُولِ اللَّهِ صلى الله عليه وسلم وَمَعَهُ النَّاسُ مُقْبِلاً مِنْ حُنَيْنٍ عَلِقَتْ رَسُولَ اللَّهِ صلى الله عليه وسلم الأَعْرَابُ يَسْأَلُونَهُ حَتَّى اضْطَرُّوهُ إِلَى سَمُرَةٍ، فَخَطِفَتْ رِدَاءَهُ، فَوَقَفَ رَسُولُ اللَّهِ صلى الله عليه وسلم فَقَالَ " أَعْطُونِي رِدَائِي، فَلَوْ كَانَ عَدَدُ هَذِهِ الْعِضَاهِ نَعَمًا لَقَسَمْتُهُ بَيْنَكُمْ، ثُمَّ لاَ تَجِدُونِي بَخِيلاً وَلاَ كَذُوبًا وَلاَ جَبَانًا "

Narrated Jubair bin Mut`im: I and `Uthman bin `Affan went to Allah's Messenger ﷺ and said, "O Allah's Messenger ﷺ! You have given to Bani Al-Muttalib and left us although they and we are of the same kinship to you." Allah's Messenger ﷺ said, "Bani Muttalib and Bani Hashim are one and the same." The Prophet ﷺ did not give a share to Bani `Abd Shams and Bani Naufai. (Ibn 'Is-haq said, "Abd Shams and Hashim and Al-Muttalib were maternal brothers and their mother was 'Atika bint Murra and Naufal was their paternal brother.). – Sahih Al-Bukhari 3140

حَدَّثَنَا عَبْدُ اللَّهِ بْنُ يُوسُفَ، حَدَّثَنَا اللَّيْثُ، عَنْ عُقَيْلٍ، عَنِ ابْنِ شِهَابٍ، عَنِ ابْنِ الْمُسَيَّبِ، عَنْ جُبَيْرِ بْنِ مُطْعِمٍ، قَالَ مَشَيْتُ أَنَا وَعُثْمَانُ بْنُ عَفَّانَ، إِلَى رَسُولِ اللَّهِ صلى الله عليه وسلم فَقُلْنَا يَا رَسُولَ اللَّهِ، أَعْطَيْتَ بَنِي الْمُطَّلِبِ وَتَرَكْتَنَا، وَنَحْنُ وَهُمْ مِنْكَ بِمَنْزِلَةٍ وَاحِدَةٍ. فَقَالَ رَسُولُ اللَّهِ صلى الله عليه وسلم " إِنَّمَا بَنُو الْمُطَّلِبِ وَبَنُو هَاشِمٍ شَىْءٌ وَاحِدٌ ". قَالَ اللَّيْثُ حَدَّثَنِي يُونُسُ وَزَادَ قَالَ جُبَيْرٌ وَلَمْ يَقْسِمِ النَّبِيُّ صلى الله عليه وسلم لِبَنِي عَبْدِ شَمْسٍ وَلاَ لِبَنِي نَوْفَلٍ. وَقَالَ ابْنُ إِسْحَاقَ عَبْدُ شَمْسٍ وَهَاشِمٌ وَالْمُطَّلِبُ إِخْوَةٌ لأُمٍّ، وَأُمُّهُمْ عَاتِكَةُ بِنْتُ مُرَّةَ، وَكَانَ نَوْفَلٌ أَخَاهُمْ لأَبِيهِمْ.

Narrated Jubair bin Mut`im: I heard Allah's Messenger ﷺ saying, 'I have several names: I am Muhammad and I am Ahmad, and I am Al- Mahi with whom Allah obliterates Kufr (disbelief), and I am Al-Hashir (gatherer) at whose feet (i.e. behind whom) the people will be gathered (on the Day of Resurrection), and I am Al-Aqib (i.e. who succeeds the other prophets in bringing about good). – Sahih Al-Bukhari 4896

حَدَّثَنَا أَبُو الْيَمَانِ، أَخْبَرَنَا شُعَيْبٌ، عَنِ الزُّهْرِيِّ، أَخْبَرَنِي مُحَمَّدُ بْنُ جُبَيْرِ بْنِ مُطْعِمٍ، عَنْ أَبِيهِ ـ رضى الله عنه ـ قَالَ سَمِعْتُ رَسُولَ اللَّهِ صلى الله عليه وسلم يَقُولُ ‏"‏ إِنَّ لِي أَسْمَاءً، أَنَا مُحَمَّدٌ، وَأَنَا أَحْمَدُ، وَأَنَا الْمَاحِي الَّذِي يَمْحُو اللَّهُ بِيَ الْكُفْرَ، وَأَنَا الْحَاشِرُ الَّذِي يُحْشَرُ النَّاسُ عَلَى قَدَمِي، وَأَنَا الْعَاقِبُ ‏"‏

Narrated Jubair bin Mut`im: I heard the Prophet ﷺ reciting Surat at-Tur in the Maghrib prayer, and when he reached the Verse: 'Were they created by nothing, Or were they themselves the creators, Or did they create the Heavens and the Earth? Nay, but they have no firm belief Or do they own the treasures of Your Lord? Or have they been given the authority to do as they like...' (52.35-37) my heart was about to fly (when I realized this firm argument). – Sahih Al-Bukhari 4854

حَدَّثَنَا الْحُمَيْدِيُّ، حَدَّثَنَا سُفْيَانُ، قَالَ حَدَّثُونِي عَنِ الزُّهْرِيِّ، عَنْ مُحَمَّدِ بْنِ جُبَيْرِ بْنِ مُطْعِمٍ، عَنْ أَبِيهِ ـ رضى الله عنه ـ قَالَ سَمِعْتُ النَّبِيَّ صلى الله عليه وسلم يَقْرَأُ فِي الْمَغْرِبِ بِالطُّورِ فَلَمَّا بَلَغَ هَذِهِ الآيَةَ ‏{‏أَمْ خُلِقُوا مِنْ غَيْرِ شَىْءٍ أَمْ هُمُ الْخَالِقُونَ * أَمْ خَلَقُوا السَّمَوَاتِ وَالأَرْضَ بَلْ لاَ يُوقِنُونَ * أَمْ عِنْدَهُمْ خَزَائِنُ رَبِّكَ أَمْ هُمُ الْمُسَيْطِرُونَ‏}‏ كَادَ قَلْبِي أَنْ يَطِيرَ‏.‏ قَالَ سُفْيَانُ فَأَمَّا أَنَا فَإِنَّمَا سَمِعْتُ الزُّهْرِيَّ يُحَدِّثُ عَنْ مُحَمَّدِ بْنِ جُبَيْرِ بْنِ مُطْعِمٍ عَنْ أَبِيهِ سَمِعْتُ النَّبِيَّ صلى الله عليه وسلم يَقْرَأُ فِي الْمَغْرِبِ بِالطُّورِ‏.‏ لَمْ أَسْمَعْهُ زَادَ الَّذِي قَالُوا لِي‏.‏

Narrated Jubair bin Mut`im: A woman came to the Prophet ﷺ and spoke to him about something and he told her to return to him. She said, "O Allah's Messenger ﷺ ! If I come and do not find you?" (As if she meant, "...if you die?") The Prophet said, "If you should not find me, then go to Abu Bakr." - Sahih al-Bukhari 7220

حَدَّثَنَا عَبْدُ الْعَزِيزِ بْنُ عَبْدِ اللَّهِ، حَدَّثَنَا إِبْرَاهِيمُ بْنُ سَعْدٍ، عَنْ أَبِيهِ، عَنْ مُحَمَّدِ بْنِ جُبَيْرِ بْنِ مُطْعِمٍ، عَنْ أَبِيهِ، قَالَ أَتَتِ النَّبِيَّ صلى الله عليه وسلم امْرَأَةٌ فَكَلَّمَتْهُ فِي شَىْءٍ فَأَمَرَهَا أَنْ تَرْجِعَ إِلَيْهِ، قَالَتْ يَا رَسُولَ اللَّهِ أَرَأَيْتَ إِنْ جِئْتُ وَلَمْ أَجِدْكَ، كَأَنَّهَا تُرِيدُ الْمَوْتَ، قَالَ ‏"‏ إِنْ لَمْ تَجِدِينِي فَأْتِي أَبَا بَكْرٍ ‏"‏‏.‏

Abu Sufyan
أَبُو سُفْيَان

Narrated Al-Bara: We faced the pagans on that day (of the battle of Uhud) and the Prophet ﷺ placed a batch of archers (at a special place) and appointed `Abdullah (bin Jubair) as their commander and said, "Do not leave this place; if you should see us conquering the enemy, do not leave this place, and if you should see them conquering us, do not (come to) help us," So, when we faced the enemy, they took to their heels till I saw their women running towards the mountain, lifting up their clothes from their legs, revealing their leg-bangles. The Muslims started saying, "The booty, the booty!" `Abdullah bin Jubair said, "The Prophet ﷺ had taken a firm promise from me not to leave this place." But his companions refused (to stay). So when they refused (to stay there), (Allah) confused them so that they could not know where to go, and they suffered seventy casualties. Abu Sufyan ascended a high place and said, "Is Muhammad present amongst the people?" The Prophet ﷺ said, "Do not answer him." Abu Sufyan said, "Is the son of Abu Quhafa present among the people?" The Prophet ﷺ said, "Do not answer him." `Abu Sufyan said, "Is the son of Al-Khattab amongst the people?" He then added, "All these people have been killed, for, were they alive, they would have replied." On that, `Umar could not help saying, "You are a liar, O enemy of Allah! Allah has kept what will make you unhappy." Abu Sufyan said, "Superior may be Hubal!" On that the Prophet said (to his companions), "Reply to him." They asked, "What may we say?" He said, "Say: Allah is More Elevated and More Majestic!" Abu Sufyan said, "We have (the idol) Al-`Uzza, whereas you have no `Uzza!" The Prophet ﷺ said (to his companions), "Reply to him." They said, "What may we say?" The Prophet ﷺ said, "Say: Allah is our Helper and you have no helper." Abu Sufyan said, "(This) day compensates for our loss at Badr and (in) the battle (the victory) is always undecided and shared in turns by the belligerents. You will see some of your dead men mutilated, but neither did I urge this action, nor am I sorry for it." Narrated Jabir: Some people took wine in the morning of the day of Uhud and were then killed as martyrs. – Sahih Al-Bukhari 4043, 4044

حَدَّثَنَا عُبَيْدُ اللَّهِ بْنُ مُوسَى، عَنْ إِسْرَائِيلَ، عَنْ أَبِي إِسْحَاقَ، عَنِ الْبَرَاءِ ـ رضى الله عنه ـ قَالَ لَقِينَا الْمُشْرِكِينَ يَوْمَئِذٍ، وَأَجْلَسَ النَّبِيُّ صلى الله عليه وسلم جَيْشًا مِنَ الرُّمَاةِ، وَأَمَّرَ عَلَيْهِمْ عَبْدَ اللَّهِ وَقَالَ " لاَ تَبْرَحُوا، إِنْ رَأَيْتُمُونَا ظَهَرْنَا عَلَيْهِمْ فَلاَ تَبْرَحُوا وَإِنْ رَأَيْتُمُوهُمْ ظَهَرُوا عَلَيْنَا فَلاَ تُعِينُونَا ". فَلَمَّا لَقِينَا هَرَبُوا حَتَّى رَأَيْتُ النِّسَاءَ يَشْتَدِدْنَ فِي الْجَبَلِ، رَفَعْنَ عَنْ سُوقِهِنَّ قَدْ بَدَتْ خَلاَخِلُهُنَّ، فَأَخَذُوا يَقُولُونَ الْغَنِيمَةَ الْغَنِيمَةَ. فَقَالَ عَبْدُ اللَّهِ عَهِدَ إِلَىَّ النَّبِيُّ صلى الله عليه وسلم أَنْ لاَ تَبْرَحُوا. فَأَبَوْا، فَلَمَّا أَبَوْا صُرِفَ وُجُوهُهُمْ، فَأُصِيبَ سَبْعُونَ قَتِيلاً، وَأَشْرَفَ أَبُو سُفْيَانَ فَقَالَ أَفِي الْقَوْمِ مُحَمَّدٌ فَقَالَ " لاَ تُجِيبُوهُ ". فَقَالَ أَفِي الْقَوْمِ ابْنُ أَبِي قُحَافَةَ قَالَ " لاَ تُجِيبُوهُ ". فَقَالَ أَفِي الْقَوْمِ ابْنُ الْخَطَّابِ فَقَالَ إِنَّ هَؤُلاَءِ قُتِلُوا، فَلَوْ كَانُوا أَحْيَاءً لأَجَابُوا، فَلَمْ يَمْلِكْ عُمَرُ نَفْسَهُ فَقَالَ كَذَبْتَ يَا عَدُوَّ اللَّهِ، أَبْقَى اللَّهُ عَلَيْكَ مَا يُخْزِيكَ. قَالَ أَبُو سُفْيَانَ أُعْلُ هُبَلْ. فَقَالَ النَّبِيُّ صلى الله عليه وسلم " أَجِيبُوهُ ". قَالُوا مَا نَقُولُ قَالَ " قُولُوا اللَّهُ أَعْلَى وَأَجَلُّ ". قَالَ أَبُو سُفْيَانَ لَنَا الْعُزَّى وَلاَ عُزَّى لَكُمْ. فَقَالَ النَّبِيُّ صلى الله عليه وسلم " أَجِيبُوهُ ". قَالُوا مَا نَقُولُ قَالَ " قُولُوا اللَّهُ مَوْلاَنَا وَلاَ مَوْلَى لَكُمْ ". قَالَ أَبُو سُفْيَانَ يَوْمٌ بِيَوْمِ بَدْرٍ، وَالْحَرْبُ سِجَالٌ، وَتَجِدُونَ مُثْلَةً لَمْ آمُرْ بِهَا وَلَمْ تَسُؤْنِي. أَخْبَرَنِي عَبْدُ اللَّهِ بْنُ مُحَمَّدٍ، حَدَّثَنَا سُفْيَانُ، عَنْ عَمْرٍو، عَنْ جَابِرٍ، قَالَ اصْطَبَحَ الْخَمْرَ يَوْمَ أُحُدٍ نَاسٌ ثُمَّ قُتِلُوا شُهَدَاءَ

Narrated `Abdullah: It (i.e., the imagined smoke) was because, when the Quraish refused to obey the Prophet, he asked Allah to afflict them with years of famine similar to those of (Prophet) Joseph. So they were stricken with famine and fatigue, so much so that they ate even bones. A man would look towards the sky and imagine seeing something like smoke between him and the sky because of extreme fatigue. So Allah revealed:-- 'Then watch you for the Day that the sky will bring forth a kind of smoke plainly visible, covering the people; this is a painfull of torment.' (44.10-11) Then someone (Abu Sufyan) came to Allah's Messenger ﷺ and said, "O Allah's Messenger ﷺ! Invoke Allah to send rain for the tribes of Mudar for they are on the verge of destruction." On that the Prophet ﷺ said (astonishingly) "Shall I invoke Allah) for the tribes of Mudar? Verily, you are a brave man!" But the Prophet prayed for rain and it rained for them. Then the Verse was revealed. 'But truly you will return (to disbelief).' (44.15) (When the famine was over and) they restored prosperity and welfare, they reverted to their ways (of heathenism) whereupon Allah revealed: 'On the Day when We shall seize you with a Mighty Grasp. We will indeed (then) exact retribution.' (44.16) The narrator said, "That was the day of the Battle of Badr.". – Sahih Al-Bukhari 4821

حَدَّثَنَا يَحْيَى، حَدَّثَنَا أَبُو مُعَاوِيَةَ، عَنِ الأَعْمَشِ، عَنْ مُسْلِمٍ، عَنْ مَسْرُوقٍ، قَالَ قَالَ عَبْدُ اللَّهِ إِنَّمَا كَانَ هَذَا لأَنَّ قُرَيْشًا لَمَّا اسْتَعْصَوْا عَلَى النَّبِيِّ صلى الله عليه وسلم دَعَا عَلَيْهِمْ بِسِنِينَ كَسِنِي يُوسُفَ، فَأَصَابَهُمْ قَحْطٌ وَجَهْدٌ حَتَّى أَكَلُوا الْعِظَامَ، فَجَعَلَ الرَّجُلُ يَنْظُرُ إِلَى السَّمَاءِ فَيَرَى مَا بَيْنَهُ وَبَيْنَهَا كَهَيْئَةِ الدُّخَانِ مِنَ الْجَهْدِ، فَأَنْزَلَ اللَّهُ تَعَالَى {فَارْتَقِبْ يَوْمَ تَأْتِي السَّمَاءُ بِدُخَانٍ مُبِينٍ * يَغْشَى النَّاسَ هَذَا عَذَابٌ أَلِيمٌ} قَالَ فَأُتِيَ رَسُولُ اللَّهِ صلى الله عليه وسلم فَقِيلَ يَا رَسُولَ اللَّهِ اسْتَسْقِ اللَّهَ لِمُضَرَ، فَإِنَّهَا قَدْ هَلَكَتْ. قَالَ " لِمُضَرَ إِنَّكَ لَجَرِيءٌ ". فَاسْتَسْقَى فَسُقُوا. فَنَزَلَتْ {إِنَّكُمْ عَائِدُونَ} فَلَمَّا أَصَابَتْهُمُ الرَّفَاهِيَةُ عَادُوا إِلَى حَالِهِمْ حِينَ أَصَابَتْهُمُ الرَّفَاهِيَةُ. فَأَنْزَلَ اللَّهُ عَزَّ وَجَلَّ {يَوْمَ نَبْطِشُ الْبَطْشَةَ الْكُبْرَى إِنَّا مُنْتَقِمُونَ} قَالَ يَعْنِي يَوْمَ بَدْرٍ.

Narrated Hisham's father: When Allah's Messenger ﷺ set out (towards Mecca) during the year of the Conquest (of Mecca) and this news reached (the infidels of Quraish), Abu Sufyan, Hakim bin Hizam and Budail bin Warqa came out to gather information about Allah's Messenger ﷺ, they proceeded on their way till they reached a place called Marr-az-Zahran (which is near Mecca). Behold! There they saw many fires as if they were the fires of `Arafat.

Abu Sufyan said, “What is this? It looked like the fires of `Arafat.” Budail bin Warqa’ said, “Banu `Amr are less in number than that.” Some of the guards of Allah’s Messenger ﷺ saw them and took them over, caught them and brought them to Allah’s Messenger ﷺ Abu Sufyan embraced Islam. When the Prophet ﷺ proceeded, he said to Al-Abbas, “Keep Abu Sufyan standing at the top of the mountain so that he would look at the Muslims. So Al-`Abbas kept him standing (at that place) and the tribes with the Prophet ﷺ started passing in front of Abu Sufyan in military batches. A batch passed and Abu Sufyan said, “O `Abbas Who are these?” `Abbas said, “They are (Banu) Ghifar.” Abu Sufyan said, I have got nothing to do with Ghifar.” Then (a batch of the tribe of) Juhaina passed by and he said similarly as above. Then (a batch of the tribe of) Sa`d bin Huzaim passed by and he said similarly as above. Then (Banu) Sulaim passed by and he said similarly as above. Then came a batch, the like of which Abu Sufyan had not seen. He said, “Who are these?” `Abbas said, “They are the Ansar headed by Sa`d bin Ubada, the one holding the flag.” Sa`d bin Ubada said, “O Abu Sufyan! Today is the day of a great battle and today (what is prohibited in) the Ka`ba will be permissible.” Abu Sufyan said., “O `Abbas! How excellent the day of destruction is! “Then came anotherr batch (of warriors) which was the smallest of all the batches, and in it there was Allah’s Messenger ﷺ and his companions and the flag of the Prophet ﷺ was carried by Az-Zubair bin Al Awwam. When Allah’s Messenger ﷺ passed by Abu Sufyan, the latter said, (to the Prophet), “Do you know what Sa`d bin ‘Ubada said?” The Prophet ﷺ said, “What did he say?” Abu Sufyan said, “He said so-and-so.” The Prophet ﷺ said, “Sa`d told a lie, but today Allah will give superiority to the Ka`ba and today the Ka`ba will be covered with a (cloth) covering.” Allah’s Messenger ﷺ ordered that his flag be fixed at Al-Hajun. Narrated `Urwa: Nafi` bin Jubair bin Mut`im said, “I heard Al-Abbas saying to Az-Zubair bin Al- `Awwam, ‘O Abu `Abdullah ! Did Allah’s Messenger ﷺ order you to fix the flag here?’ “ Allah’s Messenger ﷺ ordered Khalid bin Al-Walid to enter Mecca from its upper part from Ka’da while the Prophet ﷺ himself entered from Kuda. Two men from the cavalry of Khalid bin Al-Wahd named Hubaish bin Al-Ash’ar and Kurz bin Jabir Al-Fihri were martyred on that day. – Sahih Al-Bukhari 4280

حَدَّثَنَا عُبَيْدُ بْنُ إِسْمَاعِيلَ، حَدَّثَنَا أَبُو أُسَامَةَ، عَنْ هِشَامٍ، عَنْ أَبِيهِ، قَالَ لَمَّا سَارَ رَسُولُ اللَّهِ صلى الله عليه وسلم عَامَ الْفَتْحِ فَبَلَغَ ذَلِكَ قُرَيْشًا، خَرَجَ أَبُو سُفْيَانَ بْنُ حَرْبٍ وَحَكِيمُ بْنُ حِزَامٍ وَبُدَيْلُ بْنُ وَرْقَاءَ يَلْتَمِسُونَ الْخَبَرَ عَنْ رَسُولِ اللَّهِ صلى الله عليه وسلم فَأَقْبَلُوا يَسِيرُونَ حَتَّى أَتَوْا مَرَّ الظَّهْرَانِ، فَإِذَا هُمْ بِنِيرَانٍ كَأَنَّهَا نِيرَانُ عَرَفَةَ، فَقَالَ أَبُو سُفْيَانَ مَا هَذِهِ لَكَأَنَّهَا نِيرَانُ عَرَفَةَ. فَقَالَ بُدَيْلُ بْنُ وَرْقَاءَ نِيرَانُ بَنِي عَمْرٍو. فَقَالَ أَبُو سُفْيَانَ عَمْرٌو أَقَلُّ مِنْ ذَلِكَ. فَرَآهُمْ نَاسٌ مِنْ حَرَسِ رَسُولِ اللَّهِ صلى الله عليه وسلم فَأَدْرَكُوهُمْ فَأَخَذُوهُمْ، فَأَتَوْا بِهِمْ رَسُولَ اللَّهِ صلى الله عليه وسلم فَأَسْلَمَ أَبُو سُفْيَانَ، فَلَمَّا سَارَ قَالَ لِلْعَبَّاسِ " احْبِسْ أَبَا سُفْيَانَ عِنْدَ حَطْمِ الْخَيْلِ حَتَّى يَنْظُرَ إِلَى الْمُسْلِمِينَ ". فَحَبَسَهُ الْعَبَّاسُ، فَجَعَلَتِ الْقَبَائِلُ تَمُرُّ مَعَ النَّبِيِّ صلى الله عليه وسلم تَمُرُّ كَتِيبَةً كَتِيبَةً عَلَى أَبِي سُفْيَانَ، فَمَرَّتْ كَتِيبَةٌ قَالَ يَا عَبَّاسُ مَنْ هَذِهِ قَالَ هَذِهِ غِفَارُ. قَالَ مَا لِي وَلِغِفَارَ ثُمَّ مَرَّتْ جُهَيْنَةُ، قَالَ مِثْلَ ذَلِكَ، ثُمَّ مَرَّتْ سَعْدُ بْنُ هُذَيْمٍ، فَقَالَ مِثْلَ ذَلِكَ، وَمَرَّتْ سُلَيْمُ، فَقَالَ مِثْلَ ذَلِكَ، حَتَّى أَقْبَلَتْ كَتِيبَةٌ لَمْ يَرَ مِثْلَهَا، قَالَ مَنْ هَذِهِ قَالَ هَؤُلاَءِ الأَنْصَارُ عَلَيْهِمْ سَعْدُ بْنُ عُبَادَةَ مَعَهُ الرَّايَةُ. فَقَالَ سَعْدُ بْنُ عُبَادَةَ يَا أَبَا سُفْيَانَ الْيَوْمُ يَوْمُ الْمَلْحَمَةِ، الْيَوْمَ تُسْتَحَلُّ الْكَعْبَةُ. فَقَالَ أَبُو سُفْيَانَ يَا عَبَّاسُ حَبَّذَا يَوْمُ الذِّمَارِ. ثُمَّ جَاءَتْ كَتِيبَةٌ، وَهْىَ أَقَلُّ الْكَتَائِبِ، فِيهِمْ رَسُولُ اللَّهِ صلى الله عليه وسلم وَأَصْحَابُهُ، وَرَايَةُ النَّبِيِّ صلى الله عليه وسلم مَعَ الزُّبَيْرِ بْنِ الْعَوَّامِ، فَلَمَّا مَرَّ رَسُولُ اللَّهِ صلى الله عليه وسلم بِأَبِي سُفْيَانَ قَالَ أَلَمْ تَعْلَمْ مَا قَالَ سَعْدُ بْنُ عُبَادَةَ قَالَ " مَا قَالَ ". قَالَ كَذَا وَكَذَا. فَقَالَ " كَذَبَ سَعْدٌ، وَلَكِنْ هَذَا يَوْمٌ يُعَظِّمُ اللَّهُ فِيهِ الْكَعْبَةَ، وَيَوْمٌ تُكْسَى فِيهِ الْكَعْبَةُ ". قَالَ وَأَمَرَ رَسُولُ اللَّهِ صلى الله عليه وسلم أَنْ تُرْكَزَ رَايَتُهُ بِالْحَجُونِ. قَالَ عُرْوَةُ وَأَخْبَرَنِي نَافِعُ بْنُ جُبَيْرِ بْنِ مُطْعِمٍ قَالَ سَمِعْتُ الْعَبَّاسَ يَقُولُ لِلزُّبَيْرِ بْنِ الْعَوَّامِ يَا أَبَا عَبْدِ اللَّهِ، هَا هُنَا أَمَرَكَ رَسُولُ اللَّهِ صلى الله عليه وسلم أَنْ تَرْكُزَ الرَّايَةَ، قَالَ وَأَمَرَ رَسُولُ اللَّهِ صلى الله عليه وسلم يَوْمَئِذٍ خَالِدَ بْنَ الْوَلِيدِ أَنْ يَدْخُلَ مِنْ أَعْلَى مَكَّةَ مِنْ كَدَاءٍ، وَدَخَلَ النَّبِيُّ صلى الله عليه وسلم مِنْ كُدَا، فَقُتِلَ مِنْ خَيْلِ خَالِدٍ يَوْمَئِذٍ رَجُلاَنِ حُبَيْشُ بْنُ الأَشْعَرِ وَكُرْزُ بْنُ جَابِرٍ الْفِهْرِيُّ

Narrated Masruq: We were with `Abdullah and he said, “When the Prophet ﷺ saw the refusal of the people to accept Islam he said, “O Allah! Send (famine) years on them for (seven years) like the seven years (of famine during the time) of (Prophet) Joseph.” So famine overtook

them for one year and destroyed every kind of life to such an extent that the people started eating hides, carcasses and rotten dead animals. Whenever one of them looked towards the sky, he would (imagine himself to) see smoke because of hunger. So Abu Sufyan went to the Prophetﷺ and said, "O Muhammad! You order people to obey Allah and to keep good relations with kith and kin. No doubt the people of your tribe are dying, so please pray to Allah for them." So Allah revealed: "Then watch you For the day that The sky will bring forth a kind Of smoke Plainly visible ... Verily! You will return (to disbelief) On the day when We shall seize You with a mighty grasp. (44.10-16) Ibn Mas`ud added, "Al-Batsha (i.e. grasp) happened in the battle of Badr and no doubt smoke, Al-Batsha, Al-Lizam, and the verse of Surat Ar-Rum have all passed . – Sahih Al-Bukhari 1007
حَدَّثَنَا عُثْمَانُ بْنُ أَبِي شَيْبَةَ، قَالَ حَدَّثَنَا جَرِيرٌ، عَنْ مَنْصُورٍ، عَنْ أَبِي الضُّحَى، عَنْ مَسْرُوقٍ، قَالَ كُنَّا عِنْدَ عَبْدِ اللَّهِ فَقَالَ إِنَّ النَّبِيَّ صلى الله عليه وسلم لَمَّا رَأَى مِنَ النَّاسِ إِدْبَارًا قَالَ " اللَّهُمَّ سَبْعٌ كَسَبْعِ يُوسُفَ ". فَأَخَذَتْهُمْ سَنَةٌ حَصَّتْ كُلَّ شَىْءٍ حَتَّى أَكَلُوا الْجُلُودَ وَالْمَيْتَةَ وَالْجِيَفَ، وَيَنْظُرَ أَحَدُهُمْ إِلَى السَّمَاءِ فَيَرَى الدُّخَانَ مِنَ الْجُوعِ، فَأَتَاهُ أَبُو سُفْيَانَ فَقَالَ يَا مُحَمَّدُ إِنَّكَ تَأْمُرُ بِطَاعَةِ اللَّهِ وَبِصِلَةِ الرَّحِمِ وَإِنَّ قَوْمَكَ قَدْ هَلَكُوا، فَادْعُ اللَّهَ لَهُمْ قَالَ اللَّهُ تَعَالَى {فَارْتَقِبْ يَوْمَ تَأْتِي السَّمَاءُ بِدُخَانٍ مُبِينٍ} إِلَى قَوْلِهِ {عَائِدُونَ * يَوْمَ نَبْطِشُ الْبَطْشَةَ الْكُبْرَى} فَالْبَطْشَةُ يَوْمَ بَدْرٍ، وَقَدْ مَضَتِ الدُّخَانُ وَالْبَطْشَةُ وَاللِّزَامُ وَآيَةُ الرُّومِ.

Narrated 'Abdullah bin 'Abbas: Abu Sufyan bin Harb informed me that Heraclius had sent a messenger to him while he had been accompanying a caravan from Quraish. They were merchants doing business in Sham (Syria, Palestine, Lebanon and Jordan), at the time when Allah's Messengerﷺ had truce with Abu Sufyan and Quraish infidels. So Abu Sufyan and his companions went to Heraclius at Ilya (Jerusalem). Heraclius called them in the court and he had all the senior Roman dignitaries around him. He called for his translator who, translating Heraclius's question said to them, "Who amongst you is closely related to that man who claims to be a Prophet?" Abu Sufyan replied, "I am the nearest relative to him (amongst the group)." Heraclius said, "Bring him (Abu Sufyan) close to me and make his companions stand behind him." Abu Sufyan added, Heraclius told his translator to tell my companions that he wanted to put some questions to me regarding that man (The Prophet) and that if I told a lie they (my companions) should contradict me." Abu Sufyan added, "By Allah! Had I not been afraid of my companions labeling me a liar, I would not have spoken the truth about the Prophet. The first question he asked me about him was: 'What is his family status amongst you?' I replied, 'He belongs to a good (noble) family amongst us.' Heraclius further asked, 'Has anybody amongst you ever claimed the same (i.e. to be a Prophet) before him?' I replied, 'No.' He said, 'Was anybody amongst his ancestors a king?' I replied, 'No.' Heraclius asked, 'Do the nobles or the poor follow him?' I replied, 'It is the poor who follow him.' He said, 'Are his followers increasing decreasing (day by day)?' I replied, 'They are increasing.' He then asked, 'Does anybody amongst those who embrace his religion become displeased and renounce the religion afterwards?' I replied, 'No.' Heraclius said, 'Have you ever accused him of telling lies before his claim (to be a Prophet)?' I replied, 'No. ' Heraclius said, 'Does he break his promises?' I replied, 'No. We are at truce with him but we do not know what he will do in it.' I could not find opportunity to say anything against him except that. Heraclius asked, 'Have you ever had a war with him?' I replied, 'Yes.' Then he said, 'What was the outcome of the battles?' I replied, 'Sometimes he was victorious and sometimes we.' Heraclius said, 'What does he order you to do?' I said, 'He tells us to worship Allah and Allah alone and not to worship anything along with Him, and to renounce all that our ancestors had said. He orders us to pray, to speak the truth, to be chaste and to keep good relations with our Kith and kin.' Heraclius asked the translator to convey to me the following, I asked you about his family and your reply was that he belonged to a very noble family. In fact all the Apostles come from noble families amongst their respective peoples. I questioned you whether anybody else amongst you claimed such a thing, your reply was in the negative. If the answer had been in the affirmative, I would have thought that this man was following the previous man's statement. Then I asked you whether anyone of his ancestors was a king. Your reply was in the negative, and if it had been in the affirmative, I would have thought that this man wanted to take back his ancestral kingdom. I further asked whether he was ever accused of telling lies before he said what he said, and your reply was in the negative. So I wondered how a person who does not tell a lie about others could ever tell a lie about Allah. I, then asked you whether the rich people followed him or the poor. You replied that it was the poor who followed him. And in fact all the Apostle have been followed by this very class of people. Then I asked you whether his followers were increasing or decreasing. You replied that they were increasing, and in fact this is the way of true faith, till it is complete in all respects. I further asked you whether there was anybody, who, after embracing his religion, became displeased and discarded his religion. Your reply was in the negative, and in fact this is (the sign of) true faith, when its delight enters the hearts and mixes with them completely. I asked you whether he had ever betrayed. You replied in the negative and likewise the Apostles never betray. Then I asked you what he ordered you to do. You replied that he ordered you to worship Allah and Allah alone and not to worship any thing along with Him and forbade you to worship idols and ordered you to pray, to speak the truth and to be chaste. If what you have said is true, he will very soon occupy this place underneath my feet and I knew it (from the scriptures) that he was going to appear but I did not know that he would be from you, and if I could reach him definitely, I would go immediately to meet him and if I were with him, I would certainly wash his feet.' Heraclius then asked for the letter addressed by Allah's Apostle Which was delivered by Dihya to the Governor of Busra, who forwarded it to Heraclius to read. The contents of the letter were as follows: "In the name of Allah the Beneficent, the Merciful (This letter is) from Muhammad the slave of Allah and His Apostle to Heraclius the ruler of Byzantine. Peace be upon him, who follows the right path. Furthermore I invite you to Islam, and if you become a Muslim you will be safe, and Allah will double your reward, and if you reject this invitation of Islam you will be committing a sin of Arisiyin (tillers, farmers i.e. your people). And (Allah's Statement 'O people of the scripture! Come to a word common to you and us that we worship none but Allah and that we associate nothing in worship with Him, and that none of us shall take others as Lords beside Allah. Then, if they turn away, say: Bear witness that we are Muslims (those who have surrendered to Allah).' (3:64). Abu Sufyan then added, "When Heraclius had finished his speech and had read the letter, there was a great hue and cry in the Royal Court. So we were turned out of the court. I told my companions that the question of Ibn-Abi-Kabsha) (the Prophet ﷺMuhammad) has become so prominent that even the King of Bani Al-Asfar (Byzantine) is afraid of him. Then I started to become sure that he (the Prophet) would be the conqueror in the near future till I embraced Islam (i.e. Allah guided me to it)." The sub narrator adds, "Ibn An-Natur was the Governor of Ilya' (Jerusalem) and Heraclius was the head of the Christians of Sham. Ibn An-Natur narrates that once while Heraclius was visiting ilya' (Jerusalem), he got up in the morning with a sad mood. Some of his priests asked him why he was in that mood? Heraclius was a foreteller and an astrologer. He replied, 'At night when I looked at the stars, I saw that the leader of those who practice circumcision had appeared (become the conqueror). Who are they who practice circumcision?' The people replied, 'Except the Jews nobody practices circumcision, so you should not be afraid of them (Jews). 'Just Issue orders to kill every Jew present in the country.' While they were discussing it, a messenger sent by the king of Ghassan to convey the news of Allah's Messengerﷺ to

Heraclius was brought in. Having heard the news, he (Heraclius) ordered the people to go and see whether the messenger of Ghassan was circumcised. The people, after seeing him, told Heraclius that he was circumcised. Heraclius then asked him about the Arabs. The messenger replied, 'Arabs also practice circumcision.' (After hearing that) Heraclius remarked that sovereignty of the 'Arabs had appeared. Heraclius then wrote a letter to his friend in Rome who was as good as Heraclius in knowledge. Heraclius then left for Homs. (a town in Syrian and stayed there till he received the reply of his letter from his friend who agreed with him in his opinion about the emergence of the Prophet ﷺ and the fact that he was a Prophet. On that Heraclius invited all the heads of the Byzantines to assemble in his palace at Homs. When they assembled, he ordered that all the doors of his palace be closed. Then he came out and said, 'O Byzantines! If success is your desire and if you seek right guidance and want your empire to remain then give a pledge of allegiance to this Prophet (i.e. embrace Islam).' (On hearing the views of Heraclius) the people ran towards the gates of the palace like onagers but found the doors closed. Heraclius realized their hatred towards Islam and when he lost the hope of their embracing Islam, he ordered that they should be brought back in audience. (When they returned) he said, 'What already said was just to test the strength of your conviction and I have seen it.' The people prostrated before him and became pleased with him, and this was the end of Heraclius's story (in connection with his faith). – Sahih Al-Bukhari 7

حَدَّثَنَا أَبُو الْيَمَانِ الْحَكَمُ بْنُ نَافِعٍ، قَالَ أَخْبَرَنَا شُعَيْبٌ، عَنِ الزُّهْرِيِّ، قَالَ أَخْبَرَنِي عُبَيْدُ اللَّهِ بْنُ عَبْدِ اللَّهِ بْنِ عُتْبَةَ بْنِ مَسْعُودٍ، أَنَّ عَبْدَ اللَّهِ بْنَ عَبَّاسٍ، أَخْبَرَهُ أَنَّ أَبَا سُفْيَانَ بْنَ حَرْبٍ أَخْبَرَهُ أَنَّ هِرَقْلَ أَرْسَلَ إِلَيْهِ فِي رَكْبٍ مِنْ قُرَيْشٍ ـ وَكَانُوا تُجَّارًا بِالشَّأْمِ ـ فِي الْمُدَّةِ الَّتِي كَانَ رَسُولُ اللَّهِ صلى الله عليه وسلم مَادَّ فِيهَا أَبَا سُفْيَانَ وَكُفَّارَ قُرَيْشٍ، فَأَتَوْهُ وَهُمْ بِإِيلِيَاءَ فَدَعَاهُمْ فِي مَجْلِسِهِ، وَحَوْلَهُ عُظَمَاءُ الرُّومِ ثُمَّ دَعَاهُمْ وَدَعَا بِتَرْجُمَانِهِ فَقَالَ أَيُّكُمْ أَقْرَبُ نَسَبًا بِهَذَا الرَّجُلِ الَّذِي يَزْعُمُ أَنَّهُ نَبِيٌّ فَقَالَ أَبُو سُفْيَانَ فَقُلْتُ أَنَا أَقْرَبُهُمْ نَسَبًا. فَقَالَ أَدْنُوهُ مِنِّي، وَقَرِّبُوا أَصْحَابَهُ، فَاجْعَلُوهُمْ عِنْدَ ظَهْرِهِ. ثُمَّ قَالَ لِتَرْجُمَانِهِ قُلْ لَهُمْ إِنِّي سَائِلٌ هَذَا عَنْ هَذَا الرَّجُلِ، فَإِنْ كَذَبَنِي فَكَذِّبُوهُ. فَوَاللَّهِ لَوْلاَ الْحَيَاءُ مِنْ أَنْ يَأْثِرُوا عَلَىَّ كَذِبًا لَكَذَبْتُ عَنْهُ، ثُمَّ كَانَ أَوَّلَ مَا سَأَلَنِي عَنْهُ أَنْ قَالَ كَيْفَ نَسَبُهُ فِيكُمْ قُلْتُ هُوَ فِينَا ذُو نَسَبٍ. قَالَ فَهَلْ قَالَ هَذَا الْقَوْلَ مِنْكُمْ أَحَدٌ قَطُّ قَبْلَهُ قُلْتُ لاَ. قَالَ فَهَلْ كَانَ مِنْ آبَائِهِ مِنْ مَلِكٍ قُلْتُ لاَ. قَالَ فَأَشْرَافُ النَّاسِ يَتَّبِعُونَهُ أَمْ ضُعَفَاؤُهُمْ فَقُلْتُ بَلْ ضُعَفَاؤُهُمْ. قَالَ أَيَزِيدُونَ أَمْ يَنْقُصُونَ قُلْتُ بَلْ يَزِيدُونَ. قَالَ فَهَلْ يَرْتَدُّ أَحَدٌ مِنْهُمْ سَخْطَةً لِدِينِهِ بَعْدَ أَنْ يَدْخُلَ فِيهِ قُلْتُ لاَ. قَالَ فَهَلْ كُنْتُمْ تَتَّهِمُونَهُ بِالْكَذِبِ قَبْلَ أَنْ يَقُولَ مَا قَالَ قُلْتُ لاَ. قَالَ فَهَلْ يَغْدِرُ قُلْتُ لاَ، وَنَحْنُ مِنْهُ فِي مُدَّةٍ لاَ نَدْرِي مَا هُوَ فَاعِلٌ فِيهَا. قَالَ وَلَمْ تُمْكِنِّي كَلِمَةٌ أُدْخِلُ فِيهَا شَيْئًا غَيْرُ هَذِهِ الْكَلِمَةِ. قَالَ فَهَلْ قَاتَلْتُمُوهُ قُلْتُ نَعَمْ. قَالَ فَكَيْفَ كَانَ قِتَالُكُمْ إِيَّاهُ قُلْتُ الْحَرْبُ بَيْنَنَا وَبَيْنَهُ سِجَالٌ، يَنَالُ مِنَّا وَنَنَالُ مِنْهُ. قَالَ مَاذَا يَأْمُرُكُمْ قُلْتُ يَقُولُ اعْبُدُوا اللَّهَ وَحْدَهُ، وَلاَ تُشْرِكُوا بِهِ شَيْئًا، وَاتْرُكُوا مَا يَقُولُ آبَاؤُكُمْ، وَيَأْمُرُنَا بِالصَّلاَةِ وَالصِّدْقِ وَالْعَفَافِ وَالصِّلَةِ. فَقَالَ لِلتَّرْجُمَانِ قُلْ لَهُ سَأَلْتُكَ عَنْ نَسَبِهِ، فَذَكَرْتَ أَنَّهُ فِيكُمْ ذُو نَسَبٍ، فَكَذَلِكَ الرُّسُلُ تُبْعَثُ فِي نَسَبِ قَوْمِهَا، وَسَأَلْتُكَ هَلْ قَالَ أَحَدٌ مِنْكُمْ هَذَا الْقَوْلَ فَذَكَرْتَ أَنْ لاَ، فَقُلْتُ لَوْ كَانَ أَحَدٌ قَالَ هَذَا الْقَوْلَ قَبْلَهُ لَقُلْتُ رَجُلٌ يَأْتَسِي بِقَوْلٍ قِيلَ قَبْلَهُ، وَسَأَلْتُكَ هَلْ كَانَ مِنْ آبَائِهِ مِنْ مَلِكٍ فَذَكَرْتَ أَنْ لاَ، قُلْتُ فَلَوْ كَانَ مِنْ آبَائِهِ مِنْ مَلِكٍ قُلْتُ رَجُلٌ يَطْلُبُ مُلْكَ أَبِيهِ، وَسَأَلْتُكَ هَلْ كُنْتُمْ تَتَّهِمُونَهُ بِالْكَذِبِ قَبْلَ أَنْ يَقُولَ مَا قَالَ فَذَكَرْتَ أَنْ لاَ، فَقَدْ أَعْرِفُ أَنَّهُ لَمْ يَكُنْ لِيَذَرَ الْكَذِبَ عَلَى النَّاسِ وَيَكْذِبَ عَلَى اللَّهِ، وَسَأَلْتُكَ أَشْرَافُ النَّاسِ اتَّبَعُوهُ أَمْ ضُعَفَاؤُهُمْ فَذَكَرْتَ أَنَّ ضُعَفَاءَهُمُ اتَّبَعُوهُ، وَهُمْ أَتْبَاعُ الرُّسُلِ، وَسَأَلْتُكَ أَيَزِيدُونَ أَمْ يَنْقُصُونَ فَذَكَرْتَ أَنَّهُمْ يَزِيدُونَ، وَكَذَلِكَ أَمْرُ الإِيمَانِ حَتَّى يَتِمَّ، وَسَأَلْتُكَ أَيَرْتَدُّ أَحَدٌ سَخْطَةً لِدِينِهِ بَعْدَ أَنْ يَدْخُلَ فِيهِ فَذَكَرْتَ أَنْ لاَ، وَكَذَلِكَ الإِيمَانُ حِينَ تُخَالِطُ بَشَاشَتُهُ الْقُلُوبَ، وَسَأَلْتُكَ هَلْ يَغْدِرُ فَذَكَرْتَ أَنْ لاَ، وَكَذَلِكَ الرُّسُلُ لاَ تَغْدِرُ، وَسَأَلْتُكَ بِمَا يَأْمُرُكُمْ، فَذَكَرْتَ أَنَّهُ يَأْمُرُكُمْ أَنْ تَعْبُدُوا اللَّهَ، وَلاَ تُشْرِكُوا بِهِ شَيْئًا، وَيَنْهَاكُمْ عَنْ عِبَادَةِ الأَوْثَانِ، وَيَأْمُرُكُمْ بِالصَّلاَةِ وَالصِّدْقِ وَالْعَفَافِ. فَإِنْ كَانَ مَا تَقُولُ حَقًّا فَسَيَمْلِكُ مَوْضِعَ قَدَمَىَّ هَاتَيْنِ، وَقَدْ كُنْتُ أَعْلَمُ أَنَّهُ خَارِجٌ، لَمْ أَكُنْ أَظُنُّ أَنَّهُ مِنْكُمْ، فَلَوْ أَنِّي أَعْلَمُ أَنِّي أَخْلُصُ إِلَيْهِ لَتَجَشَّمْتُ لِقَاءَهُ، وَلَوْ كُنْتُ عِنْدَهُ لَغَسَلْتُ عَنْ قَدَمِهِ. ثُمَّ دَعَا بِكِتَابِ رَسُولِ اللَّهِ صلى الله عليه وسلم الَّذِي بَعَثَ بِهِ دِحْيَةُ إِلَى عَظِيمِ بُصْرَى، فَدَفَعَهُ إِلَى هِرَقْلَ فَقَرَأَهُ فَإِذَا فِيهِ بِسْمِ اللَّهِ الرَّحْمَنِ الرَّحِيمِ. مِنْ مُحَمَّدٍ عَبْدِ اللَّهِ وَرَسُولِهِ إِلَى هِرَقْلَ عَظِيمِ الرُّومِ. سَلاَمٌ عَلَى مَنِ اتَّبَعَ الْهُدَى، أَمَّا بَعْدُ فَإِنِّي أَدْعُوكَ بِدِعَايَةِ الإِسْلاَمِ، أَسْلِمْ تَسْلَمْ، يُؤْتِكَ اللَّهُ أَجْرَكَ مَرَّتَيْنِ، فَإِنْ تَوَلَّيْتَ فَإِنَّ عَلَيْكَ إِثْمَ الأَرِيسِيِّينَ وَ{يَا أَهْلَ الْكِتَابِ تَعَالَوْا إِلَى كَلِمَةٍ سَوَاءٍ بَيْنَنَا وَبَيْنَكُمْ أَنْ لاَ نَعْبُدَ إِلاَّ اللَّهَ وَلاَ نُشْرِكَ بِهِ شَيْئًا وَلاَ يَتَّخِذَ بَعْضُنَا بَعْضًا أَرْبَابًا مِنْ دُونِ اللَّهِ فَإِنْ تَوَلَّوْا فَقُولُوا اشْهَدُوا بِأَنَّا مُسْلِمُونَ} قَالَ أَبُو سُفْيَانَ فَلَمَّا قَالَ مَا قَالَ، وَفَرَغَ مِنْ قِرَاءَةِ الْكِتَابِ كَثُرَ عِنْدَهُ الصَّخَبُ، وَارْتَفَعَتِ الأَصْوَاتُ وَأُخْرِجْنَا، فَقُلْتُ لأَصْحَابِي حِينَ أُخْرِجْنَا لَقَدْ أَمِرَ أَمْرُ ابْنِ أَبِي كَبْشَةَ، إِنَّهُ يَخَافُهُ مَلِكُ بَنِي الأَصْفَرِ. فَمَا زِلْتُ مُوقِنًا أَنَّهُ سَيَظْهَرُ حَتَّى أَدْخَلَ اللَّهُ عَلَىَّ الإِسْلاَمَ. وَكَانَ ابْنُ النَّاظُورِ صَاحِبُ إِيلِيَاءَ وَهِرَقْلَ سُقُفًّا عَلَى نَصَارَى الشَّأْمِ، يُحَدِّثُ أَنَّ هِرَقْلَ حِينَ قَدِمَ إِيلِيَاءَ أَصْبَحَ يَوْمًا خَبِيثَ النَّفْسِ، فَقَالَ بَعْضُ بَطَارِقَتِهِ قَدِ اسْتَنْكَرْنَا هَيْئَتَكَ. قَالَ ابْنُ النَّاظُورِ وَكَانَ هِرَقْلُ حَزَّاءً يَنْظُرُ فِي النُّجُومِ، فَقَالَ لَهُمْ حِينَ سَأَلُوهُ إِنِّي رَأَيْتُ اللَّيْلَةَ حِينَ نَظَرْتُ

فِي النُّجُومِ مَلِكَ الْخِتَانِ قَدْ ظَهَرَ، فَمَنْ يَخْتَتِنُ مِنْ هَذِهِ الأُمَّةِ قَالُوا لَيْسَ يَخْتَتِنُ إِلاَّ الْيَهُودُ فَلاَ يُهِمَّنَّكَ شَأْنُهُمْ وَاكْتُبْ إِلَى مَدَايِنِ مُلْكِكَ، فَيَقْتُلُوا مَنْ فِيهِمْ مِنَ الْيَهُودِ. فَبَيْنَمَا هُمْ عَلَى أَمْرِهِمْ أُتِيَ هِرَقْلُ بِرَجُلٍ أَرْسَلَ بِهِ مَلِكُ غَسَّانَ، يُخْبِرُ عَنْ خَبَرِ رَسُولِ اللَّهِ صلى الله عليه وسلم فَلَمَّا اسْتَخْبَرَهُ هِرَقْلُ قَالَ اذْهَبُوا فَانْظُرُوا أَمُخْتَتِنٌ هُوَ أَمْ لاَ. فَنَظَرُوا إِلَيْهِ، فَحَدَّثُوهُ أَنَّهُ مُخْتَتِنٌ، وَسَأَلَهُ عَنِ الْعَرَبِ فَقَالَ هُمْ يَخْتَتِنُونَ. فَقَالَ هِرَقْلُ هَذَا مَلِكُ هَذِهِ الأُمَّةِ قَدْ ظَهَرَ. ثُمَّ كَتَبَ هِرَقْلُ إِلَى صَاحِبٍ لَهُ بِرُومِيَةَ، وَكَانَ نَظِيرَهُ فِي الْعِلْمِ، وَسَارَ هِرَقْلُ إِلَى حِمْصَ، فَلَمْ يَرِمْ حِمْصَ حَتَّى أَتَاهُ كِتَابٌ مِنْ صَاحِبِهِ يُوَافِقُ رَأْىَ هِرَقْلَ عَلَى خُرُوجِ النَّبِيِّ صلى الله عليه وسلم وَأَنَّهُ نَبِيٌّ، فَأَذِنَ هِرَقْلُ لِعُظَمَاءِ الرُّومِ فِي دَسْكَرَةٍ لَهُ بِحِمْصَ ثُمَّ أَمَرَ بِأَبْوَابِهَا فَغُلِّقَتْ، ثُمَّ اطَّلَعَ فَقَالَ يَا مَعْشَرَ الرُّومِ، هَلْ لَكُمْ فِي الْفَلاَحِ وَالرُّشْدِ وَأَنْ يَثْبُتَ مُلْكُكُمْ فَتُبَايِعُوا هَذَا النَّبِيَّ، فَحَاصُوا حَيْصَةَ حُمُرِ الْوَحْشِ إِلَى الأَبْوَابِ، فَوَجَدُوهَا قَدْ غُلِّقَتْ، فَلَمَّا رَأَى هِرَقْلُ نَفْرَتَهُمْ، وَأَيِسَ مِنَ الإِيمَانِ قَالَ رُدُّوهُمْ عَلَىَّ. وَقَالَ إِنِّي قُلْتُ مَقَالَتِي آنِفًا أَخْتَبِرُ بِهَا شِدَّتَكُمْ عَلَى دِينِكُمْ، فَقَدْ رَأَيْتُ. فَسَجَدُوا لَهُ وَرَضُوا عَنْهُ، فَكَانَ ذَلِكَ آخِرَ شَأْنِ هِرَقْلَ. رَوَاهُ صَالِحُ بْنُ كَيْسَانَ وَيُونُسُ وَمَعْمَرٌ عَنِ الزُّهْرِيِّ.

Narrated Ibn `Abbas: The Prophet ﷺ used to move his tongue when the divine Inspiration was being revealed to him. (Sufyan, a subnarrator, demonstrated (how the Prophet ﷺ used to move his lips) and added. “In order to memorize it.” So Allah revealed: “Move not your tongue concerning (the Qur’an) to make haste therewith.” (75.16). – Sahih Al-Bukhari 4927
حَدَّثَنَا الْحُمَيْدِيُّ، حَدَّثَنَا سُفْيَانُ، حَدَّثَنَا مُوسَى بْنُ أَبِي عَائِشَةَ ـ وَكَانَ ثِقَةً ـ عَنْ سَعِيدِ بْنِ جُبَيْرٍ، عَنِ ابْنِ عَبَّاسٍ ـ رضى الله عنهما ـ قَالَ كَانَ النَّبِيُّ صلى الله عليه وسلم إِذَا نَزَلَ عَلَيْهِ الْوَحْىُ حَرَّكَ بِهِ لِسَانَهُ ـ وَوَصَفَ سُفْيَانُ ـ يُرِيدُ أَنْ يَحْفَظَهُ فَأَنْزَلَ اللَّهُ {لاَ تُحَرِّكْ بِهِ لِسَانَكَ لِتَعْجَلَ بِهِ}

Narrated ‘Aishah (ra): Hind bint ‘Utba came and said, “O Allah’s Messenger! (Before I embraced Islam) there was no family on the surface of the earth I wished to see in degradation more than I did your family, but today there is no family on the surface of the earth I wish to see honored more than I did yours.” The Prophet ﷺ said, “I thought similarly, by Him in whose Hand my soul is!” She further said, “O Allah’s Messenger ! Abu Sufyan is a miser, so, is it sinful of me to feed my children from his property ?” He said, “I do not allow it unless you take for your needs what is just and reasonable.”. – Sahih Al-Bukhari 3825
وَقَالَ عَبْدَانُ أَخْبَرَنَا عَبْدُ اللَّهِ، أَخْبَرَنَا يُونُسُ، عَنِ الزُّهْرِيِّ، حَدَّثَنِي عُرْوَةُ، أَنَّ عَائِشَةَ ـ رضى الله عنها ـ قَالَتْ جَاءَتْ هِنْدٌ بِنْتُ عُتْبَةَ قَالَتْ يَا رَسُولَ اللَّهِ، مَا كَانَ عَلَى ظَهْرِ الأَرْضِ مِنْ أَهْلِ خِبَاءٍ أَحَبُّ إِلَىَّ أَنْ يَذِلُّوا مِنْ أَهْلِ خِبَائِكَ، ثُمَّ مَا أَصْبَحَ الْيَوْمَ عَلَى ظَهْرِ الأَرْضِ أَهْلُ خِبَاءٍ أَحَبَّ إِلَىَّ أَنْ يَعِزُّوا مِنْ أَهْلِ خِبَائِكَ. قَالَ وَأَيْضًا وَالَّذِي نَفْسِي بِيَدِهِ، قَالَتْ يَا رَسُولَ اللَّهِ إِنَّ أَبَا سُفْيَانَ رَجُلٌ مِسِّيكٌ، فَهَلْ عَلَىَّ حَرَجٌ أَنْ أُطْعِمَ مِنَ الَّذِي لَهُ عِيَالَنَا قَالَ " لاَ أُرَاهُ إِلاَّ بِالْمَعْرُوفِ "

Narrated Abu Huraira: Allah’s Messenger ﷺ used to seek refuge with Allah from the difficult moment of a calamity and from being overtaken by destruction and from being destined to an evil end, and from the malicious joy of enemies. Sufyan said, “This narration contained three items only, but I added one. I do not know which one that was.”. – Sahih Al-Bukhari 6347
حَدَّثَنَا عَلِيُّ بْنُ عَبْدِ اللَّهِ، حَدَّثَنَا سُفْيَانُ، حَدَّثَنِي سُمَىٌّ، عَنْ أَبِي صَالِحٍ، عَنْ أَبِي هُرَيْرَةَ، كَانَ رَسُولُ اللَّهِ صلى الله عليه وسلم يَتَعَوَّذُ مِنْ جَهْدِ الْبَلاَءِ، وَدَرَكِ الشَّقَاءِ، وَسُوءِ الْقَضَاءِ، وَشَمَاتَةِ الأَعْدَاءِ. قَالَ سُفْيَانُ الْحَدِيثُ ثَلاَثٌ زِدْتُ أَنَا وَاحِدَةً، لاَ أَدْرِي أَيَّتُهُنَّ هِيَ

Narrated ‘Amr bin Ash-Sharid: Al-Miswar bin Makhrama came and put his hand on my shoulder and I accompanied him to Sa’d. Abu Rafi’ said to Al-Miswar, “Won’t you order this (i.e. Sa’d) to buy my house which is in my yard?” Sa’d said, “I will not offer more than four hundred in installments over a fixed period.” Abu Rafi said, “I was offered five hundred cash but I refused. Had I not heard the Prophet ﷺ saying, ‘A neighbor is more entitled to receive the care of his neighbor,’ I would not have sold it to you.” The narrator said, to Sufyan: Ma’mar did not say so. Sufyan said, “But he did say so to me.” Some people said, “If someone wants to sell a house and deprived somebody of the right of preemption, he has the right to play a trick to render the preemption invalid. And that is by giving the house to the buyer as a present and marking its boundaries and giving it to him. The buyer then gives the seller one-thousand Dirham as compensation in which case the preemptor loses his right of preemption.". – Sahih Al-Bukhari 6977

حَدَّثَنَا عَلِيُّ بْنُ عَبْدِ اللَّهِ، حَدَّثَنَا سُفْيَانُ، عَنْ إِبْرَاهِيمَ بْنِ مَيْسَرَةَ، سَمِعْتُ عَمْرَو بْنَ الشَّرِيدِ، قَالَ جَاءَ الْمِسْوَرُ بْنُ مَخْرَمَةَ فَوَضَعَ يَدَهُ عَلَى مَنْكِبِي، فَانْطَلَقْتُ مَعَهُ إِلَى سَعْدٍ فَقَالَ أَبُو رَافِعٍ لِلْمِسْوَرِ أَلاَ تَأْمُرُ هَذَا أَنْ يَشْتَرِيَ مِنِّي بَيْتِي الَّذِي فِي دَارِي. فَقَالَ لاَ أَزِيدُهُ عَلَى أَرْبَعِمِائَةٍ، إِمَّا مُقَطَّعَةٍ وَإِمَّا مُنَجَّمَةٍ. قَالَ أُعْطِيتُ خَمْسَمِائَةٍ نَقْدًا، فَمَنَعْتُهُ، وَلَوْلاَ أَنِّي سَمِعْتُ النَّبِيَّ صلى الله عليه وسلم يَقُولُ " الْجَارُ أَحَقُّ بِصَقَبِهِ ". مَا بِعْتُكَهُ أَوْ قَالَ مَا أَعْطَيْتُكَهُ. قُلْتُ لِسُفْيَانَ إِنَّ مَعْمَرًا لَمْ يَقُلْ هَكَذَا. قَالَ لَكِنَّهُ قَالَ لِي هَكَذَا. وَقَالَ بَعْضُ النَّاسِ إِذَا أَرَادَ أَنْ يَبِيعَ الشُّفْعَةَ فَلَهُ أَنْ يَحْتَالَ حَتَّى يُبْطِلَ الشُّفْعَةَ فَيَهَبُ الْبَائِعُ لِلْمُشْتَرِي الدَّارَ، وَيَحُدُّهَا وَيَدْفَعُهَا إِلَيْهِ، وَيُعَوِّضُهُ الْمُشْتَرِي أَلْفَ دِرْهَمٍ، فَلاَ يَكُونُ لِلشَّفِيعِ فِيهَا شُفْعَةٌ

Narrated Um Habiba: (daughter of Abu Sufyan) I said, "O Allah's Messenger ﷺ ! Marry my sister. The daughter of Abu Sufyan." The Prophet ﷺ said, "Do you like that?" I replied, "Yes, for even now I am not your only wife and I like that my sister should share the good with me." The Prophet ﷺ said, "But that is not lawful for me." I said, We have heard that you want to marry the daughter of Abu Salama." He said, "(You mean) the daughter of Um Salama?" I said, "Yes." He said, "Even if she were not my step-daughter, she would be unlawful for me to marry as she is my foster niece. I and Abu Salama were suckled by Thuwaiba. So you should not present to me your daughters or your sisters (in marriage)." Narrated 'Urwa: Thuwaiba was the freed slave girl of Abu Lahb whom he had manumitted, and then she suckled the Prophet. When Abu Lahb died, one of his relatives saw him in a dream in a very bad state and asked him, "What have you encountered?" Abu Lahb said, "I have not found any rest since I left you, except that I have been given water to drink in this (the space between his thumb and other fingers) and that is because of my manumitting Thuwaiba.". – Sahih Al-Bukhari 5101

حَدَّثَنَا الْحَكَمُ بْنُ نَافِعٍ، أَخْبَرَنَا شُعَيْبٌ، عَنِ الزُّهْرِيِّ، قَالَ أَخْبَرَنِي عُرْوَةُ بْنُ الزُّبَيْرِ، أَنَّ زَيْنَبَ ابْنَةَ أَبِي سَلَمَةَ، أَخْبَرَتْهُ أَنَّ أُمَّ حَبِيبَةَ بِنْتَ أَبِي سُفْيَانَ أَخْبَرَتْهَا أَنَّهَا، قَالَتْ يَا رَسُولَ اللَّهِ انْكِحْ أُخْتِي بِنْتَ أَبِي سُفْيَانَ فَقَالَ " أَوَتُحِبِّينَ ذَلِكَ ". فَقُلْتُ نَعَمْ، لَسْتُ لَكَ بِمُخْلِيَةٍ، وَأَحَبُّ مَنْ شَارَكَنِي فِي خَيْرٍ أُخْتِي. فَقَالَ النَّبِيُّ صلى الله عليه وسلم " إِنَّ ذَلِكَ لاَ يَحِلُّ لِي ". قُلْتُ فَإِنَّا نُحَدَّثُ أَنَّكَ تُرِيدُ أَنْ تَنْكِحَ بِنْتَ أَبِي سَلَمَةَ. قَالَ " بِنْتَ أُمِّ سَلَمَةَ ". قُلْتُ نَعَمْ. فَقَالَ " لَوْ أَنَّهَا لَمْ تَكُنْ رَبِيبَتِي فِي حَجْرِي مَا حَلَّتْ لِي إِنَّهَا لاَبْنَةُ أَخِي مِنَ الرَّضَاعَةِ، أَرْضَعَتْنِي وَأَبَا سَلَمَةَ ثُوَيْبَةُ فَلاَ تَعْرِضْنَ عَلَىَّ بَنَاتِكُنَّ وَلاَ أَخَوَاتِكُنَّ ". قَالَ عُرْوَةُ وَثُوَيْبَةُ مَوْلاَةٌ لأَبِي لَهَبٍ كَانَ أَبُو لَهَبٍ أَعْتَقَهَا فَأَرْضَعَتِ النَّبِيَّ صلى الله عليه وسلم فَلَمَّا مَاتَ أَبُو لَهَبٍ أُرِيَهُ بَعْضُ أَهْلِهِ بِشَرِّ حِيبَةٍ قَالَ لَهُ مَاذَا لَقِيتَ قَالَ أَبُو لَهَبٍ لَمْ أَلْقَ بَعْدَكُمْ غَيْرَ أَنِّي سُقِيتُ فِي هَذِهِ بِعَتَاقَتِي ثُوَيْبَةَ.

Narrated `Abdullah bin `Abbas: Abu Sufyan told me that Heraclius said to him, "When I inquired you what he (i.e. Muhammad) ordered you, you replied that he ordered you to establish the prayer, to speak the truth, to be chaste, to keep promises and to pay back trusts." Then Heraclius added, "These are really the qualities of a prophet.". – Sahih Al-Bukhari 2681

حَدَّثَنَا إِبْرَاهِيمُ بْنُ حَمْزَةَ، حَدَّثَنَا إِبْرَاهِيمُ بْنُ سَعْدٍ، عَنْ صَالِحٍ، عَنِ ابْنِ شِهَابٍ، عَنْ عُبَيْدِ اللَّهِ بْنِ عَبْدِ اللَّهِ، أَنَّ عَبْدَ اللَّهِ بْنَ عَبَّاسٍ ـ رضى الله عنهما ـ أَخْبَرَهُ قَالَ أَخْبَرَنِي أَبُو سُفْيَانَ، أَنَّ هِرَقْلَ، قَالَ لَهُ سَأَلْتُكَ مَاذَا يَأْمُرُكُمْ فَزَعَمْتَ أَنَّهُ أَمَرَكُمْ بِالصَّلاَةِ وَالصِّدْقِ وَالْعَفَافِ وَالْوَفَاءِ بِالْعَهْدِ وَأَدَاءِ الأَمَانَةِ. قَالَ وَهَذِهِ صِفَةُ نَبِيٍّ

Abu Sufyan added, "By Allah, I remained low and was sure that his religion would be victorious till Allah converted me to Islam, though I disliked it.". – Sahih al-Bukhari 2940, 2941

قَالَ أَبُو سُفْيَانَ وَاللَّهِ مَا زِلْتُ ذَلِيلاً مُسْتَيْقِنًا بِأَنَّ أَمْرَهُ سَيَظْهَرُ، حَتَّى أَدْخَلَ اللَّهُ قَلْبِي الإِسْلاَمَ وَأَنَا كَارِهٌ.

Muʿāwiya ibn Abī Sufyān

معاوية بن أبي سفيان

Narrated `Ikrima bin Khalid: Ibn `Umar said, "I went to Hafsa while water was dribbling from her twined braids. I said, 'The condition of the people is as you see, and no authority has been given to me.' Hafsa said, (to me), 'Go to them, and as they (i.e. the people) are waiting for you, and I am afraid your absence from them will produce division amongst them.' " So Hafsa did not leave Ibn `Umar till we went to them. When the people differed. Muawiya addressed the people saying, "'If anybody wants to say anything in this matter of the Caliphate, he should show up and not conceal himself, for we are more rightful to be a Caliph than he and his father." On that, Habib bin Masalama said (to Ibn `Umar), "Why don't you reply to him (i.e. Muawiya)?" `Abdullah bin `Umar said, "I untied my garment that was going round my back and legs while I was sitting and was about to say, 'He who fought against you and against your father for the sake of Islam, is more rightful to be a Caliph,' but I was afraid that my statement might produce differences amongst the people and cause bloodshed, and my statement might be interpreted not as I intended. (So I kept quiet) remembering what Allah has prepared in the Gardens of Paradise (for those who are patient and prefer the Hereafter to this worldly life)." Habib said, "You did what kept you safe and secure (i.e. you were wise in doing so). – Sahih Al-Bukhari 4108

حَدَّثَنِي إِبْرَاهِيمُ بْنُ مُوسَى، أَخْبَرَنَا هِشَامٌ، عَنْ مَعْمَرٍ، عَنِ الزُّهْرِيِّ، عَنْ سَالِمٍ، عَنِ ابْنِ عُمَرَ، قَالَ وَأَخْبَرَنِي ابْنُ طَاوُسٍ، عَنْ عِكْرِمَةَ بْنِ خَالِدٍ، عَنِ ابْنِ عُمَرَ، قَالَ دَخَلْتُ عَلَى حَفْصَةَ وَنَسْوَاتُهَا تَنْطُفُ، قُلْتُ قَدْ كَانَ مِنْ أَمْرِ النَّاسِ مَا تَرَيْنَ، فَلَمْ يُجْعَلْ لِي مِنَ الأَمْرِ شَىْءٌ. فَقَالَتِ الْحَقْ فَإِنَّهُمْ يَنْتَظِرُونَكَ، وَأَخْشَى أَنْ يَكُونَ فِي احْتِبَاسِكَ عَنْهُمْ فُرْقَةٌ. فَلَمْ تَدَعْهُ حَتَّى ذَهَبَ، فَلَمَّا تَفَرَّقَ النَّاسُ خَطَبَ مُعَاوِيَةُ قَالَ مَنْ كَانَ يُرِيدُ أَنْ يَتَكَلَّمَ فِي هَذَا الأَمْرِ فَلْيُطْلِعْ لَنَا قَرْنَهُ، فَلَنَحْنُ أَحَقُّ بِهِ مِنْهُ وَمِنْ أَبِيهِ. قَالَ حَبِيبُ بْنُ مَسْلَمَةَ فَهَلاَّ أَجَبْتَهُ قَالَ عَبْدُ اللَّهِ فَحَلَلْتُ حُبْوَتِي وَهَمَمْتُ أَنْ أَقُولَ أَحَقُّ بِهَذَا الأَمْرِ مِنْكَ مَنْ قَاتَلَكَ وَأَبَاكَ عَلَى الإِسْلاَمِ. فَخَشِيتُ أَنْ أَقُولَ كَلِمَةً تُفَرِّقُ بَيْنَ الْجَمْعِ، وَتَسْفِكُ الدَّمَ، وَيُحْمَلُ عَنِّي غَيْرُ ذَلِكَ، فَذَكَرْتُ مَا أَعَدَّ اللَّهُ فِي الْجِنَانِ. قَالَ حَبِيبٌ حُفِظْتَ وَعُصِمْتَ. قَالَ مَحْمُودٌ عَنْ عَبْدِ الرَّزَّاقِ

Narrated Yusuf bin Mahak: Marwan had been appointed as the governor of Hijaz by Muawiya. He delivered a sermon and mentioned Yazid bin Muawiya so that the people might take the oath of allegiance to him as the successor of his father (Muawiya). Then `Abdur Rahman bin Abu Bakr told him something whereupon Marwan ordered that he be arrested. But `Abdur-Rahman entered `Aisha's house and they could not arrest him. Marwan said, "It is he (`AbdurRahman) about whom Allah revealed this Verse:-- 'And the one who says to his parents: 'Fie on you! Do you hold out the promise to me..?'" On that, `Aisha said from behind a screen, "Allah did not reveal anything from the Qur'an about us except what was connected with the declaration of my innocence (of the slander). – Sahih Al-Bukhari 4827

حَدَّثَنَا مُوسَى بْنُ إِسْمَاعِيلَ، حَدَّثَنَا أَبُو عَوَانَةَ، عَنْ أَبِي بِشْرٍ، عَنْ يُوسُفَ بْنِ مَاهَكَ، قَالَ كَانَ مَرْوَانُ عَلَى الْحِجَازِ اسْتَعْمَلَهُ مُعَاوِيَةُ، فَخَطَبَ فَجَعَلَ يَذْكُرُ يَزِيدَ بْنَ مُعَاوِيَةَ، لِكَىْ يُبَايِعَ لَهُ بَعْدَ أَبِيهِ، فَقَالَ لَهُ عَبْدُ الرَّحْمَنِ بْنُ أَبِي بَكْرٍ شَيْئًا، فَقَالَ خُذُوهُ. فَدَخَلَ بَيْتَ عَائِشَةَ فَلَمْ يَقْدِرُوا {عَلَيْهِ} فَقَالَ مَرْوَانُ إِنَّ هَذَا الَّذِي أَنْزَلَ اللَّهُ فِيهِ {وَالَّذِي قَالَ لِوَالِدَيْهِ أُفٍّ لَكُمَا أَتَعِدَانِنِي}. فَقَالَتْ عَائِشَةُ مِنْ وَرَاءِ الْحِجَابِ مَا أَنْزَلَ اللَّهُ فِينَا شَيْئًا مِنَ الْقُرْآنِ إِلاَّ أَنَّ اللَّهَ أَنْزَلَ عُذْرِي.

Asma' said to Al-Qāsim bin Muhammad and Ibn Abū Atiq, "I inherited some land in the forest from my sister Aishah, and Mu'āwiya offered _me one hundred thousand for it, but I give it to both of you as a gift. " Sahih Al-Bukhari Vol. 3 pg 447

و قالت اسماء للقائم بن محمد و ابن أبي عتيق : ورثت عن اختي عاءشة بالعتبة ، و قد اعطاني به معاوية ماءة الف فهو لكما

Narrated Ibn 'Abbas: Qariba,The daughter of Abi Umaiyya, was the wife of 'Umar bin Al-Khattab. 'Umar divorced her and then Mu'awiyya bin Abi Sufyan married her. Similarly, Um Al-Hakam, the daughter of Abi Sufyan was the wife of 'lyad bin Ghanm Al-Fihri. He divorced her and then 'Abdullah bin 'Uthman Al-Thaqafi married her – .Sahih al-Bukhari 5287
وَقَالَ عَطَاءٌ عَنِ ابْنِ عَبَّاسٍ، كَانَتْ قَرِيبَةُ بِنْتُ أَبِي أُمَيَّةَ عِنْدَ عُمَرَ بْنِ الْخَطَّابِ فَطَلَّقَهَا، فَتَزَوَّجَهَا مُعَاوِيَةُ بْنُ أَبِي سُفْيَانَ، وَكَانَتْ أُمُّ الْحَكَمِ ابْنَةُ أَبِي سُفْيَانَ تَحْتَ عِيَاضِ بْنِ غَنْمٍ الْفِهْرِيِّ فَطَلَّقَهَا، فَتَزَوَّجَهَا عَبْدُ اللَّهِ بْنُ عُثْمَانَ الثَّقَفِيُّ

Narrated Abu Umama bin Sahl bin Hunaif: I heard Muawiya bin Abi Sufyan (repeating the statements of the Adhan) while he was sitting on the pulpit. When the Mu'adh-dhin pronounced the Adhan saying, "Allahu-Akbar, Allahu Akbar", Muawiya said: "Allah Akbar, Allahu Akbar." And when the Mu'adh-dhin said, "Ash-hadu an la ilaha illal-lah (I testify that none has the right to be worshipped but Allah)", Muawiya said, "And (so do) I". When he said, "Ash-hadu anna Muhammadan Rasulullah" (I testify that Muhammad is Allah's Apostle), Muawiya said, "And (so do) I". When the Adhan was finished, Muawiya said, "O people, when the Mu'adh-dhin pronounced the Adhan I heard Allah's Messenger ﷺ on this very pulpit saying what you have just heard me saying." – Sahih al-Bukhari 914
حَدَّثَنَا ابْنُ مُقَاتِلٍ، قَالَ أَخْبَرَنَا عَبْدُ اللَّهِ، قَالَ أَخْبَرَنَا أَبُو بَكْرِ بْنُ عُثْمَانَ بْنِ سَهْلِ بْنِ حُنَيْفٍ، عَنْ أَبِي أُمَامَةَ بْنِ سَهْلِ بْنِ حُنَيْفٍ، قَالَ سَمِعْتُ مُعَاوِيَةَ بْنَ أَبِي سُفْيَانَ،، وَهُوَ جَالِسٌ عَلَى الْمِنْبَرِ، أَذَّنَ الْمُؤَذِّنُ قَالَ اللَّهُ أَكْبَرُ اللَّهُ أَكْبَرُ. قَالَ مُعَاوِيَةُ اللَّهُ أَكْبَرُ اللَّهُ أَكْبَرُ. قَالَ أَشْهَدُ أَنْ لاَ إِلَهَ إِلاَّ اللَّهُ. فَقَالَ مُعَاوِيَةُ وَأَنَا. فَقَالَ أَشْهَدُ أَنَّ مُحَمَّدًا رَسُولُ اللَّهِ. فَقَالَ مُعَاوِيَةُ وَأَنَا. فَلَمَّا أَنْ قَضَى التَّأْذِينَ قَالَ يَا أَيُّهَا النَّاسُ إِنِّي سَمِعْتُ رَسُولَ اللَّهِ صلى الله عليه وسلم عَلَى هَذَا الْمَجْلِسِ حِينَ أَذَّنَ الْمُؤَذِّنُ يَقُولُ مَا سَمِعْتُمْ مِنِّي مِنْ مَقَالَتِي

Narrated Muhammad bin `Abdur-Rahman bin Nawfal Al-Qurashi: I asked `Urwa bin Az-Zubair regarding the Hajj of the Prophet ﷺ. Urwa replied, "Aisha narrated, 'When the Prophet ﷺ reached Mecca, the first thing he started with was the ablution, then he performed Tawaf of the Ka`ba and his intention was not `Umra alone (but Hajj and `Umra together).' " Later Abu Bakr I performed the Hajj and the first thing he started with was Tawaf of the Ka`ba and it was not `Umra alone (but Hajj and `Umra together). And then `Umar did the same. Then `Uthman performed the Hajj and the first thing he started with was Tawaf of the Ka`ba and it was not `Umra alone. And then Muawiya and `Abdullah bin `Umar did the same. I performed Hajj with Ibn Az-Zubair and the first thing he started with was Tawaf of the Ka`ba and it was not `Umra alone, (but Hajj and `Umra together). Then I saw the Muhajirin (Emigrants) and Ansar doing the same and it was not `Umra alone. And the last person I saw doing the same was Ibn `Umar, and he did not do another `Umra after finishing the first. Now here is Ibn `Umar present amongst the people! They neither ask him nor anyone of the previous ones. And all these people, on entering Mecca, would not start with anything unless they had performed Tawaf of the Ka`ba, and would not finish their Ihram. And no doubt, I saw my mother and my aunt, on entering Mecca doing nothing before performing Tawaf of the Ka`ba, and they would not finish their Ihram. And my mother informed me that she, her sister, Az-Zubair and such and such persons had assumed Ihram for `Umra and after passing their hands over the Corner (the Black Stone) (i.e. finishing their Umra) they finished their Ihram." – Sahih al-Bukhari 1641, 1642
حَدَّثَنَا أَحْمَدُ بْنُ عِيسَى، حَدَّثَنَا ابْنُ وَهْبٍ، قَالَ أَخْبَرَنِي عَمْرُو بْنُ الْحَارِثِ، عَنْ مُحَمَّدِ بْنِ عَبْدِ الرَّحْمَنِ بْنِ نَوْفَلٍ الْقُرَشِيِّ، أَنَّهُ سَأَلَ عُرْوَةَ بْنَ الزُّبَيْرِ فَقَالَ قَدْ حَجَّ النَّبِيُّ صلى الله عليه وسلم فَأَخْبَرَتْنِي عَائِشَةُ ـ رضى الله عنها ـ أَنَّهُ أَوَّلُ شَىْءٍ بَدَأَ بِهِ حِينَ قَدِمَ أَنَّهُ تَوَضَّأَ ثُمَّ طَافَ بِالْبَيْتِ ثُمَّ لَمْ تَكُنْ عُمْرَةً، ثُمَّ حَجَّ أَبُو بَكْرٍ ـ رضى الله عنه ـ فَكَانَ أَوَّلَ شَىْءٍ بَدَأَ بِهِ الطَّوَافُ بِالْبَيْتِ ثُمَّ لَمْ تَكُنْ عُمْرَةً. ثُمَّ عُمَرُ ـ رضى الله عنه ـ مِثْلُ ذَلِكَ. ثُمَّ حَجَّ عُثْمَانُ ـ رضى الله عنه ـ فَرَأَيْتُهُ أَوَّلُ شَىْءٍ بَدَأَ بِهِ الطَّوَافُ بِالْبَيْتِ ثُمَّ لَمْ تَكُنْ عُمْرَةٌ، ثُمَّ مُعَاوِيَةُ وَعَبْدُ اللَّهِ بْنُ عُمَرَ، ثُمَّ حَجَجْتُ مَعَ أَبِي الزُّبَيْرِ بْنِ الْعَوَّامِ، فَكَانَ أَوَّلَ شَىْءٍ بَدَأَ بِهِ الطَّوَافُ بِالْبَيْتِ، ثُمَّ لَمْ تَكُنْ عُمْرَةٌ، ثُمَّ رَأَيْتُ الْمُهَاجِرِينَ وَالأَنْصَارَ يَفْعَلُونَ ذَلِكَ، ثُمَّ لَمْ تَكُنْ عُمْرَةٌ، ثُمَّ آخِرُ مَنْ رَأَيْتُ

فَعَلَ ذَلِكَ ابْنُ عُمَرَ ثُمَّ لَمْ يَنْقُضْهَا عُمْرَةً، وَهَذَا ابْنُ عُمَرَ عِنْدَهُمْ فَلاَ يَسْأَلُونَهُ، وَلاَ أَحَدٌ مِمَّنْ مَضَى، مَا كَانُوا يَبْدَءُونَ بِشَىْءٍ حَتَّى يَضَعُوا أَقْدَامَهُمْ مِنَ الطَّوَافِ بِالْبَيْتِ، ثُمَّ لاَ يَحِلُّونَ، وَقَدْ رَأَيْتُ أُمِّي وَخَالَتِي، حِينَ تَقْدَمَانِ لاَ تَبْتَدِئَانِ بِشَىْءٍ أَوَّلَ مِنَ الْبَيْتِ، تَطُوفَانِ بِهِ، ثُمَّ لاَ تَحِلاَّنِ. وَقَدْ أَخْبَرَتْنِي أُمِّي، أَنَّهَا أَهَلَّتْ هِيَ وَأُخْتُهَا وَالزُّبَيْرُ وَفُلاَنٌ وَفُلاَنٌ بِعُمْرَةٍ، فَلَمَّا مَسَحُوا الرُّكْنَ حَلُّوا.

Narrated Hisham Ibn `Urwa from his father who said: While I was a youngster, I asked `Aisha the wife of the Prophet. "What about the meaning of the Statement of Allah; "Verily! (the mountains) As-Safa and Al Marwa, are among the symbols of Allah. So, it is not harmful if those who perform Hajj or `Umra of the House (Ka`ba at Mecca) to perform the going (Tawaf) between them? (2.158) I understand (from that) that there is no harm if somebody does not perform the Tawaf between them." `Aisha replied, "No, for if it were as you are saying, then the recitation would have been like this: 'It is not harmful not to perform Tawaf between them.' This verse was revealed in connection with the Ansar who used to assume the Ihram for the idol Manat which was put beside a place called Qudaid and those people thought it not right to perform the Tawaf of As- Safa and Al-Marwa. When Islam came, they asked Allah's Messenger ﷺ about that, and Allah revealed:-- "Verily! (the mountains) As-Safa and Al-Marwa Are among the symbols of Allah. So, it is not harmful of those who perform Hajj or `Umra of the House (Ka`ba at Mecca) to perform the going (Tawaf) between them." (2.158) Sufyan and Abu Muawiya added from Hisham (from `Aisha): "The Hajj or `Umra of the person who does not perform the going (Tawaf) between As-Safa and Al-Marwa is incomplete in Allah's sight. – Sahih al-Bukhari 1790

حَدَّثَنَا عَبْدُ اللَّهِ بْنُ يُوسُفَ، أَخْبَرَنَا مَالِكٌ، عَنْ هِشَامِ بْنِ عُرْوَةَ، عَنْ أَبِيهِ، أَنَّهُ قَالَ قُلْتُ لِعَائِشَةَ ـ رضى الله عنها ـ زَوْجِ النَّبِيِّ صلى الله عليه وسلم وَأَنَا يَوْمَئِذٍ حَدِيثُ السِّنِّ أَرَأَيْتِ قَوْلَ اللَّهِ تَبَارَكَ وَتَعَالَى {إِنَّ الصَّفَا وَالْمَرْوَةَ مِنْ شَعَائِرِ اللَّهِ فَمَنْ حَجَّ الْبَيْتَ أَوِ اعْتَمَرَ فَلاَ جُنَاحَ عَلَيْهِ أَنْ يَطَّوَّفَ بِهِمَا} فَلاَ أُرَى عَلَى أَحَدٍ شَيْئًا أَنْ لاَ يَطَّوَّفَ بِهِمَا. فَقَالَتْ عَائِشَةُ كَلاَّ، لَوْ كَانَتْ كَمَا تَقُولُ كَانَتْ فَلاَ جُنَاحَ عَلَيْهِ أَنْ لاَ يَطَّوَّفَ بِهِمَا. إِنَّمَا أُنْزِلَتْ هَذِهِ الآيَةُ فِي الأَنْصَارِ كَانُوا يُهِلُّونَ لِمَنَاةَ، وَكَانَتْ مَنَاةُ حَذْوَ قُدَيْدٍ، وَكَانُوا يَتَحَرَّجُونَ أَنْ يَطُوفُوا بَيْنَ الصَّفَا وَالْمَرْوَةِ، فَلَمَّا جَاءَ الإِسْلاَمُ سَأَلُوا رَسُولَ اللَّهِ صلى الله عليه وسلم عَنْ ذَلِكَ، فَأَنْزَلَ اللَّهُ تَعَالَى {إِنَّ الصَّفَا وَالْمَرْوَةَ مِنْ شَعَائِرِ اللَّهِ فَمَنْ حَجَّ الْبَيْتَ أَوِ اعْتَمَرَ فَلاَ جُنَاحَ عَلَيْهِ أَنْ يَطَّوَّفَ بِهِمَا}. زَادَ سُفْيَانُ وَأَبُو مُعَاوِيَةَ عَنْ هِشَامٍ مَا أَتَمَّ اللَّهُ حَجَّ امْرِئٍ وَلاَ عُمْرَتَهُ لَمْ يَطُفْ بَيْنَ الصَّفَا وَالْمَرْوَةِ

Narrated Muhammad bin Jubair bin Mut`im: That while he was with a delegation from Quraish to Muawiya, the latter heard the news that `Abdullah bin `Amr bin Al-`As said that there would be a king from the tribe of Qahtan. On that Muawiya became angry, got up and then praised Allah as He deserved, and said, "Now then, I have heard that some men amongst you narrate things which are neither in the Holy Book, nor have been told by Allah's Messenger ﷺ. Those men are the ignorant amongst you. Beware of such hopes as make the people go astray, for I heard Allah's Messenger ﷺ saying, 'Authority of ruling will remain with Quraish, and whoever bears hostility to them, Allah will destroy him as long as they abide by the laws of the religion.' ". – Sahih Al-Bukhari 3500

حَدَّثَنَا أَبُو الْيَمَانِ، أَخْبَرَنَا شُعَيْبٌ، عَنِ الزُّهْرِيِّ، قَالَ كَانَ مُحَمَّدُ بْنُ جُبَيْرِ بْنِ مُطْعِمٍ يُحَدِّثُ أَنَّهُ بَلَغَ مُعَاوِيَةَ وَهْوَ عِنْدَهُ فِي وَفْدٍ مِنْ قُرَيْشٍ أَنَّ عَبْدَ اللَّهِ بْنَ عَمْرِو بْنِ الْعَاصِ يُحَدِّثُ أَنَّهُ سَيَكُونُ مَلِكٌ مِنْ قَحْطَانَ، فَغَضِبَ مُعَاوِيَةُ، فَقَامَ فَأَثْنَى عَلَى اللَّهِ بِمَا هُوَ أَهْلُهُ، ثُمَّ قَالَ أَمَّا بَعْدُ فَإِنَّهُ بَلَغَنِي أَنَّ رِجَالاً مِنْكُمْ يَتَحَدَّثُونَ أَحَادِيثَ لَيْسَتْ فِي كِتَابِ اللَّهِ، وَلاَ تُؤْثَرُ عَنْ رَسُولِ اللَّهِ صلى الله عليه وسلم، فَأُولَئِكَ جُهَّالُكُمْ، فَإِيَّاكُمْ وَالأَمَانِيَّ الَّتِي تُضِلُّ أَهْلَهَا، فَإِنِّي سَمِعْتُ رَسُولَ اللَّهِ صلى الله عليه وسلم يَقُولُ " إِنَّ هَذَا الأَمْرَ فِي قُرَيْشٍ، لاَ يُعَادِيهِمْ أَحَدٌ إِلاَّ كَبَّهُ اللَّهُ عَلَى وَجْهِهِ، مَا أَقَامُوا الدِّينَ "

Narrated Ibn Abu Mulaika: Muawiya offered one rak`a witr prayer after the `Isha prayer, and at that time a freed slave of Ibn `Abbas was present. He (i.e. the slave) went to Ibn `Abbas (and told him that Muawiya offered one rak`a witr prayer). Ibn `Abbas said, "Leave him, for he was in the company of Allah's Messenger. – Sahih Al-Bukhari 3764

حَدَّثَنَا الْحَسَنُ بْنُ بِشْرٍ، حَدَّثَنَا الْمُعَافَى، عَنْ عُثْمَانَ بْنِ الأَسْوَدِ، عَنِ ابْنِ أَبِي مُلَيْكَةَ، قَالَ أَوْتَرَ مُعَاوِيَةُ بَعْدَ الْعِشَاءِ بِرَكْعَةٍ وَعِنْدَهُ مَوْلًى لاِبْنِ عَبَّاسٍ، فَأَتَى ابْنَ عَبَّاسٍ فَقَالَ دَعْهُ، فَإِنَّهُ صَحِبَ رَسُولَ اللَّهِ صلى الله عليه وسلم.

Narrated Humran bin Aban: Muawiya said (to the people), "You offer a prayer which we, who were the companions of the Prophet ﷺ never saw the Prophet ﷺ offering, and he forbade its offering," i.e. the two rak`at after the compulsory `Asr prayer. – Sahih Al-Bukhari 3766
حَدَّثَنِي عَمْرُو بْنُ عَبَّاسٍ، حَدَّثَنَا مُحَمَّدُ بْنُ جَعْفَرٍ، حَدَّثَنَا شُعْبَةُ، عَنْ أَبِي التَّيَّاحِ، قَالَ سَمِعْتُ حُمْرَانَ بْنَ أَبَانَ، عَنْ مُعَاوِيَةَ ـ رضى الله عنه ـ قَالَ إِنَّكُمْ لَتُصَلُّونَ صَلاَةً لَقَدْ صَحِبْنَا النَّبِيَّ صلى الله عليه وسلم فَمَا رَأَيْنَاهُ يُصَلِّيهَا، وَلَقَدْ نَهَى عَنْهُمَا، يَعْنِي الرَّكْعَتَيْنِ بَعْدَ الْعَصْرِ.

Narrated Zaid bin Wahb: I passed by (visited) Abu Dhar at Ar-Rabadha and said to him, "What has brought you to this land?" He said, "We were at Sham and I recited the Verse: "They who hoard up gold and silver and spend them not in the way of Allah; announce to them a painful torment, " (9.34) where upon Muawiya said, 'This Verse is not for us, but for the people of the Scripture.' Then I said, 'But it is both for us (Muslim) and for them.' ". – Sahih Al-Bukhari 4660
حَدَّثَنَا قُتَيْبَةُ بْنُ سَعِيدٍ، حَدَّثَنَا جَرِيرٌ، عَنْ حُصَيْنٍ، عَنْ زَيْدِ بْنِ وَهْبٍ، قَالَ مَرَرْتُ عَلَى أَبِي ذَرٍّ بِالرَّبَذَةِ فَقُلْتُ مَا أَنْزَلَكَ بِهَذِهِ الأَرْضِ قَالَ كُنَّا بِالشَّأْمِ فَقَرَأْتُ {وَالَّذِينَ يَكْنِزُونَ الذَّهَبَ وَالْفِضَّةَ وَلاَ يُنْفِقُونَهَا فِي سَبِيلِ اللَّهِ فَبَشِّرْهُمْ بِعَذَابٍ أَلِيمٍ} قَالَ مُعَاوِيَةُ مَا هَذِهِ فِينَا، مَا هَذِهِ إِلاَّ فِي أَهْلِ الْكِتَابِ. قَالَ قُلْتُ إِنَّهَا لَفِينَا وَفِيهِمْ

Narrated `Abdullah bin Az-Zubair: When Az-Zubair got up during the battle of Al-Jamal, he called me and I stood up beside him, and he said to me, "O my son! Today one will be killed either as an oppressor or as an oppressed one. I see that I will be killed as an oppressed one. My biggest worry is my debts. Do you think, if we pay the debts, there will be something left for us from our money?" Az-Zubair added, "O my son! Sell our property and pay my debts." Az-Zubair then willed one-third of his property and willed one-third of that portion to his sons; namely, `Abdullah's sons. He said, "One-third of the one third. If any property is left after the payment of the debts, one-third (of the one-third of what is left) is to be given to your sons." (Hisham, a sub-narrator added, "Some of the sons of `Abdullah were equal in age to the sons of Az-Zubair e.g. Khubaib and `Abbas. `Abdullah had nine sons and nine daughters at that time." (The narrator `Abdullah added:) My father (Az-Zubair) went on drawing my attention to his debts saying, "If you should fail to pay part of the debts, appeal to my Master to help you." By Allah! I could not understand what he meant till I asked, "O father! Who is your Master?" He replied, "Allah (is my Master)." By Allah, whenever I had any difficulty regarding his debts, I would say, "Master of Az-Zubair! Pay his debts on his behalf ." and Allah would (help me to) pay it. Az-Zubair was martyred leaving no Dinar or Dirham but two pieces of land, one of which was (called) Al-Ghaba, and eleven houses in Medina, two in Basra, one in Kufa and one in Egypt. In fact, the source of the debt which he owed was, that if somebody brought some money to deposit with him. Az-Zubair would say, "No, (I won't keep it as a trust), but I take it as a debt, for I am afraid it might be lost." Az-Zubair was never appointed governor or collector of the tax of Kharaj or any other similar thing, but he collected his wealth (from the war booty he gained) during the holy battles he took part in, in the company of the Prophet, Abu Bakr, `Umar, and `Uthman. (`Abdullah bin Az-Zubair added: ) When I counted his debt, it turned to be two million and two hundred thousand. (The sub-narrator added: ) Hakim bin Hizam met `Abdullah bin Zubair and asked, "O my nephew! How much is the debt of my brother?" `Abdullah kept it as a secret and said, "One hundred thousand," Hakim said, "By Allah! I don't think your property will cover it." On that `Abdullah said to him, "What if it is two million and two hundred thousand?" Hakim said, "I don't think you can pay

it; so if you are unable to pay all of it, I will help you." Az- Zubair had already bought Al-Ghaba for one hundred and seventy thousand. `Abdullah sold it for one million and six hundred thousand. Then he called the people saying, "Any person who has any money claim on Az-Zubair should come to us in Al-Ghaba." There came to him `Abdullah bin Ja`far whom Az-Zubair owed four hundred thousand. He said to `Abdullah bin Az-Zubair, "If you wish I will forgive you the debt." `Abdullah (bin Az-Zubair) said, "No." Then Ibn Ja`far said, "If you wish you can defer the payment if you should defer the payment of any debt." Ibn Az-Zubair said, "No." `Abdullah bin Ja`far said, "Give me a piece of the land." `Abdullah bin AzZubair said (to him), "Yours is the land extending from this place to this place." So, `Abdullah bin Az-Zubair sold some of the property (including the houses) and paid his debt perfectly, retaining four and a half shares from the land (i.e. Al-Ghaba). He then went to Mu'awlya while `Amr bin `Uthman, Al-Mundhir bin Az- Zubair and Ibn Zam`a were sitting with him. Mu'awiya asked, "At what price have you appraised Al- Ghaba?" He said, "One hundred thousand for each share," Muawiya asked, "How many shares have been left?" `Abdullah replied, "Four and a half shares." Al-Mundhir bin Az-Zubair said, "I would like to buy one share for one hundred thousand." `Amr bin `Uthman said, "I would like to buy one share for one hundred thousand." Ibn Zam`a said, "I would like to buy one share for one hundred thousand." Muawiya said, "How much is left now?" `Abdullah replied, "One share and a half." Muawiya said, "I would like to buy it for one hundred and fifty thousand." `Abdullah also sold his part to Muawiya six hundred thousand. When Ibn AzZubair had paid all the debts. Az-Zubair's sons said to him, "Distribute our inheritance among us." He said, "No, by Allah, I will not distribute it among you till I announce in four successive Hajj seasons, 'Would those who have money claims on Az-Zubair come so that we may pay them their debt." So, he started to announce that in public in every Hajj season, and when four years had elapsed, he distributed the inheritance among the inheritors. Az-Zubair had four wives, and after the one-third of his property was excluded (according to the will), each of his wives received one million and two hundred thousand. So the total amount of his property was fifty million and two hundred thousand.
– Sahih Al-Bukhari 3129

حَدَّثَنَا إِسْحَاقُ بْنُ إِبْرَاهِيمَ، قَالَ قُلْتُ لأَبِي أُسَامَةَ أَحَدَّثَكُمْ هِشَامُ بْنُ عُرْوَةَ عَنْ أَبِيهِ عَنْ عَبْدِ اللَّهِ بْنِ الزُّبَيْرِ قَالَ لَمَّا وَقَفَ الزُّبَيْرُ يَوْمَ الْجَمَلِ دَعَانِي، فَقُمْتُ إِلَى جَنْبِهِ فَقَالَ يَا بُنَىِّ، إِنَّهُ لاَ يُقْتَلُ الْيَوْمَ إِلاَّ ظَالِمٌ أَوْ مَظْلُومٌ، وَإِنِّي لاَ أُرَانِي إِلاَّ سَأُقْتَلُ الْيَوْمَ مَظْلُومًا، وَإِنَّ مِنْ أَكْبَرِ هَمِّي لَدَيْنِي، أَفَتُرَى يُبْقِي دَيْنُنَا مِنْ مَالِنَا شَيْئًا فَقَالَ يَا بُنَىِّ بِعْ مَالَنَا فَاقْضِ دَيْنِي. وَأَوْصَى بِالثُّلُثِ، وَثُلُثِهِ لِبَنِيهِ، يَعْنِي عَبْدَ اللَّهِ بْنَ الزُّبَيْرِ يَقُولُ ثُلُثُ الثُّلُثِ، فَإِنْ فَضَلَ مِنْ مَالِنَا فَضْلٌ بَعْدَ قَضَاءِ الدَّيْنِ شَىْءٌ فَثُلُثُهُ لِوَلَدِكَ. قَالَ هِشَامٌ وَكَانَ بَعْضُ وَلَدِ عَبْدِ اللَّهِ قَدْ وَازَى بَعْضَ بَنِي الزُّبَيْرِ خُبَيْبٌ وَعَبَّادٌ، وَلَهُ يَوْمَئِذٍ تِسْعَةُ بَنِينَ وَتِسْعُ بَنَاتٍ. قَالَ عَبْدُ اللَّهِ فَجَعَلَ يُوصِينِي بِدَيْنِهِ وَيَقُولُ يَا بُنَىِّ، إِنْ عَجَزْتَ عَنْهُ فِي شَىْءٍ فَاسْتَعِنْ عَلَيْهِ مَوْلاَىَ. قَالَ فَوَاللَّهِ مَا دَرَيْتُ مَا أَرَادَ حَتَّى قُلْتُ يَا أَبَتِ مَنْ مَوْلاَكَ قَالَ اللَّهُ. قَالَ فَوَاللَّهِ مَا وَقَعْتُ فِي كُرْبَةٍ مِنْ دَيْنِهِ إِلاَّ قُلْتُ يَا مَوْلَى الزُّبَيْرِ، اقْضِ عَنْهُ دَيْنَهُ. فَيَقْضِيهِ، فَقُتِلَ الزُّبَيْرُ ـ رضى الله عنه ـ وَلَمْ يَدَعْ دِينَارًا وَلاَ دِرْهَمًا، إِلاَّ أَرَضِينَ مِنْهَا الْغَابَةُ، وَإِحْدَى عَشْرَةَ دَارًا بِالْمَدِينَةِ، وَدَارَيْنِ بِالْبَصْرَةِ، وَدَارًا بِالْكُوفَةِ، وَدَارًا بِمِصْرَ. قَالَ وَإِنَّمَا كَانَ دَيْنُهُ الَّذِي عَلَيْهِ أَنَّ الرَّجُلَ كَانَ يَأْتِيهِ بِالْمَالِ فَيَسْتَوْدِعُهُ إِيَّاهُ فَيَقُولُ الزُّبَيْرُ لاَ وَلَكِنَّهُ سَلَفٌ، فَإِنِّي أَخْشَى عَلَيْهِ الضَّيْعَةَ، وَمَا وَلِيَ إِمَارَةً قَطُّ وَلاَ جِبَايَةَ خَرَاجٍ وَلاَ شَيْئًا، إِلاَّ أَنْ يَكُونَ فِي غَزْوَةٍ مَعَ النَّبِيِّ صلى الله عليه وسلم أَوْ مَعَ أَبِي بَكْرٍ وَعُمَرَ وَعُثْمَانَ ـ رضى الله عنهم ـ قَالَ عَبْدُ اللَّهِ بْنُ الزُّبَيْرِ فَحَسَبْتُ مَا عَلَيْهِ مِنَ الدَّيْنِ فَوَجَدْتُهُ أَلْفَىْ أَلْفٍ وَمِائَتَىْ أَلْفٍ قَالَ فَلَقِيَ حَكِيمُ بْنُ حِزَامٍ عَبْدَ اللَّهِ بْنَ الزُّبَيْرِ فَقَالَ يَا ابْنَ أَخِي، كَمْ عَلَى أَخِي مِنَ الدَّيْنِ فَكَتَمَهُ. فَقَالَ مِائَةُ أَلْفٍ. فَقَالَ حَكِيمٌ وَاللَّهِ مَا أُرَى أَمْوَالَكُمْ تَسَعُ لِهَذِهِ. فَقَالَ لَهُ عَبْدُ اللَّهِ أَفَرَأَيْتَكَ إِنْ كَانَتْ أَلْفَىْ أَلْفٍ وَمِائَتَىْ أَلْفٍ قَالَ مَا أُرَاكُمْ تُطِيقُونَ هَذَا، فَإِنْ عَجَزْتُمْ عَنْ شَىْءٍ مِنْهُ فَاسْتَعِينُوا بِي. قَالَ وَكَانَ الزُّبَيْرُ اشْتَرَى الْغَابَةَ بِسَبْعِينَ وَمِائَةِ أَلْفٍ، فَبَاعَهَا عَبْدُ اللَّهِ بِأَلْفِ أَلْفٍ وَسِتِّمِائَةِ أَلْفٍ ثُمَّ قَامَ فَقَالَ مَنْ كَانَ لَهُ عَلَى الزُّبَيْرِ حَقٌّ فَلْيُوَافِنَا بِالْغَابَةِ، فَأَتَاهُ عَبْدُ اللَّهِ بْنُ جَعْفَرٍ، وَكَانَ لَهُ عَلَى الزُّبَيْرِ أَرْبَعُمِائَةِ أَلْفٍ فَقَالَ لِعَبْدِ اللَّهِ إِنْ شِئْتُمْ تَرَكْتُهَا لَكُمْ. قَالَ عَبْدُ اللَّهِ لاَ. قَالَ فَإِنْ شِئْتُمْ جَعَلْتُمُوهَا فِيمَا تُؤَخِّرُونَ إِنْ أَخَّرْتُمْ. فَقَالَ عَبْدُ اللَّهِ لاَ. قَالَ قَالَ فَاقْطَعُوا لِي قِطْعَةً. فَقَالَ عَبْدُ اللَّهِ لَكَ مِنْ هَا هُنَا إِلَى هَا هُنَا. قَالَ فَبَاعَ مِنْهَا فَقَضَى دَيْنَهُ فَأَوْفَاهُ، وَبَقِيَ مِنْهَا أَرْبَعَةُ أَسْهُمٍ وَنِصْفٌ، فَقَدِمَ عَلَى مُعَاوِيَةَ وَعِنْدَهُ عَمْرُو بْنُ عُثْمَانَ وَالْمُنْذِرُ بْنُ الزُّبَيْرِ وَابْنُ زَمْعَةَ فَقَالَ لَهُ مُعَاوِيَةُ كَمْ قُوِّمَتِ الْغَابَةُ قَالَ كُلُّ سَهْمٍ مِائَةَ أَلْفٍ. قَالَ كَمْ بَقِيَ قَالَ أَرْبَعَةُ أَسْهُمٍ وَنِصْفٌ. قَالَ الْمُنْذِرُ بْنُ الزُّبَيْرِ قَدْ أَخَذْتُ سَهْمًا بِمِائَةِ أَلْفٍ. قَالَ عَمْرُو بْنُ عُثْمَانَ قَدْ أَخَذْتُ سَهْمًا بِمِائَةِ أَلْفٍ. وَقَالَ ابْنُ زَمْعَةَ قَدْ أَخَذْتُ سَهْمًا بِمِائَةِ أَلْفٍ. فَقَالَ مُعَاوِيَةُ كَمْ بَقِيَ فَقَالَ سَهْمٌ وَنِصْفٌ. قَالَ أَخَذْتُهُ بِخَمْسِينَ وَمِائَةِ أَلْفٍ. قَالَ وَبَاعَ عَبْدُ اللَّهِ بْنُ جَعْفَرٍ نَصِيبَهُ مِنْ

مُعَاوِيَةَ بِسِتِّمِائَةِ أَلْفٍ، فَلَمَّا فَرَغَ ابْنُ الزُّبَيْرِ مِنْ قَضَاءِ دَيْنِهِ قَالَ بَنُو الزُّبَيْرِ اقْسِمْ بَيْنَنَا مِيرَاثَنَا. قَالَ لاَ، وَاللَّهِ لاَ أَقْسِمُ بَيْنَكُمْ حَتَّى أُنَادِيَ بِالْمَوْسِمِ أَرْبَعَ سِنِينَ أَلاَ مَنْ كَانَ لَهُ عَلَى الزُّبَيْرِ دَيْنٌ فَلْيَأْتِنَا فَلْنَقْضِهِ. قَالَ فَجَعَلَ كُلَّ سَنَةٍ يُنَادِي بِالْمَوْسِمِ، فَلَمَّا مَضَى أَرْبَعُ سِنِينَ قَسَمَ بَيْنَهُمْ قَالَ فَكَانَ لِلزُّبَيْرِ أَرْبَعُ نِسْوَةٍ، وَرَفَعَ الثُّلُثَ، فَأَصَابَ كُلَّ امْرَأَةٍ أَلْفُ أَلْفٍ وَمِائَتَا أَلْفٍ، فَجَمِيعُ مَالِهِ خَمْسُونَ أَلْفَ أَلْفٍ وَمِائَتَا أَلْفٍ.

Narrated Anas bin Malik: Allah's Messenger ﷺ used to visit Um Haram bint Milhan she was the wife of 'Ubada bin As-Samit. One day the Prophet ﷺ visited her and she provided him with food and started looking for lice in his head. Then Allah's Messenger ﷺ slept and afterwards woke up smiling. Um Haram asked, "What makes you smile, O Allah's Messenger He said, "Some of my followers were presented before me in my dream as fighters in Allah's Cause, sailing in the middle of the seas like kings on the thrones or like kings sitting on their thrones." (The narrator 'Is-haq is not sure as to which expression was correct). Um Haram added, 'I said, "O Allah's Messenger ﷺ ! Invoke Allah, to make me one of them;" So Allah's Messenger ﷺ invoked Allah for her and then laid his head down (and slept). Then he woke up smiling (again). (Um Haram added): I said, "What makes you smile, O Allah's Messenger ﷺ He said, "Some people of my followers were presented before me (in a dream) as fighters in Allah's Cause." He said the same as he had said before. I said, "O Allah's Messenger ﷺ! Allah to make me from them." He said, "You are among the first ones." Then Um Haram sailed over the sea during the Caliphate of Muawiya bin Abu Sufyan, and she fell down from her riding animal after coming ashore, and died.. – Sahih Al-Bukhari 7001, 7002
حَدَّثَنَا عَبْدُ اللَّهِ بْنُ يُوسُفَ، أَخْبَرَنَا مَالِكٌ، عَنْ إِسْحَاقَ بْنِ عَبْدِ اللَّهِ بْنِ أَبِي طَلْحَةَ، أَنَّهُ سَمِعَ أَنَسَ بْنَ مَالِكٍ، يَقُولُ كَانَ رَسُولُ اللَّهِ صلى الله عليه وسلم يَدْخُلُ عَلَى أُمِّ حَرَامٍ بِنْتِ مِلْحَانَ، وَكَانَتْ تَحْتَ عُبَادَةَ بْنِ الصَّامِتِ، فَدَخَلَ عَلَيْهَا يَوْمًا فَأَطْعَمَتْهُ، وَجَعَلَتْ تَفْلِي رَأْسَهُ، فَنَامَ رَسُولُ اللَّهِ صلى الله عليه وسلم ثُمَّ اسْتَيْقَظَ وَهْوَ يَضْحَكُ. قَالَتْ فَقُلْتُ مَا يُضْحِكُكَ يَا رَسُولَ اللَّهِ قَالَ " نَاسٌ مِنْ أُمَّتِي عُرِضُوا عَلَىَّ، غُزَاةً فِي سَبِيلِ اللَّهِ، يَرْكَبُونَ ثَبَجَ هَذَا الْبَحْرِ، مُلُوكًا عَلَى الأَسِرَّةِ أَوْ مِثْلَ الْمُلُوكِ عَلَى الأَسِرَّةِ ". شَكَّ إِسْحَاقُ. قَالَتْ فَقُلْتُ يَا رَسُولَ اللَّهِ ادْعُ اللَّهَ أَنْ يَجْعَلَنِي مِنْهُمْ، فَدَعَا لَهَا رَسُولُ اللَّهِ صلى الله عليه وسلم ثُمَّ وَضَعَ رَأْسَهُ ثُمَّ اسْتَيْقَظَ وَهْوَ يَضْحَكُ. فَقُلْتُ مَا يُضْحِكُكَ يَا رَسُولَ اللَّهِ قَالَ " نَاسٌ مِنْ أُمَّتِي عُرِضُوا عَلَىَّ، غُزَاةً فِي سَبِيلِ اللَّهِ ". كَمَا قَالَ فِي الأُولَى. قَالَتْ فَقُلْتُ يَا رَسُولَ اللَّهِ ادْعُ اللَّهَ أَنْ يَجْعَلَنِي مِنْهُمْ. قَالَ " أَنْتِ مِنَ الأَوَّلِينَ ". فَرَكِبَتِ الْبَحْرَ فِي زَمَانِ مُعَاوِيَةَ بْنِ أَبِي سُفْيَانَ فَصُرِعَتْ عَنْ دَابَّتِهَا حِينَ خَرَجَتْ مِنَ الْبَحْرِ، فَهَلَكَتْ.

Narrated Habib bin Abi Thabit: I went to Abu Wail to ask him (about those who had rebelled against `Ali). On that Abu Wail said, "We were at Siffin (a city on the bank of the Euphrates, the place where me battle took place between `Ali and Muawiya) A man said, "Will you be on the side of those who are called to consult Allah's Book (to settle the dispute)?" `Ali said, 'Yes (I agree that we should settle the matter in the light of the Qur'an)." ' Some people objected to `Ali's agreement and wanted to fight. On that Sahl bin Hunaif said, 'Blame yourselves! I remember how, on the day of Al-Hudaibiya (i.e. the peace treaty between the Prophet ﷺ and the Quraish pagans), if we had been allowed to choose fighting, we would have fought (the pagans). At that time `Umar came (to the Prophet) and said, "Aren't we on the right (path) and they (pagans) in the wrong? Won't our killed persons go to Paradise, and theirs in the Fire?" The Prophet replied, "Yes." `Umar further said, "Then why should we let our religion be degraded and return before Allah has settled the matter between us?" The Prophet ﷺ said, "O the son of Al-Khattab! No doubt, I am Allah's Messenger ﷺ and Allah will never neglect me." So `Umar left the place angrily and he was so impatient that he went to Abu Bakr and said, "O Abu Bakr! Aren't we on the right (path) and they (pagans) on the wrong?" Abu Bakr said, "O the son of Al-Khattab! He is Allah's Messenger ﷺ and Allah will never neglect him." Then Sura Al-Fath (The Victory) was revealed.". – Sahih Al-Bukhari 4844
حَدَّثَنَا أَحْمَدُ بْنُ إِسْحَاقَ السُّلَمِيُّ، حَدَّثَنَا يَعْلَى، حَدَّثَنَا عَبْدُ الْعَزِيزِ بْنُ سِيَاهٍ، عَنْ حَبِيبِ بْنِ أَبِي ثَابِتٍ، قَالَ أَتَيْتُ أَبَا وَائِلٍ أَسْأَلُهُ فَقَالَ كُنَّا بِصِفِّينَ فَقَالَ رَجُلٌ أَلَمْ تَرَ إِلَى الَّذِينَ يُدْعَوْنَ إِلَى كِتَابِ اللَّهِ. فَقَالَ عَلِيٌّ نَعَمْ. فَقَالَ سَهْلُ بْنُ حُنَيْفٍ اتَّهِمُوا أَنْفُسَكُمْ فَلَقَدْ

رَأَيْتُنَا يَوْمَ الْحُدَيْبِيَةِ ـ يَعْنِي الصُّلْحَ الَّذِي كَانَ بَيْنَ النَّبِيِّ صلى الله عليه وسلم وَالْمُشْرِكِينَ ـ وَلَوْ نَرَى قِتَالاً لَقَاتَلْنَا، فَجَاءَ عُمَرُ فَقَالَ أَلَسْنَا عَلَى الْحَقِّ وَهُمْ عَلَى الْبَاطِلِ أَلَيْسَ قَتْلاَنَا فِي الْجَنَّةِ وَقَتْلاَهُمْ فِي النَّارِ قَالَ " بَلَى ". قَالَ فَفِيمَ أُعْطِي الدَّنِيَّةَ فِي دِينِنَا، وَنَرْجِعُ وَلَمَّا يَحْكُمِ اللَّهُ بَيْنَنَا. فَقَالَ " يَا ابْنَ الْخَطَّابِ إِنِّي رَسُولُ اللَّهِ وَلَنْ يُضَيِّعَنِي اللَّهُ أَبَدًا ". فَرَجَعَ مُتَغَيِّظًا، فَلَمْ يَصْبِرْ حَتَّى جَاءَ أَبَا بَكْرٍ فَقَالَ يَا أَبَا بَكْرٍ أَلَسْنَا عَلَى الْحَقِّ وَهُمْ عَلَى الْبَاطِلِ قَالَ يَا ابْنَ الْخَطَّابِ إِنَّهُ رَسُولُ اللَّهِ صلى الله عليه وسلم وَلَنْ يُضَيِّعَهُ اللَّهُ أَبَدًا. فَنَزَلَتْ سُورَةُ الْفَتْحِ

Marwan ibn al-Hakam ibn Abi al-As ibn Umayya
مروان بن الحكم بن أبي العاص بن أمية

Narrated Qasim bin Muhammad and Sulaiman bin Yasar: That Yahya bin Sa`id bin Al-`As divorced the daughter of `Abdur-Rahman bin Al-Hakarn. `Abdur- Rahman took her to his house. On that `Aisha sent a message to Marwan bin Al-Hakam who was the ruler of Medina, saying, "Fear Allah, and urge your brother) to return her to her house." Marwan (in Sulaiman's version) said, "Abdur-Rahman bin Al-Hakam did not obey me (or had a convincing argument)." (In Al-Qasim's versions Marwan said, "Have you not heard of the case of Fatima bint Qais?" Aisha said, "The case of Fatima bint Qais is not in your favor.' Marwan bin Al-Hakam said to `Aisha, "The reason that made Fatima bint Qais go to her father's house is just applicable to the daughter of `Abdur-Rahman." – Sahih al-Bukhari 5321, 5322

حَدَّثَنَا إِسْمَاعِيلُ، حَدَّثَنَا مَالِكٌ، عَنْ يَحْيَى بْنِ سَعِيدٍ، عَنِ الْقَاسِمِ بْنِ مُحَمَّدٍ، أَنَّهُ سَمِعَهُ يَذْكُرُ، أَنَّ يَحْيَى بْنَ سَعِيدِ بْنِ الْعَاصِ، طَلَّقَ بِنْتَ عَبْدِ الرَّحْمَنِ بْنِ الْحَكَمِ، فَانْتَقَلَهَا عَبْدُ الرَّحْمَنِ، فَأَرْسَلَتْ عَائِشَةُ أُمُّ الْمُؤْمِنِينَ إِلَى مَرْوَانَ وَهْوَ أَمِيرُ الْمَدِينَةِ اتَّقِ اللَّهَ وَارْدُدْهَا إِلَى بَيْتِهَا. قَالَ مَرْوَانُ فِي حَدِيثِ سُلَيْمَانَ إِنَّ عَبْدَ الرَّحْمَنِ بْنَ الْحَكَمِ غَلَبَنِي. وَقَالَ الْقَاسِمُ بْنُ مُحَمَّدٍ أَوَمَا بَلَغَكِ شَأْنُ فَاطِمَةَ بِنْتِ قَيْسٍ قَالَتْ لاَ يَضُرُّكَ أَنْ لاَ تَذْكُرَ حَدِيثَ فَاطِمَةَ. فَقَالَ مَرْوَانُ بْنُ الْحَكَمِ إِنْ كَانَ بِكِ شَرٌّ فَحَسْبُكِ مَا بَيْنَ هَذَيْنِ مِنَ الشَّرِّ.

Narrated Yusuf bin Mahak: Marwan had been appointed as the governor of Hijaz by Muawiya. He delivered a sermon and mentioned Yazid bin Muawiya so that the people might take the oath of allegiance to him as the successor of his father (Muawiya). Then `Abdur Rahman bin Abu Bakr told him something whereupon Marwan ordered that he be arrested. But `Abdur-Rahman entered `Aisha's house and they could not arrest him. Marwan said, "It is he (`AbdurRahman) about whom Allah revealed this Verse:-- 'And the one who says to his parents: 'Fie on you! Do you hold out the promise to me..?'" On that, `Aisha said from behind a screen, "Allah did not reveal anything from the Qur'an about us except what was connected with the declaration of my innocence (of the slander.) – Sahih al-Bukhari 4827

حَدَّثَنَا مُوسَى بْنُ إِسْمَاعِيلَ، حَدَّثَنَا أَبُو عَوَانَةَ، عَنْ أَبِي بِشْرٍ، عَنْ يُوسُفَ بْنِ مَاهَكَ، قَالَ كَانَ مَرْوَانُ عَلَى الْحِجَازِ اسْتَعْمَلَهُ مُعَاوِيَةُ، فَخَطَبَ فَجَعَلَ يَذْكُرُ يَزِيدَ بْنَ مُعَاوِيَةَ، لِكَىْ يُبَايَعَ لَهُ بَعْدَ أَبِيهِ، فَقَالَ لَهُ عَبْدُ الرَّحْمَنِ بْنُ أَبِي بَكْرٍ شَيْئًا، فَقَالَ خُذُوهُ. فَدَخَلَ بَيْتَ عَائِشَةَ فَلَمْ يَقْدِرُوا {عَلَيْهِ} فَقَالَ مَرْوَانُ إِنَّ هَذَا الَّذِي أَنْزَلَ اللَّهُ فِيهِ {وَالَّذِي قَالَ لِوَالِدَيْهِ أُفٍّ لَكُمَا أَتَعِدَانِنِي}. فَقَالَتْ عَائِشَةُ مِنْ وَرَاءِ الْحِجَابِ مَا أَنْزَلَ اللَّهُ فِينَا شَيْئًا مِنَ الْقُرْآنِ إِلاَّ أَنَّ اللَّهَ أَنْزَلَ عُذْرِي

Narrated Sa`id Al-Umawi: I was with Marwan and Abu Huraira and heard Abu Huraira saying, "I heard the trustworthy, truly inspired one (i.e. the Prophet ﷺ) saying, 'The destruction of my followers will be brought about by the hands of some youngsters from Quraish." Marwan asked, "Youngsters?" Abu Huraira said, "If you wish, I would name them: They are the children of so-and-so and the children of so-and-so." – Sahih al-Bukhari 3605

حَدَّثَنَا أَحْمَدُ بْنُ مُحَمَّدٍ الْمَكِّيُّ، حَدَّثَنَا عَمْرُو بْنُ يَحْيَى بْنِ سَعِيدٍ الأُمَوِيُّ، عَنْ جَدِّهِ، قَالَ كُنْتُ مَعَ مَرْوَانَ وَأَبِي هُرَيْرَةَ فَسَمِعْتُ أَبَا هُرَيْرَةَ، يَقُولُ سَمِعْتُ الصَّادِقَ الْمَصْدُوقَ، يَقُولُ " هَلاَكُ أُمَّتِي عَلَى يَدَىْ غِلْمَةٍ مِنْ قُرَيْشٍ ". فَقَالَ مَرْوَانُ غِلْمَةٌ. قَالَ أَبُو هُرَيْرَةَ إِنْ شِئْتَ أَنْ أُسَمِّيَهُمْ بَنِي فُلاَنٍ وَبَنِي فُلاَنٍ

Narrated Al-Miswar bin Makhrama and Marwan bin Al-Hakam: (one of them said more than his friend): The Prophet ﷺ set out in the company of more than onethousand of his companions in the year of Al-Hudaibiya, and when he reached Dhul-Hulaifa, he garlanded his Hadi (i.e. sacrificing animal), assumed the state of Ihram for `Umra from that place and sent a spy of his from Khuzaa'ah (tribe). The Prophet ﷺ proceeded on till he reached (a village called) Ghadir-al-Ashtat. There his spy came and said, "The Quraish (infidels) have collected a great number of people against you, and they have collected against you the Ethiopians, and they will fight with you, and will stop you from entering the Ka`ba and prevent you." The Prophet ﷺ said, "O people! Give me your opinion. Do you recommend that I should destroy the families and offspring of those who want to stop us from the Ka`ba? If they should come to us (for peace) then Allah will destroy a spy from the pagans, or otherwise we will leave them in a miserable state." On that Abu Bakr said, "O Allah Apostle! You have come with the intention of visiting this House (i.e. Ka`ba) and you do not want to kill or fight anybody. So proceed to it, and whoever should stop us from it, we will fight him." On that the Prophet ﷺ said, "Proceed on, in the Name of Allah!" – Sahih al-Bukhari 4178, 4179

حَدَّثَنَا عَبْدُ اللَّهِ بْنُ مُحَمَّدٍ، حَدَّثَنَا سُفْيَانُ، قَالَ سَمِعْتُ الزُّهْرِيَّ، حِينَ حَدَّثَ هَذَا الْحَدِيثَ،، حَفِظْتُ بَعْضَهُ، وَثَبَّتَنِي مَعْمَرٌ عَنْ عُرْوَةَ بْنِ الزُّبَيْرِ، عَنِ الْمِسْوَرِ بْنِ مَخْرَمَةَ، وَمَرْوَانَ بْنِ الْحَكَمِ، يَزِيدُ أَحَدُهُمَا عَلَى صَاحِبِهِ قَالاَ خَرَجَ النَّبِيُّ صلى الله عليه وسلم عَامَ الْحُدَيْبِيَةِ فِي بِضْعَ عَشْرَةَ مِائَةً مِنْ أَصْحَابِهِ، فَلَمَّا أَتَى ذَا الْحُلَيْفَةِ قَلَّدَ الْهَدْىَ، وَأَشْعَرَهُ، وَأَحْرَمَ مِنْهَا بِعُمْرَةٍ، وَبَعَثَ عَيْنًا لَهُ مِنْ خُزَاعَةَ، وَسَارَ النَّبِيُّ صلى الله عليه وسلم حَتَّى كَانَ بِغَدِيرِ الأَشْطَاطِ، أَتَاهُ عَيْنُهُ قَالَ إِنَّ قُرَيْشًا جَمَعُوا لَكَ جُمُوعًا، وَقَدْ جَمَعُوا لَكَ الأَحَابِيشَ، وَهُمْ مُقَاتِلُوكَ وَصَادُّوكَ عَنِ الْبَيْتِ وَمَانِعُوكَ. فَقَالَ " أَشِيرُوا أَيُّهَا النَّاسُ عَلَىَّ، أَتَرَوْنَ أَنْ أَمِيلَ إِلَى عِيَالِهِمْ وَذَرَارِيِّ هَؤُلاَءِ الَّذِينَ يُرِيدُونَ أَنْ يَصُدُّونَا عَنِ الْبَيْتِ، فَإِنْ يَأْتُونَا كَانَ اللَّهُ عَزَّ وَجَلَّ قَدْ قَطَعَ عَيْنًا مِنَ الْمُشْرِكِينَ، وَإِلاَّ تَرَكْنَاهُمْ مَحْرُوبِينَ ". قَالَ أَبُو بَكْرٍ يَا رَسُولَ اللَّهِ، خَرَجْتَ عَامِدًا لِهَذَا الْبَيْتِ، لاَ تُرِيدُ قَتْلَ أَحَدٍ وَلاَ حَرْبَ أَحَدٍ، فَتَوَجَّهْ لَهُ، فَمَنْ صَدَّنَا عَنْهُ قَاتَلْنَاهُ. قَالَ " امْضُوا عَلَى اسْمِ اللَّهِ ".

Narrated `Urwa bin Az-Zubair: That he heard Marwan bin Al-Hakam and Al-Miswar bin Makhrama relating one of the events that happened to Allah's Messenger ﷺ in the `Umra of Al-Hudaibiya. They said, "When Allah's Messenger ﷺ concluded the truce with Suhail bin `Amr on the day of Al-Hudaibiya, one of the conditions which Suhail bin `Amr stipulated, was his saying (to the Prophet), "If anyone from us (i.e. infidels) ever comes to you, though he has embraced your religion, you should return him to us, and should not interfere between us and him." Suhail refused to conclude the truce with Allah's Messenger ﷺ except on this condition. The believers disliked this condition and got disgusted with it and argued about it. But when Suhail refused to conclude the truce with Allah's Messenger except on that condition, Allah's Apostle concluded it. Accordingly, Allah's Messenger ﷺ then returned Abu Jandal bin Suhail to his father, Suhail bin `Amr, and returned every man coming to him from them during that period even if he was a Muslim. The believing women Emigrants came (to Medina) and Um Kulthum, the daughter of `Uqba bin Abi Mu'ait was one of those who came to Allah's Messenger ﷺ and she was an adult at that time. Her relatives came, asking Allah's Messenger ﷺ to return her to them, and in this connection, Allah revealed the Verses dealing with the believing (women). – Sahih al-Bukhari 4180, 4181

حَدَّثَنِي إِسْحَاقُ، أَخْبَرَنَا يَعْقُوبُ، حَدَّثَنِي ابْنُ أَخِي ابْنِ شِهَابٍ، عَنْ عَمِّهِ، أَخْبَرَنِي عُرْوَةُ بْنُ الزُّبَيْرِ، أَنَّهُ سَمِعَ مَرْوَانَ بْنَ الْحَكَمِ، وَالْمِسْوَرَ بْنَ مَخْرَمَةَ، يُخْبِرَانِ خَبَرًا مِنْ خَبَرِ رَسُولِ اللَّهِ صلى الله عليه وسلم فِي عُمْرَةِ الْحُدَيْبِيَةِ فَكَانَ فِيمَا أَخْبَرَنِي عُرْوَةُ عَنْهُمَا أَنَّهُ لَمَّا كَاتَبَ رَسُولُ اللَّهِ صلى الله عليه وسلم سُهَيْلَ بْنَ عَمْرٍو، يَوْمَ الْحُدَيْبِيَةِ عَلَى قَضِيَّةِ الْمُدَّةِ، وَكَانَ فِيمَا اشْتَرَطَ سُهَيْلُ بْنُ عَمْرٍو أَنَّهُ قَالَ لاَ يَأْتِيكَ مِنَّا أَحَدٌ وَإِنْ كَانَ عَلَى دِينِكَ إِلاَّ رَدَدْتَهُ إِلَيْنَا، وَخَلَّيْتَ بَيْنَنَا وَبَيْنَهُ. وَأَبَى سُهَيْلٌ أَنْ يُقَاضِيَ رَسُولَ اللَّهِ صلى الله عليه وسلم إِلاَّ عَلَى ذَلِكَ، فَكَرِهَ الْمُؤْمِنُونَ ذَلِكَ وَامَّعَضُوا، فَتَكَلَّمُوا فِيهِ، فَلَمَّا أَبَى سُهَيْلٌ أَنْ يُقَاضِيَ رَسُولَ اللَّهِ صلى الله عليه وسلم إِلاَّ عَلَى ذَلِكَ، كَاتَبَهُ رَسُولُ اللَّهِ صلى الله عليه وسلم، فَرَدَّ رَسُولُ اللَّهِ صلى الله عليه وسلم أَبَا جَنْدَلِ بْنَ سُهَيْلٍ يَوْمَئِذٍ إِلَى أَبِيهِ سُهَيْلِ بْنِ عَمْرٍو، وَلَمْ يَأْتِ رَسُولَ اللَّهِ صلى الله عليه وسلم أَحَدٌ مِنَ الرِّجَالِ

إلاَّ رَدَّهُ فِي تِلْكَ الْمُدَّةِ، وَإِنْ كَانَ مُسْلِمًا، وَجَاءَتِ الْمُؤْمِنَاتُ مُهَاجِرَاتٍ، فَكَانَتْ أُمُّ كُلْثُومٍ بِنْتُ عُقْبَةَ بْنِ مُعَيْطٍ مِمَّنْ خَرَجَ إِلَى رَسُولِ اللَّهِ صلى الله عليه وسلم وَهْيَ عَاتِقٌ، فَجَاءَ أَهْلُهَا يَسْأَلُونَ رَسُولَ اللَّهِ صلى الله عليه وسلم أَنْ يَرْجِعَهَا إِلَيْهِمْ، حَتَّى أَنْزَلَ اللَّهُ تَعَالَى فِي الْمُؤْمِنَاتِ مَا أَنْزَلَ

Narrated Sahl bin Sa`d As-Sa`idi: I saw Marwan bin Al-Hakam sitting in the Mosque. So I came forward and sat by his side. He told us that Zaid bin Thabit had told him that Allah's Messenger ﷺ had dictated to him the Divine Verse: "Not equal are those believers who sit (at home) and those who strive hard and fight in the Cause of Allah with their wealth and lives.' (4.95) Zaid said, "Ibn-Maktum came to the Prophet ﷺ while he was dictating to me that very Verse. On that Ibn Um Maktum said, "O Allah's Messenger ! If I had power, I would surely take part in Jihad." He was a blind man. So Allah sent down revelation to His Apostle while his thigh was on mine and it became so heavy for me that I feared that my thigh would be broken. Then that state of the Prophet was over after Allah revealed "...except those who are disabled (by injury or are blind or lame etc.) (4.95) – Sahih al-Bukhari 2832
حَدَّثَنَا عَبْدُ الْعَزِيزِ بْنُ عَبْدِ اللَّهِ، حَدَّثَنَا إِبْرَاهِيمُ بْنُ سَعْدٍ الزُّهْرِيُّ، قَالَ حَدَّثَنِي صَالِحُ بْنُ كَيْسَانَ، عَنِ ابْنِ شِهَابٍ، عَنْ سَهْلِ بْنِ سَعْدٍ السَّاعِدِيِّ، أَنَّهُ قَالَ رَأَيْتُ مَرْوَانَ بْنَ الْحَكَمِ جَالِسًا فِي الْمَسْجِدِ، فَأَقْبَلْتُ حَتَّى جَلَسْتُ إِلَى جَنْبِهِ، فَأَخْبَرَنَا أَنَّ زَيْدَ بْنَ ثَابِتٍ أَخْبَرَهُ أَنَّ رَسُولَ اللَّهِ صلى الله عليه وسلم أَمْلَى عَلَيْهِ لاَ يَسْتَوِي الْقَاعِدُونَ مِنَ الْمُؤْمِنِينَ وَالْمُجَاهِدُونَ فِي سَبِيلِ اللَّهِ قَالَ فَجَاءَهُ ابْنُ أُمِّ مَكْتُومٍ وَهُوَ يُمِلُّهَا عَلَىَّ، فَقَالَ يَا رَسُولَ اللَّهِ، لَوْ أَسْتَطِيعُ الْجِهَادَ لَجَاهَدْتُ. وَكَانَ رَجُلاً أَعْمَى، فَأَنْزَلَ اللَّهُ تَبَارَكَ وَتَعَالَى عَلَى رَسُولِهِ صلى الله عليه وسلم وَفَخِذُهُ عَلَى فَخِذِي، فَثَقُلَتْ عَلَىَّ حَتَّى خِفْتُ أَنْ تَرُضَّ فَخِذِي، ثُمَّ سُرِّيَ عَنْهُ، فَأَنْزَلَ اللَّهُ عَزَّ وَجَلَّ {غَيْرُ أُولِي الضَّرَرِ}.

Narrated `Urwa bin Az-Zubair: Marwan bin Al-Hakam and Al-Miswar bin Makhrama told him that when the Muslims were permitted to set free the captives of Hawazin, Allah's Messenger ﷺ said, "I do not know who amongst you has agreed (to it) and who has not. Go back so that your 'Urafa' may submit your decision to us." So the people returned and their 'Urafa' talked to them and then came back to Allah's Messenger ﷺ and told him that the people had given their consent happily and permitted (their captives to be freed). – Sahih al-Bukhari 7176, 7177
حَدَّثَنَا إِسْمَاعِيلُ بْنُ أَبِي أُوَيْسٍ، حَدَّثَنِي إِسْمَاعِيلُ بْنُ إِبْرَاهِيمَ، عَنْ عَمِّهِ، مُوسَى بْنِ عُقْبَةَ قَالَ ابْنُ شِهَابٍ حَدَّثَنِي عُرْوَةُ بْنُ الزُّبَيْرِ، أَنَّ مَرْوَانَ بْنَ الْحَكَمِ، وَالْمِسْوَرَ بْنَ مَخْرَمَةَ، أَخْبَرَاهُ أَنَّ رَسُولَ اللَّهِ صلى الله عليه وسلم قَالَ حِينَ أَذِنَ لَهُمُ الْمُسْلِمُونَ فِي عِتْقِ سَبْيِ هَوَازِنَ "إِنِّي لاَ أَدْرِي مَنْ أَذِنَ مِنْكُمْ مِمَّنْ لَمْ يَأْذَنْ، فَارْجِعُوا حَتَّى يَرْفَعَ إِلَيْنَا عُرَفَاؤُكُمْ أَمْرَكُمْ ". فَرَجَعَ النَّاسُ فَكَلَّمَهُمْ عُرَفَاؤُهُمْ، فَرَجَعُوا إِلَى رَسُولِ اللَّهِ صلى الله عليه وسلم فَأَخْبَرُوهُ أَنَّ النَّاسَ قَدْ طَيَّبُوا وَأَذِنُوا

Narrated 'Ubaidullah bin 'Abdullah bin 'Utbah: It was narrated from 'Ubaidullah bin 'Abdullah bin 'Utbah that during the reign of Marwan, 'Abdullah bin 'Amr bin 'Uthman, who was a young man, issued a final divorce to the daughter of Sa'eed bin Zaid, whose mother was Bint Qais. Her maternal aunt, Fatimah bint Qais, sent word to her telling her to move from the house of 'Abdullah bin 'Amr. Marwan heard of that and he sent word to the daughter of Sa'eed, telling her to go back to her home, and asking her why she had moved from her home before her 'Iddah was over? She sent word to him telling him that her maternal aunt had told her to do that. Fatimah bint Qais said that she had been married to Abu 'Amr bin Hafs, and when the Messenger of Allah appointed 'Ali bin Abi Talib as governor of Yemen, he went out with him and sent word to her that she was divorced with the third Talaq. He told Al-Harith bin Hisham and 'Ayyash bin Abi Rai'ah to spend on her. She sent word to Al-Harith and 'Ayyash asking them what her husband had told them to spend on her, and they said: 'By Allah, she has no right to any maintenance from us, unless she is pregnant, and she cannot come into our home without our permission.' She said that she came to the Messenger of Allah and told him about that, and he stated that they were correct. Fatimah said: 'Where should I move to, O Messenger of Allah?' He said: 'Move to the home of Ibn Umm Maktum, the blind man whom Allah, the Mighty and Sublime, named in His Book.' Fatimah said: 'So I observed my 'Iddah there. He was a man who has lost his sight, so I used to take off my garments in his house, until the Messenger of Allah married me to Usamah bin Zaid.' Marwan criticized her for that and said: 'I have never heard this Hadith from anyone before you. I will continue to follow the ruling that the people have been following.'" – Sunan an-Nasa'I 3222

أَخْبَرَنَا كَثِيرُ بْنُ عُبَيْدٍ، قَالَ حَدَّثَنَا مُحَمَّدُ بْنُ حَرْبٍ، عَنِ الزُّبَيْدِيِّ، عَنِ الزُّهْرِيِّ، عَنْ عُبَيْدِ اللَّهِ بْنِ عَبْدِ اللَّهِ بْنِ عُتْبَةَ، أَنَّ عَبْدَ اللَّهِ بْنَ عَمْرِو بْنِ عُثْمَانَ، طَلَّقَ وَهُوَ غُلاَمٌ شَابٌّ فِي إِمَارَةِ مَرْوَانَ ابْنَةَ سَعِيدِ بْنِ زَيْدٍ وَأُمُّهَا بِنْتُ قَيْسٍ الْبَتَّةَ فَأَرْسَلَتْ إِلَيْهَا خَالَتُهَا فَاطِمَةُ بِنْتُ قَيْسٍ تَأْمُرُهَا بِالاِنْتِقَالِ مِنْ بَيْتِ عَبْدِ اللَّهِ بْنِ عَمْرٍو وَسَمِعَ بِذَلِكَ مَرْوَانُ فَأَرْسَلَ إِلَى ابْنَةِ سَعِيدٍ فَأَمَرَهَا أَنْ تَرْجِعَ إِلَى مَسْكَنِهَا وَسَأَلَهَا مَا حَمَلَهَا عَلَى الاِنْتِقَالِ مِنْ قَبْلِ أَنْ تَعْتَدَّ فِي مَسْكَنِهَا حَتَّى تَنْقَضِيَ عِدَّتُهَا فَأَرْسَلَتْ إِلَيْهِ تُخْبِرُهُ أَنَّ خَالَتَهَا أَمَرَتْهَا بِذَلِكَ فَزَعَمَتْ فَاطِمَةُ بِنْتُ قَيْسٍ أَنَّهَا كَانَتْ تَحْتَ أَبِي عَمْرِو بْنِ حَفْصٍ فَلَمَّا أَمَّرَ رَسُولُ اللَّهِ صلى الله عليه وسلم عَلِيَّ بْنَ أَبِي طَالِبٍ عَلَى الْيَمَنِ خَرَجَ مَعَهُ وَأَرْسَلَ إِلَيْهَا بِتَطْلِيقَةٍ هِيَ بَقِيَّةُ طَلاَقِهَا وَأَمَرَ لَهَا الْحَارِثَ بْنَ هِشَامٍ وَعَيَّاشَ بْنَ أَبِي رَبِيعَةَ بِنَفَقَتِهَا فَأَرْسَلَتْ – زَعَمَتْ – إِلَى الْحَارِثِ وَعَيَّاشٍ تَسْأَلُهُمَا الَّذِي أَمَرَ لَهَا بِهِ زَوْجُهَا فَقَالاَ وَاللَّهِ مَا لَهَا عِنْدَنَا نَفَقَةٌ إِلاَّ أَنْ تَكُونَ حَامِلاً وَمَا لَهَا أَنْ تَكُونَ فِي مَسْكَنِنَا إِلاَّ بِإِذْنِنَا فَزَعَمَتْ أَنَّهَا أَتَتْ رَسُولَ اللَّهِ صلى الله عليه وسلم فَذَكَرَتْ ذَلِكَ لَهُ فَصَدَّقَهُمَا . قَالَتْ فَاطِمَةُ فَأَيْنَ أَنْتَقِلُ يَا رَسُولَ اللَّهِ قَالَ " انْتَقِلِي عِنْدَ ابْنِ أُمِّ مَكْتُومٍ الأَعْمَى الَّذِي سَمَّاهُ اللَّهُ عَزَّ وَجَلَّ فِي كِتَابِهِ " . قَالَتْ فَاطِمَةُ فَاعْتَدَدْتُ عِنْدَهُ وَكَانَ رَجُلاً قَدْ ذَهَبَ بَصَرُهُ فَكُنْتُ أَضَعُ ثِيَابِي عِنْدَهُ حَتَّى أَنْكَحَهَا رَسُولُ اللَّهِ صلى الله عليه وسلم أُسَامَةَ بْنَ زَيْدٍ فَأَنْكَرَ ذَلِكَ عَلَيْهَا مَرْوَانُ وَقَالَ لَمْ أَسْمَعْ هَذَا الْحَدِيثَ مِنْ أَحَدٍ قَبْلَكِ وَسَآخُذُ بِالْقَضِيَّةِ الَّتِي وَجَدْنَا النَّاسَ عَلَيْهَا . مُخْتَصَرٌ

Narrated Marwan bin Al-Hakam and Al-Miswar bin Makhrama: When the delegates of the tribe of Hawazin came to the Prophetﷺ they requested him to return their property and their captives. He said to them, "This concerns also other people along with me as you see, and the best statement to me is the true one, so you may choose one of two alternatives; either the captives or the property and (I have not distributed the booty for) I have been waiting for you." When the Prophetﷺ had returned from Ta'if, he waited for them for more than ten nights. When they came to know that the Prophetﷺ would not return except one of the two, they chose their captives. The Prophet then stood up amongst the Muslims, Glorified and Praised Allah as He deserved, and then said, "Then after: These brothers of yours have come to you with repentance and I see it proper to return their captives, so whoever amongst you likes to do that as a favor, then he can do it, and whoever of you wants to stick to his share till we pay him from the very first Fai (i.e. war booty) which Allah will give us, then he can do so." The people said, "We return (the captives) to them willingly as a favor, O Allah's Messenger "! The Prophetﷺ said, "I do not know who of you has given his consent and who has not; so go back and your leaders may present your decision to me." The people went away, and their leaders discussed the matter with them, and then came to the Prophetﷺ to tell him that all of them had given their consent (to return the captives) willingly. (Az-Zuhn, the sub-narrator said, "This is what we know about the captives, of Hawazin.") – Sahih al-Bukhari 2607, 2608

حَدَّثَنَا يَحْيَى بْنُ بُكَيْرٍ، حَدَّثَنَا اللَّيْثُ، عَنْ عُقَيْلٍ، عَنِ ابْنِ شِهَابٍ، عَنْ عُرْوَةَ، أَنَّ مَرْوَانَ بْنَ الْحَكَمِ، وَالْمِسْوَرَ بْنَ مَخْرَمَةَ، أَخْبَرَاهُ أَنَّ النَّبِيَّ صلى الله عليه وسلم قَالَ حِينَ جَاءَهُ وَفْدُ هَوَازِنَ مُسْلِمِينَ، فَسَأَلُوهُ أَنْ يَرُدَّ إِلَيْهِمْ أَمْوَالَهُمْ وَسَبْيَهُمْ فَقَالَ لَهُمْ " مَعِي مَنْ تَرَوْنَ، وَأَحَبُّ الْحَدِيثِ إِلَىَّ أَصْدَقُهُ، فَاخْتَارُوا إِحْدَى الطَّائِفَتَيْنِ إِمَّا السَّبْىَ وَإِمَّا الْمَالَ، وَقَدْ كُنْتُ اسْتَأْنَيْتُ ". وَكَانَ النَّبِيُّ صلى الله عليه وسلم انْتَظَرَهُمْ بِضْعَ عَشْرَةَ لَيْلَةً حِينَ قَفَلَ مِنَ الطَّائِفِ، فَلَمَّا تَبَيَّنَ لَهُمْ أَنَّ النَّبِيَّ صلى الله عليه وسلم غَيْرُ رَادٍّ إِلَيْهِمْ إِلاَّ إِحْدَى الطَّائِفَتَيْنِ قَالُوا فَإِنَّا نَخْتَارُ سَبْيَنَا. فَقَامَ فِي الْمُسْلِمِينَ فَأَثْنَى عَلَى اللَّهِ بِمَا هُوَ أَهْلُهُ ثُمَّ قَالَ " أَمَّا بَعْدُ فَإِنَّ إِخْوَانَكُمْ هَؤُلاَءِ جَاءُونَا تَائِبِينَ، وَإِنِّي رَأَيْتُ أَنْ أَرُدَّ إِلَيْهِمْ سَبْيَهُمْ، فَمَنْ أَحَبَّ مِنْكُمْ أَنْ يُطَيِّبَ ذَلِكَ فَلْيَفْعَلْ، وَمَنْ أَحَبَّ أَنْ يَكُونَ عَلَى حَظِّهِ حَتَّى نُعْطِيَهُ إِيَّاهُ مِنْ أَوَّلِ مَا يُفِيءُ اللَّهُ عَلَيْنَا فَلْيَفْعَلْ ". فَقَالَ النَّاسُ طَيَّبْنَا يَا رَسُولَ اللَّهِ لَهُمْ. فَقَالَ لَهُمْ " إِنَّا لاَ نَدْرِي مَنْ أَذِنَ مِنْكُمْ فِيهِ مِمَّنْ لَمْ يَأْذَنْ، فَارْجِعُوا حَتَّى يَرْفَعَ إِلَيْنَا عُرَفَاؤُكُمْ أَمْرَكُمْ ". فَرَجَعَ النَّاسُ فَكَلَّمَهُمْ عُرَفَاؤُهُمْ، ثُمَّ رَجَعُوا إِلَى النَّبِيِّ صلى الله عليه وسلم فَأَخْبَرُوهُ أَنَّهُمْ طَيَّبُوا وَأَذِنُوا. وَهَذَا الَّذِي بَلَغَنَا مِنْ سَبْىِ هَوَازِنَ هَذَا آخِرُ قَوْلِ الزُّهْرِيِّ، يَعْنِي فَهَذَا الَّذِي بَلَغَنَا

Narrated Sahl bin Sa`d As-Sa`idi: I saw Marwan bin Al-Hakam sitting in the Mosque. So I came forward and sat by his side. He told us that Zaid bin Thabit had told him that Allah's Messenger ﷺ had dictated to him the Divine Verse: "Not equal are those believers who sit (at home) and those who strive hard and fight in the Cause of Allah with their wealth and lives.' (4.95) Zaid said, "Ibn-Maktum came to the Prophet ﷺ while he was dictating to me that very Verse. On that Ibn Um Maktum said, "O Allah's Messenger ﷺ ! If I had power, I would surely take part in Jihad." He was a blind man. So Allah sent down revelation to His Apostle while his thigh was on mine and it became so heavy for me that I feared that my thigh would be broken. Then that state of the Prophet ﷺ was over after Allah revealed "...except those who are disabled (by injury or are blind or lame etc.) (4.95). – Sahih Al-Bukhari 2832

حَدَّثَنَا عَبْدُ الْعَزِيزِ بْنُ عَبْدِ اللَّهِ، حَدَّثَنَا إِبْرَاهِيمُ بْنُ سَعْدٍ الزُّهْرِيُّ، قَالَ حَدَّثَنِي صَالِحُ بْنُ كَيْسَانَ، عَنِ ابْنِ شِهَابٍ، عَنْ سَهْلِ بْنِ سَعْدٍ السَّاعِدِيِّ، أَنَّهُ قَالَ رَأَيْتُ مَرْوَانَ بْنَ الْحَكَمِ جَالِسًا فِي الْمَسْجِدِ، فَأَقْبَلْتُ حَتَّى جَلَسْتُ إِلَى جَنْبِهِ، فَأَخْبَرَنَا أَنَّ زَيْدَ بْنَ ثَابِتٍ أَخْبَرَهُ أَنَّ رَسُولَ اللَّهِ صلى الله عليه وسلم أَمْلَى عَلَيْهِ لاَ يَسْتَوِي الْقَاعِدُونَ مِنَ الْمُؤْمِنِينَ وَالْمُجَاهِدُونَ فِي سَبِيلِ اللَّهِ قَالَ فَجَاءَهُ ابْنُ أُمِّ مَكْتُومٍ وَهُوَ يُمِلُّهَا عَلَىَّ، فَقَالَ يَا رَسُولَ اللَّهِ، لَوْ أَسْتَطِيعُ الْجِهَادَ لَجَاهَدْتُ. وَكَانَ رَجُلاً أَعْمَى، فَأَنْزَلَ اللَّهُ تَبَارَكَ وَتَعَالَى عَلَى رَسُولِهِ صلى الله عليه وسلم وَفَخِذُهُ عَلَى فَخِذِي، فَثَقُلَتْ عَلَىَّ حَتَّى خِفْتُ أَنْ تَرُضَّ فَخِذِي، ثُمَّ سُرِّيَ عَنْهُ، فَأَنْزَلَ اللَّهُ عَزَّ وَجَلَّ {غَيْرُ أُولِي الضَّرَرِ}

Narrated Marwan bin Al-Hakam: `Uthman bin `Affan was afflicted with severe nose-bleeding in the year when such illness was prevelant and that prevented him from performing Hajj, and (because of it) he made his will. A man from Quraish came to him and said, "Appoint your successor." `Uthman asked, "Did the people name him? (i.e. the successor) the man said, "Yes." `Uthman asked, "Who is that?" The man remained silent. Another man came to `Uthman and I think it was Al-Harith. He also said, "Appoint your successor." `Uthman asked, "Did the people name him?" The man replied "Yes." `Uthman said, "Who is that?" The man remained silent. `Uthman said, "Perhaps they have mentioned Az-Zubair?" The man said, "Yes." `Uthman said, "By Him in Whose Hands my life is, he is the best of them as I know, and the dearest of them to Allah's Messenger. – Sahih Al-Bukhari 3717

حَدَّثَنَا خَالِدُ بْنُ مَخْلَدٍ، حَدَّثَنَا عَلِيُّ بْنُ مُسْهِرٍ، عَنْ هِشَامِ بْنِ عُرْوَةَ، عَنْ أَبِيهِ، قَالَ أَخْبَرَنِي مَرْوَانُ بْنُ الْحَكَمِ، قَالَ أَصَابَ عُثْمَانَ بْنَ عَفَّانَ رُعَافٌ شَدِيدٌ سَنَةَ الرُّعَافِ، حَتَّى حَبَسَهُ عَنِ الْحَجِّ وَأَوْصَى، فَدَخَلَ عَلَيْهِ رَجُلٌ مِنْ قُرَيْشٍ قَالَ اسْتَخْلِفْ. قَالَ وَقَالُوهُ قَالَ نَعَمْ. قَالَ وَمَنْ فَسَكَتَ، فَدَخَلَ عَلَيْهِ رَجُلٌ آخَرُ ـ أَحْسِبُهُ الْحَارِثَ ـ فَقَالَ اسْتَخْلِفْ. فَقَالَ عُثْمَانُ وَقَالُوا فَقَالَ نَعَمْ. قَالَ وَمَنْ هُوَ فَسَكَتَ قَالَ فَلَعَلَّهُمْ قَالُوا الزُّبَيْرَ قَالَ نَعَمْ. قَالَ أَمَا وَالَّذِي نَفْسِي بِيَدِهِ إِنَّهُ لَخَيْرُهُمْ مَا عَلِمْتُ، وَإِنْ كَانَ لأَحَبَّهُمْ إِلَى رَسُولِ اللَّهِ صلى الله عليه وسلم.

Narrated Abu Sa`id: The Prophet ﷺ said, (what is ascribed to him in the following Hadith): Narrated Abu Salih As-Samman: I saw Abu Sa`id Al-Khudri praying on a Friday, behind something which acted as a Sutra. A young man from Bani Abi Mu'ait, wanted to pass in front of him, but Abu Sa`id repulsed him with a push on his chest. Finding no alternative he again tried to pass but Abu Sa`id pushed him with a greater force. The young man abused Abu Sa`id and went to Marwan and lodged a complaint against Abu Sa`id and Abu Sa`id followed the young man to Marwan who asked him, "O Abu Sa`id! What has happened between you and the son of your brother?" Abu Sa`id said to him, "I heard the Prophet ﷺ saying, 'If anybody amongst you is praying behind something as a Sutra and somebody tries to pass in front of him, then he should repulse him and if he refuses, he should use force against him for he is a Shaitan (a Satan).' ". – Sahih Al-Bukhari 509

حَدَّثَنَا أَبُو مَعْمَرٍ، قَالَ حَدَّثَنَا عَبْدُ الْوَارِثِ، قَالَ حَدَّثَنَا يُونُسُ، عَنْ حُمَيْدِ بْنِ هِلاَلٍ، عَنْ أَبِي صَالِحٍ، أَنَّ أَبَا سَعِيدٍ، قَالَ قَالَ النَّبِيُّ صلى الله عليه وسلم وَحَدَّثَنَا آدَمُ بْنُ أَبِي إِيَاسٍ قَالَ حَدَّثَنَا سُلَيْمَانُ بْنُ الْمُغِيرَةِ قَالَ حَدَّثَنَا حُمَيْدُ بْنُ هِلاَلٍ الْعَدَوِيُّ قَالَ حَدَّثَنَا أَبُو صَالِحٍ السَّمَّانُ قَالَ رَأَيْتُ أَبَا سَعِيدٍ الْخُدْرِيَّ فِي يَوْمِ جُمُعَةٍ يُصَلِّي إِلَى شَىْءٍ يَسْتُرُهُ مِنَ النَّاسِ، فَأَرَادَ شَابٌّ مِنْ بَنِي أَبِي مُعَيْطٍ أَنْ يَجْتَازَ بَيْنَ يَدَيْهِ فَدَفَعَ أَبُو سَعِيدٍ فِي صَدْرِهِ، فَنَظَرَ الشَّابُّ فَلَمْ يَجِدْ مَسَاغًا إِلاَّ بَيْنَ يَدَيْهِ، فَعَادَ لِيَجْتَازَ فَدَفَعَهُ أَبُو

سَعِيدٍ أَشَدَّ مِنَ الأُولَى، فَنَالَ مِنْ أَبِي سَعِيدٍ، ثُمَّ دَخَلَ عَلَى مَرْوَانَ فَشَكَا إِلَيْهِ مَا لَقِيَ مِنْ أَبِي سَعِيدٍ، وَدَخَلَ أَبُو سَعِيدٍ خَلْفَهُ عَلَى مَرْوَانَ فَقَالَ مَا لَكَ وَلاِبْنِ أَخِيكَ يَا أَبَا سَعِيدٍ قَالَ سَمِعْتُ النَّبِيَّ صلى الله عليه وسلم يَقُولُ " إِذَا صَلَّى أَحَدُكُمْ إِلَى شَىْءٍ يَسْتُرُهُ مِنَ النَّاسِ، فَأَرَادَ أَحَدٌ أَنْ يَجْتَازَ بَيْنَ يَدَيْهِ فَلْيَدْفَعْهُ، فَإِنْ أَبَى فَلْيُقَاتِلْهُ، فَإِنَّمَا هُوَ شَيْطَانٌ ".

Narrated Abu Al-Minhal: When Ibn Ziyad and Marwan were in Sham and Ibn Az-Zubair took over the authority in Mecca and Qurra' (the Kharijites) revolted in Basra, I went out with my father to Abu Barza Al-Aslami till we entered upon him in his house while he was sitting in the shade of a room built of cane. So we sat with him and my father started talking to him saying, "O Abu Barza! Don't you see in what dilemma the people has fallen?" The first thing heard him saying "I seek reward from Allah for myself because of being angry and scornful at the Quraish tribe. O you Arabs! You know very well that you were in misery and were few in number and misguided, and that Allah has brought you out of all that with Islam and with Muhammad till He brought you to this state (of prosperity and happiness) which you see now; and it is this worldly wealth and pleasures which has caused mischief to appear among you. The one who is in Sham (i.e., Marwan), by Allah, is not fighting except for the sake of worldly gain: and those who are among you, by Allah, are not fighting except for the sake of worldly gain; and that one who is in Mecca (i.e., Ibn Az-Zubair) by Allah, is not fighting except for the sake of worldly gain.". – Sahih Al-Bukhari 7112

حَدَّثَنَا أَحْمَدُ بْنُ يُونُسَ، حَدَّثَنَا أَبُو شِهَابٍ، عَنْ عَوْفٍ، عَنْ أَبِي الْمِنْهَالِ، قَالَ لَمَّا كَانَ ابْنُ زِيَادٍ وَمَرْوَانُ بِالشَّأْمِ، وَوَثَبَ ابْنُ الزُّبَيْرِ بِمَكَّةَ، وَوَثَبَ الْقُرَّاءُ بِالْبَصْرَةِ، فَانْطَلَقْتُ مَعَ أَبِي إِلَى أَبِي بَرْزَةَ الأَسْلَمِيِّ حَتَّى دَخَلْنَا عَلَيْهِ فِي دَارِهِ وَهْوَ جَالِسٌ فِي ظِلِّ عُلِّيَّةٍ لَهُ مِنْ قَصَبٍ، فَجَلَسْنَا إِلَيْهِ فَأَنْشَأَ أَبِي يَسْتَطْعِمُهُ الْحَدِيثَ فَقَالَ يَا أَبَا بَرْزَةَ أَلاَ تَرَى مَا وَقَعَ فِيهِ النَّاسُ فَأَوَّلُ شَىْءٍ سَمِعْتُهُ تَكَلَّمَ بِهِ إِنِّي احْتَسَبْتُ عِنْدَ اللَّهِ أَنِّي أَصْبَحْتُ سَاخِطًا عَلَى أَحْيَاءِ قُرَيْشٍ، إِنَّكُمْ يَا مَعْشَرَ الْعَرَبِ كُنْتُمْ عَلَى الْحَالِ الَّذِي عَلِمْتُمْ مِنَ الذِّلَّةِ وَالْقِلَّةِ وَالضَّلاَلَةِ، وَإِنَّ اللَّهَ أَنْقَذَكُمْ بِالإِسْلاَمِ وَبِمُحَمَّدٍ صلى الله عليه وسلم حَتَّى بَلَغَ بِكُمْ مَا تَرَوْنَ، وَهَذِهِ الدُّنْيَا الَّتِي أَفْسَدَتْ بَيْنَكُمْ، إِنَّ ذَاكَ الَّذِي بِالشَّأْمِ وَاللَّهِ إِنْ يُقَاتِلُ إِلاَّ عَلَى الدُّنْيَا

Narrated Alqama bin Waqqas: Marwan said to his gatekeeper, "Go to Ibn `Abbas, O Rafi`, and say, 'If everybody who rejoices in what he has done, and likes to be praised for what he has not done, will be punished, then all of us will be punished." Ibn `Abbas said, "What connection have you with this case? It was only that the Prophetﷺ called the Jews and asked them about something, and they hid the truth and told him something else, and showed him that they deserved praise for the favor of telling him the answer to his question, and they became happy with what they had concealed. Then Ibn `Abbas recited:-- "(And remember) when Allah took a Covenant from those who were given the Scripture..and those who rejoice in what they have done and love to be praised for what they have not done.' " (3.187-188) Humaid bin `Abdur-Rahman bin `Auf narrated that Marwan had told him (the above narration). – Sahih Al-Bukhari 4568

حَدَّثَنِي إِبْرَاهِيمُ بْنُ مُوسَى، أَخْبَرَنَا هِشَامٌ، أَنَّ ابْنَ جُرَيْجٍ، أَخْبَرَهُمْ عَنِ ابْنِ أَبِي مُلَيْكَةَ، أَنَّ عَلْقَمَةَ بْنَ وَقَّاصٍ، أَخْبَرَهُ أَنَّ مَرْوَانَ قَالَ لِبَوَّابِهِ اذْهَبْ يَا رَافِعُ إِلَى ابْنِ عَبَّاسٍ فَقُلْ لَئِنْ كَانَ كُلُّ امْرِئٍ فَرِحَ بِمَا أُوتِيَ، وَأَحَبَّ أَنْ يُحْمَدَ بِمَا لَمْ يَفْعَلْ، مُعَذَّبًا، لَنُعَذَّبَنَّ أَجْمَعُونَ. فَقَالَ ابْنُ عَبَّاسٍ وَمَا لَكُمْ وَلِهَذِهِ إِنَّمَا دَعَا النَّبِيُّ صلى الله عليه وسلم يَهُودَ فَسَأَلَهُمْ عَنْ شَىْءٍ، فَكَتَمُوهُ إِيَّاهُ، وَأَخْبَرُوهُ بِغَيْرِهِ، فَأَرَوْهُ أَنْ قَدِ اسْتَحْمَدُوا إِلَيْهِ بِمَا أَخْبَرُوهُ عَنْهُ فِيمَا سَأَلَهُمْ، وَفَرِحُوا بِمَا أُوتُوا مِنْ كِتْمَانِهِمْ، ثُمَّ قَرَأَ ابْنُ عَبَّاسٍ {وَإِذْ أَخَذَ اللَّهُ مِيثَاقَ الَّذِينَ أُوتُوا الْكِتَابَ} كَذَلِكَ حَتَّى قَوْلِهِ {يَفْرَحُونَ بِمَا أَتَوْا وَيُحِبُّونَ أَنْ يُحْمَدُوا بِمَا لَمْ يَفْعَلُوا}. تَابَعَهُ عَبْدُ الرَّزَّاقِ عَنِ ابْنِ جُرَيْجٍ. حَدَّثَنَا ابْنُ مُقَاتِلٍ، أَخْبَرَنَا الْحَجَّاجُ، عَنِ ابْنِ جُرَيْجٍ، أَخْبَرَنِي ابْنُ أَبِي مُلَيْكَةَ، عَنْ حُمَيْدِ بْنِ عَبْدِ الرَّحْمَنِ بْنِ عَوْفٍ، أَنَّهُ أَخْبَرَهُ أَنَّ مَرْوَانَ بِهَذَا.

Narrated Sa`id bin Zaid bin `Amr bin Nufail: That Arwa sued him before Marwan for a right, which she claimed, he had deprived her of. On that Sa`id said, "How should I deprive her of her right? I testify that I heard Allah's Messengerﷺ saying, 'If anyone takes a span of land unjustly, his neck will be encircled with it down seven earths on the Day of Resurrection.". – Sahih Al-Bukhari 3198

حَدَّثَنِي عُبَيْدُ بْنُ إِسْمَاعِيلَ، حَدَّثَنَا أَبُو أُسَامَةَ، عَنْ هِشَامٍ، عَنْ أَبِيهِ، عَنْ سَعِيدِ بْنِ زَيْدِ بْنِ عَمْرِو بْنِ نُفَيْلٍ، أَنَّهُ خَاصَمَتْهُ أَرْوَى فِي حَقٍّ زَعَمَتْ أَنَّهُ انْتَقَصَهُ لَهَا إِلَى مَرْوَانَ، فَقَالَ سَعِيدٌ أَنَا أَنْتَقِصُ مِنْ حَقِّهَا شَيْئًا، أَشْهَدُ لَسَمِعْتُ رَسُولَ اللَّهِ صلى الله عليه وسلم يَقُولُ " مَنْ أَخَذَ شِبْرًا مِنَ الأَرْضِ ظُلْمًا، فَإِنَّهُ يُطَوَّقُهُ يَوْمَ الْقِيَامَةِ مِنْ سَبْعِ أَرَضِينَ ". قَالَ ابْنُ أَبِي الزِّنَادِ عَنْ هِشَامٍ عَنْ أَبِيهِ قَالَ قَالَ لِي سَعِيدُ بْنُ زَيْدٍ دَخَلْتُ عَلَى النَّبِيِّ صلى الله عليه وسلم.

Narrated Marwan bin Al-Hakam: I saw `Uthman and `Ali. `Uthman used to forbid people to perform Hajj-at-Tamattu` and Hajj-al- Qiran (Hajj and `Umra together), and when `Ali saw (this act of `Uthman), he assumed Ihram for Hajj and `Umra together saying, "Lubbaik for `Umra and Hajj," and said, "I will not leave the tradition of the Prophet ﷺ on the saying of somebody.". – Sahih Al-Bukhari 1563

حَدَّثَنَا مُحَمَّدُ بْنُ بَشَّارٍ، حَدَّثَنَا غُنْدَرٌ، حَدَّثَنَا شُعْبَةُ، عَنِ الْحَكَمِ، عَنْ عَلِيِّ بْنِ حُسَيْنٍ، عَنْ مَرْوَانَ بْنِ الْحَكَمِ، قَالَ شَهِدْتُ عُثْمَانَ وَعَلِيًّا ـ رضى الله عنهما ـ وَعُثْمَانُ يَنْهَى عَنِ الْمُتْعَةِ وَأَنْ يُجْمَعَ بَيْنَهُمَا. فَلَمَّا رَأَى عَلِيٌّ، أَهَلَّ بِهِمَا لَبَّيْكَ بِعُمْرَةٍ وَحَجَّةٍ قَالَ مَا كُنْتُ لأَدَعَ سُنَّةَ النَّبِيِّ صلى الله عليه وسلم لِقَوْلِ أَحَدٍ

Narrated Abu Sa`id Al-Khudri: The Prophet ﷺ used to proceed to the Musalla on the days of Id-ul-Fitr and Id-ul-Adha; the first thing to begin with was the prayer and after that he would stand in front of the people and the people would keep sitting in their rows. Then he would preach to them, advise them and give them orders, (i.e. Khutba). And after that if he wished to send an army for an expedition, he would do so; or if he wanted to give and order, he would do so, and then depart. The people followed this tradition till I went out with Marwan, the Governor of Medina, for the prayer of Id-ul-Adha or Id-ul-Fitr. When we reached the Musalla, there was a pulpit made by Kathir bin As-Salt. Marwan wanted to get up on that pulpit before the prayer. I got hold of his clothes but he pulled them and ascended the pulpit and delivered the Khutba before the prayer. I said to him, "By Allah, you have changed (the Prophet's tradition)." He replied, "O Abu Sa`id! Gone is that which you know." I said, "By Allah! What I know is better than what I do not know." Marwan said, "People do not sit to listen to our Khutba after the prayer, so I delivered the Khutba before the prayer.". – Sahih Al-Bukhari 956

حَدَّثَنَا سَعِيدُ بْنُ أَبِي مَرْيَمَ، قَالَ حَدَّثَنَا مُحَمَّدُ بْنُ جَعْفَرٍ، قَالَ أَخْبَرَنِي زَيْدٌ، عَنْ عِيَاضِ بْنِ عَبْدِ اللَّهِ بْنِ أَبِي سَرْحٍ، عَنْ أَبِي سَعِيدٍ الْخُدْرِيِّ، قَالَ كَانَ رَسُولُ اللَّهِ صلى الله عليه وسلم يَخْرُجُ يَوْمَ الْفِطْرِ وَالأَضْحَى إِلَى الْمُصَلَّى، فَأَوَّلُ شَىْءٍ يَبْدَأُ بِهِ الصَّلاَةُ ثُمَّ يَنْصَرِفُ، فَيَقُومُ مُقَابِلَ النَّاسِ، وَالنَّاسُ جُلُوسٌ عَلَى صُفُوفِهِمْ، فَيَعِظُهُمْ وَيُوصِيهِمْ وَيَأْمُرُهُمْ، فَإِنْ كَانَ يُرِيدُ أَنْ يَقْطَعَ بَعْثًا قَطَعَهُ، أَوْ يَأْمُرَ بِشَىْءٍ أَمَرَ بِهِ، ثُمَّ يَنْصَرِفُ. قَالَ أَبُو سَعِيدٍ فَلَمْ يَزَلِ النَّاسُ عَلَى ذَلِكَ حَتَّى خَرَجْتُ مَعَ مَرْوَانَ وَهْوَ أَمِيرُ الْمَدِينَةِ فِي أَضْحًى أَوْ فِطْرٍ، فَلَمَّا أَتَيْنَا الْمُصَلَّى إِذَا مِنْبَرٌ بَنَاهُ كَثِيرُ بْنُ الصَّلْتِ، فَإِذَا مَرْوَانُ يُرِيدُ أَنْ يَرْتَقِيَهُ قَبْلَ أَنْ يُصَلِّيَ، فَجَبَذْتُ بِثَوْبِهِ فَجَبَذَنِي فَارْتَفَعَ، فَخَطَبَ قَبْلَ الصَّلاَةِ، فَقُلْتُ لَهُ غَيَّرْتُمْ وَاللَّهِ. فَقَالَ أَبَا سَعِيدٍ، قَدْ ذَهَبَ مَا تَعْلَمُ. فَقُلْتُ مَا أَعْلَمُ وَاللَّهِ خَيْرٌ مِمَّا لاَ أَعْلَمُ. فَقَالَ إِنَّ النَّاسَ لَمْ يَكُونُوا يَجْلِسُونَ لَنَا بَعْدَ الصَّلاَةِ فَجَعَلْتُهَا قَبْلَ الصَّلاَةِ.

Hakim bin Hizam

حكيم بن حزام

Narrated Hisham's father: When Allah's Messenger ﷺ set out (towards Mecca) during the year of the Conquest (of Mecca) and this news reached (the infidels of Quraish), Abu Sufyan, Hakim bin Hizam and Budail bin Warqa came out to gather information about Allah's Messenger ﷺ Proceeded on their way till they reached a place called Marr-az-Zahran (which is near Mecca). Behold! There they saw many fires as if they were the fires of `Arafat. Abu

Sufyan said, "What is this? It looked like the fires of `Arafat." Budail bin Warqa' said, "Banu `Amr are less in number than that." Some of the guards of Allah's Messenger ﷺ saw them and took them over, caught them and brought them to Allah's Messenger ﷺ Abu Sufyan embraced Islam. When the Prophet ﷺ proceeded, he said to Al-Abbas, "Keep Abu Sufyan standing at the top of the mountain so that he would look at the Muslims. So Al-`Abbas kept him standing (at that place) and the tribes with the Prophet ﷺ started passing in front of Abu Sufyan in military batches. A batch passed and Abu Sufyan said, "O `Abbas Who are these?" `Abbas said, "They are (Banu) Ghifar." Abu Sufyan said, I have got nothing to do with Ghifar." Then (a batch of the tribe of) Juhaina passed by and he said similarly as above. Then (a batch of the tribe of) Sa`d bin Huzaim passed by and he said similarly as above. Then (Banu) Sulaim passed by and he said similarly as above. Then came a batch, the like of which Abu Sufyan had not seen. He said, "Who are these?" `Abbas said, "They are the Ansar headed by Sa`d bin Ubada, the one holding the flag." Sa`d bin Ubada said, "O Abu Sufyan! Today is the day of a great battle and today (what is prohibited in) the Ka`ba will be permissible." Abu Sufyan said., "O `Abbas! How excellent the day of destruction is! "Then came another batch (of warriors) which was the smallest of all the batches, and in it there was Allah's Messenger ﷺ and his companions and the flag of the Prophet ﷺ was carried by Az-Zubair bin Al Awwam. When Allah's Messenger ﷺ passed by Abu Sufyan, the latter said, (to the Prophet), "Do you know what Sa`d bin 'Ubada said?" The Prophet ﷺ said, "What did he say?" Abu Sufyan said, "He said so-and-so." The Prophet ﷺ said, "Sa`d told a lie, but today Allah will give superiority to the Ka`ba and today the Ka`ba will be covered with a (cloth) covering." Allah's Messenger ﷺ ordered that his flag be fixed at Al-Hajun. Narrated `Urwa: Nafi` bin Jubair bin Mut`im said, "I heard Al-Abbas saying to Az-Zubair bin Al- `Awwam, 'O Abu `Abdullah ! Did Allah's Messenger ﷺ order you to fix the flag here?' " Allah's Messenger ﷺ ordered Khalid bin Al-Walid to enter Mecca from its upper part from Ka'da while the Prophet ﷺ himself entered from Kuda. Two men from the cavalry of Khalid bin Al-Wahd named Hubaish bin Al-Ash'ar and Kurz bin Jabir Al-Fihri were martyred on that day. – Sahih Al-Bukhari 4280

حَدَّثَنَا عُبَيْدُ بْنُ إِسْمَاعِيلَ، حَدَّثَنَا أَبُو أُسَامَةَ، عَنْ هِشَامٍ، عَنْ أَبِيهِ، قَالَ لَمَّا سَارَ رَسُولُ اللَّهِ صلى الله عليه وسلم عَامَ الْفَتْحِ فَبَلَغَ ذَلِكَ قُرَيْشًا، خَرَجَ أَبُو سُفْيَانَ بْنُ حَرْبٍ وَحَكِيمُ بْنُ حِزَامٍ وَبُدَيْلُ بْنُ وَرْقَاءَ يَلْتَمِسُونَ الْخَبَرَ عَنْ رَسُولِ اللَّهِ صلى الله عليه وسلم فَأَقْبَلُوا يَسِيرُونَ حَتَّى أَتَوْا مَرَّ الظَّهْرَانِ، فَإِذَا هُمْ بِنِيرَانٍ كَأَنَّهَا نِيرَانُ عَرَفَةَ، فَقَالَ أَبُو سُفْيَانَ مَا هَذِهِ لَكَأَنَّهَا نِيرَانُ عَرَفَةَ. فَقَالَ بُدَيْلُ بْنُ وَرْقَاءَ نِيرَانُ بَنِي عَمْرٍو. فَقَالَ أَبُو سُفْيَانَ عَمْرٌو أَقَلُّ مِنْ ذَلِكَ. فَرَآهُمْ نَاسٌ مِنْ حَرَسِ رَسُولِ اللَّهِ صلى الله عليه وسلم فَأَدْرَكُوهُمْ فَأَخَذُوهُمْ، فَأَتَوْا بِهِمْ رَسُولَ اللَّهِ صلى الله عليه وسلم فَأَسْلَمَ أَبُو سُفْيَانَ، فَلَمَّا سَارَ قَالَ لِلْعَبَّاسِ " احْبِسْ أَبَا سُفْيَانَ عِنْدَ حَطْمِ الْخَيْلِ حَتَّى يَنْظُرَ إِلَى الْمُسْلِمِينَ ". فَحَبَسَهُ الْعَبَّاسُ، فَجَعَلَتِ الْقَبَائِلُ تَمُرُّ مَعَ النَّبِيِّ صلى الله عليه وسلم تَمُرُّ كَتِيبَةً كَتِيبَةً عَلَى أَبِي سُفْيَانَ، فَمَرَّتْ كَتِيبَةٌ قَالَ يَا عَبَّاسُ مَنْ هَذِهِ قَالَ هَذِهِ غِفَارُ. قَالَ مَا لِي وَلِغِفَارَ ثُمَّ مَرَّتْ جُهَيْنَةُ، قَالَ مِثْلَ ذَلِكَ، ثُمَّ مَرَّتْ سَعْدُ بْنُ هُذَيْمٍ، فَقَالَ مِثْلَ ذَلِكَ، وَمَرَّتْ سُلَيْمُ، فَقَالَ مِثْلَ ذَلِكَ، حَتَّى أَقْبَلَتْ كَتِيبَةٌ لَمْ يَرَ مِثْلَهَا، قَالَ مَنْ هَذِهِ قَالَ هَؤُلاَءِ الأَنْصَارُ عَلَيْهِمْ سَعْدُ بْنُ عُبَادَةَ مَعَهُ الرَّايَةُ. فَقَالَ سَعْدُ بْنُ عُبَادَةَ يَا أَبَا سُفْيَانَ الْيَوْمُ يَوْمُ الْمَلْحَمَةِ، الْيَوْمَ تُسْتَحَلُّ الْكَعْبَةُ. فَقَالَ أَبُو سُفْيَانَ يَا عَبَّاسُ حَبَّذَا يَوْمُ الذِّمَارِ. ثُمَّ جَاءَتْ كَتِيبَةٌ، وَهْىَ أَقَلُّ الْكَتَائِبِ، فِيهِمْ رَسُولُ اللَّهِ صلى الله عليه وسلم وَأَصْحَابُهُ، وَرَايَةُ النَّبِيِّ صلى الله عليه وسلم مَعَ الزُّبَيْرِ بْنِ الْعَوَّامِ، فَلَمَّا مَرَّ رَسُولُ اللَّهِ صلى الله عليه وسلم بِأَبِي سُفْيَانَ قَالَ أَلَمْ تَعْلَمْ مَا قَالَ سَعْدُ بْنُ عُبَادَةَ قَالَ " مَا قَالَ ". قَالَ كَذَا وَكَذَا. فَقَالَ " كَذَبَ سَعْدٌ، وَلَكِنْ هَذَا يَوْمٌ يُعَظِّمُ اللَّهُ فِيهِ الْكَعْبَةَ، وَيَوْمٌ تُكْسَى فِيهِ الْكَعْبَةُ ". قَالَ وَأَمَرَ رَسُولُ اللَّهِ صلى الله عليه وسلم أَنْ تُرْكَزَ رَايَتُهُ بِالْحَجُونِ. قَالَ عُرْوَةُ وَأَخْبَرَنِي نَافِعُ بْنُ جُبَيْرِ بْنِ مُطْعِمٍ قَالَ سَمِعْتُ الْعَبَّاسَ يَقُولُ لِلزُّبَيْرِ بْنِ الْعَوَّامِ يَا أَبَا عَبْدِ اللَّهِ، هَا هُنَا أَمَرَكَ رَسُولُ اللَّهِ صلى الله عليه وسلم أَنْ تَرْكُزَ الرَّايَةَ، قَالَ وَأَمَرَ رَسُولُ اللَّهِ صلى الله عليه وسلم يَوْمَئِذٍ خَالِدَ بْنَ الْوَلِيدِ أَنْ يَدْخُلَ مِنْ أَعْلَى مَكَّةَ مِنْ كَدَاءٍ، وَدَخَلَ النَّبِيُّ صلى الله عليه وسلم مِنْ كُدَا، فَقُتِلَ مِنْ خَيْلِ خَالِدٍ يَوْمَئِذٍ رَجُلاَنِ حُبَيْشُ بْنُ الأَشْعَرِ وَكُرْزُ بْنُ جَابِرٍ الْفِهْرِيُّ.

Narrated `Umar bin Khattab: I heard Hisham bin Hakim bin Hizam reciting Surat-al-Furqan during the lifetime of Allah's Messenger ﷺ and I listened to his recitation and noticed that he recited it in several ways which Allah's Messenger ﷺ had not taught me. So I was on the point of attacking him in the prayer, but I waited till he finished his prayer, and then I seized him by the collar and said, "Who taught you this Surah which I have heard you reciting?" He replied, "Allah's Messenger taught it to me." I said, "You are telling a lie; By Allah! Allah's Messenger ﷺtaught me (in a different way) this very Surah which I have heard you reciting." So I took him, leading him to Allah's Messenger ﷺ and said, "O Allah's Messengeﷺ ! I heard this person reciting Surat-al-Furqan in a way that you did not teach me, and you have taught me Surat-al-Furqan." The Prophet said, "O Hisham, recite!" So he recited in the same way as I heard him recite it before. On that Allah's Messengerﷺ said, "It was revealed to be recited in this way." Then Allah's Messengerﷺ said, "Recite, O `Umar!" So I recited it as he had taught me. Allah's Messengerﷺ then said, "It was revealed to be recited in this way." Allah" Apostle added, "The Qur'an has been revealed to be recited in several different ways, so recite of it that which is easier for you.". – Sahih Al-Bukhari 5041

حَدَّثَنَا أَبُو الْيَمَانِ، أَخْبَرَنَا شُعَيْبٌ، عَنِ الزُّهْرِيِّ، قَالَ أَخْبَرَنِي عُرْوَةُ، عَنْ حَدِيثِ الْمِسْوَرِ بْنِ مَخْرَمَةَ، وَعَبْدِ الرَّحْمَنِ بْنِ عَبْدٍ الْقَارِيِّ، أَنَّهُمَا سَمِعَا عُمَرَ بْنَ الْخَطَّابِ، يَقُولُ سَمِعْتُ هِشَامَ بْنَ حَكِيمِ بْنِ حِزَامٍ، يَقْرَأُ سُورَةَ الْفُرْقَانِ فِي حَيَاةِ رَسُولِ اللَّهِ صلى الله عليه وسلم فَاسْتَمَعْتُ لِقِرَاءَتِهِ فَإِذَا هُوَ يَقْرَؤُهَا عَلَى حُرُوفٍ كَثِيرَةٍ لَمْ يُقْرِئْنِيهَا رَسُولُ اللَّهِ صلى الله عليه وسلم فَكِدْتُ أُسَاوِرُهُ فِي الصَّلاَةِ فَانْتَظَرْتُهُ حَتَّى سَلَّمَ فَلَبَبْتُهُ فَقُلْتُ مَنْ أَقْرَأَكَ هَذِهِ السُّورَةَ الَّتِي سَمِعْتُكَ تَقْرَأُ قَالَ أَقْرَأَنِيهَا رَسُولُ اللَّهِ صلى الله عليه وسلم. فَقُلْتُ لَهُ كَذَبْتَ فَوَاللَّهِ إِنَّ رَسُولَ اللَّهِ صلى الله عليه وسلم لَهُوَ أَقْرَأَنِي هَذِهِ السُّورَةَ الَّتِي سَمِعْتُكَ، فَانْطَلَقْتُ بِهِ إِلَى رَسُولِ اللَّهِ صلى الله عليه وسلم أَقُودُهُ فَقُلْتُ يَا رَسُولَ اللَّهِ إِنِّي سَمِعْتُ هَذَا يَقْرَأُ سُورَةَ الْفُرْقَانِ عَلَى حُرُوفٍ لَمْ تُقْرِئْنِيهَا وَإِنَّكَ أَقْرَأْتَنِي سُورَةَ الْفُرْقَانِ. فَقَالَ " يَا هِشَامُ اقْرَأْهَا ". فَقَرَأَهَا الْقِرَاءَةَ الَّتِي سَمِعْتُهُ فَقَالَ رَسُولُ اللَّهِ صلى الله عليه وسلم " هَكَذَا أُنْزِلَتْ ". ثُمَّ قَالَ " اقْرَأْ يَا عُمَرُ ". فَقَرَأْتُهَا الَّتِي أَقْرَأَنِيهَا، فَقَالَ رَسُولُ اللَّهِ صلى الله عليه وسلم " هَكَذَا أُنْزِلَتْ ". ثُمَّ قَالَ رَسُولُ اللَّهِ صلى الله عليه وسلم " إِنَّ الْقُرْآنَ أُنْزِلَ عَلَى سَبْعَةِ أَحْرُفٍ فَاقْرَءُوا مَا تَيَسَّرَ مِنْهُ ".

Narrated `Abdullah: Today a man came to me and asked me a question which I did not know how to answer. He said, "Tell me, if a wealthy active man, well-equipped with arms, goes out on military expeditions with our chiefs, and orders us to do such things as we cannot do (should we obey him?)" I replied, "By Allah, I do not know what to reply you, except that we, were in the company of the Prophetﷺ and he used to order us to do a thing once only till we finished it. And no doubt, everyone among you will remain in a good state as long as he obeys Allah. If one is in doubt as to the legality of something, he should ask somebody who would satisfy him, but soon will come a time when you will not find such a man. By Him, except Whom none has the right to be worshipped. I see that the example of what has passed of this life (to what remains thereof) is like a pond whose fresh water has been used up and nothing remains but muddy water.". – Sahih Al-Bukhari 2964

حَدَّثَنَا عُثْمَانُ بْنُ أَبِي شَيْبَةَ، حَدَّثَنَا جَرِيرٌ، عَنْ مَنْصُورٍ، عَنْ أَبِي وَائِلٍ، قَالَ قَالَ عَبْدُ اللَّهِ ـ رضى الله عنه ـ لَقَدْ أَتَانِي الْيَوْمَ رَجُلٌ فَسَأَلَنِي عَنْ أَمْرٍ مَا دَرَيْتُ مَا أَرُدُّ عَلَيْهِ، فَقَالَ أَرَأَيْتَ رَجُلاً مُؤْدِيًا نَشِيطًا، يَخْرُجُ مَعَ أُمَرَائِنَا فِي الْمَغَازِي، فَيَعْزِمُ عَلَيْنَا فِي أَشْيَاءَ لاَ نُحْصِيهَا. فَقُلْتُ لَهُ وَاللَّهِ مَا أَدْرِي مَا أَقُولُ لَكَ إِلاَّ أَنَّا كُنَّا مَعَ النَّبِيِّ صلى الله عليه وسلم فَعَسَى أَنْ لاَ يَعْزِمَ عَلَيْنَا فِي أَمْرٍ إِلاَّ مَرَّةً حَتَّى نَفْعَلَهُ، وَإِنَّ أَحَدَكُمْ لَنْ يَزَالَ بِخَيْرٍ مَا اتَّقَى اللَّهَ، وَإِذَا شَكَّ فِي نَفْسِهِ شَىْءٌ سَأَلَ رَجُلاً فَشَفَاهُ مِنْهُ، وَأَوْشَكَ أَنْ لاَ تَجِدُوهُ، وَالَّذِي لاَ إِلَهَ إِلاَّ هُوَ مَا أَذْكُرُ مَا غَبَرَ مِنَ الدُّنْيَا إِلاَّ كَالثَّغْبِ شُرِبَ صَفْوُهُ وَبَقِيَ كَدَرُهُ.

Narrated `Abdullah bin Az-Zubair: When Az-Zubair got up during the battle of Al-Jamal, he called me and I stood up beside him, and he said to me, "O my son! Today one will be killed either as an oppressor or as an oppressed one. I see that I will be killed as an oppressed one. My biggest worry is my debts. Do you think, if we pay the debts, there will be something left for us from our money?" Az-Zubair added, "O my son! Sell our property and pay my debts." Az-Zubair then willed one-third of his property and willed one-third of that portion to his sons; namely, `Abdullah's sons. He said, "One-third of the one third. If any property is left after the payment of the debts, one-third (of the one-third of what is left) is to be given to your sons." (Hisham, a sub-narrator added, "Some of the sons of `Abdullah were equal in age

to the sons of Az-Zubair e.g. Khubaib and `Abbas. `Abdullah had nine sons and nine daughters at that time." (The narrator `Abdullah added:) My father (Az-Zubair) went on drawing my attention to his debts saying, "If you should fail to pay part of the debts, appeal to my Master to help you." By Allah! I could not understand what he meant till I asked, "O father! Who is your Master?" He replied, "Allah (is my Master)." By Allah, whenever I had any difficulty regarding his debts, I would say, "Master of Az-Zubair! Pay his debts on his behalf ." and Allah would (help me to) pay it. Az-Zubair was martyred leaving no Dinar or Dirham but two pieces of land, one of which was (called) Al-Ghaba, and eleven houses in Medina, two in Basra, one in Kufa and one in Egypt. In fact, the source of the debt which he owed was, that if somebody brought some money to deposit with him. Az-Zubair would say, "No, (I won't keep it as a trust), but I take it as a debt, for I am afraid it might be lost." Az-Zubair was never appointed governor or collector of the tax of Kharaj or any other similar thing, but he collected his wealth (from the war booty he gained) during the holy battles he took part in, in the company of the Prophet, Abu Bakr, `Umar, and `Uthman. (`Abdullah bin Az-Zubair added: ) When I counted his debt, it turned to be two million and two hundred thousand. (The sub-narrator added: ) Hakim bin Hizam met `Abdullah bin Zubair and asked, "O my nephew! How much is the debt of my brother?" `Abdullah kept it as a secret and said, "One hundred thousand," Hakim said, "By Allah! I don't think your property will cover it." On that `Abdullah said to him, "What if it is two million and two hundred thousand?" Hakim said, "I don't think you can pay it; so if you are unable to pay all of it, I will help you." Az- Zubair had already bought Al-Ghaba for one hundred and seventy thousand. `Abdullah sold it for one million and six hundred thousand. Then he called the people saying, "Any person who has any money claim on Az-Zubair should come to us in Al-Ghaba." There came to him `Abdullah bin Ja`far whom Az-Zubair owed four hundred thousand. He said to `Abdullah bin Az-Zubair, "If you wish I will forgive you the debt." `Abdullah (bin Az-Zubair) said, "No." Then Ibn Ja`far said, "If you wish you can defer the payment if you should defer the payment of any debt." Ibn Az-Zubair said, "No." `Abdullah bin Ja`far said, "Give me a piece of the land." `Abdullah bin AzZubair said (to him), "Yours is the land extending from this place to this place." So, `Abdullah bin Az-Zubair sold some of the property (including the houses) and paid his debt perfectly, retaining four and a half shares from the land (i.e. Al-Ghaba). He then went to Mu'awlya while `Amr bin `Uthman, Al-Mundhir bin Az- Zubair and Ibn Zam`a were sitting with him. Mu'awiya asked, "At what price have you appraised Al- Ghaba?" He said, "One hundred thousand for each share," Muawiya asked, "How many shares have been left?" `Abdullah replied, "Four and a half shares." Al-Mundhir bin Az-Zubair said, "I would like to buy one share for one hundred thousand." `Amr bin `Uthman said, "I would like to buy one share for one hundred thousand." Ibn Zam`a said, "I would like to buy one share for one hundred thousand." Muawiya said, "How much is left now?" `Abdullah replied, "One share and a half." Muawiya said, "I would like to buy it for one hundred and fifty thousand." `Abdullah also sold his part to Muawiya six hundred thousand. When Ibn AzZubair had paid all the debts. Az-Zubair's sons said to him, "Distribute our inheritance among us." He said, "No, by Allah, I will not distribute it among you till I announce in four successive Hajj seasons, 'Would those who have money claims on Az-Zubair come so that we may pay them their debt." So, he started to announce that in public in every Hajj season, and when four years had elapsed, he distributed the inheritance among the inheritors. Az-Zubair had four wives, and after the one-third of his property was excluded (according to the will), each of his wives received one million and two hundred thousand. So the total amount of his property was fifty million and two hundred thousand.
– Sahih Al-Bukhari 3129

حَدَّثَنَا إِسْحَاقُ بْنُ إِبْرَاهِيمَ، قَالَ قُلْتُ لأَبِي أُسَامَةَ أَحَدَّثَكُمْ هِشَامُ بْنُ عُرْوَةَ عَنْ أَبِيهِ عَنْ عَبْدِ اللَّهِ بْنِ الزُّبَيْرِ قَالَ لَمَّا وَقَفَ الزُّبَيْرُ يَوْمَ الْجَمَلِ دَعَانِي، فَقُمْتُ إِلَى جَنْبِهِ فَقَالَ يَا بُنَيِّ، إِنَّهُ لاَ يُقْتَلُ الْيَوْمَ إِلاَّ ظَالِمٌ أَوْ مَظْلُومٌ، وَإِنِّي لاَ أُرَانِي إِلاَّ سَأُقْتَلُ الْيَوْمَ مَظْلُومًا، وَإِنَّ مِنْ أَكْبَرِ هَمِّي لَدَيْنِي، أَفَتُرَى يُبْقِي دَيْنُنَا مِنْ مَالِنَا شَيْئًا فَقَالَ يَا بُنَيِّ بِعْ مَالَنَا فَاقْضِ دَيْنِي. وَأَوْصَى بِالثُّلُثِ، وَثُلُثِهِ لِبَنِيهِ، يَعْنِي عَبْدَ اللَّهِ بْنَ الزُّبَيْرِ يَقُولُ ثُلُثُ الثُّلُثِ، فَإِنْ فَضَلَ مِنْ مَالِنَا فَضْلٌ بَعْدَ قَضَاءِ الدَّيْنِ شَىْءٌ فَثُلُثُهُ لِوَلَدِكَ. قَالَ هِشَامٌ وَكَانَ بَعْضُ وَلَدِ عَبْدِ اللَّهِ قَدْ وَازَى بَعْضَ بَنِي الزُّبَيْرِ خُبَيْبٌ وَعَبَّادٌ، وَلَهُ يَوْمَئِذٍ تِسْعَةُ بَنِينَ وَتِسْعُ بَنَاتٍ. قَالَ عَبْدُ اللَّهِ فَجَعَلَ يُوصِينِي بِدَيْنِهِ وَيَقُولُ يَا بُنَيِّ، إِنْ عَجَزْتَ عَنْهُ فِي شَىْءٍ فَاسْتَعِنْ عَلَيْهِ مَوْلاَىَ. قَالَ فَوَاللَّهِ مَا دَرَيْتُ مَا أَرَادَ حَتَّى قُلْتُ يَا أَبَتِ مَنْ مَوْلاَكَ قَالَ اللَّهُ. قَالَ فَوَاللَّهِ مَا وَقَعْتُ فِي كُرْبَةٍ مِنْ دَيْنِهِ إِلاَّ قُلْتُ يَا مَوْلَى الزُّبَيْرِ، اقْضِ عَنْهُ دَيْنَهُ. فَيَقْضِيهِ، فَقُتِلَ الزُّبَيْرُ ـ رضى الله عنه ـ وَلَمْ يَدَعْ دِينَارًا وَلاَ دِرْهَمًا، إِلاَّ أَرَضِينَ مِنْهَا الْغَابَةُ، وَإِحْدَى عَشْرَةَ دَارًا بِالْمَدِينَةِ، وَدَارَيْنِ بِالْبَصْرَةِ، وَدَارًا بِالْكُوفَةِ، وَدَارًا بِمِصْرَ. قَالَ وَإِنَّمَا كَانَ دَيْنُهُ الَّذِي عَلَيْهِ أَنَّ الرَّجُلَ كَانَ يَأْتِيهِ بِالْمَالِ فَيَسْتَوْدِعُهُ إِيَّاهُ فَيَقُولُ الزُّبَيْرُ لاَ وَلَكِنَّهُ سَلَفٌ، فَإِنِّي أَخْشَى عَلَيْهِ الضَّيْعَةَ، وَمَا وَلِيَ إِمَارَةً قَطُّ وَلاَ جِبَايَةَ خَرَاجٍ وَلاَ شَيْئًا، إِلاَّ أَنْ يَكُونَ فِي غَزْوَةٍ مَعَ النَّبِيِّ صلى الله عليه وسلم أَوْ مَعَ أَبِي بَكْرٍ وَعُمَرَ وَعُثْمَانَ ـ رضى الله عنهم ـ قَالَ عَبْدُ اللَّهِ بْنُ الزُّبَيْرِ فَحَسَبْتُ مَا عَلَيْهِ مِنَ الدَّيْنِ فَوَجَدْتُهُ أَلْفَىْ أَلْفٍ وَمِائَتَىْ أَلْفٍ قَالَ فَلَقِيَ حَكِيمُ بْنُ حِزَامٍ عَبْدَ اللَّهِ بْنَ الزُّبَيْرِ فَقَالَ يَا ابْنَ أَخِي، كَمْ عَلَى أَخِي مِنَ الدَّيْنِ فَكَتَمَهُ. فَقَالَ مِائَةُ أَلْفٍ. فَقَالَ حَكِيمٌ وَاللَّهِ مَا أُرَى أَمْوَالَكُمْ تَسَعُ لِهَذِهِ. فَقَالَ لَهُ عَبْدُ اللَّهِ أَفَرَأَيْتَكَ إِنْ كَانَتْ أَلْفَىْ أَلْفٍ وَمِائَتَىْ أَلْفٍ قَالَ مَا أُرَاكُمْ تُطِيقُونَ هَذَا، فَإِنْ عَجَزْتُمْ عَنْ شَىْءٍ مِنْهُ فَاسْتَعِينُوا بِي. قَالَ وَكَانَ الزُّبَيْرُ اشْتَرَى الْغَابَةَ بِسَبْعِينَ وَمِائَةِ أَلْفٍ، فَبَاعَهَا عَبْدُ اللَّهِ بِأَلْفِ أَلْفٍ وَسِتِّمِائَةِ أَلْفٍ ثُمَّ قَامَ فَقَالَ مَنْ كَانَ لَهُ عَلَى الزُّبَيْرِ حَقٌّ فَلْيُوَافِنَا بِالْغَابَةِ، فَأَتَاهُ عَبْدُ اللَّهِ بْنُ جَعْفَرٍ، وَكَانَ لَهُ عَلَى الزُّبَيْرِ أَرْبَعُمِائَةِ أَلْفٍ فَقَالَ لِعَبْدِ اللَّهِ إِنْ شِئْتُمْ تَرَكْتُهَا لَكُمْ. قَالَ عَبْدُ اللَّهِ لاَ. قَالَ فَإِنْ شِئْتُمْ جَعَلْتُمُوهَا فِيمَا تُؤَخِّرُونَ إِنْ أَخَّرْتُمْ. فَقَالَ عَبْدُ اللَّهِ لاَ. قَالَ قَالَ فَاقْطَعُوا لِي قِطْعَةً. فَقَالَ عَبْدُ اللَّهِ لَكَ مِنْ هَا هُنَا إِلَى هَا هُنَا. قَالَ فَبَاعَ مِنْهَا فَقَضَى دَيْنَهُ فَأَوْفَاهُ، وَبَقِيَ مِنْهَا أَرْبَعَةُ أَسْهُمٍ وَنِصْفٌ، فَقَدِمَ عَلَى مُعَاوِيَةَ وَعِنْدَهُ عَمْرُو بْنُ عُثْمَانَ وَالْمُنْذِرُ بْنُ الزُّبَيْرِ وَابْنُ زَمْعَةَ فَقَالَ لَهُ مُعَاوِيَةُ كَمْ قُوِّمَتِ الْغَابَةُ قَالَ كُلُّ سَهْمٍ مِائَةَ أَلْفٍ. قَالَ كَمْ بَقِيَ قَالَ أَرْبَعَةُ أَسْهُمٍ وَنِصْفٌ. قَالَ الْمُنْذِرُ بْنُ الزُّبَيْرِ قَدْ أَخَذْتُ سَهْمًا بِمِائَةِ أَلْفٍ. قَالَ عَمْرُو بْنُ عُثْمَانَ قَدْ أَخَذْتُ سَهْمًا بِمِائَةِ أَلْفٍ. وَقَالَ ابْنُ زَمْعَةَ قَدْ أَخَذْتُ سَهْمًا بِمِائَةِ أَلْفٍ. فَقَالَ مُعَاوِيَةُ كَمْ بَقِيَ فَقَالَ سَهْمٌ وَنِصْفٌ. قَالَ أَخَذْتُهُ بِخَمْسِينَ وَمِائَةِ أَلْفٍ. قَالَ وَبَاعَ عَبْدُ اللَّهِ بْنُ جَعْفَرٍ نَصِيبَهُ مِنْ مُعَاوِيَةَ بِسِتِّمِائَةِ أَلْفٍ، فَلَمَّا فَرَغَ ابْنُ الزُّبَيْرِ مِنْ قَضَاءِ دَيْنِهِ قَالَ بَنُو الزُّبَيْرِ اقْسِمْ بَيْنَنَا مِيرَاثَنَا. قَالَ لاَ، وَاللَّهِ لاَ أَقْسِمُ بَيْنَكُمْ حَتَّى أُنَادِيَ بِالْمَوْسِمِ أَرْبَعَ سِنِينَ أَلاَ مَنْ كَانَ لَهُ عَلَى الزُّبَيْرِ دَيْنٌ فَلْيَأْتِنَا فَلْنَقْضِهِ. قَالَ فَجَعَلَ كُلَّ سَنَةٍ يُنَادِي بِالْمَوْسِمِ، فَلَمَّا مَضَى أَرْبَعُ سِنِينَ قَسَمَ بَيْنَهُمْ قَالَ فَكَانَ لِلزُّبَيْرِ أَرْبَعُ نِسْوَةٍ، وَرَفَعَ الثُّلُثَ، فَأَصَابَ كُلَّ امْرَأَةٍ أَلْفُ أَلْفٍ وَمِائَتَا أَلْفٍ، فَجَمِيعُ مَالِهِ خَمْسُونَ أَلْفَ أَلْفٍ وَمِائَتَا أَلْفٍ.

Narrated `Urwa bin Az-Zubair: Hakim bin Hizam said, "I asked Allah's Messenger ﷺ for something, and he gave me, and I asked him again and he gave me and said, 'O Hakim! This wealth is green and sweet (i.e. as tempting as fruits), and whoever takes it without greed then he is blessed in it, and whoever takes it with greediness, he is not blessed in it and he is like one who eats and never gets satisfied. The upper (i.e. giving) hand is better than the lower (i.e. taking) hand." Hakim added, "I said, O Allah's Messenger ﷺ ! By Him Who has sent you with the Truth I will never demand anything from anybody after you till I die." Afterwards Abu Bakr used to call Hakim to give him something but he refused to accept anything from him. Then `Umar called him to give him (something) but he refused. Then `Umar said, "O Muslims! I offered to him (i.e. Hakim) his share which Allah has ordained for him from this booty and he refuses to take it." Thus Hakim did not ask anybody for anything after the Prophet, till he died—may Allah bestow His mercy upon him. – Sahih Al-Bukhari 2750

حَدَّثَنَا مُحَمَّدُ بْنُ يُوسُفَ، حَدَّثَنَا الأَوْزَاعِيُّ، عَنِ الزُّهْرِيِّ، عَنْ سَعِيدِ بْنِ الْمُسَيَّبِ، وَعُرْوَةَ بْنِ الزُّبَيْرِ، أَنَّ حَكِيمَ بْنَ حِزَامٍ ـ رضى الله عنه ـ قَالَ سَأَلْتُ رَسُولَ اللَّهِ صلى الله عليه وسلم فَأَعْطَانِي، ثُمَّ سَأَلْتُهُ فَأَعْطَانِي ثُمَّ قَالَ لِي " يَا حَكِيمُ، إِنَّ هَذَا الْمَالَ خَضِرٌ حُلْوٌ، فَمَنْ أَخَذَهُ بِسَخَاوَةِ نَفْسٍ بُورِكَ لَهُ فِيهِ، وَمَنْ أَخَذَهُ بِإِشْرَافِ نَفْسٍ لَمْ يُبَارَكْ لَهُ فِيهِ، وَكَانَ كَالَّذِي يَأْكُلُ وَلاَ يَشْبَعُ، وَالْيَدُ الْعُلْيَا خَيْرٌ مِنَ الْيَدِ السُّفْلَى ". قَالَ حَكِيمٌ فَقُلْتُ يَا رَسُولَ اللَّهِ، وَالَّذِي بَعَثَكَ بِالْحَقِّ لاَ أَرْزَأُ أَحَدًا بَعْدَكَ شَيْئًا حَتَّى أُفَارِقَ الدُّنْيَا. فَكَانَ أَبُو بَكْرٍ يَدْعُو حَكِيمًا لِيُعْطِيَهُ الْعَطَاءَ فَيَأْبَى أَنْ يَقْبَلَ مِنْهُ شَيْئًا، ثُمَّ إِنَّ عُمَرَ دَعَاهُ لِيُعْطِيَهُ فَيَأْبَى أَنْ يَقْبَلَهُ فَقَالَ يَا مَعْشَرَ الْمُسْلِمِينَ، إِنِّي أَعْرِضُ عَلَيْهِ حَقَّهُ الَّذِي قَسَمَ اللَّهُ لَهُ مِنْ هَذَا الْفَىْءِ فَيَأْبَى أَنْ يَأْخُذَهُ. فَلَمْ يَرْزَأْ حَكِيمٌ أَحَدًا مِنَ النَّاسِ بَعْدَ النَّبِيِّ صلى الله عليه وسلم حَتَّى تُوُفِّيَ رَحِمَهُ اللَّهُ

Narrated Hakim bin Hizam: That he said, "O Allah's Messenger ﷺ what do you think about my good deeds which I used to do during the period of ignorance (before embracing Islam) like keeping good relations with my Kith and kin, manumitting of slaves and giving alms etc; Shall

I receive the reward for that?" Allah's Messenger ﷺ said, "You have embraced Islam with all those good deeds which you did. – Sahih Al-Bukhari 5992

حَدَّثَنَا أَبُو الْيَمَانِ، أَخْبَرَنَا شُعَيْبٌ، عَنِ الزُّهْرِيِّ، قَالَ أَخْبَرَنِي عُرْوَةُ بْنُ الزُّبَيْرِ، أَنَّ حَكِيمَ بْنَ حِزَامٍ، أَخْبَرَهُ أَنَّهُ، قَالَ يَا رَسُولَ اللَّهِ أَرَأَيْتَ أُمُورًا كُنْتُ أَتَحَنَّثُ بِهَا فِي الْجَاهِلِيَّةِ مِنْ صِلَةٍ وَعَتَاقَةٍ وَصَدَقَةٍ، هَلْ لِي فِيهَا مِنْ أَجْرٍ. قَالَ حَكِيمٌ قَالَ رَسُولُ اللَّهِ صلى الله عليه وسلم " أَسْلَمْتَ عَلَى مَا سَلَفَ مِنْ خَيْرٍ ". وَيُقَالُ أَيْضًا عَنْ أَبِي الْيَمَانِ أَتَحَنَّثُ. وَقَالَ مَعْمَرٌ وَصَالِحٌ وَابْنُ الْمُسَافِرِ أَتَحَنَّثُ. وَقَالَ ابْنُ إِسْحَاقَ التَّحَنُّثُ التَّبَرُّرُ، وَتَابَعَهُمْ هِشَامٌ عَنْ أَبِيهِ.

Narrated Hakim bin Hizam: The Prophet ﷺ said, "Both the buyer and the seller have the option of canceling or confirming the bargain unless they separate." The sub-narrator, Hammam said, "I found this in my book: 'Both the buyer and the seller give the option of either confirming or canceling the bargain three times, and if they speak the truth and mention the defects, then their bargain will be blessed, and if they tell lies and conceal the defects, they might gain some financial gain but they will deprive their sale of (Allah's) blessings.". – Sahih Al-Bukhari 2114

حَدَّثَنِي إِسْحَاقُ، حَدَّثَنَا حَبَّانُ، حَدَّثَنَا هَمَّامٌ، حَدَّثَنَا قَتَادَةُ، عَنْ أَبِي الْخَلِيلِ، عَنْ عَبْدِ اللَّهِ بْنِ الْحَارِثِ، عَنْ حَكِيمِ بْنِ حِزَامٍ - رضى الله عنه - أَنَّ النَّبِيَّ صلى الله عليه وسلم قَالَ " الْبَيِّعَانِ بِالْخِيَارِ مَا لَمْ يَتَفَرَّقَا " - قَالَ هَمَّامٌ وَجَدْتُ فِي كِتَابِي يَخْتَارُ ثَلاَثَ مِرَارٍ - "فَإِنْ صَدَقَا وَبَيَّنَا بُورِكَ لَهُمَا فِي بَيْعِهِمَا، وَإِنْ كَذَبَا وَكَتَمَا فَعَسَى أَنْ يَرْبَحَا رِبْحًا، وَيُمْحَقَا بَرَكَةَ بَيْعِهِمَا ". قَالَ وَحَدَّثَنَا هَمَّامٌ، حَدَّثَنَا أَبُو التَّيَّاحِ، أَنَّهُ سَمِعَ عَبْدَ اللَّهِ بْنَ الْحَارِثِ، يُحَدِّثُ بِهَذَا الْحَدِيثِ عَنْ حَكِيمِ بْنِ حِزَامٍ، عَنِ النَّبِيِّ صلى الله عليه وسلم.

Narrated Hakim bin Hizam: The Prophet ﷺ said, "The upper hand is better than the lower hand (i.e. he who gives in charity is better than him who takes it). One should start giving first to his dependents. And the best object of charity is that which is given by a wealthy person (from the money which is left after his expenses). And whoever abstains from asking others for some financial help, Allah will give him and save him from asking others, Allah will make him self-sufficient.". – Sahih Al-Bukhari 1427, 1428

حَدَّثَنَا مُوسَى بْنُ إِسْمَاعِيلَ، حَدَّثَنَا وُهَيْبٌ، حَدَّثَنَا هِشَامٌ، عَنْ أَبِيهِ، عَنْ حَكِيمِ بْنِ حِزَامٍ - رضى الله عنه - عَنِ النَّبِيِّ صلى الله عليه وسلم قَالَ " الْيَدُ الْعُلْيَا خَيْرٌ مِنَ الْيَدِ السُّفْلَى، وَابْدَأْ بِمَنْ تَعُولُ، وَخَيْرُ الصَّدَقَةِ عَنْ ظَهْرِ غِنًى، وَمَنْ يَسْتَعْفِفْ يُعِفَّهُ اللَّهُ، وَمَنْ يَسْتَغْنِ يُغْنِهِ اللَّهُ ". وَعَنْ وُهَيْبٍ، قَالَ أَخْبَرَنَا هِشَامٌ، عَنْ أَبِيهِ، عَنْ أَبِي هُرَيْرَةَ - رضى الله عنه - بِهَذَا

Mujashi
مُجَاشِعٍ

Narrated Abu Sa`id: `Ali sent a piece of gold to the Prophet ﷺ who distributed it among four persons: Al-Aqra' bin H`Abis Al-Hanzali from the tribe of Mujashi, 'Uyaina bin Badr Al-Fazari, Zaid at-Ta'I who belonged to (the tribe of) Bani Nahban, and 'Alqama bin Ulatha Al-`Amir who belonged to (the tribe of) Bani Kilab. So the Quraish and the Ansar became angry and said, "He (i.e. the Prophet ﷺ), gives the chief of Najd and does not give us." The Prophet ﷺ said, "I give them) so as to attract their hearts (to Islam)." Then a man with sunken eyes, prominent checks, a raised forehead, a thick beard and a shaven head, came (in front of the Prophet ﷺ) and said, "Be afraid of Allah, O Muhammad!" The Prophet ﷺ said "Who would obey Allah if I disobeyed Him? (Is it fair that) Allah has trusted all the people of the earth to me while, you do not trust me?" Somebody who, I think was Khalid bin Al-Walid, requested the Prophet ﷺ to let him chop that man's head off, but he prevented him. When the man left, the Prophet ﷺ said, "Among the off-spring of this man will be some who will recite the Qur'an but the Qur'an will not reach beyond their throats (i.e. they will recite like parrots and will not understand it nor act on it), and they will renegade from the religion as an arrow goes through the game's body. They will kill the Muslims but will not disturb the idolaters. If I should live up to their time' I will kill them as the people of 'Ad were killed (i.e. I will kill all of them).". – Sahih Al-Bukhari 3344

قَالَ وَقَالَ ابْنُ كَثِيرٍ عَنْ سُفْيَانَ، عَنْ أَبِيهِ، عَنِ ابْنِ أَبِي نُعْمٍ، عَنْ أَبِي سَعِيدٍ ـ رضى الله عنه ـ قَالَ بَعَثَ عَلِيٌّ ـ رضى الله عنه ـ إِلَى النَّبِيِّ صلى الله عليه وسلم بِذُهَيْبَةٍ فَقَسَمَهَا بَيْنَ الأَرْبَعَةِ الأَقْرَعِ بْنِ حَابِسٍ الْحَنْظَلِيِّ ثُمَّ الْمُجَاشِعِيِّ، وَعُيَيْنَةَ بْنِ بَدْرٍ الْفَزَارِيِّ، وَزَيْدٍ الطَّائِيِّ ثُمَّ أَحَدِ بَنِي نَبْهَانَ، وَعَلْقَمَةَ بْنِ عُلاَثَةَ الْعَامِرِيِّ ثُمَّ أَحَدِ بَنِي كِلاَبٍ، فَغَضِبَتْ قُرَيْشٌ وَالأَنْصَارُ، قَالُوا يُعْطِي صَنَادِيدَ أَهْلِ نَجْدٍ وَيَدَعُنَا. قَالَ " إِنَّمَا أَتَأَلَّفُهُمْ ". فَأَقْبَلَ رَجُلٌ غَائِرُ الْعَيْنَيْنِ مُشْرِفُ الْوَجْنَتَيْنِ، نَاتِئُ الْجَبِينِ، كَثُّ اللِّحْيَةِ، مَحْلُوقٌ فَقَالَ اتَّقِ اللَّهَ يَا مُحَمَّدُ. فَقَالَ " مَنْ يُطِعِ اللَّهَ إِذَا عَصَيْتُ، أَيَأْمَنُنِي اللَّهُ عَلَى أَهْلِ الأَرْضِ فَلاَ تَأْمَنُونِي ". فَسَأَلَهُ رَجُلٌ قَتْلَهُ ـ أَحْسِبُهُ خَالِدَ بْنَ الْوَلِيدِ ـ فَمَنَعَهُ، فَلَمَّا وَلَّى قَالَ " إِنَّ مِنْ ضِئْضِئِ هَذَا ـ أَوْ فِي عَقِبِ هَذَا ـ قَوْمٌ يَقْرَءُونَ الْقُرْآنَ، لاَ يُجَاوِزُ حَنَاجِرَهُمْ، يَمْرُقُونَ مِنَ الدِّينِ مُرُوقَ السَّهْمِ مِنَ الرَّمِيَّةِ، يَقْتُلُونَ أَهْلَ الإِسْلاَمِ، وَيَدَعُونَ أَهْلَ الأَوْثَانِ، لَئِنْ أَنَا أَدْرَكْتُهُمْ لأَقْتُلَنَّهُمْ قَتْلَ عَادٍ ".

Narrated Mujashi: My brother and I came to the Prophetﷺ and I requested him to take the pledge of allegiance from us for migration. He said, "Migration has passed away with its people." I asked, "For what will you take the pledge of allegiance from us then?" He said, "I will take (the pledge) for Islam and Jihad.". – Sahih Al-Bukhari 2962, 2963

حَدَّثَنَا إِسْحَاقُ بْنُ إِبْرَاهِيمَ، سَمِعَ مُحَمَّدَ بْنَ فُضَيْلٍ، عَنْ عَاصِمٍ، عَنْ أَبِي عُثْمَانَ، عَنْ مُجَاشِعٍ ـ رضى الله عنه ـ قَالَ أَتَيْتُ النَّبِيَّ صلى الله عليه وسلم أَنَا وَأَخِي فَقُلْتُ بَايِعْنَا عَلَى الْهِجْرَةِ. فَقَالَ " مَضَتِ الْهِجْرَةُ لأَهْلِهَا ". فَقُلْتُ عَلاَمَ تُبَايِعُنَا قَالَ " عَلَى الإِسْلاَمِ وَالْجِهَادِ "

Narrated Abu Sa`id Al-Khudri: When `Ali was in Yemen, he sent some gold in its ore to the Prophet. The Prophetﷺ distributed it among Al-Aqra' bin H`Abis Al-Hanzali who belonged to Bani Mujashi, 'Uyaina bin Badr Al-Fazari, 'Alqama bin 'Ulatha Al-`Amiri, who belonged to the Bani Kilab tribe and Zaid Al-Khail at-Ta'I who belonged to Bani Nabhan. So the Quraish and the Ansar became angry and said, "He gives to the chiefs of Najd and leaves us!" The Prophetﷺ said, "I just wanted to attract and unite their hearts (make them firm in Islam)." Then there came a man with sunken eyes, bulging forehead, thick beard, fat raised cheeks, and clean-shaven head, and said, "O Muhammad! Be afraid of Allah! " The Prophetﷺ said, "Who would obey Allah if I disobeyed Him? (Allah). He trusts me over the people of the earth, but you do not trust me?" A man from the people (present then), who, I think, was Khalid bin Al- Walid, asked for permission to kill him, but the Prophetﷺ prevented him. When the man went away, the Prophet said, "Out of the offspring of this man, there will be people who will recite the Qur'an but it will not go beyond their throats, and they will go out of Islam as an arrow goes out through the game, and they will kill the Muslims and leave the idolators. Should I live till they appear, I would kill them as the Killing of the nation of 'Ad." – Sahih al-Bukhari 7432

حَدَّثَنَا قَبِيصَةُ، حَدَّثَنَا سُفْيَانُ، عَنْ أَبِيهِ، عَنِ ابْنِ أَبِي نُعْمٍ ـ أَوْ أَبِي نُعْمٍ شَكَّ قَبِيصَةُ ـ عَنْ أَبِي سَعِيدٍ، قَالَ بُعِثَ إِلَى النَّبِيِّ صلى الله عليه وسلم بِذُهَيْبَةٍ فَقَسَمَهَا بَيْنَ أَرْبَعَةٍ. وَحَدَّثَنِي إِسْحَاقُ بْنُ نَصْرٍ حَدَّثَنَا عَبْدُ الرَّزَّاقِ أَخْبَرَنَا سُفْيَانُ عَنْ أَبِيهِ عَنِ ابْنِ أَبِي نُعْمٍ عَنْ أَبِي سَعِيدٍ الْخُدْرِيِّ قَالَ بَعَثَ عَلِيٌّ وَهْوَ بِالْيَمَنِ إِلَى النَّبِيِّ صلى الله عليه وسلم بِذُهَيْبَةٍ فِي تُرْبَتِهَا، فَقَسَمَهَا بَيْنَ الأَقْرَعِ بْنِ حَابِسٍ الْحَنْظَلِيِّ ثُمَّ أَحَدِ بَنِي مُجَاشِعٍ، وَبَيْنَ عُيَيْنَةَ بْنِ بَدْرٍ الْفَزَارِيِّ، وَبَيْنَ عَلْقَمَةَ بْنِ عُلاَثَةَ الْعَامِرِيِّ ثُمَّ أَحَدِ بَنِي كِلاَبٍ، وَبَيْنَ زَيْدِ الْخَيْلِ الطَّائِيِّ ثُمَّ أَحَدِ بَنِي نَبْهَانَ، فَتَغَضَّبَتْ قُرَيْشٌ وَالأَنْصَارُ فَقَالُوا يُعْطِيهِ صَنَادِيدَ أَهْلِ نَجْدٍ وَيَدَعُنَا قَالَ " إِنَّمَا أَتَأَلَّفُهُمْ ". فَأَقْبَلَ رَجُلٌ غَائِرُ الْعَيْنَيْنِ، نَاتِئُ الْجَبِينِ، كَثُّ اللِّحْيَةِ، مُشْرِفُ الْوَجْنَتَيْنِ، مَحْلُوقُ الرَّأْسِ فَقَالَ يَا مُحَمَّدُ اتَّقِ اللَّهَ. فَقَالَ النَّبِيُّ صلى الله عليه وسلم " فَمَنْ يُطِيعُ اللَّهَ إِذَا عَصَيْتُهُ فَيَأْمَنِّي عَلَى أَهْلِ الأَرْضِ، وَلاَ تَأْمَنُونِي ". فَسَأَلَ رَجُلٌ مِنَ الْقَوْمِ ـ قَتْلَهُ أُرَاهُ خَالِدَ بْنَ الْوَلِيدِ ـ فَمَنَعَهُ النَّبِيُّ صلى الله عليه وسلم فَلَمَّا وَلَّى قَالَ النَّبِيُّ صلى الله عليه وسلم " إِنَّ مِنْ ضِئْضِئِ هَذَا قَوْمًا يَقْرَءُونَ الْقُرْآنَ لاَ يُجَاوِزُ حَنَاجِرَهُمْ، يَمْرُقُونَ مِنَ الإِسْلاَمِ مُرُوقَ السَّهْمِ مِنَ الرَّمِيَّةِ، يَقْتُلُونَ أَهْلَ الإِسْلاَمِ وَيَدَعُونَ أَهْلَ الأَوْثَانِ، لَئِنْ أَدْرَكْتُهُمْ لأَقْتُلَنَّهُمْ قَتْلَ عَادٍ ".

Abu sa'id al-khudri said : 'Ali sent some gold-mixed dust to the prophet (May peace be upon him). He divided it among the four : al-Aqra b. Habis al-Hanzall and then al-Mujashi, uyainah b. Badr al-fazari, zaid al-khail al-Ta'l, next to one of Banu nabhan, and 'Alqamah b. 'Ulathat al-Amiri (in general), next to one of Banu kulaib. The Quraish and the ansar became angry and said : He is giving to the chiefs of the people of Najd and leaving us. He said : I am giving them for reconciliation of their hearts. Then a man with deep-seated eyes, high cheek-bones, a projecting brow, a thick beard and a shaven head came forward and said: For Allah, Muhammad! He said : Who will obey Allah if I disobey Him? Allah entrusts me with power over the inhabitants of the earth, but you do not. A man asked to be allowed to kill him and I think he was Khalid b. al-Walid but he prevented him. Then when the man turned away, he said: From this one's stock there will be people who recite the Quran, but it will not pass down their throats. They will sever from Islam and leave the worshippers of Idols alone; but if I live up to their time I shall certainly kill them as 'Ad were killed. – Sunan Abi Dawud 4764
حَدَّثَنَا مُحَمَّدُ بْنُ كَثِيرٍ، أَخْبَرَنَا سُفْيَانُ، عَنْ أَبِيهِ، عَنِ ابْنِ أَبِي نُعْمٍ، عَنْ أَبِي سَعِيدٍ الْخُدْرِيِّ، قَالَ : بَعَثَ عَلِيٌّ عَلَيْهِ السَّلاَمُ إِلَى النَّبِيِّ صلى الله عليه وسلم بِذُهَيْبَةٍ فِي تُرْبَتِهَا، فَقَسَّمَهَا بَيْنَ أَرْبَعَةٍ بَيْنَ : الأَقْرَعِ بْنِ حَابِسٍ الْحَنْظَلِيِّ ثُمَّ الْمُجَاشِعِيِّ، وَبَيْنَ عُيَيْنَةَ بْنِ بَدْرٍ الْفَزَارِيِّ وَبَيْنَ زَيْدِ الْخَيْلِ الطَّائِيِّ ثُمَّ أَحَدِ بَنِي نَبْهَانَ وَبَيْنَ عَلْقَمَةَ بْنِ عُلاَثَةَ الْعَامِرِيِّ ثُمَّ أَحَدِ بَنِي كِلاَبٍ قَالَ فَغَضِبَتْ قُرَيْشٌ وَالأَنْصَارُ وَقَالَتْ : يُعْطِي صَنَادِيدَ أَهْلِ نَجْدٍ وَيَدَعُنَا . فَقَالَ : " إِنَّمَا أَتَأَلَّفُهُمْ " . قَالَ : فَأَقْبَلَ رَجُلٌ غَائِرُ الْعَيْنَيْنِ مُشْرِفُ الْوَجْنَتَيْنِ نَاتِئُ الْجَبِينِ كَثُّ اللِّحْيَةِ مَحْلُوقٌ قَالَ : اتَّقِ اللَّهَ يَا مُحَمَّدُ . فَقَالَ : " مَنْ يُطِعِ اللَّهَ إِذَا عَصَيْتُهُ أَيَأْمَنُنِي اللَّهُ عَلَى أَهْلِ الأَرْضِ وَلاَ تَأْمَنُونِي " . قَالَ : فَسَأَلَ رَجُلٌ قَتْلَهُ أَحْسِبُهُ خَالِدَ بْنَ الْوَلِيدِ – قَالَ – فَمَنَعَهُ . قَالَ : فَلَمَّا وَلَّى قَالَ : " إِنَّ مِنْ ضِئْضِئِ هَذَا أَوْ فِي عَقِبِ هَذَا قَوْمًا يَقْرَءُونَ الْقُرْآنَ لاَ يُجَاوِزُ حَنَاجِرَهُمْ يَمْرُقُونَ مِنَ الإِسْلاَمِ مُرُوقَ السَّهْمِ مِنَ الرَّمِيَّةِ، يَقْتُلُونَ أَهْلَ الإِسْلاَمِ وَيَدَعُونَ أَهْلَ الأَوْثَانِ لَئِنْ أَنَا أَدْرَكْتُهُمْ قَتَلْتُهُمْ قَتْلَ عَادٍ " .

Wahshi ibn Harb

وحشي بن حرب

Narrated Wahshi ibn Harb: The Companions of the Prophet ﷺ said: Messenger of Allah ﷺ we eat but we are not satisfied. He said: Perhaps you eat separately. They replied: Yes. He said: If you gather together at your food and mention Allah's name, you will be blessed in it. Abu Dawud said: If you are invited to a wedding feast before you, do not take it until the owner of the house (i.e. the host) allows you (to eat). – Sunan Abi Dawud 3764
حَدَّثَنَا إِبْرَاهِيمُ بْنُ مُوسَى الرَّازِيُّ، حَدَّثَنَا الْوَلِيدُ بْنُ مُسْلِمٍ، قَالَ حَدَّثَنِي وَحْشِيُّ بْنُ حَرْبٍ، عَنْ أَبِيهِ، عَنْ جَدِّهِ، أَنَّ أَصْحَابَ النَّبِيِّ، صلى الله عليه وسلم قَالُوا يَا رَسُولَ اللَّهِ إِنَّا نَأْكُلُ وَلاَ نَشْبَعُ . قَالَ " فَلَعَلَّكُمْ تَفْتَرِقُونَ " . قَالُوا نَعَمْ . قَالَ " فَاجْتَمِعُوا عَلَى طَعَامِكُمْ وَاذْكُرُوا اسْمَ اللَّهِ عَلَيْهِ يُبَارَكْ لَكُمْ فِيهِ " . قَالَ أَبُو دَاوُدَ إِذَا كُنْتَ فِي وَلِيمَةٍ فَوُضِعَ الْعَشَاءُ فَلاَ تَأْكُلْ حَتَّى يَأْذَنَ لَكَ صَاحِبُ الدَّارِ

Narrated Jafar bin `Amr bin Umaiya: I went out with 'Ubaidullah bin `Adi Al-Khaiyar. When we reached Hims (i.e. a town in Syria), 'Ubaidullah bin `Adi said (to me), "Would you like to see Wahshi so that we may ask him about the killing of Hamza?" I replied, "Yes." Wahshi used to live in Hims. We enquired about him and somebody said to us, "He is that in the shade of his palace, as if he were a full water skin." So we went up to him, and when we were at a short distance from him, we greeted him and he greeted us in return. 'Ubaidullah was wearing his turban and Wahshi could not see except his eyes and feet. 'Ubaidullah said, "O Wahshi! Do you know me?" Wahshi looked at him and then said, "No, by Allah! But I know that `Adi bin Al-Khiyar married a woman called Um Qital, the daughter of Abu Al-Is, and she delivered a boy for him at Mecca, and I looked for a wet nurse for that child. (Once) I carried that child along with his mother and then I handed him over to her, and your feet resemble that child's feet." Then 'Ubaidullah uncovered his face and said (to Wahshi), "Will you tell us (the story of) the killing of Hamza?" Wahshi replied "Yes, Hamza killed Tuaima bin `Adi bin Al-Khaiyar at Badr (battle) so my master, Jubair bin Mut`im said to me, 'If you kill Hamza in revenge for my uncle, then you will be set free." When the people set out (for the battle of Uhud) in the year of 'Ainain ..'Ainain is a mountain near the mountain of Uhud, and between it and Uhud there is a valley.. I went out with the people for the battle. When the army aligned for the fight, Siba' came out and said, 'Is there any (Muslim) to accept my challenge to a duel?' Hamza bin `Abdul Muttalib came out and said, 'O Siba'. O Ibn Um Anmar, the one who circumcises other ladies! Do you challenge Allah and His Apostle?' Then Hamza attacked and killed him, causing him to be non-extant like the bygone yesterday. I hid myself under a rock, and when he (i.e. Hamza) came near me, I threw my spear at him, driving it into his umbilicus so that it came out through his buttocks, causing him to die. When all the people returned to Mecca, I too returned with them. I stayed in (Mecca) till Islam spread in it (i.e. Mecca). Then I left for Taif, and when the people (of Taif) sent their messengers to Allah's Messenger ﷺ, I was told that the Prophet ﷺ did not harm the messengers; So I too went out with them till I reached Allah's Messenger ﷺ. When he saw me, he said, 'Are you Wahshi?' I said, 'Yes.' He said, 'Was it you who killed Hamza?' I replied, 'What happened is what you have been told of.' He said, 'Can you hide your face from me?' So I went out when Allah's Messenger ﷺ died, and Musailamah Al-Kadhdhab appeared (claiming to be a prophet). I said, 'I will go out to Musailamah so that I may kill him, and make amends for killing Hamza. So I went out with the people (to fight Musailamah and his followers) and then famous events took place concerning that battle. Suddenly I saw a man (i.e. Musailamah) standing near a gap in a wall. He looked like an ash-colored camel and his hair was dishevelled. So I threw my spear at him, driving it into his chest in between his breasts till it passed out through his shoulders, and then an Ansari man attacked him and struck him on the head with a sword. `Abdullah bin `Umar said, 'A slave girl on the roof of a house said: Alas! The chief of the believers (i.e. Musailamah) has been killed by a black slave.". – Sahih Al-Bukhari 4072

حَدَّثَنِي أَبُو جَعْفَرٍ، مُحَمَّدُ بْنُ عَبْدِ اللَّهِ حَدَّثَنَا حُجَيْنُ بْنُ الْمُثَنَّى، حَدَّثَنَا عَبْدُ الْعَزِيزِ بْنُ عَبْدِ اللَّهِ بْنِ أَبِي سَلَمَةَ، عَنْ عَبْدِ اللَّهِ بْنِ الْفَضْلِ، عَنْ سُلَيْمَانَ بْنِ يَسَارٍ، عَنْ جَعْفَرِ بْنِ عَمْرِو بْنِ أُمَيَّةَ الضَّمْرِيِّ، قَالَ خَرَجْتُ مَعَ عُبَيْدِ اللَّهِ بْنِ عَدِيِّ بْنِ الْخِيَارِ، فَلَمَّا قَدِمْنَا حِمْصَ قَالَ لِي عُبَيْدُ اللَّهِ هَلْ لَكَ فِي وَحْشِيٍّ نَسْأَلُهُ عَنْ قَتْلِ حَمْزَةَ قُلْتُ نَعَمْ. وَكَانَ وَحْشِيٌّ يَسْكُنُ حِمْصَ فَسَأَلْنَا عَنْهُ فَقِيلَ لَنَا هُوَ ذَاكَ فِي ظِلِّ قَصْرِهِ، كَأَنَّهُ حَمِيتٌ. قَالَ فَجِئْنَا حَتَّى وَقَفْنَا عَلَيْهِ بِيَسِيرٍ، فَسَلَّمْنَا، فَرَدَّ السَّلاَمَ، قَالَ وَعُبَيْدُ اللَّهِ مُعْتَجِرٌ بِعِمَامَتِهِ، مَا يَرَى وَحْشِيٌّ إِلاَّ عَيْنَيْهِ وَرِجْلَيْهِ، فَقَالَ عُبَيْدُ اللَّهِ يَا وَحْشِيُّ أَتَعْرِفُنِي قَالَ فَنَظَرَ إِلَيْهِ ثُمَّ قَالَ لاَ وَاللَّهِ إِلاَّ أَنِّي أَعْلَمُ أَنَّ عَدِيَّ بْنَ الْخِيَارِ تَزَوَّجَ امْرَأَةً يُقَالُ لَهَا أُمُّ قِتَالٍ بِنْتُ أَبِي الْعِيصِ، فَوَلَدَتْ لَهُ غُلاَمًا بِمَكَّةَ، فَكُنْتُ أَسْتَرْضِعُ لَهُ، فَحَمَلْتُ ذَلِكَ الْغُلاَمَ مَعَ أُمِّهِ، فَنَاوَلْتُهَا إِيَّاهُ، فَلَكَأَنِّي نَظَرْتُ إِلَى قَدَمَيْكَ. قَالَ فَكَشَفَ عُبَيْدُ اللَّهِ عَنْ وَجْهِهِ ثُمَّ قَالَ أَلاَ تُخْبِرُنَا بِقَتْلِ حَمْزَةَ قَالَ نَعَمْ، إِنَّ حَمْزَةَ قَتَلَ طُعَيْمَةَ بْنَ عَدِيِّ بْنِ الْخِيَارِ بِبَدْرٍ، فَقَالَ لِي مَوْلاَىَ جُبَيْرُ بْنُ مُطْعِمٍ إِنْ قَتَلْتَ حَمْزَةَ بِعَمِّي فَأَنْتَ حُرٌّ، قَالَ فَلَمَّا أَنْ خَرَجَ النَّاسُ عَامَ عَيْنَيْنِ ـ وَعَيْنَيْنِ جَبَلٌ بِحِيَالِ أُحُدٍ، بَيْنَهُ وَبَيْنَهُ وَادٍ ـ خَرَجْتُ مَعَ النَّاسِ إِلَى الْقِتَالِ، فَلَمَّا اصْطَفُّوا لِلْقِتَالِ خَرَجَ سِبَاعٌ فَقَالَ هَلْ مِنْ مُبَارِزٍ قَالَ فَخَرَجَ إِلَيْهِ حَمْزَةُ بْنُ عَبْدِ الْمُطَّلِبِ فَقَالَ يَا سِبَاعُ يَا ابْنَ أُمِّ أَنْمَارٍ مُقَطِّعَةِ الْبُظُورِ، أَتُحَادُّ اللَّهَ وَرَسُولَهُ صلى الله عليه وسلم قَالَ ثُمَّ شَدَّ عَلَيْهِ فَكَانَ كَأَمْسِ الذَّاهِبِ ـ قَالَ ـ وَكَمَنْتُ لِحَمْزَةَ تَحْتَ صَخْرَةٍ فَلَمَّا دَنَا مِنِّي رَمَيْتُهُ بِحَرْبَتِي، فَأَضَعُهَا فِي ثُنَّتِهِ حَتَّى خَرَجَتْ مِنْ بَيْنِ وَرِكَيْهِ ـ قَالَ ـ فَكَانَ ذَاكَ الْعَهْدَ بِهِ، فَلَمَّا رَجَعَ النَّاسُ رَجَعْتُ مَعَهُمْ فَأَقَمْتُ بِمَكَّةَ، حَتَّى فَشَا فِيهَا الإِسْلاَمُ، ثُمَّ خَرَجْتُ إِلَى الطَّائِفِ، فَأَرْسَلُوا إِلَى رَسُولِ اللَّهِ صلى الله عليه وسلم رَسُولاً، فَقِيلَ لِي إِنَّهُ لاَ يَهِيجُ الرُّسُلَ ـ قَالَ ـ فَخَرَجْتُ مَعَهُمْ حَتَّى قَدِمْتُ عَلَى رَسُولِ اللَّهِ صلى الله عليه وسلم فَلَمَّا رَآنِي قَالَ " آنْتَ وَحْشِيٌّ ". قُلْتُ نَعَمْ. قَالَ " أَنْتَ قَتَلْتَ حَمْزَةَ ". قُلْتُ قَدْ كَانَ مِنَ الأَمْرِ مَا بَلَغَكَ. قَالَ " فَهَلْ تَسْتَطِيعُ أَنْ تُغَيِّبَ وَجْهَكَ عَنِّي ". قَالَ فَخَرَجْتُ، فَلَمَّا قُبِضَ رَسُولُ اللَّهِ صلى الله عليه وسلم فَخَرَجَ مُسَيْلِمَةُ الْكَذَّابُ قُلْتُ لأَخْرُجَنَّ إِلَى مُسَيْلِمَةَ لَعَلِّي أَقْتُلُهُ فَأُكَافِئَ بِهِ حَمْزَةَ ـ قَالَ ـ فَخَرَجْتُ مَعَ النَّاسِ، فَكَانَ مِنْ أَمْرِهِ مَا كَانَ ـ قَالَ ـ فَإِذَا رَجُلٌ قَائِمٌ فِي ثَلْمَةِ جِدَارٍ، كَأَنَّهُ جَمَلٌ أَوْرَقُ ثَائِرُ الرَّأْسِ ـ قَالَ ـ فَرَمَيْتُهُ بِحَرْبَتِي، فَأَضَعُهَا بَيْنَ ثَدْيَيْهِ حَتَّى خَرَجَتْ مِنْ بَيْنِ كَتِفَيْهِ ـ قَالَ ـ وَوَثَبَ إِلَيْهِ رَجُلٌ مِنَ الأَنْصَارِ، فَضَرَبَهُ بِالسَّيْفِ عَلَى هَامَتِهِ. قَالَ قَالَ عَبْدُ اللَّهِ بْنُ الْفَضْلِ فَأَخْبَرَنِي سُلَيْمَانُ بْنُ يَسَارٍ أَنَّهُ سَمِعَ عَبْدَ اللَّهِ بْنَ عُمَرَ يَقُولُ فَقَالَتْ جَارِيَةٌ عَلَى ظَهْرِ بَيْتٍ وَا أَمِيرَ الْمُؤْمِنِينَ، قَتَلَهُ الْعَبْدُ الأَسْوَدُ

Abu Jahl
أبو جهل

Narrated Ibn `Abbas: Abu Jahl said, "If I see Muhammad praying at the Ka`ba, I will tread on his neck." When the Prophetﷺ heard of that, he said, "If he does so, the Angels will snatch him away.". – Sahih Al-Bukhari 4958

حَدَّثَنَا يَحْيَى، حَدَّثَنَا عَبْدُ الرَّزَّاقِ، عَنْ مَعْمَرٍ، عَنْ عَبْدِ الْكَرِيمِ الْجَزَرِيِّ، عَنْ عِكْرِمَةَ، قَالَ ابْنُ عَبَّاسٍ قَالَ أَبُو جَهْلٍ لَئِنْ رَأَيْتُ مُحَمَّدًا يُصَلِّي عِنْدَ الْكَعْبَةِ لأَطَأَنَّ عَلَى عُنُقِهِ. فَبَلَغَ النَّبِيَّ صلى الله عليه وسلم فَقَالَ " لَوْ فَعَلَهُ لأَخَذَتْهُ الْمَلاَئِكَةُ ". تَابَعَهُ عَمْرُو بْنُ خَالِدٍ عَنْ عُبَيْدِ اللَّهِ عَنْ عَبْدِ الْكَرِيمِ.

Narrated `Abdullah:While the Prophetﷺ was in the state of prostration, surrounded by a group of people from Quraish pagans. `Uqba bin Abi Mu'ait came and brought the intestines of a camel and threw them on the back of the Prophetﷺ. The Prophetﷺ did not raise his head from prostration till Fatima (i.e. his daughter) came and removed those intestines from his back, and invoked evil on whoever had done (the evil deed). The Prophetﷺ said, "O Allah! Destroy the chiefs of Quraish, O Allah! Destroy Abu Jahl bin Hisham, `Utba bin Rabi`a, Shaiba bin Rabi`a, `Uqba bin Abi Mu'ait, Umaiya bin Khalaf (or Ubai bin Kalaf)." Later on I saw all of them killed during the battle of Badr and their bodies were thrown into a well except the body of Umaiya or Ubai, because he was a fat person, and when he was pulled, the parts of his body got separated before he was thrown into the well. – Sahih Al-Bukhari 3185

حَدَّثَنَا عَبْدَانُ بْنُ عُثْمَانَ، قَالَ أَخْبَرَنِي أَبِي، عَنْ شُعْبَةَ، عَنْ أَبِي إِسْحَاقَ، عَنْ عَمْرِو بْنِ مَيْمُونٍ، عَنْ عَبْدِ اللَّهِ ـ رضى الله عنه ـ قَالَ بَيْنَا رَسُولُ اللَّهِ صلى الله عليه وسلم سَاجِدٌ وَحَوْلَهُ نَاسٌ مِنْ قُرَيْشٍ مِنَ الْمُشْرِكِينَ إِذْ جَاءَ عُقْبَةُ بْنُ أَبِي مُعَيْطٍ بِسَلَى جَزُورٍ، فَقَذَفَهُ عَلَى ظَهْرِ النَّبِيِّ صلى الله عليه وسلم فَلَمْ يَرْفَعْ رَأْسَهُ حَتَّى جَاءَتْ فَاطِمَةُ ـ عَلَيْهَا السَّلاَمُ ـ فَأَخَذَتْ مِنْ ظَهْرِهِ، وَدَعَتْ عَلَى مَنْ صَنَعَ ذَلِكَ، فَقَالَ النَّبِيُّ صلى الله عليه وسلم " اللَّهُمَّ عَلَيْكَ الْمَلأَ مِنْ قُرَيْشٍ، اللَّهُمَّ عَلَيْكَ أَبَا جَهْلِ بْنَ هِشَامٍ، وَعُتْبَةَ بْنَ رَبِيعَةَ، وَشَيْبَةَ بْنَ رَبِيعَةَ، وَعُقْبَةَ بْنَ أَبِي مُعَيْطٍ، وَأُمَيَّةَ بْنَ خَلَفٍ ـ أَوْ أُبَىَّ بْنَ خَلَفٍ ". فَلَقَدْ رَأَيْتُهُمْ قُتِلُوا يَوْمَ بَدْرٍ، فَأُلْقُوا فِي بِئْرٍ، غَيْرَ أُمَيَّةَ أَوْ أُبَىٍّ، فَإِنَّهُ كَانَ رَجُلاً ضَخْمًا، فَلَمَّا جَرُّوهُ تَقَطَّعَتْ أَوْصَالُهُ قَبْلَ أَنْ يُلْقَى فِي الْبِئْرِ

Narrated `Abdur-Rahman bin `Auf: While I was standing in the row on the day (of the battle) of Badr, I looked to my right and my left and saw two young Ansari boys, and I wished I had been stronger than they. One of them called my attention saying, "O Uncle! Do you know Abu Jahl?" I said, "Yes, What do you want from him, O my nephew?" He said, "I have been informed that he abuses Allah's Messengerﷺ. By Him in Whose Hands my life is, if I should see him, then my body will not leave his body till either of us meet his fate." I was astonished at that talk. Then the other boy called my attention saying the same as the other had said. After a while I saw Abu Jahl walking amongst the people. I said (to the boys), "Look! This is the man you asked me about." So, both of them attacked him with their swords and struck him to death and returned to Allah's Apostle to inform him of that. Allah's Messenger asked, "Which of you has killed him?" Each of them said, "I Have killed him." Allah's Messengerﷺ asked, "Have you cleaned your swords?" They said, "No. " He then looked at their swords and said, "No doubt, you both have killed him and the spoils of the deceased will be given to Mu`adh bin `Amr bin Al-Jamuh." The two boys were Mu`adh bin 'Afra and Mu`adh bin `Amr bin Al-Jamuh. – Sahih Al-Bukhari 3141

حَدَّثَنَا مُسَدَّدٌ، حَدَّثَنَا يُوسُفُ بْنُ الْمَاجِشُونِ، عَنْ صَالِحِ بْنِ إِبْرَاهِيمَ بْنِ عَبْدِ الرَّحْمَنِ بْنِ عَوْفٍ، عَنْ أَبِيهِ، عَنْ جَدِّهِ، قَالَ بَيْنَا أَنَا وَاقِفٌ، فِي الصَّفِّ يَوْمَ بَدْرٍ فَنَظَرْتُ عَنْ يَمِينِي، وَشِمَالِي، فَإِذَا أَنَا بِغُلاَمَيْنِ، مِنَ الأَنْصَارِ حَدِيثَةٍ أَسْنَانُهُمَا، تَمَنَّيْتُ أَنْ أَكُونَ بَيْنَ أَضْلَعَ مِنْهُمَا، فَغَمَزَنِي أَحَدُهُمَا فَقَالَ يَا عَمِّ، هَلْ تَعْرِفُ أَبَا جَهْلٍ قُلْتُ نَعَمْ، مَا حَاجَتُكَ إِلَيْهِ يَا ابْنَ أَخِي قَالَ أُخْبِرْتُ أَنَّهُ يَسُبُّ رَسُولَ اللَّهِ صلى الله عليه وسلم، وَالَّذِي نَفْسِي بِيَدِهِ لَئِنْ رَأَيْتُهُ لاَ يُفَارِقُ سَوَادِي سَوَادَهُ حَتَّى يَمُوتَ الأَعْجَلُ مِنَّا. فَتَعَجَّبْتُ لِذَلِكَ، فَغَمَزَنِي الآخَرُ فَقَالَ لِي مِثْلَهَا، فَلَمْ أَنْشَبْ أَنْ نَظَرْتُ إِلَى أَبِي جَهْلٍ يَجُولُ فِي النَّاسِ، قُلْتُ أَلاَ إِنَّ هَذَا صَاحِبُكُمَا الَّذِي سَأَلْتُمَانِي. فَابْتَدَرَاهُ بِسَيْفَيْهِمَا فَضَرَبَاهُ حَتَّى قَتَلاَهُ، ثُمَّ انْصَرَفَا إِلَى رَسُولِ اللَّهِ صلى الله عليه وسلم فَأَخْبَرَاهُ

فَقَالَ " أَيُّكُمَا قَتَلَهُ ". قَالَ كُلُّ وَاحِدٍ مِنْهُمَا أَنَا قَتَلْتُهُ. فَقَالَ " هَلْ مَسَحْتُمَا سَيْفَيْكُمَا ". قَالاَ لاَ. فَنَظَرَ فِي السَّيْفَيْنِ فَقَالَ " كِلاَكُمَا قَتَلَهُ ". سَلَبُهُ لِمُعَاذِ بْنِ عَمْرِو بْنِ الْجَمُوحِ. وَكَانَا مُعَاذَ ابْنَ عَفْرَاءَ وَمُعَاذَ بْنَ عَمْرِو بْنِ الْجَمُوحِ.
قَالَ مُحَمَّدٌ سَمِعَ يُوسُفُ صَالِحًا وَإِبْرَاهِيمَ أَبَاهُ (عَبْدِ الرَّحْمَنِ بْنِ عَوْفٍ)

Narrated `Abdullah bin Mas`ud: From Sa`d bin Mu`adh: Sa`d bin Mu`adh was an intimate friend of Umaiya bin Khalaf and whenever Umaiya passed through Medina, he used to stay with Sa`d, and whenever Sa`d went to Mecca, he used to stay with Umaiya. When Allah's Messenger ﷺ arrived at Medina, Sa`d went to perform `Umra and stayed at Umaiya's home in Mecca. He said to Umaiya, "Tell me of a time when (the Mosque) is empty so that I may be able to perform Tawaf around the Ka`ba." So Umaiya went with him about midday. Abu Jahl met them and said, "O Abu Safwan! Who is this man accompanying you?" He said, "He is Sa`d." Abu Jahl addressed Sa`d saying, "I see you wandering about safely in Mecca inspite of the fact that you have given shelter to the people who have changed their religion (i.e. became Muslims) and have claimed that you will help them and support them. By Allah, if you were not in the company of Abu Safwan, you would not be able to go your family safely." Sa`d, raising his voice, said to him, "By Allah, if you should stop me from doing this (i.e. performing Tawaf) I would certainly prevent you from something which is more valuable for you, that is, your passage through Medina." On this, Umaiya said to him, "O Sa`d do not raise your voice before Abu-l-Hakam, the chief of the people of the Valley (of Mecca)." Sa`d said, "O Umaiya, stop that! By Allah, I have heard Allah's Messenger ﷺ predicting that the Muslim will kill you." Umaiya asked, "In Mecca?" Sa`d said, "I do not know." Umaiya was greatly scared by that news. When Umaiya returned to his family, he said to his wife, "O Um Safwan! Don't you know what Sa`d told me? "She said, "What has he told you?" He replied, "He claims that Muhammad has Informed them (i.e. companions that they will kill me. I asked him, 'In Mecca?' He replied, 'I do not know." Then Umaiya added, "By Allah, I will never go out of Mecca." But when the day of (the Ghazwa of) Badr came, Abu Jahl called the people to war, saying, "Go and protect your caravan." But Umaiya disliked to go out (of Mecca). Abu Jahl came to him and said, "O Abu Safwan! If the people see you staying behind though you are the chief of the people of the Valley, then they will remain behind with you." Abu Jahl kept on urging him to go until he (i.e. Umaiya) said, "As you have forced me to change my mind, by Allah, I will buy the best camel in Mecca. Then Umaiya said (to his wife). "O Um Safwan, prepare what I need (for the journey)." She said to him, "O Abu Safwan! Have you forgotten what your Yathribi brother told you?" He said, "No, but I do not want to go with them but for a short distance." So when Umaiya went out, he used to tie his camel wherever he camped. He kept on doing that till Allah caused him to be killed at Badr. – Sahih Al-Bukhari 3950

حَدَّثَنِي أَحْمَدُ بْنُ عُثْمَانَ، حَدَّثَنَا شُرَيْحُ بْنُ مَسْلَمَةَ، حَدَّثَنَا إِبْرَاهِيمُ بْنُ يُوسُفَ، عَنْ أَبِيهِ، عَنْ أَبِي إِسْحَاقَ، قَالَ حَدَّثَنِي عَمْرُو بْنُ مَيْمُونٍ، أَنَّهُ سَمِعَ عَبْدَ اللَّهِ بْنَ مَسْعُودٍ ـ رضى الله عنه ـ حَدَّثَ عَنْ سَعْدِ بْنِ مُعَاذٍ، أَنَّهُ قَالَ كَانَ صَدِيقًا لأُمَيَّةَ بْنِ خَلَفٍ، وَكَانَ أُمَيَّةُ إِذَا مَرَّ بِالْمَدِينَةِ نَزَلَ عَلَى سَعْدٍ، وَكَانَ سَعْدٌ إِذَا مَرَّ بِمَكَّةَ نَزَلَ عَلَى أُمَيَّةَ، فَلَمَّا قَدِمَ رَسُولُ اللَّهِ صلى الله عليه وسلم الْمَدِينَةَ انْطَلَقَ سَعْدٌ مُعْتَمِرًا، فَنَزَلَ عَلَى أُمَيَّةَ بِمَكَّةَ، فَقَالَ لأُمَيَّةَ انْظُرْ لِي سَاعَةَ خَلْوَةٍ لَعَلِّي أَنْ أَطُوفَ بِالْبَيْتِ. فَخَرَجَ بِهِ قَرِيبًا مِنْ نِصْفِ النَّهَارِ فَلَقِيَهُمَا أَبُو جَهْلٍ فَقَالَ يَا أَبَا صَفْوَانَ، مَنْ هَذَا مَعَكَ فَقَالَ هَذَا سَعْدٌ. فَقَالَ لَهُ أَبُو جَهْلٍ أَلاَ أَرَاكَ تَطُوفُ بِمَكَّةَ آمِنًا، وَقَدْ أَوَيْتُمُ الصُّبَاةَ، وَزَعَمْتُمْ أَنَّكُمْ تَنْصُرُونَهُمْ وَتُعِينُونَهُمْ، أَمَا وَاللَّهِ لَوْلاَ أَنَّكَ مَعَ أَبِي صَفْوَانَ مَا رَجَعْتَ إِلَى أَهْلِكَ سَالِمًا. فَقَالَ لَهُ سَعْدٌ وَرَفَعَ صَوْتَهُ عَلَيْهِ أَمَا وَاللَّهِ لَئِنْ مَنَعْتَنِي هَذَا لأَمْنَعَنَّكَ مَا هُوَ أَشَدُّ عَلَيْكَ مِنْهُ طَرِيقَكَ عَلَى الْمَدِينَةِ. فَقَالَ لَهُ أُمَيَّةُ لاَ تَرْفَعْ صَوْتَكَ يَا سَعْدُ عَلَى أَبِي الْحَكَمِ سَيِّدِ أَهْلِ الْوَادِي. فَقَالَ سَعْدٌ دَعْنَا عَنْكَ يَا أُمَيَّةُ، فَوَاللَّهِ لَقَدْ سَمِعْتُ رَسُولَ اللَّهِ صلى الله عليه وسلم يَقُولُ إِنَّهُمْ قَاتِلُوكَ. قَالَ بِمَكَّةَ قَالَ لاَ أَدْرِي. فَفَزِعَ لِذَلِكَ أُمَيَّةُ فَزَعًا شَدِيدًا، فَلَمَّا رَجَعَ أُمَيَّةُ إِلَى أَهْلِهِ قَالَ يَا أُمَّ صَفْوَانَ، أَلَمْ تَرَىْ مَا قَالَ لِي سَعْدٌ قَالَتْ وَمَا قَالَ لَكَ قَالَ زَعَمَ أَنَّ مُحَمَّدًا أَخْبَرَهُمْ أَنَّهُمْ قَاتِلِيَّ، فَقُلْتُ لَهُ بِمَكَّةَ قَالَ لاَ أَدْرِي. فَقَالَ أُمَيَّةُ وَاللَّهِ لاَ أَخْرُجُ مِنْ مَكَّةَ، فَلَمَّا كَانَ يَوْمَ بَدْرٍ اسْتَنْفَرَ أَبُو جَهْلٍ النَّاسَ قَالَ أَدْرِكُوا عِيرَكُمْ. فَكَرِهَ أُمَيَّةُ أَنْ يَخْرُجَ، فَأَتَاهُ أَبُو جَهْلٍ فَقَالَ يَا أَبَا صَفْوَانَ، إِنَّكَ مَتَى مَا يَرَاكَ النَّاسُ قَدْ تَخَلَّفْتَ وَأَنْتَ سَيِّدُ أَهْلِ الْوَادِي تَخَلَّفُوا مَعَكَ، فَلَمْ يَزَلْ بِهِ أَبُو جَهْلٍ حَتَّى قَالَ أَمَّا إِذْ غَلَبْتَنِي، فَوَاللَّهِ لأَشْتَرِيَنَّ أَجْوَدَ بَعِيرٍ بِمَكَّةَ ثُمَّ قَالَ أُمَيَّةُ يَا أُمَّ صَفْوَانَ جَهِّزِينِي.

فَقَالَتْ لَهُ يَا أَبَا صَفْوَانَ وَقَدْ نَسِيتَ مَا قَالَ لَكَ أَخُوكَ الْيَثْرِبِيُّ قَالَ لاَ، مَا أُرِيدُ أَنْ أَجُوزَ مَعَهُمْ إِلاَّ قَرِيبًا. فَلَمَّا خَرَجَ أُمَيَّةُ أَخَذَ لاَ يَنْزِلُ مَنْزِلاً إِلاَّ عَقَلَ بَعِيرَهُ، فَلَمْ يَزَلْ بِذَلِكَ حَتَّى قَتَلَهُ اللَّهُ عَزَّ وَجَلَّ

Narrated Anas bin Malik: Abu Jahl said, "O Allah! If this (Qur'an) is indeed the Truth from You, then rain down on us a shower of stones from the sky or bring on us a painful torment." So Allah revealed:-- "But Allah would not punish them while you were amongst them, nor He will punish them while they seek (Allah's) forgiveness..." (8.33) And why Allah should not punish them while they turn away (men) from Al- Masjid-al-Haram (the Sacred Mosque of Mecca)..." (8.33-34). – Sahih Al-Bukhari 4648

حَدَّثَنِي أَحْمَدُ، حَدَّثَنَا عُبَيْدُ اللَّهِ بْنُ مُعَاذٍ، حَدَّثَنَا أَبِي، حَدَّثَنَا شُعْبَةُ، عَنْ عَبْدِ الْحَمِيدِ ـ هُوَ ابْنُ كُرْدِيدٍ صَاحِبُ الزِّيَادِيِّ ـ سَمِعَ أَنَسَ بْنَ مَالِكٍ ـ رضى الله عنه ـ قَالَ أَبُو جَهْلٍ {اللَّهُمَّ إِنْ كَانَ هَذَا هُوَ الْحَقَّ مِنْ عِنْدِكَ فَأَمْطِرْ عَلَيْنَا حِجَارَةً مِنَ السَّمَاءِ أَوِ ائْتِنَا بِعَذَابٍ أَلِيمٍ} فَنَزَلَتْ {وَمَا كَانَ اللَّهُ لِيُعَذِّبَهُمْ وَأَنْتَ فِيهِمْ وَمَا كَانَ اللَّهُ مُعَذِّبَهُمْ وَهُمْ يَسْتَغْفِرُونَ * وَمَا لَهُمْ أَنْ لاَ يُعَذِّبَهُمُ اللَّهُ وَهُمْ يَصُدُّونَ عَنِ الْمَسْجِدِ الْحَرَامِ} الآيَةَ

Narrated Al-Miswar bin Makhrama: `Ali demanded the hand of the daughter of Abu Jahl. Fatima heard of this and went to Allah's Messenger ﷺ saying, "Your people think that you do not become angry for the sake of your daughters as `Ali is now going to marry the daughter of Abu Jahl. "On that Allah's Messenger ﷺ got up and after his recitation of Tashah-hud. I heard him saying, "Then after! I married one of my daughters to Abu Al-`As bin Al- Rabi` (the husband of Zainab, the daughter of the Prophet ﷺ) before Islam and he proved truthful in whatever he said to me. No doubt, Fatima is a part of me, I hate to see her being troubled. By Allah, the daughter of Allah's Messenger ﷺ and the daughter of Allah's Enemy cannot be the wives of one man." So `Ali gave up that engagement. 'Al-Miswar further said: I heard the Prophet ﷺ talking and he mentioned a son-in-law of his belonging to the tribe of Bani `Abd-Shams. He highly praised him concerning that relationship and said (whenever) he spoke to me, he spoke the truth, and whenever he promised me, he fulfilled his promise.". – Sahih Al-Bukhari 3729

حَدَّثَنَا أَبُو الْيَمَانِ، أَخْبَرَنَا شُعَيْبٌ، عَنِ الزُّهْرِيِّ، قَالَ حَدَّثَنِي عَلِيُّ بْنُ حُسَيْنٍ، أَنَّ الْمِسْوَرَ بْنَ مَخْرَمَةَ، قَالَ إِنَّ عَلِيًّا خَطَبَ بِنْتَ أَبِي جَهْلٍ، فَسَمِعَتْ بِذَلِكَ، فَاطِمَةُ، فَأَتَتْ رَسُولَ اللَّهِ صلى الله عليه وسلم فَقَالَتْ يَزْعُمُ قَوْمُكَ أَنَّكَ لاَ تَغْضَبُ لِبَنَاتِكَ، هَذَا عَلِيٌّ نَاكِحٌ بِنْتَ أَبِي جَهْلٍ، فَقَامَ رَسُولُ اللَّهِ صلى الله عليه وسلم فَسَمِعْتُهُ حِينَ تَشَهَّدَ يَقُولُ " أَمَّا بَعْدُ أَنْكَحْتُ أَبَا الْعَاصِ بْنَ الرَّبِيعِ، فَحَدَّثَنِي وَصَدَقَنِي، وَإِنَّ فَاطِمَةَ بَضْعَةٌ مِنِّي، وَإِنِّي أَكْرَهُ أَنْ يَسُوءَهَا، وَاللَّهِ لاَ تَجْتَمِعُ بِنْتُ رَسُولِ اللَّهِ صلى الله عليه وسلم وَبِنْتُ عَدُوِّ اللَّهِ عِنْدَ رَجُلٍ وَاحِدٍ ". فَتَرَكَ عَلِيٌّ الْخِطْبَةَ. وَزَادَ مُحَمَّدُ بْنُ عَمْرِو بْنِ حَلْحَلَةَ عَنِ ابْنِ شِهَابٍ عَنْ عَلِيٍّ عَنْ مِسْوَرٍ، سَمِعْتُ النَّبِيَّ صلى الله عليه وسلم وَذَكَرَ صِهْرًا لَهُ مِنْ بَنِي عَبْدِ شَمْسٍ فَأَثْنَى عَلَيْهِ فِي مُصَاهَرَتِهِ إِيَّاهُ فَأَحْسَنَ قَالَ " حَدَّثَنِي فَصَدَقَنِي، وَوَعَدَنِي فَوَفَى لِي "

Narrated Al-Musaiyab: When Abu Talib was on his death bed, Allah's Messenger ﷺ came to him and found with him, Abu Jahl and `Abdullah bin Abi Umaiya bin Al-Mughira. Allah's Messenger ﷺ said, "O uncle! Say: None has the right to be worshipped except Allah, a sentence with which I will defend you before Allah." On that Abu Jahl and `Abdullah bin Abi Umaiya said to Abu Talib, "Will you now leave the religion of `Abdul Muttalib?" Allah's Messenger ﷺ kept on inviting him to say that sentence while the other two kept on repeating their sentence before him till Abu Talib said as the last thing he said to them, "I am on the religion of `Abdul Muttalib," and refused to say: None has the right to be worshipped except Allah. On that Allah's Messenger ﷺ said, "By Allah, I will keep on asking Allah's forgiveness for you unless I am forbidden (by Allah) to do so." So Allah revealed:-- 'It is not fitting for the Prophet ﷺ and those who believe that they should invoke (Allah) for forgiveness for pagans.' (9.113) And then Allah revealed especially about Abu Talib:--'Verily! You (O, Muhammad) guide not whom you like, but Allah guides whom He will.' (28.56). – Sahih Al-Bukhari 4772

حَدَّثَنَا أَبُو الْيَمَانِ، أَخْبَرَنَا شُعَيْبٌ، عَنِ الزُّهْرِيِّ، قَالَ أَخْبَرَنِي سَعِيدُ بْنُ الْمُسَيَّبِ، عَنْ أَبِيهِ، قَالَ لَمَّا حَضَرَتْ أَبَا طَالِبٍ الْوَفَاةُ جَاءَهُ رَسُولُ اللَّهِ صلى الله عليه وسلم فَوَجَدَ عِنْدَهُ أَبَا جَهْلٍ وَعَبْدَ اللَّهِ بْنَ أَبِي أُمَيَّةَ بْنِ الْمُغِيرَةِ، فَقَالَ " أَىْ عَمِّ قُلْ لاَ إِلَهَ إِلاَّ اللَّهُ، كَلِمَةً أُحَاجُّ لَكَ بِهَا عِنْدَ اللَّهِ ". فَقَالَ أَبُو جَهْلٍ وَعَبْدُ اللَّهِ بْنُ أَبِي أُمَيَّةَ أَتَرْغَبُ عَنْ مِلَّةِ عَبْدِ الْمُطَّلِبِ فَلَمْ يَزَلْ رَسُولُ اللَّهِ صلى الله عليه وسلم يَعْرِضُهَا عَلَيْهِ، وَيُعِيدَانِهِ بِتِلْكَ الْمَقَالَةِ حَتَّى قَالَ أَبُو طَالِبٍ آخِرَ مَا كَلَّمَهُمْ عَلَى مِلَّةِ عَبْدِ الْمُطَّلِبِ، وَأَبَى أَنْ يَقُولَ لاَ إِلَهَ إِلاَّ اللَّهُ. قَالَ قَالَ رَسُولُ اللَّهِ صلى الله عليه وسلم " وَاللَّهِ لأَسْتَغْفِرَنَّ لَكَ مَا لَمْ أُنْهَ عَنْكَ ". فَأَنْزَلَ اللَّهُ {مَا كَانَ لِلنَّبِيِّ وَالَّذِينَ آمَنُوا أَنْ يَسْتَغْفِرُوا لِلْمُشْرِكِينَ} وَأَنْزَلَ اللَّهُ فِي أَبِي طَالِبٍ، فَقَالَ لِرَسُولِ اللَّهِ صلى الله عليه وسلم {إِنَّكَ لاَ تَهْدِي مَنْ أَحْبَبْتَ وَلَكِنَّ اللَّهَ يَهْدِي مَنْ يَشَاءُ}. قَالَ ابْنُ عَبَّاسٍ {أُولِي الْقُوَّةِ} لاَ يَرْفَعُهَا الْعُصْبَةُ مِنَ الرِّجَالِ. {لَتَنُوءُ} لَتُثْقِلُ. {فَارِغًا} إِلاَّ مِنْ ذِكْرِ مُوسَى. {الْفَرِحِينَ} الْمَرِحِينَ. {قُصِّيهِ} اتَّبِعِي أَثَرَهُ، وَقَدْ يَكُونُ أَنْ يَقُصَّ الْكَلاَمَ {نَحْنُ نَقُصُّ عَلَيْكَ}. {عَنْ جُنُبٍ} عَنْ بُعْدٍ عَنْ جَنَابَةٍ وَاحِدٌ، وَعَنِ اجْتِنَابٍ أَيْضًا، يَبْطِشُ وَيَبْطُشُ. {يَأْتَمِرُونَ} يَتَشَاوَرُونَ. الْعُدْوَانُ وَالْعَدَاءُ وَالتَّعَدِّي وَاحِدٌ. {آنَسَ} أَبْصَرَ. الْجِذْوَةُ قِطْعَةٌ غَلِيظَةٌ مِنَ الْخَشَبِ، لَيْسَ فِيهَا لَهَبٌ، وَالشِّهَابُ فِيهِ لَهَبٌ. وَالْحَيَّاتُ أَجْنَاسٌ الْجَانُّ وَالأَفَاعِي وَالأَسَاوِدُ. {رِدْءًا} مُعِينًا. قَالَ ابْنُ عَبَّاسٍ {يُصَدِّقُنِي} وَقَالَ غَيْرُهُ {سَنَشُدُّ} سَنُعِينُكَ كُلَّمَا عَزَّزْتَ شَيْئًا فَقَدْ جَعَلْتَ لَهُ عَضُدًا. مَقْبُوحِينَ مُهْلَكِينَ. {وَصَّلْنَا} بَيَّنَّاهُ وَأَتْمَمْنَاهُ. {يُجْبَى} يُجْلَبُ. {بَطِرَتْ} أَشِرَتْ. {فِي أُمِّهَا رَسُولاً} أُمُّ الْقُرَى مَكَّةُ وَمَا حَوْلَهَا. {تُكِنُّ} تُخْفِي. أَكْنَنْتُ الشَّىْءَ أَخْفَيْتُهُ، وَكَنَنْتُهُ أَخْفَيْتُهُ وَأَظْهَرْتُهُ. {وَيْكَأَنَّ اللَّهَ} مِثْلُ أَلَمْ تَرَ أَنَّ اللَّهَ {يَبْسُطُ الرِّزْقَ لِمَنْ يَشَاءُ وَيَقْدِرُ} يُوَسِّعُ عَلَيْهِ وَيُضَيِّقُ عَلَيْهِ.

Narrated Anas: On the day of Badr, the Prophet ﷺ said, “Who will go and see what has happened to Abu Jahl?” Ibn Mas`ud went and found that the two sons of ‘Afra had struck him fatally. `Abdullah bin Mas`ud got hold of his beard and said, “’Are you Abu Jahl?” He replied, “Can there be a man more superior to one whom his own folk have killed (or you have killed)?”. – Sahih Al-Bukhari 3963

حَدَّثَنِي مُحَمَّدُ بْنُ الْمُثَنَّى، حَدَّثَنَا ابْنُ أَبِي عَدِيٍّ، عَنْ سُلَيْمَانَ التَّيْمِيِّ، عَنْ أَنَسٍ، رضى الله عنه قَالَ قَالَ النَّبِيُّ صلى الله عليه وسلم يَوْمَ بَدْرٍ " مَنْ يَنْظُرُ مَا فَعَلَ أَبُو جَهْلٍ ". فَانْطَلَقَ ابْنُ مَسْعُودٍ، فَوَجَدَهُ قَدْ ضَرَبَهُ ابْنَا عَفْرَاءَ حَتَّى بَرَدَ، فَأَخَذَ بِلِحْيَتِهِ فَقَالَ أَنْتَ أَبَا جَهْلٍ قَالَ وَهَلْ فَوْقَ رَجُلٍ قَتَلَهُ قَوْمُهُ أَوْ قَالَ قَتَلْتُمُوهُ

Abu Lahab
أبو لهب

Narrated Ibn `Abbas: When the Verse:--‘And warn your tribe of near-kindred, was revealed, the Prophet ﷺ ascended the Safa (mountain) and started calling, “O Bani Fihr! O Bani `Adi!” addressing various tribes of Quraish till they were assembled. Those who could not come themselves, sent their messengers to see what was there. Abu Lahab and other people from Quraish came and the Prophet ﷺ then said, “Suppose I told you that there is an (enemy) cavalry in the valley intending to attack you, would you believe me?” They said, “Yes, for we have not found you telling anything other than the truth.” He then said, “I am a warner to you in face of a terrific punishment.” Abu Lahab said (to the Prophet) “May your hands perish all this day. Is it for this purpose you have gathered us?” Then it was revealed: “Perish the hands of Abu Lahab (one of the Prophet’s uncles), and perish he! His wealth and his children will not profit him....” (111.1-5). – Sahih Al-Bukhari 4770

حَدَّثَنَا عُمَرُ بْنُ حَفْصِ بْنِ غِيَاثٍ، حَدَّثَنَا أَبِي، حَدَّثَنَا الأَعْمَشُ، قَالَ حَدَّثَنِي عَمْرُو بْنُ مُرَّةَ، عَنْ سَعِيدِ بْنِ جُبَيْرٍ، عَنِ ابْنِ عَبَّاسٍ ـ رضى الله عنهما ـ قَالَ لَمَّا نَزَلَتْ {وَأَنْذِرْ عَشِيرَتَكَ الأَقْرَبِينَ} صَعِدَ النَّبِيُّ صلى الله عليه وسلم عَلَى الصَّفَا فَجَعَلَ يُنَادِي " يَا بَنِي فِهْرٍ، يَا بَنِي عَدِيٍّ ". لِبُطُونِ قُرَيْشٍ حَتَّى اجْتَمَعُوا، فَجَعَلَ الرَّجُلُ إِذَا لَمْ يَسْتَطِعْ أَنْ يَخْرُجَ أَرْسَلَ رَسُولاً لِيَنْظُرَ مَا هُوَ، فَجَاءَ أَبُو لَهَبٍ وَقُرَيْشٌ فَقَالَ " أَرَأَيْتَكُمْ لَوْ أَخْبَرْتُكُمْ أَنَّ خَيْلاً بِالْوَادِي تُرِيدُ أَنْ تُغِيرَ عَلَيْكُمْ، أَكُنْتُمْ مُصَدِّقِيَّ ". قَالُوا نَعَمْ، مَا جَرَّبْنَا عَلَيْكَ إِلاَّ صِدْقًا. قَالَ " فَإِنِّي نَذِيرٌ لَكُمْ بَيْنَ يَدَىْ عَذَابٍ شَدِيدٍ ". فَقَالَ أَبُو لَهَبٍ تَبًّا لَكَ سَائِرَ الْيَوْمِ، أَلِهَذَا جَمَعْتَنَا فَنَزَلَتْ {تَبَّتْ يَدَا أَبِي لَهَبٍ وَتَبَّ * مَا أَغْنَى عَنْهُ مَالُهُ وَمَا كَسَبَ}

Narrated Ibn `Abbas: When the Verse:-- ‘And warn your tribe of near kindred.’ (26.214) was revealed. Allah’s Messenger ﷺ went out, and when he had ascended As-Safa mountain, he shouted, "O Sabahah!" The people said, "Who is that?" "Then they gathered around him, whereupon he said, "Do you see? If I inform you that cavalrymen are proceeding up the side of this mountain, will you believe me?" They said, "We have never heard you telling a lie." Then he said, "I am a plain warner to you of a coming severe punishment." Abu Lahab said, "May you perish! You gathered us only for this reason? " Then Abu Lahab went away. So the "Surah: Al-Lahab" 'Perish the hands of Abu Lahab!' (111.1) was revealed. – Sahih Al-Bukhari 4971

حَدَّثَنَا يُوسُفُ بْنُ مُوسَى، حَدَّثَنَا أَبُو أُسَامَةَ، حَدَّثَنَا الأَعْمَشُ، حَدَّثَنَا عَمْرُو بْنُ مُرَّةَ، عَنْ سَعِيدِ بْنِ جُبَيْرٍ، عَنِ ابْنِ عَبَّاسٍ ـ رضى الله عنهما ـ قَالَ لَمَّا نَزَلَتْ {وَأَنْذِرْ عَشِيرَتَكَ الأَقْرَبِينَ} وَرَهْطَكَ مِنْهُمُ الْمُخْلَصِينَ، خَرَجَ رَسُولُ اللَّهِ صلى الله عليه وسلم حَتَّى صَعِدَ الصَّفَا فَهَتَفَ " يَا صَبَاحَاهْ ". فَقَالُوا مَنْ هَذَا، فَاجْتَمَعُوا إِلَيْهِ. فَقَالَ " أَرَأَيْتُمْ إِنْ أَخْبَرْتُكُمْ أَنَّ خَيْلاً تَخْرُجُ مِنْ سَفْحِ هَذَا الْجَبَلِ أَكُنْتُمْ مُصَدِّقِيَّ ". قَالُوا مَا جَرَّبْنَا عَلَيْكَ كَذِبًا. قَالَ " فَإِنِّي نَذِيرٌ لَكُمْ بَيْنَ يَدَىْ عَذَابٍ شَدِيدٍ ". قَالَ أَبُو لَهَبٍ تَبًّا لَكَ مَا جَمَعْتَنَا إِلاَّ لِهَذَا ثُمَّ قَامَ فَنَزَلَتْ {تَبَّتْ يَدَا أَبِي لَهَبٍ وَتَبَّ} وَقَدْ تَبَّ هَكَذَا قَرَأَهَا الأَعْمَشُ يَوْمَئِذٍ.

Narrated Jundub bin Sufyan:Once Allah's Messenger ﷺ became sick and could not offer his night prayer (Tahajjud) for two or three nights. Then a lady (the wife of Abu Lahab) came and said, "O Muhammad! I think that your Satan has forsaken you, for I have not seen him with you for two or three nights!" On that Allah revealed: 'By the fore-noon, and by the night when it darkens, your Lord (O Muhammad) has neither forsaken you, nor hated you.' (93.1-3). – Sahih Al-Bukhari 4950

حَدَّثَنَا أَحْمَدُ بْنُ يُونُسَ، حَدَّثَنَا زُهَيْرٌ، حَدَّثَنَا الأَسْوَدُ بْنُ قَيْسٍ، قَالَ سَمِعْتُ جُنْدُبَ بْنَ سُفْيَانَ ـ رضى الله عنه ـ قَالَ اشْتَكَى رَسُولُ اللَّهِ صلى الله عليه وسلم فَلَمْ يَقُمْ لَيْلَتَيْنِ أَوْ ثَلاَثًا، فَجَاءَتِ امْرَأَةٌ فَقَالَتْ يَا مُحَمَّدُ إِنِّي لأَرْجُو أَنْ يَكُونَ شَيْطَانُكَ قَدْ تَرَكَكَ، لَمْ أَرَهُ قَرِبَكَ مُنْذُ لَيْلَتَيْنِ أَوْ ثَلاَثًا. فَأَنْزَلَ اللَّهُ عَزَّ وَجَلَّ {وَالضُّحَى * وَاللَّيْلِ إِذَا سَجَى * مَا وَدَّعَكَ رَبُّكَ وَمَا قَلَى}

Narrated Um Habiba: (the wife of the Prophet) I said, "O Allah's Messenger ﷺ! Will you marry my sister, the daughter of Abu Sufyan." The Prophet ﷺ said, "Do you like that?" I said, "Yes, for I am not your only wife, and the person I like most to share the good with me, is my sister." He said, "That is not lawful for me." I said, "O Allah's Messenger ﷺ! We have heard that you want to marry Durra, the daughter of Abu Salama." He said, "You mean the daughter of Um Salama?" I said, "Yes." He said, "Even if she were not my stepdaughter, she is unlawful for me, for she is my foster niece. Thuwaiba suckled me and Abu Salama. So you should not present to me your daughters and sisters." Narrated 'Urwa: Thuwaiba had been a slave girl whom Abu Lahab had emancipated. – Sahih Al-Bukhari 5372

حَدَّثَنَا يَحْيَى بْنُ بُكَيْرٍ، حَدَّثَنَا اللَّيْثُ، عَنْ عُقَيْلٍ، عَنِ ابْنِ شِهَابٍ، أَخْبَرَنِي عُرْوَةُ، أَنَّ زَيْنَبَ ابْنَةَ أَبِي سَلَمَةَ، أَخْبَرَتْهُ أَنَّ أُمَّ حَبِيبَةَ زَوْجَ النَّبِيِّ صلى الله عليه وسلم قَالَتْ قُلْتُ يَا رَسُولَ اللَّهِ انْكِحْ أُخْتِي ابْنَةَ أَبِي سُفْيَانَ. قَالَ " وَتُحِبِّينَ ذَلِكَ ". قُلْتُ نَعَمْ لَسْتُ لَكَ بِمُخْلِيَةٍ، وَأَحَبُّ مَنْ شَارَكَنِي فِي الْخَيْرِ أُخْتِي. فَقَالَ " إِنَّ ذَلِكَ لاَ يَحِلُّ لِي ". فَقُلْتُ يَا رَسُولَ اللَّهِ فَوَاللَّهِ إِنَّا نَتَحَدَّثُ أَنَّكَ تُرِيدُ أَنْ تَنْكِحَ دُرَّةَ ابْنَةَ أَبِي سَلَمَةَ. فَقَالَ " ابْنَةَ أُمِّ سَلَمَةَ ". فَقُلْتُ نَعَمْ. قَالَ "فَوَاللَّهِ لَوْ لَمْ تَكُنْ رَبِيبَتِي فِي حَجْرِي مَا حَلَّتْ لِي، إِنَّهَا ابْنَةُ أَخِي مِنَ الرَّضَاعَةِ، أَرْضَعَتْنِي وَأَبَا سَلَمَةَ ثُوَيْبَةُ، فَلاَ تَعْرِضْنَ عَلَىَّ بَنَاتِكُنَّ وَلاَ أَخَوَاتِكُنَّ ". وَقَالَ شُعَيْبٌ عَنِ الزُّهْرِيِّ قَالَ عُرْوَةُ ثُوَيْبَةُ أَعْتَقَهَا أَبُو لَهَبٍ

Umayyia Ibn Khalaf
أمية ابن خلف

Narrated `Aisha: When Allah's Messenger ﷺ reached Medina, Abu Bakr and Bilal became ill. When Abu Bakr's fever got worse, he would recite (this poetic verse): "Everybody is staying alive with his People, yet Death is nearer to him than His shoe laces." And Bilal, when his fever deserted him, would recite: "Would that I could stay overnight in A valley wherein I would be Surrounded by Idhkhir and Jalil (kinds of goodsmelling grass). Would that one day I could Drink the water of the Majanna, and Would that (The two mountains) Shama and Tafil would appear to me!" The Prophet ﷺ said, "O Allah! Curse Shaiba bin Rabi`a and `Utba bin Rabi`a and Umaiya bin Khalaf as they turned us out of our land to the land of epidemics." Allah's Messenger ﷺ then said, "O Allah! Make us love Medina as we love Mecca or even more than that. O Allah! Give blessings in our Sa and our Mudd (measures symbolizing food) and make the climate of Medina suitable for us, and divert its fever towards Aljuhfa." Aisha added: When we reached Medina, it was the most unhealthy of Allah's lands, and the valley of Bathan (the valley of Medina) used to flow with impure colored water. – Sahih Al-Bukhari 1889

حَدَّثَنَا عُبَيْدُ بْنُ إِسْمَاعِيلَ، حَدَّثَنَا أَبُو أُسَامَةَ، عَنْ هِشَامٍ، عَنْ أَبِيهِ، عَنْ عَائِشَةَ ـ رضى الله عنها ـ قَالَتْ لَمَّا قَدِمَ رَسُولُ اللَّهِ صلى الله عليه وسلم الْمَدِينَةَ وُعِكَ أَبُو بَكْرٍ وَبِلاَلٌ، فَكَانَ أَبُو بَكْرٍ إِذَا أَخَذَتْهُ الْحُمَّى يَقُولُ كُلُّ امْرِئٍ مُصَبَّحٌ فِي أَهْلِهِ وَالْمَوْتُ أَدْنَى مِنْ شِرَاكِ نَعْلِهِ وَكَانَ بِلاَلٌ إِذَا أُقْلِعَ عَنْهُ الْحُمَّى يَرْفَعُ عَقِيرَتَهُ يَقُولُ أَلاَ لَيْتَ شِعْرِي هَلْ أَبِيتَنَّ لَيْلَةً بِوَادٍ وَحَوْلِي إِذْخِرٌ وَجَلِيلُ وَهَلْ أَرِدَنْ يَوْمًا مِيَاهَ مَجَنَّةٍ وَهَلْ يَبْدُوَنْ لِي شَامَةٌ وَطَفِيلُ قَالَ اللَّهُمَّ الْعَنْ شَيْبَةَ بْنَ رَبِيعَةَ، وَعُتْبَةَ بْنَ رَبِيعَةَ، وَأُمَيَّةَ بْنَ خَلَفٍ، كَمَا أَخْرَجُونَا مِنْ أَرْضِنَا إِلَى أَرْضِ الْوَبَاءِ ثُمَّ قَالَ رَسُولُ اللَّهِ صلى الله عليه وسلم " اللَّهُمَّ حَبِّبْ إِلَيْنَا الْمَدِينَةَ كَحُبِّنَا مَكَّةَ أَوْ أَشَدَّ، اللَّهُمَّ بَارِكْ لَنَا فِي صَاعِنَا، وَفِي مُدِّنَا، وَصَحِّحْهَا لَنَا وَانْقُلْ حُمَّاهَا إِلَى الْجُحْفَةِ ". قَالَتْ وَقَدِمْنَا الْمَدِينَةَ، وَهْىَ أَوْبَأُ أَرْضِ اللَّهِ. قَالَتْ فَكَانَ بُطْحَانُ يَجْرِي نَجْلاً. تَعْنِي مَاءً آجِنًا

Narrated `Abdur-Rahman bin `Auf: " I had an agreement with Umaiya bin Khalaf (that he would look after my relatives and property in Mecca, and I would look after his relatives and property in Medina)." `Abdur-Rahman then mentioned the killing of Umaiya and his son on the day of Badr, and Bilal said, "Woe to me if Umaiya remains safe (i.e. alive)." – Sahih al-Bukhari 3971

حَدَّثَنَا عَبْدُ الْعَزِيزِ بْنُ عَبْدِ اللَّهِ، قَالَ حَدَّثَنِي يُوسُفُ بْنُ الْمَاجِشُونِ، عَنْ صَالِحِ بْنِ إِبْرَاهِيمَ بْنِ عَبْدِ الرَّحْمَنِ بْنِ عَوْفٍ، عَنْ أَبِيهِ، عَنْ جَدِّهِ عَبْدِ الرَّحْمَنِ، قَالَ كَاتَبْتُ أُمَيَّةَ بْنَ خَلَفٍ، فَلَمَّا كَانَ يَوْمُ بَدْرٍ، فَذَكَرَ قَتْلَهُ وَقَتْلَ ابْنِهِ، فَقَالَ بِلاَلٌ لاَ نَجَوْتُ إِنْ نَجَا أُمَيَّةُ.

Narrated `Abdullah: While the Prophet ﷺ was prostrating, surrounded by some of Quraish, `Uqba bin Abi Mu'ait brought the intestines (i.e. Abdominal contents) of a camel and put them over the back of the Prophet. The Prophet ﷺ did not raise his head, (till) Fatima, came and took it off his back and cursed the one who had done the harm. The Prophet ﷺ said, "O Allah! Destroy the chiefs of Quraish, Abu Jahl bin Hisham, `Utba bin Rabi`al, Shaba bin Rabi`a, Umaiya bin Khalaf or Ubai bin Khalaf." (The sub-narrator Shu`ba, is not sure of the last name.) I saw these people killed on the day of Badr battle and thrown in the well except Umaiya or Ubai whose body parts were mutilated but he was not thrown in the well. – Sahih al-Bukhari 3854

حَدَّثَنِي مُحَمَّدُ بْنُ بَشَّارٍ، حَدَّثَنَا غُنْدَرٌ، حَدَّثَنَا شُعْبَةُ، عَنْ أَبِي إِسْحَاقَ، عَنْ عَمْرِو بْنِ مَيْمُونٍ، عَنْ عَبْدِ اللَّهِ ـ رضى الله عنه ـ قَالَ بَيْنَا النَّبِيُّ صلى الله عليه وسلم سَاجِدٌ وَحَوْلَهُ نَاسٌ مِنْ قُرَيْشٍ جَاءَ عُقْبَةُ بْنُ أَبِي مُعَيْطٍ بِسَلَى جَزُورٍ، فَقَذَفَهُ عَلَى ظَهْرِ النَّبِيِّ صلى الله عليه وسلم، فَلَمْ يَرْفَعْ رَأْسَهُ فَجَاءَتْ فَاطِمَةُ ـ عَلَيْهَا السَّلاَمُ ـ فَأَخَذَتْهُ مِنْ ظَهْرِهِ، وَدَعَتْ عَلَى مَنْ صَنَعَ فَقَالَ النَّبِيُّ صلى الله عليه وسلم " اللَّهُمَّ عَلَيْكَ الْمَلأَ مِنْ قُرَيْشٍ أَبَا جَهْلِ بْنَ هِشَامٍ، وَعُتْبَةَ بْنَ رَبِيعَةَ، وَشَيْبَةَ بْنَ رَبِيعَةَ، وَأُمَيَّةَ بْنَ خَلَفٍ ـ أَوْ أُبَىَّ بْنَ خَلَفٍ ". شُعْبَةُ الشَّاكُّ ـ فَرَأَيْتُهُمْ قُتِلُوا يَوْمَ بَدْرٍ، فَأُلْقُوا فِي بِئْرٍ غَيْرَ أُمَيَّةَ أَوْ أُبَيِّ تَقَطَّعَتْ أَوْصَالُهُ، فَلَمْ يُلْقَ فِي الْبِئْرِ

Narrated `Abdullah: The first Sura in which a prostration was mentioned, was Sura An-Najm (The Star). Allah's Messenger ﷺ prostrated (while reciting it), and everybody behind him prostrated except a man whom I saw taking a hand-full of dust in his hand and prostrated on it. Later I saw that man killed as an infidel, and he was Umaiya bin Khalaf. – Sahih al-Bukhari 4863

حَدَّثَنَا نَصْرُ بْنُ عَلِيٍّ، أَخْبَرَنِي أَبُو أَحْمَدَ، حَدَّثَنَا إِسْرَائِيلُ، عَنْ أَبِي إِسْحَاقَ، عَنِ الأَسْوَدِ بْنِ يَزِيدَ، عَنْ عَبْدِ اللَّهِ ـ رضى الله عنه ـ قَالَ أَوَّلُ سُورَةٍ أُنْزِلَتْ فِيهَا سَجْدَةٌ {وَالنَّجْمِ}. قَالَ فَسَجَدَ رَسُولُ اللَّهِ صلى الله عليه وسلم وَسَجَدَ مَنْ خَلْفَهُ، إِلاَّ رَجُلاً رَأَيْتُهُ أَخَذَ كَفًّا مِنْ تُرَابٍ فَسَجَدَ عَلَيْهِ، فَرَأَيْتُهُ بَعْدَ ذَلِكَ قُتِلَ كَافِرًا، وَهْوَ أُمَيَّةُ بْنُ خَلَفٍ

Narrated `Abdullah: While the Prophet ﷺ was in the state of prostration, surrounded by a group of people from Quraish pagans. `Uqba bin Abi Mu'ait came and brought the intestines of a camel and threw them on the back of the Prophet ﷺ. The Prophet ﷺ did not raise his head from prostration till Fatima (i.e. his daughter) came and removed those intestines from his back, and invoked evil on whoever had done (the evil deed). The Prophet ﷺ slaid, "O Allah! Destroy the chiefs of Quraish, O Allah! Destroy Abu Jahl bin Hisham, `Utba bin Rabi`a, Shaiba bin Rabi`a, `Uqba bin Abi Mu'ait, Umaiya bin Khalaf (or Ubai bin Kalaf)." Later on I saw all of them killed during the battle of Badr and their bodies were thrown into a well except the body of Umaiya or Ubai, because he was a fat person, and when he was pulled, the parts of his body got separated before he was thrown into the well. – Sahih al-Bukhari 3185

حَدَّثَنَا عَبْدَانُ بْنُ عُثْمَانَ، قَالَ أَخْبَرَنِي أَبِي، عَنْ شُعْبَةَ، عَنْ أَبِي إِسْحَاقَ، عَنْ عَمْرِو بْنِ مَيْمُونٍ، عَنْ عَبْدِ اللَّهِ ـ رضى الله عنه ـ قَالَ بَيْنَا رَسُولُ اللَّهِ صلى الله عليه وسلم سَاجِدٌ وَحَوْلَهُ نَاسٌ مِنْ قُرَيْشٍ مِنَ الْمُشْرِكِينَ إِذْ جَاءَ عُقْبَةُ بْنُ أَبِي مُعَيْطٍ بِسَلَى جَزُورٍ، فَقَذَفَهُ عَلَى ظَهْرِ النَّبِيِّ صلى الله عليه وسلم فَلَمْ يَرْفَعْ رَأْسَهُ حَتَّى جَاءَتْ فَاطِمَةُ ـ عَلَيْهَا السَّلاَمُ ـ فَأَخَذَتْ مِنْ ظَهْرِهِ، وَدَعَتْ عَلَى مَنْ صَنَعَ ذَلِكَ، فَقَالَ النَّبِيُّ صلى الله عليه وسلم " اللَّهُمَّ عَلَيْكَ الْمَلأَ مِنْ قُرَيْشٍ، اللَّهُمَّ عَلَيْكَ أَبَا جَهْلِ بْنَ هِشَامٍ، وَعُتْبَةَ بْنَ رَبِيعَةَ، وَشَيْبَةَ بْنَ رَبِيعَةَ، وَعُقْبَةَ بْنَ أَبِي مُعَيْطٍ، وَأُمَيَّةَ بْنَ خَلَفٍ ـ أَوْ أُبَىَّ بْنَ خَلَفٍ ". فَلَقَدْ رَأَيْتُهُمْ قُتِلُوا يَوْمَ بَدْرٍ، فَأُلْقُوا فِي بِئْرٍ، غَيْرَ أُمَيَّةَ أَوْ أُبَيٍّ، فَإِنَّهُ كَانَ رَجُلاً ضَخْمًا، فَلَمَّا جَرُّوهُ تَقَطَّعَتْ أَوْصَالُهُ قَبْلَ أَنْ يُلْقَى فِي الْبِئْرِ

Narrated `Abdullah bin Mas`ud: From Sa`d bin Mu`adh: Sa`d bin Mu`adh was an intimate friend of Umaiya bin Khalaf and whenever Umaiya passed through Medina, he used to stay with Sa`d, and whenever Sa`d went to Mecca, he used to stay with Umaiya. When Allah's Messenger ﷺ arrived at Medina, Sa`d went to perform `Umra and stayed at Umaiya's home in Mecca. He said to Umaiya, "Tell me of a time when (the Mosque) is empty so that I may be able to perform Tawaf around the Ka`ba." So Umaiya went with him about midday. Abu Jahl met them and said, "O Abu Safwan! Who is this man accompanying you?" He said, "He is Sa`d." Abu Jahl addressed Sa`d saying, "I see you wandering about safely in Mecca inspite of the fact that you have given shelter to the people who have changed their religion (i.e. became Muslims) and have claimed that you will help them and support them. By Allah, if you were not in the company of Abu Safwan, you would not be able to go your family safely." Sa`d, raising his voice, said to him, "By Allah, if you should stop me from doing this (i.e. performing Tawaf) I would certainly prevent you from something which is more valuable for you, that is, your passage through Medina." On this, Umaiya said to him, "O Sa`d do not raise your voice before Abu-l-Hakam, the chief of the people of the Valley (of Mecca)." Sa`d said, "O Umaiya, stop that! By Allah, I have heard Allah's Messenger ﷺ predicting that the Muslim will kill you." Umaiya asked, "In Mecca?" Sa`d said, "I do not know." Umaiya was greatly scared by that news. When Umaiya returned to his family, he said to his wife, "O Um Safwan! Don't you know what Sa`d told me? "She said, "What has he told you?" He replied, "He claims that Muhammad has informed them (i.e. companions that they will kill me. I asked him, 'In Mecca?' He replied, 'I do not know." Then Umaiya added, "By Allah, I will never go out of Mecca." But when the day of (the Ghazwa of) Badr came, Abu Jahl called the people to war, saying, "Go and protect your caravan." But Umaiya disliked to go out (of Mecca). Abu Jahl came to him and said, "O Abu Safwan! If the people see you staying behind though you are the chief of the people of the Valley, then they will remain behind with you." Abu Jahl kept on urging him to go until he (i.e. Umaiya) said, "As you have forced me to change my mind, by Allah, I will buy the best camel in Mecca. Then Umaiya said (to his wife). "O Um Safwan, prepare what I need (for the journey)." She said to him, "O Abu Safwan! Have you forgotten what your Yathribi brother told you?" He said, "No, but I do not want to go with them but for a short distance." So when Umaiya went out, he used to tie his camel wherever he camped. He kept on doing that till Allah caused him to be killed at Badr. – Sahih al-Bukhari 3950

حَدَّثَنِي أَحْمَدُ بْنُ عُثْمَانَ، حَدَّثَنَا شُرَيْحُ بْنُ مَسْلَمَةَ، حَدَّثَنَا إِبْرَاهِيمُ بْنُ يُوسُفَ، عَنْ أَبِيهِ، عَنْ أَبِي إِسْحَاقَ، قَالَ حَدَّثَنِي عَمْرُو بْنُ مَيْمُونٍ، أَنَّهُ سَمِعَ عَبْدَ اللَّهِ بْنَ مَسْعُودٍ ـ رضى الله عنه ـ حَدَّثَ عَنْ سَعْدِ بْنِ مُعَاذٍ، أَنَّهُ قَالَ كَانَ صَدِيقًا لأُمَيَّةَ بْنِ خَلَفٍ، وَكَانَ أُمَيَّةُ إِذَا مَرَّ بِالْمَدِينَةِ نَزَلَ عَلَى سَعْدٍ، وَكَانَ سَعْدٌ إِذَا مَرَّ بِمَكَّةَ نَزَلَ عَلَى أُمَيَّةَ، فَلَمَّا قَدِمَ رَسُولُ اللَّهِ صلى الله عليه وسلم الْمَدِينَةَ انْطَلَقَ سَعْدٌ مُعْتَمِرًا، فَنَزَلَ عَلَى أُمَيَّةَ بِمَكَّةَ، فَقَالَ لأُمَيَّةَ انْظُرْ لِي سَاعَةَ خَلْوَةٍ لَعَلِّي أَنْ أَطُوفَ بِالْبَيْتِ. فَخَرَجَ بِهِ قَرِيبًا مِنْ نِصْفِ النَّهَارِ فَلَقِيَهُمَا أَبُو جَهْلٍ فَقَالَ يَا أَبَا صَفْوَانَ، مَنْ هَذَا مَعَكَ فَقَالَ هَذَا سَعْدٌ. فَقَالَ لَهُ أَبُو جَهْلٍ أَلاَ أَرَاكَ تَطُوفُ بِمَكَّةَ آمِنًا، وَقَدْ أَوَيْتُمُ الصُّبَاةَ، وَزَعَمْتُمْ أَنَّكُمْ تَنْصُرُونَهُمْ وَتُعِينُونَهُمْ، أَمَا وَاللَّهِ لَوْلاَ أَنَّكَ مَعَ أَبِي صَفْوَانَ مَا رَجَعْتَ إِلَى أَهْلِكَ سَالِمًا. فَقَالَ لَهُ سَعْدٌ وَرَفَعَ صَوْتَهُ عَلَيْهِ أَمَا وَاللَّهِ لَئِنْ مَنَعْتَنِي هَذَا لأَمْنَعَنَّكَ مَا هُوَ أَشَدُّ عَلَيْكَ مِنْهُ طَرِيقَكَ عَلَى الْمَدِينَةِ. فَقَالَ لَهُ أُمَيَّةُ لاَ تَرْفَعْ صَوْتَكَ يَا سَعْدُ عَلَى أَبِي الْحَكَمِ سَيِّدِ أَهْلِ الْوَادِي. فَقَالَ سَعْدٌ دَعْنَا عَنْكَ يَا أُمَيَّةُ، فَوَاللَّهِ لَقَدْ سَمِعْتُ رَسُولَ اللَّهِ صلى الله عليه وسلم يَقُولُ إِنَّهُمْ قَاتِلُوكَ. قَالَ بِمَكَّةَ قَالَ لاَ أَدْرِي. فَفَزِعَ لِذَلِكَ أُمَيَّةُ فَزَعًا شَدِيدًا، فَلَمَّا رَجَعَ أُمَيَّةُ إِلَى أَهْلِهِ قَالَ يَا أُمَّ صَفْوَانَ، أَلَمْ تَرَىْ مَا قَالَ لِي سَعْدٌ قَالَتْ وَمَا قَالَ لَكَ قَالَ زَعَمَ أَنَّ مُحَمَّدًا أَخْبَرَهُمْ أَنَّهُمْ قَاتِلِيَّ، فَقُلْتُ لَهُ بِمَكَّةَ قَالَ لاَ أَدْرِي. فَقَالَ أُمَيَّةُ وَاللَّهِ لاَ أَخْرُجُ مِنْ مَكَّةَ، فَلَمَّا كَانَ يَوْمَ بَدْرٍ اسْتَنْفَرَ أَبُو جَهْلٍ النَّاسَ قَالَ أَدْرِكُوا عِيرَكُمْ. فَكَرِهَ أُمَيَّةُ أَنْ يَخْرُجَ، فَأَتَاهُ أَبُو جَهْلٍ فَقَالَ يَا أَبَا صَفْوَانَ، إِنَّكَ مَتَى مَا يَرَاكَ النَّاسُ قَدْ تَخَلَّفْتَ وَأَنْتَ سَيِّدُ أَهْلِ الْوَادِي تَخَلَّفُوا مَعَكَ، فَلَمْ يَزَلْ بِهِ أَبُو جَهْلٍ حَتَّى قَالَ أَمَّا إِذْ غَلَبْتَنِي، فَوَاللَّهِ لأَشْتَرِيَنَّ أَجْوَدَ بَعِيرٍ بِمَكَّةَ ثُمَّ قَالَ أُمَيَّةُ يَا أُمَّ صَفْوَانَ جَهِّزِينِي. فَقَالَتْ لَهُ يَا أَبَا صَفْوَانَ وَقَدْ نَسِيتَ مَا قَالَ لَكَ أَخُوكَ الْيَثْرِبِيُّ قَالَ لاَ، مَا أُرِيدُ أَنْ أَجُوزَ مَعَهُمْ إِلاَّ قَرِيبًا. فَلَمَّا خَرَجَ أُمَيَّةُ أَخَذَ لاَ يَنْزِلُ مَنْزِلاً إِلاَّ عَقَلَ بَعِيرَهُ، فَلَمْ يَزَلْ بِذَلِكَ حَتَّى قَتَلَهُ اللَّهُ عَزَّ وَجَلَّ بِبَدْرٍ.

Narrated `Amr bin Maimun: `Abdullah bin Mas`ud said, "While Allah's Messenger ﷺ was praying beside the Ka`ba, there were some Quraish people sitting in a gathering. One of them said, 'Don't you see this (who does deeds just to show off)? Who amongst you can go and bring the dung, blood and the Abdominal contents (intestines, etc.) of the slaughtered camels of the family of so and so and then wait till he prostrates and put that in between his shoulders?' The most unfortunate amongst them (`Uqba bin Abi Mu'ait) went (and brought them) and when Allah's Messenger ﷺ prostrated, he put them between his shoulders. The Prophet remained in prostration and they laughed so much so that they fell on each other. A passerby went to Fatima, who was a young girl in those days. She came running and the Prophet ﷺ was still in prostration. She removed them and cursed upon the Quraish on their faces. When Allah's Messenger ﷺ completed his prayer, he said, 'O Allah! Take revenge on Quraish.' He said so thrice and added, 'O Allah! Take revenge on `Amr bin Hisham, `Utba bin Rabi`a, Shaiba bin Rabi`a, Al-Walid bin `Utba, Umaiya bin Khalaf, `Uqba bin Abi Mu'ait and `Umar a bin Al-Walid." `Abdullah added, "By Allah! I saw all of them dead in the battle field on the day of Badr and they were dragged and thrown in the Qalib (a well) at Badr: Allah's Messenger ﷺ then said, 'Allah's curse has descended upon the people of the Qalib (well). – Sahih al-Bukhari 520

حَدَّثَنَا أَحْمَدُ بْنُ إِسْحَاقَ السُّرْمَارِيُّ، قَالَ حَدَّثَنَا عُبَيْدُ اللَّهِ بْنُ مُوسَى، قَالَ حَدَّثَنَا إِسْرَائِيلُ، عَنْ أَبِي إِسْحَاقَ، عَنْ عَمْرِو بْنِ مَيْمُونٍ، عَنْ عَبْدِ اللَّهِ، قَالَ بَيْنَمَا رَسُولُ اللَّهِ صلى الله عليه وسلم قَائِمٌ يُصَلِّي عِنْدَ الْكَعْبَةِ، وَجَمْعُ قُرَيْشٍ فِي مَجَالِسِهِمْ إِذْ قَالَ قَائِلٌ مِنْهُمْ أَلاَ تَنْظُرُونَ إِلَى هَذَا الْمُرَائِي أَيُّكُمْ يَقُومُ إِلَى جَزُورِ آلِ فُلاَنٍ، فَيَعْمِدُ إِلَى فَرْثِهَا وَدَمِهَا وَسَلاَهَا فَيَجِيءُ بِهِ، ثُمَّ يُمْهِلُهُ حَتَّى إِذَا سَجَدَ وَضَعَهُ بَيْنَ كَتِفَيْهِ فَانْبَعَثَ أَشْقَاهُمْ، فَلَمَّا سَجَدَ رَسُولُ اللَّهِ صلى الله عليه وسلم وَضَعَهُ بَيْنَ كَتِفَيْهِ، وَثَبَتَ النَّبِيُّ صلى الله عليه وسلم سَاجِدًا، فَضَحِكُوا حَتَّى مَالَ بَعْضُهُمْ إِلَى بَعْضٍ مِنَ الضَّحِكِ، فَانْطَلَقَ مُنْطَلِقٌ إِلَى فَاطِمَةَ ـ عَلَيْهَا السَّلاَمُ ـ وَهْىَ جُوَيْرِيَةٌ، فَأَقْبَلَتْ تَسْعَى وَثَبَتَ النَّبِيُّ صلى الله عليه وسلم سَاجِدًا حَتَّى أَلْقَتْهُ عَنْهُ، وَأَقْبَلَتْ عَلَيْهِمْ تَسُبُّهُمْ، فَلَمَّا قَضَى رَسُولُ اللَّهِ صلى الله عليه وسلم الصَّلاَةَ قَالَ " اللَّهُمَّ عَلَيْكَ بِقُرَيْشٍ، اللَّهُمَّ عَلَيْكَ بِقُرَيْشٍ، اللَّهُمَّ عَلَيْكَ بِقُرَيْشٍ ـ ثُمَّ سَمَّى ـ اللَّهُمَّ عَلَيْكَ بِعَمْرِو بْنِ هِشَامٍ، وَعُتْبَةَ بْنِ رَبِيعَةَ، وَشَيْبَةَ بْنِ رَبِيعَةَ، وَالْوَلِيدِ بْنِ عُتْبَةَ، وَأُمَيَّةَ بْنِ خَلَفٍ، وَعُقْبَةَ بْنِ أَبِي مُعَيْطٍ، وَعُمَارَةَ بْنِ الْوَلِيدِ ". قَالَ عَبْدُ اللَّهِ فَوَاللَّهِ لَقَدْ رَأَيْتُهُمْ صَرْعَى يَوْمَ بَدْرٍ، ثُمَّ سُحِبُوا إِلَى الْقَلِيبِ قَلِيبِ بَدْرٍ، ثُمَّ قَالَ رَسُولُ اللَّهِ صلى الله عليه وسلم " وَأُتْبِعَ أَصْحَابُ الْقَلِيبِ لَعْنَةً ".

Narrated `Abdullah: While Allah's Messenger ﷺ was prostrating (as stated below). Narrated `Abdullah bin Mas`ud: Once the Prophet was offering prayers at the Ka`ba. Abu Jahl was sitting with some of his companions. One of them said to the others, "Who amongst you will bring the Abdominal contents (intestines, etc.) of a camel of Bani so and so and put it on the back of Muhammad, when he prostrates?" The most unfortunate of them got up and brought it. He waited till the Prophet ﷺ prostrated and then placed it on his back between his shoulders. I was watching but could not do any thing. I wish I had some people with me to hold out against them. They started laughing and falling on one another. Allah's Messenger ﷺ was in prostration and he did not lift his head up till Fatima (Prophet's daughter) came and threw that (camel's Abdominal contents) away from his back. He raised his head and said thrice, "O Allah! Punish Quraish." So it was hard for Abu Jahl and his companions when the Prophet invoked Allah against them as they had a conviction that the prayers and invocations were accepted in this city (Mecca). The Prophet ﷺ said, "O Allah! Punish Abu Jahl, `Utba bin Rabi`a, Shaiba bin Rabi`a, Al-Walid bin `Utba, Umaiya bin Khalaf, and `Uqba bin Al Mu'it (and he mentioned the seventh whose name I cannot recall). By Allah in Whose Hands my life is, I saw the dead bodies of those persons who were counted by Allah's Messenger ﷺ in the Qalib (one of the wells) of Badr. – Sahih al-Bukhari 240

حَدَّثَنَا عَبْدَانُ، قَالَ أَخْبَرَنِي أَبِي، عَنْ شُعْبَةَ، عَنْ أَبِي إِسْحَاقَ، عَنْ عَمْرِو بْنِ مَيْمُونٍ، عَنْ عَبْدِ اللَّهِ، قَالَ بَيْنَا رَسُولُ اللَّهِ صلى الله عليه وسلم سَاجِدٌ ح قَالَ وَحَدَّثَنِي أَحْمَدُ بْنُ عُثْمَانَ قَالَ حَدَّثَنَا شُرَيْحُ بْنُ مَسْلَمَةَ قَالَ حَدَّثَنَا إِبْرَاهِيمُ بْنُ يُوسُفَ عَنْ أَبِيهِ عَنْ أَبِي إِسْحَاقَ قَالَ حَدَّثَنِي عَمْرُو بْنُ مَيْمُونٍ أَنَّ عَبْدَ اللَّهِ بْنَ مَسْعُودٍ حَدَّثَهُ أَنَّ النَّبِيَّ صلى الله عليه وسلم كَانَ يُصَلِّي عِنْدَ الْبَيْتِ، وَأَبُو جَهْلٍ وَأَصْحَابٌ لَهُ جُلُوسٌ، إِذْ قَالَ بَعْضُهُمْ لِبَعْضٍ أَيُّكُمْ يَجِيءُ بِسَلَى جَزُورِ بَنِي فُلاَنٍ فَيَضَعُهُ عَلَى ظَهْرِ مُحَمَّدٍ إِذَا سَجَدَ فَانْبَعَثَ أَشْقَى الْقَوْمِ فَجَاءَ بِهِ، فَنَظَرَ حَتَّى إِذَا سَجَدَ النَّبِيُّ صلى الله عليه وسلم وَضَعَهُ عَلَى ظَهْرِهِ بَيْنَ كَتِفَيْهِ وَأَنَا أَنْظُرُ، لاَ أُغَيِّرُ شَيْئًا، لَوْ كَانَ لِي مَنْعَةٌ. قَالَ فَجَعَلُوا يَضْحَكُونَ وَيُحِيلُ بَعْضُهُمْ عَلَى بَعْضٍ، وَرَسُولُ اللَّهِ صلى الله عليه وسلم سَاجِدٌ لاَ يَرْفَعُ رَأْسَهُ، حَتَّى جَاءَتْهُ فَاطِمَةُ، فَطَرَحَتْ عَنْ ظَهْرِهِ، فَرَفَعَ رَأْسَهُ ثُمَّ قَالَ " اللَّهُمَّ عَلَيْكَ بِقُرَيْشٍ ". ثَلاَثَ مَرَّاتٍ، فَشَقَّ عَلَيْهِمْ إِذْ دَعَا عَلَيْهِمْ ـ قَالَ وَكَانُوا يُرَوْنَ أَنَّ الدَّعْوَةَ فِي ذَلِكَ الْبَلَدِ مُسْتَجَابَةٌ ـ ثُمَّ سَمَّى " اللَّهُمَّ عَلَيْكَ بِأَبِي جَهْلٍ، وَعَلَيْكَ بِعُتْبَةَ بْنِ رَبِيعَةَ، وَشَيْبَةَ بْنِ رَبِيعَةَ، وَالْوَلِيدِ بْنِ عُتْبَةَ، وَأُمَيَّةَ بْنِ خَلَفٍ، وَعُقْبَةَ بْنِ أَبِي مُعَيْطٍ ". وَعَدَّ السَّابِعَ فَلَمْ يَحْفَظْهُ قَالَ فَوَالَّذِي نَفْسِي بِيَدِهِ، لَقَدْ رَأَيْتُ الَّذِينَ عَدَّ رَسُولُ اللَّهِ صلى الله عليه وسلم صَرْعَى فِي الْقَلِيبِ قَلِيبِ بَدْرٍ

Narrated Sa`id bin Al-Musaiyab from his father: When the time of the death of Abu Talib approached, Allah's Messenger ﷺ went to him and found Abu Jahl bin Hisham and `Abdullah bin Abi Umaiya bin Al-Mughira by his side. Allah's Messenger ﷺ said to Abu Talib, "O uncle! Say: None has the right to be worshipped but Allah, a sentence with which I shall be a witness (i.e. argue) for you before Allah. Abu Jahl and `Abdullah bin Abi Umaiya said, "O Abu Talib! Are you going to denounce the religion of `Abdul Muttalib?" Allah's Messenger ﷺ kept on inviting Abu Talib to say it (i.e. 'None has the right to be worshipped but Allah') while they (Abu Jahl and `Abdullah) kept on repeating their statement till Abu Talib said as his last statement that he was on the religion of `Abdul Muttalib and refused to say, 'None has the right to be worshipped but Allah.' (Then Allah's Messenger ﷺ said, "I will keep on asking Allah's forgiveness for you unless I am forbidden (by Allah) to do so." So Allah revealed (the verse) concerning him (i.e. It is not fitting for the Prophet ﷺ and those who believe that they should invoke (Allah) for forgiveness for pagans even though they be of kin, after it has become clear to them that they are companions of the fire (9.113). – Sahih al-Bukhari 1360

حَدَّثَنَا إِسْحَاقُ، أَخْبَرَنَا يَعْقُوبُ بْنُ إِبْرَاهِيمَ، قَالَ حَدَّثَنِي أَبِي، عَنْ صَالِحٍ، عَنِ ابْنِ شِهَابٍ، قَالَ أَخْبَرَنِي سَعِيدُ بْنُ الْمُسَيَّبِ، عَنْ أَبِيهِ، أَنَّهُ أَخْبَرَهُ أَنَّهُ، لَمَّا حَضَرَتْ أَبَا طَالِبٍ الْوَفَاةُ جَاءَهُ رَسُولُ اللَّهِ صلى الله عليه وسلم فَوَجَدَ عِنْدَهُ أَبَا جَهْلِ بْنَ هِشَامٍ، وَعَبْدَ اللَّهِ بْنَ أَبِي أُمَيَّةَ بْنِ الْمُغِيرَةِ، قَالَ رَسُولُ اللَّهِ صلى الله عليه وسلم لأَبِي طَالِبٍ " يَا عَمِّ، قُلْ لاَ إِلَهَ إِلاَّ اللَّهُ، كَلِمَةً أَشْهَدُ لَكَ بِهَا عِنْدَ اللَّهِ ". فَقَالَ أَبُو جَهْلٍ وَعَبْدُ اللَّهِ بْنُ أَبِي أُمَيَّةَ يَا أَبَا طَالِبٍ، أَتَرْغَبُ عَنْ مِلَّةِ عَبْدِ الْمُطَّلِبِ فَلَمْ يَزَلْ رَسُولُ اللَّهِ صلى الله عليه وسلم يَعْرِضُهَا عَلَيْهِ، وَيَعُودَانِ بِتِلْكَ الْمَقَالَةِ، حَتَّى قَالَ أَبُو طَالِبٍ آخِرَ مَا كَلَّمَهُمْ هُوَ عَلَى مِلَّةِ عَبْدِ الْمُطَّلِبِ،

وَأَبَى أَنْ يَقُولَ لاَ إِلَهَ إِلاَّ اللَّهُ. فَقَالَ رَسُولُ اللَّهِ صلى الله عليه وسلم " أَمَا وَاللَّهِ لأَسْتَغْفِرَنَّ لَكَ، مَا لَمْ أُنْهَ عَنْكَ ". فَأَنْزَلَ اللَّهُ تَعَالَى فِيهِ {مَا كَانَ لِلنَّبِيِّ} الآيَةَ

Narrated `Abdullah bin Mas`ud: Sa`d bin Mu`adh came to Mecca with the intention of performing `Umra, and stayed at the house of Umaiya bin Khalaf Abi Safwan, for Umaiya himself used to stay at Sa`d's house when he passed by Medina on his way to Sham. Umaiya said to Sa`d, "Will you wait till midday when the people are (at their homes), then you may go and perform the Tawaf round the Ka`ba?" So, while Sa`d was going around the Ka`ba, Abu Jahl came and asked, "Who is that who is performing Tawaf?" Sa`d replied, "I am Sa`d." Abu Jahl said, "Are you circumambulating the Ka`ba safely although you have given refuge to Muhammad and his companions?" Sa`d said, "Yes," and they started quarreling. Umaiya said to Sa`d, "Don't shout at Abi-l-Hakam (i.e. Abu Jahl), for he is chief of the valley (of Mecca)." Sa`d then said (to Abu Jahl). 'By Allah, if you prevent me from performing the Tawaf of the Ka`ba, I will spoil your trade with Sham." Umaiya kept on saying to Sa`d, "Don't raise your voice." And kept on taking hold of him. Sa`d became furious and said, (to Umaiya), "Be away from me, for I have heard Muhammad saying that he will kill you." Umaiiya said, "Will he kill me?" Sa`d said, "Yes,." Umaiya said, "By Allah! When Muhammad says a thing, he never tells a lie." Umaiya went to his wife and said to her, "Do you know what my brother from Yathrib (i.e. Medina) has said to me?" She said, "What has he said?" He said, "He claims that he has heard Muhammad claiming that he will kill me." She said, By Allah! Muhammad never tells a lie." So when the infidels started to proceed for Badr (Battle) and declared war (against the Muslims), his wife said to him, "Don't you remember what your brother from Yathrib told you?" Umaiya decided not to go but Abu Jahl said to him, "You are from the nobles of the valley (of Mecca), so you should accompany us for a day or two." He went with them and thus Allah got him killed. – Sahih Al-Bukhari 3632

حَدَّثَنِي أَحْمَدُ بْنُ إِسْحَاقَ، حَدَّثَنَا عُبَيْدُ اللَّهِ بْنُ مُوسَى، حَدَّثَنَا إِسْرَائِيلُ، عَنْ أَبِي إِسْحَاقَ، عَنْ عَمْرِو بْنِ مَيْمُونٍ، عَنْ عَبْدِ اللَّهِ بْنِ مَسْعُودٍ ـ رضى الله عنه ـ قَالَ انْطَلَقَ سَعْدُ بْنُ مُعَاذٍ مُعْتَمِرًا ـ قَالَ ـ فَنَزَلَ عَلَى أُمَيَّةَ بْنِ خَلَفٍ أَبِي صَفْوَانَ، وَكَانَ أُمَيَّةُ إِذَا انْطَلَقَ إِلَى الشَّأْمِ فَمَرَّ بِالْمَدِينَةِ نَزَلَ عَلَى سَعْدٍ، فَقَالَ أُمَيَّةُ لِسَعْدٍ انْتَظِرْ حَتَّى إِذَا انْتَصَفَ النَّهَارُ، وَغَفَلَ النَّاسُ انْطَلَقْتُ فَطُفْتُ، فَبَيْنَا سَعْدٌ يَطُوفُ إِذَا أَبُو جَهْلٍ فَقَالَ مَنْ هَذَا الَّذِي يَطُوفُ بِالْكَعْبَةِ فَقَالَ سَعْدٌ أَنَا سَعْدٌ. فَقَالَ أَبُو جَهْلٍ تَطُوفُ بِالْكَعْبَةِ آمِنًا، وَقَدْ آوَيْتُمْ مُحَمَّدًا وَأَصْحَابَهُ فَقَالَ نَعَمْ. فَتَلاَحَيَا بَيْنَهُمَا. فَقَالَ أُمَيَّةُ لِسَعْدٍ لاَ تَرْفَعْ صَوْتَكَ عَلَى أَبِي الْحَكَمِ، فَإِنَّهُ سَيِّدُ أَهْلِ الْوَادِي. ثُمَّ قَالَ سَعْدٌ وَاللَّهِ لَئِنْ مَنَعْتَنِي أَنْ أَطُوفَ بِالْبَيْتِ لأَقْطَعَنَّ مَتْجَرَكَ بِالشَّأْمِ. قَالَ فَجَعَلَ أُمَيَّةُ يَقُولُ لِسَعْدٍ لاَ تَرْفَعْ صَوْتَكَ. وَجَعَلَ يُمْسِكُهُ، فَغَضِبَ سَعْدٌ فَقَالَ دَعْنَا عَنْكَ، فَإِنِّي سَمِعْتُ مُحَمَّدًا صلى الله عليه وسلم يَزْعُمُ أَنَّهُ قَاتِلُكَ. قَالَ إِيَّاىَ قَالَ نَعَمْ. قَالَ وَاللَّهِ مَا يَكْذِبُ مُحَمَّدٌ إِذَا حَدَّثَ. فَرَجَعَ إِلَى امْرَأَتِهِ، فَقَالَ أَمَا تَعْلَمِينَ مَا قَالَ لِي أَخِي الْيَثْرِبِيُّ قَالَتْ وَمَا قَالَ قَالَ زَعَمَ أَنَّهُ سَمِعَ مُحَمَّدًا يَزْعُمُ أَنَّهُ قَاتِلِي. قَالَتْ فَوَاللَّهِ مَا يَكْذِبُ مُحَمَّدٌ. قَالَ فَلَمَّا خَرَجُوا إِلَى بَدْرٍ، وَجَاءَ الصَّرِيخُ قَالَتْ لَهُ امْرَأَتُهُ أَمَا ذَكَرْتَ مَا قَالَ لَكَ أَخُوكَ الْيَثْرِبِيُّ قَالَ فَأَرَادَ أَنْ لاَ يَخْرُجَ، فَقَالَ لَهُ أَبُو جَهْلٍ إِنَّكَ مِنْ أَشْرَافِ الْوَادِي، فَسِرْ يَوْمًا أَوْ يَوْمَيْنِ، فَسَارَ مَعَهُمْ فَقَتَلَهُ اللَّهُ.

Narrated `Abdur-Rahman bin `Auf: I got an agreement written between me and Umaiya bin Khalaf that Umaiya would look after my property (or family) in Mecca and I would look after his in Medina. When I mentioned the word 'Ar-Rahman' in the documents, Umaiya said, "I do not know 'Ar-Rahman.' Write down to me your name, (with which you called yourself) in the Pre-Islamic Period of Ignorance." So, I wrote my name ' `Abdu `Amr'. On the day (of the battle) of Badr, when all the people went to sleep, I went up the hill to protect him. Bilal saw him (i.e. Umaiya) and went to a gathering of Ansar and said, "(Here Is) Umaiya bin Khalaf! Woe to me if he escapes!" So, a group of Ansar went out with Bilal to follow us (`Abdur-Rahman and Umaiya). Being afraid that they would catch us, I left Umaiya's son for them to keep them busy but the Ansar killed the son and insisted on following us. Umaiya was a fat man, and when they approached us, I told him to kneel down, and he knelt, and I laid myself on him to protect him, but the Ansar killed him by passing their swords underneath me, and one of them injured my foot with his sword. (The sub narrator said, " `Abdur-Rahman used to show us the trace of the wound on the back of his foot."). – Sahih Al-Bukhari 2301

حَدَّثَنَا عَبْدُ الْعَزِيزِ بْنُ عَبْدِ اللَّهِ، قَالَ حَدَّثَنِي يُوسُفُ بْنُ الْمَاجِشُونِ، عَنْ صَالِحِ بْنِ إِبْرَاهِيمَ بْنِ عَبْدِ الرَّحْمَنِ بْنِ عَوْفٍ، عَنْ أَبِيهِ، عَنْ جَدِّهِ عَبْدِ الرَّحْمَنِ بْنِ عَوْفٍ ـ رضى الله عنه ـ قَالَ كَاتَبْتُ أُمَيَّةَ بْنَ خَلَفٍ كِتَابًا بِأَنْ يَحْفَظَنِي فِي صَاغِيَتِي بِمَكَّةَ، وَأَحْفَظَهُ فِي صَاغِيَتِهِ بِالْمَدِينَةِ، فَلَمَّا ذَكَرْتُ الرَّحْمَنَ قَالَ لاَ أَعْرِفُ الرَّحْمَنَ، كَاتِبْنِي بِاسْمِكَ الَّذِي كَانَ فِي الْجَاهِلِيَّةِ.
فَكَاتَبْتُهُ عَبْدُ عَمْرٍو فَلَمَّا كَانَ فِي يَوْمِ بَدْرٍ خَرَجْتُ إِلَى جَبَلٍ لأُحْرِزَهُ حِينَ نَامَ النَّاسُ فَأَبْصَرَهُ بِلاَلٌ فَخَرَجَ حَتَّى وَقَفَ عَلَى مَجْلِسٍ مِنَ الأَنْصَارِ فَقَالَ أُمَيَّةُ بْنُ خَلَفٍ، لاَ نَجَوْتُ إِنْ نَجَا أُمَيَّةُ. فَخَرَجَ مَعَهُ فَرِيقٌ مِنَ الأَنْصَارِ فِي آثَارِنَا، فَلَمَّا خَشِيتُ أَنْ يَلْحَقُونَا خَلَّفْتُ لَهُمُ ابْنَهُ، لأَشْغَلَهُمْ فَقَتَلُوهُ ثُمَّ أَبَوْا حَتَّى يَتْبَعُونَا، وَكَانَ رَجُلاً ثَقِيلاً، فَلَمَّا أَدْرَكُونَا قُلْتُ لَهُ ابْرُكْ. فَبَرَكَ، فَأَلْقَيْتُ عَلَيْهِ نَفْسِي لأَمْنَعَهُ، فَتَخَلَّلُوهُ بِالسُّيُوفِ مِنْ تَحْتِي، حَتَّى قَتَلُوهُ، وَأَصَابَ أَحَدُهُمْ رِجْلِي بِسَيْفِهِ، وَكَانَ عَبْدُ الرَّحْمَنِ بْنُ عَوْفٍ يُرِينَا ذَلِكَ الأَثَرَ فِي ظَهْرِ قَدَمِهِ.
قَالَ أَبُو عَبْد اللَّهِ سَمِعَ يُوسُفُ صَالِحًا وَإِبْرَاهِيمُ أَبَاهُ

Narrated Ibn Abi Mulaika: There was a disagreement between them (i.e. Ibn `Abbas and Ibn Az-Zubair) so I went to Ibn `Abbas in the morning and said (to him), "Do you want to fight against Ibn Zubair and thus make lawful what Allah has made unlawful (i.e. fighting in Meccas?" Ibn `Abbas said, "Allah forbid! Allah ordained that Ibn Zubair and Bani Umaiya would permit (fighting in Mecca), but by Allah, I will never regard it as permissible." Ibn `Abbas added. "The people asked me to take the oath of allegiance to Ibn Az-Zubair. I said, 'He is really entitled to assume authority for his father, Az-Zubair was the helper of the Prophet, his (maternal) grandfather, Abu Bakr was (the Prophet's) companion in the cave, his mother, Asma' was 'Dhatun-Nitaq', his aunt, `Aisha was the mother of the Believers, his paternal aunt, Khadija was the wife of the Prophet ﷺ, and the paternal aunt of the Prophet ﷺ was his grandmother. He himself is pious and chaste in Islam, well versed in the Knowledge of the Qur'an. By Allah! (Really, I left my relatives, Bani Umaiya for his sake though) they are my close relatives, and if they should be my rulers, they are equally apt to be so and are descended from a noble family. – Sahih Al-Bukhari 4665

حَدَّثَنِي عَبْدُ اللَّهِ بْنُ مُحَمَّدٍ، قَالَ حَدَّثَنِي يَحْيَى بْنُ مَعِينٍ، حَدَّثَنَا حَجَّاجٌ، قَالَ ابْنُ جُرَيْجٍ قَالَ ابْنُ أَبِي مُلَيْكَةَ وَكَانَ بَيْنَهُمَا شَىْءٌ فَغَدَوْتُ عَلَى ابْنِ عَبَّاسٍ فَقُلْتُ أَتُرِيدُ أَنْ تُقَاتِلَ ابْنَ الزُّبَيْرِ، فَتُحِلَّ حَرَمَ اللَّهِ. فَقَالَ مَعَاذَ اللَّهِ، إِنَّ اللَّهَ كَتَبَ ابْنَ الزُّبَيْرِ وَبَنِي أُمَيَّةَ مُحِلِّينَ، وَإِنِّي وَاللَّهِ لاَ أُحِلُّهُ أَبَدًا. قَالَ قَالَ النَّاسُ بَايِعْ لاِبْنِ الزُّبَيْرِ. فَقُلْتُ وَأَيْنَ بِهَذَا الأَمْرِ عَنْهُ أَمَّا أَبُوهُ فَحَوَارِيُّ النَّبِيِّ صلى الله عليه وسلم، يُرِيدُ الزُّبَيْرَ، وَأَمَّا جَدُّهُ فَصَاحِبُ الْغَارِ، يُرِيدُ أَبَا بَكْرٍ، وَأُمُّهُ فَذَاتُ النِّطَاقِ، يُرِيدُ أَسْمَاءَ، وَأَمَّا خَالَتُهُ فَأُمُّ الْمُؤْمِنِينَ، يُرِيدُ عَائِشَةَ، وَأَمَّا عَمَّتُهُ فَزَوْجُ النَّبِيِّ صلى الله عليه وسلم، يُرِيدُ خَدِيجَةَ، وَأَمَّا عَمَّةُ النَّبِيِّ صلى الله عليه وسلم فَجَدَّتُهُ، يُرِيدُ صَفِيَّةَ، ثُمَّ عَفِيفٌ فِي الإِسْلاَمِ، قَارِئٌ لِلْقُرْآنِ. وَاللَّهِ إِنْ وَصَلُونِي وَصَلُونِي مِنْ قَرِيبٍ، وَإِنْ رَبُّونِي رَبَّنِي أَكْفَاءٌ كِرَامٌ، فَآثَرَ التُّوَيْتَاتِ وَالأُسَامَاتِ وَالْحُمَيْدَاتِ، يُرِيدُ أَبْطُنًا مِنْ بَنِي أَسَدٍ بَنِي تُوَيْتٍ وَبَنِي أُسَامَةَ وَبَنِي أَسَدٍ، إِنَّ ابْنَ أَبِي الْعَاصِ بَرَزَ يَمْشِي الْقُدَمِيَّةَ، يَعْنِي عَبْدَ الْمَلِكِ بْنَ مَرْوَانَ، وَإِنَّهُ لَوَّى ذَنَبَهُ، يَعْنِي ابْنَ الزُّبَيْرِ.

Abdullah bin Ubaiyy bin Salul
عبد الله بن أبي بن سلول

Narrated Usama bin Zaid: Allah's Messenger ﷺ rode a donkey, equipped with a thick cloth-covering made in Fadak and was riding behind him. He was going to pay visit to Sa`d bin Ubada in Banu Al-Harith bin Al-Khazraj; and this incident happened before the battle of Badr. The Prophet ﷺ passed by a gathering in which `Abdullah bin Ubai bin Salul was present, and that was before `Abdullah bin Ubai embraced Islam. Behold in that gathering there were people of different religions: there were Muslims, pagans, idol-worshippers and Jews, and in that gathering `Abdullah bin Rawaha was also present. When a cloud of dust raised by the donkey reached that gathering, `Abdullah bin Ubai covered his nose with his garment and then said, "Do not cover us with dust." Then Allah's Messenger ﷺ greeted them and stopped and dismounted and invited them to Allah (i.e. to embrace Islam) and recited to them the Holy Qur'an. On that, `Abdullah bin Ubai bin Saluil said, "O man ! There is nothing better than that what you say. If it is the truth, then do not trouble us with it in our gatherings. Return to your mount (or residence) and if somebody comes to you, relate (your tales) to him." On that `Abdullah bin Rawaha said, "Yes, O Allah's Apostle! Bring it (i.e. what you want to say) to us in our gathering, for we love that." So the Muslims, the pagans and the Jews started abusing one another till they were on the point of fighting with one another. The Prophet ﷺ kept on quietening them till they became quiet, whereupon the Prophet rode his animal (mount) and proceeded till he entered upon Sa`d bin Ubada. The Prophet ﷺ said to Sa`d, "Did you not hear what 'Abu Hub-b said?" He meant `Abdullah bin Ubai. "He said so-andso." On that Sa`d bin Ubada said, "O Allah's Messenger ﷺ! Excuse and forgive him, for by Him Who revealed the Book to you, Allah brought the Truth which was sent to you at the time when the people of this town (i.e. Medina) had decided unanimously to crown him and tie a turban on his head (electing him as chief). But when Allah opposed that (decision) through the Truth which Allah gave to you, he (i.e. `Abdullah bin Ubai) was grieved with jealously. And that caused him to do what you have seen." So Allah's Messenger ﷺ excused him, for the Prophet ﷺ and his companions used to forgive the pagans and the people of Scripture as Allah had ordered them, and they used to put up with their mischief with patience. Allah said: "And you shall certainly hear much that will grieve you from those who received the Scripture before you and from the pagans........'(3.186) And Allah also said:--"Many of the people of the Scripture wish if they could turn you away as disbelievers after you have believed, from selfish envy.." (2.109) So the Prophet ﷺ used to stick to the principle of forgiveness for them as long as Allah ordered him to do so till Allah permitted fighting them. So when Allah's Messenger ﷺ fought the battle of Badr and Allah killed the nobles of Quraish infidels through him, Ibn Ubai bin Salul and the pagans and idolaters who were with him, said, "This matter (i.e. Islam) has appeared (i.e. became victorious)." So they gave the pledge of allegiance (for embracing Islam) to Allah's Messenger ﷺ and became Muslims. – Sahih Al-Bukhari 4566

حَدَّثَنَا أَبُو الْيَمَانِ، أَخْبَرَنَا شُعَيْبٌ، عَنِ الزُّهْرِيِّ، قَالَ أَخْبَرَنِي عُرْوَةُ بْنُ الزُّبَيْرِ، أَنَّ أُسَامَةَ بْنَ زَيْدٍ ـ رضى الله عنهما ـ أَخْبَرَهُ أَنَّ رَسُولَ اللَّهِ صلى الله عليه وسلم رَكِبَ عَلَى حِمَارٍ عَلَى قَطِيفَةٍ فَدَكِيَّةٍ، وَأَرْدَفَ أُسَامَةَ بْنَ زَيْدٍ وَرَاءَهُ، يَعُودُ سَعْدَ بْنَ عُبَادَةَ فِي بَنِي الْحَارِثِ بْنِ الْخَزْرَجِ قَبْلَ وَقْعَةِ بَدْرٍ ـ قَالَ ـ حَتَّى مَرَّ بِمَجْلِسٍ فِيهِ عَبْدُ اللَّهِ بْنُ أُبَيٍّ، ابْنُ سَلُولَ، وَذَلِكَ قَبْلَ أَنْ يُسْلِمَ عَبْدُ اللَّهِ بْنُ أُبَيٍّ فَإِذَا فِي الْمَجْلِسِ أَخْلاَطٌ مِنَ الْمُسْلِمِينَ وَالْمُشْرِكِينَ عَبَدَةِ الأَوْثَانِ وَالْيَهُودِ وَالْمُسْلِمِينَ، وَفِي الْمَجْلِسِ عَبْدُ اللَّهِ بْنُ رَوَاحَةَ، فَلَمَّا غَشِيَتِ الْمَجْلِسَ عَجَاجَةُ الدَّابَّةِ خَمَّرَ عَبْدُ اللَّهِ بْنُ أُبَيٍّ أَنْفَهُ بِرِدَائِهِ، ثُمَّ قَالَ لاَ تُغَبِّرُوا عَلَيْنَا. فَسَلَّمَ رَسُولُ اللَّهِ صلى الله عليه وسلم عَلَيْهِمْ ثُمَّ وَقَفَ فَنَزَلَ فَدَعَاهُمْ إِلَى اللَّهِ، وَقَرَأَ عَلَيْهِمُ الْقُرْآنَ، فَقَالَ عَبْدُ اللَّهِ بْنُ أُبَيٍّ ابْنُ سَلُولَ أَيُّهَا الْمَرْءُ، إِنَّهُ لاَ أَحْسَنَ مِمَّا تَقُولُ، إِنْ كَانَ حَقًّا، فَلاَ تُؤْذِينَا بِهِ فِي مَجْلِسِنَا، ارْجِعْ إِلَى رَحْلِكَ، فَمَنْ جَاءَكَ فَاقْصُصْ عَلَيْهِ. فَقَالَ عَبْدُ اللَّهِ بْنُ رَوَاحَةَ بَلَى يَا رَسُولَ اللَّهِ، فَاغْشَنَا بِهِ فِي مَجَالِسِنَا، فَإِنَّا نُحِبُّ ذَلِكَ. فَاسْتَبَّ الْمُسْلِمُونَ وَالْمُشْرِكُونَ وَالْيَهُودُ حَتَّى كَادُوا يَتَثَاوَرُونَ، فَلَمْ يَزَلِ النَّبِيُّ صلى الله عليه وسلم يُخَفِّضُهُمْ حَتَّى سَكَنُوا، ثُمَّ رَكِبَ النَّبِيُّ صلى الله عليه وسلم دَابَّتَهُ فَسَارَ حَتَّى دَخَلَ عَلَى سَعْدِ بْنِ عُبَادَةَ، فَقَالَ لَهُ النَّبِيُّ صلى الله عليه وسلم " يَا سَعْدُ أَلَمْ تَسْمَعْ مَا قَالَ أَبُو حُبَابٍ ". يُرِيدُ عَبْدَ اللَّهِ بْنَ أُبَىٍّ " قَالَ كَذَا وَكَذَا " قَالَ سَعْدُ بْنُ عُبَادَةَ يَا رَسُولَ اللَّهِ اعْفُ عَنْهُ وَاصْفَحْ عَنْهُ، فَوَالَّذِي أَنْزَلَ عَلَيْكَ الْكِتَابَ، لَقَدْ جَاءَ اللَّهُ بِالْحَقِّ الَّذِي أَنْزَلَ عَلَيْكَ، لَقَدِ اصْطَلَحَ أَهْلُ هَذِهِ الْبُحَيْرَةِ عَلَى أَنْ يُتَوِّجُوهُ فَيُعَصِّبُونَهُ بِالْعِصَابَةِ، فَلَمَّا أَبَى اللَّهُ ذَلِكَ بِالْحَقِّ الَّذِي أَعْطَاكَ اللَّهُ شَرِقَ بِذَلِكَ، فَذَلِكَ فَعَلَ بِهِ مَا رَأَيْتَ. فَعَفَا عَنْهُ رَسُولُ اللَّهِ صلى الله عليه وسلم وَكَانَ النَّبِيُّ صلى الله عليه وسلم وَأَصْحَابُهُ يَعْفُونَ عَنِ الْمُشْرِكِينَ وَأَهْلِ الْكِتَابِ كَمَا أَمَرَهُمُ اللَّهُ، وَيَصْبِرُونَ عَلَى الأَذَى قَالَ اللَّهُ عَزَّ وَجَلَّ {وَلَتَسْمَعُنَّ مِنَ الَّذِينَ أُوتُوا الْكِتَابَ مِنْ قَبْلِكُمْ وَمِنَ الَّذِينَ أَشْرَكُوا أَذًى كَثِيرًا } الآيَةَ، وَقَالَ اللَّهُ {وَدَّ كَثِيرٌ مِنْ أَهْلِ الْكِتَابِ لَوْ يَرُدُّونَكُمْ مِنْ بَعْدِ إِيمَانِكُمْ كُفَّارًا حَسَدًا مِنْ عِنْدِ أَنْفُسِهِمْ} إِلَى آخِرِ الآيَةِ، وَكَانَ النَّبِيُّ صلى الله عليه وسلم يَتَأَوَّلُ الْعَفْوَ مَا أَمَرَهُ اللَّهُ بِهِ، حَتَّى أَذِنَ اللَّهُ فِيهِمْ، فَلَمَّا غَزَا رَسُولُ اللَّهِ صلى الله عليه وسلم بَدْرًا، فَقَتَلَ اللَّهُ بِهِ صَنَادِيدَ كُفَّارِ قُرَيْشٍ قَالَ ابْنُ

أُبَيٍّ ابْنُ سَلُولَ، وَمَنْ مَعَهُ مِنَ الْمُشْرِكِينَ، وَعَبَدَةِ الأَوْثَانِ هَذَا أَمْرٌ قَدْ تَوَجَّهَ. فَبَايَعُوا الرَّسُولَ صلى الله عليه وسلم عَلَى الإِسْلاَمِ فَأَسْلَمُوا.

Narrated Zaid bin Arqam: We went out with the Prophetﷺ: on a journey and the people suffered from lack of provisions. So `Abdullah bin Ubai said to his companions, "Don't spend on those who are with Allah's Messengerﷺ, that they may disperse and go away from him." He also said, "If we return to Medina, surely, the more honorable will expel therefrom the meaner. So I went to the Prophetﷺ and informed him of that. He sent for `Abdullah bin Ubai and asked him, but `Abdullah bin Ubai swore that he did not say so. The people said, "Zaid told a lie to 'Allah's Messenger." What they said distressed me very much. Later Allah revealed the confirmation of my statement in his saying:-- '(When the hypocrites come to you.' (63.1) So the Prophetﷺ called them that they might ask Allah to forgive them, but they turned their heads aside. (Concerning Allah's saying: 'Pieces of wood propped up,' Zaid said; They were the most handsome men.). – Sahih Al-Bukhari 4903

حَدَّثَنَا عَمْرُو بْنُ خَالِدٍ، حَدَّثَنَا زُهَيْرُ بْنُ مُعَاوِيَةَ، حَدَّثَنَا أَبُو إِسْحَاقَ، قَالَ سَمِعْتُ زَيْدَ بْنَ أَرْقَمَ، قَالَ خَرَجْنَا مَعَ النَّبِيِّ صلى الله عليه وسلم فِي سَفَرٍ أَصَابَ النَّاسَ فِيهِ شِدَّةٌ، فَقَالَ عَبْدُ اللَّهِ بْنُ أُبَىٍّ لأَصْحَابِهِ لاَ تُنْفِقُوا عَلَى مَنْ عِنْدَ رَسُولِ اللَّهِ حَتَّى يَنْفَضُّوا مِنْ حَوْلِهِ. وَقَالَ لَئِنْ رَجَعْنَا إِلَى الْمَدِينَةِ لَيُخْرِجَنَّ الأَعَزُّ مِنْهَا الأَذَلَّ. فَأَتَيْتُ النَّبِيَّ صلى الله عليه وسلم فَأَخْبَرْتُهُ فَأَرْسَلَ إِلَى عَبْدِ اللَّهِ بْنِ أُبَىٍّ فَسَأَلَهُ، فَاجْتَهَدَ يَمِينَهُ مَا فَعَلَ، قَالُوا كَذَبَ زَيْدٌ رَسُولَ اللَّهِ صلى الله عليه وسلم فَوَقَعَ فِي نَفْسِي مِمَّا قَالُوا شِدَّةٌ، حَتَّى أَنْزَلَ اللَّهُ عَزَّ وَجَلَّ تَصْدِيقِي فِي {إِذَا جَاءَكَ الْمُنَافِقُونَ} فَدَعَاهُمُ النَّبِيُّ صلى الله عليه وسلم لِيَسْتَغْفِرَ لَهُمْ فَلَوَّوْا رُءُوسَهُمْ. وَقَوْلُهُ {خُشُبٌ مُسَنَّدَةٌ} قَالَ كَانُوا رِجَالاً أَجْمَلَ شَىْءٍ.

Narrated Jabir bin `Abdullah: We were in a Ghazwa (Sufyan once said, in an army) and a man from the emigrants kicked an Ansari man (on the buttocks with his foot). The Ansari man said, "O the Ansar! (Help!)" and the emigrant said. "O the emigrants! (Help!) Allah's Messengerﷺ heard that and said, "What is this call for, which is characteristic of the period of ignorance?" They said, "O Allah's Messengerﷺ! A man from the emigrants kicked one of the Ansar (on the buttocks with his foot)." Allah's Messengerﷺ said, "Leave it (that call) as is a detestable thing." `Abdullah bin Ubai heard that and said, 'Have the (the emigrants) done so? By Allah, if we return Medina, surely, the more honorable will expel therefrom the meaner." When this statement reached the Prophet. `Umar got up an, said, "O Allah's Messengerﷺ! Let me chop off the head of this hypocrite (`Abdullah bin Ubai)!" The Prophetﷺ said "Leave him, lest the people say that Muhammad kills his companions." The Ansar were then more in number than the emigrants when the latter came to Medina, but later on the emigrant increased. – Sahih Al-Bukhari 4905

حَدَّثَنَا عَلِيٌّ، حَدَّثَنَا سُفْيَانُ، قَالَ عَمْرٌو سَمِعْتُ جَابِرَ بْنَ عَبْدِ اللَّهِ ـ رضى الله عنهما ـ قَالَ كُنَّا فِي غَزَاةٍ ـ قَالَ سُفْيَانُ مَرَّةً فِي جَيْشٍ ـ فَكَسَعَ رَجُلٌ مِنَ الْمُهَاجِرِينَ رَجُلاً مِنَ الأَنْصَارِ فَقَالَ الأَنْصَارِيُّ يَا لَلأَنْصَارِ. وَقَالَ الْمُهَاجِرِيُّ يَا لَلْمُهَاجِرِينَ. فَسَمِعَ ذَاكَ رَسُولُ اللَّهِ صلى الله عليه وسلم فَقَالَ " مَا بَالُ دَعْوَى جَاهِلِيَّةٍ " قَالُوا يَا رَسُولَ اللَّهِ كَسَعَ رَجُلٌ مِنَ الْمُهَاجِرِينَ رَجُلاً مِنَ الأَنْصَارِ. فَقَالَ " دَعُوهَا فَإِنَّهَا مُنْتِنَةٌ ". فَسَمِعَ بِذَلِكَ عَبْدُ اللَّهِ بْنُ أُبَىٍّ فَقَالَ فَعَلُوهَا، أَمَا وَاللَّهِ لَئِنْ رَجَعْنَا إِلَى الْمَدِينَةِ لَيُخْرِجَنَّ الأَعَزُّ مِنْهَا الأَذَلَّ. فَبَلَغَ النَّبِيَّ صلى الله عليه وسلم فَقَامَ عُمَرُ فَقَالَ يَا رَسُولَ اللَّهِ دَعْنِي أَضْرِبْ عُنُقَ هَذَا الْمُنَافِقِ. فَقَالَ النَّبِيُّ صلى الله عليه وسلم " دَعْهُ لاَ يَتَحَدَّثُ النَّاسُ أَنَّ مُحَمَّدًا يَقْتُلُ أَصْحَابَهُ " وَكَانَتِ الأَنْصَارُ أَكْثَرَ مِنَ الْمُهَاجِرِينَ حِينَ قَدِمُوا الْمَدِينَةَ، ثُمَّ إِنَّ الْمُهَاجِرِينَ كَثُرُوا بَعْدُ. قَالَ سُفْيَانُ فَحَفِظْتُهُ مِنْ عَمْرٍو قَالَ عَمْرٌو سَمِعْتُ جَابِرًا كُنَّا مَعَ النَّبِيِّ صلى الله عليه وسلم

Narrated Aisha: (the wife of the Prophet) "Whenever Allah's Messengerﷺ intended to go on a journey, he would draw lots amongst his wives and would take with him the one upon whom the lot fell. During a Ghazwa of his, he drew lots amongst us and the lot fell upon me, and I proceeded with him after Allah had decreed the use of the veil by women. I was carried in a Howdah (on the camel) and dismounted while still in it. When Allah's Messengerﷺ was through with his Ghazwa and returned home, and we approached the city of Medina, Allah's Messenger ordered us to proceed at night. When the order of setting off was given, I walked till I was past the army to answer the call of nature. After finishing I returned (to the camp) to depart (with the others) and suddenly realized that my necklace over my chest was missing. So, I returned to look for it and was delayed because of that. The people who used to carry me on the camel, came to my Howdah and put it on the back of the camel, thinking that I was in it, as, at that time, women were light in weight, and thin and lean, and did not use to eat much. So, those people did not feel the difference in the heaviness of the Howdah while lifting it, and they put it over the camel. At that time I was a young lady. They set the camel moving and proceeded on. I found my necklace after the army had gone, and came to their camp to find nobody. So, I went to the place where I used to stay, thinking that they would discover my absence and come back in my search. While in that state, I felt sleepy and slept. Safwan bin Mu'attal As-Sulami Adh-Dhakwani was behind the army and reached my abode in the morning. When he saw a sleeping person, he came to me, and he used to see me before veiling. So, I got up when I heard him saying, "Inna lil-lah-wa inn a ilaihi rajiun (We are for Allah, and we will return to Him)." He made his camel knell down. He got down from his camel, and put his leg on the front legs of the camel and then I rode and sat over it. Safwan set out walking, leading the camel by the rope till we reached the army who had halted to take rest at midday. Then whoever was meant for destruction, fell into destruction, (some people accused me falsely) and the leader of the false accusers was `Abdullah bin Ubai bin Salul. After that we returned to Medina, and I became ill for one month while the people were spreading the forged statements of the false accusers. I was feeling during my ailment as if I were not receiving the usual kindness from the Prophet which I used to receive from him when I got sick. But he would come, greet and say, 'How is that (girl)?' I did not know anything of what was going on till I recovered from my ailment and went out with Um Mistah to the Manasi where we used to answer the call of nature, and we used not to go to answer the call of nature except from night to night and that was before we had lavatories near to our houses. And this habit of ours was similar to the habit of the old 'Arabs in the open country (or away from houses). So. I and Um Mistah bint Ruhm went out walking. Um Mistah stumbled because of her long dress and on that she said, 'Let Mistah be ruined.' I said, 'You are saying a bad word. Why are you abusing a man who took part in (the battle of) Badr?' She said, 'O Hanata (you there) didn't you hear what they said?' Then she told me the rumors of the false accusers. My sickness was aggravated, and when I returned home, Allah's Messenger came to me, and after greeting he said, 'How is that (girl)?' I requested him to allow me to go to my parents. I wanted then to be sure of the news through them I Allah's Messenger allowed me, and I went to my parents and asked my mother, 'What are the people talking about?' She said, 'O my daughter! Don't worry much about this matter. By Allah, never is there a charming woman lo"ed by her husband who has other wives, but the women would forge false news about her.' I said, 'Glorified be Allah! Are the people really taking of this matter?' That night I kept on weeping and could not sleep till morning. In the morning Allah's Messenger called `Ali bin Abu Talib and Usama bin Zaid when he saw the Divine Inspiration delayed, to consul them about divorcing his wife (i.e. `Aisha). Usama bin Zaid said what he knew of the good reputation of his wives and added, 'O Allah's Messenger! Keep you wife, for, by Allah, we know nothing about her but good.' `Ali bin Abu Talib said, 'O Allah's Messenger! Allah has no imposed restrictions on you, and there are many women other than she, yet you may ask the woman-servant who will tell you the truth.' On that Allah's Messenger called Barirah and said, 'O Barirah. Did you ever see anything which roused your suspicions about her?' Barirah said, 'No, by Allah Who has sent you with the Truth, I have never seen in her anything faulty except that she is a girl of immature age, who sometimes sleeps and leaves the dough for the goats to eat.' On that day Allah's Messenger ﷺ ascended the pulpit and requested that somebody support him in punishing `Abdullah bin Ubai bin Salul. Allah's Apostle said, 'Who will support me to punish that person (`Abdullah bin Ubai bin Salul) who has hurt me by slandering the reputation of my family? By Allah, I know nothing about my family but good, and they have accused a person about whom I know nothing except good, and he never entered my house except in my company.' Sa`d bin Mu`adh got up and said, 'O Allah's Messenger ﷺ! By Allah, I will relieve you from him. If that man is from the tribe of the Aus, then we will chop his head off, and if he is from our brothers, the Khazraj, then order us, and we will fulfill your order.' On that Sa`d bin 'Ubada, the chief of the Khazraj and before this incident, he had been a pious man, got up, motivated by his zeal for his tribe and said, 'By Allah, you have told a lie; you cannot kill him, and you will never be able to kill him.' On that Usaid bin Al-Hadir got up and said (to Sa`d bin 'Ubada), 'By Allah! You are a liar. By Allah, we will kill him; and you are a hypocrite, defending the hypocrites.' On this the two tribes of Aus and Khazraj got excited and were about to fight each other, while Allah's Messenger ﷺ was standing on the pulpit. He got down and quieted them till they became silent and he kept quiet. On that day I kept on weeping so much so that neither did my tears stop, nor could I sleep. In the morning my parents were with me and I had wept for two nights and a day, till I thought my liver would burst from weeping. While they were sitting with me and I was weeping, an Ansari woman asked my permission to enter, and I allowed her to come in. She sat down and started weeping with me. While we were in this state, Allah's Messenger ﷺ came and sat down and he had never sat with me since the day they forged the accusation. No revelation regarding my case came to him for a month. He recited Tashah-hud (i.e. None has the right to be worshipped but Allah and Muhammad is His Apostle) and then said, 'O `Aisha! I have been informed such-and-such about you; if you are innocent, then Allah will soon reveal your innocence, and if you have committed a sin, then repent to Allah and ask Him to forgive you, for when a person confesses his sin and asks Allah for forgiveness, Allah accepts his repentance.' When Allah's Messenger ﷺ finished his speech my tears ceased completely and there remained not even a single drop of it. I requested my father to reply to Allah's Messenger ﷺ on my behalf. My father said, By Allah, I do not know what to say to Allah's Messenger ﷺ. I said to my mother, 'Talk to Allah's Messenger ﷺ on my behalf.' She said, 'By Allah, I do not know what to say to Allah's Apostle. I was a young girl and did not have much knowledge of the Qur'an. I said. 'I know, by Allah, that you have listened to what people are saying and that has been planted in your minds and you have taken it as a truth. Now, if I told you that I am innocent and Allah knows that I am innocent, you would not believe me and if I confessed to you falsely that I am guilty, and Allah knows that I am innocent you would believe me. By Allah, I don't compare my situation with you except to the situation of Joseph's father (i.e. Jacob) who said, 'So (for me) patience is most fitting against that which you assert and it is Allah (Alone) whose help can be sought.' Then I turned to the other side of my bed hoping that Allah would prove my innocence. By Allah I never thought that Allah would reveal Divine Inspiration in my case, as I considered myself too inferior to be talked of in the Holy Qur'an. I had hoped that Allah's Messenger ﷺ might have a dream in which Allah would prove my innocence. By Allah, Allah's Apostle had not got up and nobody had left the house before the Divine Inspiration came to Allah's Apostle. So, there overtook him the same state which used to overtake him, (when he used to have, on being inspired divinely). He was sweating so much so that the drops of the sweat were dropping like pearls though it was a (cold) wintry day. When that state of Allah's Messenger ﷺ was over, he was smiling and the first word he said, `Aisha! Thank Allah, for Allah has declared your innocence.' My mother told me to go to Allah's Messenger ﷺ. I replied, 'By Allah I will not go to him and will not thank but Allah.' So Allah revealed: "Verily! They who spread the slander are a gang among you . . ." (24.11) When Allah gave the declaration of my Innocence, Abu Bakr, who used to provide for Mistah bin Uthatha for he was his relative, said, 'By Allah, I will never provide Mistah with anything because of what he said about Aisha.' But Allah later revealed: -- "And let not those who are good and wealthy among you swear not to help their kinsmen, those in need and those who left their homes in Allah's Cause. Let them forgive and overlook. Do you not wish that Allah should forgive you? Verily! Allah is Oft-forgiving, Most Merciful." (24.22) After that Abu Bakr said, 'Yes ! By Allah! I like that Allah should forgive me,' and resumed helping Mistah whom he used to help before. Allah's Messenger ﷺ also asked Zainab bint Jahsh (i.e. the Prophet's wife about me saying, 'What do you know and what did you see?' She replied, 'O Allah's Messenger ﷺ! I refrain to claim hearing or seeing what I have not heard or seen. By Allah, I know nothing except goodness about Aisha." Aisha further added "Zainab was competing with me (in her beauty and the Prophet's love), yet Allah protected her (from being malicious), for she had piety.". – Sahih Al-Bukhari 2661

حَدَّثَنَا أَبُو الرَّبِيعِ، سُلَيْمَانُ بْنُ دَاوُدَ وَأَفْهَمَنِي بَعْضَهُ أَحْمَدُ حَدَّثَنَا فُلَيْحُ بْنُ سُلَيْمَانَ، عَنِ ابْنِ شِهَابٍ الزُّهْرِيِّ، عَنْ عُرْوَةَ بْنِ الزُّبَيْرِ، وَسَعِيدِ بْنِ الْمُسَيَّبِ، وَعَلْقَمَةَ بْنِ وَقَّاصٍ اللَّيْثِيِّ، وَعُبَيْدِ اللَّهِ بْنِ عَبْدِ اللَّهِ بْنِ عُتْبَةَ، عَنْ عَائِشَةَ ـ رضى الله عنها ـ زَوْجِ النَّبِيِّ صلى الله عليه وسلم حِينَ قَالَ لَهَا أَهْلُ الإِفْكِ مَا قَالُوا، فَبَرَّأَهَا اللَّهُ مِنْهُ، قَالَ الزُّهْرِيُّ، وَكُلُّهُمْ حَدَّثَنِي طَائِفَةً مِنْ حَدِيثِهَا وَبَعْضُهُمْ أَوْعَى مِنْ بَعْضٍ، وَأَثْبَتُ لَهُ اقْتِصَاصًا، وَقَدْ وَعَيْتُ عَنْ كُلِّ وَاحِدٍ مِنْهُمُ الْحَدِيثَ الَّذِي حَدَّثَنِي عَنْ عَائِشَةَ، وَبَعْضُ حَدِيثِهِمْ يُصَدِّقُ بَعْضًا. زَعَمُوا أَنَّ عَائِشَةَ قَالَتْ كَانَ رَسُولُ اللَّهِ صلى الله عليه وسلم إِذَا أَرَادَ أَنْ يَخْرُجَ سَفَرًا أَقْرَعَ بَيْنَ أَزْوَاجِهِ، فَأَيَّتُهُنَّ خَرَجَ سَهْمُهَا خَرَجَ بِهَا مَعَهُ، فَأَقْرَعَ بَيْنَنَا فِي غَزَاةٍ غَزَاهَا فَخَرَجَ سَهْمِي، فَخَرَجْتُ مَعَهُ بَعْدَ مَا أُنْزِلَ الْحِجَابُ، فَأَنَا أُحْمَلُ فِي هَوْدَجٍ وَأُنْزَلُ فِيهِ، فَسِرْنَا حَتَّى إِذَا فَرَغَ رَسُولُ اللَّهِ صلى الله عليه وسلم مِنْ غَزْوَتِهِ تِلْكَ، وَقَفَلَ وَدَنَوْنَا مِنَ الْمَدِينَةِ، آذَنَ لَيْلَةً بِالرَّحِيلِ، فَقُمْتُ حِينَ آذَنُوا بِالرَّحِيلِ، فَمَشَيْتُ حَتَّى جَاوَزْتُ الْجَيْشَ، فَلَمَّا قَضَيْتُ شَأْنِي أَقْبَلْتُ إِلَى الرَّحْلِ، فَلَمَسْتُ صَدْرِي، فَإِذَا عِقْدٌ لِي مِنْ جَزْعِ أَظْفَارٍ قَدِ انْقَطَعَ، فَرَجَعْتُ فَالْتَمَسْتُ عِقْدِي، فَحَبَسَنِي ابْتِغَاؤُهُ، فَأَقْبَلَ الَّذِينَ يَرْحَلُونَ لِي، فَاحْتَمَلُوا هَوْدَجِي فَرَحَلُوهُ عَلَى بَعِيرِي الَّذِي كُنْتُ أَرْكَبُ، وَهُمْ يَحْسِبُونَ أَنِّي فِيهِ، وَكَانَ النِّسَاءُ إِذْ ذَاكَ خِفَافًا لَمْ يَثْقُلْنَ وَلَمْ يَغْشَهُنَّ اللَّحْمُ، وَإِنَّمَا يَأْكُلْنَ الْعُلْقَةَ مِنَ الطَّعَامِ، فَلَمْ يَسْتَنْكِرِ الْقَوْمُ حِينَ رَفَعُوهُ ثِقَلَ الْهَوْدَجِ فَاحْتَمَلُوهُ وَكُنْتُ جَارِيَةً حَدِيثَةَ السِّنِّ، فَبَعَثُوا الْجَمَلَ وَسَارُوا، فَوَجَدْتُ عِقْدِي بَعْدَ مَا اسْتَمَرَّ الْجَيْشُ، فَجِئْتُ مَنْزِلَهُمْ وَلَيْسَ فِيهِ أَحَدٌ، فَأَمَمْتُ مَنْزِلِي الَّذِي كُنْتُ بِهِ فَظَنَنْتُ أَنَّهُمْ سَيَفْقِدُونِي فَيَرْجِعُونَ إِلَيَّ، فَبَيْنَا أَنَا جَالِسَةٌ غَلَبَتْنِي عَيْنَاىَ فَنِمْتُ، وَكَانَ صَفْوَانُ بْنُ الْمُعَطَّلِ السُّلَمِيُّ ثُمَّ الذَّكْوَانِيُّ مِنْ وَرَاءِ الْجَيْشِ، فَأَصْبَحَ عِنْدَ مَنْزِلِي فَرَأَى سَوَادَ إِنْسَانٍ نَائِمٍ فَأَتَانِي، وَكَانَ يَرَانِي قَبْلَ الْحِجَابِ فَاسْتَيْقَظْتُ بِاسْتِرْجَاعِهِ حِينَ أَنَاخَ رَاحِلَتَهُ، فَوَطِئَ يَدَهَا فَرَكِبْتُهَا فَانْطَلَقَ يَقُودُ بِي الرَّاحِلَةَ، حَتَّى أَتَيْنَا الْجَيْشَ بَعْدَ مَا نَزَلُوا مُعَرِّسِينَ فِي نَحْرِ الظَّهِيرَةِ، فَهَلَكَ مَنْ هَلَكَ، وَكَانَ الَّذِي تَوَلَّى الإِفْكَ عَبْدُ اللَّهِ بْنُ أُبَىٍّ ابْنُ سَلُولَ، فَقَدِمْنَا الْمَدِينَةَ فَاشْتَكَيْتُ بِهَا شَهْرًا، يُفِيضُونَ مِنْ قَوْلِ أَصْحَابِ الإِفْكِ، وَيَرِيبُنِي فِي وَجَعِي أَنِّي لاَ أَرَى مِنَ النَّبِيِّ صلى الله عليه وسلم اللُّطْفَ الَّذِي كُنْتُ أَرَى مِنْهُ حِينَ أَمْرَضُ، إِنَّمَا يَدْخُلُ فَيُسَلِّمُ ثُمَّ يَقُولُ " كَيْفَ تِيكُمْ ". لاَ أَشْعُرُ بِشَىْءٍ مِنْ ذَلِكَ حَتَّى نَقَهْتُ، فَخَرَجْتُ أَنَا وَأُمُّ مِسْطَحٍ قِبَلَ الْمَنَاصِعِ مُتَبَرَّزُنَا، لاَ نَخْرُجُ إِلاَّ لَيْلاً إِلَى لَيْلٍ، وَذَلِكَ قَبْلَ أَنْ نَتَّخِذَ الْكُنُفَ قَرِيبًا مِنْ بُيُوتِنَا، وَأَمْرُنَا أَمْرُ الْعَرَبِ الأُوَلِ فِي الْبَرِّيَّةِ أَوْ فِي التَّنَزُّهِ، فَأَقْبَلْتُ أَنَا وَأُمُّ مِسْطَحٍ بِنْتُ أَبِي رُهْمٍ نَمْشِي، فَعَثُرَتْ فِي مِرْطِهَا فَقَالَتْ تَعِسَ مِسْطَحٌ، فَقُلْتُ لَهَا بِئْسَ مَا قُلْتِ، أَتَسُبِّينَ رَجُلاً شَهِدَ بَدْرًا فَقَالَتْ يَا هَنْتَاهْ أَلَمْ تَسْمَعِي مَا قَالُوا فَأَخْبَرَتْنِي بِقَوْلِ أَهْلِ الإِفْكِ، فَازْدَدْتُ مَرَضًا إِلَى مَرَضِي، فَلَمَّا رَجَعْتُ إِلَى بَيْتِي دَخَلَ عَلَىَّ رَسُولُ اللَّهِ صلى الله عليه وسلم فَسَلَّمَ فَقَالَ " كَيْفَ تِيكُمْ ". فَقُلْتُ ائْذَنْ لِي إِلَى أَبَوَىَّ. قَالَتْ وَأَنَا حِينَئِذٍ أُرِيدُ أَنْ أَسْتَيْقِنَ الْخَبَرَ مِنْ قِبَلِهِمَا، فَأَذِنَ لِي رَسُولُ اللَّهِ صلى الله عليه وسلم فَأَتَيْتُ أَبَوَىَّ فَقُلْتُ لأُمِّي مَا يَتَحَدَّثُ بِهِ النَّاسُ فَقَالَتْ يَا بُنَيَّةُ هَوِّنِي عَلَى نَفْسِكِ الشَّأْنَ، فَوَاللَّهِ لَقَلَّمَا كَانَتِ امْرَأَةٌ قَطُّ وَضِيئَةٌ عِنْدَ رَجُلٍ يُحِبُّهَا وَلَهَا ضَرَائِرُ إِلاَّ أَكْثَرْنَ عَلَيْهَا. فَقُلْتُ سُبْحَانَ اللَّهِ وَلَقَدْ يَتَحَدَّثُ النَّاسُ بِهَذَا قَالَتْ فَبِتُّ تِلْكَ اللَّيْلَةَ حَتَّى أَصْبَحْتُ لاَ يَرْقَأُ لِي دَمْعٌ وَلاَ أَكْتَحِلُ بِنَوْمٍ، ثُمَّ أَصْبَحْتُ فَدَعَا رَسُولُ اللَّهِ صلى الله عليه وسلم عَلِيَّ بْنَ أَبِي طَالِبٍ وَأُسَامَةَ بْنَ زَيْدٍ حِينَ اسْتَلْبَثَ الْوَحْىُ، يَسْتَشِيرُهُمَا فِي فِرَاقِ أَهْلِهِ، فَأَمَّا أُسَامَةُ فَأَشَارَ عَلَيْهِ بِالَّذِي يَعْلَمُ فِي نَفْسِهِ مِنَ الْوُدِّ لَهُمْ، فَقَالَ أُسَامَةُ أَهْلُكَ يَا رَسُولَ اللَّهِ وَلاَ نَعْلَمُ وَاللَّهِ إِلاَّ خَيْرًا، وَأَمَّا عَلِيُّ بْنُ أَبِي طَالِبٍ فَقَالَ يَا رَسُولَ اللَّهِ لَمْ يُضَيِّقِ اللَّهُ عَلَيْكَ وَالنِّسَاءُ سِوَاهَا كَثِيرٌ، وَسَلِ الْجَارِيَةَ تَصْدُقْكَ. فَدَعَا رَسُولُ اللَّهِ صلى الله عليه وسلم بَرِيرَةَ فَقَالَ " يَا بَرِيرَةُ هَلْ رَأَيْتِ فِيهَا شَيْئًا يَرِيبُكِ ". فَقَالَتْ بَرِيرَةُ لاَ وَالَّذِي بَعَثَكَ بِالْحَقِّ، إِنْ رَأَيْتُ مِنْهَا أَمْرًا أَغْمِصُهُ عَلَيْهَا أَكْثَرَ مِنْ أَنَّهَا جَارِيَةٌ حَدِيثَةُ السِّنِّ تَنَامُ عَنِ الْعَجِينِ فَتَأْتِي الدَّاجِنُ فَتَأْكُلُهُ. فَقَامَ رَسُولُ اللَّهِ صلى الله عليه وسلم مِنْ يَوْمِهِ، فَاسْتَعْذَرَ مِنْ عَبْدِ اللَّهِ بْنِ أُبَىٍّ ابْنِ سَلُولَ فَقَالَ رَسُولُ

اللَّهِ صلى الله عليه وسلم " مَنْ يَعْذِرُنِي مِنْ رَجُلٍ بَلَغَنِي أَذَاهُ فِي أَهْلِي، فَوَاللَّهِ مَا عَلِمْتُ عَلَى أَهْلِي إِلاَّ خَيْرًا، وَقَدْ ذَكَرُوا رَجُلاً مَا عَلِمْتُ عَلَيْهِ إِلاَّ خَيْرًا، وَمَا كَانَ يَدْخُلُ عَلَى أَهْلِي إِلاَّ مَعِي ". فَقَامَ سَعْدُ بْنُ مُعَاذٍ فَقَالَ يَا رَسُولَ اللَّهِ أَنَا وَاللَّهِ أَعْذِرُكَ مِنْهُ، إِنْ كَانَ مِنَ الأَوْسِ ضَرَبْنَا عُنُقَهُ، وَإِنْ كَانَ مِنْ إِخْوَانِنَا مِنَ الْخَزْرَجِ أَمَرْتَنَا فَفَعَلْنَا فِيهِ أَمْرَكَ. فَقَامَ سَعْدُ بْنُ عُبَادَةَ وَهُوَ سَيِّدُ الْخَزْرَجِ، وَكَانَ قَبْلَ ذَلِكَ رَجُلاً صَالِحًا وَلَكِنِ احْتَمَلَتْهُ الْحَمِيَّةُ فَقَالَ كَذَبْتَ لَعَمْرُ اللَّهِ، لاَ تَقْتُلُهُ وَلاَ تَقْدِرُ عَلَى ذَلِكَ، فَقَامَ أُسَيْدُ بْنُ الْحُضَيْرِ فَقَالَ كَذَبْتَ لَعَمْرُ اللَّهِ، وَاللَّهِ لَنَقْتُلَنَّهُ، فَإِنَّكَ مُنَافِقٌ تُجَادِلُ عَنِ الْمُنَافِقِينَ. فَثَارَ الْحَيَّانِ الأَوْسُ وَالْخَزْرَجُ حَتَّى هَمُّوا، وَرَسُولُ اللَّهِ صلى الله عليه وسلم عَلَى الْمِنْبَرِ فَنَزَلَ فَخَفَّضَهُمْ حَتَّى سَكَتُوا وَسَكَتَ، وَبَكَيْتُ يَوْمِي لاَ يَرْقَأُ لِي دَمْعٌ وَلاَ أَكْتَحِلُ بِنَوْمٍ، فَأَصْبَحَ عِنْدِي أَبَوَاىَ، قَدْ بَكَيْتُ لَيْلَتَيْنِ وَيَوْمًا حَتَّى أَظُنُّ أَنَّ الْبُكَاءَ فَالِقٌ كَبِدِي ـ قَالَتْ ـ فَبَيْنَا هُمَا جَالِسَانِ عِنْدِي وَأَنَا أَبْكِي إِذِ اسْتَأْذَنَتِ امْرَأَةٌ مِنَ الأَنْصَارِ فَأَذِنْتُ لَهَا، فَجَلَسَتْ تَبْكِي مَعِي، فَبَيْنَا نَحْنُ كَذَلِكَ إِذْ دَخَلَ رَسُولُ اللَّهِ صلى الله عليه وسلم فَجَلَسَ، وَلَمْ يَجْلِسْ عِنْدِي مِنْ يَوْمِ قِيلَ فِيَّ مَا قِيلَ قَبْلَهَا، وَقَدْ مَكُثَ شَهْرًا لاَ يُوحَى إِلَيْهِ فِي شَأْنِي شَىْءٌ ـ قَالَتْ ـ فَتَشَهَّدَ ثُمَّ قَالَ " يَا عَائِشَةُ فَإِنَّهُ بَلَغَنِي عَنْكِ كَذَا وَكَذَا، فَإِنْ كُنْتِ بَرِيئَةً فَسَيُبَرِّئُكِ اللَّهُ، وَإِنْ كُنْتِ أَلْمَمْتِ فَاسْتَغْفِرِي اللَّهَ وَتُوبِي إِلَيْهِ، فَإِنَّ الْعَبْدَ إِذَا اعْتَرَفَ بِذَنْبِهِ ثُمَّ تَابَ تَابَ اللَّهُ عَلَيْهِ ". فَلَمَّا قَضَى رَسُولُ اللَّهِ صلى الله عليه وسلم مَقَالَتَهُ قَلَصَ دَمْعِي حَتَّى مَا أُحِسُّ مِنْهُ قَطْرَةً وَقُلْتُ لأَبِي أَجِبْ عَنِّي رَسُولَ اللَّهِ صلى الله عليه وسلم. قَالَ وَاللَّهِ مَا أَدْرِي مَا أَقُولُ لِرَسُولِ اللَّهِ صلى الله عليه وسلم. فَقُلْتُ لأُمِّي أَجِيبِي عَنِّي رَسُولَ اللَّهِ صلى الله عليه وسلم فِيمَا قَالَ. قَالَتْ وَاللَّهِ مَا أَدْرِي مَا أَقُولُ لِرَسُولِ اللَّهِ صلى الله عليه وسلم. قَالَتْ وَأَنَا جَارِيَةٌ حَدِيثَةُ السِّنِّ لاَ أَقْرَأُ كَثِيرًا مِنَ الْقُرْآنِ فَقُلْتُ إِنِّي وَاللَّهِ لَقَدْ عَلِمْتُ أَنَّكُمْ سَمِعْتُمْ مَا يَتَحَدَّثُ بِهِ النَّاسُ، وَوَقَرَ فِي أَنْفُسِكُمْ وَصَدَّقْتُمْ بِهِ، وَلَئِنْ قُلْتُ لَكُمْ إِنِّي بَرِيئَةٌ. وَاللَّهُ يَعْلَمُ إِنِّي لَبَرِيئَةٌ لاَ تُصَدِّقُونِي بِذَلِكَ، وَلَئِنِ اعْتَرَفْتُ لَكُمْ بِأَمْرٍ، وَاللَّهُ يَعْلَمُ أَنِّي بَرِيئَةٌ لَتُصَدِّقُنِّي وَاللَّهِ مَا أَجِدُ لِي وَلَكُمْ مَثَلاً إِلاَّ أَبَا يُوسُفَ إِذْ قَالَ {فَصَبْرٌ جَمِيلٌ وَاللَّهُ الْمُسْتَعَانُ عَلَى مَا تَصِفُونَ} ثُمَّ تَحَوَّلْتُ عَلَى فِرَاشِي، وَأَنَا أَرْجُو أَنْ يُبَرِّئَنِي اللَّهُ، وَلَكِنْ وَاللَّهِ مَا ظَنَنْتُ أَنْ يُنْزِلَ فِي شَأْنِي وَحْيًا، وَلأَنَا أَحْقَرُ فِي نَفْسِي مِنْ أَنْ يُتَكَلَّمَ بِالْقُرْآنِ فِي أَمْرِي، وَلَكِنِّي كُنْتُ أَرْجُو أَنْ يَرَى رَسُولُ اللَّهِ صلى الله عليه وسلم فِي النَّوْمِ رُؤْيَا يُبَرِّئُنِي اللَّهُ، فَوَاللَّهِ مَا رَامَ مَجْلِسَهُ وَلاَ خَرَجَ أَحَدٌ مِنْ أَهْلِ الْبَيْتِ حَتَّى أُنْزِلَ عَلَيْهِ، فَأَخَذَهُ مَا كَانَ يَأْخُذُهُ مِنَ الْبُرَحَاءِ، حَتَّى إِنَّهُ لَيَتَحَدَّرُ مِنْهُ مِثْلُ الْجُمَانِ مِنَ الْعَرَقِ فِي يَوْمٍ شَاتٍ، فَلَمَّا سُرِّيَ عَنْ رَسُولِ اللَّهِ صلى الله عليه وسلم وَهُوَ يَضْحَكُ، فَكَانَ أَوَّلَ كَلِمَةٍ تَكَلَّمَ بِهَا أَنْ قَالَ لِي " يَا عَائِشَةُ، احْمَدِي اللَّهَ فَقَدْ بَرَّأَكِ اللَّهُ ". فَقَالَتْ لِي أُمِّي قُومِي إِلَى رَسُولِ اللَّهِ صلى الله عليه وسلم. فَقُلْتُ لاَ وَاللَّهِ، لاَ أَقُومُ إِلَيْهِ، وَلاَ أَحْمَدُ إِلاَّ اللَّهَ فَأَنْزَلَ اللَّهُ تَعَالَى {إِنَّ الَّذِينَ جَاءُوا بِالإِفْكِ عُصْبَةٌ مِنْكُمْ} الآيَاتِ، فَلَمَّا أَنْزَلَ اللَّهُ هَذَا فِي بَرَاءَتِي قَالَ أَبُو بَكْرٍ الصِّدِّيقُ ـ رضى الله عنه ـ وَكَانَ يُنْفِقُ عَلَى مِسْطَحِ بْنِ أُثَاثَةَ لِقَرَابَتِهِ مِنْهُ وَاللَّهِ لاَ أُنْفِقُ عَلَى مِسْطَحٍ شَيْئًا أَبَدًا بَعْدَ مَا قَالَ لِعَائِشَةَ. فَأَنْزَلَ اللَّهُ تَعَالَى {وَلاَ يَأْتَلِ أُولُو الْفَضْلِ مِنْكُمْ وَالسَّعَةِ} إِلَى قَوْلِهِ {غَفُورٌ رَحِيمٌ} فَقَالَ أَبُو بَكْرٍ بَلَى، وَاللَّهِ إِنِّي لأُحِبُّ أَنْ يَغْفِرَ اللَّهُ لِي، فَرَجَعَ إِلَى مِسْطَحٍ الَّذِي كَانَ يُجْرِي عَلَيْهِ. وَكَانَ رَسُولُ اللَّهِ صلى الله عليه وسلم يَسْأَلُ زَيْنَبَ بِنْتَ جَحْشٍ عَنْ أَمْرِي، فَقَالَ " يَا زَيْنَبُ، مَا عَلِمْتِ مَا رَأَيْتِ ". فَقَالَتْ يَا رَسُولَ اللَّهِ، أَحْمِي سَمْعِي وَبَصَرِي، وَاللَّهِ مَا عَلِمْتُ عَلَيْهَا إِلاَّ خَيْرًا، قَالَتْ وَهْىَ الَّتِي كَانَتْ تُسَامِينِي، فَعَصَمَهَا اللَّهُ بِالْوَرَعِ. قَالَ وَحَدَّثَنَا فُلَيْحٌ، عَنْ هِشَامِ بْنِ عُرْوَةَ، عَنْ عُرْوَةَ، عَنْ عَائِشَةَ، وَعَبْدِ اللَّهِ بْنِ الزُّبَيْرِ، مِثْلَهُ. قَالَ وَحَدَّثَنَا فُلَيْحٌ، عَنْ رَبِيعَةَ بْنِ أَبِي عَبْدِ الرَّحْمَنِ، وَيَحْيَى بْنِ سَعِيدٍ، عَنِ الْقَاسِمِ بْنِ مُحَمَّدِ بْنِ أَبِي بَكْرٍ، مِثْلَهُ.

Narrated Ibn `Umar: When `Abdullah bin Ubai (the chief of hypocrites) died, his son came to the Prophet ﷺ and said, "O Allah's Messenger ﷺ! Please give me your shirt to shroud him in it, offer his funeral prayer and ask for Allah's forgiveness for him." So Allah's Messenger ﷺ gave his shirt to him and said, "Inform me (When the funeral is ready) so that I may offer the funeral prayer." So, he informed him and when the Prophet intended to offer the funeral prayer, `Umar took hold of his hand and said, "Has Allah not forbidden you to offer the funeral prayer for the hypocrites? The Prophet ﷺ said, "I have been given the choice for Allah says: '(It does not avail) Whether you (O Muhammad) ask forgiveness for them (hypocrites), or do not ask for forgiveness for them. Even though you ask for their forgiveness seventy times, Allah will not forgive them. (9.80)" So the Prophet ﷺ offered the funeral prayer and on that the revelation came: "And never (O Muhammad) pray (funeral prayer) for any of them (i.e. hypocrites) that dies." (9. 84). – Sahih Al-Bukhari 1269

حَدَّثَنَا مُسَدَّدٌ، قَالَ حَدَّثَنَا يَحْيَى بْنُ سَعِيدٍ، عَنْ عُبَيْدِ اللَّهِ، قَالَ حَدَّثَنِي نَافِعٌ، عَنِ ابْنِ عُمَرَ ـ رضى الله عنهما ـ أَنَّ عَبْدَ، اللَّهِ بْنَ أُبَىٍّ لَمَّا تُوُفِّيَ جَاءَ ابْنُهُ إِلَى النَّبِيِّ صلى الله عليه وسلم فَقَالَ يَا رَسُولَ اللَّهِ أَعْطِنِي قَمِيصَكَ أُكَفِّنْهُ فِيهِ، وَصَلِّ عَلَيْهِ وَاسْتَغْفِرْ لَهُ، فَأَعْطَاهُ النَّبِيُّ صلى الله عليه وسلم قَمِيصَهُ فَقَالَ " آذِنِّي أُصَلِّي عَلَيْهِ ". فَآذَنَهُ، فَلَمَّا أَرَادَ أَنْ يُصَلِّيَ عَلَيْهِ جَذَبَهُ عُمَرُ ـ رضى الله عنه ـ فَقَالَ أَلَيْسَ اللَّهُ نَهَاكَ أَنْ تُصَلِّيَ عَلَى الْمُنَافِقِينَ فَقَالَ " أَنَا بَيْنَ خِيرَتَيْنِ قَالَ {اسْتَغْفِرْ لَهُمْ أَوْ لاَ تَسْتَغْفِرْ لَهُمْ إِنْ تَسْتَغْفِرْ لَهُمْ سَبْعِينَ مَرَّةً فَلَنْ يَغْفِرَ اللَّهُ لَهُمْ} ". فَصَلَّى عَلَيْهِ فَنَزَلَتْ {وَلاَ تُصَلِّ عَلَى أَحَدٍ مِنْهُمْ مَاتَ أَبَدًا}

`Utba bin Rabi`a
عُتْبَةَ بْنِ رَبِيعَةَ

Narrated Qais: I heard Abu Dhar swearing that the following Holy verse:-- "These two opponents (believers and disbelievers) disputing with each other about their Lord," (22.19) was revealed concerning those men who fought on the day of Badr, namely, Hamza, `Ali, Ubaida bin Al-Harith, `Utba and Shaiba----the two sons of Rabi`a—and Al-Walid bin `Utba. – Sahih al-Bukhari 3969
حَدَّثَنَا يَعْقُوبُ بْنُ إِبْرَاهِيمَ، حَدَّثَنَا هُشَيْمٌ، أَخْبَرَنَا أَبُو هَاشِمٍ، عَنْ أَبِي مِجْلَزٍ، عَنْ قَيْسٍ، قَالَ سَمِعْتُ أَبَا ذَرٍّ، يُقْسِمُ قَسَمًا إِنَّ هَذِهِ الآيَةَ {هَذَانِ خَصْمَانِ اخْتَصَمُوا فِي رَبِّهِمْ } نَزَلَتْ فِي الَّذِينَ بَرَزُوا يَوْمَ بَدْرٍ حَمْزَةَ وَعَلِيٍّ وَعُبَيْدَةَ بْنِ الْحَارِثِ وَعُتْبَةَ وَشَيْبَةَ ابْنَىْ رَبِيعَةَ وَالْوَلِيدِ بْنِ عُتْبَةَ

Narrated Qais bin Ubad: `Ali said, "I will be the first to kneel before the Beneficent on the Day of Resurrection because of the dispute." Qais said; This Verse: 'These two opponents (believers and disbelievers dispute with each other about their Lord,' (22.19) was revealed in connection with those who came out for the Battle of Badr, i.e. `Ali, Hamza, 'Ubaida, Shaiba bin Rabi`a, `Utba bin Rabi`a and Al-Walid bin `Utba. – Sahih al-Bukhari 4744
حَدَّثَنَا حَجَّاجُ بْنُ مِنْهَالٍ، حَدَّثَنَا مُعْتَمِرُ بْنُ سُلَيْمَانَ، قَالَ سَمِعْتُ أَبِي قَالَ، حَدَّثَنَا أَبُو مِجْلَزٍ، عَنْ قَيْسِ بْنِ عُبَادٍ، عَنْ عَلِيِّ بْنِ أَبِي طَالِبٍ ـ رضى الله عنه ـ قَالَ أَنَا أَوَّلُ، مَنْ يَجْثُو بَيْنَ يَدَىِ الرَّحْمَنِ لِلْخُصُومَةِ يَوْمَ الْقِيَامَةِ‏.‏ قَالَ قَيْسٌ وَفِيهِمْ نَزَلَتْ ‏{‏هَذَانِ خَصْمَانِ اخْتَصَمُوا فِي رَبِّهِمْ‏}‏ قَالَ هُمُ الَّذِينَ بَارَزُوا يَوْمَ بَدْرٍ عَلِيٌّ وَحَمْزَةُ وَعُبَيْدَةُ وَشَيْبَةُ بْنُ رَبِيعَةَ وَعُتْبَةُ بْنُ رَبِيعَةَ وَالْوَلِيدُ بْنُ عُتْبَةَ‏.‏

Narrated `Abdullah: Once the Prophet ﷺ was offering the prayer in the shade of the Ka`ba. Abu Jahl and some Quraishi men sent somebody to bring the Abdominal contents of a shecamel which had been slaughtered somewhere in Mecca, and when he brought them, they put them over the Prophet ﷺ Then Fatima (i.e. the Prophet's daughter) came and threw them away from him, and he said, "O Allah! Destroy (the pagans of) Quraish; O Allah! Destroy Quraish; O Allah Destroy Quraish," naming especially Abu Jahl bin Hisham, `Utba bin Rabi`a, Shaiba bin Rabi`a, Al Walid bin `Utba, Ubai bin Khalaf and `Uqba bin Abi Mitt. (The narrator, `Abdullah added, "I saw them all killed and thrown in the Badr well). – Sahih al-Bukhari 2934
حَدَّثَنَا عَبْدُ اللَّهِ بْنُ أَبِي شَيْبَةَ، حَدَّثَنَا جَعْفَرُ بْنُ عَوْنٍ، حَدَّثَنَا سُفْيَانُ، عَنْ أَبِي إِسْحَاقَ، عَنْ عَمْرِو بْنِ مَيْمُونٍ، عَنْ عَبْدِ اللَّهِ ـ رضى الله عنه ـ قَالَ كَانَ النَّبِيُّ صلى الله عليه وسلم يُصَلِّي فِي ظِلِّ الْكَعْبَةِ، فَقَالَ أَبُو جَهْلٍ وَنَاسٌ مِنْ قُرَيْشٍ، وَنُحِرَتْ جَزُورٌ بِنَاحِيَةِ مَكَّةَ، فَأَرْسَلُوا فَجَاءُوا مِنْ سَلاَهَا، وَطَرَحُوهُ عَلَيْهِ، فَجَاءَتْ فَاطِمَةُ فَأَلْقَتْهُ عَنْهُ، فَقَالَ ‏"‏ اللَّهُمَّ عَلَيْكَ بِقُرَيْشٍ، اللَّهُمَّ عَلَيْكَ بِقُرَيْشٍ، اللَّهُمَّ عَلَيْكَ بِقُرَيْشٍ ‏"‏‏.‏ لأَبِي جَهْلِ بْنِ هِشَامٍ، وَعُتْبَةَ بْنِ رَبِيعَةَ، وَشَيْبَةَ بْنِ رَبِيعَةَ، وَالْوَلِيدِ بْنِ عُتْبَةَ، وَأُبَىِّ بْنِ خَلَفٍ، وَعُقْبَةَ بْنِ أَبِي مُعَيْطٍ‏.‏ قَالَ عَبْدُ اللَّهِ فَلَقَدْ رَأَيْتُهُمْ فِي قَلِيبِ بَدْرٍ قَتْلَى‏.‏ قَالَ أَبُو إِسْحَاقَ وَنَسِيتُ السَّابِعَ‏.‏ وَقَالَ يُوسُفُ بْنُ إِسْحَاقَ عَنْ أَبِي إِسْحَاقَ أُمَيَّةُ بْنُ خَلَفٍ‏.‏ وَقَالَ شُعْبَةُ أُمَيَّةُ أَوْ أُبَىٌّ‏.‏ وَالصَّحِيحُ أُمَيَّةُ

'Ali said: At the battle of Badr 'Utba b. Rabi'a came forward followed by his son and his brother and cried out, "Who will engage in single combat?" Some young men of the Helpers responded to his call, but when he asked them who they were and they told him he said, "I have no use for you; I want only my cousins on my father's side." God's Messenger then said, "Get up, Hamza; get up, 'Ali; get up, 'Ubaida b. al-Harith." Hamza went forward to 'Utba, I went forward to Shaiba, and after two blows had been exchanged between 'Ubaida and al-Walid they wounded one another severely; so we turned against al-Walid, and when we had killed him we carried 'Ubaida away. Ahmad and Abu Dawud transmitted it. – Mishkat al-Masabih 3957

وَعَنْ عَلِيٍّ رَضِيَ اللَّهُ عَنْهُ قَالَ: لَمَّا كَانَ يَوْمُ بَدْرٍ تَقَدَّمَ عُتْبَةُ بْنُ رَبِيعَةَ وَتَبِعَهُ ابْنُهُ وَأَخُوهُ فَنَادَى: مَنْ يُبَارِزُ؟ فَانْتُدِبَ لَهُ شبابٌ مِنَ الْأَنْصَارِ فَقَالَ: مَنْ أَنْتُمْ؟ فَأَخْبَرُوهُ فَقَالَ: لَا حَاجَةَ لَنَا فِيكُمْ إِنَّمَا أَرَدْنَا بَنِي عَمِّنَا فَقَالَ رَسُولُ اللَّهِ صَلَّى اللَّهُ عَلَيْهِ وَسَلَّمَ: «قُمْ يَا حَمْزَةُ قُمْ يَا عَلِيُّ قُمْ يَا عُبَيْدَةُ بْنَ الْحَارِثِ» . فَأَقْبَلَ حَمْزَةُ إِلى عتبةَ وَأَقْبَلْتُ إِلَى شَيْبَةَ وَاخْتَلَفَ بَيْنَ عُبَيْدَةَ وَالْوَلِيدِ ضَرْبَتَانِ فَأَثْخَنَ كُلُّ وَاحِدٍ مِنْهُمَا صَاحِبَهُ ثُمَّ مِلْنَا عَلَى الْوَلِيدِ فَقَتَلْنَاهُ وَاحْتَمَلْنَا عُبَيْدَةَ. رَوَاهُ أَحْمد وَأَبُو دَاوُد

Narrated `Abdullah: While the Prophet ﷺ was in the state of prostration, surrounded by a group of people from Quraish pagans. `Uqba bin Abi Mu'ait came and brought the intestines of a camel and threw them on the back of the Prophet ﷺ. The Prophet ﷺ did not raise his head from prostration till Fatima (i.e. his daughter) came and removed those intestines from his back, and invoked evil on whoever had done (the evil deed). The Prophet ﷺ said, "O Allah! Destroy the chiefs of Quraish, O Allah! Destroy Abu Jahl bin Hisham, `Utba bin Rabi`a, Shaiba bin Rabi`a, `Uqba bin Abi Mu'ait, Umaiya bin Khalaf (or Ubai bin Kalaf)." Later on I saw all of them killed during the battle of Badr and their bodies were thrown into a well except the body of Umaiya or Ubai, because he was a fat person, and when he was pulled, the parts of his body got separated before he was thrown into the well. – Sahih Al-Bukhari 3185

حَدَّثَنَا عَبْدَانُ بْنُ عُثْمَانَ، قَالَ أَخْبَرَنِي أَبِي، عَنْ شُعْبَةَ، عَنْ أَبِي إِسْحَاقَ، عَنْ عَمْرِو بْنِ مَيْمُونٍ، عَنْ عَبْدِ اللَّهِ ـ رضى الله عنه ـ قَالَ بَيْنَا رَسُولُ اللَّهِ صلى الله عليه وسلم سَاجِدٌ وَحَوْلَهُ نَاسٌ مِنْ قُرَيْشٍ مِنَ الْمُشْرِكِينَ إِذْ جَاءَ عُقْبَةُ بْنُ أَبِي مُعَيْطٍ بِسَلَى جَزُورٍ، فَقَذَفَهُ عَلَى ظَهْرِ النَّبِيِّ صلى الله عليه وسلم فَلَمْ يَرْفَعْ رَأْسَهُ حَتَّى جَاءَتْ فَاطِمَةُ ـ عَلَيْهَا السَّلاَمُ ـ فَأَخَذَتْ مِنْ ظَهْرِهِ، وَدَعَتْ عَلَى مَنْ صَنَعَ ذَلِكَ، فَقَالَ النَّبِيُّ صلى الله عليه وسلم " اللَّهُمَّ عَلَيْكَ الْمَلأَ مِنْ قُرَيْشٍ، اللَّهُمَّ عَلَيْكَ أَبَا جَهْلِ بْنَ هِشَامٍ، وَعُتْبَةَ بْنَ رَبِيعَةَ، وَشَيْبَةَ بْنَ رَبِيعَةَ، وَعُقْبَةَ بْنَ أَبِي مُعَيْطٍ، وَأُمَيَّةَ بْنَ خَلَفٍ ـ أَوْ أُبَىَّ بْنَ خَلَفٍ ". فَلَقَدْ رَأَيْتُهُمْ قُتِلُوا يَوْمَ بَدْرٍ، فَأُلْقُوا فِي بِئْرٍ، غَيْرَ أُمَيَّةَ أَوْ أُبَيٍّ، فَإِنَّهُ كَانَ رَجُلاً ضَخْمًا، فَلَمَّا جَرُّوهُ تَقَطَّعَتْ أَوْصَالُهُ قَبْلَ أَنْ يُلْقَى فِي الْبِئْرِ

Narrated Abu Dhar: The following Holy Verse:-- "These two opponents (believers & disbelievers) dispute with each other about their Lord," (22.19) was revealed concerning six men from Quraish, namely, `Ali, Hamza, 'Ubaida bin Al-Harith; Shaiba bin Rabi`a, `Utba bin Rabi`a and Al-Walid bin `Utba. – Sahih Al-Bukhari 3966

حَدَّثَنَا قَبِيصَةُ، حَدَّثَنَا سُفْيَانُ، عَنْ أَبِي هَاشِمٍ، عَنْ أَبِي مِجْلَزٍ، عَنْ قَيْسِ بْنِ عُبَادٍ، عَنْ أَبِي ذَرٍّ ـ رضى الله عنه ـ قَالَ نَزَلَتْ {هَذَانِ خَصْمَانِ اخْتَصَمُوا فِي رَبِّهِمْ} فِي سِتَّةٍ مِنْ قُرَيْشٍ عَلِيٍّ وَحَمْزَةَ وَعُبَيْدَةَ بْنِ الْحَارِثِ وَشَيْبَةَ بْنِ رَبِيعَةَ وَعُتْبَةَ بْنِ رَبِيعَةَ وَالْوَلِيدِ بْنِ عُتْبَةَ.

Narrated `Aisha: Hind bint `Utba bin Rabi`a said, "O Allah 's Apostle! (Before I embraced Islam), there was no family on the surface of the earth, I wish to have degraded more than I did your family. But today there is no family whom I wish to have honored more than I did yours." Allah's Messenger ﷺ said, "I thought similarly, by Him in Whose Hand Muhammad's soul is!" Hind said, "O Allah's Messenger! (My husband) Abu Sufyan is a miser. Is it sinful of me to feed my children from his property?" The Prophet said, "No, unless you take it for your needs what Is just and reasonable.". – Sahih Al-Bukhari 6641

حَدَّثَنَا يَحْيَى بْنُ بُكَيْرٍ، حَدَّثَنَا اللَّيْثُ، عَنْ يُونُسَ، عَنِ ابْنِ شِهَابٍ، حَدَّثَنِي عُرْوَةُ بْنُ الزُّبَيْرِ، أَنَّ عَائِشَةَ ـ رضى الله عنها ـ قَالَتْ إِنَّ هِنْدَ بِنْتَ عُتْبَةَ بْنِ رَبِيعَةَ قَالَتْ يَا رَسُولَ اللَّهِ مَا كَانَ مِمَّا عَلَى ظَهْرِ الأَرْضِ أَهْلُ أَخْبَاءٍ ـ أَوْ خِبَاءٍ ـ أَحَبَّ إِلَيَّ أَنْ يَذِلُّوا مِنْ أَهْلِ أَخْبَائِكَ ـ أَوْ خِبَائِكَ، شَكَّ يَحْيَى ـ ثُمَّ مَا أَصْبَحَ الْيَوْمَ أَهْلُ أَخْبَاءٍ ـ أَوْ خِبَاءٍ ـ أَحَبَّ إِلَيَّ مِنْ أَنْ يَعِزُّوا مِنْ أَهْلِ أَخْبَائِكَ أَوْ خِبَائِكَ. قَالَ رَسُولُ اللَّهِ صلى الله عليه وسلم " وَأَيْضًا وَالَّذِي نَفْسُ مُحَمَّدٍ بِيَدِهِ ". قَالَتْ يَا رَسُولَ اللَّهِ إِنَّ أَبَا سُفْيَانَ رَجُلٌ مِسِّيكٌ، فَهَلْ عَلَىَّ حَرَجٌ أَنْ أُطْعِمَ مِنَ الَّذِي لَهُ قَالَ " لاَ إِلاَّ بِالْمَعْرُوفِ

Narrated `Abdullah bin Mas`ud: The Prophet ﷺ faced the Ka`ba and invoked evil on some people of Quraish, on Shaiba bin Rabi`a, `Utba bin Rabi`a, Al-Walid bin `Utba and Abu Jahl bin Hisham. I bear witness, by Allah, that I saw them all dead, putrefied by the sun as that day was a very hot day. – Sahih Al-Bukhari 3960

حَدَّثَنِي عَمْرُو بْنُ خَالِدٍ، حَدَّثَنَا زُهَيْرٌ، حَدَّثَنَا أَبُو إِسْحَاقَ، عَنْ عَمْرِو بْنِ مَيْمُونٍ، عَنْ عَبْدِ اللَّهِ بْنِ مَسْعُودٍ ـ رضى الله عنه ـ قَالَ اسْتَقْبَلَ النَّبِيُّ صلى الله عليه وسلم الْكَعْبَةَ فَدَعَا عَلَى نَفَرٍ مِنْ قُرَيْشٍ، عَلَى شَيْبَةَ بْنِ رَبِيعَةَ، وَعُتْبَةَ بْنِ رَبِيعَةَ وَالْوَلِيدِ بْنِ عُتْبَةَ، وَأَبِي جَهْلِ بْنِ هِشَامٍ. فَأَشْهَدُ بِاللَّهِ لَقَدْ رَأَيْتُهُمْ صَرْعَى، قَدْ غَيَّرَتْهُمُ الشَّمْسُ، وَكَانَ يَوْمًا حَارًّا

Uqba Ibn Abi Muait
عقبة بن أبي معيط

Narrated Marwan and al-Miswar bin Makhrama: (from the companions of Allah's Messengerﷺ) When Suhail bin `Amr agreed to the Treaty (of Hudaibiya), one of the things he stipulated then, was that the Prophetﷺ should return to them (i.e. the pagans) anyone coming to him from their side, even if he was a Muslim; and would not interfere between them and that person. The Muslims did not like this condition and got disgusted with it. Suhail did not agree except with that condition. So, the Prophetﷺ agreed to that condition and returned Abu Jandal to his father Suhail bin `Amr. Thenceforward the Prophetﷺ returned everyone in that period (of truce) even if he was a Muslim. During that period some believing women emigrants including Um Kulthum bint `Uqba bin Abu Muait who came to Allah's Messengerﷺ and she was a young lady then. Her relative came to the Prophetﷺ and asked him to return her, but the Prophetﷺ did not return her to them for Allah had revealed the following Verse regarding women: "O you who believe! When the believing women come to you as emigrants. Examine them, Allah knows best as to their belief, then if you know them for true believers, Send them not back to the unbelievers, (for) they are not lawful (wives) for the disbelievers, Nor are the unbelievers lawful (husbands) for them (60.10) – Sahih al-Bukhari 2711, 2712

حَدَّثَنَا يَحْيَى بْنُ بُكَيْرٍ، حَدَّثَنَا اللَّيْثُ، عَنْ عُقَيْلٍ، عَنِ ابْنِ شِهَابٍ، قَالَ أَخْبَرَنِي عُرْوَةُ بْنُ الزُّبَيْرِ، أَنَّهُ سَمِعَ مَرْوَانَ، وَالْمِسْوَرَ بْنَ مَخْرَمَةَ، رضى الله عنهما يُخْبِرَانِ عَنْ أَصْحَابِ، رَسُولِ اللَّهِ صلى الله عليه وسلم قَالَ لَمَّا كَاتَبَ سُهَيْلُ بْنُ عَمْرٍو يَوْمَئِذٍ كَانَ فِيمَا اشْتَرَطَ سُهَيْلُ بْنُ عَمْرٍو عَلَى النَّبِيِّ صلى الله عليه وسلم أَنَّهُ لاَ يَأْتِيكَ مِنَّا أَحَدٌ وَإِنْ كَانَ عَلَى دِينِكَ إِلاَّ رَدَدْتَهُ إِلَيْنَا، وَخَلَّيْتَ بَيْنَنَا وَبَيْنَهُ. فَكَرِهَ الْمُؤْمِنُونَ ذَلِكَ، وَامْتَعَضُوا مِنْهُ، وَأَبَى سُهَيْلٌ إِلاَّ ذَلِكَ، فَكَاتَبَهُ النَّبِيُّ صلى الله عليه وسلم عَلَى ذَلِكَ، فَرَدَّ يَوْمَئِذٍ أَبَا جَنْدَلٍ عَلَى أَبِيهِ سُهَيْلِ بْنِ عَمْرٍو، وَلَمْ يَأْتِهِ أَحَدٌ مِنَ الرِّجَالِ إِلاَّ رَدَّهُ فِي تِلْكَ الْمُدَّةِ، وَإِنْ كَانَ مُسْلِمًا، وَجَاءَ الْمُؤْمِنَاتُ مُهَاجِرَاتٍ، وَكَانَتْ أُمُّ كُلْثُومٍ بِنْتُ عُقْبَةَ بْنِ أَبِي مُعَيْطٍ مِمَّنْ خَرَجَ إِلَى رَسُولِ اللَّهِ صلى الله عليه وسلم يَوْمَئِذٍ وَهْىَ عَاتِقٌ، فَجَاءَ أَهْلُهَا يَسْأَلُونَ النَّبِيَّ صلى الله عليه وسلم أَنْ يَرْجِعَهَا إِلَيْهِمْ، فَلَمْ يَرْجِعْهَا إِلَيْهِمْ لِمَا أَنْزَلَ اللَّهُ فِيهِنَّ {إِذَا جَاءَكُمُ الْمُؤْمِنَاتُ مُهَاجِرَاتٍ فَامْتَحِنُوهُنَّ اللَّهُ أَعْلَمُ بِإِيمَانِهِنَّ} إِلَى قَوْلِهِ {وَلاَ هُمْ يَحِلُّونَ لَهُنَّ}.

Umm Kulthum, the daughter of 'Uqba ibn Abi Mu'ayt, reported that she heard the Messenger of Allah, may Allah bless him and grant him peace, say, "Someone who makes peace between people by saying something good or relates something good is not a liar." - Al-Adab Al-Mufrad 385

حَدَّثَنَا عَبْدُ اللهِ بْنُ صَالِح قَالَ: حَدَّثَنِي اللَّيْثُ قَالَ: حَدَّثَنِي يُونُسُ، عَنِ ابْنِ شِهَابٍ قَالَ: أَخْبَرَنِي حُمَيْدُ بْنُ عَبْدِ الرَّحْمَنِ، أَنَّ أُمَّهُ أُمَّ كُلْثُومٍ ابْنَةَ عُقْبَةَ بْنِ أَبِي مُعَيْطٍ أَخْبَرَتْهُ، أَنَّهَا سَمِعَتْ رَسُولَ اللهِ صلى الله عليه وسلم يَقُولُ: لَيْسَ الْكَذَّابُ الَّذِي يُصْلِحُ بَيْنَ النَّاسِ، فَيَقُولُ خَيْرًا، أَوْ يَنْمِي خَيْرًا، قَالَتْ: وَلَمْ أَسْمَعْهُ يُرَخِّصُ فِي شَيْءٍ مِمَّا يَقُولُ النَّاسُ مِنَ الْكَذِبِ إِلاَّ فِي ثَلاَثٍ: الإِصْلاَحِ بَيْنَ النَّاسِ، وَحَدِيثِ الرَّجُلِ امْرَأَتَهُ، وَحَدِيثِ الْمَرْأَةِ زَوْجَهَا

Narrated `Abdullah: While the Prophetﷺ was in the state of prostration, surrounded by a group of people from Quraish pagans. `Uqba bin Abi Mu'ait came and brought the intestines of a camel and threw them on the back of the Prophetﷺ . The Prophetﷺ did not raise his head from prostration till Fatima (i.e. his daughter) came and removed those intestines from his back, and invoked evil on whoever had done (the evil deed). The Prophetﷺ said, "O Allah! Destroy the chiefs of Quraish, O Allah! Destroy Abu Jahl bin Hisham, `Utba bin Rabi`a, Shaiba bin Rabi`a, `Uqba bin Abi Mu'ait, Umaiya bin Khalaf (or Ubai bin Kalaf)." Later on I saw all of them killed during the battle of Badr and their bodies were thrown into a well except the body of Umaiya or Ubai, because he was a fat person, and when he was pulled, the parts of his body got separated before he was thrown into the well. – Sahih al-Bukhari 3185

حَدَّثَنَا عَبْدَانُ بْنُ عُثْمَانَ، قَالَ أَخْبَرَنِي أَبِي، عَنْ شُعْبَةَ، عَنْ أَبِي إِسْحَاقَ، عَنْ عَمْرِو بْنِ مَيْمُونٍ، عَنْ عَبْدِ اللَّهِ ـ رضى الله عنه ـ قَالَ بَيْنَا رَسُولُ اللَّهِ صلى الله عليه وسلم سَاجِدٌ وَحَوْلَهُ نَاسٌ مِنْ قُرَيْشٍ مِنَ الْمُشْرِكِينَ إِذْ جَاءَ عُقْبَةُ بْنُ أَبِي مُعَيْطٍ بِسَلَى جَزُورٍ، فَقَذَفَهُ عَلَى ظَهْرِ النَّبِيِّ صلى الله عليه وسلم فَلَمْ يَرْفَعْ رَأْسَهُ حَتَّى جَاءَتْ فَاطِمَةُ ـ عَلَيْهَا السَّلاَمُ ـ فَأَخَذَتْ مِنْ ظَهْرِهِ، وَدَعَتْ عَلَى مَنْ صَنَعَ ذَلِكَ، فَقَالَ النَّبِيُّ صلى الله عليه وسلم " اللَّهُمَّ عَلَيْكَ الْمَلأَ مِنْ قُرَيْشٍ، اللَّهُمَّ عَلَيْكَ أَبَا جَهْلِ بْنَ هِشَامٍ، وَعُتْبَةَ بْنَ رَبِيعَةَ، وَشَيْبَةَ بْنَ رَبِيعَةَ، وَعُقْبَةَ بْنَ أَبِي مُعَيْطٍ، وَأُمَيَّةَ بْنَ خَلَفٍ ـ أَوْ أُبَىَّ بْنَ خَلَفٍ ". فَلَقَدْ رَأَيْتُهُمْ قُتِلُوا يَوْمَ بَدْرٍ، فَأُلْقُوا فِي بِئْرٍ، غَيْرَ أُمَيَّةَ أَوْ أُبَىٍّ، فَإِنَّهُ كَانَ رَجُلاً ضَخْمًا، فَلَمَّا جَرُّوهُ تَقَطَّعَتْ أَوْصَالُهُ قَبْلَ أَنْ يُلْقَى فِي الْبِئْرِ

Narrated `Urwa bin Az-Zubair: I asked `Abdullah bin `Amr bin Al-`As to inform me of the worst thing the pagans had done to Allah's Apostle. He said: "While Allah's Messengerﷺ was praying in the courtyard of the Ka`ba, `Uqba bin Abi Mu'ait came and seized Allah's Messengerﷺ by the shoulder and twisted his garment round his neck and throttled him severely. Abu Bakr came and seized `Uqba's shoulder and threw him away from Allah's Apostle and said, "Would you kill a man because he says: 'My Lord is Allah,' and has come to you with clear Signs from your Lord?" (40.28) - Sahih al-Bukhari 4815

حَدَّثَنَا عَلِيُّ بْنُ عَبْدِ اللَّهِ، حَدَّثَنَا الْوَلِيدُ بْنُ مُسْلِمٍ، حَدَّثَنَا الأَوْزَاعِيُّ، قَالَ حَدَّثَنِي يَحْيَى بْنُ أَبِي كَثِيرٍ، قَالَ حَدَّثَنِي مُحَمَّدُ بْنُ إِبْرَاهِيمَ التَّيْمِيُّ، قَالَ حَدَّثَنِي عُرْوَةُ بْنُ الزُّبَيْرِ، قَالَ قُلْتُ لِعَبْدِ اللَّهِ بْنِ عَمْرِو بْنِ الْعَاصِ أَخْبِرْنِي بِأَشَدِّ، مَا صَنَعَ الْمُشْرِكُونَ بِرَسُولِ اللَّهِ صلى الله عليه وسلم قَالَ بَيْنَا رَسُولُ اللَّهِ صلى الله عليه وسلم يُصَلِّي بِفِنَاءِ الْكَعْبَةِ، إِذْ أَقْبَلَ عُقْبَةُ بْنُ أَبِي مُعَيْطٍ، فَأَخَذَ بِمَنْكِبِ رَسُولِ اللَّهِ صلى الله عليه وسلم وَلَوَى ثَوْبَهُ فِي عُنُقِهِ فَخَنَقَهُ خَنْقًا شَدِيدًا، فَأَقْبَلَ أَبُو بَكْرٍ فَأَخَذَ بِمَنْكِبِهِ، وَدَفَعَ عَنْ رَسُولِ اللَّهِ صلى الله عليه وسلم وَقَالَ {أَتَقْتُلُونَ رَجُلاً أَنْ يَقُولَ رَبِّيَ اللَّهُ وَقَدْ جَاءَكُمْ بِالْبَيِّنَاتِ مِنْ رَبِّكُمْ}

Narrated `Urwa bin Az-Zubair: That he heard Marwan bin Al-Hakam and Al-Miswar bin Makhrama relating one of the events that happened to Allah's Messengerﷺ in the `Umra of Al-Hudaibiya. They said, "When Allah's Messengerﷺ concluded the truce with Suhail bin `Amr on the day of Al-Hudaibiya, one of the conditions which Suhail bin `Amr stipulated, was his saying (to the Prophet), "If anyone from us (i.e. infidels) ever comes to you, though he has embraced your religion, you should return him to us, and should not interfere between us and him." Suhail refused to conclude the truce with Allah's Messengerﷺ except on this condition. The believers disliked this condition and got disgusted with it and argued about it. But when Suhail refused to conclude the truce with Allah's Messengerﷺ except on that condition, Allah's Apostle concluded it. Accordingly, Allah's Messengerﷺ then returned Abu Jandal bin Suhail to his father, Suhail bin `Amr, and returned every man coming to him from them during that period even if he was a Muslim. The believing women Emigrants came (to Medina) and Um Kulthum, the daughter of `Uqba bin Abi Mu'ait was one of those who came to Allah's Messengerﷺ and she was an adult at that time. Her relatives came, asking Allah's Messengerﷺ to return her to them, and in this connection, Allah revealed the Verses dealing with the believing (women). – Sahih Al-Bukhari 4180, 4181

حَدَّثَنِي إِسْحَاقُ، أَخْبَرَنَا يَعْقُوبُ، حَدَّثَنِي ابْنُ أَخِي ابْنِ شِهَابٍ، عَنْ عَمِّهِ، أَخْبَرَنِي عُرْوَةُ بْنُ الزُّبَيْرِ، أَنَّهُ سَمِعَ مَرْوَانَ بْنَ الْحَكَمِ، وَالْمِسْوَرَ بْنَ مَخْرَمَةَ، يُخْبِرَانِ خَبَرًا مِنْ خَبَرِ رَسُولِ اللَّهِ صلى الله عليه وسلم فِي عُمْرَةِ الْحُدَيْبِيَةِ فَكَانَ فِيمَا أَخْبَرَنِي عُرْوَةُ عَنْهُمَا أَنَّهُ لَمَّا كَاتَبَ رَسُولُ اللَّهِ صلى الله عليه وسلم سُهَيْلَ بْنَ عَمْرٍو، يَوْمَ الْحُدَيْبِيَةِ عَلَى قَضِيَّةِ الْمُدَّةِ، وَكَانَ فِيمَا اشْتَرَطَ سُهَيْلُ بْنُ عَمْرٍو أَنَّهُ قَالَ لاَ يَأْتِيكَ مِنَّا أَحَدٌ وَإِنْ كَانَ عَلَى دِينِكَ إِلاَّ رَدَدْتَهُ إِلَيْنَا، وَخَلَّيْتَ بَيْنَنَا وَبَيْنَهُ. وَأَبَى سُهَيْلٌ أَنْ يُقَاضِيَ رَسُولَ اللَّهِ صلى الله عليه وسلم إِلاَّ عَلَى ذَلِكَ، فَكَرِهَ الْمُؤْمِنُونَ ذَلِكَ وَامَّعَضُوا، فَتَكَلَّمُوا فِيهِ، فَلَمَّا أَبَى سُهَيْلٌ أَنْ

يُقَاضِيَ رَسُولَ اللَّهِ صلى الله عليه وسلم إِلاَّ عَلَى ذَلِكَ، كَاتَبَهُ رَسُولُ اللَّهِ صلى الله عليه وسلم، فَرَدَّ رَسُولُ اللَّهِ صلى الله عليه وسلم أَبَا جَنْدَلِ بْنَ سُهَيْلٍ يَوْمَئِذٍ إِلَى أَبِيهِ سُهَيْلِ بْنِ عَمْرٍو، وَلَمْ يَأْتِ رَسُولَ اللَّهِ صلى الله عليه وسلم أَحَدٌ مِنَ الرِّجَالِ إِلاَّ رَدَّهُ فِي تِلْكَ الْمُدَّةِ، وَإِنْ كَانَ مُسْلِمًا، وَجَاءَتِ الْمُؤْمِنَاتُ مُهَاجِرَاتٍ، فَكَانَتْ أُمُّ كُلْثُومٍ بِنْتُ عُقْبَةَ بْنِ مُعَيْطٍ مِمَّنْ خَرَجَ إِلَى رَسُولِ اللَّهِ صلى الله عليه وسلم وَهْىَ عَاتِقٌ، فَجَاءَ أَهْلُهَا يَسْأَلُونَ رَسُولَ اللَّهِ صلى الله عليه وسلم أَنْ يَرْجِعَهَا إِلَيْهِمْ، حَتَّى أَنْزَلَ اللَّهُ تَعَالَى فِي الْمُؤْمِنَاتِ مَا أَنْزَلَ.

Narrated `Abdullah: While the Prophetﷺ was prostrating, surrounded by some of Quraish, `Uqba bin Abi Mu'ait brought the intestines (i.e. Abdominal contents) of a camel and put them over the back of the Prophet. The Prophetﷺ did not raise his head, (till) Fatima, came and took it off his back and cursed the one who had done the harm. The Prophetﷺ said, "O Allah! Destroy the chiefs of Quraish, Abu Jahl bin Hisham, `Utba bin Rabi`al, Shaba bin Rabi`a, Umaiya bin Khalaf or Ubai bin Khalaf." (The sub-narrator Shu`ba, is not sure of the last name.) I saw these people killed on the day of Badr battle and thrown in the well except Umaiya or Ubai whose body parts were mutilated but he was not thrown in the well. – Sahih Al-Bukhari 3854

حَدَّثَنِي مُحَمَّدُ بْنُ بَشَّارٍ، حَدَّثَنَا غُنْدَرٌ، حَدَّثَنَا شُعْبَةُ، عَنْ أَبِي إِسْحَاقَ، عَنْ عَمْرِو بْنِ مَيْمُونٍ، عَنْ عَبْدِ اللَّهِ ـ رضى الله عنه ـ قَالَ بَيْنَا النَّبِيُّ صلى الله عليه وسلم سَاجِدٌ وَحَوْلَهُ نَاسٌ مِنْ قُرَيْشٍ جَاءَ عُقْبَةُ بْنُ أَبِي مُعَيْطٍ بِسَلَى جَزُورٍ، فَقَذَفَهُ عَلَى ظَهْرِ النَّبِيِّ صلى الله عليه وسلم، فَلَمْ يَرْفَعْ رَأْسَهُ فَجَاءَتْ فَاطِمَةُ ـ عَلَيْهَا السَّلاَمُ ـ فَأَخَذَتْهُ مِنْ ظَهْرِهِ، وَدَعَتْ عَلَى مَنْ صَنَعَ فَقَالَ النَّبِيُّ صلى الله عليه وسلم " اللَّهُمَّ عَلَيْكَ الْمَلأَ مِنْ قُرَيْشٍ أَبَا جَهْلِ بْنَ هِشَامٍ، وَعُتْبَةَ بْنَ رَبِيعَةَ، وَشَيْبَةَ بْنَ رَبِيعَةَ، وَأُمَيَّةَ بْنَ خَلَفٍ ـ أَوْ أُبَىَّ بْنَ خَلَفٍ ". شُعْبَةُ الشَّاكُّ ـ فَرَأَيْتُهُمْ قُتِلُوا يَوْمَ بَدْرٍ، فَأُلْقُوا فِي بِئْرٍ غَيْرَ أُمَيَّةَ أَوْ أُبَيٍّ تَقَطَّعَتْ أَوْصَالُهُ، فَلَمْ يُلْقَ فِي الْبِئْرِ.

Narrated `Urwa bin Az-Zubair: I asked Ibn `Amr bin Al-As, "Tell me of the worst thing which the pagans did to the Prophet." He said, "While the Prophetﷺ was praying in the Hijr of the Ka`ba; `Uqba bin Abi Mu'ait came and put his garment around the Prophet's neck and throttled him violently. Abu Bakr came and caught him by his shoulder and pushed him away from the Prophetﷺ and said, "Do you want to kill a man just because he says, 'My Lord is Allah?' ". – Sahih Al-Bukhari 3856

حَدَّثَنَا عَيَّاشُ بْنُ الْوَلِيدِ، حَدَّثَنَا الْوَلِيدُ بْنُ مُسْلِمٍ، حَدَّثَنِي الأَوْزَاعِيُّ، حَدَّثَنِي يَحْيَى بْنُ أَبِي كَثِيرٍ، عَنْ مُحَمَّدِ بْنِ إِبْرَاهِيمَ التَّيْمِيِّ، قَالَ حَدَّثَنِي عُرْوَةُ بْنُ الزُّبَيْرِ، قَالَ سَأَلْتُ ابْنَ عَمْرِو بْنِ الْعَاصِ أَخْبِرْنِي بِأَشَدِّ، شَىْءٍ صَنَعَهُ الْمُشْرِكُونَ بِالنَّبِيِّ صلى الله عليه وسلم قَالَ بَيْنَا النَّبِيُّ صلى الله عليه وسلم يُصَلِّي فِي حِجْرِ الْكَعْبَةِ إِذْ أَقْبَلَ عُقْبَةُ بْنُ أَبِي مُعَيْطٍ، فَوَضَعَ ثَوْبَهُ فِي عُنُقِهِ فَخَنَقَهُ خَنْقًا شَدِيدًا، فَأَقْبَلَ أَبُو بَكْرٍ حَتَّى أَخَذَ بِمَنْكِبِهِ وَدَفَعَهُ عَنِ النَّبِيِّ صلى الله عليه وسلم قَالَ {أَتَقْتُلُونَ رَجُلاً أَنْ يَقُولَ رَبِّيَ اللَّهُ} الآيَةَ. تَابَعَهُ ابْنُ إِسْحَاقَ حَدَّثَنِي يَحْيَى بْنُ عُرْوَةَ عَنْ عُرْوَةَ، قُلْتُ لِعَبْدِ اللَّهِ بْنِ عَمْرٍو. وَقَالَ عَبْدَةُ عَنْ هِشَامٍ عَنْ أَبِيهِ قِيلَ لِعَمْرِو بْنِ الْعَاصِ. وَقَالَ مُحَمَّدُ بْنُ عَمْرٍو عَنْ أَبِي سَلَمَةَ حَدَّثَنِي عَمْرُو بْنُ الْعَاصِ.

Mut'im Ibn Adi
مطعم بن عدي

Narrated Jubair bin Mut'im: I heard the Prophetﷺ reciting Surat-at-Tur in Maghrib prayer, and that was at a time when belief was first planted in my heart. The Prophetﷺ while speaking about the war prisoners of Badr, said, "Were Al-Mutim bin Adi alive and interceded with me for these filthy people, I would definitely forgive them for his sake.". – Sahih Al-Bukhari 4023

حَدَّثَنِي إِسْحَاقُ بْنُ مَنْصُورٍ، حَدَّثَنَا عَبْدُ الرَّزَّاقِ، أَخْبَرَنَا مَعْمَرٌ، عَنِ الزُّهْرِيِّ، عَنْ مُحَمَّدِ بْنِ جُبَيْرٍ، عَنْ أَبِيهِ، قَالَ سَمِعْتُ النَّبِيَّ صلى الله عليه وسلم يَقْرَأُ فِي الْمَغْرِبِ بِالطُّورِ، وَذَلِكَ أَوَّلَ مَا وَقَرَ الإِيمَانُ فِي قَلْبِي

Al-Mughira bin Shuba
المغيرة بن شعبة

Narrated Al-Miswar bin Makhrama and Marwan: (whose narrations attest each other) Allah's Messenger ﷺ set out at the time of Al-Hudaibiya (treaty), and when they proceeded for a distance, he said, "Khalid bin Al-Walid leading the cavalry of Quraish constituting the front of the army, is at a place called Al-Ghamim, so take the way on the right." By Allah, Khalid did not perceive the arrival of the Muslims till the dust arising from the march of the Muslim army reached him, and then he turned back hurriedly to inform Quraish. The Prophet ﷺ went on advancing till he reached the Thaniya (i.e. a mountainous way) through which one would go to them (i.e. people of Quraish). The she-camel of the Prophet ﷺ sat down. The people tried their best to cause the she-camel to get up but in vain, so they said, "Al-Qaswa' (i.e. the she-camel's name) has become stubborn! Al-Qaswa' has become stubborn!" The Prophet ﷺ said, "Al-Qaswa' has not become stubborn, for stubbornness is not her habit, but she was stopped by Him Who stopped the elephant." Then he said, "By the Name of Him in Whose Hands my soul is, if they (i.e. the Quraish infidels) ask me anything which will respect the ordinances of Allah, I will grant it to them." The Prophet ﷺ then rebuked the she-camel and she got up. The Prophet ﷺ changed his way till he dismounted at the farthest end of Al-Hudaibiya at a pit (i.e. well) containing a little water which the people used in small amounts, and in a short while the people used up all its water and complained to Allah's Messenger ﷺ of thirst. The Prophet ﷺ took an arrow out of his arrow-case and ordered them to put the arrow in that pit. By Allah, the water started and continued sprouting out till all the people quenched their thirst and returned with satisfaction. While they were still in that state, Budail bin Warqa-al- Khuza`l came with some persons from his tribe Khuza`a and they were the advisers of Allah's Messenger ﷺ who would keep no secret from him and were from the people of Tihama. Budail said, "I left Ka`b bin Luai and 'Amir bin Luai residing at the profuse water of Al-Hudaibiya and they had milch camels (or their women and children) with them, and will wage war against you, and will prevent you from visiting the Ka`ba." Allah's Messenger ﷺ said, "We have not come to fight anyone, but to perform the `Umra. No doubt, the war has weakened Quraish and they have suffered great losses, so if they wish, I will conclude a truce with them, during which they should refrain from interfering between me and the people (i.e. the 'Arab infidels other than Quraish), and if I have victory over those infidels, Quraish will have the option to embrace Islam as the other people do, if they wish; they will at least get strong enough to fight. But if they do not accept the truce, by Allah in Whose Hands my life is, I will fight with them defending my Cause till I get killed, but (I am sure) Allah will definitely make His Cause victorious." Budail said, "I will inform them of what you have said." So, he set off till he reached Quraish and said, "We have come from that man (i.e. Muhammad) whom we heard saying something which we will disclose to you if you should like." Some of the fools among Quraish shouted that they were not in need of this information, but the wiser among them said, "Relate what you heard him saying." Budail said, "I heard him saying so-and-so," relating what the Prophet ﷺ had told him. `Urwa bin Mas`ud got up and said, "O people! Aren't you the sons? They said, "Yes." He added, "Am I not the father?" They said, "Yes." He said, "Do you mistrust me?" They said, "No." He said, "Don't you know that I invited the people of `Ukaz for your help, and when they refused I brought my relatives and children and those who obeyed me (to help you)?" They said, "Yes." He said,

"Well, this man (i.e. the Prophet) has offered you a reasonable proposal, you'd better accept it and allow me to meet him." They said, "You may meet him." So, he went to the Prophet ﷺ and started talking to him. The Prophet ﷺ told him almost the same as he had told Budail. Then `Urwa said, "O Muhammad! Won't you feel any scruple in extirpating your relations? Have you ever heard of anyone amongst the Arabs extirpating his relatives before you? On the other hand, if the reverse should happen, (nobody will aid you, for) by Allah, I do not see (with you) dignified people, but people from various tribes who would run away leaving you alone." Hearing that, Abu Bakr abused him and said, "Do you say we would run and leave the Prophet ﷺ alone?" `Urwa said, "Who is that man?" They said, "He is Abu Bakr." `Urwa said to Abu Bakr, "By Him in Whose Hands my life is, were It not for the favor which you did to me and which I did not compensate, I would retort on you." `Urwa kept on talking to the Prophet ﷺ and seizing the Prophet's beard as he was talking while Al-Mughira bin Shu`ba was standing near the head of the Prophet, holding a sword and wearing a helmet. Whenever `Urwa stretched his hand towards the beard of the Prophet, Al-Mughira would hit his hand with the handle of the sword and say (to `Urwa), "Remove your hand from the beard of Allah's Messenger ﷺ." Urwa raised his head and asked, "Who is that?" The people said, "He is Al-Mughira bin Shu`ba." `Urwa said, "O treacherous! Am I not doing my best to prevent evil consequences of your treachery?" Before embracing Islam Al-Mughira was in the company of some people. He killed them and took their property and came (to Medina) to embrace Islam. The Prophet ﷺ said (to him, "As regards your Islam, I accept it, but as for the property I do not take anything of it. (As it was taken through treason). `Urwa then started looking at the Companions of the Prophet. By Allah, whenever Allah's Messenger ﷺ spat, the spittle would fall in the hand of one of them (i.e. the Prophet's companions) who would rub it on his face and skin; if he ordered them they would carry his orders immediately; if he performed ablution, they would struggle to take the remaining water; and when they spoke to him, they would lower their voices and would not look at his face constantly out of respect. `Urwa returned to his people and said, "O people! By Allah, I have been to the kings and to Caesar, Khosrau and An- Najashi, yet I have never seen any of them respected by his courtiers as much as Muhammad is respected by his companions. By Allah, if he spat, the spittle would fall in the hand of one of them (i.e. the Prophet's companions) who would rub it on his face and skin; if he ordered them, they would carry out his order immediately; if he performed ablution, they would struggle to take the remaining water; and when they spoke, they would lower their voices and would not look at his face constantly out of respect." `Urwa added, "No doubt, he has presented to you a good reasonable offer, so please accept it." A man from the tribe of Bani Kinana said, "Allow me to go to him," and they allowed him, and when he approached the Prophet and his companions, Allah's Messenger ﷺ said, "He is so-and-so who belongs to the tribe that respects the Budn (i.e. camels of the sacrifice). So, bring the Budn in front of him." So, the Budn were brought before him and the people received him while they were reciting Talbiya. When he saw that scene, he said, "Glorified be Allah! It is not fair to prevent these people from visiting the Ka`ba." When he returned to his people, he said, 'I saw the Budn garlanded (with colored knotted ropes) and marked (with stabs on their backs). I do not think it is advisable to prevent them from visiting the Ka`ba." Another person called Mikraz bin Hafs got up and sought their permission to go to Muhammad, and they allowed him, too. When he approached the Muslims, the Prophet ﷺ said, "Here is Mikraz and he is a vicious man." Mikraz started talking to the Prophet and as he was talking, Suhail bin `Amr came. When Suhail bin `Amr came, the Prophet ﷺ said, "Now the matter has become easy." Suhail said to the Prophet "Please conclude a peace treaty with us." So, the Prophet ﷺ called the clerk and said to him, "Write: By the Name of Allah, the most Beneficent, the most Merciful." Suhail said, "As for 'Beneficent,' by Allah, I do not know what it means. So write: By Your Name O Allah, as you used to write previously." The Muslims said, "By Allah, we will not write except: By the Name of Allah, the most Beneficent, the most Merciful." The Prophet ﷺ said, "Write: By Your Name O Allah." Then he dictated, "This is the peace treaty which Muhammad, Allah's Messenger ﷺ has concluded." Suhail said, "By Allah, if we knew that you are Allah's Messenger ﷺ we would not prevent you from visiting the Ka`ba, and would not fight with you. So, write: "Muhammad bin `Abdullah." The Prophet ﷺ said, "By Allah! I am Apostle of Allah even if you people do not believe me. Write: Muhammad bin `Abdullah." (Az-Zuhri said, "The Prophet ﷺ accepted all those things, as he had already said that he would accept everything they would demand if it respects the ordinance of Allah, (i.e. by letting him and his companions perform `Umra.)" The Prophet ﷺ said to Suhail, "On the condition that you allow us to visit the House (i.e. Ka`ba) so that we may perform Tawaf around it." Suhail said, "By Allah, we will not (allow you this year) so as not to give chance to the 'Arabs to say that we have yielded to you, but we will allow you next year." So, the Prophet ﷺ got that written. Then Suhail said, "We also stipulate that you should return to us whoever comes to you from us, even if he embraced your religion." The Muslims said, "Glorified be Allah! How will such a person be returned to the pagans after he has become a Muslim? While they were in this state Abu- Jandal bin Suhail bin `Amr came from the valley of Mecca staggering with his fetters and fell down amongst the Muslims. Suhail said, "O Muhammad! This is the very first term with which we make peace with you, i.e. you shall return Abu Jandal to me." The Prophet ﷺ said, "The peace treaty has not been written yet." Suhail said, "I will never allow you to keep him." The Prophet ﷺ said, "Yes, do." He said, "I won't do.: Mikraz said, "We allow you (to keep him)." Abu Jandal said, "O Muslims! Will I be returned to the pagans though I have come as a Muslim? Don't you see how much I have suffered?" -3.891:... ... Abu Jandal had been tortured severely for the Cause of Allah. `Umar bin Al-Khattab said, "I went to the Prophet ﷺ and said, 'Aren't you truly the Messenger of Allah?' The Prophet ﷺ said, 'Yes, indeed.' I said, 'Isn't our Cause just and the cause of the enemy unjust?' He said, 'Yes.' I said, 'Then why should we be humble in our religion?' He said, 'I am Allah's Messenger ﷺ and I do not disobey Him, and He will make me victorious.' I said, 'Didn't you tell us that we would go to the Ka`ba and perform Tawaf around it?' He said, 'Yes, but did I tell you that we would visit the Ka`ba this year?' I said, 'No.' He said, 'So you will visit it and perform Tawaf around it?' " `Umar further said, "I went to Abu Bakr and said, 'O Abu Bakr! Isn't he truly Allah's Prophet?' He replied, 'Yes.' I said, 'Then why should we be humble in our religion?' He said, 'Indeed, he is Allah's Messenger ﷺ and he does not disobey his Lord, and He will make him victorious. Adhere to him as, by Allah, he is on the right.' I said, 'Was he not telling us that we would go to the Ka`ba and perform Tawaf around it?' He said, 'Yes, but did he tell you that you would go to the Ka`ba this year?' I said, 'No.' He said, "You will go to Ka`ba and perform Tawaf around it." (Az-Zuhri said, " `Umar said, 'I performed many good deeds as expiation for the improper questions I asked them.' ") When the writing of the peace treaty was concluded, Allah's Messenger ﷺ said to his companions, "Get up and' slaughter your sacrifices and get your head shaved." By Allah none of them got up, and the Prophet repeated his order thrice. When none of them got up, he left them and went to Um Salama and told her of the people's attitudes towards him. Um Salama said, "O the Prophet ﷺ of Allah! Do you want your order to be carried out? Go out and don't say a word to anybody till you have slaughtered your sacrifice and call your barber to shave your head." So, the Prophet ﷺ went out and did not talk to anyone of them till he did that, i.e. slaughtered the sacrifice and called his barber who shaved his head. Seeing that, the companions of the Prophetﷺ got up, slaughtered their sacrifices, and started shaving the heads of one another, and there was so much rush that there was a danger of killing each other. Then some believing women came (to the Prophetﷺ); and Allah revealed the following Divine Verses:-- "O you who believe, when the believing women come to you as emigrants examine them . . ." (60.10) `Umar then divorced two wives of his who were infidels. Later on Muawiya bin Abu Sufyan married one of them, and Safwan bin Umaiya married the other. When the Prophetﷺ returned to Medina, Abu Basir, a new Muslim convert from Quraish came to him. The Infidels sent in his pursuit two men who said (to the Prophetﷺ), "Abide by the promise you gave us." So, the Prophetﷺ handed him over to them. They took him out (of the City) till they reached Dhul-Hulaifa where they dismounted to eat some dates they had with them. Abu Basir said to one of them, "By Allah, O so-and-so, I see you have a fine sword." The other drew it out (of the scabbard) and said, "By Allah, it is very fine and I have tried it many times." Abu Basir said, "Let me have a look at it." When the other gave it to him, he hit him with it till he died, and his companion ran away till he came to Medina and entered the Mosque running. When Allah's Messengerﷺ saw him he said, "This man appears to have been frightened." When he reached the Prophetﷺ he said, "My companion has been murdered and I would have been murdered too." Abu Basir came and said, "O Allah's Messengerﷺ, by Allah, Allah has made you fulfill your obligations by your returning me to them (i.e. the Infidels), but Allah has saved me from them." The Prophetﷺ said, "Woe to his mother! What excellent war kindler he would be, should he only have supporters." When Abu Basir heard that he understood that the Prophetﷺ would return him to them again, so he set off till he reached the seashore. Abu Jandal bin Suhail got himself released from them (i.e. infidels) and joined Abu Basir. So, whenever a man from Quraish embraced Islam he would follow Abu Basir till they formed a strong group. By Allah, whenever they heard about a caravan of Quraish heading towards Sham, they stopped it and attacked and killed them (i.e. infidels) and took their properties. The people of Quraish sent a message to the Prophetﷺ requesting him for the Sake of Allah and Kith and kin to send for (i.e. Abu Basir and his companions) promising that whoever (amongst them) came to the Prophetﷺ would be secure. So the Prophetﷺ sent for them (i.e. Abu Basir's companions) and Allah I revealed the following Divine Verses: "And it is He Who Has withheld their hands from you and your hands From them in the midst of Mecca, After He made you the victorious over them. ... the unbelievers had pride and haughtiness, in their hearts ... the pride and haughtiness of the time of ignorance." (48.24-26) And their pride and haughtiness was that they did not confess (write in the treaty) that he (i.e. Muhammad) was the Prophet of Allah and refused to write: "In the Name of Allah, the most Beneficent, the Most Merciful," and they (the mushriks) prevented them (the Muslims) from visiting the House (the Ka`bah). – Sahih Al-Bukhari 2731, 2732

حَدَّثَنِي عَبْدُ اللَّهِ بْنُ مُحَمَّدٍ، حَدَّثَنَا عَبْدُ الرَّزَّاقِ، أَخْبَرَنَا مَعْمَرٌ، قَالَ أَخْبَرَنِي الزُّهْرِيُّ، قَالَ أَخْبَرَنِي عُرْوَةُ بْنُ الزُّبَيْرِ، عَنِ الْمِسْوَرِ بْنِ مَخْرَمَةَ، وَمَرْوَانَ، يُصَدِّقُ كُلُّ وَاحِدٍ مِنْهُمَا حَدِيثَ صَاحِبِهِ قَالَ خَرَجَ رَسُولُ اللَّهِ صلى الله عليه وسلم زَمَنَ الْحُدَيْبِيَةِ، حَتَّى كَانُوا بِبَعْضِ الطَّرِيقِ قَالَ النَّبِيُّ صلى الله عليه وسلم " إِنَّ خَالِدَ بْنَ الْوَلِيدِ بِالْغَمِيمِ فِي خَيْلٍ لِقُرَيْشٍ طَلِيعَةً فَخُذُوا ذَاتَ الْيَمِينِ ". فَوَاللَّهِ مَا شَعَرَ بِهِمْ خَالِدٌ حَتَّى إِذَا هُمْ بِقَتَرَةِ الْجَيْشِ، فَانْطَلَقَ يَرْكُضُ نَذِيرًا لِقُرَيْشٍ، وَسَارَ النَّبِيُّ صلى الله عليه وسلم حَتَّى إِذَا كَانَ بِالثَّنِيَّةِ الَّتِي يُهْبَطُ عَلَيْهِمْ مِنْهَا، بَرَكَتْ بِهِ رَاحِلَتُهُ. فَقَالَ النَّاسُ حَلْ حَلْ. فَأَلَحَّتْ، فَقَالُوا خَلأَتِ الْقَصْوَاءُ، خَلأَتِ الْقَصْوَاءُ. فَقَالَ النَّبِيُّ صلى الله عليه وسلم " مَا خَلأَتِ الْقَصْوَاءُ، وَمَا ذَاكَ لَهَا بِخُلُقٍ، وَلَكِنْ حَبَسَهَا حَابِسُ الْفِيلِ، ثُمَّ قَالَ وَالَّذِي نَفْسِي بِيَدِهِ لاَ يَسْأَلُونِي خُطَّةً يُعَظِّمُونَ فِيهَا حُرُمَاتِ اللَّهِ إِلاَّ أَعْطَيْتُهُمْ إِيَّاهَا ". ثُمَّ زَجَرَهَا فَوَثَبَتْ، قَالَ فَعَدَلَ عَنْهُمْ حَتَّى نَزَلَ بِأَقْصَى الْحُدَيْبِيَةِ، عَلَى ثَمَدٍ قَلِيلِ الْمَاءِ يَتَبَرَّضُهُ النَّاسُ تَبَرُّضًا، فَلَمْ يُلَبِّثْهُ النَّاسُ حَتَّى نَزَحُوهُ، وَشُكِيَ إِلَى رَسُولِ اللَّهِ صلى الله عليه وسلم الْعَطَشُ، فَانْتَزَعَ سَهْمًا مِنْ كِنَانَتِهِ، ثُمَّ أَمَرَهُمْ أَنْ يَجْعَلُوهُ فِيهِ، فَوَاللَّهِ مَا زَالَ يَجِيشُ لَهُمْ بِالرِّيِّ حَتَّى صَدَرُوا عَنْهُ، فَبَيْنَمَا هُمْ كَذَلِكَ، إِذْ جَاءَ بُدَيْلُ بْنُ وَرْقَاءَ الْخُزَاعِيُّ فِي نَفَرٍ مِنْ قَوْمِهِ مِنْ خُزَاعَةَ، وَكَانُوا عَيْبَةَ نُصْحِ رَسُولِ اللَّهِ صلى الله عليه وسلم مِنْ أَهْلِ تِهَامَةَ، فَقَالَ إِنِّي تَرَكْتُ كَعْبَ بْنَ لُؤَىٍّ وَعَامِرَ بْنَ لُؤَىٍّ نَزَلُوا أَعْدَادَ مِيَاهِ

الْحُدَيْبِيَةِ، وَمَعَهُمُ الْعُوذُ الْمَطَافِيلُ، وَهُمْ مُقَاتِلُوكَ وَصَادُّوكَ عَنِ الْبَيْتِ. فَقَالَ رَسُولُ اللَّهِ صلى الله عليه وسلم " إِنَّا لَمْ نَجِئْ لِقِتَالِ أَحَدٍ، وَلَكِنَّا جِئْنَا مُعْتَمِرِينَ، وَإِنَّ قُرَيْشًا قَدْ نَهِكَتْهُمُ الْحَرْبُ، وَأَضَرَّتْ بِهِمْ، فَإِنْ شَاءُوا مَادَدْتُهُمْ مُدَّةً، وَيُخَلُّوا بَيْنِي وَبَيْنَ النَّاسِ، فَإِنْ أَظْهَرْ فَإِنْ شَاءُوا أَنْ يَدْخُلُوا فِيمَا دَخَلَ فِيهِ النَّاسُ فَعَلُوا، وَإِلاَّ فَقَدْ جَمُّوا، وَإِنْ هُمْ أَبَوْا فَوَالَّذِي نَفْسِي بِيَدِهِ، لأُقَاتِلَنَّهُمْ عَلَى أَمْرِي هَذَا حَتَّى تَنْفَرِدَ سَالِفَتِي، وَلَيُنْفِذَنَّ اللَّهُ أَمْرَهُ ". فَقَالَ بُدَيْلٌ سَأُبَلِّغُهُمْ مَا تَقُولُ. قَالَ فَانْطَلَقَ حَتَّى أَتَى قُرَيْشًا قَالَ إِنَّا قَدْ جِئْنَاكُمْ مِنْ هَذَا الرَّجُلِ، وَسَمِعْنَاهُ يَقُولُ قَوْلاً، فَإِنْ شِئْتُمْ أَنْ نَعْرِضَهُ عَلَيْكُمْ فَعَلْنَا، فَقَالَ سُفَهَاؤُهُمْ لاَ حَاجَةَ لَنَا أَنْ تُخْبِرَنَا عَنْهُ بِشَىْءٍ. وَقَالَ ذَوُو الرَّأْىِ مِنْهُمْ هَاتِ مَا سَمِعْتَهُ يَقُولُ. قَالَ سَمِعْتُهُ يَقُولُ كَذَا وَكَذَا، فَحَدَّثَهُمْ بِمَا قَالَ النَّبِيُّ صلى الله عليه وسلم. فَقَامَ عُرْوَةُ بْنُ مَسْعُودٍ فَقَالَ أَىْ قَوْمِ أَلَسْتُمْ بِالْوَالِدِ قَالُوا بَلَى. قَالَ أَوَلَسْتُ بِالْوَلَدِ قَالُوا بَلَى. قَالَ فَهَلْ تَتَّهِمُونِي. قَالُوا لاَ. قَالَ أَلَسْتُمْ تَعْلَمُونَ أَنِّي اسْتَنْفَرْتُ أَهْلَ عُكَاظٍ، فَلَمَّا بَلَّحُوا عَلَىَّ جِئْتُكُمْ بِأَهْلِي وَوَلَدِي وَمَنْ أَطَاعَنِي قَالُوا بَلَى. قَالَ فَإِنَّ هَذَا قَدْ عَرَضَ لَكُمْ خُطَّةَ رُشْدٍ، اقْبَلُوهَا وَدَعُونِي آتِهِ. قَالُوا ائْتِهِ. فَأَتَاهُ فَجَعَلَ يُكَلِّمُ النَّبِيَّ صلى الله عليه وسلم فَقَالَ النَّبِيُّ صلى الله عليه وسلم نَحْوًا مِنْ قَوْلِهِ لِبُدَيْلٍ، فَقَالَ عُرْوَةُ عِنْدَ ذَلِكَ أَىْ مُحَمَّدُ، أَرَأَيْتَ إِنِ اسْتَأْصَلْتَ أَمْرَ قَوْمِكَ هَلْ سَمِعْتَ بِأَحَدٍ مِنَ الْعَرَبِ اجْتَاحَ أَهْلَهُ قَبْلَكَ وَإِنْ تَكُنِ الأُخْرَى، فَإِنِّي وَاللَّهِ لأَرَى وُجُوهًا، وَإِنِّي لأَرَى أَوْشَابًا مِنَ النَّاسِ خَلِيقًا أَنْ يَفِرُّوا وَيَدَعُوكَ. فَقَالَ لَهُ أَبُو بَكْرٍ امْصُصْ بَظْرَ اللاَّتِ، أَنَحْنُ نَفِرُّ عَنْهُ وَنَدَعُهُ فَقَالَ مَنْ ذَا قَالُوا أَبُو بَكْرٍ. قَالَ أَمَا وَالَّذِي نَفْسِي بِيَدِهِ لَوْلاَ يَدٌ كَانَتْ لَكَ عِنْدِي لَمْ أَجْزِكَ بِهَا لأَجَبْتُكَ. قَالَ وَجَعَلَ يُكَلِّمُ النَّبِيَّ صلى الله عليه وسلم فَكُلَّمَا تَكَلَّمَ أَخَذَ بِلِحْيَتِهِ، وَالْمُغِيرَةُ بْنُ شُعْبَةَ قَائِمٌ عَلَى رَأْسِ النَّبِيِّ صلى الله عليه وسلم وَمَعَهُ السَّيْفُ وَعَلَيْهِ الْمِغْفَرُ، فَكُلَّمَا أَهْوَى عُرْوَةُ بِيَدِهِ إِلَى لِحْيَةِ النَّبِيِّ صلى الله عليه وسلم ضَرَبَ يَدَهُ بِنَعْلِ السَّيْفِ، وَقَالَ لَهُ أَخِّرْ يَدَكَ عَنْ لِحْيَةِ رَسُولِ اللَّهِ صلى الله عليه وسلم. فَرَفَعَ عُرْوَةُ رَأْسَهُ فَقَالَ مَنْ هَذَا قَالُوا الْمُغِيرَةُ بْنُ شُعْبَةَ. فَقَالَ أَىْ غُدَرُ، أَلَسْتُ أَسْعَى فِي غَدْرَتِكَ وَكَانَ الْمُغِيرَةُ صَحِبَ قَوْمًا فِي الْجَاهِلِيَّةِ، فَقَتَلَهُمْ، وَأَخَذَ أَمْوَالَهُمْ، ثُمَّ جَاءَ فَأَسْلَمَ فَقَالَ النَّبِيُّ صلى الله عليه وسلم " أَمَّا الإِسْلاَمَ فَأَقْبَلُ، وَأَمَّا الْمَالَ فَلَسْتُ مِنْهُ فِي شَىْءٍ ". ثُمَّ إِنَّ عُرْوَةَ جَعَلَ يَرْمُقُ أَصْحَابَ النَّبِيِّ صلى الله عليه وسلم بِعَيْنَيْهِ. قَالَ فَوَاللَّهِ مَا تَنَخَّمَ رَسُولُ اللَّهِ صلى الله عليه وسلم نُخَامَةً إِلاَّ وَقَعَتْ فِي كَفِّ رَجُلٍ مِنْهُمْ فَدَلَكَ بِهَا وَجْهَهُ وَجِلْدَهُ، وَإِذَا أَمَرَهُمُ ابْتَدَرُوا أَمْرَهُ، وَإِذَا تَوَضَّأَ كَادُوا يَقْتَتِلُونَ عَلَى وَضُوئِهِ، وَإِذَا تَكَلَّمَ خَفَضُوا أَصْوَاتَهُمْ عِنْدَهُ، وَمَا يُحِدُّونَ إِلَيْهِ النَّظَرَ تَعْظِيمًا لَهُ، فَرَجَعَ عُرْوَةُ إِلَى أَصْحَابِهِ، فَقَالَ أَىْ قَوْمِ، وَاللَّهِ لَقَدْ وَفَدْتُ عَلَى الْمُلُوكِ، وَوَفَدْتُ عَلَى قَيْصَرَ وَكِسْرَى وَالنَّجَاشِيِّ وَاللَّهِ إِنْ رَأَيْتُ مَلِكًا قَطُّ، يُعَظِّمُهُ أَصْحَابُهُ مَا يُعَظِّمُ أَصْحَابُ مُحَمَّدٍ صلى الله عليه وسلم مُحَمَّدًا، وَاللَّهِ إِنْ تَنَخَّمَ نُخَامَةً إِلاَّ وَقَعَتْ فِي كَفِّ رَجُلٍ مِنْهُمْ، فَدَلَكَ بِهَا وَجْهَهُ وَجِلْدَهُ، وَإِذَا أَمَرَهُمُ ابْتَدَرُوا أَمْرَهُ وَإِذَا تَوَضَّأَ كَادُوا يَقْتَتِلُونَ عَلَى وَضُوئِهِ، وَإِذَا تَكَلَّمَ خَفَضُوا أَصْوَاتَهُمْ عِنْدَهُ، وَمَا يُحِدُّونَ إِلَيْهِ النَّظَرَ تَعْظِيمًا لَهُ، وَإِنَّهُ قَدْ عَرَضَ عَلَيْكُمْ خُطَّةَ رُشْدٍ، فَاقْبَلُوهَا. فَقَالَ رَجُلٌ مِنْ بَنِي كِنَانَةَ دَعُونِي آتِهِ. فَقَالُوا ائْتِهِ. فَلَمَّا أَشْرَفَ عَلَى النَّبِيِّ صلى الله عليه وسلم وَأَصْحَابِهِ، قَالَ رَسُولُ اللَّهِ صلى الله عليه وسلم " هَذَا فُلاَنٌ، وَهْوَ مِنْ قَوْمٍ يُعَظِّمُونَ الْبُدْنَ فَابْعَثُوهَا لَهُ ". فَبُعِثَتْ لَهُ وَاسْتَقْبَلَهُ النَّاسُ يُلَبُّونَ، فَلَمَّا رَأَى ذَلِكَ قَالَ سُبْحَانَ اللَّهِ مَا يَنْبَغِي لِهَؤُلاَءِ أَنْ يُصَدُّوا عَنِ الْبَيْتِ، فَلَمَّا رَجَعَ إِلَى أَصْحَابِهِ قَالَ رَأَيْتُ الْبُدْنَ قَدْ قُلِّدَتْ وَأُشْعِرَتْ، فَمَا أَرَى أَنْ يُصَدُّوا عَنِ الْبَيْتِ. فَقَامَ رَجُلٌ مِنْهُمْ يُقَالُ لَهُ مِكْرَزُ بْنُ حَفْصٍ. فَقَالَ دَعُونِي آتِهِ. فَقَالُوا ائْتِهِ. فَلَمَّا أَشْرَفَ عَلَيْهِمْ قَالَ النَّبِيُّ صلى الله عليه وسلم " هَذَا مِكْرَزٌ وَهْوَ رَجُلٌ فَاجِرٌ ". فَجَعَلَ يُكَلِّمُ النَّبِيَّ صلى الله عليه وسلم، فَبَيْنَمَا هُوَ يُكَلِّمُهُ إِذْ جَاءَ سُهَيْلُ بْنُ عَمْرٍو. قَالَ مَعْمَرٌ فَأَخْبَرَنِي أَيُّوبُ عَنْ عِكْرِمَةَ، أَنَّهُ لَمَّا جَاءَ سُهَيْلُ بْنُ عَمْرٍو قَالَ النَّبِيُّ صلى الله عليه وسلم " لَقَدْ سَهُلَ لَكُمْ مِنْ أَمْرِكُمْ ". قَالَ مَعْمَرٌ قَالَ الزُّهْرِيُّ فِي حَدِيثِهِ فَجَاءَ سُهَيْلُ بْنُ عَمْرٍو فَقَالَ هَاتِ، اكْتُبْ بَيْنَنَا وَبَيْنَكُمْ كِتَابًا، فَدَعَا النَّبِيُّ صلى الله عليه وسلم الْكَاتِبَ، فَقَالَ النَّبِيُّ صلى الله عليه وسلم " بِسْمِ اللَّهِ الرَّحْمَنِ الرَّحِيمِ ". قَالَ سُهَيْلٌ أَمَّا الرَّحْمَنُ فَوَاللَّهِ مَا أَدْرِي مَا هُوَ وَلَكِنِ اكْتُبْ بِاسْمِكَ اللَّهُمَّ. كَمَا كُنْتَ تَكْتُبُ. فَقَالَ الْمُسْلِمُونَ وَاللَّهِ لاَ نَكْتُبُهَا إِلاَّ بِسْمِ اللَّهِ الرَّحْمَنِ الرَّحِيمِ. فَقَالَ النَّبِيُّ صلى الله عليه وسلم " اكْتُبْ بِاسْمِكَ اللَّهُمَّ ". ثُمَّ قَالَ " هَذَا مَا قَاضَى عَلَيْهِ مُحَمَّدٌ رَسُولُ اللَّهِ ". فَقَالَ سُهَيْلٌ وَاللَّهِ لَوْ كُنَّا نَعْلَمُ أَنَّكَ رَسُولُ اللَّهِ مَا صَدَدْنَاكَ عَنِ الْبَيْتِ وَلاَ قَاتَلْنَاكَ، وَلَكِنِ اكْتُبْ مُحَمَّدُ بْنُ عَبْدِ اللَّهِ. فَقَالَ النَّبِيُّ صلى الله عليه وسلم " وَاللَّهِ إِنِّي لَرَسُولُ اللَّهِ وَإِنْ كَذَّبْتُمُونِي. اكْتُبْ مُحَمَّدُ بْنُ عَبْدِ اللَّهِ ". قَالَ الزُّهْرِيُّ وَذَلِكَ لِقَوْلِهِ " لاَ يَسْأَلُونِي خُطَّةً يُعَظِّمُونَ فِيهَا حُرُمَاتِ اللَّهِ إِلاَّ أَعْطَيْتُهُمْ إِيَّاهَا ". فَقَالَ لَهُ النَّبِيُّ صلى الله عليه وسلم " عَلَى أَنْ تُخَلُّوا بَيْنَنَا وَبَيْنَ الْبَيْتِ فَنَطُوفَ بِهِ ". فَقَالَ سُهَيْلٌ وَاللَّهِ لاَ تَتَحَدَّثُ الْعَرَبُ أَنَّا أُخِذْنَا ضُغْطَةً وَلَكِنْ ذَلِكَ مِنَ الْعَامِ الْمُقْبِلِ فَكَتَبَ. فَقَالَ سُهَيْلٌ وَعَلَى أَنَّهُ لاَ يَأْتِيكَ مِنَّا رَجُلٌ، وَإِنْ كَانَ عَلَى دِينِكَ، إِلاَّ رَدَدْتَهُ إِلَيْنَا. قَالَ الْمُسْلِمُونَ سُبْحَانَ اللَّهِ كَيْفَ يُرَدُّ إِلَى الْمُشْرِكِينَ وَقَدْ جَاءَ مُسْلِمًا فَبَيْنَمَا هُمْ كَذَلِكَ إِذْ دَخَلَ أَبُو جَنْدَلِ بْنُ سُهَيْلِ بْنِ عَمْرٍو يَرْسُفُ فِي قُيُودِهِ، وَقَدْ خَرَجَ مِنْ أَسْفَلِ مَكَّةَ، حَتَّى رَمَى بِنَفْسِهِ بَيْنَ أَظْهُرِ الْمُسْلِمِينَ. فَقَالَ سُهَيْلٌ هَذَا يَا مُحَمَّدُ أَوَّلُ مَا أُقَاضِيكَ عَلَيْهِ أَنْ تَرُدَّهُ إِلَىَّ. فَقَالَ النَّبِيُّ صلى الله عليه وسلم " إِنَّا لَمْ نَقْضِ الْكِتَابَ بَعْدُ ". قَالَ فَوَاللَّهِ إِذًا لَمْ أُصَالِحْكَ عَلَى شَىْءٍ أَبَدًا. قَالَ النَّبِيُّ صلى الله عليه وسلم " فَأَجِزْهُ لِي ". قَالَ مَا أَنَا بِمُجِيزِهِ لَكَ. قَالَ " بَلَى، فَافْعَلْ ". قَالَ مَا أَنَا بِفَاعِلٍ. قَالَ مِكْرَزٌ بَلْ قَدْ أَجَزْنَاهُ لَكَ. قَالَ أَبُو جَنْدَلٍ أَىْ مَعْشَرَ الْمُسْلِمِينَ، أُرَدُّ إِلَى الْمُشْرِكِينَ وَقَدْ جِئْتُ مُسْلِمًا أَلاَ تَرَوْنَ مَا قَدْ لَقِيتُ وَكَانَ قَدْ عُذِّبَ عَذَابًا شَدِيدًا فِي اللَّهِ. قَالَ فَقَالَ عُمَرُ بْنُ الْخَطَّابِ فَأَتَيْتُ نَبِيَّ اللَّهِ صلى الله عليه وسلم فَقُلْتُ أَلَسْتَ نَبِيَّ اللَّهِ حَقًّا قَالَ " بَلَى ". قُلْتُ أَلَسْنَا عَلَى الْحَقِّ وَعَدُوُّنَا عَلَى الْبَاطِلِ قَالَ " بَلَى ". قُلْتُ فَلِمَ نُعْطِي الدَّنِيَّةَ فِي دِينِنَا إِذًا قَالَ " إِنِّي رَسُولُ اللَّهِ، وَلَسْتُ أَعْصِيهِ وَهْوَ نَاصِرِي ". قُلْتُ أَوَلَيْسَ كُنْتَ تُحَدِّثُنَا أَنَّا سَنَأْتِي الْبَيْتَ فَنَطُوفُ بِهِ قَالَ " بَلَى، فَأَخْبَرْتُكَ أَنَّا نَأْتِيهِ الْعَامَ ". قَالَ قُلْتُ لاَ. قَالَ " فَإِنَّكَ آتِيهِ وَمُطَّوِّفٌ بِهِ ". قَالَ فَأَتَيْتُ أَبَا بَكْرٍ فَقُلْتُ يَا أَبَا بَكْرٍ، أَلَيْسَ هَذَا نَبِيَّ اللَّهِ حَقًّا قَالَ بَلَى. قُلْتُ أَلَسْنَا عَلَى الْحَقِّ وَعَدُوُّنَا عَلَى الْبَاطِلِ قَالَ بَلَى. قُلْتُ فَلِمَ نُعْطِي الدَّنِيَّةَ فِي دِينِنَا إِذًا قَالَ أَيُّهَا الرَّجُلُ، إِنَّهُ لَرَسُولُ اللَّهِ صلى الله عليه وسلم وَلَيْسَ يَعْصِي رَبَّهُ وَهْوَ نَاصِرُهُ، فَاسْتَمْسِكْ بِغَرْزِهِ، فَوَاللَّهِ إِنَّهُ عَلَى الْحَقِّ. قُلْتُ أَلَيْسَ كَانَ يُحَدِّثُنَا أَنَّا سَنَأْتِي الْبَيْتَ وَنَطُوفُ بِهِ قَالَ بَلَى، أَفَأَخْبَرَكَ أَنَّكَ تَأْتِيهِ الْعَامَ قُلْتُ لاَ. قَالَ فَإِنَّكَ آتِيهِ وَمُطَّوِّفٌ بِهِ. قَالَ الزُّهْرِيِّ

قَالَ عُمَرُ فَعَمِلْتُ لِذَلِكَ أَعْمَالاً. قَالَ فَلَمَّا فَرَغَ مِنْ قَضِيَّةِ الْكِتَابِ قَالَ رَسُولُ اللَّهِ صلى الله عليه وسلم لأَصْحَابِهِ " قُومُوا فَانْحَرُوا، ثُمَّ احْلِقُوا ". قَالَ فَوَاللَّهِ مَا قَامَ مِنْهُمْ رَجُلٌ حَتَّى قَالَ ذَلِكَ ثَلاَثَ مَرَّاتٍ، فَلَمَّا لَمْ يَقُمْ مِنْهُمْ أَحَدٌ دَخَلَ عَلَى أُمِّ سَلَمَةَ، فَذَكَرَ لَهَا مَا لَقِيَ مِنَ النَّاسِ. فَقَالَتْ أُمُّ سَلَمَةَ يَا نَبِيَّ اللَّهِ، أَتُحِبُّ ذَلِكَ اخْرُجْ ثُمَّ لاَ تُكَلِّمْ أَحَدًا مِنْهُمْ كَلِمَةً حَتَّى تَنْحَرَ بُدْنَكَ، وَتَدْعُوَ حَالِقَكَ فَيَحْلِقَكَ. فَخَرَجَ فَلَمْ يُكَلِّمْ أَحَدًا مِنْهُمْ، حَتَّى فَعَلَ ذَلِكَ نَحَرَ بُدْنَهُ، وَدَعَا حَالِقَهُ فَحَلَقَهُ. فَلَمَّا رَأَوْا ذَلِكَ، قَامُوا فَنَحَرُوا، وَجَعَلَ بَعْضُهُمْ يَحْلِقُ بَعْضًا، حَتَّى كَادَ بَعْضُهُمْ يَقْتُلُ بَعْضًا غَمًّا، ثُمَّ جَاءَهُ نِسْوَةٌ مُؤْمِنَاتٌ فَأَنْزَلَ اللَّهُ تَعَالَى {يَا أَيُّهَا الَّذِينَ آمَنُوا إِذَا جَاءَكُمُ الْمُؤْمِنَاتُ مُهَاجِرَاتٍ فَامْتَحِنُوهُنَّ} حَتَّى بَلَغَ {بِعِصَمِ الْكَوَافِرِ} فَطَلَّقَ عُمَرُ يَوْمَئِذٍ امْرَأَتَيْنِ كَانَتَا لَهُ فِي الشِّرْكِ، فَتَزَوَّجَ إِحْدَاهُمَا مُعَاوِيَةُ بْنُ أَبِي سُفْيَانَ، وَالأُخْرَى صَفْوَانُ بْنُ أُمَيَّةَ، ثُمَّ رَجَعَ النَّبِيُّ صلى الله عليه وسلم إِلَى الْمَدِينَةِ، فَجَاءَهُ أَبُو بَصِيرٍ ـ رَجُلٌ مِنْ قُرَيْشٍ ـ وَهْوَ مُسْلِمٌ فَأَرْسَلُوا فِي طَلَبِهِ رَجُلَيْنِ، فَقَالُوا الْعَهْدَ الَّذِي جَعَلْتَ لَنَا. فَدَفَعَهُ إِلَى الرَّجُلَيْنِ، فَخَرَجَا بِهِ حَتَّى بَلَغَا ذَا الْحُلَيْفَةِ، فَنَزَلُوا يَأْكُلُونَ مِنْ تَمْرٍ لَهُمْ، فَقَالَ أَبُو بَصِيرٍ لأَحَدِ الرَّجُلَيْنِ وَاللَّهِ إِنِّي لأَرَى سَيْفَكَ هَذَا يَا فُلاَنُ جَيِّدًا. فَاسْتَلَّهُ الآخَرُ فَقَالَ أَجَلْ، وَاللَّهِ إِنَّهُ لَجَيِّدٌ، لَقَدْ جَرَّبْتُ بِهِ ثُمَّ جَرَّبْتُ. فَقَالَ أَبُو بَصِيرٍ أَرِنِي أَنْظُرْ إِلَيْهِ، فَأَمْكَنَهُ مِنْهُ، فَضَرَبَهُ حَتَّى بَرَدَ، وَفَرَّ الآخَرُ، حَتَّى أَتَى الْمَدِينَةَ، فَدَخَلَ الْمَسْجِدَ يَعْدُو. فَقَالَ رَسُولُ اللَّهِ صلى الله عليه وسلم حِينَ رَآهُ " لَقَدْ رَأَى هَذَا ذُعْرًا ". فَلَمَّا انْتَهَى إِلَى النَّبِيِّ صلى الله عليه وسلم قَالَ قُتِلَ وَاللَّهِ صَاحِبِي وَإِنِّي لَمَقْتُولٌ، فَجَاءَ أَبُو بَصِيرٍ فَقَالَ يَا نَبِيَّ اللَّهِ، قَدْ وَاللَّهِ أَوْفَى اللَّهُ ذِمَّتَكَ، قَدْ رَدَدْتَنِي إِلَيْهِمْ ثُمَّ أَنْجَانِي اللَّهُ مِنْهُمْ. قَالَ النَّبِيُّ صلى الله عليه وسلم " وَيْلُ أُمِّهِ مِسْعَرَ حَرْبٍ، لَوْ كَانَ لَهُ أَحَدٌ ". فَلَمَّا سَمِعَ ذَلِكَ عَرَفَ أَنَّهُ سَيَرُدُّهُ إِلَيْهِمْ، فَخَرَجَ حَتَّى أَتَى سِيفَ الْبَحْرِ. قَالَ وَيَنْفَلِتُ مِنْهُمْ أَبُو جَنْدَلِ بْنُ سُهَيْلٍ، فَلَحِقَ بِأَبِي بَصِيرٍ، فَجَعَلَ لاَ يَخْرُجُ مِنْ قُرَيْشٍ رَجُلٌ قَدْ أَسْلَمَ إِلاَّ لَحِقَ بِأَبِي بَصِيرٍ، حَتَّى اجْتَمَعَتْ مِنْهُمْ عِصَابَةٌ، فَوَاللَّهِ مَا يَسْمَعُونَ بِعِيرٍ خَرَجَتْ لِقُرَيْشٍ إِلَى الشَّأْمِ إِلاَّ اعْتَرَضُوا لَهَا، فَقَتَلُوهُمْ، وَأَخَذُوا أَمْوَالَهُمْ، فَأَرْسَلَتْ قُرَيْشٌ إِلَى النَّبِيِّ صلى الله عليه وسلم تُنَاشِدُهُ بِاللَّهِ وَالرَّحِمِ لَمَّا أَرْسَلَ، فَمَنْ أَتَاهُ فَهْوَ آمِنٌ، فَأَرْسَلَ النَّبِيُّ صلى الله عليه وسلم إِلَيْهِمْ، فَأَنْزَلَ اللَّهُ تَعَالَى {وَهُوَ الَّذِي كَفَّ أَيْدِيَهُمْ عَنْكُمْ وَأَيْدِيَكُمْ عَنْهُمْ بِبَطْنِ مَكَّةَ مِنْ بَعْدِ أَنْ أَظْفَرَكُمْ عَلَيْهِمْ} حَتَّى بَلَغَ {الْحَمِيَّةَ حَمِيَّةَ الْجَاهِلِيَّةِ} وَكَانَتْ حَمِيَّتُهُمْ أَنَّهُمْ لَمْ يُقِرُّوا أَنَّهُ نَبِيُّ اللَّهِ، وَلَمْ يُقِرُّوا بِبِسْمِ اللَّهِ الرَّحْمَنِ الرَّحِيمِ، وَحَالُوا بَيْنَهُمْ وَبَيْنَ الْبَيْتِ

Narrated Ibn Shihab: Once `Umar bin `Abdul `Aziz delayed the prayer and `Urwa bin Az-Zubair went to him and said, "Once in 'Iraq, Al-Mughira bin Shu`ba delayed his prayers and Abi Mas`ud Al-Ansari went to him and said, 'O Mughira! What is this? Don't you know that once Gabriel came and offered the prayer (Fajr prayer) and Allah's Messengerﷺ prayed too, then he prayed again (Zuhr prayer) and so did Allah's Apostle and again he prayed (`Asr prayers and Allah's Messengerﷺ did the same; again he prayed (Maghrib-prayer) and so did Allah's Messengerﷺ and again prayed (`Isha prayer) and so did Allah's Apostle and (Gabriel) said, 'I was ordered to do so (to demonstrate the prayers prescribed to you)?'" `Umar (bin `Abdul `Aziz) said to `Urwa, "Be sure of what you Say. Did Gabriel lead Allah's Messengerﷺ at the stated times of the prayers?" `Urwa replied, "Bashir bin Abi Mas`ud narrated like this on the authority of his father." `Urwa added, "Aisha told me that Allah's Messengerﷺ used to pray `Asr prayer when the sunshine was still inside her residence (during the early time of `Asr). – Sahih Al-Bukhari 521, 522

حَدَّثَنَا عَبْدُ اللَّهِ بْنُ مَسْلَمَةَ، قَالَ قَرَأْتُ عَلَى مَالِكٍ عَنِ ابْنِ شِهَابٍ، أَنَّ عُمَرَ بْنَ عَبْدِ الْعَزِيزِ، أَخَّرَ الصَّلاَةَ يَوْمًا، فَدَخَلَ عَلَيْهِ عُرْوَةُ بْنُ الزُّبَيْرِ، فَأَخْبَرَهُ أَنَّ الْمُغِيرَةَ بْنَ شُعْبَةَ أَخَّرَ الصَّلاَةَ يَوْمًا وَهْوَ بِالْعِرَاقِ، فَدَخَلَ عَلَيْهِ أَبُو مَسْعُودٍ الأَنْصَارِيُّ فَقَالَ مَا هَذَا يَا مُغِيرَةُ أَلَيْسَ قَدْ عَلِمْتَ أَنَّ جِبْرِيلَ نَزَلَ فَصَلَّى، فَصَلَّى رَسُولُ اللَّهِ صلى الله عليه وسلم ثُمَّ صَلَّى فَصَلَّى رَسُولُ اللَّهِ صلى الله عليه وسلم ثُمَّ صَلَّى فَصَلَّى رَسُولُ اللَّهِ صلى الله عليه وسلم ثُمَّ صَلَّى فَصَلَّى رَسُولُ اللَّهِ صلى الله عليه وسلم ثُمَّ صَلَّى فَصَلَّى رَسُولُ اللَّهِ صلى الله عليه وسلم ثُمَّ قَالَ " بِهَذَا أُمِرْتُ ". فَقَالَ عُمَرُ لِعُرْوَةَ اعْلَمْ مَا تُحَدِّثُ أَوَإِنَّ جِبْرِيلَ هُوَ أَقَامَ لِرَسُولِ اللَّهِ صلى الله عليه وسلم وَقْتَ الصَّلاَةِ. قَالَ عُرْوَةُ كَذَلِكَ كَانَ بَشِيرُ بْنُ أَبِي مَسْعُودٍ يُحَدِّثُ عَنْ أَبِيهِ. قَالَ عُرْوَةُ وَلَقَدْ حَدَّثَتْنِي عَائِشَةُ، أَنَّ رَسُولَ اللَّهِ صلى الله عليه وسلم كَانَ يُصَلِّي الْعَصْرَ، وَالشَّمْسُ فِي حُجْرَتِهَا قَبْلَ أَنْ تَظْهَرَ.

Narrated Al-Mughira bin Shu`ba: The Prophetﷺ went to answer the call of nature, and when he returned, I met him with water and he performed the ablution while he was wearing a Sham, cloak. He rinsed his mouth, put the water in his nose and blew it out, washed his face and tried to take his hands out of his sleeves, but they were too narrow, so he took out his hands from under his chest and washed them and then passed his wet hands over his head and Khuffs (socks made from thick fabric or leather). – Sahih Al-Bukhari 5798

حَدَّثَنَا قَيْسُ بْنُ حَفْصٍ، حَدَّثَنَا عَبْدُ الْوَاحِدِ، حَدَّثَنَا الأَعْمَشُ، قَالَ حَدَّثَنِي أَبُو الضُّحَى، قَالَ حَدَّثَنِي مَسْرُوقٌ، قَالَ حَدَّثَنِي الْمُغِيرَةُ بْنُ شُعْبَةَ، قَالَ انْطَلَقَ النَّبِيُّ صلى الله عليه وسلم لِحَاجَتِهِ ثُمَّ أَقْبَلَ، فَتَلَقَّيْتُهُ بِمَاءٍ، فَتَوَضَّأَ وَعَلَيْهِ جُبَّةٌ شَأْمِيَّةٌ،

فَمَضْمَضَ وَاسْتَنْشَقَ وَغَسَلَ وَجْهَهُ، فَذَهَبَ يُخْرِجُ يَدَيْهِ مِنْ كُمَّيْهِ فَكَانَا ضَيِّقَيْنِ، فَأَخْرَجَ يَدَيْهِ مِنْ تَحْتِ الْجُبَّةِ، فَغَسَلَهُمَا وَمَسَحَ بِرَأْسِهِ وَعَلَى خُفَّيْهِ.

Narrated Al-Mughira bin Shu`ba: `Umar bin Al-Khattab asked (the people) about the Imlas of a woman, i.e., a woman who has an abortion because of having been beaten on her `Abdomen, saying, "Who among you has heard anything about it from the Prophet?" I said, "I did." He said, "What is that?" I said, "I heard the Prophet saying, "Its Diya (blood money) is either a male or a female slave.' " `Umar said, "Do not leave till you present witness in support of your statement." So I went out, and found Muhammad bin Maslama. I brought him, and he bore witness with me that he had heard the Prophet ﷺ saying, "Its Diya (blood money) is either a male slave or a female slave.". – Sahih Al-Bukhari 7317, 7318
حَدَّثَنَا مُحَمَّدٌ، أَخْبَرَنَا أَبُو مُعَاوِيَةَ، حَدَّثَنَا هِشَامٌ، عَنْ أَبِيهِ، عَنِ الْمُغِيرَةِ بْنِ شُعْبَةَ، قَالَ سَأَلَ عُمَرُ بْنُ الْخَطَّابِ عَنْ إِمْلاَصِ الْمَرْأَةِ ـ هِيَ الَّتِي يُضْرَبُ بَطْنُهَا فَتُلْقِي جَنِينًا ـ فَقَالَ أَيُّكُمْ سَمِعَ مِنَ النَّبِيِّ صلى الله عليه وسلم فِيهِ شَيْئًا فَقُلْتُ أَنَا. فَقَالَ مَا هُوَ قُلْتُ سَمِعْتُ النَّبِيَّ صلى الله عليه وسلم يَقُولُ " فِيهِ غُرَّةٌ عَبْدٌ أَوْ أَمَةٌ ". فَقَالَ لاَ تَبْرَحْ حَتَّى تَجِيئَنِي بِالْمَخْرَجِ فِيمَا قُلْتَ.فَخَرَجْتُ فَوَجَدْتُ مُحَمَّدَ بْنَ مَسْلَمَةَ فَجِئْتُ بِهِ، فَشَهِدَ مَعِي أَنَّهُ سَمِعَ النَّبِيَّ صلى الله عليه وسلم يَقُولُ " فِيهِ غُرَّةٌ عَبْدٌ أَوْ أَمَةٌ ". تَابَعَهُ ابْنُ أَبِي الزِّنَادِ عَنْ أَبِيهِ عَنْ عُرْوَةَ عَنِ الْمُغِيرَةِ

Narrated Ziyad bin'Ilaqa: I heard Jarir bin 'Abdullah (Praising Allah). On the day when Al-Mughira bin Shu'ba died, he (Jarir) got up (on the pulpit) and thanked and praised Allah and said, "Be afraid of Allah alone Who has none along with Him to be worshipped.(You should) be calm and quiet till the (new) chief comes to you and he will come to you soon. Ask Allah's forgiveness for your (late) chief because he himself loved to forgive others." Jarir added, "Amma badu (now then), I went to the Prophet and said, 'I give my pledge of allegiance to you for Islam." The Prophet ﷺ conditioned (my pledge) for me to be sincere and true to every Muslim so I gave my pledge to him for this. By the Lord of this mosque! I am sincere and true to you (Muslims). Then Jarir asked for Allah's forgiveness and came down (from the pulpit). – Sahih Al-Bukhari 58
حَدَّثَنَا أَبُو النُّعْمَانِ، قَالَ حَدَّثَنَا أَبُو عَوَانَةَ، عَنْ زِيَادِ بْنِ عِلاَقَةَ، قَالَ سَمِعْتُ جَرِيرَ بْنَ عَبْدِ اللَّهِ، يَقُولُ يَوْمَ مَاتَ الْمُغِيرَةُ بْنُ شُعْبَةَ قَامَ فَحَمِدَ اللَّهَ وَأَثْنَى عَلَيْهِ وَقَالَ عَلَيْكُمْ بِاتِّقَاءِ اللَّهِ وَحْدَهُ لاَ شَرِيكَ لَهُ، وَالْوَقَارِ وَالسَّكِينَةِ حَتَّى يَأْتِيَكُمْ أَمِيرٌ، فَإِنَّمَا يَأْتِيكُمُ الآنَ، ثُمَّ قَالَ اسْتَعْفُوا لأَمِيرِكُمْ، فَإِنَّهُ كَانَ يُحِبُّ الْعَفْوَ. ثُمَّ قَالَ أَمَّا بَعْدُ، فَإِنِّي أَتَيْتُ النَّبِيَّ صلى الله عليه وسلم قُلْتُ أُبَايِعُكَ عَلَى الإِسْلاَمِ. فَشَرَطَ عَلَىَّ وَالنُّصْحِ لِكُلِّ مُسْلِمٍ. فَبَايَعْتُهُ عَلَى هَذَا، وَرَبِّ هَذَا الْمَسْجِدِ إِنِّي لَنَاصِحٌ لَكُمْ. ثُمَّ اسْتَغْفَرَ وَنَزَلَ.

Narrated Az-Zuhri: I heard `Urwa bin Az-Zubair talking to `Umar bin `Abdul `Aziz during the latter's Governorship (at Medina), he said, "Al-Mughira bin Shu`ba delayed the `Asr prayer when he was the ruler of Al-Kufa. On that, Abu Mas`ud. `Uqba bin `Amr Al-Ansari, the grand-father of Zaid bin Hasan, who was one of the Badr warriors, came in and said, (to Al-Mughira), 'You know that Gabriel came down and offered the prayer and Allah's Messenger ﷺ prayed five prescribed prayers, and Gabriel said (to the Prophet ﷺ), "I have been ordered to do so (i.e. offer these five prayers at these fixed stated hours of the day). – Sahih Al-Bukhari 4007
حَدَّثَنَا أَبُو الْيَمَانِ، أَخْبَرَنَا شُعَيْبٌ، عَنِ الزُّهْرِيِّ، سَمِعْتُ عُرْوَةَ بْنَ الزُّبَيْرِ، يُحَدِّثُ عُمَرَ بْنَ عَبْدِ الْعَزِيزِ فِي إِمَارَتِهِ أَخَّرَ الْمُغِيرَةُ بْنُ شُعْبَةَ الْعَصْرَ وَهْوَ أَمِيرُ الْكُوفَةِ، فَدَخَلَ أَبُو مَسْعُودٍ عُقْبَةُ بْنُ عَمْرٍو الأَنْصَارِيُّ جَدُّ زَيْدِ بْنِ حَسَنٍ شَهِدَ بَدْرًا فَقَالَ لَقَدْ عَلِمْتَ نَزَلَ جِبْرِيلُ فَصَلَّى فَصَلَّى رَسُولُ اللَّهِ صلى الله عليه وسلم خَمْسَ صَلَوَاتٍ ثُمَّ قَالَ هَكَذَا أُمِرْتَ. كَذَلِكَ كَانَ بَشِيرُ بْنُ أَبِي مَسْعُودٍ يُحَدِّثُ عَنْ أَبِيهِ

Narrated Al-Mughira bin Shu`ba: Nobody asked the Prophet ﷺ as many questions as I asked regarding Ad-Dajjal. The Prophet ﷺ said to me, "What worries you about him?" I said, "Because the people say that he will have a mountain of bread and a river of water with him (i.e. he will have abundance of food and water)" The Prophet ﷺ said, "Nay, he is too mean to

be allowed such a thing by Allah"' (but it is only to test mankind whether they believe in Allah or in Ad-Dajjal.). – Sahih Al-Bukhari 7122
حَدَّثَنَا مُسَدَّدٌ، حَدَّثَنَا يَحْيَى، حَدَّثَنَا إِسْمَاعِيلُ، حَدَّثَنِي قَيْسٌ، قَالَ قَالَ لِي الْمُغِيرَةُ بْنُ شُعْبَةَ مَا سَأَلَ أَحَدٌ النَّبِيَّ صلى الله عليه وسلم عَنِ الدَّجَّالِ مَا سَأَلْتُهُ وَإِنَّهُ قَالَ لِي " مَا يَضُرُّكَ مِنْهُ ". قُلْتُ لأَنَّهُمْ يَقُولُونَ إِنَّ مَعَهُ جَبَلَ خُبْزٍ وَنَهَرَ مَاءٍ. قَالَ " هُوَ أَهْوَنُ عَلَى اللَّهِ مِنْ ذَلِكَ ".

Narrated Al-Mughira bin Shu`ba: The Prophet ﷺ said, "Allah has forbidden for you, (1) to be undutiful to your mothers, (2) to bury your daughters alive, (3) to not to pay the rights of the others (e.g. charity, etc.) and (4) to beg of men (begging). And Allah has hated for you (1) vain, useless talk, or that you talk too much about others, (2) to ask too many questions, (in disputed religious matters) and (3) to waste the wealth (by extravagance). – Sahih Al-Bukhari 2408
حَدَّثَنَا عُثْمَانُ، حَدَّثَنَا جَرِيرٌ، عَنْ مَنْصُورٍ، عَنِ الشَّعْبِيِّ، عَنْ وَرَّادٍ، مَوْلَى الْمُغِيرَةِ بْنِ شُعْبَةَ عَنِ الْمُغِيرَةِ بْنِ شُعْبَةَ، قَالَ قَالَ النَّبِيُّ صلى الله عليه وسلم " إِنَّ اللَّهَ حَرَّمَ عَلَيْكُمْ عُقُوقَ الأُمَّهَاتِ، وَوَأْدَ الْبَنَاتِ، وَمَنَعَ وَهَاتِ، وَكَرِهَ لَكُمْ قِيلَ وَقَالَ، وَكَثْرَةَ السُّؤَالِ، وَإِضَاعَةَ الْمَالِ ".

Relative's of Muhammad ﷺ
أقارب محمد

That ⸢reward⸣ is the good news which Allah gives to His servants who believe and do good. Say, ⸢O Prophet,⸣ "I do not ask you for a reward for this ⸢message⸣—only honour for ⸢our⸣ kinship." Whoever earns a good deed, We will increase it in goodness for them. Surely Allah is All-Forgiving, Most Appreciative. – Surah Ash-Shura 42:23
ذَٰلِكَ ٱلَّذِى يُبَشِّرُ ٱللَّهُ عِبَادَهُ ٱلَّذِينَ ءَامَنُوا۟ وَعَمِلُوا۟ ٱلصَّٰلِحَٰتِ ۗ قُل لَّآ أَسْـَٔلُكُمْ عَلَيْهِ أَجْرًا إِلَّا ٱلْمَوَدَّةَ فِى ٱلْقُرْبَىٰ ۗ وَمَن يَقْتَرِفْ حَسَنَةً نَّزِدْ لَهُۥ فِيهَا حُسْنًا ۚ إِنَّ ٱللَّهَ غَفُورٌ شَكُورٌ

Narrated Isma`il: I asked Abi `Aufa, "Did you see Ibrahim, the son of the Prophet ﷺ?" He said, "Yes, but he died in his early childhood. Had there been a Prophet after Muhammad then his son would have lived, but there is no Prophet after him.". – Sahih Al-Bukhari 6194
حَدَّثَنَا ابْنُ نُمَيْرٍ، حَدَّثَنَا مُحَمَّدُ بْنُ بِشْرٍ، حَدَّثَنَا إِسْمَاعِيلُ، قُلْتُ لاِبْنِ أَبِي أَوْفَى رَأَيْتَ إِبْرَاهِيمَ ابْنَ النَّبِيِّ صلى الله عليه وسلم قَالَ مَاتَ صَغِيرًا، وَلَوْ قُضِيَ أَنْ يَكُونَ بَعْدَ مُحَمَّدٍ صلى الله عليه وسلم نَبِيٌّ عَاشَ ابْنُهُ، وَلَكِنْ لاَ نَبِيَّ بَعْدَهُ.

Narrated Abu `Aqil: That his grandfather. `Abdullah bin Hisham used to take him from the market or to the market (the narrator is in doubt) and used to buy grain and when Ibn Az-Zubair and Ibn `Umar met him, they would say to him, "Let us be your partners (in trading) as the Prophet ﷺ invoked for Allah's blessing upon you." He would then take them as partners and he would Sometimes gain a whole load carried by an animal which he would send home. – Sahih Al-Bukhari 6353
حَدَّثَنَا عَبْدُ اللَّهِ بْنُ يُوسُفَ، حَدَّثَنَا ابْنُ وَهْبٍ، حَدَّثَنَا سَعِيدُ بْنُ أَبِي أَيُّوبَ، عَنْ أَبِي عَقِيلٍ، أَنَّهُ كَانَ يَخْرُجُ بِهِ جَدُّهُ عَبْدُ اللَّهِ بْنُ هِشَامٍ مِنَ السُّوقِ أَوْ إِلَى السُّوقِ فَيَشْتَرِي الطَّعَامَ، فَيَلْقَاهُ ابْنُ الزُّبَيْرِ وَابْنُ عُمَرَ فَيَقُولاَنِ أَشْرِكْنَا فَإِنَّ النَّبِيَّ صلى الله عليه وسلم قَدْ دَعَا لَكَ بِالْبَرَكَةِ. فَرُبَّمَا أَصَابَ الرَّاحِلَةَ كَمَا هِيَ، فَيَبْعَثُ بِهَا إِلَى الْمَنْزِلِ.

Narrated Abu Humaid As-Saidi: The people said, "O Allah's Messenger How may we send Salat on you?" He said, ("Say: O Allah! Send Your Salat on Muhammad and his wives and his offspring as You sent Your Salat on the family of (Prophet) Ibrähim; and also send Your Blessing's on Mahammad and his wives and his offsprings as You sent Your Blessings on the family of Ibrahim, You are indeed the One Who deserves praises and glorifications.") "Say: Allahumma Salli 'ala- Muhammadin wa azwajihi wa dhurriyyatihi kama sal-laita 'ala `Ali Ibrahim; wa barik 'ala Muhammadin wa azwajihi wa dhurriyyatihi kamabarakta 'ala `Ali Ibrahim innaka hamidun majid.". – Sahih Al-Bukhari 6360
حَدَّثَنَا عَبْدُ اللَّهِ بْنُ مَسْلَمَةَ، عَنْ مَالِكٍ، عَنْ عَبْدِ اللَّهِ بْنِ أَبِي بَكْرٍ، عَنْ أَبِيهِ، عَنْ عَمْرِو بْنِ سُلَيْمٍ الزُّرَقِيِّ، قَالَ أَخْبَرَنِي أَبُو حُمَيْدٍ السَّاعِدِيُّ، أَنَّهُمْ قَالُوا يَا رَسُولَ اللَّهِ كَيْفَ نُصَلِّي عَلَيْكَ قَالَ " قُولُوا اللَّهُمَّ صَلِّ عَلَى مُحَمَّدٍ وَأَزْوَاجِهِ وَذُرِّيَّتِهِ، كَمَا صَلَّيْتَ عَلَى آلِ إِبْرَاهِيمَ، وَبَارِكْ عَلَى مُحَمَّدٍ وَأَزْوَاجِهِ وَذُرِّيَّتِهِ، كَمَا بَارَكْتَ عَلَى آلِ إِبْرَاهِيمَ، إِنَّكَ حَمِيدٌ مَجِيدٌ ".

Narrated Abu Huraira: Allah's Messenger ﷺ said, "O Allah! Give food to the family of Muhammad.". – Sahih Al-Bukhari 6460
حَدَّثَنَا عَبْدُ اللَّهِ بْنُ مُحَمَّدٍ، حَدَّثَنَا مُحَمَّدُ بْنُ فُضَيْلٍ، عَنْ أَبِيهِ، عَنْ عُمَارَةَ، عَنْ أَبِي زُرْعَةَ، عَنْ أَبِي هُرَيْرَةَ ـ رضى الله عنه ـ قَالَ قَالَ رَسُولُ اللَّهِ صلى الله عليه وسلم " اللَّهُمَّ ارْزُقْ آلَ مُحَمَّدٍ قُوتًا ".

Narrated `Aisha: Allah's Messenger ﷺ once entered upon me in a very happy mood, with his features glittering with joy, and said, "O `Aisha! Won't you see that Mujazziz (a Qa'if) looked just now at Zaid bin Haritha and Usama bin Zaid and said, 'These feet (of Usama and his father) belong to each other." (See Hadith No. 755, Vol. 4). – Sahih Al-Bukhari 6770

حَدَّثَنَا قُتَيْبَةُ بْنُ سَعِيدٍ، حَدَّثَنَا اللَّيْثُ، عَنِ ابْنِ شِهَابٍ، عَنْ عُرْوَةَ، عَنْ عَائِشَةَ ـ رضى الله عنها ـ قَالَتْ إِنَّ رَسُولَ اللَّهِ صلى الله عليه وسلم دَخَلَ عَلَىَّ مَسْرُورًا تَبْرُقُ أَسَارِيرُ وَجْهِهِ فَقَالَ " أَلَمْ تَرَىْ أَنَّ مُجَزِّزًا نَظَرَ آنِفًا إِلَى زَيْدِ بْنِ حَارِثَةَ وَأُسَامَةَ بْنِ زَيْدٍ، فَقَالَ إِنَّ هَذِهِ الأَقْدَامَ بَعْضُهَا مِنْ بَعْضٍ ".

Narrated `Aisha: The Quraish people became very worried about the Makhzumiya lady who had committed theft. They said, "Nobody can speak (in favor of the lady) to Allah's Messenger ﷺ and nobody dares do that except Usama who is the favorite of Allah's Messenger ﷺ." When Usama spoke to Allah's Messenger ﷺ about that matter, Allah's Messenger ﷺ said, "Do you intercede (with me) to violate one of the legal punishment of Allah?" Then he got up and addressed the people, saying, "O people! The nations before you went astray because if a noble person committed theft, they used to leave him, but if a weak person among them committed theft, they used to inflict the legal punishment on him. By Allah, if Fatima, the daughter of Muhammad committed theft, Muhammad will cut off her hand!". – Sahih Al-Bukhari 6788

حَدَّثَنَا سَعِيدُ بْنُ سُلَيْمَانَ، حَدَّثَنَا اللَّيْثُ، عَنِ ابْنِ شِهَابٍ، عَنْ عُرْوَةَ، عَنْ عَائِشَةَ ـ رضى الله عنها أَنَّ قُرَيْشًا، أَهَمَّتْهُمُ الْمَرْأَةُ الْمَخْزُومِيَّةُ الَّتِي سَرَقَتْ فَقَالُوا مَنْ يُكَلِّمُ رَسُولَ اللَّهِ صلى الله عليه وسلم وَمَنْ يَجْتَرِئُ عَلَيْهِ إِلاَّ أُسَامَةُ حِبُّ رَسُولِ اللَّهِ صلى الله عليه وسلم. فَكَلَّمَ رَسُولَ اللَّهِ صلى الله عليه وسلم فَقَالَ " أَتَشْفَعُ فِي حَدٍّ مِنْ حُدُودِ اللَّهِ ". ثُمَّ قَامَ فَخَطَبَ قَالَ " يَا أَيُّهَا النَّاسُ إِنَّمَا ضَلَّ مَنْ قَبْلَكُمْ أَنَّهُمْ كَانُوا إِذَا سَرَقَ الشَّرِيفُ تَرَكُوهُ، وَإِذَا سَرَقَ الضَّعِيفُ فِيهِمْ أَقَامُوا عَلَيْهِ الْحَدَّ، وَايْمُ اللَّهِ لَوْ أَنَّ فَاطِمَةَ بِنْتَ مُحَمَّدٍ سَرَقَتْ لَقَطَعَ مُحَمَّدٌ يَدَهَا "

Narrated `Abdur-Rahman bin `Abis: Ibn `Abbas was asked, "Did you offer the Id prayer with the Prophet?" He said, "Yes, had it not been for my close relation to the Prophet, I would not have performed it (with him) because of my being too young The Prophet ﷺ came to the mark which is near the home of Kathir bin As-Salt and offered the Id prayer and then delivered the sermon. I do not remember if any Adhan or Iqama were pronounced for the prayer. Then the Prophet ﷺ ordered (the women) to give alms, and they started stretching out their hands towards their ears and throats (giving their ornaments in charity), and the Prophet ﷺ ordered Bilal to go to them (to collect the alms), and then Bilal returned to the Prophet. – Sahih Al-Bukhari 7325

حَدَّثَنَا مُحَمَّدُ بْنُ كَثِيرٍ، أَخْبَرَنَا سُفْيَانُ، عَنْ عَبْدِ الرَّحْمَنِ بْنِ عَابِسٍ، قَالَ سُئِلَ ابْنُ عَبَّاسٍ أَشَهِدْتَ الْعِيدَ مَعَ النَّبِيِّ صلى الله عليه وسلم قَالَ نَعَمْ وَلَوْلاَ مَنْزِلَتِي مِنْهُ مَا شَهِدْتُهُ مِنَ الصِّغَرِ، فَأَتَى الْعَلَمَ الَّذِي عِنْدَ دَارِ كَثِيرِ بْنِ الصَّلْتِ فَصَلَّى ثُمَّ خَطَبَ، وَلَمْ يَذْكُرْ أَذَانًا وَلاَ إِقَامَةً، ثُمَّ أَمَرَ بِالصَّدَقَةِ فَجَعَلَ النِّسَاءُ يُشِرْنَ إِلَى آذَانِهِنَّ وَحُلُوقِهِنَّ، فَأَمَرَ بِلاَلاً فَأَتَاهُنَّ، ثُمَّ رَجَعَ إِلَى النَّبِيِّ صلى الله عليه وسلم.

Narrated `Aisha: When the Prophet ﷺ got the news of the death of Ibn Haritha, Ja`far and Ibn Rawaha he sat down and looked sad and I was looking at him through the chink of the door. A man came and told him about the crying of the women of Ja`far. The Prophet ﷺ ordered him to forbid them. The man went and came back saying that he had told them but they did not listen to him. The Prophet ﷺ said, "Forbid them." So again he went and came back for the third time and said, "O Allah's Messenger ﷺ! By Allah, they did not listen to us at all." (`Aisha added): Allah's Messenger ﷺ ordered him to go and put dust in their mouths. I said, (to that man) "May Allah stick your nose in the dust (i.e. humiliate you)! You could neither (persuade the women to) fulfill the order of Allah's Messenger ﷺ nor did you relieve Allah's Messenger ﷺ from fatigue." – Sahih Al-Bukhari 1299

حَدَّثَنَا مُحَمَّدُ بْنُ الْمُثَنَّى، حَدَّثَنَا عَبْدُ الْوَهَّابِ، قَالَ سَمِعْتُ يَحْيَى، قَالَ أَخْبَرَتْنِي عَمْرَةُ، قَالَتْ سَمِعْتُ عَائِشَةَ ـ رضى الله عنها ـ قَالَتْ لَمَّا جَاءَ النَّبِيَّ صلى الله عليه وسلم قَتْلُ ابْنِ حَارِثَةَ وَجَعْفَرٍ وَابْنِ رَوَاحَةَ جَلَسَ يُعْرَفُ فِيهِ الْحُزْنُ، وَأَنَا أَنْظُرُ مِنْ

صَائِرِ الْبَابِ ـ شَقِّ الْبَابِ ـ فَأَتَاهُ رَجُلٌ، فَقَالَ إِنَّ نِسَاءَ جَعْفَرٍ، وَذَكَرَ بُكَاءَهُنَّ، فَأَمَرَهُ أَنْ يَنْهَاهُنَّ، فَذَهَبَ ثُمَّ أَتَاهُ الثَّانِيَةَ، لَمْ يُطِعْنَهُ فَقَالَ انْهَهُنَّ. فَأَتَاهُ الثَّالِثَةَ قَالَ وَاللَّهِ غَلَبْنَنَا يَا رَسُولَ اللَّهِ فَزَعَمَتْ أَنَّهُ قَالَ " فَاحْثُ فِي أَفْوَاهِهِنَّ التُّرَابَ ". فَقُلْتُ أَرْغَمَ اللَّهُ أَنْفَكَ، لَمْ تَفْعَلْ مَا أَمَرَكَ رَسُولُ اللَّهِ صلى الله عليه وسلم وَلَمْ تَتْرُكْ رَسُولَ اللَّهِ صلى الله عليه وسلم مِنَ الْعَنَاءِ.

Narrated Abu Huraira: Dates used to be brought to Allah's Messenger ﷺ immediately after being plucked. Different persons would bring their dates till a big heap collected (in front of the Prophet). Once Al-Hasan and Al-Husain were playing with these dates. One of them took a date and put it in his mouth. Allah's Messenger ﷺ looked at him and took it out from his mouth and said, "Don't you know that Muhammad's offspring do not eat what is given in charity?". – Sahih Al-Bukhari 1485

حَدَّثَنَا عُمَرُ بْنُ مُحَمَّدِ بْنِ الْحَسَنِ الأَسَدِيُّ، حَدَّثَنَا أَبِي، حَدَّثَنَا إِبْرَاهِيمُ بْنُ طَهْمَانَ، عَنْ مُحَمَّدِ بْنِ زِيَادٍ، عَنْ أَبِي هُرَيْرَةَ ـ رضى الله عنه ـ قَالَ كَانَ رَسُولُ اللَّهِ صلى الله عليه وسلم يُؤْتَى بِالتَّمْرِ عِنْدَ صِرَامِ النَّخْلِ فَيَجِيءُ هَذَا بِتَمْرِهِ وَهَذَا مِنْ تَمْرِهِ حَتَّى يَصِيرَ عِنْدَهُ كَوْمًا مِنْ تَمْرٍ، فَجَعَلَ الْحَسَنُ وَالْحُسَيْنُ ـ رضى الله عنهما ـ يَلْعَبَانِ بِذَلِكَ التَّمْرِ، فَأَخَذَ أَحَدُهُمَا تَمْرَةً، فَجَعَلَهَا فِي فِيهِ، فَنَظَرَ إِلَيْهِ رَسُولُ اللَّهِ صلى الله عليه وسلم فَأَخْرَجَهَا مِنْ فِيهِ فَقَالَ " أَمَا عَلِمْتَ أَنَّ آلَ مُحَمَّدٍ صلى الله عليه وسلم لاَ يَأْكُلُونَ الصَّدَقَةَ ".

Narrated Anas: Whenever drought threatened them, `Umar bin Al-Khattab, used to ask Al-Abbas bin `Abdul Muttalib to invoke Allah for rain. He used to say, "O Allah! We used to ask our Prophet to invoke You for rain, and You would bless us with rain, and now we ask his uncle to invoke You for rain. O Allah ! Bless us with rain."(1) And so it would rain. – Sahih Al-Bukhari 1010

حَدَّثَنَا الْحَسَنُ بْنُ مُحَمَّدٍ، قَالَ حَدَّثَنَا مُحَمَّدُ بْنُ عَبْدِ اللَّهِ الأَنْصَارِيُّ، قَالَ حَدَّثَنِي أَبِي عَبْدُ اللَّهِ بْنُ الْمُثَنَّى، عَنْ ثُمَامَةَ بْنِ عَبْدِ اللَّهِ بْنِ أَنَسٍ، عَنْ أَنَسٍ، أَنَّ عُمَرَ بْنَ الْخَطَّابِ ـ رضى الله عنه ـ كَانَ إِذَا قَحَطُوا اسْتَسْقَى بِالْعَبَّاسِ بْنِ عَبْدِ الْمُطَّلِبِ فَقَالَ اللَّهُمَّ إِنَّا كُنَّا نَتَوَسَّلُ إِلَيْكَ بِنَبِيِّنَا فَتَسْقِينَا وَإِنَّا نَتَوَسَّلُ إِلَيْكَ بِعَمِّ نَبِيِّنَا فَاسْقِنَا. قَالَ فَيُسْقَوْنَ.

Narrated `Umar: The properties of Bani An-Nadir which Allah had transferred to His Apostle as Fai Booty were not gained by the Muslims with their horses and camels. The properties therefore, belonged especially to Allah's Messenger ﷺ who used to give his family their yearly expenditure and spend what remained thereof on arms and horses to be used in Allah's Cause. – Sahih Al-Bukhari 2904

حَدَّثَنَا عَلِيُّ بْنُ عَبْدِ اللَّهِ، حَدَّثَنَا سُفْيَانُ، عَنْ عَمْرٍو، عَنِ الزُّهْرِيِّ، عَنْ مَالِكِ بْنِ أَوْسِ بْنِ الْحَدَثَانِ، عَنْ عُمَرَ ـ رضى الله عنه ـ قَالَ كَانَتْ أَمْوَالُ بَنِي النَّضِيرِ مِمَّا أَفَاءَ اللَّهُ عَلَى رَسُولِهِ صلى الله عليه وسلم مِمَّا لَمْ يُوجِفِ الْمُسْلِمُونَ عَلَيْهِ بِخَيْلٍ وَلاَ رِكَابٍ، فَكَانَتْ لِرَسُولِ اللَّهِ صلى الله عليه وسلم خَاصَّةً، وَكَانَ يُنْفِقُ عَلَى أَهْلِهِ نَفَقَةَ سَنَتِهِ، ثُمَّ يَجْعَلُ مَا بَقِيَ فِي السِّلاَحِ وَالْكُرَاعِ، عُدَّةً فِي سَبِيلِ اللَّهِ.

Narrated Jubair bin Mut`im: I and `Uthman bin `Affan went to Allah's Messenger ﷺ and said, "O Allah's Messenger ﷺ! You have given to Bani Al-Muttalib and left us although they and we are of the same kinship to you." Allah's Messenger ﷺ said, "Bani Muttalib and Bani Hashim are one and the same." The Prophet ﷺ did not give a share to Bani `Abd Shams and Bani Naufai. (Ibn 'Is-haq said, "Abd Shams and Hashim and Al-Muttalib were maternal brothers and their mother was 'Atika bint Murra and Naufal was their paternal brother.). – Sahih Al-Bukhari 3140

حَدَّثَنَا عَبْدُ اللَّهِ بْنُ يُوسُفَ، حَدَّثَنَا اللَّيْثُ، عَنْ عُقَيْلٍ، عَنِ ابْنِ شِهَابٍ، عَنِ ابْنِ الْمُسَيَّبِ، عَنْ جُبَيْرِ بْنِ مُطْعِمٍ، قَالَ مَشَيْتُ أَنَا وَعُثْمَانُ بْنُ عَفَّانَ، إِلَى رَسُولِ اللَّهِ صلى الله عليه وسلم فَقُلْنَا يَا رَسُولَ اللَّهِ، أَعْطَيْتَ بَنِي الْمُطَّلِبِ وَتَرَكْتَنَا، وَنَحْنُ وَهُمْ مِنْكَ بِمَنْزِلَةٍ وَاحِدَةٍ. فَقَالَ رَسُولُ اللَّهِ صلى الله عليه وسلم " إِنَّمَا بَنُو الْمُطَّلِبِ وَبَنُو هَاشِمٍ شَىْءٌ وَاحِدٌ ". قَالَ اللَّيْثُ حَدَّثَنِي يُونُسُ وَزَادَ قَالَ جُبَيْرٌ وَلَمْ يَقْسِمِ النَّبِيُّ صلى الله عليه وسلم لِبَنِي عَبْدِ شَمْسٍ وَلاَ لِبَنِي نَوْفَلٍ. وَقَالَ ابْنُ إِسْحَاقَ عَبْدُ شَمْسٍ وَهَاشِمٌ وَالْمُطَّلِبُ إِخْوَةٌ لأُمٍّ، وَأُمُّهُمْ عَاتِكَةُ بِنْتُ مُرَّةَ، وَكَانَ نَوْفَلٌ أَخَاهُمْ لأَبِيهِمْ.

Narrated Ibn `Abbas: The first event of Qasama in the pre-Islamic period of ignorance was practiced by us (i.e. Banu Hashim). A man from Banu Hashim was employed by a Quraishi man from another branch-family. The (Hashimi) laborer set out with the Quraishi driving his camels. There passed by him another man from Banu Hashim. The leather rope of the latter's bag had broken so he said to the laborer, "Will you help me by giving me a rope in order to tie the handle of my bag lest the camels should run away from me?" The laborer gave him a rope and the latter tied his bag with it. When the caravan halted, all the camels' legs were tied with their fetters except one camel. The employer asked the laborer, "Why, from among all the camels has this camel not been fettered?" He replied, "There is no fetter for it." The Quraishi asked, "Where is its fetter?" and hit the laborer with a stick that caused his death (later on Just before his death) a man from Yemen passed by him. The laborer asked (him), "Will you go for the pilgrimage?" He replied, "I do not think I will attend it, but perhaps I will attend it." The (Hashimi) laborer said, "Will you please convey a message for me once in your life?" The other man said, "yes." The laborer wrote: 'When you attend the pilgrimage, call the family of Quraish, and if they respond to you, call the family of Banu Hashim, and if they respond to you, ask about Abu Talib and tell him that so-and-so has killed me for a fetter." Then the laborer expired. When the employer reached (Mecca), Abu Talib visited him and asked, "What has happened to our companion?" He said, "He became ill and I looked after him nicely (but he died) and I buried him." Then Abu Talib said, "The deceased deserved this from you." After some time, the messenger whom the laborer has asked to convey the message, reached during the pilgrimage season. He called, "O the family of Quraish!" The people replied, "This is Quraish." Then he called, "O the family of Banu Hashim!" Again the people replied, "This is Banu Hashim." He asked, "Who is Abu Talib?" The people replied, "This is Abu Talib." He said, "'So-and-so has asked me to convey a message to you that so-and-so has killed him for a fetter (of a camel)." Then Abu Talib went to the (Quraishi) killer and said to him, "Choose one of three alternatives: (i) If you wish, give us one-hundred camels because you have murdered our companion, (ii) or if you wish, fifty of your men should take an oath that you have not murdered our companion, and if you do not accept this, (iii) we will kill you in Qisas." The killer went to his people and they said, "We will take an oath." Then a woman from Banu Hashim who was married to one of them (i.e.the Quraishis) and had given birth to a child from him, came to Abu Talib and said, "O Abu Talib! I wish that my son from among the fifty men, should be excused from this oath, and that he should not take the oath where the oathtaking is carried on." Abu Talib excused him. Then another man from them came (to Abu Talib) and said, "O Abu Talib! You want fifty persons to take an oath instead of giving a hundred camels, and that means each man has to give two camels (in case he does not take an oath). So there are two camels I would like you to accept from me and excuse me from taking an oath where the oaths are taken. Abu Talib accepted them from him. Then 48 men came and took the oath. Ibn `Abbas further said:) By Him in Whose Hand my life is, before the end of that year, none of those 48 persons remained alive.
– Sahih Al-Bukhari 3845

حَدَّثَنَا أَبُو مَعْمَرٍ، حَدَّثَنَا عَبْدُ الْوَارِثِ، حَدَّثَنَا قَطَنٌ أَبُو الْهَيْثَمِ، حَدَّثَنَا أَبُو يَزِيدَ الْمَدَنِيُّ، عَنْ عِكْرِمَةَ، عَنِ ابْنِ عَبَّاسٍ ـ رضى الله عنهما ـ قَالَ إِنَّ أَوَّلَ قَسَامَةٍ كَانَتْ فِي الْجَاهِلِيَّةِ لَفِينَا بَنِي هَاشِمٍ، كَانَ رَجُلٌ مِنْ بَنِي هَاشِمٍ اسْتَأْجَرَهُ رَجُلٌ مِنْ قُرَيْشٍ مِنْ فَخِذٍ أُخْرَى، فَانْطَلَقَ مَعَهُ فِي إِبِلِهِ، فَمَرَّ رَجُلٌ بِهِ مِنْ بَنِي هَاشِمٍ قَدِ انْقَطَعَتْ عُرْوَةُ جُوَالِقِهِ فَقَالَ أَغِثْنِي بِعِقَالٍ أَشُدُّ بِهِ عُرْوَةَ جُوَالِقِي، لاَ تَنْفِرُ الإِبِلُ. فَأَعْطَاهُ عِقَالاً، فَشَدَّ بِهِ عُرْوَةَ جُوَالِقِهِ، فَلَمَّا نَزَلُوا عُقِلَتِ الإِبِلُ إِلاَّ بَعِيرًا وَاحِدًا، فَقَالَ الَّذِي اسْتَأْجَرَهُ مَا شَأْنُ هَذَا الْبَعِيرِ لَمْ يُعْقَلْ مِنْ بَيْنِ الإِبِلِ قَالَ لَيْسَ لَهُ عِقَالٌ. قَالَ فَأَيْنَ عِقَالُهُ قَالَ فَحَذَفَهُ بِعَصًا كَانَ فِيهَا أَجَلُهُ، فَمَرَّ بِهِ رَجُلٌ مِنْ أَهْلِ الْيَمَنِ، فَقَالَ أَتَشْهَدُ الْمَوْسِمَ قَالَ مَا أَشْهَدُ، وَرُبَّمَا شَهِدْتُهُ. قَالَ هَلْ أَنْتَ مُبْلِغٌ عَنِّي رِسَالَةً مَرَّةً مِنَ الدَّهْرِ قَالَ نَعَمْ. قَالَ فَكُنْتَ إِذَا أَنْتَ شَهِدْتَ الْمَوْسِمَ فَنَادِ يَا آلَ قُرَيْشٍ. فَإِذَا أَجَابُوكَ، فَنَادِ يَا آلَ بَنِي هَاشِمٍ. فَإِنْ أَجَابُوكَ فَسَلْ عَنْ أَبِي طَالِبٍ، فَأَخْبِرْهُ أَنَّ فُلاَنًا قَتَلَنِي فِي عِقَالٍ، وَمَاتَ الْمُسْتَأْجَرُ، فَلَمَّا قَدِمَ الَّذِي اسْتَأْجَرَهُ أَتَاهُ أَبُو طَالِبٍ فَقَالَ مَا فَعَلَ صَاحِبُنَا قَالَ مَرِضَ،

فَأَحْسَنْتُ الْقِيَامَ عَلَيْهِ، فَوَلِيتُ دَفْنَهُ. قَالَ قَدْ كَانَ أَهْلَ ذَاكَ مِنْكَ. فَمَكُثَ حِينًا، ثُمَّ إِنَّ الرَّجُلَ الَّذِي أَوْصَى إِلَيْهِ أَنْ يُبْلِغَ عَنْهُ وَافَى الْمَوْسِمَ فَقَالَ يَا آلَ قُرَيْشٍ. قَالُوا هَذِهِ قُرَيْشٌ. قَالَ يَا آلَ بَنِي هَاشِمٍ. قَالُوا هَذِهِ بَنُو هَاشِمٍ. قَالَ أَيْنَ أَبُو طَالِبٍ قَالُوا هَذَا أَبُو طَالِبٍ. قَالَ أَمَرَنِي فُلاَنٌ أَنْ أُبْلِغَكَ رِسَالَةً أَنَّ فُلاَنًا قَتَلَهُ فِي عِقَالٍ. فَأَتَاهُ أَبُو طَالِبٍ فَقَالَ لَهُ اخْتَرْ مِنَّا إِحْدَى ثَلاَثٍ، إِنْ شِئْتَ أَنْ تُؤَدِّيَ مِائَةً مِنَ الإِبِلِ، فَإِنَّكَ قَتَلْتَ صَاحِبَنَا، وَإِنْ شِئْتَ حَلَفَ خَمْسُونَ مِنْ قَوْمِكَ أَنَّكَ لَمْ تَقْتُلْهُ، فَإِنْ أَبَيْتَ قَتَلْنَاكَ بِهِ فَأَتَى قَوْمَهُ، فَقَالُوا نَحْلِفُ. فَأَتَتْهُ امْرَأَةٌ مِنْ بَنِي هَاشِمٍ كَانَتْ تَحْتَ رَجُلٍ مِنْهُمْ قَدْ وَلَدَتْ لَهُ. فَقَالَتْ يَا أَبَا طَالِبٍ أُحِبُّ أَنْ تُجِيزَ ابْنِي هَذَا بِرَجُلٍ مِنَ الْخَمْسِينَ وَلاَ تُصْبِرْ يَمِينَهُ حَيْثُ تُصْبَرُ الأَيْمَانُ. فَفَعَلَ فَأَتَاهُ رَجُلٌ مِنْهُمْ فَقَالَ يَا أَبَا طَالِبٍ، أَرَدْتَ خَمْسِينَ رَجُلاً أَنْ يَحْلِفُوا مَكَانَ مِائَةٍ مِنَ الإِبِلِ، يُصِيبُ كُلَّ رَجُلٍ بَعِيرَانِ، هَذَانِ بَعِيرَانِ فَاقْبَلْهُمَا عَنِّي وَلاَ تُصْبِرْ يَمِينِي حَيْثُ تُصْبَرُ الأَيْمَانُ. فَقَبِلَهُمَا، وَجَاءَ ثَمَانِيَةٌ وَأَرْبَعُونَ فَحَلَفُوا. قَالَ ابْنُ عَبَّاسٍ فَوَالَّذِي نَفْسِي بِيَدِهِ، مَا حَالَ الْحَوْلُ وَمِنَ الثَّمَانِيَةِ وَأَرْبَعِينَ عَيْنٌ تَطْرِفُ.

Narrated Ibn `Umar: Abu Bakr used to say, "Look after Muhammad ﷺ in (looking after) his family.". – Sahih Al-Bukhari 3751

حَدَّثَنِي يَحْيَى بْنُ مَعِينٍ، وَصَدَقَةُ، قَالاَ أَخْبَرَنَا مُحَمَّدُ بْنُ جَعْفَرٍ، عَنْ شُعْبَةَ، عَنْ وَاقِدِ بْنِ مُحَمَّدٍ، عَنْ أَبِيهِ، عَنِ ابْنِ عُمَرَ ـ رضى الله عنهما ـ قَالَ قَالَ أَبُو بَكْرٍ ارْقُبُوا مُحَمَّدًا صلى الله عليه وسلم فِي أَهْلِ بَيْتِهِ

Abu Bakr: Look at Muhammad through his family . – Sahih Al-Bukhari 3713

أَخْبَرَنِي عَبْدُ اللَّهِ بْنُ عَبْدِ الْوَهَّابِ، حَدَّثَنَا خَالِدٌ، حَدَّثَنَا شُعْبَةُ، عَنْ وَاقِدٍ، قَالَ سَمِعْتُ أَبِي يُحَدِّثُ، عَنِ ابْنِ عُمَرَ، عَنْ أَبِي بَكْرٍ ـ رضى الله عنهم ـ قَالَ ارْقُبُوا مُحَمَّدًا صلى الله عليه وسلم فِي أَهْلِ بَيْتِهِ

Narrated `Urwa bin Az-Zubair: `Abdullah bin Az-Zubair went with some women of the tribe of Bani Zuhra to `Aisha who used to treat them nicely because of their relation to Allah's Messenger. – Sahih Al-Bukhari 3503

وَقَالَ اللَّيْثُ حَدَّثَنِي أَبُو الأَسْوَدِ، مُحَمَّدٌ عَنْ عُرْوَةَ بْنِ الزُّبَيْرِ، قَالَ ذَهَبَ عَبْدُ اللَّهِ بْنُ الزُّبَيْرِ مَعَ أُنَاسٍ مِنْ بَنِي زُهْرَةَ إِلَى عَائِشَةَ، وَكَانَتْ أَرَقَّ شَىْءٍ لِقَرَابَتِهِمْ مِنْ رَسُولِ اللَّهِ صلى الله عليه وسلم.

Narrated Malik bin Aus Al-Hadathan An-Nasri: That once `Umar bin Al-Khattab called him and while he was sitting with him, his gatekeeper, Yarfa came and said, "Will you admit `Uthman, `Abdur-Rahman bin `Auf, AzZubair and Sa`d (bin Abi Waqqas) who are waiting for your permission?" `Umar said, "Yes, let them come in." After a while, Yarfa- came again and said, "Will you admit `Ali and `Abbas who are asking your permission?" `Umar said, "Yes." So, when the two entered, `Abbas said, "O chief of the believers! Judge between me and this (i.e. `Ali). "Both of them had a dispute regarding the property of Bani An-Nadir which Allah had given to His Apostle as Fai (i.e. booty gained without fighting), `Ali and `Abbas started reproaching each other. The (present) people (i.e. `Uthman and his companions) said, "O chief of the believers! Give your verdict in their case and relieve each from) the other." `Umar said, "Wait I beseech you, by Allah, by Whose Permission both the heaven and the earth stand fast! Do you know that Allah's Messenger ﷺ said, 'We (Prophets) our properties are not to be inherited, and whatever we leave, is to be spent in charity,' and he said it about himself?" They (i.e. `Uthman and his company) said, "He did say it. "`Umar then turned towards `Ali and `Abbas and said, "I beseech you both, by Allah! Do you know that Allah's Messenger ﷺ said this?" They replied in the affirmative. He said, "Now I am talking to you about this matter. Allah the Glorified favored His Apostle with something of this Fai (i.e. booty won without fighting) which He did not give to anybody else. Allah said:-- "And what Allah gave to His Apostle ("Fai"" Booty) from them—For which you made no expedition With either Calvary or camelry. But Allah gives power to His Apostles Over whomsoever He will And Allah is able to do all things." (59.6) So this property was especially granted to Allah's Messenger ﷺ. But by Allah, the Prophet ﷺ neither took it all for himself only, nor deprived you of it, but he gave it to all of you and distributed it amongst you till only this remained out of it. And from this

Allah's Messenger ﷺ used to spend the yearly maintenance for his family, and whatever used to remain, he used to spend it where Allah's Property is spent (i.e. in charity), Allah's Messenger ﷺ kept on acting like that during all his life, Then he died, and Abu Bakr said, 'I am the successor of Allah's Messenger ﷺ. So he (i.e. Abu Bakr) took charge of this property and disposed of it in the same manner as Allah's Messenger ﷺ used to do, and all of you (at that time) knew all about it." Then `Umar turned towards `Ali and `Abbas and said, "You both remember that Abu Bakr disposed of it in the way you have described and Allah knows that, in that matter, he was sincere, pious, rightly guided and the follower of the right. Then Allah caused Abu Bakr to die and I said, 'I am the successor of Allah's Messenger ﷺ and Abu Bakr.' So I kept this property in my possession for the first two years of my rule (i.e. Caliphate and I used to dispose of it in the same wa as Allah's Messenger ﷺ and Abu Bakr used to do; and Allah knows that I have been sincere, pious, rightly guided an the follower of the right (in this matte Later on both of you (i.e. `Ali and `Abbas) came to me, and the claim of you both was one and the same, O `Abbas! You also came to me. So I told you both that Allah's Messenger ﷺ said, "Our property is not inherited, but whatever we leave is to be given in charity.' Then when I thought that I should better hand over this property to you both or the condition that you will promise and pledge before Allah that you will dispose it off in the same way as Allah's Messenger ﷺ and Abu Bakr did and as I have done since the beginning of my caliphate or else you should not speak to me (about it).' So, both of you said to me, 'Hand it over to us on this condition.' And on this condition I handed it over to you. Do you want me now to give a decision other than that (decision)? By Allah, with Whose Permission both the sky and the earth stand fast, I will never give any decision other than that (decision) till the Last Hour is established. But if you are unable to manage it (i.e. that property), then return it to me, and I will manage on your behalf." The sub-narrator said, "I told `Urwa bin Az-Zubair of this Hadith and he said, 'Malik bin Aus has told the truth" I heard `Aisha, the wife of the Prophet ﷺ saying, 'The wives of the Prophet ﷺ sent `Uthman to Abu Bakr demanding from him their 1/8 of the Fai which Allah had granted to his Apostle. But I used to oppose them and say to them: Will you not fear Allah? Don't you know that the Prophet used to say: Our property is not inherited, but whatever we leave is to be given in charity? The Prophet ﷺ mentioned that regarding himself. He added: 'The family of Muhammad can take their sustenance from this property. So the wives of the Prophet ﷺ stopped demanding it when I told them of that.' So, this property (of Sadaqa) was in the hands of `Ali who withheld it from `Abbas and overpowered him. Then it came in the hands of Hasan bin `Ali, then in the hands of Husain bin `Ali, and then in the hands of `Ali bin Husain and Hasan bin Hasan, and each of the last two used to manage it in turn, then it came in the hands of Zaid bin Hasan, and it was truly the Sadaqa of Allah's Apostle .". – Sahih Al-Bukhari 4033, 4034

حَدَّثَنَا أَبُو الْيَمَانِ، أَخْبَرَنَا شُعَيْبٌ، عَنِ الزُّهْرِيِّ، قَالَ أَخْبَرَنِي مَالِكُ بْنُ أَوْسِ بْنِ الْحَدَثَانِ النَّصْرِيُّ، أَنَّ عُمَرَ بْنَ الْخَطَّابِ ـ رضى الله عنه ـ دَعَاهُ إِذْ جَاءَهُ حَاجِبُهُ يَرْفَا فَقَالَ هَلْ لَكَ فِي عُثْمَانَ، وَعَبْدِ الرَّحْمَنِ، وَالزُّبَيْرِ وَسَعْدٍ يَسْتَأْذِنُونَ فَقَالَ نَعَمْ، فَأَدْخِلْهُمْ. فَلَبِثَ قَلِيلاً، ثُمَّ جَاءَ فَقَالَ هَلْ لَكَ فِي عَبَّاسٍ وَعَلِيٍّ يَسْتَأْذِنَانِ قَالَ نَعَمْ. فَلَمَّا دَخَلاَ قَالَ عَبَّاسٌ يَا أَمِيرَ الْمُؤْمِنِينَ، اقْضِ بَيْنِي وَبَيْنَ هَذَا، وَهُمَا يَخْتَصِمَانِ فِي الَّذِي أَفَاءَ اللَّهُ عَلَى رَسُولِهِ صلى الله عليه وسلم مِنْ بَنِي النَّضِيرِ، فَاسْتَبَّ عَلِيٌّ وَعَبَّاسٌ، فَقَالَ الرَّهْطُ يَا أَمِيرَ الْمُؤْمِنِينَ، اقْضِ بَيْنَهُمَا وَأَرِحْ أَحَدَهُمَا مِنَ الآخَرِ. فَقَالَ عُمَرُ اتَّئِدُوا، أَنْشُدُكُمْ بِاللَّهِ الَّذِي بِإِذْنِهِ تَقُومُ السَّمَاءُ وَالأَرْضُ، هَلْ تَعْلَمُونَ أَنَّ رَسُولَ اللَّهِ صلى الله عليه وسلم قَالَ " لاَ نُورَثُ، مَا تَرَكْنَا صَدَقَةٌ ". يُرِيدُ بِذَلِكَ نَفْسَهُ. قَالُوا قَدْ قَالَ ذَلِكَ. فَأَقْبَلَ عُمَرُ عَلَى عَبَّاسٍ وَعَلِيٍّ فَقَالَ أَنْشُدُكُمَا بِاللَّهِ هَلْ تَعْلَمَانِ أَنَّ رَسُولَ اللَّهِ صلى الله عليه وسلم قَدْ قَالَ ذَلِكَ قَالاَ نَعَمْ. قَالَ فَإِنِّي أُحَدِّثُكُمْ عَنْ هَذَا الأَمْرِ، إِنَّ اللَّهَ سُبْحَانَهُ كَانَ خَصَّ رَسُولَهُ صلى الله عليه وسلم فِي هَذَا الْفَىْءِ بِشَىْءٍ لَمْ يُعْطِهِ أَحَدًا غَيْرَهُ فَقَالَ جَلَّ ذِكْرُهُ {وَمَا أَفَاءَ اللَّهُ عَلَى رَسُولِهِ مِنْهُمْ فَمَا أَوْجَفْتُمْ عَلَيْهِ مِنْ خَيْلٍ وَلاَ رِكَابٍ} إِلَى قَوْلِهِ {قَدِيرٌ} فَكَانَتْ هَذِهِ خَالِصَةً لِرَسُولِ اللَّهِ صلى الله عليه وسلم، ثُمَّ وَاللَّهِ مَا احْتَازَهَا دُونَكُمْ، وَلاَ اسْتَأْثَرَهَا عَلَيْكُمْ، لَقَدْ أَعْطَاكُمُوهَا وَقَسَمَهَا فِيكُمْ، حَتَّى بَقِيَ هَذَا الْمَالُ مِنْهَا، فَكَانَ رَسُولُ اللَّهِ صلى الله عليه وسلم يُنْفِقُ عَلَى أَهْلِهِ نَفَقَةَ سَنَتِهِمْ مِنْ هَذَا الْمَالِ، ثُمَّ يَأْخُذُ مَا بَقِيَ فَيَجْعَلُهُ مَجْعَلَ مَالِ اللَّهِ، فَعَمِلَ ذَلِكَ رَسُولُ اللَّهِ صلى الله عليه وسلم حَيَاتَهُ، ثُمَّ تُوُفِّيَ النَّبِيُّ صلى الله عليه وسلم فَقَالَ أَبُو بَكْرٍ فَأَنَا وَلِيُّ رَسُولِ اللَّهِ صلى الله عليه وسلم. فَقَبَضَهُ أَبُو بَكْرٍ، فَعَمِلَ فِيهِ بِمَا عَمِلَ بِهِ رَسُولُ اللَّهِ صلى الله عليه وسلم وَأَنْتُمْ حِينَئِذٍ. فَأَقْبَلَ عَلَى عَلِيٍّ وَعَبَّاسٍ وَقَالَ تَذْكُرَانِ أَنَّ أَبَا بَكْرٍ عَمِلَ فِيهِ كَمَا تَقُولاَنِ، وَاللَّهُ يَعْلَمُ إِنَّهُ فِيهِ لَصَادِقٌ بَارٌّ رَاشِدٌ تَابِعٌ لِلْحَقِّ ثُمَّ تَوَفَّى اللَّهُ أَبَا بَكْرٍ فَقُلْتُ أَنَا وَلِيُّ رَسُولِ اللَّهِ صلى الله عليه وسلم وَأَبِي بَكْرٍ. فَقَبَضْتُهُ سَنَتَيْنِ مِنْ إِمَارَتِي أَعْمَلُ فِيهِ بِمَا عَمِلَ رَسُولُ اللَّهِ صلى الله عليه وسلم وَأَبُو بَكْرٍ،

وَاللَّهُ يَعْلَمُ أَنِّي فِيهِ صَادِقٌ بَارٌّ رَاشِدٌ تَابِعٌ لِلْحَقِّ، ثُمَّ جِئْتُمَانِي كِلاَكُمَا وَكَلِمَتُكُمَا وَاحِدَةٌ وَأَمْرُكُمَا جَمِيعٌ، فَجِئْتَنِي - يَعْنِي عَبَّاسًا - فَقُلْتُ لَكُمَا إِنَّ رَسُولَ اللَّهِ صلى الله عليه وسلم قَالَ " لاَ نُورَثُ، مَا تَرَكْنَا صَدَقَةٌ ". فَلَمَّا بَدَا لِي أَنْ أَدْفَعَهُ إِلَيْكُمَا قُلْتُ إِنْ شِئْتُمَا دَفَعْتُهُ إِلَيْكُمَا عَلَى أَنَّ عَلَيْكُمَا عَهْدَ اللَّهِ وَمِيثَاقَهُ لَتَعْمَلاَنِ فِيهِ بِمَا عَمِلَ فِيهِ رَسُولُ اللَّهِ صلى الله عليه وسلم وَأَبُو بَكْرٍ، وَمَا عَمِلْتُ فِيهِ مُذْ وَلِيتُ، وَإِلاَّ فَلاَ تُكَلِّمَانِي، فَقُلْتُمَا ادْفَعْهُ إِلَيْنَا بِذَلِكَ. فَدَفَعْتُهُ إِلَيْكُمَا، أَفَتَلْتَمِسَانِ مِنِّي قَضَاءً غَيْرَ ذَلِكَ فَوَاللَّهِ الَّذِي بِإِذْنِهِ تَقُومُ السَّمَاءُ وَالأَرْضُ لاَ أَقْضِي فِيهِ بِقَضَاءٍ غَيْرِ ذَلِكَ حَتَّى تَقُومَ السَّاعَةُ، فَإِنْ عَجَزْتُمَا عَنْهُ، فَادْفَعَا إِلَيَّ فَأَنَا أَكْفِيكُمَاهُ. قَالَ فَحَدَّثْتُ هَذَا الْحَدِيثَ، عُرْوَةَ بْنَ الزُّبَيْرِ فَقَالَ صَدَقَ مَالِكُ بْنُ أَوْسٍ، أَنَا سَمِعْتُ عَائِشَةَ - رضى الله عنها - زَوْجَ النَّبِيِّ صلى الله عليه وسلم تَقُولُ أَرْسَلَ أَزْوَاجُ النَّبِيِّ صلى الله عليه وسلم عُثْمَانَ إِلَى أَبِي بَكْرٍ يَسْأَلْنَهُ ثُمُنَهُنَّ مِمَّا أَفَاءَ اللَّهُ عَلَى رَسُولِهِ صلى الله عليه وسلم، فَكُنْتُ أَنَا أَرُدُّهُنَّ، فَقُلْتُ لَهُنَّ أَلاَ تَتَّقِينَ اللَّهَ، أَلَمْ تَعْلَمْنَ أَنَّ النَّبِيَّ صلى الله عليه وسلم كَانَ يَقُولُ " لاَ نُورَثُ، مَا تَرَكْنَا صَدَقَةٌ - يُرِيدُ بِذَلِكَ نَفْسَهُ - إِنَّمَا يَأْكُلُ آلُ مُحَمَّدٍ صلى الله عليه وسلم فِي هَذَا الْمَالِ ". فَانْتَهَى أَزْوَاجُ النَّبِيِّ صلى الله عليه وسلم إِلَى مَا أَخْبَرَتْهُنَّ. قَالَ فَكَانَتْ هَذِهِ الصَّدَقَةُ بِيَدِ عَلِيٍّ، مَنَعَهَا عَلِيٌّ عَبَّاسًا فَغَلَبَهُ عَلَيْهَا، ثُمَّ كَانَ بِيَدِ حَسَنِ بْنِ عَلِيٍّ، ثُمَّ بِيَدِ حُسَيْنِ بْنِ عَلِيٍّ، ثُمَّ بِيَدِ عَلِيِّ بْنِ حُسَيْنٍ وَحَسَنِ بْنِ حَسَنٍ، كِلاَهُمَا كَانَا يَتَدَاوَلاَنِهَا، ثُمَّ بِيَدِ زَيْدِ بْنِ حَسَنٍ، وَهْىَ صَدَقَةُ رَسُولِ اللَّهِ صلى الله عليه وسلم حَقًّا.

Allah chose Adam, Noah, Abraham's family, and Imran's family over all people- An offspring of one another, and Allah is Ever-Hearing, Ever-Knowing Surah Al-Imran 3:33&34

إِنَّ ٱللَّهَ ٱصْطَفَىٰٓ ءَادَمَ وَنُوحًا وَءَالَ إِبْرَٰهِيمَ وَءَالَ عِمْرَٰنَ عَلَى ٱلْعَٰلَمِينَ ذُرِّيَّةًۢ بَعْضُهَا مِنۢ بَعْضٍۗ وَٱللَّهُ سَمِيعٌ عَلِيمٌ

.....Allah said, "I will make you a leader of men." He said, "And [what about] my seed?" Allah said, "My covenant does not extend to the unjust." – Surah 2:124

قَالَ إِنِّى جَاعِلُكَ لِلنَّاسِ إِمَامًاۖ قَالَ وَمِن ذُرِّيَّتِىۖ قَالَ لَا يَنَالُ عَهْدِى ٱلظَّٰلِمِينَ

They said, "Are you amazed at (the) decree (of) Allah? The Mercy (of) Allah and His blessings (be) upon you, people (of) the house. Indeed, He (is) All-Praiseworthy, All-Glorious." – Surah Hud 11:73

قَالُوٓا۟ أَتَعْجَبِينَ مِنْ أَمْرِ ٱللَّهِۖ رَحْمَتُ ٱللَّهِ وَبَرَكَٰتُهُۥ عَلَيْكُمْ أَهْلَ ٱلْبَيْتِۚ إِنَّهُۥ حَمِيدٌ مَّجِيدٌ

Lord, grant that I and some of my offspring may keep establishing prayer. "Lord, accept my supplication. – Surah Ibrahim 14:40

رَبِّ ٱجْعَلْنِى مُقِيمَ ٱلصَّلَوٰةِ وَمِن ذُرِّيَّتِىۚ رَبَّنَا وَتَقَبَّلْ دُعَآءِ

So, in no way did (anyone) believe Musa, (Moses) except (some) offspring of his people... - Surah Yu us 10:83

فَمَآ ءَامَنَ لِمُوسَىٰٓ إِلَّا ذُرِّيَّةٌ مِّن قَوْمِهِۦ

He called you Muslim

هُوَ سَمَّىٰكُمُ ٱلْمُسْلِمِينَ

And strive for Allah as He deserves. He has chosen you and has not imposed hardships on you in religion- the faith of your father, Abraham. He named you Muslims before and in this [revelation], so that the Messenger may be a witness over you, and you may be witnesses over other human beings. So, establish prayer, and give the purifying alms and hold fast to Allah. He is your Protector. How excellent a Protector and how excellent a Helper. " – Surah Al-Hajj 22:78

وَجَٰهِدُوا۟ فِى ٱللَّهِ حَقَّ جِهَادِهِۦ ۚ هُوَ ٱجْتَبَىٰكُمْ وَمَا جَعَلَ عَلَيْكُمْ فِى ٱلدِّينِ مِنْ حَرَجٍ ۚ مِّلَّةَ أَبِيكُمْ إِبْرَٰهِيمَ ۚ هُوَ سَمَّىٰكُمُ ٱلْمُسْلِمِينَ مِن قَبْلُ وَفِى هَٰذَا لِيَكُونَ ٱلرَّسُولُ شَهِيدًا عَلَيْكُمْ وَتَكُونُوا۟ شُهَدَآءَ عَلَى ٱلنَّاسِ ۚ فَأَقِيمُوا۟ ٱلصَّلَوٰةَ وَءَاتُوا۟ ٱلزَّكَوٰةَ وَٱعْتَصِمُوا۟ بِٱللَّهِ هُوَ مَوْلَىٰكُمْ ۖ فَنِعْمَ ٱلْمَوْلَىٰ وَنِعْمَ ٱلنَّصِيرُ

We have commanded people to honour their parents. Their mothers bore them in hardship and delivered them in hardship. Their ⌜period of⌝ bearing and weaning is thirty months. In time, when the child reaches their prime at the age of forty, they pray, "My Lord! Inspire me to ⌜always⌝ be thankful for Your favours which You blessed me and my parents with, and to do good deeds that please You. And instil righteousness in my offspring. I truly repent to You, and indeed I am of the Muslims." – Surah Al-Ahqaf 46:15
وَوَصَّيْنَا ٱلْإِنسَٰنَ بِوَٰلِدَيْهِ إِحْسَٰنًا ۖ حَمَلَتْهُ أُمُّهُۥ كُرْهًا وَوَضَعَتْهُ كُرْهًا ۖ وَحَمْلُهُۥ وَفِصَٰلُهُۥ ثَلَٰثُونَ شَهْرًا ۚ حَتَّىٰٓ إِذَا بَلَغَ أَشُدَّهُۥ وَبَلَغَ أَرْبَعِينَ سَنَةً قَالَ رَبِّ أَوْزِعْنِىٓ أَنْ أَشْكُرَ نِعْمَتَكَ ٱلَّتِىٓ أَنْعَمْتَ عَلَىَّ وَعَلَىٰ وَٰلِدَىَّ وَأَنْ أَعْمَلَ صَٰلِحًا تَرْضَىٰهُ وَأَصْلِحْ لِى فِى ذُرِّيَّتِىٓ ۖ إِنِّى تُبْتُ إِلَيْكَ وَإِنِّى مِنَ ٱلْمُسْلِمِينَ

Muhammad is not the father of any man among you, but he is the Messenger of Allah and the Seal of the Prophets. And Allah is Ever All-Aware of everything – .Surah Al-Ahzab 33:40
مَّا كَانَ مُحَمَّدٌ أَبَآ أَحَدٍ مِّن رِّجَالِكُمْ وَلَٰكِن رَّسُولَ ٱللَّهِ وَخَاتَمَ ٱلنَّبِيِّۦنَ ۗ وَكَانَ ٱللَّهُ بِكُلِّ شَىْءٍ عَلِيمًا

Narrated Isma`il: I asked Abi `Aufa, "Did you see Ibrahim, the son of the Prophet ﷺ?" He said, "Yes, but he died in his early childhood. Had there been a Prophet after Muhammad then his son would have lived, but there is no Prophet after him.". – Sahih al-Bukhari 6194
حَدَّثَنَا ابْنُ نُمَيْرٍ، حَدَّثَنَا مُحَمَّدُ بْنُ بِشْرٍ، حَدَّثَنَا إِسْمَاعِيلُ، قُلْتُ لاِبْنِ أَبِي أَوْفَى رَأَيْتَ إِبْرَاهِيمَ ابْنَ النَّبِيِّ صلى الله عليه وسلم قَالَ مَاتَ صَغِيرًا، وَلَوْ قُضِيَ أَنْ يَكُونَ بَعْدَ مُحَمَّدٍ صلى الله عليه وسلم نَبِيٌّ عَاشَ ابْنُهُ، وَلَكِنْ لاَ نَبِيَّ بَعْدَهُ.

And whose words are better than someone who calls ⌜others⌝ to Allah, does good, and says, "Verily, I am of the Muslims". – Surah Al-Fussilat 41:33
وَمَنْ أَحْسَنُ قَوْلًا مِّمَّن دَعَآ إِلَى ٱللَّهِ وَعَمِلَ صَٰلِحًا وَقَالَ إِنَّنِى مِنَ ٱلْمُسْلِمِينَ

Al-Abbas ibn Abd al-Muttalib
ٱلْعَبَّاسُ بْنُ عَبْدِ ٱلْمُطَّلِبِ

Narrated Jabir bin `Abdullah: Allah's Messenger ﷺ came to `Abdullah bin Ubai (a hypocrite) after his death and he has been laid in his pit (grave). He ordered (that he be taken out of the grave) and he was taken out. Then he placed him on his knees and threw some of his saliva on him and clothed him in his (the Prophet's) own shirt. Allah knows better (why he did so). `Abdullah bin Ubai had given his shirt to Al-Abbas to wear. Abu Harun said, "Allah's Messenger ﷺ at that time had two shirts and the son of `Abdullah bin Ubai said to him, 'O Allah's Messenger ﷺ! Clothe my father in your shirt which has been in contact with your skin.' ' Sufyan added, "Thus people think that the Prophet ﷺ clothed `Abdullah bin Tubal in his shirt in lieu of what he (Abdullah) had done (for Al Abbas, the Prophet's uncle.)". Sahih Al Bukhari 1350

حَدَّثَنَا عَلِيُّ بْنُ عَبْدِ اللَّهِ، حَدَّثَنَا سُفْيَانُ، قَالَ عَمْرٌو سَمِعْتُ جَابِرَ بْنَ عَبْدِ اللَّهِ ـ رضى الله عنهما ـ قَالَ أَتَى رَسُولُ اللَّهِ صلى الله عليه وسلم عَبْدَ اللَّهِ بْنَ أُبَىٍّ بَعْدَ مَا أُدْخِلَ حُفْرَتَهُ فَأَمَرَ بِهِ فَأُخْرِجَ، فَوَضَعَهُ عَلَى رُكْبَتَيْهِ، وَنَفَثَ عَلَيْهِ مِنْ رِيقِهِ، وَأَلْبَسَهُ قَمِيصَهُ، فَاللَّهُ أَعْلَمُ، وَكَانَ كَسَا عَبَّاسًا قَمِيصًا. قَالَ سُفْيَانُ وَقَالَ أَبُو هَارُونَ وَكَانَ عَلَى رَسُولِ اللَّهِ صلى الله عليه وسلم قَمِيصَانِ، فَقَالَ لَهُ ابْنُ عَبْدِ اللَّهِ يَا رَسُولَ اللَّهِ، أَلْبِسْ أَبِي قَمِيصَكَ الَّذِي يَلِي جِلْدَكَ. قَالَ سُفْيَانُ فَيُرَوْنَ أَنَّ النَّبِيَّ صلى الله عليه وسلم أَلْبَسَ عَبْدَ اللَّهِ قَمِيصَهُ مُكَافَأَةً لِمَا صَنَعَ

Narrated Jabir bin `Abdullah: When it was the day (of the battle) of Badr, prisoners of war were brought including Al-Abbas who was undressed. The Prophet ﷺ looked for a shirt for him. It was found that the shirt of `Abdullah bin Ubai would do, so the Prophet ﷺ let him wear it. That was the reason why the Prophet ﷺ took off and gave his own shirt to `Abdullah. (The narrator adds, "He had done the Prophet ﷺ some favor for which the Prophet liked to reward him.") - Sahih Al-Bukhari 3008

حَدَّثَنَا عَبْدُ اللَّهِ بْنُ مُحَمَّدٍ، حَدَّثَنَا ابْنُ عُيَيْنَةَ، عَنْ عَمْرٍو، سَمِعَ جَابِرَ بْنَ عَبْدِ اللَّهِ ـ رضى الله عنهما ـ قَالَ لَمَّا كَانَ يَوْمَ بَدْرٍ أُتِيَ بِأُسَارَى، وَأُتِيَ بِالْعَبَّاسِ وَلَمْ يَكُنْ عَلَيْهِ ثَوْبٌ، فَنَظَرَ النَّبِيُّ صلى الله عليه وسلم لَهُ قَمِيصًا فَوَجَدُوا قَمِيصَ عَبْدِ اللَّهِ بْنِ أُبَىٍّ يَقْدُرُ عَلَيْهِ، فَكَسَاهُ النَّبِيُّ صلى الله عليه وسلم إِيَّاهُ، فَلِذَلِكَ نَزَعَ النَّبِيُّ صلى الله عليه وسلم قَمِيصَهُ الَّذِي أَلْبَسَهُ. قَالَ ابْنُ عُيَيْنَةَ كَانَتْ لَهُ عِنْدَ النَّبِيِّ صلى الله عليه وسلم يَدٌ فَأَحَبَّ أَنْ يُكَافِئَهُ.

Narrated Abu Jamra: Ibn `Abbas said to us, "Shall I tell you the story of Abu Dhar's conversion to Islam?" We said, "Yes." He said, "Abu Dhar said: I was a man from the tribe of Ghifar. We heard that a man had appeared in Mecca, claiming to be a Prophet. ! said to my brother, 'Go to that man and talk to him and bring me his news.' He set out, met him and returned. I asked him, 'What is the news with you?' He said, 'By Allah, I saw a man enjoining what is good and forbidding what is evil.' I said to him, 'You have not satisfied me with this little information.' So, I took a waterskin and a stick and proceeded towards Mecca. Neither did I know him (i.e. the Prophet ﷺ), nor did I like to ask anyone about him. I Kept on drinking Zam zam water and staying in the Mosque. Then `Ali passed by me and said, 'It seems you are a stranger?' I said, 'Yes.' He proceeded to his house and I accompanied him. Neither did he ask me anything, nor did I tell him anything. Next morning I went to the Mosque to ask about the Prophet but no-one told me anything about him. `Ali passed by me again and asked, 'Hasn't the man recognized his dwelling place yet' I said, 'No.' He said, 'Come along with me.' He asked me, 'What is your business? What has brought you to this town?' I said to him, 'If you keep my secret, I will tell you.' He said, 'I will do,' I said to him, 'We have heard that a person has appeared here, claiming to be a Prophet. I sent my brother to speak to him and when he returned, he did not bring a satisfactory report; so I thought of meeting him personally.' `Ali said (to Abu Dhar), 'You have reached your goal; I am going to him just now, so follow me, and wherever I enter, enter after me. If I should see someone who may cause you trouble, I will stand near a wall pretending to mend my shoes (as a warning), and you should go away then.' `Ali proceeded and I accompanied him till he entered a place, and I entered with him to the Prophet ﷺ to whom I said, 'Present (the principles of) Islam to me.' When he did, I embraced Islam 'immediately. He said to me, 'O Abu Dhar! Keep your conversion as a secret and return to your town; and when you hear of our victory, return to us. ' I said, 'By H him Who has sent you with the Truth, I will announce my conversion to Islam publicly amongst them (i.e. the infidels),' Abu Dhar went to the Mosque, where some people from Quraish were present, and said, 'O folk of Quraish ! I testify that None has the right to be worshipped except Allah, and I (also) testify that Muhammad is Allah's Slave and His Apostle.' (Hearing that) the Quraishi men said, 'Get at this Sabi (i.e. Muslim) !' They got up and beat me nearly to death. Al `Abbas saw me and threw himself over me to protect me. He then faced them and said, 'Woe to you! You want to kill a man from the tribe of Ghifar, although your trade and your communications are through the territory of Ghifar?' They therefore left me. The next morning I returned (to the Mosque) and said the same as I have said on the previous day. They again said, 'Get at this Sabi!' I was treated in the same way as on the previous day, and again Al-Abbas found me and threw himself over me to protect me and told them the same as he had said the day before.' So, that was the conversion of Abu Dhar (may Allah be Merciful to him) to Islam.". – Sahih Al-Bukhari 3522

حَدَّثَنَا زَيْدٌ ـ هُوَ ابْنُ أَخْزَمَ ـ قَالَ أَبُو قُتَيْبَةَ سَلْمُ بْنُ قُتَيْبَةَ حَدَّثَنِي مُثَنَّى بْنُ سَعِيدٍ الْقَصِيرُ، قَالَ حَدَّثَنِي أَبُو جَمْرَةَ، قَالَ لَنَا ابْنُ عَبَّاسٍ أَلاَ أُخْبِرُكُمْ بِإِسْلاَمِ أَبِي ذَرٍّ، قَالَ قُلْنَا بَلَى. قَالَ قَالَ أَبُو ذَرٍّ كُنْتُ رَجُلاً مِنْ غِفَارٍ، فَبَلَغَنَا أَنَّ رَجُلاً قَدْ خَرَجَ بِمَكَّةَ، يَزْعُمُ أَنَّهُ نَبِيٌّ، فَقُلْتُ لأَخِي انْطَلِقْ إِلَى هَذَا الرَّجُلِ كَلِّمْهُ وَأْتِنِي بِخَبَرِهِ. فَانْطَلَقَ فَلَقِيَهُ، ثُمَّ رَجَعَ فَقُلْتُ مَا عِنْدَكَ فَقَالَ وَاللَّهِ لَقَدْ رَأَيْتُ رَجُلاً يَأْمُرُ بِالْخَيْرِ وَيَنْهَى عَنِ الشَّرِّ. فَقُلْتُ لَهُ لَمْ تَشْفِنِي مِنَ الْخَبَرِ. فَأَخَذْتُ جِرَابًا وَعَصًا، ثُمَّ أَقْبَلْتُ إِلَى مَكَّةَ فَجَعَلْتُ لاَ أَعْرِفُهُ، وَأَكْرَهُ أَنْ أَسْأَلَ عَنْهُ، وَأَشْرَبُ مِنْ مَاءِ زَمْزَمَ وَأَكُونُ فِي الْمَسْجِدِ. قَالَ فَمَرَّ بِي عَلِيٌّ فَقَالَ كَأَنَّ الرَّجُلَ غَرِيبٌ. قَالَ قُلْتُ نَعَمْ. قَالَ فَانْطَلِقْ إِلَى الْمَنْزِلِ. قَالَ فَانْطَلَقْتُ مَعَهُ لاَ يَسْأَلُنِي عَنْ شَىْءٍ، وَلاَ أُخْبِرُهُ، فَلَمَّا أَصْبَحْتُ غَدَوْتُ إِلَى الْمَسْجِدِ لأَسْأَلَ عَنْهُ، وَلَيْسَ أَحَدٌ يُخْبِرُنِي عَنْهُ بِشَىْءٍ. قَالَ فَمَرَّ بِي عَلِيٌّ فَقَالَ أَمَا نَالَ لِلرَّجُلِ يَعْرِفُ مَنْزِلَهُ بَعْدُ قَالَ قُلْتُ لاَ. قَالَ انْطَلِقْ مَعِي. قَالَ فَقَالَ مَا أَمْرُكَ وَمَا أَقْدَمَكَ هَذِهِ الْبَلْدَةَ قَالَ قُلْتُ لَهُ إِنْ كَتَمْتَ عَلَىَّ أَخْبَرْتُكَ. قَالَ فَإِنِّي أَفْعَلُ. قَالَ قُلْتُ لَهُ بَلَغَنَا أَنَّهُ قَدْ خَرَجَ هَا هُنَا رَجُلٌ يَزْعُمُ أَنَّهُ نَبِيٌّ، فَأَرْسَلْتُ أَخِي لِيُكَلِّمَهُ فَرَجَعَ وَلَمْ يَشْفِنِي مِنَ الْخَبَرِ، فَأَرَدْتُ أَنْ أَلْقَاهُ. فَقَالَ لَهُ أَمَا إِنَّكَ قَدْ رَشَدْتَ، هَذَا وَجْهِي إِلَيْهِ، فَاتَّبِعْنِي، ادْخُلْ حَيْثُ أَدْخُلُ، فَإِنِّي إِنْ رَأَيْتُ أَحَدًا أَخَافُهُ عَلَيْكَ، قُمْتُ إِلَى الْحَائِطِ، كَأَنِّي أُصْلِحُ نَعْلِي، وَامْضِ أَنْتَ، فَمَضَى وَمَضَيْتُ مَعَهُ، حَتَّى دَخَلَ وَدَخَلْتُ مَعَهُ عَلَى النَّبِيِّ صلى الله عليه وسلم فَقُلْتُ لَهُ اعْرِضْ عَلَىَّ الإِسْلاَمَ. فَعَرَضَهُ فَأَسْلَمْتُ مَكَانِي، فَقَالَ لِي " يَا أَبَا ذَرٍّ اكْتُمْ هَذَا الأَمْرَ، وَارْجِعْ إِلَى بَلَدِكَ، فَإِذَا بَلَغَكَ ظُهُورُنَا فَأَقْبِلْ ". فَقُلْتُ وَالَّذِي بَعَثَكَ بِالْحَقِّ لأَصْرُخَنَّ بِهَا بَيْنَ أَظْهُرِهِمْ. فَجَاءَ إِلَى الْمَسْجِدِ، وَقُرَيْشٌ فِيهِ فَقَالَ يَا مَعْشَرَ قُرَيْشٍ، إِنِّي أَشْهَدُ أَنْ لاَ إِلَهَ إِلاَّ اللَّهُ، وَأَشْهَدُ أَنَّ مُحَمَّدًا عَبْدُهُ وَرَسُولُهُ. فَقَالُوا قُومُوا إِلَى هَذَا الصَّابِئِ. فَقَامُوا فَضُرِبْتُ لأَمُوتَ فَأَدْرَكَنِي الْعَبَّاسُ، فَأَكَبَّ عَلَىَّ ثُمَّ أَقْبَلَ عَلَيْهِمْ، فَقَالَ وَيْلَكُمْ تَقْتُلُونَ رَجُلاً مِنْ غِفَارَ، وَمَتْجَرُكُمْ وَمَمَرُّكُمْ عَلَى غِفَارَ. فَأَقْلَعُوا عَنِّي، فَلَمَّا أَنْ أَصْبَحْتُ الْغَدَ رَجَعْتُ فَقُلْتُ مِثْلَ مَا قُلْتُ بِالأَمْسِ، فَقَالُوا قُومُوا إِلَى هَذَا الصَّابِئِ. فَصُنِعَ {بِي} مِثْلَ مَا صُنِعَ بِالأَمْسِ وَأَدْرَكَنِي الْعَبَّاسُ فَأَكَبَّ عَلَىَّ، وَقَالَ مِثْلَ مَقَالَتِهِ بِالأَمْسِ. قَالَ فَكَانَ هَذَا أَوَّلَ إِسْلاَمِ أَبِي ذَرٍّ رَحِمَهُ اللَّهُ

Narrated Malik bin Aus An-Nasri: I proceeded till I entered upon `Umar (and while I was sitting there), his gate-keeper Yarfa came to him and said, " `Uthman, `Abdur-Rahman, Az-Zubair and Sa`d ask your permission to come in." `Umar allowed them. So they entered, greeted, and sat down. (After a while the gatekeeper came) and said, "Shall I admit `Ali and `Abbas?" `Umar allowed them to enter. Al-`Abbas said "O Chief of the believers! Judge between me and the oppressor (`Ali)." Then there was a dispute (regarding the property of Bani Nadir) between them (`Abbas and `Ali). `Uthman and his companions said, "O Chief of the Believers! Judge between them and relieve one from the other." `Umar said, "Be patient! Beseech you by Allah, with Whose permission the Heaven and the Earth Exist! Do you know that Allah's Messenger ﷺ said, 'Our property is not to be inherited, and whatever we leave is to be given in charity,' and by this Allah's Messenger ﷺ meant himself?" On that the group said, "He verily said so." `Umar then faced `Ali and `Abbas and said, "I beseech you both by Allah, do you both know that Allah's Messenger ﷺ said so?" They both replied, "Yes". `Umar then said, "Now I am talking to you about this matter (in detail) . Allah favored Allah's Messenger ﷺ with some of this wealth which He did not give to anybody else, as Allah said: 'What Allah bestowed as Fai (Booty on His Apostle for which you made no expedition... ' (59.6) So that property was totally meant for Allah's Messenger ﷺ, yet he did not collect it and ignore you, nor did he withhold it with your exclusion, but he gave it to you and أَصْبَغُ distributed it among you till this much of it was left behind, and the Prophet, used to spend of this as the yearly expenditures of his family and then take what remained of it and spent it as he did with (other) Allah's wealth. The Prophet ﷺ did so during all his lifetime, and I beseech you by Allah, do you know that?" They replied, "Yes." `Umar then addressed `Ali and `Abbas, saying, "I beseech you both by Allah, do you know that?" Both of them replied, "Yes." Umar added, "Then Allah took His Apostle unto Him. Abu Bakr then said 'I am the successor of Allah's Messenger ﷺ and took over all the Prophet's property and disposed of it in the same way as Allah's Messenger ﷺ used to do, and you were present then." Then he turned to `Ali and `Abbas and said, "You both claim that Abu Bakr did so-and-so in managing the property, but Allah knows that Abu Bakr was honest, righteous, intelligent, and a follower of what is right in managing it. Then Allah took Abu Bakr unto Him, 'I said: I am the successor of Allah's Messenger ﷺ and Abu Bakr.' So I took over the property for two years and managed it in the same way as Allah's Messenger ﷺ, and Abu Bakr used to do. Then you both (`Ali and `Abbas) came to me and asked for the same thing! (O `Abbas! You came to me to ask me for your share from nephew's property; and this (`Ali) came to me asking for his wives share from her father's property, and I said to you both, 'If you wish, I will place it in your custody on condition that you both will manage it in the same way as Allah's Messenger ﷺ and Abu Bakr did and as I have been doing since I took charge of managing it; otherwise, do not speak to me anymore about it.' Then you both said, 'Give it to us on that (condition).' So I gave it to you on that condition. Now I beseech you by Allah, did I not give it to them on that condition?" The group (whom he had been addressing) replied, "Yes." `Umar then addressed `Abbas and `Ali saying, "I beseech you both by Allah, didn't I give you all that property on that condition?" They said, "Yes." `Umar then said, "Are you now seeking a verdict from me other than that? By Him with Whose Permission the Heaven and the Earth exists I will not give any verdict other than that till the Hour is established; and if you both are unable to manage this property, then you can hand it back to me, and I will be sufficient for it on your behalf." (See, Hadith No. 326, Vol. 4). – Sahih Al-Bukhari 7305

حَدَّثَنَا عَبْدُ اللَّهِ بْنُ يُوسُفَ، حَدَّثَنَا اللَّيْثُ، حَدَّثَنِي عُقَيْلٌ، عَنِ ابْنِ شِهَابٍ، قَالَ أَخْبَرَنِي مَالِكُ بْنُ أَوْسٍ النَّصْرِيُّ، وَكَانَ، مُحَمَّدُ بْنُ جُبَيْرِ بْنِ مُطْعِمٍ ذَكَرَ لِي ذِكْرًا مِنْ ذَلِكَ فَدَخَلْتُ عَلَى مَالِكٍ فَسَأَلْتُهُ فَقَالَ انْطَلَقْتُ حَتَّى أَدْخُلَ عَلَى عُمَرَ أَتَاهُ حَاجِبُهُ يَرْفَا فَقَالَ هَلْ لَكَ فِي عُثْمَانَ وَعَبْدِ الرَّحْمَنِ وَالزُّبَيْرِ وَسَعْدٍ يَسْتَأْذِنُونَ. قَالَ نَعَمْ. فَدَخَلُوا فَسَلَّمُوا وَجَلَسُوا. فَقَالَ هَلْ لَكَ فِي عَلِيٍّ وَعَبَّاسٍ. فَأَذِنَ لَهُمَا. قَالَ الْعَبَّاسُ يَا أَمِيرَ الْمُؤْمِنِينَ اقْضِ بَيْنِي وَبَيْنَ الظَّالِمِ. اسْتَبَّا. فَقَالَ الرَّهْطُ عُثْمَانُ وَأَصْحَابُهُ يَا أَمِيرَ الْمُؤْمِنِينَ اقْضِ بَيْنَهُمَا وَأَرِحْ أَحَدَهُمَا مِنَ الآخَرِ. فَقَالَ اتَّئِدُوا أَنْشُدُكُمْ بِاللَّهِ الَّذِي بِإِذْنِهِ تَقُومُ السَّمَاءُ وَالأَرْضُ، هَلْ تَعْلَمُونَ أَنَّ رَسُولَ اللَّهِ صلى الله عليه وسلم قَالَ " لاَ نُورَثُ مَا تَرَكْنَا صَدَقَةٌ ". يُرِيدُ رَسُولُ اللَّهِ صلى الله عليه وسلم نَفْسَهُ. قَالَ الرَّهْطُ قَدْ قَالَ ذَلِكَ. فَأَقْبَلَ عُمَرُ عَلَى عَلِيٍّ وَعَبَّاسٍ فَقَالَ أَنْشُدُكُمَا بِاللَّهِ هَلْ تَعْلَمَانِ أَنَّ رَسُولَ اللَّهِ صلى الله عليه وسلم قَالَ ذَلِكَ. قَالاَ نَعَمْ. قَالَ عُمَرُ فَإِنِّي مُحَدِّثُكُمْ عَنْ هَذَا الأَمْرِ، إِنَّ اللَّهَ كَانَ خَصَّ رَسُولَهُ صلى الله عليه وسلم فِي هَذَا الْمَالِ بِشَىْءٍ لَمْ يُعْطِهِ أَحَدًا غَيْرَهُ، فَإِنَّ اللَّهَ يَقُولُ {مَا أَفَاءَ اللَّهُ عَلَى رَسُولِهِ مِنْهُمْ فَمَا أَوْجَفْتُمْ} الآيَةَ، فَكَانَتْ هَذِهِ خَالِصَةً لِرَسُولِ اللَّهِ صلى الله عليه وسلم، ثُمَّ وَاللَّهِ مَا احْتَازَهَا دُونَكُمْ وَلاَ اسْتَأْثَرَ بِهَا عَلَيْكُمْ، وَقَدْ أَعْطَاكُمُوهَا وَبَثَّهَا فِيكُمْ، حَتَّى بَقِيَ مِنْهَا هَذَا الْمَالُ، وَكَانَ النَّبِيُّ صلى الله عليه وسلم يُنْفِقُ عَلَى أَهْلِهِ نَفَقَةَ سَنَتِهِمْ مِنْ هَذَا الْمَالِ، ثُمَّ يَأْخُذُ مَا بَقِيَ فَيَجْعَلُهُ مَجْعَلَ مَالِ اللَّهِ، فَعَمِلَ النَّبِيُّ صلى الله عليه وسلم بِذَلِكَ حَيَاتَهُ، أَنْشُدُكُمْ بِاللَّهِ هَلْ تَعْلَمُونَ ذَلِكَ فَقَالُوا نَعَمْ. ثُمَّ قَالَ لِعَلِيٍّ وَعَبَّاسٍ أَنْشُدُكُمَا اللَّهَ هَلْ تَعْلَمَانِ ذَلِكَ قَالاَ نَعَمْ. ثُمَّ تَوَفَّى اللَّهُ نَبِيَّهُ صلى الله عليه وسلم فَقَالَ أَبُو بَكْرٍ أَنَا وَلِيُّ رَسُولِ اللَّهِ صلى الله عليه وسلم، فَقَبَضَهَا أَبُو بَكْرٍ فَعَمِلَ فِيهَا بِمَا عَمِلَ فِيهَا رَسُولُ اللَّهِ صلى الله عليه وسلم، وَأَنْتُمَا حِينَئِذٍ ـ وَأَقْبَلَ عَلَى عَلِيٍّ وَعَبَّاسٍ ـ تَزْعُمَانِ أَنَّ أَبَا بَكْرٍ فِيهَا كَذَا، وَاللَّهُ يَعْلَمُ أَنَّهُ فِيهَا صَادِقٌ بَارٌّ رَاشِدٌ تَابِعٌ لِلْحَقِّ، ثُمَّ تَوَفَّى اللَّهُ أَبَا بَكْرٍ فَقُلْتُ أَنَا وَلِيُّ رَسُولِ اللَّهِ صلى الله عليه وسلم وَأَبِي بَكْرٍ. فَقَبَضْتُهَا سَنَتَيْنِ أَعْمَلُ فِيهَا بِمَا عَمِلَ بِهِ رَسُولُ اللَّهِ صلى الله عليه وسلم وَأَبُو بَكْرٍ، ثُمَّ جِئْتُمَانِي وَكَلِمَتُكُمَا عَلَى كَلِمَةٍ وَاحِدَةٍ وَأَمْرُكُمَا جَمِيعٌ، جِئْتَنِي تَسْأَلُنِي نَصِيبَكَ مِنِ ابْنِ أَخِيكَ، وَأَتَانِي هَذَا يَسْأَلُنِي نَصِيبَ امْرَأَتِهِ مِنْ أَبِيهَا فَقُلْتُ إِنْ شِئْتُمَا دَفَعْتُهَا إِلَيْكُمَا، عَلَى أَنَّ عَلَيْكُمَا عَهْدَ اللَّهِ وَمِيثَاقَهُ تَعْمَلاَنِ فِيهَا بِمَا عَمِلَ بِهِ رَسُولُ اللَّهِ صلى الله عليه وسلم وَبِمَا عَمِلَ فِيهَا أَبُو بَكْرٍ وَبِمَا عَمِلْتُ فِيهَا مُنْذُ وَلِيتُهَا، وَإِلاَّ فَلاَ تُكَلِّمَانِي فِيهَا. فَقُلْتُمَا ادْفَعْهَا إِلَيْنَا بِذَلِكَ. فَدَفَعْتُهَا إِلَيْكُمَا بِذَلِكَ، أَنْشُدُكُمْ بِاللَّهِ هَلْ دَفَعْتُهَا إِلَيْهِمَا بِذَلِكَ قَالَ الرَّهْطُ نَعَمْ. فَأَقْبَلَ عَلَى عَلِيٍّ وَعَبَّاسٍ فَقَالَ أَنْشُدُكُمَا بِاللَّهِ هَلْ دَفَعْتُهَا إِلَيْكُمَا بِذَلِكَ. قَالاَ نَعَمْ. قَالَ أَفَتَلْتَمِسَانِ مِنِّي قَضَاءً غَيْرَ ذَلِكَ فَوَالَّذِي بِإِذْنِهِ تَقُومُ السَّمَاءُ وَالأَرْضُ لاَ أَقْضِي فِيهَا قَضَاءً غَيْرَ ذَلِكَ حَتَّى تَقُومَ السَّاعَةُ، فَإِنْ عَجَزْتُمَا عَنْهَا فَادْفَعَاهَا إِلَيَّ، فَأَنَا أَكْفِيكُمَاهَا.

Narrated `Amr bin Maimun: I saw `Umar bin Al-Khattab a few days before he was stabbed in Medina. He was standing with Hudhaifa bin Al-Yaman and `Uthman bin Hunaif to whom he said, "What have you done? Do you think that you have imposed more taxation on the land (of As-Swad i.e. 'Iraq) than it can bear?" They replied, "We have imposed on it what it can bear because of its great yield." `Umar again said, "Check whether you have imposed on the land what it can not bear." They said, "No, (we haven't)." `Umar added, "If Allah should keep me alive I will let the widows of Iraq need no men to support them after me." But only four days had elapsed when he was stabbed (to death ). The day he was stabbed, I was standing and there was nobody between me and him (i.e. `Umar) except `Abdullah bin `Abbas.

Whenever `Umar passed between the two rows, he would say, "Stand in straight lines." When he saw no defect (in the rows), he would go forward and start the prayer with Takbir. He would recite Surat Yusuf or An-Nahl or the like in the first rak`a so that the people may have the time to Join the prayer. As soon as he said Takbir, I heard him saying, "The dog has killed or eaten me," at the time he (i.e. the murderer) stabbed him. A non-Arab infidel proceeded on carrying a double-edged knife and stabbing all the persons he passed by on the right and left (till) he stabbed thirteen persons out of whom seven died. When one of the Muslims saw that, he threw a cloak on him. Realizing that he had been captured, the non-Arab infidel killed himself, `Umar held the hand of `Abdur-Rahman bin `Auf and let him lead the prayer. Those who were standing by the side of `Umar saw what I saw, but the people who were in the other parts of the Mosque did not see anything, but they lost the voice of `Umar and they were saying, "Subhan Allah! Subhan Allah! (i.e. Glorified be Allah)." `Abdur-Rahman bin `Auf led the people a short prayer. When they finished the prayer, `Umar said, "O Ibn `Abbas! Find out who attacked me." Ibn `Abbas kept on looking here and there for a short time and came to say. "The slave of Al Mughira." On that `Umar said, "The craftsman?" Ibn `Abbas said, "Yes." `Umar said, "May Allah curse him. I did not treat him unjustly. All the Praises are for Allah Who has not caused me to die at the hand of a man who claims himself to be a Muslim. No doubt, you and your father (Abbas) used to love to have more non-Arab infidels in Medina." Al-Abbas had the greatest number of slaves. Ibn `Abbas said to `Umar. "If you wish, we will do." He meant, "If you wish we will kill them." `Umar said, "You are mistaken (for you can't kill them) after they have spoken your language, prayed towards your Qibla, and performed Hajj like yours." Then `Umar was carried to his house, and we went along with him, and the people were as if they had never suffered a calamity before. Some said, "Do not worry (he will be Alright soon)." Some said, "We are afraid (that he will die)." Then an infusion of dates was brought to him and he drank it but it came out (of the wound) of his belly. Then milk was brought to him and he drank it, and it also came out of his belly. The people realized that he would die. We went to him, and the people came, praising him. A young man came saying, "O chief of the believers! Receive the glad tidings from Allah to you due to your company with Allah's Messenger ﷺ and your superiority in Islam which you know. Then you became the ruler (i.e. Caliph) and you ruled with justice and finally you have been martyred." `Umar said, "I wish that all these privileges will counterbalance (my shortcomings) so that I will neither lose nor gain anything." When the young man turned back to leave, his clothes seemed to be touching the ground. `Umar said, "Call the young man back to me." (When he came back) `Umar said, "O son of my brother! Lift your clothes, for this will keep your clothes clean and save you from the Punishment of your Lord." `Umar further said, "O `Abdullah bin `Umar! See how much I am in debt to others." When the debt was checked, it amounted to approximately eighty-six thousand. `Umar said, "If the property of `Umar's family covers the debt, then pay the debt thereof; otherwise request it from Bani `Adi bin Ka`b, and if that too is not sufficient, ask for it from Quraish tribe, and do not ask for it from any one else, and pay this debt on my behalf." `Umar then said (to `Abdullah), "Go to `Aisha (the mother of the believers) and say: "`Umar is paying his salutation to you. But don't say: 'The chief of the believers,' because today I am not the chief of the believers. And say: "`Umar bin Al-Khattab asks the permission to be buried with his two companions (i.e. the Prophet, and Abu Bakr)." `Abdullah greeted `Aisha and asked for the permission for entering, and then entered to her and found her sitting and weeping. He said to her, "`Umar bin Al-Khattab is paying his salutations to you, and asks the permission to be buried with his two companions." She said, "I had the idea of having this place for myself, but today I prefer `Umar to myself." When he returned it was said (to `Umar), "`Abdullah bin `Umar has come." `Umar said, "Make me sit up." Somebody supported him against his body and `Umar asked (`Abdullah), "What news do you have?" He said, "O chief of the believers! It is as you wish. She has given the permission." `Umar said, "Praise be to Allah, there was nothing more important to me than this. So when I die, take me, and greet `Aisha and say: "`Umar bin Al-Khattab asks the permission (to be buried with the Prophetﷺ), and if she gives the permission, bury me there, and if she refuses, then take me to the grave-yard of the Muslims." Then Hafsa (the mother of the believers) came with many other women walking with her. When we saw her, we went away. She went in (to `Umar) and wept there for sometime. When the men asked for permission to enter, she went into another place, and we heard her weeping inside. The people said (to `Umar), "O chief of the believers! Appoint a successor." `Umar said, "I do not find anyone more suitable for the job than the following persons or group whom Allah's Messengerﷺ had been pleased with before he died." Then `Umar mentioned `Ali, `Uthman, AzZubair, Talha, Sa`d and `Abdur-Rahman (bin `Auf) and said, "Abdullah bin `Umar will be a witness to you, but he will have no share in the rule. His being a witness will compensate him for not sharing the right of ruling. If Sa`d becomes the ruler, it will be alright: otherwise, whoever becomes the ruler should seek his help, as I have not dismissed him because of disability or dishonesty." `Umar added, "I recommend that my successor takes care of the early emigrants; to know their rights and protect their honor and sacred things. I also recommend that he be kind to the Ansar who had lived in Medina before the emigrants and Belief had entered their hearts before them. I recommend that the (ruler) should accept the good of the righteous among them and excuse their wrong-doers, and I recommend that he should do good to all the people of the towns (Al-Ansar), as they are the protectors of Islam and the source of wealth and the source of annoyance to the enemy. I also recommend that nothing be taken from them except from their surplus with their consent. I also recommend that he do good to the 'Arab Bedouin, as they are the origin of the 'Arabs and the material of Islam. He should take from what is inferior, amongst their properties and distribute that to the poor amongst them. I also recommend him concerning Allah's and His Apostle's protectees (i.e. Dhimmis) to fulfill their contracts and to fight for them and not to overburden them with what is beyond their ability." So when `Umar expired, we carried him out and set out walking. `Abdullah bin `Umar greeted (`Aisha) and said, "`Umar bin Al-Khattab asks for the permission." `Aisha said, "Bring him in." He was brought in and buried beside his two companions. When he was buried, the group (recommended by `Umar) held a meeting. Then `Abdur-Rahman said, " Reduce the candidates for rulership to three of you." Az-Zubair said, "I give up my right to `Ali." Talha said, "I give up my right to `Uthman," Sa`d, 'I give up my right to `Abdur-Rahman bin `Auf." `Abdur-Rahman then said (to `Uthman and `Ali), "Now which of you is willing to give up his right of candidacy to that he may choose the better of the (remaining) two, bearing in mind that Allah and Islam will be his witnesses." So both the sheiks (i.e. `Uthman and `Ali) kept silent. `Abdur-Rahman said, "Will you both leave this matter to me, and I take Allah as my Witness that I will not choose but the better of you?" They said, "Yes." So `Abdur-Rahman took the hand of one of them (i.e. `Ali) and said, "You are related to Allah's Messengerﷺ and one of the earliest Muslims as you know well. So I ask you by Allah to promise that if I select you as a ruler you will do justice, and if I select `Uthman as a ruler you will listen to him and obey him." Then he took the other (i.e. `Uthman) aside and said the same to him. When `Abdur-Rahman secured (their agreement to) this covenant, he said, "O `Uthman! Raise your hand." So he (i.e. `Abdur-Rahman) gave him (i.e. `Uthman) the solemn pledge, and then `Ali gave him the pledge of allegiance and then all the (Medina) people gave him the pledge of allegiance. – Sahih Al-Bukhari 3700

حَدَّثَنَا مُوسَى بْنُ إِسْمَاعِيلَ، حَدَّثَنَا أَبُو عَوَانَةَ، عَنْ حُصَيْنٍ، عَنْ عَمْرِو بْنِ مَيْمُونٍ، قَالَ رَأَيْتُ عُمَرَ بْنَ الْخَطَّابِ ـ رضى الله عنه ـ قَبْلَ أَنْ يُصَابَ بِأَيَّامٍ بِالْمَدِينَةِ وَقَفَ عَلَى حُذَيْفَةَ بْنِ الْيَمَانِ وَعُثْمَانَ بْنِ حُنَيْفٍ، قَالَ كَيْفَ فَعَلْتُمَا أَتَخَافَانِ أَنْ تَكُونَا قَدْ حَمَّلْتُمَا الأَرْضَ مَا لاَ تُطِيقُ قَالاَ حَمَّلْنَاهَا أَمْرًا هِيَ لَهُ مُطِيقَةٌ، مَا فِيهَا كَبِيرُ فَضْلٍ. قَالَ انْظُرَا أَنْ تَكُونَا حَمَّلْتُمَا الأَرْضَ مَا لاَ تُطِيقُ، قَالَ قَالاَ لاَ. فَقَالَ عُمَرُ لَئِنْ سَلَّمَنِي اللَّهُ لأَدَعَنَّ أَرَامِلَ أَهْلِ الْعِرَاقِ لاَ يَحْتَجْنَ إِلَى رَجُلٍ بَعْدِي أَبَدًا. قَالَ فَمَا أَتَتْ عَلَيْهِ إِلاَّ رَابِعَةٌ حَتَّى أُصِيبَ. قَالَ إِنِّي لَقَائِمٌ مَا بَيْنِي وَبَيْنَهُ إِلاَّ عَبْدُ اللَّهِ بْنُ عَبَّاسٍ غَدَاةَ أُصِيبَ، وَكَانَ إِذَا مَرَّ بَيْنَ الصَّفَّيْنِ قَالَ اسْتَوُوا. حَتَّى إِذَا لَمْ يَرَ فِيهِنَّ خَلَلاً تَقَدَّمَ فَكَبَّرَ، وَرُبَّمَا قَرَأَ سُورَةَ يُوسُفَ، أَوِ النَّحْلَ، أَوْ نَحْوَ ذَلِكَ، فِي الرَّكْعَةِ الأُولَى حَتَّى يَجْتَمِعَ النَّاسُ، فَمَا هُوَ إِلاَّ أَنْ كَبَّرَ فَسَمِعْتُهُ يَقُولُ قَتَلَنِي ـ أَوْ أَكَلَنِي ـ الْكَلْبُ. حِينَ طَعَنَهُ، فَطَارَ الْعِلْجُ بِسِكِّينٍ ذَاتِ طَرَفَيْنِ لاَ يَمُرُّ عَلَى أَحَدٍ يَمِينًا وَلاَ شِمَالاً إِلاَّ طَعَنَهُ حَتَّى طَعَنَ ثَلاَثَةَ عَشَرَ رَجُلاً، مَاتَ مِنْهُمْ سَبْعَةٌ، فَلَمَّا رَأَى ذَلِكَ رَجُلٌ مِنَ الْمُسْلِمِينَ، طَرَحَ عَلَيْهِ بُرْنُسًا، فَلَمَّا ظَنَّ الْعِلْجُ أَنَّهُ مَأْخُوذٌ نَحَرَ نَفْسَهُ، وَتَنَاوَلَ عُمَرُ يَدَ عَبْدِ الرَّحْمَنِ بْنِ عَوْفٍ فَقَدَّمَهُ، فَمَنْ يَلِي عُمَرَ فَقَدْ رَأَى الَّذِي أَرَى، وَأَمَّا نَوَاحِي الْمَسْجِدِ فَإِنَّهُمْ لاَ يَدْرُونَ غَيْرَ أَنَّهُمْ قَدْ فَقَدُوا صَوْتَ عُمَرَ وَهُمْ يَقُولُونَ سُبْحَانَ اللَّهِ سُبْحَانَ اللَّهِ. فَصَلَّى بِهِمْ عَبْدُ الرَّحْمَنِ صَلاَةً خَفِيفَةً، فَلَمَّا انْصَرَفُوا. قَالَ يَا ابْنَ عَبَّاسٍ، انْظُرْ مَنْ قَتَلَنِي. فَجَالَ سَاعَةً، ثُمَّ جَاءَ، فَقَالَ غُلاَمُ الْمُغِيرَةِ. قَالَ الصَّنَعُ قَالَ نَعَمْ. قَالَ قَاتَلَهُ اللَّهُ لَقَدْ أَمَرْتُ بِهِ مَعْرُوفًا، الْحَمْدُ لِلَّهِ الَّذِي لَمْ يَجْعَلْ مَنِيَّتِي بِيَدِ رَجُلٍ يَدَّعِي الإِسْلاَمَ، قَدْ كُنْتَ أَنْتَ وَأَبُوكَ تُحِبَّانِ أَنْ تَكْثُرَ الْعُلُوجُ بِالْمَدِينَةِ وَكَانَ {الْعَبَّاسُ} أَكْثَرَهُمْ رَقِيقًا. فَقَالَ إِنْ شِئْتَ فَعَلْتُ. أَىْ إِنْ شِئْتَ قَتَلْنَا. قَالَ كَذَبْتَ، بَعْدَ مَا تَكَلَّمُوا بِلِسَانِكُمْ، وَصَلَّوْا قِبْلَتَكُمْ وَحَجُّوا حَجَّكُمْ فَاحْتُمِلَ إِلَى بَيْتِهِ فَانْطَلَقْنَا مَعَهُ، وَكَأَنَّ النَّاسَ لَمْ تُصِبْهُمْ مُصِيبَةٌ قَبْلَ يَوْمَئِذٍ، فَقَائِلٌ يَقُولُ لاَ بَأْسَ. وَقَائِلٌ يَقُولُ أَخَافُ عَلَيْهِ، فَأُتِيَ بِنَبِيذٍ فَشَرِبَهُ فَخَرَجَ مِنْ جَوْفِهِ، ثُمَّ أُتِيَ بِلَبَنٍ فَشَرِبَهُ فَخَرَجَ مِنْ جُرْحِهِ، فَعَلِمُوا أَنَّهُ مَيِّتٌ، فَدَخَلْنَا عَلَيْهِ، وَجَاءَ النَّاسُ يُثْنُونَ عَلَيْهِ، وَجَاءَ رَجُلٌ شَابٌّ، فَقَالَ أَبْشِرْ يَا أَمِيرَ الْمُؤْمِنِينَ بِبُشْرَى اللَّهِ لَكَ مِنْ صُحْبَةِ رَسُولِ اللَّهِ صلى الله عليه وسلم وَقَدَمٍ فِي الإِسْلاَمِ مَا قَدْ عَلِمْتَ، ثُمَّ وَلِيتَ فَعَدَلْتَ، ثُمَّ شَهَادَةٌ. قَالَ وَدِدْتُ أَنَّ ذَلِكَ كَفَافٌ لاَ عَلَيَّ وَلاَ لِي. فَلَمَّا أَدْبَرَ، إِذَا إِزَارُهُ يَمَسُّ الأَرْضَ. قَالَ رُدُّوا عَلَيَّ الْغُلاَمَ قَالَ ابْنَ أَخِي ارْفَعْ ثَوْبَكَ، فَإِنَّهُ أَبْقَى لِثَوْبِكَ وَأَتْقَى لِرَبِّكَ، يَا عَبْدَ اللَّهِ بْنَ عُمَرَ انْظُرْ مَا عَلَيَّ مِنَ الدَّيْنِ. فَحَسَبُوهُ فَوَجَدُوهُ سِتَّةً وَثَمَانِينَ أَلْفًا أَوْ نَحْوَهُ، قَالَ إِنْ وَفَى لَهُ مَالُ آلِ عُمَرَ، فَأَدِّهِ مِنْ أَمْوَالِهِمْ، وَإِلاَّ فَسَلْ فِي بَنِي عَدِيِّ بْنِ كَعْبٍ، فَإِنْ لَمْ تَفِ أَمْوَالُهُمْ فَسَلْ فِي قُرَيْشٍ، وَلاَ تَعْدُهُمْ إِلَى غَيْرِهِمْ، فَأَدِّ عَنِّي هَذَا الْمَالَ، انْطَلِقْ إِلَى عَائِشَةَ أُمِّ الْمُؤْمِنِينَ فَقُلْ يَقْرَأُ عَلَيْكِ عُمَرُ السَّلاَمَ. وَلاَ تَقُلْ أَمِيرُ الْمُؤْمِنِينَ. فَإِنِّي لَسْتُ الْيَوْمَ لِلْمُؤْمِنِينَ أَمِيرًا، وَقُلْ يَسْتَأْذِنُ عُمَرُ بْنُ الْخَطَّابِ أَنْ يُدْفَنَ مَعَ صَاحِبَيْهِ. فَسَلَّمَ وَاسْتَأْذَنَ، ثُمَّ دَخَلَ عَلَيْهَا، فَوَجَدَهَا قَاعِدَةً تَبْكِي فَقَالَ يَقْرَأُ عَلَيْكِ عُمَرُ بْنُ الْخَطَّابِ السَّلاَمَ وَيَسْتَأْذِنُ أَنْ يُدْفَنَ مَعَ صَاحِبَيْهِ. فَقَالَتْ كُنْتُ أُرِيدُهُ لِنَفْسِي، وَلأُوثِرَنَّ بِهِ الْيَوْمَ عَلَى نَفْسِي. فَلَمَّا أَقْبَلَ قِيلَ هَذَا عَبْدُ اللَّهِ بْنُ عُمَرَ قَدْ جَاءَ. قَالَ ارْفَعُونِي، فَأَسْنَدَهُ رَجُلٌ إِلَيْهِ، فَقَالَ مَا لَدَيْكَ قَالَ الَّذِي تُحِبُّ يَا أَمِيرَ الْمُؤْمِنِينَ أَذِنَتْ. قَالَ الْحَمْدُ لِلَّهِ، مَا كَانَ مِنْ شَىْءٍ أَهَمُّ إِلَىَّ مِنْ ذَلِكَ، فَإِذَا أَنَا قَضَيْتُ فَاحْمِلُونِي ثُمَّ سَلِّمْ فَقُلْ يَسْتَأْذِنُ عُمَرُ بْنُ الْخَطَّابِ، فَإِنْ أَذِنَتْ لِي فَأَدْخِلُونِي، وَإِنْ رَدَّتْنِي رُدُّونِي إِلَى مَقَابِرِ الْمُسْلِمِينَ.

وَجَاءَتْ أُمُّ الْمُؤْمِنِينَ حَفْصَةُ وَالنِّسَاءُ تَسِيرُ مَعَهَا، فَلَمَّا رَأَيْنَاهَا قُمْنَا، فَوَلَجَتْ عَلَيْهِ فَبَكَتْ عِنْدَهُ سَاعَةً، وَاسْتَأْذَنَ الرِّجَالُ، فَوَلَجَتْ دَاخِلاً لَهُمْ، فَسَمِعْنَا بُكَاءَهَا مِنَ الدَّاخِلِ. فَقَالُوا أَوْصِ يَا أَمِيرَ الْمُؤْمِنِينَ اسْتَخْلِفْ. قَالَ مَا أَجِدُ أَحَقَّ بِهَذَا الأَمْرِ مِنْ هَؤُلاَءِ النَّفَرِ أَوِ الرَّهْطِ الَّذِينَ تُوُفِّيَ رَسُولُ اللَّهِ صلى الله عليه وسلم وَهْوَ عَنْهُمْ رَاضٍ. فَسَمَّى عَلِيًّا وَعُثْمَانَ وَالزُّبَيْرَ وَطَلْحَةَ وَسَعْدًا وَعَبْدَ الرَّحْمَنِ وَقَالَ يَشْهَدُكُمْ عَبْدُ اللَّهِ بْنُ عُمَرَ وَلَيْسَ لَهُ مِنَ الأَمْرِ شَىْءٌ ـ كَهَيْئَةِ التَّعْزِيَةِ لَهُ ـ فَإِنْ أَصَابَتِ الإِمْرَةُ سَعْدًا فَهْوَ ذَاكَ، وَإِلاَّ فَلْيَسْتَعِنْ بِهِ أَيُّكُمْ مَا أُمِّرَ، فَإِنِّي لَمْ أَعْزِلْهُ عَنْ عَجْزٍ وَلاَ خِيَانَةٍ وَقَالَ أُوصِي الْخَلِيفَةَ مِنْ بَعْدِي بِالْمُهَاجِرِينَ الأَوَّلِينَ أَنْ يَعْرِفَ لَهُمْ حَقَّهُمْ، وَيَحْفَظَ لَهُمْ حُرْمَتَهُمْ، وَأُوصِيهِ بِالأَنْصَارِ خَيْرًا، الَّذِينَ تَبَوَّءُوا الدَّارَ وَالإِيمَانَ مِنْ قَبْلِهِمْ، أَنْ يُقْبَلَ مِنْ مُحْسِنِهِمْ، وَأَنْ يُعْفَى عَنْ مُسِيئِهِمْ، وَأُوصِيهِ بِأَهْلِ الأَمْصَارِ خَيْرًا فَإِنَّهُمْ رِدْءُ الإِسْلاَمِ، وَجُبَاةُ الْمَالِ، وَغَيْظُ الْعَدُوِّ، وَأَنْ لاَ يُؤْخَذَ مِنْهُمْ إِلاَّ فَضْلُهُمْ عَنْ رِضَاهُمْ، وَأُوصِيهِ بِالأَعْرَابِ خَيْرًا، فَإِنَّهُمْ أَصْلُ الْعَرَبِ وَمَادَّةُ الإِسْلاَمِ أَنْ يُؤْخَذَ مِنْ حَوَاشِي أَمْوَالِهِمْ وَتُرَدَّ عَلَى فُقَرَائِهِمْ، وَأُوصِيهِ بِذِمَّةِ اللَّهِ وَذِمَّةِ رَسُولِهِ صلى الله عليه وسلم أَنْ يُوفَى لَهُمْ بِعَهْدِهِمْ، وَأَنْ يُقَاتَلَ مِنْ وَرَائِهِمْ، وَلاَ يُكَلَّفُوا إِلاَّ طَاقَتَهُمْ. فَلَمَّا قُبِضَ خَرَجْنَا بِهِ فَانْطَلَقْنَا نَمْشِي فَسَلَّمَ عَبْدُ اللَّهِ بْنُ عُمَرَ قَالَ يَسْتَأْذِنُ عُمَرُ بْنُ الْخَطَّابِ. قَالَتْ أَدْخِلُوهُ. فَأُدْخِلَ، فَوُضِعَ هُنَالِكَ مَعَ صَاحِبَيْهِ، فَلَمَّا فُرِغَ مِنْ دَفْنِهِ اجْتَمَعَ هَؤُلاَءِ الرَّهْطُ، فَقَالَ عَبْدُ الرَّحْمَنِ اجْعَلُوا أَمْرَكُمْ إِلَى ثَلاَثَةٍ مِنْكُمْ. فَقَالَ الزُّبَيْرُ قَدْ جَعَلْتُ أَمْرِي إِلَى عَلِيٍّ. فَقَالَ طَلْحَةُ قَدْ جَعَلْتُ أَمْرِي إِلَى عُثْمَانَ. وَقَالَ سَعْدٌ قَدْ جَعَلْتُ أَمْرِي إِلَى عَبْدِ الرَّحْمَنِ بْنِ عَوْفٍ. فَقَالَ عَبْدُ الرَّحْمَنِ أَيُّكُمَا تَبَرَّأَ مِنْ هَذَا الأَمْرِ فَنَجْعَلُهُ إِلَيْهِ، وَاللَّهُ عَلَيْهِ وَالإِسْلاَمُ لَيَنْظُرَنَّ أَفْضَلَهُمْ فِي نَفْسِهِ. فَأُسْكِتَ الشَّيْخَانِ، فَقَالَ عَبْدُ الرَّحْمَنِ أَفَتَجْعَلُونَهُ إِلَىَّ، وَاللَّهُ عَلَىَّ أَنْ لاَ آلُوَ عَنْ أَفْضَلِكُمْ قَالاَ نَعَمْ، فَأَخَذَ بِيَدِ أَحَدِهِمَا فَقَالَ لَكَ قَرَابَةٌ مِنْ رَسُولِ اللَّهِ صلى الله عليه وسلم وَالْقَدَمُ فِي الإِسْلاَمِ مَا قَدْ عَلِمْتَ، فَاللَّهُ عَلَيْكَ لَئِنْ أَمَّرْتُكَ لَتَعْدِلَنَّ، وَلَئِنْ أَمَّرْتُ عُثْمَانَ لَتَسْمَعَنَّ وَلَتُطِيعَنَّ. ثُمَّ خَلاَ بِالآخَرِ فَقَالَ لَهُ مِثْلَ ذَلِكَ، فَلَمَّا أَخَذَ الْمِيثَاقَ قَالَ ارْفَعْ يَدَكَ يَا عُثْمَانُ. فَبَايَعَهُ، فَبَايَعَ لَهُ عَلِيٌّ، وَوَلَجَ أَهْلُ الدَّارِ فَبَايَعُوهُ.

Narrated `Abdullah bin `Abbas: `Ali bin Abu Talib came out of the house of the Prophet ﷺ during his fatal ailment. The people asked (`Ali), “O Abu Hasan! How is the health of Allah’s Messenger ﷺ this morning?” `Ali said, “This morning he is better, with the grace of Allah.” Al-`Abbas held `Ali by the hand and said, “Don’t you see him (about to die)? By Allah, within three days you will be the slave of the stick (i.e., under the command of another ruler). By Allah, I think that Allah's Messenger ﷺ will die from his present ailment, for I know the signs of death on the faces of the offspring of `Abdul Muttalib. So let us go to Allah's Messenger ﷺ to ask him who will take over the Caliphate. If the authority is given to us, we will know it, and if it is given to somebody else we will request him to recommend us to him. " `Ali said, "By Allah! If we ask Allah's Messenger ﷺ for the rulership and he refuses, then the people will never give it to us. Besides, I will never ask Allah's Messenger ﷺ for it." (See Hadith No 728, Vol 5). – Sahih Al-Bukhari 6266

حَدَّثَنَا إِسْحَاقُ، أَخْبَرَنَا بِشْرُ بْنُ شُعَيْبٍ، حَدَّثَنِي أَبِي، عَنِ الزُّهْرِيِّ، قَالَ أَخْبَرَنِي عَبْدُ اللَّهِ بْنُ كَعْبٍ، أَنَّ عَبْدَ اللَّهِ بْنَ عَبَّاسٍ، أَخْبَرَهُ أَنَّ عَلِيًّا ـ يَعْنِي ابْنَ أَبِي طَالِبٍ ـ خَرَجَ مِنْ عِنْدِ النَّبِيِّ صلى الله عليه وسلم وَحَدَّثَنَا أَحْمَدُ بْنُ صَالِحٍ حَدَّثَنَا عَنْبَسَةُ حَدَّثَنَا يُونُسُ عَنِ ابْنِ شِهَابٍ قَالَ أَخْبَرَنِي عَبْدُ اللَّهِ بْنُ كَعْبِ بْنِ مَالِكٍ أَنَّ عَبْدَ اللَّهِ بْنَ عَبَّاسٍ أَخْبَرَهُ أَنَّ عَلِيَّ بْنَ أَبِي طَالِبٍ ـ رضى الله عنه ـ خَرَجَ مِنْ عِنْدِ النَّبِيِّ صلى الله عليه وسلم فِي وَجَعِهِ الَّذِي تُوُفِّيَ فِيهِ فَقَالَ النَّاسُ يَا أَبَا حَسَنٍ كَيْفَ أَصْبَحَ رَسُولُ اللَّهِ صلى الله عليه وسلم قَالَ أَصْبَحَ بِحَمْدِ اللَّهِ بَارِئًا فَأَخَذَ بِيَدِهِ الْعَبَّاسُ فَقَالَ أَلاَ تَرَاهُ أَنْتَ وَاللَّهِ بَعْدَ الثَّلاَثِ عَبْدُ الْعَصَا وَاللَّهِ إِنِّي لأُرَى رَسُولَ اللَّهِ صلى الله عليه وسلم سَيُتَوَفَّى فِي وَجَعِهِ، وَإِنِّي لأَعْرِفُ فِي وُجُوهِ بَنِي عَبْدِ الْمُطَّلِبِ الْمَوْتَ، فَاذْهَبْ بِنَا إِلَى رَسُولِ اللَّهِ صلى الله عليه وسلم فَنَسْأَلَهُ فِيمَنْ يَكُونُ الأَمْرُ فَإِنْ كَانَ فِينَا عَلِمْنَا ذَلِكَ، وَإِنْ كَانَ فِي غَيْرِنَا أَمَرْنَاهُ فَأَوْصَى بِنَا. قَالَ عَلِيٌّ وَاللَّهِ لَئِنْ سَأَلْنَاهَا رَسُولَ اللَّهِ صلى الله عليه وسلم فَيَمْنَعُنَا لاَ يُعْطِينَاهَا النَّاسُ أَبَدًا، وَإِنِّي لاَ أَسْأَلُهَا رَسُولَ اللَّهِ صلى الله عليه وسلم أَبَدًا.

Narrated Abu Huraira: When Allah gave victory to His Apostle over the people of Mecca, Allah's Messenger ﷺ stood up among the people and after glorifying Allah, said, "Allah has prohibited fighting in Mecca and has given authority to His Apostle and the believers over it, so fighting was illegal for anyone before me, and was made legal for me for a part of a day, and it will not be legal for anyone after me. Its game should not be chased, its thorny bushes should not be uprooted, and picking up its fallen things is not allowed except for one who makes public announcement for it, and he whose relative is murdered has the option either to accept a compensation for it or to retaliate." Al-`Abbas said, "Except Al-Idhkhir, for we use it in our graves and houses." Allah's Messenger ﷺ said, "Except Al-Idhkhir." Abu Shah, a Yemenite, stood up and said, "O Allah's Messenger! Get it written for me." Allah's Messenger ﷺ said, "Write it for Abu Shah." (The sub-narrator asked Al-Auza'i): What did he mean by saying, "Get it written, O Allah's Apostle?" He replied, "The speech which he had heard from Allah's Messenger . – Sahih Al-Bukhari 2434

حَدَّثَنَا يَحْيَى بْنُ مُوسَى، حَدَّثَنَا الْوَلِيدُ بْنُ مُسْلِمٍ، حَدَّثَنَا الأَوْزَاعِيُّ، قَالَ حَدَّثَنِي يَحْيَى بْنُ أَبِي كَثِيرٍ، قَالَ حَدَّثَنِي أَبُو سَلَمَةَ بْنُ عَبْدِ الرَّحْمَنِ، قَالَ حَدَّثَنِي أَبُو هُرَيْرَةَ ـ رضى الله عنه ـ قَالَ لَمَّا فَتَحَ اللَّهُ عَلَى رَسُولِهِ صلى الله عليه وسلم مَكَّةَ قَامَ فِي النَّاسِ، فَحَمِدَ اللَّهَ، وَأَثْنَى عَلَيْهِ ثُمَّ قَالَ " إِنَّ اللَّهَ حَبَسَ عَنْ مَكَّةَ الْفِيلَ، وَسَلَّطَ عَلَيْهَا رَسُولَهُ وَالْمُؤْمِنِينَ، فَإِنَّهَا لاَ تَحِلُّ لأَحَدٍ كَانَ قَبْلِي، وَإِنَّهَا أُحِلَّتْ لِي سَاعَةً مِنْ نَهَارٍ، وَإِنَّهَا لاَ تَحِلُّ لأَحَدٍ بَعْدِي، فَلاَ يُنَفَّرُ صَيْدُهَا وَلاَ يُخْتَلَى شَوْكُهَا، وَلاَ تَحِلُّ سَاقِطَتُهَا إِلاَّ لِمُنْشِدٍ، وَمَنْ قُتِلَ لَهُ قَتِيلٌ فَهْوَ بِخَيْرِ النَّظَرَيْنِ، إِمَّا أَنْ يُفْدَى، وَإِمَّا أَنْ يُقِيدَ ". فَقَالَ الْعَبَّاسُ إِلاَّ الإِذْخِرَ، فَإِنَّا نَجْعَلُهُ لِقُبُورِنَا وَبُيُوتِنَا. فَقَالَ رَسُولُ اللَّهِ صلى الله عليه وسلم " إِلاَّ الإِذْخِرَ ". فَقَامَ أَبُو شَاهٍ ـ رَجُلٌ مِنْ أَهْلِ الْيَمَنِ ـ فَقَالَ اكْتُبُوا لِي يَا رَسُولَ اللَّهِ. فَقَالَ رَسُولُ اللَّهِ صلى الله عليه وسلم " اكْتُبُوا لأَبِي شَاهٍ ". قُلْتُ لِلأَوْزَاعِيِّ مَا قَوْلُهُ اكْتُبُوا لِي يَا رَسُولَ اللَّهِ قَالَ هَذِهِ الْخُطْبَةَ الَّتِي سَمِعَهَا مِنْ رَسُولِ اللَّهِ صلى الله عليه وسلم

Narrated Hisham's father: When Allah's Messenger ﷺ set out (towards Mecca) during the year of the Conquest (of Mecca) and this news reached (the infidels of Quraish), Abu Sufyan, Hakim bin Hizam and Budail bin Warqa came out to gather information about Allah's Messenger ﷺ, They proceeded on their way till they reached a place called Marr-az-Zahran (which is near Mecca). Behold! There they saw many fires as if they were the fires of `Arafat. Abu Sufyan said, "What is this? It looked like the fires of `Arafat." Budail bin Warqa' said, "Banu `Amr are less in number than that." Some of the guards of Allah's Messenger ﷺ saw them and took them over, caught them and brought them to Allah's Messenger ﷺ. Abu

Sufyan embraced Islam. When the Prophet ﷺ proceeded, he said to Al-Abbas, “Keep Abu Sufyan standing at the top of the mountain so that he would look at the Muslims. So Al-`Abbas kept him standing (at that place) and the tribes with the Prophet ﷺ started passing in front of Abu Sufyan in military batches. A batch passed and Abu Sufyan said, “O `Abbas Who are these?” `Abbas said, “They are (Banu) Ghifar.” Abu Sufyan said, I have got nothing to do with Ghifar.” Then (a batch of the tribe of) Juhaina passed by and he said similarly as above. Then (a batch of the tribe of) Sa`d bin Huzaim passed by and he said similarly as above. Then (Banu) Sulaim passed by and he said similarly as above. Then came a batch, the like of which Abu Sufyan had not seen. He said, “Who are these?” `Abbas said, “They are the Ansar headed by Sa`d bin Ubada, the one holding the flag.” Sa`d bin Ubada said, “O Abu Sufyan! Today is the day of a great battle and today (what is prohibited in) the Ka`ba will be permissible.” Abu Sufyan said., “O `Abbas! How excellent the day of destruction is! “Then came another batch (of warriors) which was the smallest of all the batches, and in it there was Allah’s Messenger ﷺ and his companions and the flag of the Prophet ﷺ was carried by Az-Zubair bin Al Awwam. When Allah’s Messenger ﷺ passed by Abu Sufyan, the latter said, (to the Prophet), “Do you know what Sa`d bin ‘Ubada said?” The Prophet ﷺ said, “What did he say?” Abu Sufyan said, “He said so-and-so.” The Prophet ﷺ said, “Sa`d told a lie, but today Allah will give superiority to the Ka`ba and today the Ka`ba will be covered with a (cloth) covering.” Allah’s Messenger ﷺ ordered that his flag be fixed at Al-Hajun. Narrated `Urwa: Nafi` bin Jubair bin Mut`im said, “I heard Al-Abbas saying to Az-Zubair bin Al- `Awwam, ‘O Abu `Abdullah ! Did Allah’s Messenger ﷺ order you to fix the flag here?’ “ Allah’s Messenger ﷺ ordered Khalid bin Al-Walid to enter Mecca from its upper part from Ka’da while the Prophet ﷺ himself entered from Kuda. Two men from the cavalry of Khalid bin Al-Wahd named Hubaish bin Al-Ash’ar and Kurz bin Jabir Al-Fihri were martyred on that day. – Sahih Al-Bukhari 4280

حَدَّثَنَا عُبَيْدُ بْنُ إِسْمَاعِيلَ، حَدَّثَنَا أَبُو أُسَامَةَ، عَنْ هِشَامٍ، عَنْ أَبِيهِ، قَالَ لَمَّا سَارَ رَسُولُ اللَّهِ صلى الله عليه وسلم عَامَ الْفَتْحِ فَبَلَغَ ذَلِكَ قُرَيْشًا، خَرَجَ أَبُو سُفْيَانَ بْنُ حَرْبٍ وَحَكِيمُ بْنُ حِزَامٍ وَبُدَيْلُ بْنُ وَرْقَاءَ يَلْتَمِسُونَ الْخَبَرَ عَنْ رَسُولِ اللَّهِ صلى الله عليه وسلم فَأَقْبَلُوا يَسِيرُونَ حَتَّى أَتَوْا مَرَّ الظَّهْرَانِ، فَإِذَا هُمْ بِنِيرَانٍ كَأَنَّهَا نِيرَانُ عَرَفَةَ، فَقَالَ أَبُو سُفْيَانَ مَا هَذِهِ لَكَأَنَّهَا نِيرَانُ عَرَفَةَ. فَقَالَ بُدَيْلُ بْنُ وَرْقَاءَ نِيرَانُ بَنِي عَمْرٍو. فَقَالَ أَبُو سُفْيَانَ عَمْرٌو أَقَلُّ مِنْ ذَلِكَ. فَرَآهُمْ نَاسٌ مِنْ حَرَسِ رَسُولِ اللَّهِ صلى الله عليه وسلم فَأَدْرَكُوهُمْ فَأَخَذُوهُمْ، فَأَتَوْا بِهِمْ رَسُولَ اللَّهِ صلى الله عليه وسلم فَأَسْلَمَ أَبُو سُفْيَانَ، فَلَمَّا سَارَ قَالَ لِلْعَبَّاسِ " احْبِسْ أَبَا سُفْيَانَ عِنْدَ حَطْمِ الْخَيْلِ حَتَّى يَنْظُرَ إِلَى الْمُسْلِمِينَ ". فَحَبَسَهُ الْعَبَّاسُ، فَجَعَلَتِ الْقَبَائِلُ تَمُرُّ مَعَ النَّبِيِّ صلى الله عليه وسلم تَمُرُّ كَتِيبَةً كَتِيبَةً عَلَى أَبِي سُفْيَانَ، فَمَرَّتْ كَتِيبَةٌ قَالَ يَا عَبَّاسُ مَنْ هَذِهِ قَالَ هَذِهِ غِفَارُ. قَالَ مَا لِي وَلِغِفَارَ ثُمَّ مَرَّتْ جُهَيْنَةُ، قَالَ مِثْلَ ذَلِكَ، ثُمَّ مَرَّتْ سَعْدُ بْنُ هُذَيْمٍ، فَقَالَ مِثْلَ ذَلِكَ، وَمَرَّتْ سُلَيْمُ، فَقَالَ مِثْلَ ذَلِكَ، حَتَّى أَقْبَلَتْ كَتِيبَةٌ لَمْ يَرَ مِثْلَهَا، قَالَ مَنْ هَذِهِ قَالَ هَؤُلاَءِ الأَنْصَارُ عَلَيْهِمْ سَعْدُ بْنُ عُبَادَةَ مَعَهُ الرَّايَةُ. فَقَالَ سَعْدُ بْنُ عُبَادَةَ يَا أَبَا سُفْيَانَ الْيَوْمُ يَوْمُ الْمَلْحَمَةِ، الْيَوْمَ تُسْتَحَلُّ الْكَعْبَةُ. فَقَالَ أَبُو سُفْيَانَ يَا عَبَّاسُ حَبَّذَا يَوْمُ الذِّمَارِ. ثُمَّ جَاءَتْ كَتِيبَةٌ، وَهْىَ أَقَلُّ الْكَتَائِبِ، فِيهِمْ رَسُولُ اللَّهِ صلى الله عليه وسلم وَأَصْحَابُهُ، وَرَايَةُ النَّبِيِّ صلى الله عليه وسلم مَعَ الزُّبَيْرِ بْنِ الْعَوَّامِ، فَلَمَّا مَرَّ رَسُولُ اللَّهِ صلى الله عليه وسلم بِأَبِي سُفْيَانَ قَالَ أَلَمْ تَعْلَمْ مَا قَالَ سَعْدُ بْنُ عُبَادَةَ قَالَ " مَا قَالَ ". قَالَ كَذَا وَكَذَا. فَقَالَ " كَذَبَ سَعْدٌ، وَلَكِنْ هَذَا يَوْمٌ يُعَظِّمُ اللَّهُ فِيهِ الْكَعْبَةَ، وَيَوْمٌ تُكْسَى فِيهِ الْكَعْبَةُ ". قَالَ وَأَمَرَ رَسُولُ اللَّهِ صلى الله عليه وسلم أَنْ تُرْكَزَ رَايَتُهُ بِالْحَجُونِ. قَالَ عُرْوَةُ وَأَخْبَرَنِي نَافِعُ بْنُ جُبَيْرِ بْنِ مُطْعِمٍ قَالَ سَمِعْتُ الْعَبَّاسَ يَقُولُ لِلزُّبَيْرِ بْنِ الْعَوَّامِ يَا أَبَا عَبْدِ اللَّهِ، هَا هُنَا أَمَرَكَ رَسُولُ اللَّهِ صلى الله عليه وسلم أَنْ تَرْكُزَ الرَّايَةَ، قَالَ وَأَمَرَ رَسُولُ اللَّهِ صلى الله عليه وسلم يَوْمَئِذٍ خَالِدَ بْنَ الْوَلِيدِ أَنْ يَدْخُلَ مِنْ أَعْلَى مَكَّةَ مِنْ كَدَاءٍ، وَدَخَلَ النَّبِيُّ صلى الله عليه وسلم مِنْ كُدَا، فَقُتِلَ مِنْ خَيْلِ خَالِدٍ يَوْمَئِذٍ رَجُلاَنِ حُبَيْشُ بْنُ الأَشْعَرِ وَكُرْزُ بْنُ جَابِرٍ الْفِهْرِيُّ

Narrated `Aisha: We poured medicine into the mouth of Allah’s Messenger ﷺ during his illness, and he pointed out to us intending to say, “Don’t pour medicine into my mouth.” We thought that his refusal was out of the aversion a patient usually has for medicine. When he improved and felt a bit better he said (to us.) “Didn’t I forbid you to pour medicine into my mouth?” We said, “We thought (you did so) because of the aversion, one usually have for medicine.” Allah’s Messenger ﷺ said, “There is none of you but will be forced to drink medicine, and I will watch you, except Al-`Abbas, for he did not witness this act of yours.". – Sahih Al-Bukhari 6897

حَدَّثَنَا مُسَدَّدٌ، حَدَّثَنَا يَحْيَى، عَنْ سُفْيَانَ، حَدَّثَنَا مُوسَى بْنُ أَبِي عَائِشَةَ، عَنْ عُبَيْدِ اللَّهِ بْنِ عَبْدِ اللَّهِ، قَالَ قَالَتْ عَائِشَةُ لَدَدْنَا رَسُولَ اللَّهِ صلى الله عليه وسلم فِي مَرَضِهِ، وَجَعَلَ يُشِيرُ إِلَيْنَا " لاَ تَلُدُّونِي ". قَالَ فَقُلْنَا كَرَاهِيَةُ الْمَرِيضِ بِالدَّوَاءِ، فَلَمَّا أَفَاقَ قَالَ " أَلَمْ أَنْهَكُمْ أَنْ تَلُدُّونِي ". قَالَ قُلْنَا كَرَاهِيَةٌ لِلدَّوَاءِ. فَقَالَ رَسُولُ اللَّهِ صلى الله عليه وسلم " لاَ يَبْقَى مِنْكُمْ أَحَدٌ إِلاَّ لُدَّ ـ وَأَنَا أَنْظُرُ ـ إِلاَّ الْعَبَّاسَ فَإِنَّهُ لَمْ يَشْهَدْكُمْ "

Narrated `Aisha: Fatima and Al `Abbas came to Abu Bakr, seeking their share from the property of Allah's Messenger ﷺ and at that time, they were asking for their land at Fadak and their share from Khaibar. Abu Bakr said to them, " I have heard from Allah's Messenger ﷺ saying, 'Our property cannot be inherited, and whatever we leave is to be spent in charity, but the family of Muhammad may take their provisions from this property." Abu Bakr added, "By Allah, I will not leave the procedure I saw Allah's Messenger ﷺ following during his lifetime concerning this property." Therefore Fatima left Abu Bakr and did not speak to him till she died. – Sahih Al-Bukhari 6725, 6726

حَدَّثَنَا عَبْدُ اللَّهِ بْنُ مُحَمَّدٍ، حَدَّثَنَا هِشَامٌ، أَخْبَرَنَا مَعْمَرٌ، عَنِ الزُّهْرِيِّ، عَنْ عُرْوَةَ، عَنْ عَائِشَةَ، أَنَّ فَاطِمَةَ، وَالْعَبَّاسَ ـ عَلَيْهِمَا السَّلاَمُ ـ أَتَيَا أَبَا بَكْرٍ يَلْتَمِسَانِ مِيرَاثَهُمَا مِنْ رَسُولِ اللَّهِ صلى الله عليه وسلم وَهُمَا حِينَئِذٍ يَطْلُبَانِ أَرْضَيْهِمَا مِنْ فَدَكَ، وَسَهْمَهُمَا مِنْ خَيْبَرَ. فَقَالَ لَهُمَا أَبُو بَكْرٍ سَمِعْتُ رَسُولَ اللَّهِ صلى الله عليه وسلم يَقُولُ " لاَ نُورَثُ، مَا تَرَكْنَا صَدَقَةٌ، إِنَّمَا يَأْكُلُ آلُ مُحَمَّدٍ مِنْ هَذَا الْمَالِ ". قَالَ أَبُو بَكْرٍ وَاللَّهِ لاَ أَدَعُ أَمْرًا رَأَيْتُ رَسُولَ اللَّهِ صلى الله عليه وسلم يَصْنَعُهُ فِيهِ إِلاَّ صَنَعْتُهُ. قَالَ فَهَجَرَتْهُ فَاطِمَةُ، فَلَمْ تُكَلِّمْهُ حَتَّى مَاتَتْ

Narrated Jabir bin `Abdullah: While Allah's Messenger ﷺ was carrying stones (along) with the people of Mecca for (the building of) the Ka`ba wearing an Izar (waist-sheet cover), his uncle Al-`Abbas said to him, "O my nephew! (It would be better) if you take off your Izar and put it over your shoulders underneath the stones." So he took off his Izar and put it over his shoulders, but he fell unconscious and since then he had never been seen naked. – Sahih Al-Bukhari 364

حَدَّثَنَا مَطَرُ بْنُ الْفَضْلِ، قَالَ حَدَّثَنَا رَوْحٌ، قَالَ حَدَّثَنَا زَكَرِيَّاءُ بْنُ إِسْحَاقَ، حَدَّثَنَا عَمْرُو بْنُ دِينَارٍ، قَالَ سَمِعْتُ جَابِرَ بْنَ عَبْدِ اللَّهِ، يُحَدِّثُ أَنَّ رَسُولَ اللَّهِ صلى الله عليه وسلم كَانَ يَنْقُلُ مَعَهُمُ الْحِجَارَةَ لِلْكَعْبَةِ وَعَلَيْهِ إِزَارُهُ. فَقَالَ لَهُ الْعَبَّاسُ عَمُّهُ يَا ابْنَ أَخِي، لَوْ حَلَلْتَ إِزَارَكَ فَجَعَلْتَ عَلَى مَنْكِبَيْكَ دُونَ الْحِجَارَةِ. قَالَ فَحَلَّهُ فَجَعَلَهُ عَلَى مَنْكِبَيْهِ، فَسَقَطَ مَغْشِيًّا عَلَيْهِ، فَمَا رُئِيَ بَعْدَ ذَلِكَ عُرْيَانًا صلى الله عليه وسلم.

Narrated Al-Abbas bin `Abdul Muttalib: That he said to the Prophet ﷺ "You have not been of any avail to your uncle (Abu Talib) (though) by Allah, he used to protect you and used to become angry on your behalf." The Prophet ﷺ said, "He is in a shallow fire, and had It not been for me, he would have been in the bottom of the (Hell) Fire.". – Sahih Al-Bukhari 3883

حَدَّثَنَا مُسَدَّدٌ، حَدَّثَنَا يَحْيَى، عَنْ سُفْيَانَ، حَدَّثَنَا عَبْدُ الْمَلِكِ، حَدَّثَنَا عَبْدُ اللَّهِ بْنُ الْحَارِثِ، حَدَّثَنَا الْعَبَّاسُ بْنُ عَبْدِ الْمُطَّلِبِ ـ رضى الله عنه ـ قَالَ لِلنَّبِيِّ صلى الله عليه وسلم مَا أَغْنَيْتَ عَنْ عَمِّكَ فَإِنَّهُ كَانَ يَحُوطُكَ وَيَغْضَبُ لَكَ. قَالَ " هُوَ فِي ضَحْضَاحٍ مِنْ نَارٍ، وَلَوْلاَ أَنَا لَكَانَ فِي الدَّرَكِ الأَسْفَلِ مِنَ النَّارِ "

Ibn Abbas
اَبْن عَبَّاس

Narrated `Amr: When I mentioned it (i.e. the narration of Rafi` 'bin Khadij: no. 532) to Tawus, he said, "It is permissible to rent the land for cultivation, for Ibn `Abbas said, 'The Prophet ﷺ did not forbid that, but said: One had better give the land to one's brother gratis rather than charge a certain amount for it.' ". – Sahih Al-Bukhari 2342

حَدَّثَنَا قَبِيصَةُ، حَدَّثَنَا سُفْيَانُ، عَنْ عَمْرٍو، قَالَ ذَكَرْتُهُ لِطَاوُسٍ فَقَالَ يُزْرِعُ، قَالَ ابْنُ عَبَّاسٍ ـ رضى الله عنهما ـ إِنَّ النَّبِيَّ صلى الله عليه وسلم لَمْ يَنْهَ عَنْهُ وَلَكِنْ قَالَ " أَنْ يَمْنَحَ أَحَدُكُمْ أَخَاهُ خَيْرٌ لَهُ مِنْ أَنْ يَأْخُذَ شَيْئًا مَعْلُومًا ".

Narrated Ibn `Abbas: The Prophet ﷺ said, "May Allah be merciful to the mother of Ishmael! If she had left the water of Zamzam (fountain) as it was, (without constructing a basin for keeping the water), (or said, "If she had not taken handfuls of its water"), it would have been a flowing stream. Jurhum (an Arab tribe) came and asked her, 'May we settle at your dwelling?' She said, 'Yes, but you have no right to possess the water.' They agreed.". – Sahih Al-Bukhari 2368

حَدَّثَنَا عَبْدُ اللَّهِ بْنُ مُحَمَّدٍ، أَخْبَرَنَا عَبْدُ الرَّزَّاقِ، أَخْبَرَنَا مَعْمَرٌ، عَنْ أَيُّوبَ، وَكَثِيرِ بْنِ كَثِيرٍ ـ يَزِيدُ أَحَدُهُمَا عَلَى الآخَرِ ـ عَنْ سَعِيدِ بْنِ جُبَيْرٍ، قَالَ قَالَ ابْنُ عَبَّاسٍ ـ رضى الله عنهما ـ قَالَ النَّبِيُّ صلى الله عليه وسلم " يَرْحَمُ اللَّهُ أُمَّ إِسْمَاعِيلَ، لَوْ تَرَكَتْ زَمْزَمَ ـ أَوْ قَالَ لَوْ لَمْ تَغْرِفْ مِنَ الْمَاءِ ـ لَكَانَتْ عَيْنًا مَعِينًا، وَأَقْبَلَ جُرْهُمُ فَقَالُوا أَتَأْذَنِينَ أَنْ نَنْزِلَ عِنْدَكِ قَالَتْ نَعَمْ وَلاَ حَقَّ لَكُمْ فِي الْمَاءِ. قَالُوا نَعَمْ ".

Narrated `Abdullah bin `Abbas: I had been eager to ask `Umar about the two ladies from among the wives of the Prophet ﷺ regarding whom Allah said (in the Qur'an saying): If you two (wives of the Prophet ﷺ namely Aisha and Hafsa) turn in repentance to Allah your hearts are indeed so inclined (to oppose what the Prophet ﷺ likes) (66.4), till performed the Hajj along with `Umar (and on our way back from Hajj) he went aside (to answer the call of nature) and I also went aside along with him carrying a tumbler of water. When he had answered the call of nature and returned. I poured water on his hands from the tumbler and he performed ablution. I said, "O Chief of the believers! ' Who were the two ladies from among the wives of the Prophet ﷺ to whom Allah said: 'If you two return in repentance (66.4)? He said, "I am astonished at your question, O Ibn `Abbas. They were Aisha and Hafsa." Then `Umar went on relating the narration and said. "I and an Ansari neighbor of mine from Bani Umaiya bin Zaid who used to live in `Awali Al-Medina, used to visit the Prophet ﷺ in turns. He used to go one day, and I another day. When I went I would bring him the news of what had happened that day regarding the instructions and orders and when he went, he used to do the same for me. We, the people of Quraish, used to have authority over women, but when we came to live with the Ansar, we noticed that the Ansari women had the upper hand over their men, so our women started acquiring the habits of the Ansari women. Once I shouted at my wife and she paid me back in my coin and I disliked that she should answer me back. She said, 'Why do you take it ill that I retort upon you? By Allah, the wives of the Prophet ﷺ retort upon him, and some of them may not speak with him for the whole day till night.' What she said scared me and I said to her, 'Whoever amongst them does so, will be a great loser.' Then I dressed myself and went to Hafsa and asked her, 'Does any of you keep Allah's Messenger ﷺ angry all the day long till night?' She replied in the affirmative. I said, 'She is a ruined losing person (and will never have success)! Doesn't she fear that Allah may get angry for the anger of Allah's Messenger ﷺ and thus she will be ruined? Don't ask Allah's Messenger ﷺ too many things, and don't retort upon him in any case, and don't desert him. Demand from me whatever you like, and don't be tempted to imitate your neighbor (i.e. `Aisha) in her behavior towards the Prophet), for she (i.e. Aisha) is more beautiful than you, and more beloved to Allah's Messenger ﷺ. In those days it was rumored that Ghassan, (a tribe living in Sham) was getting prepared their horses to invade us. My companion went (to the Prophet ﷺ on the day of his turn, went and returned to us at night and knocked at my door violently, asking whether I was sleeping. I was scared (by the hard knocking) and came out to him. He said that a great thing had happened. I asked him: What is it? Have Ghassan come? He replied that it was worse and more serious than that, and added that Allah's Apostle had divorced all his wives.

I said, Hafsa is a ruined loser! I expected that would happen some day.' So I dressed myself and offered the Fajr prayer with the Prophet. Then the Prophet ﷺ entered an upper room and stayed there alone. I went to Hafsa and found her weeping. I asked her, 'Why are you weeping? Didn't I warn you? Have Allah's Messenger ﷺ divorced you all?' She replied, 'I don't know. He is there in the upper room.' I then went out and came to the pulpit and found a group of people around it and some of them were weeping. Then I sat with them for some time, but could not endure the situation. So I went to the upper room where the Prophet ﷺ was and requested to a black slave of his: "Will you get the permission of (Allah's Apostle) for `Umar (to enter)? The slave went in, talked to the Prophet ﷺ about it and came out saying, 'I mentioned you to him but he did not reply.' So, I went and sat with the people who were sitting by the pulpit, but I could not bear the situation, so I went to the slave again and said: "Will you get he permission for `Umar? He went in and brought the same reply as before. When I was leaving, behold, the slave called me saying, "Allah's Messenger ﷺ has granted you permission." So, I entered upon the Prophet and saw him lying on a mat without wedding on it, and the mat had left its mark on the body of the Prophet, and he was leaning on a leather pillow stuffed with palm fires. I greeted him and while still standing, I said: "Have you divorced your wives?' He raised his eyes to me and replied in the negative. And then while still standing, I said chatting: "Will you heed what I say, 'O Allah's Messenger ﷺ !We, the people of Quraish used to have the upper hand over our women (wives), and when we came to the people whose women had the upper hand over them..." `Umar told the whole story (about his wife). "On that the Prophet ﷺ smiled." `Umar further said, "I then said, 'I went to Hafsa and said to her: Do not be tempted to imitate your companion (`Aisha) for she is more beautiful than you and more beloved to the Prophet.' The Prophet ﷺ smiled again. When I saw him smiling, I sat down and cast a glance at the room, and by Allah, I couldn't see anything of importance but three hides. I said (to Allah's Messenger ﷺ) "Invoke Allah to make your followers prosperous for the Persians and the Byzantines have been made prosperous and given worldly luxuries, though they do not worship Allah?' The Prophet ﷺ was leaning then (and on hearing my speech he sat straight) and said, 'O Ibn Al-Khattab! Do you have any doubt (that the Hereafter is better than this world)? These people have been given rewards of their good deeds in this world only.' I asked the Prophet' ﷺ. Please ask Allah's forgiveness for me. The Prophet ﷺ did not go to his wives because of the secret which Hafsa had disclosed to `Aisha, and he said that he would not go to his wives for one month as he was angry with them when Allah admonished him (for his oath that he would not approach Maria). When twenty-nine days had passed, the Prophet ﷺ went to Aisha first of all. She said to him, 'You took an oath that you would not come to us for one month, and today only twenty-nine days have passed, as I have been counting them day by day.' The Prophet ﷺ said, 'The month is also of twenty-nine days.' That month consisted of twenty-nine days. `Aisha said, 'When the Divine revelation of Choice was revealed, the Prophet ﷺ started with me, saying to me, 'I am telling you something, but you need not hurry to give the reply till you can consult your parents." `Aisha knew that her parents would not advise her to part with the Prophet ﷺ. The Prophet ﷺ said that Allah had said: 'O Prophet! Say To your wives; If you desire The life of this world And its glitter, ... then come! I will make a provision for you and set you free In a handsome manner. But if you seek Allah And His Apostle, and The Home of the Hereafter, then Verily, Allah has prepared For the good-doers amongst you A great reward.' (33.28) `Aisha said, 'Am I to consult my parents about this? I indeed prefer Allah, His Apostle, and the Home of the Hereafter.' After that the Prophet ﷺ gave the choice to his other wives and they also gave the same reply as `Aisha did.". – Sahih Al-Bukhari 2468

حَدَّثَنَا يَحْيَى بْنُ بُكَيْرٍ، حَدَّثَنَا اللَّيْثُ، عَنْ عُقَيْلٍ، عَنِ ابْنِ شِهَابٍ، قَالَ أَخْبَرَنِي عُبَيْدُ اللَّهِ بْنُ عَبْدِ اللَّهِ بْنِ أَبِي ثَوْرٍ، عَنْ عَبْدِ اللَّهِ بْنِ عَبَّاسٍ ـ رضى الله عنهما ـ قَالَ لَمْ أَزَلْ حَرِيصًا عَلَى أَنْ أَسْأَلَ عُمَرَ ـ رضى الله عنه ـ عَنِ الْمَرْأَتَيْنِ مِنْ أَزْوَاجِ النَّبِيِّ صلى الله عليه وسلم اللَّتَيْنِ قَالَ اللَّهُ لَهُمَا {إِنْ تَتُوبَا إِلَى اللَّهِ فَقَدْ صَغَتْ قُلُوبُكُمَا} فَحَجَجْتُ مَعَهُ فَعَدَلَ وَعَدَلْتُ مَعَهُ بِالإِدَاوَةِ، فَتَبَرَّزَ حَتَّى جَاءَ، فَسَكَبْتُ عَلَى يَدَيْهِ مِنَ الإِدَاوَةِ، فَتَوَضَّأَ فَقُلْتُ يَا أَمِيرَ الْمُؤْمِنِينَ مَنِ الْمَرْأَتَانِ مِنْ أَزْوَاجِ النَّبِيِّ صلى الله عليه وسلم اللَّتَانِ قَالَ لَهُمَا {إِنْ تَتُوبَا إِلَى اللَّهِ} فَقَالَ وَاعَجَبِي لَكَ يَا ابْنَ عَبَّاسٍ عَائِشَةُ وَحَفْصَةُ، ثُمَّ اسْتَقْبَلَ عُمَرُ الْحَدِيثَ يَسُوقُهُ، فَقَالَ إِنِّي كُنْتُ وَجَارٌ لِي مِنَ الأَنْصَارِ فِي بَنِي أُمَيَّةَ بْنِ زَيْدٍ، وَهْىَ مِنْ عَوَالِي الْمَدِينَةِ، وَكُنَّا نَتَنَاوَبُ النُّزُولَ عَلَى النَّبِيِّ صلى الله عليه وسلم فَيَنْزِلُ يَوْمًا وَأَنْزِلُ يَوْمًا، فَإِذَا نَزَلْتُ جِئْتُهُ مِنْ خَبَرِ ذَلِكَ الْيَوْمِ مِنَ الأَمْرِ وَغَيْرِهِ، وَإِذَا نَزَلَ فَعَلَ مِثْلَهُ، وَكُنَّا مَعْشَرَ قُرَيْشٍ نَغْلِبُ النِّسَاءَ، فَلَمَّا قَدِمْنَا عَلَى الأَنْصَارِ إِذَا هُمْ قَوْمٌ تَغْلِبُهُمْ نِسَاؤُهُمْ، فَطَفِقَ نِسَاؤُنَا يَأْخُذْنَ مِنْ أَدَبِ نِسَاءِ الأَنْصَارِ، فَصِحْتُ عَلَى امْرَأَتِي، فَرَاجَعَتْنِي، فَأَنْكَرْتُ أَنْ تُرَاجِعَنِي، فَقَالَتْ وَلِمَ تُنْكِرُ أَنْ أُرَاجِعَكَ فَوَاللَّهِ إِنَّ أَزْوَاجَ النَّبِيِّ صلى الله عليه وسلم لَيُرَاجِعْنَهُ، وَإِنَّ إِحْدَاهُنَّ لَتَهْجُرُهُ الْيَوْمَ حَتَّى اللَّيْلِ. فَأَفْزَعَنِي، فَقُلْتُ خَابَتْ مَنْ فَعَلَ مِنْهُنَّ بِعَظِيمٍ. ثُمَّ جَمَعْتُ عَلَىَّ ثِيَابِي، فَدَخَلْتُ عَلَى حَفْصَةَ فَقُلْتُ أَىْ حَفْصَةُ، أَتُغَاضِبُ إِحْدَاكُنَّ رَسُولَ اللَّهِ صلى الله عليه وسلم الْيَوْمَ حَتَّى اللَّيْلِ فَقَالَتْ نَعَمْ. فَقُلْتُ خَابَتْ وَخَسِرَتْ، أَفَتَأْمَنُ أَنْ يَغْضَبَ اللَّهُ لِغَضَبِ رَسُولِهِ صلى الله عليه وسلم فَتَهْلِكِينَ لاَ تَسْتَكْثِرِي عَلَى رَسُولِ اللَّهِ صلى الله عليه وسلم وَلاَ تُرَاجِعِيهِ فِي شَىْءٍ وَلاَ تَهْجُرِيهِ، وَاسْأَلِينِي مَا بَدَا لَكِ، وَلاَ يَغُرَّنَّكِ أَنْ كَانَتْ جَارَتُكِ هِيَ أَوْضَأَ مِنْكِ وَأَحَبَّ إِلَى رَسُولِ اللَّهِ صلى الله عليه وسلم ـ يُرِيدُ عَائِشَةَ ـ وَكُنَّا تَحَدَّثْنَا أَنَّ غَسَّانَ تُنْعِلُ النِّعَالَ لِغَزْوِنَا، فَنَزَلَ صَاحِبِي يَوْمَ نَوْبَتِهِ فَرَجَعَ عِشَاءً، فَضَرَبَ بَابِي ضَرْبًا شَدِيدًا، وَقَالَ أَنَائِمٌ هُوَ فَفَزِعْتُ فَخَرَجْتُ إِلَيْهِ. وَقَالَ حَدَثَ أَمْرٌ عَظِيمٌ. قُلْتُ مَا هُوَ أَجَاءَتْ غَسَّانُ قَالَ لاَ، بَلْ أَعْظَمُ مِنْهُ وَأَطْوَلُ، طَلَّقَ رَسُولُ اللَّهِ صلى الله عليه وسلم نِسَاءَهُ. قَالَ قَدْ خَابَتْ حَفْصَةُ وَخَسِرَتْ، كُنْتُ أَظُنُّ أَنَّ هَذَا يُوشِكُ أَنْ يَكُونَ، فَجَمَعْتُ عَلَىَّ ثِيَابِي، فَصَلَّيْتُ صَلاَةَ الْفَجْرِ مَعَ النَّبِيِّ صلى الله عليه وسلم فَدَخَلَ مَشْرُبَةً لَهُ فَاعْتَزَلَ فِيهَا، فَدَخَلْتُ عَلَى حَفْصَةَ، فَإِذَا هِيَ تَبْكِي. قُلْتُ مَا يُبْكِيكِ أَوَلَمْ أَكُنْ حَذَّرْتُكِ أَطَلَّقَكُنَّ رَسُولُ اللَّهِ صلى الله عليه وسلم قَالَتْ لاَ أَدْرِي هُوَ ذَا فِي الْمَشْرُبَةِ. فَخَرَجْتُ، فَجِئْتُ الْمِنْبَرَ، فَإِذَا حَوْلَهُ رَهْطٌ يَبْكِي بَعْضُهُمْ، فَجَلَسْتُ مَعَهُمْ قَلِيلاً ثُمَّ غَلَبَنِي مَا أَجِدُ، فَجِئْتُ الْمَشْرُبَةَ الَّتِي هُوَ فِيهَا فَقُلْتُ لِغُلاَمٍ لَهُ أَسْوَدَ اسْتَأْذِنْ لِعُمَرَ. فَدَخَلَ، فَكَلَّمَ النَّبِيَّ صلى الله عليه وسلم ثُمَّ خَرَجَ، فَقَالَ ذَكَرْتُكَ لَهُ، فَصَمَتَ، فَانْصَرَفْتُ حَتَّى جَلَسْتُ مَعَ الرَّهْطِ الَّذِينَ عِنْدَ الْمِنْبَرِ، ثُمَّ غَلَبَنِي مَا أَجِدُ فَجِئْتُ، فَذَكَرَ مِثْلَهُ، فَجَلَسْتُ مَعَ الرَّهْطِ الَّذِينَ عِنْدَ الْمِنْبَرِ، ثُمَّ غَلَبَنِي مَا أَجِدُ فَجِئْتُ الْغُلاَمَ. فَقُلْتُ اسْتَأْذِنْ لِعُمَرَ. فَذَكَرَ مِثْلَهُ، فَلَمَّا وَلَّيْتُ مُنْصَرِفًا، فَإِذَا الْغُلاَمُ يَدْعُونِي قَالَ أَذِنَ لَكَ رَسُولُ اللَّهِ صلى الله عليه وسلم. فَدَخَلْتُ عَلَيْهِ، فَإِذَا هُوَ مُضْطَجِعٌ عَلَى رِمَالِ حَصِيرٍ لَيْسَ بَيْنَهُ وَبَيْنَهُ فِرَاشٌ، قَدْ أَثَّرَ الرِّمَالُ بِجَنْبِهِ، مُتَّكِئٌ عَلَى وِسَادَةٍ مِنْ أَدَمٍ حَشْوُهَا لِيفٌ، فَسَلَّمْتُ عَلَيْهِ، ثُمَّ قُلْتُ وَأَنَا قَائِمٌ طَلَّقْتَ نِسَاءَكَ فَرَفَعَ بَصَرَهُ إِلَىَّ، فَقَالَ " لاَ ". ثُمَّ قُلْتُ ـ وَأَنَا قَائِمٌ أَسْتَأْنِسُ يَا رَسُولَ اللَّهِ، لَوْ رَأَيْتَنِي، وَكُنَّا مَعْشَرَ قُرَيْشٍ نَغْلِبُ النِّسَاءَ، فَلَمَّا قَدِمْنَا عَلَى قَوْمٍ تَغْلِبُهُمْ نِسَاؤُهُمْ، فَذَكَرَهُ، فَتَبَسَّمَ النَّبِيُّ صلى الله عليه وسلم، ثُمَّ قُلْتُ لَوْ رَأَيْتَنِي، وَدَخَلْتُ عَلَى حَفْصَةَ، فَقُلْتُ لاَ يَغُرَّنَّكِ أَنْ كَانَتْ جَارَتُكِ هِيَ أَوْضَأَ مِنْكِ وَأَحَبَّ إِلَى النَّبِيِّ صلى الله عليه وسلم ـ يُرِيدُ عَائِشَةَ ـ فَتَبَسَّمَ أُخْرَى، فَجَلَسْتُ حِينَ رَأَيْتُهُ تَبَسَّمَ، ثُمَّ رَفَعْتُ بَصَرِي فِي بَيْتِهِ، فَوَاللَّهِ مَا رَأَيْتُ فِيهِ شَيْئًا يَرُدُّ الْبَصَرَ غَيْرَ أَهَبَةٍ ثَلاَثَةٍ. فَقُلْتُ ادْعُ اللَّهَ فَلْيُوَسِّعْ عَلَى أُمَّتِكَ، فَإِنَّ فَارِسَ وَالرُّومَ وُسِّعَ عَلَيْهِمْ وَأُعْطُوا الدُّنْيَا، وَهُمْ لاَ يَعْبُدُونَ اللَّهَ، وَكَانَ مُتَّكِئًا. فَقَالَ " أَوَفِي شَكٍّ أَنْتَ يَا ابْنَ الْخَطَّابِ أُولَئِكَ قَوْمٌ عُجِّلَتْ لَهُمْ طَيِّبَاتُهُمْ فِي الْحَيَاةِ الدُّنْيَا ". فَقُلْتُ يَا رَسُولَ اللَّهِ اسْتَغْفِرْ لِي. فَاعْتَزَلَ النَّبِيُّ صلى الله عليه وسلم مِنْ أَجْلِ ذَلِكَ الْحَدِيثِ حِينَ أَفْشَتْهُ حَفْصَةُ إِلَى عَائِشَةَ، وَكَانَ قَدْ قَالَ " مَا أَنَا بِدَاخِلٍ عَلَيْهِنَّ شَهْرًا ". مِنْ شِدَّةِ مَوْجَدَتِهِ عَلَيْهِنَّ حِينَ عَاتَبَهُ اللَّهُ. فَلَمَّا مَضَتْ تِسْعٌ وَعِشْرُونَ دَخَلَ عَلَى عَائِشَةَ فَبَدَأَ بِهَا، فَقَالَتْ لَهُ عَائِشَةُ إِنَّكَ أَقْسَمْتَ أَنْ لاَ تَدْخُلَ عَلَيْنَا شَهْرًا، وَإِنَّا أَصْبَحْنَا لِتِسْعٍ وَعِشْرِينَ لَيْلَةً، أَعُدُّهَا عَدًّا. فَقَالَ النَّبِيُّ صلى الله عليه وسلم " الشَّهْرُ تِسْعٌ وَعِشْرُونَ ". وَكَانَ ذَلِكَ الشَّهْرُ تِسْعٌ وَعِشْرُونَ. قَالَتْ عَائِشَةُ فَأُنْزِلَتْ آيَةُ التَّخْيِيرِ فَبَدَأَ بِي أَوَّلَ امْرَأَةٍ، فَقَالَ " إِنِّي ذَاكِرٌ لَكِ أَمْرًا، وَلاَ عَلَيْكِ أَنْ لاَ تَعْجَلِي حَتَّى تَسْتَأْمِرِي أَبَوَيْكِ ". قَالَتْ قَدْ أَعْلَمُ أَنَّ أَبَوَىَّ لَمْ يَكُونَا يَأْمُرَانِي بِفِرَاقِكَ. ثُمَّ قَالَ " إِنَّ اللَّهَ قَالَ {يَا أَيُّهَا النَّبِيُّ قُلْ لأَزْوَاجِكَ} إِلَى قَوْلِهِ { عَظِيمًا} ". قُلْتُ أَفِي هَذَا أَسْتَأْمِرُ أَبَوَىَّ فَإِنِّي أُرِيدُ اللَّهَ وَرَسُولَهُ وَالدَّارَ الآخِرَةَ. ثُمَّ خَيَّرَ نِسَاءَهُ، فَقُلْنَ مِثْلَ مَا قَالَتْ عَائِشَةُ.

Narrated Ibn `Abbas: Once the Prophet ﷺ embraced me (pressed me to his chest) and said, "O Allah, teach him wisdom (i.e. the understanding of the knowledge of Qur'an). – Sahih Al-Bukhari 3756

حَدَّثَنَا مُسَدَّدٌ، حَدَّثَنَا عَبْدُ الْوَارِثِ، عَنْ خَالِدٍ، عَنْ عِكْرِمَةَ، عَنِ ابْنِ عَبَّاسٍ،، قَالَ ضَمَّنِي النَّبِيُّ صلى الله عليه وسلم إِلَى صَدْرِهِ وَقَالَ " اللَّهُمَّ عَلِّمْهُ الْحِكْمَةَ ".

Narrated 'Abdul Warith: The same but said, "O Allah, teach him (Ibn Abbas) the Book (i.e. the understanding of the knowledge of Qur'an)." Narrated Khalid: As above. – Sahih Al-Bukhari 3756b

حَدَّثَنَا أَبُو مَعْمَرٍ، حَدَّثَنَا عَبْدُ الْوَارِثِ، وَقَالَ، " عَلِّمْهُ الْكِتَابَ ". حَدَّثَنَا مُوسَى، حَدَّثَنَا وُهَيْبٌ، عَنْ خَالِدٍ، مِثْلَهُ. وَالْحِكْمَةُ الإِصَابَةُ فِي غَيْرِ النُّبُوَّةِ

Narrated Ibn Abi Mulaika: Somebody said to Ibn `Abbas, “Can you speak to the chief of the believers Mu`awiyah, as he does not pray except one rak`a as witr?” Ibn `Abbas replied, “He is a Faqih (i.e. a learned man who can give religious verdicts) .”. – Sahih Al-Bukhari 3765
حَدَّثَنَا ابْنُ أَبِي مَرْيَمَ، حَدَّثَنَا نَافِعُ بْنُ عُمَرَ، حَدَّثَنِي ابْنُ أَبِي مُلَيْكَةَ، قِيلَ لاِبْنِ عَبَّاسٍ هَلْ لَكَ فِي أَمِيرِ الْمُؤْمِنِينَ مُعَاوِيَةَ، فَإِنَّهُ مَا أَوْتَرَ إِلاَّ بِوَاحِدَةٍ. قَالَ إِنَّهُ فَقِيهٌ.

Narrated Abu As-Safar: I heard Ibn `Abbas saying, “O people! Listen to what I say to you, and let me hear whatever you say, and don’t go (without understanding), and start saying, ‘Ibn `Abbas said so-and-so, Ibn `Abbas said soand- so, Ibn `Abbas said so-and-so.’ He who wants to perform the Tawaf around the Ka`ba should go behind Al-Hijr (i.e. a portion of the Ka`ba left out unroofed) and do not call it Al-Hatim, for in the pre-Islamic period of ignorance if any man took an oath, he used to throw his whip, shoes or bow in it. – Sahih Al-Bukhari 3848
حَدَّثَنَا عَبْدُ اللَّهِ بْنُ مُحَمَّدٍ الْجُعْفِيُّ، حَدَّثَنَا سُفْيَانُ، أَخْبَرَنَا مُطَرِّفٌ، سَمِعْتُ أَبَا السَّفَرِ، يَقُولُ سَمِعْتُ ابْنَ عَبَّاسٍ ـ رضى الله عنهما ـ يَقُولُ يَا أَيُّهَا النَّاسُ، اسْمَعُوا مِنِّي مَا أَقُولُ لَكُمْ، وَأَسْمِعُونِي مَا تَقُولُونَ، وَلاَ تَذْهَبُوا فَتَقُولُوا قَالَ ابْنُ عَبَّاسٍ، قَالَ ابْنُ عَبَّاسٍ مَنْ طَافَ بِالْبَيْتِ فَلْيَطُفْ مِنْ وَرَاءِ الْحِجْرِ، وَلاَ تَقُولُوا الْحَطِيمُ، فَإِنَّ الرَّجُلَ فِي الْجَاهِلِيَّةِ كَانَ يَحْلِفُ فَيُلْقِي سَوْطَهُ أَوْ نَعْلَهُ أَوْ قَوْسَهُ

Narrated `Abdullah bin Al-Harith: Ibn `Abbas addressed us on a (rainy and) muddy day and when the Mu’adh-dhin said, “Come for the prayer” Ibn `Abbas ordered him to say, “Pray in your homes.” The people began to look at one another with surprise as if they did not like it. Ibn `Abbas said, “It seems that you thought ill of it but no doubt it was done by one who was better than I (i.e. the Prophet). It (the prayer) is a strict order and I disliked to bring you out.” Ibn `Abbas narrated the same as above but he said, “I did not like you to make you sinful (in refraining from coming to the mosque) and to come (to the mosque) covered with mud up to the knees.”. – Sahih Al-Bukhari 668
حَدَّثَنَا عَبْدُ اللَّهِ بْنُ عَبْدِ الْوَهَّابِ، قَالَ حَدَّثَنَا حَمَّادُ بْنُ زَيْدٍ، قَالَ حَدَّثَنَا عَبْدُ الْحَمِيدِ، صَاحِبُ الزِّيَادِيِّ قَالَ سَمِعْتُ عَبْدَ اللَّهِ بْنَ الْحَارِثِ، قَالَ خَطَبَنَا ابْنُ عَبَّاسٍ فِي يَوْمٍ ذِي رَدْغٍ، فَأَمَرَ الْمُؤَذِّنَ لَمَّا بَلَغَ حَىَّ عَلَى الصَّلاَةِ. قَالَ قُلِ الصَّلاَةُ فِي الرِّحَالِ، فَنَظَرَ بَعْضُهُمْ إِلَى بَعْضٍ، فَكَأَنَّهُمْ أَنْكَرُوا فَقَالَ كَأَنَّكُمْ أَنْكَرْتُمْ هَذَا إِنَّ هَذَا فَعَلَهُ مَنْ هُوَ خَيْرٌ مِنِّي ـ يَعْنِي النَّبِيَّ صلى الله عليه وسلم ـ إِنَّهَا عَزْمَةٌ، وَإِنِّي كَرِهْتُ أَنْ أُحْرِجَكُمْ. وَعَنْ حَمَّادٍ عَنْ عَاصِمٍ عَنْ عَبْدِ اللَّهِ بْنِ الْحَارِثِ عَنِ ابْنِ عَبَّاسٍ نَحْوَهُ، غَيْرَ أَنَّهُ قَالَ كَرِهْتُ أَنْ أُؤَثِّمَكُمْ، فَتَجِيئُونَ تَدُوسُونَ الطِّينَ إِلَى رُكَبِكُمْ.

Narrated Ibn Abi Mulaika: Ibn `Abbas recited:-- “Except the weak ones among men women and children,” (4.98) and said, “My mother and I were among those whom Allah had excused.”. – Sahih Al-Bukhari 4588
حَدَّثَنَا سُلَيْمَانُ بْنُ حَرْبٍ، حَدَّثَنَا حَمَّادُ بْنُ زَيْدٍ، عَنْ أَيُّوبَ، عَنِ ابْنِ أَبِي مُلَيْكَةَ، أَنَّ ابْنَ عَبَّاسٍ، تَلاَ {إِلاَّ الْمُسْتَضْعَفِينَ مِنَ الرِّجَالِ وَالنِّسَاءِ وَالْوِلْدَانِ} قَالَ كُنْتُ أَنَا وَأُمِّي مِمَّنْ عَذَرَ اللَّهُ. وَيُذْكَرُ عَنِ ابْنِ عَبَّاسٍ {حَصِرَتْ} ضَاقَتْ {تَلْوُوا} أَلْسِنَتَكُمْ بِالشَّهَادَةِ. وَقَالَ غَيْرُهُ الْمُرَاغَمُ الْمُهَاجَرُ. رَاغَمْتُ هَاجَرْتُ قَوْمِي. {مَوْقُوتًا} مُوَقَّتًا وَقْتَهُ عَلَيْهِمْ

Narrated Sa`id bin Jubair: Those Suras which you people call the Mufassal, are the Muhkam. And Ibn `Abbas said, “Allah’s Apostle died when I was a boy of ten years, and I had learnt the Muhkam (of the Qur’an). – Sahih Al-Bukhari 5035
حَدَّثَنِي مُوسَى بْنُ إِسْمَاعِيلَ، حَدَّثَنَا أَبُو عَوَانَةَ، عَنْ أَبِي بِشْرٍ، عَنْ سَعِيدِ بْنِ جُبَيْرٍ، قَالَ إِنَّ الَّذِي تَدْعُونَهُ الْمُفَصَّلَ هُوَ الْمُحْكَمُ، قَالَ وَقَالَ ابْنُ عَبَّاسٍ تُوُفِّيَ رَسُولُ اللَّهِ صلى الله عليه وسلم وَأَنَا ابْنُ عَشْرِ سِنِينَ وَقَدْ قَرَأْتُ الْمُحْكَمَ

Narrated Ibn Abi Mulaika: When there happened the disagreement between Ibn Az-Zubair and Ibn `Abbas, I said (to the latter), “(Why don’t you take the oath of allegiance to him as) his father is Az-Zubair, and his mother is Asma,’ and his aunt is `Aisha, and his maternal grandfather is Abu Bakr, and his grandmother is Safiya?”. – Sahih Al-Bukhari 4664

حَدَّثَنَا عَبْدُ اللَّهِ بْنُ مُحَمَّدٍ، حَدَّثَنَا ابْنُ عُيَيْنَةَ، عَنِ ابْنِ جُرَيْجٍ، عَنِ ابْنِ أَبِي مُلَيْكَةَ، عَنِ ابْنِ عَبَّاسٍ ـ رضى الله عنهما ـ أَنَّهُ قَالَ حِينَ وَقَعَ بَيْنَهُ وَبَيْنَ ابْنِ الزُّبَيْرِ قُلْتُ أَبُوهُ الزُّبَيْرُ، وَأُمُّهُ أَسْمَاءُ، وَخَالَتُهُ عَائِشَةُ، وَجَدُّهُ أَبُو بَكْرٍ، وَجَدَّتُهُ صَفِيَّةُ. فَقُلْتُ لِسُفْيَانَ إِسْنَادُهُ. فَقَالَ حَدَّثَنَا، فَشَغَلَهُ إِنْسَانٌ وَلَمْ يَقُلِ ابْنُ جُرَيْجٍ

Narrated Ibn `Abbas: Qur'an 28.85'...will bring you home' means to Mecca. – Sahih Al-Bukhari 4773

حَدَّثَنَا مُحَمَّدُ بْنُ مُقَاتِلٍ، أَخْبَرَنَا يَعْلَى، حَدَّثَنَا سُفْيَانُ الْعُصْفُرِيُّ، عَنْ عِكْرِمَةَ، عَنِ ابْنِ عَبَّاسٍ، {لَرَادُّكَ إِلَى مَعَادٍ} قَالَ إِلَى مَكَّةَ

Narrated Abu Jamra: I heard Ibn `Abbas (giving a verdict) when he was asked about the Mut'a with the women, and he permitted it (Nikah-al-Mut'a). On that a freed slave of his said to him, "That is only when it is very badly needed and women are scarce." On that, Ibn `Abbas said, "Yes.". – Sahih Al-Bukhari 5116

حَدَّثَنَا مُحَمَّدُ بْنُ بَشَّارٍ، حَدَّثَنَا غُنْدَرٌ، حَدَّثَنَا شُعْبَةُ، عَنْ أَبِي جَمْرَةَ، قَالَ سَمِعْتُ ابْنَ عَبَّاسٍ، سُئِلَ عَنْ مُتْعَةِ النِّسَاءِ، فَرَخَّصَ فَقَالَ لَهُ مَوْلًى لَهُ إِنَّمَا ذَلِكَ فِي الْحَالِ الشَّدِيدِ وَفِي النِّسَاءِ قِلَّةٌ أَوْ نَحْوَهُ. فَقَالَ ابْنُ عَبَّاسٍ نَعَمْ

Narrated Ibn `Abbas: While in his tent on the day the Battle of Badr, the Prophet ﷺ said, "O Allah! I request You (to fulfill) Your promise and contract. O Allah! It You wish that the Believers be destroyed). You will never be worshipped henceforth." On that, Abu Bakr held the Prophet ﷺ by the hand and said, "That is enough, O Allah's Messenger ﷺ! You have appealed to your Lord too pressingly" The Prophet ﷺ was wearing his armor and then went out reciting: 'Their multitude will be put to flight and they will show their backs. Nay, but the Hour is their appointed time (for their full recompense), and the Hour will be more previous and most bitter.' (54.45-46). – Sahih Al-Bukhari 4877

حَدَّثَنِي إِسْحَاقُ، حَدَّثَنَا خَالِدٌ، عَنْ خَالِدٍ، عَنْ عِكْرِمَةَ، عَنِ ابْنِ عَبَّاسٍ، أَنَّ النَّبِيَّ صلى الله عليه وسلم قَالَ وَهْوَ فِي قُبَّةٍ لَهُ يَوْمَ بَدْرٍ " أَنْشُدُكَ عَهْدَكَ وَوَعْدَكَ، اللَّهُمَّ إِنْ شِئْتَ لَمْ تُعْبَدْ بَعْدَ الْيَوْمِ أَبَدًا ". فَأَخَذَ أَبُو بَكْرٍ بِيَدِهِ وَقَالَ حَسْبُكَ يَا رَسُولَ اللَّهِ فَقَدْ أَلْحَحْتَ عَلَى رَبِّكَ. وَهْوَ فِي الدِّرْعِ فَخَرَجَ وَهْوَ يَقُولُ " {سَيُهْزَمُ الْجَمْعُ وَيُوَلُّونَ الدُّبُرَ * بَلِ السَّاعَةُ مَوْعِدُهُمْ وَالسَّاعَةُ أَدْهَى وَأَمَرُّ}."

Narrated `Abdullah bin `Abbas: Abu Sufyan told me that Heraclius said to him, "When I inquired you what he (i.e. Muhammad) ordered you, you replied that he ordered you to establish the prayer, to speak the truth, to be chaste, to keep promises and to pay back trusts." Then Heraclius added, "These are really the qualities of a prophet.". – Sahih Al-Bukhari 2681

حَدَّثَنَا إِبْرَاهِيمُ بْنُ حَمْزَةَ، حَدَّثَنَا إِبْرَاهِيمُ بْنُ سَعْدٍ، عَنْ صَالِحٍ، عَنِ ابْنِ شِهَابٍ، عَنْ عُبَيْدِ اللَّهِ بْنِ عَبْدِ اللَّهِ، أَنَّ عَبْدَ اللَّهِ بْنَ عَبَّاسٍ ـ رضى الله عنهما ـ أَخْبَرَهُ قَالَ أَخْبَرَنِي أَبُو سُفْيَانَ، أَنَّ هِرَقْلَ، قَالَ لَهُ سَأَلْتُكَ مَاذَا يَأْمُرُكُمْ فَزَعَمْتَ أَنَّهُ أَمَرَكُمْ بِالصَّلاَةِ وَالصِّدْقِ وَالْعَفَافِ وَالْوَفَاءِ بِالْعَهْدِ وَأَدَاءِ الأَمَانَةِ. قَالَ وَهَذِهِ صِفَةُ نَبِيٍّ

Narrated Abu Jamra Ad-Dabi: I used to sit with Ibn `Abbas in Mecca. Once I had a fever and he said (to me), "Cool your fever with Zamzam water, for Allah's Messenger ﷺ said: 'It, (the Fever) is from the heat of the (Hell) Fire; so, cool it with water (or Zamzam water). – Sahih Al Bukhari 3261

حدثني عبد الله بن مُحَمَّدٍ، حَدَّثَنَا أَبُو عَامِرٍ، حَدَّثَنَا هَمَّامٌ، عَنْ أَبِي جَمْرَةَ الضُّبَعِيِّ، قَالَ كُنْتُ أُجَالِسُ ابْنَ عَبَّاسٍ بِمَكَّةَ، فَأَخَذَتْنِي الْحُمَّى، فَقَالَ أَبْرِدْهَا عَنْكَ بِمَاءِ زَمْزَمَ، فَإِنَّ رَسُولَ اللَّهِ صلى الله عليه وسلم قَالَ " الْحُمَّى مِنْ فَيْحِ جَهَنَّمَ فَأَبْرِدُوهَا بِالْمَاءِ ". أَوْ قَالَ " بِمَاءِ زَمْزَمَ ". شَكَّ هَمَّامٌ.

Narrated Bukair: That Kuraib, the freed slave of Ibn `Abbas told him that Ibn `Abbas, `Abdur-Rahman bin Azhar and Al-Miswar bin Makhrama sent him to `Aisha saying, "Pay her our greetings and ask her about our offering of the two-rak`at after `Asr Prayer, and tell her that we have been informed that you offer these two rak`at while we have heard that the Prophet ﷺ had forbidden their offering." Ibn `Abbas said, "I and `Umar used to beat the people for their offering them." Kuraib added, "I entered upon her and delivered their message to her.' She said, 'Ask Um Salama.' So, I informed them (of `Aisha's answer) and they sent me to Um Salama for the same purpose as they sent me to `Aisha. Um Salama replied, 'I heard the Prophet ﷺ forbidding the offering of these two rak`at. Once the Prophet ﷺ offered the `Asr prayer, and then came to me. And at that time some Ansari women from the Tribe of Banu Haram were with me. Then (the Prophet ﷺ) offered those two rak`at, and I sent my (lady) servant to him, saying, 'Stand beside him and say (to him): Um Salama says, 'O Allah's Messenger ﷺ! Didn't I hear you forbidding the offering of these two rak`at (after the `Asr prayer yet I see you offering them?' And if he beckons to you with his hand, then wait behind.' So the lady slave did that and the Prophet ﷺ beckoned her with his hand, and she stayed behind, and when the Prophet ﷺ finished his prayer, he said, 'O the daughter of Abu Umaiya (i.e. Um Salama), You were asking me about these two rak`at after the `Asr prayer. In fact, some people from the tribe of `Abdul Qais came to me to embrace Islam and busied me so much that I did not offer the two rak`at which were offered after Zuhr compulsory prayer, and these two rak`at (you have seen me offering) make up for those.". – Sahih Al-Bukhari 4370

حَدَّثَنَا يَحْيَى بْنُ سُلَيْمَانَ، حَدَّثَنِي ابْنُ وَهْبٍ، أَخْبَرَنِي عَمْرٌو، وَقَالَ بَكْرُ بْنُ مُضَرَ عَنْ عَمْرِو بْنِ الْحَارِثِ، عَنْ بُكَيْرٍ، أَنَّ كُرَيْبًا، مَوْلَى ابْنِ عَبَّاسٍ حَدَّثَهُ أَنَّ ابْنَ عَبَّاسٍ وَعَبْدَ الرَّحْمَنِ بْنَ أَزْهَرَ وَالْمِسْوَرَ بْنَ مَخْرَمَةَ أَرْسَلُوا إِلَى عَائِشَةَ ـ رضى الله عنها ـ فَقَالُوا اقْرَأْ عَلَيْهَا السَّلاَمَ مِنَّا جَمِيعًا، وَسَلْهَا عَنِ الرَّكْعَتَيْنِ بَعْدَ الْعَصْرِ، وَإِنَّا أُخْبِرْنَا أَنَّكِ تُصَلِّيهَا، وَقَدْ بَلَغَنَا أَنَّ النَّبِيَّ صلى الله عليه وسلم نَهَى عَنْهَا، قَالَ ابْنُ عَبَّاسٍ وَكُنْتُ أَضْرِبُ مَعَ عُمَرَ النَّاسَ عَنْهُمَا. قَالَ كُرَيْبٌ فَدَخَلْتُ عَلَيْهَا، وَبَلَّغْتُهَا مَا أَرْسَلُونِي، فَقَالَتْ سَلْ أُمَّ سَلَمَةَ. فَأَخْبَرْتُهُمْ، فَرَدُّونِي إِلَى أُمِّ سَلَمَةَ بِمِثْلِ مَا أَرْسَلُونِي إِلَى عَائِشَةَ، فَقَالَتْ أُمُّ سَلَمَةَ سَمِعْتُ النَّبِيَّ صلى الله عليه وسلم يَنْهَى عَنْهُمَا، وَإِنَّهُ صَلَّى الْعَصْرَ ثُمَّ دَخَلَ عَلَىَّ وَعِنْدِي نِسْوَةٌ مِنْ بَنِي حَرَامٍ مِنَ الأَنْصَارِ، فَصَلاَّهُمَا، فَأَرْسَلْتُ إِلَيْهِ الْخَادِمَ فَقُلْتُ قُومِي إِلَى جَنْبِهِ فَقُولِي تَقُولُ أُمُّ سَلَمَةَ يَا رَسُولَ اللَّهِ أَلَمْ أَسْمَعْكَ تَنْهَى عَنْ هَاتَيْنِ الرَّكْعَتَيْنِ فَأَرَاكَ تُصَلِّيهِمَا. فَإِنْ أَشَارَ بِيَدِهِ فَاسْتَأْخِرِي. فَفَعَلَتِ الْجَارِيَةُ، فَأَشَارَ بِيَدِهِ، فَاسْتَأْخَرَتْ عَنْهُ، فَلَمَّا انْصَرَفَ قَالَ " يَا بِنْتَ أَبِي أُمَيَّةَ، سَأَلْتِ عَنِ الرَّكْعَتَيْنِ بَعْدَ الْعَصْرِ، إِنَّهُ أَتَانِي أُنَاسٌ مِنْ عَبْدِ الْقَيْسِ بِالإِسْلاَمِ مِنْ قَوْمِهِمْ، فَشَغَلُونِي عَنِ الرَّكْعَتَيْنِ اللَّتَيْنِ بَعْدَ الظُّهْرِ، فَهُمَا هَاتَانِ ".

Narrated Ibn `Abbas: Once I stayed overnight in the house of my aunt Maimuna bint Al-Harith and Allah's Messenger ﷺ was with her as it was her turn. Allah's Messenger ﷺ got up to offer the night prayer. I stood on his left but he took hold of my two locks of hair and made me stand on his right. Narrated Abu Bishr: (the above Hadith) but he quoted: Ibn `Abbas said, (took hold of) my two braids on my head.". – Sahih Al-Bukhari 5919

حَدَّثَنَا عَلِيُّ بْنُ عَبْدِ اللَّهِ، حَدَّثَنَا الْفَضْلُ بْنُ عَنْبَسَةَ، أَخْبَرَنَا هُشَيْمٌ، أَخْبَرَنَا أَبُو بِشْرٍ، ح وَحَدَّثَنَا قُتَيْبَةُ، حَدَّثَنَا هُشَيْمٌ، عَنْ أَبِي بِشْرٍ، عَنْ سَعِيدِ بْنِ جُبَيْرٍ، عَنِ ابْنِ عَبَّاسٍ ـ رضى الله عنهما ـ قَالَ بِتُّ لَيْلَةً عِنْدَ مَيْمُونَةَ بِنْتِ الْحَارِثِ خَالَتِي، وَكَانَ رَسُولُ اللَّهِ صلى الله عليه وسلم عِنْدَهَا فِي لَيْلَتِهَا ـ قَالَ ـ فَقَامَ رَسُولُ اللَّهِ صلى الله عليه وسلم يُصَلِّي مِنَ اللَّيْلِ، فَقُمْتُ عَنْ يَسَارِهِ ـ قَالَ ـ فَأَخَذَ بِذُؤَابَتِي فَجَعَلَنِي عَنْ يَمِينِهِ. حَدَّثَنَا عَمْرُو بْنُ مُحَمَّدٍ، حَدَّثَنَا هُشَيْمٌ، أَخْبَرَنَا أَبُو بِشْرٍ، بِهَذَا، وَقَالَ بِذُؤَابَتِي أَوْ بِرَأْسِي.

Narrated Ibn `Abbas: The Prophet ﷺ used to copy the people of the Scriptures in matters in which there was no order from Allah. The people of the Scripture used to let their hair hang down while the pagans used to part their hair. So the Prophet ﷺ let his hair hang down first, but later on he parted it. – Sahih Al-Bukhari 5917

حَدَّثَنَا أَحْمَدُ بْنُ يُونُسَ، حَدَّثَنَا إِبْرَاهِيمُ بْنُ سَعْدٍ، حَدَّثَنَا ابْنُ شِهَابٍ، عَنْ عُبَيْدِ اللَّهِ بْنِ عَبْدِ اللَّهِ، عَنِ ابْنِ عَبَّاسٍ ـ رضى الله عنهما ـ قَالَ كَانَ النَّبِيُّ صلى الله عليه وسلم يُحِبُّ مُوَافَقَةَ أَهْلِ الْكِتَابِ فِيمَا لَمْ يُؤْمَرْ فِيهِ، وَكَانَ أَهْلُ الْكِتَابِ يَسْدِلُونَ أَشْعَارَهُمْ، وَكَانَ الْمُشْرِكُونَ يَفْرُقُونَ رُءُوسَهُمْ، فَسَدَلَ النَّبِيُّ صلى الله عليه وسلم نَاصِيَتَهُ، ثُمَّ فَرَقَ بَعْدُ.

Narrated Said bin Jubair: Ibn 'Abbas was asked, "How old were you when the Prophet ﷺ died?" He replied. "At that time I had been circumcised." At that time, people did not circumcise the boys till they attained the age of puberty. Sa'id bin Jubair said, "Ibn 'Abbas said, 'When the Prophet died, I had already been circumcised. ". – Sahih Al-Bukhari 6299
حَدَّثَنَا مُحَمَّدُ بْنُ عَبْدِ الرَّحِيمِ، أَخْبَرَنَا عَبَّادُ بْنُ مُوسَى، حَدَّثَنَا إِسْمَاعِيلُ بْنُ جَعْفَرٍ، عَنْ إِسْرَائِيلَ، عَنْ أَبِي إِسْحَاقَ، عَنْ سَعِيدِ بْنِ جُبَيْرٍ، قَالَ سُئِلَ ابْنُ عَبَّاسٍ مِثْلُ مَنْ أَنْتَ حِينَ قُبِضَ النَّبِيُّ صلى الله عليه وسلم قَالَ أَنَا يَوْمَئِذٍ مَخْتُونٌ. قَالَ وَكَانُوا لاَ يَخْتِنُونَ الرَّجُلَ حَتَّى يُدْرِكَ.

Narrated Ibn `Abbas: Allah's Messenger ﷺ started receiving the Divine Inspiration at the age of forty. Then he stayed in Mecca for thirteen years, receiving the Divine Revelation. Then he was ordered to migrate and he lived as an Emigrant for ten years and then died at the age of sixty-three (years). – Sahih Al-Bukhari 3902
حَدَّثَنَا مَطَرُ بْنُ الْفَضْلِ، حَدَّثَنَا رَوْحٌ، حَدَّثَنَا هِشَامٌ، حَدَّثَنَا عِكْرِمَةُ، عَنِ ابْنِ عَبَّاسٍ ـ رضى الله عنهما ـ قَالَ بُعِثَ رَسُولُ اللَّهِ صلى الله عليه وسلم لأَرْبَعِينَ سَنَةً، فَمَكُثَ بِمَكَّةَ ثَلاَثَ عَشْرَةَ سَنَةً يُوحَى إِلَيْهِ، ثُمَّ أُمِرَ بِالْهِجْرَةِ فَهَاجَرَ عَشْرَ سِنِينَ، وَمَاتَ وَهُوَ ابْنُ ثَلاَثٍ وَسِتِّينَ.

Narrated Ibn Abbas : Abu-Sufyan said to me, "Caesar said to me, 'I asked you whether the wealthy people followed him (i.e., Muhammad)or the poor, and you said that the poor. Really, such are the followers of the Messengers.'" – Sahih Al-Bukhari Vol.4 page 99
و قال ابن عباس : أخبر ني ابو سفيان قال : فال لي قيصر : سالتك ، اشراف الناس اتبعوه ام ضعفاوهم؟ فزعمت : ضعفاءهم و هم أتباع الرسل.

Sa'id said: A man said to Ibn Abbas, "I find in the Qur'an certain things which seem to me contradictory, for example Allah says :- . ..There will be no kinship among them that Day, nor will they ask of one another.? (V,23 :101) (yet He says:) And they will turn to one another and question one another.' (V.37:27) '...But they will never be able to hide single fact from Allāh.' (V.4:42) [Yet He reports what Al-Mushrikūn (polytheists, pagans, idolaters, and disbelievers in the Oneness of Allāh and in His Messenger Muhammad will say :] '...By Allāh, our Lord, we were not those who joined others in worship with Allāh.' (V.6:23) According to this Verse, they will hide some facts. Allāh says: Or is the heaven that He constructed?.. (up to) ... He spread the earth.' (V .79: 27-30) In this Verse He mentions the creation of the heavens before the creation of the earth. Then He says: Say (O Muhammad): Do you verily, disbelieve in Him Who created the earth in two Days... (up to) ...willingly. (V.41:9-11) So He mentions in this Verse the creation of the earth before the heavens and He says: '...Verily, Allāh is Oft-Forgiving, Most Merciful.' (V.4:23) ...Allah is Ever Most Powerful, All-Wise. (V,4:56) ...Allāh is Ever All-Hearer, All-Seer,' (V 4:58) This seems to be something that was and has passed." Then Ibn ' Abbas answered, " 'There will be no relationship between them,' That is on the first blowing of the Trumpet. 'And so the Trumpet will be blown, and all who are in the heavens and all who are on the earth will swoon, away except him whom Allah wills..." (V.39:68) Then 'there will be no relationship between them, and at that time one will not ask another. Then, when the Trumpet will be blown for the second time they will turn to one another and question one another.' As for His Statement: "...We were not who joined others in worship with Allah. 'But they will not be able to hide a single fact from Allah,? Allah will forgive the sins of those who were sincere in their worship, whereupon Al-Mushrikún will say (to each other), 'Come, let's say we never worshipped others besides Allah. But their mouths will be sealed and their hands will speak (the truth). At that time it will be evident that no speech can be concealed from Allah, and those who disbelieved and disobeyed the

Messenger will wish that they were buried in the earth, but they will never be able to hide a single fact from Allah_ (V 4:42). Allāh created the earth in two days and then created the heavens, then He turned towards the heavens and gave it perfection in two (other) days. Then he spread the earth, and its spreading means the bringing of water and pasture out of it. He then created the mountains, the camels and the hillocks and whatever is in between them (the earth and the heaven) in two (other) days. That is the meaning of Allah's saying: 'He spread it.' and His Saying : 'And He created the earth in two days.' So the carth and whatever is on it, was created in four days; and the heavens were created in two days. (Concerning His Saying-) `And Allah is Oft-Forgiving.' He named Himself like that (so the naming has passed) but the contents of His Saying is still valid, for if Allah ever wants to do something, He surely fulfils what He wants. So you should not see contradiction in the Quran, for all of it is from Allāh." Sahih Al-Bukhari Vol.6 page 291-293

و قال طاوس، عن ابن عباس(اءتيا طوعا أو كرها) : أعطيا (قالتا اتينا طاءعين) : اعطينا. و قال المنهال، عن سعيد قال : قال رجل لابن عباس : اني اجد في القران الشيء تختلف علي، قال (فلا انساب بينهم يومءذ و لا يتساءلون) (و اقبل بعضهم على بعض يتساءلون ٢٧) (و لا يكتمون الله حديثا) (ربنا ما كنا مشركين) فقد كتموا في هذه الاية، و قال : (ام اسماء بنها) إلى قوله : (دحها) فذكر خلق السماء قبل خلق الارض، ثم قال : (اءنكم لتكفرون بالذى خلق الأرض فى يومين) إلى (طاءعين) فذكر في هذه خلق الأرض قبل السماء. و قال تعالى : (و كان الله غفورا رحيما) (عزيزا حكيما) (سميعا بصيرا) فكأنه كان ثم مضى. فقال : (فلا انساب بينهم) في النفخة الاولى، ثم ينفخ في الصور (فصعق من فى السموات و من فى الارض الا من شاء الله) (فلا انساب بينهم) عند ذلك ولا يتساءلون. ثم في النفخة الا خرة (و اقبل بعضهم على بعض يتساءلون ٢٧) و أما قوله : (ما كنا مشركين) (و لا يكتمون الله) فاءن الله يغفر لا هل الاخلاص ذنوبهم. و قال المشركون : تعالوا نقول : لم نكن مشركين، فختم على أفواههم فتنطق ايديهم، فعند ذلك عرف أن الله لا يكتم حديثا، و عنده (يود الذين كفروا) الآية. و خلق الأرض في يومين ثم خلق السماء، ثم استوى إلى السماء فسواهن في يومين اخرين، ثم دحا الأرض. و دحوها أن أخرج منها الماء و المرعى . و خلق الجبال و الجمال و الجمال و الكام و ما بينهما في يومين آخرين ، فذلك قوله : (دحها). و قوله : (خلق الأرض فى يومين) فجعلت الأرض و ما فيها من شيء في أربعة أيام ، و خلقت السموات في يومين. (و كان الله غفورا) سمى نفسه ذلك، و ذلك قوله، اي لم يزل كذلك فإن الله لم يرد شيءا الا أصاب به الذي اراد، فلا يختلف عليك القران، فإن كلا من عند الله. حدثنيه يوسف بن عدي : حدثنا عبيد الله بن عمرو ، عن زيد بن أبي انيسة، عن المنهال بهذا. و قال مجاهد (لهم اجر غير ممنون) محسوب . (اقوتها) : ارزاقها . (فى كل سماء أمرها) مما أمر به . (نحسات) : مشاييم. (و قيضنا لهم قرناء) قرناهم بهم (تتنزل عليهم الملكة) عند الموت. (اهتزت) بالنبات (وربت) : ارتفعت . من (أكمامها) : حين تطلع (ليقولن هذا لى) : إلى بعملي أنا محقوق بهذا . و قال غيره : (سواء للساءلين) قدرها سواء (فهدينهم) دللناهم على الخير و الشر، كقوله : (و هديته النجدين ١٠) و كقوله : (هديته السبيل) و الهدى الذي هو الإرشاد بمنزلة اسعدناه، من ذلك قوله : (اولك الذين هدى الله فبهدهم اقتده) (يوزعون) : يكفون، (من أكمامها) : قشر الكفرى هي الكم. و قال غيره : و يقال للعنب إذا خرج أيضا كافور و كفرى (ولى حميم) : القريب. (من محيص) : حاص عنه : حاد عنه. (مرية) و مرية واحد : اى امتراء . و قال مجاهد : (اعملوا ما شئتم) : الوعيد. و قال ابن عباس : (بالتى ها احسن) الصبر عند الغضب و العفو عند الإساءة فإذا فعلوه عصمهم الله و خضع لهم عدوهم (كأنه و لى حميم).

And Al-Hasan, Shuraih, Ibrahim and Qạtāda said, "If one of the parents of the boy becomes a Muslim, then the boy will be with the Muslim parent." And Ibn Abbās was with his mother who was amongst the weak and the poor people , and was not with his father who was on the religion of his nation. And said, "Islam is always superior and never inferior.". – Sahih Al-Bukhari Vol.2 page 250

و قال الحسن و شريح و ابراهيم و قتادة : إذا أسلم أحدهما فال ولد مع المسلم. و كان ابن عباس رضي الله عنهما مع أبيه على دين قومه . و قال : الاسلام يعلو و لا يعلى.

Ibn 'Abbās chained Ikrima to teach him the Quran, the Prophet's Sunna (legal ways), and the knowledge_ of Fard'id (laws of inheritance). – Sahih Al-Bukhari Vol. 3 page 347

و قيد ابن عباس عكرمة على تعلم القرآن و السنن و الفراءض .

Narrated Muhammad bin `Ali: `Ali was told that Ibn `Abbas did not see any harm in the Mut'a marriage. `Ali said, "Allah's Messenger ﷺ forbade the Mut'a marriage on the Day of the battle of Khaibar and he forbade the eating of donkey's meat." Some people said, "If one, by a tricky way, marries temporarily, his marriage is illegal." Others said, "The marriage is valid but its condition is illegal.". – Sahih Al-Bukhari 6961

حَدَّثَنَا مُسَدَّدٌ، حَدَّثَنَا يَحْيَى، عَنْ عُبَيْدِ اللَّهِ بْنِ عُمَرَ، حَدَّثَنَا الزُّهْرِيُّ، عَنِ الْحَسَنِ، وَعَبْدِ اللَّهِ، ابْنَىْ مُحَمَّدِ بْنِ عَلِيٍّ عَنْ أَبِيهِمَا، أَنَّ عَلِيًّا ـ رضى الله عنه ـ قِيلَ لَهُ إِنَّ ابْنَ عَبَّاسٍ لاَ يَرَى بِمُتْعَةِ النِّسَاءِ بَأْسًا. فَقَالَ إِنَّ رَسُولَ اللَّهِ صلى الله عليه وسلم نَهَى عَنْهَا يَوْمَ خَيْبَرَ، وَعَنْ لُحُومِ الْحُمُرِ الإِنْسِيَّةِ. وَقَالَ بَعْضُ النَّاسِ إِنِ احْتَالَ حَتَّى تَمَتَّعَ، فَالنِّكَاحُ فَاسِدٌ. وَقَالَ بَعْضُهُمُ النِّكَاحُ جَائِزٌ وَالشَّرْطُ بَاطِلٌ.

Narrated `Ikrima: The people of Medina asked Ibn `Abbas about a woman who got her menses after performing Tawafal- Ifada. He said, "She could depart (from Mecca)." They said, "We will not act on your verdict and ignore the verdict of Zaid." Ibn `Abbas said, "When you reach Medina, inquire about it." So, when they reached Medina they asked (about that). One of those whom they asked was Um Sulaim. She told them the narration of Safiya (812). – Sahih Al-Bukhari 1758, 1759

حَدَّثَنَا أَبُو النُّعْمَانِ، حَدَّثَنَا حَمَّادٌ، عَنْ أَيُّوبَ، عَنْ عِكْرِمَةَ، أَنَّ أَهْلَ الْمَدِينَةِ، سَأَلُوا ابْنَ عَبَّاسٍ ـ رضى الله عنهما ـ عَنِ امْرَأَةٍ، طَافَتْ ثُمَّ حَاضَتْ، قَالَ لَهُمْ تَنْفِرُ. قَالُوا لاَ نَأْخُذُ بِقَوْلِكَ وَنَدَعُ قَوْلَ زَيْدٍ. قَالَ إِذَا قَدِمْتُمُ الْمَدِينَةَ فَسَلُوا. فَقَدِمُوا الْمَدِينَةَ فَسَأَلُوا، فَكَانَ فِيمَنْ سَأَلُوا أُمُّ سُلَيْمٍ، فَذَكَرَتْ حَدِيثَ صَفِيَّةَ. رَوَاهُ خَالِدٌ وَقَتَادَةُ عَنْ عِكْرِمَةَ.

Narrated `Abdullah bin `Abbas: I came riding on my she-ass and had (just) then attained the age of puberty. Allah's Messenger ﷺ was praying at Mina. I passed in front of a part of the first row and then dismounted from it, and the animal started grazing. I aligned with the people behind Allah's Messenger ﷺ . The sub-narrator added that happened in Mina during the Prophet's Hajjat-al-Wada`.) – Sahih al-Bukhari 1857

حَدَّثَنَا إِسْحَاقُ، أَخْبَرَنَا يَعْقُوبُ بْنُ إِبْرَاهِيمَ، حَدَّثَنَا ابْنُ أَخِي ابْنِ شِهَابٍ، عَنْ عَمِّهِ، أَخْبَرَنِي عُبَيْدُ اللَّهِ بْنُ عَبْدِ اللَّهِ بْنِ عُتْبَةَ بْنِ مَسْعُودٍ، أَنَّ عَبْدَ اللَّهِ بْنَ عَبَّاسٍ ـ رضى الله عنهما ـ قَالَ أَقْبَلْتُ وَقَدْ نَاهَزْتُ الْحُلُمَ، أَسِيرُ عَلَى أَتَانٍ لِي، وَرَسُولُ اللَّهِ صلى الله عليه وسلم قَائِمٌ يُصَلِّي بِمِنًى، حَتَّى سِرْتُ بَيْنَ يَدَىْ بَعْضِ الصَّفِّ الأَوَّلِ، ثُمَّ نَزَلْتُ عَنْهَا فَرَتَعَتْ، فَصَفَفْتُ مَعَ النَّاسِ وَرَاءَ رَسُولِ اللَّهِ صلى الله عليه وسلم. وَقَالَ يُونُسُ عَنِ ابْنِ شِهَابٍ بِمِنًى فِي حَجَّةِ الْوَدَاعِ.

Faḍl ibn ʿAbbās
فضل بن عباس

Narrated `Abdullah bin `Abbas: Al-Fadl bin `Abbas rode behind the Prophet ﷺ as his companion rider on the back portion of his she camel on the Day of Nahr (slaughtering of sacrifice, 10th Dhul-Hijja) and Al-Fadl was a handsome man. The Prophet ﷺ stopped to give the people verdicts. In the meantime, a beautiful woman From the tribe of Khath'am came, asking the verdict of Allah's Messenger ﷺ. Al-Fadl started looking at her as her beauty attracted him. The Prophet ﷺ looked behind while Al-Fadl was looking at her; so the Prophet ﷺ held out his hand backwards and caught the chin of Al-Fadl and turned his face (to the owner sides in order that he should not gaze at her. She said, "O Allah's Messenger ﷺ! The obligation of Performing Hajj enjoined by Allah on His worshipers, has become due (compulsory) on my father who is an old man and who cannot sit firmly on the riding animal. Will it be sufficient that I perform Hajj on his behalf?" He said, "Yes.". – Sahih Al-Bukhari 6228

حَدَّثَنَا أَبُو الْيَمَانِ، أَخْبَرَنَا شُعَيْبٌ، عَنِ الزُّهْرِيِّ، قَالَ أَخْبَرَنِي سُلَيْمَانُ بْنُ يَسَارٍ، أَخْبَرَنِي عَبْدُ اللَّهِ بْنُ عَبَّاسٍ ـ رضى الله عنهما ـ قَالَ أَرْدَفَ رَسُولُ اللَّهِ صلى الله عليه وسلم الْفَضْلَ بْنَ عَبَّاسٍ يَوْمَ النَّحْرِ خَلْفَهُ عَلَى عَجُزِ رَاحِلَتِهِ، وَكَانَ الْفَضْلُ

رَجُلاً وَضِيئًا، فَوَقَفَ النَّبِيُّ صلى الله عليه وسلم لِلنَّاسِ يُفْتِيهِمْ، وَأَقْبَلَتِ امْرَأَةٌ مِنْ خَثْعَمَ وَضِيئَةٌ تَسْتَفْتِي رَسُولَ اللَّهِ صلى الله عليه وسلم فَطَفِقَ الْفَضْلُ يَنْظُرُ إِلَيْهَا، وَأَعْجَبَهُ حُسْنُهَا، فَالْتَفَتَ النَّبِيُّ صلى الله عليه وسلم يَنْظُرُ إِلَيْهَا، فَأَخْلَفَ بِيَدِهِ فَأَخَذَ بِذَقَنِ الْفَضْلِ، فَعَدَلَ وَجْهَهُ عَنِ النَّظَرِ إِلَيْهَا، فَقَالَتْ يَا رَسُولَ اللَّهِ إِنَّ فَرِيضَةَ اللَّهِ فِي الْحَجِّ عَلَى عِبَادِهِ أَدْرَكَتْ أَبِي شَيْخًا كَبِيرًا، لاَ يَسْتَطِيعُ أَنْ يَسْتَوِيَ عَلَى الرَّاحِلَةِ، فَهَلْ يَقْضِي عَنْهُ أَنْ أَحُجَّ عَنْهُ قَالَ " نَعَمْ ".

Narrated Ibn `Abbas: A woman from the tribe of Khath'am asked for the verdict of Allah's Messenger)ﷺ regarding something) during Hajjat-ul-Wada` while Al-Fadl bin `Abbas was the companion-rider behind Allah's Messengerﷺ. She asked, "Allah's ordained obligation (i.e. compulsory Hajj) enjoined on His slaves has become due on my old father who cannot sit firmly on the riding animal. Will it be sufficient if I perform the Hajj on his behalf?" He said, "Yes.". – Sahih Al-Bukhari 4399

حَدَّثَنَا أَبُو الْيَمَانِ، قَالَ حَدَّثَنِي شُعَيْبٌ، عَنِ الزُّهْرِيِّ، وَقَالَ، مُحَمَّدُ بْنُ يُوسُفَ حَدَّثَنَا الأَوْزَاعِيُّ، قَالَ أَخْبَرَنِي ابْنُ شِهَابٍ، عَنْ سُلَيْمَانَ بْنِ يَسَارٍ، عَنِ ابْنِ عَبَّاسٍ ـ رضى الله عنهما ـ أَنَّ امْرَأَةً، مِنْ خَثْعَمَ اسْتَفْتَتْ رَسُولَ اللَّهِ صلى الله عليه وسلم فِي حَجَّةِ الْوَدَاعِ وَالْفَضْلُ بْنُ عَبَّاسٍ رَدِيفُ رَسُولِ اللَّهِ صلى الله عليه وسلم فَقَالَتْ يَا رَسُولَ اللَّهِ إِنَّ فَرِيضَةَ اللَّهِ عَلَى عِبَادِهِ أَدْرَكَتْ أَبِي شَيْخًا كَبِيرًا لاَ يَسْتَطِيعُ أَنْ يَسْتَوِيَ عَلَى الرَّاحِلَةِ، فَهَلْ يَقْضِي أَنْ أَحُجَّ عَنْهُ قَالَ " نَعَمْ ".

Narrated Ibn `Abbas: Allah's Messengerﷺ came to the drinking place and asked for water. Al-Abbas said, "O Fadl! Go to your mother and bring water from her for Allah's Messengerﷺ." Allah's Messengerﷺ said, "Give me water to drink." Al-Abbas said, "O Allah's Messengerﷺ! The people put their hands in it." Allah's Messengerﷺ again said, 'Give me water to drink. So, he drank from that water and then went to the Zamzam (well) and there the people were offering water to the others and working at it (drawing water from the well). The Prophetﷺ then said to them, "Carry on! You are doing a good deed." Then he said, "Were I not afraid that other people would compete with you (in drawing water from Zamzam), I would certainly take the rope and put it over this (i.e. his shoulder) (to draw water)." On saying that the Prophetﷺ pointed to his shoulder. – Sahih Al-Bukhari 1635

حَدَّثَنَا إِسْحَاقُ، حَدَّثَنَا خَالِدٌ، عَنْ خَالِدٍ الْحَذَّاءِ، عَنْ عِكْرِمَةَ، عَنِ ابْنِ عَبَّاسٍ ـ رضى الله عنهما ـ أَنَّ رَسُولَ اللَّهِ صلى الله عليه وسلم جَاءَ إِلَى السِّقَايَةِ، فَاسْتَسْقَى، فَقَالَ الْعَبَّاسُ يَا فَضْلُ اذْهَبْ إِلَى أُمِّكَ، فَأْتِ رَسُولَ اللَّهِ صلى الله عليه وسلم بِشَرَابٍ مِنْ عِنْدِهَا. فَقَالَ " اسْقِنِي ". قَالَ يَا رَسُولَ اللَّهِ إِنَّهُمْ يَجْعَلُونَ أَيْدِيَهُمْ فِيهِ. قَالَ " اسْقِنِي ". فَشَرِبَ مِنْهُ، ثُمَّ أَتَى زَمْزَمَ، وَهُمْ يَسْقُونَ وَيَعْمَلُونَ فِيهَا، فَقَالَ " اعْمَلُوا، فَإِنَّكُمْ عَلَى عَمَلٍ صَالِحٍ ـ ثُمَّ قَالَ ـ لَوْلاَ أَنْ تُغْلَبُوا لَنَزَلْتُ حَتَّى أَضَعَ الْحَبْلَ عَلَى هَذِهِ ". ـ يَعْنِي عَاتِقَهُ ـ وَأَشَارَ إِلَى عَاتِقِهِ

Narrated 'Ubaidullah bin `Abdullah: Ibn `Abbas said, "Usama bin Zaid rode behind the Prophetﷺ from `Arafat to Al-Muzdalifa; and then from Al-Muzdalifa to Mina, Al-Fadl rode behind him." He added, "Both of them (Usama and Al-Fadl) said, 'The Prophetﷺ was constantly reciting Talbiya till he did Rami of the Jamarat-Al-`Aqaba.". – Sahih Al-Bukhari 1686, 1687

حَدَّثَنَا زُهَيْرُ بْنُ حَرْبٍ، حَدَّثَنَا وَهْبُ بْنُ جَرِيرٍ، حَدَّثَنَا أَبِي، عَنْ يُونُسَ الأَيْلِيِّ، عَنِ الزُّهْرِيِّ، عَنْ عُبَيْدِ اللَّهِ بْنِ عَبْدِ اللَّهِ، عَنِ ابْنِ عَبَّاسٍ ـ رضى الله عنهما ـ أَنَّ أُسَامَةَ بْنَ زَيْدٍ ـ رضى الله عنهما ـ كَانَ رِدْفَ النَّبِيِّ صلى الله عليه وسلم مِنْ عَرَفَةَ إِلَى الْمُزْدَلِفَةِ، ثُمَّ أَرْدَفَ الْفَضْلَ مِنَ الْمُزْدَلِفَةِ إِلَى مِنًى ـ قَالَ ـ فَكِلاَهُمَا قَالاَ لَمْ يَزَلِ النَّبِيُّ صلى الله عليه وسلم يُلَبِّي حَتَّى رَمَى جَمْرَةَ الْعَقَبَةِ

Az-Zubair bin Al-Awwam
الزُّبَيْر بْن الْعَوَّام

Narrated `Abdullah bin Az-Zubair: During the battle of Al-Ahzab, I and `Umar bin Abi-Salama were kept behind with the women. Behold! I saw (my father) Az-Zubair riding his horse, going to and coming from Bani Quraiza twice or thrice. So when I came back I said, "O my father! I saw you going to and coming from Bani Quraiza?" He said, "Did you really see me, O my son?" I said, "Yes." He said, "Allah's Messenger ﷺ said, 'Who will go to Bani Quraiza and bring me their news?' So I went, and when I came back, Allah's Apostle mentioned for me both his parents saying, "Let my father and mother be sacrificed for you."'. – Sahih Al-Bukhari 3720

حَدَّثَنَا أَحْمَدُ بْنُ مُحَمَّدٍ، أَخْبَرَنَا {عَبْدُ اللَّهِ} أَخْبَرَنَا هِشَامُ بْنُ عُرْوَةَ، عَنْ أَبِيهِ، عَنْ عَبْدِ اللَّهِ بْنِ الزُّبَيْرِ، قَالَ كُنْتُ يَوْمَ الأَحْزَابِ جُعِلْتُ أَنَا وَعُمَرُ بْنُ أَبِي سَلَمَةَ، فِي النِّسَاءِ، فَنَظَرْتُ فَإِذَا أَنَا بِالزُّبَيْرِ، عَلَى فَرَسِهِ، يَخْتَلِفُ إِلَى بَنِي قُرَيْظَةَ مَرَّتَيْنِ أَوْ ثَلاَثًا، فَلَمَّا رَجَعْتُ قُلْتُ يَا أَبَتِ، رَأَيْتُكَ تَخْتَلِفُ. قَالَ أَوَهَلْ رَأَيْتَنِي يَا بُنَىَّ قُلْتُ نَعَمْ. قَالَ كَانَ رَسُولُ اللَّهِ صلى الله عليه وسلم قَالَ " مَنْ يَأْتِ بَنِي قُرَيْظَةَ فَيَأْتِينِي بِخَبَرِهِمْ ". فَانْطَلَقْتُ، فَلَمَّا رَجَعْتُ جَمَعَ لِي رَسُولُ اللَّهِ صلى الله عليه وسلم أَبَوَيْهِ فَقَالَ " فِدَاكَ أَبِي وَأُمِّي ".

Narrated `Urwa: On the day of the battle of Al-Yarmuk, the companions of the Prophet ﷺ said to Az-Zubair, "Will you attack the enemy vigorously so that we may attack them along with you?" So Az-Zubair attacked them, and they inflicted two wounds over his shoulder, and in between these two wounds there was an old scar he had received on the day of the battle of Badr When I was a child, I used to insert my fingers into those scars in play. – Sahih Al-Bukhari 3721

حَدَّثَنَا عَلِيُّ بْنُ حَفْصٍ، حَدَّثَنَا ابْنُ الْمُبَارَكِ، أَخْبَرَنَا هِشَامُ بْنُ عُرْوَةَ، عَنْ أَبِيهِ، أَنَّ أَصْحَابَ النَّبِيِّ، صلى الله عليه وسلم قَالُوا لِلزُّبَيْرِ يَوْمَ الْيَرْمُوكِ أَلاَ تَشُدُّ فَنَشُدَّ مَعَكَ فَحَمَلَ عَلَيْهِمْ، فَضَرَبُوهُ ضَرْبَتَيْنِ عَلَى عَاتِقِهِ، بَيْنَهُمَا ضَرْبَةٌ ضُرِبَهَا يَوْمَ بَدْرٍ. قَالَ عُرْوَةُ فَكُنْتُ أُدْخِلُ أَصَابِعِي فِي تِلْكَ الضَّرَبَاتِ أَلْعَبُ وَأَنَا صَغِيرٌ

Narrated `Urwa: Az-Zubair quarrelled with a man from the Ansar because of a natural mountainous stream at Al-Harra. The Prophet ﷺ said "O Zubair! Irrigate (your lands and the let the water flow to your neighbor The Ansar said, "O Allah's Messenger ﷺ (This is because) he (Zubair) is your cousin?" At that, the Prophet's face became red (with anger) and he said "O Zubair! Irrigate (your land) and then withhold the water till it fills the land up to the walls and then let it flow to your neighbor." So the Prophet ﷺ enabled Az- Zubair to take his full right after the Ansari provoked his anger. The Prophet ﷺ had previously given a order that was in favor of both of them Az-Zubair said, "I don't think but the Verse was revealed in this connection: "But no, by your Lord, they can have no faith, until they make you judge in all disputes between them." (4.65). – Sahih Al-Bukhari 4585

حَدَّثَنَا عَلِيُّ بْنُ عَبْدِ اللَّهِ، حَدَّثَنَا مُحَمَّدُ بْنُ جَعْفَرٍ، أَخْبَرَنَا مَعْمَرٌ، عَنِ الزُّهْرِيِّ، عَنْ عُرْوَةَ، قَالَ خَاصَمَ الزُّبَيْرُ رَجُلاً مِنَ الأَنْصَارِ فِي شَرِيجٍ مِنَ الْحَرَّةِ، فَقَالَ النَّبِيُّ صلى الله عليه وسلم " اسْقِ يَا زُبَيْرُ ثُمَّ أَرْسِلِ الْمَاءَ إِلَى جَارِكَ ". فَقَالَ الأَنْصَارِيُّ يَا رَسُولَ اللَّهِ أَنْ كَانَ ابْنَ عَمَّتِكَ فَتَلَوَّنَ وَجْهُهُ ثُمَّ قَالَ " اسْقِ يَا زُبَيْرُ ثُمَّ احْبِسِ الْمَاءَ حَتَّى يَرْجِعَ إِلَى الْجَدْرِ، ثُمَّ أَرْسِلِ الْمَاءَ إِلَى جَارِكَ ". وَاسْتَوْعَى النَّبِيُّ صلى الله عليه وسلم لِلزُّبَيْرِ حَقَّهُ فِي صَرِيحِ الْحُكْمِ حِينَ أَحْفَظَهُ الأَنْصَارِيُّ، كَانَ أَشَارَ عَلَيْهِمَا بِأَمْرٍ لَهُمَا فِيهِ سَعَةٌ. قَالَ الزُّبَيْرُ فَمَا أَحْسِبُ هَذِهِ الآيَاتِ إِلاَّ نَزَلَتْ فِي ذَلِكَ {فَلاَ وَرَبِّكَ لاَ يُؤْمِنُونَ حَتَّى يُحَكِّمُوكَ فِيمَا شَجَرَ بَيْنَهُمْ}

Narrated `Ali: Allah's Messenger ﷺ sent me along with AzZubair and Al-Miqdad and said, "Proceed till you reach a place called Raudat-Khakh where there is a lady travelling in a howda on a camel. She has a letter. Take the letter from her." So we set out, and our horses ran at full pace till we reached Raudat Khakh, and behold, we saw the lady and said (to her), "Take out the letter!" She said, "I have no letter with me." We said, "Either you take out the letter or we will strip you of your clothes." So she took the letter out of her hair braid. We brought the letter to the Prophet ﷺ and behold, it was addressed by Hatib bin Abi Balta'a to some pagans at Mecca, informing them of some of the affairs of the Prophet. The Prophet ﷺ said, "What is this, O Hatib?" Hatib replied, "Do not be hasty with me, O Allah's Messenger ﷺ! I am an Ansari man and do not belong to them (Quraish infidels) while the emigrants who were with you had their relatives who used to protect their families and properties at Mecca. So, to compensate for not having blood relation with them.' I intended to do them some favor so that they might protect my relatives (at Mecca), and I did not do this out of disbelief or an inclination to desert my religion." The Prophet then said (to his companions), "He (Hatib) has told you the truth." `Umar said, "O Allah's Apostle! Allow me to chop his head off?" The Apostle said, "He is one of those who witnessed (fought in) the Battle of Badr, and what do you know, perhaps Allah looked upon the people of Badr (Badr warriors) and said, 'Do what you want as I have forgiven you.' " (`Amr, a sub-narrator, said,: This Verse was revealed about him (Hatib): 'O you who believe! Take not My enemies and your enemies as friends or protectors.' (60.1) Narrated `Ali: Sufyan was asked whether (the Verse): 'Take not My enemies and your enemies...' was revealed in connection with Hatib. Sufyan replied, "This occurs only in the narration of the people. I memorized the Hadith from `Amr, not overlooking even a single letter thereof, and I do not know of anybody who remembered it by heart other than myself.". – Sahih Al-Bukhari 4890

حَدَّثَنَا الْحُمَيْدِيُّ، حَدَّثَنَا سُفْيَانُ، حَدَّثَنَا عَمْرُو بْنُ دِينَارٍ، قَالَ حَدَّثَنِي الْحَسَنُ بْنُ مُحَمَّدِ بْنِ عَلِيٍّ، أَنَّهُ سَمِعَ عُبَيْدَ اللَّهِ بْنَ أَبِي رَافِعٍ، كَاتِبَ عَلِيٍّ يَقُولُ سَمِعْتُ عَلِيًّا ـ رضى الله عنه ـ يَقُولُ بَعَثَنِي رَسُولُ اللَّهِ صلى الله عليه وسلم أَنَا وَالزُّبَيْرَ وَالْمِقْدَادَ فَقَالَ " انْطَلِقُوا حَتَّى تَأْتُوا رَوْضَةَ خَاخٍ فَإِنَّ بِهَا ظَعِينَةً مَعَهَا كِتَابٌ فَخُذُوهُ مِنْهَا ". فَذَهَبْنَا تَعَادَى بِنَا خَيْلُنَا حَتَّى أَتَيْنَا الرَّوْضَةَ فَإِذَا نَحْنُ بِالظَّعِينَةِ فَقُلْنَا أَخْرِجِي الْكِتَابَ فَقَالَتْ مَا مَعِي مِنْ كِتَابٍ. فَقُلْنَا لَتُخْرِجِنَّ الْكِتَابَ أَوْ لَنُلْقِيَنَّ الثِّيَابَ. فَأَخْرَجَتْهُ مِنْ عِقَاصِهَا فَأَتَيْنَا بِهِ النَّبِيَّ صلى الله عليه وسلم فَإِذَا فِيهِ مِنْ حَاطِبِ بْنِ أَبِي بَلْتَعَةَ إِلَى أُنَاسٍ مِنَ الْمُشْرِكِينَ مِمَّنْ بِمَكَّةَ يُخْبِرُهُمْ بِبَعْضِ أَمْرِ النَّبِيِّ صلى الله عليه وسلم فَقَالَ النَّبِيُّ صلى الله عليه وسلم " مَا هَذَا يَا حَاطِبُ ". قَالَ لاَ تَعْجَلْ عَلَىَّ يَا رَسُولَ اللَّهِ إِنِّي كُنْتُ امْرَأً مِنْ قُرَيْشٍ وَلَمْ أَكُنْ مِنْ أَنْفُسِهِمْ وَكَانَ مَنْ مَعَكَ مِنَ الْمُهَاجِرِينَ لَهُمْ قَرَابَاتٌ يَحْمُونَ بِهَا أَهْلِيهِمْ وَأَمْوَالَهُمْ بِمَكَّةَ فَأَحْبَبْتُ إِذْ فَاتَنِي مِنَ النَّسَبِ فِيهِمْ أَنْ أَصْطَنِعَ إِلَيْهِمْ يَدًا يَحْمُونَ قَرَابَتِي وَمَا فَعَلْتُ ذَلِكَ كُفْرًا وَلاَ ارْتِدَادًا عَنْ دِينِي. فَقَالَ النَّبِيُّ صلى الله عليه وسلم " إِنَّهُ قَدْ صَدَقَكُمْ ". فَقَالَ عُمَرُ دَعْنِي يَا رَسُولَ اللَّهِ فَأَضْرِبَ عُنُقَهُ. فَقَالَ " إِنَّهُ شَهِدَ بَدْرًا وَمَا يُدْرِيكَ لَعَلَّ اللَّهَ ـ عَزَّ وَجَلَّ ـ اطَّلَعَ عَلَى أَهْلِ بَدْرٍ فَقَالَ اعْمَلُوا مَا شِئْتُمْ فَقَدْ غَفَرْتُ لَكُمْ ". قَالَ عَمْرٌو وَنَزَلَتْ فِيهِ {يَا أَيُّهَا الَّذِينَ آمَنُوا لاَ تَتَّخِذُوا عَدُوِّي وَعَدُوَّكُمْ} قَالَ لاَ أَدْرِي الآيَةَ فِي الْحَدِيثِ أَوْ قَوْلُ عَمْرٍو. حَدَّثَنَا عَلِيٌّ قِيلَ لِسُفْيَانَ فِي هَذَا فَنَزَلَتْ {لاَ تَتَّخِذُوا عَدُوِّي} قَالَ سُفْيَانُ هَذَا فِي حَدِيثِ النَّاسِ حَفِظْتُهُ مِنْ عَمْرٍو وَمَا تَرَكْتُ مِنْهُ حَرْفًا وَمَا أُرَى أَحَدًا حَفِظَهُ غَيْرِي

The nephew of Suraqa bin Ju'sham said that his father informed him that he heard Suraqa bin Ju'sham saying, "The messengers of the heathens of Quraish came to us declaring that they had assigned for the persons why would kill or arrest Allah's Messenger ﷺ and Abu Bakr, a reward equal to their blood money. While I was sitting in one of the gatherings of my tribe. Bani Mudlij, a man from them came to us and stood up while we were sitting, and said, "O Suraqa! No doubt, I have just seen some people far away on the seashore, and I think they are Muhammad and his companions." Suraqa added, "I too realized that it must have been they. But I said 'No, it is not they, but you have seen so-and-so, and so-and-so whom we saw set out.' I stayed in the gathering for a while and then got up and left for my home. And ordered my slave-girl to get my horse which was behind a hillock, and keep it ready for me. Then I took my spear and left by the back door of my house dragging the lower end of the spear on the ground and keeping it low. Then I reached my horse, mounted it and made it gallop. When I approached them (i.e. Muhammad and Abu Bakr), my horse stumbled and I fell down from it, Then I stood up, got hold of my quiver and took out the divining arrows and drew lots as to whether I should harm them (i.e. the Prophet ﷺ and Abu Bakr) or not, and the lot which I disliked came out. But I remounted my horse and let it gallop, giving no importance to the divining arrows. When I heard the recitation of the Quran by Allah's Messenger ﷺ who did not look hither and thither while Abu Bakr was doing it often, suddenly the forelegs of my horse sank into the ground up to the knees, and I fell down from it. Then I rebuked it and it got up but could hardly take out its forelegs from the ground, and when it stood up straight again, its fore-legs caused dust to rise up in the sky like smoke. Then again

I drew lots with the divining arrows, and the lot which I disliked, came out. So I called upon them to feel secure. They stopped, and I remounted my horse and went to them. When I saw how I had been hampered from harming them, it came to my mind that the cause of Allah's Messenger ﷺ (i.e. Islam) will become victorious. So I said to him, "Your people have assigned a reward equal to the blood money for your head." Then I told them all the plans the people of Mecca had made concerning them. Then I offered them some journey food and goods but they refused to take anything and did not ask for anything, but the Prophet ﷺ said, "Do not tell others about us." Then I requested him to write for me a statement of security and peace. He ordered 'Amr bin Fuhaira who wrote it for me on a parchment, and then Allah's Messenger ﷺ proceeded on his way. Narrated 'Urwa bin Az-Zubair: Allah's Messenger ﷺ met Az-Zubair in a caravan of Muslim merchants who were returning from Sham. Az-Zubair provided Allah's Messenger ﷺ and Abu Bakr with white clothes to wear. When the Muslims of Medina heard the news of the departure of Allah's Messenger ﷺ from Mecca (towards Medina), they started going to the Harra every morning . They would wait for him till the heat of the noon forced them to return. One day, after waiting for a long while, they returned home, and when they went into their houses, a Jew climbed up the roof of one of the forts of his people to look for some thing, and he saw Allah's Messenger ﷺ and his companions dressed in white clothes, emerging out of the desert mirage. The Jew could not help shouting at the top of his voice, "O you 'Arabs! Here is your great man whom you have been waiting for!" So all the Muslims rushed to their arms and received Allah's Messenger ﷺ on the summit of Harra. The Prophet ﷺ turned with them to the right and alighted at the quarters of Bani 'Amr bin 'Auf, and this was on Monday in the month of Rabi-ul-Awal. Abu Bakr stood up, receiving the people while Allah's Messenger ﷺ sat down and kept silent. Some of the Ansar who came and had not seen Allah's Messenger ﷺ before, began greeting Abu Bakr, but when the sunshine fell on Allah's Messenger ﷺ and Abu Bakr came forward and shaded him with his sheet only then the people came to know Allah's Messenger ﷺ. Allah's Messenger ﷺ stayed with Bani 'Amr bin 'Auf for ten nights and established the mosque (mosque of Quba) which was founded on piety. Allah's Messenger ﷺ prayed in it and then mounted his she-camel and proceeded on, accompanied by the people till his she-camel knelt down at (the place of) the Mosque of Allah's Messenger ﷺ at Medina. Some Muslims used to pray there in those days, and that place was a yard for drying dates belonging to Suhail and Sahl, the orphan boys who were under the guardianship of 'Asad bin Zurara. When his she-camel knelt down, Allah's Messenger ﷺ said, "This place, Allah willing, will be our abiding place." Allah's Messenger ﷺ then called the two boys and told them to suggest a price for that yard so that he might take it as a mosque. The two boys said, "No, but we will give it as a gift, O Allah's Messenger ﷺ!" Allah's Messenger ﷺ then built a mosque there. The Prophet ﷺ himself started carrying unburnt bricks for its building and while doing so, he was saying "This load is better than the load of Khaibar, for it is more pious in the Sight of Allah and purer and better rewardable." He was also saying, "O Allah! The actual reward is the reward in the Hereafter, so bestow Your Mercy on the Ansar and the Emigrants." Thus the Prophet ﷺ recited (by way of proverb) the poem of some Muslim poet whose name is unknown to me. (Ibn Shibab said, "In the Hadiths it does not occur that Allah's Apostle Recited a complete poetic verse other than this one."). – Sahih Al-Bukhari 3906

قَالَ ابْنُ شِهَابٍ وَأَخْبَرَنِي عَبْدُ الرَّحْمَنِ بْنُ مَالِكٍ الْمُدْلِجِيُّ ـ وَهْوَ ابْنُ أَخِي سُرَاقَةَ بْنِ مَالِكِ بْنِ جُعْشُمٍ ـ أَنَّ أَبَاهُ، أَخْبَرَهُ أَنَّهُ، سَمِعَ سُرَاقَةَ بْنَ جُعْشُمٍ، يَقُولُ جَاءَنَا رُسُلُ كُفَّارِ قُرَيْشٍ يَجْعَلُونَ فِي رَسُولِ اللَّهِ صلى الله عليه وسلم وَأَبِي بَكْرٍ دِيَةَ كُلِّ وَاحِدٍ مِنْهُمَا، مَنْ قَتَلَهُ أَوْ أَسَرَهُ، فَبَيْنَمَا أَنَا جَالِسٌ فِي مَجْلِسٍ مِنْ مَجَالِسِ قَوْمِي بَنِي مُدْلِجٍ أَقْبَلَ رَجُلٌ مِنْهُمْ حَتَّى قَامَ عَلَيْنَا وَنَحْنُ جُلُوسٌ، فَقَالَ يَا سُرَاقَةُ، إِنِّي قَدْ رَأَيْتُ آنِفًا أَسْوِدَةً بِالسَّاحِلِ ـ أُرَاهَا مُحَمَّدًا وَأَصْحَابَهُ. قَالَ سُرَاقَةُ فَعَرَفْتُ أَنَّهُمْ هُمْ، فَقُلْتُ لَهُ إِنَّهُمْ لَيْسُوا بِهِمْ، وَلَكِنَّكَ رَأَيْتَ فُلاَنًا وَفُلاَنًا انْطَلَقُوا بِأَعْيُنِنَا. ثُمَّ لَبِثْتُ فِي الْمَجْلِسِ سَاعَةً، ثُمَّ قُمْتُ فَدَخَلْتُ فَأَمَرْتُ جَارِيَتِي أَنْ

تَخْرُجَ بِفَرَسِي وَهْيَ مِنْ وَرَاءِ أَكَمَةٍ فَتَحْبِسَهَا عَلَيَّ، وَأَخَذْتُ رُمْحِي، فَخَرَجْتُ بِهِ مِنْ ظَهْرِ الْبَيْتِ، فَحَطَطْتُ بِزُجِّهِ الأَرْضَ، وَخَفَضْتُ عَالِيَهُ حَتَّى أَتَيْتُ فَرَسِي فَرَكِبْتُهَا، فَرَفَعْتُهَا تُقَرِّبُ بِي حَتَّى دَنَوْتُ مِنْهُمْ، فَعَثَرَتْ بِي فَرَسِي، فَخَرَرْتُ عَنْهَا فَقُمْتُ، فَأَهْوَيْتُ يَدِي إِلَى كِنَانَتِي فَاسْتَخْرَجْتُ مِنْهَا الأَزْلاَمَ، فَاسْتَقْسَمْتُ بِهَا أَضُرُّهُمْ أَمْ لاَ فَخَرَجَ الَّذِي أَكْرَهُ، فَرَكِبْتُ فَرَسِي، وَعَصَيْتُ الأَزْلاَمَ، تُقَرِّبُ بِي حَتَّى إِذَا سَمِعْتُ قِرَاءَةَ رَسُولِ اللَّهِ صلى الله عليه وسلم وَهْوَ لاَ يَلْتَفِتُ، وَأَبُو بَكْرٍ يُكْثِرُ الاِلْتِفَاتَ سَاخَتْ يَدَا فَرَسِي فِي الأَرْضِ حَتَّى بَلَغَتَا الرُّكْبَتَيْنِ، فَخَرَرْتُ عَنْهَا ثُمَّ زَجَرْتُهَا فَنَهَضَتْ، فَلَمْ تَكَدْ تُخْرِجُ يَدَيْهَا، فَلَمَّا اسْتَوَتْ قَائِمَةً، إِذَا لأَثَرِ يَدَيْهَا عُثَانٌ سَاطِعٌ فِي السَّمَاءِ مِثْلُ الدُّخَانِ، فَاسْتَقْسَمْتُ بِالأَزْلاَمِ، فَخَرَجَ الَّذِي أَكْرَهُ، فَنَادَيْتُهُمْ بِالأَمَانِ فَوَقَفُوا، فَرَكِبْتُ فَرَسِي حَتَّى جِئْتُهُمْ، وَوَقَعَ فِي نَفْسِي حِينَ لَقِيتُ مَا لَقِيتُ مِنَ الْحَبْسِ عَنْهُمْ أَنْ سَيَظْهَرُ أَمْرُ رَسُولِ اللَّهِ صلى الله عليه وسلم فَقُلْتُ لَهُ إِنَّ قَوْمَكَ قَدْ جَعَلُوا فِيكَ الدِّيَةَ. وَأَخْبَرْتُهُمْ أَخْبَارَ مَا يُرِيدُ النَّاسُ بِهِمْ، وَعَرَضْتُ عَلَيْهِمِ الزَّادَ وَالْمَتَاعَ، فَلَمْ يَرْزَآنِي وَلَمْ يَسْأَلاَنِي إِلاَّ أَنْ قَالَ أَخْفِ عَنَّا. فَسَأَلْتُهُ أَنْ يَكْتُبَ لِي كِتَابَ أَمْنٍ، فَأَمَرَ عَامِرَ بْنَ فُهَيْرَةَ، فَكَتَبَ فِي رُقْعَةٍ مِنْ أَدِيمٍ، ثُمَّ مَضَى رَسُولُ اللَّهِ صلى الله عليه وسلم. قَالَ ابْنُ شِهَابٍ فَأَخْبَرَنِي عُرْوَةُ بْنُ الزُّبَيْرِ أَنَّ رَسُولَ اللَّهِ صلى الله عليه وسلم لَقِيَ الزُّبَيْرَ فِي رَكْبٍ مِنَ الْمُسْلِمِينَ كَانُوا تِجَارًا قَافِلِينَ مِنَ الشَّأْمِ، فَكَسَا الزُّبَيْرُ رَسُولَ اللَّهِ صلى الله عليه وسلم وَأَبَا بَكْرٍ ثِيَابَ بَيَاضٍ، وَسَمِعَ الْمُسْلِمُونَ بِالْمَدِينَةِ مَخْرَجَ رَسُولِ اللَّهِ صلى الله عليه وسلم مِنْ مَكَّةَ، فَكَانُوا يَغْدُونَ كُلَّ غَدَاةٍ إِلَى الْحَرَّةِ فَيَنْتَظِرُونَهُ، حَتَّى يَرُدَّهُمْ حَرُّ الظَّهِيرَةِ، فَانْقَلَبُوا يَوْمًا بَعْدَ مَا أَطَالُوا انْتِظَارَهُمْ، فَلَمَّا أَوَوْا إِلَى بُيُوتِهِمْ، أَوْفَى رَجُلٌ مِنْ يَهُودَ عَلَى أُطُمٍ مِنْ آطَامِهِمْ لأَمْرٍ يَنْظُرُ إِلَيْهِ، فَبَصُرَ بِرَسُولِ اللَّهِ صلى الله عليه وسلم وَأَصْحَابِهِ مُبَيَّضِينَ يَزُولُ بِهِمُ السَّرَابُ، فَلَمْ يَمْلِكِ الْيَهُودِيُّ أَنْ قَالَ بِأَعْلَى صَوْتِهِ يَا مَعَاشِرَ الْعَرَبِ هَذَا جَدُّكُمُ الَّذِي تَنْتَظِرُونَ. فَثَارَ الْمُسْلِمُونَ إِلَى السِّلاَحِ، فَتَلَقَّوْا رَسُولَ اللَّهِ صلى الله عليه وسلم بِظَهْرِ الْحَرَّةِ، فَعَدَلَ بِهِمْ ذَاتَ الْيَمِينِ حَتَّى نَزَلَ بِهِمْ فِي بَنِي عَمْرِو بْنِ عَوْفٍ، وَذَلِكَ يَوْمَ الاِثْنَيْنِ مِنْ شَهْرِ رَبِيعٍ الأَوَّلِ، فَقَامَ أَبُو بَكْرٍ لِلنَّاسِ، وَجَلَسَ رَسُولُ اللَّهِ صلى الله عليه وسلم صَامِتًا، فَطَفِقَ مَنْ جَاءَ مِنَ الأَنْصَارِ مِمَّنْ لَمْ يَرَ رَسُولَ اللَّهِ صلى الله عليه وسلم يُحَيِّي أَبَا بَكْرٍ، حَتَّى أَصَابَتِ الشَّمْسُ رَسُولَ اللَّهِ صلى الله عليه وسلم فَأَقْبَلَ أَبُو بَكْرٍ حَتَّى ظَلَّلَ عَلَيْهِ بِرِدَائِهِ، فَعَرَفَ النَّاسُ رَسُولَ اللَّهِ صلى الله عليه وسلم عِنْدَ ذَلِكَ، فَلَبِثَ رَسُولُ اللَّهِ صلى الله عليه وسلم فِي بَنِي عَمْرِو بْنِ عَوْفٍ بِضْعَ عَشْرَةَ لَيْلَةً وَأُسِّسَ الْمَسْجِدُ الَّذِي أُسِّسَ عَلَى التَّقْوَى، وَصَلَّى فِيهِ رَسُولُ اللَّهِ صلى الله عليه وسلم، ثُمَّ رَكِبَ رَاحِلَتَهُ فَسَارَ يَمْشِي مَعَهُ النَّاسُ حَتَّى بَرَكَتْ عِنْدَ مَسْجِدِ الرَّسُولِ صلى الله عليه وسلم بِالْمَدِينَةِ، وَهْوَ يُصَلِّي فِيهِ يَوْمَئِذٍ رِجَالٌ مِنَ الْمُسْلِمِينَ، وَكَانَ مِرْبَدًا لِلتَّمْرِ لِسُهَيْلٍ وَسَهْلٍ غُلاَمَيْنِ يَتِيمَيْنِ فِي حَجْرِ أَسْعَدَ بْنِ زُرَارَةَ، فَقَالَ رَسُولُ اللَّهِ صلى الله عليه وسلم حِينَ بَرَكَتْ بِهِ رَاحِلَتُهُ " هَذَا إِنْ شَاءَ اللَّهُ الْمَنْزِلُ ". ثُمَّ دَعَا رَسُولُ اللَّهِ صلى الله عليه وسلم الْغُلاَمَيْنِ، فَسَاوَمَهُمَا بِالْمِرْبَدِ لِيَتَّخِذَهُ مَسْجِدًا، فَقَالاَ لاَ بَلْ نَهَبُهُ لَكَ يَا رَسُولَ اللَّهِ، ثُمَّ بَنَاهُ مَسْجِدًا، وَطَفِقَ رَسُولُ اللَّهِ صلى الله عليه وسلم يَنْقُلُ مَعَهُمُ اللَّبِنَ فِي بُنْيَانِهِ، وَيَقُولُ وَهُوَ يَنْقُلُ اللَّبِنَ " هَذَا الْحِمَالُ لاَ حِمَالَ خَيْبَرْ هَذَا أَبَرُّ رَبَّنَا وَأَطْهَرْ ". وَيَقُولُ " اللَّهُمَّ إِنَّ الأَجْرَ أَجْرُ الآخِرَهْ فَارْحَمِ الأَنْصَارَ وَالْمُهَاجِرَهْ ". فَتَمَثَّلَ بِشِعْرِ رَجُلٍ مِنَ الْمُسْلِمِينَ لَمْ يُسَمَّ لِي. قَالَ ابْنُ شِهَابٍ وَلَمْ يَبْلُغْنَا فِي الأَحَادِيثِ أَنَّ رَسُولَ اللَّهِ صلى الله عليه وسلم تَمَثَّلَ بِبَيْتِ شِعْرٍ تَامٍّ غَيْرِ هذه الآيات

Narrated Hisham's father: When Allah's Messenger ﷺ set out (towards Mecca) during the year of the Conquest (of Mecca) and this news reached (the infidels of Quraish), Abu Sufyan, Hakim bin Hizam and Budail bin Warqa came out to gather information about Allah's Messenger ﷺ, They proceeded on their way till they reached a place called Marr-az-Zahran (which is near Mecca). Behold! There they saw many fires as if they were the fires of `Arafat. Abu Sufyan said, "What is this? It looked like the fires of `Arafat." Budail bin Warqa' said, "Banu `Amr are less in number than that." Some of the guards of Allah's Messenger ﷺ saw them and took them over, caught them and brought them to Allah's Messenger ﷺ. Abu Sufyan embraced Islam. When the Prophet ﷺ proceeded, he said to Al-Abbas, "Keep Abu Sufyan standing at the top of the mountain so that he would look at the Muslims. So Al-`Abbas kept him standing (at that place) and the tribes with the Prophet ﷺ started passing in front of Abu Sufyan in military batches. A batch passed and Abu Sufyan said, "O `Abbas Who are these?" `Abbas said, "They are (Banu) Ghifar." Abu Sufyan said, I have got nothing to do with Ghifar." Then (a batch of the tribe of) Juhaina passed by and he said similarly as above. Then (a batch of the tribe of) Sa`d bin Huzaim passed by and he said similarly as above. Then (Banu) Sulaim passed by and he said similarly as above. Then came a batch, the like of which Abu Sufyan had not seen. He said, "Who are these?" `Abbas said, "They are the Ansar headed by Sa`d bin Ubada, the one holding the flag." Sa`d bin Ubada said, "O Abu Sufyan! Today is the day of a great battle and today (what is prohibited in) the Ka`ba will be permissible." Abu Sufyan said., "O `Abbas! How excellent the day of destruction is! "Then came another batch (of warriors) which was the smallest of all the batches, and in it there was Allah's Messenger ﷺ

and his companions and the flag of the Prophetﷺ was carried by Az-Zubair bin Al Awwam. When Allah's Messengerﷺ passed by Abu Sufyan, the latter said, (to the Prophet), "Do you know what Sa`d bin 'Ubada said?" The Prophetﷺ said, "What did he say?" Abu Sufyan said, "He said so-and-so." The Prophetﷺ said, "Sa`d told a lie, but today Allah will give superiority to the Ka`ba and today the Ka`ba will be covered with a (cloth) covering." Allah's Messengerﷺ ordered that his flag be fixed at Al-Hajun. Narrated `Urwa: Nafi` bin Jubair bin Mut`im said, "I heard Abbas saying to Az-Zubair bin Al-Awwam, O Abu `Abdullah! Did Allah's Messengerﷺ order you to fix the flag here?' " Allah's Messengerﷺ ordered Khalid bin Al-Walid to enter Mecca from its upper part from Ka'da while the Prophetﷺ himself entered from Kuda. Two men from the cavalry of Khalid bin Al-Wahd named Hubaish bin Al-Ash'ar and Kurz bin Jabir Al-Fihri were martyred on that day. – Sahih Al-Bukhari 4280

حَدَّثَنَا عُبَيْدُ بْنُ إِسْمَاعِيلَ، حَدَّثَنَا أَبُو أُسَامَةَ، عَنْ هِشَامٍ، عَنْ أَبِيهِ، قَالَ لَمَّا سَارَ رَسُولُ اللَّهِ صلى الله عليه وسلم عَامَ الْفَتْحِ فَبَلَغَ ذَلِكَ قُرَيْشًا، خَرَجَ أَبُو سُفْيَانَ بْنُ حَرْبٍ وَحَكِيمُ بْنُ حِزَامٍ وَبُدَيْلُ بْنُ وَرْقَاءَ يَلْتَمِسُونَ الْخَبَرَ عَنْ رَسُولِ اللَّهِ صلى الله عليه وسلم فَأَقْبَلُوا يَسِيرُونَ حَتَّى أَتَوْا مَرَّ الظَّهْرَانِ، فَإِذَا هُمْ بِنِيرَانٍ كَأَنَّهَا نِيرَانُ عَرَفَةَ، فَقَالَ أَبُو سُفْيَانَ مَا هَذِهِ لَكَأَنَّهَا نِيرَانُ عَرَفَةَ. فَقَالَ بُدَيْلُ بْنُ وَرْقَاءَ نِيرَانُ بَنِي عَمْرٍو. فَقَالَ أَبُو سُفْيَانَ عَمْرٌو أَقَلُّ مِنْ ذَلِكَ. فَرَآهُمْ نَاسٌ مِنْ حَرَسِ رَسُولِ اللَّهِ صلى الله عليه وسلم فَأَدْرَكُوهُمْ فَأَخَذُوهُمْ، فَأَتَوْا بِهِمْ رَسُولَ اللَّهِ صلى الله عليه وسلم فَأَسْلَمَ أَبُو سُفْيَانَ، فَلَمَّا سَارَ قَالَ لِلْعَبَّاسِ " احْبِسْ أَبَا سُفْيَانَ عِنْدَ حَطْمِ الْخَيْلِ حَتَّى يَنْظُرَ إِلَى الْمُسْلِمِينَ ". فَحَبَسَهُ الْعَبَّاسُ، فَجَعَلَتِ الْقَبَائِلُ تَمُرُّ مَعَ النَّبِيِّ صلى الله عليه وسلم تَمُرُّ كَتِيبَةً كَتِيبَةً عَلَى أَبِي سُفْيَانَ، فَمَرَّتْ كَتِيبَةٌ قَالَ يَا عَبَّاسُ مَنْ هَذِهِ قَالَ هَذِهِ غِفَارُ. قَالَ مَا لِي وَلِغِفَارَ ثُمَّ مَرَّتْ جُهَيْنَةُ، قَالَ مِثْلَ ذَلِكَ، ثُمَّ مَرَّتْ سَعْدُ بْنُ هُذَيْمٍ، فَقَالَ مِثْلَ ذَلِكَ، وَمَرَّتْ سُلَيْمُ، فَقَالَ مِثْلَ ذَلِكَ، حَتَّى أَقْبَلَتْ كَتِيبَةٌ لَمْ يَرَ مِثْلَهَا، قَالَ مَنْ هَذِهِ قَالَ هَؤُلاَءِ الأَنْصَارُ عَلَيْهِمْ سَعْدُ بْنُ عُبَادَةَ مَعَهُ الرَّايَةُ. فَقَالَ سَعْدُ بْنُ عُبَادَةَ يَا أَبَا سُفْيَانَ الْيَوْمُ يَوْمُ الْمَلْحَمَةِ، الْيَوْمَ تُسْتَحَلُّ الْكَعْبَةُ. فَقَالَ أَبُو سُفْيَانَ يَا عَبَّاسُ حَبَّذَا يَوْمُ الذِّمَارِ. ثُمَّ جَاءَتْ كَتِيبَةٌ، وَهْىَ أَقَلُّ الْكَتَائِبِ، فِيهِمْ رَسُولُ اللَّهِ صلى الله عليه وسلم وَأَصْحَابُهُ، وَرَايَةُ النَّبِيِّ صلى الله عليه وسلم مَعَ الزُّبَيْرِ بْنِ الْعَوَّامِ، فَلَمَّا مَرَّ رَسُولُ اللَّهِ صلى الله عليه وسلم بِأَبِي سُفْيَانَ قَالَ أَلَمْ تَعْلَمْ مَا قَالَ سَعْدُ بْنُ عُبَادَةَ قَالَ " مَا قَالَ ". قَالَ كَذَا وَكَذَا. فَقَالَ " كَذَبَ سَعْدٌ، وَلَكِنْ هَذَا يَوْمٌ يُعَظِّمُ اللَّهُ فِيهِ الْكَعْبَةَ، وَيَوْمٌ تُكْسَى فِيهِ الْكَعْبَةُ ". قَالَ وَأَمَرَ رَسُولُ اللَّهِ صلى الله عليه وسلم أَنْ تُرْكَزَ رَايَتُهُ بِالْحَجُونِ. قَالَ عُرْوَةُ وَأَخْبَرَنِي نَافِعُ بْنُ جُبَيْرِ بْنِ مُطْعِمٍ قَالَ سَمِعْتُ الْعَبَّاسَ يَقُولُ لِلزُّبَيْرِ بْنِ الْعَوَّامِ يَا أَبَا عَبْدِ اللَّهِ، هَا هُنَا أَمَرَكَ رَسُولُ اللَّهِ صلى الله عليه وسلم أَنْ تَرْكُزَ الرَّايَةَ، قَالَ وَأَمَرَ رَسُولُ اللَّهِ صلى الله عليه وسلم يَوْمَئِذٍ خَالِدَ بْنَ الْوَلِيدِ أَنْ يَدْخُلَ مِنْ أَعْلَى مَكَّةَ مِنْ كَدَاءٍ، وَدَخَلَ النَّبِيُّ صلى الله عليه وسلم مِنْ كُدَا، فَقُتِلَ مِنْ خَيْلِ خَالِدٍ يَوْمَئِذٍ رَجُلاَنِ حُبَيْشُ بْنُ الأَشْعَرِ وَكُرْزُ بْنُ جَابِرٍ الْفِهْرِيُّ

Narrated Jabir bin `Abdullah: On the day of (the battle of) the Trench, the Prophetﷺ called the people (to bring news about the enemy). Az-Zubair responded to his call. He called them again and Az-Zubair responded to his call again; then he called them for the third time and again Az-Zubair responded to his call whereupon the Prophet said, "Every prophet has his Hawairi (helper), and Az-Zubair is my Hawari.". – Sahih Al-Bukhari 7261

حَدَّثَنَا عَلِيُّ بْنُ عَبْدِ اللَّهِ، حَدَّثَنَا سُفْيَانُ، حَدَّثَنَا ابْنُ الْمُنْكَدِرِ، قَالَ سَمِعْتُ جَابِرَ بْنَ عَبْدِ اللَّهِ، قَالَ نَدَبَ النَّبِيُّ صلى الله عليه وسلم يَوْمَ الْخَنْدَقِ فَانْتَدَبَ الزُّبَيْرُ، ثُمَّ نَدَبَهُمْ فَانْتَدَبَ الزُّبَيْرُ، ثُمَّ نَدَبَهُمْ فَانْتَدَبَ الزُّبَيْرُ فَقَالَ " لِكُلِّ نَبِيٍّ حَوَارِيٌّ وَحَوَارِيِّ الزُّبَيْرُ ". قَالَ سُفْيَانُ حَفِظْتُهُ مِنِ ابْنِ الْمُنْكَدِرِ. وَقَالَ لَهُ أَيُّوبُ يَا أَبَا بَكْرٍ حَدِّثْهُمْ عَنْ جَابِرٍ، فَإِنَّ الْقَوْمَ يُعْجِبُهُمْ أَنْ تُحَدِّثَهُمْ عَنْ جَابِرٍ. فَقَالَ فِي ذَلِكَ الْمَجْلِسِ سَمِعْتُ جَابِرًا فَتَابَعَ بَيْنَ أَحَادِيثَ سَمِعْتُ جَابِرًا، قُلْتُ لِسُفْيَانَ فَإِنَّ الثَّوْرِيَّ يَقُولُ يَوْمَ قُرَيْظَةَ فَقَالَ كَذَا حَفِظْتُهُ كَمَا أَنَّكَ جَالِسٌ يَوْمَ الْخَنْدَقِ. قَالَ سُفْيَانُ هُوَ يَوْمٌ وَاحِدٌ. وَتَبَسَّمَ سُفْيَانُ.

Narrated Marwan bin Al-Hakam: `Uthman bin `Affan was afflicted with severe nose-bleeding in the year when such illness was prevelant and that prevented him from performing Hajj, and (because of it) he made his will. A man from Quraish came to him and said, "Appoint your successor." `Uthman asked, "Did the people name him? (i.e. the successor) the man said, "Yes." `Uthman asked, "Who is that?" The man remained silent. Another man came to `Uthman and I think it was Al-Harith. He also said, "Appoint your successor." `Uthman asked, "Did the people name him?" The man replied "Yes." `Uthman said, "Who is that?" The man remained silent. `Uthman said, "Perhaps they have mentioned Az-Zubair?" The man said,

"Yes." `Uthman said, "By Him in Whose Hands my life is, he is the best of them as I know, and the dearest of them to Allah's Messenger. – Sahih Al-Bukhari 3717
حَدَّثَنَا خَالِدُ بْنُ مَخْلَدٍ، حَدَّثَنَا عَلِيُّ بْنُ مُسْهِرٍ، عَنْ هِشَامِ بْنِ عُرْوَةَ، عَنْ أَبِيهِ، قَالَ أَخْبَرَنِي مَرْوَانُ بْنُ الْحَكَمِ، قَالَ أَصَابَ عُثْمَانَ بْنَ عَفَّانَ رُعَافٌ شَدِيدٌ سَنَةَ الرُّعَافِ، حَتَّى حَبَسَهُ عَنِ الْحَجِّ وَأَوْصَى، فَدَخَلَ عَلَيْهِ رَجُلٌ مِنْ قُرَيْشٍ قَالَ اسْتَخْلِفْ. قَالَ وَقَالُوهُ قَالَ نَعَمْ. قَالَ وَمَنْ فَسَكَتَ، فَدَخَلَ عَلَيْهِ رَجُلٌ آخَرُ ـ أَحْسِبُهُ الْحَارِثَ ـ فَقَالَ اسْتَخْلِفْ. فَقَالَ عُثْمَانُ وَقَالُوا فَقَالَ نَعَمْ. قَالَ وَمَنْ هُوَ فَسَكَتَ قَالَ فَلَعَلَّهُمْ قَالُوا الزُّبَيْرَ قَالَ نَعَمْ. قَالَ أَمَا وَالَّذِي نَفْسِي بِيَدِهِ إِنَّهُ لَخَيْرُهُمْ مَا عَلِمْتُ، وَإِنْ كَانَ لأَحَبَّهُمْ إِلَى رَسُولِ اللَّهِ صلى الله عليه وسلم.

Narrated Jabir: The Prophet ﷺ said, "Every prophet used to have a Hawari (i.e. disciple), and my Hawari is Az-Zubair bin Al-`Awwam." – Sahih Al-Bukhari 3719
حَدَّثَنَا مَالِكُ بْنُ إِسْمَاعِيلَ، حَدَّثَنَا عَبْدُ الْعَزِيزِ ـ هُوَ ابْنُ أَبِي سَلَمَةَ ـ عَنْ مُحَمَّدِ بْنِ الْمُنْكَدِرِ، عَنْ جَابِرٍ ـ رضى الله عنه ـ قَالَ قَالَ النَّبِيُّ صلى الله عليه وسلم " إِنَّ لِكُلِّ نَبِيٍّ حَوَارِيًّا، وَإِنَّ حَوَارِيَّ الزُّبَيْرُ بْنُ الْعَوَّامِ "

Narrated `Ali: Allah's Messenger ﷺ sent me, Az-Zubair bin Al-Awwam and Abu Marthad Al-Ghanawi, and all of us were horsemen, and he said, "Proceed till you reach Rawdat Khakh, where there is a woman from the pagans carrying a letter sent by Hatib bin Abi Balta'a to the pagans (of Mecca)." So we overtook her while she was proceeding on her camel at the same place as Allah's Messenger ﷺ told us. We said (to her) "Where is the letter which is with you?" She said, "I have no letter with me." So we made her camel kneel down and searched her mount (baggage etc) but could not find anything. My two companions said, "We do not see any letter." I said, "I know that Allah's Messenger ﷺ did not tell a lie. By Allah, if you (the lady) do not bring out the letter, I will strip you of your clothes' When she noticed that I was serious, she put her hand into the knot of her waist sheet, for she was tying a sheet round herself, and brought out the letter. So we proceeded to Allah's Messenger ﷺ with the letter. The Prophet ﷺ said (to Habib), "What made you o what you have done, O Hatib?" Hatib replied, "I have done nothing except that I believe in Allah and His Apostle, and I have not changed or altered (my religion). But I wanted to do the favor to the people (pagans of Mecca) through which Allah might protect my family and my property, as there is none among your companions but has someone in Mecca through whom Allah protects his property (against harm). The Prophet ﷺ said, "Habib has told you the truth, so do not say to him (anything) but good." `Umar bin Al-Khattab said, "Verily he has betrayed Allah, His Apostle, and the believers! Allow me to chop his neck off!" The Prophet ﷺ said, "O `Umar! What do you know; perhaps Allah looked upon the Badr warriors and said, 'Do whatever you like, for I have ordained that you will be in Paradise.'" On that `Umar wept and said, "Allah and His Apostle know best.". – Sahih Al-Bukhari 6259
حَدَّثَنَا يُوسُفُ بْنُ بُهْلُولٍ، حَدَّثَنَا ابْنُ إِدْرِيسَ، قَالَ حَدَّثَنِي حُصَيْنُ بْنُ عَبْدِ الرَّحْمَنِ، عَنْ سَعْدِ بْنِ عُبَيْدَةَ، عَنْ أَبِي عَبْدِ الرَّحْمَنِ السُّلَمِيِّ، عَنْ عَلِيٍّ ـ رضى الله عنه ـ قَالَ بَعَثَنِي رَسُولُ اللَّهِ صلى الله عليه وسلم وَالزُّبَيْرَ بْنَ الْعَوَّامِ وَأَبَا مَرْثَدٍ الْغَنَوِيَّ وَكُلُّنَا فَارِسٌ فَقَالَ " انْطَلِقُوا حَتَّى تَأْتُوا رَوْضَةَ خَاخٍ، فَإِنَّ بِهَا امْرَأَةً مِنَ الْمُشْرِكِينَ مَعَهَا صَحِيفَةٌ مِنْ حَاطِبِ بْنِ أَبِي بَلْتَعَةَ إِلَى الْمُشْرِكِينَ ". قَالَ فَأَدْرَكْنَاهَا تَسِيرُ عَلَى جَمَلٍ لَهَا حَيْثُ قَالَ لَنَا رَسُولُ اللَّهِ صلى الله عليه وسلم قَالَ قُلْنَا أَيْنَ الْكِتَابُ الَّذِي مَعَكِ قَالَتْ مَا مَعِي كِتَابٌ. فَأَنَخْنَا بِهَا، فَابْتَغَيْنَا فِي رَحْلِهَا فَمَا وَجَدْنَا شَيْئًا، قَالَ صَاحِبَاىَ مَا نَرَى كِتَابًا. قَالَ قُلْتُ لَقَدْ عَلِمْتُ مَا كَذَبَ رَسُولُ اللَّهِ صلى الله عليه وسلم وَالَّذِي يُحْلَفُ بِهِ لَتُخْرِجِنَّ الْكِتَابَ أَوْ لأُجَرِّدَنَّكِ. قَالَ فَلَمَّا رَأَتِ الْجِدَّ مِنِّي أَهْوَتْ بِيَدِهَا إِلَى حُجْزَتِهَا وَهْىَ مُحْتَجِزَةٌ بِكِسَاءٍ فَأَخْرَجَتِ الْكِتَابَ ـ قَالَ ـ فَانْطَلَقْنَا بِهِ إِلَى رَسُولِ اللَّهِ صلى الله عليه وسلم فَقَالَ " مَا حَمَلَكَ يَا حَاطِبُ عَلَى مَا صَنَعْتَ ". قَالَ مَا بِي إِلاَّ أَنْ أَكُونَ مُؤْمِنًا بِاللَّهِ وَرَسُولِهِ، وَمَا غَيَّرْتُ وَلاَ بَدَّلْتُ، أَرَدْتُ أَنْ تَكُونَ لِي عِنْدَ الْقَوْمِ يَدٌ يَدْفَعُ اللَّهُ بِهَا عَنْ أَهْلِي وَمَالِي، وَلَيْسَ مِنْ أَصْحَابِكَ هُنَاكَ إِلاَّ وَلَهُ مَنْ يَدْفَعُ اللَّهُ بِهِ عَنْ أَهْلِهِ وَمَالِهِ. قَالَ " صَدَقَ فَلاَ تَقُولُوا لَهُ إِلاَّ خَيْرًا ". قَالَ فَقَالَ عُمَرُ بْنُ الْخَطَّابِ إِنَّهُ قَدْ خَانَ اللَّهَ وَرَسُولَهُ وَالْمُؤْمِنِينَ، فَدَعْنِي فَأَضْرِبَ عُنُقَهُ. قَالَ فَقَالَ " يَا عُمَرُ وَمَا يُدْرِيكَ لَعَلَّ اللَّهَ قَدِ اطَّلَعَ عَلَى أَهْلِ بَدْرٍ فَقَالَ اعْمَلُوا مَا شِئْتُمْ فَقَدْ وَجَبَتْ لَكُمُ الْجَنَّةُ ". قَالَ فَدَمَعَتْ عَيْنَا عُمَرَ وَقَالَ اللَّهُ وَرَسُولُهُ أَعْلَمُ.

Narrated Az-Zubair bin Al-`Awwam: The Prophet ﷺ said, "It is better for anyone of you to take a rope (and cut) and bring a bundle of wood (from the forest) over his back and sell it and Allah will save his face (from the Hell-Fire) because of that, rather than to ask the people who may give him or not.". – Sahih Al-Bukhari 1471

حَدَّثَنَا مُوسَى، حَدَّثَنَا وُهَيْبٌ، حَدَّثَنَا هِشَامٌ، عَنْ أَبِيهِ، عَنِ الزُّبَيْرِ بْنِ الْعَوَّامِ ـ رضى الله عنه ـ عَنِ النَّبِيِّ صلى الله عليه وسلم قَالَ " لأَنْ يَأْخُذَ أَحَدُكُمْ حَبْلَهُ فَيَأْتِيَ بِحُزْمَةِ الْحَطَبِ عَلَى ظَهْرِهِ فَيَبِيعَهَا فَيَكُفَّ اللَّهُ بِهَا وَجْهَهُ، خَيْرٌ لَهُ مِنْ أَنْ يَسْأَلَ النَّاسَ أَعْطَوْهُ أَوْ مَنَعُوهُ ".

Narrated Abu Huraira: The Prophet ﷺ said, "O Bani `Abd Munaf! Buy yourselves from Allah; O Bani `Abdul-Muttalib! Buy yourselves from Allah; O mother of Az-Zubair bin Al-Awwam, the aunt of Allah's Messenger ﷺ , and O Fatima bint Muhammad! Buy yourselves from Allah, for I cannot defend you before Allah. You (both) can ask me from my property as much as you like. ". – Sahih Al-Bukhari 3527

حَدَّثَنَا أَبُو الْيَمَانِ، أَخْبَرَنَا شُعَيْبٌ، أَخْبَرَنَا أَبُو الزِّنَادِ، عَنِ الأَعْرَجِ، عَنْ أَبِي هُرَيْرَةَ ـ رضى الله عنه ـ أَنَّ النَّبِيَّ صلى الله عليه وسلم قَالَ " يَا بَنِي عَبْدِ مَنَافٍ، اشْتَرُوا أَنْفُسَكُمْ مِنَ اللَّهِ، يَا بَنِي عَبْدِ الْمُطَّلِبِ اشْتَرُوا أَنْفُسَكُمْ مِنَ اللَّهِ، يَا أُمَّ الزُّبَيْرِ بْنِ الْعَوَّامِ عَمَّةَ رَسُولِ اللَّهِ، يَا فَاطِمَةُ بِنْتَ مُحَمَّدٍ، اشْتَرِيَا أَنْفُسَكُمَا مِنَ اللَّهِ، لاَ أَمْلِكُ لَكُمَا مِنَ اللَّهِ شَيْئًا، سَلاَنِي مِنْ مَالِي مَا شِئْتُمَا

Narrated Sahl bin Sa`d: I witnessed the case of Lian (the case of a man who charged his wife for committing illegal sexual intercourse when I was fifteen years old. The Prophet ﷺ ordered that they be divorced, and the husband said, "If I kept her, I would be a liar." I remember that Az-Zubair also said, "(It was said) that if that woman brought forth the child with such-and-such description, her husband would prove truthful, but if she brought it with such-and-such description looking like a Wahra (a red insect), he would prove untruthful." I heard Az-Zubair also saying, "Finally she gave birth to a child of description which her husband disliked . – Sahih Al-Bukhari 6854

حَدَّثَنَا عَلِيٌّ، حَدَّثَنَا سُفْيَانُ، قَالَ الزُّهْرِيُّ عَنْ سَهْلِ بْنِ سَعْدٍ، قَالَ شَهِدْتُ الْمُتَلاَعِنَيْنِ وَأَنَا ابْنُ خَمْسَ، عَشْرَةَ، فَرَّقَ بَيْنَهُمَا فَقَالَ زَوْجُهَا كَذَبْتُ عَلَيْهَا إِنْ أَمْسَكْتُهَا. قَالَ فَحَفِظْتُ ذَاكَ مِنَ الزُّهْرِيِّ " إِنْ جَاءَتْ بِهِ كَذَا وَكَذَا فَهُوَ، وَإِنْ جَاءَتْ بِهِ كَذَا وَكَذَا كَأَنَّهُ وَحَرَةٌ فَهُوَ ". وَسَمِعْتُ الزُّهْرِيَّ يَقُولُ جَاءَتْ بِهِ لِلَّذِي يُكْرَهُ

Abd Allah ibn al-Zubayr ibn al-Awwam

عَبْدُ اللَّهِ ابْنِ الزُّبَيْرِ ابْنِ الْعَوَّامِ

Narrated Asma: That she conceived `Abdullah bin Az-Zubair. She added, "I migrated to Medina while I was at full term of pregnancy and alighted at Quba where I gave birth to him. Then I brought him to the Prophet ﷺ and put him in his lap. The Prophet ﷺ asked for a date, chewed it, and put some of its juice in the child's mouth. So, the first thing that entered the child's stomach was the saliva of Allah's Messenger ﷺ. Then the Prophet rubbed the child's palate with a date and invoked for Allah's Blessings on him, and he was the first child born amongst the Emigrants in the Islamic Land (i.e. Medina). – Sahih Al-Bukhari 3909

حَدَّثَنِي زَكَرِيَّاءُ بْنُ يَحْيَى، عَنْ أَبِي أُسَامَةَ، عَنْ هِشَامِ بْنِ عُرْوَةَ، عَنْ أَبِيهِ، عَنْ أَسماء ـ رضى الله عنها ـ أنها حَمَلَتْ بِعَبْدِ اللَّهِ بْنِ الزُّبَيْرِ، قَالَتْ فَخَرَجْتُ وَأَنَا مُتِمٌّ، فَأَتَيْتُ الْمَدِينَةَ، فَنَزَلْتُ بِقُبَاءٍ، فَوَلَدْتُهُ بِقُبَاءٍ، ثُمَّ أَتَيْتُ بِهِ النَّبِيَّ صلى الله عليه وسلم فَوَضَعْتُهُ فِي حَجْرِهِ، ثُمَّ دَعَا بِتَمْرَةٍ، فَمَضَغَهَا، ثُمَّ تَفَلَ فِي فِيهِ، فَكَانَ أَوَّلَ شَىْءٍ دَخَلَ جَوْفَهُ رِيقُ رَسُولِ اللَّهِ صلى الله عليه وسلم، ثُمَّ حَنَّكَهُ بِتَمْرَةٍ ثُمَّ دَعَا لَهُ وَبَرَّكَ عَلَيْهِ، وَكَانَ أَوَّلَ مَوْلُودٍ وُلِدَ فِي الإِسْلاَمِ. تَابَعَهُ خَالِدُ بْنُ مَخْلَدٍ عَنْ عَلِيِّ بْنِ مُسْهِرٍ عَنْ هِشَامٍ عَنْ أَبِيهِ عَنْ أَسْمَاءَ ـ رضى الله عنها ـ أَنَّهَا هَاجَرَتْ إِلَى النَّبِيِّ صلى الله عليه وسلم وَهْىَ حُبْلَى.

Narrated Muhammad bin `Abdur-Rahman Abu Al-Aswad: The people of Medina were forced to prepare an army (to fight against the people of Sham during the caliphate of `Abdullah bin Az-Zubair at Mecca), and I was enlisted in it; Then I met `Ikrima, the freed slave of Ibn `Abbas, and informed him (about it), and he forbade me strongly to do so (i.e. to enlist in that army), and then said, "Ibn `Abbas informed me that some Muslim people were with the pagans, increasing the number of the pagans against Allah's Messenger ﷺ. An arrow used to be shot which would hit one of them (the Muslims in the company of the pagans) and kill him, or he would be struck and killed (with a sword)." Then Allah revealed:-- "Verily! As for those whom the angels take (in death) while they are wronging themselves (by staying among the disbelievers)" (4.97) Abu AlAswad also narrated it. – Sahih Al-Bukhari 4596

حَدَّثَنَا عَبْدُ اللَّهِ بْنُ يَزِيدَ الْمُقْرِئُ، حَدَّثَنَا حَيْوَةُ، وَغَيْرُهُ، قَالاَ حَدَّثَنَا مُحَمَّدُ بْنُ عَبْدِ الرَّحْمَنِ أَبُو الأَسْوَدِ، قَالَ قُطِعَ عَلَى أَهْلِ الْمَدِينَةِ بَعْثٌ فَاكْتُتِبْتُ فِيهِ، فَلَقِيتُ عِكْرِمَةَ مَوْلَى ابْنِ عَبَّاسٍ فَأَخْبَرْتُهُ، فَنَهَانِي عَنْ ذَلِكَ أَشَدَّ النَّهْىِ، ثُمَّ قَالَ أَخْبَرَنِي ابْنُ عَبَّاسٍ أَنَّ نَاسًا مِنَ الْمُسْلِمِينَ كَانُوا مَعَ الْمُشْرِكِينَ يُكَثِّرُونَ سَوَادَ الْمُشْرِكِينَ عَلَى رَسُولِ اللَّهِ صلى الله عليه وسلم يَأْتِي السَّهْمُ فَيُرْمَى بِهِ، فَيُصِيبُ أَحَدَهُمْ فَيَقْتُلُهُ أَوْ يُضْرَبُ فَيُقْتَلُ، فَأَنْزَلَ اللَّهُ {إِنَّ الَّذِينَ تَوَفَّاهُمُ الْمَلاَئِكَةُ ظَالِمِي أَنْفُسِهِمْ} الآيَةَ. رَوَاهُ اللَّيْثُ عَنْ أَبِي الأَسْوَدِ.

Narrated Hisham's father: `Aisha said to `Abdullah bin Az-Zubair, "Bury me with my female companions (i.e. the wives of the Prophet) and do not bury me with the Prophet ﷺ in the house, for I do not like to be regarded as sanctified (just for being buried there)." Narrated Hisham's father: `Umar sent a message to `Aisha, saying, "Will you allow me to be buried with my two companions (the Prophet ﷺ and Abu Bakr) ?" She said, "Yes, by Allah." Though it was her habit that if a man from among the companions (of the Prophet ﷺ) sent her a message asking her to allow him to be buried there, she would say, "No, by Allah, I will never give permission to anyone to be buried with them.". – Sahih Al-Bukhari 7327, 7328

حَدَّثَنَا عُبَيْدُ بْنُ إِسْمَاعِيلَ، حَدَّثَنَا أَبُو أُسَامَةَ، عَنْ هِشَامٍ، عَنْ أَبِيهِ، عَنْ عَائِشَةَ، قَالَتْ لِعَبْدِ اللَّهِ بْنِ الزُّبَيْرِ ادْفِنِّي مَعَ صَوَاحِبِي وَلاَ تَدْفِنِّي مَعَ النَّبِيِّ صلى الله عليه وسلم فِي الْبَيْتِ، فَإِنِّي أَكْرَهُ أَنْ أُزَكَّى. وَعَنْ هِشَامٍ، عَنْ أَبِيهِ، أَنَّ عُمَرَ، أَرْسَلَ إِلَى عَائِشَةَ ائْذَنِي لِي أَنْ أُدْفَنَ مَعَ صَاحِبَىَّ فَقَالَتْ إِي وَاللَّهِ. قَالَ وَكَانَ الرَّجُلُ إِذَا أَرْسَلَ إِلَيْهَا مِنَ الصَّحَابَةِ قَالَتْ لاَ وَاللَّهِ لاَ أُوثِرُهُمْ بِأَحَدٍ أَبَدًا

Narrated Ibn Abi Mulaika: We entered upon Ibn `Abbas and he said "Are you not astonished at Ibn Az-Zubair's assuming the caliphate?" I said (to myself), "I will support him and speak of his good traits as I did not do even for Abu Bakr and `Umar though they were more entitled to receive al I good than he was." I said "He (i.e Ibn Az-Zubair) is the son of the aunt of the Prophet ﷺ and the son of Az-Zubair, and the grandson of Abu Bakr and the son of Khadija's brother, and the son of `Aisha's sister." Nevertheless, he considers himself to be superior to me and does not want me to be one of his friends. So I said, "I never expected that he would refuse my offer to support him, and I don't think he intends to do me any good, therefore, if my cousins should inevitably be my rulers, it will be better for me to be ruled by them than by some others.". – Sahih Al-Bukhari 4666

حَدَّثَنَا مُحَمَّدُ بْنُ عُبَيْدِ بْنِ مَيْمُونٍ، حَدَّثَنَا عِيسَى بْنُ يُونُسَ، عَنْ عُمَرَ بْنِ سَعِيدٍ، قَالَ أَخْبَرَنِي ابْنُ أَبِي مُلَيْكَةَ، دَخَلْنَا عَلَى ابْنِ عَبَّاسٍ فَقَالَ أَلاَ تَعْجَبُونَ لاِبْنِ الزُّبَيْرِ قَامَ فِي أَمْرِهِ هَذَا فَقُلْتُ لأُحَاسِبَنَّ نَفْسِي لَهُ مَا حَاسَبْتُهَا لأَبِي بَكْرٍ وَلاَ لِعُمَرَ، وَلَهُمَا كَانَا أَوْلَى بِكُلِّ خَيْرٍ مِنْهُ، وَقُلْتُ ابْنُ عَمَّةِ النَّبِيِّ صلى الله عليه وسلم، وَابْنُ الزُّبَيْرِ، وَابْنُ أَبِي بَكْرٍ، وَابْنُ أَخِي خَدِيجَةَ، وَابْنُ أُخْتِ عَائِشَةَ فَإِذَا هُوَ يَتَعَلَّى عَنِّي وَلاَ يُرِيدُ ذَلِكَ فَقُلْتُ مَا كُنْتُ أَظُنُّ أَنِّي أَعْرِضُ هَذَا مِنْ نَفْسِي، فَيَدَعُهُ، وَمَا أُرَاهُ يُرِيدُ خَيْرًا، وَإِنْ كَانَ لاَ بُدَّ لأَنْ يَرُبَّنِي بَنُو عَمِّي أَحَبُّ إِلَىَّ مِنْ أَنْ يَرُبَّنِي غَيْرُهُمْ

Narrated `Urwa bin Az-Zubair: `Abdullah bin Az-Zubair went with some women of the tribe of Bani Zuhra to `Aisha who used to treat them nicely because of their relation to Allah's Messenger. – Sahih Al-Bukhari 3503

وَقَالَ اللَّيْثُ حَدَّثَنِي أَبُو الأَسْوَدِ، مُحَمَّدٌ عَنْ عُرْوَةَ بْنِ الزُّبَيْرِ، قَالَ ذَهَبَ عَبْدُ اللَّهِ بْنُ الزُّبَيْرِ مَعَ أُنَاسٍ مِنْ بَنِي زُهْرَةَ إِلَى عَائِشَةَ، وَكَانَتْ أَرَقَّ شَىْءٍ لِقَرَابَتِهِمْ مِنْ رَسُولِ اللَّهِ صلى الله عليه وسلم.

Narrated Ibn Abi Mulaika: Once the two righteous men, i.e., Abu Bakr and `Umar were on the verge of destruction (and that was because): When the delegate of Bani Tamim came to the Prophet, one of them (either Abu Bakr or `Umar) recommended Al-Aqra' bin H`Abis at-Tamimi Al-Hanzali, the brother of Bani Majashi (to be appointed as their chief), while the other recommended somebody else. Abu Bakr said to `Umar, "You intended only to oppose me." `Umar said, "I did not intend to oppose you!" Then their voices grew louder in front of the Prophet ﷺ whereupon there was revealed: 'O you who believe! Do not raise your voices above the voice of the Prophet..a great reward.' (49.2-3) Ibn Az-Zubair said, 'Thence forward when `Umar talked to the Prophet, he would talk like one who whispered a secret and would even fail to make the Prophet ﷺ hear him, in which case the Prophet ﷺ would ask him (to repeat his words). – Sahih Al-Bukhari 7302

حَدَّثَنَا مُحَمَّدُ بْنُ مُقَاتِلٍ، أَخْبَرَنَا وَكِيعٌ، عَنْ نَافِعِ بْنِ عُمَرَ، عَنِ ابْنِ أَبِي مُلَيْكَةَ، قَالَ كَادَ الْخَيِّرَانِ أَنْ يَهْلِكَا أَبُو بَكْرٍ، وَعُمَرُ، لَمَّا قَدِمَ عَلَى النَّبِيِّ صلى الله عليه وسلم وَفْدُ بَنِي تَمِيمٍ، أَشَارَ أَحَدُهُمَا بِالأَقْرَعِ بْنِ حَابِسٍ الْحَنْظَلِيِّ أَخِي بَنِي مُجَاشِعٍ، وَأَشَارَ الآخَرُ بِغَيْرِهِ، فَقَالَ أَبُو بَكْرٍ لِعُمَرَ إِنَّمَا أَرَدْتَ خِلاَفِي. فَقَالَ عُمَرُ مَا أَرَدْتُ خِلاَفَكَ. فَارْتَفَعَتْ أَصْوَاتُهُمَا عِنْدَ النَّبِيِّ صلى الله عليه وسلم فَنَزَلَتْ {يَا أَيُّهَا الَّذِينَ آمَنُوا لاَ تَرْفَعُوا أَصْوَاتَكُمْ} إِلَى قَوْلِهِ {عَظِيمٌ}. قَالَ ابْنُ أَبِي مُلَيْكَةَ قَالَ ابْنُ الزُّبَيْرِ فَكَانَ عُمَرُ بَعْدُ ـ وَلَمْ يَذْكُرْ ذَلِكَ عَنْ أَبِيهِ يَعْنِي أَبَا بَكْرٍ ـ إِذَا حَدَّثَ النَّبِيَّ صلى الله عليه وسلم بِحَدِيثٍ حَدَّثَهُ كَأَخِي السِّرَارِ، لَمْ يُسْمِعْهُ حَتَّى يَسْتَفْهِمَهُ

Narrated Marwan bin Al-Hakam: `Uthman bin `Affan was afflicted with severe nose-bleeding in the year when such illness was prevelant and that prevented him from performing Hajj, and (because of it) he made his will. A man from Quraish came to him and said, "Appoint your successor." `Uthman asked, "Did the people name him? (i.e. the successor) the man said, "Yes." `Uthman asked, "Who is that?" The man remained silent. Another man came to `Uthman and I think it was Al-Harith. He also said, "Appoint your successor." `Uthman asked, "Did the people name him?" The man replied "Yes." `Uthman said, "Who is that?" The man remained silent. `Uthman said, "Perhaps they have mentioned Az-Zubair?" The man said, "Yes." `Uthman said, "By Him in Whose Hands my life is, he is the best of them as I know, and the dearest of them to Allah's Messenger. – Sahih Al-Bukhari 3717

حَدَّثَنَا خَالِدُ بْنُ مَخْلَدٍ، حَدَّثَنَا عَلِيُّ بْنُ مُسْهِرٍ، عَنْ هِشَامِ بْنِ عُرْوَةَ، عَنْ أَبِيهِ، قَالَ أَخْبَرَنِي مَرْوَانُ بْنُ الْحَكَمِ، قَالَ أَصَابَ عُثْمَانَ بْنَ عَفَّانَ رُعَافٌ شَدِيدٌ سَنَةَ الرُّعَافِ، حَتَّى حَبَسَهُ عَنِ الْحَجِّ وَأَوْصَى، فَدَخَلَ عَلَيْهِ رَجُلٌ مِنْ قُرَيْشٍ قَالَ اسْتَخْلِفْ. قَالَ وَقَالُوهُ قَالَ نَعَمْ. قَالَ وَمَنْ فَسَكَتَ، فَدَخَلَ عَلَيْهِ رَجُلٌ آخَرُ ـ أَحْسِبُهُ الْحَارِثَ ـ فَقَالَ اسْتَخْلِفْ. فَقَالَ عُثْمَانُ وَقَالُوا فَقَالَ نَعَمْ. قَالَ وَمَنْ هُوَ فَسَكَتَ قَالَ فَلَعَلَّهُمْ قَالُوا الزُّبَيْرَ قَالَ نَعَمْ. قَالَ أَمَا وَالَّذِي نَفْسِي بِيَدِهِ إِنَّهُ لَخَيْرُهُمْ مَا عَلِمْتُ، وَإِنْ كَانَ لأَحَبَّهُمْ إِلَى رَسُولِ اللَّهِ صلى الله عليه وسلم.

Ibn Shihab said: Salim said, "In the year when Al-Hajjaj bin Yusuf attacked Ibn Az-Zubair, the former asked 'Abdullah (Ibn 'Umar) what to do during the stay on the Day of 'Arafa (9th of Dhul-Hajjah). I said to him, "If you want to follow the Sunna (the legal way of the Prophet ﷺ) you should offer the Salat just after midday on the Day of the 'Arafa. 'Abdullah bin 'Umar said, 'He (Salim) has spoken the truth.' " They (the Companions of the Prophet ﷺ used to offer the Zuhr and Asr prayer together according to the Sunna, I asked Salim, "Did Allah's Messenger ﷺ do that ?" Salim said, "And in doing that do you (people) follow anything else except his ﷺ Sunna?". – Sahih Al-Bukhari 1662

وَقَالَ اللَّيْثُ حَدَّثَنِي عُقَيْلٌ، عَنِ ابْنِ شِهَابٍ، قَالَ أَخْبَرَنِي سَالِمٌ، أَنَّ الْحَجَّاجَ بْنَ يُوسُفَ، عَامَ نَزَلَ بِابْنِ الزُّبَيْرِ ـ رضى الله عنهما ـ سَأَلَ عَبْدَ اللَّهِ ـ رضى الله عنه ـ كَيْفَ تَصْنَعُ فِي الْمَوْقِفِ يَوْمَ عَرَفَةَ فَقَالَ سَالِمٌ إِنْ كُنْتَ تُرِيدُ السُّنَّةَ فَهَجِّرْ بِالصَّلاَةِ

يَوْمَ عَرَفَةَ. فَقَالَ عَبْدُ اللَّهِ بْنُ عُمَرَ صَدَقَ. إِنَّهُمْ كَانُوا يَجْمَعُونَ بَيْنَ الظُّهْرِ وَالْعَصْرِ فِي السُّنَّةِ. فَقُلْتُ لِسَالِمٍ أَفَعَلَ ذَلِكَ رَسُولُ اللَّهِ صلى الله عليه وسلم فَقَالَ سَالِمٌ وَهَلْ تَتَّبِعُونَ فِي ذَلِكَ إِلاَّ سُنَّتَهُ

Narrated Sahl bin Sa`d: I heard Ibn Az-Zubair who was on the pulpit at Mecca, delivering a sermon, saying, "O men! The Prophet used to say, "If the son of Adam were given a valley full of gold, he would love to have a second one; and if he were given the second one, he would love to have a third, for nothing fills the belly of Adam's son except dust. And Allah forgives he who repents to Him." Ubai said, "We considered this as a saying from the Qur'an till the Sura (beginning with) 'The mutual rivalry for piling up of worldly things diverts you..' (102.1) was revealed.". – Sahih Al-Bukhari 6438

حَدَّثَنَا أَبُو نُعَيْمٍ، حَدَّثَنَا عَبْدُ الرَّحْمَنِ بْنُ سُلَيْمَانَ بْنِ الْغَسِيلِ، عَنْ عَبَّاسِ بْنِ سَهْلِ بْنِ سَعْدٍ، قَالَ سَمِعْتُ ابْنَ الزُّبَيْرِ، عَلَى الْمِنْبَرِ بِمَكَّةَ فِي خُطْبَتِهِ يَقُولُ يَا أَيُّهَا النَّاسُ إِنَّ النَّبِيَّ صلى الله عليه وسلم كَانَ يَقُولُ " لَوْ أَنَّ ابْنَ آدَمَ أُعْطِيَ وَادِيًا مَلأً مِنْ ذَهَبٍ أَحَبَّ إِلَيْهِ ثَانِيًا، وَلَوْ أُعْطِيَ ثَانِيًا أَحَبَّ إِلَيْهِ ثَالِثًا، وَلاَ يَسُدُّ جَوْفَ ابْنِ آدَمَ إِلاَّ التُّرَابُ، وَيَتُوبُ اللَّهُ عَلَى مَنْ تَابَ "

Narrated Yazid bin Ruman from `Urwa: `Aisha said that the Prophet ﷺ said to her, "O Aisha! Were your nation not close to the Pre-Islamic Period of Ignorance, I would have had the Ka`ba demolished and would have included in it the portion which had been left, and would have made it at a level with the ground and would have made two doors for it, one towards the east and the other towards the west, and then by doing this it would have been built on the foundations laid by Abraham." That was what urged Ibn-Az-Zubair to demolish the Ka`ba. Jazz said, "I saw Ibn-Az-Zubair when he demolished and rebuilt the Ka`ba and included in it a portion of Al-Hijr (the unroofed portion of Ka`ba which is at present in the form of a compound towards the northwest of the Ka`ba). I saw the original foundations of Abraham which were of stones resembling the humps of camels." So Jarir asked Yazid, "Where was the place of those stones?" Jazz said, "I will just now show it to you." So Jarir accompanied Yazid and entered Al-Hijr, and Jazz pointed to a place and said, "Here it is." Jarir said, "It appeared to me about six cubits from Al-Hijr or so.". – Sahih Al-Bukhari 1586

حَدَّثَنَا بَيَانُ بْنُ عَمْرٍو، حَدَّثَنَا يَزِيدُ، حَدَّثَنَا جَرِيرُ بْنُ حَازِمٍ، حَدَّثَنَا يَزِيدُ بْنُ رُومَانَ، عَنْ عُرْوَةَ، عَنْ عَائِشَةَ ـ رضى الله عنها ـ أَنَّ النَّبِيَّ صلى الله عليه وسلم قَالَ لَهَا " يَا عَائِشَةُ لَوْلاَ أَنَّ قَوْمَكِ حَدِيثُ عَهْدٍ بِجَاهِلِيَّةٍ لأَمَرْتُ بِالْبَيْتِ فَهُدِمَ، فَأَدْخَلْتُ فِيهِ مَا أُخْرِجَ مِنْهُ وَأَلْزَقْتُهُ بِالأَرْضِ، وَجَعَلْتُ لَهُ بَابَيْنِ بَابًا شَرْقِيًّا وَبَابًا غَرْبِيًّا، فَبَلَغْتُ بِهِ أَسَاسَ إِبْرَاهِيمَ ". فَذَلِكَ الَّذِي حَمَلَ ابْنَ الزُّبَيْرِ ـ رضى الله عنهما ـ عَلَى هَدْمِهِ. قَالَ يَزِيدُ وَشَهِدْتُ ابْنَ الزُّبَيْرِ حِينَ هَدَمَهُ وَبَنَاهُ وَأَدْخَلَ فِيهِ مِنَ الْحِجْرِ، وَقَدْ رَأَيْتُ أَسَاسَ إِبْرَاهِيمَ حِجَارَةً كَأَسْنِمَةِ الإِبِلِ. قَالَ جَرِيرٌ فَقُلْتُ لَهُ أَيْنَ مَوْضِعُهُ قَالَ أُرِيكَهُ الآنَ. فَدَخَلْتُ مَعَهُ الْحِجْرَ فَأَشَارَ إِلَى مَكَانٍ فَقَالَ هَا هُنَا. قَالَ جَرِيرٌ فَحَزَرْتُ مِنَ الْحِجْرِ سِتَّةَ أَذْرُعٍ أَوْ نَحْوَهَا.

Narrated Ibn Az-Zubair: I said to `Uthman, "This Verse which is in Surat-al-Baqara: "Those of you who die and leave widows behind...without turning them out." Has been abrogated by another Verse. Why then do you write it (in the Qur'an)?" `Uthman said. "Leave it (where it is), O the son of my brother, for I will not shift anything of it (i.e. the Qur'an) from its original position.". – Sahih Al-Bukhari 4536

حَدَّثَنِي عَبْدُ اللَّهِ بْنُ أَبِي الأَسْوَدِ، حَدَّثَنَا حُمَيْدُ بْنُ الأَسْوَدِ، وَيَزِيدُ بْنُ زُرَيْعٍ، قَالاَ حَدَّثَنَا حَبِيبُ بْنُ الشَّهِيدِ، عَنِ ابْنِ أَبِي مُلَيْكَةَ، قَالَ قَالَ ابْنُ الزُّبَيْرِ قُلْتُ لِعُثْمَانَ هَذِهِ الآيَةُ الَّتِي فِي الْبَقَرَةِ {وَالَّذِينَ يُتَوَفَّوْنَ مِنْكُمْ وَيَذَرُونَ أَزْوَاجًا} إِلَى قَوْلِهِ {غَيْرَ إِخْرَاجٍ} قَدْ نَسَخَتْهَا الأُخْرَى، فَلِمَ تَكْتُبُهَا قَالَ تَدَعُهَا. يَا ابْنَ أَخِي لاَ أُغَيِّرُ شَيْئًا مِنْهُ مِنْ مَكَانِهِ. قَالَ حُمَيْدٌ أَوْ نَحْوَ هَذَا.

Narrated `Abdullah bin Az-Zubair: During the battle of Al-Ahzab, I and `Umar bin Abi-Salama were kept behind with the women. Behold! I saw (my father) Az-Zubair riding his horse, going to and coming from Bani Quraiza twice or thrice. So when I came back I said, "O my father! I saw you going to and coming from Bani Quraiza?" He said, "Did you really see me, O my son?" I said, "Yes." He said, "Allah's Messenger ﷺ said, 'Who will go to Bani Quraiza and bring me their news?' So I went, and when I came back, Allah's Apostle mentioned for me both his parents saying, "Let my father and mother be sacrificed for you."'. – Sahih Al-Bukhari 3720

حَدَّثَنَا أَحْمَدُ بْنُ مُحَمَّدٍ، أَخْبَرَنَا {عَبْدُ اللَّهِ} أَخْبَرَنَا هِشَامُ بْنُ عُرْوَةَ، عَنْ أَبِيهِ، عَنْ عَبْدِ اللَّهِ بْنِ الزُّبَيْرِ، قَالَ كُنْتُ يَوْمَ الأَحْزَابِ جُعِلْتُ أَنَا وَعُمَرُ بْنُ أَبِي سَلَمَةَ، فِي النِّسَاءِ، فَنَظَرْتُ فَإِذَا أَنَا بِالزُّبَيْرِ، عَلَى فَرَسِهِ، يَخْتَلِفُ إِلَى بَنِي قُرَيْظَةَ مَرَّتَيْنِ أَوْ ثَلاَثًا، فَلَمَّا رَجَعْتُ قُلْتُ يَا أَبَتِ، رَأَيْتُكَ تَخْتَلِفُ‏.‏ قَالَ أَوَهَلْ رَأَيْتَنِي يَا بُنَىَّ قُلْتُ نَعَمْ‏.‏ قَالَ كَانَ رَسُولُ اللَّهِ صلى الله عليه وسلم قَالَ ‏"‏ مَنْ يَأْتِ بَنِي قُرَيْظَةَ فَيَأْتِينِي بِخَبَرِهِمْ ‏"‏‏.‏ فَانْطَلَقْتُ، فَلَمَّا رَجَعْتُ جَمَعَ لِي رَسُولُ اللَّهِ صلى الله عليه وسلم أَبَوَيْهِ فَقَالَ ‏"‏ فِدَاكَ أَبِي وَأُمِّي ‏"‏‏.

Narrated Wahb bin Kaisan: The People of Sham taunted `Abdullah bin Az-Zubair by calling him "The son of Dhatin-Nataqain" (the woman who has two waist-belts). (His mother) (Asma, said to him, "O my son! They taunt you with "Nataqain". Do you know what the Nataqain were? That was my waist-belt which I divided in two parts. I tied the water skin of Allah's Messenger ﷺ with one part, and with the other part I tied his food container.". – Sahih Al-Bukhari 5388

حَدَّثَنَا مُحَمَّدٌ، أَخْبَرَنَا أَبُو مُعَاوِيَةَ، حَدَّثَنَا هِشَامٌ، عَنْ أَبِيهِ، وَعَنْ وَهْبِ بْنِ كَيْسَانَ، قَالَ كَانَ أَهْلُ الشَّأْمِ يُعَيِّرُونَ ابْنَ الزُّبَيْرِ يَقُولُونَ يَا ابْنَ ذَاتِ النِّطَاقَيْنِ‏.‏ فَقَالَتْ لَهُ أَسْمَاءُ يَا بُنَىَّ إِنَّهُمْ يُعَيِّرُونَكَ بِالنِّطَاقَيْنِ، هَلْ تَدْرِي مَا كَانَ النِّطَاقَانِ إِنَّمَا كَانَ نِطَاقِي شَقَقْتُهُ نِصْفَيْنِ، فَأَوْكَيْتُ قِرْبَةَ رَسُولِ اللَّهِ صلى الله عليه وسلم بِأَحَدِهِمَا، وَجَعَلْتُ فِي سُفْرَتِهِ آخَرَ، قَالَ فَكَانَ أَهْلُ الشَّأْمِ إِذَا عَيَّرُوهُ بِالنِّطَاقَيْنِ يَقُولُ إِيهًا وَالإِلَهْ‏.‏ تِلْكَ شَكَاةٌ ظَاهِرٌ عَنْكَ عَارُهَا‏.

Narrated `Abdullah bin Abi Mulaika :The people of Kufa sent a letter to Ibn Az-Zubair, asking about (the inheritance of) (paternal) grandfather. He replied that the right of the inheritance of (paternal) grandfather is the same as that of father if the father is dead) and added, "Allah's Messenger ﷺ said, ' If I were to take a Khalil from this nation, I would have taken him (i.e. Abu Bakr) – .Sahih Al-Bukhari 3658

حَدَّثَنَا سُلَيْمَانُ بْنُ حَرْبٍ، أَخْبَرَنَا حَمَّادُ بْنُ زَيْدٍ، عَنْ أَيُّوبَ، عَنْ عَبْدِ اللَّهِ بْنِ أَبِي مُلَيْكَةَ، قَالَ كَتَبَ أَهْلُ الْكُوفَةِ إِلَى ابْنِ الزُّبَيْرِ فِي الْجَدِّ‏.‏ فَقَالَ أَمَّا الَّذِي قَالَ رَسُولُ اللَّهِ صلى الله عليه وسلم ‏"‏ لَوْ كُنْتُ مُتَّخِذًا مِنْ هَذِهِ الأُمَّةِ خَلِيلاً لاَتَّخَذْتُهُ ‏"‏‏.‏ أَنْزَلَهُ أَبًا يَعْنِي أَبَا بَكْرٍ‏.

Narrated `Urwa bin Az-Zubair: 'Abdullah bin Az-Zubair was the most beloved person to `Aisha excluding the Prophet ﷺ and Abu Bakr, and he in his turn, was the most devoted to her, `Aisha used not to withhold the money given to her by Allah, but she used to spend it in charity. (`Abdullah) bin AzZubair said, " `Aisha should be stopped from doing so." (When `Aisha heard this), she said protestingly, "Shall I be stopped from doing so? I vow that I will never talk to `Abdullah bin Az-Zubair." On that, Ibn Az-Zubair asked some people from Quraish and particularly the two uncles of Allah's Messenger ﷺ to intercede with her, but she refused (to talk to him). Az-Zuhriyun, the uncles of the Prophet, including `Abdur-Rahman bin Al-Aswad bin `Abd Yaghuth and Al-Miswar bin Makhrama said to him, "When we ask for the permission to visit her, enter her house along with us (without taking her leave)." He did accordingly (and she accepted their intercession). He sent her ten slaves whom she manumitted as an expiation for (not keeping) her vow. `Aisha manumitted more slaves for the same purpose till she manumitted forty slaves. She said, "I wish I had specified what I would have done in case of not fulfilling my vow when I made the vow, so that I might have done it easily – .".Sahih Al-Bukhari 3505

حَدَّثَنَا عَبْدُ اللَّهِ بْنُ يُوسُفَ، حَدَّثَنَا اللَّيْثُ، قَالَ حَدَّثَنِي أَبُو الأَسْوَدِ، عَنْ عُرْوَةَ بْنِ الزُّبَيْرِ، قَالَ كَانَ عَبْدُ اللَّهِ بْنُ الزُّبَيْرِ أَحَبَّ الْبَشَرِ إِلَى عَائِشَةَ بَعْدَ النَّبِيِّ صلى الله عليه وسلم وَأَبِي بَكْرٍ، وَكَانَ أَبَرَّ النَّاسِ بِهَا، وَكَانَتْ لاَ تُمْسِكُ شَيْئًا مِمَّا جَاءَهَا مِنْ رِزْقِ اللَّهِ {إِلاَّ} تَصَدَّقَتْ‏.‏ فَقَالَ ابْنُ الزُّبَيْرِ يَنْبَغِي أَنْ يُؤْخَذَ عَلَى يَدَيْهَا‏.‏ فَقَالَتْ أَيُؤْخَذُ عَلَى يَدَىَّ عَلَىَّ نَذْرٌ إِنْ كَلَّمْتُهُ‏.‏ فَاسْتَشْفَعَ

إِلَيْهَا بِرِجَالٍ مِنْ قُرَيْشٍ، وَبِأَخْوَالِ رَسُولِ اللَّهِ صلى الله عليه وسلم خَاصَّةً فَامْتَنَعَتْ، فَقَالَ لَهُ الزُّهْرِيُّونَ أَخْوَالُ النَّبِيِّ صلى الله عليه وسلم مِنْهُمْ عَبْدُ الرَّحْمَنِ بْنُ الأَسْوَدِ بْنِ عَبْدِ يَغُوثَ وَالْمِسْوَرُ بْنُ مَخْرَمَةَ إِذَا اسْتَأْذَنَّا فَاقْتَحِمِ الْحِجَابَ. فَفَعَلَ، فَأَرْسَلَ إِلَيْهَا بِعَشْرِ رِقَابٍ، فَأَعْتَقَتْهُمْ، ثُمَّ لَمْ تَزَلْ تُعْتِقُهُمْ حَتَّى بَلَغَتْ أَرْبَعِينَ. فَقَالَتْ وَدِدْتُ أَنِّي جَعَلْتُ حِينَ حَلَفْتُ عَمَلاً أَعْمَلُهُ فَأَفْرُغَ مِنْهُ.

Narrated Jabala : " While at Medina we were struck with famine. Ibn Az-Zubair used to provide us with dates as our food. Ibn `Umar used to pass by us and say, "Don't eat two dates together at a time as the Prophet ﷺ has forbidden eating two dates together at a time (in a gathering) unless one takes the permission of one's companion brother – .".Sahih Al-Bukhari 2490

حَدَّثَنَا أَبُو الْوَلِيدِ، حَدَّثَنَا شُعْبَةُ، عَنْ جَبَلَةَ، قَالَ كُنَّا بِالْمَدِينَةِ فَأَصَابَتْنَا سَنَةٌ، فَكَانَ ابْنُ الزُّبَيْرِ يَرْزُقُنَا التَّمْرَ، وَكَانَ ابْنُ عُمَرَ يَمُرُّ بِنَا فَيَقُولُ لاَ تَقْرُنُوا فَإِنَّ النَّبِيَّ صلى الله عليه وسلم نَهَى عَنِ الإِقْرَانِ، إِلاَّ أَنْ يَسْتَأْذِنَ الرَّجُلُ مِنْكُمْ أَخَاهُ.

Narrated `Amr bin Dinar and 'Ubaidullah bin Abi Yazid :In the lifetime of the Prophet ﷺ there was no wall around the Ka`ba and the people used to pray around the Ka`ba till `Umar became the Caliph and he built the wall around it. 'Ubaidullah further said, "Its wall was low, so Ibn Az-Zubair built it – .".Sahih Al-Bukhari 3830

حَدَّثَنَا أَبُو النُّعْمَانِ، حَدَّثَنَا حَمَّادُ بْنُ زَيْدٍ، عَنْ عَمْرِو بْنِ دِينَارٍ، وَعُبَيْدِ اللَّهِ بْنِ أَبِي يَزِيدَ، قَالاَ لَمْ يَكُنْ عَلَى عَهْدِ النَّبِيِّ صلى الله عليه وسلم حَوْلَ الْبَيْتِ حَائِطٌ، كَانُوا يُصَلُّونَ حَوْلَ الْبَيْتِ، حَتَّى كَانَ عُمَرُ، فَبَنَى حَوْلَهُ حَائِطًا ـ قَالَ عُبَيْدُ اللَّهِ ـ جَدْرُهُ قَصِيرٌ، فَبَنَاهُ ابْنُ الزُّبَيْرِ.

Urwa ibn al-Zubayr ibn al-Awwam
عُرْوَة بْن الزُّبَيْر بْن الْعَوَّام الأَسَدِيّ

Narrated 'Urwa bin Az-Zubair: 'Aishah, the wife of the Prophet ﷺ told him that there were four types of marriage during Pre-Islamic period of Ignorance. One type was similar to that of the present day i.e. a man used to ask somebody else for the hand of a girl under his guardianship or for his daughter's hand, and give her Mahr and then marry her. The second type was that a man would say to his wife after she had become clean from her period. "Send for so-and-so and have sexual intercourse with him." Her husband would then keep away from her and would never sleep with her till she got pregnant from the other man with whom she was sleeping. When her pregnancy became evident, he husband would sleep with her if he wished. Her husband did so (i.e. let his wife sleep with some other man) so that he might have a child of noble breed. Such marriage was called as Al-Istibda'. Another type of marriage was that a group of less than ten men would assemble and enter upon a woman, and all of them would have sexual relation with her. If she became pregnant and delivered a child and some days had passed after delivery, she would sent for all of them and none of them would refuse to come, and when they all gathered before her, she would say to them, "You (all) know what you have done, and now I have given birth to a child. So, it is your child so-and-so!" naming whoever she liked, and her child would follow him and he could not refuse to take him. The fourth type of marriage was that many people would enter upon a lady and she would never refuse anyone who came to her. Those were the prostitutes who used to fix flags at their doors as sign, and he who would wished, could have sexual intercourse with them. If anyone of them got pregnant and delivered a child, then all those men would be gathered for her and they would call the Qa'if (persons skilled in recognizing the likeness of a child to his father) to them and would let the child follow the man (whom they recognized as his father) and she would let him adhere to him and be called his son. The man would not refuse all that. But when Muhammad ﷺ was sent with the Truth, he abolished all the types of marriages observed in pre-Islamic period of Ignorance except the type of marriage the people recognize today. – Sahih Al-Bukhari 5127

قَالَ يَحْيَى بْنُ سُلَيْمَانَ حَدَّثَنَا ابْنُ وَهْبٍ، عَنْ يُونُسَ. حَدَّثَنَا أَحْمَدُ بْنُ صَالِحٍ، حَدَّثَنَا عَنْبَسَةُ، حَدَّثَنَا يُونُسُ، عَنِ ابْنِ شِهَابٍ، قَالَ أَخْبَرَنِي عُرْوَةُ بْنُ الزُّبَيْرِ، أَنَّ عَائِشَةَ، زَوْجَ النَّبِيِّ صلى الله عليه وسلم أَخْبَرَتْهُ أَنَّ النِّكَاحَ فِي الْجَاهِلِيَّةِ كَانَ عَلَى أَرْبَعَةِ أَنْحَاءٍ فَنِكَاحٌ مِنْهَا نِكَاحُ النَّاسِ الْيَوْمَ، يَخْطُبُ الرَّجُلُ إِلَى الرَّجُلِ وَلِيَّتَهُ أَوِ ابْنَتَهُ، فَيُصْدِقُهَا ثُمَّ يَنْكِحُهَا، وَنِكَاحٌ آخَرُ كَانَ الرَّجُلُ يَقُولُ لاِمْرَأَتِهِ إِذَا طَهُرَتْ مِنْ طَمْثِهَا أَرْسِلِي إِلَى فُلاَنٍ فَاسْتَبْضِعِي مِنْهُ. وَيَعْتَزِلُهَا زَوْجُهَا، وَلاَ يَمَسُّهَا أَبَدًا، حَتَّى يَتَبَيَّنَ حَمْلُهَا مِنْ ذَلِكَ الرَّجُلِ الَّذِي تَسْتَبْضِعُ مِنْهُ، فَإِذَا تَبَيَّنَ حَمْلُهَا أَصَابَهَا زَوْجُهَا إِذَا أَحَبَّ، وَإِنَّمَا يَفْعَلُ ذَلِكَ رَغْبَةً فِي نَجَابَةِ الْوَلَدِ، فَكَانَ هَذَا النِّكَاحُ نِكَاحَ الاِسْتِبْضَاعِ، وَنِكَاحٌ آخَرُ يَجْتَمِعُ الرَّهْطُ مَا دُونَ الْعَشَرَةِ فَيَدْخُلُونَ عَلَى الْمَرْأَةِ كُلُّهُمْ يُصِيبُهَا. فَإِذَا حَمَلَتْ وَوَضَعَتْ، وَمَرَّ عَلَيْهَا لَيَالِيَ بَعْدَ أَنْ تَضَعَ حَمْلَهَا، أَرْسَلَتْ إِلَيْهِمْ فَلَمْ يَسْتَطِعْ رَجُلٌ مِنْهُمْ أَنْ يَمْتَنِعَ حَتَّى يَجْتَمِعُوا عِنْدَهَا تَقُولُ لَهُمْ قَدْ عَرَفْتُمُ الَّذِي كَانَ مِنْ أَمْرِكُمْ، وَقَدْ وَلَدْتُ فَهُوَ ابْنُكَ يَا فُلاَنُ. تُسَمِّي مَنْ أَحَبَّتْ بِاسْمِهِ، فَيَلْحَقُ بِهِ وَلَدُهَا، لاَ يَسْتَطِيعُ أَنْ يَمْتَنِعَ بِهِ الرَّجُلُ. وَنِكَاحُ الرَّابِعِ يَجْتَمِعُ النَّاسُ الْكَثِيرُ فَيَدْخُلُونَ عَلَى الْمَرْأَةِ لاَ تَمْتَنِعُ مِمَّنْ جَاءَهَا وَهُنَّ الْبَغَايَا كُنَّ يَنْصِبْنَ عَلَى أَبْوَابِهِنَّ رَايَاتٍ تَكُونُ عَلَمًا فَمَنْ أَرَادَهُنَّ دَخَلَ عَلَيْهِنَّ، فَإِذَا حَمَلَتْ إِحْدَاهُنَّ وَوَضَعَتْ حَمْلَهَا جُمِعُوا لَهَا وَدَعَوْا لَهُمُ الْقَافَةَ ثُمَّ أَلْحَقُوا وَلَدَهَا بِالَّذِي يَرَوْنَ فَالْتَاطَ بِهِ، وَدُعِيَ ابْنَهُ لاَ يَمْتَنِعُ مِنْ ذَلِكَ، فَلَمَّا بُعِثَ مُحَمَّدٌ صلى الله عليه وسلم بِالْحَقِّ هَدَمَ نِكَاحَ الْجَاهِلِيَّةِ كُلَّهُ، إِلاَّ نِكَاحَ النَّاسِ الْيَوْمَ.

Narrated Mujahid: Urwa bin Az-Zubair and I entered the Mosque (of the Prophet) and saw `Abdullah bin `Umar sitting near the dwelling place of Aisha and some people were offering the Duha prayer. We asked him about their prayer and he replied that it was a heresy. He (Urwa) then asked him how many times the Prophet ﷺ had performed `Umra. He replied, 'Four times; one of them was in the month of Rajab." We disliked to contradict him. Then we heard `Aisha, the Mother of faithful believers cleaning her teeth with Siwak in the dwelling place. 'Urwa said, "O Mother! O Mother of the believers! Don't you hear what Abu `Abdur Rahman is saying?" She said, "What does he say?" 'Urwa said, "He says that Allah's Messenger ﷺ performed four `Umra and one of them was in the month of Rajab." `Aisha said, "May Allah be merciful to Abu `Abdur Rahman! The Prophet ﷺ did not perform any `Umra except that he was with him, and he never performed any `Umra in Rajab.". – Sahih Al-Bukhari 1775, 1776

حَدَّثَنَا قُتَيْبَةُ، حَدَّثَنَا جَرِيرٌ، عَنْ مَنْصُورٍ، عَنْ مُجَاهِدٍ، قَالَ دَخَلْتُ أَنَا وَعُرْوَةُ بْنُ الزُّبَيْرِ الْمَسْجِدَ،، فَإِذَا عَبْدُ اللَّهِ بْنُ عُمَرَ ـ رضى الله عنهما ـ جَالِسٌ إِلَى حُجْرَةِ عَائِشَةَ، وَإِذَا نَاسٌ يُصَلُّونَ فِي الْمَسْجِدِ صَلاَةَ الضُّحَى. قَالَ فَسَأَلْنَاهُ عَنْ صَلاَتِهِمْ. فَقَالَ بِدْعَةٌ. ثُمَّ قَالَ لَهُ كَمِ اعْتَمَرَ رَسُولُ اللَّهِ صلى الله عليه وسلم قَالَ أَرْبَعٌ إِحْدَاهُنَّ فِي رَجَبٍ، فَكَرِهْنَا أَنْ نَرُدَّ عَلَيْهِ. قَالَ وَسَمِعْنَا اسْتِنَانَ، عَائِشَةَ أُمِّ الْمُؤْمِنِينَ فِي الْحُجْرَةِ، فَقَالَ عُرْوَةُ يَا أُمَّاهُ، يَا أُمَّ الْمُؤْمِنِينَ. أَلاَ تَسْمَعِينَ مَا يَقُولُ أَبُو عَبْدِ الرَّحْمَنِ. قَالَتْ مَا يَقُولُ قَالَ يَقُولُ إِنَّ رَسُولَ اللَّهِ صلى الله عليه وسلم اعْتَمَرَ أَرْبَعَ عُمَرَاتٍ إِحْدَاهُنَّ فِي رَجَبٍ. قَالَتْ يَرْحَمُ اللَّهُ أَبَا عَبْدِ الرَّحْمَنِ، مَا اعْتَمَرَ عُمْرَةً إِلاَّ وَهُوَ شَاهِدُهُ، وَمَا اعْتَمَرَ فِي رَجَبٍ قَطُّ.

Narrated Ibn Abu Mulaika: Ibn `Abbas recited: "(Respite will be granted) until when the Apostles gave up hope (of their people) and thought that they were denied (by their people). There came to them Our Help ...." (12.110) reading Kudhibu without doubling the sound 'dh', and that was what he understood of the Verse. Then he went on reciting: "..even the Apostle and those who believed along with him said: When (will come) Allah's Help? Yes, verily, Allah's Help is near." (2.214) Then I met `Urwa bin Az-Zubair and I mentioned that to him. He said, "Aisha said, 'Allah forbid! By Allah, Allah never promised His Apostle anything but he knew that it would certainly happen before he died. But trials were continuously presented before the Apostles till they were afraid that their followers would accuse them of telling lies. So I used to recite:-- "Till they (come to) think that they were treated as liars." Reading 'Kudh-dhibu with double 'dh.'. – Sahih Al-Bukhari 4524, 4525

حَدَّثَنَا إِبْرَاهِيمُ بْنُ مُوسَى، أَخْبَرَنَا هِشَامٌ، عَنِ ابْنِ جُرَيْجٍ، قَالَ سَمِعْتُ ابْنَ أَبِي مُلَيْكَةَ، يَقُولُ قَالَ ابْنُ عَبَّاسٍ ـ رضى الله عنهما ـ {حَتَّى إِذَا اسْتَيْأَسَ الرُّسُلُ وَظَنُّوا أَنَّهُمْ قَدْ كُذِبُوا} خَفِيفَةً، ذَهَبَ بِهَا هُنَاكَ، وَتَلاَ {حَتَّى يَقُولَ الرَّسُولُ وَالَّذِينَ آمَنُوا

مَعَهُ مَتَى نَصْرُ اللَّهِ أَلاَ إِنَّ نَصْرَ اللَّهِ قَرِيبٌ} فَلَقِيتُ عُرْوَةَ بْنَ الزُّبَيْرِ فَذَكَرْتُ لَهُ ذَلِكَ فَقَالَ قَالَتْ عَائِشَةُ مَعَاذَ اللَّهِ، وَاللَّهِ مَا وَعَدَ اللَّهُ رَسُولَهُ مِنْ شَىْءٍ قَطُّ إِلاَّ عَلِمَ أَنَّهُ كَائِنٌ قَبْلَ أَنْ يَمُوتَ، وَلَكِنْ لَمْ يَزَلِ الْبَلاَءُ بِالرُّسُلِ حَتَّى خَافُوا أَنْ يَكُونَ مَنْ مَعَهُمْ يُكَذِّبُونَهُمْ، فَكَانَتْ تَقْرَؤُهَا {وَظَنُّوا أَنَّهُمْ قَدْ كُذِّبُوا} مُثَقَّلَةً.

Narrated Az-Zuhri: I heard `Urwa bin Az-Zubair, Sa`id bin Al-Musaiyab, 'Alqama bin Waqqas and 'Ubaidullah bin `Abdullah bin `Uqba relating from `Aisha, the wife of the Prophet ﷺ the narration of the people (i.e. the liars) who spread the slander against her and they said what they said, and how Allah revealed her innocence. Each of them related to me a portion of that narration. (They said that `Aisha said), "Then Allah revealed the ten Verses starting with:--'Verily! Those who spread the slander..' (24.11-21) All these verses were in proof of my innocence. Abu Bakr As-Siddiq who used to provide for Mistah some financial aid because of his relation to him, said, "By Allah, I will never give anything (in charity) to Mistah, after what he has said about `Aisha" Then Allah revealed:-- 'And let not those among you who are good and are wealthy swear not to give (any sort of help) to their kins men....' (24.22) On that, Abu Bakr said, "Yes, by Allah, I like that Allah should forgive me." And then resumed giving Mistah the aid he used to give him and said, "By Allah! I will never withhold it from him.". – Sahih Al-Bukhari 6679

حَدَّثَنَا عَبْدُ الْعَزِيزِ، حَدَّثَنَا إِبْرَاهِيمُ، عَنْ صَالِحٍ، عَنِ ابْنِ شِهَابٍ، ح وَحَدَّثَنَا الْحَجَّاجُ، حَدَّثَنَا عَبْدُ اللَّهِ بْنُ عُمَرَ النُّمَيْرِيُّ، حَدَّثَنَا يُونُسُ بْنُ يَزِيدَ الأَيْلِيُّ، قَالَ سَمِعْتُ الزُّهْرِيَّ، قَالَ سَمِعْتُ عُرْوَةَ بْنَ الزُّبَيْرِ، وَسَعِيدَ بْنَ الْمُسَيَّبِ، وَعَلْقَمَةَ بْنَ وَقَّاصٍ، وَعُبَيْدَ اللَّهِ بْنَ عَبْدِ اللَّهِ بْنِ عُتْبَةَ، عَنْ حَدِيثِ، عَائِشَةَ زَوْجِ النَّبِيِّ صلى الله عليه وسلم حِينَ قَالَ لَهَا أَهْلُ الإِفْكِ مَا قَالُوا، فَبَرَّأَهَا اللَّهُ مِمَّا قَالُوا ـ كُلٌّ حَدَّثَنِي طَائِفَةً مِنَ الْحَدِيثِ ـ فَأَنْزَلَ اللَّهُ {إِنَّ الَّذِينَ جَاءُوا بِالإِفْكِ} الْعَشْرَ الآيَاتِ كُلَّهَا فِي بَرَاءَتِي. فَقَالَ أَبُو بَكْرٍ الصِّدِّيقُ ـ وَكَانَ يُنْفِقُ عَلَى مِسْطَحٍ لِقَرَابَتِهِ مِنْهُ ـ وَاللَّهِ لاَ أُنْفِقُ عَلَى مِسْطَحٍ شَيْئًا أَبَدًا، بَعْدَ الَّذِي قَالَ لِعَائِشَةَ. فَأَنْزَلَ اللَّهُ {وَلاَ يَأْتَلِ أُولُو الْفَضْلِ مِنْكُمْ وَالسَّعَةِ أَنْ يُؤْتُوا أُولِي الْقُرْبَى} الآيَةَ. قَالَ أَبُو بَكْرٍ بَلَى وَاللَّهِ إِنِّي لأُحِبُّ أَنْ يَغْفِرَ اللَّهُ لِي. فَرَجَعَ إِلَى مِسْطَحٍ النَّفَقَةَ الَّتِي كَانَ يُنْفِقُ عَلَيْهِ وَقَالَ وَاللَّهِ لاَ أَنْزِعُهَا عَنْهُ أَبَدًا

Narrated Ibn Shihab: Once `Umar bin `Abdul `Aziz delayed the prayer and `Urwa bin Az-Zubair went to him and said, "Once in 'Iraq, Al-Mughira bin Shu`ba delayed his prayers and Abi Mas`ud Al-Ansari went to him and said, 'O Mughira! What is this? Don't you know that once Gabriel came and offered the prayer (Fajr prayer) and Allah's Messenger ﷺ prayed too, then he prayed again (Zuhr prayer) and so did Allah's Apostle and again he prayed (`Asr prayers and Allah's Messenger ﷺ did the same; again he prayed (Maghrib-prayer) and so did Allah's Messenger ﷺ and again prayed (`Isha prayer) and so did Allah's Apostle and (Gabriel) said, 'I was ordered to do so (to demonstrate the prayers prescribed to you)?'" `Umar (bin `Abdul `Aziz) said to `Urwa, "Be sure of what you Say. Did Gabriel lead Allah's Messenger ﷺ at the stated times of the prayers?" `Urwa replied, "Bashir bin Abi Mas`ud narrated like this on the authority of his father." `Urwa added, "Aisha told me that Allah's Messenger ﷺ used to pray `Asr prayer when the sunshine was still inside her residence (during the early time of `Asr). – Sahih Al-Bukhari 521, 522

حَدَّثَنَا عَبْدُ اللَّهِ بْنُ مَسْلَمَةَ، قَالَ قَرَأْتُ عَلَى مَالِكٍ عَنِ ابْنِ شِهَابٍ، أَنَّ عُمَرَ بْنَ عَبْدِ الْعَزِيزِ، أَخَّرَ الصَّلاَةَ يَوْمًا، فَدَخَلَ عَلَيْهِ عُرْوَةُ بْنُ الزُّبَيْرِ، فَأَخْبَرَهُ أَنَّ الْمُغِيرَةَ بْنَ شُعْبَةَ أَخَّرَ الصَّلاَةَ يَوْمًا وَهُوَ بِالْعِرَاقِ، فَدَخَلَ عَلَيْهِ أَبُو مَسْعُودٍ الأَنْصَارِيُّ فَقَالَ مَا هَذَا يَا مُغِيرَةُ أَلَيْسَ قَدْ عَلِمْتَ أَنَّ جِبْرِيلَ نَزَلَ فَصَلَّى، فَصَلَّى رَسُولُ اللَّهِ صلى الله عليه وسلم ثُمَّ صَلَّى فَصَلَّى رَسُولُ اللَّهِ صلى الله عليه وسلم ثُمَّ صَلَّى فَصَلَّى رَسُولُ اللَّهِ صلى الله عليه وسلم ثُمَّ صَلَّى فَصَلَّى رَسُولُ اللَّهِ صلى الله عليه وسلم ثُمَّ صَلَّى فَصَلَّى رَسُولُ اللَّهِ صلى الله عليه وسلم ثُمَّ قَالَ " بِهَذَا أُمِرْتُ ". فَقَالَ عُمَرُ لِعُرْوَةَ اعْلَمْ مَا تُحَدِّثُ أَوَإِنَّ جِبْرِيلَ هُوَ أَقَامَ لِرَسُولِ اللَّهِ صلى الله عليه وسلم وَقْتَ الصَّلاَةِ. قَالَ عُرْوَةُ كَذَلِكَ كَانَ بَشِيرُ بْنُ أَبِي مَسْعُودٍ يُحَدِّثُ عَنْ أَبِيهِ. قَالَ عُرْوَةُ وَلَقَدْ حَدَّثَتْنِي عَائِشَةُ، أَنَّ رَسُولَ اللَّهِ صلى الله عليه وسلم كَانَ يُصَلِّي الْعَصْرَ، وَالشَّمْسُ فِي حُجْرَتِهَا قَبْلَ أَنْ تَظْهَرَ.

Narrated `Aisha: The Prophet ﷺ used to talk so clearly that if somebody wanted to count the number of his words, he could do so. Narrated `Urwa bin Az-Zubair: `Aisha said (to me),

"Don't you wonder at Abu so-and-so who came and sat by my dwelling and started relating the traditions of Allah's Messenger ﷺ intending to let me hear that, while I was performing an optional prayer. He left before I finished my optional prayer. Had I found him still there. I would have said to him, 'Allah's Messenger ﷺ never talked so quickly and vaguely as you do.' ". – Sahih Al-Bukhari 3567, 3568

حَدَّثَنِي الْحَسَنُ بْنُ صَبَّاحٍ الْبَزَّارُ، حَدَّثَنَا سُفْيَانُ، عَنِ الزُّهْرِيِّ، عَنْ عُرْوَةَ، عَنْ عَائِشَةَ ـ رضى الله عنها أَنَّ النَّبِيَّ صلى الله عليه وسلم كَانَ يُحَدِّثُ حَدِيثًا لَوْ عَدَّهُ الْعَادُّ لأَحْصَاهُ. وَقَالَ اللَّيْثُ حَدَّثَنِي يُونُسُ، عَنِ ابْنِ شِهَابٍ، أَنَّهُ قَالَ أَخْبَرَنِي عُرْوَةُ بْنُ الزُّبَيْرِ، عَنْ عَائِشَةَ، أَنَّهَا قَالَتْ أَلاَ يُعْجِبُكَ أَبُو فُلاَنٍ جَاءَ فَجَلَسَ إِلَى جَانِبِ حُجْرَتِي يُحَدِّثُ عَنْ رَسُولِ اللَّهِ صلى الله عليه وسلم، يُسْمِعُنِي ذَلِكَ وَكُنْتُ أُسَبِّحُ فَقَامَ قَبْلَ أَنْ أَقْضِيَ سُبْحَتِي، وَلَوْ أَدْرَكْتُهُ لَرَدَدْتُ عَلَيْهِ، إِنَّ رَسُولَ اللَّهِ صلى الله عليه وسلم لَمْ يَكُنْ يَسْرُدُ الْحَدِيثَ كَسَرْدِكُمْ

Narrated Az-Zuhri: I heard `Urwa bin Az-Zubair talking to `Umar bin `Abdul `Aziz during the latter's Governorship (at Medina), he said, "Al-Mughira bin Shu`ba delayed the `Asr prayer when he was the ruler of Al-Kufa. On that, Abu Mas`ud. `Uqba bin `Amr Al-Ansari, the grand-father of Zaid bin Hasan, who was one of the Badr warriors, came in and said, (to Al-Mughira), 'You know that Gabriel came down and offered the prayer and Allah's Messenger ﷺ prayed five prescribed prayers, and Gabriel said (to the Prophet ﷺ), "I have been ordered to do so (i.e. offer these five prayers at these fixed stated hours of the day). – Sahih Al-Bukhari 4007

حَدَّثَنَا أَبُو الْيَمَانِ، أَخْبَرَنَا شُعَيْبٌ، عَنِ الزُّهْرِيِّ، سَمِعْتُ عُرْوَةَ بْنَ الزُّبَيْرِ، يُحَدِّثُ عُمَرَ بْنَ عَبْدِ الْعَزِيزِ فِي إِمَارَتِهِ أَخَّرَ الْمُغِيرَةُ بْنُ شُعْبَةَ الْعَصْرَ وَهْوَ أَمِيرُ الْكُوفَةِ، فَدَخَلَ أَبُو مَسْعُودٍ عُقْبَةُ بْنُ عَمْرٍو الأَنْصَارِيُّ جَدُّ زَيْدِ بْنِ حَسَنٍ شَهِدَ بَدْرًا فَقَالَ لَقَدْ عَلِمْتَ نَزَلَ جِبْرِيلُ فَصَلَّى فَصَلَّى رَسُولُ اللَّهِ صلى الله عليه وسلم خَمْسَ صَلَوَاتٍ ثُمَّ قَالَ هَكَذَا أُمِرْتَ. كَذَلِكَ كَانَ بَشِيرُ بْنُ أَبِي مَسْعُودٍ يُحَدِّثُ عَنْ أَبِيهِ

Narrated `Urwa bin Az-Zubair: `Aisha said, "The Prophet ﷺ said during his fatal illness, "Allah cursed the Jews for they took the graves of their prophets as places for worship." `Aisha added, "Had it not been for that (statement of the Prophet) his grave would have been made conspicuous. But he was afraid that it might be taken as a place for worship.". – Sahih Al-Bukhari 4441

حَدَّثَنَا الصَّلْتُ بْنُ مُحَمَّدٍ، حَدَّثَنَا أَبُو عَوَانَةَ، عَنْ هِلاَلٍ الْوَزَّانِ، عَنْ عُرْوَةَ بْنِ الزُّبَيْرِ، عَنْ عَائِشَةَ ـ رضى الله عنها ـ قَالَتْ قَالَ النَّبِيُّ صلى الله عليه وسلم فِي مَرَضِهِ الَّذِي لَمْ يَقُمْ مِنْهُ " لَعَنَ اللَّهُ الْيَهُودَ، اتَّخَذُوا قُبُورَ أَنْبِيَائِهِمْ مَسَاجِدَ ". قَالَتْ عَائِشَةُ لَوْلاَ ذَلِكَ لأُبْرِزَ قَبْرُهُ. خَشِيَ أَنْ يُتَّخَذَ مَسْجِدًا.

Abu Talib ibn Abd al-Muttalib
أَبُو طَالِب بن عَبْد ٱلْمُطَّلِب

Narrated Ibn `Abbas: The first event of Qasama in the pre-Islamic period of ignorance was practiced by us (i.e. Banu Hashim). A man from Banu Hashim was employed by a Quraishi man from another branch-family. The (Hashimi) laborer set out with the Quraishi driving his camels. There passed by him another man from Banu Hashim. The leather rope of the latter's bag had broken so he said to the laborer, "Will you help me by giving me a rope in order to tie the handle of my bag lest the camels should run away from me?" The laborer gave him a rope and the latter tied his bag with it. When the caravan halted, all the camels' legs were tied with their fetters except one camel. The employer asked the laborer, "Why, from among all the camels has this camel not been fettered?" He replied, "There is no fetter for it." The Quraishi asked, "Where is its fetter?" and hit the laborer with a stick that caused his death (later on Just before his death) a man from Yemen passed by him. The laborer asked (him), "Will you go for the pilgrimage?" He replied, "I do not think I will attend it, but perhaps I will

attend it." The (Hashimi) laborer said, "Will you please convey a message for me once in your life?" The other man said, "yes." The laborer wrote: 'When you attend the pilgrimage, call the family of Quraish, and if they respond to you, call the family of Banu Hashim, and if they respond to you, ask about Abu Talib and tell him that so-and-so has killed me for a fetter." Then the laborer expired. When the employer reached (Mecca), Abu Talib visited him and asked, "What has happened to our companion?" He said, "He became ill and I looked after him nicely (but he died) and I buried him." Then Abu Talib said, "The deceased deserved this from you." After some time, the messenger whom the laborer has asked to convey the message, reached during the pilgrimage season. He called, "O the family of Quraish!" The people replied, "This is Quraish." Then he called, "O the family of Banu Hashim!" Again the people replied, "This is Banu Hashim." He asked, "Who is Abu Talib?" The people replied, "This is Abu Talib." He said, "'So-and-so has asked me to convey a message to you that so-and-so has killed him for a fetter (of a camel)." Then Abu Talib went to the (Quraishi) killer and said to him, "Choose one of three alternatives: (i) If you wish, give us one-hundred camels because you have murdered our companion, (ii) or if you wish, fifty of your men should take an oath that you have not murdered our companion, and if you do not accept this, (iii) we will kill you in Qisas." The killer went to his people and they said, "We will take an oath." Then a woman from Banu Hashim who was married to one of them (i.e.the Quraishis) and had given birth to a child from him, came to Abu Talib and said, "O Abu Talib! I wish that my son from among the fifty men, should be excused from this oath, and that he should not take the oath where the oathtaking is carried on." Abu Talib excused him. Then another man from them came (to Abu Talib) and said, "O Abu Talib! You want fifty persons to take an oath instead of giving a hundred camels, and that means each man has to give two camels (in case he does not take an oath). So there are two camels I would like you to accept from me and excuse me from taking an oath where the oaths are taken. Abu Talib accepted them from him. Then 48 men came and took the oath. Ibn `Abbas further said:)By Him in Whose Hand my life is, before the end of that year, none of those 48 persons remained alive.
– Sahih Al-Bukhari 3845

حَدَّثَنَا أَبُو مَعْمَرٍ، حَدَّثَنَا عَبْدُ الْوَارِثِ، حَدَّثَنَا قَطَنٌ أَبُو الْهَيْثَمِ، حَدَّثَنَا أَبُو يَزِيدَ الْمَدَنِيُّ، عَنْ عِكْرِمَةَ، عَنِ ابْنِ عَبَّاسٍ ـ رضى الله عنهما ـ قَالَ إِنَّ أَوَّلَ قَسَامَةٍ كَانَتْ فِي الْجَاهِلِيَّةِ لَفِينَا بَنِي هَاشِمٍ، كَانَ رَجُلٌ مِنْ بَنِي هَاشِمٍ اسْتَأْجَرَهُ رَجُلٌ مِنْ قُرَيْشٍ مِنْ فَخِذٍ أُخْرَى، فَانْطَلَقَ مَعَهُ فِي إِبِلِهِ، فَمَرَّ رَجُلٌ بِهِ مِنْ بَنِي هَاشِمٍ قَدِ انْقَطَعَتْ عُرْوَةُ جُوَالِقِهِ فَقَالَ أَغِثْنِي بِعِقَالٍ أَشُدُّ بِهِ عُرْوَةَ جُوَالِقِي، لاَ تَنْفِرُ الإِبِلُ. فَأَعْطَاهُ عِقَالاً، فَشَدَّ بِهِ عُرْوَةَ جُوَالِقِهِ، فَلَمَّا نَزَلُوا عُقِلَتِ الإِبِلُ إِلاَّ بَعِيرًا وَاحِدًا، فَقَالَ الَّذِي اسْتَأْجَرَهُ مَا شَأْنُ هَذَا الْبَعِيرِ لَمْ يُعْقَلْ مِنْ بَيْنِ الإِبِلِ قَالَ لَيْسَ لَهُ عِقَالٌ. قَالَ فَأَيْنَ عِقَالُهُ قَالَ فَحَذَفَهُ بِعَصًا كَانَ فِيهَا أَجَلُهُ، فَمَرَّ بِهِ رَجُلٌ مِنْ أَهْلِ الْيَمَنِ، فَقَالَ أَتَشْهَدُ الْمَوْسِمَ قَالَ مَا أَشْهَدُ، وَرُبَّمَا شَهِدْتُهُ. قَالَ هَلْ أَنْتَ مُبْلِغٌ عَنِّي رِسَالَةً مَرَّةً مِنَ الدَّهْرِ قَالَ نَعَمْ. قَالَ فَكُنْتَ إِذَا أَنْتَ شَهِدْتَ الْمَوْسِمَ فَنَادِ يَا آلَ قُرَيْشٍ. فَإِذَا أَجَابُوكَ، فَنَادِ يَا آلَ بَنِي هَاشِمٍ. فَإِنْ أَجَابُوكَ فَسَلْ عَنْ أَبِي طَالِبٍ، فَأَخْبِرْهُ أَنَّ فُلاَنًا قَتَلَنِي فِي عِقَالٍ، وَمَاتَ الْمُسْتَأْجَرُ، فَلَمَّا قَدِمَ الَّذِي اسْتَأْجَرَهُ أَتَاهُ أَبُو طَالِبٍ فَقَالَ مَا فَعَلَ صَاحِبُنَا قَالَ مَرِضَ، فَأَحْسَنْتُ الْقِيَامَ عَلَيْهِ، فَوَلِيتُ دَفْنَهُ. قَالَ قَدْ كَانَ أَهْلَ ذَاكَ مِنْكَ. فَمَكُثَ حِينًا، ثُمَّ إِنَّ الرَّجُلَ الَّذِي أَوْصَى إِلَيْهِ أَنْ يُبْلِغَ عَنْهُ وَافَى الْمَوْسِمَ فَقَالَ يَا آلَ قُرَيْشٍ. قَالُوا هَذِهِ قُرَيْشٌ. قَالَ يَا آلَ بَنِي هَاشِمٍ. قَالُوا هَذِهِ بَنُو هَاشِمٍ. قَالَ أَيْنَ أَبُو طَالِبٍ قَالُوا هَذَا أَبُو طَالِبٍ. قَالَ أَمَرَنِي فُلاَنٌ أَنْ أُبْلِغَكَ رِسَالَةً أَنَّ فُلاَنًا قَتَلَهُ فِي عِقَالٍ. فَأَتَاهُ أَبُو طَالِبٍ فَقَالَ لَهُ اخْتَرْ مِنَّا إِحْدَى ثَلاَثٍ، إِنْ شِئْتَ أَنْ تُؤَدِّيَ مِائَةً مِنَ الإِبِلِ، فَإِنَّكَ قَتَلْتَ صَاحِبَنَا، وَإِنْ شِئْتَ حَلَفَ خَمْسُونَ مِنْ قَوْمِكَ أَنَّكَ لَمْ تَقْتُلْهُ، فَإِنْ أَبَيْتَ قَتَلْنَاكَ بِهِ فَأَتَى قَوْمَهُ، فَقَالُوا نَحْلِفُ. فَأَتَتْهُ امْرَأَةٌ مِنْ بَنِي هَاشِمٍ كَانَتْ تَحْتَ رَجُلٍ مِنْهُمْ قَدْ وَلَدَتْ لَهُ. فَقَالَتْ يَا أَبَا طَالِبٍ أُحِبُّ أَنْ تُجِيزَ ابْنِي هَذَا بِرَجُلٍ مِنَ الْخَمْسِينَ وَلاَ تَصْبُرْ يَمِينَهُ حَيْثُ تُصْبَرُ الأَيْمَانُ. فَفَعَلَ فَأَتَاهُ رَجُلٌ مِنْهُمْ فَقَالَ يَا أَبَا طَالِبٍ، أَرَدْتَ خَمْسِينَ رَجُلاً أَنْ يَحْلِفُوا مَكَانَ مِائَةٍ مِنَ الإِبِلِ، يُصِيبُ كُلَّ رَجُلٍ بَعِيرَانِ، هَذَانِ بَعِيرَانِ فَاقْبَلْهُمَا عَنِّي وَلاَ تَصْبُرْ يَمِينِي حَيْثُ تُصْبَرُ الأَيْمَانُ. فَقَبِلَهُمَا، وَجَاءَ ثَمَانِيَةٌ وَأَرْبَعُونَ فَحَلَفُوا. قَالَ ابْنُ عَبَّاسٍ فَوَالَّذِي نَفْسِي بِيَدِهِ، مَا حَالَ الْحَوْلُ وَمِنَ الثَّمَانِيَةِ وَأَرْبَعِينَ عَيْنٌ تَطْرِفُ.

Narrated `Abdullah bin Dinar: My father said, "I heard Ibn `Umar reciting the poetic verses of Abu Talib: And a white (person) (i.e. the Prophet) who is requested to pray for rain and who takes care of the orphans and is the guardian of widows." Salim's father (Ibn `Umar) said, "The following poetic verse occurred to my mind while I was looking at the face of the Prophetﷺ while he was praying for rain. He did not get down till the rain water flowed profusely from every roof-gutter: And a white (person) who is requested to pray for rain and who takes care of the orphans and is the guardian of widows . . . And these were the words of Abu Talib.". – Sahih Al-Bukhari 1008, 1009

حَدَّثَنَا عَمْرُو بْنُ عَلِيٍّ، قَالَ حَدَّثَنَا أَبُو قُتَيْبَةَ، قَالَ حَدَّثَنَا عَبْدُ الرَّحْمَنِ بْنُ عَبْدِ اللَّهِ بْنِ دِينَارٍ، عَنْ أَبِيهِ، قَالَ سَمِعْتُ ابْنَ عُمَرَ، يَتَمَثَّلُ بِشِعْرِ أَبِي طَالِبٍ وَأَبْيَضَ يُسْتَسْقَى الْغَمَامُ بِوَجْهِهِ ثِمَالُ الْيَتَامَى عِصْمَةٌ لِلأَرَامِلِ وَقَالَ عُمَرُ بْنُ حَمْزَةَ حَدَّثَنَا سَالِمٌ، عَنْ أَبِيهِ، رُبَّمَا ذَكَرْتُ قَوْلَ الشَّاعِرِ وَأَنَا أَنْظُرُ، إِلَى وَجْهِ النَّبِيِّ صلى الله عليه وسلم يَسْتَسْقِي، فَمَا يَنْزِلُ حَتَّى يَجِيشَ كُلُّ مِيزَابٍ. وَأَبْيَضَ يُسْتَسْقَى الْغَمَامُ بِوَجْهِهِ ثِمَالُ الْيَتَامَى عِصْمَةٌ لِلأَرَامِلِ وَهْوَ قَوْلُ أَبِي طَالِبٍ.

Narrated Al-Musaiyab: When Abu Talib was in his death bed, the Prophetﷺ went to him while Abu Jahl was sitting beside him. The Prophetﷺ said, "O my uncle! Say: None has the right to be worshipped except Allah, an expression I will defend your case with, before Allah." Abu Jahl and `Abdullah bin Umaiya said, "O Abu Talib! Will you leave the religion of `Abdul Muttalib?" So they kept on saying this to him so that the last statement he said to them (before he died) was: "I am on the religion of `Abdul Muttalib." Then the Prophet said, " I will keep on asking for Allah's Forgiveness for you unless I am forbidden to do so." Then the following Verse was revealed:-- "It is not fitting for the Prophetﷺ and the believers to ask Allah's Forgiveness for the pagans, even if they were their near relatives, after it has become clear to them that they are the dwellers of the (Hell) Fire." (9.113) The other Verse was also revealed:-- "(O Prophet!) Verily, you guide not whom you like, but Allah guides whom He will ...." (28.56). – Sahih Al-Bukhari 3884

حَدَّثَنَا مَحْمُودٌ، حَدَّثَنَا عَبْدُ الرَّزَّاقِ، أَخْبَرَنَا مَعْمَرٌ، عَنِ الزُّهْرِيِّ، عَنِ ابْنِ الْمُسَيَّبِ، عَنْ أَبِيهِ، أَنَّ أَبَا طَالِبٍ، لَمَّا حَضَرَتْهُ الْوَفَاةُ دَخَلَ عَلَيْهِ النَّبِيُّ صلى الله عليه وسلم وَعِنْدَهُ أَبُو جَهْلٍ فَقَالَ " أَىْ عَمِّ، قُلْ لاَ إِلَهَ إِلاَّ اللَّهُ. كَلِمَةً أُحَاجُّ لَكَ بِهَا عِنْدَ اللَّهِ ". فَقَالَ أَبُو جَهْلٍ وَعَبْدُ اللَّهِ بْنُ أَبِي أُمَيَّةَ يَا أَبَا طَالِبٍ، تَرْغَبُ عَنْ مِلَّةِ عَبْدِ الْمُطَّلِبِ فَلَمْ يَزَالاَ يُكَلِّمَانِهِ حَتَّى قَالَ آخِرَ شَىْءٍ كَلَّمَهُمْ بِهِ عَلَى مِلَّةِ عَبْدِ الْمُطَّلِبِ. فَقَالَ النَّبِيُّ صلى الله عليه وسلم " لأَسْتَغْفِرَنَّ لَكَ مَا لَمْ أُنْهَ عَنْهُ ". فَنَزَلَتْ {مَا كَانَ لِلنَّبِيِّ وَالَّذِينَ آمَنُوا أَنْ يَسْتَغْفِرُوا لِلْمُشْرِكِينَ وَلَوْ كَانُوا أُولِي قُرْبَى مِنْ بَعْدِ مَا تَبَيَّنَ لَهُمْ أَنَّهُمْ أَصْحَابُ الْجَحِيمِ} وَنَزَلَتْ {إِنَّكَ لاَ تَهْدِي مَنْ أَحْبَبْتَ}

Narrated `Abdullah bin Al-Harith bin Naufal: `Abbas bin `Abdul Muttalib said, "O Allah's Messenger ﷺ !Did you benefit Abu Talib with anything as he used to protect and take care of you, and used to become angry for you?" The Prophetﷺ said, "Yes, he is in a shallow place of Fire. Were it not for me, he would have been in the bottom-most depth of the Fire.". – Sahih Al-Bukhari 6208

حَدَّثَنَا مُوسَى بْنُ إِسْمَاعِيلَ، حَدَّثَنَا أَبُو عَوَانَةَ، حَدَّثَنَا عَبْدُ الْمَلِكِ، عَنْ عَبْدِ اللَّهِ بْنِ الْحَارِثِ بْنِ نَوْفَلٍ، عَنْ عَبَّاسِ بْنِ عَبْدِ الْمُطَّلِبِ، قَالَ يَا رَسُولَ اللَّهِ هَلْ نَفَعْتَ أَبَا طَالِبٍ بِشَىْءٍ، فَإِنَّهُ كَانَ يَحُوطُكَ وَيَغْضَبُ لَكَ قَالَ " نَعَمْ هُوَ فِي ضَحْضَاحٍ مِنْ نَارٍ، لَوْلاَ أَنَا لَكَانَ فِي الدَّرَكِ الأَسْفَلِ مِنَ النَّارِ

Narrated 'Usama bin Zaid: I asked, "O Allah's Messengerﷺ! Where will you stay in Mecca? Will you stay in your house in Mecca?" He replied, "Has `Aqil left any property or house?" 'Aqil along with Talib had inherited the property of Abu Talib. Jafar and `Ali did not inherit anything as they were Muslims and the other two were non-believers. `Umar bin Al-Khattab used to say, "A believer cannot inherit (anything from an) infidel." Ibn Shihab, (a sub-narrator) said, "They (`Umar and others) derived the above verdict from Allah's Statement: "Verily! Those who believed and Emigrated and strove with their life And property in Allah's Cause, And those who helped (the emigrants) And gave them their places to live in, These are (all) allies to one another." (8.72). – Sahih Al-Bukhari 1588

حَدَّثَنَا أَصْبَغُ، قَالَ أَخْبَرَنِي ابْنُ وَهْبٍ، عَنْ يُونُسَ، عَنِ ابْنِ شِهَابٍ، عَنْ عَلِيِّ بْنِ حُسَيْنٍ، عَنْ عَمْرِو بْنِ عُثْمَانَ، عَنْ أُسَامَةَ بْنِ زَيْدٍ ـ رضى الله عنهما ـ أَنَّهُ قَالَ يَا رَسُولَ اللَّهِ، أَيْنَ تَنْزِلُ فِي دَارِكَ بِمَكَّةَ. فَقَالَ " وَهَلْ تَرَكَ عَقِيلٌ مِنْ رِبَاعٍ أَوْ دُورٍ ". وَكَانَ عَقِيلٌ وَرِثَ أَبَا طَالِبٍ هُوَ وَطَالِبٌ وَلَمْ يَرِثْهُ جَعْفَرٌ وَلاَ عَلِيٌّ ـ رضى الله عنهما ـ شَيْئًا لأَنَّهُمَا كَانَا مُسْلِمَيْنِ، وَكَانَ عَقِيلٌ وَطَالِبٌ كَافِرَيْنِ، فَكَانَ عُمَرُ بْنُ الْخَطَّابِ ـ رضى الله عنه ـ يَقُولُ لاَ يَرِثُ الْمُؤْمِنُ الْكَافِرَ. قَالَ ابْنُ شِهَابٍ وَكَانُوا يَتَأَوَّلُونَ قَوْلَ اللَّهِ تَعَالَى {إِنَّ الَّذِينَ آمَنُوا وَهَاجَرُوا وَجَاهَدُوا بِأَمْوَالِهِمْ وَأَنْفُسِهِمْ فِي سَبِيلِ اللَّهِ وَالَّذِينَ آوَوْا وَنَصَرُوا أُولَئِكَ بَعْضُهُمْ أَوْلِيَاءُ بَعْضٍ} الآيَةَ.

It was narrated that Ibn ‘Abbas said: “The first instance of Qasamah during the Jahiliyyah involved a man from Banu Hashim who was employed by a man from Quraish, from another branch of the tribe. He went out with him, driving his camels and another man from Banu Hashim passed by them. The leather rope of that man’s bag broke, so he said (to the hired worker): ‘Help me by giving me a rope with which to tie the handle of my bag, lest the camels run away from me. ‘So he gave him a rope and he tied his gab with it. When they halted, all the camels’ legs were hobbled except one camel. The one who had hired him said: ‘Why is his camel, out of all of them, not hobbled? He said: ‘There is no rope for it. He said: ‘Where is its rope? He said: A man from Banu Hashim passed by and the leather rope of his bag had broken, and he asked me to help him; he said: “Help me by giving me a rope with which to tie the handle of my bag lest the camels run away from me, so I gave him a rope . “ He struck him with a stick, which led to his death.Then a man from Yemen passed by him (the man from Banu Hashim, (the man from Banu Hashim, just before he died) and he (the Hashimi man) said: ‘Are you going to attend the Pilgrimage? He said: ‘I do not think I will attend it, but perhaps I will attend it.’ He said: ‘Will you convey a message from me once in your lifetime? He said: ‘Yes. ‘He said: ‘If you attend the pilgrimage, then call out, O family of Quraish! If they respond, then call out, O family of Hashim! If they respond, then ask for Abu Talib, and tell him that so and so killed me for a rope.’ Then the hired worker died. When the one who had hired him cam, Abu Talib went to him and said: ‘What happened to our companion? He said: ‘He fell sick and I took good care of him, but he died, so I stopped and buried him.’ He said: ‘He deserved that from you. ‘Some time passed, then the Yemeni man who had been asked to convey the message arrived at the time of the pilgrimage. He said: ‘O family of Quraish! And they said: ‘Here is Quraish.’ He said: ‘O family of Banu Hashim! They said: ‘Here is Banu Hashim.’ He said” ‘Where is Abu Talib? He said: ‘Here is Abu Talib.’ He said: ‘so and so asked me to convey a message to you, that so and so killed him for a camel’s rope.’ Abu Talib went to him and said” ‘Choose one of three alternatives that we are offering you. If you wish, you may give us one hundred camels, because you killed our companion by mistake: or if you wish, fifty of your men may swear an oath that you did not kill him; or if you wish, we will kill you in retaliation. ‘He went to his people and told them about that, and they said: ‘We will swear the oath.’ Then a woman from Banu Hashim, who was married to one of their men and had born him a child, came to Abu Talib and said:’ O Abu Talib, I wish that my son, who is one of these fifty men, should be excused from having to take the oath., So the excused him. Then one of the men came to him and said: ‘O Abu Talib, you want fifty men to take the oath in lieu of one hundred camels, which means that each man may give two camels instead, so here are two camels; take them from me, and do not make me take the oath.’ So he accepted them, and did not make him take the oath. Then forty-eight men came and took the oath.” Ibn ‘Abbas said: “By the One in Whose hand is my soul, by the time a year has passed, none of those forty-eight men remained alive.” - Sunan an-Nasa’I 4706

أَخْبَرَنَا مُحَمَّدُ بْنُ يَحْيَى، قَالَ حَدَّثَنَا أَبُو مَعْمَرٍ، قَالَ حَدَّثَنَا عَبْدُ الْوَارِثِ، قَالَ حَدَّثَنَا قَطَنٌ أَبُو الْهَيْثَمِ، قَالَ حَدَّثَنَا أَبُو يَزِيدَ الْمَدَنِيُّ، عَنْ عِكْرِمَةَ، عَنِ ابْنِ عَبَّاسٍ، قَالَ أَوَّلُ قَسَامَةٍ كَانَتْ فِي الْجَاهِلِيَّةِ كَانَ رَجُلٌ مِنْ بَنِي هَاشِمٍ اسْتَأْجَرَ رَجُلاً مِنْ قُرَيْشٍ مِنْ فَخِذِ أَحَدِهِمْ – قَالَ – فَانْطَلَقَ مَعَهُ فِي إِبِلِهِ فَمَرَّ بِهِ رَجُلٌ مِنْ بَنِي هَاشِمٍ قَدِ انْقَطَعَتْ عُرْوَةُ جُوَالِقِهِ فَقَالَ أَغِثْنِي

بِعِقَالٍ أَشُدُّ بِهِ عُرْوَةَ جُوَالِقِي لاَ تَنْفِرُ الإِبِلُ فَأَعْطَاهُ عِقَالاً يَشُدُّ بِهِ عُرْوَةَ جُوَالِقِهِ فَلَمَّا نَزَلُوا وَعُقِلَتِ الإِبِلُ إِلاَّ بَعِيرًا وَاحِدًا فَقَالَ الَّذِي اسْتَأْجَرَهُ مَا شَأْنُ هَذَا الْبَعِيرِ لَمْ يُعْقَلْ مِنْ بَيْنِ الإِبِلِ قَالَ لَيْسَ لَهُ عِقَالٌ . قَالَ فَأَيْنَ عِقَالُهُ قَالَ مَرَّ بِي رَجُلٌ مِنْ بَنِي هَاشِمٍ قَدِ انْقَطَعَتْ عُرْوَةُ جُوَالِقِهِ فَاسْتَغَاثَنِي فَقَالَ أَغِثْنِي بِعِقَالٍ أَشُدُّ بِهِ عُرْوَةَ جُوَالِقِي لاَ تَنْفِرُ الإِبِلُ . فَأَعْطَيْتُهُ عِقَالاً فَحَذَفَهُ بِعَصًا كَانَ فِيهَا أَجَلُهُ فَمَرَّ بِهِ رَجُلٌ مِنْ أَهْلِ الْيَمَنِ فَقَالَ أَتَشْهَدُ الْمَوْسِمَ قَالَ مَا أَشْهَدُ وَرُبَّمَا شَهِدْتُ . قَالَ هَلْ أَنْتَ مُبَلِّغٌ عَنِّي رِسَالَةً مَرَّةً مِنَ الدَّهْرِ قَالَ نَعَمْ . قَالَ إِذَا شَهِدْتَ الْمَوْسِمَ فَنَادِ يَا آلَ قُرَيْشٍ فَإِذَا أَجَابُوكَ فَنَادِ يَا آلَ هَاشِمٍ فَإِذَا أَجَابُوكَ فَسَلْ عَنْ أَبِي طَالِبٍ فَأَخْبِرْهُ أَنَّ فُلاَنًا قَتَلَنِي فِي عِقَالٍ وَمَاتَ الْمُسْتَأْجَرُ فَلَمَّا قَدِمَ الَّذِي اسْتَأْجَرَهُ أَتَاهُ أَبُو طَالِبٍ فَقَالَ مَا فَعَلَ صَاحِبُنَا قَالَ مَرِضَ فَأَحْسَنْتُ الْقِيَامَ عَلَيْهِ ثُمَّ مَاتَ فَنَزَلْتُ فَدَفَنْتُهُ . فَقَالَ كَانَ ذَا أَهْلَ ذَاكَ مِنْكَ . فَمَكُثَ حِينًا ثُمَّ إِنَّ الرَّجُلَ الْيَمَانِيَّ الَّذِي كَانَ أَوْصَى إِلَيْهِ أَنْ يُبَلِّغَ عَنْهُ وَافَى الْمَوْسِمَ قَالَ يَا آلَ قُرَيْشٍ . قَالُوا هَذِهِ قُرَيْشٌ . قَالَ يَا آلَ بَنِي هَاشِمٍ . قَالُوا هَذِهِ بَنُو هَاشِمٍ . قَالَ أَيْنَ أَبُو طَالِبٍ قَالَ هَذَا أَبُو طَالِبٍ . قَالَ أَمَرَنِي فُلاَنٌ أَنْ أُبَلِّغَكَ رِسَالَةً أَنَّ فُلاَنًا قَتَلَهُ فِي عِقَالٍ . فَأَتَاهُ أَبُو طَالِبٍ فَقَالَ اخْتَرْ مِنَّا إِحْدَى ثَلاَثٍ إِنْ شِئْتَ أَنْ تُؤَدِّيَ مِائَةً مِنَ الإِبِلِ فَإِنَّكَ قَتَلْتَ صَاحِبَنَا خَطَأً وَإِنْ شِئْتَ يَحْلِفْ خَمْسُونَ مِنْ قَوْمِكَ أَنَّكَ لَمْ تَقْتُلْهُ فَإِنْ أَبَيْتَ قَتَلْنَاكَ بِهِ . فَأَتَى قَوْمَهُ فَذَكَرَ ذَلِكَ لَهُمْ فَقَالُوا نَحْلِفُ . فَأَتَتْهُ امْرَأَةٌ مِنْ بَنِي هَاشِمٍ كَانَتْ تَحْتَ رَجُلٍ مِنْهُمْ قَدْ وَلَدَتْ لَهُ فَقَالَتْ يَا أَبَا طَالِبٍ أُحِبُّ أَنْ تُجِيزَ ابْنِي هَذَا بِرَجُلٍ مِنَ الْخَمْسِينَ وَلاَ تُصْبِرْ يَمِينَهُ . فَفَعَلَ فَأَتَاهُ رَجُلٌ مِنْهُمْ فَقَالَ يَا أَبَا طَالِبٍ أَرَدْتَ خَمْسِينَ رَجُلاً أَنْ يَحْلِفُوا مَكَانَ مِائَةٍ مِنَ الإِبِلِ يُصِيبُ كُلَّ رَجُلٍ بَعِيرَانِ فَهَذَانِ بَعِيرَانِ فَاقْبَلْهُمَا عَنِّي وَلاَ تُصْبِرْ يَمِينِي حَيْثُ تُصْبَرُ الأَيْمَانُ . فَقَبِلَهُمَا وَجَاءَ ثَمَانِيَةٌ وَأَرْبَعُونَ رَجُلاً حَلَفُوا . قَالَ ابْنُ عَبَّاسٍ فَوَالَّذِي نَفْسِي بِيَدِهِ مَا حَالَ الْحَوْلُ وَمِنَ الثَّمَانِيَةِ وَالأَرْبَعِينَ عَيْنٌ تَطْرِفُ

Narrated Abu Sa`id Al-Khudri: I heard Allah's Messenger's ﷺ when his uncle, Abu Talib had been mentioned in his presence, saying, "May be my intercession will help him (Abu Talib) on the Day of Resurrection so that he may be put in a shallow place in the Fire, with fire reaching his ankles and causing his brain to boil.". – Sahih al-Bukhari 6564

حَدَّثَنَا إِبْرَاهِيمُ بْنُ حَمْزَةَ، حَدَّثَنَا ابْنُ أَبِي حَازِمٍ، وَالدَّرَاوَرْدِيُّ، عَنْ يَزِيدَ، عَنْ عَبْدِ اللَّهِ بْنِ خَبَّابٍ، عَنْ أَبِي سَعِيدٍ الْخُدْرِيِّ - رضى الله عنه - أَنَّهُ سَمِعَ رَسُولَ اللَّهِ صلى الله عليه وسلم وَذُكِرَ عِنْدَهُ عَمُّهُ أَبُو طَالِبٍ فَقَالَ " لَعَلَّهُ تَنْفَعُهُ شَفَاعَتِي يَوْمَ الْقِيَامَةِ فَيُجْعَلُ فِي ضَحْضَاحٍ مِنَ النَّارِ، يَبْلُغُ كَعْبَيْهِ، يَغْلِي مِنْهُ أُمُّ دِمَاغِهِ "

Narrated `Amr bin `Uthman: Usama bin Zaid said during the Conquest (of Mecca), "O Allah's Messenger ﷺ ! Where will we encamp tomorrow?" The Prophet ﷺ said, "But has `Aqil left for us any house to lodge in?" He then added, "No believer will inherit an infidel's property, and no infidel will inherit the property of a believer." Az- Zuhri was asked, "Who inherited Abu Talib?" Az-Zuhri replied, "Ail and Talib inherited him - ".Sahih al-Bukhari 4282, 4283

حَدَّثَنَا سُلَيْمَانُ بْنُ عَبْدِ الرَّحْمَنِ، حَدَّثَنَا سَعْدَانُ بْنُ يَحْيَى، حَدَّثَنَا مُحَمَّدُ بْنُ أَبِي حَفْصَةَ، عَنِ الزُّهْرِيِّ، عَنْ عَلِيِّ بْنِ حُسَيْنٍ، عَنْ عَمْرِو بْنِ عُثْمَانَ، عَنْ أُسَامَةَ بْنِ زَيْدٍ، أَنَّهُ قَالَ زَمَنَ الْفَتْحِ يَا رَسُولَ اللَّهِ، أَيْنَ تَنْزِلُ غَدًا قَالَ النَّبِيُّ صلى الله عليه وسلم " وَهَلْ تَرَكَ لَنَا عَقِيلٌ مِنْ مَنْزِلٍ ". ثُمَّ قَالَ " لاَ يَرِثُ الْمُؤْمِنُ الْكَافِرَ، وَلاَ يَرِثُ الْكَافِرُ الْمُؤْمِنَ ". قِيلَ لِلزُّهْرِيِّ وَمَنْ وَرِثَ أَبَا طَالِبٍ قَالَ وَرِثَهُ عَقِيلٌ وَطَالِبٌ. قَالَ مَعْمَرٌ عَنِ الزُّهْرِيِّ أَيْنَ تَنْزِلُ غَدًا. فِي حَجَّتِهِ، وَلَمْ يَقُلْ يُونُسُ حَجَّتِهِ وَلاَ زَمَنَ الْفَتْحِ.

Ali Ibn Abu Talib
عَلِيّ بْن أَبِي طَالِب

Narrated Sahl bin Sa`d: That he heard the Prophet ﷺ on the day (of the battle) of Khaibar saying, "I will give the flag to a person at whose hands Allah will grant victory." So, the companions of the Prophet ﷺ got up, wishing eagerly to see to whom the flag will be given, and everyone of them wished to be given the flag. But the Prophet asked for `Ali. Someone informed him that he was suffering from eye-trouble. So, he ordered them to bring `Ali in front of him. Then the Prophet ﷺ spat in his eyes and his eyes were cured immediately as if he had never any eye-trouble. `Ali said, "We will fight with them (i.e. infidels) till they become like us (i.e. Muslims)." The Prophet ﷺ said, "Be patient, till you face them and invite them to

Islam and inform them of what Allah has enjoined upon them. By Allah! If a single person embraces Islam at your hands (i.e. through you), that will be better for you than the red camels.". – Sahih Al-Bukhari 2942

حَدَّثَنَا عَبْدُ اللَّهِ بْنُ مَسْلَمَةَ الْقَعْنَبِيُّ، حَدَّثَنَا عَبْدُ الْعَزِيزِ بْنُ أَبِي حَازِمٍ، عَنْ أَبِيهِ، عَنْ سَهْلِ بْنِ سَعْدٍ ـ رضى الله عنه ـ سَمِعَ النَّبِيَّ صلى الله عليه وسلم يَقُولُ يَوْمَ خَيْبَرَ " لأُعْطِيَنَّ الرَّايَةَ رَجُلاً يَفْتَحُ اللَّهُ عَلَى يَدَيْهِ ". فَقَامُوا يَرْجُونَ لِذَلِكَ أَيُّهُمْ يُعْطَى، فَغَدَوْا وَكُلُّهُمْ يَرْجُو أَنْ يُعْطَى فَقَالَ " أَيْنَ عَلِيٌّ ". فَقِيلَ يَشْتَكِي عَيْنَيْهِ، فَأَمَرَ فَدُعِيَ لَهُ، فَبَصَقَ فِي عَيْنَيْهِ، فَبَرَأَ مَكَانَهُ حَتَّى كَأَنَّهُ لَمْ يَكُنْ بِهِ شَىْءٌ فَقَالَ نُقَاتِلُهُمْ حَتَّى يَكُونُوا مِثْلَنَا. فَقَالَ " عَلَى رِسْلِكَ حَتَّى تَنْزِلَ بِسَاحَتِهِمْ، ثُمَّ ادْعُهُمْ إِلَى الإِسْلاَمِ، وَأَخْبِرْهُمْ بِمَا يَجِبُ عَلَيْهِمْ، فَوَاللَّهِ لأَنْ يُهْدَى بِكَ رَجُلٌ وَاحِدٌ خَيْرٌ لَكَ مِنْ حُمْرِ النَّعَمِ "

Narrated `Ali: I got a she-camel in my share of the war booty on the day (of the battle) of Badr, and the Prophet ﷺ had given me a she-camel from the Khumus. When I intended to marry Fatima, the daughter of Allah's Apostle, I had an appointment with a goldsmith from the tribe of Bani Qainuqa' to go with me to bring Idhkhir (i.e. grass of pleasant smell) and sell it to the goldsmiths and spend its price on my wedding party. I was collecting for my she-camels equipment of saddles, sacks and ropes while my two shecamels were kneeling down beside the room of an Ansari man. I returned after collecting whatever I collected, to see the humps of my two she-camels cut off and their flanks cut open and some portion of their livers was taken out. When I saw that state of my two she-camels, I could not help weeping. I asked, "Who has done this?" The people replied, "Hamza bin `Abdul Muttalib who is staying with some Ansari drunks in this house." I went away till I reached the Prophet ﷺ and Zaid bin Haritha was with him. The Prophet ﷺ noticed on my face the effect of what I had suffered, so the Prophet ﷺ asked. "What is wrong with you." I replied, "O Allah's Messenger ﷺ! I have never seen such a day as today. Hamza attacked my two she-camels, cut off their humps, and ripped open their flanks, and he is sitting there in a house in the company of some drunks." The Prophet ﷺ then asked for his covering sheet, put it on, and set out walking followed by me and Zaid bin Haritha till he came to the house where Hamza was. He asked permission to enter, and they allowed him, and they were drunk. Allah's Messenger ﷺ started rebuking Hamza for what he had done, but Hamza was drunk and his eyes were red. Hamza looked at Allah's Messenger ﷺ and then he raised his eyes, looking at his knees, then he raised up his eyes looking at his umbilicus, and again he raised up his eyes look in at his face. Hamza then said, "Aren't you but the slaves of my father?" Allah's Messenger ﷺ realized that he was drunk, so Allah's Messenger ﷺ retreated, and we went out with him. – Sahih Al-Bukhari 3091

حَدَّثَنَا عَبْدَانُ، أَخْبَرَنَا عَبْدُ اللَّهِ، أَخْبَرَنَا يُونُسُ، عَنِ الزُّهْرِيِّ، قَالَ أَخْبَرَنِي عَلِيُّ بْنُ الْحُسَيْنِ، أَنَّ حُسَيْنَ بْنَ عَلِيٍّ، عَلَيْهِمَا السَّلاَمُ أَخْبَرَهُ أَنَّ عَلِيًّا قَالَ كَانَتْ لِي شَارِفٌ مِنْ نَصِيبِي مِنَ الْمَغْنَمِ يَوْمَ بَدْرٍ، وَكَانَ النَّبِيُّ صلى الله عليه وسلم أَعْطَانِي شَارِفًا مِنَ الْخُمُسِ، فَلَمَّا أَرَدْتُ أَنْ أَبْتَنِيَ بِفَاطِمَةَ بِنْتِ رَسُولِ اللَّهِ صلى الله عليه وسلم وَاعَدْتُ رَجُلاً صَوَّاغًا مِنْ بَنِي قَيْنُقَاعَ، أَنْ يَرْتَحِلَ مَعِيَ فَنَأْتِيَ بِإِذْخِرٍ أَرَدْتُ أَنْ أَبِيعَهُ الصَّوَّاغِينَ، وَأَسْتَعِينَ بِهِ فِي وَلِيمَةِ عُرْسِي، فَبَيْنَا أَنَا أَجْمَعُ لِشَارِفَىَّ مَتَاعًا مِنَ الأَقْتَابِ وَالْغَرَائِرِ وَالْحِبَالِ، وَشَارِفَاىَ مُنَاخَانِ إِلَى جَنْبِ حُجْرَةِ رَجُلٍ مِنَ الأَنْصَارِ، رَجَعْتُ حِينَ جَمَعْتُ مَا جَمَعْتُ، فَإِذَا شَارِفَاىَ قَدِ اجْتُبَّ أَسْنِمَتُهُمَا وَبُقِرَتْ خَوَاصِرُهُمَا، وَأُخِذَ مِنْ أَكْبَادِهِمَا، فَلَمْ أَمْلِكْ عَيْنَىَّ حِينَ رَأَيْتُ ذَلِكَ الْمَنْظَرَ مِنْهُمَا، فَقُلْتُ مَنْ فَعَلَ هَذَا فَقَالُوا فَعَلَ حَمْزَةُ بْنُ عَبْدِ الْمُطَّلِبِ، وَهْوَ فِي هَذَا الْبَيْتِ فِي شَرْبٍ مِنَ الأَنْصَارِ. فَانْطَلَقْتُ حَتَّى أَدْخُلَ عَلَى النَّبِيِّ صلى الله عليه وسلم وَعِنْدَهُ زَيْدُ بْنُ حَارِثَةَ، فَعَرَفَ النَّبِيُّ صلى الله عليه وسلم فِي وَجْهِي الَّذِي لَقِيتُ، فَقَالَ النَّبِيُّ صلى الله عليه وسلم " مَا لَكَ " فَقُلْتُ يَا رَسُولَ اللَّهِ، مَا رَأَيْتُ كَالْيَوْمِ قَطُّ، عَدَا حَمْزَةُ عَلَى نَاقَتَىَّ، فَأَجَبَّ أَسْنِمَتَهُمَا وَبَقَرَ خَوَاصِرَهُمَا، وَهَا هُوَ ذَا فِي بَيْتٍ مَعَهُ شَرْبٌ. فَدَعَا النَّبِيُّ صلى الله عليه وسلم بِرِدَائِهِ فَارْتَدَى ثُمَّ انْطَلَقَ يَمْشِي، وَاتَّبَعْتُهُ أَنَا وَزَيْدُ بْنُ حَارِثَةَ حَتَّى جَاءَ الْبَيْتَ الَّذِي فِيهِ حَمْزَةُ، فَاسْتَأْذَنَ فَأَذِنُوا لَهُمْ فَإِذَا هُمْ شَرْبٌ، فَطَفِقَ رَسُولُ اللَّهِ صلى الله عليه وسلم يَلُومُ حَمْزَةَ فِيمَا فَعَلَ، فَإِذَا حَمْزَةُ قَدْ ثَمِلَ مُحْمَرَّةً عَيْنَاهُ، فَنَظَرَ حَمْزَةُ إِلَى رَسُولِ اللَّهِ صلى الله عليه وسلم، ثُمَّ صَعَّدَ النَّظَرَ فَنَظَرَ إِلَى رُكْبَتِهِ، ثُمَّ صَعَّدَ النَّظَرَ فَنَظَرَ إِلَى سُرَّتِهِ، ثُمَّ صَعَّدَ النَّظَرَ فَنَظَرَ إِلَى وَجْهِهِ ثُمَّ قَالَ حَمْزَةُ هَلْ أَنْتُمْ إِلاَّ عَبِيدٌ لأَبِي فَعَرَفَ رَسُولُ اللَّهِ صلى الله عليه وسلم أَنَّهُ قَدْ ثَمِلَ، فَنَكَصَ رَسُولُ اللَّهِ صلى الله عليه وسلم عَلَى عَقِبَيْهِ الْقَهْقَرَى وَخَرَجْنَا مَعَهُ.

Narrated Sa`d bin 'Ubaida: A man came to Ibn `Umar and asked about `Uthman and Ibn `Umar mentioned his good deeds and said to the questioner. "Perhaps these facts annoy you?" The other said, "Yes." Ibn `Umar said, "May Allah stick your nose in the dust (i.e. degrade you)!' Then the man asked him about `Ali. Ibn `Umar mentioned his good deeds and said, "It is all true, and that is his house in the midst of the houses of the Prophet. Perhaps these facts have hurt you?" The questioner said, "Yes." Ibn `Umar said, "May Allah stick your nose in the dust (i.e. degrade you or make you do things which you hate) ! Go away and do whatever you can against me.". – Sahih Al-Bukhari 3704

حَدَّثَنَا مُحَمَّدُ بْنُ رَافِعٍ، حَدَّثَنَا حُسَيْنٌ، عَنْ زَائِدَةَ، عَنْ أَبِي حَصِينٍ، عَنْ سَعْدِ بْنِ عُبَيْدَةَ، قَالَ جَاءَ رَجُلٌ إِلَى ابْنِ عُمَرَ، فَسَأَلَهُ عَنْ عُثْمَانَ،، فَذَكَرَ عَنْ مَحَاسِنِ، عَمَلِهِ، قَالَ لَعَلَّ ذَاكَ يَسُوؤُكَ. قَالَ نَعَمْ. قَالَ فَأَرْغَمَ اللَّهُ بِأَنْفِكَ. ثُمَّ سَأَلَهُ عَنْ عَلِيٍّ، فَذَكَرَ مَحَاسِنَ عَمَلِهِ قَالَ هُوَ ذَاكَ، بَيْتُهُ أَوْسَطُ بُيُوتِ النَّبِيِّ صلى الله عليه وسلم. ثُمَّ قَالَ لَعَلَّ ذَاكَ يَسُوؤُكَ. قَالَ أَجَلْ. قَالَ فَأَرْغَمَ اللَّهُ بِأَنْفِكَ، انْطَلِقْ فَاجْهَدْ عَلَىَّ جَهْدَكَ

And narrated Sad That the Prophetﷺ said to 'Ali, "Will you not be pleased from this that you are to me like Aaron was to Moses?". – Sahih Al-Bukhari 3706

حَدَّثَنِي مُحَمَّدُ بْنُ بَشَّارٍ، حَدَّثَنَا غُنْدَرٌ، حَدَّثَنَا شُعْبَةُ، عَنْ سَعْدٍ، قَالَ سَمِعْتُ إِبْرَاهِيمَ بْنَ سَعْدٍ، عَنْ أَبِيهِ، قَالَ النَّبِيُّ صلى الله عليه وسلم لِعَلِيٍّ " أَمَا تَرْضَى أَنْ تَكُونَ مِنِّي بِمَنْزِلَةِ هَارُونَ مِنْ مُوسَى "

Narrated Ibn Maqal: `Ali led the funeral prayer of Sahl bin Hunaif and said, "He was one of the warriors of Badr.". – Sahih Al-Bukhari 4004

حَدَّثَنِي مُحَمَّدُ بْنُ عَبَّادٍ، أَخْبَرَنَا ابْنُ عُيَيْنَةَ، قَالَ أَنْفَذَهُ لَنَا ابْنُ الأَصْبَهَانِيِّ سَمِعَهُ مِنِ ابْنِ مَعْقِلٍ، أَنَّ عَلِيًّا ـ رضى الله عنه ـ كَبَّرَ عَلَى سَهْلِ بْنِ حُنَيْفٍ فَقَالَ إِنَّهُ شَهِدَ بَدْرًا.

Narrated Abu Hazim: That he heard Sahl bin Sa`d being asked about the wounds of Allah's Messengerﷺ saying, "By Allah, I know who washed the wounds of Allah's Messengerﷺ and who poured water (for washing them), and with what he was treated." Sahl added, "Fatima, the daughter of Allah's Messengerﷺ used to wash the wounds, and `Ali bin Abi Talib used to pour water from a shield. When Fatima saw that the water aggravated the bleeding, she took a piece of a mat, burnt it, and inserted its ashes into the wound so that the blood was congealed (and bleeding stopped). His canine tooth got broken on that day, and face was wounded, and his helmet was broken on his head." – Sahih Al-Bukhari 4075

حَدَّثَنَا قُتَيْبَةُ بْنُ سَعِيدٍ، حَدَّثَنَا يَعْقُوبُ، عَنْ أَبِي حَازِمٍ، أَنَّهُ سَمِعَ سَهْلَ بْنَ سَعْدٍ، وَهْوَ يُسْأَلُ عَنْ جُرْحِ رَسُولِ اللَّهِ صلى الله عليه وسلم فَقَالَ أَمَا وَاللَّهِ إِنِّي لأَعْرِفُ مَنْ كَانَ يَغْسِلُ جُرْحَ رَسُولِ اللَّهِ صلى الله عليه وسلم وَمَنْ كَانَ يَسْكُبُ الْمَاءَ وَبِمَا دُووِيَ ـ قَالَ كَانَتْ فَاطِمَةُ ـ عَلَيْهَا السَّلاَمُ ـ بِنْتُ رَسُولِ اللَّهِ صلى الله عليه وسلم تَغْسِلُهُ وَعَلِيٌّ يَسْكُبُ الْمَاءَ بِالْمِجَنِّ، فَلَمَّا رَأَتْ فَاطِمَةُ أَنَّ الْمَاءَ لاَ يَزِيدُ الدَّمَ إِلاَّ كَثْرَةً أَخَذَتْ قِطْعَةً مِنْ حَصِيرٍ، فَأَحْرَقَتْهَا وَأَلْصَقَتْهَا فَاسْتَمْسَكَ الدَّمُ، وَكُسِرَتْ رَبَاعِيَتُهُ يَوْمَئِذٍ، وَجُرِحَ وَجْهُهُ، وَكُسِرَتِ الْبَيْضَةُ عَلَى رَأْسِهِ.

Narrated Az-Zuhri: Al-Walid bin `Abdul Malik said to me, "Have you heard that `Ali' was one of those who slandered `Aisha?" I replied, "No, but two men from your people (named) Abu Salama bin `Abdur-Rahman and Abu Bakr bin `Abdur-Rahman bin Al-Harith have informed me that Aisha told them that `Ali remained silent about her case.". – Sahih Al-Bukhari 4142

حَدَّثَنِي عَبْدُ اللَّهِ بْنُ مُحَمَّدٍ، قَالَ أَمْلَى عَلَىَّ هِشَامُ بْنُ يُوسُفَ مِنْ حِفْظِهِ أَخْبَرَنَا مَعْمَرٌ، عَنِ الزُّهْرِيِّ، قَالَ قَالَ لِي الْوَلِيدُ بْنُ عَبْدِ الْمَلِكِ أَبَلَغَكَ أَنَّ عَلِيًّا، كَانَ فِيمَنْ قَذَفَ عَائِشَةَ قُلْتُ لاَ. وَلَكِنْ قَدْ أَخْبَرَنِي رَجُلاَنِ مِنْ قَوْمِكِ أَبُو سَلَمَةَ بْنُ عَبْدِ الرَّحْمَنِ وَأَبُو بَكْرِ بْنُ عَبْدِ الرَّحْمَنِ بْنِ الْحَارِثِ أَنَّ عَائِشَةَ ـ رضى الله عنها ـ قَالَتْ لَهُمَا كَانَ عَلِيٌّ مُسَلِّمًا فِي شَأْنِهَا. فَرَاجَعُوهُ فَلَمْ يَرْجِعْ وَقَالَ مُسَلِّمًا بِلاَ شَكٍّ فِيهِ وَعَلَيْهِ كَانَ فِي أَصْلِ الْعَتِيقِ كَذَلِكَ

Narrated Al-Bara: When the Prophetﷺ went out for the `Umra in the month of Dhal-Qa'da, the people of Mecca did not allow him to enter Mecca till he agreed to conclude a peace treaty with them by virtue of which he would stay in Mecca for three days only (in the following year). When the agreement was being written, the Muslims wrote: "This is the peace treaty, which Muhammad, Apostle of Allah has concluded." The infidels said (to the Prophet), "We do not agree with you on this, for if we knew that you are Apostle of Allah we would not have prevented you for anything (i.e. entering Mecca, etc.), but you are Muhammad, the son of `Abdullah." Then he said to `Ali, "Erase (the name of) 'Apostle of Allah'." `Ali said, "No, by Allah, I will never erase you (i.e. your name)." Then Allah's Messenger ﷺ took the writing sheet...and he did not know a better writing..and he wrote or got it the following written! "This is the peace treaty which Muhammad, the son of `Abdullah, has concluded: "Muhammad should not bring arms into Mecca except sheathed swords, and should not take with him any person of the people of Mecca even if such a person wanted to follow him, and if any of his companions wants to stay in Mecca, he should not forbid him." (In the next year) when the Prophet ﷺ entered Mecca and the allowed period of stay elapsed, the infidels came to `Ali and said "Tell your companion (Muhammad) to go out, as the allowed period of his stay has finished." So the Prophet ﷺ departed (from Mecca) and the daughter of Hamza followed him shouting "O Uncle, O Uncle!" `Ali took her by the hand and said to Fatima, "Take the daughter of your uncle." So she made her ride (on her horse). (When they reached Medina) `Ali, Zaid and Ja`far quarreled about her. `Ali said, "I took her for she is the daughter of my uncle." Ja`far said, "She is the daughter of my uncle and her aunt is my wife." Zaid said, "She is the daughter of my brother." On that, the Prophet ﷺ gave her to her aunt and said, "The aunt is of the same status as the mother." He then said to `Ali, "You are from me, and I am from you," and said to Ja`far, "You resemble me in appearance and character," and said to Zaid, "You are our brother and our freed slave." `Ali said to the Prophet 'Won't you marry the daughter of Hamza?" The Prophet ﷺ said, "She is the daughter of my foster brother.". – Sahih Al-Bukhari 4251

حَدَّثَنِي عُبَيْدُ اللَّهِ بْنُ مُوسَى، عَنْ إِسْرَائِيلَ، عَنْ أَبِي إِسْحَاقَ، عَنِ الْبَرَاءِ ـ رضى الله عنه ـ قَالَ لَمَّا اعْتَمَرَ النَّبِيُّ صلى الله عليه وسلم فِي ذِي الْقَعْدَةِ، فَأَبَى أَهْلُ مَكَّةَ أَنْ يَدَعُوهُ يَدْخُلُ مَكَّةَ، حَتَّى قَاضَاهُمْ عَلَى أَنْ يُقِيمَ بِهَا ثَلاَثَةَ أَيَّامٍ، فَلَمَّا كَتَبُوا الْكِتَابَ كَتَبُوا، هَذَا مَا قَاضَى عَلَيْهِ مُحَمَّدٌ رَسُولُ اللَّهِ. قَالُوا لاَ نُقِرُّ بِهَذَا، لَوْ نَعْلَمُ أَنَّكَ رَسُولُ اللَّهِ مَا مَنَعْنَاكَ شَيْئًا، وَلَكِنْ أَنْتَ مُحَمَّدُ بْنُ عَبْدِ اللَّهِ. فَقَالَ " أَنَا رَسُولُ اللَّهِ، وَأَنَا مُحَمَّدُ بْنُ عَبْدِ اللَّهِ ". ثُمَّ قَالَ لِعَلِيٍّ " امْحُ رَسُولَ اللَّهِ ". قَالَ عَلِيٌّ لاَ وَاللَّهِ لاَ أَمْحُوكَ أَبَدًا. فَأَخَذَ رَسُولُ اللَّهِ صلى الله عليه وسلم الْكِتَابَ، وَلَيْسَ يُحْسِنُ يَكْتُبُ، فَكَتَبَ هَذَا مَا قَاضَى مُحَمَّدُ بْنُ عَبْدِ اللَّهِ لاَ يُدْخِلُ مَكَّةَ السِّلاَحَ، إِلاَّ السَّيْفَ فِي الْقِرَابِ، وَأَنْ لاَ يَخْرُجَ مِنْ أَهْلِهَا بِأَحَدٍ، إِنْ أَرَادَ أَنْ يَتْبَعَهُ، وَأَنْ لاَ يَمْنَعَ مِنْ أَصْحَابِهِ أَحَدًا، إِنْ أَرَادَ أَنْ يُقِيمَ بِهَا. فَلَمَّا دَخَلَهَا وَمَضَى الأَجَلُ أَتَوْا عَلِيًّا فَقَالُوا قُلْ لِصَاحِبِكَ اخْرُجْ عَنَّا، فَقَدْ مَضَى الأَجَلُ. فَخَرَجَ النَّبِيُّ صلى الله عليه وسلم فَتَبِعَتْهُ ابْنَةُ حَمْزَةَ تُنَادِي يَا عَمِّ يَا عَمِّ. فَتَنَاوَلَهَا عَلِيٌّ، فَأَخَذَ بِيَدِهَا وَقَالَ لِفَاطِمَةَ ـ عَلَيْهَا السَّلاَمُ ـ دُونَكِ ابْنَةَ عَمِّكِ. حَمَلَتْهَا فَاخْتَصَمَ فِيهَا عَلِيٌّ وَزَيْدٌ وَجَعْفَرٌ. قَالَ عَلِيٌّ أَنَا أَخَذْتُهَا وَهْىَ بِنْتُ عَمِّي. وَقَالَ جَعْفَرٌ ابْنَةُ عَمِّي وَخَالَتُهَا تَحْتِي. وَقَالَ زَيْدٌ ابْنَةُ أَخِي. فَقَضَى بِهَا النَّبِيُّ صلى الله عليه وسلم لِخَالَتِهَا وَقَالَ " الْخَالَةُ بِمَنْزِلَةِ الأُمِّ ". وَقَالَ لِعَلِيٍّ " أَنْتَ مِنِّي وَأَنَا مِنْكَ ". وَقَالَ لِجَعْفَرٍ " أَشْبَهْتَ خَلْقِي وَخُلُقِي ". وَقَالَ لِزَيْدٍ " أَنْتَ أَخُونَا وَمَوْلاَنَا ". وَقَالَ عَلِيٌّ أَلاَ تَتَزَوَّجُ بِنْتَ حَمْزَةَ. قَالَ " إِنَّهَا ابْنَةُ أَخِي مِنَ الرَّضَاعَةِ ".

Narrated `Ali: The Prophet ﷺ sent a Sariya under the command of a man from the Ansar and ordered the soldiers to obey him. He (i.e. the commander) became angry and said "Didn't the Prophet ﷺ order you to obey me!" They replied, "Yes." He said, "Collect fire-wood for me." So they collected it. He said, "Make a fire." When they made it, he said, "Enter it (i.e. the fire)." So they intended to do that and started holding each other and saying, "We run towards (i.e. take refuge with) the Prophet ﷺ from the fire." They kept on saying that till the fire was extinguished and the anger of the commander abated. When that news reached the Prophet ﷺ he said, "If they had entered it (i.e. the fire), they would not have come out of it till the Day of Resurrection. Obedience (to somebody) is required when he enjoins what is good.". – Sahih Al-Bukhari 4340

حَدَّثَنَا مُسَدَّدٌ، حَدَّثَنَا عَبْدُ الْوَاحِدِ، حَدَّثَنَا الأَعْمَشُ، قَالَ حَدَّثَنِي سَعْدُ بْنُ عُبَيْدَةَ، عَنْ أَبِي عَبْدِ الرَّحْمَنِ، عَنْ عَلِيٍّ ـ رضى الله عنه ـ قَالَ بَعَثَ النَّبِيُّ صلى الله عليه وسلم سَرِيَّةً فَاسْتَعْمَلَ رَجُلاً مِنَ الأَنْصَارِ، وَأَمَرَهُمْ أَنْ يُطِيعُوهُ، فَغَضِبَ فَقَالَ أَلَيْسَ أَمَرَكُمُ النَّبِيُّ صلى الله عليه وسلم أَنْ تُطِيعُونِي. قَالُوا بَلَى. قَالَ فَاجْمَعُوا لِي حَطَبًا. فَجَمَعُوا، فَقَالَ أَوْقِدُوا نَارًا. فَأَوْقَدُوهَا، فَقَالَ ادْخُلُوهَا. فَهَمُّوا، وَجَعَلَ بَعْضُهُمْ يُمْسِكُ بَعْضًا، وَيَقُولُونَ فَرَرْنَا إِلَى النَّبِيِّ صلى الله عليه وسلم مِنَ النَّارِ. فَمَا زَالُوا حَتَّى خَمَدَتِ النَّارُ، فَسَكَنَ غَضَبُهُ، فَبَلَغَ النَّبِيَّ صلى الله عليه وسلم فَقَالَ " لَوْ دَخَلُوهَا مَا خَرَجُوا مِنْهَا إِلَى يَوْمِ الْقِيَامَةِ، الطَّاعَةُ فِي الْمَعْرُوفِ "

Narrated Al-Aswad: It was mentioned in the presence of `Aisha that the Prophetﷺ had appointed `Ali as successor by will. Thereupon she said, "Who said so? I saw the Prophet, while I was supporting him against my chest. He asked for a tray, and then fell on one side and expired, and I did not feel it. So how (do the people say) he appointed `Ali as his successor?" – Sahih Al-Bukhari 4459

حَدَّثَنَا عَبْدُ اللَّهِ بْنُ مُحَمَّدٍ، أَخْبَرَنَا أَزْهَرُ، أَخْبَرَنَا ابْنُ عَوْنٍ، عَنْ إِبْرَاهِيمَ، عَنِ الأَسْوَدِ، قَالَ ذُكِرَ عِنْدَ عَائِشَةَ أَنَّ النَّبِيَّ صلى الله عليه وسلم أَوْصَى إِلَى عَلِيٍّ، فَقَالَتْ مَنْ قَالَهُ لَقَدْ رَأَيْتُ النَّبِيَّ صلى الله عليه وسلم وَإِنِّي لَمُسْنِدَتُهُ إِلَى صَدْرِي، فَدَعَا بِالطَّسْتِ فَانْخَنَثَ فَمَاتَ، فَمَا شَعَرْتُ، فَكَيْفَ أَوْصَى إِلَى عَلِيٍّ

Narrated Buraida: The Prophetﷺ sent `Ali to Khalid to bring the Khumus (of the booty) and I hated `Ali, and `Ali had taken a bath (after a sexual act with a slave-girl from the Khumus). I said to Khalid, "Don't you see this (i.e. `Ali)?" When we reached the Prophetﷺ I mentioned that to him. He said, "O Buraida! Do you hate `Ali?" I said, "Yes." He said, "Do you hate him, for he deserves more than that from the Khumlus." – Sahih Al-Bukhari 4350

حَدَّثَنِي مُحَمَّدُ بْنُ بَشَّارٍ، حَدَّثَنَا رَوْحُ بْنُ عُبَادَةَ، حَدَّثَنَا عَلِيُّ بْنُ سُوَيْدِ بْنِ مَنْجُوفٍ، عَنْ عَبْدِ اللَّهِ بْنِ بُرَيْدَةَ، عَنْ أَبِيهِ ـ رضى الله عنه ـ قَالَ بَعَثَ النَّبِيُّ صلى الله عليه وسلم عَلِيًّا إِلَى خَالِدٍ لِيَقْبِضَ الْخُمُسَ وَكُنْتُ أُبْغِضُ عَلِيًّا، وَقَدِ اغْتَسَلَ، فَقُلْتُ لِخَالِدٍ أَلاَ تَرَى إِلَى هَذَا فَلَمَّا قَدِمْنَا عَلَى النَّبِيِّ صلى الله عليه وسلم ذَكَرْتُ ذَلِكَ لَهُ فَقَالَ " يَا بُرَيْدَةُ أَتُبْغِضُ عَلِيًّا ". فَقُلْتُ نَعَمْ. قَالَ " لاَ تُبْغِضْهُ فَإِنَّ لَهُ فِي الْخُمُسِ أَكْثَرَ مِنْ ذَلِكَ ".

Narrated Sa`d: Allah's Messengerﷺ set out for Tabuk. Appointing `Ali as his deputy (in Medina). `Ali said, "Do you want to leave me with the children and women?" The Prophetﷺ said, "Will you not be pleased that you will be to me like Aaron to Moses? But there will be no prophet after me.". – Sahih Al-Bukhari 4416

حَدَّثَنَا مُسَدَّدٌ، حَدَّثَنَا يَحْيَى، عَنْ شُعْبَةَ، عَنِ الْحَكَمِ، عَنْ مُصْعَبِ بْنِ سَعْدٍ، عَنْ أَبِيهِ، أَنَّ رَسُولَ اللَّهِ صلى الله عليه وسلم خَرَجَ إِلَى تَبُوكَ، وَاسْتَخْلَفَ عَلِيًّا فَقَالَ أَتُخَلِّفُنِي فِي الصِّبْيَانِ وَالنِّسَاءِ قَالَ " أَلاَ تَرْضَى أَنْ تَكُونَ مِنِّي بِمَنْزِلَةِ هَارُونَ مِنْ مُوسَى إِلاَّ أَنَّهُ لَيْسَ نَبِيٌّ بَعْدِي ". وَقَالَ أَبُو دَاوُدَ حَدَّثَنَا شُعْبَةُ عَنِ الْحَكَمِ سَمِعْتُ مُصْعَبًا.

Narrated Ibn `Abbas: `Umar said, "Our best Qur'an reciter is Ubai and our best judge is `Ali; and in spite of this, we leave some of the statements of Ubai because Ubai says, 'I do not leave anything that I have heard from Allah's Messengerﷺ while Allah: "Whatever verse (Revelations) do We abrogate or cause to be forgotten but We bring a better one or similar to it." (2.106). – Sahih Al-Bukhari 4481

حَدَّثَنَا عَمْرُو بْنُ عَلِيٍّ، حَدَّثَنَا يَحْيَى، حَدَّثَنَا سُفْيَانُ، عَنْ حَبِيبٍ، عَنْ سَعِيدِ بْنِ جُبَيْرٍ، عَنِ ابْنِ عَبَّاسٍ، قَالَ قَالَ عُمَرُ ـ رضى الله عنه ـ أَقْرَؤُنَا أُبَيٌّ، وَأَقْضَانَا عَلِيٌّ، وَإِنَّا لَنَدَعُ مِنْ قَوْلِ أُبَيٍّ، وَذَاكَ أَنَّ أُبَيًّا يَقُولُ لاَ أَدَعُ شَيْئًا سَمِعْتُهُ مِنْ رَسُولِ اللَّهِ صلى الله عليه وسلم وَقَدْ قَالَ اللَّهُ تَعَالَى {مَا نَنْسَخْ مِنْ آيَةٍ أَوْ نَنْسَأْهَا}

Narrated Marwan bin Al-Hakam: I saw `Uthman and `Ali. `Uthman used to forbid people to perform Hajj-at-Tamattu` and Hajj-al- Qiran (Hajj and `Umra together), and when `Ali saw (this act of `Uthman), he assumed Ihram for Hajj and `Umra together saying, "Lubbaik for `Umra and Hajj," and said, "I will not leave the tradition of the Prophetﷺ on the saying of somebody." – Sahih Al-Bukhari 1563

حَدَّثَنَا مُحَمَّدُ بْنُ بَشَّارٍ، حَدَّثَنَا غُنْدَرٌ، حَدَّثَنَا شُعْبَةُ، عَنِ الْحَكَمِ، عَنْ عَلِيِّ بْنِ حُسَيْنٍ، عَنْ مَرْوَانَ بْنِ الْحَكَمِ، قَالَ شَهِدْتُ عُثْمَانَ وَعَلِيًّا ـ رضى الله عنهما ـ وَعُثْمَانُ يَنْهَى عَنِ الْمُتْعَةِ وَأَنْ يُجْمَعَ بَيْنَهُمَا. فَلَمَّا رَأَى عَلِيٌّ، أَهَلَّ بِهِمَا لَبَّيْكَ بِعُمْرَةٍ وَحَجَّةٍ قَالَ مَا كُنْتُ لأَدَعَ سُنَّةَ النَّبِيِّ صلى الله عليه وسلم لِقَوْلِ أَحَدٍ

Narrated `Ali: We have nothing except the Book of Allah and this written paper from the Prophet (wherein is written:) Medina is a sanctuary from the 'Air Mountain to such and such a place, and whoever innovates in it an heresy or commits a sin, or gives shelter to such an innovator in it will incur the curse of Allah, the angels, and all the people, none of his compulsory or optional good deeds of worship will be accepted. And the asylum (of protection) granted by any Muslim is to be secured (respected) by all the other Muslims; and whoever betrays a Muslim in this respect incurs the curse of Allah, the angels, and all the people, and none of his compulsory or optional good deeds of worship will be accepted, and whoever (freed slave) befriends (take as masters) other than his manumitters without their permission incurs the curse of Allah, the angels, and all the people, and none of his compulsory or optional good deeds of worship will be accepted. – Sahih Al-Bukhari 1870

حَدَّثَنَا مُحَمَّدُ بْنُ بَشَّارٍ، حَدَّثَنَا عَبْدُ الرَّحْمَنِ، حَدَّثَنَا سُفْيَانُ، عَنِ الأَعْمَشِ، عَنْ إِبْرَاهِيمَ التَّيْمِيِّ، عَنْ أَبِيهِ، عَنْ عَلِيٍّ ـ رضى الله عنه ـ قَالَ مَا عِنْدَنَا شَىْءٌ إِلاَّ كِتَابُ اللَّهِ، وَهَذِهِ الصَّحِيفَةُ عَنِ النَّبِيِّ صلى الله عليه وسلم " الْمَدِينَةُ حَرَمٌ، مَا بَيْنَ عَائِرٍ إِلَى كَذَا، مَنْ أَحْدَثَ فِيهَا حَدَثًا، أَوْ آوَى مُحْدِثًا، فَعَلَيْهِ لَعْنَةُ اللَّهِ وَالْمَلاَئِكَةِ وَالنَّاسِ أَجْمَعِينَ، لاَ يُقْبَلُ مِنْهُ صَرْفٌ وَلاَ عَدْلٌ ". وَقَالَ " ذِمَّةُ الْمُسْلِمِينَ وَاحِدَةٌ، فَمَنْ أَخْفَرَ مُسْلِمًا فَعَلَيْهِ لَعْنَةُ اللَّهِ وَالْمَلاَئِكَةِ وَالنَّاسِ أَجْمَعِينَ، لاَ يُقْبَلُ مِنْهُ صَرْفٌ وَلاَ عَدْلٌ، وَمَنْ تَوَلَّى قَوْمًا بِغَيْرِ إِذْنِ مَوَالِيهِ، فَعَلَيْهِ لَعْنَةُ اللَّهِ وَالْمَلاَئِكَةِ وَالنَّاسِ أَجْمَعِينَ، لاَ يُقْبَلُ مِنْهُ صَرْفٌ وَلاَ عَدْلٌ "

Narrated `Ali: I got an old she-camel as my share from the booty, and the Prophet ﷺ had given me another from Al- Khumus. And when I intended to marry Fatima (daughter of the Prophet), I arranged that a goldsmith from the tribe of Bani Qainuqa' would accompany me in order to bring Idhkhir and then sell it to the goldsmiths and use its price for my marriage banquet. – Sahih Al-Bukhari 2089

حَدَّثَنَا عَبْدَانُ، أَخْبَرَنَا عَبْدُ اللَّهِ، أَخْبَرَنَا يُونُسُ، عَنِ ابْنِ شِهَابٍ، قَالَ أَخْبَرَنِي عَلِيُّ بْنُ حُسَيْنٍ، أَنَّ حُسَيْنَ بْنَ عَلِيٍّ ـ رضى الله عنهما ـ أَخْبَرَهُ أَنَّ عَلِيًّا ـ عَلَيْهِ السَّلاَمُ ـ قَالَ كَانَتْ لِي شَارِفٌ مِنْ نَصِيبِي مِنَ الْمَغْنَمِ، وَكَانَ النَّبِيُّ صلى الله عليه وسلم أَعْطَانِي شَارِفًا مِنَ الْخُمْسِ، فَلَمَّا أَرَدْتُ أَنْ أَبْتَنِيَ بِفَاطِمَةَ ـ عَلَيْهَا السَّلاَمُ ـ بِنْتِ رَسُولِ اللَّهِ صلى الله عليه وسلم وَاعَدْتُ رَجُلاً صَوَّاغًا مِنْ بَنِي قَيْنُقَاعَ أَنْ يَرْتَحِلَ مَعِي فَنَأْتِيَ بِإِذْخِرٍ أَرَدْتُ أَنْ أَبِيعَهُ مِنَ الصَّوَّاغِينَ، وَأَسْتَعِينَ بِهِ فِي وَلِيمَةِ عُرُسِي

Narrated Al-Bara: When the Prophet ﷺ intended to perform `Umra in the month of Dhul-Qada, the people of Mecca did not let him enter Mecca till he settled the matter with them by promising to stay in it for three days only. When the document of treaty was written, the following was mentioned: 'These are the terms on which Muhammad, Allah's Messenger ﷺ agreed (to make peace).' They said, "We will not agree to this, for if we believed that you are Allah's Messenger ﷺ we would not prevent you, but you are Muhammad bin `Abdullah." The Prophet ﷺ said, "I am Allah's Messenger ﷺ and also Muhammad bin `Abdullah." Then he said to `Ali, "Rub off (the words) 'Allah's Messenger ﷺ,' " But `Ali said, "No, by Allah, I will never rub off your name." So, Allah's Messenger ﷺ took the document and wrote, 'This is what Muhammad bin `Abdullah has agreed upon: No arms will be brought into Mecca except in their cases, and nobody from the people of Mecca will be allowed to go with him (i.e. the Prophet ﷺ) even if he wished to follow him and he (the Prophet ﷺ) will not prevent any of his companions from staying in Mecca if the latter wants to stay.' When the Prophet ﷺ entered Mecca and the time limit passed, the Meccans went to `Ali and said, "Tell your Friend (i.e. the Prophet ﷺ) to go out, as the period (agreed to) has passed." So, the Prophet ﷺ went out of Mecca. The daughter of Hamza ran after them (i.e. the Prophet ﷺ and his companions), calling, "O Uncle! O Uncle!" `Ali received her and led her by the hand and said to Fatima,

"Take your uncle's daughter." Zaid and Ja`far quarreled about her. `Ali said, "I have more right to her as she is my uncle's daughter." Ja`far said, "She is my uncle's daughter, and her aunt is my wife." Zaid said, "She is my brother's daughter." The Prophet ﷺ judged that she should be given to her aunt, and said that the aunt was like the mother. He then said to 'All, "You are from me and I am from you", and said to Ja`far, "You resemble me both in character and appearance", and said to Zaid, "You are our brother (in faith) and our freed slave.". – Sahih Al-Bukhari 2699

حَدَّثَنَا عُبَيْدُ اللَّهِ بْنُ مُوسَى، عَنْ إِسْرَائِيلَ، عَنْ أَبِي إِسْحَاقَ، عَنِ الْبَرَاءِ ـ رضى الله عنه ـ قَالَ اعْتَمَرَ النَّبِيُّ صلى الله عليه وسلم فِي ذِي الْقَعْدَةِ، فَأَبَى أَهْلُ مَكَّةَ أَنْ يَدَعُوهُ يَدْخُلُ مَكَّةَ، حَتَّى قَاضَاهُمْ عَلَى أَنْ يُقِيمَ بِهَا ثَلاَثَةَ أَيَّامٍ، فَلَمَّا كَتَبُوا الْكِتَابَ كَتَبُوا هَذَا مَا قَاضَى عَلَيْهِ مُحَمَّدٌ رَسُولُ اللَّهِ صلى الله عليه وسلم. فَقَالُوا لاَ نُقِرُّ بِهَا، فَلَوْ نَعْلَمُ أَنَّكَ رَسُولُ اللَّهِ مَا مَنَعْنَاكَ، لَكِنْ أَنْتَ مُحَمَّدُ بْنُ عَبْدِ اللَّهِ. قَالَ " أَنَا رَسُولُ اللَّهِ وَأَنَا مُحَمَّدُ بْنُ عَبْدِ اللَّهِ ". ثُمَّ قَالَ لِعَلِيٍّ " امْحُ رَسُولُ اللَّهِ ". قَالَ لاَ، وَاللَّهِ لاَ أَمْحُوكَ أَبَدًا، فَأَخَذَ رَسُولُ اللَّهِ صلى الله عليه وسلم الْكِتَابَ، فَكَتَبَ هَذَا مَا قَاضَى عَلَيْهِ مُحَمَّدُ بْنُ عَبْدِ اللَّهِ، لاَ يَدْخُلُ مَكَّةَ سِلاَحٌ إِلاَّ فِي الْقِرَابِ، وَأَنْ لاَ يَخْرُجَ مِنْ أَهْلِهَا بِأَحَدٍ، إِنْ أَرَادَ أَنْ يَتَّبِعَهُ، وَأَنْ لاَ يَمْنَعَ أَحَدًا مِنْ أَصْحَابِهِ أَرَادَ أَنْ يُقِيمَ بِهَا. فَلَمَّا دَخَلَهَا، وَمَضَى الأَجَلُ أَتَوْا عَلِيًّا، فَقَالُوا قُلْ لِصَاحِبِكَ اخْرُجْ عَنَّا فَقَدْ مَضَى الأَجَلُ. فَخَرَجَ النَّبِيُّ صلى الله عليه وسلم فَتَبِعَتْهُمُ ابْنَةُ حَمْزَةَ يَا عَمِّ يَا عَمِّ. فَتَنَاوَلَهَا عَلِيٌّ فَأَخَذَ بِيَدِهَا، وَقَالَ لِفَاطِمَةَ عَلَيْهَا السَّلاَمُ دُونَكِ ابْنَةَ عَمِّكِ، احْمِلِيهَا. فَاخْتَصَمَ فِيهَا عَلِيٌّ وَزَيْدٌ وَجَعْفَرٌ، فَقَالَ عَلِيٌّ أَنَا أَحَقُّ بِهَا وَهْىَ ابْنَةُ عَمِّي. وَقَالَ جَعْفَرٌ ابْنَةُ عَمِّي وَخَالَتُهَا تَحْتِي. وَقَالَ زَيْدٌ ابْنَةُ أَخِي. فَقَضَى بِهَا النَّبِيُّ صلى الله عليه وسلم لِخَالَتِهَا. وَقَالَ " الْخَالَةُ بِمَنْزِلَةِ الأُمِّ ". وَقَالَ لِعَلِيٍّ " أَنْتَ مِنِّي وَأَنَا مِنْكَ ". وَقَالَ لِجَعْفَرٍ " أَشْبَهْتَ خَلْقِي وَخُلُقِي ". وَقَالَ لِزَيْدٍ " أَنْتَ أَخُونَا وَمَوْلاَنَا "

Narrated `Ali: The Prophet ﷺ gave me a silken dress as a gift and I wore it. When I saw the signs of anger on his face, I cut it into pieces and distributed it among my wives.". – Sahih Al-Bukhari 2614

حَدَّثَنَا حَجَّاجُ بْنُ مِنْهَالٍ، حَدَّثَنَا شُعْبَةُ، قَالَ أَخْبَرَنِي عَبْدُ الْمَلِكِ بْنُ مَيْسَرَةَ، قَالَ سَمِعْتُ زَيْدَ بْنَ وَهْبٍ، عَنْ عَلِيٍّ ـ رضى الله عنه ـ قَالَ أَهْدَى إِلَىَّ النَّبِيُّ صلى الله عليه وسلم حُلَّةَ سِيَرَاءَ فَلَبِسْتُهَا، فَرَأَيْتُ الْغَضَبَ فِي وَجْهِهِ، فَشَقَّقْتُهَا بَيْنَ نِسَائِي.

Narrated Al-Bara: When the Prophet ﷺ intended to perform the `Umra he sent a person to the people of Mecca asking their permission to enter Mecca. They stipulated that he would not stay for more than three days and would not enter it except with sheathed arms and would not preach (Islam) to any of them. So `Ali bin Abi- Talib started writing the treaty between them. He wrote, "This is what Muhammad, Apostle of Allah has agreed to." The (Meccans) said, "If we knew that you (Muhammad) are the Messenger of Allah, then we would not have prevented you and would have followed you. But write, 'This is what Muhammad bin `Abdullah has agreed to..' " On that Allah's Messenger ﷺ said, "By Allah, I am Muhammad bin `Abdullah, and, by Allah, I am Apostle of 'Allah." Allah's Messenger ﷺ used not to write; so he asked `Ali to erase the expression of Apostle of Allah. On that `Ali said, "By Allah I will never erase it." Allah's Apostle said (to `Ali), "Let me see the paper." When `Ali showed him the paper, the Prophet ﷺ erased the expression with his own hand. When Allah's Messenger ﷺ had entered Mecca and three days had elapsed, the Meccans came to `Ali and said, "Let your friend (i.e. the Prophet) quit Mecca." `Ali informed Allah's Messenger ﷺ about it and Allah's Messenger ﷺ said, "Yes," and then he departed. – Sahih Al-Bukhari 3184

حَدَّثَنَا أَحْمَدُ بْنُ عُثْمَانَ بْنِ حَكِيمٍ، حَدَّثَنَا شُرَيْحُ بْنُ مَسْلَمَةَ، حَدَّثَنَا إِبْرَاهِيمُ بْنُ يُوسُفَ بْنِ أَبِي إِسْحَاقَ، قَالَ حَدَّثَنِي أَبِي، عَنْ أَبِي إِسْحَاقَ، قَالَ حَدَّثَنِي الْبَرَاءُ ـ رضى الله عنه أَنَّ النَّبِيَّ صلى الله عليه وسلم لَمَّا أَرَادَ أَنْ يَعْتَمِرَ أَرْسَلَ إِلَى أَهْلِ مَكَّةَ يَسْتَأْذِنُهُمْ لِيَدْخُلَ مَكَّةَ، فَاشْتَرَطُوا عليهِ أن لا يُقِيمَ بِهَا إِلاَّ ثَلاَثَ لَيَالٍ، وَلاَ يَدْخُلَهَا إِلاَّ بِجُلُبَّانِ السِّلاَحِ، وَلاَ يَدْعُوَ مِنْهُمْ أَحَدًا، قَالَ فَأَخَذَ يَكْتُبُ الشَّرْطَ بَيْنَهُمْ عَلِيُّ بْنُ أَبِي طَالِبٍ، فَكَتَبَ هَذَا مَا قَاضَى عَلَيْهِ مُحَمَّدٌ رَسُولُ اللَّهِ. فَقَالُوا لَوْ عَلِمْنَا أَنَّكَ رَسُولُ اللَّهِ لَمْ نَمْنَعْكَ وَلَبَايَعْنَاكَ، وَلَكِنِ اكْتُبْ هَذَا مَا قَاضَى عَلَيْهِ مُحَمَّدُ بْنُ عَبْدِ اللَّهِ. فَقَالَ " أَنَا وَاللَّهِ مُحَمَّدُ بْنُ عَبْدِ اللَّهِ وَأَنَا وَاللَّهِ رَسُولُ اللَّهِ ". قَالَ وَكَانَ لاَ يَكْتُبُ قَالَ فَقَالَ لِعَلِيٍّ " امْحُ رَسُولَ اللَّهِ ". فَقَالَ عَلِيٌّ وَاللَّهِ لاَ أَمْحَاهُ أَبَدًا. قَالَ " فَأَرِنِيهِ ". قَالَ فَأَرَاهُ إِيَّاهُ، فَمَحَاهُ النَّبِيُّ صلى الله عليه وسلم بِيَدِهِ، فَلَمَّا دَخَلَ وَمَضَى الأَيَّامُ أَتَوْا عَلِيًّا فَقَالُوا مُرْ صَاحِبَكَ فَلْيَرْتَحِلْ. فَذَكَرَ ذَلِكَ لِرَسُولِ اللَّهِ صلى الله عليه وسلم فَقَالَ " نَعَمْ " ثُمَّ ارْتَحَلَ

Narrated `Ikrima bin Khalid: Ibn `Umar said, "I went to Hafsa while water was dribbling from her twined braids. I said, 'The condition of the people is as you see, and no authority has been given to me.' Hafsa said, (to me), 'Go to them, and as they (i.e. the people) are waiting for you, and I am afraid your absence from them will produce division amongst them.' " So Hafsa did not leave Ibn `Umar till we went to them. When the people differed. Muawiya addressed the people saying, "'If anybody wants to say anything in this matter of the Caliphate, he should show up and not conceal himself, for we are more rightful to be a Caliph than he and his father." On that, Habib bin Masalama said (to Ibn `Umar), "Why don't you reply to him (i.e. Muawiya)?" `Abdullah bin `Umar said, "I untied my garment that was going round my back and legs while I was sitting and was about to say, 'He who fought against you and against your father for the sake of Islam, is more rightful to be a Caliph,' but I was afraid that my statement might produce differences amongst the people and cause bloodshed, and my statement might be interpreted not as I intended. (So I kept quiet) remembering what Allah has prepared in the Gardens of Paradise (for those who are patient and prefer the Hereafter to this worldly life)." Habib said, "You did what kept you safe and secure (i.e. you were wise in doing so). – Sahih Al-Bukhari 4108

حَدَّثَنِي إِبْرَاهِيمُ بْنُ مُوسَى، أَخْبَرَنَا هِشَامٌ، عَنْ مَعْمَرٍ، عَنِ الزُّهْرِيِّ، عَنْ سَالِمٍ، عَنِ ابْنِ عُمَرَ، قَالَ وَأَخْبَرَنِي ابْنُ طَاوُسٍ، عَنْ عِكْرِمَةَ بْنِ خَالِدٍ، عَنِ ابْنِ عُمَرَ، قَالَ دَخَلْتُ عَلَى حَفْصَةَ وَنَسْوَاتُهَا تَنْطُفُ، قُلْتُ قَدْ كَانَ مِنْ أَمْرِ النَّاسِ مَا تَرَيْنَ، فَلَمْ يُجْعَلْ لِي مِنَ الأَمْرِ شَىْءٌ. فَقَالَتِ الْحَقْ فَإِنَّهُمْ يَنْتَظِرُونَكَ، وَأَخْشَى أَنْ يَكُونَ فِي احْتِبَاسِكَ عَنْهُمْ فُرْقَةٌ. فَلَمْ تَدَعْهُ حَتَّى ذَهَبَ، فَلَمَّا تَفَرَّقَ النَّاسُ خَطَبَ مُعَاوِيَةُ قَالَ مَنْ كَانَ يُرِيدُ أَنْ يَتَكَلَّمَ فِي هَذَا الأَمْرِ فَلْيُطْلِعْ لَنَا قَرْنَهُ، فَلَنَحْنُ أَحَقُّ بِهِ مِنْهُ وَمِنْ أَبِيهِ. قَالَ حَبِيبُ بْنُ مَسْلَمَةَ فَهَلاَّ أَجَبْتَهُ قَالَ عَبْدُ اللَّهِ فَحَلَلْتُ حُبْوَتِي وَهَمَمْتُ أَنْ أَقُولَ أَحَقُّ بِهَذَا الأَمْرِ مِنْكَ مَنْ قَاتَلَكَ وَأَبَاكَ عَلَى الإِسْلاَمِ. فَخَشِيتُ أَنْ أَقُولَ كَلِمَةً تُفَرِّقُ بَيْنَ الْجَمْعِ، وَتَسْفِكُ الدَّمَ، وَيُحْمَلُ عَنِّي غَيْرُ ذَلِكَ، فَذَكَرْتُ مَا أَعَدَّ اللَّهُ فِي الْجِنَانِ. قَالَ حَبِيبٌ حُفِظْتَ وَعُصِمْتَ. قَالَ مَحْمُودٌ عَنْ عَبْدِ الرَّزَّاقِ وَنَوْسَاتُهَا

Narrated `Aisha: Fatima the daughter of the Prophet ﷺ sent someone to Abu Bakr (when he was a caliph), asking for her inheritance of what Allah's Messenger ﷺ had left of the property bestowed on him by Allah from the Fai (i.e. booty gained without fighting) in Medina, and Fadak, and what remained of the Khumus of the Khaibar booty. On that, Abu Bakr said, "Allah's Messenger ﷺ said, "Our property is not inherited. Whatever we leave, is Sadaqa, but the family of (the Prophet) Muhammad can eat of this property.' By Allah, I will not make any change in the state of the Sadaqa of Allah's Messenger ﷺ and will leave it as it was during the lifetime of Allah's Messenger ﷺ, and will dispose of it as Allah's Messenger ﷺ used to do." So Abu Bakr refused to give anything of that to Fatima. So she became angry with Abu Bakr and kept away from him, and did not task to him till she died. She remained alive for six months after the death of the Prophet. When she died, her husband `Ali, buried her at night without informing Abu Bakr and he said the funeral prayer by himself. When Fatima was alive, the people used to respect `Ali much, but after her death, `Ali noticed a change in the people's attitude towards him. So `Ali sought reconciliation with Abu Bakr and gave him an oath of allegiance. `Ali had not given the oath of allegiance during those months (i.e. the period between the Prophet's death and Fatima's death). `Ali sent someone to Abu Bakr saying, "Come to us, but let nobody come with you," as he disliked that `Umar should come, `Umar said (to Abu Bakr), "No, by Allah, you shall not enter upon them alone " Abu Bakr said, "What do you think they will do to me? By Allah, I will go to them' So Abu Bakr entered upon them, and then `Ali uttered Tashah-hud and said (to Abu Bakr), "We know well your superiority and what Allah has given you, and we are not jealous of the good what Allah has bestowed upon you, but you did not consult us in the question of the rule and we thought that we have got a right in it because of our near relationship to Allah's Messenger ﷺ." Thereupon Abu Bakr's eyes flowed with tears. And when Abu Bakr spoke, he said, "By Him in Whose Hand my soul is to keep good relations with the relatives of Allah's Messenger ﷺ is dearer to me than to keep good relations with my own relatives. But as for the trouble which arose between me and you about his property, I will do my best to spend it according to what is good, and will not leave any rule or regulation which I saw Allah's Messenger ﷺ following, in disposing of it, but I will follow." On that `Ali said to Abu Bakr, "I promise to give you the oath of allegiance in this after noon." So when Abu Bakr had offered the Zuhr prayer, he ascended the pulpit and uttered the Tashah-hud and then mentioned the story of `Ali and his failure to give the oath of allegiance, and excused him, accepting what excuses he had offered; Then `Ali (got up) and praying (to Allah) for forgiveness, he uttered Tashah-hud, praised Abu Bakr's right, and said, that he had not done what he had done because of jealousy of Abu Bakr or as a protest of that Allah had favored him with. `Ali added, "But we used to consider that we too had some right in this affair (of rulership) and that he (i.e. Abu Bakr) did not consult us in this matter, and therefore caused us to feel sorry." On that all the Muslims became happy and said, "You have done the right thing." The Muslims then became friendly with `Ali as he returned to what the people had done (i.e. giving the oath of allegiance to Abu Bakr). – Sahih Al-Bukhari 4240, 4241

حَدَّثَنَا يَحْيَى بْنُ بُكَيْرٍ، حَدَّثَنَا اللَّيْثُ، عَنْ عُقَيْلٍ، عَنِ ابْنِ شِهَابٍ، عَنْ عُرْوَةَ، عَنْ عَائِشَةَ، أَنَّ فَاطِمَةَ ـ عَلَيْهَا السَّلاَمُ ـ بِنْتَ النَّبِيِّ صلى الله عليه وسلم أَرْسَلَتْ إِلَى أَبِي بَكْرٍ تَسْأَلُهُ مِيرَاثَهَا مِنْ رَسُولِ اللَّهِ صلى الله عليه وسلم مِمَّا أَفَاءَ اللَّهُ عَلَيْهِ بِالْمَدِينَةِ وَفَدَكَ، وَمَا بَقِيَ مِنْ خُمُسِ خَيْبَرَ، فَقَالَ أَبُو بَكْرٍ إِنَّ رَسُولَ اللَّهِ صلى الله عليه وسلم قَالَ " لاَ نُورَثُ، مَا تَرَكْنَا صَدَقَةٌ، إِنَّمَا يَأْكُلُ آلُ مُحَمَّدٍ صلى الله عليه وسلم فِي هَذَا الْمَالِ ". وَإِنِّي وَاللَّهِ لاَ أُغَيِّرُ شَيْئًا مِنْ صَدَقَةِ رَسُولِ اللَّهِ صلى الله عليه وسلم عَنْ حَالِهَا الَّتِي كَانَ عَلَيْهَا فِي عَهْدِ رَسُولِ اللَّهِ صلى الله عليه وسلم وَلأَعْمَلَنَّ فِيهَا بِمَا عَمِلَ بِهِ رَسُولُ اللَّهِ صلى الله عليه وسلم فَأَبَى أَبُو بَكْرٍ أَنْ يَدْفَعَ إِلَى فَاطِمَةَ مِنْهَا شَيْئًا فَوَجَدَتْ فَاطِمَةُ عَلَى أَبِي بَكْرٍ فِي ذَلِكَ فَهَجَرَتْهُ، فَلَمْ تُكَلِّمْهُ حَتَّى تُوُفِّيَتْ، وَعَاشَتْ بَعْدَ النَّبِيِّ صلى الله عليه وسلم سِتَّةَ أَشْهُرٍ، فَلَمَّا تُوُفِّيَتْ، دَفَنَهَا زَوْجُهَا عَلِيٌّ لَيْلاً، وَلَمْ يُؤْذِنْ بِهَا أَبَا بَكْرٍ وَصَلَّى عَلَيْهَا، وَكَانَ لِعَلِيٍّ مِنَ النَّاسِ وَجْهٌ حَيَاةَ فَاطِمَةَ، فَلَمَّا تُوُفِّيَتِ اسْتَنْكَرَ عَلِيٌّ وُجُوهَ النَّاسِ، فَالْتَمَسَ مُصَالَحَةَ أَبِي بَكْرٍ وَمُبَايَعَتَهُ، وَلَمْ يَكُنْ يُبَايِعُ تِلْكَ الأَشْهُرَ، فَأَرْسَلَ إِلَى أَبِي بَكْرٍ أَنِ ائْتِنَا، وَلاَ يَأْتِنَا أَحَدٌ مَعَكَ، كَرَاهِيَةً لِمَحْضَرِ عُمَرَ. فَقَالَ عُمَرُ لاَ وَاللَّهِ لاَ تَدْخُلُ عَلَيْهِمْ وَحْدَكَ. فَقَالَ أَبُو بَكْرٍ وَمَا عَسَيْتَهُمْ أَنْ يَفْعَلُوا بِي، وَاللَّهِ لآتِيَنَّهُمْ. فَدَخَلَ عَلَيْهِمْ أَبُو بَكْرٍ، فَتَشَهَّدَ عَلِيٌّ فَقَالَ إِنَّا قَدْ عَرَفْنَا فَضْلَكَ، وَمَا أَعْطَاكَ، اللَّهُ وَلَمْ نَنْفَسْ عَلَيْكَ خَيْرًا سَاقَهُ اللَّهُ إِلَيْكَ، وَلَكِنَّكَ اسْتَبْدَدْتَ عَلَيْنَا بِالأَمْرِ، وَكُنَّا نَرَى لِقَرَابَتِنَا مِنْ رَسُولِ اللَّهِ صلى الله عليه وسلم نَصِيبًا. حَتَّى فَاضَتْ عَيْنَا أَبِي بَكْرٍ، فَلَمَّا تَكَلَّمَ أَبُو بَكْرٍ قَالَ وَالَّذِي نَفْسِي بِيَدِهِ لَقَرَابَةُ رَسُولِ اللَّهِ صلى الله عليه وسلم أَحَبُّ إِلَىَّ أَنْ أَصِلَ مِنْ قَرَابَتِي، وَأَمَّا الَّذِي شَجَرَ بَيْنِي وَبَيْنَكُمْ مِنْ هَذِهِ الأَمْوَالِ، فَلَمْ آلُ فِيهَا عَنِ الْخَيْرِ، وَلَمْ أَتْرُكْ أَمْرًا رَأَيْتُ رَسُولَ اللَّهِ صلى الله عليه وسلم يَصْنَعُهُ فِيهَا إِلاَّ صَنَعْتُهُ. فَقَالَ عَلِيٌّ لأَبِي بَكْرٍ مَوْعِدُكَ الْعَشِيَّةُ لِلْبَيْعَةِ. فَلَمَّا صَلَّى أَبُو بَكْرٍ الظُّهْرَ رَقِيَ عَلَى الْمِنْبَرِ، فَتَشَهَّدَ وَذَكَرَ شَأْنَ عَلِيٍّ، وَتَخَلُّفَهُ عَنِ الْبَيْعَةِ، وَعُذْرَهُ بِالَّذِي اعْتَذَرَ إِلَيْهِ، ثُمَّ اسْتَغْفَرَ، وَتَشَهَّدَ عَلِيٌّ فَعَظَّمَ حَقَّ أَبِي بَكْرٍ، وَحَدَّثَ أَنَّهُ لَمْ يَحْمِلْهُ عَلَى الَّذِي صَنَعَ نَفَاسَةً عَلَى أَبِي بَكْرٍ، وَلاَ إِنْكَارًا لِلَّذِي فَضَّلَهُ اللَّهُ بِهِ، وَلَكِنَّا نَرَى لَنَا فِي هَذَا الأَمْرِ نَصِيبًا، فَاسْتَبَدَّ عَلَيْنَا، فَوَجَدْنَا فِي أَنْفُسِنَا، فَسُرَّ بِذَلِكَ الْمُسْلِمُونَ وَقَالُوا أَصَبْتَ. وَكَانَ الْمُسْلِمُونَ إِلَى عَلِيٍّ قَرِيبًا، حِينَ رَاجَعَ الأَمْرَ الْمَعْرُوفَ.

Narrated Muhammad bin Al-Hanafiya: I asked my father (`Ali bin Abi Talib), "Who are the best people after Allah's Messenger ﷺ?" He said, "Abu Bakr." I asked, "Who then?" He said, "Then `Umar. " I was afraid he would say "Uthman, so I said, "Then you?" He said, "I am only an ordinary person. – Sahih Al-Bukhari 3671

حَدَّثَنَا مُحَمَّدُ بْنُ كَثِيرٍ، أَخْبَرَنَا سُفْيَانُ، حَدَّثَنَا جَامِعُ بْنُ أَبِي رَاشِدٍ، حَدَّثَنَا أَبُو يَعْلَى، عَنْ مُحَمَّدِ ابْنِ الْحَنَفِيَّةِ، قَالَ قُلْتُ لأَبِي أَىُّ النَّاسِ خَيْرٌ بَعْدَ رَسُولِ اللَّهِ صلى الله عليه وسلم قَالَ أَبُو بَكْرٍ. قُلْتُ ثُمَّ مَنْ قَالَ ثُمَّ عُمَرُ. وَخَشِيتُ أَنْ يَقُولَ عُثْمَانُ قُلْتُ ثُمَّ أَنْتَ قَالَ مَا أَنَا إِلاَّ رَجُلٌ مِنَ الْمُسْلِمِينَ

Narrated Ibn `Abbas: While I was standing amongst the people who were invoking Allah for `Umar bin Al-Khattab who was lying (dead) on his bed, a man behind me rested his elbows on my shoulder and said, "(O `Umar!) May Allah bestow His Mercy on you. I always hoped that Allah will keep you with your two companions, for I often heard Allah's Messenger ﷺ saying, "I, Abu Bakr and `Umar were (somewhere). I, Abu Bakr and `Umar did (something). I,

Abu Bakr and `Umar set out.' So I hoped that Allah will keep you with both of them." I turned back to see that the speaker was `Ali bin Abi Talib. – Sahih Al-Bukhari 3677
حَدَّثَنِي الْوَلِيدُ بْنُ صَالِحٍ، حَدَّثَنَا عِيسَى بْنُ يُونُسَ، حَدَّثَنَا عُمَرُ بْنُ سَعِيدِ بْنِ أَبِي الْحُسَيْنِ الْمَكِّيُّ، عَنِ ابْنِ أَبِي مُلَيْكَةَ، عَنِ ابْنِ عَبَّاسٍ ـ رضى الله عنهما ـ قَالَ إِنِّي لَوَاقِفٌ فِي قَوْمٍ، فَدَعَوُا اللَّهَ لِعُمَرَ بْنِ الْخَطَّابِ وَقَدْ وُضِعَ عَلَى سَرِيرِهِ، إِذَا رَجُلٌ مِنْ خَلْفِي قَدْ وَضَعَ مِرْفَقَهُ عَلَى مَنْكِبِي، يَقُولُ رَحِمَكَ اللَّهُ، إِنْ كُنْتُ لأَرْجُو أَنْ يَجْعَلَكَ اللَّهُ مَعَ صَاحِبَيْكَ، لأَنِّي كَثِيرًا مِمَّا كُنْتُ أَسْمَعُ رَسُولَ اللَّهِ صلى الله عليه وسلم يَقُولُ كُنْتُ وَأَبُو بَكْرٍ وَعُمَرُ، وَفَعَلْتُ وَأَبُو بَكْرٍ وَعُمَرُ، وَانْطَلَقْتُ وَأَبُو بَكْرٍ وَعُمَرُ. فَإِنْ كُنْتُ لأَرْجُو أَنْ يَجْعَلَكَ اللَّهُ مَعَهُمَا. فَالْتَفَتُّ فَإِذَا هُوَ عَلِيُّ بْنُ أَبِي طَالِبٍ.

Salama bin Al-Akwa` said: Allah's Messenger ﷺ said, "If a man and a woman agree (to marry temporarily), their marriage should last for three nights, and if they like to continue, they can do so; and if they want to separate, they can do so." I do not know whether that was only for us or for all the people in general. Abu `Abdullah (Al-Bukhari) said: `Ali made it clear that the Prophet said, "The Mut'a marriage has been cancelled (made unlawful). – Sahih Al-Bukhari 5119
وَقَالَ ابْنُ أَبِي ذِئْبٍ حَدَّثَنِي إِيَاسُ بْنُ سَلَمَةَ بْنِ الأَكْوَعِ، عَنْ أَبِيهِ، عَنْ رَسُولِ اللَّهِ صلى الله عليه وسلم " أَيُّمَا رَجُلٍ وَامْرَأَةٍ تَوَافَقَا فَعِشْرَةُ مَا بَيْنَهُمَا ثَلاَثُ لَيَالٍ فَإِنْ أَحَبَّا أَنْ يَتَزَايَدَا أَوْ يَتَتَارَكَا تَتَارَكَا ". فَمَا أَدْرِي أَشَىْءٌ كَانَ لَنَا خَاصَّةً أَمْ لِلنَّاسِ عَامَّةً. قَالَ أَبُو عَبْدِ اللَّهِ وَبَيَّنَهُ عَلِيٌّ عَنِ النَّبِيِّ صلى الله عليه وسلم أَنَّهُ مَنْسُوخٌ.

Narrated Malik bin Aus bin Al-Hadathan: Once I set out to visit `Umar (bin Al-Khattab). (While I was sitting there with him his gate-keeper, Yarfa, came and said, "Uthman `AbdurRahman (bin `Auf), Az-Zubair and Sa`d (bin Abi Waqqas) are seeking permission (to meet you)." `Umar said, "Yes. So he admitted them and they entered, greeted, and sat down. After a short while Yarfa came again and said to `Umar 'Shall I admit `Ali and `Abbas?" `Umar said, "Yes." He admitted them and when they entered, they greeted and sat down. `Abbas said, "O Chief of the Believers! Judge between me and this (`Ali)." The group, `Uthman and his companions Sa`d, 'O Chief of the Believers! Judge between them and relieve one from the other." `Umar said. Wait! I beseech you by Allah, by Whose permission both the Heaven and the Earth stand fast ! Do you know that Allah's Messenger ﷺ said. 'We (Apostles) do not bequeath anything to our heirs, but whatever we leave is to be given in charity.' And by that Allah's Messenger ﷺ meant himself?" The group said, "He did say so." `Umar then turned towards 'All and `Abbas and said. "I beseech you both by Allah, do you know that Allah's Messenger ﷺ said that?" They said, 'Yes " `Umar said, "Now, let me talk to you about this matter. Allah favored His Apostle with something of this property (war booty) which He did not give to anybody else. And Allah said:-- 'And what Allah has bestowed on His Apostle (as Fai Booty) from them for which you made no expedition with either cavalry or camelry . . . Allah is Able to do all things.' (59.6) So this property was especially granted to Allah's Messenger ﷺ. But by Allah he neither withheld it from you, nor did he keep it for himself and deprive you of it, but he gave it all to you and distributed it among you till only this remained out of it. And out of this property Allah's Messenger ﷺ used to provide his family with their yearly needs, and whatever remained, he would spend where Allah's Property (the revenues of Zakat) used to be spent. Allah's Messenger ﷺ kept on acting like this throughout his lifetime. Now I beseech you by Allah, do you know that?" They said, "Yes." Then `Umar said to `Ali and `Abbas, "I beseech you by Allah, do you both know that?" They said, "Yes." `Umar added, "When Allah had taken His Apostle unto Him, Abu Bakr said, 'I am the successor of Allah's Messenger ﷺ. So he took charge of that property and did with it the same what Allah's Messenger ﷺ used to do, and both of you knew all about it then." Then `Umar turned towards `Ali and `Abbas and said, "You both claim that Abu- Bakr was so-and-so! But Allah knows that he was honest, sincere, pious and right (in that matter). Then Allah caused Abu Bakr to die, and I said, 'I am the successor of Allah's Messenger ﷺ and Abu Bakr.' So I kept this property in my possession for the first two years of my rule, and I used to do the same with it as Allah's Messenger ﷺ and Abu Bakr used to do. Later both of you (`Ali and `Abbas) came to me with the same claim and the same problem. (O `Abbas!) You came to me demanding your share from (the inheritance of) the son of your brother, and he (`Ali) came to me demanding his wives share from (the inheritance of) her father. So I said to you, 'If you wish I will hand over this property to you, on condition that you both promise me before Allah that you will manage it in the same way as Allah's Messenger ﷺ and Abu Bakr did, and as I have done since the beginning of my rule; otherwise you should not speak to me about it.' So you both said, 'Hand over this property to us on this condition.' And on this condition I handed it over to you. I beseech you by Allah, did I hand it over to them on that condition?" The group said, "Yes." `Umar then faced `Ali and `Abbas and said, "I beseech you both by Allah, did I hand it over to you both on that condition?" They both said, "Yes." `Umar added, "Do you want me now to give a decision other than that? By Him with Whose permission (order) both the Heaven and the Earth stand fast, I will never give any decision other than that till the Hour is established! But if you are unable to manage it (that property), then return it to me and I will be sufficient for it on your behalf . ". – Sahih Al-Bukhari 5358

حَدَّثَنَا سَعِيدُ بْنُ عُفَيْرٍ، قَالَ حَدَّثَنِي اللَّيْثُ، قَالَ حَدَّثَنِي عُقَيْلٌ، عَنِ ابْنِ شِهَابٍ، قَالَ أَخْبَرَنِي مَالِكُ بْنُ أَوْسِ بْنِ الْحَدَثَانِ، وَكَانَ، مُحَمَّدُ بْنُ جُبَيْرِ بْنِ مُطْعِمٍ ذَكَرَ لِي ذِكْرًا مِنْ حَدِيثِهِ، فَانْطَلَقْتُ حَتَّى دَخَلْتُ عَلَى مَالِكِ بْنِ أَوْسٍ فَسَأَلْتُهُ فَقَالَ مَالِكٌ انْطَلَقْتُ حَتَّى أَدْخُلَ عَلَى عُمَرَ، إِذْ أَتَاهُ حَاجِبُهُ يَرْفَا فَقَالَ هَلْ لَكَ فِي عُثْمَانَ وَعَبْدِ الرَّحْمَنِ وَالزُّبَيْرِ وَسَعْدٍ يَسْتَأْذِنُونَ قَالَ نَعَمْ. فَأَذِنَ لَهُمْ ـ قَالَ ـ فَدَخَلُوا وَسَلَّمُوا فَجَلَسُوا، ثُمَّ لَبِثَ يَرْفَا قَلِيلاً فَقَالَ لِعُمَرَ هَلْ لَكَ فِي عَلِيٍّ وَعَبَّاسٍ قَالَ نَعَمْ. فَأَذِنَ لَهُمَا، فَلَمَّا دَخَلاَ سَلَّمَا وَجَلَسَا، فَقَالَ عَبَّاسٌ يَا أَمِيرَ الْمُؤْمِنِينَ اقْضِ بَيْنِي وَبَيْنَ هَذَا. فَقَالَ الرَّهْطُ عُثْمَانُ وَأَصْحَابُهُ يَا أَمِيرَ الْمُؤْمِنِينَ اقْضِ بَيْنَهُمَا، وَأَرِحْ أَحَدَهُمَا مِنَ الآخَرِ. فَقَالَ عُمَرُ اتَّئِدُوا أَنْشُدُكُمْ بِاللَّهِ الَّذِي بِهِ تَقُومُ السَّمَاءُ وَالأَرْضُ، هَلْ تَعْلَمُونَ أَنَّ رَسُولَ اللَّهِ صلى الله عليه وسلم قَالَ " لاَ نُورَثُ مَا تَرَكْنَا صَدَقَةٌ ". يُرِيدُ رَسُولُ اللَّهِ صلى الله عليه وسلم نَفْسَهُ. قَالَ الرَّهْطُ قَدْ قَالَ ذَلِكَ. فَأَقْبَلَ عُمَرُ عَلَى عَلِيٍّ وَعَبَّاسٍ فَقَالَ أَنْشُدُكُمَا بِاللَّهِ هَلْ تَعْلَمَانِ أَنَّ رَسُولَ اللَّهِ صلى الله عليه وسلم قَالَ ذَلِكَ قَالاَ قَدْ قَالَ ذَلِكَ. قَالَ عُمَرُ فَإِنِّي أُحَدِّثُكُمْ عَنْ هَذَا الأَمْرِ، إِنَّ اللَّهَ كَانَ خَصَّ رَسُولَهُ صلى الله عليه وسلم فِي هَذَا الْمَالِ بِشَىْءٍ لَمْ يُعْطِهِ أَحَدًا غَيْرَهُ، قَالَ اللَّهُ {مَا أَفَاءَ اللَّهُ عَلَى رَسُولِهِ مِنْهُمْ فَمَا أَوْجَفْتُمْ عَلَيْهِ مِنْ خَيْلٍ} إِلَى قَوْلِهِ {قَدِيرٌ}. فَكَانَتْ هَذِهِ خَالِصَةً لِرَسُولِ اللَّهِ صلى الله عليه وسلم وَاللَّهِ مَا احْتَازَهَا دُونَكُمْ وَلاَ اسْتَأْثَرَ بِهَا عَلَيْكُمْ، لَقَدْ أَعْطَاكُمُوهَا وَبَثَّهَا فِيكُمْ، حَتَّى بَقِيَ مِنْهَا هَذَا الْمَالُ، فَكَانَ رَسُولُ اللَّهِ صلى الله عليه وسلم يُنْفِقُ عَلَى أَهْلِهِ نَفَقَةَ سَنَتِهِمْ مِنْ هَذَا الْمَالِ، ثُمَّ يَأْخُذُ مَا بَقِيَ، فَيَجْعَلُهُ مَجْعَلَ مَالِ اللَّهِ، فَعَمِلَ بِذَلِكَ رَسُولُ اللَّهِ صلى الله عليه وسلم حَيَاتَهُ، أَنْشُدُكُمْ بِاللَّهِ، هَلْ تَعْلَمُونَ ذَلِكَ قَالُوا نَعَمْ. قَالَ لِعَلِيٍّ وَعَبَّاسٍ أَنْشُدُكُمَا بِاللَّهِ هَلْ تَعْلَمَانِ ذَلِكَ قَالاَ نَعَمْ. ثُمَّ تَوَفَّى اللَّهُ نَبِيَّهُ صلى الله عليه وسلم فَقَالَ أَبُو بَكْرٍ أَنَا وَلِيُّ رَسُولِ اللَّهِ صلى الله عليه وسلم فَقَبَضَهَا أَبُو بَكْرٍ يَعْمَلُ فِيهَا بِمَا عَمِلَ بِهِ فِيهَا رَسُولُ اللَّهِ صلى الله عليه وسلم وَأَنْتُمَا حِينَئِذٍ ـ وَأَقْبَلَ عَلَى عَلِيٍّ وَعَبَّاسٍ ـ تَزْعُمَانِ أَنَّ أَبَا بَكْرٍ كَذَا وَكَذَا، وَاللَّهُ يَعْلَمُ أَنَّهُ فِيهَا صَادِقٌ بَارٌّ رَاشِدٌ تَابِعٌ لِلْحَقِّ، ثُمَّ تَوَفَّى اللَّهُ أَبَا بَكْرٍ فَقُلْتُ أَنَا وَلِيُّ رَسُولِ اللَّهِ صلى الله عليه وسلم وَأَبِي بَكْرٍ، فَقَبَضْتُهَا سَنَتَيْنِ أَعْمَلُ فِيهَا بِمَا عَمِلَ رَسُولُ اللَّهِ صلى الله عليه وسلم وَأَبُو بَكْرٍ، ثُمَّ جِئْتُمَانِي وَكَلِمَتُكُمَا وَاحِدَةٌ وَأَمْرُكُمَا جَمِيعٌ، جِئْتَنِي تَسْأَلُنِي نَصِيبَكَ مِنِ ابْنِ أَخِيكَ، وَأَتَى هَذَا يَسْأَلُنِي نَصِيبَ امْرَأَتِهِ مِنْ أَبِيهَا، فَقُلْتُ إِنْ شِئْتُمَا دَفَعْتُهُ إِلَيْكُمَا عَلَى أَنَّ عَلَيْكُمَا عَهْدَ اللَّهِ وَمِيثَاقَهُ لَتَعْمَلاَنِ فِيهَا بِمَا عَمِلَ بِهِ رَسُولُ اللَّهِ صلى الله عليه وسلم وَبِمَا عَمِلَ بِهِ فِيهَا أَبُو بَكْرٍ، وَبِمَا عَمِلْتُ بِهِ فِيهَا، مُنْذُ وُلِّيتُهَا، وَإِلاَّ فَلاَ تُكَلِّمَانِي فِيهَا فَقُلْتُمَا ادْفَعْهَا إِلَيْنَا بِذَلِكَ. فَدَفَعْتُهَا إِلَيْكُمَا بِذَلِكَ، أَنْشُدُكُمْ بِاللَّهِ هَلْ دَفَعْتُهَا إِلَيْهِمَا بِذَلِكَ فَقَالَ الرَّهْطُ نَعَمْ. قَالَ فَأَقْبَلَ عَلَى عَلِيٍّ وَعَبَّاسٍ فَقَالَ أَنْشُدُكُمَا بِاللَّهِ هَلْ دَفَعْتُهَا إِلَيْكُمَا بِذَلِكَ قَالاَ نَعَمْ. قَالَ أَفَتَلْتَمِسَانِ مِنِّي قَضَاءً غَيْرَ ذَلِكَ، فَوَالَّذِي بِإِذْنِهِ تَقُومُ السَّمَاءُ وَالأَرْضُ لاَ أَقْضِي فِيهَا قَضَاءً غَيْرَ ذَلِكَ، حَتَّى تَقُومَ السَّاعَةُ، فَإِنْ عَجَزْتُمَا عَنْهَا فَادْفَعَاهَا فَأَنَا أَكْفِيكُمَاهَا

Narrated Aisha: (the wife of the Prophet) "Whenever Allah's Messenger ﷺ intended to go on a journey, he would draw lots amongst his wives and would take with him the one upon whom the lot fell. During a Ghazwa of his, he drew lots amongst us and the lot fell upon me, and I proceeded with him after Allah had decreed the use of the veil by women. I was carried in a Howdah (on the camel) and dismounted while still in it. When Allah's Messenger ﷺ was through with his Ghazwa and returned home, and we approached the city of Medina, Allah's Messenger ﷺ ordered us to proceed at night. When the order of setting off was given, I walked till I was past the army to answer the call of nature. After finishing I returned (to the camp) to depart (with the others) and suddenly realized that my necklace over my chest was missing. So, I returned to look for it and was delayed because of that. The people who used to carry me on the camel, came to my Howdah and put it on the back of the camel, thinking that I was in it, as, at that time, women were light in weight, and thin and lean, and did not use to eat much. So, those people did not feel the difference in the heaviness of the Howdah while lifting it, and they put it over the camel. At that time I was a young lady. They set the camel moving and proceeded on. I found my necklace after the army had gone, and came to their camp to find nobody. So, I went to the place where I used to stay, thinking that they would discover my absence and come back in my search. While in that state, I felt sleepy and slept. Safwan bin Mu'attal As-Sulami Adh-Dhakwani was behind the army and reached my abode in the morning. When he saw a sleeping person, he came to me, and he used to see me before veiling. So, I got up when I heard him saying, "Inna lil-lah-wa inn a ilaihi rajiun (We are for Allah, and we will return to Him)." He made his camel knell down. He got down from his camel, and put his leg on the front legs of the camel and then I rode and sat over it. Safwan set out walking, leading the camel by the rope till we reached the army who had halted to take rest at midday. Then whoever was meant for destruction, fell into destruction, (some people accused me falsely) and the leader of the false accusers was `Abdullah bin Ubai bin Salul. After that we returned to Medina, and I became ill for one month while the people were spreading the forged statements of the false accusers. I was feeling during my ailment as if I were not receiving the usual kindness from the Prophetﷺ which I used to receive from him when I got sick. But he would come, greet and say, 'How is that (girl)?' I did not know anything of what was going on till I recovered from my ailment and went out with Um Mistah to the Manasi where we used to answer the call of nature, and we used not to go to answer the call of nature except from night to night and that was before we had lavatories near to our houses. And this habit of ours was similar to the habit of the old 'Arabs in the open country (or away from houses). So. I and Um Mistah bint Ruhm went out walking. Um Mistah stumbled because of her long dress and on that she said, 'Let Mistah be ruined.' I said, 'You are saying a bad word. Why are you abusing a man who took part in (the battle of) Badr?' She said, 'O Hanata (you there) didn't you hear what they said?' Then she told me the rumors of the false accusers. My sickness was aggravated, and when I returned home, Allah's Messengerﷺ came to me, and after greeting he said, 'How is that (girl)?' I requested him to allow me to go to my parents. I wanted then to be sure of the news through them I Allah's Messengerﷺ allowed me, and I went to my parents and asked my mother, 'What are the people talking about?' She said, 'O my daughter! Don't worry much about this matter. By Allah, never is there a charming woman loved by her husband who has other wives, but the women would forge false news about her.' I said, 'Glorified be Allah! Are the people really taking of this matter?' That night I kept on weeping and could not sleep till morning. In the morning Allah's Messengerﷺ called `Ali bin Abu Talib and Usama bin Zaid when he saw the Divine Inspiration delayed, to consul them about divorcing his wife (i.e. `Aisha). Usama bin Zaid said what he knew of the good reputation of his wives and added, 'O Allah's Messengerﷺ! Keep you wife, for, by Allah, we know nothing about her but good.' `Ali bin Abu Talib said, 'O Allah's Messengerﷺ! Allah has no imposed restrictions on you, and there are many women other than she, yet you may ask the woman-servant who will tell you the truth.' On that Allah's Messengerﷺ called Barirah and said, 'O Barirah. Did you ever see anything which roused your suspicions about her?' Barirah said, 'No, by Allah Who has sent you with the Truth, I have never seen in her anything faulty except that she is a girl of immature age, who sometimes sleeps and leaves the dough for the goats to eat.' On that day Allah's

Messenger‎ﷺ ascended the pulpit and requested that somebody support him in punishing `Abdullah bin Ubai bin Salul. Allah's Apostle said, 'Who will support me to punish that person (`Abdullah bin Ubai bin Salul) who has hurt me by slandering the reputation of my family? By Allah, I know nothing about my family but good, and they have accused a person about whom I know nothing except good, and he never entered my house except in my company.' Sa`d bin Mu`adh got up and said, 'O Allah's Messengerﷺ! By Allah, I will relieve you from him. If that man is from the tribe of the Aus, then we will chop his head off, and if he is from our brothers, the Khazraj, then order us, and we will fulfill your order.' On that Sa`d bin 'Ubada, the chief of the Khazraj and before this incident, he had been a pious man, got up, motivated by his zeal for his tribe and said, 'By Allah, you have told a lie; you cannot kill him, and you will never be able to kill him.' On that Usaid bin Al-Hadir got up and said (to Sa`d bin 'Ubada), 'By Allah! You are a liar. By Allah, we will kill him; and you are a hypocrite, defending the hypocrites.' On this the two tribes of Aus and Khazraj got excited and were about to fight each other, while Allah's Messengerﷺ was standing on the pulpit. He got down and quieted them till they became silent and he kept quiet. On that day I kept on weeping so much so that neither did my tears stop, nor could I sleep. In the morning my parents were with me and I had wept for two nights and a day, till I thought my liver would burst from weeping. While they were sitting with me and I was weeping, an Ansari woman asked my permission to enter, and I allowed her to come in. She sat down and started weeping with me. While we were in this state, Allah's Messengerﷺ came and sat down and he had never sat with me since the day they forged the accusation. No revelation regarding my case came to him for a month. He recited Tashah-hud (i.e. None has the right to be worshipped but Allah and Muhammad is His Apostle) and then said, 'O `Aisha! I have been informed such-and-such about you; if you are innocent, then Allah will soon reveal your Innocence, and if you have committed a sin, then repent to Allah and ask Him to forgive you, for when a person confesses his sin and asks Allah for forgiveness, Allah accepts his repentance.' When Allah's Messengerﷺ finished his speech my tears ceased completely and there remained not even a single drop of it. I requested my father to reply to Allah's Messengerﷺ on my behalf. My father said, By Allah, I do not know what to say to Allah's Messengerﷺ. I said to my mother, 'Talk to Allah's Messengerﷺ on my behalf.' She said, 'By Allah, I do not know what to say to Allah's Apostle. I was a young girl and did not have much knowledge of the Qur'an. I said. 'I know, by Allah, that you have listened to what people are saying and that has been planted in your minds and you have taken it as a truth. Now, if I told you that I am innocent and Allah knows that I am innocent, you would not believe me and if I confessed to you falsely that I am guilty, and Allah knows that I am innocent you would believe me. By Allah, I don't compare my situation with you except to the situation of Joseph's father (i.e. Jacob) who said, 'So (for me) patience is most fitting against that which you assert and it is Allah (Alone) whose help can be sought.' Then I turned to the other side of my bed hoping that Allah would prove my innocence. By Allah I never thought that Allah would reveal Divine Inspiration in my case, as I considered myself too inferior to be talked of in the Holy Qur'an. I had hoped that Allah's Messengerﷺ might have a dream in which Allah would prove my innocence. By Allah, Allah's Apostle had not got up and nobody had left the house before the Divine Inspiration came to Allah's Apostle. So, there overtook him the same state which used to overtake him, (when he used to have, on being inspired divinely). He was sweating so much so that the drops of the sweat were dropping like pearls though it was a (cold) wintry day. When that state of Allah's Messengerﷺ was over, he was smiling and the first word he said, `Aisha! Thank Allah, for Allah has declared your innocence.' My mother told me to go to Allah's Messengerﷺ. I replied, 'By Allah I will not go to him and will not thank but Allah.' So Allah revealed: "Verily! They who spread the slander are a gang among you . . ." (24.11) When Allah gave the declaration of my Innocence, Abu Bakr, who used to provide for Mistah bin Uthatha for he was his relative, said, 'By Allah, I will never provide Mistah with anything because of what he said about Aisha.' But Allah later revealed: -- "And let not those who are good and wealthy among you swear not to help their kinsmen, those in need and those who left their homes in Allah's Cause. Let them forgive and overlook. Do you not wish that Allah should forgive you? Verily! Allah is Oft-forgiving, Most Merciful." (24.22) After that Abu Bakr said, 'Yes ! By Allah! I like that Allah should forgive me,' and resumed helping Mistah whom he used to help before. Allah's Messenger ﷺ also asked Zainab bint Jahsh (i.e. the Prophet's wife about me saying, 'What do you know and what did you see?' She replied, 'O Allah's Messenger ﷺ! I refrain to claim hearing or seeing what I have not heard or seen. By Allah, I know nothing except goodness about Aisha." Aisha further added "Zainab was competing with me (in her beauty and the Prophet's love), yet Allah protected her (from being malicious), for she had piety.". – Sahih Al-Bukhari 2661

حَدَّثَنَا أَبُو الرَّبِيعِ، سُلَيْمَانُ بْنُ دَاوُدَ وَأَفْهَمَنِي بَعْضَهُ أَحْمَدُ حَدَّثَنَا فُلَيْحُ بْنُ سُلَيْمَانَ، عَنِ ابْنِ شِهَابٍ الزُّهْرِيِّ، عَنْ عُرْوَةَ بْنِ الزُّبَيْرِ، وَسَعِيدِ بْنِ الْمُسَيَّبِ، وَعَلْقَمَةَ بْنِ وَقَّاصٍ اللَّيْثِيِّ، وَعُبَيْدِ اللَّهِ بْنِ عَبْدِ اللَّهِ بْنِ عُتْبَةَ، عَنْ عَائِشَةَ ـ رضى الله عنها ـ زَوْجِ النَّبِيِّ صلى الله عليه وسلم حِينَ قَالَ لَهَا أَهْلُ الإِفْكِ مَا قَالُوا، فَبَرَّأَهَا اللَّهُ مِنْهُ، قَالَ الزُّهْرِيُّ، وَكُلُّهُمْ حَدَّثَنِي طَائِفَةً مِنْ حَدِيثِهَا وَبَعْضُهُمْ أَوْعَى مِنْ بَعْضٍ، وَأَثْبَتُ لَهُ اقْتِصَاصًا، وَقَدْ وَعَيْتُ عَنْ كُلِّ وَاحِدٍ مِنْهُمُ الْحَدِيثَ الَّذِي حَدَّثَنِي عَنْ عَائِشَةَ، وَبَعْضُ حَدِيثِهِمْ يُصَدِّقُ بَعْضًا. زَعَمُوا أَنَّ عَائِشَةَ قَالَتْ كَانَ رَسُولُ اللَّهِ صلى الله عليه وسلم إِذَا أَرَادَ أَنْ يَخْرُجَ سَفَرًا أَقْرَعَ بَيْنَ أَزْوَاجِهِ، فَأَيَّتُهُنَّ خَرَجَ سَهْمُهَا خَرَجَ بِهَا مَعَهُ، فَأَقْرَعَ بَيْنَنَا فِي غَزَاةٍ غَزَاهَا فَخَرَجَ سَهْمِي، فَخَرَجْتُ مَعَهُ بَعْدَ مَا أُنْزِلَ الْحِجَابُ، فَأَنَا أُحْمَلُ فِي هَوْدَجٍ وَأُنْزَلُ فِيهِ، فَسِرْنَا حَتَّى إِذَا فَرَغَ رَسُولُ اللَّهِ صلى الله عليه وسلم مِنْ غَزْوَتِهِ تِلْكَ، وَقَفَلَ وَدَنَوْنَا مِنَ الْمَدِينَةِ، آذَنَ لَيْلَةً بِالرَّحِيلِ، فَقُمْتُ حِينَ آذَنُوا بِالرَّحِيلِ، فَمَشَيْتُ حَتَّى جَاوَزْتُ الْجَيْشَ، فَلَمَّا قَضَيْتُ شَأْنِي أَقْبَلْتُ إِلَى الرَّحْلِ، فَلَمَسْتُ صَدْرِي، فَإِذَا عِقْدٌ لِي مِنْ جَزْعِ أَظْفَارٍ قَدِ انْقَطَعَ، فَرَجَعْتُ فَالْتَمَسْتُ عِقْدِي، فَحَبَسَنِي ابْتِغَاؤُهُ، فَأَقْبَلَ الَّذِينَ يَرْحَلُونَ لِي، فَاحْتَمَلُوا هَوْدَجِي فَرَحَلُوهُ عَلَى بَعِيرِي الَّذِي كُنْتُ أَرْكَبُ، وَهُمْ يَحْسِبُونَ أَنِّي فِيهِ، وَكَانَ النِّسَاءُ إِذْ ذَاكَ خِفَافًا لَمْ يَثْقُلْنَ وَلَمْ يَغْشَهُنَّ اللَّحْمُ، وَإِنَّمَا يَأْكُلْنَ الْعُلْقَةَ مِنَ الطَّعَامِ، فَلَمْ يَسْتَنْكِرِ الْقَوْمُ حِينَ رَفَعُوهُ ثِقَلَ الْهَوْدَجِ فَاحْتَمَلُوهُ وَكُنْتُ جَارِيَةً حَدِيثَةَ السِّنِّ، فَبَعَثُوا الْجَمَلَ وَسَارُوا، فَوَجَدْتُ عِقْدِي بَعْدَ مَا اسْتَمَرَّ الْجَيْشُ، فَجِئْتُ مَنْزِلَهُمْ وَلَيْسَ فِيهِ أَحَدٌ، فَأَمَمْتُ مَنْزِلِي الَّذِي كُنْتُ بِهِ فَظَنَنْتُ أَنَّهُمْ سَيَفْقِدُونِي فَيَرْجِعُونَ إِلَىَّ، فَبَيْنَا أَنَا جَالِسَةٌ غَلَبَتْنِي عَيْنَاىَ فَنِمْتُ، وَكَانَ صَفْوَانُ بْنُ الْمُعَطَّلِ السُّلَمِيُّ ثُمَّ الذَّكْوَانِيُّ مِنْ وَرَاءِ الْجَيْشِ، فَأَصْبَحَ عِنْدَ مَنْزِلِي فَرَأَى سَوَادَ إِنْسَانٍ نَائِمٍ فَأَتَانِي، وَكَانَ يَرَانِي قَبْلَ الْحِجَابِ فَاسْتَيْقَظْتُ بِاسْتِرْجَاعِهِ حِينَ أَنَاخَ رَاحِلَتَهُ، فَوَطِئَ يَدَهَا فَرَكِبْتُهَا فَانْطَلَقَ يَقُودُ بِي الرَّاحِلَةَ، حَتَّى أَتَيْنَا الْجَيْشَ بَعْدَ مَا نَزَلُوا مُعَرِّسِينَ فِي نَحْرِ الظَّهِيرَةِ، فَهَلَكَ مَنْ هَلَكَ، وَكَانَ الَّذِي تَوَلَّى الإِفْكَ عَبْدُ اللَّهِ بْنُ أُبَىٍّ ابْنُ سَلُولَ، فَقَدِمْنَا الْمَدِينَةَ فَاشْتَكَيْتُ بِهَا شَهْرًا، يُفِيضُونَ مِنْ قَوْلِ أَصْحَابِ الإِفْكِ، وَيَرِيبُنِي فِي وَجَعِي أَنِّي لاَ أَرَى مِنَ النَّبِيِّ صلى الله عليه وسلم اللُّطْفَ الَّذِي كُنْتُ أَرَى مِنْهُ حِينَ أَمْرَضُ، إِنَّمَا يَدْخُلُ فَيُسَلِّمُ ثُمَّ يَقُولُ " كَيْفَ تِيكُمْ ". لاَ أَشْعُرُ بِشَىْءٍ مِنْ ذَلِكَ حَتَّى نَقَهْتُ، فَخَرَجْتُ أَنَا وَأُمُّ مِسْطَحٍ قِبَلَ الْمَنَاصِعِ مُتَبَرَّزُنَا، لاَ نَخْرُجُ إِلاَّ لَيْلاً إِلَى لَيْلٍ، وَذَلِكَ قَبْلَ أَنْ نَتَّخِذَ الْكُنُفَ قَرِيبًا مِنْ بُيُوتِنَا، وَأَمْرُنَا أَمْرُ الْعَرَبِ الأُوَلِ فِي الْبَرِّيَّةِ أَوْ فِي التَّنَزُّهِ، فَأَقْبَلْتُ أَنَا وَأُمُّ مِسْطَحٍ بِنْتُ أَبِي رُهْمٍ نَمْشِي، فَعَثُرَتْ فِي مِرْطِهَا فَقَالَتْ تَعِسَ مِسْطَحٌ، فَقُلْتُ لَهَا بِئْسَ مَا قُلْتِ، أَتَسُبِّينَ رَجُلاً شَهِدَ بَدْرًا فَقَالَتْ يَا هَنْتَاهْ أَلَمْ تَسْمَعِي مَا قَالُوا فَأَخْبَرَتْنِي بِقَوْلِ أَهْلِ الإِفْكِ، فَازْدَدْتُ مَرَضًا إِلَى مَرَضِي، فَلَمَّا رَجَعْتُ إِلَى بَيْتِي دَخَلَ عَلَىَّ رَسُولُ اللَّهِ صلى الله عليه وسلم فَسَلَّمَ فَقَالَ " كَيْفَ تِيكُمْ ". فَقُلْتُ ائْذَنْ لِي إِلَى أَبَوَىَّ. قَالَتْ وَأَنَا حِينَئِذٍ أُرِيدُ أَنْ أَسْتَيْقِنَ الْخَبَرَ مِنْ قِبَلِهِمَا، فَأَذِنَ لِي رَسُولُ اللَّهِ صلى الله عليه وسلم فَأَتَيْتُ أَبَوَىَّ فَقُلْتُ لأُمِّي مَا يَتَحَدَّثُ بِهِ النَّاسُ فَقَالَتْ يَا بُنَيَّةُ هَوِّنِي عَلَى نَفْسِكِ الشَّأْنَ، فَوَاللَّهِ لَقَلَّمَا كَانَتِ امْرَأَةٌ قَطُّ وَضِيئَةٌ عِنْدَ رَجُلٍ يُحِبُّهَا وَلَهَا ضَرَائِرُ إِلاَّ أَكْثَرْنَ عَلَيْهَا. فَقُلْتُ سُبْحَانَ اللَّهِ وَلَقَدْ يَتَحَدَّثُ النَّاسُ بِهَذَا قَالَتْ فَبِتُّ تِلْكَ اللَّيْلَةَ حَتَّى أَصْبَحْتُ لاَ يَرْقَأُ لِي دَمْعٌ وَلاَ أَكْتَحِلُ بِنَوْمٍ، ثُمَّ أَصْبَحْتُ فَدَعَا رَسُولُ اللَّهِ صلى الله عليه وسلم عَلِيَّ بْنَ أَبِي طَالِبٍ وَأُسَامَةَ بْنَ زَيْدٍ حِينَ اسْتَلْبَثَ الْوَحْىُ، يَسْتَشِيرُهُمَا فِي فِرَاقِ أَهْلِهِ، فَأَمَّا أُسَامَةُ فَأَشَارَ عَلَيْهِ بِالَّذِي يَعْلَمُ فِي نَفْسِهِ مِنَ الْوُدِّ لَهُمْ، فَقَالَ أُسَامَةُ أَهْلُكَ يَا رَسُولَ اللَّهِ وَلاَ نَعْلَمُ وَاللَّهِ إِلاَّ خَيْرًا، وَأَمَّا عَلِيُّ بْنُ أَبِي طَالِبٍ فَقَالَ يَا رَسُولَ اللَّهِ لَمْ يُضَيِّقِ اللَّهُ عَلَيْكَ وَالنِّسَاءُ سِوَاهَا كَثِيرٌ، وَسَلِ الْجَارِيَةَ تَصْدُقْكَ. فَدَعَا رَسُولُ اللَّهِ صلى الله عليه وسلم بَرِيرَةَ فَقَالَ " يَا بَرِيرَةُ هَلْ رَأَيْتِ فِيهَا شَيْئًا يَرِيبُكِ ". فَقَالَتْ بَرِيرَةُ لاَ وَالَّذِي بَعَثَكَ بِالْحَقِّ، إِنْ رَأَيْتُ مِنْهَا أَمْرًا أَغْمِصُهُ عَلَيْهَا أَكْثَرَ مِنْ أَنَّهَا جَارِيَةٌ حَدِيثَةُ السِّنِّ تَنَامُ عَنِ الْعَجِينِ فَتَأْتِي الدَّاجِنُ فَتَأْكُلُهُ. فَقَامَ رَسُولُ اللَّهِ صلى الله عليه وسلم مِنْ يَوْمِهِ، فَاسْتَعْذَرَ مِنْ عَبْدِ اللَّهِ بْنِ أُبَىٍّ ابْنِ سَلُولَ فَقَالَ رَسُولُ اللَّهِ صلى الله عليه وسلم " مَنْ يَعْذِرُنِي مِنْ رَجُلٍ بَلَغَنِي أَذَاهُ فِي أَهْلِي، فَوَاللَّهِ مَا عَلِمْتُ عَلَى أَهْلِي إِلاَّ خَيْرًا، وَقَدْ ذَكَرُوا رَجُلاً مَا عَلِمْتُ عَلَيْهِ إِلاَّ خَيْرًا، وَمَا كَانَ يَدْخُلُ عَلَى أَهْلِي إِلاَّ مَعِي ". فَقَامَ سَعْدُ بْنُ مُعَاذٍ فَقَالَ يَا رَسُولَ اللَّهِ أَنَا وَاللَّهِ أَعْذِرُكَ مِنْهُ، إِنْ كَانَ مِنَ الأَوْسِ ضَرَبْنَا عُنُقَهُ، وَإِنْ كَانَ مِنْ إِخْوَانِنَا مِنَ الْخَزْرَجِ أَمَرْتَنَا فَفَعَلْنَا فِيهِ أَمْرَكَ. فَقَامَ سَعْدُ بْنُ عُبَادَةَ وَهُوَ

سَيِّدُ الْخَزْرَجِ، وَكَانَ قَبْلَ ذَلِكَ رَجُلاً صَالِحًا وَلَكِنِ احْتَمَلَتْهُ الْحَمِيَّةُ فَقَالَ كَذَبْتَ لَعَمْرُ اللَّهِ، لاَ تَقْتُلُهُ وَلاَ تَقْدِرُ عَلَى ذَلِكَ، فَقَامَ أُسَيْدُ بْنُ الْحُضَيْرِ فَقَالَ كَذَبْتَ لَعَمْرُ اللَّهِ، وَاللَّهِ لَنَقْتُلَنَّهُ، فَإِنَّكَ مُنَافِقٌ تُجَادِلُ عَنِ الْمُنَافِقِينَ. فَثَارَ الْحَيَّانِ الأَوْسُ وَالْخَزْرَجُ حَتَّى هَمُّوا، وَرَسُولُ اللَّهِ صلى الله عليه وسلم عَلَى الْمِنْبَرِ فَنَزَلَ فَخَفَّضَهُمْ حَتَّى سَكَتُوا وَسَكَتَ، وَبَكَيْتُ يَوْمِي لاَ يَرْقَأُ لِي دَمْعٌ وَلاَ أَكْتَحِلُ بِنَوْمٍ، فَأَصْبَحَ عِنْدِي أَبَوَاىَ، قَدْ بَكَيْتُ لَيْلَتَيْنِ وَيَوْمًا حَتَّى أَظُنُّ أَنَّ الْبُكَاءَ فَالِقٌ كَبِدِي ـ قَالَتْ ـ فَبَيْنَا هُمَا جَالِسَانِ عِنْدِي وَأَنَا أَبْكِي إِذِ اسْتَأْذَنَتِ امْرَأَةٌ مِنَ الأَنْصَارِ فَأَذِنْتُ لَهَا، فَجَلَسَتْ تَبْكِي مَعِي، فَبَيْنَا نَحْنُ كَذَلِكَ إِذْ دَخَلَ رَسُولُ اللَّهِ صلى الله عليه وسلم فَجَلَسَ، وَلَمْ يَجْلِسْ عِنْدِي مِنْ يَوْمِ قِيلَ فِيَّ مَا قِيلَ قَبْلَهَا، وَقَدْ مَكُثَ شَهْرًا لاَ يُوحَى إِلَيْهِ فِي شَأْنِي شَىْءٌ ـ قَالَتْ ـ فَتَشَهَّدَ ثُمَّ قَالَ " يَا عَائِشَةُ فَإِنَّهُ بَلَغَنِي عَنْكِ كَذَا وَكَذَا، فَإِنْ كُنْتِ بَرِيئَةً فَسَيُبَرِّئُكِ اللَّهُ، وَإِنْ كُنْتِ أَلْمَمْتِ فَاسْتَغْفِرِي اللَّهَ وَتُوبِي إِلَيْهِ، فَإِنَّ الْعَبْدَ إِذَا اعْتَرَفَ بِذَنْبِهِ ثُمَّ تَابَ تَابَ اللَّهُ عَلَيْهِ ". فَلَمَّا قَضَى رَسُولُ اللَّهِ صلى الله عليه وسلم مَقَالَتَهُ قَلَصَ دَمْعِي حَتَّى مَا أُحِسُّ مِنْهُ قَطْرَةً وَقُلْتُ لأَبِي أَجِبْ عَنِّي رَسُولَ اللَّهِ صلى الله عليه وسلم. قَالَ وَاللَّهِ مَا أَدْرِي مَا أَقُولُ لِرَسُولِ اللَّهِ صلى الله عليه وسلم. فَقُلْتُ لأُمِّي أَجِيبِي عَنِّي رَسُولَ اللَّهِ صلى الله عليه وسلم فِيمَا قَالَ. قَالَتْ وَاللَّهِ مَا أَدْرِي مَا أَقُولُ لِرَسُولِ اللَّهِ صلى الله عليه وسلم. قَالَتْ وَأَنَا جَارِيَةٌ حَدِيثَةُ السِّنِّ لاَ أَقْرَأُ كَثِيرًا مِنَ الْقُرْآنِ فَقُلْتُ إِنِّي وَاللَّهِ لَقَدْ عَلِمْتُ أَنَّكُمْ سَمِعْتُمْ مَا يَتَحَدَّثُ بِهِ النَّاسُ، وَوَقَرَ فِي أَنْفُسِكُمْ وَصَدَّقْتُمْ بِهِ، وَلَئِنْ قُلْتُ لَكُمْ إِنِّي بَرِيئَةٌ. وَاللَّهُ يَعْلَمُ إِنِّي لَبَرِيئَةٌ لاَ تُصَدِّقُونِي بِذَلِكَ، وَلَئِنِ اعْتَرَفْتُ لَكُمْ بِأَمْرٍ، وَاللَّهُ يَعْلَمُ أَنِّي بَرِيئَةٌ لَتُصَدِّقُنِّي وَاللَّهِ مَا أَجِدُ لِي وَلَكُمْ مَثَلاً إِلاَّ أَبَا يُوسُفَ إِذْ قَالَ {فَصَبْرٌ جَمِيلٌ وَاللَّهُ الْمُسْتَعَانُ عَلَى مَا تَصِفُونَ} ثُمَّ تَحَوَّلْتُ عَلَى فِرَاشِي، وَأَنَا أَرْجُو أَنْ يُبَرِّئَنِي اللَّهُ، وَلَكِنْ وَاللَّهِ مَا ظَنَنْتُ أَنْ يُنْزِلَ فِي شَأْنِي وَحْيًا، وَلأَنَا أَحْقَرُ فِي نَفْسِي مِنْ أَنْ يُتَكَلَّمَ بِالْقُرْآنِ فِي أَمْرِي، وَلَكِنِّي كُنْتُ أَرْجُو أَنْ يَرَى رَسُولُ اللَّهِ صلى الله عليه وسلم فِي النَّوْمِ رُؤْيَا يُبَرِّئُنِي اللَّهُ، فَوَاللَّهِ مَا رَامَ مَجْلِسَهُ وَلاَ خَرَجَ أَحَدٌ مِنْ أَهْلِ الْبَيْتِ حَتَّى أُنْزِلَ عَلَيْهِ، فَأَخَذَهُ مَا كَانَ يَأْخُذُهُ مِنَ الْبُرَحَاءِ، حَتَّى إِنَّهُ لَيَتَحَدَّرُ مِنْهُ مِثْلُ الْجُمَانِ مِنَ الْعَرَقِ فِي يَوْمٍ شَاتٍ، فَلَمَّا سُرِّيَ عَنْ رَسُولِ اللَّهِ صلى الله عليه وسلم وَهُوَ يَضْحَكُ، فَكَانَ أَوَّلَ كَلِمَةٍ تَكَلَّمَ بِهَا أَنْ قَالَ لِي " يَا عَائِشَةُ، احْمَدِي اللَّهَ فَقَدْ بَرَّأَكِ اللَّهُ ". فَقَالَتْ لِي أُمِّي قُومِي إِلَى رَسُولِ اللَّهِ صلى الله عليه وسلم. فَقُلْتُ لاَ وَاللَّهِ، لاَ أَقُومُ إِلَيْهِ، وَلاَ أَحْمَدُ إِلاَّ اللَّهَ فَأَنْزَلَ اللَّهُ تَعَالَى {إِنَّ الَّذِينَ جَاءُوا بِالإِفْكِ عُصْبَةٌ مِنْكُمْ} الآيَاتِ، فَلَمَّا أَنْزَلَ اللَّهُ هَذَا فِي بَرَاءَتِي قَالَ أَبُو بَكْرٍ الصِّدِّيقُ ـ رضى الله عنه ـ وَكَانَ يُنْفِقُ عَلَى مِسْطَحِ بْنِ أُثَاثَةَ لِقَرَابَتِهِ مِنْهُ وَاللَّهِ لاَ أُنْفِقُ عَلَى مِسْطَحٍ شَيْئًا أَبَدًا بَعْدَ مَا قَالَ لِعَائِشَةَ. فَأَنْزَلَ اللَّهُ تَعَالَى {وَلاَ يَأْتَلِ أُولُو الْفَضْلِ مِنْكُمْ وَالسَّعَةِ} إِلَى قَوْلِهِ {غَفُورٌ رَحِيمٌ} فَقَالَ أَبُو بَكْرٍ بَلَى، وَاللَّهِ إِنِّي لأُحِبُّ أَنْ يَغْفِرَ اللَّهُ لِي، فَرَجَعَ إِلَى مِسْطَحٍ الَّذِي كَانَ يُجْرِي عَلَيْهِ. وَكَانَ رَسُولُ اللَّهِ صلى الله عليه وسلم يَسْأَلُ زَيْنَبَ بِنْتَ جَحْشٍ عَنْ أَمْرِي، فَقَالَ " يَا زَيْنَبُ، مَا عَلِمْتِ مَا رَأَيْتِ ". فَقَالَتْ يَا رَسُولَ اللَّهِ، أَحْمِي سَمْعِي وَبَصَرِي، وَاللَّهِ مَا عَلِمْتُ عَلَيْهَا إِلاَّ خَيْرًا، قَالَتْ وَهْىَ الَّتِي كَانَتْ تُسَامِينِي، فَعَصَمَهَا اللَّهُ بِالْوَرَعِ. قَالَ وَحَدَّثَنَا فُلَيْحٌ، عَنْ هِشَامِ بْنِ عُرْوَةَ، عَنْ عُرْوَةَ، عَنْ عَائِشَةَ، وَعَبْدِ اللَّهِ بْنِ الزُّبَيْرِ، مِثْلَهُ. قَالَ وَحَدَّثَنَا فُلَيْحٌ، عَنْ رَبِيعَةَ بْنِ أَبِي عَبْدِ الرَّحْمَنِ، وَيَحْيَى بْنِ سَعِيدٍ، عَنِ الْقَاسِمِ بْنِ مُحَمَّدِ بْنِ أَبِي بَكْرٍ، مِثْلَهُ.

Narrated Al-Miswar bin Makhrama: `Ali demanded the hand of the daughter of Abu Jahl. Fatima heard of this and went to Allah's Messenger ﷺ saying, "Your people think that you do not become angry for the sake of your daughters as `Ali is now going to marry the daughter of Abu Jahl. "On that Allah's Messenger ﷺ got up and after his recitation of Tashah-hud. I heard him saying, "Then after! I married one of my daughters to Abu Al-`As bin Al- Rabi` (the husband of Zainab, the daughter of the Prophet ﷺ before Islam and he proved truthful in whatever he said to me. No doubt, Fatima is a part of me, I hate to see her being troubled. By Allah, the daughter of Allah's Messenger ﷺ and the daughter of Allah's Enemy cannot be the wives of one man." So `Ali gave up that engagement. 'Al-Miswar further said: I heard the Prophet ﷺ talking and he mentioned a son-in-law of his belonging to the tribe of Bani `Abd-Shams. He highly praised him concerning that relationship and said (whenever) he spoke to me, he spoke the truth, and whenever he promised me, he fulfilled his promise.". – Sahih Al-Bukhari 3729

حَدَّثَنَا أَبُو الْيَمَانِ، أَخْبَرَنَا شُعَيْبٌ، عَنِ الزُّهْرِيِّ، قَالَ حَدَّثَنِي عَلِيُّ بْنُ حُسَيْنٍ، أَنَّ الْمِسْوَرَ بْنَ مَخْرَمَةَ، قَالَ إِنَّ عَلِيًّا خَطَبَ بِنْتَ أَبِي جَهْلٍ، فَسَمِعَتْ بِذَلِكَ، فَاطِمَةُ، فَأَتَتْ رَسُولَ اللَّهِ صلى الله عليه وسلم فَقَالَتْ يَزْعُمُ قَوْمُكَ أَنَّكَ لاَ تَغْضَبُ لِبَنَاتِكَ، هَذَا عَلِيٌّ نَاكِحٌ بِنْتَ أَبِي جَهْلٍ، فَقَامَ رَسُولُ اللَّهِ صلى الله عليه وسلم فَسَمِعْتُهُ حِينَ تَشَهَّدَ يَقُولُ " أَمَّا بَعْدُ أَنْكَحْتُ أَبَا الْعَاصِ بْنَ الرَّبِيعِ، فَحَدَّثَنِي وَصَدَقَنِي، وَإِنَّ فَاطِمَةَ بَضْعَةٌ مِنِّي، وَإِنِّي أَكْرَهُ أَنْ يَسُوءَهَا، وَاللَّهِ لاَ تَجْتَمِعُ بِنْتُ رَسُولِ اللَّهِ صلى الله عليه وسلم وَبِنْتُ عَدُوِّ اللَّهِ عِنْدَ رَجُلٍ وَاحِدٍ ". فَتَرَكَ عَلِيٌّ الْخِطْبَةَ. وَزَادَ مُحَمَّدُ بْنُ عَمْرِو بْنِ حَلْحَلَةَ عَنِ ابْنِ شِهَابٍ عَنْ عَلِيٍّ عَنْ مِسْوَرٍ، سَمِعْتُ النَّبِيَّ صلى الله عليه وسلم وَذَكَرَ صِهْرًا لَهُ مِنْ بَنِي عَبْدِ شَمْسٍ فَأَثْنَى عَلَيْهِ فِي مُصَاهَرَتِهِ إِيَّاهُ فَأَحْسَنَ قَالَ " حَدَّثَنِي فَصَدَقَنِي، وَوَعَدَنِي فَوَفَى لِي "

Narrated Al-Miswar bin Makhrama: I heard Allah's Messenger ﷺ who was on the pulpit, saying, "Banu Hisham bin Al-Mughira have requested me to allow them to marry their daughter to `Ali bin Abu Talib, but I don't give permission, and will not give permission unless `Ali bin Abi Talib divorces my daughter in order to marry their daughter, because Fatima is a part of my body, and I hate what she hates to see, and what hurts her, hurts me." – Sahih al-Bukhari 5230

حَدَّثَنَا قُتَيْبَةُ، حَدَّثَنَا اللَّيْثُ، عَنِ ابْنِ أَبِي مُلَيْكَةَ، عَنِ الْمِسْوَرِ بْنِ مَخْرَمَةَ، قَالَ سَمِعْتُ رَسُولَ اللَّهِ صلى الله عليه وسلم يَقُولُ وَهُوَ عَلَى الْمِنْبَرِ " إِنَّ بَنِي هِشَامِ بْنِ الْمُغِيرَةِ اسْتَأْذَنُوا فِي أَنْ يُنْكِحُوا ابْنَتَهُمْ عَلِيَّ بْنَ أَبِي طَالِبٍ فَلاَ آذَنُ، ثُمَّ لاَ آذَنُ، ثُمَّ لاَ آذَنُ، إِلاَّ أَنْ يُرِيدَ ابْنُ أَبِي طَالِبٍ أَنْ يُطَلِّقَ ابْنَتِي وَيَنْكِحَ ابْنَتَهُمْ، فَإِنَّمَا هِيَ بَضْعَةٌ مِنِّي، يُرِيبُنِي مَا أَرَابَهَا وَيُؤْذِينِي مَا آذَاهَا ". هَكَذَا قَالَ

Narrated `Ali bin Abi Talib: On the day of Khaibar, Allah's Messenger ﷺ forbade the Mut'a (i.e. temporary marriage) and the eating of donkey-meat. – Sahih al-Bukhari 4216

حَدَّثَنِي يَحْيَى بْنُ قَزَعَةَ، حَدَّثَنَا مَالِكٌ، عَنِ ابْنِ شِهَابٍ، عَنْ عَبْدِ اللَّهِ، وَالْحَسَنِ، ابْنَىْ مُحَمَّدِ بْنِ عَلِيٍّ عَنْ أَبِيهِمَا، عَنْ عَلِيِّ بْنِ أَبِي طَالِبٍ ـ رضى الله عنه ـ أَنَّ رَسُولَ اللَّهِ صلى الله عليه وسلم نَهَى عَنْ مُتْعَةِ النِّسَاءِ يَوْمَ خَيْبَرَ، وَعَنْ أَكْلِ الْحُمُرِ الإِنْسِيَّةِ

Narrated 'Usama bin Zaid: I asked, "O Allah's Messenger ﷺ ! There will you stay in Mecca? Will you stay in your house in Mecca?" He replied, "Has `Aqil left any property or house?" `Aqil along with Talib had inherited the property of Abu Talib. Jafar and `Ali did not inherit anything as they were Muslims and the other two were non-believers. `Umar bin Al-Khattab used to say, "A believer cannot inherit (anything from an) infidel." Ibn Shihab, (a sub-narrator) said, "They (`Umar and others) derived the above verdict from Allah's Statement: "Verily! Those who believed and Emigrated and strove with their life And property in Allah's Cause, And those who helped (the emigrants) And gave them their places to live in, These are (all) allies to one another." (8.72). – Sahih al-Bukhari 1588

حَدَّثَنَا أَصْبَغُ، قَالَ أَخْبَرَنِي ابْنُ وَهْبٍ، عَنْ يُونُسَ، عَنِ ابْنِ شِهَابٍ، عَنْ عَلِيِّ بْنِ حُسَيْنٍ، عَنْ عَمْرِو بْنِ عُثْمَانَ، عَنْ أُسَامَةَ بْنِ زَيْدٍ ـ رضى الله عنهما ـ أَنَّهُ قَالَ يَا رَسُولَ اللَّهِ، أَيْنَ تَنْزِلُ فِي دَارِكَ بِمَكَّةَ. فَقَالَ " وَهَلْ تَرَكَ عَقِيلٌ مِنْ رِبَاعٍ أَوْ دُورٍ ". وَكَانَ عَقِيلٌ وَرِثَ أَبَا طَالِبٍ هُوَ وَطَالِبٌ وَلَمْ يَرِثْهُ جَعْفَرٌ وَلاَ عَلِيٌّ ـ رضى الله عنهما ـ شَيْئًا لأَنَّهُمَا كَانَا مُسْلِمَيْنِ، وَكَانَ عَقِيلٌ وَطَالِبٌ كَافِرَيْنِ، فَكَانَ عُمَرُ بْنُ الْخَطَّابِ ـ رضى الله عنه ـ يَقُولُ لاَ يَرِثُ الْمُؤْمِنُ الْكَافِرَ. قَالَ ابْنُ شِهَابٍ وَكَانُوا يَتَأَوَّلُونَ قَوْلَ اللَّهِ تَعَالَى {إِنَّ الَّذِينَ آمَنُوا وَهَاجَرُوا وَجَاهَدُوا بِأَمْوَالِهِمْ وَأَنْفُسِهِمْ فِي سَبِيلِ اللَّهِ وَالَّذِينَ آوَوْا وَنَصَرُوا أُولَئِكَ بَعْضُهُمْ أَوْلِيَاءُ بَعْضٍ} الآيَةَ

Narrated Al-Bara bin `Azib: When Allah's Messenger ﷺ concluded a peace treaty with the people of Hudaibiya, `Ali bin Abu Talib wrote the document and he mentioned in it, "Muhammad, Allah's Messenger ﷺ ". The pagans said, "Don't write: 'Muhammad, Allah's Messenger ﷺ ' For if you were an apostle we would not fight with you." Allah's Apostle asked `Ali to rub it out, but `Ali said, "I will not be the person to rub it out." Allah's Messenger ﷺ rubbed it out and made peace with them on the condition that the Prophet ﷺ and his companions would enter Mecca and stay there for three days, and that they would enter with their weapons in cases. – Sahih al-Bukhari 2698

حَدَّثَنَا مُحَمَّدُ بْنُ بَشَّارٍ، حَدَّثَنَا غُنْدَرٌ، حَدَّثَنَا شُعْبَةُ، عَنْ أَبِي إِسْحَاقَ، قَالَ سَمِعْتُ الْبَرَاءَ بْنَ عَازِبٍ ـ رضى الله عنهما ـ قَالَ لَمَّا صَالَحَ رَسُولُ اللَّهِ صلى الله عليه وسلم أَهْلَ الْحُدَيْبِيَةِ كَتَبَ عَلِيٌّ بَيْنَهُمْ كِتَابًا فَكَتَبَ مُحَمَّدٌ رَسُولُ اللَّهِ صلى الله عليه وسلم. فَقَالَ الْمُشْرِكُونَ لاَ تَكْتُبْ مُحَمَّدٌ رَسُولُ اللَّهِ، لَوْ كُنْتَ رَسُولاً لَمْ نُقَاتِلْكَ. فَقَالَ لِعَلِيٍّ " امْحُهُ ". فَقَالَ عَلِيٌّ مَا أَنَا بِالَّذِي أَمْحَاهُ. فَمَحَاهُ رَسُولُ اللَّهِ صلى الله عليه وسلم بِيَدِهِ، وَصَالَحَهُمْ عَلَى أَنْ يَدْخُلَ هُوَ وَأَصْحَابُهُ ثَلاَثَةَ أَيَّامٍ، وَلاَ يَدْخُلُوهَا إِلاَّ بِجُلُبَّانِ السِّلاَحِ، فَسَأَلُوهُ مَا جُلُبَّانُ السِّلاَحِ فَقَالَ الْقِرَابُ بِمَا فِيهِ

Narrated `Ali bin Abi Talib: The Prophetﷺ gave me a silk suit. I went out wearing it, but seeing the signs of anger on his face, I tore it and distributed it among my wives. – Sahih al-Bukhari 5840

حَدَّثَنَا سُلَيْمَانُ بْنُ حَرْبٍ، حَدَّثَنَا شُعْبَةُ، ح وَحَدَّثَنِي مُحَمَّدُ بْنُ بَشَّارٍ، حَدَّثَنَا غُنْدَرٌ، حَدَّثَنَا شُعْبَةُ، عَنْ عَبْدِ الْمَلِكِ بْنِ مَيْسَرَةَ، عَنْ زَيْدِ بْنِ وَهْبٍ، عَنْ عَلِيٍّ ـ رضى الله عنه ـ قَالَ كَسَانِي النَّبِيُّ صلى الله عليه وسلم حُلَّةً سِيَرَاءَ، فَخَرَجْتُ فِيهَا، فَرَأَيْتُ الْغَضَبَ فِي وَجْهِهِ، فَشَقَّقْتُهَا بَيْنَ نِسَائِي.

Jafar bin Abi Talib
جَعْفَر ٱبْن أَبِي طَالِب

Narrated Al-Bara: When the Prophetﷺ intended to perform `Umra in the month of Dhul-Qada, the people of Mecca did not let him enter Mecca till he settled the matter with them by promising to stay in it for three days only. When the document of treaty was written, the following was mentioned: 'These are the terms on which Muhammad, Allah's Messengerﷺ agreed (to make peace).' They said, "We will not agree to this, for if we believed that you are Allah's Messengerﷺ we would not prevent you, but you are Muhammad bin `Abdullah." The Prophetﷺ said, "I am Allah's Messengerﷺ and also Muhammad bin `Abdullah." Then he said to `Ali, "Rub off (the words) 'Allah's Messengerﷺ'," But `Ali said, "No, by Allah, I will never rub off your name." So, Allah's Messengerﷺ took the document and wrote, 'This is what Muhammad bin `Abdullah has agreed upon: No arms will be brought into Mecca except in their cases, and nobody from the people of Mecca will be allowed to go with him (i.e. the Prophetﷺ) even if he wished to follow him and he (the Prophetﷺ) will not prevent any of his companions from staying in Mecca if the latter wants to stay.' When the Prophetﷺ entered Mecca and the time limit passed, the Meccans went to `Ali and said, "Tell your Friend (i.e. the Prophetﷺ) to go out, as the period (agreed to) has passed." So, the Prophetﷺ went out of Mecca. The daughter of Hamza ran after them (i.e. the Prophetﷺ and his companions), calling, "O Uncle! O Uncle!" `Ali received her and led her by the hand and said to Fatima, "Take your uncle's daughter." Zaid and Ja`far quarreled about her. `Ali said, "I have more right to her as she is my uncle's daughter." Ja`far said, "She is my uncle's daughter, and her aunt is my wife." Zaid said, "She is my brother's daughter." The Prophetﷺ judged that she should be given to her aunt, and said that the aunt was like the mother. He then said to 'All, "You are from me and I am from you", and said to Ja`far, "You resemble me both in character and appearance", and said to Zaid, "You are our brother (in faith) and our freed slave.". – Sahih Al-Bukhari 2699

حَدَّثَنَا عُبَيْدُ اللَّهِ بْنُ مُوسَى، عَنْ إِسْرَائِيلَ، عَنْ أَبِي إِسْحَاقَ، عَنِ الْبَرَاءِ ـ رضى الله عنه ـ قَالَ اعْتَمَرَ النَّبِيُّ صلى الله عليه وسلم فِي ذِي الْقَعْدَةِ، فَأَبَى أَهْلُ مَكَّةَ أَنْ يَدَعُوهُ يَدْخُلُ مَكَّةَ، حَتَّى قَاضَاهُمْ عَلَى أَنْ يُقِيمَ بِهَا ثَلاَثَةَ أَيَّامٍ، فَلَمَّا كَتَبُوا الْكِتَابَ كَتَبُوا هَذَا مَا قَاضَى عَلَيْهِ مُحَمَّدٌ رَسُولُ اللَّهِ صلى الله عليه وسلم. فَقَالُوا لاَ نُقِرُّ بِهَا، فَلَوْ نَعْلَمُ أَنَّكَ رَسُولُ اللَّهِ مَا مَنَعْنَاكَ، لَكِنْ أَنْتَ مُحَمَّدُ بْنُ عَبْدِ اللَّهِ. قَالَ " أَنَا رَسُولُ اللَّهِ وَأَنَا مُحَمَّدُ بْنُ عَبْدِ اللَّهِ ". ثُمَّ قَالَ لِعَلِيٍّ " امْحُ رَسُولُ اللَّهِ ". قَالَ لاَ، وَاللَّهِ لاَ أَمْحُوكَ أَبَدًا، فَأَخَذَ رَسُولُ اللَّهِ صلى الله عليه وسلم الْكِتَابَ، فَكَتَبَ هَذَا مَا قَاضَى عَلَيْهِ مُحَمَّدُ بْنُ عَبْدِ اللَّهِ، لاَ يَدْخُلُ مَكَّةَ سِلاَحٌ إِلاَّ فِي الْقِرَابِ، وَأَنْ لاَ يَخْرُجَ مِنْ أَهْلِهَا بِأَحَدٍ، إِنْ أَرَادَ أَنْ يَتَّبِعَهُ، وَأَنْ لاَ يَمْنَعَ أَحَدًا مِنْ أَصْحَابِهِ أَرَادَ أَنْ يُقِيمَ بِهَا. فَلَمَّا دَخَلَهَا، وَمَضَى الأَجَلُ أَتَوْا عَلِيًّا، فَقَالُوا قُلْ لِصَاحِبِكَ اخْرُجْ عَنَّا فَقَدْ مَضَى الأَجَلُ. فَخَرَجَ النَّبِيُّ صلى الله عليه وسلم فَتَبِعَتْهُمُ ابْنَةُ حَمْزَةَ يَا عَمِّ يَا عَمِّ. فَتَنَاوَلَهَا عَلِيٌّ فَأَخَذَ بِيَدِهَا، وَقَالَ لِفَاطِمَةَ عَلَيْهَا السَّلاَمُ دُونَكِ ابْنَةَ عَمِّكِ، احْمِلِيهَا. فَاخْتَصَمَ فِيهَا عَلِيٌّ وَزَيْدٌ وَجَعْفَرٌ، فَقَالَ عَلِيٌّ أَنَا أَحَقُّ بِهَا وَهْىَ ابْنَةُ عَمِّي. وَقَالَ جَعْفَرٌ ابْنَةُ عَمِّي وَخَالَتُهَا تَحْتِي. وَقَالَ زَيْدٌ ابْنَةُ أَخِي. فَقَضَى بِهَا النَّبِيُّ صلى الله عليه وسلم لِخَالَتِهَا. وَقَالَ " الْخَالَةُ بِمَنْزِلَةِ الأُمِّ ". وَقَالَ لِعَلِيٍّ " أَنْتَ مِنِّي وَأَنَا مِنْكَ ". وَقَالَ لِجَعْفَرٍ " أَشْبَهْتَ خَلْقِي وَخُلُقِي ". وَقَالَ لِزَيْدٍ " أَنْتَ أَخُونَا وَمَوْلاَنَا "

Narrated Ash-Shu`bi: Whenever Ibn `Umar greeted Ibn Jafar, he used to say: "As-salamu-'Alaika (i.e. Peace be on you) O son of Dhu-l-Janahain (son of the two-winged person). – Sahih Al-Bukhari 3709
حَدَّثَنِي عَمْرُو بْنُ عَلِيٍّ، حَدَّثَنَا يَزِيدُ بْنُ هَارُونَ، أَخْبَرَنَا إِسْمَاعِيلُ بْنُ أَبِي خَالِدٍ، عَنِ الشَّعْبِيِّ، أَنَّ ابْنَ عُمَرَ ـ رضى الله عنهما ـ كَانَ إِذَا سَلَّمَ عَلَى ابْنِ جَعْفَرٍ قَالَ السَّلاَمُ عَلَيْكَ يَا ابْنَ ذِي الْجَنَاحَيْنِ

Narrated Anas: The Prophet ﷺ had informed the people of the martyrdom of Zaid, Ja`far and Ibn Rawaha before the news of their death reached. The Prophet ﷺ said, "Zaid took the flag (as the commander of the army) and was martyred, then Ja`far took it and was martyred, and then Ibn Rawaha took it and was martyred." At that time the Prophet's eyes were shedding tears. He added, "Then the flag was taken by a Sword amongst the Swords of Allah (i.e. Khalid) and Allah made them (i.e. the Muslims) victorious.". – Sahih Al-Bukhari 4262
حَدَّثَنَا أَحْمَدُ بْنُ وَاقِدٍ، حَدَّثَنَا حَمَّادُ بْنُ زَيْدٍ، عَنْ أَيُّوبَ، عَنْ حُمَيْدِ بْنِ هِلاَلٍ، عَنْ أَنَسٍ ـ رضى الله عنه ـ أَنَّ النَّبِيَّ صلى الله عليه وسلم نَعَى زَيْدًا وَجَعْفَرًا وَابْنَ رَوَاحَةَ لِلنَّاسِ، قَبْلَ أَنْ يَأْتِيَهُمْ خَبَرُهُمْ فَقَالَ " أَخَذَ الرَّايَةَ زَيْدٌ فَأُصِيبَ، ثُمَّ أَخَذَ جَعْفَرٌ فَأُصِيبَ، ثُمَّ أَخَذَ ابْنُ رَوَاحَةَ فَأُصِيبَ ـ وَعَيْنَاهُ تَذْرِفَانِ ـ حَتَّى أَخَذَ الرَّايَةَ سَيْفٌ مِنْ سُيُوفِ اللَّهِ حَتَّى فَتَحَ اللَّهُ عَلَيْهِمْ "

Narrated 'Usama bin Zaid: I asked, "O Allah's Messenger ﷺ! Where will you stay in Mecca? Will you stay in your house in Mecca?" He replied, "Has `Aqil left any property or house?" `Aqil along with Talib had inherited the property of Abu Talib. Jafar and `Ali did not inherit anything as they were Muslims and the other two were non-believers. `Umar bin Al-Khattab used to say, "A believer cannot inherit (anything from an) infidel." Ibn Shihab, (a sub-narrator) said, "They (`Umar and others) derived the above verdict from Allah's Statement: "Verily! Those who believed and Emigrated and strove with their life And property in Allah's Cause, And those who helped (the emigrants) And gave them their places to live in, These are (all) allies to one another." (8.72). – Sahih Al-Bukhari 1588
حَدَّثَنَا ، قَالَ أَخْبَرَنِي ابْنُ وَهْبٍ، عَنْ يُونُسَ، عَنِ ابْنِ شِهَابٍ، عَنْ عَلِيِّ بْنِ حُسَيْنٍ، عَنْ عَمْرِو بْنِ عُثْمَانَ، عَنْ أُسَامَةَ بْنِ زَيْدٍ ـ رضى الله عنهما ـ أَنَّهُ قَالَ يَا رَسُولَ اللَّهِ، أَيْنَ تَنْزِلُ فِي دَارِكَ بِمَكَّةَ. فَقَالَ " وَهَلْ تَرَكَ عَقِيلٌ مِنْ رِبَاعٍ أَوْ دُورٍ ". وَكَانَ عَقِيلٌ وَرِثَ أَبَا طَالِبٍ هُوَ وَطَالِبٌ وَلَمْ يَرِثْهُ جَعْفَرٌ وَلاَ عَلِيٌّ ـ رضى الله عنهما ـ شَيْئًا لأَنَّهُمَا كَانَا مُسْلِمَيْنِ، وَكَانَ عَقِيلٌ وَطَالِبٌ كَافِرَيْنِ، فَكَانَ عُمَرُ بْنُ الْخَطَّابِ ـ رضى الله عنه ـ يَقُولُ لاَ يَرِثُ الْمُؤْمِنُ الْكَافِرَ. قَالَ ابْنُ شِهَابٍ وَكَانُوا يَتَأَوَّلُونَ قَوْلَ اللَّهِ تَعَالَى {إِنَّ الَّذِينَ آمَنُوا وَهَاجَرُوا وَجَاهَدُوا بِأَمْوَالِهِمْ وَأَنْفُسِهِمْ فِي سَبِيلِ اللَّهِ وَالَّذِينَ آوَوْا وَنَصَرُوا أُولَئِكَ بَعْضُهُمْ أَوْلِيَاءُ بَعْضٍ} الآيَةَ.

Narrated Anas bin Malik: The Prophet ﷺ said, "Zaid took over the flag and was martyred. Then it was taken by Jafar who was martyred as well. Then `Abdullah bin Rawaha took the flag but he too was martyred and at that time the eyes of Allah's Messenger ﷺ were full of tears. Then Khalid bin Al-Walid took the flag without being nominated as a chief (before hand) and was blessed with victory.". – Sahih Al-Bukhari 1246
حَدَّثَنَا أَبُو مَعْمَرٍ، حَدَّثَنَا عَبْدُ الْوَارِثِ، حَدَّثَنَا أَيُّوبُ، عَنْ حُمَيْدِ بْنِ هِلاَلٍ، عَنْ أَنَسِ بْنِ مَالِكٍ ـ رضى الله عنه ـ قَالَ قَالَ النَّبِيُّ صلى الله عليه وسلم " أَخَذَ الرَّايَةَ زَيْدٌ فَأُصِيبَ، ثُمَّ أَخَذَهَا جَعْفَرٌ فَأُصِيبَ، ثُمَّ أَخَذَهَا عَبْدُ اللَّهِ بْنُ رَوَاحَةَ فَأُصِيبَ ـ وَإِنَّ عَيْنَىْ رَسُولِ اللَّهِ صلى الله عليه وسلم لَتَذْرِفَانِ ـ ثُمَّ أَخَذَهَا خَالِدُ بْنُ الْوَلِيدِ مِنْ غَيْرِ إِمْرَةٍ فَفُتِحَ لَهُ

Narrated Abu Musa: The news of the migration of the Prophet (from Mecca to Medina) reached us while we were in Yemen. So we set out as emigrants towards him. We were (three) I and my two brothers. I was the youngest of them, and one of the two was Abu Burda, and the other, Abu Ruhm, and our total number was either 53 or 52 men from my people. We got on board a boat and our boat took us to Negus in Ethiopia. There we met Ja`far bin Abi Talib and stayed with him. Then we all came (to Medina) and met the Prophet ﷺ at the time of the conquest of Khaibar. Some of the people used to say to us, namely the people of the ship, "We have migrated before you." Asma' bint 'Umais who was one of those who had come with us, came as a visitor to Hafsa, the wife the Prophet ﷺ. She had migrated along with those other Muslims who migrated to Negus. `Umar came to Hafsa while Asma' bint 'Umais was with her. `Umar, on seeing Asma,' said, "Who is this?" She said, "Asma' bint 'Umais," `Umar said, "Is she the Ethiopian? Is she the sea-faring lady?" Asma' replied, "Yes." `Umar said, "We have migrated before you (people of the boat), so we have got more right than you over Allah's Messenger ﷺ" On that Asma' became angry and said, "No, by Allah, while you were with Allah's Messenger ﷺ who was feeding the hungry ones amongst you, and advised the ignorant ones amongst you, we were in the far-off hated land of Ethiopia, and all that was for the sake of Allah's Messenger ﷺ. By Allah, I will neither eat any food nor drink anything till I inform Allah's Messenger ﷺ of all that you have said. There we were harmed and frightened. I will mention this to the Prophet ﷺ and will not tell a lie or curtail your saying or add something to it.". – Sahih Al-Bukhari 4230

حَدَّثَنِي مُحَمَّدُ بْنُ الْعَلاَءِ، حَدَّثَنَا أَبُو أُسَامَةَ، حَدَّثَنَا بُرَيْدُ بْنُ عَبْدِ اللَّهِ، عَنْ أَبِي بُرْدَةَ، عَنْ أَبِي مُوسَى ـ رضى الله عنه ـ قَالَ بَلَغَنَا مَخْرَجُ النَّبِيِّ صلى الله عليه وسلم وَنَحْنُ بِالْيَمَنِ، فَخَرَجْنَا مُهَاجِرِينَ إِلَيْهِ أَنَا، وَأَخَوَانِ لِي أَنَا أَصْغَرُهُمْ، أَحَدُهُمَا أَبُو بُرْدَةَ، وَالآخَرُ أَبُو رُهْمٍ ـ إِمَّا قَالَ بِضْعٌ وَإِمَّا قَالَ ـ فِي ثَلاَثَةٍ وَخَمْسِينَ أَوِ اثْنَيْنِ وَخَمْسِينَ رَجُلاً مِنْ قَوْمِي، فَرَكِبْنَا سَفِينَةً، فَأَلْقَتْنَا سَفِينَتُنَا إِلَى النَّجَاشِيِّ بِالْحَبَشَةِ، فَوَافَقْنَا جَعْفَرَ بْنَ أَبِي طَالِبٍ فَأَقَمْنَا مَعَهُ حَتَّى قَدِمْنَا جَمِيعًا، فَوَافَقْنَا النَّبِيَّ صلى الله عليه وسلم حِينَ افْتَتَحَ خَيْبَرَ، وَكَانَ أُنَاسٌ مِنَ النَّاسِ يَقُولُونَ لَنَا ـ يَعْنِي لأَهْلِ السَّفِينَةِ ـ سَبَقْنَاكُمْ بِالْهِجْرَةِ، وَدَخَلَتْ أَسْمَاءُ بِنْتُ عُمَيْسٍ، وَهْىَ مِمَّنْ قَدِمَ مَعَنَا، عَلَى حَفْصَةَ زَوْجِ النَّبِيِّ صلى الله عليه وسلم زَائِرَةً، وَقَدْ كَانَتْ هَاجَرَتْ إِلَى النَّجَاشِيِّ فِيمَنْ هَاجَرَ، فَدَخَلَ عُمَرُ عَلَى حَفْصَةَ وَأَسْمَاءُ عِنْدَهَا، فَقَالَ عُمَرُ حِينَ رَأَى أَسْمَاءَ مَنْ هَذِهِ قَالَتْ أَسْمَاءُ بِنْتُ عُمَيْسٍ. قَالَ عُمَرُ الْحَبَشِيَّةُ هَذِهِ الْبَحْرِيَّةُ هَذِهِ قَالَتْ أَسْمَاءُ نَعَمْ. قَالَ سَبَقْنَاكُمْ بِالْهِجْرَةِ، فَنَحْنُ أَحَقُّ بِرَسُولِ اللَّهِ صلى الله عليه وسلم مِنْكُمْ. فَغَضِبَتْ وَقَالَتْ كَلاَّ وَاللَّهِ، كُنْتُمْ مَعَ رَسُولِ اللَّهِ صلى الله عليه وسلم يُطْعِمُ جَائِعَكُمْ، وَيَعِظُ جَاهِلَكُمْ، وَكُنَّا فِي دَارِ أَوْ فِي أَرْضِ الْبُعَدَاءِ الْبُغَضَاءِ بِالْحَبَشَةِ، وَذَلِكَ فِي اللَّهِ وَفِي رَسُولِهِ صلى الله عليه وسلم وَايْمُ اللَّهِ، لاَ أَطْعَمُ طَعَامًا، وَلاَ أَشْرَبُ شَرَابًا حَتَّى أَذْكُرَ مَا قُلْتَ لِرَسُولِ اللَّهِ صلى الله عليه وسلم وَنَحْنُ كُنَّا نُؤْذَى وَنُخَافُ، وَسَأَذْكُرُ ذَلِكَ لِلنَّبِيِّ صلى الله عليه وسلم وَأَسْأَلُهُ، وَاللَّهِ لاَ أَكْذِبُ وَلاَ أَزِيغُ وَلاَ أَزِيدُ عَلَيْهِ.

Narrated Abu Huraira: I used to accompany Allah's Messenger ﷺ to fill my stomach; and that was when I did not eat baked bread, nor wear silk. Neither a male nor a female slave used to serve me, and I used to bind stones over my belly and ask somebody to recite a Qur'anic Verse for me though I knew it, so that he might take me to his house and feed me. Ja`far bin Abi Talib was very kind to the poor, and he used to take us and feed us with what ever was available in his house, (and if nothing was available), he used to give us the empty (honey or butter) skin which we would tear and lick whatever was in it. – Sahih Al-Bukhari 5432

حَدَّثَنَا عَبْدُ الرَّحْمَنِ بْنُ شَيْبَةَ، قَالَ أَخْبَرَنِي ابْنُ أَبِي الْفُدَيْكِ، عَنِ ابْنِ أَبِي ذِئْبٍ، عَنِ الْمَقْبُرِيِّ، عَنْ أَبِي هُرَيْرَةَ، قَالَ كُنْتُ أَلْزَمُ النَّبِيَّ صلى الله عليه وسلم لِشِبَعِ بَطْنِي حِينَ لاَ آكُلُ الْخَمِيرَ، وَلاَ أَلْبَسُ الْحَرِيرَ، وَلاَ يَخْدُمُنِي فُلاَنٌ وَلاَ فُلاَنَةُ، وَأُلْصِقُ بَطْنِي بِالْحَصْبَاءِ، وَأَسْتَقْرِئُ الرَّجُلَ الآيَةَ وَهْىَ مَعِي كَىْ يَنْقَلِبَ بِي فَيُطْعِمَنِي، وَخَيْرُ النَّاسِ لِلْمَسَاكِينِ جَعْفَرُ بْنُ أَبِي طَالِبٍ، يَنْقَلِبُ بِنَا فَيُطْعِمُنَا مَا كَانَ فِي بَيْتِهِ، حَتَّى إِنْ كَانَ لَيُخْرِجُ إِلَيْنَا الْعُكَّةَ لَيْسَ فِيهَا شَىْءٌ، فَنَشْتَقُّهَا فَنَلْعَقُ مَا فِيهَا.

Narrated `Amra: I heard `Aisha saying, "When the news of the martyrdom of Ibn Haritha, Ja`far bin Abi Talib and `Abdullah bin Rawaka reached, Allah's Messenger ﷺ sat with sorrow explicit on his face." `Aisha added, "I was then peeping through a chink in the door. A man came to him and said, "O Allah's Messenger ﷺ! The women of Ja`far are crying.' Thereupon the Prophet ﷺ told him to forbid them to do so. So the man went away and returned saying, "I forbade them but they did not listen to me." The Prophet ﷺ ordered him again to go (and forbid them). He went again and came saying, 'By Allah, they overpowered me (i.e. did not listen to me)." `Aisha said that Allah's Messenger ﷺ said (to him), "Go and throw dust into their mouths." Aisha added, "I said, May Allah put your nose in the dust! By Allah, neither have you done what you have been ordered, nor have you relieved Allah's Messenger ﷺ from trouble.". – Sahih Al-Bukhari 4263

حَدَّثَنَا قُتَيْبَةُ، حَدَّثَنَا عَبْدُ الْوَهَّابِ، قَالَ سَمِعْتُ يَحْيَى بْنَ سَعِيدٍ، قَالَ أَخْبَرَتْنِي عَمْرَةُ، قَالَتْ سَمِعْتُ عَائِشَةَ ـ رضى الله عنها ـ تَقُولُ لَمَّا جَاءَ قَتْلُ ابْنِ حَارِثَةَ وَجَعْفَرِ بْنِ أَبِي طَالِبٍ وَعَبْدِ اللَّهِ بْنِ رَوَاحَةَ ـ رضى الله عنهم ـ جَلَسَ رَسُولُ اللَّهِ صلى الله عليه وسلم يُعْرَفُ فِيهِ الْحُزْنُ ـ قَالَتْ عَائِشَةُ ـ وَأَنَا أَطَّلِعُ مِنْ صَائِرِ الْبَابِ ـ تَعْنِي مِنْ شَقِّ الْبَابِ ـ فَأَتَاهُ رَجُلٌ فَقَالَ أَىْ رَسُولَ اللَّهِ إِنَّ نِسَاءَ جَعْفَرٍ قَالَ وَذَكَرَ بُكَاءَهُنَّ، فَأَمَرَهُ أَنْ يَنْهَاهُنَّ قَالَ فَذَهَبَ الرَّجُلُ ثُمَّ أَتَى فَقَالَ قَدْ نَهَيْتُهُنَّ. وَذَكَرَ أَنَّهُ لَمْ يُطِعْنَهُ قَالَ فَأَمَرَ أَيْضًا فَذَهَبَ ثُمَّ أَتَى فَقَالَ وَاللَّهِ لَقَدْ غَلَبْنَنَا.

فزَعَمَتْ أنَّ رَسُولَ اللَّهِ صلى الله عليه وسلم قَالَ " فَاحْثُ فِي أَفْوَاهِهِنَّ مِنَ التُّرَابِ " قَالَتْ عَائِشَةُ فَقُلْتُ أَرْغَمَ اللَّهُ أَنْفَكَ، فَوَاللَّهِ مَا أَنْتَ تَفْعَلُ، وَمَا تَرَكْتَ رَسُولَ اللَّهِ صلى الله عليه وسلم مِنَ الْعَنَاءِ.

Narrated Nafi`: Ibn `Umar informed me that on the day (of Mu'tah) he stood beside Ja`far who was dead (i.e. killed in the battle), and he counted fifty wounds in his body, caused by stabs or strokes, and none of those wounds was in his back. – Sahih Al-Bukhari 4260
حَدَّثَنَا أَحْمَدُ، حَدَّثَنَا ابْنُ وَهْبٍ، عَنْ عَمْرٍو، عَنِ ابْنِ أَبِي هِلاَلٍ، قَالَ وَأَخْبَرَنِي نَافِعٌ، أَنَّ ابْنَ عُمَرَ، أَخْبَرَهُ أَنَّهُ، وَقَفَ عَلَى جَعْفَرٍ يَوْمَئِذٍ وَهْوَ قَتِيلٌ، فَعَدَدْتُ بِهِ خَمْسِينَ بَيْنَ طَعْنَةٍ وَضَرْبَةٍ، لَيْسَ مِنْهَا شَىْءٌ فِي دُبُرِهِ. يَعْنِي فِي ظَهْرِهِ.

Fatima bint Muhammad
فَاطِمَة بِنْت مُحَمَّد

Narrated Husain bin `Ali: `Ali bin Abi Talib said: "I got a she-camel as my share of the war booty on the day (of the battle) of Badr, and Allah's Messenger ﷺ gave me another she-camel. I let both of them kneel at the door of one of the Ansar, intending to carry Idhkhir on them to sell it and use its price for my wedding banquet on marrying Fatima. A goldsmith from Bani Qainqa' was with me. Hamza bin `Abdul-Muttalib was in that house drinking wine and a lady singer was reciting: "O Hamza! (Kill) the (two) fat old she camels (and serve them to your guests). So Hamza took his sword and went towards the two she-camels and cut off their humps and opened their flanks and took a part of their livers." (I said to Ibn Shihab, "Did he take part of the humps?" He replied, "He cut off their humps and carried them away.") `Ali further said, "When I saw that dreadful sight, I went to the Prophet ﷺ and told him the news. The Prophet ﷺ came out in the company of Zaid bin Haritha who was with him then, and I too went with them. He went to Hamza and spoke harshly to him. Hamza looked up and said, 'Aren't you only the slaves of my forefathers?' The Prophet ﷺ retreated and went out. This incident happened before the prohibition of drinking.". – Sahih Al-Bukhari 2375
حَدَّثَنَا إِبْرَاهِيمُ بْنُ مُوسَى، أَخْبَرَنَا هِشَامٌ، أَنَّ ابْنَ جُرَيْجٍ، أَخْبَرَهُمْ قَالَ أَخْبَرَنِي ابْنُ شِهَابٍ، عَنْ عَلِيِّ بْنِ حُسَيْنِ بْنِ عَلِيٍّ، عَنْ أَبِيهِ، حُسَيْنِ بْنِ عَلِيٍّ عَنْ عَلِيِّ بْنِ أَبِي طَالِبٍ ـ رضى الله عنهم ـ أَنَّهُ قَالَ أَصَبْتُ شَارِفًا مَعَ رَسُولِ اللَّهِ صلى الله عليه وسلم فِي مَغْنَمٍ يَوْمَ بَدْرٍ قَالَ وَأَعْطَانِي رَسُولُ اللَّهِ صلى الله عليه وسلم شَارِفًا أُخْرَى، فَأَنَخْتُهُمَا يَوْمًا عِنْدَ باب رَجُلٍ مِنَ الأَنْصَارِ، وَأَنَا أُرِيدُ أَنْ أَحْمِلَ عَلَيْهِمَا إِذْخِرًا لأَبِيعَهُ، وَمَعِي صَائِغٌ مِنْ بَنِي قَيْنُقَاعَ فَأَسْتَعِينَ بِهِ عَلَى وَلِيمَةِ فَاطِمَةَ، وَحَمْزَةُ بْنُ عَبْدِ الْمُطَّلِبِ يَشْرَبُ فِي ذَلِكَ الْبَيْتِ مَعَهُ قَيْنَةٌ، فَقَالَتْ أَلاَ يَا حَمْزَ لِلشُّرُفِ النِّوَاءِ. فَثَارَ إِلَيْهِمَا حَمْزَةُ بِالسَّيْفِ، فَجَبَّ أَسْنِمَتَهُمَا، وَبَقَرَ خَوَاصِرَهُمَا، ثُمَّ أَخَذَ مِنْ أَكْبَادِهِمَا. قُلْتُ لاِبْنِ شِهَابٍ وَمِنَ السَّنَامِ قَالَ قَدْ جَبَّ أَسْنِمَتَهُمَا فَذَهَبَ بِهَا. قَالَ ابْنُ شِهَابٍ قَالَ عَلِيٌّ ـ رضى الله عنه ـ فَنَظَرْتُ إِلَى مَنْظَرٍ أَفْظَعَنِي فَأَتَيْتُ نَبِيَّ اللَّهِ صلى الله عليه وسلم وَعِنْدَهُ زَيْدُ بْنُ حَارِثَةَ فَأَخْبَرْتُهُ الْخَبَرَ فَخَرَجَ وَمَعَهُ زَيْدٌ، فَانْطَلَقْتُ مَعَهُ، فَدَخَلَ عَلَى حَمْزَةَ فَتَغَيَّظَ عَلَيْهِ فَرَفَعَ حَمْزَةُ بَصَرَهُ وَقَالَ هَلْ أَنْتُمْ إِلاَّ عَبِيدٌ لآبَائِي فَرَجَعَ رَسُولُ اللَّهِ صلى الله عليه وسلم يُقَهْقِرُ حَتَّى خَرَجَ عَنْهُمْ، وَذَلِكَ قَبْلَ تَحْرِيمِ الْخَمْرِ

Narrated `Amr bin Maimun: `Abdullah bin Mas`ud said, "While Allah's Messenger ﷺ was praying beside the Ka`ba, there were some Quraish people sitting in a gathering. One of them said, 'Don't you see this (who does deeds just to show off)? Who amongst you can go and bring the dung, blood and the Abdominal contents (intestines, etc.) of the slaughtered camels of the family of so and so and then wait till he prostrates and put that in between his shoulders?' The most unfortunate amongst them (`Uqba bin Abi Mu'ait) went (and brought them) and when Allah's Messenger ﷺ prostrated, he put them between his shoulders. The Prophet remained in prostration and they laughed so much so that they fell on each other. A passerby went to Fatima, who was a young girl in those days. She came running and the Prophet ﷺ was still in prostration. She removed them and cursed upon the Quraish on their faces. When Allah's Messenger ﷺ completed his prayer, he said, 'O Allah! Take revenge on Quraish.' He said so thrice and added, 'O Allah! Take revenge on `Amr bin Hisham, `Utba bin Rabi`a, Shaiba bin Rabi`a, Al-Walid bin `Utba, Umaiya bin Khalaf, `Uqba bin Abi Mu'ait and `Umar a bin Al-Walid." `Abdullah added, "By Allah! I saw all of them dead in the battle field on the day of Badr and they were dragged and thrown in the Qalib (a well) at Badr: Allah's Messenger ﷺ then said, 'Allah's curse has descended upon the people of the Qalib (well). – Sahih Al-Bukhari 520

حَدَّثَنَا أَحْمَدُ بْنُ إِسْحَاقَ السُّرْمَارِيُّ، قَالَ حَدَّثَنَا عُبَيْدُ اللَّهِ بْنُ مُوسَى، قَالَ حَدَّثَنَا إِسْرَائِيلُ، عَنْ أَبِي إِسْحَاقَ، عَنْ عَمْرِو بْنِ مَيْمُونٍ، عَنْ عَبْدِ اللَّهِ، قَالَ بَيْنَمَا رَسُولُ اللَّهِ صلى الله عليه وسلم قَائِمٌ يُصَلِّي عِنْدَ الْكَعْبَةِ، وَجَمْعُ قُرَيْشٍ فِي مَجَالِسِهِمْ إِذْ قَالَ قَائِلٌ مِنْهُمْ أَلاَ تَنْظُرُونَ إِلَى هَذَا الْمُرَائِي أَيُّكُمْ يَقُومُ إِلَى جَزُورِ آلِ فُلاَنٍ، فَيَعْمِدُ إِلَى فَرْثِهَا وَدَمِهَا وَسَلاَهَا فَيَجِيءُ بِهِ، ثُمَّ يُمْهِلُهُ حَتَّى إِذَا سَجَدَ وَضَعَهُ بَيْنَ كَتِفَيْهِ فَانْبَعَثَ أَشْقَاهُمْ، فَلَمَّا سَجَدَ رَسُولُ اللَّهِ صلى الله عليه وسلم وَضَعَهُ بَيْنَ كَتِفَيْهِ، وَثَبَتَ النَّبِيُّ صلى الله عليه وسلم سَاجِدًا، فَضَحِكُوا حَتَّى مَالَ بَعْضُهُمْ إِلَى بَعْضٍ مِنَ الضَّحِكِ، فَانْطَلَقَ مُنْطَلِقٌ إِلَى فَاطِمَةَ ـ عَلَيْهَا السَّلاَمُ ـ وَهْىَ جُوَيْرِيَةٌ، فَأَقْبَلَتْ تَسْعَى وَثَبَتَ النَّبِيُّ صلى الله عليه وسلم سَاجِدًا حَتَّى أَلْقَتْهُ عَنْهُ، وَأَقْبَلَتْ عَلَيْهِمْ تَسُبُّهُمْ، فَلَمَّا قَضَى رَسُولُ اللَّهِ صلى الله عليه وسلم الصَّلاَةَ قَالَ " اللَّهُمَّ عَلَيْكَ بِقُرَيْشٍ، اللَّهُمَّ عَلَيْكَ بِقُرَيْشٍ، اللَّهُمَّ عَلَيْكَ بِقُرَيْشٍ ـ ثُمَّ سَمَّى ـ اللَّهُمَّ عَلَيْكَ بِعَمْرِو بْنِ هِشَامٍ، وَعُتْبَةَ بْنِ رَبِيعَةَ، وَشَيْبَةَ بْنِ رَبِيعَةَ، وَالْوَلِيدِ بْنِ عُتْبَةَ، وَأُمَيَّةَ بْنِ خَلَفٍ، وَعُقْبَةَ بْنِ أَبِي مُعَيْطٍ، وَعُمَارَةَ بْنِ الْوَلِيدِ ". قَالَ عَبْدُ اللَّهِ فَوَاللَّهِ لَقَدْ رَأَيْتُهُمْ صَرْعَى يَوْمَ بَدْرٍ، ثُمَّ سُحِبُوا إِلَى الْقَلِيبِ قَلِيبِ بَدْرٍ، ثُمَّ قَالَ رَسُولُ اللَّهِ صلى الله عليه وسلم " وَأُتْبِعَ أَصْحَابُ الْقَلِيبِ لَعْنَةً ".

Narrated `Aisha: (mother of the believers) After the death of Allah 's Apostle Fatima the daughter of Allah's Messenger ﷺ asked Abu Bakr As-Siddiq to give her, her share of inheritance from what Allah's Messenger ﷺ had left of the Fai (i.e. booty gained without fighting) which Allah had given him. Abu Bakr said to her, "Allah's Apostle said, 'Our property will not be inherited, whatever we (i.e. prophets) leave is Sadaqa (to be used for charity)." Fatima, the daughter of Allah's Messenger ﷺ got angry and stopped speaking to Abu Bakr, and continued assuming that attitude till she died. Fatima remained alive for six months after the death of Allah's Messenger ﷺ. She used to ask Abu Bakr for her share from the property of Allah's Messenger ﷺ which he left at Khaibar, and Fadak, and his property at Medina (devoted for charity). Abu Bakr refused to give her that property and said, "I will not leave anything Allah's Messenger ﷺ used to do, because I am afraid that if I left something from the Prophet's tradition, then I would go astray." (Later on) `Umar gave the Prophet's property (of Sadaqa) at Medina to `Ali and `Abbas, but he withheld the properties of Khaibar and Fadak in his custody and said, "These two properties are the Sadaqa which Allah's Apostle used to use for his expenditures and urgent needs. Now their management is to be entrusted to the ruler." (Az-Zuhri said, "They have been managed in this way till today."). – Sahih Al-Bukhari 3092, 3093

حَدَّثَنَا عَبْدُ الْعَزِيزِ بْنُ عَبْدِ اللَّهِ، حَدَّثَنَا إِبْرَاهِيمُ بْنُ سَعْدٍ، عَنْ صَالِحٍ، عَنِ ابْنِ شِهَابٍ، قَالَ أَخْبَرَنِي عُرْوَةُ بْنُ الزُّبَيْرِ، أَنَّ عَائِشَةَ أُمَّ الْمُؤْمِنِينَ ـ رضى الله عنها ـ أَخْبَرَتْهُ أَنَّ فَاطِمَةَ ـ عَلَيْهَا السَّلاَمُ ـ ابْنَةَ رَسُولِ اللَّهِ صلى الله عليه وسلم سَأَلَتْ أَبَا بَكْرٍ الصِّدِّيقَ بَعْدَ وَفَاةِ رَسُولِ اللَّهِ صلى الله عليه وسلم أَنْ يَقْسِمَ لَهَا مِيرَاثَهَا، مَا تَرَكَ رَسُولُ اللَّهِ صلى الله عليه وسلم مِمَّا أَفَاءَ اللَّهُ عَلَيْهِ. فَقَالَ لَهَا أَبُو بَكْرٍ إِنَّ رَسُولَ اللَّهِ صلى الله عليه وسلم قَالَ " لاَ نُورَثُ مَا تَرَكْنَا صَدَقَةٌ ". فَغَضِبَتْ فَاطِمَةُ بِنْتُ رَسُولِ اللَّهِ صلى الله عليه وسلم فَهَجَرَتْ أَبَا بَكْرٍ، فَلَمْ تَزَلْ مُهَاجِرَتَهُ حَتَّى تُوُفِّيَتْ وَعَاشَتْ بَعْدَ رَسُولِ اللَّهِ صلى الله عليه وسلم سِتَّةَ أَشْهُرٍ. قَالَتْ وَكَانَتْ فَاطِمَةُ تَسْأَلُ أَبَا بَكْرٍ نَصِيبَهَا مِمَّا تَرَكَ رَسُولُ اللَّهِ صلى الله عليه وسلم مِنْ خَيْبَرَ وَفَدَكٍ وَصَدَقَتِهِ بِالْمَدِينَةِ، فَأَبَى أَبُو بَكْرٍ عَلَيْهَا ذَلِكَ، وَقَالَ لَسْتُ تَارِكًا شَيْئًا كَانَ رَسُولُ اللَّهِ صلى الله عليه وسلم يَعْمَلُ بِهِ إِلاَّ عَمِلْتُ بِهِ، فَإِنِّي أَخْشَى إِنْ تَرَكْتُ شَيْئًا مِنْ أَمْرِهِ أَنْ أَزِيغَ. فَأَمَّا صَدَقَتُهُ بِالْمَدِينَةِ فَدَفَعَهَا عُمَرُ إِلَى عَلِيٍّ وَعَبَّاسٍ، فَأَمَّا خَيْبَرُ وَفَدَكٌ فَأَمْسَكَهَا عُمَرُ وَقَالَ هُمَا صَدَقَةُ رَسُولِ اللَّهِ صلى الله عليه وسلم كَانَتَا لِحُقُوقِهِ الَّتِي تَعْرُوهُ وَنَوَائِبِهِ، وَأَمْرُهُمَا إِلَى مَنْ وَلِيَ الأَمْرَ. قَالَ فَهُمَا عَلَى ذَلِكَ إِلَى الْيَوْمِ. قَالَ أَبُو عَبْد اللَّهِ اعْتَرَاكَ افْتَعَلْتَ مِنْ عَرَوْتُهُ فَأَصَبْتُهُ وَمِنْهُ يَعْرُوهُ وَاعْتَرَانِي

Narrated Malik bin Aus: While I was at home, the sun rose high and it got hot. Suddenly the messenger of `Umar bin Al- Khattab came to me and said, "The chief of the believers has sent for you." So, I went along with him till I entered the place where `Umar was sitting on a bedstead made of date-palm leaves and covered with no mattress, and he was leaning over a leather pillow. I greeted him and sat down. He said, "O Mali! Some persons of your people who have families came to me and I have ordered that a gift should be given to them, so take it and distribute it among them." I said, "O chief of the believers! I wish that you order someone else to do it." He said, "O man! Take it." While I was sitting there with him, his doorman Yarfa' came saying, "`Uthman, `Abdur-Rahman bin `Auf, Az-Zubair and Sa`d bin Abi Waqqas are asking your permission (to see you); may I admit them?" `Umar said, "Yes", So they were admitted and they came in, greeted him, and sat down. After a while Yarfa' came again and said, "May I admit `Ali and `Abbas?" `Umar said, "yes." So, they were admitted and they came in and greeted (him) and sat down. Then `Abbas said, "O chief of the believers! Judge between me and this (i.e. `Ali)." They had a dispute regarding the property of Bani An-Nadir which Allah had given to His Apostle as Fai. The group (i.e. `Uthman and his companions) said, "O chief of the believers! Judge between them and relieve both of them front each other." `Umar said, "Be patient! I beseech you by Allah by Whose Permission the Heaven and the Earth exist, do you know that Allah's Messenger ﷺ said, 'Our (i.e. prophets') property will not be inherited, and whatever we leave, is Sadaqa (to be used for charity),' and Allah's Messenger ﷺ meant himself (by saying "we")?" The group said, "He said so." `Umar then turned to `Ali and `Abbas and said, "I beseech you by Allah, do you know that Allah's Messenger ﷺ said so?" They replied, " He said so." `Umar then said, "So, I will talk to you about this matter. Allah bestowed on His Apostle with a special favor of something of this Fai (booty) which he gave to nobody else." `Umar then recited the Holy Verses: "What Allah bestowed as (Fai) Booty on his Apostle (Muhammad) from them --- for this you made no expedition with either cavalry or camelry: But Allah gives power to His Apostles over whomever He will 'And Allah is able to do all things." 9:6) `Umar added "So this property was especially given to Allah's Messenger ﷺ, but, by Allah, neither did he take possession of it and leave your, nor did he favor himself with it to your exclusion, but he gave It to all of you and distributed it amongst you till this property remained out of it. Allah's Messenger ﷺ used to spend the yearly expenses of his family out of this property and used to keep the rest of its revenue to be spent on Allah 's Cause. Allah 's Apostle kept on doing this during all his lifetime. I ask you by Allah do you know this?" They replies in the affirmative. `Umar then said to `Ali and `Abbas. "I ask you by Allah, do you know this?" `Umar added, "When Allah had taken His Prophet unto Him, 'Abu Bakr said, 'I am the successor of Allah's Messenger ﷺ so, Abu Bakr took over that property and managed it in the same way as Allah's Messenger ﷺ used to do, and Allah knows that he was true, pious and rightlyguided, and he was a follower of what was right. Then Allah took Abu Bakr unto Him and I became Abu Bakr's successor, and I kept that property in my possession for the first two years of my Caliphate, managing it in the same way as Allah's Messenger ﷺ used to do and as Abu Bakr used to do, and Allah knows that I have been true, pious, rightly guided, and a follower of what is right. Now you both (i.e. 'Ah and `Abbas) came to talk to me, bearing the same claim and presenting the same case; you, `Abbas, came to me asking for your share from your nephew's property, and this man, i.e. `Ali, came to me asking for his wife's share from her father's property. I told you both that Allah's Messenger ﷺ said, 'Our (prophets') properties are not to be inherited, but what we leave is Sadaqa (to be used for charity).' When I thought it right that I should hand over this property to you, I said to you, 'I am ready to hand over this property to you if you wish, on the condition that you would take Allah's Pledge and Convention that you would manage it in the same way as Allah's Messenger ﷺ used to, and as Abu Bakr used to do, and as I have done since I was in charge of it.' So, both of you said (to me), 'Hand it over to us,' and on that condition I handed it over to you. So, I ask you by Allah, did I hand it over to them on this condition?" The group aid, "Yes." Then `Umar faced `Ali and `Abbas saying, "I ask you by Allah, did I hand it over to you on this condition?" They said, "Yes. " He said, " Do you want now to give a different decision? By Allah, by Whose Leave both the Heaven and the Earth exist, I will never give any decision other than that (I have already given). And if you are unable to manage it, then return it to me, and I will do the job on your behalf.". – Sahih Al-Bukhari 3094

حَدَّثَنَا إِسْحَاقُ بْنُ مُحَمَّدٍ الْفَرْوِيُّ، حَدَّثَنَا مَالِكُ بْنُ أَنَسٍ، عَنِ ابْنِ شِهَابٍ، عَنْ مَالِكِ بْنِ أَوْسِ بْنِ الْحَدَثَانِ،، وَكَانَ، مُحَمَّدُ بْنُ جُبَيْرٍ ذَكَرَ لِي ذِكْرًا مِنْ حَدِيثِهِ ذَلِكَ، فَانْطَلَقْتُ حَتَّى أَدْخُلَ عَلَى مَالِكِ بْنِ أَوْسٍ، فَسَأَلْتُهُ عَنْ ذَلِكَ الْحَدِيثِ فَقَالَ مَالِكٌ بَيْنَا أَنَا جَالِسٌ فِي أَهْلِي حِينَ مَتَعَ النَّهَارُ، إِذَا رَسُولُ عُمَرَ بْنِ الْخَطَّابِ يَأْتِينِي فَقَالَ أَجِبْ أَمِيرَ الْمُؤْمِنِينَ. فَانْطَلَقْتُ مَعَهُ حَتَّى أَدْخُلَ عَلَى عُمَرَ، فَإِذَا هُوَ جَالِسٌ عَلَى رِمَالِ سَرِيرٍ، لَيْسَ بَيْنَهُ وَبَيْنَهُ فِرَاشٌ مُتَّكِئٌ عَلَى وِسَادَةٍ مِنْ أَدَمٍ، فَسَلَّمْتُ عَلَيْهِ ثُمَّ جَلَسْتُ فَقَالَ يَا مَالِ، إِنَّهُ قَدِمَ عَلَيْنَا مِنْ قَوْمِكَ أَهْلُ أَبْيَاتٍ، وَقَدْ أَمَرْتُ فِيهِمْ بِرَضْخٍ فَاقْبِضْهُ فَاقْسِمْهُ بَيْنَهُمْ. فَقُلْتُ يَا أَمِيرَ الْمُؤْمِنِينَ، لَوْ أَمَرْتَ بِهِ غَيْرِي. قَالَ اقْبِضْهُ أَيُّهَا الْمَرْءُ. فَبَيْنَا أَنَا جَالِسٌ عِنْدَهُ أَتَاهُ حَاجِبُهُ يَرْفَا فَقَالَ هَلْ لَكَ فِي عُثْمَانَ وَعَبْدِ الرَّحْمَنِ بْنِ عَوْفٍ وَالزُّبَيْرِ وَسَعْدِ بْنِ أَبِي وَقَّاصٍ يَسْتَأْذِنُونَ قَالَ نَعَمْ. فَأَذِنَ لَهُمْ فَدَخَلُوا فَسَلَّمُوا وَجَلَسُوا، ثُمَّ جَلَسَ يَرْفَا يَسِيرًا ثُمَّ قَالَ هَلْ لَكَ فِي عَلِيٍّ وَعَبَّاسٍ قَالَ نَعَمْ. فَأَذِنَ لَهُمَا، فَدَخَلاَ فَسَلَّمَا فَجَلَسَا، فَقَالَ عَبَّاسٌ يَا أَمِيرَ الْمُؤْمِنِينَ، اقْضِ بَيْنِي وَبَيْنَ هَذَا. وَهُمَا يَخْتَصِمَانِ فِيمَا أَفَاءَ اللَّهُ عَلَى رَسُولِهِ صلى الله عليه وسلم مِنْ بَنِي النَّضِيرِ. فَقَالَ الرَّهْطُ عُثْمَانُ وَأَصْحَابُهُ يَا أَمِيرَ الْمُؤْمِنِينَ، اقْضِ بَيْنَهُمَا وَأَرِحْ أَحَدَهُمَا مِنَ الآخَرِ. قَالَ عُمَرُ تَيْدَكُمْ، أَنْشُدُكُمْ بِاللَّهِ الَّذِي بِإِذْنِهِ تَقُومُ السَّمَاءُ وَالأَرْضُ، هَلْ تَعْلَمُونَ أَنَّ رَسُولَ اللَّهِ صلى الله عليه وسلم قَالَ " لاَ نُورَثُ مَا تَرَكْنَا صَدَقَةٌ ". يُرِيدُ رَسُولُ اللَّهِ صلى الله عليه وسلم نَفْسَهُ. قَالَ الرَّهْطُ قَدْ قَالَ ذَلِكَ. فَأَقْبَلَ عُمَرُ عَلَى عَلِيٍّ وَعَبَّاسٍ فَقَالَ أَنْشُدُكُمَا اللَّهَ، أَتَعْلَمَانِ أَنَّ رَسُولَ اللَّهِ صلى الله عليه وسلم قَدْ قَالَ ذَلِكَ قَالاَ قَدْ قَالَ ذَلِكَ. قَالَ عُمَرُ فَإِنِّي أُحَدِّثُكُمْ عَنْ هَذَا الأَمْرِ، إِنَّ اللَّهَ قَدْ خَصَّ رَسُولَهُ صلى الله عليه وسلم فِي هَذَا الْفَىْءِ بِشَىْءٍ لَمْ يُعْطِهِ أَحَدًا غَيْرَهُ ـ ثُمَّ قَرَأَ {وَمَا أَفَاءَ اللَّهُ عَلَى رَسُولِهِ مِنْهُمْ} إِلَى قَوْلِهِ {قَدِيرٌ} ـ فَكَانَتْ هَذِهِ خَالِصَةً لِرَسُولِ اللَّهِ صلى الله عليه وسلم. وَاللَّهِ مَا احْتَازَهَا دُونَكُمْ، وَلاَ اسْتَأْثَرَ بِهَا عَلَيْكُمْ قَدْ أَعْطَاكُمُوهُ، وَبَثَّهَا فِيكُمْ حَتَّى بَقِيَ مِنْهَا هَذَا الْمَالُ، فَكَانَ رَسُولُ اللَّهِ صلى الله عليه وسلم يُنْفِقُ عَلَى أَهْلِهِ نَفَقَةَ سَنَتِهِمْ مِنْ هَذَا الْمَالِ، ثُمَّ يَأْخُذُ مَا بَقِيَ فَيَجْعَلُهُ مَجْعَلَ مَالِ اللَّهِ، فَعَمِلَ رَسُولُ اللَّهِ صلى الله عليه وسلم بِذَلِكَ حَيَاتَهُ، أَنْشُدُكُمْ بِاللَّهِ هَلْ تَعْلَمُونَ ذَلِكَ قَالُوا نَعَمْ. ثُمَّ قَالَ لِعَلِيٍّ وَعَبَّاسٍ أَنْشُدُكُمَا بِاللَّهِ هَلْ تَعْلَمَانِ ذَلِكَ قَالَ عُمَرُ ثُمَّ تَوَفَّى اللَّهُ نَبِيَّهُ صلى الله عليه وسلم فَقَالَ أَبُو بَكْرٍ أَنَا وَلِيُّ رَسُولِ اللَّهِ صلى الله عليه وسلم. فَقَبَضَهَا أَبُو بَكْرٍ، فَعَمِلَ فِيهَا بِمَا عَمِلَ رَسُولُ اللَّهِ صلى الله عليه وسلم، وَاللَّهُ يَعْلَمُ إِنَّهُ فِيهَا لَصَادِقٌ بَارٌّ رَاشِدٌ تَابِعٌ لِلْحَقِّ، ثُمَّ تَوَفَّى اللَّهُ أَبَا بَكْرٍ، فَكُنْتُ أَنَا وَلِيَّ أَبِي بَكْرٍ، فَقَبَضْتُهَا سَنَتَيْنِ مِنْ إِمَارَتِي، أَعْمَلُ فِيهَا بِمَا عَمِلَ رَسُولُ اللَّهِ صلى الله عليه وسلم وَمَا عَمِلَ فِيهَا أَبُو بَكْرٍ، وَاللَّهُ يَعْلَمُ إِنِّي فِيهَا لَصَادِقٌ بَارٌّ رَاشِدٌ تَابِعٌ لِلْحَقِّ، ثُمَّ جِئْتُمَانِي تُكَلِّمَانِي وَكَلِمَتُكُمَا وَاحِدَةٌ، وَأَمْرُكُمَا وَاحِدٌ، جِئْتَنِي يَا عَبَّاسُ تَسْأَلُنِي نَصِيبَكَ مِنِ ابْنِ أَخِيكَ، وَجَاءَنِي هَذَا ـ يُرِيدُ عَلِيًّا ـ يُرِيدُ نَصِيبَ امْرَأَتِهِ مِنْ أَبِيهَا، فَقُلْتُ لَكُمَا إِنَّ رَسُولَ اللَّهِ صلى الله عليه وسلم قَالَ " لاَ نُورَثُ مَا تَرَكْنَا صَدَقَةٌ ". فَلَمَّا بَدَا لِي أَنْ أَدْفَعَهُ إِلَيْكُمَا قُلْتُ إِنْ شِئْتُمَا دَفَعْتُهَا إِلَيْكُمَا عَلَى أَنَّ عَلَيْكُمَا عَهْدَ اللَّهِ وَمِيثَاقَهُ لَتَعْمَلاَنِ فِيهَا بِمَا عَمِلَ فِيهَا رَسُولُ اللَّهِ صلى الله عليه وسلم، وَبِمَا عَمِلَ فِيهَا أَبُو بَكْرٍ، وَبِمَا عَمِلْتُ فِيهَا مُنْذُ وَلِيتُهَا، فَقُلْتُمَا ادْفَعْهَا إِلَيْنَا. فَبِذَلِكَ دَفَعْتُهَا إِلَيْكُمَا، فَأَنْشُدُكُمْ بِاللَّهِ، هَلْ دَفَعْتُهَا إِلَيْهِمَا بِذَلِكَ قَالَ الرَّهْطُ نَعَمْ. ثُمَّ أَقْبَلَ عَلَى عَلِيٍّ وَعَبَّاسٍ فَقَالَ أَنْشُدُكُمَا بِاللَّهِ هَلْ دَفَعْتُهَا إِلَيْكُمَا بِذَلِكَ قَالاَ نَعَمْ. قَالَ فَتَلْتَمِسَانِ مِنِّي قَضَاءً غَيْرَ ذَلِكَ فَوَاللَّهِ الَّذِي بِإِذْنِهِ تَقُومُ السَّمَاءُ وَالأَرْضُ، لاَ أَقْضِي فِيهَا قَضَاءً غَيْرَ ذَلِكَ، فَإِنْ عَجَزْتُمَا عَنْهَا فَادْفَعَاهَا إِلَىَّ، فَإِنِّي أَكْفِيكُمَاهَا.

Narrated Al-Miswar bin Makhrama: Allah's Messenger ﷺ said, "Fatima is a part of me, and he who makes her angry, makes me angry.". – Sahih Al-Bukhari 3714

حَدَّثَنَا أَبُو الْوَلِيدِ، حَدَّثَنَا ابْنُ عُيَيْنَةَ، عَنْ عَمْرِو بْنِ دِينَارٍ، عَنِ ابْنِ أَبِي مُلَيْكَةَ، عَنِ الْمِسْوَرِ بْنِ مَخْرَمَةَ، أَنَّ رَسُولَ اللَّهِ صلى الله عليه وسلم قَالَ " فَاطِمَةُ بَضْعَةٌ مِنِّي، فَمَنْ أَغْضَبَهَا أَغْضَبَنِي "

Narrated Ibn `Umar: Once the Prophet ﷺ went to the house of Fatima but did not enter it. `Ali came and she told him about that. When 'Ali asked the Prophet ﷺ about it, he said, "I saw a (multicolored) decorated curtain on her door. I am not interested in worldly things." `Ali went to Fatima and told her about it. Fatima said, "I am ready to dispense with it in the way he suggests." The Prophet ﷺ ordered her to send it to such-andsuch needy people. ". – Sahih Al-Bukhari 2613

حَدَّثَنَا مُحَمَّدُ بْنُ جَعْفَرٍ أَبُو جَعْفَرٍ، حَدَّثَنَا ابْنُ فُضَيْلٍ، عَنْ أَبِيهِ، عَنْ نَافِعٍ، عَنِ ابْنِ عُمَرَ ـ رضى الله عنهما ـ قَالَ أَتَى النَّبِيُّ صلى الله عليه وسلم بَيْتَ فَاطِمَةَ فَلَمْ يَدْخُلْ عَلَيْهَا، وَجَاءَ عَلِيٌّ فَذَكَرَتْ لَهُ ذَلِكَ فَذَكَرَهُ لِلنَّبِيِّ صلى الله عليه وسلم قَالَ " إِنِّي

رَأَيْتُ عَلَى بَابِهَا سِتْرًا مَوْشِيًّا ". فَقَالَ " مَا لِي وَلِلدُّنْيَا ". فَأَتَاهَا عَلِيٌّ فَذَكَرَ ذَلِكَ لَهَا فَقَالَتْ لِيَأْمُرْنِي فِيهِ بِمَا شَاءَ. قَالَ تُرْسِلُ بِهِ إِلَى فُلاَنٍ. أَهْلِ بَيْتٍ بِهِمْ حَاجَةٌ.

Narrated Sahl: When the helmet of the Prophet ﷺ was smashed on his head and blood covered his face and one of his front teeth got broken, `Ali brought the water in his shield and Fatima the Prophet's daughter) washed him. But when she saw that the bleeding increased more by the water, she took a mat, burnt it, and placed the ashes on the wound of the Prophet ﷺ and so the blood stopped oozing out. – Sahih Al-Bukhari 2903

حَدَّثَنَا سَعِيدُ بْنُ عُفَيْرٍ، حَدَّثَنَا يَعْقُوبُ بْنُ عَبْدِ الرَّحْمَنِ، عَنْ أَبِي حَازِمٍ، عَنْ سَهْلٍ، قَالَ لَمَّا كُسِرَتْ بَيْضَةُ النَّبِيِّ صلى الله عليه وسلم عَلَى رَأْسِهِ وَأُدْمِيَ وَجْهُهُ، وَكُسِرَتْ رَبَاعِيَتُهُ، وَكَانَ عَلِيٌّ يَخْتَلِفُ بِالْمَاءِ فِي الْمِجَنِّ، وَكَانَتْ فَاطِمَةُ تَغْسِلُهُ، فَلَمَّا رَأَتِ الدَّمَ يَزِيدُ عَلَى الْمَاءِ كَثْرَةً عَمَدَتْ إِلَى حَصِيرٍ، فَأَحْرَقَتْهَا وَأَلْصَقَتْهَا عَلَى جُرْحِهِ، فَرَقَأَ الدَّمُ.

Narrated `Aisha: The people of Quraish worried about the lady from Bani Makhzum who had committed theft. They asked, "Who will intercede for her with Allah's Messenger ﷺ?" Some said, "No one dare to do so except Usama bin Zaid the beloved one to Allah's Messenger ﷺ." When Usama spoke about that to Allah's Apostle Allah's Messenger ﷺ said, (to him), "Do you try to intercede for somebody in a case connected with Allah's Prescribed Punishments?" Then he got up and delivered a sermon saying, "What destroyed the nations preceding you, was that if a noble amongst them stole, they would forgive him, and if a poor person amongst them stole, they would inflict Allah's Legal punishment on him. By Allah, if Fatima, the daughter of Muhammad stole, I would cut off her hand.". – Sahih Al-Bukhari 3475

حَدَّثَنَا قُتَيْبَةُ بْنُ سَعِيدٍ، حَدَّثَنَا لَيْثٌ، عَنِ ابْنِ شِهَابٍ، عَنْ عُرْوَةَ، عَنْ عَائِشَةَ ـ رضى الله عنها أَنَّ قُرَيْشًا، أَهَمَّهُمْ شَأْنُ الْمَرْأَةِ الْمَخْزُومِيَّةِ الَّتِي سَرَقَتْ، فَقَالَ وَمَنْ يُكَلِّمُ فِيهَا رَسُولَ اللَّهِ صلى الله عليه وسلم فَقَالُوا وَمَنْ يَجْتَرِئُ عَلَيْهِ إِلاَّ أُسَامَةُ بْنُ زَيْدٍ، حِبُّ رَسُولِ اللَّهِ صلى الله عليه وسلم، فَكَلَّمَهُ أُسَامَةُ، فَقَالَ رَسُولُ اللَّهِ صلى الله عليه وسلم " أَتَشْفَعُ فِي حَدٍّ مِنْ حُدُودِ اللَّهِ ". ثُمَّ قَامَ فَاخْتَطَبَ، ثُمَّ قَالَ " إِنَّمَا أَهْلَكَ الَّذِينَ قَبْلَكُمْ أَنَّهُمْ كَانُوا إِذَا سَرَقَ فِيهِمُ الشَّرِيفُ تَرَكُوهُ، وَإِذَا سَرَقَ فِيهِمُ الضَّعِيفُ أَقَامُوا عَلَيْهِ الْحَدَّ، وَايْمُ اللَّهِ، لَوْ أَنَّ فَاطِمَةَ ابْنَةَ مُحَمَّدٍ سَرَقَتْ لَقَطَعْتُ يَدَهَا ".

Narrated `Aisha: Once Fatima came walking and her gait resembled the gait of the Prophet ﷺ. The Prophet ﷺ said, "Welcome, O my daughter!" Then he made her sit on his right or on his left side, and then he told her a secret and she started weeping. I asked her, "Why are you weeping?" He again told her a secret and she started laughing. I said, "I never saw happiness so near to sadness as I saw today." I asked her what the Prophet ﷺ had told her. She said, "I would never disclose the secret of Allah's Messenger." When the Prophet ﷺ died, I asked her about it. She replied. "The Prophet ﷺ said: 'Every year Gabriel used to revise the Qur'an with me once only, but this year he has done so twice. I think this portends my death, and you will be the first of my family to follow me.' So I started weeping. Then he said. 'Don't you like to be the chief of all the ladies of Paradise or the chief of the believing women? So I laughed for that.". – Sahih Al-Bukhari 3623, 3624

حَدَّثَنَا أَبُو نُعَيْمٍ، حَدَّثَنَا زَكَرِيَّاءُ، عَنْ فِرَاسٍ، عَنْ عَامِرٍ، عَنْ مَسْرُوقٍ، عَنْ عَائِشَةَ ـ رضى الله عنها ـ قَالَتْ أَقْبَلَتْ فَاطِمَةُ تَمْشِي، كَأَنَّ مِشْيَتَهَا مَشْىُ النَّبِيِّ صلى الله عليه وسلم فَقَالَ النَّبِيُّ صلى الله عليه وسلم " مَرْحَبًا بِابْنَتِي ". ثُمَّ أَجْلَسَهَا عَنْ يَمِينِهِ أَوْ عَنْ شِمَالِهِ، ثُمَّ أَسَرَّ إِلَيْهَا حَدِيثًا، فَبَكَتْ فَقُلْتُ لَهَا لِمَ تَبْكِينَ ثُمَّ أَسَرَّ إِلَيْهَا حَدِيثًا فَضَحِكَتْ فَقُلْتُ مَا رَأَيْتُ كَالْيَوْمِ فَرَحًا أَقْرَبَ مِنْ حُزْنٍ، فَسَأَلْتُهَا عَمَّا قَالَ. فَقَالَتْ مَا كُنْتُ لأُفْشِيَ سِرَّ رَسُولِ اللَّهِ صلى الله عليه وسلم حَتَّى قُبِضَ النَّبِيُّ صلى الله عليه وسلم فَسَأَلْتُهَا فَقَالَتْ أَسَرَّ إِلَىَّ " إِنَّ جِبْرِيلَ كَانَ يُعَارِضُنِي الْقُرْآنَ كُلَّ سَنَةٍ مَرَّةً، وَإِنَّهُ عَارَضَنِي الْعَامَ مَرَّتَيْنِ، وَلاَ أُرَاهُ إِلاَّ حَضَرَ أَجَلِي، وَإِنَّكِ أَوَّلُ أَهْلِ بَيْتِي لَحَاقًا بِي ". فَبَكَيْتُ فَقَالَ " أَمَا تَرْضَيْنَ أَنْ تَكُونِي سَيِّدَةَ نِسَاءِ أَهْلِ الْجَنَّةِ ـ أَوْ نِسَاءِ الْمُؤْمِنِينَ ". فَضَحِكْتُ لِذَلِكَ.

Narrated Anas: When the ailment of the Prophet ﷺ got aggravated, he became unconscious whereupon Fatima said, "Oh, how distressed my father is!" He said, "Your father will have no more distress after today." When he expired, she said, "O Father! Who has responded to the call of the Lord Who has invited him! O Father, whose dwelling place is the Garden of Paradise (i.e. Al-Firdaus)! O Father! We convey this news (of your death) to Gabriel." When he was buried, Fatima said, "O Anas! Do you feel pleased to throw earth over Allah's Messenger?" – Sahih Al-Bukhari 4462

حَدَّثَنَا سُلَيْمَانُ بْنُ حَرْبٍ، حَدَّثَنَا حَمَّادٌ، عَنْ ثَابِتٍ، عَنْ أَنَسٍ، قَالَ لَمَّا ثَقُلَ النَّبِيُّ صلى الله عليه وسلم جَعَلَ يَتَغَشَّاهُ، فَقَالَتْ فَاطِمَةُ ـ عَلَيْهَا السَّلاَمُ ـ وَاكَرْبَ أَبَاهُ. فَقَالَ لَهَا " لَيْسَ عَلَى أَبِيكِ كَرْبٌ بَعْدَ الْيَوْمِ ". فَلَمَّا مَاتَ قَالَتْ يَا أَبَتَاهْ، أَجَابَ رَبًّا دَعَاهُ، يَا أَبَتَاهْ مَنْ جَنَّةُ الْفِرْدَوْسِ مَأْوَاهُ، يَا أَبَتَاهْ إِلَى جِبْرِيلَ نَنْعَاهْ. فَلَمَّا دُفِنَ قَالَتْ فَاطِمَةُ ـ عَلَيْهَا السَّلاَمُ ـ يَا أَنَسُ، أَطَابَتْ أَنْفُسُكُمْ أَنْ تَحْثُوا عَلَى رَسُولِ اللَّهِ صلى الله عليه وسلم التُّرَابَ

Narrated `Aisha: Mother of the Believers: We, the wives of the Prophet ﷺ were all sitting with the Prophet ﷺ and none of us had left when Fatima came walking, and by Allah, her gait was very similar to that of Allah's Messenger ﷺ. When he saw her, he welcomed her, saying, "Welcome, O my daughter!" Then he made her sit on his right or his left, confided something to her, whereupon she wept bitterly. When he noticed her sorrow, he confided something else to her for the second time, and she started laughing. Only I from among the Prophet's wives said to her, "(O Fatima), Allah's Messenger ﷺ selected you from among us for the secret talk and still you weep?" When Allah's Messenger ﷺ got up (and went away), I asked her, "What did he confide to you?" She said, "I wouldn't disclose the secrets of Allah's Messenger" But when he died I asked her, "I beseech you earnestly by what right I have on you, to tell me (that secret talk which the Prophet had with you)" She said, "As you ask me now, yes, (I will tell you)." She informed me, saying, "When he talked to me secretly the first time, he said that Gabriel used to review the Qur'an with him once every year. He added, 'But this year he reviewed it with me twice, and therefore I think that my time of death has approached. So, be afraid of Allah, and be patient, for I am the best predecessor for you (in the Hereafter).' " Fatima added, "So I wept as you (`Aisha) witnessed. And when the Prophet ﷺ saw me in this sorrowful state, he confided the second secret to me saying, 'O Fatima! Will you not be pleased that you will be chief of all the believing women (or chief of the women of this nation i.e. my followers?"). – Sahih Al-Bukhari 6285, 6286

حَدَّثَنَا مُوسَى، عَنْ أَبِي عَوَانَةَ، حَدَّثَنَا فِرَاسٌ، عَنْ عَامِرٍ، عَنْ مَسْرُوقٍ، حَدَّثَتْنِي عَائِشَةُ أُمُّ الْمُؤْمِنِينَ، قَالَتْ إِنَّا كُنَّا أَزْوَاجَ النَّبِيِّ صلى الله عليه وسلم عِنْدَهُ جَمِيعًا، لَمْ تُغَادَرْ مِنَّا وَاحِدَةٌ، فَأَقْبَلَتْ فَاطِمَةُ ـ عَلَيْهَا السَّلاَمُ ـ تَمْشِي، لاَ وَاللَّهِ مَا تَخْفَى مِشْيَتُهَا مِنْ مِشْيَةِ رَسُولِ اللَّهِ صلى الله عليه وسلم فَلَمَّا رَآهَا رَحَّبَ قَالَ " مَرْحَبًا بِابْنَتِي ". ثُمَّ أَجْلَسَهَا عَنْ يَمِينِهِ أَوْ عَنْ شِمَالِهِ، ثُمَّ سَارَّهَا فَبَكَتْ بُكَاءً شَدِيدًا، فَلَمَّا رَأَى حُزْنَهَا سَارَّهَا الثَّانِيَةَ إِذَا هِيَ تَضْحَكُ. فَقُلْتُ لَهَا أَنَا مِنْ بَيْنِ نِسَائِهِ خَصَّكِ رَسُولُ اللَّهِ صلى الله عليه وسلم بِالسِّرِّ مِنْ بَيْنِنَا، ثُمَّ أَنْتِ تَبْكِينَ، فَلَمَّا قَامَ رَسُولُ اللَّهِ صلى الله عليه وسلم سَأَلْتُهَا عَمَّا سَارَّكِ قَالَتْ مَا كُنْتُ لأُفْشِيَ عَلَى رَسُولِ اللَّهِ صلى الله عليه وسلم سِرَّهُ. فَلَمَّا تُوُفِّيَ قُلْتُ لَهَا عَزَمْتُ عَلَيْكِ بِمَا لِي عَلَيْكِ مِنَ الْحَقِّ لَمَّا أَخْبَرْتِنِي. قَالَتْ أَمَّا الآنَ فَنَعَمْ. فَأَخْبَرَتْنِي قَالَتْ أَمَّا حِينَ سَارَّنِي فِي الأَمْرِ الأَوَّلِ، فَإِنَّهُ أَخْبَرَنِي أَنَّ جِبْرِيلَ كَانَ يُعَارِضُهُ بِالْقُرْآنِ كُلَّ سَنَةٍ مَرَّةً " وَإِنَّهُ قَدْ عَارَضَنِي بِهِ الْعَامَ مَرَّتَيْنِ، وَلاَ أَرَى الأَجَلَ إِلاَّ قَدِ اقْتَرَبَ، فَاتَّقِي اللَّهَ وَاصْبِرِي، فَإِنِّي نِعْمَ السَّلَفُ أَنَا لَكِ ". قَالَتْ فَبَكَيْتُ بُكَائِي الَّذِي رَأَيْتِ، فَلَمَّا رَأَى جَزَعِي سَارَّنِي الثَّانِيَةَ قَالَ " يَا فَاطِمَةُ أَلاَ تَرْضَيْنَ أَنْ تَكُونِي سَيِّدَةَ نِسَاءِ الْمُؤْمِنِينَ ـ أَوْ ـ سَيِّدَةَ نِسَاءِ هَذِهِ الأُمَّةِ "

Narrated `Urwa from `Aisha: The wives of Allah's Messenger ﷺ were in two groups. One group consisted of `Aisha, Hafsa, Safiyya and Sauda; and the other group consisted of Um Salama and the other wives of Allah's Messenger ﷺ. The Muslims knew that Allah's Messenger ﷺ loved `Aisha, so if any of them had a gift and wished to give to Allah's Messenger ﷺ, he would delay it, till Allah's Messenger ﷺ had come to `Aisha's home and then he would send his gift to Allah's Messenger ﷺ in her home. The group of Um Salama discussed the matter together and decided that Um Salama should request Allah's Messenger ﷺ to tell the people to send their gifts to him in whatever wife's house he was. Um Salama told Allah's Messenger ﷺ of what they had said, but he did not reply. Then they (those wives) asked Um Salama about it. She said, "He did not say anything to me." They asked her to talk to him again. She talked to him again when she met him on her day, but he gave no reply. When they asked her, she replied that he had given no reply. They said to her, "Talk to him till he gives you a reply." When it was her turn, she talked to him again. He then said to her, "Do not hurt me regarding Aisha, as the Divine Inspirations do not come to me on any of the beds except that of Aisha." On that Um Salama said, "I repent to Allah for hurting you." Then the group of Um Salama called Fatima, the daughter of Allah's Messenger ﷺ and sent her to Allah's Messenger ﷺ to say to him, "Your wives request to treat them and the daughter of Abu Bakr on equal terms." Then Fatima conveyed the message to him. The Prophet ﷺ said, "O my daughter! Don't you love whom I love?" She replied in the affirmative and returned and told them of the situation. They requested her to go to him again but she refused. They then sent Zainab bint Jahsh who went to him and used harsh words saying, "Your wives request you to treat them and the daughter of Ibn Abu Quhafa on equal terms." On that she raised her voice and abused `Aisha to her face so much so that Allah's Messenger ﷺ looked at `Aisha to see whether she would retort. `Aisha started replying to Zainab till she silenced her. The Prophet ﷺ then looked at `Aisha and said, "She is really the daughter of Abu Bakr.". – Sahih Al-Bukhari 2581

حَدَّثَنَا إِسْمَاعِيلُ، قَالَ حَدَّثَنِي أَخِي، عَنْ سُلَيْمَانَ، عَنْ هِشَامِ بْنِ عُرْوَةَ، عَنْ أَبِيهِ، عَنْ عَائِشَةَ ـ رضى الله عنها ـ أَنَّ نِسَاءَ رَسُولِ اللَّهِ صلى الله عليه وسلم كُنَّ حِزْبَيْنِ فَحِزْبٌ فِيهِ عَائِشَةُ وَحَفْصَةُ وَصَفِيَّةُ وَسَوْدَةُ، وَالْحِزْبُ الآخَرُ أُمُّ سَلَمَةَ وَسَائِرُ نِسَاءِ رَسُولِ اللَّهِ صلى الله عليه وسلم، وَكَانَ الْمُسْلِمُونَ قَدْ عَلِمُوا حُبَّ رَسُولِ اللَّهِ صلى الله عليه وسلم عَائِشَةَ، فَإِذَا كَانَتْ عِنْدَ أَحَدِهِمْ هَدِيَّةٌ يُرِيدُ أَنْ يُهْدِيَهَا إِلَى رَسُولِ اللَّهِ صلى الله عليه وسلم أَخَّرَهَا، حَتَّى إِذَا كَانَ رَسُولُ اللَّهِ صلى الله عليه وسلم فِي بَيْتِ عَائِشَةَ بَعَثَ صَاحِبُ الْهَدِيَّةِ إِلَى رَسُولِ اللَّهِ صلى الله عليه وسلم فِي بَيْتِ عَائِشَةَ، فَكَلَّمَ حِزْبُ أُمِّ سَلَمَةَ، فَقُلْنَ لَهَا كَلِّمِي رَسُولَ اللَّهِ صلى الله عليه وسلم يُكَلِّمُ النَّاسَ، فَيَقُولُ مَنْ أَرَادَ أَنْ يُهْدِيَ إِلَى رَسُولِ اللَّهِ صلى الله عليه وسلم هَدِيَّةً فَلْيُهْدِهِ إِلَيْهِ حَيْثُ كَانَ مِنْ بُيُوتِ نِسَائِهِ، فَكَلَّمَتْهُ أُمُّ سَلَمَةَ بِمَا قُلْنَ، فَلَمْ يَقُلْ لَهَا شَيْئًا، فَسَأَلْنَهَا. فَقَالَتْ مَا قَالَ لِي شَيْئًا. فَقُلْنَ لَهَا فَكَلِّمِيهِ. قَالَتْ فَكَلَّمَتْهُ حِينَ دَارَ إِلَيْهَا أَيْضًا، فَلَمْ يَقُلْ لَهَا شَيْئًا، فَسَأَلْنَهَا. فَقَالَتْ مَا قَالَ لِي شَيْئًا. فَقُلْنَ لَهَا كَلِّمِيهِ حَتَّى يُكَلِّمَكِ. فَدَارَ إِلَيْهَا فَكَلَّمَتْهُ. فَقَالَ لَهَا " لاَ تُؤْذِينِي فِي عَائِشَةَ، فَإِنَّ الْوَحْىَ لَمْ يَأْتِنِي، وَأَنَا فِي ثَوْبِ امْرَأَةٍ إِلاَّ عَائِشَةَ ". قَالَتْ فَقَالَتْ أَتُوبُ إِلَى اللَّهِ مِنْ أَذَاكَ يَا رَسُولَ اللَّهِ. ثُمَّ إِنَّهُنَّ دَعَوْنَ فَاطِمَةَ بِنْتَ رَسُولِ اللَّهِ صلى الله عليه وسلم فَأَرْسَلْنَ إِلَى رَسُولِ اللَّهِ صلى الله عليه وسلم تَقُولُ إِنَّ نِسَاءَكَ يَنْشُدْنَكَ اللَّهَ الْعَدْلَ فِي بِنْتِ أَبِي بَكْرٍ. فَكَلَّمَتْهُ. فَقَالَ " يَا بُنَيَّةُ، أَلاَ تُحِبِّينَ مَا أُحِبُّ ". قَالَتْ بَلَى. فَرَجَعَتْ إِلَيْهِنَّ، فَأَخْبَرَتْهُنَّ. فَقُلْنَ ارْجِعِي إِلَيْهِ. فَأَبَتْ أَنْ تَرْجِعَ، فَأَرْسَلْنَ زَيْنَبَ بِنْتَ جَحْشٍ، فَأَتَتْهُ فَأَغْلَظَتْ، وَقَالَتْ إِنَّ نِسَاءَكَ يَنْشُدْنَكَ اللَّهَ الْعَدْلَ فِي بِنْتِ ابْنِ أَبِي قُحَافَةَ. فَرَفَعَتْ صَوْتَهَا، حَتَّى تَنَاوَلَتْ عَائِشَةَ. وَهْىَ قَاعِدَةٌ، فَسَبَّتْهَا حَتَّى إِنَّ رَسُولَ اللَّهِ صلى الله عليه وسلم لَيَنْظُرُ إِلَى عَائِشَةَ هَلْ تَكَلَّمُ قَالَ فَتَكَلَّمَتْ عَائِشَةُ تَرُدُّ عَلَى زَيْنَبَ، حَتَّى أَسْكَتَتْهَا. قَالَتْ فَنَظَرَ النَّبِيُّ صلى الله عليه وسلم إِلَى عَائِشَةَ، وَقَالَ " إِنَّهَا بِنْتُ أَبِي بَكْرٍ ". قَالَ الْبُخَارِيُّ الْكَلاَمُ الأَخِيرُ قِصَّةُ فَاطِمَةَ يُذْكَرُ عَنْ هِشَامِ بْنِ عُرْوَةَ عَنْ رَجُلٍ عَنِ الزُّهْرِيِّ عَنْ مُحَمَّدِ بْنِ عَبْدِ الرَّحْمَنِ. وَقَالَ أَبُو مَرْوَانَ عَنْ هِشَامٍ عَنْ عُرْوَةَ كَانَ النَّاسُ يَتَحَرَّوْنَ بِهَدَايَاهُمْ يَوْمَ عَائِشَةَ. وَعَنْ هِشَامٍ عَنْ رَجُلٍ مِنْ قُرَيْشٍ، وَرَجُلٍ مِنَ الْمَوَالِي، عَنِ الزُّهْرِيِّ عَنْ مُحَمَّدِ بْنِ عَبْدِ الرَّحْمَنِ بْنِ الْحَارِثِ بْنِ هِشَامٍ قَالَتْ عَائِشَةُ كُنْتُ عِنْدَ النَّبِيِّ صلى الله عليه وسلم فَاسْتَأْذَنَتْ فَاطِمَةُ

Narrated `Ali: Fatima complained about the blisters on her hand because of using a millstone. She went to ask the Prophet for servant, but she did not find him (at home) and had to inform `Aisha of her need. When he came, `Aisha informed him about it. `Ali added: The Prophet ﷺ came to us when we had gone to our beds. When I was going to get up, he said, "'Stay in your places," and sat between us, till I felt the coolness of the feet on my chest. The Prophet ﷺ then said, "Shall I not tell you of a thing which is better for you than a servant? When you (both) go to your beds, say 'Allahu Akbar' thirty-three times, and 'Subhan Allah' thirty-three times, 'Al hamdu 'illah' thirty-three times, for that is better for you than a servant." Ibn Seereen said, "Subhan Allah' (is to be said for) thirty-four times." - Sahih Al-Bukhari 6318

حَدَّثَنَا سُلَيْمَانُ بْنُ حَرْبٍ، حَدَّثَنَا شُعْبَةُ، عَنِ الْحَكَمِ، عَنِ ابْنِ أَبِي لَيْلَى، عَنْ عَلِيٍّ، أَنَّ فَاطِمَةَ ـ عَلَيْهِمَا السَّلاَمُ ـ شَكَتْ مَا تَلْقَى فِي يَدِهَا مِنَ الرَّحَى، فَأَتَتِ النَّبِيَّ صلى الله عليه وسلم تَسْأَلُهُ خَادِمًا، فَلَمْ تَجِدْهُ، فَذَكَرَتْ ذَلِكَ لِعَائِشَةَ، فَلَمَّا جَاءَ أَخْبَرَتْهُ. قَالَ

فَجَاءَنَا وَقَدْ أَخَذْنَا مَضَاجِعَنَا، فَذَهَبْتُ أَقُومُ فَقَالَ " مَكَانَكِ ". فَجَلَسَ بَيْنَنَا حَتَّى وَجَدْتُ بَرْدَ قَدَمَيْهِ عَلَى صَدْرِي فَقَالَ " أَلاَ أَدُلُّكُمَا عَلَى مَا هُوَ خَيْرٌ لَكُمَا مِنْ خَادِمٍ، إِذَا أَوَيْتُمَا إِلَى فِرَاشِكُمَا، أَوْ أَخَذْتُمَا مَضَاجِعَكُمَا، فَكَبِّرَا ثَلاَثًا وَثَلاَثِينَ، وَسَبِّحَا ثَلاَثًا وَثَلاَثِينَ، وَاحْمَدَا ثَلاَثًا وَثَلاَثِينَ، فَهَذَا خَيْرٌ لَكُمَا مِنْ خَادِمٍ ". وَعَنْ شُعْبَةَ عَنْ خَالِدٍ عَنِ ابْنِ سِيرِينَ قَالَ التَّسْبِيحُ أَرْبَعٌ وَثَلاَثُونَ.

Narrated Sahl bin Sa`d: There was no name dearer to `Ali than his nickname Abu Turab (the father of dust). He used to feel happy whenever he was called by this name. Once Allah's Messenger ﷺ came to the house of Fatima but did not find `Ali in the house. So he asked "Where is your cousin?" She replied, "There was something (a quarrel) between me and him whereupon he got angry with me and went out without having a midday nap in my house." Allah's Messenger ﷺ asked a person to look for him. That person came, and said, "O Allah's Messenger ﷺ !He (Ali) is sleeping in the mosque." So Allah's Messenger ﷺ went there and found him lying. His upper body cover had fallen off to one side of his body, and so he was covered with dust. Allah's Messenger ﷺ started cleaning the dust from him, saying, "Get up, O Abu Turab! Get up, Abu Turab!" (See Hadith No. 432, Vol 1). – Sahih Al-Bukhari 6280
حَدَّثَنَا قُتَيْبَةُ بْنُ سَعِيدٍ، حَدَّثَنَا عَبْدُ الْعَزِيزِ بْنُ أَبِي حَازِمٍ، عَنْ أَبِي حَازِمٍ، عَنْ سَهْلِ بْنِ سَعْدٍ، قَالَ مَا كَانَ لِعَلِيٍّ اسْمٌ أَحَبَّ إِلَيْهِ مِنْ أَبِي تُرَابٍ، وَإِنْ كَانَ لَيَفْرَحُ بِهِ إِذَا دُعِيَ بِهَا، جَاءَ رَسُولُ اللَّهِ صلى الله عليه وسلم بَيْتَ فَاطِمَةَ ـ عَلَيْهَا السَّلاَمُ ـ فَلَمْ يَجِدْ عَلِيًّا فِي الْبَيْتِ فَقَالَ " أَيْنَ ابْنُ عَمِّكِ ". فَقَالَتْ كَانَ بَيْنِي وَبَيْنَهُ شَىْءٌ، فَغَاضَبَنِي فَخَرَجَ فَلَمْ يَقِلْ عِنْدِي. فَقَالَ رَسُولُ اللَّهِ صلى الله عليه وسلم لإِنْسَانٍ " انْظُرْ أَيْنَ هُوَ " فَجَاءَ فَقَالَ يَا رَسُولَ اللَّهِ هُوَ فِي الْمَسْجِدِ رَاقِدٌ. فَجَاءَ رَسُولُ اللَّهِ صلى الله عليه وسلم وَهْوَ مُضْطَجِعٌ، قَدْ سَقَطَ رِدَاؤُهُ عَنْ شِقِّهِ، فَأَصَابَهُ تُرَابٌ، فَجَعَلَ رَسُولُ اللَّهِ صلى الله عليه وسلم يَمْسَحُهُ عَنْهُ ـ وَهْوَ يَقُولُ " قُمْ أَبَا تُرَابٍ، قُمْ أَبَا تُرَابٍ ".

Husayn ibn Ali ibn Abi Talib
الْحُسَيْنُ بْنُ عَلِيِّ بْنِ أَبِي طَالِبٍ

Narrated Ibn Abi Na'm: I was present when a man asked Ibn `Umar about the blood of mosquitoes. Ibn `Umar said, "From where are you?" The man replied. "From Iraq." Ibn `Umar said, "Look at that! He is asking me about the blood of Mosquitoes while they (the Iraqis) have killed the (grand) son of the Prophet. I have heard the Prophet ﷺ saying, "They (Hasan and Husain) are my two sweet-smelling flowers in this world.". – Sahih Al-Bukhari 5994
حَدَّثَنَا مُوسَى بْنُ إِسْمَاعِيلَ، حَدَّثَنَا مَهْدِيٌّ، حَدَّثَنَا ابْنُ أَبِي يَعْقُوبَ، عَنِ ابْنِ أَبِي نُعْمٍ، قَالَ كُنْتُ شَاهِدًا لاِبْنِ عُمَرَ وَسَأَلَهُ رَجُلٌ عَنْ دَمِ الْبَعُوضِ. فَقَالَ مِمَّنْ أَنْتَ فَقَالَ مِنْ أَهْلِ الْعِرَاقِ. قَالَ انْظُرُوا إِلَى هَذَا، يَسْأَلُنِي عَنْ دَمِ الْبَعُوضِ وَقَدْ قَتَلُوا ابْنَ النَّبِيِّ صلى الله عليه وسلم وَسَمِعْتُ النَّبِيَّ صلى الله عليه وسلم يَقُولُ " هُمَا رَيْحَانَتَاىَ مِنَ الدُّنْيَا "

Narrated Muhammad: Anas bin Malik said, "The head of Al-Husain was brought to 'Ubaidullah bin Ziyad and was put in a tray, and then Ibn Ziyad started playing with a stick at the nose and mouth of Al-Husain's head and saying something about his handsome features." Anas then said (to him), "Al-Husain resembled the Prophet more than the others did." Anas added, "His (i.e. Al-Husain's) hair was dyed with Wasma (i.e. a kind of plant used as a dye). – Sahih Al-Bukhari 3748
حَدَّثَنِي مُحَمَّدُ بْنُ الْحُسَيْنِ بْنِ إِبْرَاهِيمَ، قَالَ حَدَّثَنِي حُسَيْنُ بْنُ مُحَمَّدٍ، حَدَّثَنَا جَرِيرٌ، عَنْ مُحَمَّدٍ، عَنْ أَنَسِ بْنِ مَالِكٍ ـ رضى الله عنه ـ أُتِيَ عُبَيْدُ اللَّهِ بْنُ زِيَادٍ بِرَأْسِ الْحُسَيْنِ ـ عَلَيْهِ السَّلاَمُ ـ فَجُعِلَ فِي طَسْتٍ، فَجَعَلَ يَنْكُتُ، وَقَالَ فِي حُسْنِهِ شَيْئًا. فَقَالَ أَنَسٌ كَانَ أَشْبَهَهُمْ بِرَسُولِ اللَّهِ صلى الله عليه وسلم، وَكَانَ مَخْضُوبًا بِالْوَسْمَةِ

Narrated Ibn Abi Na'm: I was present when a man asked Ibn `Umar about the blood of mosquitoes. Ibn `Umar said, "From where are you?" The man replied. "From Iraq." Ibn `Umar said, "Look at that! He is asking me about the blood of Mosquitoes while they (the Iraqis)

have killed the (grand) son of the Prophet. I have heard the Prophet ﷺ saying, "They (Hasan and Husain) are my two sweet-smelling flowers in this world.". – Sahih Al-Bukhari 5994
حَدَّثَنَا مُوسَى بْنُ إِسْمَاعِيلَ، حَدَّثَنَا مَهْدِيٌّ، حَدَّثَنَا ابْنُ أَبِي يَعْقُوبَ، عَنِ ابْنِ أَبِي نُعْمٍ، قَالَ كُنْتُ شَاهِدًا لاِبْنِ عُمَرَ وَسَأَلَهُ رَجُلٌ عَنْ دَمِ الْبَعُوضِ. فَقَالَ مِمَّنْ أَنْتَ فَقَالَ مِنْ أَهْلِ الْعِرَاقِ. قَالَ انْظُرُوا إِلَى هَذَا، يَسْأَلُنِي عَنْ دَمِ الْبَعُوضِ وَقَدْ قَتَلُوا ابْنَ النَّبِيِّ صلى الله عليه وسلم وَسَمِعْتُ النَّبِيَّ صلى الله عليه وسلم يَقُولُ " هُمَا رَيْحَانَتَاىَ مِنَ الدُّنْيَا ".

Narrated Ibn `Abbas: The Prophet ﷺ used to seek Refuge with Allah for Al-Hasan and Al-Husain and say: "Your forefather (i.e. Abraham) used to seek Refuge with Allah for Ishmael and Isaac by reciting the following: 'O Allah! I seek Refuge with Your Perfect Words from every devil and from poisonous pests and from every evil, harmful, envious eye.' ". – Sahih Al-Bukhari 3371
حَدَّثَنَا عُثْمَانُ بْنُ أَبِي شَيْبَةَ، حَدَّثَنَا جَرِيرٌ، عَنْ مَنْصُورٍ، عَنِ الْمِنْهَالِ، عَنْ سَعِيدِ بْنِ جُبَيْرٍ، عَنِ ابْنِ عَبَّاسٍ ـ رضى الله عنهما ـ قَالَ كَانَ النَّبِيُّ صلى الله عليه وسلم يُعَوِّذُ الْحَسَنَ وَالْحُسَيْنَ وَيَقُولُ " إِنَّ أَبَاكُمَا كَانَ يُعَوِّذُ بِهَا إِسْمَاعِيلَ وَإِسْحَاقَ، أَعُوذُ بِكَلِمَاتِ اللَّهِ التَّامَّةِ مِنْ كُلِّ شَيْطَانٍ وَهَامَّةٍ، وَمِنْ كُلِّ عَيْنٍ لاَمَّةٍ ".

Narrated Abu Huraira: Dates used to be brought to Allah's Messenger ﷺ immediately after being plucked. Different persons would bring their dates till a big heap collected (in front of the Prophet). Once Al-Hasan and Al-Husain were playing with these dates. One of them took a date and put it in his mouth. Allah's Messenger ﷺ looked at him and took it out from his mouth and said, "Don't you know that Muhammad's offspring do not eat what is given in charity?". – Sahih Al-Bukhari 1485
حَدَّثَنَا عُمَرُ بْنُ مُحَمَّدِ بْنِ الْحَسَنِ الأَسَدِيُّ، حَدَّثَنَا أَبِي، حَدَّثَنَا إِبْرَاهِيمُ بْنُ طَهْمَانَ، عَنْ مُحَمَّدِ بْنِ زِيَادٍ، عَنْ أَبِي هُرَيْرَةَ ـ رضى الله عنه ـ قَالَ كَانَ رَسُولُ اللَّهِ صلى الله عليه وسلم يُؤْتَى بِالتَّمْرِ عِنْدَ صِرَامِ النَّخْلِ فَيَجِيءُ هَذَا بِتَمْرِهِ وَهَذَا مِنْ تَمْرِهِ حَتَّى يَصِيرَ عِنْدَهُ كَوْمًا مِنْ تَمْرٍ، فَجَعَلَ الْحَسَنُ وَالْحُسَيْنُ ـ رضى الله عنهما ـ يَلْعَبَانِ بِذَلِكَ التَّمْرِ، فَأَخَذَ أَحَدُهُمَا تَمْرَةً، فَجَعَلَهَا فِي فِيهِ، فَنَظَرَ إِلَيْهِ رَسُولُ اللَّهِ صلى الله عليه وسلم فَأَخْرَجَهَا مِنْ فِيهِ فَقَالَ " أَمَا عَلِمْتَ أَنَّ آلَ مُحَمَّدٍ صلى الله عليه وسلم لاَ يَأْكُلُونَ الصَّدَقَةَ ".

Hasan ibn Ali ibn Abi Talib
الْحَسَنِ بْن عَلِيِّ بْن أَبِي طَالِب

Narrated Ma`bad bin Hilal Al-`Anzi: We, i.e., some people from Basra gathered and went to Anas bin Malik, and we went in company with Thabit Al-Bunnani so that he might ask him about the Hadith of Intercession on our behalf. Behold, Anas was in his palace, and our arrival coincided with his Duha prayer. We asked permission to enter and he admitted us while he was sitting on his bed. We said to Thabit, "Do not ask him about anything else first but the Hadith of Intercession." He said, "O Abu Hamza! There are your brethren from Basra coming to ask you about the Hadith of Intercession." Anas then said, "Muhammad talked to us saying, 'On the Day of Resurrection the people will surge with each other like waves, and then they will come to Adam and say, 'Please intercede for us with your Lord.' He will say, 'I am not fit for that but you'd better go to Abraham as he is the Khalil of the Beneficent.' They will go to Abraham and he will say, 'I am not fit for that, but you'd better go to Moses as he is the one to whom Allah spoke directly.' So they will go to Moses and he will say, 'I am not fit for that, but you'd better go to Jesus as he is a soul created by Allah and His Word.' (Be: And it was) they will go to Jesus and he will say, 'I am not fit for that, but you'd better go to Muhammad.' They would come to me and I would say, 'I am for that.' Then I will ask for my Lord's permission, and it will be given, and then He will inspire me to praise Him with such praises as I do not know now. So I will praise Him with those praises and will fall down, prostrate before Him. Then it will be said, 'O Muhammad, raise your head and speak, for you will be listened to; and ask, for your will be granted (your request); and intercede, for your intercession will be accepted.' I will say, 'O Lord, my followers! My followers!' And then it will be said, 'Go and take out of Hell (Fire) all those who have faith in their hearts, equal to the weight of a barley grain.' I will go and do so and return to praise Him with the same praises, and fall down (prostrate) before Him. Then it will be said, 'O Muhammad, raise your head and speak, for you will be listened to, and ask, for you will be granted (your request); and intercede, for your intercession will be accepted.' I will say, 'O Lord, my followers! My followers!' It will be said, 'Go and take out of it all those who have faith in their hearts equal to the weight of a small ant or a mustard seed.' I will go and do so and return to praise Him with the same praises, and fall down in prostration before Him. It will be said, 'O, Muhammad, raise your head and speak, for you will be listened to, and ask, for you will be granted (your request); and intercede, for your intercession will be accepted.' I will say, 'O Lord, my followers!' Then He will say, 'Go and take out (all those) in whose hearts there is faith even to the lightest, lightest mustard seed. (Take them) out of the Fire.' I will go and do so."' When we left Anas, I said to some of my companions, "Let's pass by Al-Hasan who is hiding himself in the house of Abi Khalifa and request him to tell us what Anas bin Malik has told us." So we went to him and we greeted him and he admitted us. We said to him, "O Abu Sa`id! We came to you from your brother Anas Bin Malik and he related to us a Hadith about the Intercession the like of which I have never heard." He said, "What is that?" Then we told him of the Hadith and said, "He stopped at this point (of the Hadith)." He said, "What then?" We said, "He did not add anything to that." He said, Anas related the Hadith to me twenty years ago when he was a young fellow. I don't know whether he forgot or if he did not like to let you depend on what he might have said." We said, "O Abu Sa`id ! Let us know that." He smiled and said, "Man was created hasty. I did not mention that, but that I wanted to inform you of it. Anas told me the same as he told you and said that the Prophet ﷺ added, 'I then return for a fourth time and praise Him similarly and prostrate before Him me the same as he 'O Muhammad, raise your head and speak, for you will be listened to; and ask, for you will be granted (your request): and intercede, for your intercession will be accepted .' I will say, 'O Lord, allow me to intercede for whoever said, 'None has the right to be worshiped except Allah.' Then Allah will say, 'By my Power, and my Majesty, and by My Supremacy, and by My Greatness, I will take out of Hell (Fire) whoever said: 'None has the right to be worshipped except Allah.' ". – Sahih Al-Bukhari 7510

حَدَّثَنَا سُلَيْمَانُ بْنُ حَرْبٍ، حَدَّثَنَا حَمَّادُ بْنُ زَيْدٍ، حَدَّثَنَا مَعْبَدُ بْنُ هِلاَلٍ الْعَنَزِيُّ، قَالَ اجْتَمَعْنَا نَاسٌ مِنْ أَهْلِ الْبَصْرَةِ فَذَهَبْنَا إِلَى أَنَسِ بْنِ مَالِكٍ وَذَهَبْنَا مَعَنَا بِثَابِتٍ إِلَيْهِ يَسْأَلُهُ لَنَا عَنْ حَدِيثِ الشَّفَاعَةِ، فَإِذَا هُوَ فِي قَصْرِهِ فَوَافَقْنَاهُ يُصَلِّي الضُّحَى، فَاسْتَأْذَنَّا، فَأَذِنَ لَنَا وَهْوَ قَاعِدٌ عَلَى فِرَاشِهِ فَقُلْنَا لِثَابِتٍ لاَ تَسْأَلْهُ عَنْ شَىْءٍ أَوَّلَ مِنْ حَدِيثِ الشَّفَاعَةِ فَقَالَ يَا أَبَا حَمْزَةَ هَؤُلاَءِ إِخْوَانُكَ مِنْ أَهْلِ الْبَصْرَةِ جَاءُوكَ يَسْأَلُونَكَ عَنْ حَدِيثِ الشَّفَاعَةِ. فَقَالَ حَدَّثَنَا مُحَمَّدٌ صلى الله عليه وسلم قَالَ " إِذَا كَانَ يَوْمُ الْقِيَامَةِ مَاجَ النَّاسُ بَعْضُهُمْ فِي بَعْضٍ فَيَأْتُونَ آدَمَ فَيَقُولُونَ اشْفَعْ لَنَا إِلَى رَبِّكَ. فَيَقُولُ لَسْتُ لَهَا وَلَكِنْ عَلَيْكُمْ بِإِبْرَاهِيمَ فَإِنَّهُ خَلِيلُ الرَّحْمَنِ. فَيَأْتُونَ إِبْرَاهِيمَ فَيَقُولُ لَسْتُ لَهَا وَلَكِنْ عَلَيْكُمْ بِمُوسَى فَإِنَّهُ كَلِيمُ اللَّهِ. فَيَأْتُونَ مُوسَى فَيَقُولُ لَسْتُ لَهَا وَلَكِنْ عَلَيْكُمْ بِعِيسَى فَإِنَّهُ رُوحُ اللَّهِ وَكَلِمَتُهُ. فَيَأْتُونَ عِيسَى فَيَقُولُ لَسْتُ لَهَا وَلَكِنْ عَلَيْكُمْ بِمُحَمَّدٍ صلى الله عليه وسلم فَيَأْتُونِي فَأَقُولُ أَنَا لَهَا. فَأَسْتَأْذِنُ عَلَى رَبِّي فَيُؤْذَنُ لِي وَيُلْهِمُنِي مَحَامِدَ أَحْمَدُهُ بِهَا لاَ تَحْضُرُنِي الآنَ، فَأَحْمَدُهُ بِتِلْكَ الْمَحَامِدِ وَأَخِرُّ لَهُ سَاجِدًا فَيُقَالُ يا محمد ارْفَعْ رَأْسَكَ، وَقُلْ يُسْمَعْ لَكَ، وَسَلْ تُعْطَ، وَاشْفَعْ تُشَفَّعْ. فَأَقُولُ يَا رَبِّ أُمَّتِي أُمَّتِي. فَيُقَالُ انْطَلِقْ فَأَخْرِجْ مَنْ كَانَ فِي قَلْبِهِ مِثْقَالُ شَعِيرَةٍ مِنْ إِيمَانٍ. فَأَنْطَلِقُ فَأَفْعَلُ ثُمَّ أَعُودُ فَأَحْمَدُهُ بِتِلْكَ الْمَحَامِدِ، ثُمَّ أَخِرُّ لَهُ سَاجِدًا فَيُقَالُ يَا مُحَمَّدُ ارْفَعْ رَأْسَكَ، وَقُلْ يُسْمَعْ لَكَ، وَسَلْ تُعْطَ، وَاشْفَعْ تُشَفَّعْ، فَأَقُولُ يَا رَبِّ أُمَّتِي أُمَّتِي. فَيُقَالُ انْطَلِقْ فَأَخْرِجْ مِنْهَا مَنْ كَانَ فِي قَلْبِهِ مِثْقَالُ ذَرَّةٍ أَوْ خَرْدَلَةٍ مِنْ إِيمَانٍ. فَأَنْطَلِقُ فَأَفْعَلُ ثُمَّ أَعُودُ فَأَحْمَدُهُ بِتِلْكَ الْمَحَامِدِ، ثُمَّ أَخِرُّ لَهُ سَاجِدًا فَيُقَالُ يَا مُحَمَّدُ ارْفَعْ رَأْسَكَ، وَقُلْ يُسْمَعْ لَكَ، وَسَلْ تُعْطَ، وَاشْفَعْ تُشَفَّعْ. فَأَقُولُ يَا رَبِّ أُمَّتِي أُمَّتِي. فَيَقُولُ انْطَلِقْ فَأَخْرِجْ مَنْ كَانَ فِي قَلْبِهِ أَدْنَى أَدْنَى أَدْنَى مِثْقَالِ حَبَّةِ خَرْدَلٍ مِنْ إِيمَانٍ، فَأَخْرِجْهُ مِنَ النَّارِ. فَأَنْطَلِقُ فَأَفْعَلُ ". فَلَمَّا خَرَجْنَا مِنْ عِنْدِ أَنَسٍ قُلْتُ لِبَعْضِ أَصْحَابِنَا لَوْ مَرَرْنَا بِالْحَسَنِ

وَهْوَ مُتَوَارٍ فِي مَنْزِلِ أَبِي خَلِيفَةَ فَحَدَّثَنَا بِمَا حَدَّثَنَا أَنَسُ بْنُ مَالِكٍ، فَأَتَيْنَاهُ فَسَلَّمْنَا عَلَيْهِ فَأَذِنَ لَنَا فَقُلْنَا لَهُ يَا أَبَا سَعِيدٍ جِئْنَاكَ مِنْ عِنْدِ أَخِيكَ أَنَسِ بْنِ مَالِكٍ فَلَمْ نَرَ مِثْلَ مَا حَدَّثَنَا فِي الشَّفَاعَةِ، فَقَالَ هِيهِ، فَحَدَّثْنَاهُ بِالْحَدِيثِ فَانْتَهَى إِلَى هَذَا الْمَوْضِعِ فَقَالَ هِيهِ، فَقُلْنَا لَمْ يَزِدْ لَنَا عَلَى هَذَا. فَقَالَ لَقَدْ حَدَّثَنِي وَهْوَ جَمِيعٌ مُنْذُ عِشْرِينَ سَنَةً فَلاَ أَدْرِي أَنَسِيَ أَمْ كَرِهَ أَنْ تَتَّكِلُوا. قُلْنَا يَا أَبَا سَعِيدٍ فَحَدِّثْنَا، فَضَحِكَ وَقَالَ خُلِقَ الإِنْسَانُ عَجُولاً مَا ذَكَرْتُهُ إِلاَّ وَأَنَا أُرِيدُ أَنْ أُحَدِّثَكُمْ حَدَّثَنِي كَمَا حَدَّثَكُمْ بِهِ قَالَ " ثُمَّ أَعُودُ الرَّابِعَةَ فَأَحْمَدُهُ بِتِلْكَ، ثُمَّ أَخِرُّ لَهُ سَاجِدًا فَيُقَالُ يَا مُحَمَّدُ ارْفَعْ رَأْسَكَ وَقُلْ يُسْمَعْ، وَسَلْ تُعْطَهْ، وَاشْفَعْ تُشَفَّعْ. فَأَقُولُ يَا رَبِّ ائْذَنْ لِي فِيمَنْ قَالَ لاَ إِلَهَ إِلاَّ اللَّهُ. فَيَقُولُ وَعِزَّتِي وَجَلاَلِي وَكِبْرِيَائِي وَعَظَمَتِي لأُخْرِجَنَّ مِنْهَا مَنْ قَالَ لاَ إِلَهَ إِلاَّ اللَّهُ "

Narrated Al-Hasan: Concerning the Verse: 'Do not prevent them' (2.232) Ma'qil bin Yasar told me that it was revealed in his connection. He said, "I married my sister to a man and he divorced her, and when her days of 'Idda (three menstrual periods) were over, the man came again and asked for her hand, but I said to him, 'I married her to you and made her your bed (your wife) and favored you with her, but you divorced her. Now you come to ask for her hand again? No, by Allah, she will never go back to you (again)!' That man was not a bad man and his wife wanted to go back to him. So Allah revealed this Verse: 'Do not prevent them.' (2.232) So I said, 'Now I will do it (let her go back to him), O Allah's Messenger ﷺ." So he married her to him again. – Sahih Al-Bukhari 5130
حَدَّثَنَا أَحْمَدُ بْنُ أَبِي عَمْرٍو، قَالَ حَدَّثَنِي أَبِي قَالَ، حَدَّثَنِي إِبْرَاهِيمُ، عَنْ يُونُسَ، عَنِ الْحَسَنِ، {فَلاَ تَعْضُلُوهُنَّ} قَالَ حَدَّثَنِي مَعْقِلُ بْنُ يَسَارٍ، أَنَّهَا نَزَلَتْ فِيهِ قَالَ زَوَّجْتُ أُخْتًا لِي مِنْ رَجُلٍ فَطَلَّقَهَا، حَتَّى إِذَا انْقَضَتْ عِدَّتُهَا جَاءَ يَخْطُبُهَا، فَقُلْتُ لَهُ زَوَّجْتُكَ وَفَرَشْتُكَ وَأَكْرَمْتُكَ، فَطَلَّقْتَهَا، ثُمَّ جِئْتَ تَخْطُبُهَا، لاَ وَاللَّهِ لاَ تَعُودُ إِلَيْكَ أَبَدًا، وَكَانَ رَجُلاً لاَ بَأْسَ بِهِ وَكَانَتِ الْمَرْأَةُ تُرِيدُ أَنْ تَرْجِعَ إِلَيْهِ فَأَنْزَلَ اللَّهُ هَذِهِ الآيَةَ {فَلاَ تَعْضُلُوهُنَّ} فَقُلْتُ الآنَ أَفْعَلُ يَا رَسُولَ اللَّهِ. قَالَ فَزَوَّجَهَا إِيَّاهُ

Narrated Abu Huraira Ad-Dausi: Once the Prophet ﷺ went out during the day. Neither did he talk to me nor I to him till he reached the market of Bani Qainuqa and then he sat in the compound of Fatima's house and asked about the small boy (his grandson Al-Hasan) but Fatima kept the boy in for a while. I thought she was either changing his clothes or giving the boy a bath. After a while the boy came out running and the Prophet ﷺ embraced and kissed him and then said, 'O Allah! Love him, and love whoever loves him.'. – Sahih Al-Bukhari 2122
حَدَّثَنَا عَلِيُّ بْنُ عَبْدِ اللَّهِ، حَدَّثَنَا سُفْيَانُ، عَنْ عُبَيْدِ اللَّهِ بْنِ أَبِي يَزِيدَ، عَنْ نَافِعِ بْنِ جُبَيْرِ بْنِ مُطْعِمٍ، عَنْ أَبِي هُرَيْرَةَ الدَّوْسِيِّ - رضى الله عنه - قَالَ خَرَجَ النَّبِيُّ صلى الله عليه وسلم فِي طَائِفَةِ النَّهَارِ لاَ يُكَلِّمُنِي وَلاَ أُكَلِّمُهُ حَتَّى أَتَى سُوقَ بَنِي قَيْنُقَاعَ، فَجَلَسَ بِفِنَاءِ بَيْتِ فَاطِمَةَ فَقَالَ " أَثَمَّ لُكَعُ أَثَمَّ لُكَعُ ". فَحَبَسَتْهُ شَيْئًا فَظَنَنْتُ أَنَّهَا تُلْبِسُهُ سِخَابًا أَوْ تُغَسِّلُهُ، فَجَاءَ يَشْتَدُّ حَتَّى عَانَقَهُ وَقَبَّلَهُ، وَقَالَ " اللَّهُمَّ أَحْبِبْهُ وَأَحِبَّ مَنْ يُحِبُّهُ ". قَالَ سُفْيَانُ قَالَ عُبَيْدُ اللَّهِ أَخْبَرَنِي أَنَّهُ رَأَى نَافِعَ بْنَ جُبَيْرٍ أَوْتَرَ بِرَكْعَةٍ.

Ibn 'Abbas further said, "Seven types of marriages are unlawful because of blood relations, and seven because of marriage relations." Then Ibn 'Abbas recited the Verse: "Forbidden for you (for marriages) are your mothers..." (4:23). 'Abdullah bin Ja'far married the daughter and wife of 'Ali at the same time (they were step-daughter and mother). Ibn Sirin said, "There is no harm in that." But Al-Hasan Al-Basri disapproved of it at first, but then said that there was no harm in it. Al-Hasan bin Al-Hasan bin 'Ali married two of his cousins in one night. Ja'far bin Zaid disapproved of that because of it would bring hatred (between the two cousins), but it is not unlawful, as Allah said, "Lawful to you are all others [beyond those (mentioned)]. (4:24). Ibn 'Abbas said: "If somebody commits illegal sexual intercourse with his wife's sister, his wife does not become unlawful for him." And narrated Abu Ja'far, "If a person commits homosexuality with a boy, then the mother of that boy is unlawful for him to marry." Narrated Ibn 'Abbas, "If one commits illegal sexual intercourse with his mother in law, then his married relation to his wife does not become unlawful." Abu Nasr reported to have said that Ibn 'Abbas in the above case, regarded his marital relation to his wife unlawful, but Abu Nasr is not known well for hearing Hadith from Ibn 'Abbas. Imran bin Hussain, Jabir b. Zaid, Al-Hasan and some other Iraqi's, are reported to have judged that his marital relations to his wife would be unlawful. In the above case Abu Hurairah said, “The marital relation to one’s wife does not become unlawful except if one as had sexual intercourse (with her mother).” Ibn Al-Musaiyab, ‘Urwa, and Az-Zuhri allows such person to keep his wife. ‘Ali said, “His marital relations to his wife does not become unlawful.”. – Sahih Al-Bukhari 5105

وَقَالَ لَنَا أَحْمَدُ بْنُ حَنْبَلٍ حَدَّثَنَا يَحْيَى بْنُ سَعِيدٍ، عَنْ سُفْيَانَ، حَدَّثَنِي حَبِيبٌ، عَنْ سَعِيدٍ، عَنِ ابْنِ عَبَّاسٍ، حَرُمَ مِنَ النَّسَبِ سَبْعٌ، وَمِنَ الصِّهْرِ سَبْعٌ. ثُمَّ قَرَأَ {حُرِّمَتْ عَلَيْكُمْ أُمَّهَاتُكُمْ} الآيَةَ. وَجَمَعَ عَبْدُ اللَّهِ بْنُ جَعْفَرٍ بَيْنَ ابْنَةِ عَلِيٍّ وَامْرَأَةِ عَلِيٍّ. وَقَالَ ابْنُ سِيرِينَ لاَ بَأْسَ بِهِ. وَكَرِهَهُ الْحَسَنُ مَرَّةً ثُمَّ قَالَ لاَ بَأْسَ بِهِ. وَجَمَعَ الْحَسَنُ بْنُ الْحَسَنِ بْنِ عَلِيٍّ بَيْنَ ابْنَتَىْ عَمٍّ فِي لَيْلَةٍ، وَكَرِهَهُ جَابِرُ بْنُ زَيْدٍ لِلْقَطِيعَةِ، وَلَيْسَ فِيهِ تَحْرِيمٌ لِقَوْلِهِ تَعَالَى {وَأُحِلَّ لَكُمْ مَا وَرَاءَ ذَلِكُمْ} وَقَالَ عِكْرِمَةُ عَنِ ابْنِ عَبَّاسٍ إِذَا زَنَى بِأُخْتِ امْرَأَتِهِ لَمْ تَحْرُمْ عَلَيْهِ امْرَأَتُهُ. وَيُرْوَى عَنْ يَحْيَى الْكِنْدِيِّ عَنِ الشَّعْبِيِّ وَأَبِي جَعْفَرٍ، فِيمَنْ يَلْعَبُ بِالصَّبِيِّ إِنْ أَدْخَلَهُ فِيهِ، فَلاَ يَتَزَوَّجَنَّ أُمَّهُ، وَيَحْيَى هَذَا غَيْرُ مَعْرُوفٍ، لَمْ يُتَابَعْ عَلَيْهِ. وَقَالَ عِكْرِمَةُ عَنِ ابْنِ عَبَّاسٍ إِذَا زَنَى بِهَا لَمْ تَحْرُمْ عَلَيْهِ امْرَأَتُهُ. وَيُذْكَرُ عَنْ أَبِي نَصْرٍ أَنَّ ابْنَ عَبَّاسٍ حَرَّمَهُ. وَأَبُو نَصْرٍ هَذَا لَمْ يُعْرَفْ بِسَمَاعِهِ مِنِ ابْنِ عَبَّاسٍ. وَيُرْوَى عَنْ عِمْرَانَ بْنِ حُصَيْنٍ وَجَابِرِ بْنِ زَيْدٍ وَالْحَسَنِ وَبَعْضِ أَهْلِ الْعِرَاقِ تَحْرُمُ عَلَيْهِ. وَقَالَ أَبُو هُرَيْرَةَ لاَ تَحْرُمُ حَتَّى يُلْزِقَ بِالأَرْضِ يَعْنِي يُجَامِعَ. وَجَوَّزَهُ ابْنُ الْمُسَيَّبِ وَعُرْوَةُ وَالزُّهْرِيُّ. وَقَالَ الزُّهْرِيُّ قَالَ عَلِيٌّ لاَ تَحْرُمُ. وَهَذَا مُرْسَلٌ

Narrated Abu Huraira: Allah’s Messenger ﷺ kissed Al-Hasan bin `Ali while Al-Aqra’ bin H`Abis at-Tamim was sitting beside him. Al-Aqra said, “I have ten children and I have never kissed anyone of them,” Allah’s Messenger ﷺ cast a look at him and said, “Whoever is not merciful to others will not be treated mercifully.”. – Sahih Al-Bukhari 5997

حَدَّثَنَا أَبُو الْيَمَانِ، أَخْبَرَنَا شُعَيْبٌ، عَنِ الزُّهْرِيِّ، حَدَّثَنَا أَبُو سَلَمَةَ بْنُ عَبْدِ الرَّحْمَنِ، أَنَّ أَبَا هُرَيْرَةَ ـ رضى الله عنه ـ قَالَ قَبَّلَ رَسُولُ اللَّهِ صلى الله عليه وسلم الْحَسَنَ بْنَ عَلِيٍّ وَعِنْدَهُ الأَقْرَعُ بْنُ حَابِسٍ التَّمِيمِيُّ جَالِسًا. فَقَالَ الأَقْرَعُ إِنَّ لِي عَشَرَةً مِنَ الْوَلَدِ مَا قَبَّلْتُ مِنْهُمْ أَحَدًا. فَنَظَرَ إِلَيْهِ رَسُولُ اللَّهِ صلى الله عليه وسلم ثُمَّ قَالَ " مَنْ لاَ يَرْحَمُ لاَ يُرْحَمُ ".

Narrated Abu Wail: When `Ali sent `Ammar and Al-Hasan to (the people of) Kufa to urge them to fight, `Ammar addressed them saying, “I know that she (i.e. `Aisha) is the wife of the Prophet ﷺ in this world and in the Hereafter (world to come), but Allah has put you to test, whether you will follow Him (i.e. Allah) or her.”. – Sahih Al-Bukhari 3772

حَدَّثَنَا مُحَمَّدُ بْنُ بَشَّارٍ، حَدَّثَنَا غُنْدَرٌ، حَدَّثَنَا شُعْبَةُ، عَنِ الْحَكَمِ، سَمِعْتُ أَبَا وَائِلٍ، قَالَ لَمَّا بَعَثَ عَلِيٌّ عَمَّارًا وَالْحَسَنَ إِلَى الْكُوفَةِ لِيَسْتَنْفِرَهُمْ خَطَبَ عَمَّارٌ فَقَالَ إِنِّي لأَعْلَمُ أَنَّهَا زَوْجَتُهُ فِي الدُّنْيَا وَالآخِرَةِ، وَلَكِنَّ اللَّهَ ابْتَلاَكُمْ لِتَتَّبِعُوهُ أَوْ إِيَّاهَا

Narrated Isma`il bin Abi Khalid: I heard Abii Juhaifa saying, “I saw the Prophet, and Al-Hasan bin `Ali resembled him.” I said to Abu- Juhaifa, “Describe him for me.” He said, “He was white and his beard was black with some white hair. He promised to give us 13 young she-camels, but he expired before we could get them.”. – Sahih Al-Bukhari 3544

حَدَّثَنِي عَمْرُو بْنُ عَلِيٍّ، حَدَّثَنَا ابْنُ فُضَيْلٍ، حَدَّثَنَا إِسْمَاعِيلُ بْنُ أَبِي خَالِدٍ، قَالَ سَمِعْتُ أَبَا جُحَيْفَةَ ـ رضى الله عنه ـ قَالَ رَأَيْتُ النَّبِيَّ صلى الله عليه وسلم وَكَانَ الْحَسَنُ بْنُ عَلِيٍّ ـ عَلَيْهِمَا السَّلاَمُ ـ يُشْبِهُهُ قُلْتُ لأَبِي جُحَيْفَةَ صِفْهُ لِي. قَالَ كَانَ أَبْيَضَ قَدْ شَمِطَ. وَأَمَرَ لَنَا النَّبِيُّ صلى الله عليه وسلم بِثَلاَثَ عَشْرَةَ قَلُوصًا قَالَ فَقُبِضَ النَّبِيُّ صلى الله عليه وسلم قَبْلَ أَنْ نَقْبِضَهَا.

Narrated Abu Huraira: Dates used to be brought to Allah’s Messenger ﷺ immediately after being plucked. Different persons would bring their dates till a big heap collected (in front of the Prophet). Once Al-Hasan and Al-Husain were playing with these dates. One of them took a date and put it in his mouth. Allah’s Messenger ﷺ looked at him and took it out from his mouth and said, “Don’t you know that Muhammad’s offspring do not eat what is given in charity?”. – Sahih Al-Bukhari 1485

حَدَّثَنَا عُمَرُ بْنُ مُحَمَّدِ بْنِ الْحَسَنِ الأَسَدِيُّ، حَدَّثَنَا أَبِي، حَدَّثَنَا إِبْرَاهِيمُ بْنُ طَهْمَانَ، عَنْ مُحَمَّدِ بْنِ زِيَادٍ، عَنْ أَبِي هُرَيْرَةَ ـ رضى الله عنه ـ قَالَ كَانَ رَسُولُ اللَّهِ صلى الله عليه وسلم يُؤْتَى بِالتَّمْرِ عِنْدَ صِرَامِ النَّخْلِ فَيَجِيءُ هَذَا بِتَمْرِهِ وَهَذَا مِنْ تَمْرِهِ حَتَّى يَصِيرَ عِنْدَهُ كَوْمًا مِنْ تَمْرٍ، فَجَعَلَ الْحَسَنُ وَالْحُسَيْنُ ـ رضى الله عنهما ـ يَلْعَبَانِ بِذَلِكَ التَّمْرِ، فَأَخَذَ أَحَدُهُمَا تَمْرَةً، فَجَعَلَهَا فِي فِيهِ، فَنَظَرَ إِلَيْهِ رَسُولُ اللَّهِ صلى الله عليه وسلم فَأَخْرَجَهَا مِنْ فِيهِ فَقَالَ " أَمَا عَلِمْتَ أَنَّ آلَ مُحَمَّدٍ صلى الله عليه وسلم لاَ يَأْكُلُونَ الصَّدَقَةَ ".

Narrated Abu Ja`far: Jabir bin `Abdullah said to me, "Your cousin (Hasan bin Muhammad bin Al-Hanafiya) came to me and asked about the bath of Janaba. I replied, 'The Prophet ﷺ uses to take three handfuls of water, pour them on his head and then pour more water over his body.' Al-Hasan said to me, 'I am a hairy man.' I replied, 'The Prophet ﷺ had more hair than you'. ". – Sahih Al-Bukhari 256

حَدَّثَنَا أَبُو نُعَيْمٍ، قَالَ حَدَّثَنَا مَعْمَرُ بْنُ يَحْيَى بْنِ سَامٍ، حَدَّثَنِي أَبُو جَعْفَرٍ، قَالَ قَالَ لِي جَابِرٌ أَتَانِي ابْنُ عَمِّكَ يُعَرِّضُ بِالْحَسَنِ بْنِ مُحَمَّدٍ ابْنِ الْحَنَفِيَّةِ قَالَ كَيْفَ الْغُسْلُ مِنَ الْجَنَابَةِ فَقُلْتُ كَانَ النَّبِيُّ صلى الله عليه وسلم يَأْخُذُ ثَلاَثَةَ أَكُفٍّ وَيُفِيضُهَا عَلَى رَأْسِهِ، ثُمَّ يُفِيضُ عَلَى سَائِرِ جَسَدِهِ. فَقَالَ لِي الْحَسَنُ إِنِّي رَجُلٌ كَثِيرُ الشَّعَرِ. فَقُلْتُ كَانَ النَّبِيُّ صلى الله عليه وسلم أَكْثَرَ مِنْكَ شَعَرًا.

Narrated Abu Maryam `Abdullah bin Ziyad Al-Aasadi: When Talha, AzZubair and `Aisha moved to Basra, `Ali sent `Ammar bin Yasir and Hasan bin `Ali who came to us at Kufa and ascended the pulpit. Al-Hasan bin `Ali was at the top of the pulpit and `Ammar was below Al-Hasan. We all gathered before him. I heard `Ammar saying, "`Aisha has moved to Al-Busra. By Allah! She is the wife of your Prophet in this world and in the Hereafter. But Allah has put you to test whether you obey Him (Allah) or her (`Aisha). – Sahih Al-Bukhari 7100

حَدَّثَنَا عَبْدُ اللَّهِ بْنُ مُحَمَّدٍ، حَدَّثَنَا يَحْيَى بْنُ آدَمَ، حَدَّثَنَا أَبُو بَكْرِ بْنُ عَيَّاشٍ، حَدَّثَنَا أَبُو حَصِينٍ، حَدَّثَنَا أَبُو مَرْيَمَ عَبْدُ اللَّهِ بْنُ زِيَادٍ الأَسَدِيُّ، قَالَ لَمَّا سَارَ طَلْحَةُ وَالزُّبَيْرُ وَعَائِشَةُ إِلَى الْبَصْرَةِ بَعَثَ عَلِيٌّ عَمَّارَ بْنَ يَاسِرٍ وَحَسَنَ بْنَ عَلِيٍّ، فَقَدِمَا عَلَيْنَا الْكُوفَةَ فَصَعِدَا الْمِنْبَرَ، فَكَانَ الْحَسَنُ بْنُ عَلِيٍّ فَوْقَ الْمِنْبَرِ فِي أَعْلاَهُ، وَقَامَ عَمَّارٌ أَسْفَلَ مِنَ الْحَسَنِ، فَاجْتَمَعْنَا إِلَيْهِ فَسَمِعْتُ عَمَّارًا يَقُولُ إِنَّ عَائِشَةَ قَدْ سَارَتْ إِلَى الْبَصْرَةِ، وَوَاللَّهِ إِنَّهَا لَزَوْجَةُ نَبِيِّكُمْ صلى الله عليه وسلم فِي الدُّنْيَا وَالآخِرَةِ، وَلَكِنَّ اللَّهَ تَبَارَكَ وَتَعَالَى ابْتَلاَكُمْ، لِيَعْلَمَ إِيَّاهُ تُطِيعُونَ أَمْ هِيَ

Narrated Usama bin Zaid: Allah's Messenger ﷺ used to put me on (one of) his thighs and put Al-Hasan bin `Ali on his other thigh, and then embrace us and say, "O Allah! Please be Merciful to them, as I am merciful to them. ". – Sahih Al-Bukhari 6003

حَدَّثَنَا عَبْدُ اللَّهِ بْنُ مُحَمَّدٍ، حَدَّثَنَا عَارِمٌ، حَدَّثَنَا الْمُعْتَمِرُ بْنُ سُلَيْمَانَ، يُحَدِّثُ عَنْ أَبِيهِ، قَالَ سَمِعْتُ أَبَا تَمِيمَةَ، يُحَدِّثُ عَنْ أَبِي عُثْمَانَ النَّهْدِيِّ، يُحَدِّثُهُ أَبُو عُثْمَانَ عَنْ أُسَامَةَ بْنِ زَيْدٍ ـ رضى الله عنهما كَانَ رَسُولُ اللَّهِ صلى الله عليه وسلم يَأْخُذُنِي فَيُقْعِدُنِي عَلَى فَخِذِهِ، وَيُقْعِدُ الْحَسَنَ عَلَى فَخِذِهِ الأُخْرَى، ثُمَّ يَضُمُّهُمَا ثُمَّ يَقُولُ " اللَّهُمَّ ارْحَمْهُمَا فَإِنِّي أَرْحَمُهُمَا ". وَعَنْ عَلِيٍّ، قَالَ حَدَّثَنَا يَحْيَى، حَدَّثَنَا سُلَيْمَانُ، عَنْ أَبِي عُثْمَانَ، قَالَ التَّيْمِيُّ فَوَقَعَ فِي قَلْبِي مِنْهُ شَىْءٌ، قُلْتُ حَدَّثْتُ بِهِ كَذَا وَكَذَا، فَلَمْ أَسْمَعْهُ مِنْ أَبِي عُثْمَانَ، فَنَظَرْتُ فَوَجَدْتُهُ عِنْدِي مَكْتُوبًا فِيمَا سَمِعْتُ.

Narrated Al-Hasan Al-Basri: By Allah, Al-Hasan bin `Ali led large battalions like mountains against Muawiya. `Amr bin Al-As said (to Muawiya), "I surely see battalions which will not turn back before killing their opponents." Muawiya who was really the best of the two men said to him, "O `Amr! If these killed those and those killed these, who would be left with me for the jobs of the public, who would be left with me for their women, who would be left with me for their children?" Then Muawiya sent two Quraishi men from the tribe of `Abd-i-Shams called `Abdur Rahman bin Sumura and `Abdullah bin 'Amir bin Kuraiz to Al-Hasan saying to them, "Go to this man (i.e. Al-Hasan) and negotiate peace with him and talk and appeal to him." So, they went to Al-Hasan and talked and appealed to him to accept peace. Al-Hasan said, "We, the offspring of `Abdul Muttalib, have got wealth and people have indulged in killing and corruption (and money only will appease them)." They said to Al-Hasan, "Muawiya offers you so and so, and appeals to you and entreats you to accept peace." Al-Hasan said to them, "But who will be responsible for what you have said?" They said, "We will be responsible for it." So, whatever Al- Hasan asked they said, "We will be responsible for it for you." So, Al-Hasan concluded a peace treaty with Muawiya. Al-Hasan (Al-Basri) said: I heard Abu Bakr saying, "I saw Allah's Messenger ﷺ on the pulpit and Al-Hasan bin `Ali was by his side. The Prophet ﷺ was looking once at the people and once at Al-Hasan bin `Ali saying, 'This son of mine is a Saiyid (i.e. a noble) and may Allah make peace between two big groups of Muslims through him.". – Sahih Al-Bukhari 2704

حَدَّثَنَا عَبْدُ اللَّهِ بْنُ مُحَمَّدٍ، حَدَّثَنَا سُفْيَانُ، عَنْ أَبِي مُوسَى، قَالَ سَمِعْتُ الْحَسَنَ، يَقُولُ اسْتَقْبَلَ وَاللَّهِ الْحَسَنُ بْنُ عَلِيٍّ مُعَاوِيَةَ بِكَتَائِبَ أَمْثَالِ الْجِبَالِ فَقَالَ عَمْرُو بْنُ الْعَاصِ إِنِّي لأَرَى كَتَائِبَ لاَ تُوَلِّي حَتَّى تَقْتُلَ أَقْرَانَهَا. فَقَالَ لَهُ مُعَاوِيَةُ ـ وَكَانَ وَاللَّهِ خَيْرَ الرَّجُلَيْنِ ـ أَىْ عَمْرُو إِنْ قَتَلَ هَؤُلاَءِ هَؤُلاَءِ وَهَؤُلاَءِ هَؤُلاَءِ مَنْ لِي بِأُمُورِ النَّاسِ مَنْ لِي بِنِسَائِهِمْ، مَنْ لِي بِضَيْعَتِهِمْ فَبَعَثَ إِلَيْهِ رَجُلَيْنِ مِنْ قُرَيْشٍ مِنْ بَنِي عَبْدِ شَمْسٍ عَبْدَ الرَّحْمَنِ بْنَ سَمُرَةَ وَعَبْدَ اللَّهِ بْنَ عَامِرِ بْنِ كُرَيْزٍ، فَقَالَ اذْهَبَا إِلَى هَذَا الرَّجُلِ فَاعْرِضَا عَلَيْهِ، وَقُولاَ لَهُ، وَاطْلُبَا إِلَيْهِ. فَأَتَيَاهُ، فَدَخَلاَ عَلَيْهِ فَتَكَلَّمَا، وَقَالاَ لَهُ، فَطَلَبَا إِلَيْهِ، فَقَالَ لَهُمَا الْحَسَنُ بْنُ عَلِيٍّ إِنَّا بَنُو عَبْدِ الْمُطَّلِبِ، قَدْ أَصَبْنَا مِنْ هَذَا الْمَالِ، وَإِنَّ هَذِهِ الأُمَّةَ قَدْ عَاثَتْ فِي دِمَائِهَا. قَالاَ فَإِنَّهُ يَعْرِضُ عَلَيْكَ كَذَا وَكَذَا وَيَطْلُبُ إِلَيْكَ وَيَسْأَلُكَ. قَالَ فَمَنْ لِي بِهَذَا قَالاَ نَحْنُ لَكَ بِهِ. فَمَا سَأَلَهُمَا شَيْئًا إِلاَّ قَالاَ نَحْنُ لَكَ بِهِ. فَصَالَحَهُ، فَقَالَ الْحَسَنُ وَلَقَدْ سَمِعْتُ أَبَا بَكْرَةَ يَقُولُ رَأَيْتُ رَسُولَ اللَّهِ صلى الله عليه وسلم عَلَى الْمِنْبَرِ وَالْحَسَنُ بْنُ عَلِيٍّ إِلَى جَنْبِهِ، وَهْوَ يُقْبِلُ عَلَى النَّاسِ مَرَّةً وَعَلَيْهِ أُخْرَى وَيَقُولُ " إِنَّ ابْنِي هَذَا سَيِّدٌ، وَلَعَلَّ اللَّهَ أَنْ يُصْلِحَ بِهِ بَيْنَ فِئَتَيْنِ عَظِيمَتَيْنِ مِنَ الْمُسْلِمِينَ ". قَالَ لِي عَلِيُّ بْنُ عَبْدِ اللَّهِ إِنَّمَا ثَبَتَ لَنَا سَمَاعُ الْحَسَنِ مِنْ أَبِي بَكْرَةَ بِهَذَا الْحَدِيثِ.

Narrated `Uqba bin Al-Harith: (Once) Abu Bakr offered the `Asr prayer and then went out walking and saw Al-Hasan playing with the boys. He lifted him on to his shoulders and said, " Let my parents be sacrificed for your sake! (You) resemble the Prophet ﷺ and not `Ali," while `Ali was smiling. – Sahih Al-Bukhari 3542

حَدَّثَنَا أَبُو عَاصِمٍ، عَنْ عُمَرَ بْنِ سَعِيدِ بْنِ أَبِي حُسَيْنٍ، عَنِ ابْنِ أَبِي مُلَيْكَةَ، عَنْ عُقْبَةَ بْنِ الْحَارِثِ، قَالَ صَلَّى أَبُو بَكْرٍ ـ رضى الله عنه ـ الْعَصْرَ، ثُمَّ خَرَجَ يَمْشِي فَرَأَى الْحَسَنَ يَلْعَبُ مَعَ الصِّبْيَانِ، فَحَمَلَهُ عَلَى عَاتِقِهِ وَقَالَ بِأَبِي شَبِيهٌ بِالنَّبِيِّ لاَ شَبِيهٌ بِعَلِيٍّ. وَعَلِيٌّ يَضْحَكُ

Narrated Abu Huraira: Al-Hasan bin 'All took a date from the dates of the Sadaqa and put it in his mouth. The Prophet ﷺ said (to him) in Persian, "Kakh, kakh! (i.e. Don't you know that we do not eat the Sadaqa (i.e. what is given in charity) (charity is the dirt of the people). – Sahih Al-Bukhari 3072

حَدَّثَنَا مُحَمَّدُ بْنُ بَشَّارٍ، حَدَّثَنَا غُنْدَرٌ، حَدَّثَنَا شُعْبَةُ، عَنْ مُحَمَّدِ بْنِ زِيَادٍ، عَنْ أَبِي هُرَيْرَةَ ـ رضى الله عنه أَنَّ الْحَسَنَ بْنَ عَلِيٍّ، أَخَذَ تَمْرَةً مِنْ تَمْرِ الصَّدَقَةِ، فَجَعَلَهَا فِي فِيهِ، فَقَالَ النَّبِيُّ صلى الله عليه وسلم بِالْفَارِسِيَّةِ " كَخٍ كَخٍ، أَمَا تَعْرِفُ أَنَّا لاَ نَأْكُلُ الصَّدَقَةَ "

Narrated Qurra bin Khalid: Once he waited for Al-Hasan and he did not show up till it was about the usual time for him to start his speech; then he came and apologized saying, "Our neighbors invited us." Then he added, "Narrated Anas, 'Once we waited for the Prophet ﷺ till it was midnight or about midnight. He came and led the prayer, and after finishing it, he addressed us and said, 'All the people prayed and then slept and you had been in prayer as long as you were waiting for it." Al-Hasan said, "The people are regarded as performing good deeds as long as they are waiting for doing good deeds." Al-Hasan's statement is a portion of Anas's Hadith from the Prophet. – Sahih Al-Bukhari 600

حَدَّثَنَا عَبْدُ اللَّهِ بْنُ الصَّبَّاحِ، قَالَ حَدَّثَنَا أَبُو عَلِيٍّ الْحَنَفِيُّ، حَدَّثَنَا قُرَّةُ بْنُ خَالِدٍ، قَالَ انْتَظَرْنَا الْحَسَنَ وَرَاثَ عَلَيْنَا حَتَّى قَرُبْنَا مِنْ وَقْتِ قِيَامِهِ، فَجَاءَ فَقَالَ دَعَانَا جِيرَانُنَا هَؤُلاَءِ. ثُمَّ قَالَ قَالَ أَنَسٌ نَظَرْنَا النَّبِيَّ صلى الله عليه وسلم ذَاتَ لَيْلَةٍ حَتَّى كَانَ شَطْرُ اللَّيْلِ يَبْلُغُهُ، فَجَاءَ فَصَلَّى لَنَا، ثُمَّ خَطَبَنَا فَقَالَ " أَلاَ إِنَّ النَّاسَ قَدْ صَلَّوْا ثُمَّ رَقَدُوا، وَإِنَّكُمْ لَمْ تَزَالُوا فِي صَلاَةٍ مَا انْتَظَرْتُمُ الصَّلاَةَ ". قَالَ الْحَسَنُ وَإِنَّ الْقَوْمَ لاَ يَزَالُونَ بِخَيْرٍ مَا انْتَظَرُوا الْخَيْرَ. قَالَ قُرَّةُ هُوَ مِنْ حَدِيثِ أَنَسٍ عَنِ النَّبِيِّ صلى الله عليه وسلم.

Narrated Abu Bakra: I heard the Prophet ﷺ talking at the pulpit while Al-Hasan was sitting beside him, and he (i.e. the Prophet) was once looking at the people and at another time Al-Hasan, and saying, "This son of mine is a Saiyid (i.e. chief) and perhaps Allah will bring about an agreement between two sects of the Muslims through him." - Sahih al-Bukhari 3746

حَدَّثَنَا صَدَقَةُ، حَدَّثَنَا ابْنُ عُيَيْنَةَ، حَدَّثَنَا أَبُو مُوسَى، عَنِ الْحَسَنِ، سَمِعَ أَبَا بَكْرَةَ، سَمِعْتُ النَّبِيَّ صلى الله عليه وسلم عَلَى الْمِنْبَرِ وَالْحَسَنُ إِلَى جَنْبِهِ، يَنْظُرُ إِلَى النَّاسِ مَرَّةً وَإِلَيْهِ مَرَّةً، وَيَقُولُ " ابْنِي هَذَا سَيِّدٌ، وَلَعَلَّ اللَّهَ أَنْ يُصْلِحَ بِهِ بَيْنَ فِئَتَيْنِ مِنَ الْمُسْلِمِينَ

Narrated Ibn Abi Nu'm: A person asked `Abdullah bin `Umar whether a Muslim could kill flies. I heard him saying (in reply). "The people of Iraq are asking about the killing of flies while they themselves murdered the son of the daughter of Allah's Messenger ﷺ. The Prophet ﷺ said, They (i.e. Hasan and Husain) are my two sweet basils in this world." – Sahih al-Bukhari 3753

حَدَّثَنِي مُحَمَّدُ بْنُ بَشَّارٍ، حَدَّثَنَا غُنْدَرٌ، حَدَّثَنَا شُعْبَةُ، عَنْ مُحَمَّدِ بْنِ أَبِي يَعْقُوبَ، سَمِعْتُ ابْنَ أَبِي نُعْمٍ، سَمِعْتُ عَبْدَ اللَّهِ بْنَ عُمَرَ، وَسَأَلَهُ، عَنِ الْمُحْرِمِ،، قَالَ شُعْبَةُ أَحْسِبُهُ يَقْتُلُ الذُّبَابَ فَقَالَ أَهْلُ الْعِرَاقِ يَسْأَلُونَ عَنِ الذُّبَابِ وَقَدْ قَتَلُوا ابْنَ ابْنَةِ رَسُولِ اللَّهِ صلى الله عليه وسلم، وَقَالَ النَّبِيُّ صلى الله عليه وسلم " هُمَا رَيْحَانَتَاىَ مِنَ الدُّنْيَا

Hamza ibn ʿAbd al-Muṭṭalib
حَمْزَة إبْن عَبْد ٱلْمُطَّلِب

Narrated Ibn `Abbas: It was said to the Prophet, "Won't you marry the daughter of Hamza?" He said, "She is my foster niece (brother's daughter). ". – Sahih Al-Bukhari 5100

حَدَّثَنَا مُسَدَّدٌ، حَدَّثَنَا يَحْيَى، عَنْ شُعْبَةَ، عَنْ قَتَادَةَ، عَنْ جَابِرِ بْنِ زَيْدٍ، عَنِ ابْنِ عَبَّاسٍ، قَالَ قِيلَ لِلنَّبِيِّ صلى الله عليه وسلم أَلاَ تَزَوَّجُ ابْنَةَ حَمْزَةَ قَالَ " إِنَّهَا ابْنَةُ أَخِي مِنَ الرَّضَاعَةِ ". وَقَالَ بِشْرُ بْنُ عُمَرَ حَدَّثَنَا شُعْبَةُ سَمِعْتُ قَتَادَةَ سَمِعْتُ جَابِرَ بْنَ زَيْدٍ مِثْلَهُ

Narrated Al-Bara: When the Prophet ﷺ intended to perform `Umra in the month of Dhul-Qada, the people of Mecca did not let him enter Mecca till he settled the matter with them by promising to stay in it for three days only. When the document of treaty was written, the following was mentioned: 'These are the terms on which Muhammad, Allah's Messenger ﷺ agreed (to make peace).' They said, "We will not agree to this, for if we believed that you are Allah's Messenger ﷺ we would not prevent you, but you are Muhammad bin `Abdullah." The Prophet ﷺ said, "I am Allah's Messenger ﷺ and also Muhammad bin `Abdullah." Then he said to `Ali, "Rub off (the words) 'Allah's Messenger ﷺ'," but `Ali said, "No, by Allah, I will never rub off your name." So, Allah's Messenger ﷺ took the document and wrote, 'This is what Muhammad bin `Abdullah has agreed upon: No arms will be brought into Mecca except in their cases, and nobody from the people of Mecca will be allowed to go with him (i.e. the Prophet ﷺ) even if he wished to follow him and he (the Prophet ﷺ) will not prevent any of his companions from staying in Mecca if the latter wants to stay.' When the Prophet ﷺ entered Mecca and the time limit passed, the Meccans went to `Ali and said, "Tell your Friend (i.e. the Prophet ﷺ) to go out, as the period (agreed to) has passed." So, the Prophet ﷺ went out of Mecca. The daughter of Hamza ran after them (i.e. the Prophet ﷺ and his companions), calling, "O Uncle! O Uncle!" `Ali received her and led her by the hand and said to Fatima, "Take your uncle's daughter." Zaid and Ja`far quarreled about her. `Ali said, "I have more right to her as she is my uncle's daughter." Ja`far said, "She is my uncle's daughter, and her aunt is my wife." Zaid said, "She is my brother's daughter." The Prophet ﷺ judged that she should be given to her aunt, and said that the aunt was like the mother. He then said to 'All, "You are from me and I am from you", and said to Ja`far, "You resemble me both in character and appearance", and said to Zaid, "You are our brother (in faith) and our freed slave.". – Sahih Al-Bukhari 2699

حَدَّثَنَا عُبَيْدُ اللَّهِ بْنُ مُوسَى، عَنْ إِسْرَائِيلَ، عَنْ أَبِي إِسْحَاقَ، عَنِ الْبَرَاءِ ـ رضى الله عنه ـ قَالَ اعْتَمَرَ النَّبِيُّ صلى الله عليه وسلم فِي ذِي الْقَعْدَةِ، فَأَبَى أَهْلُ مَكَّةَ أَنْ يَدَعُوهُ يَدْخُلُ مَكَّةَ، حَتَّى قَاضَاهُمْ عَلَى أَنْ يُقِيمَ بِهَا ثَلاَثَةَ أَيَّامٍ، فَلَمَّا كَتَبُوا الْكِتَابَ كَتَبُوا هَذَا مَا قَاضَى عَلَيْهِ مُحَمَّدٌ رَسُولُ اللَّهِ صلى الله عليه وسلم. فَقَالُوا لاَ نُقِرُّ بِهَا، فَلَوْ نَعْلَمُ أَنَّكَ رَسُولُ اللَّهِ مَا مَنَعْنَاكَ، لَكِنْ أَنْتَ مُحَمَّدُ بْنُ عَبْدِ اللَّهِ. قَالَ " أَنَا رَسُولُ اللَّهِ وَأَنَا مُحَمَّدُ بْنُ عَبْدِ اللَّهِ ". ثُمَّ قَالَ لِعَلِيٍّ " امْحُ رَسُولُ اللَّهِ ". قَالَ لاَ، وَاللَّهِ لاَ أَمْحُوكَ أَبَدًا، فَأَخَذَ رَسُولُ اللَّهِ صلى الله عليه وسلم الْكِتَابَ، فَكَتَبَ هَذَا مَا قَاضَى عَلَيْهِ مُحَمَّدُ بْنُ عَبْدِ اللَّهِ، لاَ يَدْخُلُ مَكَّةَ سِلاَحٌ إِلاَّ فِي الْقِرَابِ، وَأَنْ لاَ يَخْرُجَ مِنْ أَهْلِهَا بِأَحَدٍ، إِنْ أَرَادَ أَنْ يَتَّبِعَهُ، وَأَنْ لاَ يَمْنَعَ أَحَدًا مِنْ أَصْحَابِهِ أَرَادَ أَنْ يُقِيمَ بِهَا. فَلَمَّا دَخَلَهَا، وَمَضَى الأَجَلُ أَتَوْا عَلِيًّا، فَقَالُوا قُلْ لِصَاحِبِكَ اخْرُجْ عَنَّا فَقَدْ مَضَى الأَجَلُ. فَخَرَجَ النَّبِيُّ صلى الله عليه وسلم فَتَبِعَتْهُمُ ابْنَةُ حَمْزَةَ يَا عَمِّ يَا عَمِّ. فَتَنَاوَلَهَا عَلِيٌّ فَأَخَذَ بِيَدِهَا، وَقَالَ لِفَاطِمَةَ عَلَيْهَا السَّلاَمُ دُونَكِ ابْنَةَ عَمِّكِ، احْمِلِيهَا. فَاخْتَصَمَ فِيهَا عَلِيٌّ وَزَيْدٌ وَجَعْفَرٌ، فَقَالَ عَلِيٌّ أَنَا أَحَقُّ بِهَا وَهْىَ ابْنَةُ عَمِّي. وَقَالَ جَعْفَرٌ ابْنَةُ عَمِّي وَخَالَتُهَا تَحْتِي. وَقَالَ زَيْدٌ ابْنَةُ أَخِي. فَقَضَى بِهَا النَّبِيُّ صلى الله عليه وسلم لِخَالَتِهَا. وَقَالَ " الْخَالَةُ بِمَنْزِلَةِ الأُمِّ ". وَقَالَ لِعَلِيٍّ " أَنْتَ مِنِّي وَأَنَا مِنْكَ ". وَقَالَ لِجَعْفَرٍ " أَشْبَهْتَ خَلْقِي وَخُلُقِي ". وَقَالَ لِزَيْدٍ " أَنْتَ أَخُونَا وَمَوْلاَنَا "

Narrated Sa`d bin Ibrahim: A meal was brought to `Abdur-Rahman bin `Auf while he was fasting. He said, "Mus`ab bin `Umar was martyred, and he was better than I, yet he was shrouded in a Burda (i.e. a sheet) so that, if his head was covered, his feet became naked, and if his feet were covered, his head became naked." `Abdur-Rahman added, "Hamza was martyred and he was better than I. Then worldly wealth was bestowed upon us and we were given thereof too much. We are afraid that the reward of our deeds have been given to us in this life." `Abdur-Rahman then started weeping so much that he left the food. – Sahih Al-Bukhari 4045

حَدَّثَنَا عَبْدَانُ، حَدَّثَنَا عَبْدُ اللَّهِ، أَخْبَرَنَا شُعْبَةُ، عَنْ سَعْدِ بْنِ إِبْرَاهِيمَ، عَنْ أَبِيهِ، إِبْرَاهِيمَ أَنَّ عَبْدَ الرَّحْمَنِ بْنَ عَوْفٍ، أُتِيَ بِطَعَامٍ، وَكَانَ صَائِمًا فَقَالَ قُتِلَ مُصْعَبُ بْنُ عُمَيْرٍ، وَهْوَ خَيْرٌ مِنِّي، كُفِّنَ فِي بُرْدَةٍ، إِنْ غُطِّيَ رَأْسُهُ بَدَتْ رِجْلاَهُ، وَإِنْ غُطِّيَ رِجْلاَهُ بَدَا رَأْسُهُ ـ وَأُرَاهُ قَالَ ـ وَقُتِلَ حَمْزَةُ وَهْوَ خَيْرٌ مِنِّي، ثُمَّ بُسِطَ لَنَا مِنَ الدُّنْيَا مَا بُسِطَ، أَوْ قَالَ أُعْطِينَا مِنَ الدُّنْيَا مَا أُعْطِينَا، وَقَدْ خَشِينَا أَنْ تَكُونَ حَسَنَاتُنَا عُجِّلَتْ لَنَا. ثُمَّ جَعَلَ يَبْكِي حَتَّى تَرَكَ الطَّعَامَ.

Narrated Jafar bin `Amr bin Umaiya: I went out with 'Ubaidullah bin `Adi Al-Khaiyar. When we reached Hims (i.e. a town in Syria), 'Ubaidullah bin `Adi said (to me), "Would you like to see Wahshi so that we may ask him about the killing of Hamza?" I replied, "Yes." Wahshi used to live in Hims. We enquired about him and somebody said to us, "He is that in the shade of his palace, as if he were a full water skin." So we went up to him, and when we were at a short distance from him, we greeted him and he greeted us in return. 'Ubaidullah was wearing his turban and Wahshi could not see except his eyes and feet. 'Ubaidullah said, "O Wahshi! Do you know me?" Wahshi looked at him and then said, "No, by Allah! But I know that `Adi bin Al-Khiyar married a woman called Um Qital, the daughter of Abu Al-Is, and she delivered a boy for him at Mecca, and I looked for a wet nurse for that child. (Once) I carried that child along with his mother and then I handed him over to her, and your feet resemble that child's feet." Then 'Ubaidullah uncovered his face and said (to Wahshi), "Will you tell us (the story of) the killing of Hamza?" Wahshi replied "Yes, Hamza killed Tuaima bin `Adi bin Al-Khaiyar at Badr (battle) so my master, Jubair bin Mut`im said to me, 'If you kill Hamza in revenge for my uncle, then you will be set free." When the people set out (for the battle of Uhud) in the year of 'Ainain ..'Ainain is a mountain near the mountain of Uhud, and between it and Uhud there is a valley.. I went out with the people for the battle. When the army aligned for the fight, Siba' came out and said, 'Is there any (Muslim) to accept my challenge to a duel?' Hamza bin `Abdul Muttalib came out and said, 'O Siba'. O Ibn Um Anmar, the one who circumcises other ladies! Do you challenge Allah and His Apostle?' Then Hamza attacked and killed him, causing him to be non-extant like the bygone yesterday. I hid myself under a rock, and when he (i.e. Hamza) came near me, I threw my spear at him, driving it into his umbilicus so that it came out through his buttocks, causing him to die. When all the people returned to Mecca, I too returned with them. I stayed in (Mecca) till Islam spread in it (i.e. Mecca). Then I left for Taif, and when the people (of Taif) sent their messengers to Allah's Messenger ﷺ, I was told that the Prophet ﷺ did not harm the messengers; So I too went out with them till I reached Allah's Messenger ﷺ. When he saw me, he said, 'Are you Wahshi?' I said, 'Yes.' He said, 'Was it you who killed Hamza?' I replied, 'What happened is what you have been told of.' He said, 'Can you hide your face from me?' So I went out when Allah's Messenger ﷺ died, and Musailamah Al-Kadhdhab appeared (claiming to be a prophet). I said, 'I will go out to Musailamah so that I may kill him, and make amends for killing Hamza. So I went out with the people (to fight Musailamah and his followers) and then famous events took place concerning that battle. Suddenly I saw a man (i.e. Musailamah) standing near a gap in a wall. He looked like an ash-colored camel and his hair was dishevelled. So I threw my spear at him, driving it into his chest in between his breasts till it passed out through his shoulders, and then an Ansari man attacked him and struck him on the head with a sword. `Abdullah bin `Umar said, 'A slave girl on the roof of a house said: Alas! The chief of the believers (i.e. Musailamah) has been killed by a black slave.". – Sahih Al-Bukhari 4072

حَدَّثَنِي أَبُو جَعْفَرٍ، مُحَمَّدُ بْنُ عَبْدِ اللَّهِ حَدَّثَنَا حُجَيْنُ بْنُ الْمُثَنَّى، حَدَّثَنَا عَبْدُ الْعَزِيزِ بْنُ عَبْدِ اللَّهِ بْنِ أَبِي سَلَمَةَ، عَنْ عَبْدِ اللَّهِ بْنِ الْفَضْلِ، عَنْ سُلَيْمَانَ بْنِ يَسَارٍ، عَنْ جَعْفَرِ بْنِ عَمْرِو بْنِ أُمَيَّةَ الضَّمْرِيِّ، قَالَ خَرَجْتُ مَعَ عُبَيْدِ اللَّهِ بْنِ عَدِيِّ بْنِ الْخِيَارِ، فَلَمَّا قَدِمْنَا حِمْصَ قَالَ لِي عُبَيْدُ اللَّهِ هَلْ لَكَ فِي وَحْشِيٍّ نَسْأَلُهُ عَنْ قَتْلِ حَمْزَةَ قُلْتُ نَعَمْ. وَكَانَ وَحْشِيٌّ يَسْكُنُ حِمْصَ فَسَأَلْنَا عَنْهُ فَقِيلَ لَنَا هُوَ ذَاكَ فِي ظِلِّ قَصْرِهِ، كَأَنَّهُ حَمِيتٌ. قَالَ فَجِئْنَا حَتَّى وَقَفْنَا عَلَيْهِ بِيَسِيرٍ، فَسَلَّمْنَا، فَرَدَّ السَّلاَمَ، قَالَ وَعُبَيْدُ اللَّهِ مُعْتَجِرٌ بِعِمَامَتِهِ، مَا يَرَى وَحْشِيٌّ إِلاَّ عَيْنَيْهِ وَرِجْلَيْهِ، فَقَالَ عُبَيْدُ اللَّهِ يَا وَحْشِيُّ أَتَعْرِفُنِي قَالَ فَنَظَرَ إِلَيْهِ ثُمَّ قَالَ لاَ وَاللَّهِ إِلاَّ أَنِّي أَعْلَمُ أَنَّ عَدِيَّ بْنَ الْخِيَارِ تَزَوَّجَ امْرَأَةً يُقَالُ لَهَا أُمُّ قِتَالٍ بِنْتُ أَبِي الْعِيصِ، فَوَلَدَتْ لَهُ غُلاَمًا بِمَكَّةَ، فَكُنْتُ أَسْتَرْضِعُ لَهُ، فَحَمَلْتُ ذَلِكَ الْغُلاَمَ مَعَ أُمِّهِ، فَنَاوَلْتُهَا إِيَّاهُ، فَلَكَأَنِّي نَظَرْتُ إِلَى قَدَمَيْكَ. قَالَ فَكَشَفَ عُبَيْدُ اللَّهِ عَنْ وَجْهِهِ ثُمَّ قَالَ أَلاَ تُخْبِرُنَا بِقَتْلِ حَمْزَةَ قَالَ نَعَمْ، إِنَّ حَمْزَةَ قَتَلَ طُعَيْمَةَ بْنَ عَدِيِّ بْنِ الْخِيَارِ بِبَدْرٍ، فَقَالَ لِي مَوْلاَىَ جُبَيْرُ بْنُ مُطْعِمٍ إِنْ قَتَلْتَ حَمْزَةَ بِعَمِّي فَأَنْتَ حُرٌّ، قَالَ فَلَمَّا أَنْ خَرَجَ النَّاسُ عَامَ عَيْنَيْنِ ـ وَعَيْنَيْنِ جَبَلٌ بِحِيَالِ أُحُدٍ، بَيْنَهُ وَبَيْنَهُ وَادٍ ـ خَرَجْتُ مَعَ النَّاسِ إِلَى الْقِتَالِ، فَلَمَّا اصْطَفُّوا لِلْقِتَالِ خَرَجَ سِبَاعٌ فَقَالَ هَلْ مِنْ مُبَارِزٍ قَالَ فَخَرَجَ إِلَيْهِ حَمْزَةُ بْنُ عَبْدِ الْمُطَّلِبِ فَقَالَ يَا سِبَاعُ يَا ابْنَ أُمِّ أَنْمَارٍ مُقَطِّعَةِ الْبُظُورِ، أَتُحَادُّ اللَّهَ وَرَسُولَهُ صلى الله عليه وسلم قَالَ ثُمَّ شَدَّ عَلَيْهِ فَكَانَ كَأَمْسِ الذَّاهِبِ ـ قَالَ ـ وَكَمَنْتُ لِحَمْزَةَ تَحْتَ صَخْرَةٍ فَلَمَّا دَنَا مِنِّي رَمَيْتُهُ بِحَرْبَتِي، فَأَضَعُهَا فِي ثُنَّتِهِ حَتَّى خَرَجَتْ مِنْ بَيْنِ وَرِكَيْهِ ـ قَالَ ـ فَكَانَ ذَاكَ الْعَهْدَ بِهِ، فَلَمَّا رَجَعَ النَّاسُ رَجَعْتُ مَعَهُمْ فَأَقَمْتُ بِمَكَّةَ، حَتَّى فَشَا فِيهَا الإِسْلاَمُ، ثُمَّ خَرَجْتُ إِلَى الطَّائِفِ، فَأَرْسَلُوا إِلَى رَسُولِ اللَّهِ صلى الله عليه وسلم رَسُولاً، فَقِيلَ لِي إِنَّهُ لاَ يَهِيجُ الرُّسُلَ ـ قَالَ ـ فَخَرَجْتُ مَعَهُمْ حَتَّى قَدِمْتُ عَلَى رَسُولِ اللَّهِ صلى الله عليه وسلم فَلَمَّا رَآنِي قَالَ " آنْتَ وَحْشِيٌّ ". قُلْتُ نَعَمْ. قَالَ " أَنْتَ قَتَلْتَ حَمْزَةَ ". قُلْتُ قَدْ كَانَ مِنَ الأَمْرِ مَا بَلَغَكَ. قَالَ " فَهَلْ تَسْتَطِيعُ أَنْ تُغَيِّبَ وَجْهَكَ عَنِّي ". قَالَ فَخَرَجْتُ، فَلَمَّا قُبِضَ رَسُولُ اللَّهِ صلى الله عليه وسلم فَخَرَجَ مُسَيْلِمَةُ الْكَذَّابُ قُلْتُ لأَخْرُجَنَّ إِلَى مُسَيْلِمَةَ لَعَلِّي أَقْتُلُهُ فَأُكَافِئَ بِهِ حَمْزَةَ ـ قَالَ ـ فَخَرَجْتُ مَعَ النَّاسِ، فَكَانَ مِنْ أَمْرِهِ مَا كَانَ ـ قَالَ ـ فَإِذَا رَجُلٌ قَائِمٌ فِي ثَلْمَةِ جِدَارٍ، كَأَنَّهُ جَمَلٌ أَوْرَقُ ثَائِرُ الرَّأْسِ ـ قَالَ ـ فَرَمَيْتُهُ بِحَرْبَتِي، فَأَضَعُهَا بَيْنَ ثَدْيَيْهِ حَتَّى خَرَجَتْ مِنْ بَيْنِ كَتِفَيْهِ ـ قَالَ ـ وَوَثَبَ إِلَيْهِ رَجُلٌ مِنَ الأَنْصَارِ، فَضَرَبَهُ بِالسَّيْفِ عَلَى هَامَتِهِ. قَالَ قَالَ عَبْدُ اللَّهِ بْنُ الْفَضْلِ فَأَخْبَرَنِي سُلَيْمَانُ بْنُ يَسَارٍ أَنَّهُ سَمِعَ عَبْدَ اللَّهِ بْنَ عُمَرَ يَقُولُ فَقَالَتْ جَارِيَةٌ عَلَى ظَهْرِ بَيْتٍ وَا أَمِيرَ الْمُؤْمِنِينَ، قَتَلَهُ الْعَبْدُ الأَسْوَدُ

Narrated Husain bin `Ali: `Ali bin Abi Talib said: "I got a she-camel as my share of the war booty on the day (of the battle) of Badr, and Allah's Messenger ﷺ gave me another she-camel. I let both of them kneel at the door of one of the Ansar, intending to carry Idhkhir on them to sell it and use its price for my wedding banquet on marrying Fatima. A goldsmith from Bani Qainqa' was with me. Hamza bin `Abdul-Muttalib was in that house drinking wine and a lady singer was reciting: "O Hamza! (Kill) the (two) fat old she camels (and serve them to your guests). So Hamza took his sword and went towards the two she-camels and cut off their humps and opened their flanks and took a part of their livers." (I said to Ibn Shihab, "Did he take part of the humps?" He replied, "He cut off their humps and carried them away.") `Ali further said, "When I saw that dreadful sight, I went to the Prophet ﷺ and told him the news. The Prophet ﷺ came out in the company of Zaid bin Haritha who was with him then, and I too went with them. He went to Hamza and spoke harshly to him. Hamza looked up and said, 'Aren't you only the slaves of my forefathers?' The Prophet ﷺ retreated and went out. This incident happened before the prohibition of drinking.". – Sahih Al-Bukhari 2375

حَدَّثَنَا إِبْرَاهِيمُ بْنُ مُوسَى، أَخْبَرَنَا هِشَامٌ، أَنَّ ابْنَ جُرَيْجٍ، أَخْبَرَهُمْ قَالَ أَخْبَرَنِي ابْنُ شِهَابٍ، عَنْ عَلِيِّ بْنِ حُسَيْنِ بْنِ عَلِيٍّ، عَنْ أَبِيهِ، حُسَيْنِ بْنِ عَلِيٍّ عَنْ عَلِيِّ بْنِ أَبِي طَالِبٍ ـ رضى الله عنهم ـ أَنَّهُ قَالَ أَصَبْتُ شَارِفًا مَعَ رَسُولِ اللَّهِ صلى الله عليه وسلم فِي مَغْنَمٍ يَوْمَ بَدْرٍ قَالَ وَأَعْطَانِي رَسُولُ اللَّهِ صلى الله عليه وسلم شَارِفًا أُخْرَى، فَأَنَخْتُهُمَا يَوْمًا عِنْدَ بَابِ رَجُلٍ مِنَ الأَنْصَارِ، وَأَنَا أُرِيدُ أَنْ أَحْمِلَ عَلَيْهِمَا إِذْخِرًا

لأبِيعَهُ، وَمَعِي صَائِغٌ مِنْ بَنِي قَيْنُقَاعَ فَأَسْتَعِينَ بِهِ عَلَى وَلِيمَةِ فَاطِمَةَ، وَحَمْزَةُ بْنُ عَبْدِ الْمُطَّلِبِ يَشْرَبُ فِي ذَلِكَ الْبَيْتِ مَعَهُ قَيْنَةٌ، فَقَالَتْ أَلاَ يَا حَمْزَ لِلشُّرُفِ النِّوَاءِ. فَثَارَ إِلَيْهِمَا حَمْزَةُ بِالسَّيْفِ، فَجَبَّ أَسْنِمَتَهُمَا، وَبَقَرَ خَوَاصِرَهُمَا، ثُمَّ أَخَذَ مِنْ أَكْبَادِهِمَا. قُلْتُ لاِبْنِ شِهَابٍ وَمِنَ السَّنَامِ قَالَ قَدْ جَبَّ أَسْنِمَتَهُمَا فَذَهَبَ بِهَا. قَالَ ابْنُ شِهَابٍ قَالَ عَلِيٌّ ـ رضى الله عنه ـ فَنَظَرْتُ إِلَى مَنْظَرٍ أَفْظَعَنِي فَأَتَيْتُ نَبِيَّ اللَّهِ صلى الله عليه وسلم وَعِنْدَهُ زَيْدُ بْنُ حَارِثَةَ فَأَخْبَرْتُهُ الْخَبَرَ فَخَرَجَ وَمَعَهُ زَيْدٌ، فَانْطَلَقْتُ مَعَهُ، فَدَخَلَ عَلَى حَمْزَةَ فَتَغَيَّظَ عَلَيْهِ فَرَفَعَ حَمْزَةُ بَصَرَهُ وَقَالَ هَلْ أَنْتُمْ إِلاَّ عَبِيدٌ لآبَائِي فَرَجَعَ رَسُولُ اللَّهِ صلى الله عليه وسلم يُقَهْقِرُ حَتَّى خَرَجَ عَنْهُمْ، وَذَلِكَ قَبْلَ تَحْرِيمِ الْخَمْرِ.

Narrated Qais bin Ubad: `Ali said, "I will be the first to kneel before the Beneficent on the Day of Resurrection because of the dispute." Qais said; This Verse: 'These two opponents (believers and disbelievers dispute with each other about their Lord,' (22.19) was revealed in connection with those who came out for the Battle of Badr, i.e. `Ali, Hamza, 'Ubaida, Shaiba bin Rabi`a, `Utba bin Rabi`a and Al-Walid bin `Utba. – Sahih Al-Bukhari 4744

حَدَّثَنَا حَجَّاجُ بْنُ مِنْهَالٍ، حَدَّثَنَا مُعْتَمِرُ بْنُ سُلَيْمَانَ، قَالَ سَمِعْتُ أَبِي قَالَ، حَدَّثَنَا أَبُو مِجْلَزٍ، عَنْ قَيْسِ بْنِ عُبَادٍ، عَنْ عَلِيِّ بْنِ أَبِي طَالِبٍ ـ رضى الله عنه ـ قَالَ أَنَا أَوَّلُ، مَنْ يَجْثُو بَيْنَ يَدَىِ الرَّحْمَنِ لِلْخُصُومَةِ يَوْمَ الْقِيَامَةِ. قَالَ قَيْسٌ وَفِيهِمْ نَزَلَتْ {هَذَانِ خَصْمَانِ اخْتَصَمُوا فِي رَبِّهِمْ} قَالَ هُمُ الَّذِينَ بَارَزُوا يَوْمَ بَدْرٍ عَلِيٌّ وَحَمْزَةُ وَعُبَيْدَةُ وَشَيْبَةُ بْنُ رَبِيعَةَ وَعُتْبَةُ بْنُ رَبِيعَةَ وَالْوَلِيدُ بْنُ عُتْبَةَ

Zayd ibn Ḥāritha al-Kalbī
زيد بن حارثة الكلبي

Call them after their fathers; that is more equitable with Allah. But if you do not know their fathers, then your brethren in faith and your friends. There is no blame on you if you err therein, barring what your hearts premeditates. Allah is Forgiving and Merciful. – Surah Al-Ahzab 33:5

ٱدْعُوهُمْ لِءَابَآئِهِمْ هُوَ أَقْسَطُ عِندَ ٱللَّهِ ۚ فَإِن لَّمْ تَعْلَمُوٓا۟ ءَابَآءَهُمْ فَإِخْوَٰنُكُمْ فِى ٱلدِّينِ وَمَوَٰلِيكُمْ ۚ وَلَيْسَ عَلَيْكُمْ جُنَاحٌ فِيمَآ أَخْطَأْتُم بِهِۦ وَلَٰكِن مَّا تَعَمَّدَتْ قُلُوبُكُمْ ۚ وَكَانَ ٱللَّهُ غَفُورًا رَّحِيمًا

Narrated `Abdullah bin `Umar: We used not to call Zaid bin Haritha the freed slave of Allah's Messenger ﷺ except Zaid bin Muhammad till the Qu'anic Verse was revealed: "Call them (adopted sons) by (the names of) their fathers. That is more than just in the Sight of Allah." (33.5) - Sahih Al-Bukhari 4782

حَدَّثَنَا مُعَلَّى بْنُ أَسَدٍ، حَدَّثَنَا عَبْدُ الْعَزِيزِ بْنُ الْمُخْتَارِ، حَدَّثَنَا مُوسَى بْنُ عُقْبَةَ، قَالَ حَدَّثَنِي سَالِمٌ، عَنْ عَبْدِ اللَّهِ بْنِ عُمَرَ ـ رضى الله عنهما ـ أَنَّ زَيْدَ بْنَ حَارِثَةَ، مَوْلَى رَسُولِ اللَّهِ صلى الله عليه وسلم مَا كُنَّا نَدْعُوهُ إِلاَّ زَيْدَ ابْنَ مُحَمَّدٍ حَتَّى نَزَلَ الْقُرْآنُ {ادْعُوهُمْ لآبَائِهِمْ هُوَ أَقْسَطُ عِنْدَ اللَّهِ}.

Narrated `Aisha: Abu Hudhaifa bin `Utba bin Rabi`a bin `Abdi Shams who had witnessed the battle of Badr along with the Prophet ﷺ adopted Salim as his son, to whom he married his niece, Hind bint Al-Walid bin `Utba bin Rabi`a; and Salim was the freed slave of an Ansar woman, just as the Prophet ﷺ had adopted Zaid as his son. It was the custom in the Pre-Islamic Period that if somebody adopted a boy, the people would call him the son of the adoptive father and he would be the latter's heir. But when Allah revealed the Divine Verses: 'Call them by (the names of) their fathers . . . your freed-slaves,' (33.5) the adopted persons were called by their fathers' names. The one whose father was not known, would be regarded as a Maula and your brother in religion. Later on Sahla bint Suhail bin `Amr Al-Quraishi Al-`Amiri—and she was the wife of Abu- Hudhaifa bin `Utba—came to the Prophet ﷺ and said, "O Allah's Messenger ﷺ! We used to consider Salim as our (adopted) son, and now Allah has revealed what you know (regarding adopted sons)." The sub-narrator then mentioned the rest of the narration. – Sahih Al-Bukhari 5088

حَدَّثَنَا أَبُو الْيَمَانِ، أَخْبَرَنَا شُعَيْبٌ، عَنِ الزُّهْرِيِّ، قَالَ أَخْبَرَنِي عُرْوَةُ بْنُ الزُّبَيْرِ، عَنْ عَائِشَةَ ـ رضى الله عنها ـ أَنَّ أَبَا حُذَيْفَةَ بْنَ عُتْبَةَ بْنِ رَبِيعَةَ بْنِ عَبْدِ شَمْسٍ،، وَكَانَ، مِمَّنْ شَهِدَ بَدْرًا مَعَ النَّبِيِّ صلى الله عليه وسلم تَبَنَّى سَالِمًا، وَأَنْكَحَهُ بِنْتَ أَخِيهِ

هِنْدَ بِنْتَ الْوَلِيدِ بْنِ عُتْبَةَ بْنِ رَبِيعَةَ وَهْوَ مَوْلًى لاِمْرَأَةٍ مِنَ الأَنْصَارِ، كَمَا تَبَنَّى النَّبِيُّ صلى الله عليه وسلم زَيْدًا، وَكَانَ مَنْ تَبَنَّى رَجُلاً فِي الْجَاهِلِيَّةِ دَعَاهُ النَّاسُ إِلَيْهِ وَوَرِثَ مِنْ مِيرَاثِهِ حَتَّى أَنْزَلَ اللَّهُ {ادْعُوهُمْ لآبَائِهِمْ} إِلَى قَوْلِهِ {وَمَوَالِيكُمْ} فَرُدُّوا إِلَى آبَائِهِمْ، فَمَنْ لَمْ يُعْلَمْ لَهُ أَبٌ كَانَ مَوْلًى وَأَخًا فِي الدِّينِ، فَجَاءَتْ سَهْلَةُ بِنْتُ سُهَيْلِ بْنِ عَمْرٍو الْقُرَشِيِّ ثُمَّ الْعَامِرِيِّ ـ وَهْىَ امْرَأَةُ أَبِي حُذَيْفَةَ ـ النَّبِيَّ صلى الله عليه وسلم فَقَالَتْ يَا رَسُولَ اللَّهِ إِنَّا كُنَّا نَرَى سَالِمًا وَلَدًا وَقَدْ أَنْزَلَ اللَّهُ فِيهِ مَا قَدْ عَلِمْتَ فَذَكَرَ الْحَدِيثَ

Narrated `Ali: The Prophet ﷺ asked for his Rida, put it on and set out walking. Zaid bin Haritha and I followed him till he reached the house where Harnza (bin `Abdul Muttalib) was present and asked for permission to enter, and they gave us permission. – Sahih Al-Bukhari 5793

حَدَّثَنَا عَبْدَانُ، أَخْبَرَنَا عَبْدُ اللَّهِ، أَخْبَرَنَا يُونُسُ، عَنِ الزُّهْرِيِّ، أَخْبَرَنِي عَلِيُّ بْنُ حُسَيْنٍ، أَنَّ حُسَيْنَ بْنَ عَلِيٍّ، أَخْبَرَهُ أَنَّ عَلِيًّا ـ رضى الله عنه ـ قَالَ فَدَعَا النَّبِيُّ صلى الله عليه وسلم بِرِدَائِهِ، ثُمَّ انْطَلَقَ يَمْشِي، وَاتَّبَعْتُهُ أَنَا وَزَيْدُ بْنُ حَارِثَةَ، حَتَّى جَاءَ الْبَيْتَ الَّذِي فِيهِ حَمْزَةُ، فَاسْتَأْذَنَ فَأَذِنُوا لَهُمْ

Narrated `Urwa: Aisha said, "A Qaif (i.e. one skilled in recognizing the lineage of a person through Physiognomy and through examining the body parts of an infant) came to me while the Prophet ﷺ was present, and Usama bin Zaid and Zaid bin Haritha were Lying asleep. The Qa'if said. These feet (of Usama and his father) are of persons belonging to the same lineage.' " The Prophet ﷺ was pleased with that saying which won his admiration, and he told `Aisha of it. – Sahih Al-Bukhari 3731

حَدَّثَنَا يَحْيَى بْنُ قَزَعَةَ، حَدَّثَنَا إِبْرَاهِيمُ بْنُ سَعْدٍ، عَنِ الزُّهْرِيِّ، عَنْ عُرْوَةَ، عَنْ عَائِشَةَ ـ رضى الله عنها ـ قَالَتْ دَخَلَ عَلَىَّ قَائِفٌ وَالنَّبِيُّ صلى الله عليه وسلم شَاهِدٌ، وَأُسَامَةُ بْنُ زَيْدٍ وَزَيْدُ بْنُ حَارِثَةَ مُضْطَجِعَانِ، فَقَالَ إِنَّ هَذِهِ الأَقْدَامَ بَعْضُهَا مِنْ بَعْضٍ. قَالَ فَسُرَّ بِذَلِكَ النَّبِيُّ صلى الله عليه وسلم وَأَعْجَبَهُ، فَأَخْبَرَ بِهِ عَائِشَةَ.

Narrated `Ali: I got a she-camel in my share of the war booty on the day (of the battle) of Badr, and the Prophet ﷺ had given me a she-camel from the Khumus. When I intended to marry Fatima, the daughter of Allah's Apostle, I had an appointment with a goldsmith from the tribe of Bani Qainuqa' to go with me to bring Idhkhir (i.e. grass of pleasant smell) and sell it to the goldsmiths and spend its price on my wedding party. I was collecting for my she-camels equipment of saddles, sacks and ropes while my two shecamels were kneeling down beside the room of an Ansari man. I returned after collecting whatever I collected, to see the humps of my two she-camels cut off and their flanks cut open and some portion of their livers was taken out. When I saw that state of my two she-camels, I could not help weeping. I asked, "Who has done this?" The people replied, "Hamza bin `Abdul Muttalib who is staying with some Ansari drunks in this house." I went away till I reached the Prophet ﷺ and Zaid bin Haritha was with him. The Prophet ﷺ noticed on my face the effect of what I had suffered, so the Prophet ﷺ asked. "What is wrong with you." I replied, "O Allah's Messenger! I have never seen such a day as today. Hamza attacked my two she-camels, cut off their humps, and ripped open their flanks, and he is sitting there in a house in the company of some drunks." The Prophet ﷺ then asked for his covering sheet, put it on, and set out walking followed by me and Zaid bin Haritha till he came to the house where Hamza was. He asked permission to enter, and they allowed him, and they were drunk. Allah's Messenger ﷺ started rebuking Hamza for what he had done, but Hamza was drunk and his eyes were red. Hamza looked at Allah's Messenger ﷺ and then he raised his eyes, looking at his knees, then he raised up his eyes looking at his umbilicus, and again he raised up his eyes look in at his face. Hamza then said, "Aren't you but the slaves of my father?" Allah's Messenger ﷺ realized that he was drunk, so Allah's Messenger ﷺ retreated, and we went out with him. – Sahih Al-Bukhari 3091

حَدَّثَنَا عَبْدَانُ، أَخْبَرَنَا عَبْدُ اللَّهِ، أَخْبَرَنَا يُونُسُ، عَنِ الزُّهْرِيِّ، قَالَ أَخْبَرَنِي عَلِيُّ بْنُ الْحُسَيْنِ، أَنَّ حُسَيْنَ بْنَ عَلِيٍّ، عَلَيْهِمَا السَّلاَمُ أَخْبَرَهُ أَنَّ عَلِيًّا قَالَ كَانَتْ لِي شَارِفٌ مِنْ نَصِيبِي مِنَ الْمَغْنَمِ يَوْمَ بَدْرٍ، وَكَانَ النَّبِيُّ صلى الله عليه وسلم أَعْطَانِي شَارِفًا مِنَ الْخُمُسِ، فَلَمَّا أَرَدْتُ أَنْ

أَبْتَنِيَ بِفَاطِمَةَ بِنْتِ رَسُولِ اللَّهِ صلى الله عليه وسلم وَاعَدْتُ رَجُلاً صَوَّاغًا مِنْ بَنِي قَيْنُقَاعٍ، أَنْ يَرْتَحِلَ مَعِيَ فَنَأْتِيَ بِإِذْخِرٍ أَرَدْتُ أَنْ أَبِيعَهُ الصَّوَّاغِينَ، وَأَسْتَعِينَ بِهِ فِي وَلِيمَةِ عُرْسِي، فَبَيْنَا أَنَا أَجْمَعُ لِشَارِفَىَّ مَتَاعًا مِنَ الأَقْتَابِ وَالْغَرَائِرِ وَالْحِبَالِ، وَشَارِفَاىَ مُنَاخَانِ إِلَى جَنْبِ حُجْرَةِ رَجُلٍ مِنَ الأَنْصَارِ، رَجَعْتُ حِينَ جَمَعْتُ مَا جَمَعْتُ، فَإِذَا شَارِفَاىَ قَدِ اجْتُبَّ أَسْنِمَتُهُمَا وَبُقِرَتْ خَوَاصِرُهُمَا، وَأُخِذَ مِنْ أَكْبَادِهِمَا، فَلَمْ أَمْلِكْ عَيْنَىَّ حِينَ رَأَيْتُ ذَلِكَ الْمَنْظَرَ مِنْهُمَا، فَقُلْتُ مَنْ فَعَلَ هَذَا فَقَالُوا فَعَلَ حَمْزَةُ بْنُ عَبْدِ الْمُطَّلِبِ، وَهْوَ فِي هَذَا الْبَيْتِ فِي شَرْبٍ مِنَ الأَنْصَارِ. فَانْطَلَقْتُ حَتَّى أَدْخُلَ عَلَى النَّبِيِّ صلى الله عليه وسلم وَعِنْدَهُ زَيْدُ بْنُ حَارِثَةَ، فَعَرَفَ النَّبِيُّ صلى الله عليه وسلم فِي وَجْهِي الَّذِي لَقِيتُ، فَقَالَ النَّبِيُّ صلى الله عليه وسلم " مَا لَكَ " فَقُلْتُ يَا رَسُولَ اللَّهِ، مَا رَأَيْتُ كَالْيَوْمِ قَطُّ، عَدَا حَمْزَةُ عَلَى نَاقَتَىَّ، فَأَجَبَّ أَسْنِمَتَهُمَا وَبَقَرَ خَوَاصِرَهُمَا، وَهَا هُوَ ذَا فِي بَيْتٍ مَعَهُ شَرْبٌ. فَدَعَا النَّبِيُّ صلى الله عليه وسلم بِرِدَائِهِ فَارْتَدَى ثُمَّ انْطَلَقَ يَمْشِي، وَاتَّبَعْتُهُ أَنَا وَزَيْدُ بْنُ حَارِثَةَ حَتَّى جَاءَ الْبَيْتَ الَّذِي فِيهِ حَمْزَةُ، فَاسْتَأْذَنَ فَأَذِنُوا لَهُمْ فَإِذَا هُمْ شَرْبٌ، فَطَفِقَ رَسُولُ اللَّهِ صلى الله عليه وسلم يَلُومُ حَمْزَةَ فِيمَا فَعَلَ، فَإِذَا حَمْزَةُ قَدْ ثَمِلَ مُحْمَرَّةً عَيْنَاهُ، فَنَظَرَ حَمْزَةُ إِلَى رَسُولِ اللَّهِ صلى الله عليه وسلم، ثُمَّ صَعَّدَ النَّظَرَ فَنَظَرَ إِلَى رُكْبَتِهِ، ثُمَّ صَعَّدَ النَّظَرَ فَنَظَرَ إِلَى سُرَّتِهِ، ثُمَّ صَعَّدَ النَّظَرَ فَنَظَرَ إِلَى وَجْهِهِ ثُمَّ قَالَ حَمْزَةُ هَلْ أَنْتُمْ إِلاَّ عَبِيدٌ لأَبِي فَعَرَفَ رَسُولُ اللَّهِ صلى الله عليه وسلم أَنَّهُ قَدْ ثَمِلَ، فَنَكَصَ رَسُولُ اللَّهِ صلى الله عليه وسلم عَلَى عَقِبَيْهِ الْقَهْقَرَى وَخَرَجْنَا مَعَهُ.

When you said to him whom Allah had blessed, and you had favored, “Keep your wife to yourself, and fear Allah.” But you hid within yourself what Allah was to reveal. And you feared the people, but it was Allah you were supposed to fear. Then, when Zaid ended his relationship with her, We gave her to you in marriage, that there may be no restriction for believers regarding the wives of their adopted sons, when their relationship has ended. The command of Allah was fulfilled. – Surah Al-Ahzab 33:37
وَإِذْ تَقُولُ لِلَّذِىٓ أَنْعَمَ ٱللَّهُ عَلَيْهِ وَأَنْعَمْتَ عَلَيْهِ أَمْسِكْ عَلَيْكَ زَوْجَكَ وَٱتَّقِ ٱللَّهَ وَتُخْفِى فِى نَفْسِكَ مَا ٱللَّهُ مُبْدِيهِ وَتَخْشَى ٱلنَّاسَ وَٱللَّهُ أَحَقُّ أَن تَخْشَىٰهُ فَلَمَّا قَضَىٰ زَيْدٌ مِّنْهَا وَطَرًا زَوَّجْنَـٰكَهَا لِكَىْ لَا يَكُونَ عَلَى ٱلْمُؤْمِنِينَ حَرَجٌ فِىٓ أَزْوَٰجِ أَدْعِيَآئِهِمْ إِذَا قَضَوْا۟ مِنْهُنَّ وَطَرًا ۚ وَكَانَ أَمْرُ ٱللَّهِ مَفْعُولًا

Narrated Anas: Zaid bin Haritha came to the Prophet ﷺ complaining about his wife. The Prophet ﷺ kept on saying (to him), “Be afraid of Allah and keep your wife.” Aisha said, “If Allah’s Messenger ﷺ were to conceal anything (of the Qur’an he would have concealed this Verse.” Zainab used to boast before the wives of the Prophet ﷺ and used to say, “You were given in marriage by your families, while I was married (to the Prophet) by Allah from over seven Heavens.” And Thabit recited, “The Verse:-- ‘But (O Muhammad) you did hide in your heart that which Allah was about to make manifest, you did fear the people,’ (33.37) was revealed in connection with Zainab and Zaid bin Haritha.”. – Sahih Al-Bukhari 7420
حَدَّثَنَا أَحْمَدُ، حَدَّثَنَا مُحَمَّدُ بْنُ أَبِي بَكْرٍ الْمُقَدَّمِيُّ، حَدَّثَنَا حَمَّادُ بْنُ زَيْدٍ، عَنْ ثَابِتٍ، عَنْ أَنَسٍ، قَالَ جَاءَ زَيْدُ بْنُ حَارِثَةَ يَشْكُو فَجَعَلَ النَّبِيُّ صلى الله عليه وسلم يَقُولُ " اتَّقِ اللَّهَ، وَأَمْسِكْ عَلَيْكَ زَوْجَكَ ". قَالَتْ عَائِشَةُ لَوْ كَانَ رَسُولُ اللَّهِ صلى الله عليه وسلم كَاتِمًا شَيْئًا لَكَتَمَ هَذِهِ. قَالَ فَكَانَتْ زَيْنَبُ تَفْخَرُ عَلَى أَزْوَاجِ النَّبِيِّ صلى الله عليه وسلم تَقُولُ زَوَّجَكُنَّ أَهَالِيكُنَّ، وَزَوَّجَنِي اللَّهُ تَعَالَى مِنْ فَوْقِ سَبْعِ سَمَوَاتٍ. وَعَنْ ثَابِتٍ {وَتُخْفِي فِي نَفْسِكَ مَا اللَّهُ مُبْدِيهِ وَتَخْشَى النَّاسَ} نَزَلَتْ فِي شَأْنِ زَيْنَبَ وَزَيْدِ بْنِ حَارِثَةَ.

`Abdullah bin `Umar said: “Allah’s Messenger ﷺ appointed Zaid bin Haritha as the commander of the army during the Ghazwa of Mu’tah and said, “If Zaid is martyred, Ja`far should take over his position, and if Ja`far is martyred, `Abdullah bin Rawaha should take over his position.’ “ `Abdulla-h bin `Umar further said, “I was present amongst them in that battle and we searched for Ja`far bin Abi Talib and found his body amongst the bodies of the martyred ones, and found over ninety wounds over his body, caused by stabs or shots (of arrows). – Sahih Al-Bukhari 4261
أَخْبَرَنَا أَحْمَدُ بْنُ أَبِي بَكْرٍ، حَدَّثَنَا مُغِيرَةُ بْنُ عَبْدِ الرَّحْمَنِ، عَنْ عَبْدِ اللَّهِ بْنِ سَعِيدٍ، عَنْ نَافِعٍ، عَنْ عَبْدِ اللَّهِ بْنِ عُمَرَ ـ رضى الله عنهما ـ قَالَ أَمَّرَ رَسُولُ اللَّهِ صلى الله عليه وسلم فِي غَزْوَةِ مُوتَةَ زَيْدَ بْنَ حَارِثَةَ، فَقَالَ رَسُولُ اللَّهِ صلى الله عليه وسلم " إِنْ قُتِلَ زَيْدٌ فَجَعْفَرٌ، وَإِنْ قُتِلَ جَعْفَرٌ فَعَبْدُ اللَّهِ بْنُ رَوَاحَةَ ". قَالَ عَبْدُ اللَّهِ كُنْتُ فِيهِمْ فِي تِلْكَ الْغَزْوَةِ فَالْتَمَسْنَا جَعْفَرَ بْنَ أَبِي طَالِبٍ، فَوَجَدْنَاهُ فِي الْقَتْلَى، وَوَجَدْنَا مَا فِي جَسَدِهِ بِضْعًا وَتِسْعِينَ مِنْ طَعْنَةٍ وَرَمْيَةٍ

Narrated Aisha: When the news of the martyrdom of Zaid bin Haritha, Ja`far and `Abdullah bin Rawaha came, the Prophet sat down looking sad, and I was looking through the chink of the door. A man came and said, “O Allah’s Messenger ﷺ! The women of Ja`far,” and then he mentioned their crying . The Prophet ﷺ ordered him to stop them from crying. The man went and came back and said, "I tried to stop them but they disobeyed." The Prophet ﷺ ordered him for the second time to forbid them. He went again and came back and said, "They did not listen to me, (or "us": the sub-narrator Muhammad bin Haushab is in doubt as to which is right). " (`Aisha added: The Prophet ﷺ said, "Put dust in their mouths." I said (to that man), "May Allah stick your nose in the dust (i.e. humiliate you)." By Allah, you could not (stop the women from crying) to fulfill the order, besides you did not relieve Allah's Apostle from fatigue.". – Sahih Al-Bukhari 1305

حَدَّثَنَا مُحَمَّدُ بْنُ عَبْدِ اللَّهِ بْنِ حَوْشَبٍ، حَدَّثَنَا عَبْدُ الْوَهَّابِ، حَدَّثَنَا يَحْيَى بْنُ سَعِيدٍ، قَالَ أَخْبَرَتْنِي عَمْرَةُ، قَالَتْ سَمِعْتُ عَائِشَةَ ـ رضى الله عنها ـ تَقُولُ لَمَّا جَاءَ قَتْلُ زَيْدِ بْنِ حَارِثَةَ وَجَعْفَرٍ وَعَبْدِ اللَّهِ بْنِ رَوَاحَةَ، جَلَسَ النَّبِيُّ صلى الله عليه وسلم يُعْرَفُ فِيهِ الْحُزْنُ، وَأَنَا أَطَّلِعُ مِنْ شَقِّ الْبَابِ، فَأَتَاهُ رَجُلٌ فَقَالَ يَا رَسُولَ اللَّهِ إِنَّ نِسَاءَ جَعْفَرٍ وَذَكَرَ بُكَاءَهُنَّ فَأَمَرَهُ بِأَنْ يَنْهَاهُنَّ، فَذَهَبَ الرَّجُلُ ثُمَّ أَتَى فَقَالَ قَدْ نَهَيْتُهُنَّ، وَذَكَرَ أَنَّهُنَّ لَمْ يُطِعْنَهُ، فَأَمَرَهُ الثَّانِيَةَ أَنْ يَنْهَاهُنَّ، فَذَهَبَ، ثُمَّ أَتَى، فَقَالَ وَاللَّهِ لَقَدْ غَلَبْنَنِي أَوْ غَلَبْنَنَا الشَّكُّ مِنْ مُحَمَّدِ بْنِ حَوْشَبٍ ـ فَزَعَمَتْ أَنَّ النَّبِيَّ صلى الله عليه وسلم قَالَ " فَاحْثُ فِي أَفْوَاهِهِنَّ التُّرَابَ ". فَقُلْتُ أَرْغَمَ اللَّهُ أَنْفَكَ، فَوَاللَّهِ مَا أَنْتَ بِفَاعِلٍ وَمَا تَرَكْتَ رَسُولَ اللَّهِ صلى الله عليه وسلم مِنَ الْعَنَاءِ.

Usāma ibn Zayd
أُسَامَة بن زَيْد

Narrated `Aisha :After the slanderers had given a forged statement against her, Allah's Messenger ﷺ called `Ali bin Abi Talib and Usama bin Zaid when the Divine Inspiration was delayed. He wanted to ask them and consult them about the question of divorcing me. Usama gave his evidence that was based on what he knew about my innocence, but `Ali said, "Allah has not put restrictions on you and there are many women other than her. Furthermore you may ask the slave girl who will tell you the truth." So the Prophet ﷺ asked Barira (my salve girl), "Have you seen anything that may arouse your suspicion?" She replied, "I have not seen anything more than that she is a little girl who sleeps, leaving the dough of her family (unguarded) that the domestic goats come and eat it." Then the Prophet ﷺ stood on the pulpit and said, "O Muslims! Who will help me against the man who has harmed me by slandering my wife? By Allah, I know nothing about my family except good." The narrator added: Then the Prophet ﷺ mentioned the innocence of `Aisha. (See Hadith No. 274, Vol. 6). – Sahih Al-Bukhari 7369

حَدَّثَنَا الأُوَيْسِيُّ، حَدَّثَنَا إِبْرَاهِيمُ، عَنْ صَالِحٍ، عَنِ ابْنِ شِهَابٍ، حَدَّثَنِي عُرْوَةُ، وَابْنُ الْمُسَيَّبِ، وَعَلْقَمَةُ بْنُ وَقَّاصٍ، وَعُبَيْدُ اللَّهِ، عَنْ عَائِشَةَ ـ رضى الله عنها ـ حِينَ قَالَ لَهَا أَهْلُ الإِفْكِ قَالَتْ وَدَعَا رَسُولُ اللَّهِ صلى الله عليه وسلم عَلِيَّ بْنَ أَبِي طَالِبٍ وَأُسَامَةَ بْنَ زَيْدٍ حِينَ اسْتَلْبَثَ الْوَحْىُ يَسْأَلُهُمَا، وَهْوَ يَسْتَشِيرُهُمَا فِي فِرَاقِ أَهْلِهِ، فَأَمَّا أُسَامَةُ فَأَشَارَ بِالَّذِي يَعْلَمُ مِنْ بَرَاءَةِ أَهْلِهِ، وَأَمَّا عَلِيٌّ فَقَالَ لَمْ يُضَيِّقِ اللَّهُ عَلَيْكَ، وَالنِّسَاءُ سِوَاهَا كَثِيرٌ، وَسَلِ الْجَارِيَةَ تَصْدُقْكَ. فَقَالَ " هَلْ رَأَيْتِ مِنْ شَىْءٍ يَرِيبُكِ ". قَالَتْ مَا رَأَيْتُ أَمْرًا أَكْثَرَ مِنْ أَنَّهَا جَارِيَةٌ حَدِيثَةُ السِّنِّ تَنَامُ عَنْ عَجِينِ أَهْلِهَا فَتَأْتِي الدَّاجِنُ فَتَأْكُلُهُ. فَقَامَ عَلَى الْمِنْبَرِ فَقَالَ " يَا مَعْشَرَ الْمُسْلِمِينَ مَنْ يَعْذِرُنِي مِنْ رَجُلٍ بَلَغَنِي أَذَاهُ فِي أَهْلِي، وَاللَّهِ مَا عَلِمْتُ عَلَى أَهْلِي إِلاَّ خَيْرًا ". فَذَكَرَ بَرَاءَةَ عَائِشَةَ. وَقَالَ أَبُو أُسَامَةَ عَنْ هِشَامٍ.

Narrated Ibn Shihab Az-Zuhri :Anas bin Malik said, "When the emigrants came Medina, they had nothing whereas the Ansar had land and property. The Ansar gave them their land on condition that the emigrants would give them half the yearly yield and work on the land and provide the necessaries for cultivation." His (i.e. Anas's mother who was also the mother of `Abdullah bin Abu Talha, gave some date-palms to Allah' Apostle who gave them to his freed slave-girl (Um Aiman) who was also the mother of Usama bin Zaid. When the Prophet ﷺ finished from the fighting against the people of Khaibar and returned to Medina, the emigrants returned to the Ansar the fruit gifts which the Ansar had given them. The

Prophet ﷺ also returned to Anas's mother the date-palms. Allah's Messenger ﷺ gave Um Aiman other trees from his garden in lieu of the old gift – .Sahih Al-Bukhari 2630

حَدَّثَنَا عَبْدُ اللَّهِ بْنُ يُوسُفَ، أَخْبَرَنَا ابْنُ وَهْبٍ، حَدَّثَنَا يُونُسُ، عَنِ ابْنِ شِهَابٍ، عَنْ أَنَسِ بْنِ مَالِكٍ ـ رضى الله عنه ـ قَالَ لَمَّا قَدِمَ الْمُهَاجِرُونَ الْمَدِينَةَ مِنْ مَكَّةَ وَلَيْسَ بِأَيْدِيهِمْ ـ يَعْنِي شَيْئًا ـ وَكَانَتِ الأَنْصَارُ أَهْلَ الأَرْضِ وَالْعَقَارِ، فَقَاسَمَهُمُ الأَنْصَارُ عَلَى أَنْ يُعْطُوهُمْ ثِمَارَ أَمْوَالِهِمْ كُلَّ عَامٍ وَيَكْفُوهُمُ الْعَمَلَ وَالْمَئُونَةَ، وَكَانَتْ أُمُّهُ أُمُّ أَنَسٍ أُمُّ سُلَيْمٍ كَانَتْ أُمَّ عَبْدِ اللَّهِ بْنِ أَبِي طَلْحَةَ، فَكَانَتْ أَعْطَتْ أُمُّ أَنَسٍ رَسُولَ اللَّهِ صلى الله عليه وسلم عِذَاقًا فَأَعْطَاهُنَّ النَّبِيُّ صلى الله عليه وسلم أُمَّ أَيْمَنَ مَوْلاَتَهُ أُمَّ أُسَامَةَ بْنِ زَيْدٍ. قَالَ ابْنُ شِهَابٍ فَأَخْبَرَنِي أَنَسُ بْنُ مَالِكٍ أَنَّ النَّبِيَّ صلى الله عليه وسلم لَمَّا فَرَغَ مِنْ قَتْلِ أَهْلِ خَيْبَرَ فَانْصَرَفَ إِلَى الْمَدِينَةِ، رَدَّ الْمُهَاجِرُونَ إِلَى الأَنْصَارِ مَنَائِحَهُمُ الَّتِي كَانُوا مَنَحُوهُمْ مِنْ ثِمَارِهِمْ فَرَدَّ النَّبِيُّ صلى الله عليه وسلم إِلَى أُمِّهِ عِذَاقَهَا، وَأَعْطَى رَسُولُ اللَّهِ صلى الله عليه وسلم أُمَّ أَيْمَنَ مَكَانَهُنَّ مِنْ حَائِطِهِ. وَقَالَ أَحْمَدُ بْنُ شَبِيبٍ أَخْبَرَنَا أَبِي عَنْ يُونُسَ بِهَذَا، وَقَالَ مَكَانَهُنَّ مِنْ خَالِصِهِ.

Narrated Safiya bint Huyay :While Allah's Messenger ﷺ was in I`tikaf, I called on him at night and having had a talk with him, I got up to depart. He got up also to accompany me to my dwelling place, which was then in the house of Usama bin Zaid. Two Ansari men passed by, and when they saw the Prophet ﷺ they hastened away. The Prophet said (to them). "Don't hurry! It is Safiya, the daughter of Huyay (i.e. my wife)." They said, "Glorified be Allah! O Allah's Messenger ﷺ! (How dare we suspect you?)" He said, "Satan circulates in the human mind as blood circulates in it, and I was afraid that Satan might throw an evil thought (or something) into your hearts – .".Sahih Al-Bukhari 3281

حَدَّثَنِي مَحْمُودُ بْنُ غَيْلاَنَ، حَدَّثَنَا عَبْدُ الرَّزَّاقِ، أَخْبَرَنَا مَعْمَرٌ، عَنِ الزُّهْرِيِّ، عَنْ عَلِيِّ بْنِ حُسَيْنٍ، عَنْ صَفِيَّةَ ابْنَةِ حُيَيٍّ، قَالَتْ كَانَ رَسُولُ اللَّهِ صلى الله عليه وسلم مُعْتَكِفًا، فَأَتَيْتُهُ أَزُورُهُ لَيْلاً فَحَدَّثْتُهُ ثُمَّ قُمْتُ، فَانْقَلَبْتُ فَقَامَ مَعِي لِيَقْلِبَنِي. وَكَانَ مَسْكَنُهَا فِي دَارِ أُسَامَةَ بْنِ زَيْدٍ، فَمَرَّ رَجُلاَنِ مِنَ الأَنْصَارِ، فَلَمَّا رَأَيَا النَّبِيَّ صلى الله عليه وسلم أَسْرَعَا، فَقَالَ النَّبِيُّ صلى الله عليه وسلم " عَلَى رِسْلِكُمَا إِنَّهَا صَفِيَّةُ بِنْتُ حُيَيٍّ ". فَقَالاَ سُبْحَانَ اللَّهِ يَا رَسُولَ اللَّهِ. قَالَ " إِنَّ الشَّيْطَانَ يَجْرِي مِنَ الإِنْسَانِ مَجْرَى الدَّمِ، وَإِنِّي خَشِيتُ أَنْ يَقْذِفَ فِي قُلُوبِكُمَا سُوءًا ـ أَوْ قَالَ ـ شَيْئًا ".

Narrated Usama bin Zaid bin Haritha: Allah's Messenger ﷺ sent us (to fight) against Al-Huraqa (one of the sub-tribes) of Juhaina. We reached those people in the morning and defeated them. A man from the Ansar and I chased one of their men and when we attacked him, he said, "None has the right to be worshipped but Allah." The Ansari refrained from killing him but I stabbed him with my spear till I killed him. When we reached (Medina), this news reached the Prophet. He said to me, "O Usama! You killed him after he had said, 'None has the right to be worshipped but Allah?"' I said, "O Allah's Messenger ﷺ! He said so in order to save himself." The Prophet ﷺ said, "You killed him after he had said, 'None has the right to be worshipped but Allah." The Prophet ﷺ kept on repeating that statement till I wished I had not been a Muslim before that day. – Sahih Al-Bukhari 6872

حَدَّثَنَا عَمْرُو بْنُ زُرَارَةَ، حَدَّثَنَا هُشَيْمٌ، حَدَّثَنَا حُصَيْنٌ، حَدَّثَنَا أَبُو ظَبْيَانَ، قَالَ سَمِعْتُ أُسَامَةَ بْنَ زَيْدِ بْنِ حَارِثَةَ ـ رضى الله عنهما ـ يُحَدِّثُ قَالَ بَعَثَنَا رَسُولُ اللَّهِ صلى الله عليه وسلم إِلَى الْحُرَقَةِ مِنْ جُهَيْنَةَ ـ قَالَ ـ فَصَبَّحْنَا الْقَوْمَ فَهَزَمْنَاهُمْ ـ قَالَ ـ وَلَحِقْتُ أَنَا وَرَجُلٌ مِنَ الأَنْصَارِ رَجُلاً مِنْهُمْ ـ قَالَ ـ فَلَمَّا غَشِينَاهُ قَالَ لاَ إِلَهَ إِلاَّ اللَّهُ ـ قَالَ ـ فَكَفَّ عَنْهُ الأَنْصَارِيُّ، فَطَعَنْتُهُ بِرُمْحِي حَتَّى قَتَلْتُهُ ـ قَالَ ـ فَلَمَّا قَدِمْنَا بَلَغَ ذَلِكَ النَّبِيَّ صلى الله عليه وسلم قَالَ فَقَالَ لِي " يَا أُسَامَةُ أَقَتَلْتَهُ بَعْدَ مَا قَالَ لاَ إِلَهَ إِلاَّ اللَّهُ ". قَالَ قُلْتُ يَا رَسُولَ اللَّهِ إِنَّمَا كَانَ مُتَعَوِّذًا. قَالَ " أَقَتَلْتَهُ بَعْدَ أَنْ قَالَ لاَ إِلَهَ إِلاَّ اللَّهُ ". قَالَ فَمَا زَالَ يُكَرِّرُهَا عَلَىَّ حَتَّى تَمَنَّيْتُ أَنِّي لَمْ أَكُنْ أَسْلَمْتُ قَبْلَ ذَلِكَ الْيَوْمِ.

Narrated Usama bin Zaid: Allah's Messenger ﷺ proceeded from `Arafat and dismounted at the mountainous pass and then urinated and performed a light ablution. I said to him, "(Shall we offer) the prayer?" He replied, "The prayer is ahead of you (i.e. at Al-Muzdalifa)." When he came to Al-Muzdalifa, he performed a perfect ablution. Then Iqama for the prayer was pronounced and he offered the Maghrib prayer and then every person made his camel kneel at his place; and then Iqama for the prayer was pronounced and he offered the (`Isha') prayer and he did not offer any prayer in between them (i.e. Maghrib and `Isha' prayers). – Sahih Al-Bukhari 1672

حَدَّثَنَا عَبْدُ اللَّهِ بْنُ يُوسُفَ، أَخْبَرَنَا مَالِكٌ، عَنْ مُوسَى بْنِ عُقْبَةَ، عَنْ كُرَيْبٍ، عَنْ أُسَامَةَ بْنِ زَيْدٍ ـ رضى الله عنهما ـ أَنَّهُ سَمِعَهُ يَقُولُ دَفَعَ رَسُولُ اللَّهِ صلى الله عليه وسلم مِنْ عَرَفَةَ، فَنَزَلَ الشِّعْبَ، فَبَالَ ثُمَّ تَوَضَّأَ، وَلَمْ يُسْبِغِ الْوُضُوءَ. فَقُلْتُ لَهُ الصَّلاَةَ. فَقَالَ " الصَّلاَةُ أَمَامَكَ ". فَجَاءَ الْمُزْدَلِفَةَ، فَتَوَضَّأَ، فَأَسْبَغَ، ثُمَّ أُقِيمَتِ الصَّلاَةُ، فَصَلَّى الْمَغْرِبَ، ثُمَّ أَنَاخَ كُلُّ إِنْسَانٍ بَعِيرَهُ فِي مَنْزِلِهِ، ثُمَّ أُقِيمَتِ الصَّلاَةُ فَصَلَّى، وَلَمْ يُصَلِّ بَيْنَهُمَا

Narrated `Aisha :The people of Quraish worried about the lady from Bani Makhzum who had committed theft. They asked, "Who will intercede for her with Allah's Messenger ﷺ?" Some said, "No one dare to do so except Usama bin Zaid the beloved one to Allah's Messenger ﷺ." When Usama spoke about that to Allah's Apostle Allah's Messenger ﷺ said, (to him), "Do you try to intercede for somebody in a case connected with Allah's Prescribed Punishments?" Then he got up and delivered a sermon saying, "What destroyed the nations preceding you, was that if a noble amongst them stole, they would forgive him, and if a poor person amongst them stole, they would inflict Allah's Legal punishment on him. By Allah, if Fatima, the daughter of Muhammad stole, I would cut off her hand – .".Sahih Al-Bukhari 3475

حَدَّثَنَا قُتَيْبَةُ بْنُ سَعِيدٍ، حَدَّثَنَا لَيْثٌ، عَنِ ابْنِ شِهَابٍ، عَنْ عُرْوَةَ، عَنْ عَائِشَةَ ـ رضى الله عنها أَنَّ قُرَيْشًا، أَهَمَّهُمْ شَأْنُ الْمَرْأَةِ الْمَخْزُومِيَّةِ الَّتِي سَرَقَتْ، فَقَالَ وَمَنْ يُكَلِّمُ فِيهَا رَسُولَ اللَّهِ صلى الله عليه وسلم فَقَالُوا وَمَنْ يَجْتَرِئُ عَلَيْهِ إِلاَّ أُسَامَةُ بْنُ زَيْدٍ، حِبُّ رَسُولِ اللَّهِ صلى الله عليه وسلم، فَكَلَّمَهُ أُسَامَةُ، فَقَالَ رَسُولُ اللَّهِ صلى الله عليه وسلم " أَتَشْفَعُ فِي حَدٍّ مِنْ حُدُودِ اللَّهِ ". ثُمَّ قَامَ فَاخْتَطَبَ، ثُمَّ قَالَ " إِنَّمَا أَهْلَكَ الَّذِينَ قَبْلَكُمْ أَنَّهُمْ كَانُوا إِذَا سَرَقَ فِيهِمُ الشَّرِيفُ تَرَكُوهُ، وَإِذَا سَرَقَ فِيهِمُ الضَّعِيفُ أَقَامُوا عَلَيْهِ الْحَدَّ، وَايْمُ اللَّهِ، لَوْ أَنَّ فَاطِمَةَ ابْنَةَ مُحَمَّدٍ سَرَقَتْ لَقَطَعْتُ يَدَهَا ".

Narrated Nafi :`Abdullah bin `Umar said, "Allah's Messenger ﷺ entered the Ka`ba along with Usama bin Zaid, Bilal and `Uthman bin Talha Al-Hajabi and closed the door and stayed there for some time. I asked Bilal when he came out, 'What did the Prophet ﷺ do?' He replied, 'He offered prayer with one pillar to his left and one to his right and three behind.' In those days the Ka`ba was supported by six pillars." Malik said: "There were two pillars on his (the Prophet's) right side – .".Sahih Al-Bukhari 505

حَدَّثَنَا عَبْدُ اللَّهِ بْنُ يُوسُفَ، قَالَ أَخْبَرَنَا مَالِكٌ، عَنْ نَافِعٍ، عَنْ عَبْدِ اللَّهِ بْنِ عُمَرَ، أَنَّ رَسُولَ اللَّهِ صلى الله عليه وسلم دَخَلَ الْكَعْبَةَ وَأُسَامَةُ بْنُ زَيْدٍ وَبِلاَلٌ وَعُثْمَانُ بْنُ طَلْحَةَ الْحَجَبِيُّ فَأَغْلَقَهَا عَلَيْهِ وَمَكَثَ فِيهَا، فَسَأَلْتُ بِلاَلاً حِينَ خَرَجَ مَا صَنَعَ النَّبِيُّ صلى الله عليه وسلم قَالَ جَعَلَ عَمُودًا عَنْ يَسَارِهِ، وَعَمُودًا عَنْ يَمِينِهِ، وَثَلاَثَةَ أَعْمِدَةٍ وَرَاءَهُ، وَكَانَ الْبَيْتُ يَوْمَئِذٍ عَلَى سِتَّةِ أَعْمِدَةٍ، ثُمَّ صَلَّى. وَقَالَ لَنَا إِسْمَاعِيلُ حَدَّثَنِي مَالِكٌ وَقَالَ عَمُودَيْنِ عَنْ يَمِينِهِ.

Narrated Usama bin Zaid: That Allah's Messenger ﷺ rode over a donkey covered with a Fadakiya (velvet sheet) and Usama was riding behind him. He was visiting Sa`d bin 'Ubada (who was sick) in the dwelling place of Bani Al-Harith bin Al-Khazraj and this incident happened before the battle of Badr. They proceeded till they passed by a gathering in which `Abdullah bin Ubai bin Salul was present., and that was before `Abdullah bin Ubat embraced Islam. In that gathering there were Muslims, pagan idolators and Jews, and among the Muslims there was `Abdullah bin Rawaha. When a cloud of dust raised by (the movement of) the animal covered that gathering, `Abdullah bin Ubai covered his nose with his garment and said, "Do not cover us with dust." Allah's Messenger ﷺ greeted them, stopped, dismounted and invited them to Allah (i.e. to embrace Islam) and recited to them the Holy Qur'an. On that `Abdullah bin Ubai bin Salul said to him, "O man! There is nothing better than what you say, if it is the truth. So do not trouble us with it in our gatherings, but if somebody comes to you, you can preach to him." On that `Abdullah bin Rawaha said "Yes, O Allah's Messenger ﷺ! Call on us in our gathering, for we love that." So the Muslims, the pagans and the Jews started abusing one another till they were about to fight with one another.

Allah's Messenger ﷺ kept on quietening them till all of them became quiet, and then Allah's Messenger ﷺ rode his animal and proceeded till he entered upon Sa`d bin 'Ubada. Allah's Messenger ﷺ said, "O Sa`d! Didn't you hear what Abu Habab said?" (meaning `Abdullah bin Unbar). "He said so-and-so." Sa`d bin Ubada said, "O Allah's Messenger ﷺ! Let my father be sacrificed for you ! Excuse and forgive him for, by Him Who revealed to you the Book, Allah sent the Truth which was revealed to you at the time when the people of this town had decided to crown him (`Abdullah bin Ubai) as their ruler. So when Allah had prevented that with the Truth He had given you, he was choked by that, and that caused him to behave in such an impolite manner which you had noticed." So Allah's Messenger ﷺ excused him. (It was the custom of) Allah's Messenger ﷺ and his companions to excuse the pagans and the people of the scripture (Christians and Jews) as Allah ordered them, and they used to be patient when annoyed (by them). Allah said: 'You shall certainly hear much that will grieve you from those who received the Scripture before you.....and from the pagans (3.186) He also said: 'Many of the people of the scripture wish that if they could turn you away as disbelievers after you have believed. .... (2.109) So Allah's Messenger ﷺ used to apply what Allah had ordered him by excusing them till he was allowed to fight against them. When Allah's Messenger ﷺ had fought the battle of Badr and Allah killed whomever He killed among the chiefs of the infidels and the nobles of Quraish, and Allah's Messenger ﷺ and his companions had returned with victory and booty, bringing with them some of the chiefs of the infidels and the nobles of the Quraish as captives. `Abdullah bin Ubai bin Salul and the pagan idolators who were with him, said, "This matter (Islam) has now brought out its face (triumphed), so give Allah's Messenger ﷺ the pledge of allegiance (for embracing Islam.)". Then they became Muslims. – Sahih Al-Bukhari 6207

حَدَّثَنَا أَبُو الْيَمَانِ، أَخْبَرَنَا شُعَيْبٌ، عَنِ الزُّهْرِيِّ، حَدَّثَنَا إِسْمَاعِيلُ، قَالَ حَدَّثَنِي أَخِي، عَنْ سُلَيْمَانَ، عَنْ مُحَمَّدِ بْنِ أَبِي عَتِيقٍ، عَنِ ابْنِ شِهَابٍ، عَنْ عُرْوَةَ بْنِ الزُّبَيْرِ، أَنَّ أُسَامَةَ بْنَ زَيْدٍ ـ رضى الله عنهما ـ أَخْبَرَهُ أَنَّ رَسُولَ اللَّهِ صلى الله عليه وسلم رَكِبَ عَلَى حِمَارٍ عَلَيْهِ قَطِيفَةٌ فَدَكِيَّةٌ وَأُسَامَةُ وَرَاءَهُ، يَعُودُ سَعْدَ بْنَ عُبَادَةَ فِي بَنِي حَارِثِ بْنِ الْخَزْرَجِ قَبْلَ وَقْعَةِ بَدْرٍ، فَسَارَا حَتَّى مَرَّا بِمَجْلِسٍ فِيهِ عَبْدُ اللَّهِ بْنُ أُبَىٍّ ابْنُ سَلُولَ، وَذَلِكَ قَبْلَ أَنْ يُسْلِمَ عَبْدُ اللَّهِ بْنُ أُبَىٍّ، فَإِذَا فِي الْمَجْلِسِ أَخْلاَطٌ مِنَ الْمُسْلِمِينَ وَالْمُشْرِكِينَ عَبَدَةِ الأَوْثَانِ وَالْيَهُودِ، وَفِي الْمُسْلِمِينَ عَبْدُ اللَّهِ بْنُ رَوَاحَةَ، فَلَمَّا غَشِيَتِ الْمَجْلِسَ عَجَاجَةُ الدَّابَّةِ خَمَّرَ ابْنُ أُبَىٍّ أَنْفَهُ بِرِدَائِهِ وَقَالَ لاَ تُغَبِّرُوا عَلَيْنَا. فَسَلَّمَ رَسُولُ اللَّهِ صلى الله عليه وسلم عَلَيْهِمْ، ثُمَّ وَقَفَ فَنَزَلَ فَدَعَاهُمْ إِلَى اللَّهِ وَقَرَأَ عَلَيْهِمُ الْقُرْآنَ، فَقَالَ لَهُ عَبْدُ اللَّهِ بْنُ أُبَىٍّ ابْنُ سَلُولَ أَيُّهَا الْمَرْءُ لاَ أَحْسَنَ مِمَّا تَقُولُ إِنْ كَانَ حَقًّا، فَلاَ تُؤْذِنَا بِهِ فِي مَجَالِسِنَا، فَمَنْ جَاءَكَ فَاقْصُصْ عَلَيْهِ. قَالَ عَبْدُ اللَّهِ بْنُ رَوَاحَةَ بَلَى يَا رَسُولَ اللَّهِ فَاغْشَنَا فِي مَجَالِسِنَا فَإِنَّا نُحِبُّ ذَلِكَ. فَاسْتَبَّ الْمُسْلِمُونَ وَالْمُشْرِكُونَ وَالْيَهُودُ حَتَّى كَادُوا يَتَثَاوَرُونَ فَلَمْ يَزَلْ رَسُولُ اللَّهِ صلى الله عليه وسلم يُخَفِّضُهُمْ حَتَّى سَكَتُوا، ثُمَّ رَكِبَ رَسُولُ اللَّهِ صلى الله عليه وسلم دَابَّتَهُ فَسَارَ حَتَّى دَخَلَ عَلَى سَعْدِ بْنِ عُبَادَةَ، فَقَالَ رَسُولُ اللَّهِ صلى الله عليه وسلم " أَىْ سَعْدُ أَلَمْ تَسْمَعْ مَا قَالَ أَبُو حُبَابٍ ـ يُرِيدُ عَبْدَ اللَّهِ بْنَ أُبَىٍّ ـ قَالَ كَذَا وَكَذَا ". فَقَالَ سَعْدُ بْنُ عُبَادَةَ أَىْ رَسُولَ اللَّهِ بِأَبِي أَنْتَ، اعْفُ عَنْهُ وَاصْفَحْ، فَوَالَّذِي أَنْزَلَ عَلَيْكَ الْكِتَابَ لَقَدْ جَاءَ اللَّهُ بِالْحَقِّ الَّذِي أَنْزَلَ عَلَيْكَ، وَلَقَدِ اصْطَلَحَ أَهْلُ هَذِهِ الْبَحْرَةِ عَلَى أَنْ يُتَوِّجُوهُ وَيُعَصِّبُوهُ بِالْعِصَابَةِ، فَلَمَّا رَدَّ اللَّهُ ذَلِكَ بِالْحَقِّ الَّذِي أَعْطَاكَ شَرِقَ بِذَلِكَ فَذَلِكَ فَعَلَ بِهِ مَا رَأَيْتَ. فَعَفَا عَنْهُ رَسُولُ اللَّهِ صلى الله عليه وسلم وَكَانَ رَسُولُ اللَّهِ صلى الله عليه وسلم وَأَصْحَابُهُ يَعْفُونَ عَنِ الْمُشْرِكِينَ وَأَهْلِ الْكِتَابِ كَمَا أَمَرَهُمُ اللَّهُ، وَيَصْبِرُونَ عَلَى الأَذَى، قَالَ اللَّهُ تَعَالَى {وَلَتَسْمَعُنَّ مِنَ الَّذِينَ أُوتُوا الْكِتَابَ} الآيَةَ، وَقَالَ {وَدَّ كَثِيرٌ مِنْ أَهْلِ الْكِتَابِ} فَكَانَ رَسُولُ اللَّهِ صلى الله عليه وسلم يَتَأَوَّلُ فِي الْعَفْوِ عَنْهُمْ مَا أَمَرَهُ اللَّهُ بِهِ حَتَّى أَذِنَ لَهُ فِيهِمْ، فَلَمَّا غَزَا رَسُولُ اللَّهِ صلى الله عليه وسلم بَدْرًا، فَقَتَلَ اللَّهُ بِهَا مَنْ قَتَلَ مِنْ صَنَادِيدِ الْكُفَّارِ، وَسَادَةِ قُرَيْشٍ، فَقَفَلَ رَسُولُ اللَّهِ صلى الله عليه وسلم وَأَصْحَابُهُ مَنْصُورِينَ غَانِمِينَ مَعَهُمْ أُسَارَى مِنْ صَنَادِيدِ الْكُفَّارِ وَسَادَةِ قُرَيْشٍ قَالَ ابْنُ أُبَىٍّ ابْنُ سَلُولَ، وَمَنْ مَعَهُ مِنَ الْمُشْرِكِينَ عَبَدَةِ الأَوْثَانِ هَذَا أَمْرٌ قَدْ تَوَجَّهَ فَبَايِعُوا رَسُولَ اللَّهِ صلى الله عليه وسلم عَلَى الإِسْلاَمِ فَأَسْلَمُوا.

Narrated Abu `Uthman: Usama bin Zaid said that while he. Sa`d and Ubai bin Ka`b were with the Prophet ﷺ a daughter of the Prophet sent a message to him, saying. 'My daughter is dying; please come to us." The Prophet ﷺ sent her his greetings and added "It is for Allah what He takes, and what He gives; and everything before His sight has a limited period. So she should hope for Allah's reward and remain patient." She again sent a message, beseeching him by Allah, to come. So the Prophetﷺ got up. And so did we (and went there). The child was placed on his lap while his breath was irregular. Tears flowed from the eyes of the Prophet. Sa`d said to him, "What is this, O Allah's Messengerﷺ?" He said. "This Is Mercy which Allah has embedded in the hearts of whomever He wished of His slaves. And Allah does not bestow His Mercy, except on the merciful among His slaves. (See Hadith No. 373 Vol. 2). – Sahih Al-Bukhari 5655

حَدَّثَنَا حَجَّاجُ بْنُ مِنْهَالٍ، حَدَّثَنَا شُعْبَةُ، قَالَ أَخْبَرَنِي عَاصِمٌ، قَالَ سَمِعْتُ أَبَا عُثْمَانَ، عَنْ أُسَامَةَ بْنِ زَيْدٍ ـ رضى الله عنهما ـ أَنَّ ابْنَةً لِلنَّبِيِّ، صلى الله عليه وسلم أَرْسَلَتْ إِلَيْهِ وَهْوَ مَعَ النَّبِيِّ صلى الله عليه وسلم وَسَعْدٍ وَأُبَىٍّ نَحْسِبُ أَنَّ ابْنَتِي قَدْ حُضِرَتْ فَاشْهَدْنَا فَأَرْسَلَ إِلَيْهَا السَّلاَمَ وَيَقُولُ " إِنَّ لِلَّهِ مَا أَخَذَ وَمَا أَعْطَى وَكُلُّ شَىْءٍ عِنْدَهُ مُسَمًّى فَلْتَحْتَسِبْ وَلْتَصْبِرْ ". فَأَرْسَلَتْ تُقْسِمُ عَلَيْهِ، فَقَامَ النَّبِيُّ صلى الله عليه وسلم وَقُمْنَا، فَرُفِعَ الصَّبِيُّ فِي حَجْرِ النَّبِيِّ صلى الله عليه وسلم وَنَفْسُهُ تَقَعْقَعُ فَفَاضَتْ عَيْنَا النَّبِيِّ صلى الله عليه وسلم فَقَالَ لَهُ سَعْدٌ مَا هَذَا يَا رَسُولَ اللَّهِ قَالَ " هَذِهِ رَحْمَةٌ وَضَعَهَا اللَّهُ فِي قُلُوبِ مَنْ شَاءَ مِنْ عِبَادِهِ، وَلاَ يَرْحَمُ اللَّهُ مِنْ عِبَادِهِ إِلاَّ الرُّحَمَاءَ "

Narrated Usama bin Zaid: Allah's Messengerﷺ said, "Plague was a means of torture sent on a group of Israelis (or on some people before you). So if you hear of its spread in a land, don't approach it, and if a plague should appear in a land where you are present, then don't leave that land in order to run away from it (i.e. plague). – Sahih Al-Bukhari 3473

حَدَّثَنَا عَبْدُ الْعَزِيزِ بْنُ عَبْدِ اللَّهِ، قَالَ حَدَّثَنِي مَالِكٌ، عَنْ مُحَمَّدِ بْنِ الْمُنْكَدِرِ، وَعَنْ أَبِي النَّضْرِ، مَوْلَى عُمَرَ بْنِ عُبَيْدِ اللَّهِ عَنْ عَامِرِ بْنِ سَعْدِ بْنِ أَبِي وَقَّاصٍ، عَنْ أَبِيهِ، أَنَّهُ سَمِعَهُ يَسْأَلُ، أُسَامَةَ بْنَ زَيْدٍ مَاذَا سَمِعْتَ مِنْ، رَسُولِ اللَّهِ صلى الله عليه وسلم فِي الطَّاعُونِ فَقَالَ أُسَامَةُ قَالَ رَسُولُ اللَّهِ صلى الله عليه وسلم " الطَّاعُونُ رِجْسٌ أُرْسِلَ عَلَى طَائِفَةٍ مِنْ بَنِي إِسْرَائِيلَ أَوْ عَلَى مَنْ كَانَ قَبْلَكُمْ، فَإِذَا سَمِعْتُمْ بِهِ بِأَرْضٍ فَلاَ تَقْدَمُوا عَلَيْهِ، وَإِذَا وَقَعَ بِأَرْضٍ وَأَنْتُمْ بِهَا فَلاَ تَخْرُجُوا فِرَارًا مِنْهُ ". قَالَ أَبُو النَّضْرِ " لاَ يُخْرِجُكُمْ إِلاَّ فِرَارًا مِنْهُ "

Narrated Harmala: (Usama's Maula) Usama (bin Zaid) sent me to `Ali (at Kufa) and said, "`Ali will ask you, 'What has prevented your companion from joining me?' You then should say to him, 'If you (`Ali) were in the mouth of a lion, I would like to be with you, but in this matter I won't take any part.' " Harmala added: "`Ali didn't give me anything (when I conveyed the message to him) so I went to Hasan, Hussain and Ibn Ja`far and they loaded my camels with much (wealth). – Sahih Al-Bukhari 7110

حَدَّثَنَا عَلِيُّ بْنُ عَبْدِ اللَّهِ، حَدَّثَنَا سُفْيَانُ، قَالَ قَالَ عَمْرٌو أَخْبَرَنِي مُحَمَّدُ بْنُ عَلِيٍّ، أَنَّ حَرْمَلَةَ، مَوْلَى أُسَامَةَ أَخْبَرَهُ قَالَ عَمْرٌو وَقَدْ رَأَيْتُ حَرْمَلَةَ قَالَ أَرْسَلَنِي أُسَامَةُ إِلَى عَلِيٍّ وَقَالَ إِنَّهُ سَيَسْأَلُكَ الآنَ فَيَقُولُ مَا خَلَّفَ صَاحِبَكَ فَقُلْ لَهُ يَقُولُ لَكَ لَوْ كُنْتَ فِي شِدْقِ الأَسَدِ لأَحْبَبْتُ أَنْ أَكُونَ مَعَكَ فِيهِ، وَلَكِنَّ هَذَا أَمْرٌ لَمْ أَرَهُ، فَلَمْ يُعْطِنِي شَيْئًا، فَذَهَبْتُ إِلَى حَسَنٍ وَحُسَيْنٍ وَابْنِ جَعْفَرٍ فَأَوْقَرُوا لِي رَاحِلَتِي.

Narrated Usama bin Zaid: Once the Prophetﷺ stood over one of the high buildings of Medina and then said (to the people), "Do you see what I see?" They said, "No." He said, "I see afflictions falling among your houses as rain drops fall.". – Sahih Al-Bukhari 7060

حَدَّثَنَا أَبُو نُعَيْمٍ، حَدَّثَنَا ابْنُ عُيَيْنَةَ، عَنِ الزُّهْرِيِّ. وَحَدَّثَنِي مَحْمُودٌ، أَخْبَرَنَا عَبْدُ الرَّزَّاقِ، أَخْبَرَنَا مَعْمَرٌ، عَنِ الزُّهْرِيِّ، عَنْ عُرْوَةَ، عَنْ أُسَامَةَ بْنِ زَيْدٍ ـ رضى الله عنهما ـ قَالَ أَشْرَفَ النَّبِيُّ صلى الله عليه وسلم عَلَى أُطُمٍ مِنْ آطَامِ الْمَدِينَةِ فَقَالَ " هَلْ تَرَوْنَ مَا أَرَى ". قَالُوا لاَ. قَالَ " فَإِنِّي لأَرَى الْفِتَنَ تَقَعُ خِلاَلَ بُيُوتِكُمْ كَوَقْعِ الْقَطْرِ ".

The Book of

We used to compare the people as to who was better during the lifetime of Allah's Messenger

ابْنِ عُمَرَ ـ رضى الله عنهما ـ قَالَ كُنَّا نُخَيِّرُ بَيْنَ النَّاسِ فِي زَمَنِ النَّبِيِّ صلى الله عليه وسلم

The Pioneers—The first of the Migrants and the Supporters, and those who followed them in righteousness. Allah is pleased with them, and they are pleased with Him. He has prepared for them Gardens beneath which rivers flow, where they will abide forever. That is the sublime triumph. – Surah At-Taubah 9:100

وَٱلسَّٰبِقُونَ ٱلْأَوَّلُونَ مِنَ ٱلْمُهَٰجِرِينَ وَٱلْأَنصَارِ وَٱلَّذِينَ ٱتَّبَعُوهُم بِإِحْسَٰنٍ رَّضِىَ ٱللَّهُ عَنْهُمْ وَرَضُوا۟ عَنْهُ وَأَعَدَّ لَهُمْ جَنَّٰتٍ تَجْرِى تَحْتَهَا ٱلْأَنْهَٰرُ خَٰلِدِينَ فِيهَآ أَبَدًا ذَٰلِكَ ٱلْفَوْزُ ٱلْعَظِيمُ

And you become three classes. Those on the Right—what of those on the Right? And those on the Left—what of those on the Left? And the forerunners, the forerunners. Those are the nearest. In the Gardens of Bliss. A throng from the ancients. And a small band from the latecomers. – Surah Al-Waqi'ah 56:7-14

وَكُنتُمْ أَزْوَٰجًا ثَلَٰثَةً فَأَصْحَٰبُ ٱلْمَيْمَنَةِ مَآ أَصْحَٰبُ ٱلْمَيْمَنَةِ وَأَصْحَٰبُ ٱلْمَشْـَٔمَةِ مَآ أَصْحَٰبُ ٱلْمَشْـَٔمَةِ وَٱلسَّٰبِقُونَ ٱلسَّٰبِقُونَ أُو۟لَٰٓئِكَ ٱلْمُقَرَّبُونَ فِى جَنَّٰتِ ٱلنَّعِيمِ ثُلَّةٌ مِّنَ ٱلْأَوَّلِينَ وَقَلِيلٌ مِّنَ ٱلْءَاخِرِينَ

To the poor refugees who were driven out of their homes and their possessions, as they sought the favor of Allah and His approval, and came to the aid of Allah and His Messenger. These are the sincere. And those who, before them, had settled in the homeland, and had accepted faith. They love those who emigrated to them, and find no hesitation in their hearts in helping them. They give them priority over themselves, even if they themselves are needy. Whoever is protected from his natural greed—it is they who are the successful. And those who came after them, saying, "Our Lord, forgive us, and our brethren who preceded us in faith, and leave no malice in our hearts towards those who believe. Our Lord, You are Clement and Merciful." Have you not considered those who act hypocritically? They say to their brethren who disbelieved among the People of the Book, "If you are evicted, we will leave with you, and will not obey anyone against you; and should anyone fight you, we will certainly support you." But Allah bears witness that they are liars. If they are evicted, they will not leave with them; and if anyone fights them, they will not support them; and if they go to their aid, they will turn their backs and flee; then they will receive no support. – Surah Al-Hashr 59:8-12

لِلْفُقَرَآءِ ٱلْمُهَٰجِرِينَ ٱلَّذِينَ أُخْرِجُوا۟ مِن دِيَٰرِهِمْ وَأَمْوَٰلِهِمْ يَبْتَغُونَ فَضْلًا مِّنَ ٱللَّهِ وَرِضْوَٰنًا وَيَنصُرُونَ ٱللَّهَ وَرَسُولَهُۥٓ ۚ أُو۟لَٰٓئِكَ هُمُ ٱلصَّٰدِقُونَ وَٱلَّذِينَ تَبَوَّءُو ٱلدَّارَ وَٱلْإِيمَٰنَ مِن قَبْلِهِمْ يُحِبُّونَ مَنْ هَاجَرَ إِلَيْهِمْ وَلَا يَجِدُونَ فِى صُدُورِهِمْ حَاجَةً مِّمَّآ أُوتُوا۟ وَيُؤْثِرُونَ عَلَىٰٓ أَنفُسِهِمْ وَلَوْ كَانَ بِهِمْ خَصَاصَةٌ وَمَن يُوقَ شُحَّ نَفْسِهِۦ فَأُو۟لَٰٓئِكَ هُمُ ٱلْمُفْلِحُونَ وَٱلَّذِينَ جَآءُو مِنۢ بَعْدِهِمْ يَقُولُونَ رَبَّنَا ٱغْفِرْ لَنَا وَلِإِخْوَٰنِنَا ٱلَّذِينَ سَبَقُونَا بِٱلْإِيمَٰنِ وَلَا تَجْعَلْ فِى قُلُوبِنَا غِلًّا لِّلَّذِينَ ءَامَنُوا۟ رَبَّنَآ إِنَّكَ رَءُوفٌ رَّحِيمٌ أَلَمْ تَرَ إِلَى ٱلَّذِينَ نَافَقُوا۟ يَقُولُونَ لِإِخْوَٰنِهِمُ ٱلَّذِينَ كَفَرُوا۟ مِنْ أَهْلِ ٱلْكِتَٰبِ لَئِنْ أُخْرِجْتُمْ لَنَخْرُجَنَّ مَعَكُمْ وَلَا نُطِيعُ فِيكُمْ أَحَدًا أَبَدًا وَإِن قُوتِلْتُمْ لَنَنصُرَنَّكُمْ وَٱللَّهُ يَشْهَدُ إِنَّهُمْ لَكَٰذِبُونَ لَئِنْ أُخْرِجُوا۟ لَا يَخْرُجُونَ مَعَهُمْ وَلَئِن قُوتِلُوا۟ لَا يَنصُرُونَهُمْ وَلَئِن نَّصَرُوهُمْ لَيُوَلُّنَّ ٱلْأَدْبَٰرَ ثُمَّ لَا يُنصَرُونَ

A throng from the ancients. And a throng from the latecomers. – Surah Al-Waqi'ah 56:39-40

ثُلَّةٌ مِّنَ ٱلْأَوَّلِينَ وَثُلَّةٌ مِّنَ ٱلْءَاخِرِينَ

And why is it that you do not spend in the cause of Allah, when to Allah belongs the inheritance of the heavens and the earth? Not equal among you are those who contributed before the conquest, and fought. Those are higher in rank than those who contributed afterwards, and fought. But Allah promises both a good reward. Allah is Well Experienced in what you do. – Surah Al-Hadid 57:10
وَمَا لَكُمْ أَلَّا تُنفِقُوا۟ فِى سَبِيلِ ٱللَّهِ وَلِلَّهِ مِيرَٰثُ ٱلسَّمَٰوَٰتِ وَٱلْأَرْضِ ۚ لَا يَسْتَوِى مِنكُم مَّنْ أَنفَقَ مِن قَبْلِ ٱلْفَتْحِ وَقَٰتَلَ ۚ أُو۟لَٰٓئِكَ أَعْظَمُ دَرَجَةً مِّنَ ٱلَّذِينَ أَنفَقُوا۟ مِنۢ بَعْدُ وَقَٰتَلُوا۟ ۚ وَكُلًّا وَعَدَ ٱللَّهُ ٱلْحُسْنَىٰ ۚ وَٱللَّهُ بِمَا تَعْمَلُونَ خَبِيرٌ

O you who believe! When believing women come to you emigrating, test them. Allah is Aware of their faith. And if you find them to be faithful, do not send them back to the unbelievers. They are not lawful for them, nor are they lawful for them. But give them what they have spent. You are not at fault if you marry them, provided you give them their compensation. And do not hold on to ties with unbelieving women, but demand what you have spent, and let them demand what they have spent. This is the rule of Allah; He rules among you. Allah is Knowing and Wise. – Surah Al-Mumtahinah 60:10
يَٰٓأَيُّهَا ٱلَّذِينَ ءَامَنُوٓا۟ إِذَا جَآءَكُمُ ٱلْمُؤْمِنَٰتُ مُهَٰجِرَٰتٍ فَٱمْتَحِنُوهُنَّ ۖ ٱللَّهُ أَعْلَمُ بِإِيمَٰنِهِنَّ ۖ فَإِنْ عَلِمْتُمُوهُنَّ مُؤْمِنَٰتٍ فَلَا تَرْجِعُوهُنَّ إِلَى ٱلْكُفَّارِ ۖ لَا هُنَّ حِلٌّ لَّهُمْ وَلَا هُمْ يَحِلُّونَ لَهُنَّ ۖ وَءَاتُوهُم مَّآ أَنفَقُوا۟ ۚ وَلَا جُنَاحَ عَلَيْكُمْ أَن تَنكِحُوهُنَّ إِذَآ ءَاتَيْتُمُوهُنَّ أُجُورَهُنَّ ۚ وَلَا تُمْسِكُوا۟ بِعِصَمِ ٱلْكَوَافِرِ وَسْـَٔلُوا۟ مَآ أَنفَقْتُمْ وَلْيَسْـَٔلُوا۟ مَآ أَنفَقُوا۟ ۚ ذَٰلِكُمْ حُكْمُ ٱللَّهِ ۖ يَحْكُمُ بَيْنَكُمْ ۚ وَٱللَّهُ عَلِيمٌ حَكِيمٌ

Narrated Sa`d from his father: Once the meal of `Abdur-Rahman bin `Auf was brought in front of him, and he said, "Mus`ab bin `Umair was martyred and he was better than I, and he had nothing except his Burd (a black square narrow dress) to be shrouded in. Hamza or another person was martyred and he was also better than I and he had nothing to be shrouded in except his Burd. No doubt, I fear that the rewards of my deeds might have been given early in this world." Then he started weeping. – Sahih Al-Bukhari 1274
حَدَّثَنَا أَحْمَدُ بْنُ مُحَمَّدٍ الْمَكِّيُّ، حَدَّثَنَا إِبْرَاهِيمُ بْنُ سَعْدٍ، عَنْ سَعْدٍ، عَنْ أَبِيهِ، قَالَ أُتِيَ عَبْدُ الرَّحْمَنِ بْنُ عَوْفٍ ـ رضى الله عنه ـ يَوْمًا بِطَعَامِهِ فَقَالَ قُتِلَ مُصْعَبُ بْنُ عُمَيْرٍ ـ وَكَانَ خَيْرًا مِنِّي ـ فَلَمْ يُوجَدْ لَهُ مَا يُكَفَّنُ فِيهِ إِلاَّ بُرْدَةٌ، وَقُتِلَ حَمْزَةُ أَوْ رَجُلٌ آخَرُ خَيْرٌ مِنِّي فَلَمْ يُوجَدْ لَهُ مَا يُكَفَّنُ فِيهِ إِلاَّ بُرْدَةٌ، لَقَدْ خَشِيتُ أَنْ يَكُونَ قَدْ عُجِّلَتْ لَنَا طَيِّبَاتُنَا فِي حَيَاتِنَا الدُّنْيَا، ثُمَّ جَعَلَ يَبْكِي

So when the Prophet ﷺ came, she said, "O Allah's Prophet `Umar has said so-and-so." He said (to Asma'), "What did you say to him?" Asma's aid, "I told him so-and-so." The Prophet ﷺ said, "He (i.e. `Umar) has not got more right than you people over me, as he and his companions have (the reward of) only one migration, and you, the people of the boat, have (the reward of) two migrations." Asma' later on said, "I saw Abu Musa and the other people of the boat coming to me in successive groups, asking me about this narration,, and to them nothing in the world was more cheerful and greater than what the Prophet ﷺ had said about them." Narrated Abu Burda: Asma' said, "I saw Abu Musa requesting me to repeat this narration again and again.". – Sahih Al-Bukhari 4231
فَلَمَّا جَاءَ النَّبِيُّ صلى الله عليه وسلم قَالَتْ يَا نَبِيَّ اللَّهِ إِنَّ عُمَرَ قَالَ كَذَا وَكَذَا. قَالَ " فَمَا قُلْتِ لَهُ ". قَالَتْ قُلْتُ لَهُ كَذَا وَكَذَا. قَالَ " لَيْسَ بِأَحَقَّ بِي مِنْكُمْ، وَلَهُ وَلأَصْحَابِهِ هِجْرَةٌ وَاحِدَةٌ، وَلَكُمْ أَنْتُمْ أَهْلَ السَّفِينَةِ هِجْرَتَانِ ". قَالَتْ فَلَقَدْ رَأَيْتُ أَبَا مُوسَى وَأَصْحَابَ السَّفِينَةِ يَأْتُونِي أَرْسَالاً، يَسْأَلُونِي عَنْ هَذَا الْحَدِيثِ، مَا مِنَ الدُّنْيَا شَىْءٌ هُمْ بِهِ أَفْرَحُ وَلاَ أَعْظَمُ فِي أَنْفُسِهِمْ مِمَّا قَالَ لَهُمُ النَّبِيُّ صلى الله عليه وسلم. قَالَ أَبُو بُرْدَةَ قَالَتْ أَسْمَاءُ فَلَقَدْ رَأَيْتُ أَبَا مُوسَى وَإِنَّهُ لَيَسْتَعِيدُ هَذَا الْحَدِيثَ مِنِّي

Narrated Zaid bin Thabit: Abu Bakr sent for me owing to the large number of casualties in the battle of Al-Yamama, while `Umar was sitting with him. Abu Bakr said (to me), `Umar has come to my and said, 'A great number of Qaris of the Holy Qur'an were killed on the day of the battle of Al-Yamama, and I am afraid that the casualties among the Qaris of the Qur'an may increase on other battle-fields whereby a large part of the Qur'an may be lost. Therefore I consider it advisable that you (Abu Bakr) should have the Qur'an collected.' I said, 'How dare I do something which Allah's Messenger ﷺ did not do?' `Umar said, By Allah, it is something beneficial.' `Umar kept on pressing me for that till Allah opened my chest for that for which He had opened the chest of `Umar and I had in that matter, the same opinion as `Umar had." Abu Bakr then said to me (Zaid), "You are a wise young man and we do not have any suspicion about you, and you used to write the Divine Inspiration for Allah's Messenger ﷺ. So you should search for the fragmentary scripts of the Qur'an and collect it (in one Book)." Zaid further said: By Allah, if Abu Bakr had ordered me to shift a mountain among the mountains from one place to another it would not have been heavier for me than this ordering me to collect the Qur'an. Then I said (to `Umar and Abu Bakr), "How can you do something which Allah's Messenger ﷺ did not do?" Abu Bakr said, "By Allah, it is something beneficial." Zaid added: So he (Abu Bakr) kept on pressing me for that until Allah opened my chest for that for which He had opened the chests of Abu Bakr and `Umar, and I had in that matter, the same opinion as theirs. So I started compiling the Qur'an by collecting it from the leafless stalks of the date-palm tree and from the pieces of leather and hides and from the stones, and from the chests of men (who had memorized the Qur'an). I found the last verses of Sirat-at-Tauba: ("Verily there has come unto you an Apostle (Muhammad) from amongst yourselves—' (9.128-129)) from Khuza`ima or Abi Khuza`ima and I added to it the rest of the Sura. The manuscripts of the Qur'an remained with Abu Bakr till Allah took him unto Him. Then it remained with `Umar till Allah took him unto Him, and then with Hafsa bint `Umar. – Sahih Al-Bukhari 7191

حَدَّثَنَا مُحَمَّدُ بْنُ عُبَيْدِ اللَّهِ أَبُو ثَابِتٍ، حَدَّثَنَا إِبْرَاهِيمُ بْنُ سَعْدٍ، عَنِ ابْنِ شِهَابٍ، عَنْ عُبَيْدِ بْنِ السَّبَّاقِ، عَنْ زَيْدِ بْنِ ثَابِتٍ، قَالَ بَعَثَ إِلَىَّ أَبُو بَكْرٍ لِمَقْتَلِ أَهْلِ الْيَمَامَةِ وَعِنْدَهُ عُمَرُ فَقَالَ أَبُو بَكْرٍ إِنَّ عُمَرَ أَتَانِي فَقَالَ إِنَّ الْقَتْلَ قَدِ اسْتَحَرَّ يَوْمَ الْيَمَامَةِ بِقُرَّاءِ الْقُرْآنِ، وَإِنِّي أَخْشَى أَنْ يَسْتَحِرَّ الْقَتْلُ بِقُرَّاءِ الْقُرْآنِ فِي الْمَوَاطِنِ كُلِّهَا، فَيَذْهَبَ قُرْآنٌ كَثِيرٌ، وَإِنِّي أَرَى أَنْ تَأْمُرَ بِجَمْعِ الْقُرْآنِ. قُلْتُ كَيْفَ أَفْعَلُ شَيْئًا لَمْ يَفْعَلْهُ رَسُولُ اللَّهِ صلى الله عليه وسلم فَقَالَ عُمَرُ هُوَ وَاللَّهِ خَيْرٌ. فَلَمْ يَزَلْ عُمَرُ يُرَاجِعُنِي فِي ذَلِكَ حَتَّى شَرَحَ اللَّهُ صَدْرِي لِلَّذِي شَرَحَ لَهُ صَدْرَ عُمَرَ، وَرَأَيْتُ فِي ذَلِكَ الَّذِي رَأَى عُمَرُ. قَالَ زَيْدٌ قَالَ أَبُو بَكْرٍ وَإِنَّكَ رَجُلٌ شَابٌّ عَاقِلٌ لاَ نَتَّهِمُكَ، قَدْ كُنْتَ تَكْتُبُ الْوَحْىَ لِرَسُولِ اللَّهِ صلى الله عليه وسلم فَتَتَبَّعِ الْقُرْآنَ فَاجْمَعْهُ. قَالَ زَيْدٌ فَوَاللَّهِ لَوْ كَلَّفَنِي نَقْلَ جَبَلٍ مِنَ الْجِبَالِ مَا كَانَ بِأَثْقَلَ عَلَىَّ مِمَّا كَلَّفَنِي مِنْ جَمْعِ الْقُرْآنِ. قُلْتُ كَيْفَ تَفْعَلاَنِ شَيْئًا لَمْ يَفْعَلْهُ رَسُولُ اللَّهِ صلى الله عليه وسلم قَالَ أَبُو بَكْرٍ هُوَ وَاللَّهِ خَيْرٌ. فَلَمْ يَزَلْ يَحُثُّ مُرَاجَعَتِي حَتَّى شَرَحَ اللَّهُ صَدْرِي لِلَّذِي شَرَحَ اللَّهُ لَهُ صَدْرَ أَبِي بَكْرٍ وَعُمَرَ، وَرَأَيْتُ فِي ذَلِكَ الَّذِي رَأَيَا، فَتَتَبَّعْتُ الْقُرْآنَ أَجْمَعُهُ مِنَ الْعُسُبِ وَالرِّقَاعِ وَاللِّخَافِ وَصُدُورِ الرِّجَالِ، فَوَجَدْتُ آخِرَ سُورَةِ التَّوْبَةِ {لَقَدْ جَاءَكُمْ رَسُولٌ مِنْ أَنْفُسِكُمْ} إِلَى آخِرِهَا مَعَ خُزَيْمَةَ أَوْ أَبِي خُزَيْمَةَ فَأَلْحَقْتُهَا فِي سُورَتِهَا، وَكَانَتِ الصُّحُفُ عِنْدَ أَبِي بَكْرٍ حَيَاتَهُ حَتَّى تَوَفَّاهُ اللَّهُ عَزَّ وَجَلَّ، ثُمَّ عِنْدَ عُمَرَ حَيَاتَهُ حَتَّى تَوَفَّاهُ اللَّهُ، ثُمَّ عِنْدَ حَفْصَةَ بِنْتِ عُمَرَ. قَالَ مُحَمَّدُ بْنُ عُبَيْدِ اللَّهِ اللِّخَافُ يَعْنِي الْخَزَفَ.

Narrated Abu Ad-Darda: There was a dispute between Abu Bakr and `Umar, and Abu Bakr made `Umar angry. So `Umar left angrily. Abu Bakr followed him, requesting him to ask forgiveness (of Allah) for him, but `Umar refused to do so and closed his door in Abu Bakr's face. So Abu Bakr went to Allah's Messenger ﷺ while we were with him. Allah's Messengeraid, "This friend of yours must have quarrelled (with somebody)." In the meantime `Umar repented and felt sorry for what he had done, so he came, greeted (those who were present) and sat with the Prophet ﷺ and related the story to him. Allah's Messenger ﷺ became angry and Abu Bakr started saying, "O Allah's Messenger ﷺ! By Allah, I was more at fault (than `Umar)." Allah's Apostle said, "Are you (people) leaving for me my companion? (Abu Bakr), Are you (people) leaving for me my companion? When I said, 'O people I am sent to you all as the Messenger of Allah,' you said, 'You tell a lie.' While Abu Bakr said, 'You have spoken the truth .". – Sahih Al-Bukhari 4640

حَدَّثَنَا عَبْدُ اللَّهِ، حَدَّثَنَا سُلَيْمَانُ بْنُ عَبْدِ الرَّحْمَنِ، وَمُوسَى بْنُ هَارُونَ، قَالاَ حَدَّثَنَا الْوَلِيدُ بْنُ مُسْلِمٍ، حَدَّثَنَا عَبْدُ اللَّهِ بْنُ الْعَلاَءِ بْنِ زَبْرٍ، قَالَ حَدَّثَنِي بُسْرُ بْنُ عُبَيْدِ اللَّهِ، قَالَ حَدَّثَنِي أَبُو إِدْرِيسَ الْخَوْلاَنِيُّ، قَالَ سَمِعْتُ أَبَا الدَّرْدَاءِ، يَقُولُ كَانَتْ بَيْنَ أَبِي بَكْرٍ وَعُمَرَ مُحَاوَرَةٌ، فَأَغْضَبَ أَبُو بَكْرٍ عُمَرَ، فَانْصَرَفَ عَنْهُ عُمَرُ مُغْضَبًا، فَاتَّبَعَهُ أَبُو بَكْرٍ يَسْأَلُهُ أَنْ يَسْتَغْفِرَ لَهُ، فَلَمْ يَفْعَلْ حَتَّى أَغْلَقَ بَابَهُ فِي وَجْهِهِ، فَأَقْبَلَ أَبُو بَكْرٍ إِلَى رَسُولِ اللَّهِ صلى الله عليه وسلم فَقَالَ أَبُو الدَّرْدَاءِ وَنَحْنُ عِنْدَهُ فَقَالَ رَسُولُ اللَّهِ صلى الله عليه وسلم " أَمَّا صَاحِبُكُمْ هَذَا فَقَدْ غَامَرَ ". قَالَ وَنَدِمَ عُمَرُ عَلَى مَا كَانَ مِنْهُ فَأَقْبَلَ حَتَّى سَلَّمَ وَجَلَسَ إِلَى النَّبِيِّ صلى الله عليه وسلم وَقَصَّ عَلَى رَسُولِ اللَّهِ صلى الله عليه وسلم الْخَبَرَ. قَالَ أَبُو الدَّرْدَاءِ وَغَضِبَ رَسُولُ اللَّهِ صلى الله عليه وسلم وَجَعَلَ أَبُو بَكْرٍ يَقُولُ وَاللَّهِ يَا رَسُولَ اللَّهِ لأَنَا كُنْتُ أَظْلَمَ فَقَالَ رَسُولُ اللَّهِ صلى الله عليه وسلم " هَلْ أَنْتُمْ تَارِكُو لِي صَاحِبِي هَلْ أَنْتُمْ تَارِكُو لِي صَاحِبِي إِنِّي قُلْتُ يَا أَيُّهَا النَّاسُ إِنِّي رَسُولُ اللَّهِ إِلَيْكُمْ جَمِيعًا فَقُلْتُمْ كَذَبْتَ. وَقَالَ أَبُو بَكْرٍ صَدَقْتَ قَالَ أَبُو عَبْدِ اللَّهِ غَامَرَ سَبَقَ بِالْخَيْرِ"

Narrated `Umar: I recommend that my successor should take care of and secure the rights of the early emigrants; and I also advise my successor to be kind to the Ansar who had homes (in Medina) and had adopted the Faith, before the Prophet ﷺ migrated to them, and to accept the good from their good ones and excuse their wrong doers. – Sahih Al-Bukhari 4888

حَدَّثَنَا أَحْمَدُ بْنُ يُونُسَ، حَدَّثَنَا أَبُو بَكْرٍ، عَنْ حُصَيْنٍ، عَنْ عَمْرِو بْنِ مَيْمُونٍ، قَالَ قَالَ عُمَرُ رضى الله عنه أُوصِي الْخَلِيفَةَ بِالْمُهَاجِرِينَ الأَوَّلِينَ أَنْ يَعْرِفَ لَهُمْ حَقَّهُمْ، وَأُوصِي الْخَلِيفَةَ بِالأَنْصَارِ الَّذِينَ تَبَوَّءُوا الدَّارَ وَالإِيمَانَ مِنْ قَبْلِ أَنْ يُهَاجِرَ النَّبِيُّ صلى الله عليه وسلم أَنْ يَقْبَلَ مِنْ مُحْسِنِهِمْ وَيَعْفُوَ عَنْ مُسِيئِهِمْ.

Narrated Ibn `Umar: We used to compare the people as to who was better during the lifetime of Allah's Messenger ﷺ. We used to regard Abu Bakr as the best, then `Umar, and then `Uthman . – Sahih Al-Bukhari 3655

حَدَّثَنَا عَبْدُ الْعَزِيزِ بْنُ عَبْدِ اللَّهِ، حَدَّثَنَا سُلَيْمَانُ، عَنْ يَحْيَى بْنِ سَعِيدٍ، عَنْ نَافِعٍ، عَنِ ابْنِ عُمَرَ ـ رضى الله عنهما ـ قَالَ كُنَّا نُخَيِّرُ بَيْنَ النَّاسِ فِي زَمَنِ النَّبِيِّ صلى الله عليه وسلم فَنُخَيِّرُ أَبَا بَكْرٍ، ثُمَّ عُمَرَ بْنَ الْخَطَّابِ، ثُمَّ عُثْمَانَ بْنَ عَفَّانَ رضى الله عنهم.

Narrated Ibrahim: 'Alaqama went to Sham and came to the mosque and offered a two-rak`at prayer, and invoked Allah: "O Allah! Bless me with a (pious) good companion." So he sat beside Abu Ad-Darda' who asked, "From where are you?" He said, "From the people of Kufa." Abu Darda' said, "Wasn't there among you the person who keeps the secrets (of the Prophet ﷺ) which nobody knew except him (i.e., Hudhaifa (bin Al-Yaman). And isn't there among you the person whom Allah gave refuge from Satan through the request (tongue) of Allah's Messenger ﷺ? (i.e., `Ammar). Isn't there among you the one who used to carry the Siwak and the cushion (or pillows (of the Prophets)? (i.e., Ibn Mas`ud). How did Ibn Mas`ud use to recite 'By the night as it conceals (the light)?" (Sura 92). 'Alqama said, "Wadhdhakari Wal Untha' (And by male and female.") Abu Ad-Darda added. 'These people continued to argue with me regarding it till they were about to cause me to have doubts although I heard it from Allah's Messenger." – Sahih Al-Bukhari 6278

حَدَّثَنَا يَحْيَى بْنُ جَعْفَرٍ، حَدَّثَنَا يَزِيدُ، عَنْ شُعْبَةَ، عَنْ مُغِيرَةَ، عَنْ إِبْرَاهِيمَ، عَنْ عَلْقَمَةَ، أَنَّهُ قَدِمَ الشَّأْمَ. وَحَدَّثَنَا أَبُو الْوَلِيدِ، حَدَّثَنَا شُعْبَةُ، عَنْ مُغِيرَةَ، عَنْ إِبْرَاهِيمَ، قَالَ ذَهَبَ عَلْقَمَةُ إِلَى الشَّأْمِ، فَأَتَى الْمَسْجِدَ فَصَلَّى رَكْعَتَيْنِ فَقَالَ اللَّهُمَّ ارْزُقْنِي جَلِيسًا. فَقَعَدَ إِلَى أَبِي الدَّرْدَاءِ فَقَالَ مِمَّنْ أَنْتَ قَالَ مِنْ أَهْلِ الْكُوفَةِ. قَالَ أَلَيْسَ فِيكُمْ صَاحِبُ السِّرِّ الَّذِي كَانَ لاَ يَعْلَمُهُ غَيْرُهُ ـ يَعْنِي حُذَيْفَةَ ـ أَلَيْسَ فِيكُمْ ـ أَوْ كَانَ فِيكُمُ ـ الَّذِي أَجَارَهُ اللَّهُ عَلَى لِسَانِ رَسُولِهِ صلى الله عليه وسلم مِنَ الشَّيْطَانِ ـ يَعْنِي عَمَّارًا ـ أَوَلَيْسَ فِيكُمْ صَاحِبُ السِّوَاكِ وَالْوِسَادِ ـ يَعْنِي ابْنَ مَسْعُودٍ ـ كَيْفَ كَانَ عَبْدُ اللَّهِ يَقْرَأُ {وَاللَّيْلِ إِذَا يَغْشَى}. قَالَ {وَالذَّكَرِ وَالأُنْثَى}. فَقَالَ مَا زَالَ هَؤُلاَءِ حَتَّى كَادُوا يُشَكِّكُونِي، وَقَدْ سَمِعْتُهَا مِنْ رَسُولِ اللَّهِ صلى الله عليه وسلم.

Narrated Al-Bara: When the Divine Inspiration: "Those of the believers who sit (at home), was revealed the Prophet ﷺ sent for Zaid (bin Thabit) who came with a shoulder-blade and wrote on it. Ibn Um-Maktum complained about his blindness and on that the following revelation came: "Not equal are those believers who sit (at home) except those who are

disabled (by injury, or are blind or lame etc.) and those who strive hard and fight in the Way of Allah with their wealth and lives)." (4.95). – Sahih Al-Bukhari 2831
حَدَّثَنَا أَبُو الْوَلِيدِ، حَدَّثَنَا شُعْبَةُ، عَنْ أَبِي إِسْحَاقَ، قَالَ سَمِعْتُ الْبَرَاءَ ـ رضى الله عنه ـ يَقُولُ لَمَّا نَزَلَتْ {لاَ يَسْتَوِي الْقَاعِدُونَ مِنَ الْمُؤْمِنِينَ} دَعَا رَسُولُ اللَّهِ صلى الله عليه وسلم زَيْدًا، فَجَاءَ بِكَتِفٍ فَكَتَبَهَا، وَشَكَا ابْنُ أُمِّ مَكْتُومٍ ضَرَارَتَهُ فَنَزَلَتْ {لاَ يَسْتَوِي الْقَاعِدُونَ مِنَ الْمُؤْمِنِينَ غَيْرُ أُولِي الضَّرَرِ }

Narrated Ibn `Abbas: The believers who failed to join the Ghazwa of Badr and those who took part in it are not equal (in reward). – Sahih Al-Bukhari 3954
حَدَّثَنِي إِبْرَاهِيمُ بْنُ مُوسَى، أَخْبَرَنَا هِشَامٌ، أَنَّ ابْنَ جُرَيْجٍ، أَخْبَرَهُمْ قَالَ أَخْبَرَنِي عَبْدُ الْكَرِيمِ، أَنَّهُ سَمِعَ مِقْسَمًا، مَوْلَى عَبْدِ اللَّهِ بْنِ الْحَارِثِ يُحَدِّثُ عَنِ ابْنِ عَبَّاسٍ، أَنَّهُ سَمِعَهُ يَقُولُ {لاَ يَسْتَوِي الْقَاعِدُونَ مِنَ الْمُؤْمِنِينَ} عَنْ بَدْرٍ، وَالْخَارِجُونَ، إِلَى بَدْرٍ

Narrated Rifaa: (who was one of the Badr warriors) Gabriel came to the Prophet ﷺ and said, "How do you look upon the warriors of Badr among yourselves?" The Prophet ﷺ said, "As the best of the Muslims." Or said a similar statement. On that, Gabriel said, "And so are the Angels who participated in the Badr (battle). – Sahih Al-Bukhari 3992
حَدَّثَنِي إِسْحَاقُ بْنُ إِبْرَاهِيمَ، أَخْبَرَنَا جَرِيرٌ، عَنْ يَحْيَى بْنِ سَعِيدٍ، عَنْ مُعَاذِ بْنِ رِفَاعَةَ بْنِ رَافِعٍ الزُّرَقِيِّ، عَنْ أَبِيهِ ـ وَكَانَ أَبُوهُ مِنْ أَهْلِ بَدْرٍ ـ قَالَ جَاءَ جِبْرِيلُ إِلَى النَّبِيِّ صلى الله عليه وسلم فَقَالَ " مَا تَعُدُّونَ أَهْلَ بَدْرٍ فِيكُمْ قَالَ مِنْ أَفْضَلِ الْمُسْلِمِينَ ـ أَوْ كَلِمَةً نَحْوَهَا ـ قَالَ وَكَذَلِكَ مَنْ شَهِدَ بَدْرًا مِنَ الْمَلاَئِكَةِ ".

Narrated Qais: The Badr warriors were given five thousand (Dirhams) each, yearly. `Umar said, "I will surely give them more than what I will give to others.". – Sahih Al-Bukhari 4022
حَدَّثَنَا إِسْحَاقُ بْنُ إِبْرَاهِيمَ، سَمِعَ مُحَمَّدَ بْنَ فُضَيْلٍ، عَنْ إِسْمَاعِيلَ، عَنْ قَيْسٍ، كَانَ عَطَاءُ الْبَدْرِيِّينَ خَمْسَةَ آلاَفٍ خَمْسَةَ آلاَفٍ. وَقَالَ عُمَرُ لأُفَضِّلَنَّهُمْ عَلَى مَنْ بَعْدَهُمْ

Narrated Abu `Uthman: Allah's Messenger ﷺ sent `Amr bin Al As as the commander of the troops of Dhat-us-Salasil. `Amr bin Al- `As said, "(On my return) I came to the Prophet ﷺ and said, 'Which people do you love most?' He replied, `Aisha.' I said, 'From amongst the men?' He replied, 'Her father (Abu Bakr)'. I said, 'Whom (do you love) next?' He replied, "`Umar.' Then he counted the names of many men, and I became silent for fear that he might regard me as the last of them.". – Sahih Al-Bukhari 4358
حَدَّثَنَا إِسْحَاقُ، أَخْبَرَنَا خَالِدُ بْنُ عَبْدِ اللَّهِ، عَنْ خَالِدٍ الْحَذَّاءِ، عَنْ أَبِي عُثْمَانَ، أَنَّ رَسُولَ اللَّهِ صلى الله عليه وسلم بَعَثَ عَمْرَو بْنَ الْعَاصِ عَلَى جَيْشِ ذَاتِ السَّلاَسِلِ قَالَ فَأَتَيْتُهُ فَقُلْتُ أَىُّ النَّاسِ أَحَبُّ إِلَيْكَ قَالَ " عَائِشَةُ ". قُلْتُ مِنَ الرِّجَالِ قَالَ " أَبُوهَا ". قُلْتُ ثُمَّ مَنْ قَالَ " عُمَرُ ". فَعَدَّ رِجَالاً فَسَكَتُّ مَخَافَةَ أَنْ يَجْعَلَنِي فِي آخِرِهِمْ

Narrated Abu Huraira: By Allah except Whom none has the right to- be worshipped, (sometimes) I used to lay (sleep) on the ground on my liver (abdomen) because of hunger, and (sometimes) I used to bind a stone over my belly because of hunger. One day I sat by the way from where they (the Prophet ﷺ and his companions) used to come out. When Abu Bakr passed by, I asked him about a Verse from Allah's Book and I asked him only that he might satisfy my hunger, but he passed by and did not do so. Then `Umar passed by me and I asked him about a Verse from Allah's Book, and I asked him only that he might satisfy my hunger, but he passed by without doing so. Finally Abu-l-Qasim (the Prophet ﷺ) passed by me and he smiled when he saw me, for he knew what was in my heart and on my face. He said, "O Aba Hirr (Abu Huraira)!" I replied, "Labbaik, O Allah's Messenger ﷺ!" He said to me, "Follow me." He left and I followed him. Then he entered the house and I asked permission to enter and was admitted. He found milk in a bowl and said, "From where is this milk?" They said, "It has been presented to you by such-and-such man (or by such and such woman)." He said, "O Aba Hirr!" I said, "Labbaik, O Allah's Messenger ﷺ!" He said, "Go and call the people of Suffa to me." These people of Suffa were the guests of Islam who had no families, nor money, nor anybody to depend upon, and whenever an object of charity was brought to the Prophet, he would send it to them and would not take anything from it, and whenever any present was given to him, he used to send some for them and take some of it for himself. The order of the Prophet upset me, and I said to myself, "How will this little milk be enough for the people of As- Suffa? Though I was more entitled to drink from that milk in order to strengthen myself", but behold! The Prophet ﷺ came to order me to give that milk to them. I wondered what will remain of that milk for me, but anyway, I could not but obey Allah and His Apostle so I went to the people of As-Suffa and called them, and they came and asked the Prophet's permission to enter. They were admitted and took their seats in the house. The Prophet ﷺ said, "O Aba-Hirr!" I said, "Labbaik, O Allah's Messenger ﷺ!" He said, "Take it and give it to them." So I took the bowl (of milk) and started giving it to one man who would drink his fill and return it to me, whereupon I would give it to another man who, in his turn, would drink his fill and return it to me, and I would then offer it to another man who would drink his fill and return it to me. Finally, after the whole group had drunk their fill, I reached the Prophet ﷺ who took the bowl and put it on his hand, looked at me and smiled and said. "O Aba Hirr!" I replied, "Labbaik, O Allah's Messenger ﷺ!" He said, "There remain you and I." I said, "You have said the truth, O Allah's Messenger ﷺ!" He said, "Sit down and drink." I sat down and drank. He said, "Drink," and I drank. He kept on telling me repeatedly to drink, till I said, "No. by Allah Who sent you with the Truth, I have no space for it (in my stomach)." He said, "Hand it over to me." When I gave him the bowl, he praised Allah and pronounced Allah's Name on it and drank the remaining milk. – Sahih Al-Bukhari 6452

حَدَّثَنِي أَبُو نُعَيْمٍ، بِنَحْوٍ مِنْ نِصْفِ هَذَا الْحَدِيثِ حَدَّثَنَا عُمَرُ بْنُ ذَرٍّ، حَدَّثَنَا مُجَاهِدٌ، أَنَّ أَبَا هُرَيْرَةَ، كَانَ يَقُولُ آللَّهِ الَّذِي لاَ إِلَهَ إِلاَّ هُوَ إِنْ كُنْتُ لأَعْتَمِدُ بِكَبِدِي عَلَى الأَرْضِ مِنَ الْجُوعِ، وَإِنْ كُنْتُ لأَشُدُّ الْحَجَرَ عَلَى بَطْنِي مِنَ الْجُوعِ، وَلَقَدْ قَعَدْتُ يَوْمًا عَلَى طَرِيقِهِمُ الَّذِي يَخْرُجُونَ مِنْهُ، فَمَرَّ أَبُو بَكْرٍ، فَسَأَلْتُهُ عَنْ آيَةٍ مِنْ كِتَابِ اللَّهِ، مَا سَأَلْتُهُ إِلاَّ لِيُشْبِعَنِي، فَمَرَّ وَلَمْ يَفْعَلْ، ثُمَّ مَرَّ بِي عُمَرُ فَسَأَلْتُهُ عَنْ آيَةٍ مِنْ كِتَابِ اللَّهِ، مَا سَأَلْتُهُ إِلاَّ لِيُشْبِعَنِي، فَمَرَّ فَلَمْ يَفْعَلْ، ثُمَّ مَرَّ بِي أَبُو الْقَاسِمِ صلى الله عليه وسلم فَتَبَسَّمَ حِينَ رَآنِي وَعَرَفَ، مَا فِي نَفْسِي وَمَا فِي وَجْهِي ثُمَّ قَالَ " أَبَا هِرٍّ ". قُلْتُ لَبَّيْكَ يَا رَسُولَ اللَّهِ. قَالَ " الْحَقْ ". وَمَضَى فَتَبِعْتُهُ، فَدَخَلَ فَاسْتَأْذَنَ، فَأَذِنَ لِي، فَدَخَلَ فَوَجَدَ لَبَنًا فِي قَدَحٍ فَقَالَ " مِنْ أَيْنَ هَذَا اللَّبَنُ ". قَالُوا أَهْدَاهُ لَكَ فُلاَنٌ أَوْ فُلاَنَةُ. قَالَ " أَبَا هِرٍّ ". قُلْتُ لَبَّيْكَ يَا رَسُولَ اللَّهِ. قَالَ " الْحَقْ إِلَى أَهْلِ الصُّفَّةِ فَادْعُهُمْ لِي ". قَالَ وَأَهْلُ الصُّفَّةِ أَضْيَافُ الإِسْلاَمِ، لاَ يَأْوُونَ إِلَى أَهْلٍ وَلاَ مَالٍ، وَلاَ عَلَى أَحَدٍ، إِذَا أَتَتْهُ صَدَقَةٌ بَعَثَ بِهَا إِلَيْهِمْ، وَلَمْ يَتَنَاوَلْ مِنْهَا شَيْئًا، وَإِذَا أَتَتْهُ هَدِيَّةٌ أَرْسَلَ إِلَيْهِمْ، وَأَصَابَ مِنْهَا وَأَشْرَكَهُمْ فِيهَا، فَسَاءَنِي ذَلِكَ فَقُلْتُ وَمَا هَذَا اللَّبَنُ فِي أَهْلِ الصُّفَّةِ كُنْتُ أَحَقُّ أَنَا أَنْ أُصِيبَ مِنْ هَذَا اللَّبَنِ شَرْبَةً أَتَقَوَّى بِهَا، فَإِذَا جَاءَ أَمَرَنِي فَكُنْتُ أَنَا أُعْطِيهِمْ، وَمَا عَسَى أَنْ يَبْلُغَنِي مِنْ هَذَا اللَّبَنِ، وَلَمْ يَكُنْ مِنْ طَاعَةِ اللَّهِ وَطَاعَةِ رَسُولِهِ صلى الله عليه وسلم بُدٌّ، فَأَتَيْتُهُمْ فَدَعَوْتُهُمْ فَأَقْبَلُوا، فَاسْتَأْذَنُوا فَأَذِنَ لَهُمْ، وَأَخَذُوا مَجَالِسَهُمْ مِنَ الْبَيْتِ قَالَ " يَا أَبَا هِرٍّ ". قُلْتُ لَبَّيْكَ يَا رَسُولَ اللَّهِ. قَالَ " خُذْ فَأَعْطِهِمْ ". قَالَ فَأَخَذْتُ الْقَدَحَ فَجَعَلْتُ أُعْطِيهِ الرَّجُلَ فَيَشْرَبُ حَتَّى يَرْوَى، ثُمَّ يَرُدُّ عَلَىَّ الْقَدَحَ، فَأُعْطِيهِ الرَّجُلَ فَيَشْرَبُ حَتَّى يَرْوَى، ثُمَّ يَرُدُّ عَلَىَّ الْقَدَحَ فَيَشْرَبُ حَتَّى يَرْوَى، ثُمَّ يَرُدُّ عَلَىَّ الْقَدَحَ، حَتَّى انْتَهَيْتُ إِلَى النَّبِيِّ صلى الله عليه وسلم وَقَدْ رَوِيَ الْقَوْمُ كُلُّهُمْ، فَأَخَذَ الْقَدَحَ فَوَضَعَهُ عَلَى يَدِهِ فَنَظَرَ إِلَىَّ فَتَبَسَّمَ فَقَالَ " أَبَا هِرٍّ ". قُلْتُ لَبَّيْكَ يَا رَسُولَ اللَّهِ. قَالَ " بَقِيتُ أَنَا وَأَنْتَ ". قُلْتُ صَدَقْتَ يَا رَسُولَ اللَّهِ. قَالَ " اقْعُدْ فَاشْرَبْ ". فَقَعَدْتُ فَشَرِبْتُ. فَقَالَ " اشْرَبْ ". فَشَرِبْتُ، فَمَا زَالَ يَقُولُ " اشْرَبْ ". حَتَّى قُلْتُ لاَ وَالَّذِي بَعَثَكَ بِالْحَقِّ، مَا أَجِدُ لَهُ مَسْلَكًا. قَالَ " فَأَرِنِي ". فَأَعْطَيْتُهُ الْقَدَحَ فَحَمِدَ اللَّهَ وَسَمَّى، وَشَرِبَ الْفَضْلَةَ

Narrated Anas: The Prophet ﷺ said, "Every nation has an Amin (i.e. the most honest man), and the Amin of this nation is Abu 'Ubaida bin Al-Jarrah.". – Sahih Al-Bukhari 4382

حَدَّثَنَا أَبُو الْوَلِيدِ، حَدَّثَنَا شُعْبَةُ، عَنْ خَالِدٍ، عَنْ أَبِي قِلاَبَةَ، عَنْ أَنَسٍ، عَنِ النَّبِيِّ صلى الله عليه وسلم قَالَ " لِكُلِّ أُمَّةٍ أَمِينٌ، وَأَمِينُ هَذِهِ الأُمَّةِ أَبُو عُبَيْدَةَ بْنُ الْجَرَّاحِ "

Narrated `Adi bin Hatim: We came to `Umar in a delegation (during his rule). He started calling the men one by one, calling each by his name. (As he did not call me early) I said to him. "Don't you know me, O chief of the Believers?" He said, "Yes, you embraced Islam when

they (i.e. your people) disbelieved; you have come (to the Truth) when they ran away; you fulfilled your promises when they broke theirs; and you recognized it (i.e. the Truth of Islam) when they denied it." On that, `Adi said, "I therefore don't care.". – Sahih Al-Bukhari 4394
حَدَّثَنَا مُوسَى بْنُ إِسْمَاعِيلَ، حَدَّثَنَا أَبُو عَوَانَةَ، حَدَّثَنَا عَبْدُ الْمَلِكِ، عَنْ عَمْرِو بْنِ حُرَيْثٍ، عَنْ عَدِيِّ بْنِ حَاتِمٍ، قَالَ أَتَيْنَا عُمَرَ فِي وَفْدٍ، فَجَعَلَ يَدْعُو رَجُلاً رَجُلاً وَيُسَمِّيهِمْ فَقُلْتُ أَمَا تَعْرِفُنِي يَا أَمِيرَ الْمُؤْمِنِينَ قَالَ بَلَى، أَسْلَمْتَ إِذْ كَفَرُوا، وَأَقْبَلْتَ إِذْ أَدْبَرُوا، وَوَفَيْتَ إِذْ غَدَرُوا، وَعَرَفْتَ إِذْ أَنْكَرُوا. فَقَالَ عَدِيٌّ فَلاَ أُبَالِي إِذًا.

Narrated Khabbab bin Al-Art: We complained to Allah's Messenger ﷺ (about our state) while he was leaning against his sheet cloak in the shade of the Ka`ba. We said, "Will you ask Allah to help us? Will you invoke Allah for us?" He said, "Among those who were before you a (believer) used to be seized and, a pit used to be dug for him and then he used to be placed in it. Then a saw used to be brought and put on his head which would be split into two halves. His flesh might be combed with iron combs and removed from his bones, yet, all that did not cause him to revert from his religion. By Allah! This religion (Islam) will be completed (and triumph) till a rider (traveler) goes from San`a' (the capital of Yemen) to Hadramout fearing nobody except Allah and the wolf lest it should trouble his sheep, but you are impatient." (See Hadith No. 191, Vol. 5). – Sahih Al-Bukhari 6943
حَدَّثَنَا مُسَدَّدٌ، حَدَّثَنَا يَحْيَى، عَنْ إِسْمَاعِيلَ، حَدَّثَنَا قَيْسٌ، عَنْ خَبَّابِ بْنِ الأَرَتِّ، قَالَ شَكَوْنَا إِلَى رَسُولِ اللَّهِ صلى الله عليه وسلم وَهْوَ مُتَوَسِّدٌ بُرْدَةً لَهُ فِي ظِلِّ الْكَعْبَةِ فَقُلْنَا أَلاَ تَسْتَنْصِرُ لَنَا أَلاَ تَدْعُو لَنَا. فَقَالَ " قَدْ كَانَ مَنْ قَبْلَكُمْ يُؤْخَذُ الرَّجُلُ فَيُحْفَرُ لَهُ فِي الأَرْضِ فَيُجْعَلُ فِيهَا، فَيُجَاءُ بِالْمِنْشَارِ فَيُوضَعُ عَلَى رَأْسِهِ فَيُجْعَلُ نِصْفَيْنِ، وَيُمَشَّطُ بِأَمْشَاطِ الْحَدِيدِ مَا دُونَ لَحْمِهِ وَعَظْمِهِ، فَمَا يَصُدُّهُ ذَلِكَ عَنْ دِينِهِ، وَاللَّهِ لَيَتِمَّنَّ هَذَا الأَمْرُ، حَتَّى يَسِيرَ الرَّاكِبُ مِنْ صَنْعَاءَ إِلَى حَضْرَمَوْتَ لاَ يَخَافُ إِلاَّ اللَّهَ وَالذِّئْبَ عَلَى غَنَمِهِ، وَلَكِنَّكُمْ تَسْتَعْجِلُونَ ".

Narrated Qais bin Abi Hazim: We went to pay a visit to Khabbab (who was sick) and he had been branded (cauterized) at seven places in his body. He said, "Our companions who died (during the lifetime of the Prophet) left (this world) without having their rewards reduced through enjoying the pleasures of this life, but we have got (so much) wealth that we find no way to spend It except on the construction of buildings Had the Prophet not forbidden us to wish for death, I would have wished for it.' We visited him for the second time while he was building a wall. He said, A Muslim is rewarded (in the Hereafter) for whatever he spends except for something that he spends on building." – Sahih Al-Bukhari 5672
حَدَّثَنَا آدَمُ، حَدَّثَنَا شُعْبَةُ، عَنْ إِسْمَاعِيلَ بْنِ أَبِي خَالِدٍ، عَنْ قَيْسِ بْنِ أَبِي حَازِمٍ، قَالَ دَخَلْنَا عَلَى خَبَّابٍ نَعُودُهُ وَقَدِ اكْتَوَى سَبْعَ كَيَّاتٍ فَقَالَ إِنَّ أَصْحَابَنَا الَّذِينَ سَلَفُوا مَضَوْا وَلَمْ تَنْقُصْهُمُ الدُّنْيَا وَإِنَّا أَصَبْنَا مَا لاَ نَجِدُ لَهُ مَوْضِعًا إِلاَّ التُّرَابَ وَلَوْلاَ أَنَّ النَّبِيَّ صلى الله عليه وسلم نَهَانَا أَنْ نَدْعُوَ بِالْمَوْتِ لَدَعَوْتُ بِهِ، ثُمَّ أَتَيْنَاهُ مَرَّةً أُخْرَى وَهْوَ يَبْنِي حَائِطًا لَهُ فَقَالَ إِنَّ الْمُسْلِمَ لَيُوجَرُ فِي كُلِّ شَىْءٍ يُنْفِقُهُ إِلاَّ فِي شَىْءٍ يَجْعَلُهُ فِي هَذَا التُّرَابِ.

Narrated `Abdullah: Today a man came to me and asked me a question which I did not know how to answer. He said, "Tell me, if a wealthy active man, well-equipped with arms, goes out on military expeditions with our chiefs, and orders us to do such things as we cannot do (should we obey him?)" I replied, "By Allah, I do not know what to reply you, except that we, were in the company of the Prophet ﷺ and he used to order us to do a thing once only till we finished it. And no doubt, everyone among you will remain in a good state as long as he obeys Allah. If one is in doubt as to the legality of something, he should ask somebody who would satisfy him, but soon will come a time when you will not find such a man. By Him, except Whom none has the right to be worshipped. I see that the example of what has passed of this life (to what remains thereof) is like a pond whose fresh water has been used up and nothing remains but muddy water.". – Sahih Al-Bukhari 2964

حَدَّثَنَا عُثْمَانُ بْنُ أَبِي شَيْبَةَ، حَدَّثَنَا جَرِيرٌ، عَنْ مَنْصُورٍ، عَنْ أَبِي وَائِلٍ، قَالَ قَالَ عَبْدُ اللَّهِ ـ رضى الله عنه ـ لَقَدْ أَتَانِي الْيَوْمَ رَجُلٌ فَسَأَلَنِي عَنْ أَمْرٍ مَا دَرَيْتُ مَا أَرُدُّ عَلَيْهِ، فَقَالَ أَرَأَيْتَ رَجُلاً مُؤْدِيًا نَشِيطًا، يَخْرُجُ مَعَ أُمَرَائِنَا فِي الْمَغَازِي، فَيَعْزِمُ عَلَيْنَا فِي أَشْيَاءَ لاَ نُحْصِيهَا. فَقُلْتُ لَهُ وَاللَّهِ مَا أَدْرِي مَا أَقُولُ لَكَ إِلاَّ أَنَّا كُنَّا مَعَ النَّبِيِّ صلى الله عليه وسلم فَعَسَى أَنْ لاَ يَعْزِمَ عَلَيْنَا فِي أَمْرٍ إِلاَّ مَرَّةً حَتَّى نَفْعَلَهُ، وَإِنَّ أَحَدَكُمْ لَنْ يَزَالَ بِخَيْرٍ مَا اتَّقَى اللَّهَ، وَإِذَا شَكَّ فِي نَفْسِهِ شَىْءٌ سَأَلَ رَجُلاً فَشَفَاهُ مِنْهُ، وَأَوْشَكَ أَنْ لاَ تَجِدُوهُ، وَالَّذِي لاَ إِلَهَ إِلاَّ هُوَ مَا أَذْكُرُ مَا غَبَرَ مِنَ الدُّنْيَا إِلاَّ كَالثَّغْبِ شُرِبَ صَفْوُهُ وَبَقِيَ كَدَرُهُ.

The Desert-Arabs say, "We have believed." Say, "You have not believed; but say, 'We have submitted,' for faith has not yet entered into your hearts. But if you obey Allah and His Messenger, He will not diminish any of your deeds. Allah is Forgiving and Merciful." – Surah Al-Hujurat 49:14

قَالَتِ ٱلْأَعْرَابُ ءَامَنَّا ۖ قُل لَّمْ تُؤْمِنُوا۟ وَلَـٰكِن قُولُوٓا۟ أَسْلَمْنَا وَلَمَّا يَدْخُلِ ٱلْإِيمَـٰنُ فِى قُلُوبِكُمْ ۖ وَإِن تُطِيعُوا۟ ٱللَّهَ وَرَسُولَهُۥ لَا يَلِتْكُم مِّنْ أَعْمَـٰلِكُمْ شَيْـًٔا ۚ إِنَّ ٱللَّهَ غَفُورٌ رَّحِيمٌ

They say, "If we return to the City, the more powerful therein will evict the weak." But power belongs to Allah, and His Messenger, and the believers; but the hypocrites do not know. – Surah Al-Munafiqun 63:8

يَقُولُونَ لَئِن رَّجَعْنَآ إِلَى ٱلْمَدِينَةِ لَيُخْرِجَنَّ ٱلْأَعَزُّ مِنْهَا ٱلْأَذَلَّ ۚ وَلِلَّهِ ٱلْعِزَّةُ وَلِرَسُولِهِۦ وَلِلْمُؤْمِنِينَ وَلَـٰكِنَّ ٱلْمُنَـٰفِقِينَ لَا يَعْلَمُونَ

Narrated Anas: I saw the most famous people amongst the companions of the Prophet ﷺ hurrying towards the pillars at the Maghrib prayer before the Prophet ﷺ came for the prayer. – Sahih al-Bukhari 503

حَدَّثَنَا قَبِيصَةُ، قَالَ حَدَّثَنَا سُفْيَانُ، عَنْ عَمْرِو بْنِ عَامِرٍ، عَنْ أَنَسٍ، قَالَ لَقَدْ رَأَيْتُ كِبَارَ أَصْحَابِ النَّبِيِّ صلى الله عليه وسلم يَبْتَدِرُونَ السَّوَارِيَ عِنْدَ الْمَغْرِبِ. وَزَادَ شُعْبَةُ عَنْ عَمْرٍو عَنْ أَنَسٍ حَتَّى يَخْرُجَ النَّبِيُّ صلى الله عليه وسلم.

The Book of
Influential Arabian Tribes
القبائل العربية المؤثرة

Banu Hashim and Banu Al-Muttalib only are one and the same
"إِنَّمَا بَنُو هَاشِمٍ وَبَنُو الْمُطَّلِبِ شَىْءٌ وَاحِدٌ

Narrated Anas bin Malik: While we were sitting with the Prophet ﷺ in the mosque, a man came riding on a camel. He made his camel kneel down in the mosque, tied its foreleg and then said: "Who amongst you is Muhammad?" At that time the Prophet ﷺ was sitting amongst us (his companions) leaning on his arm. We replied, "This white man reclining on his arm." The man then addressed him, "O Son of `Abdul Muttalib." The Prophet ﷺ said, "I am here to answer your questions." The man said to the Prophet, "I want to ask you something and will be hard in questioning. So do not get angry." The Prophet ﷺ said, "Ask whatever you want." The man said, "I ask you by your Lord, and the Lord of those who were before you, has Allah sent you as an Apostle to all the mankind?" The Prophet ﷺ replied, "By Allah, yes." The man further said, "I ask you by Allah. Has Allah ordered you to offer five prayers in a day and night (24 hours).? He replied, "By Allah, Yes." The man further said, "I ask you by Allah! Has Allah ordered you to observe fasts during this month of the year (i.e. Ramadan)?" He replied, "By Allah, Yes." The man further said, "I ask you by Allah. Has Allah ordered you to take Zakat (obligatory charity) from our rich people and distribute it amongst our poor people?" The Prophet ﷺ replied, "By Allah, yes." Thereupon that man said, "I have believed in all that with which you have been sent, and I have been sent by my people as a messenger, and I am Dimam bin Tha`laba from the brothers of Bani Sa`d bin Bakr.". – Sahih Al-Bukhari 63

حَدَّثَنَا عَبْدُ اللَّهِ بْنُ يُوسُفَ، قَالَ حَدَّثَنَا اللَّيْثُ، عَنْ سَعِيدٍ ـ هُوَ الْمَقْبُرِيُّ ـ عَنْ شَرِيكِ بْنِ عَبْدِ اللَّهِ بْنِ أَبِي نَمِرٍ، أَنَّهُ سَمِعَ أَنَسَ بْنَ مَالِكٍ، يَقُولُ بَيْنَمَا نَحْنُ جُلُوسٌ مَعَ النَّبِيِّ صلى الله عليه وسلم فِي الْمَسْجِدِ، دَخَلَ رَجُلٌ عَلَى جَمَلٍ فَأَنَاخَهُ فِي الْمَسْجِدِ، ثُمَّ عَقَلَهُ، ثُمَّ قَالَ لَهُمْ أَيُّكُمْ مُحَمَّدٌ وَالنَّبِيُّ صلى الله عليه وسلم مُتَّكِئٌ بَيْنَ ظَهْرَانَيْهِمْ. فَقُلْنَا هَذَا الرَّجُلُ الأَبْيَضُ الْمُتَّكِئُ. فَقَالَ لَهُ الرَّجُلُ ابْنَ عَبْدِ الْمُطَّلِبِ فَقَالَ لَهُ النَّبِيُّ صلى الله عليه وسلم " قَدْ أَجَبْتُكَ ". فَقَالَ الرَّجُلُ لِلنَّبِيِّ صلى الله عليه وسلم إِنِّي سَائِلُكَ فَمُشَدِّدٌ عَلَيْكَ فِي الْمَسْأَلَةِ فَلاَ تَجِدْ عَلَىَّ فِي نَفْسِكَ. فَقَالَ " سَلْ عَمَّا بَدَا لَكَ ". فَقَالَ أَسْأَلُكَ بِرَبِّكَ وَرَبِّ مَنْ قَبْلَكَ، آللَّهُ أَرْسَلَكَ إِلَى النَّاسِ كُلِّهِمْ فَقَالَ " اللَّهُمَّ نَعَمْ ". قَالَ أَنْشُدُكَ بِاللَّهِ، آللَّهُ أَمَرَكَ أَنْ نُصَلِّيَ الصَّلَوَاتِ الْخَمْسَ فِي الْيَوْمِ وَاللَّيْلَةِ قَالَ " اللَّهُمَّ نَعَمْ ". قَالَ أَنْشُدُكَ بِاللَّهِ، آللَّهُ أَمَرَكَ أَنْ نَصُومَ هَذَا الشَّهْرَ مِنَ السَّنَةِ قَالَ " اللَّهُمَّ نَعَمْ ". قَالَ أَنْشُدُكَ بِاللَّهِ، آللَّهُ أَمَرَكَ أَنْ تَأْخُذَ هَذِهِ الصَّدَقَةَ مِنْ أَغْنِيَائِنَا فَتَقْسِمَهَا عَلَى فُقَرَائِنَا فَقَالَ النَّبِيُّ صلى الله عليه وسلم " اللَّهُمَّ نَعَمْ ". فَقَالَ الرَّجُلُ آمَنْتُ بِمَا جِئْتَ بِهِ، وَأَنَا رَسُولُ مَنْ وَرَائِي مِنْ قَوْمِي، وَأَنَا ضِمَامُ بْنُ ثَعْلَبَةَ أَخُو بَنِي سَعْدِ بْنِ بَكْرٍ. رَوَاهُ مُوسَى وَعَلِيُّ بْنُ عَبْدِ الْحَمِيدِ عَنْ سُلَيْمَانَ عَنْ ثَابِتٍ عَنْ أَنَسٍ عَنِ النَّبِيِّ صلى الله عليه وسلم بِهَذَا

Narrated Jubair bin Mut`im: `Uthman bin `Affan and I went to the Prophet ﷺ and said, "You had given Banu Al-Muttalib from the Khumus of Khaibar's booty and left us in spite of the fact that we and Banu Al-Muttalib are similarly related to you." The Prophet ﷺ said, "Banu Hashim and Banu Al-Muttalib only are one and the same." So the Prophet ﷺ did not give anything to Banu `Abd Shams and Banu Nawfal. – Sahih Al-Bukhari 4229

حدثنا يحيى بن بكير، حدثنا اللَّيْثُ، عَنْ يُونُسَ، عَنِ ابْنِ شِهَابٍ، عَنْ سَعِيدِ بْنِ الْمُسَيَّبِ، أَنَّ جُبَيْرَ بْنَ مُطْعِمٍ، أَخْبَرَهُ قَالَ مَشَيْتُ أَنَا وَعُثْمَانُ بْنُ عَفَّانَ، إِلَى النَّبِيِّ صلى الله عليه وسلم فَقُلْنَا أَعْطَيْتَ بَنِي الْمُطَّلِبِ مِنْ خُمْسِ خَيْبَرَ، وَتَرَكْتَنَا، وَنَحْنُ بِمَنْزِلَةٍ وَاحِدَةٍ مِنْكَ. فَقَالَ " إِنَّمَا بَنُو هَاشِمٍ وَبَنُو الْمُطَّلِبِ شَىْءٌ وَاحِدٌ ". قَالَ جُبَيْرٌ وَلَمْ يَقْسِمِ النَّبِيُّ صلى الله عليه وسلم لِبَنِي عَبْدِ شَمْسٍ وَبَنِي نَوْفَلٍ شَيْئًا

Narrated Al-Hasan Al-Basri: By Allah, Al-Hasan bin `Ali led large battalions like mountains against Muawiya. `Amr bin Al-As said (to Muawiya), "I surely see battalions which will not turn back before killing their opponents." Muawiya who was really the best of the two men said to him, "O `Amr! If these killed those and those killed these, who would be left with me for the jobs of the public, who would be left with me for their women, who would be left with me for their children?" Then Muawiya sent two Quraishi men from the tribe of `Abd-i-Shams called `Abdur Rahman bin Sumura and `Abdullah bin 'Amir bin Kuraiz to Al-Hasan saying to them, "Go to this man (i.e. Al-Hasan) and negotiate peace with him and talk and appeal to him." So, they went to Al-Hasan and talked and appealed to him to accept peace. Al-Hasan said, "We, the offspring of `Abdul Muttalib, have got wealth and people have indulged in killing and corruption (and money only will appease them)." They said to Al-Hasan, "Muawiya offers you so and so, and appeals to you and entreats you to accept peace." Al-Hasan said to them, "But who will be responsible for what you have said?" They said, "We will be responsible for it." So, whatever Al- Hasan asked they said, "We will be responsible for it for you." So, Al-Hasan concluded a peace treaty with Muawiya. Al-Hasan (Al-Basri) said: I heard Abu Bakr saying, "I saw Allah's Messenger ﷺ on the pulpit and Al-Hasan bin `Ali was by his side. The Prophet ﷺ was looking once at the people and once at Al-Hasan bin `Ali saying, 'This son of mine is a Saiyid (i.e. a noble) and may Allah make peace between two big groups of Muslims through him." – Sahih Al-Bukhari 2704

حَدَّثَنَا عَبْدُ اللَّهِ بْنُ مُحَمَّدٍ، حَدَّثَنَا سُفْيَانُ، عَنْ أَبِي مُوسَى، قَالَ سَمِعْتُ الْحَسَنَ، يَقُولُ اسْتَقْبَلَ وَاللَّهِ الْحَسَنُ بْنُ عَلِيٍّ مُعَاوِيَةَ بِكَتَائِبَ أَمْثَالِ الْجِبَالِ فَقَالَ عَمْرُو بْنُ الْعَاصِ إِنِّي لأَرَى كَتَائِبَ لاَ تُوَلِّي حَتَّى تَقْتُلَ أَقْرَانَهَا. فَقَالَ لَهُ مُعَاوِيَةُ ـ وَكَانَ وَاللَّهِ خَيْرَ الرَّجُلَيْنِ ـ أَىْ عَمْرُو إِنْ قَتَلَ هَؤُلاَءِ هَؤُلاَءِ وَهَؤُلاَءِ هَؤُلاَءِ مَنْ لِي بِأُمُورِ النَّاسِ مَنْ لِي بِنِسَائِهِمْ، مَنْ لِي بِضَيْعَتِهِمْ فَبَعَثَ إِلَيْهِ رَجُلَيْنِ مِنْ قُرَيْشٍ مِنْ بَنِي عَبْدِ شَمْسٍ عَبْدَ الرَّحْمَنِ بْنَ سَمُرَةَ وَعَبْدَ اللَّهِ بْنَ عَامِرِ بْنِ كُرَيْزٍ، فَقَالَ اذْهَبَا إِلَى هَذَا الرَّجُلِ فَاعْرِضَا عَلَيْهِ، وَقُولاَ لَهُ، وَاطْلُبَا إِلَيْهِ. فَأَتَيَاهُ، فَدَخَلاَ عَلَيْهِ فَتَكَلَّمَا، وَقَالاَ لَهُ، فَطَلَبَا إِلَيْهِ، فَقَالَ لَهُمَا الْحَسَنُ بْنُ عَلِيٍّ إِنَّا بَنُو عَبْدِ الْمُطَّلِبِ، قَدْ أَصَبْنَا مِنْ هَذَا الْمَالِ، وَإِنَّ هَذِهِ الأُمَّةَ قَدْ عَاثَتْ فِي دِمَائِهَا. قَالاَ فَإِنَّهُ يَعْرِضُ عَلَيْكَ كَذَا وَكَذَا وَيَطْلُبُ إِلَيْكَ وَيَسْأَلُكَ. قَالَ فَمَنْ لِي بِهَذَا قَالاَ نَحْنُ لَكَ بِهِ. فَمَا سَأَلَهُمَا شَيْئًا إِلاَّ قَالاَ نَحْنُ لَكَ بِهِ. فَصَالَحَهُ، فَقَالَ الْحَسَنُ وَلَقَدْ سَمِعْتُ أَبَا بَكْرَةَ يَقُولُ رَأَيْتُ رَسُولَ اللَّهِ صلى الله عليه وسلم عَلَى الْمِنْبَرِ وَالْحَسَنُ بْنُ عَلِيٍّ إِلَى جَنْبِهِ، وَهْوَ يُقْبِلُ عَلَى النَّاسِ مَرَّةً وَعَلَيْهِ أُخْرَى وَيَقُولُ " إِنَّ ابْنِي هَذَا سَيِّدٌ، وَلَعَلَّ اللَّهَ أَنْ يُصْلِحَ بِهِ بَيْنَ فِئَتَيْنِ عَظِيمَتَيْنِ مِنَ الْمُسْلِمِينَ ". قَالَ لِي عَلِيُّ بْنُ عَبْدِ اللَّهِ إِنَّمَا ثَبَتَ لَنَا سَمَاعُ الْحَسَنِ مِنْ أَبِي بَكْرَةَ بِهَذَا الْحَدِيثِ.

Narrated `Abdullah bin `Abbas: `Ali bin Abu Talib came out of the house of the Prophet ﷺ during his fatal ailment. The people asked (`Ali), "O Abu Hasan! How is the health of Allah's Messenger ﷺ this morning?" `Ali said, "This morning he is better, with the grace of Allah." Al-`Abbas held `Ali by the hand and said, "Don't you see him (about to die)? By Allah, within three days you will be the slave of the stick (i.e., under the command of another ruler). By Allah, I think that Allah's Messenger ﷺ will die from his present ailment, for I know the signs of death on the faces of the offspring of `Abdul Muttalib. So let us go to Allah's Messenger ﷺ to ask him who will take over the Caliphate. If the authority is given to us, we will know it, and if it is given to somebody else we will request him to recommend us to him. " `Ali said, "By Allah! If we ask Allah's Messenger ﷺ for the rulership and he refuses, then the people will never give it to us. Besides, I will never ask Allah's Messenger ﷺ for it." (See Hadith No 728, Vol 5). – Sahih Al-Bukhari 6266

حَدَّثَنَا إِسْحَاقُ، أَخْبَرَنَا بِشْرُ بْنُ شُعَيْبٍ، حَدَّثَنِي أَبِي، عَنِ الزُّهْرِيِّ، قَالَ أَخْبَرَنِي عَبْدُ اللَّهِ بْنُ كَعْبٍ، أَنَّ عَبْدَ اللَّهِ بْنَ عَبَّاسٍ، أَخْبَرَهُ أَنَّ عَلِيًّا ـ يَعْنِي ابْنَ أَبِي طَالِبٍ ـ خَرَجَ مِنْ عِنْدِ النَّبِيِّ صلى الله عليه وسلم وَحَدَّثَنَا أَحْمَدُ بْنُ صَالِحٍ حَدَّثَنَا عَنْبَسَةُ حَدَّثَنَا يُونُسُ عَنِ ابْنِ شِهَابٍ قَالَ أَخْبَرَنِي عَبْدُ اللَّهِ بْنُ كَعْبِ بْنِ مَالِكٍ أَنَّ عَبْدَ اللَّهِ بْنَ عَبَّاسٍ أَخْبَرَهُ أَنَّ عَلِيَّ بْنَ أَبِي طَالِبٍ ـ رضى الله عنه ـ خَرَجَ مِنْ عِنْدِ النَّبِيِّ صلى الله عليه وسلم فِي وَجَعِهِ الَّذِي تُوُفِّيَ فِيهِ فَقَالَ النَّاسُ يَا أَبَا حَسَنٍ كَيْفَ أَصْبَحَ رَسُولُ اللَّهِ صلى الله عليه وسلم قَالَ أَصْبَحَ بِحَمْدِ اللَّهِ بَارِئًا فَأَخَذَ بِيَدِهِ الْعَبَّاسُ فَقَالَ أَلاَ تَرَاهُ أَنْتَ وَاللَّهِ بَعْدَ الثَّلاَثِ عَبْدُ الْعَصَا وَاللَّهِ إِنِّي لأُرَى رَسُولَ اللَّهِ صلى الله عليه وسلم سَيُتَوَفَّى فِي وَجَعِهِ، وَإِنِّي لأَعْرِفُ فِي وُجُوهِ بَنِي عَبْدِ الْمُطَّلِبِ الْمَوْتَ، فَاذْهَبْ بِنَا إِلَى رَسُولِ اللَّهِ صلى الله عليه وسلم فَنَسْأَلَهُ فِيمَنْ يَكُونُ الأَمْرُ فَإِنْ كَانَ فِينَا عَلِمْنَا ذَلِكَ، وَإِنْ كَانَ فِي غَيْرِنَا أَمَرْنَاهُ فَأَوْصَى بِنَا. قَالَ عَلِيٌّ وَاللَّهِ لَئِنْ سَأَلْنَاهَا رَسُولَ اللَّهِ صلى الله عليه وسلم فَيَمْنَعُنَا لاَ يُعْطِينَاهَا النَّاسُ أَبَدًا، وَإِنِّي لاَ أَسْأَلُهَا رَسُولَ اللَّهِ صلى الله عليه وسلم أَبَدًا.

Narrated Abu Huraira: Allah's Messenger ﷺ got up when the Verse:--'And warn your tribe of near kindred...." (26.214) was revealed and said, "O Quraish people! (or he said a similar word) Buy yourselves! I cannot save you from Allah (if you disobey Him) O Bani Abu Manaf! I cannot save you from Allah (if you disobey Him). O `Abbas! The son of `Abdul Muttalib! I cannot save you from Allah (if you disobey Him) O Safiya, (the aunt of Allah's Messenger ﷺ) I cannot save you from Allah (if you disobey Him). O Fatima, the daughter of Muhammad ! Ask what you wish from my property, but I cannot save you from Allah (if you disobey Him). – Sahih Al-Bukhari 4771

حَدَّثَنَا أَبُو الْيَمَانِ، أَخْبَرَنَا شُعَيْبٌ، عَنِ الزُّهْرِيِّ، قَالَ أَخْبَرَنِي سَعِيدُ بْنُ الْمُسَيَّبِ، وَأَبُو سَلَمَةَ بْنُ عَبْدِ الرَّحْمَنِ أَنَّ أَبَا هُرَيْرَةَ، قَالَ قَامَ رَسُولُ اللَّهِ صلى الله عليه وسلم حِينَ أَنْزَلَ اللَّهُ {وَأَنْذِرْ عَشِيرَتَكَ الأَقْرَبِينَ} قَالَ " يَا مَعْشَرَ قُرَيْشٍ ـ أَوْ كَلِمَةً نَحْوَهَا ـ اشْتَرُوا أَنْفُسَكُمْ، لاَ أُغْنِي عَنْكُمْ مِنَ اللَّهِ شَيْئًا، يَا بَنِي عَبْدِ مَنَافٍ، لاَ أُغْنِي عَنْكُمْ مِنَ اللَّهِ شَيْئًا، يَا عَبَّاسُ بْنَ عَبْدِ الْمُطَّلِبِ، لاَ أُغْنِي عَنْكَ مِنَ اللَّهِ شَيْئًا، وَيَا صَفِيَّةُ عَمَّةَ رَسُولِ اللَّهِ، لاَ أُغْنِي عَنْكِ مِنَ اللَّهِ شَيْئًا وَيَا فَاطِمَةُ بِنْتَ مُحَمَّدٍ سَلِينِي مَا شِئْتِ مِنْ مَالِي، لاَ أُغْنِي عَنْكِ مِنَ اللَّهِ شَيْئًا ". تَابَعَهُ أَصْبَغُ عَنِ ابْنِ وَهْبٍ عَنْ يُونُسَ عَنِ ابْنِ شِهَابٍ

Narrated Al-Musaiyab: When Abu Talib's death approached, the Prophet ﷺ went to him while Abu Jahl and `Abdullah bin Abi Umaiya were present with him. The Prophet ﷺ said, "O uncle, say: None has the right to be worshipped except Allah, so that I may argue for your case with it before Allah." On that, Abu Jahl and `Abdullah bin Abu Umaiya said, "O Abu Talib! Do you want to renounce `Abdul Muttalib's religion?" Then the Prophet said, "I will keep on asking (Allah for) forgiveness for you unless I am forbidden to do so." Then there was revealed:-- 'It is not fitting for the Prophet ﷺ and those who believe that they should invoke (Allah) for forgiveness for pagans even though they be of kin, after it has become clear to them that they are companions of the Fire.' (9.113). – Sahih Al-Bukhari 4675

حَدَّثَنَا إِسْحَاقُ بْنُ إِبْرَاهِيمَ، حَدَّثَنَا عَبْدُ الرَّزَّاقِ، أَخْبَرَنَا مَعْمَرٌ، عَنِ الزُّهْرِيِّ، عَنْ سَعِيدِ بْنِ الْمُسَيَّبِ، عَنْ أَبِيهِ، قَالَ لَمَّا حَضَرَتْ أَبَا طَالِبٍ الْوَفَاةُ دَخَلَ عَلَيْهِ النَّبِيُّ صلى الله عليه وسلم وَعِنْدَهُ أَبُو جَهْلٍ وَعَبْدُ اللَّهِ بْنُ أَبِي أُمَيَّةَ، فَقَالَ النَّبِيُّ صلى الله عليه وسلم " أَىْ عَمِّ قُلْ لاَ إِلَهَ إِلاَّ اللَّهُ. أُحَاجُّ لَكَ بِهَا عِنْدَ اللَّهِ ". فَقَالَ أَبُو جَهْلٍ وَعَبْدُ اللَّهِ بْنُ أَبِي أُمَيَّةَ يَا أَبَا طَالِبٍ، أَتَرْغَبُ عَنْ مِلَّةِ عَبْدِ الْمُطَّلِبِ. فَقَالَ النَّبِيُّ صلى الله عليه وسلم " لأَسْتَغْفِرَنَّ لَكَ مَا لَمْ أُنْهَ عَنْكَ ". فَنَزَلَتْ {مَا كَانَ لِلنَّبِيِّ وَالَّذِينَ آمَنُوا أَنْ يَسْتَغْفِرُوا لِلْمُشْرِكِينَ وَلَوْ كَانُوا أُولِي قُرْبَى مِنْ بَعْدِ مَا تَبَيَّنَ لَهُمْ أَنَّهُمْ أَصْحَابُ الْجَحِيمِ}

Narrated Abu 'Is-haq: Somebody asked Al-Bar-a bin `Azib, "Did you flee deserting Allah's Messenger ﷺ during the battle of Hunain?" Al-Bara replied, "But Allah's Messenger ﷺ did not flee. The people of the Tribe of Hawazin were good archers. When we met them, we attacked them, and they fled. When the Muslims started collecting the war booty, the pagans faced us with arrows, but Allah's Messenger ﷺ did not flee. No doubt, I saw him on his white mule and Abu Sufyan was holding its reins and the Prophet ﷺ was saying, 'I am the Prophet ﷺ in truth: I am the son of `Abdul Muttalib.' ". – Sahih Al-Bukhari 2864

حَدَّثَنَا قُتَيْبَةُ، حَدَّثَنَا سَهْلُ بْنُ يُوسُفَ، عَنْ شُعْبَةَ، عَنْ أَبِي إِسْحَاقَ. قَالَ رَجُلٌ لِلْبَرَاءِ بْنِ عَازِبٍ ـ رضى الله عنهما ـ أَفَرَرْتُمْ عَنْ رَسُولِ اللَّهِ صلى الله عليه وسلم يَوْمَ حُنَيْنٍ قَالَ لَكِنَّ رَسُولَ اللَّهِ صلى الله عليه وسلم لَمْ يَفِرَّ، إِنَّ هَوَازِنَ كَانُوا قَوْمًا رُمَاةً، وَإِنَّا لَمَّا لَقِينَاهُمْ حَمَلْنَا عَلَيْهِمْ فَانْهَزَمُوا، فَأَقْبَلَ الْمُسْلِمُونَ عَلَى الْغَنَائِمِ وَاسْتَقْبَلُونَا بِالسِّهَامِ، فَأَمَّا رَسُولُ اللَّهِ صلى الله عليه وسلم فَلَمْ يَفِرَّ، فَلَقَدْ رَأَيْتُهُ وَإِنَّهُ لَعَلَى بَغْلَتِهِ الْبَيْضَاءِ وَإِنَّ أَبَا سُفْيَانَ آخِذٌ بِلِجَامِهَا، وَالنَّبِيُّ صلى الله عليه وسلم يَقُولُ " أَنَا النَّبِيُّ لاَ كَذِبْ أَنَا ابْنُ عَبْدِ الْمُطَّلِبْ ".

Narrated Abu Huraira: On the Day of Nahr at Mina, the Prophet ﷺ said, "Tomorrow we shall stay at Khaif Bani Kinana where the pagans had taken the oath of Kufr (heathenism)." He meant (by that place) Al-Muhassab where the Quraish tribe and Bani Kinana concluded a contract against Bani Hashim and Bani `Abdul-Muttalib or Bani Al-Muttalib that they would not intermarry with them or deal with them in business until they handed over the Prophet ﷺ to them. – Sahih Al-Bukhari 1590

حَدَّثَنَا الْحُمَيْدِيُّ، حَدَّثَنَا الْوَلِيدُ، حَدَّثَنَا الأَوْزَاعِيُّ، قَالَ حَدَّثَنِي الزُّهْرِيُّ، عَنْ أَبِي سَلَمَةَ، عَنْ أَبِي هُرَيْرَةَ ـ رضى الله عنه ـ قَالَ قَالَ النَّبِيُّ صلى الله عليه وسلم مِنَ الْغَدِ يَوْمَ النَّحْرِ وَهُوَ بِمِنًى " نَحْنُ نَازِلُونَ غَدًا بِخَيْفِ بَنِي كِنَانَةَ حَيْثُ تَقَاسَمُوا عَلَى

الْكُفْرِ ". يَعْنِي ذَلِكَ الْمُحَصَّبَ، وَذَلِكَ أَنَّ قُرَيْشًا وَكِنَانَةَ تَحَالَفَتْ عَلَى بَنِي هَاشِمٍ وَبَنِي عَبْدِ الْمُطَّلِبِ، أَوْ بَنِي الْمُطَّلِبِ أَنْ لاَ يُنَاكِحُوهُمْ، وَلاَ يُبَايِعُوهُمْ حَتَّى يُسْلِمُوا إِلَيْهِمُ النَّبِيَّ صلى الله عليه وسلم. وَقَالَ سَلاَمَةُ عَنْ عُقَيْلٍ وَيَحْيَى بْنُ الضَّحَّاكِ عَنِ الأَوْزَاعِيِّ أَخْبَرَنِي ابْنُ شِهَابٍ وَقَالاَ بَنِي هَاشِمٍ وَبَنِي الْمُطَّلِبِ. قَالَ أَبُو عَبْدِ اللَّهِ بَنِي الْمُطَّلِبِ أَشْبَهُ.

Narrated Ibn `Abbas: When the Prophet ﷺ arrived at Mecca, the children of Bani `Abdul Muttalib received him. He then mounted one of them in front of him and the other behind him. – Sahih Al-Bukhari 5965

حَدَّثَنَا مُسَدَّدٌ، حَدَّثَنَا يَزِيدُ بْنُ زُرَيْعٍ، حَدَّثَنَا خَالِدٌ، عَنْ عِكْرِمَةَ، عَنِ ابْنِ عَبَّاسٍ ـ رضى الله عنهما ـ قَالَ لَمَّا قَدِمَ النَّبِيُّ صلى الله عليه وسلم مَكَّةَ اسْتَقْبَلَهُ أُغَيْلِمَةُ بَنِي عَبْدِ الْمُطَّلِبِ، فَحَمَلَ وَاحِدًا بَيْنَ يَدَيْهِ وَالآخَرَ خَلْفَهُ.

Yazid b. Hayyan reported, I went along with Husain b. Sabra and 'Umar b. Muslim to Zaid b. Arqam and, as we sat by his side, Husain said to him: Zaid. You have been able to acquire a great virtue that you saw Allah's Messenger ﷺ listened to his talk, fought by his side in (different) battles, offered prayer behind me. Zaid, you have in fact earned a great virtue. Zaid, narrate to us what you heard from Allah's Messenger ﷺ. He said: I have grown old and have almost spent my age and I have forgotten some of the things which I remembered in connection with Allah's Messenger ﷺ, so accept whatever I narrate to you, and which I do not narrate do not compel me to do that. He then said: One day Allah's Messenger ﷺ stood up to deliver sermon at a watering place known as Khumm situated between Mecca and Medina. He praised Allah, extolled Him and delivered the sermon and. Exhorted (us) and said: Now to our purpose. O people, I am a human being. I am about to receive a messenger (the angel of death) from my Lord and I, in response to Allah's call, (would bid good-bye to you), but I am leaving among you two weighty things: the one being the Book of Allah in which there is right guidance and light, so hold fast to the Book of Allah and adhere to it. He exhorted (us) (to hold fast) to the Book of Allah and then said: The second are the members of my household I remind you (of your duties) to the members of my family. He (Husain) said to Zaid: Who are the members of his household? Aren't his wives the members of his family? Thereupon he said: His wives are the members of his family (but here) the members of his family are those for whom acceptance of Zakat is forbidden. And he said: Who are they? Thereupon he said: 'Ali and the offspring of 'Ali, 'Aqil and the offspring of 'Aqil and the offspring of Ja'far and the offspring of 'Abbas. Husain said: These are those for whom the acceptance of Zakat is forbidden. Zaid said: Yes. – Sahih Muslim 2408 a

حَدَّثَنِي زُهَيْرُ بْنُ حَرْبٍ، وَشُجَاعُ بْنُ مَخْلَدٍ، جَمِيعًا عَنِ ابْنِ عُلَيَّةَ، قَالَ زُهَيْرٌ حَدَّثَنَا إِسْمَاعِيلُ بْنُ إِبْرَاهِيمَ، حَدَّثَنِي أَبُو حَيَّانَ، حَدَّثَنِي يَزِيدُ بْنُ حَيَّانَ، قَالَ انْطَلَقْتُ أَنَا وَحُصَيْنُ، بْنُ سَبْرَةَ وَعُمَرُ بْنُ مُسْلِمٍ إِلَى زَيْدِ بْنِ أَرْقَمَ فَلَمَّا جَلَسْنَا إِلَيْهِ قَالَ لَهُ حُصَيْنٌ لَقَدْ لَقِيتَ يَا زَيْدُ خَيْرًا كَثِيرًا رَأَيْتَ رَسُولَ اللَّهِ صلى الله عليه وسلم وَسَمِعْتَ حَدِيثَهُ وَغَزَوْتَ مَعَهُ وَصَلَّيْتَ خَلْفَهُ لَقَدْ لَقِيتَ يَا زَيْدُ خَيْرًا كَثِيرًا حَدِّثْنَا يَا زَيْدُ مَا سَمِعْتَ مِنْ رَسُولِ اللَّهِ صلى الله عليه وسلم – قَالَ – يَا ابْنَ أَخِي وَاللَّهِ لَقَدْ كَبِرَتْ سِنِّي وَقَدُمَ عَهْدِي وَنَسِيتُ بَعْضَ الَّذِي كُنْتُ أَعِي مِنْ رَسُولِ اللَّهِ صلى الله عليه وسلم فَمَا حَدَّثْتُكُمْ فَاقْبَلُوا وَمَا لاَ فَلاَ تُكَلِّفُونِيهِ . ثُمَّ قَالَ قَامَ رَسُولُ اللَّهِ صلى الله عليه وسلم يَوْمًا فِينَا خَطِيبًا بِمَاءٍ يُدْعَى خُمًّا بَيْنَ مَكَّةَ وَالْمَدِينَةِ فَحَمِدَ اللَّهَ وَأَثْنَى عَلَيْهِ وَوَعَظَ وَذَكَّرَ ثُمَّ قَالَ " أَمَّا بَعْدُ أَلاَ أَيُّهَا النَّاسُ فَإِنَّمَا أَنَا بَشَرٌ يُوشِكُ أَنْ يَأْتِيَ رَسُولُ رَبِّي فَأُجِيبَ وَأَنَا تَارِكٌ فِيكُمْ ثَقَلَيْنِ أَوَّلُهُمَا كِتَابُ اللَّهِ فِيهِ الْهُدَى وَالنُّورُ فَخُذُوا بِكِتَابِ اللَّهِ وَاسْتَمْسِكُوا بِهِ " . فَحَثَّ عَلَى كِتَابِ اللَّهِ وَرَغَّبَ فِيهِ ثُمَّ قَالَ " وَأَهْلُ بَيْتِي أُذَكِّرُكُمُ اللَّهَ فِي أَهْلِ بَيْتِي أُذَكِّرُكُمُ اللَّهَ فِي أَهْلِ بَيْتِي أُذَكِّرُكُمُ اللَّهَ فِي أَهْلِ بَيْتِي " . فَقَالَ لَهُ حُصَيْنٌ وَمَنْ أَهْلُ بَيْتِهِ يَا زَيْدُ أَلَيْسَ نِسَاؤُهُ مِنْ أَهْلِ بَيْتِهِ قَالَ نِسَاؤُهُ مِنْ أَهْلِ بَيْتِهِ وَلَكِنْ أَهْلُ بَيْتِهِ مَنْ حُرِمَ الصَّدَقَةَ بَعْدَهُ . قَالَ وَمَنْ هُمْ قَالَ هُمْ آلُ عَلِيٍّ وَآلُ عَقِيلٍ وَآلُ جَعْفَرٍ وَآلُ عَبَّاسٍ . قَالَ كُلُّ هَؤُلاَءِ حُرِمَ الصَّدَقَةَ قَالَ نَعَمْ

Banu Tamim

بَنِي تَمِيمٍ

Narrated Abu Sa`id Al-Khudri: While the Prophetﷺ was distributing (war booty etc.) one day, Dhul Khawaisira, a man from the tribe of Bani Tamim, said, "O Allah's Messengerﷺ! Act justly." The Prophets said, "Woe to you! Who else would act justly if I did not act justly?" `Umar said (to the Prophetﷺ), "Allow me to chop his neck off." The Prophet said, "No, for he has companions (who are apparently so pious that) if anyone of (you compares his prayer with) their prayer, he will consider his prayer inferior to theirs, and similarly his fasting inferior to theirs, but they will desert Islam (go out of religion) as an arrow goes through the victim's body (games etc.) in which case if its Nasl is examined nothing will be seen thereon, and if its Nady is examined, nothing will be seen thereon, and if its Qudhadh is examined, nothing will be seen thereon, for the arrow has gone out too fast even for the excretions and blood to smear over it. Such people will come out at the time of difference among the (Muslim) people and the sign by which they will be recognized, will be a man whose one of the two hands will look like the breast of a woman or a lump of flesh moving loosely." Abu Sa`id added, "I testify that I heard that from the Prophetﷺ and also testify that I was with `Ali when `Ali fought against those people. The man described by the Prophet was searched for among the killed, and was found, and he was exactly as the Prophetﷺ had described him." (See Hadith No. 807, Vol. 4). – Sahih Al-Bukhari 6163

حَدَّثَنِي عَبْدُ الرَّحْمَنِ بْنُ إِبْرَاهِيمَ، حَدَّثَنَا الْوَلِيدُ، عَنِ الأَوْزَاعِيِّ، عَنِ الزُّهْرِيِّ، عَنْ أَبِي سَلَمَةَ، وَالضَّحَّاكِ، عَنْ أَبِي سَعِيدٍ الْخُدْرِيِّ، قَالَ بَيْنَا النَّبِيُّ صلى الله عليه وسلم يَقْسِمُ ذَاتَ يَوْمٍ قِسْمًا فَقَالَ ذُو الْخُوَيْصِرَةِ ـ رَجُلٌ مِنْ بَنِي تَمِيمٍ ـ يَا رَسُولَ اللَّهِ اعْدِلْ. قَالَ " وَيْلَكَ مَنْ يَعْدِلُ إِذَا لَمْ أَعْدِلْ ". فَقَالَ عُمَرُ ائْذَنْ لِي فَلأَضْرِبْ عُنُقَهُ. قَالَ " لاَ، إِنَّ لَهُ أَصْحَابًا يَحْقِرُ أَحَدُكُمْ صَلاَتَهُ مَعَ صَلاَتِهِمْ، وَصِيَامَهُ مَعَ صِيَامِهِمْ، يَمْرُقُونَ مِنَ الدِّينِ كَمُرُوقِ السَّهْمِ مِنَ الرَّمِيَّةِ، يُنْظَرُ إِلَى نَصْلِهِ فَلاَ يُوجَدُ فِيهِ شَىْءٌ، ثُمَّ يُنْظَرُ إِلَى رِصَافِهِ فَلاَ يُوجَدُ فِيهِ شَىْءٌ، ثُمَّ يُنْظَرُ إِلَى نَضِيِّهِ فَلاَ يُوجَدُ فِيهِ شَىْءٌ، ثُمَّ يُنْظَرُ إِلَى قُذَذِهِ فَلاَ يُوجَدُ فِيهِ شَىْءٌ، سَبَقَ الْفَرْثَ وَالدَّمَ، يَخْرُجُونَ عَلَى حِينِ فُرْقَةٍ مِنَ النَّاسِ، آيَتُهُمْ رَجُلٌ إِحْدَى يَدَيْهِ مِثْلُ ثَدْىِ الْمَرْأَةِ، أَوْ مِثْلُ الْبَضْعَةِ تَدَرْدَرُ ". قَالَ أَبُو سَعِيدٍ أَشْهَدُ لَسَمِعْتُهُ مِنَ النَّبِيِّ صلى الله عليه وسلم وَأَشْهَدُ أَنِّي كُنْتُ مَعَ عَلِيٍّ حِينَ قَاتَلَهُمْ، فَالْتُمِسَ فِي الْقَتْلَى، فَأُتِيَ بِهِ عَلَى النَّعْتِ الَّذِي نَعَتَ النَّبِيُّ صلى الله عليه وسلم.

Narrated Ibn Abi Mulaika: `Abdullah bin Az-Zubair said that a group of riders belonging to Banu Tamim came to the Prophet, Abu Bakr said (to the Prophetﷺ), "Appoint Al-Qa'qa bin Mabad bin Zurara as (their) ruler." `Umar said (to the Prophet). "No! But appoint Al-Aqra bin H`Abis." Thereupon Abu Bakr said (to `Umar). "You just wanted to oppose me." `Umar replied. "I did not want to oppose you." So both of them argued so much that their voices became louder, and then the following Divine Verses were revealed in that connection:-- "O you who believe ! Do not be forward in the presence of Allah and His Apostle..." (till the end of Verse)...(49.1). – Sahih Al-Bukhari 4367

حَدَّثَنِي إِبْرَاهِيمُ بْنُ مُوسَى، حَدَّثَنَا هِشَامُ بْنُ يُوسُفَ، أَنَّ ابْنَ جُرَيْجٍ، أَخْبَرَهُمْ عَنِ ابْنِ أَبِي مُلَيْكَةَ، أَنَّ عَبْدَ اللَّهِ بْنَ الزُّبَيْرِ، أَخْبَرَهُمْ أَنَّهُ، قَدِمَ رَكْبٌ مِنْ بَنِي تَمِيمٍ عَلَى النَّبِيِّ صلى الله عليه وسلم فَقَالَ أَبُو بَكْرٍ أَمِّرِ الْقَعْقَاعَ بْنَ مَعْبَدِ بْنِ زُرَارَةَ. قَالَ عُمَرُ بَلْ أَمِّرِ الأَقْرَعَ بْنَ حَابِسٍ. قَالَ أَبُو بَكْرٍ مَا أَرَدْتَ إِلاَّ خِلاَفِي. قَالَ عُمَرُ مَا أَرَدْتُ خِلاَفَكَ. فَتَمَارَيَا حَتَّى ارْتَفَعَتْ أَصْوَاتُهُمَا فَنَزَلَ فِي ذَلِكَ {يَا أَيُّهَا الَّذِينَ آمَنُوا لاَ تُقَدِّمُوا} حَتَّى انْقَضَتْ.

Narrated Abu Bakra: Al-Aqra' bin Habis said to the Prophetﷺ "Nobody gave you the pledge of allegiance but the robbers of the pilgrims (i.e. those who used to rob the pilgrims) from the tribes of Aslam, Ghifar, Muzaina." (Ibn Abi Ya'qub is in doubt whether Al-Aqra' added. 'And Juhaina.') The Prophetﷺ said, "Don't you think that the tribes of Aslam, Ghifar, Muzaina (and also perhaps) Juhaina are better than the tribes of Bani Tamim, Bani Amir, Asad, and Ghatafan?" Somebody said, "They were unsuccessful and losers!" The Prophet said, "Yes, by

Him in Whose Hands my life is, they (i.e. the former) are better than they (i.e. the latter). – Sahih Al-Bukhari 3516
حَدَّثَنِي مُحَمَّدُ بْنُ بَشَّارٍ، حَدَّثَنَا غُنْدَرٌ، حَدَّثَنَا شُعْبَةُ، عَنْ مُحَمَّدِ بْنِ أَبِي يَعْقُوبَ، قَالَ سَمِعْتُ عَبْدَ الرَّحْمَنِ بْنَ أَبِي بَكْرَةَ، عَنْ أَبِيهِ، أَنَّ الأَقْرَعَ بْنَ حَابِسٍ، قَالَ لِلنَّبِيِّ صلى الله عليه وسلم إِنَّمَا بَايَعَكَ سُرَّاقُ الْحَجِيجِ مِنْ أَسْلَمَ وَغِفَارَ وَمُزَيْنَةَ ـ وَأَحْسِبُهُ وَجُهَيْنَةَ ابْنُ أَبِي يَعْقُوبَ شَكَّ ـ قَالَ النَّبِيُّ صلى الله عليه وسلم " أَرَأَيْتَ إِنْ كَانَ أَسْلَمُ وَغِفَارُ وَمُزَيْنَةُ ـ وَأَحْسِبُهُ ـ وَجُهَيْنَةُ خَيْرًا مِنْ بَنِي تَمِيمٍ وَبَنِي عَامِرٍ وَأَسَدٍ وَغَطَفَانَ، خَابُوا وَخَسِرُوا ". قَالَ نَعَمْ. قَالَ " وَالَّذِي نَفْسِي بِيَدِهِ، إِنَّهُمْ لَخَيْرٌ مِنْهُمْ "

Narrated Imran bin Husain: I went to the Prophet ﷺ and tied my she-camel at the gate. The people of Bani Tamim came to the Prophet ﷺ who said "O Bani Tamim! Accept the good tidings." They said twice, 'You have given us the good tidings, now give us something" Then some Yemenites came to him and he said, "Accept the good tidings, O people of Yemem, for Bani Tamim refused them." They said, "We accept it, O Allah's Messenger ﷺ! We have come to ask you about this matter (i.e. the start of creations)." He said, "First of all, there was nothing but Allah, and (then He created His Throne). His throne was over the water, and He wrote everything in the Book (in the Heaven) and created the Heavens and the Earth." Then a man shouted, "O Ibn Husain! Your she-camel has gone away!" So, I went away and could not see the she-camel because of the mirage. By Allah, I wished I had left that she-camel (but not that gathering). – Sahih Al-Bukhari 3191
حَدَّثَنَا عُمَرُ بْنُ حَفْصِ بْنِ غِيَاثٍ، حَدَّثَنَا أَبِي، حَدَّثَنَا الأَعْمَشُ، حَدَّثَنَا جَامِعُ بْنُ شَدَّادٍ، عَنْ صَفْوَانَ بْنِ مُحْرِزٍ، أَنَّهُ حَدَّثَهُ عَنْ عِمْرَانَ بْنِ حُصَيْنٍ ـ رضى الله عنهما ـ قَالَ دَخَلْتُ عَلَى النَّبِيِّ صلى الله عليه وسلم وَعَقَلْتُ نَاقَتِي بِالْبَابِ، فَأَتَاهُ نَاسٌ مِنْ بَنِي تَمِيمٍ فَقَالَ " اقْبَلُوا الْبُشْرَى يَا بَنِي تَمِيمٍ ". قَالُوا قَدْ بَشَّرْتَنَا فَأَعْطِنَا. مَرَّتَيْنِ، ثُمَّ دَخَلَ عَلَيْهِ نَاسٌ مِنْ أَهْلِ الْيَمَنِ فَقَالَ " اقْبَلُوا الْبُشْرَى يَا أَهْلَ الْيَمَنِ، إِذْ لَمْ يَقْبَلْهَا بَنُو تَمِيمٍ ". قَالُوا قَدْ قَبِلْنَا يَا رَسُولَ اللَّهِ، قَالُوا جِئْنَاكَ نَسْأَلُكَ عَنْ هَذَا الأَمْرِ قَالَ " كَانَ اللَّهُ وَلَمْ يَكُنْ شَىْءٌ غَيْرُهُ، وَكَانَ عَرْشُهُ عَلَى الْمَاءِ، وَكَتَبَ فِي الذِّكْرِ كُلَّ شَىْءٍ، وَخَلَقَ السَّمَوَاتِ وَالأَرْضَ ". فَنَادَى مُنَادٍ ذَهَبَتْ نَاقَتُكَ يَا ابْنَ الْحُصَيْنِ. فَانْطَلَقْتُ فَإِذَا هِيَ يَقْطَعُ دُونَهَا السَّرَابُ، فَوَاللَّهِ لَوَدِدْتُ أَنِّي كُنْتُ تَرَكْتُهَا

Banu Adi
بَنِي عَدِيٍّ

Narrated Ibn `Abbas: When the Verse:--'And warn your tribe of near-kindred, was revealed, the Prophet ﷺ ascended the Safa (mountain) and started calling, "O Bani Fihr! O Bani `Adi!" addressing various tribes of Quraish till they were assembled. Those who could not come themselves, sent their messengers to see what was there. Abu Lahab and other people from Quraish came and the Prophet ﷺ then said, "Suppose I told you that there is an (enemy) cavalry in the valley intending to attack you, would you believe me?" They said, "Yes, for we have not found you telling anything other than the truth." He then said, "I am a warner to you in face of a terrific punishment." Abu Lahab said (to the Prophet) "May your hands perish all this day. Is it for this purpose you have gathered us?" Then it was revealed: "Perish the hands of Abu Lahab (one of the Prophet's uncles), and perish he! His wealth and his children will not profit him...." (111.1-5). – Sahih Al-Bukhari 4770
حَدَّثَنَا عُمَرُ بْنُ حَفْصِ بْنِ غِيَاثٍ، حَدَّثَنَا أَبِي، حَدَّثَنَا الأَعْمَشُ، قَالَ حَدَّثَنِي عَمْرُو بْنُ مُرَّةَ، عَنْ سَعِيدِ بْنِ جُبَيْرٍ، عَنِ ابْنِ عَبَّاسٍ ـ رضى الله عنهما ـ قَالَ لَمَّا نَزَلَتْ {وَأَنْذِرْ عَشِيرَتَكَ الأَقْرَبِينَ} صَعِدَ النَّبِيُّ صلى الله عليه وسلم عَلَى الصَّفَا فَجَعَلَ يُنَادِي " يَا بَنِي فِهْرٍ، يَا بَنِي عَدِيٍّ ". لِبُطُونِ قُرَيْشٍ حَتَّى اجْتَمَعُوا، فَجَعَلَ الرَّجُلُ إِذَا لَمْ يَسْتَطِعْ أَنْ يَخْرُجَ أَرْسَلَ رَسُولاً لِيَنْظُرَ مَا هُوَ، فَجَاءَ أَبُو لَهَبٍ وَقُرَيْشٌ فَقَالَ " أَرَأَيْتَكُمْ لَوْ أَخْبَرْتُكُمْ أَنَّ خَيْلاً بِالْوَادِي تُرِيدُ أَنْ تُغِيرَ عَلَيْكُمْ، أَكُنْتُمْ مُصَدِّقِيَّ ". قَالُوا نَعَمْ، مَا جَرَّبْنَا عَلَيْكَ إِلاَّ صِدْقًا. قَالَ " فَإِنِّي نَذِيرٌ لَكُمْ بَيْنَ يَدَىْ عَذَابٍ شَدِيدٍ ". فَقَالَ أَبُو لَهَبٍ تَبًّا لَكَ سَائِرَ الْيَوْمِ، أَلِهَذَا جَمَعْتَنَا فَنَزَلَتْ {تَبَّتْ يَدَا أَبِي لَهَبٍ وَتَبَّ * مَا أَغْنَى عَنْهُ مَالُهُ وَمَا كَسَبَ}

Narrated Abu Sa`id Al-Khudri and Abu Huraira: Allah's Messenger ﷺ sent the brother of the tribe of Bani Adi Al-Ansari as governor of Khaibar. Then the man returned, bringing Janib (a good kind of date). Allah's Messenger ﷺ asked him, "Are all the dates of Khaibar like that?" He replied, "No, by Allah, O Allah's Messenger ﷺ! We take one Sa' of these (good) dates for two Sas of mixed dates." Allah's Messenger ﷺ then said, "Do not do so. You should either take one Sa of this (kind) for one Sa' of the other; or sell one kind and then buy with its price the other kind (of dates), and you should do the same in weighing.". – Sahih Al-Bukhari 7350, 7351

حَدَّثَنَا إِسْمَاعِيلُ، عَنْ أَخِيهِ، عَنْ سُلَيْمَانَ بْنِ بِلاَلٍ، عَنْ عَبْدِ الْمَجِيدِ بْنِ سُهَيْلِ بْنِ عَبْدِ الرَّحْمَنِ بْنِ عَوْفٍ، أَنَّهُ سَمِعَ سَعِيدَ بْنَ الْمُسَيَّبِ، يُحَدِّثُ أَنَّ أَبَا سَعِيدٍ الْخُدْرِيَّ، وَأَبَا، هُرَيْرَةَ حَدَّثَاهُ أَنَّ رَسُولَ اللَّهِ صلى الله عليه وسلم بَعَثَ أَخَا بَنِي عَدِيٍّ الأَنْصَارِيَّ وَاسْتَعْمَلَهُ عَلَى خَيْبَرَ، فَقَدِمَ بِتَمْرٍ جَنِيبٍ فَقَالَ لَهُ رَسُولُ اللَّهِ صلى الله عليه وسلم " أَكُلُّ تَمْرِ خَيْبَرَ هَكَذَا ". قَالَ لاَ وَاللَّهِ يَا رَسُولَ اللَّهِ إِنَّا لَنَشْتَرِي الصَّاعَ بِالصَّاعَيْنِ مِنَ الْجَمْعِ. فَقَالَ رَسُولُ اللَّهِ صلى الله عليه وسلم " لاَ تَفْعَلُوا، وَلَكِنْ مِثْلاً بِمِثْلٍ، أَوْ بِيعُوا هَذَا وَاشْتَرُوا بِثَمَنِهِ مِنْ هَذَا وَكَذَلِكَ الْمِيزَانُ "

Narrated Aisha: Allah's Messenger ﷺ offered prayer while he was wearing a Khamisa of his that had printed marks. He looked at its marks and when he finished prayer, he said, "Take this Khamisa of mine to Abu Jahm, for it has just now diverted my attention from my prayer, and bring to me the Anbijania (a plain thick sheet) of Abu Jahm bin Hudhaifa bin Ghanim who belonged to Bani Adi bin Ka`b.". – Sahih Al-Bukhari 5817

حَدَّثَنَا مُوسَى بْنُ إِسْمَاعِيلَ، حَدَّثَنَا إِبْرَاهِيمُ بْنُ سَعْدٍ، حَدَّثَنَا ابْنُ شِهَابٍ، عَنْ عُرْوَةَ، عَنْ عَائِشَةَ، قَالَتْ صَلَّى رَسُولُ اللَّهِ صلى الله عليه وسلم فِي خَمِيصَةٍ لَهُ لَهَا أَعْلاَمٌ، فَنَظَرَ إِلَى أَعْلاَمِهَا نَظْرَةً، فَلَمَّا سَلَّمَ قَالَ " اذْهَبُوا بِخَمِيصَتِي هَذِهِ إِلَى أَبِي جَهْمٍ، فَإِنَّهَا أَلْهَتْنِي آنِفًا عَنْ صَلاَتِي، وَائْتُونِي بِأَنْبِجَانِيَّةِ أَبِي جَهْمِ بْنِ حُذَيْفَةَ بْنِ غَانِمٍ مِنْ بَنِي عَدِيِّ بْنِ كَعْبٍ ".

Narrated `Abdullah bin `Amr bin Rabi`a: Who was one of the leaders of Bani `Adi and his father participated in the battle of Badr in the company of the Prophet. `Umar appointed Qudama bin Maz'un as ruler of Bahrain, Qudama was one of the warriors of the battle of Badr and was the maternal uncle of `Abdullah bin `Umar and Hafsa. – Sahih Al-Bukhari 4011

حَدَّثَنَا أَبُو الْيَمَانِ، أَخْبَرَنَا شُعَيْبٌ، عَنِ الزُّهْرِيِّ، قَالَ أَخْبَرَنِي عَبْدُ اللَّهِ بْنُ عَامِرِ بْنِ رَبِيعَةَ، وَكَانَ، مِنْ أَكْبَرِ بَنِي عَدِيٍّ وَكَانَ أَبُوهُ شَهِدَ بَدْرًا مَعَ النَّبِيِّ صلى الله عليه وسلم أَنَّ عُمَرَ اسْتَعْمَلَ قُدَامَةَ بْنَ مَظْعُونٍ عَلَى الْبَحْرَيْنِ، وَكَانَ شَهِدَ بَدْرًا، وَهُوَ خَالُ عَبْدِ اللَّهِ بْنِ عُمَرَ وَحَفْصَةَ رضى الله عنهم

Abu Sa`id and Abu Huraira said: "The Prophet ﷺ made the brother of Bani Adi from the Ansar as the ruler of Khaibar. – Sahih Al-Bukhari 4246, 4247

وَقَالَ عَبْدُ الْعَزِيزِ بْنُ مُحَمَّدٍ عَنْ عَبْدِ الْمَجِيدِ، عَنْ سَعِيدٍ، أَنَّ أَبَا سَعِيدٍ، وَأَبَا، هُرَيْرَةَ حَدَّثَاهُ أَنَّ النَّبِيَّ صلى الله عليه وسلم بَعَثَ أَخَا بَنِي عَدِيٍّ مِنَ الأَنْصَارِ إِلَى خَيْبَرَ فَأَمَّرَهُ عَلَيْهَا. وَعَنْ عَبْدِ الْمَجِيدِ عَنْ أَبِي صَالِحٍ السَّمَّانِ عَنْ أَبِي هُرَيْرَةَ وَأَبِي سَعِيدٍ مِثْلَهُ.

Coalition of Mudar
ائتلاف مضر

Narrated Ibn `Abbas: When the delegate of `Abd Al-Qais came to Allah's Messenger ﷺ, he said, "Who are the delegate?" They said, "The delegate are from the tribe of Rabi`a." The Prophet ﷺ said, "Welcome, O the delegate, and welcome! O people! Neither you will have any disgrace nor will you regret." They said, "O Allah's Apostle! Between you and us there are the infidels of the tribe of Mudar, so please order us to do something good (religious deeds) that by acting on them we may enter Paradise, and that we may inform (our people) whom we have left behind, about it." They also asked (the Prophet) about drinks. He forbade them from four things and ordered them to do four things. He ordered them to believe in Allah, and asked them, "Do you know what is meant by belief in Allah?" They said, "Allah and His Apostle know best." He said, "To testify that none has the right to be worshipped except Allah, the One, Who has no partners with Him, and that Muhammad is Allah's Messenger ﷺ; and to offer prayers perfectly and to pay Zakat." (the narrator thinks that fasting in Ramadan is included), "and to give one-fifth of the war booty (to the state)." Then he forbade four (drinking utensils): Ad-Duba', Al56 Hantam, Al-Mazaffat and An-Naqir, or probably, Al-Muqaiyar. And then the Prophet ﷺ said, "Remember all these things by heart and preach it to those whom you have left behind.". – Sahih Al-Bukhari 7266

حَدَّثَنَا عَلِيُّ بْنُ الْجَعْدِ، أَخْبَرَنَا شُعْبَةُ، وَحَدَّثَنِي إِسْحَاقُ، أَخْبَرَنَا النَّضْرُ، أَخْبَرَنَا شُعْبَةُ، عَنْ أَبِي جَمْرَةَ، قَالَ كَانَ ابْنُ عَبَّاسٍ يُقْعِدُنِي عَلَى سَرِيرِهِ فَقَالَ إِنَّ وَفْدَ عَبْدِ الْقَيْسِ لَمَّا أَتَوْا رَسُولَ اللَّهِ صلى الله عليه وسلم قَالَ " مَنِ الْوَفْدُ ". قَالُوا رَبِيعَةُ. قَالَ " مَرْحَبًا بِالْوَفْدِ وَالْقَوْمِ، غَيْرَ خَزَايَا وَلاَ نَدَامَى ". قَالُوا يَا رَسُولَ اللَّهِ إِنَّ بَيْنَنَا وَبَيْنَكَ كُفَّارَ مُضَرَ، فَمُرْنَا بِأَمْرٍ نَدْخُلُ بِهِ الْجَنَّةَ، وَنُخْبِرُ بِهِ مَنْ وَرَاءَنَا فَسَأَلُوا عَنِ الأَشْرِبَةِ، فَنَهَاهُمْ عَنْ أَرْبَعٍ وَأَمَرَهُمْ بِأَرْبَعٍ أَمَرَهُمْ بِالإِيمَانِ بِاللَّهِ قَالَ " هَلْ تَدْرُونَ مَا الإِيمَانُ بِاللَّهِ ". قَالُوا اللَّهُ وَرَسُولُهُ أَعْلَمُ. قَالَ " شَهَادَةُ أَنْ لاَ إِلَهَ إِلاَّ اللَّهُ وَحْدَهُ لاَ شَرِيكَ لَهُ وَأَنَّ مُحَمَّدًا رَسُولُ اللَّهِ، وَإِقَامُ الصَّلاَةِ، وَإِيتَاءُ الزَّكَاةِ ـ وَأَظُنُّ فِيهِ ـ صِيَامُ رَمَضَانَ، وَتُؤْتُوا مِنَ الْمَغَانِمِ الْخُمُسَ ". وَنَهَاهُمْ عَنِ الدُّبَّاءِ، وَالْحَنْتَمِ، وَالْمُزَفَّتِ، وَالنَّقِيرِ، وَرُبَّمَا قَالَ الْمُقَيَّرِ. قَالَ " احْفَظُوهُنَّ، وَأَبْلِغُوهُنَّ مَنْ وَرَاءَكُمْ "

Narrated Abu Huraira: Whenever Allah's Messenger ﷺ intended to invoke evil upon somebody or invoke good upon somebody, he used to invoke (Allah after bowing (in the prayer). Sometimes after saying, "Allah hears him who sends his praises to Him, all praise is for You, O our Lord," he would say, "O Allah. Save Al-Walid bin Al-Walid and Salama bin Hisham, and `Aiyash bin Abu Rabi`a. O Allah! Inflict Your Severe Torture on Mudar (tribe) and strike them with (famine) years like the years of Joseph." The Prophet ﷺ used to say in a loud voice, and he also used to say in some of his Fajr prayers, "O Allah! Curse soand- so and so-and-so." Naming some of the Arab tribes till Allah revealed:--"Not for you (O Muhammad) (but for Allah) is the decision." (3.128). – Sahih Al-Bukhari 4560

حَدَّثَنَا مُوسَى بْنُ إِسْمَاعِيلَ، حَدَّثَنَا إِبْرَاهِيمُ بْنُ سَعْدٍ، حَدَّثَنَا ابْنُ شِهَابٍ، عَنْ سَعِيدِ بْنِ الْمُسَيَّبِ، وَأَبِي، سَلَمَةَ بْنِ عَبْدِ الرَّحْمَنِ عَنْ أَبِي هُرَيْرَةَ ـ رضى الله عنه ـ أَنَّ رَسُولَ اللَّهِ صلى الله عليه وسلم كَانَ إِذَا أَرَادَ أَنْ يَدْعُوَ عَلَى أَحَدٍ أَوْ يَدْعُوَ لأَحَدٍ قَنَتَ بَعْدَ الرُّكُوعِ، فَرُبَّمَا قَالَ إِذَا قَالَ " سَمِعَ اللَّهُ لِمَنْ حَمِدَهُ، اللَّهُمَّ رَبَّنَا لَكَ الْحَمْدُ، اللَّهُمَّ أَنْجِ الْوَلِيدَ بْنَ الْوَلِيدِ، وَسَلَمَةَ بْنَ هِشَامٍ، وَعَيَّاشَ بْنَ أَبِي رَبِيعَةَ، اللَّهُمَّ اشْدُدْ وَطْأَتَكَ عَلَى مُضَرَ وَاجْعَلْهَا سِنِينَ كَسِنِي يُوسُفَ ". يَجْهَرُ بِذَلِكَ وَكَانَ يَقُولُ فِي بَعْضِ صَلاَتِهِ فِي صَلاَةِ الْفَجْرِ " اللَّهُمَّ الْعَنْ فُلاَنًا وَفُلاَنًا ". لأَحْيَاءٍ مِنَ الْعَرَبِ، حَتَّى أَنْزَلَ اللَّهُ {لَيْسَ لَكَ مِنَ الأَمْرِ شَىْءٌ} الآيَةَ.

Narrated `Abdullah: It (i.e., the imagined smoke) was because, when the Quraish refused to obey the Prophet, he asked Allah to afflict them with years of famine similar to those of (Prophet) Joseph. So they were stricken with famine and fatigue, so much so that they ate even bones. A man would look towards the sky and imagine seeing something like smoke between him and the sky because of extreme fatigue. So Allah revealed:-- 'Then watch you for the Day that the sky will bring forth a kind of smoke plainly visible, covering the people; this is a painfull of torment.' (44.10-11) Then someone (Abu Sufyan) came to Allah's Messenger ﷺ and said, "O Allah's Messenger ﷺ! Invoke Allah to send rain for the tribes of Mudar for they are on the verge of destruction." On that the Prophet ﷺ said (astonishingly) "Shall I invoke Allah) for the tribes of Mudar? Verily, you are a brave man!" But the Prophet prayed for rain and it rained for them. Then the Verse was revealed. 'But truly you will return (to disbelief).' (44.15) (When the famine was over and) they restored prosperity and welfare, they reverted to their ways (of heathenism) whereupon Allah revealed: 'On the Day when We shall seize you with a Mighty Grasp. We will indeed (then) exact retribution.' (44.16) The narrator said, "That was the day of the Battle of Badr.". – Sahih Al-Bukhari 4821

حَدَّثَنَا يَحْيَى، حَدَّثَنَا أَبُو مُعَاوِيَةَ، عَنِ الأَعْمَشِ، عَنْ مُسْلِمٍ، عَنْ مَسْرُوقٍ، قَالَ قَالَ عَبْدُ اللَّهِ إِنَّمَا كَانَ هَذَا لأَنَّ قُرَيْشًا لَمَّا اسْتَعْصَوْا عَلَى النَّبِيِّ صلى الله عليه وسلم دَعَا عَلَيْهِمْ بِسِنِينَ كَسِنِي يُوسُفَ، فَأَصَابَهُمْ قَحْطٌ وَجَهْدٌ حَتَّى أَكَلُوا الْعِظَامَ، فَجَعَلَ الرَّجُلُ يَنْظُرُ إِلَى السَّمَاءِ فَيَرَى مَا بَيْنَهُ وَبَيْنَهَا كَهَيْئَةِ الدُّخَانِ مِنَ الْجَهْدِ، فَأَنْزَلَ اللَّهُ تَعَالَى {فَارْتَقِبْ يَوْمَ تَأْتِي السَّمَاءُ بِدُخَانٍ مُبِينٍ * يَغْشَى النَّاسَ هَذَا عَذَابٌ أَلِيمٌ} قَالَ فَأُتِيَ رَسُولُ اللَّهِ صلى الله عليه وسلم فَقِيلَ يَا رَسُولَ اللَّهِ اسْتَسْقِ اللَّهَ لِمُضَرَ، فَإِنَّهَا قَدْ هَلَكَتْ. قَالَ " لِمُضَرَ إِنَّكَ لَجَرِيءٌ ". فَاسْتَسْقَى فَسُقُوا. فَنَزَلَتْ {إِنَّكُمْ عَائِدُونَ} فَلَمَّا أَصَابَتْهُمُ الرَّفَاهِيَةُ عَادُوا إِلَى حَالِهِمْ حِينَ أَصَابَتْهُمُ الرَّفَاهِيَةُ. فَأَنْزَلَ اللَّهُ عَزَّ وَجَلَّ {يَوْمَ نَبْطِشُ الْبَطْشَةَ الْكُبْرَى إِنَّا مُنْتَقِمُونَ} قَالَ يَعْنِي يَوْمَ بَدْرٍ.

Banu Asad
بَنِي أَسَدٍ

Narrated Abu Humaid Al-Sa`idi: The Prophetﷺ appointed a man from the tribe of Bani Asad, called Ibn Al-Utabiyya to collect the Zakat. When he returned (with the money) he said (to the Prophet), "This is for you and this has been given to me as a gift." The Prophetﷺ stood up on the pulpit (Sufyan said he ascended the pulpit), and after glorifying and praising Allah, he said, "What is wrong with the employee whom we send (to collect Zakat from the public) that he returns to say, 'This is for you and that is for me?' Why didn't he stay at his father's and mother's house to see whether he will be given gifts or not? By Him in Whose Hand my life is, whoever takes anything illegally will bring it on the Day of Resurrection by carrying it over his neck: if it is a camel, it will be grunting: if it is a cow, it will be mooing: and if it is a sheep it will be bleating!" The Prophetﷺ then raised both his hands till we saw the whiteness of his armpits (and he said), "No doubt! Haven't I conveyed Allah's Message?" And he repeated it three times. – Sahih Al-Bukhari 7174

حَدَّثَنَا عَلِيُّ بْنُ عَبْدِ اللَّهِ، حَدَّثَنَا سُفْيَانُ، عَنِ الزُّهْرِيِّ، أَنَّهُ سَمِعَ عُرْوَةَ، أَخْبَرَنَا أَبُو حُمَيْدٍ السَّاعِدِيُّ، قَالَ اسْتَعْمَلَ النَّبِيُّ صلى الله عليه وسلم رَجُلاً مِنْ بَنِي أَسَدٍ يُقَالُ لَهُ ابْنُ الأُتَبِيَّةِ عَلَى صَدَقَةٍ فَلَمَّا قَدِمَ قَالَ هَذَا لَكُمْ وَهَذَا أُهْدِيَ لِي. فَقَامَ النَّبِيُّ صلى الله عليه وسلم عَلَى الْمِنْبَرِ ـ قَالَ سُفْيَانُ أَيْضًا فَصَعِدَ الْمِنْبَرَ ـ فَحَمِدَ اللَّهَ وَأَثْنَى عَلَيْهِ ثُمَّ قَالَ " مَا بَالُ الْعَامِلِ نَبْعَثُهُ، فَيَأْتِي يَقُولُ هَذَا لَكَ وَهَذَا لِي. فَهَلاَّ جَلَسَ فِي بَيْتِ أَبِيهِ وَأُمِّهِ فَيَنْظُرُ أَيُهْدَى لَهُ أَمْ لاَ، وَالَّذِي نَفْسِي بِيَدِهِ لاَ يَأْتِي بِشَىْءٍ إِلاَّ جَاءَ بِهِ يَوْمَ الْقِيَامَةِ يَحْمِلُهُ عَلَى رَقَبَتِهِ، إِنْ كَانَ بَعِيرًا لَهُ رُغَاءٌ، أَوْ بَقَرَةً لَهَا خُوَارٌ، أَوْ شَاةً تَيْعَرُ ". ثُمَّ رَفَعَ يَدَيْهِ حَتَّى رَأَيْنَا عُفْرَتَىْ إِبْطَيْهِ " أَلاَ هَلْ بَلَّغْتُ " ثَلاَثًا. قَالَ سُفْيَانُ قَصَّهُ عَلَيْنَا الزُّهْرِيُّ. وَزَادَ هِشَامٌ عَنْ أَبِيهِ عَنْ أَبِي حُمَيْدٍ قَالَ سَمِعَ أُذُنَاىَ وَأَبْصَرَتْهُ عَيْنِي، وَسَلُوا زَيْدَ بْنَ ثَابِتٍ فَإِنَّهُ سَمِعَهُ مَعِي. وَلَمْ يَقُلِ الزُّهْرِيُّ سَمِعَ أُذُنِي. {خُوَارٌ} صَوْتٌ، وَالْجُؤَارُ مِنْ تَجْأَرُونَ كَصَوْتِ الْبَقَرَةِ.

Narrated Qais: I heard Sa`d saying, "I was the first amongst the 'Arabs who shot an arrow for Allah's Cause. We used to fight along with the Prophets, while we had nothing to eat except the leaves of trees so that one's excrete would look like the excrete balls of camel or a sheep, containing nothing to mix them together. Today Banu Asad tribe blame me for not having understood Islam. I would be a loser if my deeds were in vain." Those people complained about Sa`d to `Umar, claiming that he did not offer his prayers perfectly. – Sahih Al-Bukhari 3728

حَدَّثَنَا عَمْرُو بْنُ عَوْنٍ، حَدَّثَنَا خَالِدُ بْنُ عَبْدِ اللَّهِ، عَنْ إِسْمَاعِيلَ، عَنْ قَيْسٍ، قَالَ سَمِعْتُ سَعْدًا ـ رضى الله عنه ـ يَقُولُ إِنِّي لأَوَّلُ الْعَرَبِ رَمَى بِسَهْمٍ فِي سَبِيلِ اللَّهِ، وَكُنَّا نَغْزُو مَعَ النَّبِيِّ صلى الله عليه وسلم وَمَا لَنَا طَعَامٌ إِلاَّ وَرَقُ الشَّجَرِ، حَتَّى إِنَّ أَحَدَنَا لَيَضَعُ كَمَا يَضَعُ الْبَعِيرُ أَوِ الشَّاةُ، مَا لَهُ خِلْطٌ، ثُمَّ أَصْبَحَتْ بَنُو أَسَدٍ تُعَزِّرُنِي عَلَى الإِسْلاَمِ، لَقَدْ خِبْتُ إِذًا وَضَلَّ عَمَلِي. وَكَانُوا وَشَوْا بِهِ إِلَى عُمَرَ، قَالُوا لاَ يُحْسِنُ يُصَلِّي.

Narrated Abu Bakra: The Prophetﷺ said, "Do you think if the tribes of Aslam, Ghifar, Muzaina and Juhaina are better than the tribes of Tamim, 'Amir bin Sa'sa'a, Ghatfan and Asad, they (the second group) are despairing and losing?" They (the Prophet's companions) said, "Yes,

(they are)." He said, "By Him in Whose Hand my soul is, they (the first group) are better than them (the second group). – Sahih Al-Bukhari 6635
حَدَّثَنِي عَبْدُ اللَّهِ بْنُ مُحَمَّدٍ، حَدَّثَنَا وَهْبٌ، حَدَّثَنَا شُعْبَةُ، عَنْ مُحَمَّدِ بْنِ أَبِي يَعْقُوبَ، عَنْ عَبْدِ الرَّحْمَنِ بْنِ أَبِي بَكْرَةَ، عَنْ أَبِيهِ، عَنِ النَّبِيِّ صلى الله عليه وسلم قَالَ " أَرَأَيْتُمْ إِنْ كَانَ أَسْلَمُ وَغِفَارُ وَمُزَيْنَةُ وَجُهَيْنَةُ خَيْرًا مِنْ تَمِيمٍ وَعَامِرِ بْنِ صَعْصَعَةَ وَغَطَفَانَ وَأَسَدٍ، خَابُوا وَخَسِرُوا ". قَالُوا نَعَمْ. فَقَالَ " وَالَّذِي نَفْسِي بِيَدِهِ إِنَّهُمْ خَيْرٌ مِنْهُمْ ".

Narrated 'Aisha: A woman from the tribe of Bani Asad was sitting with me and Allah's Apostleﷺ came to my house and said, "Who is this?" I said, "(She is) So and so. She does not sleep at night because she is engaged in prayer." The Prophetﷺ said disapprovingly: Do (good) deeds which is within your capacity as Allah never gets tired of giving rewards till you get tired of doing good deeds.". – Sahih Al-Bukhari 1151
قَالَ وَقَالَ عَبْدُ اللَّهِ بْنِ مَسْلَمَةَ عَنْ مَالِكٍ، عَنْ هِشَامِ بْنِ عُرْوَةَ، عَنْ أَبِيهِ، عَنْ عَائِشَةَ ـ رضى الله عنها ـ قَالَتْ كَانَتْ عِنْدِي امْرَأَةٌ مِنْ بَنِي أَسَدٍ فَدَخَلَ عَلَىَّ رَسُولُ اللَّهِ صلى الله عليه وسلم فَقَالَ " مَنْ هَذِهِ ". قُلْتُ فُلاَنَةُ لاَ تَنَامُ بِاللَّيْلِ. فَذُكِرَ مِنْ صَلاَتِهَا فَقَالَ " مَهْ عَلَيْكُمْ مَا تُطِيقُونَ مِنَ الأَعْمَالِ، فَإِنَّ اللَّهَ لاَ يَمَلُّ حَتَّى تَمَلُّوا "

Banu Ghifar
بنو غفار

Narrated Ibn `Abbas: When Abu Dhar received the news of the Advent of the Prophetﷺ he said to his brother, "Ride to this valley (of Mecca) and try to find out the truth of the person who claims to be a prophet who is informed of the news of Heaven. Listen to what he says and come back to me." So his brother set out and came to the Prophetﷺ and listened to some of his talks, and returned to Abu Dhar and said to him. "I have seen him enjoining virtuous behavior and saying something that is not poetry." Abu Dhar said, "You have not satisfied me as to what I wanted." He then took his journey-food and carried a waterskin of his, containing some water till be reached Mecca. He went to the Mosque and searched for the Prophet and though he did not know him, he hated to ask anybody about him. When a part of the night had passed away, `Ali saw him and knew that he was a stranger. So when Abu Dhar saw `Ali, he followed him, and none of them asked his companion about anything, and when it was dawn, Abu Dhar took his journey food and his water-skin to the Mosque and stayed there all the day long without being perceived by the Prophet, and when it was evening, he came back to his retiring place. `Ali passed by him and said, "Has the man not known his dwelling place yet?" So `Ali awakened him and took him with him and none of them spoke to the other about anything. When it was the third day. `Ali did the same and Abu Dhar stayed with him. Then `Ali said "Will you tell me what has brought you here?" Abu Dhar said, "If you give me a firm promise that you will guide me, then I will tell you." `Ali promised him, and he informed `Ali about the matter. `Ali said, "It is true, and he is the Messenger of Allah. Next morning when you get up, accompany me, and if I see any danger for you, I will stop as if to pass water, but if I go on, follow me and enter the place which I will enter." Abu Dhar did so, and followed `Ali till he entered the place of the Prophet, and Abu Dhar went in with him, Abu Dhar listened to some of the Prophet's talks and embraced Islam on the spot. The Prophetﷺ said to him, "Go back to your people and inform them (about it) till you receive my order." Abu Dhar said, "By Him in Whose Hand my life is, I will proclaim my conversion loudly amongst them (i.e. the pagans)." So he went out, and when he reached the Mosque, he said as loudly as possible, "I bear witness that None has the right to be worshipped except Allah, and Muhammad is the Messenger of Allah." The People got up and beat him painfully. Then Al-Abbas came and knelt over him (to protect him) and said (to the people), "Woe to you! Don't you know that this man belongs to the tribe of Ghifar and your trade to Sha'm is through their way?" So he rescued him from them. Abu Dhar again did the same the next day. They beat him and took vengeance on him and again Al-Abbas knelt over him (to protect him). – Sahih Al-Bukhari 3861

حَدَّثَنِي عَمْرُو بْنُ عَبَّاسٍ، حَدَّثَنَا عَبْدُ الرَّحْمَنِ بْنُ مَهْدِيٍّ، حَدَّثَنَا الْمُثَنَّى، عَنْ أَبِي جَمْرَةَ، عَنِ ابْنِ عَبَّاسٍ ـ رضى الله عنهما ـ قَالَ لَمَّا بَلَغَ أَبَا ذَرٍّ مَبْعَثُ النَّبِيِّ صلى الله عليه وسلم قَالَ لأَخِيهِ ارْكَبْ إِلَى هَذَا الْوَادِي، فَاعْلَمْ لِي عِلْمَ هَذَا الرَّجُلِ الَّذِي يَزْعُمُ أَنَّهُ نَبِيٌّ، يَأْتِيهِ الْخَبَرُ مِنَ السَّمَاءِ، وَاسْمَعْ مِنْ قَوْلِهِ، ثُمَّ ائْتِنِي. فَانْطَلَقَ الأَخُ حَتَّى قَدِمَهُ وَسَمِعَ مِنْ قَوْلِهِ، ثُمَّ رَجَعَ إِلَى أَبِي ذَرٍّ، فَقَالَ لَهُ رَأَيْتُهُ يَأْمُرُ بِمَكَارِمِ الأَخْلاَقِ، وَكَلاَمًا مَا هُوَ بِالشِّعْرِ. فَقَالَ مَا شَفَيْتَنِي مِمَّا أَرَدْتُ، فَتَزَوَّدَ وَحَمَلَ شَنَّةً لَهُ فِيهَا مَاءٌ حَتَّى قَدِمَ مَكَّةَ، فَأَتَى الْمَسْجِدَ، فَالْتَمَسَ النَّبِيَّ صلى الله عليه وسلم وَلاَ يَعْرِفُهُ، وَكَرِهَ أَنْ يَسْأَلَ عَنْهُ حَتَّى أَدْرَكَهُ بَعْضُ اللَّيْلِ، فَرَآهُ عَلِيٌّ فَعَرَفَ أَنَّهُ غَرِيبٌ. فَلَمَّا رَآهُ تَبِعَهُ، فَلَمْ يَسْأَلْ وَاحِدٌ مِنْهُمَا صَاحِبَهُ عَنْ شَىْءٍ حَتَّى أَصْبَحَ، ثُمَّ احْتَمَلَ قِرْبَتَهُ وَزَادَهُ إِلَى الْمَسْجِدِ، وَظَلَّ ذَلِكَ الْيَوْمَ وَلاَ يَرَاهُ النَّبِيُّ صلى الله عليه وسلم حَتَّى أَمْسَى، فَعَادَ إِلَى مَضْجَعِهِ، فَمَرَّ بِهِ عَلِيٌّ فَقَالَ أَمَا نَالَ لِلرَّجُلِ أَنْ يَعْلَمَ مَنْزِلَهُ فَأَقَامَهُ، فَذَهَبَ بِهِ مَعَهُ لاَ يَسْأَلُ وَاحِدٌ مِنْهُمَا صَاحِبَهُ عَنْ شَىْءٍ، حَتَّى إِذَا كَانَ يَوْمَ الثَّالِثِ، فَعَادَ عَلِيٌّ مِثْلَ ذَلِكَ، فَأَقَامَ مَعَهُ ثُمَّ قَالَ أَلاَ تُحَدِّثُنِي مَا الَّذِي أَقْدَمَكَ قَالَ إِنْ أَعْطَيْتَنِي عَهْدًا وَمِيثَاقًا لَتُرْشِدَنَّنِي فَعَلْتُ فَفَعَلَ فَأَخْبَرَهُ. قَالَ فَإِنَّهُ حَقٌّ وَهُوَ رَسُولُ اللَّهِ صلى الله عليه وسلم، فَإِذَا أَصْبَحْتَ فَاتْبَعْنِي، فَإِنِّي إِنْ رَأَيْتُ شَيْئًا أَخَافُ عَلَيْكَ قُمْتُ كَأَنِّي أُرِيقُ الْمَاءَ، فَإِنْ مَضَيْتُ فَاتْبَعْنِي حَتَّى تَدْخُلَ مَدْخَلِي. فَفَعَلَ، فَانْطَلَقَ يَقْفُوهُ حَتَّى دَخَلَ عَلَى النَّبِيِّ صلى الله عليه وسلم وَدَخَلَ مَعَهُ، فَسَمِعَ مِنْ قَوْلِهِ، وَأَسْلَمَ مَكَانَهُ فَقَالَ لَهُ النَّبِيُّ صلى الله عليه وسلم " ارْجِعْ إِلَى قَوْمِكَ، فَأَخْبِرْهُمْ حَتَّى يَأْتِيَكَ أَمْرِي ". قَالَ وَالَّذِي نَفْسِي بِيَدِهِ لأَصْرُخَنَّ بِهَا بَيْنَ ظَهْرَانَيْهِمْ، فَخَرَجَ حَتَّى أَتَى الْمَسْجِدَ فَنَادَى بِأَعْلَى صَوْتِهِ أَشْهَدُ أَنْ لاَ إِلَهَ إِلاَّ اللَّهُ، وَأَنَّ مُحَمَّدًا رَسُولُ اللَّهِ. ثُمَّ قَامَ الْقَوْمُ فَضَرَبُوهُ حَتَّى أَضْجَعُوهُ، وَأَتَى الْعَبَّاسُ فَأَكَبَّ عَلَيْهِ قَالَ وَيْلَكُمْ أَلَسْتُمْ تَعْلَمُونَ أَنَّهُ مِنْ غِفَارٍ وَأَنَّ طَرِيقَ تِجَارِكُمْ إِلَى الشَّأْمِ فَأَنْقَذَهُ مِنْهُمْ، ثُمَّ عَادَ مِنَ الْغَدِ لِمِثْلِهَا، فَضَرَبُوهُ وَثَارُوا إِلَيْهِ، فَأَكَبَّ الْعَبَّاسُ عَلَيْهِ.

Narrated `Abdullah bin Abu Qatada: That his father said "We proceeded with the Prophet ﷺ in the year of Al-Hudaibiya and his companions assumed Ihram but I did not. We were informed that some enemies were at Ghaiqa and so we went on towards them. My companions saw an onager and some of them started laughing among themselves. I looked and saw it. I chased it with my horse and stabbed and caught it. I wanted some help from my companions but they refused. (I slaughtered it all alone). We all ate from it (i.e. its meat). Then I followed Allah's Messenger ﷺ lest we should be left behind. At times I urged my horse to run at a galloping speed and at other times at an ordinary slow speed. On the way I met a man from the tribe of Bani Ghifar at midnight. I asked him where he had left Allah's Messenger ﷺ. The man replied that he had left the Prophet ﷺ at a place called Ta'hun and he had the intention of having the midday rest at As-Suqya. So, I followed Allah's Messenger ﷺ till I reached him and said, "O Allah's Messenger ﷺ! I have been sent by my companions who send you their greetings and compliments and ask for Allah's Mercy and Blessings upon you. They were afraid lest the enemy might intervene between you and them; so please wait for them." So he did. Then I said, "O Allah's Messenger ﷺ! We have hunted an onager and have some of it (i.e. its meat) left over." Allah's Messenger ﷺ told his companions to eat the meat although all of them were in a state of Ihram.". – Sahih Al-Bukhari 1822

حَدَّثَنَا سَعِيدُ بْنُ الرَّبِيعِ، حَدَّثَنَا عَلِيُّ بْنُ الْمُبَارَكِ، عَنْ يَحْيَى، عَنْ عَبْدِ اللَّهِ بْنِ أَبِي قَتَادَةَ، أَنَّ أَبَاهُ، حَدَّثَهُ قَالَ انْطَلَقْنَا مَعَ النَّبِيِّ صلى الله عليه وسلم عَامَ الْحُدَيْبِيَةِ فَأَحْرَمَ أَصْحَابُهُ، وَلَمْ أُحْرِمْ، فَأُنْبِئْنَا بِعَدُوٍّ بِغَيْقَةَ فَتَوَجَّهْنَا نَحْوَهُمْ، فَبَصُرَ أَصْحَابِي بِحِمَارِ وَحْشٍ، فَجَعَلَ بَعْضُهُمْ يَضْحَكُ إِلَى بَعْضٍ، فَنَظَرْتُ فَرَأَيْتُهُ فَحَمَلْتُ عَلَيْهِ الْفَرَسَ، فَطَعَنْتُهُ، فَأَثْبَتُّهُ، فَاسْتَعَنْتُهُمْ، فَأَبَوْا أَنْ يُعِينُونِي، فَأَكَلْنَا مِنْهُ، ثُمَّ لَحِقْتُ بِرَسُولِ اللَّهِ صلى الله عليه وسلم وَخَشِينَا أَنْ نُقْتَطَعَ، أَرْفَعُ فَرَسِي شَأْوًا، وَأَسِيرُ عَلَيْهِ شَأْوًا، فَلَقِيتُ رَجُلاً مِنْ بَنِي غِفَارٍ فِي جَوْفِ اللَّيْلِ فَقُلْتُ أَيْنَ تَرَكْتَ رَسُولَ اللَّهِ صلى الله عليه وسلم فَقَالَ تَرَكْتُهُ بِتَعْهِنَ وَهُوَ قَائِلٌ السُّقْيَا. فَلَحِقْتُ بِرَسُولِ اللَّهِ صلى الله عليه وسلم حَتَّى أَتَيْتُهُ فَقُلْتُ يَا رَسُولَ اللَّهِ، إِنَّ أَصْحَابَكَ أَرْسَلُوا يَقْرَءُونَ عَلَيْكَ السَّلاَمَ وَرَحْمَةَ اللَّهِ وَبَرَكَاتِهِ، وَإِنَّهُمْ قَدْ خَشُوا أَنْ يَقْتَطِعَهُمُ الْعَدُوُّ دُونَكَ، فَانْظُرْهُمْ، فَفَعَلَ فَقُلْتُ يَا رَسُولَ اللَّهِ، إِنَّا اصَّدْنَا حِمَارَ وَحْشٍ، وَإِنَّ عِنْدَنَا فَاضِلَةً. فَقَالَ رَسُولُ اللَّهِ صلى الله عليه وسلم لأَصْحَابِهِ " كُلُوا ". وَهُمْ مُحْرِمُونَ

Narrated `Aisha: Sa`d was wounded on the day of Khandaq (i.e. Trench) when a man from Quraish, called Hibban bin Al-`Araqa hit him (with an arrow). The man was Hibban bin Qais from (the tribe of) Bani Mais bin 'Amir bin Lu'ai who shot an arrow at Sa`d's medial arm vein (or main artery of the arm). The Prophetﷺ pitched a tent (for Sa`d) in the Mosque so that he might be near to the Prophetﷺ to visit. When the Prophet returned from the (battle) of Al-Khandaq (i.e. Trench) and laid down his arms and took a bath Gabriel came to him while he (i.e. Gabriel) was shaking the dust off his head, and said, "You have laid down the arms?" By Allah, I have not laid them down. Go out to them (to attack them)." The Prophetﷺ said, "Where?" Gabriel pointed towards Bani Quraiza. So Allah's Messengerﷺ went to them (i.e. Banu Quraiza) (i.e. besieged them). They then surrendered to the Prophet's judgment but he directed them to Sa`d to give his verdict concerning them. Sa`d said, "I give my judgment that their warriors should be killed, their women and children should be taken as captives, and their properties distributed." Narrated Hisham: My father informed me that `Aisha said, "Sa`d said, "O Allah! You know that there is nothing more beloved to me than to fight in Your Cause against those who disbelieved Your Apostle and turned him out (of Mecca). O Allah! I think you have put to an end the fight between us and them (i.e. Quraish infidels). And if there still remains any fight with the Quraish (infidels), then keep me alive till I fight against them for Your Sake. But if you have brought the war to an end, then let this wound burst and cause my death thereby.' So blood gushed from the wound. There was a tent in the Mosque belonging to Banu Ghifar who were surprised by the blood flowing towards them . They said, 'O people of the tent! What is this thing which is coming to us from your side?' Behold! Blood was flowing profusely out of Sa`d's wound. Sa`d then died because of that.". – Sahih Al-Bukhari 4122

حَدَّثَنَا زَكَرِيَّاءُ بْنُ يَحْيَى، حَدَّثَنَا عَبْدُ اللَّهِ بْنُ نُمَيْرٍ، حَدَّثَنَا هِشَامٌ، عَنْ أَبِيهِ، عَنْ عَائِشَةَ ـ رضى الله عنها ـ قَالَتْ أُصِيبَ سَعْدٌ يَوْمَ الْخَنْدَقِ، رَمَاهُ رَجُلٌ مِنْ قُرَيْشٍ يُقَالُ لَهُ حِبَّانُ ابْنُ الْعَرِقَةِ، رَمَاهُ فِي الأَكْحَلِ، فَضَرَبَ النَّبِيُّ صلى الله عليه وسلم خَيْمَةً فِي الْمَسْجِدِ لِيَعُودَهُ مِنْ قَرِيبٍ، فَلَمَّا رَجَعَ رَسُولُ اللَّهِ صلى الله عليه وسلم مِنَ الْخَنْدَقِ وَضَعَ السِّلاَحَ وَاغْتَسَلَ، فَأَتَاهُ جِبْرِيلُ ـ عَلَيْهِ السَّلاَمُ ـ وَهْوَ يَنْفُضُ رَأْسَهُ مِنَ الْغُبَارِ فَقَالَ قَدْ وَضَعْتَ السِّلاَحَ وَاللَّهِ مَا وَضَعْتُهُ، اخْرُجْ إِلَيْهِمْ. قَالَ النَّبِيُّ صلى الله عليه وسلم " فَأَيْنَ ". فَأَشَارَ إِلَى بَنِي قُرَيْظَةَ، فَأَتَاهُمْ رَسُولُ اللَّهِ صلى الله عليه وسلم فَنَزَلُوا عَلَى حُكْمِهِ، فَرَدَّ الْحُكْمَ إِلَى سَعْدٍ، قَالَ فَإِنِّي أَحْكُمُ فِيهِمْ أَنْ تُقْتَلَ الْمُقَاتِلَةُ، وَأَنْ تُسْبَى النِّسَاءُ وَالذُّرِّيَّةُ، وَأَنْ تُقْسَمَ أَمْوَالُهُمْ. قَالَ هِشَامٌ فَأَخْبَرَنِي أَبِي عَنْ عَائِشَةَ أَنَّ سَعْدًا قَالَ اللَّهُمَّ إِنَّكَ تَعْلَمُ أَنَّهُ لَيْسَ أَحَدٌ أَحَبَّ إِلَىَّ أَنْ أُجَاهِدَهُمْ فِيكَ مِنْ قَوْمٍ كَذَّبُوا رَسُولَكَ صلى الله عليه وسلم وَأَخْرَجُوهُ، اللَّهُمَّ فَإِنِّي أَظُنُّ أَنَّكَ قَدْ وَضَعْتَ الْحَرْبَ بَيْنَنَا وَبَيْنَهُمْ، فَإِنْ كَانَ بَقِيَ مِنْ حَرْبِ قُرَيْشٍ شَىْءٌ، فَأَبْقِنِي لَهُ حَتَّى أُجَاهِدَهُمْ فِيكَ، وَإِنْ كُنْتَ وَضَعْتَ الْحَرْبَ فَافْجُرْهَا، وَاجْعَلْ مَوْتَتِي فِيهَا. فَانْفَجَرَتْ مِنْ لَبَّتِهِ، فَلَمْ يَرُعْهُمْ وَفِي الْمَسْجِدِ خَيْمَةٌ مِنْ بَنِي غِفَارٍ إِلاَّ الدَّمُ يَسِيلُ إِلَيْهِمْ فَقَالُوا يَا أَهْلَ الْخَيْمَةِ مَا هَذَا الَّذِي يَأْتِينَا مِنْ قِبَلِكُمْ فَإِذَا سَعْدٌ يَغْذُو جُرْحُهُ دَمًا، فَمَاتَ مِنْهَا رضى الله عنه.

Narrated Abu Dhar Al-Ghifar: We were with the Prophetﷺ on a journey and the Mu'adh-dhin (call maker for the prayer) wanted to pronounce the Adhan (call) for the Zuhr prayer. The Prophetﷺ said, 'Let it become cooler." He again (after a while) wanted to pronounce the Adhan but the Prophetﷺ said to him, "Let it become cooler till we see the shadows of hillocks." The Prophetﷺ added, "The severity of heat is from the raging of the Hell-fire, and in very hot weather pray (Zuhr) when it becomes cooler.". – Sahih Al-Bukhari 539

حَدَّثَنَا آدَمُ بْنُ أَبِي إِيَاسٍ، قَالَ حَدَّثَنَا شُعْبَةُ، قَالَ حَدَّثَنَا مُهَاجِرٌ أَبُو الْحَسَنِ، مَوْلًى لِبَنِي تَيْمِ اللَّهِ قَالَ سَمِعْتُ زَيْدَ بْنَ وَهْبٍ، عَنْ أَبِي ذَرٍّ الْغِفَارِيِّ، قَالَ كُنَّا مَعَ النَّبِيِّ صلى الله عليه وسلم فِي سَفَرٍ، فَأَرَادَ الْمُؤَذِّنُ أَنْ يُؤَذِّنَ لِلظُّهْرِ فَقَالَ النَّبِيُّ صلى الله عليه وسلم " أَبْرِدْ ". ثُمَّ أَرَادَ أَنْ يُؤَذِّنَ فَقَالَ لَهُ " أَبْرِدْ ". حَتَّى رَأَيْنَا فَىْءَ التُّلُولِ، فَقَالَ النَّبِيُّ صلى الله عليه وسلم " إِنَّ شِدَّةَ الْحَرِّ مِنْ فَيْحِ جَهَنَّمَ، فَإِذَا اشْتَدَّ الْحَرُّ فَأَبْرِدُوا بِالصَّلاَةِ ". وَقَالَ ابْنُ عَبَّاسٍ تَتَفَيَّأُ تَتَمَيَّلُ.

Narrated Hisham's father: When Allah's Messengerﷺ set out (towards Mecca) during the year of the Conquest (of Mecca) and this news reached (the infidels of Quraish), Abu Sufyan, Hakim bin Hizam and Budail bin Warqa came out to gather information about Allah's Messengerﷺ, They proceeded on their way till they reached a place called Marr-az-Zahran (which is near Mecca). Behold! There they saw many fires as if they were the fires of `Arafat. Abu Sufyan said, "What is this? It looked like the fires of `Arafat." Budail bin Warqa' said, "Banu `Amr are less in number than that." Some of the guards of Allah's Messenger ﷺ saw them and took them over, caught them and brought them to Allah's Messenger ﷺ. Abu Sufyan embraced Islam. When the Prophet ﷺ proceeded, he said to Al-Abbas, "Keep Abu Sufyan standing at the top of the mountain so that he would look at the Muslims. So Al-`Abbas kept him standing (at that place) and the tribes with the Prophet ﷺ started passing in front of Abu Sufyan in military batches. A batch passed and Abu Sufyan said, "O `Abbas Who are these?" `Abbas said, "They are (Banu) Ghifar." Abu Sufyan said, I have got nothing to do with Ghifar." Then (a batch of the tribe of) Juhaina passed by and he said similarly as above. Then (a batch of the tribe of) Sa`d bin Huzaim passed by and he said similarly as above. Then (Banu) Sulaim passed by and he said similarly as above. Then came a batch, the like of which Abu Sufyan had not seen. He said, "Who are these?" `Abbas said, "They are the Ansar headed by Sa`d bin Ubada, the one holding the flag." Sa`d bin Ubada said, "O Abu Sufyan! Today is the day of a great battle and today (what is prohibited in) the Ka`ba will be permissible." Abu Sufyan said., "O `Abbas! How excellent the day of destruction is! "Then came another batch (of warriors) which was the smallest of all the batches, and in it there was Allah's Messenger ﷺ and his companions and the flag of the Prophet ﷺ was carried by Az-Zubair bin Al Awwam. When Allah's Messenger ﷺ passed by Abu Sufyan, the latter said, (to the Prophet), "Do you know what Sa`d bin 'Ubada said?" The Prophet ﷺ said, "What did he say?" Abu Sufyan said, "He said so-and-so." The Prophet ﷺ said, "Sa`d told a lie, but today Allah will give superiority to the Ka`ba and today the Ka`ba will be covered with a (cloth) covering." Allah's Messenger ﷺ ordered that his flag be fixed at Al-Hajun. Narrated `Urwa: Nafi` bin Jubair bin Mut`im said, "I heard Al-Abbas saying to Az-Zubair bin Al- `Awwam, 'O Abu `Abdullah! Did Allah's Messenger ﷺ order you to fix the flag here?' " Allah's Messenger ﷺ ordered Khalid bin Al-Walid to enter Mecca from its upper part from Ka'da while the Prophet ﷺ himself entered from Kuda. Two men from the cavalry of Khalid bin Al-Wahd named Hubaish bin Al-Ash'ar and Kurz bin Jabir Al-Fihri were martyred on that day. – Sahih Al-Bukhari 4280

حَدَّثَنَا عُبَيْدُ بْنُ إِسْمَاعِيلَ، حَدَّثَنَا أَبُو أُسَامَةَ، عَنْ هِشَامٍ، عَنْ أَبِيهِ، قَالَ لَمَّا سَارَ رَسُولُ اللَّهِ صلى الله عليه وسلم عَامَ الْفَتْحِ فَبَلَغَ ذَلِكَ قُرَيْشًا، خَرَجَ أَبُو سُفْيَانَ بْنُ حَرْبٍ وَحَكِيمُ بْنُ حِزَامٍ وَبُدَيْلُ بْنُ وَرْقَاءَ يَلْتَمِسُونَ الْخَبَرَ عَنْ رَسُولِ اللَّهِ صلى الله عليه وسلم فَأَقْبَلُوا يَسِيرُونَ حَتَّى أَتَوْا مَرَّ الظَّهْرَانِ، فَإِذَا هُمْ بِنِيرَانٍ كَأَنَّهَا نِيرَانُ عَرَفَةَ، فَقَالَ أَبُو سُفْيَانَ مَا هَذِهِ لَكَأَنَّهَا نِيرَانُ عَرَفَةَ. فَقَالَ بُدَيْلُ بْنُ وَرْقَاءَ نِيرَانُ بَنِي عَمْرٍو. فَقَالَ أَبُو سُفْيَانَ عَمْرٌو أَقَلُّ مِنْ ذَلِكَ. فَرَآهُمْ نَاسٌ مِنْ حَرَسِ رَسُولِ اللَّهِ صلى الله عليه وسلم فَأَدْرَكُوهُمْ فَأَخَذُوهُمْ، فَأَتَوْا بِهِمْ رَسُولَ اللَّهِ صلى الله عليه وسلم فَأَسْلَمَ أَبُو سُفْيَانَ، فَلَمَّا سَارَ قَالَ لِلْعَبَّاسِ " احْبِسْ أَبَا سُفْيَانَ عِنْدَ حَطْمِ الْخَيْلِ حَتَّى يَنْظُرَ إِلَى الْمُسْلِمِينَ ". فَحَبَسَهُ الْعَبَّاسُ، فَجَعَلَتِ الْقَبَائِلُ تَمُرُّ مَعَ النَّبِيِّ صلى الله عليه وسلم تَمُرُّ كَتِيبَةً كَتِيبَةً عَلَى أَبِي سُفْيَانَ، فَمَرَّتْ كَتِيبَةٌ قَالَ يَا عَبَّاسُ مَنْ هَذِهِ قَالَ هَذِهِ غِفَارُ. قَالَ مَا لِي وَلِغِفَارَ ثُمَّ مَرَّتْ جُهَيْنَةُ، قَالَ مِثْلَ ذَلِكَ، ثُمَّ مَرَّتْ سَعْدُ بْنُ هُذَيْمٍ، فَقَالَ مِثْلَ ذَلِكَ، وَمَرَّتْ سُلَيْمُ، فَقَالَ مِثْلَ ذَلِكَ، حَتَّى أَقْبَلَتْ كَتِيبَةٌ لَمْ يَرَ مِثْلَهَا، قَالَ مَنْ هَذِهِ قَالَ هَؤُلاَءِ الأَنْصَارُ عَلَيْهِمْ سَعْدُ بْنُ عُبَادَةَ مَعَهُ الرَّايَةُ. فَقَالَ سَعْدُ بْنُ عُبَادَةَ يَا أَبَا سُفْيَانَ الْيَوْمُ يَوْمُ الْمَلْحَمَةِ، الْيَوْمَ تُسْتَحَلُّ الْكَعْبَةُ. فَقَالَ أَبُو سُفْيَانَ يَا عَبَّاسُ حَبَّذَا يَوْمُ الذِّمَارِ. ثُمَّ جَاءَتْ كَتِيبَةٌ، وَهْىَ أَقَلُّ الْكَتَائِبِ، فِيهِمْ رَسُولُ اللَّهِ صلى الله عليه وسلم وَأَصْحَابُهُ، وَرَايَةُ النَّبِيِّ صلى الله عليه وسلم مَعَ الزُّبَيْرِ بْنِ الْعَوَّامِ، فَلَمَّا مَرَّ رَسُولُ اللَّهِ صلى الله عليه وسلم بِأَبِي سُفْيَانَ قَالَ أَلَمْ تَعْلَمْ مَا قَالَ سَعْدُ بْنُ عُبَادَةَ قَالَ " مَا قَالَ ". قَالَ كَذَا وَكَذَا. فَقَالَ " كَذَبَ سَعْدٌ، وَلَكِنْ هَذَا يَوْمٌ يُعَظِّمُ اللَّهُ فِيهِ الْكَعْبَةَ، وَيَوْمٌ تُكْسَى فِيهِ الْكَعْبَةُ ". قَالَ وَأَمَرَ رَسُولُ اللَّهِ صلى الله عليه وسلم أَنْ تُرْكَزَ رَايَتُهُ بِالْحَجُونِ. قَالَ عُرْوَةُ وَأَخْبَرَنِي نَافِعُ بْنُ جُبَيْرِ بْنِ مُطْعِمٍ قَالَ سَمِعْتُ الْعَبَّاسَ يَقُولُ لِلزُّبَيْرِ بْنِ الْعَوَّامِ يَا أَبَا عَبْدِ اللَّهِ، هَا هُنَا أَمَرَكَ رَسُولُ اللَّهِ صلى الله عليه وسلم أَنْ تَرْكُزَ الرَّايَةَ، قَالَ وَأَمَرَ رَسُولُ اللَّهِ صلى الله عليه وسلم يَوْمَئِذٍ خَالِدَ بْنَ الْوَلِيدِ أَنْ يَدْخُلَ مِنْ أَعْلَى مَكَّةَ مِنْ كَدَاءٍ، وَدَخَلَ النَّبِيُّ صلى الله عليه وسلم مِنْ كُدَا، فَقُتِلَ مِنْ خَيْلِ خَالِدٍ يَوْمَئِذٍ رَجُلاَنِ حُبَيْشُ بْنُ الأَشْعَرِ وَكُرْزُ بْنُ جَابِرٍ الْفِهْرِيُّ

Narrated Abu Huraira;: Whenever the Prophet ﷺ lifted his head from the bowing in the last rak`a he used to say: "O Allah! Save `Aiyash bin Abi Rabi`a. O Allah! Save Salama bin Hisham.

O Allah! Save Walid bin Walid. O Allah! Save the weak faithful believers. O Allah! Be hard on the tribes of Mudar and send (famine) years on them like the famine years of (Prophet) Joseph ." The Prophet ﷺ further said, "Allah forgive the tribes of Ghifar and save the tribes of Aslam." Abu Az-Zinad (a sub-narrator) said, "The Qunut used to be recited by the Prophet ﷺ in the Fajr prayer.". – Sahih Al-Bukhari 1006

حَدَّثَنَا قُتَيْبَةُ، حَدَّثَنَا مُغِيرَةُ بْنُ عَبْدِ الرَّحْمَنِ، عَنْ أَبِي الزِّنَادِ، عَنِ الأَعْرَجِ، عَنْ أَبِي هُرَيْرَةَ، أَنَّ النَّبِيَّ صلى الله عليه وسلم كَانَ إِذَا رَفَعَ رَأْسَهُ مِنَ الرَّكْعَةِ الآخِرَةِ يَقُولُ " اللَّهُمَّ أَنْجِ عَيَّاشَ بْنَ أَبِي رَبِيعَةَ، اللَّهُمَّ أَنْجِ سَلَمَةَ بْنَ هِشَامٍ، اللَّهُمَّ أَنْجِ الْوَلِيدَ بْنَ الْوَلِيدِ، اللَّهُمَّ أَنْجِ الْمُسْتَضْعَفِينَ مِنَ الْمُؤْمِنِينَ، اللَّهُمَّ اشْدُدْ وَطْأَتَكَ عَلَى مُضَرَ، اللَّهُمَّ اجْعَلْهَا سِنِينَ كَسِنِي يُوسُفَ ". وَأَنَّ النَّبِيَّ صلى الله عليه وسلم قَالَ " غِفَارُ غَفَرَ اللَّهُ لَهَا، وَأَسْلَمُ سَالَمَهَا اللَّهُ ". قَالَ ابْنُ أَبِي الزِّنَادِ عَنْ أَبِيهِ هَذَا كُلُّهُ فِي الصُّبْحِ

Narrated Abu Hurairah (ra): The Prophet ﷺ said, (The people of) Aslam, Ghifar and some people of Muzaina and Juhaina or said (some people of Juhaina or Muzaina) are better with Allah or said (on the Day of resurrection) than the tribe of Asad, Tamim, Hawazin and Ghatafan. – Sahih Al-Bukhari 3523

حَدَّثَنَا سُلَيْمَانُ بْنُ حَرْبٍ، حَدَّثَنَا حَمَّادٌ، عَنْ أَيُّوبَ، عَنْ مُحَمَّدٍ، عَنْ أَبِي هُرَيْرَةَ ـ رضى الله عنه ـ قَالَ قَالَ أَسْلَمُ وَغِفَارُ وَشَىْءٌ مِنْ مُزَيْنَةَ وَجُهَيْنَةَ ـ أَوْ قَالَ شَىْءٌ مِنْ جُهَيْنَةَ أَوْ مُزَيْنَةَ ـ خَيْرٌ عِنْدَ اللَّهِ ـ أَوْ قَالَ ـ يَوْمَ الْقِيَامَةِ مِنْ أَسَدٍ وَتَمِيمٍ وَهَوَازِنَ وَغَطَفَانَ

Coalition of Ghatafan
ائتلاف غطفان

Narrated Anas: That the Prophet ﷺ sent his uncle, the brother of Um Sulaim at the head of seventy riders. The chief of the pagans, 'Amir bin at-Tufail proposed three suggestions (to the Prophet ﷺ) saying, "Choose one of three alternatives: (1) that the bedouins will be under your command and the townspeople will be under my command; (2) or that I will be your successor, (3) or otherwise I will attack you with two thousand from Bani Ghatafan." But 'Amir was infected with plague in the House of Um so-and-so. He said, "Shall I stay in the house of a lady from the family of so-and-so after having a (swelled) gland like that she-camel? Get me my horse." So he died on the back of his horse. Then Haram, the brother of Um Sulaim and a lame man along with another man from so-and-so (tribe) went towards the pagans (i.e. the tribe of 'Amir). Haram said (to his companions), "Stay near to me, for I will go to them. If they (i.e. infidels) should give me protection, you will be near to me, and if they should kill me, then you should go back to your companions. Then Haram went to them and said, "Will you give me protection so as to convey the message of Allah's Messenger "?ﷺ So, he started talking to them' but they signalled to a man (to kill him) and he went behind him and stabbed him (with a spear). He (i.e. Haram) said, "Allahu Akbar! I have succeeded, by the Lord of the Ka`ba!" The companion of Haram was pursued by the infidels, and then they (i.e. Haram's companions) were all killed except the lame man who was at the top of a mountain. Then Allah revealed to us a verse that was among the cancelled ones later on. It was: 'We have met our Lord and He is pleased with us and has made us pleased.' (After this event) the Prophet ﷺ invoked evil on the infidels every morning for 30 days. He invoked evil upon the (tribes of) Ril, Dhakwan, Bani Lihyan and Usaiya who disobeyed Allah and His Apostle. – Sahih Al-Bukhari 4091

حَدَّثَنَا مُوسَى بْنُ إِسْمَاعِيلَ، حَدَّثَنَا هَمَّامٌ، عَنْ إِسْحَاقَ بْنِ عَبْدِ اللَّهِ بْنِ أَبِي طَلْحَةَ، قَالَ حَدَّثَنِي أَنَسٌ، أَنَّ النَّبِيَّ صلى الله عليه وسلم بَعَثَ خَالَهُ أَخٌ لأُمِّ سُلَيْمٍ فِي سَبْعِينَ رَاكِبًا، وَكَانَ رَئِيسَ الْمُشْرِكِينَ عَامِرُ بْنُ الطُّفَيْلِ خَيَّرَ بَيْنَ ثَلاَثِ خِصَالٍ فَقَالَ يَكُونُ لَكَ أَهْلُ السَّهْلِ، وَلِي أَهْلُ الْمَدَرِ، أَوْ أَكُونُ خَلِيفَتَكَ، أَوْ أَغْزُوكَ بِأَهْلِ غَطَفَانَ بِأَلْفٍ وَأَلْفٍ، فَطُعِنَ عَامِرٌ فِي بَيْتِ أُمِّ فُلاَنٍ فَقَالَ غُدَّةٌ كَغُدَّةِ الْبَكْرِ فِي بَيْتِ امْرَأَةٍ مِنْ آلِ فُلاَنٍ ائْتُونِي بِفَرَسِي. فَمَاتَ عَلَى ظَهْرِ فَرَسِهِ، فَانْطَلَقَ حَرَامٌ أَخُو أُمِّ سُلَيْمٍ هُوَ {وَ} رَجُلٌ أَعْرَجُ وَرَجُلٌ مِنْ بَنِي فُلاَنٍ قَالَ كُونَا قَرِيبًا حَتَّى آتِيَهُمْ، فَإِنْ آمَنُونِي كُنْتُمْ، وَإِنْ قَتَلُونِي أَتَيْتُمْ أَصْحَابَكُمْ. فَقَالَ

أَتُؤْمِنُونِي أُبَلِّغْ رِسَالَةَ رَسُولِ اللَّهِ صلى الله عليه وسلم. فَجَعَلَ يُحَدِّثُهُمْ وَأَوْمَئُوا إِلَى رَجُلٍ، فَأَتَاهُ مِنْ خَلْفِهِ فَطَعَنَهُ ـ قَالَ هَمَّامٌ أَحْسِبُهُ حَتَّى أَنْفَذَهُ ـ بِالرُّمْحِ، قَالَ اللَّهُ أَكْبَرُ فُزْتُ وَرَبِّ الْكَعْبَةِ. فَلُحِقَ الرَّجُلُ، فَقُتِلُوا كُلُّهُمْ غَيْرَ الأَعْرَجِ كَانَ فِي رَأْسِ جَبَلٍ، فَأَنْزَلَ اللَّهُ عَلَيْنَا، ثُمَّ كَانَ مِنَ الْمَنْسُوخِ إِنَّا قَدْ لَقِينَا رَبَّنَا فَرَضِيَ عَنَّا وَأَرْضَانَا. فَدَعَا النَّبِيُّ صلى الله عليه وسلم عَلَيْهِمْ ثَلاَثِينَ صَبَاحًا، عَلَى رِعْلٍ وَذَكْوَانَ وَبَنِي لَحْيَانَ وَعُصَيَّةَ، الَّذِينَ عَصَوُا اللَّهَ وَرَسُولَهُ صلى الله عليه وسلم.

Narrated Anas Bin Malik: When it was the day (of the battle) of Hunain, the tributes of Hawazin and Ghatafan and others, along with their animals and offspring (and wives) came to fight against the Prophet ﷺ The Prophet ﷺ had with him, ten thousand men and some of the Tulaqa. The companions fled, leaving the Prophet ﷺ alone. The Prophet then made two calls which were clearly distinguished from each other. He turned right and said, "O the group of Ansar!" They said, "Labbaik, O Allah's Messenger ﷺ! Rejoice, for we are with you!" Then he turned left and said, "O the group of Ansar!" They said, "Labbaik! O Allah's Messenger ﷺ! Rejoice, for we are with you!" The Prophet ﷺ at that time, was riding on a white mule; then he dismounted and said, "I am Allah's Slave and His Apostle." The infidels then were defeated, and on that day the Prophet ﷺ gained a large amount of booty which he distributed amongst the Muhajirin and the Tulaqa and did not give anything to the Ansar. The Ansar said, "When there is a difficulty, we are called, but the booty is given to other than us." The news reached the Prophet ﷺ and he gathered them in a leather tent and said, "What is this news reaching me from you, O the group of Ansar?" They kept silent, He added," O the group of Ansar! Won't you be happy that the people take the worldly things and you take Allah's Messenger ﷺ to your homes reserving him for yourself?" They said, "Yes." Then the Prophet said, "If the people took their way through a valley, and the Ansar took their way through a mountain pass, surely, I would take the Ansar's mountain pass." Hisham said, "O Abu Hamza (i.e. Anas)! Did you witness that? " He replied, "And how could I be absent from him?". – Sahih Al-Bukhari 4337

حَدَّثَنَا مُحَمَّدُ بْنُ بَشَّارٍ، حَدَّثَنَا مُعَاذُ بْنُ مُعَاذٍ، حَدَّثَنَا ابْنُ عَوْنٍ، عَنْ هِشَامِ بْنِ زَيْدِ بْنِ أَنَسِ بْنِ مَالِكٍ، عَنْ أَنَسِ بْنِ مَالِكٍ ـ رضى الله عنه ـ قَالَ لَمَّا كَانَ يَوْمُ حُنَيْنٍ أَقْبَلَتْ هَوَازِنُ وَغَطَفَانُ وَغَيْرُهُمْ بِنَعَمِهِمْ وَذَرَارِيِّهِمْ، وَمَعَ النَّبِيِّ صلى الله عليه وسلم عَشَرَةُ آلاَفٍ وَمِنَ الطُّلَقَاءِ، فَأَدْبَرُوا عَنْهُ حَتَّى بَقِيَ وَحْدَهُ، فَنَادَى يَوْمَئِذٍ نِدَاءَيْنِ لَمْ يَخْلِطْ بَيْنَهُمَا، الْتَفَتَ عَنْ يَمِينِهِ، فَقَالَ " يَا مَعْشَرَ الأَنْصَارِ ". قَالُوا لَبَّيْكَ يَا رَسُولَ اللَّهِ، أَبْشِرْ نَحْنُ مَعَكَ. ثُمَّ الْتَفَتَ عَنْ يَسَارِهِ، فَقَالَ " يَا مَعْشَرَ الأَنْصَارِ ". قَالُوا لَبَّيْكَ يَا رَسُولَ اللَّهِ، أَبْشِرْ نَحْنُ مَعَكَ. وَهْوَ عَلَى بَغْلَةٍ بَيْضَاءَ، فَنَزَلَ فَقَالَ " أَنَا عَبْدُ اللَّهِ وَرَسُولُهُ "، فَانْهَزَمَ الْمُشْرِكُونَ، فَأَصَابَ يَوْمَئِذٍ غَنَائِمَ كَثِيرَةً، فَقَسَمَ فِي الْمُهَاجِرِينَ وَالطُّلَقَاءِ وَلَمْ يُعْطِ الأَنْصَارَ شَيْئًا، فَقَالَتِ الأَنْصَارُ إِذَا كَانَتْ شَدِيدَةٌ فَنَحْنُ نُدْعَى، وَيُعْطَى الْغَنِيمَةَ غَيْرُنَا. فَبَلَغَهُ ذَلِكَ، فَجَمَعَهُمْ فِي قُبَّةٍ، فَقَالَ " يَا مَعْشَرَ الأَنْصَارِ مَا حَدِيثٌ بَلَغَنِي عَنْكُمْ ". فَسَكَتُوا فَقَالَ " يَا مَعْشَرَ الأَنْصَارِ أَلاَ تَرْضَوْنَ أَنْ يَذْهَبَ النَّاسُ بِالدُّنْيَا، وَتَذْهَبُونَ بِرَسُولِ اللَّهِ صلى الله عليه وسلم تَحُوزُونَهُ إِلَى بُيُوتِكُمْ ". قَالُوا بَلَى. فَقَالَ رَسُولُ اللَّهِ صلى الله عليه وسلم " لَوْ سَلَكَ النَّاسُ وَادِيًا، وَسَلَكَتِ الأَنْصَارُ شِعْبًا لأَخَذْتُ شِعْبَ الأَنْصَارِ ". فَقَالَ هِشَامٌ يَا أَبَا حَمْزَةَ، وَأَنْتَ شَاهِدٌ ذَاكَ قَالَ وَأَيْنَ أَغِيبُ عَنْهُ

Narrated Salama bin Al-Akwa`: Once I went (from Medina) towards (Al-Ghaba) before the first Adhan of the Fajr Prayer. The shecamels of Allah's Messenger ﷺ used to graze at a place called Dhi-Qarad. A slave of `Abdur-Rahman bin `Auf met me (on the way) and said, "The she-camels of Allah's Messenger ﷺ had been taken away by force." I asked, "Who had taken them?" He replied "(The people of) Ghatafan." I made three loud cries (to the people of Medina) saying, "O Sabahah!" I made the people between the two mountains of Medina hear me. Then I rushed onward and caught up with the robbers while they were watering the camels. I started throwing arrows at them as I was a good archer and I was saying, "I am the son of Al-Akwa`, and today will perish the wicked people." I kept on saying like that till I restored the shecamels (of the Prophet), I also snatched thirty Burda (i.e. garments) from them. Then the Prophet ﷺ and the other people came there, and I said, "O Allah's Prophet! I have stopped the people (of Ghatafan) from taking water and they are thirsty now. So send (some people) after them now." On that the Prophet said, "O the son of Al-Akwa`! You have over-powered them, so forgive them." Then we all came back and Allah's Messenger ﷺ seated me behind him on his she-camel till we entered Medina. – Sahih Al-Bukhari 4194

حَدَّثَنَا قُتَيْبَةُ بْنُ سَعِيدٍ، حَدَّثَنَا حَاتِمٌ، عَنْ يَزِيدَ بْنِ أَبِي عُبَيْدٍ، قَالَ سَمِعْتُ سَلَمَةَ بْنَ الأَكْوَعِ، يَقُولُ خَرَجْتُ قَبْلَ أَنْ يُؤَذَّنَ، بِالأُولَى، وَكَانَتْ لِقَاحُ رَسُولِ اللَّهِ صلى الله عليه وسلم تَرْعَى بِذِي قَرَدٍ ـ قَالَ ـ فَلَقِيَنِي غُلاَمٌ لِعَبْدِ الرَّحْمَنِ بْنِ عَوْفٍ فَقَالَ أُخِذَتْ لِقَاحُ رَسُولِ اللَّهِ صلى الله عليه وسلم قُلْتُ مَنْ أَخَذَهَا قَالَ غَطَفَانُ. قَالَ فَصَرَخْتُ ثَلاَثَ صَرَخَاتٍ ـ يَا صَبَاحَاهْ ـ قَالَ فَأَسْمَعْتُ مَا بَيْنَ لاَبَتَىِ الْمَدِينَةِ، ثُمَّ انْدَفَعْتُ عَلَى وَجْهِي حَتَّى أَدْرَكْتُهُمْ وَقَدْ أَخَذُوا يَسْتَقُونَ مِنَ الْمَاءِ، فَجَعَلْتُ أَرْمِيهِمْ بِنَبْلِي، وَكُنْتُ رَامِيًا، وَأَقُولُ أَنَا ابْنُ الأَكْوَعِ، الْيَوْمُ يَوْمُ الرُّضَّعْ. وَأَرْتَجِزُ حَتَّى اسْتَنْقَذْتُ اللِّقَاحَ مِنْهُمْ، وَاسْتَلَبْتُ مِنْهُمْ ثَلاَثِينَ بُرْدَةً، قَالَ وَجَاءَ النَّبِيُّ صلى الله عليه وسلم وَالنَّاسُ فَقُلْتُ يَا نَبِيَّ اللَّهِ قَدْ حَمَيْتُ الْقَوْمَ الْمَاءَ وَهُمْ عِطَاشٌ، فَابْعَثْ إِلَيْهِمُ السَّاعَةَ. فَقَالَ " يَا ابْنَ الأَكْوَعِ، مَلَكْتَ فَأَسْجِحْ ". قَالَ ثُمَّ رَجَعْنَا وَيُرْدِفُنِي رَسُولُ اللَّهِ صلى الله عليه وسلم عَلَى نَاقَتِهِ حَتَّى دَخَلْنَا الْمَدِينَةَ

Jabir added: "The Prophet ﷺ set out for the battle of Dhat-ur-Riqa' at a place called Nakhl and he met a group of people from Ghatafan, but there was no clash (between them); the people were afraid of each other and the Prophet ﷺ offered the two raka'at of the Fear prayer." Narrated Salama: "I fought in the company of the Prophet ﷺ on the day of al-Qarad.". – Sahih Al-Bukhari 4127

وَقَالَ ابْنُ إِسْحَاقَ سَمِعْتُ وَهْبَ بْنَ كَيْسَانَ، سَمِعْتُ جَابِرًا، خَرَجَ النَّبِيُّ صلى الله عليه وسلم إِلَى ذَاتِ الرِّقَاعِ مِنْ نَخْلٍ فَلَقِيَ جَمْعًا مِنْ غَطَفَانَ، فَلَمْ يَكُنْ قِتَالٌ، وَأَخَافَ النَّاسُ بَعْضُهُمْ بَعْضًا فَصَلَّى النَّبِيُّ صلى الله عليه وسلم رَكْعَتَىِ الْخَوْفِ. وَقَالَ يَزِيدُ عَنْ سَلَمَةَ غَزَوْتُ مَعَ النَّبِيِّ صلى الله عليه وسلم يَوْمَ الْقَرَدِ.

Banū Khuzāʿah
بنو خزاعة

Narrated `Abdullah bin `Umar: Allah's Messenger ﷺ said. "While I was sleeping, I saw myself (in a dream) performing Tawaf around the Ka`ba. Behold, I saw a reddish-white man with lank hair, and water was dropping from his head. I asked, "Who is this?' They replied, 'The son of Mary.' Then I turned my face to see another man with a huge body, red complexion and curly hair and blind in one eye. His eye looked like a protruding out grape. They said (to me), He is Ad-Dajjal." The Prophet ﷺ added, "The man he resembled most is Ibn Qatan, a man from the tribe of Khuza`a. ". – Sahih Al-Bukhari 7128

حَدَّثَنَا يَحْيَى بْنُ بُكَيْرٍ، حَدَّثَنَا اللَّيْثُ، عَنْ عُقَيْلٍ، عَنِ ابْنِ شِهَابٍ، عَنْ سَالِمٍ، عَنْ عَبْدِ اللَّهِ بْنِ عُمَرَ، أَنَّ رَسُولَ اللَّهِ صلى الله عليه وسلم قَالَ " بَيْنَا أَنَا نَائِمٌ أَطُوفُ بِالْكَعْبَةِ، فَإِذَا رَجُلٌ آدَمُ سَبْطُ الشَّعَرِ يَنْطُفُ ـ أَوْ يُهَرَاقُ ـ رَأْسُهُ مَاءً قُلْتُ مَنْ هَذَا قَالُوا ابْنُ مَرْيَمَ. ثُمَّ ذَهَبْتُ أَلْتَفِتُ، فَإِذَا رَجُلٌ جَسِيمٌ أَحْمَرُ جَعْدُ الرَّأْسِ أَعْوَرُ الْعَيْنِ، كَأَنَّ عَيْنَهُ عِنَبَةٌ طَافِيَةٌ قَالُوا هَذَا الدَّجَّالُ. أَقْرَبُ النَّاسِ بِهِ شَبَهًا ابْنُ قَطَنٍ ". رَجُلٌ مِنْ خُزَاعَةَ

Narrated Abu Huraira: In the year of the Conquest of Mecca, the tribe of Khuza`a killed a man from the tribe of Bani Laith in revenge for a killed person, belonging to them. They informed the Prophet ﷺ about it. So he rode his Rahila (she-camel for riding) and addressed the people saying, "Allah held back the killing from Mecca. (The sub-narrator is in doubt whether the Prophet ﷺ said "elephant or killing," as the Arabic words standing for these words have great similarity in shape), but He (Allah) let His Apostle and the believers over power the infidels of Mecca. Beware! (Mecca is a sanctuary) Verily! Fighting in Mecca was not permitted for anyone before me nor will it be permitted for anyone after me. It (war) in it was made legal for me for few hours or so on that day. No doubt it is at this moment a sanctuary, it is not allowed to uproot its thorny shrubs or to uproot its trees or to pick up its Luqat (fallen things) except by a person who will look for its owner (announce it publicly). And if somebody is killed, then his closest relative has the right to choose one of the two—the blood money

(Diyya) or retaliation having the killer killed. In the meantime a man from Yemen came and said, "O Allah's Messenger ﷺ! Get that written for me." The Prophet ﷺ ordered his companions to write that for him. Then a man from Quraish said, "Except Al-Idhkhir (a type of grass that has good smell) O Allah's Messenger ﷺ, as we use it in our houses and graves." The Prophet ﷺ said, "Except Al-Idhkhir i.e. Al-Idhkhir is allowed to be plucked.". – Sahih Al-Bukhari 112

حَدَّثَنَا أَبُو نُعَيْمٍ الْفَضْلُ بْنُ دُكَيْنٍ، قَالَ حَدَّثَنَا شَيْبَانُ، عَنْ يَحْيَى، عَنْ أَبِي سَلَمَةَ، عَنْ أَبِي هُرَيْرَةَ، أَنَّ خُزَاعَةَ، قَتَلُوا رَجُلاً مِنْ بَنِي لَيْثٍ عَامَ فَتْحِ مَكَّةَ بِقَتِيلٍ مِنْهُمْ قَتَلُوهُ، فَأُخْبِرَ بِذَلِكَ النَّبِيُّ صلى الله عليه وسلم فَرَكِبَ رَاحِلَتَهُ، فَخَطَبَ فَقَالَ " إِنَّ اللَّهَ حَبَسَ عَنْ مَكَّةَ الْقَتْلَ ـ أَوِ الْفِيلَ شَكَّ أَبُو عَبْدِ اللَّهِ ـ وَسَلَّطَ عَلَيْهِمْ رَسُولَ اللَّهِ صلى الله عليه وسلم وَالْمُؤْمِنِينَ، أَلاَ وَإِنَّهَا لَمْ تَحِلَّ لأَحَدٍ قَبْلِي، وَلاَ تَحِلُّ لأَحَدٍ بَعْدِي أَلاَ وَإِنَّهَا حَلَّتْ لِي سَاعَةً مِنْ نَهَارٍ، أَلاَ وَإِنَّهَا سَاعَتِي هَذِهِ حَرَامٌ، لاَ يُخْتَلَى شَوْكُهَا، وَلاَ يُعْضَدُ شَجَرُهَا، وَلاَ تُلْتَقَطُ سَاقِطَتُهَا إِلاَّ لِمُنْشِدٍ، فَمَنْ قُتِلَ فَهُوَ بِخَيْرِ النَّظَرَيْنِ إِمَّا أَنْ يُعْقَلَ، وَإِمَّا أَنْ يُقَادَ أَهْلُ الْقَتِيلِ ". فَجَاءَ رَجُلٌ مِنْ أَهْلِ الْيَمَنِ فَقَالَ اكْتُبْ لِي يَا رَسُولَ اللَّهِ. فَقَالَ " اكْتُبُوا لأَبِي فُلاَنٍ ". فَقَالَ رَجُلٌ مِنْ قُرَيْشٍ إِلاَّ الإِذْخِرَ يَا رَسُولَ اللَّهِ، فَإِنَّا نَجْعَلُهُ فِي بُيُوتِنَا وَقُبُورِنَا. فَقَالَ النَّبِيُّ صلى الله عليه وسلم " إِلاَّ الإِذْخِرَ، إِلاَّ الإِذْخِرَ ". قَالَ أَبُو عَبْدِ اللَّهِ يُقَالُ يُقَادُ بِالْقَافِ. فَقِيلَ لأَبِي عَبْدِ اللَّهِ أَىُّ شَىْءٍ كَتَبَ لَهُ قَالَ كَتَبَ لَهُ هَذِهِ الْخُطْبَةَ

Narrated Sa`id bin Al-Musaiyab: Bahira is a she-camel whose milk is kept for the idols and nobody is allowed to milk it; Sa'iba was the she-camel which they used to set free for their gods and nothing was allowed to be carried on it. Abu Huraira said: Allah's Messenger ﷺ said, "I saw `Amr bin 'Amir Al-Khuza`I (in a dream) dragging his intestines in the Fire, and he was the first person to establish the tradition of setting free the animals (for the sake of their deities)," Wasila is the she-camel which gives birth to a she-camel as its first delivery, and then gives birth to another she-camel as its second delivery. People (in the Pre-Islamic periods of ignorance) used to let that she camel loose for their idols if it gave birth to two she-camels successively without giving birth to a male camel in between. 'Ham' was the male camel which was used for copulation. When it had finished the number of copulations assigned for it, they would let it loose for their idols and excuse it from burdens so that nothing would be carried on it, and they called it the 'Hami.' Abu Huraira said, "I heard the Prophet ﷺ saying so.". – Sahih Al-Bukhari 4623

حَدَّثَنَا مُوسَى بْنُ إِسْمَاعِيلَ، حَدَّثَنَا إِبْرَاهِيمُ بْنُ سَعْدٍ، عَنْ صَالِحِ بْنِ كَيْسَانَ، عَنِ ابْنِ شِهَابٍ، عَنْ سَعِيدِ بْنِ الْمُسَيَّبِ، قَالَ الْبَحِيرَةُ الَّتِي يُمْنَعُ دَرُّهَا لِلطَّوَاغِيتِ فَلاَ يَحْلُبُهَا أَحَدٌ مِنَ النَّاسِ. وَالسَّائِبَةُ كَانُوا يُسَيِّبُونَهَا لآلِهَتِهِمْ لاَ يُحْمَلُ عَلَيْهَا شَىْءٌ. قَالَ وَقَالَ أَبُو هُرَيْرَةَ قَالَ رَسُولُ اللَّهِ صلى الله عليه وسلم " رَأَيْتُ عَمْرَو بْنَ عَامِرٍ الْخُزَاعِيَّ يَجُرُّ قُصْبَهُ فِي النَّارِ، كَانَ أَوَّلَ مَنْ سَيَّبَ السَّوَائِبَ ". وَالْوَصِيلَةُ النَّاقَةُ الْبِكْرُ تُبَكِّرُ فِي أَوَّلِ نِتَاجِ الإِبِلِ، ثُمَّ تُثَنِّي بَعْدُ بِأُنْثَى. وَكَانُوا يُسَيِّبُونَهُمْ لِطَوَاغِيتِهِمْ إِنْ وَصَلَتْ إِحْدَاهُمَا بِالأُخْرَى لَيْسَ بَيْنَهُمَا ذَكَرٌ. وَالْحَامِ فَحْلُ الإِبِلِ يَضْرِبُ الضِّرَابَ الْمَعْدُودَ، فَإِذَا قَضَى ضِرَابَهُ وَدَعُوهُ لِلطَّوَاغِيتِ وَأَعْفَوْهُ مِنَ الْحَمْلِ فَلَمْ يُحْمَلْ عَلَيْهِ شَىْءٌ وَسَمَّوْهُ الْحَامِيَ. وَقَالَ لِي أَبُو الْيَمَانِ أَخْبَرَنَا شُعَيْبٌ، عَنِ الزُّهْرِيِّ، سَمِعْتُ سَعِيدًا، قَالَ يُخْبِرُهُ بِهَذَا قَالَ وَقَالَ أَبُو هُرَيْرَةَ سَمِعْتُ النَّبِيَّ صلى الله عليه وسلم نَحْوَهُ. وَرَوَاهُ ابْنُ الْهَادِ عَنِ ابْنِ شِهَابٍ عَنْ سَعِيدٍ عَنْ أَبِي هُرَيْرَةَ ـ رضى الله عنه ـ سَمِعْتُ النَّبِيَّ صلى الله عليه وسلم.

Narrated Abu Huraira: Allah's Messenger ﷺ said, "`Amr bin Luhai bin Qam'a bin Khindif was the father of Khuza`a.'. – Sahih Al-Bukhari 3520

حَدَّثَنِي إِسْحَاقُ بْنُ إِبْرَاهِيمَ، حَدَّثَنَا يَحْيَى بْنُ آدَمَ، أَخْبَرَنَا إِسْرَائِيلُ، عَنْ أَبِي حَصِينٍ، عَنْ أَبِي صَالِحٍ، عَنْ أَبِي هُرَيْرَةَ ـ رضى الله عنه ـ أَنَّ رَسُولَ اللَّهِ صلى الله عليه وسلم قَالَ " عَمْرُو بْنُ لُحَيِّ بْنِ قَمَعَةَ بْنِ خِنْدِفَ أَبُو خُزَاعَةَ ".

Banu Daus
بنو دوس

Narrated Abu Huraira: Allah's Messenger ﷺ said, "The Hour will not be established till the buttocks of the women of the tribe of Daus move while going round Dhi-al-Khalasa." Dhi-al-

Khalasa was the idol of the Daus tribe which they used to worship in the Pre Islamic Period of ignorance. – Sahih Al-Bukhari 7116

حَدَّثَنَا أَبُو الْيَمَانِ، أَخْبَرَنَا شُعَيْبٌ، عَنِ الزُّهْرِيِّ، قَالَ قَالَ سَعِيدُ بْنُ الْمُسَيَّبِ أَخْبَرَنِي أَبُو هُرَيْرَةَ ـ رضى الله عنه ـ أَنَّ رَسُولَ اللَّهِ صلى الله عليه وسلم قَالَ " لاَ تَقُومُ السَّاعَةُ حَتَّى تَضْطَرِبَ أَلَيَاتُ نِسَاءِ دَوْسٍ عَلَى ذِي الْخَلَصَةِ ". وَذُو الْخَلَصَةِ طَاغِيَةُ دَوْسٍ الَّتِي كَانُوا يَعْبُدُونَ فِي الْجَاهِلِيَّةِ

Narrated Abu Huraira: Tufail bin `Amr came to the Prophet ﷺ and said, "The Daus (nation) have perished as they disobeyed and refused to accept Islam. So invoke Allah against them." But the Prophet ﷺ said, "O Allah! Give guidance to the Daus (tribe) and bring them (to Islam)!". – Sahih Al-Bukhari 4392

حَدَّثَنَا أَبُو نُعَيْمٍ، حَدَّثَنَا سُفْيَانُ، عَنِ ابْنِ ذَكْوَانَ، عَنْ عَبْدِ الرَّحْمَنِ الأَعْرَجِ، عَنْ أَبِي هُرَيْرَةَ ـ رضى الله عنه ـ قَالَ جَاءَ الطُّفَيْلُ بْنُ عَمْرٍو إِلَى النَّبِيِّ صلى الله عليه وسلم فَقَالَ إِنَّ دَوْسًا قَدْ هَلَكَتْ، عَصَتْ وَأَبَتْ، فَادْعُ اللَّهَ عَلَيْهِمْ. فَقَالَ " اللَّهُمَّ اهْدِ دَوْسًا وَأْتِ بِهِمْ ".

Banu Nadir
بَنُو ٱلنَّضِير

Narrated `Abdul `Aziz: Anas said, 'When Allah's Messenger ﷺ invaded Khaibar, we offered the Fajr prayer there (early in the morning) when it was still dark. The Prophet ﷺ rode and Abu Talha rode too and I was riding behind Abu Talha. The Prophet ﷺ passed through the lane of Khaibar quickly and my knee was touching the thigh of the Prophet ﷺ. He uncovered his thigh and I saw the whiteness of the thigh of the Prophet. When he entered the town, he said, 'Allahu Akbar! Khaibar is ruined. Whenever we approach near a (hostile) nation (to fight) then evil will be the morning of those who have been warned.' He repeated this thrice. The people came out for their jobs and some of them said, 'Muhammad (has come).' (Some of our companions added, "With his army.") We conquered Khaibar, took the captives, and the booty was collected. Dihya came and said, 'O Allah's Prophet! Give me a slave girl from the captives.' The Prophet said, 'Go and take any slave girl.' He took Safiya bint Huyai. A man came to the Prophet ﷺ and said, 'O Allah's Messenger ﷺ! You gave Safiya bint Huyai to Dihya and she is the chief mistress of the tribes of Quraidha and An-Nadir and she befits none but you.' So the Prophet ﷺ said, 'Bring him along with her.' So Dihya came with her and when Prophet ﷺ saw her, he said to Dihya, 'Take any slave girl other than her from the captives.' Anas added: The Prophet ﷺ then manumitted her and married her." Thabit asked Anas, "O Abu Hamza! What did the Prophet ﷺ pay her (as Mahr)?" He said, "Her self was her Mahr for he manumitted her and then married her." Anas added, "While on the way, Um Sulaim dressed her for marriage (ceremony) and at night she sent her as a bride to the Prophet ﷺ. So the Prophet was a bridegroom and he said, 'Whoever has anything (food) should bring it.' He spread out a leather sheet (for the food) and some brought dates and others cooking butter. (I think he (Anas) mentioned As-Sawaq). So they prepared a dish of Hais (a kind of meal). And that was Walima (the marriage banquet) of Allah's Messenger ﷺ." - Sahih Al-Bukhari 371

حَدَّثَنَا يَعْقُوبُ بْنُ إِبْرَاهِيمَ، قَالَ حَدَّثَنَا إِسْمَاعِيلُ ابْنُ عُلَيَّةَ، قَالَ حَدَّثَنَا عَبْدُ الْعَزِيزِ بْنُ صُهَيْبٍ، عَنْ أَنَسٍ، أَنَّ رَسُولَ اللَّهِ صلى الله عليه وسلم غَزَا خَيْبَرَ، فَصَلَّيْنَا عِنْدَهَا صَلاَةَ الْغَدَاةِ بِغَلَسٍ، فَرَكِبَ نَبِيُّ اللَّهِ صلى الله عليه وسلم وَرَكِبَ أَبُو طَلْحَةَ، وَأَنَا رَدِيفُ أَبِي طَلْحَةَ، فَأَجْرَى نَبِيُّ اللَّهِ صلى الله عليه وسلم فِي زُقَاقِ خَيْبَرَ، وَإِنَّ رُكْبَتِي لَتَمَسُّ فَخِذَ نَبِيِّ اللَّهِ صلى الله عليه وسلم، ثُمَّ حَسَرَ الإِزَارَ عَنْ فَخِذِهِ حَتَّى إِنِّي أَنْظُرُ إِلَى بَيَاضِ فَخِذِ نَبِيِّ اللَّهِ صلى الله عليه وسلم، فَلَمَّا دَخَلَ الْقَرْيَةَ قَالَ " اللَّهُ أَكْبَرُ، خَرِبَتْ خَيْبَرُ، إِنَّا إِذَا نَزَلْنَا بِسَاحَةِ قَوْمٍ فَسَاءَ صَبَاحُ الْمُنْذَرِينَ ". قَالَهَا ثَلاَثًا. قَالَ وَخَرَجَ الْقَوْمُ إِلَى أَعْمَالِهِمْ فَقَالُوا مُحَمَّدٌ ـ قَالَ عَبْدُ الْعَزِيزِ وَقَالَ بَعْضُ أَصْحَابِنَا ـ وَالْخَمِيسُ. يَعْنِي الْجَيْشَ، قَالَ فَأَصَبْنَاهَا عَنْوَةً، فَجُمِعَ السَّبْىُ، فَجَاءَ دِحْيَةُ

فَقَالَ يَا نَبِيَّ اللَّهِ، أَعْطِنِي جَارِيَةً مِنَ السَّبْىِ. قَالَ " اذْهَبْ فَخُذْ جَارِيَةً ". فَأَخَذَ صَفِيَّةَ بِنْتَ حُيَىٍّ، فَجَاءَ رَجُلٌ إِلَى النَّبِيِّ صلى الله عليه وسلم فَقَالَ يَا نَبِيَّ اللَّهِ، أَعْطَيْتَ دِحْيَةَ صَفِيَّةَ بِنْتَ حُيَىٍّ سَيِّدَةَ قُرَيْظَةَ وَالنَّضِيرِ، لاَ تَصْلُحُ إِلاَّ لَكَ. قَالَ " ادْعُوهُ بِهَا ". فَجَاءَ بِهَا، فَلَمَّا نَظَرَ إِلَيْهَا النَّبِيُّ صلى الله عليه وسلم قَالَ " خُذْ جَارِيَةً مِنَ السَّبْىِ غَيْرَهَا ". قَالَ فَأَعْتَقَهَا النَّبِيُّ صلى الله عليه وسلم وَتَزَوَّجَهَا. فَقَالَ لَهُ ثَابِتٌ يَا أَبَا حَمْزَةَ، مَا أَصْدَقَهَا قَالَ نَفْسَهَا، أَعْتَقَهَا وَتَزَوَّجَهَا، حَتَّى إِذَا كَانَ بِالطَّرِيقِ جَهَّزَتْهَا لَهُ أُمُّ سُلَيْمٍ فَأَهْدَتْهَا لَهُ مِنَ اللَّيْلِ، فَأَصْبَحَ النَّبِيُّ صلى الله عليه وسلم عَرُوسًا فَقَالَ " مَنْ كَانَ عِنْدَهُ شَىْءٌ فَلْيَجِئْ بِهِ ". وَبَسَطَ نِطَعًا، فَجَعَلَ الرَّجُلُ يَجِيءُ بِالتَّمْرِ، وَجَعَلَ الرَّجُلُ يَجِيءُ بِالسَّمْنِ ـ قَالَ وَأَحْسِبُهُ قَدْ ذَكَرَ السَّوِيقَ ـ قَالَ فَحَاسُوا حَيْسًا، فَكَانَتْ وَلِيمَةَ رَسُولِ اللَّهِ صلى الله عليه وسلم.

Narrated Malik bin Aus Al-Hadathan An-Nasri: That once `Umar bin Al-Khattab called him and while he was sitting with him, his gatekeeper, Yarfa came and said, "Will you admit `Uthman, `Abdur-Rahman bin `Auf, AzZubair and Sa`d (bin Abi Waqqas) who are waiting for your permission?" `Umar said, "Yes, let them come in." After a while, Yarfa- came again and said, "Will you admit `Ali and `Abbas who are asking your permission?" `Umar said, "Yes." So, when the two entered, `Abbas said, "O chief of the believers! Judge between me and this (i.e. `Ali). "Both of them had a dispute regarding the property of Bani An-Nadir which Allah had given to His Apostle as Fai (i.e. booty gained without fighting), `Ali and `Abbas started reproaching each other. The (present) people (i.e. `Uthman and his companions) said, "O chief of the believers! Give your verdict in their case and relieve each from) the other." `Umar said, "Wait I beseech you, by Allah, by Whose Permission both the heaven and the earth stand fast! Do you know that Allah's Messenger ﷺ said, 'We (Prophets) our properties are not to be inherited, and whatever we leave, is to be spent in charity,' and he said it about himself?" They (i.e. `Uthman and his company) said, "He did say it. "`Umar then turned towards `Ali and `Abbas and said, "I beseech you both, by Allah! Do you know that Allah's Messenger ﷺ said this?" They replied in the affirmative. He said, "Now I am talking to you about this matter. Allah the Glorified favored His Apostle with something of this Fai (i.e. booty won without fighting) which He did not give to anybody else. Allah said:-- "And what Allah gave to His Apostle ("Fai"" Booty) from them—For which you made no expedition With either Calvary or camelry. But Allah gives power to His Apostles Over whomsoever He will And Allah is able to do all things." (59.6) So this property was especially granted to Allah's Messenger ﷺ. But by Allah, the Prophet ﷺ neither took it all for himself only, nor deprived you of it, but he gave it to all of you and distributed it amongst you till only this remained out of it. And from this Allah's Messenger ﷺ used to spend the yearly maintenance for his family, and whatever used to remain, he used to spend it where Allah's Property is spent (i.e. in charity), Allah's Messenger ﷺ kept on acting like that during all his life, Then he died, and Abu Bakr said, 'I am the successor of Allah's Messenger ﷺ. So he (i.e. Abu Bakr) took charge of this property and disposed of it in the same manner as Allah's Messenger ﷺ used to do, and all of you (at that time) knew all about it." Then `Umar turned towards `Ali and `Abbas and said, "You both remember that Abu Bakr disposed of it in the way you have described and Allah knows that, in that matter, he was sincere, pious, rightly guided and the follower of the right. Then Allah caused Abu Bakr to die and I said, 'I am the successor of Allah's Messenger ﷺ and Abu Bakr.' So I kept this property in my possession for the first two years of my rule (i.e. Caliphate and I used to dispose of it in the same wa as Allah's Messenger ﷺ and Abu Bakr used to do) and Allah knows that I have been sincere, pious, rightly guided an the follower of the right (in this matte Later on both of you (i.e. `Ali and `Abbas) came to me, and the claim of you both was one and the same, O `Abbas! You also came to me. So I told you both that Allah's Messenger ﷺ said, "Our property is not inherited, but whatever we leave is to be given in charity.' Then when I thought that I should better hand over this property to you both or the condition that you will promise and pledge before Allah that you will dispose it off in the same way as Allah's

Messenger ﷺ and Abu Bakr did and as I have done since the beginning of my caliphate or else you should not speak to me (about it).' So, both of you said to me, 'Hand it over to us on this condition.' And on this condition I handed it over to you. Do you want me now to give a decision other than that (decision)? By Allah, with Whose Permission both the sky and the earth stand fast, I will never give any decision other than that (decision) till the Last Hour is established. But if you are unable to manage it (i.e. that property), then return it to me, and I will manage on your behalf." The sub-narrator said, "I told `Urwa bin Az-Zubair of this Hadith and he said, 'Malik bin Aus has told the truth" I heard `Aisha, the wife of the Prophet ﷺ saying, 'The wives of the Prophet ﷺ sent `Uthman to Abu Bakr demanding from him their 1/8 of the Fai which Allah had granted to his Apostle. But I used to oppose them and say to them: Will you not fear Allah? Don't you know that the Prophet used to say: Our property is not inherited, but whatever we leave is to be given in charity? The Prophet ﷺ mentioned that regarding himself. He added: 'The family of Muhammad can take their sustenance from this property. So the wives of the Prophet ﷺ stopped demanding it when I told them of that.' So, this property (of Sadaqa) was in the hands of `Ali who withheld it from `Abbas and overpowered him. Then it came in the hands of Hasan bin `Ali, then in the hands of Husain bin `Ali, and then in the hands of `Ali bin Husain and Hasan bin Hasan, and each of the last two used to manage it in turn, then it came in the hands of Zaid bin Hasan, and it was truly the Sadaqa of Allah's Apostle .". – Sahih Al-Bukhari 4033, 4034

حَدَّثَنَا أَبُو الْيَمَانِ، أَخْبَرَنَا شُعَيْبٌ، عَنِ الزُّهْرِيِّ، قَالَ أَخْبَرَنِي مَالِكُ بْنُ أَوْسِ بْنِ الْحَدَثَانِ النَّصْرِيُّ، أَنَّ عُمَرَ بْنَ الْخَطَّابِ ـ رضى الله عنه ـ دَعَاهُ إِذْ جَاءَهُ حَاجِبُهُ يَرْفَا فَقَالَ هَلْ لَكَ فِي عُثْمَانَ، وَعَبْدِ الرَّحْمَنِ، وَالزُّبَيْرِ وَسَعْدٍ يَسْتَأْذِنُونَ فَقَالَ نَعَمْ، فَأَدْخِلْهُمْ. فَلَبِثَ قَلِيلاً، ثُمَّ جَاءَ فَقَالَ هَلْ لَكَ فِي عَبَّاسٍ وَعَلِيٍّ يَسْتَأْذِنَانِ قَالَ نَعَمْ. فَلَمَّا دَخَلاَ قَالَ عَبَّاسٌ يَا أَمِيرَ الْمُؤْمِنِينَ، اقْضِ بَيْنِي وَبَيْنَ هَذَا، وَهُمَا يَخْتَصِمَانِ فِي الَّذِي أَفَاءَ اللَّهُ عَلَى رَسُولِهِ صلى الله عليه وسلم مِنْ بَنِي النَّضِيرِ، فَاسْتَبَّ عَلِيٌّ وَعَبَّاسٌ، فَقَالَ الرَّهْطُ يَا أَمِيرَ الْمُؤْمِنِينَ، اقْضِ بَيْنَهُمَا وَأَرِحْ أَحَدَهُمَا مِنَ الآخَرِ. فَقَالَ عُمَرُ اتَّئِدُوا، أَنْشُدُكُمْ بِاللَّهِ الَّذِي بِإِذْنِهِ تَقُومُ السَّمَاءُ وَالأَرْضُ، هَلْ تَعْلَمُونَ أَنَّ رَسُولَ اللَّهِ صلى الله عليه وسلم قَالَ " لاَ نُورَثُ، مَا تَرَكْنَا صَدَقَةٌ ". يُرِيدُ بِذَلِكَ نَفْسَهُ. قَالُوا قَدْ قَالَ ذَلِكَ. فَأَقْبَلَ عُمَرُ عَلَى عَبَّاسٍ وَعَلِيٍّ فَقَالَ أَنْشُدُكُمَا بِاللَّهِ هَلْ تَعْلَمَانِ أَنَّ رَسُولَ اللَّهِ صلى الله عليه وسلم قَدْ قَالَ ذَلِكَ قَالاَ نَعَمْ. قَالَ فَإِنِّي أُحَدِّثُكُمْ عَنْ هَذَا الأَمْرِ، إِنَّ اللَّهَ سُبْحَانَهُ كَانَ خَصَّ رَسُولَهُ صلى الله عليه وسلم فِي هَذَا الْفَىْءِ بِشَىْءٍ لَمْ يُعْطِهِ أَحَدًا غَيْرَهُ فَقَالَ جَلَّ ذِكْرُهُ {وَمَا أَفَاءَ اللَّهُ عَلَى رَسُولِهِ مِنْهُمْ فَمَا أَوْجَفْتُمْ عَلَيْهِ مِنْ خَيْلٍ وَلاَ رِكَابٍ} إِلَى قَوْلِهِ {قَدِيرٌ} فَكَانَتْ هَذِهِ خَالِصَةً لِرَسُولِ اللَّهِ صلى الله عليه وسلم، ثُمَّ وَاللَّهِ مَا احْتَازَهَا دُونَكُمْ، وَلاَ اسْتَأْثَرَهَا عَلَيْكُمْ، لَقَدْ أَعْطَاكُمُوهَا وَقَسَمَهَا فِيكُمْ، حَتَّى بَقِيَ هَذَا الْمَالُ مِنْهَا، فَكَانَ رَسُولُ اللَّهِ صلى الله عليه وسلم يُنْفِقُ عَلَى أَهْلِهِ نَفَقَةَ سَنَتِهِمْ مِنْ هَذَا الْمَالِ، ثُمَّ يَأْخُذُ مَا بَقِيَ فَيَجْعَلُهُ مَجْعَلَ مَالِ اللَّهِ، فَعَمِلَ ذَلِكَ رَسُولُ اللَّهِ صلى الله عليه وسلم حَيَاتَهُ، ثُمَّ تُوُفِّيَ النَّبِيُّ صلى الله عليه وسلم فَقَالَ أَبُو بَكْرٍ فَأَنَا وَلِيُّ رَسُولِ اللَّهِ صلى الله عليه وسلم. فَقَبَضَهُ أَبُو بَكْرٍ، فَعَمِلَ فِيهِ بِمَا عَمِلَ بِهِ رَسُولُ اللَّهِ صلى الله عليه وسلم وَأَنْتُمْ حِينَئِذٍ. فَأَقْبَلَ عَلَى عَلِيٍّ وَعَبَّاسٍ وَقَالَ تَذْكُرَانِ أَنَّ أَبَا بَكْرٍ عَمِلَ فِيهِ كَمَا تَقُولاَنِ، وَاللَّهُ يَعْلَمُ إِنَّهُ فِيهِ لَصَادِقٌ بَارٌّ رَاشِدٌ تَابِعٌ لِلْحَقِّ ثُمَّ تَوَفَّى اللَّهُ أَبَا بَكْرٍ فَقُلْتُ أَنَا وَلِيُّ رَسُولِ اللَّهِ صلى الله عليه وسلم وَأَبِي بَكْرٍ. فَقَبَضْتُهُ سَنَتَيْنِ مِنْ إِمَارَتِي أَعْمَلُ فِيهِ بِمَا عَمِلَ رَسُولُ اللَّهِ صلى الله عليه وسلم وَأَبُو بَكْرٍ، وَاللَّهُ يَعْلَمُ أَنِّي فِيهِ صَادِقٌ بَارٌّ رَاشِدٌ تَابِعٌ لِلْحَقِّ، ثُمَّ جِئْتُمَانِي كِلاَكُمَا وَكَلِمَتُكُمَا وَاحِدَةٌ وَأَمْرُكُمَا جَمِيعٌ، فَجِئْتَنِي ـ يَعْنِي عَبَّاسًا ـ فَقُلْتُ لَكُمَا إِنَّ رَسُولَ اللَّهِ صلى الله عليه وسلم قَالَ " لاَ نُورَثُ، مَا تَرَكْنَا صَدَقَةٌ ". فَلَمَّا بَدَا لِي أَنْ أَدْفَعَهُ إِلَيْكُمَا قُلْتُ إِنْ شِئْتُمَا دَفَعْتُهُ إِلَيْكُمَا عَلَى أَنَّ عَلَيْكُمَا عَهْدَ اللَّهِ وَمِيثَاقَهُ لَتَعْمَلاَنِ فِيهِ بِمَا عَمِلَ فِيهِ رَسُولُ اللَّهِ صلى الله عليه وسلم وَأَبُو بَكْرٍ، وَمَا عَمِلْتُ فِيهِ مُذْ وَلِيتُ، وَإِلاَّ فَلاَ تُكَلِّمَانِي، فَقُلْتُمَا ادْفَعْهُ إِلَيْنَا بِذَلِكَ. فَدَفَعْتُهُ إِلَيْكُمَا، أَفَتَلْتَمِسَانِ مِنِّي قَضَاءً غَيْرَ ذَلِكَ فَوَاللَّهِ الَّذِي بِإِذْنِهِ تَقُومُ السَّمَاءُ وَالأَرْضُ لاَ أَقْضِي فِيهِ بِقَضَاءٍ غَيْرِ ذَلِكَ حَتَّى تَقُومَ السَّاعَةُ، فَإِنْ عَجَزْتُمَا عَنْهُ، فَادْفَعَا إِلَىَّ فَأَنَا أَكْفِيكُمَاهُ. قَالَ فَحَدَّثْتُ هَذَا الْحَدِيثَ، عُرْوَةَ بْنَ الزُّبَيْرِ فَقَالَ صَدَقَ مَالِكُ بْنُ أَوْسٍ، أَنَا سَمِعْتُ عَائِشَةَ ـ رضى الله عنها ـ زَوْجَ النَّبِيِّ صلى الله عليه وسلم تَقُولُ أَرْسَلَ أَزْوَاجُ النَّبِيِّ صلى الله عليه وسلم عُثْمَانَ إِلَى أَبِي بَكْرٍ يَسْأَلْنَهُ ثُمُنَهُنَّ مِمَّا أَفَاءَ اللَّهُ عَلَى رَسُولِهِ صلى الله عليه وسلم، فَكُنْتُ أَنَا أَرُدُّهُنَّ، فَقُلْتُ لَهُنَّ أَلاَ تَتَّقِينَ اللَّهَ، أَلَمْ تَعْلَمْنَ أَنَّ النَّبِيَّ صلى الله عليه وسلم كَانَ يَقُولُ " لاَ نُورَثُ، مَا تَرَكْنَا صَدَقَةٌ ـ يُرِيدُ بِذَلِكَ نَفْسَهُ ـ إِنَّمَا يَأْكُلُ آلُ مُحَمَّدٍ صلى الله عليه وسلم فِي هَذَا الْمَالِ ". فَانْتَهَى أَزْوَاجُ النَّبِيِّ صلى الله عليه وسلم إِلَى مَا أَخْبَرَتْهُنَّ. قَالَ فَكَانَتْ هَذِهِ الصَّدَقَةُ بِيَدِ عَلِيٍّ، مَنَعَهَا عَلِيٌّ عَبَّاسًا فَغَلَبَهُ عَلَيْهَا، ثُمَّ كَانَ بِيَدِ حَسَنِ بْنِ عَلِيٍّ، ثُمَّ بِيَدِ حُسَيْنِ بْنِ عَلِيٍّ، ثُمَّ بِيَدِ عَلِيِّ بْنِ حُسَيْنٍ وَحَسَنِ بْنِ حَسَنٍ، كِلاَهُمَا كَانَا يَتَدَاوَلاَنِهَا، ثُمَّ بِيَدِ زَيْدِ بْنِ حَسَنٍ، وَهْىَ صَدَقَةُ رَسُولِ اللَّهِ صلى الله عليه وسلم حَقًّا.

Narrated Anas: Some (of the Ansar) used to present date palm trees to the Prophet ﷺ till Banu Quraiza and Banu An- Nadir were conquered (then he returned to the people their date palms). My people ordered me to ask the Prophet ﷺ to return some or all the date palms they had given to him, but the Prophet ﷺ had given those trees to Um Aiman. On that, Um Aiman came and put the garment around my neck and said, "No, by Him except Whom none has the right to be worshipped, he will not return those trees to you as he (i.e. the Prophet ﷺ) has given them to me." The Prophet ﷺ go said (to her), "Return those trees and I will give you so much (instead of them)." But she kept on refusing, saying, "No, by Allah," till he gave her ten times the number of her date palms. – Sahih Al-Bukhari 4120
حَدَّثَنَا ابْنُ أَبِي الأَسْوَدِ، حَدَّثَنَا مُعْتَمِرٌ، وَحَدَّثَنِي خَلِيفَةُ، حَدَّثَنَا مُعْتَمِرٌ، قَالَ سَمِعْتُ أَبِي، عَنْ أَنَسٍ ـ رضى الله عنه ـ قَالَ كَانَ الرَّجُلُ يَجْعَلُ لِلنَّبِيِّ صلى الله عليه وسلم النَّخَلاَتِ حَتَّى افْتَتَحَ قُرَيْظَةَ وَالنَّضِيرَ، وَإِنَّ أَهْلِي أَمَرُونِي أَنْ آتِيَ النَّبِيَّ صلى الله عليه وسلم فَأَسْأَلَهُ الَّذِينَ كَانُوا أَعْطَوْهُ أَوْ بَعْضَهُ. وَكَانَ النَّبِيُّ صلى الله عليه وسلم قَدْ أَعْطَاهُ أُمَّ أَيْمَنَ، فَجَاءَتْ أُمُّ أَيْمَنَ فَجَعَلَتِ الثَّوْبَ فِي عُنُقِي تَقُولُ كَلاَّ وَالَّذِي لاَ إِلَهَ إِلاَّ هُوَ لاَ يُعْطِيكَهُمْ وَقَدْ أَعْطَانِيهَا، أَوْ كَمَا قَالَتْ، وَالنَّبِيُّ صلى الله عليه وسلم يَقُولُ " لَكِ كَذَا ". وَتَقُولُ كَلاَّ وَاللَّهِ. حَتَّى أَعْطَاهَا، حَسِبْتُ أَنَّهُ قَالَ " عَشَرَةَ أَمْثَالِهِ ". أَوْ كَمَا قَالَ.

Narrated Sa`id bin Jubair: I asked Ibn `Abbas about Surat Al-Tauba, and he said, "Surat Al-Tauba? It is exposure (of all the evils of the infidels and the hypocrites). And it continued revealing (that the oft-repeated expression): '...and of them ...and of them.' Till they started thinking that none would be left unmentioned therein." I said, "What about) Surat Al-Anfal?" He replied, "Surat Al-Anfal was revealed in connection with the Badr Battle." I said, "(What about) Surat Al-Hashr?" He replied, "It was revealed in connection with Bani an-Nadir.". – Sahih Al-Bukhari 4882
حَدَّثَنَا مُحَمَّدُ بْنُ عَبْدِ الرَّحِيمِ، حَدَّثَنَا سَعِيدُ بْنُ سُلَيْمَانَ، حَدَّثَنَا هُشَيْمٌ، أَخْبَرَنَا أَبُو بِشْرٍ، عَنْ سَعِيدِ بْنِ جُبَيْرٍ، قَالَ قُلْتُ لاِبْنِ عَبَّاسٍ سُورَةُ التَّوْبَةِ قَالَ التَّوْبَةُ هِيَ الْفَاضِحَةُ، مَا زَالَتْ تَنْزِلُ وَمِنْهُمْ وَمِنْهُمْ، حَتَّى ظَنُّوا أَنَّهَا لَمْ تُبْقِ أَحَدًا مِنْهُمْ إِلاَّ ذُكِرَ فِيهَا. قَالَ قُلْتُ سُورَةُ الأَنْفَالِ. قَالَ نَزَلَتْ فِي بَدْرٍ. قَالَ قُلْتُ سُورَةُ الْحَشْرِ. قَالَ نَزَلَتْ فِي بَنِي النَّضِيرِ.

Narrated `Umar: The properties of Bam An-Nadir were among the booty that Allah gave to His Apostle such Booty were not obtained by any expedition on the part of Muslims, neither with cavalry, nor with camelry. So those properties were for Allah's Messenger ﷺ only, and he used to provide thereof the yearly expenditure for his wives, and dedicate the rest of its revenues for purchasing arms and horses as war material to be used in Allah's Cause. – Sahih Al-Bukhari 4885
حَدَّثَنَا عَلِيُّ بْنُ عَبْدِ اللَّهِ، حَدَّثَنَا سُفْيَانُ ـ غَيْرَ مَرَّةٍ ـ عَنْ عَمْرٍو، عَنِ الزُّهْرِيِّ، عَنْ مَالِكِ بْنِ أَوْسِ بْنِ الْحَدَثَانِ، عَنْ عُمَرَ ـ رضى الله عنه ـ قَالَ كَانَتْ أَمْوَالُ بَنِي النَّضِيرِ مِمَّا أَفَاءَ اللَّهُ عَلَى رَسُولِهِ صلى الله عليه وسلم مِمَّا لَمْ يُوجِفِ الْمُسْلِمُونَ عَلَيْهِ بِخَيْلٍ وَلاَ رِكَابٍ، فَكَانَتْ لِرَسُولِ اللَّهِ صلى الله عليه وسلم خَاصَّةً، يُنْفِقُ عَلَى أَهْلِهِ مِنْهَا نَفَقَةَ سَنَتِهِ، ثُمَّ يَجْعَلُ مَا بَقِيَ فِي السِّلاَحِ وَالْكُرَاعِ، عُدَّةً فِي سَبِيلِ اللَّهِ

Narrated Ibn `Umar: 'Allah's Messenger ﷺ burnt and cut down the palm trees of Bani An-Nadir which were at Al-Buwair (a place near Medina). There upon Allah revealed: 'What you (O Muslims) cut down of the palm trees (of the enemy) or you left them standing on their stems, it was by the leave of Allah, so that He might cover with shame the rebellious.' (59.5).
Sahih Al Bukhari 4884
حَدَّثَنَا قُتَيْبَةُ، حَدَّثَنَا لَيْثٌ، عَنْ نَافِعٍ، عَنِ ابْنِ عُمَرَ ـ رضى الله عنهما ـ أَنَّ رَسُولَ اللَّهِ صلى الله عليه وسلم حَرَّقَ نَخْلَ بَنِي النَّضِيرِ وَقَطَعَ، وَهْىَ الْبُوَيْرَةُ، فَأَنْزَلَ اللَّهُ تَعَالَى {مَا قَطَعْتُمْ مِنْ لِينَةٍ أَوْ تَرَكْتُمُوهَا قَائِمَةً عَلَى أُصُولِهَا فَبِإِذْنِ اللَّهِ وَلِيُخْزِيَ الْفَاسِقِينَ}

Narrated Asma bint Abu Bakr: I used to carry the date stones on my head from the land of Az-Zubair which Allah's Messenger ﷺ had given to him, and it was at a distance of 2/3 of a

Farsakh from my house. Narrated Hisham's father: The Prophet ﷺ gave Az-Zubair a piece of land from the property of Bani An- Nadir (gained as war booty). – Sahih Al-Bukhari 3151
حَدَّثَنَا مَحْمُودُ بْنُ غَيْلاَنَ، حَدَّثَنَا أَبُو أُسَامَةَ، حَدَّثَنَا هِشَامٌ، قَالَ أَخْبَرَنِي أَبِي، عَنْ أَسْمَاءَ ابْنَةِ أَبِي بَكْرٍ ـ رضى الله عنهما ـ قَالَتْ كُنْتُ أَنْقُلُ النَّوَى مِنْ أَرْضِ الزُّبَيْرِ الَّتِي أَقْطَعَهُ رَسُولُ اللَّهِ صلى الله عليه وسلم عَلَى رَأْسِي، وَهْىَ مِنِّي عَلَى ثُلُثَىْ فَرْسَخٍ. وَقَالَ أَبُو ضَمْرَةَ عَنْ هِشَامٍ عَنْ أَبِيهِ أَنَّ النَّبِيَّ صلى الله عليه وسلم أَقْطَعَ الزُّبَيْرَ أَرْضًا مِنْ أَمْوَالِ بَنِي النَّضِيرِ

Narrated Ibn `Umar: Bani An-Nadir and Bani Quraiza fought (against the Prophet ﷺ violating their peace treaty), so the Prophet exiled Bani An-Nadir and allowed Bani Quraiza to remain at their places (in Medina) taking nothing from them till they fought against the Prophet ﷺ again. He then killed their men and distributed their women, children and property among the Muslims, but some of them came to the Prophet ﷺ and he granted them safety, and they embraced Islam. He exiled all the Jews from Medina. They were the Jews of Bani Qainuqa', the tribe of `Abdullah bin Salam and the Jews of Bani Haritha and all the other Jews of Medina. – Sahih Al-Bukhari 4028
حَدَّثَنَا إِسْحَاقُ بْنُ نَصْرٍ، حَدَّثَنَا عَبْدُ الرَّزَّاقِ، أَخْبَرَنَا ابْنُ جُرَيْجٍ، عَنْ مُوسَى بْنِ عُقْبَةَ، عَنْ نَافِعٍ، عَنِ ابْنِ عُمَرَ ـ رضى الله عنهما ـ قَالَ حَارَبَتِ النَّضِيرُ وَقُرَيْظَةُ، فَأَجْلَى بَنِي النَّضِيرِ، وَأَقَرَّ قُرَيْظَةَ وَمَنَّ عَلَيْهِمْ، حَتَّى حَارَبَتْ قُرَيْظَةُ فَقَتَلَ رِجَالَهُمْ وَقَسَمَ نِسَاءَهُمْ وَأَوْلاَدَهُمْ وَأَمْوَالَهُمْ بَيْنَ الْمُسْلِمِينَ إِلاَّ بَعْضَهُمْ لَحِقُوا بِالنَّبِيِّ صلى الله عليه وسلم فَآمَنَهُمْ وَأَسْلَمُوا، وَأَجْلَى يَهُودَ الْمَدِينَةِ كُلَّهُمْ بَنِي قَيْنُقَاعَ وَهُمْ رَهْطُ عَبْدِ اللَّهِ بْنِ سَلاَمٍ وَيَهُودَ بَنِي حَارِثَةَ، وَكُلَّ يَهُودِ الْمَدِينَةِ.

Narrated Anas bin Malik: People used to give some of their datepalms to the Prophet (as a gift), till he conquered Bani Quraiza and Bani An-Nadir, whereupon he started returning their favors. – Sahih Al-Bukhari 3128
حَدَّثَنَا عَبْدُ اللَّهِ بْنُ أَبِي الأَسْوَدِ، حَدَّثَنَا مُعْتَمِرٌ، عَنْ أَبِيهِ، قَالَ سَمِعْتُ أَنَسَ بْنَ مَالِكٍ ـ رضى الله عنه ـ يَقُولُ كَانَ الرَّجُلُ يَجْعَلُ لِلنَّبِيِّ صلى الله عليه وسلم النَّخَلاَتِ حَتَّى افْتَتَحَ قُرَيْظَةَ وَالنَّضِيرَ، فَكَانَ بَعْدَ ذَلِكَ يَرُدُّ عَلَيْهِمْ.

Narrated Anas: We think that the Verse: 'Among the Believers are men who have been true to their covenant with Allah.' Was revealed in favor of Anas bin An-Nadir. – Sahih Al-Bukhari 4783
حَدَّثَنِي مُحَمَّدُ بْنُ بَشَّارٍ، حَدَّثَنَا مُحَمَّدُ بْنُ عَبْدِ اللَّهِ الأَنْصَارِيُّ، قَالَ حَدَّثَنِي أَبِي، عَنْ ثُمَامَةَ، عَنْ أَنَسِ بْنِ مَالِكٍ ـ رضى الله عنه ـ قَالَ نُرَى هَذِهِ الآيَةَ نَزَلَتْ فِي أَنَسِ بْنِ النَّضْرِ {مِنَ الْمُؤْمِنِينَ رِجَالٌ صَدَقُوا مَا عَاهَدُوا اللَّهَ عَلَيْهِ}

Narrated Sa`id bin Jubair: I mentioned to Ibn `Abbas Surat-Hashr. He said, "Call it Surat-an-Nadir." – Sahih Al-Bukhari 4029
حَدَّثَنِي الْحَسَنُ بْنُ مُدْرِكٍ، حَدَّثَنَا يَحْيَى بْنُ حَمَّادٍ، أَخْبَرَنَا أَبُو عَوَانَةَ، عَنْ أَبِي بِشْرٍ، عَنْ سَعِيدِ بْنِ جُبَيْرٍ، قَالَ قُلْتُ لاِبْنِ عَبَّاسٍ سُورَةُ الْحَشْرِ. قَالَ قُلْ سُورَةُ النَّضِيرِ. تَابَعَهُ هُشَيْمٌ عَنْ أَبِي بِشْرٍ

Banu Lihyan
بنو لحيان

Narrated Abu Huraira: The Prophet ﷺ sent a Sariya of spies and appointed `Asim bin Thabit, the grandfather of `Asim bin `Umar bin Al-Khattab, as their leader. So they set out, and when they reached (a place) between 'Usfan and Mecca, they were mentioned to one of the branch tribes of Bani Hudhail called Lihyan. So, about one-hundred archers followed their traces till they (i.e. the archers) came to a journey station where they (i.e. `Asim and his companions) had encamped and found stones of dates they had brought as journey food from Medina. The archers said, "These are the dates of Medina," and followed their traces till they took them over. When `Asim and his companions were not able to go ahead, they went up a high place, and their pursuers encircled them and said, "You have a covenant and a promise that if you come down to us, we will not kill anyone of you." `Asim said, "As for me, I will never come down on the security of an infidel. O Allah! Inform Your Prophet about us." So they fought with them till they killed `Asim along with seven of his companions with arrows, and there remained Khubaib, Zaid and another man to whom they gave a promise and a covenant. So when the infidels gave them the covenant and promise, they came down. When they captured them, they opened the strings of their arrow bows and tied them with it. The third man who was with them said, "This is the first breach in the covenant," and refused to accompany them. They dragged him and tried to make him accompany them, but he refused, and they killed him. Then they proceeded on taking Khubaib and Zaid till they sold them in Mecca. The sons of Al-Harith bin `Amr bin Naufal bought Khubaib. It was Khubaib who had killed Al-Harith bin `Amr on the day of Badr. Khubaib stayed with them for a while as a captive till they decided unanimously to kill him. (At that time) Khubaib borrowed a razor from one of the daughters of Al- Harith to shave his pubic hair. She gave it to him. She said later on, "I was heedless of a little baby of mine, who moved towards Khubaib, and when it reached him, he put it on his thigh. When I saw it, I got scared so much that Khubaib noticed my distress while he was carrying the razor in his hand. He said 'Are you afraid that I will kill it? Allah willing, I will never do that,' " Later on she used to say, "I have never seen a captive better than Khubaib Once I saw him eating from a bunch of grapes although at that time no fruits were available at Mecca, and he was fettered with iron chains, and in fact, it was nothing but food bestowed upon him by Allah." So they took him out of the Sanctuary (of Mecca) to kill him. He said, "Allow me to offer a two-rak`at prayer." Then he went to them and said, "Had I not been afraid that you would think I was afraid of death, I would have prayed for a longer time." So it was Khubaib who first set the tradition of praying two rak`at before being executed. He then said, "O Allah! Count them one by one," and added, 'When I am being martyred as a Muslim, I do not care in what way I receive my death for Allah's Sake, because this death is in Allah's Cause. If He wishes, He will bless the cut limbs." Then `Uqba bin Al-Harith got up and martyred him. The narrator added: The Quraish (infidels) sent some people to `Asim in order to bring a part of his body so that his death might be known for certain, for `Asim had killed one of their chiefs on the day of Badr. But Allah sent a cloud of wasps which protected his body from their messengers who could not harm his body consequently. – Sahih Al-Bukhari 4086

حَدَّثَنِي إِبْرَاهِيمُ بْنُ مُوسَى، أَخْبَرَنَا هِشَامُ بْنُ يُوسُفَ، عَنْ مَعْمَرٍ، عَنِ الزُّهْرِيِّ، عَنْ عَمْرِو بْنِ أَبِي سُفْيَانَ الثَّقَفِيِّ، عَنْ أَبِي هُرَيْرَةَ ـ رضى الله عنه ـ قَالَ بَعَثَ النَّبِيُّ صلى الله عليه وسلم سَرِيَّةً عَيْنًا، وَأَمَّرَ عَلَيْهِمْ عَاصِمَ بْنَ ثَابِتٍ ـ وَهْوَ جَدُّ عَاصِمِ بْنِ عُمَرَ بْنِ الْخَطَّابِ ـ فَانْطَلَقُوا حَتَّى إِذَا كَانَ بَيْنَ عُسْفَانَ وَمَكَّةَ ذُكِرُوا لِحَيٍّ مِنْ هُذَيْلٍ، يُقَالُ لَهُمْ بَنُو لَحْيَانَ، فَتَبِعُوهُمْ بِقَرِيبٍ مِنْ مِائَةِ رَامٍ، فَاقْتَصُّوا آثَارَهُمْ حَتَّى أَتَوْا مَنْزِلاً نَزَلُوهُ فَوَجَدُوا فِيهِ نَوَى تَمْرٍ تَزَوَّدُوهُ مِنَ الْمَدِينَةِ فَقَالُوا هَذَا تَمْرُ يَثْرِبَ. فَتَبِعُوا آثَارَهُمْ حَتَّى لَحِقُوهُمْ، فَلَمَّا انْتَهَى عَاصِمٌ وَأَصْحَابُهُ لَجَئُوا إِلَى فَدْفَدٍ، وَجَاءَ الْقَوْمُ فَأَحَاطُوا بِهِمْ، فَقَالُوا لَكُمُ الْعَهْدُ وَالْمِيثَاقُ إِنْ نَزَلْتُمْ إِلَيْنَا أَنْ لاَ نَقْتُلَ مِنْكُمْ رَجُلاً. فَقَالَ عَاصِمٌ أَمَّا أَنَا فَلاَ أَنْزِلُ فِي ذِمَّةِ كَافِرٍ، اللَّهُمَّ أَخْبِرْ عَنَّا نَبِيَّكَ. فَقَاتَلُوهُمْ حَتَّى قَتَلُوا عَاصِمًا فِي سَبْعَةِ نَفَرٍ بِالنَّبْلِ، وَبَقِيَ خُبَيْبٌ، وَزَيْدٌ وَرَجُلٌ آخَرُ، فَأَعْطَوْهُمُ الْعَهْدَ وَالْمِيثَاقَ، فَلَمَّا أَعْطَوْهُمُ الْعَهْدَ وَالْمِيثَاقَ نَزَلُوا إِلَيْهِمْ، فَلَمَّا اسْتَمْكَنُوا مِنْهُمْ حَلُّوا أَوْتَارَ قِسِيِّهِمْ فَرَبَطُوهُمْ بِهَا. فَقَالَ الرَّجُلُ الثَّالِثُ الَّذِي مَعَهُمَا هَذَا أَوَّلُ الْغَدْرِ. فَأَبَى أَنْ يَصْحَبَهُمْ فَجَرَّرُوهُ وَعَالَجُوهُ عَلَى أَنْ يَصْحَبَهُمْ، فَلَمْ يَفْعَلْ، فَقَتَلُوهُ، وَانْطَلَقُوا بِخُبَيْبٍ وَزَيْدٍ حَتَّى بَاعُوهُمَا بِمَكَّةَ، فَاشْتَرَى خُبَيْبًا بَنُو الْحَارِثِ بْنِ عَامِرِ بْنِ نَوْفَلٍ، وَكَانَ خُبَيْبٌ هُوَ قَتَلَ الْحَارِثَ يَوْمَ بَدْرٍ، فَمَكَثَ عِنْدَهُمْ أَسِيرًا حَتَّى إِذَا أَجْمَعُوا قَتْلَهُ اسْتَعَارَ مُوسَى مِنْ بَعْضِ بَنَاتِ الْحَارِثِ أَسْتَحِدُّ بِهَا فَأَعَارَتْهُ، قَالَتْ فَغَفَلْتُ عَنْ صَبِيٍّ لِي فَدَرَجَ إِلَيْهِ حَتَّى أَتَاهُ، فَوَضَعَهُ عَلَى فَخِذِهِ، فَلَمَّا رَأَيْتُهُ فَزِعْتُ فَزْعَةً عَرَفَ ذَاكَ مِنِّي، وَفِي يَدِهِ الْمُوسَى فَقَالَ أَتَخْشَيْنَ أَنْ أَقْتُلَهُ مَا كُنْتُ لأَفْعَلَ ذَاكِ إِنْ شَاءَ اللَّهُ. وَكَانَتْ تَقُولُ مَا رَأَيْتُ أَسِيرًا قَطُّ خَيْرًا مِنْ خُبَيْبٍ، لَقَدْ رَأَيْتُهُ يَأْكُلُ مِنْ قِطْفِ عِنَبٍ، وَمَا بِمَكَّةَ يَوْمَئِذٍ ثَمَرَةٌ، وَإِنَّهُ لَمُوثَقٌ فِي الْحَدِيدِ، وَمَا كَانَ إِلاَّ رِزْقٌ رَزَقَهُ اللَّهُ، فَخَرَجُوا بِهِ مِنَ الْحَرَمِ، لِيَقْتُلُوهُ فَقَالَ دَعُونِي أُصَلِّي رَكْعَتَيْنِ. ثُمَّ انْصَرَفَ إِلَيْهِمْ فَقَالَ لَوْلاَ أَنْ تَرَوْا أَنَّ مَا بِي جَزَعٌ مِنَ الْمَوْتِ، لَزِدْتُ. فَكَانَ أَوَّلَ مَنْ سَنَّ الرَّكْعَتَيْنِ عِنْدَ الْقَتْلِ هُوَ، ثُمَّ قَالَ اللَّهُمَّ أَحْصِهِمْ عَدَدًا ثُمَّ قَالَ مَا أُبَالِي حِينَ أُقْتَلُ مُسْلِمًا عَلَى أَىِّ شِقٍّ كَانَ لِلَّهِ مَصْرَعِي وَذَلِكَ فِي ذَاتِ الإِلَهِ وَإِنْ يَشَأْ يُبَارِكْ عَلَى

أَوْصَالِ شِلْوٍ مُمَزَّعِ ثُمَّ قَامَ إِلَيْهِ عُقْبَةُ بْنُ الْحَارِثِ فَقَتَلَهُ، وَبَعَثَ قُرَيْشٌ إِلَى عَاصِمٍ لِيُؤْتَوْا بِشَيْءٍ مِنْ جَسَدِهِ يَعْرِفُونَهُ، وَكَانَ عَاصِمٌ قَتَلَ عَظِيمًا مِنْ عُظَمَائِهِمْ يَوْمَ بَدْرٍ، فَبَعَثَ اللَّهُ عَلَيْهِ مِثْلَ الظُّلَّةِ مِنَ الدَّبْرِ، فَحَمَتْهُ مِنْ رُسُلِهِمْ، فَلَمْ يَقْدِرُوا مِنْهُ عَلَى شَيْءٍ.

Narrated Anas: The Prophet ﷺ sent seventy men from the tribe of Bani Salim to the tribe of Bani Amir. When they reached there, my maternal uncle said to them, "I will go ahead of you, and if they allow me to convey the message of Allah's Messenger ﷺ (it will be all right); otherwise you will remain close to me." So he went ahead of them and the pagans granted him security But while he was reporting the message of the Prophet ﷺ, they beckoned to one of their men who stabbed him to death. My maternal uncle said, "Allah is Greater! By the Lord of the Ka`ba, I am successful." After that they attached the rest of the party and killed them all except a lame man who went up to the top of the mountain. (Hammam, a sub-narrator said, "I think another man was saved along with him)." Gabriel informed the Prophet ﷺ that they (i.e the martyrs) met their Lord, and He was pleased with them and made them pleased. We used to recite, "Inform our people that we have met our Lord, He is pleased with us and He has made us pleased " Later on this Qur'anic Verse was cancelled. The Prophet ﷺ invoked Allah for forty days to curse the murderers from the tribe of Ral, Dhakwan, Bani Lihyan and Bam Usaiya who disobeyed Allah and his Apostle. – Sahih Al-Bukhari 2801

حَدَّثَنَا حَفْصُ بْنُ عُمَرَ الْحَوْضِيُّ، حَدَّثَنَا هَمَّامٌ، عَنْ إِسْحَاقَ، عَنْ أَنَسٍ ـ رضى الله عنه ـ قَالَ بَعَثَ النَّبِيُّ صلى الله عليه وسلم أَقْوَامًا مِنْ بَنِي سُلَيْمٍ إِلَى بَنِي عَامِرٍ فِي سَبْعِينَ، فَلَمَّا قَدِمُوا، قَالَ لَهُمْ خَالِي أَتَقَدَّمُكُمْ، فَإِنْ أَمَّنُونِي حَتَّى أُبَلِّغَهُمْ عَنْ رَسُولِ اللَّهِ صلى الله عليه وسلم وَإِلاَّ كُنْتُمْ مِنِّي قَرِيبًا. فَتَقَدَّمَ، فَأَمَّنُوهُ، فَبَيْنَمَا يُحَدِّثُهُمْ عَنِ النَّبِيِّ صلى الله عليه وسلم إِذْ أَوْمَئُوا إِلَى رَجُلٍ مِنْهُمْ، فَطَعَنَهُ فَأَنْفَذَهُ فَقَالَ اللَّهُ أَكْبَرُ، فُزْتُ وَرَبِّ الْكَعْبَةِ. ثُمَّ مَالُوا عَلَى بَقِيَّةِ أَصْحَابِهِ فَقَتَلُوهُمْ، إِلاَّ رَجُلاً أَعْرَجَ صَعِدَ الْجَبَلَ. قَالَ هَمَّامٌ فَأُرَاهُ آخَرَ مَعَهُ، فَأَخْبَرَ جِبْرِيلُ ـ عَلَيْهِ السَّلاَمُ ـ النَّبِيَّ صلى الله عليه وسلم أَنَّهُمْ قَدْ لَقُوا رَبَّهُمْ، فَرَضِيَ عَنْهُمْ وَأَرْضَاهُمْ، فَكُنَّا نَقْرَأُ أَنْ بَلِّغُوا قَوْمَنَا أَنْ قَدْ لَقِينَا رَبَّنَا فَرَضِيَ عَنَّا وَأَرْضَانَا. ثُمَّ نُسِخَ بَعْدُ، فَدَعَا عَلَيْهِمْ أَرْبَعِينَ صَبَاحًا، عَلَى رِعْلٍ وَذَكْوَانَ وَبَنِي لِحْيَانَ وَبَنِي عُصَيَّةَ الَّذِينَ عَصَوُا اللَّهَ وَرَسُولَهُ صلى الله عليه وسلم.

Narrated Abu Huraira: Allah's Messenger ﷺ gave a verdict regarding an aborted fetus of a woman from Bani Lihyan that the killer (of the fetus) should give a male or female slave (as a Diya) but the woman who was required to give the slave, died, so Allah's Messenger ﷺ gave the verdict that her inheritance be given to her children and her husband and the Diya be paid by her 'Asaba. – Sahih Al-Bukhari 6909

حَدَّثَنَا عَبْدُ اللَّهِ بْنُ يُوسُفَ، حَدَّثَنَا اللَّيْثُ، عَنِ ابْنِ شِهَابٍ، عَنْ سَعِيدِ بْنِ الْمُسَيَّبِ، عَنْ أَبِي هُرَيْرَةَ، أَنَّ رَسُولَ اللَّهِ صلى الله عليه وسلم قَضَى فِي جَنِينِ امْرَأَةٍ مِنْ بَنِي لِحْيَانَ بِغُرَّةٍ عَبْدٍ أَوْ أَمَةٍ، ثُمَّ إِنَّ الْمَرْأَةَ الَّتِي قَضَى عَلَيْهَا بِالْغُرَّةِ تُوُفِّيَتْ، فَقَضَى رَسُولُ اللَّهِ صلى الله عليه وسلم أَنَّ مِيرَاثَهَا لِبَنِيهَا وَزَوْجِهَا، وَأَنَّ الْعَقْلَ عَلَى عَصَبَتِهَا

Banu Quraiza
بنو قريظة

Narrated `Aisha: Sa`d was wounded on the day of Khandaq (i.e. Trench) when a man from Quraish, called Hibban bin Al-`Araqa hit him (with an arrow). The man was Hibban bin Qais from (the tribe of) Bani Mais bin 'Amir bin Lu'ai who shot an arrow at Sa'd's medial arm vein (or main artery of the arm). The Prophet ﷺ pitched a tent (for Sa`d) in the Mosque so that he might be near to the Prophet ﷺ to visit. When the Prophet returned from the (battle) of Al-Khandaq (i.e. Trench) and laid down his arms and took a bath Gabriel came to him while he (i.e. Gabriel) was shaking the dust off his head, and said, "You have laid down the arms?" By Allah, I have not laid them down. Go out to them (to attack them)." The Prophet ﷺ said,

"Where?" Gabriel pointed towards Bani Quraiza. So Allah's Messenger ﷺ went to them (i.e. Banu Quraiza) (i.e. besieged them). They then surrendered to the Prophet's judgment but he directed them to Sa`d to give his verdict concerning them. Sa`d said, "I give my judgment that their warriors should be killed, their women and children should be taken as captives, and their properties distributed." Narrated Hisham: My father informed me that `Aisha said, "Sa`d said, "O Allah! You know that there is nothing more beloved to me than to fight in Your Cause against those who disbelieved Your Apostle and turned him out (of Mecca). O Allah! I think you have put to an end the fight between us and them (i.e. Quraish infidels). And if there still remains any fight with the Quraish (infidels), then keep me alive till I fight against them for Your Sake. But if you have brought the war to an end, then let this wound burst and cause my death thereby.' So blood gushed from the wound. There was a tent in the Mosque belonging to Banu Ghifar who were surprised by the blood flowing towards them . They said, 'O people of the tent! What is this thing which is coming to us from your side?' Behold! Blood was flowing profusely out of Sa`d's wound. Sa`d then died because of that.". – Sahih Al-Bukhari 4122

حَدَّثَنَا زَكَرِيَّاءُ بْنُ يَحْيَى، حَدَّثَنَا عَبْدُ اللَّهِ بْنُ نُمَيْرٍ، حَدَّثَنَا هِشَامٌ، عَنْ أَبِيهِ، عَنْ عَائِشَةَ ـ رضى الله عنها ـ قَالَتْ أُصِيبَ سَعْدٌ يَوْمَ الْخَنْدَقِ، رَمَاهُ رَجُلٌ مِنْ قُرَيْشٍ يُقَالُ لَهُ حِبَّانُ ابْنُ الْعَرِقَةِ، رَمَاهُ فِي الأَكْحَلِ، فَضَرَبَ النَّبِيُّ صلى الله عليه وسلم خَيْمَةً فِي الْمَسْجِدِ لِيَعُودَهُ مِنْ قَرِيبٍ، فَلَمَّا رَجَعَ رَسُولُ اللَّهِ صلى الله عليه وسلم مِنَ الْخَنْدَقِ وَضَعَ السِّلاَحَ وَاغْتَسَلَ، فَأَتَاهُ جِبْرِيلُ ـ عَلَيْهِ السَّلاَمُ ـ وَهْوَ يَنْفُضُ رَأْسَهُ مِنَ الْغُبَارِ فَقَالَ قَدْ وَضَعْتَ السِّلاَحَ وَاللَّهِ مَا وَضَعْتُهُ، اخْرُجْ إِلَيْهِمْ. قَالَ النَّبِيُّ صلى الله عليه وسلم " فَأَيْنَ ". فَأَشَارَ إِلَى بَنِي قُرَيْظَةَ، فَأَتَاهُمْ رَسُولُ اللَّهِ صلى الله عليه وسلم فَنَزَلُوا عَلَى حُكْمِهِ، فَرَدَّ الْحُكْمَ إِلَى سَعْدٍ، قَالَ فَإِنِّي أَحْكُمُ فِيهِمْ أَنْ تُقْتَلَ الْمُقَاتِلَةُ، وَأَنْ تُسْبَى النِّسَاءُ وَالذُّرِّيَّةُ، وَأَنْ تُقْسَمَ أَمْوَالُهُمْ. قَالَ هِشَامٌ فَأَخْبَرَنِي أَبِي عَنْ عَائِشَةَ أَنَّ سَعْدًا قَالَ اللَّهُمَّ إِنَّكَ تَعْلَمُ أَنَّهُ لَيْسَ أَحَدٌ أَحَبَّ إِلَىَّ أَنْ أُجَاهِدَهُمْ فِيكَ مِنْ قَوْمٍ كَذَّبُوا رَسُولَكَ صلى الله عليه وسلم وَأَخْرَجُوهُ، اللَّهُمَّ فَإِنِّي أَظُنُّ أَنَّكَ قَدْ وَضَعْتَ الْحَرْبَ بَيْنَنَا وَبَيْنَهُمْ، فَإِنْ كَانَ بَقِيَ مِنْ حَرْبِ قُرَيْشٍ شَىْءٌ، فَأَبْقِنِي لَهُ حَتَّى أُجَاهِدَهُمْ فِيكَ، وَإِنْ كُنْتَ وَضَعْتَ الْحَرْبَ فَافْجُرْهَا، وَاجْعَلْ مَوْتَتِي فِيهَا. فَانْفَجَرَتْ مِنْ لَبَّتِهِ، فَلَمْ يَرُعْهُمْ وَفِي الْمَسْجِدِ خَيْمَةٌ مِنْ بَنِي غِفَارٍ إِلاَّ الدَّمُ يَسِيلُ إِلَيْهِمْ فَقَالُوا يَا أَهْلَ الْخَيْمَةِ مَا هَذَا الَّذِي يَأْتِينَا مِنْ قِبَلِكُمْ فَإِذَا سَعْدٌ يَغْذُو جُرْحُهُ دَمًا، فَمَاتَ مِنْهَا رضى الله عنه.

Narrated Anas :Some (of the Ansar) used to present date palm trees to the Prophet ﷺ till Banu Quraiza and Banu An- Nadir were conquered (then he returned to the people their date palms). My people ordered me to ask the Prophet ﷺ to return some or all the date palms they had given to him, but the Prophet ﷺ had given those trees to Um Aiman. On that, Um Aiman came and put the garment around my neck and said, "No, by Him except Whom none has the right to be worshipped, he will not return those trees to you as he (i.e. the Prophet ﷺ) has given them to me." The Prophet ﷺ go said (to her), "Return those trees and I will give you so much (instead of them)." But she kept on refusing, saying, "No, by Allah," till he gave her ten times the number of her date palms – .Sahih Al-Bukhari 4120

حَدَّثَنَا ابْنُ أَبِي الأَسْوَدِ، حَدَّثَنَا مُعْتَمِرٌ، وَحَدَّثَنِي خَلِيفَةُ، حَدَّثَنَا مُعْتَمِرٌ، قَالَ سَمِعْتُ أَبِي، عَنْ أَنَسٍ ـ رضى الله عنه ـ قَالَ كَانَ الرَّجُلُ يَجْعَلُ لِلنَّبِيِّ صلى الله عليه وسلم النَّخَلاَتِ حَتَّى افْتَتَحَ قُرَيْظَةَ وَالنَّضِيرَ، وَإِنَّ أَهْلِي أَمَرُونِي أَنْ آتِيَ النَّبِيَّ صلى الله عليه وسلم فَأَسْأَلَهُ الَّذِينَ كَانُوا أَعْطَوْهُ أَوْ بَعْضَهُ. وَكَانَ النَّبِيُّ صلى الله عليه وسلم قَدْ أَعْطَاهُ أُمَّ أَيْمَنَ، فَجَاءَتْ أُمُّ أَيْمَنَ فَجَعَلَتِ الثَّوْبَ فِي عُنُقِي تَقُولُ كَلاَّ وَالَّذِي لاَ إِلَهَ إِلاَّ هُوَ لاَ يُعْطِيكَهُمْ وَقَدْ أَعْطَانِيهَا، أَوْ كَمَا قَالَتْ، وَالنَّبِيُّ صلى الله عليه وسلم يَقُولُ " لَكِ كَذَا ". وَتَقُولُ كَلاَّ وَاللَّهِ. حَتَّى أَعْطَاهَا، حَسِبْتُ أَنَّهُ قَالَ " عَشَرَةَ أَمْثَالِهِ ". أَوْ كَمَا قَالَ.

Narrated Abu Sa`id Al-Khudri :Some people (i.e. the Jews of Bani bin Quraiza) agreed to accept the verdict of Sa`d bin Mu`adh so the Prophet ﷺ sent for him (i.e. Sa`d bin Mu`adh). He came riding a donkey, and when he approached the Mosque, the Prophet ﷺ said, "Get up for the best amongst you." Or said, "Get up for your chief." Then the Prophet ﷺ said, "O Sa`d! These people have agreed to accept your verdict." Sa`d said, "I judge that their warriors should be killed and their children and women should be taken as captives." The Prophet said, “You have given a judgment similar to Allah’s Judgment (or the King’s judgment) – . Sahih Al-Bukhari 3804

حَدَّثَنَا مُحَمَّدُ بْنُ عَرْعَرَةَ، حَدَّثَنَا شُعْبَةُ، عَنْ سَعْدِ بْنِ إِبْرَاهِيمَ، عَنْ أَبِي أُمَامَةَ بْنِ سَهْلِ بْنِ حُنَيْفٍ، عَنْ أَبِي سَعِيدٍ الْخُدْرِيِّ - رضى الله عنه - أَنَّ أُنَاسًا نَزَلُوا عَلَى حُكْمِ سَعْدِ بْنِ مُعَاذٍ، فَأَرْسَلَ إِلَيْهِ فَجَاءَ عَلَى حِمَارٍ، فَلَمَّا بَلَغَ قَرِيبًا مِنَ الْمَسْجِدِ قَالَ النَّبِيُّ صلى الله عليه وسلم " قُومُوا إِلَى خَيْرِكُمْ أَوْ سَيِّدِكُمْ ". فَقَالَ " يَا سَعْدُ، إِنَّ هَؤُلاَءِ نَزَلُوا عَلَى حُكْمِكَ ". قَالَ فَإِنِّي أَحْكُمُ فِيهِمْ أَنْ تُقْتَلَ مُقَاتِلَتُهُمْ وَتُسْبَى ذَرَارِيُّهُمْ. قَالَ " حَكَمْتَ بِحُكْمِ اللَّهِ، أَوْ بِحُكْمِ الْمَلِكِ ".

Narrated Al-Bara :The Prophet ﷺ said to Hassan, “Abuse them (with your poems), and Gabriel is with you (i.e, supports you).” (Through another group of sub narrators) Al-Bara bin Azib said, “On the day of Quraiza’s (besiege), Allah’s Messenger ﷺ said to Hassan bin Thabit, ‘Abuse them (with your poems), and Gabriel is with you (i.e. supports you) – ." '.Sahih Al-Bukhari 4123

حَدَّثَنَا الْحَجَّاجُ بْنُ مِنْهَالٍ، أَخْبَرَنَا شُعْبَةُ، قَالَ أَخْبَرَنِي عَدِيٌّ، أَنَّهُ سَمِعَ الْبَرَاءَ - رضى الله عنه - قَالَ قَالَ النَّبِيُّ صلى الله عليه وسلم لِحَسَّانَ اهْجُهُمْ - أَوْ هَاجِهِمْ - وَجِبْرِيلُ مَعَكَ ".

Narrated Anas :As if I am just now looking at the dust rising in the street of Banu Ghanm (in Medina) because of the marching of Gabriel’s regiment when Allah’s Messenger ﷺ set out to Banu Quraiza (to attack them) – .Sahih Al-Bukhari 4118

حَدَّثَنَا مُوسَى، حَدَّثَنَا جَرِيرُ بْنُ حَازِمٍ، عَنْ حُمَيْدِ بْنِ هِلاَلٍ، عَنْ أَنَسٍ - رضى الله عنه - قَالَ كَأَنِّي أَنْظُرُ إِلَى الْغُبَارِ سَاطِعًا فِي زُقَاقِ بَنِي غَنْمٍ مَوْكِبِ جِبْرِيلَ حِينَ سَارَ رَسُولُ اللَّهِ صلى الله عليه وسلم إِلَى بَنِي قُرَيْظَةَ.

Narrated `Abdullah bin Az-Zubair :During the battle of Al-Ahzab, I and `Umar bin Abi-Salama were kept behind with the women. Behold! I saw (my father) Az-Zubair riding his horse, going to and coming from Bani Quraiza twice or thrice. So when I came back I said, “O my father! I saw you going to and coming from Bani Quraiza?” He said, “Did you really see me, O my son?” I said, “Yes.” He said, “Allah’s Messenger ﷺ said, ‘Who will go to Bani Quraiza and bring me their news?’ So I went, and when I came back, Allah’s Apostle mentioned for me both his parents saying, “Let my father and mother be sacrificed for you – .'".Sahih Al-Bukhari 3720

حَدَّثَنَا أَحْمَدُ بْنُ مُحَمَّدٍ، أَخْبَرَنَا {عَبْدُ اللَّهِ} أَخْبَرَنَا هِشَامُ بْنُ عُرْوَةَ، عَنْ أَبِيهِ، عَنْ عَبْدِ اللَّهِ بْنِ الزُّبَيْرِ، قَالَ كُنْتُ يَوْمَ الأَحْزَابِ جُعِلْتُ أَنَا وَعُمَرُ بْنُ أَبِي سَلَمَةَ، فِي النِّسَاءِ، فَنَظَرْتُ فَإِذَا أَنَا بِالزُّبَيْرِ، عَلَى فَرَسِهِ، يَخْتَلِفُ إِلَى بَنِي قُرَيْظَةَ مَرَّتَيْنِ أَوْ ثَلاَثًا، فَلَمَّا رَجَعْتُ قُلْتُ يَا أَبَتِ، رَأَيْتُكَ تَخْتَلِفُ. قَالَ أَوَهَلْ رَأَيْتَنِي يَا بُنَىَّ قُلْتُ نَعَمْ. قَالَ كَانَ رَسُولُ اللَّهِ صلى الله عليه وسلم قَالَ " مَنْ يَأْتِ بَنِي قُرَيْظَةَ فَيَأْتِينِي بِخَبَرِهِمْ ". فَانْطَلَقْتُ، فَلَمَّا رَجَعْتُ جَمَعَ لِي رَسُولُ اللَّهِ صلى الله عليه وسلم أَبَوَيْهِ فَقَالَ " فِدَاكَ أَبِي وَأُمِّي ".

The Book of

Medina & Jewish Tribes

المدينة المنورة والقبائل اليهودية

Banu Al-Harith-ibn-Khazraj

بنو الحارث بن الخزرج

Narrated Anas bin Malik: Allah's Messenger ﷺ said, "Shall I tell you of the best families among the Ansar?" They (the people) said, "Yes, O Allah's Messenger ﷺ ! The Prophet ﷺ said, "The best are Banu- An-Najjar, and after them are Banu `Abdil Ash-hal, and after them are Banu Al-Harith bin Al-Khazraj, and after them are Banu Sa`ida." The Prophet ﷺ then moved his hand by closing his fingers and then opening them like one throwing something, and then said, "Anyhow, there is good in all the families of the Ansar. " – Sahih al-Bukhari 5300

حَدَّثَنَا قُتَيْبَةُ، حَدَّثَنَا لَيْثٌ، عَنْ يَحْيَى بْنِ سَعِيدٍ الأَنْصَارِيِّ، أَنَّهُ سَمِعَ أَنَسَ بْنَ مَالِكٍ، يَقُولُ قَالَ رَسُولُ اللَّهِ صلى الله عليه وسلم " أَلاَ أُخْبِرُكُمْ بِخَيْرِ دُورِ الأَنْصَارِ ". قَالُوا بَلَى يَا رَسُولَ اللَّهِ. قَالَ " بَنُو النَّجَّارِ، ثُمَّ الَّذِينَ يَلُونَهُمْ بَنُو عَبْدِ الأَشْهَلِ، ثُمَّ الَّذِينَ يَلُونَهُمْ بَنُو الْحَارِثِ بْنِ الْخَزْرَجِ، ثُمَّ الَّذِينَ يَلُونَهُمْ بَنُو سَاعِدَةَ ". ثُمَّ قَالَ بِيَدِهِ، فَقَبَضَ أَصَابِعَهُ، ثُمَّ بَسَطَهُنَّ كَالرَّامِي بِيَدِهِ ثُمَّ قَالَ " وَفِي كُلِّ دُورِ الأَنْصَارِ خَيْرٌ "

Narrated Aisha: The Prophet ﷺ engaged me when I was a girl of six (years). We went to Medina and stayed at the home of Bani-al-Harith bin Khazraj. Then I got ill and my hair fell down. Later on my hair grew (again) and my mother, Um Ruman, came to me while I was playing in a swing with some of my girl friends. She called me, and I went to her, not knowing what she wanted to do to me. She caught me by the hand and made me stand at the door of the house. I was breathless then, and when my breathing became Allright, she took some water and rubbed my face and head with it. Then she took me into the house. There in the house I saw some Ansari women who said, "Best wishes and Allah's Blessing and a good luck." Then she entrusted me to them and they prepared me (for the marriage). Unexpectedly Allah's Apostle came to me in the forenoon and my mother handed me over to him, and at that time I was a girl of nine years of age. – Sahih al-Bukhari 3894

حَدَّثَنِي فَرْوَةُ بْنُ أَبِي الْمَغْرَاءِ، حَدَّثَنَا عَلِيُّ بْنُ مُسْهِرٍ، عَنْ هِشَامٍ، عَنْ أَبِيهِ، عَنْ عَائِشَةَ ـ رضى الله عنها ـ قَالَتْ تَزَوَّجَنِي النَّبِيُّ صلى الله عليه وسلم وَأَنَا بِنْتُ سِتِّ سِنِينَ، فَقَدِمْنَا الْمَدِينَةَ فَنَزَلْنَا فِي بَنِي الْحَارِثِ بْنِ خَزْرَجٍ، فَوُعِكْتُ فَتَمَرَّقَ شَعَرِي فَوَفَى جُمَيْمَةً، فَأَتَتْنِي أُمِّي أُمُّ رُومَانَ وَإِنِّي لَفِي أُرْجُوحَةٍ وَمَعِي صَوَاحِبُ لِي، فَصَرَخَتْ بِي فَأَتَيْتُهَا لاَ أَدْرِي مَا تُرِيدُ بِي فَأَخَذَتْ بِيَدِي حَتَّى أَوْقَفَتْنِي عَلَى بَابِ الدَّارِ، وَإِنِّي لأُنْهِجُ، حَتَّى سَكَنَ بَعْضُ نَفَسِي، ثُمَّ أَخَذَتْ شَيْئًا مِنْ مَاءٍ فَمَسَحَتْ بِهِ وَجْهِي وَرَأْسِي ثُمَّ أَدْخَلَتْنِي الدَّارَ فَإِذَا نِسْوَةٌ مِنَ الأَنْصَارِ فِي الْبَيْتِ فَقُلْنَ عَلَى الْخَيْرِ وَالْبَرَكَةِ، وَعَلَى خَيْرِ طَائِرٍ. فَأَسْلَمَتْنِي إِلَيْهِنَّ فَأَصْلَحْنَ مِنْ شَأْنِي، فَلَمْ يَرُعْنِي إِلاَّ رَسُولُ اللَّهِ صلى الله عليه وسلم ضُحًى، فَأَسْلَمَتْنِي إِلَيْهِ، وَأَنَا يَوْمَئِذٍ بِنْتُ تِسْعِ سِنِينَ.

Narrated `Aisha: The day of Bu'ath (i.e. Day of fighting between the two tribes of the Ansar, the Aus and Khazraj) was brought about by Allah for the good of His Apostle so that when Allah's Messenger ﷺ reached (Medina), the tribes of Medina had already divided and their chiefs had been killed and wounded. So Allah had brought about the battle for the good of His Apostle in order that they (i.e. the Ansar) might embrace Islam. – Sahih al-Bukhari 3777

حَدَّثَنِي عُبَيْدُ بْنُ إِسْمَاعِيلَ، حَدَّثَنَا أَبُو أُسَامَةَ، عَنْ هِشَامٍ، عَنْ أَبِيهِ، عَنْ عَائِشَةَ ـ رضى الله عنها ـ قَالَتْ كَانَ يَوْمُ بُعَاثَ يَوْمًا قَدَّمَهُ اللَّهُ لِرَسُولِهِ صلى الله عليه وسلم فَقَدِمَ رَسُولُ اللَّهِ صلى الله عليه وسلم وَقَدِ افْتَرَقَ مَلَؤُهُمْ، وَقُتِلَتْ سَرَوَاتُهُمْ، وَجُرِّحُوا، فَقَدَّمَهُ اللَّهُ لِرَسُولِهِ صلى الله عليه وسلم فِي دُخُولِهِمْ فِي الإِسْلاَمِ

Narrated `Urwa-bin Az-Zubair: Usama bin Zaid said, "The Prophet ﷺ rode over a donkey with a saddle underneath which there was a thick soft Fadakiya velvet sheet. Usama bin Zaid was his companion rider, and he was going to pay a visit to Sa`d bin Ubada (who was sick) at the dwelling place of Bani Al-Harith bin Al-Khazraj, and this incident happened before the battle of Badr. The Prophet ﷺ passed by a gathering in which there were Muslims and pagan idolators and Jews, and among them there was `Abdullah bin Ubai bin Salul, and there was `Abdullah bin Rawaha too. When a cloud of dust raised by the animal covered that gathering, `Abdullah bin Ubai covered his nose with his Rida (sheet) and said (to the Prophet), "Don't cover us with dust." The Prophet ﷺ greeted them and then stopped, dismounted and invited them to Allah (i.e., to embrace Islam) and also recited to them the Holy Qur'an. `Abdullah bin Ubai' bin Salul said, "O man! There is nothing better than what you say, if what you say is the truth. So do not trouble us in our gatherings. Go back to your mount (or house,) and if anyone of us comes to you, tell (your tales) to him." On that `Abdullah bin Rawaha said, "(O Allah's Messenger ﷺ ! Come to us and bring it(what you want to say) in our gatherings, for we love that." So the Muslims, the pagans and the Jews started quarreling till they were about to fight and clash with one another. The Prophet ﷺ kept on quietening them (till they all became quiet). He then rode his animal, and proceeded till he entered upon Sa`d bin 'Ubada, he said, "O Sa`d, didn't you hear what Abu Habbab said? (He meant `Abdullah bin Ubai). He said so-and-so." Sa`d bin 'Ubada said, "O Allah's Messenger ﷺ ! Excuse and forgive him, for by Allah, Allah has given you what He has given you. The people of this town decided to crown him (as their chief) and make him their king. But when Allah prevented that with the Truth which He had given you, it choked him, and that was what made him behave in the way you saw him behaving." So the Prophet excused him. – Sahih al-Bukhari 6254

حَدَّثَنَا إِبْرَاهِيمُ بْنُ مُوسَى، أَخْبَرَنَا هِشَامٌ، عَنْ مَعْمَرٍ، عَنِ الزُّهْرِيِّ، عَنْ عُرْوَةَ بْنِ الزُّبَيْرِ، قَالَ أَخْبَرَنِي أُسَامَةُ بْنُ زَيْدٍ، أَنَّ النَّبِيَّ صلى الله عليه وسلم رَكِبَ حِمَارًا عَلَيْهِ إِكَافٌ، تَحْتَهُ قَطِيفَةٌ فَدَكِيَّةٌ، وَأَرْدَفَ وَرَاءَهُ أُسَامَةَ بْنَ زَيْدٍ وَهْوَ يَعُودُ سَعْدَ بْنَ عُبَادَةَ فِي بَنِي الْحَارِثِ بْنِ الْخَزْرَجِ، وَذَلِكَ قَبْلَ وَقْعَةِ بَدْرٍ حَتَّى مَرَّ فِي مَجْلِسٍ فِيهِ أَخْلاَطٌ مِنَ الْمُسْلِمِينَ وَالْمُشْرِكِينَ عَبَدَةِ الأَوْثَانِ وَالْيَهُودِ، وَفِيهِمْ عَبْدُ اللَّهِ بْنُ أُبَىٍّ ابْنُ سَلُولَ، وَفِي الْمَجْلِسِ عَبْدُ اللَّهِ بْنُ رَوَاحَةَ، فَلَمَّا غَشِيَتِ الْمَجْلِسَ عَجَاجَةُ الدَّابَّةِ خَمَّرَ عَبْدُ اللَّهِ بْنُ أُبَىٍّ أَنْفَهُ بِرِدَائِهِ ثُمَّ قَالَ لاَ تُغَبِّرُوا عَلَيْنَا. فَسَلَّمَ عَلَيْهِمُ النَّبِيُّ صلى الله عليه وسلم ثُمَّ وَقَفَ فَنَزَلَ، فَدَعَاهُمْ إِلَى اللَّهِ وَقَرَأَ عَلَيْهِمُ الْقُرْآنَ فَقَالَ عَبْدُ اللَّهِ بْنُ أُبَىٍّ ابْنُ سَلُولَ أَيُّهَا الْمَرْءُ لاَ أَحْسَنَ مِنْ هَذَا، إِنْ كَانَ مَا تَقُولُ حَقًّا، فَلاَ تُؤْذِنَا فِي مَجَالِسِنَا، وَارْجِعْ إِلَى رَحْلِكَ، فَمَنْ جَاءَكَ مِنَّا فَاقْصُصْ عَلَيْهِ. قَالَ ابْنُ رَوَاحَةَ اغْشَنَا فِي مَجَالِسِنَا، فَإِنَّا نُحِبُّ ذَلِكَ. فَاسْتَبَّ الْمُسْلِمُونَ وَالْمُشْرِكُونَ وَالْيَهُودُ حَتَّى هَمُّوا أَنْ يَتَوَاثَبُوا، فَلَمْ يَزَلِ النَّبِيُّ صلى الله عليه وسلم يُخَفِّضُهُمْ، ثُمَّ رَكِبَ دَابَّتَهُ حَتَّى دَخَلَ عَلَى سَعْدِ بْنِ عُبَادَةَ فَقَالَ " أَىْ سَعْدُ أَلَمْ تَسْمَعْ مَا قَالَ أَبُو حُبَابٍ ". يُرِيدُ عَبْدَ اللَّهِ بْنَ أُبَىٍّ قَالَ كَذَا وَكَذَا قَالَ اعْفُ عَنْهُ يَا رَسُولَ اللَّهِ وَاصْفَحْ فَوَاللَّهِ لَقَدْ أَعْطَاكَ اللَّهُ الَّذِي أَعْطَاكَ، وَلَقَدِ اصْطَلَحَ أَهْلُ هَذِهِ الْبَحْرَةِ عَلَى أَنْ يُتَوِّجُوهُ فَيُعَصِّبُونَهُ بِالْعِصَابَةِ، فَلَمَّا رَدَّ اللَّهُ ذَلِكَ بِالْحَقِّ الَّذِي أَعْطَاكَ شَرِقَ بِذَلِكَ، فَذَلِكَ فَعَلَ بِهِ مَا رَأَيْتَ، فَعَفَا عَنْهُ النَّبِيُّ صلى الله عليه وسلم

Banu Saida
بنو ساعدة

Narrated 'Aisha: (the wife of the Prophet) Allah's Messenger ﷺ died while Abu Bakr was at a place called As-Sunah (Al-'Aliya) 'Umar stood up and said, "By Allah! Allah's Messenger ﷺ is not dead!" 'Umar (later on) said, "By Allah! Nothing occurred to my mind except that." He said, "Verily! Allah will resurrect him and he will cut the hands and legs of some men." Then Abu Bakr came and uncovered the face of Allah's Messenger ﷺ , kissed him and said, "Let my mother and father be sacrificed for you, (O Allah's Messenger ﷺ), you are good in life and in death. By Allah in Whose Hands my life is, Allah will never make you taste death twice." Then he went out and said, "O oath-taker! Don't be hasty." When Abu Bakr spoke, 'Umar sat down.

Abu Bakr praised and glorified Allah and said, No doubt! Whoever worshipped Muhammad, then Muhammad is dead, but whoever worshipped Allah, then Allah is Alive and shall never die." Then he recited Allah's Statement.:-- "(O Muhammad) Verily you will die, and they also will die." (39.30) He also recited:- "Muhammad is no more than an Apostle; and indeed many Apostles have passed away, before him, If he dies Or is killed, will you then Turn back on your heels? And he who turns back On his heels, not the least Harm will he do to Allah And Allah will give reward to those Who are grateful." (3.144) The people wept loudly, and the Ansar were assembled with Sad bin 'Ubada in the shed of Bani Saida. They said (to the emigrants). "There should be one 'Amir from us and one from you." Then Abu Bakr, Umar bin Al-Khattab and Abu 'baida bin Al-Jarrah went to them. 'Umar wanted to speak but Abu Bakr stopped him. 'Umar later on used to say, "By Allah, I intended only to say something that appealed to me and I was afraid that Abu Bakr would not speak so well. Then Abu Bakr spoke and his speech was very eloquent. He said in his statement, "We are the rulers and you (Ansars) are the ministers (i.e. advisers)," Hubab bin Al-Mundhir said, "No, by Allah we won't accept this. But there must be a ruler from us and a ruler from you." Abu Bakr said, "No, we will be the rulers and you will be the ministers, for they (i.e. Quarish) are the best family amongst the 'Arabs and of best origin. So you should elect either 'Umar or Abu 'Ubaida bin Al-Jarrah as your ruler." 'Umar said (to Abu Bakr), "No but we elect you, for you are our chief and the best amongst us and the most beloved of all of us to Allah's Messenger ﷺ." So 'Umar took Abu Bakr's hand and gave the pledge of allegiance and the people too gave the pledge of allegiance to Abu Bakr. Someone said, "You have killed Sad bin Ubada." 'Umar said, "Allah has killed him.". – Sahih Al-Bukhari 3667, 3668

حَدَّثَنَا إِسْمَاعِيلُ بْنُ عَبْدِ اللَّهِ، حَدَّثَنَا سُلَيْمَانُ بْنُ بِلاَلٍ، عَنْ هِشَامِ بْنِ عُرْوَةَ، عَنْ عُرْوَةَ بْنِ الزُّبَيْرِ، عَنْ عَائِشَةَ ـ رضى الله عنها ـ زَوْجِ النَّبِيِّ صلى الله عليه وسلم أَنَّ رَسُولَ اللَّهِ صلى الله عليه وسلم مَاتَ وَأَبُو بَكْرٍ بِالسُّنْحِ ـ قَالَ إِسْمَاعِيلُ يَعْنِي بِالْعَالِيَةِ ـ فَقَامَ عُمَرُ يَقُولُ وَاللَّهِ مَا مَاتَ رَسُولُ اللَّهِ صلى الله عليه وسلم. قَالَتْ وَقَالَ عُمَرُ وَاللَّهِ مَا كَانَ يَقَعُ فِي نَفْسِي إِلاَّ ذَاكَ وَلَيَبْعَثَنَّهُ اللَّهُ فَلَيَقْطَعَنَّ أَيْدِيَ رِجَالٍ وَأَرْجُلَهُمْ. فَجَاءَ أَبُو بَكْرٍ فَكَشَفَ عَنْ رَسُولِ اللَّهِ صلى الله عليه وسلم فَقَبَّلَهُ قَالَ بِأَبِي أَنْتَ وَأُمِّي طِبْتَ حَيًّا وَمَيِّتًا، وَالَّذِي نَفْسِي بِيَدِهِ لاَ يُذِيقُكَ اللَّهُ الْمَوْتَتَيْنِ أَبَدًا. ثُمَّ خَرَجَ فَقَالَ أَيُّهَا الْحَالِفُ عَلَى رِسْلِكَ. فَلَمَّا تَكَلَّمَ أَبُو بَكْرٍ جَلَسَ عُمَرُ. فَحَمِدَ اللَّهَ أَبُو بَكْرٍ وَأَثْنَى عَلَيْهِ وَقَالَ أَلاَ مَنْ كَانَ يَعْبُدُ مُحَمَّدًا صلى الله عليه وسلم فَإِنَّ مُحَمَّدًا قَدْ مَاتَ، وَمَنْ كَانَ يَعْبُدُ اللَّهَ فَإِنَّ اللَّهَ حَيٌّ لاَ يَمُوتُ. وَقَالَ {إِنَّكَ مَيِّتٌ وَإِنَّهُمْ مَيِّتُونَ} وَقَالَ {وَمَا مُحَمَّدٌ إِلاَّ رَسُولٌ قَدْ خَلَتْ مِنْ قَبْلِهِ الرُّسُلُ أَفَإِنْ مَاتَ أَوْ قُتِلَ انْقَلَبْتُمْ عَلَى أَعْقَابِكُمْ وَمَنْ يَنْقَلِبْ عَلَى عَقِبَيْهِ فَلَنْ يَضُرَّ اللَّهَ شَيْئًا وَسَيَجْزِي اللَّهُ الشَّاكِرِينَ} قَالَ فَنَشَجَ النَّاسُ يَبْكُونَ ـ قَالَ ـ وَاجْتَمَعَتِ الأَنْصَارُ إِلَى سَعْدِ بْنِ عُبَادَةَ فِي سَقِيفَةِ بَنِي سَاعِدَةَ فَقَالُوا مِنَّا أَمِيرٌ وَمِنْكُمْ أَمِيرٌ، فَذَهَبَ إِلَيْهِمْ أَبُو بَكْرٍ وَعُمَرُ بْنُ الْخَطَّابِ وَأَبُو عُبَيْدَةَ بْنُ الْجَرَّاحِ، فَذَهَبَ عُمَرُ يَتَكَلَّمُ فَأَسْكَتَهُ أَبُو بَكْرٍ، وَكَانَ عُمَرُ يَقُولُ وَاللَّهِ مَا أَرَدْتُ بِذَلِكَ إِلاَّ أَنِّي قَدْ هَيَّأْتُ كَلاَمًا قَدْ أَعْجَبَنِي خَشِيتُ أَنْ لاَ يَبْلُغَهُ أَبُو بَكْرٍ، ثُمَّ تَكَلَّمَ أَبُو بَكْرٍ فَتَكَلَّمَ أَبْلَغَ النَّاسِ فَقَالَ فِي كَلاَمِهِ نَحْنُ الأُمَرَاءُ وَأَنْتُمُ الْوُزَرَاءُ. فَقَالَ حُبَابُ بْنُ الْمُنْذِرِ لاَ وَاللَّهِ لاَ نَفْعَلُ، مِنَّا أَمِيرٌ وَمِنْكُمْ أَمِيرٌ. فَقَالَ أَبُو بَكْرٍ لاَ، وَلَكِنَّا الأُمَرَاءُ وَأَنْتُمُ الْوُزَرَاءُ هُمْ أَوْسَطُ الْعَرَبِ دَارًا، وَأَعْرَبُهُمْ أَحْسَابًا فَبَايِعُوا عُمَرَ أَوْ أَبَا عُبَيْدَةَ. فَقَالَ عُمَرُ بَلْ نُبَايِعُكَ أَنْتَ، فَأَنْتَ سَيِّدُنَا وَخَيْرُنَا وَأَحَبُّنَا إِلَى رَسُولِ اللَّهِ صلى الله عليه وسلم. فَأَخَذَ عُمَرُ بِيَدِهِ فَبَايَعَهُ، وَبَايَعَهُ النَّاسُ، فَقَالَ قَائِلٌ قَتَلْتُمْ سَعْدَ بْنَ عُبَادَةَ. فَقَالَ عُمَرُ قَتَلَهُ اللَّهُ

Narrated Abu Humaid: The Prophet ﷺ said, "The best of the Ansar families (homes) are the families (homes) of Banu An- Najjar, and then that of Banu `Abdul Ash-hal, and then that of Banu Al-Harith, and then that of Banu Saida; and there is good in all the families (homes) of the Ansar." Sa`d bin 'Ubada followed us and said, "O Abu Usaid ! Don't you see that the Prophet ﷺ compared the Ansar and made us the last of them in superiority? Then Sa`d met the Prophet ﷺ and said, "O Allah's Messenger ﷺ ! In comparing the Ansar's families (homes) as to the degree of superiority, you have made us the last of them." Allah's Messenger ﷺ replied, "Isn't it sufficient that you are regarded amongst the best?". – Sahih Al-Bukhari 3791

حَدَّثَنَا خَالِدُ بْنُ مَخْلَدٍ، حَدَّثَنَا سُلَيْمَانُ، قَالَ حَدَّثَنِي عَمْرُو بْنُ يَحْيَى، عَنْ عَبَّاسِ بْنِ سَهْلٍ، عَنْ أَبِي حُمَيْدٍ، عَنِ النَّبِيِّ صلى الله عليه وسلم قَالَ " إِنَّ خَيْرَ دُورِ الأَنْصَارِ دَارُ بَنِي النَّجَّارِ، ثُمَّ عَبْدِ الأَشْهَلِ، ثُمَّ دَارُ بَنِي الْحَارِثِ، ثُمَّ بَنِي سَاعِدَةَ، وَفِي كُلِّ

دُورِ الأَنْصَارِ خَيْرٌ ". فَلَحِقْنَا سَعْدَ بْنَ عُبَادَةَ فَقَالَ أَبَا أُسَيْدٍ أَلَمْ تَرَ أَنَّ نَبِيَّ اللَّهِ صلى الله عليه وسلم خَيَّرَ الأَنْصَارَ فَجَعَلَنَا أَخِيرًا فَأَدْرَكَ سَعْدٌ النَّبِيَّ صلى الله عليه وسلم فَقَالَ يَا رَسُولَ اللَّهِ، خُيِّرَ دُورُ الأَنْصَارِ فَجُعِلْنَا آخِرًا. فَقَالَ " أَوَلَيْسَ بِحَسْبِكُمْ أَنْ تَكُونُوا مِنَ الْخِيَارِ "

Narrated Ibn `Abbas: That the mother of Sa`d bin Ubada the brother of Bani Saida died in Sa`d's absence, so he came to the Prophet saying, "O Allah's Messenger ﷺ ! My mother died in my absence, will it benefit her if I give in charity on her behalf?" The Prophet ﷺ said, "Yes." Sa`d said, "I take you as my witness that I give my garden Al-Makhraf in charity on her behalf.". – Sahih Al-Bukhari 2762

حَدَّثَنَا إِبْرَاهِيمُ بْنُ مُوسَى، أَخْبَرَنَا هِشَامُ بْنُ يُوسُفَ، أَنَّ ابْنَ جُرَيْجٍ، أَخْبَرَهُمْ قَالَ أَخْبَرَنِي يَعْلَى، أَنَّهُ سَمِعَ عِكْرِمَةَ، مَوْلَى ابْنِ عَبَّاسٍ يَقُولُ أَنْبَأَنَا ابْنُ عَبَّاسٍ، أَنَّ سَعْدَ بْنَ عُبَادَةَ ـ رضى الله عنهم ـ أَخَا بَنِي سَاعِدَةَ تُوُفِّيَتْ أُمُّهُ وَهْوَ غَائِبٌ، فَأَتَى النَّبِيَّ صلى الله عليه وسلم فَقَالَ يَا رَسُولَ اللَّهِ إِنَّ أُمِّي تُوُفِّيَتْ وَأَنَا غَائِبٌ عَنْهَا، فَهَلْ يَنْفَعُهَا شَىْءٌ إِنْ تَصَدَّقْتُ بِهِ عَنْهَا قَالَ " نَعَمْ ". قَالَ فَإِنِّي أُشْهِدُكَ أَنَّ حَائِطِي الْمِخْرَافَ صَدَقَةٌ عَلَيْهَا

Banu Jusham
بنو جشم

It was narrated that Al-Hasan said: "Aqil bin Abi Talib married a woman from Banu Jusham, and it was said to him: 'May you live in harmony and have many sons.' He said: 'Say what the Messenger of Allah said: Barak Allahu fikum, wa baraka lakum. (May Allah bless you and bestow blessings upon you.)'" – Sunan an-Nasa'I 3371

حَدَّثَنَا عَمْرُو بْنُ عَلِيٍّ، وَمُحَمَّدُ بْنُ عَبْدِ الأَعْلَى، قَالاَ حَدَّثَنَا خَالِدٌ، عَنْ أَشْعَثَ، عَنِ الْحَسَنِ، قَالَ تَزَوَّجَ عَقِيلُ بْنُ أَبِي طَالِبٍ امْرَأَةً مِنْ بَنِي جُشَمٍ فَقِيلَ لَهُ بِالرِّفَاءِ وَالْبَنِينِ . قَالَ قُولُوا كَمَا قَالَ رَسُولُ اللَّهِ صلى الله عليه وسلم " بَارَكَ اللَّهُ فِيكُمْ وَبَارَكَ لَكُمْ "

Abu Burda reported on the authority of his father that when Allah's Apostle ﷺ had been free from the Battle of Hunain, he sent Abu 'Amir as the head of the army of Autas. He had an encounter with Duraid b. as_Simma. Duraid was killed and Allah gave defeat to his friends. Abu Musa said: He (the Holy Prophet) sent me along with Abu 'Amir and Abu 'Amir received a wound in his knee from the arrow, (shot by) a person of Bani Jusham. It stuck in his knee. I went to him and said: Uncle, who shot an arrow upon you? Abu 'Amir pointed out to Abu Musa and said: Verily that one who shot an arrow upon me in fact killed me. Abu Musa said: I followed him with the determination to kill him and overtook him and when he saw me he turned upon his heels. I followed him and I said to him: Don't you feel ashamed (that you run), aren't you an Arab? Why don't you stop? He stopped and I had an encounter with him and we exchanged the strokes of (swords). I struck him with the sword and killed him. Then I came back to Abu Amir and said: Verily Allah has killed the one who killed you. And he said: Now draw out this arrow. I drew out the arrow and there came out from that (wound) water. Abu 'Amir said: My nephew, go to Allah's Messenger ﷺ and convey my greetings to him and tell him that Abu Amir begs you to ask forgiveness for him. And Abu Amir appointed me as the chief of the people and he died after a short time. When I came to Allah's Apostle ﷺ I visited him and he had been lying on the cot woven by strings and there was (no) bed over it and so there had been marks of the strings on the back of Allah's Messenger ﷺ and on his sides. I narrated to him what had happened to us and narrated to him about Abu Amir and said to him that he had made a request to the effect that forgiveness should be sought for him (from Allah). Thereupon Allah's Messenger (may peace be. Upon him) called for water and performed ablution with it. He then lifted his hands and said. O Allah, grant pardon to

Thy servant Abu Amir. (The Prophet had raised his hands so high for supplication) that I saw the whiteness of his armpits. He again said: O Allah, grant him distinction amongst the majority of Thine created beings or from amongst the people. I said: Allah's Messenger, ask forgiveness for me too. Thereupon Allah's Apostle ﷺ said: Allah, forgive the sins of Abdullah b. Qais (Abu Musa Ash'ari) and admit him to an elevated place on the Day of Resurrection. Abu Burda said: One prayer is for abu 'Amir and the other is tor Abu Musa. – Sahih Muslim 2498

حَدَّثَنَا عَبْدُ اللَّهِ بْنُ بَرَّادٍ أَبُو عَامِرٍ الأَشْعَرِيُّ، وَأَبُو كُرَيْبٍ مُحَمَّدُ بْنُ الْعَلاَءِ – وَاللَّفْظُ لأَبِي عَامِرٍ – قَالاَ حَدَّثَنَا أَبُو أُسَامَةَ، عَنْ بُرَيْدٍ، عَنْ أَبِي بُرْدَةَ، عَنْ أَبِيهِ، قَالَ لَمَّا فَرَغَ النَّبِيُّ صلى الله عليه وسلم مِنْ حُنَيْنٍ بَعَثَ أَبَا عَامِرٍ عَلَى جَيْشٍ إِلَى أَوْطَاسٍ فَلَقِيَ دُرَيْدَ بْنَ الصِّمَّةِ فَقُتِلَ دُرَيْدٌ وَهَزَمَ اللَّهُ أَصْحَابَهُ فَقَالَ أَبُو مُوسَى وَبَعَثَنِي مَعَ أَبِي عَامِرٍ – قَالَ – فَرُمِيَ أَبُو عَامِرٍ فِي رُكْبَتِهِ رَمَاهُ رَجُلٌ مِنْ بَنِي جُشَمٍ بِسَهْمٍ فَأَثْبَتَهُ فِي رُكْبَتِهِ فَانْتَهَيْتُ إِلَيْهِ فَقُلْتُ يَا عَمِّ مَنْ رَمَاكَ فَأَشَارَ أَبُو عَامِرٍ إِلَى أَبِي مُوسَى فَقَالَ إِنَّ ذَاكَ قَاتِلِي تَرَاهُ ذَلِكَ الَّذِي رَمَانِي . قَالَ أَبُو مُوسَى فَقَصَدْتُ لَهُ فَاعْتَمَدْتُهُ فَلَحِقْتُهُ فَلَمَّا رَآنِي وَلَّى عَنِّي ذَاهِبًا فَاتَّبَعْتُهُ وَجَعَلْتُ أَقُولُ لَهُ أَلاَ تَسْتَحْيِي أَلَسْتَ عَرَبِيًّا أَلاَ تَثْبُتُ فَكَفَّ فَالْتَقَيْتُ أَنَا وَهُوَ فَاخْتَلَفْنَا أَنَا وَهُوَ ضَرْبَتَيْنِ فَضَرَبْتُهُ بِالسَّيْفِ فَقَتَلْتُهُ ثُمَّ رَجَعْتُ إِلَى أَبِي عَامِرٍ فَقُلْتُ إِنَّ اللَّهَ قَدْ قَتَلَ صَاحِبَكَ . قَالَ فَانْزِعْ هَذَا السَّهْمَ فَنَزَعْتُهُ فَنَزَا مِنْهُ الْمَاءُ فَقَالَ يَا ابْنَ أَخِي انْطَلِقْ إِلَى رَسُولِ اللَّهِ صلى الله عليه وسلم فَأَقْرِئْهُ مِنِّي السَّلاَمَ وَقُلْ لَهُ يَقُولُ لَكَ أَبُو عَامِرٍ اسْتَغْفِرْ لِي . قَالَ وَاسْتَعْمَلَنِي أَبُو عَامِرٍ عَلَى النَّاسِ وَمَكَثَ يَسِيرًا ثُمَّ إِنَّهُ مَاتَ فَلَمَّا رَجَعْتُ إِلَى النَّبِيِّ صلى الله عليه وسلم دَخَلْتُ عَلَيْهِ وَهُوَ فِي بَيْتٍ عَلَى سَرِيرٍ مُرْمَلٍ وَعَلَيْهِ فِرَاشٌ وَقَدْ أَثَّرَ رِمَالُ السَّرِيرِ بِظَهْرِ رَسُولِ اللَّهِ صلى الله عليه وسلم وَجَنْبَيْهِ فَأَخْبَرْتُهُ بِخَبَرِنَا وَخَبَرِ أَبِي عَامِرٍ وَقُلْتُ لَهُ قَالَ قُلْ لَهُ يَسْتَغْفِرْ لِي . فَدَعَا رَسُولُ اللَّهِ صلى الله عليه وسلم بِمَاءٍ فَتَوَضَّأَ مِنْهُ ثُمَّ رَفَعَ يَدَيْهِ ثُمَّ قَالَ " اللَّهُمَّ اغْفِرْ لِعُبَيْدٍ أَبِي عَامِرٍ " . حَتَّى رَأَيْتُ بَيَاضَ إِبْطَيْهِ ثُمَّ قَالَ " اللَّهُمَّ اجْعَلْهُ يَوْمَ الْقِيَامَةِ فَوْقَ كَثِيرٍ مِنْ خَلْقِكَ أَوْ مِنَ النَّاسِ " . فَقُلْتُ وَلِي يَا رَسُولَ اللَّهِ فَاسْتَغْفِرْ . فَقَالَ النَّبِيُّ صلى الله عليه وسلم " اللَّهُمَّ اغْفِرْ لِعَبْدِ اللَّهِ بْنِ قَيْسٍ ذَنْبَهُ وَأَدْخِلْهُ يَوْمَ الْقِيَامَةِ مُدْخَلاً كَرِيمًا " . قَالَ أَبُو بُرْدَةَ إِحْدَاهُمَا لأَبِي عَامِرٍ وَالأُخْرَى لأَبِي مُوسَى .

Banu Amir
بنو عامر

Narrated Anas: The Prophet ﷺ sent seventy men from the tribe of Bani Salim to the tribe of Bani Amir. When they reached there, my maternal uncle said to them, "I will go ahead of you, and if they allow me to convey the message of Allah's Messenger ﷺ (it will be all right); otherwise you will remain close to me." So he went ahead of them and the pagans granted him security But while he was reporting the message of the Prophet ﷺ , they beckoned to one of their men who stabbed him to death. My maternal uncle said, "Allah is Greater! By the Lord of the Ka`ba, I am successful." After that they attached the rest of the party and killed them all except a lame man who went up to the top of the mountain. (Hammam, a sub-narrator said, "I think another man was saved along with him)." Gabriel informed the Prophet ﷺ that they (i.e the martyrs) met their Lord, and He was pleased with them and made them pleased. We used to recite, "Inform our people that we have met our Lord, He is pleased with us and He has made us pleased " Later on this Qur'anic Verse was cancelled. The Prophet ﷺ invoked Allah for forty days to curse the murderers from the tribe of Ral, Dhakwan, Bani Lihyan and Bam Usaiya who disobeyed Allah and his Apostle. – Sahih Al-Bukhari 2801.

حَدَّثَنَا حَفْصُ بْنُ عُمَرَ الْحَوْضِيُّ، حَدَّثَنَا هَمَّامٌ، عَنْ إِسْحَاقَ، عَنْ أَنَسٍ ـ رضى الله عنه ـ قَالَ بَعَثَ النَّبِيُّ صلى الله عليه وسلم أَقْوَامًا مِنْ بَنِي سُلَيْمٍ إِلَى بَنِي عَامِرٍ فِي سَبْعِينَ، فَلَمَّا قَدِمُوا، قَالَ لَهُمْ خَالِي أَتَقَدَّمُكُمْ، فَإِنْ أَمَّنُونِي حَتَّى أُبَلِّغَهُمْ عَنْ رَسُولِ اللَّهِ صلى الله عليه وسلم وَإِلاَّ كُنْتُمْ مِنِّي قَرِيبًا. فَتَقَدَّمَ، فَأَمَّنُوهُ، فَبَيْنَمَا يُحَدِّثُهُمْ عَنِ النَّبِيِّ صلى الله عليه وسلم إِذْ أَوْمَئُوا إِلَى رَجُلٍ مِنْهُمْ، فَطَعَنَهُ فَأَنْفَذَهُ فَقَالَ اللَّهُ أَكْبَرُ، فُزْتُ وَرَبِّ الْكَعْبَةِ. ثُمَّ مَالُوا عَلَى بَقِيَّةِ أَصْحَابِهِ فَقَتَلُوهُمْ، إِلاَّ رَجُلاً أَعْرَجَ صَعِدَ الْجَبَلَ. قَالَ هَمَّامٌ فَأُرَاهُ آخَرَ مَعَهُ، فَأَخْبَرَ جِبْرِيلُ ـ عَلَيْهِ السَّلاَمُ ـ النَّبِيَّ صلى الله عليه وسلم أَنَّهُمْ قَدْ لَقُوا رَبَّهُمْ، فَرَضِيَ عَنْهُمْ وَأَرْضَاهُمْ، فَكُنَّا نَقْرَأُ أَنْ بَلِّغُوا قَوْمَنَا أَنْ قَدْ لَقِينَا رَبَّنَا فَرَضِيَ عَنَّا وَأَرْضَانَا. ثُمَّ نُسِخَ بَعْدُ، فَدَعَا عَلَيْهِمْ أَرْبَعِينَ صَبَاحًا، عَلَى رِعْلٍ وَذَكْوَانَ وَبَنِي لِحْيَانَ وَبَنِي عُصَيَّةَ الَّذِينَ عَصَوُا اللَّهَ وَرَسُولَهُ صلى الله عليه وسلم.

Narrated Abu Bakra: Al-Aqra' bin Habis said to the Prophetﷺ "Nobody gave you the pledge of allegiance but the robbers of the pilgrims (i.e. those who used to rob the pilgrims) from the tribes of Aslam, Ghifar, Muzaina." (Ibn Abi Ya'qub is in doubt whether Al-Aqra' added. 'And Juhaina.') The Prophetﷺ said, "Don't you think that the tribes of Aslam, Ghifar, Muzaina (and also perhaps) Juhaina are better than the tribes of Bani Tamim, Bani Amir, Asad, and Ghatafan?" Somebody said, "They were unsuccessful and losers!" The Prophet said, "Yes, by Him in Whose Hands my life is, they (i.e. the former) are better than they (i.e. the latter). – Sahih Al-Bukhari 3516

حَدَّثَنِي مُحَمَّدُ بْنُ بَشَّارٍ، حَدَّثَنَا غُنْدَرٌ، حَدَّثَنَا شُعْبَةُ، عَنْ مُحَمَّدِ بْنِ أَبِي يَعْقُوبَ، قَالَ سَمِعْتُ عَبْدَ الرَّحْمَنِ بْنَ أَبِي بَكْرَةَ، عَنْ أَبِيهِ، أَنَّ الأَقْرَعَ بْنَ حَابِسٍ، قَالَ لِلنَّبِيِّ صلى الله عليه وسلم إِنَّمَا بَايَعَكَ سُرَّاقُ الْحَجِيجِ مِنْ أَسْلَمَ وَغِفَارَ وَمُزَيْنَةَ ـ وَأَحْسِبُهُ وَجُهَيْنَةَ ابْنُ أَبِي يَعْقُوبَ شَكَّ ـ قَالَ النَّبِيُّ صلى الله عليه وسلم " أَرَأَيْتَ إِنْ كَانَ أَسْلَمُ وَغِفَارُ وَمُزَيْنَةُ ـ وَأَحْسِبُهُ ـ وَجُهَيْنَةُ ”خَيْرًا مِنْ بَنِي تَمِيمٍ وَبَنِي عَامِرٍ وَأَسَدٍ وَغَطَفَانَ، خَابُوا وَخَسِرُوا ". قَالَ نَعَمْ. قَالَ " وَالَّذِي نَفْسِي بِيَدِهِ، إِنَّهُمْ لَخَيْرٌ مِنْهُمْ

Banu Najjar (A Yemen tribe of Khazraj)
بَنُو نَجَّار

Narrated Anas: The Prophetﷺ said (at the time of building the Mosque), "O Ban, An-Najjar! Suggest to me a price for your garden." They replied, "We do not ask its price except from Allah." – Sahih Al-Bukhari 2779

حَدَّثَنَا مُسَدَّدٌ، حَدَّثَنَا عَبْدُ الْوَارِثِ، عَنْ أَبِي التَّيَّاحِ، عَنْ أَنَسٍ ـ رضى الله عنه ـ قَالَ النَّبِيُّ صلى الله عليه وسلم " يَا بَنِي النَّجَّارِ ثَامِنُونِي بِحَائِطِكُمْ ". قَالُوا لاَ نَطْلُبُ ثَمَنَهُ إِلاَّ إِلَى اللَّهِ

Narrated Anas bin Malik: When Allah's Messengerﷺ arrived at Medina, he alighted at the upper part of Medina among the people called Bani `Amr bin `Auf and he stayed with them for fourteen nights. Then he sent for the chiefs of Bani An-Najjar, and they came, carrying their swords. As if I am just now looking at Allah's Messengerﷺ on his she-camel with Abu Bakr riding behind him (on the same camel) and the chiefs of Bani An- Najjar around him till he dismounted in the courtyard of Abu Aiyub's home. The Prophetﷺ used to offer the prayer wherever the prayer was due, and he would pray even in sheepfolds. Then he ordered that the mosque be built. He sent for the chiefs of Banu An-Najjar, and when they came, he said, "O Banu An-Najjar! Suggest to me the price of this garden of yours." They replied "No! By Allah, we do not demand its price except from Allah." In that garden there were the (following) things that I will tell you: Graves of pagans, unleveled land with holes and pits etc., and date-palm trees. Allah's Messengerﷺ ordered that the graves of the pagans be dug up and, the unleveled land be leveled and the date-palm trees be cut down. The trunks of the trees were arranged so as to form the wall facing the Qibla. The Stone pillars were built at the sides of its gate. The companions of the Prophetﷺ were carrying the stones and reciting some lyrics, and Allah's Messengerﷺ was with them and they were saying, "O Allah! There is no good Excel the good of the Hereafter, so bestow victory on the Ansar and the Emigrants. ". – Sahih Al-Bukhari 3932

حَدَّثَنَا مُسَدَّدٌ، حَدَّثَنَا عَبْدُ الْوَارِثِ. وَحَدَّثَنَا إِسْحَاقُ بْنُ مَنْصُورٍ، أَخْبَرَنَا عَبْدُ الصَّمَدِ، قَالَ سَمِعْتُ أَبِي يُحَدِّثُ، حَدَّثَنَا أَبُو التَّيَّاحِ، يَزِيدُ بْنُ حُمَيْدٍ الضُّبَعِيُّ قَالَ حَدَّثَنِي أَنَسُ بْنُ مَالِكٍ ـ رضى الله عنه ـ قَالَ لَمَّا قَدِمَ رَسُولُ اللَّهِ صلى الله عليه وسلم الْمَدِينَةَ، نَزَلَ فِي عُلْوِ الْمَدِينَةِ فِي حَيٍّ يُقَالُ لَهُمْ بَنُو عَمْرِو بْنِ عَوْفٍ ـ قَالَ ـ فَأَقَامَ فِيهِمْ أَرْبَعَ عَشْرَةَ لَيْلَةً، ثُمَّ أَرْسَلَ إِلَى مَلإِ بَنِي النَّجَّارِ ـ قَالَ ـ فَجَاءُوا مُتَقَلِّدِي سُيُوفِهِمْ، قَالَ وَكَأَنِّي أَنْظُرُ إِلَى رَسُولِ اللَّهِ صلى الله عليه وسلم عَلَى رَاحِلَتِهِ، وَأَبُو بَكْرٍ رِدْفَهُ، وَمَلأُ بَنِي النَّجَّارِ حَوْلَهُ حَتَّى أَلْقَى بِفِنَاءِ أَبِي أَيُّوبَ، قَالَ فَكَانَ يُصَلِّي حَيْثُ أَدْرَكَتْهُ الصَّلاَةُ، وَيُصَلِّي فِي مَرَابِضِ الْغَنَمِ، قَالَ ثُمَّ إِنَّهُ أَمَرَ بِبِنَاءِ الْمَسْجِدِ، فَأَرْسَلَ إِلَى مَلإِ بَنِي النَّجَّارِ، فَجَاءُوا فَقَالَ " يَا بَنِي النَّجَّارِ، ثَامِنُونِي حَائِطَكُمْ هَذَا ".

فَقَالُوا لاَ، وَاللَّهِ لاَ نَطْلُبُ ثَمَنَهُ إِلاَّ إِلَى اللَّهِ. قَالَ فَكَانَ فِيهِ مَا أَقُولُ لَكُمْ كَانَتْ فِيهِ قُبُورُ الْمُشْرِكِينَ، وَكَانَتْ فِيهِ خِرَبٌ، وَكَانَ فِيهِ نَخْلٌ، فَأَمَرَ رَسُولُ اللَّهِ صلى الله عليه وسلم بِقُبُورِ الْمُشْرِكِينَ فَنُبِشَتْ، وَبِالْخِرَبِ فَسُوِّيَتْ، وَبِالنَّخْلِ فَقُطِعَ، قَالَ فَصَفُّوا النَّخْلَ قِبْلَةَ الْمَسْجِدِ ـ قَالَ ـ وَجَعَلُوا عِضَادَتَيْهِ حِجَارَةً. قَالَ قَالَ جَعَلُوا يَنْقُلُونَ ذَاكَ الصَّخْرَ وَهُمْ يَرْتَجِزُونَ، وَرَسُولُ اللَّهِ صلى الله عليه وسلم مَعَهُمْ يَقُولُونَ اللَّهُمَّ إِنَّهُ لاَ خَيْرَ إِلاَّ خَيْرُ الآخِرَهْ فَانْصُرِ الأَنْصَارَ وَالْمُهَاجِرَهْ

Narrated Abu Humaid As-Sa`idi: We took part in the holy battle of Tabuk in the company of the Prophet ﷺ and when we arrived at the Wadi-al-Qura, there was a woman in her garden. The Prophet ﷺ asked his companions to estimate the amount of the fruits in the garden, and Allah's Messenger ﷺ estimated it at ten Awsuq (One Wasaq = 60 Sa's) and 1 Sa'= 3 kg. approximately). The Prophet ﷺ said to that lady, "Check what your garden will yield." When we reached Tabuk, the Prophet ﷺ said, "There will be a strong wind tonight and so no one should stand and whoever has a camel, should fasten it." So we fastened our camels. A strong wind blew at night and a man stood up and he was blown away to a mountain called Taiy, The King of Aila sent a white mule and a sheet for wearing to the Prophet ﷺ as a present, and wrote to the Prophet ﷺ that his people would stay in their place (and will pay Jizya taxation.) (1) When the Prophet ﷺ reached Wadi-al- Qura he asked that woman how much her garden had yielded. She said, "Ten Awsuq," and that was what Allah's Messenger ﷺ had estimated. Then the Prophet ﷺ said, "I want to reach Medina quickly, and whoever among you wants to accompany me, should hurry up." The sub-narrator Ibn Bakkar said something which meant: When the Prophet ﷺ saw Medina he said, "This is Taba." And when he saw the mountain of Uhud, he said, "This mountain loves us and we love it. Shall I tell you of the best amongst the Ansar?" They replied in the affirmative. He said, "The family of Bani-n-Najjar, and then the family of Bani Sa`ida or Bani Al-Harith bin Al-Khazraj. (The above-mentioned are the best) but there is goodness in all the families of Ansar.". – Sahih Al-Bukhari 1481, 1482

حَدَّثَنَا سَهْلُ بْنُ بَكَّارٍ، حَدَّثَنَا وُهَيْبٌ، عَنْ عَمْرِو بْنِ يَحْيَى، عَنْ عَبَّاسٍ السَّاعِدِيِّ، عَنْ أَبِي حُمَيْدٍ السَّاعِدِيِّ، قَالَ غَزَوْنَا مَعَ النَّبِيِّ صلى الله عليه وسلم غَزْوَةَ تَبُوكَ فَلَمَّا جَاءَ وَادِيَ الْقُرَى إِذَا امْرَأَةٌ فِي حَدِيقَةٍ لَهَا فَقَالَ النَّبِيُّ صلى الله عليه وسلم لأَصْحَابِهِ " اخْرُصُوا ". وَخَرَصَ رَسُولُ اللَّهِ صلى الله عليه وسلم عَشَرَةَ أَوْسُقٍ فَقَالَ لَهَا " أَحْصِي مَا يَخْرُجُ مِنْهَا ". فَلَمَّا أَتَيْنَا تَبُوكَ قَالَ " أَمَا إِنَّهَا سَتَهُبُّ اللَّيْلَةَ رِيحٌ شَدِيدَةٌ فَلاَ يَقُومَنَّ أَحَدٌ، وَمَنْ كَانَ مَعَهُ بَعِيرٌ فَلْيَعْقِلْهُ ". فَعَقَلْنَاهَا وَهَبَّتْ رِيحٌ شَدِيدَةٌ فَقَامَ رَجُلٌ فَأَلْقَتْهُ بِجَبَلِ طَيِّئٍ ـ وَأَهْدَى مَلِكُ أَيْلَةَ لِلنَّبِيِّ صلى الله عليه وسلم بَغْلَةً بَيْضَاءَ، وَكَسَاهُ بُرْدًا وَكَتَبَ لَهُ بِبَحْرِهِمْ ـ فَلَمَّا أَتَى وَادِيَ الْقُرَى قَالَ لِلْمَرْأَةِ " كَمْ جَاءَ حَدِيقَتُكِ ". قَالَتْ عَشَرَةَ أَوْسُقٍ خَرْصَ رَسُولِ اللَّهِ صلى الله عليه وسلم فَقَالَ النَّبِيُّ صلى الله عليه وسلم " إِنِّي مُتَعَجِّلٌ إِلَى الْمَدِينَةِ، فَمَنْ أَرَادَ مِنْكُمْ أَنْ يَتَعَجَّلَ مَعِي فَلْيَتَعَجَّلْ ". فَلَمَّا ـ قَالَ ابْنُ بَكَّارٍ كَلِمَةً مَعْنَاهَا ـ أَشْرَفَ عَلَى الْمَدِينَةِ قَالَ " هَذِهِ طَابَةُ ". فَلَمَّا رَأَى أُحُدًا قَالَ " هَذَا جُبَيْلٌ يُحِبُّنَا وَنُحِبُّهُ، أَلاَ أُخْبِرُكُمْ بِخَيْرِ دُورِ الأَنْصَارِ ". قَالُوا بَلَى. قَالَ " دُورُ بَنِي النَّجَّارِ، ثُمَّ دُورُ بَنِي عَبْدِ الأَشْهَلِ، ثُمَّ دُورُ بَنِي سَاعِدَةَ، أَوْ دُورُ بَنِي الْحَارِثِ بْنِ الْخَزْرَجِ، وَفِي كُلِّ دُورِ الأَنْصَارِ ـ يَعْنِي ـ خَيْرًا ". وَقَالَ سُلَيْمَانُ بْنُ بِلاَلٍ حَدَّثَنِي عَمْرٌو، " ثُمَّ دَارُ بَنِي الْحَارِثِ، ثُمَّ بَنِي سَاعِدَةَ ". وَقَالَ سُلَيْمَانُ عَنْ سَعْدِ بْنِ سَعِيدٍ، عَنْ عُمَارَةَ بْنِ غَزِيَّةَ، عَنْ عَبَّاسٍ، عَنْ أَبِيهِ، عَنِ النَّبِيِّ صلى الله عليه وسلم قَالَ " أُحُدٌ جَبَلٌ يُحِبُّنَا وَنُحِبُّهُ ". قَالَ أَبُو عَبْدِ اللَّهِ كُلُّ بُسْتَانٍ عَلَيْهِ حَائِطٌ فَهْوَ حَدِيقَةٌ، وَمَا لَمْ يَكُنْ عَلَيْهِ حَائِطٌ لَمْ يَقُلْ حَدِيقَةٌ.

Narrated Abu Humaid: The Prophet ﷺ said, "The best of the Ansar families (homes) are the families (homes) of Banu An- Najjar, and then that of Banu `Abdul Ash-hal, and then that of Banu Al-Harith, and then that of Banu Saida; and there is good in all the families (homes) of the Ansar." Sa`d bin 'Ubada followed us and said, "O Abu Usaid ! Don't you see that the Prophet ﷺ compared the Ansar and made us the last of them in superiority? Then Sa`d met the Prophet ﷺ and said, "O Allah's Messenger ﷺ ! In comparing the Ansar's families (homes) as to the degree of superiority, you have made us the last of them." Allah's Messenger ﷺ replied, "Isn't it sufficient that you are regarded amongst the best?". – Sahih Al-Bukhari 3791

حَدَّثَنَا خَالِدُ بْنُ مَخْلَدٍ، حَدَّثَنَا سُلَيْمَانُ، قَالَ حَدَّثَنِي عَمْرُو بْنُ يَحْيَى، عَنْ عَبَّاسِ بْنِ سَهْلٍ، عَنْ أَبِي حُمَيْدٍ، عَنِ النَّبِيِّ صلى الله عليه وسلم قَالَ " إِنَّ خَيْرَ دُورِ الأَنْصَارِ دَارُ بَنِي النَّجَّارِ، ثُمَّ عَبْدِ الأَشْهَلِ، ثُمَّ دَارُ بَنِي الْحَارِثِ، ثُمَّ بَنِي سَاعِدَةَ، وَفِي كُلِّ دُورِ الأَنْصَارِ خَيْرٌ ". فَلَحِقَنَا سَعْدُ بْنُ عُبَادَةَ فَقَالَ أَبَا أُسَيْدٍ أَلَمْ تَرَ أَنَّ نَبِيَّ اللَّهِ صلى الله عليه وسلم خَيَّرَ الأَنْصَارَ فَجَعَلَنَا

أَخِيرًا فَأَدْرَكَ سَعْدٌ النَّبِيَّ صلى الله عليه وسلم فَقَالَ يَا رَسُولَ اللَّهِ، خُيِّرَ دُورُ الأَنْصَارِ فَجُعِلْنَا آخِرًا. فَقَالَ " أَوَلَيْسَ بِحَسْبِكُمْ أَنْ تَكُونُوا مِنَ الْخِيَارِ "

Yemen
اليمن

Narrated Abu Huraira: The Prophet ﷺ said, “The people of Yemen have come to you and they are more gentle and soft-hearted. Belief is Yemenite and Wisdom is Yemenite, while pride and haughtiness are the qualities of the owners of camels (i.e. bedouins). Calmness and solemnity are the characters of the owners of sheep.” – Sahih al-Bukhari 4388

حَدَّثَنَا مُحَمَّدُ بْنُ بَشَّارٍ، حَدَّثَنَا ابْنُ أَبِي عَدِيٍّ، عَنْ شُعْبَةَ، عَنْ سُلَيْمَانَ، عَنْ ذَكْوَانَ، عَنْ أَبِي هُرَيْرَةَ ـ رضى الله عنه ـ عَنِ النَّبِيِّ صلى الله عليه وسلم قَالَ " أَتَاكُمْ أَهْلُ الْيَمَنِ، هُمْ أَرَقُّ أَفْئِدَةً وَأَلْيَنُ قُلُوبًا، الإِيمَانُ يَمَانٍ وَالْحِكْمَةُ يَمَانِيَةٌ، وَالْفَخْرُ وَالْخُيَلاَءُ فِي أَصْحَابِ الإِبِلِ، وَالسَّكِينَةُ وَالْوَقَارُ فِي أَهْلِ الْغَنَمِ ". وَقَالَ غُنْدَرٌ عَنْ شُعْبَةَ، عَنْ سُلَيْمَانَ، سَمِعْتُ ذَكْوَانَ، عَنْ أَبِي هُرَيْرَةَ، عَنِ النَّبِيِّ صلى الله عليه وسلم.

Narrated Abu Masud: The Prophet ﷺ beckoned with his hand towards Yemen and said, “Belief is there.” The harshness and mercilessness are the qualities of those farmers etc, who are busy with their camels and pay no attention to the religion (is towards the east) from where the side of the head of Satan will appear; those are the tribes of Rabi`a and Mudar. – Sahih al-Bukhari 4387

حَدَّثَنِي عَبْدُ اللَّهِ بْنُ مُحَمَّدٍ الْجُعْفِيُّ، حَدَّثَنَا وَهْبُ بْنُ جَرِيرٍ، حَدَّثَنَا شُعْبَةُ، عَنْ إِسْمَاعِيلَ بْنِ أَبِي خَالِدٍ، عَنْ قَيْسِ بْنِ أَبِي حَازِمٍ، عَنْ أَبِي مَسْعُودٍ، أَنَّ النَّبِيَّ صلى الله عليه وسلم قَالَ " الإِيمَانُ هَا هُنَا ". وَأَشَارَ بِيَدِهِ إِلَى الْيَمَنِ " وَالْجَفَاءُ وَغِلَظُ الْقُلُوبِ فِي الْفَدَّادِينَ، عِنْدَ أُصُولِ أَذْنَابِ الإِبِلِ مِنْ حَيْثُ يَطْلُعُ قَرْنَا الشَّيْطَانِ رَبِيعَةَ وَمُضَرَ ".

Narrated Ibn `Umar: (The Prophet) said, “O Allah! Bless our Sham and our Yemen.” People said, “Our Najd as well.” The Prophet again said, “O Allah! Bless our Sham and Yemen.” They said again, “Our Najd as well.” On that the Prophet ﷺ said, “There will appear earthquakes and afflictions, and from there will come out the side of the head of Satan.” - Sahih al-Bukhari 1037

حَدَّثَنَا مُحَمَّدُ بْنُ الْمُثَنَّى، قَالَ حَدَّثَنَا حُسَيْنُ بْنُ الْحَسَنِ، قَالَ حَدَّثَنَا ابْنُ عَوْنٍ، عَنْ نَافِعٍ، عَنِ ابْنِ عُمَرَ، قَالَ اللَّهُمَّ بَارِكْ لَنَا فِي شَامِنَا وَفِي يَمَنِنَا. قَالَ قَالُوا وَفِي نَجْدِنَا قَالَ قَالَ اللَّهُمَّ بَارِكْ لَنَا فِي شَامِنَا وَفِي يَمَنِنَا. قَالَ قَالُوا وَفِي نَجْدِنَا قَالَ قَالَ هُنَاكَ الزَّلاَزِلُ وَالْفِتَنُ، وَبِهَا يَطْلُعُ قَرْنُ الشَّيْطَانِ.

Narrated `Imran bin Husain: Some people of Bani Tamim came to the Prophet ﷺ and he said (to them), “O Bani Tamim! Rejoice with glad tidings.” They said, “You have given us glad tidings, now give us something.” On hearing that the color of his face changed then the people of Yemen came to him and he said, “O people of Yemen ! Accept the good tidings, as Bani Tamim has refused them.” The Yemenites said, “We accept them. Then the Prophet ﷺ started taking about the beginning of creation and about Allah’s Throne. In the mean time a man came saying, “O `Imran! Your she-camel has run away!'' (I got up and went away), but I wish I had not left that place (for I missed what Allah’s Messenger ﷺ had said.) – Sahih al-Bukhari 3190

حَدَّثَنَا مُحَمَّدُ بْنُ كَثِيرٍ، أَخْبَرَنَا سُفْيَانُ، عَنْ جَامِعِ بْنِ شَدَّادٍ، عَنْ صَفْوَانَ بْنِ مُحْرِزٍ، عَنْ عِمْرَانَ بْنِ حُصَيْنٍ ـ رضى الله عنهما ـ قَالَ جَاءَ نَفَرٌ مِنْ بَنِي تَمِيمٍ إِلَى النَّبِيِّ صلى الله عليه وسلم فَقَالَ " يَا بَنِي تَمِيمٍ، أَبْشِرُوا ". قَالُوا بَشَّرْتَنَا فَأَعْطِنَا. فَتَغَيَّرَ وَجْهُهُ، فَجَاءَهُ أَهْلُ الْيَمَنِ، فَقَالَ " يَا أَهْلَ الْيَمَنِ، اقْبَلُوا الْبُشْرَى إِذْ لَمْ يَقْبَلْهَا بَنُو تَمِيمٍ ". قَالُوا قَبِلْنَا. فَأَخَذَ النَّبِيُّ صلى الله عليه وسلم يُحَدِّثُ بَدْءَ الْخَلْقِ وَالْعَرْشِ، فَجَاءَ رَجُلٌ فَقَالَ يَا عِمْرَانُ، رَاحِلَتُكَ تَفَلَّتَتْ، لَيْتَنِي لَمْ أَقُمْ

Narrated Abu Huraira: I heard Allah's Messenger ﷺ saying, "Pride and arrogance are characteristics of the rural bedouins while calmness is found among the owners of sheep. Belief is Yemenite, and wisdom is also Yemenite i.e. the Yemenites are well-known for their true belief and wisdom)." Abu `Abdullah (Al-Bukhari) said, "Yemen was called so because it is situated to the right of the Ka`ba, and Sham was called so because it is situated to the left of the Ka`ba." – Sahih al-Bukhari 3499

حَدَّثَنَا أَبُو الْيَمَانِ، أَخْبَرَنَا شُعَيْبٌ، عَنِ الزُّهْرِيِّ، قَالَ أَخْبَرَنِي أَبُو سَلَمَةَ بْنُ عَبْدِ الرَّحْمَنِ، أَنَّ أَبَا هُرَيْرَةَ ـ رضى الله عنه ـ قَالَ سَمِعْتُ رَسُولَ اللَّهِ صلى الله عليه وسلم يَقُولُ " الْفَخْرُ وَالْخُيَلاَءُ فِي الْفَدَّادِينَ أَهْلِ الْوَبَرِ، وَالسَّكِينَةُ فِي أَهْلِ الْغَنَمِ، وَالإِيمَانُ يَمَانٍ، وَالْحِكْمَةُ يَمَانِيَةٌ ". سُمِّيَتِ الْيَمَنَ لأَنَّهَا عَنْ يَمِينِ الْكَعْبَةِ، وَالشَّأْمَ عَنْ يَسَارِ الْكَعْبَةِ، وَالْمَشْأَمَةُ الْمَيْسَرَةُ، وَالْيَدُ الْيُسْرَى الشُّؤْمَى، وَالْجَانِبُ الأَيْسَرُ الأَشْأَمُ

Banu Nabit
بنو نبيط

It has been reported on the authority of Bara! ' who stated: A man from Banu Nabit (one of the Ansar tribes) came to the Prophet ﷺ and said: I testify that there is no god except Allah and that thou art His bondman and Messenger. Then he went forward and fought until he was killed. The Prophet ﷺ said: He has done a little but shall be given a great reward. – Sahih Muslim 1900

حَدَّثَنَا أَبُو بَكْرِ بْنُ أَبِي شَيْبَةَ، حَدَّثَنَا أَبُو أُسَامَةَ، عَنْ زَكَرِيَّاءَ، عَنْ أَبِي إِسْحَاقَ، عَنِ الْبَرَاءِ، قَالَ جَاءَ رَجُلٌ مِنْ بَنِي النَّبِيتِ إِلَى النَّبِيِّ صلى الله عليه وسلم ح وَحَدَّثَنَا أَحْمَدُ بْنُ جَنَابٍ الْمِصِّيصِيُّ حَدَّثَنَا عِيسَى – يَعْنِي ابْنَ يُونُسَ – عَنْ زَكَرِيَّاءَ عَنْ أَبِي إِسْحَاقَ عَنِ الْبَرَاءِ قَالَ جَاءَ رَجُلٌ مِنْ بَنِي النَّبِيتِ – قَبِيلٍ مِنَ الأَنْصَارِ – فَقَالَ أَشْهَدُ أَنْ لاَ إِلَهَ إِلاَّ اللَّهُ وَأَنَّكَ عَبْدُهُ وَرَسُولُهُ . ثُمَّ تَقَدَّمَ فَقَاتَلَ حَتَّى قُتِلَ فَقَالَ النَّبِيُّ صلى الله عليه وسلم " عَمِلَ هَذَا يَسِيرًا وَأُجِرَ كَثِيرًا " .

Banu Al-Aus
بنو أوس

Narrated `Aisha: Allah's Messenger ﷺ came to my house while two girls were singing beside me the songs of Bu'ath (a story about the war between the two tribes of the Ansar, i.e. Khazraj and Aus, before Islam.) The Prophet ﷺ reclined on the bed and turned his face to the other side. Abu Bakr came and scolded me and said protestingly, "Instrument of Satan in the presence of Allah's Messenger ﷺ ?" Allah's Messenger ﷺ turned his face towards him and said, "Leave them." When Abu Bakr became inattentive, I waved the two girls to go away and they left. It was the day of `Id when negroes used to play with leather shields and spears. Either I requested Allah's Messenger ﷺ or he himself asked me whether I would like to see the display. I replied in the affirmative. Then he let me stand behind him and my cheek was touching his cheek and he was saying, "Carry on, O Bani Arfida (i.e. negroes)!" When I got tired, he asked me if that was enough. I replied in the affirmative and he told me to leave. – Sahih al-Bukhari 2906, 2907

حَدَّثَنَا إِسْمَاعِيلُ، قَالَ حَدَّثَنِي ابْنُ وَهْبٍ، قَالَ عَمْرٌو حَدَّثَنِي أَبُو الأَسْوَدِ، عَنْ عُرْوَةَ، عَنْ عَائِشَةَ ـ رضى الله عنها ـ دَخَلَ عَلَىَّ رَسُولُ اللَّهِ صلى الله عليه وسلم وَعِنْدِي جَارِيَتَانِ تُغَنِّيَانِ بِغِنَاءِ بُعَاثَ، فَاضْطَجَعَ عَلَى الْفِرَاشِ وَحَوَّلَ وَجْهَهُ، فَدَخَلَ أَبُو بَكْرٍ فَانْتَهَرَنِي وَقَالَ مِزْمَارَةُ الشَّيْطَانِ عِنْدَ رَسُولِ اللَّهِ صلى الله عليه وسلم. فَأَقْبَلَ عَلَيْهِ رَسُولُ اللَّهِ صلى الله عليه وسلم فَقَالَ " دَعْهُمَا ". فَلَمَّا غَفَلَ غَمَزْتُهُمَا فَخَرَجَتَا. قَالَتْ وَكَانَ يَوْمُ عِيدٍ يَلْعَبُ السُّودَانُ بِالدَّرَقِ وَالْحِرَابِ، فَإِمَّا سَأَلْتُ رَسُولَ اللَّهِ صلى الله عليه وسلم وَإِمَّا قَالَ " تَشْتَهِينَ تَنْظُرِينَ ". فَقَالَتْ نَعَمْ. فَأَقَامَنِي وَرَاءَهُ خَدِّي عَلَى خَدِّهِ وَيَقُولُ " دُونَكُمْ بَنِي أَرْفِدَةَ ". حَتَّى إِذَا مَلِلْتُ قَالَ " حَسْبُكِ ". قُلْتُ نَعَمْ. قَالَ " فَاذْهَبِي ". قَالَ أَحْمَدُ عَنِ ابْنِ وَهْبٍ، فَلَمَّا غَفَلَ.

The Book of
Surely I am making in the earth a successor
إِنِّى جَاعِلٌ فِى ٱلْأَرْضِ خَلِيفَةً

When your Lord told the angels, “I will place a successor on Earth,” they said, “Will you put someone there who will corrupt it and shed blood while we glorify, praise, and sanctify You?” He said, “I know what you do not know.” He taught Adam the names of all things and then showed them to the angels. He said, “Tell me the names of these if you are so sure of what you know.” They said, “May You be exalted in your glory! We know nothing except what You have taught us . You are the All-Knowing, the Wise.” He said, “Adam, tell them their names.” When he told them their names , He said, “Did I not tell you that I know the hidden reality of the heavens and the Earth, and I know what you show and what you hide.” When We told the angels, “Bow down in respect to Adam,” they all bowed down, except for Iblīs , who refused out of arrogance and became among the ungrateful. We said, “Adam, live with your spouse in the Heavenly Garden and eat whatever you want, but do not come near this tree , or you will be unjust.” But Satan made them slip and caused them to be expelled from where they were, and We said, “Go down, you will be enemies to one another, and on Earth, you will have a temporary abode and livelihood.” Then Adam received words from his Lord, and He accepted his repentance . He alone is the Accepter of Repentance, the Mercy Giver. We said, “All of you go down from it [the Garden]. When my guidance comes to you, whoever follows my guidance will not have fear or grieve” Those who deny the truth and reject Our revelations will be heading for Hell, where they will remain forever. – Surah Al-Baqarah 2:30-39

وَإِذْ قَالَ رَبُّكَ لِلْمَلَـٰٓئِكَةِ إِنِّى جَاعِلٌ فِى ٱلْأَرْضِ خَلِيفَةً ۖ قَالُوٓا۟ أَتَجْعَلُ فِيهَا مَن يُفْسِدُ فِيهَا وَيَسْفِكُ ٱلدِّمَآءَ وَنَحْنُ نُسَبِّحُ بِحَمْدِكَ وَنُقَدِّسُ لَكَ ۖ قَالَ إِنِّىٓ أَعْلَمُ مَا لَا تَعْلَمُونَ وَعَلَّمَ ءَادَمَ ٱلْأَسْمَآءَ كُلَّهَا ثُمَّ عَرَضَهُمْ عَلَى ٱلْمَلَـٰٓئِكَةِ فَقَالَ أَنۢبِـُٔونِى بِأَسْمَآءِ هَـٰٓؤُلَآءِ إِن كُنتُمْ صَـٰدِقِينَ قَالُوا۟ سُبْحَـٰنَكَ لَا عِلْمَ لَنَآ إِلَّا مَا عَلَّمْتَنَآ ۖ إِنَّكَ أَنتَ ٱلْعَلِيمُ ٱلْحَكِيمُ قَالَ يَـٰٓـَٔادَمُ أَنۢبِئْهُم بِأَسْمَآئِهِمْ ۖ فَلَمَّآ أَنۢبَأَهُم بِأَسْمَآئِهِمْ قَالَ أَلَمْ أَقُل لَّكُمْ إِنِّىٓ أَعْلَمُ غَيْبَ ٱلسَّمَـٰوَٰتِ وَٱلْأَرْضِ وَأَعْلَمُ مَا تُبْدُونَ وَمَا كُنتُمْ تَكْتُمُونَ وَإِذْ قُلْنَا لِلْمَلَـٰٓئِكَةِ ٱسْجُدُوا۟ لِـَٔادَمَ فَسَجَدُوٓا۟ إِلَّآ إِبْلِيسَ أَبَىٰ وَٱسْتَكْبَرَ وَكَانَ مِنَ ٱلْكَـٰفِرِينَ وَقُلْنَا يَـٰٓـَٔادَمُ ٱسْكُنْ أَنتَ وَزَوْجُكَ ٱلْجَنَّةَ وَكُلَا مِنْهَا رَغَدًا حَيْثُ شِئْتُمَا وَلَا تَقْرَبَا هَـٰذِهِ ٱلشَّجَرَةَ فَتَكُونَا مِنَ ٱلظَّـٰلِمِينَ فَأَزَلَّهُمَا ٱلشَّيْطَـٰنُ عَنْهَا فَأَخْرَجَهُمَا مِمَّا كَانَا فِيهِ ۖ وَقُلْنَا ٱهْبِطُوا۟ بَعْضُكُمْ لِبَعْضٍ عَدُوٌّ ۖ وَلَكُمْ فِى ٱلْأَرْضِ مُسْتَقَرٌّ وَمَتَـٰعٌ إِلَىٰ حِينٍ فَتَلَقَّىٰٓ ءَادَمُ مِن رَّبِّهِۦ كَلِمَـٰتٍ فَتَابَ عَلَيْهِ ۚ إِنَّهُۥ هُوَ ٱلتَّوَّابُ ٱلرَّحِيمُ قُلْنَا ٱهْبِطُوا۟ مِنْهَا جَمِيعًا ۖ فَإِمَّا يَأْتِيَنَّكُم مِّنِّى هُدًى فَمَن تَبِعَ هُدَاىَ فَلَا خَوْفٌ عَلَيْهِمْ وَلَا هُمْ يَحْزَنُونَ وَٱلَّذِينَ كَفَرُوا۟ وَكَذَّبُوا۟ بِـَٔايَـٰتِنَآ أُو۟لَـٰٓئِكَ أَصْحَـٰبُ ٱلنَّارِ ۖ هُمْ فِيهَا خَـٰلِدُونَ

And as your Lord said to the Angels, “Surely I am creating a mortal of dry clay of mud modeled So, when I have molded him and breathed into him of My Spirit, fall down to him prostrating!” So the Angels prostrated themselves, all of them together Except Iblis; he refused to be among the prostrate Said He, “O Iblis, what about you, that you are not among the prostrate?” Said he, “Indeed I did not have to prostrate myself to a mortal whom You created of dry clay of mud modeled.” Said He, “Then get out (Literally: go out) of it; so, surely you are outcast And surely the curse will be upon you till the Day of Doom.” Said he, “Lord! Then respite me till the Day they will be made to rise again.” Said He, “Then surely you are among the respited To the Day of a known time.” Said he, “Lord! For (the fact) that You misguided me, indeed I will definitely adorn for them (i.e., make “evil” attractive to them) in the earth; and indeed I will definitely misguide them all together Excepting Your bondmen among them, who are most faithful.” Said He, “This is for Me a straight Path Surely over My bondmen you will have no all-binding authority, except the ones who closely follow you of the misguided ones." And surely Hell will be indeed their promised (abode) all together It has seven gates; and each gate has an appointed part (Literally: divided) Surely the pious will be amidst Gardens and Springs." "Enter them, in peace, secure!" And We will draw out from them whatever rancor may be in their breasts; as brethren they will be upon settees facing one another No toil will touch them therein, and in no way will they be made to go out of it Fully inform My bondmen that I, Ever I, am The Ever-Forgiving, The Ever-Merciful And that My torment is the (most) painful torment – Surah Al-Hijr 15:28-50

وَإِذْ قَالَ رَبُّكَ لِلْمَلَٰٓئِكَةِ إِنِّى خَٰلِقٌۢ بَشَرًا مِّن صَلْصَٰلٍ مِّنْ حَمَإٍ مَّسْنُونٍ فَإِذَا سَوَّيْتُهُۥ وَنَفَخْتُ فِيهِ مِن رُّوحِى فَقَعُوا۟ لَهُۥ سَٰجِدِينَ فَسَجَدَ ٱلْمَلَٰٓئِكَةُ كُلُّهُمْ أَجْمَعُونَ إِلَّآ إِبْلِيسَ أَبَىٰٓ أَن يَكُونَ مَعَ ٱلسَّٰجِدِينَ قَالَ يَٰٓإِبْلِيسُ مَا لَكَ أَلَّا تَكُونَ مَعَ ٱلسَّٰجِدِينَ قَالَ لَمْ أَكُن لِّأَسْجُدَ لِبَشَرٍ خَلَقْتَهُۥ مِن صَلْصَٰلٍ مِّنْ حَمَإٍ مَّسْنُونٍ قَالَ فَٱخْرُجْ مِنْهَا فَإِنَّكَ رَجِيمٌ وَإِنَّ عَلَيْكَ ٱللَّعْنَةَ إِلَىٰ يَوْمِ ٱلدِّينِ قَالَ رَبِّ فَأَنظِرْنِىٓ إِلَىٰ يَوْمِ يُبْعَثُونَ قَالَ فَإِنَّكَ مِنَ ٱلْمُنظَرِينَ إِلَىٰ يَوْمِ ٱلْوَقْتِ ٱلْمَعْلُومِ قَالَ رَبِّ بِمَآ أَغْوَيْتَنِى لَأُزَيِّنَنَّ لَهُمْ فِى ٱلْأَرْضِ وَلَأُغْوِيَنَّهُمْ أَجْمَعِينَ إِلَّا عِبَادَكَ مِنْهُمُ ٱلْمُخْلَصِينَ قَالَ هَٰذَا صِرَٰطٌ عَلَىَّ مُسْتَقِيمٌ إِنَّ عِبَادِى لَيْسَ لَكَ عَلَيْهِمْ سُلْطَٰنٌ إِلَّا مَنِ ٱتَّبَعَكَ مِنَ ٱلْغَاوِينَ وَإِنَّ جَهَنَّمَ لَمَوْعِدُهُمْ أَجْمَعِينَ لَهَا سَبْعَةُ أَبْوَٰبٍ لِّكُلِّ بَابٍ مِّنْهُمْ جُزْءٌ مَّقْسُومٌ إِنَّ ٱلْمُتَّقِينَ فِى جَنَّٰتٍ وَعُيُونٍ ٱدْخُلُوهَا بِسَلَٰمٍ ءَامِنِينَ وَنَزَعْنَا مَا فِى صُدُورِهِم مِّنْ غِلٍّ إِخْوَٰنًا عَلَىٰ سُرُرٍ مُّتَقَٰبِلِينَ لَا يَمَسُّهُمْ فِيهَا نَصَبٌ وَمَا هُم مِّنْهَا بِمُخْرَجِينَ نَبِّئْ عِبَادِىٓ أَنِّىٓ أَنَا ٱلْغَفُورُ ٱلرَّحِيمُ وَأَنَّ عَذَابِى هُوَ ٱلْعَذَابُ ٱلْأَلِيمُ

Allah has promised the ones of you who have believed and done deeds of righteous- ness that indeed He will definitely make them successors in the earth, (even) as He made the ones who were before them successors, and that indeed He will definitely establish for them their religion that He is Divinely satisfied with (i.e., that He approves of) for them, and that indeed He will definitely give them in exchange, even after their fear, security. "They shall worship Me, not associating with Me anything." And whoever disbelieves after that, then those are they (who are) the immoral. Surah An-Nur 24:55

وَعَدَ ٱللَّهُ ٱلَّذِينَ ءَامَنُوا۟ مِنكُمْ وَعَمِلُوا۟ ٱلصَّٰلِحَٰتِ لَيَسْتَخْلِفَنَّهُمْ فِى ٱلْأَرْضِ كَمَا ٱسْتَخْلَفَ ٱلَّذِينَ مِن قَبْلِهِمْ وَلَيُمَكِّنَنَّ لَهُمْ دِينَهُمُ ٱلَّذِى ٱرْتَضَىٰ لَهُمْ وَلَيُبَدِّلَنَّهُم مِّنۢ بَعْدِ خَوْفِهِمْ أَمْنًا ۚ يَعْبُدُونَنِى لَا يُشْرِكُونَ بِى شَيْـًٔا ۚ وَمَن كَفَرَ بَعْدَ ذَٰلِكَ فَأُو۟لَٰٓئِكَ هُمُ ٱلْفَٰسِقُونَ

The Book of
Caliphate of Abu Bakr
خلافة أبي بكر

Narrated `Umar: When Allah took away the soul of His Prophet at his death, the Ansar assembled In the shed of Bani Sa`ida. I said to Abu Bakr, "Let us go." So, we come to them (i.e. to Ansar) at the shed of Bani Sa`ida. – Sahih al-Bukhari 2462

حَدَّثَنَا يَحْيَى بْنُ سُلَيْمَانَ، قَالَ حَدَّثَنِي ابْنُ وَهْبٍ، قَالَ حَدَّثَنِي مَالِكٌ. وَأَخْبَرَنِي يُونُسُ، عَنِ ابْنِ شِهَابٍ، أَخْبَرَنِي عُبَيْدُ اللَّهِ بْنُ عَبْدِ اللَّهِ بْنِ عُتْبَةَ، أَنَّ ابْنَ عَبَّاسٍ، أَخْبَرَهُ عَنْ عُمَرَ ـ رضى الله عنهم ـ قَالَ حِينَ تَوَفَّى اللَّهُ نَبِيَّهُ صلى الله عليه وسلم إِنَّ الأَنْصَارَ اجْتَمَعُوا فِي سَقِيفَةِ بَنِي سَاعِدَةَ، فَقُلْتُ لأَبِي بَكْرٍ انْطَلِقْ بِنَا. فَجِئْنَاهُمْ فِي سَقِيفَةِ بَنِي سَاعِدَةَ.

Narrated Anas bin Malik: That he heard `Umar's second speech he delivered when he sat on the pulpit on the day following the death of the Prophet ﷺ `Umar recited the Tashahhud while Abu Bakr was silent. `Umar said, "I wish that Allah's Messenger ﷺ had outlived all of us, i.e., had been the last (to die). But if Muhammad is dead, Allah nevertheless has kept the light amongst you from which you can receive the same guidance as Allah guided Muhammad with that. And Abu Bakr is the companion of Allah's Messenger ﷺ He is the second of the two in the cave. He is the most entitled person among the Muslims to manage your affairs. Therefore get up and swear allegiance to him." Some people had already taken the oath of allegiance to him in the shed of Bani Sa`ida but the oath of allegiance taken by the public was taken at the pulpit. I heard `Umar saying to Abu Bakr on that day. "Please ascend the pulpit," and kept on urging him till he ascended the pulpit whereupon, all the people swore allegiance to him. – Sahih Al-Bukhari 7219

حَدَّثَنَا إِبْرَاهِيمُ بْنُ مُوسَى، أَخْبَرَنَا هِشَامٌ، عَنْ مَعْمَرٍ، عَنِ الزُّهْرِيِّ، أَخْبَرَنِي أَنَسُ بْنُ مَالِكٍ ـ رضى الله عنه ـ أَنَّهُ سَمِعَ خُطْبَةَ، عُمَرَ الآخِرَةَ حِينَ جَلَسَ عَلَى الْمِنْبَرِ، وَذَلِكَ الْغَدُ مِنْ يَوْمِ تُوُفِّيَ النَّبِيُّ صلى الله عليه وسلم فَتَشَهَّدَ وَأَبُو بَكْرٍ صَامِتٌ لاَ يَتَكَلَّمُ قَالَ كُنْتُ أَرْجُو أَنْ يَعِيشَ رَسُولُ اللَّهِ صلى الله عليه وسلم حَتَّى يَدْبُرَنَا ـ يُرِيدُ بِذَلِكَ أَنْ يَكُونَ آخِرَهُمْ ـ فَإِنْ يَكُ مُحَمَّدٌ صلى الله عليه وسلم قَدْ مَاتَ، فَإِنَّ اللَّهَ تَعَالَى قَدْ جَعَلَ بَيْنَ أَظْهُرِكُمْ نُورًا تَهْتَدُونَ بِهِ بِمَا هَدَى اللَّهُ مُحَمَّدًا صلى الله عليه وسلم وَإِنَّ أَبَا بَكْرٍ صَاحِبُ رَسُولِ اللَّهِ صلى الله عليه وسلم ثَانِي اثْنَيْنِ، فَإِنَّهُ أَوْلَى الْمُسْلِمِينَ بِأُمُورِكُمْ، فَقُومُوا فَبَايِعُوهُ. وَكَانَتْ طَائِفَةٌ مِنْهُمْ قَدْ بَايَعُوهُ قَبْلَ ذَلِكَ فِي سَقِيفَةِ بَنِي سَاعِدَةَ، وَكَانَتْ بَيْعَةُ الْعَامَّةِ عَلَى الْمِنْبَرِ. قَالَ الزُّهْرِيُّ عَنْ أَنَسِ بْنِ مَالِكٍ سَمِعْتُ عُمَرَ يَقُولُ لأَبِي بَكْرٍ يَوْمَئِذٍ اصْعَدِ الْمِنْبَرَ. فَلَمْ يَزَلْ بِهِ حَتَّى صَعِدَ الْمِنْبَرَ، فَبَايَعَهُ النَّاسُ عَامَّةً

Narrated Ibn `Abbas: I used to teach (the Qur'an to) some people of the Muhajirln (emigrants), among whom there was `Abdur Rahman bin `Auf. While I was in his house at Mina, and he was with `Umar bin Al-Khattab during `Umar's last Hajj, `Abdur-Rahman came to me and said, "Would that you had seen the man who came today to the Chief of the Believers (`Umar), saying, 'O Chief of the Believers! What do you think about so-and-so who says, 'If `Umar should die, I will give the pledge of allegiance to such-andsuch person, as by Allah, the pledge of allegiance to Abu Bakr was nothing but a prompt sudden action which got established afterwards.' `Umar became angry and then said, 'Allah willing, I will stand before the people tonight and warn them against those people who want to deprive the others of their rights (the question of rulership). `Abdur-Rahman said, "I said, 'O Chief of the believers! Do not do that, for the season of Hajj gathers the riff-raff and the rubble, and it will be they who will gather around you when you stand to address the people. And I am afraid that you will get up and say something, and some people will spread your statement and may not say what you have actually said and may not understand its meaning, and may interpret it incorrectly, so you should wait till you reach Medina, as it is the place of emigration and the place of Prophet's Traditions, and there you can come in touch with the learned and noble people, and tell them your ideas with confidence; and the learned people will understand your statement and put it in its proper place.' On that, `Umar said, 'By Allah! Allah willing, I will do this in the first speech I will deliver before the people in Medina." Ibn `Abbas added: We reached Medina by the end of the month of Dhul-Hijja, and when it was Friday, we went quickly (to the mosque) as soon as the sun had declined, and I saw Sa`id bin Zaid bin `Amr bin Nufail sitting at the corner of the pulpit, and I too sat close to him so that my knee was touching his knee, and after a short while `Umar bin Al-Khattab came out, and when I saw him coming towards us, I said to Sa`id bin Zaid bin `Amr bin Nufail "Today `Umar will say such a thing as he has never said since he was chosen as Caliph." Sa`id denied my statement with astonishment and said, "What thing do you expect `Umar to say the like of which he has never said before?" In the meantime, `Umar sat on the pulpit and when the callmakers for the prayer had finished their call, `Umar stood up, and having glorified and praised Allah as He deserved, he said, "Now then, I am going to tell you something which (Allah) has written for me to say. I do not know; perhaps it portends my death, so whoever understands and remembers it, must narrate it to the others wherever his mount takes him, but if somebody is afraid that he does not understand it, then it is unlawful for him to tell lies about me. Allah sent Muhammad with the Truth and revealed the Holy Book to him, and among what Allah revealed, was the Verse of the Rajam (the stoning of married person (male & female) who commits illegal sexual intercourse, and we did recite this Verse and understood and memorized it. Allah's Messenger ﷺ did carry out the punishment of stoning and so did we after him. I am afraid that after a long time has passed, somebody will say, 'By Allah, we do not find the Verse of the Rajam in Allah's Book,' and thus they will go astray by leaving an obligation which Allah has revealed. And the punishment of the Rajam is to be inflicted to any married person (male & female), who commits illegal sexual intercourse, if the required evidence is available or there is conception or confession. And then we used to recite among the Verses in Allah's Book: 'O people! Do not claim to be the offspring of other than your fathers, as it is disbelief (unthankfulness) on your part that you claim to be the offspring of other than your real father.' Then Allah's Messenger ﷺ said, 'Do not praise me excessively as Jesus, son of Marry was praised, but call me Allah's Slave and His Apostles.' (O people!) I have been informed that a speaker amongst you says, 'By Allah, if `Umar should die, I will give the pledge of allegiance to such-and-such person.' One should not deceive oneself by saying that the pledge of allegiance given to Abu Bakr was given suddenly and it was successful. No doubt, it was like that, but Allah saved (the people) from its evil, and there is none among you who has the qualities of Abu Bakr. Remember that whoever gives the pledge of allegiance to anybody among you without consulting the other Muslims, neither that person, nor the person to whom the pledge of allegiance was given, are to be supported, lest they both should be killed. And no doubt after the death of the Prophet ﷺ we were informed that the Ansar disagreed with us and gathered in the shed of Bani Sa`da. `Ali and Zubair and whoever was with them, opposed us, while the emigrants gathered with Abu Bakr. I said to Abu Bakr, 'Let's go to these Ansari brothers of ours.' So we set out seeking them, and when we approached them, two pious men of theirs met us and informed us of the final decision of the Ansar, and said, 'O group of Muhajirin (emigrants) ! Where are you going?' We replied, 'We are going to these Ansari brothers of ours.' They said to us, 'You shouldn't go near them. Carry out whatever we have already decided.' I said, 'By Allah, we will go to them.' And so we proceeded until we reached them at the shed of Bani Sa`da. Behold! There was a man sitting amongst them and wrapped in something. I asked, 'Who is that man?' They said, 'He is Sa`d bin 'Ubada.' I asked, 'What is wrong with him?' They said, 'He is sick.' After we sat for a while, the Ansar's speaker said, 'None has the right to be worshipped but Allah,' and praising Allah as He deserved, he added, 'To proceed, we are Allah's Ansar (helpers) and the majority of the Muslim army, while you, the emigrants, are a small group and some people among you came with the intention of preventing us from practicing this matter (of caliphate) and depriving us of it.' When the speaker had finished, I intended to speak as I had prepared a speech which I liked and which I wanted to deliver in the presence of Abu Bakr, and I used to avoid provoking him. So, when I wanted to speak, Abu Bakr said, 'Wait a while.' I disliked to make him angry. So Abu Bakr himself gave a speech, and he was wiser and more patient than I. By Allah, he never missed a sentence that I liked in my own prepared speech, but he said the like of it or better than it spontaneously. After a pause he said, 'O Ansar! You deserve all (the qualities that you have attributed to yourselves, but this question (of Caliphate) is only for the Quraish as they are the best of the Arabs as regards descent and home, and I am pleased to suggest that you choose either of these two men, so take the oath of allegiance to either of them as you wish. And then Abu Bakr held my hand and Abu Ubaida bin al-Jarrah's hand who was sitting amongst us. I hated nothing of what he had said except that proposal, for by Allah, I would rather have my neck chopped off as expiator for a sin than become the ruler of a nation, one of whose members is Abu Bakr, unless at the time of my death my own-self suggests something I don't feel at present.' And then one of the Ansar said, 'I am the pillar on which the camel with a skin disease (eczema) rubs itself to satisfy the itching (i.e., I am a noble), and I am as a high class palm tree! O Quraish. There should be one ruler from us and one from you.' Then there was a hue and cry among the gathering and their voices rose so that I was afraid there might be great disagreement, so I said, 'O Abu Bakr! Hold your hand out.' He held his hand out and I pledged allegiance to him, and then all the emigrants gave the Pledge of allegiance and so did the Ansar afterwards. And so we became victorious over Sa`d bin Ubada (whom Al-Ansar wanted to make a ruler). One of the Ansar said, 'You have killed Sa`d bin Ubada.' I replied, 'Allah has killed Sa`d bin Ubada.' `Umar added, "By Allah, apart from the great tragedy that had happened to us (i.e. the death of the Prophet), there was no greater problem than the allegiance pledged to Abu Bakr because we were afraid that if we left the people, they might give the Pledge of allegiance after us to one of their men, in which case we would have given them our consent for something against our real wish, or would have opposed them and caused great trouble. So if any person gives the Pledge of allegiance to somebody (to become a Caliph) without consulting the other Muslims, then the one he has selected should not be granted allegiance, lest both of them should be killed.". – Sahih Al-Bukhari 6830

حَدَّثَنَا عَبْدُ الْعَزِيزِ بْنُ عَبْدِ اللَّهِ، حَدَّثَنِي إِبْرَاهِيمُ بْنُ سَعْدٍ، عَنْ صَالِحٍ، عَنِ ابْنِ شِهَابٍ، عَنْ عُبَيْدِ اللَّهِ بْنِ عَبْدِ اللَّهِ بْنِ عُتْبَةَ بْنِ مَسْعُودٍ، عَنِ ابْنِ عَبَّاسٍ، قَالَ كُنْتُ أُقْرِئُ رِجَالاً مِنَ الْمُهَاجِرِينَ مِنْهُمْ عَبْدُ الرَّحْمَنِ بْنُ عَوْفٍ، فَبَيْنَمَا أَنَا فِي مَنْزِلِهِ بِمِنًى، وَهْوَ عِنْدَ عُمَرَ بْنِ الْخَطَّابِ فِي آخِرِ حَجَّةٍ حَجَّهَا، إِذْ رَجَعَ إِلَىَّ عَبْدُ الرَّحْمَنِ فَقَالَ لَوْ رَأَيْتَ رَجُلاً أَتَى أَمِيرَ الْمُؤْمِنِينَ الْيَوْمَ فَقَالَ يَا أَمِيرَ الْمُؤْمِنِينَ هَلْ لَكَ فِي فُلاَنٍ يَقُولُ لَوْ قَدْ مَاتَ عُمَرُ لَقَدْ بَايَعْتُ فُلاَنًا، فَوَاللَّهِ مَا كَانَتْ بَيْعَةُ أَبِي بَكْرٍ إِلاَّ فَلْتَةً، فَتَمَّتْ. فَغَضِبَ عُمَرُ ثُمَّ قَالَ إِنِّي إِنْ شَاءَ اللَّهُ لَقَائِمٌ الْعَشِيَّةَ فِي النَّاسِ، فَمُحَذِّرُهُمْ هَؤُلاَءِ الَّذِينَ يُرِيدُونَ أَنْ يَغْصِبُوهُمْ أُمُورَهُمْ. قَالَ عَبْدُ الرَّحْمَنِ فَقُلْتُ يَا أَمِيرَ الْمُؤْمِنِينَ لاَ تَفْعَلْ فَإِنَّ الْمَوْسِمَ يَجْمَعُ رَعَاعَ النَّاسِ وَغَوْغَاءَهُمْ، فَإِنَّهُمْ هُمُ الَّذِينَ يَغْلِبُونَ عَلَى قُرْبِكَ حِينَ تَقُومُ فِي النَّاسِ، وَأَنَا أَخْشَى أَنْ تَقُومَ فَتَقُولَ مَقَالَةً يُطَيِّرُهَا عَنْكَ كُلُّ مُطَيِّرٍ، وَأَنْ لاَ يَعُوهَا، وَأَنْ لاَ يَضَعُوهَا عَلَى مَوَاضِعِهَا، فَأَمْهِلْ حَتَّى تَقْدَمَ الْمَدِينَةَ فَإِنَّهَا دَارُ الْهِجْرَةِ وَالسُّنَّةِ، فَتَخْلُصَ بِأَهْلِ الْفِقْهِ وَأَشْرَافِ النَّاسِ، فَتَقُولَ مَا قُلْتَ مُتَمَكِّنًا، فَيَعِي أَهْلُ الْعِلْمِ مَقَالَتَكَ، وَيَضَعُونَهَا عَلَى مَوَاضِعِهَا. فَقَالَ عُمَرُ أَمَا وَاللَّهِ إِنْ شَاءَ اللَّهُ لأَقُومَنَّ بِذَلِكَ أَوَّلَ مَقَامٍ أَقُومُهُ بِالْمَدِينَةِ. قَالَ ابْنُ عَبَّاسٍ فَقَدِمْنَا الْمَدِينَةَ فِي عَقِبِ ذِي الْحَجَّةِ، فَلَمَّا كَانَ يَوْمُ الْجُمُعَةِ عَجَّلْنَا الرَّوَاحَ حِينَ زَاغَتِ الشَّمْسُ، حَتَّى أَجِدَ سَعِيدَ بْنَ زَيْدِ بْنِ عَمْرِو بْنِ نُفَيْلٍ جَالِسًا إِلَى رُكْنِ الْمِنْبَرِ، فَجَلَسْتُ حَوْلَهُ تَمَسُّ رُكْبَتِي رُكْبَتَهُ، فَلَمْ أَنْشَبْ أَنْ خَرَجَ عُمَرُ بْنُ الْخَطَّابِ، فَلَمَّا رَأَيْتُهُ مُقْبِلاً قُلْتُ لِسَعِيدِ بْنِ زَيْدِ بْنِ عَمْرِو بْنِ نُفَيْلٍ، لَيَقُولَنَّ الْعَشِيَّةَ مَقَالَةً لَمْ يَقُلْهَا مُنْذُ اسْتُخْلِفَ، فَأَنْكَرَ عَلَىَّ وَقَالَ مَا عَسَيْتَ أَنْ يَقُولَ مَا لَمْ يَقُلْ. قَبْلَهُ فَجَلَسَ عُمَرُ عَلَى الْمِنْبَرِ، فَلَمَّا سَكَتَ الْمُؤَذِّنُونَ قَامَ فَأَثْنَى عَلَى اللَّهِ بِمَا هُوَ أَهْلُهُ قَالَ أَمَّا بَعْدُ فَإِنِّي قَائِلٌ لَكُمْ مَقَالَةً قَدْ قُدِّرَ لِي أَنْ أَقُولَهَا، لاَ أَدْرِي لَعَلَّهَا بَيْنَ يَدَىْ أَجَلِي، فَمَنْ عَقَلَهَا وَوَعَاهَا فَلْيُحَدِّثْ بِهَا حَيْثُ انْتَهَتْ بِهِ رَاحِلَتُهُ، وَمَنْ خَشِيَ أَنْ لاَ يَعْقِلَهَا فَلاَ أُحِلُّ لأَحَدٍ أَنْ يَكْذِبَ عَلَىَّ، إِنَّ اللَّهَ بَعَثَ مُحَمَّدًا صلى الله عليه وسلم بِالْحَقِّ وَأَنْزَلَ عَلَيْهِ الْكِتَابَ فَكَانَ مِمَّا أَنْزَلَ اللَّهُ آيَةُ الرَّجْمِ، فَقَرَأْنَاهَا وَعَقَلْنَاهَا وَوَعَيْنَاهَا، رَجَمَ رَسُولُ اللَّهِ صلى الله عليه وسلم وَرَجَمْنَا بَعْدَهُ، فَأَخْشَى إِنْ طَالَ بِالنَّاسِ زَمَانٌ أَنْ يَقُولَ قَائِلٌ وَاللَّهِ مَا نَجِدُ آيَةَ الرَّجْمِ فِي كِتَابِ اللَّهِ، فَيَضِلُّوا بِتَرْكِ فَرِيضَةٍ أَنْزَلَهَا اللَّهُ، وَالرَّجْمُ فِي كِتَابِ اللَّهِ حَقٌّ عَلَى مَنْ زَنَى إِذَا أُحْصِنَ مِنَ الرِّجَالِ وَالنِّسَاءِ، إِذَا قَامَتِ الْبَيِّنَةُ أَوْ كَانَ الْحَبَلُ أَوِ الاِعْتِرَافُ، ثُمَّ إِنَّا كُنَّا نَقْرَأُ فِيمَا نَقْرَأُ مِنْ كِتَابِ اللَّهِ أَنْ لاَ تَرْغَبُوا عَنْ آبَائِكُمْ، فَإِنَّهُ كُفْرٌ بِكُمْ أَنْ تَرْغَبُوا عَنْ آبَائِكُمْ، أَوْ إِنَّ كُفْرًا بِكُمْ أَنْ تَرْغَبُوا عَنْ آبَائِكُمْ، أَلاَ ثُمَّ إِنَّ رَسُولَ اللَّهِ صلى الله عليه وسلم قَالَ " لاَ تُطْرُونِي كَمَا أُطْرِيَ عِيسَى ابْنُ مَرْيَمَ وَقُولُوا عَبْدُ اللَّهِ وَرَسُولُهُ ". ثُمَّ إِنَّهُ بَلَغَنِي أَنَّ قَائِلاً مِنْكُمْ يَقُولُ وَاللَّهِ لَوْ مَاتَ عُمَرُ بَايَعْتُ فُلاَنًا. فَلاَ يَغْتَرَّنَّ امْرُؤٌ أَنْ يَقُولَ إِنَّمَا كَانَتْ بَيْعَةُ أَبِي بَكْرٍ فَلْتَةً وَتَمَّتْ أَلاَ وَإِنَّهَا قَدْ كَانَتْ كَذَلِكَ وَلَكِنَّ اللَّهَ وَقَى شَرَّهَا، وَلَيْسَ مِنْكُمْ مَنْ تُقْطَعُ الأَعْنَاقُ إِلَيْهِ مِثْلُ أَبِي بَكْرٍ، مَنْ بَايَعَ رَجُلاً عَنْ غَيْرِ مَشُورَةٍ مِنَ الْمُسْلِمِينَ فَلاَ يُبَايَعُ هُوَ وَلاَ الَّذِي بَايَعَهُ تَغِرَّةً أَنْ يُقْتَلاَ، وَإِنَّهُ قَدْ كَانَ مِنْ خَبَرِنَا حِينَ تَوَفَّى اللَّهُ نَبِيَّهُ صلى الله عليه وسلم إِلاَّ أَنَّ الأَنْصَارَ خَالَفُونَا وَاجْتَمَعُوا بِأَسْرِهِمْ فِي سَقِيفَةِ بَنِي سَاعِدَةَ، وَخَالَفَ عَنَّا عَلِيٌّ وَالزُّبَيْرُ وَمَنْ مَعَهُمَا، وَاجْتَمَعَ الْمُهَاجِرُونَ إِلَى أَبِي بَكْرٍ فَقُلْتُ لأَبِي بَكْرٍ يَا أَبَا بَكْرٍ انْطَلِقْ بِنَا إِلَى إِخْوَانِنَا هَؤُلاَءِ مِنَ الأَنْصَارِ. فَانْطَلَقْنَا نُرِيدُهُمْ فَلَمَّا دَنَوْنَا مِنْهُمْ لَقِيَنَا مِنْهُمْ رَجُلاَنِ صَالِحَانِ، فَذَكَرَا مَا تَمَالَى عَلَيْهِ الْقَوْمُ فَقَالاَ أَيْنَ تُرِيدُونَ يَا مَعْشَرَ الْمُهَاجِرِينَ فَقُلْنَا نُرِيدُ إِخْوَانَنَا هَؤُلاَءِ مِنَ الأَنْصَارِ. فَقَالاَ لاَ عَلَيْكُمْ أَنْ لاَ تَقْرَبُوهُمُ اقْضُوا أَمْرَكُمْ. فَقُلْتُ وَاللَّهِ لَنَأْتِيَنَّهُمْ. فَانْطَلَقْنَا حَتَّى أَتَيْنَاهُمْ فِي سَقِيفَةِ بَنِي سَاعِدَةَ، فَإِذَا رَجُلٌ مُزَمَّلٌ بَيْنَ ظَهْرَانَيْهِمْ فَقُلْتُ مَنْ هَذَا فَقَالُوا هَذَا سَعْدُ بْنُ عُبَادَةَ. فَقُلْتُ مَا لَهُ قَالُوا يُوعَكُ. فَلَمَّا جَلَسْنَا قَلِيلاً تَشَهَّدَ خَطِيبُهُمْ، فَأَثْنَى عَلَى اللَّهِ بِمَا هُوَ أَهْلُهُ ثُمَّ قَالَ أَمَّا بَعْدُ فَنَحْنُ أَنْصَارُ اللَّهِ وَكَتِيبَةُ الإِسْلاَمِ، وَأَنْتُمْ مَعْشَرَ الْمُهَاجِرِينَ رَهْطٌ، وَقَدْ دَفَّتْ دَافَّةٌ مِنْ قَوْمِكُمْ، فَإِذَا هُمْ يُرِيدُونَ أَنْ يَخْتَزِلُونَا مِنْ أَصْلِنَا وَأَنْ يَحْضُنُونَا مِنَ الأَمْرِ. فَلَمَّا سَكَتَ أَرَدْتُ أَنْ أَتَكَلَّمَ وَكُنْتُ زَوَّرْتُ مَقَالَةً أَعْجَبَتْنِي أُرِيدُ أَنْ أُقَدِّمَهَا بَيْنَ يَدَىْ أَبِي بَكْرٍ، وَكُنْتُ أُدَارِي مِنْهُ بَعْضَ الْحَدِّ، فَلَمَّا أَرَدْتُ أَنْ أَتَكَلَّمَ قَالَ أَبُو بَكْرٍ عَلَى رِسْلِكَ. فَكَرِهْتُ أَنْ أُغْضِبَهُ، فَتَكَلَّمَ أَبُو بَكْرٍ فَكَانَ هُوَ أَحْلَمَ مِنِّي وَأَوْقَرَ، وَاللَّهِ مَا تَرَكَ مِنْ كَلِمَةٍ أَعْجَبَتْنِي فِي تَزْوِيرِي إِلاَّ قَالَ فِي بَدِيهَتِهِ مِثْلَهَا أَوْ أَفْضَلَ مِنْهَا حَتَّى سَكَتَ فَقَالَ مَا ذَكَرْتُمْ فِيكُمْ مِنْ خَيْرٍ فَأَنْتُمْ لَهُ أَهْلٌ، وَلَنْ يُعْرَفَ هَذَا الأَمْرُ إِلاَّ لِهَذَا الْحَىِّ مِنْ قُرَيْشٍ، هُمْ أَوْسَطُ الْعَرَبِ نَسَبًا وَدَارًا، وَقَدْ رَضِيتُ لَكُمْ أَحَدَ هَذَيْنِ الرَّجُلَيْنِ، فَبَايِعُوا أَيَّهُمَا شِئْتُمْ. فَأَخَذَ بِيَدِي وَبِيَدِ أَبِي عُبَيْدَةَ بْنِ الْجَرَّاحِ وَهْوَ جَالِسٌ بَيْنَنَا، فَلَمْ أَكْرَهْ مِمَّا قَالَ غَيْرَهَا، كَانَ

وَاللَّهِ أَنْ أُقَدَّمَ فَتُضْرَبَ عُنُقِي لاَ يُقَرِّبُنِي ذَلِكَ مِنْ إِثْمٍ، أَحَبَّ إِلَيَّ مِنْ أَنْ أَتَأَمَّرَ عَلَى قَوْمٍ فِيهِمْ أَبُو بَكْرٍ، اللَّهُمَّ إِلاَّ أَنْ تُسَوِّلَ إِلَيَّ نَفْسِي عِنْدَ الْمَوْتِ شَيْئًا لاَ أَجِدُهُ الآنَ. فَقَالَ قَائِلٌ مِنَ الأَنْصَارِ أَنَا جُذَيْلُهَا الْمُحَكَّكُ، وَعُذَيْقُهَا الْمُرَجَّبُ، مِنَّا أَمِيرٌ، وَمِنْكُمْ أَمِيرٌ، يَا مَعْشَرَ قُرَيْشٍ. فَكَثُرَ اللَّغَطُ، وَارْتَفَعَتِ الأَصْوَاتُ حَتَّى فَرِقْتُ مِنَ الاِخْتِلاَفِ. فَقُلْتُ ابْسُطْ يَدَكَ يَا أَبَا بَكْرٍ. فَبَسَطَ يَدَهُ فَبَايَعْتُهُ، وَبَايَعَهُ الْمُهَاجِرُونَ، ثُمَّ بَايَعَتْهُ الأَنْصَارُ، وَنَزَوْنَا عَلَى سَعْدِ بْنِ عُبَادَةَ فَقَالَ قَائِلٌ مِنْهُمْ قَتَلْتُمْ سَعْدَ بْنَ عُبَادَةَ. فَقُلْتُ قَتَلَ اللَّهُ سَعْدَ بْنَ عُبَادَةَ. قَالَ عُمَرُ وَإِنَّا وَاللَّهِ مَا وَجَدْنَا فِيمَا حَضَرْنَا مِنْ أَمْرٍ أَقْوَى مِنْ مُبَايَعَةِ أَبِي بَكْرٍ خَشِينَا إِنْ فَارَقْنَا الْقَوْمَ وَلَمْ تَكُنْ بَيْعَةٌ أَنْ يُبَايِعُوا رَجُلاً مِنْهُمْ بَعْدَنَا، فَإِمَّا بَايَعْنَاهُمْ عَلَى مَا لاَ نَرْضَى، وَإِمَّا نُخَالِفُهُمْ فَيَكُونُ فَسَادٌ، فَمَنْ بَايَعَ رَجُلاً عَلَى غَيْرِ مَشُورَةٍ مِنَ الْمُسْلِمِينَ فَلاَ يُتَابَعُ هُوَ وَلاَ الَّذِي بَايَعَهُ تَغِرَّةً أَنْ يُقْتَلاَ.

Narrated `Aisha: Fatima the daughter of the Prophetﷺ sent someone to Abu Bakr (when he was a caliph), asking for her inheritance of what Allah's Messengerﷺ had left of the property bestowed on him by Allah from the Fai (i.e. booty gained without fighting) in Medina, and Fadak, and what remained of the Khumus of the Khaibar booty. On that, Abu Bakr said, "Allah's Messengerﷺ said, "Our property is not inherited. Whatever we leave, is Sadaqa, but the family of (the Prophet) Muhammad can eat of this property.' By Allah, I will not make any change in the state of the Sadaqa of Allah's Messengerﷺ and will leave it as it was during the lifetime of Allah's Messengerﷺ, and will dispose of it as Allah's Messengerﷺ used to do." So Abu Bakr refused to give anything of that to Fatima. So she became angry with Abu Bakr and kept away from him, and did not task to him till she died. She remained alive for six months after the death of the Prophet. When she died, her husband `Ali, buried her at night without informing Abu Bakr and he said the funeral prayer by himself. When Fatima was alive, the people used to respect `Ali much, but after her death, `Ali noticed a change in the people's attitude towards him. So `Ali sought reconciliation with Abu Bakr and gave him an oath of allegiance. `Ali had not given the oath of allegiance during those months (i.e. the period between the Prophet's death and Fatima's death). `Ali sent someone to Abu Bakr saying, "Come to us, but let nobody come with you," as he disliked that `Umar should come, `Umar said (to Abu Bakr), "No, by Allah, you shall not enter upon them alone " Abu Bakr said, "What do you think they will do to me? By Allah, I will go to them' So Abu Bakr entered upon them, and then `Ali uttered Tashah-hud and said (to Abu Bakr), "We know well your superiority and what Allah has given you, and we are not jealous of the good what Allah has bestowed upon you, but you did not consult us in the question of the rule and we thought that we have got a right in it because of our near relationship to Allah's Messengerﷺ." Thereupon Abu Bakr's eyes flowed with tears. And when Abu Bakr spoke, he said, "By Him in Whose Hand my soul is to keep good relations with the relatives of Allah's Messengerﷺ is dearer to me than to keep good relations with my own relatives. But as for the trouble which arose between me and you about his property, I will do my best to spend it according to what is good, and will not leave any rule or regulation which I saw Allah's Messengerﷺ following, in disposing of it, but I will follow." On that `Ali said to Abu Bakr, "I promise to give you the oath of allegiance in this after noon." So when Abu Bakr had offered the Zuhr prayer, he ascended the pulpit and uttered the Tashah-hud and then mentioned the story of `Ali and his failure to give the oath of allegiance, and excused him, accepting what excuses he had offered; Then `Ali (got up) and praying (to Allah) for forgiveness, he uttered Tashah-hud, praised Abu Bakr's right, and said, that he had not done what he had done because of jealousy of Abu Bakr or as a protest of that Allah had favored him with. `Ali added, "But we used to consider that we too had some right in this affair (of rulership) and that he (i.e. Abu Bakr) did not consult us in this matter, and therefore caused us to feel sorry." On that all the Muslims became happy and said, "You have done the right thing." The Muslims then became friendly with `Ali as he returned to what the people had done (i.e. giving the oath of allegiance to Abu Bakr). – Sahih Al-Bukhari 4240, 4241

حَدَّثَنَا يَحْيَى بْنُ بُكَيْرٍ، حَدَّثَنَا اللَّيْثُ، عَنْ عُقَيْلٍ، عَنِ ابْنِ شِهَابٍ، عَنْ عُرْوَةَ، عَنْ عَائِشَةَ، أَنَّ فَاطِمَةَ ـ عَلَيْهَا السَّلاَمُ ـ بِنْتَ النَّبِيِّ صلى الله عليه وسلم أَرْسَلَتْ إِلَى أَبِي بَكْرٍ تَسْأَلُهُ مِيرَاثَهَا مِنْ رَسُولِ اللَّهِ صلى الله عليه وسلم مِمَّا أَفَاءَ اللَّهُ عَلَيْهِ بِالْمَدِينَةِ وَفَدَكَ، وَمَا بَقِيَ مِنْ خُمُسِ خَيْبَرَ، فَقَالَ أَبُو بَكْرٍ إِنَّ رَسُولَ اللَّهِ صلى الله عليه وسلم قَالَ " لاَ نُورَثُ، مَا تَرَكْنَا صَدَقَةٌ، إِنَّمَا يَأْكُلُ آلُ مُحَمَّدٍ صلى الله عليه وسلم فِي هَذَا الْمَالِ ". وَإِنِّي وَاللَّهِ لاَ أُغَيِّرُ شَيْئًا مِنْ صَدَقَةِ رَسُولِ اللَّهِ صلى الله عليه وسلم عَنْ حَالِهَا الَّتِي كَانَ عَلَيْهَا فِي عَهْدِ رَسُولِ اللَّهِ صلى الله عليه وسلم وَلأَعْمَلَنَّ فِيهَا بِمَا عَمِلَ بِهِ رَسُولُ اللَّهِ صلى الله عليه وسلم فَأَبَى أَبُو بَكْرٍ أَنْ يَدْفَعَ إِلَى فَاطِمَةَ مِنْهَا شَيْئًا فَوَجَدَتْ فَاطِمَةُ عَلَى أَبِي بَكْرٍ فِي ذَلِكَ فَهَجَرَتْهُ، فَلَمْ تُكَلِّمْهُ حَتَّى تُوُفِّيَتْ، وَعَاشَتْ بَعْدَ النَّبِيِّ صلى الله عليه وسلم سِتَّةَ أَشْهُرٍ، فَلَمَّا تُوُفِّيَتْ، دَفَنَهَا زَوْجُهَا عَلِيٌّ لَيْلاً، وَلَمْ يُؤْذِنْ بِهَا أَبَا بَكْرٍ وَصَلَّى عَلَيْهَا، وَكَانَ لِعَلِيٍّ مِنَ النَّاسِ وَجْهٌ حَيَاةَ فَاطِمَةَ، فَلَمَّا تُوُفِّيَتِ اسْتَنْكَرَ عَلِيٌّ وُجُوهَ النَّاسِ، فَالْتَمَسَ مُصَالَحَةَ أَبِي بَكْرٍ وَمُبَايَعَتَهُ، وَلَمْ يَكُنْ يُبَايِعُ تِلْكَ الأَشْهُرَ، فَأَرْسَلَ إِلَى أَبِي بَكْرٍ أَنِ ائْتِنَا، وَلاَ يَأْتِنَا أَحَدٌ مَعَكَ، كَرَاهِيَةً لِمَحْضَرِ عُمَرَ. فَقَالَ عُمَرُ لاَ وَاللَّهِ لاَ تَدْخُلُ عَلَيْهِمْ وَحْدَكَ. فَقَالَ أَبُو بَكْرٍ وَمَا عَسَيْتَهُمْ أَنْ يَفْعَلُوا بِي، وَاللَّهِ لآتِيَنَّهُمْ. فَدَخَلَ عَلَيْهِمْ أَبُو بَكْرٍ، فَتَشَهَّدَ عَلِيٌّ فَقَالَ إِنَّا قَدْ عَرَفْنَا فَضْلَكَ، وَمَا أَعْطَاكَ، اللَّهُ وَلَمْ نَنْفَسْ عَلَيْكَ خَيْرًا سَاقَهُ اللَّهُ إِلَيْكَ، وَلَكِنَّكَ اسْتَبْدَدْتَ عَلَيْنَا بِالأَمْرِ، وَكُنَّا نَرَى لِقَرَابَتِنَا مِنْ رَسُولِ اللَّهِ صلى الله عليه وسلم نَصِيبًا. حَتَّى فَاضَتْ عَيْنَا أَبِي بَكْرٍ، فَلَمَّا تَكَلَّمَ أَبُو بَكْرٍ قَالَ وَالَّذِي نَفْسِي بِيَدِهِ لَقَرَابَةُ رَسُولِ اللَّهِ صلى الله عليه وسلم أَحَبُّ إِلَيَّ أَنْ أَصِلَ مِنْ قَرَابَتِي، وَأَمَّا الَّذِي شَجَرَ بَيْنِي وَبَيْنَكُمْ مِنْ هَذِهِ الأَمْوَالِ، فَلَمْ آلُ فِيهَا عَنِ الْخَيْرِ، وَلَمْ أَتْرُكْ أَمْرًا رَأَيْتُ رَسُولَ اللَّهِ صلى الله عليه وسلم يَصْنَعُهُ فِيهَا إِلاَّ صَنَعْتُهُ. فَقَالَ عَلِيٌّ لأَبِي بَكْرٍ مَوْعِدُكَ الْعَشِيَّةُ لِلْبَيْعَةِ. فَلَمَّا صَلَّى أَبُو بَكْرٍ الظُّهْرَ رَقِيَ عَلَى الْمِنْبَرِ، فَتَشَهَّدَ وَذَكَرَ شَأْنَ عَلِيٍّ، وَتَخَلُّفَهُ عَنِ الْبَيْعَةِ، وَعُذْرَهُ بِالَّذِي اعْتَذَرَ إِلَيْهِ، ثُمَّ اسْتَغْفَرَ، وَتَشَهَّدَ عَلِيٌّ فَعَظَّمَ حَقَّ أَبِي بَكْرٍ، وَحَدَّثَ أَنَّهُ لَمْ يَحْمِلْهُ عَلَى الَّذِي صَنَعَ نَفَاسَةً عَلَى أَبِي بَكْرٍ، وَلاَ إِنْكَارًا لِلَّذِي فَضَّلَهُ اللَّهُ بِهِ، وَلَكِنَّا نَرَى لَنَا فِي هَذَا الأَمْرِ نَصِيبًا، فَاسْتَبَدَّ عَلَيْنَا، فَوَجَدْنَا فِي أَنْفُسِنَا، فَسُرَّ بِذَلِكَ الْمُسْلِمُونَ وَقَالُوا أَصَبْتَ. وَكَانَ الْمُسْلِمُونَ إِلَى عَلِيٍّ قَرِيبًا، حِينَ رَاجَعَ الأَمْرَ الْمَعْرُوفَ.

Buzakha
بُزَاخَةَ

Narrated Tariq bin Shihab: Abu Bakr said to the delegate of Buzakha. "Follow the tails of the camels till Allah shows the Caliph (successor) of His Prophet and Al-Muhajirin (emigrants) something because of which you may excuse yourselves.". – Sahih Al-Bukhari 7221

حَدَّثَنَا مُسَدَّدٌ، حَدَّثَنَا يَحْيَى، عَنْ سُفْيَانَ، حَدَّثَنِي قَيْسُ بْنُ مُسْلِمٍ، عَنْ طَارِقِ بْنِ شِهَابٍ، عَنْ أَبِي بَكْرٍ ـ رضى الله عنه ـ قَالَ لِوَفْدِ بُزَاخَةَ تَتْبَعُونَ أَذْنَابَ الإِبِلِ حَتَّى يُرِيَ اللَّهُ خَلِيفَةَ نَبِيِّهِ صلى الله عليه وسلم وَالْمُهَاجِرِينَ أَمْرًا يَعْذِرُونَكُمْ بِهِ.

Narrated Abu Huraira: When Allah's Messenger ﷺ died and Abu Bakr became the caliph some Arabs renegade (reverted to disbelief) (Abu Bakr decided to declare war against them), `Umar, said to Abu Bakr, "How can you fight with these people although Allah's Messenger ﷺ said, 'I have been ordered (by Allah) to fight the people till they say: "None has the right to be worshipped but Allah, and whoever said it then he will save his life and property from me except on trespassing the law (rights and conditions for which he will be punished justly), and his accounts will be with Allah.' " Abu Bakr said, "By Allah! I will fight those who differentiate between the prayer and the Zakat as Zakat is the compulsory right to be taken from the property (according to Allah's orders) By Allah! If they refuse to pay me even a she-kid which they used to pay at the time of Allah's Messenger ﷺ. I would fight with them for withholding it" Then `Umar said, "By Allah, it was nothing, but Allah opened Abu Bakr's chest towards the decision (to fight) and I came to know that his decision was right.". – Sahih al-Bukhari 1399, 1400

حَدَّثَنَا أَبُو الْيَمَانِ الْحَكَمُ بْنُ نَافِعٍ، أَخْبَرَنَا شُعَيْبُ بْنُ أَبِي حَمْزَةَ، عَنِ الزُّهْرِيِّ، حَدَّثَنَا عُبَيْدُ اللَّهِ بْنُ عَبْدِ اللَّهِ بْنِ عُتْبَةَ بْنِ مَسْعُودٍ، أَنَّ أَبَا هُرَيْرَةَ ـ رضى الله عنه ـ قَالَ لَمَّا تُوُفِّيَ رَسُولُ اللَّهِ صلى الله عليه وسلم وَكَانَ أَبُو بَكْرٍ ـ رضى الله عنه ـ وَكَفَرَ مَنْ كَفَرَ مِنَ الْعَرَبِ فَقَالَ عُمَرُ ـ رضى الله عنه كَيْفَ تُقَاتِلُ النَّاسَ، وَقَدْ قَالَ رَسُولُ اللَّهِ صلى الله عليه وسلم " أُمِرْتُ أَنْ أُقَاتِلَ النَّاسَ حَتَّى يَقُولُوا لاَ إِلَهَ إِلاَّ اللَّهُ. فَمَنْ قَالَهَا فَقَدْ عَصَمَ مِنِّي مَالَهُ وَنَفْسَهُ إِلاَّ بِحَقِّهِ، وَحِسَابُهُ عَلَى اللَّهِ ". فَقَالَ وَاللَّهِ لأُقَاتِلَنَّ مَنْ فَرَّقَ بَيْنَ الصَّلاَةِ وَالزَّكَاةِ، فَإِنَّ الزَّكَاةَ حَقُّ الْمَالِ، وَاللَّهِ لَوْ مَنَعُونِي عَنَاقًا كَانُوا يُؤَدُّونَهَا إِلَى رَسُولِ اللَّهِ صلى الله عليه وسلم لَقَاتَلْتُهُمْ عَلَى مَنْعِهَا. قَالَ عُمَرُ ـ رضى الله عنه ـ فَوَاللَّهِ مَا هُوَ إِلاَّ أَنْ قَدْ شَرَحَ اللَّهُ صَدْرَ أَبِي بَكْرٍ ـ رضى الله عنه ـ فَعَرَفْتُ أَنَّهُ الْحَقُّ.

Narrated Abu Huraira: When the Prophet ﷺ died and Abu Bakr became his successor and some of the Arabs reverted to disbelief, `Umar said, "O Abu Bakr! How can you fight these people although Allah's Messenger ﷺ said, 'I have been ordered to fight the people till they say: 'None has the right to be worshipped but Allah, 'and whoever said, 'None has the right to be worshipped but Allah', Allah will save his property and his life from me, unless (he does something for which he receives legal punishment) justly, and his account will be with Allah?' "Abu Bakr said, "By Allah! I will fight whoever differentiates between prayers and Zakat as Zakat is the right to be taken from property (according to Allah's Orders). By Allah! If they refused to pay me even a kid they used to pay to Allah's Messenger ﷺ . I would fight with them for withholding it." `Umar said, "By Allah: It was nothing, but I noticed that Allah opened Abu Bakr's chest towards the decision to fight, therefore I realized that his decision was right.". – Sahih al-Bukhari 6924, 6925
حَدَّثَنَا يَحْيَى بْنُ بُكَيْرٍ، حَدَّثَنَا اللَّيْثُ، عَنْ عُقَيْلٍ، عَنِ ابْنِ شِهَابٍ، أَخْبَرَنِي عُبَيْدُ اللَّهِ بْنُ عَبْدِ اللَّهِ بْنِ عُتْبَةَ، أَنَّ أَبَا هُرَيْرَةَ، قَالَ لَمَّا تُوُفِّيَ النَّبِيُّ صلى الله عليه وسلم وَاسْتُخْلِفَ أَبُو بَكْرٍ، وَكَفَرَ مَنْ كَفَرَ مِنَ الْعَرَبِ، قَالَ عُمَرُ يَا أَبَا بَكْرٍ، كَيْفَ تُقَاتِلُ النَّاسَ، وَقَدْ قَالَ رَسُولُ اللَّهِ صلى الله عليه وسلم " أُمِرْتُ أَنْ أُقَاتِلَ النَّاسَ حَتَّى يَقُولُوا لاَ إِلَهَ إِلاَّ اللَّهُ. فَمَنْ قَالَ لاَ إِلَهَ إِلاَّ اللَّهُ. عَصَمَ مِنِّي مَالَهُ وَنَفْسَهُ، إِلاَّ بِحَقِّهِ، وَحِسَابُهُ عَلَى اللَّهِ ". قَالَ أَبُو بَكْرٍ وَاللَّهِ لأُقَاتِلَنَّ مَنْ فَرَّقَ بَيْنَ الصَّلاَةِ وَالزَّكَاةِ، فَإِنَّ الزَّكَاةَ حَقُّ الْمَالِ، وَاللَّهِ لَوْ مَنَعُونِي عَنَاقًا كَانُوا يُؤَدُّونَهَا إِلَى رَسُولِ اللَّهِ صلى الله عليه وسلم لَقَاتَلْتُهُمْ عَلَى مَنْعِهَا. قَالَ عُمَرُ فَوَاللَّهِ مَا هُوَ إِلاَّ أَنْ رَأَيْتُ أَنْ قَدْ شَرَحَ اللَّهُ صَدْرَ أَبِي بَكْرٍ لِلْقِتَالِ فَعَرَفْتُ أَنَّهُ الْحَقُّ.

Ghazwa Yamama
غزوة اليمامة

Narrated Zaid bin Thabit: Abu Bakr sent for me owing to the large number of casualties in the battle of Al-Yamama, while `Umar was sitting with him. Abu Bakr said (to me), `Umar has come to my and said, 'A great number of Qaris of the Holy Qur'an were killed on the day of the battle of Al-Yamama, and I am afraid that the casualties among the Qaris of the Qur'an may increase on other battle-fields whereby a large part of the Qur'an may be lost. Therefore I consider it advisable that you (Abu Bakr) should have the Qur'an collected.' I said, 'How dare I do something which Allah's Messenger ﷺ did not do?' `Umar said, By Allah, it is something beneficial.' `Umar kept on pressing me for that till Allah opened my chest for that for which He had opened the chest of `Umar and I had in that matter, the same opinion as `Umar had." Abu Bakr then said to me (Zaid), "You are a wise young man and we do not have any suspicion about you, and you used to write the Divine Inspiration for Allah's Messenger ﷺ. So you should search for the fragmentary scripts of the Qur'an and collect it (in one Book)." Zaid further said: By Allah, if Abu Bakr had ordered me to shift a mountain among the mountains from one place to another it would not have been heavier for me than this ordering me to collect the Qur'an. Then I said (to `Umar and Abu Bakr), "How can you do something which Allah's Messenger ﷺ did not do?" Abu Bakr said, "By Allah, it is something beneficial." Zaid added: So he (Abu Bakr) kept on pressing me for that until Allah opened my chest for that for which He had opened the chests of Abu Bakr and `Umar, and I had in that matter, the same opinion as theirs. So I started compiling the Qur'an by collecting it from the leafless stalks of the date-palm tree and from the pieces of leather and hides and from the stones, and from the chests of men (who had memorized the Qur'an). I found the last verses of Sirat-at-Tauba: ["Verily there has come unto you an Apostle (Muhammad) from amongst yourselves—' (9.128-129)] from Khuza`ima or Abi Khuza`ima and I added to it the rest of the Sura. The manuscripts of the Qur'an remained with Abu Bakr till Allah took him unto Him. Then it remained with `Umar till Allah took him unto Him, and then with Hafsa bint `Umar. – Sahih Al-Bukhari 7191

حَدَّثَنَا مُحَمَّدُ بْنُ عُبَيْدِ اللَّهِ أَبُو ثَابِتٍ، حَدَّثَنَا إِبْرَاهِيمُ بْنُ سَعْدٍ، عَنِ ابْنِ شِهَابٍ، عَنْ عُبَيْدِ بْنِ السَّبَّاقِ، عَنْ زَيْدِ بْنِ ثَابِتٍ، قَالَ بَعَثَ إِلَيَّ أَبُو بَكْرٍ لِمَقْتَلِ أَهْلِ الْيَمَامَةِ وَعِنْدَهُ عُمَرُ فَقَالَ أَبُو بَكْرٍ إِنَّ عُمَرَ أَتَانِي فَقَالَ إِنَّ الْقَتْلَ قَدِ اسْتَحَرَّ يَوْمَ الْيَمَامَةِ بِقُرَّاءِ الْقُرْآنِ، وَإِنِّي أَخْشَى أَنْ يَسْتَحِرَّ الْقَتْلُ بِقُرَّاءِ الْقُرْآنِ فِي الْمَوَاطِنِ كُلِّهَا، فَيَذْهَبَ قُرْآنٌ كَثِيرٌ، وَإِنِّي أَرَى أَنْ تَأْمُرَ بِجَمْعِ الْقُرْآنِ. قُلْتُ كَيْفَ أَفْعَلُ شَيْئًا لَمْ يَفْعَلْهُ رَسُولُ اللَّهِ صلى الله عليه وسلم فَقَالَ عُمَرُ هُوَ وَاللَّهِ خَيْرٌ. فَلَمْ يَزَلْ عُمَرُ يُرَاجِعُنِي فِي ذَلِكَ حَتَّى شَرَحَ اللَّهُ صَدْرِي لِلَّذِي شَرَحَ لَهُ صَدْرَ عُمَرَ، وَرَأَيْتُ فِي ذَلِكَ الَّذِي رَأَى عُمَرُ. قَالَ زَيْدٌ قَالَ أَبُو بَكْرٍ وَإِنَّكَ رَجُلٌ شَابٌّ عَاقِلٌ لاَ نَتَّهِمُكَ، قَدْ كُنْتَ تَكْتُبُ الْوَحْىَ لِرَسُولِ اللَّهِ صلى الله عليه وسلم فَتَتَبَّعِ الْقُرْآنَ فَاجْمَعْهُ. قَالَ زَيْدٌ فَوَاللَّهِ لَوْ كَلَّفَنِي نَقْلَ جَبَلٍ مِنَ الْجِبَالِ مَا كَانَ بِأَثْقَلَ عَلَىَّ مِمَّا كَلَّفَنِي مِنْ جَمْعِ الْقُرْآنِ. قُلْتُ كَيْفَ تَفْعَلاَنِ شَيْئًا لَمْ يَفْعَلْهُ رَسُولُ اللَّهِ صلى الله عليه وسلم قَالَ أَبُو بَكْرٍ هُوَ وَاللَّهِ خَيْرٌ. فَلَمْ يَزَلْ يَحُثُّ مُرَاجَعَتِي حَتَّى شَرَحَ اللَّهُ صَدْرِي لِلَّذِي شَرَحَ اللَّهُ لَهُ صَدْرَ أَبِي بَكْرٍ وَعُمَرَ، وَرَأَيْتُ فِي ذَلِكَ الَّذِي رَأَيَا، فَتَتَبَّعْتُ الْقُرْآنَ أَجْمَعُهُ مِنَ الْعُسُبِ وَالرِّقَاعِ وَاللِّخَافِ وَصُدُورِ الرِّجَالِ، فَوَجَدْتُ آخِرَ سُورَةِ التَّوْبَةِ {لَقَدْ جَاءَكُمْ رَسُولٌ مِنْ أَنْفُسِكُمْ} إِلَى آخِرِهَا مَعَ خُزَيْمَةَ أَوْ أَبِي خُزَيْمَةَ فَأَلْحَقْتُهَا فِي سُورَتِهَا، وَكَانَتِ الصُّحُفُ عِنْدَ أَبِي بَكْرٍ حَيَاتَهُ حَتَّى تَوَفَّاهُ اللَّهُ عَزَّ وَجَلَّ، ثُمَّ عِنْدَ عُمَرَ حَيَاتَهُ حَتَّى تَوَفَّاهُ اللَّهُ، ثُمَّ عِنْدَ حَفْصَةَ بِنْتِ عُمَرَ. قَالَ مُحَمَّدُ بْنُ عُبَيْدِ اللَّهِ اللِّخَافُ يَعْنِي الْخَزَفَ.

Narrated Qatada: We do not know of any tribe amongst the 'Arab tribes who lost more martyrs than Al-Ansar, and they will have superiority on the Day of Resurrection. Anas bin Malik told us that seventy from the Ansar were martyred on the day of Uhud, and seventy on the day (of the battle of) Bir Ma'una, and seventy on the day of Al-Yamama. Anas added, "The battle of Bir Ma'una took place during the lifetime of Allah's Messenger ﷺ and the battle of Al-Yamama, during the caliphate of Abu Bakr, and it was the day when Musailamah Al-Kadhdhab was killed.". – Sahih Al-Bukhari 4078

حَدَّثَنِي عَمْرُو بْنُ عَلِيٍّ، حَدَّثَنَا مُعَاذُ بْنُ هِشَامٍ، قَالَ حَدَّثَنِي أَبِي، عَنْ قَتَادَةَ، قَالَ مَا نَعْلَمُ حَيًّا مِنْ أَحْيَاءِ الْعَرَبِ أَكْثَرَ شَهِيدًا أَعَزَّ يَوْمَ الْقِيَامَةِ مِنَ الأَنْصَارِ. قَالَ قَتَادَةُ وَحَدَّثَنَا أَنَسُ بْنُ مَالِكٍ أَنَّهُ قُتِلَ مِنْهُمْ يَوْمَ أُحُدٍ سَبْعُونَ، وَيَوْمَ بِئْرِ مَعُونَةَ سَبْعُونَ، وَيَوْمَ الْيَمَامَةِ سَبْعُونَ، قَالَ وَكَانَ بِئْرُ مَعُونَةَ عَلَى عَهْدِ رَسُولِ اللَّهِ صلى الله عليه وسلم، وَيَوْمُ الْيَمَامَةِ عَلَى عَهْدِ أَبِي بَكْرٍ يَوْمَ مُسَيْلِمَةَ الْكَذَّابِ.

Narrated Zaid bin Thabit Al-Ansari: Who was one of those who used to write the Divine Revelation: Abu Bakr sent for me after the (heavy) casualties among the warriors (of the battle) of Yamama (where a great number of Qurra' were killed). `Umar was present with Abu Bakr who said, `Umar has come to me and said, The people have suffered heavy casualties on the day of (the battle of) Yamama, and I am afraid that there will be more casualties among the Qurra' (those who know the Qur'an by heart) at other battle-fields, whereby a large part of the Qur'an may be lost, unless you collect it. And I am of the opinion that you should collect the Qur'an." Abu Bakr added, "I said to `Umar, 'How can I do something which Allah's Apostle has not done?' `Umar said (to me), 'By Allah, it is (really) a good thing.' So `Umar kept on pressing, trying to persuade me to accept his proposal, till Allah opened my bosom for it and I had the same opinion as `Umar." (Zaid bin Thabit added:)`Umar was sitting with him (Abu Bakr) and was not speaking. Me). "You are a wise young man and we do not suspect you (of telling lies or of forgetfulness): and you used to write the Divine Inspiration for Allah's Messenger ﷺ. Therefore, look for the Qur'an and collect it (in one manuscript). " By Allah, if he (Abu Bakr) had ordered me to shift one of the mountains (from its place) it would not have been harder for me than what he had ordered me concerning the collection of the Qur'an. I said to both of them, "How dare you do a thing which the Prophet has not done?" Abu Bakr said, "By Allah, it is (really) a good thing. So I kept on arguing with him about it till Allah opened my bosom for that which He had opened the bosoms of Abu Bakr and `Umar. So I started locating Qur'anic material and collecting it from parchments, scapula, leaf-stalks of date palms and from the memories of men (who knew it by heart). I found with Khuza`ima two Verses of Surat-at-Tauba which I had not found with anybody else, (and they were):-- "Verily there has come to you an Apostle (Muhammad) from amongst yourselves. It grieves him that you should receive any injury or difficulty He (Muhammad) is ardently anxious over you (to be rightly guided)" (9.128) The manuscript on which the Qur'an was collected, remained with Abu Bakr till Allah took him unto Him, and then with `Umar till Allah took him unto Him, and finally it remained with Hafsa, `Umar's daughter. – Sahih Al-Bukhari 4679

حَدَّثَنَا أَبُو الْيَمَانِ، أَخْبَرَنَا شُعَيْبٌ، عَنِ الزُّهْرِيِّ، قَالَ أَخْبَرَنِي ابْنُ السَّبَّاقِ، أَنَّ زَيْدَ بْنَ ثَابِتٍ الأَنْصَارِيَّ ـ رضى الله عنه ـ وَكَانَ مِمَّنْ يَكْتُبُ الْوَحْىَ قَالَ أَرْسَلَ إِلَىَّ أَبُو بَكْرٍ مَقْتَلَ أَهْلِ الْيَمَامَةِ وَعِنْدَهُ عُمَرُ، فَقَالَ أَبُو بَكْرٍ إِنَّ عُمَرَ أَتَانِي فَقَالَ إِنَّ الْقَتْلَ قَدِ اسْتَحَرَّ يَوْمَ الْيَمَامَةِ بِالنَّاسِ، وَإِنِّي أَخْشَى أَنْ يَسْتَحِرَّ الْقَتْلُ بِالْقُرَّاءِ فِي الْمَوَاطِنِ فَيَذْهَبَ كَثِيرٌ مِنَ الْقُرْآنِ، إِلاَّ أَنْ تَجْمَعُوهُ، وَإِنِّي لأَرَى أَنْ تَجْمَعَ الْقُرْآنَ. قَالَ أَبُو بَكْرٍ قُلْتُ لِعُمَرَ كَيْفَ أَفْعَلُ شَيْئًا لَمْ يَفْعَلْهُ رَسُولُ اللَّهِ صلى الله عليه وسلم فَقَالَ عُمَرُ هُوَ وَاللَّهِ خَيْرٌ. فَلَمْ يَزَلْ عُمَرُ يُرَاجِعُنِي فِيهِ حَتَّى شَرَحَ اللَّهُ لِذَلِكَ صَدْرِي، وَرَأَيْتُ الَّذِي رَأَى عُمَرُ. قَالَ زَيْدُ بْنُ ثَابِتٍ وَعُمَرُ عِنْدَهُ جَالِسٌ لاَ يَتَكَلَّمُ. فَقَالَ أَبُو بَكْرٍ إِنَّكَ رَجُلٌ شَابٌّ عَاقِلٌ وَلاَ نَتَّهِمُكَ، كُنْتَ تَكْتُبُ الْوَحْىَ لِرَسُولِ اللَّهِ صلى الله عليه وسلم فَتَتَبَّعِ الْقُرْآنَ فَاجْمَعْهُ. فَوَاللَّهِ لَوْ كَلَّفَنِي نَقْلَ جَبَلٍ مِنَ الْجِبَالِ مَا كَانَ أَثْقَلَ عَلَىَّ مِمَّا أَمَرَنِي بِهِ مِنْ جَمْعِ الْقُرْآنِ قُلْتُ كَيْفَ تَفْعَلاَنِ شَيْئًا لَمْ يَفْعَلْهُ النَّبِيُّ صلى الله عليه وسلم فَقَالَ أَبُو بَكْرٍ هُوَ وَاللَّهِ خَيْرٌ، فَلَمْ أَزَلْ أُرَاجِعُهُ حَتَّى شَرَحَ اللَّهُ صَدْرِي لِلَّذِي شَرَحَ اللَّهُ لَهُ صَدْرَ أَبِي بَكْرٍ وَعُمَرَ، فَقُمْتُ فَتَتَبَّعْتُ الْقُرْآنَ أَجْمَعُهُ مِنَ الرِّقَاعِ وَالأَكْتَافِ وَالْعُسُبِ وَصُدُورِ الرِّجَالِ، حَتَّى وَجَدْتُ مِنْ سُورَةِ التَّوْبَةِ آيَتَيْنِ مَعَ خُزَيْمَةَ الأَنْصَارِيِّ، لَمْ أَجِدْهُمَا مَعَ أَحَدٍ غَيْرِهِ {لَقَدْ جَاءَكُمْ رَسُولٌ مِنْ أَنْفُسِكُمْ عَزِيزٌ عَلَيْهِ مَا عَنِتُّمْ حَرِيصٌ عَلَيْكُمْ} إِلَى آخِرِهِمَا، وَكَانَتِ الصُّحُفُ الَّتِي جُمِعَ فِيهَا الْقُرْآنُ عِنْدَ أَبِي بَكْرٍ حَتَّى تَوَفَّاهُ اللَّهُ، ثُمَّ عِنْدَ عُمَرَ حَتَّى تَوَفَّاهُ اللَّهُ، ثُمَّ عِنْدَ حَفْصَةَ بِنْتِ عُمَرَ. تَابَعَهُ عُثْمَانُ بْنُ عُمَرَ وَاللَّيْثُ عَنْ يُونُسَ عَنِ ابْنِ شِهَابٍ. وَقَالَ اللَّيْثُ حَدَّثَنِي عَبْدُ الرَّحْمَنِ بْنُ خَالِدٍ عَنِ ابْنِ شِهَابٍ وَقَالَ مَعَ أَبِي خُزَيْمَةَ الأَنْصَارِيِّ. وَقَالَ مُوسَى عَنْ إِبْرَاهِيمَ حَدَّثَنَا ابْنُ شِهَابٍ مَعَ أَبِي خُزَيْمَةَ. وَتَابَعَهُ يَعْقُوبُ بْنُ إِبْرَاهِيمَ عَنْ أَبِيهِ. وَقَالَ أَبُو ثَابِتٍ حَدَّثَنَا إِبْرَاهِيمُ وَقَالَ مَعَ خُزَيْمَةَ، أَوْ أَبِي خُزَيْمَةَ

Narrated Hisham's father: Aisha said, "I went to Abu Bakr (during his fatal illness) and he asked me, 'In how many garments was the Prophet ﷺ shrouded?' She replied, 'In three Suhuliya pieces of white cloth of cotton, and there was neither a shirt nor a turban among them.' Abu Bakr further asked her, 'On which day did the Prophet die?' She replied, 'He died on Monday.' He asked, 'What is today?' She replied, 'Today is Monday.' He added, 'I hope I shall die sometime between this morning and tonight.' Then he looked at a garment that he was wearing during his illness and it had some stains of saffron. Then he said, 'Wash this garment of mine and add two more garments and shroud me in them.' I said, 'This is worn out.' He said, 'A living person has more right to wear new clothes than a dead one; the shroud is only for the body's pus.' He did not die till it was the night of Tuesday and was buried before the morning.". – Sahih Al-Bukhari 1387

حَدَّثَنَا مُعَلَّى بْنُ أَسَدٍ، حَدَّثَنَا وُهَيْبٌ، عَنْ هِشَامٍ، عَنْ أَبِيهِ، عَنْ عَائِشَةَ ـ رضى الله عنها ـ قَالَتْ دَخَلْتُ عَلَى أَبِي بَكْرٍ ـ رضى الله عنه ـ فَقَالَ فِي كَمْ كَفَّنْتُمُ النَّبِيَّ صلى الله عليه وسلم قَالَتْ فِي ثَلاَثَةِ أَثْوَابٍ بِيضٍ سَحُولِيَّةٍ، لَيْسَ فِيهَا قَمِيصٌ وَلاَ عِمَامَةٌ. وَقَالَ لَهَا فِي أَىِّ يَوْمٍ تُوُفِّيَ رَسُولُ اللَّهِ صلى الله عليه وسلم قَالَتْ يَوْمَ الاِثْنَيْنِ. قَالَ فَأَىُّ يَوْمٍ هَذَا قَالَتْ يَوْمُ الاِثْنَيْنِ. قَالَ أَرْجُو فِيمَا بَيْنِي وَبَيْنَ اللَّيْلِ. فَنَظَرَ إِلَى ثَوْبٍ عَلَيْهِ كَانَ يُمَرَّضُ فِيهِ، بِهِ رَدْعٌ مِنْ زَعْفَرَانٍ فَقَالَ اغْسِلُوا ثَوْبِي هَذَا، وَزِيدُوا عَلَيْهِ ثَوْبَيْنِ فَكَفِّنُونِي فِيهَا. قُلْتُ إِنَّ هَذَا خَلَقٌ. قَالَ إِنَّ الْحَىَّ أَحَقُّ بِالْجَدِيدِ مِنَ الْمَيِّتِ، إِنَّمَا هُوَ لِلْمُهْلَةِ. فَلَمْ يُتَوَفَّ حَتَّى أَمْسَى مِنْ لَيْلَةِ الثُّلاَثَاءِ وَدُفِنَ قَبْلَ أَنْ يُصْبِحَ.

The Book of
Caliphate of Umar ibn al-Khattab
خلافة عُمَر بْن الْخَطَّاب

Narrated Malik bin Aus An-Nasri: I proceeded till I entered upon `Umar (and while I was sitting there), his gate-keeper Yarfa came to him and said, " `Uthman, `Abdur-Rahman, Az-Zubair and Sa`d ask your permission to come in." `Umar allowed them. So they entered, greeted, and sat down. (After a while the gatekeeper came) and said, "Shall I admit `Ali and `Abbas?" `Umar allowed them to enter. Al-`Abbas said "O Chief of the believers! Judge between me and the oppressor (`Ali)." Then there was a dispute (regarding the property of Bani Nadir) between them (`Abbas and `Ali). `Uthman and his companions said, "O Chief of the Believers! Judge between them and relieve one from the other." `Umar said, "Be patient! Beseech you by Allah, with Whose permission the Heaven and the Earth Exist! Do you know that Allah's Messenger ﷺ said, 'Our property is not to be inherited, and whatever we leave is to be given in charity,' and by this Allah's Messenger ﷺ meant himself?" On that the group said, "He verily said so." `Umar then faced `Ali and `Abbas and said, "I beseech you both by Allah, do you both know that Allah's Messenger ﷺ said so?" They both replied, "Yes". `Umar then said, "Now I am talking to you about this matter (in detail) . Allah favored Allah's Messenger ﷺ with some of this wealth which He did not give to anybody else, as Allah said: 'What Allah bestowed as Fai (Booty on His Apostle for which you made no expedition... ' (59.6) So that property was totally meant for Allah's Messenger ﷺ, yet he did not collect it and ignore you, nor did he withhold it with your exclusion, but he gave it to you and distributed it among you till this much of it was left behind, and the Prophet, used to spend of this as the yearly expenditures of his family and then take what remained of it and spent it as he did with (other) Allah's wealth. The Prophet ﷺ did so during all his lifetime, and I beseech you by Allah, do you know that?" They replied, "Yes." `Umar then addressed `Ali and `Abbas, saying, "I beseech you both by Allah, do you know that?" Both of them replied, "Yes." `Umar added, "Then Allah took His Apostle unto Him. Abu Bakr then said 'I am the successor of Allah's Messenger ﷺ and took over all the Prophet's property and disposed of it in the same way as Allah's Messenger ﷺ used to do, and you were present then." Then he turned to `Ali and `Abbas and said, "You both claim that Abu Bakr did so-and-so in managing the property, but Allah knows that Abu Bakr was honest, righteous, intelligent, and a follower of what is right in managing it. Then Allah took Abu Bakr unto Him, 'I said: I am the successor of Allah's Messenger ﷺ and Abu Bakr.' So I took over the property for two years and managed it in the same way as Allah's Messenger ﷺ, and Abu Bakr used to do. Then you both (`Ali and `Abbas) came to me and asked for the same thing! (O `Abbas! You came to me to ask me for your share from nephew's property; and this (`Ali) came to me asking for his wives share from her father's property, and I said to you both, 'If you wish, I will place it in your custody on condition that you both will manage it in the same way as Allah's Messenger ﷺ and Abu Bakr did and as I have been doing since I took charge of managing it; otherwise, do not speak to me anymore about it.' Then you both said, 'Give it to us on that (condition).' So I gave it to you on that condition. Now I beseech you by Allah, did I not give it to them on that condition?" The group (whom he had been addressing) replied, "Yes." `Umar then addressed `Abbas and `Ali saying, "I beseech you both by Allah, didn't I give you all that property on that condition?" They said, "Yes." `Umar then said, "Are you now seeking a verdict from me other than that? By Him with Whose Permission the Heaven and the Earth exists I will not give any verdict other than that till the Hour is established; and if you both are unable to manage this property, then you can hand it back to me, and I will be sufficient for it on your behalf.” (See, Hadith No. 326, Vol. 4). – Sahih Al-Bukhari 7305

حَدَّثَنَا عَبْدُ اللَّهِ بْنُ يُوسُفَ، حَدَّثَنَا اللَّيْثُ، حَدَّثَنِي عُقَيْلٌ، عَنِ ابْنِ شِهَابٍ، قَالَ أَخْبَرَنِي مَالِكُ بْنُ أَوْسٍ النَّصْرِيُّ، وَكَانَ، مُحَمَّدُ بْنُ جُبَيْرِ بْنِ مُطْعِمٍ ذَكَرَ لِي ذِكْرًا مِنْ ذَلِكَ فَدَخَلْتُ عَلَى مَالِكٍ فَسَأَلْتُهُ فَقَالَ انْطَلَقْتُ حَتَّى أَدْخُلَ عَلَى عُمَرَ أَتَاهُ حَاجِبُهُ يَرْفَا فَقَالَ هَلْ لَكَ فِي عُثْمَانَ وَعَبْدِ الرَّحْمَنِ وَالزُّبَيْرِ وَسَعْدٍ يَسْتَأْذِنُونَ. قَالَ نَعَمْ. فَدَخَلُوا فَسَلَّمُوا وَجَلَسُوا. فَقَالَ هَلْ لَكَ فِي عَلِيٍّ وَعَبَّاسٍ. فَأَذِنَ لَهُمَا. قَالَ الْعَبَّاسُ يَا أَمِيرَ الْمُؤْمِنِينَ اقْضِ بَيْنِي وَبَيْنَ الظَّالِمِ. اسْتَبَّا. فَقَالَ الرَّهْطُ عُثْمَانُ وَأَصْحَابُهُ يَا أَمِيرَ الْمُؤْمِنِينَ اقْضِ بَيْنَهُمَا وَأَرِحْ أَحَدَهُمَا مِنَ الآخَرِ. فَقَالَ اتَّئِدُوا أَنْشُدُكُمْ بِاللَّهِ الَّذِي بِإِذْنِهِ تَقُومُ السَّمَاءُ وَالأَرْضُ، هَلْ تَعْلَمُونَ أَنَّ رَسُولَ اللَّهِ صلى الله عليه وسلم قَالَ " لاَ نُورَثُ مَا تَرَكْنَا صَدَقَةٌ ". يُرِيدُ رَسُولُ اللَّهِ صلى الله عليه وسلم نَفْسَهُ. قَالَ الرَّهْطُ قَدْ قَالَ ذَلِكَ. فَأَقْبَلَ عُمَرُ عَلَى عَلِيٍّ وَعَبَّاسٍ فَقَالَ أَنْشُدُكُمَا بِاللَّهِ هَلْ تَعْلَمَانِ أَنَّ رَسُولَ اللَّهِ صلى الله عليه وسلم قَالَ ذَلِكَ. قَالاَ نَعَمْ. قَالَ عُمَرُ فَإِنِّي مُحَدِّثُكُمْ عَنْ هَذَا الأَمْرِ، إِنَّ اللَّهَ كَانَ خَصَّ رَسُولَهُ صلى الله عليه وسلم فِي هَذَا الْمَالِ بِشَىْءٍ لَمْ يُعْطِهِ أَحَدًا غَيْرَهُ، فَإِنَّ اللَّهَ يَقُولُ {مَا أَفَاءَ اللَّهُ عَلَى رَسُولِهِ مِنْهُمْ فَمَا أَوْجَفْتُمْ} الآيَةَ، فَكَانَتْ هَذِهِ خَالِصَةً لِرَسُولِ اللَّهِ صلى الله عليه وسلم، ثُمَّ وَاللَّهِ مَا احْتَازَهَا دُونَكُمْ وَلاَ اسْتَأْثَرَ بِهَا عَلَيْكُمْ، وَقَدْ أَعْطَاكُمُوهَا وَبَثَّهَا فِيكُمْ، حَتَّى بَقِيَ مِنْهَا هَذَا الْمَالُ، وَكَانَ النَّبِيُّ صلى الله عليه وسلم يُنْفِقُ عَلَى أَهْلِهِ نَفَقَةَ سَنَتِهِمْ مِنْ هَذَا الْمَالِ، ثُمَّ يَأْخُذُ مَا بَقِيَ فَيَجْعَلُهُ مَجْعَلَ مَالِ اللَّهِ، فَعَمِلَ النَّبِيُّ صلى الله عليه وسلم بِذَلِكَ حَيَاتَهُ، أَنْشُدُكُمْ بِاللَّهِ هَلْ تَعْلَمُونَ ذَلِكَ فَقَالُوا نَعَمْ. ثُمَّ قَالَ لِعَلِيٍّ وَعَبَّاسٍ أَنْشُدُكُمَا اللَّهَ هَلْ تَعْلَمَانِ ذَلِكَ قَالاَ نَعَمْ. ثُمَّ تَوَفَّى اللَّهُ نَبِيَّهُ صلى الله عليه وسلم فَقَالَ أَبُو بَكْرٍ أَنَا وَلِيُّ رَسُولِ اللَّهِ صلى الله عليه وسلم، فَقَبَضَهَا أَبُو بَكْرٍ فَعَمِلَ فِيهَا بِمَا عَمِلَ فِيهَا رَسُولُ اللَّهِ صلى الله عليه وسلم، وَأَنْتُمَا حِينَئِذٍ ـ وَأَقْبَلَ عَلَى عَلِيٍّ وَعَبَّاسٍ ـ تَزْعُمَانِ أَنَّ أَبَا بَكْرٍ فِيهَا كَذَا، وَاللَّهُ يَعْلَمُ أَنَّهُ فِيهَا صَادِقٌ بَارٌّ رَاشِدٌ تَابِعٌ لِلْحَقِّ، ثُمَّ تَوَفَّى اللَّهُ أَبَا بَكْرٍ فَقُلْتُ أَنَا وَلِيُّ رَسُولِ اللَّهِ صلى الله عليه وسلم وَأَبِي بَكْرٍ. فَقَبَضْتُهَا سَنَتَيْنِ أَعْمَلُ فِيهَا بِمَا عَمِلَ بِهِ رَسُولُ اللَّهِ صلى الله عليه وسلم وَأَبُو بَكْرٍ، ثُمَّ جِئْتُمَانِي وَكَلِمَتُكُمَا عَلَى كَلِمَةٍ وَاحِدَةٍ وَأَمْرُكُمَا جَمِيعٌ، جِئْتَنِي تَسْأَلُنِي نَصِيبَكَ مِنِ ابْنِ أَخِيكَ، وَأَتَانِي هَذَا يَسْأَلُنِي نَصِيبَ امْرَأَتِهِ مِنْ أَبِيهَا فَقُلْتُ إِنْ شِئْتُمَا دَفَعْتُهَا إِلَيْكُمَا، عَلَى أَنَّ عَلَيْكُمَا عَهْدَ اللَّهِ وَمِيثَاقَهُ تَعْمَلاَنِ فِيهَا بِمَا عَمِلَ بِهِ رَسُولُ اللَّهِ صلى الله عليه وسلم وَبِمَا عَمِلَ فِيهَا أَبُو بَكْرٍ وَبِمَا عَمِلْتُ فِيهَا مُنْذُ وَلِيتُهَا، وَإِلاَّ فَلاَ تُكَلِّمَانِي فِيهَا. فَقُلْتُمَا ادْفَعْهَا إِلَيْنَا بِذَلِكَ. فَدَفَعْتُهَا إِلَيْكُمَا بِذَلِكَ، أَنْشُدُكُمْ بِاللَّهِ هَلْ دَفَعْتُهَا إِلَيْهِمَا بِذَلِكَ قَالَ الرَّهْطُ نَعَمْ. فَأَقْبَلَ عَلَى عَلِيٍّ وَعَبَّاسٍ فَقَالَ أَنْشُدُكُمَا بِاللَّهِ هَلْ دَفَعْتُهَا إِلَيْكُمَا بِذَلِكَ. قَالاَ نَعَمْ. قَالَ أَفَتَلْتَمِسَانِ مِنِّي قَضَاءً غَيْرَ ذَلِكَ فَوَالَّذِي بِإِذْنِهِ تَقُومُ السَّمَاءُ وَالأَرْضُ لاَ أَقْضِي فِيهَا قَضَاءً غَيْرَ ذَلِكَ حَتَّى تَقُومَ السَّاعَةُ، فَإِنْ عَجَزْتُمَا عَنْهَا فَادْفَعَاهَا إِلَىَّ، فَأَنَا أَكْفِيكُمَاهَا.

Narrated Zaid bin Aslam from his father: `Umar said, “But for the future Muslim generations, I would have distributed the land of the villages I conquer among the soldiers as the Prophetﷺ distributed the land of Khaibar.”. – Sahih Al-Bukhari 2334

حَدَّثَنَا صَدَقَةُ، أَخْبَرَنَا عَبْدُ الرَّحْمَنِ، عَنْ مَالِكٍ، عَنْ زَيْدِ بْنِ أَسْلَمَ، عَنْ أَبِيهِ، قَالَ قَالَ عُمَرُ ـ رضى الله عنه ـ لَوْلاَ آخِرُ الْمُسْلِمِينَ مَا فَتَحْتُ قَرْيَةً إِلاَّ قَسَمْتُهَا بَيْنَ أَهْلِهَا كَمَا قَسَمَ النَّبِيُّ صلى الله عليه وسلم خَيْبَرَ.

Narrated Ibn `Umar: When the people of Khaibar dislocated `Abdullah bin `Umar’s hands and feet, `Umar got up delivering a sermon saying, “No doubt, Allah’s Messengerﷺ made a contract with the Jews concerning their properties, and said to them, ‘We allow you (to stand in your land) as long as Allah allows you.’ Now `Abdullah bin `Umar went to his land and was attacked at night, and his hands and feet were dislocated, and as we have no enemies there except those Jews, they are our enemies and the only people whom we suspect, I have made up my mind to exile them.” When `Umar decided to carry out his decision, a son of Abu Al-Haqiq’s came and addressed `Umar, “O chief of the believers, will you exile us although Muhammad allowed us to stay at our places, and made a contract with us about our properties, and accepted the condition of our residence in our land?” `Umar said, “Do you think that I have forgotten the statement of Allah’s Messengerﷺ, i.e.: What will your condition be when you are expelled from Khaibar and your camel will be carrying you night after night?” The Jew replied, “That was joke from Abul-Qasim.” `Umar said, “O the enemy of Allah! You are telling a lie.” `Umar then drove them out and paid them the price of their properties in the form of fruits, money, camel saddles and ropes, etc.” – Sahih Al-Bukhari 2730

حَدَّثَنَا أَبُو أَحْمَدَ، حَدَّثَنَا مُحَمَّدُ بْنُ يَحْيَى أَبُو غَسَّانَ الْكِنَانِيُّ، أَخْبَرَنَا مَالِكٌ، عَنْ نَافِعٍ، عَنِ ابْنِ عُمَرَ ـ رضى الله عنهما ـ قَالَ لَمَّا فَدَعَ أَهْلُ خَيْبَرَ عَبْدَ اللَّهِ بْنَ عُمَرَ، قَامَ عُمَرُ خَطِيبًا فَقَالَ إِنَّ رَسُولَ اللَّهِ صلى الله عليه وسلم كَانَ عَامَلَ يَهُودَ خَيْبَرَ عَلَى أَمْوَالِهِمْ، وَقَالَ " نُقِرُّكُمْ مَا أَقَرَّكُمُ اللَّهُ ". وَإِنَّ عَبْدَ اللَّهِ بْنَ عُمَرَ خَرَجَ إِلَى مَالِهِ هُنَاكَ فَعُدِيَ عَلَيْهِ مِنَ اللَّيْلِ، فَفُدِعَتْ يَدَاهُ وَرِجْلاَهُ، وَلَيْسَ لَنَا هُنَاكَ عَدُوٌّ غَيْرُهُمْ، هُمْ عَدُوُّنَا وَتُهَمَتُنَا، وَقَدْ رَأَيْتُ إِجْلاَءَهُمْ، فَلَمَّا أَجْمَعَ عُمَرُ عَلَى ذَلِكَ أَتَاهُ أَحَدُ بَنِي أَبِي الْحُقَيْقِ، فَقَالَ يَا أَمِيرَ الْمُؤْمِنِينَ، أَتُخْرِجُنَا وَقَدْ أَقَرَّنَا مُحَمَّدٌ صلى الله عليه وسلم وَعَامَلَنَا عَلَى الأَمْوَالِ، وَشَرَطَ ذَلِكَ لَنَا فَقَالَ عُمَرُ أَظَنَنْتَ أَنِّي نَسِيتُ قَوْلَ رَسُولِ اللَّهِ صلى الله عليه وسلم " كَيْفَ بِكَ إِذَا أُخْرِجْتَ مِنْ خَيْبَرَ تَعْدُو بِكَ قَلُوصُكَ، لَيْلَةً بَعْدَ لَيْلَةٍ ". فَقَالَ كَانَتْ هَذِهِ هُزَيْلَةً مِنْ أَبِي الْقَاسِمِ. قَالَ كَذَبْتَ يَا عَدُوَّ اللَّهِ. فَأَجْلاَهُمْ عُمَرُ وَأَعْطَاهُمْ قِيمَةَ مَا كَانَ لَهُمْ مِنَ الثَّمَرِ مَالاً وَإِبِلاً وَعُرُوضًا، مِنْ أَقْتَابٍ وَحِبَالٍ وَغَيْرِ ذَلِكَ. رَوَاهُ حَمَّادُ بْنُ سَلَمَةَ عَنْ عُبَيْدِ اللَّهِ، أَحْسِبُهُ عَنْ نَافِعٍ، عَنِ ابْنِ عُمَرَ، عَنْ عُمَرَ، عَنِ النَّبِيِّ صلى الله عليه وسلم، اخْتَصَرَهُ.

Narrated Ibn `Abbas: During the last Hajj led by `Umar, `Abdur-Rahman bin `Auf returned to his family at Mina and met me there. `AbdurRahman said (to `Umar), "O chief of the believers! The season of Hajj is the season when there comes the scum of the people (besides the good amongst them), so I recommend that you should wait till you go back to Medina, for it is the place of Migration and Sunna (i.e. the Prophet's tradition), and there you will be able to refer the matter to the religious scholars and the nobles and the people of wise opinions." `Umar said, "I will speak of it in Medina on my very first sermon I will deliver there." – Sahih al-Bukhari 3928

حَدَّثَنَا يَحْيَى بْنُ سُلَيْمَانَ، حَدَّثَنِي ابْنُ وَهْبٍ، حَدَّثَنَا مَالِكٌ. وَأَخْبَرَنِي يُونُسُ، عَنِ ابْنِ شِهَابٍ، قَالَ أَخْبَرَنِي عُبَيْدُ اللَّهِ بْنُ عَبْدِ اللَّهِ، أَنَّ ابْنَ عَبَّاسٍ، أَخْبَرَهُ أَنَّ عَبْدَ الرَّحْمَنِ بْنَ عَوْفٍ رَجَعَ إِلَى أَهْلِهِ وَهْوَ بِمِنًى، فِي آخِرِ حَجَّةٍ حَجَّهَا عُمَرُ، فَوَجَدَنِي، فَقَالَ عَبْدُ الرَّحْمَنِ فَقُلْتُ يَا أَمِيرَ الْمُؤْمِنِينَ إِنَّ الْمَوْسِمَ يَجْمَعُ رَعَاعَ النَّاسِ، وَإِنِّي أَرَى أَنْ تُمْهِلَ حَتَّى تَقْدَمَ الْمَدِينَةَ، فَإِنَّهَا دَارُ الْهِجْرَةِ وَالسُّنَّةِ، وَتَخْلُصَ لأَهْلِ الْفِقْهِ وَأَشْرَافِ النَّاسِ وَذَوِي رَأْيِهِمْ. قَالَ عُمَرُ لأَقُومَنَّ فِي أَوَّلِ مَقَامٍ أَقُومُهُ بِالْمَدِينَةِ

Narrated Jabir bin Samura: The People of Kufa complained against Sa`d to `Umar and the latter dismissed him and appointed `Ammar as their chief . They lodged many complaints against Sa`d and even they alleged that he did not pray properly. `Umar sent for him and said, "O Aba 'Is-haq! These people claim that you do not pray properly." Abu 'Is-haq said, "By Allah, I used to pray with them a prayer similar to that of Allah's Apostle and I never reduced anything of it. I used to prolong the first two rak`at of `Isha prayer and shorten the last two rak`at." `Umar said, "O Aba 'Is-haq, this was what I thought about you." And then he sent one or more persons with him to Kufa so as to ask the people about him. So they went there and did not leave any mosque without asking about him. All the people praised him till they came to the mosque of the tribe of Bani `Abs; one of the men called Usama bin Qatada with a surname of Aba Sa`da stood up and said, "As you have put us under an oath; I am bound to tell you that Sa`d never went himself with the army and never distributed (the war booty) equally and never did justice in legal verdicts." (On hearing it) Sa`d said, "I pray to Allah for three things: O Allah! If this slave of yours is a liar and got up for showing off, give him a long life, increase his poverty and put him to trials." (And so it happened). Later on when that person was asked how he was, he used to reply that he was an old man in trial as the result of Sa`d's curse. `Abdul Malik, the sub narrator, said that he had seen him afterwards and his eyebrows were overhanging his eyes owing to old age and he used to tease and assault the small girls in the way. – Sahih al-Bukhari 755

حَدَّثَنَا مُوسَى، قَالَ حَدَّثَنَا أَبُو عَوَانَةَ، قَالَ حَدَّثَنَا عَبْدُ الْمَلِكِ بْنُ عُمَيْرٍ، عَنْ جَابِرِ بْنِ سَمُرَةَ، قَالَ شَكَا أَهْلُ الْكُوفَةِ سَعْدًا إِلَى عُمَرَ ـ رضى الله عنه ـ فَعَزَلَهُ وَاسْتَعْمَلَ عَلَيْهِمْ عَمَّارًا، فَشَكَوْا حَتَّى ذَكَرُوا أَنَّهُ لاَ يُحْسِنُ يُصَلِّي، فَأَرْسَلَ إِلَيْهِ فَقَالَ يَا أَبَا إِسْحَاقَ إِنَّ هَؤُلاَءِ يَزْعُمُونَ أَنَّكَ لاَ تُحْسِنُ تُصَلِّي قَالَ أَبُو إِسْحَاقَ أَمَّا أَنَا وَاللَّهِ فَإِنِّي كُنْتُ أُصَلِّي بِهِمْ صَلاَةَ رَسُولِ اللَّهِ صلى الله عليه وسلم مَا أَخْرِمُ عَنْهَا، أُصَلِّي صَلاَةَ الْعِشَاءِ فَأَرْكُدُ فِي الأُولَيَيْنِ وَأُخِفُّ فِي الأُخْرَيَيْنِ. قَالَ ذَاكَ الظَّنُّ بِكَ يَا أَبَا إِسْحَاقَ. فَأَرْسَلَ مَعَهُ رَجُلاً أَوْ رِجَالاً إِلَى الْكُوفَةِ، فَسَأَلَ عَنْهُ أَهْلَ الْكُوفَةِ، وَلَمْ يَدَعْ مَسْجِدًا إِلاَّ سَأَلَ عَنْهُ، وَيُثْنُونَ مَعْرُوفًا، حَتَّى دَخَلَ مَسْجِدًا لِبَنِي عَبْسٍ، فَقَامَ رَجُلٌ مِنْهُمْ يُقَالُ لَهُ أُسَامَةُ بْنُ قَتَادَةَ يُكْنَى أَبَا سَعْدَةَ قَالَ أَمَّا إِذْ نَشَدْتَنَا فَإِنَّ سَعْدًا كَانَ لاَ يَسِيرُ بِالسَّرِيَّةِ، وَلاَ يَقْسِمُ بِالسَّوِيَّةِ، وَلاَ يَعْدِلُ فِي الْقَضِيَّةِ. قَالَ سَعْدٌ أَمَا وَاللَّهِ لأَدْعُوَنَّ بِثَلاَثٍ، اللَّهُمَّ إِنْ كَانَ عَبْدُكَ هَذَا كَاذِبًا،

قَامَ رِيَاءً وَسُمْعَةً فَأَطِلْ عُمْرَهُ، وَأَطِلْ فَقْرَهُ، وَعَرِّضْهُ بِالْفِتَنِ، وَكَانَ بَعْدُ إِذَا سُئِلَ يَقُولُ شَيْخٌ كَبِيرٌ مَفْتُونٌ، أَصَابَتْنِي دَعْوَةُ سَعْدٍ. قَالَ عَبْدُ الْمَلِكِ فَأَنَا رَأَيْتُهُ بَعْدُ قَدْ سَقَطَ حَاجِبَاهُ عَلَى عَيْنَيْهِ مِنَ الْكِبَرِ، وَإِنَّهُ لَيَتَعَرَّضُ لِلْجَوَارِي فِي الطُّرُقِ يَغْمِزُهُنَّ

Ghazwa of Al-Yarmuk
غزوة اليرموك

Narrated Ibn `Umar: When the people of Khaibar dislocated `Abdullah bin `Umar's hands and feet, `Umar got up delivering a sermon saying, "No doubt, Allah's Messenger ﷺ made a contract with the Jews concerning their properties, and said to them, 'We allow you (to stand in your land) as long as Allah allows you.' Now `Abdullah bin `Umar went to his land and was attacked at night, and his hands and feet were dislocated, and as we have no enemies there except those Jews, they are our enemies and the only people whom we suspect, I have made up my mind to exile them." When `Umar decided to carry out his decision, a son of Abu Al-Haqiq's came and addressed `Umar, "O chief of the believers, will you exile us although Muhammad allowed us to stay at our places, and made a contract with us about our properties, and accepted the condition of our residence in our land?" `Umar said, "Do you think that I have forgotten the statement of Allah's Messenger ﷺ, i.e.: What will your condition be when you are expelled from Khaibar and your camel will be carrying you night after night?" The Jew replied, "That was joke from Abul-Qasim." `Umar said, "O the enemy of Allah! You are telling a lie." `Umar then drove them out and paid them the price of their properties in the form of fruits, money, camel saddles and ropes, etc." - Sahih al-Bukhari 2730
حَدَّثَنَا أَبُو أَحْمَدَ، حَدَّثَنَا مُحَمَّدُ بْنُ يَحْيَى أَبُو غَسَّانَ الْكِنَانِيُّ، أَخْبَرَنَا مَالِكٌ، عَنْ نَافِعٍ، عَنِ ابْنِ عُمَرَ ـ رضى الله عنهما ـ قَالَ لَمَّا فَدَعَ أَهْلُ خَيْبَرَ عَبْدَ اللَّهِ بْنَ عُمَرَ، قَامَ عُمَرُ خَطِيبًا فَقَالَ إِنَّ رَسُولَ اللَّهِ صلى الله عليه وسلم كَانَ عَامَلَ يَهُودَ خَيْبَرَ عَلَى أَمْوَالِهِمْ، وَقَالَ " نُقِرُّكُمْ مَا أَقَرَّكُمُ اللَّهُ ". وَإِنَّ عَبْدَ اللَّهِ بْنَ عُمَرَ خَرَجَ إِلَى مَالِهِ هُنَاكَ فَعُدِيَ عَلَيْهِ مِنَ اللَّيْلِ، فَفُدِعَتْ يَدَاهُ وَرِجْلاَهُ، وَلَيْسَ لَنَا هُنَاكَ عَدُوٌّ غَيْرُهُمْ، هُمْ عَدُوُّنَا وَتُهَمَتُنَا، وَقَدْ رَأَيْتُ إِجْلاَءَهُمْ، فَلَمَّا أَ

And had it not been that Allah had decreed exile for them, He would certainly have punished them in this world, and in the Hereafter theirs shall be the torment of the Fire. – Surah Al-Hashr 59:3
وَلَوْلَآ أَن كَتَبَ ٱللَّهُ عَلَيْهِمُ ٱلْجَلَآءَ لَعَذَّبَهُمْ فِى ٱلدُّنْيَا ۖ وَلَهُمْ فِى ٱلْءَاخِرَةِ عَذَابُ ٱلنَّارِ

Narrated Ibn `Umar: `Umar expelled the Jews and the Christians from Hijaz. When Allah's Messenger ﷺ had conquered Khaibar, he wanted to expel the Jews from it as its land became the property of Allah, His Apostle, and the Muslims. Allah's Messenger ﷺ intended to expel the Jews but they requested him to let them stay there on the condition that they would do the labor and get half of the fruits. Allah's Messenger ﷺ told them, "We will let you stay on thus condition, as long as we wish." So, they (i.e. Jews) kept on living there until `Umar forced them to go towards Taima' and Ariha'. – Sahih Al-Bukhari 2338
حَدَّثَنَا أَحْمَدُ بْنُ الْمِقْدَامِ، حَدَّثَنَا فُضَيْلُ بْنُ سُلَيْمَانَ، حَدَّثَنَا مُوسَى، أَخْبَرَنَا نَافِعٌ، عَنِ ابْنِ عُمَرَ ـ رضى الله عنهما ـ قَالَ كَانَ رَسُولُ اللَّهِ صلى الله عليه وسلم. وَقَالَ عَبْدُ الرَّزَّاقِ أَخْبَرَنَا ابْنُ جُرَيْجٍ قَالَ حَدَّثَنِي مُوسَى بْنُ عُقْبَةَ عَنْ نَافِعٍ عَنِ ابْنِ عُمَرَ أَنَّ عُمَرَ بْنَ الْخَطَّابِ ـ رضى الله عنهما ـ أَجْلَى الْيَهُودَ وَالنَّصَارَى مِنْ أَرْضِ الْحِجَازِ، وَكَانَ رَسُولُ اللَّهِ صلى الله عليه وسلم لَمَّا ظَهَرَ عَلَى خَيْبَرَ أَرَادَ إِخْرَاجَ الْيَهُودِ مِنْهَا، وَكَانَتِ الأَرْضُ حِينَ ظَهَرَ عَلَيْهَا لِلَّهِ وَلِرَسُولِهِ صلى الله عليه وسلم وَلِلْمُسْلِمِينَ، وَأَرَادَ إِخْرَاجَ الْيَهُودِ، مِنْهَا فَسَأَلَتِ الْيَهُودُ رَسُولَ اللَّهِ صلى الله عليه وسلم لِيُقِرَّهُمْ بِهَا أَنْ يَكْفُوا عَمَلَهَا وَلَهُمْ نِصْفُ الثَّمَرِ، فَقَالَ لَهُمْ رَسُولُ اللَّهِ صلى الله عليه وسلم " نُقِرُّكُمْ بِهَا عَلَى ذَلِكَ مَا شِئْنَا ". فَقَرُّوا بِهَا حَتَّى أَجْلاَهُمْ عُمَرُ إِلَى تَيْمَاءَ وَأَرِيحَاءَ

Narrated `Urwa: On the day of (the battle) of Al-Yarmuk, the companions of Allah's Messenger ﷺ said to Az-Zubair, "Will you attack the enemy so that we shall attack them with you?" Az-Zubair replied, "If I attack them, you people would not support me." They said, "No, we will support you." So Az-Zubair attacked them (i.e. Byzantine) and pierced through their lines, and went beyond them and none of his companions was with him. Then he returned and the enemy got hold of the bridle of his (horse) and struck him two blows (with the sword) on his shoulder. Between these two wounds there was a scar caused by a blow, he had received on the day of Badr (battle). When I was a child I used to play with those scars by putting my fingers in them. On that day (my brother) "Abdullah bin Az-Zubair was also with him and he was ten years old. Az-Zubair had carried him on a horse and let him to the care of some men. – Sahih Al-Bukhari 3975

حَدَّثَنَا أَحْمَدُ بْنُ مُحَمَّدٍ، حَدَّثَنَا عَبْدُ اللَّهِ، أَخْبَرَنَا هِشَامُ بْنُ عُرْوَةَ، عَنْ أَبِيهِ، أَنَّ أَصْحَابَ، رَسُولِ اللَّهِ صلى الله عليه وسلم قَالُوا لِلزُّبَيْرِ يَوْمَ الْيَرْمُوكِ أَلاَ تَشُدُّ فَنَشُدَّ مَعَكَ فَقَالَ إِنِّي إِنْ شَدَدْتُ كَذَبْتُمْ. فَقَالُوا لاَ نَفْعَلُ، فَحَمَلَ عَلَيْهِمْ حَتَّى شَقَّ صُفُوفَهُمْ، فَجَاوَزَهُمْ وَمَا مَعَهُ أَحَدٌ، ثُمَّ رَجَعَ مُقْبِلاً، فَأَخَذُوا بِلِجَامِهِ، فَضَرَبُوهُ ضَرْبَتَيْنِ عَلَى عَاتِقِهِ بَيْنَهُمَا ضَرْبَةٌ ضُرِبَهَا يَوْمَ بَدْرٍ. قَالَ عُرْوَةُ كُنْتُ أُدْخِلُ أَصَابِعِي فِي تِلْكَ الضَّرَبَاتِ أَلْعَبُ وَأَنَا صَغِيرٌ. قَالَ عُرْوَةُ وَكَانَ مَعَهُ عَبْدُ اللَّهِ بْنُ الزُّبَيْرِ يَوْمَئِذٍ وَهْوَ ابْنُ عَشْرِ سِنِينَ، فَحَمَلَهُ عَلَى فَرَسٍ وَكَّلَ بِهِ رَجُلاً.

Narrated 'Urwa (the son of Az- Zubair): Az-Zubair had three scars caused by the sword, one of which was over his shoulder and I used to insert my fingers in it. He received two of those wounds on the day of Badr and one on the day of Al-Yarmuk. When 'Abdullah bin Zubair was killed, 'Abdul-Malik bin Marwan said to me, "O 'Urwa, do you recognize the sword of Az-Zubair?" I said, "Yes." He said, "What marks does it have?" I replied, "It has a dent in its sharp edge which was caused in it on the day of Badr." 'Abdul- Malik said, "You are right! (i.e. their swords) have dents because of clashing with the regiments of the enemies Then 'Abdul-Malik returned that sword to me (i.e. Urwa). (Hisham, 'Urwa's son said, "We estimated the price of the sword as three-thousand (Dinars) and after that it was taken by one of us (i.e. the inheritors) and I wish I could have had it."). – Sahih Al-Bukhari 3973

أَخْبَرَنِي إِبْرَاهِيمُ بْنُ مُوسَى، حَدَّثَنَا هِشَامُ بْنُ يُوسُفَ، عَنْ مَعْمَرٍ، عَنْ هِشَامٍ، عَنْ عُرْوَةَ، قَالَ كَانَ فِي الزُّبَيْرِ ثَلاَثُ ضَرَبَاتٍ بِالسَّيْفِ، إِحْدَاهُنَّ فِي عَاتِقِهِ، قَالَ إِنْ كُنْتُ لأُدْخِلُ أَصَابِعِي فِيهَا. قَالَ ضُرِبَ ثِنْتَيْنِ يَوْمَ بَدْرٍ، وَوَاحِدَةً يَوْمَ الْيَرْمُوكِ. قَالَ عُرْوَةُ وَقَالَ لِي عَبْدُ الْمَلِكِ بْنُ مَرْوَانَ حِينَ قُتِلَ عَبْدُ اللَّهِ بْنُ الزُّبَيْرِ يَا عُرْوَةُ، هَلْ تَعْرِفُ سَيْفَ الزُّبَيْرِ قُلْتُ نَعَمْ. قَالَ فَمَا فِيهِ قُلْتُ فِيهِ فَلَّةٌ فُلَّهَا يَوْمَ بَدْرٍ. قَالَ صَدَقْتَ. بِهِنَّ فُلُولٌ مِنْ قِرَاعِ الْكَتَائِبِ ثُمَّ رَدَّهُ عَلَى عُرْوَةَ. قَالَ هِشَامٌ فَأَقَمْنَاهُ بَيْنَنَا ثَلاَثَةَ آلاَفٍ، وَأَخَذَهُ بَعْضُنَا، وَلَوَدِدْتُ أَنِّي كُنْتُ أَخَذْتُهُ.

Narrated Safwan bin Ya`la bin Umaiya: That his father said, "I participated in Al-Usra (i.e. Tabuk) along with the Prophet." Ya`la added, "(My participation in) that Ghazwa was the best of my deeds to me." Ya`la said, "I had a laborer who quarrelled with somebody, and one of the two bit the hand of the other (`Ata', the sub-narrator, said, "Safwan told me who bit whom but I forgot it"), and the one who was bitten, pulled his hand out of the mouth of the biter, so one of the incisors of the biter was broken. So we came to the Prophet ﷺ and he considered the biter's claim as invalid (i.e. the biter did not get a recompense for his broken incisor). The Prophet ﷺ said, "Should he leave his hand in your mouth so that you might snap it as if it were in the mouth of a male camel to snap it?". – Sahih Al-Bukhari 4417

حَدَّثَنَا عُبَيْدُ اللَّهِ بْنُ سَعِيدٍ، حَدَّثَنَا مُحَمَّدُ بْنُ بَكْرٍ، أَخْبَرَنَا ابْنُ جُرَيْجٍ، قَالَ سَمِعْتُ عَطَاءً، يُخْبِرُ قَالَ أَخْبَرَنِي صَفْوَانُ بْنُ يَعْلَى بْنِ أُمَيَّةَ، عَنْ أَبِيهِ، قَالَ غَزَوْتُ مَعَ النَّبِيِّ صلى الله عليه وسلم الْعُسْرَةَ قَالَ كَانَ يَعْلَى يَقُولُ تِلْكَ الْغَزْوَةُ أَوْثَقُ أَعْمَالِي عِنْدِي. قَالَ عَطَاءٌ فَقَالَ صَفْوَانُ قَالَ يَعْلَى فَكَانَ لِي أَجِيرٌ فَقَاتَلَ إِنْسَانًا فَعَضَّ أَحَدُهُمَا يَدَ الآخَرِ، قَالَ عَطَاءٌ فَلَقَدْ أَخْبَرَنِي صَفْوَانُ أَيُّهُمَا عَضَّ الآخَرَ فَنَسِيتُهُ، قَالَ فَانْتَزَعَ الْمَعْضُوضُ يَدَهُ مِنْ فِي الْعَاضِّ، فَانْتَزَعَ إِحْدَى ثَنِيَّتَيْهِ، فَأَتَيَا النَّبِيَّ صلى الله عليه وسلم فَأَهْدَرَ ثَنِيَّتَهُ. قَالَ عَطَاءٌ وَحَسِبْتُ أَنَّهُ قَالَ قَالَ النَّبِيُّ صلى الله عليه وسلم " أَفَيَدَعُ يَدَهُ فِي فِيكَ تَقْضَمُهَا، كَأَنَّهَا فِي فِي فَحْلٍ يَقْضَمُهَا ".

Narrated `Abdullah bin Ka`b: I heard Ka`b bin Malik who was one of the three who were forgiven, saying that he had never remained behind Allah's Messenger ﷺ in any Ghazwa which he had fought except two Ghazwat Ghazwat- Al-`Usra (Tabuk) and Ghazwat-Badr. He added. "I decided to tell the truth to Allah's Messenger ﷺ in the forenoon, and scarcely did he return from a journey he made, except in the forenoon, he would go first to the mosque and offer a two-rak`at prayer. The Prophet ﷺ forbade others to speak to me or to my two companions, but he did not prohibit speaking to any of those who had remained behind excepting us. So the people avoided speaking to us, and I stayed in that state till I could no longer bear it, and the only thing that worried me was that I might die and the Prophet ﷺ would not offer the funeral prayer for me, or Allah's Messenger ﷺ might die and I would be left in that social status among the people that nobody would speak to me or offer the funeral prayer for me. But Allah revealed His Forgiveness for us to the Prophet ﷺ in the last third of the night while Allah's Messenger ﷺ was with Um Salama. Um Salama sympathized with me and helped me in my disaster. Allah's Messenger ﷺ said, 'O Um Salama! Ka`b has been forgiven!' She said, 'Shall I send someone to him to give him the good tidings?' He said, 'If you did so, the people would not let you sleep the rest of the night.' So when the Prophet ﷺ had offered the Fajr prayer, he announced Allah's Forgiveness for us. His face used to look as bright as a piece of the (full) moon whenever he was pleased. When Allah revealed His Forgiveness for us, we were the three whose case had been deferred while the excuse presented by those who had apologized had been accepted. But when there were mentioned those who had told the Prophet ﷺ lies and remained behind (the battle of Tabuk) and had given false excuses, they were described with the worse description one may be described with. Allah said: 'They will present their excuses to you (Muslims) when you return to them. Say: Present no excuses; we shall not believe you. Allah has already informed us of the true state of matters concerning you. Allah and His Apostle will observe your actions." (9.94). – Sahih Al-Bukhari 4677

حَدَّثَنِي مُحَمَّدٌ، حَدَّثَنَا أَحْمَدُ بْنُ أَبِي شُعَيْبٍ، حَدَّثَنَا مُوسَى بْنُ أَعْيَنَ، حَدَّثَنَا إِسْحَاقُ بْنُ رَاشِدٍ، أَنَّ الزُّهْرِيَّ، حَدَّثَهُ قَالَ أَخْبَرَنِي عَبْدُ الرَّحْمَنِ بْنُ عَبْدِ اللَّهِ بْنِ كَعْبِ بْنِ مَالِكٍ، عَنْ أَبِيهِ، قَالَ سَمِعْتُ أَبِي كَعْبَ بْنَ مَالِكٍ،، وَهْوَ أَحَدُ الثَّلاَثَةِ الَّذِينَ تِيبَ عَلَيْهِمْ أَنَّهُ لَمْ يَتَخَلَّفْ عَنْ رَسُولِ اللَّهِ صلى الله عليه وسلم فِي غَزْوَةٍ غَزَاهَا قَطُّ غَيْرَ غَزْوَتَيْنِ غَزْوَةِ الْعُسْرَةِ وَغَزْوَةِ بَدْرٍ. قَالَ فَأَجْمَعْتُ صِدْقَ رَسُولِ اللَّهِ صلى الله عليه وسلم ضُحًى، وَكَانَ قَلَّمَا يَقْدَمُ مِنْ سَفَرٍ سَافَرَهُ إِلاَّ ضُحًى وَكَانَ يَبْدَأُ بِالْمَسْجِدِ، فَيَرْكَعُ رَكْعَتَيْنِ، وَنَهَى النَّبِيُّ صلى الله عليه وسلم عَنْ كَلاَمِي وَكَلاَمِ صَاحِبَىَّ، وَلَمْ يَنْهَ عَنْ كَلاَمِ أَحَدٍ مِنَ الْمُتَخَلِّفِينَ غَيْرِنَا، فَاجْتَنَبَ النَّاسُ كَلاَمَنَا، فَلَبِثْتُ كَذَلِكَ حَتَّى طَالَ عَلَىَّ الأَمْرُ، وَمَا مِنْ شَىْءٍ أَهَمُّ إِلَىَّ مِنْ أَنْ أَمُوتَ فَلاَ يُصَلِّي عَلَىَّ النَّبِيُّ صلى الله عليه وسلم أَوْ يَمُوتَ رَسُولُ اللَّهِ صلى الله عليه وسلم فَأَكُونَ مِنَ النَّاسِ بِتِلْكَ الْمَنْزِلَةِ، فَلاَ يُكَلِّمُنِي أَحَدٌ مِنْهُمْ، وَلاَ يُصَلِّي عَلَىَّ، فَأَنْزَلَ اللَّهُ تَوْبَتَنَا عَلَى نَبِيِّهِ صلى الله عليه وسلم حِينَ بَقِيَ الثُّلُثُ الآخِرُ مِنَ اللَّيْلِ، وَرَسُولُ اللَّهِ صلى الله عليه وسلم عِنْدَ أُمِّ سَلَمَةَ، وَكَانَتْ أُمُّ سَلَمَةَ مُحْسِنَةً فِي شَأْنِي مَعْنِيَّةً فِي أَمْرِي، فَقَالَ رَسُولُ اللَّهِ صلى الله عليه وسلم " يَا أُمَّ سَلَمَةَ تِيبَ عَلَى كَعْبٍ ". قَالَتْ أَفَلاَ أُرْسِلُ إِلَيْهِ فَأُبَشِّرَهُ قَالَ " إِذًا يَحْطِمَكُمُ النَّاسُ فَيَمْنَعُونَكُمُ النَّوْمَ سَائِرَ اللَّيْلَةِ ". حَتَّى إِذَا صَلَّى رَسُولُ اللَّهِ صلى الله عليه وسلم صَلاَةَ الْفَجْرِ آذَنَ بِتَوْبَةِ اللَّهِ عَلَيْنَا، وَكَانَ إِذَا اسْتَبْشَرَ اسْتَنَارَ وَجْهُهُ حَتَّى كَأَنَّهُ قِطْعَةٌ مِنَ الْقَمَرِ، وَكُنَّا أَيُّهَا الثَّلاَثَةُ الَّذِينَ خُلِّفُوا عَنِ الأَمْرِ الَّذِي قُبِلَ مِنْ هَؤُلاَءِ الَّذِينَ اعْتَذَرُوا حِينَ أَنْزَلَ اللَّهُ لَنَا التَّوْبَةَ، فَلَمَّا ذُكِرَ الَّذِينَ كَذَبُوا رَسُولَ اللَّهِ صلى الله عليه وسلم مِنَ الْمُتَخَلِّفِينَ، وَاعْتَذَرُوا بِالْبَاطِلِ، ذُكِرُوا بِشَرِّ مَا ذُكِرَ بِهِ أَحَدٌ قَالَ اللَّهُ سُبْحَانَهُ {يَعْتَذِرُونَ إِلَيْكُمْ إِذَا رَجَعْتُمْ إِلَيْهِمْ قُلْ لاَ تَعْتَذِرُوا لَنْ نُؤْمِنَ لَكُمْ قَدْ نَبَّأَنَا اللَّهُ مِنْ أَخْبَارِكُمْ وَسَيَرَى اللَّهُ عَمَلَكُمْ وَرَسُولُهُ} الآيَةَ

And Anas bin Malik said, "I reached at dawn during the siege of Tustar and the fighting was at its peak. The Muslims were not able to offer the Fajr prayer and we did not offered Salāt (prayer) till a part of the day had passed and then we offered the Salat with Abū Musa and we were granted victory By Allah." Anas further said, "It would not make me happy even if I got the whole world and whatever is in it instead of that Salāt (prayer) (I,e, the one they missed because of Fighting). Bukhari vol. 2 pg 53

و قال أنس بن مالك : حضرت عند مناهضة حصن تستر عند إضاءة الفجر و اشتد اشتعال القتال فلم تقدروا على الصلاة فلم نصل الا بعد ارتفاع النهار، فصليناها ونحن مع أبي موسى ففتح لنا . قال أنس : و ما يسرني بتلك الصلاة الدنيا و ما فيها .

Narrated As-Sa'ib bin Yazid: We used to strike the drunks with our hands, shoes, clothes (by twisting it into the shape of lashes) during the lifetime of the Prophet, Abu Bakr and the early part of `Umar's caliphate. But during the last period of `Umar's caliphate, he used to give the drunk forty lashes; and when drunks became mischievous and disobedient, he used to scourge them eighty lashes. – Sahih Al-Bukhari 6779

حَدَّثَنَا مَكِّيُّ بْنُ إِبْرَاهِيمَ، عَنِ الْجُعَيْدِ، عَنْ يَزِيدَ بْنِ خُصَيْفَةَ، عَنِ السَّائِبِ بْنِ يَزِيدَ، قَالَ كُنَّا نُؤْتَى بِالشَّارِبِ عَلَى عَهْدِ رَسُولِ اللَّهِ صلى الله عليه وسلم وَإِمْرَةِ أَبِي بَكْرٍ وَصَدْرًا مِنْ خِلاَفَةِ عُمَرَ، فَنَقُومُ إِلَيْهِ بِأَيْدِينَا وَنِعَالِنَا وَأَرْدِيَتِنَا، حَتَّى كَانَ آخِرُ إِمْرَةِ عُمَرَ، فَجَلَدَ أَرْبَعِينَ، حَتَّى إِذَا عَتَوْا وَفَسَقُوا جَلَدَ ثَمَانِينَ.

Narrated `Abdullah bin `Umar: It was said to `Umar, "Will you appoint your successor?" `Umar said, "If I appoint a Caliph (as my successor) it is true that somebody who was better than I (i.e., Abu Bakr) did so, and if I leave the matter undecided, it is true that somebody who was better than I (i.e., Allah's Messenger ﷺ) did so." On this, the people praised him. `Umar said, "People are of two kinds: Either one who is keen to take over the Caliphate or one who is afraid of assuming such a responsibility. I wish I could be free from its responsibility in that I would receive neither reward nor retribution I won't bear the burden of the caliphate in my death as I do in my life.". – Sahih Al-Bukhari 7218

حَدَّثَنَا مُحَمَّدُ بْنُ يُوسُفَ، أَخْبَرَنَا سُفْيَانُ، عَنْ هِشَامِ بْنِ عُرْوَةَ، عَنْ أَبِيهِ، عَنْ عَبْدِ اللَّهِ بْنِ عُمَرَ ـ رضى الله عنهما ـ قَالَ قِيلَ لِعُمَرَ أَلاَ تَسْتَخْلِفُ قَالَ إِنْ أَسْتَخْلِفْ فَقَدِ اسْتَخْلَفَ مَنْ هُوَ خَيْرٌ مِنِّي أَبُو بَكْرٍ، وَإِنْ أَتْرُكْ فَقَدْ تَرَكَ مَنْ هُوَ خَيْرٌ مِنِّي رَسُولُ اللَّهِ صلى الله عليه وسلم فَأَثْنَوْا عَلَيْهِ فَقَالَ رَاغِبٌ رَاهِبٌ، وَدِدْتُ أَنِّي نَجَوْتُ مِنْهَا كَفَافًا لاَ لِي وَلاَ عَلَىَّ لاَ أَتَحَمَّلُهَا حَيًّا وَمَيِّتًا.

Narrated Ibn `Abbas: When (the dead body of) `Umar was put on his deathbed, the people gathered around him and invoked (Allah) and prayed for him before the body was taken away, and I was amongst them. Suddenly I felt somebody taking hold of my shoulder and found out that he was `Ali bin Abi Talib. `Ali invoked Allah's Mercy for `Umar and said, "O `Umar! You have not left behind you a person whose deeds I like to imitate and meet Allah with more than I like your deeds. By Allah! I always thought that Allah would keep you with your two companions, for very often I used to hear the Prophet ﷺ saying, 'I, Abu Bakr and `Umar went (somewhere); I, Abu Bakr and `Umar entered (somewhere); and I, Abu Bakr and `Umar went out."' – Sahih al-Bukhari 3685

حَدَّثَنَا عَبْدَانُ، أَخْبَرَنَا عَبْدُ اللَّهِ، حَدَّثَنَا عُمَرُ بْنُ سَعِيدٍ، عَنِ ابْنِ أَبِي مُلَيْكَةَ، أَنَّهُ سَمِعَ ابْنَ عَبَّاسٍ، يَقُولُ وُضِعَ عُمَرُ عَلَى سَرِيرِهِ، فَتَكَنَّفَهُ النَّاسُ يَدْعُونَ وَيُصَلُّونَ قَبْلَ أَنْ يُرْفَعَ، وَأَنَا فِيهِمْ، فَلَمْ يَرُعْنِي إِلاَّ رَجُلٌ آخِذٌ مَنْكِبِي، فَإِذَا عَلِيٌّ فَتَرَحَّمَ عَلَى عُمَرَ، وَقَالَ مَا خَلَّفْتَ أَحَدًا أَحَبَّ إِلَىَّ أَنْ أَلْقَى اللَّهَ بِمِثْلِ عَمَلِهِ مِنْكَ، وَايْمُ اللَّهِ، إِنْ كُنْتُ لأَظُنُّ أَنْ يَجْعَلَكَ اللَّهُ مَعَ صَاحِبَيْكَ، وَحَسِبْتُ أَنِّي كُنْتُ كَثِيرًا أَسْمَعُ النَّبِيَّ صلى الله عليه وسلم يَقُولُ ذَهَبْتُ أَنَا وَأَبُو بَكْرٍ وَعُمَرُ، وَدَخَلْتُ أَنَا وَأَبُو بَكْرٍ وَعُمَرُ، وَخَرَجْتُ أَنَا وَأَبُو بَكْرٍ وَعُمَرُ

The Book of
Caliphate of Uthman bin Affan bin Abi Al-Aas
خلافة عُثْمَان بْن عَفَّان بْن أَبِي الْعَاص

Narrated `Amr bin Maimun: I saw `Umar bin Al-Khattab a few days before he was stabbed in Medina. He was standing with Hudhaifa bin Al-Yaman and `Uthman bin Hunaif to whom he said, "What have you done? Do you think that you have imposed more taxation on the land (of As-Swad i.e. 'Iraq) than it can bear?" They replied, "We have imposed on it what it can bear because of its great yield." `Umar again said, "Check whether you have imposed on the land what it can not bear." They said, "No, (we haven't)." `Umar added, "If Allah should keep me alive I will let the widows of Iraq need no men to support them after me." But only four days had elapsed when he was stabbed (to death ). The day he was stabbed, I was standing and there was nobody between me and him (i.e. `Umar) except `Abdullah bin `Abbas. Whenever `Umar passed between the two rows, he would say, "Stand in straight lines." When he saw no defect (in the rows), he would go forward and start the prayer with Takbir. He would recite Surat Yusuf or An-Nahl or the like in the first rak`a so that the people may have the time to Join the prayer. As soon as he said Takbir, I heard him saying, "The dog has killed or eaten me," at the time he (i.e. the murderer) stabbed him. A non-Arab infidel proceeded on carrying a double-edged knife and stabbing all the persons he passed by on the right and left (till) he stabbed thirteen persons out of whom seven died. When one of the Muslims saw that, he threw a cloak on him. Realizing that he had been captured, the non-Arab infidel killed himself, `Umar held the hand of `Abdur-Rahman bin `Auf and let him lead the prayer. Those who were standing by the side of `Umar saw what I saw, but the people who were in the other parts of the Mosque did not see anything, but they lost the voice of `Umar and they were saying, "Subhan Allah! Subhan Allah! (i.e. Glorified be Allah)." `Abdur-Rahman bin `Auf led the people a short prayer. When they finished the prayer, `Umar said, "O Ibn `Abbas! Find out who attacked me." Ibn `Abbas kept on looking here and there for a short time and came to say. "The slave of Al Mughira." On that `Umar said, "The craftsman?" Ibn `Abbas said, "Yes." `Umar said, "May Allah curse him. I did not treat him unjustly. All the Praises are for Allah Who has not caused me to die at the hand of a man who claims himself to be a Muslim. No doubt, you and your father (Abbas) used to love to have more non-Arab infidels in Medina." Al-Abbas had the greatest number of slaves. Ibn `Abbas said to `Umar. "If you wish, we will do." He meant, "If you wish we will kill them." `Umar said, "You are mistaken (for you can't kill them) after they have spoken your language, prayed towards your Qibla, and performed Hajj like yours." Then `Umar was carried to his house, and we went along with him, and the people were as if they had never suffered a calamity before. Some said, "Do not worry (he will be Alright soon)." Some said, "We are afraid (that he will die)." Then an infusion of dates was brought to him and he drank it but it came out (of the wound) of his belly. Then milk was brought to him and he drank it, and it also came out of his belly. The people realized that he would die. We went to him, and the people came, praising him. A young man came saying, "O chief of the believers! Receive the glad tidings from Allah to you due to your company with Allah's Messenger ﷺ and your superiority in Islam which you know. Then you became the ruler (i.e. Caliph) and you ruled with justice and finally you have been martyred." `Umar said, "I wish that all these privileges will counterbalance (my shortcomings) so that I will neither lose nor gain anything." When the young man turned back to leave, his clothes seemed to be touching the ground. `Umar said, "Call the young man back to me." (When he came back) `Umar said, "O son of my brother! Lift your clothes, for this will keep your clothes clean and save you from the Punishment of your Lord." `Umar further said, "O `Abdullah bin `Umar! See how much I am in debt to others." When the debt was checked, it amounted to approximately eighty-six thousand. `Umar said, "If the property of `Umar's family covers the debt, then pay the debt thereof; otherwise request it from Bani `Adi bin Ka`b, and if that too is not sufficient, ask for it from Quraish tribe, and do not ask for it from any one else, and pay this debt on my behalf." `Umar then said (to `Abdullah), "Go to `Aisha (the mother of the believers) and say: "`Umar is paying his salutation to you. But don't say: 'The chief of the believers,' because today I am not the chief of the believers. And say: "`Umar bin Al-Khattab asks the permission to be buried with his two companions (i.e. the Prophet, and Abu Bakr)." `Abdullah greeted `Aisha and asked for the permission for entering, and then entered to her and found her sitting and weeping. He said to her, "`Umar bin Al-Khattab is paying his salutations to you, and asks the permission to be buried with his two companions." She said, "I had the idea of having this place for myself, but today I prefer `Umar to myself." When he returned it was said (to `Umar), "`Abdullah bin `Umar has come." `Umar said, "Make me sit up." Somebody supported him against his body and `Umar asked (`Abdullah), "What news do you have?" He said, "O chief of the believers! It is as you wish. She has given the permission." `Umar said, "Praise be to Allah, there was nothing more important to me than this. So when I die, take me, and greet `Aisha and say: "`Umar bin Al-Khattab asks the permission (to be buried with the Prophetﷺ), and if she gives the permission, bury me there, and if she refuses, then take me to the grave-yard of the Muslims." Then Hafsa (the mother of the believers) came with many other women walking with her. When we saw her, we went away. She went in (to `Umar) and wept there for sometime. When the men asked for permission to enter, she went into another place, and we heard her weeping inside. The people said (to `Umar), "O chief of the believers! Appoint a successor." `Umar said, "I do not find anyone more suitable for the job than the following persons or group whom Allah's Messengerﷺ had been pleased with before he died." Then `Umar mentioned `Ali, `Uthman, AzZubair, Talha, Sa`d and `Abdur-Rahman (bin `Auf) and said, "Abdullah bin `Umar will be a witness to you, but he will have no share in the rule. His being a witness will compensate him for not sharing the right of ruling. If Sa`d becomes the ruler, it will be alright: otherwise, whoever becomes the ruler should seek his help, as I have not dismissed him because of disability or dishonesty." `Umar added, "I recommend that my successor takes care of the early emigrants; to know their rights and protect their honor and sacred things. I also recommend that he be kind to the Ansar who had lived in Medina before the emigrants and Belief had entered their hearts before them. I recommend that the (ruler) should accept the good of the righteous among them and excuse their wrong-doers, and I recommend that he should do good to all the people of the towns (Al-Ansar), as they are the protectors of Islam and the source of wealth and the source of annoyance to the enemy. I also recommend that nothing be taken from them except from their surplus with their consent. I also recommend that he do good to the 'Arab bedouin, as they are the origin of the 'Arabs and the material of Islam. He should take from what is inferior, amongst their properties and distribute that to the poor amongst them. I also recommend him concerning Allah's and His Apostle's protectees (i.e. Dhimmis) to fulfill their contracts and to fight for them and not to overburden them with what is beyond their ability." So when `Umar expired, we carried him out and set out walking. `Abdullah bin `Umar greeted (`Aisha) and said, "`Umar bin Al-Khattab asks for the permission." `Aisha said, "Bring him in." He was brought in and buried beside his two companions. When he was buried, the group (recommended by `Umar) held a meeting. Then

\`Abdur-Rahman said, " Reduce the candidates for rulership to three of you." Az-Zubair said, "I give up my right to \`Ali." Talha said, "I give up my right to \`Uthman," Sa\`d, 'I give up my right to \`Abdur-Rahman bin \`Auf." \`Abdur-Rahman then said (to \`Uthman and \`Ali), "Now which of you is willing to give up his right of candidacy to that he may choose the better of the (remaining) two, bearing in mind that Allah and Islam will be his witnesses." So both the sheiks (i.e. \`Uthman and \`Ali) kept silent. \`Abdur-Rahman said, "Will you both leave this matter to me, and I take Allah as my Witness that I will not choose but the better of you?" They said, "Yes." So \`Abdur-Rahman took the hand of one of them (i.e. \`Ali) and said, "You are related to Allah's Messenger ﷺ and one of the earliest Muslims as you know well. So I ask you by Allah to promise that if I select you as a ruler you will do justice, and if I select \`Uthman as a ruler you will listen to him and obey him." Then he took the other (i.e. \`Uthman) aside and said the same to him. When \`Abdur-Rahman secured (their agreement to) this covenant, he said, "O \`Uthman! Raise your hand." So he (i.e. \`Abdur-Rahman) gave him (i.e. \`Uthman) the solemn pledge, and then \`Ali gave him the pledge of allegiance and then all the (Medina) people gave him the pledge of allegiance. – Sahih Al-Bukhari 3700

حَدَّثَنَا مُوسَى بْنُ إِسْمَاعِيلَ، حَدَّثَنَا أَبُو عَوَانَةَ، عَنْ حُصَيْنٍ، عَنْ عَمْرِو بْنِ مَيْمُونٍ، قَالَ رَأَيْتُ عُمَرَ بْنَ الْخَطَّابِ ـ رضى الله عنه ـ قَبْلَ أَنْ يُصَابَ بِأَيَّامٍ بِالْمَدِينَةِ وَقَفَ عَلَى حُذَيْفَةَ بْنِ الْيَمَانِ وَعُثْمَانَ بْنِ حُنَيْفٍ، قَالَ كَيْفَ فَعَلْتُمَا أَتَخَافَانِ أَنْ تَكُونَا قَدْ حَمَّلْتُمَا الأَرْضَ مَا لاَ تُطِيقُ قَالاَ حَمَّلْنَاهَا أَمْرًا هِيَ لَهُ مُطِيقَةٌ، مَا فِيهَا كَبِيرُ فَضْلٍ. قَالَ انْظُرَا أَنْ تَكُونَا حَمَّلْتُمَا الأَرْضَ مَا لاَ تُطِيقُ، قَالَ قَالاَ لاَ. فَقَالَ عُمَرُ لَئِنْ سَلَّمَنِي اللَّهُ لأَدَعَنَّ أَرَامِلَ أَهْلِ الْعِرَاقِ لاَ يَحْتَجْنَ إِلَى رَجُلٍ بَعْدِي أَبَدًا. قَالَ فَمَا أَتَتْ عَلَيْهِ إِلاَّ رَابِعَةٌ حَتَّى أُصِيبَ. قَالَ إِنِّي لَقَائِمٌ مَا بَيْنِي وَبَيْنَهُ إِلاَّ عَبْدُ اللَّهِ بْنُ عَبَّاسٍ غَدَاةَ أُصِيبَ، وَكَانَ إِذَا مَرَّ بَيْنَ الصَّفَّيْنِ قَالَ اسْتَوُوا. حَتَّى إِذَا لَمْ يَرَ فِيهِنَّ خَلَلاً تَقَدَّمَ فَكَبَّرَ، وَرُبَّمَا قَرَأَ سُورَةَ يُوسُفَ، أَوِ النَّحْلَ، أَوْ نَحْوَ ذَلِكَ، فِي الرَّكْعَةِ الأُولَى حَتَّى يَجْتَمِعَ النَّاسُ، فَمَا هُوَ إِلاَّ أَنْ كَبَّرَ فَسَمِعْتُهُ يَقُولُ قَتَلَنِي ـ أَوْ أَكَلَنِي ـ الْكَلْبُ. حِينَ طَعَنَهُ، فَطَارَ الْعِلْجُ بِسِكِّينٍ ذَاتِ طَرَفَيْنِ لاَ يَمُرُّ عَلَى أَحَدٍ يَمِينًا وَلاَ شِمَالاً إِلاَّ طَعَنَهُ حَتَّى طَعَنَ ثَلاَثَةَ عَشَرَ رَجُلاً، مَاتَ مِنْهُمْ سَبْعَةٌ، فَلَمَّا رَأَى ذَلِكَ رَجُلٌ مِنَ الْمُسْلِمِينَ، طَرَحَ عَلَيْهِ بُرْنُسًا، فَلَمَّا ظَنَّ الْعِلْجُ أَنَّهُ مَأْخُوذٌ نَحَرَ نَفْسَهُ، وَتَنَاوَلَ عُمَرُ يَدَ عَبْدِ الرَّحْمَنِ بْنِ عَوْفٍ فَقَدَّمَهُ، فَمَنْ يَلِي عُمَرَ فَقَدْ رَأَى الَّذِي أَرَى، وَأَمَّا نَوَاحِي الْمَسْجِدِ فَإِنَّهُمْ لاَ يَدْرُونَ غَيْرَ أَنَّهُمْ قَدْ فَقَدُوا صَوْتَ عُمَرَ وَهُمْ يَقُولُونَ سُبْحَانَ اللَّهِ. فَصَلَّى بِهِمْ عَبْدُ الرَّحْمَنِ صَلاَةً خَفِيفَةً، فَلَمَّا انْصَرَفُوا. قَالَ يَا ابْنَ عَبَّاسٍ، انْظُرْ مَنْ قَتَلَنِي. فَجَالَ سَاعَةً، ثُمَّ جَاءَ، فَقَالَ غُلاَمُ الْمُغِيرَةِ. قَالَ الصَّنَعُ قَالَ نَعَمْ. قَالَ قَاتَلَهُ اللَّهُ لَقَدْ أَمَرْتُ بِهِ مَعْرُوفًا، الْحَمْدُ لِلَّهِ الَّذِي لَمْ يَجْعَلْ مَنِيَّتِي بِيَدِ رَجُلٍ يَدَّعِي الإِسْلاَمَ، قَدْ كُنْتَ أَنْتَ وَأَبُوكَ تُحِبَّانِ أَنْ تَكْثُرَ الْعُلُوجُ بِالْمَدِينَةِ وَكَانَ {الْعَبَّاسُ} أَكْثَرَهُمْ رَقِيقًا. فَقَالَ إِنْ شِئْتَ فَعَلْتُ. أَىْ إِنْ شِئْتَ قَتَلْنَا. قَالَ كَذَبْتَ، بَعْدَ مَا تَكَلَّمُوا بِلِسَانِكُمْ، وَصَلَّوْا قِبْلَتَكُمْ وَحَجُّوا حَجَّكُمْ فَاحْتُمِلَ إِلَى بَيْتِهِ فَانْطَلَقْنَا مَعَهُ، وَكَأَنَّ النَّاسَ لَمْ تُصِبْهُمْ مُصِيبَةٌ قَبْلَ يَوْمَئِذٍ، فَقَائِلٌ يَقُولُ لاَ بَأْسَ. وَقَائِلٌ يَقُولُ أَخَافُ عَلَيْهِ، فَأُتِيَ بِنَبِيذٍ فَشَرِبَهُ فَخَرَجَ مِنْ جَوْفِهِ، ثُمَّ أُتِيَ بِلَبَنٍ فَشَرِبَهُ فَخَرَجَ مِنْ جُرْحِهِ، فَعَلِمُوا أَنَّهُ مَيِّتٌ، فَدَخَلْنَا عَلَيْهِ، وَجَاءَ النَّاسُ يُثْنُونَ عَلَيْهِ، وَجَاءَ رَجُلٌ شَابٌّ، فَقَالَ أَبْشِرْ يَا أَمِيرَ الْمُؤْمِنِينَ بِبُشْرَى اللَّهِ لَكَ مِنْ صُحْبَةِ رَسُولِ اللَّهِ صلى الله عليه وسلم وَقَدَمٍ فِي الإِسْلاَمِ مَا قَدْ عَلِمْتَ، ثُمَّ وَلِيتَ فَعَدَلْتَ، ثُمَّ شَهَادَةٌ. قَالَ وَدِدْتُ أَنَّ ذَلِكَ كَفَافٌ لاَ عَلَىَّ وَلاَ لِي. فَلَمَّا أَدْبَرَ، إِذَا إِزَارُهُ يَمَسُّ الأَرْضَ. قَالَ رُدُّوا عَلَىَّ الْغُلاَمَ قَالَ ابْنَ أَخِي ارْفَعْ ثَوْبَكَ، فَإِنَّهُ أَبْقَى لِثَوْبِكَ وَأَتْقَى لِرَبِّكَ، يَا عَبْدَ اللَّهِ بْنَ عُمَرَ انْظُرْ مَا عَلَىَّ مِنَ الدَّيْنِ. فَحَسَبُوهُ فَوَجَدُوهُ سِتَّةً وَثَمَانِينَ أَلْفًا أَوْ نَحْوَهُ، قَالَ إِنْ وَفَى لَهُ مَالُ آلِ عُمَرَ، فَأَدِّهِ مِنْ أَمْوَالِهِمْ، وَإِلاَّ فَسَلْ فِي بَنِي عَدِيِّ بْنِ كَعْبٍ، فَإِنْ لَمْ تَفِ أَمْوَالُهُمْ فَسَلْ فِي قُرَيْشٍ، وَلاَ تَعْدُهُمْ إِلَى غَيْرِهِمْ، فَأَدِّ عَنِّي هَذَا الْمَالَ، انْطَلِقْ إِلَى عَائِشَةَ أُمِّ الْمُؤْمِنِينَ فَقُلْ يَقْرَأُ عَلَيْكِ عُمَرُ السَّلاَمَ. وَلاَ تَقُلْ أَمِيرُ الْمُؤْمِنِينَ. فَإِنِّي لَسْتُ الْيَوْمَ لِلْمُؤْمِنِينَ أَمِيرًا، وَقُلْ يَسْتَأْذِنُ عُمَرُ بْنُ الْخَطَّابِ أَنْ يُدْفَنَ مَعَ صَاحِبَيْهِ. فَسَلَّمَ وَاسْتَأْذَنَ، ثُمَّ دَخَلَ عَلَيْهَا، فَوَجَدَهَا قَاعِدَةً تَبْكِي فَقَالَ يَقْرَأُ عَلَيْكِ عُمَرُ بْنُ الْخَطَّابِ السَّلاَمَ وَيَسْتَأْذِنُ أَنْ يُدْفَنَ مَعَ صَاحِبَيْهِ. فَقَالَتْ كُنْتُ أُرِيدُهُ لِنَفْسِي، وَلأُوثِرَنَّ بِهِ الْيَوْمَ عَلَى نَفْسِي. فَلَمَّا أَقْبَلَ قِيلَ هَذَا عَبْدُ اللَّهِ بْنُ عُمَرَ قَدْ جَاءَ. قَالَ ارْفَعُونِي، فَأَسْنَدَهُ رَجُلٌ إِلَيْهِ، فَقَالَ مَا لَدَيْكَ قَالَ الَّذِي تُحِبُّ يَا أَمِيرَ الْمُؤْمِنِينَ أَذِنَتْ. قَالَ الْحَمْدُ لِلَّهِ، مَا كَانَ مِنْ شَىْءٍ أَهَمُّ إِلَىَّ مِنْ ذَلِكَ، فَإِذَا أَنَا قَضَيْتُ فَاحْمِلُونِي ثُمَّ سَلِّمْ فَقُلْ يَسْتَأْذِنُ عُمَرُ بْنُ الْخَطَّابِ، فَإِنْ أَذِنَتْ لِي فَأَدْخِلُونِي، وَإِنْ رَدَّتْنِي رُدُّونِي إِلَى مَقَابِرِ الْمُسْلِمِينَ. وَجَاءَتْ أُمُّ الْمُؤْمِنِينَ حَفْصَةُ وَالنِّسَاءُ تَسِيرُ مَعَهَا، فَلَمَّا رَأَيْنَاهَا قُمْنَا، فَوَلَجَتْ عَلَيْهِ فَبَكَتْ عِنْدَهُ سَاعَةً، وَاسْتَأْذَنَ الرِّجَالُ، فَوَلَجَتْ دَاخِلاً لَهُمْ، فَسَمِعْنَا بُكَاءَهَا مِنَ الدَّاخِلِ. فَقَالُوا أَوْصِ يَا أَمِيرَ الْمُؤْمِنِينَ اسْتَخْلِفْ. قَالَ مَا أَجِدُ أَحَقَّ بِهَذَا الأَمْرِ مِنْ هَؤُلاَءِ النَّفَرِ أَوِ الرَّهْطِ الَّذِينَ تُوُفِّيَ رَسُولُ اللَّهِ صلى الله عليه وسلم وَهْوَ عَنْهُمْ رَاضٍ. فَسَمَّى عَلِيًّا وَعُثْمَانَ وَالزُّبَيْرَ وَطَلْحَةَ وَسَعْدًا وَعَبْدَ الرَّحْمَنِ وَقَالَ يَشْهَدُكُمْ عَبْدُ اللَّهِ بْنُ عُمَرَ وَلَيْسَ لَهُ مِنَ الأَمْرِ شَىْءٌ ـ كَهَيْئَةِ التَّعْزِيَةِ لَهُ ـ فَإِنْ أَصَابَتِ الإِمْرَةُ سَعْدًا فَهْوَ ذَاكَ، وَإِلاَّ فَلْيَسْتَعِنْ بِهِ أَيُّكُمْ مَا أُمِّرَ، فَإِنِّي لَمْ أَعْزِلْهُ عَنْ عَجْزٍ وَلاَ خِيَانَةٍ وَقَالَ أُوصِي الْخَلِيفَةَ مِنْ بَعْدِي بِالْمُهَاجِرِينَ الأَوَّلِينَ أَنْ يَعْرِفَ لَهُمْ حَقَّهُمْ، وَيَحْفَظَ لَهُمْ حُرْمَتَهُمْ، وَأُوصِيهِ بِالأَنْصَارِ خَيْرًا، الَّذِينَ تَبَوَّءُوا الدَّارَ وَالإِيمَانَ مِنْ قَبْلِهِمْ، أَنْ يُقْبَلَ مِنْ مُحْسِنِهِمْ، وَأَنْ يُعْفَى عَنْ مُسِيئِهِمْ، وَأُوصِيهِ بِأَهْلِ الأَمْصَارِ خَيْرًا فَإِنَّهُمْ رِدْءُ الإِسْلاَمِ، وَجُبَاةُ الْمَالِ، وَغَيْظُ الْعَدُوِّ، وَأَنْ لاَ يُؤْخَذَ مِنْهُمْ إِلاَّ فَضْلُهُمْ عَنْ رِضَاهُمْ، وَأُوصِيهِ بِالأَعْرَابِ خَيْرًا، فَإِنَّهُمْ أَصْلُ الْعَرَبِ وَمَادَّةُ الإِسْلاَمِ أَنْ يُؤْخَذَ مِنْ حَوَاشِي أَمْوَالِهِمْ وَيُرَدَّ عَلَى فُقَرَائِهِمْ، وَأُوصِيهِ بِذِمَّةِ اللَّهِ وَذِمَّةِ رَسُولِهِ صلى الله عليه وسلم أَنْ يُوفَى لَهُمْ بِعَهْدِهِمْ، وَأَنْ يُقَاتَلَ مِنْ وَرَائِهِمْ، وَلاَ يُكَلَّفُوا إِلاَّ طَاقَتَهُمْ. فَلَمَّا قُبِضَ خَرَجْنَا بِهِ فَانْطَلَقْنَا نَمْشِي فَسَلَّمَ عَبْدُ اللَّهِ بْنُ عُمَرَ قَالَ يَسْتَأْذِنُ عُمَرُ بْنُ الْخَطَّابِ. قَالَتْ أَدْخِلُوهُ. فَأُدْخِلَ، فَوُضِعَ هُنَالِكَ مَعَ صَاحِبَيْهِ، فَلَمَّا فُرِغَ مِنْ دَفْنِهِ اجْتَمَعَ هَؤُلاَءِ الرَّهْطُ، فَقَالَ عَبْدُ الرَّحْمَنِ اجْعَلُوا أَمْرَكُمْ إِلَى ثَلاَثَةٍ مِنْكُمْ. فَقَالَ الزُّبَيْرُ قَدْ جَعَلْتُ أَمْرِي إِلَى عَلِيٍّ. فَقَالَ طَلْحَةُ قَدْ جَعَلْتُ أَمْرِي إِلَى عُثْمَانَ. وَقَالَ سَعْدٌ قَدْ جَعَلْتُ أَمْرِي إِلَى عَبْدِ الرَّحْمَنِ بْنِ عَوْفٍ. فَقَالَ عَبْدُ الرَّحْمَنِ أَيُّكُمَا تَبَرَّأَ مِنْ هَذَا الأَمْرِ فَنَجْعَلُهُ إِلَيْهِ، وَاللَّهُ عَلَيْهِ وَالإِسْلاَمُ لَيَنْظُرَنَّ أَفْضَلَهُمْ فِي نَفْسِهِ. فَأُسْكِتَ الشَّيْخَانِ، فَقَالَ عَبْدُ الرَّحْمَنِ أَفَتَجْعَلُونَهُ إِلَىَّ، وَاللَّهُ عَلَىَّ أَنْ لاَ آلُوَ عَنْ أَفْضَلِكُمْ قَالاَ نَعَمْ، فَأَخَذَ بِيَدِ أَحَدِهِمَا فَقَالَ لَكَ قَرَابَةٌ مِنْ رَسُولِ اللَّهِ صلى الله عليه وسلم وَالْقَدَمُ فِي الإِسْلاَمِ مَا قَدْ عَلِمْتَ، فَاللَّهُ عَلَيْكَ لَئِنْ أَمَّرْتُكَ لَتَعْدِلَنَّ، وَلَئِنْ

أَمَّرْتُ عُثْمَانَ لَتَسْمَعَنَّ وَلَتُطِيعَنَّ. ثُمَّ خَلاَ بِالآخَرِ فَقَالَ لَهُ مِثْلَ ذَلِكَ، فَلَمَّا أَخَذَ الْمِيثَاقَ قَالَ ارْفَعْ يَدَكَ يَا عُثْمَانُ. فَبَايَعَهُ، فَبَايَعَ لَهُ عَلِيٌّ، وَوَلَجَ أَهْلُ الدَّارِ فَبَايَعُوهُ.

Narrated Nafi`: During the affliction of Ibn Az-Zubair, two men came to Ibn `Umar and said, "The people are lost, and you are the son of `Umar, and the companion of the Prophet, so what forbids you from coming out?" He said, "What forbids me is that Allah has prohibited the shedding of my brother's blood." They both said, "Didn't Allah say, 'And fight then until there is no more affliction?" He said "We fought until there was no more affliction and the worship is for Allah (Alone while you want to fight until there is affliction and until the worship become for other than Allah." Narrated Nafi` (through another group of sub-narrators): A man came to Ibn `Umar and said, "O Abu `Abdur Rahman! What made you perform Hajj in one year and Umra in another year and leave the Jihad for Allah' Cause though you know how much Allah recommends it?" Ibn `Umar replied, "O son of my brother! Islam is founded on five principles, i.e. believe in Allah and His Apostle, the five compulsory prayers, the fasting of the month of Ramadan, the payment of Zakat, and the Hajj to the House (of Allah)." The man said, "O Abu `Abdur Rahman! Won't you listen to why Allah has mentioned in His Book: 'If two groups of believers fight each other, then make peace between them, but if one of then transgresses beyond bounds against the other, then you all fight against the one that transgresses. (49.9) and:--"And fight them till there is no more affliction (i.e. no more worshiping of others along with Allah)." Ibn `Umar said, "We did it, during the lifetime of Allah's Messenger ﷺ when Islam had only a few followers. A man would be put to trial because of his religion; he would either be killed or tortured. But when the Muslims increased, there was no more afflictions or oppressions." The man said, "What is your opinion about `Uthman and `Ali?" Ibn `Umar said, "As for `Uthman, it seems that Allah has forgiven him, but you people dislike that he should be forgiven. And as for `Ali, he is the cousin of Allah's Messenger ﷺ and his son-in-law." Then he pointed with his hand and said, "That is his house which you see." – Sahih Al-Bukhari 4513, 4514, 4515

حَدَّثَنَا مُحَمَّدُ بْنُ بَشَّارٍ، حَدَّثَنَا عَبْدُ الْوَهَّابِ، حَدَّثَنَا عُبَيْدُ اللَّهِ، عَنْ نَافِعٍ، عَنِ ابْنِ عُمَرَ ـ رضى الله عنهما ـ أَتَاهُ رَجُلاَنِ فِي فِتْنَةِ ابْنِ الزُّبَيْرِ فَقَالاَ إِنَّ النَّاسَ قَدْ ضُيِّعُوا، وَأَنْتَ ابْنُ عُمَرَ وَصَاحِبُ النَّبِيِّ صلى الله عليه وسلم فَمَا يَمْنَعُكَ أَنْ تَخْرُجَ فَقَالَ يَمْنَعُنِي أَنَّ اللَّهَ حَرَّمَ دَمَ أَخِي. فَقَالاَ أَلَمْ يَقُلِ اللَّهُ {وَقَاتِلُوهُمْ حَتَّى لاَ تَكُونَ فِتْنَةٌ } فَقَالَ قَاتَلْنَا حَتَّى لَمْ تَكُنْ فِتْنَةٌ، وَكَانَ الدِّينُ لِلَّهِ، وَأَنْتُمْ تُرِيدُونَ أَنْ تُقَاتِلُوا حَتَّى تَكُونَ فِتْنَةٌ، وَيَكُونَ الدِّينُ لِغَيْرِ اللَّهِ. وَزَادَ عُثْمَانُ بْنُ صَالِحٍ عَنِ ابْنِ وَهْبٍ، قَالَ أَخْبَرَنِي فُلاَنٌ، وَحَيْوَةُ بْنُ شُرَيْحٍ، عَنْ بَكْرِ بْنِ عَمْرٍو الْمَعَافِرِيِّ، أَنَّ بُكَيْرَ بْنَ عَبْدِ اللَّهِ، حَدَّثَهُ عَنْ نَافِعٍ، أَنَّ رَجُلاً، أَتَى ابْنَ عُمَرَ فَقَالَ يَا أَبَا عَبْدِ الرَّحْمَنِ مَا حَمَلَكَ عَلَى أَنْ تَحُجَّ عَامًا وَتَعْتَمِرَ عَامًا، وَتَتْرُكَ الْجِهَادَ فِي سَبِيلِ اللَّهِ عَزَّ وَجَلَّ، وَقَدْ عَلِمْتَ مَا رَغَّبَ اللَّهُ فِيهِ قَالَ يَا ابْنَ أَخِي بُنِيَ الإِسْلاَمُ عَلَى خَمْسٍ إِيمَانٍ بِاللَّهِ وَرَسُولِهِ، وَالصَّلاَةِ الْخَمْسِ، وَصِيَامِ رَمَضَانَ، وَأَدَاءِ الزَّكَاةِ، وَحَجِّ الْبَيْتِ. قَالَ يَا أَبَا عَبْدِ الرَّحْمَنِ، أَلاَ تَسْمَعُ مَا ذَكَرَ اللَّهُ فِي كِتَابِهِ {وَإِنْ طَائِفَتَانِ مِنَ الْمُؤْمِنِينَ اقْتَتَلُوا فَأَصْلِحُوا بَيْنَهُمَا} {إِلَى أَمْرِ اللَّهِ} {قَاتِلُوهُمْ حَتَّى لاَ تَكُونَ فِتْنَةٌ} قَالَ فَعَلْنَا عَلَى عَهْدِ رَسُولِ اللَّهِ صلى الله عليه وسلم وَكَانَ الإِسْلاَمُ قَلِيلاً، فَكَانَ الرَّجُلُ يُفْتَنُ فِي دِينِهِ إِمَّا قَتَلُوهُ، وَإِمَّا يُعَذِّبُوهُ، حَتَّى كَثُرَ الإِسْلاَمُ فَلَمْ تَكُنْ فِتْنَةٌ. قَالَ فَمَا قَوْلُكَ فِي عَلِيٍّ وَعُثْمَانَ قَالَ أَمَّا عُثْمَانُ فَكَأَنَّ اللَّهَ عَفَا عَنْهُ، وَأَمَّا أَنْتُمْ فَكَرِهْتُمْ أَنْ تَعْفُوا عَنْهُ، وَأَمَّا عَلِيٌّ فَابْنُ عَمِّ رَسُولِ اللَّهِ صلى الله عليه وسلم وَخَتَنُهُ. وَأَشَارَ بِيَدِهِ فَقَالَ هَذَا بَيْتُهُ حَيْثُ تَرَوْنَ.

Narrated Al-Miswar bin Makhrama: The group of people whom `Umar had selected as candidates for the Caliphate gathered and consulted each other. `Abdur-Rahman said to them, "I am not going to compete with you in this matter, but if you wish, I would select for you a caliph from among you." So all of them agreed to let `Abdur-Rahman decide the case. So when the candidates placed the case in the hands of `Abdur-Rahman, the people went towards him and nobody followed the rest of the group nor obeyed any after him. So the people followed `Abdur-Rahman and consulted him all those nights till there came the night we gave the oath of allegiance to `Uthman. Al-Miswar (bin Makhrama) added: `Abdur-

Rahman called on me after a portion of the night had passed and knocked on my door till I got up, and he said to me, "I see you have been sleeping! By Allah, during the last three nights I have not slept enough. Go and call Az-Zubair and Sa`d.' So I called them for him and he consulted them and then called me saying, 'Call `Ali for me." I called `Ali and he held a private talk with him till very late at night, and then 'Al, got up to leave having had much hope (to be chosen as a Caliph) but `Abdur-Rahman was afraid of something concerning `Ali. `Abdur-Rahman then said to me, "Call `Uthman for me." I called him and he kept on speaking to him privately till the Mu'adh-dhin put an end to their talk by announcing the Adhan for the Fajr prayer. When the people finished their morning prayer and that (six men) group gathered near the pulpit, `Abdur-Rahman sent for all the Muhajirin (emigrants) and the Ansar present there and sent for the army chief who had performed the Hajj with `Umar that year. When all of them had gathered, `Abdur- Rahman said, "None has the right to be worshipped but Allah," and added, "Now then, O `Ali, I have looked at the people's tendencies and noticed that they do not consider anybody equal to `Uthman, so you should not incur blame (by disagreeing)." Then `Abdur-Rahman said (to `Uthman), "I gave the oath of allegiance to you on condition that you will follow Allah's Laws and the traditions of Allah's Apostle and the traditions of the two Caliphs after him." So `Abdur-Rahman gave the oath of allegiance to him, and so did the people including the Muhajirin (emigrants) and the Ansar and the chiefs of the army staff and all the Muslims. – Sahih Al-Bukhari 7207

حَدَّثَنَا عَبْدُ اللَّهِ بْنُ مُحَمَّدِ بْنِ أَسْمَاءَ، حَدَّثَنَا جُوَيْرِيَةُ، عَنْ مَالِكٍ، عَنِ الزُّهْرِيِّ، أَنَّ حُمَيْدَ بْنَ عَبْدِ الرَّحْمَنِ، أَخْبَرَهُ أَنَّ الْمِسْوَرَ بْنَ مَخْرَمَةَ أَخْبَرَهُ. أَنَّ الرَّهْطَ الَّذِينَ وَلاَّهُمْ عُمَرُ اجْتَمَعُوا فَتَشَاوَرُوا، قَالَ لَهُمْ عَبْدُ الرَّحْمَنِ لَسْتُ بِالَّذِي أُنَافِسُكُمْ عَلَى هَذَا الأَمْرِ، وَلَكِنَّكُمْ إِنْ شِئْتُمُ اخْتَرْتُ لَكُمْ مِنْكُمْ. فَجَعَلُوا ذَلِكَ إِلَى عَبْدِ الرَّحْمَنِ، فَلَمَّا وَلَّوْا عَبْدَ الرَّحْمَنِ أَمْرَهُمْ فَمَالَ النَّاسُ عَلَى عَبْدِ الرَّحْمَنِ، حَتَّى مَا أَرَى أَحَدًا مِنَ النَّاسِ يَتْبَعُ أُولَئِكَ الرَّهْطَ وَلاَ يَطَأُ عَقِبَهُ، وَمَالَ النَّاسُ عَلَى عَبْدِ الرَّحْمَنِ يُشَاوِرُونَهُ تِلْكَ اللَّيَالِيَ حَتَّى إِذَا كَانَتِ اللَّيْلَةُ الَّتِي أَصْبَحْنَا مِنْهَا، فَبَايَعْنَا عُثْمَانَ قَالَ الْمِسْوَرُ طَرَقَنِي عَبْدُ الرَّحْمَنِ بَعْدَ هَجْعٍ مِنَ اللَّيْلِ فَضَرَبَ الْبَابَ حَتَّى اسْتَيْقَظْتُ فَقَالَ أَرَاكَ نَائِمًا، فَوَاللَّهِ مَا اكْتَحَلْتُ هَذِهِ اللَّيْلَةَ بِكَبِيرِ نَوْمٍ، انْطَلِقْ فَادْعُ الزُّبَيْرَ وَسَعْدًا، فَدَعَوْتُهُمَا لَهُ فَشَاوَرَهُمَا ثُمَّ دَعَانِي فَقَالَ ادْعُ لِي عَلِيًّا. فَدَعَوْتُهُ فَنَاجَاهُ حَتَّى ابْهَارَّ اللَّيْلُ، ثُمَّ قَامَ عَلِيٌّ مِنْ عِنْدِهِ، وَهْوَ عَلَى طَمَعٍ، وَقَدْ كَانَ عَبْدُ الرَّحْمَنِ يَخْشَى مِنْ عَلِيٍّ شَيْئًا، ثُمَّ قَالَ ادْعُ لِي عُثْمَانَ، فَدَعَوْتُهُ فَنَاجَاهُ حَتَّى فَرَّقَ بَيْنَهُمَا الْمُؤَذِّنُ بِالصُّبْحِ، فَلَمَّا صَلَّى لِلنَّاسِ الصُّبْحَ وَاجْتَمَعَ أُولَئِكَ الرَّهْطُ عِنْدَ الْمِنْبَرِ، فَأَرْسَلَ إِلَى مَنْ كَانَ حَاضِرًا مِنَ الْمُهَاجِرِينَ وَالأَنْصَارِ، وَأَرْسَلَ إِلَى أُمَرَاءِ الأَجْنَادِ وَكَانُوا وَافَوْا تِلْكَ الْحَجَّةَ مَعَ عُمَرَ، فَلَمَّا اجْتَمَعُوا تَشَهَّدَ عَبْدُ الرَّحْمَنِ ثُمَّ قَالَ أَمَّا بَعْدُ يَا عَلِيُّ، إِنِّي قَدْ نَظَرْتُ فِي أَمْرِ النَّاسِ فَلَمْ أَرَهُمْ يَعْدِلُونَ بِعُثْمَانَ، فَلاَ تَجْعَلَنَّ عَلَى نَفْسِكَ سَبِيلاً. فَقَالَ أُبَايِعُكَ عَلَى سُنَّةِ اللَّهِ وَرَسُولِهِ وَالْخَلِيفَتَيْنِ مِنْ بَعْدِهِ. فَبَايَعَهُ عَبْدُ الرَّحْمَنِ، وَبَايَعَهُ النَّاسُ الْمُهَاجِرُونَ وَالأَنْصَارُ وَأُمَرَاءُ الأَجْنَادِ وَالْمُسْلِمُونَ

Narrated As-Saib bin Yazid: The person who increased the number of Adhans for the Jumua prayers to three was `Uthman bin `Affan and it was when the number of the (Muslim) people of Medina had increased. In the lifetime of the Prophet ﷺ there was only one Mu'adh-dhin and the Adhan used to be pronounced only after the Imam had taken his seat (i.e. on the pulpit). – Sahih al-Bukhari 913

حَدَّثَنَا أَبُو نُعَيْمٍ، قَالَ حَدَّثَنَا عَبْدُ الْعَزِيزِ بْنُ أَبِي سَلَمَةَ الْمَاجِشُونُ، عَنِ الزُّهْرِيِّ، عَنِ السَّائِبِ بْنِ يَزِيدَ، أَنَّ الَّذِي، زَادَ التَّأْذِينَ الثَّالِثَ يَوْمَ الْجُمُعَةِ عُثْمَانُ بْنُ عَفَّانَ ـ رضى الله عنه ـ حِينَ كَثُرَ أَهْلُ الْمَدِينَةِ، وَلَمْ يَكُنْ لِلنَّبِيِّ صلى الله عليه وسلم مُؤَذِّنٌ غَيْرَ وَاحِدٍ، وَكَانَ التَّأْذِينُ يَوْمَ الْجُمُعَةِ حِينَ يَجْلِسُ الإِمَامُ، يَعْنِي عَلَى الْمِنْبَرِ.

Narrated `Abdullah bin `Umar: In the lifetime of Allah's Messenger ﷺ the mosque was built of adobes, its roof of the leaves of date-palms and its pillars of the stems of date-palms. Abu Bakr did not alter it. `Umar expanded it on the same pattern as it was in the lifetime of Allah's Messenger ﷺ by using adobes, leaves of date-palms and changing the pillars into wooden ones. `Uthman changed it by expanding it to a great extent and built its walls with engraved stones and lime and made its pillars of engraved stones and its roof of teak wood. – Sahih al-Bukhari 446

حَدَّثَنَا عَلِيُّ بْنُ عَبْدِ اللَّهِ، قَالَ حَدَّثَنَا يَعْقُوبُ بْنُ إِبْرَاهِيمَ بْنِ سَعْدٍ، قَالَ حَدَّثَنِي أَبِي، عَنْ صَالِحِ بْنِ كَيْسَانَ، قَالَ حَدَّثَنَا نَافِعٌ، أَنَّ عَبْدَ اللَّهِ، أَخْبَرَهُ أَنَّ الْمَسْجِدَ كَانَ عَلَى عَهْدِ رَسُولِ اللَّهِ صلى الله عليه وسلم مَبْنِيًّا بِاللَّبِنِ، وَسَقْفُهُ الْجَرِيدُ، وَعُمُدُهُ خَشَبُ النَّخْلِ، فَلَمْ يَزِدْ فِيهِ أَبُو بَكْرٍ شَيْئًا، وَزَادَ فِيهِ عُمَرُ وَبَنَاهُ عَلَى بُنْيَانِهِ فِي عَهْدِ رَسُولِ اللَّهِ صلى الله عليه وسلم بِاللَّبِنِ وَالْجَرِيدِ، وَأَعَادَ عُمُدَهُ خَشَبًا، ثُمَّ غَيَّرَهُ عُثْمَانُ، فَزَادَ فِيهِ زِيَادَةً كَثِيرَةً، وَبَنَى جِدَارَهُ بِالْحِجَارَةِ الْمَنْقُوشَةِ وَالْقَصَّةِ، وَجَعَلَ عُمُدَهُ مِنْ حِجَارَةٍ مَنْقُوشَةٍ، وَسَقَفَهُ بِالسَّاجِ.

Narrated Ibn. `Umar: Allah's Messenger ﷺ wore a gold ring or a silver ring and placed its stone towards the palm of his hand and had the name 'Muhammad, the Messenger of Allah' engraved on it. The people also started wearing gold rings like it, but when the Prophet ﷺ saw them wearing such rings, he threw away his own ring and said. "I will never wear it," and then wore a silver ring, whereupon the people too started wearing silver rings. Ibn `Umar added: After the Prophet ﷺ Abu Bakr wore the ring, and then `Umar and then `Uthman wore it till it fell in the Aris well from `Uthman. – Sahih al-Bukhari 5866

حَدَّثَنَا يُوسُفُ بْنُ مُوسَى، حَدَّثَنَا أَبُو أُسَامَةَ، حَدَّثَنَا عُبَيْدُ اللَّهِ، عَنْ نَافِعٍ، عَنِ ابْنِ عُمَرَ ـ رضى الله عنهما أَنَّ رَسُولَ اللَّهِ صلى الله عليه وسلم اتَّخَذَ خَاتَمًا مِنْ ذَهَبٍ أَوْ فِضَّةٍ، وَجَعَلَ فَصَّهُ مِمَّا يَلِي كَفَّهُ، وَنَقَشَ فِيهِ مُحَمَّدٌ رَسُولُ اللَّهِ. فَاتَّخَذَ النَّاسُ مِثْلَهُ، فَلَمَّا رَآهُمْ قَدِ اتَّخَذُوهَا رَمَى بِهِ، وَقَالَ " لاَ أَلْبَسُهُ أَبَدًا ". ثُمَّ اتَّخَذَ خَاتَمًا مِنْ فِضَّةٍ، فَاتَّخَذَ النَّاسُ خَوَاتِيمَ الْفِضَّةِ. قَالَ ابْنُ عُمَرَ فَلَبِسَ الْخَاتَمَ بَعْدَ النَّبِيِّ صلى الله عليه وسلم أَبُو بَكْرٍ ثُمَّ عُمَرُ ثُمَّ عُثْمَانُ، حَتَّى وَقَعَ مِنْ عُثْمَانَ فِي بِئْرِ أَرِيسَ.

Conquest of Armenia
احتلال أرمينيا

Narrated Anas bin Malik: Hudhaifa bin Al-Yaman came to `Uthman at the time when the people of Sham and the people of Iraq were Waging war to conquer Arminya and Adharbijan. Hudhaifa was afraid of their (the people of Sham and Iraq) differences in the recitation of the Qur'an, so he said to `Uthman, "O chief of the Believers! Save this nation before they differ about the Book (Qur'an) as Jews and the Christians did before." So `Uthman sent a message to Hafsa saying, "Send us the manuscripts of the Qur'an so that we may compile the Qur'anic materials in perfect copies and return the manuscripts to you." Hafsa sent it to `Uthman. `Uthman then ordered Zaid bin Thabit, `Abdullah bin AzZubair, Sa`id bin Al-As and `AbdurRahman bin Harith bin Hisham to rewrite the manuscripts in perfect copies. `Uthman said to the three Quraishi men, "In case you disagree with Zaid bin Thabit on any point in the Qur'an, then write it in the dialect of Quraish, the Qur'an was revealed in their tongue." They did so, and when they had written many copies, `Uthman returned the original manuscripts to Hafsa. `Uthman sent to every Muslim province one copy of what they had copied, and ordered that all the other Qur'anic materials, whether written in fragmentary manuscripts or whole copies, be burnt. – Sahih Al-Bukhari 4987

حَدَّثَنَا مُوسَى، حَدَّثَنَا إِبْرَاهِيمُ، حَدَّثَنَا ابْنُ شِهَابٍ، أَنَّ أَنَسَ بْنَ مَالِكٍ، حَدَّثَهُ أَنَّ حُذَيْفَةَ بْنَ الْيَمَانِ قَدِمَ عَلَى عُثْمَانَ وَكَانَ يُغَازِي أَهْلَ الشَّأْمِ فِي فَتْحِ إِرْمِينِيَةَ وَأَذْرَبِيجَانَ مَعَ أَهْلِ الْعِرَاقِ فَأَفْزَعَ حُذَيْفَةَ اخْتِلاَفُهُمْ فِي الْقِرَاءَةِ فَقَالَ حُذَيْفَةُ لِعُثْمَانَ يَا أَمِيرَ الْمُؤْمِنِينَ أَدْرِكْ هَذِهِ الأُمَّةَ قَبْلَ أَنْ يَخْتَلِفُوا فِي الْكِتَابِ اخْتِلاَفَ الْيَهُودِ وَالنَّصَارَى فَأَرْسَلَ عُثْمَانُ إِلَى حَفْصَةَ أَنْ أَرْسِلِي إِلَيْنَا بِالصُّحُفِ نَنْسَخُهَا فِي الْمَصَاحِفِ ثُمَّ نَرُدُّهَا إِلَيْكِ فَأَرْسَلَتْ بِهَا حَفْصَةُ إِلَى عُثْمَانَ فَأَمَرَ زَيْدَ بْنَ ثَابِتٍ وَعَبْدَ اللَّهِ بْنَ الزُّبَيْرِ وَسَعِيدَ بْنَ الْعَاصِ وَعَبْدَ الرَّحْمَنِ بْنَ الْحَارِثِ بْنِ هِشَامٍ فَنَسَخُوهَا فِي الْمَصَاحِفِ وَقَالَ عُثْمَانُ لِلرَّهْطِ الْقُرَشِيِّينَ الثَّلاَثَةِ إِذَا اخْتَلَفْتُمْ أَنْتُمْ وَزَيْدُ بْنُ ثَابِتٍ فِي شَىْءٍ مِنَ الْقُرْآنِ فَاكْتُبُوهُ بِلِسَانِ قُرَيْشٍ فَإِنَّمَا نَزَلَ بِلِسَانِهِمْ فَفَعَلُوا حَتَّى إِذَا نَسَخُوا الصُّحُفَ فِي الْمَصَاحِفِ رَدَّ عُثْمَانُ الصُّحُفَ إِلَى حَفْصَةَ وَأَرْسَلَ إِلَى كُلِّ أُفُقٍ بِمُصْحَفٍ مِمَّا نَسَخُوا وَأَمَرَ بِمَا سِوَاهُ مِنَ الْقُرْآنِ فِي كُلِّ صَحِيفَةٍ أَوْ مُصْحَفٍ أَنْ يُحْرَقَ.

Anas added: The ring of the Prophet ﷺ was in his hand, and after him, in Abu Bakr's hand, and then in `Umar's hand after Abu Bakr. When `Uthman was the Caliph, once he was sitting at the well of Aris. He removed the ring from his hand and while he was trifling with it, dropped into the well. We kept on going to the well with `Uthman for three days looking for the ring, and finally the well was drained, but the ring was not found. – Sahih Al-Bukhari 5879

وَزَادَنِي أَحْمَدُ حَدَّثَنَا الأَنْصَارِيُّ، قَالَ حَدَّثَنِي أَبِي، عَنْ ثُمَامَةَ، عَنْ أَنَسٍ، قَالَ كَانَ خَاتَمُ النَّبِيِّ صلى الله عليه وسلم فِي يَدِهِ، وَفِي يَدِ أَبِي بَكْرٍ بَعْدَهُ، وَفِي يَدِ عُمَرَ بَعْدَ أَبِي بَكْرٍ، فَلَمَّا كَانَ عُثْمَانُ جَلَسَ عَلَى بِئْرِ أَرِيسَ ـ قَالَ ـ فَأَخْرَجَ الْخَاتَمَ، فَجَعَلَ يَعْبَثُ بِهِ فَسَقَطَ قَالَ فَاخْتَلَفْنَا ثَلاَثَةَ أَيَّامٍ مَعَ عُثْمَانَ فَنَنْزَحُ الْبِئْرَ فَلَمْ نَجِدْهُ

Narrated Marwan bin Al-Hakam: I saw `Uthman and `Ali. `Uthman used to forbid people to perform Hajj-at-Tamattu` and Hajj-al- Qiran (Hajj and `Umra together), and when `Ali saw (this act of `Uthman), he assumed Ihram for Hajj and `Umra together saying, "Lubbaik for `Umra and Hajj," and said, "I will not leave the tradition of the Prophet ﷺ on the saying of somebody.". – Sahih Al-Bukhari 1563

حَدَّثَنَا مُحَمَّدُ بْنُ بَشَّارٍ، حَدَّثَنَا غُنْدَرٌ، حَدَّثَنَا شُعْبَةُ، عَنِ الْحَكَمِ، عَنْ عَلِيِّ بْنِ حُسَيْنٍ، عَنْ مَرْوَانَ بْنِ الْحَكَمِ، قَالَ شَهِدْتُ عُثْمَانَ وَعَلِيًّا ـ رضى الله عنهما ـ وَعُثْمَانُ يَنْهَى عَنِ الْمُتْعَةِ وَأَنْ يُجْمَعَ بَيْنَهُمَا. فَلَمَّا رَأَى عَلِيٌّ، أَهَلَّ بِهِمَا لَبَّيْكَ بِعُمْرَةٍ وَحَجَّةٍ قَالَ مَا كُنْتُ لأَدَعَ سُنَّةَ النَّبِيِّ صلى الله عليه وسلم لِقَوْلِ أَحَدٍ

Narrated `Abdullah bin `Umar: In the lifetime of Allah's Messenger ﷺ the mosque was built of adobes, its roof of the leaves of date-palms and its pillars of the stems of date-palms. Abu Bakr did not alter it. `Umar expanded it on the same pattern as it was in the lifetime of Allah's Messenger ﷺ by using adobes, leaves of date-palms and changing the pillars into wooden ones. `Uthman changed it by expanding it to a great extent and built its walls with engraved stones and lime and made its pillars of engraved stones and its roof of teak wood. – Sahih Al-Bukhari 446

حَدَّثَنَا عَلِيُّ بْنُ عَبْدِ اللَّهِ، قَالَ حَدَّثَنَا يَعْقُوبُ بْنُ إِبْرَاهِيمَ بْنِ سَعْدٍ، قَالَ حَدَّثَنِي أَبِي، عَنْ صَالِحِ بْنِ كَيْسَانَ، قَالَ حَدَّثَنَا نَافِعٌ، أَنَّ عَبْدَ اللَّهِ، أَخْبَرَهُ أَنَّ الْمَسْجِدَ كَانَ عَلَى عَهْدِ رَسُولِ اللَّهِ صلى الله عليه وسلم مَبْنِيًّا بِاللَّبِنِ، وَسَقْفُهُ الْجَرِيدُ، وَعُمُدُهُ خَشَبُ النَّخْلِ، فَلَمْ يَزِدْ فِيهِ أَبُو بَكْرٍ شَيْئًا، وَزَادَ فِيهِ عُمَرُ وَبَنَاهُ عَلَى بُنْيَانِهِ فِي عَهْدِ رَسُولِ اللَّهِ صلى الله عليه وسلم بِاللَّبِنِ وَالْجَرِيدِ، وَأَعَادَ عُمُدَهُ خَشَبًا، ثُمَّ غَيَّرَهُ عُثْمَانُ، فَزَادَ فِيهِ زِيَادَةً كَثِيرَةً، وَبَنَى جِدَارَهُ بِالْحِجَارَةِ الْمَنْقُوشَةِ وَالْقَصَّةِ، وَجَعَلَ عُمُدَهُ مِنْ حِجَارَةٍ مَنْقُوشَةٍ، وَسَقَفَهُ بِالسَّاجِ

The Book of
Khawarij
الخوارج

Narrated Abu Sa`id Al-Khudri: `Ali bin Abi Talib sent a piece of gold not yet taken out of its ore, in a tanned leather container to Allah's Messenger ﷺ. Allah's Messenger ﷺ distributed that amongst four Persons: 'Uyaina bin Badr, Aqra bin H`Abis, Zaid Al-Khail and the fourth was either Alqama or Amir bin at-Tufail. On that, one of his companions said, "We are more deserving of this (gold) than these (persons)." When that news reached the Prophet ﷺ, he said, "Don't you trust me though I am the truth worthy man of the One in the Heavens, and I receive the news of Heaven (i.e. Divine Inspiration) both in the morning and in the evening?" There got up a man with sunken eyes, raised cheek bones, raised forehead, a thick beard, a shaven head and a waist sheet that was tucked up and he said, "O Allah's Messenger ﷺ! Be afraid of Allah." The Prophet ﷺ said, "Woe to you! Am I not of all the people of the earth the most entitled to fear Allah?" Then that man went away. Khalid bin Al-Wahd said, "O Allah's Messenger ﷺ! Shall I chop his neck off?" The Prophet ﷺ said, "No, for he may offer prayers." Khalid said, "Numerous are those who offer prayers and say by their tongues (i.e. mouths) what is not in their hearts." Allah's Messenger ﷺ said, "I have not been ordered (by Allah) to search the hearts of the people or cut open their bellies." Then the Prophet looked at him (i.e. that man) while the latter was going away and said, "From the offspring of this (man there will come out (people) who will recite the Qur'an continuously and elegantly but it will not exceed their throats. (They will neither understand it nor act upon it). They would go out of the religion (i.e. Islam) as an arrow goes through a game's body." I think he also said, "If I should be present at their time I would kill them as the nations a Thamud were killed.". – Sahih Al-Bukhari 4351

حَدَّثَنَا قُتَيْبَةُ، حَدَّثَنَا عَبْدُ الْوَاحِدِ، عَنْ عُمَارَةَ بْنِ الْقَعْقَاعِ بْنِ شُبْرُمَةَ، حَدَّثَنَا عَبْدُ الرَّحْمَنِ بْنِ أَبِي نُعْمٍ، قَالَ سَمِعْتُ أَبَا سَعِيدٍ الْخُدْرِيَّ، يَقُولُ بَعَثَ عَلِيُّ بْنُ أَبِي طَالِبٍ ـ رضى الله عنه ـ إِلَى رَسُولِ اللَّهِ صلى الله عليه وسلم مِنَ الْيَمَنِ بِذُهَيْبَةٍ فِي أَدِيمٍ مَقْرُوظٍ لَمْ تُحَصَّلْ مِنْ تُرَابِهَا، قَالَ فَقَسَمَهَا بَيْنَ أَرْبَعَةِ نَفَرٍ بَيْنَ عُيَيْنَةَ بْنِ بَدْرٍ، وَأَقْرَعَ بْنِ حَابِسٍ وَزَيْدِ الْخَيْلِ، وَالرَّابِعُ إِمَّا عَلْقَمَةُ وَإِمَّا عَامِرُ بْنُ الطُّفَيْلِ، فَقَالَ رَجُلٌ مِنْ أَصْحَابِهِ كُنَّا نَحْنُ أَحَقَّ بِهَذَا مِنْ هَؤُلاَءِ. قَالَ فَبَلَغَ ذَلِكَ النَّبِيَّ صلى الله عليه وسلم فَقَالَ " أَلاَ تَأْمَنُونِي وَأَنَا أَمِينُ مَنْ فِي السَّمَاءِ، يَأْتِينِي خَبَرُ السَّمَاءِ صَبَاحًا وَمَسَاءً ". قَالَ فَقَامَ رَجُلٌ غَائِرُ الْعَيْنَيْنِ، مُشْرِفُ الْوَجْنَتَيْنِ، نَاشِزُ الْجَبْهَةِ، كَثُّ اللِّحْيَةِ، مَحْلُوقُ الرَّأْسِ، مُشَمَّرُ الإِزَارِ، فَقَالَ يَا رَسُولَ اللَّهِ، اتَّقِ اللَّهَ. قَالَ " وَيْلَكَ أَوَلَسْتُ أَحَقَّ أَهْلِ الأَرْضِ أَنْ يَتَّقِيَ اللَّهَ ". قَالَ ثُمَّ وَلَّى الرَّجُلُ، قَالَ خَالِدُ بْنُ الْوَلِيدِ يَا رَسُولَ اللَّهِ، أَلاَ أَضْرِبُ عُنُقَهُ قَالَ " لاَ، لَعَلَّهُ أَنْ يَكُونَ يُصَلِّي ". فَقَالَ خَالِدٌ وَكَمْ مِنْ مُصَلٍّ يَقُولُ بِلِسَانِهِ مَا لَيْسَ فِي قَلْبِهِ. قَالَ رَسُولُ اللَّهِ صلى الله عليه وسلم " إِنِّي لَمْ أُومَرْ أَنْ أَنْقُبَ قُلُوبَ النَّاسِ، وَلاَ أَشُقَّ بُطُونَهُمْ " قَالَ ثُمَّ نَظَرَ إِلَيْهِ وَهْوَ مُقَفٍّ فَقَالَ " إِنَّهُ يَخْرُجُ مِنْ ضِئْضِئِ هَذَا قَوْمٌ يَتْلُونَ كِتَابَ اللَّهِ رَطْبًا، لاَ يُجَاوِزُ حَنَاجِرَهُمْ، يَمْرُقُونَ مِنَ الدِّينِ كَمَا يَمْرُقُ السَّهْمُ مِنَ الرَّمِيَّةِ ". وَأَظُنُّهُ قَالَ " لَئِنْ أَدْرَكْتُهُمْ لأَقْتُلَنَّهُمْ قَتْلَ ثَمُودَ ".

We were at Al-Ahwaz fighting the Al-Haruriya (tribe). While I was at the bank of a river a man was praying and the reins of his animal were in his hands and the animal was struggling and he was following the animal. (Shu`ba, a sub-narrator, said that man was Abu Barza Al-Aslami). A man from the Khawarij said, "O Allah! Be harsh to this sheik." And when the sheik (Abu Barza) finished his prayer, he said, "I heard your remark. No doubt, I participated with Allah's Messenger ﷺ in six or seven or eight holy battles and saw his leniency, and no doubt, I would rather retain my animal than let it return to its stable, as it would cause me much trouble. "
Narrated Al-Azraq bin Qais: We were at Al-Ahwaz fighting the Al-Haruriya (tribe). While I was at the bank of a river a man was praying and the reins of his animal were in his hands and the animal was struggling and he was following the animal. (Shu`ba, a sub-narrator, said that

man was Abu Barza Al-Aslami). A man from the Khawarij said, “O Allah! Be harsh to this sheik.” And when the sheik (Abu Barza) finished his prayer, he said, “I heard your remark. No doubt, I participated with Allah’s Messenger ﷺ in six or seven or eight holy battles and saw his leniency, and no doubt, I would rather retain my animal than let it return to its stable, as it would cause me much trouble. “. – Sahih Al-Bukhari 1211

حَدَّثَنَا آدَمُ، حَدَّثَنَا شُعْبَةُ، حَدَّثَنَا الأَزْرَقُ بْنُ قَيْسٍ، قَالَ كُنَّا بِالأَهْوَازِ نُقَاتِلُ الْحَرُورِيَّةَ، فَبَيْنَا أَنَا عَلَى جُرُفِ نَهَرٍ إِذَا رَجُلٌ يُصَلِّي، وَإِذَا لِجَامُ دَابَّتِهِ بِيَدِهِ فَجَعَلَتِ الدَّابَّةُ تُنَازِعُهُ، وَجَعَلَ يَتْبَعُهَا ـ قَالَ شُعْبَةُ ـ هُوَ أَبُو بَرْزَةَ الأَسْلَمِيُّ ـ فَجَعَلَ رَجُلٌ مِنَ الْخَوَارِجِ يَقُولُ اللَّهُمَّ افْعَلْ بِهَذَا الشَّيْخِ. فَلَمَّا انْصَرَفَ الشَّيْخُ قَالَ إِنِّي سَمِعْتُ قَوْلَكُمْ، وَإِنِّي غَزَوْتُ مَعَ رَسُولِ اللَّهِ صلى الله عليه وسلم سِتَّ غَزَوَاتٍ أَوْ سَبْعَ غَزَوَاتٍ وَثَمَانِيًا، وَشَهِدْتُ تَيْسِيرَهُ، وَإِنِّي أَنْ كُنْتُ أَنْ أُرَاجِعَ مَعَ دَابَّتِي أَحَبُّ إِلَيَّ مِنْ أَنْ أَدَعَهَا تَرْجِعُ إِلَى مَأْلَفِهَا فَيَشُقَّ عَلَىَّ.

Narrated Abu Sa`id Al-Khudri: The Prophet ﷺ said, “There will emerge from the East some people who will recite the Qur’an but it will not exceed their throats and who will go out of (renounce) the religion (Islam) as an arrow passes through the game, and they will never come back to it unless the arrow, comes back to the middle of the bow (by itself) (i.e., impossible). The people asked, “What will their signs be?” He said, “Their sign will be the habit of shaving (of their beards and their heads). (Fath-ul-Bari, Page 322, Vol. 17th). – Sahih Al-Bukhari 7562

حَدَّثَنَا أَبُو النُّعْمَانِ، حَدَّثَنَا مَهْدِيُّ بْنُ مَيْمُونٍ، سَمِعْتُ مُحَمَّدَ بْنَ سِيرِينَ، يُحَدِّثُ عَنْ مَعْبَدِ بْنِ سِيرِينَ، عَنْ أَبِي سَعِيدٍ الْخُدْرِيِّ ـ رضى الله عنه ـ عَنِ النَّبِيِّ صلى الله عليه وسلم قَالَ " يَخْرُجُ نَاسٌ مِنْ قِبَلِ الْمَشْرِقِ وَيَقْرَءُونَ الْقُرْآنَ لاَ يُجَاوِزُ تَرَاقِيَهُمْ، يَمْرُقُونَ مِنَ الدِّينِ كَمَا يَمْرُقُ السَّهْمُ مِنَ الرَّمِيَّةِ، ثُمَّ لاَ يَعُودُونَ فِيهِ حَتَّى يَعُودَ السَّهْمُ إِلَى فُوقِهِ ". قِيلَ مَا سِيمَاهُمْ. قَالَ " سِيمَاهُمُ التَّحْلِيقُ ". أَوْ قَالَ " التَّسْبِيدُ ".

Narrated Abu Sa`id Al-Khudri: While we were with Allah’s Messenger ﷺ who was distributing (i.e. some property), there came Dhu-l- Khuwaisira, a man from the tribe of Bani Tamim and said, “O Allah’s Messenger ﷺ ! Do Justice.” The Prophet said, “Woe to you! Who could do justice if I did not? I would be a desperate loser if I did not do justice.” `Umar said, “O Allah’s Messengerr ﷺ ! Allow me to chop his head off.” The Prophet ﷺ said, “Leave him, for he has companions who pray and fast in such a way that you will consider your fasting negligible in comparison to theirs. They recite Qur’an but it does not go beyond their throats (i.e. they do not act on it) and they will desert Islam as an arrow goes through a victim’s body, so that the hunter, on looking at the arrow’s blade, would see nothing on it; he would look at its Risaf and see nothing: he would look at its Na,di and see nothing, and he would look at its Qudhadh (1) and see nothing (neither meat nor blood), for the arrow has been too fast even for the blood and excretions to smear. The sign by which they will be recognized is that among them there will be a black man, one of whose arms will resemble a woman’s breast or a lump of meat moving loosely. Those people will appear when there will be differences amongst the people.” I testify that I heard this narration from Allah’s Messenger ﷺ and I testify that `Ali bin Abi Talib fought with such people, and I was in his company. He ordered that the man (described by the Prophet ﷺ) should be looked for. The man was brought and I looked at him and noticed that he looked exactly as the Prophet ﷺ had described him – .Sahih al-Bukhari 3610

حَدَّثَنَا أَبُو الْيَمَانِ، أَخْبَرَنَا شُعَيْبٌ، عَنِ الزُّهْرِيِّ، قَالَ أَخْبَرَنِي أَبُو سَلَمَةَ بْنُ عَبْدِ الرَّحْمَنِ، أَنَّ أَبَا سَعِيدٍ الْخُدْرِيَّ ـ رضى الله عنه ـ قَالَ بَيْنَمَا نَحْنُ عِنْدَ رَسُولِ اللَّهِ صلى الله عليه وسلم وَهْوَ يَقْسِمُ قَسْمًا أَتَاهُ ذُو الْخُوَيْصِرَةِ ـ وَهْوَ رَجُلٌ مِنْ بَنِي تَمِيمٍ ـ فَقَالَ يَا رَسُولَ اللَّهِ اعْدِلْ. فَقَالَ " وَيْلَكَ، وَمَنْ يَعْدِلُ إِذَا لَمْ أَعْدِلْ قَدْ خِبْتَ وَخَسِرْتَ إِنْ لَمْ أَكُنْ أَعْدِلُ ". فَقَالَ عُمَرُ يَا رَسُولَ اللَّهِ ائْذَنْ لِي فِيهِ، فَأَضْرِبَ عُنُقَهُ. فَقَالَ " دَعْهُ فَإِنَّ لَهُ أَصْحَابًا، يَحْقِرُ أَحَدُكُمْ صَلاَتَهُ مَعَ صَلاَتِهِمْ وَصِيَامَهُ مَعَ صِيَامِهِمْ، يَقْرَءُونَ الْقُرْآنَ لاَ يُجَاوِزُ تَرَاقِيَهُمْ، يَمْرُقُونَ مِنَ الدِّينِ كَمَا يَمْرُقُ السَّهْمُ مِنَ الرَّمِيَّةِ، يُنْظَرُ إِلَى نَصْلِهِ فَلاَ يُوجَدُ فِيهِ شَىْءٌ، ثُمَّ يُنْظَرُ إِلَى رِصَافِهِ فَمَا يُوجَدُ فِيهِ شَىْءٌ، ثُمَّ يُنْظَرُ إِلَى نَضِيِّهِ ـ وَهْوَ قِدْحُهُ ـ فَلاَ يُوجَدُ فِيهِ شَىْءٌ، ثُمَّ يُنْظَرُ إِلَى قُذَذِهِ فَلاَ يُوجَدُ

فِيهِ شَىْءٌ، قَدْ سَبَقَ الْفَرْثَ وَالدَّمَ، آيَتُهُمْ رَجُلٌ أَسْوَدُ إِحْدَى عَضُدَيْهِ مِثْلُ ثَدْىِ الْمَرْأَةِ، أَوْ مِثْلُ الْبَضْعَةِ تَدَرْدَرُ وَيَخْرُجُونَ عَلَى حِينِ فُرْقَةٍ مِنَ النَّاسِ ". قَالَ أَبُو سَعِيدٍ فَأَشْهَدُ أَنِّي سَمِعْتُ هَذَا الْحَدِيثَ مِنْ رَسُولِ اللَّهِ صلى الله عليه وسلم، وَأَشْهَدُ أَنَّ عَلِيَّ بْنَ أَبِي طَالِبٍ قَاتَلَهُمْ وَأَنَا مَعَهُ، فَأَمَرَ بِذَلِكَ الرَّجُلِ، فَالْتُمِسَ فَأُتِيَ بِهِ حَتَّى نَظَرْتُ إِلَيْهِ عَلَى نَعْتِ النَّبِيِّ صلى الله عليه وسلم الَّذِي نَعَتَهُ.

Narrated Yusair bin `Amr: I asked Sahl bin Hunaif, "Did you hear the Prophetﷺ saying anything about Al-Khawarij?" He said, "I heard him saying while pointing his hand towards Iraq. "There will appear in it (i.e, Iraq) some people who will recite the Qur'an but it will not go beyond their throats, and they will go out from (leave) Islam as an arrow darts through the game's body.' ". – Sahih Al-Bukhari 6934

حَدَّثَنَا مُوسَى بْنُ إِسْمَاعِيلَ، حَدَّثَنَا عَبْدُ الْوَاحِدِ، حَدَّثَنَا الشَّيْبَانِيُّ، حَدَّثَنَا يُسَيْرُ بْنُ عَمْرٍو، قَالَ قُلْتُ لِسَهْلِ بْنِ حُنَيْفٍ هَلْ سَمِعْتَ النَّبِيَّ صلى الله عليه وسلم يَقُولُ فِي الْخَوَارِجِ شَيْئًا قَالَ سَمِعْتُهُ يَقُولُ ـ وَأَهْوَى بِيَدِهِ قِبَلَ الْعِرَاقِ ـ " يَخْرُجُ مِنْهُ قَوْمٌ يَقْرَءُونَ الْقُرْآنَ لاَ يُجَاوِزُ تَرَاقِيَهُمْ، يَمْرُقُونَ مِنَ الإِسْلاَمِ مُرُوقَ السَّهْمِ مِنَ الرَّمِيَّةِ "

Narrated Abu Al-Minhal: When Ibn Ziyad and Marwan were in Sham and Ibn Az-Zubair took over the authority in Mecca and Qurra' (the Kharijites) revolted in Basra, I went out with my father to Abu Barza Al-Aslami till we entered upon him in his house while he was sitting in the shade of a room built of cane. So we sat with him and my father started talking to him saying, "O Abu Barza! Don't you see in what dilemma the people has fallen?" The first thing heard him saying "I seek reward from Allah for myself because of being angry and scornful at the Quraish tribe. O you Arabs! You know very well that you were in misery and were few in number and misguided, and that Allah has brought you out of all that with Islam and with Muhammad till He brought you to this state (of prosperity and happiness) which you see now; and it is this worldly wealth and pleasures which has caused mischief to appear among you. The one who is in Sham (i.e., Marwan), by Allah, is not fighting except for the sake of worldly gain: and those who are among you, by Allah, are not fighting except for the sake of worldly gain; and that one who is in Mecca (i.e., Ibn Az-Zubair) by Allah, is not fighting except for the sake of worldly gain.". – Sahih Al-Bukhari 7112

حَدَّثَنَا أَحْمَدُ بْنُ يُونُسَ، حَدَّثَنَا أَبُو شِهَابٍ، عَنْ عَوْفٍ، عَنْ أَبِي الْمِنْهَالِ، قَالَ لَمَّا كَانَ ابْنُ زِيَادٍ وَمَرْوَانُ بِالشَّأْمِ، وَوَثَبَ ابْنُ الزُّبَيْرِ بِمَكَّةَ، وَوَثَبَ الْقُرَّاءُ بِالْبَصْرَةِ، فَانْطَلَقْتُ مَعَ أَبِي إِلَى أَبِي بَرْزَةَ الأَسْلَمِيِّ حَتَّى دَخَلْنَا عَلَيْهِ فِي دَارِهِ وَهْوَ جَالِسٌ فِي ظِلِّ عُلِّيَّةٍ لَهُ مِنْ قَصَبٍ، فَجَلَسْنَا إِلَيْهِ فَأَنْشَأَ أَبِي يَسْتَطْعِمُهُ الْحَدِيثَ فَقَالَ يَا أَبَا بَرْزَةَ أَلاَ تَرَى مَا وَقَعَ فِيهِ النَّاسُ فَأَوَّلُ شَىْءٍ سَمِعْتُهُ تَكَلَّمَ بِهِ إِنِّي احْتَسَبْتُ عِنْدَ اللَّهِ أَنِّي أَصْبَحْتُ سَاخِطًا عَلَى أَحْيَاءِ قُرَيْشٍ، إِنَّكُمْ يَا مَعْشَرَ الْعَرَبِ كُنْتُمْ عَلَى الْحَالِ الَّذِي عَلِمْتُمْ مِنَ الذِّلَّةِ وَالْقِلَّةِ وَالضَّلاَلَةِ، وَإِنَّ اللَّهَ أَنْقَذَكُمْ بِالإِسْلاَمِ وَبِمُحَمَّدٍ صلى الله عليه وسلم حَتَّى بَلَغَ بِكُمْ مَا تَرَوْنَ، وَهَذِهِ الدُّنْيَا الَّتِي أَفْسَدَتْ بَيْنَكُمْ، إِنَّ ذَاكَ الَّذِي بِالشَّأْمِ وَاللَّهِ إِنْ يُقَاتِلُ إِلاَّ عَلَى الدُّنْيَا

Narrated Ibn Abi Na'm: I was present when a man asked Ibn `Umar about the blood of mosquitoes. Ibn `Umar said, "From where are you?" The man replied. "From Iraq." Ibn `Umar said, "Look at that! He is asking me about the blood of Mosquitoes while they (the Iraqis) have killed the (grand) son of the Prophet. I have heard the Prophetﷺ saying, "They (Hasan and Husain) are my two sweet-smelling flowers in this world." – Sahih Al-Bukhari 5994

حَدَّثَنَا مُوسَى بْنُ إِسْمَاعِيلَ، حَدَّثَنَا مَهْدِيٌّ، حَدَّثَنَا ابْنُ أَبِي يَعْقُوبَ، عَنِ ابْنِ أَبِي نُعْمٍ، قَالَ كُنْتُ شَاهِدًا لاِبْنِ عُمَرَ وَسَأَلَهُ رَجُلٌ عَنْ دَمِ الْبَعُوضِ. فَقَالَ مِمَّنْ أَنْتَ فَقَالَ مِنْ أَهْلِ الْعِرَاقِ. قَالَ انْظُرُوا إِلَى هَذَا، يَسْأَلُنِي عَنْ دَمِ الْبَعُوضِ وَقَدْ قَتَلُوا ابْنَ النَّبِيِّ صلى الله عليه وسلم وَسَمِعْتُ النَّبِيَّ صلى الله عليه وسلم يَقُولُ " هُمَا رَيْحَانَتَاىَ مِنَ الدُّنْيَا "

And Ibn Umar used to consider them (Al- Khawārij and Al-Mulhidūn) the worst of Allah's creatures and said "These people took some Verses that had been revealed concerning the disbelievers and interpreted them as describing the believers. Bukhari Vol.9 page 49

و كان ابن عمر يراهم شرار خلق الله، و قال : أنهم انطلقوا الى ايات نزلت في الكفار فخعلوها على المومنين

The Book of
Al-Mulhidun
الملحون

Those who despise Our revelations are not hidden from Us. Is he who is hurled into the Fire better? Or he who arrives safely on the Day of Resurrection? Do as you please; He is Seeing of everything you do. – Surah Al-Fussilat 41:40

إِنَّ ٱلَّذِينَ يُلۡحِدُونَ فِيٓ ءَايَٰتِنَا لَا يَخۡفَوۡنَ عَلَيۡنَآۗ أَفَمَن يُلۡقَىٰ فِي ٱلنَّارِ خَيۡرٌ أَم مَّن يَأۡتِيٓ ءَامِنٗا يَوۡمَ ٱلۡقِيَٰمَةِۚ ٱعۡمَلُواْ مَا شِئۡتُمۡ إِنَّهُۥ بِمَا تَعۡمَلُونَ بَصِيرٌ

But whoever turns away and disbelieves. Allah will punish him with the greatest punishment. – Surah Al-Ghashiyah 88:23&24

إِلَّا مَن تَوَلَّىٰ وَكَفَرَ فَيُعَذِّبُهُ ٱللَّهُ ٱلۡعَذَابَ ٱلۡأَكۡبَرَ

Had they kept true to the Path, We would have given them plenty water to drink. To test them with it. Whoever turns away from the remembrance of his Lord, He will direct him to torment ever mounting. – Surah Al-Jinn 72:16&17

لِّنَفۡتِنَهُمۡ فِيهِۚ وَمَن يُعۡرِضۡ عَن ذِكۡرِ رَبِّهِۦ يَسۡلُكۡهُ عَذَابٗا صَعَدٗا وَأَلَّوِ ٱسۡتَقَٰمُواْ عَلَى ٱلطَّرِيقَةِ لَأَسۡقَيۡنَٰهُم مَّآءً غَدَقٗا

Who does greater wrong than he, who, when reminded of his Lord's revelations, turns away from them, and forgets what his hands have put forward? We have placed coverings over their hearts, lest they understand it, and heaviness in their ears. And if you call them to guidance, they will not be guided, ever. – Surah Al-Kahf 18:57

وَمَنۡ أَظۡلَمُ مِمَّن ذُكِّرَ بِـَٔايَٰتِ رَبِّهِۦ فَأَعۡرَضَ عَنۡهَا وَنَسِيَ مَا قَدَّمَتۡ يَدَاهُۚ إِنَّا جَعَلۡنَا عَلَىٰ قُلُوبِهِمۡ أَكِنَّةً أَن يَفۡقَهُوهُ وَفِيٓ ءَاذَانِهِمۡ وَقۡرٗاۖ وَإِن تَدۡعُهُمۡ إِلَى ٱلۡهُدَىٰ فَلَن يَهۡتَدُوٓاْ إِذًا أَبَدٗا

Narrated Abu Burda: That the Prophet ﷺ sent his (i.e. Abu Burda's) grandfather, Abu Musa and Mu`adh to Yemen and said to both of them "Facilitate things for the people (Be kind and lenient) and do not make things difficult (for people), and give them good tidings, and do not repulse them and both of you should obey each other." Abu Musa said, "O Allah's Prophet! In our land there is an alcoholic drink (prepared) from barley called Al-Mizr, and another (prepared) from honey, called Al-Bit"' The Prophet ﷺ said, "All intoxicants are prohibited." Then both of them proceeded and Mu`adh asked Abu Musa, "How do you recite the Qur'an?" Abu Musa replied, "I recite it while I am standing, sitting or riding my riding animals, at intervals and piecemeal." Mu`adh said, "But I sleep and then get up. I sleep and hope for Allah's Reward for my sleep as I seek His Reward for my night prayer." Then he (i.e. Mu`adh) pitched a tent and they started visiting each other. Once Mu`adh paid a visit to Abu Musa and saw a chained man. Mu`adh asked, "What is this?" Abu Musa said, "(He was) a Jew who embraced Islam and has now turned apostate." Mu`adh said, "I will surely chop off his neck!". – Sahih Al-Bukhari 4344, 4345

حَدَّثَنَا مُسْلِمٌ، حَدَّثَنَا شُعْبَةُ، حَدَّثَنَا سَعِيدُ بْنُ أَبِي بُرْدَةَ، عَنْ أَبِيهِ، قَالَ بَعَثَ النَّبِيُّ صلى الله عليه وسلم جَدَّهُ أَبَا مُوسَى، وَمُعَاذًا إِلَى الْيَمَنِ فَقَالَ " يَسِّرَا وَلاَ تُعَسِّرَا، وَبَشِّرَا وَلاَ تُنَفِّرَا، وَتَطَاوَعَا ". فَقَالَ أَبُو مُوسَى يَا نَبِيَّ اللَّهِ، إِنَّ أَرْضَنَا بِهَا شَرَابٌ مِنَ الشَّعِيرِ الْمِزْرُ، وَشَرَابٌ مِنَ الْعَسَلِ الْبِتْعُ. فَقَالَ " كُلُّ مُسْكِرٍ حَرَامٌ ". فَانْطَلَقَا فَقَالَ مُعَاذٌ لأَبِي مُوسَى كَيْفَ تَقْرَأُ الْقُرْآنَ قَالَ قَائِمًا وَقَاعِدًا وَعَلَى رَاحِلَتِهِ وَأَتَفَوَّقُهُ تَفَوُّقًا. قَالَ أَمَّا أَنَا فَأَنَامُ وَأَقُومُ، فَأَحْتَسِبُ نَوْمَتِي كَمَا أَحْتَسِبُ قَوْمَتِي، وَضَرَبَ فُسْطَاطًا، فَجَعَلاَ يَتَزَاوَرَانِ، فَزَارَ مُعَاذٌ أَبَا مُوسَى، فَإِذَا رَجُلٌ مُوثَقٌ، فَقَالَ مَا هَذَا فَقَالَ أَبُو مُوسَى يَهُودِيٌّ أَسْلَمَ ثُمَّ ارْتَدَّ. فَقَالَ مُعَاذٌ لأَضْرِبَنَّ عُنُقَهُ. تَابَعَهُ الْعَقَدِيُّ وَوَهْبٌ عَنْ شُعْبَةَ. وَقَالَ وَكِيعٌ وَالنَّضْرُ وَأَبُو دَاوُدَ عَنْ شُعْبَةَ، عَنْ سَعِيدٍ، عَنْ أَبِيهِ، عَنْ جَدِّهِ، عَنِ النَّبِيِّ صلى الله عليه وسلم. رَوَاهُ جَرِيرُ بْنُ عَبْدِ الْحَمِيدِ عَنِ الشَّيْبَانِيِّ عَنْ أَبِي بُرْدَةَ.

Narrated Anas bin Malik: A group of people from `Ukl (or `Uraina) tribe ----but I think he said that they were from `Ukl came to Medina and (they became ill, so) the Prophet ﷺ ordered them to go to the herd of (Milch) she-camels and told them to go out and drink the camels' urine and milk (as a medicine). So they went and drank it, and when they became healthy, they killed the shepherd and drove away the camels. This news reached the Prophet ﷺ early in the morning, so he sent (some) men in their pursuit and they were captured and brought to the Prophet ﷺ before midday. He ordered to cut off their hands and legs and their eyes to be branded with heated iron pieces and they were thrown at Al-Harra, and when they asked for water to drink, they were not given water. (Abu Qilaba said, "Those were the people who committed theft and murder and reverted to disbelief after being believers (Muslims), and fought against Allah and His Apostle"). – Sahih Al-Bukhari 6805

حَدَّثَنَا قُتَيْبَةُ بْنُ سَعِيدٍ، حَدَّثَنَا حَمَّادٌ، عَنْ أَيُّوبَ، عَنْ أَبِي قِلاَبَةَ، عَنْ أَنَسِ بْنِ مَالِكٍ، أَنَّ رَهْطًا، مِنْ عُكْلٍ ـ أَوْ قَالَ عُرَيْنَةَ وَلاَ أَعْلَمُهُ إِلاَّ قَالَ مِنْ عُكْلٍ ـ قَدِمُوا الْمَدِينَةَ، فَأَمَرَ لَهُمُ النَّبِيُّ صلى الله عليه وسلم بِلِقَاحٍ، وَأَمَرَهُمْ أَنْ يَخْرُجُوا فَيَشْرَبُوا مِنْ أَبْوَالِهَا وَأَلْبَانِهَا، فَشَرِبُوا حَتَّى إِذَا بَرِئُوا قَتَلُوا الرَّاعِيَ وَاسْتَاقُوا النَّعَمَ، فَبَلَغَ النَّبِيَّ صلى الله عليه وسلم غُدْوَةً فَبَعَثَ الطَّلَبَ فِي إِثْرِهِمْ، فَمَا ارْتَفَعَ النَّهَارُ حَتَّى جِيءَ بِهِمْ، فَأَمَرَ بِهِمْ فَقَطَعَ أَيْدِيَهُمْ وَأَرْجُلَهُمْ وَسَمَرَ أَعْيُنَهُمْ، فَأُلْقُوا بِالْحَرَّةِ يَسْتَسْقُونَ فَلاَ يُسْقَوْنَ. قَالَ أَبُو قِلاَبَةَ هَؤُلاَءِ قَوْمٌ سَرَقُوا، وَقَتَلُوا، وَكَفَرُوا بَعْدَ إِيمَانِهِمْ، وَحَارَبُوا اللَّهَ وَرَسُولَهُ

And Ibn Umar used to consider them (Al- Khawārij and Al-Mulhidūn) the worst of Allah's creatures and said "These people took some Verses that had been revealed concerning the disbelievers and interpreted them as describing the believers. Bukhari Vol.9 page 49

و كان ابن عمر يراهم شرار خلق الله، و قال : أنهم انطلقوا الى ايات نزلت في الكفار فخعلوها على المومنين

When the hypocrites come to you, they say, "We bear witness that you are Allah's Messenger." Allah knows that you are His Messenger, and Allah bears witness that the hypocrites are liars. They treat their oaths as a cover, and so they repel others from Allah's path. Evil is what they do. That is because they believed, and then disbelieved; so their hearts were sealed, and they cannot understand. When you see them, their appearance impresses you. And when they speak, you listen to what they say. They are like propped-up timber. They think every shout is aimed at them. They are the enemy, so beware of them. Allah condemns them; how deluded they are! And when it is said to them, "Come, the Messenger of Allah will ask forgiveness for you," they bend their heads, and you see them turning away arrogantly. It is the same for them, whether you ask forgiveness for them, or do not ask forgiveness for them; Allah will not forgive them. Allah does not guide the sinful people. - Surah Al-Munafiqun 63:1-6

إِذَا جَآءَكَ ٱلْمُنَـٰفِقُونَ قَالُوا۟ نَشْهَدُ إِنَّكَ لَرَسُولُ ٱللَّهِ ۗ وَٱللَّهُ يَعْلَمُ إِنَّكَ لَرَسُولُهُۥ وَٱللَّهُ يَشْهَدُ إِنَّ ٱلْمُنَـٰفِقِينَ لَكَـٰذِبُونَ ٱتَّخَذُوٓا۟ أَيْمَـٰنَهُمْ جُنَّةً فَصَدُّوا۟ عَن سَبِيلِ ٱللَّهِ ۚ إِنَّهُمْ سَآءَ مَا كَانُوا۟ يَعْمَلُونَ ذَٰلِكَ بِأَنَّهُمْ ءَامَنُوا۟ ثُمَّ كَفَرُوا۟ فَطُبِعَ عَلَىٰ قُلُوبِهِمْ فَهُمْ لَا يَفْقَهُونَ وَإِذَا رَأَيْتَهُمْ تُعْجِبُكَ أَجْسَامُهُمْ ۖ وَإِن يَقُولُوا۟ تَسْمَعْ لِقَوْلِهِمْ ۖ كَأَنَّهُمْ خُشُبٌ مُّسَنَّدَةٌ ۖ يَحْسَبُونَ كُلَّ صَيْحَةٍ عَلَيْهِمْ ۚ هُمُ ٱلْعَدُوُّ فَٱحْذَرْهُمْ ۚ قَـٰتَلَهُمُ ٱللَّهُ ۖ أَنَّىٰ يُؤْفَكُونَ وَإِذَا قِيلَ لَهُمْ تَعَالَوْا۟ يَسْتَغْفِرْ لَكُمْ رَسُولُ ٱللَّهِ لَوَّوْا۟ رُءُوسَهُمْ وَرَأَيْتَهُمْ يَصُدُّونَ وَهُم مُّسْتَكْبِرُونَ سَوَآءٌ عَلَيْهِمْ أَسْتَغْفَرْتَ لَهُمْ أَمْ لَمْ تَسْتَغْفِرْ لَهُمْ لَن يَغْفِرَ ٱللَّهُ لَهُمْ ۚ إِنَّ ٱللَّهَ لَا يَهْدِى ٱلْقَوْمَ ٱلْفَـٰسِقِينَ

The Book of
Al-Harariyya
الْحَرُورِيَّة

Narrated `Abdullah bin `Amr bin Yasar: That they visited Abu Sa`id Al-Khudri and asked him about Al-Harauriyya, a special unorthodox religious sect, “Did you hear the Prophetﷺ saying anything about them?” Abu Sa`id said, “I do not know what Al-Harauriyya is, but I heard the Prophetﷺ saying, “There will appear in this nation---- he did not say: From this nation ---- a group of people so pious apparently that you will consider your prayers inferior to their prayers, but they will recite the Qur’an, the teachings of which will not go beyond their throats and will go out of their religion as an arrow darts through the game, whereupon the archer may look at his arrow, its Nasl at its Risaf and its Fuqa to see whether it is blood-stained or not (i.e. they will have not even a trace of Islam in them). – Sahih Al-Bukhari 6931

حَدَّثَنَا مُحَمَّدُ بْنُ الْمُثَنَّى، حَدَّثَنَا عَبْدُ الْوَهَّابِ، قَالَ سَمِعْتُ يَحْيَى بْنَ سَعِيدٍ، قَالَ أَخْبَرَنِي مُحَمَّدُ بْنُ إِبْرَاهِيمَ، عَنْ أَبِي سَلَمَةَ، وَعَطَاءِ بْنِ يَسَارٍ، أَنَّهُمَا أَتَيَا أَبَا سَعِيدٍ الْخُدْرِيَّ فَسَأَلاَهُ عَنِ الْحَرُورِيَّةِ، أَسَمِعْتَ النَّبِيَّ صلى الله عليه وسلم. قَالَ لاَ أَدْرِي مَا الْحَرُورِيَّةُ سَمِعْتُ النَّبِيَّ صلى الله عليه وسلم يَقُولُ " يَخْرُجُ فِي هَذِهِ الأُمَّةِ - وَلَمْ يَقُلْ مِنْهَا - قَوْمٌ تَحْقِرُونَ صَلاَتَكُمْ مَعَ صَلاَتِهِمْ، يَقْرَءُونَ الْقُرْآنَ لاَ يُجَاوِزُ حُلُوقَهُمْ - أَوْ حَنَاجِرَهُمْ - يَمْرُقُونَ مِنَ الدِّينِ مُرُوقَ السَّهْمِ مِنَ الرَّمِيَّةِ، فَيَنْظُرُ الرَّامِي إِلَى سَهْمِهِ إِلَى نَصْلِهِ إِلَى رِصَافِهِ، فَيَتَمَارَى فِي الْفُوقَةِ، هَلْ عَلِقَ بِهَا مِنَ الدَّمِ شَىْءٌ "

Narrated Mus`ab: I asked my father, “Was the Verse:-- ‘Say: (O Muhammad) Shall We tell you the greatest losers in respect of their deeds?’(18.103) revealed regarding Al-Haruriyya?” He said, “No, but regarding the Jews and the Christians, for the Jews disbelieved Muhammad and the Christians disbelieved in Paradise and say that there are neither meals nor drinks therein. Al- Hururiyya are those people who break their pledge to Allah after they have confirmed that they will fulfill it, and Sa`d used to call them ‘Al-Fasiqin (evildoers who forsake Allah’s obedience). – Sahih Al-Bukhari 4728

حَدَّثَنِي مُحَمَّدُ بْنُ بَشَّارٍ، حَدَّثَنَا مُحَمَّدُ بْنُ جَعْفَرٍ، حَدَّثَنَا شُعْبَةُ، عَنْ عَمْرٍو، عَنْ مُصْعَبٍ، قَالَ سَأَلْتُ أَبِي {قُلْ هَلْ نُنَبِّئُكُمْ بِالأَخْسَرِينَ أَعْمَالاً} هُمُ الْحَرُورِيَّةُ قَالَ لاَ، هُمُ الْيَهُودُ وَالنَّصَارَى، أَمَّا الْيَهُودُ فَكَذَّبُوا مُحَمَّدًا صلى الله عليه وسلم وَأَمَّا النَّصَارَى كَفَرُوا بِالْجَنَّةِ وَقَالُوا لاَ طَعَامَ فِيهَا وَلاَ شَرَابَ، وَالْحَرُورِيَّةُ الَّذِينَ يَنْقُضُونَ عَهْدَ اللَّهِ مِنْ بَعْدِ مِيثَاقِهِ، وَكَانَ سَعْدٌ يُسَمِّيهِمُ الْفَاسِقِينَ

Narrated `Abdullah bin `Umar: Regarding Al-Harauriyya: The Prophetﷺ said, “They will go out of Islam as an arrow darts out of the game’s body.’. – Sahih Al-Bukhari 6932

حَدَّثَنَا يَحْيَى بْنُ سُلَيْمَانُ، حَدَّثَنِي ابْنُ وَهْبٍ، قَالَ حَدَّثَنِي عُمَرُ، أَنَّ أَبَاهُ، حَدَّثَهُ عَنْ عَبْدِ اللَّهِ بْنِ عُمَرَ - وَذَكَرَ الْحَرُورِيَّةَ - فَقَالَ قَالَ النَّبِيُّ صلى الله عليه وسلم " يَمْرُقُونَ مِنَ الإِسْلاَمِ مُرُوقَ السَّهْمِ مِنَ الرَّمِيَّةِ ".

Narrated Al-Azraq bin Qais: We were at Al-Ahwaz fighting the Al-Haruriya (tribe). While I was at the bank of a river a man was praying and the reins of his animal were in his hands and the animal was struggling and he was following the animal. (Shu`ba, a sub-narrator, said that man was Abu Barza Al-Aslami). A man from the Khawarij said, “O Allah! Be harsh to this sheik.” And when the sheik (Abu Barza) finished his prayer, he said, "I heard your remark. No doubt, I participated with Allah’s Messengerﷺ in six or seven or eight holy battles and saw his leniency, and no doubt, I would rather retain my animal than let it return to its stable, as it would cause me much trouble. “. – Sahih Al-Bukhari 1211

حَدَّثَنَا آدَمُ، حَدَّثَنَا شُعْبَةُ، حَدَّثَنَا الأَزْرَقُ بْنُ قَيْسٍ، قَالَ كُنَّا بِالأَهْوَازِ نُقَاتِلُ الْحَرُورِيَّةَ، فَبَيْنَا أَنَا عَلَى جُرُفِ نَهَرٍ إِذَا رَجُلٌ يُصَلِّي، وَإِذَا لِجَامُ دَابَّتِهِ بِيَدِهِ فَجَعَلَتِ الدَّابَّةُ تُنَازِعُهُ، وَجَعَلَ يَتْبَعُهَا - قَالَ شُعْبَةُ - هُوَ أَبُو بَرْزَةَ الأَسْلَمِيُّ - فَجَعَلَ رَجُلٌ مِنَ الْخَوَارِجِ يَقُولُ اللَّهُمَّ افْعَلْ بِهَذَا الشَّيْخِ. فَلَمَّا انْصَرَفَ الشَّيْخُ قَالَ إِنِّي سَمِعْتُ قَوْلَكُمْ، وَإِنِّي غَزَوْتُ مَعَ رَسُولِ اللَّهِ صلى الله

عليه وسلم سِتَّ غَزَوَاتٍ أَوْ سَبْعَ غَزَوَاتٍ وَثَمَانِيًا، وَشَهِدْتُ تَيْسِيرَهُ، وَإِنِّي أَنْ كُنْتُ أَنْ أُرَاجِعَ مَعَ دَابَّتِي أَحَبُّ إِلَيَّ مِنْ أَنْ أَدَعَهَا تَرْجِعُ إِلَى مَأْلَفِهَا فَيَشُقُّ عَلَيَّ.

Narrated Salim Abu An-Nadr: (the freed slave of 'Umar bin 'Ubaidullah) I was Umar's clerk. Once Abdullah bin Abi Aufa wrote a letter to 'Umar when he proceeded to Al-Haruriya. I read in it that Allah's Messenger ﷺ in one of his military expeditions against the enemy, waited till the sun declined and then he got up amongst the people saying, "O people! Do not wish to meet the enemy, and ask Allah for safety, but when you face the enemy, be patient, and remember that Paradise is under the shades of swords." Then he said, "O Allah, the Revealer of the Holy Book, and the Mover of the clouds and the Defeater of the clans, defeat them, and grant us victory over them.". – Sahih Al-Bukhari 3024, 3025

حَدَّثَنَا يُوسُفُ بْنُ مُوسَى، حَدَّثَنَا عَاصِمُ بْنُ يُوسُفَ الْيَرْبُوعِيُّ، حَدَّثَنَا أَبُو إِسْحَاقَ الْفَزَارِيُّ، عَنْ مُوسَى بْنِ عُقْبَةَ، قَالَ حَدَّثَنِي سَالِمٌ أَبُو النَّضْرِ، مَوْلَى عُمَرَ بْنِ عُبَيْدِ اللَّهِ كُنْتُ كَاتِبًا لَهُ قَالَ كَتَبَ إِلَيْهِ عَبْدُ اللَّهِ بْنُ أَبِي أَوْفَى حِينَ خَرَجَ إِلَى الْحَرُورِيَّةِ فَقَرَأْتُهُ فَإِذَا فِيهِ إِنَّ رَسُولَ اللَّهِ صلى الله عليه وسلم فِي بَعْضِ أَيَّامِهِ الَّتِي لَقِيَ فِيهَا الْعَدُوَّ انْتَظَرَ حَتَّى مَالَتِ الشَّمْسُ. ثُمَّ قَامَ فِي النَّاسِ فَقَالَ " أَيُّهَا النَّاسُ لاَ تَمَنَّوْا لِقَاءَ الْعَدُوِّ وَسَلُوا اللَّهَ الْعَافِيَةَ، فَإِذَا لَقِيتُمُوهُمْ فَاصْبِرُوا وَاعْلَمُوا أَنَّ الْجَنَّةَ تَحْتَ ظِلاَلِ السُّيُوفِ ـ ثُمَّ قَالَ ـ اللَّهُمَّ مُنْزِلَ الْكِتَابِ وَمُجْرِيَ السَّحَابِ وَهَازِمَ الأَحْزَابِ اهْزِمْهُمْ وَانْصُرْنَا عَلَيْهِمْ ". وَقَالَ مُوسَى بْنُ عُقْبَةَ حَدَّثَنِي سَالِمٌ أَبُو النَّضْرِ كُنْتُ كَاتِبًا لِعُمَرَ بْنِ عُبَيْدِ اللَّهِ فَأَتَاهُ كِتَابُ عَبْدِ اللَّهِ بْنِ أَبِي أَوْفَى ـ رضى الله عنهما أَنَّ رَسُولَ اللَّهِ صلى الله عليه وسلم قَالَ " لاَ تَمَنَّوْا لِقَاءَ الْعَدُوِّ ".

The Book of
Al-Qurra
الْقُرَّاءِ

Narrated Hammam: Hudhaifa said, "O the Group of Al-Qurra! Follow the straight path, for then you have taken a great lead (and will be the leaders), but if you divert right or left, then you will go astray far away.". – Sahih Al-Bukhari 7282

حَدَّثَنَا أَبُو نُعَيْمٍ، حَدَّثَنَا سُفْيَانُ، عَنِ الأَعْمَشِ، عَنْ إِبْرَاهِيمَ، عَنْ هَمَّامٍ، عَنْ حُذَيْفَةَ، قَالَ يَا مَعْشَرَ الْقُرَّاءِ اسْتَقِيمُوا فَقَدْ سُبِقْتُمْ سَبْقًا بَعِيدًا فَإِنْ أَخَذْتُمْ يَمِينًا وَشِمَالاً، لَقَدْ ضَلَلْتُمْ ضَلاَلاً بَعِيدًا

Narrated `Abdullah bin `Abbas: Uyaina bin Hisn bin Hudhaifa bin Badr came and stayed (at Medina) with his nephew Al-Hurr bin Qais bin Hisn who was one of those whom `Umar used to keep near him, as the Qurra' (learned men knowing Qur'an by heart) were the people of `Umar's meetings and his advisors whether they were old or young. 'Uyaina said to his nephew, "O my nephew! Have you an approach to this chief so as to get for me the permission to see him?" His nephew said, "I will get the permission for you to see him." (Ibn `Abbas added: ) So he took the permission for 'Uyaina, and when the latter entered, he said, "O the son of Al-Khattab! By Allah, you neither give us sufficient provision nor judge among us with justice." On that `Umar became so furious that he intended to harm him. Al-Hurr, said, "O Chief of the Believers!" Allah said to His Apostle 'Hold to forgiveness, command what is good (right), and leave the foolish (i.e. do not punish them).' (7.199) and this person is among the foolish." By Allah, `Umar did not overlook that Verse when Al-Hurr recited it before him, and `Umar said to observe (the orders of) Allah's Book strictly." (See Hadith No. 166, Vol. 6). – Sahih Al-Bukhari 7286

حَدَّثَنِي إِسْمَاعِيلُ، حَدَّثَنِي ابْنُ وَهْبٍ، عَنْ يُونُسَ، عَنِ ابْنِ شِهَابٍ، حَدَّثَنِي عُبَيْدُ اللَّهِ بْنُ عَبْدِ اللَّهِ بْنِ عُتْبَةَ، أَنَّ عَبْدَ اللَّهِ بْنَ عَبَّاسٍ ـ رضى الله عنهما ـ قَالَ قَدِمَ عُيَيْنَةُ بْنُ حِصْنِ بْنِ حُذَيْفَةَ بْنِ بَدْرٍ فَنَزَلَ عَلَى ابْنِ أَخِيهِ الْحُرِّ بْنِ قَيْسِ بْنِ حِصْنٍ، وَكَانَ مِنَ النَّفَرِ الَّذِينَ يُدْنِيهِمْ عُمَرُ، وَكَانَ الْقُرَّاءُ أَصْحَابَ مَجْلِسِ عُمَرَ وَمُشَاوَرَتِهِ كُهُولاً كَانُوا أَوْ شُبَّانًا فَقَالَ عُيَيْنَةُ لاِبْنِ أَخِيهِ يَا ابْنَ أَخِي هَلْ لَكَ وَجْهٌ عِنْدَ هَذَا الأَمِيرِ فَتَسْتَأْذِنَ لِي عَلَيْهِ قَالَ سَأَسْتَأْذِنُ لَكَ عَلَيْهِ. قَالَ ابْنُ عَبَّاسٍ فَاسْتَأْذَنَ لِعُيَيْنَةَ فَلَمَّا دَخَلَ قَالَ يَا ابْنَ الْخَطَّابِ وَاللَّهِ مَا تُعْطِينَا الْجَزْلَ، وَمَا تَحْكُمُ بَيْنَنَا بِالْعَدْلِ. فَغَضِبَ عُمَرُ حَتَّى هَمَّ بِأَنْ يَقَعَ بِهِ فَقَالَ الْحُرُّ يَا أَمِيرَ الْمُؤْمِنِينَ إِنَّ اللَّهَ تَعَالَى قَالَ لِنَبِيِّهِ صلى الله عليه وسلم {خُذِ الْعَفْوَ وَأْمُرْ بِالْعُرْفِ وَأَعْرِضْ عَنِ الْجَاهِلِينَ} وَإِنَّ هَذَا مِنَ الْجَاهِلِينَ. فَوَاللَّهِ مَا جَاوَزَهَا عُمَرُ حِينَ تَلاَهَا عَلَيْهِ، وَكَانَ وَقَّافًا عِنْدَ كِتَابِ اللَّهِ

Narrated Anas: When the reciters of Qur'an were martyred, Allah's Messenger ﷺ recited Qunut for one month and I never saw him (i.e. Allah's Messenger ﷺ so sad as he was on that day. – Sahih Al-Bukhari 1300

حَدَّثَنَا عَمْرُو بْنُ عَلِيٍّ، حَدَّثَنَا مُحَمَّدُ بْنُ فُضَيْلٍ، حَدَّثَنَا عَاصِمٌ الأَحْوَلُ، عَنْ أَنَسٍ ـ رضى الله عنه ـ قَالَ قَنَتَ رَسُولُ اللَّهِ صلى الله عليه وسلم شَهْرًا حِينَ قُتِلَ الْقُرَّاءُ، فَمَا رَأَيْتُ رَسُولَ اللَّهِ صلى الله عليه وسلم حَزِنَ حُزْنًا قَطُّ أَشَدَّ مِنْهُ.

Narrated `Ali: We have nothing except the Book of Allah and this written paper from the Prophet (wherein is written:)Medina is a sanctuary from the 'Air Mountain to such and such a place, and whoever innovates in it an heresy or commits a sin, or gives shelter to such an innovator in it will incur the curse of Allah, the angels, and all the people, none of his compulsory or optional good deeds of worship will be accepted. And the asylum (of protection) granted by any Muslim is to be secured (respected) by all the other Muslims; and whoever betrays a Muslim in this respect incurs the curse of Allah, the angels, and all the people, and none of his compulsory or optional good deeds of worship will be accepted, and whoever (freed slave) befriends (take as masters) other than his manumitters without their permission incurs the curse of Allah, the angels, and all the people, and none of his compulsory or optional good deeds of worship will be accepted. – Sahih Al-Bukhari 1870

حَدَّثَنَا مُحَمَّدُ بْنُ بَشَّارٍ، حَدَّثَنَا عَبْدُ الرَّحْمَنِ، حَدَّثَنَا سُفْيَانُ، عَنِ الأَعْمَشِ، عَنْ إِبْرَاهِيمَ التَّيْمِيِّ، عَنْ أَبِيهِ، عَنْ عَلِيٍّ ـ رضى الله عنه ـ قَالَ مَا عِنْدَنَا شَىْءٌ إِلاَّ كِتَابُ اللَّهِ، وَهَذِهِ الصَّحِيفَةُ عَنِ النَّبِيِّ صلى الله عليه وسلم " الْمَدِينَةُ حَرَمٌ، مَا بَيْنَ عَائِرٍ إِلَى كَذَا، مَنْ أَحْدَثَ فِيهَا حَدَثًا، أَوْ آوَى مُحْدِثًا، فَعَلَيْهِ لَعْنَةُ اللَّهِ وَالْمَلاَئِكَةِ وَالنَّاسِ أَجْمَعِينَ، لاَ يُقْبَلُ مِنْهُ صَرْفٌ وَلاَ عَدْلٌ ". وَقَالَ " ذِمَّةُ الْمُسْلِمِينَ وَاحِدَةٌ، فَمَنْ أَخْفَرَ مُسْلِمًا فَعَلَيْهِ لَعْنَةُ اللَّهِ وَالْمَلاَئِكَةِ وَالنَّاسِ أَجْمَعِينَ، لاَ يُقْبَلُ مِنْهُ صَرْفٌ وَلاَ عَدْلٌ، وَمَنْ تَوَلَّى قَوْمًا بِغَيْرِ إِذْنِ مَوَالِيهِ، فَعَلَيْهِ لَعْنَةُ اللَّهِ وَالْمَلاَئِكَةِ وَالنَّاسِ أَجْمَعِينَ، لاَ يُقْبَلُ مِنْهُ صَرْفٌ وَلاَ عَدْلٌ ".

Narrated Abu Musa Al-Ash`ari: I came to the Prophet ﷺ at Al-Batha' while his camel was kneeling down and he asked me, "Have you intended to perform the Hajj?" I replied in the affirmative. He asked me, 'With what intention have you assumed Ihram?" I replied, "I have assumed Ihram with the same intention as that of the Prophet. He said, "You have done well. Perform the Tawaf of the Ka`ba and (the Sai) between As-Safa and Al- Marwa and then finish the Ihram." So, I performed the Tawaf around the Ka`ba and the Sai) between As-Safa and Al-Marwa and then went to a woman of the tribe of Qais who cleaned my head from lice. Later I assumed the Ihram for Hajj. I used to give the verdict of doing the same till the caliphate of `Umar who said, "If you follow the Holy Book then it orders you to remain in the state of Ihram till you finish from Hajj, if you follow the Prophet ﷺ then he did not finish his Ihram till the Hadi (sacrifice) had reached its place of slaughtering (Hajj-al-Qiran). – Sahih Al-Bukhari 1795

حَدَّثَنَا مُحَمَّدُ بْنُ بَشَّارٍ، حَدَّثَنَا غُنْدَرٌ، حَدَّثَنَا شُعْبَةُ، عَنْ قَيْسِ بْنِ مُسْلِمٍ، عَنْ طَارِقِ بْنِ شِهَابٍ، عَنْ أَبِي مُوسَى الأَشْعَرِيِّ ـ رضى الله عنه ـ قَالَ قَدِمْتُ عَلَى النَّبِيِّ صلى الله عليه وسلم بِالْبَطْحَاءِ وَهُوَ مُنِيخٌ فَقَالَ " أَحَجَجْتَ ". قُلْتُ نَعَمْ. قَالَ " بِمَا أَهْلَلْتَ ". قُلْتُ لَبَّيْكَ بِإِهْلاَلٍ كَإِهْلاَلِ النَّبِيِّ صلى الله عليه وسلم قَالَ " أَحْسَنْتَ. طُفْ بِالْبَيْتِ وَبِالصَّفَا وَالْمَرْوَةِ ثُمَّ أَحِلَّ ". فَطُفْتُ بِالْبَيْتِ، وَبِالصَّفَا وَالْمَرْوَةِ، ثُمَّ أَتَيْتُ امْرَأَةً مِنْ قَيْسٍ، فَفَلَتْ رَأْسِي، ثُمَّ أَهْلَلْتُ بِالْحَجِّ. فَكُنْتُ أُفْتِي بِهِ، حَتَّى كَانَ فِي خِلاَفَةِ عُمَرَ فَقَالَ إِنْ أَخَذْنَا بِكِتَابِ اللَّهِ فَإِنَّهُ يَأْمُرُنَا بِالتَّمَامِ، وَإِنْ أَخَذْنَا بِقَوْلِ النَّبِيِّ صلى الله عليه وسلم فَإِنَّهُ لَمْ يَحِلَّ حَتَّى يَبْلُغَ الْهَدْىُ مَحِلَّهُ

Narrated Abu Huraira: Allah's Messenger ﷺ said, "Not to wish to be the like except of two men. A man whom Allah has given the (knowledge of the) Qur'an and he recites it during the hours of night and day and the one who wishes says: If I were given the same as this (man) has been given, I would do what he does, and a man whom Allah has given wealth and he spends it in the just and right way, in which case the one who wishes says, 'If I were given the same as he has been given, I would do what he does.' " (See Hadith 5025 and 5026). – Sahih Al-Bukhari 7232

حَدَّثَنَا عُثْمَانُ بْنُ أَبِي شَيْبَةَ، حَدَّثَنَا جَرِيرٌ، عَنِ الأَعْمَشِ، عَنْ أَبِي صَالِحٍ، عَنْ أَبِي هُرَيْرَةَ، قَالَ قَالَ رَسُولُ اللَّهِ صلى الله عليه وسلم " لاَ تَحَاسُدَ إِلاَّ فِي اثْنَتَيْنِ رَجُلٌ آتَاهُ اللَّهُ الْقُرْآنَ، فَهُوَ يَتْلُوهُ آنَاءَ اللَّيْلِ وَالنَّهَارِ يَقُولُ لَوْ أُوتِيتُ مِثْلَ مَا أُوتِيَ هَذَا لَفَعَلْتُ كَمَا يَفْعَلُ، وَرَجُلٌ آتَاهُ اللَّهُ مَالاً يُنْفِقُهُ فِي حَقِّهِ فَيَقُولُ لَوْ أُوتِيتُ مِثْلَ مَا أُوتِيَ لَفَعَلْتُ كَمَا يَفْعَلُ ".
حَدَّثَنَا قُتَيْبَةُ، حَدَّثَنَا جَرِيرٌ، بِهَذَا.

How many a prophet fought alongside him numerous godly people? They did not waver for what afflicted them in the cause of Allah, nor did they weaken, nor did they give in. Allah loves those who endure.– Surah Al-Imran 3:146

وَكَأَيِّن مِّن نَّبِيٍّ قَـٰتَلَ مَعَهُۥ رِبِّيُّونَ كَثِيرٌ فَمَا وَهَنُوا۟ لِمَآ أَصَابَهُمْ فِى سَبِيلِ ٱللَّهِ وَمَا ضَعُفُوا۟ وَمَا ٱسْتَكَانُوا۟ ۗ وَٱللَّهُ يُحِبُّ ٱلصَّـٰبِرِينَ

Narrated `Abdul `Aziz: Anas said, "The Prophet ﷺ sent seventy men, called Al-Qurra 'for some purpose. The two groups of Bani Sulaim called Ri'l and Dhakwan, appeared to them near a well called Bir Ma'una. The people (i.e. Al- Qurra) said, 'By Allah, we have not come to harm you, but we are passing by you on our way to do something for the Prophet.' But (the infidels) killed them. The Prophet ﷺ therefore invoked evil upon them for a month during the morning prayer. That was the beginning of Al Qunut and we used not to say Qunut before that." A man asked Anas about Al-Qunut, "Is it to be said after the Bowing (in the prayer) or after finishing the Recitation (i.e. before Bowing)?" Anas replied, "No, but (it is to be said) after finishing the Recitation.". – Sahih Al-Bukhari 4088

حَدَّثَنَا أَبُو مَعْمَرٍ، حَدَّثَنَا عَبْدُ الْوَارِثِ، حَدَّثَنَا عَبْدُ الْعَزِيزِ، عَنْ أَنَسٍ ـ رضى الله عنه ـ قَالَ بَعَثَ النَّبِيُّ صلى الله عليه وسلم سَبْعِينَ رَجُلاً لِحَاجَةٍ يُقَالُ لَهُمُ الْقُرَّاءُ، فَعَرَضَ لَهُمْ حَيَّانِ مِنْ بَنِي سُلَيْمٍ رِعْلٌ وَذَكْوَانُ، عِنْدَ بِئْرٍ يُقَالُ لَهَا بِئْرُ مَعُونَةَ، فَقَالَ الْقَوْمُ وَاللَّهِ مَا إِيَّاكُمْ أَرَدْنَا، إِنَّمَا نَحْنُ مُجْتَازُونَ فِي حَاجَةٍ لِلنَّبِيِّ صلى الله عليه وسلم، فَقَتَلُوهُمْ فَدَعَا النَّبِيُّ صلى الله عليه وسلم عَلَيْهِمْ شَهْرًا فِي صَلاَةِ الْغَدَاةِ، وَذَلِكَ بَدْءُ الْقُنُوتِ وَمَا كُنَّا نَقْنُتُ. قَالَ عَبْدُ الْعَزِيزِ وَسَأَلَ رَجُلٌ أَنَسًا عَنِ الْقُنُوتِ أَبَعْدَ الرُّكُوعِ، أَوْ عِنْدَ فَرَاغٍ مِنَ الْقِرَاءَةِ قَالَ لاَ بَلْ عِنْدَ فَرَاغٍ مِنَ الْقِرَاءَةِ

Narrated Anas: The Prophet ﷺ sent a Sariya (an army detachment) consisting of men called Al-Qurra', and all of them were martyred. I had never seen the Prophet ﷺ so sad over anything as he was over them. So he said Qunut (invocation in the prayer) for one month in the Fajr prayer, invoking for Allah's wrath upon the tribe of 'Usaiya, and he used to say, "The people of 'Usaiya have disobeyed Allah and His Apostle.". – Sahih Al-Bukhari 6394

حَدَّثَنَا الْحَسَنُ بْنُ الرَّبِيعِ، حَدَّثَنَا أَبُو الأَحْوَصِ، عَنْ عَاصِمٍ، عَنْ أَنَسٍ ـ رضى الله عنه ـ قَالَ بَعَثَ النَّبِيُّ صلى الله عليه وسلم سَرِيَّةً يُقَالُ لَهُمُ الْقُرَّاءُ فَأُصِيبُوا، فَمَا رَأَيْتُ النَّبِيَّ صلى الله عليه وسلم وَجَدَ عَلَى شَىْءٍ مَا وَجَدَ عَلَيْهِمْ، فَقَنَتَ شَهْرًا فِي صَلاَةِ الْفَجْرِ وَيَقُولُ " إِنَّ عُصَيَّةَ عَصَوُا اللَّهَ وَرَسُولَهُ "

Narrated `Asim Al-Ahwal: I asked Anas bin Malik regarding Al-Qunut during the prayer. Anas replied, "Yes (Al-Qunut was said by the Prophet ﷺ in the prayer)." I said, "Is it before Bowing or after Bowing?" Anas replied, "(It was said) before (Bowing)." I said, "So-and-so informed me that you told him that it was said after Bowing." Anas replied, "He was mistaken, for Allah's Messenger ﷺ said Al-Qunut after Bowing for one month. The Prophet ﷺ had sent some people called Al-Qurra who were seventy in number, to some pagan people who had concluded a peace treaty with Allah's Messenger ﷺ. But those who had concluded the treaty with Allah's Messenger ﷺ violated the treaty (and martyred all the seventy men). So Allah's Apostle said Al-Qunut after Bowing (in the prayer) for one month, invoking evil upon them. – Sahih Al-Bukhari 4096

حَدَّثَنَا مُوسَى بْنُ إِسْمَاعِيلَ، حَدَّثَنَا عَبْدُ الْوَاحِدِ، حَدَّثَنَا عَاصِمٌ الأَحْوَلُ، قَالَ سَأَلْتُ أَنَسَ بْنَ مَالِكٍ ـ رضى الله عنه ـ عَنِ الْقُنُوتِ، فِي الصَّلاَةِ فَقَالَ نَعَمْ. فَقُلْتُ كَانَ قَبْلَ الرُّكُوعِ أَوْ بَعْدَهُ قَالَ قَبْلَهُ. قُلْتُ فَإِنَّ فُلاَنًا أَخْبَرَنِي عَنْكَ أَنَّكَ قُلْتَ بَعْدَهُ، قَالَ كَذَبَ إِنَّمَا قَنَتَ رَسُولُ اللَّهِ صلى الله عليه وسلم بَعْدَ الرُّكُوعِ شَهْرًا، أَنَّهُ كَانَ بَعَثَ نَاسًا يُقَالُ لَهُمُ الْقُرَّاءُ، وَهُمْ سَبْعُونَ رَجُلاً إِلَى نَاسٍ مِنَ الْمُشْرِكِينَ، وَبَيْنَهُمْ وَبَيْنَ رَسُولِ اللَّهِ صلى الله عليه وسلم عَهْدٌ قِبَلَهُمْ، فَظَهَرَ هَؤُلاَءِ الَّذِينَ كَانَ بَيْنَهُمْ وَبَيْنَ رَسُولِ اللَّهِ صلى الله عليه وسلم عَهْدٌ، فَقَنَتَ رَسُولُ اللَّهِ صلى الله عليه وسلم بَعْدَ الرُّكُوعِ شَهْرًا يَدْعُو عَلَيْهِمْ

The Book of
As-Suffa
الصُّفَّةِ

Narrated Abu Huraira: By Allah except Whom none has the right to- be worshipped, (sometimes) I used to lay (sleep) on the ground on my liver (abdomen) because of hunger, and (sometimes) I used to bind a stone over my belly because of hunger. One day I sat by the way from where they (the Prophetﷺ and his companions) used to come out. When Abu Bakr passed by, I asked him about a Verse from Allah's Book and I asked him only that he might satisfy my hunger, but he passed by and did not do so. Then `Umar passed by me and I asked him about a Verse from Allah's Book, and I asked him only that he might satisfy my hunger, but he passed by without doing so. Finally Abu-l-Qasim (the Prophetﷺ) passed by me and he smiled when he saw me, for he knew what was in my heart and on my face. He said, "O Aba Hirr (Abu Huraira)!" I replied, "Labbaik, O Allah's Messengerﷺ!" He said to me, "Follow me." He left and I followed him. Then he entered the house and I asked permission to enter and was admitted. He found milk in a bowl and said, "From where is this milk?" They said, "It has been presented to you by such-and-such man (or by such and such woman)." He said, "O Aba Hirr!" I said, "Labbaik, O Allah's Messengerﷺ!" He said, "Go and call the people of Suffa to me." These people of Suffa were the guests of Islam who had no families, nor money, nor anybody to depend upon, and whenever an object of charity was brought to the Prophet, he would send it to them and would not take anything from It, and whenever any present was given to him, he used to send some for them and take some of it for himself. The order of the Prophet upset me, and I said to myself, "How will this little milk be enough for the people of As- Suffa? Though I was more entitled to drink from that milk in order to strengthen myself", but behold! The Prophetﷺ came to order me to give that milk to them. I wondered what will remain of that milk for me, but anyway, I could not but obey Allah and His Apostle so I went to the people of As-Suffa and called them, and they came and asked the Prophet's permission to enter. They were admitted and took their seats in the house. The Prophet said, "O Aba-Hirr!" I said, "Labbaik, O Allah's Messengerﷺ!" He said, "Take it and give it to them." So I took the bowl (of milk) and started giving it to one man who would drink his fill and return it to me, whereupon I would give it to another man who, in his turn, would drink his fill and return it to me, and I would then offer it to another man who would drink his fill and return it to me. Finally, after the whole group had drunk their fill, I reached the Prophetﷺ who took the bowl and put it on his hand, looked at me and smiled and said. "O Aba Hirr!" I replied, "Labbaik, O Allah's Messengerﷺ!" He said, "There remain you and I." I said, "You have said the truth, O Allah's Messengerﷺ!" He said, "Sit down and drink." I sat down and drank. He said, "Drink," and I drank. He kept on telling me repeatedly to drink, till I said, "No. by Allah Who sent you with the Truth, I have no space for it (in my stomach)." He said, "Hand it over to me." When I gave him the bowl, he praised Allah and pronounced Allah's Name on it and drank the remaining milk. – Sahih Al-Bukhari 6452

حَدَّثَنِي أَبُو نُعَيْمٍ، بِنَحْوٍ مِنْ نِصْفِ هَذَا الْحَدِيثِ حَدَّثَنَا عُمَرُ بْنُ ذَرٍّ، حَدَّثَنَا مُجَاهِدٌ، أَنَّ أَبَا هُرَيْرَةَ، كَانَ يَقُولُ آللَّهِ الَّذِي لاَ إِلَهَ إِلاَّ هُوَ إِنْ كُنْتُ لأَعْتَمِدُ بِكَبِدِي عَلَى الأَرْضِ مِنَ الْجُوعِ، وَإِنْ كُنْتُ لأَشُدُّ الْحَجَرَ عَلَى بَطْنِي مِنَ الْجُوعِ، وَلَقَدْ قَعَدْتُ يَوْمًا عَلَى طَرِيقِهِمُ الَّذِي يَخْرُجُونَ مِنْهُ، فَمَرَّ أَبُو بَكْرٍ، فَسَأَلْتُهُ عَنْ آيَةٍ مِنْ كِتَابِ اللَّهِ، مَا سَأَلْتُهُ إِلاَّ لِيُشْبِعَنِي، فَمَرَّ وَلَمْ يَفْعَلْ، ثُمَّ مَرَّ بِي عُمَرُ فَسَأَلْتُهُ عَنْ آيَةٍ مِنْ كِتَابِ اللَّهِ، مَا سَأَلْتُهُ إِلاَّ لِيُشْبِعَنِي، فَمَرَّ فَلَمْ يَفْعَلْ، ثُمَّ مَرَّ بِي أَبُو الْقَاسِمِ صلى الله عليه وسلم فَتَبَسَّمَ حِينَ رَآنِي وَعَرَفَ، مَا فِي نَفْسِي وَمَا فِي وَجْهِي ثُمَّ قَالَ " أَبَا هِرٍّ ". قُلْتُ لَبَّيْكَ يَا رَسُولَ اللَّهِ. قَالَ " الْحَقْ ". وَمَضَى فَتَبِعْتُهُ، فَدَخَلَ فَاسْتَأْذَنَ، فَأَذِنَ لِي، فَدَخَلَ فَوَجَدَ لَبَنًا فِي قَدَحٍ فَقَالَ " مِنْ أَيْنَ هَذَا اللَّبَنُ ". قَالُوا أَهْدَاهُ لَكَ فُلاَنٌ أَوْ فُلاَنَةُ. قَالَ " أَبَا هِرٍّ ". قُلْتُ لَبَّيْكَ يَا رَسُولَ اللَّهِ. قَالَ " الْحَقْ إِلَى أَهْلِ الصُّفَّةِ فَادْعُهُمْ لِي ". قَالَ وَأَهْلُ الصُّفَّةِ أَضْيَافُ الإِسْلاَمِ، لاَ يَأْوُونَ

إِلَى أَهْلٍ وَلاَ مَالٍ، وَلاَ عَلَى أَحَدٍ، إِذَا أَتَتْهُ صَدَقَةٌ بَعَثَ بِهَا إِلَيْهِمْ، وَلَمْ يَتَنَاوَلْ مِنْهَا شَيْئًا، وَإِذَا أَتَتْهُ هَدِيَّةٌ أَرْسَلَ إِلَيْهِمْ، وَأَصَابَ مِنْهَا وَأَشْرَكَهُمْ فِيهَا، فَسَاءَنِي ذَلِكَ فَقُلْتُ وَمَا هَذَا اللَّبَنُ فِي أَهْلِ الصُّفَّةِ كُنْتُ أَحَقُّ أَنَا أَنْ أُصِيبَ مِنْ هَذَا اللَّبَنِ شَرْبَةً أَتَقَوَّى بِهَا، فَإِذَا جَاءَ أَمَرَنِي فَكُنْتُ أَنَا أُعْطِيهِمْ، وَمَا عَسَى أَنْ يَبْلُغَنِي مِنْ هَذَا اللَّبَنِ، وَلَمْ يَكُنْ مِنْ طَاعَةِ اللَّهِ وَطَاعَةِ رَسُولِهِ صلى الله عليه وسلم بُدٌّ، فَأَتَيْتُهُمْ فَدَعَوْتُهُمْ فَأَقْبَلُوا، فَاسْتَأْذَنُوا فَأَذِنَ لَهُمْ، وَأَخَذُوا مَجَالِسَهُمْ مِنَ الْبَيْتِ قَالَ " يَا أَبَا هِرٍّ ". قُلْتُ لَبَّيْكَ يَا رَسُولَ اللَّهِ. قَالَ " خُذْ فَأَعْطِهِمْ ". قَالَ فَأَخَذْتُ الْقَدَحَ فَجَعَلْتُ أُعْطِيهِ الرَّجُلَ فَيَشْرَبُ حَتَّى يَرْوَى، ثُمَّ يَرُدُّ عَلَيَّ الْقَدَحَ، فَأُعْطِيهِ الرَّجُلَ فَيَشْرَبُ حَتَّى يَرْوَى، ثُمَّ يَرُدُّ عَلَيَّ الْقَدَحَ فَيَشْرَبُ حَتَّى يَرْوَى، ثُمَّ يَرُدُّ عَلَيَّ الْقَدَحَ، حَتَّى انْتَهَيْتُ إِلَى النَّبِيِّ صلى الله عليه وسلم وَقَدْ رَوِيَ الْقَوْمُ كُلُّهُمْ، فَأَخَذَ الْقَدَحَ فَوَضَعَهُ عَلَى يَدِهِ فَنَظَرَ إِلَىَّ فَتَبَسَّمَ فَقَالَ " أَبَا هِرٍّ ". قُلْتُ لَبَّيْكَ يَا رَسُولَ اللَّهِ. قَالَ " بَقِيتُ أَنَا وَأَنْتَ ". قُلْتُ صَدَقْتَ يَا رَسُولَ اللَّهِ. قَالَ " اقْعُدْ فَاشْرَبْ ". فَقَعَدْتُ فَشَرِبْتُ. فَقَالَ " اشْرَبْ ". فَشَرِبْتُ، فَمَا زَالَ يَقُولُ " اشْرَبْ ". حَتَّى قُلْتُ لاَ وَالَّذِي بَعَثَكَ بِالْحَقِّ، مَا أَجِدُ لَهُ مَسْلَكًا. قَالَ " فَأَرِنِي ". فَأَعْطَيْتُهُ الْقَدَحَ فَحَمِدَ اللَّهَ وَسَمَّى، وَشَرِبَ الْفَضْلَةَ

Narrated Abu `Uthman: `Abdur Rahman bin Abi Bakr said, "The Suffa Companions were poor people and the Prophet ﷺ said, 'Whoever has food for two persons should take a third one from them (Suffa companions). And whosoever has food for four persons he should take one or two from them' Abu Bakr took three men and the Prophet ﷺ took ten of them." `Abdur Rahman added, my father my mother and I were there (in the house). (The sub-narrator is in doubt whether `Abdur Rahman also said, 'My wife and our servant who was common for both my house and Abu Bakr's house). Abu Bakr took his supper with the Prophet ﷺ and remained there till the `Isha' prayer was offered. Abu Bakr went back and stayed with the Prophet ﷺ till the Prophet ﷺ took his meal and then Abu Bakr returned to his house after a long portion of the night had passed. Abu Bakr's wife said, 'What detained you from your guests (or guest)?' He said, 'Have you not served them yet?' She said, 'They refused to eat until you come. The food was served for them but they refused." `Abdur Rahman added, "I went away and hid myself (being afraid of Abu Bakr) and in the meantime he (Abu Bakr) called me, 'O Ghunthar (a harsh word)!' and also called me bad names and abused me and then said (to his family), 'Eat. No welcome for you.' Then (the supper was served). Abu Bakr took an oath that he would not eat that food. The narrator added: By Allah, whenever any one of us (myself and the guests of Suffa companions) took anything from the food, it increased from underneath. We all ate to our fill and the food was more than it was before its serving. Abu Bakr looked at it (the food) and found it as it was before serving or even more than that. He addressed his wife (saying) 'O the sister of Bani Firas! What is this?' She said, 'O the pleasure of my eyes! The food is now three times more than it was before.' Abu Bakr ate from it, and said, 'That (oath) was from Satan' meaning his oath (not to eat). Then he again took a morsel (mouthful) from it and then took the rest of it to the Prophet. So that meal was with the Prophet. There was a treaty between us and some people, and when the period of that treaty had elapsed the Prophet ﷺ divided us into twelve (groups) (the Prophet's companions) each being headed by a man. Allah knows how many men were under the command of each (leader). So all of them (12 groups of men) ate of that meal.". – Sahih Al-Bukhari 602

حَدَّثَنَا أَبُو النُّعْمَانِ، قَالَ حَدَّثَنَا مُعْتَمِرُ بْنُ سُلَيْمَانَ، قَالَ حَدَّثَنَا أَبِي، حَدَّثَنَا أَبُو عُثْمَانَ، عَنْ عَبْدِ الرَّحْمَنِ بْنِ أَبِي بَكْرٍ، أَنَّ أَصْحَابَ الصُّفَّةِ، كَانُوا أُنَاسًا فُقَرَاءَ، وَأَنَّ النَّبِيَّ صلى الله عليه وسلم قَالَ " مَنْ كَانَ عِنْدَهُ طَعَامُ اثْنَيْنِ فَلْيَذْهَبْ بِثَالِثٍ، وَإِنْ أَرْبَعٌ فَخَامِسٌ أَوْ سَادِسٌ ". وَأَنَّ أَبَا بَكْرٍ جَاءَ بِثَلاَثَةٍ فَانْطَلَقَ النَّبِيُّ صلى الله عليه وسلم بِعَشَرَةٍ، قَالَ فَهْوَ أَنَا وَأَبِي وَأُمِّي، فَلاَ أَدْرِي قَالَ وَامْرَأَتِي وَخَادِمٌ بَيْنَنَا وَبَيْنَ بَيْتِ أَبِي بَكْرٍ. وَإِنَّ أَبَا بَكْرٍ تَعَشَّى عِنْدَ النَّبِيِّ صلى الله عليه وسلم ثُمَّ لَبِثَ حَيْثُ صُلِّيَتِ الْعِشَاءُ، ثُمَّ رَجَعَ فَلَبِثَ حَتَّى تَعَشَّى النَّبِيُّ صلى الله عليه وسلم فَجَاءَ بَعْدَ مَا مَضَى مِنَ اللَّيْلِ مَا شَاءَ اللَّهُ، قَالَتْ لَهُ امْرَأَتُهُ وَمَا حَبَسَكَ عَنْ أَضْيَافِكَ ـ أَوْ قَالَتْ ضَيْفِكَ ـ قَالَ أَوَمَا عَشَّيْتِيهِمْ قَالَتْ أَبَوْا حَتَّى تَجِيءَ، قَدْ عُرِضُوا فَأَبَوْا. قَالَ فَذَهَبْتُ أَنَا فَاخْتَبَأْتُ فَقَالَ يَا غُنْثَرُ، فَجَدَّعَ وَسَبَّ، وَقَالَ كُلُوا لاَ هَنِيئًا. فَقَالَ وَاللَّهِ لاَ أَطْعَمُهُ أَبَدًا، وَايْمُ اللَّهِ مَا كُنَّا نَأْخُذُ مِنْ لُقْمَةٍ إِلاَّ رَبَا مِنْ أَسْفَلِهَا أَكْثَرُ مِنْهَا. قَالَ يَعْنِي حَتَّى شَبِعُوا وَصَارَتْ أَكْثَرَ مِمَّا كَانَتْ قَبْلَ ذَلِكَ، فَنَظَرَ إِلَيْهَا أَبُو بَكْرٍ فَإِذَا هِيَ كَمَا هِيَ أَوْ أَكْثَرُ مِنْهَا. فَقَالَ لاِمْرَأَتِهِ يَا أُخْتَ بَنِي فِرَاسٍ مَا هَذَا قَالَتْ لاَ وَقُرَّةِ عَيْنِي لَهِيَ الآنَ أَكْثَرُ مِنْهَا قَبْلَ ذَلِكَ بِثَلاَثِ مَرَّاتٍ. فَأَكَلَ مِنْهَا أَبُو بَكْرٍ وَقَالَ إِنَّمَا كَانَ ذَلِكَ مِنَ الشَّيْطَانِ ـ يَعْنِي يَمِينَهُ ـ ثُمَّ أَكَلَ مِنْهَا لُقْمَةً، ثُمَّ حَمَلَهَا إِلَى النَّبِيِّ صلى الله عليه وسلم

فَأَصْبَحَتْ عِنْدَهُ، وَكَانَ بَيْنَنَا وَبَيْنَ قَوْمٍ عَقْدٌ، فَمَضَى الأَجَلُ، فَفَرَّقَنَا اثْنَا عَشَرَ رَجُلاً، مَعَ كُلِّ رَجُلٍ مِنْهُمْ أُنَاسٌ، اللَّهُ أَعْلَمُ كَمْ مَعَ كُلِّ رَجُلٍ فَأَكَلُوا مِنْهَا أَجْمَعُونَ، أَوْ كَمَا قَالَ.

Narrated Abu Huraira: I saw seventy of As-Suffa men and none of them had a Rida' (a garment covering the upper part of the body). They had either Izars (only) or sheets which they tied round their necks. Some of these sheets reached the middle of their legs and some reached their heels and they used to gather them with their hands lest their private parts should become naked. – Sahih Al-Bukhari 442
حَدَّثَنَا يُوسُفُ بْنُ عِيسَى، قَالَ حَدَّثَنَا ابْنُ فُضَيْلٍ، عَنْ أَبِيهِ، عَنْ أَبِي حَازِمٍ، عَنْ أَبِي هُرَيْرَةَ، قَالَ رَأَيْتُ سَبْعِينَ مِنْ أَصْحَابِ الصُّفَّةِ، مَا مِنْهُمْ رَجُلٌ عَلَيْهِ رِدَاءٌ، إِمَّا إِزَارٌ وَإِمَّا كِسَاءٌ، قَدْ رَبَطُوا فِي أَعْنَاقِهِمْ، فَمِنْهَا مَا يَبْلُغُ نِصْفَ السَّاقَيْنِ، وَمِنْهَا مَا يَبْلُغُ الْكَعْبَيْنِ، فَيَجْمَعُهُ بِيَدِهِ، كَرَاهِيَةَ أَنْ تُرَى عَوْرَتُهُ.

Do not spread corruption in the land after it has been set in order.
وَلَا تُفْسِدُوا۟ فِى ٱلْأَرْضِ بَعْدَ إِصْلَـٰحِهَا

(Allah) Said He , "O Iblis, what about you, that you are not among the prostrate?" Said he, "Indeed I did not have to prostrate myself to a mortal whom You created of dry clay of mud modeled." Said He, "Then get out (Literally: go out) of it; so, surely you are outcast And surely the curse will be upon you till the Day of Doom." Said he, "Lord! Then respite me till the Day they will be made to rise again." Said He, "Then surely you are among the respited To the Day of a known time." Said he, "Lord! For (the fact) that You misguided me, indeed I will definitely adorn for them (i.e., make "evil" attractive to them) in the earth; and indeed I will definitely misguide them all together Excepting Your bondmen among them, who are most faithful." Said He, "This is for Me a straight Path Surely over My servants you will have no all-binding authority, except the ones who closely follow you of the misguided ones. Surah Al-Hijr 15:32-42
قَالَ يَـٰٓإِبْلِيسُ مَا لَكَ أَلَّا تَكُونَ مَعَ ٱلسَّـٰجِدِينَ قَالَ لَمْ أَكُن لِّأَسْجُدَ لِبَشَرٍ خَلَقْتَهُۥ مِن صَلْصَـٰلٍ مِّنْ حَمَإٍ مَّسْنُونٍ قَالَ فَٱخْرُجْ مِنْهَا فَإِنَّكَ رَجِيمٌ وَإِنَّ عَلَيْكَ ٱللَّعْنَةَ إِلَىٰ يَوْمِ ٱلدِّينِ قَالَ رَبِّ فَأَنظِرْنِىٓ إِلَىٰ يَوْمِ يُبْعَثُونَ قَالَ فَإِنَّكَ مِنَ ٱلْمُنظَرِينَ إِلَىٰ يَوْمِ ٱلْوَقْتِ ٱلْمَعْلُومِ قَالَ رَبِّ بِمَآ أَغْوَيْتَنِى لَأُزَيِّنَنَّ لَهُمْ فِى ٱلْأَرْضِ وَلَأُغْوِيَنَّهُمْ أَجْمَعِينَ إِلَّا عِبَادَكَ مِنْهُمُ ٱلْمُخْلَصِينَ قَالَ هَـٰذَا صِرَٰطٌ عَلَىَّ مُسْتَقِيمٌ إِنَّ عِبَادِى لَيْسَ لَكَ عَلَيْهِمْ سُلْطَـٰنٌ إِلَّا مَنِ ٱتَّبَعَكَ مِنَ ٱلْغَاوِينَ

And when your Lord said to the angels, "I am placing a deputy on earth," they said, "Will you put someone who will cause trouble there and shed blood? And while we sing Your praise and glorify You?" God said, "I know what you do not know." And God taught Adam the names, all of them; then set the1n before the angels and said, "Tell me these names. If you speak the truth." They said, "Glory to You! No knowledge is ours but what you have taught us. For You are most knowing, most wise." God said, "Adam, tell them their names." And when he had told them their names, God said, "Did I not tell you I know the mysteries of the heavens and the earth? And I know what you disclose, and what you have been concealing." And when We said to the angels, '"Bow to Adam," they bowed, except one, Ibliis: he refused, and showed arrogance; and he was of the ungrateful. – Surah Al-Baqarah 2:30-34
وَإِذْ قَالَ رَبُّكَ لِلْمَلَـٰٓئِكَةِ إِنِّى جَاعِلٌ فِى ٱلْأَرْضِ خَلِيفَةً ۖ قَالُوٓا۟ أَتَجْعَلُ فِيهَا مَن يُفْسِدُ فِيهَا وَيَسْفِكُ ٱلدِّمَآءَ وَنَحْنُ نُسَبِّحُ بِحَمْدِكَ وَنُقَدِّسُ لَكَ ۖ قَالَ إِنِّىٓ أَعْلَمُ مَا لَا تَعْلَمُونَ وَعَلَّمَ ءَادَمَ ٱلْأَسْمَآءَ كُلَّهَا ثُمَّ عَرَضَهُمْ عَلَى ٱلْمَلَـٰٓئِكَةِ فَقَالَ أَنۢبِـُٔونِى بِأَسْمَآءِ هَـٰٓؤُلَآءِ إِن كُنتُمْ صَـٰدِقِينَ قَالُوا۟ سُبْحَـٰنَكَ لَا عِلْمَ لَنَآ إِلَّا مَا عَلَّمْتَنَآ ۖ إِنَّكَ أَنتَ ٱلْعَلِيمُ ٱلْحَكِيمُ قَالَ يَـٰٓـَٔادَمُ أَنۢبِئْهُم بِأَسْمَآئِهِمْ ۖ فَلَمَّآ أَنۢبَأَهُم بِأَسْمَآئِهِمْ

قَالَ أَلَمْ أَقُل لَّكُمْ إِنِّيٓ أَعْلَمُ غَيْبَ ٱلسَّمَـٰوَٰتِ وَٱلْأَرْضِ وَأَعْلَمُ مَا تُبْدُونَ وَمَا كُنتُمْ تَكْتُمُونَ وَإِذْ قُلْنَا لِلْمَلَـٰٓئِكَةِ ٱسْجُدُوا۟ لِءَادَمَ فَسَجَدُوٓا۟ إِلَّآ إِبْلِيسَ أَبَىٰ وَٱسْتَكْبَرَ وَكَانَ مِنَ ٱلْكَـٰفِرِينَ

....Do not follow Satan's steps; he is clearly your enemy. – Surah Al-Baqarah 2:126

....وَلَا تَتَّبِعُوا۟ خُطُوَٰتِ ٱلشَّيْطَـٰنِ ۚ إِنَّهُۥ لَكُمْ عَدُوٌّ مُّبِينٌ

Indeed I will definitely fill Hell with you and with whoever of them follows you all together." – Surah Sad 38:85

لَأَمْلَأَنَّ جَهَنَّمَ مِنكَ وَمِمَّن تَبِعَكَ مِنْهُمْ أَجْمَعِينَ

Said He, "Go! So, whoever of them follows you, then surely Hell will be your recompense, an ample recompense – Surah Al-Isra 17:63

قَالَ ٱذْهَبْ فَمَن تَبِعَكَ مِنْهُمْ فَإِنَّ جَهَنَّمَ جَزَآؤُكُمْ جَزَآءً مَّوْفُورًا

And ⌜remember⌝ when Moses prayed for water for his people, We said, "Strike the rock with your staff." Then twelve springs gushed out, ⌜and⌝ each tribe knew its drinking place. ⌜We then said,⌝ "Eat and drink of Allah's provisions, and do not go about spreading corruption in the land." – Surah Al-Baqarah 2:60

وَإِذِ ٱسْتَسْقَىٰ مُوسَىٰ لِقَوْمِهِۦ فَقُلْنَا ٱضْرِب بِّعَصَاكَ ٱلْحَجَرَ ۖ فَٱنفَجَرَتْ مِنْهُ ٱثْنَتَا عَشْرَةَ عَيْنًا ۖ قَدْ عَلِمَ كُلُّ أُنَاسٍ مَّشْرَبَهُمْ ۖ كُلُوا۟ وَٱشْرَبُوا۟ مِن رِّزْقِ ٱللَّهِ وَلَا تَعْثَوْا۟ فِى ٱلْأَرْضِ مُفْسِدِينَ

And to the people of Midian We sent their brother Shu'aib. He said, "O my people! Worship Allah—you have no other god except Him. A clear proof has already come to you from your Lord. So give just measure and weight, do not defraud people of their property, nor spread corruption in the land after it has been set in order. This is for your own good, if you are ⌜truly⌝ believers. – Surah Al-A'raf 7:85

وَإِلَىٰ مَدْيَنَ أَخَاهُمْ شُعَيْبًا ۗ قَالَ يَـٰقَوْمِ ٱعْبُدُوا۟ ٱللَّهَ مَا لَكُم مِّنْ إِلَـٰهٍ غَيْرُهُۥ ۖ قَدْ جَآءَتْكُم بَيِّنَةٌ مِّن رَّبِّكُمْ ۖ فَأَوْفُوا۟ ٱلْكَيْلَ وَٱلْمِيزَانَ وَلَا تَبْخَسُوا۟ ٱلنَّاسَ أَشْيَآءَهُمْ وَلَا تُفْسِدُوا۟ فِى ٱلْأَرْضِ بَعْدَ إِصْلَـٰحِهَا ۚ ذَٰلِكُمْ خَيْرٌ لَّكُمْ إِن كُنتُم مُّؤْمِنِينَ

Do not spread corruption in the land after it has been set in order. And call upon Him with hope and fear. Indeed, Allah's mercy is always close to the good-doers. – Surah Al-A'raf 7:56

وَلَا تُفْسِدُوا۟ فِى ٱلْأَرْضِ بَعْدَ إِصْلَـٰحِهَا وَٱدْعُوهُ خَوْفًا وَطَمَعًا ۚ إِنَّ رَحْمَتَ ٱللَّهِ قَرِيبٌ مِّنَ ٱلْمُحْسِنِينَ

The Book of **First Fitnah** الفتنة الأولى

Narrated 'Ubaidullah bin `Adi bin Al-Khiyar: That Al-Miswar bin Makhrama and `Abdur-Rahman bin Al-Aswad bin 'Abu Yaghuth had said to him, "What prevents you from speaking to your uncle `Uthman regarding his brother Al-Walid bin `Uqba?" The people were speaking against the latter for what he had done. 'Ubaidullah said, "So I kept waiting for `Uthman, and when he went out for the prayer, I said to him, 'I have got something to say to you as a piece of advice.' `Uthman said, 'O man! I seek Refuge with Allah from you. So I went away. When I finished my prayer, I sat with Al-Miswar and Ibn 'Abu Yaghutb and talked to both of them of what I had said to `Uthman and what he had said to me. They said, 'You have done your duty.' So while I was sitting with them. `Uthman's Messenger came to me. They said, 'Allah has put you to trial." I set out and when I reached `Uthman, he said, 'What is your advice which you mentioned a while ago?' I recited Tashahhud and added, 'Allah has sent Muhammad and has revealed the Holy Book (i.e. Qur'an) to him. You (O `Uthman!) were amongst those who responded to the call of Allah and His Apostle and had faith in him. And you took part in the first two migrations (to Ethiopia and to Medina), and you enjoyed the company of Allah's Messenger ﷺ and learned his traditions and advice. Now the people are talking much about Al-Walid bin `Uqba and so it is your duty to impose on him the legal punishment.' `Uthman then said to me, 'O my nephew! Did you ever meet Allah's Messenger ﷺ?' I said, 'No, but his knowledge has reached me as it has reached the virgin in her seclusion.' `Uthman then recited Tashahhud and said, 'No doubt, Allah has sent Muhammad with the Truth and has revealed to him His Holy Book (i.e. Qur'an) and I was amongst those who responded to the call of Allah and His Apostle and I had faith in Muhammad's Mission, and I had performed the first two migrations as you have said, and I enjoyed the company of Allah's Messenger ﷺ and gave the pledge of allegiance to him. By Allah, I never disobeyed him and never cheated him till Allah caused him to die. Then Allah made Abu Bakr Caliph, and by Allah, I was never disobedient to him, nor did I cheat him. Then `Umar became Caliph, and by Allah, I was never disobedient to him, nor did I cheat him. Then I became Caliph. Have I not then the same rights over you as they had over me?' I replied in the affirmative. `Uthman further said, 'The what are these talks which are reaching me from you? As for what you ha mentioned about Al-Walid bin 'Uqb; Allah willing, I shall give him the leg; punishment justly. Then `Uthman ordered that Al-Walid be flogged fort lashes. He ordered `Ali to flog him an he himself flogged him as well.". – Sahih Al-Bukhari 3872

حَدَّثَنَا عَبْدُ اللَّهِ بْنُ مُحَمَّدٍ الْجُعْفِيُّ، حَدَّثَنَا هِشَامٌ، أَخْبَرَنَا مَعْمَرٌ، عَنِ الزُّهْرِيِّ، حَدَّثَنَا عُرْوَةُ بْنُ الزُّبَيْرِ، أَنَّ عُبَيْدَ اللَّهِ بْنَ عَدِيِّ بْنِ الْخِيَارِ، أَخْبَرَهُ أَنَّ الْمِسْوَرَ بْنَ مَخْرَمَةَ وَعَبْدَ الرَّحْمَنِ بْنَ الأَسْوَدِ بْنِ عَبْدِ يَغُوثَ قَالاَ لَهُ مَا يَمْنَعُكَ أَنْ تُكَلِّمَ خَالَكَ عُثْمَانَ فِي أَخِيهِ الْوَلِيدِ بْنِ عُقْبَةَ وَكَانَ أَكْثَرَ النَّاسُ فِيمَا فَعَلَ بِهِ. قَالَ عُبَيْدُ اللَّهِ فَانْتَصَبْتُ لِعُثْمَانَ حِينَ خَرَجَ إِلَى الصَّلاَةِ فَقُلْتُ لَهُ إِنَّ لِي إِلَيْكَ حَاجَةً وَهْىَ نَصِيحَةٌ. فَقَالَ أَيُّهَا الْمَرْءُ، أَعُوذُ بِاللَّهِ مِنْكَ، فَانْصَرَفْتُ، فَلَمَّا قَضَيْتُ الصَّلاَةَ جَلَسْتُ إِلَى الْمِسْوَرِ وَإِلَى ابْنِ عَبْدِ يَغُوثَ، فَحَدَّثْتُهُمَا بِالَّذِي قُلْتُ لِعُثْمَانَ وَقَالَ لِي. فَقَالاَ قَدْ قَضَيْتَ الَّذِي كَانَ عَلَيْكَ. فَبَيْنَمَا أَنَا جَالِسٌ مَعَهُمَا، إِذْ جَاءَنِي رَسُولُ عُثْمَانَ، فَقَالاَ لِي قَدِ ابْتَلاَكَ اللَّهُ. فَانْطَلَقْتُ حَتَّى دَخَلْتُ عَلَيْهِ، فَقَالَ مَا نَصِيحَتُكَ الَّتِي ذَكَرْتَ آنِفًا قَالَ فَتَشَهَّدْتُ ثُمَّ قُلْتُ إِنَّ اللَّهَ بَعَثَ مُحَمَّدًا صلى الله عليه وسلم وَأَنْزَلَ عَلَيْهِ الْكِتَابَ، وَكُنْتَ مِمَّنِ اسْتَجَابَ لِلَّهِ وَرَسُولِهِ صلى الله عليه وسلم وَآمَنْتَ بِهِ، وَهَاجَرْتَ الْهِجْرَتَيْنِ الأُولَيَيْنِ، وَصَحِبْتَ رَسُولَ اللَّهِ صلى الله عليه وسلم وَرَأَيْتَ هَدْيَهُ، وَقَدْ أَكْثَرَ النَّاسُ فِي شَأْنِ الْوَلِيدِ بْنِ عُقْبَةَ، فَحَقٌّ عَلَيْكَ أَنْ تُقِيمَ عَلَيْهِ الْحَدَّ. فَقَالَ لِي يَا ابْنَ أَخِي أَدْرَكْتَ رَسُولَ اللَّهِ صلى الله عليه وسلم قَالَ قُلْتُ لاَ، وَلَكِنْ قَدْ خَلَصَ إِلَيَّ مِنْ عِلْمِهِ مَا خَلَصَ إِلَى الْعَذْرَاءِ فِي سِتْرِهَا. قَالَ فَتَشَهَّدَ عُثْمَانُ فَقَالَ إِنَّ اللَّهَ قَدْ بَعَثَ مُحَمَّدًا صلى الله عليه وسلم بِالْحَقِّ وَأَنْزَلَ عَلَيْهِ الْكِتَابَ، وَكُنْتُ مِمَّنِ اسْتَجَابَ لِلَّهِ وَرَسُولِهِ صلى الله عليه وسلم وَآمَنْتُ بِمَا بُعِثَ بِهِ مُحَمَّدٌ صلى الله عليه وسلم. وَهَاجَرْتُ الْهِجْرَتَيْنِ الأُولَيَيْنِ كَمَا قُلْتَ، وَصَحِبْتُ رَسُولَ اللَّهِ صلى الله عليه وسلم وَبَايَعْتُهُ، وَاللَّهِ مَا عَصَيْتُهُ وَلاَ

غَشَشْتُهُ حَتَّى تَوَفَّاهُ اللَّهُ، ثُمَّ اسْتَخْلَفَ اللَّهُ أَبَا بَكْرٍ فَوَاللَّهِ مَا عَصَيْتُهُ وَلاَ غَشَشْتُهُ، ثُمَّ اسْتُخْلِفَ عُمَرُ، فَوَاللَّهِ مَا عَصَيْتُهُ وَلاَ غَشَشْتُهُ، ثُمَّ اسْتُخْلِفْتُ، أَفَلَيْسَ لِي عَلَيْكُمْ مِثْلُ الَّذِي كَانَ لَهُمْ عَلَىَّ قَالَ بَلَى. قَالَ فَمَا هَذِهِ الأَحَادِيثُ الَّتِي تَبْلُغُنِي عَنْكُمْ فَأَمَّا مَا ذَكَرْتَ مِنْ شَأْنِ الْوَلِيدِ بْنِ عُقْبَةَ، فَسَنَأْخُذُ فِيهِ إِنْ شَاءَ اللَّهُ بِالْحَقِّ قَالَ فَجَلَدَ الْوَلِيدَ أَرْبَعِينَ جَلْدَةً، وَأَمَرَ عَلِيًّا أَنْ يَجْلِدَهُ، وَكَانَ هُوَ يَجْلِدُهُ. وَقَالَ يُونُسُ وَابْنُ أَخِي الزُّهْرِيِّ عَنِ الزُّهْرِيِّ أَفَلَيْسَ لِي عَلَيْكُمْ مِنَ الْحَقِّ مِثْلُ الَّذِي كَانَ لَهُمْ.
قَالَ أَبُو عَبْد اللَّهِ بَلاَءٌ مِنْ رَبِّكُمْ مَا ابْتُلِيتُمْ بِهِ مِنْ شِدَّةٍ وَفِي مَوْضِعِ الْبَلاَءُ الاِبْتِلاَءُ وَالتَّمْحِيصُ مَنْ بَلَوْتُهُ وَمَحَّصْتُهُ أَيْ اسْتَخْرَجْتُ مَا عِنْدَهُ يَبْلُو يَخْتَبِرُ مُبْتَلِيكُمْ مُخْتَبِرُكُمْ وَأَمَّا قَوْلُهُ بَلاَءٌ عَظِيمٌ النِّعَمُ وَهِيَ مِنْ أَبْلَيْتُهُ وَتِلْكَ مِنِ ابْتَلَيْتُهُ

Narrated ‘Ubaid-Ullah bin Adi bin Khiyar: I went to ‘Uthman bin Affan while he was besieged, and said to him, “You are the chief of all Muslims in general and you see what has befallen you. We are led in the Salat (prayer) by a leader of Al-Fitan (trials and afflictions etc.) and we are afraid of being sinful in following him.” ‘Uthman said. “As-Salat (the prayers) is the best of all deeds so when the people do good deeds do the same with them and when they do bad deeds, avoid those bad deeds.” Az-Zuhri said, “In our opinion one should not offer Salat behind an effeminate person unless there is no alternative.”. – Sahih Al-Bukhari 695
قَالَ أَبُو عَبْدِ اللَّهِ وَقَالَ لَنَا مُحَمَّدُ بْنُ يُوسُفَ حَدَّثَنَا الأَوْزَاعِيُّ، حَدَّثَنَا الزُّهْرِيُّ، عَنْ حُمَيْدِ بْنِ عَبْدِ الرَّحْمَنِ، عَنْ عُبَيْدِ اللَّهِ بْنِ عَدِيِّ بْنِ خِيَارٍ، أَنَّهُ دَخَلَ عَلَى عُثْمَانَ بْنِ عَفَّانَ ـ رضى الله عنه ـ وَهْوَ مَحْصُورٌ فَقَالَ إِنَّكَ إِمَامُ عَامَّةٍ، وَنَزَلَ بِكَ مَا تَرَى وَيُصَلِّي لَنَا إِمَامُ فِتْنَةٍ وَنَتَحَرَّجُ. فَقَالَ الصَّلاَةُ أَحْسَنُ مَا يَعْمَلُ النَّاسُ، فَإِذَا أَحْسَنَ النَّاسُ فَأَحْسِنْ مَعَهُمْ، وَإِذَا أَسَاءُوا فَاجْتَنِبْ إِسَاءَتَهُمْ. وَقَالَ الزُّبَيْدِيُّ قَالَ الزُّهْرِيُّ لاَ نَرَى أَنْ يُصَلَّى خَلْفَ الْمُخَنَّثِ إِلاَّ مِنْ ضَرُورَةٍ لاَ بُدَّ مِنْهَا.

Conflict of Jamal
مَعْرَكَةُ الْجَمَلِ

Narrated Abu Maryam `Abdullah bin Ziyad Al-Aasadi: When Talha, AzZubair and `Aisha moved to Basra, `Ali sent `Ammar bin Yasir and Hasan bin `Ali who came to us at Kufa and ascended the pulpit. Al-Hasan bin `Ali was at the top of the pulpit and `Ammar was below Al-Hasan. We all gathered before him. I heard `Ammar saying, “`Aisha has moved to Al-Busra. By Allah! She is the wife of your Prophet in this world and in the Hereafter. But Allah has put you to test whether you obey Him (Allah) or her (`Aisha). – Sahih Al-Bukhari 7100
حَدَّثَنَا عَبْدُ اللَّهِ بْنُ مُحَمَّدٍ، حَدَّثَنَا يَحْيَى بْنُ آدَمَ، حَدَّثَنَا أَبُو بَكْرِ بْنُ عَيَّاشٍ، حَدَّثَنَا أَبُو حَصِينٍ، حَدَّثَنَا أَبُو مَرْيَمَ عَبْدُ اللَّهِ بْنُ زِيَادٍ الأَسَدِيُّ، قَالَ لَمَّا سَارَ طَلْحَةُ وَالزُّبَيْرُ وَعَائِشَةُ إِلَى الْبَصْرَةِ بَعَثَ عَلِيٌّ عَمَّارَ بْنَ يَاسِرٍ وَحَسَنَ بْنَ عَلِيٍّ، فَقَدِمَا عَلَيْنَا الْكُوفَةَ فَصَعِدَا الْمِنْبَرَ، فَكَانَ الْحَسَنُ بْنُ عَلِيٍّ فَوْقَ الْمِنْبَرِ فِي أَعْلاَهُ، وَقَامَ عَمَّارٌ أَسْفَلَ مِنَ الْحَسَنِ، فَاجْتَمَعْنَا إِلَيْهِ فَسَمِعْتُ عَمَّارًا يَقُولُ إِنَّ عَائِشَةَ قَدْ سَارَتْ إِلَى الْبَصْرَةِ، وَوَاللَّهِ إِنَّهَا لَزَوْجَةُ نَبِيِّكُمْ صلى الله عليه وسلم فِي الدُّنْيَا وَالآخِرَةِ، وَلَكِنَّ اللَّهَ تَبَارَكَ وَتَعَالَى ابْتَلاَكُمْ، لِيَعْلَمَ إِيَّاهُ تُطِيعُونَ أَمْ هِيَ

Narrated `Abdullah bin Az-Zubair: When Az-Zubair got up during the battle of Al-Jamal, he called me and I stood up beside him, and he said to me, “O my son! Today one will be killed either as an oppressor or as an oppressed one. I see that I will be killed as an oppressed one. My biggest worry is my debts. Do you think, if we pay the debts, there will be something left for us from our money?” Az-Zubair added, “O my son! Sell our property and pay my debts.” Az-Zubair then willed one-third of his property and willed one-third of that portion to his sons; namely, 'Abdullah's sons. He said, “One third of the one third. If any property is left after the payment of the debts, one-third (of the one-third of what is left) is to be given to your sons.” (Hisham, a sub-narrator added, “Some of the sons of `Abdullah were equal in age to the sons of Az-Zubair e.g. Khubaib and `Abbas. `Abdullah had nine sons and nine daughters at that time.” (The narrator `Abdullah added:)My father (Az-Zubair) went on drawing my attention to his debts saying, “If you should fail to pay part of the debts, appeal to my Master to help you.” By Allah! I could not understand what he meant till I asked, “O father! Who is

your Master?" He replied, "Allah (is my Master)." By Allah, whenever I had any difficulty regarding his debts, I would say, "Master of Az-Zubair! Pay his debts on his behalf ." and Allah would (help me to) pay it. Az-Zubair was martyred leaving no Dinar or Dirham but two pieces of land, one of which was (called) Al-Ghaba, and eleven houses in Medina, two in Basra, one in Kufa and one in Egypt. In fact, the source of the debt which he owed was, that if somebody brought some money to deposit with him. Az-Zubair would say, "No, (I won't keep it as a trust), but I take it as a debt, for I am afraid it might be lost." Az-Zubair was never appointed governor or collector of the tax of Kharaj or any other similar thing, but he collected his wealth (from the war booty he gained) during the holy battles he took part in, in the company of the Prophet, Abu Bakr, `Umar, and `Uthman. (`Abdullah bin Az-Zubair added: )When I counted his debt, it turned to be two million and two hundred thousand. (The sub-narrator added: )Hakim bin Hizam met `Abdullah bin Zubair and asked, "O my nephew! How much is the debt of my brother?" `Abdullah kept it as a secret and said, "One hundred thousand," Hakim said, "By Allah! I don't think your property will cover it." On that `Abdullah said to him, "What if it is two million and two hundred thousand?" Hakim said, "I don't think you can pay it; so if you are unable to pay all of it, I will help you." Az- Zubair had already bought Al-Ghaba for one hundred and seventy thousand. `Abdullah sold it for one million and six hundred thousand. Then he called the people saying, "Any person who has any money claim on Az-Zubair should come to us in Al-Ghaba." There came to him `Abdullah bin Ja`far whom Az-Zubair owed four hundred thousand. He said to `Abdullah bin Az-Zubair, "If you wish I will forgive you the debt." `Abdullah (bin Az-Zubair) said, "No." Then Ibn Ja`far said, "If you wish you can defer the payment if you should defer the payment of any debt." Ibn Az-Zubair said, "No." `Abdullah bin Ja`far said, "Give me a piece of the land." `Abdullah bin AzZubair said (to him), "Yours is the land extending from this place to this place." So, `Abdullah bin Az-Zubair sold some of the property (including the houses) and paid his debt perfectly, retaining four and a half shares from the land (i.e. Al-Ghaba). He then went to Mu'awlya while `Amr bin `Uthman, Al-Mundhir bin Az- Zubair and Ibn Zam`a were sitting with him. Mu'awiya asked, "At what price have you appraised Al- Ghaba?" He said, "One hundred thousand for each share," Muawiya asked, "How many shares have been left?" `Abdullah replied, "Four and a half shares." Al-Mundhir bin Az-Zubair said, "I would like to buy one share for one hundred thousand." `Amr bin `Uthman said, "I would like to buy one share for one hundred thousand." Ibn Zam`a said, "I would like to buy one share for one hundred thousand." Muawiya said, "How much is left now?" `Abdullah replied, "One share and a half." Muawiya said, "I would like to buy it for one hundred and fifty thousand." `Abdullah also sold his part to Muawiya six hundred thousand. When Ibn AzZubair had paid all the debts. Az-Zubair's sons said to him, "Distribute our inheritance among us." He said, "No, by Allah, I will not distribute it among you till I announce in four successive Hajj seasons, 'Would those who have money claims on Az-Zubair come so that we may pay them their debt." So, he started to announce that in public in every Hajj season, and when four years had elapsed, he distributed the inheritance among the inheritors. Az-Zubair had four wives, and after the one-third of his property was excluded (according to the will), each of his wives received one million and two hundred thousand. So the total amount of his property was fifty million and two hundred thousand.
– Sahih Al-Bukhari 3129

حَدَّثَنَا إِسْحَاقُ بْنُ إِبْرَاهِيمَ، قَالَ قُلْتُ لأَبِي أُسَامَةَ أَحَدَّثَكُمْ هِشَامُ بْنُ عُرْوَةَ عَنْ أَبِيهِ عَنْ عَبْدِ اللَّهِ بْنِ الزُّبَيْرِ قَالَ لَمَّا وَقَفَ الزُّبَيْرُ يَوْمَ الْجَمَلِ دَعَانِي، فَقُمْتُ إِلَى جَنْبِهِ فَقَالَ يَا بُنَىِّ، إِنَّهُ لاَ يُقْتَلُ الْيَوْمَ إِلاَّ ظَالِمٌ أَوْ مَظْلُومٌ، وَإِنِّي لاَ أُرَانِي إِلاَّ سَأُقْتَلُ الْيَوْمَ مَظْلُومًا، وَإِنَّ مِنْ أَكْبَرِ هَمِّي لَدَيْنِي، أَفَتُرَى يُبْقِي دَيْنُنَا مِنْ مَالِنَا شَيْئًا فَقَالَ يَا بُنَىِّ بِعْ مَالَنَا فَاقْضِ دَيْنِي. وَأَوْصَى بِالثُّلُثِ، وَثُلُثِهِ لِبَنِيهِ، يَعْنِي عَبْدَ اللَّهِ بْنَ الزُّبَيْرِ يَقُولُ ثُلُثُ الثُّلُثِ، فَإِنْ فَضَلَ مِنْ مَالِنَا فَضْلٌ بَعْدَ قَضَاءِ الدَّيْنِ شَىْءٌ فَثُلُثُهُ لِوَلَدِكَ. قَالَ هِشَامٌ وَكَانَ بَعْضُ وَلَدِ عَبْدِ اللَّهِ قَدْ وَازَى بَعْضَ بَنِي الزُّبَيْرِ خُبَيْبٌ وَعَبَّادٌ، وَلَهُ يَوْمَئِذٍ تِسْعَةُ بَنِينَ وَتِسْعُ بَنَاتٍ.

قَالَ عَبْدُ اللَّهِ فَجَعَلَ يُوصِينِي بِدَيْنِهِ وَيَقُولُ يَا بُنَىِّ، إِنْ عَجَزْتَ عَنْهُ فِي شَىْءٍ فَاسْتَعِنْ عَلَيْهِ مَوْلاَىَ. قَالَ فَوَاللَّهِ مَا دَرَيْتُ مَا أَرَادَ حَتَّى قُلْتُ يَا أَبَتِ مَنْ مَوْلاَكَ قَالَ اللَّهُ. قَالَ فَوَاللَّهِ مَا وَقَعْتُ فِي كُرْبَةٍ مِنْ دَيْنِهِ إِلاَّ قُلْتُ يَا مَوْلَى الزُّبَيْرِ، اقْضِ عَنْهُ دَيْنَهُ. فَيَقْضِيهِ، فَقُتِلَ الزُّبَيْرُ ـ رضى الله عنه ـ وَلَمْ يَدَعْ دِينَارًا وَلاَ دِرْهَمًا، إِلاَّ أَرَضِينَ مِنْهَا الْغَابَةُ، وَإِحْدَى عَشْرَةَ دَارًا بِالْمَدِينَةِ، وَدَارَيْنِ بِالْبَصْرَةِ، وَدَارًا بِالْكُوفَةِ، وَدَارًا بِمِصْرَ. قَالَ وَإِنَّمَا كَانَ دَيْنُهُ الَّذِي عَلَيْهِ أَنَّ الرَّجُلَ كَانَ يَأْتِيهِ بِالْمَالِ فَيَسْتَوْدِعُهُ إِيَّاهُ فَيَقُولُ الزُّبَيْرُ لاَ وَلَكِنَّهُ سَلَفٌ، فَإِنِّي أَخْشَى عَلَيْهِ الضَّيْعَةَ، وَمَا وَلِيَ إِمَارَةً قَطُّ وَلاَ جِبَايَةَ خَرَاجٍ وَلاَ شَيْئًا، إِلاَّ أَنْ يَكُونَ فِي غَزْوَةٍ مَعَ النَّبِيِّ صلى الله عليه وسلم أَوْ مَعَ أَبِي بَكْرٍ وَعُمَرَ وَعُثْمَانَ ـ رضى الله عنهم ـ قَالَ عَبْدُ اللَّهِ بْنُ الزُّبَيْرِ فَحَسَبْتُ مَا عَلَيْهِ مِنَ الدَّيْنِ فَوَجَدْتُهُ أَلْفَىْ أَلْفٍ وَمِائَتَىْ أَلْفٍ قَالَ فَلَقِيَ حَكِيمُ بْنُ حِزَامٍ عَبْدَ اللَّهِ بْنَ الزُّبَيْرِ فَقَالَ يَا ابْنَ أَخِي، كَمْ عَلَى أَخِي مِنَ الدَّيْنِ فَكَتَمَهُ. فَقَالَ مِائَةُ أَلْفٍ. فَقَالَ حَكِيمٌ وَاللَّهِ مَا أُرَى أَمْوَالَكُمْ تَسَعُ لِهَذِهِ. فَقَالَ لَهُ عَبْدُ اللَّهِ أَفَرَأَيْتَكَ إِنْ كَانَتْ أَلْفَىْ أَلْفٍ وَمِائَتَىْ أَلْفٍ قَالَ مَا أُرَاكُمْ تُطِيقُونَ هَذَا، فَإِنْ عَجَزْتُمْ عَنْ شَىْءٍ مِنْهُ فَاسْتَعِينُوا بِي. قَالَ وَكَانَ الزُّبَيْرُ اشْتَرَى الْغَابَةَ بِسَبْعِينَ وَمِائَةِ أَلْفٍ، فَبَاعَهَا عَبْدُ اللَّهِ بِأَلْفِ أَلْفٍ وَسِتِّمِائَةِ أَلْفٍ ثُمَّ قَامَ فَقَالَ مَنْ كَانَ لَهُ عَلَى الزُّبَيْرِ حَقٌّ فَلْيُوَافِنَا بِالْغَابَةِ، فَأَتَاهُ عَبْدُ اللَّهِ بْنُ جَعْفَرٍ، وَكَانَ لَهُ عَلَى الزُّبَيْرِ أَرْبَعُمِائَةِ أَلْفٍ فَقَالَ لِعَبْدِ اللَّهِ إِنْ شِئْتُمْ تَرَكْتُهَا لَكُمْ. قَالَ عَبْدُ اللَّهِ لاَ. قَالَ فَإِنْ شِئْتُمْ جَعَلْتُمُوهَا فِيمَا تُؤَخِّرُونَ إِنْ أَخَّرْتُمْ. فَقَالَ عَبْدُ اللَّهِ لاَ. قَالَ قَالَ فَاقْطَعُوا لِي قِطْعَةً. فَقَالَ عَبْدُ اللَّهِ لَكَ مِنْ هَا هُنَا إِلَى هَا هُنَا. قَالَ فَبَاعَ مِنْهَا فَقَضَى دَيْنَهُ فَأَوْفَاهُ، وَبَقِيَ مِنْهَا أَرْبَعَةُ أَسْهُمٍ وَنِصْفٌ، فَقَدِمَ عَلَى مُعَاوِيَةَ وَعِنْدَهُ عَمْرُو بْنُ عُثْمَانَ وَالْمُنْذِرُ بْنُ الزُّبَيْرِ وَابْنُ زَمْعَةَ فَقَالَ لَهُ مُعَاوِيَةُ كَمْ قُوِّمَتِ الْغَابَةُ قَالَ كُلُّ سَهْمٍ مِائَةَ أَلْفٍ. قَالَ كَمْ بَقِيَ قَالَ أَرْبَعَةُ أَسْهُمٍ وَنِصْفٌ. قَالَ الْمُنْذِرُ بْنُ الزُّبَيْرِ قَدْ أَخَذْتُ سَهْمًا بِمِائَةِ أَلْفٍ. قَالَ عَمْرُو بْنُ عُثْمَانَ قَدْ أَخَذْتُ سَهْمًا بِمِائَةِ أَلْفٍ. وَقَالَ ابْنُ زَمْعَةَ قَدْ أَخَذْتُ سَهْمًا بِمِائَةِ أَلْفٍ. فَقَالَ مُعَاوِيَةُ كَمْ بَقِيَ فَقَالَ سَهْمٌ وَنِصْفٌ. قَالَ أَخَذْتُهُ بِخَمْسِينَ وَمِائَةِ أَلْفٍ. قَالَ وَبَاعَ عَبْدُ اللَّهِ بْنُ جَعْفَرٍ نَصِيبَهُ مِنْ مُعَاوِيَةَ بِسِتِّمِائَةِ أَلْفٍ، فَلَمَّا فَرَغَ ابْنُ الزُّبَيْرِ مِنْ قَضَاءِ دَيْنِهِ قَالَ بَنُو الزُّبَيْرِ اقْسِمْ بَيْنَنَا مِيرَاثَنَا. قَالَ لاَ، وَاللَّهِ لاَ أَقْسِمُ بَيْنَكُمْ حَتَّى أُنَادِيَ بِالْمَوْسِمِ أَرْبَعَ سِنِينَ أَلاَ مَنْ كَانَ لَهُ عَلَى الزُّبَيْرِ دَيْنٌ فَلْيَأْتِنَا فَلْنَقْضِهِ. قَالَ فَجَعَلَ كُلَّ سَنَةٍ يُنَادِي بِالْمَوْسِمِ، فَلَمَّا مَضَى أَرْبَعُ سِنِينَ قَسَمَ بَيْنَهُمْ قَالَ فَكَانَ لِلزُّبَيْرِ أَرْبَعُ نِسْوَةٍ، وَرَفَعَ الثُّلُثَ، فَأَصَابَ كُلَّ امْرَأَةٍ أَلْفُ أَلْفٍ وَمِائَتَا أَلْفٍ، فَجَمِيعُ مَالِهِ خَمْسُونَ أَلْفَ أَلْفٍ وَمِائَتَا أَلْفٍ.

Narrated Abu Bakra: During the battle of Al-Jamal, Allah benefited me with a Word (I heard from the Prophet). When the Prophet heard the news that the people of the Persia had made the daughter of Khosrau their Queen (ruler), he said, "Never will succeed such a nation as makes a woman their ruler." - Sahih Al-Bukhari 7099

حَدَّثَنَا عُثْمَانُ بْنُ الْهَيْثَمِ، حَدَّثَنَا عَوْفٌ، عَنِ الْحَسَنِ، عَنْ أَبِي بَكْرَةَ، قَالَ لَقَدْ نَفَعَنِي اللَّهُ بِكَلِمَةٍ أَيَّامَ الْجَمَلِ لَمَّا بَلَغَ النَّبِيَّ صلى الله عليه وسلم أَنَّ فَارِسًا مَلَّكُوا ابْنَةَ كِسْرَى قَالَ " لَنْ يُفْلِحَ قَوْمٌ وَلَّوْا أَمْرَهُمُ امْرَأَةً ".

Narrated Abu Bakra: During the days (of the battle) of Al-Jamal, Allah benefited me with a word I had heard from Allah's Apostle after I had been about to join the Companions of Al-Jamal (i.e. the camel) and fight along with them. When Allah's Messenger ﷺ was informed that the Persians had crowned the daughter of Khosrau as their ruler, he said, "Such people as ruled by a lady will never be successful." – Sahih Al-Bukhari 4425

حَدَّثَنَا عُثْمَانُ بْنُ الْهَيْثَمِ، حَدَّثَنَا عَوْفٌ، عَنِ الْحَسَنِ، عَنْ أَبِي بَكْرَةَ، قَالَ لَقَدْ نَفَعَنِي اللَّهُ بِكَلِمَةٍ سَمِعْتُهَا مِنْ، رَسُولِ اللَّهِ صلى الله عليه وسلم أَيَّامَ الْجَمَلِ، بَعْدَ مَا كِدْتُ أَنْ أَلْحَقَ بِأَصْحَابِ الْجَمَلِ فَأُقَاتِلَ مَعَهُمْ قَالَ لَمَّا بَلَغَ رَسُولَ اللَّهِ صلى الله عليه وسلم أَنَّ أَهْلَ فَارِسَ قَدْ مَلَّكُوا عَلَيْهِمْ بِنْتَ كِسْرَى قَالَ " لَنْ يُفْلِحَ قَوْمٌ وَلَّوْا أَمْرَهُمُ امْرَأَةً ".

Battle of Siffin
مَعْرَكَة صِفِّينَ

Narrated Harmala: (Usama's Maula) Usama (bin Zaid) sent me to `Ali (at Kufa) and said, "`Ali will ask you, 'What has prevented your companion from joining me?' You then should say to him, 'If you (`Ali) were in the mouth of a lion, I would like to be with you, but in this matter I won't take any part.' " Harmala added: "`Ali didn't give me anything (when I conveyed the message to him) so I went to Hasan, Hussain and Ibn Ja`far and they loaded my camels with much (wealth). – Sahih Al-Bukhari 7110

حَدَّثَنَا عَلِيُّ بْنُ عَبْدِ اللَّهِ، حَدَّثَنَا سُفْيَانُ، قَالَ قَالَ عَمْرٌو أَخْبَرَنِي مُحَمَّدُ بْنُ عَلِيٍّ، أَنَّ حَرْمَلَةَ، مَوْلَى أُسَامَةَ أَخْبَرَهُ قَالَ عَمْرٌو وَقَدْ رَأَيْتُ حَرْمَلَةَ قَالَ أَرْسَلَنِي أُسَامَةُ إِلَى عَلِيٍّ وَقَالَ إِنَّهُ سَيَسْأَلُكَ الآنَ فَيَقُولُ مَا خَلَّفَ صَاحِبَكَ فَقُلْ لَهُ يَقُولُ لَكَ لَوْ كُنْتَ فِي شِدْقِ الأَسَدِ لأَحْبَبْتُ أَنْ أَكُونَ مَعَكَ فِيهِ، وَلَكِنَّ هَذَا أَمْرٌ لَمْ أَرَهُ، فَلَمْ يُعْطِنِي شَيْئًا، فَذَهَبْتُ إِلَى حَسَنٍ وَحُسَيْنٍ وَابْنِ جَعْفَرٍ فَأَوْقَرُوا لِي رَاحِلَتِي.

Narrated Al-A`mash: I asked Abu Wail, "Did you witness the battle of Siffin between `Ali and Muawiya?" He said, "Yes," and added, "Then I heard Sahl bin Hunaif saying, 'O people! Blame your personal opinions in your religion. No doubt, I remember myself on the day of Abi Jandal; if I had the power to refuse the order of Allah's Messenger ﷺ, I would have refused it. We have never put our swords on our shoulders to get involved in a situation that might have been horrible for us, but those swords brought us to victory and peace, except this present situation.' " Abu Wail said, "I witnessed the battle of Siffin, and how nasty Siffin was!". – Sahih Al-Bukhari 7308

حَدَّثَنَا عَبْدَانُ، أَخْبَرَنَا أَبُو حَمْزَةَ، سَمِعْتُ الأَعْمَشَ، قَالَ سَأَلْتُ أَبَا وَائِلٍ هَلْ شَهِدْتَ صِفِّينَ قَالَ نَعَمْ. فَسَمِعْتُ سَهْلَ بْنَ حُنَيْفٍ، يَقُولُ ح وَحَدَّثَنَا مُوسَى بْنُ إِسْمَاعِيلَ، حَدَّثَنَا أَبُو عَوَانَةَ، عَنِ الأَعْمَشِ، عَنْ أَبِي وَائِلٍ، قَالَ قَالَ سَهْلُ بْنُ حُنَيْفٍ يَا أَيُّهَا النَّاسُ اتَّهِمُوا رَأْيَكُمْ عَلَى دِينِكُمْ، لَقَدْ رَأَيْتُنِي يَوْمَ أَبِي جَنْدَلٍ وَلَوْ أَسْتَطِيعُ أَنْ أَرُدَّ أَمْرَ رَسُولِ اللَّهِ صلى الله عليه وسلم لَرَدَدْتُهُ، وَمَا وَضَعْنَا سُيُوفَنَا عَلَى عَوَاتِقِنَا إِلَى أَمْرٍ يُفْظِعُنَا إِلاَّ أَسْهَلْنَ بِنَا إِلَى أَمْرٍ نَعْرِفُهُ غَيْرَ هَذَا الأَمْرِ. قَالَ وَقَالَ أَبُو وَائِلٍ شَهِدْتُ صِفِّينَ وَبِئْسَتْ صِفُّونَ

Narrated Habib bin Abi Thabit: I went to Abu Wail to ask him (about those who had rebelled against `Ali). On that Abu Wail said, "We were at Siffin (a city on the bank of the Euphrates, the place where me battle took place between `Ali and Muawiya) A man said, "Will you be on the side of those who are called to consult Allah's Book (to settle the dispute)?" `Ali said, 'Yes (I agree that we should settle the matter in the light of the Qur'an)." ' Some people objected to `Ali's agreement and wanted to fight. On that Sahl bin Hunaif said, 'Blame yourselves! I remember how, on the day of Al-Hudaibiya (i.e. the peace treaty between the Prophet ﷺ and the Quraish pagans), if we had been allowed to choose fighting, we would have fought (the pagans). At that time `Umar came (to the Prophet) and said, "Aren't we on the right (path) and they (pagans) in the wrong? Won't our killed persons go to Paradise, and theirs in the Fire?" The Prophet replied, "Yes." `Umar further said, "Then why should we let our religion be degraded and return before Allah has settled the matter between us?" The Prophet ﷺ said, "O the son of Al-Khattab! No doubt, I am Allah's Messenger ﷺ and Allah will never neglect me." So `Umar left the place angrily and he was so impatient that he went to Abu Bakr and said, "O Abu Bakr! Aren't we on the right (path) and they (pagans) on the wrong?" Abu Bakr said, "O the son of Al-Khattab! He Is Allah's Messenger, and Allah will never neglect him." Then Sura Al-Fath (The Victory) was revealed." :- Sahih Al-Bukhari 4844

حَدَّثَنَا أَحْمَدُ بْنُ إِسْحَاقَ السُّلَمِيُّ، حَدَّثَنَا يَعْلَى، حَدَّثَنَا عَبْدُ الْعَزِيزِ بْنُ سِيَاهٍ، عَنْ حَبِيبِ بْنِ أَبِي ثَابِتٍ، قَالَ أَتَيْتُ أَبَا وَائِلٍ أَسْأَلُهُ فَقَالَ كُنَّا بِصِفِّينَ فَقَالَ رَجُلٌ أَلَمْ تَرَ إِلَى الَّذِينَ يُدْعَوْنَ إِلَى كِتَابِ اللَّهِ. فَقَالَ عَلِيٌّ نَعَمْ. فَقَالَ سَهْلُ بْنُ حُنَيْفٍ اتَّهِمُوا أَنْفُسَكُمْ فَلَقَدْ رَأَيْتُنَا يَوْمَ الْحُدَيْبِيَةِ ـ يَعْنِي الصُّلْحَ الَّذِي كَانَ بَيْنَ النَّبِيِّ صلى الله عليه وسلم وَالْمُشْرِكِينَ ـ وَلَوْ نَرَى قِتَالاً لَقَاتَلْنَا، فَجَاءَ عُمَرُ فَقَالَ أَلَسْنَا عَلَى الْحَقِّ وَهُمْ عَلَى الْبَاطِلِ أَلَيْسَ قَتْلاَنَا فِي الْجَنَّةِ وَقَتْلاَهُمْ فِي النَّارِ قَالَ " بَلَى ". قَالَ فَفِيمَ أُعْطِي الدَّنِيَّةَ فِي دِينِنَا، وَنَرْجِعُ وَلَمَّا يَحْكُمِ اللَّهُ بَيْنَنَا. فَقَالَ " يَا ابْنَ الْخَطَّابِ إِنِّي رَسُولُ اللَّهِ وَلَنْ يُضَيِّعَنِي اللَّهُ أَبَدًا ". فَرَجَعَ مُتَغَيِّظًا، فَلَمْ يَصْبِرْ حَتَّى جَاءَ أَبَا بَكْرٍ فَقَالَ يَا أَبَا بَكْرٍ أَلَسْنَا عَلَى الْحَقِّ وَهُمْ عَلَى الْبَاطِلِ قَالَ يَا ابْنَ الْخَطَّابِ إِنَّهُ رَسُولُ اللَّهِ صلى الله عليه وسلم وَلَنْ يُضَيِّعَهُ اللَّهُ أَبَدًا. فَنَزَلَتْ سُورَةُ الْفَتْحِ

Narrated `Ikrima bin Khalid: Ibn `Umar said, "I went to Hafsa while water was dribbling from her twined braids. I said, 'The condition of the people is as you see, and no authority has been given to me.' Hafsa said, (to me), 'Go to them, and as they (i.e. the people) are waiting for you, and I am afraid your absence from them will produce division amongst them.' " So

Hafsa did not leave Ibn `Umar till we went to them. When the people differed. Muawiya addressed the people saying, "'If anybody wants to say anything in this matter of the Caliphate, he should show up and not conceal himself, for we are more rightful to be a Caliph than he and his father." On that, Habib bin Masalama said (to Ibn `Umar), "Why don't you reply to him (i.e. Muawiya)?" `Abdullah bin `Umar said, "I untied my garment that was going round my back and legs while I was sitting and was about to say, 'He who fought against you and against your father for the sake of Islam, is more rightful to be a Caliph,' but I was afraid that my statement might produce differences amongst the people and cause bloodshed, and my statement might be interpreted not as I intended. (So I kept quiet) remembering what Allah has prepared in the Gardens of Paradise (for those who are patient and prefer the Hereafter to this worldly life)." Habib said, "You did what kept you safe and secure (i.e. you were wise in doing so). – Sahih Al-Bukhari 4108

حَدَّثَنِي إِبْرَاهِيمُ بْنُ مُوسَى، أَخْبَرَنَا هِشَامٌ، عَنْ مَعْمَرٍ، عَنِ الزُّهْرِيِّ، عَنْ سَالِمٍ، عَنِ ابْنِ عُمَرَ، قَالَ وَأَخْبَرَنِي ابْنُ طَاوُسٍ، عَنْ عِكْرِمَةَ بْنِ خَالِدٍ، عَنِ ابْنِ عُمَرَ، قَالَ دَخَلْتُ عَلَى حَفْصَةَ وَنَسْوَاتُهَا تَنْطُفُ، قُلْتُ قَدْ كَانَ مِنْ أَمْرِ النَّاسِ مَا تَرَيْنَ، فَلَمْ يُجْعَلْ لِي مِنَ الأَمْرِ شَىْءٌ. فَقَالَتِ الْحَقْ فَإِنَّهُمْ يَنْتَظِرُونَكَ، وَأَخْشَى أَنْ يَكُونَ فِي احْتِبَاسِكَ عَنْهُمْ فُرْقَةٌ. فَلَمْ تَدَعْهُ حَتَّى ذَهَبَ، فَلَمَّا تَفَرَّقَ النَّاسُ خَطَبَ مُعَاوِيَةُ قَالَ مَنْ كَانَ يُرِيدُ أَنْ يَتَكَلَّمَ فِي هَذَا الأَمْرِ فَلْيُطْلِعْ لَنَا قَرْنَهُ، فَلَنَحْنُ أَحَقُّ بِهِ مِنْهُ وَمِنْ أَبِيهِ. قَالَ حَبِيبُ بْنُ مَسْلَمَةَ فَهَلاَّ أَجَبْتَهُ قَالَ عَبْدُ اللَّهِ فَحَلَلْتُ حُبْوَتِي وَهَمَمْتُ أَنْ أَقُولَ أَحَقُّ بِهَذَا الأَمْرِ مِنْكَ مَنْ قَاتَلَكَ وَأَبَاكَ عَلَى الإِسْلاَمِ. فَخَشِيتُ أَنْ أَقُولَ كَلِمَةً تُفَرِّقُ بَيْنَ الْجَمْعِ، وَتَسْفِكُ الدَّمَ، وَيُحْمَلُ عَنِّي غَيْرُ ذَلِكَ، فَذَكَرْتُ مَا أَعَدَّ اللَّهُ فِي الْجِنَانِ. قَالَ حَبِيبٌ حُفِظْتَ وَعُصِمْتَ. قَالَ مَحْمُودٌ عَنْ عَبْدِ الرَّزَّاقِ وَنَوْسَاتُهَا

Agreement to end Siffin
اتفاق معاهدة إنهاء صفين

Narrated Al-Hasan Al-Basri: By Allah, Al-Hasan bin `Ali led large battalions like mountains against Muawiya. `Amr bin Al-As said (to Muawiya), "I surely see battalions which will not turn back before killing their opponents." Muawiya who was really the best of the two men said to him, "O `Amr! If these killed those and those killed these, who would be left with me for the jobs of the public, who would be left with me for their women, who would be left with me for their children?" Then Muawiya sent two Quraishi men from the tribe of `Abd-i-Shams called `Abdur Rahman bin Sumura and `Abdullah bin 'Amir bin Kuraiz to Al-Hasan saying to them, "Go to this man (i.e. Al-Hasan) and negotiate peace with him and talk and appeal to him." So, they went to Al-Hasan and talked and appealed to him to accept peace. Al-Hasan said, "We, the offspring of `Abdul Muttalib, have got wealth and people have indulged in killing and corruption (and money only will appease them)." They said to Al-Hasan, "Muawiya offers you so and so, and appeals to you and entreats you to accept peace." Al-Hasan said to them, "But who will be responsible for what you have said?" They said, "We will be responsible for it." So, whatever Al- Hasan asked they said, "We will be responsible for it for you." So, Al-Hasan concluded a peace treaty with Muawiya. Al-Hasan (Al-Basri) said: I heard Abu Bakr saying, "I saw Allah's Messenger ﷺ on the pulpit and Al-Hasan bin `Ali was by his side. The Prophet ﷺ was looking once at the people and once at Al-Hasan bin `Ali saying, 'This son of mine is a Saiyid (i.e. a noble) and may Allah make peace between two big groups of Muslims through him.". – Sahih Al-Bukhari 2704

حَدَّثَنَا عَبْدُ اللَّهِ بْنُ مُحَمَّدٍ، حَدَّثَنَا سُفْيَانُ، عَنْ أَبِي مُوسَى، قَالَ سَمِعْتُ الْحَسَنَ، يَقُولُ اسْتَقْبَلَ وَاللَّهِ الْحَسَنُ بْنُ عَلِيٍّ مُعَاوِيَةَ بِكَتَائِبَ أَمْثَالِ الْجِبَالِ فَقَالَ عَمْرُو بْنُ الْعَاصِ إِنِّي لأَرَى كَتَائِبَ لاَ تُوَلِّي حَتَّى تَقْتُلَ أَقْرَانَهَا. فَقَالَ لَهُ مُعَاوِيَةُ ـ وَكَانَ وَاللَّهِ خَيْرَ الرَّجُلَيْنِ ـ أَىْ عَمْرُو إِنْ قَتَلَ هَؤُلاَءِ هَؤُلاَءِ وَهَؤُلاَءِ هَؤُلاَءِ مَنْ لِي بِأُمُورِ النَّاسِ مَنْ لِي بِنِسَائِهِمْ، مَنْ لِي بِضَيْعَتِهِمْ فَبَعَثَ إِلَيْهِ رَجُلَيْنِ مِنْ قُرَيْشٍ مِنْ بَنِي عَبْدِ شَمْسٍ عَبْدَ الرَّحْمَنِ بْنَ سَمُرَةَ وَعَبْدَ اللَّهِ بْنَ عَامِرِ بْنِ كُرَيْزٍ، فَقَالَ اذْهَبَا إِلَى هَذَا الرَّجُلِ فَاعْرِضَا عَلَيْهِ، وَقُولاَ لَهُ، وَاطْلُبَا إِلَيْهِ. فَأَتَيَاهُ، فَدَخَلاَ عَلَيْهِ فَتَكَلَّمَا، وَقَالاَ لَهُ، فَطَلَبَا إِلَيْهِ، فَقَالَ لَهُمَا الْحَسَنُ بْنُ عَلِيٍّ إِنَّا بَنُو

عَبْدِ الْمُطَّلِبِ، قَدْ أَصَبْنَا مِنْ هَذَا الْمَالِ، وَإِنَّ هَذِهِ الأُمَّةَ قَدْ عَاثَتْ فِي دِمَائِهَا. قَالاَ فَإِنَّهُ يَعْرِضُ عَلَيْكَ كَذَا وَكَذَا وَيَطْلُبُ إِلَيْكَ وَيَسْأَلُكَ. قَالَ فَمَنْ لِي بِهَذَا قَالاَ نَحْنُ لَكَ بِهِ. فَمَا سَأَلَهُمَا شَيْئًا إِلاَّ قَالاَ نَحْنُ لَكَ بِهِ. فَصَالَحَهُ، فَقَالَ الْحَسَنُ وَلَقَدْ سَمِعْتُ أَبَا بَكْرَةَ يَقُولُ رَأَيْتُ رَسُولَ اللَّهِ صلى الله عليه وسلم عَلَى الْمِنْبَرِ وَالْحَسَنُ بْنُ عَلِيٍّ إِلَى جَنْبِهِ، وَهْوَ يُقْبِلُ عَلَى النَّاسِ مَرَّةً وَعَلَيْهِ أُخْرَى وَيَقُولُ " إِنَّ ابْنِي هَذَا سَيِّدٌ، وَلَعَلَّ اللَّهَ أَنْ يُصْلِحَ بِهِ بَيْنَ فِئَتَيْنِ عَظِيمَتَيْنِ مِنَ الْمُسْلِمِينَ ". قَالَ لِي عَلِيُّ بْنُ عَبْدِ اللَّهِ إِنَّمَا ثَبَتَ لَنَا سَمَاعُ الْحَسَنِ مِنْ أَبِي بَكْرَةَ بِهَذَا الْحَدِيثِ.

Narrated `Ali bin Al-Husain: That when they reached Medina after returning from Yazid bin Mu'awaiya after the martyrdom of Husain bin `Ali (may Allah bestow His Mercy upon him), Al-Miswar bin Makhrama met him and said to him, "Do you have any need you may order me to satisfy?" `Ali said, "No." Al-Miswar said, Will you give me the sword of Allah's Messenger ﷺ for I am afraid that people may take it from you by force? By Allah, if you give it to me, they will never be able to take it till I die." When `Ali bin Abu Talib demanded the hand of the daughter of Abi Jahal to be his wife besides Fatima, I heard Allah's Messenger ﷺ on his pulpit delivering a sermon in this connection before the people, and I had then attained my age of puberty. Allah's Messenger ﷺ said, "Fatima is from me, and I am afraid she will be subjected to trials in her religion (because of jealousy)." The Prophet ﷺ then mentioned one of his son-in-law who was from the tribe of 'Abu Shams, and he praised him as a good son-in-law, saying, "Whatever he said was the truth, and he promised me and fulfilled his promise. I do not make a legal thing illegal, nor do I make an illegal thing legal, but by Allah, the daughter of Allah's Messenger ﷺ and the daughter of the enemy of Allah, (i.e. Abu Jahl) can never get together (as the wives of one man) (See Hadith No. 76, Vo. 5). – Sahih Al-Bukhari 3110

حَدَّثَنَا سَعِيدُ بْنُ مُحَمَّدٍ الْجَرْمِيُّ، حَدَّثَنَا يَعْقُوبُ بْنُ إِبْرَاهِيمَ، حَدَّثَنَا أَبِي أَنَّ الْوَلِيدَ بْنَ كَثِيرٍ، حَدَّثَهُ عَنْ مُحَمَّدِ بْنِ عَمْرِو بْنِ حَلْحَلَةَ الدُّؤَلِيِّ، حَدَّثَهُ أَنَّ ابْنَ شِهَابٍ حَدَّثَهُ أَنَّ عَلِيَّ بْنَ حُسَيْنٍ حَدَّثَهُ أَنَّهُمْ، حِينَ قَدِمُوا الْمَدِينَةَ مِنْ عِنْدِ يَزِيدَ بْنِ مُعَاوِيَةَ مَقْتَلَ حُسَيْنِ بْنِ عَلِيٍّ رَحْمَةُ اللَّهِ عَلَيْهِ لَقِيَهُ الْمِسْوَرُ بْنُ مَخْرَمَةَ فَقَالَ لَهُ هَلْ لَكَ إِلَىَّ مِنْ حَاجَةٍ تَأْمُرُنِي بِهَا فَقُلْتُ لَهُ لاَ. فَقَالَ لَهُ فَهَلْ أَنْتَ مُعْطِيَّ سَيْفَ رَسُولِ اللَّهِ صلى الله عليه وسلم فَإِنِّي أَخَافُ أَنْ يَغْلِبَكَ الْقَوْمُ عَلَيْهِ، وَايْمُ اللَّهِ، لَئِنْ أَعْطَيْتَنِيهِ لاَ يُخْلَصُ إِلَيْهِمْ أَبَدًا حَتَّى تُبْلَغَ نَفْسِي، إِنَّ عَلِيَّ بْنَ أَبِي طَالِبٍ خَطَبَ ابْنَةَ أَبِي جَهْلٍ عَلَى فَاطِمَةَ - عَلَيْهَا السَّلاَمُ - فَسَمِعْتُ رَسُولَ اللَّهِ صلى الله عليه وسلم يَخْطُبُ النَّاسَ فِي ذَلِكَ عَلَى مِنْبَرِهِ هَذَا وَأَنَا يَوْمَئِذٍ مُحْتَلِمٌ فَقَالَ " إِنَّ فَاطِمَةَ مِنِّي، وَأَنَا أَتَخَوَّفُ أَنْ تُفْتَنَ فِي دِينِهَا ". ثُمَّ ذَكَرَ صِهْرًا لَهُ مِنْ بَنِي عَبْدِ شَمْسٍ، فَأَثْنَى عَلَيْهِ فِي مُصَاهَرَتِهِ إِيَّاهُ قَالَ " حَدَّثَنِي فَصَدَقَنِي، وَوَعَدَنِي فَوَفَى لِي، وَإِنِّي لَسْتُ أُحَرِّمُ حَلاَلاً وَلاَ أُحِلُّ حَرَامًا، وَلَكِنْ وَاللَّهِ لاَ تَجْتَمِعُ بِنْتُ رَسُولِ اللَّهِ صلى الله عليه وسلم وَبِنْتُ عَدُوِّ اللَّهِ أَبَدًا ".

Warrad
وَرَّادٍ

Narrated Warrad: (The clerk of Al-Mughira) Muawiya wrote to Al-Mughira 'Write to me what you have heard from Allah's Messenger ﷺ.' So he (Al-Mughira) wrote to him: Allah's Prophet used to say at the end of each prayer: "La ilaha illalla-h wahdahu la sharika lahu, lahul Mulku, wa lahul Hamdu wa hula ala kulli shai'in qadir. 'Allahumma la mani' a lima a'taita, wala mu'tiya lima mana'ta, wala yanfa'u dhuljadd minkal-jadd." He also wrote to him that the Prophet ﷺ used to forbid (1) Qil and Qal (idle useless talk or that you talk too much about others), (2) Asking too many questions (in disputed Religious matters); (3) And wasting one's wealth by extravagance; (4) and to be undutiful to one's mother (5) and to bury the daughters alive (6) and to prevent your favors (benevolence to others (i.e. not to pay the rights of others (7) And asking others for something (except when it is unavoidable). – Sahih Al-Bukhari 7292

حَدَّثَنَا مُوسَى، حَدَّثَنَا أَبُو عَوَانَةَ، حَدَّثَنَا عَبْدُ الْمَلِكِ، عَنْ وَرَّادٍ، كَاتِبِ الْمُغِيرَةِ قَالَ كَتَبَ مُعَاوِيَةُ إِلَى الْمُغِيرَةِ اكْتُبْ إِلَيَّ مَا سَمِعْتَ مِنْ رَسُولِ اللَّهِ صلى الله عليه وسلم. فَكَتَبَ إِلَيْهِ إِنَّ نَبِيَّ اللَّهِ صلى الله عليه وسلم كَانَ يَقُولُ فِي دُبُرِ كُلِّ صَلاَةٍ " لاَ إِلَهَ إِلاَّ اللَّهُ، وَحْدَهُ لاَ شَرِيكَ لَهُ، لَهُ الْمُلْكُ وَلَهُ الْحَمْدُ، وَهْوَ عَلَى كُلِّ شَىْءٍ قَدِيرٌ، اللَّهُمَّ لاَ مَانِعَ لِمَا أَعْطَيْتَ، وَلاَ مُعْطِيَ لِمَا

مَنَعْتَ، وَلاَ يَنْفَعُ ذَا الْجَدِّ مِنْكَ الْجَدُّ ". وَكَتَبَ إِلَيْهِ إِنَّهُ كَانَ يَنْهَى عَنْ قِيلَ وَقَالَ، وَكَثْرَةِ السُّؤَالِ، وَإِضَاعَةِ الْمَالِ، وَكَانَ يَنْهَى عَنْ عُقُوقِ الأُمَّهَاتِ وَوَأْدِ الْبَنَاتِ وَمَنْعٍ وَهَاتِ

Narrated Warrad: (the freed slave of Al-Mughira bin Shu`ba) Muawiya wrote to Mughira. 'Write to me what you heard the Prophet ﷺ saying after his prayer.' So Al-Mughira dictated to me and said, "I heard the Prophet ﷺ saying after the prayer, 'None has the right to be worshipped but Allah Alone Who has no partner. O Allah! No-one can withhold what You give, and none can give what You withhold, and the fortune of a man of means is useless before You (i.e., only good deeds are of value). – Sahih Al-Bukhari 6615
حَدَّثَنَا مُحَمَّدُ بْنُ سِنَانٍ، حَدَّثَنَا فُلَيْحٌ، حَدَّثَنَا عَبْدَةُ بْنُ أَبِي لُبَابَةَ، عَنْ وَرَّادٍ، مَوْلَى الْمُغِيرَةِ بْنِ شُعْبَةَ قَالَ كَتَبَ مُعَاوِيَةُ إِلَى الْمُغِيرَةِ اكْتُبْ إِلَيَّ مَا سَمِعْتَ النَّبِيَّ صلى الله عليه وسلم يَقُولُ خَلْفَ الصَّلاَةِ. فَأَمْلَى عَلَىَّ الْمُغِيرَةُ قَالَ سَمِعْتُ النَّبِيَّ صلى الله عليه وسلم يَقُولُ خَلْفَ الصَّلاَةِ " لاَ إِلَهَ إِلاَّ اللَّهُ، وَحْدَهُ لاَ شَرِيكَ لَهُ، اللَّهُمَّ لاَ مَانِعَ لِمَا أَعْطَيْتَ، وَلاَ مُعْطِيَ لِمَا مَنَعْتَ، وَلاَ يَنْفَعُ ذَا الْجَدِّ مِنْكَ الْجَدُّ ". وَقَالَ ابْنُ جُرَيْجٍ أَخْبَرَنِي عَبْدَةُ أَنَّ وَرَّادًا أَخْبَرَهُ بِهَذَا. ثُمَّ وَفَدْتُ بَعْدُ إِلَى مُعَاوِيَةَ فَسَمِعْتُهُ يَأْمُرُ النَّاسَ بِذَلِكَ الْقَوْلِ

Narrated Muawiya :You offer a prayer which I did not see being offered by Allah's Messenger (ﷺ)when we were in his company and he certainly had forbidden it (i.e. two rak`at after the `Asr prayer). Sahih al-Bukhari 587
حَدَّثَنَا مُحَمَّدُ بْنُ أَبَانَ، قَالَ حَدَّثَنَا غُنْدَرٌ، قَالَ حَدَّثَنَا شُعْبَةُ، عَنْ أَبِي التَّيَّاحِ، قَالَ سَمِعْتُ حُمْرَانَ بْنَ أَبَانَ، يُحَدِّثُ عَنْ مُعَاوِيَةَ، قَالَ إِنَّكُمْ لَتُصَلُّونَ صَلاَةً، لَقَدْ صَحِبْنَا رَسُولَ اللَّهِ صلى الله عليه وسلم فَمَا رَأَيْنَاهُ يُصَلِّيهَا، وَلَقَدْ نَهَى عَنْهُمَا، يَعْنِي الرَّكْعَتَيْنِ بَعْدَ الْعَصْرِ.

Narrated Abu Huraira :Allah's Messenger (ﷺ) forbade the offering of two prayers: -1. After the morning prayer till the sunrises. -2. After the `Asr prayer till the sun sets. Al-Bukhari 588
حَدَّثَنَا مُحَمَّدُ بْنُ سَلاَمٍ، قَالَ حَدَّثَنَا عَبْدَةُ، عَنْ عُبَيْدِ اللَّهِ، عَنْ خُبَيْبٍ، عَنْ حَفْصِ بْنِ عَاصِمٍ، عَنْ أَبِي هُرَيْرَةَ، قَالَ نَهَى رَسُولُ اللَّهِ صلى الله عليه وسلم عَنْ صَلاَتَيْنِ بَعْدَ الْفَجْرِ حَتَّى تَطْلُعَ الشَّمْسُ، وَبَعْدَ الْعَصْرِ حَتَّى تَغْرُبَ الشَّمْسُ.

Narrated Ibn `Umar :I pray as I saw my companions praying. I do not forbid praying at any time during the day or night except at sunset and sunrise. - Sahih al-Bukhari 589
حَدَّثَنَا أَبُو النُّعْمَانِ، حَدَّثَنَا حَمَّادُ بْنُ زَيْدٍ، عَنْ أَيُّوبَ، عَنْ نَافِعٍ، عَنِ ابْنِ عُمَرَ، قَالَ أُصَلِّي كَمَا رَأَيْتُ أَصْحَابِي يُصَلُّونَ، لاَ أَنْهَى أَحَدًا يُصَلِّي بِلَيْلٍ وَلاَ نَهَارٍ مَا شَاءَ، غَيْرَ أَنْ لاَ تَحَرَّوْا طُلُوعَ الشَّمْسِ وَلاَ غُرُوبَهَا.

Narrated `Aisha :By Allah, Who took away the Prophet. The Prophet (ﷺ) never missed them (two rak`at) after the `Asr prayer till he met Allah and he did not meet Allah till it became heavy for him to pray while standing so he used to offer most of the prayers while sitting. (She meant the two rak`at after `Asr) He used to pray them in the house and never prayed them in the mosque lest it might be hard for his followers and he loved what was easy for them. - Sahih al-Bukhari 590 [20]
حَدَّثَنَا أَبُو نُعَيْمٍ، قَالَ حَدَّثَنَا عَبْدُ الْوَاحِدِ بْنُ أَيْمَنَ، قَالَ حَدَّثَنِي أَبِي أَنَّهُ، سَمِعَ عَائِشَةَ، قَالَتْ وَالَّذِي ذَهَبَ بِهِ مَا تَرَكَهُمَا حَتَّى لَقِيَ اللَّهَ، وَمَا لَقِيَ اللَّهَ تَعَالَى حَتَّى ثَقُلَ عَنِ الصَّلاَةِ، وَكَانَ يُصَلِّي كَثِيرًا مِنْ صَلاَتِهِ قَاعِدًا ـ تَعْنِي الرَّكْعَتَيْنِ بَعْدَ الْعَصْرِ ـ وَكَانَ النَّبِيُّ صلى الله عليه وسلم يُصَلِّيهِمَا، وَلاَ يُصَلِّيهِمَا فِي الْمَسْجِدِ مَخَافَةَ أَنْ يُثَقِّلَ عَلَى أُمَّتِهِ، وَكَانَ يُحِبُّ مَا يُخَفِّفُ عَنْهُمْ.

---

[20] Bukhari 587-590 Division between Aisha and the caliphate of Mu'awiya . With the imprisonment of Abdur Rahman bin Bakr Sahih Al-Bukhari 4827, and Asama bint Bakr refused to sale her land to Mu'awiya Sahih Al-Bukhari Vol. 3 pg 447.

It was narrated that Saeed bin Jubair said: "I was with Ibn Abbas in Arafat and he said: 'Why do I not hear the people reciting Talbiyah?' I said: They are afraid of Muawiyah.' So Ibn Abbas went out of his tent and said: "Labbaik Allahumma Labbaik, Labbaik! They are only forsaking the Sunnah out of hatred for Ali.'" - Sunan an-Nasa'I 3006

أَخْبَرَنَا أَحْمَدُ بْنُ عُثْمَانَ بْنِ حَكِيمٍ الأَوْدِيُّ، قَالَ حَدَّثَنَا خَالِدُ بْنُ مَخْلَدٍ، قَالَ حَدَّثَنَا عَلِيُّ بْنُ صَالِحٍ، عَنْ مَيْسَرَةَ بْنِ حَبِيبٍ، عَنِ الْمِنْهَالِ بْنِ عَمْرٍو، عَنْ سَعِيدِ بْنِ جُبَيْرٍ، قَالَ كُنْتُ مَعَ ابْنِ عَبَّاسٍ بِعَرَفَاتٍ فَقَالَ مَا لِي لاَ أَسْمَعُ النَّاسَ يُلَبُّونَ قُلْتُ يَخَافُونَ مِنْ مُعَاوِيَةَ . فَخَرَجَ ابْنُ عَبَّاسٍ مِنْ فُسْطَاطِهِ فَقَالَ لَبَّيْكَ اللَّهُمَّ لَبَّيْكَ لَبَّيْكَ فَإِنَّهُمْ قَدْ تَرَكُوا السُّنَّةَ مِنْ بُغْضِ عَلِيٍّ.

The second Fitnah
الفتنة الثانية

Caliphate Yazid ibn Mu'awiya ibn Abi Sufyan
يزيد بن معاوية بن أبي سفيان

Ubaidullah bin Ziyad
عُبَيْدُ اللَّهِ بْنُ زِيَادٍ

Narrated Muhammad: Anas bin Malik said, "The head of Al-Husain was brought to 'Ubaidullah bin Ziyad and was put in a tray, and then Ibn Ziyad started playing with a stick at the nose and mouth of Al-Husain's head and saying something about his handsome features." Anas then said (to him), "Al-Husain resembled the Prophet more than the others did." Anas added, "His (i.e. Al-Husain's) hair was dyed with Wasma (i.e. a kind of plant used as a dye). – Sahih Al-Bukhari 3748

حَدَّثَنِي مُحَمَّدُ بْنُ الْحُسَيْنِ بْنِ إِبْرَاهِيمَ، قَالَ حَدَّثَنِي حُسَيْنُ بْنُ مُحَمَّدٍ، حَدَّثَنَا جَرِيرٌ، عَنْ مُحَمَّدٍ، عَنْ أَنَسِ بْنِ مَالِكٍ ـ رضى الله عنه ـ أُتِيَ عُبَيْدُ اللَّهِ بْنُ زِيَادٍ بِرَأْسِ الْحُسَيْنِ ـ عَلَيْهِ السَّلاَمُ ـ فَجُعِلَ فِي طَسْتٍ، فَجَعَلَ يَنْكُتُ، وَقَالَ فِي حُسْنِهِ شَيْئًا. فَقَالَ أَنَسٌ كَانَ أَشْبَهَهُمْ بِرَسُولِ اللَّهِ صلى الله عليه وسلم، وَكَانَ مَخْضُوبًا بِالْوَسْمَةِ

Karbala
كربلاء المقدسة

Narrated `Ali bin Al-Husain: That when they reached Medina after returning from Yazid bin Mu'awaiya after the martyrdom of Husain bin `Ali (may Allah bestow His Mercy upon him), Al-Miswar bin Makhrama met him and said to him, "Do you have any need you may order me to satisfy?" `Ali said, "No." Al-Miswar said, Will you give me the sword of Allah's Messenger ﷺ for I am afraid that people may take it from you by force? By Allah, if you give it to me, they will never be able to take it till I die." When `Ali bin Abu Talib demanded the hand of the daughter of Abi Jahal to be his wife besides Fatima, I heard Allah's Messenger ﷺ on his pulpit delivering a sermon in this connection before the people, and I had then attained my age of puberty. Allah's Messenger ﷺ said, "Fatima is from me, and I am afraid she will be subjected to trials in her religion (because of jealousy)." The Prophet ﷺ then mentioned one of his son-in-law who was from the tribe of 'Abu Shams, and he praised him as a good son-in-law, saying, "Whatever he said was the truth, and he promised me and fulfilled his promise. I do not make a legal thing illegal, nor do I make an illegal thing legal, but by Allah, the daughter of Allah's Messenger ﷺ and the daughter of the enemy of Allah, (i.e. Abu Jahl) can never get together (as the wives of one man). – Sahih Al-Bukhari 3110

حَدَّثَنَا سَعِيدُ بْنُ مُحَمَّدٍ الْجَرْمِيُّ، حَدَّثَنَا يَعْقُوبُ بْنُ إِبْرَاهِيمَ، حَدَّثَنَا أَبِي أَنَّ الْوَلِيدَ بْنَ كَثِيرٍ، حَدَّثَهُ عَنْ مُحَمَّدِ بْنِ عَمْرِو بْنِ حَلْحَلَةَ الدُّؤَلِيِّ، حَدَّثَهُ أَنَّ ابْنَ شِهَابٍ حَدَّثَهُ أَنَّ عَلِيَّ بْنَ حُسَيْنٍ حَدَّثَهُ أَنَّهُمْ، حِينَ قَدِمُوا الْمَدِينَةَ مِنْ عِنْدِ يَزِيدَ بْنِ مُعَاوِيَةَ مَقْتَلَ حُسَيْنِ بْنِ عَلِيٍّ رَحْمَةُ اللَّهِ عَلَيْهِ لَقِيَهُ الْمِسْوَرُ بْنُ مَخْرَمَةَ فَقَالَ لَهُ هَلْ لَكَ إِلَىَّ مِنْ حَاجَةٍ تَأْمُرُنِي بِهَا فَقُلْتُ لَهُ لاَ. فَقَالَ لَهُ فَهَلْ أَنْتَ مُعْطِيَّ سَيْفَ رَسُولِ اللَّهِ صلى الله عليه وسلم فَإِنِّي أَخَافُ أَنْ يَغْلِبَكَ الْقَوْمُ عَلَيْهِ، وَايْمُ اللَّهِ، لَئِنْ أَعْطَيْتَنِيهِ لاَ يُخْلَصُ إِلَيْهِمْ أَبَدًا حَتَّى تُبْلَغَ نَفْسِي، إِنَّ عَلِيَّ بْنَ أَبِي طَالِبٍ خَطَبَ ابْنَةَ أَبِي جَهْلٍ عَلَى فَاطِمَةَ ـ عَلَيْهَا السَّلاَمُ ـ فَسَمِعْتُ رَسُولَ اللَّهِ صلى الله عليه وسلم يَخْطُبُ النَّاسَ فِي ذَلِكَ عَلَى مِنْبَرِهِ هَذَا وَأَنَا يَوْمَئِذٍ مُحْتَلِمٌ فَقَالَ " إِنَّ فَاطِمَةَ مِنِّي، وَأَنَا أَتَخَوَّفُ أَنْ تُفْتَنَ فِي دِينِهَا ". ثُمَّ ذَكَرَ صِهْرًا لَهُ مِنْ بَنِي عَبْدِ شَمْسٍ، فَأَثْنَى عَلَيْهِ فِي مُصَاهَرَتِهِ إِيَّاهُ قَالَ " حَدَّثَنِي فَصَدَقَنِي، وَوَعَدَنِي فَوَفَى لِي، وَإِنِّي لَسْتُ أُحَرِّمُ حَلاَلاً وَلاَ أُحِلُّ حَرَامًا، وَلَكِنْ وَاللَّهِ لاَ تَجْتَمِعُ بِنْتُ رَسُولِ اللَّهِ صلى الله عليه وسلم وَبِنْتُ عَدُوِّ اللَّهِ أَبَدًا ".

Narrated ‘Ata: We presented ourselves along with Ibn `Abbas at the funeral procession of Maimuna at a place called Sarif. Ibn `Abbas said, “This is the wife of the Prophetﷺ so when you lift her bier, do not Jerk it or shake it much, but walk smoothly because the Prophetﷺ had nine wives and he used to observe the night turns with eight of them, and for one of them there was no night turn.”. – Sahih Al-Bukhari 5067

حَدَّثَنَا إِبْرَاهِيمُ بْنُ مُوسَى، أَخْبَرَنَا هِشَامُ بْنُ يُوسُفَ، أَنَّ ابْنَ جُرَيْجٍ، أَخْبَرَهُمْ قَالَ أَخْبَرَنِي عَطَاءٌ، قَالَ حَضَرْنَا مَعَ ابْنِ عَبَّاسٍ جَنَازَةَ مَيْمُونَةَ بِسَرِفَ، فَقَالَ ابْنُ عَبَّاسٍ هَذِهِ زَوْجَةُ النَّبِيِّ صلى الله عليه وسلم فَإِذَا رَفَعْتُمْ نَعْشَهَا فَلاَ تُزَعْزِعُوهَا وَلاَ تُزَلْزِلُوهَا وَارْفُقُوا، فَإِنَّهُ كَانَ عِنْدَ النَّبِيِّ صلى الله عليه وسلم تِسْعٌ، كَانَ يَقْسِمُ لِثَمَانٍ وَلاَ يَقْسِمُ لِوَاحِدَةٍ.

Narrated Shaqiq: While we were waiting for `Abdullah (bin Mas`ud). Yazid bin Muawiya came. I said (to him), “Will you sit down?” He said, “No, but I will go into the house (of Ibn Mas`ud) and let your companion (Ibn Mas`ud) come out to you; and if he should not (come out), I will come out and sit (with you).” Then `Abdullah came out, holding the hand of Yazid, addressed us, saying, “I know that you are assembled here, but the reason that prevents me from coming out to you, is that Allah’s Messengerﷺ used to preach to us at intervals during the days, lest we should become bored.”. – Sahih Al-Bukhari 6411

حَدَّثَنَا عُمَرُ بْنُ حَفْصٍ، حَدَّثَنَا أَبِي، حَدَّثَنَا الأَعْمَشُ، قَالَ حَدَّثَنِي شَقِيقٌ، قَالَ كُنَّا نَنْتَظِرُ عَبْدَ اللَّهِ إِذْ جَاءَ يَزِيدُ بْنُ مُعَاوِيَةَ فَقُلْنَا أَلاَ تَجْلِسُ قَالَ لاَ وَلَكِنْ أَدْخُلُ فَأُخْرِجُ إِلَيْكُمْ صَاحِبَكُمْ، وَإِلاَّ جِئْتُ أَنَا. فَجَلَسْتُ فَخَرَجَ عَبْدُ اللَّهِ وَهْوَ آخِذٌ بِيَدِهِ فَقَامَ عَلَيْنَا فَقَالَ أَمَا إِنِّي أُخْبَرُ بِمَكَانِكُمْ، وَلَكِنَّهُ يَمْنَعُنِي مِنَ الْخُرُوجِ إِلَيْكُمْ أَنَّ رَسُولَ اللَّهِ صلى الله عليه وسلم كَانَ يَتَخَوَّلُنَا بِالْمَوْعِظَةِ فِي الأَيَّامِ، كَرَاهِيَةَ السَّآمَةِ عَلَيْنَا

Narrated Sa`id: Abu Shuraih said, “When `Amr bin Sa`id was sending the troops to Mecca (to fight `Abdullah bin Az- Zubair) I said to him, ‘O chief! Allow me to tell you what the Prophetﷺ said on the day following the conquests of Mecca. My ears heard and my heart comprehended, and I saw him with my own eyes, when he said it. He glorified and praised Allah and then said, “Allah and not the people has made Mecca a sanctuary. So anybody who has belief in Allah and the Last Day (i.e. a Muslim) should neither shed blood in it nor cut down its trees. If anybody argues that fighting is allowed in Mecca as Allah’s Messengerﷺ did fight (in Mecca), tell him that Allah gave permission to His Apostle, but He did not give it to you. The Prophetﷺ added: Allah allowed me only for a few hours on that day (of the conquest) and today (now) its sanctity is the same (valid) as it was before. So it is Incumbent upon those who are present to convey it (this information) to those who are absent.” Abu-Shuraih was asked, “What did `Amr reply?” He said `Amr said, “O Abu Shuraih! I know better than you (in this respect). Mecca does not give protection to one who disobeys (Allah) or runs after committing murder, or theft (and takes refuge in Mecca). – Sahih Al-Bukhari 104

حَدَّثَنَا عَبْدُ اللَّهِ بْنُ يُوسُفَ، قَالَ حَدَّثَنِي اللَّيْثُ، قَالَ حَدَّثَنِي سَعِيدٌ، عَنْ أَبِي شُرَيْحٍ، أَنَّهُ قَالَ لِعَمْرِو بْنِ سَعِيدٍ وَهُوَ يَبْعَثُ الْبُعُوثَ إِلَى مَكَّةَ ائْذَنْ لِي أَيُّهَا الأَمِيرُ أُحَدِّثْكَ قَوْلاً قَامَ بِهِ النَّبِيُّ صلى الله عليه وسلم الْغَدَ مِنْ يَوْمِ الْفَتْحِ، سَمِعَتْهُ أُذُنَاىَ وَوَعَاهُ قَلْبِي، وَأَبْصَرَتْهُ عَيْنَاىَ، حِينَ تَكَلَّمَ بِهِ، حَمِدَ اللَّهَ وَأَثْنَى عَلَيْهِ ثُمَّ قَالَ " إِنَّ مَكَّةَ حَرَّمَهَا اللَّهُ، وَلَمْ يُحَرِّمْهَا النَّاسُ، فَلاَ يَحِلُّ لاِمْرِئٍ يُؤْمِنُ بِاللَّهِ وَالْيَوْمِ الآخِرِ أَنْ يَسْفِكَ بِهَا دَمًا، وَلاَ يَعْضِدَ بِهَا شَجَرَةً، فَإِنْ أَحَدٌ تَرَخَّصَ لِقِتَالِ رَسُولِ اللَّهِ صلى الله عليه وسلم فِيهَا فَقُولُوا إِنَّ اللَّهَ قَدْ أَذِنَ لِرَسُولِهِ، وَلَمْ يَأْذَنْ لَكُمْ. وَإِنَّمَا أَذِنَ لِي فِيهَا سَاعَةً مِنْ نَهَارٍ، ثُمَّ عَادَتْ حُرْمَتُهَا الْيَوْمَ كَحُرْمَتِهَا بِالأَمْسِ، وَلْيُبَلِّغِ الشَّاهِدُ الْغَائِبَ ". فَقِيلَ لأَبِي شُرَيْحٍ مَا قَالَ عَمْرٌو قَالَ أَنَا أَعْلَمُ مِنْكَ يَا أَبَا شُرَيْحٍ، لاَ يُعِيذُ عَاصِيًا، وَلاَ فَارًّا بِدَمٍ، وَلاَ فَارًّا بِخَرْبَةٍ.

Narrated Muhammad bin `Abdur-Rahman Abu Al-Aswad: The people of Medina were forced to prepare an army (to fight against the people of Sham during the caliphate of `Abdullah bin Az-Zubair at Mecca), and I was enlisted in it; Then I met `Ikrima, the freed slave of Ibn `Abbas, and informed him (about it), and he forbade me strongly to do so (i.e. to enlist in that army), and then said, "Ibn `Abbas informed me that some Muslim people were with the pagans, increasing the number of the pagans against Allah's Messenger ﷺ. An arrow used to be shot which would hit one of them (the Muslims in the company of the pagans) and kill him, or he would be struck and killed (with a sword)." Then Allah revealed:-- "Verily! As for those whom the angels take (in death) while they are wronging themselves (by staying among the disbelievers)" (4.97) Abu AlAswad also narrated it. – Sahih Al-Bukhari 4596

حَدَّثَنَا عَبْدُ اللَّهِ بْنُ يَزِيدَ الْمُقْرِئُ، حَدَّثَنَا حَيْوَةُ، وَغَيْرُهُ، قَالاَ حَدَّثَنَا مُحَمَّدُ بْنُ عَبْدِ الرَّحْمَنِ أَبُو الأَسْوَدِ، قَالَ قُطِعَ عَلَى أَهْلِ الْمَدِينَةِ بَعْثٌ فَاكْتُتِبْتُ فِيهِ، فَلَقِيتُ عِكْرِمَةَ مَوْلَى ابْنِ عَبَّاسٍ فَأَخْبَرْتُهُ، فَنَهَانِي عَنْ ذَلِكَ أَشَدَّ النَّهْىِ، ثُمَّ قَالَ أَخْبَرَنِي ابْنُ عَبَّاسٍ أَنَّ نَاسًا مِنَ الْمُسْلِمِينَ كَانُوا مَعَ الْمُشْرِكِينَ يُكَثِّرُونَ سَوَادَ الْمُشْرِكِينَ عَلَى رَسُولِ اللَّهِ صلى الله عليه وسلم يَأْتِي السَّهْمُ فَيُرْمَى بِهِ، فَيُصِيبُ أَحَدَهُمْ فَيَقْتُلُهُ أَوْ يُضْرَبُ فَيُقْتَلُ، فَأَنْزَلَ اللَّهُ {إِنَّ الَّذِينَ تَوَفَّاهُمُ الْمَلاَئِكَةُ ظَالِمِي أَنْفُسِهِمْ} الآيَةَ. رَوَاهُ اللَّيْثُ عَنْ أَبِي الأَسْوَدِ

Narrated Ibn Abi Mulaika: When there happened the disagreement between Ibn Az-Zubair and Ibn `Abbas, I said (to the latter), "(Why don't you take the oath of allegiance to him as) his father is Az-Zubair, and his mother is Asma,' and his aunt is `Aisha, and his maternal grandfather is Abu Bakr, and his grandmother is Safiya?". – Sahih Al-Bukhari 4664

حَدَّثَنَا عَبْدُ اللَّهِ بْنُ مُحَمَّدٍ، حَدَّثَنَا ابْنُ عُيَيْنَةَ، عَنِ ابْنِ جُرَيْجٍ، عَنِ ابْنِ أَبِي مُلَيْكَةَ، عَنِ ابْنِ عَبَّاسٍ ـ رضى الله عنهما ـ أَنَّهُ قَالَ حِينَ وَقَعَ بَيْنَهُ وَبَيْنَ ابْنِ الزُّبَيْرِ قُلْتُ أَبُوهُ الزُّبَيْرُ، وَأُمُّهُ أَسْمَاءُ، وَخَالَتُهُ عَائِشَةُ، وَجَدُّهُ أَبُو بَكْرٍ، وَجَدَّتُهُ صَفِيَّةُ. فَقُلْتُ لِسُفْيَانَ إِسْنَادُهُ. فَقَالَ حَدَّثَنَا، فَشَغَلَهُ إِنْسَانٌ وَلَمْ يَقُلِ ابْنُ جُرَيْجٍ

Narrated Ibn Abi Mulaika: There was a disagreement between them (i.e. Ibn `Abbas and Ibn Az-Zubair) so I went to Ibn `Abbas in the morning and said (to him), "Do you want to fight against Ibn Zubair and thus make lawful what Allah has made unlawful (i.e. fighting in Meccas?" Ibn `Abbas said, "Allah forbid! Allah ordained that Ibn Zubair and Bani Umaiya would permit (fighting in Mecca), but by Allah, I will never regard it as permissible." Ibn `Abbas added. "The people asked me to take the oath of allegiance to Ibn AzZubair. I said, 'He is really entitled to assume authority for his father, Az-Zubair was the helper of the Prophet, his (maternal) grandfather, Abu Bakr was (the Prophet's) companion in the cave, his mother, Asma' was 'Dhatun-Nitaq', his aunt, `Aisha was the mother of the Believers, his paternal aunt, Khadija was the wife of the Prophet ﷺ, and the paternal aunt of the Prophet ﷺ was his grandmother. He himself is pious and chaste in Islam, well versed in the Knowledge of the Qur'an. By Allah! (Really, I left my relatives, Bani Umaiya for his sake though) they are my close relatives, and if they should be my rulers, they are equally apt to be so and are descended from a noble family. – Sahih Al-Bukhari 4665

حَدَّثَنِي عَبْدُ اللَّهِ بْنُ مُحَمَّدٍ، قَالَ حَدَّثَنِي يَحْيَى بْنُ مَعِينٍ، حَدَّثَنَا حَجَّاجٌ، قَالَ ابْنُ جُرَيْجٍ قَالَ ابْنُ أَبِي مُلَيْكَةَ وَكَانَ بَيْنَهُمَا شَىْءٌ فَغَدَوْتُ عَلَى ابْنِ عَبَّاسٍ فَقُلْتُ أَتُرِيدُ أَنْ تُقَاتِلَ ابْنَ الزُّبَيْرِ، فَتُحِلُّ حَرَمَ اللَّهِ. فَقَالَ مَعَاذَ اللَّهِ، إِنَّ اللَّهَ كَتَبَ ابْنَ الزُّبَيْرِ وَبَنِي أُمَيَّةَ مُحِلِّينَ، وَإِنِّي وَاللَّهِ لاَ أُحِلُّهُ أَبَدًا. قَالَ قَالَ النَّاسُ بَايِعْ لاِبْنِ الزُّبَيْرِ. فَقُلْتُ وَأَيْنَ بِهَذَا الأَمْرِ عَنْهُ أَمَّا أَبُوهُ فَحَوَارِيُّ النَّبِيِّ صلى الله عليه وسلم، يُرِيدُ الزُّبَيْرَ، وَأَمَّا جَدُّهُ فَصَاحِبُ الْغَارِ، يُرِيدُ أَبَا بَكْرٍ، وَأُمُّهُ فَذَاتُ النِّطَاقِ، يُرِيدُ أَسْمَاءَ، وَأَمَّا خَالَتُهُ فَأُمُّ الْمُؤْمِنِينَ، يُرِيدُ عَائِشَةَ، وَأَمَّا عَمَّتُهُ فَزَوْجُ النَّبِيِّ صلى الله عليه وسلم، يُرِيدُ خَدِيجَةَ، وَأَمَّا عَمَّةُ النَّبِيِّ صلى الله عليه وسلم فَجَدَّتُهُ، يُرِيدُ صَفِيَّةَ، ثُمَّ عَفِيفٌ فِي الإِسْلاَمِ، قَارِئٌ لِلْقُرْآنِ. وَاللَّهِ إِنْ وَصَلُونِي وَصَلُونِي مِنْ قَرِيبٍ، وَإِنْ رَبُّونِي رَبَّنِي أَكْفَاءٌ كِرَامٌ، فَآثَرَ التُّوَيْتَاتِ وَالأُسَامَاتِ وَالْحُمَيْدَاتِ، يُرِيدُ أَبْطُنًا مِنْ بَنِي أَسَدٍ بَنِي تُوَيْتٍ وَبَنِي أُسَامَةَ وَبَنِي أَسَدٍ، إِنَّ ابْنَ أَبِي الْعَاصِ بَرَزَ يَمْشِي الْقُدَمِيَّةَ، يَعْنِي عَبْدَ الْمَلِكِ بْنَ مَرْوَانَ، وَإِنَّهُ لَوَّى ذَنَبَهُ، يَعْنِي ابْنَ الزُّبَيْرِ.

Narrated Ibn Abi Mulaika: We entered upon Ibn `Abbas and he said "Are you not astonished at Ibn Az-Zubair's assuming the caliphate?" I said (to myself), "I will support him and speak of his good traits as I did not do even for Abu Bakr and `Umar though they were more entitled to receive al l good than he was." I said "He (i.e Ibn Az-Zubair) is the son of the aunt of the Prophet ﷺ and the son of AzZubair, and the grandson of Abu Bakr and the son of Khadija's

brother, and the son of `Aisha's sister." Nevertheless, he considers himself to be superior to me and does not want me to be one of his friends. So I said, "I never expected that he would refuse my offer to support him, and I don't think he intends to do me any good, therefore, if my cousins should inevitably be my rulers, it will be better for me to be ruled by them than by some others.". – Sahih Al-Bukhari 4666
حَدَّثَنَا مُحَمَّدُ بْنُ عُبَيْدِ بْنِ مَيْمُونٍ، حَدَّثَنَا عِيسَى بْنُ يُونُسَ، عَنْ عُمَرَ بْنِ سَعِيدٍ، قَالَ أَخْبَرَنِي ابْنُ أَبِي مُلَيْكَةَ، دَخَلْنَا عَلَى ابْنِ عَبَّاسٍ فَقَالَ أَلاَ تَعْجَبُونَ لاِبْنِ الزُّبَيْرِ قَامَ فِي أَمْرِهِ هَذَا فَقُلْتُ لأُحَاسِبَنَّ نَفْسِي لَهُ مَا حَاسَبْتُهَا لأَبِي بَكْرٍ وَلاَ لِعُمَرَ، وَلَهُمَا كَانَا أَوْلَى بِكُلِّ خَيْرٍ مِنْهُ، وَقُلْتُ ابْنُ عَمَّةِ النَّبِيِّ صلى الله عليه وسلم، وَابْنُ الزُّبَيْرِ، وَابْنُ أَبِي بَكْرٍ، وَابْنُ أَخِي خَدِيجَةَ، وَابْنُ أُخْتِ عَائِشَةَ فَإِذَا هُوَ يَتَعَلَّى عَنِّي وَلاَ يُرِيدُ ذَلِكَ فَقُلْتُ مَا كُنْتُ أَظُنُّ أَنِّي أَعْرِضُ هَذَا مِنْ نَفْسِي، فَيَدَعُهُ، وَمَا أُرَاهُ يُرِيدُ خَيْرًا، وَإِنْ كَانَ لاَ بُدَّ لأَنْ يَرُبَّنِي بَنُو عَمِّي أَحَبُّ إِلَىَّ مِنْ أَنْ يَرُبَّنِي غَيْرُهُمْ

Narrated Nafi`: When the people of Medina dethroned Yazid bin Muawiya, Ibn `Umar gathered his special friends and children and said, "I heard the Prophetﷺ saying, 'A flag will be fixed for every betrayer on the Day of Resurrection,' and we have given the oath of allegiance to this person (Yazid) in accordance with the conditions enjoined by Allah and His Apostle and I do not know of anything more faithless than fighting a person who has been given the oath of allegiance in accordance with the conditions enjoined by Allah and His Apostle , and if ever I learn that any person among you has agreed to dethrone Yazid, by giving the oath of allegiance (to somebody else) then there will be separation between him and me.". – Sahih Al-Bukhari 7111
حَدَّثَنَا سُلَيْمَانُ بْنُ حَرْبٍ، حَدَّثَنَا حَمَّادُ بْنُ زَيْدٍ، عَنْ أَيُّوبَ، عَنْ نَافِعٍ، قَالَ لَمَّا خَلَعَ أَهْلُ الْمَدِينَةِ يَزِيدَ بْنَ مُعَاوِيَةَ جَمَعَ ابْنُ عُمَرَ حَشَمَهُ وَوَلَدَهُ فَقَالَ إِنِّي سَمِعْتُ النَّبِيَّ صلى الله عليه وسلم يَقُولُ " يُنْصَبُ لِكُلِّ غَادِرٍ لِوَاءٌ يَوْمَ الْقِيَامَةِ ". وَإِنَّا قَدْ بَايَعْنَا هَذَا الرَّجُلَ عَلَى بَيْعِ اللَّهِ وَرَسُولِهِ، وَإِنِّي لاَ أَعْلَمُ غَدْرًا أَعْظَمَ مِنْ أَنْ يُبَايَعَ رَجُلٌ عَلَى بَيْعِ اللَّهِ وَرَسُولِهِ، ثُمَّ يُنْصَبُ لَهُ الْقِتَالُ، وَإِنِّي لاَ أَعْلَمُ أَحَدًا مِنْكُمْ خَلَعَهُ، وَلاَ بَايَعَ فِي هَذَا الأَمْرِ، إِلاَّ كَانَتِ الْفَيْصَلَ بَيْنِي وَبَيْنَهُ

Marwan
مَرْوَانُ

First Siege of Mecca
الحصار الأول لمكة

Narrated Yusuf bin Mahak: Marwan had been appointed as the governor of Hijaz by Muawiya. He delivered a sermon and mentioned Yazid bin Muawiya so that the people might take the oath of allegiance to him as the successor of his father (Muawiya). Then `Abdur Rahman bin Abu Bakr told him something whereupon Marwan ordered that he be arrested. But `Abdur-Rahman entered `Aisha's house and they could not arrest him. Marwan said, "It is he (`AbdurRahman) about whom Allah revealed this Verse:-- 'And the one who says to his parents: 'Fie on you! Do you hold out the promise to me..?'" On that, `Aisha said from behind a screen, "Allah did not reveal anything from the Qur'an about us except what was connected with the declaration of my innocence (of the slander). – Sahih Al-Bukhari 4827
حَدَّثَنَا مُوسَى بْنُ إِسْمَاعِيلَ، حَدَّثَنَا أَبُو عَوَانَةَ، عَنْ أَبِي بِشْرٍ، عَنْ يُوسُفَ بْنِ مَاهَكَ، قَالَ كَانَ مَرْوَانُ عَلَى الْحِجَازِ اسْتَعْمَلَهُ مُعَاوِيَةُ، فَخَطَبَ فَجَعَلَ يَذْكُرُ يَزِيدَ بْنَ مُعَاوِيَةَ، لِكَىْ يُبَايَعَ لَهُ بَعْدَ أَبِيهِ، فَقَالَ لَهُ عَبْدُ الرَّحْمَنِ بْنُ أَبِي بَكْرٍ شَيْئًا، فَقَالَ خُذُوهُ. فَدَخَلَ بَيْتَ عَائِشَةَ فَلَمْ يَقْدِرُوا {عَلَيْهِ} فَقَالَ مَرْوَانُ إِنَّ هَذَا الَّذِي أَنْزَلَ اللَّهُ فِيهِ {وَالَّذِي قَالَ لِوَالِدَيْهِ أُفٍّ لَكُمَا أَتَعِدَانِنِي}. فَقَالَتْ عَائِشَةُ مِنْ وَرَاءِ الْحِجَابِ مَا أَنْزَلَ اللَّهُ فِينَا شَيْئًا مِنَ الْقُرْآنِ إِلاَّ أَنَّ اللَّهَ أَنْزَلَ عُذْرِي.

Narrated Abu Al-Minhal: When Ibn Ziyad and Marwan were in Sham and Ibn Az-Zubair took over the authority in Mecca and Qurra' (the Kharijites) revolted in Basra, I went out with my father to Abu Barza Al-Aslami till we entered upon him in his house while he was sitting in the shade of a room built of cane. So we sat with him and my father started talking to him saying, “O Abu Barza! Don’t you see in what dilemma the people has fallen?” The first thing heard him saying “I seek reward from Allah for myself because of being angry and scornful at the Quraish tribe. O you Arabs! You know very well that you were in misery and were few in number and misguided, and that Allah has brought you out of all that with Islam and with Muhammad till He brought you to this state (of prosperity and happiness) which you see now; and it is this worldly wealth and pleasures which has caused mischief to appear among you. The one who is in Sham (i.e., Marwan), by Allah, is not fighting except for the sake of worldly gain: and those who are among you, by Allah, are not fighting except for the sake of worldly gain; and that one who is in Mecca (i.e., Ibn Az-Zubair) by Allah, is not fighting except for the sake of worldly gain.”. – Sahih Al-Bukhari 7112

حَدَّثَنَا أَحْمَدُ بْنُ يُونُسَ، حَدَّثَنَا أَبُو شِهَابٍ، عَنْ عَوْفٍ، عَنْ أَبِي الْمِنْهَالِ، قَالَ لَمَّا كَانَ ابْنُ زِيَادٍ وَمَرْوَانُ بِالشَّأْمِ، وَوَثَبَ ابْنُ الزُّبَيْرِ بِمَكَّةَ، وَوَثَبَ الْقُرَّاءُ بِالْبَصْرَةِ، فَانْطَلَقْتُ مَعَ أَبِي إِلَى أَبِي بَرْزَةَ الأَسْلَمِيِّ حَتَّى دَخَلْنَا عَلَيْهِ فِي دَارِهِ وَهْوَ جَالِسٌ فِي ظِلِّ عُلِّيَّةٍ لَهُ مِنْ قَصَبٍ، فَجَلَسْنَا إِلَيْهِ فَأَنْشَأَ أَبِي يَسْتَطْعِمُهُ الْحَدِيثَ فَقَالَ يَا أَبَا بَرْزَةَ أَلاَ تَرَى مَا وَقَعَ فِيهِ النَّاسُ فَأَوَّلُ شَىْءٍ سَمِعْتُهُ تَكَلَّمَ بِهِ إِنِّي احْتَسَبْتُ عِنْدَ اللَّهِ أَنِّي أَصْبَحْتُ سَاخِطًا عَلَى أَحْيَاءِ قُرَيْشٍ، إِنَّكُمْ يَا مَعْشَرَ الْعَرَبِ كُنْتُمْ عَلَى الْحَالِ الَّذِي عَلِمْتُمْ مِنَ الذِّلَّةِ وَالْقِلَّةِ وَالضَّلاَلَةِ، وَإِنَّ اللَّهَ أَنْقَذَكُمْ بِالإِسْلاَمِ وَبِمُحَمَّدٍ صلى الله عليه وسلم حَتَّى بَلَغَ بِكُمْ مَا تَرَوْنَ، وَهَذِهِ الدُّنْيَا الَّتِي أَفْسَدَتْ بَيْنَكُمْ، إِنَّ ذَاكَ الَّذِي بِالشَّأْمِ وَاللَّهِ إِنْ يُقَاتِلُ إِلاَّ عَلَى الدُّنْيَا

Narrated Abu Sa`id Al-Khudri: The Prophet ﷺ used to proceed to the Musalla on the days of Id-ul-Fitr and Id-ul-Adha; the first thing to begin with was the prayer and after that he would stand in front of the people and the people would keep sitting in their rows. Then he would preach to them, advise them and give them orders. And after that if he wished to send an army for an expedition, he would do so; or if he wanted to give and order, he would do so, and then depart. The people followed this tradition till I went out with Marwan, the Governor of Medina, for the prayer of Id-ul-Adha or Id-ul-Fitr. When we reached the Musalla, there was a pulpit made by Kathir bin As-Salt. Marwan wanted to get up on that pulpit before the prayer. I got hold of his clothes but he pulled them and ascended the pulpit and delivered the Khutba before the prayer. I said to him, “By Allah, you have changed (the Prophet’s tradition).” He replied, “O Abu Sa`id! Gone is that which you know.” I said, “By Allah! What I know is better than what I do not know.” Marwan said, “People do not sit to listen to our Khutba after the prayer, so I delivered the Khutba before the prayer.”. – Sahih Al-Bukhari 956

حَدَّثَنَا سَعِيدُ بْنُ أَبِي مَرْيَمَ، قَالَ حَدَّثَنَا مُحَمَّدُ بْنُ جَعْفَرٍ، قَالَ أَخْبَرَنِي زَيْدٌ، عَنْ عِيَاضِ بْنِ عَبْدِ اللَّهِ بْنِ أَبِي سَرْحٍ، عَنْ أَبِي سَعِيدٍ الْخُدْرِيِّ، قَالَ كَانَ رَسُولُ اللَّهِ صلى الله عليه وسلم يَخْرُجُ يَوْمَ الْفِطْرِ وَالأَضْحَى إِلَى الْمُصَلَّى، فَأَوَّلُ شَىْءٍ يَبْدَأُ بِهِ الصَّلاَةُ ثُمَّ يَنْصَرِفُ، فَيَقُومُ مُقَابِلَ النَّاسِ، وَالنَّاسُ جُلُوسٌ عَلَى صُفُوفِهِمْ، فَيَعِظُهُمْ وَيُوصِيهِمْ وَيَأْمُرُهُمْ، فَإِنْ كَانَ يُرِيدُ أَنْ يَقْطَعَ بَعْثًا قَطَعَهُ، أَوْ يَأْمُرَ بِشَىْءٍ أَمَرَ بِهِ، ثُمَّ يَنْصَرِفُ. قَالَ أَبُو سَعِيدٍ فَلَمْ يَزَلِ النَّاسُ عَلَى ذَلِكَ حَتَّى خَرَجْتُ مَعَ مَرْوَانَ وَهْوَ أَمِيرُ الْمَدِينَةِ فِي أَضْحًى أَوْ فِطْرٍ، فَلَمَّا أَتَيْنَا الْمُصَلَّى إِذَا مِنْبَرٌ بَنَاهُ كَثِيرُ بْنُ الصَّلْتِ، فَإِذَا مَرْوَانُ يُرِيدُ أَنْ يَرْتَقِيَهُ قَبْلَ أَنْ يُصَلِّيَ، فَجَبَذْتُ بِثَوْبِهِ فَجَبَذَنِي فَارْتَفَعَ، فَخَطَبَ قَبْلَ الصَّلاَةِ، فَقُلْتُ لَهُ غَيَّرْتُمْ وَاللَّهِ. فَقَالَ أَبَا سَعِيدٍ، قَدْ ذَهَبَ مَا تَعْلَمُ. فَقُلْتُ مَا أَعْلَمُ وَاللَّهِ خَيْرٌ مِمَّا لاَ أَعْلَمُ. فَقَالَ إِنَّ النَّاسَ لَمْ يَكُونُوا يَجْلِسُونَ لَنَا بَعْدَ الصَّلاَةِ فَجَعَلْتُهَا قَبْلَ الصَّلاَةِ.

Narrated Jabala: “While at Medina we were struck with famine. Ibn Az-Zubair used to provide us with dates as our food. Ibn `Umar used to pass by us and say, “Don’t eat two dates together at a time as the Prophet ﷺ has forbidden eating two dates together at a time (in a gathering) unless one takes the permission of one’s companion brother.”. – Sahih Al-Bukhari 2490

حَدَّثَنَا أَبُو الْوَلِيدِ، حَدَّثَنَا شُعْبَةُ، عَنْ جَبَلَةَ، قَالَ كُنَّا بِالْمَدِينَةِ فَأَصَابَتْنَا سَنَةٌ، فَكَانَ ابْنُ الزُّبَيْرِ يَرْزُقُنَا التَّمْرَ، وَكَانَ ابْنُ عُمَرَ يَمُرُّ بِنَا فَيَقُولُ لاَ تَقْرُنُوا فَإِنَّ النَّبِيَّ صلى الله عليه وسلم نَهَى عَنِ الإِقْرَانِ، إِلاَّ أَنْ يَسْتَأْذِنَ الرَّجُلُ مِنْكُمْ أَخَاهُ

Narrated Abu Al-Minhal: When Ibn Ziyad and Marwan were in Sham and Ibn Az-Zubair took over the authority in Mecca and Qurra’ (the Kharijites) revolted in Basra, I went out with my father to Abu Barza Al-Aslami till we entered upon him in his house while he was sitting in the shade of a room built of cane. So we sat with him and my father started talking to him saying, "O Abu Barza! Don't you see in what dilemma the people has fallen?" The first thing heard him saying "I seek reward from Allah for myself because of being angry and scornful at the Quraish tribe. O you Arabs! You know very well that you were in misery and were few in number and misguided, and that Allah has brought you out of all that with Islam and with Muhammad till He brought you to this state (of prosperity and happiness) which you see now; and it is this worldly wealth and pleasures which has caused mischief to appear among you. The one who is in Sham (i.e., Marwan), by Allah, is not fighting except for the sake of worldly gain: and those who are among you, by Allah, are not fighting except for the sake of worldly gain; and that one who is in Mecca (i.e., Ibn Az-Zubair) by Allah, is not fighting except for the sake of worldly gain.". – Sahih Al-Bukhari 7112

حَدَّثَنَا أَحْمَدُ بْنُ يُونُسَ، حَدَّثَنَا أَبُو شِهَابٍ، عَنْ عَوْفٍ، عَنْ أَبِي الْمِنْهَالِ، قَالَ لَمَّا كَانَ ابْنُ زِيَادٍ وَمَرْوَانُ بِالشَّأْمِ، وَوَثَبَ ابْنُ الزُّبَيْرِ بِمَكَّةَ، وَوَثَبَ الْقُرَّاءُ بِالْبَصْرَةِ، فَانْطَلَقْتُ مَعَ أَبِي إِلَى أَبِي بَرْزَةَ الأَسْلَمِيِّ حَتَّى دَخَلْنَا عَلَيْهِ فِي دَارِهِ وَهْوَ جَالِسٌ فِي ظِلِّ عُلِّيَّةٍ لَهُ مِنْ قَصَبٍ، فَجَلَسْنَا إِلَيْهِ فَأَنْشَأَ أَبِي يَسْتَطْعِمُهُ الْحَدِيثَ فَقَالَ يَا أَبَا بَرْزَةَ أَلاَ تَرَى مَا وَقَعَ فِيهِ النَّاسُ فَأَوَّلُ شَىْءٍ سَمِعْتُهُ تَكَلَّمَ بِهِ إِنِّي احْتَسَبْتُ عِنْدَ اللَّهِ أَنِّي أَصْبَحْتُ سَاخِطًا عَلَى أَحْيَاءِ قُرَيْشٍ، إِنَّكُمْ يَا مَعْشَرَ الْعَرَبِ كُنْتُمْ عَلَى الْحَالِ الَّذِي عَلِمْتُمْ مِنَ الذِّلَّةِ وَالْقِلَّةِ وَالضَّلاَلَةِ، وَإِنَّ اللَّهَ أَنْقَذَكُمْ بِالإِسْلاَمِ وَبِمُحَمَّدٍ صلى الله عليه وسلم حَتَّى بَلَغَ بِكُمْ مَا تَرَوْنَ، وَهَذِهِ الدُّنْيَا الَّتِي أَفْسَدَتْ بَيْنَكُمْ، إِنَّ ذَاكَ الَّذِي بِالشَّأْمِ وَاللَّهِ إِنْ يُقَاتِلُ إِلاَّ عَلَى الدُّنْيَا

Narrated Nafi`: Ibn `Umar intended to perform Hajj in the year of the Hajj of Al-Harawriya during the rule of Ibn Az- Zubair. Some people said to him, "It is very likely that there will be a fight among the people, and we are afraid that they might prevent you (from performing Hajj)." He replied, "Verily, in Allah's Messenger ﷺ there is a good example for you (to follow). In this case I would do the same as he had done. I make you witness that I have intended to perform `Umra." When he reached Al-Baida', he said, "The conditions for both Hajj and `Umra are the same. I make you witness that I have intended to perform Hajj along with `Umra." After that he took a garlanded Hadi (to Mecca) which he bought (on the way). When he reached (Mecca), he performed Tawaf of the Ka`ba and of Safa (and Marwa) and did not do more than that. He did not make legal for himself the things which were illegal for a Muhrim till it was the Day of Nahr (sacrifice), when he had his head shaved and slaughtered (the sacrifice) and considered sufficient his first Tawaf (between Safa and Marwa), as a (Sa`i) for his Hajj and `Umra both. He then said, "The Prophet ﷺ used to do like that.". – Sahih Al-Bukhari 1708

حَدَّثَنَا إِبْرَاهِيمُ بْنُ الْمُنْذِرِ، حَدَّثَنَا أَبُو ضَمْرَةَ، حَدَّثَنَا مُوسَى بْنُ عُقْبَةَ، عَنْ نَافِعٍ، قَالَ أَرَادَ ابْنُ عُمَرَ ـ رضى الله عنهما ـ الْحَجَّ عَامَ حَجَّةِ الْحَرُورِيَّةِ فِي عَهْدِ ابْنِ الزُّبَيْرِ ـ رضى الله عنهما ـ فَقِيلَ لَهُ إِنَّ النَّاسَ كَائِنٌ بَيْنَهُمْ قِتَالٌ، وَنَخَافُ أَنْ يَصُدُّوكَ. فَقَالَ {لَقَدْ كَانَ لَكُمْ فِي رَسُولِ اللَّهِ أُسْوَةٌ حَسَنَةٌ} إِذًا أَصْنَعَ كَمَا صَنَعَ، أُشْهِدُكُمْ أَنِّي أَوْجَبْتُ عُمْرَةً. حَتَّى كَانَ بِظَاهِرِ الْبَيْدَاءِ قَالَ مَا شَأْنُ الْحَجِّ وَالْعُمْرَةِ إِلاَّ وَاحِدٌ، أُشْهِدُكُمْ أَنِّي جَمَعْتُ حَجَّةً مَعَ عُمْرَةٍ. وَأَهْدَى هَدْيًا مُقَلَّدًا اشْتَرَاهُ حَتَّى قَدِمَ، فَطَافَ بِالْبَيْتِ وَبِالصَّفَا، وَلَمْ يَزِدْ عَلَى ذَلِكَ، وَلَمْ يَحْلِلْ مِنْ شَىْءٍ حَرُمَ مِنْهُ حَتَّى يَوْمِ النَّحْرِ، فَحَلَقَ وَنَحَرَ وَرَأَى أَنْ قَدْ قَضَى طَوَافَهُ الْحَجَّ وَالْعُمْرَةَ بِطَوَافِهِ الأَوَّلِ، ثُمَّ قَالَ كَذَلِكَ صَنَعَ النَّبِيُّ صلى الله عليه وسلم.

Narrated Muhammad bin `Abdur-Rahman Abu Al-Aswad: The people of Medina were forced to prepare an army (to fight against the people of Sham during the caliphate of `Abdullah bin Az-Zubair at Mecca), and I was enlisted in it; Then I met `Ikrima, the freed slave of Ibn `Abbas, and informed him (about it), and he forbade me strongly to do so (i.e. to enlist in that army), and then said, "Ibn `Abbas informed me that some Muslim people were with the pagans, increasing the number of the pagans against Allah's Messenger ﷺ. An arrow used to be shot which would hit one of them (the Muslims in the company of the pagans) and kill him, or he would be struck and killed (with a sword)." Then Allah revealed:-- "Verily! As for those whom the angels take (in death) while they are wronging themselves (by staying among the disbelievers)" (4.97) Abu AlAswad also narrated it. – Sahih Al-Bukhari 4596

حَدَّثَنَا عَبْدُ اللَّهِ بْنُ يَزِيدَ الْمُقْرِئُ، حَدَّثَنَا حَيْوَةُ، وَغَيْرُهُ، قَالاَ حَدَّثَنَا مُحَمَّدُ بْنُ عَبْدِ الرَّحْمَنِ أَبُو الأَسْوَدِ، قَالَ قُطِعَ عَلَى أَهْلِ الْمَدِينَةِ بَعْثٌ فَاكْتُتِبْتُ فِيهِ، فَلَقِيتُ عِكْرِمَةَ مَوْلَى ابْنِ عَبَّاسٍ فَأَخْبَرْتُهُ، فَنَهَانِي عَنْ ذَلِكَ أَشَدَّ النَّهْىِ، ثُمَّ قَالَ أَخْبَرَنِي ابْنُ عَبَّاسٍ أَنَّ نَاسًا مِنَ الْمُسْلِمِينَ

كَانُوا مَعَ الْمُشْرِكِينَ يُكَثِّرُونَ سَوَادَ الْمُشْرِكِينَ عَلَى رَسُولِ اللَّهِ صلى الله عليه وسلم يَأْتِي السَّهْمُ فَيُرْمَى بِهِ، فَيُصِيبُ أَحَدَهُمْ فَيَقْتُلُهُ أَوْ يُضْرَبُ فَيُقْتَلُ، فَأَنْزَلَ اللَّهُ {إِنَّ الَّذِينَ تَوَفَّاهُمُ الْمَلاَئِكَةُ ظَالِمِي أَنْفُسِهِمْ} الآيَةَ. رَوَاهُ اللَّيْثُ عَنْ أَبِي الأَسْوَدِ

Narrated Nafi`: During the affliction of Ibn Az-Zubair, two men came to Ibn `Umar and said, "The people are lost, and you are the son of `Umar, and the companion of the Prophet, so what forbids you from coming out?" He said, "What forbids me is that Allah has prohibited the shedding of my brother's blood." They both said, "Didn't Allah say, 'And fight then until there is no more affliction?" He said "We fought until there was no more affliction and the worship is for Allah (Alone while you want to fight until there is affliction and until the worship become for other than Allah." Narrated Nafi` (through another group of sub-narrators): A man came to Ibn `Umar and said, "O Abu `Abdur Rahman! What made you perform Hajj in one year and Umra in another year and leave the Jihad for Allah' Cause though you know how much Allah recommends it?" Ibn `Umar replied, "O son of my brother! Islam is founded on five principles, i.e. believe in Allah and His Apostle, the five compulsory prayers, the fasting of the month of Ramadan, the payment of Zakat, and the Hajj to the House (of Allah)." The man said, "O Abu `Abdur Rahman! Won't you listen to why Allah has mentioned in His Book: 'If two groups of believers fight each other, then make peace between them, but if one of then transgresses beyond bounds against the other, then you all fight against the one that transgresses. (49.9) and:--"And fight them till there is no more affliction (i.e. no more worshiping of others along with Allah)." Ibn `Umar said, "We did it, during the lifetime of Allah's Messenger ﷺ when Islam had only a few followers. A man would be put to trial because of his religion; he would either be killed or tortured. But when the Muslims increased, there was no more afflictions or oppressions." The man said, "What is your opinion about `Uthman and `Ali?" Ibn `Umar said, "As for `Uthman, it seems that Allah has forgiven him, but you people dislike that he should be forgiven. And as for `Ali, he is the cousin of Allah's Messenger ﷺ and his son-in-law." Then he pointed with his hand and said, "That is his house which you see.". – Sahih Al-Bukhari 4513, 4514, 4515

حَدَّثَنَا مُحَمَّدُ بْنُ بَشَّارٍ، حَدَّثَنَا عَبْدُ الْوَهَّابِ، حَدَّثَنَا عُبَيْدُ اللَّهِ، عَنْ نَافِعٍ، عَنِ ابْنِ عُمَرَ ـ رضى الله عنهما ـ أَتَاهُ رَجُلاَنِ فِي فِتْنَةِ ابْنِ الزُّبَيْرِ فَقَالاَ إِنَّ النَّاسَ قَدْ ضُيِّعُوا، وَأَنْتَ ابْنُ عُمَرَ وَصَاحِبُ النَّبِيِّ صلى الله عليه وسلم فَمَا يَمْنَعُكَ أَنْ تَخْرُجَ فَقَالَ يَمْنَعُنِي أَنَّ اللَّهَ حَرَّمَ دَمَ أَخِي. فَقَالاَ أَلَمْ يَقُلِ اللَّهُ {وَقَاتِلُوهُمْ حَتَّى لاَ تَكُونَ فِتْنَةٌ } فَقَالَ قَاتَلْنَا حَتَّى لَمْ تَكُنْ فِتْنَةٌ، وَكَانَ الدِّينُ لِلَّهِ، وَأَنْتُمْ تُرِيدُونَ أَنْ تُقَاتِلُوا حَتَّى تَكُونَ فِتْنَةٌ، وَيَكُونَ الدِّينُ لِغَيْرِ اللَّهِ. وَزَادَ عُثْمَانُ بْنُ صَالِحٍ عَنِ ابْنِ وَهْبٍ، قَالَ أَخْبَرَنِي فُلاَنٌ، وَحَيْوَةُ بْنُ شُرَيْحٍ، عَنْ بَكْرِ بْنِ عَمْرٍو الْمَعَافِرِيِّ، أَنَّ بُكَيْرَ بْنَ عَبْدِ اللَّهِ، حَدَّثَهُ عَنْ نَافِعٍ، أَنَّ رَجُلاً، أَتَى ابْنَ عُمَرَ فَقَالَ يَا أَبَا عَبْدِ الرَّحْمَنِ مَا حَمَلَكَ عَلَى أَنْ تَحُجَّ عَامًا وَتَعْتَمِرَ عَامًا، وَتَتْرُكَ الْجِهَادَ فِي سَبِيلِ اللَّهِ عَزَّ وَجَلَّ، وَقَدْ عَلِمْتَ مَا رَغَّبَ اللَّهُ فِيهِ قَالَ يَا ابْنَ أَخِي بُنِيَ الإِسْلاَمُ عَلَى خَمْسٍ إِيمَانٍ بِاللَّهِ وَرَسُولِهِ، وَالصَّلاَةِ الْخَمْسِ، وَصِيَامِ رَمَضَانَ، وَأَدَاءِ الزَّكَاةِ، وَحَجِّ الْبَيْتِ. قَالَ يَا أَبَا عَبْدِ الرَّحْمَنِ، أَلاَ تَسْمَعُ مَا ذَكَرَ اللَّهُ فِي كِتَابِهِ {وَإِنْ طَائِفَتَانِ مِنَ الْمُؤْمِنِينَ اقْتَتَلُوا فَأَصْلِحُوا بَيْنَهُمَا} {إِلَى أَمْرِ اللَّهِ} {قَاتِلُوهُمْ حَتَّى لاَ تَكُونَ فِتْنَةٌ} قَالَ فَعَلْنَا عَلَى عَهْدِ رَسُولِ اللَّهِ صلى الله عليه وسلم وَكَانَ الإِسْلاَمُ قَلِيلاً، فَكَانَ الرَّجُلُ يُفْتَنُ فِي دِينِهِ إِمَّا قَتَلُوهُ، وَإِمَّا يُعَذِّبُوهُ، حَتَّى كَثُرَ الإِسْلاَمُ فَلَمْ تَكُنْ فِتْنَةٌ. قَالَ فَمَا قَوْلُكَ فِي عَلِيٍّ وَعُثْمَانَ قَالَ أَمَّا عُثْمَانُ فَكَأَنَّ اللَّهَ عَفَا عَنْهُ، وَأَمَّا أَنْتُمْ فَكَرِهْتُمْ أَنْ تَعْفُوا عَنْهُ، وَأَمَّا عَلِيٌّ فَابْنُ عَمِّ رَسُولِ اللَّهِ صلى الله عليه وسلم وَخَتَنُهُ. وَأَشَارَ بِيَدِهِ فَقَالَ هَذَا بَيْتُهُ حَيْثُ تَرَوْنَ.

Al-Hajjaj
الحجاج

Narrated Nafi`: Ibn `Umar intended to perform Hajj in the year when Al-Hajjaj attacked Ibn Az-Zubair. Somebody said to Ibn `Umar, "There is a danger of an impending war between them." Ibn `Umar said, "Verily, in Allah's Messenger ﷺ you have a good example. (And if it happened as you say) then I would do the same as Allah's Messenger ﷺ had done. I make you witness that I have decided to perform `Umra." Then he set out and when he reached Al-Baida', he said, "The ceremonies of both Hajj and `Umra are similar. I make you witness that

I have made Hajj compulsory for me along with `Umra." He drove (to Mecca) a Hadi which he had bought from (a place called) Qudaid and did not do more than that. He did not slaughter the Hadi or finish his Ihram, or shave or cut short his hair till the day of slaughtering the sacrifices (10th Dhul-Hijja). Then he slaughtered his Hadi and shaved his head and considered the first Tawaf (of Safa and Marwa) as sufficient for Hajj and `Umra. Ibn `Umar said, "Allah's Messenger ﷺ did the same.". – Sahih Al-Bukhari 1640

حَدَّثَنَا قُتَيْبَةُ، حَدَّثَنَا اللَّيْثُ، عَنْ نَافِعٍ، أَنَّ ابْنَ عُمَرَ ـ رضى الله عنهما ـ أَرَادَ الْحَجَّ عَامَ نَزَلَ الْحَجَّاجُ بِابْنِ الزُّبَيْرِ. فَقِيلَ لَهُ إِنَّ النَّاسَ كَائِنٌ بَيْنَهُمْ قِتَالٌ، وَإِنَّا نَخَافُ أَنْ يَصُدُّوكَ. فَقَالَ {لَقَدْ كَانَ لَكُمْ فِي رَسُولِ اللَّهِ أُسْوَةٌ حَسَنَةٌ} إِذًا أَصْنَعَ كَمَا صَنَعَ رَسُولُ اللَّهِ صلى الله عليه وسلم، إِنِّي أُشْهِدُكُمْ أَنِّي قَدْ أَوْجَبْتُ عُمْرَةً. ثُمَّ خَرَجَ حَتَّى إِذَا كَانَ بِظَاهِرِ الْبَيْدَاءِ قَالَ مَا شَأْنُ الْحَجِّ وَالْعُمْرَةِ إِلاَّ وَاحِدٌ، أُشْهِدُكُمْ أَنِّي قَدْ أَوْجَبْتُ حَجًّا مَعَ عُمْرَتِي. وَأَهْدَى هَدْيًا اشْتَرَاهُ بِقُدَيْدٍ وَلَمْ يَزِدْ عَلَى ذَلِكَ، فَلَمْ يَنْحَرْ، وَلَمْ يَحِلَّ مِنْ شَىْءٍ حَرُمَ مِنْهُ، وَلَمْ يَحْلِقْ وَلَمْ يُقَصِّرْ حَتَّى كَانَ يَوْمُ النَّحْرِ، فَنَحَرَ وَحَلَقَ، وَرَأَى أَنْ قَدْ قَضَى طَوَافَ الْحَجِّ، وَالْعُمْرَةِ بِطَوَافِهِ الأَوَّلِ. وَقَالَ ابْنُ عُمَرَ ـ رضى الله عنهما ـ كَذَلِكَ فَعَلَ رَسُولُ اللَّهِ صلى الله عليه وسلم.

Narrated Anas: The Prophet ﷺ paid a visit to Um-Sulaim and she placed before him dates and ghee. The Prophet ﷺ said, "Replace the ghee and dates in their respective containers for I am fasting." Then he stood somewhere in her house and offered an optional prayer and then he invoked good on Um-Sulaim and her family. Then Um-Sulaim said, "O Allah's Messenger ﷺ! I have a special request (today)." He said, "What is it?" She replied, "(Please invoke for) your servant Anas." So Allah's Messenger ﷺ did not leave anything good in the world or the Hereafter which he did not invoke (Allah to bestow) on me and said, "O Allah! Give him (i.e. Anas) property and children and bless him." Thus I am one of the richest among the Ansar and my daughter Umaina told me that when Al-Hajjaj came to Basra, more than 120 of my offspring had been buried. – Sahih Al-Bukhari 1982

حَدَّثَنَا مُحَمَّدُ بْنُ الْمُثَنَّى، قَالَ حَدَّثَنِي خَالِدٌ ـ هُوَ ابْنُ الْحَارِثِ ـ حَدَّثَنَا حُمَيْدٌ، عَنْ أَنَسٍ ـ رضى الله عنه ـ دَخَلَ النَّبِيُّ صلى الله عليه وسلم عَلَى أُمِّ سُلَيْمٍ، فَأَتَتْهُ بِتَمْرٍ وَسَمْنٍ، قَالَ " أَعِيدُوا سَمْنَكُمْ فِي سِقَائِهِ، وَتَمْرَكُمْ فِي وِعَائِهِ، فَإِنِّي صَائِمٌ ". ثُمَّ قَامَ إِلَى نَاحِيَةٍ مِنَ الْبَيْتِ، فَصَلَّى غَيْرَ الْمَكْتُوبَةِ، فَدَعَا لأُمِّ سُلَيْمٍ، وَأَهْلِ بَيْتِهَا، فَقَالَتْ أُمُّ سُلَيْمٍ يَا رَسُولَ اللَّهِ، إِنَّ لِي خُوَيْصَةً، قَالَ " مَا هِيَ ". قَالَتْ خَادِمُكَ أَنَسٌ. فَمَا تَرَكَ خَيْرَ آخِرَةٍ وَلاَ دُنْيَا إِلاَّ دَعَا لِي بِهِ قَالَ " اللَّهُمَّ ارْزُقْهُ مَالاً وَوَلَدًا وَبَارِكْ لَهُ ". فَإِنِّي لَمِنْ أَكْثَرِ الأَنْصَارِ مَالاً. وَحَدَّثَتْنِي ابْنَتِي أُمَيْنَةُ أَنَّهُ دُفِنَ لِصُلْبِي مَقْدَمَ حَجَّاجٍ الْبَصْرَةَ بِضْعٌ وَعِشْرُونَ وَمِائَةٌ. حَدَّثَنَا ابْنُ أَبِي مَرْيَمَ، أَخْبَرَنَا يَحْيَى، قَالَ حَدَّثَنِي حُمَيْدٌ، سَمِعَ أَنَسًا ـ رضى الله عنه ـ عَنِ النَّبِيِّ صلى الله عليه وسلم

Narrated Al-A`mash: I heard Al-Hajjaj saying on the pulpit, "The Sura in which Al-Baqara (the cow) is mentioned and the Sura in which the family of `Imran is mentioned and the Sura in which the women (An-Nisa) is mentioned." I mentioned this to Ibrahim, and he said, `Abdur-Rahman bin Yazid told me, 'I was with Ibn Mas`ud, when he did the Rami of the Jamrat-ul-Aqaba. He went down the middle of the valley, and when he came near the tree (which was near the Jamra) he stood opposite to it and threw seven small pebbles and said: 'Allahu-Akbar' on throwing every pebble.' Then he said, 'By Him, except Whom none has the right to be worshipped, here (at this place) stood the one on whom Surat-al-Baqra was revealed (i.e. Allah's Messenger". – Sahih Al-Bukhari 1750

حَدَّثَنَا مُسَدَّدٌ، عَنْ عَبْدِ الْوَاحِدِ، حَدَّثَنَا الأَعْمَشُ، قَالَ سَمِعْتُ الْحَجَّاجَ، يَقُولُ عَلَى الْمِنْبَرِ السُّورَةُ الَّتِي يُذْكَرُ فِيهَا الْبَقَرَةُ، وَالسُّورَةُ الَّتِي يُذْكَرُ فِيهَا آلُ عِمْرَانَ، وَالسُّورَةُ الَّتِي يُذْكَرُ فِيهَا النِّسَاءُ. قَالَ فَذَكَرْتُ ذَلِكَ لإِبْرَاهِيمَ، فَقَالَ حَدَّثَنِي عَبْدُ الرَّحْمَنِ بْنُ يَزِيدَ أَنَّهُ كَانَ مَعَ ابْنِ مَسْعُودٍ ـ رضى الله عنه ـ حِينَ رَمَى جَمْرَةَ الْعَقَبَةِ، فَاسْتَبْطَنَ الْوَادِيَ، حَتَّى إِذَا حَاذَى بِالشَّجَرَةِ اعْتَرَضَهَا، فَرَمَى بِسَبْعِ حَصَيَاتٍ، يُكَبِّرُ مَعَ كُلِّ حَصَاةٍ، ثُمَّ قَالَ مِنْ هَا هُنَا وَالَّذِي لاَ إِلَهَ غَيْرُهُ قَامَ الَّذِي أُنْزِلَتْ عَلَيْهِ سُورَةُ الْبَقَرَةِ صلى الله عليه وسلم.

Narrated Az-Zubair bin `Adi: We went to Anas bin Malik and complained about the wrong we were suffering at the hand of Al- Hajjaj. Anas bin Malik said, "Be patient till you meet your

Lord, for no time will come upon you but the time following it will be worse than it. I heard that from the Prophet." - Sahih Al-Bukhari 7068

حَدَّثَنَا مُحَمَّدُ بْنُ يُوسُفَ، حَدَّثَنَا سُفْيَانُ، عَنِ الزُّبَيْرِ بْنِ عَدِيٍّ، قَالَ أَتَيْنَا أَنَسَ بْنَ مَالِكٍ فَشَكَوْنَا إِلَيْهِ مَا نَلْقَى مِنَ الْحَجَّاجِ فَقَالَ " اصْبِرُوا، فَإِنَّهُ لاَ يَأْتِي عَلَيْكُمْ زَمَانٌ إِلاَّ الَّذِي بَعْدَهُ شَرٌّ مِنْهُ، حَتَّى تَلْقَوْا رَبَّكُمْ ". سَمِعْتُهُ مِنْ نَبِيِّكُمْ صلى الله عليه وسلم.

Narrated Salama bin Al-Akwa`: That he visited Al-Hajjaj (bin Yusuf). Al-Hajjaj said, "O son of Al-Akwa`! You have turned on your heels (i.e., deserted Islam) by staying (in the desert) with the bedouins." Salama replied, "No, but Allah's Messenger ﷺ allowed me to stay with the bedouin in the desert." Narrated Yazid bin Abi Ubaid: When `Uthman bin `Affan was killed (martyred), Salama bin Al-Akwa` went out to a place called Ar- Rabadha and married there and begot children, and he stayed there till a few nights before his death when he came to Medina. – Sahih Al-Bukhari 7087

حَدَّثَنَا قُتَيْبَةُ بْنُ سَعِيدٍ، حَدَّثَنَا حَاتِمٌ، عَنْ يَزِيدَ بْنِ أَبِي عُبَيْدٍ، عَنْ سَلَمَةَ بْنِ الأَكْوَعِ، أَنَّهُ دَخَلَ عَلَى الْحَجَّاجِ فَقَالَ يَا ابْنَ الأَكْوَعِ ارْتَدَدْتَ عَلَى عَقِبَيْكَ تَعَرَّبْتَ قَالَ لاَ وَلَكِنَّ رَسُولَ اللَّهِ صلى الله عليه وسلم أَذِنَ لِي فِي الْبَدْوِ. وَعَنْ يَزِيدَ بْنِ أَبِي عُبَيْدٍ قَالَ لَمَّا قُتِلَ عُثْمَانُ بْنُ عَفَّانَ خَرَجَ سَلَمَةُ بْنُ الأَكْوَعِ إِلَى الرَّبَذَةِ، وَتَزَوَّجَ هُنَاكَ امْرَأَةً وَوَلَدَتْ لَهُ أَوْلاَدًا، فَلَمْ يَزَلْ بِهَا حَتَّى قَبْلَ أَنْ يَمُوتَ بِلَيَالٍ، فَنَزَلَ الْمَدِينَةَ

Narrated Sa`id bin Jubair: I was with Ibn `Umar when a spear head pierced the sole of his foot and his foot stuck to the paddle of the saddle and I got down and pulled his foot out, and that happened in Mina. Al-Hajjaj got the news and came to inquire about his health and said, "Alas! If we could only know the man who wounded you!" Ibn `Umar said, "You are the one who wounded me." Al-Hajjaj said, "How is that?" Ibn `Umar said, "You have allowed the arms to be carried on a day on which nobody used to carry them and you allowed arms to be carried in the Haram even though it was not allowed before.". – Sahih Al-Bukhari 966

حَدَّثَنَا زَكَرِيَّاءُ بْنُ يَحْيَى أَبُو السُّكَيْنِ، قَالَ حَدَّثَنَا الْمُحَارِبِيُّ، قَالَ حَدَّثَنَا مُحَمَّدُ بْنُ سُوقَةَ، عَنْ سَعِيدِ بْنِ جُبَيْرٍ، قَالَ كُنْتُ مَعَ ابْنِ عُمَرَ حِينَ أَصَابَهُ سِنَانُ الرُّمْحِ فِي أَخْمَصِ قَدَمِهِ، فَلَزِقَتْ قَدَمُهُ بِالرِّكَابِ، فَنَزَلْتُ فَنَزَعْتُهَا وَذَلِكَ بِمِنًى، فَبَلَغَ الْحَجَّاجَ فَجَعَلَ يَعُودُهُ فَقَالَ الْحَجَّاجُ لَوْ نَعْلَمُ مَنْ أَصَابَكَ. فَقَالَ ابْنُ عُمَرَ أَنْتَ أَصَبْتَنِي. قَالَ وَكَيْفَ قَالَ حَمَلْتَ السِّلاَحَ فِي يَوْمٍ لَمْ يَكُنْ يُحْمَلُ فِيهِ، وَأَدْخَلْتَ السِّلاَحَ الْحَرَمَ وَلَمْ يَكُنِ السِّلاَحُ يُدْخَلُ الْحَرَمَ.

Narrated Salim: `Abdul Malik wrote to Al-Hajjaj that he should not differ from Ibn `Umar during Hajj. On the Day of `Arafat, when the sun declined at midday, Ibn `Umar came along with me and shouted near Al- Hajjaj's cotton (cloth) tent. Al-Hajjaj came Out, wrapping himself with a waist-sheet dyed with safflower, and said, "O Abu `Abdur-Rahman! What is the matter?" He said, If you want to follow the Sunna (the tradition of the Prophet ﷺ) then proceed (to `Arafat)." Al-Hajjaj asked, "At this very hour?" Ibn `Umar said, "Yes." He replied, "Please wait for me till I pour some water over my head (i.e. take a bath) and come out." Then Ibn `Umar dismounted and waited till Al-Hajjaj came out. So, he (Al-Hajjaj) walked in between me and my father (Ibn `Umar). I said to him, "If you want to follow the Sunna then deliver a brief sermon and hurry up for the stay at `Arafat." He started looking at `Abdullah (Ibn `Umar) (inquiringly), and when `Abdullah noticed that, he said that he had told the truth. – Sahih Al-Bukhari 1660

حَدَّثَنَا عَبْدُ اللَّهِ بْنُ يُوسُفَ، أَخْبَرَنَا مَالِكٌ، عَنِ ابْنِ شِهَابٍ، عَنْ سَالِمٍ، قَالَ كَتَبَ عَبْدُ الْمَلِكِ إِلَى الْحَجَّاجِ أَنْ لاَ يُخَالِفَ ابْنَ عُمَرَ فِي الْحَجِّ، فَجَاءَ ابْنُ عُمَرَ ـ رضى الله عنه ـ وَأَنَا مَعَهُ يَوْمَ عَرَفَةَ حِينَ زَالَتِ الشَّمْسُ، فَصَاحَ عِنْدَ سُرَادِقِ الْحَجَّاجِ، فَخَرَجَ وَعَلَيْهِ مِلْحَفَةٌ مُعَصْفَرَةٌ فَقَالَ مَا لَكَ يَا أَبَا عَبْدِ الرَّحْمَنِ فَقَالَ الرَّوَاحَ إِنْ كُنْتَ تُرِيدُ السُّنَّةَ. قَالَ هَذِهِ السَّاعَةَ قَالَ نَعَمْ. قَالَ فَأَنْظِرْنِي حَتَّى أُفِيضَ عَلَى رَأْسِي ثُمَّ أَخْرُجَ. فَنَزَلَ حَتَّى خَرَجَ الْحَجَّاجُ، فَسَارَ بَيْنِي وَبَيْنَ أَبِي، فَقُلْتُ إِنْ كُنْتَ تُرِيدُ السُّنَّةَ فَاقْصُرِ الْخُطْبَةَ وَعَجِّلِ الْوُقُوفَ. فَجَعَلَ يَنْظُرُ إِلَى عَبْدِ اللَّهِ، فَلَمَّا رَأَى ذَلِكَ عَبْدُ اللَّهِ قَالَ صَدَقَ

Narrated Sa`id bin Jubair: `Abdullah bin `Umar came to us and we hoped that he would narrate to us a good Hadith. But before we asked him, a man got up and said to him, "O Abu `Abdur-Rahman! Narrate to us about the battles during the time of the afflictions, as Allah says:-- 'And fight them until there is no more afflictions (i.e. no more worshipping of others besides Allah).'" (2.193) Ibn `Umar said (to the man), "Do you know what is meant by afflictions? Let your mother bereave you! Muhammad used to fight against the pagans, for a Muslim was put to trial in his religion (The pagans will either kill him or chain him as a captive). His fighting was not like your fighting which is carried on for the sake of ruling.". – Sahih Al-Bukhari 7095

حَدَّثَنَا إِسْحَاقُ الْوَاسِطِيُّ، حَدَّثَنَا خَالِدٌ، عَنْ بَيَانٍ، عَنْ وَبَرَةَ بْنِ عَبْدِ الرَّحْمَنِ، عَنْ سَعِيدِ بْنِ جُبَيْرٍ، قَالَ خَرَجَ عَلَيْنَا عَبْدُ اللَّهِ بْنُ عُمَرَ فَرَجَوْنَا أَنْ يُحَدِّثَنَا، حَدِيثًا حَسَنًا ـ قَالَ ـ فَبَادَرَنَا إِلَيْهِ رَجُلٌ فَقَالَ يَا أَبَا عَبْدِ الرَّحْمَنِ حَدِّثْنَا عَنِ الْقِتَالِ فِي الْفِتْنَةِ وَاللَّهُ يَقُولُ {وَقَاتِلُوهُمْ حَتَّى لاَ تَكُونَ فِتْنَةٌ} فَقَالَ هَلْ تَدْرِي مَا الْفِتْنَةُ ثَكِلَتْكَ أُمُّكَ، إِنَّمَا كَانَ مُحَمَّدٌ صلى الله عليه وسلم يُقَاتِلُ الْمُشْرِكِينَ، وَكَانَ الدُّخُولُ فِي دِينِهِمْ فِتْنَةً، وَلَيْسَ كَقِتَالِكُمْ عَلَى الْمُلْكِ

Caliphate of Al-Walid bin `Abdul Malik
خلافة الوليد بن عبد الملك

Narrated `Urwa: When the wall fell on them (i.e. graves) during the caliphate of Al-Walid bin `Abdul Malik, the people started repairing it, and a foot appeared to them. The people got scared and thought that it was the foot of the Prophet. No one could be found who could tell them about it till I (`Urwa) said to them, "By Allah, this is not the foot of the Prophet ﷺ but it is the foot of `Umar.". – Sahih Al-Bukhari 1390c

حَدَّثَنَا فَرْوَةُ، حَدَّثَنَا عَلِيٌّ، عَنْ هِشَامِ بْنِ عُرْوَةَ، عَنْ أَبِيهِ، لَمَّا سَقَطَ عَلَيْهِمُ الْحَائِطُ فِي زَمَانِ الْوَلِيدِ بْنِ عَبْدِ الْمَلِكِ أَخَذُوا فِي بِنَائِهِ، فَبَدَتْ لَهُمْ قَدَمٌ فَفَزِعُوا، وَظَنُّوا أَنَّهَا قَدَمُ النَّبِيِّ صلى الله عليه وسلم فَمَا وَجَدُوا أَحَدًا يَعْلَمُ ذَلِكَ حَتَّى قَالَ لَهُمْ عُرْوَةُ لاَ وَاللَّهِ مَا هِيَ قَدَمُ النَّبِيِّ صلى الله عليه وسلم مَا هِيَ إِلاَّ قَدَمُ عُمَرَ ـ رضى الله عنه ـ.

Narrated Az-Zuhri: Al-Walid bin `Abdul Malik said to me, "Have you heard that `Ali' was one of those who slandered `Aisha?" I replied, "No, but two men from your people (named) Abu Salama bin `Abdur-Rahman and Abu Bakr bin `Abdur-Rahman bin Al-Harith have informed me that Aisha told them that `Ali remained silent about her case." – Sahih al-Bukhari 4142

حَدَّثَنِي عَبْدُ اللَّهِ بْنُ مُحَمَّدٍ، قَالَ أَمْلَى عَلَىَّ هِشَامُ بْنُ يُوسُفَ مِنْ حِفْظِهِ أَخْبَرَنَا مَعْمَرٌ، عَنِ الزُّهْرِيِّ، قَالَ قَالَ لِي الْوَلِيدُ بْنُ عَبْدِ الْمَلِكِ أَبَلَغَكَ أَنَّ عَلِيًّا، كَانَ فِيمَنْ قَذَفَ عَائِشَةَ قُلْتُ لاَ. وَلَكِنْ قَدْ أَخْبَرَنِي رَجُلاَنِ مِنْ قَوْمِكِ أَبُو سَلَمَةَ بْنُ عَبْدِ الرَّحْمَنِ وَأَبُو بَكْرِ بْنُ عَبْدِ الرَّحْمَنِ بْنِ الْحَارِثِ أَنَّ عَائِشَةَ ـ رضى الله عنها ـ قَالَتْ لَهُمَا كَانَ عَلِيٌّ مُسَلِّمًا فِي شَأْنِهَا. فَرَاجَعُوهُ فَلَمْ يَرْجِعْ وَقَالَ مُسَلِّمًا بِلاَ شَكٍّ فِيهِ وَعَلَيْهِ كَانَ فِي أَصْلِ الْعَتِيقِ كَذَلِكَ

Narrated Abi Huraira: The Prophet ﷺ used to invoke Allah in his prayer, "O Allah! Save `Aiyash bin Abi Rabi`a and Salama bin Hisham and Al-Walid bin Al-Walid; O Allah! Save the weak among the believers; O Allah! Be hard upon the tribe of Mudar and inflict years (of famine) upon them like the (famine) years of Joseph.". – Sahih al-Bukhari 6940

حَدَّثَنَا يَحْيَى بْنُ بُكَيْرٍ، حَدَّثَنَا اللَّيْثُ، عَنْ خَالِدِ بْنِ يَزِيدَ، عَنْ سَعِيدِ بْنِ أَبِي هِلاَلٍ، عَنْ هِلاَلِ بْنِ أُسَامَةَ، أَنَّ أَبَا سَلَمَةَ بْنَ عَبْدِ الرَّحْمَنِ، أَخْبَرَهُ عَنْ أَبِي هُرَيْرَةَ، أَنَّ النَّبِيَّ صلى الله عليه وسلم كَانَ يَدْعُو فِي الصَّلاَةِ " اللَّهُمَّ أَنْجِ عَيَّاشَ بْنَ أَبِي رَبِيعَةَ، وَسَلَمَةَ بْنَ هِشَامٍ، وَالْوَلِيدَ بْنَ الْوَلِيدِ، اللَّهُمَّ أَنْجِ الْمُسْتَضْعَفِينَ مِنَ الْمُؤْمِنِينَ، اللَّهُمَّ اشْدُدْ وَطْأَتَكَ عَلَى مُضَرَ، وَابْعَثْ عَلَيْهِمْ سِنِينَ كَسِنِي يُوسُفَ ".

Caliphate `Umar bin `Abdul `Aziz
الخليفة عمر بن عبد العزيز

Narrated Az-Zuhri: I heard `Urwa bin Az-Zubair talking to `Umar bin `Abdul `Aziz during the latter's Governorship (at Medina), he said, "Al-Mughira bin Shu`ba delayed the `Asr prayer when he was the ruler of Al-Kufa. On that, Abu Mas`ud. `Uqba bin `Amr Al-Ansari, the grandfather of Zaid bin Hasan, who was one of the Badr warriors, came in and said, (to Al-Mughira), 'You know that Gabriel came down and offered the prayer and Allah's Messenger ﷺ prayed five prescribed prayers, and Gabriel said (to the Prophet ﷺ), "I have been ordered to do so (i.e. offer these five prayers at these fixed stated hours of the day). – Sahih Al-Bukhari 4007

حَدَّثَنَا أَبُو الْيَمَانِ، أَخْبَرَنَا شُعَيْبٌ، عَنِ الزُّهْرِيِّ، سَمِعْتُ عُرْوَةَ بْنَ الزُّبَيْرِ، يُحَدِّثُ عُمَرَ بْنَ عَبْدِ الْعَزِيزِ فِي إِمَارَتِهِ أَخَّرَ الْمُغِيرَةُ بْنُ شُعْبَةَ الْعَصْرَ وَهْوَ أَمِيرُ الْكُوفَةِ، فَدَخَلَ أَبُو مَسْعُودٍ عُقْبَةُ بْنُ عَمْرٍو الأَنْصَارِيُّ جَدُّ زَيْدِ بْنِ حَسَنٍ شَهِدَ بَدْرًا فَقَالَ لَقَدْ عَلِمْتَ نَزَلَ جِبْرِيلُ فَصَلَّى فَصَلَّى رَسُولُ اللَّهِ صلى الله عليه وسلم خَمْسَ صَلَوَاتٍ ثُمَّ قَالَ هَكَذَا أُمِرْتَ. كَذَلِكَ كَانَ بَشِيرُ بْنُ أَبِي مَسْعُودٍ يُحَدِّثُ عَنْ أَبِيهِ

Narrated Sahl bin Sa`d: An Arab lady was mentioned to the Prophet ﷺ so he asked Abu Usaid As-Sa`idi to send for her, and he sent for her and she came and stayed in the castle of Bani Sa`ida. The Prophet ﷺ came out and went to her and entered upon her. Behold, it was a lady sitting with a drooping head. When the Prophet ﷺ spoke to her, she said, "I seek refuge with Allah from you." He said, "I grant you refuge from me." They said to her, "Do you know who this is?" She said, "No." They said, "This is Allah's Messenger ﷺ who has come to command your hand in marriage." She said, "I am very unlucky to lose this chance." Then the Prophet and his companions went towards the shed of Bani Sa`ida and sat there. Then he said, "Give us water, O Sahl!" So I took out this drinking bowl and gave them water in it. The sub-narrator added: Sahl took out for us that very drinking bowl and we all drank from it. Later on `Umar bin `Abdul `Aziz requested Sahl to give it to him as a present, and he gave it to him as a present. – Sahih Al-Bukhari 5637

حَدَّثَنَا سَعِيدُ بْنُ أَبِي مَرْيَمَ، حَدَّثَنَا أَبُو غَسَّانَ، قَالَ حَدَّثَنِي أَبُو حَازِمٍ، عَنْ سَهْلِ بْنِ سَعْدٍ ـ رضى الله عنه ـ قَالَ ذُكِرَ لِلنَّبِيِّ صلى الله عليه وسلم امْرَأَةٌ مِنَ الْعَرَبِ، فَأَمَرَ أَبَا أُسَيْدٍ السَّاعِدِيَّ أَنْ يُرْسِلَ إِلَيْهَا فَأَرْسَلَ إِلَيْهَا، فَقَدِمَتْ فَنَزَلَتْ فِي أُجُمِ بَنِي سَاعِدَةَ، فَخَرَجَ النَّبِيُّ صلى الله عليه وسلم حَتَّى جَاءَهَا فَدَخَلَ عَلَيْهَا فَإِذَا امْرَأَةٌ مُنَكِّسَةٌ رَأْسَهَا، فَلَمَّا كَلَّمَهَا النَّبِيُّ صلى الله عليه وسلم قَالَتْ أَعُوذُ بِاللَّهِ مِنْكَ. فَقَالَ " قَدْ أَعَذْتُكِ مِنِّي ". فَقَالُوا لَهَا أَتَدْرِينَ مَنْ هَذَا قَالَتْ لاَ. قَالُوا هَذَا رَسُولُ اللَّهِ صلى الله عليه وسلم جَاءَ لِيَخْطُبَكِ. قَالَتْ كُنْتُ أَنَا أَشْقَى مِنْ ذَلِكَ. فَأَقْبَلَ النَّبِيُّ صلى الله عليه وسلم يَوْمَئِذٍ حَتَّى جَلَسَ فِي سَقِيفَةِ بَنِي سَاعِدَةَ هُوَ وَأَصْحَابُهُ، ثُمَّ قَالَ " اسْقِنَا يَا سَهْلُ ". فَخَرَجْتُ لَهُمْ بِهَذَا الْقَدَحِ فَأَسْقَيْتُهُمْ فِيهِ، فَأَخْرَجَ لَنَا سَهْلٌ ذَلِكَ الْقَدَحَ فَشَرِبْنَا مِنْهُ. قَالَ ثُمَّ اسْتَوْهَبَهُ عُمَرُ بْنُ عَبْدِ الْعَزِيزِ بَعْدَ ذَلِكَ فَوَهَبَهُ لَهُ.

Narrated Abu Qilaba: Once `Umar bin `Abdul `Aziz sat on his throne in the courtyard of his house so that the people might gather before him. Then he admitted them and (when they came in), he said, "What do you think of Al-Qasama?" They said, "We say that it is lawful to depend on Al-Qasama in Qisas, as the previous Muslim Caliphs carried out Qisas depending on it." Then he said to me, "O Abu Qilaba! What do you say about it?" He let me appear before the people and I said, "O Chief of the Believers! You have the chiefs of the army staff and the nobles of the Arabs. If fifty of them testified that a married man had committed illegal sexual intercourse in Damascus but they had not seen him (doing so), would you stone him?" He said, "No." I said, "If fifty of them testified that a man had committed theft in Hums, would you cut off his hand though they did not see him?" He replied, "No." I said, "By Allah, Allah's Messenger ﷺ never killed anyone except in one of the following three situations: (1) A person who killed somebody unjustly, was killed (in Qisas,) (2) a married person who committed illegal sexual intercourse and (3) a man who fought against Allah and His Apostle and deserted Islam and became an apostate." Then the people said, "Didn't Anas bin Malik narrate that Allah's Messenger ﷺ cut off the hands of the thieves, branded their eyes and then, threw them in the sun?" I said, "I shall tell you the narration of Anas. Anas said: "Eight persons from the tribe of `Ukl came to Allah's Messenger ﷺ and gave the Pledge of allegiance for Islam (became Muslim). The climate of the place (Medina) did not suit them, so they became sick and complained about that to Allah's Messenger ﷺ. He said (to them), "Won't you go out with the shepherd of our camels and drink of the camels' milk and urine (as medicine)?" They said, "Yes." So they went out and drank the camels' milk and urine, and after they became healthy, they killed the shepherd of Allah's Messenger ﷺ and took away all the camels. This news reached Allah's Messenger ﷺ, so he sent (men) to follow their traces and they were captured and brought (to the Prophet). He then ordered to cut their hands and feet, and their eyes were branded with heated pieces of iron, and then he threw them in the sun till they died." I said, "What can be worse than what those people did? They deserted Islam, committed murder and theft." Then 'Anbasa bin Sa`id said, "By Allah, I never heard a narration like this of today." I said, "O 'Anbasa! You deny my narration?" 'Anbasa said, "No, but you have related the narration in the way it should be related. By Allah, these people are in welfare as long as this Sheikh (Abu Qilaba) is among them." I added, "Indeed in this event there has been a tradition set by Allah's Messenger ﷺ. The narrator added: Some Ansari people came to the Prophet ﷺ and discussed some matters with him, a man from amongst them went out and was murdered. Those people went out after him, and behold, their companion was swimming in blood. They returned to Allah's Messenger ﷺ and said to him, "O Allah's Apostle, we have found our companion who had talked with us and gone out before us, swimming in blood (killed)." Allah's Messenger ﷺ went out and asked them, "Whom do you suspect or whom do you think has killed him?" They said, "We think that the Jews have killed him." The Prophet ﷺ sent for the Jews and asked them, "Did you kill this (person)?" They replied, "No." He asked the Al-Ansars, "Do you agree that I let fifty Jews take an oath that they have not killed him?" They said, "It matters little for the Jews to kill us all and then take false oaths." He said, "Then would you like to receive the Diya after fifty of you have taken an oath (that the Jews have killed your man)?" They said, "We will not take the oath." Then the Prophet ﷺ himself paid them the Diya (Blood-money)." The narrator added, "The tribe of Hudhail repudiated one of their men (for his evil conduct) in the Pre-Islamic period of Ignorance. Then, at a place called Al-Batha' (near Mecca), the man attacked a Yemenite family at night to steal from them, but a. man from the family noticed him and struck him with his sword and killed him. The tribe of Hudhail came and captured the Yemenite and brought him to `Umar during the Hajj season and said, "He has killed our companion." The Yemenite said, "But these people had repudiated him (i.e., their companion)." `Umar said, "Let fifty persons of Hudhail swear that they had not repudiated him." So forty-nine of them took the oath and then a person belonging to them, came from Sham and they requested him to swear similarly, but he paid one-thousand Dirhams instead of taking the oath. They called another man instead of him and the new man shook hands with the brother of the deceased. Some people said, "We and those fifty men who had taken false oaths (Al-Qasama) set out, and when they reached a place called Nakhlah, it started raining so they entered a cave in the mountain, and the cave collapsed on those fifty men who took the false oath, and all of them died except the two persons who had shaken hands with each other. They escaped death but a stone fell on the leg of the brother of the deceased and broke it, whereupon he survived for one year and then died." I further said, "`Abdul Malik bin Marwan sentenced a man to death in Qisas (equality in punishment) for murder, basing his judgment on Al-Qasama, but later on he regretted that judgment and ordered that the names of the fifty persons who had taken the oath (Al-Qasama), be erased from the register, and he exiled them in Sham.". – Sahih Al-Bukhari 6899

حَدَّثَنَا قُتَيْبَةُ بْنُ سَعِيدٍ، حَدَّثَنَا أَبُو بِشْرٍ، إِسْمَاعِيلُ بْنُ إِبْرَاهِيمَ الأَسَدِيُّ حَدَّثَنَا الْحَجَّاجُ بْنُ أَبِي عُثْمَانَ، حَدَّثَنِي أَبُو رَجَاءٍ، مِنْ آلِ أَبِي قِلاَبَةَ حَدَّثَنِي أَبُو قِلاَبَةَ، أَنَّ عُمَرَ بْنَ عَبْدِ الْعَزِيزِ، أَبْرَزَ سَرِيرَهُ يَوْمًا لِلنَّاسِ، ثُمَّ أَذِنَ لَهُمْ فَدَخَلُوا فَقَالَ مَا تَقُولُونَ فِي الْقَسَامَةِ قَالَ نَقُولُ الْقَسَامَةُ الْقَوَدُ بِهَا حَقٌّ، وَقَدْ أَقَادَتْ بِهَا الْخُلَفَاءُ. قَالَ لِي مَا تَقُولُ يَا أَبَا قِلاَبَةَ وَنَصَبَنِي لِلنَّاسِ. فَقُلْتُ يَا أَمِيرَ الْمُؤْمِنِينَ عِنْدَكَ رُءُوسُ الأَجْنَادِ وَأَشْرَافُ الْعَرَبِ، أَرَأَيْتَ لَوْ أَنَّ خَمْسِينَ مِنْهُمْ شَهِدُوا عَلَى رَجُلٍ مُحْصَنٍ بِدِمَشْقَ أَنَّهُ قَدْ زَنَى، لَمْ يَرَوْهُ أَكُنْتَ تَرْجُمُهُ قَالَ لاَ. قُلْتُ أَرَأَيْتَ لَوْ أَنَّ خَمْسِينَ مِنْهُمْ شَهِدُوا عَلَى رَجُلٍ بِحِمْصَ أَنَّهُ سَرَقَ أَكُنْتَ تَقْطَعُهُ وَلَمْ يَرَوْهُ قَالَ لاَ. قُلْتُ فَوَاللَّهِ مَا قَتَلَ رَسُولُ اللَّهِ صلى الله عليه وسلم قَطُّ، إِلاَّ فِي إِحْدَى ثَلاَثِ خِصَالٍ رَجُلٌ قَتَلَ بِجَرِيرَةِ نَفْسِهِ فَقُتِلَ، أَوْ رَجُلٌ زَنَى بَعْدَ إِحْصَانٍ، أَوْ رَجُلٌ حَارَبَ اللَّهَ وَرَسُولَهُ وَارْتَدَّ عَنِ الإِسْلاَمِ. فَقَالَ الْقَوْمُ أَوَلَيْسَ قَدْ حَدَّثَ أَنَسُ بْنُ مَالِكٍ أَنَّ رَسُولَ اللَّهِ صلى الله عليه وسلم قَطَعَ فِي السَّرَقِ وَسَمَرَ الأَعْيُنَ، ثُمَّ نَبَذَهُمْ فِي الشَّمْسِ. فَقُلْتُ أَنَا أُحَدِّثُكُمْ حَدِيثَ أَنَسٍ، حَدَّثَنِي أَنَسٌ أَنَّ نَفَرًا مِنْ عُكْلٍ ثَمَانِيَةً قَدِمُوا عَلَى رَسُولِ اللَّهِ صلى الله عليه وسلم فَبَايَعُوهُ عَلَى الإِسْلاَمِ، فَاسْتَوْخَمُوا الأَرْضَ فَسَقِمَتْ أَجْسَامُهُمْ، فَشَكَوْا ذَلِكَ إِلَى رَسُولِ اللَّهِ صلى الله عليه وسلم قَالَ " أَفَلاَ تَخْرُجُونَ مَعَ رَاعِينَا فِي إِبِلِهِ، فَتُصِيبُونَ مِنْ أَلْبَانِهَا وَأَبْوَالِهَا ". قَالُوا بَلَى، فَخَرَجُوا فَشَرِبُوا مِنْ أَلْبَانِهَا وَأَبْوَالِهَا فَصَحُّوا، فَقَتَلُوا رَاعِيَ رَسُولِ اللَّهِ صلى الله عليه وسلم وَأَطْرَدُوا النَّعَمَ، فَبَلَغَ ذَلِكَ رَسُولَ اللَّهِ صلى الله عليه وسلم فَأَرْسَلَ فِي آثَارِهِمْ، فَأُدْرِكُوا فَجِيءَ بِهِمْ، فَأَمَرَ بِهِمْ فَقُطِّعَتْ أَيْدِيهِمْ وَأَرْجُلُهُمْ، وَسَمَرَ أَعْيُنَهُمْ، ثُمَّ نَبَذَهُمْ فِي الشَّمْسِ حَتَّى مَاتُوا. قُلْتُ وَأَىُّ شَىْءٍ أَشَدُّ مِمَّا صَنَعَ هَؤُلاَءِ ارْتَدُّوا عَنِ الإِسْلاَمِ وَقَتَلُوا وَسَرَقُوا. فَقَالَ عَنْبَسَةُ بْنُ سَعِيدٍ وَاللَّهِ إِنْ سَمِعْتُ كَالْيَوْمِ قَطُّ. فَقُلْتُ أَتَرُدُّ عَلَىَّ حَدِيثِي يَا عَنْبَسَةُ قَالَ لاَ، وَلَكِنْ جِئْتَ بِالْحَدِيثِ عَلَى وَجْهِهِ، وَاللَّهِ لاَ يَزَالُ هَذَا الْجُنْدُ بِخَيْرٍ مَا عَاشَ هَذَا الشَّيْخُ بَيْنَ أَظْهُرِهِمْ. قُلْتُ وَقَدْ كَانَ فِي هَذَا سُنَّةٌ مِنْ رَسُولِ اللَّهِ صلى الله عليه وسلم دَخَلَ عَلَيْهِ نَفَرٌ مِنَ الأَنْصَارِ فَتَحَدَّثُوا عِنْدَهُ، فَخَرَجَ رَجُلٌ مِنْهُمْ بَيْنَ أَيْدِيهِمْ فَقُتِلَ، فَخَرَجُوا بَعْدَهُ، فَإِذَا هُمْ بِصَاحِبِهِمْ يَتَشَحَّطُ فِي الدَّمِ، فَرَجَعُوا إِلَى رَسُولِ اللَّهِ صلى الله عليه وسلم فَقَالُوا يَا رَسُولَ اللَّهِ صَاحِبُنَا كَانَ تَحَدَّثَ مَعَنَا، فَخَرَجَ بَيْنَ أَيْدِينَا، فَإِذَا نَحْنُ بِهِ يَتَشَحَّطُ فِي الدَّمِ. فَخَرَجَ رَسُولُ اللَّهِ صلى الله عليه وسلم فَقَالَ " بِمَنْ تَظُنُّونَ أَوْ تَرَوْنَ قَتَلَهُ ". قَالُوا نَرَى أَنَّ الْيَهُودَ قَتَلَتْهُ. فَأَرْسَلَ إِلَى الْيَهُودِ فَدَعَاهُمْ. فَقَالَ " آنْتُمْ قَتَلْتُمْ هَذَا ". قَالُوا لاَ. قَالَ " أَتَرْضَوْنَ نَفَلَ خَمْسِينَ مِنَ الْيَهُودِ مَا قَتَلُوهُ ". فَقَالُوا مَا يُبَالُونَ أَنْ يَقْتُلُونَا أَجْمَعِينَ ثُمَّ يَنْتَفِلُونَ. قَالَ " أَفَتَسْتَحِقُّونَ الدِّيَةَ بِأَيْمَانِ خَمْسِينَ مِنْكُمْ ". قَالُوا مَا كُنَّا لِنَحْلِفَ، فَوَدَاهُ مِنْ عِنْدِهِ. قُلْتُ وَقَدْ كَانَتْ هُذَيْلٌ خَلَعُوا خَلِيعًا لَهُمْ فِي الْجَاهِلِيَّةِ فَطَرَقَ أَهْلَ بَيْتٍ مِنَ الْيَمَنِ بِالْبَطْحَاءِ فَانْتَبَهَ لَهُ رَجُلٌ مِنْهُمْ فَحَذَفَهُ بِالسَّيْفِ فَقَتَلَهُ، فَجَاءَتْ هُذَيْلٌ فَأَخَذُوا الْيَمَانِيَ فَرَفَعُوهُ إِلَى عُمَرَ بِالْمَوْسِمِ وَقَالُوا قَتَلَ صَاحِبَنَا. فَقَالَ إِنَّهُمْ قَدْ خَلَعُوهُ. فَقَالَ يُقْسِمُ خَمْسُونَ مِنْ هُذَيْلٍ مَا خَلَعُوهُ. قَالَ فَأَقْسَمَ مِنْهُمْ تِسْعَةٌ وَأَرْبَعُونَ رَجُلاً، وَقَدِمَ رَجُلٌ مِنْهُمْ مِنَ الشَّأْمِ فَسَأَلُوهُ أَنْ يُقْسِمَ فَافْتَدَى يَمِينَهُ مِنْهُمْ بِأَلْفِ دِرْهَمٍ، فَأَدْخَلُوا مَكَانَهُ رَجُلاً آخَرَ، فَدَفَعَهُ إِلَى أَخِي الْمَقْتُولِ فَقُرِنَتْ يَدُهُ بِيَدِهِ، قَالُوا فَانْطَلَقَا وَالْخَمْسُونَ الَّذِينَ أَقْسَمُوا حَتَّى إِذَا كَانُوا بِنَخْلَةَ، أَخَذَتْهُمُ السَّمَاءُ فَدَخَلُوا فِي غَارٍ فِي الْجَبَلِ، فَانْهَجَمَ الْغَارُ عَلَى الْخَمْسِينَ الَّذِينَ أَقْسَمُوا فَمَاتُوا جَمِيعًا، وَأَفْلَتَ الْقَرِينَانِ وَاتَّبَعَهُمَا حَجَرٌ فَكَسَرَ رِجْلَ أَخِي الْمَقْتُولِ، فَعَاشَ حَوْلاً ثُمَّ مَاتَ. قُلْتُ وَقَدْ كَانَ عَبْدُ الْمَلِكِ بْنُ مَرْوَانَ أَقَادَ رَجُلاً بِالْقَسَامَةِ ثُمَّ نَدِمَ بَعْدَ مَا صَنَعَ، فَأَمَرَ بِالْخَمْسِينَ الَّذِينَ أَقْسَمُوا فَمُحُوا مِنَ الدِّيوَانِ وَسَيَّرَهُمْ إِلَى الشَّأْمِ

Narrated Ibn `Umar :Allah's Messenger ﷺ called me to present myself in front of him or the eve of the battle of Uhud, while I was fourteen years of age at that time, and he did not allow me to take part in that battle, but he called me in front of him on the eve of the battle of the Trench when I was fifteen years old, and he allowed me (to join the battle)." Nafi` said, "I went to `Umar bin `Abdul `Aziz who was Caliph at that time and related the above narration to him, He said, "This age (fifteen) is the limit between childhood and manhood," and wrote to his governors to give salaries to those who reached the age of fifteen – .Sahih Al-Bukhari 2664

حَدَّثَنَا عُبَيْدُ اللَّهِ بْنُ سَعِيدٍ، حَدَّثَنَا أَبُو أُسَامَةَ، قَالَ حَدَّثَنِي عُبَيْدُ اللَّهِ، قَالَ حَدَّثَنِي نَافِعٌ، قَالَ حَدَّثَنِي ابْنُ عُمَرَ ـ رضى الله عنهما ـ أَنَّ رَسُولَ اللَّهِ صلى الله عليه وسلم عَرَضَهُ يَوْمَ أُحُدٍ وَهْوَ ابْنُ أَرْبَعَ عَشْرَةَ سَنَةً، فَلَمْ يُجِزْنِي، ثُمَّ عَرَضَنِي يَوْمَ الْخَنْدَقِ وَأَنَا ابْنُ خَمْسَ عَشْرَةَ فَأَجَازَنِي. قَالَ نَافِعٌ فَقَدِمْتُ عَلَى عُمَرَ بْنِ عَبْدِ الْعَزِيزِ وَهْوَ خَلِيفَةٌ، فَحَدَّثْتُهُ هَذَا الْحَدِيثَ، فَقَالَ إِنَّ هَذَا لَحَدٌّ بَيْنَ الصَّغِيرِ وَالْكَبِيرِ. وَكَتَبَ إِلَى عُمَّالِهِ أَنْ يَفْرِضُوا لِمَنْ بَلَغَ خَمْسَ عَشْرَةَ.

Narrated Ibn Shihab :Once `Umar bin `Abdul `Aziz delayed the prayer and `Urwa bin Az-Zubair went to him and said, "Once in 'Iraq, Al-Mughira bin Shu`ba delayed his prayers and Abi Mas`ud Al-Ansari went to him and said, 'O Mughira! What is this? Don't you know that once Gabriel came and offered the prayer (Fajr prayer) and Allah's Messenger ﷺ prayed too, then he prayed again (Zuhr prayer) and so did Allah's Apostle and again he prayed (`Asr prayers and Allah's Messenger ﷺ did the same; again he prayed (Maghrib-prayer) and so did Allah's Messenger ﷺ and again prayed (`Isha prayer) and so did Allah's Apostle and (Gabriel) said, 'I was ordered to do so (to demonstrate the prayers prescribed to you)?'" `Umar (bin `Abdul `Aziz) said to `Urwa, "Be sure of what you Say. Did Gabriel lead Allah's Messenger ﷺ at the stated times of the prayers?" `Urwa replied, "Bashir bin Abi Mas`ud narrated like this on the authority of his father." `Urwa added, "Aisha told me that Allah's Messenger ﷺ used to pray `Asr prayer when the sunshine was still inside her residence (during the early time of `Asr) – .Sahih Al-Bukhari 521, 522

حَدَّثَنَا عَبْدُ اللَّهِ بْنُ مَسْلَمَةَ، قَالَ قَرَأْتُ عَلَى مَالِكٍ عَنِ ابْنِ شِهَابٍ، أَنَّ عُمَرَ بْنَ عَبْدِ الْعَزِيزِ، أَخَّرَ الصَّلاَةَ يَوْمًا، فَدَخَلَ عَلَيْهِ عُرْوَةُ بْنُ الزُّبَيْرِ، فَأَخْبَرَهُ أَنَّ الْمُغِيرَةَ بْنَ شُعْبَةَ أَخَّرَ الصَّلاَةَ يَوْمًا وَهُوَ بِالْعِرَاقِ، فَدَخَلَ عَلَيْهِ أَبُو مَسْعُودٍ الأَنْصَارِيُّ فَقَالَ مَا هَذَا يَا مُغِيرَةُ أَلَيْسَ قَدْ عَلِمْتَ أَنَّ جِبْرِيلَ نَزَلَ فَصَلَّى، فَصَلَّى رَسُولُ اللَّهِ صلى الله عليه وسلم ثُمَّ صَلَّى فَصَلَّى رَسُولُ اللَّهِ صلى الله عليه وسلم ثُمَّ صَلَّى فَصَلَّى رَسُولُ اللَّهِ صلى الله عليه وسلم ثُمَّ صَلَّى فَصَلَّى رَسُولُ اللَّهِ صلى الله عليه وسلم ثُمَّ صَلَّى فَصَلَّى رَسُولُ اللَّهِ صلى الله عليه وسلم ثُمَّ قَالَ " بِهَذَا أُمِرْتُ ". فَقَالَ عُمَرُ لِعُرْوَةَ اعْلَمْ مَا تُحَدِّثُ أَوَإِنَّ جِبْرِيلَ هُوَ أَقَامَ لِرَسُولِ اللَّهِ صلى الله عليه وسلم وَقْتَ الصَّلاَةِ. قَالَ عُرْوَةُ كَذَلِكَ كَانَ بَشِيرُ بْنُ أَبِي مَسْعُودٍ يُحَدِّثُ عَنْ أَبِيهِ. قَالَ عُرْوَةُ وَلَقَدْ حَدَّثَتْنِي عَائِشَةُ، أَنَّ رَسُولَ اللَّهِ صلى الله عليه وسلم كَانَ يُصَلِّي الْعَصْرَ، وَالشَّمْسُ فِي حُجْرَتِهَا قَبْلَ أَنْ تَظْهَرَ.

Narrated `Abdur-Rahman bin Humaid Az-Zuhri :I heard `Umar bin `Abdul-Aziz asking As-Sa'ib, the nephew of An-Nimr. "What have you heard about residing in Mecca?" The other said, "I heard Al-Ala bin Al-Hadrami saying, Allah's Messenger ﷺ said: An Emigrant is allowed to stay in Mecca for three days after departing from Mina (i.e. after performing all the ceremonies of Hajj) – ."Sahih Al-Bukhari 3933

حَدَّثَنِي إِبْرَاهِيمُ بْنُ حَمْزَةَ، حَدَّثَنَا حَاتِمٌ، عَنْ عَبْدِ الرَّحْمَنِ بْنِ حُمَيْدٍ الزُّهْرِيِّ، قَالَ سَمِعْتُ عُمَرَ بْنَ عَبْدِ الْعَزِيزِ، يَسْأَلُ السَّائِبَ ابْنَ أُخْتِ النَّمِرِ مَا سَمِعْتَ فِي، سُكْنَى مَكَّةَ قَالَ سَمِعْتُ الْعَلاَءَ بْنَ الْحَضْرَمِيِّ، قَالَ قَالَ رَسُولُ اللَّهِ صلى الله عليه وسلم " ثَلاَثٌ لِلْمُهَاجِرِ بَعْدَ الصَّدَرِ ".

Narrated Al-Ju'aid bin `Abdur-Rahman :As-Sa'ib bin Yazid said, "The Sa' at the time of the Prophet ﷺ was equal to one Mudd plus one-third of a Mudd of your time, and then it was increased in the time of Caliph `Umar bin `Abdul `Aziz – .".Sahih Al-Bukhari 6712

حَدَّثَنَا عُثْمَانُ بْنُ أَبِي شَيْبَةَ، حَدَّثَنَا الْقَاسِمُ بْنُ مَالِكٍ الْمُزَنِيُّ، حَدَّثَنَا الْجُعَيْدُ بْنُ عَبْدِ الرَّحْمَنِ، عَنِ السَّائِبِ بْنِ يَزِيدَ، قَالَ كَانَ الصَّاعُ عَلَى عَهْدِ النَّبِيِّ صلى الله عليه وسلم مُدًّا وَثُلُثًا بِمُدِّكُمُ الْيَوْمَ فَزِيدَ فِيهِ فِي زَمَنِ عُمَرَ بْنِ عَبْدِ الْعَزِيزِ.

Narrated Said bin Al-Musaiyab :When the first civil strife (in Islam) took place because of the murder of 'Uthman, it left none of the Badr warriors alive. When the second civil strife, that is the battle of Al-Harra, took place, it left none of the Hudaibiya treaty companions alive. Then the third civil strife took place and it did not subside till it had exhausted all the strength of the people – .Sahih Al-Bukhari 4024

وَعَنِ الزُّهْرِيِّ، عَنْ مُحَمَّدِ بْنِ جُبَيْرِ بْنِ مُطْعِمٍ، عَنْ أَبِيهِ، أَنَّ النَّبِيَّ صلى الله عليه وسلم قَالَ فِي أُسَارَى بَدْرٍ " لَوْ كَانَ الْمُطْعِمُ بْنُ عَدِيٍّ حَيًّا ثُمَّ كَلَّمَنِي فِي هَؤُلاَءِ النَّتْنَى لَتَرَكْتُهُمْ لَهُ ". وَقَالَ اللَّيْثُ عَنْ يَحْيَى، عَنْ سَعِيدِ بْنِ الْمُسَيَّبِ، وَقَعَتِ الْفِتْنَةُ الأُولَى ـ يَعْنِي مَقْتَلَ عُثْمَانَ ـ فَلَمْ تُبْقِ مِنْ أَصْحَابِ بَدْرٍ أَحَدًا، ثُمَّ وَقَعَتِ الْفِتْنَةُ الثَّانِيَةُ ـ يَعْنِي الْحَرَّةَ ـ فَلَمْ تُبْقِ مِنْ أَصْحَابِ الْحُدَيْبِيَةِ أَحَدًا ثُمَّ وَقَعَتِ الثَّالِثَةُ فَلَمْ تَرْتَفِعْ وَلِلنَّاسِ طَبَاخٌ.

The Book of
.....and establish Salah for My remembrance. – Surah Ta-Ha 20:14
....وَأَقِمِ ٱلصَّلَوٰةَ لِذِكْرِىٓ

Narrated `Abbas bin Malik: Malik bin Sasaa said that Allah's Messenger ﷺ described to them his Night Journey saying, "While I was lying in Al-Hatim or Al-Hijr, suddenly someone came to me and cut my body open from here to here." I asked Al-Jarud who was by my side, "What does he mean?" He said, "It means from his throat to his pubic area," or said, "From the top of the chest." The Prophet ﷺ further said, "He then took out my heart. Then a gold tray of Belief was brought to me and my heart was washed and was filled (with Belief) and then returned to its original place. Then a white animal which was smaller than a mule and bigger than a donkey was brought to me." (On this Al-Jarud asked, "Was it the Buraq, O Abu Hamza?" I (i.e. Anas) replied in the affirmative). The Prophet ﷺ said, "The animal's step (was so wide that it) reached the farthest point within the reach of the animal's sight. I was carried on it, and Gabriel set out with me till we reached the nearest heaven. When he asked for the gate to be opened, it was asked, 'Who is it?' Gabriel answered, 'Gabriel.' It was asked, 'Who is accompanying you?' Gabriel replied, 'Muhammad.' It was asked, 'Has Muhammad been called?' Gabriel replied In the affirmative. Then it was said, 'He is welcomed. What an excellent visit his is!' The gate was opened, and when I went over the first heaven, I saw Adam there. Gabriel said (to me). 'This is your father, Adam; pay him your greetings.' So I greeted him and he returned the greeting to me and said, 'You are welcomed, O pious son and pious Prophet.' Then Gabriel ascended with me till we reached the second heaven. Gabriel asked for the gate to be opened. It was asked, 'Who is it?' Gabriel answered, 'Gabriel.' It was asked, 'Who is accompanying you?' Gabriel replied, 'Muhammad.' It was asked, 'Has he been called?' Gabriel answered In the affirmative. Then it was said, 'He is welcomed. What an excellent visit his is!' The gate was opened. When I went over the second heaven, there I saw Yahya (i.e. John) and `Isa (i.e. Jesus) who were cousins of each other. Gabriel said (to me), 'These are John and Jesus; pay them your greetings.' So I greeted them and both of them returned my greetings to me and said, 'You are welcomed, O pious brother and pious Prophet.' Then Gabriel ascended with me to the third heaven and asked for its gate to be opened. It was asked, 'Who is it?' Gabriel replied, 'Gabriel.' It was asked, 'Who is accompanying you?' Gabriel replied, 'Muhammad.' It was asked, 'Has he been called?' Gabriel replied in the affirmative. Then it was said, 'He is welcomed, what an excellent visit his is!' The gate was opened, and when I went over the third heaven there I saw Joseph. Gabriel said (to me), 'This is Joseph; pay him your greetings.' So I greeted him and he returned the greeting to me and said, 'You are welcomed, O pious brother and pious Prophet.' Then Gabriel ascended with me to the fourth heaven and asked for its gate to be opened. It was asked, 'Who is it?' Gabriel replied, 'Gabriel' It was asked, 'Who is accompanying you?' Gabriel replied, 'Muhammad.' It was asked, 'Has he been called?' Gabriel replied in the affirmative. Then it was said, 'He is welcomed, what an excel lent visit his is!' The gate was opened, and when I went over the fourth heaven, there I saw Idris. Gabriel said (to me), 'This is Idris; pay him your greetings.' So I greeted him and he returned the greeting to me and said, 'You are welcomed, O pious brother and pious Prophet.' Then Gabriel ascended with me to the fifth heaven and asked for its gate to be opened. It was asked, 'Who is it?' Gabriel replied,

'Gabriel.' It was asked. 'Who is accompanying you?' Gabriel replied, 'Muhammad.' It was asked, 'Has he been called?' Gabriel replied in the affirmative. Then it was said He is welcomed, what an excellent visit his is! So when I went over the fifth heaven, there I saw Harun (i.e. Aaron), Gabriel said, (to me). This is Aaron; pay him your greetings.' I greeted him and he returned the greeting to me and said, 'You are welcomed, O pious brother and pious Prophet.' Then Gabriel ascended with me to the sixth heaven and asked for its gate to be opened. It was asked. 'Who is it?' Gabriel replied, 'Gabriel.' It was asked, 'Who Is accompanying you?' Gabriel replied, 'Muhammad.' It was asked, 'Has he been called?' Gabriel replied In the affirmative. It was said, 'He is welcomed. What an excellent visit his is!' When I went (over the sixth heaven), there I saw Moses. Gabriel said (to me),' This is Moses; pay him your greeting. So I greeted him and he returned the greetings to me and said, 'You are welcomed, O pious brother and pious Prophet.' When I left him (i.e. Moses) he wept. Someone asked him, 'What makes you weep?' Moses said, 'I weep because after me there has been sent (as Prophet) a young man whose followers will enter Paradise In greater numbers than my followers.' Then Gabriel ascended with me to the seventh heaven and asked for its gate to be opened. It was asked, 'Who is it?' Gabriel replied, 'Gabriel.' It was asked,' Who is accompanying you?' Gabriel replied, 'Muhammad.' It was asked, 'Has he been called?' Gabriel replied in the affirmative. Then it was said, 'He is welcomed. What an excellent visit his is!' So when I went (over the seventh heaven), there I saw Abraham. Gabriel said (to me), 'This is your father; pay your greetings to him.' So I greeted him and he returned the greetings to me and said, 'You are welcomed, O pious son and pious Prophet.' Then I was made to ascend to Sidrat-ul-Muntaha (i.e. the Lote Tree of the utmost boundary) Behold! Its fruits were like the jars of Hajr (i.e. a place near Medina) and its leaves were as big as the ears of elephants. Gabriel said, 'This is the Lote Tree of the utmost boundary) . Behold ! There ran four rivers, two were hidden and two were visible, I asked, 'What are these two kinds of rivers, O Gabriel?' He replied,' As for the hidden rivers, they are two rivers in Paradise and the visible rivers are the Nile and the Euphrates.' Then Al-Bait-ul-Ma'mur (i.e. the Sacred House) was shown to me and a container full of wine and another full of milk and a third full of honey were brought to me. I took the milk. Gabriel remarked, 'This is the Islamic religion which you and your followers are following.' Then the prayers were enjoined on me: They were fifty prayers a day. When I returned, I passed by Moses who asked (me), 'What have you been ordered to do?' I replied, 'I have been ordered to offer fifty prayers a day.' Moses said, 'Your followers cannot bear fifty prayers a day, and by Allah, I have tested people before you, and I have tried my level best with Bani Israel (in vain). Go back to your Lord and ask for reduction to lessen your followers' burden.' So I went back, and Allah reduced ten prayers for me. Then again I came to Moses, but he repeated the same as he had said before. Then again I went back to Allah and He reduced ten more prayers. When I came back to Moses he said the same, I went back to Allah and He ordered me to observe ten prayers a day. When I came back to Moses, he repeated the same advice, so I went back to Allah and was ordered to observe five prayers a day. When I came back to Moses, he said, 'What have you been ordered?' I replied, 'I have been ordered to observe five prayers a day.' He said, 'Your followers cannot bear five prayers a day, and no doubt, I have got an experience of the people before you, and I have tried my level best with Bani Israel, so go back to your Lord and ask for reduction to lessen your follower's burden.' I said, 'I have requested so much of my Lord that I feel ashamed, but I am satisfied now and surrender to Allah's Order.' When I left, I heard a voice saying, 'I have passed My Order and have lessened the burden of My Worshipers.". – Sahih Al-Bukhari 3887

حَدَّثَنَا هُدْبَةُ بْنُ خَالِدٍ، حَدَّثَنَا هَمَّامُ بْنُ يَحْيَى، حَدَّثَنَا قَتَادَةُ، عَنْ أَنَسِ بْنِ مَالِكٍ، عَنْ مَالِكِ بْنِ صَعْصَعَةَ ـ رضى الله عنهما ـ أَنَّ نَبِيَّ اللَّهِ صلى الله عليه وسلم حَدَّثَهُمْ عَنْ لَيْلَةَ أُسْرِيَ بِهِ " بَيْنَمَا أَنَا فِي الْحَطِيمِ ـ وَرُبَّمَا قَالَ فِي الْحِجْرِ ـ مُضْطَجِعًا، إِذْ أَتَانِي آتٍ فَقَدَّ ـ قَالَ وَسَمِعْتُهُ يَقُولُ فَشَقَّ ـ مَا بَيْنَ هَذِهِ إِلَى هَذِهِ ـ فَقُلْتُ لِلْجَارُودِ وَهْوَ إِلَى جَنْبِي مَا يَعْنِي بِهِ قَالَ مِنْ ثُغْرَةِ نَحْرِهِ إِلَى شِعْرَتِهِ، وَسَمِعْتُهُ يَقُولُ مِنْ قَصِّهِ إِلَى شِعْرَتِهِ ـ فَاسْتَخْرَجَ قَلْبِي، ثُمَّ أُتِيتُ بِطَسْتٍ مِنْ ذَهَبٍ مَمْلُوءَةٍ إِيمَانًا، فَغُسِلَ قَلْبِي ثُمَّ حُشِيَ، ثُمَّ أُوتِيتُ بِدَابَّةٍ دُونَ الْبَغْلِ وَفَوْقَ الْحِمَارِ أَبْيَضَ ". ـ فَقَالَ لَهُ الْجَارُودُ هُوَ الْبُرَاقُ يَا أَبَا حَمْزَةَ قَالَ أَنَسٌ نَعَمْ، يَضَعُ خَطْوَهُ عِنْدَ أَقْصَى طَرْفِهِ ـ " فَحُمِلْتُ عَلَيْهِ، فَانْطَلَقَ بِي جِبْرِيلُ حَتَّى أَتَى السَّمَاءَ الدُّنْيَا فَاسْتَفْتَحَ، فَقِيلَ مَنْ هَذَا قَالَ جِبْرِيلُ. قِيلَ وَمَنْ مَعَكَ قَالَ مُحَمَّدٌ. قِيلَ وَقَدْ أُرْسِلَ إِلَيْهِ قَالَ نَعَمْ. قِيلَ مَرْحَبًا بِهِ، فَنِعْمَ الْمَجِيءُ جَاءَ فَفَتَحَ، فَلَمَّا خَلَصْتُ، فَإِذَا فِيهَا آدَمُ، فَقَالَ هَذَا أَبُوكَ آدَمُ فَسَلِّمْ عَلَيْهِ. فَسَلَّمْتُ عَلَيْهِ فَرَدَّ السَّلاَمَ ثُمَّ قَالَ مَرْحَبًا بِالاِبْنِ الصَّالِحِ وَالنَّبِيِّ الصَّالِحِ. ثُمَّ صَعِدَ حَتَّى أَتَى السَّمَاءَ الثَّانِيَةَ فَاسْتَفْتَحَ، قِيلَ مَنْ هَذَا قَالَ جِبْرِيلُ. قِيلَ وَمَنْ مَعَكَ قَالَ مُحَمَّدٌ. قِيلَ وَقَدْ أُرْسِلَ إِلَيْهِ قَالَ نَعَمْ. قِيلَ مَرْحَبًا بِهِ فَنِعْمَ الْمَجِيءُ جَاءَ. فَفَتَحَ، فَلَمَّا خَلَصْتُ، إِذَا يَحْيَى وَعِيسَى، وَهُمَا ابْنَا الْخَالَةِ قَالَ هَذَا يَحْيَى وَعِيسَى فَسَلِّمْ عَلَيْهِمَا. فَسَلَّمْتُ فَرَدَّا، ثُمَّ قَالاَ مَرْحَبًا بِالأَخِ الصَّالِحِ وَالنَّبِيِّ الصَّالِحِ. ثُمَّ صَعِدَ بِي إِلَى السَّمَاءِ الثَّالِثَةِ، فَاسْتَفْتَحَ قِيلَ مَنْ هَذَا قَالَ جِبْرِيلُ. قِيلَ وَمَنْ مَعَكَ قَالَ مُحَمَّدٌ. قِيلَ وَقَدْ أُرْسِلَ إِلَيْهِ قَالَ نَعَمْ. قِيلَ مَرْحَبًا بِهِ، فَنِعْمَ الْمَجِيءُ جَاءَ. فَفُتِحَ، فَلَمَّا خَلَصْتُ إِذَا يُوسُفُ. قَالَ هَذَا يُوسُفُ فَسَلِّمْ عَلَيْهِ. فَسَلَّمْتُ عَلَيْهِ فَرَدَّ، ثُمَّ قَالَ مَرْحَبًا بِالأَخِ الصَّالِحِ وَالنَّبِيِّ الصَّالِحِ، ثُمَّ صَعِدَ بِي حَتَّى أَتَى السَّمَاءَ الرَّابِعَةَ، فَاسْتَفْتَحَ، قِيلَ مَنْ هَذَا قَالَ جِبْرِيلُ. قِيلَ وَمَنْ مَعَكَ قَالَ مُحَمَّدٌ. قِيلَ أَوَقَدْ أُرْسِلَ إِلَيْهِ قَالَ نَعَمْ. قِيلَ مَرْحَبًا بِهِ، فَنِعْمَ الْمَجِيءُ جَاءَ. فَفُتِحَ، فَلَمَّا خَلَصْتُ إِلَى إِدْرِيسَ قَالَ هَذَا إِدْرِيسُ فَسَلِّمْ عَلَيْهِ. فَسَلَّمْتُ عَلَيْهِ فَرَدَّ ثُمَّ قَالَ مَرْحَبًا بِالأَخِ الصَّالِحِ وَالنَّبِيِّ الصَّالِحِ. ثُمَّ صَعِدَ بِي حَتَّى أَتَى السَّمَاءَ الْخَامِسَةَ، فَاسْتَفْتَحَ، قِيلَ مَنْ هَذَا قَالَ جِبْرِيلُ. قِيلَ وَمَنْ مَعَكَ قَالَ مُحَمَّدٌ صلى الله عليه وسلم. قِيلَ وَقَدْ أُرْسِلَ إِلَيْهِ قَالَ نَعَمْ. قِيلَ مَرْحَبًا بِهِ، فَنِعْمَ الْمَجِيءُ جَاءَ. فَلَمَّا خَلَصْتُ فَإِذَا هَارُونُ قَالَ هَذَا هَارُونُ فَسَلِّمْ عَلَيْهِ. فَسَلَّمْتُ عَلَيْهِ فَرَدَّ ثُمَّ قَالَ مَرْحَبًا بِالأَخِ الصَّالِحِ وَالنَّبِيِّ الصَّالِحِ. ثُمَّ صَعِدَ بِي حَتَّى أَتَى السَّمَاءَ السَّادِسَةَ، فَاسْتَفْتَحَ، قِيلَ مَنْ هَذَا قَالَ جِبْرِيلُ. قِيلَ مَنْ مَعَكَ قَالَ مُحَمَّدٌ. قِيلَ وَقَدْ أُرْسِلَ إِلَيْهِ قَالَ نَعَمْ. قَالَ مَرْحَبًا بِهِ، فَنِعْمَ الْمَجِيءُ جَاءَ، فَلَمَّا خَلَصْتُ، فَإِذَا مُوسَى قَالَ هَذَا مُوسَى فَسَلِّمْ عَلَيْهِ، فَسَلَّمْتُ عَلَيْهِ فَرَدَّ ثُمَّ قَالَ مَرْحَبًا بِالأَخِ الصَّالِحِ وَالنَّبِيِّ الصَّالِحِ. فَلَمَّا تَجَاوَزْتُ بَكَى، قِيلَ لَهُ مَا يُبْكِيكَ قَالَ أَبْكِي لأَنَّ غُلاَمًا بُعِثَ بَعْدِي، يَدْخُلُ الْجَنَّةَ مِنْ أُمَّتِهِ أَكْثَرُ مَنْ يَدْخُلُهَا مِنْ أُمَّتِي. ثُمَّ صَعِدَ بِي إِلَى السَّمَاءِ السَّابِعَةِ، فَاسْتَفْتَحَ جِبْرِيلُ، قِيلَ مَنْ هَذَا قَالَ جِبْرِيلُ. قِيلَ وَمَنْ مَعَكَ قَالَ مُحَمَّدٌ. قِيلَ وَقَدْ بُعِثَ إِلَيْهِ. قَالَ نَعَمْ. قَالَ مَرْحَبًا بِهِ، فَنِعْمَ الْمَجِيءُ جَاءَ فَلَمَّا خَلَصْتُ، فَإِذَا إِبْرَاهِيمُ قَالَ هَذَا أَبُوكَ فَسَلِّمْ عَلَيْهِ. قَالَ فَسَلَّمْتُ عَلَيْهِ، فَرَدَّ السَّلاَمَ قَالَ مَرْحَبًا بِالاِبْنِ الصَّالِحِ وَالنَّبِيِّ الصَّالِحِ. ثُمَّ رُفِعَتْ لِي سِدْرَةُ الْمُنْتَهَى، فَإِذَا نَبِقُهَا مِثْلُ قِلاَلِ هَجَرَ، وَإِذَا وَرَقُهَا مِثْلُ آذَانِ الْفِيَلَةِ قَالَ هَذِهِ سِدْرَةُ الْمُنْتَهَى، وَإِذَا أَرْبَعَةُ أَنْهَارٍ نَهْرَانِ بَاطِنَانِ، وَنَهْرَانِ ظَاهِرَانِ. فَقُلْتُ مَا هَذَانِ يَا جِبْرِيلُ قَالَ أَمَّا الْبَاطِنَانِ، فَنَهَرَانِ فِي الْجَنَّةِ، وَأَمَّا الظَّاهِرَانِ فَالنِّيلُ وَالْفُرَاتُ. ثُمَّ رُفِعَ لِي الْبَيْتُ الْمَعْمُورُ، ثُمَّ أُتِيتُ بِإِنَاءٍ مِنْ خَمْرٍ، وَإِنَاءٍ مِنْ لَبَنٍ وَإِنَاءٍ مِنْ عَسَلٍ، فَأَخَذْتُ اللَّبَنَ، فَقَالَ هِيَ الْفِطْرَةُ أَنْتَ عَلَيْهَا وَأُمَّتُكَ. ثُمَّ فُرِضَتْ عَلَىَّ الصَّلَوَاتُ خَمْسِينَ صَلاَةً كُلَّ يَوْمٍ. فَرَجَعْتُ فَمَرَرْتُ عَلَى مُوسَى، فَقَالَ بِمَا أُمِرْتَ قَالَ أُمِرْتُ بِخَمْسِينَ صَلاَةً كُلَّ يَوْمٍ. قَالَ إِنَّ أُمَّتَكَ لاَ تَسْتَطِيعُ خَمْسِينَ صَلاَةً كُلَّ يَوْمٍ، وَإِنِّي وَاللَّهِ قَدْ جَرَّبْتُ النَّاسَ قَبْلَكَ، وَعَالَجْتُ بَنِي إِسْرَائِيلَ أَشَدَّ الْمُعَالَجَةِ، فَارْجِعْ إِلَى رَبِّكَ فَاسْأَلْهُ التَّخْفِيفَ لأُمَّتِكَ. فَرَجَعْتُ، فَوَضَعَ عَنِّي عَشْرًا، فَرَجَعْتُ إِلَى مُوسَى فَقَالَ مِثْلَهُ، فَرَجَعْتُ فَوَضَعَ عَنِّي عَشْرًا، فَرَجَعْتُ إِلَى مُوسَى فَقَالَ مِثْلَهُ، فَرَجَعْتُ فَوَضَعَ عَنِّي عَشْرًا، فَرَجَعْتُ إِلَى مُوسَى فَقَالَ مِثْلَهُ، فَرَجَعْتُ فَأُمِرْتُ بِعَشْرِ صَلَوَاتٍ كُلَّ يَوْمٍ، فَرَجَعْتُ فَقَالَ مِثْلَهُ، فَرَجَعْتُ فَأُمِرْتُ بِخَمْسِ صَلَوَاتٍ كُلَّ يَوْمٍ، فَرَجَعْتُ إِلَى مُوسَى، فَقَالَ بِمَا أُمِرْتَ قُلْتُ أُمِرْتُ بِخَمْسِ صَلَوَاتٍ كُلَّ يَوْمٍ. قَالَ إِنَّ أُمَّتَكَ لاَ تَسْتَطِيعُ خَمْسَ صَلَوَاتٍ كُلَّ يَوْمٍ، وَإِنِّي قَدْ جَرَّبْتُ النَّاسَ قَبْلَكَ، وَعَالَجْتُ بَنِي إِسْرَائِيلَ أَشَدَّ الْمُعَالَجَةِ، فَارْجِعْ إِلَى رَبِّكَ فَاسْأَلْهُ التَّخْفِيفَ لأُمَّتِكَ. قَالَ سَأَلْتُ رَبِّي حَتَّى اسْتَحْيَيْتُ، وَلَكِنْ أَرْضَى وَأُسَلِّمُ ـ قَالَ ـ فَلَمَّا جَاوَزْتُ نَادَى مُنَادٍ أَمْضَيْتُ فَرِيضَتِي وَخَفَّفْتُ عَنْ عِبَادِي "

Wudu
الوضوء

O you who have believed, when you rise up for prayer, then wash your faces, and your hands up to the elbows, and wipe your heads, (Or: "part of" the head) and (wash) your legs to the ankles. And in case you are ritually unclean, (i.e., from the emission of semea or "for women" sexual discharge) then totally purify yourselves; and in case you are sick or on a journey, or (in case) any of you has come up from the privy, or you have had contact with women, yet you cannot find water, then have recourse to good (i.e. a mounting place, high and dry) soil (and) so wipe (most of) your faces and hands with (some) of it. In no way does Allah indeed will to make any restriction for you, but indeed He wills to purify you and perfect His favor on you, indeed, that possibly you would thank (Him) – Surah Al-Ma'idah 5:6

يَـٰٓأَيُّهَا ٱلَّذِينَ ءَامَنُوٓاْ إِذَا قُمۡتُمۡ إِلَى ٱلصَّلَوٰةِ فَٱغۡسِلُواْ وُجُوهَكُمۡ وَأَيۡدِيَكُمۡ إِلَى ٱلۡمَرَافِقِ وَٱمۡسَحُواْ بِرُءُوسِكُمۡ وَأَرۡجُلَكُمۡ إِلَى ٱلۡكَعۡبَيۡنِۚ وَإِن كُنتُمۡ جُنُبٗا فَٱطَّهَّرُواْۚ وَإِن كُنتُم مَّرۡضَىٰٓ أَوۡ عَلَىٰ سَفَرٍ أَوۡ جَآءَ أَحَدٞ مِّنكُم مِّنَ ٱلۡغَآئِطِ أَوۡ لَـٰمَسۡتُمُ ٱلنِّسَآءَ فَلَمۡ تَجِدُواْ مَآءٗ فَتَيَمَّمُواْ صَعِيدٗا طَيِّبٗا فَٱمۡسَحُواْ بِوُجُوهِكُمۡ وَأَيۡدِيكُم مِّنۡهُۚ مَا يُرِيدُ ٱللَّهُ لِيَجۡعَلَ عَلَيۡكُم مِّنۡ حَرَجٖ وَلَـٰكِن يُرِيدُ لِيُطَهِّرَكُمۡ وَلِيُتِمَّ نِعۡمَتَهُۥ عَلَيۡكُمۡ لَعَلَّكُمۡ تَشۡكُرُونَ

And so your clothes purify – Surah Al-Mudathir 74:4

وَثِيَابَكَ فَطَهِّرۡ

......Indeed a mosque that was founded on piety from the first day is worthier for you to rise up therein; in it are men who love to purify themselves; and Allah loves the ones who keep themselves pure – Surah At-Taubah 9:108

....لَّمَسۡجِدٌ أُسِّسَ عَلَى ٱلتَّقۡوَىٰ مِنۡ أَوَّلِ يَوۡمٍ أَحَقُّ أَن تَقُومَ فِيهِۚ فِيهِ رِجَالٞ يُحِبُّونَ أَن يَتَطَهَّرُواْۚ وَٱللَّهُ يُحِبُّ ٱلۡمُطَّهِّرِينَ

Children of Adam, We have sent down clothes to you to cover your nakedness and as a thing of beauty, but the garment of awareness of Allah is the best of all. These are blessings from Allah so that you may remember. – Surah Al-A'raf 7:26

يَـٰبَنِيٓ ءَادَمَ قَدۡ أَنزَلۡنَا عَلَيۡكُمۡ لِبَاسٗا يُوَٰرِي سَوۡءَٰتِكُمۡ وَرِيشٗاۖ وَلِبَاسُ ٱلتَّقۡوَىٰ ذَٰلِكَ خَيۡرٞۚ ذَٰلِكَ مِنۡ ءَايَٰتِ ٱللَّهِ لَعَلَّهُمۡ يَذَّكَّرُونَ

Narrated `Amr bin Yahya: (on the authority of his father) `Abdullah bin Zaid poured water on his hands from a utensil containing water and washed them and then with one handful of water he rinsed his mouth and cleaned his nose by putting water in it and then blowing it out. He repeated it thrice. He, then, washed his hands and forearms up to the elbows twice and passed wet hands over his head, both forwards and backwards, and washed his feet up to the ankles and said, "This is the ablution of Allah's Messenger ﷺ." – Sahih al-Bukhari 191

حَدَّثَنَا مُسَدَّدٌ، قَالَ حَدَّثَنَا خَالِدُ بْنُ عَبْدِ اللَّهِ، قَالَ حَدَّثَنَا عَمْرُو بْنُ يَحْيَى، عَنْ أَبِيهِ، عَنْ عَبْدِ اللَّهِ بْنِ زَيْدٍ، أَنَّهُ أَفْرَغَ مِنَ الإِنَاءِ عَلَى يَدَيْهِ فَغَسَلَهُمَا، ثُمَّ غَسَلَ أَوْ مَضْمَضَ، وَاسْتَنْشَقَ مِنْ كَفَّةٍ وَاحِدَةٍ، فَفَعَلَ ذَلِكَ ثَلاَثًا، فَغَسَلَ يَدَيْهِ إِلَى الْمِرْفَقَيْنِ مَرَّتَيْنِ مَرَّتَيْنِ، وَمَسَحَ بِرَأْسِهِ مَا أَقْبَلَ وَمَا أَدْبَرَ، وَغَسَلَ رِجْلَيْهِ إِلَى الْكَعْبَيْنِ، ثُمَّ قَالَ هَكَذَا وُضُوءُ رَسُولِ اللَّهِ صلى الله عليه وسلم

Ghusl
غسل

Narrated Maimuna: I placed water for the bath of the Prophet. He washed his hands twice or thrice and then poured water on his left hand and washed his private parts. He rubbed his hands over the earth (and cleaned them), rinsed his mouth, washed his nose by putting water in it and blowing it out, washed his face and both forearms and then poured water over his body. Then he withdrew from that place and washed his feet. – Sahih al-Bukhari 257

حَدَّثَنَا مُوسَى، قَالَ حَدَّثَنَا عَبْدُ الْوَاحِدِ، عَنِ الأَعْمَشِ، عَنْ سَالِمِ بْنِ أَبِي الْجَعْدِ، عَنْ كُرَيْبٍ، عَنِ ابْنِ عَبَّاسٍ، قَالَ قَالَتْ مَيْمُونَةُ وَضَعْتُ لِلنَّبِيِّ صلى الله عليه وسلم مَاءً لِلْغُسْلِ، فَغَسَلَ يَدَيْهِ مَرَّتَيْنِ أَوْ ثَلاَثًا، ثُمَّ أَفْرَغَ عَلَى شِمَالِهِ فَغَسَلَ مَذَاكِيرَهُ، ثُمَّ مَسَحَ يَدَهُ بِالأَرْضِ، ثُمَّ مَضْمَضَ وَاسْتَنْشَقَ وَغَسَلَ وَجْهَهُ وَيَدَيْهِ، ثُمَّ أَفَاضَ عَلَى جَسَدِهِ، ثُمَّ تَحَوَّلَ مِنْ مَكَانِهِ فَغَسَلَ قَدَمَيْهِ

Narrated Maimuna bint Al-Harith: I placed water for the bath of Allah's Messenger ﷺ and put a screen. He poured water over his hands, and washed them once or twice. (The sub-narrator added that he did not remember if she had said thrice or not). Then he poured water with his right hand over his left one and washed his private parts. He rubbed his hand over the earth or the wall and washed it. He rinsed his mouth and washed his nose by putting water in it and blowing it out. He washed his face, forearms and head. He poured water over his body and then withdrew from that place and washed his feet. I presented him a piece of cloth (towel) and he pointed with his hand (that he does not want it) and did not take it. – Sahih al-Bukhari 266

حَدَّثَنَا مُوسَى بْنُ إِسْمَاعِيلَ، قَالَ حَدَّثَنَا أَبُو عَوَانَةَ، حَدَّثَنَا الأَعْمَشُ، عَنْ سَالِمِ بْنِ أَبِي الْجَعْدِ، عَنْ كُرَيْبٍ، مَوْلَى ابْنِ عَبَّاسٍ عَنِ ابْنِ عَبَّاسٍ، عَنْ مَيْمُونَةَ بِنْتِ الْحَارِثِ، قَالَتْ وَضَعْتُ لِرَسُولِ اللَّهِ صلى الله عليه وسلم غُسْلاً وَسَتَرْتُهُ، فَصَبَّ عَلَى يَدِهِ، فَغَسَلَهَا مَرَّةً أَوْ مَرَّتَيْنِ ـ قَالَ سُلَيْمَانُ لاَ أَدْرِي أَذَكَرَ الثَّالِثَةَ أَمْ لاَ ـ ثُمَّ أَفْرَغَ بِيَمِينِهِ عَلَى شِمَالِهِ، فَغَسَلَ فَرْجَهُ، ثُمَّ دَلَكَ يَدَهُ بِالأَرْضِ أَوْ بِالْحَائِطِ، ثُمَّ تَمَضْمَضَ وَاسْتَنْشَقَ، وَغَسَلَ وَجْهَهُ وَيَدَيْهِ، وَغَسَلَ رَأْسَهُ، ثُمَّ صَبَّ عَلَى جَسَدِهِ، ثُمَّ تَنَحَّى فَغَسَلَ قَدَمَيْهِ، فَنَاوَلْتُهُ خِرْقَةً، فَقَالَ بِيَدِهِ هَكَذَا، وَلَمْ يُرِدْهَا.

And the earth has been made for me a place of prostration and purification

وَجُعِلَتْ لِيَ الأَرْضُ مَسْجِدًا وَطَهُورًا

Narrated Jabir bin `Abdullah: Allah's Messenger ﷺ said, "I have been given five things which were not given to any amongst the Prophets before me. These are: -1. Allah made me victorious by awe (by His frightening my enemies) for a distance of one month's journey. -2. The earth has been made for me (and for my followers) a place for praying and a thing to perform Tayammum. Therefore my followers can pray wherever the time of a prayer is due. -3. The booty has been made Halal (lawful) for me (and was not made so for anyone else). -4. Every Prophet used to be sent to his nation exclusively but I have been sent to all mankind. -5. I have been given the right of intercession (on the Day of Resurrection.). – Sahih al-Bukhari 438

حَدَّثَنَا مُحَمَّدُ بْنُ سِنَانٍ، قَالَ حَدَّثَنَا هُشَيْمٌ، قَالَ حَدَّثَنَا سَيَّارٌ ـ هُوَ أَبُو الْحَكَمِ ـ قَالَ حَدَّثَنَا يَزِيدُ الْفَقِيرُ، قَالَ حَدَّثَنَا جَابِرُ بْنُ عَبْدِ اللَّهِ، قَالَ قَالَ رَسُولُ اللَّهِ صلى الله عليه وسلم " أُعْطِيتُ خَمْسًا لَمْ يُعْطَهُنَّ أَحَدٌ مِنَ الأَنْبِيَاءِ قَبْلِي، نُصِرْتُ بِالرُّعْبِ مَسِيرَةَ شَهْرٍ، وَجُعِلَتْ لِيَ الأَرْضُ مَسْجِدًا وَطَهُورًا، وَأَيُّمَا رَجُلٍ مِنْ أُمَّتِي أَدْرَكَتْهُ الصَّلاَةُ فَلْيُصَلِّ، وَأُحِلَّتْ لِيَ الْغَنَائِمُ، وَكَانَ النَّبِيُّ يُبْعَثُ إِلَى قَوْمِهِ خَاصَّةً، وَبُعِثْتُ إِلَى النَّاسِ كَافَّةً، وَأُعْطِيتُ الشَّفَاعَةَ ".

Ibn Mughaffal reported: The Messenger of Allah ﷺ ordered killing of the dogs, and then said: What about them, i. e. about other dogs? And then granted concession (to keep) the dog for hunting and the dog for (the security) of the herd, and said: When the dog licks the utensil, wash it seven times, and rub it with earth the eighth time. – Sahih Muslim 280a

وَحَدَّثَنَا عُبَيْدُ اللَّهِ بْنُ مُعَاذٍ، حَدَّثَنَا أَبِي، حَدَّثَنَا شُعْبَةُ، عَنْ أَبِي التَّيَّاحِ، سَمِعَ مُطَرِّفَ بْنَ عَبْدِ اللَّهِ، يُحَدِّثُ عَنِ ابْنِ الْمُغَفَّلِ، قَالَ أَمَرَ رَسُولُ اللَّهِ صلى الله عليه وسلم بِقَتْلِ الْكِلاَبِ ثُمَّ قَالَ " مَا بَالُهُمْ وَبَالُ الْكِلاَبِ " . ثُمَّ رَخَّصَ فِي كَلْبِ الصَّيْدِ وَكَلْبِ الْغَنَمِ وَقَالَ " إِذَا وَلَغَ الْكَلْبُ فِي الإِنَاءِ فَاغْسِلُوهُ سَبْعَ مَرَّاتٍ وَعَفِّرُوهُ الثَّامِنَةَ فِي التُّرَابِ ".

Narrated `Imran: Once we were traveling with the Prophet ((ﷺ and we carried on traveling till the last part of the night and then we (halted at a place) and slept (deeply). There is nothing sweeter than sleep for a traveler in the last part of the night. So it was only the heat of the sun that made us to wake up and the first to wake up was so and so, then so and so and then so and so (the narrator `Auf said that Abu Raja' had told him their names but he had forgotten them) and the fourth person to wake up was `Umar bin Al- Khattab. And whenever the Prophet ﷺ used to sleep, nobody would wake up him till he himself used to get up as we did not know what was happening (being revealed) to him in his sleep. So, `Umar got up and saw the condition of the people, and he was a strict man, so he said, "Allahu Akbar" and raised his voice with Takbir, and kept on saying loudly till the Prophet ﷺ got up because of it. When he got up, the people informed him about what had happened to them.

He said, "There is no harm (or it will not be harmful). Depart!" So they departed from that place, and after covering some distance the Prophet ((ﷺstopped and asked for some water to perform the ablution. So he performed the ablution and the call for the prayer was pronounced and he led the people in prayer. After he finished from the prayer, he saw a man sitting aloof who had not prayed with the people. He asked, "O so and so! What has prevented you from praying with us?" He replied, "I am Junub and there is no water. " The Prophetﷺ said, "Perform Tayammum with (clean) earth and that is sufficient for you." Then the Prophetﷺ proceeded on and the people complained to him of thirst. Thereupon he got down and called a person (the narrator `Auf added that Abu Raja' had named him but he had forgotten) and `Ali, and ordered them to go and bring water. So they went in search of water and met a woman who was sitting on her camel between two bags of water. They asked, "Where can we find water?" She replied, "I was there (at the place of water) this hour yesterday and my people are behind me." They requested her to accompany them. She asked, "Where?" They said, "To Allah's Messengerﷺ ". She said, "Do you mean the man who is called the Sabi, (with a new religion)?" They replied, "Yes, the same person. So come along." They brought her to the Prophetﷺ and narrated the whole story. He said, "Help her to dismount." The Prophetﷺ asked for a pot, then he opened the mouths of the bags and poured some water into the pot. Then he closed the big openings of the bags and opened the small ones and the people were called upon to drink and water their animals. So they all watered their animals and they (too) all quenched their thirst and also gave water to others and last of all the Prophetﷺ gave a pot full of water to the person who was Junub and told him to pour it over his body. The woman was standing and watching all that which they were doing with her water. By Allah, when her water bags were returned the looked like as if they were more full (of water) than they had been before (Miracle of Allah's Messengerﷺ Then the Prophetﷺ ordered us to collect something for her; so dates, flour and Sawiq were collected which amounted to a good meal that was put in a piece of cloth. She was helped to ride on her camel and that cloth full of foodstuff was also placed in front of her and then the Prophetﷺ said to her, "We have not taken your water but Allah has given water to us." She returned home late. Her relatives asked her: "O so and so what has delayed you?" She said, "A strange thing! Two men met me and took me to the man who is called the Sabi' and he did such and such a thing. By Allah, he is either the greatest magician between this and this (gesturing with her index and middle fingers raising them towards the sky indicating the heaven and the earth) or he is Allah's true Apostle." Afterwards the Muslims used to attack the pagans around her abode but never touched her village. One day she said to her people, "I think that these people leave you purposely. Have you got any inclination to Islam?" They obeyed her and all of them embraced Islam. Abu `Abdullah said: The word Saba'a means "The one who has deserted his old religion and embraced a new religion." Abul 'Ailya [??] said, "The S`Abis are a sect of people of the Scripture who recite the Book of Psalms.". – Sahih al-Bukhari 344

حَدَّثَنَا مُسَدَّدٌ، قَالَ حَدَّثَنِي يَحْيَى بْنُ سَعِيدٍ، قَالَ حَدَّثَنَا عَوْفٌ، قَالَ حَدَّثَنَا أَبُو رَجَاءٍ، عَنْ عِمْرَانَ، قَالَ كُنَّا فِي سَفَرٍ مَعَ النَّبِيِّ صلى الله عليه وسلم وَإِنَّا أَسْرَيْنَا، حَتَّى كُنَّا فِي آخِرِ اللَّيْلِ، وَقَعْنَا وَقْعَةً وَلاَ وَقْعَةَ أَحْلَى عِنْدَ الْمُسَافِرِ مِنْهَا، فَمَا أَيْقَظَنَا إِلاَّ حَرُّ الشَّمْسِ، وَكَانَ أَوَّلَ مَنِ اسْتَيْقَظَ فُلاَنٌ ثُمَّ فُلاَنٌ ثُمَّ فُلاَنٌ - يُسَمِّيهِمْ أَبُو رَجَاءٍ فَنَسِيَ عَوْفٌ - ثُمَّ عُمَرُ بْنُ الْخَطَّابِ الرَّابِعُ، وَكَانَ النَّبِيُّ صلى الله عليه وسلم إِذَا نَامَ لَمْ يُوقَظْ حَتَّى يَكُونَ هُوَ يَسْتَيْقِظُ، لأَنَّا لاَ نَدْرِي مَا يَحْدُثُ لَهُ فِي نَوْمِهِ، فَلَمَّا اسْتَيْقَظَ عُمَرُ، وَرَأَى مَا أَصَابَ النَّاسَ، وَكَانَ رَجُلاً جَلِيدًا، فَكَبَّرَ وَرَفَعَ صَوْتَهُ بِالتَّكْبِيرِ، فَمَا زَالَ يُكَبِّرُ وَيَرْفَعُ صَوْتَهُ بِالتَّكْبِيرِ حَتَّى اسْتَيْقَظَ لِصَوْتِهِ النَّبِيُّ صلى الله عليه وسلم فَلَمَّا اسْتَيْقَظَ شَكَوْا إِلَيْهِ الَّذِي أَصَابَهُمْ قَالَ " لاَ ضَيْرَ - أَوْ لاَ يَضِيرُ - ارْتَحِلُوا ". فَارْتَحَلَ فَسَارَ غَيْرَ بَعِيدٍ ثُمَّ نَزَلَ، فَدَعَا بِالْوَضُوءِ، فَتَوَضَّأَ وَنُودِيَ بِالصَّلاَةِ فَصَلَّى بِالنَّاسِ، فَلَمَّا انْفَتَلَ مِنْ صَلاَتِهِ إِذَا هُوَ بِرَجُلٍ مُعْتَزِلٍ لَمْ يُصَلِّ مَعَ الْقَوْمِ قَالَ " مَا مَنَعَكَ يَا فُلاَنُ أَنْ تُصَلِّيَ مَعَ الْقَوْمِ ". قَالَ أَصَابَتْنِي جَنَابَةٌ وَلاَ مَاءَ. قَالَ " عَلَيْكَ بِالصَّعِيدِ، فَإِنَّهُ يَكْفِيكَ ". ثُمَّ سَارَ النَّبِيُّ صلى الله عليه وسلم فَاشْتَكَى إِلَيْهِ النَّاسُ مِنَ الْعَطَشِ فَنَزَلَ، فَدَعَا فُلاَنًا - كَانَ يُسَمِّيهِ

أَبُو رَجَاءٍ نَسِيَهُ عَوْفٌ ـ وَدَعَا عَلِيًّا فَقَالَ " اذْهَبَا فَابْتَغِيَا الْمَاءَ ". فَانْطَلَقَا فَتَلَقَّيَا امْرَأَةً بَيْنَ مَزَادَتَيْنِ ـ أَوْ سَطِيحَتَيْنِ ـ مِنْ مَاءٍ عَلَى بَعِيرٍ لَهَا، فَقَالاَ لَهَا أَيْنَ الْمَاءُ قَالَتْ عَهْدِي بِالْمَاءِ أَمْسِ هَذِهِ السَّاعَةَ، وَنَفَرُنَا خُلُوفًا. قَالاَ لَهَا انْطَلِقِي إِذًا. قَالَتْ إِلَى أَيْنَ قَالاَ إِلَى رَسُولِ اللَّهِ صلى الله عليه وسلم. قَالَتِ الَّذِي يُقَالُ لَهُ الصَّابِئُ قَالاَ هُوَ الَّذِي تَعْنِينَ فَانْطَلِقِي. فَجَاءَا بِهَا إِلَى النَّبِيِّ صلى الله عليه وسلم وَحَدَّثَاهُ الْحَدِيثَ قَالَ فَاسْتَنْزَلُوهَا عَنْ بَعِيرِهَا وَدَعَا النَّبِيُّ صلى الله عليه وسلم بِإِنَاءٍ، فَفَرَّغَ فِيهِ مِنْ أَفْوَاهِ الْمَزَادَتَيْنِ ـ أَوِ السَّطِيحَتَيْنِ ـ وَأَوْكَأَ أَفْوَاهَهُمَا، وَأَطْلَقَ الْعَزَالِيَ، وَنُودِيَ فِي النَّاسِ اسْقُوا وَاسْتَقُوا. فَسَقَى مَنْ شَاءَ، وَاسْتَقَى مَنْ شَاءَ، وَكَانَ آخِرَ ذَاكَ أَنْ أَعْطَى الَّذِي أَصَابَتْهُ الْجَنَابَةُ إِنَاءً مِنْ مَاءٍ قَالَ " اذْهَبْ، فَأَفْرِغْهُ عَلَيْكَ ". وَهْىَ قَائِمَةٌ تَنْظُرُ إِلَى مَا يُفْعَلُ بِمَائِهَا، وَايْمُ اللَّهِ لَقَدْ أُقْلِعَ عَنْهَا، وَإِنَّهُ لَيُخَيَّلُ إِلَيْنَا أَنَّهَا أَشَدُّ مِلأَةً مِنْهَا حِينَ ابْتَدَأَ فِيهَا، فَقَالَ النَّبِيُّ صلى الله عليه وسلم " اجْمَعُوا لَهَا ". فَجَمَعُوا لَهَا مِنْ بَيْنِ عَجْوَةٍ وَدَقِيقَةٍ وَسَوِيقَةٍ، حَتَّى جَمَعُوا لَهَا طَعَامًا، فَجَعَلُوهَا فِي ثَوْبٍ، وَحَمَلُوهَا عَلَى بَعِيرِهَا، وَوَضَعُوا الثَّوْبَ بَيْنَ يَدَيْهَا قَالَ لَهَا " تَعْلَمِينَ مَا رَزِئْنَا مِنْ مَائِكِ شَيْئًا، وَلَكِنَّ اللَّهَ هُوَ الَّذِي أَسْقَانَا ". فَأَتَتْ أَهْلَهَا، وَقَدِ احْتَبَسَتْ عَنْهُمْ قَالُوا مَا حَبَسَكِ يَا فُلاَنَةُ قَالَتِ الْعَجَبُ، لَقِيَنِي رَجُلاَنِ فَذَهَبَا بِي إِلَى هَذَا الَّذِي يُقَالُ لَهُ الصَّابِئُ، فَفَعَلَ كَذَا وَكَذَا، فَوَاللَّهِ إِنَّهُ لأَسْحَرُ النَّاسِ مِنْ بَيْنِ هَذِهِ وَهَذِهِ. وَقَالَتْ بِإِصْبَعَيْهَا الْوُسْطَى وَالسَّبَّابَةِ، فَرَفَعَتْهُمَا إِلَى السَّمَاءِ ـ تَعْنِي السَّمَاءَ وَالأَرْضَ ـ أَوْ إِنَّهُ لَرَسُولُ اللَّهِ حَقًّا، فَكَانَ الْمُسْلِمُونَ بَعْدَ ذَلِكَ يُغِيرُونَ عَلَى مَنْ حَوْلَهَا مِنَ الْمُشْرِكِينَ، وَلاَ يُصِيبُونَ الصِّرْمَ الَّذِي هِيَ مِنْهُ، فَقَالَتْ يَوْمًا لِقَوْمِهَا مَا أُرَى أَنَّ هَؤُلاَءِ الْقَوْمَ يَدَعُونَكُمْ عَمْدًا، فَهَلْ لَكُمْ فِي الإِسْلاَمِ فَأَطَاعُوهَا فَدَخَلُوا فِي الإِسْلاَمِ.

Narrated Al-A`mash: Shaqiq said, “While I was sitting with `Abdullah and Abu Musa Al-Ash`ari, the latter asked the former, ‘If a person becomes Junub and does not find water for one month, can he perform Tayammum and offer his prayer?’ (He applied in the negative). Abu Musa said, ‘What do you say about this verse from Sura “Al-Ma’ida”: When you do not find water then perform Tayammum with clean earth? `Abdullah replied, ‘If we allowed it then they would probably perform Tayammum with clean earth even if water were available but cold.’ I said to Shaqiq, ‘You then disliked to perform Tayammum because of this?’ Shaqiq said, ‘Yes.’ (Shaqiq added), “Abu Musa said, ‘Haven’t you heard the statement of `Ammar to `Umar? He said: I was sent out by Allah’s Messenger ﷺ for some job and I became Junub and could not find water so I rolled myself over the dust (clean earth) like an animal does, and when I told the Prophet ﷺ of that he said, ‘Like this would have been sufficient.’ The Prophet ﷺ (saying so) lightly stroked the earth with his hand once and blew it off, then passed his (left) hand over the back of his right hand or his (right) hand over the back of his left hand and then passed them over his face.’ So `Abdullah said to Abu- Musa, ‘Don’t you know that `Umar was not satisfied with `Ammar’s statement?’ “ Narrated Shaqiq: While I was with `Abdullah and Abu Musa, the latter said to the former, “Haven’t you heard the statement of `Ammar to `Umar? He said, “Allah’s Messenger ﷺ sent you and me out and I became Junub and rolled myself in the dust (clean earth) (for Tayammum). When we came to Allah’s Apostle I told him about it and he said, ‘This would have been sufficient,’ passing his hands over his face and the backs of his hands once only.' " - Sahih al-Bukhari 347

حَدَّثَنَا مُحَمَّدُ بْنُ سَلاَمٍ، قَالَ أَخْبَرَنَا أَبُو مُعَاوِيَةَ، عَنِ الأَعْمَشِ، عَنْ شَقِيقٍ، قَالَ كُنْتُ جَالِسًا مَعَ عَبْدِ اللَّهِ وَأَبِي مُوسَى الأَشْعَرِيِّ فَقَالَ لَهُ أَبُو مُوسَى لَوْ أَنَّ رَجُلاً أَجْنَبَ، فَلَمْ يَجِدِ الْمَاءَ شَهْرًا، أَمَا كَانَ يَتَيَمَّمُ وَيُصَلِّي فَكَيْفَ تَصْنَعُونَ بِهَذِهِ الآيَةِ فِي سُورَةِ الْمَائِدَةِ {فَلَمْ تَجِدُوا مَاءً فَتَيَمَّمُوا صَعِيدًا طَيِّبًا} فَقَالَ عَبْدُ اللَّهِ لَوْ رُخِّصَ لَهُمْ فِي هَذَا لأَوْشَكُوا إِذَا بَرَدَ عَلَيْهِمُ الْمَاءُ أَنْ يَتَيَمَّمُوا الصَّعِيدَ. قُلْتُ وَإِنَّمَا كَرِهْتُمْ هَذَا لِذَا قَالَ نَعَمْ. فَقَالَ أَبُو مُوسَى أَلَمْ تَسْمَعْ قَوْلَ عَمَّارٍ لِعُمَرَ بَعَثَنِي رَسُولُ اللَّهِ صلى الله عليه وسلم فِي حَاجَةٍ فَأَجْنَبْتُ، فَلَمْ أَجِدِ الْمَاءَ، فَتَمَرَّغْتُ فِي الصَّعِيدِ كَمَا تَمَرَّغُ الدَّابَّةُ، فَذَكَرْتُ ذَلِكَ لِلنَّبِيِّ صلى الله عليه وسلم فَقَالَ " إِنَّمَا كَانَ يَكْفِيكَ أَنْ تَصْنَعَ هَكَذَا ". فَضَرَبَ بِكَفِّهِ ضَرْبَةً عَلَى الأَرْضِ ثُمَّ نَفَضَهَا، ثُمَّ مَسَحَ بِهَا ظَهْرَ كَفِّهِ بِشِمَالِهِ، أَوْ ظَهْرَ شِمَالِهِ بِكَفِّهِ، ثُمَّ مَسَحَ بِهِمَا وَجْهَهُ فَقَالَ عَبْدُ اللَّهِ أَفَلَمْ تَرَ عُمَرَ لَمْ يَقْنَعْ بِقَوْلِ عَمَّارٍ وَزَادَ يَعْلَى عَنِ الأَعْمَشِ عَنْ شَقِيقٍ كُنْتُ مَعَ عَبْدِ اللَّهِ وَأَبِي مُوسَى فَقَالَ أَبُو مُوسَى أَلَمْ تَسْمَعْ قَوْلَ عَمَّارٍ لِعُمَرَ إِنَّ رَسُولَ اللَّهِ صلى الله عليه وسلم بَعَثَنِي أَنَا وَأَنْتَ فَأَجْنَبْتُ فَتَمَعَّكْتُ بِالصَّعِيدِ، فَأَتَيْنَا رَسُولَ اللَّهِ صلى الله عليه وسلم فَأَخْبَرْنَاهُ فَقَالَ " إِنَّمَا كَانَ يَكْفِيكَ هَكَذَا ". وَمَسَحَ وَجْهَهُ وَكَفَّيْهِ وَاحِدَةً

Congregational prayer
صلاة الجماعة

Narrated Zaid bin Thabit: The Prophetﷺ took a room made of date palm leaves mats in the mosque. Allah's Messengerﷺ prayed in it for a few nights till the people gathered (to pray the night prayer (Tarawih) (behind him.) Then on the 4th night the people did not hear his voice and they thought he had slept, so some of them started humming in order that he might come out. The Prophetﷺ then said, "You continued doing what I saw you doing till I was afraid that this (Tarawih prayer) might be enjoined on you, and if it were enjoined on you, you would not continue performing it. Therefore, O people! Perform your prayers at your homes, for the best prayer of a person is what is performed at his home except the compulsory congregational prayer." (See Hadith No. 229,Vol. 3) (See Hadith No. 134, Vol. 8) – Al-Bukhari 7290 (also Bukhari #6113)

حَدَّثَنَا إِسْحَاقُ، أَخْبَرَنَا عَفَّانُ، حَدَّثَنَا وُهَيْبٌ، حَدَّثَنَا مُوسَى بْنُ عُقْبَةَ، سَمِعْتُ أَبَا النَّضْرِ، يُحَدِّثُ عَنْ بُسْرِ بْنِ سَعِيدٍ، عَنْ زَيْدِ بْنِ ثَابِتٍ، أَنَّ النَّبِيَّ صلى الله عليه وسلم اتَّخَذَ حُجْرَةً فِي الْمَسْجِدِ مِنْ حَصِيرٍ، فَصَلَّى رَسُولُ اللَّهِ صلى الله عليه وسلم فِيهَا لَيَالِيَ، حَتَّى اجْتَمَعَ إِلَيْهِ نَاسٌ، ثُمَّ فَقَدُوا صَوْتَهُ لَيْلَةً فَظَنُّوا أَنَّهُ قَدْ نَامَ، فَجَعَلَ بَعْضُهُمْ يَتَنَحْنَحُ لِيَخْرُجَ إِلَيْهِمْ فَقَالَ " مَا زَالَ بِكُمُ الَّذِي رَأَيْتُ مِنْ صَنِيعِكُمْ، حَتَّى خَشِيتُ أَنْ يُكْتَبَ عَلَيْكُمْ، وَلَوْ كُتِبَ عَلَيْكُمْ مَا قُمْتُمْ بِهِ فَصَلُّوا أَيُّهَا النَّاسُ فِي بُيُوتِكُمْ، فَإِنَّ أَفْضَلَ صَلاَةِ الْمَرْءِ فِي بَيْتِهِ، إِلاَّ الصَّلاَةَ الْمَكْتُوبَةَ

Narrated `Abdullah bin `Umar: The reward of the congregational prayer is twenty seven times greater (than that of the prayer offered by a person alone). – Sahih Al-Bukhari 649

قَالَ شُعَيْبٌ وَحَدَّثَنِي نَافِعٌ، عَنْ عَبْدِ اللَّهِ بْنِ عُمَرَ، قَالَ تَفْضُلُهَا بِسَبْعٍ وَعِشْرِينَ دَرَجَةً

It has been narrated on the authority of Abu Mas'ud al-Ansari who said: A man came to the Messenger of Allahﷺ and said: My riding beast has been killed, so give me some animal to ride upon. He (the Holy Prophet) said: I have none with me. A man said: Messenger of Allah, I can guide him to one who will provide him with a riding beast. The Messenger of Allahﷺ said: One who guides to something good has a reward similar to that of its doer. – Sahih Muslim 1893 a

وَحَدَّثَنَا أَبُو بَكْرِ بْنُ أَبِي شَيْبَةَ، وَأَبُو كُرَيْبٍ وَابْنُ أَبِي عُمَرَ – وَاللَّفْظُ لأَبِي كُرَيْبٍ – قَالُوا حَدَّثَنَا أَبُو مُعَاوِيَةَ، عَنِ الأَعْمَشِ، عَنْ أَبِي عَمْرٍو الشَّيْبَانِيِّ، عَنْ أَبِي مَسْعُودٍ الأَنْصَارِيِّ، قَالَ جَاءَ رَجُلٌ إِلَى النَّبِيِّ صلى الله عليه وسلم فَقَالَ إِنِّي أُبْدِعَ بِي فَاحْمِلْنِي فَقَالَ " مَا عِنْدِي " . فَقَالَ رَجُلٌ يَا رَسُولَ اللَّهِ أَنَا أَدُلُّهُ عَلَى مَنْ يَحْمِلُهُ فَقَالَ رَسُولُ اللَّهِ صلى الله عليه وسلم " مَنْ دَلَّ عَلَى خَيْرٍ فَلَهُ مِثْلُ أَجْرِ فَاعِلِهِ " .

And let the one amongst you who knows Qur'an most should, lead the prayer.
وَلْيَؤُمَّكُمْ أَكْثَرُكُمْ قُرْآنًا

Narrated `Amr bin Salama: We were at a place which was a thoroughfare for the people, and the caravans used to pass by us and we would ask them, "What is wrong with the people? What is wrong with the people? Who is that man? They would say, "That man claims that Allah has sent him (as an Apostle), that he has been divinely inspired, that Allah has revealed to him such-and-such." I used to memorize that (Divine) Talk, and feel as if it was inculcated in my chest (i.e. mind) And the 'Arabs (other than Quraish) delayed their conversion to Islam till the Conquest (of Mecca). They used to say." "Leave him (i.e. Muhammad) and his people Quraish: if he overpowers them then he is a true Prophet. So, when Mecca was conquered, then every tribe rushed to embrace Islam, and my father hurried to embrace Islam before (the other members of) my tribe. When my father returned (from the Prophet) to his tribe, he said, "By Allah, I have come to you from the Prophet ﷺ for sure!" The Prophet ﷺ afterwards said to them, 'Offer such-and-such prayer at such-and-such time, and when the time for the prayer becomes due, then one of you should pronounce the Adhan (for the prayer), and let the one amongst you who knows Qur'an most should, lead the prayer." So they looked for such a person and found none who knew more Qur'an than I because of the Qur'anic material which I used to learn from the caravans. They therefore made me their Imam (to lead the prayer) and at that time I was a boy of six or seven years, wearing a Burda (i.e. a black square garment) proved to be very short for me (and my body became partly naked). A lady from the tribe said, "Won't you cover the anus of your reciter for us?" So they bought (a piece of cloth) and made a shirt for me. I had never been so happy with anything before as I was with that shirt. – Al-Bukhari 4302

حَدَّثَنَا سُلَيْمَانُ بْنُ حَرْبٍ، حَدَّثَنَا حَمَّادُ بْنُ زَيْدٍ، عَنْ أَيُّوبَ، عَنْ أَبِي قِلاَبَةَ، عَنْ عَمْرِو بْنِ سَلِمَةَ، قَالَ قَالَ لِي أَبُو قِلاَبَةَ أَلاَ تَلْقَاهُ فَتَسْأَلَهُ، قَالَ فَلَقِيتُهُ فَسَأَلْتُهُ فَقَالَ كُنَّا بِمَاءٍ مَمَرَّ النَّاسِ، وَكَانَ يَمُرُّ بِنَا الرُّكْبَانُ فَنَسْأَلُهُمْ مَا لِلنَّاسِ مَا لِلنَّاسِ مَا هَذَا الرَّجُلُ فَيَقُولُونَ يَزْعُمُ أَنَّ اللَّهَ أَرْسَلَهُ أَوْحَى إِلَيْهِ، أَوْ أَوْحَى اللَّهُ بِكَذَا. فَكُنْتُ أَحْفَظُ ذَلِكَ الْكَلاَمَ، وَكَأَنَّمَا يُغْرَى فِي صَدْرِي، وَكَانَتِ الْعَرَبُ تَلَوَّمُ بِإِسْلاَمِهِمِ الْفَتْحَ، فَيَقُولُونَ اتْرُكُوهُ وَقَوْمَهُ، فَإِنَّهُ إِنْ ظَهَرَ عَلَيْهِمْ فَهْوَ نَبِيٌّ صَادِقٌ. فَلَمَّا كَانَتْ وَقْعَةُ أَهْلِ الْفَتْحِ بَادَرَ كُلُّ قَوْمٍ بِإِسْلاَمِهِمْ، وَبَدَرَ أَبِي قَوْمِي بِإِسْلاَمِهِمْ، فَلَمَّا قَدِمَ قَالَ جِئْتُكُمْ وَاللَّهِ مِنْ عِنْدِ النَّبِيِّ صلى الله عليه وسلم حَقًّا فَقَالَ " صَلُّوا صَلاَةَ كَذَا فِي حِينِ كَذَا، وَصَلُّوا كَذَا فِي حِينِ كَذَا، فَإِذَا حَضَرَتِ الصَّلاَةُ، فَلْيُؤَذِّنْ أَحَدُكُمْ، وَلْيَؤُمَّكُمْ أَكْثَرُكُمْ قُرْآنًا ". فَنَظَرُوا فَلَمْ يَكُنْ أَحَدٌ أَكْثَرَ قُرْآنًا مِنِّي، لِمَا كُنْتُ أَتَلَقَّى مِنَ الرُّكْبَانِ، فَقَدَّمُونِي بَيْنَ أَيْدِيهِمْ، وَأَنَا ابْنُ سِتٍّ أَوْ سَبْعِ، سِنِينَ وَكَانَتْ عَلَيَّ بُرْدَةٌ، كُنْتُ إِذَا سَجَدْتُ تَقَلَّصَتْ عَنِّي، فَقَالَتِ امْرَأَةٌ مِنَ الْحَيِّ أَلاَ تُغَطُّوا عَنَّا اسْتَ قَارِئِكُمْ. فَاشْتَرَوْا فَقَطَعُوا لِي قَمِيصًا، فَمَا فَرِحْتُ بِشَىْءٍ فَرَحِي بِذَلِكَ الْقَمِيصِ.

Aishah, was led in the Saldt prayer) by her slave Dhakwan who used to recite from the Mushaf [the written Qur'an (not from memory)]. Can an illegitimate boy a bedouin or a boy who has not reached the age of puberty lead the Salāt? (It is permissible according to) the statement of the Prophet that the Imām should be a person who knows the Our'an more than the others. – Al-Bukhari Vol.1 page395

و كانت عاءشة يومها بعدها ذكوان من المصحف، و ولد البغي و الأعرابي و الغلام الذي لم يحتمل لقول النبي ﷺ : "يومهم اقروهم لكتاب الله"، و لا يمنع العبر من الجماعة بغير علة.

How much of the Qur'an do you know
فَمَا عِنْدَكَ مِنَ الْقُرْآنِ

Narrated Ibrahim: The companions of `Abdullah (bin Mas`ud) came to Abu Darda', (and before they arrived at his home), he looked for them and found them. Then he asked them,: 'Who among you can recite (Qur'an) as `Abdullah recites it?" They replied, "All of us." He asked, "Who among you knows it by heart?" They pointed at 'Alqama. Then he asked Alqama. "How did you hear `Abdullah bin Mas`ud reciting Surat Al-Lail (The Night)?" Alqama recited: 'By the male and the female.' Abu Ad-Darda said, "I testify that I heard me Prophet reciting it likewise, but these people want me to recite it:-- 'And by Him Who created male and female.' But by Allah, I will not follow them.". – Sahih Al-Bukhari 4944

حَدَّثَنَا عُمَرُ، حَدَّثَنَا أَبِي، حَدَّثَنَا الأَعْمَشُ، عَنْ إِبْرَاهِيمَ، قَالَ قَدِمَ أَصْحَابُ عَبْدِ اللَّهِ عَلَى أَبِي الدَّرْدَاءِ فَطَلَبَهُمْ فَوَجَدَهُمْ فَقَالَ أَيُّكُمْ يَقْرَأُ عَلَى قِرَاءَةِ عَبْدِ اللَّهِ قَالَ كُلُّنَا. قَالَ فَأَيُّكُمْ يَحْفَظُ وَأَشَارُوا إِلَى عَلْقَمَةَ. قَالَ كَيْفَ سَمِعْتَهُ يَقْرَأُ {وَاللَّيْلِ إِذَا يَغْشَى}. قَالَ عَلْقَمَةُ {وَالذَّكَرِ وَالأُنْثَى}. قَالَ أَشْهَدُ أَنِّي سَمِعْتُ النَّبِيَّ صلى الله عليه وسلم يَقْرَأُ هَكَذَا، وَهَؤُلاَءِ يُرِيدُونِي عَلَى أَنْ أَقْرَأَ {وَمَا خَلَقَ الذَّكَرَ وَالأُنْثَى} وَاللَّهِ لاَ أُتَابِعُهُمْ

Narrated Sahl: A woman came to the Prophet,, and presented herself to him (for marriage). He said, "I am not in need of women these days." Then a man said, "O Allah's Messenger ﷺ! Marry her to me." The Prophet ﷺ asked him, "What have you got?" He said, "I have got nothing." The Prophet ﷺ said, "Give her something, even an iron ring." He said, "I have got nothing." The Prophet ﷺ asked (him), "How much of the Qur'an do you know (by heart)?" He said, "So much and so much." The Prophet ﷺ said, "I have married her to you for what you know of the Qur'an.". – Sahih Al-Bukhari 5141
حَدَّثَنَا أَبُو النُّعْمَانِ، حَدَّثَنَا حَمَّادُ بْنُ زَيْدٍ، عَنْ أَبِي حَازِمٍ، عَنْ سَهْلٍ، أَنَّ امْرَأَةً، أَتَتِ النَّبِيَّ صلى الله عليه وسلم فَعَرَضَتْ عَلَيْهِ نَفْسَهَا فَقَالَ " مَا لِي الْيَوْمَ فِي النِّسَاءِ مِنْ حَاجَةٍ ". فَقَالَ رَجُلٌ يَا رَسُولَ اللَّهِ زَوِّجْنِيهَا. قَالَ " مَا عِنْدَكَ ". قَالَ مَا عِنْدِي شَىْءٌ. قَالَ " أَعْطِهَا وَلَوْ خَاتَمًا مِنْ حَدِيدٍ ". قَالَ مَا عِنْدِي شَىْءٌ. قَالَ " فَمَا عِنْدَكَ مِنَ الْقُرْآنِ ". قَالَ عِنْدِي كَذَا وَكَذَا. قَالَ " فَقَدْ مَلَّكْتُكَهَا بِمَا مَعَكَ مِنَ الْقُرْآنِ ".

And Ibn Mas'ūd asked Tamim bin Hadhlam, while he was a boy, to recite Sūrah and said to him, "Prostrate as you are our Imam." Sahih Al-Bukhari vol. 2 pg 120
و قال ابن مسعود لتصميم بن حذلم و هو غلام فقرا عليه سجدة فقال : أسجد فانك أمامنا.

Then do not stand for the prayer till you see me and do it calmly
فَلاَ تَقُومُوا حَتَّى تَرَوْنِي وَعَلَيْكُمْ بِالسَّكِينَةِ

Narrated Abu Huraira: The Prophet ﷺ said, "When you hear the Iqama, proceed to offer the prayer with calmness and solemnity and do not make haste. And pray whatever you are able to pray and complete whatever you have missed. – Al-Bukhari 636
حَدَّثَنَا آدَمُ، قَالَ حَدَّثَنَا ابْنُ أَبِي ذِئْبٍ، قَالَ حَدَّثَنَا الزُّهْرِيُّ، عَنْ سَعِيدِ بْنِ الْمُسَيَّبِ، عَنْ أَبِي هُرَيْرَةَ، عَنِ النَّبِيِّ صلى الله عليه وسلم. وَعَنِ الزُّهْرِيِّ، عَنْ أَبِي سَلَمَةَ، عَنْ أَبِي هُرَيْرَةَ، عَنِ النَّبِيِّ صلى الله عليه وسلم قَالَ " إِذَا سَمِعْتُمُ الإِقَامَةَ فَامْشُوا إِلَى الصَّلاَةِ، وَعَلَيْكُمْ بِالسَّكِينَةِ وَالْوَقَارِ وَلاَ تُسْرِعُوا، فَمَا أَدْرَكْتُمْ فَصَلُّوا وَمَا فَاتَكُمْ فَأَتِمُّوا "

Narrated `Abdullah bin Abi Qatada: My father said. "Allah's Messenger ﷺ said, 'If the Iqama is pronounced then do not stand for the prayer till you see me (in front of you).' " – Al-Bukhari 637
حَدَّثَنَا مُسْلِمُ بْنُ إِبْرَاهِيمَ، قَالَ حَدَّثَنَا هِشَامٌ، قَالَ كَتَبَ إِلَىَّ يَحْيَى عَنْ عَبْدِ اللَّهِ بْنِ أَبِي قَتَادَةَ، عَنْ أَبِيهِ، قَالَ قَالَ رَسُولُ اللَّهِ صلى الله عليه وسلم " إِذَا أُقِيمَتِ الصَّلاَةُ فَلاَ تَقُومُوا حَتَّى تَرَوْنِي "

Narrated `Abdullah bin Abi Qatada: My father said, "Allah's Messenger ﷺ said, 'If the Iqama is pronounced, then do not stand for the prayer till you see me (in front of you) and do it calmly.' " – Al-Bukhari 638
حَدَّثَنَا أَبُو نُعَيْمٍ، قَالَ حَدَّثَنَا شَيْبَانُ، عَنْ يَحْيَى، عَنْ عَبْدِ اللَّهِ بْنِ أَبِي قَتَادَةَ، عَنْ أَبِيهِ، قَالَ قَالَ رَسُولُ اللَّهِ صلى الله عليه وسلم " إِذَا أُقِيمَتِ الصَّلاَةُ فَلاَ تَقُومُوا حَتَّى تَرَوْنِي وَعَلَيْكُمْ بِالسَّكِينَةِ ". تَابَعَهُ عَلِيُّ بْنُ الْمُبَارَكِ.

Takbiratul Ihram
تكبيرة الإحرام

Narrated Nafi`: Whenever Ibn `Umar started the prayer with Takbir, he used to raise his hands: whenever he bowed, he used to raise his hands (before bowing) and also used to raise his hands on saying, "Sami`a l-lahu liman hamidah", and he used to do the same on rising from the second rak`a (for the 3rd rak`a). Ibn `Umar said: "The Prophet ﷺ used to do the same."- Al-Bukhari 739

حَدَّثَنَا عَيَّاشٌ، قَالَ حَدَّثَنَا عَبْدُ الأَعْلَى، قَالَ حَدَّثَنَا عُبَيْدُ اللَّهِ، عَنْ نَافِعٍ، أَنَّ ابْنَ عُمَرَ، كَانَ إِذَا دَخَلَ فِي الصَّلاَةِ كَبَّرَ وَرَفَعَ يَدَيْهِ، وَإِذَا رَكَعَ رَفَعَ يَدَيْهِ، وَإِذَا قَالَ سَمِعَ اللَّهُ لِمَنْ حَمِدَهُ. رَفَعَ يَدَيْهِ، وَإِذَا قَامَ مِنَ الرَّكْعَتَيْنِ رَفَعَ يَدَيْهِ. وَرَفَعَ ذَلِكَ ابْنُ عُمَرَ إِلَى نَبِيِّ اللَّهِ صلى الله عليه وسلم. رَوَاهُ حَمَّادُ بْنُ سَلَمَةَ عَنْ أَيُّوبَ عَنْ نَافِعٍ عَنِ ابْنِ عُمَرَ عَنِ النَّبِيِّ صلى الله عليه وسلم. وَرَوَاهُ ابْنُ طَهْمَانَ عَنْ أَيُّوبَ وَمُوسَى بْنِ عُقْبَةَ مُخْتَصَرًا

And narrated Abu Huraira: Whenever Allah's Messenger ﷺ stood for the prayer, he said Takbir on starting the prayer and then on bowing. On rising from bowing he said, "Sami`a llahu liman hamidah," and then while standing straight he used to say, "Rabbana laka-l hamd" (Al- Laith said, "(The Prophet ﷺ said), 'Wa laka l-hamd'." He used to say Takbir on prostrating and on raising his head from prostration; again he would Say Takbir on prostrating and raising his head. He would then do the same in the whole of the prayer till it was completed. On rising from the second rak`a (after sitting for at-Tahiyyat), he used to say Takbir. – Al-Bukhari 789

حَدَّثَنَا يَحْيَى بْنُ بُكَيْرٍ، قَالَ حَدَّثَنَا اللَّيْثُ، عَنْ عُقَيْلٍ، عَنِ ابْنِ شِهَابٍ، قَالَ أَخْبَرَنِي أَبُو بَكْرِ بْنُ عَبْدِ الرَّحْمَنِ بْنِ الْحَارِثِ، أَنَّهُ سَمِعَ أَبَا هُرَيْرَةَ، يَقُولُ كَانَ رَسُولُ اللَّهِ صلى الله عليه وسلم إِذَا قَامَ إِلَى الصَّلاَةِ يُكَبِّرُ حِينَ يَقُومُ، ثُمَّ يُكَبِّرُ حِينَ يَرْكَعُ، ثُمَّ يَقُولُ سَمِعَ اللَّهُ لِمَنْ حَمِدَهُ. حِينَ يَرْفَعُ صُلْبَهُ مِنَ الرَّكْعَةِ، ثُمَّ يَقُولُ وَهُوَ قَائِمٌ رَبَّنَا لَكَ الْحَمْدُ ـ قَالَ عَبْدُ اللَّهِ {بْنُ صَالِحٍ عَنِ اللَّيْثِ} وَلَكَ الْحَمْدُ ـ ثُمَّ يُكَبِّرُ حِينَ يَهْوِي، ثُمَّ يُكَبِّرُ حِينَ يَرْفَعُ رَأْسَهُ، ثُمَّ يُكَبِّرُ حِينَ يَسْجُدُ، ثُمَّ يُكَبِّرُ حِينَ يَرْفَعُ رَأْسَهُ، ثُمَّ يَفْعَلُ ذَلِكَ فِي الصَّلاَةِ كُلِّهَا حَتَّى يَقْضِيَهَا، وَيُكَبِّرُ حِينَ يَقُومُ مِنَ الثِّنْتَيْنِ بَعْدَ الْجُلُوسِ.

I saw that every one of us used to put his heel with the heel of his companion

رأيت الرجل منا يلزق كبعه بكعب صاحبه .

Narrated Anas bin Malik: The Prophet ﷺ said, "Straighten your rows for I see you from behind my back." Anas added, "Everyone of us used to put his shoulder with the shoulder of his companion and his foot with the foot of his companion." – Al-Bukhari 725

حَدَّثَنَا عَمْرُو بْنُ خَالِدٍ، قَالَ حَدَّثَنَا زُهَيْرٌ، عَنْ حُمَيْدٍ، عَنْ أَنَسٍ، عَنِ النَّبِيِّ صلى الله عليه وسلم قَالَ " أَقِيمُوا صُفُوفَكُمْ فَإِنِّي أَرَاكُمْ مِنْ وَرَاءِ ظَهْرِي ". وَكَانَ أَحَدُنَا يُلْزِقُ مَنْكِبَهُ بِمَنْكِبِ صَاحِبِهِ وَقَدَمَهُ بِقَدَمِهِ

And An-Nu'mân bin Bashir said, "I saw that every one of us used to put his heel with the heel of his companion. – Al-Bukhari Vol.1 page 409

و قال النعمان بن بشير : رأيت الرجل منا يلزق كبعه بكعب صاحبه .

Bismillahir Rahmanir Raheem

بِسۡمِ ٱللَّهِ ٱلرَّحۡمَـٰنِ ٱلرَّحِيمِ

Narrated Qatada: Anas was asked, "How was the recitation (of the Qur'an) of the Prophet?' He replied, "It was characterized by the prolongation of certain sounds." He then recited: In the Name of Allah, the Most Beneficent, the Most Merciful prolonging the pronunciation of 'In the Name of Allah, 'the most Beneficent,' and 'the Most Merciful. – Al-Bukhari 5046

حَدَّثَنَا عَمْرُو بْنُ عَاصِمٍ، حَدَّثَنَا هَمَّامٌ، عَنْ قَتَادَةَ، قَالَ سُئِلَ أَنَسٌ كَيْفَ كَانَتْ قِرَاءَةُ النَّبِيِّ صلى الله عليه وسلم. فَقَالَ كَانَتْ مَدًّا. ثُمَّ قَرَأَ بِسْمِ اللَّهِ الرَّحْمَنِ الرَّحِيمِ، يَمُدُّ بِبِسْمِ اللَّهِ، وَيَمُدُّ بِالرَّحْمَنِ، وَيَمُدُّ بِالرَّحِيمِ

And We have given you seven of the oft-repeated [verses], and this glorious Qur'an. – Surah Al-Hijr 15:87

وَلَقَدْ ءَاتَيْنَـٰكَ سَبْعًا مِّنَ ٱلْمَثَانِى وَٱلْقُرْءَانَ ٱلْعَظِيمَ

In The Name of Allah, The All-Merciful, The Ever-Merciful Praise be to Allah, The Lord of the worlds The All-Merciful, The Ever-Merciful The Possessor of the Day of Doom You only do we worship, and You only do we beseech for help Guide us in the straight Path The Path of the ones whom You have favored, other than that of the ones against whom You are angered, and not (that of) the erring. – Surah Al-Fatihah
بِسْمِ ٱللَّهِ ٱلرَّحْمَـٰنِ ٱلرَّحِيمِ ٱلْحَمْدُ لِلَّهِ رَبِّ ٱلْعَـٰلَمِينَ ٱلرَّحْمَـٰنِ ٱلرَّحِيمِ مَـٰلِكِ يَوْمِ ٱلدِّينِ إِيَّاكَ نَعْبُدُ وَإِيَّاكَ نَسْتَعِينُ ٱهْدِنَا ٱلصِّرَٰطَ ٱلْمُسْتَقِيمَ صِرَٰطَ ٱلَّذِينَ أَنْعَمْتَ عَلَيْهِمْ غَيْرِ ٱلْمَغْضُوبِ عَلَيْهِمْ وَلَا ٱلضَّآلِّينَ

....I never saw him pray a shorter prayer..... – Sahih al-Bukhari 1103

فَمَا رَأَيْتُهُ صَلَّى صَلاَةً أَخَفَّ

Narrated Shaqiq: `Abdullah said, "I learnt An-Naza'ir which the Prophetﷺ used to recite in pairs in each rak`a." Then `Abdullah got up and Alqama accompanied him to his house, and when Alqama came out, we asked him (about those Suras). He said, "They are twenty Suras that start from the beginning of Al- Mufassal, according to the arrangement done be Ibn Mas`ud, and end with the Suras starting with Ha Mim, e.g. Ha Mim (the Smoke). And "About what they question one another?" (78.1) – Al-Bukhari 4996
حَدَّثَنَا عَبْدَانُ، عَنْ أَبِي حَمْزَةَ، عَنِ الأَعْمَشِ، عَنْ شَقِيقٍ، قَالَ قَالَ عَبْدُ اللَّهِ قَدْ عَلِمْتُ النَّظَائِرَ الَّتِي كَانَ النَّبِيُّ صلى الله عليه وسلم يَقْرَؤُهُنَّ اثْنَيْنِ اثْنَيْنِ فِي كُلِّ رَكْعَةٍ. فَقَامَ عَبْدُ اللَّهِ وَدَخَلَ مَعَهُ عَلْقَمَةُ وَخَرَجَ عَلْقَمَةُ فَسَأَلْنَاهُ فَقَالَ عِشْرُونَ سُورَةً مِنْ أَوَّلِ الْمُفَصَّلِ عَلَى تَأْلِيفِ ابْنِ مَسْعُودٍ آخِرُهُنَّ الْحَوَامِيمُ حم الدُّخَانُ وَعَمَّ يَتَسَاءَلُونَ.

Narrated Abu Al-Minhal: Abu Barza said, "The Prophetﷺ used to offer the Fajr (prayer) when one could recognize the person sitting by him (after the prayer) and he used to recite between 60 to 100 Ayat (verses) of the Qur'an. He used to offer the Zuhr prayer as soon as the sun declined (at noon) and the `Asr at a time when a man might go and return from the farthest place in Medina and find the sun still hot. (The sub-narrator forgot what was said about the Maghrib). He did not mind delaying the `Isha prayer to one third of the night or the middle of the night.". – Sahih Al-Bukhari 541
حَدَّثَنَا حَفْصُ بْنُ عُمَرَ، قَالَ حَدَّثَنَا شُعْبَةُ، عَنْ أَبِي الْمِنْهَالِ، عَنْ أَبِي بَرْزَةَ، كَانَ النَّبِيُّ صلى الله عليه وسلم يُصَلِّي الصُّبْحَ وَأَحَدُنَا يَعْرِفُ جَلِيسَهُ، وَيَقْرَأُ فِيهَا مَا بَيْنَ السِّتِّينَ إِلَى الْمِائَةِ، وَيُصَلِّي الظُّهْرَ إِذَا زَالَتِ الشَّمْسُ، وَالْعَصْرَ وَأَحَدُنَا يَذْهَبُ إِلَى أَقْصَى الْمَدِينَةِ ثُمَّ يَرْجِعُ وَالشَّمْسُ حَيَّةٌ، وَنَسِيتُ مَا قَالَ فِي الْمَغْرِبِ، وَلاَ يُبَالِي بِتَأْخِيرِ الْعِشَاءِ إِلَى ثُلُثِ اللَّيْلِ. ثُمَّ قَالَ إِلَى شَطْرِ اللَّيْلِ. وَقَالَ مُعَاذٌ قَالَ شُعْبَةُ ثُمَّ لَقِيتُهُ مَرَّةً فَقَالَ أَوْ ثُلُثِ اللَّيْلِ.

Narrated Abu Huraira: The Prophetﷺ used to recite the following in the Fajr prayer of Friday, "Alif, Lam, Mim, Tanzil" (Suratas- Sajda #32) and "Hal-ata-ala-l-Insani" (i.e. Surah-Ad-Dahr #76). – Sahih al-Bukhari 891
حَدَّثَنَا أَبُو نُعَيْمٍ، قَالَ حَدَّثَنَا سُفْيَانُ، عَنْ سَعْدِ بْنِ إِبْرَاهِيمَ، عَنْ عَبْدِ الرَّحْمَنِ ـ هُوَ ابْنُ هُرْمُزَ ـ عَنْ أَبِي هُرَيْرَةَ ـ رضى الله عنه ـ قَالَ كَانَ النَّبِيُّ صلى الله عليه وسلم يَقْرَأُ فِي الْجُمُعَةِ فِي صَلاَةِ الْفَجْرِ {الم * تَنْزِيلُ} السَّجْدَةَ وَ{هَلْ أَتَى عَلَى الإِنْسَانِ}

Narrated Marwan bin Al-Hakam: Zaid bin Thabit said to me, "Why do you recite very short Suras in the Maghrib prayer while I heard the Prophetﷺ reciting the longer of the two long Suras?" – Sahih al-Bukhari 764
حَدَّثَنَا أَبُو عَاصِمٍ، عَنِ ابْنِ جُرَيْجٍ، عَنِ ابْنِ أَبِي مُلَيْكَةَ، عَنْ عُرْوَةَ بْنِ الزُّبَيْرِ، عَنْ مَرْوَانَ بْنِ الْحَكَمِ، قَالَ قَالَ لِي زَيْدُ بْنُ ثَابِتٍ مَا لَكَ تَقْرَأُ فِي الْمَغْرِبِ بِقِصَارٍ، وَقَدْ سَمِعْتُ النَّبِيَّ صلى الله عليه وسلم يَقْرَأُ بِطُولِ الطُّولَيَيْنِ

Narrated Abu Wa'il: A man came to Ibn Mas`ud and said, "I recited the Mufassal (Suras) at night in one rak`a." Ibn Mas`ud said, "This recitation is (too quick) like the recitation of poetry. I know the identical Suras which the Prophet ﷺ used to recite in pairs." Ibn Mas`ud then mentioned 20 Mufassal Suras including two Suras from the family of (i.e. those verses which begin with) Ha, Meem [??] (which the Prophet ﷺ used to recite) in each rak`a. – Sahih al-Bukhari 775

حَدَّثَنَا آدَمُ، قَالَ حَدَّثَنَا شُعْبَةُ، عَنْ عَمْرِو بْنِ مُرَّةَ، قَالَ سَمِعْتُ أَبَا وَائِلٍ، قَالَ جَاءَ رَجُلٌ إِلَى ابْنِ مَسْعُودٍ فَقَالَ قَرَأْتُ الْمُفَصَّلَ اللَّيْلَةَ فِي رَكْعَةٍ‏.‏ فَقَالَ هَذًّا كَهَذِّ الشِّعْرِ لَقَدْ عَرَفْتُ النَّظَائِرَ الَّتِي كَانَ النَّبِيُّ صلى الله عليه وسلم يَقْرِنُ بَيْنَهُنَّ فَذَكَرَ عِشْرِينَ سُورَةً مِنَ الْمُفَصَّلِ سُورَتَيْنِ فِي كُلِّ رَكْعَةٍ

Ruku
رُكَّعًا

Muhammad is the Messenger of Allah. Those with him are stern against the disbelievers, yet compassionate amongst themselves. You see them kneeling, prostrating, seeking blessings from Allah and approval. Their marks are on their faces from the effects of prostration. Such is their description in the Torah, and their description in the Gospel: like a plant that sprouts, becomes strong, grows thick, and rests on its stem, impressing thefarmers. Through them He enrages the disbelievers. Allah has promised those among them who believe and do good deeds forgiveness and a great reward. – Surah Al-Fath 48:29

مُّحَمَّدٌ رَّسُولُ ٱللَّهِ ۚ وَٱلَّذِينَ مَعَهُۥٓ أَشِدَّآءُ عَلَى ٱلْكُفَّارِ رُحَمَآءُ بَيْنَهُمْ ۖ تَرَىٰهُمْ رُكَّعًا سُجَّدًا يَبْتَغُونَ فَضْلًا مِّنَ ٱللَّهِ وَرِضْوَٰنًا ۖ سِيمَاهُمْ فِى وُجُوهِهِم مِّنْ أَثَرِ ٱلسُّجُودِ ۚ ذَٰلِكَ مَثَلُهُمْ فِى ٱلتَّوْرَىٰةِ ۚ وَمَثَلُهُمْ فِى ٱلْإِنجِيلِ كَزَرْعٍ أَخْرَجَ شَطْـَٔهُۥ فَـَٔازَرَهُۥ فَٱسْتَغْلَظَ فَٱسْتَوَىٰ عَلَىٰ سُوقِهِۦ يُعْجِبُ ٱلزُّرَّاعَ لِيَغِيظَ بِهِمُ ٱلْكُفَّارَ ۗ وَعَدَ ٱللَّهُ ٱلَّذِينَ ءَامَنُوا۟ وَعَمِلُوا۟ ٱلصَّـٰلِحَـٰتِ مِنْهُم مَّغْفِرَةً وَأَجْرًا عَظِيمًۢا

Those who repent, those who worship, those who praise, those who journey, those who kneel, those who bow down, those who advocate righteousness and forbid evil, and those who keep Allah's limits—give good news to the believers.. – Surah At-Taubah 9:112

ٱلتَّـٰٓئِبُونَ ٱلْعَـٰبِدُونَ ٱلْحَـٰمِدُونَ ٱلسَّـٰٓئِحُونَ ٱلرَّٰكِعُونَ ٱلسَّـٰجِدُونَ ٱلْـَٔامِرُونَ بِٱلْمَعْرُوفِ وَٱلنَّاهُونَ عَنِ ٱلْمُنكَرِ وَٱلْحَـٰفِظُونَ لِحُدُودِ ٱللَّهِ ۗ وَبَشِّرِ ٱلْمُؤْمِنِينَ

Place his knees on the ground before his hands
ضَعَ رُكْبَتَيْهِ قَبْلَ يَدَيْهِ

The same narration was told by Majzaa from a man called Uhban bin Aus who was one of those who had witnessed (the Pledge of allegiance beneath) the Tree., and who had some trouble in his knee so that while doing prostrations, he used to put a pillow underneath his knee. – Al-Bukhari 4174 [21]

---

[21] "When the Prophet ﷺ prayed, he would place his knees (on the floor) before his hands, then his hands, his forehead and nose. This is what is authentic and has been related by Shuraik from 'Asim ibn Kulaib on the authority of his father from Wa'il ibn Hajr." (Quoted from commentary of Ibn al-Qayyim) "Ibn Taymiyyah (may Allah have mercy on him) made a valuable comment on this matter in Al-Fatawa (22/449): 'Praying in both ways is permissible, according to the consensus of the scholars. If a person wants to go down knees first or hands first, his prayer is valid in either case, according to the consensus of the scholars, but they disputed as to which is preferable."

وَعَنْ مَجْزَأَةَ، عَنْ رَجُلٍ، مِنْهُمْ مِنْ أَصْحَابِ الشَّجَرَةِ اسْمُهُ أُهْبَانُ بْنُ أَوْسٍ وَكَانَ اشْتَكَى رُكْبَتَهُ، وَكَانَ إِذَا سَجَدَ جَعَلَ تَحْتَ رُكْبَتِهِ وِسَادَةً.

It was narrated that Wa'il bin Hujr said: 'I saw the Messenger of Allah ﷺ when he prostrated, place his knees on the ground before his hands, and when he got up, he lifted his hands before his knees." – Sunan an-Nasa'I 1154

أَخْبَرَنَا إِسْحَاقُ بْنُ مَنْصُورٍ، قَالَ أَنْبَأَنَا يَزِيدُ بْنُ هَارُونَ، قَالَ أَنْبَأَنَا شَرِيكٌ، عَنْ عَاصِمِ بْنِ كُلَيْبٍ، عَنْ أَبِيهِ، عَنْ وَائِلِ بْنِ حُجْرٍ، قَالَ رَأَيْتُ رَسُولَ اللَّهِ صلى الله عليه وسلم إِذَا سَجَدَ وَضَعَ رُكْبَتَيْهِ قَبْلَ يَدَيْهِ وَإِذَا نَهَضَ رَفَعَ يَدَيْهِ قَبْلَ رُكْبَتَيْهِ . قَالَ أَبُو عَبْدِ الرَّحْمَنِ لَمْ يَقُلْ هَذَا عَنْ شَرِيكٍ غَيْرُ يَزِيدَ بْنِ هَارُونَ وَاللَّهُ تَعَالَى أَعْلَمُ

Nafi said: 'Ibn 'Umar used to place Hands (on the ground) before his knees." Al-Bukhari vol.1 pg 144

و قال نافع: كان ابن عمر يضع يديه قبل ركبتيه.

Narrated `Abdullah bin `Abdullah: I saw `Abdullah bin `Umar crossing his legs while sitting in the prayer and I, a mere youngster in those days, did the same. Ibn `Umar forbade me to do so, and said, "The proper way is to keep the right foot propped up and bend the left in the prayer." I said questioningly, "But you are doing so (crossing the legs)." He said, "My feet cannot bear my weight.". – Sahih al-Bukhari 827

حَدَّثَنَا عَبْدُ اللَّهِ بْنُ مَسْلَمَةَ، عَنْ مَالِكٍ، عَنْ عَبْدِ الرَّحْمَنِ بْنِ الْقَاسِمِ، عَنْ عَبْدِ اللَّهِ بْنِ عَبْدِ اللَّهِ، أَنَّهُ أَخْبَرَهُ أَنَّهُ، كَانَ يَرَى عَبْدَ اللَّهِ بْنَ عُمَرَ ـ رضى الله عنهما ـ يَتَرَبَّعُ فِي الصَّلاَةِ إِذَا جَلَسَ، فَفَعَلْتُهُ وَأَنَا يَوْمَئِذٍ حَدِيثُ السِّنِّ، فَنَهَانِي عَبْدُ اللَّهِ بْنُ عُمَرَ وَقَالَ إِنَّمَا سُنَّةُ الصَّلاَةِ أَنْ تَنْصِبَ رِجْلَكَ الْيُمْنَى وَتَثْنِيَ الْيُسْرَى. فَقُلْتُ إِنَّكَ تَفْعَلُ ذَلِكَ. فَقَالَ إِنَّ رِجْلَىَّ لاَ تَحْمِلاَنِي

It was narrated that Abu Hurairah said: "The Messenger of Allah ﷺ said: 'When one of you prostrates, let him put his hands down before his knees, and not kneel like a camel.'" – Sunan an-Nasa'I 1091

أَخْبَرَنَا هَارُونُ بْنُ مُحَمَّدِ بْنِ بَكَّارِ بْنِ بِلاَلٍ، مِنْ كِتَابِهِ قَالَ حَدَّثَنَا مَرْوَانُ بْنُ مُحَمَّدٍ، قَالَ حَدَّثَنَا عَبْدُ الْعَزِيزِ بْنُ مُحَمَّدٍ، قَالَ حَدَّثَنَا مُحَمَّدُ بْنُ عَبْدِ اللَّهِ بْنِ الْحَسَنِ، عَنْ أَبِي الزِّنَادِ، عَنِ الأَعْرَجِ، عَنْ أَبِي هُرَيْرَةَ، قَالَ قَالَ رَسُولُ اللَّهِ صلى الله عليه وسلم " إِذَا سَجَدَ أَحَدُكُمْ فَلْيَضَعْ يَدَيْهِ قَبْلَ رُكْبَتَيْهِ وَلاَ يَبْرُكْ بُرُوكَ الْبَعِيرِ " .

Narrated Abu Huraira: A man entered the mosque and started praying while Allah's Messenger ﷺ was sitting somewhere in the mosque. Then (after finishing the prayer) the man came to the Prophet ﷺ and greeted him. The Prophet ﷺ said to him, "Go back and pray, for you have not prayed. The man went back, and having prayed, he came and greeted the Prophet. The Prophet ﷺ after returning his greetings said, "Go back and pray, for you did not pray." On the third time the man said, "(O Allah's Messenger ﷺ!) Teach me (how to pray)." The Prophet said, "When you get up for the prayer, perform the ablution properly and then face the Qibla and say Takbir (Allahu Akbar), and then recite of what you know of the Qur'an, and then bow, and remain in this state till you feel at rest in bowing, and then raise your head and stand straight; and then prostrate till you feel at rest in prostration, and then sit up till you feel at rest while sitting; and then prostrate again till you feel at rest in prostration; and then get up and stand straight, and do all this in all your prayers." – Al-Bukhari 6667

حَدَّثَنِي إِسْحَاقُ بْنُ مَنْصُورٍ، حَدَّثَنَا أَبُو أُسَامَةَ، حَدَّثَنَا عُبَيْدُ اللَّهِ بْنُ عُمَرَ، عَنْ سَعِيدِ بْنِ أَبِي سَعِيدٍ، عَنْ أَبِي هُرَيْرَةَ، أَنَّ رَجُلاً، دَخَلَ الْمَسْجِدَ يُصَلِّي وَرَسُولُ اللَّهِ صلى الله عليه وسلم فِي نَاحِيَةِ الْمَسْجِدِ، فَجَاءَ فَسَلَّمَ عَلَيْهِ فَقَالَ لَهُ " ارْجِعْ فَصَلِّ، فَإِنَّكَ لَمْ تُصَلِّ ". فَرَجَعَ فَصَلَّى، ثُمَّ سَلَّمَ فَقَالَ " وَعَلَيْكَ، ارْجِعْ فَصَلِّ، فَإِنَّكَ لَمْ تُصَلِّ ". قَالَ فِي الثَّالِثَةِ فَأَعْلِمْنِي. قَالَ " إِذَا قُمْتَ إِلَى الصَّلاَةِ فَأَسْبِغِ الْوُضُوءَ، ثُمَّ اسْتَقْبِلِ الْقِبْلَةَ فَكَبِّرْ، وَاقْرَأْ بِمَا تَيَسَّرَ مَعَكَ مِنَ الْقُرْآنِ، ثُمَّ ارْكَعْ حَتَّى تَطْمَئِنَّ رَاكِعًا، ثُمَّ ارْفَعْ رَأْسَكَ حَتَّى تَعْتَدِلَ قَائِمًا، ثُمَّ اسْجُدْ حَتَّى تَطْمَئِنَّ، سَاجِدًا ثُمَّ ارْفَعْ حَتَّى تَسْتَوِيَ وَتَطْمَئِنَّ جَالِسًا، ثُمَّ اسْجُدْ حَتَّى تَطْمَئِنَّ "سَاجِدًا، ثُمَّ ارْفَعْ حَتَّى تَسْتَوِيَ قَائِمًا، ثُمَّ افْعَلْ ذَلِكَ فِي صَلاَتِكَ كُلِّهَا

They fall upon their faces in prostration
يَخِرُّونَ لِلْأَذْقَانِ سُجَّدً

Muḥammad is the Messenger of Allah. And those with him are firm with the disbelievers and compassionate with one another. You see them bowing and prostrating ˹in prayer˺, seeking Allah's bounty and pleasure. The sign ˹of brightness can be seen˺ on their faces from the trace of prostrating ˹in prayer˺. This is their description in the Torah. And their parable in the Gospel is that of a seed that sprouts its ˹tiny˺ branches, making it strong. Then it becomes thick, standing firmly on its stem, to the delight of the planters—in this way Allah makes the believers a source of dismay for the disbelievers. To those of them who believe and do good, Allah has promised forgiveness and a great reward. - Surah Al-Fath 48:29
مُّحَمَّدٌ رَّسُولُ ٱللَّهِ ۚ وَٱلَّذِينَ مَعَهُۥٓ أَشِدَّآءُ عَلَى ٱلْكُفَّارِ رُحَمَآءُ بَيْنَهُمْ ۖ تَرَىٰهُمْ رُكَّعًا سُجَّدًا يَبْتَغُونَ فَضْلًا مِّنَ ٱللَّهِ وَرِضْوَٰنًا ۖ سِيمَاهُمْ فِى وُجُوهِهِم مِّنْ أَثَرِ ٱلسُّجُودِ ۚ ذَٰلِكَ مَثَلُهُمْ فِى ٱلتَّوْرَىٰةِ ۚ وَمَثَلُهُمْ فِى ٱلْإِنجِيلِ كَزَرْعٍ أَخْرَجَ شَطْـَٔهُۥ فَـَٔازَرَهُۥ فَٱسْتَغْلَظَ فَٱسْتَوَىٰ عَلَىٰ سُوقِهِۦ يُعْجِبُ ٱلزُّرَّاعَ لِيَغِيظَ بِهِمُ ٱلْكُفَّارَ ۗ وَعَدَ ٱللَّهُ ٱلَّذِينَ ءَامَنُوا۟ وَعَمِلُوا۟ ٱلصَّٰلِحَٰتِ مِنْهُم مَّغْفِرَةً وَأَجْرًا عَظِيمًۢا

Say, ˹O Prophet,˺ "Believe in this ˹Quran˺, or do not. Indeed, when it is recited to those who were gifted with knowledge before it ˹was revealed˺, they fall upon their faces in prostration, - Surah Al-Isra 17:107
قُلْ آمِنُوا بِهِ أَوْ لَا تُؤْمِنُوا إِنَّ الَّذِينَ أُوتُوا الْعِلْمَ مِن قَبْلِهِ إِذَا يُتْلَىٰ عَلَيْهِمْ يَخِرُّونَ لِلْأَذْقَانِ سُجَّدً

Narrated Ibn `Abbas: The Prophetﷺ was ordered (by Allah) to prostrate on seven parts and not to tuck up the clothes or hair (while praying). Those parts are: the forehead (along with the tip of nose), both hands, both knees, and (toes of) both feet. – Sahih al-Bukhari 809
حَدَّثَنَا قَبِيصَةُ، قَالَ حَدَّثَنَا سُفْيَانُ، عَنْ عَمْرِو بْنِ دِينَارٍ، عَنْ طَاوُسٍ، عَنِ ابْنِ عَبَّاسٍ، أُمِرَ النَّبِيُّ صلى الله عليه وسلم أَنْ يَسْجُدَ عَلَى سَبْعَةِ أَعْضَاءٍ، وَلاَ يَكُفَّ شَعَرًا وَلاَ ثَوْبًا الْجَبْهَةِ وَالْيَدَيْنِ وَالرُّكْبَتَيْنِ وَالرِّجْلَيْنِ.

'Abdur-Rahman bin Shibl said: The Messenger of Allahﷺ forbade three things: "Pecking like a crow, resting one's forearms on the ground like a predator, and allocating the same place for prayer like a camel gets used to a certain place.". – Sunan an-Nasa'I 1112
أَخْبَرَنَا مُحَمَّدُ بْنُ عَبْدِ اللَّهِ بْنِ عَبْدِ الْحَكَمِ، عَنْ شُعَيْبٍ، عَنِ اللَّيْثِ، قَالَ حَدَّثَنَا خَالِدٌ، عَنِ ابْنِ أَبِي هِلاَلٍ، عَنْ جَعْفَرِ بْنِ عَبْدِ اللَّهِ، أَنَّ تَمِيمَ بْنَ مَحْمُودٍ، أَخْبَرَهُ أَنَّ عَبْدَ الرَّحْمَنِ بْنَ شِبْلٍ أَخْبَرَهُ أَنَّ رَسُولَ اللَّهِ صلى الله عليه وسلم نَهَى عَنْ ثَلاَثٍ عَنْ نَقْرَةِ الْغُرَابِ وَافْتِرَاشِ السَّبُعِ وَأَنْ يُوطِنَ الرَّجُلُ الْمُقَامَ لِلصَّلاَةِ كَمَا يُوطِنُ الْبَعِيرُ.

Rise from sujud into qiyam first and third raka
النهوض من السجود إلى الركعة الأولى والثالثة

Narrated Nafi`: Whenever Ibn `Umar started the prayer with Takbir, he used to raise his hands: whenever he bowed, he used to raise his hands (before bowing) and also used to raise his hands on saying, "Sami`a l-lahu liman hamidah", and he used to do the same on rising from the second rak`a (for the 3rd rak`a). Ibn `Umar said: "The Prophetﷺ used to do the same." – Sahih al-Bukhari 739
حَدَّثَنَا عَيَّاشٌ، قَالَ حَدَّثَنَا عَبْدُ الأَعْلَى، قَالَ حَدَّثَنَا عُبَيْدُ اللَّهِ، عَنْ نَافِعٍ، أَنَّ ابْنَ عُمَرَ، كَانَ إِذَا دَخَلَ فِي الصَّلاَةِ كَبَّرَ وَرَفَعَ يَدَيْهِ، وَإِذَا رَكَعَ رَفَعَ يَدَيْهِ، وَإِذَا قَالَ سَمِعَ اللَّهُ لِمَنْ حَمِدَهُ. رَفَعَ يَدَيْهِ، وَإِذَا قَامَ مِنَ الرَّكْعَتَيْنِ رَفَعَ يَدَيْهِ. وَرَفَعَ ذَلِكَ ابْنُ عُمَرَ إِلَى نَبِيِّ اللَّهِ صلى الله عليه وسلم. رَوَاهُ حَمَّادُ بْنُ سَلَمَةَ عَنْ أَيُّوبَ عَنْ نَافِعٍ عَنِ ابْنِ عُمَرَ عَنِ النَّبِيِّ صلى الله عليه وسلم. وَرَوَاهُ ابْنُ طَهْمَانَ عَنْ أَيُّوبَ وَمُوسَى بْنِ عُقْبَةَ مُخْتَصَرًا

Narrated `Aisha: Originally, two rak`at were prescribed in every prayer. When the Prophet ﷺmigrated (to Medina) four rak`at were enjoined, while the journey prayer remained unchanged(i.e. two rak`at). – Al-Bukhari 3935

حَدَّثَنَا مُسَدَّدٌ، حَدَّثَنَا يَزِيدُ بْنُ زُرَيْعٍ، حَدَّثَنَا مَعْمَرٌ، عَنِ الزُّهْرِيِّ، عَنْ عُرْوَةَ، عَنْ عَائِشَةَ ـ رضى الله عنها ـ قَالَتْ فُرِضَتِ الصَّلاَةُ رَكْعَتَيْنِ، ثُمَّ هَاجَرَ النَّبِيُّ صلى الله عليه وسلم فَفُرِضَتْ أَرْبَعًا، وَتُرِكَتْ صَلاَةُ السَّفَرِ عَلَى الأُولَى. تَابَعَهُ عَبْدُ الرَّزَّاقِ عَنْ مَعْمَرٍ

Sitting during tashahhud
الجلوس أثناء التشهد

Narrated Abu Qilaba: Once Malik bin Huwairith said to his friends, "Shall I show you how Allah's Messengerﷺ used to offer his prayers?" And it was not the time for any of the compulsory congregational prayers. So he stood up (for the prayer) bowed and said the Takbir, then he raised his head and remained standing for a while and then prostrated and raised his head for a while (sat up for a while). He prayed like our Sheikh `Amr Ibn Salama. (Aiyub said, "The latter used to do a thing which I did not see the people doing i.e. he used to sit between the third and the fourth rak`a). Malik bin Huwairith said, "We came to the Prophet (after embracing Islam) and stayed with him. He said to us, 'When you go back to your families, pray such and such a prayer at such and such a time, pray such and such a prayer at such and such a time, and when there is the time for the prayer then only of you should pronounce the Adhan for the prayer and the oldest of you should lead the prayer." – Al-Bukhari 818, 819

حَدَّثَنَا أَبُو النُّعْمَانِ، قَالَ حَدَّثَنَا حَمَّادٌ، عَنْ أَيُّوبَ، عَنْ أَبِي قِلاَبَةَ، أَنَّ مَالِكَ بْنَ الْحُوَيْرِثِ، قَالَ لأَصْحَابِهِ أَلاَ أُنَبِّئُكُمْ صَلاَةَ رَسُولِ اللَّهِ صلى الله عليه وسلم قَالَ وَذَاكَ فِي غَيْرِ حِينِ صَلاَةٍ، فَقَامَ، ثُمَّ رَكَعَ فَكَبَّرَ ثُمَّ رَفَعَ رَأْسَهُ، فَقَامَ هُنَيَّةً، ثُمَّ سَجَدَ ثُمَّ رَفَعَ رَأْسَهُ هُنَيَّةً، فَصَلَّى صَلاَةَ عَمْرِو بْنِ سَلِمَةَ شَيْخِنَا هَذَا. قَالَ أَيُّوبُ كَانَ يَفْعَلُ شَيْئًا لَمْ أَرَهُمْ يَفْعَلُونَهُ، كَانَ يَقْعُدُ فِي الثَّالِثَةِ وَالرَّابِعَةِ. قَالَ فَأَتَيْنَا النَّبِيَّ صلى الله عليه وسلم فَأَقَمْنَا عِنْدَهُ فَقَالَ " لَوْ رَجَعْتُمْ إِلَى أَهْلِيكُمْ صَلُّوا صَلاَةَ كَذَا فِي حِينِ كَذَا، صَلُّوا صَلاَةَ كَذَا فِي حِينِ كَذَا، فَإِذَا حَضَرَتِ الصَّلاَةُ فَلْيُؤَذِّنْ أَحَدُكُمْ وَلْيَؤُمَّكُمْ أَكْبَرُكُمْ"

Narrated `Abdullah bin `Abdullah: I saw `Abdullah bin `Umar crossing his legs while sitting in the prayer and I, a mere youngster in those days, did the same. Ibn `Umar forbade me to do so, and said, "The proper way is to keep the right foot propped up and bend the left in the prayer." I said questioningly, "But you are doing so (crossing the legs)." He said, "My feet cannot bear my weight." – Al-Bukhari 827

حَدَّثَنَا عَبْدُ اللَّهِ بْنُ مَسْلَمَةَ، عَنْ مَالِكٍ، عَنْ عَبْدِ الرَّحْمَنِ بْنِ الْقَاسِمِ، عَنْ عَبْدِ اللَّهِ بْنِ عَبْدِ اللَّهِ، أَنَّهُ أَخْبَرَهُ أَنَّهُ، كَانَ يَرَى عَبْدَ اللَّهِ بْنَ عُمَرَ ـ رضى الله عنهما ـ يَتَرَبَّعُ فِي الصَّلاَةِ إِذَا جَلَسَ، فَفَعَلْتُهُ وَأَنَا يَوْمَئِذٍ حَدِيثُ السِّنِّ، فَنَهَانِي عَبْدُ اللَّهِ بْنُ عُمَرَ وَقَالَ إِنَّمَا سُنَّةُ الصَّلاَةِ أَنْ تَنْصِبَ رِجْلَكَ الْيُمْنَى وَتَثْنِيَ الْيُسْرَى. فَقُلْتُ إِنَّكَ تَفْعَلُ ذَلِكَ. فَقَالَ إِنَّ رِجْلَىَّ لاَ تَحْمِلاَنِي

Equal in duration
قَرِيبًا مِنَ السَّوَاءِ

Narrated Al-Bara: The bowing, the prostration the sitting in between the two prostrations and the standing after the bowing of the Prophetﷺ but not qiyam (standing in the prayer) and qu`ud (sitting in the prayer) used to be approximately equal (in duration). – Al-Bukhari 792

حَدَّثَنَا بَدَلُ بْنُ الْمُحَبَّرِ، قَالَ حَدَّثَنَا شُعْبَةُ، قَالَ أَخْبَرَنِي الْحَكَمُ، عَنِ ابْنِ أَبِي لَيْلَى، عَنِ الْبَرَاءِ، قَالَ كَانَ رُكُوعُ النَّبِيِّ صلى الله عليه وسلم وَسُجُودُهُ وَبَيْنَ السَّجْدَتَيْنِ وَإِذَا رَفَعَ مِنَ الرُّكُوعِ، مَا خَلاَ الْقِيَامَ وَالْقُعُودَ، قَرِيبًا مِنَ السَّوَاءِ.

Narrated Al-Bara': The bowing, the prostrations, the period of standing after bowing and the interval between the two prostrations of the Prophet ﷺ used to be equal in duration . – Al-Bukhari 801
حَدَّثَنَا أَبُو الْوَلِيدِ، قَالَ حَدَّثَنَا شُعْبَةُ، عَنِ الْحَكَمِ، عَنِ ابْنِ أَبِي لَيْلَى، عَنِ الْبَرَاءِ ـ رضى الله عنه ـ قَالَ كَانَ رُكُوعُ النَّبِيِّ صلى الله عليه وسلم وَسُجُودُهُ وَإِذَا رَفَعَ رَأْسَهُ مِنَ الرُّكُوعِ وَبَيْنَ السَّجْدَتَيْنِ قَرِيبًا مِنَ السَّوَاءِ.

To testify that None has the right to be worshipped except Allah." The Prophet ﷺ pointed with finger indicating one

شَهَادَةِ أَنْ لاَ إِلَهَ إِلاَّ اللَّهُ ـ وَعَقَدَ وَاحِدَةً

Narrated Ibn `Abbas: The delegation of `Abdul Qais came to the Prophet ﷺ and said, "O Allah's Messenger ﷺ We belong to the tribe of Rabi`a. The infidels of Mudar tribe intervened between us and you so that we cannot come to you except in the Sacred Months, so please order us some things we may act on and invite those left behind to act on. The Prophet ﷺ said, "I order you to observe four things and forbid you from four things: (I order you) to believe in Allah, i.e. to testify that None has the right to be worshipped except Allah." The Prophet ﷺ pointed with finger indicating one and added, "To offer prayers perfectly: to give Zakat, and to give one-fifth of the booty you win (for Allah's Sake). I forbid you to use Ad-Dubba', An-Naquir, Al-Hantam and Al-Muzaffat, (Utensils used for preparing alcoholic liquors and drinks). – Al-Bukhari 4369
حَدَّثَنَا سُلَيْمَانُ بْنُ حَرْبٍ، حَدَّثَنَا حَمَّادُ بْنُ زَيْدٍ، عَنْ أَبِي جَمْرَةَ، قَالَ سَمِعْتُ ابْنَ عَبَّاسٍ، يَقُولُ قَدِمَ وَفْدُ عَبْدِ الْقَيْسِ عَلَى النَّبِيِّ صلى الله عليه وسلم فَقَالُوا يَا رَسُولَ اللَّهِ إِنَّا هَذَا الْحَىَّ مِنْ رَبِيعَةَ، وَقَدْ حَالَتْ بَيْنَنَا وَبَيْنَكَ كُفَّارُ مُضَرَ، فَلَسْنَا نَخْلُصُ إِلَيْكَ إِلاَّ فِي شَهْرٍ حَرَامٍ، فَمُرْنَا بِأَشْيَاءَ نَأْخُذُ بِهَا وَنَدْعُو إِلَيْهَا مَنْ وَرَاءَنَا. قَالَ " آمُرُكُمْ بِأَرْبَعٍ وَأَنْهَاكُمْ عَنْ أَرْبَعٍ، الإِيمَانِ بِاللَّهِ شَهَادَةِ أَنْ لاَ إِلَهَ إِلاَّ اللَّهُ ـ وَعَقَدَ وَاحِدَةً ـ وَإِقَامِ الصَّلاَةِ، وَإِيتَاءِ الزَّكَاةِ، وَأَنْ تُؤَدُّوا لِلَّهِ خُمُسَ مَا غَنِمْتُمْ، وَأَنْهَاكُمْ عَنِ الدُّبَّاءِ، وَالنَّقِيرِ وَالْحَنْتَمِ وَالْمُزَفَّتِ ".

Narrated Sa'd ibn AbuWaqqas: The Prophet ﷺ passed by me while I was supplicating by pointing with two fingers of mine. He said: Point with one finger; point with one finger. He then himself pointed with the forefinger. – Sunan Abi Dawud 1499
حَدَّثَنَا زُهَيْرُ بْنُ حَرْبٍ، حَدَّثَنَا أَبُو مُعَاوِيَةَ، حَدَّثَنَا الأَعْمَشُ، عَنْ أَبِي صَالِحٍ، عَنْ سَعْدِ بْنِ أَبِي وَقَّاصٍ، قَالَ مَرَّ عَلَىَّ النَّبِيُّ صلى الله عليه وسلم وَأَنَا أَدْعُو بِأُصْبُعَىَّ فَقَالَ " أَحِّدْ أَحِّدْ " . وَأَشَارَ بِالسَّبَّابَةِ .

In another narration of Muslim: 'and he clenched all his (right hand) fingers and pointed with the index finger.' – Bulugh al-Maram - The Book of Prayer
وَفِي رِوَايَةٍ لَهُ : وَقَبَضَ أَصَابِعَهُ كُلَّهَا , وَأَشَارَ بِالَّتِي تَلِي اَلْإِبْهَامَ

'Abdallah b. az-Zubair said that the Prophet used to point with his [fore] finger when he made supplication, but did not move it. Abu Dawud and Nasa'I transmitted it, Abu Dawud adding that he kept his look fixed on the finger he was pointing. – Mishkat al-Masabih 912
وَعَن عبد الله بن الزبير قَالَ: كَانَ النَّبِيُّ صَلَّى اللَّهُ عَلَيْهِ وَسَلَّمَ يُشِيرُ بِأُصْبُعِهِ إِذَا دَعَا وَلَا يُحَرِّكُهَا. رَوَاهُ أَبُو دَاوُدَ وَالنَّسَائِيّ وَزَاد أَبُو دَاوُد وَلَا يُجَاوز بَصَره إِشَارَته

It was narrated from 'Amir bin Abdullah bin Az-Zubair, from his father, that: When the Messenger of Allah ﷺ sat to say the tashahhud, he placed his left hand on his left thigh and pointed with his forefinger, and his gaze did not go beyond he finger with which he was pointing. – Sunan an-Nasa'I 1275

أَخْبَرَنَا يَعْقُوبُ بْنُ إِبْرَاهِيمَ، قَالَ حَدَّثَنَا يَحْيَى، عَنِ ابْنِ عَجْلاَنَ، عَنْ عَامِرِ بْنِ عَبْدِ اللَّهِ بْنِ الزُّبَيْرِ، عَنْ أَبِيهِ، أَنَّ رَسُولَ اللَّهِ صلى الله عليه وسلم كَانَ إِذَا قَعَدَ فِي التَّشَهُّدِ وَضَعَ كَفَّهُ الْيُسْرَى عَلَى فَخِذِهِ الْيُسْرَى وَأَشَارَ بِالسَّبَّابَةِ لاَ يُجَاوِزُ بَصَرُهُ إِشَارَتَهُ

'Amr bin 'Abdullah bin Az-Zubair narrated that: His father said: "When the Messenger of Allah ﷺ sat in the second or fourth rak'ah, he would place his hands on his knees and point with his finger." – Sunan an-Nasa'I 1161 [22]

أَخْبَرَنَا زَكَرِيَّا بْنُ يَحْيَى السِّجْزِيُّ، - يُعْرَفُ بِخَيَّاطِ السُّنَّةِ نَزَلَ بِدِمَشْقَ أَحَدُ الثِّقَاتِ – قَالَ حَدَّثَنَا الْحَسَنُ بْنُ عِيسَى قَالَ أَنْبَأَنَا ابْنُ الْمُبَارَكِ قَالَ حَدَّثَنَا مَخْرَمَةُ بْنُ بُكَيْرٍ قَالَ أَنْبَأَنَا عَامِرُ بْنُ عَبْدِ اللَّهِ بْنِ الزُّبَيْرِ عَنْ أَبِيهِ قَالَ كَانَ رَسُولُ اللَّهِ صلى الله عليه وسلم إِذَا جَلَسَ فِي الثِّنْتَيْنِ أَوْ فِي الأَرْبَعِ يَضَعُ يَدَيْهِ عَلَى رُكْبَتَيْهِ ثُمَّ أَشَارَ بِأُصْبُعِهِ .

Narrated Samura bin Jundub: The Prophet ﷺ used to face us on completion of the prayer. – Al-Bukhari 845

حَدَّثَنَا مُوسَى بْنُ إِسْمَاعِيلَ، قَالَ حَدَّثَنَا جَرِيرُ بْنُ حَازِمٍ، قَالَ حَدَّثَنَا أَبُو رَجَاءٍ، عَنْ سَمُرَةَ بْنِ جُنْدُبٍ، قَالَ كَانَ النَّبِيُّ صلى الله عليه وسلم إِذَا صَلَّى صَلاَةً أَقْبَلَ عَلَيْنَا بِوَجْهِهِ.

Narrated Zaid bin Khalid Al-Juhani: The Prophet ﷺ led us in the Fajr prayer at Hudaibiya after a rainy night. On completion of the prayer, he faced the people and said, "Do you know what your Lord has said (revealed)?" The people replied, "Allah and His Apostle know better." He said, "Allah has said, 'In this morning some of my slaves remained as true believers and some became non-believers; whoever said that the rain was due to the Blessings and the Mercy of Allah had belief in Me and he disbelieves in the stars, and whoever said that it rained because of a particular star had no belief in Me but believes in that star.' " – Al-Bukhari 846

حَدَّثَنَا عَبْدُ اللَّهِ بْنُ مَسْلَمَةَ، عَنْ مَالِكٍ، عَنْ صَالِحِ بْنِ كَيْسَانَ، عَنْ عُبَيْدِ اللَّهِ بْنِ عَبْدِ اللَّهِ بْنِ عُتْبَةَ بْنِ مَسْعُودٍ، عَنْ زَيْدِ بْنِ خَالِدٍ الْجُهَنِيِّ، أَنَّهُ قَالَ صَلَّى لَنَا رَسُولُ اللَّهِ صلى الله عليه وسلم صَلاَةَ الصُّبْحِ بِالْحُدَيْبِيَةِ عَلَى إِثْرِ سَمَاءٍ كَانَتْ مِنَ اللَّيْلَةِ، فَلَمَّا انْصَرَفَ أَقْبَلَ عَلَى النَّاسِ فَقَالَ " هَلْ تَدْرُونَ مَاذَا قَالَ رَبُّكُمْ ". قَالُوا اللَّهُ وَرَسُولُهُ أَعْلَمُ. قَالَ " أَصْبَحَ مِنْ عِبَادِي مُؤْمِنٌ بِي وَكَافِرٌ، فَأَمَّا مَنْ قَالَ مُطِرْنَا بِفَضْلِ اللَّهِ وَرَحْمَتِهِ فَذَلِكَ مُؤْمِنٌ بِي وَكَافِرٌ بِالْكَوْكَبِ، وَأَمَّا مَنْ قَالَ بِنَوْءِ كَذَا وَكَذَا فَذَلِكَ كَافِرٌ بِي وَمُؤْمِنٌ بِالْكَوْكَبِ ".

Narrated Ibn `Abbas: I used to recognize the completion of the prayer of the Prophet ﷺ by hearing Takbir. – Al-Bukhari 842

حَدَّثَنَا عَلِيُّ بْنُ عَبْدِ اللَّهِ، قَالَ حَدَّثَنَا سُفْيَانُ، {عَنْ عَمْرٍو،} قَالَ أَخْبَرَنِي أَبُو مَعْبَدٍ، عَنِ ابْنِ عَبَّاسٍ - رضى الله عنهما - قَالَ كُنْتُ أَعْرِفُ انْقِضَاءَ صَلاَةِ النَّبِيِّ صلى الله عليه وسلم بِالتَّكْبِيرِ.

Narrated Abu Ma`bad: (the freed slave of Ibn `Abbas) Ibn `Abbas told me, "In the lifetime of the Prophet ﷺ it was the custom to celebrate Allah's praises aloud after the compulsory

---

22 Al-Albani initially interpreted certain narrations to suggest a back-and-forth movement, but after further research and re-evaluation of the hadith literature, particularly the hadith of Wa'il ibn Hujr, he concluded that the Prophet Muhammad's action was to point the finger without swaying. He explicitly corrected his earlier position in later editions of his works, such as Sifat Salat al-Nabi (The Prophet's Prayer Described), clarifying that the pointing should be continuous without movement

congregational prayers." Ibn `Abbas further said, "When I heard the Dhikr, I would learn that the compulsory congregational prayer had ended." – Al-Bukhari 841

حَدَّثَنَا إِسْحَاقُ بْنُ نَصْرٍ، قَالَ حَدَّثَنَا عَبْدُ الرَّزَّاقِ، قَالَ أَخْبَرَنَا ابْنُ جُرَيْجٍ، قَالَ أَخْبَرَنِي عَمْرٌو، أَنَّ أَبَا مَعْبَدٍ، مَوْلَى ابْنِ عَبَّاسٍ أَخْبَرَهُ أَنَّ ابْنَ عَبَّاسٍ ـ رضى الله عنهما ـ أَخْبَرَهُ أَنَّ رَفْعَ الصَّوْتِ بِالذِّكْرِ حِينَ يَنْصَرِفُ النَّاسُ مِنَ الْمَكْتُوبَةِ كَانَ عَلَى عَهْدِ النَّبِيِّ صلى الله عليه وسلم. وَقَالَ ابْنُ عَبَّاسٍ كُنْتُ أَعْلَمُ إِذَا انْصَرَفُوا بِذَلِكَ إِذَا سَمِعْتُهُ.

Salah Sadl and Salah Qabd

صلاح سدل وصلاح قبد

And so We have made you ⌜believers⌝ an upright community so that you may be witnesses over humanity and that the Messenger may be a witness over you. We assigned your former direction of prayer only to distinguish those who would remain faithful to the Messenger from those who would lose faith. It was certainly a difficult test except for those ⌜rightly⌝ guided by Allah. And Allah would never discount your ⌜previous acts of⌝ faith. Surely Allah is Ever Gracious and Most Merciful to humanity. – Al-Baqarah 2:143

وَكَذَٰلِكَ جَعَلْنَٰكُمْ أُمَّةً وَسَطًا لِّتَكُونُوا۟ شُهَدَآءَ عَلَى ٱلنَّاسِ وَيَكُونَ ٱلرَّسُولُ عَلَيْكُمْ شَهِيدًا ۗ وَمَا جَعَلْنَا ٱلْقِبْلَةَ ٱلَّتِى كُنتَ عَلَيْهَآ إِلَّا لِنَعْلَمَ مَن يَتَّبِعُ ٱلرَّسُولَ مِمَّن يَنقَلِبُ عَلَىٰ عَقِبَيْهِ ۚ وَإِن كَانَتْ لَكَبِيرَةً إِلَّا عَلَى ٱلَّذِينَ هَدَى ٱللَّهُ ۗ وَمَا كَانَ ٱللَّهُ لِيُضِيعَ إِيمَٰنَكُمْ ۚ إِنَّ ٱللَّهَ بِٱلنَّاسِ لَرَءُوفٌ رَّحِيمٌ

Narrated Bara' bin `Azib: Allah's Messenger ﷺ prayed facing Baitul-Maqdis for sixteen or seventeen months but he loved to face the Ka`ba (at Mecca) so Allah revealed: "Verily, We have seen the turning of your face to the heaven!" (2:144) So the Prophet ﷺ faced the Ka`ba and the fools amongst the people namely "the Jews" said, "What has turned them from their Qibla (Baitul-Maqdis) which they formerly observed"" (Allah revealed): "Say: 'To Allah belongs the East and the West. He guides whom he will to a straight path'." (2:142) A man prayed with the Prophet (facing the Ka`ba) and went out. He saw some of the Ansar praying the `Asr prayer with their faces towards Baitul-Maqdis, he said, "I bear witness that I prayed with Allah's Messenger ﷺ facing the Ka`ba." So all the people turned their faces towards the Ka`ba. – Al-Bukhari 399

حَدَّثَنَا عَبْدُ اللَّهِ بْنُ رَجَاءٍ، قَالَ حَدَّثَنَا إِسْرَائِيلُ، عَنْ أَبِي إِسْحَاقَ، عَنِ الْبَرَاءِ بْنِ عَازِبٍ ـ رضى الله عنهما ـ قَالَ كَانَ رَسُولُ اللَّهِ صلى الله عليه وسلم صَلَّى نَحْوَ بَيْتِ الْمَقْدِسِ سِتَّةَ عَشَرَ أَوْ سَبْعَةَ عَشَرَ شَهْرًا، وَكَانَ رَسُولُ اللَّهِ صلى الله عليه وسلم يُحِبُّ أَنْ يُوَجَّهَ إِلَى الْكَعْبَةِ، فَأَنْزَلَ اللَّهُ ‏{‏قَدْ نَرَى تَقَلُّبَ وَجْهِكَ فِي السَّمَاءِ‏}‏ فَتَوَجَّهَ نَحْوَ الْكَعْبَةِ، وَقَالَ السُّفَهَاءُ مِنَ النَّاسِ ـ وَهُمُ الْيَهُودُ ـ مَا وَلاَّهُمْ عَنْ قِبْلَتِهِمُ الَّتِي كَانُوا عَلَيْهَا ‏{‏قُلْ لِلَّهِ الْمَشْرِقُ وَالْمَغْرِبُ يَهْدِي مَنْ يَشَاءُ إِلَى صِرَاطٍ مُسْتَقِيمٍ‏}‏ فَصَلَّى مَعَ النَّبِيِّ صلى الله عليه وسلم رَجُلٌ ثُمَّ خَرَجَ بَعْدَ مَا صَلَّى، فَمَرَّ عَلَى قَوْمٍ مِنَ الأَنْصَارِ فِي صَلاَةِ الْعَصْرِ نَحْوَ بَيْتِ الْمَقْدِسِ فَقَالَ هُوَ يَشْهَدُ أَنَّهُ صَلَّى مَعَ رَسُولِ اللَّهِ صلى الله عليه وسلم، وَأَنَّهُ تَوَجَّهَ نَحْوَ الْكَعْبَةِ‏.‏ فَتَحَرَّفَ الْقَوْمُ حَتَّى تَوَجَّهُوا نَحْوَ الْكَعْبَةِ‏.‏

Narrated Al-Bara' (bin 'Azib): When the Prophet ﷺ came to Medina, he stayed first with his grandfathers or maternal uncles from Ansar. He offered his prayers facing Baitul-Maqdis (Jerusalem) for sixteen or seventeen months, but he wished that he could pray facing the Ka'ba (at Mecca). The first prayer which he offered facing the Ka'ba was the 'Asr prayer in the company of some people. Then one of those who had offered that prayer with him came out and passed by some people in a mosque who were bowing during their prayers (facing Jerusalem). He said addressing them, "By Allah, I testify that I have prayed with Allah's Messenger ﷺ facing Mecca (Ka'ba).' Hearing that, those people changed their direction towards the Ka'ba immediately. Jews and the people of the scriptures used to be pleased to see the Prophet ﷺ facing Jerusalem in prayers but when he changed his direction towards the

Ka'ba, during the prayers, they disapproved of it. Al-Bara' added, "Before we changed our direction towards the Ka'ba (Mecca) in prayers, some Muslims had died or had been killed and we did not know what to say about them (regarding their prayers.) Allah then revealed: And Allah would never make your faith (prayers) to be lost (i.e. the prayers of those Muslims were valid).' " (2:143). – Al-Bukhari 40

حَدَّثَنَا عَمْرُو بْنُ خَالِدٍ، قَالَ حَدَّثَنَا زُهَيْرٌ، قَالَ حَدَّثَنَا أَبُو إِسْحَاقَ، عَنِ الْبَرَاءِ، أَنَّ النَّبِيَّ صلى الله عليه وسلم كَانَ أَوَّلَ مَا قَدِمَ الْمَدِينَةَ نَزَلَ عَلَى أَجْدَادِهِ ـ أَوْ قَالَ أَخْوَالِهِ ـ مِنَ الأَنْصَارِ، وَأَنَّهُ صَلَّى قِبَلَ بَيْتِ الْمَقْدِسِ سِتَّةَ عَشَرَ شَهْرًا، أَوْ سَبْعَةَ عَشَرَ شَهْرًا، وَكَانَ يُعْجِبُهُ أَنْ تَكُونَ قِبْلَتُهُ قِبَلَ الْبَيْتِ، وَأَنَّهُ صَلَّى أَوَّلَ صَلاَةٍ صَلاَّهَا صَلاَةَ الْعَصْرِ، وَصَلَّى مَعَهُ قَوْمٌ، فَخَرَجَ رَجُلٌ مِمَّنْ صَلَّى مَعَهُ، فَمَرَّ عَلَى أَهْلِ مَسْجِدٍ، وَهُمْ رَاكِعُونَ فَقَالَ أَشْهَدُ بِاللَّهِ لَقَدْ صَلَّيْتُ مَعَ رَسُولِ اللَّهِ صلى الله عليه وسلم قِبَلَ مَكَّةَ، فَدَارُوا كَمَا هُمْ قِبَلَ الْبَيْتِ، وَكَانَتِ الْيَهُودُ قَدْ أَعْجَبَهُمْ إِذْ كَانَ يُصَلِّي قِبَلَ بَيْتِ الْمَقْدِسِ، وَأَهْلُ الْكِتَابِ، فَلَمَّا وَلَّى وَجْهَهُ قِبَلَ الْبَيْتِ أَنْكَرُوا ذَلِكَ. قَالَ زُهَيْرٌ حَدَّثَنَا أَبُو إِسْحَاقَ عَنِ الْبَرَاءِ فِي حَدِيثِهِ هَذَا أَنَّهُ مَاتَ عَلَى الْقِبْلَةِ قَبْلَ أَنْ تُحَوَّلَ رِجَالٌ وَقُتِلُوا، فَلَمْ نَدْرِ مَا نَقُولُ فِيهِمْ، فَأَنْزَلَ اللَّهُ تَعَالَى {وَمَا كَانَ اللَّهُ لِيُضِيعَ إِيمَانَكُمْ

Narrated Ibn Shihab from `Urwa: `Aisha said, "Once Allah's Messenger ﷺ delayed the `Isha' prayer till `Umar reminded him by saying, "The prayer!" The women and children have slept. Then the Prophet ﷺ came out and said, 'None amongst the dwellers of the earth has been waiting for it (the prayer) except you." `Urwa said, "Nowhere except in Medina the prayer used to be offered (in those days)[23]." He further said, "The Prophet ﷺ used to offer the `Isha' prayer in the period between the disappearance of the twilight and the end of the first third of the night." – Sahih al-Bukhari 569

حَدَّثَنَا أَيُّوبُ بْنُ سُلَيْمَانَ، قَالَ حَدَّثَنِي أَبُو بَكْرٍ، عَنْ سُلَيْمَانَ، قَالَ صَالِحُ بْنُ كَيْسَانَ أَخْبَرَنِي ابْنُ شِهَابٍ، عَنْ عُرْوَةَ، أَنَّ عَائِشَةَ، قَالَتْ أَعْتَمَ رَسُولُ اللَّهِ صلى الله عليه وسلم بِالْعِشَاءِ حَتَّى نَادَاهُ عُمَرُ الصَّلاَةَ، نَامَ النِّسَاءُ وَالصِّبْيَانُ. فَخَرَجَ فَقَالَ " مَا يَنْتَظِرُهَا أَحَدٌ مِنْ أَهْلِ الأَرْضِ غَيْرُكُمْ ". قَالَ وَلاَ يُصَلَّى يَوْمَئِذٍ إِلاَّ بِالْمَدِينَةِ، وَكَانُوا يُصَلُّونَ فِيمَا بَيْنَ أَنْ يَغِيبَ الشَّفَقُ إِلَى ثُلُثِ اللَّيْلِ الأَوَّلِ

Narrated Ibn `Umar: When the Muslims arrived at Medina, they used to assemble for the prayer, and used to guess the time for it. During those days, the practice of Adhan for the prayers had not been introduced yet. Once they discussed this problem regarding the call for prayer. Some people suggested the use of a bell like the Christians, others proposed a trumpet like the horn used by the Jews, but `Umar was the first to suggest that a man should call (the people) for the prayer; so Allah's Messenger ﷺ ordered Bilal to get up and pronounce the Adhan for prayers. – Sahih al-Bukhari 604

حَدَّثَنَا مَحْمُودُ بْنُ غَيْلاَنَ، قَالَ حَدَّثَنَا عَبْدُ الرَّزَّاقِ، قَالَ أَخْبَرَنَا ابْنُ جُرَيْجٍ، قَالَ أَخْبَرَنِي نَافِعٌ، أَنَّ ابْنَ عُمَرَ، كَانَ يَقُولُ كَانَ الْمُسْلِمُونَ حِينَ قَدِمُوا الْمَدِينَةَ يَجْتَمِعُونَ فَيَتَحَيَّنُونَ الصَّلاَةَ، لَيْسَ يُنَادَى لَهَا، فَتَكَلَّمُوا يَوْمًا فِي ذَلِكَ، فَقَالَ بَعْضُهُمُ اتَّخِذُوا نَاقُوسًا مِثْلَ نَاقُوسِ النَّصَارَى. وَقَالَ بَعْضُهُمْ بَلْ بُوقًا مِثْلَ قَرْنِ الْيَهُودِ. فَقَالَ عُمَرُ أَوَلاَ تَبْعَثُونَ رَجُلاً يُنَادِي بِالصَّلاَةِ. فَقَالَ رَسُولُ اللَّهِ صلى الله عليه وسلم " يَا بِلاَلُ قُمْ فَنَادِ بِالصَّلاَةِ "

Yet, in case you fear (the enemy), then (pray) afoot or riding; so when you are secure, then remember Allah, as He taught you that (i.e., the prayers) which you did not know. – Surah Al-Baqarah 2:239

فَإِنْ خِفْتُمْ فَرِجَالًا أَوْ رُكْبَانًا ۖ فَإِذَآ أَمِنتُمْ فَٱذْكُرُوا۟ ٱللَّهَ كَمَا عَلَّمَكُم مَّا لَمْ تَكُونُوا۟ تَعْلَمُونَ

Narrated Abu Huraira :It was forbidden to pray with the hands over one's hips – .Sahih al-Bukhari 1220

---

[23] And in no way is their prayer at the Home anything except a whistling and a clapping of hands……. – Surah Al-Anfal 8:35

وَمَا كَانَ صَلَاتُهُمْ عِندَ ٱلْبَيْتِ إِلَّا مُكَآءً وَتَصْدِيَةً

حَدَّثَنَا عَمْرُو بْنُ عَلِيٍّ، حَدَّثَنَا يَحْيَى، حَدَّثَنَا هِشَامٌ، حَدَّثَنَا مُحَمَّدٌ، عَنْ أَبِي هُرَيْرَةَ، رضى الله عنه قَالَ نُهِيَ أَنْ يُصَلِّيَ الرَّجُلُ مُخْتَصِرًا.

He has ordained for you ⸢believers⸣ the Way which He decreed for Noah, and what We have revealed to you ⸢O Prophet⸣ and what We decreed for Abraham, Moses, and Jesus, ⸢commanding:⸣ "Uphold the faith, and make no divisions in it." What you call the polytheists to is unbearable for them. Allah chooses for Himself whoever He wills, and guides to Himself whoever turns ⸢to Him⸣. – Surah Ash-Shura 42:13
شَرَعَ لَكُم مِّنَ ٱلدِّينِ مَا وَصَّىٰ بِهِۦ نُوحًا وَٱلَّذِىٓ أَوْحَيْنَآ إِلَيْكَ وَمَا وَصَّيْنَا بِهِۦٓ إِبْرَٰهِيمَ وَمُوسَىٰ وَعِيسَىٰٓ ۖ أَنْ أَقِيمُوا۟ ٱلدِّينَ وَلَا تَتَفَرَّقُوا۟ فِيهِ ۚ كَبُرَ عَلَى ٱلْمُشْرِكِينَ مَا تَدْعُوهُمْ إِلَيْهِ ۚ ٱللَّهُ يَجْتَبِىٓ إِلَيْهِ مَن يَشَآءُ وَيَهْدِىٓ إِلَيْهِ مَن يُنِيبُ

Narrated Mujahid: I asked Ibn `Abbas, "Should we perform a prostration on reciting Surat-Sa`d?" He recited (the Sura) including: 'And among his progeny, David, Solomon..(up to)...so follow their guidance (6.84-91) And then he said, "Your Prophet is amongst those people who have been ordered to follow them (i.e. the preceding apostles). – Al-Bukhari 3421
حَدَّثَنَا مُحَمَّدٌ، حَدَّثَنَا سَهْلُ بْنُ يُوسُفَ، قَالَ سَمِعْتُ الْعَوَّامَ، عَنْ مُجَاهِدٍ، قَالَ قُلْتُ لاِبْنِ عَبَّاسٍ أَسْجُدُ فِي {ص} فَقَرَأَ {وَمِنْ ذُرِّيَّتِهِ دَاوُدَ وَسُلَيْمَانَ} حَتَّى أَتَى {فَبِهُدَاهُمُ اقْتَدِهْ} فَقَالَ نَبِيُّكُمْ صلى الله عليه وسلم مِمَّنْ أُمِرَ أَنْ يَقْتَدِيَ بِهِمْ.

Narrated Ibn `Abbas: The Prophet ﷺ used to copy the people of the Scriptures in matters in which there was no order from Allah. The people of the Scripture used to let their hair hang down while the pagans used to part their hair. So the Prophet ﷺ let his hair hang down first, but later on he parted it. – Al-Bukhari 5917
حَدَّثَنَا أَحْمَدُ بْنُ يُونُسَ، حَدَّثَنَا إِبْرَاهِيمُ بْنُ سَعْدٍ، حَدَّثَنَا ابْنُ شِهَابٍ، عَنْ عُبَيْدِ اللَّهِ بْنِ عَبْدِ اللَّهِ، عَنِ ابْنِ عَبَّاسٍ ـ رضى الله عنهما ـ قَالَ كَانَ النَّبِيُّ صلى الله عليه وسلم يُحِبُّ مُوَافَقَةَ أَهْلِ الْكِتَابِ فِيمَا لَمْ يُؤْمَرْ فِيهِ، وَكَانَ أَهْلُ الْكِتَابِ يَسْدِلُونَ أَشْعَارَهُمْ، وَكَانَ الْمُشْرِكُونَ يَفْرُقُونَ رُءُوسَهُمْ، فَسَدَلَ النَّبِيُّ صلى الله عليه وسلم نَاصِيَتَهُ، ثُمَّ فَرَقَ بَعْدُ.

The tradition of the messengers We sent before you—you will find no change in Our rules – Surah Al-Isra 17:77
سُنَّةَ مَن قَدْ أَرْسَلْنَا قَبْلَكَ مِن رُّسُلِنَا ۖ وَلَا تَجِدُ لِسُنَّتِنَا تَحْوِيلًا

...When I returned, I passed by Moses who asked (me), 'What have you been ordered to do?' I replied, 'I have been ordered to offer fifty prayers a day.' Moses said, 'Your followers cannot bear fifty prayers a day, and by Allah, I have tested people before you, and I have tried my level best with Bani Israel (in vain). Go back to your Lord and ask for reduction to lessen your followers' burden.' So I went back, and Allah reduced ten prayers for me. Then again I came to Moses, but he repeated the same as he had said before. Then again I went back to Allah and He reduced ten more prayers. When I came back to Moses he said the same, I went back to Allah and He ordered me to observe ten prayers a day. When I came back to Moses, he repeated the same advice, so I went back to Allah and was ordered to observe five prayers a day. When I came back to Moses, he said, 'What have you been ordered?' I replied, 'I have been ordered to observe five prayers a day.' He said, 'Your followers cannot bear five prayers a day, and no doubt, I have got an experience of the people before you..., - Sahih Al-Bukhari 3887
فَرَجَعْتُ فَمَرَرْتُ عَلَى مُوسَى، فَقَالَ بِمَا أُمِرْتَ قَالَ أُمِرْتُ بِخَمْسِينَ صَلاَةً كُلَّ يَوْمٍ. قَالَ إِنَّ أُمَّتَكَ لاَ تَسْتَطِيعُ خَمْسِينَ صَلاَةً كُلَّ يَوْمٍ، وَإِنِّي وَاللَّهِ قَدْ جَرَّبْتُ النَّاسَ قَبْلَكَ، وَعَالَجْتُ بَنِي إِسْرَائِيلَ أَشَدَّ الْمُعَالَجَةِ، فَارْجِعْ إِلَى رَبِّكَ فَاسْأَلْهُ التَّخْفِيفَ لأُمَّتِكَ. فَرَجَعْتُ، فَوَضَعَ عَنِّي عَشْرًا، فَرَجَعْتُ إِلَى مُوسَى فَقَالَ مِثْلَهُ، فَرَجَعْتُ فَوَضَعَ عَنِّي عَشْرًا، فَرَجَعْتُ إِلَى مُوسَى فَقَالَ مِثْلَهُ، فَرَجَعْتُ فَوَضَعَ عَنِّي عَشْرًا، فَرَجَعْتُ إِلَى مُوسَى فَقَالَ مِثْلَهُ، فَرَجَعْتُ فَأُمِرْتُ بِعَشْرِ صَلَوَاتٍ كُلَّ يَوْمٍ، فَرَجَعْتُ فَقَالَ مِثْلَهُ، فَرَجَعْتُ فَأُمِرْتُ بِخَمْسِ صَلَوَاتٍ كُلَّ يَوْمٍ، فَرَجَعْتُ إِلَى مُوسَى، فَقَالَ بِمَا أُمِرْتَ قُلْتُ أُمِرْتُ بِخَمْسِ صَلَوَاتٍ كُلَّ يَوْمٍ. قَالَ

إِنَّ أُمَّتَكَ لاَ تَسْتَطِيعُ خَمْسَ صَلَوَاتٍ كُلَّ يَوْمٍ، وَإِنِّي قَدْ جَرَّبْتُ النَّاسَ قَبْلَكَ، وَعَالَجْتُ بَنِي إِسْرَائِيلَ أَشَدَّ الْمُعَالَجَةِ، فَارْجِعْ إِلَى رَبِّكَ فَاسْأَلْهُ التَّخْفِيفَ لأُمَّتِكَ....

Narrated Sahl bin Sa`d: The people were ordered to place the right hand on the left forearm in the prayer. Abu Hazim[24] said: I do not know except that it is attributed to the Prophetﷺ." Al-Bukhari 740

حَدَّثَنَا عَبْدُ اللَّهِ بْنُ مَسْلَمَةَ، عَنْ مَالِكٍ، عَنْ أَبِي حَازِمٍ، عَنْ سَهْلِ بْنِ سَعْدٍ، قَالَ كَانَ النَّاسُ يُؤْمَرُونَ أَنْ يَضَعَ الرَّجُلُ الْيَدَ الْيُمْنَى عَلَى ذِرَاعِهِ الْيُسْرَى فِي الصَّلاَةِ. قَالَ أَبُو حَازِمٍ لاَ أَعْلَمُهُ إِلاَّ يَنْمِي ذَلِكَ إِلَى النَّبِيِّ صلى الله عليه وسلم. قَالَ إِسْمَاعِيلُ يُنْمَى ذَلِكَ. وَلَمْ يَقُلْ يَنْمِي

Narrated Abu Huraira: Once the Prophetﷺ entered the mosque, a man came in, offered the prayer and greeted the Prophet. The Prophet returned his greeting and said to him, "Go back and pray again for you have not prayed." The man offered the prayer again, came back and greeted the Prophet. He said to him thrice, "Go back and pray again for you have not prayed." The man said, "By Him Who has sent you with the truth! I do not know a better way of praying. Kindly teach Me how to pray." He said, "When you stand for the prayer, say Takbir and then recite from the Qur'an what you know and then bow with calmness till you feel at ease, then rise from bowing till you stand straight. Afterwards prostrate calmly till you feel at ease and then raise (your head) and sit with Calmness till you feel at ease and then prostrate with calmness till you feel at ease in prostration and do the same in the whole of your prayer." - Sahih al-Bukhari 793

حَدَّثَنَا مُسَدَّدٌ، قَالَ أَخْبَرَنِي يَحْيَى بْنُ سَعِيدٍ، عَنْ عُبَيْدِ اللَّهِ، قَالَ حَدَّثَنَا سَعِيدٌ الْمَقْبُرِيُّ، عَنْ أَبِيهِ، عَنْ أَبِي هُرَيْرَةَ، أَنَّ النَّبِيَّ صلى الله عليه وسلم دَخَلَ الْمَسْجِدَ فَدَخَلَ رَجُلٌ فَصَلَّى ثُمَّ جَاءَ فَسَلَّمَ عَلَى النَّبِيِّ صلى الله عليه وسلم فَرَدَّ النَّبِيُّ صلى الله عليه وسلم عَلَيْهِ السَّلاَمَ فَقَالَ " ارْجِعْ فَصَلِّ فَإِنَّكَ لَمْ تُصَلِّ " فَصَلَّى، ثُمَّ جَاءَ فَسَلَّمَ عَلَى النَّبِيِّ صلى الله عليه وسلم فَقَالَ " ارْجِعْ فَصَلِّ فَإِنَّكَ لَمْ تُصَلِّ ". ثَلاَثًا. فَقَالَ وَالَّذِي بَعَثَكَ بِالْحَقِّ فَمَا أُحْسِنُ غَيْرَهُ فَعَلِّمْنِي. قَالَ " إِذَا قُمْتَ إِلَى الصَّلاَةِ فَكَبِّرْ، ثُمَّ اقْرَأْ مَا تَيَسَّرَ مَعَكَ مِنَ الْقُرْآنِ، ثُمَّ ارْكَعْ حَتَّى تَطْمَئِنَّ رَاكِعًا، ثُمَّ ارْفَعْ حَتَّى تَعْتَدِلَ قَائِمًا، ثُمَّ اسْجُدْ حَتَّى تَطْمَئِنَّ سَاجِدًا، ثُمَّ ارْفَعْ حَتَّى تَطْمَئِنَّ جَالِسًا، ثُمَّ اسْجُدْ حَتَّى تَطْمَئِنَّ سَاجِدًا، ثُمَّ افْعَلْ ذَلِكَ فِي صَلاَتِكَ كُلِّهَا ".

Abu Huraira reported from the Messenger of Allahﷺ that he forbade keeping one's hand on one's waist while praying, and in the narration of Abu Bakr (the words are): The Messenger of Allah ﷺforbade to do so. – Sahih Muslim 545

وَحَدَّثَنِي الْحَكَمُ بْنُ مُوسَى الْقَنْطَرِيُّ، حَدَّثَنَا عَبْدُ اللَّهِ بْنُ الْمُبَارَكِ، ح قَالَ وَحَدَّثَنَا أَبُو بَكْرِ بْنُ أَبِي شَيْبَةَ، حَدَّثَنَا أَبُو خَالِدٍ، وَأَبُو أُسَامَةَ جَمِيعًا عَنْ هِشَامٍ، عَنْ مُحَمَّدٍ، عَنْ أَبِي هُرَيْرَةَ، عَنِ النَّبِيِّ صلى الله عليه وسلم أَنَّهُ نَهَى أَنْ يُصَلِّيَ الرَّجُلُ مُخْتَصِرًا . وَفِي رِوَايَةِ أَبِي بَكْرٍ قَالَ نَهَى رَسُولُ اللَّهِ صلى الله عليه وسلم .

Narrated `Aisha: That she used to hate that one should keep his hands on his flanks while praying. She said that the Jew used to do so. – Al-Bukhari 3458 [25]

حَدَّثَنَا مُحَمَّدُ بْنُ يُوسُفَ، حَدَّثَنَا سُفْيَانُ، عَنِ الأَعْمَشِ، عَنْ أَبِي الضُّحَى، عَنْ مَسْرُوقٍ، عَنْ عَائِشَةَ ـ رضى الله عنها كَانَتْ تَكْرَهُ أَنْ يَجْعَلَ {الْمُصَلِّي} يَدَهُ فِي خَاصِرَتِهِ وَتَقُولُ إِنَّ الْيَهُودَ تَفْعَلُهُ. تَابَعَهُ شُعْبَةُ عَنِ الأَعْمَشِ.

---

[24] Salamah Ibn Dinar al-Madani , also known as Abu Hazim Al-A'raj, was a prominent Muslim ascetic and jurist from the taba'een generation. (died c. 757 or 781) , Sahl bin Sa`d died in 91 AH, He was a young boy at the Battle of Uhud (3 AH / 625 CE)

[25] Note Salah had been established as a Sunnah pre revelation, both Jews and early Muslims offered Salah Sadl (hands at sides) . Narrated Ibn `Abbas: The Prophet ﷺused to copy the people of the Scriptures in matters in which there was no order from Allah.

Yet they are not all alike: there are some among the People of the Book who are upright, who recite Allah's revelations throughout the night, prostrating ⌜in prayer⌝. – Surah Al-Imran 3113
لَيْسُوا۟ سَوَآءً ۗ مِّنْ أَهْلِ ٱلْكِتَـٰبِ أُمَّةٌ قَآئِمَةٌ يَتْلُونَ ءَايَـٰتِ ٱللَّهِ ءَانَآءَ ٱلَّيْلِ وَهُمْ يَسْجُدُونَ

They asked, "O Shu'aib! Does your prayer command you that we should abandon what our forefathers worshipped or give up managing our wealth as we please? Indeed, you are such a tolerant, sensible man!"
Surah Hud 11:87
قَالُوا۟ يَـٰشُعَيْبُ أَصَلَوٰتُكَ تَأْمُرُكَ أَن نَّتْرُكَ مَا يَعْبُدُ ءَابَآؤُنَآ أَوْ أَن نَّفْعَلَ فِىٓ أَمْوَٰلِنَا مَا نَشَـٰٓؤُا۟ ۖ إِنَّكَ لَأَنتَ ٱلْحَلِيمُ ٱلرَّشِيدُ

So, the Angels called out to him (as) he was upright praying in the Chamber, " Allah gives you the good tidings of Yahya, (John) sincerely (verifying previous scriptures) with a Word from Allah, and a master, and chaste, and a Prophet, one of the righteous." – Al-Imran 3:39
فَنَادَتْهُ ٱلْمَلَـٰٓئِكَةُ وَهُوَ قَآئِمٌ يُصَلِّى فِى ٱلْمِحْرَابِ أَنَّ ٱللَّهَ يُبَشِّرُكَ بِيَحْيَىٰ مُصَدِّقًۢا بِكَلِمَةٍ مِّنَ ٱللَّهِ وَسَيِّدًا وَحَصُورًا وَنَبِيًّا مِّنَ ٱلصَّـٰلِحِينَ

And when We assigned to Abraham the site of the House, "Do not associate anything with Me and purify My House for those who circle ⌜the Ka'bah⌝, stand ⌜in prayer⌝, and bow and prostrate themselves. – Surah Al-Hajj 22:26
وَإِذْ بَوَّأْنَا لِإِبْرَٰهِيمَ مَكَانَ ٱلْبَيْتِ أَن لَّا تُشْرِكْ بِى شَيْـًۭٔا وَطَهِّرْ بَيْتِىَ لِلطَّآئِفِينَ وَٱلْقَآئِمِينَ وَٱلرُّكَّعِ ٱلسُّجُودِ

These were the people Allah guided. Follow their guidance and say, "I ask no reward for it from you. It is a reminder to all people." – Surah Al-An'am 6:90
أُو۟لَـٰٓئِكَ ٱلَّذِينَ هَدَى ٱللَّهُ ۖ فَبِهُدَىٰهُمُ ٱقْتَدِهْ ۗ قُل لَّآ أَسْـَٔلُكُمْ عَلَيْهِ أَجْرًا ۖ إِنْ هُوَ إِلَّا ذِكْرَىٰ لِلْعَـٰلَمِينَ

Narrated Abu Huraira: Once the Prophet ﷺ entered the mosque, a man came in, offered the prayer and greeted the Prophet. The Prophet returned his greeting and said to him, "Go back and pray again for you have not prayed." The man offered the prayer again, came back and greeted the Prophet. He said to him thrice, "Go back and pray again for you have not prayed." The man said, "By Him Who has sent you with the truth! I do not know a better way of praying. Kindly teach Me how to pray." He said, "When you stand for the prayer, say Takbir and then recite from the Qur'an what you know and then bow with calmness till you feel at ease, then rise from bowing till you stand straight. Afterwards prostrate calmly till you feel at ease and then raise (your head) and sit with Calmness till you feel at ease and then prostrate with calmness till you feel at ease in prostration and do the same in the whole of your prayer.".
– Sahih Al-Bukhari 793
حَدَّثَنَا مُسَدَّدٌ، قَالَ أَخْبَرَنِي يَحْيَى بْنُ سَعِيدٍ، عَنْ عُبَيْدِ اللَّهِ، قَالَ حَدَّثَنَا سَعِيدٌ الْمَقْبُرِيُّ، عَنْ أَبِيهِ، عَنْ أَبِي هُرَيْرَةَ، أَنَّ النَّبِيَّ صلى الله عليه وسلم دَخَلَ الْمَسْجِدَ فَدَخَلَ رَجُلٌ فَصَلَّى ثُمَّ جَاءَ فَسَلَّمَ عَلَى النَّبِيِّ صلى الله عليه وسلم فَرَدَّ النَّبِيُّ صلى الله عليه وسلم عَلَيْهِ السَّلاَمَ فَقَالَ " ارْجِعْ فَصَلِّ فَإِنَّكَ لَمْ تُصَلِّ " فَصَلَّى، ثُمَّ جَاءَ فَسَلَّمَ عَلَى النَّبِيِّ صلى الله عليه وسلم فَقَالَ " ارْجِعْ فَصَلِّ فَإِنَّكَ لَمْ تُصَلِّ ". ثَلاَثًا. فَقَالَ وَالَّذِي بَعَثَكَ بِالْحَقِّ فَمَا أُحْسِنُ غَيْرَهُ فَعَلِّمْنِي. قَالَ " إِذَا قُمْتَ إِلَى الصَّلاَةِ فَكَبِّرْ، ثُمَّ اقْرَأْ مَا تَيَسَّرَ مَعَكَ مِنَ الْقُرْآنِ، ثُمَّ ارْكَعْ حَتَّى تَطْمَئِنَّ رَاكِعًا، ثُمَّ ارْفَعْ حَتَّى تَعْتَدِلَ قَائِمًا، ثُمَّ اسْجُدْ حَتَّى تَطْمَئِنَّ سَاجِدًا، ثُمَّ ارْفَعْ حَتَّى تَطْمَئِنَّ جَالِسًا، ثُمَّ اسْجُدْ حَتَّى تَطْمَئِنَّ سَاجِدًا، ثُمَّ افْعَلْ ذَلِكَ فِي صَلاَتِكَ كُلِّهَا ".

Narrated Ghailan: Anas said, "I do not find (now-a-days) things as they were (practiced) at the time of the Prophet." Somebody said "The prayer (is as it was.)" Anas said, "Have you not done in the prayer what you have done? – Al-Bukhari 529
حَدَّثَنَا مُوسَى بْنُ إِسْمَاعِيلَ، قَالَ حَدَّثَنَا مَهْدِيٌّ، عَنْ غَيْلاَنَ، عَنْ أَنَسٍ، قَالَ مَا أَعْرِفُ شَيْئًا مِمَّا كَانَ عَلَى عَهْدِ النَّبِيِّ صلى الله عليه وسلم. قِيلَ الصَّلاَةُ. قَالَ أَلَيْسَ ضَيَّعْتُمْ مَا ضَيَّعْتُمْ فِيهَا

Narrated Az-Zuhri that he visited Anas bin Malik at Damascus and found him weeping and asked him why he was weeping. He replied, "I do not know anything which I used to know during the life-time of Allah's Apostle except this prayer which is being lost (not offered as it should be)." – Al-Bukhari 530

حَدَّثَنَا عَمْرُو بْنُ زُرَارَةَ، قَالَ أَخْبَرَنَا عَبْدُ الْوَاحِدِ بْنُ وَاصِلٍ أَبُو عُبَيْدَةَ الْحَدَّادُ، عَنْ عُثْمَانَ بْنِ أَبِي رَوَّادٍ، أَخِي عَبْدِ الْعَزِيزِ قَالَ سَمِعْتُ الزُّهْرِيَّ، يَقُولُ دَخَلْتُ عَلَى أَنَسِ بْنِ مَالِكٍ بِدِمَشْقَ وَهُوَ يَبْكِي فَقُلْتُ مَا يُبْكِيكَ فَقَالَ لاَ أَعْرِفُ شَيْئًا مِمَّا أَدْرَكْتُ إِلاَّ هَذِهِ الصَّلاَةَ، وَهَذِهِ الصَّلاَةُ قَدْ ضُيِّعَتْ. وَقَالَ بَكْرٌ حَدَّثَنَا مُحَمَّدُ بْنُ بَكْرٍ الْبُرْسَانِيُّ أَخْبَرَنَا عُثْمَانُ بْنُ أَبِي رَوَّادٍ نَحْوَهُ.

Narrated `Abdullah: The Prophet ﷺ prayed (and the sub-narrator Ibrahim said, "I do not know whether he prayed more or less than usual"), and when he had finished the prayers he was asked, "O Allah's Messenger ﷺ ! Has there been any change in the prayers?" He said, "What is it?' The people said, "You have prayed so much and so much." So the Prophet ﷺ bent his legs, faced the Qibla and performed two prostration's (of Sahu) and finished his prayers with Taslim (by turning his face to right and left saying: 'As-Salamu `Alaikum- Warahmat-ullah'). When he turned his face to us he said, "If there had been anything changed in the prayer, surely I would have informed you but I am a human being like you and liable to forget like you. So if I forget remind me and if anyone of you is doubtful about his prayer, he should follow what he thinks to be correct and complete his prayer accordingly and finish it and do two prostrations (of Sahu). – Sahih al-Bukhari 401

حَدَّثَنَا عُثْمَانُ، قَالَ حَدَّثَنَا جَرِيرٌ، عَنْ مَنْصُورٍ، عَنْ إِبْرَاهِيمَ، عَنْ عَلْقَمَةَ، قَالَ قَالَ عَبْدُ اللَّهِ صَلَّى النَّبِيُّ صلى الله عليه وسلم ـ قَالَ إِبْرَاهِيمُ لاَ أَدْرِي زَادَ أَوْ نَقَصَ ـ فَلَمَّا سَلَّمَ قِيلَ لَهُ يَا رَسُولَ اللَّهِ، أَحَدَثَ فِي الصَّلاَةِ شَىْءٌ قَالَ " وَمَا ذَاكَ ". قَالُوا صَلَّيْتَ كَذَا وَكَذَا. فَثَنَى رِجْلَيْهِ وَاسْتَقْبَلَ الْقِبْلَةَ، وَسَجَدَ سَجْدَتَيْنِ ثُمَّ سَلَّمَ، فَلَمَّا أَقْبَلَ عَلَيْنَا بِوَجْهِهِ قَالَ " إِنَّهُ لَوْ حَدَثَ فِي الصَّلاَةِ شَىْءٌ لَنَبَّأْتُكُمْ بِهِ، وَلَكِنْ إِنَّمَا أَنَا بَشَرٌ مِثْلُكُمْ، أَنْسَى كَمَا تَنْسَوْنَ، فَإِذَا نَسِيتُ فَذَكِّرُونِي، وَإِذَا شَكَّ أَحَدُكُمْ فِي صَلاَتِهِ فَلْيَتَحَرَّى الصَّوَابَ، فَلْيُتِمَّ عَلَيْهِ ثُمَّ يُسَلِّمْ، ثُمَّ يَسْجُدْ سَجْدَتَيْنِ "

Narrated Hudhaifa: The Prophet ﷺ said (to us), " List the names of those people who have announced that they are Muslims." So, we listed one thousand and five hundred men. Then we wondered, "Should we be afraid (of infidels) although we are one thousand and five hundred in number?" No doubt, we witnessed ourselves being afflicted with such bad trials that one would have to offer the prayer alone in fear. Narrated Al-A`mash: "We (listed the Muslims and) found them five hundred." And Abu Muawiya said, "Between six hundred to seven hundred." – Al-Bukhari 3060

حَدَّثَنَا مُحَمَّدُ بْنُ يُوسُفَ، حَدَّثَنَا سُفْيَانُ، عَنِ الأَعْمَشِ، عَنْ أَبِي وَائِلٍ، عَنْ حُذَيْفَةَ ـ رضى الله عنه ـ قَالَ قَالَ النَّبِيُّ صلى الله عليه وسلم " اكْتُبُوا لِي مَنْ تَلَفَّظَ بِالإِسْلاَمِ مِنَ النَّاسِ ". فَكَتَبْنَا لَهُ أَلْفًا وَخَمْسَمِائَةِ رَجُلٍ، فَقُلْنَا نَخَافُ وَنَحْنُ أَلْفٌ وَخَمْسُمِائَةٍ فَلَقَدْ رَأَيْتُنَا ابْتُلِينَا حَتَّى إِنَّ الرَّجُلَ لَيُصَلِّي وَحْدَهُ وَهْوَ خَائِفٌ.
حَدَّثَنَا عَبْدَانُ، عَنْ أَبِي حَمْزَةَ، عَنِ الأَعْمَشِ، فَوَجَدْنَاهُمْ خَمْسَمِائَةٍ. قَالَ أَبُو مُعَاوِيَةَ مَا بَيْنَ سِتِّمِائَةٍ إِلَى سَبْعِمِائَةٍ

Righteousness does not consist of turning your faces towards the East and the West. But righteous is he who believes in Allah, and the Last Day, and the angels, and the Scripture, and the prophets. Who gives money, though dear, to near relatives, and orphans, and the needy, and the homeless, and the beggars, and for the freeing of slaves; those who perform the prayers, and pay the obligatory charity, and fulfill their promise when they promise, and patiently persevere in the face of persecution, hardship, and in the time of conflict. These are the sincere; these are the pious. – Surah Al-Baqarah 2:177

لَّيْسَ ٱلْبِرَّ أَن تُوَلُّوا۟ وُجُوهَكُمْ قِبَلَ ٱلْمَشْرِقِ وَٱلْمَغْرِبِ وَلَـٰكِنَّ ٱلْبِرَّ مَنْ ءَامَنَ بِٱللَّهِ وَٱلْيَوْمِ ٱلْـَٔاخِرِ وَٱلْمَلَـٰٓئِكَةِ وَٱلْكِتَـٰبِ وَٱلنَّبِيِّـۧنَ وَءَاتَى ٱلْمَالَ عَلَىٰ حُبِّهِۦ ذَوِى ٱلْقُرْبَىٰ وَٱلْيَتَـٰمَىٰ وَٱلْمَسَـٰكِينَ وَٱبْنَ ٱلسَّبِيلِ وَٱلسَّآئِلِينَ وَفِى ٱلرِّقَابِ وَأَقَامَ ٱلصَّلَوٰةَ وَءَاتَى ٱلزَّكَوٰةَ وَٱلْمُوفُونَ بِعَهْدِهِمْ إِذَا عَـٰهَدُوا۟ ۖ وَٱلصَّـٰبِرِينَ فِى ٱلْبَأْسَآءِ وَٱلضَّرَّآءِ وَحِينَ ٱلْبَأْسِ ۗ أُو۟لَـٰٓئِكَ ٱلَّذِينَ صَدَقُوا۟ ۖ وَأُو۟لَـٰٓئِكَ هُمُ ٱلْمُتَّقُونَ

For every congregation We have appointed acts of devotion, which they observe. So do not let them dispute with you in this matter. And invite to your Lord; you are upon a straight guidance. – Surah Al-Hajj 22:67

لِّكُلِّ أُمَّةٍ جَعَلْنَا مَنسَكًا هُمْ نَاسِكُوهُ ۖ فَلَا يُنَـٰزِعُنَّكَ فِى ٱلْأَمْرِ ۚ وَٱدْعُ إِلَىٰ رَبِّكَ ۖ إِنَّكَ لَعَلَىٰ هُدًى مُّسْتَقِيمٍ

On the Day when We call every people with their leader. Whoever is given his record in his right hand—these will read their record, and they will not be wronged one bit. – Surah Al-Isra 17:71 [26] [27] [28] [29]

يَوْمَ نَدْعُوا۟ كُلَّ أُنَاسٍۭ بِإِمَـٰمِهِمْ ۖ فَمَنْ أُوتِىَ كِتَـٰبَهُۥ بِيَمِينِهِۦ فَأُو۟لَـٰٓئِكَ يَقْرَءُونَ كِتَـٰبَهُمْ وَلَا يُظْلَمُونَ فَتِيلًا

Wa'il b. Hujr reported: He saw the Messenger of Allahﷺ raising his hands at the time of beginning the prayer and reciting takbir, and according to Hammam (the narrator), the hands were lifted opposite to ears. He (the Holy Prophet) then wrapped his hands in his cloth and placed his right hand over his left hand. And when he was about to bow down, he brought out his hands from the cloth, and then lifted them, and then recited takbir and bowed down,

---

[26] Ibn Taymiyyah stated that "It is not required of any Muslim to follow a particular scholar in all that he says," and "anyone's view may be accepted or rejected, except that of the Messenger of Allah".

ليس على أحد من المسلمين أن يتبع عالماً بعينه في كل ما يقوله، وكل يؤخذ من قوله ويترك إلا رسول الله صلى الله عليه وسلم"

[27] Ibn Abi Shayba, in his Musannaf, recorded the practice of irsaal (also called sadl)—praying with one's hands at one's sides—from several prominent early Muslim figures. The individuals mentioned, including Al-Hasan Al-Basri, Ibrahim an-Nakha'i, Ibn Sireen, Sa'id ibn al-Musayyib, and Sa'id ibn Jubayr, were all among the Tabi'in, the generation of Muslims that succeeded the Companions of the Prophet. - Ibn Abi Shaybah recorded these narrations in his Musannaf, Volume 2

[28] Ibn Jurayj said: "When Ibn Zubayr prayed, he would leave his hands (by his sides) and not place one of them over the other.") Ibn Abi Shaybah's Al-Musannaf, specifically in Volume 2, Page 482, Hadith number 3762

".عَنِ ابْنِ جُرَيْجٍ قَالَ: كَانَ ابْنُ الزُّبَيْرِ إِذَا صَلَّى تَرَكَ يَدَيْهِ، وَلَمْ يَضَعْ إِحْدَاهُمَا عَلَى الْأُخْرَى"

[29] Zayd ibn Thabit "When you see the people of Madina doing something, know that it is the sunna". - Imam al-Harawi's Al-Ma'rifah wat-Tarikh.

إذا رأيت أهل المدينة يفعلون شيئًا، فاعلم أنه السنة.

"In the generations which the Messenger of Allah صلى الله عليه وسلم praised, the Madh-hab of the people of Madinah was the soundest of the madh-habs of the people of the cities….." – Ibn Taymiyyah – The authenticity of the principles of the Madinan school of thought

وفى القرون التي أثنى عليها رسول الله صلى الله تعالى عليه وسلم، كان مذهب أهل المدينة أصح مذاهب أهل المدائن

Imam Malik and other scholars noted that the people of Madinah, during their time, were observed praying with Sadl. – (amalahlal-Madinah)

and when (he came back to the erect position) he recited:" Allah listened to him who praised Him." And when he prostrated, he prostrated between his two palms. – Sahih Muslim 401 [30]
حَدَّثَنَا زُهَيْرُ بْنُ حَرْبٍ، حَدَّثَنَا عَفَّانُ، حَدَّثَنَا هَمَّامٌ، حَدَّثَنَا مُحَمَّدُ بْنُ جُحَادَةَ، حَدَّثَنِي عَبْدُ الْجَبَّارِ بْنُ وَائِلٍ، عَنْ عَلْقَمَةَ بْنِ وَائِلٍ، وَمَوْلًى، لَهُمْ أَنَّهُمَا حَدَّثَاهُ عَنْ أَبِيهِ، وَائِلِ بْنِ حُجْرٍ، أَنَّهُ رَأَى النَّبِيَّ صلى الله عليه وسلم رَفَعَ يَدَيْهِ حِينَ دَخَلَ فِي الصَّلاَةِ كَبَّرَ – وَصَفَ هَمَّامٌ حِيَالَ أُذُنَيْهِ – ثُمَّ الْتَحَفَ بِثَوْبِهِ ثُمَّ وَضَعَ يَدَهُ الْيُمْنَى عَلَى الْيُسْرَى فَلَمَّا أَرَادَ أَنْ يَرْكَعَ أَخْرَجَ يَدَيْهِ مِنَ الثَّوْبِ ثُمَّ رَفَعَهُمَا ثُمَّ كَبَّرَ فَرَكَعَ فَلَمَّا قَالَ " سَمِعَ اللَّهُ لِمَنْ حَمِدَهُ " . رَفَعَ يَدَيْهِ فَلَمَّا سَجَدَ سَجَدَ بَيْنَ كَفَّيْهِ

It was narrated that Wa'il bin Hujr said: "I said: 'I am going to watch the Messenger of Allahﷺ and see how he prays.' The Messenger of Allahﷺ stood up and faced the Qiblah, then he raised his hands until they were in level with his ears, then he held his left hand with his right. When he wanted to bow, he raised them (his hands) likewise, then placed his hands on his knees. When he raised his head from bowing, he raised them (his hands) likewise. When he prostrated he put his hands in the same position in relation to his head, then he sat up and lay his left foot on the ground. He placed his left hand on his left thigh and his right elbow on his right thigh, and made a circle with two of his fingers. And I saw him doing like this"- Bishr (one of the narrators) pointed with the forefinger of his right hand and made a circle with the thumb and middle finger. – Sunan an-Nasa'I 1265
أَخْبَرَنَا إِسْمَاعِيلُ بْنُ مَسْعُودٍ، قَالَ أَنْبَأَنَا بِشْرُ بْنُ الْمُفَضَّلِ، قَالَ حَدَّثَنَا عَاصِمُ بْنُ كُلَيْبٍ، عَنْ أَبِيهِ، عَنْ وَائِلِ بْنِ حُجْرٍ، قَالَ قُلْتُ لأَنْظُرَنَّ إِلَى صَلاَةِ رَسُولِ اللَّهِ صلى الله عليه وسلم كَيْفَ يُصَلِّي فَقَامَ رَسُولُ اللَّهِ صلى الله عليه وسلم فَاسْتَقْبَلَ الْقِبْلَةَ فَرَفَعَ يَدَيْهِ حَتَّى حَاذَتَا أُذُنَيْهِ ثُمَّ أَخَذَ شِمَالَهُ بِيَمِينِهِ فَلَمَّا أَرَادَ أَنْ يَرْكَعَ رَفَعَهُمَا مِثْلَ ذَلِكَ وَوَضَعَ يَدَيْهِ عَلَى رُكْبَتَيْهِ فَلَمَّا رَفَعَ رَأْسَهُ مِنَ الرُّكُوعِ رَفَعَهُمَا مِثْلَ ذَلِكَ فَلَمَّا سَجَدَ وَضَعَ رَأْسَهُ بِذَلِكَ الْمَنْزِلِ مِنْ يَدَيْهِ ثُمَّ جَلَسَ فَافْتَرَشَ رِجْلَهُ الْيُسْرَى وَوَضَعَ يَدَهُ الْيُسْرَى عَلَى فَخِذِهِ الْيُسْرَى وَحَدَّ مِرْفَقَهُ الأَيْمَنَ عَلَى فَخِذِهِ الْيُمْنَى وَقَبَضَ ثِنْتَيْنِ وَحَلَّقَ وَرَأَيْتُهُ يَقُولُ هَكَذَا وَأَشَارَ بِشْرٌ بِالسَّبَّابَةِ مِنَ الْيُمْنَى وَحَلَّقَ الإِبْهَامَ وَالْوُسْطَى

Narrated Abdullah ibn Mas'ud: AbuUthman an-Nahdi said: When Ibn Mas'ud prayed he placed his left hand on the right. The Prophetﷺ saw him and placed his right hand on his left one . - Sunan Abi Dawud 755
حَدَّثَنَا مُحَمَّدُ بْنُ بَكَّارِ بْنِ الرَّيَّانِ، عَنْ هُشَيْمِ بْنِ بَشِيرٍ، عَنِ الْحَجَّاجِ بْنِ أَبِي زَيْنَبَ، عَنْ أَبِي عُثْمَانَ النَّهْدِيِّ، عَنِ ابْنِ مَسْعُودٍ، أَنَّهُ كَانَ يُصَلِّي فَوَضَعَ يَدَهُ الْيُسْرَى عَلَى الْيُمْنَى فَرَآهُ النَّبِيُّ صلى الله عليه وسلم فَوَضَعَ يَدَهُ الْيُمْنَى عَلَى الْيُسْرَىالْيُسْرَى عَلَى فَخِذِهِ الْيُسْرَى وَحَدَّ مِرْفَقَهُ الأَيْمَنَ عَلَى فَخِذِهِ الْيُمْنَى وَقَبَضَ ثِنْتَيْنِ وَحَلَّقَ حَلْقَةً وَرَأَيْتُهُ يَقُولُ هَكَذَا وَحَلَّقَ بِشْرٌ الإِبْهَامَ وَالْوُسْطَى وَأَشَارَ بِالسَّبَّابَةِ

[30] The practice of offering salah in the Qabd format—where the hands are placed on the chest or upper abdomen during prayer—is often supported by a narration from Wa'il ibn Hujr (RA). According to this narration, he observed the Prophet Muhammadﷺ during salah and reported that the Prophet placed his right hand over his left hand on his chest. This hadith has been cited particularly by scholars of the Hanbali school and some Salafi traditions to support the Qabd method. They consider it a sunnah based on this authentic or at least acceptable narration found in collections such as Musnad Ahmad and Sunan al-Daraqutni, though its grading varies among scholars. Thus, for those who follow this practice, the act of placing the hands in Qabd is seen as an imitation of the Prophet'sﷺ method as reported by Wa'il ibn Hujr. According to classical Islamic historians such as Ibn Sa'd (Ṭabaqāt al-Kubrā), Ibn Hajar al-'Asqalānī (al-Iṣābah fī Tamyīz al-Ṣaḥābah), and Ibn 'Abd al-Barr (al-Istī'āb), Wa'il ibn Hujr al-Hadrami accepted Islam around the 9th year after Hijrah (9 AH) — corresponding roughly to 630 CE.

Do not recite your prayers too loudly or silently

وَلَا تَجۡهَرۡ بِصَلَاتِكَ وَلَا تُخَافِتۡ بِهَا

Say, "Call Him Allah, or call Him the Most Merciful. Whichever name you use, to Him belong the Best Names." And be neither loud in your prayer, nor silent in it, but follow a course in between. – Surah Al-Isra 17:110

قُلِ ٱدۡعُواْ ٱللَّهَ أَوِ ٱدۡعُواْ ٱلرَّحۡمَٰنَۖ أَيّٗا مَّا تَدۡعُواْ فَلَهُ ٱلۡأَسۡمَآءُ ٱلۡحُسۡنَىٰۚ وَلَا تَجۡهَرۡ بِصَلَاتِكَ وَلَا تُخَافِتۡ بِهَا وَٱبۡتَغِ بَيۡنَ ذَٰلِكَ سَبِيلٗا

Narrated Aisha: (wife of the Prophet) Since I reached the age when I could remember things, I have seen my parents worshipping according to the right faith of Islam. Not a single day passed but Allah's Messenger ﷺ visited us both in the morning and in the evening. When the Muslims were persecuted, Abu Bakr set out for Ethiopia as an emigrant. When he reached a place called Bark-al-Ghimad, he met Ibn Ad-Daghna, the chief of the Qara tribe, who asked Abu Bakr, "Where are you going?" Abu Bakr said, "My people have turned me out of the country and I would like to tour the world and worship my Lord." Ibn Ad- Daghna said, "A man like you will not go out, nor will he be turned out as you help the poor earn their living, keep good relation with your Kith and kin, help the disabled (or the dependents), provide guests with food and shelter, and help people during their troubles. I am your protector. So, go back and worship your Lord at your home." Ibn Ad-Daghna went along with Abu Bakr and took him to the chiefs of Quraish saying to them, "A man like Abu Bakr will not go out, nor will he be turned out. Do you turn out a man who helps the poor earn their living, keeps good relations with Kith and kin, helps the disabled, provides guests with food and shelter, and helps the people during their troubles?" So, Quraish allowed Ibn Ad-Daghna's guarantee of protection and told Abu- Bakr that he was secure, and said to Ibn Ad-Daghna, "Advise Abu Bakr to worship his Lord in his house and to pray and read what he liked and not to hurt us and not to do these things publicly, for we fear that our sons and women may follow him." Ibn Ad-Daghna told Abu Bakr of all that, so Abu- Bakr continued worshipping his Lord in his house and did not pray or recite Qur'an aloud except in his house. Later on Abu Bakr had an Idea of building a mosque in the court yard of his house. He fulfilled that idea and started praying and reciting Qur'an there publicly. The women and the offspring of the pagans started gathering around him and looking at him astonishingly. Abu Bakr was a softhearted person and could not help weeping while reciting Qur'an. This horrified the pagan chiefs of Quraish. They sent for Ibn Ad-Daghna and when he came, they said, "We have given Abu Bakr protection on condition that he will worship his Lord in his house, but he has transgressed that condition and has built a mosque in the court yard of his house and offered his prayer and recited Qur'an in public. We are afraid lest he mislead our women and offspring. So, go to him and tell him that if he wishes he can worship his Lord in his house only, and if not, then tell him to return your pledge of protection as we do not like to betray you by revoking your pledge, nor can we tolerate Abu Bakr's public declaration of Islam (his worshipping). `Aisha added: Ibn Ad-Daghna came to Abu Bakr and said, "You know the conditions on which I gave you protection, so you should either abide by those conditions or revoke my protection, as I do not like to hear the 'Arabs saying that Ibn Ad-Daghna gave the pledge of protection to a person and his people did not respect it." Abu Bakr said, "I revoke your pledge of protection and am satisfied with Allah's protection." At that time Allah's Messenger ﷺ was still in Mecca and he said to his companions, "Your place of emigration has been shown to me. I have seen salty land, planted with date-palms and situated between two mountains which are the two ,Harras." So, when the Prophet ﷺ told it, some of the companions migrated to Medina, and some of those who had migrated to Ethiopia returned to Medina. When Abu Bakr prepared for emigration, Allah's Messenger ﷺ said to him, "Wait, for I expect to be permitted to emigrate." Abu Bakr asked, "May my father be sacrificed for your sake, do you really expect that?" Allah's Messenger ﷺ replied in the affirmative. So, Abu Bakr postponed his departure in order to accompany Allah's Messenger ﷺ and fed two camels which he had, with the leaves of Samor trees for four months. – Al-Bukhari 2297

حَدَّثَنَا يَحْيَى بْنُ بُكَيْرٍ، حَدَّثَنَا اللَّيْثُ، عَنْ عُقَيْلٍ، قَالَ ابْنُ شِهَابٍ فَأَخْبَرَنِي عُرْوَةُ بْنُ الزُّبَيْرِ، أَنَّ عَائِشَةَ ـ رضى الله عنها ـ زَوْجَ النَّبِيِّ صلى الله عليه وسلم قَالَتْ لَمْ أَعْقِلْ أَبَوَىَّ إِلاَّ وَهُمَا يَدِينَانِ الدِّينَ. وَقَالَ أَبُو صَالِحٍ حَدَّثَنِي عَبْدُ اللَّهِ عَنْ يُونُسَ عَنِ الزُّهْرِيِّ قَالَ أَخْبَرَنِي عُرْوَةُ بْنُ الزُّبَيْرِ أَنَّ عَائِشَةَ ـ رضى الله عنها ـ قَالَتْ لَمْ أَعْقِلْ أَبَوَىَّ قَطُّ، إِلاَّ وَهُمَا يَدِينَانِ الدِّينَ، وَلَمْ يَمُرَّ عَلَيْنَا يَوْمٌ إِلاَّ يَأْتِينَا فِيهِ رَسُولُ اللَّهِ صلى الله عليه وسلم طَرَفَىِ النَّهَارِ بُكْرَةً وَعَشِيَّةً، فَلَمَّا ابْتُلِيَ الْمُسْلِمُونَ خَرَجَ أَبُو بَكْرٍ مُهَاجِرًا قِبَلَ الْحَبَشَةِ، حَتَّى إِذَا بَلَغَ بَرْكَ الْغِمَادِ لَقِيَهُ ابْنُ الدَّغِنَةِ ـ وَهْوَ سَيِّدُ الْقَارَةِ ـ فَقَالَ أَيْنَ تُرِيدُ يَا أَبَا بَكْرٍ فَقَالَ أَبُو بَكْرٍ أَخْرَجَنِي قَوْمِي فَأَنَا أُرِيدُ أَنْ أَسِيحَ فِي الأَرْضِ فَأَعْبُدَ رَبِّي. قَالَ ابْنُ الدَّغِنَةِ إِنَّ مِثْلَكَ لاَ يَخْرُجُ وَلاَ يُخْرَجُ، فَإِنَّكَ تَكْسِبُ الْمَعْدُومَ، وَتَصِلُ الرَّحِمَ، وَتَحْمِلُ الْكَلَّ، وَتَقْرِي الضَّيْفَ، وَتُعِينُ عَلَى نَوَائِبِ الْحَقِّ، وَأَنَا لَكَ جَارٌ فَارْجِعْ فَاعْبُدْ رَبَّكَ بِبِلاَدِكَ. فَارْتَحَلَ ابْنُ الدَّغِنَةِ، فَرَجَعَ مَعَ أَبِي بَكْرٍ، فَطَافَ فِي أَشْرَافِ كُفَّارِ قُرَيْشٍ، فَقَالَ لَهُمْ إِنَّ أَبَا بَكْرٍ لاَ يَخْرُجُ مِثْلُهُ، وَلاَ يُخْرَجُ، أَتُخْرِجُونَ رَجُلاً يُكْسِبُ الْمَعْدُومَ، وَيَصِلُ الرَّحِمَ، وَيَحْمِلُ الْكَلَّ، وَيَقْرِي الضَّيْفَ، وَيُعِينُ عَلَى نَوَائِبِ الْحَقِّ. فَأَنْفَذَتْ قُرَيْشٌ جِوَارَ ابْنِ الدَّغِنَةِ وَآمَنُوا أَبَا بَكْرٍ وَقَالُوا لاِبْنِ الدَّغِنَةِ مُرْ أَبَا بَكْرٍ فَلْيَعْبُدْ رَبَّهُ فِي دَارِهِ، فَلْيُصَلِّ وَلْيَقْرَأْ مَا شَاءَ، وَلاَ يُؤْذِينَا بِذَلِكَ، وَلاَ يَسْتَعْلِنْ بِهِ، فَإِنَّا قَدْ خَشِينَا أَنْ يَفْتِنَ أَبْنَاءَنَا وَنِسَاءَنَا. قَالَ ذَلِكَ ابْنُ الدَّغِنَةِ لأَبِي بَكْرٍ، فَطَفِقَ أَبُو بَكْرٍ يَعْبُدُ رَبَّهُ فِي دَارِهِ، وَلاَ يَسْتَعْلِنُ بِالصَّلاَةِ وَلاَ الْقِرَاءَةِ فِي غَيْرِ دَارِهِ، ثُمَّ بَدَا لأَبِي بَكْرٍ فَابْتَنَى مَسْجِدًا بِفِنَاءِ دَارِهِ، وَبَرَزَ فَكَانَ يُصَلِّي فِيهِ، وَيَقْرَأُ الْقُرْآنَ، فَيَتَقَصَّفُ عَلَيْهِ نِسَاءُ الْمُشْرِكِينَ وَأَبْنَاؤُهُمْ، يَعْجَبُونَ وَيَنْظُرُونَ إِلَيْهِ، وَكَانَ أَبُو بَكْرٍ رَجُلاً بَكَّاءً لاَ يَمْلِكُ دَمْعَهُ حِينَ يَقْرَأُ الْقُرْآنَ، فَأَفْزَعَ ذَلِكَ أَشْرَافَ قُرَيْشٍ مِنَ الْمُشْرِكِينَ، فَأَرْسَلُوا إِلَى ابْنِ الدَّغِنَةِ فَقَدِمَ عَلَيْهِمْ، فَقَالُوا لَهُ إِنَّا كُنَّا أَجَرْنَا أَبَا بَكْرٍ عَلَى أَنْ يَعْبُدَ رَبَّهُ فِي دَارِهِ، وَإِنَّهُ جَاوَزَ ذَلِكَ، فَابْتَنَى مَسْجِدًا بِفِنَاءِ دَارِهِ، وَأَعْلَنَ الصَّلاَةَ وَالْقِرَاءَةَ، وَقَدْ خَشِينَا أَنْ يَفْتِنَ أَبْنَاءَنَا وَنِسَاءَنَا، فَأْتِهِ فَإِنْ أَحَبَّ أَنْ يَقْتَصِرَ عَلَى أَنْ يَعْبُدَ رَبَّهُ فِي دَارِهِ فَعَلَ، وَإِنْ أَبَى إِلاَّ أَنْ يُعْلِنَ ذَلِكَ فَسَلْهُ أَنْ يَرُدَّ إِلَيْكَ ذِمَّتَكَ، فَإِنَّا كَرِهْنَا أَنْ نُخْفِرَكَ، وَلَسْنَا مُقِرِّينَ لأَبِي بَكْرٍ الاِسْتِعْلاَنَ. قَالَتْ عَائِشَةُ فَأَتَى ابْنُ الدَّغِنَةِ أَبَا بَكْرٍ، فَقَالَ قَدْ عَلِمْتَ الَّذِي عَقَدْتُ لَكَ عَلَيْهِ، فَإِمَّا أَنْ تَقْتَصِرَ عَلَى ذَلِكَ وَإِمَّا أَنْ تَرُدَّ إِلَىَّ ذِمَّتِي، فَإِنِّي لاَ أُحِبُّ أَنْ تَسْمَعَ الْعَرَبُ أَنِّي أُخْفِرْتُ فِي رَجُلٍ عَقَدْتُ لَهُ. قَالَ أَبُو بَكْرٍ إِنِّي أَرُدُّ إِلَيْكَ جِوَارَكَ، وَأَرْضَى بِجِوَارِ اللَّهِ. وَرَسُولُ اللَّهِ صلى الله عليه وسلم يَوْمَئِذٍ بِمَكَّةَ، فَقَالَ رَسُولُ اللَّهِ صلى الله عليه وسلم " قَدْ أُرِيتُ دَارَ هِجْرَتِكُمْ، رَأَيْتُ سَبْخَةً ذَاتَ نَخْلٍ بَيْنَ لاَبَتَيْنِ ". وَهُمَا الْحَرَّتَانِ، فَهَاجَرَ مَنْ هَاجَرَ قِبَلَ الْمَدِينَةِ حِينَ ذَكَرَ ذَلِكَ رَسُولُ اللَّهِ صلى الله عليه وسلم، وَرَجَعَ إِلَى الْمَدِينَةِ بَعْضُ مَنْ كَانَ هَاجَرَ إِلَى أَرْضِ الْحَبَشَةِ، وَتَجَهَّزَ أَبُو بَكْرٍ مُهَاجِرًا، فَقَالَ لَهُ رَسُولُ اللَّهِ صلى الله عليه وسلم " عَلَى رِسْلِكَ فَإِنِّي أَرْجُو أَنْ يُؤْذَنَ لِي ". قَالَ أَبُو بَكْرٍ هَلْ تَرْجُو ذَلِكَ بِأَبِي أَنْتَ قَالَ " نَعَمْ ". فَحَبَسَ أَبُو بَكْرٍ نَفْسَهُ عَلَى رَسُولِ اللَّهِ صلى الله عليه وسلم لِيَصْحَبَهُ وَعَلَفَ رَاحِلَتَيْنِ كَانَتَا عِنْدَهُ وَرَقَ السَّمُرِ أَرْبَعَةَ أَشْهُرٍ.

Those who disbelieve say, "Do not listen to this Quran, and talk over it, so that you may prevail." – Surah Al-Fussilat 41:26

وَقَالَ ٱلَّذِينَ كَفَرُوا۟ لَا تَسْمَعُوا۟ لِهَـٰذَا ٱلْقُرْءَانِ وَٱلْغَوْا۟ فِيهِ لَعَلَّكُمْ تَغْلِبُونَ

Narrated Ibn `Abbas: Regarding the explanation of the Verse:-- '(O Muhammad!) Neither say your prayer aloud, nor say it in a low tone.' (17.110) This Verse was revealed while Allah's Messenger ﷺ was hiding himself at Mecca. At that time, when he led his companions in prayer, he used to raise his voice while reciting the Qur'an, and if the pagans heard him, they would abuse the Qur'an, its Revealer, and the one who brought it. So Allah said to His Prophet: "Neither say your prayer aloud. i.e., your recitation (of Qur'an) lest the pagans should hear (it) and abuse the Qur'an" nor say it in a low tone, "lest your voice should fail to reach your companions, "but follow a way between." (17.110) – Al-Bukhari 7525

حَدَّثَنِي عَمْرُو بْنُ زُرَارَةَ، عَنْ هُشَيْمٍ، أَخْبَرَنَا أَبُو بِشْرٍ، عَنْ سَعِيدِ بْنِ جُبَيْرٍ، عَنِ ابْنِ عَبَّاسٍ ـ رضى الله عنهما ـ فِي قَوْلِهِ تَعَالَى {وَلاَ تَجْهَرْ بِصَلاَتِكَ وَلاَ تُخَافِتْ بِهَا} قَالَ نَزَلَتْ وَرَسُولُ اللَّهِ صلى الله عليه وسلم مُخْتَفٍ بِمَكَّةَ، فَكَانَ إِذَا صَلَّى

بِأَصْحَابِهِ رَفَعَ صَوْتَهُ بِالْقُرْآنِ، فَإِذَا سَمِعَهُ الْمُشْرِكُونَ سَبُّوا الْقُرْآنَ وَمَنْ أَنْزَلَهُ وَمَنْ جَاءَ بِهِ، فَقَالَ اللَّهُ لِنَبِيِّهِ صلى الله عليه وسلم {وَلاَ تَجْهَرْ بِصَلاَتِكَ} أَىْ بِقِرَاءَتِكَ، فَيَسْمَعَ الْمُشْرِكُونَ، فَيَسُبُّوا الْقُرْآنَ {وَلاَ تُخَافِتْ بِهَا} عَنْ أَصْحَابِكَ فَلاَ تُسْمِعُهُمْ {وَابْتَغِ بَيْنَ ذَلِكَ سَبِيلاً}

Narrated Zaid bin Thabit: The Prophetﷺ took a room made of date palm leaves mats in the mosque. Allah's Messengerﷺ prayed in it for a few nights till the people gathered (to pray the night prayer (Tarawih) (behind him.) Then on the 4th night the people did not hear his voice and they thought he had slept, so some of them started humming in order that he might come out. The Prophetﷺ then said, "You continued doing what I saw you doing till I was afraid that this (Tarawih prayer) might be enjoined on you, and if it were enjoined on you, you would not continue performing it. Therefore, O people! Perform your prayers at your homes, for the best prayer of a person is what is performed at his home except the compulsory congregational) prayer." (See Hadith No. 229,Vol. 3) (See Hadith No. 134, Vol. 8). – Sahih Al-Bukhari 7290

حَدَّثَنَا إِسْحَاقُ، أَخْبَرَنَا عَفَّانُ، حَدَّثَنَا وُهَيْبٌ، حَدَّثَنَا مُوسَى بْنُ عُقْبَةَ، سَمِعْتُ أَبَا النَّضْرِ، يُحَدِّثُ عَنْ بُسْرِ بْنِ سَعِيدٍ، عَنْ زَيْدِ بْنِ ثَابِتٍ، أَنَّ النَّبِيَّ صلى الله عليه وسلم اتَّخَذَ حُجْرَةً فِي الْمَسْجِدِ مِنْ حَصِيرٍ، فَصَلَّى رَسُولُ اللَّهِ صلى الله عليه وسلم فِيهَا لَيَالِيَ، حَتَّى اجْتَمَعَ إِلَيْهِ نَاسٌ، ثُمَّ فَقَدُوا صَوْتَهُ لَيْلَةً فَظَنُّوا أَنَّهُ قَدْ نَامَ، فَجَعَلَ بَعْضُهُمْ يَتَنَحْنَحُ لِيَخْرُجَ إِلَيْهِمْ فَقَالَ " مَا زَالَ بِكُمُ الَّذِي رَأَيْتُ مِنْ صَنِيعِكُمْ، حَتَّى خَشِيتُ أَنْ يُكْتَبَ عَلَيْكُمْ، وَلَوْ كُتِبَ عَلَيْكُمْ مَا قُمْتُمْ بِهِ فَصَلُّوا أَيُّهَا النَّاسُ فِي بُيُوتِكُمْ، فَإِنَّ أَفْضَلَ صَلاَةِ الْمَرْءِ فِي بَيْتِهِ، إِلاَّ الصَّلاَةَ الْمَكْتُوبَةَ

Narrated `Abdullah bin Abi Qatada: My father said, "The Prophetﷺ used to recite Al-Fatiha along with another Sura in the first two rak`at of the Zuhr and the `Asr prayers and at times a verse or so was audible to us.". – Sahih al-Bukhari 762

حَدَّثَنَا الْمَكِّيُّ بْنُ إِبْرَاهِيمَ، عَنْ هِشَامٍ، عَنْ يَحْيَى بْنِ أَبِي كَثِيرٍ، عَنْ عَبْدِ اللَّهِ بْنِ أَبِي قَتَادَةَ، عَنْ أَبِيهِ، قَالَ كَانَ النَّبِيُّ صلى الله عليه وسلم يَقْرَأُ فِي الرَّكْعَتَيْنِ مِنَ الظُّهْرِ وَالْعَصْرِ بِفَاتِحَةِ الْكِتَابِ، وَسُورَةٍ سُورَةٍ، وَيُسْمِعُنَا الآيَةَ أَحْيَانًا.

And remember all Allah's messages and Wisdom that are recited in your homes. Allah is Most-Subtle and All-Aware. - Surah Al-Ahzab 33:34 [31]

وَٱذْكُرْنَ مَا يُتْلَىٰ فِى بُيُوتِكُنَّ مِنْ ءَايَـٰتِ ٱللَّهِ وَٱلْحِكْمَةِ ۚ إِنَّ ٱللَّهَ كَانَ لَطِيفًا خَبِيرًا

And those who recite the Reminder! - Surah As-Saffat 37:3

فَٱلتَّـٰلِيَـٰتِ ذِكْرًا

And as for those who disbelieved, ˹they will be told,˺ "Were My revelations not recited to you, yet you acted arrogantly and were a wicked people? - Surah Al-Jathiyah 45:31

وَأَمَّا ٱلَّذِينَ كَفَرُوٓا۟ أَفَلَمْ تَكُنْ ءَايَـٰتِى تُتْلَىٰ عَلَيْكُمْ فَٱسْتَكْبَرْتُمْ وَكُنتُمْ قَوْمًا مُّجْرِمِينَ

Say, "Come; let me tell you what Allah has forbidden you.....
Surah Al-An'am 6:151

قُلْ تَعَالَوْا۟ أَتْلُ مَا حَرَّمَ رَبُّكُمْ عَلَيْكُمْ....

So profess openly what you have been commanded and veer away from the associators. – Surah Al-Hijr 15:94

فَٱصْدَعْ بِمَا تُؤْمَرُ وَأَعْرِضْ عَنِ ٱلْمُشْرِكِينَ

---

[31] Ayat Al-Ahzab 33:34, As-Saffat 37:3, Al-Jathiyah 45:31, Al-An'am 6:151 the Arabic word used to recite is in an audible manner.

Giving good news and admonition: yet most of them turn away, and so they hear not. – Surah Al-Fussilat 41:4
بَشِيرًا وَنَذِيرًا فَأَعْرَضَ أَكْثَرُهُمْ فَهُمْ لَا يَسْمَعُونَ

And the ones who have disbelieved say, "Do not give ear to this Qur'an, and talk idly about it, that possibly you would overcome.". – Surah Al-Fussilat 41:26
وَقَالَ ٱلَّذِينَ كَفَرُواْ لَا تَسْمَعُواْ لِهَٰذَا ٱلْقُرْءَانِ وَٱلْغَوْاْ فِيهِ لَعَلَّكُمْ تَغْلِبُونَ

And do not be as the ones who have said, "We hear, " and they do not hear. – Surah Al-Anfal 8:21
وَلَا تَكُونُواْ كَٱلَّذِينَ قَالُواْ سَمِعْنَا وَهُمْ لَا يَسْمَعُونَ

When the Qur'an is recited, pay attention and listen to it in silence, so that you might be graced with [Allah's] mercy." – Surah Al-A'raf 7:204
وَإِذَا قُرِئَ ٱلْقُرْءَانُ فَٱسْتَمِعُواْ لَهُۥ وَأَنصِتُواْ لَعَلَّكُمْ تُرْحَمُونَ

And when Our ayat (Verses or signs) are recited to him, he turns away, waxing proud, as though he did not hear them, as though in his ears were obstruction. So give him (good) tiding (s) of a painful torment. – Surah Luqman 31:7
وَإِذَا تُتْلَىٰ عَلَيْهِ ءَايَٰتُنَا وَلَّىٰ مُسْتَكْبِرًا كَأَن لَّمْ يَسْمَعْهَا كَأَنَّ فِيٓ أُذُنَيْهِ وَقْرًاۖ فَبَشِّرْهُ بِعَذَابٍ أَلِيمٍ

You have not prayed and if you should die you would die on a religion other than that of Muhammad ﷺ
مَا صَلَّيْتَ، وَلَوْ مُتَّ مُتَّ عَلَى غَيْرِ الْفِطْرَةِ الَّتِي فَطَرَ اللَّهُ مُحَمَّدًا صلى الله عليه وسلم

Narrated Hudhaifa that he saw a person bowing and prostrating imperfectly. When he finished his Salat, Hudhaifa told him that he had not offered Salat. The subnarrator added, "I think that Hudhaifa also said: Were you to die you would die on a "Sunna" (legal way) other than that of Muhammad - Al-Bukhari 389
أَخْبَرَنَا الصَّلْتُ بْنُ مُحَمَّدٍ، أَخْبَرَنَا مَهْدِيٌّ، عَنْ وَاصِلٍ، عَنْ أَبِي وَائِلٍ، عَنْ حُذَيْفَةَ، رَأَى رَجُلاً لاَ يُتِمُّ رُكُوعَهُ وَلاَ سُجُودَهُ، فَلَمَّا قَضَى صَلاَتَهُ قَالَ لَهُ حُذَيْفَةُ مَا صَلَّيْتَ ـ قَالَ وَأَحْسِبُهُ قَالَ ـ لَوْ مُتَّ مُتَّ عَلَى غَيْرِ سُنَّةِ مُحَمَّدٍ صلى الله عليه وسلم.

Narrated Zaid bin Wahb: Hudhaifa saw a person who was not performing the bowing and prostration perfectly. He said to him, "You have not prayed and if you should die you would die on a religion other than that of Muhammad." – Al-Bukhari 791
حَدَّثَنَا حَفْصُ بْنُ عُمَرَ، قَالَ حَدَّثَنَا شُعْبَةُ، عَنْ سُلَيْمَانَ، قَالَ سَمِعْتُ زَيْدَ بْنَ وَهْبٍ، قَالَ رَأَى حُذَيْفَةُ رَجُلاً لاَ يُتِمُّ الرُّكُوعَ وَالسُّجُودَ قَالَ مَا صَلَّيْتَ، وَلَوْ مُتَّ مُتَّ عَلَى غَيْرِ الْفِطْرَةِ الَّتِي فَطَرَ اللَّهُ مُحَمَّدًا صلى الله عليه وسلم.

Narrated Anas bin Malik: A group of three men came to the houses of the wives of the Prophet ﷺ asking how the Prophet ﷺ worshipped (Allah), and when they were informed about that, they considered their worship insufficient and said, "Where are we from the Prophet ﷺ as his past and future sins have been forgiven." Then one of them said, "I will offer the prayer throughout the night forever." The other said, "I will fast throughout the year and will not break my fast." The third said, "I will keep away from the women and will not marry forever." Allah's Messenger ﷺ came to them and said, "Are you the same people who said so-and-so? By Allah, I am more submissive to Allah and more afraid of Him than you; yet I fast and break my fast, I do sleep and I also marry women. So he who does not follow my tradition in religion, is not from me (not one of my followers). – Al-Bukhari 5063

حَدَّثَنَا سَعِيدُ بْنُ أَبِي مَرْيَمَ، أَخْبَرَنَا مُحَمَّدُ بْنُ جَعْفَرٍ، أَخْبَرَنَا حُمَيْدُ بْنُ أَبِي حُمَيْدٍ الطَّوِيلُ، أَنَّهُ سَمِعَ أَنَسَ بْنَ مَالِكٍ ـ رضى الله عنه ـ يَقُولُ جَاءَ ثَلاَثَةُ رَهْطٍ إِلَى بُيُوتِ أَزْوَاجِ النَّبِيِّ صلى الله عليه وسلم يَسْأَلُونَ عَنْ عِبَادَةِ النَّبِيِّ صلى الله عليه وسلم فَلَمَّا أُخْبِرُوا كَأَنَّهُمْ تَقَالُّوهَا فَقَالُوا وَأَيْنَ نَحْنُ مِنَ النَّبِيِّ صلى الله عليه وسلم قَدْ غُفِرَ لَهُ مَا تَقَدَّمَ مِنْ ذَنْبِهِ وَمَا تَأَخَّرَ. قَالَ أَحَدُهُمْ أَمَّا أَنَا فَإِنِّي أُصَلِّي اللَّيْلَ أَبَدًا. وَقَالَ آخَرُ أَنَا أَصُومُ الدَّهْرَ وَلاَ أُفْطِرُ. وَقَالَ آخَرُ أَنَا أَعْتَزِلُ النِّسَاءَ فَلاَ أَتَزَوَّجُ أَبَدًا. فَجَاءَ رَسُولُ اللَّهِ صلى الله عليه وسلم فَقَالَ " أَنْتُمُ الَّذِينَ قُلْتُمْ كَذَا وَكَذَا أَمَا وَاللَّهِ إِنِّي لأَخْشَاكُمْ لِلَّهِ وَأَتْقَاكُمْ لَهُ، لَكِنِّي أَصُومُ وَأُفْطِرُ، وَأُصَلِّي وَأَرْقُدُ وَأَتَزَوَّجُ النِّسَاءَ، فَمَنْ رَغِبَ عَنْ سُنَّتِي فَلَيْسَ مِنِّي

"Save your heels from the fire."

وَيْلٌ لِلأَعْقَابِ مِنَ النَّارِ

Narrated `Abdullah bin `Amr: Once the Prophet ﷺ remained behind us in a journey. He joined us while we were performing ablution for the prayer which was over-due. We were just passing wet hands over our feet (and not washing them properly) so the Prophet ﷺ addressed us in a loud voice and said twice or thrice: "Save your heels from the fire." – Al-Bukhari 60 (also #96 & 163)

حَدَّثَنَا أَبُو النُّعْمَانِ، عَارِمُ بْنُ الْفَضْلِ قَالَ حَدَّثَنَا أَبُو عَوَانَةَ، عَنْ أَبِي بِشْرٍ، عَنْ يُوسُفَ بْنِ مَاهَكَ، عَنْ عَبْدِ اللَّهِ بْنِ عَمْرٍو، قَالَ تَخَلَّفَ عَنَّا النَّبِيُّ صلى الله عليه وسلم فِي سَفْرَةٍ سَافَرْنَاهَا، فَأَدْرَكَنَا وَقَدْ أَرْهَقَتْنَا الصَّلاَةُ وَنَحْنُ نَتَوَضَّأُ، فَجَعَلْنَا نَمْسَحُ عَلَى أَرْجُلِنَا، فَنَادَى بِأَعْلَى صَوْتِهِ " وَيْلٌ لِلأَعْقَابِ مِنَ النَّارِ ". مَرَّتَيْنِ أَوْ ثَلاَثًا

Narrated Muhammad Ibn Ziyad: I heard Abu Huraira saying as he passed by us while the people were performing ablution from a utensil containing water, "Perform ablution perfectly and thoroughly for Abul-Qasim (the Prophet) said, 'Save your heels from the Hell-fire.' " – Al-Bukhari 165

حَدَّثَنَا آدَمُ بْنُ أَبِي إِيَاسٍ، قَالَ حَدَّثَنَا شُعْبَةُ، قَالَ حَدَّثَنَا مُحَمَّدُ بْنُ زِيَادٍ، قَالَ سَمِعْتُ أَبَا هُرَيْرَةَ ـ وَكَانَ يَمُرُّ بِنَا وَالنَّاسُ يَتَوَضَّئُونَ مِنَ الْمِطْهَرَةِ ـ قَالَ أَسْبِغُوا الْوُضُوءَ فَإِنَّ أَبَا الْقَاسِمِ صلى الله عليه وسلم قَالَ " وَيْلٌ لِلأَعْقَابِ مِنَ النَّارِ ".

O you who believe! When you rise to pray, wash your faces and your hands and arms to the elbows, and wipe your heads, and your feet to the ankles. If you had intercourse, then purify yourselves. If you are ill, or travelling, or one of you returns from the toilet, or you had contact with women, and could not find water, then use some clean sand and wipe your faces and hands with it. Allah does not intend to burden you, but He intends to purify you, and to complete His blessing upon you, that you may be thankful. Surah Al-Ma'idah 5:6

يَـٰٓأَيُّهَا ٱلَّذِينَ ءَامَنُوٓاْ إِذَا قُمْتُمْ إِلَى ٱلصَّلَوٰةِ فَٱغْسِلُواْ وُجُوهَكُمْ وَأَيْدِيَكُمْ إِلَى ٱلْمَرَافِقِ وَٱمْسَحُواْ بِرُءُوسِكُمْ وَأَرْجُلَكُمْ إِلَى ٱلْكَعْبَيْنِ ۚ وَإِن كُنتُمْ جُنُبًا فَٱطَّهَّرُواْ ۚ وَإِن كُنتُم مَّرْضَىٰٓ أَوْ عَلَىٰ سَفَرٍ أَوْ جَآءَ أَحَدٌ مِّنكُم مِّنَ ٱلْغَآئِطِ أَوْ لَـٰمَسْتُمُ ٱلنِّسَآءَ فَلَمْ تَجِدُواْ مَآءً فَتَيَمَّمُواْ صَعِيدًا طَيِّبًا فَٱمْسَحُواْ بِوُجُوهِكُمْ وَأَيْدِيكُم مِّنْهُ ۚ مَا يُرِيدُ ٱللَّهُ لِيَجْعَلَ عَلَيْكُم مِّنْ حَرَجٍ وَلَـٰكِن يُرِيدُ لِيُطَهِّرَكُمْ وَلِيُتِمَّ نِعْمَتَهُۥ عَلَيْكُمْ لَعَلَّكُمْ تَشْكُرُونَ

At-Tahiyatu
التَّحِيَّاتُ

Narrated Shaqiq bin Salama: `Abdullah said, "Whenever we prayed behind the Prophetﷺ we used to recite (in sitting) 'Peace be on Gabriel, Michael, peace be on so and so. Once Allah's Messengerﷺ looked back at us and said, 'Allah Himself is As-Salam (Peace), and if anyone of you prays then he should say, at-Tahiyatu li l-lahi wa ssalawatu wa t-taiyibat. As-salamu `alalika aiyuha n-Nabiyu wa rahmatu l-lahi wa barakatuh. Assalamu `alaina wa `ala `ibadi l-lahi s-salihin. (All the compliments, prayers and good things are due to Allah; peace be on you, O Prophet, and Allah's mercy and blessings [be on you]. Peace be on us an on the pious subjects of Allah). (If you say that, it will reach all the subjects in the heaven and the earth). Ash-hadu al-la ilaha illa l-lah, wa ash-hadu anna Muhammadan `Abduhu wa Rasuluh. (I testify that there is no Deity [worthy of worship] but Allah, and I testify that Muhammad is His slave and His Apostle). – Sahih al-Bukhari 831
حَدَّثَنَا أَبُو نُعَيْمٍ، قَالَ حَدَّثَنَا الأَعْمَشُ، عَنْ شَقِيقِ بْنِ سَلَمَةَ، قَالَ قَالَ عَبْدُ اللَّهِ كُنَّا إِذَا صَلَّيْنَا خَلْفَ النَّبِيِّ صلى الله عليه وسلم قُلْنَا السَّلاَمُ عَلَى جِبْرِيلَ وَمِيكَائِيلَ، السَّلاَمُ عَلَى فُلاَنٍ وَفُلاَنٍ. فَالْتَفَتَ إِلَيْنَا رَسُولُ اللَّهِ صلى الله عليه وسلم فَقَالَ " إِنَّ اللَّهَ هُوَ السَّلاَمُ، فَإِذَا صَلَّى أَحَدُكُمْ فَلْيَقُلِ التَّحِيَّاتُ لِلَّهِ، وَالصَّلَوَاتُ وَالطَّيِّبَاتُ، السَّلاَمُ عَلَيْكَ أَيُّهَا النَّبِيُّ وَرَحْمَةُ اللَّهِ وَبَرَكَاتُهُ، السَّلاَمُ عَلَيْنَا وَعَلَى عِبَادِ اللَّهِ الصَّالِحِينَ. فَإِنَّكُمْ إِذَا قُلْتُمُوهَا أَصَابَتْ كُلَّ عَبْدٍ لِلَّهِ صَالِحٍ فِي السَّمَاءِ وَالأَرْضِ، أَشْهَدُ أَنْ لاَ إِلَهَ إِلاَّ اللَّهُ، وَأَشْهَدُ أَنَّ مُحَمَّدًا عَبْدُهُ وَرَسُولُهُ ".

Narrated `Abdullah: When we prayed with the Prophetﷺ we used to say: As-Salam be on Allah from His worshipers, As- Salam be on Gabriel, As-Salam be on Michael, As-Salam be on so-and-so. When the Prophetﷺ finished his prayer, he faced us and said, "Allah Himself is As-Salam (Peace), so when one sits in the prayer, one should say, 'at-Tahiyatu-li l-lahi Was-Salawatu, Wat-Taiyibatu, As-Salamu 'Alaika aiyuhan- Nabiyyu wa Rah-matul-iahi wa Barakatuhu, As-Salamu 'Alaina wa 'ala 'Ibadillahi assalihin, for if he says so, then it will be for all the pious slave of Allah in the Heavens and the Earth. (Then he should say), 'Ash-hadu an la ilaha illalllahu wa ash-hadu anna Muhammadan `Abduhu wa rasulu-hu,' and then he can choose whatever speech (i.e. invocation) he wishes " (See Hadith No. 797, Vol. 1). – Sahih al-Bukhari 6230
حَدَّثَنَا عُمَرُ بْنُ حَفْصٍ، حَدَّثَنَا أَبِي، حَدَّثَنَا الأَعْمَشُ، قَالَ حَدَّثَنِي شَقِيقٌ، عَنْ عَبْدِ اللَّهِ، قَالَ كُنَّا إِذَا صَلَّيْنَا مَعَ النَّبِيِّ صلى الله عليه وسلم قُلْنَا السَّلاَمُ عَلَى اللَّهِ قَبْلَ عِبَادِهِ، السَّلاَمُ عَلَى جِبْرِيلَ، السَّلاَمُ عَلَى مِيكَائِيلَ، السَّلاَمُ عَلَى فُلاَنٍ، فَلَمَّا انْصَرَفَ النَّبِيُّ صلى الله عليه وسلم أَقْبَلَ عَلَيْنَا بِوَجْهِهِ فَقَالَ " إِنَّ اللَّهَ هُوَ السَّلاَمُ، فَإِذَا جَلَسَ أَحَدُكُمْ فِي الصَّلاَةِ فَلْيَقُلِ التَّحِيَّاتُ لِلَّهِ، وَالصَّلَوَاتُ وَالطَّيِّبَاتُ السَّلاَمُ عَلَيْكَ أَيُّهَا النَّبِيُّ وَرَحْمَةُ اللَّهِ وَبَرَكَاتُهُ، السَّلاَمُ عَلَيْنَا وَعَلَى عِبَادِ اللَّهِ الصَّالِحِينَ. فَإِنَّهُ إِذَا قَالَ ذَلِكَ أَصَابَ كُلَّ عَبْدٍ صَالِحٍ فِي السَّمَاءِ وَالأَرْضِ، أَشْهَدُ أَنْ لاَ إِلَهَ إِلاَّ اللَّهُ وَأَشْهَدُ أَنَّ مُحَمَّدًا عَبْدُهُ وَرَسُولُهُ. ثُمَّ يَتَخَيَّرْ بَعْدُ مِنَ الْكَلاَمِ مَا شَاءَ ".

How shall we send blessings on you?
كَيْفَ نُصَلِّي عَلَيْكَ

Narrated Abu Humaid As-Sa`idi: The people asked, "O Allah's Messengerﷺ ! How shall we (ask Allah to) send blessings on you?" Allah's Apostle replied, "Say: O Allah! Send Your Mercy on Muhammad and on his wives and on his off spring, as You sent Your Mercy on Abraham's family; and send Your Blessings on Muhammad and on his offspring, as You sent Your Blessings on Abraham's family, for You are the Most Praiseworthy, the Most Glorious." - Sahih al-Bukhari 3369

حَدَّثَنَا عَبْدُ اللَّهِ بْنُ يُوسُفَ، أَخْبَرَنَا مَالِكُ بْنُ أَنَسٍ، عَنْ عَبْدِ اللَّهِ بْنِ أَبِي بَكْرِ بْنِ مُحَمَّدِ بْنِ عَمْرِو بْنِ حَزْمٍ، عَنْ أَبِيهِ، عَنْ عَمْرِو بْنِ سُلَيْمٍ الزُّرَقِيِّ، أَخْبَرَنِي أَبُو حُمَيْدٍ السَّاعِدِيُّ ـ رضى الله عنه ـ أَنَّهُمْ قَالُوا يَا رَسُولَ اللَّهِ كَيْفَ نُصَلِّي عَلَيْكَ فَقَالَ رَسُولُ اللَّهِ صلى الله عليه وسلم " قُولُوا اللَّهُمَّ صَلِّ عَلَى مُحَمَّدٍ وَأَزْوَاجِهِ وَذُرِّيَّتِهِ، كَمَا صَلَّيْتَ عَلَى آلِ إِبْرَاهِيمَ، وَبَارِكْ عَلَى مُحَمَّدٍ وَأَزْوَاجِهِ وَذُرِّيَّتِهِ، كَمَا بَارَكْتَ عَلَى آلِ إِبْرَاهِيمَ، إِنَّكَ حَمِيدٌ مَجِيدٌ ".

Narrated `Abdur-Rahman bin Abi Laila: Ka`b bin Ujrah met me and said, “Shall I not give you a present I got from the Prophet?” `Abdur- Rahman said, “Yes, give it to me.” I said, “We asked Allah’s Messenger ﷺ saying, ‘O Allah’s Messenger ﷺ ! How should one (ask Allah to) send blessings on you, the members of the family, for Allah has taught us how to salute you (in the prayer)?’ He said, ‘Say: O Allah! Send Your Mercy on Muhammad and on the family of Muhammad, as You sent Your Mercy on Abraham and on the family of Abraham, for You are the Most Praise-worthy, the Most Glorious. O Allah! Send Your Blessings on Muhammad and the family of Muhammad, as You sent your Blessings on Abraham and on the family of Abraham, for You are the Most Praise-worthy, the Most Glorious.’ “ - Sahih al-Bukhari 3370

حَدَّثَنَا قَيْسُ بْنُ حَفْصٍ، وَمُوسَى بْنُ إِسْمَاعِيلَ، قَالاَ حَدَّثَنَا عَبْدُ الْوَاحِدِ بْنُ زِيَادٍ، حَدَّثَنَا أَبُو قُرَّةَ، مُسْلِمُ بْنُ سَالِمٍ الْهَمْدَانِيُّ قَالَ حَدَّثَنِي عَبْدُ اللَّهِ بْنُ عِيسَى، سَمِعَ عَبْدَ الرَّحْمَنِ بْنَ أَبِي لَيْلَى، قَالَ لَقِيَنِي كَعْبُ بْنُ عُجْرَةَ فَقَالَ أَلاَ أُهْدِي لَكَ هَدِيَّةً سَمِعْتُهَا مِنَ النَّبِيِّ، صلى الله عليه وسلم فَقُلْتُ بَلَى، فَأَهْدِهَا لِي. فَقَالَ سَأَلْنَا رَسُولَ اللَّهِ صلى الله عليه وسلم فَقُلْنَا يَا رَسُولَ اللَّهِ كَيْفَ الصَّلاَةُ عَلَيْكُمْ أَهْلَ الْبَيْتِ فَإِنَّ اللَّهَ قَدْ عَلَّمَنَا كَيْفَ نُسَلِّمُ. قَالَ " قُولُوا اللَّهُمَّ صَلِّ عَلَى مُحَمَّدٍ، وَعَلَى آلِ مُحَمَّدٍ، كَمَا صَلَّيْتَ عَلَى إِبْرَاهِيمَ وَعَلَى آلِ إِبْرَاهِيمَ، إِنَّكَ حَمِيدٌ مَجِيدٌ، اللَّهُمَّ بَارِكْ عَلَى مُحَمَّدٍ، وَعَلَى آلِ مُحَمَّدٍ، كَمَا بَارَكْتَ عَلَى إِبْرَاهِيمَ، وَعَلَى آلِ إِبْرَاهِيمَ، إِنَّكَ حَمِيدٌ مَجِيدٌ ".

Istikhara
الاستخارة

Narrated Jabir bin `Abdullah: The Prophet ﷺ used to teach us the way of doing Istikhara (Istikhara means to ask Allah to guide one to the right sort of action concerning any job or a deed), in all matters as he taught us the Suras of the Qur’an. He said, “If anyone of you thinks of doing any job he should offer a two rak`at prayer other than the compulsory ones and say (after the prayer): -- ‘Allahumma inni astakhiruka bi’ilmika, Wa astaqdiruka bi-qudratika, Wa as’alaka min fadlika Al-`azlm Fa-innaka taqdiru Wala aqdiru, Wa ta’lamu Wala a’lamu, Wa anta ‘allamu l-ghuyub. Allahumma, in kunta ta’lam anna hadha-lamra Khairun li fi dini wa ma’ashi wa’aqibati `Amri (or ‘ajili `Amri wa’ajilihi) Faqdirhu wa yas-sirhu li thumma barik li Fihi, Wa in kunta ta’lamu anna hadha-lamra shar-run li fi dini wa ma’ashi wa’aqibati `Amri (or fi’ajili `Amri wa ajilihi) Fasrifhu anni was-rifni anhu. Waqdir li al-khaira haithu kana Thumma ardini bihi.’ (O Allah! I ask guidance from Your knowledge, And Power from Your Might and I ask for Your great blessings. You are capable and I am not. You know and I do not and You know the unseen. O Allah! If You know that this job is good for my religion and my subsistence and in my Hereafter—(or said: If it is better for my present and later needs)—Then You ordain it for me and make it easy for me to get, And then bless me in it, and if You know that this job is harmful to me In my religion and subsistence and in the Hereafter—(or said: If it is worse for my present and later needs)—Then keep it away from me and let me be away from it. And ordain for me whatever is good for me, And make me satisfied with it). The Prophet ﷺ added that then the person should name (mention) his need. – Sahih al-Bukhari 1166

حَدَّثَنَا قُتَيْبَةُ، قَالَ حَدَّثَنَا عَبْدُ الرَّحْمَنِ بْنُ أَبِي الْمَوَالِي، عَنْ مُحَمَّدِ بْنِ الْمُنْكَدِرِ، عَنْ جَابِرِ بْنِ عَبْدِ اللَّهِ ـ رضى الله عنهما ـ قَالَ كَانَ رَسُولُ اللَّهِ صلى الله عليه وسلم يُعَلِّمُنَا الاِسْتِخَارَةَ فِي الأُمُورِ كَمَا يُعَلِّمُنَا السُّورَةَ مِنَ الْقُرْآنِ يَقُولُ " إِذَا هَمَّ أَحَدُكُمْ بِالأَمْرِ فَلْيَرْكَعْ رَكْعَتَيْنِ مِنْ غَيْرِ الْفَرِيضَةِ ثُمَّ لِيَقُلِ اللَّهُمَّ إِنِّي أَسْتَخِيرُكَ بِعِلْمِكَ وَأَسْتَقْدِرُكَ بِقُدْرَتِكَ، وَأَسْأَلُكَ مِنْ فَضْلِكَ الْعَظِيمِ، فَإِنَّكَ تَقْدِرُ وَلاَ أَقْدِرُ وَتَعْلَمُ وَلاَ أَعْلَمُ وَأَنْتَ عَلاَّمُ الْغُيُوبِ، اللَّهُمَّ إِنْ كُنْتَ تَعْلَمُ أَنَّ هَذَا الأَمْرَ خَيْرٌ لِي فِي دِينِي وَمَعَاشِي وَعَاقِبَةِ أَمْرِي ـ أَوْ قَالَ عَاجِلِ أَمْرِي وَآجِلِهِ ـ فَاقْدُرْهُ لِي

وَيَسِّرْهُ لِي ثُمَّ بَارِكْ لِي فِيهِ، وَإِنْ كُنْتَ تَعْلَمُ أَنَّ هَذَا الأَمْرَ شَرٌّ لِي فِي دِينِي وَمَعَاشِي وَعَاقِبَةِ أَمْرِي ـ أَوْ قَالَ فِي عَاجِلِ أَمْرِي وَآجِلِهِ ـ فَاصْرِفْهُ عَنِّي وَاصْرِفْنِي عَنْهُ، وَاقْدُرْ لِي الْخَيْرَ حَيْثُ كَانَ ثُمَّ أَرْضِنِي بِهِ ـ قَالَ ـ وَيُسَمِّي حَاجَتَهُ ".

Narrated Jabir bin `Abdullah: As-Salami: Allah's Messenger ﷺ used to teach his companions to perform the prayer of Istikhara for each and every matter just as he used to teach them the Suras from the Qur'an He used to say, "If anyone of you intends to do some thing, he should offer a two rak`at prayer other than the compulsory prayers, and after finishing it, he should say: O Allah! I consult You, for You have all knowledge, and appeal to You to support me with Your Power and ask for Your Bounty, for You are able to do things while I am not, and You know while I do not; and You are the Knower of the Unseen. O Allah If You know It this matter (name your matter) is good for me both at present and in the future, (or in my religion), in my this life and in the Hereafter, then fulfill it for me and make it easy for me, and then bestow Your Blessings on me in that matter. O Allah! If You know that this matter is not good for me in my religion, in my this life and in my coming Hereafter (or at present or in the future), then divert me from it and choose for me what is good wherever it may be, and make me be pleased with it." (See Hadith No. 391, Vol. 8) – Sahih al-Bukhari 7390

حَدَّثَنِي إِبْرَاهِيمُ بْنُ الْمُنْذِرِ، حَدَّثَنَا مَعْنُ بْنُ عِيسَى، حَدَّثَنِي عَبْدُ الرَّحْمَنِ بْنُ أَبِي الْمَوَالِي، قَالَ سَمِعْتُ مُحَمَّدَ بْنَ الْمُنْكَدِرِ، يُحَدِّثُ عَبْدَ اللَّهِ بْنَ الْحَسَنِ يَقُولُ أَخْبَرَنِي جَابِرُ بْنُ عَبْدِ اللَّهِ السَّلَمِيُّ، قَالَ كَانَ رَسُولُ اللَّهِ صلى الله عليه وسلم يُعَلِّمُ أَصْحَابَهُ الاِسْتِخَارَةَ فِي الأُمُورِ كُلِّهَا، كَمَا يُعَلِّمُ السُّورَةَ مِنَ الْقُرْآنِ يَقُولُ " إِذَا هَمَّ أَحَدُكُمْ بِالأَمْرِ فَلْيَرْكَعْ رَكْعَتَيْنِ مِنْ غَيْرِ الْفَرِيضَةِ ثُمَّ لِيَقُلِ اللَّهُمَّ إِنِّي أَسْتَخِيرُكَ بِعِلْمِكَ، وَأَسْتَقْدِرُكَ بِقُدْرَتِكَ، وَأَسْأَلُكَ مِنْ فَضْلِكَ، فَإِنَّكَ تَقْدِرُ وَلاَ أَقْدِرُ، وَتَعْلَمُ وَلاَ أَعْلَمُ، وَأَنْتَ عَلاَّمُ الْغُيُوبِ، اللَّهُمَّ فَإِنْ كُنْتَ تَعْلَمُ هَذَا الأَمْرَ ـ ثُمَّ تُسَمِّيهِ بِعَيْنِهِ ـ خَيْرًا لِي فِي عَاجِلِ أَمْرِي وَآجِلِهِ ـ قَالَ أَوْ فِي دِينِي وَمَعَاشِي وَعَاقِبَةِ أَمْرِي ـ فَاقْدُرْهُ لِي، وَيَسِّرْهُ لِي، ثُمَّ بَارِكْ لِي فِيهِ، اللَّهُمَّ وَإِنْ كُنْتَ تَعْلَمُ أَنَّهُ شَرٌّ لِي فِي دِينِي وَمَعَاشِي وَعَاقِبَةِ أَمْرِي ـ أَوْ قَالَ فِي عَاجِلِ أَمْرِي وَآجِلِهِ ـ فَاصْرِفْنِي عَنْهُ، وَاقْدُرْ لِيَ الْخَيْرَ حَيْثُ كَانَ، ثُمَّ رَضِّنِي بِهِ "

Narrated Jabir: The Prophet ﷺ used to teach us the Istikhara for each and every matter as he used to teach us the Suras from the Holy Qur'an. (He used to say), "If anyone of you intends to do something, he should offer a two-rak`at prayer other than the obligatory prayer, and then say: 'Allahumma inni astakhiruka bi'ilmika, wa astaqdiruka biqudratika, wa as'aluka min fadlika-l-'azim, fa innaka taqdiru wala aqdiru, wa ta'lamu wala a'lamu, wa anta'allamu-l-ghuyub. Allahumma in kunta ta'lamu anna hadha-lamra khairun li fi dini wa ma'ashi wa 'aqibati `Amri (or said, fi 'ajili `Amri wa ajilihi) fa-qdurhu li, Wa in kunta ta'lamu anna ha-dha-l-amra sharrun li fi dini wa ma'ashi wa 'aqibati `Amri (or said, fi ajili `Amri wa ajilihi) fasrifhu 'anni was-rifni 'anhu wa aqdur li alkhaira haithu kana, thumma Raddani bihi," Then he should mention his matter (need). – Sahih al-Bukhari 6382

حَدَّثَنَا مُطَرِّفُ بْنُ عَبْدِ اللَّهِ أَبُو مُصْعَبٍ، حَدَّثَنَا عَبْدُ الرَّحْمَنِ بْنُ أَبِي الْمَوَالِ، عَنْ مُحَمَّدِ بْنِ الْمُنْكَدِرِ، عَنْ جَابِرٍ ـ رضى الله عنه ـ قَالَ كَانَ النَّبِيُّ صلى الله عليه وسلم يُعَلِّمُنَا الإِسْتِخَارَةَ فِي الأُمُورِ كُلِّهَا كَالسُّورَةِ مِنَ الْقُرْآنِ " إِذَا هَمَّ بِالأَمْرِ فَلْيَرْكَعْ رَكْعَتَيْنِ، ثُمَّ يَقُولُ اللَّهُمَّ إِنِّي أَسْتَخِيرُكَ بِعِلْمِكَ، وَأَسْتَقْدِرُكَ بِقُدْرَتِكَ، وَأَسْأَلُكَ مِنْ فَضْلِكَ الْعَظِيمِ، فَإِنَّكَ تَقْدِرُ وَلاَ أَقْدِرُ، وَتَعْلَمُ وَلاَ أَعْلَمُ، وَأَنْتَ عَلاَّمُ الْغُيُوبِ، اللَّهُمَّ إِنْ كُنْتَ تَعْلَمُ أَنَّ هَذَا الأَمْرَ خَيْرٌ لِي فِي دِينِي وَمَعَاشِي وَعَاقِبَةِ أَمْرِي ـ أَوْ قَالَ عَاجِلِ أَمْرِي وَآجِلِهِ ـ فَاقْدُرْهُ لِي، وَإِنْ كُنْتَ تَعْلَمُ أَنَّ هَذَا الأَمْرَ شَرٌّ لِي فِي دِينِي وَمَعَاشِي وَعَاقِبَةِ أَمْرِي ـ أَوْ قَالَ فِي عَاجِلِ أَمْرِي وَآجِلِهِ ـ فَاصْرِفْهُ عَنِّي وَاصْرِفْنِي عَنْهُ، وَاقْدُرْ لِيَ الْخَيْرَ حَيْثُ كَانَ، ثُمَّ رَضِّنِي بِهِ. وَيُسَمِّي حَاجَتَهُ ".

Pray during the night, an extra voluntary prayer, as it may well be that your Lord will elevate you to a praiseworthy status. – Surah Al-Israel 17:79

وَمِنَ ٱلَّيْلِ فَتَهَجَّدْ بِهِۦ نَافِلَةً لَّكَ عَسَىٰٓ أَن يَبْعَثَكَ رَبُّكَ مَقَامًا مَّحْمُودًا

O you enwrapped (in your raiment) Rise up (to pray during) the night, except a little A half of it, or diminish a little thereof Or increase thereto; and recite the Qur'an (in a distinct) recitation Surely We will soon cast upon you a weighty Saying Surely (prayer) by night is more intense in performance and more upright in (devotional) oration Surely in the daytime you have long employment And remember the Name of your Lord, and devote yourself to Him with complete devotion The Lord of the east and the west; there is no god except He; so take Him to yourself for an Ever-Trusted Trustee And (endure) patiently what they (The disbelievers) say, and forsake them with a becoming forsaking And leave Me away (to deal) with the beliers, the ones endowed with (earthly) comfort, and give them more leisure for a little (while) Surely, close to Us are manacles and a (raging) Hell And food that chokes, (Literally: comprising choking) and a painful torment On the Day when the earth and the mountains will be in commotion, and the mountains become a heap of sand let loose Surely We have sent to you a Messenger as a witness over you, as We sent to Firaawn (Pharaoh) a Messenger Yet Firaawn disobeyed the Messenger, so We took him (away) a baneful (The root of the Arabic word implies death by droning) taking So, in case you disbelieve, how will you protect yourselves against a Day that will make the- newborn hoary-headed Whereby the heaven will be rent asunder; His promise has (always) been performed Surely this is a Reminder; so let him who decides take for (himself) to his Lord a way Surely your Lord knows that you (rise) up (for prayer) nearly two thirds of the night, and (sometimes) a half of it, and (sometimes) a third of it, and a section of the ones with you (also rise for prayer); and Allah determines (precisely) the night and the daytime. He knows that you (The believers, This and the following pronouns are plural) will never enumerate it; so He has relented towards you. Then read of the Qur'an that which is easy (for you). He knows that (some) of you are sick, and others striking in the earth, (i.e., traveling) seeking a share of the Grace of Allah, and others fighting in the way of Allah. So read of it that which is easy (for you). And keep up the prayer, and bring the Zakat, and lend to Allah a fair loan. And whatever charity you will forward to your selves, you will find (it) in the Providence of Allah; it will be more charitable (i.e., better) and more magnificent in reward. And ask the forgiveness of Allah; surely Allah is Ever-Forgiving, Ever-Merciful. – Surah Al-Muzammil 73

يَـٰٓأَيُّهَا ٱلْمُزَّمِّلُ قُمِ ٱلَّيْلَ إِلَّا قَلِيلًا نِّصْفَهُۥٓ أَوِ ٱنقُصْ مِنْهُ قَلِيلًا أَوْ زِدْ عَلَيْهِ وَرَتِّلِ ٱلْقُرْءَانَ تَرْتِيلًا إِنَّا سَنُلْقِى عَلَيْكَ قَوْلًا ثَقِيلًا إِنَّ نَاشِئَةَ ٱلَّيْلِ هِىَ أَشَدُّ وَطْـًٔا وَأَقْوَمُ قِيلًا إِنَّ لَكَ فِى ٱلنَّهَارِ سَبْحًا طَوِيلًا وَٱذْكُرِ ٱسْمَ رَبِّكَ وَتَبَتَّلْ إِلَيْهِ تَبْتِيلًا رَّبُّ ٱلْمَشْرِقِ وَٱلْمَغْرِبِ لَآ إِلَـٰهَ إِلَّا هُوَ فَٱتَّخِذْهُ وَكِيلًا وَٱصْبِرْ عَلَىٰ مَا يَقُولُونَ وَٱهْجُرْهُمْ هَجْرًا جَمِيلًا وَذَرْنِى وَٱلْمُكَذِّبِينَ أُو۟لِى ٱلنَّعْمَةِ وَمَهِّلْهُمْ قَلِيلًا إِنَّ لَدَيْنَآ أَنكَالًا وَجَحِيمًا وَطَعَامًا ذَا غُصَّةٍ وَعَذَابًا أَلِيمًا يَوْمَ تَرْجُفُ ٱلْأَرْضُ وَٱلْجِبَالُ وَكَانَتِ ٱلْجِبَالُ كَثِيبًا مَّهِيلًا إِنَّآ أَرْسَلْنَآ إِلَيْكُمْ رَسُولًا شَـٰهِدًا عَلَيْكُمْ كَمَآ أَرْسَلْنَآ إِلَىٰ فِرْعَوْنَ رَسُولًا فَعَصَىٰ فِرْعَوْنُ ٱلرَّسُولَ فَأَخَذْنَـٰهُ أَخْذًا وَبِيلًا فَكَيْفَ تَتَّقُونَ إِن كَفَرْتُمْ يَوْمًا يَجْعَلُ ٱلْوِلْدَٰنَ شِيبًا ٱلسَّمَآءُ مُنفَطِرٌۢ بِهِۦ ۚ كَانَ وَعْدُهُۥ مَفْعُولًا إِنَّ هَـٰذِهِۦ تَذْكِرَةٌ ۖ فَمَن شَآءَ ٱتَّخَذَ إِلَىٰ رَبِّهِۦ سَبِيلًا إِنَّ رَبَّكَ يَعْلَمُ أَنَّكَ تَقُومُ أَدْنَىٰ مِن ثُلُثَىِ ٱلَّيْلِ وَنِصْفَهُۥ وَثُلُثَهُۥ وَطَآئِفَةٌ مِّنَ ٱلَّذِينَ مَعَكَ ۚ وَٱللَّهُ يُقَدِّرُ ٱلَّيْلَ وَٱلنَّهَارَ ۚ عَلِمَ أَن لَّن تُحْصُوهُ فَتَابَ عَلَيْكُمْ ۖ فَٱقْرَءُوا۟ مَا تَيَسَّرَ مِنَ ٱلْقُرْءَانِ ۚ عَلِمَ أَن سَيَكُونُ مِنكُم مَّرْضَىٰ ۙ وَءَاخَرُونَ يَضْرِبُونَ فِى ٱلْأَرْضِ يَبْتَغُونَ مِن فَضْلِ ٱللَّهِ ۙ وَءَاخَرُونَ يُقَـٰتِلُونَ فِى سَبِيلِ ٱللَّهِ ۖ فَٱقْرَءُوا۟ مَا تَيَسَّرَ مِنْهُ ۚ وَأَقِيمُوا۟ ٱلصَّلَوٰةَ وَءَاتُوا۟ ٱلزَّكَوٰةَ وَأَقْرِضُوا۟ ٱللَّهَ قَرْضًا حَسَنًا ۚ وَمَا تُقَدِّمُوا۟ لِأَنفُسِكُم مِّنْ خَيْرٍ تَجِدُوهُ عِندَ ٱللَّهِ هُوَ خَيْرًا وَأَعْظَمَ أَجْرًا ۚ وَٱسْتَغْفِرُوا۟ ٱللَّهَ ۖ إِنَّ ٱللَّهَ غَفُورٌ رَّحِيمٌۢ.

Narrated `A'isha: Allah's Messenger ﷺ used to pray eleven rak`at at night and that was his night prayer and each of his prostrations lasted for a period enough for one of you to recite fifty verses before Allah's Messenger ﷺ raised his head. He also used to pray two rak`at (Sunnah) before the (compulsory) Fajr prayer and then lie down on his right side till the Mu'adh-dhin came to him for the prayer. – Sahih al-Bukhari 994

حَدَّثَنَا أَبُو الْيَمَانِ، قَالَ أَخْبَرَنَا شُعَيْبٌ، عَنِ الزُّهْرِيِّ، عَنْ عُرْوَةَ، أَنَّ عَائِشَةَ، أَخْبَرَتْهُ أَنَّ رَسُولَ اللَّهِ صلى الله عليه وسلم كَانَ يُصَلِّي إِحْدَى عَشْرَةَ رَكْعَةً، كَانَتْ تِلْكَ صَلاَتَهُ ـ تَعْنِي بِاللَّيْلِ ـ فَيَسْجُدُ السَّجْدَةَ مِنْ ذَلِكَ قَدْرَ مَا يَقْرَأُ أَحَدُكُمْ خَمْسِينَ آيَةً قَبْلَ أَنْ يَرْفَعَ رَأْسَهُ، وَيَرْكَعُ رَكْعَتَيْنِ قَبْلَ صَلاَةِ الْفَجْرِ، ثُمَّ يَضْطَجِعُ عَلَى شِقِّهِ الأَيْمَنِ حَتَّى يَأْتِيَهُ الْمُؤَذِّنُ لِلصَّلاَةِ

Narrated Kuraib Maula Ibn `Abbas: `Abdullah bin `Abbas said that he had passed a night in the house of Maimuna the mother of the faithful believers , who was his aunt. He said, "I slept across the bed, and Allah's Messenger ﷺ along with his wife slept lengthwise. Allah's Messenger ﷺ slept till midnight or slightly before or after it. Then Allah's Apostle woke up, sat, and removed the traces of sleep by rubbing his hands over his face. Then he recited the last ten verses of Surat-Al `Imran (2). Then he went towards a hanging leather watercontainer and performed a perfect ablution and then stood up for prayer." `Abdullah bin `Abbas added, "I got up and did the same as Allah's Messenger ﷺ had done and then went and stood by his side. Allah's Messenger ﷺ then put his right hand over my head and caught my right ear and twisted it. He offered two rak`at, then two rak`at, then two rak`at, then two rak`at, then two rak`at, then two rak`at and then offered one rak`a witr. Then he lay down till the Mu'adh-dhin came and then he prayed two light rak`at and went out and offered the early morning (Fajr) prayer.". – Sahih al-Bukhari 1198

حَدَّثَنَا عَبْدُ اللَّهِ بْنُ يُوسُفَ، أَخْبَرَنَا مَالِكٌ، عَنْ مَخْرَمَةَ بْنِ سُلَيْمَانَ، عَنْ كُرَيْبٍ، مَوْلَى ابْنِ عَبَّاسٍ أَنَّهُ أَخْبَرَهُ عَنْ عَبْدِ اللَّهِ بْنِ عَبَّاسٍ ـ رضى الله عنهما ـ أَنَّهُ بَاتَ عِنْدَ مَيْمُونَةَ أُمِّ الْمُؤْمِنِينَ ـ رضى الله عنها ـ وَهْىَ خَالَتُهُ ـ قَالَ فَاضْطَجَعْتُ عَلَى عَرْضِ الْوِسَادَةِ، وَاضْطَجَعَ رَسُولُ اللَّهِ صلى الله عليه وسلم وَأَهْلُهُ فِي طُولِهَا، فَنَامَ رَسُولُ اللَّهِ صلى الله عليه وسلم حَتَّى انْتَصَفَ اللَّيْلُ أَوْ قَبْلَهُ بِقَلِيلٍ أَوْ بَعْدَهُ بِقَلِيلٍ، ثُمَّ اسْتَيْقَظَ رَسُولُ اللَّهِ صلى الله عليه وسلم فَجَلَسَ، فَمَسَحَ النَّوْمَ عَنْ وَجْهِهِ بِيَدِهِ، ثُمَّ قَرَأَ الْعَشْرَ آيَاتٍ خَوَاتِيمَ سُورَةِ آلِ عِمْرَانَ، ثُمَّ قَامَ إِلَى شَنٍّ مُعَلَّقَةٍ فَتَوَضَّأَ مِنْهَا، فَأَحْسَنَ وُضُوءَهُ، ثُمَّ قَامَ يُصَلِّي. قَالَ عَبْدُ اللَّهِ بْنُ عَبَّاسٍ ـ رضى الله عنهما ـ فَقُمْتُ فَصَنَعْتُ مِثْلَ مَا صَنَعَ، ثُمَّ ذَهَبْتُ فَقُمْتُ إِلَى جَنْبِهِ، فَوَضَعَ رَسُولُ اللَّهِ صلى الله عليه وسلم يَدَهُ الْيُمْنَى عَلَى رَأْسِي، وَأَخَذَ بِأُذُنِي الْيُمْنَى يَفْتِلُهَا بِيَدِهِ، فَصَلَّى رَكْعَتَيْنِ، ثُمَّ رَكْعَتَيْنِ، ثُمَّ رَكْعَتَيْنِ، ثُمَّ رَكْعَتَيْنِ، ثُمَّ رَكْعَتَيْنِ، ثُمَّ رَكْعَتَيْنِ، ثُمَّ أَوْتَرَ، ثُمَّ اضْطَجَعَ حَتَّى جَاءَهُ الْمُؤَذِّنُ، فَقَامَ فَصَلَّى رَكْعَتَيْنِ خَفِيفَتَيْنِ، ثُمَّ خَرَجَ فَصَلَّى الصُّبْحَ.

Narrated `Aisha;: Allah's Messenger ﷺ offered the `Isha' prayer (and then got up at the Tahajjud time) and offered eight rak`at and then offered two rak`at while sitting. He then offered two rak`at in between the Adhan and Iqama (of the Fajr prayer) and he never missed them. – Sahih al-Bukhari 1159

حَدَّثَنَا عَبْدُ اللَّهِ بْنُ يَزِيدَ، حَدَّثَنَا سَعِيدٌ ـ هُوَ ابْنُ أَبِي أَيُّوبَ ـ قَالَ حَدَّثَنِي جَعْفَرُ بْنُ رَبِيعَةَ، عَنْ عِرَاكِ بْنِ مَالِكٍ، عَنْ أَبِي سَلَمَةَ، عَنْ عَائِشَةَ ـ رضى الله عنها ـ قَالَتْ صَلَّى النَّبِيُّ صلى الله عليه وسلم الْعِشَاءَ ثُمَّ صَلَّى ثَمَانَ رَكَعَاتٍ وَرَكْعَتَيْنِ جَالِسًا وَرَكْعَتَيْنِ بَيْنَ النِّدَاءَيْنِ، وَلَمْ يَكُنْ يَدَعُهُمَا أَبَدًا

Narrated `Aisha: Allah's Messenger ﷺ offered witr prayer at different nights at various hours extending (from the `Isha' prayer) up to the last hour of the night. – Sahih al-Bukhari 996

حَدَّثَنَا عُمَرُ بْنُ حَفْصٍ، قَالَ حَدَّثَنَا أَبِي قَالَ، حَدَّثَنَا الأَعْمَشُ، قَالَ حَدَّثَنِي مُسْلِمٌ، عَنْ مَسْرُوقٍ، عَنْ عَائِشَةَ، قَالَتْ كُلَّ اللَّيْلِ أَوْتَرَ رَسُولُ اللَّهِ صلى الله عليه وسلم وَانْتَهَى وِتْرُهُ إِلَى السَّحَرِ.

Narrated Ibn `Abbas: Once I passed the night in the house of my aunt Maimuna. Allah's Messenger ﷺ offered the `Isha' prayer and then came to the house and offered four rak`at an slept. Later on, he woke up and stood for the prayer and I stood on his left side. He drew me to his right and prayed five rak`at and then two. He then slept till I heard him snoring (or heard his breath sounds). Afterwards he went out for the morning prayer. – Sahih al-Bukhari 697

حَدَّثَنَا سُلَيْمَانُ بْنُ حَرْبٍ، قَالَ حَدَّثَنَا شُعْبَةُ، عَنِ الْحَكَمِ، قَالَ سَمِعْتُ سَعِيدَ بْنَ جُبَيْرٍ، عَنِ ابْنِ عَبَّاسٍ ـ رضى الله عنهما ـ قَالَ بِتُّ فِي بَيْتِ خَالَتِي مَيْمُونَةَ فَصَلَّى رَسُولُ اللَّهِ صلى الله عليه وسلم الْعِشَاءَ، ثُمَّ جَاءَ فَصَلَّى أَرْبَعَ رَكَعَاتٍ ثُمَّ نَامَ، ثُمَّ قَامَ فَجِئْتُ فَقُمْتُ عَنْ يَسَارِهِ، فَجَعَلَنِي عَنْ يَمِينِهِ، فَصَلَّى خَمْسَ رَكَعَاتٍ، ثُمَّ صَلَّى رَكْعَتَيْنِ، ثُمَّ نَامَ حَتَّى سَمِعْتُ غَطِيطَهُ ـ أَوْ قَالَ خَطِيطَهُ ـ ثُمَّ خَرَجَ إِلَى الصَّلاَةِ

They used to slumber (only) little of the night And before dawn, it is they (who) would seek forgiveness. – Surah Adh-Dhariyat 51:17&18

كَانُواْ قَلِيلًا مِّنَ ٱلَّيۡلِ مَا يَهۡجَعُونَ وَبِٱلۡأَسۡحَارِ هُمۡ يَسۡتَغۡفِرُونَ

And (part) of the night; so prostrate yourself to Him, and extol Him through the long night. – Surah Al-Insan 76:26

وَمِنَ ٱلَّيْلِ فَٱسْجُدْ لَهُۥ وَسَبِّحْهُ لَيْلًا طَوِيلًا

.....who pray before dawn for forgiveness. – Surah Al-Imran 3:17

وَٱلْمُسْتَغْفِرِينَ بِٱلْأَسْحَارِ

If anyone of you enters a mosque, he should pray two rak`at before sitting
إِذَا دَخَلَ أَحَدُكُمُ الْمَسْجِدَ فَلْيَرْكَعْ رَكْعَتَيْنِ قَبْلَ أَنْ يَجْلِسَ

Narrated Abu Qatada Al-Aslami: Allah's Messenger ﷺ said, "If anyone of you enters a mosque, he should pray two rak`at before sitting.". – Sahih al-Bukhari 444 [32]

حَدَّثَنَا عَبْدُ اللَّهِ بْنُ يُوسُفَ، قَالَ أَخْبَرَنَا مَالِكٌ، عَنْ عَامِرِ بْنِ عَبْدِ اللَّهِ بْنِ الزُّبَيْرِ، عَنْ عَمْرِو بْنِ سُلَيْمٍ الزُّرَقِيِّ، عَنْ أَبِي قَتَادَةَ السَّلَمِيِّ، أَنَّ رَسُولَ اللَّهِ صلى الله عليه وسلم قَالَ " إِذَا دَخَلَ أَحَدُكُمُ الْمَسْجِدَ فَلْيَرْكَعْ رَكْعَتَيْنِ قَبْلَ أَنْ يَجْلِسَ ".

Narrated Ka`b: Whenever the Prophet ﷺ returned from a journey in the forenoon, he would enter the Mosque and offer two rak`at before sitting. – Sahih al-Bukhari 3088

حَدَّثَنَا أَبُو عَاصِمٍ، عَنِ ابْنِ جُرَيْجٍ، عَنِ ابْنِ شِهَابٍ، عَنْ عَبْدِ الرَّحْمَنِ بْنِ عَبْدِ اللَّهِ بْنِ كَعْبٍ، عَنْ أَبِيهِ، وَعَمِّهِ، عُبَيْدِ اللَّهِ بْنِ كَعْبٍ عَنْ كَعْبٍ ـ رضى الله عنه ـ أَنَّ النَّبِيَّ صلى الله عليه وسلم كَانَ إِذَا قَدِمَ مِنْ سَفَرٍ ضُحًى دَخَلَ الْمَسْجِدَ، فَصَلَّى رَكْعَتَيْنِ قَبْلَ أَنْ يَجْلِسَ

Narrated Jabir: A man entered the Mosque while the Prophet ﷺ was delivering the Khutba. The Prophet ﷺ said to him, "Have you prayed?" The man replied in the negative. The Prophet ﷺ said, "Pray two rak`at.". – Sahih al-Bukhari 931

حَدَّثَنَا عَلِيُّ بْنُ عَبْدِ اللَّهِ، قَالَ حَدَّثَنَا سُفْيَانُ، عَنْ عَمْرٍو، سَمِعَ جَابِرًا، قَالَ دَخَلَ رَجُلٌ يَوْمَ الْجُمُعَةِ وَالنَّبِيُّ صلى الله عليه وسلم يَخْطُبُ فَقَالَ " أَصَلَّيْتَ ". قَالَ لاَ. قَالَ " فَصَلِّ رَكْعَتَيْنِ "

Narrated Jabir bin `Abdullah: I went to the Prophet ﷺ while he was in the Mosque. (Mas`ar thinks, that Jabir went in the forenoon.) After the Prophet ﷺ told me to pray two rak`at, he repaid me the debt he owed me and gave me an extra amount. – Sahih al-Bukhari 2394

حَدَّثَنَا خَلاَّدٌ، حَدَّثَنَا مِسْعَرٌ، حَدَّثَنَا مُحَارِبُ بْنُ دِثَارٍ، عَنْ جَابِرِ بْنِ عَبْدِ اللَّهِ ـ رضى الله عنهما ـ قَالَ أَتَيْتُ النَّبِيَّ صلى الله عليه وسلم وَهْوَ فِي الْمَسْجِدِ ـ قَالَ مِسْعَرٌ أُرَاهُ قَالَ ضُحًى ـ فَقَالَ " صَلِّ رَكْعَتَيْنِ ". وَكَانَ لِي عَلَيْهِ دَيْنٌ فَقَضَانِي وَزَادَنِي

Prostration of Tilawa
آيات السجدة

Narrated Rabi`a: `Umar bin Al-Khattab recited Surat-an-Nahl on a Friday on the pulpit and when he reached the verse of Sajda he got down from the pulpit and prostrated and the people also prostrated. The next Friday `Umar bin Al-Khattab recited the same Sura and when he reached the verse of Sajda he said, "O people! When we recite the verses of Sajda (during

---

[32] Praying the two rak'ahs of Tahiyyat al-Masjid (greeting the mosque) upon entering is a highly emphasized Sunnah. Some scholars even considered it to be obligatory (wajib). – Shaykh Muhammad ibn al-Uthaymeen

the sermon) whoever prostrates does the right thing, yet it is no sin for the one who does not prostrate." And `Umar did not prostrate (that day). Added Ibn `Umar "Allah has not made the prostration of recitation compulsory but if we wish we can do it." – Sahih al-Bukhari 1077
حَدَّثَنَا إِبْرَاهِيمُ بْنُ مُوسَى، قَالَ أَخْبَرَنَا هِشَامُ بْنُ يُوسُفَ، أَنَّ ابْنَ جُرَيْجٍ، أَخْبَرَهُمْ قَالَ أَخْبَرَنِي أَبُو بَكْرِ بْنُ أَبِي مُلَيْكَةَ، عَنْ عُثْمَانَ بْنِ عَبْدِ الرَّحْمَنِ التَّيْمِيِّ، عَنْ رَبِيعَةَ بْنِ عَبْدِ اللَّهِ بْنِ الْهُدَيْرِ التَّيْمِيِّ ـ قَالَ أَبُو بَكْرٍ وَكَانَ رَبِيعَةُ مِنْ خِيَارِ النَّاسِ عَمَّا حَضَرَ رَبِيعَةُ مِنْ عُمَرَ بْنِ الْخَطَّابِ ـ رضى الله عنه ـ قَرَأَ يَوْمَ الْجُمُعَةِ عَلَى الْمِنْبَرِ بِسُورَةِ النَّحْلِ حَتَّى إِذَا جَاءَ السَّجْدَةَ نَزَلَ فَسَجَدَ وَسَجَدَ النَّاسُ، حَتَّى إِذَا كَانَتِ الْجُمُعَةُ الْقَابِلَةُ قَرَأَ بِهَا حَتَّى إِذَا جَاءَ السَّجْدَةَ قَالَ يَا أَيُّهَا النَّاسُ إِنَّا نَمُرُّ بِالسُّجُودِ فَمَنْ سَجَدَ فَقَدْ أَصَابَ، وَمَنْ لَمْ يَسْجُدْ فَلاَ إِثْمَ عَلَيْهِ. وَلَمْ يَسْجُدْ عُمَرُ ـ رضى الله عنه. وَزَادَ نَافِعٌ عَنِ ابْنِ عُمَرَ ـ رضى الله عنهما إِنَّ اللَّهَ لَمْ يَفْرِضِ السُّجُودَ إِلاَّ أَنْ نَشَاءَ.

It was narrated from Abdullah bin Umar : That when the Messenger of Allah ((ﷺstarted to pray, he would raise his hands in level with his shoulders, and when he bowed and when he raised his head from bowing, he would raise them likewise and say "Sami Allahu liman hamidah, Rabbana wa lakal-hamd (Allah hears those who praise Him, our Lord, to You be praise." And he did not do that when he prostrated. – Sunan an-Nasa'I 878
أَخْبَرَنَا قُتَيْبَةُ، عَنْ مَالِكٍ، عَنِ ابْنِ شِهَابٍ، عَنْ سَالِمٍ، عَنْ عَبْدِ اللَّهِ بْنِ عُمَرَ، أَنَّ رَسُولَ اللَّهِ صلى الله عليه وسلم كَانَ إِذَا افْتَتَحَ الصَّلاَةَ رَفَعَ يَدَيْهِ حَذْوَ مَنْكِبَيْهِ وَإِذَا رَكَعَ وَإِذَا رَفَعَ رَأْسَهُ مِنَ الرُّكُوعِ رَفَعَهُمَا كَذَلِكَ وَقَالَ " سَمِعَ اللَّهُ لِمَنْ حَمِدَهُ رَبَّنَا وَلَكَ الْحَمْدُ " . وَكَانَ لاَ يَفْعَلُ ذَلِكَ فِي السُّجُودِ

Prostrations of Sahu
سَجْدَتَيِ السَّهْوِ

Narrated `Abdullah bin Buhaina: Allah's Messengerﷺ got up after the second rak`a of the Zuhr prayer without sitting in between (the second and the third rak`at). When he finished the prayer he performed two prostrations (of Sahu) and then finished the prayer with Taslim. – Sahih al-Bukhari 1225
حَدَّثَنَا عَبْدُ اللَّهِ بْنُ يُوسُفَ، أَخْبَرَنَا مَالِكٌ، عَنْ يَحْيَى بْنِ سَعِيدٍ، عَنْ عَبْدِ الرَّحْمَنِ الأَعْرَجِ، عَنْ عَبْدِ اللَّهِ ابْنِ بُحَيْنَةَ ـ رضى الله عنه ـ أَنَّهُ قَالَ إِنَّ رَسُولَ اللَّهِ صلى الله عليه وسلم قَامَ مِنِ اثْنَتَيْنِ مِنَ الظُّهْرِ لَمْ يَجْلِسْ بَيْنَهُمَا، فَلَمَّا قَضَى صَلاَتَهُ سَجَدَ سَجْدَتَيْنِ ثُمَّ سَلَّمَ بَعْدَ ذَلِكَ

Narrated Salama bin 'Alqama: I asked Muhammad (bin Seereen) whether Tashah-hud should be recited after the two prostrations of Sahu. He replied, "It is not (mentioned) in Abu Huraira's narration . " - Sahih al-Bukhari 1228b
حَدَّثَنَا سُلَيْمَانُ بْنُ حَرْبٍ، حَدَّثَنَا حَمَّادٌ، عَنْ سَلَمَةَ بْنِ عَلْقَمَةَ، قَالَ قُلْتُ لِمُحَمَّدٍ فِي سَجْدَتَىِ السَّهْوِ تَشَهُّدٌ قَالَ لَيْسَ فِي حَدِيثِ أَبِي هُرَيْرَةَ

Narrated Abu Huraira: The Prophetﷺ said, "When the call for the prayer is pronounced, Satan takes to his heels, passing wind with noise, When the call for the prayer is finished, he comes back. And when the Iqama is pronounced, he again takes to his heels, and after its completion, he returns again to interfere between the (praying) person and his heart, saying to him. 'Remember this or that thing.' Till the person forgets whether he has offered three or four rak`at: so if one forgets whether he has prayed three or four rak`at, he should perform two prostrations of Sahu (i.e. forgetfulness). – Sahih al-Bukhari 3285
حَدَّثَنَا مُحَمَّدُ بْنُ يُوسُفَ، حَدَّثَنَا الأَوْزَاعِيُّ، عَنْ يَحْيَى بْنِ أَبِي كَثِيرٍ، عَنْ أَبِي سَلَمَةَ، عَنْ أَبِي هُرَيْرَةَ ـ رضى الله عنه ـ قَالَ قَالَ النَّبِيُّ صلى الله عليه وسلم " إِذَا نُودِيَ بِالصَّلاَةِ أَدْبَرَ الشَّيْطَانُ وَلَهُ ضُرَاطٌ، فَإِذَا قُضِيَ أَقْبَلَ، فَإِذَا ثُوِّبَ بِهَا أَدْبَرَ، فَإِذَا قُضِيَ أَقْبَلَ، حَتَّى يَخْطِرَ بَيْنَ الإِنْسَانِ وَقَلْبِهِ، فَيَقُولُ اذْكُرْ كَذَا وَكَذَا. حَتَّى لاَ يَدْرِي أَثَلاَثًا صَلَّى أَمْ أَرْبَعًا فَإِذَا لَمْ يَدْرِ ثَلاَثًا صَلَّى أَوْ أَرْبَعًا سَجَدَ سَجْدَتَىِ السَّهْوِ "

Narrated `Abdullah bin Malik bin Buhaina: Once Allah's Messenger ﷺ led us in the Zuhr prayer and got up (after the prostrations of the second rak`a) although he should have sat (for the Tashahhud). So at the end of the prayer, he prostrated twice while sitting (prostrations of Sahu). – Sahih al-Bukhari 830

حَدَّثَنَا قُتَيْبَةُ بْنُ سَعِيدٍ، قَالَ حَدَّثَنَا بَكْرٌ، عَنْ جَعْفَرِ بْنِ رَبِيعَةَ، عَنِ الأَعْرَجِ، عَنْ عَبْدِ اللَّهِ بْنِ مَالِكٍ ابْنِ بُحَيْنَةَ، قَالَ صَلَّى بِنَا رَسُولُ اللَّهِ صلى الله عليه وسلم الظُّهْرَ فَقَامَ وَعَلَيْهِ جُلُوسٌ، فَلَمَّا كَانَ فِي آخِرِ صَلاَتِهِ سَجَدَ سَجْدَتَيْنِ وَهْوَ جَالِسٌ.

Narrated `Abdullah: "Once the Prophet ﷺ offered five rak`at in Zuhr prayer. He was asked, "Is there an increase in the prayer?" The Prophet ﷺ said, "And what is it?" They said, "You have prayed five rak`at.' So he bent his legs and performed two prostrations (of Sahu). – Sahih al-Bukhari 404

حَدَّثَنَا مُسَدَّدٌ، قَالَ حَدَّثَنَا يَحْيَى، عَنْ شُعْبَةَ، عَنِ الْحَكَمِ، عَنْ إِبْرَاهِيمَ، عَنْ عَلْقَمَةَ، عَنْ عَبْدِ اللَّهِ، قَالَ صَلَّى النَّبِيُّ صلى الله عليه وسلم الظُّهْرَ خَمْسًا فَقَالُوا أَزِيدَ فِي الصَّلاَةِ قَالَ " وَمَا ذَاكَ ". قَالُوا صَلَّيْتَ خَمْسًا. فَثَنَى رِجْلَيْهِ وَسَجَدَ سَجْدَتَيْنِ

Qunut
القنوت

Narrated `Abdul `Aziz: Anas said, "The Prophet ﷺ sent seventy men, called Al-Qurra 'for some purpose. The two groups of Bani Sulaim called Ri'l and Dhakwan, appeared to them near a well called Bir Ma'una. The people (i.e. Al- Qurra) said, 'By Allah, we have not come to harm you, but we are passing by you on our way to do something for the Prophet.' But (the infidels) killed them. The Prophet ﷺ therefore invoked evil upon them for a month during the morning prayer. That was the beginning of Al Qunut and we used not to say Qunut before that." A man asked Anas about Al-Qunut, "Is it to be said after the Bowing (in the prayer) or after finishing the Recitation (i.e. before Bowing)?" Anas replied, "No, but (it is to be said) after finishing the Recitation.". – Sahih al-Bukhari 4088

حَدَّثَنَا أَبُو مَعْمَرٍ، حَدَّثَنَا عَبْدُ الْوَارِثِ، حَدَّثَنَا عَبْدُ الْعَزِيزِ، عَنْ أَنَسٍ ـ رضى الله عنه ـ قَالَ بَعَثَ النَّبِيُّ صلى الله عليه وسلم سَبْعِينَ رَجُلاً لِحَاجَةٍ يُقَالُ لَهُمُ الْقُرَّاءُ، فَعَرَضَ لَهُمْ حَيَّانِ مِنْ بَنِي سُلَيْمٍ رِعْلٌ وَذَكْوَانُ، عِنْدَ بِئْرٍ يُقَالُ لَهَا بِئْرُ مَعُونَةَ، فَقَالَ الْقَوْمُ وَاللَّهِ مَا إِيَّاكُمْ أَرَدْنَا، إِنَّمَا نَحْنُ مُجْتَازُونَ فِي حَاجَةٍ لِلنَّبِيِّ صلى الله عليه وسلم، فَقَتَلُوهُمْ فَدَعَا النَّبِيُّ صلى الله عليه وسلم عَلَيْهِمْ شَهْرًا فِي صَلاَةِ الْغَدَاةِ، وَذَلِكَ بَدْءُ الْقُنُوتِ وَمَا كُنَّا نَقْنُتُ. قَالَ عَبْدُ الْعَزِيزِ وَسَأَلَ رَجُلٌ أَنَسًا عَنِ الْقُنُوتِ أَبَعْدَ الرُّكُوعِ، أَوْ عِنْدَ فَرَاغٍ مِنَ الْقِرَاءَةِ قَالَ لاَ بَلْ عِنْدَ فَرَاغٍ مِنَ الْقِرَاءَةِ

It was narrated from Anas: "The Messenger of Allah ﷺ said the Qunut for a month."- (One of the narrators) Shu'bah said: "He cursed some men." Hisham said: "He supplicated against some of the tribes of Arabs."-"Then he stopped doing that after bowing." This is what Hisham said. Shu'bah said, narrating from Qatadah, from Anas that the Prophet ﷺ said the Qunut for a month, cursing Ri'l, Dhawkan and Lihyan. – Sunan an-Nasa'I 1077

أَخْبَرَنَا مُحَمَّدُ بْنُ الْمُثَنَّى، قَالَ حَدَّثَنَا أَبُو دَاوُدَ، قَالَ حَدَّثَنَا شُعْبَةُ، عَنْ قَتَادَةَ، عَنْ أَنَسٍ، وَهِشَامٌ، عَنْ قَتَادَةَ، عَنْ أَنَسٍ، أَنَّ رَسُولَ اللَّهِ صلى الله عليه وسلم قَنَتَ شَهْرًا – قَالَ شُعْبَةُ لَعَنَ رِجَالاً وَقَالَ هِشَامٌ يَدْعُو عَلَى أَحْيَاءٍ مِنْ أَحْيَاءِ الْعَرَبِ – ثُمَّ تَرَكَهُ بَعْدَ الرُّكُوعِ . هَذَا قَوْلُ هِشَامٍ وَقَالَ شُعْبَةُ عَنْ قَتَادَةَ عَنْ أَنَسٍ أَنَّ النَّبِيَّ صلى الله عليه وسلم قَنَتَ شَهْرًا يَلْعَنُ رِعْلاً وَذَكْوَانَ وَلِحْيَانَ

Narrated Anas: The Qunut used to be recited in the Maghrib and the Fajr prayers. – Sahih al-Bukhari 1004

حَدَّثَنَا مُسَدَّدٌ، قَالَ حَدَّثَنَا إِسْمَاعِيلُ، قَالَ حَدَّثَنَا خَالِدٌ، عَنْ أَبِي قِلاَبَةَ، عَنْ أَنَسٍ، قَالَ كَانَ الْقُنُوتُ فِي الْمَغْرِبِ وَالْفَجْرِ.

Narrated `Asim Al-Ahwal: I asked Anas bin Malik regarding Al-Qunut during the prayer. Anas replied, "Yes (Al-Qunut was said by the Prophet ﷺ (in the prayer)." I said, "Is it before Bowing or after Bowing?" Anas replied, "(It was said) before (Bowing)." I said, "So-and-so informed me that you told him that it was said after Bowing." Anas replied, "He was mistaken, for Allah's Messenger ﷺ said Al-Qunut after Bowing for one month. The Prophet ﷺ had sent some people called Al-Qurra who were seventy in number, to some pagan people who had concluded a peace treaty with Allah's Messenger ﷺ. But those who had concluded the treaty with Allah's Messenger ﷺ violated the treaty (and martyred all the seventy men). So Allah's Apostle said Al-Qunut after Bowing (in the prayer) for one month, invoking evil upon them. – Sahih al-Bukhari 4096

حَدَّثَنَا مُوسَى بْنُ إِسْمَاعِيلَ، حَدَّثَنَا عَبْدُ الْوَاحِدِ، حَدَّثَنَا عَاصِمٌ الأَحْوَلُ، قَالَ سَأَلْتُ أَنَسَ بْنَ مَالِكٍ ـ رضى الله عنه ـ عَنِ الْقُنُوتِ، فِي الصَّلاَةِ فَقَالَ نَعَمْ. فَقُلْتُ كَانَ قَبْلَ الرُّكُوعِ أَوْ بَعْدَهُ قَالَ قَبْلَهُ. قُلْتُ فَإِنَّ فُلاَنًا أَخْبَرَنِي عَنْكَ أَنَّكَ قُلْتَ بَعْدَهُ، قَالَ كَذَبَ إِنَّمَا قَنَتَ رَسُولُ اللَّهِ صلى الله عليه وسلم بَعْدَ الرُّكُوعِ شَهْرًا، أَنَّهُ كَانَ بَعَثَ نَاسًا يُقَالُ لَهُمُ الْقُرَّاءُ، وَهُمْ سَبْعُونَ رَجُلاً إِلَى نَاسٍ مِنَ الْمُشْرِكِينَ، وَبَيْنَهُمْ وَبَيْنَ رَسُولِ اللَّهِ صلى الله عليه وسلم عَهْدٌ قِبَلَهُمْ، فَظَهَرَ هَؤُلاَءِ الَّذِينَ كَانَ بَيْنَهُمْ وَبَيْنَ رَسُولِ اللَّهِ صلى الله عليه وسلم عَهْدٌ، فَقَنَتَ رَسُولُ اللَّهِ صلى الله عليه وسلم بَعْدَ الرُّكُوعِ شَهْرًا يَدْعُو عَلَيْهِمْ

Narrated Muhammad bin Seereen: Anas was asked, "Did the Prophet ﷺ recite Qunut in the Fajr prayer?" Anas replied in the affirmative. He was further asked, "Did he recite Qunut before bowing?" Anas replied, "He recited Qunut after bowing for some time (for one month)." – Sahih al-Bukhari 1001

حَدَّثَنَا مُسَدَّدٌ، قَالَ حَدَّثَنَا حَمَّادُ بْنُ زَيْدٍ، عَنْ أَيُّوبَ، عَنْ مُحَمَّدٍ، قَالَ سُئِلَ أَنَسٌ أَقَنَتَ النَّبِيُّ صلى الله عليه وسلم فِي الصُّبْحِ قَالَ نَعَمْ. فَقِيلَ لَهُ أَوَقَنَتَ قَبْلَ الرُّكُوعِ قَالَ بَعْدَ الرُّكُوعِ يَسِيرًا

It was narrated from Abu Malik Al-Ashja'l that his father said: "I prayed behind the Messenger of Allah ﷺ and he did not say the Qunut, and I prayed behind Abu Bakr and he did not say the Qunut, and I prayed behind Umar and he did not say the Qunut, and I prayed behind Uthman and he did not say the Qunut, and I prayed behind Ali and he did not say the Qunut." Then he said: "O my son, this is an innovation.". – Sunan an-Nasa'I 1080

أَخْبَرَنَا قُتَيْبَةُ، عَنْ خَلَفٍ، - وَهُوَ ابْنُ خَلِيفَةَ – عَنْ أَبِي مَالِكٍ الأَشْجَعِيِّ، عَنْ أَبِيهِ، قَالَ صَلَّيْتُ خَلْفَ رَسُولِ اللَّهِ صلى الله عليه وسلم فَلَمْ يَقْنُتْ وَصَلَّيْتُ خَلْفَ أَبِي بَكْرٍ فَلَمْ يَقْنُتْ وَصَلَّيْتُ خَلْفَ عُمَرَ فَلَمْ يَقْنُتْ وَصَلَّيْتُ خَلْفَ عُثْمَانَ فَلَمْ يَقْنُتْ وَصَلَّيْتُ خَلْفَ عَلِيٍّ فَلَمْ يَقْنُتْ ثُمَّ قَالَ يَا بُنَىَّ إِنَّهَا بِدْعَةٌ .

Two rak`at before the Fajr prayer
الرَّكْعَتَيْنِ اللَّتَيْنِ قَبْلَ صَلاَةِ الصُّبْحِ

Narrated Hafsa: When the Mu'adh-dhin pronounced the Adhan for Fajr prayer and the dawn became evident the Prophet ordered a two rak`at light prayer (Sunna) before the Iqama of the compulsory (congregational) prayer. – Sahih al-Bukhari 618

حَدَّثَنَا عَبْدُ اللَّهِ بْنُ يُوسُفَ، قَالَ أَخْبَرَنَا مَالِكٌ، عَنْ نَافِعٍ، عَنْ عَبْدِ اللَّهِ بْنِ عُمَرَ، قَالَ أَخْبَرَتْنِي حَفْصَةُ، أَنَّ رَسُولَ اللَّهِ صلى الله عليه وسلم كَانَ إِذَا اعْتَكَفَ الْمُؤَذِّنُ لِلصُّبْحِ وَبَدَا الصُّبْحُ صَلَّى رَكْعَتَيْنِ خَفِيفَتَيْنِ قَبْلَ أَنْ تُقَامَ الصَّلاَةُ

Narrated `Aisha: The Prophet (p.b.u.h) used to make the two rak`at before the Fajr prayer so light that I would wonder whether he recited Al-Fatiha (or not). – Sahih al-Bukhari 1165

حَدَّثَنَا مُحَمَّدُ بْنُ بَشَّارٍ، قَالَ حَدَّثَنَا مُحَمَّدُ بْنُ جَعْفَرٍ، حَدَّثَنَا شُعْبَةُ، عَنْ مُحَمَّدِ بْنِ عَبْدِ الرَّحْمَنِ، عَنْ عَمَّتِهِ، عَمْرَةَ عَنْ عَائِشَةَ ـ رضى الله عنها ـ قَالَتْ كَانَ النَّبِيُّ صلى الله عليه وسلم ح وَحَدَّثَنَا أَحْمَدُ بْنُ يُونُسَ حَدَّثَنَا زُهَيْرٌ حَدَّثَنَا يَحْيَى ـ هُوَ ابْنُ سَعِيدٍ ـ عَنْ مُحَمَّدِ بْنِ عَبْدِ الرَّحْمَنِ عَنْ عَمْرَةَ عَنْ عَائِشَةَ ـ رضى الله عنها ـ قَالَتْ كَانَ النَّبِيُّ صلى الله عليه وسلم يُخَفِّفُ الرَّكْعَتَيْنِ اللَّتَيْنِ قَبْلَ صَلاَةِ الصُّبْحِ حَتَّى إِنِّي لأَقُولُ هَلْ قَرَأَ بِأُمِّ الْكِتَابِ

Narrated `Aisha: Allah's Messenger ﷺ never missed two rak`at before the Fajr prayer and after the `Asr prayer openly and secretly. – Sahih al-Bukhari 592

حَدَّثَنَا مُوسَى بْنُ إِسْمَاعِيلَ، قَالَ حَدَّثَنَا عَبْدُ الْوَاحِدِ، قَالَ حَدَّثَنَا الشَّيْبَانِيُّ، قَالَ حَدَّثَنَا عَبْدُ الرَّحْمَنِ بْنُ الأَسْوَدِ، عَنْ أَبِيهِ، عَنْ عَائِشَةَ، قَالَتْ رَكْعَتَانِ لَمْ يَكُنْ رَسُولُ اللَّهِ صلى الله عليه وسلم يَدَعُهُمَا سِرًّا وَلاَ عَلاَنِيَةً رَكْعَتَانِ قَبْلَ صَلاَةِ الصُّبْحِ، وَرَكْعَتَانِ بَعْدَ الْعَصْرِ.

Narrated Ibn `Umar: I offered with the Prophet ( (ﷺ two rak`at before the Zuhr and two rak`at after the Zuhr prayer; two rak`at after Maghrib, `Isha' and the Jumua prayers. Those of the Maghrib and `Isha' were offered in his house. My sister Hafsa told me that the Prophet ﷺ used to offer two light rak`at after dawn and it was the time when I never went to the Prophet." - Sahih al-Bukhari 1172, 1173

حَدَّثَنَا مُسَدَّدٌ، قَالَ حَدَّثَنَا يَحْيَى بْنُ سَعِيدٍ، عَنْ عُبَيْدِ اللَّهِ، قَالَ أَخْبَرَنَا نَافِعٌ، عَنِ ابْنِ عُمَرَ ـ رضى الله عنهما ـ قَالَ صَلَّيْتُ مَعَ النَّبِيِّ صلى الله عليه وسلم سَجْدَتَيْنِ قَبْلَ الظُّهْرِ، وَسَجْدَتَيْنِ بَعْدَ الظُّهْرِ، وَسَجْدَتَيْنِ بَعْدَ الْمَغْرِبِ، وَسَجْدَتَيْنِ بَعْدَ الْعِشَاءِ، وَسَجْدَتَيْنِ بَعْدَ الْجُمُعَةِ، فَأَمَّا الْمَغْرِبُ وَالْعِشَاءُ فَفِي بَيْتِهِ. قَالَ ابْنُ أَبِي الزِّنَادِ عَنْ مُوسَى بْنِ عُقْبَةَ عَنْ نَافِعٍ بَعْدَ الْعِشَاءِ فِي أَهْلِهِ. تَابَعَهُ كَثِيرُ بْنُ فَرْقَدٍ وَأَيُّوبُ عَنْ نَافِعٍ. وَحَدَّثَتْنِي أُخْتِي، حَفْصَةُ أَنَّ النَّبِيَّ صلى الله عليه وسلم كَانَ يُصَلِّي سَجْدَتَيْنِ خَفِيفَتَيْنِ بَعْدَ مَا يَطْلُعُ الْفَجْرُ، وَكَانَتْ سَاعَةً لاَ أَدْخُلُ عَلَى النَّبِيِّ صلى الله عليه وسلم فِيهَا. تَابَعَهُ كَثِيرُ بْنُ فَرْقَدٍ وَأَيُّوبُ عَنْ نَافِعٍ. وَقَالَ ابْنُ أَبِي الزِّنَادِ عَنْ مُوسَى بْنِ عُقْبَةَ عَنْ نَافِعٍ بَعْدَ الْعِشَاءِ فِي أَهْلِهِ.

Narrated Anas bin Seereen: I asked Ibn `Umar, "What is your opinion about the two rak`at before the Fajr (compulsory) prayer, as to prolonging the recitation in them?" He said, "The Prophet ﷺ used to pray at night two rak`at followed by two and so on, and end the prayer by one rak`ah witr. He used to offer two rak`at before the Fajr prayer immediately after the Adhan." (Hammad, the sub-narrator said, "That meant (that he prayed) quickly.)". – Sahih al-Bukhari 995

حَدَّثَنَا أَبُو النُّعْمَانِ، قَالَ حَدَّثَنَا حَمَّادُ بْنُ زَيْدٍ، قَالَ حَدَّثَنَا أَنَسُ بْنُ سِيرِينَ، قَالَ قُلْتُ لاِبْنِ عُمَرَ أَرَأَيْتَ الرَّكْعَتَيْنِ قَبْلَ صَلاَةِ الْغَدَاةِ أُطِيلُ فِيهِمَا الْقِرَاءَةَ فَقَالَ كَانَ النَّبِيُّ صلى الله عليه وسلم يُصَلِّي مِنَ اللَّيْلِ مَثْنَى مَثْنَى، وَيُوتِرُ بِرَكْعَةٍ وَيُصَلِّي الرَّكْعَتَيْنِ قَبْلَ صَلاَةِ الْغَدَاةِ وَكَأَنَّ الأَذَانَ بِأُذُنَيْهِ. قَالَ حَمَّادٌ أَىْ سُرْعَةً

Eclipse Salah
كسوف صلاح

Narrated `Aisha: On the day of a solar eclipse, Allah's Messenger ﷺ stood up (to offer the eclipse prayer). He recited Takbir, recited a long recitation (of Holy Verses), bowed a long bowing, and then he raised h is head saying. "Allah hears him who sends his praises to Him." Then he stayed standing, recited a long recitation again, but shorter than the former, bowed a long bowing, but shorter than the first, performed a long prostration and then performed the second rak`a in the same way as he had done the first. By the time he had finished his prayer with Taslim, the solar eclipse had been over. Then he addressed the people referring to the solar and lunar eclipses saying, "These are two signs amongst the Signs of Allah, and they do not eclipse because of anyone's death or life. So, if you see them, hasten for the Prayer." - Sahih al-Bukhari 3203

حَدَّثَنَا يَحْيَى بْنُ بُكَيْرٍ، حَدَّثَنَا اللَّيْثُ، عَنْ عُقَيْلٍ، عَنِ ابْنِ شِهَابٍ، قَالَ أَخْبَرَنِي عُرْوَةُ، أَنَّ عَائِشَةَ ـ رضى الله عنها ـ أَخْبَرَتْهُ أَنَّ رَسُولَ اللَّهِ صلى الله عليه وسلم يَوْمَ خَسَفَتِ الشَّمْسُ قَامَ فَكَبَّرَ وَقَرَأَ قِرَاءَةً طَوِيلَةً، ثُمَّ رَكَعَ رُكُوعًا طَوِيلاً ثُمَّ رَفَعَ رَأْسَهُ فَقَالَ " سَمِعَ اللَّهُ لِمَنْ حَمِدَهُ " وَقَامَ كَمَا هُوَ، فَقَرَأَ قِرَاءَةً طَوِيلَةً وَهْىَ أَدْنَى مِنَ الْقِرَاءَةِ الأُولَى، ثُمَّ رَكَعَ رُكُوعًا طَوِيلاً وَهْىَ أَدْنَى مِنَ الرَّكْعَةِ الأُولَى، ثُمَّ سَجَدَ سُجُودًا طَوِيلاً، ثُمَّ فَعَلَ فِي الرَّكْعَةِ الآخِرَةِ مِثْلَ ذَلِكَ، ثُمَّ سَلَّمَ وَقَدْ تَجَلَّتِ الشَّمْسُ، فَخَطَبَ

النَّاسَ، فَقَالَ فِي كُسُوفِ الشَّمْسِ وَالْقَمَرِ " إِنَّهُمَا آيَتَانِ مِنْ آيَاتِ اللَّهِ، لاَ يَخْسِفَانِ لِمَوْتِ أَحَدٍ، وَلاَ لِحَيَاتِهِ، فَإِذَا رَأَيْتُمُوهُمَا فَافْزَعُوا إِلَى الصَّلاَةِ "

Narrated `Aisha: The Prophet (p.b.u.h) recited (the Qur'an) aloud during the eclipse prayer and when he had finished the eclipse prayer he said the Takbir and bowed. When he stood straight from bowing he would say "Sami 'allahu liman hamidah Rabbana wa laka l-hamd." And he would again start reciting. In the eclipse prayer there are four bowing and four prostrations in two rak`at. Al-Auza'I and others said that they had heard Az-Zuhri from 'Urwa from `Aisha saying, "In the lifetime of Allah's Messenger ﷺ the sun eclipsed, and he made a person to announce: 'Prayer in congregation.' He led the prayer and performed four bowing and four prostrations in two rak`at." Narrated Al-Walid that `Abdur-Rahman bin Namir had informed him that he had heard the same. Ibn Shihab heard the same. Az-Zuhri said, "I asked ('Urwa), 'What did your brother `Abdullah bin Az-Zubair do? He prayed two rak`at (of the eclipse prayer) like the morning prayer, when he offered the (eclipse) prayer in Medina.' 'Urwa replied that he had missed (i.e. did not pray according to) the Prophet's tradition." Sulaiman bin Kathir and Sufyan bin Husain narrated from Az-Zuhri that the prayer for the eclipse used to be offered with loud recitation. – Sahih al-Bukhari 1065, 1066

حَدَّثَنَا مُحَمَّدُ بْنُ مِهْرَانَ، قَالَ حَدَّثَنَا الْوَلِيدُ، قَالَ أَخْبَرَنَا ابْنُ نَمِرٍ، سَمِعَ ابْنَ شِهَابٍ، عَنْ عُرْوَةَ، عَنْ عَائِشَةَ ـ رضى الله عنها ـ جَهَرَ النَّبِيُّ صلى الله عليه وسلم فِي صَلاَةِ الْخُسُوفِ بِقِرَاءَتِهِ، فَإِذَا فَرَغَ مِنْ قِرَاءَتِهِ كَبَّرَ فَرَكَعَ، وَإِذَا رَفَعَ مِنَ الرَّكْعَةِ قَالَ سَمِعَ اللَّهُ لِمَنْ حَمِدَهُ، رَبَّنَا وَلَكَ الْحَمْدُ. ثُمَّ يُعَاوِدُ الْقِرَاءَةَ فِي صَلاَةِ الْكُسُوفِ، أَرْبَعَ رَكَعَاتٍ فِي رَكْعَتَيْنِ وَأَرْبَعَ سَجَدَاتٍ.
وَقَالَ الأَوْزَاعِيُّ وَغَيْرُهُ سَمِعْتُ الزُّهْرِيَّ، عَنْ عُرْوَةَ، عَنْ عَائِشَةَ ـ رضى الله عنها ـ أَنَّ الشَّمْسَ، خَسَفَتْ عَلَى عَهْدِ رَسُولِ اللَّهِ صلى الله عليه وسلم فَبَعَثَ مُنَادِيًا بِالصَّلاَةُ جَامِعَةٌ، فَتَقَدَّمَ فَصَلَّى أَرْبَعَ رَكَعَاتٍ فِي رَكْعَتَيْنِ وَأَرْبَعَ سَجَدَاتٍ. وَأَخْبَرَنِي عَبْدُ الرَّحْمَنِ بْنُ نَمِرٍ سَمِعَ ابْنَ شِهَابٍ مِثْلَهُ. قَالَ الزُّهْرِيُّ فَقُلْتُ مَا صَنَعَ أَخُوكَ ذَلِكَ، عَبْدُ اللَّهِ بْنُ الزُّبَيْرِ مَا صَلَّى إِلاَّ رَكْعَتَيْنِ مِثْلَ الصُّبْحِ إِذْ صَلَّى بِالْمَدِينَةِ. قَالَ أَجَلْ، إِنَّهُ أَخْطَأَ السُّنَّةَ. تَابَعَهُ سُفْيَانُ بْنُ حُسَيْنٍ وَسُلَيْمَانُ بْنُ كَثِيرٍ عَنِ الزُّهْرِيِّ فِي الْجَهْرِ

Narrated Aisha: (the wife of the Prophet) On the day when the sun Khasafat (eclipsed) Allah's Messenger ﷺ prayed; he stood up and said Takbir and recited a prolonged recitation, then he performed a prolonged bowing, then he raised his head and said, "Sami`a l-lahu Lyman Hamidah," and then remained standing and recited a prolonged recitation which was shorter than the first. Then he performed a prolonged bowing which was shorter than the first. Then he prostrated and prolonged the prostration and he did the same in the second rak`a as in the first and then finished the prayer with Taslim. By that time the sun (eclipse) had cleared He addressed the people and said, "The sun and the moon are two of the signs of Allah; they do not eclipse (Yakhsifan) because of the death or the life (i.e. birth) of someone. So when you see them make haste for the prayer." - Sahih al-Bukhari 1047

حَدَّثَنَا سَعِيدُ بْنُ عُفَيْرٍ، قَالَ حَدَّثَنَا اللَّيْثُ، حَدَّثَنِي عُقَيْلٌ، عَنِ ابْنِ شِهَابٍ، قَالَ أَخْبَرَنِي عُرْوَةُ بْنُ الزُّبَيْرِ، أَنَّ عَائِشَةَ، زَوْجَ النَّبِيِّ صلى الله عليه وسلم أَخْبَرَتْهُ. أَنَّ رَسُولَ اللَّهِ صلى الله عليه وسلم صَلَّى يَوْمَ خَسَفَتِ الشَّمْسُ، فَقَامَ فَكَبَّرَ، فَقَرَأَ قِرَاءَةً طَوِيلَةً، ثُمَّ رَكَعَ رُكُوعًا طَوِيلاً، ثُمَّ رَفَعَ رَأْسَهُ، فَقَالَ سَمِعَ اللَّهُ لِمَنْ حَمِدَهُ. وَقَامَ كَمَا هُوَ، ثُمَّ قَرَأَ قِرَاءَةً طَوِيلَةً، وَهْىَ أَدْنَى مِنَ الْقِرَاءَةِ الأُولَى، ثُمَّ رَكَعَ رُكُوعًا طَوِيلاً، وَهْىَ أَدْنَى مِنَ الرَّكْعَةِ الأُولَى، ثُمَّ سَجَدَ سُجُودًا طَوِيلاً، ثُمَّ فَعَلَ فِي الرَّكْعَةِ الآخِرَةِ مِثْلَ ذَلِكَ، ثُمَّ سَلَّمَ وَقَدْ تَجَلَّتِ الشَّمْسُ، فَخَطَبَ النَّاسَ، فَقَالَ فِي كُسُوفِ الشَّمْسِ وَالْقَمَرِ " إِنَّهُمَا آيَتَانِ مِنْ آيَاتِ اللَّهِ، لاَ يَخْسِفَانِ لِمَوْتِ أَحَدٍ وَلاَ لِحَيَاتِهِ، فَإِذَا رَأَيْتُمُوهُمَا فَافْزَعُوا إِلَى الصَّلاَةِ "

Narrated `Abdullah bin `Abbas: During the lifetime of Allah's Messenger ﷺ, the sun eclipsed. Allah's Messenger ﷺ offered the prayer of (the) eclipse) and so did the people along with him. He performed a long Qiyam (standing posture) during which Surat-al-Baqara could have been recited; then he performed a pro-longed bowing, then raised his head and stood for a long time which was slightly less than that of the first Qiyam (and recited Qur'an). Then he

performed a prolonged bowing again but the period was shorter than the period of the first bowing, then he stood up and then prostrated. Again he stood up, but this time the period of standing was less than the first standing. Then he performed a prolonged bowing but of a lesser duration than the first, then he stood up again for a long time but for a lesser duration than the first. Then he performed a prolonged bowing but of lesser duration than the first, and then he again stood up, and then prostrated and then finished his prayer. By then the sun eclipse had cleared. The Prophetﷺ then said, "The sun and the moon are two signs among the signs of Allah, and they do not eclipse because of the death or birth of someone, so when you observe the eclipse, remember Allah (offer the eclipse prayer)." They (the people) said, "O Allah's Messengerﷺ ! We saw you stretching your hand to take something at this place of yours, then we saw you stepping backward." He said, "I saw Paradise (or Paradise was shown to me), and I stretched my hand to pluck a bunch (of grapes), and had I plucked it, you would have eaten of it as long as this world exists. Then I saw the (Hell) Fire, and I have never before, seen such a horrible sight as that, and I saw that the majority of its dwellers were women." The people asked, "O Allah's Messengerﷺ ! What is the reason for that?" He replied, "Because of their ungratefulness." It was said. "Do they disbelieve in Allah (are they ungrateful to Allah)?" He replied, "They are not thankful to their husbands and are ungrateful for the favors done to them. Even if you do good to one of them all your life, when she seems some harshness from you, she will say, "I have never seen any good from you.' "
- Sahih al-Bukhari 5197

حَدَّثَنَا عَبْدُ اللَّهِ بْنُ يُوسُفَ، أَخْبَرَنَا مَالِكٌ، عَنْ زَيْدِ بْنِ أَسْلَمَ، عَنْ عَطَاءِ بْنِ يَسَارٍ، عَنْ عَبْدِ اللَّهِ بْنِ عَبَّاسٍ، أَنَّهُ قَالَ خَسَفَتِ الشَّمْسُ عَلَى عَهْدِ رَسُولِ اللَّهِ صلى الله عليه وسلم فَصَلَّى رَسُولُ اللَّهِ صلى الله عليه وسلم وَالنَّاسُ مَعَهُ، فَقَامَ قِيَامًا طَوِيلاً نَحْوًا مِنْ سُورَةِ الْبَقَرَةِ، ثُمَّ رَكَعَ رُكُوعًا طَوِيلاً، ثُمَّ رَفَعَ فَقَامَ قِيَامًا طَوِيلاً وَهْوَ دُونَ الْقِيَامِ الأَوَّلِ، ثُمَّ رَكَعَ رُكُوعًا طَوِيلاً وَهْوَ دُونَ الرُّكُوعِ الأَوَّلِ، ثُمَّ سَجَدَ، ثُمَّ قَامَ فَقَامَ قِيَامًا طَوِيلاً وَهْوَ دُونَ الْقِيَامِ الأَوَّلِ، ثُمَّ رَكَعَ رُكُوعًا طَوِيلاً وَهْوَ دُونَ الرُّكُوعِ الأَوَّلِ، ثُمَّ رَفَعَ فَقَامَ قِيَامًا طَوِيلاً وَهْوَ دُونَ الْقِيَامِ الأَوَّلِ، ثُمَّ رَكَعَ رُكُوعًا طَوِيلاً وَهْوَ دُونَ الرُّكُوعِ الأَوَّلِ، ثُمَّ رَفَعَ ثُمَّ سَجَدَ، ثُمَّ انْصَرَفَ، وَقَدْ تَجَلَّتِ الشَّمْسُ، فَقَالَ " إِنَّ الشَّمْسَ وَالْقَمَرَ آيَتَانِ مِنْ آيَاتِ اللَّهِ لاَ يَخْسِفَانِ لِمَوْتِ أَحَدٍ وَلاَ لِحَيَاتِهِ، فَإِذَا رَأَيْتُمْ ذَلِكَ فَاذْكُرُوا اللَّهَ ". قَالُوا يَا رَسُولَ اللَّهِ رَأَيْنَاكَ تَنَاوَلْتَ شَيْئًا فِي مَقَامِكَ هَذَا، ثُمَّ رَأَيْنَاكَ تَكَعْكَعْتَ. فَقَالَ " إِنِّي رَأَيْتُ الْجَنَّةَ ـ أَوْ أُرِيتُ الْجَنَّةَ ـ فَتَنَاوَلْتُ مِنْهَا عُنْقُودًا وَلَوْ أَخَذْتُهُ لأَكَلْتُمْ مِنْهُ مَا بَقِيَتِ الدُّنْيَا، وَرَأَيْتُ النَّارَ فَلَمْ أَرَ كَالْيَوْمِ مَنْظَرًا قَطُّ وَرَأَيْتُ أَكْثَرَ أَهْلِهَا النِّسَاءَ ". قَالُوا لِمَ يَا رَسُولَ اللَّهِ قَالَ " بِكُفْرِهِنَّ ". قِيلَ يَكْفُرْنَ بِاللَّهِ قَالَ " يَكْفُرْنَ الْعَشِيرَ، وَيَكْفُرْنَ الإِحْسَانَ، وَلَوْ أَحْسَنْتَ إِلَى إِحْدَاهُنَّ الدَّهْرَ، ثُمَّ رَأَتْ مِنْكَ شَيْئًا قَالَتْ مَا رَأَيْتُ مِنْكَ خَيْرًا قَطُّ ".

Narrated `Aisha: (the wife of the Prophet (p.b.u.h) In the lifetime of the Prophetﷺ the sun eclipsed and he went to the Mosque and the people aligned behind him. He said the Takbir (starting the prayer) and prolonged the recitation (from the Qur'an) and then said Takbir and performed a prolonged bowing; then he (lifted his head and) said, "Sami allahu liman hamidah" (Allah heard him who sent his praises to Him). He then did not prostrate but stood up and recited a prolonged recitation which was shorter than the first recitation. He again said Takbir and then bowed a prolonged bowing but shorter than the first one and then said, "Sami`a l-lahu Lyman hamidah Rabbana walak-lhamd, (Allah heard him who sent his praises to Him. O our Sustainer! All the praises are for You)" and then prostrated and did the same in the second rak`a; thus he completed four bowing and four prostrations. The sun (eclipse) had cleared before he finished the prayer. (After the prayer) he stood up, glorified and praised Allah as He deserved and then said, "The sun and the moon are two of the signs of Allah. They do not eclipse because of the death or the life (i.e. birth) of someone. When you see them make haste for the prayer." Narrated Az-Zuhri: I said to 'Urwa, "When the sun eclipsed at Medina your brother (`Abdullah bin Az-Zubair) offered only a two-rak`at prayer like that of the morning (Fajr) prayer." 'Urwa replied, "Yes, for he missed the Prophet's tradition (concerning this matter)." - Sahih al-Bukhari 1046

حَدَّثَنَا يَحْيَى بْنُ بُكَيْرٍ، قَالَ حَدَّثَنِي اللَّيْثُ، عَنْ عُقَيْلٍ، عَنِ ابْنِ شِهَابٍ، ح وَحَدَّثَنِي أَحْمَدُ بْنُ صَالِحٍ، قَالَ حَدَّثَنَا عَنْبَسَةُ، قَالَ حَدَّثَنَا يُونُسُ، عَنِ ابْنِ شِهَابٍ، حَدَّثَنِي عُرْوَةُ، عَنْ عَائِشَةَ، زَوْجِ النَّبِيِّ صلى الله عليه وسلم قَالَتْ خَسَفَتِ الشَّمْسُ فِي حَيَاةِ النَّبِيِّ صلى الله عليه وسلم فَخَرَجَ إِلَى الْمَسْجِدِ فَصَفَّ النَّاسُ وَرَاءَهُ، فَكَبَّرَ فَاقْتَرَأَ رَسُولُ اللَّهِ صلى الله عليه وسلم قِرَاءَةً طَوِيلَةً، ثُمَّ كَبَّرَ فَرَكَعَ رُكُوعًا طَوِيلاً، ثُمَّ قَالَ سَمِعَ اللَّهُ لِمَنْ حَمِدَهُ. فَقَامَ وَلَمْ يَسْجُدْ، وَقَرَأَ قِرَاءَةً طَوِيلَةً، هِيَ أَدْنَى مِنَ الْقِرَاءَةِ الأُولَى، ثُمَّ كَبَّرَ وَرَكَعَ رُكُوعًا طَوِيلاً، وَهْوَ أَدْنَى مِنَ الرُّكُوعِ الأَوَّلِ، ثُمَّ قَالَ سَمِعَ اللَّهُ لِمَنْ حَمِدَهُ، رَبَّنَا وَلَكَ الْحَمْدُ. ثُمَّ سَجَدَ، ثُمَّ قَالَ فِي الرَّكْعَةِ الآخِرَةِ مِثْلَ ذَلِكَ، فَاسْتَكْمَلَ أَرْبَعَ رَكَعَاتٍ فِي أَرْبَعِ سَجَدَاتٍ، وَانْجَلَتِ الشَّمْسُ قَبْلَ أَنْ يَنْصَرِفَ، ثُمَّ قَامَ فَأَثْنَى عَلَى اللَّهِ بِمَا هُوَ أَهْلُهُ ثُمَّ قَالَ " هُمَا آيَتَانِ مِنْ آيَاتِ اللَّهِ، لاَ يَخْسِفَانِ لِمَوْتِ أَحَدٍ وَلاَ لِحَيَاتِهِ، فَإِذَا رَأَيْتُمُوهُمَا فَافْزَعُوا إِلَى الصَّلاَةِ ". وَكَانَ يُحَدِّثُ كَثِيرُ بْنُ عَبَّاسٍ أَنَّ عَبْدَ اللَّهِ بْنَ عَبَّاسٍ ـ رضى الله عنهما ـ كَانَ يُحَدِّثُ يَوْمَ خَسَفَتِ الشَّمْسُ بِمِثْلِ حَدِيثِ عُرْوَةَ عَنْ عَائِشَةَ. فَقُلْتُ لِعُرْوَةَ إِنَّ أَخَاكَ يَوْمَ خَسَفَتْ بِالْمَدِينَةِ لَمْ يَزِدْ عَلَى رَكْعَتَيْنِ مِثْلَ الصُّبْحِ. قَالَ أَجَلْ لأَنَّهُ أَخْطَأَ السُّنَّةَ

Salat al-Jumuha
صلاة الجمعة

Narrated `Abdullah bin `Umar Abu: I offered with Allah's Messenger ﷺ a two rak`at prayer before the Zuhr prayer and two rak`at after the Zuhr prayer, two rak`at after Jumua, Maghrib and `Isha' prayers. – Sahih al-Bukhari 1169

حَدَّثَنَا يَحْيَى بْنُ بُكَيْرٍ، حَدَّثَنَا اللَّيْثُ، عَنْ عُقَيْلٍ، عَنِ ابْنِ شِهَابٍ، قَالَ أَخْبَرَنِي سَالِمٌ، عَنْ عَبْدِ اللَّهِ بْنِ عُمَرَ ـ رضى الله عنهما ـ قَالَ صَلَّيْتُ مَعَ رَسُولِ اللَّهِ صلى الله عليه وسلم رَكْعَتَيْنِ قَبْلَ الظُّهْرِ، وَرَكْعَتَيْنِ بَعْدَ الظُّهْرِ، وَرَكْعَتَيْنِ بَعْدَ الْجُمُعَةِ، وَرَكْعَتَيْنِ بَعْدَ الْمَغْرِبِ، وَرَكْعَتَيْنِ بَعْدَ الْعِشَاءِ.

Narrated Salman Al-Farsi: Allah's Messenger ﷺ said, "Anyone who takes a bath on Friday and cleans himself as much as he can and puts oil (on his hair) or scents himself; and then proceeds for the prayer and does not force his way between two persons (assembled in the mosque for the Friday prayer), and prays as much as is written for him and remains quiet when the Imam delivers the Khutba, all his sins in between the present and the last Friday will be forgiven.". – Sahih al-Bukhari 910

حَدَّثَنَا عَبْدَانُ، قَالَ أَخْبَرَنَا عَبْدُ اللَّهِ، قَالَ أَخْبَرَنَا ابْنُ أَبِي ذِئْبٍ، عَنْ سَعِيدٍ الْمَقْبُرِيِّ، عَنْ أَبِيهِ، عَنِ ابْنِ وَدِيعَةَ، عَنْ سَلْمَانَ الْفَارِسِيِّ، قَالَ قَالَ رَسُولُ اللَّهِ صلى الله عليه وسلم " مَنِ اغْتَسَلَ يَوْمَ الْجُمُعَةِ، وَتَطَهَّرَ بِمَا اسْتَطَاعَ مِنْ طُهْرٍ، ثُمَّ ادَّهَنَ أَوْ مَسَّ مِنْ طِيبٍ، ثُمَّ رَاحَ فَلَمْ يُفَرِّقْ بَيْنَ اثْنَيْنِ، فَصَلَّى مَا كُتِبَ لَهُ، ثُمَّ إِذَا خَرَجَ الإِمَامُ أَنْصَتَ، غُفِرَ لَهُ مَا بَيْنَهُ وَبَيْنَ الْجُمُعَةِ الأُخْرَى "

Narrated Ibn Juraij: I heard Nazi' saying, "Ibn `Umar, said, 'The Prophet ﷺ forbade that a man should make another man to get up to sit in his place' ". I said to Nafi`, 'Is it for Jumua prayer only?' He replied, "For Jumua prayer and any other (prayer)." - Sahih al-Bukhari 911

حَدَّثَنَا مُحَمَّدٌ، قَالَ أَخْبَرَنَا مَخْلَدُ بْنُ يَزِيدَ، قَالَ أَخْبَرَنَا ابْنُ جُرَيْجٍ، قَالَ سَمِعْتُ نَافِعًا، يَقُولُ سَمِعْتُ ابْنَ عُمَرَ ـ رضى الله عنهما ـ يَقُولُ نَهَى النَّبِيُّ صلى الله عليه وسلم أَنْ يُقِيمَ الرَّجُلُ أَخَاهُ مِنْ مَقْعَدِهِ وَيَجْلِسَ فِيهِ. قُلْتُ لِنَافِعٍ الْجُمُعَةَ قَالَ الْجُمُعَةَ وَغَيْرَهَا

Narrated Anas: We used to offer the Jumua prayer early and then have the afternoon nap. – Sahih al-Bukhari 940

حَدَّثَنَا مُحَمَّدُ بْنُ عُقْبَةَ الشَّيْبَانِيُّ، قَالَ حَدَّثَنَا أَبُو إِسْحَاقَ الْفَزَارِيُّ، عَنْ حُمَيْدٍ، قَالَ سَمِعْتُ أَنَسًا، يَقُولُ كُنَّا نُبَكِّرُ إِلَى الْجُمُعَةِ ثُمَّ نَقِيلُ

Narrated Abu Huraira: While `Umar (bin Al-Khattab) was delivering the Khutba on a Friday, a man entered (the mosque). `Umar asked him, "What has detained you from the prayer?" The man said, "It was only that when I heard the Adhan I performed ablution (for the prayer)."

On that `Umar said, “Did you not hear the Prophet saying: ‘Anyone of you going out for the Jumua prayer should take a bath’?”. – Sahih al-Bukhari 882
حَدَّثَنَا أَبُو نُعَيْمٍ، قَالَ حَدَّثَنَا شَيْبَانُ، عَنْ يَحْيَى، عَنْ أَبِي سَلَمَةَ، عَنْ أَبِي هُرَيْرَةَ، أَنَّ عُمَرَ ـ رضى الله عنه ـ بَيْنَمَا هُوَ يَخْطُبُ يَوْمَ الْجُمُعَةِ إِذْ دَخَلَ رَجُلٌ فَقَالَ عُمَرُ لِمَ تَحْتَبِسُونَ عَنِ الصَّلاَةِ فَقَالَ الرَّجُلُ مَا هُوَ إِلاَّ سَمِعْتُ النِّدَاءَ تَوَضَّأْتُ. فَقَالَ أَلَمْ تَسْمَعُوا النَّبِيَّ صلى الله عليه وسلم قَالَ " إِذَا رَاحَ أَحَدُكُمْ إِلَى الْجُمُعَةِ فَلْيَغْتَسِلْ

Narrated Sahl bin Sa`d: We used to be very happy on Friday as an old lady used to cut some roots of the Silq, which we used to plant on the banks of our small water streams, and cook them in a pot of her’s, adding to them, some grains of barley. (Ya’qub, the sub-narrator said, “I think the narrator mentioned that the food did not contain fat or melted fat (taken from meat).”) When we offered the Friday prayer we would go to her and she would serve us with the dish. So, we used to be happy on Fridays because of that. We used not to take our meals or the midday nap except after the Jumua prayer (i.e. Friday prayer). – Sahih al-Bukhari 2349
حَدَّثَنَا قُتَيْبَةُ بْنُ سَعِيدٍ، حَدَّثَنَا يَعْقُوبُ، عَنْ أَبِي حَازِمٍ، عَنْ سَهْلِ بْنِ سَعْدٍ ـ رضى الله عنه ـ أَنَّهُ قَالَ إِنَّا كُنَّا نَفْرَحُ بِيَوْمِ الْجُمُعَةِ، كَانَتْ لَنَا عَجُوزٌ تَأْخُذُ مِنْ أُصُولِ سِلْقٍ لَنَا كُنَّا نَغْرِسُهُ فِي أَرْبِعَائِنَا فَتَجْعَلُهُ فِي قِدْرٍ لَهَا فَتَجْعَلُ فِيهِ حَبَّاتٍ مِنْ شَعِيرٍ لاَ أَعْلَمُ إِلاَّ أَنَّهُ قَالَ لَيْسَ فِيهِ شَحْمٌ وَلاَ وَدَكٌ، فَإِذَا صَلَّيْنَا الْجُمُعَةَ زُرْنَاهَا فَقَرَّبَتْهُ، إِلَيْنَا فَكُنَّا نَفْرَحُ بِيَوْمِ الْجُمُعَةِ مِنْ أَجْلِ ذَلِكَ وَمَا كُنَّا نَتَغَدَّى وَلاَ نَقِيلُ إِلاَّ بَعْدَ الْجُمُعَةِ.

The Book of

For all believers, prayer is a sacred duty to be performed at prescribed times. – Surah An-Nisa 4:103

إِنَّ ٱلصَّلَوٰةَ كَانَتْ عَلَى ٱلْمُؤْمِنِينَ كِتَـٰبًا مَّوْقُوتًا

Establish prayer from the time the sun declines until the darkening of the night, and also [remember] the [Qur'an) recitation at dawn. The dawn recitation is indeed witnessed [by Us]. – Al-Isra 17:78

أَقِمِ ٱلصَّلَوٰةَ لِدُلُوكِ ٱلشَّمْسِ إِلَىٰ غَسَقِ ٱلَّيْلِ وَقُرْءَانَ ٱلْفَجْرِ ۖ إِنَّ قُرْءَانَ ٱلْفَجْرِ كَانَ مَشْهُودًا

So (endure) patiently under what they say, and extol (with) the praise of your Lord before the rising of the sun and before its setting; and then extol (Him) at various times of the night and at the two extremes of the daytime, that possibly you would be satisfied. – Surah TaHa 20:130

فَٱصْبِرْ عَلَىٰ مَا يَقُولُونَ وَسَبِّحْ بِحَمْدِ رَبِّكَ قَبْلَ طُلُوعِ ٱلشَّمْسِ وَقَبْلَ غُرُوبِهَا ۖ وَمِنْ ءَانَآئِ ٱلَّيْلِ فَسَبِّحْ وَأَطْرَافَ ٱلنَّهَارِ لَعَلَّكَ تَرْضَىٰ

Narrated `Abdullah: I never saw the Prophet ﷺ offering any prayer not at its stated time except two; he prayed the Maghrib and the `Isha' together and he offered the morning prayer before its usual time. – Sahih al-Bukhari 1682

حَدَّثَنَا عُمَرُ بْنُ حَفْصِ بْنِ غِيَاثٍ، حَدَّثَنَا أَبِي، حَدَّثَنَا الأَعْمَشُ، قَالَ حَدَّثَنِي عُمَارَةُ، عَنْ عَبْدِ الرَّحْمَنِ، عَنْ عَبْدِ اللَّهِ ـ رضى الله عنه ـ قَالَ مَا رَأَيْتُ النَّبِيَّ صلى الله عليه وسلم صَلَّى صَلاَةً بِغَيْرِ مِيقَاتِهَا إِلاَّ صَلاَتَيْنِ جَمَعَ بَيْنَ الْمَغْرِبِ وَالْعِشَاءِ، وَصَلَّى الْفَجْرَ قَبْلَ مِيقَاتِهَا

Fajr prayer
صلاة الفجر

Narrated Abu Huraira: Allah's Messenger ﷺ said, "Whoever could get one rak`a (of the Fajr prayer) before sunrise, he has got the (morning) prayer and whoever could get one rak`a of the `Asr prayer before sunset, he has got the (`Asr) prayer.". – Sahih al-Bukhari 579

حَدَّثَنَا عَبْدُ اللَّهِ بْنُ مَسْلَمَةَ، عَنْ مَالِكٍ، عَنْ زَيْدِ بْنِ أَسْلَمَ، عَنْ عَطَاءِ بْنِ يَسَارٍ، وَعَنْ بُسْرِ بْنِ سَعِيدٍ، وَعَنِ الأَعْرَجِ، يُحَدِّثُونَهُ عَنْ أَبِي هُرَيْرَةَ، أَنَّ رَسُولَ اللَّهِ صلى الله عليه وسلم قَالَ " مَنْ أَدْرَكَ مِنَ الصُّبْحِ رَكْعَةً قَبْلَ أَنْ تَطْلُعَ الشَّمْسُ فَقَدْ أَدْرَكَ الصُّبْحَ، وَمَنْ أَدْرَكَ رَكْعَةً مِنَ الْعَصْرِ قَبْلَ أَنْ تَغْرُبَ الشَّمْسُ فَقَدْ أَدْرَكَ الْعَصْرَ "

Narrated `Aisha: Allah's Messenger ﷺ used to offer the Fajr prayer when it was still dark and the believing women used to return (after finishing their prayer) and nobody could recognize them owing to darkness, or they could not recognize one another. – Sahih al-Bukhari 872

حَدَّثَنَا يَحْيَى بْنُ مُوسَى، حَدَّثَنَا سَعِيدُ بْنُ مَنْصُورٍ، حَدَّثَنَا فُلَيْحٌ، عَنْ عَبْدِ الرَّحْمَنِ بْنِ الْقَاسِمِ، عَنْ أَبِيهِ، عَنْ عَائِشَةَ، رضى الله عنها أَنَّ رَسُولَ اللَّهِ صلى الله عليه وسلم كَانَ يُصَلِّي الصُّبْحَ بِغَلَسٍ فَيَنْصَرِفْنَ نِسَاءُ الْمُؤْمِنِينَ، لاَ يُعْرَفْنَ مِنَ الْغَلَسِ، أَوْ لاَ يَعْرِفُ بَعْضُهُنَّ بَعْضًا.

Narrated Anas bin Malik: Allah's Messenger ﷺ offered the Fajr prayer when it was still dark, then he rode and said, 'Allah Akbar! Khaibar is ruined. When we approach near to a nation, the most unfortunate is the morning of those who have been warned." The people came out into the streets saying, "Muhammad and his army." Allah's Messenger ﷺ vanquished them by force and their warriors were killed; the children and women were taken as captives. Safiya was taken by Dihya Al-Kalbi and later she belonged to Allah's Apostle go who married her and her Mahr was her manumission. – Sahih al-Bukhari 947

حَدَّثَنَا مُسَدَّدٌ، قَالَ حَدَّثَنَا حَمَّادٌ، عَنْ عَبْدِ الْعَزِيزِ بْنِ صُهَيْبٍ، وَثَابِتٍ الْبُنَانِيِّ، عَنْ أَنَسِ بْنِ مَالِكٍ، أَنَّ رَسُولَ اللَّهِ صلى الله عليه وسلم صَلَّى الصُّبْحَ بِغَلَسٍ ثُمَّ رَكِبَ فَقَالَ " اللَّهُ أَكْبَرُ خَرِبَتْ خَيْبَرُ، إِنَّا إِذَا نَزَلْنَا بِسَاحَةِ قَوْمٍ فَسَاءَ صَبَاحُ الْمُنْذَرِينَ ". فَخَرَجُوا يَسْعَوْنَ فِي السِّكَكِ وَيَقُولُونَ مُحَمَّدٌ وَالْخَمِيسُ ـ قَالَ وَالْخَمِيسُ الْجَيْشُ ـ فَظَهَرَ عَلَيْهِمْ رَسُولُ اللَّهِ صلى الله عليه وسلم فَقَتَلَ الْمُقَاتِلَةَ وَسَبَى الذَّرَارِيَّ، فَصَارَتْ صَفِيَّةُ لِدِحْيَةَ الْكَلْبِيِّ، وَصَارَتْ لِرَسُولِ اللَّهِ صلى الله عليه وسلم ثُمَّ تَزَوَّجَهَا وَجَعَلَ صَدَاقَهَا عِتْقَهَا. فَقَالَ عَبْدُ الْعَزِيزِ لِثَابِتٍ يَا أَبَا مُحَمَّدٍ، أَنْتَ سَأَلْتَ أَنَسًا مَا أَمْهَرَهَا قَالَ أَمْهَرَهَا نَفْسَهَا. فَتَبَسَّمَ.

Narrated Abu Al-Minhal: Abu Barza said, "The Prophet ﷺ used to offer the Fajr (prayer) when one could recognize the person sitting by him (after the prayer) and he used to recite between 60 to 100 Ayat (verses) of the Qur'an. He used to offer the Zuhr prayer as soon as the sun declined (at noon) and the `Asr at a time when a man might go and return from the farthest place in Medina and find the sun still hot. (The sub-narrator forgot what was said about the Maghrib). He did not mind delaying the `Isha prayer to one third of the night or the middle of the night.". – Sahih al-Bukhari 541

حَدَّثَنَا حَفْصُ بْنُ عُمَرَ، قَالَ حَدَّثَنَا شُعْبَةُ، عَنْ أَبِي الْمِنْهَالِ، عَنْ أَبِي بَرْزَةَ، كَانَ النَّبِيُّ صلى الله عليه وسلم يُصَلِّي الصُّبْحَ وَأَحَدُنَا يَعْرِفُ جَلِيسَهُ، وَيَقْرَأُ فِيهَا مَا بَيْنَ السِّتِّينَ إِلَى الْمِائَةِ، وَيُصَلِّي الظُّهْرَ إِذَا زَالَتِ الشَّمْسُ، وَالْعَصْرَ وَأَحَدُنَا يَذْهَبُ إِلَى أَقْصَى الْمَدِينَةِ ثُمَّ يَرْجِعُ وَالشَّمْسُ حَيَّةٌ، وَنَسِيتُ مَا قَالَ فِي الْمَغْرِبِ، وَلاَ يُبَالِي بِتَأْخِيرِ الْعِشَاءِ إِلَى ثُلُثِ اللَّيْلِ. ثُمَّ قَالَ إِلَى شَطْرِ اللَّيْلِ. وَقَالَ مُعَاذٌ قَالَ شُعْبَةُ ثُمَّ لَقِيتُهُ مَرَّةً فَقَالَ أَوْ ثُلُثِ اللَّيْلِ

Zuhr prayer
صلاة الظهر

Narrated Muhammad bin `Amr: We asked Jabir bin `Abdullah about the prayers of the Prophet ﷺ . He said, "He used to pray Zuhr prayer at midday, the `Asr when the sun was still hot, and the Maghrib after sunset (at its stated time). The `Isha was offered early if the people gathered, and used to be delayed if their number was less; and the morning prayer was offered when it was still dark. ". – Sahih al-Bukhari 565

حَدَّثَنَا مُسْلِمُ بْنُ إِبْرَاهِيمَ، قَالَ حَدَّثَنَا شُعْبَةُ، عَنْ سَعْدِ بْنِ إِبْرَاهِيمَ، عَنْ مُحَمَّدِ بْنِ عَمْرٍو ـ هُوَ ابْنُ الْحَسَنِ بْنِ عَلِيٍّ ـ قَالَ سَأَلْنَا جَابِرَ بْنَ عَبْدِ اللَّهِ عَنْ صَلاَةِ النَّبِيِّ، صلى الله عليه وسلم فَقَالَ كَانَ يُصَلِّي الظُّهْرَ بِالْهَاجِرَةِ، وَالْعَصْرَ وَالشَّمْسُ حَيَّةٌ، وَالْمَغْرِبَ إِذَا وَجَبَتْ، وَالْعِشَاءَ إِذَا كَثُرَ النَّاسُ عَجَّلَ، وَإِذَا قَلُّوا أَخَّرَ، وَالصُّبْحَ بِغَلَسٍ

Narrated Jabir bin `Abdullah: The Prophet ﷺ used to pray the Zuhr at midday, and the `Asr at a time when the sun was still bright, the Maghrib after sunset (at its stated time) and the `Isha at a variable time. Whenever he saw the people assembled (for `Isha' prayer) he would pray earlier and if the people delayed, he would delay the prayer. And they or the Prophet ﷺ used to offer the Fajr Prayers when it still dark. – Sahih al-Bukhari 560

حَدَّثَنَا مُحَمَّدُ بْنُ بَشَّارٍ، قَالَ حَدَّثَنَا مُحَمَّدُ بْنُ جَعْفَرٍ، قَالَ حَدَّثَنَا شُعْبَةُ، عَنْ سَعْدٍ، عَنْ مُحَمَّدِ بْنِ عَمْرِو بْنِ الْحَسَنِ بْنِ عَلِيٍّ، قَالَ قَدِمَ الْحَجَّاجُ فَسَأَلْنَا جَابِرَ بْنَ عَبْدِ اللَّهِ فَقَالَ كَانَ النَّبِيُّ صلى الله عليه وسلم يُصَلِّي الظُّهْرَ بِالْهَاجِرَةِ، وَالْعَصْرَ وَالشَّمْسُ نَقِيَّةٌ، وَالْمَغْرِبَ إِذَا وَجَبَتْ، وَالْعِشَاءَ أَحْيَانًا وَأَحْيَانًا، إِذَا رَآهُمُ اجْتَمَعُوا عَجَّلَ، وَإِذَا رَآهُمْ أَبْطَوْا أَخَّرَ، وَالصُّبْحَ كَانُوا ـ أَوْ كَانَ النَّبِيُّ صلى الله عليه وسلم يُصَلِّيهَا بِغَلَسٍ

Narrated Abu Al-Minhal: Abu Barza said, "The Prophet ﷺ used to offer the Fajr (prayer) when one could recognize the person sitting by him (after the prayer) and he used to recite between 60 to 100 Ayat (verses) of the Qur'an. He used to offer the Zuhr prayer as soon as the sun declined (at noon) and the `Asr at a time when a man might go and return from the farthest place in Medina and find the sun still hot. (The sub-narrator forgot what was said about the Maghrib). He did not mind delaying the `Isha prayer to one third of the night or the middle of the night.". – Sahih al-Bukhari 541
حَدَّثَنَا حَفْصُ بْنُ عُمَرَ، قَالَ حَدَّثَنَا شُعْبَةُ، عَنْ أَبِي الْمِنْهَالِ، عَنْ أَبِي بَرْزَةَ، كَانَ النَّبِيُّ صلى الله عليه وسلم يُصَلِّي الصُّبْحَ وَأَحَدُنَا يَعْرِفُ جَلِيسَهُ، وَيَقْرَأُ فِيهَا مَا بَيْنَ السِّتِّينَ إِلَى الْمِائَةِ، وَيُصَلِّي الظُّهْرَ إِذَا زَالَتِ الشَّمْسُ، وَالْعَصْرَ وَأَحَدُنَا يَذْهَبُ إِلَى أَقْصَى الْمَدِينَةِ ثُمَّ يَرْجِعُ وَالشَّمْسُ حَيَّةٌ، وَنَسِيتُ مَا قَالَ فِي الْمَغْرِبِ، وَلاَ يُبَالِي بِتَأْخِيرِ الْعِشَاءِ إِلَى ثُلُثِ اللَّيْلِ. ثُمَّ قَالَ إِلَى شَطْرِ اللَّيْلِ. وَقَالَ مُعَاذٌ قَالَ شُعْبَةُ ثُمَّ لَقِيتُهُ مَرَّةً فَقَالَ أَوْ ثُلُثِ اللَّيْلِ

It was narrated from Az-Zuhri he said: "Anas told me that the Messenger of Allah ﷺ went out when the sun had passed its zenith, and led them in Zuhr prayer." - Sunan an-Nasa'I 496
أَخْبَرَنَا كَثِيرُ بْنُ عُبَيْدٍ، قَالَ حَدَّثَنَا مُحَمَّدُ بْنُ حَرْبٍ، عَنِ الزُّبَيْدِيِّ، عَنِ الزُّهْرِيِّ، قَالَ أَخْبَرَنِي أَنَسٌ، أَنَّ رَسُولَ اللَّهِ صلى الله عليه وسلم خَرَجَ حِينَ زَاغَتِ الشَّمْسُ فَصَلَّى بِهِمْ صَلاَةَ الظُّهْرِ

'Uqbah bin 'Amir Al-Juhani said: "There are three times at which the Messenger of Allah forbade us to pray or to bury our dead: When the sun has risen fully until it is higher, when it reaches its zenith until it has passed the zenith, and when the sun starts to set" (Sahib). – Sunan an-Nasa'I 2013
أَخْبَرَنَا عَمْرُو بْنُ عَلِيٍّ، قَالَ حَدَّثَنَا عَبْدُ الرَّحْمَنِ، قَالَ حَدَّثَنَا مُوسَى بْنُ عُلَيِّ بْنِ رَبَاحٍ، قَالَ سَمِعْتُ أَبِي قَالَ، سَمِعْتُ عُقْبَةَ بْنَ عَامِرٍ الْجُهَنِيَّ، قَالَ : ثَلاَثُ سَاعَاتٍ كَانَ رَسُولُ اللَّهِ صلى الله عليه وسلم يَنْهَانَا أَنْ نُصَلِّيَ فِيهِنَّ، أَوْ نَقْبُرَ فِيهِنَّ مَوْتَانَا : حِينَ تَطْلُعُ الشَّمْسُ بَازِغَةً حَتَّى تَرْتَفِعَ، وَحِينَ يَقُومُ قَائِمُ الظَّهِيرَةِ حَتَّى تَزُولَ الشَّمْسُ، وَحِينَ تَضَيَّفُ الشَّمْسُ لِلْغُرُوبِ

Asr prayer
صلاة العصر

Yahya related to me from Malik from Hisham ibn Urwa from his father that Umar ibn al-Khattab wrote to Abu Musa al-Ashari that he should pray asr when the sun was still pure white so that a man could ride three farsakhs (before maghrib) and that he should pray Isha during the first third of the night, or, if he delayed it, then up until the middle of the night, and he warned him not to be forgetful. – Muwatta Malik – The Times of Prayer
وَحَدَّثَنِي عَنْ مَالِكٍ، عَنْ هِشَامِ بْنِ عُرْوَةَ، عَنْ أَبِيهِ، أَنَّ عُمَرَ بْنَ الْخَطَّابِ، كَتَبَ إِلَى أَبِي مُوسَى الأَشْعَرِيِّ أَنْ صَلِّ الْعَصْرَ، وَالشَّمْسُ، بَيْضَاءُ نَقِيَّةٌ قَدْرَ مَا يَسِيرُ الرَّاكِبُ ثَلاَثَةَ فَرَاسِخَ وَأَنْ صَلِّ الْعِشَاءَ مَا بَيْنَكَ وَبَيْنَ ثُلُثِ اللَّيْلِ فَإِنْ أَخَّرْتَ فَإِلَى شَطْرِ اللَّيْلِ وَلاَ تَكُنْ مِنَ الْغَافِلِينَ .

Narrated Aisha: The Prophet ﷺ used to pray the `Asr prayers at a time when the sunshine was still inside my chamber and no shadow had yet appeared in it. – Sahih al-Bukhari 546
حَدَّثَنَا أَبُو نُعَيْمٍ، قَالَ أَخْبَرَنَا ابْنُ عُيَيْنَةَ، عَنِ الزُّهْرِيِّ، عَنْ عُرْوَةَ، عَنْ عَائِشَةَ، قَالَتْ كَانَ النَّبِيُّ صلى الله عليه وسلم يُصَلِّي صَلاَةَ الْعَصْرِ وَالشَّمْسُ طَالِعَةٌ فِي حُجْرَتِي لَمْ يَظْهَرِ الْفَىْءُ بَعْدُ. وَقَالَ مَالِكٌ وَيَحْيَى بْنُ سَعِيدٍ وَشُعَيْبٌ وَابْنُ أَبِي حَفْصَةَ وَالشَّمْسُ قَبْلَ أَنْ تَظْهَرَ

Maghrib prayer
صلاة المغرب

Narrated `Abdullah bin `Umar: The Prophet ((ﷺprayed one of the `Isha' prayer in his last days and after finishing it with Taslim, he stood up and said, "Do you realize (the importance of) this night? Nobody present on the surface of the earth tonight would be living after the completion of one hundred years from this night." The people made a mistake in grasping the meaning of this statement of Allah's Messenger ((ﷺand they indulged in those things which are said about these narrators (i.e. some said that the Day of Resurrection will be established after 100 years etc.) But the Prophet ((ﷺsaid, "Nobody present on the surface of earth tonight would be living after the completion of 100 years from this night"; he meant "When that century (people of that century) would pass away.". – Sahih al-Bukhari 601
حَدَّثَنَا أَبُو الْيَمَانِ، قَالَ أَخْبَرَنَا شُعَيْبٌ، عَنِ الزُّهْرِيِّ، قَالَ حَدَّثَنِي سَالِمُ بْنُ عَبْدِ اللَّهِ بْنِ عُمَرَ، وَأَبُو بَكْرِ بْنُ أَبِي حَثْمَةَ أَنَّ عَبْدَ اللَّهِ بْنَ عُمَرَ، قَالَ صَلَّى النَّبِيُّ صلى الله عليه وسلم صَلاَةَ الْعِشَاءِ فِي آخِرِ حَيَاتِهِ، فَلَمَّا سَلَّمَ قَامَ النَّبِيُّ صلى الله عليه وسلم فَقَالَ " أَرَأَيْتَكُمْ لَيْلَتَكُمْ هَذِهِ فَإِنَّ رَأْسَ مِائَةٍ لاَ يَبْقَى مِمَّنْ هُوَ الْيَوْمَ عَلَى ظَهْرِ الأَرْضِ أَحَدٌ ". فَوَهِلَ النَّاسُ فِي مَقَالَةِ رَسُولِ اللَّهِ ـ عَلَيْهِ السَّلاَمُ ـ إِلَى مَا يَتَحَدَّثُونَ مِنْ هَذِهِ الأَحَادِيثِ عَنْ مِائَةِ سَنَةٍ، وَإِنَّمَا قَالَ النَّبِيُّ صلى الله عليه وسلم " لاَ يَبْقَى مِمَّنْ هُوَ الْيَوْمَ عَلَى ظَهْرِ الأَرْضِ " يُرِيدُ بِذَلِكَ أَنَّهَا تَخْرِمُ ذَلِكَ الْقَرْنَ.

Narrated Rafi` bin Khadij: We used to offer the Maghrib prayer with the Prophetﷺ and after finishing the prayer one of us may go away and could still see as Par as the spots where one's arrow might reach when shot by a bow. – Sahih al-Bukhari 559
حَدَّثَنَا مُحَمَّدُ بْنُ مِهْرَانَ، قَالَ حَدَّثَنَا الْوَلِيدُ، قَالَ حَدَّثَنَا الأَوْزَاعِيُّ، قَالَ حَدَّثَنَا أَبُو النَّجَاشِيِّ، صُهَيْبٌ مَوْلَى رَافِعِ بْنِ خَدِيجٍ قَالَ سَمِعْتُ رَافِعَ بْنَ خَدِيجٍ، يَقُولُ كُنَّا نُصَلِّي الْمَغْرِبَ مَعَ النَّبِيِّ صلى الله عليه وسلم فَيَنْصَرِفُ أَحَدُنَا وَإِنَّهُ لَيُبْصِرُ مَوَاقِعَ نَبْلِهِ

`Isha' prayer
صلاة العشاء

Narrated `Abdullah bin `Umar: The Prophetﷺ prayed one of the `Isha' prayer in his last days and after finishing it with Taslim, he stood up and said, "Do you realize (the importance of) this night? Nobody present on the surface of the earth tonight would be living after the completion of one hundred years from this night." The people made a mistake in grasping the meaning of this statement of Allah's Messengerﷺ and they indulged in those things which are said about these narrators (i.e. some said that the Day of Resurrection will be established after 100 years etc.) But the Prophetﷺ said, "Nobody present on the surface of earth tonight would be living after the completion of 100 years from this night"; he meant "When that century (people of that century) would pass away.". – Sahih al-Bukhari 601
حَدَّثَنَا أَبُو الْيَمَانِ، قَالَ أَخْبَرَنَا شُعَيْبٌ، عَنِ الزُّهْرِيِّ، قَالَ حَدَّثَنِي سَالِمُ بْنُ عَبْدِ اللَّهِ بْنِ عُمَرَ، وَأَبُو بَكْرِ بْنُ أَبِي حَثْمَةَ أَنَّ عَبْدَ اللَّهِ بْنَ عُمَرَ، قَالَ صَلَّى النَّبِيُّ صلى الله عليه وسلم صَلاَةَ الْعِشَاءِ فِي آخِرِ حَيَاتِهِ، فَلَمَّا سَلَّمَ قَامَ النَّبِيُّ صلى الله عليه وسلم فَقَالَ " أَرَأَيْتَكُمْ لَيْلَتَكُمْ هَذِهِ فَإِنَّ رَأْسَ مِائَةٍ لاَ يَبْقَى مِمَّنْ هُوَ الْيَوْمَ عَلَى ظَهْرِ الأَرْضِ أَحَدٌ ". فَوَهِلَ النَّاسُ فِي مَقَالَةِ رَسُولِ اللَّهِ ـ عَلَيْهِ السَّلاَمُ ـ إِلَى مَا يَتَحَدَّثُونَ مِنْ هَذِهِ الأَحَادِيثِ عَنْ مِائَةِ سَنَةٍ، وَإِنَّمَا قَالَ النَّبِيُّ صلى الله عليه وسلم " لاَ يَبْقَى مِمَّنْ هُوَ الْيَوْمَ عَلَى ظَهْرِ الأَرْضِ " يُرِيدُ بِذَلِكَ أَنَّهَا تَخْرِمُ ذَلِكَ الْقَرْنَ.

It was narrated from 'Abdullah bin 'Amr that the Prophetﷺ said: "When you pray Fajr, its time is until the first part of the sun appears. When you pray Zuhr, its time is until 'Asr comes. When you pray 'Asr, its time is until the sun turns yellow. When you pray Maghrib, its time is until the twilight has disappeared. When you pray 'Isha, its time is until half of the night has passed.". – Sahih Muslim 612 a

حَدَّثَنَا أَبُو غَسَّانَ الْمِسْمَعِيُّ، وَمُحَمَّدُ بْنُ الْمُثَنَّى، قَالاَ حَدَّثَنَا مُعَاذٌ، - وَهُوَ ابْنُ هِشَامٍ - حَدَّثَنِي أَبِي، عَنْ قَتَادَةَ، عَنْ أَبِي أَيُّوبَ، عَنْ عَبْدِ اللَّهِ بْنِ عَمْرٍو، أَنَّ نَبِيَّ اللَّهِ صلى الله عليه وسلم قَالَ " إِذَا صَلَّيْتُمُ الْفَجْرَ فَإِنَّهُ وَقْتٌ إِلَى أَنْ يَطْلُعَ قَرْنُ الشَّمْسِ الأَوَّلُ ثُمَّ إِذَا صَلَّيْتُمُ الظُّهْرَ فَإِنَّهُ وَقْتٌ إِلَى أَنْ يَحْضُرَ الْعَصْرُ فَإِذَا صَلَّيْتُمُ الْعَصْرَ فَإِنَّهُ وَقْتٌ إِلَى أَنْ تَصْفَرَّ الشَّمْسُ فَإِذَا صَلَّيْتُمُ الْمَغْرِبَ فَإِنَّهُ وَقْتٌ إِلَى أَنْ يَسْقُطَ الشَّفَقُ فَإِذَا صَلَّيْتُمُ الْعِشَاءَ فَإِنَّهُ وَقْتٌ إِلَى نِصْفِ اللَّيْلِ "

It was narrated that Abu Hurairah said: "The Messenger of Allahﷺ said: This is 'Jibril, peace be upon you, he came to teach you your religion. He prayed Subh when the dawn appeared, and he prayed Zuhr when the sun had (passed its zenith), and he prayed 'Asr when he saw that the shadow of a thing was equal to its height, then he prayed Maghrib when the sub had set and it is permissible for the fasting person to eat. Then he prayed 'Isha' when the twilight had disappeared. Then he came to him the following day and prayed Subh when it had got a little lighter, then he prayed Zuhr when the shadow of a thing was equal to its height, then he prayed 'Asr when the shadow of a thing was equal to twice its height, then he prayed Maghrib at the same time as before, then he prayed 'Isha' when a short period of the night had passed. Then he said: 'The prayer is between the times when you prayed yesterday and the times when you prayed today.'". – Sunan an-Nasa'I 502

أَخْبَرَنَا الْحُسَيْنُ بْنُ حُرَيْثٍ، قَالَ أَنْبَأَنَا الْفَضْلُ بْنُ مُوسَى، عَنْ مُحَمَّدِ بْنِ عَمْرٍو، عَنْ أَبِي سَلَمَةَ، عَنْ أَبِي هُرَيْرَةَ، قَالَ قَالَ رَسُولُ اللَّهِ صلى الله عليه وسلم " هَذَا جِبْرِيلُ عَلَيْهِ السَّلاَمُ جَاءَكُمْ يُعَلِّمُكُمْ دِينَكُمْ " . فَصَلَّى الصُّبْحَ حِينَ طَلَعَ الْفَجْرُ وَصَلَّى الظُّهْرَ حِينَ زَاغَتِ الشَّمْسُ ثُمَّ صَلَّى الْعَصْرَ حِينَ رَأَى الظِّلَّ مِثْلَهُ ثُمَّ صَلَّى الْمَغْرِبَ حِينَ غَرَبَتِ الشَّمْسُ وَحَلَّ فِطْرُ الصَّائِمِ ثُمَّ صَلَّى الْعِشَاءَ حِينَ ذَهَبَ شَفَقُ اللَّيْلِ ثُمَّ جَاءَهُ الْغَدَ فَصَلَّى بِهِ الصُّبْحَ حِينَ أَسْفَرَ قَلِيلاً ثُمَّ صَلَّى بِهِ الظُّهْرَ حِينَ كَانَ الظِّلُّ مِثْلَهُ ثُمَّ صَلَّى الْعَصْرَ حِينَ كَانَ الظِّلُّ مِثْلَيْهِ ثُمَّ صَلَّى الْمَغْرِبَ بِوَقْتٍ وَاحِدٍ حِينَ غَرَبَتِ الشَّمْسُ وَحَلَّ فِطْرُ الصَّائِمِ ثُمَّ صَلَّى الْعِشَاءَ حِينَ ذَهَبَ سَاعَةٌ مِنَ اللَّيْلِ ثُمَّ قَالَ " الصَّلاَةُ مَا بَيْنَ صَلاَتِكَ أَمْسِ وَصَلاَتِكَ الْيَوْمَ " .

The Book of

....Fasting is ordained for you as it was ordained for those before you, so that you would be pious. Surah Al-Baqarah 2:183

كُتِبَ عَلَيْكُمُ ٱلصِّيَامُ كَمَا كُتِبَ عَلَى ٱلَّذِينَ مِن قَبْلِكُمْ لَعَلَّكُمْ تَتَّقُونَ

Whoever of you lives to see this month (Ramadan) shall fast throughout it

فَمَن شَهِدَ مِنكُمُ ٱلشَّهْرَ فَلْيَصُمْهُ

O you who have believed, prescribed for you is the Fast, as it was prescribed for (the ones) who were before you, that possibly you would be pious (The fast is) (for) a prescribed number of days. So, whoever of you is sick or is on a journey, then a (fixed) number of other days; and against the ones who can afford it, there should be a ransom of food for an indigent man; (yet) whoever volunteers charitably, then it is most charitable on his part; and to fast is more charitable for you, in case you know The month of Ramadan (is the month) in which the Qur'an All-Supreme Reading) was sent down: a guidance to mankind, and supreme evidences of the guidance and the all-distinctive Criterion; So, whoever of you is present (Literally: witnesses the month) at the month, then he should fast it; and whoever is sick or on a journey, then a (fixed) number of other days. Allah wills for you ease, and He does not will difficulty for you (He wills) and that you should complete the (fixed) number. And magnify Allah for having guided you, and that possibly you would thank (Him) And when My bondmen ask you concerning Me, then, surely I am near; I answer the invocation of the invoker when he invokes Me; so let them respond (to) Me, and let them believe in Me, so that possibly they would respond right-mindedly It is made lawful to you, upon the night of the Fast, to lie (Literally: lying) with your wives; they are a garment (i.e. vestment, mutual protection) for you, and you are a garment for them. Allah knows that you have been betraying yourselves, so He has relented toward you and has been clement to you. So now go in to them, and seek whatever Allah has prescribed for you. And eat and drink until the white thread becomes evident to you from the black thread at dawn; thereafter complete (Literally: perfect) the Fast to the night, and do not go in to them while you are consecrating yourselves in the mosques. Such are the bounds of Allah, so do not draw near them. Thus Allah makes His signs evident to mankind, that possibly they would be pious. Surah Al-Baqarah 2:183-187

يَٰٓأَيُّهَا ٱلَّذِينَ ءَامَنُواْ كُتِبَ عَلَيْكُمُ ٱلصِّيَامُ كَمَا كُتِبَ عَلَى ٱلَّذِينَ مِن قَبْلِكُمْ لَعَلَّكُمْ تَتَّقُونَ أَيَّامًا مَّعْدُودَٰتٍ فَمَن كَانَ مِنكُم مَّرِيضًا أَوْ عَلَىٰ سَفَرٍ فَعِدَّةٌ مِّنْ أَيَّامٍ أُخَرَ وَعَلَى ٱلَّذِينَ يُطِيقُونَهُۥ فِدْيَةٌ طَعَامُ مِسْكِينٍ فَمَن تَطَوَّعَ خَيْرًا فَهُوَ خَيْرٌ لَّهُۥ وَأَن تَصُومُواْ خَيْرٌ لَّكُمْ إِن كُنتُمْ تَعْلَمُونَ شَهْرُ رَمَضَانَ ٱلَّذِىٓ أُنزِلَ فِيهِ ٱلْقُرْءَانُ هُدًى لِّلنَّاسِ وَبَيِّنَٰتٍ مِّنَ ٱلْهُدَىٰ وَٱلْفُرْقَانِ فَمَن شَهِدَ مِنكُمُ ٱلشَّهْرَ فَلْيَصُمْهُ وَمَن كَانَ مَرِيضًا أَوْ عَلَىٰ سَفَرٍ فَعِدَّةٌ مِّنْ أَيَّامٍ أُخَرَ يُرِيدُ ٱللَّهُ بِكُمُ ٱلْيُسْرَ وَلَا يُرِيدُ بِكُمُ ٱلْعُسْرَ وَلِتُكْمِلُواْ ٱلْعِدَّةَ وَلِتُكَبِّرُواْ ٱللَّهَ عَلَىٰ مَا هَدَىٰكُمْ وَلَعَلَّكُمْ تَشْكُرُونَ وَإِذَا سَأَلَكَ عِبَادِى عَنِّى فَإِنِّى قَرِيبٌ أُجِيبُ دَعْوَةَ ٱلدَّاعِ إِذَا دَعَانِ فَلْيَسْتَجِيبُواْ لِى وَلْيُؤْمِنُواْ بِى لَعَلَّهُمْ يَرْشُدُونَ أُحِلَّ لَكُمْ لَيْلَةَ ٱلصِّيَامِ ٱلرَّفَثُ إِلَىٰ نِسَآئِكُمْ هُنَّ لِبَاسٌ لَّكُمْ وَأَنتُمْ لِبَاسٌ لَّهُنَّ عَلِمَ ٱللَّهُ أَنَّكُمْ كُنتُمْ تَخْتَانُونَ أَنفُسَكُمْ فَتَابَ عَلَيْكُمْ وَعَفَا عَنكُمْ فَٱلْـَٰٔنَ بَٰشِرُوهُنَّ وَٱبْتَغُواْ مَا كَتَبَ ٱللَّهُ لَكُمْ وَكُلُواْ وَٱشْرَبُواْ حَتَّىٰ يَتَبَيَّنَ لَكُمُ ٱلْخَيْطُ ٱلْأَبْيَضُ مِنَ ٱلْخَيْطِ ٱلْأَسْوَدِ مِنَ ٱلْفَجْرِ ثُمَّ أَتِمُّواْ ٱلصِّيَامَ إِلَى ٱلَّيْلِ وَلَا تُبَٰشِرُوهُنَّ وَأَنتُمْ عَٰكِفُونَ فِى ٱلْمَسَٰجِدِ تِلْكَ حُدُودُ ٱللَّهِ فَلَا تَقْرَبُوهَا كَذَٰلِكَ يُبَيِّنُ ٱللَّهُ ءَايَٰتِهِۦ لِلنَّاسِ لَعَلَّهُمْ يَتَّقُونَ

Narrated Al-Bara': When the order of compulsory fasting of Ramadan was revealed, the people did not have sexual relations with their wives for the whole month of Ramadan, but some men cheated themselves (by violating that restriction). So Allah revealed: "Allah is aware that you were deceiving yourselves but He accepted your repentance and forgave you.." (2.187). – Sahih al-Bukhari 4508

حَدَّثَنَا عُبَيْدُ اللَّهِ، عَنْ إِسْرَائِيلَ، عَنْ أَبِي إِسْحَاقَ، عَنِ الْبَرَاءِ، وَحَدَّثَنَا أَحْمَدُ بْنُ عُثْمَانَ، حَدَّثَنَا شُرَيْحُ بْنُ مَسْلَمَةَ، قَالَ حَدَّثَنِي إِبْرَاهِيمُ بْنُ يُوسُفَ، عَنْ أَبِيهِ، عَنْ أَبِي إِسْحَاقَ، قَالَ سَمِعْتُ الْبَرَاءَ ـ رضى الله عنه ـ لَمَّا نَزَلَ صَوْمُ رَمَضَانَ كَانُوا لاَ يَقْرَبُونَ النِّسَاءَ رَمَضَانَ كُلَّهُ، وَكَانَ رِجَالٌ يَخُونُونَ أَنْفُسَهُمْ، فَأَنْزَلَ اللَّهُ {عَلِمَ اللَّهُ أَنَّكُمْ كُنْتُمْ تَخْتَانُونَ أَنْفُسَكُمْ فَتَابَ عَلَيْكُمْ وَعَفَا عَنْكُمْ}.

Narrated Ibn `Umar: I heard Allah's Messenger ﷺ saying, "When you see the crescent (of the month of Ramadan), start fasting, and when you see the crescent (of the month of Shawwal), stop fasting; and if the sky is overcast (and you can't see it) then regard the month of Ramadan as of 30 days.". – Sahih al-Bukhari 1900

حَدَّثَنَا يَحْيَى بْنُ بُكَيْرٍ، قَالَ حَدَّثَنِي اللَّيْثُ، عَنْ عُقَيْلٍ، عَنِ ابْنِ شِهَابٍ، قَالَ أَخْبَرَنِي سَالِمٌ، أَنَّ ابْنَ عُمَرَ ـ رضى الله عنهما ـ قَالَ سَمِعْتُ رَسُولَ اللَّهِ صلى الله عليه وسلم يَقُولُ " إِذَا رَأَيْتُمُوهُ فَصُومُوا، وَإِذَا رَأَيْتُمُوهُ فَأَفْطِرُوا، فَإِنْ غُمَّ عَلَيْكُمْ فَاقْدُرُوا لَهُ ". وَقَالَ غَيْرُهُ عَنِ اللَّيْثِ حَدَّثَنِي عُقَيْلٌ وَيُونُسُ لِهِلاَلِ رَمَضَانَ.

Narrated Abu Huraira: I heard Allah's Messenger ﷺ saying regarding Ramadan, "Whoever prayed at night in it (the month of Ramadan) out of sincere Faith and hoping for a reward from Allah, then all his previous sins will be forgiven.". – Sahih al-Bukhari 2008

حَدَّثَنَا يَحْيَى بْنُ بُكَيْرٍ، حَدَّثَنَا اللَّيْثُ، عَنْ عُقَيْلٍ، عَنِ ابْنِ شِهَابٍ، قَالَ أَخْبَرَنِي أَبُو سَلَمَةَ، أَنَّ أَبَا هُرَيْرَةَ ـ رضى الله عنه ـ قَالَ سَمِعْتُ رَسُولَ اللَّهِ صلى الله عليه وسلم يَقُولُ لِرَمَضَانَ " مَنْ قَامَهُ إِيمَانًا وَاحْتِسَابًا غُفِرَ لَهُ مَا تَقَدَّمَ مِنْ ذَنْبِهِ ".

Narrated Abu Salama bin `Abdur-Rahman: I asked Abu Sa`id Al-Khudri, "Did you hear Allah's Messenger ﷺ talking about the Night of Qadr?" He replied in the affirmative and said, "Once we were in I`tikaf with Allah's Messenger ﷺ in the middle ten days of (Ramadan) and we came out of it in the morning of the twentieth, and Allah's Messenger ﷺ delivered a sermon on the 20th (of Ramadan) and said, 'I was informed (of the date) of the Night of Qadr (in my dream) but had forgotten it. So, look for it in the odd nights of the last ten nights of the month of Ramadan. I saw myself prostrating in mud and water on that night (as a sign of the Night of Qadr). So, whoever had been in I`tikaf with Allah's Messenger ﷺ should return for it.' The people returned to the mosque (for I`tikaf). There was no trace of clouds in the sky. But all of a sudden a cloud came and it rained. Then the prayer was established (they stood for the prayer) and Allah's Messenger ﷺ prostrated in mud and water and I saw mud over the forehead and the nose of the Prophet. – Sahih al-Bukhari 2036

حَدَّثَنِي عَبْدُ اللَّهِ بْنُ مُنِيرٍ، سَمِعَ هَارُونَ بْنَ إِسْمَاعِيلَ، حَدَّثَنَا عَلِيُّ بْنُ الْمُبَارَكِ، قَالَ حَدَّثَنِي يَحْيَى بْنُ أَبِي كَثِيرٍ، قَالَ سَمِعْتُ أَبَا سَلَمَةَ بْنَ عَبْدِ الرَّحْمَنِ، قَالَ سَأَلْتُ أَبَا سَعِيدٍ الْخُدْرِيَّ ـ رضى الله عنه ـ قُلْتُ هَلْ سَمِعْتَ رَسُولَ اللَّهِ صلى الله عليه وسلم يَذْكُرُ لَيْلَةَ الْقَدْرِ قَالَ نَعَمِ، اعْتَكَفْنَا مَعَ رَسُولِ اللَّهِ صلى الله عليه وسلم الْعَشْرَ الأَوْسَطَ مِنْ رَمَضَانَ ـ قَالَ ـ فَخَرَجْنَا صَبِيحَةَ عِشْرِينَ، قَالَ فَخَطَبَنَا رَسُولُ اللَّهِ صلى الله عليه وسلم صَبِيحَةَ عِشْرِينَ فَقَالَ " إِنِّي أُرِيتُ لَيْلَةَ الْقَدْرِ، وَإِنِّي نُسِّيتُهَا، فَالْتَمِسُوهَا فِي الْعَشْرِ الأَوَاخِرِ فِي وِتْرٍ، فَإِنِّي رَأَيْتُ أَنِّي أَسْجُدُ فِي مَاءٍ وَطِينٍ، وَمَنْ كَانَ اعْتَكَفَ مَعَ رَسُولِ اللَّهِ صلى الله عليه وسلم فَلْيَرْجِعْ ". فَرَجَعَ النَّاسُ إِلَى الْمَسْجِدِ، وَمَا نَرَى فِي السَّمَاءِ قَزَعَةً ـ قَالَ ـ فَجَاءَتْ سَحَابَةٌ فَمَطَرَتْ، وَأُقِيمَتِ الصَّلاَةُ، فَسَجَدَ رَسُولُ اللَّهِ صلى الله عليه وسلم فِي الطِّينِ وَالْمَاءِ، حَتَّى رَأَيْتُ الطِّينَ فِي أَرْنَبَتِهِ وَجَبْهَتِهِ.

Surely We sent it down on the Night of Determination And what makes you realize what the Night of Determination is The Night of Determination is more charitable (i.e., better) than a thousand months The Angels and the Spirit keep coming down therein, by the permission of their Lord, with (Literally: from) every Command Peace it is, till the rising of the dawn. Surah Al-Qadr 97

إِنَّا أَنزَلْنَاهُ فِي لَيْلَةِ الْقَدْرِ وَمَا أَدْرَاكَ مَا لَيْلَةُ الْقَدْرِ لَيْلَةُ الْقَدْرِ خَيْرٌ مِّنْ أَلْفِ شَهْرٍ تَنَزَّلُ الْمَلَائِكَةُ وَالرُّوحُ فِيهَا بِإِذْنِ رَبِّهِم مِّن كُلِّ أَمْرٍ سَلَامٌ هِيَ حَتَّىٰ مَطْلَعِ الْفَجْرِ

Narrated Ibn 'Abbas: Allah's Messenger ﷺ was the most generous of all the people, and he used to reach the peak in generosity in the month of Ramadan when Gabriel met him. Gabriel used to meet him every night of Ramadan to teach him the Qur'an. Allah's Messenger ﷺ was the most generous person, even more generous than the strong uncontrollable wind (in readiness and haste to do charitable deeds). – Sahih al-Bukhari 6

حَدَّثَنَا عَبْدَانُ، قَالَ أَخْبَرَنَا عَبْدُ اللَّهِ، قَالَ أَخْبَرَنَا يُونُسُ، عَنِ الزُّهْرِيِّ، ح وَحَدَّثَنَا بِشْرُ بْنُ مُحَمَّدٍ، قَالَ أَخْبَرَنَا عَبْدُ اللَّهِ، قَالَ أَخْبَرَنَا يُونُسُ، وَمَعْمَرٌ، عَنِ الزُّهْرِيِّ، نَحْوَهُ قَالَ أَخْبَرَنِي عُبَيْدُ اللَّهِ بْنُ عَبْدِ اللَّهِ، عَنِ ابْنِ عَبَّاسٍ، قَالَ كَانَ رَسُولُ اللَّهِ صلى الله عليه وسلم أَجْوَدَ النَّاسِ، وَكَانَ أَجْوَدُ مَا يَكُونُ فِي رَمَضَانَ حِينَ يَلْقَاهُ جِبْرِيلُ، وَكَانَ يَلْقَاهُ فِي كُلِّ لَيْلَةٍ مِنْ رَمَضَانَ فَيُدَارِسُهُ الْقُرْآنَ، فَلَرَسُولُ اللَّهِ صلى الله عليه وسلم أَجْوَدُ بِالْخَيْرِ مِنَ الرِّيحِ الْمُرْسَلَةِ.

Narrated Ata: I heard Ibn `Abbas saying, "Allah's Messengerﷺ asked an Ansari woman (Ibn `Abbas named her but `Ata' forgot her name), 'What prevented you from performing Hajj with us?' She replied, 'We have a camel and the father of so-and-so and his son (i.e. her husband and her son) rode it and left one camel for us to use for irrigation.' He said (to her), 'Perform `Umra when Ramadan comes, for `Umra in Ramadan is equal to Hajj (in reward),' or said something similar.". – Sahih al-Bukhari 1782

حَدَّثَنَا مُسَدَّدٌ، حَدَّثَنَا يَحْيَى، عَنِ ابْنِ جُرَيْجٍ، عَنْ عَطَاءٍ، قَالَ سَمِعْتُ ابْنَ عَبَّاسٍ ـ رضى الله عنهما ـ يُخْبِرُنَا يَقُولُ قَالَ رَسُولُ اللَّهِ صلى الله عليه وسلم لاِمْرَأَةٍ مِنَ الأَنْصَارِ سَمَّاهَا ابْنُ عَبَّاسٍ، فَنَسِيتُ اسْمَهَا " مَا مَنَعَكِ أَنْ تَحُجِّي مَعَنَا ". قَالَتْ كَانَ لَنَا نَاضِحٌ فَرَكِبَهُ أَبُو فُلاَنٍ وَابْنُهُ ـ لِزَوْجِهَا وَابْنِهَا ـ وَتَرَكَ نَاضِحًا نَنْضَحُ عَلَيْهِ قَالَ " فَإِذَا كَانَ رَمَضَانُ اعْتَمِرِي فِيهِ فَإِنَّ عُمْرَةً فِي رَمَضَانَ حَجَّةٌ ". أَوْ نَحْوًا مِمَّا قَالَ.

Narrated Ibn `Abbas: The Prophetﷺ left Medina (for Mecca) in the company of ten-thousand (Muslim warriors) in (the month of) Ramadan, and that was eight and a half years after his migration to Medina. He and the Muslims who were with him, proceeded on their way to Mecca. He was fasting and they were fasting, but when they reached a place called Al-Kadid which was a place of water between 'Usfan and Kudaid, he broke his fast and so did they. (Az-Zuhri said, "One should take the last action of Allah's Messengerﷺ and leave his early action (while taking a verdict."[33]) – Sahih al-Bukhari 4276

حَدَّثَنِي مَحْمُودٌ، أَخْبَرَنَا عَبْدُ الرَّزَّاقِ، أَخْبَرَنِي مَعْمَرٌ، قَالَ أَخْبَرَنِي الزُّهْرِيُّ، عَنْ عُبَيْدِ اللَّهِ بْنِ عَبْدِ اللَّهِ، عَنِ ابْنِ عَبَّاسٍ ـ رضى الله عنهما ـ أَنَّ النَّبِيَّ صلى الله عليه وسلم خَرَجَ فِي رَمَضَانَ مِنَ الْمَدِينَةِ، وَمَعَهُ عَشَرَةُ آلاَفٍ، وَذَلِكَ عَلَى رَأْسِ ثَمَانِ سِنِينَ وَنِصْفٍ مِنْ مَقْدَمِهِ الْمَدِينَةَ، فَسَارَ هُوَ وَمَنْ مَعَهُ مِنَ الْمُسْلِمِينَ إِلَى مَكَّةَ، يَصُومُ وَيَصُومُونَ حَتَّى بَلَغَ الْكَدِيدَ ـ وَهْوَ مَاءٌ بَيْنَ عُسْفَانَ وَقُدَيْدٍ ـ أَفْطَرَ وَأَفْطَرُوا. قَالَ الزُّهْرِيُّ وَإِنَّمَا يُؤْخَذُ مِنْ أَمْرِ رَسُولِ اللَّهِ صلى الله عليه وسلم الآخِرُ فَالآخِرُ.

Fasting in Shawwal
صيام شوال

Narrated Mutarrif from `Imran Ibn Husain: That the Prophetﷺ asked him (Imran) or asked a man and `Imran was listening, "O Abu so-and-so! Have you fasted the last days of this month?" (The narrator thought that he said, "the month of Ramadan"). The man replied, "No, O Allah's Messengerﷺ ! The Prophetﷺ said to him, "When you finish your fasting (of Ramadan) fast two days (in Shawwal)." Through another series of narrators `Imran said, "The Prophetﷺ said, '(Have you fasted) the last days of Sha'ban?". – Sahih al-Bukhari 1983

حَدَّثَنَا الصَّلْتُ بْنُ مُحَمَّدٍ، حَدَّثَنَا مَهْدِيٌّ، عَنْ غَيْلاَنَ،. وَحَدَّثَنَا أَبُو النُّعْمَانِ، حَدَّثَنَا مَهْدِيُّ بْنُ مَيْمُونٍ، حَدَّثَنَا غَيْلاَنُ بْنُ جَرِيرٍ، عَنْ مُطَرِّفٍ، عَنْ عِمْرَانَ بْنِ حُصَيْنٍ ـ رضى الله عنهما ـ عَنِ النَّبِيِّ صلى الله عليه وسلم. أَنَّهُ سَأَلَهُ ـ أَوْ سَأَلَ رَجُلاً وَعِمْرَانُ يَسْمَعُ ـ فَقَالَ " يَا أَبَا فُلاَنٍ أَمَا صُمْتَ سَرَرَ هَذَا الشَّهْرِ ". قَالَ أَظُنُّهُ قَالَ يَعْنِي رَمَضَانَ. قَالَ الرَّجُلُ لاَ يَا رَسُولَ اللَّهِ. قَالَ " فَإِذَا أَفْطَرْتَ فَصُمْ يَوْمَيْنِ ". لَمْ يَقُلِ الصَّلْتُ أَظُنُّهُ يَعْنِي رَمَضَانَ. قَالَ أَبُو عَبْدِ اللَّهِ وَقَالَ ثَابِتٌ عَنْ مُطَرِّفٍ عَنْ عِمْرَانَ عَنِ النَّبِيِّ صلى الله عليه وسلم " مِنْ سَرَرِ شَعْبَانَ ".

---

[33] Az-Zuhri said, "One should take the last action of Allah's Messengerﷺ and leave his early action (while taking a verdict.")

قَالَ الزُّهْرِيُّ وَإِنَّمَا يُؤْخَذُ مِنْ أَمْرِ رَسُولِ اللَّهِ صلى الله عليه وسلم الآخِرُ فَالآخِرُ.

Abu Ayyub al-Ansari (Allah be pleased with him) reported Allah's Messenger ﷺ as saying: He who observed the fast of Ramadan and then followed it with six (fasts) of Shawwal. It would be as if he fasted perpetually. – Sahih Muslim 1164 a

حَدَّثَنَا يَحْيَى بْنُ أَيُّوبَ، وَقُتَيْبَةُ بْنُ سَعِيدٍ، وَعَلِيُّ بْنُ حُجْرٍ، جَمِيعًا عَنْ إِسْمَاعِيلَ، - قَالَ ابْنُ أَيُّوبَ حَدَّثَنَا إِسْمَاعِيلُ بْنُ جَعْفَرٍ، - أَخْبَرَنِي سَعْدُ بْنُ سَعِيدِ بْنِ قَيْسٍ، عَنْ عُمَرَ، بْنِ ثَابِتِ بْنِ الْحَارِثِ الْخَزْرَجِيِّ عَنْ أَبِي أَيُّوبَ الأَنْصَارِيِّ، - رضى الله عنه – أَنَّهُ حَدَّثَهُ أَنَّ رَسُولَ اللَّهِ صلى الله عليه وسلم قَالَ " مَنْ صَامَ رَمَضَانَ ثُمَّ أَتْبَعَهُ سِتًّا مِنْ شَوَّالٍ كَانَ كَصِيَامِ الدَّهْرِ"

Fasting of Dhul-Hijjah
صيام ذي الحجة

Ibn 'Abbas said that he has been asked regarding Hajj-at-Tamattu' on which he said: "The Muhajirin and the Ansar and the wives of the Prophet ﷺ and we did the same. When we reached Makkah, Allah's Messenger ﷺ said, "Give up your intention of doing the Hajj (at this moment) and perform 'Umra, except the one who had garlanded the Hady." So, we performed Tawaf round the Ka'bah and [Sa'y] between As-safa and Al-MArwa, slept with our wives and wore ordinary (stitched) clothes. The Prophet ﷺ added, "Whoever has garlanded his Hady is not allowed to finish the Ihram till the Hady has reached its destination (has been sacrificed)". Then on the night of Tarwiya (8th Dhul Hijjah, in the afternoon) he ordered us to assume Ihram for Hajj and when we have performed all the ceremonies of Hajj, we came and performed Tawaf round the Ka'bah and (Sa'y) between As-Safa and Al-Marwa, and then our Hajj was complete, and we had to sacrifice a Hady according to the statement of Allah:
"... He must slaughter a Hady such as he can afford, but if he cannot afford it, he should observer Saum (fasts) three days during the Hajj and seven days after his return (to his home)...." (V. 2:196).
And the sacrifice of the sheep is sufficient. So, the Prophet ﷺ and his Companions joined the two religious deeds, (i.e. Hajj and 'Umra) in one year, for Allah revealed (the permissibility) of such practice in His book and in the Sunna (legal ways) of His Prophet ﷺ and rendered it permissible for all the people except those living in Makkah. Allah says: "This is for him whose family is not present at the Al-Masjid-Al-Haram, (i.e. non resident of Makkah)." The months of Hajj which Allah mentioned in His book are: Shawwal, Dhul-Qa'da and Dhul-Hijjah. Whoever performed Hajj-at-Tamattu' in those months, then slaughtering or fasting is compulsory for him. The words: 1. Ar-Rafatha means sexual intercourse. 2. Al-Fasuq means all kinds of sin, and 3. Al-Jidal means to dispute. – Sahih al-Bukhari 1572

وَقَالَ أَبُو كَامِلٍ فُضَيْلُ بْنُ حُسَيْنٍ الْبَصْرِيُّ حَدَّثَنَا أَبُو مَعْشَرٍ، حَدَّثَنَا عُثْمَانُ بْنُ غِيَاثٍ، عَنْ عِكْرِمَةَ، عَنِ ابْنِ عَبَّاسٍ ـ رضى الله عنهما ـ أَنَّهُ سُئِلَ عَنْ مُتْعَةِ الْحَجِّ، فَقَالَ أَهَلَّ الْمُهَاجِرُونَ وَالأَنْصَارُ وَأَزْوَاجُ النَّبِيِّ صلى الله عليه وسلم فِي حَجَّةِ الْوَدَاعِ وَأَهْلَلْنَا، فَلَمَّا قَدِمْنَا مَكَّةَ قَالَ رَسُولُ اللَّهِ صلى الله عليه وسلم " اجْعَلُوا إِهْلاَلَكُمْ بِالْحَجِّ عُمْرَةً إِلاَّ مَنْ قَلَّدَ الْهَدْىَ ". فَطُفْنَا بِالْبَيْتِ وَبِالصَّفَا وَالْمَرْوَةِ وَأَتَيْنَا النِّسَاءَ، وَلَبِسْنَا الثِّيَابَ وَقَالَ " مَنْ قَلَّدَ الْهَدْىَ فَإِنَّهُ لاَ يَحِلُّ لَهُ حَتَّى يَبْلُغَ الْهَدْىُ مَحِلَّهُ ". ثُمَّ أَمَرَنَا عَشِيَّةَ التَّرْوِيَةِ أَنْ نُهِلَّ بِالْحَجِّ، فَإِذَا فَرَغْنَا مِنَ الْمَنَاسِكِ جِئْنَا فَطُفْنَا بِالْبَيْتِ وَبِالصَّفَا وَالْمَرْوَةِ فَقَدْ تَمَّ حَجُّنَا، وَعَلَيْنَا الْهَدْىُ كَمَا قَالَ اللَّهُ تَعَالَى {فَمَا اسْتَيْسَرَ مِنَ الْهَدْىِ فَمَنْ لَمْ يَجِدْ فَصِيَامُ ثَلاَثَةِ أَيَّامٍ فِي الْحَجِّ وَسَبْعَةٍ إِذَا رَجَعْتُمْ} إِلَى أَمْصَارِكُمْ. الشَّاةُ تَجْزِي، فَجَمَعُوا نُسُكَيْنِ فِي عَامٍ بَيْنَ الْحَجِّ وَالْعُمْرَةِ، فَإِنَّ اللَّهَ تَعَالَى أَنْزَلَهُ فِي كِتَابِهِ وَسَنَّهُ نَبِيُّهُ صلى الله عليه وسلم وَأَبَاحَهُ لِلنَّاسِ غَيْرَ أَهْلِ مَكَّةَ، قَالَ اللَّهُ {ذَلِكَ لِمَنْ لَمْ يَكُنْ أَهْلُهُ حَاضِرِي الْمَسْجِدِ الْحَرَامِ} وَأَشْهُرُ الْحَجِّ الَّتِي ذَكَرَ اللَّهُ تَعَالَى شَوَّالٌ وَذُو الْقَعْدَةِ وَذُو الْحَجَّةِ، فَمَنْ تَمَتَّعَ فِي هَذِهِ الأَشْهُرِ فَعَلَيْهِ دَمٌ أَوْ صَوْمٌ، وَالرَّفَثُ الْجِمَاعُ، وَالْفُسُوقُ الْمَعَاصِي، وَالْجِدَالُ الْمِرَاءُ

Narrated Ibn `Abbas: A man who wants to perform the Hajj (from Mecca) can perform the Tawaf around the Ka`ba as long as he is not in the state of Ihram till he assumes the Ihram for Hajj. Then, if he rides and proceeds to `Arafat, he should take a Hadi (i.e. animal for sacrifice), either a camel or a cow or a sheep, whatever he can afford; but if he cannot afford it, he should fast for three days during the Hajj before the day of `Arafat, but if the third day of his fasting happens to be the day of `Arafat (i.e. 9th of Dhul-Hijja) then it is no sin for him (to fast on it). Then he should proceed to `Arafat and stay there from the time of the `Asr prayer till darkness falls. Then the pilgrims should proceed from `Arafat, and when they have departed from it, they reach Jam' (i.e. Al-Muzdalifa) where they ask Allah to help them to be righteous and dutiful to Him, and there they remember Allah greatly or say Takbir (i.e. Allah is Greater) and Tahlil (i.e. None has the right to be worshipped but Allah) repeatedly before dawn breaks. Then, after offering the morning (Fajr) prayer you should pass on (to Mina) for the people used to do so and Allah said:-- "Then depart from the place whence all the people depart. And ask for Allah's Forgiveness. Truly! Allah is Oft-Forgiving, Most Merciful." (2.199) Then you should go on doing so till you throw pebbles over the Jamra. – Sahih al-Bukhari 4521

حَدَّثَنِي مُحَمَّدُ بْنُ أَبِي بَكْرٍ، حَدَّثَنَا فُضَيْلُ بْنُ سُلَيْمَانَ، حَدَّثَنَا مُوسَى بْنُ عُقْبَةَ، أَخْبَرَنِي كُرَيْبٌ، عَنِ ابْنِ عَبَّاسٍ، قَالَ يَطَوَّفُ الرَّجُلُ بِالْبَيْتِ مَا كَانَ حَلاَلاً حَتَّى يُهِلَّ بِالْحَجِّ، فَإِذَا رَكِبَ إِلَى عَرَفَةَ فَمَنْ تَيَسَّرَ لَهُ هَدِيَّةٌ مِنَ الإِبِلِ أَوِ الْبَقَرِ أَوِ الْغَنَمِ، مَا تَيَسَّرَ لَهُ مِنْ ذَلِكَ أَىَّ ذَلِكَ شَاءَ، غَيْرَ إِنْ لَمْ يَتَيَسَّرْ لَهُ فَعَلَيْهِ ثَلاَثَةُ أَيَّامٍ فِي الْحَجِّ، وَذَلِكَ قَبْلَ يَوْمِ عَرَفَةَ، فَإِنْ كَانَ آخِرُ يَوْمٍ مِنَ الأَيَّامِ الثَّلاَثَةِ يَوْمَ عَرَفَةَ فَلاَ جُنَاحَ عَلَيْهِ، ثُمَّ لِيَنْطَلِقْ حَتَّى يَقِفَ بِعَرَفَاتٍ مِنْ صَلاَةِ الْعَصْرِ إِلَى أَنْ يَكُونَ الظَّلاَمُ، ثُمَّ لِيَدْفَعُوا مِنْ عَرَفَاتٍ إِذَا أَفَاضُوا مِنْهَا حَتَّى يَبْلُغُوا جَمْعًا الَّذِي يُتَبَرَّرُ فِيهِ، ثُمَّ لِيَذْكُرُوا اللَّهَ كَثِيرًا، أَوْ أَكْثِرُوا التَّكْبِيرَ وَالتَّهْلِيلَ قَبْلَ أَنْ تُصْبِحُوا ثُمَّ أَفِيضُوا، فَإِنَّ النَّاسَ كَانُوا يُفِيضُونَ، وَقَالَ اللَّهُ تَعَالَى {ثُمَّ أَفِيضُوا مِنْ حَيْثُ أَفَاضَ النَّاسُ وَاسْتَغْفِرُوا اللَّهَ إِنَّ اللَّهَ غَفُورٌ رَحِيمٌ} حَتَّى تَرْمُوا الْجَمْرَةَ.

Narrated Yahya: Hisham said, "My father said that 'Aishah (ra) used to observe Saum (fast) on the days of Mina." His (i.e., Hisham's) father also used to observe Saum on those days. – Sahih al-Bukhari 1996

وَقَالَ لِي مُحَمَّدُ بْنُ الْمُثَنَّى حَدَّثَنَا يَحْيَى، عَنْ هِشَامٍ، قَالَ أَخْبَرَنِي أَبِي كَانَتْ، عَائِشَةُ ـ رضى الله عنها ـ تَصُومُ أَيَّامَ مِنًى، وَكَانَ أَبُوهَا يَصُومُهَا.

It was narrated from Hunaidah bin Khalid, from his wife, from one of the wives of the Prophet, that: The Messenger of Allah used to fast nine days of Dhul-Hijjah, the day of 'Ashura', and three days of each month: The first Monday of the month, and two Thursday. – Sunan an-Nasa'I 2417

أَخْبَرَنِي أَحْمَدُ بْنُ يَحْيَى، عَنْ أَبِي نُعَيْمٍ، قَالَ حَدَّثَنَا أَبُو عَوَانَةَ، عَنِ الْحُرِّ بْنِ الصَّيَّاحِ، عَنْ هُنَيْدَةَ بْنِ خَالِدٍ، عَنِ امْرَأَتِهِ، عَنْ بَعْضِ، أَزْوَاجِ النَّبِيِّ صلى الله عليه وسلم أَنَّ رَسُولَ اللَّهِ صلى الله عليه وسلم كَانَ يَصُومُ تِسْعًا مِنْ ذِي الْحِجَّةِ وَيَوْمَ عَاشُورَاءَ وَثَلاَثَةَ أَيَّامٍ مِنْ كُلِّ شَهْرٍ أَوَّلَ اثْنَيْنِ مِنَ الشَّهْرِ وَخَمِيسَيْنِ

What if fasting happens to be the day of `Arafat
ماذا لو صادف صيام يوم عرفة؟

Narrated Ibn `Abbas: A man who wants to perform the Hajj (from Mecca) can perform the Tawaf around the Ka`ba as long as he is not in the state of Ihram till he assumes the Ihram for Hajj. Then, if he rides and proceeds to `Arafat, he should take a Hadi (i.e. animal for sacrifice), either a camel or a cow or a sheep, whatever he can afford; but if he cannot afford it, he should fast for three days during the Hajj before the day of `Arafat, but if the third day of his fasting happens to be the day of `Arafat (i.e. 9th of Dhul-Hijja) then it is no sin for him (to fast on it). Then he should proceed to `Arafat and stay there from the time of the `Asr prayer till darkness falls. Then the pilgrims should proceed from `Arafat, and when they have departed from it, they reach Jam' (i.e. Al-Muzdalifa) where they ask Allah to help them to be righteous and dutiful to Him, and there they remember Allah greatly or say Takbir (i.e. Allah is Greater) and Tahlil (i.e. None has the right to be worshipped but Allah) repeatedly before dawn breaks. Then, after offering the morning (Fajr) prayer you should pass on (to Mina) for the people used to do so and Allah said:-- "Then depart from the place whence all the people depart. And ask for Allah's Forgiveness. Truly! Allah is Oft-Forgiving, Most Merciful." (2.199) Then you should go on doing so till you throw pebbles over the Jamra. – Sahih al-Bukhari 4521

حَدَّثَنِي مُحَمَّدُ بْنُ أَبِي بَكْرٍ، حَدَّثَنَا فُضَيْلُ بْنُ سُلَيْمَانَ، حَدَّثَنَا مُوسَى بْنُ عُقْبَةَ، أَخْبَرَنِي كُرَيْبٌ، عَنِ ابْنِ عَبَّاسٍ، قَالَ يَطَوَّفُ الرَّجُلُ بِالْبَيْتِ مَا كَانَ حَلاَلاً حَتَّى يُهِلَّ بِالْحَجِّ، فَإِذَا رَكِبَ إِلَى عَرَفَةَ فَمَنْ تَيَسَّرَ لَهُ هَدِيَّةٌ مِنَ الإِبِلِ أَوِ الْبَقَرِ أَوِ الْغَنَمِ، مَا تَيَسَّرَ لَهُ مِنْ ذَلِكَ أَىَّ ذَلِكَ شَاءَ، غَيْرَ إِنْ لَمْ يَتَيَسَّرْ لَهُ فَعَلَيْهِ ثَلاَثَةُ أَيَّامٍ فِي الْحَجِّ، وَذَلِكَ قَبْلَ يَوْمِ عَرَفَةَ، فَإِنْ كَانَ آخِرُ يَوْمٍ مِنَ الأَيَّامِ الثَّلاَثَةِ يَوْمَ عَرَفَةَ فَلاَ جُنَاحَ عَلَيْهِ، ثُمَّ لِيَنْطَلِقْ حَتَّى يَقِفَ بِعَرَفَاتٍ مِنْ صَلاَةِ الْعَصْرِ إِلَى أَنْ يَكُونَ الظَّلاَمُ، ثُمَّ لِيَدْفَعُوا مِنْ عَرَفَاتٍ إِذَا أَفَاضُوا مِنْهَا حَتَّى يَبْلُغُوا جَمْعًا الَّذِي يُتَبَرَّرُ فِيهِ، ثُمَّ لِيَذْكُرُوا اللَّهَ كَثِيرًا، أَوْ أَكْثِرُوا التَّكْبِيرَ وَالتَّهْلِيلَ قَبْلَ أَنْ تُصْبِحُوا ثُمَّ أَفِيضُوا، فَإِنَّ النَّاسَ كَانُوا يُفِيضُونَ، وَقَالَ اللَّهُ تَعَالَى {ثُمَّ أَفِيضُوا مِنْ حَيْثُ أَفَاضَ النَّاسُ وَاسْتَغْفِرُوا اللَّهَ إِنَّ اللَّهَ غَفُورٌ رَحِيمٌ} حَتَّى تَرْمُوا الْجَمْرَةَ.

Narrated `Aisha: On the 1st of Dhul-Hijja we set out with the intention of performing Hajj. Allah's Messenger ﷺ said, "Any one who likes to assume the Ihram for `Umra he can do so. Had I not brought the Hadi with me, I would have assumed the Ihram for `Umra. "Some of us assumed the Ihram for `Umra while the others assumed the Ihram for Hajj. I was one of those who assumed the Ihram for `Umra. I got menses and kept on menstruating until the day of `Arafat and complained of that to the Prophet. He told me to postpone my `Umra, undo and comb my hair, and to assume the Ihram of Hajj and I did so. On the night of Hasba, he sent my brother `Abdur-Rahman bin Abi Bakr with me to at-Tan`im, where I assumed the Ihram for `Umra in lieu of the previous one. Hisham said, "For that (`Umra) no Hadi, fasting or alms were required. – Sahih al-Bukhari 317

حَدَّثَنَا عُبَيْدُ بْنُ إِسْمَاعِيلَ، قَالَ حَدَّثَنَا أَبُو أُسَامَةَ، عَنْ هِشَامٍ، عَنْ أَبِيهِ، عَنْ عَائِشَةَ، قَالَتْ خَرَجْنَا مُوَافِينَ لِهِلاَلِ ذِي الْحِجَّةِ، فَقَالَ رَسُولُ اللَّهِ صلى الله عليه وسلم " مَنْ أَحَبَّ أَنْ يُهِلَّ بِعُمْرَةٍ فَلْيُهْلِلْ، فَإِنِّي لَوْلاَ أَنِّي أَهْدَيْتُ لأَهْلَلْتُ بِعُمْرَةٍ ". فَأَهَلَّ بَعْضُهُمْ بِعُمْرَةٍ، وَأَهَلَّ بَعْضُهُمْ بِحَجٍّ، وَكُنْتُ أَنَا مِمَّنْ أَهَلَّ بِعُمْرَةٍ، فَأَدْرَكَنِي يَوْمُ عَرَفَةَ وَأَنَا حَائِضٌ، فَشَكَوْتُ إِلَى النَّبِيِّ صلى الله عليه وسلم فَقَالَ " دَعِي عُمْرَتَكِ، وَانْقُضِي رَأْسَكِ وَامْتَشِطِي، وَأَهِلِّي بِحَجٍّ ". فَفَعَلْتُ حَتَّى إِذَا كَانَ لَيْلَةُ الْحَصْبَةِ أَرْسَلَ مَعِي أَخِي عَبْدَ الرَّحْمَنِ بْنَ أَبِي بَكْرٍ، فَخَرَجْتُ إِلَى التَّنْعِيمِ، فَأَهْلَلْتُ بِعُمْرَةٍ مَكَانَ عُمْرَتِي. قَالَ هِشَامٌ وَلَمْ يَكُنْ فِي شَىْءٍ مِنْ ذَلِكَ هَدْىٌ وَلاَ صَوْمٌ وَلاَ صَدَقَةٌ

Narrated Um Al-Fadl bint Al-Harith: "While the people were with me on the day of `Arafat they differed as to whether the Prophet ﷺ was fasting or not; some said that he was fasting while others said that he was not fasting. So, I sent to him a bowl full of milk while he was riding over his camel and he drank it.". – Sahih al-Bukhari 1988

حَدَّثَنَا مُسَدَّدٌ، حَدَّثَنَا يَحْيَى، عَنْ مَالِكٍ، قَالَ حَدَّثَنِي سَالِمٌ، قَالَ حَدَّثَنِي عُمَيْرٌ، مَوْلَى أُمِّ الْفَضْلِ أَنَّ أُمَّ، الْفَضْلِ حَدَّثَتْهُ ح وَحَدَّثَنَا عَبْدُ اللَّهِ بْنُ يُوسُفَ أَخْبَرَنَا مَالِكٌ عَنْ أَبِي النَّضْرِ مَوْلَى عُمَرَ بْنِ عُبَيْدِ اللَّهِ عَنْ عُمَيْرٍ مَوْلَى عَبْدِ اللَّهِ بْنِ الْعَبَّاسِ عَنْ أُمِّ الْفَضْلِ بِنْتِ الْحَارِثِ أَنَّ نَاسًا تَمَارَوْا عِنْدَهَا يَوْمَ عَرَفَةَ فِي صَوْمِ النَّبِيِّ صلى الله عليه وسلم فَقَالَ بَعْضُهُمْ هُوَ صَائِمٌ. وَقَالَ بَعْضُهُمْ لَيْسَ بِصَائِمٍ. فَأَرْسَلَتْ إِلَيْهِ بِقَدَحِ لَبَنٍ وَهْوَ وَاقِفٌ عَلَى بَعِيرِهِ فَشَرِبَهُ

Fasting on the day of 'Ashura'
صيام يوم عاشوراء

Narrated Ibn `Abbas: When the Prophet ﷺ arrived at Medina he found that the Jews observed fast on the day of 'Ashura'. They were asked the reason for the fast. They replied, "This is the day when Allah caused Moses and the children of Israel to have victory over Pharaoh, so we fast on this day as a sign of glorifying it." Allah's Messenger ﷺ said, "We are closer to Moses than you." Then he ordered that fasting on this day should be observed. – Sahih al-Bukhari 3943

حَدَّثَنَا زِيَادُ بْنُ أَيُّوبَ، حَدَّثَنَا هُشَيْمٌ، حَدَّثَنَا أَبُو بِشْرٍ، عَنْ سَعِيدِ بْنِ جُبَيْرٍ، عَنِ ابْنِ عَبَّاسٍ ـ رضى الله عنهما ـ قَالَ لَمَّا قَدِمَ النَّبِيُّ صلى الله عليه وسلم الْمَدِينَةَ وَجَدَ الْيَهُودَ يَصُومُونَ عَاشُورَاءَ، فَسُئِلُوا عَنْ ذَلِكَ، فَقَالُوا هَذَا الْيَوْمُ الَّذِي أَظْفَرَ اللَّهُ فِيهِ مُوسَى وَبَنِي إِسْرَائِيلَ عَلَى فِرْعَوْنَ، وَنَحْنُ نَصُومُهُ تَعْظِيمًا لَهُ، فَقَالَ رَسُولُ اللَّهِ صلى الله عليه وسلم " نَحْنُ أَوْلَى بِمُوسَى مِنْكُمْ ". ثُمَّ أَمَرَ بِصَوْمِهِ.

Narrated Ibn `Abbas: When the Prophet ﷺ arrived at Medina, the Jews were observing the fast on 'Ashura' (10th of Muharram) and they said, "This is the day when Moses became victorious over Pharaoh," On that, the Prophet ﷺ said to his companions, "You (Muslims) have more right to celebrate Moses' victory than they have, so observe the fast on this day.". – Sahih al-Bukhari 4680

حَدَّثَنِي مُحَمَّدُ بْنُ بَشَّارٍ، حَدَّثَنَا غُنْدَرٌ، حَدَّثَنَا شُعْبَةُ، عَنْ أَبِي بِشْرٍ، عَنْ سَعِيدِ بْنِ جُبَيْرٍ، عَنِ ابْنِ عَبَّاسٍ، قَالَ قَدِمَ النَّبِيُّ صلى الله عليه وسلم الْمَدِينَةَ وَالْيَهُودُ تَصُومُ عَاشُورَاءَ فَقَالُوا هَذَا يَوْمٌ ظَهَرَ فِيهِ مُوسَى عَلَى فِرْعَوْنَ. فَقَالَ النَّبِيُّ صلى الله عليه وسلم لأَصْحَابِهِ " أَنْتُمْ أَحَقُّ بِمُوسَى مِنْهُمْ، فَصُومُوا ".

Narrated `Aisha: The people used to fast on 'Ashura (the tenth day of the month of Muharram) before the fasting of Ramadan was made obligatory. And on that day the Ka`ba used to be covered with a cover. When Allah made the fasting of the month of Ramadan compulsory, Allah's Messenger ﷺ said, "Whoever wishes to fast (on the day of 'Ashura') may do so; and whoever wishes to leave it can do so.". – Sahih al-Bukhari 1592

حَدَّثَنَا يَحْيَى بْنُ بُكَيْرٍ، حَدَّثَنَا اللَّيْثُ، عَنْ عُقَيْلٍ، عَنِ ابْنِ شِهَابٍ، عَنْ عُرْوَةَ، عَنْ عَائِشَةَ ـ رضى الله عنها ـ. وَحَدَّثَنِي مُحَمَّدُ بْنُ مُقَاتِلٍ، قَالَ أَخْبَرَنِي عَبْدُ اللَّهِ ـ هُوَ ابْنُ الْمُبَارَكِ ـ قَالَ أَخْبَرَنَا مُحَمَّدُ بْنُ أَبِي حَفْصَةَ، عَنِ الزُّهْرِيِّ، عَنْ عُرْوَةَ، عَنْ عَائِشَةَ ـ رضى الله عنها ـ قَالَتْ كَانُوا يَصُومُونَ عَاشُورَاءَ قَبْلَ أَنْ يُفْرَضَ رَمَضَانُ، وَكَانَ يَوْمًا تُسْتَرُ فِيهِ الْكَعْبَةُ، فَلَمَّا فَرَضَ اللَّهُ رَمَضَانَ قَالَ رَسُولُ اللَّهِ صلى الله عليه وسلم " مَنْ شَاءَ أَنْ يَصُومَهُ فَلْيَصُمْهُ، وَمَنْ شَاءَ أَنْ يَتْرُكَهُ فَلْيَتْرُكْهُ ".

Misunderstanding of Ayyam al-Beed

سوء فهم أيام البيض

Abu Dharr (May Allah be pleased with him) reported: The Messenger of Allah ﷺ said, "If you want to observe Saum on three days in a month, then fast on the thirteenth, fourteenth and fifteenth of the (lunar) month."
[At-Tirmidhi]. – Riyad as-Salihin 1262

وعن أبي ذر رضي الله عنه، قال: قال رسول الله صلى الله عليه وسلم: "إذا صمت من الشهر ثلاثًا، فصم ثلاث عشرة، وأربع عشرة وخمس عشرة" رواه الترمذي وقال: حديث حسن.

Mu'adhah (al-'Adawiyyah) said: I asked 'Aishah: Would the Messenger of Allah ﷺ fast three days every month ? She replied: Yes. I asked: Which days in the month he used to fast ? She replied: He did not care which days of the month he fasted. – Sunan Abi Dawud 2453

حَدَّثَنَا مُسَدَّدٌ، حَدَّثَنَا عَبْدُ الْوَارِثِ، عَنْ يَزِيدَ الرِّشْكِ، عَنْ مُعَاذَةَ، قَالَتْ قُلْتُ لِعَائِشَةَ أَكَانَ رَسُولُ اللَّهِ صلى الله عليه وسلم يَصُومُ مِنْ كُلِّ شَهْرٍ ثَلاَثَةَ أَيَّامٍ قَالَتْ نَعَمْ . قُلْتُ مِنْ أَىِّ شَهْرٍ كَانَ يَصُومُ قَالَتْ مَا كَانَ يُبَالِي مِنْ أَىِّ أَيَّامِ الشَّهْرِ كَانَ يَصُومُ

Mu'adha al-'Adawiyya reported that she asked 'A'isha, the wife of the Messenger of Allah ﷺ, whether the Messenger of Allah ﷺ observed fasts for three days during every month. She said: Yes I said to her: Which were (the particular) days of the month on which he observed fast? She said: He was not particular about the days of the month on which to observe fast. – Sahih Muslim 1160

حَدَّثَنَا شَيْبَانُ بْنُ فَرُّوخَ، حَدَّثَنَا عَبْدُ الْوَارِثِ، عَنْ يَزِيدَ الرِّشْكِ، قَالَ حَدَّثَتْنِي مُعَاذَةُ، الْعَدَوِيَّةُ أَنَّهَا سَأَلَتْ عَائِشَةَ زَوْجَ النَّبِيِّ صلى الله عليه وسلم أَكَانَ رَسُولُ اللَّهِ صلى الله عليه وسلم يَصُومُ مِنْ كُلِّ شَهْرٍ ثَلاَثَةَ أَيَّامٍ قَالَتْ نَعَمْ . فَقُلْتُ لَهَا مِنْ أَىِّ أَيَّامِ الشَّهْرِ كَانَ يَصُومُ قَالَتْ لَمْ يَكُنْ يُبَالِي مِنْ أَىِّ أَيَّامِ الشَّهْرِ يَصُومُ .

But we (Imam Muslim) did not mention Thursday for we found it as an error (in reporting)

فَسَكَتْنَا عَنْ ذِكْرِ الْخَمِيسِ لَمَّا نَرَاهُ وَهْمًا

It was narrated that Umm Salamah said: "The Messenger of Allah used to enjoin fasting three days: The first Thursday, and Monday and Monday." – Sunan an-Nasa'I 2419

أَخْبَرَنَا إِبْرَاهِيمُ بْنُ سَعِيدٍ الْجَوْهَرِيُّ، قَالَ حَدَّثَنَا مُحَمَّدُ بْنُ فُضَيْلٍ، عَنِ الْحَسَنِ بْنِ عُبَيْدِ اللَّهِ، عَنْ هُنَيْدَةَ الْخُزَاعِيِّ، عَنْ أُمِّهِ، عَنْ أُمِّ سَلَمَةَ، قَالَتْ كَانَ رَسُولُ اللَّهِ صلى الله عليه وسلم يَأْمُرُ بِصِيَامِ ثَلاَثَةِ أَيَّامٍ أَوَّلِ خَمِيسٍ وَالاِثْنَيْنِ وَالاِثْنَيْنِ .

Abu Qatada al-Ansari (Allah be pleased with him) reported that the Messenger of Allahﷺ was asked about his fasting. The Messenger of Allahﷺ felt annoyed. Thereupon 'Umar (Allah be pleased with him) said: We are pleased with Allah as the Lord, with Islam as our Code of Life, with Muhammad as the Messenger and with our pledge (to you for willing and cheerful submission) as a (sacred) commitment. He was then asked about perpetual fasting, whereupon he said: He neither fasted nor did he break it, or he did not fast and he did not break it. He was then asked about fasting for two days and breaking one day. He (the Holy Prophet) said: And who has strength enough to do it? He was asked about fasting for a day and breaking for two days, whereupon he said: May Allah bestow upon us strength to do it. He was then asked about fasting for a day and breaking on the other, whereupon he said: That is the fasting of my brother David (peace be upon him). He was then asked about fasting on Monday, whereupon he said: It was the day on which I was born. On which I was commissioned with prophethood or revelation was sent to me, (and he further) said: Three days' fasting every month and of the whole of Ramadan every year is a perpetual fast. He was asked about fasting on the day of 'Arafa (9th of Dhu'l-Hijja), whereupon he said: It expiates the sins of the preceding year and the coming year. He was asked about fasting on the day of 'Ashura (10th of Muharram), whereupon be said: It expiates the sins of the preceding year. (Imam Muslim said that in this hadith there is a) narration of Imam Shu'ba that he was asked about fasting on Monday and Thursday, but we (Imam Muslim) did not mention Thursday for we found it as an error (in reporting). [34] – Sahih Muslim 1162 b

حَدَّثَنَا مُحَمَّدُ بْنُ الْمُثَنَّى، وَمُحَمَّدُ بْنُ بَشَّارٍ، - وَاللَّفْظُ لاِبْنِ الْمُثَنَّى – قَالاَ حَدَّثَنَا مُحَمَّدُ بْنُ جَعْفَرٍ، حَدَّثَنَا شُعْبَةُ، عَنْ غَيْلاَنَ بْنِ جَرِيرٍ، سَمِعَ عَبْدَ اللَّهِ بْنَ مَعْبَدٍ الزِّمَّانِيَّ، عَنْ أَبِي قَتَادَةَ الأَنْصَارِيِّ، رضى الله عنه أَنَّ رَسُولَ اللَّهِ صلى الله عليه وسلم سُئِلَ عَنْ صَوْمِهِ قَالَ فَغَضِبَ رَسُولُ اللَّهِ صلى الله عليه وسلم فَقَالَ عُمَرُ رضى الله عنه رَضِينَا بِاللَّهِ رَبًّا وَبِالإِسْلاَمِ دِينًا وَبِمُحَمَّدٍ رَسُولاً وَبِبَيْعَتِنَا بَيْعَةً . قَالَ فَسُئِلَ عَنْ صِيَامِ الدَّهْرِ فَقَالَ " لاَ صَامَ وَلاَ أَفْطَرَ " . أَوْ " مَا صَامَ وَمَا أَفْطَرَ " . قَالَ فَسُئِلَ عَنْ صَوْمِ يَوْمَيْنِ وَإِفْطَارِ يَوْمٍ قَالَ " وَمَنْ يُطِيقُ ذَلِكَ " . قَالَ وَسُئِلَ عَنْ صَوْمِ يَوْمٍ وَإِفْطَارِ يَوْمَيْنِ قَالَ " لَيْتَ أَنَّ اللَّهَ قَوَّانَا لِذَلِكَ " . قَالَ وَسُئِلَ عَنْ صَوْمِ يَوْمٍ وَإِفْطَارِ يَوْمٍ قَالَ " ذَاكَ صَوْمُ أَخِي دَاوُدَ عَلَيْهِ السَّلاَمُ " . قَالَ وَسُئِلَ عَنْ صَوْمِ يَوْمِ الاِثْنَيْنِ قَالَ " ذَاكَ يَوْمٌ وُلِدْتُ فِيهِ وَيَوْمٌ بُعِثْتُ أَوْ أُنْزِلَ عَلَىَّ فِيهِ " . قَالَ فَقَالَ " صَوْمُ ثَلاَثَةٍ مِنْ كُلِّ شَهْرٍ وَرَمَضَانَ إِلَى رَمَضَانَ صَوْمُ الدَّهْرِ " . قَالَ وَسُئِلَ عَنْ صَوْمِ يَوْمِ عَرَفَةَ فَقَالَ " يُكَفِّرُ السَّنَةَ الْمَاضِيَةَ وَالْبَاقِيَةَ " . قَالَ وَسُئِلَ عَنْ صَوْمِ يَوْمِ عَاشُورَاءَ فَقَالَ " يُكَفِّرُ السَّنَةَ الْمَاضِيَةَ " . وَفِي هَذَا الْحَدِيثِ مِنْ رِوَايَةِ شُعْبَةَ قَالَ وَسُئِلَ عَنْ صَوْمِ يَوْمِ الاِثْنَيْنِ وَالْخَمِيسِ فَسَكَتْنَا عَنْ ذِكْرِ الْخَمِيسِ لَمَّا نَرَاهُ وَهْمًا

---

[34] Ilm al-hadith

This process involves examining the chain of narrators (isnad), the content of the hadith (matn), and other factors to determine the hadith's classification.

Iftar
إفطار

Narrated Sahl bin Sa`d: Allah's Messenger ﷺ said, "The people will remain on the right path as long as they hasten the breaking of the fast.". – Sahih al-Bukhari 1957
حَدَّثَنَا عَبْدُ اللَّهِ بْنُ يُوسُفَ، أَخْبَرَنَا مَالِكٌ، عَنْ أَبِي حَازِمٍ، عَنْ سَهْلِ بْنِ سَعْدٍ، أَنَّ رَسُولَ اللَّهِ صلى الله عليه وسلم قَالَ " لاَ يَزَالُ النَّاسُ بِخَيْرٍ مَا عَجَّلُوا الْفِطْرَ "

It was narrated that Abu 'Atiyyah said: "I said to 'Aishah: 'Among us there are two men, one of whom hastens Iftar and delays Sahur, and the other delays Iftar and hastens Sahur.' She said; 'Which of them is the one who hastens Iftar and delays Sahur?' I said: "Abdullah bin Masud.' She said; 'This is what the Messenger of Allah used to do."'. – Sunan an-Nasa'I 2159
أَخْبَرَنَا مُحَمَّدُ بْنُ بَشَّارٍ، قَالَ حَدَّثَنَا عَبْدُ الرَّحْمَنِ، قَالَ حَدَّثَنَا سُفْيَانُ، عَنِ الأَعْمَشِ، عَنْ خَيْثَمَةَ، عَنْ أَبِي عَطِيَّةَ، قَالَ قُلْتُ لِعَائِشَةَ فِينَا رَجُلاَنِ أَحَدُهُمَا يُعَجِّلُ الإِفْطَارَ وَيُؤَخِّرُ السُّحُورَ وَالآخَرُ يُؤَخِّرُ الْفِطْرَ وَيُعَجِّلُ السُّحُورَ . قَالَتْ أَيُّهُمَا الَّذِي يُعَجِّلُ الإِفْطَارَ وَيُؤَخِّرُ السُّحُورَ قُلْتُ عَبْدُ اللَّهِ بْنُ مَسْعُودٍ . قَالَتْ هَكَذَا كَانَ رَسُولُ اللَّهِ صلى الله عليه وسلم يَصْنَعُ.

Anas bin Malik narrated: "The Messenger of Allah would break the fast with fresh dates before performing Salat. If there were no fresh dates then (he would break the fast) with dried dates, and if there were no dried dates then he would take a few sips of water.". – Jami` at-Tirmidhi 696
حَدَّثَنَا مُحَمَّدُ بْنُ رَافِعٍ، حَدَّثَنَا عَبْدُ الرَّزَّاقِ، أَخْبَرَنَا جَعْفَرُ بْنُ سُلَيْمَانَ، عَنْ ثَابِتٍ، عَنْ أَنَسِ بْنِ مَالِكٍ، قَالَ " كَانَ النَّبِيُّ صلى الله عليه وسلم يُفْطِرُ قَبْلَ أَنْ يُصَلِّيَ عَلَى رُطَبَاتٍ فَإِنْ لَمْ تَكُنْ رُطَبَاتٌ فَتُمَيْرَاتٍ فَإِنْ لَمْ تَكُنْ تُمَيْرَاتٌ حَسَا حَسَوَاتٍ مِنْ مَاءٍ " . قَالَ أَبُو عِيسَى هَذَا حَدِيثٌ حَسَنٌ غَرِيبٌ . قَالَ أَبُو عِيسَى وَرُوِيَ أَنَّ رَسُولَ اللَّهِ صلى الله عليه وسلم كَانَ يُفْطِرُ فِي الشِّتَاءِ عَلَى تَمَرَاتٍ وَفِي الصَّيْفِ عَلَى الْمَاءِ

Suhur
السحور

Narrated Anas: Zaid bin Thabit said, "We took the "Suhur" (the meal taken before dawn while fasting is observed) with the Prophet ﷺ and then stood up for the (morning) prayer." I asked him how long the interval between the two (Suhur and prayer) was. He replied, 'The interval between the two was just sufficient to recite fifty to Sixth 'Ayat.". – Sahih al-Bukhari 575
حَدَّثَنَا عَمْرُو بْنُ عَاصِمٍ، قَالَ حَدَّثَنَا هَمَّامٌ، عَنْ قَتَادَةَ، عَنْ أَنَسٍ، أَنَّ زَيْدَ بْنَ ثَابِتٍ، حَدَّثَهُ أَنَّهُمْ، تَسَحَّرُوا مَعَ النَّبِيِّ صلى الله عليه وسلم ثُمَّ قَامُوا إِلَى الصَّلاَةِ. قُلْتُ كَمْ بَيْنَهُمَا قَالَ قَدْرُ خَمْسِينَ أَوْ سِتِّينَ - يَعْنِي آيَةً - ح.

Narrated Qatada: Anas bin Malik said, "The Prophet (p.b.u.h) and Zaid bin Thabit took their Suhur together. When they finished it, the Prophet ﷺ stood for the (Fajr) prayer and offered it." We asked Anas, "What was the interval between their finishing the Suhur and the starting of the morning prayer?" Anas replied, "It was equal to the time taken by a person in reciting fifty verses of the Qur'an.". – Sahih al-Bukhari 1134

حَدَّثَنَا يَعْقُوبُ بْنُ إِبْرَاهِيمَ، قَالَ حَدَّثَنَا رَوْحٌ، قَالَ حَدَّثَنَا سَعِيدٌ، عَنْ قَتَادَةَ، عَنْ أَنَسِ بْنِ مَالِكٍ ـ رضى الله عنه ـ أَنَّ نَبِيَّ اللَّهِ صلى الله عليه وسلم وَزَيْدَ بْنَ ثَابِتٍ ـ رضى الله عنه ـ تَسَحَّرَا، فَلَمَّا فَرَغَا مِنْ سَحُورِهِمَا قَامَ نَبِيُّ اللَّهِ صلى الله عليه وسلم إِلَى الصَّلاَةِ فَصَلَّى. قُلْنَا لأَنَسٍ كَمْ كَانَ بَيْنَ فَرَاغِهِمَا مِنْ سَحُورِهِمَا وَدُخُولِهِمَا فِي الصَّلاَةِ قَالَ كَقَدْرِ مَا يَقْرَأُ الرَّجُلُ خَمْسِينَ آيَةً

Narrated Ibn Mas`ud: Allah's Messenger ﷺ said, "The (call for prayer) Adhan of Bilal should not stop anyone of you from taking his Suhur for he pronounces the Adhan in order that whoever among you is praying the night prayer, may return (to eat his Suhur) and whoever among you is sleeping, may get up, for it is not yet dawn (when it is like this)." (Yahya, the sub-narrator stretched his two index fingers side ways). – Sahih al-Bukhari 7247

حَدَّثَنَا مُسَدَّدٌ، عَنْ يَحْيَى، عَنِ التَّيْمِيِّ، عَنْ أَبِي عُثْمَانَ، عَنِ ابْنِ مَسْعُودٍ، قَالَ قَالَ رَسُولُ اللَّهِ صلى الله عليه وسلم " لاَ يَمْنَعَنَّ أَحَدَكُمْ أَذَانُ بِلاَلٍ مِنْ سَحُورِهِ، فَإِنَّهُ يُؤَذِّنُ ـ أَوْ قَالَ يُنَادِي ـ لِيَرْجِعَ قَائِمَكُمْ، وَيُنَبِّهَ نَائِمَكُمْ، وَلَيْسَ الْفَجْرُ أَنْ يَقُولَ هَكَذَا ـ وَجَمَعَ يَحْيَى كَفَّيْهِ ـ حَتَّى يَقُولَ هَكَذَا ". وَمَدَّ يَحْيَى إِصْبَعَيْهِ السَّبَّابَتَيْنِ.

Narrated `Aisha: The Prophet ﷺ said, "Bilal pronounces the Adhan at night, so eat and drink (Suhur) till Ibn Um Maktum pronounces the Adhan.". – Sahih al-Bukhari 622, 623

حَدَّثَنَا إِسْحَاقُ، قَالَ أَخْبَرَنَا أَبُو أُسَامَةَ، قَالَ عُبَيْدُ اللَّهِ حَدَّثَنَا عَنِ الْقَاسِمِ بْنِ مُحَمَّدٍ، عَنْ عَائِشَةَ. وَعَنْ نَافِعٍ، عَنِ ابْنِ عُمَرَ، أَنَّ رَسُولَ اللَّهِ صلى الله عليه وسلم قَالَ. ح وَحَدَّثَنِي يُوسُفُ بْنُ عِيسَى الْمَرْوَزِيُّ، قَالَ حَدَّثَنَا الْفَضْلُ، قَالَ حَدَّثَنَا عُبَيْدُ اللَّهِ بْنُ عُمَرَ، عَنِ الْقَاسِمِ بْنِ مُحَمَّدٍ، عَنْ عَائِشَةَ، عَنِ النَّبِيِّ صلى الله عليه وسلم أَنَّهُ قَالَ " إِنَّ بِلاَلاً يُؤَذِّنُ بِلَيْلٍ، فَكُلُوا وَاشْرَبُوا حَتَّى يُؤَذِّنَ ابْنُ أُمِّ مَكْتُومٍ ".

Narrated Salim bin `Abdullah: My father said that Allah s Apostle said, "Bilal pronounces 'Adhan at night, so keep on eating and drinking (Suhur) till Ibn Um Maktum pronounces Adhan." Salim added, "He was a blind man who would not pronounce the Adhan unless he was told that the day had dawned.". – Sahih al-Bukhari 617

حَدَّثَنَا عَبْدُ اللَّهِ بْنُ مَسْلَمَةَ، عَنْ مَالِكٍ، عَنِ ابْنِ شِهَابٍ، عَنْ سَالِمِ بْنِ عَبْدِ اللَّهِ، عَنْ أَبِيهِ، أَنَّ رَسُولَ اللَّهِ صلى الله عليه وسلم قَالَ " إِنَّ بِلاَلاً يُؤَذِّنُ بِلَيْلٍ، فَكُلُوا وَاشْرَبُوا حَتَّى يُنَادِيَ ابْنُ أُمِّ مَكْتُومٍ ". ثُمَّ قَالَ وَكَانَ رَجُلاً أَعْمَى لاَ يُنَادِي حَتَّى يُقَالَ لَهُ أَصْبَحْتَ أَصْبَحْتَ

'Narrated Abu Sa`id: That he had heard the Prophet ﷺ saying, "Do not fast continuously (practice Al-Wisal), and if you intend to lengthen your fast, then carry it on only till the Suhur (before the following dawn)." The people said to him, "But you practice (Al-Wisal), O Allah's Messenger ﷺ ! He replied, "I am not similar to you, for during my sleep I have One Who makes me eat and drink.". – Sahih al-Bukhari 1963

حَدَّثَنَا عَبْدُ اللَّهِ بْنُ يُوسُفَ، حَدَّثَنَا اللَّيْثُ، حَدَّثَنِي ابْنُ الْهَادِ، عَنْ عَبْدِ اللَّهِ بْنِ خَبَّابٍ، عَنْ أَبِي سَعِيدٍ ـ رضى الله عنه ـ أَنَّهُ سَمِعَ النَّبِيَّ صلى الله عليه وسلم يَقُولُ " لاَ تُوَاصِلُوا، فَأَيُّكُمْ إِذَا أَرَادَ أَنْ يُوَاصِلَ فَلْيُوَاصِلْ حَتَّى السَّحَرِ ". قَالُوا فَإِنَّكَ تُوَاصِلُ يَا رَسُولَ اللَّهِ. قَالَ " إِنِّي لَسْتُ كَهَيْئَتِكُمْ، إِنِّي أَبِيتُ لِي مُطْعِمٌ يُطْعِمُنِي وَسَاقٍ يَسْقِينِ ".

The Book of
Zakat
زكاة

Those who do not pay alms-tax and are in denial of the Hereafter. – Surah Al-Fussilat 41:7
ٱلَّذِينَ لَا يُؤْتُونَ ٱلزَّكَوٰةَ وَهُم بِٱلْـَٔاخِرَةِ هُمْ كَـٰفِرُونَ

Here you are, being invited to donate ˹a little˺ in the cause of Allah. Still some of you withhold. And whoever does so, it is only to their own loss. For Allah is the Self-Sufficient, whereas you stand in need ˹of Him˺. If you ˹still˺ turn away, He will replace you with another people. And they will not be like you Surah Muhammad 47:38
هَـٰٓأَنتُمْ هَـٰٓؤُلَآءِ تُدْعَوْنَ لِتُنفِقُوا۟ فِى سَبِيلِ ٱللَّهِ فَمِنكُم مَّن يَبْخَلُ ۖ وَمَن يَبْخَلْ فَإِنَّمَا يَبْخَلُ عَن نَّفْسِهِۦ ۚ وَٱللَّهُ ٱلْغَنِىُّ وَأَنتُمُ ٱلْفُقَرَآءُ ۚ وَإِن تَتَوَلَّوْا۟ يَسْتَبْدِلْ قَوْمًا غَيْرَكُمْ ثُمَّ لَا يَكُونُوٓا۟ أَمْثَـٰلَكُم

(It is) for the poor who are detained in the way of Allah, (and) are unable to strike (i.e. journey in the land) in the earth. The ignorant man reckons them rich because of (their) regular abstinence. You recognize them by their mark; they do not ask of mankind importunately, and whatever charity you expend, then surely Allah is Ever-Knowing of it. – Surah Al-Baqarah 2:273
لِلْفُقَرَآءِ ٱلَّذِينَ أُحْصِرُوا۟ فِى سَبِيلِ ٱللَّهِ لَا يَسْتَطِيعُونَ ضَرْبًا فِى ٱلْأَرْضِ يَحْسَبُهُمُ ٱلْجَاهِلُ أَغْنِيَآءَ مِنَ ٱلتَّعَفُّفِ تَعْرِفُهُم بِسِيمَـٰهُمْ لَا يَسْـَٔلُونَ ٱلنَّاسَ إِلْحَافًا ۗ وَمَا تُنفِقُوا۟ مِنْ خَيْرٍ فَإِنَّ ٱللَّهَ بِهِۦ عَلِيمٌ

Narrated Abu Mas`ud Al-Ansari: Whenever Allah's Messenger ﷺ ordered us to give in charity, we used to go to the market and work as porters and get a Mudd (a special measure of grain) and then give it in charity. (Those were the days of poverty) and today some of us have one hundred thousand. – Sahih Al-Bukhari 1416
حَدَّثَنَا سَعِيدُ بْنُ يَحْيَى، حَدَّثَنَا أَبِي، حَدَّثَنَا الأَعْمَشُ، عَنْ شَقِيقٍ، عَنْ أَبِي مَسْعُودٍ الأَنْصَارِيِّ ـ رضى الله عنه ـ قَالَ كَانَ رَسُولُ اللَّهِ صلى الله عليه وسلم إِذَا أَمَرَنَا بِالصَّدَقَةِ انْطَلَقَ أَحَدُنَا إِلَى السُّوقِ فَتَحَامَلَ فَيُصِيبُ الْمُدَّ، وَإِنَّ لِبَعْضِهِمُ الْيَوْمَ لَمِائَةَ أَلْفٍ.

Narrated Abu Mas`ud: When the verses of charity were revealed, we used to work as porters. A man came and distributed objects of charity in abundance. And they (the people) said, "He is showing off." And another man came and gave a Sa (a small measure of food grains); they said, "Allah is not in need of this small amount of charity." And then the Divine Inspiration came: "Those who criticize such of the believers who give in charity voluntarily and those who could not find to give in charity except what is available to them." (9.79). – Sahih Al-Bukhari 1415
حَدَّثَنَا عُبَيْدُ اللَّهِ بْنُ سَعِيدٍ، حَدَّثَنَا أَبُو النُّعْمَانِ الْحَكَمُ ـ هُوَ ابْنُ عَبْدِ اللَّهِ الْبَصْرِيُّ ـ حَدَّثَنَا شُعْبَةُ، عَنْ سُلَيْمَانَ، عَنْ أَبِي وَائِلٍ، عَنْ أَبِي مَسْعُودٍ ـ رضى الله عنه ـ قَالَ لَمَّا نَزَلَتْ آيَةُ الصَّدَقَةِ كُنَّا نُحَامِلُ، فَجَاءَ رَجُلٌ فَتَصَدَّقَ بِشَىْءٍ كَثِيرٍ فَقَالُوا مُرَائِي. وَجَاءَ رَجُلٌ فَتَصَدَّقَ بِصَاعٍ فَقَالُوا إِنَّ اللَّهَ لَغَنِيٌّ عَنْ صَاعِ هَذَا. فَنَزَلَتِ {الَّذِينَ يَلْمِزُونَ الْمُطَّوِّعِينَ مِنَ الْمُؤْمِنِينَ فِي الصَّدَقَاتِ وَالَّذِينَ لاَ يَجِدُونَ إِلاَّ جُهْدَهُمْ} الآيَةَ

Narrated Salama bin Al-Aqwa: We went out with Allah's Messenger ﷺ to Khaibar and we travelled during the night. A man amongst the people said to 'Amir bin Al-Aqwa', "Won't you let us hear your poetry?" 'Amir was a poet, and so he got down and started (chanting Huda) reciting for the people, poetry that keep pace with the camel's foot steps, saying, "O Allah!

Without You we would not have been guided on the right path, neither would we have given in charity, nor would we have prayed. So please forgive us what we have committed. Let all of us be sacrificed for Your cause and when we meet our enemy, make our feet firm and bestow peace and calmness on us and if they (our enemy) will call us towards an unjust thing we will refuse. The infidels have made a hue and cry to ask others help against us. Allah's Messenger ﷺ said, "Who is that driver (of the camels)?" They said, "He is 'Amir bin Al-Aqwa."' He said, "May Allah bestow His mercy on him." A man among the people said, Has Martyrdom been granted to him, O Allah's Prophet! Would that you let us enjoy his company longer." We reached (the people of) Khaibar and besieged them till we were stricken with severe hunger but Allah helped the Muslims conquer Khaibar. In the evening of its conquest the people made many fires. Allah's Messenger ﷺ asked, "What are those fires? For what are you making fires?" They said, "For cooking meat." He asked, "What kind of meat?" They said, "Donkeys' meat." Allah's Messenger ﷺ said, "Throw away the meat and break the cooking pots." A man said, O Allah's Messenger ﷺ! Shall we throw away the meat and wash the cooking pots?" He said, "You can do that too." When the army files aligned in rows (for the battle), 'Amir's sword was a short one, and while attacking a Jew with it in order to hit him, the sharp edge of the sword turned back and hit 'Amir's knee and caused him to die. When the Muslims returned (from the battle), Salama said, Allah's Messenger ﷺ saw me pale and said, 'What is wrong with you?"' I said, "Let my parents be sacrificed for you! The people claim that all the deeds of Amir have been annulled." The Prophet ﷺ asked, "Who said so?" I replied, "So-and-so and soand- so and Usaid bin Al-Hudair Al-Ansari said, 'Whoever says so is telling a lie. Verily, 'Amir will have double reward."' (While speaking) the Prophet ﷺ put two of his fingers together to indicate that, and added, "He was really a hard-working man and a Mujahid (devout fighter in Allah's Cause) and rarely have there lived in it (i.e., Medina or the battle-field) an "Arab like him.". – Sahih Al-Bukhari 6148

حَدَّثَنَا قُتَيْبَةُ بْنُ سَعِيدٍ، حَدَّثَنَا حَاتِمُ بْنُ إِسْمَاعِيلَ، عَنْ يَزِيدَ بْنِ أَبِي عُبَيْدٍ، عَنْ سَلَمَةَ بْنِ الأَكْوَعِ، قَالَ خَرَجْنَا مَعَ رَسُولِ اللَّهِ صلى الله عليه وسلم إِلَى خَيْبَرَ فَسِرْنَا لَيْلاً، فَقَالَ رَجُلٌ مِنَ الْقَوْمِ لِعَامِرِ بْنِ الأَكْوَعِ أَلاَ تُسْمِعُنَا مِنْ هُنَيْهَاتِكَ، قَالَ وَكَانَ عَامِرٌ رَجُلاً شَاعِرًا، فَنَزَلَ يَحْدُو بِالْقَوْمِ يَقُولُ اللَّهُمَّ لَوْلاَ أَنْتَ مَا اهْتَدَيْنَا وَلاَ تَصَدَّقْنَا وَلاَ صَلَّيْنَا فَاغْفِرْ فِدَاءٌ لَكَ مَا اقْتَفَيْنَا وَثَبِّتِ الأَقْدَامَ إِنْ لاَقَيْنَا وَأَلْقِيَنْ سَكِينَةً عَلَيْنَا إِنَّا إِذَا صِيحَ بِنَا أَتَيْنَا وَبِالصِّيَاحِ عَوَّلُوا عَلَيْنَا فَقَالَ رَسُولُ اللَّهِ صلى الله عليه وسلم " مَنْ هَذَا السَّائِقُ ". قَالُوا عَامِرُ بْنُ الأَكْوَعِ. فَقَالَ " يَرْحَمُهُ اللَّهُ ". فَقَالَ رَجُلٌ مِنَ الْقَوْمِ وَجَبَتْ يَا نَبِيَّ اللَّهِ، لَوْ أَمْتَعْتَنَا بِهِ. قَالَ فَأَتَيْنَا خَيْبَرَ فَحَاصَرْنَاهُمْ حَتَّى أَصَابَتْنَا مَخْمَصَةٌ شَدِيدَةٌ، ثُمَّ إِنَّ اللَّهَ فَتَحَهَا عَلَيْهِمْ، فَلَمَّا أَمْسَى النَّاسُ الْيَوْمَ الَّذِي فُتِحَتْ عَلَيْهِمْ أَوْقَدُوا نِيرَانًا كَثِيرَةً. فَقَالَ رَسُولُ اللَّهِ صلى الله عليه وسلم " مَا هَذِهِ النِّيرَانُ، عَلَى أَىِّ شَىْءٍ تُوقِدُونَ ". قَالُوا عَلَى لَحْمٍ. قَالَ " عَلَى أَىِّ لَحْمٍ ". قَالُوا عَلَى لَحْمِ حُمُرٍ إِنْسِيَّةٍ. فَقَالَ رَسُولُ اللَّهِ صلى الله عليه وسلم " أَهْرِقُوهَا وَاكْسِرُوهَا ". فَقَالَ رَجُلٌ يَا رَسُولَ اللَّهِ أَوْ نُهَرِيقُهَا وَنَغْسِلُهَا قَالَ " أَوْ ذَاكَ ". فَلَمَّا تَصَافَّ الْقَوْمُ كَانَ سَيْفُ عَامِرٍ فِيهِ قِصَرٌ، فَتَنَاوَلَ بِهِ يَهُودِيًّا لِيَضْرِبَهُ، وَيَرْجِعُ ذُبَابُ سَيْفِهِ فَأَصَابَ رُكْبَةَ عَامِرٍ فَمَاتَ مِنْهُ، فَلَمَّا قَفَلُوا قَالَ سَلَمَةُ رَآنِي رَسُولُ اللَّهِ صلى الله عليه وسلم شَاحِبًا. فَقَالَ لِي " مَا لَكَ ". فَقُلْتُ فِدًى لَكَ أَبِي وَأُمِّي زَعَمُوا أَنَّ عَامِرًا حَبِطَ عَمَلُهُ. قَالَ " مَنْ قَالَهُ ". قُلْتُ قَالَهُ فُلاَنٌ وَفُلاَنٌ وَفُلاَنٌ وَأُسَيْدُ بْنُ الْحُضَيْرِ الأَنْصَارِيُّ. فَقَالَ رَسُولُ اللَّهِ صلى الله عليه وسلم " كَذَبَ مَنْ قَالَهُ، إِنَّ لَهُ لأَجْرَيْنِ - وَجَمَعَ بَيْنَ إِصْبَعَيْهِ - إِنَّهُ لَجَاهِدٌ مُجَاهِدٌ، قَلَّ عَرَبِيٌّ نَشَأَ بِهَا مِثْلَهُ ".

Narrated Zaid bin Wahab: I passed by a place called Ar-Rabadha and by chance I met Abu Dhar and asked him, "What has brought you to this place?" He said, "I was in Sham and differed with Muawiya on the meaning of (the following verses of the Qur'an): 'They who hoard up gold and silver and spend them not in the way of Allah.' (9.34). Muawiya said, 'This verse is revealed regarding the people of the scriptures." I said, It was revealed regarding us and also the people of the scriptures." So we had a quarrel and Mu'awiya sent a complaint against me to `Uthman. `Uthman wrote to me to come to Medina, and I came to Medina. Many people came to me as if they had not seen me before. So I told this to `Uthman who said to me, "You may depart and live nearby if you wish." That was the reason for my being here for even if an Ethiopian had been nominated as my ruler, I would have obeyed him . – Sahih Al-Bukhari 1406

حَدَّثَنَا عَلِيٌّ، سَمِعَ هُشَيْمًا، أَخْبَرَنَا حُصَيْنٌ، عَنْ زَيْدِ بْنِ وَهْبٍ، قَالَ مَرَرْتُ بِالرَّبَذَةِ فَإِذَا أَنَا بِأَبِي، ذَرٍّ ـ رضى الله عنه ـ فَقُلْتُ لَهُ مَا أَنْزَلَكَ مَنْزِلَكَ هَذَا قَالَ كُنْتُ بِالشَّأْمِ، فَاخْتَلَفْتُ أَنَا وَمُعَاوِيَةُ فِي الَّذِينَ يَكْنِزُونَ الذَّهَبَ وَالْفِضَّةَ وَلاَ يُنْفِقُونَهَا فِي سَبِيلِ اللَّهِ. قَالَ مُعَاوِيَةُ نَزَلَتْ فِي أَهْلِ الْكِتَابِ. فَقُلْتُ نَزَلَتْ فِينَا وَفِيهِمْ. فَكَانَ بَيْنِي وَبَيْنَهُ فِي ذَاكَ، وَكَتَبَ إِلَى عُثْمَانَ ـ رضى الله عنه ـ يَشْكُونِي، فَكَتَبَ إِلَىَّ عُثْمَانُ أَنِ اقْدَمِ الْمَدِينَةَ. فَقَدِمْتُهَا فَكَثُرَ عَلَىَّ النَّاسُ حَتَّى كَأَنَّهُمْ لَمْ يَرَوْنِي قَبْلَ ذَلِكَ، فَذَكَرْتُ ذَاكَ لِعُثْمَانَ فَقَالَ لِي إِنْ شِئْتَ تَنَحَّيْتَ فَكُنْتَ قَرِيبًا. فَذَاكَ الَّذِي أَنْزَلَنِي هَذَا الْمَنْزِلَ، وَلَوْ أَمَّرُوا عَلَىَّ حَبَشِيًّا لَسَمِعْتُ وَأَطَعْتُ.

Verily, spendthrifts are brothers of the Shayatin
إِنَّ ٱلْمُبَذِّرِينَ كَانُوٓا۟ إِخْوَٰنَ ٱلشَّيَٰطِينِ

It is He who produces gardens, both cultivated and wild, and date-palms, and crops of diverse tastes, and olives and pomegranates, similar and dissimilar. Eat of its fruit when it yields, and give its due on the day of its harvest, and do not waste. He does not love the wasteful. - Surah An-An'am 6:141

وَهُوَ ٱلَّذِىٓ أَنشَأَ جَنَّٰتٍ مَّعْرُوشَٰتٍ وَغَيْرَ مَعْرُوشَٰتٍ وَٱلنَّخْلَ وَٱلزَّرْعَ مُخْتَلِفًا أُكُلُهُۥ وَٱلزَّيْتُونَ وَٱلرُّمَّانَ مُتَشَٰبِهًا وَغَيْرَ مُتَشَٰبِهٍ ۚ كُلُوا۟ مِن ثَمَرِهِۦٓ إِذَآ أَثْمَرَ وَءَاتُوا۟ حَقَّهُۥ يَوْمَ حَصَادِهِۦ ۖ وَلَا تُسْرِفُوٓا۟ ۚ إِنَّهُۥ لَا يُحِبُّ ٱلْمُسْرِفِينَ

O Children of Adam! Dress properly at every place of worship, and eat and drink, but do not be excessive. He does not love the excessive. – Surah Al-A'raf 7:31

يَٰبَنِىٓ ءَادَمَ خُذُوا۟ زِينَتَكُمْ عِندَ كُلِّ مَسْجِدٍ وَكُلُوا۟ وَٱشْرَبُوا۟ وَلَا تُسْرِفُوٓا۟ ۚ إِنَّهُۥ لَا يُحِبُّ ٱلْمُسْرِفِينَ

The extravagant are brethren of the devils, and the devil is ever ungrateful to his Lord.– Surah Al-Isra 17:27

إِنَّ ٱلْمُبَذِّرِينَ كَانُوٓا۟ إِخْوَٰنَ ٱلشَّيَٰطِينِ ۖ وَكَانَ ٱلشَّيْطَٰنُ لِرَبِّهِۦ كَفُورًا

No calamity occurs on earth, or in your souls, but it is in a Book, even before We make it happen. That is easy for Allah. That you may not sorrow over what eludes you, nor exult over what He has given you. Allah does not love the proud snob.– Surah Al-Hadid 57:22&23

مَآ أَصَابَ مِن مُّصِيبَةٍ فِى ٱلْأَرْضِ وَلَا فِىٓ أَنفُسِكُمْ إِلَّا فِى كِتَٰبٍ مِّن قَبْلِ أَن نَّبْرَأَهَآ ۚ إِنَّ ذَٰلِكَ عَلَى ٱللَّهِ يَسِيرٌ لِّكَيْلَا تَأْسَوْا۟ عَلَىٰ مَا فَاتَكُمْ وَلَا تَفْرَحُوا۟ بِمَآ ءَاتَىٰكُمْ ۗ وَٱللَّهُ لَا يُحِبُّ كُلَّ مُخْتَالٍ فَخُورٍ

And those who, before them, had settled in the homeland, and had accepted faith. They love those who emigrated to them, and find no hesitation in their hearts in helping them. They give them priority over themselves, even if they themselves are needy. Whoever is protected from his natural greed—it is they who are the successful. – Surah Al-Hashr 59:9

وَٱلَّذِينَ تَبَوَّءُو ٱلدَّارَ وَٱلْإِيمَٰنَ مِن قَبْلِهِمْ يُحِبُّونَ مَنْ هَاجَرَ إِلَيْهِمْ وَلَا يَجِدُونَ فِى صُدُورِهِمْ حَاجَةً مِّمَّآ أُوتُوا۟ وَيُؤْثِرُونَ عَلَىٰٓ أَنفُسِهِمْ وَلَوْ كَانَ بِهِمْ خَصَاصَةٌ ۚ وَمَن يُوقَ شُحَّ نَفْسِهِۦ فَأُو۟لَٰٓئِكَ هُمُ ٱلْمُفْلِحُونَ

O you who believe! Do not feed on usury
يَٰٓأَيُّهَا ٱلَّذِينَ ءَامَنُوا۟ لَا تَأْكُلُوا۟ ٱلرِّبَوٰٓا۟

"O my people! Give full measure and full weight, in all fairness, and do not cheat the people out of their rights, and do not spread corruption in the land. Surah Hud 11:85

وَيَٰقَوْمِ أَوْفُوا۟ ٱلْمِكْيَالَ وَٱلْمِيزَانَ بِٱلْقِسْطِ ۖ وَلَا تَبْخَسُوا۟ ٱلنَّاسَ أَشْيَآءَهُمْ وَلَا تَعْثَوْا۟ فِى ٱلْأَرْضِ مُفْسِدِينَ

Those who swallow usury will not rise, except as someone driven mad by Satan's touch. That is because they say, "Commerce is like usury." But Allah has permitted commerce, and has forbidden usury. Whoever, on receiving advice from his Lord, refrains, may keep his past earnings, and his case rests with Allah. But whoever resumes—these are the dwellers of the Fire, wherein they will abide forever. Allah condemns usury, and He blesses charities. Allah does not love any sinful ingrate. Those who believe, and do good deeds, and pray regularly, and give charity—they will have their reward with their Lord; they will have no fear, nor shall they grieve. O you who believe! Fear Allah, and forgo what remains of usury, if you are believers. If you do not, then take notice of a war by Allah and His Messenger. But if you repent, you may keep your capital, neither wronging, nor being wronged. But if he is in hardship, then deferment until a time of ease. But to remit it as charity is better for you, if you only knew. Surah Al-Baqarah 2:275-280

ٱلَّذِينَ يَأْكُلُونَ ٱلرِّبَوٰاْ لَا يَقُومُونَ إِلَّا كَمَا يَقُومُ ٱلَّذِى يَتَخَبَّطُهُ ٱلشَّيْطَـٰنُ مِنَ ٱلْمَسِّ ذَٰلِكَ بِأَنَّهُمْ قَالُوٓاْ إِنَّمَا ٱلْبَيْعُ مِثْلُ ٱلرِّبَوٰاْ ۗ وَأَحَلَّ ٱللَّهُ ٱلْبَيْعَ وَحَرَّمَ ٱلرِّبَوٰاْ ۚ فَمَن جَآءَهُۥ مَوْعِظَةٌ مِّن رَّبِّهِۦ فَٱنتَهَىٰ فَلَهُۥ مَا سَلَفَ وَأَمْرُهُۥٓ إِلَى ٱللَّهِ ۖ وَمَنْ عَادَ فَأُو۟لَـٰٓئِكَ أَصْحَـٰبُ ٱلنَّارِ ۖ هُمْ فِيهَا خَـٰلِدُونَ يَمْحَقُ ٱللَّهُ ٱلرِّبَوٰاْ وَيُرْبِى ٱلصَّدَقَـٰتِ ۗ وَٱللَّهُ لَا يُحِبُّ كُلَّ كَفَّارٍ أَثِيمٍ إِنَّ ٱلَّذِينَ ءَامَنُواْ وَعَمِلُواْ ٱلصَّـٰلِحَـٰتِ وَأَقَامُواْ ٱلصَّلَوٰةَ وَءَاتَوُاْ ٱلزَّكَوٰةَ لَهُمْ أَجْرُهُمْ عِندَ رَبِّهِمْ وَلَا خَوْفٌ عَلَيْهِمْ وَلَا هُمْ يَحْزَنُونَ يَـٰٓأَيُّهَا ٱلَّذِينَ ءَامَنُواْ ٱتَّقُواْ ٱللَّهَ وَذَرُواْ مَا بَقِىَ مِنَ ٱلرِّبَوٰٓاْ إِن كُنتُم مُّؤْمِنِينَ فَإِن لَّمْ تَفْعَلُواْ فَأْذَنُواْ بِحَرْبٍ مِّنَ ٱللَّهِ وَرَسُولِهِۦ ۖ وَإِن تُبْتُمْ فَلَكُمْ رُءُوسُ أَمْوَٰلِكُمْ لَا تَظْلِمُونَ وَلَا تُظْلَمُونَ وَإِن كَانَ ذُو عُسْرَةٍ فَنَظِرَةٌ إِلَىٰ مَيْسَرَةٍ ۚ وَأَن تَصَدَّقُواْ خَيْرٌ لَّكُمْ إِن كُنتُمْ تَعْلَمُونَ

O you who believe! Do not feed on usury, compounded over and over, and fear Allah, so that you may prosper. Surah Al-imran 3:130

يَـٰٓأَيُّهَا ٱلَّذِينَ ءَامَنُواْ لَا تَأْكُلُواْ ٱلرِّبَوٰٓاْ أَضْعَـٰفًا مُّضَـٰعَفَةً ۖ وَٱتَّقُواْ ٱللَّهَ لَعَلَّكُمْ تُفْلِحُونَ

And for their taking usury, although they were forbidden it; and for their consuming people's wealth dishonestly. We have prepared for the faithless among them a painful torment. Surah An-Nisa 4:161

وَأَخْذِهِمُ الرِّبَا وَقَدْ نُهُوا عَنْهُ وَأَكْلِهِمْ أَمْوَالَ النَّاسِ بِالْبَاطِلِ وَأَعْتَدْنَا لِلْكَافِرِينَ مِنْهُمْ عَذَابًا أَلِيمً

The usury you practice, seeking thereby to multiply people's wealth, will not multiply with Allah. But what you give in charity, desiring Allah's approval—these are the multipliers. Surah Ar-Rum 30:39

وَمَآ ءَاتَيْتُم مِّن رِّبًا لِّيَرْبُوَاْ فِىٓ أَمْوَٰلِ ٱلنَّاسِ فَلَا يَرْبُواْ عِندَ ٱللَّهِ ۖ وَمَآ ءَاتَيْتُم مِّن زَكَوٰةٍ تُرِيدُونَ وَجْهَ ٱللَّهِ فَأُو۟لَـٰٓئِكَ هُمُ ٱلْمُضْعِفُونَ

Narrated Ibn `Umar: The Prophet ﷺ said, "The selling of wheat for wheat is Riba (usury) except if it is handed from hand to hand and equal in amount. Similarly the selling of barley for barley, is Riba except if it is from hand to hand and equal in amount, and dates for dates is usury except if it is from hand to hand and equal in amount. (See Riba-Fadl in the glossary).. – Sahih al-Bukhari 2170

حَدَّثَنَا أَبُو الْوَلِيدِ، حَدَّثَنَا اللَّيْثُ، عَنِ ابْنِ شِهَابٍ، عَنْ مَالِكِ بْنِ أَوْسٍ، سَمِعَ عُمَرَ ـ رضى الله عنهما ـ عَنِ النَّبِيِّ صلى الله عليه وسلم قَالَ " الْبُرُّ بِالْبُرِّ رِبًا إِلاَّ هَاءَ وَهَاءَ، وَالشَّعِيرُ بِالشَّعِيرِ رِبًا إِلاَّ هَاءَ وَهَاءَ، وَالتَّمْرُ بِالتَّمْرِ رِبًا إِلاَّ هَاءَ وَهَاءَ ".

Narrated Ibn `Abbas: The last Verse (in the Qur'an) revealed to the Prophet ﷺ was the Verse dealing with usury (i.e. Riba). – Sahih al-Bukhari 4544

حَدَّثَنَا قَبِيصَةُ بْنُ عُقْبَةَ، حَدَّثَنَا سُفْيَانُ، عَنْ عَاصِمٍ، عَنِ الشَّعْبِيِّ، عَنِ ابْنِ عَبَّاسٍ ـ رضى الله عنهما ـ قَالَ آخِرُ آيَةٍ نَزَلَتْ عَلَى النَّبِيِّ صلى الله عليه وسلم آيَةُ الرِّبَا.

Jabir said that Allah's Messenger ﷺ cursed the accepter of interest and its payer, and one who records it, and the two witnesses, and he said: They are all equal. – Sahih Muslim 1598
حَدَّثَنَا مُحَمَّدُ بْنُ الصَّبَّاحِ، وَزُهَيْرُ بْنُ حَرْبٍ، وَعُثْمَانُ بْنُ أَبِي شَيْبَةَ، قَالُوا حَدَّثَنَا هُشَيْمٌ، أَخْبَرَنَا أَبُو الزُّبَيْرِ، عَنْ جَابِرٍ، قَالَ لَعَنَ رَسُولُ اللَّهِ صلى الله عليه وسلم آكِلَ الرِّبَا وَمُوكِلَهُ وَكَاتِبَهُ وَشَاهِدَيْهِ وَقَالَ هُمْ سَوَاءٌ

And We made Mary's son and his mother a sign, and We sheltered them on high ground with security and flowing springs. Surah Al-Mu'minun 23:10
وَجَعَلْنَا ٱبْنَ مَرْيَمَ وَأُمَّهُۥٓ ءَايَةً وَءَاوَيْنَـٰهُمَآ إِلَىٰ رَبْوَةٍ ذَاتِ قَرَارٍ وَمَعِينٍ

But they disobeyed the messenger of their Lord, so He seized them with an overpowering grip. Surah Al-Haqqah 69:10
فَعَصَوْا۟ رَسُولَ رَبِّهِمْ فَأَخَذَهُمْ أَخْذَةً رَّابِيَةً

And of His signs is that you see the land still. But when We send down water upon it, it stirs and grows. Surely, He Who revived it will revive the dead. He is Able to do all things. Surah Fussilat 41:39
وَمِنْ ءَايَـٰتِهِۦٓ أَنَّكَ تَرَى ٱلْأَرْضَ خَـٰشِعَةً فَإِذَآ أَنزَلْنَا عَلَيْهَا ٱلْمَآءَ ٱهْتَزَّتْ وَرَبَتْ ۚ إِنَّ ٱلَّذِىٓ أَحْيَاهَا لَمُحْىِ ٱلْمَوْتَىٰٓ ۚ إِنَّهُۥ عَلَىٰ كُلِّ شَىْءٍ قَدِيرٌ

He sends down water from the sky, and riverbeds flow according to their capacity. The current carries swelling froth. And from what they heat in fire of ornaments or utensils comes a similar froth. Thus Allah exemplifies truth and falsehood. As for the froth, it is swept away, but what benefits the people remains in the ground. Thus Allah presents the analogies. – Surah Ar-Ra'd 13:17
أَنزَلَ مِنَ السَّمَاءِ مَاءً فَسَالَتْ أَوْدِيَةٌ بِقَدَرِهَا فَاحْتَمَلَ السَّيْلُ زَبَدًا رَّابِيًا وَمِمَّا يُوقِدُونَ عَلَيْهِ فِي النَّارِ ابْتِغَاءَ حِلْيَةٍ أَوْ مَتَاعٍ زَبَدٌ مِّثْلُهُ كَذَٰلِكَ يَضْرِبُ اللَّهُ الْحَقَّ وَالْبَاطِلَ فَأَمَّا الزَّبَدُ فَيَذْهَبُ جُفَاءً وَأَمَّا مَا يَنفَعُ النَّاسَ فَيَمْكُثُ فِي الْأَرْضِ كَذَٰلِكَ يَضْرِبُ اللَّهُ الْأَمْثَالَ

He said, "Did we not raise you among us as a child, and you stayed among us for many of your years? – Surah Ash-Shu'ara 26:18
قَالَ أَلَمْ نُرَبِّكَ فِينَا وَلِيدًا وَلَبِثْتَ فِينَا مِنْ عُمُرِكَ سِنِينَ

And lower to them the wing of humility, out of mercy, and say, "My Lord, have mercy on them, as they raised me when I was a child." – Surah Al-Isra 17:24
وَٱخْفِضْ لَهُمَا جَنَاحَ ٱلذُّلِّ مِنَ ٱلرَّحْمَةِ وَقُل رَّبِّ ٱرْحَمْهُمَا كَمَا رَبَّيَانِى صَغِيرًا

.....We send down rain upon it, it begins to stir ⌜to life⌝ and swell, producing every type of pleasant plant. Surah Al-Hajj 22:5 [35]
...فَإِذَآ أَنزَلْنَا عَلَيْهَا ٱلْمَآءَ ٱهْتَزَّتْ وَرَبَتْ وَأَنۢبَتَتْ مِن كُلِّ زَوْجٍۭ بَهِيجٍ

[35] The root word (ر ب و) of Riba should be understood to better understand Riba. High; Al-Mu'23:10 overpowering; Al-Haqqah 69:10 , growth; Fussilat 41:39, swelling; Ar-Ra'd 13:17, raise; Ash-Shu'ara 26:18, raised; Al-Isra 17:24, swell; Al-Hajj 22:5

And weigh with the straight equitableness
وَزِنُوا۟ بِٱلْقِسْطَاسِ ٱلْمُسْتَقِيمِ

How terrible it is to those who give short measures, Who, when they measure against mankind, (i.e., when they take from others) take full (measure) And when they measure for them or weigh for them, (i.e., when they give to others) they cause them loss. – Surah Al-Mutaffifin 83:1-3

وَيْلٌ لِّلْمُطَفِّفِينَ الَّذِينَ إِذَا اكْتَالُوا عَلَى النَّاسِ يَسْتَوْفُونَ وَإِذَا كَالُوهُمْ أَو وَّزَنُوهُمْ يُخْسِرُونَ

And fill up the measure when you measure, and weigh with the straight equitableness; that is more charitable and fairest in interpretation (Or: determination, outcome). – Surah Al-Isra 17:35

وَأَوْفُوا۟ ٱلْكَيْلَ إِذَا كِلْتُمْ وَزِنُوا۟ بِٱلْقِسْطَاسِ ٱلْمُسْتَقِيمِ ذَٰلِكَ خَيْرٌ وَأَحْسَنُ تَأْوِيلًا

Fill up the measure, and do not be of them who make others losers And weigh with the straight equitableness And do not depreciate for mankind (the value) of their things, (i.e., their goods) and do not perpetrate (mischief) in the earth (as) corruptors. – Surah Ash-Shu'ara 26:181-183

أَوْفُوا۟ ٱلْكَيْلَ وَلَا تَكُونُوا۟ مِنَ ٱلْمُخْسِرِينَ وَزِنُوا۟ بِٱلْقِسْطَاسِ ٱلْمُسْتَقِيمِ وَلَا تَبْخَسُوا۟ ٱلنَّاسَ أَشْيَآءَهُمْ وَلَا تَعْثَوْا۟ فِى ٱلْأَرْضِ مُفْسِدِينَ

And to Madyan (We sent) their brother Shuaayb. He said, "O my people! Worship Allah! In no way do you have any god other than He. A supreme evidence has already come to you from your Lord; so fill up the measure and the balance, and do not depreciate mankind their things; (i.e., their goods) and do not corrupt in the earth after its being righteous. That (Literally: those "orders") is most charitable for you, in case you are believers. – Surah Al-A'raf 7:85

وَإِلَىٰ مَدْيَنَ أَخَاهُمْ شُعَيْبًا ۗ قَالَ يَٰقَوْمِ ٱعْبُدُوا۟ ٱللَّهَ مَا لَكُم مِّنْ إِلَٰهٍ غَيْرُهُۥ ۖ قَدْ جَآءَتْكُم بَيِّنَةٌ مِّن رَّبِّكُمْ ۖ فَأَوْفُوا۟ ٱلْكَيْلَ وَٱلْمِيزَانَ وَلَا تَبْخَسُوا۟ ٱلنَّاسَ أَشْيَآءَهُمْ وَلَا تُفْسِدُوا۟ فِى ٱلْأَرْضِ بَعْدَ إِصْلَٰحِهَا ۚ ذَٰلِكُمْ خَيْرٌ لَّكُمْ إِن كُنتُم مُّؤْمِنِينَ

And to Madyan (We sent) their brother Shuaayb. He said, "O my people, worship Allah! In no way do you have any god other than He. And do not diminish the measuring and the balance. Surely I see you are in charitable (circumstances); and surely I fear for you the torment of an encompassing Day And my people, fill up the measuring and the balance with equity and do not depreciate the things of mankind, and do not perpetrate (mischief) in the land as corruptors. – Surah Hud 11:84&85

وَإِلَىٰ مَدْيَنَ أَخَاهُمْ شُعَيْبًا ۚ قَالَ يَٰقَوْمِ ٱعْبُدُوا۟ ٱللَّهَ مَا لَكُم مِّنْ إِلَٰهٍ غَيْرُهُۥ ۖ وَلَا تَنقُصُوا۟ ٱلْمِكْيَالَ وَٱلْمِيزَانَ ۚ إِنِّىٓ أَرَىٰكُم بِخَيْرٍ وَإِنِّىٓ أَخَافُ عَلَيْكُمْ عَذَابَ يَوْمٍ مُّحِيطٍ وَيَٰقَوْمِ أَوْفُوا۟ ٱلْمِكْيَالَ وَٱلْمِيزَانَ بِٱلْقِسْطِ ۖ وَلَا تَبْخَسُوا۟ ٱلنَّاسَ أَشْيَآءَهُمْ وَلَا تَعْثَوْا۟ فِى ٱلْأَرْضِ مُفْسِدِى

You will never attain benignancy until you expend of whatever you love
لَن تَنَالُوا۟ ٱلْبِرَّ حَتَّىٰ تُنفِقُوا۟ مِمَّا تُحِبُّونَ

Who is he that will lend to Allah a fair loan, so He will double it for him, and he will have an honorable reward. – Surah Al-Hadid 57:11
مَّن ذَا ٱلَّذِى يُقْرِضُ ٱللَّهَ قَرْضًا حَسَنًا فَيُضَـٰعِفَهُۥ لَهُۥ وَلَهُۥٓ أَجْرٌ كَرِيمٌ

The unbelievers spend their wealth to turn people away from Allah's path. They will continue to spend it until it becomes a source of sorrow for them: in the end, they will be overcome and will be gathered in Hell, - Surah Al-Anfal 8:36
إِنَّ ٱلَّذِينَ كَفَرُوا۟ يُنفِقُونَ أَمْوَٰلَهُمْ لِيَصُدُّوا۟ عَن سَبِيلِ ٱللَّهِ ۚ فَسَيُنفِقُونَهَا ثُمَّ تَكُونُ عَلَيْهِمْ حَسْرَةً ثُمَّ يُغْلَبُونَ ۗ وَٱلَّذِينَ كَفَرُوٓا۟ إِلَىٰ جَهَنَّمَ يُحْشَرُونَ

Prepare whatever forces you can so that you might frighten Allah's enemies and yours and to frighten others unknown to you but known to Allah. Whatever you may do in Allah's cause will be repaid to you in full, and you will be justly rewarded. – Surah Al-Anfal 8:60
وَأَعِدُّوا۟ لَهُم مَّا ٱسْتَطَعْتُم مِّن قُوَّةٍ وَمِن رِّبَاطِ ٱلْخَيْلِ تُرْهِبُونَ بِهِۦ عَدُوَّ ٱللَّهِ وَعَدُوَّكُمْ وَءَاخَرِينَ مِن دُونِهِمْ لَا تَعْلَمُونَهُمُ ٱللَّهُ يَعْلَمُهُمْ ۚ وَمَا تُنفِقُوا۟ مِن شَىْءٍ فِى سَبِيلِ ٱللَّهِ يُوَفَّ إِلَيْكُمْ وَأَنتُمْ لَا تُظْلَمُونَ

Nor do they expend any expense, small or great, nor do they cut across any valley, except that it is written for them, (i.e., written o their account) that Allah may recompense them for the fairest of whatever they were doing – Surah At-Taubah 9:121
وَلَا يُنفِقُونَ نَفَقَةً صَغِيرَةً وَلَا كَبِيرَةً وَلَا يَقْطَعُونَ وَادِيًا إِلَّا كُتِبَ لَهُمْ لِيَجْزِيَهُمُ ٱللَّهُ أَحْسَنَ مَا كَانُوا۟ يَعْمَلُونَ

You will never attain benignancy until you expend of whatever you love; and whatever thing you expend, then surely Allah is Ever-Knowing of it. – Surah Al-Imran 3:92
لَن تَنَالُوا۟ ٱلْبِرَّ حَتَّىٰ تُنفِقُوا۟ مِمَّا تُحِبُّونَ ۚ وَمَا تُنفِقُوا۟ مِن شَىْءٍ فَإِنَّ ٱللَّهَ بِهِۦ عَلِيمٌ

The Book of
Nikah
نكاح

Narrated 'Urwa bin Az-Zubair: 'Aishah, the wife of the Prophet ﷺ told him that there were four types of marriage during Pre-Islamic period of Ignorance. One type was similar to that of the present day i.e. a man used to ask somebody else for the hand of a girl under his guardianship or for his daughter's hand, and give her Mahr and then marry her. The second type was that a man would say to his wife after she had become clean from her period. "Send for so-and-so and have sexual intercourse with him." Her husband would then keep away from her and would never sleep with her till she got pregnant from the other man with whom she was sleeping. When her pregnancy became evident, he husband would sleep with her if he wished. Her husband did so (i.e. let his wife sleep with some other man) so that he might have a child of noble breed. Such marriage was called as Al-Istibda'. Another type of marriage was that a group of less than ten men would assemble and enter upon a woman, and all of them would have sexual relation with her. If she became pregnant and delivered a child and some days had passed after delivery, she would sent for all of them and none of them would refuse to come, and when they all gathered before her, she would say to them, "You (all) know what you have done, and now I have given birth to a child. So, it is your child so-and-so!" naming whoever she liked, and her child would follow him and he could not refuse to take him. The fourth type of marriage was that many people would enter upon a lady and she would never refuse anyone who came to her. Those were the prostitutes who used to fix flags at their doors as sign, and he who would wished, could have sexual intercourse with them. If anyone of them got pregnant and delivered a child, then all those men would be gathered for her and they would call the Qa'if (persons skilled in recognizing the likeness of a child to his father) to them and would let the child follow the man (whom they recognized as his father) and she would let him adhere to him and be called his son. The man would not refuse all that. But when Muhammad ﷺ was sent with the Truth, he abolished all the types of marriages observed in pre-Islamic period of Ignorance except the type of marriage the people recognize today. – Sahih Al-Bukhari 5127

قَالَ يَحْيَى بْنُ سُلَيْمَانَ حَدَّثَنَا ابْنُ وَهْبٍ، عَنْ يُونُسَ. حَدَّثَنَا أَحْمَدُ بْنُ صَالِحٍ، حَدَّثَنَا عَنْبَسَةُ، حَدَّثَنَا يُونُسُ، عَنِ ابْنِ شِهَابٍ، قَالَ أَخْبَرَنِي عُرْوَةُ بْنُ الزُّبَيْرِ، أَنَّ عَائِشَةَ، زَوْجَ النَّبِيِّ صلى الله عليه وسلم أَخْبَرَتْهُ أَنَّ النِّكَاحَ فِي الْجَاهِلِيَّةِ كَانَ عَلَى أَرْبَعَةِ أَنْحَاءٍ فَنِكَاحٌ مِنْهَا نِكَاحُ النَّاسِ الْيَوْمَ، يَخْطُبُ الرَّجُلُ إِلَى الرَّجُلِ وَلِيَّتَهُ أَوِ ابْنَتَهُ، فَيُصْدِقُهَا ثُمَّ يَنْكِحُهَا، وَنِكَاحٌ آخَرُ كَانَ الرَّجُلُ يَقُولُ لاِمْرَأَتِهِ إِذَا طَهُرَتْ مِنْ طَمْثِهَا أَرْسِلِي إِلَى فُلاَنٍ فَاسْتَبْضِعِي مِنْهُ. وَيَعْتَزِلُهَا زَوْجُهَا، وَلاَ يَمَسُّهَا أَبَدًا، حَتَّى يَتَبَيَّنَ حَمْلُهَا مِنْ ذَلِكَ الرَّجُلِ الَّذِي تَسْتَبْضِعُ مِنْهُ، فَإِذَا تَبَيَّنَ حَمْلُهَا أَصَابَهَا زَوْجُهَا إِذَا أَحَبَّ، وَإِنَّمَا يَفْعَلُ ذَلِكَ رَغْبَةً فِي نَجَابَةِ الْوَلَدِ، فَكَانَ هَذَا النِّكَاحُ نِكَاحَ الاِسْتِبْضَاعِ، وَنِكَاحٌ آخَرُ يَجْتَمِعُ الرَّهْطُ مَا دُونَ الْعَشَرَةِ فَيَدْخُلُونَ عَلَى الْمَرْأَةِ كُلُّهُمْ يُصِيبُهَا. فَإِذَا حَمَلَتْ وَوَضَعَتْ، وَمَرَّ عَلَيْهَا لَيَالِيَ بَعْدَ أَنْ تَضَعَ حَمْلَهَا، أَرْسَلَتْ إِلَيْهِمْ فَلَمْ يَسْتَطِعْ رَجُلٌ مِنْهُمْ أَنْ يَمْتَنِعَ حَتَّى يَجْتَمِعُوا عِنْدَهَا تَقُولُ لَهُمْ قَدْ عَرَفْتُمُ الَّذِي كَانَ مِنْ أَمْرِكُمْ، وَقَدْ وَلَدْتُ فَهُوَ ابْنُكَ يَا فُلاَنُ. تُسَمِّي مَنْ أَحَبَّتْ بِاسْمِهِ، فَيَلْحَقُ بِهِ وَلَدُهَا، لاَ يَسْتَطِيعُ أَنْ يَمْتَنِعَ بِهِ الرَّجُلُ. وَنِكَاحُ الرَّابِعِ يَجْتَمِعُ النَّاسُ الْكَثِيرُ فَيَدْخُلُونَ عَلَى الْمَرْأَةِ لاَ تَمْتَنِعُ مِمَّنْ جَاءَهَا وَهُنَّ الْبَغَايَا كُنَّ يَنْصِبْنَ عَلَى أَبْوَابِهِنَّ رَايَاتٍ تَكُونُ عَلَمًا فَمَنْ أَرَادَهُنَّ دَخَلَ عَلَيْهِنَّ، فَإِذَا حَمَلَتْ إِحْدَاهُنَّ وَوَضَعَتْ حَمْلَهَا جُمِعُوا لَهَا وَدَعَوْا لَهُمُ الْقَافَةَ ثُمَّ أَلْحَقُوا وَلَدَهَا بِالَّذِي يَرَوْنَ فَالْتَاطَ بِهِ، وَدُعِيَ ابْنَهُ لاَ يَمْتَنِعُ مِنْ ذَلِكَ، فَلَمَّا بُعِثَ مُحَمَّدٌ صلى الله عليه وسلم بِالْحَقِّ هَدَمَ نِكَاحَ الْجَاهِلِيَّةِ كُلَّهُ، إِلاَّ نِكَاحَ النَّاسِ الْيَوْمَ.

Narrated `Abdullah: We were with the Prophet ﷺ while we were young and had no wealth. So Allah's Messenger ﷺ said, "O young people! Whoever among you can marry, should marry, because it helps him lower his gaze and guard his modesty (i.e. his private parts from committing illegal sexual intercourse etc.), and whoever is not able to marry, should fast, as fasting diminishes his sexual power.". – Sahih Al-Bukhari 5066

حَدَّثَنَا عُمَرُ بْنُ حَفْصِ بْنِ غِيَاثٍ، حَدَّثَنَا أَبِي، حَدَّثَنَا الأَعْمَشُ، قَالَ حَدَّثَنِي عُمَارَةُ، عَنْ عَبْدِ الرَّحْمَنِ بْنِ يَزِيدَ، قَالَ دَخَلْتُ مَعَ عَلْقَمَةَ وَالأَسْوَدِ عَلَى عَبْدِ اللَّهِ فَقَالَ عَبْدُ اللَّهِ كُنَّا مَعَ النَّبِيِّ صلى الله عليه وسلم شَبَابًا لاَ نَجِدُ شَيْئًا فَقَالَ لَنَا رَسُولُ اللَّهُ صلى الله عليه وسلم " يَا مَعْشَرَ الشَّبَابِ مَنِ اسْتَطَاعَ الْبَاءَةَ فَلْيَتَزَوَّجْ، فَإِنَّهُ أَغَضُّ لِلْبَصَرِ، وَأَحْصَنُ لِلْفَرْجِ، وَمَنْ لَمْ يَسْتَطِعْ فَعَلَيْهِ بِالصَّوْمِ، فَإِنَّهُ لَهُ وِجَاءٌ ".

O you who believe! It is not permitted for you to inherit women against their will. And do not coerce them in order to take away some of what you had given them, unless they commit a proven adultery. And live with them in kindness. If you dislike them, it may be that you dislike something in which Allah has placed much good. – Surah An-Nisa 4:19

يَا أَيُّهَا الَّذِينَ آمَنُوا لَا يَحِلُّ لَكُمْ أَن تَرِثُوا النِّسَاءَ كَرْهًا وَلَا تَعْضُلُوهُنَّ لِتَذْهَبُوا بِبَعْضِ مَا آتَيْتُمُوهُنَّ إِلَّا أَن يَأْتِينَ بِفَاحِشَةٍ مُّبَيِّنَةٍ وَعَاشِرُوهُنَّ بِالْمَعْرُوفِ فَإِن كَرِهْتُمُوهُنَّ فَعَسَىٰ أَن تَكْرَهُوا شَيْئًا وَيَجْعَلَ اللَّهُ فِيهِ خَيْرًا كَثِيرًا

Narrated Sahl: A man passed by Allah's Messenger ﷺ and Allah s Apostle asked (his companions) "What do you say about this (man)?" They replied "If he asks for a lady's hand, he ought to be given her in marriage; and if he intercedes (for someone) his intercessor should be accepted; and if he speaks, he should be listened to." Allah's Messenger ﷺ kept silent, and then a man from among the poor Muslims passed by, an Allah's Apostle asked (them) "What do you say about this man?" They replied, "If he asks for a lady's hand in marriage he does not deserve to be married, and he intercedes (for someone), his intercession should not be accepted; And if he speaks, he should not be listened to.' Allah's Messenger ﷺ said, "This poor man is better than so many of the first as filling the earth.' - Sahih Al-Bukhari 5091

حَدَّثَنَا إِبْرَاهِيمُ بْنُ حَمْزَةَ، حَدَّثَنَا ابْنُ أَبِي حَازِمٍ، عَنْ أَبِيهِ، عَنْ سَهْلٍ، قَالَ مَرَّ رَجُلٌ عَلَى رَسُولِ اللَّهِ صلى الله عليه وسلم فَقَالَ " مَا تَقُولُونَ فِي هَذَا ". قَالُوا حَرِيٌّ إِنْ خَطَبَ أَنْ يُنْكَحَ، وَإِنْ شَفَعَ أَنْ يُشَفَّعَ، وَإِنْ قَالَ أَنْ يُسْتَمَعَ. قَالَ ثُمَّ سَكَتَ فَمَرَّ رَجُلٌ مِنْ فُقَرَاءِ الْمُسْلِمِينَ فَقَالَ " مَا تَقُولُونَ فِي هَذَا ". قَالُوا حَرِيٌّ إِنْ خَطَبَ أَنْ لاَ يُنْكَحَ وَإِنْ شَفَعَ أَنْ لاَ يُشَفَّعَ، وَإِنْ قَالَ أَنْ لاَ يُسْتَمَعَ. فَقَالَ رَسُولُ اللَّهِ صلى الله عليه وسلم " هَذَا خَيْرٌ مِنْ مِلْءِ الأَرْضِ مِثْلَ هَذَا "

Marry off those among you who are unmarried and those who are righteous among your male and female slaves.

وَأَنكِحُوا۟ ٱلْأَيَـٰمَىٰ مِنكُمْ وَٱلصَّـٰلِحِينَ مِنْ عِبَادِكُمْ وَإِمَآئِكُمْ فَضْلِهِۦ

Marry off those among you who are unmarried and those who are righteous among your male and female slaves. If they should be poor, God will enrich them from His favor; God is All-Encompassing and All-Knowing. – Surah An-Nur 24:32

وَأَنكِحُوا۟ ٱلْأَيَـٰمَىٰ مِنكُمْ وَٱلصَّـٰلِحِينَ مِنْ عِبَادِكُمْ وَإِمَآئِكُمْ إِن يَكُونُوا۟ فُقَرَآءَ يُغْنِهِمُ ٱللَّهُ مِن فَضْلِهِۦ

Narrated 'Abdullah bin Buraidah: It was narrated from 'Abdullah bin Buraidah that his father said: "Abu Bakr and 'Umar, may Allah be pleased with them, proposed marriage to Fatimah but the Messenger of Allah said: 'She is young.' Then 'Ali proposed marriage to her and he married her to him." – Sunan an-Nasa'I 3221

أَخْبَرَنَا الْحُسَيْنُ بْنُ حُرَيْثٍ، قَالَ حَدَّثَنَا الْفَضْلُ بْنُ مُوسَى، عَنِ الْحُسَيْنِ بْنِ وَاقِدٍ، عَنْ عَبْدِ اللَّهِ بْنِ بُرَيْدَةَ، عَنْ أَبِيهِ، قَالَ خَطَبَ أَبُو بَكْرٍ وَعُمَرُ رضى الله عنهما فَاطِمَةَ فَقَالَ رَسُولُ اللَّهِ صلى الله عليه وسلم " إِنَّهَا صَغِيرَةٌ " . فَخَطَبَهَا عَلِيٌّ فَزَوَّجَهَا مِنْهُ .

Narrated 'Urwa: The Prophet ﷺ asked Abu Bakr for `Aisha's hand in marriage. Abu Bakr said "But I am your brother." The Prophet ﷺ said, "You are my brother in Allah's religion and His Book, but she (Aisha) is lawful for me to marry.". – Sahih al-Bukhari 5081

حَدَّثَنَا عَبْدُ اللَّهِ بْنُ يُوسُفَ، حَدَّثَنَا اللَّيْثُ، عَنْ يَزِيدَ، عَنْ عِرَاكٍ، عَنْ عُرْوَةَ، أَنَّ النَّبِيَّ صلى الله عليه وسلم خَطَبَ عَائِشَةَ إِلَى أَبِي بَكْرٍ فَقَالَ لَهُ أَبُو بَكْرٍ إِنَّمَا أَنَا أَخُوكَ، فَقَالَ " أَنْتَ أَخِي فِي دِينِ اللَّهِ وَكِتَابِهِ وَهْىَ لِي حَلاَلٌ ".

Narrated `Abdullah bin `Umar: `Umar bin Al-Khattab said, "When (my daughter) Hafsa bint `Umar lost her husband Khunais bin Hudhaifa As-Sahrni who was one of the companions of Allah's Messenger ﷺ and had fought in the battle of Badr and had died in Medina, I met `Uthman bin `Affan and suggested that he should marry Hafsa saying, "If you wish, I will marry Hafsa bint `Umar to you,' on that, he said, 'I will think it over.' I waited for a few days and then he said to me. 'I am of the opinion that I shall not marry at present.' Then I met Abu Bakr and said, 'if you wish, I will marry you, Hafsa bint `Umar.' He kept quiet and did not give me any reply and I became more angry with him than I was with `Uthman . Some days later, Allah's Messenger ﷺ demanded her hand in marriage and I married her to him. Later on Abu Bakr met me and said, "Perhaps you were angry with me when you offered me Hafsa for marriage and I gave no reply to you?' I said, 'Yes.' Abu Bakr said, 'Nothing prevented me from accepting your offer except that I learnt that Allah's Messenger ﷺ had referred to the issue of Hafsa and I did not want to disclose the secret of Allah's Messenger ﷺ , but had he (i.e. the Prophet) given her up I would surely have accepted her.". – Sahih al-Bukhari 4005

حَدَّثَنَا أَبُو الْيَمَانِ، أَخْبَرَنَا شُعَيْبٌ، عَنِ الزُّهْرِيِّ، قَالَ أَخْبَرَنِي سَالِمُ بْنُ عَبْدِ اللَّهِ، أَنَّهُ سَمِعَ عَبْدَ اللَّهِ بْنَ عُمَرَ ـ رضى الله عنهما ـ يُحَدِّثُ أَنَّ عُمَرَ بْنَ الْخَطَّابِ حِينَ تَأَيَّمَتْ حَفْصَةُ بِنْتُ عُمَرَ مِنْ خُنَيْسِ بْنِ حُذَافَةَ السَّهْمِيِّ وَكَانَ مِنْ أَصْحَابِ رَسُولِ اللَّهِ صلى الله عليه وسلم قَدْ شَهِدَ بَدْرًا تُوُفِّيَ بِالْمَدِينَةِ قَالَ عُمَرُ فَلَقِيتُ عُثْمَانَ بْنَ عَفَّانَ فَعَرَضْتُ عَلَيْهِ حَفْصَةَ فَقُلْتُ إِنْ شِئْتَ أَنْكَحْتُكَ حَفْصَةَ بِنْتَ عُمَرَ. قَالَ سَأَنْظُرُ فِي أَمْرِي. فَلَبِثْتُ لَيَالِيَ، فَقَالَ قَدْ بَدَا لِي أَنْ لاَ أَتَزَوَّجَ يَوْمِي هَذَا. قَالَ عُمَرُ فَلَقِيتُ أَبَا بَكْرٍ فَقُلْتُ إِنْ شِئْتَ أَنْكَحْتُكَ حَفْصَةَ بِنْتَ عُمَرَ. فَصَمَتَ أَبُو بَكْرٍ، فَلَمْ يَرْجِعْ إِلَيَّ شَيْئًا، فَكُنْتُ عَلَيْهِ أَوْجَدَ مِنِّي عَلَى عُثْمَانَ، فَلَبِثْتُ لَيَالِيَ، ثُمَّ خَطَبَهَا رَسُولُ اللَّهِ صلى الله عليه وسلم فَأَنْكَحْتُهَا إِيَّاهُ، فَلَقِيَنِي أَبُو بَكْرٍ فَقَالَ لَعَلَّكَ وَجَدْتَ عَلَىَّ حِينَ عَرَضْتَ عَلَىَّ حَفْصَةَ فَلَمْ أَرْجِعْ إِلَيْكَ قُلْتُ نَعَمْ. قَالَ فَإِنَّهُ لَمْ يَمْنَعْنِي أَنْ أَرْجِعَ إِلَيْكَ فِيمَا عَرَضْتَ إِلاَّ أَنِّي قَدْ عَلِمْتُ أَنَّ رَسُولَ اللَّهِ صلى الله عليه وسلم قَدْ ذَكَرَهَا، فَلَمْ أَكُنْ لأُفْشِيَ سِرَّ رَسُولِ اللَّهِ صلى الله عليه وسلم، وَلَوْ تَرَكَهَا لَقَبِلْتُهَا.

And to wedlock women of to whom the Book was brought
وَٱلْمُحْصَنَـٰتُ مِنَ ٱلَّذِينَ أُوتُوا۟ ٱلْكِتَـٰبَ

Today the good things are made lawful for you, and the food of the ones to whom the Book was brought is lawful to you, and your food is made lawful to them. And (so) are believing women in wedlock, and in wedlock women of (the ones) to whom the Book was brought even before you when you have brought them their rewards in wedlock, other than in fornication, neither taking them to yourselves as mates (i.e., girl-friends). And whoever disbelieves in belief, (i.e., the religion) then his deed has been frustrated and in the Hereafter he is among the losers. Surah Al-Ma'idah 5:5

ٱلْيَوْمَ أُحِلَّ لَكُمُ ٱلطَّيِّبَـٰتُ ۖ وَطَعَامُ ٱلَّذِينَ أُوتُوا۟ ٱلْكِتَـٰبَ حِلٌّ لَّكُمْ وَطَعَامُكُمْ حِلٌّ لَّهُمْ ۖ وَٱلْمُحْصَنَـٰتُ مِنَ ٱلْمُؤْمِنَـٰتِ وَٱلْمُحْصَنَـٰتُ مِنَ ٱلَّذِينَ أُوتُوا۟ ٱلْكِتَـٰبَ مِن قَبْلِكُمْ إِذَآ ءَاتَيْتُمُوهُنَّ أُجُورَهُنَّ مُحْصِنِينَ غَيْرَ مُسَـٰفِحِينَ وَلَا مُتَّخِذِىٓ أَخْدَانٍ ۗ وَمَن يَكْفُرْ بِٱلْإِيمَـٰنِ فَقَدْ حَبِطَ عَمَلُهُۥ وَهُوَ فِى ٱلْـَٔاخِرَةِ مِنَ ٱلْخَـٰسِرِينَ

Indeed they have already disbelieved, the ones who have said, "Surely Allah, He is the Masih son of Maryam." (The Missiah) And the Masih said, "O Seeds of worship Allah, my Lord, and your Lord; surely whoever associates with Allah (anything), Allah has already prohibited him (entrance to) the Garden, and his abode will be the Fire; and in no way will the unjust have any vindicators."

Indeed they have already disbelieved, the ones who have said, "Surely Allah is the third of three." And in no way is there any god except One God. And in case they do not refrain from what they say, indeed there will definitely touch the ones of them that have disbelieved a painful torment. – Surah Al-Ma'idah 5:72&73

لَقَدْ كَفَرَ ٱلَّذِينَ قَالُوٓا۟ إِنَّ ٱللَّهَ هُوَ ٱلْمَسِيحُ ٱبْنُ مَرْيَمَ ۖ وَقَالَ ٱلْمَسِيحُ يَـٰبَنِىٓ إِسْرَٰٓءِيلَ ٱعْبُدُوا۟ ٱللَّهَ رَبِّى وَرَبَّكُمْ ۖ إِنَّهُۥ مَن يُشْرِكْ بِٱللَّهِ فَقَدْ حَرَّمَ ٱللَّهُ
عَلَيْهِ ٱلْجَنَّةَ وَمَأْوَىٰهُ ٱلنَّارُ ۖ وَمَا لِلظَّـٰلِمِينَ مِنْ أَنصَارٍ لَّقَدْ كَفَرَ ٱلَّذِينَ قَالُوٓا۟ إِنَّ ٱللَّهَ ثَالِثُ ثَلَـٰثَةٍ ۘ وَمَا مِنْ إِلَـٰهٍ إِلَّآ إِلَـٰهٌ وَٰحِدٌ ۚ وَإِن لَّمْ يَنتَهُوا۟ عَمَّا
يَقُولُونَ لَيَمَسَّنَّ ٱلَّذِينَ كَفَرُوا۟ مِنْهُمْ عَذَابٌ أَلِيمٌ

Say (O Muslims), "We have believed in Allah, and whatever has been sent down to us, and whatever was sent down to Ibrahim, and Shuaayb, and Ishaq and Yaaqub (Abraham, Ishmael, Isaac and Jacob, respectively) and the Grandsons, (i.e., the Tribes) and whatever was brought down to Musa and Isa, (Moses and Jesus, respectively) and whatever was brought to the Prophets from their Lord. We make no distinction between any of them, and to Him we are Muslims."
So, in case they believe in the like of whatever you have believed in, then they are readily guided; and in case they turn away, then surely they are only in opposition; so Allah will soon suffice you for them; and He is The Ever-Hearing, The Ever-Knowing – Surah Al-Baqarah 2:136&137

قُولُوٓا۟ ءَامَنَّا بِٱللَّهِ وَمَآ أُنزِلَ إِلَيْنَا وَمَآ أُنزِلَ إِلَىٰٓ إِبْرَٰهِـۧمَ وَإِسْمَـٰعِيلَ وَإِسْحَـٰقَ وَيَعْقُوبَ وَٱلْأَسْبَاطِ وَمَآ أُوتِىَ مُوسَىٰ وَعِيسَىٰ وَمَآ أُوتِىَ ٱلنَّبِيُّونَ
مِن رَّبِّهِمْ لَا نُفَرِّقُ بَيْنَ أَحَدٍ مِّنْهُمْ وَنَحْنُ لَهُۥ مُسْلِمُونَ فَإِنْ ءَامَنُوا۟ بِمِثْلِ مَآ ءَامَنتُم بِهِۦ فَقَدِ ٱهْتَدَوا۟ ۖ وَّإِن تَوَلَّوْا۟ فَإِنَّمَا هُمْ فِى شِقَاقٍ ۖ فَسَيَكْفِيكَهُمُ
ٱللَّهُ ۚ وَهُوَ ٱلسَّمِيعُ ٱلْعَلِيمُ

The adulterer shall marry none but an adulteress or an idolatress; and the adulteress shall marry none but an adulterer or an idolater. That has been prohibited for the believers. – Surah An-Nur 24:3

ٱلزَّانِى لَا يَنكِحُ إِلَّا زَانِيَةً أَوْ مُشْرِكَةً وَٱلزَّانِيَةُ لَا يَنكِحُهَآ إِلَّا زَانٍ أَوْ مُشْرِكٌ ۚ وَحُرِّمَ ذَٰلِكَ عَلَى ٱلْمُؤْمِنِينَ

And do not marry female associators (Those who associate others with Allah) until they believe; and indeed a believing bondwoman is more charitable than a female associator, even if you may admire her. And do not (allow) associators to marry (your females) until they believe. And indeed a believing bondman is more charitable than an associator, even if you may admire him. Those call to the Fire, and Allah calls to the Garden and forgiveness, by His permission, and He makes evident His signs to mankind, that possibly they would remind themselves. Surah Al-Baqarah 2:221

وَلَا تَنكِحُوا۟ ٱلْمُشْرِكَـٰتِ حَتَّىٰ يُؤْمِنَّ ۚ وَلَأَمَةٌ مُّؤْمِنَةٌ خَيْرٌ مِّن مُّشْرِكَةٍ وَلَوْ أَعْجَبَتْكُمْ ۗ وَلَا تُنكِحُوا۟ ٱلْمُشْرِكِينَ حَتَّىٰ يُؤْمِنُوا۟ ۚ وَلَعَبْدٌ
مُّؤْمِنٌ خَيْرٌ مِّن مُّشْرِكٍ وَلَوْ أَعْجَبَكُمْ ۗ أُو۟لَـٰٓئِكَ يَدْعُونَ إِلَى ٱلنَّارِ ۖ وَٱللَّهُ يَدْعُوٓا۟ إِلَى ٱلْجَنَّةِ وَٱلْمَغْفِرَةِ بِإِذْنِهِۦ ۖ وَيُبَيِّنُ ءَايَـٰتِهِۦ لِلنَّاسِ
لَعَلَّهُمْ يَتَذَكَّرُونَ

The believers, both men, and women support each other; they order what is obviously right and forbid what is obviously wrong, and they establish prayers, pay the prescribed purifying alms, and obey God and His Messenger. God will have mercy on them. He is Revered, Wise. Surah At-Taubah 9:71

وَٱلْمُؤْمِنُونَ وَٱلْمُؤْمِنَـٰتُ بَعْضُهُمْ أَوْلِيَآءُ بَعْضٍ ۚ يَأْمُرُونَ بِٱلْمَعْرُوفِ وَيَنْهَوْنَ عَنِ ٱلْمُنكَرِ وَيُقِيمُونَ ٱلصَّلَوٰةَ وَيُؤْتُونَ ٱلزَّكَوٰةَ
وَيُطِيعُونَ ٱللَّهَ وَرَسُولَهُۥٓ ۚ أُو۟لَـٰٓئِكَ سَيَرْحَمُهُمُ ٱللَّهُ ۗ إِنَّ ٱللَّهَ عَزِيزٌ حَكِيمٌ

......And do not hold to marriage bonds with unbelieving women,..... Surah Al-Mumtahinah 60:10

وَلَا تُمْسِكُوا۟ بِعِصَمِ ٱلْكَوَافِرِ

O you who have attained to faith! Those who ascribe divinity to aught beside Allah are nothing but impure..... 9:28

يَـٰٓأَيُّهَا ٱلَّذِينَ ءَامَنُوٓا۟ إِنَّمَا ٱلْمُشْرِكُونَ نَجَسٌ

Then marry such women as is good to you
فَٱنكِحُواْ مَا طَابَ لَكُم مِّنَ ٱلنِّسَآءِ

Narrated Sa`id bin Jubair: Ibn `Abbas asked me, "Are you married?" I replied, "No." He said, "Marry, for the best person of this (Muslim) nation (i.e., Muhammad) of all other Muslims, had the largest number of wives.". – Sahih Al-Bukhari 5069
حَدَّثَنَا عَلِيُّ بْنُ الْحَكَمِ الأَنْصَارِيُّ، حَدَّثَنَا أَبُو عَوَانَةَ، عَنْ رَقَبَةَ، عَنْ طَلْحَةَ الْيَامِيِّ، عَنْ سَعِيدِ بْنِ جُبَيْرٍ، قَالَ قَالَ لِي ابْنُ عَبَّاسٍ هَلْ تَزَوَّجْتَ قُلْتُ لاَ. قَالَ فَتَزَوَّجْ فَإِنَّ خَيْرَ هَذِهِ الأُمَّةِ أَكْثَرُهَا نِسَاءً

And, in case you fear that you will not act equitably towards the orphans, then marry such women as is good to you, two, three, four, (Literally: in twos and threes and fours) then, in case you fear that you will not do justice, then one (only), or what your right hands possess. That (way) is likelier you will not be in want (Or: you will have too many dependents). – Surah An-Nisa 4:3
وَإِنْ خِفْتُمْ أَلَّا تُقْسِطُواْ فِى ٱلْيَتَـٰمَىٰ فَٱنكِحُواْ مَا طَابَ لَكُم مِّنَ ٱلنِّسَآءِ مَثْنَىٰ وَثُلَـٰثَ وَرُبَـٰعَ ۖ فَإِنْ خِفْتُمْ أَلَّا تَعْدِلُواْ فَوَٰحِدَةً أَوْ مَا مَلَكَتْ أَيْمَـٰنُكُمْ ۚ ذَٰلِكَ أَدْنَىٰٓ أَلَّا تَعُولُواْ

And they ask you for your pronouncement concerning women. Say, " Allah pronounces concerning them, and what is recited to you in the Book concerning the orphan women (Or (possibly): women who have orphans. And Allah knows bests) to whom you do not bring what is prescribed for them, and (yet) you desire to marry them, and the (ones) deemed weak of the children (Literally: newborns) (and) that you keep up equity (Literally: set "things" up with equity) for orphans. And whatever charity you perform, then surely Allah has been Ever-Knowing of it. – Surah An-Nisa 4:127
وَيَسْتَفْتُونَكَ فِى ٱلنِّسَآءِ ۖ قُلِ ٱللَّهُ يُفْتِيكُمْ فِيهِنَّ وَمَا يُتْلَىٰ عَلَيْكُمْ فِى ٱلْكِتَـٰبِ فِى يَتَـٰمَى ٱلنِّسَآءِ ٱلَّـٰتِى لَا تُؤْتُونَهُنَّ مَا كُتِبَ لَهُنَّ وَتَرْغَبُونَ أَن تَنكِحُوهُنَّ وَٱلْمُسْتَضْعَفِينَ مِنَ ٱلْوِلْدَٰنِ وَأَن تَقُومُواْ لِلْيَتَـٰمَىٰ بِٱلْقِسْطِ ۚ وَمَا تَفْعَلُواْ مِنْ خَيْرٍ فَإِنَّ ٱللَّهَ كَانَ بِهِۦ عَلِيمًا

Narrated `Urwa bin Az-Zubair: That he asked `Aisha regarding the Statement of Allah: "If you fear that you shall not be able to deal justly with the orphan girls..." (4.3) She said, "O son of my sister! An Orphan girl used to be under the care of a guardian with whom she shared property. Her guardian, being attracted by her wealth and beauty, would intend to marry her without giving her a just Mahr, i.e. the same Mahr as any other person might give her (in case he married her). So such guardians were forbidden to do that unless they did justice to their female wards and gave them the highest Mahr their peers might get. They were ordered (by Allah, to marry women of their choice other than those orphan girls." `Aisha added," The people asked Allah's Messenger ﷺ his instructions after the revelation of this Divine Verse whereupon Allah revealed: "They ask your instruction regarding women " (4.127) `Aisha further said, "And the Statement of Allah: "And yet whom you desire to marry." (4.127) as anyone of you refrains from marrying an orphan girl (under his guardianship) when she is lacking in property and beauty." `Aisha added, "So they were forbidden to marry those orphan girls for whose wealth and beauty they had a desire unless with justice, and that was because they would refrain from marrying them if they were lacking in property and beauty." – Sahih al-Bukhari 4574
حَدَّثَنَا عَبْدُ الْعَزِيزِ بْنُ عَبْدِ اللَّهِ، حَدَّثَنَا إِبْرَاهِيمُ بْنُ سَعْدٍ، عَنْ صَالِحِ بْنِ كَيْسَانَ، عَنِ ابْنِ شِهَابٍ، قَالَ أَخْبَرَنِي عُرْوَةُ بْنُ الزُّبَيْرِ، أَنَّهُ سَأَلَ عَائِشَةَ عَنْ قَوْلِ اللَّهِ، تَعَالَى {وَإِنْ خِفْتُمْ أَنْ لاَ تُقْسِطُوا فِي الْيَتَامَى}. فَقَالَتْ يَا ابْنَ أُخْتِي، هَذِهِ الْيَتِيمَةُ تَكُونُ فِي حَجْرِ وَلِيِّهَا، تَشْرَكُهُ فِي مَالِهِ وَيُعْجِبُهُ مَالُهَا وَجَمَالُهَا، فَيُرِيدُ وَلِيُّهَا أَنْ يَتَزَوَّجَهَا، بِغَيْرِ أَنْ يُقْسِطَ فِي صَدَاقِهَا، فَيُعْطِيَهَا مِثْلَ مَا يُعْطِيهَا غَيْرُهُ، فَنُهُوا عَنْ أَنْ يَنْكِحُوهُنَّ، إِلاَّ أَنْ يُقْسِطُوا لَهُنَّ، وَيَبْلُغُوا لَهُنَّ أَعْلَى سُنَّتِهِنَّ فِي الصَّدَاقِ، فَأُمِرُوا أَنْ يَنْكِحُوا مَا طَابَ لَهُمْ مِنَ النِّسَاءِ سِوَاهُنَّ. قَالَ عُرْوَةُ قَالَتْ عَائِشَةُ وَإِنَّ النَّاسَ اسْتَفْتَوْا رَسُولَ اللَّهِ صلى الله عليه وسلم بَعْدَ هَذِهِ الآيَةِ فَأَنْزَلَ اللَّهُ {وَيَسْتَفْتُونَكَ فِي النِّسَاءِ} قَالَتْ عَائِشَةُ وَقَوْلُ اللَّهِ تَعَالَى فِي آيَةٍ أُخْرَى {وَتَرْغَبُونَ أَنْ تَنْكِحُوهُنَّ} رَغْبَةُ أَحَدِكُمْ عَنْ يَتِيمَتِهِ حِينَ تَكُونُ قَلِيلَةَ الْمَالِ وَالْجَمَالِ قَالَتْ فَنُهُوا أَنْ يَنْكِحُوا عَنْ مَنْ رَغِبُوا فِي مَالِهِ وَجَمَالِهِ فِي يَتَامَى النِّسَاءِ، إِلاَّ بِالْقِسْطِ، مِنْ أَجْلِ رَغْبَتِهِمْ عَنْهُنَّ إِذَا كُنَّ قَلِيلاَتِ الْمَالِ وَالْجَمَالِ.

8459 – Al-Muthanna narrated to me, saying: Abu Salih narrated to us, saying: Al-Layth narrated to me, saying: Yunus narrated to me, on the authority of Ibn Shihab, saying: Urwah ibn al-Zubayr narrated to me that he asked Aisha, the wife of the Prophet, peace and blessings be upon him, and mentioned a hadith similar to that of Yunus, on the authority of Ibn Wahb.

8460 – Al-Hasan ibn Yahya narrated to us, saying: Abd al-Razzaq narrated to us, saying: Muammar narrated to us, on the authority of al-Zuhri, on the authority of Urwah, on the authority of Aisha, similar to the hadith of Ibn Humayd, on the authority of Ibn al-Mubarak.
8461 – Al-Qasim narrated to us, saying: Al-Husayn narrated to us, saying: Hajjaj narrated to me, on the authority of Ibn Jurayj, on the authority of Hisham, on the authority of his father, on the authority of Aisha, who said: The verse, "And if you fear that you will not be able to deal justly with the orphan girls," was revealed about an orphan girl who is with a man and she has wealth, so he might marry her for her wealth, but she does not please him, then he beats her and treats her badly, so he was admonished for that. * * *
Abu Ja'far said: According to this interpretation, the answer to his statement, "And if you fear that you will not be able to deal justly," is his statement, "then marry."

Others said: Rather, the meaning of this is the prohibition against marrying more than four, out of concern for the orphans' wealth, lest their guardians waste it. This is because a Quraysh man would marry up to ten women, or more or less. If he became destitute, he would use the wealth of his orphan in his care, spending it or marrying with it. They were forbidden from doing this, and it was said to them: If you fear that you will not be able to deal justly with your orphans' wealth, then do not exceed four in the number of women you marry. If you also fear that you will not be able to deal justly with their wealth, then limit your marriage to one, or to what your right hands possess. * Mention of those who said that:
8462 – Muhammad ibn al-Muthanna narrated to us, he said: Muhammad ibn Ja`far narrated to us, he said: Shu`bah narrated to us, on the authority of Samak, he said: I heard `Ikrimah say about this verse: "And if you fear that you will not be just toward the orphan girls," he said: A man from Quraysh would have wives and orphan girls, and his wealth would be lost, and he would be inclined toward the orphan girls' wealth. He said: So this verse was revealed: "And if you fear that you will not be just toward the orphan girls, then marry those that please you of [other] women." 8463 – Hannad bin Al-Sarri narrated: Abu Al-Ahwas narrated to us, on the authority of Samak, on the authority of Ikrimah, regarding the statement of Allah, "And if you fear that you will not be able to deal justly with the orphan girls, then marry such women as seem good to you, two, three, or four. But if you fear that you will not be able to deal justly, then [marry only] one or those your right hands possess," he said: A man would marry four, five, six, or ten, and another man would say, "What prevents me from marrying as so-and-so married?" So he would take his orphan's money and marry with it, so they were forbidden to marry more than four. – Tafsīr al-Ṭabarī – Surah An-Nisa 4:3

٨٤٥٩ – حدثني المثنى قال، حدثنا أبو صالح قال، حدثني الليث قال، حدثني يونس، عن ابن شهاب قال، حدثني عروة بن الزبير: أنه سأل عائشة زوجَ النبي ﷺ، فذكر مثل حديث يونس، عن ابن وهب.
٨٤٦٠ – حدثنا الحسن بن يحيى قال، أخبرنا عبد الرزاق قال، أخبرنا معمر، عن الزهري عن عروة، عن عائشة، مثل حديث ابن حميد، عن ابن المبارك.
٨٤٦١ – حدثنا القاسم قال، حدثنا الحسين قال، حدثني حجاج، عن ابن جريج، عن هشام، عن أبيه، عن عائشة قالت: نزل= تعني قوله:"وإن خفتم ألا تقسطوا في اليتامى"، الآية= في اليتيمة تكون عند الرجل، وهي ذات مال، فلعله ينكحها لمالها، وهي لا تعجبه، ثم يضربها، ويسيء صحبتها، فوُعظ في ذلك.

• **

قال أبو جعفر: فعلى هذا التأويل، جواب قوله:"وإن خفتم ألا تقسطوا"، قوله:"فانكحوا".

• **

وقال آخرون: بل معنى ذلك: النهي عن نكاح ما فوق الأربع، حِذارًا على أموال اليتامى أن يتلفها أولياؤهم. وذلك أن قريشًا كان الرجل منهم يتزوج العشر من النساء والأكثر والأقل، فإذا صار معدمًا، مال على مال يتيمه الذي في حجره فأنفقه أو تزوج به. فنهوا عن ذلك، وقيل لهم: إن أنتم خفتم على أموال أيتامكم أن تنفقوها= فلا تعدلوا فيها، من أجل حاجتكم إليها لما يلزمكم من مُؤن نسائكم، فلا تجاوزوا فيما تنكحون من عدد النساء على أربعٍ= وإن خفتم أيضًا من الأربع أن لا تعدلوا في أموالهم، فاقتصروا على الواحدة، أو على ما ملكت أيمانكم.

ذكر من قال ذلك: •

٨٤٦٢ – حدثنا محمد بن المثنى قال، حدثنا محمد بن جعفر قال، حدثنا شعبة، عن سماك قال، سمعت عكرمة يقول في هذه الآية:"وإن خفتم ألا تقسطوا في اليتامى"، قال: كان الرجل من قريش يكون عنده النِّسوة، ويكون عنده الأيتام، فيذهب ماله، فيميل على مال الأيتام، قال: فنزلت هذه الآية:"وإن خفتم ألا تقسطوا في اليتامى فانكحوا ما طاب لكم من النساء".

٨٤٦٣ – حدثنا هناد بن السري قال: حدثنا أبو الأحوص، عن سماك، عن عكرمة في قوله:"وإن خفتم ألا تقسطوا في اليتامى فانكحوا ما طاب لكم من النساء مثنى وثلاث ورباع فإن خفتم ألا تعدلوا فواحدة أو ما ملكت أيمانكم"، قال: كان الرجل يتزوج الأربع والخمس والستَّ والعشر، فيقول الرجل:"ما يمنعني أن أتزوج كما تزوج فلان"؟ فيأخذ مال يتيمه فيتزوج به، فنهوا أن يتزوجوا فوق الأربع.

Narrated Qatada: Anas bin Malik said, "The Prophet ﷺ used to visit all his wives in a round, during the day and night and they were eleven in number." I asked Anas, "Had the Prophet ﷺ the strength for it?" Anas replied, "We used to say that the Prophet ﷺ was given the strength of thirty (men)." And Sa`id said on the authority of Qatada that Anas had told him about nine wives only (not eleven). – Sahih al-Bukhari 268

حَدَّثَنَا مُحَمَّدُ بْنُ بَشَّارٍ، قَالَ حَدَّثَنَا مُعَاذُ بْنُ هِشَامٍ، قَالَ حَدَّثَنِي أَبِي، عَنْ قَتَادَةَ، قَالَ حَدَّثَنَا أَنَسُ بْنُ مَالِكٍ، قَالَ كَانَ النَّبِيُّ صلى الله عليه وسلم يَدُورُ عَلَى نِسَائِهِ فِي السَّاعَةِ الْوَاحِدَةِ مِنَ اللَّيْلِ وَالنَّهَارِ، وَهُنَّ إِحْدَى عَشْرَةَ. قَالَ قُلْتُ لأَنَسٍ أَوَكَانَ يُطِيقُهُ قَالَ كُنَّا نَتَحَدَّثُ أَنَّهُ أُعْطِيَ قُوَّةَ ثَلاَثِينَ.
وَقَالَ سَعِيدٌ عَنْ قَتَادَةَ إِنَّ أَنَسًا حَدَّثَهُمْ تِسْعُ نِسْوَةٍ.

Narrated Abu Huraira: (The Prophet) Solomon son of (the Prophet) David said, "Tonight I will go round (i.e. have sexual relations with) one hundred women (my wives) everyone of whom will deliver a male child who will fight in Allah's Cause." On that an Angel said to him, "Say: 'If Allah will.' " But Solomon did not say it and forgot to say it. Then he had sexual relations with them but none of them delivered any child except one who delivered a half person. The Prophet ﷺ said, "If Solomon had said: 'If Allah will,' Allah would have fulfilled his (above) desire and that saying would have made him more hopeful.". – Sahih al-Bukhari 5242

حَدَّثَنِي مَحْمُودٌ، حَدَّثَنَا عَبْدُ الرَّزَّاقِ، أَخْبَرَنَا مَعْمَرٌ، عَنِ ابْنِ طَاوُسٍ، عَنْ أَبِيهِ، عَنْ أَبِي هُرَيْرَةَ، قَالَ " قَالَ سُلَيْمَانُ بْنُ دَاوُدَ ـ عَلَيْهِمَا السَّلاَمُ ـ لأَطُوفَنَّ اللَّيْلَةَ بِمِائَةِ امْرَأَةٍ، تَلِدُ كُلُّ امْرَأَةٍ غُلاَمًا، يُقَاتِلُ فِي سَبِيلِ اللَّهِ، فَقَالَ لَهُ الْمَلَكُ قُلْ إِنْ شَاءَ اللَّهُ. فَلَمْ يَقُلْ وَنَسِيَ، فَأَطَافَ بِهِنَّ، وَلَمْ تَلِدْ مِنْهُنَّ إِلاَّ امْرَأَةٌ نِصْفَ إِنْسَانٍ ". قَالَ النَّبِيُّ صلى الله عليه وسلم " لَوْ قَالَ إِنْ شَاءَ اللَّهُ لَمْ يَحْنَثْ، وَكَانَ أَرْجَى لِحَاجَتِهِ ".

Narrated Anas: The Prophet ﷺ paid a visit to Um-Sulaim and she placed before him dates and ghee. The Prophet ﷺ said, "Replace the ghee and dates in their respective containers for I am fasting." Then he stood somewhere in her house and offered an optional prayer and then he invoked good on Um-Sulaim and her family. Then Um-Sulaim said, "O Allah's Messenger ﷺ ! I have a special request (today)." He said, "What is it?" She replied, "(Please invoke for) your servant Anas." So Allah's Messenger ﷺ did not leave anything good in the world or the Hereafter which he did not invoke (Allah to bestow) on me and said, "O Allah! Give him (i.e. Anas) property and children and bless him." Thus I am one of the richest among the Ansar and my daughter Umaina told me that when Al-Hajjaj came to Basra, more than 120 of my offspring had been buried. -;Sahih al-Bukhari 1982

حَدَّثَنَا مُحَمَّدُ بْنُ الْمُثَنَّى، قَالَ حَدَّثَنِي خَالِدٌ ـ هُوَ ابْنُ الْحَارِثِ ـ حَدَّثَنَا حُمَيْدٌ، عَنْ أَنَسٍ ـ رضى الله عنه ـ دَخَلَ النَّبِيُّ صلى الله عليه وسلم عَلَى أُمِّ سُلَيْمٍ، فَأَتَتْهُ بِتَمْرٍ وَسَمْنٍ، قَالَ " أَعِيدُوا سَمْنَكُمْ فِي سِقَائِهِ، وَتَمْرَكُمْ فِي وِعَائِهِ، فَإِنِّي صَائِمٌ ". ثُمَّ قَامَ إِلَى نَاحِيَةٍ مِنَ الْبَيْتِ، فَصَلَّى غَيْرَ الْمَكْتُوبَةِ، فَدَعَا لأُمِّ سُلَيْمٍ، وَأَهْلِ بَيْتِهَا، فَقَالَتْ أُمُّ سُلَيْمٍ يَا رَسُولَ اللَّهِ، إِنَّ لِي خُوَيْصَةً، قَالَ " مَا هِيَ ". قَالَتْ خَادِمُكَ أَنَسٌ. فَمَا تَرَكَ خَيْرَ آخِرَةٍ وَلاَ دُنْيَا إِلاَّ دَعَا لِي بِهِ قَالَ " اللَّهُمَّ ارْزُقْهُ مَالاً وَوَلَدًا وَبَارِكْ لَهُ ". فَإِنِّي لَمِنْ أَكْثَرِ الأَنْصَارِ مَالاً. وَحَدَّثَتْنِي ابْنَتِي أُمَيْنَةُ أَنَّهُ دُفِنَ لِصُلْبِي مَقْدَمَ حَجَّاجٍ الْبَصْرَةَ بِضْعٌ وَعِشْرُونَ وَمِائَةٌ. حَدَّثَنَا ابْنُ أَبِي مَرْيَمَ، أَخْبَرَنَا يَحْيَى، قَالَ حَدَّثَنِي حُمَيْدٌ، سَمِعَ أَنَسًا ـ رضى الله عنه ـ عَنِ النَّبِيِّ صلى الله عليه وسلم.

When a man marries he has fulfilled half of the religion
إِذَا تَزَوَّجَ الْعَبْدُ فَقَدِ اسْتَكْمَلَ نِصْفَ الدِّينِ

......and she has received a Solemn pledge from you. -Shrah An-Nisa 4:21

وَأَخَذْنَ مِنكُم مِّيثَـٰقًا غَلِيظًا

Anas reported Allah's Messenger as saying, "When a man marries he has fulfilled half of the religion; so let him fear Allah regarding the remaining half." – Mishkat al-Masabih 3096 Baihaqi transmitted in Shu'ab al-iman.

وَعَنْ أَنَسٍ قَالَ: قَالَ رَسُولُ اللَّهِ صَلَّى اللَّهُ عَلَيْهِ وَسَلَّمَ: «إِذَا تَزَوَّجَ الْعَبْدُ فَقَدِ اسْتَكْمَلَ نِصْفَ الدِّينِ فَلْيَتَّقِ اللَّهَ فِي النِّصْفِ الْبَاقِي

......And do not hold to marriage bonds with unbelieving women,.... -Surah Al-Mutahinah 60:10

....وَلَا تُمْسِكُوا۟ بِعِصَمِ ٱلْكَوَافِرِ....

Do not marry polytheistic women until they believe; for a believing slave-woman is better than a free polytheist, even though she may look pleasant to you. And do not marry your women to polytheistic men until they believe, for a believing slave-man is better than a free polytheist, even though he may look pleasant to you. They invite ˹you˺ to the Fire while Allah invites ˹you˺ to Paradise and forgiveness by His grace. He makes His revelations clear to the people so perhaps they will be mindful. – Surah Al-Baqarah 2:221

وَلَا تَنكِحُوا الْمُشْرِكَاتِ حَتَّىٰ يُؤْمِنَّ وَلَأَمَةٌ مُّؤْمِنَةٌ خَيْرٌ مِّن مُّشْرِكَةٍ وَلَوْ أَعْجَبَتْكُمْ وَلَا تُنكِحُوا الْمُشْرِكِينَ حَتَّىٰ يُؤْمِنُوا وَلَعَبْدٌ مُّؤْمِنٌ خَيْرٌ مِّن مُّشْرِكٍ وَلَوْ أَعْجَبَكُمْ أُولَٰئِكَ يَدْعُونَ إِلَى النَّارِ وَاللَّهُ يَدْعُو إِلَى الْجَنَّةِ وَالْمَغْفِرَةِ بِإِذْنِهِ وَيُبَيِّنُ آيَاتِهِ لِلنَّاسِ لَعَلَّهُمْ يَتَذَكَّرُونَ

Who believed in Our signs and ˹fully˺ submitted ˹to Us˺. Enter Paradise, you and your spouses, rejoicing." Surah Az-Zukhruf 43:69&70

ٱلَّذِينَ ءَامَنُوا۟ بِـَٔايَـٰتِنَا وَكَانُوا۟ مُسْلِمِينَ ٱدْخُلُوا۟ ٱلْجَنَّةَ أَنتُمْ وَأَزْوَٰجُكُمْ تُحْبَرُونَ

Assemble those who did wrong, together with their wives and what they used to worship – As-Saffat 37:22

ٱحْشُرُوا۟ ٱلَّذِينَ ظَلَمُوا۟ وَأَزْوَٰجَهُمْ وَمَا كَانُوا۟ يَعْبُدُونَ

Mahram
مَحْرَم

Do not marry idolatresses, unless They have believed. A believing maid Is better than an idolatress, even if You like her. And do not marry Idolaters, unless they have believed. A believing servant is better than an Idolater, even if you like him. These Call to the Fire, but Allah calls to the Garden and to forgiveness, by His Leave. He makes clear His Communications to the people, that They may be mindful. – Surah Al-Baqarah 2:221

وَلَا تَنكِحُوا۟ ٱلْمُشْرِكَـٰتِ حَتَّىٰ يُؤْمِنَّ ۚ وَلَأَمَةٌ مُّؤْمِنَةٌ خَيْرٌ مِّن مُّشْرِكَةٍ وَلَوْ أَعْجَبَتْكُمْ ۗ وَلَا تُنكِحُوا۟ ٱلْمُشْرِكِينَ حَتَّىٰ يُؤْمِنُوا۟ ۚ وَلَعَبْدٌ مُّؤْمِنٌ خَيْرٌ مِّن مُّشْرِكٍ وَلَوْ أَعْجَبَكُمْ ۗ أُو۟لَـٰٓئِكَ يَدْعُونَ إِلَى ٱلنَّارِ ۖ وَٱللَّهُ يَدْعُوٓا۟ إِلَى ٱلْجَنَّةِ وَٱلْمَغْفِرَةِ بِإِذْنِهِۦ ۖ وَيُبَيِّنُ ءَايَـٰتِهِۦ لِلنَّاسِ لَعَلَّهُمْ يَتَذَكَّرُونَ

If any of you lack the means to marry free believing women, he may marry one of the believing maids under your control. Allah is well aware of your faith. You are from one another. Marry them with the permission of their guardians, and give them their recompense fairly—to be protected—neither committing adultery, nor taking secret lovers. When they are married, if they commit adultery, their punishment shall be half that of free women. That is for those among you who fear falling into decadence. But to practice self-restraint is better for you. Allah is Most Forgiving, Most Merciful – Surah An-Nisa 4:25

وَمَن لَّمْ يَسْتَطِعْ مِنكُمْ طَوْلًا أَن يَنكِحَ ٱلْمُحْصَنَـٰتِ ٱلْمُؤْمِنَـٰتِ فَمِن مَّا مَلَكَتْ أَيْمَـٰنُكُم مِّن فَتَيَـٰتِكُمُ ٱلْمُؤْمِنَـٰتِ ۚ وَٱللَّهُ أَعْلَمُ بِإِيمَـٰنِكُم ۚ بَعْضُكُم مِّنۢ بَعْضٍ ۚ فَٱنكِحُوهُنَّ بِإِذْنِ أَهْلِهِنَّ وَءَاتُوهُنَّ أُجُورَهُنَّ بِٱلْمَعْرُوفِ مُحْصَنَـٰتٍ غَيْرَ مُسَـٰفِحَـٰتٍ وَلَا مُتَّخِذَٰتِ أَخْدَانٍ ۚ فَإِذَآ أُحْصِنَّ فَإِنْ أَتَيْنَ بِفَـٰحِشَةٍ فَعَلَيْهِنَّ نِصْفُ مَا عَلَى ٱلْمُحْصَنَـٰتِ مِنَ ٱلْعَذَابِ ۚ ذَٰلِكَ لِمَنْ خَشِىَ ٱلْعَنَتَ مِنكُمْ ۚ وَأَن تَصْبِرُوا۟ خَيْرٌ لَّكُمْ ۗ وَٱللَّهُ غَفُورٌ رَّحِيمٌ

Narrated 'Urwa: The Prophetﷺ asked Abu Bakr for `Aisha's hand in marriage. Abu Bakr said "But I am your brother." The Prophetﷺ said, "You are my brother in Allah's religion and His Book, but she (Aisha) is lawful for me to marry.". – Sahih Al-Bukhari 5081

حَدَّثَنَا عَبْدُ اللَّهِ بْنُ يُوسُفَ، حَدَّثَنَا اللَّيْثُ، عَنْ يَزِيدَ، عَنْ عِرَاكٍ، عَنْ عُرْوَةَ، أَنَّ النَّبِيَّ صلى الله عليه وسلم خَطَبَ عَائِشَةَ إِلَى أَبِي بَكْرٍ فَقَالَ لَهُ أَبُو بَكْرٍ إِنَّمَا أَنَا أَخُوكَ، فَقَالَ " أَنْتَ أَخِي فِي دِينِ اللَّهِ وَكِتَابِهِ وَهْىَ لِي حَلاَلٌ ".

Narrated `Abdullah bin `Umar: `Umar bin Al-Khattab said, "When Hafsa bint `Umar became a widow after the death of (her husband) Khunais bin Hudhafa As-Sahmi who had been one of the companions of the Prophet, and he died at Medina. I went to `Uthman bin `Affan and presented Hafsa (for marriage) to him. He said, "I will think it over.' I waited for a few days, then he met me and said, 'It seems that it is not possible for me to marry at present.' " `Umar further said, "I met Abu Bakr As-Siddique and said to him, 'If you wish, I will marry my daughter Hafsa to you." Abu Bakr kept quiet and did not say anything to me in reply. I became more angry with him than with `Uthman. I waited for a few days and then Allah's Messenger ﷺasked for her hand, and I gave her in marriage to him. Afterwards I met Abu Bakr who said, 'Perhaps you became angry with me when you presented Hafsa to me and I did not give you a reply?' I said, 'Yes.' Abu Bakr said, 'Nothing stopped me to respond to your offer except that I knew that Allah's Apostle had mentioned her, and I never wanted to let out the secret of Allah's Messengerﷺ. And if Allah's Apostle had refused her, I would have accepted her.' " - Sahih Al-Bukhari 5122

حَدَّثَنَا عَبْدُ الْعَزِيزِ بْنُ عَبْدِ اللَّهِ، حَدَّثَنَا إِبْرَاهِيمُ بْنُ سَعْدٍ، عَنْ صَالِحِ بْنِ كَيْسَانَ، عَنِ ابْنِ شِهَابٍ، قَالَ أَخْبَرَنِي سَالِمُ بْنُ عَبْدِ اللَّهِ، أَنَّهُ سَمِعَ عَبْدَ اللَّهِ بْنَ عُمَرَ ـ رضى الله عنهما ـ يُحَدِّثُ أَنَّ عُمَرَ بْنَ الْخَطَّابِ حِينَ تَأَيَّمَتْ حَفْصَةُ بِنْتُ عُمَرَ مِنْ خُنَيْسِ بْنِ حُذَافَةَ السَّهْمِيِّ ـ وَكَانَ مِنْ أَصْحَابِ رَسُولِ اللَّهِ صلى الله عليه وسلم فَتُوُفِّيَ بِالْمَدِينَةِ ـ فَقَالَ عُمَرُ بْنُ الْخَطَّابِ أَتَيْتُ عُثْمَانَ بْنَ عَفَّانَ فَعَرَضْتُ عَلَيْهِ حَفْصَةَ فَقَالَ سَأَنْظُرُ فِي أَمْرِي. فَلَبِثْتُ لَيَالِيَ ثُمَّ لَقِيَنِي فَقَالَ قَدْ بَدَا لِي أَنْ لاَ أَتَزَوَّجَ يَوْمِي هَذَا. قَالَ عُمَرُ فَلَقِيتُ أَبَا بَكْرٍ الصِّدِّيقَ فَقُلْتُ إِنْ شِئْتَ زَوَّجْتُكَ حَفْصَةَ بِنْتَ عُمَرَ. فَصَمَتَ أَبُو بَكْرٍ فَلَمْ يَرْجِعْ إِلَيَّ شَيْئًا، وَكُنْتُ أَوْجَدَ عَلَيْهِ مِنِّي عَلَى عُثْمَانَ، فَلَبِثْتُ لَيَالِيَ ثُمَّ خَطَبَهَا رَسُولُ اللَّهِ صلى الله عليه وسلم فَأَنْكَحْتُهَا إِيَّاهُ، فَلَقِيَنِي أَبُو بَكْرٍ فَقَالَ لَعَلَّكَ وَجَدْتَ عَلَىَّ حِينَ عَرَضْتَ عَلَىَّ حَفْصَةَ فَلَمْ أَرْجِعْ إِلَيْكَ شَيْئًا. قَالَ عُمَرُ قُلْتُ نَعَمْ. قَالَ أَبُو بَكْرٍ فَإِنَّهُ لَمْ يَمْنَعْنِي أَنْ أَرْجِعَ إِلَيْكَ فِيمَا عَرَضْتَ عَلَىَّ إِلاَّ أَنِّي كُنْتُ عَلِمْتُ أَنَّ رَسُولَ اللَّهِ صلى الله عليه وسلم قَدْ ذَكَرَهَا، فَلَمْ أَكُنْ لأُفْشِيَ سِرَّ رَسُولِ اللَّهِ صلى الله عليه وسلم وَلَوْ تَرَكَهَا رَسُولُ اللَّهِ صلى الله عليه وسلم قَبِلْتُهَا

Narrated Abu Sa`id Al-Khudri: (who fought in twelve Ghazawat in the company of the Prophet). I heard four things from the Prophet and they won my admiration. He said; -1. "No lady should travel on a journey of two days except with her husband or a Dhi-Mahram; -2. "No fasting is permissible on the two days of Id-ul-Fitr and `Id-ul-Adha; -3. "No prayer (may be offered) after the morning compulsory prayer until the sun rises; and no prayer after the `Asr prayer till the sun sets; -4. "One should travel only for visiting three Masjid (Mosques): Masjid-al-Haram (Mecca), Masjid-al- Aqsa (Jerusalem), and this (my) Mosque (at Medina). - Sahih Al-Bukhari 1995

حَدَّثَنَا حَجَّاجُ بْنُ مِنْهَالٍ، حَدَّثَنَا شُعْبَةُ، حَدَّثَنَا عَبْدُ الْمَلِكِ بْنُ عُمَيْرٍ، قَالَ سَمِعْتُ قَزَعَةَ، قَالَ سَمِعْتُ أَبَا سَعِيدٍ الْخُدْرِيَّ ـ رضى الله عنه ـ وَكَانَ غَزَا مَعَ النَّبِيِّ صلى الله عليه وسلم ثِنْتَىْ عَشْرَةَ غَزْوَةً قَالَ سَمِعْتُ أَرْبَعًا مِنَ النَّبِيِّ صلى الله عليه وسلم فَأَعْجَبْنَنِي قَالَ " لاَ تُسَافِرِ الْمَرْأَةُ مَسِيرَةَ يَوْمَيْنِ إِلاَّ وَمَعَهَا زَوْجُهَا أَوْ ذُو مَحْرَمٍ، وَلاَ صَوْمَ فِي يَوْمَيْنِ الْفِطْرِ وَالأَضْحَى، وَلاَ صَلاَةَ بَعْدَ الصُّبْحِ حَتَّى تَطْلُعَ الشَّمْسُ، وَلاَ بَعْدَ الْعَصْرِ حَتَّى تَغْرُبَ، وَلاَ تُشَدُّ الرِّحَالُ إِلاَّ إِلَى ثَلاَثَةِ مَسَاجِدَ مَسْجِدِ الْحَرَامِ، وَمَسْجِدِ الأَقْصَى، وَمَسْجِدِي هَذَا ".

We used to avoid chatting leisurely and freely with our wives

كُنَّا نَتَّقِي الْكَلاَمَ وَالاِنْبِسَاطَ إِلَى نِسَائِنَا

Narrated `Uqba bin 'Amir: Allah's Messengerﷺ said, "Beware of entering upon the ladies." A man from the Ansar said, "Allah's Apostle! What about Al-Hamu the in-laws of the wife (the brothers of her husband or his nephews etc.)?" The Prophetﷺ replied: The in-laws of the wife are death itself. – Sahih Al-Bukhari 5232

حَدَّثَنَا قُتَيْبَةُ بْنُ سَعِيدٍ، حَدَّثَنَا لَيْثٌ، عَنْ يَزِيدَ بْنِ أَبِي حَبِيبٍ، عَنْ أَبِي الْخَيْرِ، عَنْ عُقْبَةَ بْنِ عَامِرٍ، أَنَّ رَسُولَ اللَّهِ صلى الله عليه وسلم قَالَ " إِيَّاكُمْ وَالدُّخُولَ عَلَى النِّسَاءِ ". فَقَالَ رَجُلٌ مِنَ الأَنْصَارِ يَا رَسُولَ اللَّهِ أَفَرَأَيْتَ الْحَمْوَ. قَالَ " الْحَمْوُ الْمَوْتُ

Tell the believing men to restrain their looks, and to guard their privates. That is purer for them. Allah is cognizant of what they do.– Surah An-Nur 24:30

قُل لِّلْمُؤْمِنِينَ يَغُضُّوا۟ مِنْ أَبْصَـٰرِهِمْ وَيَحْفَظُوا۟ فُرُوجَهُمْ ۚ ذَٰلِكَ أَزْكَىٰ لَهُمْ ۗ إِنَّ ٱللَّهَ خَبِيرٌۢ بِمَا يَصْنَعُونَ

And tell the believing women to restrain their looks, and to guard their privates, and not display their beauty except what is apparent thereof, and to draw their coverings over their breasts, and not expose their beauty except to their husbands, their fathers, their husbands' fathers, their sons, their husbands' sons, their brothers, their brothers' sons, their sisters' sons, their women, what their right hands possess, their male attendants who have no sexual desires, or children who are not yet aware of the nakedness of women. And they should not strike their feet to draw attention to their hidden beauty. And repent to Allah, all of you believers, so that you may succeed. – Surah An-Nur 24:31

وَقُل لِّلْمُؤْمِنَـٰتِ يَغْضُضْنَ مِنْ أَبْصَـٰرِهِنَّ وَيَحْفَظْنَ فُرُوجَهُنَّ وَلَا يُبْدِينَ زِينَتَهُنَّ إِلَّا مَا ظَهَرَ مِنْهَا ۖ وَلْيَضْرِبْنَ بِخُمُرِهِنَّ عَلَىٰ جُيُوبِهِنَّ ۖ وَلَا
يُبْدِينَ زِينَتَهُنَّ إِلَّا لِبُعُولَتِهِنَّ أَوْ ءَابَآئِهِنَّ أَوْ ءَابَآءِ بُعُولَتِهِنَّ أَوْ أَبْنَآئِهِنَّ أَوْ أَبْنَآءِ بُعُولَتِهِنَّ أَوْ إِخْوَٰنِهِنَّ أَوْ بَنِىٓ إِخْوَٰنِهِنَّ أَوْ بَنِىٓ أَخَوَٰتِهِنَّ أَوْ
نِسَآئِهِنَّ أَوْ مَا مَلَكَتْ أَيْمَـٰنُهُنَّ أَوِ ٱلتَّـٰبِعِينَ غَيْرِ أُو۟لِى ٱلْإِرْبَةِ مِنَ ٱلرِّجَالِ أَوِ ٱلطِّفْلِ ٱلَّذِينَ لَمْ يَظْهَرُوا۟ عَلَىٰ عَوْرَٰتِ ٱلنِّسَآءِ ۖ وَلَا يَضْرِبْنَ
بِأَرْجُلِهِنَّ لِيُعْلَمَ مَا يُخْفِينَ مِن زِينَتِهِنَّ ۚ وَتُوبُوٓا۟ إِلَى ٱللَّهِ جَمِيعًا أَيُّهَ ٱلْمُؤْمِنُونَ لَعَلَّكُمْ تُفْلِحُونَ

Narrated Ibn `Abbas: I am a witness that Allah's Messenger ﷺ offered the Id prayer before delivering the sermon and then he thought that the women would not be able to hear him (because of the distance), so he went to them along with Bilal who was spreading his garment. The Prophet ﷺ advised and ordered them to give in charity. So the women started giving their ornaments (in charity). (The sub-narrator Aiyub pointed towards his ears and neck meaning that they gave ornaments from those places such as earrings and necklaces.). – Sahih Al-Bukhari 1449

حَدَّثَنَا مُؤَمَّلٌ، حَدَّثَنَا إِسْمَاعِيلُ، عَنْ أَيُّوبَ، عَنْ عَطَاءِ بْنِ أَبِي رَبَاحٍ، قَالَ قَالَ ابْنُ عَبَّاسٍ ـ رضى الله عنهما ـ أَشْهَدُ عَلَى رَسُولِ اللَّهِ صلى الله عليه وسلم لَصَلَّى قَبْلَ الْخُطْبَةِ، فَرَأَى أَنَّهُ لَمْ يُسْمِعِ النِّسَاءَ، فَأَتَاهُنَّ وَمَعَهُ بِلاَلٌ نَاشِرَ ثَوْبِهِ فَوَعَظَهُنَّ، وَأَمَرَهُنَّ أَنْ يَتَصَدَّقْنَ، فَجَعَلَتِ الْمَرْأَةُ تُلْقِي، وَأَشَارَ أَيُّوبُ إِلَى أُذُنِهِ وَإِلَى حَلْقِهِ

Narrated Ibn `Abbas: That he heard the Prophet ﷺ saying, "It is not permissible for a man to be alone with a woman, and no lady should travel except with a Muhram (i.e. her husband or a person whom she cannot marry in any case for ever; e.g. her father, brother, etc.)." Then a man got up and said, "O Allah's Messenger ﷺ !I have enlisted in the army for such-and-such Ghazwa and my wife is proceeding for Hajj." Allah's Messenger ﷺ said, "Go, and perform the Hajj with your wife.". – Sahih Al-Bukhari 3006

حَدَّثَنَا قُتَيْبَةُ بْنُ سَعِيدٍ، حَدَّثَنَا سُفْيَانُ، عَنْ عَمْرٍو، عَنْ أَبِي مَعْبَدٍ، عَنِ ابْنِ عَبَّاسٍ ـ رضى الله عنهما ـ أَنَّهُ سَمِعَ النَّبِيَّ صلى الله عليه وسلم يَقُولُ " لاَ يَخْلُوَنَّ رَجُلٌ بِامْرَأَةٍ، وَلاَ تُسَافِرَنَّ امْرَأَةٌ إِلاَّ وَمَعَهَا مَحْرَمٌ ". فَقَامَ رَجُلٌ فَقَالَ يَا رَسُولَ اللَّهِ، اكْتُتِبْتُ فِي غَزْوَةِ كَذَا وَكَذَا، وَخَرَجَتِ امْرَأَتِي حَاجَّةً. قَالَ " اذْهَبْ فَحُجَّ مَعَ امْرَأَتِكَ ".

Narrated Ibn `Umar: During the lifetime of the Prophet ﷺ we used to avoid chatting leisurely and freely with our wives lest some Divine inspiration might be revealed concerning us. But when the Prophet ﷺ had died, we started chatting leisurely and freely (with them). – Sahih Al-Bukhari 5187

حَدَّثَنَا أَبُو نُعَيْمٍ، حَدَّثَنَا سُفْيَانُ، عَنْ عَبْدِ اللَّهِ بْنِ دِينَارٍ، عَنِ ابْنِ عُمَرَ ـ رضى الله عنهما ـ قَالَ كُنَّا نَتَّقِي الْكَلاَمَ وَالاِنْبِسَاطَ إِلَى نِسَائِنَا عَلَى عَهْدِ النَّبِيِّ صلى الله عليه وسلم هَيْبَةَ أَنْ يُنْزَلَ فِينَا شَىْءٌ فَلَمَّا تُوُفِّيَ النَّبِيُّ صلى الله عليه وسلم تَكَلَّمْنَا وَانْبَسَطْنَا.

You will not be able to treat women with equal fairness, no matter how much you desire it. But do not be so biased as to leave another suspended. If you make amends, and act righteously—Allah is Forgiving and Merciful. – Surah An-Nisa 4:129

وَلَن تَسْتَطِيعُوٓا۟ أَن تَعْدِلُوا۟ بَيْنَ ٱلنِّسَآءِ وَلَوْ حَرَصْتُمْ ۖ فَلَا تَمِيلُوا۟ كُلَّ ٱلْمَيْلِ فَتَذَرُوهَا كَٱلْمُعَلَّقَةِ ۚ وَإِن تُصْلِحُوا۟ وَتَتَّقُوا۟ فَإِنَّ ٱللَّهَ كَانَ غَفُورًا رَّحِيمًا

Narrated `Urwa: Aisha told me, "Allah's Messenger ﷺ used to examine them according to this Verse: "O you who believe! When the believing women come to you, as emigrants test them . . . for Allah is Oft- Forgiving, Most Merciful." (60.10-12) Aisha said, "When any of them agreed to that condition Allah's Apostle would say to her, 'I have accepted your pledge of allegiance.' He would only say that, but, by Allah he never touched the hand of any women (i.e. never shook hands with them) while taking the pledge of allegiance and he never took their pledge of allegiance except by his words (only). – Sahih Al-Bukhari 2713

قَالَ عُرْوَةُ فَأَخْبَرَتْنِي عَائِشَةُ، أَنَّ رَسُولَ اللَّهِ صلى الله عليه وسلم كَانَ يَمْتَحِنُهُنَّ بِهَذِهِ الآيَةِ {يَا أَيُّهَا الَّذِينَ آمَنُوا إِذَا جَاءَكُمُ الْمُؤْمِنَاتُ مُهَاجِرَاتٍ فَامْتَحِنُوهُنَّ } إِلَى {غَفُورٌ رَحِيمٌ}. قَالَ عُرْوَةُ قَالَتْ عَائِشَةُ فَمَنْ أَقَرَّ بِهَذَا الشَّرْطِ مِنْهُنَّ قَالَ لَهَا رَسُولُ اللَّهِ صلى الله عليه وسلم " قَدْ بَايَعْتُكِ ". كَلاَمًا يُكَلِّمُهَا بِهِ، وَاللَّهِ مَا مَسَّتْ يَدُهُ يَدَ امْرَأَةٍ قَطُّ فِي الْمُبَايَعَةِ، وَمَا بَايَعَهُنَّ إِلاَّ بِقَوْلِهِ

Narrated Anas: The Prophet ﷺ used not to enter any house in Medina except the house of Um Sulaim besides those of his wives when he was asked why, he said, "I take pity on her as her brother was killed in my company. ". – Sahih Al-Bukhari 2844

حَدَّثَنَا مُوسَى، حَدَّثَنَا هَمَّامٌ، عَنْ إِسْحَاقَ بْنِ عَبْدِ اللَّهِ، عَنْ أَنَسٍ ـ رضى الله عنه ـ أَنَّ النَّبِيَّ صلى الله عليه وسلم لَمْ يَكُنْ يَدْخُلُ بَيْتًا بِالْمَدِينَةِ غَيْرَ بَيْتِ أُمِّ سُلَيْمٍ، إِلاَّ عَلَى أَزْوَاجِهِ فَقِيلَ لَهُ، فَقَالَ " إِنِّي أَرْحَمُهَا، قُتِلَ أَخُوهَا مَعِي ".

Then the angels called out to him, as he stood praying in the sanctuary: "Allah gives you good news of John; confirming a Word from Allah, and honorable, and moral, and a prophet; one of the upright."– Surah Al-Imran 3:39

فَنَادَتْهُ ٱلْمَلَٰٓئِكَةُ وَهُوَ قَآئِمٌ يُصَلِّى فِى ٱلْمِحْرَابِ أَنَّ ٱللَّهَ يُبَشِّرُكَ بِيَحْيَىٰ مُصَدِّقًۢا بِكَلِمَةٍ مِّنَ ٱللَّهِ وَسَيِّدًا وَحَصُورًا وَنَبِيًّا مِّنَ ٱلصَّٰلِحِينَ

That you seek after (them) with your riches
وَرَآءَ ذَٰلِكُمْ أَن تَبْتَغُوا۟ بِأَمْوَٰلِكُم

And bring the women their dowries as an endowment, so in case they are good to you concerning any portion of it, (Literally: in case they feel good in themselves to you about anything of it) then eat it up rejoicing with wholesome appetite (i.e., take it and make use of it to your profit and advantage). – Surah An-Nisa 4:4

وَءَاتُوا۟ ٱلنِّسَآءَ صَدُقَٰتِهِنَّ نِحْلَةً ۚ فَإِن طِبْنَ لَكُمْ عَن شَىْءٍ مِّنْهُ نَفْسًا فَكُلُوهُ هَنِيٓـًٔا مَّرِيٓـًٔا

And in case you are willing to exchange a spouse in place of (another) spouse, and you have brought one of them a hundredweight, (Literally: a Kantar) then do not take anything of it. Will you take it by way of all-malicious (calumny) and evident vice. Surah An-Nisa 4:20

وَإِنْ أَرَدتُّمُ ٱسْتِبْدَالَ زَوْجٍ مَّكَانَ زَوْجٍ وَءَاتَيْتُمْ إِحْدَىٰهُنَّ قِنطَارًا فَلَا تَأْخُذُوا۟ مِنْهُ شَيْـًٔا ۚ أَتَأْخُذُونَهُۥ بُهْتَٰنًا وَإِثْمًا مُّبِينًا

....lawful for you, beyond all that, is that you seek after (them) with your riches (i.e., that you pay them a dowry) in wedlock, other than in fornication. So (with) whomever of these (women) you enjoy the privilege of marriage, then bring them their rewards as an ordinance.... Surah An-Nisa 4:24

....أُحِلَّ لَكُم مَّا وَرَآءَ ذَٰلِكُمْ أَن تَبْتَغُوا۟ بِأَمْوَٰلِكُم مُّحْصِنِينَ غَيْرَ مُسَٰفِحِينَ ۚ فَمَا ٱسْتَمْتَعْتُم بِهِۦ مِنْهُنَّ فَـَٔاتُوهُنَّ أُجُورَهُنَّ فَرِيضَةً.....

.....and there is no fault in you to marry them (The female believers) when you have brought them (The female believers) their (due) rewards....
Surah Al-Mumtahinah 60:10

...وَلَا جُنَاحَ عَلَيْكُمْ أَن تَنكِحُوهُنَّ إِذَآ ءَاتَيْتُمُوهُنَّ أُجُورَهُنَّ ۚ...

Narrated Sahl bin Sa`d: While we were sitting in the company of the Prophet ﷺ a woman came to him and presented herself (for marriage) to him. The Prophet ﷺ looked at her, lowering his eyes and raising them, but did not give a reply. One of his companions said, "Marry her to me O Allah's Messenger ﷺ ! " The Prophet ﷺ asked (him), "Have you got anything?" He said, "I have got nothing." The Prophet said, "Not even an iron ring?" He Sa`d, "Not even an iron ring, but I will tear my garment into two halves and give her one half and keep the other half." The Prophet; said, "No. Do you know some of the Qur'an (by heart)?" He said, "Yes." The Prophet ﷺ said, "Go, I have agreed to marry her to you with what you know of the Qur'an (as her Mahr).". – Sahih al-Bukhari 5132

حَدَّثَنَا أَحْمَدُ بْنُ الْمِقْدَامِ، حَدَّثَنَا فُضَيْلُ بْنُ سُلَيْمَانَ، حَدَّثَنَا أَبُو حَازِمٍ، حَدَّثَنَا سَهْلُ بْنُ سَعْدٍ، كُنَّا عِنْدَ النَّبِيِّ صلى الله عليه وسلم جُلُوسًا فَجَاءَتْهُ امْرَأَةٌ تَعْرِضُ نَفْسَهَا عَلَيْهِ فَخَفَّضَ فِيهَا النَّظَرَ وَرَفَعَهُ فَلَمْ يُرِدْهَا، فَقَالَ رَجُلٌ مِنْ أَصْحَابِهِ زَوِّجْنِيهَا يَا رَسُولَ اللَّهِ. قَالَ " أَعِنْدَكَ مِنْ شَىْءٍ ". قَالَ مَا عِنْدِي مِنْ شَىْءٍ. قَالَ " وَلاَ خَاتَمًا مِنْ حَدِيدٍ ". قَالَ وَلاَ خَاتَمًا مِنْ حَدِيدٍ وَلَكِنْ أَشُقُّ بُرْدَتِي هَذِهِ فَأُعْطِيهَا النِّصْفَ، وَآخُذُ النِّصْفَ. قَالَ " لاَ، هَلْ مَعَكَ مِنَ الْقُرْآنِ شَىْءٌ ". قَالَ نَعَمْ. قَالَ " اذْهَبْ فَقَدْ زَوَّجْتُكَهَا بِمَا مَعَكَ مِنَ الْقُرْآنِ ".

In order that he might enjoy the pleasure of living with her
زَوْجَهَا لِيَسْكُنَ إِلَيْهَا

It is He who created you from a single person, and made from it its mate, that he may find comfort with her. Then, when he has covered her, she conceives a light load, and she carries it around. But when she has grown heavy, they pray to Allah their Lord, "if You give us a good child, we will be among the thankful."- Surah Al-A'raf 7:189

هُوَ ٱلَّذِى خَلَقَكُم مِّن نَّفْسٍ وَٰحِدَةٍ وَجَعَلَ مِنْهَا زَوْجَهَا لِيَسْكُنَ إِلَيْهَا ۖ فَلَمَّا تَغَشَّىٰهَا حَمَلَتْ حَمْلًا خَفِيفًا فَمَرَّتْ بِهِۦ ۖ فَلَمَّآ أَثْقَلَت دَّعَوَا ٱللَّهَ رَبَّهُمَا لَئِنْ ءَاتَيْتَنَا صَٰلِحًا لَّنَكُونَنَّ مِنَ ٱلشَّٰكِرِينَ

And of His signs is that He created for you mates from among yourselves, so that you may find tranquility in them; and He planted love and compassion between you. In this are signs for people who reflect.– Surah Ar-Rum 30:21

وَمِنْ ءَايَٰتِهِۦٓ أَنْ خَلَقَ لَكُم مِّنْ أَنفُسِكُمْ أَزْوَٰجًا لِّتَسْكُنُوٓا۟ إِلَيْهَا وَجَعَلَ بَيْنَكُم مَّوَدَّةً وَرَحْمَةً ۚ إِنَّ فِى ذَٰلِكَ لَءَايَٰتٍ لِّقَوْمٍ يَتَفَكَّرُونَ

Your wives are a tilth for you, so go to your tilth, when or how you will[36]
نِسَآؤُكُمْ حَرْثٌ لَّكُمْ فَأْتُوا۟ حَرْثَكُمْ أَنَّىٰ شِئْتُمْ

Their who safeguard Those chastity. Except from their spouses, or their dependents—for then they are free from blame.- Surah Al-Mu'minun 23:5&6

وَٱلَّذِينَ هُمْ لِفُرُوجِهِمْ حَٰفِظُونَ إِلَّا عَلَىٰٓ أَزْوَٰجِهِمْ أَوْ مَا مَلَكَتْ أَيْمَٰنُهُمْ فَإِنَّهُمْ غَيْرُ مَلُومِينَ

And those who guard their chastity. Except from their spouses or those living under their control, for then they are free of blame. - Surah Al-Ma'arij 70:29&30

وَٱلَّذِينَ هُمْ لِفُرُوجِهِمْ حَٰفِظُونَ إِلَّا عَلَىٰٓ أَزْوَٰجِهِمْ أَوْ مَا مَلَكَتْ أَيْمَٰنُهُمْ فَإِنَّهُمْ غَيْرُ مَلُومِينَ

Do you lust after men instead of women? You are truly ignorant people." – Surah An-Naml 27:55

أَئِنَّكُمْ لَتَأْتُونَ ٱلرِّجَالَ شَهْوَةً مِّن دُونِ ٱلنِّسَآءِ ۚ بَلْ أَنتُمْ قَوْمٌ تَجْهَلُونَ

---

[36] In Al-Quran 2:187 Allah use's the word ٱلرَّفَثُ . The Arabic term Al-Rafath ٱلرَّفَثُ, implies desire, the term generally refers to pursuing sexual intimacy and pleasure , Lascivious speech.

"You lust after men rather than women. You are an excessive people." – Surah Al-A'raf 7:81
إِنَّكُمْ لَتَأْتُونَ ٱلرِّجَالَ شَهْوَةً مِّن دُونِ ٱلنِّسَآءِ ۚ بَلْ أَنتُمْ قَوْمٌ مُّسْرِفُونَ

Do you approach the males of the world? And forsake the wives your Lord created for you? Indeed, you are intrusive people." – Surah Ash-Shu'ara 26:165&166
أَتَأْتُونَ ٱلذُّكْرَانَ مِنَ ٱلْعَٰلَمِينَ وَتَذَرُونَ مَا خَلَقَ لَكُمْ رَبُّكُم مِّنْ أَزْوَٰجِكُم ۚ بَلْ أَنتُمْ قَوْمٌ عَادُونَ

And his people came rushing towards him—they were in the habit of committing sins. He said, "O my people, these are my daughters; they are purer for you. So fear Allah, and do not embarrass me before my guests. Is there not one reasonable man among you?" – Surah Al-Huh 11:78
وَجَآءَهُۥ قَوْمُهُۥ يُهْرَعُونَ إِلَيْهِ وَمِن قَبْلُ كَانُوا۟ يَعْمَلُونَ ٱلسَّيِّـَٔاتِ ۚ قَالَ يَٰقَوْمِ هَٰٓؤُلَآءِ بَنَاتِى هُنَّ أَطْهَرُ لَكُمْ ۖ فَٱتَّقُوا۟ ٱللَّهَ وَلَا تُخْزُونِ فِى ضَيْفِىٓ ۖ أَلَيْسَ مِنكُمْ رَجُلٌ رَّشِيدٌ

[Lout (Lot)] said, "These are my daughters, if you must." – Surah Al-Hihr 15:71
قَالَ هَٰٓؤُلَآءِ بَنَاتِىٓ إِن كُنتُمْ فَٰعِلِينَ

Narrated Nafi`: Whenever Ibn `Umar recited the Qur'an, he would not speak to anyone till he had finished his recitation. Once I held the Qur'an and he recited Surat-al-Baqara from his memory and then stopped at a certain Verse and said, "Do you know in what connection this Verse was revealed? " I replied, "No." He said, "It was revealed in such-and-such connection." Ibn `Umar then resumed his recitation. Nafi` added regarding the Verse:--"So go to your tilth when or how you will" Ibn `Umar said, "It means one should approach his wife in ..". – Sahih Al-Bukhari 4526, 4527
حَدَّثَنَا إِسْحَاقُ، أَخْبَرَنَا النَّضْرُ بْنُ شُمَيْلٍ، أَخْبَرَنَا ابْنُ عَوْنٍ، عَنْ نَافِعٍ، قَالَ كَانَ ابْنُ عُمَرَ ـ رضى الله عنهما ـ إِذَا قَرَأَ الْقُرْآنَ لَمْ يَتَكَلَّمْ حَتَّى يَفْرُغَ مِنْهُ، فَأَخَذْتُ عَلَيْهِ يَوْمًا، فَقَرَأَ سُورَةَ الْبَقَرَةِ حَتَّى انْتَهَى إِلَى مَكَانٍ قَالَ تَدْرِي فِيمَا أُنْزِلَتْ‏.‏ قُلْتُ لاَ‏.‏ قَالَ أُنْزِلَتْ فِي كَذَا وَكَذَا‏.‏ ثُمَّ مَضَى‏.‏ وَعَنْ عَبْدِ الصَّمَدِ، حَدَّثَنِي أَبِي، حَدَّثَنِي أَيُّوبُ، عَنْ نَافِعٍ، عَنِ ابْنِ عُمَرَ، ‏{‏فَأْتُوا حَرْثَكُمْ أَنَّى شِئْتُمْ‏}‏ قَالَ يَأْتِيهَا فِي‏.‏ رَوَاهُ مُحَمَّدُ بْنُ يَحْيَى بْنِ سَعِيدٍ عَنْ أَبِيهِ عَنْ عُبَيْدِ اللَّهِ عَنْ نَافِعٍ عَنِ ابْنِ عُمَرَ‏.‏

Narrated Jabir: Jews used to say: "If one has sexual intercourse with his wife from the back, then she will deliver a squint-eyed child." So this Verse was revealed:-- "Your wives are a tilth unto you; so go to your tilth when or how you will." (2.223). – Sahih Al-Bukhari 4528 [37]
حَدَّثَنَا أَبُو نُعَيْمٍ، حَدَّثَنَا سُفْيَانُ، عَنِ ابْنِ الْمُنْكَدِرِ، سَمِعْتُ جَابِرًا ـ رضى الله عنه ـ قَالَ كَانَتِ الْيَهُودُ تَقُولُ إِذَا جَامَعَهَا مِنْ وَرَائِهَا جَاءَ الْوَلَدُ أَحْوَلَ‏.‏ فَنَزَلَتْ ‏{‏نِسَاؤُكُمْ حَرْثٌ لَكُمْ فَأْتُوا حَرْثَكُمْ أَنَّى شِئْتُمْ‏}‏
Your women are cultivation for you; so approach your cultivation whenever you like, and send ahead for yourselves. And fear Allah, and know that you will meet Him. And give good news to the believers.– Surah Al-Baqarah 2:223
نِسَآؤُكُمْ حَرْثٌ لَّكُمْ فَأْتُوا۟ حَرْثَكُمْ أَنَّىٰ شِئْتُمْ ۖ وَقَدِّمُوا۟ لِأَنفُسِكُمْ ۚ وَٱتَّقُوا۟ ٱللَّهَ وَٱعْلَمُوٓا۟ أَنَّكُم مُّلَٰقُوهُ ۗ وَبَشِّرِ ٱلْمُؤْمِنِينَ

Al-Hasan found no harm in her master's kissing or fondling with her. Ibn 'Umar said, "If a slave-girl who is suitable to have sexual relations is given to somebody as a gift, or sold or manumitted, her master should not have sexual intercourse with her before she gets one menstruation so as to be sure of absence of pregnancy, and there is no such necessity for a virgin." Ata said, "There is no harm in fondling with one's pregnant slave-girl without having

---

[37] Anal intercourse is not permitted without the wife's consent. If it is consensual, then according to the rulings of some Twelver Shia jurists — including Sistani's position as reported — it is permissible but strongly disliked (makrūh jiddan). – Ayatollah Ali al-Husayni al-Sistani's fatwā
لا يجوز وطء الزوجة دُبُرًا احتياطيًا بدون رضاها، وإذا رضيت فهو مكروه بشدة.

sexual intercourse with her. Allah said : 'Except with their wives and the (woman slaves) whom their right hands possess...' " (V.70:30) – Sahih Bukhari volume 3 pg 241 chapter 111
و لم ير الحسن بأسا أن يقبلها أو يباشرها. و قال ابن عمر رضي الله عنهما: إذا وهبت الوليدة التي توطا أو بتعت أو عتقت فليستبرا رحمها بحيضة، و لا تستبرا العذراء. وقال عطاء: لا بأس أن يصيب من خاريته الحامل ما دون الفرج. و قال الله تعالى: { إلا على ازواجهم أو ما ملكت إيمانهم } [المؤمنين: ٦].

What is the right?

مَا حَقٌّ

Narrated Ibn `Umar: The Prophet ﷺ said, "If your women ask permission to go to the mosque at night, allow them.". – Sahih Al-Bukhari 865
حَدَّثَنَا عُبَيْدُ اللَّهِ بْنُ مُوسَى، عَنْ حَنْظَلَةَ، عَنْ سَالِمِ بْنِ عَبْدِ اللَّهِ، عَنِ ابْنِ عُمَرَ ـ رضى الله عنهما ـ عَنِ النَّبِيِّ صلى الله عليه وسلم قَالَ " إِذَا اسْتَأْذَنَكُمْ نِسَاؤُكُمْ بِاللَّيْلِ إِلَى الْمَسْجِدِ فَأْذَنُوا لَهُنَّ ". تَابَعَهُ شُعْبَةُ عَنِ الأَعْمَشِ عَنْ مُجَاهِدٍ عَنِ ابْنِ عُمَرَ عَنِ النَّبِيِّ صلى الله عليه وسلم.

Narrated `Aisha: Aflah, the brother of Abi Al-Qu`ais, asked permission to visit me after the order of Al-Hijab was revealed. I said, "I will not permit him unless I take permission of the Prophet ﷺ about him for it was not the brother of Abi Al-Qu`ais but the wife of Abi Al-Qu`ais that nursed me." The Prophet ﷺ entered upon me, and I said to him, "O Allah's Messenger ! ﷺ Aflah, the brother of Abi Al-Qu`ais asked permission to visit me but I refused to permit him unless I took your permission." The Prophet ﷺ said, "What stopped you from permitting him? He is your uncle." I said, "O Allah's Messenger ﷺ! The man was not the person who had nursed me, but the woman, the wife of Abi Al-Qu`ais had nursed me." He said, "Admit him, for he is your uncle. Taribat Yaminuki (may your right hand be saved)" `Urwa, the sub-narrator added: For that `Aisha used to say, "Consider those things which are illegal because of blood relations as illegal because of the corresponding foster relations.". – Sahih Al-Bukhari 4796
حَدَّثَنَا أَبُو الْيَمَانِ، أَخْبَرَنَا شُعَيْبٌ، عَنِ الزُّهْرِيِّ، حَدَّثَنِي عُرْوَةُ بْنُ الزُّبَيْرِ، أَنَّ عَائِشَةَ ـ رضى الله عنها ـ قَالَتِ اسْتَأْذَنَ عَلَىَّ أَفْلَحُ أَخُو أَبِي الْقُعَيْسِ بَعْدَ مَا أُنْزِلَ الْحِجَابُ، فَقُلْتُ لاَ آذَنُ لَهُ حَتَّى أَسْتَأْذِنَ فِيهِ النَّبِيَّ صلى الله عليه وسلم فَإِنَّ أَخَاهُ أَبَا الْقُعَيْسِ لَيْسَ هُوَ أَرْضَعَنِي، وَلَكِنْ أَرْضَعَتْنِي امْرَأَةُ أَبِي الْقُعَيْسِ، فَدَخَلَ عَلَىَّ النَّبِيُّ صلى الله عليه وسلم فَقُلْتُ لَهُ يَا رَسُولَ اللَّهِ، إِنَّ أَفْلَحَ أَخَا أَبِي الْقُعَيْسِ اسْتَأْذَنَ، فَأَبَيْتُ أَنْ آذَنَ حَتَّى أَسْتَأْذِنَكَ فَقَالَ النَّبِيُّ صلى الله عليه وسلم " وَمَا مَنَعَكِ أَنْ تَأْذَنِي عَمُّكِ ". قُلْتُ يَا رَسُولَ اللَّهِ إِنَّ الرَّجُلَ لَيْسَ هُوَ أَرْضَعَنِي، وَلَكِنْ أَرْضَعَتْنِي امْرَأَةُ أَبِي الْقُعَيْسِ. فَقَالَ " ائْذَنِي لَهُ فَإِنَّهُ عَمُّكِ، تَرِبَتْ يَمِينُكِ ". قَالَ عُرْوَةُ فَلِذَلِكَ كَانَتْ عَائِشَةُ تَقُولُ حَرِّمُوا مِنَ الرَّضَاعَةِ مَا تُحَرِّمُونَ مِنَ النَّسَبِ

Narrated Ibn `Umar: The Prophet ﷺ said, "All of you are guardians and are responsible for your wards. The ruler is a guardian and the man is a guardian of his family; the lady is a guardian and is responsible for her husband's house and his offspring; and so all of you are guardians and are responsible for your wards.". – Sahih Al-Bukhari 5200
حَدَّثَنَا عَبْدَانُ، أَخْبَرَنَا عَبْدُ اللَّهِ، أَخْبَرَنَا مُوسَى بْنُ عُقْبَةَ، عَنْ نَافِعٍ، عَنِ ابْنِ عُمَرَ ـ رضى الله عنهما ـ عَنِ النَّبِيِّ صلى الله عليه وسلم قَالَ " كُلُّكُمْ رَاعٍ، وَكُلُّكُمْ مَسْئُولٌ عَنْ رَعِيَّتِهِ، وَالأَمِيرُ رَاعٍ، وَالرَّجُلُ رَاعٍ عَلَى أَهْلِ بَيْتِهِ، وَالْمَرْأَةُ رَاعِيَةٌ عَلَى بَيْتِ زَوْجِهَا وَوَلَدِهِ، فَكُلُّكُمْ رَاعٍ وَكُلُّكُمْ مَسْئُولٌ عَنْ رَعِيَّتِهِ ".

Men are the protectors and maintainers of women, as Allah has given some of them an advantage over others, and because they spend out of their wealth. The good women are obedient, guarding what Allah would have them guard. As for those from whom you fear disloyalty, admonish them, and abandon them in their beds, then strike them. But if they obey you, seek no way against them. Allah is Sublime, Great. – Surah An-Nisa 4:34
ٱلرِّجَالُ قَوَّٰمُونَ عَلَى ٱلنِّسَآءِ بِمَا فَضَّلَ ٱللَّهُ بَعْضَهُمْ عَلَىٰ بَعْضٍ وَبِمَآ أَنفَقُوا۟ مِنْ أَمْوَٰلِهِمْ ۚ فَٱلصَّٰلِحَٰتُ قَٰنِتَٰتٌ حَٰفِظَٰتٌ لِّلْغَيْبِ بِمَا حَفِظَ ٱللَّهُ ۚ وَٱلَّٰتِى تَخَافُونَ نُشُوزَهُنَّ فَعِظُوهُنَّ وَٱهْجُرُوهُنَّ فِى ٱلْمَضَاجِعِ وَٱضْرِبُوهُنَّ ۖ فَإِنْ أَطَعْنَكُمْ فَلَا تَبْغُوا۟ عَلَيْهِنَّ سَبِيلًا ۗ إِنَّ ٱللَّهَ كَانَ عَلِيًّا كَبِيرًا

Narrated Aisha: Regarding the Verse: 'If a wife fears cruelty or desertion on her husband's part ...') (4.128) It concerns the woman whose husband does not want to keep her with him any longer, but wants to divorce her and marry some other lady, so she says to him: 'Keep me and do not divorce me, and then marry another woman, and you may neither spend on me, nor sleep with me.' This is indicated by the Statement of Allah: 'There is no blame on them if they arrange an amicable settlement between them both, and (such) settlement is better." (4.128). – Sahih Al-Bukhari 5206

حَدَّثَنَا ابْنُ سَلاَمٍ، أَخْبَرَنَا أَبُو مُعَاوِيَةَ، عَنْ هِشَامٍ، عَنْ أَبِيهِ، عَنْ عَائِشَةَ ـ رضى الله عنها ـ {وَإِنِ امْرَأَةٌ خَافَتْ مِنْ بَعْلِهَا نُشُوزًا أَوْ إِعْرَاضًا} قَالَتْ هِيَ الْمَرْأَةُ تَكُونُ عِنْدَ الرَّجُلِ، لاَ يَسْتَكْثِرُ مِنْهَا فَيُرِيدُ طَلاَقَهَا، وَيَتَزَوَّجُ غَيْرَهَا، تَقُولُ لَهُ أَمْسِكْنِي وَلاَ تُطَلِّقْنِي، ثُمَّ تَزَوَّجْ غَيْرِي، فَأَنْتَ فِي حِلٍّ مِنَ النَّفَقَةِ عَلَىَّ وَالْقِسْمَةِ لِي، فَذَلِكَ قَوْلُهُ تَعَالَى {فَلاَ جُنَاحَ عَلَيْهِمَا أَنْ يَصَّالَحَا بَيْنَهُمَا صُلْحًا وَالصُّلْحُ خَيْرٌ}

Narrated Abu Huraira: Allah's Messenger ﷺ said, "If a husband calls his wife to his bed (i.e. to have sexual relation) and she refuses and causes him to sleep in anger, the angels will curse her till morning.". – Sahih Al-Bukhari 3237

حَدَّثَنَا مُسَدَّدٌ، حَدَّثَنَا أَبُو عَوَانَةَ، عَنِ الأَعْمَشِ، عَنْ أَبِي حَازِمٍ، عَنْ أَبِي هُرَيْرَةَ ـ رضى الله عنه ـ قَالَ قَالَ رَسُولُ اللَّهِ صلى الله عليه وسلم " إِذَا دَعَا الرَّجُلُ امْرَأَتَهُ إِلَى فِرَاشِهِ فَأَبَتْ، فَبَاتَ غَضْبَانَ عَلَيْهَا، لَعَنَتْهَا الْمَلاَئِكَةُ حَتَّى تُصْبِحَ ". تَابَعَهُ شُعْبَةُ وَأَبُو حَمْزَةَ وَابْنُ دَاوُدَ وَأَبُو مُعَاوِيَةَ عَنِ الأَعْمَشِ.

It was narrated from Hakim bin Muawiyah, from his father, that: A man asked the Prophet ﷺ : "What are the right of the woman over her husband?" He said: "That he should feed her as he feeds himself and clothe her as he clothes himself; he should not strike her on the face nor disfigure her, and he should not abandon her except in the house (as a form of discipline)." – Sunan Ibn Majah 1850

حَدَّثَنَا أَبُو بَكْرِ بْنُ أَبِي شَيْبَةَ، حَدَّثَنَا يَزِيدُ بْنُ هَارُونَ، عَنْ شُعْبَةَ، عَنْ أَبِي قَزَعَةَ، عَنْ حَكِيمِ بْنِ مُعَاوِيَةَ، عَنْ أَبِيهِ، أَنَّ رَجُلاً، سَأَلَ النَّبِيَّ ـ صلى الله عليه وسلم ـ مَا حَقُّ الْمَرْأَةِ عَلَى الزَّوْجِ قَالَ " أَنْ يُطْعِمَهَا إِذَا طَعِمَ وَأَنْ يَكْسُوَهَا إِذَا اكْتَسَى وَلاَ يَضْرِبِ الْوَجْهَ وَلاَ يُقَبِّحْ وَلاَ يَهْجُرْ إِلاَّ فِي الْبَيْتِ " .

O wives of the Prophet! You are not like any other women, if you observe piety. So do not speak too softly, lest the sick at heart lusts after you, but speak in an appropriate manner. And settle in your homes; and do not display yourselves, as in the former days of ignorance. And perform the prayer, and give regular charity, and obey Allah and His Messenger. Allah desires to remove all impurity from you, O People of the Household, and to purify you thoroughly. And remember what is recited in your homes of Allah's revelations and wisdom. Allah is Kind and Informed. – Surah Al-Ahzab 33:32-34

وَلَمَّا رَءَا ٱلْمُؤْمِنُونَ ٱلْأَحْزَابَ قَالُوا۟ هَٰذَا مَا وَعَدَنَا ٱللَّهُ وَرَسُولُهُۥ وَصَدَقَ ٱللَّهُ وَرَسُولُهُۥ ۚ وَمَا زَادَهُمْ إِلَّآ إِيمَٰنًا وَتَسْلِيمًا مِّنَ ٱلْمُؤْمِنِينَ رِجَالٌ صَدَقُوا۟ مَا عَٰهَدُوا۟ ٱللَّهَ عَلَيْهِ ۖ فَمِنْهُم مَّن قَضَىٰ نَحْبَهُۥ وَمِنْهُم مَّن يَنتَظِرُ ۖ وَمَا بَدَّلُوا۟ تَبْدِيلًا لِّيَجْزِىَ ٱللَّهُ ٱلصَّٰدِقِينَ بِصِدْقِهِمْ وَيُعَذِّبَ ٱلْمُنَٰفِقِينَ إِن شَآءَ أَوْ يَتُوبَ عَلَيْهِمْ ۚ إِنَّ ٱللَّهَ كَانَ غَفُورًا رَّحِيمًا

My Lord, have mercy on them, as they raised me when I was a child.

رَّبِّ ٱرْحَمْهُمَا كَمَا رَبَّيَانِى صَغِيرًا

Narrated 'Urwa: Aisha said, "While the Ethiopians were playing with their small spears, Allah's Messenger ﷺ screened me behind him and I watched (that display) and kept on watching till I left on my own." So you may estimate of what age a little girl may listen to amusement. – Sahih Al-Bukhari 5190

حَدَّثَنَا عَبْدُ اللَّهِ بْنُ مُحَمَّدٍ، حَدَّثَنَا هِشَامٌ، أَخْبَرَنَا مَعْمَرٌ، عَنِ الزُّهْرِيِّ، عَنْ عُرْوَةَ، عَنْ عَائِشَةَ، قَالَتْ كَانَ الْحَبَشُ يَلْعَبُونَ بِحِرَابِهِمْ، فَسَتَرَنِي رَسُولُ اللَّهِ صلى الله عليه وسلم وَأَنَا أَنْظُرُ، فَمَا زِلْتُ أَنْظُرُ حَتَّى كُنْتُ أَنَا أَنْصَرِفُ فَاقْدُرُوا قَدْرَ الْجَارِيَةِ الْحَدِيثَةِ السِّنِّ تَسْمَعُ اللَّهْوَ.

Narrated Sahl bin Sa`d: A man came to Allah's Messenger ﷺ and said, "O Allah's Messenger ﷺ! Suppose a man saw another man with his wife, should he kill him whereupon you might kill him (i.e. the killer) (in Qisas) or what should he do?" So Allah revealed concerning their case what is mentioned of the order of Mula'ana. Allah's Apostle said to the man, "The matter between you and your wife has been decided." So they did Mula'ana in the presence of Allah's Messenger ﷺ and I was present there, and then the man divorced his wife. So it became a tradition to dissolve the marriage of those spouses who were involved in a case of Mula'ana. The woman was pregnant and the husband denied that he was the cause of her pregnancy, so the son was (later) ascribed to her. Then it became a tradition that such a son would be the heir of his mother, and she would inherit of him what Allah prescribed for her. – Sahih Al-Bukhari 4746

حَدَّثَنِي سُلَيْمَانُ بْنُ دَاوُدَ أَبُو الرَّبِيعِ، حَدَّثَنَا فُلَيْحٌ، عَنِ الزُّهْرِيِّ، عَنْ سَهْلِ بْنِ سَعْدٍ، أَنَّ رَجُلاً، أَتَى رَسُولَ اللَّهِ صلى الله عليه وسلم فَقَالَ يَا رَسُولَ اللَّهِ، أَرَأَيْتَ رَجُلاً رَأَى مَعَ امْرَأَتِهِ رَجُلاً أَيَقْتُلُهُ فَتَقْتُلُونَهُ أَمْ كَيْفَ يَفْعَلُ فَأَنْزَلَ اللَّهُ فِيهِمَا مَا ذُكِرَ فِي الْقُرْآنِ مِنَ التَّلاَعُنِ، فَقَالَ لَهُ رَسُولُ اللَّهِ صلى الله عليه وسلم " قَدْ قُضِيَ فِيكَ وَفِي امْرَأَتِكَ ". قَالَ فَتَلاَعَنَا، وَأَنَا شَاهِدٌ عِنْدَ رَسُولِ اللَّهِ صلى الله عليه وسلم فَفَارَقَهَا فَكَانَتْ سُنَّةً أَنْ يُفَرَّقَ بَيْنَ الْمُتَلاَعِنَيْنِ وَكَانَتْ حَامِلاً، فَأَنْكَرَ حَمْلَهَا وَكَانَ ابْنُهَا يُدْعَى إِلَيْهَا، ثُمَّ جَرَتِ السُّنَّةُ فِي الْمِيرَاثِ أَنْ يَرِثَهَا، وَتَرِثَ مِنْهُ مَا فَرَضَ اللَّهُ لَهَا

Narrated Ibn Shihab: The funeral prayer should be offered for every child even if he were the son of a prostitute as he was born with a true faith of Islam (i.e. to worship none but Allah Alone). If his parents are Muslims, particularly the father, even if his mother were a non-Muslim, and if he after the delivery cries (even once) before his death (i.e. born alive) then the funeral prayer must be offered. And if the child does not cry after his delivery (i.e. born dead) then his funeral prayer should not be offered, and he will be considered as a miscarriage. Abu Huraira, narrated that the Prophet ﷺ said, "Every child is born with a true faith (i.e. to worship none but Allah Alone) but his parents convert him to Judaism or to Christianity or to Magainism, as an animal delivers a perfect baby animal. Do you find it mutilated?" Then Abu Huraira recited the holy verses: 'The pure Allah's Islamic nature (true faith i.e. to worship none but Allah Alone), with which He has created human beings.' " (30.30). – Sahih Al-Bukhari 1358

حَدَّثَنَا أَبُو الْيَمَانِ، أَخْبَرَنَا شُعَيْبٌ، قَالَ ابْنُ شِهَابٍ يُصَلَّى عَلَى كُلِّ مَوْلُودٍ مُتَوَفًّى وَإِنْ كَانَ لِغَيَّةٍ، مِنْ أَجْلِ أَنَّهُ وُلِدَ عَلَى فِطْرَةِ الإِسْلاَمِ، يَدَّعِي أَبَوَاهُ الإِسْلاَمَ أَوْ أَبُوهُ خَاصَّةً، وَإِنْ كَانَتْ أُمُّهُ عَلَى غَيْرِ الإِسْلاَمِ، إِذَا اسْتَهَلَّ صَارِخًا صُلِّيَ عَلَيْهِ، وَلاَ يُصَلَّى عَلَى مَنْ لاَ يَسْتَهِلُّ مِنْ أَجْلِ أَنَّهُ سِقْطٌ، فَإِنَّ أَبَا هُرَيْرَةَ ـ رضى الله عنه ـ كَانَ يُحَدِّثُ قَالَ النَّبِيُّ صلى الله عليه وسلم " مَا مِنْ مَوْلُودٍ إِلاَّ يُولَدُ عَلَى الْفِطْرَةِ، فَأَبَوَاهُ يُهَوِّدَانِهِ أَوْ يُنَصِّرَانِهِ أَوْ يُمَجِّسَانِهِ، كَمَا تُنْتَجُ الْبَهِيمَةُ بَهِيمَةً جَمْعَاءَ هَلْ تُحِسُّونَ فِيهَا مِنْ جَدْعَاءَ ". ثُمَّ يَقُولُ أَبُو هُرَيْرَةَ ـ رضى الله عنه ـ {فِطْرَةَ اللَّهِ الَّتِي فَطَرَ النَّاسَ عَلَيْهَا} الآيَةَ.

And Al-Hasan, Shuraih, Ibrahim and Qaṭāda said, "If one of the parents of the boy becomes a Muslim, then the boy will be with the Muslim parent." And Ibn Abbās was with his mother who was amongst the weak and the poor people , and was not with his father who was on the religion of his nation. And said, "Islam is always superior and never inferior.". – Sahih Al-Bukhari Vol.2 page 250

و قال الحسن و شريح و ابراهيم و قتادة : إذا أسلم أحدهما فال ولد مع المسلم. و كان ابن عباس رضي الله عنهما مع أبيه على دين قومه . و قال : الاسلام يعلو و لا يعلى.

Call them after their fathers; that is more equitable with Allah. But if you do not know their fathers, then your brethren in faith and your friends. There is no blame on you if you err therein, barring what your hearts premeditates. Allah is Forgiving and Merciful. – Surah Al-Ahzab 33:5

ٱدْعُوهُمْ لِءَابَآئِهِمْ هُوَ أَقْسَطُ عِندَ ٱللَّهِ فَإِن لَّمْ تَعْلَمُوٓا۟ ءَابَآءَهُمْ فَإِخْوَٰنُكُمْ فِى ٱلدِّينِ وَمَوَٰلِيكُمْ وَلَيْسَ عَلَيْكُمْ جُنَاحٌ فِيمَآ أَخْطَأْتُم بِهِۦ وَلَٰكِن مَّا تَعَمَّدَتْ قُلُوبُكُمْ وَكَانَ ٱللَّهُ غَفُورًا رَّحِيمًا

Allow them to reside where you reside, according to your means, and do not harass them in order to make things difficult for them. If they are pregnant, spend on them until they give birth. And if they nurse your infant, give them their payment. And conduct your relation in amity. But if you disagree, then let another woman nurse him. – Surah At-Talaq 65:6

أَسْكِنُوهُنَّ مِنْ حَيْثُ سَكَنتُم مِّن وُجْدِكُمْ وَلَا تُضَآرُّوهُنَّ لِتُضَيِّقُوا۟ عَلَيْهِنَّ ۚ وَإِن كُنَّ أُو۟لَـٰتِ حَمْلٍ فَأَنفِقُوا۟ عَلَيْهِنَّ حَتَّىٰ يَضَعْنَ حَمْلَهُنَّ ۚ فَإِنْ
أَرْضَعْنَ لَكُمْ فَـَٔاتُوهُنَّ أُجُورَهُنَّ ۖ وَأْتَمِرُوا۟ بَيْنَكُم بِمَعْرُوفٍ ۖ وَإِن تَعَاسَرْتُمْ فَسَتُرْضِعُ لَهُۥٓ أُخْرَىٰ

Mothers may nurse their infants for two whole years, for those who desire to complete the nursingperiod. It is the duty of the father to provide for them and clothe them in a proper manner. No soul shall be burdened beyond its capacity. No mother shall be harmed on account of her child, and no father shall be harmed on account of his child. The same duty rests upon the heir. If the couple desire weaning, by mutual consent and consultation, they commit no error by doing so. You commit no error by hiring nursingmothers, as long as you pay them fairly. And be wary of Allah, and know that Allah is Seeing of what you do. – Surah Al-Baqarah 2:233

وَٱلْوَٰلِدَٰتُ يُرْضِعْنَ أَوْلَـٰدَهُنَّ حَوْلَيْنِ كَامِلَيْنِ ۖ لِمَنْ أَرَادَ أَن يُتِمَّ ٱلرَّضَاعَةَ ۚ وَعَلَى ٱلْمَوْلُودِ لَهُۥ رِزْقُهُنَّ وَكِسْوَتُهُنَّ بِٱلْمَعْرُوفِ ۚ لَا
تُكَلَّفُ نَفْسٌ إِلَّا وُسْعَهَا ۚ لَا تُضَآرَّ وَٰلِدَةٌۢ بِوَلَدِهَا وَلَا مَوْلُودٌ لَّهُۥ بِوَلَدِهِۦ ۚ وَعَلَى ٱلْوَارِثِ مِثْلُ ذَٰلِكَ ۗ فَإِنْ أَرَادَا فِصَالًا عَن تَرَاضٍ
مِّنْهُمَا وَتَشَاوُرٍ فَلَا جُنَاحَ عَلَيْهِمَا ۗ وَإِنْ أَرَدتُّمْ أَن تَسْتَرْضِعُوٓا۟ أَوْلَـٰدَكُمْ فَلَا جُنَاحَ عَلَيْكُمْ إِذَا سَلَّمْتُم مَّآ ءَاتَيْتُم بِٱلْمَعْرُوفِ ۗ وَٱتَّقُوا۟
ٱللَّهَ وَٱعْلَمُوٓا۟ أَنَّ ٱللَّهَ بِمَا تَعْمَلُونَ بَصِيرٌ

And your Lord has decreed that you should not worship any except Him (only) and (to show) fairest companionship to parents; in case ever one or both of them reaches old age (Literally: being great "in years") in your presence, do not say to them, "Fie!" nor scold them; and speak to them respectful words (Literally: say to them an honorable saying).- Surah Al-Isra 17:23

وَقَضَىٰ رَبُّكَ أَلَّا تَعْبُدُوٓا۟ إِلَّآ إِيَّاهُ وَبِٱلْوَٰلِدَيْنِ إِحْسَـٰنًا ۚ إِمَّا يَبْلُغَنَّ عِندَكَ ٱلْكِبَرَ أَحَدُهُمَآ أَوْ كِلَاهُمَا فَلَا تَقُل لَّهُمَآ أُفٍّ وَلَا تَنْهَرْهُمَا
وَقُل لَّهُمَا قَوْلًا كَرِيمًا

And (remember) as We took Compact with the Seeds (or: sons)of Israel) (that), "You shall not worship any (god) except Allah, and (show) fairest companionship to parents, and near kinsmen, and to orphans, and to the indigent; and speak fair to mankind, and keep up the prayer, and bring the Zakat. (i.e., pay the obligatory poor-dues)" (But) thereafter you turned away excepting for a few of you, and you are (still) veering away. Surah Al-Baqarah 2:83

وَإِذْ أَخَذْنَا مِيثَـٰقَ بَنِىٓ إِسْرَٰٓءِيلَ لَا تَعْبُدُونَ إِلَّا ٱللَّهَ وَبِٱلْوَٰلِدَيْنِ إِحْسَانًا وَذِى ٱلْقُرْبَىٰ وَٱلْيَتَـٰمَىٰ وَٱلْمَسَـٰكِينِ وَقُولُوا۟ لِلنَّاسِ حُسْنًا
وَأَقِيمُوا۟ ٱلصَّلَوٰةَ وَءَاتُوا۟ ٱلزَّكَوٰةَ ثُمَّ تَوَلَّيْتُمْ إِلَّا قَلِيلًا مِّنكُمْ وَأَنتُم مُّعْرِضُونَ

Abortion

إجهاض

And do not kill your children for fear of poverty. We provide for them, and for you. Killing them is a grave sin. – Surah Al-Isra 17:31

وَلَا تَقْتُلُوٓا۟ أَوْلَـٰدَكُمْ خَشْيَةَ إِمْلَـٰقٍ ۖ نَّحْنُ نَرْزُقُهُمْ وَإِيَّاكُمْ ۚ إِنَّ قَتْلَهُمْ كَانَ خِطْـًٔا كَبِيرًا

Say, "Come, let me tell you what your Lord has forbidden you: that you associate nothing with Him; that you honor your parents; that you do not kill your children because of poverty—We provide for you and for them; that you do not come near indecencies, whether outward or inward; and that you do not kill the soul which Allah has sanctified— except in the course of justice. All this He has enjoined upon you, so that you may understand." – Surah Al-An'am 6:151

قُلْ تَعَالَوْا۟ أَتْلُ مَا حَرَّمَ رَبُّكُمْ عَلَيْكُمْ ۖ أَلَّا تُشْرِكُوا۟ بِهِۦ شَيْـًۭٔا ۖ وَبِٱلْوَٰلِدَيْنِ إِحْسَـٰنًۭا ۖ وَلَا تَقْتُلُوٓا۟ أَوْلَـٰدَكُم مِّنْ إِمْلَـٰقٍۢ ۖ نَّحْنُ نَرْزُقُكُمْ وَإِيَّاهُمْ ۖ وَلَا تَقْرَبُوا۟ ٱلْفَوَٰحِشَ مَا ظَهَرَ مِنْهَا وَمَا بَطَنَ ۖ وَلَا تَقْتُلُوا۟ ٱلنَّفْسَ ٱلَّتِى حَرَّمَ ٱللَّهُ إِلَّا بِٱلْحَقِّ ۚ ذَٰلِكُمْ وَصَّىٰكُم بِهِۦ لَعَلَّكُمْ تَعْقِلُونَ

Narrated Abu Huraira: Two ladies (had a fight) and one of them hit the other with a stone on the `Abdomen and caused her to abort. The Prophet ﷺ judged that the victim be given either a slave or a female slave (as blood-money). Narrated Ibn Shihab: Sa`id bin Al-Musayyab said, "Allah's Messenger ﷺ judged that in case of child killed in the womb of its mother, the offender should give the mother a slave or a female slave in recompense The offender said, How can I be fined for killing one who neither ate nor drank, neither spoke nor cried: a case like that should be denied ' On that Allah's Messenger ﷺ said 'He is one of the brothers of the foretellers. – Sahih Al-Bukhari 5759, 5760

حَدَّثَنَا قُتَيْبَةُ، عَنْ مَالِكٍ، عَنِ ابْنِ شِهَابٍ، عَنْ أَبِي سَلَمَةَ، عَنْ أَبِي هُرَيْرَةَ ـ رضى الله عنه ـ أَنَّ امْرَأَتَيْنِ، رَمَتْ إِحْدَاهُمَا الأُخْرَى بِحَجَرٍ فَطَرَحَتْ جَنِينَهَا، فَقَضَى فِيهِ النَّبِيُّ صلى الله عليه وسلم بِغُرَّةٍ عَبْدٍ أَوْ وَلِيدَةٍ. وَعَنِ ابْنِ شِهَابٍ، عَنْ سَعِيدِ بْنِ الْمُسَيَّبِ، أَنَّ رَسُولَ اللَّهِ صلى الله عليه وسلم قَضَى فِي الْجَنِينِ يُقْتَلُ فِي بَطْنِ أُمِّهِ بِغُرَّةٍ عَبْدٍ أَوْ وَلِيدَةٍ. فَقَالَ الَّذِي قُضِيَ عَلَيْهِ كَيْفَ أَغْرَمُ مَنْ لاَ أَكَلَ، وَلاَ شَرِبَ، وَلاَ نَطَقَ، وَلاَ اسْتَهَلَّ، وَمِثْلُ ذَلِكَ بَطَلَ فَقَالَ رَسُولُ اللَّهِ صلى الله عليه وسلم " إِنَّمَا هَذَا مِنْ إِخْوَانِ الْكُهَّانِ ".

Narrated Abu Huraira: Allah's Messenger ﷺ gave his verdict about two ladies of the Hudhail tribe who had fought each other and one of them had hit the other with a stone. The stone hit her `Abdomen and as she was pregnant, the blow killed the child in her womb. They both filed their case with the Prophet ﷺ and he judged that the blood money for what was in her womb. Was a slave or a female slave. The guardian of the lady who was fined said, "O Allah's Messenger ﷺ! Shall I be fined for a creature that has neither drunk nor eaten, neither spoke nor cried? A case like that should be nullified." On that the Prophet ﷺ said, "This is one of the brothers of soothsayers. – Sahih Al-Bukhari 5758

حَدَّثَنَا سَعِيدُ بْنُ عُفَيْرٍ، حَدَّثَنَا اللَّيْثُ، قَالَ حَدَّثَنَا عَبْدُ الرَّحْمَنِ بْنُ خَالِدٍ، عَنِ ابْنِ شِهَابٍ، عَنْ أَبِي سَلَمَةَ، عَنْ أَبِي هُرَيْرَةَ، أَنَّ رَسُولَ اللَّهِ صلى الله عليه وسلم قَضَى فِي امْرَأَتَيْنِ مِنْ هُذَيْلٍ اقْتَتَلَتَا، فَرَمَتْ إِحْدَاهُمَا الأُخْرَى بِحَجَرٍ، فَأَصَابَ بَطْنَهَا وَهْىَ حَامِلٌ، فَقَتَلَتْ وَلَدَهَا الَّذِي فِي بَطْنِهَا فَاخْتَصَمُوا إِلَى النَّبِيِّ صلى الله عليه وسلم فَقَضَى أَنَّ دِيَةَ مَا فِي بَطْنِهَا غُرَّةٌ عَبْدٌ أَوْ أَمَةٌ، فَقَالَ وَلِيُّ الْمَرْأَةِ الَّتِي غَرِمَتْ كَيْفَ أَغْرَمُ يَا رَسُولَ اللَّهِ مَنْ لاَ شَرِبَ، وَلاَ أَكَلَ، وَلاَ نَطَقَ، وَلاَ اسْتَهَلَّ، فَمِثْلُ ذَلِكَ ي
ُطَلّ فَقَالَ النَّبِيُّ صلى الله عليه وسلم " إِنَّمَا هَذَا مِنْ إِخْوَانِ الْكُهَّانِ ".

Narrated Abu Huraira: Allah's Messenger ﷺ gave the judgment that a male or female slave should be given in Qisas for an abortion case of a woman from the tribe of Bani Lihyan (as blood money for the fetus) but the lady on whom the penalty had been imposed died, so the Prophets ordered that her property be inherited by her offspring and her husband and that the penalty be paid by her Asaba. – Sahih Al-Bukhari 6740

حَدَّثَنَا قُتَيْبَةُ، حَدَّثَنَا اللَّيْثُ، عَنِ ابْنِ شِهَابٍ، عَنِ ابْنِ الْمُسَيَّبِ، عَنْ أَبِي هُرَيْرَةَ، أَنَّهُ قَالَ قَضَى رَسُولُ اللَّهِ صلى الله عليه وسلم فِي جَنِينِ امْرَأَةٍ مِنْ بَنِي لَحْيَانَ سَقَطَ مَيِّتًا بِغُرَّةٍ عَبْدٍ أَوْ أَمَةٍ. ثُمَّ إِنَّ الْمَرْأَةَ الَّتِي قَضَى عَلَيْهَا بِالْغُرَّةِ تُوُفِّيَتْ، فَقَضَى رَسُولُ اللَّهِ صلى الله عليه وسلم " بِأَنَّ مِيرَاثَهَا لِبَنِيهَا وَزَوْجِهَا، وَأَنَّ الْعَقْلَ عَلَى عَصَبَتِهَا ".

Verily, We have created all things with Divine preordainment

إِنَّا كُلَّ شَىْءٍ خَلَقْنَـٰهُ بِقَدَرٍ

So He made him of two spouses, the male and the female. – Surah Al-Qiyamah 75:39

فَجَعَلَ مِنْهُ ٱلزَّوْجَيْنِ ٱلذَّكَرَ وَٱلْأُنثَىٰٓ

And that He created the two pairs, the male and the female. – Surah An-Najm 53:45

وَأَنَّهُۥ خَلَقَ ٱلزَّوْجَيْنِ ٱلذَّكَرَ وَٱلْأُنثَىٰ

Or He gives both male and female [to whomever He wills], and causes to be barren whomever He wills: for, verily, He is all-knowing, infinite in His power. Surah Ash-Shura 42:50
أَوْ يُزَوِّجُهُمْ ذُكْرَانًا وَإِنَاثًا ۖ وَيَجْعَلُ مَن يَشَاءُ عَقِيمًا ۚ إِنَّهُ عَلِيمٌ قَدِيرٌ

"And I (Satan) will mislead them, and I will entice them, and I will prompt them to slit the ears of cattle, and I will prompt them to alter the creation of Allah." Whoever takes Satan as a lord, instead of Allah, has surely suffered a profound loss. – Surah An-Nisa 4:119
وَلَأُضِلَّنَّهُمْ وَلَأُمَنِّيَنَّهُمْ وَلَآمُرَنَّهُمْ فَلَيُبَتِّكُنَّ آذَانَ الْأَنْعَامِ وَلَآمُرَنَّهُمْ فَلَيُغَيِّرُنَّ خَلْقَ اللَّهِ ۚ وَمَن يَتَّخِذِ الشَّيْطَانَ وَلِيًّا مِّن دُونِ اللَّهِ فَقَدْ خَسِرَ خُسْرَانًا مُّبِينًا

Narrated Ibn `Abbas: The Prophet ﷺ cursed the effeminate men and those women who assume the similitude (manners) of men. He also said, "Turn them out of your houses." He turned such-and-such person out, and `Umar also turned out such-and-such person. – Sahih Al-Bukhari 6834
حَدَّثَنَا مُسْلِمُ بْنُ إِبْرَاهِيمَ، حَدَّثَنَا هِشَامٌ، حَدَّثَنَا يَحْيَى، عَنْ عِكْرِمَةَ، عَنِ ابْنِ عَبَّاسٍ ـ رضى الله عنهما ـ قَالَ لَعَنَ النَّبِيُّ صلى الله عليه وسلم الْمُخَنَّثِينَ مِنَ الرِّجَالِ، وَالْمُتَرَجِّلاَتِ مِنَ النِّسَاءِ، وَقَالَ " أَخْرِجُوهُمْ مِنْ بُيُوتِكُمْ ". وَأَخْرَجَ فُلاَنًا، وَأَخْرَجَ عُمَرُ فُلاَنًا.

Narrated Ibn `Abbas: Allah's Messenger ﷺ cursed those men who are in the similitude (assume the manners) of women and those women who are in the similitude (assume the manners) of men. – Sahih Al-Bukhari 5885
حَدَّثَنَا مُحَمَّدُ بْنُ بَشَّارٍ، حَدَّثَنَا غُنْدَرٌ، حَدَّثَنَا شُعْبَةُ، عَنْ قَتَادَةَ، عَنْ عِكْرِمَةَ، عَنِ ابْنِ عَبَّاسٍ ـ رضى الله عنهما ـ قَالَ لَعَنَ رَسُولُ اللَّهِ صلى الله عليه وسلم الْمُتَشَبِّهِينَ مِنَ الرِّجَالِ بِالنِّسَاءِ، وَالْمُتَشَبِّهَاتِ مِنَ النِّسَاءِ بِالرِّجَالِ. تَابَعَهُ عَمْرٌو أَخْبَرَنَا شُعْبَةُ

Narrated Um Salama: The Prophet ﷺ came to me while there was an effeminate man sitting with me, and I heard him (i.e. the effeminate man) saying to `Abdullah bin Abi Umaiya, "O `Abdullah! See if Allah should make you conquer Ta'if tomorrow, then take the daughter of Ghailan (in marriage) as (she is so beautiful and fat that) she shows four folds of flesh when facing you, and eight when she turns her back." The Prophet ﷺ then said, "These (effeminate men) should never enter upon you (O women!)." Ibn Juraij said, "That effeminate man was called Hit." Narrated Hisham: The above narration and added extra, that at that time, the Prophet, was besieging Taif. – Sahih Al-Bukhari 4324
حَدَّثَنَا الْحُمَيْدِيُّ، سَمِعَ سُفْيَانَ، حَدَّثَنَا هِشَامٌ، عَنْ أَبِيهِ، عَنْ زَيْنَبَ ابْنَةِ أَبِي سَلَمَةَ، عَنْ أُمِّهَا أُمِّ سَلَمَةَ ـ رضى الله عنها ـ دَخَلَ عَلَىَّ النَّبِيُّ صلى الله عليه وسلم وَعِنْدِي مُخَنَّثٌ فَسَمِعْتُهُ يَقُولُ لِعَبْدِ اللَّهِ بْنِ أَبِي أُمَيَّةَ يَا عَبْدَ اللَّهِ أَرَأَيْتَ إِنْ فَتَحَ اللَّهُ عَلَيْكُمُ الطَّائِفَ غَدًا فَعَلَيْكَ بِابْنَةِ غَيْلاَنَ، فَإِنَّهَا تُقْبِلُ بِأَرْبَعٍ وَتُدْبِرُ بِثَمَانٍ. وَقَالَ النَّبِيُّ صلى الله عليه وسلم " لاَ يَدْخُلَنَّ هَؤُلاَءِ عَلَيْكُنَّ ". قَالَ ابْنُ عُيَيْنَةَ وَقَالَ ابْنُ جُرَيْجٍ الْمُخَنَّثُ هِيتٌ. حَدَّثَنَا مَحْمُودٌ حَدَّثَنَا أَبُو أُسَامَةَ عَنْ هِشَامٍ بِهَذَا، وَزَادَ وَهْوَ مُحَاصِرٌ الطَّائِفَ يَوْمَئِذٍ.

Narrated `Abdullah bin `Umar: I never heard `Umar saying about something that he thought it would be so-and-so, but he was quite right. Once, while `Umar was sitting, a handsome man passed by him, `Umar said, "If I am not wrong, this person is still on his religion of the pre-Islamic period of ignorance or he was their foreteller. Call the man to me." When the man was called to him, he told him of his thought. The man said, "I have never seen such a day on which a Muslim is faced with such an accusation." `Umar said, "I am determined that you should tell me the truth." He said, "I was a foreteller in the pre-Islamic period of ignorance." Then `Umar said, "Tell me the most astonishing thing your female Jinn has told you of." He said, "One-day while I was in the market, she came to me scared and said, 'Haven't you seen the Jinns and their despair and they were overthrown after their defeat (and prevented from listening to the news of the heaven) so that they (stopped going to the sky and) kept following camel-riders (i.e. 'Arabs)?" `Umar said, "He is right." And added, "One day while I was near their idols, there came a man with a calf and slaughtered it as a sacrifice (for the idols). An (unseen) creature shouted at him, and I have never heard harsher than his voice. He was crying, 'O you bold evil-doer! A matter of success! An eloquent man is saying: None has the right to be worshipped except you (O Allah).' On that the people fled, but I said, 'I shall not go away till I know what is behind this.' Then the cry came again: 'O you bold evil-doer! A matter of success! An eloquent man is saying: None has the right to be worshipped except Allah.' I then went away and a few days later it was said, "A prophet has appeared." – Sahih Al-Bukhari 3866

حَدَّثَنَا يَحْيَى بْنُ سُلَيْمَانَ، قَالَ حَدَّثَنِي ابْنُ وَهْبٍ، قَالَ حَدَّثَنِي عُمَرُ، أَنَّ سَالِمًا، حَدَّثَهُ عَنْ عَبْدِ اللَّهِ بْنِ عُمَرَ، قَالَ مَا سَمِعْتُ عُمَرَ، لِشَىْءٍ قَطُّ يَقُولُ إِنِّي لأَظُنُّهُ كَذَا. إِلاَّ كَانَ كَمَا يَظُنُّ، بَيْنَمَا عُمَرُ جَالِسٌ إِذْ مَرَّ بِهِ رَجُلٌ جَمِيلٌ فَقَالَ لَقَدْ أَخْطَأَ ظَنِّي، أَوْ إِنَّ هَذَا عَلَى دِينِهِ فِي الْجَاهِلِيَّةِ، أَوْ لَقَدْ كَانَ كَاهِنَهُمْ، عَلَىَّ الرَّجُلَ، فَدُعِيَ لَهُ، فَقَالَ لَهُ ذَلِكَ، فَقَالَ مَا رَأَيْتُ كَالْيَوْمِ اسْتُقْبِلَ بِهِ رَجُلٌ مُسْلِمٌ، قَالَ فَإِنِّي أَعْزِمُ عَلَيْكَ إِلاَّ مَا أَخْبَرْتَنِي. قَالَ كُنْتُ كَاهِنَهُمْ فِي الْجَاهِلِيَّةِ. قَالَ فَمَا أَعْجَبُ مَا جَاءَتْكَ بِهِ جِنِّيَّتُكَ قَالَ بَيْنَمَا أَنَا يَوْمًا فِي السُّوقِ جَاءَتْنِي أَعْرِفُ فِيهَا الْفَزَعَ، فَقَالَتْ أَلَمْ تَرَ الْجِنَّ وَإِبْلاَسَهَا وَيَأْسَهَا مِنْ بَعْدِ إِنْكَاسِهَا وَلُحُوقَهَا بِالْقِلاَصِ وَأَحْلاَسِهَا قَالَ عُمَرُ صَدَقَ، بَيْنَمَا أَنَا عِنْدَ آلِهَتِهِمْ إِذْ جَاءَ رَجُلٌ بِعِجْلٍ فَذَبَحَهُ، فَصَرَخَ بِهِ صَارِخٌ، لَمْ أَسْمَعْ صَارِخًا قَطُّ أَشَدَّ صَوْتًا مِنْهُ يَقُولُ يَا جَلِيحْ، أَمْرٌ نَجِيحْ رَجُلٌ فَصِيحْ يَقُولُ لاَ إِلَهَ إِلاَّ أَنْتَ. فَوَثَبَ الْقَوْمُ قُلْتُ لاَ أَبْرَحُ حَتَّى أَعْلَمَ مَا وَرَاءَ هَذَا ثُمَّ نَادَى يَا جَلِيحْ، أَمْرٌ نَجِيحْ، رَجُلٌ فَصِيحْ، يَقُولُ لاَ إِلَهَ إِلاَّ اللَّهُ. فَقُمْتُ فَمَا نَشِبْنَا أَنْ قِيلَ هَذَا نَبِيٌّ.

Narrated `Abdullah: Allah has cursed those women who practise tattooing and those who get themselves tattooed, and those who remove their face hairs, and those who create a space between their teeth artificially to look beautiful, and such women as change the features created by Allah. Why then should I not curse those whom the Prophet ﷺ has cursed? And that is in Allah's Book. i.e. His Saying: 'And what the Apostle gives you take it and what he forbids you abstain (from it).' (59.7) – Sahih Al-Bukhari 5931

حَدَّثَنَا عُثْمَانُ، حَدَّثَنَا جَرِيرٌ، عَنْ مَنْصُورٍ، عَنْ إِبْرَاهِيمَ، عَنْ عَلْقَمَةَ، عَنْ عَبْدِ اللَّهِ، لَعَنَ اللَّهُ الْوَاشِمَاتِ، وَالْمُسْتَوْشِمَاتِ، وَالْمُتَنَمِّصَاتِ وَالْمُتَفَلِّجَاتِ لِلْحُسْنِ، الْمُغَيِّرَاتِ خَلْقَ اللَّهِ تَعَالَى، مَالِي لاَ أَلْعَنُ مَنْ لَعَنَ النَّبِيُّ صلى الله عليه وسلم وَهْوَ فِي كِتَابِ اللَّهِ {وَمَا آتَاكُمُ الرَّسُولُ فَخُذُوهُ}.

Narrated Ibn `Umar: I heard the Prophet ﷺ saying, (or the Prophet ﷺ said), "Allah has cursed the lady who practices tattooing and that who gets it done for herself, and also the lady who lengthens hair artificially and that who gets her hair lengthened artificially." The Prophet ﷺ has cursed such ladies. – Sahih Al-Bukhari 5942

حَدَّثَنِي يُوسُفُ بْنُ مُوسَى، حَدَّثَنَا الْفَضْلُ بْنُ دُكَيْنٍ، حَدَّثَنَا صَخْرُ بْنُ جُوَيْرِيَةَ، عَنْ نَافِعٍ، عَنْ عَبْدِ اللَّهِ بْنِ عُمَرَ - رضى الله عنهما - سَمِعْتُ النَّبِيَّ صلى الله عليه وسلم أَوْ قَالَ النَّبِيُّ صلى الله عليه وسلم " الْوَاشِمَةُ وَالْمُوتَشِمَةُ، وَالْوَاصِلَةُ وَالْمُسْتَوْصِلَةُ ". يَعْنِي لَعَنَ النَّبِيُّ صلى الله عليه وسلم

Verily, those who believe not in the Hereafter, name the angels with female names

إِنَّ ٱلَّذِينَ لَا يُؤْمِنُونَ بِٱلْـَٔاخِرَةِ لَيُسَمُّونَ ٱلْمَلَـٰٓئِكَةَ تَسْمِيَةَ ٱلْأُنثَىٰ

Have you considered al-Lat and al-Uzza? And Manat, the third one,(3 female idol's of the pagan Arabs), the other third? Are you to have the males, and He the females? What a bizarre distribution. – Surah An-Najm 53:19-22

أَفَرَءَيْتُمُ ٱللَّـٰتَ وَٱلْعُزَّىٰ وَمَنَوٰةَ ٱلثَّالِثَةَ ٱلْأُخْرَىٰٓ أَلَكُمُ ٱلذَّكَرُ وَلَهُ ٱلْأُنثَىٰ تِلْكَ إِذًا قِسْمَةٌ ضِيزَىٰٓ

Adorned for the people is the love of desires, such as women, and children, and piles upon piles of gold and silver, and branded horses, and livestock, and fields. These are the conveniences of the worldly life, but with Allah lies the finest resort. – Surah Al-Imran 3:14

زُيِّنَ لِلنَّاسِ حُبُّ ٱلشَّهَوَٰتِ مِنَ ٱلنِّسَآءِ وَٱلْبَنِينَ وَٱلْقَنَـٰطِيرِ ٱلْمُقَنطَرَةِ مِنَ ٱلذَّهَبِ وَٱلْفِضَّةِ وَٱلْخَيْلِ ٱلْمُسَوَّمَةِ وَٱلْأَنْعَـٰمِ وَٱلْحَرْثِ ۗ ذَٰلِكَ مَتَـٰعُ ٱلْحَيَوٰةِ ٱلدُّنْيَا ۖ وَٱللَّهُ عِندَهُۥ حُسْنُ ٱلْمَـَٔابِ

Has your Lord favored you with sons, while choosing for Himself daughters from among the angels? You are indeed saying a terrible thing. – Surah Al-Isra 17:40
أَفَأَصۡفَىٰكُمۡ رَبُّكُم بِٱلۡبَنِينَ وَٱتَّخَذَ مِنَ ٱلۡمَلَٰٓئِكَةِ إِنَٰثًاۚ إِنَّكُمۡ لَتَقُولُونَ قَوۡلًا عَظِيمٗا

So He preferred girls over boys? What is the matter with you? How do you judge? – Surah As-Saffaat 37:153&154

أَصۡطَفَى ٱلۡبَنَاتِ عَلَى ٱلۡبَنِينَ مَا لَكُمۡ كَيۡفَ تَحۡكُمُونَ

Or has He chosen for Himself daughters from what He creates, and favored you with sons? Yet when one of them is given news of what he attributes to the Most Gracious, his face darkens, and he suppresses grief. "Someone brought up to be beautiful, and unable to help in a fight?" And they appoint the angels, who are servants to the Most Gracious, as females. Have they witnessed their creation? Their claim will be recorded, and they will be questioned. – Surah Az-Zukhruf 43:16-19
أَمِ ٱتَّخَذَ مِمَّا يَخۡلُقُ بَنَاتٖ وَأَصۡفَىٰكُم بِٱلۡبَنِينَ وَإِذَا بُشِّرَ أَحَدُهُم بِمَا ضَرَبَ لِلرَّحۡمَٰنِ مَثَلٗا ظَلَّ وَجۡهُهُۥ مُسۡوَدّٗا وَهُوَ كَظِيمٌ أَوَ مَن يُنَشَّؤُاْ فِي ٱلۡحِلۡيَةِ وَهُوَ فِي ٱلۡخِصَامِ غَيۡرُ مُبِينٖ وَجَعَلُواْ ٱلۡمَلَٰٓئِكَةَ ٱلَّذِينَ هُمۡ عِبَٰدُ ٱلرَّحۡمَٰنِ إِنَٰثًاۚ أَشَهِدُواْ خَلۡقَهُمۡۚ سَتُكۡتَبُ شَهَٰدَتُهُمۡ وَيُسۡـَٔلُونَ

Those who do not believe in the Hereafter give the angels the names of females. – Surah An-Najm 53:27
إِنَّ ٱلَّذِينَ لَا يُؤۡمِنُونَ بِٱلۡأٓخِرَةِ لَيُسَمُّونَ ٱلۡمَلَٰٓئِكَةَ تَسۡمِيَةَ ٱلۡأُنثَىٰ

Narrated Abu Bakra: During the days (of the battle) of Al-Jamal, Allah benefited me with a word I had heard from Allah's Apostle after I had been about to join the Companions of Al-Jamal (i.e. the camel) and fight along with them. When Allah's Messenger ﷺ was informed that the Persians had crowned the daughter of Khosrau as their ruler, he said, "Such people as ruled by a lady will never be successful.". – Sahih Al-Bukhari 4425
حَدَّثَنَا عُثْمَانُ بْنُ الْهَيْثَمِ، حَدَّثَنَا عَوْفٌ، عَنِ الْحَسَنِ، عَنْ أَبِي بَكْرَةَ، قَالَ لَقَدْ نَفَعَنِي اللَّهُ بِكَلِمَةٍ سَمِعْتُهَا مِنْ، رَسُولِ اللَّهِ صلى الله عليه وسلم أَيَّامَ الْجَمَلِ، بَعْدَ مَا كِدْتُ أَنْ أَلْحَقَ بِأَصْحَابِ الْجَمَلِ فَأُقَاتِلَ مَعَهُمْ قَالَ لَمَّا بَلَغَ رَسُولَ اللَّهِ صلى الله عليه وسلم أَنَّ أَهْلَ فَارِسَ قَدْ مَلَّكُوا عَلَيْهِمْ بِنْتَ كِسْرَى قَالَ " لَنْ يُفْلِحَ قَوْمٌ وَلَّوْا أَمْرَهُمُ امْرَأَةً "

Narrated Ibn 'Abbas: The Prophet ﷺ said: "I was shown the Hell-fire and that the majority of its dwellers were women who were ungrateful." It was asked, "Do they disbelieve in Allah?" (or are they ungrateful to Allah?) He replied, "They are ungrateful to their husbands and are ungrateful for the favors and the good (charitable deeds) done to them. If you have always been good (benevolent) to one of them and then she sees something in you (not of her liking), she will say, 'I have never received any good from you.". – Sahih Al-Bukhari 29
حَدَّثَنَا عَبْدُ اللَّهِ بْنُ مَسْلَمَةَ، عَنْ مَالِكٍ، عَنْ زَيْدِ بْنِ أَسْلَمَ، عَنْ عَطَاءِ بْنِ يَسَارٍ، عَنِ ابْنِ عَبَّاسٍ، قَالَ قَالَ النَّبِيُّ صلى الله عليه وسلم " أُرِيتُ النَّارَ فَإِذَا أَكْثَرُ أَهْلِهَا النِّسَاءُ يَكْفُرْنَ ". قِيلَ أَيَكْفُرْنَ بِاللَّهِ قَالَ " يَكْفُرْنَ الْعَشِيرَ، وَيَكْفُرْنَ الإِحْسَانَ، لَوْ أَحْسَنْتَ إِلَى إِحْدَاهُنَّ الدَّهْرَ ثُمَّ رَأَتْ مِنْكَ شَيْئًا قَالَتْ مَا رَأَيْتُ مِنْكَ خَيْرًا قَطُّ ".

Narrated Usama bin Zaid: The Prophet ﷺ said, "After me I have not left any trial more severe to men than women.". – Sahih Al-Bukhari 5096
حَدَّثَنَا آدَمُ، حَدَّثَنَا شُعْبَةُ، عَنْ سُلَيْمَانَ التَّيْمِيِّ، قَالَ سَمِعْتُ أَبَا عُثْمَانَ النَّهْدِيَّ، عَنْ أُسَامَةَ بْنِ زَيْدٍ ـ رضى الله عنهما ـ عَنِ النَّبِيِّ صلى الله عليه وسلم قَالَ " مَا تَرَكْتُ بَعْدِي فِتْنَةً أَضَرَّ عَلَى الرِّجَالِ مِنَ النِّسَاءِ "

Narrated Abu Sa`id Al-Khudri: Once Allah's Messenger ﷺ went out to the Musalla (to offer the prayer) of `Id-al-Adha or Al-Fitr prayer. Then he passed by the women and said, "O women! Give alms, as I have seen that the majority of the dwellers of Hell-fire were you (women)." They asked, "Why is it so, O Allah's Messenger ﷺ?" He replied, "You curse frequently and are ungrateful to your husbands. I have not seen anyone more deficient in intelligence and religion than you. A cautious sensible man could be led astray by some of you." The women asked, "O Allah's Messenger ﷺ! What is deficient in our intelligence and religion?" He said, "Is not the evidence of two women equal to the witness of one man?" They replied in the affirmative. He said, "This is the deficiency in her intelligence. Isn't it true that a woman can neither pray nor fast during her menses?" The women replied in the affirmative. He said, "This is the deficiency in her religion.". – Sahih Al-Bukhari 304

حَدَّثَنَا سَعِيدُ بْنُ أَبِي مَرْيَمَ، قَالَ أَخْبَرَنَا مُحَمَّدُ بْنُ جَعْفَرٍ، قَالَ أَخْبَرَنِي زَيْدٌ ـ هُوَ ابْنُ أَسْلَمَ ـ عَنْ عِيَاضِ بْنِ عَبْدِ اللَّهِ، عَنْ أَبِي سَعِيدٍ الْخُدْرِيِّ، قَالَ خَرَجَ رَسُولُ اللَّهِ صلى الله عليه وسلم فِي أَضْحًى ـ أَوْ فِطْرٍ ـ إِلَى الْمُصَلَّى، فَمَرَّ عَلَى النِّسَاءِ فَقَالَ " يَا مَعْشَرَ النِّسَاءِ تَصَدَّقْنَ، فَإِنِّي أُرِيتُكُنَّ أَكْثَرَ أَهْلِ النَّارِ ". فَقُلْنَ وَبِمَ يَا رَسُولَ اللَّهِ قَالَ " تُكْثِرْنَ اللَّعْنَ، وَتَكْفُرْنَ الْعَشِيرَ، مَا رَأَيْتُ مِنْ نَاقِصَاتِ عَقْلٍ وَدِينٍ أَذْهَبَ لِلُبِّ الرَّجُلِ الْحَازِمِ مِنْ إِحْدَاكُنَّ ". قُلْنَ وَمَا نُقْصَانُ دِينِنَا وَعَقْلِنَا يَا رَسُولَ اللَّهِ قَالَ " أَلَيْسَ شَهَادَةُ الْمَرْأَةِ مِثْلَ نِصْفِ شَهَادَةِ الرَّجُلِ ". قُلْنَ بَلَى. قَالَ " فَذَلِكِ مِنْ نُقْصَانِ عَقْلِهَا، أَلَيْسَ إِذَا حَاضَتْ لَمْ تُصَلِّ وَلَمْ تَصُمْ ". قُلْنَ بَلَى. قَالَ " فَذَلِكِ مِنْ نُقْصَانِ دِينِهَا ".

Narrated Alqama: Abdullah (bin Masud) said. "Allah curses those ladies who practice tattooing and those who get themselves tattooed, and those ladies who remove the hair from their faces and those who make artificial spaces between their teeth in order to look more beautiful whereby they change Allah's creation." His saying reached a lady from Bani Asd called Um Yaqub who came (to `Abdullah) and said, "I have come to know that you have cursed such-and-such (ladies)?" He replied, "Why should I not curse these whom Allah's Messenger ﷺ has cursed and who are (cursed) in Allah's Book!" Um Yaqub said, "I have read the whole Qur'an, but I did not find in it what you say." He said, "Verily, if you have read it (i.e. the Qur'an), you have found it. Didn't you read: 'And whatsoever the Apostle gives you take it and whatsoever he forbids you, you abstain (from it). (59.7) She replied, "Yes, I did," He said, "Verily, Allah's Messenger ﷺ forbade such things." "She said, "But I see your wife doing these things?" He said, "Go and watch her." She went and watched her but could not see anything in support of her statement. On that he said, "If my wife was as you thought, I would not keep her in my company – .".Sahih al-Bukhari 4886

حَدَّثَنَا مُحَمَّدُ بْنُ يُوسُفَ، حَدَّثَنَا سُفْيَانُ، عَنْ مَنْصُورٍ، عَنْ إِبْرَاهِيمَ، عَنْ عَلْقَمَةَ، عَنْ عَبْدِ اللَّهِ، قَالَ لَعَنَ اللَّهُ الْوَاشِمَاتِ وَالْمُوتَشِمَاتِ وَالْمُتَنَمِّصَاتِ وَالْمُتَفَلِّجَاتِ لِلْحُسْنِ الْمُغَيِّرَاتِ خَلْقَ اللَّهِ. فَبَلَغَ ذَلِكَ امْرَأَةً مِنْ بَنِي أَسَدٍ يُقَالُ لَهَا أُمُّ يَعْقُوبَ، فَجَاءَتْ فَقَالَتْ إِنَّهُ بَلَغَنِي أَنَّكَ لَعَنْتَ كَيْتَ وَكَيْتَ. فَقَالَ وَمَا لِي لاَ أَلْعَنُ مَنْ لَعَنَ رَسُولُ اللَّهِ صلى الله عليه وسلم وَمَنْ هُوَ فِي كِتَابِ اللَّهِ فَقَالَتْ لَقَدْ قَرَأْتُ مَا بَيْنَ اللَّوْحَيْنِ فَمَا وَجَدْتُ فِيهِ مَا تَقُولُ. قَالَ لَئِنْ كُنْتِ قَرَأْتِيهِ لَقَدْ وَجَدْتِيهِ، أَمَا قَرَأْتِ {وَمَا آتَاكُمُ الرَّسُولُ فَخُذُوهُ وَمَا نَهَاكُمْ عَنْهُ فَانْتَهُوا}. قَالَتْ بَلَى. قَالَ فَإِنَّهُ قَدْ نَهَى عَنْهُ. قَالَتْ فَإِنِّي أَرَى أَهْلَكَ يَفْعَلُونَهُ. قَالَ فَاذْهَبِي فَانْظُرِي. فَذَهَبَتْ فَنَظَرَتْ فَلَمْ تَرَ مِنْ حَاجَتِهَا شَيْئًا، فَقَالَ لَوْ كَانَتْ كَذَلِكَ مَا جَامَعْتُهَا.

Narrated Abu Huraira: Allah's Messenger ﷺ said, "The woman is like a rib; if you try to straighten her, she will break. So if you want to get benefit from her, do so while she still has some crookedness.". – Sahih Al-Bukhari 5184

حَدَّثَنَا عَبْدُ الْعَزِيزِ بْنُ عَبْدِ اللَّهِ، قَالَ حَدَّثَنِي مَالِكٌ، عَنْ أَبِي الزِّنَادِ، عَنِ الأَعْرَجِ، عَنْ أَبِي هُرَيْرَةَ، أَنَّ رَسُولَ اللَّهِ صلى الله عليه وسلم قَالَ " الْمَرْأَةُ كَالضِّلَعِ، إِنْ أَقَمْتَهَا كَسَرْتَهَا، وَإِنِ اسْتَمْتَعْتَ بِهَا اسْتَمْتَعْتَ بِهَا وَفِيهَا عِوَجٌ "

Narrated `Aisha: Had Allah's Messenger ﷺ known what the women were doing, he would have forbidden them from going to the mosque as the women of Bani Israel had been

forbidden. Yahya bin Sa`id (a sub-narrator) asked `Amra (another sub-narrator), "Were the women of Bani Israel forbidden?" She replied "Yes.". – Sahih Al-Bukhari 869
حَدَّثَنَا عَبْدُ اللَّهِ بْنُ يُوسُفَ، قَالَ أَخْبَرَنَا مَالِكٌ، عَنْ يَحْيَى بْنِ سَعِيدٍ، عَنْ عَمْرَةَ، عَنْ عَائِشَةَ ـ رضى الله عنها ـ قَالَتْ لَوْ أَدْرَكَ رَسُولُ اللَّهِ صلى الله عليه وسلم مَا أَحْدَثَ النِّسَاءُ لَمَنَعَهُنَّ كَمَا مُنِعَتْ نِسَاءُ بَنِي إِسْرَائِيلَ. قُلْتُ لِعَمْرَةَ أَوَ مُنِعْنَ قَالَتْ نَعَمْ.

Can we believe a woman if she says she is menstruating or pregnant, and whatever is related to menses as is referred to by the Statement of Allah " ....And it is not lawful for them to conceal what Allāh has created in their wombs ..." (V.2:228). Bukhari Vol. 1 pg 221
و ما يصدق النساء في الحيض و الحمل، و فيما يمكن من الحيض لقول الله تعالى ...وَلَا يَحِلُّ لَهُنَّ أَن يَكْتُمْنَ مَا خَلَقَ ٱللَّهُ فِىٓ أَرْحَامِهِنَّ....

Or one who is raised up in jewelry
أَوَ مَن يُنَشَّؤُا۟ فِى ٱلْحِلْيَةِ

Narrated Ibn 'Abbas: Once Allah's Messenger ﷺ came out while Bilal was accompanying him. He went towards the women thinking that they had not heard him (i.e. his sermon). So he preached them and ordered them to pay alms. (Hearing that) the women started giving alms; some donated their ear-rings, some gave their rings and Bilal was collecting them in the corner of his garment. – Sahih Al-Bukhari 98
حَدَّثَنَا سُلَيْمَانُ بْنُ حَرْبٍ، قَالَ حَدَّثَنَا شُعْبَةُ، عَنْ أَيُّوبَ، قَالَ سَمِعْتُ عَطَاءً، قَالَ سَمِعْتُ ابْنَ عَبَّاسٍ، قَالَ أَشْهَدُ عَلَى النَّبِيِّ صلى الله عليه وسلم ـ أَوْ قَالَ عَطَاءٌ أَشْهَدُ عَلَى ابْنِ عَبَّاسٍ ـ أَنَّ رَسُولَ اللَّهِ صلى الله عليه وسلم خَرَجَ وَمَعَهُ بِلاَلٌ، فَظَنَّ أَنَّهُ لَمْ يُسْمِعِ النِّسَاءَ فَوَعَظَهُنَّ، وَأَمَرَهُنَّ بِالصَّدَقَةِ، فَجَعَلَتِ الْمَرْأَةُ تُلْقِي الْقُرْطَ وَالْخَاتَمَ، وَبِلاَلٌ يَأْخُذُ فِي طَرَفِ ثَوْبِهِ.
وَقَالَ إِسْمَاعِيلُ عَنْ أَيُّوبَ عَنْ عَطَاءٍ وَقَالَ عَنِ ابْنِ عَبَّاسٍ أَشْهَدُ عَلَى النَّبِيِّ صلى الله عليه وسلم.

Al-Hasan bin Muslim told me that Ibn `Abbas had said, "I joined the Prophet, Abu Bakr, `Umar and `Uthman in the `Id ul Fitr prayers. They used to offer the prayer before the Khutba and then they used to deliver the Khutba afterwards. Once the Prophet ﷺ I came out (for the `Id prayer) as if I were just observing him waving to the people to sit down. He, then accompanied by Bilal, came crossing the rows till he reached the women. He recited the following verse: 'O Prophet! When the believing women come to you to take the oath of fealty to you . . . (to the end of the verse) (60.12).' After finishing the recitation he said, "O ladies! Are you fulfilling your covenant?" None except one woman said, "Yes." Hasan did not know who was that woman. The Prophet ﷺ said, "Then give alms." Bilal spread his garment and said, "Keep on giving alms. Let my father and mother sacrifice their lives for you (ladies)." So the ladies kept on putting their Fatkhs (big rings) and other kinds of rings in Bilal's garment." `Abdur-Razaq said, " 'Fatkhs' is a big ring which used to be worn in the (Pre-Islamic) period of ignorance. – Sahih Al-Bukhari 979
قَالَ ابْنُ جُرَيْجٍ وَأَخْبَرَنِي الْحَسَنُ بْنُ مُسْلِمٍ، عَنْ طَاوُسٍ، عَنِ ابْنِ عَبَّاسٍ ـ رضى الله عنهما ـ قَالَ شَهِدْتُ الْفِطْرَ مَعَ النَّبِيِّ صلى الله عليه وسلم وَأَبِي بَكْرٍ وَعُمَرَ وَعُثْمَانَ ـ رضى الله عنهم ـ يُصَلُّونَهَا قَبْلَ الْخُطْبَةِ، ثُمَّ يُخْطَبُ بَعْدُ، خَرَجَ النَّبِيُّ صلى الله عليه وسلم كَأَنِّي أَنْظُرُ إِلَيْهِ حِينَ يُجْلِسُ بِيَدِهِ، ثُمَّ أَقْبَلَ يَشُقُّهُمْ حَتَّى جَاءَ النِّسَاءَ مَعَهُ بِلاَلٌ فَقَالَ {يَا أَيُّهَا النَّبِيُّ إِذَا جَاءَكَ الْمُؤْمِنَاتُ يُبَايِعْنَكَ} الآيَةَ ثُمَّ قَالَ حِينَ فَرَغَ مِنْهَا " آنْتُنَّ عَلَى ذَلِكِ ". قَالَتِ امْرَأَةٌ وَاحِدَةٌ مِنْهُنَّ لَمْ يُجِبْهُ غَيْرُهَا نَعَمْ. لاَ يَدْرِي حَسَنٌ مَنْ هِيَ. قَالَ " فَتَصَدَّقْنَ " فَبَسَطَ بِلاَلٌ ثَوْبَهُ ثُمَّ قَالَ هَلُمَّ لَكُنَّ فِدَاءٌ أَبِي وَأُمِّي، فَيُلْقِينَ الْفَتَخَ وَالْخَوَاتِيمَ فِي ثَوْبِ بِلاَلٍ. قَالَ عَبْدُ الرَّزَّاقِ الْفَتَخُ الْخَوَاتِيمُ الْعِظَامُ كَانَتْ فِي الْجَاهِلِيَّةِ

Narrated Anas: On the day of the battle of Uhud, the people ran away, leaving the Prophet ﷺ, but Abu- Talha was shielding the Prophet ﷺ with his shield in front of him. Abu Talha was a strong, experienced archer who used to keep his arrow bow strong and well stretched. On that day he broke two or three arrow bows. If any man passed by carrying a quiver full of arrows, the Prophet ﷺ would say to him, "Empty it in front of Abu Talha." When the Prophet ﷺ stated looking at the enemy by raising his head, Abu Talha said, "O Allah's Prophet! Let my parents be sacrificed for your sake! Please don't raise your head and make it visible, lest an arrow of the enemy should hit you. Let my neck and chest be wounded instead of yours." (On that day) I saw `Aisha, the daughter of Abu Bakr and Um Sulaim both lifting their dresses up so that I was able to see the ornaments of their legs, and they were carrying the water skins of their arms to pour the water into the mouths of the thirsty people and then go back and fill them and come to pour the water into the mouths of the people again. (On that day) Abu Talha's sword fell from his hand twice or thrice. – Sahih Al-Bukhari 3811

حَدَّثَنَا أَبُو مَعْمَرٍ، حَدَّثَنَا عَبْدُ الْوَارِثِ، حَدَّثَنَا عَبْدُ الْعَزِيزِ، عَنْ أَنَسٍ ـ رضى الله عنه ـ قَالَ لَمَّا كَانَ يَوْمُ أُحُدٍ انْهَزَمَ النَّاسُ عَنِ النَّبِيِّ صلى الله عليه وسلم وَأَبُو طَلْحَةَ بَيْنَ يَدَىِ النَّبِيِّ صلى الله عليه وسلم مُجَوِّبٌ بِهِ عَلَيْهِ بِحَجَفَةٍ لَهُ، وَكَانَ أَبُو طَلْحَةَ رَجُلاً رَامِيًا شَدِيدَ الْقِدِّ، يَكْسِرُ يَوْمَئِذٍ قَوْسَيْنِ أَوْ ثَلاَثًا، وَكَانَ الرَّجُلُ يَمُرُّ مَعَهُ الْجَعْبَةُ مِنَ النَّبْلِ فَيَقُولُ انْشُرْهَا لأَبِي طَلْحَةَ. فَأَشْرَفَ النَّبِيُّ صلى الله عليه وسلم يَنْظُرُ إِلَى الْقَوْمِ، فَيَقُولُ أَبُو طَلْحَةَ يَا نَبِيَّ اللَّهِ بِأَبِي أَنْتَ وَأُمِّي، لاَ تُشْرِفْ يُصِيبُكَ سَهْمٌ مِنْ سِهَامِ الْقَوْمِ، نَحْرِي دُونَ نَحْرِكَ. وَلَقَدْ رَأَيْتُ عَائِشَةَ بِنْتَ أَبِي بَكْرٍ وَأُمَّ سُلَيْمٍ وَإِنَّهُمَا لَمُشَمِّرَتَانِ، أَرَى خَدَمَ سُوقِهِمَا، تُنْقِزَانِ الْقِرَبَ عَلَى مُتُونِهِمَا، تُفْرِغَانِهِ فِي أَفْوَاهِ الْقَوْمِ، ثُمَّ تَرْجِعَانِ فَتَمْلآنِهَا، ثُمَّ تَجِيآنِ فَتُفْرِغَانِهِ فِي أَفْوَاهِ الْقَوْمِ، وَلَقَدْ وَقَعَ السَّيْفُ مِنْ يَدَىْ أَبِي طَلْحَةَ إِمَّا مَرَّتَيْنِ، وَإِمَّا ثَلاَثًا

Narrated Um 'Atiyya: The Prophet ﷺ said, "It is not lawful for a lady who believes in Allah and the Last Day, to mourn for more than three days for a dead person, except for her husband, in which case she should neither put kohl in her eyes, nor perfume herself, nor wear dyed clothes, except a garment of 'Asb". – Sahih Al-Bukhari 5342

حَدَّثَنَا الْفَضْلُ بْنُ دُكَيْنٍ، حَدَّثَنَا عَبْدُ السَّلاَمِ بْنُ حَرْبٍ، عَنْ هِشَامٍ، عَنْ حَفْصَةَ، عَنْ أُمِّ عَطِيَّةَ، قَالَتْ قَالَ النَّبِيُّ صلى الله عليه وسلم " لاَ يَحِلُّ لاِمْرَأَةٍ تُؤْمِنُ بِاللَّهِ وَالْيَوْمِ الآخِرِ أَنْ تُحِدَّ فَوْقَ ثَلاَثٍ، إِلاَّ عَلَى زَوْجٍ، فَإِنَّهَا لاَ تَكْتَحِلُ وَلاَ تَلْبَسُ ثَوْبًا مَصْبُوغًا إِلاَّ ثَوْبَ عَصْبٍ ".

And settle in your homes; and do not display yourselves, as in the former days of ignorance. And perform the prayer, and give regular charity, and obey Allah and His Messenger. Allah desires to remove all impurity from you, O People of the Household, and to purify you thoroughly. – Surah Al-Azhab 33:33

وَقَرْنَ فِى بُيُوتِكُنَّ وَلَا تَبَرَّجْنَ تَبَرُّجَ ٱلْجَـٰهِلِيَّةِ ٱلْأُولَىٰ ۖ وَأَقِمْنَ ٱلصَّلَوٰةَ وَءَاتِينَ ٱلزَّكَوٰةَ وَأَطِعْنَ ٱللَّهَ وَرَسُولَهُۥٓ ۚ إِنَّمَا يُرِيدُ ٱللَّهُ لِيُذْهِبَ عَنكُمُ ٱلرِّجْسَ أَهْلَ ٱلْبَيْتِ وَيُطَهِّرَكُمْ تَطْهِيرًا

"Allow women to go to the Mosques".
ائْذَنُوا لِلنِّسَاءِ بِاللَّيْلِ إِلَى الْمَسَاجِدِ

Narrated Ibn `Umar: The Prophet (p.b.u.h) said, "Allow women to go to the Mosques at night." - Sahih al-Bukhari 899

حَدَّثَنَا عَبْدُ اللَّهِ بْنُ مُحَمَّدٍ، حَدَّثَنَا شَبَابَةُ، حَدَّثَنَا وَرْقَاءُ، عَنْ عَمْرِو بْنِ دِينَارٍ، عَنْ مُجَاهِدٍ، عَنِ ابْنِ عُمَرَ، عَنِ النَّبِيِّ صلى الله عليه وسلم قَالَ " ائْذَنُوا لِلنِّسَاءِ بِاللَّيْلِ إِلَى الْمَسَاجِدِ ".

Narrated Ibn `Umar: One of the wives of `Umar (bin Al-Khattab) used to offer the Fajr and the `Isha' prayer in congregation in the Mosque. She was asked why she had come out for the prayer as she knew that `Umar disliked it, and he has great ghaira (self-respect). She replied, "What prevents him from stopping me from this act?" The other replied, "The statement of Allah's Messenger ﷺ : 'Do not stop Allah's women-slaves from going to Allah's Mosques' prevents him.". – Sahih al-Bukhari 900

حَدَّثَنَا يُوسُفُ بْنُ مُوسَى، حَدَّثَنَا أَبُو أُسَامَةَ، حَدَّثَنَا عُبَيْدُ اللَّهِ بْنُ عُمَرَ، عَنْ نَافِعٍ، عَنِ ابْنِ عُمَرَ، قَالَ كَانَتِ امْرَأَةٌ لِعُمَرَ تَشْهَدُ صَلاَةَ الصُّبْحِ وَالْعِشَاءِ فِي الْجَمَاعَةِ فِي الْمَسْجِدِ، فَقِيلَ لَهَا لِمَ تَخْرُجِينَ وَقَدْ تَعْلَمِينَ أَنَّ عُمَرَ يَكْرَهُ ذَلِكَ وَيَغَارُ قَالَتْ وَمَا يَمْنَعُهُ أَنْ يَنْهَانِي قَالَ يَمْنَعُهُ قَوْلُ رَسُولِ اللَّهِ صلى الله عليه وسلم " لاَ تَمْنَعُوا إِمَاءَ اللَّهِ مَسَاجِدَ اللَّهِ ".

Narrated `Aisha: The Prophet ﷺ said to his wives, "You are allowed to go out to answer the call of nature. ". – Sahih al-Bukhari 147
حَدَّثَنَا زَكَرِيَّاءُ، قَالَ حَدَّثَنَا أَبُو أُسَامَةَ، عَنْ هِشَامِ بْنِ عُرْوَةَ، عَنْ أَبِيهِ، عَنْ عَائِشَةَ، عَنِ النَّبِيِّ صلى الله عليه وسلم قَالَ " قَدْ أُذِنَ أَنْ تَخْرُجْنَ فِي حَاجَتِكُنَّ ". قَالَ هِشَامٌ يَعْنِي الْبَرَازَ

Narrated Um-`Atiya: We were forbidden to mourn for a dead person for more than three days except in the case of a husband for whom mourning was allowed for four months and ten days. (During that time) we were not allowed to put kohl (Antimony eye power) in our eyes or to use perfumes or to put on colored clothes except a dress made of `Asr (a kind of Yemen cloth, very coarse and rough). We were allowed very light perfumes at the time of taking a bath after menses and also we were forbidden to go with the funeral procession . – Sahih al-Bukhari 313
حَدَّثَنَا عَبْدُ اللَّهِ بْنُ عَبْدِ الْوَهَّابِ، قَالَ حَدَّثَنَا حَمَّادُ بْنُ زَيْدٍ، عَنْ أَيُّوبَ، عَنْ حَفْصَةَ ـ قَالَ أَبُو عَبْدِ اللَّهِ أَوْ هِشَامِ بْنِ حَسَّانَ عَنْ حَفْصَةَ، عَنْ أُمِّ عَطِيَّةَ ـ قَالَتْ كُنَّا نُنْهَى أَنْ نُحِدَّ عَلَى مَيِّتٍ فَوْقَ ثَلاَثٍ، إِلاَّ عَلَى زَوْجٍ أَرْبَعَةَ أَشْهُرٍ وَعَشْرًا، وَلاَ نَكْتَحِلَ وَلاَ نَتَطَيَّبَ وَلاَ نَلْبَسَ ثَوْبًا مَصْبُوغًا إِلاَّ ثَوْبَ عَصْبٍ، وَقَدْ رُخِّصَ لَنَا عِنْدَ الطُّهْرِ إِذَا اغْتَسَلَتْ إِحْدَانَا مِنْ مَحِيضِهَا فِي نُبْذَةٍ مِنْ كُسْتِ أَظْفَارٍ، وَكُنَّا نُنْهَى عَنِ اتِّبَاعِ الْجَنَائِزِ. قَالَ رَوَاهُ هِشَامُ بْنُ حَسَّانَ عَنْ حَفْصَةَ عَنْ أُمِّ عَطِيَّةَ عَنِ النَّبِيِّ صلى الله عليه وسلم.

Narrated `Aisha: The Prophet ﷺ said to his wives, "You are allowed to go out to answer the call of nature. ". – Sahih al-Bukhari 147
حَدَّثَنَا زَكَرِيَّاءُ، قَالَ حَدَّثَنَا أَبُو أُسَامَةَ، عَنْ هِشَامِ بْنِ عُرْوَةَ، عَنْ أَبِيهِ، عَنْ عَائِشَةَ، عَنِ النَّبِيِّ صلى الله عليه وسلم قَالَ " قَدْ أُذِنَ أَنْ تَخْرُجْنَ فِي حَاجَتِكُنَّ ". قَالَ هِشَامٌ يَعْنِي الْبَرَازَ

Narrated Abu Huraira: The Prophet ﷺ said, "It is not permissible for a woman who believes in Allah and the Last Day to travel for one day and night except with a Mahram.". – Sahih al-Bukhari 1088
حَدَّثَنَا آدَمُ، قَالَ حَدَّثَنَا ابْنُ أَبِي ذِئْبٍ، قَالَ حَدَّثَنَا سَعِيدٌ الْمَقْبُرِيُّ، عَنْ أَبِيهِ، عَنْ أَبِي هُرَيْرَةَ ـ رضى الله عنهما ـ قَالَ قَالَ النَّبِيُّ صلى الله عليه وسلم " لاَ يَحِلُّ لاِمْرَأَةٍ تُؤْمِنُ بِاللَّهِ وَالْيَوْمِ الآخِرِ أَنْ تُسَافِرَ مَسِيرَةَ يَوْمٍ وَلَيْلَةٍ لَيْسَ مَعَهَا حُرْمَةٌ ". تَابَعَهُ يَحْيَى بْنُ أَبِي كَثِيرٍ وَسُهَيْلٌ وَمَالِكٌ عَنِ الْمَقْبُرِيِّ عَنْ أَبِي هُرَيْرَةَ ـ رضى الله عنه.

Narrated Anas bin Malik: My grandmother Mulaika invited Allah's Messenger ﷺ for a meal which she had prepared specially for him. He ate some of it and said, "Get up. I shall lead you in the prayer." I brought a mat that had become black owing to excessive use and I sprinkled water on it. Allah's Messenger ﷺ stood on it and prayed two rak`at; and the orphan was with me (in the first row), and the old lady stood behind us. – Sahih al-Bukhari 860
حَدَّثَنَا إِسْمَاعِيلُ، قَالَ حَدَّثَنِي مَالِكٌ، عَنْ إِسْحَاقَ بْنِ عَبْدِ اللَّهِ بْنِ أَبِي طَلْحَةَ، عَنْ أَنَسِ بْنِ مَالِكٍ، أَنَّ جَدَّتَهُ، مُلَيْكَةَ دَعَتْ رَسُولَ اللَّهِ صلى الله عليه وسلم لِطَعَامٍ صَنَعَتْهُ، فَأَكَلَ مِنْهُ فَقَالَ " قُومُوا فَلأُصَلِّيَ بِكُمْ ". فَقُمْتُ إِلَى حَصِيرٍ لَنَا قَدِ اسْوَدَّ مِنْ طُولِ مَا لُبِسَ، فَنَضَحْتُهُ بِمَاءٍ فَقَامَ رَسُولُ اللَّهِ صلى الله عليه وسلم وَالْيَتِيمُ مَعِي، وَالْعَجُوزُ مِنْ وَرَائِنَا، فَصَلَّى بِنَا رَكْعَتَيْنِ

Narrated 'Aishah (ra): Hind bint 'Utba came and said, "O Allah's Messenger! (Before I embraced Islam) there was no family on the surface of the earth I wished to see in degradation more than I did your family, but today there is no family on the surface of the earth I wish to see honored more than I did yours." The Prophet ﷺ said, "I thought similarly, by Him in whose Hand my soul is!" She further said, "O Allah's Messenger ! Abu Sufyan is a miser, so, is it sinful of me to feed my children from his property ?" He said, "I do not allow it unless you take for your needs what is just and reasonable." – Sahih al-Bukhari 3825

وَقَالَ عَبْدَانُ أَخْبَرَنَا عَبْدُ اللَّهِ، أَخْبَرَنَا يُونُسُ، عَنِ الزُّهْرِيِّ، حَدَّثَنِي عُرْوَةُ، أَنَّ عَائِشَةَ ـ رضى الله عنها ـ قَالَتْ جَاءَتْ هِنْدٌ بِنْتُ عُتْبَةَ قَالَتْ يَا رَسُولَ اللَّهِ، مَا كَانَ عَلَى ظَهْرِ الأَرْضِ مِنْ أَهْلِ خِبَاءٍ أَحَبُّ إِلَىَّ أَنْ يَذِلُّوا مِنْ أَهْلِ خِبَائِكَ، ثُمَّ مَا أَصْبَحَ الْيَوْمَ عَلَى ظَهْرِ الأَرْضِ أَهْلُ خِبَاءٍ أَحَبَّ إِلَىَّ أَنْ يَعِزُّوا مِنْ أَهْلِ خِبَائِكَ. قَالَ وَأَيْضًا وَالَّذِي نَفْسِي بِيَدِهِ، قَالَتْ يَا رَسُولَ اللَّهِ إِنَّ أَبَا سُفْيَانَ رَجُلٌ مِسِّيكٌ، فَهَلْ عَلَىَّ حَرَجٌ أَنْ أُطْعِمَ مِنَ الَّذِي لَهُ عِيَالَنَا قَالَ " لاَ أُرَاهُ إِلاَّ بِالْمَعْرُوفِ

Mary, be dedicated to your Lord; bow down and kneel with those who are kneeling in prayer."
- Surah Al-Imran 3:43

يَٰمَرْيَمُ ٱقْنُتِى لِرَبِّكِ وَٱسْجُدِى وَٱرْكَعِى مَعَ ٱلرَّٰكِعِينَ

Except for her husband
إلاَّ عَلَى زَوْجِهَا

And the ones of you who are taken up, (i.e., those who die) and leave behind (them) spouses, (the spouses) (i.e., the widows. The following verb is in the feminine plural) shall await by themselves for four months and ten (days); (This is the Iddah "term" for a widowed woman before she can remarry) so, when they have reached their term, then there is no fault in you whatever they perform (with) themselves with beneficence; and Allah is Ever-Cognizant of whatever you do. – Surah Al-Baqarah 2:234

وَٱلَّذِينَ يُتَوَفَّوْنَ مِنكُمْ وَيَذَرُونَ أَزْوَٰجًا يَتَرَبَّصْنَ بِأَنفُسِهِنَّ أَرْبَعَةَ أَشْهُرٍ وَعَشْرًا ۖ فَإِذَا بَلَغْنَ أَجَلَهُنَّ فَلَا جُنَاحَ عَلَيْكُمْ فِيمَا فَعَلْنَ فِىٓ أَنفُسِهِنَّ بِٱلْمَعْرُوفِ ۗ وَٱللَّهُ بِمَا تَعْمَلُونَ خَبِيرٌ

Narrated Um Habiba: The Prophetﷺ said, "It is not lawful for a Muslim woman who believes in Allah and the Last Day to mourn for more than three days, except for her husband, for whom she should mourn for four months and ten days.". – Sahih Al-Bukhari 5339

وَسَمِعْتُ زَيْنَبَ ابْنَةَ أُمِّ سَلَمَةَ، تُحَدِّثُ عَنْ أُمِّ حَبِيبَةَ، أَنَّ النَّبِيَّ صلى الله عليه وسلم قَالَ " لاَ يَحِلُّ لاِمْرَأَةٍ مُسْلِمَةٍ تُؤْمِنُ بِاللَّهِ وَالْيَوْمِ الآخِرِ أَنْ تُحِدَّ فَوْقَ ثَلاَثَةِ أَيَّامٍ، إِلاَّ عَلَى زَوْجِهَا أَرْبَعَةَ أَشْهُرٍ وَعَشْرًا ".

Narrated Um 'Atiyya: We were forbidden to mourn for more than three days for a dead person, except for a husband, for whom a wife should mourn for four months and ten days (while in the mourning period) we were not allowed to put kohl in our eyes, nor perfume our-selves, nor wear dyed clothes, except a garment of 'Asb (special clothes made in Yemen). But it was permissible for us that when one of us became clean from her menses and took a bath, she could use a piece of a certain kind of incense. And it was forbidden for us to follow funeral processions. – Sahih Al-Bukhari 5341

حَدَّثَنِي عَبْدُ اللَّهِ بْنُ عَبْدِ الْوَهَّابِ، حَدَّثَنَا حَمَّادُ بْنُ زَيْدٍ، عَنْ أَيُّوبَ، عَنْ حَفْصَةَ، عَنْ أُمِّ عَطِيَّةَ، قَالَتْ كُنَّا نُنْهَى أَنْ نُحِدَّ عَلَى مَيِّتٍ فَوْقَ ثَلاَثٍ، إِلاَّ عَلَى زَوْجٍ أَرْبَعَةَ أَشْهُرٍ وَعَشْرًا، وَلاَ نَكْتَحِلَ، وَلاَ نَطَّيَّبَ، وَلاَ نَلْبَسَ ثَوْبًا مَصْبُوغًا، إِلاَّ ثَوْبَ عَصْبٍ، وَقَدْ رُخِّصَ لَنَا عِنْدَ الطُّهْرِ إِذَا اغْتَسَلَتْ إِحْدَانَا مِنْ مَحِيضِهَا فِي نُبْذَةٍ مِنْ كُسْتِ أَظْفَارٍ، وَكُنَّا نُنْهَى عَنِ اتِّبَاعِ الْجَنَائِزِ.

Narrated Zainab bint Abi Salama: I went to Um Habiba, the wife of Prophet, who said, "I heard the Prophets saying, 'It is not legal for a woman who believes in Allah and the Last Day to mourn for any dead person for more than three days except for her husband, (for whom she should mourn) for four months and ten days'." Later I went to Zainab bint Jahsh when her brother died; she asked for some scent, and after using it she said, "I am not in need of scent but I heard Allah's Messengerﷺ saying, 'It is not legal for a woman who believes in Allah and the Last Day to mourn for more than three days for any dead person except her husband, (for whom she should mourn) for four months and ten days.' ". – Sahih Al-Bukhari 1281, 1282

حَدَّثَنَا إِسْمَاعِيلُ، حَدَّثَنِي مَالِكٌ، عَنْ عَبْدِ اللَّهِ بْنِ أَبِي بَكْرِ بْنِ مُحَمَّدِ بْنِ عَمْرِو بْنِ حَزْمٍ، عَنْ حُمَيْدِ بْنِ نَافِعٍ، عَنْ زَيْنَبَ بِنْتِ أَبِي سَلَمَةَ، أَخْبَرَتْهُ قَالَتْ، دَخَلْتُ عَلَى أُمِّ حَبِيبَةَ زَوْجِ النَّبِيِّ صلى الله عليه وسلم فَقَالَتْ سَمِعْتُ رَسُولَ اللَّهِ صلى الله عليه وسلم يَقُولُ " لاَ يَحِلُّ

لاِمْرَأَةٍ تُؤْمِنُ بِاللَّهِ وَالْيَوْمِ الآخِرِ تُحِدُّ عَلَى مَيِّتٍ فَوْقَ ثَلاَثٍ، إِلاَّ عَلَى زَوْجٍ أَرْبَعَةَ أَشْهُرٍ وَعَشْرًا ". ثُمَّ دَخَلْتُ عَلَى زَيْنَبَ بِنْتِ جَحْشٍ حِينَ تُوُفِّيَ أَخُوهَا، فَدَعَتْ بِطِيبٍ فَمَسَّتْ ثُمَّ قَالَتْ مَا لِي بِالطِّيبِ مِنْ حَاجَةٍ، غَيْرَ أَنِّي سَمِعْتُ رَسُولَ اللَّهِ صلى الله عليه وسلم عَلَى الْمِنْبَرِ يَقُولُ " لاَ يَحِلُّ لاِمْرَأَةٍ تُؤْمِنُ بِاللَّهِ وَالْيَوْمِ الآخِرِ تُحِدُّ عَلَى مَيِّتٍ فَوْقَ ثَلاَثٍ، إِلاَّ عَلَى زَوْجٍ أَرْبَعَةَ أَشْهُرٍ وَعَشْرًا "

Narrated Um-`Atiya: We were forbidden to mourn for a dead person for more than three days except in the case of a husband for whom mourning was allowed for four months and ten days. (During that time) we were not allowed to put kohl (Antimony eye power) in our eyes or to use perfumes or to put on colored clothes except a dress made of `Asr (a kind of Yemen cloth, very coarse and rough). We were allowed very light perfumes at the time of taking a bath after menses and also we were forbidden to go with the funeral procession . – Sahih al-Bukhari 313

حَدَّثَنَا عَبْدُ اللَّهِ بْنُ عَبْدِ الْوَهَّابِ، قَالَ حَدَّثَنَا حَمَّادُ بْنُ زَيْدٍ، عَنْ أَيُّوبَ، عَنْ حَفْصَةَ ـ قَالَ أَبُو عَبْدِ اللَّهِ أَوْ هِشَامِ بْنِ حَسَّانَ عَنْ حَفْصَةَ، عَنْ أُمِّ عَطِيَّةَ ـ قَالَتْ كُنَّا نُنْهَى أَنْ نُحِدَّ عَلَى مَيِّتٍ فَوْقَ ثَلاَثٍ، إِلاَّ عَلَى زَوْجٍ أَرْبَعَةَ أَشْهُرٍ وَعَشْرًا، وَلاَ نَكْتَحِلَ وَلاَ نَتَطَيَّبَ وَلاَ نَلْبَسَ ثَوْبًا مَصْبُوغًا إِلاَّ ثَوْبَ عَصْبٍ، وَقَدْ رُخِّصَ لَنَا عِنْدَ الطُّهْرِ إِذَا اغْتَسَلَتْ إِحْدَانَا مِنْ مَحِيضِهَا فِي نُبْذَةٍ مِنْ كُسْتِ أَظْفَارٍ، وَكُنَّا نُنْهَى عَنِ اتِّبَاعِ الْجَنَائِزِ. قَالَ رَوَاهُ هِشَامُ بْنُ حَسَّانَ عَنْ حَفْصَةَ عَنْ أُمِّ عَطِيَّةَ عَنِ النَّبِيِّ صلى الله عليه وسلم

Narrated Qays ibn Sa'd: I went to al-Hirah and saw them (the people) prostrating themselves before a satrap of theirs, so I said: The Messenger of Allah ﷺ has most right to have prostration made before him. When I came to the Prophet ﷺ, I said: I went to al-Hirah and saw them prostrating themselves before a satrap of theirs, but you have most right, Messenger of Allah, to have (people) prostrating themselves before you. He said: Tell me , if you were to pass my grave, would you prostrate yourself before it? I said: No. He then said: Do not do so. If I were to command anyone to make prostration before another I would command women to prostrate themselves before their husbands, because of the special right over them given to husbands by Allah. – Sunan Abi Dawud 2140

حَدَّثَنَا عَمْرُو بْنُ عَوْنٍ، أَخْبَرَنَا إِسْحَاقُ بْنُ يُوسُفَ، عَنْ شَرِيكٍ، عَنْ حُصَيْنٍ، عَنِ الشَّعْبِيِّ، عَنْ قَيْسِ بْنِ سَعْدٍ، قَالَ أَتَيْتُ الْحِيرَةَ فَرَأَيْتُهُمْ يَسْجُدُونَ لِمَرْزُبَانٍ لَهُمْ فَقُلْتُ رَسُولُ اللَّهِ أَحَقُّ أَنْ يُسْجَدَ لَهُ قَالَ فَأَتَيْتُ النَّبِيَّ صلى الله عليه وسلم فَقُلْتُ إِنِّي أَتَيْتُ الْحِيرَةَ فَرَأَيْتُهُمْ يَسْجُدُونَ لِمَرْزُبَانٍ لَهُمْ فَأَنْتَ يَا رَسُولَ اللَّهِ أَحَقُّ أَنْ نَسْجُدَ لَكَ . قَالَ " أَرَأَيْتَ لَوْ مَرَرْتَ بِقَبْرِي أَكُنْتَ تَسْجُدُ لَهُ " . قَالَ قُلْتُ لاَ . قَالَ " فَلاَ تَفْعَلُوا لَوْ كُنْتُ آمِرًا أَحَدًا أَنْ يَسْجُدَ لأَحَدٍ لأَمَرْتُ النِّسَاءَ أَنْ يَسْجُدْنَ لأَزْوَاجِهِنَّ لِمَا جَعَلَ اللَّهُ لَهُمْ عَلَيْهِنَّ مِنَ الْحَقِّ "

He ﷺ said, 'Aqiqa is to be offered for a boy.
قَالَ مَعَ الْغُلاَمِ عَقِيقَةٌ

Narrated Anas bin Malik: That he passed by a group of boys and greeted them and said, "The Prophet ﷺ used to do so.". – Sahih Al-Bukhari 6247

حَدَّثَنَا عَلِيُّ بْنُ الْجَعْدِ، أَخْبَرَنَا شُعْبَةُ، عَنْ سَيَّارٍ، عَنْ ثَابِتٍ الْبُنَانِيِّ، عَنْ أَنَسِ بْنِ مَالِكٍ ـ رضى الله عنه أَنَّهُ مَرَّ عَلَى صِبْيَانٍ فَسَلَّمَ عَلَيْهِمْ وَقَالَ كَانَ النَّبِيُّ صلى الله عليه وسلم يَفْعَلُهُ

Narrated `Aisha: A boy was brought to the Prophet ﷺ to do Tahnik for him, but the boy urinated on him, whereupon the Prophet had water poured on the place of urine. – Sahih Al-Bukhari 5468

حَدَّثَنَا مُسَدَّدٌ، حَدَّثَنَا يَحْيَى، عَنْ هِشَامٍ، عَنْ أَبِيهِ، عَنْ عَائِشَةَ ـ رضى الله عنها ـ قَالَتْ أُتِيَ النَّبِيُّ صلى الله عليه وسلم بِصَبِيٍّ يُحَنِّكُهُ، فَبَالَ عَلَيْهِ، فَأَتْبَعَهُ الْمَاءَ

Narrated Asma' bint Abu Bakr: I conceived `Abdullah bin AzZubair at Mecca and went out (of Mecca) while I was about to give birth. I came to Medina and encamped at Quba', and gave birth at Quba'. Then I brought the child to Allah's Messenger ﷺ and placed it (on his lap). He asked for a date, chewed it, and put his saliva in the mouth of the child. So the first thing to enter its stomach was the saliva of Allah's Messenger ﷺ. Then he did its Tahnik with a date, and invoked Allah to bless him. It was the first child born in the Islamic era, therefore they (Muslims) were very happy with its birth, for it had been said to them that the Jews had bewitched them, and so they would not produce any offspring. – Sahih Al-Bukhari 5469

حَدَّثَنَا إِسْحَاقُ بْنُ نَصْرٍ، حَدَّثَنَا أَبُو أُسَامَةَ، حَدَّثَنَا هِشَامُ بْنُ عُرْوَةَ، عَنْ أَبِيهِ، عَنْ أَسْمَاءَ بِنْتِ أَبِي بَكْرٍ ـ رضى الله عنهما ـ أَنَّهَا حَمَلَتْ بِعَبْدِ اللَّهِ بْنِ الزُّبَيْرِ بِمَكَّةَ قَالَتْ فَخَرَجْتُ وَأَنَا مُتِمٌّ، فَأَتَيْتُ الْمَدِينَةَ فَنَزَلْتُ قُبَاءً فَوَلَدْتُ بِقُبَاءٍ، ثُمَّ أَتَيْتُ بِهِ رَسُولَ اللَّهِ صلى الله عليه وسلم فَوَضَعْتُهُ فِي حَجْرِهِ، ثُمَّ دَعَا بِتَمْرَةٍ فَمَضَغَهَا، ثُمَّ تَفَلَ فِي فِيهِ فَكَانَ أَوَّلَ شَىْءٍ دَخَلَ جَوْفَهُ رِيقُ رَسُولِ اللَّهِ صلى الله عليه وسلم ثُمَّ حَنَّكَهُ بِالتَّمْرَةِ، ثُمَّ دَعَا لَهُ فَبَرَّكَ عَلَيْهِ، وَكَانَ أَوَّلَ مَوْلُودٍ وُلِدَ فِي الإِسْلاَمِ، فَفَرِحُوا بِهِ فَرَحًا شَدِيدًا، لأَنَّهُمْ قِيلَ لَهُمْ إِنَّ الْيَهُودَ قَدْ سَحَرَتْكُمْ فَلاَ يُولَدُ لَكُمْ.

Narrated Salman bin 'Amri Ad-Dabbi, the Prophet ﷺ said, 'Aqiqa is to be offered for a (newly born) boy. – Sahih Al-Bukhari 5471

حَدَّثَنَا أَبُو النُّعْمَانِ، حَدَّثَنَا حَمَّادُ بْنُ زَيْدٍ، عَنْ أَيُّوبَ، عَنْ مُحَمَّدٍ، عَنْ سَلْمَانَ بْنِ عَامِرٍ، قَالَ مَعَ الْغُلاَمِ عَقِيقَةٌ. وَقَالَ حَجَّاجٌ حَدَّثَنَا حَمَّادٌ أَخْبَرَنَا أَيُّوبُ وَقَتَادَةُ وَهِشَامٌ وَحَبِيبٌ عَنِ ابْنِ سِيرِينَ عَنْ سَلْمَانَ عَنِ النَّبِيِّ صلى الله عليه وسلم.

Narrated Salman bin 'Amir Ad-Dabbi: I heard Allah's Messenger ﷺ saying, "'Aqiqa is to be offered for a (newly born) boy, so slaughter (an animal) for him, and relieve him of his suffering." Narrated Habib bin Ash-Shahid: Ibn Seereen told me to ask Al-Hassan from whom he had heard the narration of 'Aqiqa. I asked him and he said, "From Samura bin Jundab.". – Sahih Al-Bukhari 5472

وَقَالَ غَيْرُ وَاحِدٍ عَنْ عَاصِمٍ، وَهِشَامٍ، عَنْ حَفْصَةَ بِنْتِ سِيرِينَ، عَنِ الرَّبَابِ، عَنْ سَلْمَانَ، عَنِ النَّبِيِّ صلى الله عليه وسلم. وَرَوَاهُ يَزِيدُ بْنُ إِبْرَاهِيمَ عَنِ ابْنِ سِيرِينَ عَنْ سَلْمَانَ قَوْلَهُ. وَقَالَ أَصْبَغُ أَخْبَرَنِي ابْنُ وَهْبٍ عَنْ جَرِيرِ بْنِ حَازِمٍ عَنْ أَيُّوبَ السَّخْتِيَانِيِّ عَنْ مُحَمَّدِ بْنِ سِيرِينَ حَدَّثَنَا سَلْمَانُ بْنُ عَامِرٍ الضَّبِّيُّ قَالَ سَمِعْتُ رَسُولَ اللَّهِ صلى الله عليه وسلم يَقُولُ " مَعَ الْغُلاَمِ عَقِيقَةٌ، فَأَهْرِيقُوا عَنْهُ دَمًا وَأَمِيطُوا عَنْهُ الأَذَى ". حَدَّثَنِي عَبْدُ اللَّهِ بْنُ أَبِي الأَسْوَدِ، حَدَّثَنَا قُرَيْشُ بْنُ أَنَسٍ، عَنْ حَبِيبِ بْنِ الشَّهِيدِ، قَالَ أَمَرَنِي ابْنُ سِيرِينَ أَنْ أَسْأَلَ الْحَسَنَ، مِمَّنْ سَمِعَ حَدِيثَ الْعَقِيقَةِ، فَسَأَلْتُهُ فَقَالَ مِنْ سَمُرَةَ بْنِ جُنْدَبٍ.

Tahnik
تهنيك

Narrated Abu Musa: A son was born to me and I took him to the Prophet ﷺ who named him Ibrahim, did Tahnik for him with a date, invoked Allah to bless him and returned him to me. (The narrator added: That was Abu Musa's eldest son.) – Sahih al-Bukhari 5467

حَدَّثَنِي إِسْحَاقُ بْنُ نَصْرٍ، حَدَّثَنَا أَبُو أُسَامَةَ، قَالَ حَدَّثَنِي بُرَيْدٌ، عَنْ أَبِي بُرْدَةَ، عَنْ أَبِي مُوسَى ـ رضى الله عنه ـ قَالَ وُلِدَ لِي غُلاَمٌ، فَأَتَيْتُ بِهِ النَّبِيَّ صلى الله عليه وسلم فَسَمَّاهُ إِبْرَاهِيمَ، فَحَنَّكَهُ بِتَمْرَةٍ، وَدَعَا لَهُ بِالْبَرَكَةِ وَدَفَعَهُ إِلَىَّ، وَكَانَ أَكْبَرَ وَلَدِ أَبِي مُوسَى

Narrated `Aisha: A boy was brought to the Prophet ﷺ to do Tahnik for him, but the boy urinated on him, whereupon the Prophet had water poured on the place of urine. – Sahih al-Bukhari 5468

حَدَّثَنَا مُسَدَّدٌ، حَدَّثَنَا يَحْيَى، عَنْ هِشَامٍ، عَنْ أَبِيهِ، عَنْ عَائِشَةَ ـ رضى الله عنها ـ قَالَتْ أُتِيَ النَّبِيُّ صلى الله عليه وسلم بِصَبِيٍّ يُحَنِّكُهُ، فَبَالَ عَلَيْهِ، فَأَتْبَعَهُ الْمَاءَ.

Narrated Anas bin Malik: Abu Talha had a child who was sick. Once, while Abu Talha was out, the child died. When Abu Talha returned home, he asked, "How does my son fare?" Um Salaim (his wife) replied, "He is quieter than he has ever been." Then she brought supper for him and he took his supper and slept with her. When he had finished, she said (to him), "Bury the child (as he's dead)." Next morning Abu Talha came to Allah's Messenger ﷺ and told him about that. The Prophet ﷺ said (to him), "Did you sleep with your wife last night?" Abu Talha said, "Yes". The Prophet ﷺ said, "O Allah! Bestow your blessing on them as regards that night of theirs." Um Sulaim gave birth to a boy. Abu Talha told me to take care of the child till it was taken to the Prophet. Then Abu Talha took the child to the Prophet ﷺ and Um Sulaim sent some dates along with the child. The Prophet ﷺ took the child (on his lap) and asked if there was something with him. The people replied, "Yes, a few dates." The Prophet took a date, chewed it, took some of it out of his mouth, put it into the child's mouth and did Tahnik for him with that, and named him 'Abdullah. – Sahih al-Bukhari 5470

حَدَّثَنَا مَطَرُ بْنُ الْفَضْلِ، حَدَّثَنَا يَزِيدُ بْنُ هَارُونَ، أَخْبَرَنَا عَبْدُ اللَّهِ بْنُ عَوْنٍ، عَنْ أَنَسِ بْنِ سِيرِينَ، عَنْ أَنَسِ بْنِ مَالِكٍ ـ رضى الله عنه ـ قَالَ كَانَ ابْنٌ لأَبِي طَلْحَةَ يَشْتَكِي، فَخَرَجَ أَبُو طَلْحَةَ، فَقُبِضَ الصَّبِيُّ فَلَمَّا رَجَعَ أَبُو طَلْحَةَ قَالَ مَا فَعَلَ ابْنِي قَالَتْ أُمُّ سُلَيْمٍ هُوَ أَسْكَنُ مَا كَانَ. فَقَرَّبَتْ إِلَيْهِ الْعَشَاءَ فَتَعَشَّى، ثُمَّ أَصَابَ مِنْهَا، فَلَمَّا فَرَغَ قَالَتْ وَارِ الصَّبِيَّ. فَلَمَّا أَصْبَحَ أَبُو طَلْحَةَ أَتَى رَسُولَ اللَّهِ صلى الله عليه وسلم فَأَخْبَرَهُ فَقَالَ " أَعْرَسْتُمُ اللَّيْلَةَ ". قَالَ نَعَمْ. قَالَ " اللَّهُمَّ بَارِكْ لَهُمَا ". فَوَلَدَتْ غُلاَمًا قَالَ لِي أَبُو طَلْحَةَ احْفَظْهُ حَتَّى تَأْتِيَ بِهِ النَّبِيَّ صلى الله عليه وسلم فَأَتَى بِهِ النَّبِيَّ صلى الله عليه وسلم وَأَرْسَلَتْ مَعَهُ بِتَمَرَاتٍ، فَأَخَذَهُ النَّبِيُّ صلى الله عليه وسلم فَقَالَ " أَمَعَهُ شَىْءٌ ". قَالُوا نَعَمْ تَمَرَاتٌ. فَأَخَذَهَا النَّبِيُّ صلى الله عليه وسلم فَمَضَغَهَا، ثُمَّ أَخَذَ مِنْ فِيهِ فَجَعَلَهَا فِي فِي الصَّبِيِّ، وَحَنَّكَهُ بِهِ، وَسَمَّاهُ عَبْدَ اللَّهِ

Discharge first
الخروج أولا

Narrated Anas: When `Abdullah bin Salam heard the arrival of the Prophet ﷺ at Medina, he came to him and said, "I am going to ask you about three things which nobody knows except a prophet: What is the first portent of the Hour? What will be the first meal taken by the people of Paradise? Why does a child resemble its father, and why does it resemble its maternal uncle" Allah's Messenge ﷺ said, "Gabriel has just now told me of their answers." `Abdullah said, "He (i.e. Gabriel), from amongst all the angels, is the enemy of the Jews." Allah's Messenger ﷺ said, "The first portent of the Hour will be a fire that will bring together the people from the east to the west; the first meal of the people of Paradise will be Extra-lobe (caudate lobe) of fish-liver. As for the resemblance of the child to its parents: If a man has sexual intercourse with his wife and gets discharge first, the child will resemble the father, and if the woman gets discharge first, the child will resemble her." On that `Abdullah bin Salam said, "I testify that you are the Messenger of Allah." `Abdullah bin Salam further said, "O Allah's Messenge ﷺ! The Jews are liars, and if they should come to know about my conversion to Islam before you ask them (about me), they would tell a lie about me." The Jews came to Allah's Messenger ﷺ and `Abdullah went inside the house. Allah's Apostle asked (the Jews), "What kind of man is `Abdullah bin Salam amongst you?" They replied, "He is the most learned person amongst us, and the best amongst us, and the son of the best amongst us." Allah's Messenge ﷺ said, "What do you think if he embraces Islam (will you do as he does)?" The Jews said, "May Allah save him from it." Then `Abdullah bin Salam came out in front of them saying, "I testify that None has the right to be worshipped but Allah and that Muhammad is the Apostle of Allah." Thereupon they said, "He is the evilest among us, and the son of the evilest amongst us," and continued talking badly of him. – Sahih al-Bukhari 3329

حَدَّثَنَا مُحَمَّدُ بْنُ سَلاَمٍ، أَخْبَرَنَا الْفَزَارِيُّ، عَنْ حُمَيْدٍ، عَنْ أَنَسٍ ـ رضى الله عنه ـ قَالَ بَلَغَ عَبْدَ اللَّهِ بْنَ سَلاَمٍ مَقْدَمُ رَسُولِ اللَّهِ صلى الله عليه وسلم الْمَدِينَةَ، فَأَتَاهُ، فَقَالَ إِنِّي سَائِلُكَ عَنْ ثَلاَثٍ لاَ يَعْلَمُهُنَّ إِلاَّ نَبِيٌّ، {قَالَ مَا} أَوَّلُ أَشْرَاطِ السَّاعَةِ وَمَا أَوَّلُ طَعَامٍ يَأْكُلُهُ أَهْلُ الْجَنَّةِ وَمِنْ أَىِّ شَىْءٍ يَنْزِعُ الْوَلَدُ إِلَى أَبِيهِ وَمِنْ أَىِّ شَىْءٍ يَنْزِعُ إِلَى أَخْوَالِهِ فَقَالَ رَسُولُ اللَّهِ صلى الله عليه وسلم " خَبَّرَنِي بِهِنَّ آنِفًا جِبْرِيلُ ". قَالَ فَقَالَ عَبْدُ اللَّهِ ذَاكَ عَدُوُّ الْيَهُودِ مِنَ الْمَلاَئِكَةِ. فَقَالَ رَسُولُ اللَّهِ صلى الله عليه وسلم "

أَمَّا أَوَّلُ أَشْرَاطِ السَّاعَةِ فَنَارٌ تَحْشُرُ النَّاسَ مِنَ الْمَشْرِقِ إِلَى الْمَغْرِبِ. وَأَمَّا أَوَّلُ طَعَامٍ يَأْكُلُهُ أَهْلُ الْجَنَّةِ فَزِيَادَةُ كَبِدِ حُوتٍ. وَأَمَّا الشَّبَهُ فِي الْوَلَدِ فَإِنَّ الرَّجُلَ إِذَا غَشِيَ الْمَرْأَةَ فَسَبَقَهَا مَاؤُهُ كَانَ الشَّبَهُ لَهُ، وَإِذَا سَبَقَ مَاؤُهَا كَانَ الشَّبَهُ لَهَا ". قَالَ أَشْهَدُ أَنَّكَ رَسُولُ اللَّهِ. ثُمَّ قَالَ يَا رَسُولَ اللَّهِ إِنَّ الْيَهُودَ قَوْمٌ بُهُتٌ، إِنْ عَلِمُوا بِإِسْلاَمِي قَبْلَ أَنْ تَسْأَلَهُمْ بَهَتُونِي عِنْدَكَ، فَجَاءَتِ الْيَهُودُ وَدَخَلَ عَبْدُ اللَّهِ الْبَيْتَ، فَقَالَ رَسُولُ اللَّهِ صلى الله عليه وسلم " أَىُّ رَجُلٍ فِيكُمْ عَبْدُ اللَّهِ بْنُ سَلاَمٍ ". قَالُوا أَعْلَمُنَا وَابْنُ أَعْلَمِنَا وَأَخْبَرُنَا وَابْنُ أَخْيَرِنَا. فَقَالَ رَسُولُ اللَّهِ صلى الله عليه وسلم " أَفَرَأَيْتُمْ إِنْ أَسْلَمَ عَبْدُ اللَّهِ ". قَالُوا أَعَاذَهُ اللَّهُ مِنْ ذَلِكَ. فَخَرَجَ عَبْدُ اللَّهِ إِلَيْهِمْ فَقَالَ أَشْهَدُ أَنْ لاَ إِلَهَ إِلاَّ اللَّهُ، وَأَشْهَدُ أَنَّ مُحَمَّدًا رَسُولُ اللَّهِ. فَقَالُوا شَرُّنَا وَابْنُ شَرِّنَا. وَوَقَعُوا فِيهِ.

Narrated Zainab bint Abi Salama: Um Salama said, “Um Sulaim said, ‘O Allah’s Messenger ﷺ! Allah does not refrain from saying the truth! Is it obligatory for a woman to take a bath after she gets nocturnal discharge?’ He said, ‘Yes, if she notices the water (i.e. discharge).’ Um Salama smiled and said, ‘Does a woman get discharge?’ Allah’s Apostle said. ‘Then why does a child resemble (its mother)?” - Sahih al-Bukhari 3328

حَدَّثَنَا مُسَدَّدٌ، حَدَّثَنَا يَحْيَى، عَنْ هِشَامِ بْنِ عُرْوَةَ، عَنْ أَبِيهِ، عَنْ زَيْنَبَ بِنْتِ أَبِي سَلَمَةَ، عَنْ أُمِّ سَلَمَةَ، أَنَّ أُمَّ سُلَيْمٍ، قَالَتْ يَا رَسُولَ اللَّهِ، إِنَّ اللَّهَ لاَ يَسْتَحْيِي مِنَ الْحَقِّ، فَهَلْ عَلَى الْمَرْأَةِ الْغُسْلُ إِذَا احْتَلَمَتْ قَالَ " نَعَمْ، إِذَا رَأَتِ الْمَاءَ ". فَضَحِكَتْ أُمُّ سَلَمَةَ، فَقَالَتْ تَحْتَلِمُ الْمَرْأَةُ فَقَالَ رَسُولُ اللَّهِ صلى الله عليه وسلم " فَبِمَا يُشْبِهُ الْوَلَدُ ".

.... “What is your name?” Sahih al-Bukhari 6190
" مَا اسْمُكَ ".

Narrated Al-Musaiyab: That his father (Hazn bin Wahb) went to the Prophet ﷺ and the Prophet ﷺ asked (him), “What is your name?” He replied, “My name is Hazn.” The Prophet ﷺ said, “You are Sahl.” Hazn said, “I will not change the name with which my father has named me.” Ibn Al-Musaiyab added: We have had roughness (in character) ever since.
Narrated Al-Musaiyab: On the authority of his father similarly as above (i.e., 209). – Sahih al-Bukhari 6190

حَدَّثَنَا إِسْحَاقُ بْنُ نَصْرٍ، حَدَّثَنَا عَبْدُ الرَّزَّاقِ، أَخْبَرَنَا مَعْمَرٌ، عَنِ الزُّهْرِيِّ، عَنِ ابْنِ الْمُسَيَّبِ، عَنْ أَبِيهِ، أَنَّ أَبَاهُ، جَاءَ إِلَى النَّبِيِّ صلى الله عليه وسلم فَقَالَ " مَا اسْمُكَ ". قَالَ حَزْنٌ. قَالَ " أَنْتَ سَهْلٌ ". قَالَ لاَ أُغَيِّرُ اسْمًا سَمَّانِيهِ أَبِي. قَالَ ابْنُ الْمُسَيَّبِ فَمَا زَالَتِ الْحُزُونَةُ فِينَا بَعْدُ. حَدَّثَنَا عَلِيُّ بْنُ عَبْدِ اللَّهِ، وَمَحْمُودٌ، قَالاَ حَدَّثَنَا عَبْدُ الرَّزَّاقِ، أَخْبَرَنَا مَعْمَرٌ، عَنِ الزُّهْرِيِّ، عَنِ ابْنِ الْمُسَيَّبِ، عَنْ أَبِيهِ، عَنْ جَدِّهِ، بِهَذَا.

Narrated Abu Huraira: Zainab’s original name was “Barrah,” but it was said’ “By that she is giving herself the prestige of piety.” So the Prophet ﷺ changed her name to Zainab. – Sahih al-Bukhari 6192

حَدَّثَنَا صَدَقَةُ بْنُ الْفَضْلِ، أَخْبَرَنَا مُحَمَّدُ بْنُ جَعْفَرٍ، عَنْ شُعْبَةَ، عَنْ عَطَاءِ بْنِ أَبِي مَيْمُونَةَ، عَنْ أَبِي رَافِعٍ، عَنْ أَبِي هُرَيْرَةَ، أَنَّ زَيْنَبَ، كَانَ اسْمُهَا بَرَّةَ، فَقِيلَ تُزَكِّي نَفْسَهَا. فَسَمَّاهَا رَسُولُ اللَّهِ صلى الله عليه وسلم زَيْنَبَ.

.....So do not attest to your own virtues; He knows best those who are mindful of Him. – Surah An-Najm 53:32

فَلَا تُزَكُّوٓا۟ أَنفُسَكُمْ ۖ هُوَ أَعْلَمُ بِمَنِ ٱتَّقَىٰٓ

Narrated Abu Huraira: The Prophet ﷺ said, “Name yourselves with my name (use my name) but do not name yourselves with my Kunya name (i.e. Abul Qasim). And whoever sees me in a dream then surely he has seen me for Satan cannot impersonate me. And whoever tells a lie against me (intentionally), then (surely) let him occupy his seat in Hell-fire.”. – Sahih al-Bukhari 110

حَدَّثَنَا مُوسَى، قَالَ حَدَّثَنَا أَبُو عَوَانَةَ، عَنْ أَبِي حَصِينٍ، عَنْ أَبِي صَالِحٍ، عَنْ أَبِي هُرَيْرَةَ، عَنِ النَّبِيِّ صلى الله عليه وسلم قَالَ " تَسَمَّوْا بِاسْمِي وَلاَ تَكْتَنُوا بِكُنْيَتِي، وَمَنْ رَآنِي فِي الْمَنَامِ فَقَدْ رَآنِي، فَإِنَّ الشَّيْطَانَ لاَ يَتَمَثَّلُ فِي صُورَتِي، وَمَنْ كَذَبَ عَلَىَّ مُتَعَمِّدًا فَلْيَتَبَوَّأْ مَقْعَدَهُ مِنَ النَّارِ ".

Narrated Abu Huraira: The Prophet ﷺ said, "The most awful (meanest) name in Allah's sight." Sufyan said more than once, "The most awful (meanest) name in Allah's sight is (that of) a man calling himself king of kings." Sufyan said, "Somebody else (i.e. other than Abu Az-Zinad, a sub-narrator) says: What is meant by 'The king of kings' is 'Shahan Shah.,". – Sahih al-Bukhari 6206

حَدَّثَنَا عَلِيُّ بْنُ عَبْدِ اللَّهِ، حَدَّثَنَا سُفْيَانُ، عَنْ أَبِي الزِّنَادِ، عَنِ الأَعْرَجِ، عَنْ أَبِي هُرَيْرَةَ، رِوَايَةً قَالَ " أَخْنَعُ اسْمٍ عِنْدَ اللَّهِ ـ وَقَالَ سُفْيَانُ غَيْرَ مَرَّةٍ أَخْنَعُ الأَسْمَاءِ عِنْدَ اللَّهِ ـ رَجُلٌ تَسَمَّى بِمَلِكِ الأَمْلاَكِ ". قَالَ سُفْيَانُ يَقُولُ غَيْرُهُ تَفْسِيرُهُ شَاهَانْ شَاهْ.

Narrated Jabir bin `Abdullah: A man among us begot a boy whom he named Al-Qasim. The people said (to him), "We will not call you Abul-l-Qasim, nor will we please you by calling you so." The man came to the Prophet ﷺ and mentioned that to him. The Prophet ﷺ said to him, "Name your son `Abdur-Rahman.". – Sahih al-Bukhari 6189

حَدَّثَنَا عَبْدُ اللَّهِ بْنُ مُحَمَّدٍ، حَدَّثَنَا سُفْيَانُ، قَالَ سَمِعْتُ ابْنَ الْمُنْكَدِرِ، قَالَ سَمِعْتُ جَابِرَ بْنَ عَبْدِ اللَّهِ ـ رضى الله عنهما وُلِدَ لِرَجُلٍ مِنَّا غُلاَمٌ فَسَمَّاهُ الْقَاسِمَ فَقَالُوا لاَ نَكْنِيكَ بِأَبِي الْقَاسِمِ، وَلاَ نُنْعِمُكَ عَيْنًا. فَأَتَى النَّبِيَّ صلى الله عليه وسلم فَذَكَرَ ذَلِكَ لَهُ فَقَالَ " أَسْمِ ابْنَكَ عَبْدَ الرَّحْمَنِ ".

Narrated Abu Dhar: The Prophet ﷺ said, "If somebody claims to be the son of any other than his real father knowingly, he but disbelieves in Allah, and if somebody claims to belong to some folk to whom he does not belong, let such a person take his place in the (Hell) Fire.". – Sahih al-Bukhari 3508

حَدَّثَنَا أَبُو مَعْمَرٍ، حَدَّثَنَا عَبْدُ الْوَارِثِ، عَنِ الْحُسَيْنِ، عَنْ عَبْدِ اللَّهِ بْنِ بُرَيْدَةَ، قَالَ حَدَّثَنِي يَحْيَى بْنُ يَعْمَرَ، أَنَّ أَبَا الأَسْوَدِ الدِّيلِيَّ، حَدَّثَهُ عَنْ أَبِي ذَرٍّ ـ رضى الله عنه ـ أَنَّهُ سَمِعَ النَّبِيَّ صلى الله عليه وسلم يَقُولُ " لَيْسَ مِنْ رَجُلٍ ادَّعَى لِغَيْرِ أَبِيهِ وَهْوَ يَعْلَمُهُ إِلاَّ كَفَرَ، وَمَنِ ادَّعَى قَوْمًا لَيْسَ لَهُ فِيهِمْ فَلْيَتَبَوَّأْ مَقْعَدَهُ مِنَ النَّارِ ".

Call them after their (true) fathers; (that) is more equitable in the Reckoning with Allah.... Surah Al-Ahzab 33:5

ٱدْعُوهُمْ لِءَابَآئِهِمْ هُوَ أَقْسَطُ عِندَ ٱللَّهِ

Sa'id b. Musayyab told that his father said on the authority of his grandfather (Hazn): The Prophet ﷺ asked: What is your name? He replied: Hazn (rugged). He said: You are Sahl (smooth). He said: No, smooth is trodden upon and disgraced. Sa'id said: I then thought that ruggedness would remain among us after it.

AbuDawud said: The Prophet ﷺ changed the names al-'As, Aziz, Atalah, Shaytan, al-Hakam, Ghurab, Hubab, and Shihab and called him Hisham. He changed the name Harb (war) and called him Silm (peace). He changed the name al-Munba'ith (one who lies) and called him al-Mudtaji' (one who stands up). He changed the name of a land Afrah (barren) and called it Khadrah (green). He changed the name Shi'b ad-Dalalah (the mountain path of a stray), the name of a mountain path and called it Shi'b al-Huda (mountain path of guidance). He changed the name Banu az-Zinyah (children of fornication) and called them Banu ar-Rushdah (children of those who are on the right path), and changed the name Banu Mughwiyah (children of a woman who allures and goes astray), and called them Banu Rushdah (children of a woman who is on the right path). – Sunan Abi Dawud 4956

AbuDawud said: I omitted the chains of these for the sake of brevity.

حَدَّثَنَا أَحْمَدُ بْنُ صَالِحٍ، حَدَّثَنَا عَبْدُ الرَّزَّاقِ، عَنْ مَعْمَرٍ، عَنِ الزُّهْرِيِّ، عَنْ سَعِيدِ بْنِ الْمُسَيَّبِ، عَنْ أَبِيهِ، عَنْ جَدِّهِ، أَنَّ النَّبِيَّ صلى الله عليه وسلم قَالَ لَهُ " مَا اسْمُكَ " . قَالَ حَزْنٌ . قَالَ " أَنْتَ سَهْلٌ " . قَالَ لاَ السَّهْلُ يُوطَأُ وَيُمْتَهَنُ . قَالَ سَعِيدٌ فَظَنَنْتُ أَنَّهُ سَيُصِيبُنَا بَعْدَهُ حُزُونَةٌ . قَالَ أَبُو دَاوُدَ وَغَيَّرَ النَّبِيُّ صلى الله عليه وسلم اسْمَ الْعَاصِ وَعَزِيزٍ وَعَتَلَةَ وَشَيْطَانٍ وَالْحَكَمِ وَغُرَابٍ وَحُبَابٍ وَشِهَابٍ فَسَمَّاهُ هِشَامًا وَسَمَّى حَرْبًا سَلْمًا وَسَمَّى الْمُضْطَجِعَ الْمُنْبَعِثَ وَأَرْضًا تُسَمَّى عَفِرَةَ سَمَّاهَا خَضِرَةَ وَشِعْبَ الضَّلاَلَةِ سَمَّاهُ شِعْبَ الْهُدَى وَبَنُو الزِّنْيَةِ سَمَّاهُمْ بَنِي الرِّشْدَةِ وَسَمَّى بَنِي مُغْوِيَةَ بَنِي رِشْدَةَ . قَالَ أَبُو دَاوُدَ تَرَكْتُ أَسَانِيدَهَا لِلاِخْتِصَارِ .

And whoever does (enough) deeds of righteousness, be it male or female, and he is a believer
وَمَن يَعْمَلْ مِنَ ٱلصَّٰلِحَٰتِ مِن ذَكَرٍ أَوْ أُنثَىٰ وَهُوَ مُؤْمِنٌ

Whoever does an odious (deed), then he will be recompensed with (nothing) except the like of it; and whoever does righteousness, male or female, and is a believer, then those will enter the Garden, provided therein without reckoning. Surah Ghafir 40:40
مَنْ عَمِلَ سَيِّئَةً فَلَا يُجْزَىٰٓ إِلَّا مِثْلَهَا ۖ وَمَنْ عَمِلَ صَٰلِحًا مِّن ذَكَرٍ أَوْ أُنثَىٰ وَهُوَ مُؤْمِنٌ فَأُو۟لَٰٓئِكَ يَدْخُلُونَ ٱلْجَنَّةَ يُرْزَقُونَ فِيهَا بِغَيْرِ حِسَابٍ

Then their Lord responded to them, "I do not waste the deed of any doer among you, any male or female. The one of you is as the other (Literally: some of you from some others). So, the ones who emigrated, and were driven out of their residences, and were hurt in My way, and fought, and were killed, indeed I will definitely expiate them of their odious deeds, and indeed I will definitely cause them to enter Gardens from beneath which Rivers run." A requital from (the Providence of) Allah; and Allah has in His Providence the fairest requital. – Surah Al-Imran 3:195
فَٱسْتَجَابَ لَهُمْ رَبُّهُمْ أَنِّى لَآ أُضِيعُ عَمَلَ عَٰمِلٍ مِّنكُم مِّن ذَكَرٍ أَوْ أُنثَىٰ ۖ بَعْضُكُم مِّنۢ بَعْضٍ ۖ فَٱلَّذِينَ هَاجَرُوا۟ وَأُخْرِجُوا۟ مِن دِيَٰرِهِمْ وَأُوذُوا۟ فِى سَبِيلِى وَقَٰتَلُوا۟ وَقُتِلُوا۟ لَأُكَفِّرَنَّ عَنْهُمْ سَيِّـَٔاتِهِمْ وَلَأُدْخِلَنَّهُمْ جَنَّٰتٍ تَجْرِى مِن تَحْتِهَا ٱلْأَنْهَٰرُ ثَوَابًا مِّنْ عِندِ ٱللَّهِ ۗ وَٱللَّهُ عِندَهُۥ حُسْنُ ٱلثَّوَابِ

Whoever does righteousness, be it male or female, and he is a believer, then indeed We will definitely (give him to) live a goodly life; and indeed We will definitely recompense them their reward, according to the fairest of whatever they were doing. – Surah An-Nahl 16:97
مَنْ عَمِلَ صَٰلِحًا مِّن ذَكَرٍ أَوْ أُنثَىٰ وَهُوَ مُؤْمِنٌ فَلَنُحْيِيَنَّهُۥ حَيَوٰةً طَيِّبَةً ۖ وَلَنَجْزِيَنَّهُمْ أَجْرَهُم بِأَحْسَنِ مَا كَانُوا۟ يَعْمَلُونَ

And whoever does (enough) deeds of righteousness, be it male or female, and he is a believer, then those will enter the Garden and will not be done an injustice even as a groove in a datestone (i.e., not even a small amount). – Surah An-Nisa 4:124
وَمَن يَعْمَلْ مِنَ ٱلصَّٰلِحَٰتِ مِن ذَكَرٍ أَوْ أُنثَىٰ وَهُوَ مُؤْمِنٌ فَأُو۟لَٰٓئِكَ يَدْخُلُونَ ٱلْجَنَّةَ وَلَا يُظْلَمُونَ نَقِيرًا

And the male thief and the female thief: then cut (off) the hands of both, as a recompense for what they (both) have earned, as a torture from Allah; and Allah is Ever-Mighty, Ever-Wise. Surah Al-Ma'idah 5:38
وَٱلسَّارِقُ وَٱلسَّارِقَةُ فَٱقْطَعُوٓا۟ أَيْدِيَهُمَا جَزَآءًۢ بِمَا كَسَبَا نَكَٰلًا مِّنَ ٱللَّهِ ۗ وَٱللَّهُ عَزِيزٌ حَكِيمٌ

And I advise you to take care of the women
وَاسْتَوْصُوا بِالنِّسَاءِ خَيْرًا

Narrated Anas bin Malik: That he and Abu Talha were coming in the company of the Prophet (towards Medina), while Safiya (the Prophet's wife) was riding behind him on his she-camel. After they had covered a portion of the way suddenly the foot of the she-camel slipped and both the Prophet ((ﷺand the woman (i.e., his wife, Safiya) fell down. Abu Talha jumped quickly off his camel and came to the Prophet (saying.) "O Allah's Messengerﷺ ! Let Allah sacrifice me for you! Have you received any injury?" The Prophetﷺ said, "No, but take care of the woman (my wife)." Abu Talha covered his face with his garment and went towards her and threw his garment over her. Then the woman got up and Abu Talha prepared their she-camel (by tightening its saddle, etc.) and both of them (the Prophetﷺ (and Safiya) mounted it. Then all of them proceeded and when they approached near Medina, or saw Medina, the Prophetﷺ said, "Ayibun, taibun, `abidun, liRabbina hamidun (We are coming back (to Medina) with repentance, worshiping (our Lord) and celebrating His (our Lord's) praises". The Prophetﷺ continued repeating these words till he entered the city of Medina. – Sahih al-Bukhari 6185

حَدَّثَنَا عَلِيُّ بْنُ عَبْدِ اللَّهِ، حَدَّثَنَا بِشْرُ بْنُ الْمُفَضَّلِ، حَدَّثَنَا يَحْيَى بْنُ أَبِي إِسْحَاقَ، عَنْ أَنَسِ بْنِ مَالِكٍ، أَنَّهُ أَقْبَلَ هُوَ وَأَبُو طَلْحَةَ مَعَ النَّبِيِّ صلى الله عليه وسلم وَمَعَ النَّبِيِّ صلى الله عليه وسلم صَفِيَّةُ، مُرْدِفُهَا عَلَى رَاحِلَتِهِ، فَلَمَّا كَانُوا بِبَعْضِ الطَّرِيقِ عَثَرَتِ النَّاقَةُ، فَصُرِعَ النَّبِيُّ صلى الله عليه وسلم وَالْمَرْأَةُ، وَأَنَّ أَبَا طَلْحَةَ ـ قَالَ أَحْسِبُ ـ اقْتَحَمَ عَنْ بَعِيرِهِ، فَأَتَى رَسُولَ اللَّهِ صلى الله عليه وسلم فَقَالَ يَا نَبِيَّ اللَّهِ جَعَلَنِي اللَّهُ فِدَاكَ، هَلْ أَصَابَكَ مِنْ شَىْءٍ. قَالَ " لاَ وَلَكِنْ عَلَيْكَ بِالْمَرْأَةِ ". فَأَلْقَى أَبُو طَلْحَةَ ثَوْبَهُ عَلَى وَجْهِهِ فَقَصَدَ قَصْدَهَا، فَأَلْقَى ثَوْبَهُ عَلَيْهَا فَقَامَتِ الْمَرْأَةُ، فَشَدَّ لَهُمَا عَلَى رَاحِلَتِهِمَا فَرَكِبَا، فَسَارُوا حَتَّى إِذَا كَانُوا بِظَهْرِ الْمَدِينَةِ ـ أَوْ قَالَ أَشْرَفُوا عَلَى الْمَدِينَةِ ـ قَالَ النَّبِيُّ صلى الله عليه وسلم " آيِبُونَ تَائِبُونَ، عَابِدُونَ لِرَبِّنَا حَامِدُونَ ". فَلَمْ يَزَلْ يَقُولُهَا حَتَّى دَخَلَ الْمَدِينَةَ.

Narrated Abu Huraira: The Prophetﷺ said, "Whoever believes in Allah and the Last Day should not hurt (trouble) his neighbor. And I advise you to take care of the women, for they are created from a rib and the most crooked portion of the rib is its upper part; if you try to straighten it, it will break, and if you leave it, it will remain crooked, so I urge you to take care of the women.". – Sahih al-Bukhari 5185, 5186

حَدَّثَنَا إِسْحَاقُ بْنُ نَصْرٍ، حَدَّثَنَا حُسَيْنٌ الْجُعْفِيُّ، عَنْ زَائِدَةَ، عَنْ مَيْسَرَةَ، عَنْ أَبِي حَازِمٍ، عَنْ أَبِي هُرَيْرَةَ، عَنِ النَّبِيِّ صلى الله عليه وسلم قَالَ " مَنْ كَانَ يُؤْمِنُ بِاللَّهِ وَالْيَوْمِ الآخِرِ فَلاَ يُؤْذِي جَارَهُ ". وَاسْتَوْصُوا بِالنِّسَاءِ خَيْرًا فَإِنَّهُنَّ خُلِقْنَ مِنْ ضِلَعٍ وَإِنَّ أَعْوَجَ شَىْءٍ فِي الضِّلَعِ أَعْلاَهُ فَإِنْ ذَهَبْتَ تُقِيمُهُ كَسَرْتَهُ وَإِنْ تَرَكْتَهُ لَمْ يَزَلْ أَعْوَجَ فَاسْتَوْصُوا بِالنِّسَاءِ خَيْرًا

Narrated Anas bin Malik: We arrived at Khaibar, and when Allah helped His Apostle to open the fort, the beauty of Safiya bint Huyai bin Akhtaq whose husband had been killed while she was a bride, was mentioned to Allah's Apostle. The Prophetﷺ selected her for himself, and set out with her, and when we reached a place called Sidd-as-Sahba,' Safiya became clean from her menses then Allah's Messengerﷺ married her. Hais (i.e. an 'Arabian dish) was prepared on a small leather mat. Then the Prophetﷺ said to me, "I invite the people around you." So that was the marriage banquet of the Prophetﷺ and Safiya. Then we proceeded towards Medina, and I saw the Prophet, making for her a kind of cushion with his cloak behind him (on his camel). He then sat beside his camel and put his knee for Safiya to put her foot on, in order to ride (on the camel). – Sahih al-Bukhari 4211

حَدَّثَنَا عَبْدُ الْغَفَّارِ بْنُ دَاوُدَ، حَدَّثَنَا يَعْقُوبُ بْنُ عَبْدِ الرَّحْمَنِ، ح وَحَدَّثَنِي أَحْمَدُ، حَدَّثَنَا ابْنُ وَهْبٍ، قَالَ أَخْبَرَنِي يَعْقُوبُ بْنُ عَبْدِ الرَّحْمَنِ الزُّهْرِيُّ، عَنْ عَمْرٍو، مَوْلَى الْمُطَّلِبِ عَنْ أَنَسِ بْنِ مَالِكٍ ـ رضى الله عنه ـ قَالَ قَدِمْنَا خَيْبَرَ، فَلَمَّا فَتَحَ اللَّهُ عَلَيْهِ الْحِصْنَ ذُكِرَ لَهُ جَمَالُ صَفِيَّةَ بِنْتِ حُيَىِّ بْنِ أَخْطَبَ، وَقَدْ قُتِلَ زَوْجُهَا وَكَانَتْ عَرُوسًا، فَاصْطَفَاهَا النَّبِيُّ صلى الله عليه وسلم لِنَفْسِهِ، فَخَرَجَ بِهَا، حَتَّى بَلَغْنَا سَدَّ الصَّهْبَاءِ حَلَّتْ، فَبَنَى بِهَا رَسُولُ اللَّهِ صلى الله عليه وسلم، ثُمَّ صَنَعَ حَيْسًا فِي نِطَعٍ صَغِيرٍ، ثُمَّ قَالَ لِي " آذِنْ مَنْ حَوْلَكَ ". فَكَانَتْ تِلْكَ

وَلِيمَتَهُ عَلَى صَفِيَّةَ، ثُمَّ خَرَجْنَا إِلَى الْمَدِينَةِ، فَرَأَيْتُ النَّبِيَّ صلى الله عليه وسلم يُحَوِّي لَهَا وَرَاءَهُ بِعَبَاءَةٍ، ثُمَّ يَجْلِسُ عِنْدَ بَعِيرِهِ، فَيَضَعُ رُكْبَتَهُ، وَتَضَعُ صَفِيَّةُ رِجْلَهَا عَلَى رُكْبَتِهِ حَتَّى تَرْكَبَ

Narrated Anas bin Malik: Once the Prophet ﷺ was on one of his journeys, and the driver of the camels started chanting (to let the camels go fast). The Prophet ﷺ said to him. "(Take care) Drive slowly with the glass vessels, O Anjasha! Waihaka (May Allah be Merciful to you). – Sahih al-Bukhari 6209

حَدَّثَنَا آدَمُ، حَدَّثَنَا شُعْبَةُ، عَنْ ثَابِتٍ الْبُنَانِيِّ، عَنْ أَنَسِ بْنِ مَالِكٍ، قَالَ كَانَ النَّبِيُّ صلى الله عليه وسلم فِي مَسِيرٍ لَهُ فَحَدَا الْحَادِي، فَقَالَ النَّبِيُّ صلى الله عليه وسلم " ارْفُقْ يَا أَنْجَشَةُ، وَيْحَكَ، بِالْقَوَارِيرِ

Narrated Abu Salama: `Aisha said, "Once Allah's Messenger ﷺ said (to me), 'O Aish (`Aisha)! This is Gabriel greeting you.' I said, 'Peace and Allah's Mercy and Blessings be on him, you see what I don't see' " She was addressing Allah 's Apostle. – Sahih al-Bukhari 3768

حَدَّثَنَا يَحْيَى بْنُ بُكَيْرٍ، حَدَّثَنَا اللَّيْثُ، عَنْ يُونُسَ، عَنِ ابْنِ شِهَابٍ، قَالَ أَبُو سَلَمَةَ إِنَّ عَائِشَةَ ـ رضى الله عنها ـ قَالَتْ قَالَ رَسُولُ اللَّهِ صلى الله عليه وسلم يَوْمًا " يَا عَائِشُ، هَذَا جِبْرِيلُ يُقْرِئُكِ السَّلاَمَ ". فَقُلْتُ وَعَلَيْهِ السَّلاَمُ وَرَحْمَةُ اللَّهِ وَبَرَكَاتُهُ، تَرَى مَا لاَ أَرَى. تُرِيدُ رَسُولَ اللَّهِ صلى الله عليه وسلم.

[As Soon as Joseph's interpretation was conveyed to him,] the King said, "Bring him before me." When the [King's] messenger came to him, [Joseph] said, "Go back to your master and ask him [first to find out the truth] about those women who cut their hands—my Lord knows all about their treachery.". – Surah Yusuf 12:50

وَقَالَ ٱلْمَلِكُ ٱئْتُونِى بِهِۦ ۖ فَلَمَّا جَآءَهُ ٱلرَّسُولُ قَالَ ٱرْجِعْ إِلَىٰ رَبِّكَ فَسْـَٔلْهُ مَا بَالُ ٱلنِّسْوَةِ ٱلَّـٰتِى قَطَّعْنَ أَيْدِيَهُنَّ ۚ إِنَّ رَبِّى بِكَيْدِهِنَّ عَلِيمٌ

She said, "I have never been jealous of any woman as much as I have been jealous of any other woman."
قَالَتْ مَا غِرْتُ عَلَى امْرَأَةٍ مَا غِرْتُ عَلَى

Narrated `Aisha: The Prophet ﷺ used to stay (for a period) in the house of Zainab bint Jahsh (one of the wives of the Prophet) and he used to drink honey in her house. Hafsa and I decided that when the Prophet ﷺ entered upon either of us, she would say, "I smell in you the bad smell of Maghafir (a bad smelling raisin). Have you eaten Maghafir?" When he entered upon one of us, she said that to him. He replied (to her), "No, but I have drunk honey in the house of Zainab bint Jahsh, and I will never drink it again." Then the following verse was revealed: 'O Prophet ! Why do you ban (for you) that which Allah has made lawful for you?. ..(up to) If you two (wives of the Prophet ﷺ turn in repentance to Allah.' (66.1-4) The two were `Aisha and Hafsa And also the Statement of Allah: 'And (Remember) when the Prophet ﷺ disclosed a matter in confidence to one of his wives!' (66.3) i.e., his saying, "But I have drunk honey." Hisham said: It also meant his saying, "I will not drink anymore, and I have taken an oath, so do not inform anybody of that." - Sahih al-Bukhari 6691

حَدَّثَنَا الْحَسَنُ بْنُ مُحَمَّدٍ، حَدَّثَنَا الْحَجَّاجُ، عَنِ ابْنِ جُرَيْجٍ، قَالَ زَعَمَ عَطَاءٌ أَنَّهُ سَمِعَ عُبَيْدَ بْنَ عُمَيْرٍ، يَقُولُ سَمِعْتُ عَائِشَةَ، تَزْعُمُ أَنَّ النَّبِيَّ صلى الله عليه وسلم كَانَ يَمْكُثُ عِنْدَ زَيْنَبَ بِنْتِ جَحْشٍ، وَيَشْرَبُ عِنْدَهَا عَسَلاً، فَتَوَاصَيْتُ أَنَا وَحَفْصَةُ أَنَّ أَيَّتَنَا دَخَلَ عَلَيْهَا النَّبِيُّ صلى الله عليه وسلم فَلْتَقُلْ إِنِّي أَجِدُ مِنْكَ رِيحَ مَغَافِيرَ، أَكَلْتَ مَغَافِيرَ، فَدَخَلَ عَلَى إِحْدَاهُمَا فَقَالَتْ ذَلِكَ لَهُ. فَقَالَ " لاَ بَلْ شَرِبْتُ عَسَلاً عِنْدَ زَيْنَبَ بِنْتِ جَحْشٍ، وَلَنْ أَعُودَ لَهُ ". فَنَزَلَتْ {يَا أَيُّهَا النَّبِيُّ لِمَ تُحَرِّمُ مَا أَحَلَّ اللَّهُ لَكَ}، {إِنْ تَتُوبَا إِلَى اللَّهِ}، لِعَائِشَةَ وَحَفْصَةَ، {وَإِذْ أَسَرَّ النَّبِيُّ إِلَى بَعْضِ أَزْوَاجِهِ حَدِيثًا} لِقَوْلِهِ " بَلْ شَرِبْتُ عَسَلاً ". وَقَالَ لِي إِبْرَاهِيمُ بْنُ مُوسَى عَنْ هِشَامٍ، " وَلَنْ أَعُودَ لَهُ، وَقَدْ حَلَفْتُ، فَلاَ تُخْبِرِي بِذَلِكَ أَحَدًا "

Narrated 'Aisha: Once Hala bint Khuwailid, Khadija's sister, asked the permission of the Prophet ﷺ to enter. On that, the Prophet ﷺ remembered the way Khadija used to ask permission, and that upset him. He said, "O Allah! Hala!" So I became jealous and said, "What makes you remember an old woman amongst the old women of Quraish an old woman (with a teethless mouth) of red gums who died long ago, and in whose place Allah has given you somebody better than her?" - Sahih al-Bukhari 3821

وَقَالَ إِسْمَاعِيلُ بْنُ خَلِيلٍ أَخْبَرَنَا عَلِيُّ بْنُ مُسْهِرٍ، عَنْ هِشَامٍ، عَنْ أَبِيهِ، عَنْ عَائِشَةَ ـ رضى الله عنها ـ قَالَتِ اسْتَأْذَنَتْ هَالَةُ بِنْتُ خُوَيْلِدٍ أُخْتُ خَدِيجَةَ عَلَى رَسُولِ اللَّهِ صلى الله عليه وسلم، فَعَرَفَ اسْتِئْذَانَ خَدِيجَةَ فَارْتَاعَ لِذَلِكَ، فَقَالَ " اللَّهُمَّ هَالَةَ ". قَالَتْ فَغِرْتُ فَقُلْتُ مَا تَذْكُرُ مِنْ عَجُوزٍ مِنْ عَجَائِزِ قُرَيْشٍ، حَمْرَاءِ الشِّدْقَيْنِ، هَلَكَتْ فِي الدَّهْرِ، قَدْ، أَبْدَلَكَ اللَّهُ خَيْرًا مِنْهَا

Narrated Anas: While the Prophet ﷺ was with one of his wives, one of the mothers of the believers (i.e. one of his wives) sent a wooden bowl containing food with a servant. The wife (in whose house he was sitting) stroke the bowl with her hand and broke it. The Prophet ﷺ collected the shattered pieces and put the food back in it and said, "Eat." He kept the servant and the bowl till he had eaten the food. Then the Prophet gave another unbroken. Bowl to the servant and kept the broken one. – Sahih al-Bukhari 2481

حَدَّثَنَا مُسَدَّدٌ، حَدَّثَنَا يَحْيَى بْنُ سَعِيدٍ، عَنْ حُمَيْدٍ، عَنْ أَنَسٍ ـ رضى الله عنه ـ أَنَّ النَّبِيَّ صلى الله عليه وسلم كَانَ عِنْدَ بَعْضِ نِسَائِهِ، فَأَرْسَلَتْ إِحْدَى أُمَّهَاتِ الْمُؤْمِنِينَ مَعَ خَادِمٍ بِقَصْعَةٍ فِيهَا طَعَامٌ فَضَرَبَتْ بِيَدِهَا، فَكَسَرَتِ الْقَصْعَةَ، فَضَمَّهَا، وَجَعَلَ فِيهَا الطَّعَامَ وَقَالَ " كُلُوا ". وَحَبَسَ الرَّسُولَ وَالْقَصْعَةَ حَتَّى فَرَغُوا، فَدَفَعَ الْقَصْعَةَ الصَّحِيحَةَ وَحَبَسَ الْمَكْسُورَةَ. وَقَالَ ابْنُ أَبِي مَرْيَمَ أَخْبَرَنَا يَحْيَى بْنُ أَيُّوبَ، حَدَّثَنَا حُمَيْدٌ، حَدَّثَنَا أَنَسٌ، عَنِ النَّبِيِّ صلى الله عليه وسلم

Narrated `Aisha: I never felt so jealous of any woman as I did of Khadija, though she had died three years before the Prophet married me, and that was because I heard him mentioning her too often, and because his Lord had ordered him to give her the glad tidings that she would have a palace in Paradise, made of Qasab and because he used to slaughter a sheep and distribute its meat among her friends. – Sahih al-Bukhari 6004

حَدَّثَنَا عُبَيْدُ بْنُ إِسْمَاعِيلَ، حَدَّثَنَا أَبُو أُسَامَةَ، عَنْ هِشَامٍ، عَنْ أَبِيهِ، عَنْ عَائِشَةَ ـ رضى الله عنها ـ قَالَتْ مَا غِرْتُ عَلَى امْرَأَةٍ مَا غِرْتُ عَلَى خَدِيجَةَ، وَلَقَدْ هَلَكَتْ قَبْلَ أَنْ يَتَزَوَّجَنِي بِثَلاَثِ سِنِينَ، لِمَا كُنْتُ أَسْمَعُهُ يَذْكُرُهَا، وَلَقَدْ أَمَرَهُ رَبُّهُ أَنْ يُبَشِّرَهَا بِبَيْتٍ فِي الْجَنَّةِ مِنْ قَصَبٍ، وَإِنْ كَانَ لَيَذْبَحُ الشَّاةَ ثُمَّ يُهْدِي فِي خُلَّتِهَا مِنْهَا

Narrated al-Qasim: Aisha said that whenever the Prophet ﷺ intended to go on a journey, he drew lots among his wives (so as to take one of them along with him). During one of his journeys the lot fell on `Aisha and Hafsa. When night fell the Prophet ﷺ would ride beside `Aisha and talk with her. One night Hafsa said to `Aisha, "Won't you ride my camel tonight and I ride yours, so that you may see (me) and I see (you) (in new situation)?" `Aisha said, "Yes, (I agree.)" So `Aisha rode, and then the Prophet ﷺ came towards `Aisha's camel on which Hafsa was riding. He greeted Hafsa and then proceeded (beside her) till they dismounted (on the way). `Aisha missed him, and so, when they dismounted, she put her legs in the Idhkhir and said, "O Lord (Allah)! Send a scorpion or a snake to bite me for I am not to blame him (the Prophet ﷺ . – Sahih al-Bukhari 5211

حَدَّثَنَا أَبُو نُعَيْمٍ، حَدَّثَنَا عَبْدُ الْوَاحِدِ بْنُ أَيْمَنَ، قَالَ حَدَّثَنِي ابْنُ أَبِي مُلَيْكَةَ، عَنِ الْقَاسِمِ، عَنْ عَائِشَةَ، أَنَّ النَّبِيَّ صلى الله عليه وسلم كَانَ إِذَا خَرَجَ أَقْرَعَ بَيْنَ نِسَائِهِ، فَطَارَتِ الْقُرْعَةُ لِعَائِشَةَ وَحَفْصَةَ، وَكَانَ النَّبِيُّ صلى الله عليه وسلم إِذَا كَانَ بِاللَّيْلِ سَارَ مَعَ عَائِشَةَ يَتَحَدَّثُ، فَقَالَتْ حَفْصَةُ أَلاَ تَرْكَبِينَ اللَّيْلَةَ بَعِيرِي وَأَرْكَبُ بَعِيرَكِ تَنْظُرِينَ وَأَنْظُرُ، فَقَالَتْ بَلَى فَرَكِبَتْ فَجَاءَ النَّبِيُّ صلى الله عليه وسلم إِلَى جَمَلِ عَائِشَةَ وَعَلَيْهِ حَفْصَةُ فَسَلَّمَ عَلَيْهَا ثُمَّ سَارَ حَتَّى نَزَلُوا وَافْتَقَدَتْهُ عَائِشَةُ، فَلَمَّا نَزَلُوا جَعَلَتْ رِجْلَيْهَا بَيْنَ الإِذْخِرِ وَتَقُولُ يَا رَبِّ سَلِّطْ عَلَىَّ عَقْرَبًا أَوْ حَيَّةً تَلْدَغُنِي، وَلاَ أَسْتَطِيعُ أَنْ أَقُولَ لَهُ شَيْئًا.

Narrated Ibn `Abbas: When Abraham had differences with his wife), (because of her jealousy of Hajar, Ishmael's mother), he took Ishmael and his mother and went away. They had a water-skin with them containing some water, Ishmael's mother used to drink water from the water-skin so that her milk would increase for her child. When Abraham reached Mecca, he made her sit under a tree and afterwards returned home. Ishmael's mother followed him, and when they reached Kada', she called him from behind, 'O Abraham! To whom are you

leaving us?' He replied, '(I am leaving you) to Allah's (Care).' She said, 'I am satisfied to be with Allah.'......... - Sahih al-Bukhari 3365
لَمَّا كَانَ بَيْنَ إِبْرَاهِيمَ وَبَيْنَ أَهْلِهِ مَا كَانَ، خَرَجَ بِإِسْمَاعِيلَ وَأُمِّ إِسْمَاعِيلَ، وَمَعَهُمْ شَنَّةٌ فِيهَا مَاءٌ، فَجَعَلَتْ أُمُّ إِسْمَاعِيلَ تَشْرَبُ مِنَ الشَّنَّةِ فَيَدِرُّ لَبَنُهَا عَلَى صَبِيِّهَا حَتَّى قَدِمَ مَكَّةَ، فَوَضَعَهَا تَحْتَ دَوْحَةٍ، ثُمَّ رَجَعَ إِبْرَاهِيمُ إِلَى أَهْلِهِ، فَاتَّبَعَتْهُ أُمُّ إِسْمَاعِيلَ، حَتَّى لَمَّا بَلَغُوا كَدَاءً نَادَتْهُ مِنْ وَرَائِهِ يَا إِبْرَاهِيمُ إِلَى مَنْ تَتْرُكُنَا قَالَ إِلَى اللَّهِ. قَالَتْ رَضِيتُ بِاللَّهِ

You will never be able to treat your wives with equal fairness, regardless of how much you desire to do So. Do not allow yourself to incline more towards one and exclude the other, potentially leaving her dangling [between marriage and divorce). If you make amends and remain mindful of Allah, He's the most Forgiving, the Mercy Giver. – Surah An-Nisa 4:129
وَلَن تَسْتَطِيعُوٓا۟ أَن تَعْدِلُوا۟ بَيْنَ ٱلنِّسَآءِ وَلَوْ حَرَصْتُمْ ۖ فَلَا تَمِيلُوا۟ كُلَّ ٱلْمَيْلِ فَتَذَرُوهَا كَٱلْمُعَلَّقَةِ ۚ وَإِن تُصْلِحُوا۟ وَتَتَّقُوا۟ فَإِنَّ ٱللَّهَ كَانَ غَفُورًا رَّحِيمًا

Do not desire that which Allah has given more abundantly to Some of you in preference to others
وَلَا تَتَمَنَّوْا۟ مَا فَضَّلَ ٱللَّهُ بِهِۦ بَعْضَكُمْ عَلَىٰ بَعْضٍ

To the men is an assignment of whatever the parents and the nearest kin have left, and to the women is an assignment of whatever the parents and the nearest kin have left, of whatever it be, little or much, an ordained assignment. – Surah An-Nisa 4:7
لِّلرِّجَالِ نَصِيبٌ مِّمَّا تَرَكَ ٱلْوَٰلِدَانِ وَٱلْأَقْرَبُونَ وَلِلنِّسَآءِ نَصِيبٌ مِّمَّا تَرَكَ ٱلْوَٰلِدَانِ وَٱلْأَقْرَبُونَ مِمَّا قَلَّ مِنْهُ أَوْ كَثُرَ ۚ نَصِيبًا مَّفْرُوضًا

Allah enjoins you concerning your children: to the male the like of the portion of two females; so in case they are women above two, then for them is two-thirds of whatever he has left; and in case she be one, then to her is the half. And to (both) his (i.e., the deceased's) parents, to each one of the two is the sixth of whatever he has left in case he has children; then in case he has no children, and his parents are his heirs, then a third is to his mother; (yet) in case he has brothers, then to his mother is the sixth, even after any bequest he may bequeath, or any debt. Your fathers and your sons (Or: children) – you do not realize which of them is nearer in profit to you. (This is) an ordinance from Allah; surely Allah has been Ever-Knowing, Ever-Wise. – Surah An-Nisa 4:11
يُوصِيكُمُ ٱللَّهُ فِىٓ أَوْلَٰدِكُمْ ۖ لِلذَّكَرِ مِثْلُ حَظِّ ٱلْأُنثَيَيْنِ ۚ فَإِن كُنَّ نِسَآءً فَوْقَ ٱثْنَتَيْنِ فَلَهُنَّ ثُلُثَا مَا تَرَكَ ۖ وَإِن كَانَتْ وَٰحِدَةً فَلَهَا ٱلنِّصْفُ ۚ وَلِأَبَوَيْهِ لِكُلِّ وَٰحِدٍ مِّنْهُمَا ٱلسُّدُسُ مِمَّا تَرَكَ إِن كَانَ لَهُۥ وَلَدٌ ۚ فَإِن لَّمْ يَكُن لَّهُۥ وَلَدٌ وَوَرِثَهُۥٓ أَبَوَاهُ فَلِأُمِّهِ ٱلثُّلُثُ ۚ فَإِن كَانَ لَهُۥٓ إِخْوَةٌ فَلِأُمِّهِ ٱلسُّدُسُ ۚ مِنۢ بَعْدِ وَصِيَّةٍ يُوصِى بِهَآ أَوْ دَيْنٍ ۗ ءَابَآؤُكُمْ وَأَبْنَآؤُكُمْ لَا تَدْرُونَ أَيُّهُمْ أَقْرَبُ لَكُمْ نَفْعًا ۚ فَرِيضَةً مِّنَ ٱللَّهِ ۗ إِنَّ ٱللَّهَ كَانَ عَلِيمًا حَكِيمًا

Do not desire that which Allah has given more abundantly to Some of you in preference to others. Men will profit from what they earned, and women will profit from what they earned. Ask Allah to give to you out of His favor. Allah has full knowledge of everything. – Surah An-Nisa 4:32
وَلَا تَتَمَنَّوْا۟ مَا فَضَّلَ ٱللَّهُ بِهِۦ بَعْضَكُمْ عَلَىٰ بَعْضٍ ۚ لِّلرِّجَالِ نَصِيبٌ مِّمَّا ٱكْتَسَبُوا۟ ۖ وَلِلنِّسَآءِ نَصِيبٌ مِّمَّا ٱكْتَسَبْنَ ۚ وَسْـَٔلُوا۟ ٱللَّهَ مِن فَضْلِهِۦٓ ۗ إِنَّ ٱللَّهَ كَانَ بِكُلِّ شَىْءٍ عَلِيمًا

The Book of
And in case they resolve on divorce – Surah Al-Baqarah 2:227
وَإِنۡ عَزَمُواْ ٱلطَّلَـٰقَ

And they followed what the devils taught during the reign of Solomon. It was not Solomon who disbelieved, but it was the devils who disbelieved. They taught the people witchcraft and what was revealed in Babylon to the two angels Harut and Marut. They did not teach anybody until they had said, "We are a test, so do not lose faith." But they learned from them the means to cause separation between man and his wife. But they cannot harm anyone except with Allah's permission. And they learned what would harm them and not benefit them. Yet they knew that whoever deals in it will have no share in the Hereafter. Miserable is what they sold their souls for, if they only knew.– Surah Al-Baqarah 2:102

وَٱتَّبَعُواْ مَا تَتۡلُواْ ٱلشَّيَـٰطِينُ عَلَىٰ مُلۡكِ سُلَيۡمَـٰنَۖ وَمَا كَفَرَ سُلَيۡمَـٰنُ وَلَـٰكِنَّ ٱلشَّيَـٰطِينَ كَفَرُواْ يُعَلِّمُونَ ٱلنَّاسَ ٱلسِّحۡرَ وَمَآ أُنزِلَ عَلَى
ٱلۡمَلَكَيۡنِ بِبَابِلَ هَـٰرُوتَ وَمَـٰرُوتَۚ وَمَا يُعَلِّمَانِ مِنۡ أَحَدٍ حَتَّىٰ يَقُولَآ إِنَّمَا نَحۡنُ فِتۡنَةٞ فَلَا تَكۡفُرۡۖ فَيَتَعَلَّمُونَ مِنۡهُمَا مَا يُفَرِّقُونَ بِهِۦ بَيۡنَ
ٱلۡمَرۡءِ وَزَوۡجِهِۦۚ وَمَا هُم بِضَآرِّينَ بِهِۦ مِنۡ أَحَدٍ إِلَّا بِإِذۡنِ ٱللَّهِۚ وَيَتَعَلَّمُونَ مَا يَضُرُّهُمۡ وَلَا يَنفَعُهُمۡۚ وَلَقَدۡ عَلِمُواْ لَمَنِ ٱشۡتَرَىٰهُ مَا لَهُۥ
فِي ٱلۡأٓخِرَةِ مِنۡ خَلَـٰقٖۚ وَلَبِئۡسَ مَا شَرَوۡاْ بِهِۦٓ أَنفُسَهُمۡۚ لَوۡ كَانُواْ يَعۡلَمُونَ

If a woman fears maltreatment or desertion from her husband, there is no fault in them if they reconcile their differences, for reconciliation is best. Souls are prone to avarice; yet if you do what is good, and practice piety Allah is Cognizant of what you do.– Surah An-Nisa 4:128

وَإِنِ امْرَأَةٌ خَافَتْ مِن بَعْلِهَا نُشُوزًا أَوْ إِعْرَاضًا فَلَا جُنَاحَ عَلَيْهِمَا أَن يُصْلِحَا بَيْنَهُمَا صُلْحًا وَالصُّلْحُ خَيْرٌ وَأُحْضِرَتِ الْأَنفُسُ
الشُّحَّ وَإِن تُحْسِنُوا وَتَتَّقُوا فَإِنَّ اللهَ كَانَ بِمَا

Iddah
ٱلۡعِدَّةَ

O Prophet! If any of you divorce women, divorce them during their period of purity, and calculate their term. And be pious before Allah, your Lord. And do not evict them from their homes, nor shall they leave, unless they have committed a proven adultery. These are the limits of Allah—whoever oversteps Allah's limits has wronged his own soul. You never know; Allah may afterwards bring about a new situation. – Surah At-Talaq 65:1

يَـٰٓأَيُّهَا ٱلنَّبِيُّ إِذَا طَلَّقۡتُمُ ٱلنِّسَآءَ فَطَلِّقُوهُنَّ لِعِدَّتِهِنَّ وَأَحۡصُواْ ٱلۡعِدَّةَۖ وَٱتَّقُواْ ٱللَّهَ رَبَّكُمۡۖ لَا تُخۡرِجُوهُنَّ مِنۢ بُيُوتِهِنَّ وَلَا يَخۡرُجۡنَ إِلَّآ أَن
يَأۡتِينَ بِفَـٰحِشَةٖ مُّبَيِّنَةٖۚ وَتِلۡكَ حُدُودُ ٱللَّهِۚ وَمَن يَتَعَدَّ حُدُودَ ٱللَّهِ فَقَدۡ ظَلَمَ نَفۡسَهُۥۚ لَا تَدۡرِي لَعَلَّ ٱللَّهَ يُحۡدِثُ بَعۡدَ ذَٰلِكَ أَمۡرٗا

And the ones of you who are taken up, (i.e., those who die) and leave behind (them) spouses, (the spouses) (i.e., the widows. The following verb is in the feminine plural) shall await by themselves for four months and ten (days); (This is the Iddah "term" for a widowed woman before she can remarry) so, when they have reached their term, then there is no fault in you whatever they perform (with) themselves with beneficence; and Allah is Ever-Cognizant of whatever you do. – Surah Al-Baqarah 2:234

وَٱلَّذِينَ يُتَوَفَّوۡنَ مِنكُمۡ وَيَذَرُونَ أَزۡوَٰجٗا يَتَرَبَّصۡنَ بِأَنفُسِهِنَّ أَرۡبَعَةَ أَشۡهُرٖ وَعَشۡرٗاۖ فَإِذَا بَلَغۡنَ أَجَلَهُنَّ فَلَا جُنَاحَ عَلَيۡكُمۡ فِيمَا فَعَلۡنَ
فِيٓ أَنفُسِهِنَّ بِٱلۡمَعۡرُوفِۗ وَٱللَّهُ بِمَا تَعۡمَلُونَ خَبِيرٞ

Narrated Zainab bint Abi Salama: I went to Um Habiba, the wife of Prophet, who said, "I heard the Prophets saying, 'It is not legal for a woman who believes in Allah and the Last Day to mourn for any dead person for more than three days except for her husband, (for whom she should mourn) for four months and ten days'." Later I went to Zainab bint Jahsh when her brother died; she asked for some scent, and after using it she said, "I am not in need of scent but I heard Allah's Messenger ﷺ saying, 'It is not legal for a woman who believes in Allah and the Last Day to mourn for more than three days for any dead person except her husband, (for whom she should mourn) for four months and ten days.' ". – Sahih Al-Bukhari 1281, 1282
حَدَّثَنَا إِسْمَاعِيلُ، حَدَّثَنِي مَالِكٌ، عَنْ عَبْدِ اللَّهِ بْنِ أَبِي بَكْرِ بْنِ مُحَمَّدِ بْنِ عَمْرِو بْنِ حَزْمٍ، عَنْ حُمَيْدِ بْنِ نَافِعٍ، عَنْ زَيْنَبَ بِنْتِ أَبِي سَلَمَةَ، أَخْبَرَتْهُ قَالَتْ، دَخَلْتُ عَلَى أُمِّ حَبِيبَةَ زَوْجِ النَّبِيِّ صلى الله عليه وسلم فَقَالَتْ سَمِعْتُ رَسُولَ اللَّهِ صلى الله عليه وسلم يَقُولُ " لاَ يَحِلُّ لاِمْرَأَةٍ تُؤْمِنُ بِاللَّهِ وَالْيَوْمِ الآخِرِ تُحِدُّ عَلَى مَيِّتٍ فَوْقَ ثَلاَثٍ، إِلاَّ عَلَى زَوْجٍ أَرْبَعَةَ أَشْهُرٍ وَعَشْرًا ". ثُمَّ دَخَلْتُ عَلَى زَيْنَبَ بِنْتِ جَحْشٍ حِينَ تُوُفِّيَ أَخُوهَا، فَدَعَتْ بِطِيبٍ فَمَسَّتْ ثُمَّ قَالَتْ مَا لِي بِالطِّيبِ مِنْ حَاجَةٍ، غَيْرَ أَنِّي سَمِعْتُ رَسُولَ اللَّهِ صلى الله عليه وسلم عَلَى الْمِنْبَرِ يَقُولُ " لاَ يَحِلُّ لاِمْرَأَةٍ تُؤْمِنُ بِاللَّهِ وَالْيَوْمِ الآخِرِ تُحِدُّ عَلَى مَيِّتٍ فَوْقَ ثَلاَثٍ، إِلاَّ عَلَى زَوْجٍ أَرْبَعَةَ أَشْهُرٍ وَعَشْرًا"

If you fear a breach between the two, appoint an arbiter from his family and an arbiter from her family. If they wish to reconcile, Allah will bring them together. Allah is Knowledgeable, Expert. – Surah An-Nisa 4:35
وَإِنْ خِفْتُمْ شِقَاقَ بَيْنِهِمَا فَٱبْعَثُوا۟ حَكَمًا مِّنْ أَهْلِهِۦ وَحَكَمًا مِّنْ أَهْلِهَآ إِن يُرِيدَآ إِصْلَـٰحًا يُوَفِّقِ ٱللَّهُ بَيْنَهُمَآ ۗ إِنَّ ٱللَّهَ كَانَ عَلِيمًا خَبِيرًا

Tahleel
تَحْلِيل

Divorced women shall wait by themselves for three periods. And it is not lawful for them to conceal what Allah has created in their wombs, if they believe in Allah and the Last Day. Meanwhile, their husbands have the better right to take them back, if they desire reconciliation. And women have rights similar to their obligations, according to what is fair. But men have a degree over them. Allah is Mighty and Wise. Divorce is allowed twice. Then, either honorable retention, or setting free kindly. It is not lawful for you to take back anything you have given them, unless they fear that they cannot maintain Allah's limits. If you fear that they cannot maintain Allah's limits, then there is no blame on them if she sacrifices something for her release. These are Allah's limits, so do not transgress them. Those who transgress Allah's limits are the unjust. If he divorces her, she shall not be lawful for him again until she has married another husband. If the latter divorces her, then there is no blame on them for reuniting, provided they think they can maintain Allah's limits. These are Allah's limits; He makes them clear to people who know. When you divorce women, and they have reached their term, either retain them amicably, or release them amicably. But do not retain them to hurt them and commit aggression. Whoever does that has wronged himself. And do not take Allah's revelations for a joke. And remember Allah's favor to you, and that He revealed to you the Scripture and Wisdom to teach you. And fear Allah, and know that Allah is aware of everything. When you divorce women, and they have reached their term, do not prevent them from marrying their husbands, provided they agree on Qfair terms. Thereby is advised whoever among you believes in Allah and the Last Day. That is better and more decent for you. Allah knows, and you do not know – Surah Al-Baqarah 2:228-232

وَإِنْ عَزَمُوا۟ ٱلطَّلَـٰقَ فَإِنَّ ٱللَّهَ سَمِيعٌ عَلِيمٌ وَٱلْمُطَلَّقَـٰتُ يَتَرَبَّصْنَ بِأَنفُسِهِنَّ ثَلَـٰثَةَ قُرُوٓءٍ ۚ وَلَا يَحِلُّ لَهُنَّ أَن يَكْتُمْنَ مَا خَلَقَ ٱللَّهُ فِىٓ أَرْحَامِهِنَّ إِن كُنَّ يُؤْمِنَّ بِٱللَّهِ وَٱلْيَوْمِ ٱلْـَٔاخِرِ ۚ وَبُعُولَتُهُنَّ أَحَقُّ بِرَدِّهِنَّ فِى ذَٰلِكَ إِنْ أَرَادُوٓا۟ إِصْلَـٰحًا ۚ وَلَهُنَّ مِثْلُ ٱلَّذِى عَلَيْهِنَّ بِٱلْمَعْرُوفِ ۚ وَلِلرِّجَالِ عَلَيْهِنَّ دَرَجَةٌ ۗ وَٱللَّهُ عَزِيزٌ حَكِيمٌ ٱلطَّلَـٰقُ مَرَّتَانِ ۖ فَإِمْسَاكٌۢ بِمَعْرُوفٍ أَوْ تَسْرِيحٌۢ بِإِحْسَـٰنٍ ۗ وَلَا يَحِلُّ لَكُمْ أَن تَأْخُذُوا۟ مِمَّآ ءَاتَيْتُمُوهُنَّ شَيْـًٔا إِلَّآ أَن يَخَافَآ أَلَّا يُقِيمَا حُدُودَ ٱللَّهِ ۖ فَإِنْ خِفْتُمْ أَلَّا يُقِيمَا حُدُودَ ٱللَّهِ فَلَا جُنَاحَ عَلَيْهِمَا فِيمَا ٱفْتَدَتْ بِهِۦ ۗ تِلْكَ حُدُودُ ٱللَّهِ فَلَا تَعْتَدُوهَا ۚ وَمَن يَتَعَدَّ حُدُودَ ٱللَّهِ فَأُو۟لَـٰٓئِكَ هُمُ ٱلظَّـٰلِمُونَ فَإِن طَلَّقَهَا فَلَا تَحِلُّ لَهُۥ مِنۢ بَعْدُ حَتَّىٰ تَنكِحَ زَوْجًا غَيْرَهُۥ ۗ فَإِن طَلَّقَهَا فَلَا جُنَاحَ عَلَيْهِمَآ أَن يَتَرَاجَعَآ إِن ظَنَّآ أَن يُقِيمَا حُدُودَ ٱللَّهِ ۗ وَتِلْكَ حُدُودُ ٱللَّهِ يُبَيِّنُهَا لِقَوْمٍ يَعْلَمُونَ وَإِذَا طَلَّقْتُمُ ٱلنِّسَآءَ فَبَلَغْنَ أَجَلَهُنَّ فَأَمْسِكُوهُنَّ بِمَعْرُوفٍ أَوْ سَرِّحُوهُنَّ بِمَعْرُوفٍ ۚ وَلَا تُمْسِكُوهُنَّ ضِرَارًا لِّتَعْتَدُوا۟ ۚ وَمَن يَفْعَلْ ذَٰلِكَ فَقَدْ ظَلَمَ نَفْسَهُۥ ۚ وَلَا تَتَّخِذُوٓا۟ ءَايَـٰتِ ٱللَّهِ هُزُوًا ۚ وَٱذْكُرُوا۟ نِعْمَتَ ٱللَّهِ عَلَيْكُمْ وَمَآ أَنزَلَ عَلَيْكُم مِّنَ ٱلْكِتَـٰبِ وَٱلْحِكْمَةِ يَعِظُكُم بِهِۦ ۚ وَٱتَّقُوا۟ ٱللَّهَ وَٱعْلَمُوٓا۟ أَنَّ ٱللَّهَ بِكُلِّ شَىْءٍ عَلِيمٌ وَإِذَا طَلَّقْتُمُ ٱلنِّسَآءَ فَبَلَغْنَ أَجَلَهُنَّ فَلَا تَعْضُلُوهُنَّ أَن يَنكِحْنَ أَزْوَٰجَهُنَّ إِذَا تَرَٰضَوْا۟ بَيْنَهُم بِٱلْمَعْرُوفِ ۗ ذَٰلِكَ يُوعَظُ بِهِۦ مَن كَانَ مِنكُمْ يُؤْمِنُ بِٱللَّهِ وَٱلْيَوْمِ ٱلْـَٔاخِرِ ۗ ذَٰلِكُمْ أَزْكَىٰ لَكُمْ وَأَطْهَرُ ۗ وَٱللَّهُ يَعْلَمُ وَأَنتُمْ لَا تَعْلَمُونَ

Ibn `Umar added: "When the period of four months has expired, the husband should be put in prison so that he should divorce his wife, but the divorce does not occur unless the husband himself declares it. This has been mentioned by `Uthman, `Ali, Abu Ad-Darda, `Aisha and twelve other companions of the Prophet ﷺ .". – Sahih al-Bukhari 5291

وَقَالَ لِي إِسْمَاعِيلُ حَدَّثَنِي مَالِكٌ، عَنْ نَافِعٍ، عَنِ ابْنِ عُمَرَ، إِذَا مَضَتْ أَرْبَعَةُ أَشْهُرٍ يُوقَفُ حَتَّى يُطَلِّقَ، وَلاَ يَقَعُ عَلَيْهِ الطَّلاَقُ حَتَّى يُطَلِّقَ. وَيُذْكَرُ ذَلِكَ عَنْ عُثْمَانَ وَعَلِيٍّ وَأَبِي الدَّرْدَاءِ وَعَائِشَةَ وَاثْنَىْ عَشَرَ رَجُلاً مِنْ أَصْحَابِ النَّبِيِّ صلى الله عليه وسلم

Narrated `Aisha: Rifa`a Al-Qurazi divorced his wife irrevocably (i.e. that divorce was the final). Later on `Abdur- Rahman bin Az-Zubair married her after him. She came to the Prophet ﷺ and said, "O Allah's Messenger ﷺ! I was Rifa`a's wife and he divorced me thrice, and then I was married to `Abdur-Rahman bin AzZubair, who, by Allah has nothing with him except something like this fringe, O Allah's Messenger ﷺ," showing a fringe she had taken from her covering sheet. Abu Bakr was sitting with the Prophet ﷺ while Khalid Ibn Sa`id bin Al-As was sitting at the gate of the room waiting for admission. Khalid started calling Abu Bakr, "O Abu Bakr! Why don't you reprove this lady from what she is openly saying before Allah's Apostle?" Allah's Messenger ﷺ did nothing except smiling, and then said (to the lady), "Perhaps you want to go back to Rifa`a? No, (it is not possible), unless and until you enjoy the sexual relation with him (`Abdur Rahman), and he enjoys the sexual relation with you.". – Sahih Al-Bukhari 6084

حَدَّثَنَا حِبَّانُ بْنُ مُوسَى، أَخْبَرَنَا عَبْدُ اللَّهِ، أَخْبَرَنَا مَعْمَرٌ، عَنِ الزُّهْرِيِّ، عَنْ عُرْوَةَ، عَنْ عَائِشَةَ ـ رضى الله عنها ـ أَنَّ رِفَاعَةَ، الْقُرَظِيَّ طَلَّقَ امْرَأَتَهُ فَبَتَّ طَلاَقَهَا، فَتَزَوَّجَهَا بَعْدَهُ عَبْدُ الرَّحْمَنِ بْنُ الزَّبِيرِ، فَجَاءَتِ النَّبِيَّ صلى الله عليه وسلم فَقَالَتْ يَا رَسُولَ اللَّهِ إِنَّهَا كَانَتْ عِنْدَ رِفَاعَةَ فَطَلَّقَهَا آخِرَ ثَلاَثِ تَطْلِيقَاتٍ، فَتَزَوَّجَهَا بَعْدَهُ عَبْدُ الرَّحْمَنِ بْنُ الزَّبِيرِ، وَإِنَّهُ وَاللَّهِ مَا مَعَهُ يَا رَسُولَ اللَّهِ إِلاَّ مِثْلُ هَذِهِ الْهُدْبَةِ، لِهُدْبَةٍ أَخَذَتْهَا مِنْ جِلْبَابِهَا. قَالَ وَأَبُو بَكْرٍ جَالِسٌ عِنْدَ النَّبِيِّ صلى الله عليه وسلم وَابْنُ سَعِيدِ بْنِ الْعَاصِ جَالِسٌ بِبَابِ الْحُجْرَةِ لِيُؤْذَنَ لَهُ، فَطَفِقَ خَالِدٌ يُنَادِي أَبَا بَكْرٍ، يَا أَبَا بَكْرٍ أَلاَ تَزْجُرُ هَذِهِ عَمَّا تَجْهَرُ بِهِ عِنْدَ رَسُولِ اللَّهِ صلى الله عليه وسلم وَمَا يَزِيدُ رَسُولُ اللَّهِ صلى الله عليه وسلم عَلَى التَّبَسُّمِ ثُمَّ قَالَ " لَعَلَّكِ تُرِيدِينَ أَنْ تَرْجِعِي إِلَى رِفَاعَةَ، لاَ، حَتَّى تَذُوقِي عُسَيْلَتَهُ، وَيَذُوقَ عُسَيْلَتَكِ "

Narrated Al-Hasan: The sister of Ma'qal bin Yasar was divorced by her husband who left her till she had fulfilled her term of 'Iddat (i.e. the period which should elapse before she can Remarry) and then he wanted to remarry her but Maqal refused, so this Verse was revealed:-- "Do not prevent them from marrying their (former) husbands." (2.232). – Sahih Al-Bukhari 4529

حَدَّثَنَا عُبَيْدُ اللَّهِ بْنُ سَعِيدٍ، حَدَّثَنَا أَبُو عَامِرٍ الْعَقَدِيُّ، حَدَّثَنَا عَبَّادُ بْنُ رَاشِدٍ، حَدَّثَنَا الْحَسَنُ، قَالَ حَدَّثَنِي مَعْقِلُ بْنُ يَسَارٍ، قَالَ كَانَتْ لِي أُخْتٌ تُخْطَبُ إِلَىَّ. وَقَالَ إِبْرَاهِيمُ عَنْ يُونُسَ، عَنِ الْحَسَنِ، حَدَّثَنِي مَعْقِلُ بْنُ يَسَارٍ. حَدَّثَنَا أَبُو مَعْمَرٍ، حَدَّثَنَا عَبْدُ

الْوَارِثِ، حَدَّثَنَا يُونُسُ، عَنِ الْحَسَنِ، أَنَّ أُخْتَ، مَعْقِلِ بْنِ يَسَارٍ طَلَّقَهَا زَوْجُهَا، فَتَرَكَهَا حَتَّى انْقَضَتْ عِدَّتُهَا، فَخَطَبَهَا فَأَبَى مَعْقِلٌ، فَنَزَلَتْ {فَلاَ تَعْضُلُوهُنَّ أَنْ يَنْكِحْنَ أَزْوَاجَهُنَّ}.

If you divorce them before you have touched them, but after you had set the dowry for them, give them half of what you specified—unless they forego the right, or the one in whose hand is the marriage contract foregoes it. But to forego is nearer to piety. And do not forget generosity between one another. Allah is seeing of everything you do – Surah Al-Baqarah 2:237

وَإِن طَلَّقْتُمُوهُنَّ مِن قَبْلِ أَن تَمَسُّوهُنَّ وَقَدْ فَرَضْتُمْ لَهُنَّ فَرِيضَةً فَنِصْفُ مَا فَرَضْتُمْ إِلَّآ أَن يَعْفُونَ أَوْ يَعْفُوَا۟ ٱلَّذِى بِيَدِهِۦ عُقْدَةُ ٱلنِّكَاحِ وَأَن تَعْفُوٓا۟ أَقْرَبُ لِلتَّقْوَىٰ وَلَا تَنسَوُا۟ ٱلْفَضْلَ بَيْنَكُمْ إِنَّ ٱللَّهَ بِمَا تَعْمَلُونَ بَصِيرٌ

Allow them to reside where you reside, according to your means, and do not harass them in order to make things difficult for them. If they are pregnant, spend on them until they give birth. And if they nurse your infant, give them their payment. And conduct your relation in amity. But if you disagree, then let another woman nurse him. The wealthy shall spend according to his means; and he whose resources are restricted shall spend according to what Allah has givenhim. Allah never burdens a soul beyond what He has given it. Allah will bring ease after hardship. Surah At-Talaq 65:6&7

أَسْكِنُوهُنَّ مِنْ حَيْثُ سَكَنتُم مِّن وُجْدِكُمْ وَلَا تُضَآرُّوهُنَّ لِتُضَيِّقُوا۟ عَلَيْهِنَّ وَإِن كُنَّ أُو۟لَٰتِ حَمْلٍ فَأَنفِقُوا۟ عَلَيْهِنَّ حَتَّىٰ يَضَعْنَ حَمْلَهُنَّ فَإِنْ أَرْضَعْنَ لَكُمْ فَـَٔاتُوهُنَّ أُجُورَهُنَّ وَأْتَمِرُوا۟ بَيْنَكُم بِمَعْرُوفٍ وَإِن تَعَاسَرْتُمْ فَسَتُرْضِعُ لَهُۥٓ أُخْرَىٰ لِيُنفِقْ ذُو سَعَةٍ مِّن سَعَتِهِۦ وَمَن قُدِرَ عَلَيْهِ رِزْقُهُۥ فَلْيُنفِقْ مِمَّآ ءَاتَىٰهُ ٱللَّهُ لَا يُكَلِّفُ ٱللَّهُ نَفْسًا إِلَّا مَآ ءَاتَىٰهَا سَيَجْعَلُ ٱللَّهُ بَعْدَ عُسْرٍ يُسْرًا

And divorced women shall be provided for, equitably—a duty upon the righteous. – Surah Al-Baqarah 2:241

وَلِلْمُطَلَّقَٰتِ مَتَٰعٌۢ بِٱلْمَعْرُوفِ حَقًّا عَلَى ٱلْمُتَّقِينَ

Lian
لاَعَنَ

Narrated Sahl bin Sa`d As-Sa`idi: 'Uwaimir Al-`Ajlani came to `Asim bin `Adi and said, "If a man found another man with his wife and killed him, would you sentence the husband to death (in Qisas,) i.e., equality in punishment)? O `Asim! Please ask Allah's Messenger ﷺ about this matter on my behalf." `Asim asked the Prophet ﷺ but the Prophet disliked the question and disapproved of it. `Asim returned and informed 'Uwaimir that the Prophet disliked that type of question. 'Uwaimir said, "By Allah, I will go (personally) to the Prophet." 'Uwaimir came to the Prophet ﷺ when Allah had already revealed Qur'anic Verses (in that respect), after `Asim had left the Prophet ﷺ.So the Prophet ﷺ said to 'Uwaimir, "Allah has revealed Qur'anic Verses regarding you and your wife." The Prophet ﷺ then called for them, and they came and carried out the order of Lian. Then 'Uwaimir said, "O Allah's Messenger ﷺ! Now if I kept her with me, I would be accused of telling a lie." So 'Uwaimir divorced her although the Prophet ﷺ did not order him to do so. Later on this practice of divorcing became the tradition of couples involved in a case of Li'an. The Prophet ﷺ said (to the people). "Wait for her! If she delivers a red short (small) child like a Wahra (a short red animal). Then I will be of the opinion that he ('Uwaimir) has told a lie but if she delivered a black big-eyed one with big buttocks, then I will be of the opinion that he has told the truth about her." 'Ultimately she gave birth to a child that proved the accusation. (See Hadith No. 269, Vol. 6). – Sahih Al-Bukhari 7304

حَدَّثَنَا آدَمُ، حَدَّثَنَا ابْنُ أَبِي ذِئْبٍ، حَدَّثَنَا الزُّهْرِيُّ، عَنْ سَهْلِ بْنِ سَعْدٍ السَّاعِدِيِّ، قَالَ جَاءَ عُوَيْمِرٌ إِلَى عَاصِمِ بْنِ عَدِيٍّ فَقَالَ أَرَأَيْتَ رَجُلاً وَجَدَ مَعَ امْرَأَتِهِ رَجُلاً فَيَقْتُلُهُ، أَتَقْتُلُونَهُ بِهِ سَلْ لِي يَا عَاصِمُ رَسُولَ اللَّهِ صلى الله عليه وسلم فَسَأَلَهُ فَكَرِهَ النَّبِيُّ صلى الله عليه وسلم الْمَسَائِلَ وَعَابَ، فَرَجَعَ عَاصِمٌ فَأَخْبَرَهُ أَنَّ النَّبِيَّ صلى الله عليه وسلم كَرِهَ الْمَسَائِلَ فَقَالَ عُوَيْمِرٌ وَاللَّهِ لآتِيَنَّ النَّبِيَّ صلى الله عليه وسلم، فَجَاءَ وَقَدْ أَنْزَلَ اللَّهُ تَعَالَى الْقُرْآنَ خَلْفَ عَاصِمٍ فَقَالَ لَهُ " قَدْ أَنْزَلَ اللَّهُ فِيكُمْ قُرْآنًا ". فَدَعَا بِهِمَا فَتَقَدَّمَا فَتَلاَعَنَا، ثُمَّ قَالَ عُوَيْمِرٌ كَذَبْتُ عَلَيْهَا يَا رَسُولَ اللَّهِ، إِنْ أَمْسَكْتُهَا. فَفَارَقَهَا وَلَمْ يَأْمُرْهُ النَّبِيُّ صلى الله عليه وسلم بِفِرَاقِهَا، فَجَرَتِ السُّنَّةُ فِي الْمُتَلاَعِنَيْنِ. وَقَالَ النَّبِيُّ صلى الله عليه وسلم " انْظُرُوهَا فَإِنْ جَاءَتْ بِهِ أَحْمَرَ قَصِيرًا مِثْلَ وَحَرَةٍ فَلاَ أُرَاهُ إِلاَّ قَدْ كَذَبَ، وَإِنْ جَاءَتْ بِهِ أَسْحَمَ أَعْيَنَ ذَا أَلْيَتَيْنِ فَلاَ أَحْسِبُ إِلاَّ قَدْ صَدَقَ عَلَيْهَا ". فَجَاءَتْ بِهِ عَلَى الأَمْرِ الْمَكْرُوهِ.

Narrated Sa`id bin Jubair: I asked Ibn `Umar about those who were involved in a case of Lien. He said, “The Prophet ﷺ said to those who were involved in a case of Lien, ‘Your accounts are with Allah. One of you two is a liar, and you (the husband) have no right over her (she is divorced).” The man said, ‘What about my property (Mahr) ?’ The Prophet ﷺ said, ‘You have no right to get back your property. If you have told the truth about her then your property was for the consummation of your marriage with her; and if you told a lie about her, then you are less rightful to get your property back.’ “ Sufyan, a sub-narrator said: I learned the Hadith from `Amr. Narrated Aiyub: I heard Sa`id bin Jubair saying, “I asked Ibn `Umar, ‘If a man (accuses his wife for an illegal sexual intercourse and) carries out the process of Lian (what will happen)?’ Ibn `Umar set two of his fingers apart. (Sufyan set his index finger and middle finger apart.) Ibn `Umar said, ‘The Prophet ﷺ separated the couple of Bani Al-Ajlan by divorce and said thrice, “Allah knows that one of you two is a liar; so will one of you repent (to Allah)?’ “. – Sahih Al-Bukhari 5312

حَدَّثَنَا عَلِيُّ بْنُ عَبْدِ اللَّهِ، حَدَّثَنَا سُفْيَانُ، قَالَ عَمْرٌو سَمِعْتُ سَعِيدَ بْنَ جُبَيْرٍ، قَالَ سَأَلْتُ ابْنَ عُمَرَ عَنِ الْمُتَلاَعِنَيْنِ،، فَقَالَ قَالَ النَّبِيُّ صلى الله عليه وسلم لِلْمُتَلاَعِنَيْنِ " حِسَابُكُمَا عَلَى اللَّهِ أَحَدُكُمَا كَاذِبٌ، لاَ سَبِيلَ لَكَ عَلَيْهَا ". قَالَ مَالِي قَالَ " لاَ مَالَ لَكَ، إِنْ كُنْتَ صَدَقْتَ عَلَيْهَا، فَهْوَ بِمَا اسْتَحْلَلْتَ مِنْ فَرْجِهَا، وَإِنْ كُنْتَ كَذَبْتَ عَلَيْهَا، فَذَاكَ أَبْعَدُ لَكَ ". قَالَ سُفْيَانُ حَفِظْتُهُ مِنْ عَمْرٍو. وَقَالَ أَيُّوبُ سَمِعْتُ سَعِيدَ بْنَ جُبَيْرٍ قَالَ قُلْتُ لاِبْنِ عُمَرَ رَجُلٌ لاَعَنَ امْرَأَتَهُ فَقَالَ بِإِصْبَعَيْهِ ـ وَفَرَّقَ سُفْيَانُ بَيْنَ إِصْبَعَيْهِ السَّبَّابَةِ وَالْوُسْطَى ـ فَرَّقَ النَّبِيُّ صلى الله عليه وسلم بَيْنَ أَخَوَىْ بَنِي الْعَجْلاَنِ، وَقَالَ " اللَّهُ يَعْلَمُ إِنَّ أَحَدَكُمَا كَاذِبٌ فَهَلْ مِنْكُمَا تَائِبٌ ". ثَلاَثَ مَرَّاتٍ. قَالَ سُفْيَانُ حَفِظْتُهُ مِنْ عَمْرٍو وَأَيُّوبَ كَمَا أَخْبَرْتُكَ

Narrated Ibn `Abbas: Those involved in a case of Lian were mentioned before Allah’s Messenger ﷺ Asim bin Adi said something about that and then left. Later on a man from his tribe came to him and told him that he had found another man with his wife. On that `Asim said, “I have not been put to task except for what I have said (about Lian).” `Asim took the man to Allah’s Messenger ﷺ and he told him of the state in which he found his wife. The man was pale, thin and lank-haired, while the other man whom he had found with his wife was brown, fat with thick calves and curly hair. Allah’s Messenger ﷺ said, “O Allah! Reveal the truth.” Then the lady delivered a child resembling the man whom her husband had mentioned he had found with her. So Allah’s Messenger ﷺ ordered them to carry out Lien. A man from that gathering said to Ibn `Abbas, “Was she the same lady regarding whom Allah’s Messenger ﷺ said, ‘If I were to stone to death someone without witnesses, I would have stoned this lady’?” Ibn `Abbas said, “No, that was another lady who, though being a Muslim, used to arouse suspicion because of her outright misbehavior.”. – Sahih Al-Bukhari 5316

حَدَّثَنَا إِسْمَاعِيلُ، قَالَ حَدَّثَنِي سُلَيْمَانُ بْنُ بِلاَلٍ، عَنْ يَحْيَى بْنِ سَعِيدٍ، قَالَ أَخْبَرَنِي عَبْدُ الرَّحْمَنِ بْنُ الْقَاسِمِ، عَنِ الْقَاسِمِ بْنِ مُحَمَّدٍ، عَنِ ابْنِ عَبَّاسٍ، أَنَّهُ قَالَ ذُكِرَ الْمُتَلاَعِنَانِ عِنْدَ رَسُولِ اللَّهِ صلى الله عليه وسلم فَقَالَ عَاصِمُ بْنُ عَدِيٍّ فِي ذَلِكَ قَوْلاً، ثُمَّ انْصَرَفَ فَأَتَاهُ رَجُلٌ مِنْ قَوْمِهِ، فَذَكَرَ لَهُ أَنَّهُ وَجَدَ مَعَ امْرَأَتِهِ رَجُلاً، فَقَالَ عَاصِمٌ مَا ابْتُلِيتُ بِهَذَا الأَمْرِ إِلاَّ لِقَوْلِي. فَذَهَبَ بِهِ إِلَى رَسُولِ اللَّهِ صلى الله عليه وسلم فَأَخْبَرَهُ بِالَّذِي وَجَدَ عَلَيْهِ امْرَأَتَهُ، وَكَانَ ذَلِكَ الرَّجُلُ مُصْفَرًّا قَلِيلَ اللَّحْمِ سَبْطَ الشَّعَرِ، وَكَانَ الَّذِي وَجَدَ عِنْدَ أَهْلِهِ آدَمَ خَدْلاً كَثِيرَ اللَّحْمِ جَعْدًا قَطَطًا، فَقَالَ رَسُولُ اللَّهِ صلى الله عليه وسلم " اللَّهُمَّ بَيِّنْ ". فَوَضَعَتْ

شَبِيهًا بِالرَّجُلِ الَّذِي ذَكَرَ زَوْجُهَا أَنَّهُ وَجَدَ عِنْدَهَا، فَلاَعَنَ رَسُولُ اللَّهِ صلى الله عليه وسلم بَيْنَهُمَا، فَقَالَ رَجُلٌ لاِبْنِ عَبَّاسٍ فِي الْمَجْلِسِ هِيَ الَّتِي قَالَ رَسُولُ اللَّهِ صلى الله عليه وسلم " لَوْ رَجَمْتُ أَحَدًا بِغَيْرِ بَيِّنَةٍ لَرَجَمْتُ هَذِهِ ". فَقَالَ ابْنُ عَبَّاسٍ لاَ تِلْكَ امْرَأَةٌ كَانَتْ تُظْهِرُ السُّوءَ فِي الإِسْلاَمِ

Narrated Sahl bin Sa`d: I witnessed the case of Lian (the case of a man who charged his wife for committing illegal sexual intercourse when I was fifteen years old. The Prophetﷺ ordered that they be divorced, and the husband said, "If I kept her, I would be a liar." I remember that Az-Zubair also said, "(It was said) that if that woman brought forth the child with such-and-such description, her husband would prove truthful, but if she brought it with such-and-such description looking like a Wahra (a red insect), he would prove untruthful." I heard Az-Zubair also saying, "Finally she gave birth to a child of description which her husband disliked . – Sahih Al-Bukhari 6854

حَدَّثَنَا عَلِيٌّ، حَدَّثَنَا سُفْيَانُ، قَالَ الزُّهْرِيُّ عَنْ سَهْلِ بْنِ سَعْدٍ، قَالَ شَهِدْتُ الْمُتَلاَعِنَيْنِ وَأَنَا ابْنُ خَمْسَ، عَشْرَةَ، فَرَّقَ بَيْنَهُمَا فَقَالَ زَوْجُهَا كَذَبْتُ عَلَيْهَا إِنْ أَمْسَكْتُهَا. قَالَ فَحَفِظْتُ ذَاكَ مِنَ الزُّهْرِيِّ " إِنْ جَاءَتْ بِهِ كَذَا وَكَذَا فَهْوَ، وَإِنْ جَاءَتْ بِهِ كَذَا وَكَذَا كَأَنَّهُ وَحَرَةٌ فَهْوَ ". وَسَمِعْتُ الزُّهْرِيَّ يَقُولُ جَاءَتْ بِهِ لِلَّذِي يُكْرَهُ

Narrated Ibn `Abbas: Hilal bin Umaiya accused his wife before the Prophetﷺ of committing illegal sexual intercourse with Sharik bin Sahma.' The Prophetﷺ said, "Produce a proof, or else you would get the legal punishment (by being lashed) on your back." Hilal said, "O Allah's Messengerﷺ! If anyone of us saw another man over his wife, would he go to search for a proof." The Prophetﷺ went on saying, "Produce a proof or else you would get the legal punishment (by being lashed) on your back." The Prophetﷺ then mentioned the narration of Lian (as in the Holy Book). (Surat-al-Nur: 24). – Sahih Al-Bukhari 2671

حَدَّثَنَا مُحَمَّدُ بْنُ بَشَّارٍ، حَدَّثَنَا ابْنُ أَبِي عَدِيٍّ، عَنْ هِشَامٍ، حَدَّثَنَا عِكْرِمَةُ، عَنِ ابْنِ عَبَّاسٍ ـ رضى الله عنهما ـ أَنَّ هِلاَلَ بْنَ أُمَيَّةَ، قَذَفَ امْرَأَتَهُ عِنْدَ النَّبِيِّ صلى الله عليه وسلم بِشَرِيكِ بْنِ سَحْمَاءَ، فَقَالَ النَّبِيُّ صلى الله عليه وسلم " الْبَيِّنَةُ أَوْ حَدٌّ فِي ظَهْرِكَ ". فَقَالَ يَا رَسُولَ اللَّهِ إِذَا رَأَى أَحَدُنَا عَلَى امْرَأَتِهِ رَجُلاً يَنْطَلِقُ يَلْتَمِسُ الْبَيِّنَةَ فَجَعَلَ يَقُولُ " الْبَيِّنَةَ وَإِلاَّ حَدٌّ فِي ظَهْرِكَ فَذَكَرَ حَدِيثَ اللِّعَانِ.

Narrated Ibn `Umar: A man and his wife had a case of Lian (or Mula'ana) during the lifetime of the Prophetﷺ and the man denied the paternity of her child. The Prophetﷺ gave his verdict for their separation (divorce) and then the child was regarded as belonging to the wife only. – Sahih Al-Bukhari 6748

حَدَّثَنِي يَحْيَى بْنُ قَزَعَةَ، حَدَّثَنَا مَالِكٌ، عَنْ نَافِعٍ، عَنِ ابْنِ عُمَرَ ـ رضى الله عنهما أَنَّ رَجُلاً، لاَعَنَ امْرَأَتَهُ فِي زَمَنِ النَّبِيِّ صلى الله عليه وسلم وَانْتَفَى مِنْ وَلَدِهَا فَفَرَّقَ النَّبِيُّ صلى الله عليه وسلم بَيْنَهُمَا، وَأَلْحَقَ الْوَلَدَ بِالْمَرْأَةِ

The Book of

Hijab

حجاب

And tell the believing women to restrain their looks, and to guard their privates, and not display their beauty except what is apparent thereof, and to draw their coverings over their breasts, and not expose their beauty except to their husbands, their fathers, their husbands' fathers, their sons, their husbands' sons, their brothers, their brothers' sons, their sisters' sons, their women, what their right hands possess, their male attendants who have no sexual desires, or children who are not yet aware of the nakedness of women. And they should not strike their feet to draw attention to their hidden beauty. And repent to Allah, all of you believers, so that you may succeed. – Surah An-Nur 24:31

أَبْصَـٰرِهِنَّ وَيَحْفَظْنَ فُرُوجَهُنَّ وَلَا يُبْدِينَ زِينَتَهُنَّ إِلَّا مَا ظَهَرَ مِنْهَا ۖ وَلْيَضْرِبْنَ بِخُمُرِهِنَّ عَلَىٰ جُيُوبِهِنَّ ۖ وَلَا يُبْدِينَ زِينَتَهُنَّ إِلَّا لِبُعُولَتِهِنَّ أَوْ ءَابَآئِهِنَّ أَوْ ءَابَآءِ بُعُولَتِهِنَّ أَوْ أَبْنَآئِهِنَّ أَوْ أَبْنَآءِ بُعُولَتِهِنَّ أَوْ إِخْوَٰنِهِنَّ أَوْ بَنِىٓ إِخْوَٰنِهِنَّ أَوْ بَنِىٓ أَخَوَٰتِهِنَّ أَوْ نِسَآئِهِنَّ أَوْ مَا مَلَكَتْ أَيْمَـٰنُهُنَّ أَوِ ٱلتَّـٰبِعِينَ غَيْرِ أُو۟لِى ٱلْإِرْبَةِ مِنَ ٱلرِّجَالِ أَوِ ٱلطِّفْلِ ٱلَّذِينَ لَمْ يَظْهَرُوا۟ عَلَىٰ عَوْرَٰتِ ٱلنِّسَآءِ ۖ وَلَا يَضْرِبْنَ بِأَرْجُلِهِنَّ لِيُعْلَمَ مَا يُخْفِينَ مِن زِينَتِهِنَّ ۚ وَتُوبُوٓا۟ إِلَى ٱللَّهِ جَمِيعًا أَيُّهَ ٱلْمُؤْمِنُونَ لَعَلَّكُمْ تُفْلِحُونَ

O Prophet! Tell your wives, and your daughters, and the women of the believers, to lengthen their garments. That is more proper, so they will be recognized and not harassed. Allah is Forgiving and Merciful. – Surah Al-Azhab 33:59

يَـٰٓأَيُّهَا ٱلنَّبِىُّ قُل لِّأَزْوَٰجِكَ وَبَنَاتِكَ وَنِسَآءِ ٱلْمُؤْمِنِينَ يُدْنِينَ عَلَيْهِنَّ مِن جَلَـٰبِيبِهِنَّ ۚ ذَٰلِكَ أَدْنَىٰٓ أَن يُعْرَفْنَ فَلَا يُؤْذَيْنَ ۗ وَكَانَ ٱللَّهُ غَفُورًا رَّحِيمًا

Narrated `Aishah: May Allah bestow His Mercy on the early emigrant women. When Allah revealed: "... and to draw their veils all over their Juyubihinna (i.e., their bodies, faces, necks and bosoms)..." (V.24:31) they tore their Murat (woolen dresses or waist-binding clothes or aprons etc.) and covered their heads and faces with those torn Muruts. – Sahih Al-Bukhari 4758

وَقَالَ أَحْمَدُ بْنُ شَبِيبٍ حَدَّثَنَا أَبِي، عَنْ يُونُسَ، قَالَ ابْنُ شِهَابٍ عَنْ عُرْوَةَ، عَنْ عَائِشَةَ ـ رضى الله عنها ـ قَالَتْ يَرْحَمُ اللَّهُ نِسَاءَ الْمُهَاجِرَاتِ الأُوَلَ، لَمَّا أَنْزَلَ اللَّهُ {وَلْيَضْرِبْنَ بِخُمُرِهِنَّ عَلَى جُيُوبِهِنَّ} شَقَّقْنَ مُرُوطَهُنَّ فَاخْتَمَرْنَ بِها.

Narrated Safiya bint Shaiba: `Aisha used to say: "When (the Verse): "They should draw their veils over their necks and bosoms," was revealed, (the ladies) cut their waist sheets at the edges and covered their heads and faces with those cut pieces of cloth.". – Sahih Al-Bukhari 4759

حَدَّثَنَا أَبُو نُعَيْمٍ، حَدَّثَنَا إِبْرَاهِيمُ بْنُ نَافِعٍ، عَنِ الْحَسَنِ بْنِ مُسْلِمٍ، عَنْ صَفِيَّةَ بِنْتِ شَيْبَةَ، أَنَّ عَائِشَةَ ـ رضى الله عنها ـ كَانَتْ تَقُولُ لَمَّا نَزَلَتْ هَذِهِ الآيَةُ {وَلْيَضْرِبْنَ بِخُمُرِهِنَّ عَلَى جُيُوبِهِنَّ} أَخَذْنَ أُزْرَهُنَّ فَشَقَّقْنَهَا مِنْ قِبَلِ الْحَوَاشِي فَاخْتَمَرْنَ بِهَا.

Narrated `Aisha: Allah's Messenger ﷺ used to offer the Fajr prayer and some believing women covered with their veiling sheets used to attend the Fajr prayer with him and then they would return to their homes unrecognized . – Sahih Al-Bukhari 372

حَدَّثَنَا أَبُو الْيَمَانِ، قَالَ أَخْبَرَنَا شُعَيْبٌ، عَنِ الزُّهْرِيِّ، قَالَ أَخْبَرَنِي عُرْوَةُ، أَنَّ عَائِشَةَ، قَالَتْ لَقَدْ كَانَ رَسُولُ اللَّهِ صلى الله عليه وسلم يُصَلِّي الْفَجْرَ، فَيَشْهَدُ مَعَهُ نِسَاءٌ مِنَ الْمُؤْمِنَاتِ مُتَلَفِّعَاتٍ فِي مُرُوطِهِنَّ ثُمَّ يَرْجِعْنَ إِلَى بُيُوتِهِنَّ مَا يَعْرِفُهُنَّ أَحَدٌ.

Narrated `Aisha: Once I saw Allah's Messenger ﷺ at the door of my house while some Ethiopians were playing in the mosque (displaying their skill with spears). Allah's

Messenger ﷺ was screening me with his Rida' so as to enable me to see their display. (`Urwa said that `Aisha said, "I saw the Prophet ﷺ and the Ethiopians were playing with their spears."). – Sahih Al-Bukhari 454, 455

حَدَّثَنَا عَبْدُ الْعَزِيزِ بْنُ عَبْدِ اللَّهِ، قَالَ حَدَّثَنَا إِبْرَاهِيمُ بْنُ سَعْدٍ، عَنْ صَالِحٍ، عَنِ ابْنِ شِهَابٍ، قَالَ أَخْبَرَنِي عُرْوَةُ بْنُ الزُّبَيْرِ، أَنَّ عَائِشَةَ، قَالَتْ لَقَدْ رَأَيْتُ رَسُولَ اللَّهِ صلى الله عليه وسلم يَوْمًا عَلَى باب حُجْرَتِي، وَالْحَبَشَةُ يَلْعَبُونَ فِي الْمَسْجِدِ وَرَسُولُ اللَّهِ صلى الله عليه وسلم يَسْتُرُنِي بِرِدَائِهِ، أَنْظُرُ إِلَى لَعِبِهِمْ. زَادَ إِبْرَاهِيمُ بْنُ الْمُنْذِرِ حَدَّثَنَا ابْنُ وَهْبٍ، أَخْبَرَنِي يُونُسُ، عَنِ ابْنِ شِهَابٍ، عَنْ عُرْوَةَ، عَنْ عَائِشَةَ، قَالَتْ رَأَيْتُ النَّبِيَّ صلى الله عليه وسلم وَالْحَبَشَةُ يَلْعَبُونَ بِحِرَابِهِمْ.

Narrated Aiyub: Hafsa bint Seereen said, "On Id we used to forbid our girls to go out for `Id prayer. A lady came and stayed at the palace of Bani Khalaf and I went to her. She said, 'The husband of my sister took part in twelve holy battles along with the Prophet ﷺ and my sister was with her husband in six of them. My sister said that they used to nurse the sick and treat the wounded. Once she asked, 'O Allah's Messenger ﷺ! If a woman has no veil, is there any harm if she does not come out (on `Id day)?' The Prophet ﷺ said, 'Her companion should let her share her veil with her, and the women should participate in the good deeds and in the religious gatherings of the believers.' " Hafsa added, "When Um-`Atiya came, I went to her and asked her, 'Did you hear anything about so-and-so?' Um-`Atiya said, 'Yes, let my father be sacrificed for the Prophet ﷺ. (And whenever she mentioned the name of the Prophet ﷺ she always used to say, 'Let my father be' sacrificed for him). He said, 'Virgin mature girls staying often screened (or said, 'Mature girls and virgins staying often screened—Aiyub is not sure as which was right) and menstruating women should come out (on the `Id day). But the menstruating women should keep away from the Musalla. And all the women should participate in the good deeds and in the religious gatherings of the believers'." Hafsa said, "On that I said to Um-`Atiya, 'Also those who are menstruating?' " Um-`Atiya replied, "Yes. Do they not present themselves at `Arafat and elsewhere?". – Sahih Al-Bukhari 980

حَدَّثَنَا أَبُو مَعْمَرٍ، قَالَ حَدَّثَنَا عَبْدُ الْوَارِثِ، قَالَ حَدَّثَنَا أَيُّوبُ، عَنْ حَفْصَةَ بِنْتِ سِيرِينَ، قَالَتْ كُنَّا نَمْنَعُ جَوَارِيَنَا أَنْ يَخْرُجْنَ يَوْمَ الْعِيدِ، فَجَاءَتِ امْرَأَةٌ فَنَزَلَتْ قَصْرَ بَنِي خَلَفٍ فَأَتَيْتُهَا فَحَدَّثَتْ أَنَّ زَوْجَ أُخْتِهَا غَزَا مَعَ النَّبِيِّ صلى الله عليه وسلم ثِنْتَىْ عَشْرَةَ غَزْوَةً فَكَانَتْ أُخْتُهَا مَعَهُ فِي سِتِّ غَزَوَاتٍ. فَقَالَتْ فَكُنَّا نَقُومُ عَلَى الْمَرْضَى وَنُدَاوِي الْكَلْمَى، فَقَالَتْ يَا رَسُولَ اللَّهِ، عَلَى إِحْدَانَا بَأْسٌ إِذَا لَمْ يَكُنْ لَهَا جِلْبَابٌ أَنْ لاَ تَخْرُجَ فَقَالَ " لِتُلْبِسْهَا صَاحِبَتُهَا مِنْ جِلْبَابِهَا فَلْيَشْهَدْنَ الْخَيْرَ وَدَعْوَةَ الْمُؤْمِنِينَ ". قَالَتْ حَفْصَةُ فَلَمَّا قَدِمَتْ أُمُّ عَطِيَّةَ أَتَيْتُهَا، فَسَأَلْتُهَا أَسَمِعْتِ فِي كَذَا وَكَذَا قَالَتْ نَعَمْ، بِأَبِي ـ وَقَلَّمَا ذَكَرَتِ النَّبِيَّ صلى الله عليه وسلم إِلاَّ قَالَتْ بِأَبِي ـ قَالَ " لِيَخْرُجِ الْعَوَاتِقُ ذَوَاتُ الْخُدُورِ ـ أَوْ قَالَ الْعَوَاتِقُ وَذَوَاتُ الْخُدُورِ شَكَّ أَيُّوبُ ـ وَالْحُيَّضُ، وَيَعْتَزِلُ الْحُيَّضُ الْمُصَلَّى، وَلْيَشْهَدْنَ الْخَيْرَ وَدَعْوَةَ الْمُؤْمِنِينَ ". قَالَتْ فَقُلْتُ لَهَا آلْحُيَّضُ قَالَتْ نَعَمْ، أَلَيْسَ الْحَائِضُ تَشْهَدُ عَرَفَاتٍ وَتَشْهَدُ كَذَا وَتَشْهَدُ كَذَا

Narrated `Abdullah bin `Abbas: Al-Fadl (his brother) was riding behind Allah's Messenger ﷺ and a woman from the tribe of Khath'am came and Al-Fadl started looking at her and she started looking at him. The Prophet ﷺ turned Al-Fadl's face to the other side. The woman said, "O Allah's Messenger! The obligation of Hajj enjoined by Allah on His devotees has become due on my father and he is old and weak, and he cannot sit firm on the Mount; may I perform Hajj on his behalf?" The Prophet ﷺ replied, "Yes, you may." That happened during the Hajj-al-Wida (of the Prophet. – Sahih Al-Bukhari 1513

حَدَّثَنَا عَبْدُ اللَّهِ بْنُ يُوسُفَ، أَخْبَرَنَا مَالِكٌ، عَنِ ابْنِ شِهَابٍ، عَنْ سُلَيْمَانَ بْنِ يَسَارٍ، عَنْ عَبْدِ اللَّهِ بْنِ عَبَّاسٍ ـ رضى الله عنهما ـ قَالَ كَانَ الْفَضْلُ رَدِيفَ رَسُولِ اللَّهِ صلى الله عليه وسلم فَجَاءَتِ امْرَأَةٌ مِنْ خَثْعَمَ، فَجَعَلَ الْفَضْلُ يَنْظُرُ إِلَيْهَا وَتَنْظُرُ إِلَيْهِ، وَجَعَلَ النَّبِيُّ صلى الله عليه وسلم يَصْرِفُ وَجْهَ الْفَضْلِ إِلَى الشِّقِّ الآخَرِ فَقَالَتْ يَا رَسُولَ اللَّهِ إِنَّ فَرِيضَةَ اللَّهِ عَلَى عِبَادِهِ فِي الْحَجِّ أَدْرَكَتْ أَبِي شَيْخًا كَبِيرًا، لاَ يَثْبُتُ عَلَى الرَّاحِلَةِ، أَفَأَحُجُّ عَنْهُ قَالَ " نَعَمْ ". وَذَلِكَ فِي حَجَّةِ الْوَدَاعِ

Narrated `Abdullah bin `Umar: A person stood up and asked, "O Allah's: Apostle! What clothes may be worn in the state of Ihram?" The Prophet ﷺ replied, "Do not wear a shirt or trousers, or any headgear (e.g. a turban), or a hooded cloak; but if somebody has no shoes he can wear leather stockings provided they are cut short off the ankles, and also, do not wear anything perfumed with Wars or saffron, and the Muhrima (a woman in the state of Ihram) should not cover her face, or wear gloves.". – Sahih Al-Bukhari 1838

حَدَّثَنَا عَبْدُ اللَّهِ بْنُ يَزِيدَ، حَدَّثَنَا اللَّيْثُ، حَدَّثَنَا نَافِعٌ، عَنْ عَبْدِ اللَّهِ بْنِ عُمَرَ ـ رضى الله عنهما ـ قَالَ قَامَ رَجُلٌ فَقَالَ يَا رَسُولَ اللَّهِ مَاذَا تَأْمُرُنَا أَنْ نَلْبَسَ مِنَ الثِّيَابِ فِي الإِحْرَامِ فَقَالَ النَّبِيُّ صلى الله عليه وسلم " لاَ تَلْبَسُوا الْقَمِيصَ وَلاَ السَّرَاوِيلاَتِ وَلاَ الْعَمَائِمَ، وَلاَ الْبَرَانِسَ إِلاَّ أَنْ يَكُونَ أَحَدٌ لَيْسَتْ لَهُ نَعْلاَنِ، فَلْيَلْبَسِ الْخُفَّيْنِ، وَلْيَقْطَعْ أَسْفَلَ مِنَ الْكَعْبَيْنِ، وَلاَ تَلْبَسُوا شَيْئًا مَسَّهُ زَعْفَرَانٌ، وَلاَ الْوَرْسُ، وَلاَ تَنْتَقِبِ الْمَرْأَةُ الْمُحْرِمَةُ وَلاَ تَلْبَسِ الْقُفَّازَيْنِ ". تَابَعَهُ مُوسَى بْنُ عُقْبَةَ وَإِسْمَاعِيلُ بْنُ إِبْرَاهِيمَ بْنِ عُقْبَةَ وَجُوَيْرِيَةُ وَابْنُ إِسْحَاقَ فِي النِّقَابِ وَالْقُفَّازَيْنِ. وَقَالَ عُبَيْدُ اللَّهِ وَلاَ وَرْسٌ وَكَانَ يَقُولُ لاَ تَتَنَقَّبِ الْمُحْرِمَةُ، وَلاَ تَلْبَسِ الْقُفَّازَيْنِ. وَقَالَ مَالِكٌ عَنْ نَافِعٍ عَنِ ابْنِ عُمَرَ لاَ تَتَنَقَّبِ الْمُحْرِمَةُ. وَتَابَعَهُ لَيْثُ بْنُ أَبِي سُلَيْمٍ.

Narrated `Aisha: `Utba bin Abi Waqqas authorized his brother Sa`d to take the son of the slave-girl of Zam`a into his custody. `Utba said (to him). "He is my son." When Allah's Messenger ﷺ arrived in Mecca during the Conquest (of Mecca), Sa`d bin Abi Waqqas took the son of the slave-girl of Zam`a and took him to the Prophet ﷺ Abd bin Zam`a too came along with him. Sa`d said. "This is the son of my brother and the latter has informed me that he is his son." `Abd bin Zam`a said, "O Allah's Messenger ﷺ! This is my brother who is the son of the slave-girl of Zam`a and was born on his (i.e. Zam'as) bed.' Allah's Apostle looked at the son of the slave-girl of Zam`a and noticed that he, of all the people had the greatest resemblance to `Utba bin Abi Waqqas. Allah's Messenger ﷺ then said (to `Abd), " He is yours; he is your brother, O `Abd bin Zam`a, he was born on the bed (of your father)." (At the same time) Allah's Messenger ﷺ said (to his wife Sauda), "Veil yourself before him (i.e. the son of the slave-girl) O Sauda," because of the resemblance he noticed between him and `Utba bin Abi Waqqas. Allah's Apostle added, "The boy is for the bed (i.e. for the owner of the bed where he was born), and stone is for the adulterer." (Ibn Shihab said, "Abu Huraira used to say that (i.e. the last statement of the Prophet in the above Hadith 596, publicly."). – Sahih Al-Bukhari 4303

حَدَّثَنِي عَبْدُ اللَّهِ بْنُ مَسْلَمَةَ، عَنْ مَالِكٍ، عَنِ ابْنِ شِهَابٍ، عَنْ عُرْوَةَ بْنِ الزُّبَيْرِ، عَنْ عَائِشَةَ ـ رضى الله عنها ـ عَنِ النَّبِيِّ صلى الله عليه وسلم. وَقَالَ اللَّيْثُ حَدَّثَنِي يُونُسُ عَنِ ابْنِ شِهَابٍ أَخْبَرَنِي عُرْوَةُ بْنُ الزُّبَيْرِ أَنَّ عَائِشَةَ قَالَتْ كَانَ عُتْبَةُ بْنُ أَبِي وَقَّاصٍ عَهِدَ إِلَى أَخِيهِ سَعْدٍ أَنْ يَقْبِضَ ابْنَ وَلِيدَةِ زَمْعَةَ، وَقَالَ عُتْبَةُ إِنَّهُ ابْنِي. فَلَمَّا قَدِمَ رَسُولُ اللَّهِ صلى الله عليه وسلم مَكَّةَ فِي الْفَتْحِ أَخَذَ سَعْدُ بْنُ أَبِي وَقَّاصٍ ابْنَ وَلِيدَةِ زَمْعَةَ، فَأَقْبَلَ بِهِ إِلَى رَسُولِ اللَّهِ صلى الله عليه وسلم، وَأَقْبَلَ مَعَهُ عَبْدُ بْنُ زَمْعَةَ، فَقَالَ سَعْدُ بْنُ أَبِي وَقَّاصٍ هَذَا ابْنُ أَخِي، عَهِدَ إِلَيَّ أَنَّهُ ابْنُهُ. قَالَ عَبْدُ بْنُ زَمْعَةَ يَا رَسُولَ اللَّهِ، هَذَا أَخِي، هَذَا ابْنُ زَمْعَةَ، وُلِدَ عَلَى فِرَاشِهِ. فَنَظَرَ رَسُولُ اللَّهِ صلى الله عليه وسلم إِلَى ابْنِ وَلِيدَةِ زَمْعَةَ، فَإِذَا أَشْبَهُ النَّاسِ بِعُتْبَةَ بْنِ أَبِي وَقَّاصٍ، فَقَالَ رَسُولُ اللَّهِ صلى الله عليه وسلم " هُوَ لَكَ، هُوَ أَخُوكَ يَا عَبْدُ بْنَ زَمْعَةَ ". مِنْ أَجْلِ أَنَّهُ وُلِدَ عَلَى فِرَاشِهِ، وَقَالَ رَسُولُ اللَّهِ صلى الله عليه وسلم " احْتَجِبِي مِنْهُ يَا سَوْدَةُ ". لِمَا رَأَى مِنْ شَبَهِ عُتْبَةَ بْنِ أَبِي وَقَّاصٍ. قَالَ ابْنُ شِهَابٍ قَالَتْ عَائِشَةُ قَالَ رَسُولُ اللَّهِ صلى الله عليه وسلم " الْوَلَدُ لِلْفِرَاشِ وَلِلْعَاهِرِ الْحَجَرُ ". وَقَالَ ابْنُ شِهَابٍ وَكَانَ أَبُو هُرَيْرَةَ يَصِيحُ بِذَلِكَ

Narrated Aisha: Aflah asked the permission to visit me but I did not allow him. He said, "Do you veil yourself before me although I am your uncle?" `Aisha said, "How is that?" Aflah replied, "You were suckled by my brother's wife with my brother's milk." I asked Allah's Messenger ﷺ about it, and he said, "Aflah is right, so permit him to visit you.". – Sahih Al-Bukhari 2644

حَدَّثَنَا آدَمُ، حَدَّثَنَا شُعْبَةُ، أَخْبَرَنَا الْحَكَمُ، عَنْ عِرَاكِ بْنِ مَالِكٍ، عَنْ عُرْوَةَ بْنِ الزُّبَيْرِ، عَنْ عَائِشَةَ ـ رضى الله عنها ـ قَالَتِ اسْتَأْذَنَ عَلَىَّ أَفْلَحُ فَلَمْ آذَنْ لَهُ، فَقَالَ أَتَحْتَجِبِينَ مِنِّي وَأَنَا عَمُّكِ فَقُلْتُ وَكَيْفَ ذَلِكَ قَالَ أَرْضَعَتْكِ امْرَأَةُ أَخِي بِلَبَنِ أَخِي. فَقَالَتْ سَأَلْتُ عَنْ ذَلِكَ رَسُولَ اللَّهِ صلى الله عليه وسلم فَقَالَ " صَدَقَ أَفْلَحُ، ائْذَنِي لَهُ ".

Narrated Aisha: Once the Prophet ﷺ came to me while a man was in my house. He said, "O `Aisha! Who is this (man)?" I replied, "My foster brothers" He said, "O `Aisha! Be sure about your foster brothers, as fostership is only valid if it takes place in the suckling period (before two years of age). – Sahih Al-Bukhari 2647

حَدَّثَنَا مُحَمَّدُ بْنُ كَثِيرٍ، أَخْبَرَنَا سُفْيَانُ، عَنْ أَشْعَثَ بْنِ أَبِي الشَّعْثَاءِ، عَنْ أَبِيهِ، عَنْ مَسْرُوقٍ، أَنَّ عَائِشَةَ ـ رضى الله عنها ـ قَالَتْ دَخَلَ عَلَىَّ النَّبِيُّ صلى الله عليه وسلم وَعِنْدِي رَجُلٌ، قَالَ " يَا عَائِشَةُ مَنْ هَذَا ". قُلْتُ أَخِي مِنَ الرَّضَاعَةِ. قَالَ " يَا عَائِشَةُ، انْظُرْنَ مَنْ إِخْوَانُكُنَّ، فَإِنَّمَا الرَّضَاعَةُ مِنَ الْمَجَاعَةِ ". تَابَعَهُ ابْنُ مَهْدِيٍّ عَنْ سُفْيَانَ

Narrated Aisha: (The wife of the Prophet) Whenever Allah's Messenger ﷺ intended to go on a journey, he used to draw lots among his wives and would take with him the one on whom the lot had fallen. Once he drew lots when he wanted to carry out a Ghazwa, and the lot came upon me. So I proceeded with Allah's Apostle after Allah's order of veiling (the women) had been revealed and thus I was carried in my howdah (on a camel) and dismounted while still in it. We carried on our journey, and when Allah's Apostle had finished his Ghazwa and returned and we approached Medina, Allah's Messenger ﷺ ordered to proceed at night. When the army was ordered to resume the homeward journey, I got up and walked on till I left the army (camp) behind. When I had answered the call of nature, I went towards my howdah, but behold ! A necklace of mine made of Jaz Azfar (a kind of black bead) was broken and I looked for it and my search for it detained me. The group of people who used to carry me, came and carried my howdah on to the back of my camel on which I was riding, considering that I was therein. At that time women were light in weight and were not fleshy for they used to eat little (food), so those people did not feel the lightness of the howdah while raising it up, and I was still a young lady. They drove away the camel and proceeded. Then I found my necklace after the army had gone. I came to their camp but found nobody therein so I went to the place where I used to stay, thinking that they would miss me and come back in my search. While I was sitting at my place, I felt sleepy and slept. Safwan bin Al-Mu'attil As-Sulami Adh- Dhakw-ani was behind the army. He had started in the last part of the night and reached my stationing place in the morning and saw the figure of a sleeping person. He came to me and recognized me on seeing me for he used to see me before veiling. I got up because of his saying: "Inna Li l-lahi wa inna ilaihi rajiun," which he uttered on recognizing me. I covered my face with my garment, and by Allah, he did not say to me a single word except, "Inna Li l-lahi wa inna ilaihi rajiun," till he made his shecamel kneel down whereupon he trod on its forelegs and I mounted it. Then Safwan set out, leading the she-camel that was carrying me, till we met the army while they were resting during the hot midday. Then whoever was meant for destruction, fell in destruction, and the leader of the Ifk (forged statement) was `Abdullah bin Ubai bin Salul. After this we arrived at Medina and I became ill for one month while the people were spreading the forged statements of the people of the Ifk, and I was not aware of anything thereof. But what aroused my doubt while I was sick, was that I was no longer receiving from Allah's Messenger ﷺ the same kindness as I used to receive when I fell sick. Allah's Messenger ﷺ would enter upon me, say a greeting and add, "How is that (lady)?" and then depart. That aroused my suspicion but I was not aware of the propagated evil till I recovered from my ailment. I went out with Um Mistah to answer the call of nature towards Al-Manasi, the place where we used to relieve ourselves, and used not to go out for this purpose except from night to night, and that was before we had lavatories close to our houses. And this habit of ours was similar to the habit of the old 'Arabs (in the deserts or in the tents) concerning the evacuation of the bowels, for we considered it troublesome and harmful to take lavatories in the houses. So I went out with Um Mistah who was the daughter of Abi Ruhm bin `Abd Manaf, and her mother was daughter of Sakhr bin Amir who was the aunt of Abi Bakr As-Siddiq, and her son was Mistah bin Uthatha. When we had finished our affair, Um Mistah and I came back towards my house.

Um Mistah stumbled over her robe whereupon she said, "Let Mistah be ruined ! " I said to her, "What a bad word you have said! Do you abuse a man who has taken part in the Battle of Badr?' She said, "O you there! Didn't you hear what he has said?" I said, "And what did he say?" She then told me the statement of the people of the Ifk (forged statement) which added to my ailment. When I returned home, Allah's Messenger came to me, and after greeting, he said, "How is that (lady)?" I said, "Will you allow me to go to my parents?" At that time I intended to be sure of the news through them. Allah's Messenger allowed me and I went to my parents and asked my mother, "O my mother! What are the people talking about?" My mother said, "O my daughter! Take it easy, for by Allah, there is no charming lady who is loved by her husband who has other wives as well, but that those wives would find fault with her." I said, "Subhan Allah! Did the people really talk about that?" That night I kept on weeping the whole night till the morning. My tears never stopped, nor did I sleep, and morning broke while I was still weeping, Allah's Messenger called `Ali bin Abi Talib and Usama bin Zaid when the Divine Inspiration delayed, in order to consult them as to the idea of divorcing his wife. Usama bin Zaid told Allah's Messenger of what he knew about the innocence of his wife and of his affection he kept for her. He said, "O Allah's Messenger ! She is your wife, and we do not know anything about her except good." But `Ali bin Abi Talib said, "O Allah's Messenger! Allah does not impose restrictions on you; and there are plenty of women other than her. If you however, ask (her) slave girl, she will tell you the truth." `Aisha added: So Allah's Messenger called for Barira and said, "O Barira! Did you ever see anything which might have aroused your suspicion? (as regards Aisha). Barira said, "By Allah Who has sent you with the truth, I have never seen anything regarding Aisha which I would blame her for except that she is a girl of immature age who sometimes sleeps and leaves the dough of her family unprotected so that the domestic goats come and eat it." So Allah's Messenger got up (and addressed) the people an asked for somebody who would take revenge on `Abdullah bin Ubai bin Salul then. Allah's Messenger, while on the pulpit, said, "O Muslims! Who will help me against a man who has hurt me by slandering my family? By Allah, I know nothing except good about my family, and people have blamed a man of whom I know nothing except good, and he never used to visit my family except with me," Sa`d bin Mu`adh Al-Ansari got up and said, "O Allah's Messenger! By Allah, I will relieve you from him. If he be from the tribe of (Bani) Al-Aus, then I will chop his head off; and if he be from our brethren, the Khazraj, then you give us your order and we will obey it." On that, Sa`d bin 'Ubada got up, and he was the chief of the Khazraj, and before this incident he had been a pious man but he was incited by his zeal for his tribe. He said to Sa`d (bin Mu`adh), "By Allah the Eternal, you have told a lie! You shall not kill him and you will never be able to kill him!" On that, Usaid bin Hudair, the cousin of Sa`d (bin Mu`adh) got up and said to Sa`d bin 'Ubada, "You are a liar! By Allah the Eternal, we will surely kill him; and you are a hypocrite defending the hypocrites!" So the two tribes of Al-Aus and Al-Khazraj got excited till they were on the point of fighting with each other while Allah's Messenger was standing on the pulpit. Allah's Messenger continued quietening them till they became silent whereupon he became silent too. On that day I kept on weeping so much that neither did my tears stop, nor could I sleep. In the morning my parents were with me, and I had wept for two nights and a day without sleeping and with incessant tears till they thought that my liver would burst with weeping. While they were with me and I was weeping, an Ansari woman asked permission to see me. I admitted her and she sat and started weeping with me. While I was in that state, Allah's Apostle came to us, greeted, and sat down,. He had never sat with me since the day what was said, was said. He had stayed a month without receiving any Divine Inspiration concerning my case. Allah's Messenger ﷺ recited the Tashahhud after he had sat down, and then said, "Thereafter, O `Aisha! I have been informed such and-such a thing about you; and if you are innocent, Allah will reveal your innocence, and if you have committed a sin, then ask for Allah's forgiveness and repent to Him, for when a slave confesses his sin and then repents to Allah, Allah accepts his repentance." When Allah's Apostle had finished his speech, my tears ceased completely so that I no longer felt even a drop thereof. Then I said to my father, "Reply to Allah's Messenger ﷺ on my behalf as to what he said." He said, "By Allah, I do not know what to say to Allah's Messenger ﷺ." Then I said to my mother, "Reply to Allah's Apostle." She said, "I do not know what to say to Allah's Messenger ﷺ." Still a young girl as I was and though I had little knowledge of Qur'an, I said, "By Allah, I know that you heard this story (of the Ifk) so much so that it has been planted in your minds and you have believed it. So now, if I tell you that I am innocent, and Allah knows that I am innocent, you will not believe me; and if I confess something, and Allah knows that I am innocent of it, you will believe me. By Allah, I cannot find of you an example except that of Joseph's father: "So (for me) patience is most fitting against that which you assert and it is Allah (Alone) Whose help can be sought. Then I turned away and lay on my bed, and at that time I knew that I was innocent and that Allah would reveal my innocence. But by Allah, I never thought that Allah would sent down about my affair, Divine Inspiration that would be recited (forever), as I considered myself too unworthy to be talked of by Allah with something that was to be recited: but I hoped that Allah's Messenger ﷺ might have a vision in which Allah would prove my innocence. By Allah, Allah's Messenger ﷺ had not left his seat and nobody had left the house when the Divine Inspiration came to Allah's Messenger ﷺ. So there overtook him the same hard condition which used to overtake him (when he was Divinely Inspired) so that the drops of his sweat were running down, like pearls, though it was a (cold) winter day, and that was because of the heaviness of the Statement which was revealed to him. When that state of Allah's Messenger ﷺ was over, and he was smiling when he was relieved, the first word he said was, "Aisha, Allah has declared your innocence." My mother said to me, "Get up and go to him." I said, "By Allah, I will not go to him and I will not thank anybody but Allah." So Allah revealed: "Verily! They who spread the Slander are a gang among you. Think it not...." (24.11-20). When Allah revealed this to confirm my innocence, Abu Bakr As-Siddiq who used to provide for Mistah bin Uthatha because of the latter's kinship to him and his poverty, said, "By Allah, I will never provide for Mistah anything after what he has said about Aisha". So Allah revealed: (continued...) (continuing... 1): -6.274:... ... "Let not those among you who are good and are wealthy swear not to give (help) to their kinsmen, those in need, and those who have left their homes for Allah's Cause. Let them Pardon and forgive (i.e. do not punish them). Do you not love that should forgive you? Verily Allah is Oft-forgiving. Most Merciful." (24.22) Abu Bakr said, "Yes, by Allah, I wish that Allah should forgive me." So he resumed giving Mistah the aid he used to give him before and said, "By Allah, I will never withold it from him at all." Aisha further said: Allah's Messenger ﷺ also asked Zainab bint Jahsh about my case. He said, "O Zainab! What have you seen?" She replied, "O Allah's Messenger ﷺ ! I protect my hearing and my sight (by refraining from telling lies). I know nothing but good (about Aisha)." Of all the wives of Allah's Messenger ﷺ, it was Zainab who aspired to receive from him the same favor as I used to receive, yet, Allah saved her (from telling lies) because of her piety. But her sister, Hamna, kept on fighting on her behalf so she was destroyed as were those who invented and spread the slander. – Sahih Al-Bukhari 4750

حَدَّثَنَا يَحْيَى بْنُ بُكَيْرٍ، حَدَّثَنَا اللَّيْثُ، عَنْ يُونُسَ، عَنِ ابْنِ شِهَابٍ، قَالَ أَخْبَرَنِي عُرْوَةُ بْنُ الزُّبَيْرِ، وَسَعِيدُ بْنُ الْمُسَيَّبِ، وَعَلْقَمَةُ بْنُ وَقَّاصٍ، وَعُبَيْدُ اللَّهِ بْنُ عَبْدِ اللَّهِ بْنِ عُتْبَةَ بْنِ مَسْعُودٍ، عَنْ حَدِيثِ، عَائِشَةَ ـ رضى الله عنها ـ زَوْجِ النَّبِيِّ صلى الله عليه وسلم حِينَ قَالَ لَهَا أَهْلُ الإِفْكِ مَا قَالُوا، فَبَرَّأَهَا اللَّهُ مِمَّا قَالُوا وَكُلٌّ حَدَّثَنِي طَائِفَةً مِنَ الْحَدِيثِ، وَبَعْضُ حَدِيثِهِمْ

يُصَدِّقُ بَعْضًا، وَإِنْ كَانَ بَعْضُهُمْ أَوْعَى لَهُ مِنْ بَعْضٍ الَّذِي حَدَّثَنِي عُرْوَةُ عَنْ عَائِشَةَ ـ رضى الله عنها ـ أَنَّ عَائِشَةَ ـ رضى الله عنها ـ زَوْجَ النَّبِيِّ صلى الله عليه وسلم قَالَتْ كَانَ رَسُولُ اللَّهِ صلى الله عليه وسلم إِذَا أَرَادَ أَنْ يَخْرُجَ أَقْرَعَ بَيْنَ أَزْوَاجِهِ، فَأَيَّتُهُنَّ خَرَجَ سَهْمُهَا خَرَجَ بِهَا رَسُولُ اللَّهِ صلى الله عليه وسلم مَعَهُ، قَالَتْ عَائِشَةُ فَأَقْرَعَ بَيْنَنَا فِي غَزْوَةٍ غَزَاهَا، فَخَرَجَ سَهْمِي، فَخَرَجْتُ مَعَ رَسُولِ اللَّهِ صلى الله عليه وسلم بَعْدَ مَا نَزَلَ الْحِجَابُ، فَأَنَا أُحْمَلُ فِي هَوْدَجِي وَأُنْزَلُ فِيهِ فَسِرْنَا حَتَّى إِذَا فَرَغَ رَسُولُ اللَّهِ صلى الله عليه وسلم مِنْ غَزْوَتِهِ تِلْكَ وَقَفَلَ، وَدَنَوْنَا مِنَ الْمَدِينَةِ قَافِلِينَ آذَنَ لَيْلَةً بِالرَّحِيلِ، فَقُمْتُ حِينَ آذَنُوا بِالرَّحِيلِ، فَمَشَيْتُ حَتَّى جَاوَزْتُ الْجَيْشَ، فَلَمَّا قَضَيْتُ شَأْنِي أَقْبَلْتُ إِلَى رَحْلِي، فَإِذَا عِقْدٌ لِي مِنْ جَزْعِ ظَفَارِ قَدِ انْقَطَعَ فَالْتَمَسْتُ عِقْدِي وَحَبَسَنِي ابْتِغَاؤُهُ وَأَقْبَلَ الرَّهْطُ الَّذِينَ كَانُوا يَرْحَلُونَ لِي، فَاحْتَمَلُوا هَوْدَجِي، فَرَحَلُوهُ عَلَى بَعِيرِي الَّذِي كُنْتُ رَكِبْتُ، وَهُمْ يَحْسِبُونَ أَنِّي فِيهِ، وَكَانَ النِّسَاءُ إِذْ ذَاكَ خِفَافًا لَمْ يُثْقِلْهُنَّ اللَّحْمُ، إِنَّمَا تَأْكُلُ الْعُلْقَةَ مِنَ الطَّعَامِ فَلَمْ يَسْتَنْكِرِ الْقَوْمُ خِفَّةَ الْهَوْدَجِ حِينَ رَفَعُوهُ، وَكُنْتُ جَارِيَةً حَدِيثَةَ السِّنِّ، فَبَعَثُوا الْجَمَلَ وَسَارُوا، فَوَجَدْتُ عِقْدِي بَعْدَ مَا اسْتَمَرَّ الْجَيْشُ، فَجِئْتُ مَنَازِلَهُمْ، وَلَيْسَ بِهَا دَاعٍ وَلاَ مُجِيبٌ، فَأَمَمْتُ مَنْزِلِي الَّذِي كُنْتُ بِهِ وَظَنَنْتُ أَنَّهُمْ سَيَفْقِدُونِي فَيَرْجِعُونَ إِلَيَّ فَبَيْنَا أَنَا جَالِسَةٌ فِي مَنْزِلِي غَلَبَتْنِي عَيْنِي فَنِمْتُ، وَكَانَ صَفْوَانُ بْنُ الْمُعَطَّلِ السُّلَمِيُّ ثُمَّ الذَّكْوَانِيُّ مِنْ وَرَاءِ الْجَيْشِ، فَأَدْلَجَ فَأَصْبَحَ عِنْدَ مَنْزِلِي، فَرَأَى سَوَادَ إِنْسَانٍ نَائِمٍ، فَأَتَانِي فَعَرَفَنِي حِينَ رَآنِي، وَكَانَ يَرَانِي قَبْلَ الْحِجَابِ، فَاسْتَيْقَظْتُ بِاسْتِرْجَاعِهِ حِينَ عَرَفَنِي فَخَمَّرْتُ وَجْهِي بِجِلْبَابِي، وَاللَّهِ مَا كَلَّمَنِي كَلِمَةً وَلاَ سَمِعْتُ مِنْهُ كَلِمَةً غَيْرَ اسْتِرْجَاعِهِ، حَتَّى أَنَاخَ رَاحِلَتَهُ فَوَطِئَ عَلَى يَدَيْهَا فَرَكِبْتُهَا فَانْطَلَقَ يَقُودُ بِي الرَّاحِلَةَ حَتَّى أَتَيْنَا الْجَيْشَ، بَعْدَ مَا نَزَلُوا مُوغِرِينَ فِي نَحْرِ الظَّهِيرَةِ، فَهَلَكَ مَنْ هَلَكَ، وَكَانَ الَّذِي تَوَلَّى الإِفْكَ عَبْدَ اللَّهِ بْنَ أُبَىٍّ ابْنَ سَلُولَ فَقَدِمْنَا الْمَدِينَةَ، فَاشْتَكَيْتُ حِينَ قَدِمْتُ شَهْرًا، وَالنَّاسُ يُفِيضُونَ فِي قَوْلِ أَصْحَابِ الإِفْكِ، لاَ أَشْعُرُ بِشَىْءٍ مِنْ ذَلِكَ، وَهْوَ يَرِيبُنِي فِي وَجَعِي أَنِّي لاَ أَعْرِفُ مِنْ رَسُولِ اللَّهِ صلى الله عليه وسلم اللُّطْفَ الَّذِي كُنْتُ أَرَى مِنْهُ حِينَ أَشْتَكِي، إِنَّمَا يَدْخُلُ عَلَيَّ رَسُولُ اللَّهِ صلى الله عليه وسلم فَيُسَلِّمُ ثُمَّ يَقُولُ " كَيْفَ تِيكُمْ ". ثُمَّ يَنْصَرِفُ، فَذَاكَ الَّذِي يَرِيبُنِي، وَلاَ أَشْعُرُ حَتَّى خَرَجْتُ بَعْدَ مَا نَقَهْتُ، فَخَرَجَتْ مَعِي أُمُّ مِسْطَحٍ قِبَلَ الْمَنَاصِعِ، وَهْوَ مُتَبَرَّزُنَا، وَكُنَّا لاَ نَخْرُجُ إِلاَّ لَيْلاً إِلَى لَيْلٍ، وَذَلِكَ قَبْلَ أَنْ نَتَّخِذَ الْكُنُفَ قَرِيبًا مِنْ بُيُوتِنَا، وَأَمْرُنَا أَمْرُ الْعَرَبِ الأُوَلِ فِي التَّبَرُّزِ قِبَلَ الْغَائِطِ، فَكُنَّا نَتَأَذَّى بِالْكُنُفِ أَنْ نَتَّخِذَهَا عِنْدَ بُيُوتِنَا فَانْطَلَقْتُ أَنَا وَأُمُّ مِسْطَحٍ، وَهْيَ ابْنَةُ أَبِي رُهْمِ بْنِ عَبْدِ مَنَافٍ، وَأُمُّهَا بِنْتُ صَخْرِ بْنِ عَامِرٍ خَالَةُ أَبِي بَكْرٍ الصِّدِّيقِ، وَابْنُهَا مِسْطَحُ بْنُ أُثَاثَةَ، فَأَقْبَلْتُ أَنَا وَأُمُّ مِسْطَحٍ قِبَلَ بَيْتِي، قَدْ فَرَغْنَا مِنْ شَأْنِنَا، فَعَثَرَتْ أُمُّ مِسْطَحٍ فِي مِرْطِهَا فَقَالَتْ تَعِسَ مِسْطَحٌ. فَقُلْتُ لَهَا بِئْسَ مَا قُلْتِ أَتَسُبِّينَ رَجُلاً شَهِدَ بَدْرًا قَالَتْ أَىْ هَنْتَاهْ، أَوَلَمْ تَسْمَعِي مَا قَالَ قَالَتْ قُلْتُ وَمَا قَالَ فَأَخْبَرَتْنِي بِقَوْلِ أَهْلِ الإِفْكِ فَازْدَدْتُ مَرَضًا عَلَى مَرَضِي، فَلَمَّا رَجَعْتُ إِلَى بَيْتِي وَدَخَلَ عَلَيَّ رَسُولُ اللَّهِ صلى الله عليه وسلم تَعْنِي سَلَّمَ ثُمَّ قَالَ " كَيْفَ تِيكُمْ ". فَقُلْتُ أَتَأْذَنُ لِي أَنْ آتِيَ أَبَوَىَّ قَالَتْ وَأَنَا حِينَئِذٍ أُرِيدُ أَنْ أَسْتَيْقِنَ الْخَبَرَ مِنْ قِبَلِهِمَا، قَالَتْ فَأَذِنَ لِي رَسُولُ اللَّهِ صلى الله عليه وسلم فَجِئْتُ أَبَوَىَّ فَقُلْتُ لأُمِّي يَا أُمَّتَاهْ، مَا يَتَحَدَّثُ النَّاسُ قَالَتْ يَا بُنَيَّةُ، هَوِّنِي عَلَيْكِ فَوَاللَّهِ، لَقَلَّمَا كَانَتِ امْرَأَةٌ قَطُّ وَضِيئَةً عِنْدَ رَجُلٍ يُحِبُّهَا وَلَهَا ضَرَائِرُ إِلاَّ كَثَّرْنَ عَلَيْهَا. قَالَتْ فَقُلْتُ سُبْحَانَ اللَّهِ وَلَقَدْ تَحَدَّثَ النَّاسُ بِهَذَا قَالَتْ فَبَكَيْتُ تِلْكَ اللَّيْلَةَ حَتَّى أَصْبَحْتُ لاَ يَرْقَأُ لِي دَمْعٌ، وَلاَ أَكْتَحِلُ بِنَوْمٍ حَتَّى أَصْبَحْتُ أَبْكِي فَدَعَا رَسُولُ اللَّهِ صلى الله عليه وسلم عَلِيَّ بْنَ أَبِي طَالِبٍ، وَأُسَامَةَ بْنَ زَيْدٍ ـ رضى الله عنهما ـ حِينَ اسْتَلْبَثَ الْوَحْىُ، يَسْتَأْمِرُهُمَا فِي فِرَاقِ أَهْلِهِ، قَالَتْ فَأَمَّا أُسَامَةُ بْنُ زَيْدٍ فَأَشَارَ عَلَى رَسُولِ اللَّهِ صلى الله عليه وسلم بِالَّذِي يَعْلَمُ مِنْ بَرَاءَةِ أَهْلِهِ، وَبِالَّذِي يَعْلَمُ لَهُمْ فِي نَفْسِهِ مِنَ الْوُدِّ، فَقَالَ يَا رَسُولَ اللَّهِ، أَهْلَكَ، وَمَا نَعْلَمُ إِلاَّ خَيْرًا، وَأَمَّا عَلِيُّ بْنُ أَبِي طَالِبٍ فَقَالَ يَا رَسُولَ اللَّهِ، لَمْ يُضَيِّقِ اللَّهُ عَلَيْكَ وَالنِّسَاءُ سِوَاهَا كَثِيرٌ، وَإِنْ تَسْأَلِ الْجَارِيَةَ تَصْدُقْكَ، قَالَتْ فَدَعَا رَسُولُ اللَّهِ صلى الله عليه وسلم بَرِيرَةَ فَقَالَ " أَىْ بَرِيرَةُ، هَلْ رَأَيْتِ عَلَيْهَا مِنْ شَىْءٍ يَرِيبُكِ ". قَالَتْ بَرِيرَةُ لاَ وَالَّذِي بَعَثَكَ بِالْحَقِّ، إِنْ رَأَيْتُ عَلَيْهَا أَمْرًا أَغْمِصُهُ عَلَيْهَا أَكْثَرَ مِنْ أَنَّهَا جَارِيَةٌ حَدِيثَةُ السِّنِّ، تَنَامُ عَنْ عَجِينِ أَهْلِهَا، فَتَأْتِي الدَّاجِنُ فَتَأْكُلُهُ فَقَامَ رَسُولُ اللَّهِ صلى الله عليه وسلم فَاسْتَعْذَرَ يَوْمَئِذٍ مِنْ عَبْدِ اللَّهِ بْنِ أُبَىٍّ ابْنِ سَلُولَ، قَالَتْ، فَقَالَ رَسُولُ اللَّهِ صلى الله عليه وسلم وَهْوَ عَلَى الْمِنْبَرِ " يَا مَعْشَرَ الْمُسْلِمِينَ مَنْ يَعْذِرُنِي مِنْ رَجُلٍ، قَدْ بَلَغَنِي أَذَاهُ فِي أَهْلِ بَيْتِي، فَوَاللَّهِ مَا عَلِمْتُ عَلَى أَهْلِي إِلاَّ خَيْرًا، وَلَقَدْ ذَكَرُوا رَجُلاً، مَا عَلِمْتُ عَلَيْهِ إِلاَّ خَيْرًا، وَمَا كَانَ يَدْخُلُ عَلَى أَهْلِي إِلاَّ مَعِي ". فَقَامَ سَعْدُ بْنُ مُعَاذٍ الأَنْصَارِيُّ، فَقَالَ يَا رَسُولَ اللَّهِ أَنَا أَعْذِرُكَ مِنْهُ، إِنْ كَانَ مِنَ الأَوْسِ، ضَرَبْتُ عُنُقَهُ، وَإِنْ كَانَ مِنْ إِخْوَانِنَا مِنَ الْخَزْرَجِ، أَمَرْتَنَا، فَفَعَلْنَا أَمْرَكَ، قَالَتْ فَقَامَ سَعْدُ بْنُ عُبَادَةَ وَهْوَ سَيِّدُ الْخَزْرَجِ، وَكَانَ قَبْلَ ذَلِكَ رَجُلاً صَالِحًا، وَلَكِنِ احْتَمَلَتْهُ الْحَمِيَّةُ فَقَالَ لِسَعْدٍ كَذَبْتَ، لَعَمْرُ اللَّهِ لاَ تَقْتُلُهُ، وَلاَ تَقْدِرُ عَلَى قَتْلِهِ، فَقَامَ أُسَيْدُ بْنُ حُضَيْرٍ وَهْوَ ابْنُ عَمِّ سَعْدٍ، فَقَالَ لِسَعْدِ بْنِ عُبَادَةَ كَذَبْتَ، لَعَمْرُ اللَّهِ لَنَقْتُلَنَّهُ، فَإِنَّكَ مُنَافِقٌ تُجَادِلُ عَنِ الْمُنَافِقِينَ، فَتَثَاوَرَ الْحَيَّانِ الأَوْسُ وَالْخَزْرَجُ حَتَّى هَمُّوا أَنْ يَقْتَتِلُوا، وَرَسُولُ اللَّهِ صلى الله عليه وسلم قَائِمٌ عَلَى الْمِنْبَرِ، فَلَمْ يَزَلْ رَسُولُ اللَّهِ صلى الله عليه وسلم يُخَفِّضُهُمْ حَتَّى سَكَتُوا وَسَكَتَ، قَالَتْ فَمَكُثْتُ يَوْمِي ذَلِكَ لاَ يَرْقَأُ لِي دَمْعٌ وَلاَ أَكْتَحِلُ بِنَوْمٍ، قَالَتْ فَأَصْبَحَ أَبَوَاىَ عِنْدِي ـ وَقَدْ بَكَيْتُ لَيْلَتَيْنِ وَيَوْمًا لاَ أَكْتَحِلُ بِنَوْمٍ وَلاَ يَرْقَأُ لِي دَمْعٌ ـ يَظُنَّانِ أَنَّ الْبُكَاءَ فَالِقٌ كَبِدِي، قَالَتْ فَبَيْنَمَا هُمَا جَالِسَانِ عِنْدِي وَأَنَا أَبْكِي، فَاسْتَأْذَنَتْ عَلَيَّ امْرَأَةٌ مِنَ الأَنْصَارِ، فَأَذِنْتُ لَهَا، فَجَلَسَتْ تَبْكِي مَعِي، قَالَتْ فَبَيْنَا نَحْنُ عَلَى ذَلِكَ دَخَلَ عَلَيْنَا رَسُولُ اللَّهِ صلى الله عليه وسلم فَسَلَّمَ ثُمَّ جَلَسَ قَالَتْ وَلَمْ يَجْلِسْ عِنْدِي مُنْذُ قِيلَ مَا قِيلَ قَبْلَهَا، وَقَدْ لَبِثَ شَهْرًا، لاَ يُوحَى إِلَيْهِ فِي شَأْنِي، قَالَتْ فَتَشَهَّدَ رَسُولُ اللَّهِ صلى الله عليه وسلم حِينَ جَلَسَ ثُمَّ قَالَ " أَمَّا بَعْدُ يَا عَائِشَةُ، فَإِنَّهُ قَدْ بَلَغَنِي عَنْكِ كَذَا وَكَذَا، فَإِنْ كُنْتِ بَرِيئَةً فَسَيُبَرِّئُكِ اللَّهُ، وَإِنْ كُنْتِ أَلْمَمْتِ بِذَنْبٍ فَاسْتَغْفِرِي اللَّهَ وَتُوبِي إِلَيْهِ، فَإِنَّ الْعَبْدَ إِذَا اعْتَرَفَ بِذَنْبِهِ ثُمَّ تَابَ إِلَى اللَّهِ تَابَ اللَّهُ عَلَيْهِ ". قَالَتْ فَلَمَّا قَضَى رَسُولُ اللَّهِ صلى الله عليه وسلم مَقَالَتَهُ، قَلَصَ دَمْعِي حَتَّى مَا أُحِسُّ مِنْهُ قَطْرَةً، فَقُلْتُ لأَبِي أَجِبْ رَسُولَ اللَّهِ صلى الله عليه وسلم فِيمَا قَالَ. قَالَ وَاللَّهِ مَا أَدْرِي مَا أَقُولُ لِرَسُولِ اللَّهِ صلى الله عليه وسلم فَقُلْتُ لأُمِّي أَجِيبِي رَسُولَ اللَّهِ صلى الله عليه وسلم. قَالَتْ مَا أَدْرِي مَا أَقُولُ لِرَسُولِ اللَّهِ صلى الله عليه وسلم قَالَتْ فَقُلْتُ وَأَنَا جَارِيَةٌ حَدِيثَةُ السِّنِّ لاَ أَقْرَأُ كَثِيرًا مِنَ الْقُرْآنِ، إِنِّي وَاللَّهِ لَقَدْ عَلِمْتُ لَقَدْ سَمِعْتُمْ هَذَا

الْحَدِيثَ حَتَّى اسْتَقَرَّ فِي أَنْفُسِكُمْ، وَصَدَّقْتُمْ بِهِ فَلَئِنْ قُلْتُ لَكُمْ إِنِّي بَرِيئَةٌ وَاللَّهُ يَعْلَمُ أَنِّي بَرِيئَةٌ لاَ تُصَدِّقُونِي بِذَلِكَ، وَلَئِنِ اعْتَرَفْتُ لَكُمْ بِأَمْرٍ، وَاللَّهُ يَعْلَمُ أَنِّي مِنْهُ بَرِيئَةٌ لَتُصَدِّقُنِّي، وَاللَّهِ مَا أَجِدُ لَكُمْ مَثَلاً إِلاَّ قَوْلَ أَبِي يُوسُفَ قَالَ {فَصَبْرٌ جَمِيلٌ وَاللَّهُ الْمُسْتَعَانُ عَلَى مَا تَصِفُونَ} قَالَتْ ثُمَّ تَحَوَّلْتُ فَاضْطَجَعْتُ عَلَى فِرَاشِي، قَالَتْ وَأَنَا حِينَئِذٍ أَعْلَمُ أَنِّي بَرِيئَةٌ، وَأَنَّ اللَّهَ مُبَرِّئِي بِبَرَاءَتِي، وَلَكِنْ وَاللَّهِ مَا كُنْتُ أَظُنُّ أَنَّ اللَّهَ مُنْزِلٌ فِي شَأْنِي وَحْيًا يُتْلَى، وَلَشَأْنِي فِي نَفْسِي كَانَ أَحْقَرَ مِنْ أَنْ يَتَكَلَّمَ اللَّهُ فِيَّ بِأَمْرٍ يُتْلَى، وَلَكِنْ كُنْتُ أَرْجُو أَنْ يَرَى رَسُولُ اللَّهِ صلى الله عليه وسلم فِي النَّوْمِ رُؤْيَا يُبَرِّئُنِي اللَّهُ بِهَا، قَالَتْ فَوَاللَّهِ مَا رَامَ رَسُولُ اللَّهِ صلى الله عليه وسلم وَلاَ خَرَجَ أَحَدٌ مِنْ أَهْلِ الْبَيْتِ حَتَّى أُنْزِلَ عَلَيْهِ، فَأَخَذَهُ مَا كَانَ يَأْخُذُهُ مِنَ الْبُرَحَاءِ حَتَّى إِنَّهُ لَيَتَحَدَّرُ مِنْهُ مِثْلُ الْجُمَانِ مِنَ الْعَرَقِ، وَهْوَ فِي يَوْمٍ شَاتٍ مِنْ ثِقَلِ الْقَوْلِ الَّذِي يُنْزَلُ عَلَيْهِ، قَالَتْ فَلَمَّا سُرِّيَ عَنْ رَسُولِ اللَّهِ صلى الله عليه وسلم سُرِّيَ عَنْهُ وَهْوَ يَضْحَكُ، فَكَانَتْ أَوَّلُ كَلِمَةٍ تَكَلَّمَ بِهَا " يَا عَائِشَةُ، أَمَّا اللَّهُ عَزَّ وَجَلَّ فَقَدْ بَرَّأَكِ ". فَقَالَتْ أُمِّي قُومِي إِلَيْهِ. قَالَتْ فَقُلْتُ وَاللَّهِ، لاَ أَقُومُ إِلَيْهِ، وَلاَ أَحْمَدُ إِلاَّ اللَّهَ عَزَّ وَجَلَّ. وَأَنْزَلَ اللَّهُ {إِنَّ الَّذِينَ جَاءُوا بِالإِفْكِ عُصْبَةٌ مِنْكُمْ لاَ تَحْسِبُوهُ} الْعَشْرَ الآيَاتِ كُلَّهَا، فَلَمَّا أَنْزَلَ اللَّهُ هَذَا فِي بَرَاءَتِي قَالَ أَبُو بَكْرٍ الصِّدِّيقُ ـ رضى الله عنه ـ وَكَانَ يُنْفِقُ عَلَى مِسْطَحِ بْنِ أُثَاثَةَ لِقَرَابَتِهِ مِنْهُ، وَفَقْرِهِ وَاللَّهِ لاَ أُنْفِقُ عَلَى مِسْطَحٍ شَيْئًا أَبَدًا بَعْدَ الَّذِي قَالَ لِعَائِشَةَ مَا قَالَ، فَأَنْزَلَ اللَّهُ {وَلاَ يَأْتَلِ أُولُو الْفَضْلِ مِنْكُمْ وَالسَّعَةِ أَنْ يُؤْتُوا أُولِي الْقُرْبَى وَالْمَسَاكِينَ وَالْمُهَاجِرِينَ فِي سَبِيلِ اللَّهِ وَلْيَعْفُوا وَلْيَصْفَحُوا أَلاَ تُحِبُّونَ أَنْ يَغْفِرَ اللَّهُ لَكُمْ وَاللَّهُ غَفُورٌ رَحِيمٌ} قَالَ أَبُو بَكْرٍ بَلَى، وَاللَّهِ إِنِّي أُحِبُّ أَنْ يَغْفِرَ اللَّهُ لِي، فَرَجَعَ إِلَى مِسْطَحٍ النَّفَقَةَ الَّتِي كَانَ يُنْفِقُ عَلَيْهِ، وَقَالَ وَاللَّهِ لاَ أَنْزِعُهَا مِنْهُ أَبَدًا. قَالَتْ عَائِشَةُ وَكَانَ رَسُولُ اللَّهِ صلى الله عليه وسلم يَسْأَلُ زَيْنَبَ ابْنَةَ جَحْشٍ عَنْ أَمْرِي، فَقَالَ " يَا زَيْنَبُ مَاذَا عَلِمْتِ أَوْ رَأَيْتِ ". فَقَالَتْ يَا رَسُولَ اللَّهِ، أَحْمِي سَمْعِي وَبَصَرِي، مَا عَلِمْتُ إِلاَّ خَيْرًا. قَالَتْ وَهْيَ الَّتِي كَانَتْ تُسَامِينِي مِنْ أَزْوَاجِ رَسُولِ اللَّهِ صلى الله عليه وسلم فَعَصَمَهَا اللَّهُ بِالْوَرَعِ، وَطَفِقَتْ أُخْتُهَا حَمْنَةُ تُحَارِبُ لَهَا فَهَلَكَتْ فِيمَنْ هَلَكَ مِنْ أَصْحَابِ الإِفْكِ

Narrated Anas: The Prophetﷺ said, “A single endeavor (of fighting) in Allah’s Cause in the afternoon or in the forenoon is better than all the world and whatever is in it. A place in Paradise as small as the bow or lash of one of you is better than all the world and whatever is in it. And if a houri from Paradise appeared to the people of the earth, she would fill the space between Heaven and the Earth with light and pleasant scent and her head cover is better than the world and whatever is in it.”. – Sahih Al-Bukhari 2796

وَسَمِعْتُ أَنَسَ بْنَ مَالِكٍ، عَنِ النَّبِيِّ صلى الله عليه وسلم " لَرَوْحَةٌ فِي سَبِيلِ اللَّهِ أَوْ غَدْوَةٌ خَيْرٌ مِنَ الدُّنْيَا وَمَا فِيهَا، وَلَقَابُ قَوْسِ أَحَدِكُمْ مِنَ الْجَنَّةِ أَوْ مَوْضِعُ قِيدٍ ـ يَعْنِي سَوْطَهُ ـ خَيْرٌ مِنَ الدُّنْيَا وَمَا فِيهَا، وَلَوْ أَنَّ امْرَأَةً مِنْ أَهْلِ الْجَنَّةِ اطَّلَعَتْ إِلَى أَهْلِ الأَرْضِ لأَضَاءَتْ مَا بَيْنَهُمَا وَلَمَلأَتْهُ رِيحًا، وَلَنَصِيفُهَا عَلَى رَأْسِهَا خَيْرٌ مِنَ الدُّنْيَا وَمَا فِيهَا "

Narrated Anas bin Malik: We were in the company of the Prophetﷺ while returning from ‘Usfan, and Allah’s Messengerﷺ was riding his she-camel keeping Safiya bint Huyay riding behind him. His she-camel slipped and both of them fell down. Abu Talha jumped from his camel and said, “O Allah’s Messengerﷺ! May Allah sacrifice me for you.” The Prophetﷺ said, “Take care of the lady.” So, Abu Talha covered his face with a garment and went to Safiya and covered her with it, and then he set right the condition of their shecamel so that both of them rode, and we were encircling Allah’s Messengerﷺ like a cover. When we approached Medina, the Prophetﷺ said, “We are returning with repentance and worshipping and praising our Lord.” He kept on saying this till he entered Medina. – Sahih Al-Bukhari 3085

حَدَّثَنَا أَبُو مَعْمَرٍ، حَدَّثَنَا عَبْدُ الْوَارِثِ، قَالَ حَدَّثَنِي يَحْيَى بْنُ أَبِي إِسْحَاقَ، عَنْ أَنَسِ بْنِ مَالِكٍ ـ رضى الله عنه ـ قَالَ كُنَّا مَعَ النَّبِيِّ صلى الله عليه وسلم مَقْفَلَهُ مِنْ عُسْفَانَ، وَرَسُولُ اللَّهِ صلى الله عليه وسلم عَلَى رَاحِلَتِهِ، وَقَدْ أَرْدَفَ صَفِيَّةَ بِنْتَ حُيَيٍّ، فَعَثَرَتْ نَاقَتُهُ فَصُرِعَا جَمِيعًا، فَاقْتَحَمَ أَبُو طَلْحَةَ فَقَالَ يَا رَسُولَ اللَّهِ، جَعَلَنِي اللَّهُ فِدَاءَكَ. قَالَ " عَلَيْكَ الْمَرْأَةَ ". فَقَلَبَ ثَوْبًا عَلَى وَجْهِهِ وَأَتَاهَا، فَأَلْقَاهَا عَلَيْهَا وَأَصْلَحَ لَهُمَا مَرْكَبَهُمَا فَرَكِبَا، وَاكْتَنَفْنَا رَسُولَ اللَّهِ صلى الله عليه وسلم، فَلَمَّا أَشْرَفْنَا عَلَى الْمَدِينَةِ قَالَ " آيِبُونَ تَائِبُونَ عَابِدُونَ لِرَبِّنَا حَامِدُونَ ". فَلَمْ يَزَلْ يَقُولُ ذَلِكَ حَتَّى دَخَلَ الْمَدِينَةَ.

Narrated Sa`d bin Abi Waqqas: `Umar bin Al-Khattab asked the permission of Allah’s Messengerﷺ to see him while some Quraishi women were sitting with him, talking to him and asking him for more expenses, raising their voices above the voice of Allah’s Messengerﷺ. When `Umar asked for the permission to enter, the women quickly put on their veils. Allah’sf Apostle allowed him to enter and `Umar came in while Allah’s Messengerﷺ was smiling, `Umar said “O Allah’s Apostle! May Allah always keep you smiling.” The Prophetﷺ

said, “These women who have been here, roused my wonder, for as soon as they heard your voice, they quickly put on their veils. “`Umar said, “O Allah’s Messenger ﷺ! You have more right to be feared by them than I.” Then `Umar addressed the women saying, “O enemies of yourselves! You fear me more than you do Allah’s Messenger ﷺ?” They said, “Yes, for you are harsher and sterner than Allah’s Messenger ﷺ.” Then Allah’s Messenger ﷺ said, “O Ibn Al-Khattab! By Him in Whose Hands my life is! Never does Satan find you going on a way, but he takes another way other than yours.”. – Sahih Al-Bukhari 3683

حَدَّثَنَا عَلِيُّ بْنُ عَبْدِ اللَّهِ، حَدَّثَنَا يَعْقُوبُ بْنُ إِبْرَاهِيمَ، قَالَ حَدَّثَنِي أَبِي، عَنْ صَالِحٍ، عَنِ ابْنِ شِهَابٍ، أَخْبَرَنِي عَبْدُ الْحَمِيدِ، أَنَّ مُحَمَّدَ بْنَ سَعْدٍ، أَخْبَرَهُ أَنَّ أَبَاهُ قَالَ ح حَدَّثَنِي عَبْدُ الْعَزِيزِ بْنُ عَبْدِ اللَّهِ، حَدَّثَنَا إِبْرَاهِيمُ بْنُ سَعْدٍ، عَنْ صَالِحٍ، عَنِ ابْنِ شِهَابٍ، عَنْ عَبْدِ الْحَمِيدِ بْنِ عَبْدِ الرَّحْمَنِ بْنِ زَيْدٍ، عَنْ مُحَمَّدِ بْنِ سَعْدِ بْنِ أَبِي وَقَّاصٍ، عَنْ أَبِيهِ، قَالَ اسْتَأْذَنَ عُمَرُ بْنُ الْخَطَّابِ عَلَى رَسُولِ اللَّهِ صلى الله عليه وسلم، وَعِنْدَهُ نِسْوَةٌ مِنْ قُرَيْشٍ يُكَلِّمْنَهُ وَيَسْتَكْثِرْنَهُ، عَالِيَةً أَصْوَاتُهُنَّ عَلَى صَوْتِهِ فَلَمَّا اسْتَأْذَنَ عُمَرُ بْنُ الْخَطَّابِ قُمْنَ فَبَادَرْنَ الْحِجَابَ فَأَذِنَ لَهُ رَسُولُ اللَّهِ صلى الله عليه وسلم فَدَخَلَ عُمَرُ وَرَسُولُ اللَّهِ صلى الله عليه وسلم يَضْحَكُ، فَقَالَ عُمَرُ أَضْحَكَ اللَّهُ سِنَّكَ يَا رَسُولَ اللَّهِ. فَقَالَ النَّبِيُّ صلى الله عليه وسلم " عَجِبْتُ مِنْ هَؤُلاَءِ اللاَّتِي كُنَّ عِنْدِي فَلَمَّا سَمِعْنَ صَوْتَكَ ابْتَدَرْنَ الْحِجَابِ ". فَقَالَ عُمَرُ فَأَنْتَ أَحَقُّ أَنْ يَهَبْنَ يَا رَسُولَ اللَّهِ. ثُمَّ قَالَ عُمَرُ يَا عَدُوَّاتِ أَنْفُسِهِنَّ، أَتَهَبْنَنِي وَلاَ تَهَبْنَ رَسُولَ اللَّهِ صلى الله عليه وسلم فَقُلْنَ نَعَمْ، أَنْتَ أَفَظُّ وَأَغْلَظُ مِنْ رَسُولِ اللَّهِ صلى الله عليه وسلم. فَقَالَ رَسُولُ اللَّهِ صلى الله عليه وسلم " إِيهًا يَا ابْنَ الْخَطَّابِ وَالَّذِي نَفْسِي بِيَدِهِ مَا لَقِيَكَ الشَّيْطَانُ سَالِكًا فَجًّا قَطُّ إِلاَّ سَلَكَ فَجًّا غَيْرَ فَجِّكَ ".

Narrated `Aisha: (the wife of the Prophet) that she was told that `Abdullah bin Az-Zubair (on hearing that she was selling or giving something as a gift) said, “By Allah, if `Aisha does not give up this, I will declare her incompetent to dispose of her wealth.” I said, “Did he (`Abdullah bin Az-Zubair) say so?” They (people) said, “Yes.” `Aisha said, “I vow to Allah that I will never speak to Ibn Az-Zubair.” When this desertion lasted long, `Abdullah bin Az-Zubair sought intercession with her, but she said, “By Allah, I will not accept the intercession of anyone for him, and will not commit a sin by breaking my vow.” When this state of affairs was prolonged on Ibn Az-Zubair (he felt it hard on him), he said to Al- Miswar bin Makhrama and `Abdur-Rahman bin Al-Aswad bin ‘Abu Yaghuth, who were from the tribe of Bani Zahra, “I beseech you, by Allah, to let me enter upon `Aisha, for it is unlawful for her to vow to cut the relation with me.” So Al-Miswar and `Abdur-Rahman, wrapping their sheets around themselves, asked `Aisha’s permission saying, “Peace and Allah’s Mercy and Blessings be upon you! Shall we come in?” `Aisha said, “Come in.” They said, “All of us?” She said, “Yes, come in all of you,” not knowing that Ibn Az- Zubair was also with them. So when they entered, Ibn Az-Zubair entered the screened place and got hold of `Aisha and started requesting her to excuse him, and wept. Al-Miswar and `Abdur Rahman also started requesting her to speak to him and to accept his repentance. They said (to her), “The Prophet ﷺ forbade what you know of deserting (not speaking to your Muslim Brethren), for it is unlawful for any Muslim not to talk to his brother for more than three nights (days).” So when they increased their reminding her (of the superiority of having good relation with Kith and kin, and of excusing others’ sins), and brought her down to a critical situation, she started reminding them, and wept, saying, “I have made a vow, and (the question of) vow is a difficult one.” They (Al-Miswar and `Abdur-Rahman) persisted in their appeal till she spoke with `Abdullah bin Az- Zubair and she manumitted forty slaves as an expiation for her vow. Later on, whenever she remembered her vow, she used to weep so much that her veil used to become wet with her tears. – Sahih Al-Bukhari 6073-6075

حَدَّثَنَا أَبُو الْيَمَانِ، أَخْبَرَنَا شُعَيْبٌ، عَنِ الزُّهْرِيِّ، قَالَ حَدَّثَنِي عَوْفُ بْنُ مَالِكِ بْنِ الطُّفَيْلِ ـ هُوَ ابْنُ الْحَارِثِ وَهْوَ ابْنُ أَخِي عَائِشَةَ زَوْجِ النَّبِيِّ صلى الله عليه وسلم لأُمِّهَا ـ أَنَّ عَائِشَةَ حُدِّثَتْ أَنَّ عَبْدَ اللَّهِ بْنَ الزُّبَيْرِ قَالَ فِي بَيْعٍ أَوْ عَطَاءٍ أَعْطَتْهُ عَائِشَةُ وَاللَّهِ لَتَنْتَهِيَنَّ عَائِشَةُ، أَوْ لأَحْجُرَنَّ عَلَيْهَا. فَقَالَتْ أَهُوَ قَالَ هَذَا قَالُوا نَعَمْ. قَالَتْ هُوَ لِلَّهِ عَلَىَّ نَذْرٌ، أَنْ لاَ أُكَلِّمَ ابْنَ الزُّبَيْرِ أَبَدًا. فَاسْتَشْفَعَ ابْنُ الزُّبَيْرِ إِلَيْهَا، حِينَ طَالَتِ الْهِجْرَةُ فَقَالَتْ لاَ وَاللَّهِ لاَ أُشَفِّعُ فِيهِ أَبَدًا، وَلاَ أَتَحَنَّثُ إِلَى نَذْرِي. فَلَمَّا طَالَ ذَلِكَ عَلَى

ابْنِ الزُّبَيْرِ كَلَّمَ الْمِسْوَرَ بْنَ مَخْرَمَةَ وَعَبْدَ الرَّحْمَنِ بْنَ الأَسْوَدِ بْنِ عَبْدِ يَغُوثَ، وَهُمَا مِنْ بَنِي زُهْرَةَ، وَقَالَ لَهُمَا أَنْشُدُكُمَا بِاللَّهِ لَمَّا أَدْخَلْتُمَانِي عَلَى عَائِشَةَ، فَإِنَّهَا لاَ يَحِلُّ لَهَا أَنْ تَنْذُرَ قَطِيعَتِي. فَأَقْبَلَ بِهِ الْمِسْوَرُ وَعَبْدُ الرَّحْمَنِ مُشْتَمِلَيْنِ بِأَرْدِيَتِهِمَا حَتَّى اسْتَأْذَنَا عَلَى عَائِشَةَ فَقَالاَ السَّلاَمُ عَلَيْكِ وَرَحْمَةُ اللَّهِ وَبَرَكَاتُهُ، أَنَدْخُلُ قَالَتْ عَائِشَةُ ادْخُلُوا. قَالُوا كُلُّنَا قَالَتْ نَعَمِ ادْخُلُوا كُلُّكُمْ. وَلاَ تَعْلَمُ أَنَّ مَعَهُمَا ابْنَ الزُّبَيْرِ، فَلَمَّا دَخَلُوا دَخَلَ ابْنُ الزُّبَيْرِ الْحِجَابَ، فَاعْتَنَقَ عَائِشَةَ وَطَفِقَ يُنَاشِدُهَا وَيَبْكِي، وَطَفِقَ الْمِسْوَرُ وَعَبْدُ الرَّحْمَنِ يُنَاشِدَانِهَا إِلاَّ مَا كَلَّمَتْهُ وَقَبِلَتْ مِنْهُ، وَيَقُولاَنِ إِنَّ النَّبِيَّ صلى الله عليه وسلم نَهَى عَمَّا قَدْ عَلِمْتِ مِنَ الْهِجْرَةِ، فَإِنَّهُ لاَ يَحِلُّ لِمُسْلِمٍ أَنْ يَهْجُرَ أَخَاهُ فَوْقَ ثَلاَثِ لَيَالٍ. فَلَمَّا أَكْثَرُوا عَلَى عَائِشَةَ مِنَ التَّذْكِرَةِ وَالتَّحْرِيجِ طَفِقَتْ تُذَكِّرُهُمَا نَذْرَهَا وَتَبْكِي وَتَقُولُ إِنِّي نَذَرْتُ، وَالنَّذْرُ شَدِيدٌ. فَلَمْ يَزَالاَ بِهَا حَتَّى كَلَّمَتِ ابْنَ الزُّبَيْرِ، وَأَعْتَقَتْ فِي نَذْرِهَا ذَلِكَ أَرْبَعِينَ رَقَبَةً. وَكَانَتْ تَذْكُرُ نَذْرَهَا بَعْدَ ذَلِكَ فَتَبْكِي، حَتَّى تَبُلَّ دُمُوعُهَا خِمَارَهَا.

Narrated Anas: Um (the mother of) Haritha came to Allah's Messenger ﷺ after Haritha had been martyred on the Day (of the battle) of Badr by an arrow thrown by an unknown person. She said, "O Allah's Messenger ﷺ! You know the position of Haritha in my heart (i.e. how dear to me he was), so if he is in Paradise, I will not weep for him, or otherwise, you will see what I will do." The Prophet ﷺ said, "Are you mad? Is there only one Paradise? There are many Paradises, and he is in the highest Paradise of Firdaus." The Prophet added, "A forenoon journey or an after noon journey in Allah's Cause is better than the whole world and whatever is in it; and a place equal to an arrow bow of anyone of you, or a place equal to a foot in Paradise is better than the whole world and whatever is in it; and if one of the women of Paradise looked at the earth, she would fill the whole space between them (the earth and the heaven) with light, and would fill whatever is in between them, with perfume, and the veil of her face is better than the whole world and whatever is in it.". – Sahih Al-Bukhari 6567, 6568

حَدَّثَنَا قُتَيْبَةُ، حَدَّثَنَا إِسْمَاعِيلُ بْنُ جَعْفَرٍ، عَنْ حُمَيْدٍ، عَنْ أَنَسٍ، أَنَّ أُمَّ حَارِثَةَ، أَتَتْ رَسُولَ اللَّهِ صلى الله عليه وسلم وَقَدْ هَلَكَ حَارِثَةُ يَوْمَ بَدْرٍ، أَصَابَهُ غَرْبُ سَهْمٍ. فَقَالَتْ يَا رَسُولَ اللَّهِ قَدْ عَلِمْتَ مَوْقِعَ حَارِثَةَ مِنْ قَلْبِي، فَإِنْ كَانَ فِي الْجَنَّةِ لَمْ أَبْكِ عَلَيْهِ، وَإِلاَّ سَوْفَ تَرَى مَا أَصْنَعُ. فَقَالَ لَهَا " هَبِلْتِ، أَجَنَّةٌ وَاحِدَةٌ هِيَ إِنَّهَا جِنَانٌ كَثِيرَةٌ، وَإِنَّهُ فِي الْفِرْدَوْسِ الأَعْلَى ". (وَقَالَ: غَدْوَةٌ فِي سَبِيلِ اللَّهِ أَوْ رَوْحَةٌ خَيْرٌ مِنَ الدُّنْيَا وَمَا فِيهَا، وَلَقَابُ قَوْسِ أَحَدِكُمْ أَوْ مَوْضِعُ قَدَمٍ مِنَ الْجَنَّةِ خَيْرٌ مِنَ الدُّنْيَا وَمَا فِيهَا، وَلَوْ أَنَّ امْرَأَةً مِنْ نِسَاءِ أَهْلِ الْجَنَّةِ اطَّلَعَتْ إِلَى الأَرْضِ، لأَضَاءَتْ مَا بَيْنَهُمَا، وَلَمَلأَتْ مَا بَيْنَهُمَا رِيحًا، وَلَنَصِيفُهَا - يَعْنِي الْخِمَارَ - خَيْرٌ مِنَ الدُّنْيَا وَمَا فِيهَا)

Ibn Juraij said, " `Ata informed us that when Ibn Hisham forbade women to perform Tawaf with men he said to him, 'How do you forbid them while the wives of the Prophet ﷺ used to perform Tawaf with the men?' I said, 'Was this before decreeing of the use of the veil or after it? `Ata took an oath and said, 'I saw it after the order of veil.' I said, 'How did they mix with the men?' `Ata said, 'The women never mixed with the men, and `A'ishah used to perform Tawaf separately and never mixed with men. Once it happened that `A'ishah was performing the Tawaf and woman said to her, 'O Mother of believers! Let us touch the Black stone.' `A'ishah said to her, 'Go yourself,' and she herself refused to do so. The wives of the Prophet ﷺ used to come out in night, in disguise and used to perform Tawaf with men. But whenever they intended to enter the Ka`bah, they would stay outside till the men had gone out. I and `Ubaid bin `Umair used to visit `A'ishah while she was residing at Jauf Thabir." I asked, "What was her veil?" `Ata said, "She was wearing an old Turkish veil, and that was the only thing (veil) which was screen between us and her. I saw a pink cover on her.". – Sahih Al-Bukhari 1618

وَقَالَ لِي عَمْرُو بْنُ عَلِيٍّ حَدَّثَنَا أَبُو عَاصِمٍ، قَالَ ابْنُ جُرَيْجٍ أَخْبَرَنَا قَالَ أَخْبَرَنِي عَطَاءٌ، إِذْ مَنَعَ ابْنُ هِشَامٍ النِّسَاءَ الطَّوَافَ مَعَ الرِّجَالِ قَالَ كَيْفَ يَمْنَعُهُنَّ، وَقَدْ طَافَ نِسَاءُ النَّبِيِّ صلى الله عليه وسلم مَعَ الرِّجَالِ قُلْتُ أَبَعْدَ الْحِجَابِ أَوْ قَبْلُ قَالَ إِي لَعَمْرِي لَقَدْ أَدْرَكْتُهُ بَعْدَ الْحِجَابِ. قُلْتُ كَيْفَ يُخَالِطْنَ الرِّجَالَ قَالَ لَمْ يَكُنَّ يُخَالِطْنَ كَانَتْ عَائِشَةُ - رضى الله عنها - تَطُوفُ حَجْرَةً مِنَ الرِّجَالِ لاَ تُخَالِطُهُمْ، فَقَالَتِ امْرَأَةٌ انْطَلِقِي نَسْتَلِمْ يَا أُمَّ الْمُؤْمِنِينَ. قَالَتْ {انْطَلِقِي} عَنْكِ. وَأَبَتْ. {وَكُنَّ} يَخْرُجْنَ مُتَنَكِّرَاتٍ بِاللَّيْلِ، فَيَطُفْنَ مَعَ الرِّجَالِ، وَلَكِنَّهُنَّ كُنَّ إِذَا دَخَلْنَ الْبَيْتَ قُمْنَ حَتَّى يَدْخُلْنَ وَأُخْرِجَ الرِّجَالُ، وَكُنْتُ آتِي عَائِشَةَ أَنَا

وَعُبَيْدُ بْنُ عُمَيْرٍ وَهِيَ مُجَاوِرَةٌ فِي جَوْفِ ثَبِيرٍ. قُلْتُ وَمَا حِجَابُهَا قَالَ هِيَ فِي قُبَّةٍ تُرْكِيَّةٍ لَهَا غِشَاءٌ، وَمَا بَيْنَنَا وَبَيْنَهَا غَيْرُ ذَلِكَ، وَرَأَيْتُ عَلَيْهَا دِرْعًا مُوَرَّدًا

Narrated Hafsa: (On `Id) We used to forbid our virgins to go out (for `Id prayer). A lady came and stayed at the fortress of Bani Khalaf. She mentioned that her sister was married to one of the companions of Allah's Messenger ﷺ who participated in twelve Ghazawats along with Allah's Messenger ﷺ and her sister was with him in six of them. She said, "We used to dress the wounded and look after the patients." She (her sister) asked Allah's Messenger ﷺ, "Is there any harm for a woman to stay at home if she doesn't have a veil?" He said, "She should cover herself with the veil of her companion and she should take part in the good deeds and in the religious gatherings of the believers." When Um 'Atiyya came, I asked her. "Did you hear anything about that?" Um 'Atiyya said, "Bi Abi" and she never mentioned the name of Allah's Messenger ﷺ without saying "Bi Abi" (i.e. 'Let my father be sacrificed for you'). We asked her, "Have you heard Allah's Messenger ﷺ saying so and so (about women)?" She replied in the affirmative and said, "Let my father be sacrificed for him. He told us that unmarried mature virgins who stay often screened or unmarried young virgins and mature girls who stay often screened should come out and take part in the good deeds and in the religious gatherings of the believers. But the menstruating women should keep away from the Musalla (praying place)." I asked her, "The menstruating women?" She replied, "Don't they present themselves at `Arafat and at such and such places?". – Sahih Al-Bukhari 1652

حَدَّثَنَا مُؤَمَّلُ بْنُ هِشَامٍ، حَدَّثَنَا إِسْمَاعِيلُ، عَنْ أَيُّوبَ، عَنْ حَفْصَةَ، قَالَتْ كُنَّا نَمْنَعُ عَوَاتِقَنَا أَنْ يَخْرُجْنَ، فَقَدِمَتِ امْرَأَةٌ فَنَزَلَتْ قَصْرَ بَنِي خَلَفٍ، فَحَدَّثَتْ أَنَّ أُخْتَهَا كَانَتْ تَحْتَ رَجُلٍ مِنْ أَصْحَابِ رَسُولِ اللَّهِ صلى الله عليه وسلم قَدْ غَزَا مَعَ رَسُولِ اللَّهِ صلى الله عليه وسلم ثِنْتَىْ عَشْرَةَ غَزْوَةً، وَكَانَتْ أُخْتِي مَعَهُ فِي سِتِّ غَزَوَاتٍ، قَالَتْ كُنَّا نُدَاوِي الْكَلْمَى وَنَقُومُ عَلَى الْمَرْضَى. فَسَأَلَتْ أُخْتِي رَسُولَ اللَّهِ صلى الله عليه وسلم فَقَالَتْ هَلْ عَلَى إِحْدَانَا بَأْسٌ إِنْ لَمْ يَكُنْ لَهَا جِلْبَابٌ أَنْ لاَ تَخْرُجَ قَالَ " لِتُلْبِسْهَا صَاحِبَتُهَا مِنْ جِلْبَابِهَا، وَلْتَشْهَدِ الْخَيْرَ، وَدَعْوَةَ الْمُؤْمِنِينَ ". فَلَمَّا قَدِمَتْ أُمُّ عَطِيَّةَ ـ رضى الله عنها ـ سَأَلْنَهَا ـ أَوْ قَالَتْ سَأَلْنَاهَا ـ فَقَالَتْ وَكَانَتْ لاَ تَذْكُرُ رَسُولَ اللَّهِ صلى الله عليه وسلم إِلاَّ قَالَتْ بِأَبِي. فَقُلْنَا أَسَمِعْتِ رَسُولَ اللَّهِ صلى الله عليه وسلم يَقُولُ كَذَا وَكَذَا قَالَتْ نَعَمْ بِأَبِي. فَقَالَ " لِتَخْرُجِ الْعَوَاتِقُ ذَوَاتُ الْخُدُورِ ـ أَوِ الْعَوَاتِقُ وَذَوَاتُ الْخُدُورِ ـ وَالْحُيَّضُ، فَيَشْهَدْنَ الْخَيْرَ، وَدَعْوَةَ الْمُسْلِمِينَ، وَيَعْتَزِلُ الْحُيَّضُ الْمُصَلَّى ". فَقُلْتُ الْحَائِضُ. فَقَالَتْ أَوَ لَيْسَ تَشْهَدُ عَرَفَةَ، وَتَشْهَدُ كَذَا وَتَشْهَدُ كَذَا

Narrated Anas: The Prophet ﷺ stayed for three days between Khaibar and Medina, and there he consummated his marriage to Safiyya bint Huyai. I invited the Muslims to the wedding banquet in which neither meat nor bread was offered. He ordered for leather dining-sheets to be spread, and dates, dried yoghurt and butter were laid on it, and that was the Prophet's wedding banquet. The Muslims wondered, "Is she (Saffiyya) considered as his wife or his slave girl?" Then they said, "If he orders her to veil herself, she will be one of the mothers of the Believers; but if he does not order her to veil herself, she will be a slave girl. So when the Prophet ﷺ proceeded from there, he spared her a space behind him (on his shecamel) and put a screening veil between her and the people. – Sahih Al-Bukhari 5085

حَدَّثَنَا قُتَيْبَةُ، حَدَّثَنَا إِسْمَاعِيلُ بْنُ جَعْفَرٍ، عَنْ حُمَيْدٍ، عَنْ أَنَسٍ ـ رضى الله عنه ـ قَالَ أَقَامَ النَّبِيُّ صلى الله عليه وسلم بَيْنَ خَيْبَرَ وَالْمَدِينَةِ ثَلاَثًا يُبْنَى عَلَيْهِ بِصَفِيَّةَ بِنْتِ حُيَىٍّ فَدَعَوْتُ الْمُسْلِمِينَ إِلَى وَلِيمَتِهِ فَمَا كَانَ فِيهَا مِنْ خُبْزٍ وَلاَ لَحْمٍ، أُمِرَ بِالأَنْطَاعِ فَأَلْقَى فِيهَا مِنَ التَّمْرِ وَالأَقِطِ وَالسَّمْنِ فَكَانَتْ وَلِيمَتَهُ، فَقَالَ الْمُسْلِمُونَ إِحْدَى أُمَّهَاتِ الْمُؤْمِنِينَ أَوْ مِمَّا مَلَكَتْ يَمِينُهُ، فَقَالُوا إِنْ حَجَبَهَا فَهْىَ مِنْ أُمَّهَاتِ الْمُؤْمِنِينَ، وَإِنْ لَمْ يَحْجُبْهَا فَهْىَ مِمَّا مَلَكَتْ يَمِينُهُ، فَلَمَّا ارْتَحَلَ وَطَّى لَهَا خَلْفَهُ وَمَدَّ الْحِجَابَ بَيْنَهَا وَبَيْنَ النَّاسِ

..... Samurai bin Jundab accepted the evidence of a veiled woman. – Sahih Al-Bukhari vol. 3 page 475

و اخاز سمرة بن جندب شهادة امرأة منتقبة

And Sa'id bin Abi Hasan said to Al-Hasan, "The non-Arab women expose their cheat and grade heads." Al-Hasan said (to Sa'id) "Avert your eyes from them. For Allah says: "Tell the believing men e lower their gaze (from looking at forbidden things), and protect their private parts (from illegal sexual acts)."."" (V.24:30) And Qatada added (in the explanation of the above verse), ""Guard (their modesty) Against what is unlawful for them." And Allah also said: "And tell the believing women to lower their gaze (from looking at forbidden things) and protect their private parts (from illegal sexual acts)..." (V,24:31) And the dishonesty of eyes means to gaze at a forbidden thing. And Az-Zuhri said, "It is not right to look at any of those girls at whom one has a desire to look, even if she is of very young age. And Atå disliked to look at those slave-girls who used to be sold in Makkah unless he wanted to buy. – Sahih Al-Bukhari Vol. 8 page 139

و قال يعيد بن أبي الحسن للحسن : أن نساء العجم يكشفن صدورهن وروسهن ، قال : اصرف بصرك عنهن ، يقول الله عز وجل : (قل للمؤمنين يغضوا من أبصارهم و يحفظوا فروجهم) قال قتادة : عما لا يحل لهم (و قل للمؤمنين يغضضن من أبصارهم و يحفظنا فروجهن) (خاءنة الأعين) من النظر إلى ما نهي عنه ، و قال الزهري في النظر إلى التي لم تحضر من النساء : لا يصلح النظر إلى شيء منهن ممن يشتهى النظر إليه و إن كانت صغيرة . وكره عطاء النظر إلى الجواري التي يبعت بمكة إلا أن يريد أن يشتري .

O you who have believed, do not enter the homes of the Prophet except (when you are permitted in for food, without waiting for its dueness. (i.e., its hour, its time) But when you are invited, then enter. So, when you have had food, then disperse yourselves, neither (announcing yourselves) into familiar discourse. Surely that (Literally: those) hurts the Prophet, so he (feels) shy before you; and Allah does not shy from the truth. And when you ask (his wives) for any article, then ask them from behind a curtain; that is purer for your hearts and their hearts. And in no way should you hurt the Messenger of Allah, nor marry his spouses even after him at all. Surely that would, in the Reckoning of Allah, be a monstrous (thing) Surah Al-Ahzab 33:53

يَـٰٓأَيُّهَا ٱلَّذِينَ ءَامَنُواْ لَا تَدْخُلُواْ بُيُوتَ ٱلنَّبِيِّ إِلَّآ أَن يُؤْذَنَ لَكُمْ إِلَىٰ طَعَامٍ غَيْرَ نَـٰظِرِينَ إِنَىٰهُ وَلَـٰكِنْ إِذَا دُعِيتُمْ فَٱدْخُلُواْ فَإِذَا طَعِمْتُمْ فَٱنتَشِرُواْ وَلَا مُسْتَـْٔنِسِينَ لِحَدِيثٍ إِنَّ ذَٰلِكُمْ كَانَ يُؤْذِى ٱلنَّبِىَّ فَيَسْتَحْىِۦ مِنكُمْ وَٱللَّهُ لَا يَسْتَحْىِۦ مِنَ ٱلْحَقِّ وَإِذَا سَأَلْتُمُوهُنَّ مَتَـٰعًا فَسْـَٔلُوهُنَّ مِن وَرَآءِ حِجَابٍ ذَٰلِكُمْ أَطْهَرُ لِقُلُوبِكُمْ وَقُلُوبِهِنَّ وَمَا كَانَ لَكُمْ أَن تُؤْذُواْ رَسُولَ ٱللَّهِ وَلَآ أَن تَنكِحُوٓاْ أَزْوَٰجَهُۥ مِنۢ بَعْدِهِۦٓ أَبَدًا إِنَّ ذَٰلِكُمْ كَانَ عِندَ ٱللَّهِ عَظِيمًا

There will be a barrier between Paradise and Hell. And on the heights ⌜of that barrier⌝ will be people who will recognize ⌜the residents of⌝ both by their appearance. They will call out to the residents of Paradise, "Peace be upon you!" They will have not yet entered Paradise, but eagerly hope to.[38] - Surah Al-A'raf 7:46

وَبَيْنَهُمَا حِجَابٌ وَعَلَى ٱلْأَعْرَافِ رِجَالٌ يَعْرِفُونَ كُلًّا بِسِيمَـٰهُمْ وَنَادَوْاْ أَصْحَـٰبَ ٱلْجَنَّةِ أَن سَلَـٰمٌ عَلَيْكُمْ لَمْ يَدْخُلُوهَا وَهُمْ يَطْمَعُونَ

He then proclaimed, "I am truly in love with ⌜these⌝ fine things out of remembrance for Allah," until they went out of sight. - Surah Sad 38:32

فَقَالَ إِنِّىٓ أَحْبَبْتُ حُبَّ ٱلْخَيْرِ عَن ذِكْرِ رَبِّى حَتَّىٰ تَوَارَتْ بِٱلْحِجَابِ

---

[38] Surah Al-Ahzab 33:53 Al-A'raf 7:46, Sad 38:32, Al-Isra 17:45, Maryam 19:17 Fussilat 41:5, Ash-Shura 42:51, & Al-Mutaffifin 83:15 indicate the way Allah used the Arabic word hijab in Al-Quran.

When you recite the Quran, We put a hidden barrier between you and those who do not believe in the Hereafter. – Surah Al-Isra 17:45
وَإِذَا قَرَأْتَ ٱلْقُرْءَانَ جَعَلْنَا بَيْنَكَ وَبَيْنَ ٱلَّذِينَ لَا يُؤْمِنُونَ بِٱلْـَٔاخِرَةِ حِجَابًا مَّسْتُورًا

Screening herself off from them. Then We sent to her Our angel, appearing before her as a man, perfectly formed. – Surah Maryam 19:17
فَٱتَّخَذَتْ مِن دُونِهِمْ حِجَابًا فَأَرْسَلْنَآ إِلَيْهَا رُوحَنَا فَتَمَثَّلَ لَهَا بَشَرًا سَوِيًّا

Say, "Who (shayatin) has forbidden the adornments and lawful provisions Allah has brought forth for His servants?" Say, "They are for those who believe, in this present world, but exclusively theirs on the Day of Resurrection." We thus detail the revelations for people who know. – Surah Al-A'raf 7:32
قُلْ مَنْ حَرَّمَ زِينَةَ ٱللَّهِ ٱلَّتِىٓ أَخْرَجَ لِعِبَادِهِۦ وَٱلطَّيِّبَٰتِ مِنَ ٱلرِّزْقِ ۚ قُلْ هِىَ لِلَّذِينَ ءَامَنُوا۟ فِى ٱلْحَيَوٰةِ ٱلدُّنْيَا خَالِصَةً يَوْمَ ٱلْقِيَٰمَةِ ۗ كَذَٰلِكَ نُفَصِّلُ ٱلْـَٔايَٰتِ لِقَوْمٍ يَعْلَمُونَ

And they say, "Our hearts are screened from what you call us to, and in our ears is deafness, and between us and you is a barrier. So do what you want, and so will we." - Surah Fussilat 41:5
وَقَالُوا۟ قُلُوبُنَا فِىٓ أَكِنَّةٍ مِّمَّا تَدْعُونَآ إِلَيْهِ وَفِىٓ ءَاذَانِنَا وَقْرٌ وَمِنۢ بَيْنِنَا وَبَيْنِكَ حِجَابٌ فَٱعْمَلْ إِنَّنَا عَٰمِلُونَ

It is not for any human that Allah should speak to him, except by inspiration, or from behind a veil, or by sending a messenger to reveal by His permission whatever He wills. He is All-High, All-Wise. – Surah Ash-Shura 42:51
وَمَا كَانَ لِبَشَرٍ أَن يُكَلِّمَهُ ٱللَّهُ إِلَّا وَحْيًا أَوْ مِن وَرَآئِ حِجَابٍ أَوْ يُرْسِلَ رَسُولًا فَيُوحِىَ بِإِذْنِهِۦ مَا يَشَآءُ ۚ إِنَّهُۥ عَلِىٌّ حَكِيمٌ

Not at all. On that Day, they will be screened from their Lord. Surah Al-Mutaffifin 83:15
كَلَّآ إِنَّهُمْ عَن رَّبِّهِمْ يَوْمَئِذٍ لَّمَحْجُوبُونَ

Al-Hamu
الحمو

Narrated `Uqba bin 'Amir: Allah's Messenger ﷺ said, "Beware of entering upon the ladies." A man from the Ansar said, "Allah's Apostle! What about Al-Hamu the in-laws of the wife (the brothers of her husband or his nephews etc.)?" The Prophet ﷺ replied: The in-laws of the wife are death itself. – Sahih al-Bukhari 5232
حَدَّثَنَا قُتَيْبَةُ بْنُ سَعِيدٍ، حَدَّثَنَا لَيْثٌ، عَنْ يَزِيدَ بْنِ أَبِي حَبِيبٍ، عَنْ أَبِي الْخَيْرِ، عَنْ عُقْبَةَ بْنِ عَامِرٍ، أَنَّ رَسُولَ اللَّهِ صلى الله عليه وسلم قَالَ " إِيَّاكُمْ وَالدُّخُولَ عَلَى النِّسَاءِ ". فَقَالَ رَجُلٌ مِنَ الأَنْصَارِ يَا رَسُولَ اللَّهِ أَفَرَأَيْتَ الْحَمْوَ. قَالَ " الْحَمْوُ الْمَوْتُ

And say to the female believers to cast down their be holdings, and preserve their private parts, and not display their adornment except such as is outward, and let them fix (Literally: strike) closely their veils over their bosoms, and not display their adornment except to their husbands, or their fathers, or their husbands' fathers, or their sons, or their husbands' sons, or their brothers, or their brothers's sons, or their sisters' sons, or their women, or what their right hands possess, or (male) followers, men without desire (Literally: without being endowed with "sexual" desire) or young children who have not yet attained knowledge of women's privacies, and they should not strike their legs (i.e., stamp their feet) so that whatever adornment they hide may be known. And repent to Allah altogether, (O) you believers, that possibly you would prosper. Surah An-Nur 24:31

وَقُل لِّلْمُؤْمِنَٰتِ يَغْضُضْنَ مِنْ أَبْصَٰرِهِنَّ وَيَحْفَظْنَ فُرُوجَهُنَّ وَلَا يُبْدِينَ زِينَتَهُنَّ إِلَّا مَا ظَهَرَ مِنْهَا ۖ وَلْيَضْرِبْنَ بِخُمُرِهِنَّ عَلَىٰ جُيُوبِهِنَّ ۖ وَلَا يُبْدِينَ زِينَتَهُنَّ إِلَّا لِبُعُولَتِهِنَّ أَوْ ءَابَآئِهِنَّ أَوْ ءَابَآءِ بُعُولَتِهِنَّ أَوْ أَبْنَآئِهِنَّ أَوْ أَبْنَآءِ بُعُولَتِهِنَّ أَوْ إِخْوَٰنِهِنَّ أَوْ بَنِىٓ إِخْوَٰنِهِنَّ أَوْ بَنِىٓ أَخَوَٰتِهِنَّ أَوْ نِسَآئِهِنَّ أَوْ مَا مَلَكَتْ أَيْمَٰنُهُنَّ أَوِ ٱلتَّٰبِعِينَ غَيْرِ أُوْلِى ٱلْإِرْبَةِ مِنَ ٱلرِّجَالِ أَوِ ٱلطِّفْلِ ٱلَّذِينَ لَمْ يَظْهَرُوا۟ عَلَىٰ عَوْرَٰتِ ٱلنِّسَآءِ ۖ وَلَا يَضْرِبْنَ بِأَرْجُلِهِنَّ لِيُعْلَمَ مَا يُخْفِينَ مِن زِينَتِهِنَّ ۚ وَتُوبُوٓا۟ إِلَى ٱللَّهِ جَمِيعًا أَيُّهَ ٱلْمُؤْمِنُونَ لَعَلَّكُمْ تُفْلِحُونَ

Uqbah bin Amir narrated that The Messenger of Allah said: "Beware of entering upon women." So a man from the Ansar said: '"O Messenger of Allah! What do you think about Hamu? So he said: "The Hamu is death." – Jami` at-Tirmidhi 1171

حَدَّثَنَا قُتَيْبَةُ، حَدَّثَنَا اللَّيْثُ، عَنْ يَزِيدَ بْنِ أَبِي حَبِيبٍ، عَنْ أَبِي الْخَيْرِ، عَنْ عُقْبَةَ بْنِ عَامِرٍ، أَنَّ رَسُولَ اللَّهِ صلى الله عليه وسلم قَالَ " إِيَّاكُمْ وَالدُّخُولَ عَلَى النِّسَاءِ " . فَقَالَ رَجُلٌ مِنَ الأَنْصَارِ يَا رَسُولَ اللَّهِ أَفَرَأَيْتَ الْحَمْوَ قَالَ " الْحَمْوُ الْمَوْتُ " . قَالَ وَفِي الْبَابِ عَنْ عُمَرَ وَجَابِرٍ وَعَمْرِو بْنِ الْعَاصِ . قَالَ أَبُو عِيسَى حَدِيثُ عُقْبَةَ بْنِ عَامِرٍ حَدِيثٌ حَسَنٌ صَحِيحٌ . وَإِنَّمَا مَعْنَى كَرَاهِيَةِ الدُّخُولِ عَلَى النِّسَاءِ عَلَى نَحْوِ مَا رُوِيَ عَنِ النَّبِيِّ صلى الله عليه وسلم قَالَ " لاَ يَخْلُوَنَّ رَجُلٌ بِامْرَأَةٍ إِلاَّ كَانَ ثَالِثَهُمَا الشَّيْطَانُ " . وَمَعْنَى قَوْلِهِ " الْحَمْوُ " . يُقَالُ هُوَ أَخُو الزَّوْجِ كَأَنَّهُ كَرِهَ لَهُ أَنْ يَخْلُوَ بِهَا .

The Book of
Eat of the lawful things that We have provided you with
كُلُوا۟ مِن طَيِّبَٰتِ مَا رَزَقْنَٰكُمْ

And eat of the lawful and good things Allah has provided for you; and be conscious of Allah, in whom you are believers. – Surah Al-Ma'idah 5:88

وَكُلُوا۟ مِمَّا رَزَقَكُمُ ٱللَّهُ حَلَٰلًا طَيِّبًا ۚ وَٱتَّقُوا۟ ٱللَّهَ ٱلَّذِىٓ أَنتُم بِهِۦ مُؤْمِنُونَ

We divided them into twelve tribal communities. And We inspired Moses, when his people asked him for something to drink: "Strike the rock with your staff." Whereupon twelve springs gushed from it. Each group recognized its drinking-place. And We shaded them with clouds, and We sent down upon them manna and quails: "Eat of the good things We have provided for you." They did not wrong Us, but they used to wrong their own selves. – Surah Al-A'raf 7:160

وَقَطَّعْنَٰهُمُ ٱثْنَتَىْ عَشْرَةَ أَسْبَاطًا أُمَمًا ۚ وَأَوْحَيْنَآ إِلَىٰ مُوسَىٰٓ إِذِ ٱسْتَسْقَىٰهُ قَوْمُهُۥٓ أَنِ ٱضْرِب بِّعَصَاكَ ٱلْحَجَرَ ۖ فَٱنۢبَجَسَتْ مِنْهُ ٱثْنَتَا عَشْرَةَ عَيْنًا ۖ قَدْ عَلِمَ كُلُّ أُنَاسٍ مَّشْرَبَهُمْ ۚ وَظَلَّلْنَا عَلَيْهِمُ ٱلْغَمَٰمَ وَأَنزَلْنَا عَلَيْهِمُ ٱلْمَنَّ وَٱلسَّلْوَىٰ ۖ كُلُوا۟ مِن طَيِّبَٰتِ مَا رَزَقْنَٰكُمْ ۚ وَمَا ظَلَمُونَا وَلَٰكِن كَانُوٓا۟ أَنفُسَهُمْ يَظْلِمُونَ

O you who believe! Eat of the good things We have provided for you, and give thanks to Allah, if it is Him that you serve. – Surah Al-Baqarah 2:172

يَٰٓأَيُّهَا ٱلَّذِينَ ءَامَنُوا۟ كُلُوا۟ مِن طَيِّبَٰتِ مَا رَزَقْنَٰكُمْ وَٱشْكُرُوا۟ لِلَّهِ إِن كُنتُمْ إِيَّاهُ تَعْبُدُونَ

O people! Eat of what is lawful and good on earth, and do not follow the footsteps of Satan. He is to you an open enemy. – Surah Al-Baqarah 2:168

يَٰٓأَيُّهَا ٱلنَّاسُ كُلُوا۟ مِمَّا فِى ٱلْأَرْضِ حَلَٰلًا طَيِّبًا وَلَا تَتَّبِعُوا۟ خُطُوَٰتِ ٱلشَّيْطَٰنِ ۚ إِنَّهُۥ لَكُمْ عَدُوٌّ مُّبِينٌ

Eat of the lawful and good things Allah has provided for you, and be thankful for Allah's blessings, if it is Him that you serve. – Surah An-Nahl 16:114

فَكُلُوا۟ مِمَّا رَزَقَكُمُ ٱللَّهُ حَلَٰلًا طَيِّبًا وَٱشْكُرُوا۟ نِعْمَتَ ٱللَّهِ إِن كُنتُمْ إِيَّاهُ تَعْبُدُونَ

It is He Who sends down for you from the sky water. From it is drink, and with it grows vegetation for grazing. - Surah An-Nahl 16:10

هُوَ ٱلَّذِىٓ أَنزَلَ مِنَ ٱلسَّمَآءِ مَآءً ۖ لَّكُم مِّنْهُ شَرَابٌ وَمِنْهُ شَجَرٌ فِيهِ تُسِيمُونَ

And set on it lofty mountains, and given you pure water to drink? – Surah Al-Mursalaat 77:27

وَجَعَلْنَا فِيهَا رَوَٰسِىَ شَٰمِخَٰتٍ وَأَسْقَيْنَٰكُم مَّآءً فُرَاتًا

So, let (man) look into his food (For) that We poured water in abundance, (Literally: with abundant pouring Thereafter We clove the earth in fissures, (Literally: in cloven "fissures") So, therein We caused (the) grain to grow And vines, and clover, (Or: reeds) And olives and palm trees And enclosed orchards with dense trees And fruits, and grass, (Or: fodder An enjoyment for you and your cattle (includes cattle, camels, sheep and goats) – Surah 'Abasa 80:24-32

فَلْيَنظُرِ الْإِنسَانُ إِلَىٰ طَعَامِهِ أَنَّا صَبَبْنَا الْمَاءَ صَبًّا ثُمَّ شَقَقْنَا الْأَرْضَ شَقًّا فَأَنبَتْنَا فِيهَا حَبًّا وَعِنَبًا وَقَضْبًا وَزَيْتُونًا وَنَخْلًا وَحَدَائِقَ غُلْبًا وَفَاكِهَةً وَأَبًّا مَّتَاعًا لَّكُمْ وَلِأَنْعَامِكُمْ

And after that, the earth: wide has He spread its expanse and has caused its waters to come out of it, and its pastures and has made the mountains firm [all this] as a means of livelihood for you and your animals – Surah An'Nazi'at 79:30-33
وَالْأَرْضَ بَعْدَ ذَٰلِكَ دَحَاهَا أَخْرَجَ مِنْهَا مَاءَهَا وَمَرْعَاهَا وَالْجِبَالَ أَرْسَاهَا مَتَاعًا لَّكُمْ وَلِأَنْعَامِكُمْ

And We shaded you with clouds, and We sent down to you manna and quails: "Eat of the good things We have provided for you." They did not wrong Us, but they used to wrong their own souls. – Surah Al-Baqarah 2:57
وَظَلَّلْنَا عَلَيْكُمُ ٱلْغَمَامَ وَأَنزَلْنَا عَلَيْكُمُ ٱلْمَنَّ وَٱلسَّلْوَىٰ ۖ كُلُوا۟ مِن طَيِّبَٰتِ مَا رَزَقْنَٰكُمْ ۖ وَمَا ظَلَمُونَا وَلَٰكِن كَانُوٓا۟ أَنفُسَهُمْ يَظْلِمُونَ

Narrated Abu Huraira: Allah's Messenger ﷺ was presented with two cups one containing wine and the other milk on the night of his night journey at Jerusalem. He looked at it and took the milk. Gabriel said, "Thanks to Allah Who guided you to the Fitra (i.e. Islam); if you had taken the wine, your followers would have gone astray. – Sahih Al-Bukhari 4709
حَدَّثَنَا عَبْدَانُ، حَدَّثَنَا عَبْدُ اللَّهِ، أَخْبَرَنَا يُونُسُ، ح وَحَدَّثَنَا أَحْمَدُ بْنُ صَالِحٍ، حَدَّثَنَا عَنْبَسَةُ، حَدَّثَنَا يُونُسُ، عَنِ ابْنِ شِهَابٍ، قَالَ ابْنُ الْمُسَيَّبِ قَالَ أَبُو هُرَيْرَةَ أُتِيَ رَسُولُ اللَّهِ صلى الله عليه وسلم لَيْلَةَ أُسْرِيَ بِهِ بِإِيلِيَاءَ بِقَدَحَيْنِ مِنْ خَمْرٍ وَلَبَنٍ، فَنَظَرَ إِلَيْهِمَا فَأَخَذَ اللَّبَنَ قَالَ جِبْرِيلُ الْحَمْدُ لِلَّهِ الَّذِي هَدَاكَ لِلْفِطْرَةِ، لَوْ أَخَذْتَ الْخَمْرَ غَوَتْ أُمَّتُكَ

The Prophet ﷺ added: I was raised to the Lote Tree and saw four rivers, two of which were coming out and two going in. Those which were coming out were the Nile and the Euphrates, and those which were going in were two rivers in paradise. Then I was given three bowls, one containing milk, and another containing honey, and a third containing wine. I took the bowl containing milk and drank it. It was said to me, "You and your followers will be on the right path (of Islam).". – Sahih Al-Bukhari 5610
وَقَالَ إِبْرَاهِيمُ بْنُ طَهْمَانَ عَنْ شُعْبَةَ، عَنْ قَتَادَةَ، عَنْ أَنَسِ بْنِ مَالِكٍ، قَالَ قَالَ رَسُولُ اللَّهِ صلى الله عليه وسلم " رُفِعْتُ إِلَى السِّدْرَةِ فَإِذَا أَرْبَعَةُ أَنْهَارٍ، نَهَرَانِ ظَاهِرَانِ، وَنَهَرَانِ بَاطِنَانِ، فَأَمَّا الظَّاهِرَانِ النِّيلُ وَالْفُرَاتُ، وَأَمَّا الْبَاطِنَانِ فَنَهَرَانِ فِي الْجَنَّةِ فَأُتِيتُ بِثَلاَثَةِ أَقْدَاحٍ، قَدَحٌ فِيهِ لَبَنٌ، وَقَدَحٌ فِيهِ عَسَلٌ، وَقَدَحٌ فِيهِ خَمْرٌ، فَأَخَذْتُ الَّذِي فِيهِ اللَّبَنُ فَشَرِبْتُ فَقِيلَ لِي أَصَبْتَ الْفِطْرَةَ أَنْتَ وَأُمَّتُكَ ". قَالَ هِشَامٌ وَسَعِيدٌ وَهَمَّامٌ عَنْ قَتَادَةَ عَنْ أَنَسِ بْنِ مَالِكٍ عَنْ مَالِكِ بْنِ صَعْصَعَةَ عَنِ النَّبِيِّ صلى الله عليه وسلم فِي الأَنْهَارِ نَحْوَهُ، وَلَمْ يَذْكُرُوا ثَلاَثَةَ أَقْدَاحٍ

Narrated Abu Tha`laba Al-Khushani: I said, "O Allah's Prophet! We are living in a land ruled by the people of the Scripture; Can we take our meals in their utensils? In that land there is plenty of game and I hunt the game with my bow and with my hound that is not trained and with my trained hound. Then what is lawful for me to eat?" He said, "As for what you have mentioned about the people of the Scripture, if you can get utensils other than theirs, do not eat out of theirs, but if you cannot get other than theirs, wash their utensils and eat out of It. If you hunt an animal with your bow after mentioning Allah's Name, eat of it. And if you hunt something with your trained hound after mentioning Allah's Name, eat of it, and if you hunt something with your untrained hound (and get it before it dies) and slaughter it, eat of It.". – Sahih Al-Bukhari 5478
حَدَّثَنَا عَبْدُ اللَّهِ بْنُ يَزِيدَ، حَدَّثَنَا حَيْوَةُ، قَالَ أَخْبَرَنِي رَبِيعَةُ بْنُ يَزِيدَ الدِّمَشْقِيُّ، عَنْ أَبِي إِدْرِيسَ، عَنْ أَبِي ثَعْلَبَةَ الْخُشَنِيِّ، قَالَ قُلْتُ يَا نَبِيَّ اللَّهِ إِنَّا بِأَرْضِ قَوْمٍ أَهْلِ الْكِتَابِ، أَفَنَأْكُلُ فِي آنِيَتِهِمْ وَبِأَرْضِ صَيْدٍ، أَصِيدُ بِقَوْسِي وَبِكَلْبِي الَّذِي لَيْسَ بِمُعَلَّمٍ، وَبِكَلْبِي الْمُعَلَّمِ، فَمَا يَصْلُحُ لِي قَالَ " أَمَّا مَا ذَكَرْتَ مِنْ أَهْلِ الْكِتَابِ فَإِنْ وَجَدْتُمْ غَيْرَهَا فَلاَ تَأْكُلُوا فِيهَا، وَإِنْ لَمْ تَجِدُوا فَاغْسِلُوهَا وَكُلُوا فِيهَا، وَمَا صِدْتَ بِقَوْسِكَ فَذَكَرْتَ اسْمَ اللَّهِ فَكُلْ، وَمَا صِدْتَ بِكَلْبِكَ الْمُعَلَّمِ فَذَكَرْتَ اسْمَ اللَّهِ فَكُلْ، وَمَا صِدْتَ بِكَلْبِكَ غَيْرَ مُعَلَّمٍ فَأَدْرَكْتَ ذَكَاتَهُ فَكُلْ ".

Narrated `Aisha: The Prophet ﷺ in his ailment in which he died, used to say, "O `Aisha! I still feel the pain caused by the food I ate at Khaibar, and at this time, I feel as if my aorta is being cut from that poison.". – Sahih Al-Bukhari 4428

وَقَالَ يُونُسُ عَنِ الزُّهْرِيِّ، قَالَ عُرْوَةُ قَالَتْ عَائِشَةُ ـ رضى الله عنها ـ كَانَ النَّبِيُّ صلى الله عليه وسلم يَقُولُ فِي مَرَضِهِ الَّذِي مَاتَ فِيهِ " يَا عَائِشَةُ مَا أَزَالُ أَجِدُ أَلَمَ الطَّعَامِ الَّذِي أَكَلْتُ بِخَيْبَرَ، فَهَذَا أَوَانُ وَجَدْتُ انْقِطَاعَ أَبْهَرِي مِنْ ذَلِكَ السَّمِّ"

Narrated Abaya bin Rifaa: My grandfather, Rafi` said, "We were in the company of the Prophet ﷺ at DhulHulaifa, and the people suffered from hunger. We got some camels and sheep (as booty) and the Prophet ﷺ was still behind the people. They hurried and put the cooking pots on the fire. (When he came) he ordered that the cooking pots should be upset and then he distributed the booty (amongst the people) regarding ten sheep as equal to one camel then a camel fled and the people chased it till they got tired, as they had a few horses (for chasing it). So a man threw an arrow at it and caused it to stop (with Allah's Permission). On that the Prophet ﷺ said, 'Some of these animals behave like wild beasts, so, if any animal flee from you, deal with it in the same way." My grandfather asked (the Prophet ﷺ), "We hope (or are afraid) that we may meet the enemy tomorrow and we have no knives. Can we slaughter our animals with canes?" Allah's Messenger ﷺ replied, "If the instrument used for killing causes the animal to bleed profusely and if Allah's Name is mentioned on killing it, then eat its meat (i.e. it is lawful) but won't use a tooth or a nail and I am telling you the reason: A tooth is a bone (and slaughtering with a bone is forbidden), and a nail is the slaughtering instrument of the Ethiopians.". – Sahih al-Bukhari 3075

حَدَّثَنَا مُوسَى بْنُ إِسْمَاعِيلَ، حَدَّثَنَا أَبُو عَوَانَةَ، عَنْ سَعِيدِ بْنِ مَسْرُوقٍ، عَنْ عَبَايَةَ بْنِ رِفَاعَةَ، عَنْ جَدِّهِ، رَافِعٍ قَالَ كُنَّا مَعَ النَّبِيِّ صلى الله عليه وسلم بِذِي الْحُلَيْفَةِ، فَأَصَابَ النَّاسَ جُوعٌ وَأَصَبْنَا إِبِلاً وَغَنَمًا، وَكَانَ النَّبِيُّ صلى الله عليه وسلم فِي أُخْرَيَاتِ النَّاسِ، فَعَجِلُوا فَنَصَبُوا الْقُدُورَ، فَأَمَرَ بِالْقُدُورِ فَأُكْفِئَتْ، ثُمَّ قَسَمَ فَعَدَلَ عَشَرَةً مِنَ الْغَنَمِ بِبَعِيرٍ، فَنَدَّ مِنْهَا بَعِيرٌ، وَفِي الْقَوْمِ خَيْلٌ يَسِيرٌ فَطَلَبُوهُ فَأَعْيَاهُمْ، فَأَهْوَى إِلَيْهِ رَجُلٌ بِسَهْمٍ، فَحَبَسَهُ اللَّهُ فَقَالَ " هَذِهِ الْبَهَائِمُ لَهَا أَوَابِدُ كَأَوَابِدِ الْوَحْشِ، فَمَا نَدَّ عَلَيْكُمْ فَاصْنَعُوا بِهِ هَكَذَا ". فَقَالَ جَدِّي إِنَّا نَرْجُو ـ أَوْ نَخَافُ ـ أَنْ نَلْقَى الْعَدُوَّ غَدًا وَلَيْسَ مَعَنَا مُدًى، أَفَنَذْبَحُ بِالْقَصَبِ فَقَالَ " مَا أَنْهَرَ الدَّمَ وَذُكِرَ اسْمُ اللَّهِ فَكُلْ، لَيْسَ السِّنَّ وَالظُّفُرَ، وَسَأُحَدِّثُكُمْ عَنْ ذَلِكَ، أَمَّا السِّنُّ فَعَظْمٌ، وَأَمَّا الظُّفُرُ فَمُدَى الْحَبَشَةِ "

Narrated Abaya bin Rifaa: My grandfather, Rafi` bin Khadij said, "We were in the valley of Dhul-Hulaifa of Tuhama in the company of the Prophet ﷺ and had some camels and sheep (of the booty). The people hurried (in slaughtering the animals) and put their meat in the pots and started cooking. Allah's Messenger ﷺ came and ordered them to upset the pots, and distributed the booty considering one camel as equal to ten sheep. One of the camels fled and the people had only a few horses, so they got worried. (The camel was chased and) a man slopped the camel by throwing an arrow at it. Allah's Messenger ﷺ said, 'Some of these animals are untamed like wild animals, so if anyone of them went out of your control, then you should treat it as you have done now.' " My grandfather said, "O Allah's Messenger ﷺ! We fear that we may meet our enemy tomorrow and we have no knives, could we slaughter the animals with reeds?" The Prophet ﷺ said, "Yes, or you can use what would make blood flow (slaughter) and you can eat what is slaughtered and the Name of Allah is mentioned at the time of slaughtering. But don't use teeth or fingernails (in slaughtering). I will tell you why, as for teeth, they are bones, and fingernails are used by Ethiopians for slaughtering. (See Hadith 668). – Sahih al-Bukhari 2507

حَدَّثَنَا مُحَمَّدٌ، أَخْبَرَنَا وَكِيعٌ، عَنْ سُفْيَانَ، عَنْ أَبِيهِ، عَنْ عَبَايَةَ بْنِ رِفَاعَةَ، عَنْ جَدِّهِ، رَافِعِ بْنِ خَدِيجٍ ـ رضى الله عنه ـ قَالَ كُنَّا مَعَ النَّبِيِّ صلى الله عليه وسلم بِذِي الْحُلَيْفَةِ مِنْ تِهَامَةَ، فَأَصَبْنَا غَنَمًا وَإِبِلاً، فَعَجِلَ الْقَوْمُ، فَأَغْلَوْا بِهَا الْقُدُورَ، فَجَاءَ رَسُولُ اللَّهِ صلى الله عليه وسلم فَأَمَرَ بِهَا فَأُكْفِئَتْ، ثُمَّ عَدَلَ عَشْرًا مِنَ الْغَنَمِ بِجَزُورٍ، ثُمَّ إِنَّ بَعِيرًا نَدَّ وَلَيْسَ فِي الْقَوْمِ إِلاَّ خَيْلٌ يَسِيرَةٌ فَرَمَاهُ رَجُلٌ فَحَبَسَهُ بِسَهْمٍ، فَقَالَ رَسُولُ اللَّهِ صلى الله عليه وسلم " إِنَّ لِهَذِهِ الْبَهَائِمِ أَوَابِدَ كَأَوَابِدِ الْوَحْشِ، فَمَا غَلَبَكُمْ مِنْهَا فَاصْنَعُوا بِهِ هَكَذَا ". قَالَ قَالَ جَدِّي يَا رَسُولَ اللَّهِ إِنَّا نَرْجُو ـ أَوْ نَخَافُ ـ أَنْ نَلْقَى الْعَدُوَّ غَدًا وَلَيْسَ مَعَنَا مُدًى، فَنَذْبَحُ

بِالْقَصَبِ فَقَالَ " اعْجَلْ أَوْ أَرْنِي، مَا أَنْهَرَ الدَّمَ وَذُكِرَ اسْمُ اللَّهِ عَلَيْهِ فَكُلُوا، لَيْسَ السِّنَّ وَالظُّفُرَ، وَسَأُحَدِّثُكُمْ عَنْ ذَلِكَ، أَمَّا السِّنُّ فَعَظْمٌ، وَأَمَّا الظُّفُرُ فَمُدَى الْحَبَشَةِ "

Narrated Abu Tha`laba Al-Khushani: I came to Allah's Messenger ﷺ and said, "O Allah's Messenger ﷺ! We are living in the land of the people of the Scripture and we take our meals in their utensils, and in the land there is game and I hunt with my bow and trained or untrained hounds; please tell me what is lawful for us of that." He said, "As for your saying that you are living in the land of the people of the Scripture and that you eat in their utensils, if you can get utensils other than theirs, do not eat in their utensils, but if you do not find (other than theirs), then wash their utensils and eat in them. As for your saying that you are in the land of game, if you hung something with your bow, and have mentioned Allah's Name while hunting, then you can eat (the game). And if you hunt something with your trained hound, and have mentioned Allah's Name on sending it for hunting then you can eat (the game). But if you hunt something with your untrained hound and you were able to slaughter it before its death, you can eat of it.". – Sahih Al-Bukhari 5488

حَدَّثَنَا أَبُو عَاصِمٍ، عَنْ حَيْوَةَ، . وَحَدَّثَنِي أَحْمَدُ بْنُ أَبِي رَجَاءٍ، حَدَّثَنَا سَلَمَةُ بْنُ سُلَيْمَانَ، عَنِ ابْنِ الْمُبَارَكِ، عَنْ حَيْوَةَ بْنِ شُرَيْحٍ، قَالَ سَمِعْتُ رَبِيعَةَ بْنَ يَزِيدَ الدِّمَشْقِيَّ، قَالَ أَخْبَرَنِي أَبُو إِدْرِيسَ، عَائِذُ اللَّهِ قَالَ سَمِعْتُ أَبَا ثَعْلَبَةَ الْخُشَنِيَّ ـ رضى الله عنه ـ يَقُولُ أَتَيْتُ رَسُولَ اللَّهِ صلى الله عليه وسلم فَقُلْتُ يَا رَسُولَ اللَّهِ إِنَّا بِأَرْضِ قَوْمٍ أَهْلِ الْكِتَابِ، نَأْكُلُ فِي آنِيَتِهِمْ، وَأَرْضِ صَيْدٍ أَصِيدُ بِقَوْسِي، وَأَصِيدُ بِكَلْبِي الْمُعَلَّمِ، وَالَّذِي لَيْسَ مُعَلَّمًا، فَأَخْبِرْنِي مَا الَّذِي يَحِلُّ لَنَا مِنْ ذَلِكَ فَقَالَ " أَمَّا مَا ذَكَرْتَ أَنَّكَ بِأَرْضِ قَوْمٍ أَهْلِ الْكِتَابِ، تَأْكُلُ فِي آنِيَتِهِمْ، فَإِنْ وَجَدْتُمْ غَيْرَ آنِيَتِهِمْ، فَلاَ تَأْكُلُوا فِيهَا، وَإِنْ لَمْ تَجِدُوا فَاغْسِلُوهَا ثُمَّ كُلُوا فِيهَا، وَأَمَّا مَا ذَكَرْتَ أَنَّكَ بِأَرْضِ صَيْدٍ، فَمَا صِدْتَ بِقَوْسِكَ، فَاذْكُرِ اسْمَ اللَّهِ، ثُمَّ كُلْ، وَمَا صِدْتَ بِكَلْبِكَ الْمُعَلَّمِ، فَاذْكُرِ اسْمَ اللَّهِ، ثُمَّ كُلْ، وَمَا صِدْتَ بِكَلْبِكَ الَّذِي لَيْسَ مُعَلَّمًا فَأَدْرَكْتَ ذَكَاتَهُ، فَكُلْ ".

Narrated `Amr: I said to Jabir bin Zaid, "The people claim that Allah's Messenger ﷺ forbade the eating of donkey's meat." He said, "Al-Hakam bin `Amr Al-Ghifari used to say so when he was with us, but Ibn `Abbas, the great religious learned man, refused to give a final verdict and recited:-- 'Say: I find not in that which has been inspired to me anything forbidden to be eaten by one who wishes to eat it, unless it be carrion, blood poured forth or the flesh of swine...' (6.145). – Sahih al-Bukhari 5529

حَدَّثَنَا عَلِيُّ بْنُ عَبْدِ اللَّهِ، حَدَّثَنَا سُفْيَانُ، قَالَ عَمْرٌو قُلْتُ لِجَابِرِ بْنِ زَيْدٍ يَزْعُمُونَ أَنَّ رَسُولَ اللَّهِ صلى الله عليه وسلم نَهَى عَنْ حُمُرِ الأَهْلِيَّةِ فَقَالَ قَدْ كَانَ يَقُولُ ذَاكَ الْحَكَمُ بْنُ عَمْرٍو الْغِفَارِيُّ عِنْدَنَا بِالْبَصْرَةِ، وَلَكِنْ أَبَى ذَاكَ الْبَحْرُ ابْنُ عَبَّاسٍ وَقَرَأَ {قُلْ لاَ أَجِدُ فِيمَا أُوحِيَ إِلَيَّ مُحَرَّمًا}

The Prophet ﷺ never took his meals at a dining table
مَا أَكَلَ النَّبِيُّ صلى الله عليه وسلم عَلَى خِوَانٍ

Narrated Anas bin Malik: The Prophet ﷺ never took his meals at a dining table, nor in small plates, and he never ate thin wellbaked bread. (The sub-narrator asked Qatada, "Over what did they use to take their meals?" Qatada said, "On leather dining sheets." - Sahih al-Bukhari 5415

حَدَّثَنَا عَبْدُ اللَّهِ بْنُ أَبِي الأَسْوَدِ، حَدَّثَنَا مُعَاذٌ، حَدَّثَنِي أَبِي، عَنْ يُونُسَ، عَنْ قَتَادَةَ، عَنْ أَنَسِ بْنِ مَالِكٍ، قَالَ مَا أَكَلَ النَّبِيُّ صلى الله عليه وسلم عَلَى خِوَانٍ، وَلاَ فِي سُكْرُجَةٍ، وَلاَ خُبِزَ لَهُ مُرَقَّقٌ. قُلْتُ لِقَتَادَةَ عَلَى مَا يَأْكُلُونَ قَالَ عَلَى السُّفَرِ

Narrated Anas: The Prophet ﷺ halted to consummate his marriage with Safiyya. I invited the Muslims to his wedding banquet. He ordered that leather dining sheets be spread. Then dates, dried yoghurt and butter were put on those sheets. Anas added: The Prophet ﷺ

consummated his marriage with Safiyya (during a journey) whereupon Hais (sweet dish) was served on a leather dining sheet. – Sahih al-Bukhari 5387

حَدَّثَنَا ابْنُ أَبِي مَرْيَمَ، أَخْبَرَنَا مُحَمَّدُ بْنُ جَعْفَرٍ، أَخْبَرَنِي حُمَيْدٌ، أَنَّهُ سَمِعَ أَنَسًا، يَقُولُ قَامَ النَّبِيُّ صلى الله عليه وسلم يَبْنِي بِصَفِيَّةَ فَدَعَوْتُ الْمُسْلِمِينَ إِلَى وَلِيمَتِهِ أَمَرَ بِالأَنْطَاعِ فَبُسِطَتْ فَأُلْقِيَ عَلَيْهَا التَّمْرُ وَالأَقِطُ وَالسَّمْنُ. وَقَالَ عَمْرٌو عَنْ أَنَسٍ بَنَى بِهَا النَّبِيُّ صلى الله عليه وسلم ثُمَّ صَنَعَ حَيْسًا فِي نِطَعٍ.

Narrated Ibn `Abbas: That his aunt, Um Hufaid bint Al-Harith bin Hazn, presented to the Prophet ﷺ butter, dried yoghurt and mastigures. The Prophet ﷺ invited the people to those mastigures and they were eaten on his dining sheet, but the Prophet ﷺ did not eat of it, as if he disliked it. Nevertheless. If it was unlawful to eat that, the people would not have eaten it on the dining sheet of the Prophet ﷺ nor would he have ordered that they be eaten. – Sahih al-Bukhari 5389

حَدَّثَنَا أَبُو النُّعْمَانِ، حَدَّثَنَا أَبُو عَوَانَةَ، عَنْ أَبِي بِشْرٍ، عَنْ سَعِيدِ بْنِ جُبَيْرٍ، عَنِ ابْنِ عَبَّاسٍ، أَنَّ أُمَّ حُفَيْدٍ بِنْتَ الْحَارِثِ بْنِ حَزْنٍ ـ خَالَةَ ابْنِ عَبَّاسٍ ـ أَهْدَتْ إِلَى النَّبِيِّ صلى الله عليه وسلم سَمْنًا وَأَقِطًا وَأَضُبًّا، فَدَعَا بِهِنَّ فَأُكِلْنَ عَلَى مَائِدَتِهِ، وَتَرَكَهُنَّ النَّبِيُّ صلى الله عليه وسلم كَالْمُسْتَقْذِرِ لَهُنَّ، وَلَوْ كُنَّ حَرَامًا مَا أُكِلْنَ عَلَى مَائِدَةِ النَّبِيِّ صلى الله عليه وسلم وَلاَ أَمَرَ بِأَكْلِهِنَّ

Utensils
آنِيَةِ

Narrated Ibn `Abbas: "Once a delegation of `Abdul Qais came to Allah's Messenger ﷺ and said, "We belong to such and such branch of the tribe of Rabi'ah and we can only come to you in the sacred months. Order us to do something good so that we may take it from you and also invite to it those whom we have left behind (at home)." So he said, "I order you to do four things and forbid you from four things: To believe in Allah" – and then he explained it to them "to testify that none has the right to be worshipped but Allah and that I am Allah's Messenger ﷺ , to establish the prayers (at the stated times), to pay the Zakat (obligatory charity), to hand me the Khumus (fifth) if you acquire spoils of war. And I forbid from (using) Dubba, Hantam, Muqaiyyar, and Naqir (all these were utensils used for the preparation of alcoholic drinks). – Sahih al-Bukhari 523

حَدَّثَنَا قُتَيْبَةُ بْنُ سَعِيدٍ، قَالَ حَدَّثَنَا عَبَّادٌ ـ هُوَ ابْنُ عَبَّادٍ ـ عَنْ أَبِي جَمْرَةَ، عَنِ ابْنِ عَبَّاسٍ، قَالَ قَدِمَ وَفْدُ عَبْدِ الْقَيْسِ عَلَى رَسُولِ اللَّهِ صلى الله عليه وسلم فَقَالُوا إِنَّا مِنْ هَذَا الْحَىِّ مِنْ رَبِيعَةَ، وَلَسْنَا نَصِلُ إِلَيْكَ إِلاَّ فِي الشَّهْرِ الْحَرَامِ، فَمُرْنَا بِشَىْءٍ نَأْخُذْهُ عَنْكَ، وَنَدْعُو إِلَيْهِ مَنْ وَرَاءَنَا. فَقَالَ " آمُرُكُمْ بِأَرْبَعٍ، وَأَنْهَاكُمْ عَنْ أَرْبَعٍ الإِيمَانِ بِاللَّهِ ـ ثُمَّ فَسَّرَهَا لَهُمْ شَهَادَةُ أَنْ لاَ إِلَهَ إِلاَّ اللَّهُ، وَأَنِّي رَسُولُ اللَّهِ، وَإِقَامُ الصَّلاَةِ، وَإِيتَاءُ الزَّكَاةِ، وَأَنْ تُؤَدُّوا إِلَىَّ خُمُسَ مَا غَنِمْتُمْ، وَأَنْهَى عَنِ الدُّبَّاءِ وَالْحَنْتَمِ وَالْمُقَيَّرِ وَالنَّقِيرِ ".

Narrated Abu Qatada: Allah's Messenger ﷺ said, "Whenever anyone of you drinks water, he should not breathe in the drinking utensil, and whenever anyone of you goes to a lavatory, he should neither touch his penis nor clean his private parts with his right hand." – Sahih al-Bukhari 153

حَدَّثَنَا مُعَاذُ بْنُ فَضَالَةَ، قَالَ حَدَّثَنَا هِشَامٌ ـ هُوَ الدَّسْتَوَائِيُّ ـ عَنْ يَحْيَى بْنِ أَبِي كَثِيرٍ، عَنْ عَبْدِ اللَّهِ بْنِ أَبِي قَتَادَةَ، عَنْ أَبِيهِ، قَالَ قَالَ رَسُولُ اللَّهِ صلى الله عليه وسلم " إِذَا شَرِبَ أَحَدُكُمْ فَلاَ يَتَنَفَّسْ فِي الإِنَاءِ، وَإِذَا أَتَى الْخَلاَءَ فَلاَ يَمَسَّ ذَكَرَهُ بِيَمِينِهِ، وَلاَ يَتَمَسَّحْ بِيَمِينِهِ

Narrated Jabir bin `Abdullah: Allah's Messenger ﷺ said, "(At bedtime) cover the utensils, close the doors, and put out the lights, lest the evil creature (the rat) should pull away the wick and thus burn the people of the house." – Sahih al-Bukhari 6295

حَدَّثَنَا قُتَيْبَةُ، حَدَّثَنَا حَمَّادٌ، عَنْ كَثِيرٍ، عَنْ عَطَاءٍ، عَنْ جَابِرِ بْنِ عَبْدِ اللَّهِ ـ رضى الله عنهما ـ قَالَ قَالَ رَسُولُ اللَّهِ صلى الله عليه وسلم " خَمِّرُوا الآنِيَةَ وَأَجِيفُوا الأَبْوَابَ، وَأَطْفِئُوا الْمَصَابِيحَ، فَإِنَّ الْفُوَيْسِقَةَ رُبَّمَا جَرَّتِ الْفَتِيلَةَ فَأَحْرَقَتْ أَهْلَ الْبَيْتِ ".

Narrated Hudhaifa: The Prophet ﷺ said, "Do not drink in gold or silver utensils, and do not wear clothes of silk or Dibaj, for these things are for them (unbelievers) in this world and for you in the Hereafter." – Sahih al-Bukhari 5633

حَدَّثَنَا مُحَمَّدُ بْنُ الْمُثَنَّى، حَدَّثَنَا ابْنُ أَبِي عَدِيٍّ، عَنِ ابْنِ عَوْنٍ، عَنْ مُجَاهِدٍ، عَنِ ابْنِ أَبِي لَيْلَى، قَالَ خَرَجْنَا مَعَ حُذَيْفَةَ وَذَكَرَ النَّبِيَّ صلى الله عليه وسلم قَالَ " لاَ تَشْرَبُوا فِي آنِيَةِ الذَّهَبِ وَالْفِضَّةِ، وَلاَ تَلْبَسُوا الْحَرِيرَ وَالدِّيبَاجَ، فَإِنَّهَا لَهُمْ فِي الدُّنْيَا وَلَكُمْ فِي الآخِرَةِ "

Narrated Um Salama: (the wife of the Prophet) Allah's Messenger ﷺ said, "He who drinks in silver utensils is only filling his `Abdomen with Hell Fire.". – Sahih al-Bukhari 5634

حَدَّثَنَا إِسْمَاعِيلُ، قَالَ حَدَّثَنِي مَالِكُ بْنُ أَنَسٍ، عَنْ نَافِعٍ، عَنْ زَيْدِ بْنِ عَبْدِ اللَّهِ بْنِ عُمَرَ، عَنْ عَبْدِ اللَّهِ بْنِ عَبْدِ الرَّحْمَنِ بْنِ أَبِي بَكْرٍ الصِّدِّيقِ، عَنْ أُمِّ سَلَمَةَ، زَوْجِ النَّبِيِّ صلى الله عليه وسلم أَنَّ رَسُولَ اللَّهِ صلى الله عليه وسلم قَالَ " الَّذِي يَشْرَبُ فِي إِنَاءِ الْفِضَّةِ إِنَّمَا يُجَرْجِرُ فِي بَطْنِهِ نَارَ جَهَنَّمَ ".

Narrated Jabir: The Prophet ﷺ said, "When nightfalls, then keep your children close to you, for the devil spread out then. An hour later you can let them free; and close the gates of your house (at night), and mention Allah's Name thereupon, and cover your utensils, and mention Allah's Name thereupon, (and if you don't have something to cover your utensil) you may put across it something (e.g. a piece of wood etc.). – Sahih al-Bukhari 3280

حَدَّثَنَا يَحْيَى بْنُ جَعْفَرٍ، حَدَّثَنَا مُحَمَّدُ بْنُ عَبْدِ اللَّهِ الأَنْصَارِيُّ، حَدَّثَنَا ابْنُ جُرَيْجٍ، قَالَ أَخْبَرَنِي عَطَاءٌ، عَنْ جَابِرٍ ـ رضى الله عنه ـ عَنِ النَّبِيِّ صلى الله عليه وسلم قَالَ " إِذَا اسْتَجْنَحَ {اللَّيْلُ} ـ أَوْ كَانَ جُنْحُ اللَّيْلِ ـ فَكُفُّوا صِبْيَانَكُمْ، فَإِنَّ الشَّيَاطِينَ تَنْتَشِرُ حِينَئِذٍ، فَإِذَا ذَهَبَ سَاعَةٌ مِنَ الْعِشَاءِ فَخَلُّوهُمْ وَأَغْلِقْ بَابَكَ، وَاذْكُرِ اسْمَ اللَّهِ، وَأَطْفِئْ مِصْبَاحَكَ، وَاذْكُرِ اسْمَ اللَّهِ، وَأَوْكِ سِقَاءَكَ، وَاذْكُرِ اسْمَ اللَّهِ، وَخَمِّرْ إِنَاءَكَ، وَاذْكُرِ اسْمَ اللَّهِ، وَلَوْ تَعْرُضُ عَلَيْهِ شَيْئًا ".

they eat like cattle eat
كَمَا تَأْكُلُ ٱلْأَنْعَٰمُ

...... those who disbelieved, who enjoyed themselves, and eat like cattle eat, the Fire will be their final dwelling. – Surah Muhammad 47:12

....وَٱلَّذِينَ كَفَرُوا۟ يَتَمَتَّعُونَ وَيَأْكُلُونَ كَمَا تَأْكُلُ ٱلْأَنْعَٰمُ وَٱلنَّارُ مَثْوًى لَّهُمْ

Narrated Ibn `Abbas: Allah's Messenger ﷺ drank milk, rinsed his mouth and said, "It has fat." - Sahih al-Bukhari 211

حَدَّثَنَا يَحْيَى بْنُ بُكَيْرٍ، وَقُتَيْبَةُ، قَالاَ حَدَّثَنَا اللَّيْثُ، عَنْ عُقَيْلٍ، عَنِ ابْنِ شِهَابٍ، عَنْ عُبَيْدِ اللَّهِ بْنِ عَبْدِ اللَّهِ بْنِ عُتْبَةَ، عَنِ ابْنِ عَبَّاسٍ، أَنَّ رَسُولَ اللَّهِ صلى الله عليه وسلم شَرِبَ لَبَنًا، فَمَضْمَضَ وَقَالَ " إِنَّ لَهُ دَسَمًا "

Narrated `Aisha: The Prophet ﷺ died when we had satisfied our hunger with the two black things, i.e. dates and water. – Sahih al-Bukhari 5383

حَدَّثَنَا مُسْلِمٌ، حَدَّثَنَا وُهَيْبٌ، حَدَّثَنَا مَنْصُورٌ، عَنْ أُمِّهِ، عَنْ عَائِشَةَ ـ رضى الله عنها ـ تُوُفِّيَ النَّبِيُّ صلى الله عليه وسلم حِينَ شَبِعْنَا مِنَ الأَسْوَدَيْنِ التَّمْرِ وَالْمَاءِ.

Narrated Anas: To the best of my knowledge, the Prophet ﷺ did not take his meals in a big tray at all, nor did he ever eat well-baked thin bread, nor did he ever eat at a dining table. – Sahih Al-Bukhari 5386

حَدَّثَنَا عَلِيُّ بْنُ عَبْدِ اللَّهِ، حَدَّثَنَا مُعَاذُ بْنُ هِشَامٍ، قَالَ حَدَّثَنِي أَبِي، عَنْ يُونُسَ ـ قَالَ عَلِيٌّ هُوَ الإِسْكَافُ ـ عَنْ قَتَادَةَ، عَنْ أَنَسٍ، رضى الله عنه قَالَ مَا عَلِمْتُ النَّبِيَّ صلى الله عليه وسلم أَكَلَ عَلَى سُكُرُّجَةٍ قَطُّ، وَلاَ خُبِزَ لَهُ مُرَقَّقٌ قَطُّ، وَلاَ أَكَلَ عَلَى خِوَانٍ. قِيلَ لِقَتَادَةَ فَعَلَى مَا كَانُوا يَأْكُلُونَ قَالَ عَلَى السُّفَرِ

Narrated Abu Huraira: The people used to say, “Abu Huraira narrates too many narrations.” In fact I used to keep close to Allah’s Messenger and was satisfied with what filled my stomach. I ate no leavened bread and dressed no decorated striped clothes, and never did a man or a woman serve me, and I often used to press my belly against gravel because of hunger, and I used to ask a man to recite a Qur’anic Verse to me although I knew it, so that he would take me to his home and feed me. And the most generous of all the people to the poor was Ja`far bin Abi Talib. He used to take us to his home and offer us what was available therein. He would even offer us an empty folded leather container (of butter) which we would split and lick whatever was in it. – Sahih al-Bukhari 3708

حَدَّثَنَا أَحْمَدُ بْنُ أَبِي بَكْرٍ، حَدَّثَنَا مُحَمَّدُ بْنُ إِبْرَاهِيمَ بْنِ دِينَارٍ أَبُو عَبْدِ اللَّهِ الْجُهَنِيُّ، عَنِ ابْنِ أَبِي ذِئْبٍ، عَنْ سَعِيدٍ الْمَقْبُرِيِّ، عَنْ أَبِي هُرَيْرَةَ ـ رضى الله عنه ـ أَنَّ النَّاسَ، كَانُوا يَقُولُونَ أَكْثَرَ أَبُو هُرَيْرَةَ. وَإِنِّي كُنْتُ أَلْزَمُ رَسُولَ اللَّهِ صلى الله عليه وسلم بِشِبَعِ بَطْنِي، حَتَّى لاَ آكُلُ الْخَمِيرَ، وَلاَ أَلْبَسُ الْحَبِيرَ، وَلاَ يَخْدُمُنِي فُلاَنٌ وَلاَ فُلاَنَةُ، وَكُنْتُ أُلْصِقُ بَطْنِي بِالْحَصْبَاءِ مِنَ الْجُوعِ، وَإِنْ كُنْتُ لأَسْتَقْرِئُ الرَّجُلَ الآيَةَ هِيَ مَعِي كَىْ يَنْقَلِبَ بِي فَيُطْعِمَنِي، وَكَانَ أَخْيَرَ النَّاسِ لِلْمِسْكِينِ جَعْفَرُ بْنُ أَبِي طَالِبٍ، كَانَ يَنْقَلِبُ بِنَا فَيُطْعِمُنَا مَا كَانَ فِي بَيْتِهِ، حَتَّى إِنْ كَانَ لَيُخْرِجُ إِلَيْنَا الْعُكَّةَ الَّتِي لَيْسَ فِيهَا شَىْءٌ، فَنَشُقُّهَا فَنَلْعَقُ مَا فِيهَا

The Book of
Allah has sent down the best of narrations
ٱللَّهُ نَزَّلَ أَحۡسَنَ ٱلۡحَدِيثِ

And of mankind is he who purchases idle talks (i.e.music, singing, etc.) to mislead (men) from the Path of Allah without knowledge, and takes it (the Path of Allah, the Verses of the Qur'an) by way of mockery. For such there will be a humiliating torment (in the Hell-fire). – Surah Luqman 31:6
وَمِنَ ٱلنَّاسِ مَن يَشۡتَرِى لَهۡوَ ٱلۡحَدِيثِ لِيُضِلَّ عَن سَبِيلِ ٱللَّهِ بِغَيۡرِ عِلۡمٍ وَيَتَّخِذَهَا هُزُوًاۚ أُوْلَـٰٓئِكَ لَهُمۡ عَذَابٌ مُّهِينٌ

And as for the poets—the deviators follow them. – Surah Ash-Shu'ara 26:224
وَٱلشُّعَرَآءُ يَتَّبِعُهُمُ ٱلۡغَاوُۥنَ

And He has already been sending down upon you in the Book that, "When you hear the signs of Allah being disbelieved and mocked at, then do not sit with them until they wade into (i.e., take up "a subject") (some) other discourse; surely (in that case) you are like them. Surely Allah will be gathering the hypocrites and the disbelievers altogether in Hell. – Surah An-Nisa 4:140
وَقَدۡ نَزَّلَ عَلَيۡكُمۡ فِي ٱلۡكِتَـٰبِ أَنۡ إِذَا سَمِعۡتُمۡ ءَايَـٰتِ ٱللَّهِ يُكۡفَرُ بِهَا وَيُسۡتَهۡزَأُ بِهَا فَلَا تَقۡعُدُواْ مَعَهُمۡ حَتَّىٰ يَخُوضُواْ فِى حَدِيثٍ غَيۡرِهِۦٓ إِنَّكُمۡ إِذًا مِّثۡلُهُمۡۗ إِنَّ ٱللَّهَ جَامِعُ ٱلۡمُنَـٰفِقِينَ وَٱلۡكَـٰفِرِينَ فِى جَهَنَّمَ جَمِيعًا

Constant listeners to lies, constant eaters of illicit gain, so in case they come to you, then judge between them or veer away from them; and in case you veer away from them, then they will never harm you anything; and in case you judge, then judge with equity between them. Surely Allah loves the equitable. – Surah Al-Ma'idah 5:42
سَمَّـٰعُونَ لِلۡكَذِبِ أَكَّـٰلُونَ لِلسُّحۡتِۚ فَإِن جَآءُوكَ فَٱحۡكُم بَيۡنَهُمۡ أَوۡ أَعۡرِضۡ عَنۡهُمۡۖ وَإِن تُعۡرِضۡ عَنۡهُمۡ فَلَن يَضُرُّوكَ شَيۡـًٔاۖ وَإِنۡ حَكَمۡتَ فَٱحۡكُم بَيۡنَهُم بِٱلۡقِسۡطِۚ إِنَّ ٱللَّهَ يُحِبُّ ٱلۡمُقۡسِطِينَ

Whenever you encounter those who speak with disrespect about Our revelations, turn away from them until they move on to another topic, and if Satan should ever cause you to forget, then do not remain with those unjust people after realizing what they are doing. – Surah Al-An'am 6:68
وَإِذَا رَأَيۡتَ ٱلَّذِينَ يَخُوضُونَ فِىٓ ءَايَـٰتِنَا فَأَعۡرِضۡ عَنۡهُمۡ حَتَّىٰ يَخُوضُواْ فِى حَدِيثٍ غَيۡرِهِۦۚ وَإِمَّا يُنسِيَنَّكَ ٱلشَّيۡطَـٰنُ فَلَا تَقۡعُدۡ بَعۡدَ ٱلذِّكۡرَىٰ مَعَ ٱلۡقَوۡمِ ٱلظَّـٰلِمِينَ

And do not pursue what you have no knowledge of; surely hearing and beholding and heart-sight, (Or: perception) all of those will be questioned of. – Surah Al-Isra 17:36
وَلَا تَقۡفُ مَا لَيۡسَ لَكَ بِهِۦ عِلۡمٌۚ إِنَّ ٱلسَّمۡعَ وَٱلۡبَصَرَ وَٱلۡفُؤَادَ كُلُّ أُوْلَـٰٓئِكَ كَانَ عَنۡهُ مَسۡـُٔولًا

Allah has sent down fairest discourse as a Book, of similar signs (and) oft-repeated, (literally: doubly fair) whereat shiver the skins of the ones who are apprehensive of their Lord; thereafter their skins and their hearts soften to the Remembrance of Allah. That is the guidance of Allah whereby He guides whomever He decides; and whomever Allah leads into error, then in no way will he have any guide. – Surah Az-Zumar 39:23
ٱللَّهُ نَزَّلَ أَحۡسَنَ ٱلۡحَدِيثِ كِتَـٰبًا مُّتَشَـٰبِهًا مَّثَانِىَ تَقۡشَعِرُّ مِنۡهُ جُلُودُ ٱلَّذِينَ يَخۡشَوۡنَ رَبَّهُمۡ ثُمَّ تَلِينُ جُلُودُهُمۡ وَقُلُوبُهُمۡ إِلَىٰ ذِكۡرِ ٱللَّهِۚ ذَٰلِكَ هُدَى ٱللَّهِ يَهۡدِى بِهِۦ مَن يَشَآءُۚ وَمَن يُضۡلِلِ ٱللَّهُ فَمَا لَهُۥ مِنۡ هَادٍ

Narrated `Abdullah: The Prophetﷺ got the date palm trees of the tribe of Bani-An-Nadir burnt and the trees cut down at a place called Al-Buwaira . Hassan bin Thabit said in a poetic verse: "The chiefs of Bani Lu'ai found it easy to watch fire spreading at Al-Buwaira.". – Sahih Al-Bukhari 2326

حَدَّثَنَا مُوسَى بْنُ إِسْمَاعِيلَ، حَدَّثَنَا جُوَيْرِيَةُ، عَنْ نَافِعٍ، عَنْ عَبْدِ اللَّهِ ـ رضى الله عنه ـ عَنِ النَّبِيِّ صلى الله عليه وسلم أَنَّهُ حَرَّقَ نَخْلَ بَنِي النَّضِيرِ وَقَطَعَ، وَهْىَ الْبُوَيْرَةُ، وَلَهَا يَقُولُ حَسَّانُ وَهَانَ عَلَى سَرَاةِ بَنِي لُؤَىٍّ حَرِيقٌ بِالْبُوَيْرَةِ مُسْتَطِيرٌ

Narrated Anas: When the Prophetﷺ arrived Medina he dismounted at `Awali-i-Medina amongst a tribe called Banu `Amr bin `Auf. He stayed there For fourteen nights. Then he sent for Bani An-Najjar and they came armed with their swords. As if I am looking (just now) as the Prophetﷺ was sitting over his Rahila (Mount) with Abu Bakr riding behind him and all Banu An-Najjar around him till he dismounted at the courtyard of Abu Aiyub's house. The Prophetﷺ loved to pray wherever the time for the prayer was due even at sheep-folds. Later on he ordered that a mosque should be built and sent for some people of Banu-An-Najjar and said, "O Banu An-Najjar! Suggest to me the price of this (walled) piece of land of yours." They replied, "No! By Allah! We do not demand its price except from Allah." Anas added: There were graves of pagans in it and some of it was unleveled and there were some date-palm trees in it. The Prophetﷺ ordered that the graves of the pagans be dug out and the unleveled land be level led and the date-palm trees be cut down . (So all that was done). They aligned these cut date-palm trees towards the Qibla of the mosque (as a wall) and they also built two stone side-walls (of the mosque). His companions brought the stones while reciting some poetic verses. The Prophetﷺ was with them and he kept on saying, "There is no goodness except that of the Hereafter, O Allah! So please forgive the Ansars and the emigrants. ". – Sahih Al-Bukhari 428

حَدَّثَنَا مُسَدَّدٌ، قَالَ حَدَّثَنَا عَبْدُ الْوَارِثِ، عَنْ أَبِي التَّيَّاحِ، عَنْ أَنَسٍ، قَالَ قَدِمَ النَّبِيُّ صلى الله عليه وسلم الْمَدِينَةَ فَنَزَلَ أَعْلَى الْمَدِينَةِ، فِي حَىٍّ يُقَالُ لَهُمْ بَنُو عَمْرِو بْنِ عَوْفٍ. فَأَقَامَ النَّبِيُّ صلى الله عليه وسلم فِيهِمْ أَرْبَعَ عَشْرَةَ لَيْلَةً، ثُمَّ أَرْسَلَ إِلَى بَنِي النَّجَّارِ فَجَاءُوا مُتَقَلِّدِي السُّيُوفِ، كَأَنِّي أَنْظُرُ إِلَى النَّبِيِّ صلى الله عليه وسلم عَلَى رَاحِلَتِهِ، وَأَبُو بَكْرٍ رِدْفُهُ، وَمَلأُ بَنِي النَّجَّارِ حَوْلَهُ، حَتَّى أَلْقَى بِفِنَاءِ أَبِي أَيُّوبَ، وَكَانَ يُحِبُّ أَنْ يُصَلِّيَ حَيْثُ أَدْرَكَتْهُ الصَّلاَةُ، وَيُصَلِّي فِي مَرَابِضِ الْغَنَمِ، وَأَنَّهُ أَمَرَ بِبِنَاءِ الْمَسْجِدِ، فَأَرْسَلَ إِلَى مَلإٍ مِنْ بَنِي النَّجَّارِ فَقَالَ " يَا بَنِي النَّجَّارِ ثَامِنُونِي بِحَائِطِكُمْ هَذَا ". قَالُوا لاَ وَاللَّهِ، لاَ نَطْلُبُ ثَمَنَهُ إِلاَّ إِلَى اللَّهِ. فَقَالَ أَنَسٌ فَكَانَ فِيهِ مَا أَقُولُ لَكُمْ، قُبُورُ الْمُشْرِكِينَ، وَفِيهِ خَرِبٌ، وَفِيهِ نَخْلٌ، فَأَمَرَ النَّبِيُّ صلى الله عليه وسلم بِقُبُورِ الْمُشْرِكِينَ فَنُبِشَتْ، ثُمَّ بِالْخَرِبِ فَسُوِّيَتْ، وَبِالنَّخْلِ فَقُطِعَ، فَصَفُّوا النَّخْلَ قِبْلَةَ الْمَسْجِدِ، وَجَعَلُوا عِضَادَتَيْهِ الْحِجَارَةَ، وَجَعَلُوا يَنْقُلُونَ الصَّخْرَ، وَهُمْ يَرْتَجِزُونَ، وَالنَّبِيُّ صلى الله عليه وسلم مَعَهُمْ وَهُوَ يَقُولُ " اللَّهُمَّ لاَ خَيْرَ إِلاَّ خَيْرُ الآخِرَهْ فَاغْفِرْ لِلأَنْصَارِ وَالْمُهَاجِرَهْ."

Narrated Sa`id bin Al-Musaiyab: `Umar came to the Mosque while Hassan was reciting a poem. (`Umar disapproved of that). On that Hassan said, "I used to recite poetry in this very Mosque in the presence of one (i.e. the Prophetﷺ) who was better than you." Then he turned towards Abu Huraira and said (to him), "I ask you by Allah, did you hear Allah's Messengerﷺ saying (to me), "Retort on my behalf. O Allah! Support him (i.e. Hassan) with the Holy Spirit?" Abu Huraira said, "Yes.". – Sahih Al-Bukhari 3212

حَدَّثَنَا عَلِيُّ بْنُ عَبْدِ اللَّهِ، حَدَّثَنَا سُفْيَانُ، حَدَّثَنَا الزُّهْرِيُّ، عَنْ سَعِيدِ بْنِ الْمُسَيَّبِ، قَالَ مَرَّ عُمَرُ فِي الْمَسْجِدِ وَحَسَّانُ يُنْشِدُ، فَقَالَ كُنْتُ أُنْشِدُ فِيهِ وَفِيهِ مَنْ هُوَ خَيْرٌ مِنْكَ، ثُمَّ الْتَفَتَ إِلَى أَبِي هُرَيْرَةَ فَقَالَ أَنْشُدُكَ بِاللَّهِ، أَسَمِعْتَ رَسُولَ اللَّهِ صلى الله عليه وسلم يَقُولُ " أَجِبْ عَنِّي، اللَّهُمَّ أَيِّدْهُ بِرُوحِ الْقُدُسِ ". قَالَ نَعَمْ

Narrated Abu Huraira: Allah's Messengerﷺ sent a Sariya of ten men as spies under the leadership of `Asim bin Thabit al-Ansari, the grandfather of `Asim bin `Umar Al-Khattab. They proceeded till they reached Hadaa, a place between 'Usfan, and Mecca, and their news reached a branch of the tribe of Hudhail called Bani Lihyan. About two-hundred men, who were all archers, hurried to follow their tracks till they found the place where they had eaten dates they had brought with them from Medina. They said, "These are the dates of Yathrib (i.e. Medina), "and continued following their tracks When `Asim and his companions saw their pursuers, they went up a high place and the infidels circled them. The infidels said to them, "Come down and surrender, and we promise and guarantee you that we will not kill any one of you" `Asim bin Thabit; the leader of the Sariya said, "By Allah! I will not come down to be under the protection of infidels. O Allah! Convey our news to Your Prophet. Then the infidels threw arrows at them till they martyred `Asim along with six other men, and three men came down accepting their promise and convention, and they were Khubaib-al-Ansari and Ibn Dathina and another man So, when the infidels captured them, they undid the strings of their bows and tied them. Then the third (of the captives) said, "This is the first betrayal. By Allah! I will not go with you. No doubt these, namely the martyred, have set a good example to us." So, they dragged him and tried to compel him to accompany them, but as he refused, they killed him. They took Khubaid and Ibn Dathina with them and sold them (as slaves) in Mecca (and all that took place) after the battle of Badr. Khubaib was bought by the sons of Al-Harith bin 'Amir bin Naufal bin `Abd Manaf. It was Khubaib who had killed Al-Harith bin 'Amir on the day (of the battle of) Badr. So, Khubaib remained a prisoner with those people. Narrated Az-Zuhri: 'Ubaidullah bin 'Iyyad said that the daughter of Al-Harith had told him, "When those people gathered (to kill Khubaib) he borrowed a razor from me to shave his pubes and I gave it to him. Then he took a son of mine while I was unaware when he came upon him. I saw him placing my son on his thigh and the razor was in his hand. I got scared so much that Khubaib noticed the agitation on my face and said, 'Are you afraid that I will kill him? No, I will never do so.' By Allah, I never saw a prisoner better than Khubaib. By Allah, one day I saw him eating of a bunch of grapes in his hand while he was chained in irons, and there was no fruit at that time in Mecca." The daughter of Al-Harith used to say, "It was a boon Allah bestowed upon Khubaib." When they took him out of the Sanctuary (of Mecca) to kill him outside its boundaries, Khubaib requested them to let him offer two rak`at (prayer). They allowed him and he offered Two rak`at and then said, "Hadn't I been afraid that you would think that I was afraid (of being killed), I would have prolonged the prayer. O Allah, kill them all with no exception." (He then recited the poetic verse):-- "I being martyred as a Muslim, Do not mind how I am killed in Allah's Cause, For my killing is for Allah's Sake, And if Allah wishes, He will bless the amputated parts of a torn body" Then the son of Al Harith killed him. So, it was Khubaib who set the tradition for any Muslim sentenced to death in captivity, to offer a two-rak`at prayer (before being killed). Allah fulfilled the invocation of `Asim bin Thabit on that very day on which he was martyred. The Prophet ﷺ informed his companions of their news and what had happened to them. Later on when some infidels from Quraish were informed that `Asim had been killed, they sent some people to fetch a part of his body (i.e. his head) by which he would be recognized. (That was because) `Asim had killed one of their chiefs on the day (of the battle) of Badr. So, a swarm of wasps, resembling a shady cloud, were sent to hover over `Asim and protect him from their messenger and thus they could not cut off anything from his flesh. – Sahih Al-Bukhari 3045

حَدَّثَنَا أَبُو الْيَمَانِ، أَخْبَرَنَا شُعَيْبٌ، عَنِ الزُّهْرِيِّ، قَالَ أَخْبَرَنِي عَمْرُو بْنُ أَبِي سُفْيَانَ بْنِ أَسِيدِ بْنِ جَارِيَةَ الثَّقَفِيُّ ـ وَهْوَ حَلِيفٌ لِبَنِي زُهْرَةَ وَكَانَ مِنْ أَصْحَابِ أَبِي هُرَيْرَةَ ـ أَنَّ أَبَا هُرَيْرَةَ ـ رضى الله عنه ـ قَالَ بَعَثَ رَسُولُ اللَّهِ صلى الله عليه وسلم عَشَرَةَ رَهْطٍ سَرِيَّةً عَيْنًا، وَأَمَّرَ عَلَيْهِمْ عَاصِمَ بْنَ ثَابِتٍ الأَنْصَارِيَّ جَدَّ عَاصِمِ بْنِ عُمَرَ، فَانْطَلَقُوا حَتَّى إِذَا كَانُوا بِالْهَدَأَةِ وَهْوَ بَيْنَ عُسْفَانَ وَمَكَّةَ ذُكِرُوا لِحَىٍّ مِنْ هُذَيْلٍ يُقَالُ لَهُمْ بَنُو لِحْيَانَ، فَنَفَرُوا لَهُمْ قَرِيبًا مِنْ مِائَتَىْ رَجُلٍ، كُلُّهُمْ رَامٍ، فَاقْتَصُّوا آثَارَهُمْ حَتَّى وَجَدُوا مَأْكَلَهُمْ تَمْرًا تَزَوَّدُوهُ مِنَ الْمَدِينَةِ فَقَالُوا هَذَا تَمْرُ يَثْرِبَ. فَاقْتَصُّوا آثَارَهُمْ، فَلَمَّا رَآهُمْ عَاصِمٌ وَأَصْحَابُهُ لَجَئُوا إِلَى فَدْفَدٍ، وَأَحَاطَ بِهِمُ الْقَوْمُ فَقَالُوا لَهُمُ انْزِلُوا وَأَعْطُونَا بِأَيْدِيكُمْ، وَلَكُمُ الْعَهْدُ وَالْمِيثَاقُ، وَلاَ نَقْتُلُ مِنْكُمْ أَحَدًا. قَالَ عَاصِمُ بْنُ ثَابِتٍ أَمِيرُ السَّرِيَّةِ أَمَّا أَنَا فَوَاللَّهِ لاَ أَنْزِلُ الْيَوْمَ فِي ذِمَّةِ كَافِرٍ، اللَّهُمَّ أَخْبِرْ عَنَّا نَبِيَّكَ. فَرَمَوْهُمْ بِالنَّبْلِ، فَقَتَلُوا عَاصِمًا فِي سَبْعَةٍ،

فَنَزَلَ إِلَيْهِمْ ثَلاَثَةُ رَهْطٍ بِالْعَهْدِ وَالْمِيثَاقِ، مِنْهُمْ خُبَيْبٌ الأَنْصَارِيُّ وَابْنُ دَثِنَةَ وَرَجُلٌ آخَرُ، فَلَمَّا اسْتَمْكَنُوا مِنْهُمْ أَطْلَقُوا أَوْتَارَ قِسِيِّهِمْ فَأَوْثَقُوهُمْ فَقَالَ الرَّجُلُ الثَّالِثُ هَذَا أَوَّلُ الْغَدْرِ، وَاللَّهِ لاَ أَصْحَبُكُمْ، إِنَّ فِي هَؤُلاَءِ لأُسْوَةً. يُرِيدُ الْقَتْلَى، فَجَرَّرُوهُ وَعَالَجُوهُ عَلَى أَنْ يَصْحَبَهُمْ فَأَبَى فَقَتَلُوهُ، فَانْطَلَقُوا بِخُبَيْبٍ وَابْنِ دَثِنَةَ حَتَّى بَاعُوهُمَا بِمَكَّةَ بَعْدَ وَقْعَةِ بَدْرٍ، فَابْتَاعَ خُبَيْبًا بَنُو الْحَارِثِ بْنِ عَامِرِ بْنِ نَوْفَلِ بْنِ عَبْدِ مَنَافٍ، وَكَانَ خُبَيْبٌ هُوَ قَتَلَ الْحَارِثَ بْنَ عَامِرٍ يَوْمَ بَدْرٍ، فَلَبِثَ خُبَيْبٌ عِنْدَهُمْ أَسِيرًا، فَأَخْبَرَنِي عُبَيْدُ اللَّهِ بْنُ عِيَاضٍ أَنَّ بِنْتَ الْحَارِثِ أَخْبَرَتْهُ أَنَّهُمْ حِينَ اجْتَمَعُوا اسْتَعَارَ مِنْهَا مُوسَى يَسْتَحِدُّ بِهَا فَأَعَارَتْهُ، فَأَخَذَ ابْنًا لِي وَأَنَا غَافِلَةٌ حِينَ أَتَاهُ قَالَتْ فَوَجَدْتُهُ مُجْلِسَهُ عَلَى فَخِذِهِ وَالْمُوسَى بِيَدِهِ، فَفَزِعْتُ فَزْعَةً عَرَفَهَا خُبَيْبٌ فِي وَجْهِي فَقَالَ تَخْشَيْنَ أَنْ أَقْتُلَهُ مَا كُنْتُ لأَفْعَلَ ذَلِكَ. وَاللَّهِ مَا رَأَيْتُ أَسِيرًا قَطُّ خَيْرًا مِنْ خُبَيْبٍ، وَاللَّهِ لَقَدْ وَجَدْتُهُ يَوْمًا يَأْكُلُ مِنْ قِطْفِ عِنَبٍ فِي يَدِهِ، وَإِنَّهُ لَمُوثَقٌ فِي الْحَدِيدِ، وَمَا بِمَكَّةَ مِنْ ثَمَرٍ وَكَانَتْ تَقُولُ إِنَّهُ لَرِزْقٌ مِنَ اللَّهِ رَزَقَهُ خُبَيْبًا، فَلَمَّا خَرَجُوا مِنَ الْحَرَمِ لِيَقْتُلُوهُ فِي الْحِلِّ، قَالَ لَهُمْ خُبَيْبٌ ذَرُونِي أَرْكَعْ رَكْعَتَيْنِ. فَتَرَكُوهُ، فَرَكَعَ رَكْعَتَيْنِ ثُمَّ قَالَ لَوْلاَ أَنْ تَظُنُّوا أَنَّ مَا بِي جَزَعٌ لَطَوَّلْتُهَا اللَّهُمَّ أَحْصِهِمْ عَدَدًا. وَلَسْتُ أُبَالِي حِينَ أُقْتَلُ مُسْلِمًا عَلَى أَىِّ شِقٍّ كَانَ لِلَّهِ مَصْرَعِي وَذَلِكَ فِي ذَاتِ الإِلَهِ وَإِنْ يَشَأْ يُبَارِكْ عَلَى أَوْصَالِ شِلْوٍ مُمَزَّعِ فَقَتَلَهُ ابْنُ الْحَارِثِ، فَكَانَ خُبَيْبٌ هُوَ سَنَّ الرَّكْعَتَيْنِ لِكُلِّ امْرِئٍ مُسْلِمٍ قُتِلَ صَبْرًا، فَاسْتَجَابَ اللَّهُ لِعَاصِمِ بْنِ ثَابِتٍ يَوْمَ أُصِيبَ، فَأَخْبَرَ النَّبِيُّ صلى الله عليه وسلم أَصْحَابَهُ خَبَرَهُمْ وَمَا أُصِيبُوا، وَبَعَثَ نَاسٌ مِنْ كُفَّارِ قُرَيْشٍ إِلَى عَاصِمٍ حِينَ حُدِّثُوا أَنَّهُ قُتِلَ لِيُؤْتَوْا بِشَىْءٍ مِنْهُ يُعْرَفُ، وَكَانَ قَدْ قَتَلَ رَجُلاً مِنْ عُظَمَائِهِمْ يَوْمَ بَدْرٍ، فَبُعِثَ عَلَى عَاصِمٍ مِثْلُ الظُّلَّةِ مِنَ الدَّبْرِ، فَحَمَتْهُ مِنْ رَسُولِهِمْ، فَلَمْ يَقْدِرُوا عَلَى أَنْ يَقْطَعَ مِنْ لَحْمِهِ شَيْئًا

Narrated Al-Bara:bI saw Allah’s Messenger ﷺ on the day (of the battle) of the Trench carrying earth till the hair of his chest were covered with dust and he was a hairy man. He was reciting the following verses of `Abdullah (bin Rawaha): “O Allah, were it not for You, We would not have been guided, Nor would we have given in charity, nor prayed. So, bestow on us calmness, and when we meet the enemy. Then make our feet firm, for indeed, Yet if they want to put us in affliction, (i.e. want to fight against us) we would not (flee but withstand them).” The Prophet ﷺ used to raise his voice while reciting these verses. (See Hadith No. 432, Vol. 5). – Sahih Al-Bukhari 3034

حَدَّثَنَا مُسَدَّدٌ، حَدَّثَنَا أَبُو الأَحْوَصِ، حَدَّثَنَا أَبُو إِسْحَاقَ، عَنِ الْبَرَاءِ ـ رضى الله عنه ـ قَالَ رَأَيْتُ النَّبِيَّ صلى الله عليه وسلم يَوْمَ الْخَنْدَقِ وَهُوَ يَنْقُلُ التُّرَابَ حَتَّى وَارَى التُّرَابُ شَعَرَ صَدْرِهِ، وَكَانَ رَجُلاً كَثِيرَ الشَّعَرِ وَهْوَ يَرْتَجِزُ بِرَجَزِ عَبْدِ اللَّهِ اللَّهُمَّ لَوْلاَ أَنْتَ مَا اهْتَدَيْنَا وَلاَ تَصَدَّقْنَا وَلاَ صَلَّيْنَا فَأَنْزِلَنْ سَكِينَةً عَلَيْنَا وَثَبِّتِ الأَقْدَامَ إِنْ لاَقَيْنَا إِنَّ الأَعْدَاءَ قَدْ بَغَوْا عَلَيْنَا إِذَا أَرَادُوا فِتْنَةً أَبَيْنَا يَرْفَعُ بِهَا صَوْتَهُ

Narrated `Aisha: Once Hassan bin Thabit asked the permission of the Prophet ﷺ to lampoon (i.e. compose satirical poetry defaming) the infidels. The Prophet ﷺ said, “What about the fact that I have common descent with them?” Hassan replied, “I shall take you out of them as a hair is taken out of dough.” Narrated `Urwa: I started abusing Hassan in front of `Aisha, whereupon she said. “Don’t abuse him, for he used to defend the Prophet (with his poetry). – Sahih Al-Bukhari 3531

حَدَّثَنِي عُثْمَانُ بْنُ أَبِي شَيْبَةَ، حَدَّثَنَا عَبْدَةُ، عَنْ هِشَامٍ، عَنْ أَبِيهِ، عَنْ عَائِشَةَ ـ رضى الله عنها ـ قَالَتِ اسْتَأْذَنَ حَسَّانُ النَّبِيَّ صلى الله عليه وسلم فِي هِجَاءِ الْمُشْرِكِينَ، قَالَ " كَيْفَ بِنَسَبِي ". فَقَالَ حَسَّانُ لأَسُلَّنَّكَ مِنْهُمْ كَمَا تُسَلُّ الشَّعَرَةُ مِنَ الْعَجِينِ. وَعَنْ أَبِيهِ قَالَ ذَهَبْتُ أَسُبُّ حَسَّانَ عِنْدَ عَائِشَةَ فَقَالَتْ لاَ تَسُبُّهُ فَإِنَّهُ كَانَ يُنَافِحُ عَنِ النَّبِيِّ صلى الله عليه وسلم.

Narrated `Aisha: That during the Mina days, Abu Bakr came to her, while there where two girls with her, beating drums, and the Prophet ﷺ was (lying) covering himself with his garment. Abu Bakr rebuked the two girls, but the Prophet ﷺ uncovered his face and said, “O Abu Bakr! Leave them, for these are the days of Id (festival).” Those days were the days of Mina-. `Aisha added, “I was being screened by the Prophet ﷺ while I was watching the Ethiopians playing in the Mosque. `Umar rebuked them, but the Prophet ﷺ said, “Leave them, O Bani Arfida! Play. (for) you are safe.”. – Sahih Al-Bukhari 3529, 3530

حَدَّثَنَا يَحْيَى بْنُ بُكَيْرٍ، حَدَّثَنَا اللَّيْثُ، عَنْ عُقَيْلٍ، عَنِ ابْنِ شِهَابٍ، عَنْ عُرْوَةَ، عَنْ عَائِشَةَ، أَنَّ أَبَا بَكْرٍ ـ رضى الله عنه ـ دَخَلَ عَلَيْهَا وَعِنْدَهَا جَارِيَتَانِ فِي أَيَّامِ مِنًى تُدَفِّفَانِ وَتَضْرِبَانِ، وَالنَّبِيُّ صلى الله عليه وسلم مُتَغَشٍّ بِثَوْبِهِ، فَانْتَهَرَهُمَا أَبُو بَكْرٍ، فَكَشَفَ النَّبِيُّ صلى الله عليه وسلم عَنْ وَجْهِهِ، فَقَالَ " دَعْهُمَا يَا أَبَا بَكْرٍ، فَإِنَّهَا أَيَّامُ عِيدٍ، وَتِلْكَ الأَيَّامُ أَيَّامُ مِنًى ". وَقَالَتْ

عَائِشَةُ رَأَيْتُ النَّبِيَّ صلى الله عليه وسلم يَسْتُرُنِي، وَأَنَا أَنْظُرُ إِلَى الْحَبَشَةِ، وَهُمْ يَلْعَبُونَ فِي الْمَسْجِدِ فَزَجَرَهُمْ {عُمَرُ} فَقَالَ النَّبِيُّ صلى الله عليه وسلم " دَعْهُمْ أَمْنًا بَنِي أَرْفِدَةَ ". يَعْنِي مِنَ الأَمْنِ

Narrated Ar-Rubai bint Muauwidh: The Prophet ﷺ came to me the night my marriage was consummated and sat down on my bed as you (the sub-narrator) are sitting now, and small girls were beating the tambourine and singing in lamentation of my father who had been killed on the day of the battle of Badr. Then one of the girls said, "There is a Prophet amongst us who knows what will happen tomorrow." The Prophet ﷺ said (to her)," Do not say this, but go on saying what you have spoken before.". – Sahih Al-Bukhari 4001
حَدَّثَنَا عَلِيٌّ، حَدَّثَنَا بِشْرُ بْنُ الْمُفَضَّلِ، حَدَّثَنَا خَالِدُ بْنُ ذَكْوَانَ، عَنِ الرُّبَيِّعِ بِنْتِ مُعَوِّذٍ، قَالَتْ دَخَلَ عَلَىَّ النَّبِيُّ صلى الله عليه وسلم غَدَاةَ بُنِيَ عَلَىَّ، فَجَلَسَ عَلَى فِرَاشِي كَمَجْلِسِكَ مِنِّي، وَجُوَيْرِيَاتٌ يَضْرِبْنَ بِالدُّفِّ، يَنْدُبْنَ مَنْ قُتِلَ مِنْ آبَائِهِنَّ يَوْمَ بَدْرٍ حَتَّى قَالَتْ جَارِيَةٌ وَفِينَا نَبِيٌّ يَعْلَمُ مَا فِي غَدٍ. فَقَالَ النَّبِيُّ صلى الله عليه وسلم " لاَ تَقُولِي هَكَذَا، وَقُولِي مَا كُنْتِ تَقُولِينَ ".

Narrated Al-Bara: When it was the day of Al-Ahzab (i.e. the clans) and Allah's Messenger ﷺ dug the trench, I saw him carrying earth out of the trench till dust made the skin of his `Abdomen out of my sight and he was a hairy man. I heard him reciting the poetic verses composed by Ibn Rawaha while he was carrying the earth, "O Allah! Without You we would not have been guided, nor would we have given in charity, nor would we have prayed. So, (O Allah), please send Sakina (i.e. calmness) upon us and make our feet firm if we meet the enemy, as they have rebelled against us. And if they intend affliction (i.e. want to frighten us, and fight against us) then we would not (flee but withstand them)." The Prophet ﷺ would then prolong his voice at the last words. – Sahih Al-Bukhari 4106
حَدَّثَنِي أَحْمَدُ بْنُ عُثْمَانَ، حَدَّثَنَا شُرَيْحُ بْنُ مَسْلَمَةَ، قَالَ حَدَّثَنِي إِبْرَاهِيمُ بْنُ يُوسُفَ، قَالَ حَدَّثَنِي أَبِي، عَنْ أَبِي إِسْحَاقَ، قَالَ سَمِعْتُ الْبَرَاءَ، يُحَدِّثُ قَالَ لَمَّا كَانَ يَوْمُ الأَحْزَابِ، وَخَنْدَقَ رَسُولُ اللَّهِ صلى الله عليه وسلم رَأَيْتُهُ يَنْقُلُ مِنْ تُرَابِ الْخَنْدَقِ حَتَّى وَارَى عَنِّي الْغُبَارُ جِلْدَةَ بَطْنِهِ، وَكَانَ كَثِيرَ الشَّعَرِ، فَسَمِعْتُهُ يَرْتَجِزُ بِكَلِمَاتِ ابْنِ رَوَاحَةَ، وَهْوَ يَنْقُلُ مِنَ التُّرَابِ يَقُولُ اللَّهُمَّ لَوْلاَ أَنْتَ مَا اهْتَدَيْنَا وَلاَ تَصَدَّقْنَا وَلاَ صَلَّيْنَا فَأَنْزِلَنْ سَكِينَةً عَلَيْنَا وَثَبِّتِ الأَقْدَامَ إِنْ لاَقَيْنَا إِنَّ الأُلَى قَدْ بَغَوْا عَلَيْنَا وَإِنْ أَرَادُوا فِتْنَةً أَبَيْنَا قَالَ ثُمَّ يَمُدُّ صَوْتَهُ بِآخِرِهَا

Al-Bara' bin `Azib said (through another chain of sub-narrators): "On the day of Quraiza's (siege), Allah's Messenger ﷺ said to Hassan bin Thabit, 'Abuse them (with your poems), and Jibril is with you.'". – Sahih Al-Bukhari 4124
وَزَادَ إِبْرَاهِيمُ بْنُ طَهْمَانَ عَنِ الشَّيْبَانِيِّ، عَنْ عَدِيِّ بْنِ ثَابِتٍ، عَنِ الْبَرَاءِ بْنِ عَازِبٍ، قَالَ رَسُولُ اللَّهِ صلى الله عليه وسلم يَوْمَ قُرَيْظَةَ لِحَسَّانَ بْنِ ثَابِتٍ " اهْجُ الْمُشْرِكِينَ، فَإِنَّ جِبْرِيلَ مَعَكَ ".

Narrated Salama bin Al-Akwa`: We went out to Khaibar in the company of the Prophet. While we were proceeding at night, a man from the group said to 'Amir, "O 'Amir! Won't you let us hear your poetry?" 'Amir was a poet, so he got down and started reciting for the people poetry that kept pace with the camels' footsteps, saying:-- "O Allah! Without You we Would not have been guided On the right path Neither would be have given In charity, nor would We have prayed. So please forgive us, what we have committed (i.e. our defects); let all of us Be sacrificed for Your Cause And send Sakina (i.e. calmness) Upon us to make our feet firm When we meet our enemy, and If they will call us towards An unjust thing, We will refuse. The infidels have made a hue and Cry to ask others' help Against us." The Prophet ﷺ on that, asked, "Who is that (camel) driver (reciting poetry)?" The people said, "He is 'Amir bin Al-Akwa`." Then the Prophet ﷺ said, "May Allah bestow His Mercy on him." A man amongst the people said, "O Allah's Prophet! Has (martyrdom) been granted to him. Would that you let us enjoy his company longer." Then we reached and besieged Khaibar till we were afflicted with severe hunger. Then Allah helped the Muslims conquer it (i.e. Khaibar). In the evening of the day of the conquest of the city, the Muslims made huge fires. The Prophet ﷺ said, "What are these fires? For cooking what, are you making the fire?" The people replied, "(For cooking) meat." He asked, "What kind of meat?" They (i.e. people) said, "The meat of donkeys." The Prophet ﷺ said, "Throw away the meat and break the pots!" Some man said, "O Allah's Messenger ﷺ! Shall we throw away the meat and wash the pots instead?" He said, "(Yes, you can do) that too." So when the army files were arranged in rows (for the clash), 'Amir's sword was short and he aimed at the leg of a Jew to strike it, but the sharp blade of the sword returned to him and injured his own knee, and that caused him to die. When they returned from the battle, Allah's Messenger ﷺ saw me (in a sad mood). He took my hand and said, "What is bothering you?" I replied, "Let my father and mother be sacrificed for you! The people say that the deeds of 'Amir are lost." The Prophet ﷺ said, "Whoever says so, is mistaken, for 'Amir has got a double reward." The Prophet raised two fingers and added, "He (i.e. Amir) was a persevering struggler in the Cause of Allah and there are few 'Arabs who achieved the like of (good deeds) 'Amir had done.". – Sahih Al-Bukhari 4196

حَدَّثَنَا عَبْدُ اللَّهِ بْنُ مَسْلَمَةَ، حَدَّثَنَا حَاتِمُ بْنُ إِسْمَاعِيلَ، عَنْ يَزِيدَ بْنِ أَبِي عُبَيْدٍ، عَنْ سَلَمَةَ بْنِ الأَكْوَعِ ـ رضى الله عنه ـ قَالَ خَرَجْنَا مَعَ النَّبِيِّ صلى الله عليه وسلم إِلَى خَيْبَرَ فَسِرْنَا لَيْلاً، فَقَالَ رَجُلٌ مِنَ الْقَوْمِ لِعَامِرٍ يَا عَامِرُ أَلاَ تُسْمِعُنَا مِنْ هُنَيْهَاتِكَ. وَكَانَ عَامِرٌ رَجُلاً شَاعِرًا فَنَزَلَ يَحْدُو بِالْقَوْمِ يَقُولُ: اللَّهُمَّ لَوْلاَ أَنْتَ مَا اهْتَدَيْنَا وَلاَ تَصَدَّقْنَا وَلاَ صَلَّيْنَا فَاغْفِرْ فِدَاءً لَكَ مَا أَبْقَيْنَا وَثَبِّتِ الأَقْدَامَ إِنْ لاَقَيْنَا وَأَلْقِيَنْ سَكِينَةً عَلَيْنَا إِنَّا إِذَا صِيحَ بِنَا أَبَيْنَا وَبِالصِّيَاحِ عَوَّلُوا عَلَيْنَا فَقَالَ رَسُولُ اللَّهِ صلى الله عليه وسلم " مَنْ هَذَا السَّائِقُ ". قَالُوا عَامِرُ بْنُ الأَكْوَعِ. قَالَ " يَرْحَمُهُ اللَّهُ ". قَالَ رَجُلٌ مِنَ الْقَوْمِ وَجَبَتْ يَا نَبِيَّ اللَّهِ، لَوْلاَ أَمْتَعْتَنَا بِهِ. فَأَتَيْنَا خَيْبَرَ، فَحَاصَرْنَاهُمْ حَتَّى أَصَابَتْنَا مَخْمَصَةٌ شَدِيدَةٌ، ثُمَّ إِنَّ اللَّهَ تَعَالَى فَتَحَهَا عَلَيْهِمْ، فَلَمَّا أَمْسَى النَّاسُ مَسَاءَ الْيَوْمِ الَّذِي فُتِحَتْ عَلَيْهِمْ أَوْقَدُوا نِيرَانًا كَثِيرَةً، فَقَالَ النَّبِيُّ صلى الله عليه وسلم " مَا هَذِهِ النِّيرَانُ عَلَى أَىِّ شَىْءٍ تُوقِدُونَ ". قَالُوا عَلَى لَحْمٍ. قَالَ " عَلَى أَىِّ لَحْمٍ ". قَالُوا لَحْمِ حُمُرِ الإِنْسِيَّةِ. قَالَ النَّبِيُّ صلى الله عليه وسلم " أَهْرِيقُوهَا وَاكْسِرُوهَا ". فَقَالَ رَجُلٌ يَا رَسُولَ اللَّهِ، أَوْ نُهَرِيقُهَا وَنَغْسِلُهَا قَالَ " أَوْ ذَاكَ ". فَلَمَّا تَصَافَّ الْقَوْمُ كَانَ سَيْفُ عَامِرٍ قَصِيرًا فَتَنَاوَلَ بِهِ سَاقَ يَهُودِيٍّ لِيَضْرِبَهُ، وَيَرْجِعُ ذُبَابُ سَيْفِهِ، فَأَصَابَ عَيْنَ رُكْبَةِ عَامِرٍ، فَمَاتَ مِنْهُ قَالَ فَلَمَّا قَفَلُوا، قَالَ سَلَمَةُ رَآنِي رَسُولُ اللَّهِ صلى الله عليه وسلم وَهْوَ آخِذٌ بِيَدِي، قَالَ " مَا لَكَ ". قُلْتُ لَهُ فِدَاكَ أَبِي وَأُمِّي، زَعَمُوا أَنَّ عَامِرًا حَبِطَ عَمَلُهُ. قَالَ النَّبِيُّ صلى الله عليه وسلم " كَذَبَ مَنْ قَالَهُ، إِنَّ لَهُ لأَجْرَيْنِ ـ وَجَمَعَ بَيْنَ إِصْبَعَيْهِ ـ إِنَّهُ لَجَاهِدٌ مُجَاهِدٌ قَلَّ عَرَبِيٌّ مَشَى بِهَا مِثْلَهُ ". حَدَّثَنَا قُتَيْبَةُ حَدَّثَنَا حَاتِمٌ قَالَ " نَشَأَ بِهَا "

Narrated 'Aisha: That she prepared a lady for a man from the Ansar as his bride and the Prophet said, "O 'Aisha! Haven't you got any amusement (during the marriage ceremony) as the Ansar like amusement?". – Sahih Al-Bukhari 5162

حَدَّثَنَا الْفَضْلُ بْنُ يَعْقُوبَ، حَدَّثَنَا مُحَمَّدُ بْنُ سَابِقٍ، حَدَّثَنَا إِسْرَائِيلُ، عَنْ هِشَامِ بْنِ عُرْوَةَ، عَنْ أَبِيهِ، عَنْ عَائِشَةَ، أَنَّهَا زَفَّتِ امْرَأَةً إِلَى رَجُلٍ مِنَ الأَنْصَارِ فَقَالَ نَبِيُّ اللَّهِ صلى الله عليه وسلم " يَا عَائِشَةُ مَا كَانَ مَعَكُمْ لَهْوٌ فَإِنَّ الأَنْصَارَ يُعْجِبُهُمُ اللَّهْوُ

Narrated Ubai bin Ka`b: Allah's Messenger ﷺ said, "Some poetry contains wisdom.". – Sahih Al-Bukhari 6145

حَدَّثَنَا أَبُو الْيَمَانِ، أَخْبَرَنَا شُعَيْبٌ، عَنِ الزُّهْرِيِّ، قَالَ أَخْبَرَنِي أَبُو بَكْرِ بْنُ عَبْدِ الرَّحْمَنِ، أَنَّ مَرْوَانَ بْنَ الْحَكَمِ، أَخْبَرَهُ أَنَّ عَبْدَ الرَّحْمَنِ بْنَ الأَسْوَدِ بْنِ عَبْدِ يَغُوثَ أَخْبَرَهُ أَنَّ أُبَىَّ بْنَ كَعْبٍ أَخْبَرَهُ أَنَّ رَسُولَ اللَّهِ صلى الله عليه وسلم قَالَ " إِنَّ مِنَ الشِّعْرِ حِكْمَةً "

Narrated Jundub: While the Prophet ﷺ was walking, a stone hit his foot and stumbled and his toe was injured. He then (quoting a poetic verse) said, "You are not more than a toe which has been bathed in blood in Allah's Cause.". – Sahih Al-Bukhari 6146

حَدَّثَنَا أَبُو نُعَيْمٍ، حَدَّثَنَا سُفْيَانُ، عَنِ الأَسْوَدِ بْنِ قَيْسٍ، سَمِعْتُ جُنْدَبًا، يَقُولُ بَيْنَمَا النَّبِيُّ صلى الله عليه وسلم يَمْشِي إِذْ أَصَابَهُ حَجَرٌ فَعَثَرَ فَدَمِيَتْ إِصْبَعُهُ فَقَالَ " هَلْ أَنْتِ إِلاَّ إِصْبَعٌ دَمِيتِ وَفِي سَبِيلِ اللَّهِ مَا لَقِيتِ ".

Narrated Abu Huraira: The Prophet ﷺ said, "The most true words said by a poet were the words of Labid. He said, i.e. 'Verily, everything except Allah is perishable and Umaiya bin Abi As-Salt was about to embrace Islam . – Sahih Al-Bukhari 6147

حَدَّثَنَا ابْنُ بَشَّارٍ، حَدَّثَنَا ابْنُ مَهْدِيٍّ، حَدَّثَنَا سُفْيَانُ، عَنْ عَبْدِ الْمَلِكِ، حَدَّثَنَا أَبُو سَلَمَةَ، عَنْ أَبِي هُرَيْرَةَ ـ رضى الله عنه ـ قَالَ النَّبِيُّ صلى الله عليه وسلم " أَصْدَقُ كَلِمَةٍ قَالَهَا الشَّاعِرُ كَلِمَةُ لَبِيدٍ أَلاَ كُلُّ شَىْءٍ مَا خَلاَ اللَّهَ بَاطِلُ ". وَكَادَ أُمَيَّةُ بْنُ أَبِي الصَّلْتِ أَنْ يُسْلِمَ

Narrated Salama bin Al-Aqwa: We went out with Allah's Messenger ﷺ to Khaibar and we travelled during the night. A man amongst the people said to 'Amir bin Al-Aqwa', "Won't you let us hear your poetry?" 'Amir was a poet, and so he got down and started (chanting Huda) reciting for the people, poetry that keep pace with the camel's foot steps, saying, "O Allah! Without You we would not have been guided on the right path, neither would we have given in charity, nor would we have prayed. So please forgive us what we have committed. Let all of us be sacrificed for Your cause and when we meet our enemy, make our feet firm and bestow peace and calmness on us and if they (our enemy) will call us towards an unjust thing we will refuse. The infidels have made a hue and cry to ask others help against us. Allah's Messenger ﷺ said, "Who is that driver (of the camels)?" They said, "He is 'Amir bin Al-Aqwa."' He said, "May Allah bestow His mercy on him." A man among the people said, Has Martyrdom been granted to him, O Allah's Prophet! Would that you let us enjoy his company longer." We reached (the people of) Khaibar and besieged them till we were stricken with severe hunger but Allah helped the Muslims conquer Khaibar. In the evening of its conquest the people made many fires. Allah's Messenger ﷺ asked, "What are those fires? For what are you making fires?" They said, "For cooking meat." He asked, "What kind of meat?" They said, "Donkeys' meat." Allah's Messenger ﷺ said, "Throw away the meat and break the cooking pots." A man said, O Allah's Messenger ﷺ! Shall we throw away the meat and wash the cooking pots?" He said, "You can do that too." When the army files aligned In rows (for the battle), 'Amir's sword was a short one, and while attacking a Jew with it in order to hit him, the sharp edge of the sword turned back and hit 'Amir's knee and caused him to die. When the Muslims returned (from the battle), Salama said, Allah's Messenger ﷺ saw me pale and said, 'What is wrong with you?"' I said, "Let my parents be sacrificed for you! The people claim that all the deeds of Amir have been annulled." The Prophet ﷺ asked, "Who said so?" I replied, "So-and-so and soand- so and Usaid bin Al-Hudair Al-Ansari said, 'Whoever says so is telling a lie. Verily, 'Amir will have double reward."' (While speaking) the Prophet ﷺ put two of his fingers together to indicate that, and added, "He was really a hard-working man and a Mujahid (devout fighter in Allah's Cause) and rarely have there lived in it (i.e., Medina or the battle-field) an "Arab like him.". – Sahih Al-Bukhari 6148

حَدَّثَنَا قُتَيْبَةُ بْنُ سَعِيدٍ، حَدَّثَنَا حَاتِمُ بْنُ إِسْمَاعِيلَ، عَنْ يَزِيدَ بْنِ أَبِي عُبَيْدٍ، عَنْ سَلَمَةَ بْنِ الأَكْوَعِ، قَالَ خَرَجْنَا مَعَ رَسُولِ اللَّهِ صلى الله عليه وسلم إِلَى خَيْبَرَ فَسِرْنَا لَيْلاً، فَقَالَ رَجُلٌ مِنَ الْقَوْمِ لِعَامِرِ بْنِ الأَكْوَعِ أَلاَ تُسْمِعُنَا مِنْ هُنَيْهَاتِكَ، قَالَ وَكَانَ عَامِرٌ رَجُلاً شَاعِرًا، فَنَزَلَ يَحْدُو بِالْقَوْمِ يَقُولُ اللَّهُمَّ لَوْلاَ أَنْتَ مَا اهْتَدَيْنَا وَلاَ تَصَدَّقْنَا وَلاَ صَلَّيْنَا فَاغْفِرْ فِدَاءٌ لَكَ مَا اقْتَفَيْنَا وَثَبِّتِ الأَقْدَامَ إِنْ لاَقَيْنَا وَأَلْقِيَنْ سَكِينَةً عَلَيْنَا إِنَّا إِذَا صِيحَ بِنَا أَتَيْنَا وَبِالصِّيَاحِ عَوَّلُوا عَلَيْنَا فَقَالَ رَسُولُ اللَّهِ صلى الله عليه وسلم " مَنْ هَذَا السَّائِقُ ". قَالُوا عَامِرُ بْنُ الأَكْوَعِ. فَقَالَ " يَرْحَمُهُ اللَّهُ ". فَقَالَ رَجُلٌ مِنَ الْقَوْمِ وَجَبَتْ يَا نَبِيَّ اللَّهِ، لَوْ أَمْتَعْتَنَا بِهِ. قَالَ فَأَتَيْنَا خَيْبَرَ فَحَاصَرْنَاهُمْ حَتَّى أَصَابَتْنَا مَخْمَصَةٌ شَدِيدَةٌ، ثُمَّ إِنَّ اللَّهَ فَتَحَهَا عَلَيْهِمْ، فَلَمَّا أَمْسَى النَّاسُ الْيَوْمَ الَّذِي فُتِحَتْ عَلَيْهِمْ أَوْقَدُوا نِيرَانًا كَثِيرَةً. فَقَالَ رَسُولُ اللَّهِ صلى الله عليه وسلم " مَا هَذِهِ النِّيرَانُ، عَلَى أَىِّ شَىْءٍ تُوقِدُونَ ". قَالُوا عَلَى لَحْمٍ. قَالَ " عَلَى أَىِّ لَحْمٍ ". قَالُوا عَلَى لَحْمِ حُمُرٍ إِنْسِيَّةٍ. فَقَالَ رَسُولُ اللَّهِ صلى الله عليه وسلم " أَهْرِقُوهَا وَاكْسِرُوهَا ". فَقَالَ رَجُلٌ يَا رَسُولَ اللَّهِ أَوْ نُهَرِيقُهَا وَنَغْسِلُهَا قَالَ " أَوْ ذَاكَ ". فَلَمَّا تَصَافَّ الْقَوْمُ كَانَ سَيْفُ عَامِرٍ فِيهِ قِصَرٌ، فَتَنَاوَلَ بِهِ يَهُودِيًّا لِيَضْرِبَهُ، وَيَرْجِعُ ذُبَابُ سَيْفِهِ فَأَصَابَ رُكْبَةَ عَامِرٍ فَمَاتَ مِنْهُ، فَلَمَّا قَفَلُوا قَالَ سَلَمَةُ رَآنِي رَسُولُ اللَّهِ صلى الله عليه وسلم شَاحِبًا. فَقَالَ لِي " مَا لَكَ ". فَقُلْتُ فِدًى لَكَ أَبِي وَأُمِّي زَعَمُوا أَنَّ عَامِرًا حَبِطَ عَمَلُهُ. قَالَ " مَنْ قَالَهُ ". قُلْتُ قَالَهُ فُلاَنٌ وَفُلاَنٌ وَفُلاَنٌ وَأُسَيْدُ بْنُ الْحُضَيْرِ الأَنْصَارِيُّ. فَقَالَ رَسُولُ اللَّهِ صلى الله عليه وسلم " كَذَبَ مَنْ قَالَهُ، إِنَّ لَهُ لأَجْرَيْنِ ـ وَجَمَعَ بَيْنَ إِصْبَعَيْهِ ـ إِنَّهُ لَجَاهِدٌ مُجَاهِدٌ، قَلَّ عَرَبِيٌّ نَشَأَ بِهَا مِثْلَهُ ".

Narrated `Aisha: When Allah's Messenger ﷺ reached Medina, Abu Bakr and Bilal became ill. When Abu Bakr's fever got worse, he would recite (this poetic verse): "Everybody is staying alive with his People, yet Death is nearer to him than His shoe laces." And Bilal, when his fever deserted him, would recite: "Would that I could stay overnight in A valley wherein I would be Surrounded by Idhkhir and Jalil (kinds of goodsmelling grass). Would that one day I could Drink the water of the Majanna, and Would that (The two mountains) Shama and Tafil would appear to me!" The Prophet ﷺ said, "O Allah! Curse Shaiba bin Rabi`a and `Utba bin Rabi`a and Umaiya bin Khalaf as they turned us out of our land to the land of epidemics." Allah's Messenger ﷺ then said, "O Allah! Make us love Medina as we love Mecca or even more than that. O Allah! Give blessings in our Sa and our Mudd (measures symbolizing food) and make the climate of Medina suitable for us, and divert its fever towards Aljuhfa." Aisha added: When we reached Medina, it was the most unhealthy of Allah's lands, and the valley of Bathan (the valley of Medina) used to flow with impure colored water. – Sahih Al-Bukhari 1889

حَدَّثَنَا عُبَيْدُ بْنُ إِسْمَاعِيلَ، حَدَّثَنَا أَبُو أُسَامَةَ، عَنْ هِشَامٍ، عَنْ أَبِيهِ، عَنْ عَائِشَةَ ـ رضى الله عنها ـ قَالَتْ لَمَّا قَدِمَ رَسُولُ اللَّهِ صلى الله عليه وسلم الْمَدِينَةَ وُعِكَ أَبُو بَكْرٍ وَبِلاَلٌ، فَكَانَ أَبُو بَكْرٍ إِذَا أَخَذَتْهُ الْحُمَّى يَقُولُ كُلُّ امْرِئٍ مُصَبَّحٌ فِي أَهْلِهِ وَالْمَوْتُ أَدْنَى مِنْ شِرَاكِ نَعْلِهِ وَكَانَ بِلاَلٌ إِذَا أُقْلِعَ عَنْهُ الْحُمَّى يَرْفَعُ عَقِيرَتَهُ يَقُولُ أَلاَ لَيْتَ شِعْرِي هَلْ أَبِيتَنَّ لَيْلَةً بِوَادٍ وَحَوْلِي إِذْخِرٌ وَجَلِيلُ وَهَلْ أَرِدَنْ يَوْمًا مِيَاهَ مَجَنَّةٍ وَهَلْ يَبْدُوَنْ لِي شَامَةٌ وَطَفِيلُ قَالَ اللَّهُمَّ الْعَنْ شَيْبَةَ بْنَ رَبِيعَةَ، وَعُتْبَةَ بْنَ رَبِيعَةَ، وَأُمَيَّةَ بْنَ خَلَفٍ، كَمَا أَخْرَجُونَا مِنْ أَرْضِنَا إِلَى أَرْضِ الْوَبَاءِ ثُمَّ قَالَ رَسُولُ اللَّهِ صلى الله عليه وسلم " اللَّهُمَّ حَبِّبْ إِلَيْنَا الْمَدِينَةَ كَحُبِّنَا مَكَّةَ أَوْ أَشَدَّ، اللَّهُمَّ بَارِكْ لَنَا فِي صَاعِنَا، وَفِي مُدِّنَا، وَصَحِّحْهَا لَنَا وَانْقُلْ حُمَّاهَا إِلَى الْجُحْفَةِ ". قَالَتْ وَقَدِمْنَا الْمَدِينَةَ، وَهْىَ أَوْبَأُ أَرْضِ اللَّهِ. قَالَتْ فَكَانَ بُطْحَانُ يَجْرِي نَجْلاً. تَعْنِي مَاءً آجِنًا

Narrated 'Urwa: Aisha said, "While the Ethiopians were playing with their small spears, Allah's Messenger ﷺ screened me behind him and I watched (that display) and kept on watching till I left on my own." So you may estimate of what age a little girl may listen to amusement. – Sahih Al-Bukhari 5190

حَدَّثَنَا عَبْدُ اللَّهِ بْنُ مُحَمَّدٍ، حَدَّثَنَا هِشَامٌ، أَخْبَرَنَا مَعْمَرٌ، عَنِ الزُّهْرِيِّ، عَنْ عُرْوَةَ، عَنْ عَائِشَةَ، قَالَتْ كَانَ الْحَبَشُ يَلْعَبُونَ بِحِرَابِهِمْ، فَسَتَرَنِي رَسُولُ اللَّهِ صلى الله عليه وسلم وَأَنَا أَنْظُرُ، فَمَا زِلْتُ أَنْظُرُ حَتَّى كُنْتُ أَنَا أَنْصَرِفُ فَاقْدُرُوا قَدْرَ الْجَارِيَةِ الْحَدِيثَةِ السِّنِّ تَسْمَعُ اللَّهْوَ.

Narrated Abu 'Amir or Abu Malik Al-Ash'ari: That he heard the Prophet ﷺ saying, "From among my followers there will be some people who will consider illegal sexual intercourse, the wearing of silk, the drinking of alcoholic drinks and the use of musical instruments, as lawful. And there will be some people who will stay near the side of a mountain and in the evening their shepherd will come to them with their sheep and ask them for something, but they will say to him, 'Return to us tomorrow.' Allah will destroy them during the night and will let the mountain fall on them, and He will transform the rest of them into monkeys and pigs and they will remain so till the Day of Resurrection.". – Sahih Al-Bukhari 5590

وَقَالَ هِشَامُ بْنُ عَمَّارٍ حَدَّثَنَا صَدَقَةُ بْنُ خَالِدٍ، حَدَّثَنَا عَبْدُ الرَّحْمَنِ بْنُ يَزِيدَ بْنِ جَابِرٍ، حَدَّثَنَا عَطِيَّةُ بْنُ قَيْسٍ الْكِلاَبِيُّ، حَدَّثَنَا عَبْدُ الرَّحْمَنِ بْنُ غَنْمٍ الأَشْعَرِيُّ، قَالَ حَدَّثَنِي أَبُو عَامِرٍ ـ أَوْ أَبُو مَالِكٍ ـ الأَشْعَرِيُّ وَاللَّهِ مَا كَذَبَنِي سَمِعَ النَّبِيَّ صلى الله عليه وسلم يَقُولُ " لَيَكُونَنَّ مِنْ أُمَّتِي أَقْوَامٌ يَسْتَحِلُّونَ الْحِرَ وَالْحَرِيرَ وَالْخَمْرَ وَالْمَعَازِفَ، وَلَيَنْزِلَنَّ أَقْوَامٌ إِلَى جَنْبِ عَلَمٍ يَرُوحُ عَلَيْهِمْ بِسَارِحَةٍ لَهُمْ، يَأْتِيهِمْ ـ يَعْنِي الْفَقِيرَ ـ لِحَاجَةٍ فَيَقُولُوا ارْجِعْ إِلَيْنَا غَدًا فَيُبَيِّتُهُمُ اللَّهُ وَيَضَعُ الْعَلَمَ، وَيَمْسَخُ آخَرِينَ قِرَدَةً وَخَنَازِيرَ إِلَى يَوْمِ الْقِيَامَةِ "

Narrated Salama: We went out with the Prophet ﷺ to Khaibar. A man (from the companions) said, "O 'Amir! Let us hear some of your Huda (camel-driving songs.)" So he sang some of them (i.e. a lyric in harmony with the camels walk). The Prophet ﷺ said, "Who is the driver (of these camels)?" They said, "Amir." The Prophet said, "May Allah bestow His Mercy on him

!" The people said, "O Allah's Messenger ﷺ! Would that you let us enjoy his company longer!" Then 'Amir was killed the following morning. The people said, "The good deeds of 'Amir are lost as he has killed himself." I returned at the time while they were talking about that. I went to the Prophet ﷺ and said, "O Allah's Prophet! Let my father be sacrificed for you! The people claim that 'Amir's good deeds are lost." The Prophet ﷺ said, "Whoever says so is a liar, for 'Amir will have a double reward as he exerted himself to obey Allah and fought in Allah's Cause. No other way of killing would have granted him greater reward.". – Sahih Al-Bukhari 6891

حَدَّثَنَا الْمَكِّيُّ بْنُ إِبْرَاهِيمَ، حَدَّثَنَا يَزِيدُ بْنُ أَبِي عُبَيْدٍ، عَنْ سَلَمَةَ، قَالَ خَرَجْنَا مَعَ النَّبِيِّ صلى الله عليه وسلم إِلَى خَيْبَرَ فَقَالَ رَجُلٌ مِنْهُمْ أَسْمِعْنَا يَا عَامِرُ مِنْ هُنَيْهَاتِكَ. فَحَدَا بِهِمْ، فَقَالَ النَّبِيُّ صلى الله عليه وسلم " مَنِ السَّائِقُ " قَالُوا عَامِرٌ. فَقَالَ " رَحِمَهُ اللَّهُ ". فَقَالُوا يَا رَسُولَ اللَّهِ هَلاَّ أَمْتَعْتَنَا بِهِ. فَأُصِيبَ صَبِيحَةَ لَيْلَتِهِ فَقَالَ الْقَوْمُ حَبِطَ عَمَلُهُ، قَتَلَ نَفْسَهُ. فَلَمَّا رَجَعْتُ وَهُمْ يَتَحَدَّثُونَ أَنَّ عَامِرًا حَبِطَ عَمَلُهُ، فَجِئْتُ إِلَى النَّبِيِّ صلى الله عليه وسلم فَقُلْتُ يَا نَبِيَّ اللَّهِ فَدَاكَ أَبِي وَأُمِّي، زَعَمُوا أَنَّ عَامِرًا حَبِطَ عَمَلُهُ. فَقَالَ " كَذَبَ مَنْ قَالَهَا، إِنَّ لَهُ لأَجْرَيْنِ اثْنَيْنِ، إِنَّهُ لَجَاهِدٌ مُجَاهِدٌ، وَأَىُّ قَتْلٍ يَزِيدُهُ عَلَيْهِ ".

And the ones who from idle talk are veering away. – Surah Al-Mu'minun 23:3

وَٱلَّذِينَ هُمْ عَنِ ٱللَّغْوِ مُعْرِضُونَ

Therein they will not hear any idle talk, nor any cause for vice. – Surah Al-Waqi'ah 56:25

لَا يَسْمَعُونَ فِيهَا لَغْوًا وَلَا تَأْثِيمًا

Where they will hear no idle talk. – Surah Al-Ghashiyah 88:11

لَّا تَسْمَعُ فِيهَا لَاغِيَةً

Therein they will hear no idle talk nor cry of lies. – Surah An-Naba 78:35

لَّا يَسْمَعُونَ فِيهَا لَغْوًا وَلَا كِذَّٰبًا

Whoever has disbelieved in Allah even after his belief excepting him who has been compelled and his heart is (still) composed with belief-but whoever has his breast expanded in disbelief, then upon them is anger from Allah and they will have a tremendous torment. -Shrah An:Nahl 16:106

مَن كَفَرَ بِٱللَّهِ مِنۢ بَعْدِ إِيمَـٰنِهِۦٓ إِلَّا مَنْ أُكْرِهَ وَقَلْبُهُۥ مُطْمَئِنٌّۢ بِٱلْإِيمَـٰنِ وَلَـٰكِن مَّن شَرَحَ بِٱلْكُفْرِ صَدْرًا فَعَلَيْهِمْ غَضَبٌ مِّنَ ٱللَّهِ وَلَهُمْ عَذَابٌ عَظِيمٌ

Religion is sincerity, religion is sincerity (Al-Nasihah)
إِنَّ الدِّينَ النَّصِيحَةُ إِنَّ الدِّينَ النَّصِيحَةُ إِنَّ الدِّينَ النَّصِيحَةُ

So he turned away from them and said, "O my people! Indeed I have already proclaimed the Messages of my Lord and advised you (sincerely), so how should I feel sad for a disbelieving people?". - Surah Al-A'raf 7:93

فَتَوَلَّىٰ عَنْهُمْ وَقَالَ يَـٰقَوْمِ لَقَدْ أَبْلَغْتُكُمْ رِسَـٰلَـٰتِ رَبِّى وَنَصَحْتُ لَكُمْ ۖ فَكَيْفَ ءَاسَىٰ عَلَىٰ قَوْمٍ كَـٰفِرِينَ

So he turned away from them and said, "O my people! Indeed I have already proclaimed to you the Message of my Lord and advised you (sincerely), but you do not love (sincere) advisers.". – Surah Al-A'raf 7:79

فَتَوَلَّىٰ عَنۡهُمۡ وَقَالَ يَٰقَوۡمِ لَقَدۡ أَبۡلَغۡتُكُمۡ رِسَالَةَ رَبِّي وَنَصَحۡتُ لَكُمۡ وَلَٰكِن لَّا تُحِبُّونَ ٱلنَّٰصِحِينَ

I constantly proclaim to you the Messages of my Lord, and I advise you (sincerely), and I know from Allah what you do not know. – Surah Al-A'raf 7:62
أُبَلِّغُكُمۡ رِسَٰلَٰتِ رَبِّي وَأَنصَحُ لَكُمۡ وَأَعۡلَمُ مِنَ ٱللَّهِ مَا لَا تَعۡلَمُونَ

I constantly proclaim to you the Messages of my Lord, and I am for you a devoted adviser. – Surah Al-A'raf 7:68
أُبَلِّغُكُمۡ رِسَٰلَٰتِ رَبِّي وَأَنَا۠ لَكُمۡ نَاصِحٌ أَمِينٌ

And as a (certain) nation of them said, "Why do you admonish a people whom Allah (is) causing to perish or tormenting with a strict torment?" They said, " (As) a (possible) excuse to your Lord, and that possibly they would be pious.". - Surah Al-A'raf 7:164
وَإِذۡ قَالَتۡ أُمَّةٞ مِّنۡهُمۡ لِمَ تَعِظُونَ قَوۡمًا ٱللَّهُ مُهۡلِكُهُمۡ أَوۡ مُعَذِّبُهُمۡ عَذَابٗا شَدِيدٗاۖ قَالُواْ مَعۡذِرَةً إِلَىٰ رَبِّكُمۡ وَلَعَلَّهُمۡ يَتَّقُونَ

And my advice will not profit you, in case I am willing to advise you, in case Allah wills to misguide you; He is your Lord, and to Him you will be returned.". – Surah Hud 11:34
وَلَا يَنفَعُكُمۡ نُصۡحِيٓ إِنۡ أَرَدتُّ أَنۡ أَنصَحَ لَكُمۡ إِن كَانَ ٱللَّهُ يُرِيدُ أَن يُغۡوِيَكُمۡۚ هُوَ رَبُّكُمۡ وَإِلَيۡهِ تُرۡجَعُونَ

Call people to the path of your Lord with wisdom and good advice and reason with them most courteously, for your Lord knows best who strays from His path and knows best those who are guided. – Surah An-Nahl 16:125
ٱدۡعُ إِلَىٰ سَبِيلِ رَبِّكَ بِٱلۡحِكۡمَةِ وَٱلۡمَوۡعِظَةِ ٱلۡحَسَنَةِۖ وَجَٰدِلۡهُم بِٱلَّتِي هِيَ أَحۡسَنُۚ إِنَّ رَبَّكَ هُوَ أَعۡلَمُ بِمَن ضَلَّ عَن سَبِيلِهِۦ وَهُوَ أَعۡلَمُ بِٱلۡمُهۡتَدِينَ

Those (are they) whom Allah knows whatever is in their hearts; so veer away from them, and admonish them, and say to them consummate words (Literally: saying) about themselves. – Surah An-Nisa 4:63
أُوْلَٰٓئِكَ ٱلَّذِينَ يَعۡلَمُ ٱللَّهُ مَا فِي قُلُوبِهِمۡ فَأَعۡرِضۡ عَنۡهُمۡ وَعِظۡهُمۡ وَقُل لَّهُمۡ فِيٓ أَنفُسِهِمۡ قَوۡلَۢا بَلِيغٗا

It was narrated from Abu Hurairah that the Messenger of Allah said: "Religion is sincerity, religion is sincerity (Al-Nasihah), religion is sincerity." They said; "To whom, O Messenger of Allah?" He said: "To Allah, to His Book, to His Messenger, to the imams of the Muslims and to their common folk." - Sunan an-Nasa'I 4199
أَخْبَرَنَا الرَّبِيعُ بْنُ سُلَيْمَانَ، قَالَ حَدَّثَنَا شُعَيْبُ بْنُ اللَّيْثِ، قَالَ حَدَّثَنَا اللَّيْثُ، عَنِ ابْنِ عَجْلاَنَ، عَنْ زَيْدِ بْنِ أَسْلَمَ، عَنِ الْقَعْقَاعِ بْنِ حَكِيمٍ، عَنْ أَبِي صَالِحٍ، عَنْ أَبِي هُرَيْرَةَ، عَنْ رَسُولِ اللَّهِ صلى الله عليه وسلم قَالَ " إِنَّ الدِّينَ النَّصِيحَةُ إِنَّ الدِّينَ النَّصِيحَةُ إِنَّ الدِّينَ النَّصِيحَةُ " . قَالُوا لِمَنْ يَا رَسُولَ اللَّهِ قَالَ " لِلَّهِ وَلِكِتَابِهِ وَلِرَسُولِهِ وَلأَئِمَّةِ الْمُسْلِمِينَ وَعَامَّتِهِمْ " .

you command beneficence, and forbid maleficence
تَأۡمُرُونَ بِٱلۡمَعۡرُوفِ وَتَنۡهَوۡنَ عَنِ ٱلۡمُنكَرِ

But as for him who feared to stand one day in front of his Lord and therefore restrained himself from following his whims and desires, - Surah An-Nazi'at 79:40
وَأَمَّا مَنْ خَافَ مَقَامَ رَبِّهِ وَنَهَى النَّفْسَ عَنِ الْهَوَىٰ

The ones who closely follow the Messenger, the Prophet, the illiterate one, whom they find written down in their presence in the Tawrah (the Book revealed to Musa (Moses) and the Injil, (the Book revealed to Isa (Jesus) commanding them to beneficence, and forbidding them maleficence, making lawful for them the good things, and prohibiting for them the wicked things, and ridding them of their obligation and the shackles that were upon them. So the ones who believe in him, and rally to him (in assistance) and vindicate him, and closely follow the light that has been sent down with him, those are they (who) are the prosperers." – Surah Al-A'raf 7:157

ٱلَّذِينَ يَتَّبِعُونَ ٱلرَّسُولَ ٱلنَّبِىَّ ٱلْأُمِّىَّ ٱلَّذِى يَجِدُونَهُۥ مَكْتُوبًا عِندَهُمْ فِى ٱلتَّوْرَىٰةِ وَٱلْإِنجِيلِ يَأْمُرُهُم بِٱلْمَعْرُوفِ وَيَنْهَىٰهُمْ عَنِ ٱلْمُنكَرِ وَيُحِلُّ لَهُمُ ٱلطَّيِّبَٰتِ وَيُحَرِّمُ عَلَيْهِمُ ٱلْخَبَٰٓئِثَ وَيَضَعُ عَنْهُمْ إِصْرَهُمْ وَٱلْأَغْلَٰلَ ٱلَّتِى كَانَتْ عَلَيْهِمْ ۚ فَٱلَّذِينَ ءَامَنُوا۟ بِهِۦ وَعَزَّرُوهُ وَنَصَرُوهُ وَٱتَّبَعُوا۟ ٱلنُّورَ ٱلَّذِىٓ أُنزِلَ مَعَهُۥٓ ۙ أُو۟لَٰٓئِكَ هُمُ ٱلْمُفْلِحُونَ

If only their rabbis and scholars would stop them from speaking sinfully and accepting illicit payments. Their deeds are So evil! – Surah Al-Ma'idah 5:63

لَوْلَا يَنْهَىٰهُمُ ٱلرَّبَّٰنِيُّونَ وَٱلْأَحْبَارُ عَن قَوْلِهِمُ ٱلْإِثْمَ وَأَكْلِهِمُ ٱلسُّحْتَ ۚ لَبِئْسَ مَا كَانُوا۟ يَصْنَعُونَ

They did not prevent each other from doing hateful things. Their deeds were So evil! – Surah Al-Ma'idah 5:79

كَانُوا۟ لَا يَتَنَاهَوْنَ عَن مُّنكَرٍ فَعَلُوهُ ۚ لَبِئْسَ مَا كَانُوا۟ يَفْعَلُونَ

[Moses] said, "Aaron, what prevented you, when you saw them going astray – Surah TaHa 20:92

قَالَ يَٰهَٰرُونُ مَا مَنَعَكَ إِذْ رَأَيْتَهُمْ ضَلُّوٓا۟

(Those) who, in case We establish them in the earth, keep up the prayer, and bring the Zakat (i.e., pay the poor-dues) and command beneficence and forbid malfeasance; and to Allah belongs the end of the Commands (Or: the issues of all affairs). – Al-Hajj 22:41

ٱلَّذِينَ إِن مَّكَّنَّٰهُمْ فِى ٱلْأَرْضِ أَقَامُوا۟ ٱلصَّلَوٰةَ وَءَاتَوُا۟ ٱلزَّكَوٰةَ وَأَمَرُوا۟ بِٱلْمَعْرُوفِ وَنَهَوْا۟ عَنِ ٱلْمُنكَرِ ۗ وَلِلَّهِ عَٰقِبَةُ ٱلْأُمُورِ

You have been the most charitable nation brought out to mankind: you command beneficence, and forbid maleficence, and believe in Allah. And if the population of the Book believed, it would indeed have been charitable for them; (some) of them are the believers, and the majority of them are the immoral. – Surah Al-Imran 3:110

كُنتُمْ خَيْرَ أُمَّةٍ أُخْرِجَتْ لِلنَّاسِ تَأْمُرُونَ بِٱلْمَعْرُوفِ وَتَنْهَوْنَ عَنِ ٱلْمُنكَرِ وَتُؤْمِنُونَ بِٱللَّهِ ۗ وَلَوْ ءَامَنَ أَهْلُ ٱلْكِتَٰبِ لَكَانَ خَيْرًا لَّهُم ۚ مِّنْهُمُ ٱلْمُؤْمِنُونَ وَأَكْثَرُهُمُ ٱلْفَٰسِقُونَ

O you who have believed, be constantly upright with equity (with others), witnesses for Allah, even if it be against yourselves or (your) parents and nearest kin. In case (the person) is rich or poor, then Allah is the Best Patron for both. So do not ever follow prejudice, so as to do justice; and in case you twist or veer away, then surely Allah has been Ever-Cognizant of whatever you do – Surah An-Nisa 4:135

يَٰٓأَيُّهَا ٱلَّذِينَ ءَامَنُوا۟ كُونُوا۟ قَوَّٰمِينَ بِٱلْقِسْطِ شُهَدَآءَ لِلَّهِ وَلَوْ عَلَىٰٓ أَنفُسِكُمْ أَوِ ٱلْوَٰلِدَيْنِ وَٱلْأَقْرَبِينَ ۚ إِن يَكُنْ غَنِيًّا أَوْ فَقِيرًا فَٱللَّهُ أَوْلَىٰ بِهِمَا ۖ فَلَا تَتَّبِعُوا۟ ٱلْهَوَىٰٓ أَن تَعْدِلُوا۟ ۚ وَإِن تَلْوُۥٓا۟ أَوْ تُعْرِضُوا۟ فَإِنَّ ٱللَّهَ كَانَ بِمَا تَعْمَلُونَ خَبِيرًا

(Triumphant are) the repentant (ones), the worshipers, the ones praising (Him), wandering (in His way), bowing down, prostrating themselves, the ones commanding beneficence and forbidding male-ficence, and the ones preserving the bounds of Allah; and give good tidings to the believers. – Surah At-Taubah 9:112

ٱلتَّٰٓئِبُونَ ٱلْعَٰبِدُونَ ٱلْحَٰمِدُونَ ٱلسَّٰٓئِحُونَ ٱلرَّٰكِعُونَ ٱلسَّٰجِدُونَ ٱلْءَامِرُونَ بِٱلْمَعْرُوفِ وَٱلنَّاهُونَ عَنِ ٱلْمُنكَرِ وَٱلْحَٰفِظُونَ لِحُدُودِ ٱللَّهِ ۗ وَبَشِّرِ ٱلْمُؤْمِنِينَ

The Book of
Qabr
قبر

Narrated Al-Bara' bin `Azib: Allah's Messengerﷺ ordered us to do seven things and forbade us from seven. He ordered us to visit the sick, to follow funeral processions, (to say) to a sneezer, (May Allah bestow His Mercy on you, if he says, Praise be to Allah), to accept invitations, to greet (everybody), to help the oppressed and to help others to fulfill their oaths. He forbade us to wear gold rings, to drink in silver (utensils), to use Mayathir (silken carpets placed on saddles), to wear Al-Qissi (a kind of silken cloth), to wear silk, Dibaj or Istabraq (two kinds of silk). – Sahih Al-Bukhari 5635

حَدَّثَنَا مُوسَى بْنُ إِسْمَاعِيلَ، حَدَّثَنَا أَبُو عَوَانَةَ، عَنِ الأَشْعَثِ بْنِ سُلَيْمٍ، عَنْ مُعَاوِيَةَ بْنِ سُوَيْدِ بْنِ مُقَرِّنٍ، عَنِ الْبَرَاءِ بْنِ عَازِبٍ، قَالَ أَمَرَنَا رَسُولُ اللَّهِ صلى الله عليه وسلم بِسَبْعٍ، وَنَهَانَا عَنْ سَبْعٍ، أَمَرَنَا بِعِيَادَةِ الْمَرِيضِ، وَاتِّبَاعِ الْجِنَازَةِ، وَتَشْمِيتِ الْعَاطِسِ، وَإِجَابَةِ الدَّاعِي، وَإِفْشَاءِ السَّلاَمِ، وَنَصْرِ الْمَظْلُومِ وَإِبْرَارِ الْمُقْسِمِ، وَنَهَانَا عَنْ خَوَاتِيمِ الذَّهَبِ، وَعَنِ الشُّرْبِ فِي الْفِضَّةِ ـ أَوْ قَالَ آنِيَةِ الْفِضَّةِ ـ وَعَنِ الْمَيَاثِرِ وَالْقَسِّيِّ، وَعَنْ لُبْسِ الْحَرِيرِ وَالدِّيبَاجِ وَالإِسْتَبْرَقِ.

Narrated Muawiya bin Suwaid: I heard Al-Bara' bin `Azib saying, "The Prophetﷺ orders us to do seven things and prohibited us from doing seven other things." Then Al-Bara' mentioned the following:-- (1) To pay a visit to the sick (inquiring about his health), (2) to follow funeral processions, (3) to say to a sneezer, "May Allah be merciful to you" (if he says, "Praise be to Allah!"), (4) to return greetings, (5) to help the oppressed, (6) to accept invitations, (7) to help others to fulfill their oaths. (See Hadith No. 753, Vol. 7). – Sahih Al-Bukhari 2445

حَدَّثَنَا سَعِيدُ بْنُ الرَّبِيعِ، حَدَّثَنَا شُعْبَةُ، عَنِ الأَشْعَثِ بْنِ سُلَيْمٍ، قَالَ سَمِعْتُ مُعَاوِيَةَ بْنَ سُوَيْدٍ، سَمِعْتُ الْبَرَاءَ بْنَ عَازِبٍ ـ رضى الله عنهما ـ قَالَ أَمَرَنَا النَّبِيُّ صلى الله عليه وسلم بِسَبْعٍ، وَنَهَانَا عَنْ سَبْعٍ. فَذَكَرَ عِيَادَةَ الْمَرِيضِ، وَاتِّبَاعَ الْجَنَائِزِ، وَتَشْمِيتَ الْعَاطِسِ، وَرَدَّ السَّلاَمِ، وَنَصْرَ الْمَظْلُومِ، وَإِجَابَةَ الدَّاعِي، وَإِبْرَارَ الْمُقْسِمِ.

Narrated `Ali: We were in the company of the Prophetﷺ in a funeral procession at Baqi Al-Gharqad. He said, "There is none of you but has his place written for him in Paradise or in the Hell- Fire." They said, "O Allah's Apostle! Shall we depend (on this fact and give up work)?" He said, "Carry on doing (good deeds), for every body will find it easy to do (what will lead him to his destined place)." Then he recited: 'As for him who gives (in charity) and keeps his duty to Allah, and believes in the Best reward from Allah (i.e. Allah will compensate him for what he will spend in Allah's way). So, We will make smooth for him the path of ease. But he who is a greedy miser....for him, the path for evil.' (92.5-10). – Sahih Al-Bukhari 4945

حَدَّثَنَا أَبُو نُعَيْمٍ، حَدَّثَنَا سُفْيَانُ، عَنِ الأَعْمَشِ، عَنْ سَعْدِ بْنِ عُبَيْدَةَ، عَنْ أَبِي عَبْدِ الرَّحْمَنِ السُّلَمِيِّ، عَنْ عَلِيٍّ ـ رضى الله عنه ـ قَالَ كُنَّا مَعَ النَّبِيِّ صلى الله عليه وسلم فِي بَقِيعِ الْغَرْقَدِ فِي جَنَازَةٍ فَقَالَ " مَا مِنْكُمْ مِنْ أَحَدٍ إِلاَّ وَقَدْ كُتِبَ مَقْعَدُهُ مِنَ الْجَنَّةِ وَمَقْعَدُهُ مِنَ النَّارِ ". فَقَالُوا يَا رَسُولَ اللَّهِ أَفَلاَ نَتَّكِلُ فَقَالَ " اعْمَلُوا فَكُلٌّ مُيَسَّرٌ ". ثُمَّ قَرَأَ {فَأَمَّا مَنْ أَعْطَى وَاتَّقَى * وَصَدَّقَ بِالْحُسْنَى} إِلَى قَوْلِهِ {لِلْعُسْرَى}

Narrated Jabir bin `Abdullah: A funeral procession passed in front of us and the Prophetﷺ stood up and we too stood up. We said, 'O Allah's Messengerﷺ! This is the funeral procession of a Jew." He said, "Whenever you see a funeral procession, you should stand up.". – Sahih Al-Bukhari 1311

حَدَّثَنَا مُعَاذُ بْنُ فَضَالَةَ، حَدَّثَنَا هِشَامٌ، عَنْ يَحْيَى، عَنْ عُبَيْدِ اللَّهِ بْنِ مِقْسَمٍ، عَنْ جَابِرِ بْنِ عَبْدِ اللَّهِ ـ رضى الله عنهما ـ قَالَ مَرَّ بِنَا جَنَازَةٌ فَقَامَ لَهَا النَّبِيُّ صلى الله عليه وسلم وَقُمْنَا بِهِ. فَقُلْنَا يَا رَسُولَ اللَّهِ، إِنَّهَا جَنَازَةُ يَهُودِيٍّ. قَالَ " إِذَا رَأَيْتُمُ الْجَنَازَةَ فَقُومُوا "

If Allah brings you back to a party of them, and they ask your permission to go out, say, "You will not go out with me, ever, nor will you ever fight an enemy with me. You were content to sit back the first time, so sit back with those who stay behind." You are never to pray over anyone of them who dies, nor are you to stand at his graveside. They rejectedAllah and His Messenger, and died while they were sinners. Do not let their possessions and their children impress you. Allah desires to torment them through them in this world, and their souls expire while they are disbelievers. – Surah At-Taubah 9:83-85

فَإِن رَّجَعَكَ ٱللَّهُ إِلَىٰ طَآئِفَةٍ مِّنْهُمْ فَٱسْتَـْٔذَنُوكَ لِلْخُرُوجِ فَقُل لَّن تَخْرُجُوا۟ مَعِىَ أَبَدًا وَلَن تُقَـٰتِلُوا۟ مَعِىَ عَدُوًّا ۖ إِنَّكُمْ رَضِيتُم بِٱلْقُعُودِ أَوَّلَ مَرَّةٍ فَٱقْعُدُوا۟ مَعَ ٱلْخَـٰلِفِينَ وَلَا تُصَلِّ عَلَىٰٓ أَحَدٍ مِّنْهُم مَّاتَ أَبَدًا وَلَا تَقُمْ عَلَىٰ قَبْرِهِۦٓ ۖ إِنَّهُمْ كَفَرُوا۟ بِٱللَّهِ وَرَسُولِهِۦ وَمَاتُوا۟ وَهُمْ فَـٰسِقُونَ وَلَا تُعْجِبْكَ أَمْوَٰلُهُمْ وَأَوْلَـٰدُهُمْ ۚ إِنَّمَا يُرِيدُ ٱللَّهُ أَن يُعَذِّبَهُم بِهَا فِى ٱلدُّنْيَا وَتَزْهَقَ أَنفُسُهُمْ وَهُمْ كَـٰفِرُونَ

Narrated Salama bin Al-Akwa`: A dead person was brought to the Prophet ﷺ so that he might lead the funeral prayer for him. He asked, "Is he in debt?" When the people replied in the negative, he led the funeral prayer. Another dead person was brought and he asked, "Is he in debt?" They said, "Yes." He (refused to lead the prayer and) said, "Lead the prayer of your friend." Abu Qatada said, "O Allah's Messenger ﷺ! I undertake to pay his debt." Allah's Messenger ﷺ then led his funeral prayer. – Sahih Al-Bukhari 2295

حَدَّثَنَا أَبُو عَاصِمٍ، عَنْ يَزِيدَ بْنِ أَبِي عُبَيْدٍ، عَنْ سَلَمَةَ بْنِ الأَكْوَعِ ـ رضى الله عنه ـ أَنَّ النَّبِيَّ صلى الله عليه وسلم أُتِيَ بِجَنَازَةٍ، لِيُصَلِّيَ عَلَيْهَا، فَقَالَ " هَلْ عَلَيْهِ مِنْ دَيْنٍ ". قَالُوا لاَ. فَصَلَّى عَلَيْهِ، ثُمَّ أُتِيَ بِجَنَازَةٍ أُخْرَى، فَقَالَ " هَلْ عَلَيْهِ مِنْ دَيْنٍ ". قَالُوا نَعَمْ. قَالَ " صَلُّوا عَلَى صَاحِبِكُمْ ". قَالَ أَبُو قَتَادَةَ عَلَىَّ دَيْنُهُ يَا رَسُولَ اللَّهِ. فَصَلَّى عَلَيْهِ.

Narrated `Amra: I heard `Aisha saying, "When the news of the martyrdom of Ibn Haritha, Ja`far bin Abi Talib and `Abdullah bin Rawaka reached, Allah's Messenger ﷺ sat with sorrow explicit on his face." `Aisha added, "I was then peeping through a chink in the door. A man came to him and said, "O Allah's Messenger ﷺ! The women of Ja`far are crying.' Thereupon the Prophet ﷺ told him to forbid them to do so. So the man went away and returned saying, "I forbade them but they did not listen to me." The Prophet ﷺ ordered him again to go (and forbid them). He went again and came saying, 'By Allah, they overpowered me (i.e. did not listen to me)." `Aisha said that Allah's Messenger ﷺ said (to him), "Go and throw dust into their mouths." Aisha added, "I said, May Allah put your nose in the dust! By Allah, neither have you done what you have been ordered, nor have you relieved Allah's Messenger ﷺ from trouble.". – Sahih Al-Bukhari 4263

حَدَّثَنَا قُتَيْبَةُ، حَدَّثَنَا عَبْدُ الْوَهَّابِ، قَالَ سَمِعْتُ يَحْيَى بْنَ سَعِيدٍ، قَالَ أَخْبَرَتْنِي عَمْرَةُ، قَالَتْ سَمِعْتُ عَائِشَةَ ـ رضى الله عنها ـ تَقُولُ لَمَّا جَاءَ قَتْلُ ابْنِ حَارِثَةَ وَجَعْفَرِ بْنِ أَبِي طَالِبٍ وَعَبْدِ اللَّهِ بْنِ رَوَاحَةَ ـ رضى الله عنهم ـ جَلَسَ رَسُولُ اللَّهِ صلى الله عليه وسلم يُعْرَفُ فِيهِ الْحُزْنُ ـ قَالَتْ عَائِشَةُ ـ وَأَنَا أَطَّلِعُ مِنْ صَائِرِ الْبَابِ ـ تَعْنِي مِنْ شَقِّ الْبَابِ ـ فَأَتَاهُ رَجُلٌ فَقَالَ أَىْ رَسُولَ اللَّهِ إِنَّ نِسَاءَ جَعْفَرٍ قَالَ وَذَكَرَ بُكَاءَهُنَّ، فَأَمَرَهُ أَنْ يَنْهَاهُنَّ قَالَ فَذَهَبَ الرَّجُلُ ثُمَّ أَتَى فَقَالَ قَدْ نَهَيْتُهُنَّ. وَذَكَرَ أَنَّهُ لَمْ يُطِعْنَهُ قَالَ فَأَمَرَ أَيْضًا فَذَهَبَ ثُمَّ أَتَى فَقَالَ وَاللَّهِ لَقَدْ غَلَبْنَنَا. فَزَعَمَتْ أَنَّ رَسُولَ اللَّهِ صلى الله عليه وسلم قَالَ " فَاحْثُ فِي أَفْوَاهِهِنَّ مِنَ التُّرَابِ " قَالَتْ عَائِشَةُ فَقُلْتُ أَرْغَمَ اللَّهُ أَنْفَكَ، فَوَاللَّهِ مَا أَنْتَ تَفْعَلُ، وَمَا تَرَكْتَ رَسُولَ اللَّهِ صلى الله عليه وسلم مِنَ الْعَنَاءِ

Narrated `Aisha: When the Prophet ﷺ became ill, some of his wives talked about a church which they had seen in Ethiopia and it was called Mariya. Um Salma and Um Habiba had been to Ethiopia, and both of them narrated its (the Church's) beauty and the pictures it contained. The Prophet ﷺ raised his head and said, "Those are the people who, whenever a pious man dies amongst them, make a place of worship at his grave and then they make those pictures in it. Those are the worst creatures in the Sight of Allah.". – Sahih Al-Bukhari 1341

حَدَّثَنَا إِسْمَاعِيلُ، قَالَ حَدَّثَنِي مَالِكٌ، عَنْ هِشَامٍ، عَنْ أَبِيهِ، عَنْ عَائِشَةَ ـ رضى الله عنها ـ قَالَتْ لَمَّا اشْتَكَى النَّبِيُّ صلى الله عليه وسلم ذَكَرَتْ بَعْضُ نِسَائِهِ كَنِيسَةً رَأَيْنَهَا بِأَرْضِ الْحَبَشَةِ، يُقَالُ لَهَا مَارِيَةُ، وَكَانَتْ أُمُّ سَلَمَةَ وَأُمُّ حَبِيبَةَ ـ رضى الله عنهما ـ أَتَتَا أَرْضَ الْحَبَشَةِ، فَذَكَرَتَا مِنْ حُسْنِهَا وَتَصَاوِيرَ فِيهَا، فَرَفَعَ رَأْسَهُ فَقَالَ " أُولَئِكَ إِذَا مَاتَ مِنْهُمُ الرَّجُلُ الصَّالِحُ بَنَوْا عَلَى قَبْرِهِ مَسْجِدًا، ثُمَّ صَوَّرُوا فِيهِ تِلْكَ الصُّورَةَ، أُولَئِكَ شِرَارُ الْخَلْقِ عِنْدَ اللَّهِ "

Narrated Um 'Atiyya: We were forbidden to mourn for more than three days for a dead person, except for a husband, for whom a wife should mourn for four months and ten days (while in the mourning period) we were not allowed to put kohl in our eyes, nor perfume our-selves, nor wear dyed clothes, except a garment of 'Asb (special clothes made in Yemen). But it was permissible for us that when one of us became clean from her menses and took a bath, she could use a piece of a certain kind of incense. And it was forbidden for us to follow funeral processions. – Sahih Al-Bukhari 5341

حَدَّثَنِي عَبْدُ اللَّهِ بْنُ عَبْدِ الْوَهَّابِ، حَدَّثَنَا حَمَّادُ بْنُ زَيْدٍ، عَنْ أَيُّوبَ، عَنْ حَفْصَةَ، عَنْ أُمِّ عَطِيَّةَ، قَالَتْ كُنَّا نُنْهَى أَنْ نُحِدَّ عَلَى مَيِّتٍ فَوْقَ ثَلاَثٍ، إِلاَّ عَلَى زَوْجٍ أَرْبَعَةَ أَشْهُرٍ وَعَشْرًا، وَلاَ نَكْتَحِلَ، وَلاَ نَطَّيَّبَ، وَلاَ نَلْبَسَ ثَوْبًا مَصْبُوغًا، إِلاَّ ثَوْبَ عَصْبٍ، وَقَدْ رُخِّصَ لَنَا عِنْدَ الطُّهْرِ إِذَا اغْتَسَلَتْ إِحْدَانَا مِنْ مَحِيضِهَا فِي نُبْذَةٍ مِنْ كُسْتِ أَظْفَارٍ، وَكُنَّا نُنْهَى عَنِ اتِّبَاعِ الْجَنَائِزِ.

Narrated Um Atiyya: We gave the Pledge of allegiance to the Prophetﷺ and he recited to me the verse (60.12). That they will not associate anything in worship with Allah (60.12). And he also prevented us from wailing and lamenting over the dead. A woman from us held her hand out and said, "Such-and-such a woman cried over a dead person belonging to my family and I want to compensate her for that crying" The Prophet did not say anything in reply and she left and returned. None of those women abided by her pledge except Um Sulaim, Um Al-`Ala', and the daughter of Abi Sabra, the wife of Al-Mu`adh or the daughter of Abi Sabra, and the wife of Mu`adh. – Sahih Al-Bukhari 7215

حَدَّثَنَا مُسَدَّدٌ، حَدَّثَنَا عَبْدُ الْوَارِثِ، عَنْ أَيُّوبَ، عَنْ حَفْصَةَ، عَنْ أُمِّ عَطِيَّةَ، قَالَتْ بَايَعْنَا النَّبِيَّ صلى الله عليه وسلم فَقَرَأَ عَلَىَّ {أَنْ لاَ يُشْرِكْنَ بِاللَّهِ شَيْئًا} وَنَهَانَا عَنِ النِّيَاحَةِ، فَقَبَضَتِ امْرَأَةٌ مِنَّا يَدَهَا فَقَالَتْ فُلاَنَةُ أَسْعَدَتْنِي وَأَنَا أُرِيدُ أَنْ أَجْزِيَهَا، فَلَمْ يَقُلْ شَيْئًا، ثُمَّ رَجَعَتْ، فَمَا وَفَتِ امْرَأَةٌ إِلاَّ أُمُّ سُلَيْمٍ وَأُمُّ الْعَلاَءِ، وَابْنَةُ أَبِي سَبْرَةَ امْرَأَةُ مُعَاذٍ أَوِ ابْنَةُ أَبِي سَبْرَةَ وَامْرَأَةُ مُعَاذٍ

Narrated Hisham's father: It was mentioned before `Aisha that Ibn `Umar attributed the following statement to the Prophetﷺ The dead person is punished in the grave because of the crying and lamentation Of his family." On that, `Aisha said, "But Allah's Messengerﷺ said, 'The dead person is punished for his crimes and sins while his family cry over him then." She added, "And this is similar to the statement of Allah's Messengerﷺ when he stood by the (edge of the) well which contained the corpses of the pagans killed at Badr, 'They hear what I say.' She added, "But he said now they know very well what I used to tell them was the truth." `Aisha then recited: 'You cannot make the dead hear.' (30.52) and 'You cannot make those who are in their Graves, hear you.' (35.22) that is, when they had taken their places in the (Hell) Fire. – Sahih al-Bukhari 3978, 3979

حَدَّثَنِي عُبَيْدُ بْنُ إِسْمَاعِيلَ، حَدَّثَنَا أَبُو أُسَامَةَ، عَنْ هِشَامٍ، عَنْ أَبِيهِ، قَالَ ذُكِرَ عِنْدَ عَائِشَةَ ـ رضى الله عنها ـ أَنَّ ابْنَ عُمَرَ رَفَعَ إِلَى النَّبِيِّ صلى الله عليه وسلم " إِنَّ الْمَيِّتَ يُعَذَّبُ فِي قَبْرِهِ بِبُكَاءِ أَهْلِهِ ". فَقَالَتْ إِنَّمَا قَالَ رَسُولُ اللَّهِ صلى الله عليه وسلم " إِنَّهُ لَيُعَذَّبُ بِخَطِيئَتِهِ وَذَنْبِهِ، وَإِنَّ أَهْلَهُ لَيَبْكُونَ عَلَيْهِ الآنَ ". قَالَتْ وَذَاكَ مِثْلُ قَوْلِهِ إِنَّ رَسُولَ اللَّهِ صلى الله عليه وسلم قَامَ عَلَى الْقَلِيبِ وَفِيهِ قَتْلَى بَدْرٍ مِنَ الْمُشْرِكِينَ، فَقَالَ لَهُمْ مَا قَالَ إِنَّهُمْ لَيَسْمَعُونَ مَا أَقُولُ. إِنَّمَا قَالَ " إِنَّهُمُ الآنَ لَيَعْلَمُونَ أَنَّ مَا كُنْتُ أَقُولُ لَهُمْ حَقٌّ ". ثُمَّ قَرَأَتْ {إِنَّكَ لاَ تُسْمِعُ الْمَوْتَى} {وَمَا أَنْتَ بِمُسْمِعٍ مَنْ فِي الْقُبُورِ} تَقُولُ حِينَ تَبَوَّءُوا مَقَاعِدَهُمْ مِنَ النَّارِ

Narrated `Aisha: Allah's Messengerﷺ in his fatal illness said, "Allah cursed the Jews and the Christians, for they built the places of worship at the graves of their prophets." And if that had not been the case, then the Prophet's grave would have been made prominent before

the people. So the Prophetﷺ was afraid, or the people were afraid that his grave might be taken as a place for worship. – Sahih al-Bukhari 1390
حَدَّثَنَا مُوسَى بْنُ إِسْمَاعِيلَ، حَدَّثَنَا أَبُو عَوَانَةَ، عَنْ هِلاَلٍ، عَنْ عُرْوَةَ، عَنْ عَائِشَةَ ـ رضى الله عنها ـ قَالَتْ قَالَ رَسُولُ اللَّهِ صلى الله عليه وسلم فِي مَرَضِهِ الَّذِي لَمْ يَقُمْ مِنْهُ " لَعَنَ اللَّهُ الْيَهُودَ وَالنَّصَارَى، اتَّخَذُوا قُبُورَ أَنْبِيَائِهِمْ مَسَاجِدَ ". لَوْلاَ ذَلِكَ أُبْرِزَ قَبْرُهُ، غَيْرَ أَنَّهُ خَشِيَ أَوْ خُشِيَ أَنْ يُتَّخَذَ مَسْجِدًا. وَعَنْ هِلاَلٍ قَالَ كَنَّانِي عُرْوَةُ بْنُ الزُّبَيْرِ وَلَمْ يُولَدْ لِي.

Narrated Abu Huraira: Allah's Messenerﷺ said, "May Allah's curse be on the Jews for they built the places of worship at the graves of their Prophets.". – Sahih al-Bukhari 437
حَدَّثَنَا عَبْدُ اللَّهِ بْنُ مَسْلَمَةَ، عَنْ مَالِكٍ، عَنِ ابْنِ شِهَابٍ، عَنْ سَعِيدِ بْنِ الْمُسَيَّبِ، عَنْ أَبِي هُرَيْرَةَ، أَنَّ رَسُولَ اللَّهِ صلى الله عليه وسلم قَالَ " قَاتَلَ اللَّهُ الْيَهُودَ اتَّخَذُوا قُبُورَ أَنْبِيَائِهِمْ مَسَاجِدَ ".

Funeral prayer
صلاة الجنازة

Narrated Abu Huraira: That Allah's Messengerﷺ said, "Whoever attends the funeral procession till he offers the funeral prayer for it, will get a reward equal to one Qirat, and whoever accompanies it till burial, will get a reward equal to two Qirats." It was asked, "What are two Qirats?" He replied, "Like two huge mountains.". – Sahih al-Bukhari 1325
حَدَّثَنَا عَبْدُ اللَّهِ بْنُ مَسْلَمَةَ، قَالَ قَرَأْتُ عَلَى ابْنِ أَبِي ذِئْبٍ عَنْ سَعِيدِ بْنِ أَبِي سَعِيدٍ الْمَقْبُرِيِّ، عَنْ أَبِيهِ، أَنَّهُ سَأَلَ أَبَا هُرَيْرَةَ ـ رضى الله عنه ـ فَقَالَ سَمِعْتُ النَّبِيَّ صلى الله عليه وسلم. حَدَّثَنَا أَحْمَدُ بْنُ شَبِيبِ بْنِ سَعِيدٍ، قَالَ حَدَّثَنِي أَبِي، حَدَّثَنَا يُونُسُ، قَالَ ابْنُ شِهَابٍ وَحَدَّثَنِي عَبْدُ الرَّحْمَنِ الأَعْرَجُ، أَنَّ أَبَا هُرَيْرَةَ ـ رضى الله عنه ـ قَالَ قَالَ رَسُولُ اللَّهِ صلى الله عليه وسلم " مَنْ شَهِدَ الْجَنَازَةَ حَتَّى يُصَلِّيَ عَلَيْهَا فَلَهُ قِيرَاطٌ، وَمَنْ شَهِدَ حَتَّى تُدْفَنَ كَانَ لَهُ قِيرَاطَانِ ". قِيلَ وَمَا الْقِيرَاطَانِ قَالَ " مِثْلُ الْجَبَلَيْنِ الْعَظِيمَيْنِ ".

Narrated Jabir: The Prophetﷺ offered the funeral prayer of As-Hama An-Najash and said four Takbir. – Sahih al-Bukhari 1334
حَدَّثَنَا مُحَمَّدُ بْنُ سِنَانٍ، حَدَّثَنَا سَلِيمُ بْنُ حَيَّانَ، حَدَّثَنَا سَعِيدُ بْنُ مِينَاءَ، عَنْ جَابِرٍ ـ رضى الله عنه ـ أَنَّ النَّبِيَّ صلى الله عليه وسلم صَلَّى عَلَى أَصْحَمَةَ النَّجَاشِيِّ فَكَبَّرَ أَرْبَعًا. وَقَالَ يَزِيدُ بْنُ هَارُونَ وَعَبْدُ الصَّمَدِ عَنْ سَلِيمٍ أَصْحَمَةَ. وَتَابَعَهُ عَبْدُ الصَّمَدِ

Jubair b. Nufair says: I heard it from 'Auf b. Malik that the Prophetﷺ said prayer on the dead body, and I remembered his prayer:" O Allah! Forgive him, have mercy upon him, give him peace and absolve him. Receive him with honour and make his grave spacious; wash him with water, snow and hail. Cleanse him from faults as Thou wouldst cleanse a white garment from impurity. Requite him with an abode more excellent than his abode, with a family better than his family, and with a mate better than his mate. Admit him to the Garden, and protect him from the torment of the grave and the torment of the Fire." ('Auf bin Malik) said: I earnestly desired that I were this dead body. – Sahih Muslim 963 a, 963 b
وَحَدَّثَنِي هَارُونُ بْنُ سَعِيدٍ الأَيْلِيُّ، أَخْبَرَنَا ابْنُ وَهْبٍ، أَخْبَرَنِي مُعَاوِيَةُ بْنُ صَالِحٍ، عَنْ حَبِيبِ بْنِ عُبَيْدٍ، عَنْ جُبَيْرِ بْنِ نُفَيْرٍ، سَمِعَهُ يَقُولُ سَمِعْتُ عَوْفَ بْنَ مَالِكٍ، يَقُولُ صَلَّى رَسُولُ اللَّهِ صلى الله عليه وسلم عَلَى جَنَازَةٍ فَحَفِظْتُ مِنْ دُعَائِهِ وَهُوَ يَقُولُ " اللَّهُمَّ اغْفِرْ لَهُ وَارْحَمْهُ وَعَافِهِ وَاعْفُ عَنْهُ وَأَكْرِمْ نُزُلَهُ وَوَسِّعْ مُدْخَلَهُ وَاغْسِلْهُ بِالْمَاءِ وَالثَّلْجِ وَالْبَرَدِ وَنَقِّهِ مِنَ الْخَطَايَا كَمَا نَقَّيْتَ الثَّوْبَ الأَبْيَضَ مِنَ الدَّنَسِ وَأَبْدِلْهُ دَارًا خَيْرًا مِنْ دَارِهِ وَأَهْلاً خَيْرًا مِنْ أَهْلِهِ وَزَوْجًا خَيْرًا مِنْ زَوْجِهِ وَأَدْخِلْهُ الْجَنَّةَ وَأَعِذْهُ مِنْ عَذَابِ الْقَبْرِ أَوْ مِنْ عَذَابِ النَّارِ " . قَالَ حَتَّى تَمَنَّيْتُ أَنْ أَكُونَ أَنَا ذَلِكَ الْمَيِّتَ . قَالَ وَحَدَّثَنِي عَبْدُ الرَّحْمَنِ بْنُ جُبَيْرٍ حَدَّثَهُ عَنْ أَبِيهِ عَنْ عَوْفِ بْنِ مَالِكٍ عَنِ النَّبِيِّ صلى الله عليه وسلم بِنَحْوِ هَذَا الْحَدِيثِ أَيْضًا .

Narrated Samura bin Jundab: I offered the funeral prayer behind the Prophet ﷺ for a woman who had died during childbirth and he stood up by the middle of the coffin. – Sahih al-Bukhari 1332

حَدَّثَنَا عِمْرَانُ بْنُ مَيْسَرَةَ، حَدَّثَنَا عَبْدُ الْوَارِثِ، حَدَّثَنَا حُسَيْنٌ، عَنِ ابْنِ بُرَيْدَةَ، حَدَّثَنَا سَمُرَةُ بْنُ جُنْدُبٍ ـ رضى الله عنه ـ قَالَ صَلَّيْتُ وَرَاءَ النَّبِيِّ صلى الله عليه وسلم عَلَى امْرَأَةٍ مَاتَتْ فِي نِفَاسِهَا فَقَامَ عَلَيْهَا وَسَطَهَا

Narrated `Abdur Rahman bin Abi Laila: Sahl bin Hunaif and Qais bin Sa`d were sitting in the city of Al-Qadisiya. A funeral procession passed in front of them and they stood up. They were told that funeral procession was of one of the inhabitants of the land i.e. of a non-believer, under the protection of Muslims. They said, "A funeral procession passed in front of the Prophet ﷺ and he stood up. When he was told that it was the coffin of a Jew, he said, "Is it not a living being (soul)?" - Sahih al-Bukhari 1312, 1313

حَدَّثَنَا آدَمُ، حَدَّثَنَا شُعْبَةُ، حَدَّثَنَا عَمْرُو بْنُ مُرَّةَ، قَالَ سَمِعْتُ عَبْدَ الرَّحْمَنِ بْنَ أَبِي لَيْلَى، قَالَ كَانَ سَهْلُ بْنُ حُنَيْفٍ وَقَيْسُ بْنُ سَعْدٍ قَاعِدَيْنِ بِالْقَادِسِيَّةِ، فَمَرُّوا عَلَيْهِمَا بِجَنَازَةٍ فَقَامَا. فَقِيلَ لَهُمَا إِنَّهَا مِنْ أَهْلِ الأَرْضِ، أَىْ مِنْ أَهْلِ الذِّمَّةِ فَقَالاَ إِنَّ النَّبِيَّ صلى الله عليه وسلم مَرَّتْ بِهِ جَنَازَةٌ فَقَامَ فَقِيلَ لَهُ إِنَّهَا جَنَازَةُ يَهُودِيٍّ. فَقَالَ " أَلَيْسَتْ نَفْسًا ". وَقَالَ أَبُو حَمْزَةَ عَنِ الأَعْمَشِ، عَنْ عَمْرٍو، عَنِ ابْنِ أَبِي لَيْلَى، قَالَ كُنْتُ مَعَ قَيْسٍ وَسَهْلٍ ـ رضى الله عنهما ـ فَقَالاَ كُنَّا مَعَ النَّبِيِّ صلى الله عليه وسلم. وَقَالَ زَكَرِيَّاءُ عَنِ الشَّعْبِيِّ عَنِ ابْنِ أَبِي لَيْلَى كَانَ أَبُو مَسْعُودٍ وَقَيْسٌ يَقُومَانِ لِلْجِنَازَةِ.

Narrated Salama bin Al-Akwa: Once, while we were sitting in the company of Prophet, a dead man was brought. The Prophet ﷺ was requested to lead the funeral prayer for the deceased. He said, "Is he in debt?" The people replied in the negative. He said, "Has he left any wealth?" They said, "No." So, he led his funeral prayer. Another dead man was brought and the people said, "O Allah's Messenger ﷺ ! Lead his funeral prayer." The Prophet ﷺ said, "Is he in debt?" They said, "Yes." He said, "Has he left any wealth?" They said, "Three Dinars." So, he led the prayer. Then a third dead man was brought and the people said (to the Prophet ﷺ) , Please lead his funeral prayer." He said, "Has he left any wealth?" They said, "No." He asked, "Is he in debt?" They said, ("Yes! He has to pay) three Diners.', He (refused to pray and) said, "Then pray for your (dead) companion." Abu Qatada said, "O Allah's Messenger ﷺ ! Lead his funeral prayer, and I will pay his debt." So, he led the prayer. – Sahih al-Bukhari 2289

حَدَّثَنَا الْمَكِّيُّ بْنُ إِبْرَاهِيمَ، حَدَّثَنَا يَزِيدُ بْنُ أَبِي عُبَيْدٍ، عَنْ سَلَمَةَ بْنِ الأَكْوَعِ ـ رضى الله عنه ـ قَالَ كُنَّا جُلُوسًا عِنْدَ النَّبِيِّ صلى الله عليه وسلم إِذْ أُتِيَ بِجَنَازَةٍ، فَقَالُوا صَلِّ عَلَيْهَا. فَقَالَ " هَلْ عَلَيْهِ دَيْنٌ ". قَالُوا لاَ. قَالَ " فَهَلْ تَرَكَ شَيْئًا ". قَالُوا لاَ. فَصَلَّى عَلَيْهِ ثُمَّ أُتِيَ بِجَنَازَةٍ أُخْرَى، فَقَالُوا يَا رَسُولَ اللَّهِ، صَلِّ عَلَيْهَا. قَالَ " هَلْ عَلَيْهِ دَيْنٌ ". قِيلَ نَعَمْ. قَالَ " فَهَلْ تَرَكَ شَيْئًا ". قَالُوا ثَلاَثَةَ دَنَانِيرَ. فَصَلَّى عَلَيْهَا، ثُمَّ أُتِيَ بِالثَّالِثَةِ، فَقَالُوا صَلِّ عَلَيْهَا. قَالَ " هَلْ تَرَكَ شَيْئًا ". قَالُوا لاَ. قَالَ " فَهَلْ عَلَيْهِ دَيْنٌ . قَالُوا ثَلاَثَةُ دَنَانِيرَ. قَالَ " صَلُّوا عَلَى صَاحِبِكُمْ ". قَالَ أَبُو قَتَادَةَ صَلِّ عَلَيْهِ يَا رَسُولَ اللَّهِ، وَعَلَىَّ دَيْنُهُ. فَصَلَّى عَلَيْهِ

Al-Faraid
الفرائض

Narrated Ibn `Abbas: The custom (in old days) was that the property of the deceased would be inherited by his offspring; as for the parents (of the deceased), they would inherit by the will of the deceased. Then Allah cancelled from that custom whatever He wished and fixed for the male double the amount inherited by the female, and for each parent a sixth (of the whole legacy) and for the wife an eighth or a fourth and for the husband a half or a fourth. – Sahih Al-Bukhari 2747

حَدَّثَنَا مُحَمَّدُ بْنُ يُوسُفَ، عَنْ وَرْقَاءَ، عَنِ ابْنِ أَبِي نَجِيحٍ، عَنْ عَطَاءٍ، عَنِ ابْنِ عَبَّاسٍ ـ رضى الله عنهما ـ قَالَ كَانَ الْمَالُ لِلْوَلَدِ، وَكَانَتِ الْوَصِيَّةُ لِلْوَالِدَيْنِ، فَنَسَخَ اللَّهُ مِنْ ذَلِكَ مَا أَحَبَّ، فَجَعَلَ لِلذَّكَرِ مِثْلَ حَظِّ الأُنْثَيَيْنِ، وَجَعَلَ لِلأَبَوَيْنِ لِكُلِّ وَاحِدٍ مِنْهُمَا السُّدُسَ، وَجَعَلَ لِلْمَرْأَةِ الثُّمُنَ وَالرُّبُعَ، وَلِلزَّوْجِ الشَّطْرَ وَالرُّبُعَ.

Men receive a share of what their parents and relatives leave, and women receive a share of what their parents and relatives leave; be it little or much—a legal share. If the distribution is attended by the relatives, and the orphans, and the needy, give them something out of it, and speak to them kindly. Those who are concerned about the fate of their weak children, in case they leave them behind, should fear Allah, and speak appropriate words. Those who consume the wealth of orphans illicitly consume only fire into their bellies; and they will roast in a Blaze. Allah instructs you regarding your children: The male receives the equivalent of the share of two females. If they are daughters, more than two, they get two-thirds of what he leaves. If there is only one, she gets one-half. As for the parents, each gets one-sixth of what he leaves, if he had children. If he had no children, and his parents inherit from him, his mother gets one-third. If he has siblings, his mother gets one-sixth. After fulfilling any bequest and paying off debts. Your parents and your children—you do not know which are closer to you in welfare. This is Allah's Law. Allah is Knowing and Judicious. You get one-half of what your wives leave behind, if they had no children. If they had children, you get one-fourth of what they leave. After fulfilling any bequest and paying off debts. They get one-fourth of what you leave behind, if you have no children. If you have children, they get one-eighth of what you leave. After fulfilling any bequest and paying off debts. If a man or woman leaves neither parents nor children, but has a brother or sister, each of them gets one-sixth. If there are more siblings, they share one-third. After fulfilling any bequest and paying off debts, without any prejudice. This is a will from Allah. Allah is Knowing and Clement. These are the bounds set by Allah. Whoever obeys Allah and His Messenger, He will admit him into Gardens beneath which rivers flow, to abide therein forever. That is the great attainment. . – Surah An-Nisa 4:7-13

لِّلرِّجَالِ نَصِيبٌ مِّمَّا تَرَكَ ٱلْوَٰلِدَانِ وَٱلْأَقْرَبُونَ وَلِلنِّسَآءِ نَصِيبٌ مِّمَّا تَرَكَ ٱلْوَٰلِدَانِ وَٱلْأَقْرَبُونَ مِمَّا قَلَّ مِنْهُ أَوْ كَثُرَ ۚ نَصِيبًا مَّفْرُوضًا وَإِذَا حَضَرَ ٱلْقِسْمَةَ أُو۟لُوا۟ ٱلْقُرْبَىٰ وَٱلْيَتَـٰمَىٰ وَٱلْمَسَـٰكِينُ فَٱرْزُقُوهُم مِّنْهُ وَقُولُوا۟ لَهُمْ قَوْلًا مَّعْرُوفًا وَلْيَخْشَ ٱلَّذِينَ لَوْ تَرَكُوا۟ مِنْ خَلْفِهِمْ ذُرِّيَّةً ضِعَـٰفًا خَافُوا۟ عَلَيْهِمْ فَلْيَتَّقُوا۟ ٱللَّهَ وَلْيَقُولُوا۟ قَوْلًا سَدِيدًا إِنَّ ٱلَّذِينَ يَأْكُلُونَ أَمْوَٰلَ ٱلْيَتَـٰمَىٰ ظُلْمًا إِنَّمَا يَأْكُلُونَ فِى بُطُونِهِمْ نَارًا ۖ وَسَيَصْلَوْنَ سَعِيرًا يُوصِيكُمُ ٱللَّهُ فِىٓ أَوْلَـٰدِكُمْ ۖ لِلذَّكَرِ مِثْلُ حَظِّ ٱلْأُنثَيَيْنِ ۚ فَإِن كُنَّ نِسَآءً فَوْقَ ٱثْنَتَيْنِ فَلَهُنَّ ثُلُثَا مَا تَرَكَ ۖ وَإِن كَانَتْ وَٰحِدَةً فَلَهَا ٱلنِّصْفُ ۚ وَلِأَبَوَيْهِ لِكُلِّ وَٰحِدٍ مِّنْهُمَا ٱلسُّدُسُ مِمَّا تَرَكَ إِن كَانَ لَهُۥ وَلَدٌ ۚ فَإِن لَّمْ يَكُن لَّهُۥ وَلَدٌ وَوَرِثَهُۥٓ أَبَوَاهُ فَلِأُمِّهِ ٱلثُّلُثُ ۚ فَإِن كَانَ لَهُۥٓ إِخْوَةٌ فَلِأُمِّهِ ٱلسُّدُسُ ۚ مِنۢ بَعْدِ وَصِيَّةٍ يُوصِى بِهَآ أَوْ دَيْنٍ ۗ ءَابَآؤُكُمْ وَأَبْنَآؤُكُمْ لَا تَدْرُونَ أَيُّهُمْ أَقْرَبُ لَكُمْ نَفْعًا ۚ فَرِيضَةً مِّنَ ٱللَّهِ ۗ إِنَّ ٱللَّهَ كَانَ عَلِيمًا حَكِيمًا وَلَكُمْ نِصْفُ مَا تَرَكَ أَزْوَٰجُكُمْ إِن لَّمْ يَكُن لَّهُنَّ وَلَدٌ ۚ فَإِن كَانَ لَهُنَّ وَلَدٌ فَلَكُمُ ٱلرُّبُعُ مِمَّا تَرَكْنَ ۚ مِنۢ بَعْدِ وَصِيَّةٍ يُوصِينَ بِهَآ أَوْ دَيْنٍ ۚ وَلَهُنَّ ٱلرُّبُعُ مِمَّا تَرَكْتُمْ إِن لَّمْ يَكُن لَّكُمْ وَلَدٌ ۚ فَإِن كَانَ لَكُمْ وَلَدٌ فَلَهُنَّ ٱلثُّمُنُ مِمَّا تَرَكْتُم ۚ مِّنۢ بَعْدِ وَصِيَّةٍ تُوصُونَ بِهَآ أَوْ دَيْنٍ ۗ وَإِن كَانَ رَجُلٌ يُورَثُ كَلَـٰلَةً أَوِ ٱمْرَأَةٌ وَلَهُۥٓ أَخٌ أَوْ أُخْتٌ فَلِكُلِّ وَٰحِدٍ مِّنْهُمَا ٱلسُّدُسُ ۚ فَإِن كَانُوٓا۟ أَكْثَرَ مِن ذَٰلِكَ فَهُمْ شُرَكَآءُ فِى ٱلثُّلُثِ ۚ مِنۢ بَعْدِ وَصِيَّةٍ يُوصَىٰ بِهَآ أَوْ دَيْنٍ غَيْرَ مُضَآرٍّ ۚ وَصِيَّةً مِّنَ ٱللَّهِ ۗ وَٱللَّهُ عَلِيمٌ حَلِيمٌ تِلْكَ حُدُودُ ٱللَّهِ ۚ وَمَن يُطِعِ

They ask you for a ruling. Say, "Allah gives you a ruling concerning the person who has neither parents nor children." If a man dies, and leaves no children, and he had a sister, she receives one-half of what he leaves. And he inherits from her if she leaves no children. But if there are two sisters, they receive twothirds of what he leaves. If the siblings are men and women, the male receives the share of two females." Allah makes things clear for you, lest you err. Allah is Aware of everything. – Surah An-Nisa 4:176

يَسْتَفْتُونَكَ قُلِ ٱللَّهُ يُفْتِيكُمْ فِى ٱلْكَلَـٰلَةِ ۚ إِنِ ٱمْرُؤٌا۟ هَلَكَ لَيْسَ لَهُۥ وَلَدٌ وَلَهُۥٓ أُخْتٌ فَلَهَا نِصْفُ مَا تَرَكَ ۚ وَهُوَ يَرِثُهَآ إِن لَّمْ يَكُن لَّهَا وَلَدٌ ۚ فَإِن كَانَتَا ٱثْنَتَيْنِ فَلَهُمَا ٱلثُّلُثَانِ مِمَّا تَرَكَ ۚ وَإِن كَانُوٓا۟ إِخْوَةً رِّجَالًا وَنِسَآءً فَلِلذَّكَرِ مِثْلُ حَظِّ ٱلْأُنثَيَيْنِ ۗ يُبَيِّنُ ٱللَّهُ لَكُمْ أَن تَضِلُّوا۟ ۗ وَٱللَّهُ بِكُلِّ شَىْءٍ عَلِيمٌ

Narrated Abu Huraira: The Prophetﷺ said, “There is no believer but I, of all the people, I am the closest to him both in this world and in the Hereafter. Recite if you wish: ‘The Prophetﷺ is closer to the believers than their own selves.’ (33.6) so if a believer (dies) leaves some property then his relatives will inherit that property; but if he is in debt or he leaves poor children, let those (creditors and children) come to me (that I may pay the debt and provide for the children), for them I am his sponsor (surely). – Sahih al-Bukhari 4781

حَدَّثَنِي إِبْرَاهِيمُ بْنُ الْمُنْذِرِ، حَدَّثَنَا مُحَمَّدُ بْنُ فُلَيْحٍ، حَدَّثَنَا أَبِي، عَنْ هِلاَلِ بْنِ عَلِيٍّ، عَنْ عَبْدِ الرَّحْمَنِ بْنِ أَبِي عَمْرَةَ، عَنْ أَبِي هُرَيْرَةَ ـ رضى الله عنه ـ عَنِ النَّبِيِّ صلى الله عليه وسلم قَالَ " مَا مِنْ مُؤْمِنٍ إِلاَّ وَأَنَا أَوْلَى النَّاسِ بِهِ فِي الدُّنْيَا وَالآخِرَةِ، اقْرَءُوا إِنْ شِئْتُمْ ‏{‏النَّبِيُّ أَوْلَى بِالْمُؤْمِنِينَ مِنْ أَنْفُسِهِمْ‏}‏ فَأَيُّمَا مُؤْمِنٍ تَرَكَ مَالاً فَلْيَرِثْهُ عَصَبَتُهُ مَنْ كَانُوا، فَإِنْ تَرَكَ دَيْنًا أَوْ ضِيَاعًا فَلْيَأْتِنِي وَأَنَا مَوْلاَهُ ".

Narrated ‘Usama bin Zaid: I asked, “O Allah’s Messengerﷺ ! Where will you stay in Mecca? Will you stay in your house in Mecca?” He replied, “Has `Aqil left any property or house?” `Aqil along with Talib had inherited the property of Abu Talib. Jafar and `Ali did not inherit anything as they were Muslims and the other two were non-believers. `Umar bin Al-Khattab used to say, “A believer cannot inherit (anything from an) infidel.” Ibn Shihab, (a sub-narrator) said, “They (`Umar and others) derived the above verdict from Allah’s Statement: “Verily! Those who believed and Emigrated and strove with their life And property in Allah’s Cause, And those who helped (the emigrants) And gave them their places to live in, These are (all) allies to one another.” (8.72) – Sahih al-Bukhari 1588

حَدَّثَنَا أَصْبَغُ، قَالَ أَخْبَرَنِي ابْنُ وَهْبٍ، عَنْ يُونُسَ، عَنِ ابْنِ شِهَابٍ، عَنْ عَلِيِّ بْنِ حُسَيْنٍ، عَنْ عَمْرِو بْنِ عُثْمَانَ، عَنْ أُسَامَةَ بْنِ زَيْدٍ ـ رضى الله عنهما ـ أَنَّهُ قَالَ يَا رَسُولَ اللَّهِ، أَيْنَ تَنْزِلُ فِي دَارِكَ بِمَكَّةَ‏.‏ فَقَالَ " وَهَلْ تَرَكَ عَقِيلٌ مِنْ رِبَاعٍ أَوْ دُورٍ ".‏ وَكَانَ عَقِيلٌ وَرِثَ أَبَا طَالِبٍ هُوَ وَطَالِبٌ وَلَمْ يَرِثْهُ جَعْفَرٌ وَلاَ عَلِيٌّ ـ رضى الله عنهما ـ شَيْئًا لأَنَّهُمَا كَانَا مُسْلِمَيْنِ، وَكَانَ عَقِيلٌ وَطَالِبٌ كَافِرَيْنِ، فَكَانَ عُمَرُ بْنُ الْخَطَّابِ ـ رضى الله عنه ـ يَقُولُ لاَ يَرِثُ الْمُؤْمِنُ الْكَافِرَ‏.‏ قَالَ ابْنُ شِهَابٍ وَكَانُوا يَتَأَوَّلُونَ قَوْلَ اللَّهِ تَعَالَى ‏{‏إِنَّ الَّذِينَ آمَنُوا وَهَاجَرُوا وَجَاهَدُوا بِأَمْوَالِهِمْ وَأَنْفُسِهِمْ فِي سَبِيلِ اللَّهِ وَالَّذِينَ آوَوْا وَنَصَرُوا أُولَئِكَ بَعْضُهُمْ أَوْلِيَاءُ بَعْضٍ‏}‏ الآيَةَ‏.‏

Wasiyyah
وَصِيَّة

O you who have believed, the testimony between you, when death is present to any of you while bequeathing, shall be two (men) with (i.e. owning) a sense of justice or two others from other (folk), in case you are striking in the earth (i.e., traveling) so the affliction of death afflicts you. You shall detain them (both) after the prayer (s), then they shall swear by Allah, in case you are suspicious, “We will not trade it for a price, even if it were a near kinsman, nor will we keep back the testimony of Allah, (for) lo, surely in that case we are indeed of the vicious (people).” Yet, in case it be discovered that both of them have truly merited (the accusation of) vice, then two others shall rise up in place (Literally: in both their stations) of the ones nearest of the most concerned, (Literally: truly merit the right to witness, or near kinship, or who claim a lawful right) then they both shall swear by Allah, “Indeed our testimony is truer than their testimony, and in no way have we transgressed, (for), surely in that case we are indeed of the unjust (people).” So, it is likelier that they will bear testimony in proper form (Literally: come up with the testimony at its “proper” face) or fear that after their (other) oaths may be turned back to. And be pious to Allah and give ear (obediently); and Allah does not guide the immoral people - Surah Al-Ma’idah 5:106-108

يَٰٓأَيُّهَا ٱلَّذِينَ ءَامَنُوا۟ شَهَٰدَةُ بَيْنِكُمْ إِذَا حَضَرَ أَحَدَكُمُ ٱلْمَوْتُ حِينَ ٱلْوَصِيَّةِ ٱثْنَانِ ذَوَا عَدْلٍ مِّنكُمْ أَوْ ءَاخَرَانِ مِنْ غَيْرِكُمْ إِنْ أَنتُمْ ضَرَبْتُمْ فِى ٱلْأَرْضِ فَأَصَٰبَتْكُم مُّصِيبَةُ ٱلْمَوْتِ ۚ تَحْبِسُونَهُمَا مِنۢ بَعْدِ ٱلصَّلَوٰةِ فَيُقْسِمَانِ بِٱللَّهِ إِنِ ٱرْتَبْتُمْ لَا نَشْتَرِى بِهِۦ ثَمَنًا وَلَوْ كَانَ ذَا قُرْبَىٰ ۙ وَلَا نَكْتُمُ شَهَٰدَةَ ٱللَّهِ إِنَّآ إِذًا لَّمِنَ ٱلْءَاثِمِينَ فَإِنْ عُثِرَ عَلَىٰٓ أَنَّهُمَا ٱسْتَحَقَّآ إِثْمًا فَـَٔاخَرَانِ يَقُومَانِ مَقَامَهُمَا مِنَ ٱلَّذِينَ ٱسْتَحَقَّ عَلَيْهِمُ ٱلْأَوْلَيَٰنِ فَيُقْسِمَانِ بِٱللَّهِ لَشَهَٰدَتُنَآ أَحَقُّ مِن شَهَٰدَتِهِمَا وَمَا ٱعْتَدَيْنَآ إِنَّآ إِذًا لَّمِنَ ٱلظَّٰلِمِينَ ذَٰلِكَ أَدْنَىٰٓ أَن يَأْتُوا۟ بِٱلشَّهَٰدَةِ عَلَىٰ وَجْهِهَآ أَوْ يَخَافُوٓا۟ أَن تُرَدَّ أَيْمَٰنٌۢ بَعْدَ أَيْمَٰنِهِمْ ۗ وَٱتَّقُوا۟ ٱللَّهَ وَٱسْمَعُوا۟ ۗ وَٱللَّهُ لَا يَهْدِى ٱلْقَوْمَ ٱلْفَٰسِقِينَ

Narrated Sa`d: Allah's Messenger ﷺ came to visit me during my ailment which had been aggravated during Hajjat-al- Wada`. I said to him, "You see how sick I am. I have much property but have no heir except my only daughter May I give two thirds of my property in charity?"! He said, "No." I said, "Half of it?" He said, "No." I said "One third?" He said, "One third is too much, for to leave your heirs rich is better than to leave them poor, begging of others. Nothing you spend seeking Allah's pleasure but you shall get a reward for it, even for what you put in the mouth of your wife." – Sahih al-Bukhari 5668
حَدَّثَنَا مُوسَى بْنُ إِسْمَاعِيلَ، حَدَّثَنَا عَبْدُ الْعَزِيزِ بْنُ عَبْدِ اللَّهِ بْنِ أَبِي سَلَمَةَ، أَخْبَرَنَا الزُّهْرِيُّ، عَنْ عَامِرِ بْنِ سَعْدٍ، عَنْ أَبِيهِ، قَالَ جَاءَنَا رَسُولُ اللَّهِ صلى الله عليه وسلم يَعُودُنِي مِنْ وَجَعٍ اشْتَدَّ بِي زَمَنَ حَجَّةِ الْوَدَاعِ فَقُلْتُ بَلَغَ بِي مَا تَرَى وَأَنَا ذُو مَالٍ وَلاَ يَرِثُنِي إِلاَّ ابْنَةٌ لِي أَفَأَتَصَدَّقُ بِثُلُثَىْ مَالِي قَالَ " لاَ ". قُلْتُ بِالشَّطْرِ قَالَ " لاَ ". قُلْتُ الثُّلُثُ قَالَ " الثُّلُثُ كَثِيرٌ، أَنْ تَدَعَ وَرَثَتَكَ أَغْنِيَاءَ خَيْرٌ مِنْ أَنْ تَذَرَهُمْ عَالَةً يَتَكَفَّفُونَ النَّاسَ وَلَنْ تُنْفِقَ نَفَقَةً تَبْتَغِي بِهَا وَجْهَ اللَّهِ إِلاَّ أُجِرْتَ عَلَيْهَا حَتَّى مَا تَجْعَلُ فِي فِي امْرَأَتِكَ ".

Narrated Ibn `Abbas: I recommend that people reduce the proportion of what they bequeath by will to the fourth (of the whole legacy), for Allah's Messenger ﷺ said, "One-third, yet even one third is too much.". – Sahih al-Bukhari 2743 [39]
حَدَّثَنَا قُتَيْبَةُ بْنُ سَعِيدٍ، حَدَّثَنَا سُفْيَانُ، عَنْ هِشَامِ بْنِ عُرْوَةَ، عَنْ أَبِيهِ، عَنِ ابْنِ عَبَّاسٍ ـ رضى الله عنهما ـ قَالَ لَوْ غَضَّ النَّاسُ إِلَى الرُّبْعِ، لأَنَّ رَسُولَ اللَّهِ صلى الله عليه وسلم قَالَ " الثُّلُثُ، وَالثُّلُثُ كَثِيرٌ أَوْ كَبِيرٌ ".

---

[39] In Islam, farā'iḍ refers to the fixed shares of inheritance that the Qur'an prescribes for heirs, which cannot be changed, ensuring justice for family members. Wasiyyah, on the other hand, is a voluntary will allowing a Muslim to give up to one-third of their estate to non-heirs or for charity. While farā'iḍ secures the rights of heirs, wasiyyah provides flexibility for personal wishes and generosity, all within the limits set by Shariah.

The Book of

And it is (a duty) upon mankind towards Allah (to come) to the Home on Pilgrimage

وَلِلَّهِ عَلَى ٱلنَّاسِ حِجُّ ٱلْبَيْتِ

Surely the first Home laid down for mankind was indeed at Bakkah, (Another name of Makkah) a blessed (place) and a guidance to the worlds Therein are supremely evident signs: the station of Ibrahim. (Abraham) And whoever enters it is secure. And it is (a duty) upon mankind towards Allah (to come) to the Home on Pilgrimage, for whomever is able to make a way to it. And (as for) him who has disbelieved, then surely Allah is Ever-Affluent, (Literally: Ever-Rich) (dispensing) with the worlds. – Surah Al-Imran 3:96&97

إِنَّ أَوَّلَ بَيْتٍ وُضِعَ لِلنَّاسِ لَلَّذِى بِبَكَّةَ مُبَارَكًا وَهُدًى لِّلْعَٰلَمِينَ فِيهِ ءَايَٰتٌۢ بَيِّنَٰتٌ مَّقَامُ إِبْرَٰهِيمَ ۖ وَمَن دَخَلَهُۥ كَانَ ءَامِنًا ۗ وَلِلَّهِ عَلَى ٱلنَّاسِ حِجُّ ٱلْبَيْتِ مَنِ ٱسْتَطَاعَ إِلَيْهِ سَبِيلًا ۚ وَمَن كَفَرَ فَإِنَّ ٱللَّهَ غَنِىٌّ عَنِ ٱلْعَٰلَمِينَ

They ask you about the phases of the moon. Say, "They indicate times for people and for the Pilgrimage." ...... Surah Al-Baqarah 2:189

يَسْـَٔلُونَكَ عَنِ ٱلْأَهِلَّةِ ۖ قُلْ هِىَ مَوَٰقِيتُ لِلنَّاسِ وَٱلْحَجِّ ۗ

Do your Hajj and the Umrah for Allah. If you are prevented, then send what offerings for sacrifice are possible, and do not shave your heads until the offerings arrive. If one of you is sick or has a head injury, then one can be redeemed by fasting, giving the purifying alms, or offering a sacrifice. When you are secure, whoever breaks one's purification between the Umrah until the Hajj should offer whatever sacrifice one can; or, if one cannot, one should fast three days during the Hajj, and then seven when one returns, ten days in all. This [observance] is for those whose families are not present at the Sacred Sanctuary. Be mindful of Allah, and know that Allah is severe in punishment. – Surah Al-Baqarah 2:196

وَأَتِمُّوا۟ ٱلْحَجَّ وَٱلْعُمْرَةَ لِلَّهِ ۚ فَإِنْ أُحْصِرْتُمْ فَمَا ٱسْتَيْسَرَ مِنَ ٱلْهَدْىِ ۖ وَلَا تَحْلِقُوا۟ رُءُوسَكُمْ حَتَّىٰ يَبْلُغَ ٱلْهَدْىُ مَحِلَّهُۥ ۚ فَمَن كَانَ مِنكُم مَّرِيضًا أَوْ بِهِۦٓ أَذًى مِّن رَّأْسِهِۦ فَفِدْيَةٌ مِّن صِيَامٍ أَوْ صَدَقَةٍ أَوْ نُسُكٍ ۚ فَإِذَآ أَمِنتُمْ فَمَن تَمَتَّعَ بِٱلْعُمْرَةِ إِلَى ٱلْحَجِّ فَمَا ٱسْتَيْسَرَ مِنَ ٱلْهَدْىِ ۚ فَمَن لَّمْ يَجِدْ فَصِيَامُ ثَلَٰثَةِ أَيَّامٍ فِى ٱلْحَجِّ وَسَبْعَةٍ إِذَا رَجَعْتُمْ ۗ تِلْكَ عَشَرَةٌ كَامِلَةٌ ۗ ذَٰلِكَ لِمَن لَّمْ يَكُنْ أَهْلُهُۥ حَاضِرِى ٱلْمَسْجِدِ ٱلْحَرَامِ ۚ وَٱتَّقُوا۟ ٱللَّهَ وَٱعْلَمُوٓا۟ أَنَّ ٱللَّهَ شَدِيدُ ٱلْعِقَابِ

O you who have believed, do not violate the way marks of Allah, nor the Inviolable Month, nor the offering, nor the garlands, nor the ones repairing to the Inviolable Home seeking from their Lord Grace and all-blessed Satisfaction; and when you are not on pilgrimage, (Literally: when you have become legally permissible, i.e., no longer in the sanctified state of a pilgrim) then (go game) hunting. And do not let antagonism of a people who barred you from the Inviolable Mosque provoke you to transgress. And help one another to benignancy and piety, and do not help one another to vice and hostility, and be pious to Allah; surely Allah is strict in punishment. – Surah Al-Ma'idah 5:2

يَٰٓأَيُّهَا ٱلَّذِينَ ءَامَنُوا۟ لَا تُحِلُّوا۟ شَعَٰٓئِرَ ٱللَّهِ وَلَا ٱلشَّهْرَ ٱلْحَرَامَ وَلَا ٱلْهَدْىَ وَلَا ٱلْقَلَٰٓئِدَ وَلَآ ءَآمِّينَ ٱلْبَيْتَ ٱلْحَرَامَ يَبْتَغُونَ فَضْلًا مِّن رَّبِّهِمْ وَرِضْوَٰنًا ۚ وَإِذَا حَلَلْتُمْ فَٱصْطَادُوا۟ ۚ وَلَا يَجْرِمَنَّكُمْ شَنَـَٔانُ قَوْمٍ أَن صَدُّوكُمْ عَنِ ٱلْمَسْجِدِ ٱلْحَرَامِ أَن تَعْتَدُوا۟ ۘ وَتَعَاوَنُوا۟ عَلَى ٱلْبِرِّ وَٱلتَّقْوَىٰ ۖ وَلَا تَعَاوَنُوا۟ عَلَى ٱلْإِثْمِ وَٱلْعُدْوَٰنِ ۚ وَٱتَّقُوا۟ ٱللَّهَ ۖ إِنَّ ٱللَّهَ شَدِيدُ ٱلْعِقَابِ

O you who have believed, do not kill the game (while) you are in pilgrim sanctity; (i.e., in the sacred precints or in the sanctified) and whoever of you kills it premeditatedly, then the

recompense is the like of what he has killed, in (grazing) livestock as shall be judged by two men of justice (Literally: possessing "a sense of" justice) among you, an offering to reach the Kacbah, or expiation food for indigent persons, or the just equivalent of that in fasting, so that he may taste the pernicious result of His Command. (i.e. the Command of Allah) Allah has been clement towards what Is bygone; and whoever goes back (to offense), then Allah will take vengeance on him; and Allah is Ever-Mighty, Owner of vengeance The game of the sea and the food of It are made lawful for you, as (a necessary) enjoyment for you and the travellers; and prohibited to you is the game of the land, so long as you are in pilgrim sanctity; (i.e., in the sacred precincts or in the sanctified state of a pilgrim) and be pious to Allah, to Whom you will be mustered Allah has made the Kacbah, the Inviolable Home, an upright (in-gathering) for mankind, and (likewise He has made) the in- violable month, and the offering, and the garlands. That (is so) that you may know that Allah knows whatever is in the heavens and whatever is in the earth, and that Allah is Ever-Knowing of everything. – Surah Al-Ma'idah 5:95-97
يَـٰٓأَيُّهَا ٱلَّذِينَ ءَامَنُوا۟ لَا تَقْتُلُوا۟ ٱلصَّيْدَ وَأَنتُمْ حُرُمٌ ۚ وَمَن قَتَلَهُۥ مِنكُم مُّتَعَمِّدًا فَجَزَآءٌ مِّثْلُ مَا قَتَلَ مِنَ ٱلنَّعَمِ يَحْكُمُ بِهِۦ ذَوَا عَدْلٍ مِّنكُمْ هَدْيًۢا بَـٰلِغَ ٱلْكَعْبَةِ أَوْ كَفَّـٰرَةٌ طَعَامُ مَسَـٰكِينَ أَوْ عَدْلُ ذَٰلِكَ صِيَامًا لِّيَذُوقَ وَبَالَ أَمْرِهِۦ ۗ عَفَا ٱللَّهُ عَمَّا سَلَفَ ۚ وَمَنْ عَادَ فَيَنتَقِمُ ٱللَّهُ مِنْهُ ۗ وَٱللَّهُ عَزِيزٌ ذُو ٱنتِقَامٍ أُحِلَّ لَكُمْ صَيْدُ ٱلْبَحْرِ وَطَعَامُهُۥ مَتَـٰعًا لَّكُمْ وَلِلسَّيَّارَةِ ۖ وَحُرِّمَ عَلَيْكُمْ صَيْدُ ٱلْبَرِّ مَا دُمْتُمْ حُرُمًا ۗ وَٱتَّقُوا۟ ٱللَّهَ ٱلَّذِىٓ إِلَيْهِ تُحْشَرُونَ جَعَلَ ٱللَّهُ ٱلْكَعْبَةَ ٱلْبَيْتَ ٱلْحَرَامَ قِيَـٰمًا لِّلنَّاسِ وَٱلشَّهْرَ ٱلْحَرَامَ وَٱلْهَدْىَ وَٱلْقَلَـٰٓئِدَ ۚ ذَٰلِكَ لِتَعْلَمُوٓا۟ أَنَّ ٱللَّهَ يَعْلَمُ مَا فِى ٱلسَّمَـٰوَٰتِ وَمَا فِى ٱلْأَرْضِ وَأَنَّ ٱللَّهَ بِكُلِّ شَىْءٍ عَلِيمٌ

Narrated `Abdullah bin Abu Qatada: That his father had told him that Allah's Messenger ﷺ set out for Hajj and so did his companions. He sent a batch of his companions by another route and Abu Qatada was one of them. The Prophet ﷺ said to them, "Proceed along the seashore till we meet all together." So, they took the route of the seashore, and when they started all of them assumed Ihram except Abu Qatada. While they were proceeding on, his companions saw a group of onagers. Abu Qatada chased the onagers and attacked and wounded a sheonager. They got down and ate some of its meat and said to each other: "How do we eat the meat of the game while we are in a state of Ihram?" So, we (they) carried the rest of the she-onager's meat, and when they met Allah's Messengr ﷺ they asked, saying, "O Allah's Messenger ﷺ ! We assumed Ihram with the exception of Abu Qatada and we saw (a group) of onagers. Abu Qatada attacked them and wounded a she-onager from them. Then we got down and ate from its meat. Later, we said, (to each other), 'How do we eat the meat of the game and we are in a state of Ihram?' So, we carried the rest of its meat. The Prophet asked, "Did anyone of you order Abu Qatada to attack it or point at it?" They replied in the negative. He said, "Then eat what is left of its meat.". – Sahih al-Bukhari 1824
حَدَّثَنَا مُوسَى بْنُ إِسْمَاعِيلَ، حَدَّثَنَا أَبُو عَوَانَةَ، حَدَّثَنَا عُثْمَانُ ـ هُوَ ابْنُ مَوْهَبٍ ـ قَالَ أَخْبَرَنِي عَبْدُ اللَّهِ بْنُ أَبِي قَتَادَةَ، أَنَّ أَبَاهُ، أَخْبَرَهُ أَنَّ رَسُولَ اللَّهِ صلى الله عليه وسلم خَرَجَ حَاجًّا، فَخَرَجُوا مَعَهُ فَصَرَفَ طَائِفَةً مِنْهُمْ، فِيهِمْ أَبُو قَتَادَةَ فَقَالَ خُذُوا سَاحِلَ الْبَحْرِ حَتَّى نَلْتَقِيَ. فَأَخَذُوا سَاحِلَ الْبَحْرِ، فَلَمَّا انْصَرَفُوا أَحْرَمُوا كُلُّهُمْ إِلاَّ أَبُو قَتَادَةَ لَمْ يُحْرِمْ، فَبَيْنَمَا هُمْ يَسِيرُونَ إِذْ رَأَوْا حُمُرَ وَحْشٍ، فَحَمَلَ أَبُو قَتَادَةَ عَلَى الْحُمُرِ، فَعَقَرَ مِنْهَا أَتَانًا، فَنَزَلُوا فَأَكَلُوا مِنْ لَحْمِهَا، وَقَالُوا أَنَأْكُلُ لَحْمَ صَيْدٍ وَنَحْنُ مُحْرِمُونَ فَحَمَلْنَا مَا بَقِيَ مِنْ لَحْمِ الأَتَانِ، فَلَمَّا أَتَوْا رَسُولَ اللَّهِ صلى الله عليه وسلم قَالُوا يَا رَسُولَ اللَّهِ، إِنَّا كُنَّا أَحْرَمْنَا وَقَدْ كَانَ أَبُو قَتَادَةَ لَمْ يُحْرِمْ، فَرَأَيْنَا حُمُرَ وَحْشٍ فَحَمَلَ عَلَيْهَا أَبُو قَتَادَةَ، فَعَقَرَ مِنْهَا أَتَانًا، فَنَزَلْنَا فَأَكَلْنَا مِنْ لَحْمِهَا ثُمَّ قُلْنَا أَنَأْكُلُ لَحْمَ صَيْدٍ وَنَحْنُ مُحْرِمُونَ فَحَمَلْنَا مَا بَقِيَ مِنْ لَحْمِهَا. قَالَ " مِنْكُمْ أَحَدٌ أَمَرَهُ أَنْ يَحْمِلَ عَلَيْهَا، أَوْ أَشَارَ إِلَيْهَا ". قَالُوا لاَ. قَالَ " فَكُلُوا مَا بَقِيَ مِنْ لَحْمِهَا ".

Narrated Jabir bin `Abdullah: "Allah's Messenger ﷺ sent an army towards the east coast and appointed Abu 'Ubaida bin Al-Jarrah as their chief, and the army consisted of three-hundred men including myself. We marched on till we reached a place where our food was about to finish. Abu- 'Ubaida ordered us to collect all the journey food and it was collected. My (our) journey food was dates. Abu 'Ubaida kept on giving us our daily ration in small amounts from it, till it was exhausted. The share of everyone of us used to be one date only." I said, "How could one date benefit you?" Jabir replied, "We came to know its value when even that too finished." Jabir added, "When we reached the sea-shore, we saw a huge fish which was like a small mountain. The army ate from it for eighteen days. Then Abu 'Ubaida ordered that two of its ribs be fixed and they were fixed in the ground. Then he ordered that a she-camel be ridden and it passed under the two ribs (forming an arch) without touching them." – Sahih al-Bukhari 2483

حَدَّثَنَا عَبْدُ اللَّهِ بْنُ يُوسُفَ، أَخْبَرَنَا مَالِكٌ، عَنْ وَهْبِ بْنِ كَيْسَانَ، عَنْ جَابِرِ بْنِ عَبْدِ اللَّهِ ـ رضى الله عنهما ـ أَنَّهُ قَالَ بَعَثَ رَسُولُ اللَّهِ صلى الله عليه وسلم بَعْثًا قِبَلَ السَّاحِلِ، فَأَمَّرَ عَلَيْهِمْ أَبَا عُبَيْدَةَ بْنَ الْجَرَّاحِ وَهُمْ ثَلاَثُمِائَةٍ وَأَنَا فِيهِمْ، فَخَرَجْنَا حَتَّى إِذَا كُنَّا بِبَعْضِ الطَّرِيقِ فَنِيَ الزَّادُ، فَأَمَرَ أَبُو عُبَيْدَةَ بِأَزْوَادِ ذَلِكَ الْجَيْشِ فَجُمِعَ ذَلِكَ كُلُّهُ فَكَانَ مِزْوَدَىْ تَمْرٍ، فَكَانَ يُقَوِّتُنَا كُلَّ يَوْمٍ قَلِيلاً قَلِيلاً، حَتَّى فَنِيَ فَلَمْ يَكُنْ يُصِيبُنَا إِلاَّ تَمْرَةٌ تَمْرَةٌ. فَقُلْتُ وَمَا تُغْنِي تَمْرَةٌ فَقَالَ لَقَدْ وَجَدْنَا فَقْدَهَا حِينَ فَنِيَتْ. قَالَ ثُمَّ انْتَهَيْنَا إِلَى الْبَحْرِ فَإِذَا حُوتٌ مِثْلُ الظَّرِبِ، فَأَكَلَ مِنْهُ ذَلِكَ الْجَيْشُ ثَمَانِيَ عَشْرَةَ لَيْلَةً، ثُمَّ أَمَرَ أَبُو عُبَيْدَةَ بِضِلَعَيْنِ مِنْ أَضْلاَعِهِ فَنُصِبَا، ثُمَّ أَمَرَ بِرَاحِلَةٍ فَرُحِلَتْ ثُمَّ مَرَّتْ تَحْتَهُمَا فَلَمْ تُصِبْهُمَا

Al-Masjid Al-Haram
ٱلْمَسْجِدَ ٱلْحَرَامَ

Surely the first Home laid down for mankind was indeed at Bakkah, (Another name of Makkah) a blessed (place) and a guidance to the worlds – Surah Al-Imran 3:96

إِنَّ أَوَّلَ بَيْتٍ وُضِعَ لِلنَّاسِ لَلَّذِى بِبَكَّةَ مُبَارَكًا وَهُدًى لِّلْعَٰلَمِينَ

Narrated Ibn `Abbas: The first lady to use a girdle was the mother of Ishmael. She used a girdle so that she might hide her tracks from Sarah. Abraham brought her and her son Ishmael while she was suckling him, to a place near the Ka`ba under a tree on the spot of Zamzam, at the highest place in the mosque. During those days there was nobody in Mecca, nor was there any water So he made them sit over there and placed near them a leather bag containing some dates, and a small water-skin containing some water, and set out homeward. Ishmael's mother followed him saying, "O Abraham! Where are you going, leaving us in this valley where there is no person whose company we may enjoy, nor is there anything (to enjoy)?" She repeated that to him many times, but he did not look back at her Then she asked him, "Has Allah ordered you to do so?" He said, "Yes." She said, "Then He will not neglect us," and returned while Abraham proceeded onwards, and on reaching the Thaniya where they could not see him, he faced the Ka`ba, and raising both hands, invoked Allah saying the following prayers: 'O our Lord! I have made some of my offspring dwell in a valley without cultivation, by Your Sacred House (Ka`ba at Mecca) in order, O our Lord, that they may offer prayer perfectly. So fill some hearts among men with love towards them, and (O Allah) provide them with fruits, so that they may give thanks.' (14.37) Ishmael's mother went on suckling Ishmael and drinking from the water (she had). When the water in the water-skin had all been used up, she became thirsty and her child also became thirsty. She started looking at him (i.e. Ishmael) tossing in agony; She left him, for she could not endure looking at him, and found that the mountain of Safa was the nearest mountain to her on that land. She stood on it and started looking at the valley keenly so that she might see somebody, but she could not see anybody. Then she descended from Safa and when she reached the valley, she tucked up her robe and ran in the valley like a person in distress and trouble, till she crossed the valley and reached the Marwa mountain where she stood and started looking, expecting to see somebody, but she could not see anybody. She repeated that (running between Safa and Marwa) seven times." The Prophet ((ﷺsaid, "This is the source of the tradition of the walking of people between them (i.e. Safa and Marwa). When she reached the Marwa (for the last time) she heard a voice and she asked herself to be quiet and listened attentively. She heard the voice again and said, 'O, (whoever you may be)! You have made me hear your voice; have you got something to help me?" And behold! She saw an angel at the place of Zamzam, digging the earth with his heel (or his wing), till water flowed from that place. She started to make something like a basin around it, using her hand in this way, and started filling her water-skin with water with her hands, and the water was flowing out after she had scooped some of it." The Prophet ((ﷺadded, "May Allah bestow Mercy on Ishmael's mother! Had she let the Zamzam (flow without trying to control it) (or had she not scooped from that water) (to fill her water-skin), Zamzam would have been a stream flowing on the surface of the earth." The Prophet ((ﷺfurther added, "Then she drank (water) and suckled her child. The angel said to her, 'Don't be afraid of being neglected, for this is the House of Allah which will be built by this boy and his father, and Allah never neglects His people.' The House (i.e. Ka`ba) at that time was on a high place resembling a hillock, and when torrents came, they flowed to its right and left. She lived in that way till some people from the tribe of Jurhum or a family from Jurhum passed by her and her child, as they (i.e. the Jurhum people) were coming through the way of Kada'. They landed in the lower part of Mecca where they saw a bird that had the habit of flying around water and not leaving it. They said, 'This bird must be flying around water, though we know that there is no water in this valley.' They sent one or two messengers who discovered the source of water, and returned to inform them of the water. So, they all came (towards the water)." The Prophet ((ﷺadded, "Ishmael's mother was sitting near the water. They asked her, 'Do you allow us to stay with you?" She replied, 'Yes, but you will have no right to possess the water.' They agreed to that." The Prophet ((ﷺfurther said, "Ishmael's mother was pleased with the whole situation as she used to love to enjoy the company of the people. So, they settled there, and later on they sent for their families who came and settled with them so that some families became permanent residents there. The child (i.e. Ishmael) grew up and learnt Arabic from them and (his virtues) caused them to love and admire him as he grew up, and when he reached the age of puberty they made him marry a woman from amongst them. After Ishmael's mother had died, Abraham came after Ishmael's marriage in order to see his family that he had left before, but he did not find Ishmael there. When he asked Ishmael's wife about him, she replied, 'He has gone in search of our livelihood.' Then he asked her about their way of living and their condition, and she replied, 'We are living in misery; we are living in hardship and destitution,' complaining to him. He said, 'When your husband returns, convey my salutation to him and tell him to change the threshold of the gate (of his house).' When Ishmael came, he seemed to have felt something unusual, so he asked his wife, 'Has anyone visited you?' She replied, 'Yes, an old man of so-and-so description came and asked me about you and I informed him, and he asked about our state of living, and I told him that we were living in a hardship and poverty.' On that Ishmael said, 'Did he advise you anything?' She replied, 'Yes, he told me to convey his salutation to you and to tell you to change the threshold of your gate.' Ishmael said, 'It was my father, and he has ordered me to divorce you. Go back to your family.' So, Ishmael divorced her and married another woman from amongst them (i.e. Jurhum). Then Abraham stayed away from them for a period as long as Allah wished and called on them again but did not find Ishmael. So he came to Ishmael's wife

and asked her about Ishmael. She said, 'He has gone in search of our livelihood.' Abraham asked her, 'How are you getting on?' asking her about their sustenance and living. She replied, 'We are prosperous and well-off (i.e. we have everything in abundance).' Then she thanked Allah' Abraham said, 'What kind of food do you eat?' She said. 'Meat.' He said, 'What do you drink?' She said, 'Water." He said, "O Allah! Bless their meat and water." The Prophet added, "At that time they did not have grain, and if they had grain, he would have also invoked Allah to bless it." The Prophet ((ﷺadded, "If somebody has only these two things as his sustenance, his health and disposition will be badly affected, unless he lives in Mecca." The Prophet ((ﷺadded," Then Abraham said Ishmael's wife, "When your husband comes, give my regards to him and tell him that he should keep firm the threshold of his gate.' When Ishmael came back, he asked his wife, 'Did anyone call on you?' She replied, 'Yes, a good-looking old man came to me,' so she praised him and added. 'He asked about you, and I informed him, and he asked about our livelihood and I told him that we were in a good condition.' Ishmael asked her, 'Did he give you any piece of advice?' She said, 'Yes, he told me to give his regards to you and ordered that you should keep firm the threshold of your gate.' On that Ishmael said, 'It was my father, and you are the threshold (of the gate). He has ordered me to keep you with me.' Then Abraham stayed away from them for a period as long as Allah wished, and called on them afterwards. He saw Ishmael under a tree near Zamzam, sharpening his arrows. When he saw Abraham, he rose up to welcome him (and they greeted each other as a father does with his son or a son does with his father). Abraham said, 'O Ishmael! Allah has given me an order.' Ishmael said, 'Do what your Lord has ordered you to do.' Abraham asked, 'Will you help me?' Ishmael said, 'I will help you.' Abraham said, Allah has ordered me to build a house here,' pointing to a hillock higher than the land surrounding it." The Prophet ((ﷺadded, "Then they raised the foundations of the House (i.e. the Ka`ba). Ishmael brought the stones and Abraham was building, and when the walls became high, Ishmael brought this stone and put it for Abraham who stood over it and carried on building, while Ishmael was handing him the stones, and both of them were saying, 'O our Lord! Accept (this service) from us, Verily, You are the All-Hearing, the All-Knowing.' The Prophet ((ﷺadded, "Then both of them went on building and going round the Ka`ba saying: O our Lord ! Accept (this service) from us, Verily, You are the All-Hearing, the All-Knowing." (2.127).
– Sahih al-Bukhari 3364

وَحَدَّثَنِي عَبْدُ اللَّهِ بْنُ مُحَمَّدٍ، حَدَّثَنَا عَبْدُ الرَّزَّاقِ، أَخْبَرَنَا مَعْمَرٌ، عَنْ أَيُّوبَ السَّخْتِيَانِيِّ، وَكَثِيرِ بْنِ كَثِيرِ بْنِ الْمُطَّلِبِ بْنِ أَبِي وَدَاعَةَ،، يَزِيدُ أَحَدُهُمَا عَلَى الآخَرِ عَنْ سَعِيدِ بْنِ جُبَيْرٍ، قَالَ ابْنُ عَبَّاسٍ أَوَّلَ مَا اتَّخَذَ النِّسَاءُ الْمِنْطَقَ مِنْ قِبَلِ أُمِّ إِسْمَاعِيلَ، اتَّخَذَتْ مِنْطَقًا لَتُعَفِّيَ أَثَرَهَا عَلَى سَارَةَ، ثُمَّ جَاءَ بِهَا إِبْرَاهِيمُ، وَبِابْنِهَا إِسْمَاعِيلَ وَهْىَ تُرْضِعُهُ حَتَّى وَضَعَهُمَا عِنْدَ الْبَيْتِ عِنْدَ دَوْحَةٍ، فَوْقَ زَمْزَمَ فِي أَعْلَى الْمَسْجِدِ، وَلَيْسَ بِمَكَّةَ يَوْمَئِذٍ أَحَدٌ، وَلَيْسَ بِهَا مَاءٌ، فَوَضَعَهُمَا هُنَالِكَ، وَوَضَعَ عِنْدَهُمَا جِرَابًا فِيهِ تَمْرٌ وَسِقَاءً فِيهِ مَاءٌ، ثُمَّ قَفَّى إِبْرَاهِيمُ مُنْطَلِقًا فَتَبِعَتْهُ أُمُّ إِسْمَاعِيلَ فَقَالَتْ يَا إِبْرَاهِيمُ أَيْنَ تَذْهَبُ وَتَتْرُكُنَا بِهَذَا الْوَادِي الَّذِي لَيْسَ فِيهِ إِنْسٌ وَلاَ شَىْءٌ فَقَالَتْ لَهُ ذَلِكَ

Surely the ones who have disbelieved and bar from the way of Allah and the Inviolable Mosque that We have made equal to mankind- (alike are) him who consecrates himself therein and the nomad- (The Sabaeans) and whoever would (dare) blasphemy therein unjustly, (Christians) We will let him taste (his share) of a painful torment – Surah Al-Hajj 22:25

إِنَّ ٱلَّذِينَ كَفَرُوا۟ وَيَصُدُّونَ عَن سَبِيلِ ٱللَّهِ وَٱلْمَسْجِدِ ٱلْحَرَامِ ٱلَّذِى جَعَلْنَـٰهُ لِلنَّاسِ سَوَآءً ٱلْعَـٰكِفُ فِيهِ وَٱلْبَادِ ۚ وَمَن يُرِدْ فِيهِ بِإِلْحَادٍۭ بِظُلْمٍ نُّذِقْهُ مِنْ عَذَابٍ أَلِيمٍ

In no way should the associators (Those who associate others with Allah) tend the mosques of Allah, witnessing against themselves disbelief; those, their deeds are frustrated, and in the Fire they are eternally (abiding). Surely he only shall tend the mosques of Allah who has believed in Allah and the Last Day, and kept up the prayer, and brought the Zakat, (i.e., paid the obligatoery poor-dues) and is apprehensive of none except Allah; so, it may be that those will be among the right-guided. – Surah At-Taubah 9:17&18

مَا كَانَ لِلْمُشْرِكِينَ أَن يَعْمُرُوا۟ مَسَـٰجِدَ ٱللَّهِ شَـٰهِدِينَ عَلَىٰٓ أَنفُسِهِم بِٱلْكُفْرِ ۚ أُو۟لَـٰٓئِكَ حَبِطَتْ أَعْمَـٰلُهُمْ وَفِى ٱلنَّارِ هُمْ خَـٰلِدُونَ إِنَّمَا يَعْمُرُ مَسَـٰجِدَ ٱللَّهِ مَنْ ءَامَنَ بِٱللَّهِ وَٱلْيَوْمِ ٱلْـَٔاخِرِ وَأَقَامَ ٱلصَّلَوٰةَ وَءَاتَى ٱلزَّكَوٰةَ وَلَمْ يَخْشَ إِلَّا ٱللَّهَ ۖ فَعَسَىٰٓ أُو۟لَـٰٓئِكَ أَن يَكُونُوا۟ مِنَ ٱلْمُهْتَدِينَ

Believers: idolaters are impure. From this year on, do not let them come near the Sacred House. If you fear poverty, then Allah if He wills, will enrich you out of His favor. Allah knows everything and is wise. – Surah At-Taubah 9:28

يَـٰٓأَيُّهَا ٱلَّذِينَ ءَامَنُوٓا۟ إِنَّمَا ٱلْمُشْرِكُونَ نَجَسٌ فَلَا يَقْرَبُوا۟ ٱلْمَسْجِدَ ٱلْحَرَامَ بَعْدَ عَامِهِمْ هَـٰذَا ۚ وَإِنْ خِفْتُمْ عَيْلَةً فَسَوْفَ يُغْنِيكُمُ ٱللَّهُ مِن فَضْلِهِۦٓ إِن شَآءَ ۚ إِنَّ ٱللَّهَ عَلِيمٌ حَكِيمٌ

And slay them wherever you may come upon them, and drive them away from wherever they drove you away – for oppression is even worse than killing. And fight not against them near the Inviolable House of Worship unless they fight against you there first; but if they fight against you, slay them: such shall be the recompense of those who deny the truth – Surah Al-Baqarah 2:191

وَٱقْتُلُوهُمْ حَيْثُ ثَقِفْتُمُوهُمْ وَأَخْرِجُوهُم مِّنْ حَيْثُ أَخْرَجُوكُمْ ۚ وَٱلْفِتْنَةُ أَشَدُّ مِنَ ٱلْقَتْلِ ۚ وَلَا تُقَـٰتِلُوهُمْ عِندَ ٱلْمَسْجِدِ ٱلْحَرَامِ حَتَّىٰ يُقَـٰتِلُوكُمْ فِيهِ ۖ فَإِن قَـٰتَلُوكُمْ فَٱقْتُلُوهُمْ ۗ كَذَٰلِكَ جَزَآءُ ٱلْكَـٰفِرِينَ

And what (plea) have they, that Allah should not torment them, and they are barring from the Inviolable Mosque, and in no way have they been its patrons? Decidedly none (could be) its patrons except the pious ones; but most of them do not know – Surah Al-Anfal 8:34

وَمَا لَهُمْ أَلَّا يُعَذِّبَهُمُ ٱللَّهُ وَهُمْ يَصُدُّونَ عَنِ ٱلْمَسْجِدِ ٱلْحَرَامِ وَمَا كَانُوٓا۟ أَوْلِيَآءَهُۥٓ ۚ إِنْ أَوْلِيَآؤُهُۥٓ إِلَّا ٱلْمُتَّقُونَ وَلَـٰكِنَّ أَكْثَرَهُمْ لَا يَعْلَمُونَ

Miqat
ميقات

Narrated Ibn `Abbas: The Prophet ﷺ fixed Dhul-Hulaifa as the Miqat for the people of Medina, Al-Juhfa for the people of Sham, Qarn-al-Manazil for the people of Najd, and Yalamlam for the people of Yemen; and these Mawaqit are for those living at those very places, and besides them for those whom come through them with the intention of performing Hajj and Umra; and whoever is living within these Mawaqit should assume Ihram from where he starts, and the people of Mecca can assume Ihram from Mecca. – Sahih al-Bukhari 1530

حَدَّثَنَا مُعَلَّى بْنُ أَسَدٍ، حَدَّثَنَا وُهَيْبٌ، عَنْ عَبْدِ اللَّهِ بْنِ طَاوُسٍ، عَنْ أَبِيهِ، عَنِ ابْنِ عَبَّاسٍ، رضى الله عنهما أَنَّ النَّبِيَّ صلى الله عليه وسلم وَقَّتَ لأَهْلِ الْمَدِينَةِ ذَا الْحُلَيْفَةِ، وَلأَهْلِ الشَّأْمِ الْجُحْفَةَ، وَلأَهْلِ نَجْدٍ قَرْنَ الْمَنَازِلِ، وَلأَهْلِ الْيَمَنِ يَلَمْلَمَ، هُنَّ لأَهْلِهِنَّ وَلِكُلِّ آتٍ أَتَى عَلَيْهِنَّ مِنْ غَيْرِهِمْ مِمَّنْ أَرَادَ الْحَجَّ وَالْعُمْرَةَ فَمَنْ كَانَ دُونَ ذَلِكَ، فَمِنْ حَيْثُ أَنْشَأَ حَتَّى أَهْلُ مَكَّةَ مِنْ مَكَّةَ.

Narrated Abu Shihab: I left for Mecca for Hajj-at-Tamattu` assuming Ihram for `Umra. I reached Mecca three days before the day of Tarwiya (8th Dhul-Hijja). Some people of Mecca said to me, "Your Hajj will be like the Hajj performed by the people of Mecca (i.e. you will lose the superiority of assuming Ihram from the Miqat). So I went to `Ata' asking him his view about it. He said, "Jabir bin `Abdullah narrated to me, 'I performed Hajj with Allah's Messenger ﷺ on the day when he drove camels with him. The people had assumed Ihram for Hajj-al-Ifrad. The Prophet ﷺ ordered them to finish their Ihram after Tawaf round the Ka`ba, and between Safa and Marwa and to cut short their hair and then to stay there (in Mecca) as non-Muhrims till the day of Tarwiya (i.e. 8th of Dhul-Hijja) when they would assume Ihram for Hajj and they were ordered to make the Ihram with which they had come as for `Umra only. They asked, 'How can we make it `Umra (Tamattu`) as we have intended to perform Hajj?' The Prophet ﷺ said, 'Do what I have ordered you. Had I not brought the Hadi with me, I would have done the same, but I cannot finish my Ihram till the Hadi reaches its destination (i.e. is slaughtered).' So, they did (what he ordered them to do)." – Sahih al-Bukhari 1568

حَدَّثَنَا أَبُو نُعَيْمٍ، حَدَّثَنَا أَبُو شِهَابٍ، قَالَ قَدِمْتُ مُتَمَتِّعًا مَكَّةَ بِعُمْرَةٍ فَدَخَلْنَا قَبْلَ التَّرْوِيَةِ بِثَلاَثَةِ أَيَّامٍ، فَقَالَ لِي أُنَاسٌ مِنْ أَهْلِ مَكَّةَ تَصِيرُ الآنَ حَجَّتُكَ مَكِّيَّةً. فَدَخَلْتُ عَلَى عَطَاءٍ أَسْتَفْتِيهِ فَقَالَ حَدَّثَنِي جَابِرُ بْنُ عَبْدِ اللَّهِ ـ رضى الله عنهما ـ أَنَّهُ حَجَّ مَعَ النَّبِيِّ صلى الله عليه وسلم يَوْمَ سَاقَ الْبُدْنَ مَعَهُ، وَقَدْ أَهَلُّوا بِالْحَجِّ مُفْرَدًا، فَقَالَ لَهُمْ " أَحِلُّوا مِنْ إِحْرَامِكُمْ بِطَوَافِ الْبَيْتِ وَبَيْنَ الصَّفَا وَالْمَرْوَةِ، وَقَصِّرُوا ثُمَّ أَقِيمُوا حَلاَلاً، حَتَّى إِذَا كَانَ يَوْمُ التَّرْوِيَةِ فَأَهِلُّوا بِالْحَجِّ، وَاجْعَلُوا الَّتِي قَدِمْتُمْ بِهَا مُتْعَةً ". فَقَالُوا كَيْفَ نَجْعَلُهَا مُتْعَةً وَقَدْ سَمَّيْنَا الْحَجَّ فَقَالَ " افْعَلُوا مَا أَمَرْتُكُمْ، فَلَوْلاَ أَنِّي سُقْتُ الْهَدْىَ لَفَعَلْتُ مِثْلَ الَّذِي أَمَرْتُكُمْ، وَلَكِنْ لاَ يَحِلُّ مِنِّي حَرَامٌ حَتَّى يَبْلُغَ الْهَدْىُ مَحِلَّهُ ". فَفَعَلُوا. قَالَ أَبُو عَبْد اللَّهِ أَبُو شِهَابٍ لَيْسَ لَهُ مُسْنَدٌ إِلاَّ هَذَا

Narrated `Abdullah bin Dinar: Ibn `Umar said, "The Prophet ﷺ fixed Qarn as the Miqat (for assuming the Ihram) for the people of Najd, and Al-Juhfa for the people of Sham, and Dhul-Hulaifa for the people of Medina." Ibn `Umar added, "I heard this from the Prophet, and I have been informed that the Prophet ﷺ said, 'The Miqat for the Yemenites is Yalamlam.' "When Iraq was mentioned, he said, "At that time it was not a Muslim country." – Sahih al-Bukhari 7344

حَدَّثَنَا مُحَمَّدُ بْنُ يُوسُفَ، حَدَّثَنَا سُفْيَانُ، عَنْ عَبْدِ اللَّهِ بْنِ دِينَارٍ، عَنِ ابْنِ عُمَرَ، وَقَّتَ النَّبِيُّ صلى الله عليه وسلم قَرْنًا لأَهْلِ نَجْدٍ، وَالْجُحْفَةَ لأَهْلِ الشَّأْمِ، وَذَا الْحُلَيْفَةِ لأَهْلِ الْمَدِينَةِ. قَالَ سَمِعْتُ هَذَا مِنَ النَّبِيِّ صلى الله عليه وسلم وَبَلَغَنِي أَنَّ النَّبِيَّ صلى الله عليه وسلم قَالَ " وَلأَهْلِ الْيَمَنِ يَلَمْلَمُ ". وَذُكِرَ الْعِرَاقُ فَقَالَ لَمْ يَكُنْ عِرَاقٌ يَوْمَئِذٍ

Mina
مينا

And announce to mankind the Pilgrimage; they shall come up (hurriedly) to you on foot and upon every slender (conveyance); they shall definitely come up from every deep ravine That they may witness (things) profitable to them and mention the Name of Allah on days well-known over such brute cattle as He has provided them. So eat thereof, and feed the miserable poor." – Surah Al-Hajj 22:28&29

لِّيَشْهَدُوا۟ مَنَـٰفِعَ لَهُمْ وَيَذْكُرُوا۟ ٱسْمَ ٱللَّهِ فِىٓ أَيَّامٍ مَّعْلُومَـٰتٍ عَلَىٰ مَا رَزَقَهُم مِّنۢ بَهِيمَةِ ٱلْأَنْعَـٰمِ ۖ فَكُلُوا۟ مِنْهَا وَأَطْعِمُوا۟ ٱلْبَآئِسَ ٱلْفَقِيرَ ثُمَّ لْيَقْضُوا۟ تَفَثَهُمْ وَلْيُوفُوا۟ نُذُورَهُمْ وَلْيَطَّوَّفُوا۟ بِٱلْبَيْتِ ٱلْعَتِيقِ

You have benefits in these animals marked for sacrifice for a specified time; then, their place of sacrifice is at the Ancient House. – Surah Al-Hajj 22:33

لَكُمْ فِيهَا مَنَـٰفِعُ إِلَىٰٓ أَجَلٍ مُّسَمًّى ثُمَّ مَحِلُّهَآ إِلَى ٱلْبَيْتِ ٱلْعَتِيقِ

Narrated Salim: `Abdullah bin `Umar used to send the weak among his family early to Mina. So they used to depart from Al-Mash'ar Al-Haram (that is Al-Muzdalifa) at night (when the moon had set) and invoke Allah as much as they could, and then they would return (to Mina) before the Imam had started from Al- Muzdalifa to Mina. So some of them would reach Mina at the time of the Fajr prayer and some of them would come later. When they reached Mina they would throw pebbles on the Jamra (Jamrat-Al- `Aqaba) Ibn `Umar used to say, "Allah's Messenger ﷺ gave the permission to them (weak people) to do so." – Sahih al-Bukhari 1676

حَدَّثَنَا يَحْيَى بْنُ بُكَيْرٍ، حَدَّثَنَا اللَّيْثُ، عَنْ يُونُسَ، عَنِ ابْنِ شِهَابٍ، قَالَ سَالِمٌ وَكَانَ عَبْدُ اللَّهِ بْنُ عُمَرَ ـ رضى الله عنهما ـ يُقَدِّمُ ضَعَفَةَ أَهْلِهِ، فَيَقِفُونَ عِنْدَ الْمَشْعَرِ الْحَرَامِ بِالْمُزْدَلِفَةِ بِلَيْلٍ، فَيَذْكُرُونَ اللَّهَ مَا بَدَا لَهُمْ، ثُمَّ يَرْجِعُونَ قَبْلَ أَنْ يَقِفَ الإِمَامُ، وَقَبْلَ أَنْ يَدْفَعَ، فَمِنْهُمْ مَنْ يَقْدَمُ مِنًى لِصَلاَةِ الْفَجْرِ، وَمِنْهُمْ مَنْ يَقْدَمُ بَعْدَ ذَلِكَ، فَإِذَا قَدِمُوا رَمَوُا الْجَمْرَةَ، وَكَانَ ابْنُ عُمَرَ ـ رضى الله عنهما ـ يَقُولُ أَرْخَصَ فِي أُولَئِكَ رَسُولُ اللَّهِ صلى الله عليه وسلم.

Narrated `Abdullah bin `Abbas: I came riding on my she-ass and had (just) then attained the age of puberty. Allah's Messenger ﷺ was praying at Mina. I passed in front of a part of the first row and then dismounted from it, and the animal started grazing. I aligned with the people behind Allah's Messenger ﷺ . The sub-narrator added that happened in Mina during the Prophet's Hajjat-al-Wada`.) – Sahih al-Bukhari 1857

حَدَّثَنَا إِسْحَاقُ، أَخْبَرَنَا يَعْقُوبُ بْنُ إِبْرَاهِيمَ، حَدَّثَنَا ابْنُ أَخِي ابْنِ شِهَابٍ، عَنْ عَمِّهِ، أَخْبَرَنِي عُبَيْدُ اللَّهِ بْنُ عَبْدِ اللَّهِ بْنِ عُتْبَةَ بْنِ مَسْعُودٍ، أَنَّ عَبْدَ اللَّهِ بْنَ عَبَّاسٍ ـ رضى الله عنهما ـ قَالَ أَقْبَلْتُ وَقَدْ نَاهَزْتُ الْحُلُمَ، أَسِيرُ عَلَى أَتَانٍ لِي، وَرَسُولُ اللَّهِ صلى الله عليه وسلم قَائِمٌ يُصَلِّي بِمِنًى، حَتَّى سِرْتُ بَيْنَ يَدَىْ بَعْضِ الصَّفِّ الأَوَّلِ، ثُمَّ نَزَلْتُ عَنْهَا فَرَتَعَتْ، فَصَفَفْتُ مَعَ النَّاسِ وَرَاءَ رَسُولِ اللَّهِ صلى الله عليه وسلم. وَقَالَ يُونُسُ عَنِ ابْنِ شِهَابٍ بِمِنًى فِي حَجَّةِ الْوَدَاعِ.

Narrated Ibn `Umar: The Prophet ﷺ permitted the people who provided the pilgrims with water to stay at Mecca during the nights of Mina. – Sahih al-Bukhari 1743

حَدَّثَنَا مُحَمَّدُ بْنُ عُبَيْدِ بْنِ مَيْمُونٍ، حَدَّثَنَا عِيسَى بْنُ يُونُسَ، عَنْ عُبَيْدِ اللَّهِ، عَنْ نَافِعٍ، عَنِ ابْنِ عُمَرَ ـ رضى الله عنهما ـ رَخَّصَ النَّبِيُّ صلى الله عليه وسلم.

Narrated Haritha bin Wahab: The Prophet ﷺ led us in the prayer at Mina during the peace period by offering two rak`at. – Sahih al-Bukhari 1083

حَدَّثَنَا أَبُو الْوَلِيدِ، قَالَ حَدَّثَنَا شُعْبَةُ، أَنْبَأَنَا أَبُو إِسْحَاقَ، قَالَ سَمِعْتُ حَارِثَةَ بْنَ وَهْبٍ، قَالَ صَلَّى بِنَا النَّبِيُّ صلى الله عليه وسلم آمَنَ مَا كَانَ بِمِنًى رَكْعَتَيْنِ.

Narrated `Abdur Rahman bin Yazid: We offered a four rak`at prayer at Mina behind Ibn `Affan . `Abdullah bin Mas`ud was informed about it. He said sadly, "Truly to Allah we belong and truly to Him we shall return." And added, "I prayed two rak`at with Allah's Messenger ﷺ at Mina and similarly with Abu Bakr and with `Umar (during their caliphates)." He further said, "May I be lucky enough to have two of the four rak`at accepted (by Allah)." – Sahih al-Bukhari 1084

حَدَّثَنَا قُتَيْبَةُ، قَالَ حَدَّثَنَا عَبْدُ الْوَاحِدِ، عَنِ الأَعْمَشِ، قَالَ حَدَّثَنَا إِبْرَاهِيمُ، قَالَ سَمِعْتُ عَبْدَ الرَّحْمَنِ بْنَ يَزِيدَ، يَقُولُ صَلَّى بِنَا عُثْمَانُ بْنُ عَفَّانَ ـ رضى الله عنه ـ بِمِنًى أَرْبَعَ رَكَعَاتٍ، فَقِيلَ ذَلِكَ لِعَبْدِ اللَّهِ بْنِ مَسْعُودٍ ـ رضى الله عنه ـ فَاسْتَرْجَعَ ثُمَّ قَالَ صَلَّيْتُ مَعَ رَسُولِ اللَّهِ صلى الله عليه وسلم بِمِنًى رَكْعَتَيْنِ، وَصَلَّيْتُ مَعَ أَبِي بَكْرٍ ـ رضى الله عنه ـ بِمِنًى رَكْعَتَيْنِ، وَصَلَّيْتُ مَعَ عُمَرَ بْنِ الْخَطَّابِ ـ رضى الله عنه ـ بِمِنًى رَكْعَتَيْنِ، فَلَيْتَ حَظِّي مِنْ أَرْبَعِ رَكَعَاتٍ رَكْعَتَانِ مُتَقَبَّلَتَانِ.

Day of Arafat
يَوْمَ عَرَفَةَ

Narrated Maimuna: The people doubted whether the Prophet ﷺ was fasting on the day of `Arafat or not, so I sent milk while he was standing at `Arafat, he drank it and the people were looking at him. – Sahih al-Bukhari 1989

حَدَّثَنَا يَحْيَى بْنُ سُلَيْمَانَ، حَدَّثَنَا ابْنُ وَهْبٍ ـ أَوْ قُرِئَ عَلَيْهِ ـ قَالَ أَخْبَرَنِي عَمْرٌو، عَنْ بُكَيْرٍ، عَنْ كُرَيْبٍ، عَنْ مَيْمُونَةَ ـ رضى الله عنها ـ أَنَّ النَّاسَ، شَكُّوا فِي صِيَامِ النَّبِيِّ صلى الله عليه وسلم يَوْمَ عَرَفَةَ، فَأَرْسَلَتْ إِلَيْهِ بِحِلاَبٍ وَهْوَ وَاقِفٌ فِي الْمَوْقِفِ، فَشَرِبَ مِنْهُ، وَالنَّاسُ يَنْظُرُونَ.

Narrated Um Al-Fadl: (daughter of Al-Harith) that she sent a bowl of milk to the Prophet ﷺ while he was standing (at `Arafat) in the afternoon of the Day of `Arafat. He took it in his hands and drank it. Narrated Abu Nadr: The Prophet was on the back of his camel. – Sahih al-Bukhari 5618

حَدَّثَنَا مَالِكُ بْنُ إِسْمَاعِيلَ، حَدَّثَنَا عَبْدُ الْعَزِيزِ بْنُ أَبِي سَلَمَةَ، أَخْبَرَنَا أَبُو النَّضْرِ، عَنْ عُمَيْرٍ، مَوْلَى ابْنِ عَبَّاسٍ عَنْ أُمِّ الْفَضْلِ بِنْتِ الْحَارِثِ، أَنَّهَا أَرْسَلَتْ إِلَى النَّبِيِّ صلى الله عليه وسلم بِقَدَحِ لَبَنٍ، وَهُوَ وَاقِفٌ عَشِيَّةَ عَرَفَةَ، فَأَخَذَ بِيَدِهِ فَشَرِبَهُ. زَادَ مَالِكٌ عَنْ أَبِي النَّضْرِ عَلَى بَعِيرِهِ

Proceeds to `Arafat
إِلَى عَرَفَةَ

Narrated `Aisha: The Quraish people and those who embraced their religion, used to stay at Muzdalifa and used to call themselves Al-Hums, while the rest of the Arabs used to stay at `Arafat. When Islam came, Allah ordered His Prophet to go to `Arafat and stay at it, and then pass on from there, and that is what is meant by the Statement of Allah:--"Then depart from the place whence all the people depart......" (2.199). – Sahih al-Bukhari 4520

حَدَّثَنَا عَلِيُّ بْنُ عَبْدِ اللَّهِ، حَدَّثَنَا مُحَمَّدُ بْنُ خَازِمٍ، حَدَّثَنَا هِشَامٌ، عَنْ أَبِيهِ، عَنْ عَائِشَةَ ـ رضى الله عنها ـ كَانَتْ قُرَيْشٌ وَمَنْ دَانَ دِينَهَا يَقِفُونَ بِالْمُزْدَلِفَةِ، وَكَانُوا يُسَمَّوْنَ الْحُمْسَ، وَكَانَ سَائِرُ الْعَرَبِ يَقِفُونَ بِعَرَفَاتٍ، فَلَمَّا جَاءَ الإِسْلاَمُ أَمَرَ اللَّهُ نَبِيَّهُ صلى الله عليه وسلم أَنْ يَأْتِيَ عَرَفَاتٍ، ثُمَّ يَقِفَ بِهَا ثُمَّ يُفِيضَ مِنْهَا، فَذَلِكَ قَوْلُهُ تَعَالَى {ثُمَّ أَفِيضُوا مِنْ حَيْثُ أَفَاضَ النَّاسُ}

It is no fault in you that you constantly seek Grace from your Lord; so when you press on from Arafat, then remember Allah at the Inviolable Emblem, and remember Him as He has guided you, and decidedly you were even before it (i.e. before Islam) indeed of the erring Thereafter, press on from where the multitude (Literally: mankind) press on, and ask for forgiveness from Allah; surely Allah is Ever-Forgiving, Ever-Merciful. Surah Al-Baqarah 2:198&199

لَيْسَ عَلَيْكُمْ جُنَاحٌ أَن تَبْتَغُواْ فَضْلًا مِّن رَّبِّكُمْۚ فَإِذَآ أَفَضْتُم مِّنْ عَرَفَٰتٍ فَٱذْكُرُواْ ٱللَّهَ عِندَ ٱلْمَشْعَرِ ٱلْحَرَامِۖ وَٱذْكُرُوهُ كَمَا هَدَىٰكُمْ وَإِن كُنتُم مِّن قَبْلِهِۦ لَمِنَ ٱلضَّآلِّينَ ثُمَّ أَفِيضُواْ مِنْ حَيْثُ أَفَاضَ ٱلنَّاسُ وَٱسْتَغْفِرُواْ ٱللَّهَۚ إِنَّ ٱللَّهَ غَفُورٌ رَّحِيمٌ

Narrated Ibn `Abbas: A man who wants to perform the Hajj (from Mecca) can perform the Tawaf around the Ka`ba as long as he is not in the state of Ihram till he assumes the Ihram for Hajj. Then, if he rides and proceeds to `Arafat, he should take a Hadi (i.e. animal for sacrifice), either a camel or a cow or a sheep, whatever he can afford; but if he cannot afford it, he should fast for three days during the Hajj before the day of `Arafat, but if the third day of his fasting happens to be the day of `Arafat (i.e. 9th of Dhul-Hijja) then it is no sin for him (to fast on it). Then he should proceed to `Arafat and stay there from the time of the `Asr prayer till darkness falls. Then the pilgrims should proceed from `Arafat, and when they have

departed from it, they reach Jam' (i.e. Al-Muzdalifa) where they ask Allah to help them to be righteous and dutiful to Him, and there they remember Allah greatly or say Takbir (i.e. Allah is Greater) and Tahlil (i.e. None has the right to be worshipped but Allah) repeatedly before dawn breaks. Then, after offering the morning (Fajr) prayer you should pass on (to Mina) for the people used to do so and Allah said:-- "Then depart from the place whence all the people depart. And ask for Allah's Forgiveness. Truly! Allah is Oft-Forgiving, Most Merciful." (2.199) Then you should go on doing so till you throw pebbles over the Jamra. – Sahih al-Bukhari 4521
حَدَّثَنِي مُحَمَّدُ بْنُ أَبِي بَكْرٍ، حَدَّثَنَا فُضَيْلُ بْنُ سُلَيْمَانَ، حَدَّثَنَا مُوسَى بْنُ عُقْبَةَ، أَخْبَرَنِي كُرَيْبٌ، عَنِ ابْنِ عَبَّاسٍ، قَالَ يَطَوَّفُ الرَّجُلُ بِالْبَيْتِ مَا كَانَ حَلاَلاً حَتَّى يُهِلَّ بِالْحَجِّ، فَإِذَا رَكِبَ إِلَى عَرَفَةَ فَمَنْ تَيَسَّرَ لَهُ هَدِيَّةٌ مِنَ الإِبِلِ أَوِ الْبَقَرِ أَوِ الْغَنَمِ، مَا تَيَسَّرَ لَهُ مِنْ ذَلِكَ أَىَّ ذَلِكَ شَاءَ، غَيْرَ إِنْ لَمْ يَتَيَسَّرْ لَهُ فَعَلَيْهِ ثَلاَثَةُ أَيَّامٍ فِي الْحَجِّ، وَذَلِكَ قَبْلَ يَوْمِ عَرَفَةَ، فَإِنْ كَانَ آخِرُ يَوْمٍ مِنَ الأَيَّامِ الثَّلاَثَةِ يَوْمَ عَرَفَةَ فَلاَ جُنَاحَ عَلَيْهِ، ثُمَّ لِيَنْطَلِقْ حَتَّى يَقِفَ بِعَرَفَاتٍ مِنْ صَلاَةِ الْعَصْرِ إِلَى أَنْ يَكُونَ الظَّلاَمُ، ثُمَّ لِيَدْفَعُوا مِنْ عَرَفَاتٍ إِذَا أَفَاضُوا مِنْهَا حَتَّى يَبْلُغُوا جَمْعًا الَّذِي يُتَبَرَّرُ فِيهِ، ثُمَّ لِيَذْكُرُوا اللَّهَ كَثِيرًا، أَوْ أَكْثِرُوا التَّكْبِيرَ وَالتَّهْلِيلَ قَبْلَ أَنْ تُصْبِحُوا ثُمَّ أَفِيضُوا، فَإِنَّ النَّاسَ كَانُوا يُفِيضُونَ، وَقَالَ اللَّهُ تَعَالَى {ثُمَّ أَفِيضُوا مِنْ حَيْثُ أَفَاضَ النَّاسُ وَاسْتَغْفِرُوا اللَّهَ إِنَّ اللَّهَ غَفُورٌ رَحِيمٌ} حَتَّى تَرْمُوا الْجَمْرَةَ.

Ihram
الإحرام

Narrated `Aisha: On the 1st of Dhul-Hijja we set out with the intention of performing Hajj. Allah's Messenger ﷺ said, "Any one who likes to assume the Ihram for `Umra he can do so. Had I not brought the Hadi with me, I would have assumed the Ihram for `Umra. "Some of us assumed the Ihram for `Umra while the others assumed the Ihram for Hajj. I was one of those who assumed the Ihram for `Umra. I got menses and kept on menstruating until the day of `Arafat and complained of that to the Prophet. He told me to postpone my `Umra, undo and comb my hair, and to assume the Ihram of Hajj and I did so. On the night of Hasba, he sent my brother `Abdur-Rahman bin Abi Bakr with me to at-Tan`im, where I assumed the Ihram for `Umra in lieu of the previous one. Hisham said, "For that (`Umra) no Hadi, fasting or alms were required. – Sahih al-Bukhari 317
حَدَّثَنَا عُبَيْدُ بْنُ إِسْمَاعِيلَ، قَالَ حَدَّثَنَا أَبُو أُسَامَةَ، عَنْ هِشَامٍ، عَنْ أَبِيهِ، عَنْ عَائِشَةَ، قَالَتْ خَرَجْنَا مُوَافِينَ لِهِلاَلِ ذِي الْحِجَّةِ، فَقَالَ رَسُولُ اللَّهِ صلى الله عليه وسلم " مَنْ أَحَبَّ أَنْ يُهِلَّ بِعُمْرَةٍ فَلْيُهْلِلْ، فَإِنِّي لَوْلاَ أَنِّي أَهْدَيْتُ لأَهْلَلْتُ بِعُمْرَةٍ ". فَأَهَلَّ بَعْضُهُمْ بِعُمْرَةٍ، وَأَهَلَّ بَعْضُهُمْ بِحَجٍّ، وَكُنْتُ أَنَا مِمَّنْ أَهَلَّ بِعُمْرَةٍ، فَأَدْرَكَنِي يَوْمُ عَرَفَةَ وَأَنَا حَائِضٌ، فَشَكَوْتُ إِلَى النَّبِيِّ صلى الله عليه وسلم فَقَالَ " دَعِي عُمْرَتَكِ، وَانْقُضِي رَأْسَكِ وَامْتَشِطِي، وَأَهِلِّي بِحَجٍّ ". فَفَعَلْتُ حَتَّى إِذَا كَانَ لَيْلَةُ الْحَصْبَةِ أَرْسَلَ مَعِي أَخِي عَبْدَ الرَّحْمَنِ بْنَ أَبِي بَكْرٍ، فَخَرَجْتُ إِلَى التَّنْعِيمِ، فَأَهْلَلْتُ بِعُمْرَةٍ مَكَانَ عُمْرَتِي. قَالَ هِشَامٌ وَلَمْ يَكُنْ فِي شَىْءٍ مِنْ ذَلِكَ هَدْىٌ وَلاَ صَوْمٌ وَلاَ صَدَقَةٌ

Narrated Aisha: We set out along with Allah's Messenger ﷺ shortly before the appearance of the new moon (crescent) of the month of Dhi-l-Hijja and he said to us, "Whoever wants to assume Ihram for Hajj may do so; and whoever wants to assume Ihram for `Umra may do so. Hadn't I brought the Hadi (animal for sacrificing) (with me), I would have assumed Ihram for `Umra." (`Aisha added,): So some of us assumed Ihram for `Umra while the others for Hajj. I was amongst those who assumed Ihram for `Umra. The day of `Arafat approached and I was still menstruating. I complained to the Prophet ﷺ (about that) and he said, "Abandon your `Umra, undo and comb your hair, and assume Ihram for Hajj;." When it was the night of Hasba, he sent `Abdur Rahman with me to at-Tan`im and I assumed Ihram for `Umra (and performed it) in lieu of my missed `Umra. – Sahih al-Bukhari 1783

حَدَّثَنَا مُحَمَّدُ بْنُ سَلاَمٍ، أَخْبَرَنَا أَبُو مُعَاوِيَةَ، حَدَّثَنَا هِشَامٌ، عَنْ أَبِيهِ، عَنْ عَائِشَةَ ـ رضى الله عنها ـ خَرَجْنَا مَعَ رَسُولِ اللَّهِ صلى الله عليه وسلم مُوَافِينَ لِهِلاَلِ ذِي الْحَجَّةِ فَقَالَ لَنَا " مَنْ أَحَبَّ مِنْكُمْ أَنْ يُهِلَّ بِالْحَجِّ فَلْيُهِلَّ وَمَنْ أَحَبَّ أَنْ يُهِلَّ بِعُمْرَةٍ فَلْيُهِلَّ بِعُمْرَةٍ، فَلَوْلاَ أَنِّي أَهْدَيْتُ لأَهْلَلْتُ بِعُمْرَةٍ ". قَالَتْ فَمِنَّا مَنْ أَهَلَّ بِعُمْرَةٍ، وَمِنَّا مَنْ أَهَلَّ بِحَجٍّ، وَكُنْتُ مِمَّنْ أَهَلَّ بِعُمْرَةٍ، فَأَظَلَّنِي يَوْمُ عَرَفَةَ، وَأَنَا حَائِضٌ، فَشَكَوْتُ إِلَى النَّبِيِّ صلى الله عليه وسلم فَقَالَ " ارْفُضِي عُمْرَتَكِ، وَانْقُضِي رَأْسَكِ وَامْتَشِطِي، وَأَهِلِّي بِالْحَجِّ ". فَلَمَّا كَانَ لَيْلَةُ الْحَصْبَةِ أَرْسَلَ مَعِي عَبْدَ الرَّحْمَنِ إِلَى التَّنْعِيمِ، فَأَهْلَلْتُ بِعُمْرَةٍ مَكَانَ عُمْرَتِي.

Narrated Abu Musa Al-Ash`ari: I came to the Prophet ﷺ at Al-Batha' while his camel was kneeling down and he asked me, "Have you intended to perform the Hajj?" I replied in the affirmative. He asked me, 'With what intention have you assumed Ihram?" I replied, "I have assumed Ihram with the same intention as that of the Prophet. He said, "You have done well. Perform the Tawaf of the Ka`ba and (the Sai) between As-Safa and Al- Marwa and then finish the Ihram." So, I performed the Tawaf around the Ka`ba and the Sai) between As-Safa and Al-Marwa and then went to a woman of the tribe of Qais who cleaned my head from lice. Later I assumed the Ihram for Hajj. I used to give the verdict of doing the same till the caliphate of `Umar who said, "If you follow the Holy Book then it orders you to remain in the state of Ihram till you finish from Hajj, if you follow the Prophet ﷺ then he did not finish his Ihram till the Hadi (sacrifice) had reached its place of slaughtering (Hajj-al-Qiran). – Sahih al-Bukhari 1795

حَدَّثَنَا مُحَمَّدُ بْنُ بَشَّارٍ، حَدَّثَنَا غُنْدَرٌ، حَدَّثَنَا شُعْبَةُ، عَنْ قَيْسِ بْنِ مُسْلِمٍ، عَنْ طَارِقِ بْنِ شِهَابٍ، عَنْ أَبِي مُوسَى الأَشْعَرِيِّ ـ رضى الله عنه ـ قَالَ قَدِمْتُ عَلَى النَّبِيِّ صلى الله عليه وسلم بِالْبَطْحَاءِ وَهُوَ مُنِيخٌ فَقَالَ " أَحَجَجْتَ ". قُلْتُ نَعَمْ. قَالَ " بِمَا أَهْلَلْتَ ". قُلْتُ لَبَّيْكَ بِإِهْلاَلٍ كَإِهْلاَلِ النَّبِيِّ صلى الله عليه وسلم قَالَ " أَحْسَنْتَ. طُفْ بِالْبَيْتِ وَبِالصَّفَا وَالْمَرْوَةِ ثُمَّ أَحِلَّ ". فَطُفْتُ بِالْبَيْتِ، وَبِالصَّفَا وَالْمَرْوَةِ، ثُمَّ أَتَيْتُ امْرَأَةً مِنْ قَيْسٍ، فَفَلَتْ رَأْسِي، ثُمَّ أَهْلَلْتُ بِالْحَجِّ. فَكُنْتُ أُفْتِي بِهِ، حَتَّى كَانَ فِي خِلاَفَةِ عُمَرَ فَقَالَ إِنْ أَخَذْنَا بِكِتَابِ اللَّهِ فَإِنَّهُ يَأْمُرُنَا بِالتَّمَامِ، وَإِنْ أَخَذْنَا بِقَوْلِ النَّبِيِّ صلى الله عليه وسلم فَإِنَّهُ لَمْ يَحِلَّ حَتَّى يَبْلُغَ الْهَدْىُ مَحِلَّهُ.

Narrated `Abdullah bin `Umar: A person stood up and asked, "O Allah's: Apostle! What clothes may be worn in the state of Ihram?" The Prophet ﷺ replied, "Do not wear a shirt or trousers, or any headgear (e.g. a turban), or a hooded cloak; but if somebody has no shoes he can wear leather stockings provided they are cut short off the ankles, and also, do not wear anything perfumed with Wars or saffron, and the Muhrima (a woman in the state of Ihram) should not cover her face, or wear gloves." – Sahih al-Bukhari 1838

حَدَّثَنَا عَبْدُ اللَّهِ بْنُ يَزِيدَ، حَدَّثَنَا اللَّيْثُ، حَدَّثَنَا نَافِعٌ، عَنْ عَبْدِ اللَّهِ بْنِ عُمَرَ ـ رضى الله عنهما ـ قَالَ قَامَ رَجُلٌ فَقَالَ يَا رَسُولَ اللَّهِ مَاذَا تَأْمُرُنَا أَنْ نَلْبَسَ مِنَ الثِّيَابِ فِي الإِحْرَامِ فَقَالَ النَّبِيُّ صلى الله عليه وسلم " لاَ تَلْبَسُوا الْقَمِيصَ وَلاَ السَّرَاوِيلاَتِ وَلاَ الْعَمَائِمَ، وَلاَ الْبَرَانِسَ إِلاَّ أَنْ يَكُونَ أَحَدٌ لَيْسَتْ لَهُ نَعْلاَنِ، فَلْيَلْبَسِ الْخُفَّيْنِ، وَلْيَقْطَعْ أَسْفَلَ مِنَ الْكَعْبَيْنِ، وَلاَ تَلْبَسُوا شَيْئًا مَسَّهُ زَعْفَرَانٌ، وَلاَ الْوَرْسُ، وَلاَ تَنْتَقِبِ الْمَرْأَةُ الْمُحْرِمَةُ وَلاَ تَلْبَسِ الْقُفَّازَيْنِ ". تَابَعَهُ مُوسَى بْنُ عُقْبَةَ وَإِسْمَاعِيلُ بْنُ إِبْرَاهِيمَ بْنِ عُقْبَةَ وَجُوَيْرِيَةُ وَابْنُ إِسْحَاقَ فِي النِّقَابِ وَالْقُفَّازَيْنِ. وَقَالَ عُبَيْدُ اللَّهِ وَلاَ وَرْسٌ وَكَانَ يَقُولُ لاَ تَتَنَقَّبِ الْمُحْرِمَةُ، وَلاَ تَلْبَسِ الْقُفَّازَيْنِ. وَقَالَ مَالِكٌ عَنْ نَافِعٍ عَنِ ابْنِ عُمَرَ لاَ تَتَنَقَّبِ الْمُحْرِمَةُ. وَتَابَعَهُ لَيْثُ بْنُ أَبِي سُلَيْمٍ.

Tawaf during Al-Hajj
طَافَ فِي الْحَجِّ

Narrated `Urwa: I asked `Aisha : "How do you interpret the statement of Allah,. : Verily! (the mountains) As-Safa and Al-Marwa are among the symbols of Allah, and whoever performs the Hajj to the Ka`ba or performs `Umra, it is not harmful for him to perform Tawaf between them (Safa and Marwa.) (2.158). By Allah! (it is evident from this revelation) there is no harm if one does not perform Tawaf between Safa and Marwa." `Aisha said, "O, my nephew! Your interpretation is not true. Had this interpretation of yours been correct, the statement of

Allah should have been, 'It is not harmful for him if he does not perform Tawaf between them.' But in fact, this divine inspiration was revealed concerning the Ansar who used to assume Ihram for worship ping an idol called "Manat" which they used to worship at a place called Al-Mushallal before they embraced Islam, and whoever assumed Ihram (for the idol), would consider it not right to perform Tawaf between Safa and Marwa. When they embraced Islam, they asked Allah's Messenger ﷺ regarding it, saying, "O Allah's Apostle! We used to refrain from Tawaf between Safa and Marwa." So Allah revealed: 'Verily; (the mountains) As-Safa and Al-Marwa are among the symbols of Allah.' " Aisha added, "Surely, Allah's Apostle set the tradition of Tawaf between Safa and Marwa, so nobody is allowed to omit the Tawaf between them." Later on I (`Urwa) told Abu Bakr bin `Abdur-Rahman (of `Aisha's narration) and he said, 'I have not heard of such information, but I heard learned men saying that all the people, except those whom `Aisha mentioned and who used to assume Ihram for the sake of Manat, used to perform Tawaf between Safa and Marwa. When Allah referred to the Tawaf of the Ka`ba and did not mention Safa and Marwa in the Qur'an, the people asked, 'O Allah's Messenger ﷺ ! We used to perform Tawaf between Safa and Marwa and Allah has revealed (the verses concerning) Tawaf of the Ka`ba and has not mentioned Safa and Marwa. Is there any harm if we perform Tawaf between Safa and Marwa?' So Allah revealed: "Verily As-Safa and Al- Marwa are among the symbols of Allah." Abu Bakr said, "It seems that this verse was revealed concerning the two groups, those who used to refrain from Tawaf between Safa and Marwa in the Pre- Islamic Period of ignorance and those who used to perform the Tawaf then, and after embracing Islam they refrained from the Tawaf between them as Allah had enjoined Tawaf of the Ka`ba and did not mention Tawaf (of Safa and Marwa) till later after mentioning the Tawaf of the Ka`ba.'. – Sahih al-Bukhari 1643

حَدَّثَنَا أَبُو الْيَمَانِ، أَخْبَرَنَا شُعَيْبٌ، عَنِ الزُّهْرِيِّ، قَالَ عُرْوَةُ سَأَلْتُ عَائِشَةَ ـ رضى الله عنها ـ فَقُلْتُ لَهَا أَرَأَيْتِ قَوْلَ اللَّهِ تَعَالَى {إِنَّ الصَّفَا وَالْمَرْوَةَ مِنْ شَعَائِرِ اللَّهِ فَمَنْ حَجَّ الْبَيْتَ أَوِ اعْتَمَرَ فَلاَ جُنَاحَ عَلَيْهِ أَنْ يَطَّوَّفَ بِهِمَا} فَوَاللَّهِ مَا عَلَى أَحَدٍ جُنَاحٌ أَنْ لاَ يَطُوفَ بِالصَّفَا وَالْمَرْوَةِ. قَالَتْ بِئْسَ مَا قُلْتَ يَا ابْنَ أُخْتِي إِنَّ هَذِهِ لَوْ كَانَتْ كَمَا أَوَّلْتَهَا عَلَيْهِ كَانَتْ لاَ جُنَاحَ عَلَيْهِ أَنْ لاَ يَتَطَوَّفَ بِهِمَا، وَلَكِنَّهَا أُنْزِلَتْ فِي الأَنْصَارِ، كَانُوا قَبْلَ أَنْ يُسْلِمُوا يُهِلُّونَ لِمَنَاةَ الطَّاغِيَةِ الَّتِي كَانُوا يَعْبُدُونَهَا عِنْدَ الْمُشَلَّلِ، فَكَانَ مَنْ أَهَلَّ يَتَحَرَّجُ أَنْ يَطُوفَ بِالصَّفَا وَالْمَرْوَةِ، فَلَمَّا أَسْلَمُوا سَأَلُوا رَسُولَ اللَّهِ صلى الله عليه وسلم عَنْ ذَلِكَ قَالُوا يَا رَسُولَ اللَّهِ، إِنَّا كُنَّا نَتَحَرَّجُ أَنْ نَطُوفَ بَيْنَ الصَّفَا وَالْمَرْوَةِ، فَأَنْزَلَ اللَّهُ تَعَالَى {إِنَّ الصَّفَا وَالْمَرْوَةَ مِنْ شَعَائِرِ اللَّهِ} الآيَةَ. قَالَتْ عَائِشَةُ ـ رضى الله عنها ـ وَقَدْ سَنَّ رَسُولُ اللَّهِ صلى الله عليه وسلم الطَّوَافَ بَيْنَهُمَا، فَلَيْسَ لأَحَدٍ أَنْ يَتْرُكَ الطَّوَافَ بَيْنَهُمَا. ثُمَّ أَخْبَرْتُ أَبَا بَكْرِ بْنَ عَبْدِ الرَّحْمَنِ، فَقَالَ إِنَّ هَذَا لَعِلْمٌ مَا كُنْتُ سَمِعْتُهُ، وَلَقَدْ سَمِعْتُ رِجَالاً مِنْ أَهْلِ الْعِلْمِ، يَذْكُرُونَ أَنَّ النَّاسَ إِلاَّ مَنْ ذَكَرَتْ عَائِشَةُ مِمَّنْ كَانَ يُهِلُّ بِمَنَاةَ، كَانُوا يَطُوفُونَ كُلُّهُمْ بِالصَّفَا وَالْمَرْوَةِ، فَلَمَّا ذَكَرَ اللَّهُ تَعَالَى الطَّوَافَ بِالْبَيْتِ، وَلَمْ يَذْكُرِ الصَّفَا وَالْمَرْوَةَ فِي الْقُرْآنِ قَالُوا يَا رَسُولَ اللَّهِ كُنَّا نَطُوفُ بِالصَّفَا وَالْمَرْوَةِ، وَإِنَّ اللَّهَ أَنْزَلَ الطَّوَافَ بِالْبَيْتِ، فَلَمْ يَذْكُرِ الصَّفَا فَهَلْ عَلَيْنَا مِنْ حَرَجٍ أَنْ نَطَّوَّفَ بِالصَّفَا وَالْمَرْوَةِ فَأَنْزَلَ اللَّهُ تَعَالَى {إِنَّ الصَّفَا وَالْمَرْوَةَ مِنْ شَعَائِرِ اللَّهِ} الآيَةَ. قَالَ أَبُو بَكْرٍ فَأَسْمَعُ هَذِهِ الآيَةَ نَزَلَتْ فِي الْفَرِيقَيْنِ كِلَيْهِمَا فِي الَّذِينَ كَانُوا يَتَحَرَّجُونَ أَنْ يَطُوفُوا بِالْجَاهِلِيَّةِ بِالصَّفَا وَالْمَرْوَةِ، وَالَّذِينَ يَطُوفُونَ ثُمَّ تَحَرَّجُوا أَنْ يَطُوفُوا بِهِمَا فِي الإِسْلاَمِ مِنْ أَجْلِ أَنَّ اللَّهَ تَعَالَى أَمَرَ بِالطَّوَافِ بِالْبَيْتِ، وَلَمْ يَذْكُرِ الصَّفَا حَتَّى ذَكَرَ ذَلِكَ بَعْدَ مَا ذَكَرَ الطَّوَافَ بِالْبَيْتِ.

Narrated `Amr bin Dinar: I asked Ibn `Umar, "Can a person who has performed the Tawaf around the Ka`ba for `Umra but has not performed the (Sa`i) Tawaf of Safa and Marwa, have a sexual relation with his wife?" Ibn `Umar replied "When the Prophet ﷺ reached Mecca he performed the Tawaf around the Ka`ba (circumambulated it seven times) and offered a two-rak`at prayer (at the place) behind the station (of Abraham) and then performed the Tawaf (Sa`i) of Safa and Marwa, and verily in Allah's Messenger ﷺ you have a good example." Then we put the same question to Jabir bin `Abdullah and he too replied, "He should not go near his wife (for sexual relation) till he has finished the Tawaf of Safa and Marwa.". – Sahih al-Bukhari 395, 396

حَدَّثَنَا الْحُمَيْدِيُّ، قَالَ حَدَّثَنَا سُفْيَانُ، قَالَ حَدَّثَنَا عَمْرُو بْنُ دِينَارٍ، قَالَ سَأَلْنَا ابْنَ عُمَرَ عَنْ رَجُلٍ، طَافَ بِالْبَيْتِ الْعُمْرَةَ، وَلَمْ يَطُفْ بَيْنَ الصَّفَا وَالْمَرْوَةِ، أَيَأْتِي امْرَأَتَهُ فَقَالَ قَدِمَ النَّبِيُّ صلى الله عليه وسلم فَطَافَ بِالْبَيْتِ سَبْعًا، وَصَلَّى خَلْفَ الْمَقَامِ رَكْعَتَيْنِ، وَطَافَ بَيْنَ الصَّفَا وَالْمَرْوَةِ، وَقَدْ كَانَ لَكُمْ فِي رَسُولِ اللَّهِ أُسْوَةٌ حَسَنَةٌ. وَسَأَلْنَا جَابِرَ بْنَ عَبْدِ اللَّهِ فَقَالَ لاَ يَقْرَبَنَّهَا حَتَّى يَطُوفَ بَيْنَ الصَّفَا وَالْمَرْوَةِ.

Narrated `Abdullah bin `Umar: When Allah's Messenger ﷺ performed Tawaf of the Ka`ba for Hajj or `Umra, he used to do Ramal during the first three rounds, and in the last four rounds he used to walk; then after the Tawaf he used to offer two rak`at and then performed Tawaf between Safa and Marwa. – Sahih al-Bukhari 1616

حَدَّثَنَا إِبْرَاهِيمُ بْنُ الْمُنْذِرِ، حَدَّثَنَا أَبُو ضَمْرَةَ، أَنَسٌ حَدَّثَنَا مُوسَى بْنُ عُقْبَةَ، عَنْ نَافِعٍ، عَنْ عَبْدِ اللَّهِ بْنِ عُمَرَ ـ رضى الله عنهما ـ أَنَّ رَسُولَ اللَّهِ صلى الله عليه وسلم كَانَ إِذَا طَافَ فِي الْحَجِّ أَوِ الْعُمْرَةِ أَوَّلَ مَا يَقْدَمُ سَعَى ثَلاَثَةَ أَطْوَافٍ، وَمَشَى أَرْبَعَةً، ثُمَّ سَجَدَ سَجْدَتَيْنِ، ثُمَّ يَطُوفُ بَيْنَ الصَّفَا وَالْمَرْوَةِ

Narrated Um Salama: I complained to Allah's Messenger ﷺ that I was sick, so he said, "Perform the Tawaf (of Ka`ba at Mecca) while riding behind the people (who are performing the Tawaf on foot)." So I performed the Tawaf while Allah's Messenger ﷺ was offering the prayer by the side of the Ka`ba and was reciting: 'By the Mount (Saini) and by a Decree Inscribed.'. – Sahih al-Bukhari 4853

حَدَّثَنَا عَبْدُ اللَّهِ بْنُ يُوسُفَ، أَخْبَرَنَا مَالِكٌ، عَنْ مُحَمَّدِ بْنِ عَبْدِ الرَّحْمَنِ بْنِ نَوْفَلٍ، عَنْ عُرْوَةَ، عَنْ زَيْنَبَ ابْنَةِ أَبِي سَلَمَةَ، عَنْ أُمِّ سَلَمَةَ، قَالَتْ شَكَوْتُ إِلَى رَسُولِ اللَّهِ صلى الله عليه وسلم أَنِّي أَشْتَكِي فَقَالَ " طُوفِي مِنْ وَرَاءِ النَّاسِ، وَأَنْتِ رَاكِبَةٌ ". فَطُفْتُ وَرَسُولُ اللَّهِ صلى الله عليه وسلم يُصَلِّي إِلَى جَنْبِ الْبَيْتِ يَقْرَأُ بِالطُّورِ وَكِتَابٍ مَسْطُورٍ

Narrated `Amr bin Dinar: We asked Ibn `Umar whether a man who, while performing `Umra, had performed Tawaf of the Ka`ba; and had not yet performed Tawaf between Safa and Marwa, could have sexual relation with his wife, Ibn `Umar replied "The Prophet (p.b.u.h) reached Mecca and performed the seven rounds (of Tawaf) of the Ka`ba and then offered a two-rak`at prayer behind Maqam Ibrahim and then performed the seven rounds (of Tawaf) between Safa and Marwa." He added, "Verily! In Allah's Messenger ﷺ you have a good example." We asked Jabir bin `Abdullah (the same question) and he said, "He (that man) should not come near (his wife) till he has completed Tawaf between Safa and Marwa." - Sahih al-Bukhari 1645, 1646

حَدَّثَنَا عَلِيُّ بْنُ عَبْدِ اللَّهِ، حَدَّثَنَا سُفْيَانُ، عَنْ عَمْرِو بْنِ دِينَارٍ، قَالَ سَأَلْنَا ابْنَ عُمَرَ ـ رضى الله عنه ـ عَنْ رَجُلٍ، طَافَ بِالْبَيْتِ فِي عُمْرَةٍ، وَلَمْ يَطُفْ بَيْنَ الصَّفَا وَالْمَرْوَةِ أَيَأْتِي امْرَأَتَهُ فَقَالَ قَدِمَ النَّبِيُّ صلى الله عليه وسلم فَطَافَ بِالْبَيْتِ سَبْعًا، وَصَلَّى خَلْفَ الْمَقَامِ رَكْعَتَيْنِ، فَطَافَ بَيْنَ الصَّفَا وَالْمَرْوَةِ سَبْعًا {لَقَدْ كَانَ لَكُمْ فِي رَسُولِ اللَّهِ أُسْوَةٌ حَسَنَةٌ}. وَسَأَلْنَا جَابِرَ بْنَ عَبْدِ اللَّهِ ـ رضى الله عنهما ـ فَقَالَ لاَ يَقْرَبَنَّهَا حَتَّى يَطُوفَ بَيْنَ الصَّفَا وَالْمَرْوَةِ

Sa'i
السعي

Ibn 'Abbas said that he has been asked regarding Hajj-at-Tamattu' on which he said: "The Muhajirin and the Ansar and the wives of the Prophet ﷺ and we did the same. When we reached Makkah, Allah's Messenger ﷺ said, "Give up your intention of doing the Hajj (at this moment) and perform 'Umra, except the one who had garlanded the Hady." So, we performed Tawaf round the Ka'bah and [Sa'y] between As-safa and Al-MArwa, slept with our wives and wore ordinary (stitched) clothes. The Prophet ﷺ added, "Whoever has garlanded his Hady is not allowed to finish the Ihram till the Hady has reached its destination (has been sacrificed)". Then on the night of Tarwiya (8th Dhul Hijjah, in the afternoon) he ordered us to assume Ihram for Hajj and when we have performed all the ceremonies of Hajj, we came and performed Tawaf round the Ka'bah and (Sa'y) between As-Safa and Al-Marwa, and then our Hajj was complete, and we had to sacrifice a Hady according to the statement of Allah: "... He must slaughter a Hady such as he can afford, but if he cannot afford it, he should observer Saum (fasts) three days during the Hajj and seven days after his return (to his home)…." (V. 2:196). And the sacrifice of the sheep is sufficient. So, the Prophet ﷺ and his Companions joined the two religious deeds, (i.e. Hajj and 'Umra) in one year, for Allah revealed (the permissibility) of such practice in His book and in the Sunna (legal ways) of His Prophet ﷺ and rendered it permissible for all the people except those living in Makkah. Allah says: "This is for him whose family is not present at the Al-Masjid-Al-Haram, (i.e. non resident of Makkah)." The months of Hajj which Allah mentioned in His book are: Shawwal, Dhul-Qa'da and Dhul-Hijjah. Whoever performed Hajj-at-Tamattu' in those months, then slaughtering or fasting is compulsory for him. – Sahih al-Bukhari 1572

The words: 1. Ar-Rafatha means sexual intercourse. 2. Al-Fasuq means all kinds of sin, and 3. Al-Jidal means to dispute.

وَقَالَ أَبُو كَامِلٍ فُضَيْلُ بْنُ حُسَيْنٍ الْبَصْرِيُّ حَدَّثَنَا أَبُو مَعْشَرٍ، حَدَّثَنَا عُثْمَانُ بْنُ غِيَاثٍ، عَنْ عِكْرِمَةَ، عَنِ ابْنِ عَبَّاسٍ ـ رضى الله عنهما ـ أَنَّهُ سُئِلَ عَنْ مُتْعَةِ الْحَجِّ، فَقَالَ أَهَلَّ الْمُهَاجِرُونَ وَالأَنْصَارُ وَأَزْوَاجُ النَّبِيِّ صلى الله عليه وسلم فِي حَجَّةِ الْوَدَاعِ وَأَهْلَلْنَا، فَلَمَّا قَدِمْنَا مَكَّةَ قَالَ رَسُولُ اللَّهِ صلى الله عليه وسلم " اجْعَلُوا إِهْلاَلَكُمْ بِالْحَجِّ عُمْرَةً إِلاَّ مَنْ قَلَّدَ الْهَدْىَ ". فَطُفْنَا بِالْبَيْتِ وَبِالصَّفَا وَالْمَرْوَةِ وَأَتَيْنَا النِّسَاءَ، وَلَبِسْنَا الثِّيَابَ وَقَالَ " مَنْ قَلَّدَ الْهَدْىَ فَإِنَّهُ لاَ يَحِلُّ لَهُ حَتَّى يَبْلُغَ الْهَدْىُ مَحِلَّهُ ". ثُمَّ أَمَرَنَا عَشِيَّةَ التَّرْوِيَةِ أَنْ نُهِلَّ بِالْحَجِّ، فَإِذَا فَرَغْنَا مِنَ الْمَنَاسِكِ جِئْنَا فَطُفْنَا بِالْبَيْتِ وَبِالصَّفَا وَالْمَرْوَةِ فَقَدْ تَمَّ حَجُّنَا، وَعَلَيْنَا الْهَدْىُ كَمَا قَالَ اللَّهُ تَعَالَى {فَمَا اسْتَيْسَرَ مِنَ الْهَدْىِ فَمَنْ لَمْ يَجِدْ فَصِيَامُ ثَلاَثَةِ أَيَّامٍ فِي الْحَجِّ وَسَبْعَةٍ إِذَا رَجَعْتُمْ} إِلَى أَمْصَارِكُمْ. الشَّاةُ تَجْزِي، فَجَمَعُوا نُسُكَيْنِ فِي عَامٍ بَيْنَ الْحَجِّ وَالْعُمْرَةِ، فَإِنَّ اللَّهَ تَعَالَى أَنْزَلَهُ فِي كِتَابِهِ وَسَنَّهُ نَبِيُّهُ صلى الله عليه وسلم وَأَبَاحَهُ لِلنَّاسِ غَيْرَ أَهْلِ مَكَّةَ، قَالَ اللَّهُ {ذَلِكَ لِمَنْ لَمْ يَكُنْ أَهْلُهُ حَاضِرِي الْمَسْجِدِ الْحَرَامِ} وَأَشْهُرُ الْحَجِّ الَّتِي ذَكَرَ اللَّهُ تَعَالَى شَوَّالٌ وَذُو الْقَعْدَةِ وَذُو الْحَجَّةِ، فَمَنْ تَمَتَّعَ فِي هَذِهِ الأَشْهُرِ فَعَلَيْهِ دَمٌ أَوْ صَوْمٌ، وَالرَّفَثُ الْجِمَاعُ، وَالْفُسُوقُ الْمَعَاصِي، وَالْجِدَالُ الْمِرَاءُ

It was narrated from Nafi that: Ibn 'Umar wanted to perform Hajj in the year when Al-Hajjaj was besieging Ibn Az-Zubair, and it was said to him: "It seems that there will be fighting between them, and I am afraid that you will prevented from performing Hajj." He said: "In the messenger of Allah you have a good example. I am going to do what the Messenger of Allah did. I bear witness to you that I have resolved to perform 'Umrah." Then he set out, and when he was in Zahir Al-Baida, he said: "Hajj and Umrah are the same thing; I bear witness to you that I have resolved to perform Hajj with my 'Umrah." And he brought along a Hadi (sacrificial animal) that he had bought in Qudaid. Then he set out and entered Ihram for them both. When he came to Makkah he circumambulated the House and (did sa'i) between As-Safa and Al-Marwah. Then he did not do any thing more than that, and he did not offer a sacrifice, or shave his head, or cut his hair; he remained in Ihram until the Day of Sacrifice. Then he slaughtered his Hadi and shaved his head, and he thought that he had completed the Tawaf of Hajj and 'Umrah in the first Tawaf. Ibn 'Umar said: "That is what the Messenger of Allah did. – Sunan an-Nasa'I 2746

أَخْبَرَنَا قُتَيْبَةُ، قَالَ حَدَّثَنَا اللَّيْثُ، عَنْ نَافِعٍ، أَنَّ ابْنَ عُمَرَ، أَرَادَ الْحَجَّ عَامَ نَزَلَ الْحَجَّاجُ بِابْنِ الزُّبَيْرِ فَقِيلَ لَهُ إِنَّهُ كَائِنٌ بَيْنَهُمْ قِتَالٌ وَأَنَا أَخَافُ أَنْ يَصُدُّوكَ . قَالَ لَقَدْ كَانَ لَكُمْ فِي رَسُولِ اللَّهِ أُسْوَةٌ حَسَنَةٌ إِذًا أَصْنَعَ كَمَا صَنَعَ رَسُولُ اللَّهِ صلى الله عليه وسلم إِنِّي أُشْهِدُكُمْ أَنِّي قَدْ أَوْجَبْتُ عُمْرَةً . ثُمَّ خَرَجَ حَتَّى إِذَا كَانَ بِظَاهِرِ الْبَيْدَاءِ قَالَ مَا شَأْنُ الْحَجِّ وَالْعُمْرَةِ إِلاَّ وَاحِدٌ أُشْهِدُكُمْ أَنِّي قَدْ أَوْجَبْتُ حَجًّا مَعَ عُمْرَتِي . وَأَهْدَى هَدْيًا اشْتَرَاهُ بِقُدَيْدٍ ثُمَّ انْطَلَقَ يُهِلُّ بِهِمَا جَمِيعًا حَتَّى قَدِمَ مَكَّةَ فَطَافَ بِالْبَيْتِ وَبِالصَّفَا وَالْمَرْوَةِ وَلَمْ يَزِدْ عَلَى ذَلِكَ وَلَمْ يَنْحَرْ وَلَمْ يَحْلِقْ وَلَمْ يُقَصِّرْ وَلَمْ يَحِلَّ مِنْ شَىْءٍ حَرُمَ مِنْهُ حَتَّى كَانَ يَوْمُ النَّحْرِ فَنَحَرَ وَحَلَقَ فَرَأَى أَنْ قَدْ قَضَى طَوَافَ الْحَجِّ وَالْعُمْرَةِ بِطَوَافِهِ الأَوَّلِ وَقَالَ ابْنُ عُمَرَ كَذَلِكَ فَعَلَ رَسُولُ اللَّهِ صلى الله عليه وسلم .

As-safa and Al-Marwa
ٱلصَّفَا وَٱلْمَرْوَةَ

Surely, As-safa and Al-Marwah (i.e. two hills near the Kacbah) are among the way marks of Allah. So whoever makes the Pilgrimage (i.e. Hajj) to the Home, or makes the Visitation, (cUmrah, sometimes called the minor pilgrimage) then there is no fault in him to circumambulate them; and whoever volunteers any (optional) charity, then surely Allah is Thankful, Ever-Knowing – Surah Al-Baqarah 2:158
إِنَّ ٱلصَّفَا وَٱلْمَرْوَةَ مِن شَعَآئِرِ ٱللَّهِۖ فَمَنْ حَجَّ ٱلْبَيْتَ أَوِ ٱعْتَمَرَ فَلَا جُنَاحَ عَلَيْهِ أَن يَطَّوَّفَ بِهِمَاۚ وَمَن تَطَوَّعَ خَيْرًا فَإِنَّ ٱللَّهَ شَاكِرٌ عَلِيمٌ

Narrated `Urwa: I asked `Aisha : "How do you interpret the statement of Allah,. : Verily! (the mountains) As-Safa and Al-Marwa are among the symbols of Allah, and whoever performs the Hajj to the Ka`ba or performs `Umra, it is not harmful for him to perform Tawaf between them (Safa and Marwa.) (2.158). By Allah! (it is evident from this revelation) there is no harm if one does not perform Tawaf between Safa and Marwa." `Aisha said, "O, my nephew! Your interpretation is not true. Had this interpretation of yours been correct, the statement of Allah should have been, 'It is not harmful for him if he does not perform Tawaf between them.' But in fact, this divine inspiration was revealed concerning the Ansar who used to assume Ihram for worship ping an idol called "Manat" which they used to worship at a place called Al-Mushallal before they embraced Islam, and whoever assumed Ihram (for the idol), would consider it not right to perform Tawaf between Safa and Marwa. When they embraced Islam, they asked Allah's Messenger ﷺ regarding it, saying, "O Allah's Apostle! We used to refrain from Tawaf between Safa and Marwa." So Allah revealed: 'Verily; (the mountains) As-Safa and Al-Marwa are among the symbols of Allah.' " Aisha added, "Surely, Allah's Apostle set the tradition of Tawaf between Safa and Marwa, so nobody is allowed to omit the Tawaf between them." Later on I (`Urwa) told Abu Bakr bin `Abdur-Rahman (of `Aisha's narration) and he said, 'I have not heard of such information, but I heard learned men saying that all the people, except those whom `Aisha mentioned and who used to assume Ihram for the sake of Manat, used to perform Tawaf between Safa and Marwa. When Allah referred to the Tawaf of the Ka`ba and did not mention Safa and Marwa in the Qur'an, the people asked, 'O Allah's Messenger ﷺ ! We used to perform Tawaf between Safa and Marwa and Allah has revealed (the verses concerning) Tawaf of the Ka`ba and has not mentioned Safa and Marwa. Is there any harm if we perform Tawaf between Safa and Marwa?' So Allah revealed: "Verily As-Safa and Al- Marwa are among the symbols of Allah." Abu Bakr said, "It seems that this verse was revealed concerning the two groups, those who used to refrain from Tawaf between Safa and Marwa in the Pre- Islamic Period of ignorance and those who used to perform the Tawaf then, and after embracing Islam they refrained from the Tawaf between them as Allah had enjoined Tawaf of the Ka`ba and did not mention Tawaf (of Safa and Marwa) till later after mentioning the Tawaf of the Ka`ba.'. – Sahih al-Bukhari 1643
حَدَّثَنَا أَبُو الْيَمَانِ، أَخْبَرَنَا شُعَيْبٌ، عَنِ الزُّهْرِيِّ، قَالَ عُرْوَةُ سَأَلْتُ عَائِشَةَ ـ رضى الله عنها ـ فَقُلْتُ لَهَا أَرَأَيْتِ قَوْلَ اللَّهِ تَعَالَى {إِنَّ الصَّفَا وَالْمَرْوَةَ مِنْ شَعَائِرِ اللَّهِ فَمَنْ حَجَّ الْبَيْتَ أَوِ اعْتَمَرَ فَلاَ جُنَاحَ عَلَيْهِ أَنْ يَطَّوَّفَ بِهِمَا} فَوَاللَّهِ مَا عَلَى أَحَدٍ جُنَاحٌ أَنْ لاَ يَطُوفَ بِالصَّفَا وَالْمَرْوَةِ. قَالَتْ بِئْسَ مَا قُلْتَ يَا ابْنَ أُخْتِي إِنَّ هَذِهِ لَوْ كَانَتْ كَمَا أَوَّلْتَهَا عَلَيْهِ كَانَتْ لاَ جُنَاحَ عَلَيْهِ أَنْ لاَ يَتَطَوَّفَ بِهِمَا، وَلَكِنَّهَا أُنْزِلَتْ فِي الأَنْصَارِ، كَانُوا قَبْلَ أَنْ يُسْلِمُوا يُهِلُّونَ لِمَنَاةَ الطَّاغِيَةِ الَّتِي كَانُوا يَعْبُدُونَهَا عِنْدَ الْمُشَلَّلِ، فَكَانَ مَنْ أَهَلَّ يَتَحَرَّجُ أَنْ يَطُوفَ بِالصَّفَا وَالْمَرْوَةِ، فَلَمَّا أَسْلَمُوا سَأَلُوا رَسُولَ اللَّهِ صلى الله عليه وسلم عَنْ ذَلِكَ قَالُوا يَا رَسُولَ اللَّهِ، إِنَّا كُنَّا نَتَحَرَّجُ أَنْ نَطُوفَ بَيْنَ الصَّفَا وَالْمَرْوَةِ، فَأَنْزَلَ اللَّهُ تَعَالَى {إِنَّ الصَّفَا وَالْمَرْوَةَ مِنْ شَعَائِرِ اللَّهِ} الآيَةَ. قَالَتْ

عَائِشَةُ ـ رضى الله عنها ـ وَقَدْ سَنَّ رَسُولُ اللَّهِ صلى الله عليه وسلم الطَّوَافَ بَيْنَهُمَا، فَلَيْسَ لأَحَدٍ أَنْ يَتْرُكَ الطَّوَافَ بَيْنَهُمَا. ثُمَّ أَخْبَرْتُ أَبَا بَكْرِ بْنَ عَبْدِ الرَّحْمَنِ، فَقَالَ إِنَّ هَذَا لَعِلْمٌ مَا كُنْتُ سَمِعْتُهُ، وَلَقَدْ سَمِعْتُ رِجَالاً مِنْ أَهْلِ الْعِلْمِ، يَذْكُرُونَ أَنَّ النَّاسَ إِلاَّ مَنْ ذَكَرَتْ عَائِشَةُ مِمَّنْ كَانَ يُهِلُّ بِمَنَاةَ، كَانُوا يَطُوفُونَ كُلُّهُمْ بِالصَّفَا وَالْمَرْوَةِ، فَلَمَّا ذَكَرَ اللَّهُ تَعَالَى الطَّوَافَ بِالْبَيْتِ، وَلَمْ يَذْكُرِ الصَّفَا وَالْمَرْوَةَ فِي الْقُرْآنِ قَالُوا يَا رَسُولَ اللَّهِ كُنَّا نَطُوفُ بِالصَّفَا وَالْمَرْوَةِ، وَإِنَّ اللَّهَ أَنْزَلَ الطَّوَافَ بِالْبَيْتِ، فَلَمْ يَذْكُرِ الصَّفَا فَهَلْ عَلَيْنَا مِنْ حَرَجٍ أَنْ نَطَّوَّفَ بِالصَّفَا وَالْمَرْوَةِ فَأَنْزَلَ اللَّهُ تَعَالَى {إِنَّ الصَّفَا وَالْمَرْوَةَ مِنْ شَعَائِرِ اللَّهِ} الآيَةَ. قَالَ أَبُو بَكْرٍ فَأَسْمَعُ هَذِهِ الآيَةَ نَزَلَتْ فِي الْفَرِيقَيْنِ كِلَيْهِمَا فِي الَّذِينَ كَانُوا يَتَحَرَّجُونَ أَنْ يَطُوفُوا بِالْجَاهِلِيَّةِ بِالصَّفَا وَالْمَرْوَةِ، وَالَّذِينَ يَطُوفُونَ ثُمَّ تَحَرَّجُوا أَنْ يَطُوفُوا بِهِمَا فِي الإِسْلاَمِ مِنْ أَجْلِ أَنَّ اللَّهَ تَعَالَى أَمَرَ بِالطَّوَافِ بِالْبَيْتِ، وَلَمْ يَذْكُرِ الصَّفَا حَتَّى ذَكَرَ ذَلِكَ بَعْدَ مَا ذَكَرَ الطَّوَافَ بِالْبَيْتِ

Narrated `Urwa: I asked `Aisha (regarding the Sai between As Safa and Al-Marwa). She said, "Out of reverence to the idol Manat which was placed in Al-Mushailal, those who used to assume Ihram in its name, used not to perform Sai between As-Safa and Al-Marwa, so Allah revealed: 'Verily! The As-Safa and Al-Marwa (two mountains at Mecca) are among the symbols of Allah.' (2.158). Thereupon, Allah's Messenger ﷺ and the Muslims used to perform Sai (between them)." Sufyan said: The (idol) Manat was at Al-Mushailal in Qudaid. `Aisha added, "The Verse was revealed in connection with the Ansar. They and (the tribe of) Ghassan used to assume Ihram in the name of Manat before they embraced Islam." `Aisha added, "There were men from the Ansar who used to assume Ihram in the name of Manat which was an idol between Mecca and Medina. They said, "O Allah's Messenger ﷺ ! We used not to perform the Tawaf (Sai) between As-Safa and Al-Marwa out of reverence to Manat.". – Sahih al-Bukhari 4861

حَدَّثَنَا الْحُمَيْدِيُّ، حَدَّثَنَا سُفْيَانُ، حَدَّثَنَا الزُّهْرِيُّ، سَمِعْتُ عُرْوَةَ، قُلْتُ لِعَائِشَةَ ـ رضى الله عنها ـ فَقَالَتْ إِنَّمَا كَانَ مَنْ أَهَلَّ بِمَنَاةَ الطَّاغِيَةِ الَّتِي بِالْمُشَلَّلِ لاَ يَطُوفُونَ بَيْنَ الصَّفَا وَالْمَرْوَةِ، فَأَنْزَلَ اللَّهُ تَعَالَى {إِنَّ الصَّفَا وَالْمَرْوَةَ مِنْ شَعَائِرِ اللَّهِ} فَطَافَ رَسُولُ اللَّهِ صلى الله عليه وسلم وَالْمُسْلِمُونَ. قَالَ سُفْيَانُ مَنَاةُ بِالْمُشَلَّلِ مِنْ قُدَيْدٍ. وَقَالَ عَبْدُ الرَّحْمَنِ بْنُ خَالِدٍ عَنِ ابْنِ شِهَابٍ قَالَ عُرْوَةُ قَالَتْ عَائِشَةُ نَزَلَتْ فِي الأَنْصَارِ كَانُوا هُمْ وَغَسَّانُ قَبْلَ أَنْ يُسْلِمُوا يُهِلُّونَ لِمَنَاةَ. مِثْلَهُ. وَقَالَ مَعْمَرٌ عَنِ الزُّهْرِيِّ عَنْ عُرْوَةَ عَنْ عَائِشَةَ كَانَ رِجَالٌ مِنَ الأَنْصَارِ مِمَّنْ كَانَ يُهِلُّ لِمَنَاةَ ـ وَمَنَاةُ صَنَمٌ بَيْنَ مَكَّةَ وَالْمَدِينَةِ ـ قَالُوا يَا نَبِيَّ اللَّهِ كُنَّا لاَ نَطُوفُ بَيْنَ الصَّفَا وَالْمَرْوَةِ تَعْظِيمًا لِمَنَاةَ. نَحْوَهُ

Narrated `Amr: We asked Ibn `Umar: "May a man have sexual relations with his wife during the Umra before performing Tawaf between Safa and Marwa?" He said, "Allah's Messenger ﷺ arrived (in Mecca) and circumambulated the Ka`ba seven times, then offered two rak`at behind Maqam Ibrahim (the station of Abraham), then performed Tawaf between Safa and Marwa." Ibn `Umar added, "Verily! In Allah's Apostle you have a good example." And I asked Jabir bin `Abdullah (the same question), and he replied, "You should not go near your wives (have sexual relations) till you have finished Tawaf between Safa and Marwa. ". – Sahih al-Bukhari 1623, 1624

حَدَّثَنَا قُتَيْبَةُ بْنُ سَعِيدٍ، حَدَّثَنَا سُفْيَانُ، عَنْ عَمْرٍو، سَأَلْنَا ابْنَ عُمَرَ ـ رضى الله عنهما ـ أَيَقَعُ الرَّجُلُ عَلَى امْرَأَتِهِ فِي الْعُمْرَةِ قَبْلَ أَنْ يَطُوفَ بَيْنَ الصَّفَا وَالْمَرْوَةِ قَالَ قَدِمَ رَسُولُ اللَّهِ صلى الله عليه وسلم فَطَافَ بِالْبَيْتِ سَبْعًا، ثُمَّ صَلَّى خَلْفَ الْمَقَامِ رَكْعَتَيْنِ، وَطَافَ بَيْنَ الصَّفَا وَالْمَرْوَةِ، وَقَالَ {لَقَدْ كَانَ لَكُمْ فِي رَسُولِ اللَّهِ أُسْوَةٌ حَسَنَةٌ}. قَالَ وَسَأَلْتُ جَابِرَ بْنَ عَبْدِ اللَّهِ ـ رضى الله عنهما ـ فَقَالَ لاَ يَقْرَبِ امْرَأَتَهُ حَتَّى يَطُوفَ بَيْنَ الصَّفَا وَالْمَرْوَةِ

Narrated `Amr bin Dinar: We asked Ibn `Umar whether a man who had performed the Tawaf of the Ka`ba but had not performed the Tawaf between As-Safa and Al-Marwa yet, was permitted to have sexual relation with his wife. He replied, "The Prophet ﷺ arrived (at Mecca) and circumambulated the Ka`ba seven times and then offered a two rak`at prayer behind Maqam-Ibrahim and then performed the going (Tawaf) between As-Safa and Al-Marwa (seven times) (and verily, in Allah's Messenger ﷺ you have a good example." And we asked

Jabir bin `Abdullah (the same question) and he replied, “He should not go near her till he has finished the going (Tawaf) between As-Safa and Al-Marwa.”. – Sahih al-Bukhari 1793, 1794

حَدَّثَنَا الْحُمَيْدِيُّ، حَدَّثَنَا سُفْيَانُ، عَنْ عَمْرِو بْنِ دِينَارٍ، قَالَ سَأَلْنَا ابْنَ عُمَرَ ـ رضى الله عنهما ـ عَنْ رَجُلٍ، طَافَ بِالْبَيْتِ فِي عُمْرَةٍ، وَلَمْ يَطُفْ بَيْنَ الصَّفَا وَالْمَرْوَةِ، أَيَأْتِي امْرَأَتَهُ فَقَالَ قَدِمَ النَّبِيُّ صلى الله عليه وسلم فَطَافَ بِالْبَيْتِ سَبْعًا، وَصَلَّى خَلْفَ الْمَقَامِ رَكْعَتَيْنِ، وَطَافَ بَيْنَ الصَّفَا وَالْمَرْوَةِ سَبْعًا، وَقَدْ كَانَ لَكُمْ فِي رَسُولِ اللَّهِ أُسْوَةٌ حَسَنَةٌ. قَالَ وَسَأَلْنَا جَابِرَ بْنَ عَبْدِ اللَّهِ ـ رضى الله عنهما ـ فَقَالَ لاَ يَقْرَبَنَّهَا حَتَّى يَطُوفَ بَيْنَ الصَّفَا وَالْمَرْوَةِ.

Narrated `Amr bin Dinar: I asked Ibn `Umar, “Can a person who has performed the Tawaf around the Ka`ba for `Umra but has not performed the (Sa`i) Tawaf of Safa and Marwa, have a sexual relation with his wife?” Ibn `Umar replied “When the Prophet ﷺ reached Mecca he performed the Tawaf around the Ka`ba (circumambulated it seven times) and offered a two-rak`at prayer (at the place) behind the station (of Abraham) and then performed the Tawaf (Sa`i) of Safa and Marwa, and verily in Allah’s Messenger ﷺ you have a good example.” Then we put the same question to Jabir bin `Abdullah and he too replied, “He should not go near his wife (for sexual relation) till he has finished the Tawaf of Safa and Marwa.”. – Sahih al-Bukhari 395, 396

حَدَّثَنَا الْحُمَيْدِيُّ، قَالَ حَدَّثَنَا سُفْيَانُ، قَالَ حَدَّثَنَا عَمْرُو بْنُ دِينَارٍ، قَالَ سَأَلْنَا ابْنَ عُمَرَ عَنْ رَجُلٍ، طَافَ بِالْبَيْتِ الْعُمْرَةَ، وَلَمْ يَطُفْ بَيْنَ الصَّفَا وَالْمَرْوَةِ، أَيَأْتِي امْرَأَتَهُ فَقَالَ قَدِمَ النَّبِيُّ صلى الله عليه وسلم فَطَافَ بِالْبَيْتِ سَبْعًا، وَصَلَّى خَلْفَ الْمَقَامِ رَكْعَتَيْنِ، وَطَافَ بَيْنَ الصَّفَا وَالْمَرْوَةِ، وَقَدْ كَانَ لَكُمْ فِي رَسُولِ اللَّهِ أُسْوَةٌ حَسَنَةٌ. وَسَأَلْنَا جَابِرَ بْنَ عَبْدِ اللَّهِ فَقَالَ لاَ يَقْرَبَنَّهَا حَتَّى يَطُوفَ بَيْنَ الصَّفَا وَالْمَرْوَةِ.

Ramy
رامي

Narrated ‘Ubaidullah bin `Abdullah: Ibn `Abbas said, “Usama bin Zaid rode behind the Prophet ﷺ from `Arafat to Al-Muzdalifa; and then from Al-Muzdalifa to Mina, Al-Fadl rode behind him.” He added, “Both of them (Usama and Al-Fadl) said, ‘The Prophet ﷺ was constantly reciting Talbiya till he did Rami of the Jamarat-Al-`Aqaba.”. – Sahih al-Bukhari 1686, 1687

حَدَّثَنَا زُهَيْرُ بْنُ حَرْبٍ، حَدَّثَنَا وَهْبُ بْنُ جَرِيرٍ، حَدَّثَنَا أَبِي، عَنْ يُونُسَ الأَيْلِيِّ، عَنِ الزُّهْرِيِّ، عَنْ عُبَيْدِ اللَّهِ بْنِ عَبْدِ اللَّهِ، عَنِ ابْنِ عَبَّاسٍ ـ رضى الله عنهما ـ أَنَّ أُسَامَةَ بْنَ زَيْدٍ ـ رضى الله عنهما ـ كَانَ رِدْفَ النَّبِيِّ صلى الله عليه وسلم مِنْ عَرَفَةَ إِلَى الْمُزْدَلِفَةِ، ثُمَّ أَرْدَفَ الْفَضْلَ مِنَ الْمُزْدَلِفَةِ إِلَى مِنًى ـ قَالَ ـ فَكِلاَهُمَا قَالاَ لَمْ يَزَلِ النَّبِيُّ صلى الله عليه وسلم يُلَبِّي حَتَّى رَمَى جَمْرَةَ الْعَقَبَةِ

Narrated `Abdur-Rahman bin Yazid: `Abdullah, did the Rami from the middle of the valley. So, I said, “O, Abu `Abdur-Rahman! Some people do the Rami (of the Jamra) from above it (i.e. from the top of the valley).” He said, “By Him except whom none has the right to be worshipped, this is the place from where the one on whom Surat-al-Baqara was revealed (i.e. Allah’s Messenger ﷺ) did the Rami.”. – Sahih al-Bukhari 1747

حَدَّثَنَا مُحَمَّدُ بْنُ كَثِيرٍ، أَخْبَرَنَا سُفْيَانُ، عَنِ الأَعْمَشِ، عَنْ إِبْرَاهِيمَ، عَنْ عَبْدِ الرَّحْمَنِ بْنِ يَزِيدَ، قَالَ رَمَى عَبْدُ اللَّهِ مِنْ بَطْنِ الْوَادِي، فَقُلْتُ يَا أَبَا عَبْدِ الرَّحْمَنِ، إِنَّ نَاسًا يَرْمُونَهَا مِنْ فَوْقِهَا، فَقَالَ وَالَّذِي لاَ إِلَهَ غَيْرُهُ هَذَا مَقَامُ الَّذِي أُنْزِلَتْ عَلَيْهِ سُورَةُ الْبَقَرَةِ صلى الله عليه وسلم. وَقَالَ عَبْدُ اللَّهِ بْنُ الْوَلِيدِ حَدَّثَنَا سُفْيَانُ حَدَّثَنَا الأَعْمَشُ بِهَذَا

Narrated Wabra: I asked Ibn `Umar, “When should I do the Rami of the Jimar?” He replied, “When your leader does that.” I asked him again the same question. He replied, “We used to wait till the sun declined and then we would do the Rami (i.e. on the 11th and 12th of Dhul-Hijja).”. – Sahih al-Bukhari 1746

حَدَّثَنَا أَبُو نُعَيْمٍ، حَدَّثَنَا مِسْعَرٌ، عَنْ وَبَرَةَ، قَالَ سَأَلْتُ ابْنَ عُمَرَ ـ رضى الله عنهما ـ مَتَى أَرْمِي الْجِمَارَ قَالَ إِذَا رَمَى إِمَامُكَ فَارْمِهْ. فَأَعَدْتُ عَلَيْهِ الْمَسْأَلَةَ، قَالَ كُنَّا نَتَحَيَّنُ، فَإِذَا زَالَتِ الشَّمْسُ رَمَيْنَا

Narrated Ibn `Abbas: A man said to the Prophe ﷺ t I performed the Tawaf-al-Ifada before the Rami (throwing pebbles at the Jamra)." The Prophet ﷺ replied, "There is no harm." The man said, "I had my head shaved before slaughtering." The Proph ﷺ et replied, "There is no harm." He said, "I have slaughtered the Hadi before the Rami." The Prophet ﷺ replied, "There is no harm.". – Sahih al-Bukhari 1722

حَدَّثَنَا أَحْمَدُ بْنُ يُونُسَ، أَخْبَرَنَا أَبُو بَكْرٍ، عَنْ عَبْدِ الْعَزِيزِ بْنِ رُفَيْعٍ، عَنْ عَطَاءٍ، عَنِ ابْنِ عَبَّاسٍ ـ رضى الله عنهما ـ قَالَ رَجُلٌ لِلنَّبِيِّ صلى الله عليه وسلم زُرْتُ قَبْلَ أَنْ أَرْمِيَ. قَالَ " لاَ حَرَجَ ". قَالَ حَلَقْتُ قَبْلَ أَنْ أَذْبَحَ. قَالَ " لاَ حَرَجَ ". قَالَ ذَبَحْتُ قَبْلَ أَنْ أَرْمِيَ. قَالَ " لاَ حَرَجَ ". وَقَالَ عَبْدُ الرَّحِيمِ الرَّازِيُّ عَنِ ابْنِ خُثَيْمٍ أَخْبَرَنِي عَطَاءٌ عَنِ ابْنِ عَبَّاسٍ ـ رضى الله عنهما ـ عَنِ النَّبِيِّ صلى الله عليه وسلم. وَقَالَ الْقَاسِمُ بْنُ يَحْيَى حَدَّثَنِي ابْنُ خُثَيْمٍ عَنْ عَطَاءٍ عَنِ ابْنِ عَبَّاسٍ ـ رضى الله عنهما ـ عَنِ النَّبِيِّ صلى الله عليه وسلم. وَقَالَ عَفَّانُ أُرَاهُ عَنْ وُهَيْبٍ، حَدَّثَنَا ابْنُ خُثَيْمٍ، عَنْ سَعِيدِ بْنِ جُبَيْرٍ، عَنِ ابْنِ عَبَّاسٍ ـ رضى الله عنهما ـ عَنِ النَّبِيِّ صلى الله عليه وسلم. وَقَالَ حَمَّادٌ عَنْ قَيْسِ بْنِ سَعْدٍ وَعَبَّادِ بْنِ مَنْصُورٍ عَنْ عَطَاءٍ عَنْ جَابِرٍ ـ رضى الله عنه ـ عَنِ النَّبِيِّ صلى الله عليه وسلم

Narrated Salim bin `Abdullah: `Abdullah bin `Umar used to do Rami of the Jamrat-ud-Dunya with seven small pebbles and used to recite Takbir on throwing each stone. He, then, would proceed further till he reached the level ground, where he would stay for a long time, facing the Qibla to invoke (Allah) while raising his hands. Then he would do Rami of the Jamrat-ul-Wusta similarly and would go to the left towards the level ground, where he would stand for a long time facing the Qibla to invoke (Allah) while raising his hands. Then he would do Rami of the Jamrat-ul-Aqaba from the middle of the valley, but he would not stay by it. Ibn `Umar used to say, "I saw Allah's Messenger ﷺ doing like that.". – Sahih al-Bukhari 1752

حَدَّثَنَا إِسْمَاعِيلُ بْنُ عَبْدِ اللَّهِ، قَالَ حَدَّثَنِي أَخِي، عَنْ سُلَيْمَانَ، عَنْ يُونُسَ بْنِ يَزِيدَ، عَنِ ابْنِ شِهَابٍ، عَنْ سَالِمِ بْنِ عَبْدِ اللَّهِ، أَنَّ عَبْدَ اللَّهِ بْنَ عُمَرَ ـ رضى الله عنهما ـ كَانَ يَرْمِي الْجَمْرَةَ الدُّنْيَا بِسَبْعِ حَصَيَاتٍ، ثُمَّ يُكَبِّرُ عَلَى إِثْرِ كُلِّ حَصَاةٍ، ثُمَّ يَتَقَدَّمُ فَيُسْهِلُ، فَيَقُومُ مُسْتَقْبِلَ الْقِبْلَةِ قِيَامًا طَوِيلاً، فَيَدْعُو وَيَرْفَعُ يَدَيْهِ، ثُمَّ يَرْمِي الْجَمْرَةَ الْوُسْطَى كَذَلِكَ، فَيَأْخُذُ ذَاتَ الشِّمَالِ فَيُسْهِلُ، وَيَقُومُ مُسْتَقْبِلَ الْقِبْلَةِ قِيَامًا طَوِيلاً، فَيَدْعُو وَيَرْفَعُ يَدَيْهِ، ثُمَّ يَرْمِي الْجَمْرَةَ ذَاتَ الْعَقَبَةِ مِنْ بَطْنِ الْوَادِي، وَلاَ يَقِفُ عِنْدَهَا، وَيَقُولُ هَكَذَا رَأَيْتُ رَسُولَ اللَّهِ صلى الله عليه وسلم يَفْعَلُ.

Narrated Ibn `Abbas: A man said to the Prophet (while he was delivering a sermon on the Day of Nahr), "I have performed the Tawaf round the Ka`ba before the Rami (throwing pebbles) at the Jamra." The Prophet ﷺ said, "There is no harm (therein)." Another man said, "I had my head shaved before slaughtering (the sacrifice)." The Prophet ﷺ said, "There is no harm." A third said, "I have slaughtered (the sacrifice) before the Rami (throwing pebbles) at the Jamra." The Prophet ﷺ said, "There is no harm.". – Sahih al-Bukhari 6666

حَدَّثَنَا أَحْمَدُ بْنُ يُونُسَ، حَدَّثَنَا أَبُو بَكْرٍ، عَنْ عَبْدِ الْعَزِيزِ بْنِ رُفَيْعٍ، عَنْ عَطَاءٍ، عَنِ ابْنِ عَبَّاسٍ ـ رضى الله عنهما ـ قَالَ قَالَ رَجُلٌ لِلنَّبِيِّ صلى الله عليه وسلم زُرْتُ قَبْلَ أَنْ أَرْمِيَ. قَالَ " لاَ حَرَجَ ". قَالَ آخَرُ حَلَقْتُ قَبْلَ أَنْ أَذْبَحَ. قَالَ " لاَ حَرَجَ ". قَالَ آخَرُ ذَبَحْتُ قَبْلَ أَنْ أَرْمِيَ. قَالَ " لاَ حَرَجَ ".

Narrated Salim: Ibn `Umar used to do Rami of the Jamrat-ud-Dunya (the Jamra near to the Khaif mosque) with seven small stones and used to recite Takbir on throwing every pebble. He then would go ahead till he reached the level ground where he would stand facing the Qibla for a long time to invoke (Allah) while raising his hands (while invoking). Then he would do Rami of the Jamrat-ul-Wusta (middle Jamra) and then he would go to the left towards the middle ground, where he would stand facing the Qibla. He would remain standing there for a long period to invoke (Allah) while raising his hands, and would stand there for a long period. Then he would do Rami of the Jamrat-ul-Aqaba from the middle of the valley, but he would not stay by it, and then he would leave and say, “I saw the Prophet ﷺ doing like this.” – Sahih al-Bukhari 1751

حَدَّثَنَا عُثْمَانُ بْنُ أَبِي شَيْبَةَ، حَدَّثَنَا طَلْحَةُ بْنُ يَحْيَى، حَدَّثَنَا يُونُسُ، عَنِ الزُّهْرِيِّ، عَنْ سَالِمٍ، عَنِ ابْنِ عُمَرَ ـ رضى الله عنهما ـ أَنَّهُ كَانَ يَرْمِي الْجَمْرَةَ الدُّنْيَا بِسَبْعِ حَصَيَاتٍ، يُكَبِّرُ عَلَى إِثْرِ كُلِّ حَصَاةٍ، ثُمَّ يَتَقَدَّمُ حَتَّى يُسْهِلَ فَيَقُومَ مُسْتَقْبِلَ الْقِبْلَةِ فَيَقُومُ طَوِيلاً، وَيَدْعُو وَيَرْفَعُ يَدَيْهِ، ثُمَّ يَرْمِي الْوُسْطَى، ثُمَّ يَأْخُذُ ذَاتَ الشِّمَالِ فَيَسْتَهِلُ وَيَقُومُ مُسْتَقْبِلَ الْقِبْلَةِ فَيَقُومُ طَوِيلاً وَيَدْعُو وَيَرْفَعُ يَدَيْهِ، وَيَقُومُ طَوِيلاً، ثُمَّ يَرْمِي جَمْرَةَ ذَاتِ الْعَقَبَةِ مِنْ بَطْنِ الْوَادِي، وَلاَ يَقِفُ عِنْدَهَا ثُمَّ يَنْصَرِفُ فَيَقُولُ هَكَذَا رَأَيْتُ النَّبِيَّ صلى الله عليه وسلم يَفْعَلُهُ

Narrated Ibn `Abbas: The Prophet ﷺ was asked about the slaughtering, shaving (of the head), and the doing of Rami before or after the due times. He said, “There is no harm in that.”. – Sahih al-Bukhari 1734

حَدَّثَنَا مُوسَى بْنُ إِسْمَاعِيلَ، حَدَّثَنَا وُهَيْبٌ، حَدَّثَنَا ابْنُ طَاوُسٍ، عَنْ أَبِيهِ، عَنِ ابْنِ عَبَّاسٍ ـ رضى الله عنهما ـ أَنَّ النَّبِيَّ صلى الله عليه وسلم قِيلَ لَهُ فِي الذَّبْحِ وَالْحَلْقِ وَالرَّمْىِ وَالتَّقْدِيمِ وَالتَّأْخِيرِ فَقَالَ " لاَ حَرَجَ "

Qurbani
قُرْبَان

Narrated Ibn Juraij: `Ata' said, “Ibn `Abbas said, ‘If he (i.e. the one intending to perform `Umra) has performed the Tawaf around the Ka`ba, his Ihram is considered to have finished.’ Said, ‘What proof does Ibn `Abbas has as to this saying?” `Ata' said, “(The proof is taken) from the Statement of Allah:-- “And afterwards they are brought For sacrifice unto Ancient House (Ka`ba at Mecca)” (22.33) and from the order of the Prophet to his companions to finish their Ihram during Hajjat-ul-Wada`.” I said (to `Ata’), “That (i.e. finishing the Ihram) was after coming form `Arafat.” `Ata’ said, “Ibn `Abbas used to allow it before going to `Arafat (after finishing the `Umra) and after coming from it (i.e. after performing the Hajj). – Sahih al-Bukhari 4396

حَدَّثَنِي عَمْرُو بْنُ عَلِيٍّ، حَدَّثَنَا يَحْيَى بْنُ سَعِيدٍ، حَدَّثَنَا ابْنُ جُرَيْجٍ، قَالَ حَدَّثَنِي عَطَاءٌ، عَنِ ابْنِ عَبَّاسٍ، إِذَا طَافَ بِالْبَيْتِ فَقَدْ حَلَّ. فَقُلْتُ مِنْ أَيْنَ قَالَ هَذَا ابْنُ عَبَّاسٍ قَالَ مِنْ قَوْلِ اللَّهِ تَعَالَى ‏{‏ثُمَّ مَحِلُّهَا إِلَى الْبَيْتِ الْعَتِيقِ‏}‏ وَمِنْ أَمْرِ النَّبِيِّ صلى الله عليه وسلم أَصْحَابَهُ أَنْ يَحِلُّوا فِي حَجَّةِ الْوَدَاعِ‏.‏ قُلْتُ إِنَّمَا كَانَ ذَلِكَ بَعْدَ الْمُعَرَّفِ‏.‏ قَالَ كَانَ ابْنُ عَبَّاسٍ يَرَاهُ قَبْلُ وَبَعْدُ

Narrated `Aisha: In the last Hajj of Allah’s Messengr ﷺ I assumed the Ihram for Hajj along with Allah Apostle. I was one of those who intended Tamattu` (to perform Hajj and `Umra) and did not take the Hadi (animal for sacrifice) with me. I got my menses and was not clean till the night of `Arafa I said, “O Allah’s Apostle! It is the night of the day of `Arafat and I intended to perform the Hajj Tamattu` with `Umra. Allah’s Messenger ﷺ told me to undo my hair and comb it and to postpone the `Umra. I did the same and completed the Hajj. On the night of Al-Hasba (i.e. place outside Mecca where the pilgrims go after finishing all the ceremonies of Hajj at Mina) he (the Prophet) ordered `Abdur

Rahman (`Aisha's brother) to take me to at-Tan`im to assume the Ihram for `Umra in lieu of that of Hajj-at-Tamattu` which I had intended to perform. – Sahih al-Bukhari 316

حَدَّثَنَا مُوسَى بْنُ إِسْمَاعِيلَ، حَدَّثَنَا إِبْرَاهِيمُ، حَدَّثَنَا ابْنُ شِهَابٍ، عَنْ عُرْوَةَ، أَنَّ عَائِشَةَ، قَالَتْ أَهْلَلْتُ مَعَ رَسُولِ اللَّهِ صلى الله عليه وسلم فِي حَجَّةِ الْوَدَاعِ، فَكُنْتُ مِمَّنْ تَمَتَّعَ، وَلَمْ يَسُقِ الْهَدْىَ، فَزَعَمَتْ أَنَّهَا حَاضَتْ، وَلَمْ تَطْهُرْ حَتَّى دَخَلَتْ لَيْلَةُ عَرَفَةَ فَقَالَتْ يَا رَسُولَ اللَّهِ، هَذِهِ لَيْلَةُ عَرَفَةَ، وَإِنَّمَا كُنْتُ تَمَتَّعْتُ بِعُمْرَةٍ. فَقَالَ لَهَا رَسُولُ اللَّهِ صلى الله عليه وسلم " انْقُضِي رَأْسَكِ، وَامْتَشِطِي، وَأَمْسِكِي عَنْ عُمْرَتِكِ ". فَفَعَلْتُ، فَلَمَّا قَضَيْتُ الْحَجَّ أَمَرَ عَبْدَ الرَّحْمَنِ لَيْلَةَ الْحَصْبَةِ فَأَعْمَرَنِي مِنَ التَّنْعِيمِ مَكَانَ عُمْرَتِي الَّتِي نَسَكْتُ.

Halq or Taqsir
الحَلْق أو التقصير

Narrated Ibn `Umar: The Prophet ﷺ got his head shaved during Hajjat-ul-Wada`. – Sahih al-Bukhari 4410

حَدَّثَنِي إِبْرَاهِيمُ بْنُ الْمُنْذِرِ، حَدَّثَنَا أَبُو ضَمْرَةَ، حَدَّثَنَا مُوسَى بْنُ عُقْبَةَ، عَنْ نَافِعٍ، أَنَّ ابْنَ عُمَرَ ـ رضى الله عنهما ـ أَخْبَرَهُمْ أَنَّ رَسُولَ اللَّهِ صلى الله عليه وسلم حَلَقَ رَأْسَهُ فِي حَجَّةِ الْوَدَاعِ

Narrated Ibn `Umar: During Hajjat-ul-Wada`, the Prophet ﷺ and some of his companions got their heads shaved while some of his companions got their head-hair cut short. – Sahih al-Bukhari 4411

حَدَّثَنَا عُبَيْدُ اللَّهِ بْنُ سَعِيدٍ، حَدَّثَنَا مُحَمَّدُ بْنُ بَكْرٍ، حَدَّثَنَا ابْنُ جُرَيْجٍ، أَخْبَرَنِي مُوسَى بْنُ عُقْبَةَ، عَنْ نَافِعٍ، أَخْبَرَهُ ابْنُ عُمَرَ، أَنَّ صلى الله عليه وسلم حَلَقَ فِي حَجَّةِ الْوَدَاعِ وَأُنَاسٌ مِنْ أَصْحَابِهِ وَقَصَّرَ بَعْضُهُمْ

النَّبِيَّ

Narrated Ibn `Umar: Allah's Messenger ﷺ (got) his head shaved after performing his Hajj. – Sahih al-Bukhari 1726

حَدَّثَنَا أَبُو الْيَمَانِ، أَخْبَرَنَا شُعَيْبُ بْنُ أَبِي حَمْزَةَ، قَالَ نَافِعٌ كَانَ ابْنُ عُمَرَ ـ رضى الله عنهما ـ يَقُولُ حَلَقَ رَسُولُ اللَّهِ صلى الله عليه وسلم فِي حَجَّتِهِ

Narrated `Abdullah: The Prophet ﷺ and some of his companions got their heads shaved and some others got their hair cut short. – Sahih al-Bukhari 1729

حَدَّثَنَا عَبْدُ اللَّهِ بْنُ مُحَمَّدِ بْنِ أَسْمَاءَ، حَدَّثَنَا جُوَيْرِيَةُ بْنُ أَسْمَاءَ، عَنْ نَافِعٍ، أَنَّ عَبْدَ اللَّهِ، قَالَ حَلَقَ النَّبِيُّ صلى الله عليه وسلم وَطَائِفَةٌ مِنْ أَصْحَابِهِ، وَقَصَّرَ بَعْضُهُمْ

Narrated Anas: When Allah's Messenger ﷺ got his head shaved, Abu- Talha was the first to take some of his hair. – Sahih al-Bukhari 171

حَدَّثَنَا مُحَمَّدُ بْنُ عَبْدِ الرَّحِيمِ، قَالَ أَخْبَرَنَا سَعِيدُ بْنُ سُلَيْمَانَ، قَالَ حَدَّثَنَا عَبَّادٌ، عَنِ ابْنِ عَوْنٍ، عَنِ ابْنِ سِيرِينَ، عَنْ أَنَسٍ، أَنَّ رَسُولَ اللَّهِ صلى الله عليه وسلم لَمَّا حَلَقَ رَأْسَهُ كَانَ أَبُو طَلْحَةَ أَوَّلَ مَنْ أَخَذَ مِنْ شَعَرِهِ

Tawaf Al-Wada'
طَوَاف الْوَدَاع

Narrated Ibn `Abbas: The people were ordered to perform the Tawaf of the Ka`ba (Tawaf-al-Wada`) as the lastly thing, before leaving (Mecca), except the menstruating women who were excused. – Sahih al-Bukhari 1755

حَدَّثَنَا مُسَدَّدٌ، حَدَّثَنَا سُفْيَانُ، عَنِ ابْنِ طَاوُسٍ، عَنْ أَبِيهِ، عَنِ ابْنِ عَبَّاسٍ ـ رضى الله عنهما ـ قَالَ أُمِرَ النَّاسُ أَنْ يَكُونَ آخِرُ عَهْدِهِمْ بِالْبَيْتِ، إِلاَّ أَنَّهُ خُفِّفَ عَنِ الْحَائِضِ.

Narrated Anas bin Malik: The Prophet ﷺ offered the Zuhr, `Asr, Maghrib and `Isha' prayers and slept for a while at a place called Al-Mahassab and then he rode towards the Ka`ba and performed Tawaf (al-Wada`). – Sahih al-Bukhari 1764

حَدَّثَنَا عَبْدُ الْمُتَعَالِ بْنُ طَالِبٍ، حَدَّثَنَا ابْنُ وَهْبٍ، قَالَ أَخْبَرَنِي عَمْرُو بْنُ الْحَارِثِ، أَنَّ قَتَادَةَ، حَدَّثَهُ عَنْ أَنَسِ بْنِ مَالِكٍ ـ رضى الله عنه ـ حَدَّثَهُ عَنِ النَّبِيِّ صلى الله عليه وسلم أَنَّهُ صَلَّى الظُّهْرَ وَالْعَصْرَ، وَالْمَغْرِبَ وَالْعِشَاءَ، وَرَقَدَ رَقْدَةً بِالْمُحَصَّبِ، ثُمَّ رَكِبَ إِلَى الْبَيْتِ فَطَافَ بِهِ.

Day of An-Nafr
يَوْمَ النَّفْرِ

Narrated `Abdul `Aziz bin Rufai: I asked Anas bin Malik, "Tell me what you remember from Allah's Messenger ﷺ (regarding these questions): Where did he offer the Zuhr and `Asr prayers on the day of Tarwiya (8th day of Dhul- Hijja)?" He relied, "(He offered these prayers) at Mina." I asked, "Where did he offer the `Asr prayer on the day of Nafr (i.e. departure from Mina on the 12th or 13th of Dhul-Hijja)?" He replied, "At Al- Abtah," and then added, "You should do as your chiefs do.". – Sahih al-Bukhari 1653

حَدَّثَنِي عَبْدُ اللَّهِ بْنُ مُحَمَّدٍ، حَدَّثَنَا إِسْحَاقُ الأَزْرَقُ، حَدَّثَنَا سُفْيَانُ، عَنْ عَبْدِ الْعَزِيزِ بْنِ رُفَيْعٍ، قَالَ سَأَلْتُ أَنَسَ بْنَ مَالِكٍ ـ رضى الله عنه ـ قُلْتُ أَخْبِرْنِي بِشَىْءٍ، عَقَلْتَهُ عَنِ النَّبِيِّ صلى الله عليه وسلم أَيْنَ صَلَّى الظُّهْرَ وَالْعَصْرَ يَوْمَ التَّرْوِيَةِ قَالَ بِمِنًى. قُلْتُ فَأَيْنَ صَلَّى الْعَصْرَ يَوْمَ النَّفْرِ قَالَ بِالأَبْطَحِ. ثُمَّ قَالَ افْعَلْ كَمَا يَفْعَلُ أُمَرَاؤُكَ

Narrated `Aisha: Safiya got her menses on the night of Nafr (departure from Hajj), and she said, "I see that I will detain you." The Prophet ﷺ said, "Aqra Halqa! Did she perform the Tawaf on the Day of Nahr (slaughtering)?" Somebody replied in the affirmative. He said, "Then depart." (Different narrators mentioned that) `Aisha said, "We set out with Allah''s Apostle (from Medina) with the intention of performing Hajj only. When we reached Mecca, he ordered us to finish the Ihram. When it was the night of Nafr (departure), Safiya bint Huyay got her menses. The Prophet ﷺ said, "Halqa Aqra! I think that she will detain you," and added, "Did you perform the Tawaf (Al-Ifada) on the Day of Nahr (slaughtering)?" She replied, "Yes." He said, "Then depart." I said, "O Allah''s Apostle! I have not (done the Umra)." He replied, "Perform `Umra from Tan`im." My brother went with me and we came across the Prophet ﷺ in the last part of the night. He said, "Wait at such and such a place." – Sahih al-Bukhari 1771, 1772

حَدَّثَنَا عُمَرُ بْنُ حَفْصٍ، حَدَّثَنَا أَبِي، حَدَّثَنَا الأَعْمَشُ، حَدَّثَنِي إِبْرَاهِيمُ، عَنِ الأَسْوَدِ، عَنْ عَائِشَةَ ـ رضى الله عنها ـ قَالَتْ حَاضَتْ صَفِيَّةُ لَيْلَةَ النَّفْرِ، فَقَالَتْ مَا أُرَانِي إِلاَّ حَابِسَتَكُمْ. قَالَ النَّبِيُّ صلى الله عليه وسلم " عَقْرَى حَلْقَى أَطَافَتْ يَوْمَ النَّحْرِ ". قِيلَ نَعَمْ. قَالَ " فَانْفِرِي ". قَالَ أَبُو عَبْدِ اللَّهِ وَزَادَنِي مُحَمَّدٌ حَدَّثَنَا مُحَاضِرٌ، حَدَّثَنَا الأَعْمَشُ، عَنْ إِبْرَاهِيمَ، عَنِ الأَسْوَدِ، عَنْ عَائِشَةَ ـ رضى الله عنها ـ قَالَتْ خَرَجْنَا مَعَ رَسُولِ اللَّهِ صلى الله عليه وسلم لاَ نَذْكُرُ إِلاَّ الْحَجَّ، فَلَمَّا قَدِمْنَا أَمَرَنَا أَنْ نَحِلَّ، فَلَمَّا كَانَتْ لَيْلَةُ النَّفْرِ حَاضَتْ صَفِيَّةُ بِنْتُ حُيَىٍّ، فَقَالَ النَّبِيُّ صلى الله عليه وسلم " حَلْقَى عَقْرَى، مَا أُرَاهَا إِلاَّ حَابِسَتَكُمْ

". ثُمَّ قَالَ " كُنْتِ طُفْتِ يَوْمَ النَّحْرِ ". قَالَتْ نَعَمْ. قَالَ " فَانْفِرِي ". قُلْتُ يَا رَسُولَ اللَّهِ. إِنِّي لَمْ أَكُنْ حَلَلْتُ. قَالَ " فَاعْتَمِرِي مِنَ التَّنْعِيمِ ". فَخَرَجَ مَعَهَا أَخُوهَا، فَلَقِينَاهُ مُدَّلِجًا. فَقَالَ " مَوْعِدُكِ مَكَانَ كَذَا وَكَذَا

It was narrated that Abdul-Aziz bin Rafi said: "I asked anas bin Malik: 'Tell me of something that you learned from the Messenger of Allah; where did he pray Zuhr on the day of At-Tarwiyah?' He said: 'In Mina.' I said: 'Where did he pray Asr on the day of An-Nafr?' He said: 'In Al-Abtah.'" – Sunan an-Nasa'I 2997

أَخْبَرَنَا مُحَمَّدُ بْنُ إِسْمَاعِيلَ بْنِ إِبْرَاهِيمَ، وَعَبْدُ الرَّحْمَنِ بْنُ مُحَمَّدِ بْنِ سَلاَّمٍ، قَالاَ حَدَّثَنَا إِسْحَاقُ الأَزْرَقُ، عَنْ سُفْيَانَ الثَّوْرِيِّ، عَنْ عَبْدِ الْعَزِيزِ بْنِ رُفَيْعٍ، قَالَ سَأَلْتُ أَنَسَ بْنَ مَالِكٍ فَقُلْتُ أَخْبِرْنِي بِشَىْءٍ، عَقَلْتَهُ عَنْ رَسُولِ اللَّهِ صلى الله عليه وسلم أَيْنَ صَلَّى الظُّهْرَ يَوْمَ التَّرْوِيَةِ قَالَ بِمِنًى . فَقُلْتُ أَيْنَ صَلَّى الْعَصْرَ يَوْمَ النَّفْرِ قَالَ بِالأَبْطَحِ

The Book of

Mahdi

الْمَهْدِيُّ

Narrated AbuSa'id al-Khudri: The Prophet ﷺ said: The Mahdi will be of my stock, and will have a broad forehead a prominent nose. He will fill the earth will equity and justice as it was filled with oppression and tyranny, and he will rule for seven years. – Sunan Abi Dawud 4285

حَدَّثَنَا سَهْلُ بْنُ تَمَّامِ بْنِ بَزِيعٍ، حَدَّثَنَا عِمْرَانُ الْقَطَّانُ، عَنْ قَتَادَةَ، عَنْ أَبِي نَضْرَةَ، عَنْ أَبِي سَعِيدٍ الْخُدْرِيِّ، قَالَ قَالَ رَسُولُ اللَّهِ صلى الله عليه وسلم " الْمَهْدِيُّ مِنِّي أَجْلَى الْجَبْهَةِ أَقْنَى الأَنْفِ يَمْلأُ الأَرْضَ قِسْطًا وَعَدْلاً كَمَا مُلِئَتْ جَوْرًا وَظُلْمًا يَمْلِكُ سَبْعَ سِنِينَ

Narrated Umm Salamah, Ummul Mu'minin: The Prophet ﷺ said: The Mahdi will be of my family, of the descendants of Fatimah. Abdullah ibn Ja'far said: I heard AbulMalih praising Ali ibn Nufayl and describing his good qualities. – Sunan Abi Dawud 4284

حَدَّثَنَا أَحْمَدُ بْنُ إِبْرَاهِيمَ، حَدَّثَنَا عَبْدُ اللَّهِ بْنُ جَعْفَرٍ الرَّقِّيُّ، حَدَّثَنَا أَبُو الْمَلِيحِ الْحَسَنُ بْنُ عُمَرَ، عَنْ زِيَادِ بْنِ بَيَانٍ، عَنْ عَلِيِّ بْنِ نُفَيْلٍ، عَنْ سَعِيدِ بْنِ الْمُسَيَّبِ، عَنْ أُمِّ سَلَمَةَ، قَالَتْ سَمِعْتُ رَسُولَ اللَّهِ صلى الله عليه وسلم يَقُولُ " الْمَهْدِيُّ مِنْ عِتْرَتِي مِنْ وَلَدِ فَاطِمَةَ " . قَالَ عَبْدُ اللَّهِ بْنُ جَعْفَرٍ وَسَمِعْتُ أَبَا الْمَلِيحِ يُثْنِي عَلَى عَلِيِّ بْنِ نُفَيْلٍ وَيَذْكُرُ مِنْهُ صَلاَحًا .

It was narrated from Anas bin Malik that the Messenger of Allah ﷺ said: "Adhering to religion will only become harder and worldly affairs will only become more difficult, and people will only become more stingy, and the Hour will only come upon the worst of people, and the only Mahdi (after Muhammad ﷺ) is 'Eisa bin Maryam." – Sunan Ibn Majah 4039

حَدَّثَنَا يُونُسُ بْنُ عَبْدِ الأَعْلَى، حَدَّثَنَا مُحَمَّدُ بْنُ إِدْرِيسَ الشَّافِعِيُّ، حَدَّثَنِي مُحَمَّدُ بْنُ خَالِدٍ الْجَنَدِيُّ، عَنْ أَبَانَ بْنِ صَالِحٍ، عَنِ الْحَسَنِ، عَنْ أَنَسِ بْنِ مَالِكٍ، أَنَّ رَسُولَ اللَّهِ ـ صلى الله عليه وسلم ـ قَالَ " لاَ يَزْدَادُ الأَمْرُ إِلاَّ شِدَّةً وَلاَ الدُّنْيَا إِلاَّ إِدْبَارًا وَلاَ النَّاسُ إِلاَّ شُحًّا وَلاَ تَقُومُ السَّاعَةُ إِلاَّ عَلَى شِرَارِ النَّاسِ وَلاَ الْمَهْدِيُّ إِلاَّ عِيسَى ابْنُ مَرْيَمَ ".

He (Eisa bin Maryam) is a portent of the Hour, so have no doubt about it, and follow Me. This is a straight way. – Surah Az-Zukhruf 43:61

وَإِنَّهُۥ لَعِلْمٌ لِّلسَّاعَةِ فَلَا تَمْتَرُنَّ بِهَا وَٱتَّبِعُونِ ۚ هَـٰذَا صِرَٰطٌ مُّسْتَقِيمٌ

Narrated Abu Huraira: Allah's Messenger ﷺ said, "By Him in Whose Hands my soul is, surely (Jesus,) the son of Mary will soon descend amongst you and will judge mankind justly (as a Just Ruler); he will break the Cross and kill the pigs and there will be no Jizya (i.e. taxation taken from non Muslims). Money will be in abundance so that nobody will accept it, and a single prostration to Allah (in prayer) will be better than the whole world and whatever is in it." Abu Huraira added "If you wish, you can recite (this verse of the Holy Book): -- 'And there is none Of the people of the Scriptures (Jews and Christians) But must believe in him (i.e Jesus as an Apostle of Allah and a human being) Before his death. And on the Day of Judgment He will be a witness Against them." (4.159) (See Fath-ul-Bari, Page 302 Vol 7) – Sahih al-Bukhari 3448

حَدَّثَنَا إِسْحَاقُ، أَخْبَرَنَا يَعْقُوبُ بْنُ إِبْرَاهِيمَ، حَدَّثَنَا أَبِي، عَنْ صَالِحٍ، عَنِ ابْنِ شِهَابٍ، أَنَّ سَعِيدَ بْنَ الْمُسَيَّبِ، سَمِعَ أَبَا هُرَيْرَةَ ـ رضى الله عنه ـ قَالَ قَالَ رَسُولُ اللَّهِ صلى الله عليه وسلم " وَالَّذِي نَفْسِي بِيَدِهِ، لَيُوشِكَنَّ أَنْ يَنْزِلَ فِيكُمُ ابْنُ مَرْيَمَ حَكَمًا عَدْلاً، فَيَكْسِرَ الصَّلِيبَ، وَيَقْتُلَ الْخِنْزِيرَ، وَيَضَعَ الْجِزْيَةَ، وَيَفِيضَ الْمَالُ حَتَّى لاَ يَقْبَلَهُ أَحَدٌ، حَتَّى تَكُونَ السَّجْدَةُ الْوَاحِدَةُ خَيْرًا مِنَ الدُّنْيَا وَمَا فِيهَا ". ثُمَّ يَقُولُ أَبُو هُرَيْرَةَ وَاقْرَءُوا إِنْ شِئْتُمْ {وَإِنْ مِنْ أَهْلِ الْكِتَابِ إِلاَّ لَيُؤْمِنَنَّ بِهِ قَبْلَ مَوْتِهِ وَيَوْمَ الْقِيَامَةِ يَكُونُ عَلَيْهِمْ شَهِيدًا}.

The Hour will not be established till

لاَ تَقُومُ السَّاعَةُ حَتَّى

Narrated Abu Huraira: The Propht ﷺ said, "The Hour (Last Day) will not be established until (religious) knowledge will be taken away (by the death of religious learned men), earthquakes will be very frequent, time will pass quickly, afflictions will appear, murders will increase and money will overflow amongst you." (See Hadith No. 85 Vol 1). – Sahih al-Bukhari 1036

حَدَّثَنَا أَبُو الْيَمَانِ، قَالَ أَخْبَرَنَا شُعَيْبٌ، قَالَ أَخْبَرَنَا أَبُو الزِّنَادِ، عَنْ عَبْدِ الرَّحْمَنِ الأَعْرَجِ، عَنْ أَبِي هُرَيْرَةَ، قَالَ قَالَ النَّبِيُّ صلى الله عليه وسلم " لاَ تَقُومُ السَّاعَةُ حَتَّى يُقْبَضَ الْعِلْمُ، وَتَكْثُرَ الزَّلاَزِلُ، وَيَتَقَارَبَ الزَّمَانُ، وَتَظْهَرَ الْفِتَنُ، وَيَكْثُرَ الْهَرْجُ ـ وَهْوَ الْقَتْلُ الْقَتْلُ ـ حَتَّى يَكْثُرَ فِيكُمُ الْمَالُ فَيَفِيضُ "

Narrated Abu Huraira: Allah's Messenger ﷺ said, "The Hour will not be established till a fire will come out of the land of Hijaz, and it will throw light on the necks of the camels at Busra.". – Sahih al-Bukhari 7118

حَدَّثَنَا أَبُو الْيَمَانِ، أَخْبَرَنَا شُعَيْبٌ، عَنِ الزُّهْرِيِّ، قَالَ سَعِيدُ بْنُ الْمُسَيَّبِ أَخْبَرَنِي أَبُو هُرَيْرَةَ، أَنَّ رَسُولَ اللَّهِ صلى الله عليه وسلم قَالَ " لاَ تَقُومُ السَّاعَةُ حَتَّى تَخْرُجَ نَارٌ مِنْ أَرْضِ الْحِجَازِ، تُضِيءُ أَعْنَاقَ الإِبِلِ بِبُصْرَى ".

Narrated Abu Huraira: Allah's Messenger ﷺ said, "The Hour will not be established (1) till two big groups fight each other whereupon there will be a great number of casualties on both sides and they will be following one and the same religious doctrine, (2) till about thirty Dajjals (liars) appear, and each one of them will claim that he is Allah's Messenger ﷺ (3) ,till the religious knowledge is taken away (by the death of Religious scholars) (4) earthquakes will increase in number (5) time will pass quickly, (6) afflictions will appear, (7) Al-Harj, (i.e., killing) will increase, (8) till wealth will be in abundance ---- so abundant that a wealthy person will worry lest nobody should accept his Zakat, and whenever he will present it to someone, that person (to whom it will be offered) will say, 'I am not in need of it, (9) till the people compete with one another in constructing high buildings, (10) till a man when passing by a grave of someone will say, 'Would that I were in his place (11) and till the sun rises from the West. So when the sun will rise and the people will see it (rising from the West) they will all believe (embrace Islam) but that will be the time when: (As Allah said,) 'No good will it do to a soul to believe then, if it believed not before, nor earned good (by deeds of righteousness) through its Faith.' (6.158) And the Hour will be established while two men spreading a garment in front of them but they will not be able to sell it, nor fold it up; and the Hour will be established when a man has milked his she-camel and has taken away the milk but he will not be able to drink it; and the Hour will be established before a man repairing a tank (for his livestock) is able to water (his animals) in it; and the Hour will be established when a person has raised a morsel (of food) to his mouth but will not be able to eat it.". – Sahih al-Bukhari 7121

حَدَّثَنَا أَبُو الْيَمَانِ، أَخْبَرَنَا شُعَيْبٌ، حَدَّثَنَا أَبُو الزِّنَادِ، عَنْ عَبْدِ الرَّحْمَنِ، عَنْ أَبِي هُرَيْرَةَ، أَنَّ رَسُولَ اللَّهِ صلى الله عليه وسلم قَالَ " لاَ تَقُومُ السَّاعَةُ حَتَّى تَقْتَتِلَ فِئَتَانِ عَظِيمَتَانِ، يَكُونُ بَيْنَهُمَا مَقْتَلَةٌ عَظِيمَةٌ، دَعْوَتُهُمَا وَاحِدَةٌ، وَحَتَّى يُبْعَثَ دَجَّالُونَ كَذَّابُونَ، قَرِيبٌ مِنْ ثَلاَثِينَ، كُلُّهُمْ يَزْعُمُ أَنَّهُ رَسُولُ اللَّهِ، وَحَتَّى يُقْبَضَ الْعِلْمُ، وَتَكْثُرَ الزَّلاَزِلُ، وَيَتَقَارَبَ الزَّمَانُ، وَتَظْهَرَ الْفِتَنُ، وَيَكْثُرَ الْهَرْجُ وَهْوَ الْقَتْلُ، وَحَتَّى يَكْثُرَ فِيكُمُ الْمَالُ فَيَفِيضَ، حَتَّى يُهِمَّ رَبَّ الْمَالِ مَنْ يَقْبَلُ صَدَقَتَهُ، وَحَتَّى يَعْرِضَهُ فَيَقُولَ الَّذِي يَعْرِضُهُ عَلَيْهِ لاَ أَرَبَ لِي بِهِ. وَحَتَّى يَتَطَاوَلَ النَّاسُ فِي الْبُنْيَانِ، وَحَتَّى يَمُرَّ الرَّجُلُ بِقَبْرِ الرَّجُلِ فَيَقُولُ يَا لَيْتَنِي مَكَانَهُ. وَحَتَّى تَطْلُعَ الشَّمْسُ مِنْ مَغْرِبِهَا، فَإِذَا طَلَعَتْ وَرَآهَا النَّاسُ ـ يَعْنِي ـ آمَنُوا أَجْمَعُونَ، فَذَلِكَ حِينَ لاَ يَنْفَعُ نَفْسًا إِيمَانُهَا لَمْ تَكُنْ آمَنَتْ مِنْ قَبْلُ، أَوْ كَسَبَتْ فِي إِيمَانِهَا خَيْرًا، وَلَتَقُومَنَّ السَّاعَةُ وَقَدْ نَشَرَ الرَّجُلاَنِ ثَوْبَهُمَا بَيْنَهُمَا، فَلاَ يَتَبَايَعَانِهِ وَلاَ يَطْوِيَانِهِ، وَلَتَقُومَنَّ السَّاعَةُ وَقَدِ انْصَرَفَ الرَّجُلُ بِلَبَنِ لِقْحَتِهِ فَلاَ يَطْعَمُهُ، وَلَتَقُومَنَّ السَّاعَةُ وَهْوَ يُلِيطُ حَوْضَهُ فَلاَ يَسْقِي فِيهِ، وَلَتَقُومَنَّ السَّاعَةُ وَقَدْ رَفَعَ أُكْلَتَهُ إِلَى فِيهِ فَلاَ يَطْعَمُهَا

Narrated Abu Huraira: One day while the Prophet ﷺ was sitting in the company of some people, (The angel) Gabriel came and asked, "What is faith?" Allah's Messenger ﷺ replied, 'Faith is to believe in Allah, His angels, (the) meeting with Him, His Apostles, and to believe in Resurrection." Then he further asked, "What is Islam?" Allah's Messenger ﷺ replied, "To worship Allah Alone and none else, to offer prayers perfectly to pay the compulsory charity (Zakat) and to observe fasts during the month of Ramadan." Then he further asked, "What is Ihsan (perfection)?" Allah's Messenger ﷺ replied, "To worship Allah as if you see Him, and if you cannot achieve this state of devotion then you must consider that He is looking at you." Then he further a"ked, "When will the Hour be established?" Allah's Messenger ﷺ replied, "The answerer has no better knowledge than the questioner. But I will inform you about its portents. 1 When a slave (lady) gives birth to her master. 2 When the shepherds of black camels start boasting and competing with others in the construction of higher buildings. And the Hour is one of five things which nobody knows except Allah. The Prophet ﷺ then recited: "Verily, with Allah (Alone) is the knowledge of the Hour--." (31. 34) Then that man (Gabriel) left and the Prophet ﷺ asked his companions to call him back, but they could not see him. Then the Prophet ﷺ said, "That was Gabriel who came to teach the people their religion." Abu 'Abdullah said: He (the Prophet) considered all that as a part of faith. – Sahih al-Bukhari 50

حَدَّثَنَا مُسَدَّدٌ، قَالَ حَدَّثَنَا إِسْمَاعِيلُ بْنُ إِبْرَاهِيمَ، أَخْبَرَنَا أَبُو حَيَّانَ التَّيْمِيُّ، عَنْ أَبِي زُرْعَةَ، عَنْ أَبِي هُرَيْرَةَ، قَالَ كَانَ النَّبِيُّ صلى الله عليه وسلم بَارِزًا يَوْمًا لِلنَّاسِ، فَأَتَاهُ جِبْرِيلُ فَقَالَ مَا الإِيمَانُ قَالَ " الإِيمَانُ أَنْ تُؤْمِنَ بِاللَّهِ وَمَلاَئِكَتِهِ وَبِلِقَائِهِ وَرُسُلِهِ، وَتُؤْمِنَ بِالْبَعْثِ ". قَالَ مَا الإِسْلاَمُ قَالَ " الإِسْلاَمُ أَنْ تَعْبُدَ اللَّهَ وَلاَ تُشْرِكَ بِهِ، وَتُقِيمَ الصَّلاَةَ، وَتُؤَدِّيَ الزَّكَاةَ الْمَفْرُوضَةَ، وَتَصُومَ رَمَضَانَ ". قَالَ مَا الإِحْسَانُ قَالَ " أَنْ تَعْبُدَ اللَّهَ كَأَنَّكَ تَرَاهُ، فَإِنْ لَمْ تَكُنْ تَرَاهُ فَإِنَّهُ يَرَاكَ ". قَالَ مَتَى السَّاعَةُ قَالَ " مَا الْمَسْئُولُ عَنْهَا بِأَعْلَمَ مِنَ السَّائِلِ، وَسَأُخْبِرُكَ عَنْ أَشْرَاطِهَا إِذَا وَلَدَتِ الأَمَةُ رَبَّهَا، وَإِذَا تَطَاوَلَ رُعَاةُ الإِبِلِ الْبُهْمُ فِي الْبُنْيَانِ، فِي خَمْسٍ لاَ يَعْلَمُهُنَّ إِلاَّ اللَّهُ ". ثُمَّ تَلاَ النَّبِيُّ صلى الله عليه وسلم {إِنَّ اللَّهَ عِنْدَهُ عِلْمُ السَّاعَةِ} الآيَةَ. ثُمَّ أَدْبَرَ فَقَالَ " رُدُّوهُ ". فَلَمْ يَرَوْا شَيْئًا. فَقَالَ " هَذَا جِبْرِيلُ جَاءَ يُعَلِّمُ النَّاسَ دِينَهُمْ ". قَالَ أَبُو عَبْدِ اللَّهِ جَعَلَ ذَلِكَ كُلَّهُ مِنَ الإِيمَانِ

Narrated Abu Huraira: While the Prophet was saying something in a gathering, a Bedouin came and asked him, "When would the Hour (Doomsday) take place?" Allah's Messenger ﷺ continued his talk, so some people said that Allah's Messenger ﷺ had heard the question, but did not like what that Bedouin had asked. Some of them said that Allah's Messenger ﷺ had not heard it. When the Prophet ﷺ finished his speech, he said, "Where is the questioner, who inquired about the Hour (Doomsday)?" The Bedouin said, "I am here, O Allah's Apostle ." Then the Prophet ﷺ said, "When honesty is lost, then wait for the Hour (Doomsday)." The Bedouin said, "How will that be lost?" The Prophet ﷺ said, "When the power or authority comes in the hands of unfit persons, then wait for the Hour (Doomsday.)". – Sahih al-Bukhari 59

حَدَّثَنَا مُحَمَّدُ بْنُ سِنَانٍ، قَالَ حَدَّثَنَا فُلَيْحٌ، ح وَحَدَّثَنِي إِبْرَاهِيمُ بْنُ الْمُنْذِرِ، قَالَ حَدَّثَنَا مُحَمَّدُ بْنُ فُلَيْحٍ، قَالَ حَدَّثَنِي أَبِي قَالَ، حَدَّثَنِي هِلاَلُ بْنُ عَلِيٍّ، عَنْ عَطَاءِ بْنِ يَسَارٍ، عَنْ أَبِي هُرَيْرَةَ، قَالَ بَيْنَمَا النَّبِيُّ صلى الله عليه وسلم فِي مَجْلِسٍ يُحَدِّثُ الْقَوْمَ جَاءَهُ أَعْرَابِيٌّ فَقَالَ مَتَى السَّاعَةُ فَمَضَى رَسُولُ اللَّهِ صلى الله عليه وسلم يُحَدِّثُ، فَقَالَ بَعْضُ الْقَوْمِ سَمِعَ مَا قَالَ، فَكَرِهَ مَا قَالَ، وَقَالَ بَعْضُهُمْ بَلْ لَمْ يَسْمَعْ، حَتَّى إِذَا قَضَى حَدِيثَهُ قَالَ " أَيْنَ ـ أُرَاهُ ـ السَّائِلُ عَنِ السَّاعَةِ ". قَالَ هَا أَنَا يَا رَسُولَ اللَّهِ. قَالَ " فَإِذَا ضُيِّعَتِ الأَمَانَةُ فَانْتَظِرِ السَّاعَةَ ". قَالَ كَيْفَ إِضَاعَتُهَا قَالَ " إِذَا وُسِّدَ الأَمْرُ إِلَى غَيْرِ أَهْلِهِ فَانْتَظِرِ السَّاعَةَ ".

Al-Masih Ad-Dajjal
الْمَسِيحِ الدَّجَّالِ

Narrated Anas bin Malik: The Prophet ﷺ said, "There will be no town which Ad-Dajjal will not enter except Mecca and Medina, and there will be no entrance (road) (of both Mecca and Medina) but the angels will be standing in rows guarding it against him, and then Medina will shake with its inhabitants thrice (i.e. three earthquakes will take place) and Allah will expel all the non-believers and the hypocrites from it.". – Sahih al-Bukhari 1881

حَدَّثَنَا إِبْرَاهِيمُ بْنُ الْمُنْذِرِ، حَدَّثَنَا الْوَلِيدُ، حَدَّثَنَا أَبُو عَمْرٍو، حَدَّثَنَا إِسْحَاقُ، حَدَّثَنِي أَنَسُ بْنُ مَالِكٍ ـ رضى الله عنه ـ عَنِ النَّبِيِّ صلى الله عليه وسلم قَالَ " لَيْسَ مِنْ بَلَدٍ إِلاَّ سَيَطَؤُهُ الدَّجَّالُ، إِلاَّ مَكَّةَ وَالْمَدِينَةَ، لَيْسَ لَهُ مِنْ نِقَابِهَا نَقْبٌ إِلاَّ عَلَيْهِ الْمَلاَئِكَةُ صَافِّينَ، يَحْرُسُونَهَا، ثُمَّ تَرْجُفُ الْمَدِينَةُ بِأَهْلِهَا ثَلاَثَ رَجَفَاتٍ، فَيُخْرِجُ اللَّهُ كُلَّ كَافِرٍ وَمُنَافِقٍ "

Narrated `Aisha: The Prophet ﷺ used to say, "O Allah! I seek refuge with You from laziness and geriatric old age, from all kinds of sins and from being in debt; from the trial and affliction of the grave and from the punishment in the grave; from the affliction of the Fire and from the punishment of the Fire; and from the evil of the affliction of wealth; and I seek refuge with You from the affliction of poverty, and I seek refuge with You from the affliction of Al-Mesiah Ad-Dajjal. O Allah! Wash away my sins with the water of snow and hail, and cleanse my heart from all the sins as a white garment is cleansed from the filth, and let there be a long distance between me and my sins, as You made East and West far from each other.". – Sahih al-Bukhari 6368

حَدَّثَنَا مُعَلَّى بْنُ أَسَدٍ، حَدَّثَنَا وُهَيْبٌ، عَنْ هِشَامِ بْنِ عُرْوَةَ، عَنْ أَبِيهِ، عَنْ عَائِشَةَ ـ رضى الله عنها ـ أَنَّ النَّبِيَّ صلى الله عليه وسلم كَانَ يَقُولُ " اللَّهُمَّ إِنِّي أَعُوذُ بِكَ مِنَ الْكَسَلِ وَالْهَرَمِ، وَالْمَأْثَمِ وَالْمَغْرَمِ، وَمِنْ فِتْنَةِ الْقَبْرِ وَعَذَابِ الْقَبْرِ، وَمِنْ فِتْنَةِ النَّارِ وَعَذَابِ النَّارِ، وَمِنْ شَرِّ فِتْنَةِ الْغِنَى، وَأَعُوذُ بِكَ مِنْ فِتْنَةِ الْفَقْرِ، وَأَعُوذُ بِكَ مِنْ فِتْنَةِ الْمَسِيحِ الدَّجَّالِ، اللَّهُمَّ اغْسِلْ عَنِّي خَطَايَاىَ بِمَاءِ الثَّلْجِ وَالْبَرَدِ، وَنَقِّ قَلْبِي مِنَ الْخَطَايَا، كَمَا نَقَّيْتَ الثَّوْبَ الأَبْيَضَ مِنَ الدَّنَسِ، وَبَاعِدْ بَيْنِي وَبَيْنَ خَطَايَاىَ كَمَا بَاعَدْتَ بَيْنَ الْمَشْرِقِ وَالْمَغْرِبِ "

Narrated Mujahid: I was in the company of Ibn `Abbas and the people talked about Ad-Dajjal and said, "Ad-Dajjal will come with the word Kafir (non-believer) written in between his eyes." On that Ibn `Abbas said, "I have not heard this from the Prophet ﷺ but I heard him saying, 'As if I saw Moses just now entering the valley reciting Talbyia. ' ". – Sahih al-Bukhari 1555

حَدَّثَنَا مُحَمَّدُ بْنُ الْمُثَنَّى، قَالَ حَدَّثَنِي ابْنُ أَبِي عَدِيٍّ، عَنِ ابْنِ عَوْنٍ، عَنْ مُجَاهِدٍ، قَالَ كُنَّا عِنْدَ ابْنِ عَبَّاسٍ ـ رضى الله عنهما ـ فَذَكَرُوا الدَّجَّالَ أَنَّهُ قَالَ " مَكْتُوبٌ بَيْنَ عَيْنَيْهِ كَافِرٌ ". فَقَالَ ابْنُ عَبَّاسٍ لَمْ أَسْمَعْهُ وَلَكِنَّهُ قَالَ " أَمَّا مُوسَى كَأَنِّي أَنْظُرُ إِلَيْهِ إِذِ انْحَدَرَ فِي الْوَادِي يُلَبِّي ".

Narrated Anas: The Prophet ﷺ said, "Allah did not send any prophet but that he warned his nation of the one-eyed liar (Ad-Dajjal). He is one-eyed while your Lord is not one-eyed, The word 'Kafir' (unbeliever) is written between his two eyes.". – Sahih al-Bukhari 7408

حَدَّثَنَا حَفْصُ بْنُ عُمَرَ، حَدَّثَنَا شُعْبَةُ، أَخْبَرَنَا قَتَادَةُ، قَالَ سَمِعْتُ أَنَسًا ـ رضى الله عنه ـ عَنِ النَّبِيِّ صلى الله عليه وسلم قَالَ " مَا بَعَثَ اللَّهُ مِنْ نَبِيٍّ إِلاَّ أَنْذَرَ قَوْمَهُ الأَعْوَرَ الْكَذَّابَ، إِنَّهُ أَعْوَرُ، وَإِنَّ رَبَّكُمْ لَيْسَ بِأَعْوَرَ، مَكْتُوبٌ بَيْنَ عَيْنَيْهِ كَافِرٌ ".

Narrated Ibn `Umar: Once Allah's Messenger ﷺ stood amongst the people, glorified and praised Allah as He deserved and then mentioned the Dajjal saying, "I warn you against him (i.e. the Dajjal) and there was no prophet but warned his nation against him. No doubt, Noah warned his nation against him but I tell you about him something of which no prophet told his nation before me. You should know that he is one-eyed, and Allah is not one-eyed.". – Sahih al-Bukhari 3337

حَدَّثَنَا عَبْدَانُ، أَخْبَرَنَا عَبْدُ اللَّهِ، عَنْ يُونُسَ، عَنِ الزُّهْرِيِّ، قَالَ سَالِمٌ وَقَالَ ابْنُ عُمَرَ ـ رضى الله عنهما قَامَ رَسُولُ اللَّهِ صلى الله عليه وسلم فِي النَّاسِ فَأَثْنَى عَلَى اللَّهِ بِمَا هُوَ أَهْلُهُ، ثُمَّ ذَكَرَ الدَّجَّالَ، فَقَالَ " إِنِّي لأُنْذِرُكُمُوهُ، وَمَا مِنْ نَبِيٍّ إِلاَّ أَنْذَرَهُ قَوْمَهُ، لَقَدْ أَنْذَرَ نُوحٌ قَوْمَهُ، وَلَكِنِّي أَقُولُ لَكُمْ فِيهِ قَوْلاً لَمْ يَقُلْهُ نَبِيٌّ لِقَوْمِهِ، تَعْلَمُونَ أَنَّهُ أَعْوَرُ، وَأَنَّ اللَّهَ لَيْسَ بِأَعْوَرَ "

Narrated Abu Bakra: The Prophet ﷺ said, "The terror caused by Al-Masih Ad-Dajjal will not enter Medina and at that time Medina will have seven gates and there will be two angels at each gate (guarding them). – Sahih al-Bukhari 7125

حَدَّثَنَا عَبْدُ الْعَزِيزِ بْنُ عَبْدِ اللَّهِ، حَدَّثَنَا إِبْرَاهِيمُ بْنُ سَعْدٍ، عَنْ أَبِيهِ، عَنْ جَدِّهِ، عَنْ أَبِي بَكْرَةَ، عَنِ النَّبِيِّ صلى الله عليه وسلم قَالَ " لاَ يَدْخُلُ الْمَدِينَةَ رُعْبُ الْمَسِيحِ الدَّجَّالِ، وَلَهَا يَوْمَئِذٍ سَبْعَةُ أَبْوَابٍ، عَلَى كُلِّ باب مَلَكَانِ ".

The Book of
If Allah were to hold mankind for their injustices, He would not leave upon it (Earth) a single creature
وَلَوْ يُؤَاخِذُ ٱللَّهُ ٱلنَّاسَ بِظُلْمِهِم مَّا تَرَكَ عَلَيْهَا مِن دَآبَّةٍ

If Allah were to hold mankind for their injustices, He would not leave upon it a single creature, but He postpones them until an appointed time. Then, when their time arrives, they will not delay it by one hour, nor will they advance it.
Surah An-Nahl 16:61
وَلَوْ يُؤَاخِذُ ٱللَّهُ ٱلنَّاسَ بِظُلْمِهِم مَّا تَرَكَ عَلَيْهَا مِن دَآبَّةٍ وَلَـٰكِن يُؤَخِّرُهُمْ إِلَىٰٓ أَجَلٍ مُّسَمًّى ۖ فَإِذَا جَآءَ أَجَلُهُمْ لَا يَسْتَـْٔخِرُونَ سَاعَةً وَلَا يَسْتَقْدِمُونَ

(Yusuf said) "Yet I do not claim to be innocent. The soul commands evil, except those on whom my Lord has mercy. Truly my Lord is Forgiving and Merciful." - Surah Yusuf 12:53
وَمَآ أُبَرِّئُ نَفْسِىٓ ۚ إِنَّ ٱلنَّفْسَ لَأَمَّارَةٌۢ بِٱلسُّوٓءِ إِلَّا مَا رَحِمَ رَبِّىٓ ۚ إِنَّ رَبِّى غَفُورٌ رَّحِيمٌ

And Noah called to his Lord. He said, "O My Lord, my son is of my family, and Your promise is true, and You are the Wisest of the wise." He said, "O Noah, he is not of your family. It is an unrighteous deed. So do not ask Me about something you know nothing about. I admonish you, lest you be one of the ignorant." - Surah Hud 11:45&46
وَنَادَىٰ نُوحٌ رَّبَّهُۥ فَقَالَ رَبِّ إِنَّ ٱبْنِى مِنْ أَهْلِى وَإِنَّ وَعْدَكَ ٱلْحَقُّ وَأَنتَ أَحْكَمُ ٱلْحَـٰكِمِينَ قَالَ يَـٰنُوحُ إِنَّهُۥ لَيْسَ مِنْ أَهْلِكَ ۖ إِنَّهُۥ عَمَلٌ غَيْرُ صَـٰلِحٍ ۖ فَلَا تَسْـَٔلْنِ مَا لَيْسَ لَكَ بِهِۦ عِلْمٌ ۖ إِنِّىٓ أَعِظُكَ أَن تَكُونَ مِنَ ٱلْجَـٰهِلِينَ

(Musa) said, "I did it then, when I was of those astray. – Ash-Shu'ara' 26:20
قَالَ فَعَلْتُهَآ إِذًا وَأَنَا۠ مِنَ ٱلضَّآلِّينَ

He said, "He has done you wrong by asking your ewe in addition to his ewes. Many partners take advantage of one another, except those who believe and do good deeds, but these are so few." David realized that We were testing him, so he sought forgiveness from his Lord, and fell down to his knees, and repented. – Sad 38:24
قَالَ لَقَدْ ظَلَمَكَ بِسُؤَالِ نَعْجَتِكَ إِلَىٰ نِعَاجِهِۦ ۖ وَإِنَّ كَثِيرًا مِّنَ ٱلْخُلَطَآءِ لَيَبْغِى بَعْضُهُمْ عَلَىٰ بَعْضٍ إِلَّا ٱلَّذِينَ ءَامَنُوا۟ وَعَمِلُوا۟ ٱلصَّـٰلِحَـٰتِ وَقَلِيلٌ مَّا هُمْ ۗ وَظَنَّ دَاوُۥدُ أَنَّمَا فَتَنَّـٰهُ فَٱسْتَغْفَرَ رَبَّهُۥ وَخَرَّ رَاكِعًا وَأَنَابَ

And We granted David, Solomon, an excellent servant. He was penitent. When the beautiful horses were paraded before him in the evening. He said, "I have preferred the love of niceties to the remembrance of my Lord—until it disappeared behind the veil. Bring them back to me." And he began caressing their legs and necks. We tested Solomon, and placed a body on his throne; then he repented. He said, "My Lord, forgive me, and grant me a kingdom never to be attained by anyone after me. You are the Giver." – Surah Sad 38:30-35
وَوَهَبْنَا لِدَاوُۥدَ سُلَيْمَـٰنَ ۚ نِعْمَ ٱلْعَبْدُ ۖ إِنَّهُۥٓ أَوَّابٌ إِذْ عُرِضَ عَلَيْهِ بِٱلْعَشِىِّ ٱلصَّـٰفِنَـٰتُ ٱلْجِيَادُ فَقَالَ إِنِّىٓ أَحْبَبْتُ حُبَّ ٱلْخَيْرِ عَن ذِكْرِ رَبِّى حَتَّىٰ تَوَارَتْ بِٱلْحِجَابِ رُدُّوهَا عَلَىَّ ۖ فَطَفِقَ مَسْحًۢا بِٱلسُّوقِ وَٱلْأَعْنَاقِ وَلَقَدْ فَتَنَّا سُلَيْمَـٰنَ وَأَلْقَيْنَا عَلَىٰ كُرْسِيِّهِۦ جَسَدًا ثُمَّ أَنَابَ قَالَ رَبِّ ٱغْفِرْ لِى وَهَبْ لِى مُلْكًا لَّا يَنۢبَغِى لِأَحَدٍ مِّنۢ بَعْدِىٓ ۖ إِنَّكَ أَنتَ ٱلْوَهَّابُ

Then the fish swallowed him, and he was to blame. Had he not been one of those who praised. He would have stayed in its belly until the Day they are raised. – Surah As-Saffat 37:142-144

فَٱلْتَقَمَهُ ٱلْحُوتُ وَهُوَ مُلِيمٌ فَلَوْلَآ أَنَّهُۥ كَانَ مِنَ ٱلْمُسَبِّحِينَ لَلَبِثَ فِى بَطْنِهِۦٓ إِلَىٰ يَوْمِ يُبْعَثُونَ

May Allah pardon you (Muhammad)! Why did you give them permission before it became clear to you who are the truthful ones, and who are the liars? – Surah At-Taubah 9:43

عَفَا ٱللَّهُ عَنكَ لِمَ أَذِنتَ لَهُمْ حَتَّىٰ يَتَبَيَّنَ لَكَ ٱلَّذِينَ صَدَقُوا۟ وَتَعْلَمَ ٱلْكَٰذِبِينَ

Narrated Ibn `Umar: When `Abdullah bin Ubai died, his son `Abdullah bin `Abdullah came to Allah's Messenger ﷺ who gave his shirt to him and ordered him to shroud his father in it. Then he stood up to offer the funeral prayer for the deceased, but `Umar bin Al-Khattab took hold of his garment and said, "Do you offer the funeral prayer for him though he was a hypocrite and Allah has forbidden you to ask forgiveness for hypocrites?" The Prophet ﷺ said, "Allah has given me the choice (or Allah has informed me) saying: "Whether you, O Muhammad, ask forgiveness for them, or do not ask forgiveness for them, even if you ask forgiveness for them seventy times, Allah will not forgive them," (9.80) The he added, "I will (appeal to Allah for his sake) more than seventy times." So Allah's Messenger ﷺ offered the funeral prayer for him and we too, offered the prayer along with him. Then Allah revealed: "And never, O Muhammad, pray (funeral prayer) for anyone of them that dies, nor stand at his grave. Certainly they disbelieved in Allah and His Apostle and died in a state of rebellion." (9.84) – Sahih al-Bukhari 4672

حَدَّثَنِي إِبْرَاهِيمُ بْنُ الْمُنْذِرِ، حَدَّثَنَا أَنَسُ بْنُ عِيَاضٍ، عَنْ عُبَيْدِ اللَّهِ، عَنْ نَافِعٍ، عَنِ ابْنِ عُمَرَ ـ رضى الله عنهما ـ أَنَّهُ قَالَ لَمَّا تُوُفِّيَ عَبْدُ اللَّهِ بْنُ أُبَىٍّ جَاءَ ابْنُهُ عَبْدُ اللَّهِ بْنُ عَبْدِ اللَّهِ إِلَى رَسُولِ اللَّهِ صلى الله عليه وسلم فَأَعْطَاهُ قَمِيصَهُ وَأَمَرَهُ أَنْ يُكَفِّنَهُ فِيهِ ثُمَّ قَامَ يُصَلِّي عَلَيْهِ، فَأَخَذَ عُمَرُ بْنُ الْخَطَّابِ بِثَوْبِهِ فَقَالَ تُصَلِّي عَلَيْهِ وَهْوَ مُنَافِقٌ وَقَدْ نَهَاكَ اللَّهُ أَنْ تَسْتَغْفِرَ لَهُمْ. قَالَ " إِنَّمَا خَيَّرَنِي اللَّهُ أَوْ أَخْبَرَنِي فَقَالَ {اسْتَغْفِرْ لَهُمْ أَوْ لاَ تَسْتَغْفِرْ لَهُمْ إِنْ تَسْتَغْفِرْ لَهُمْ سَبْعِينَ مَرَّةً فَلَنْ يَغْفِرَ اللَّهُ لَهُمْ} فَقَالَ سَأَزِيدُهُ عَلَى سَبْعِينَ ". قَالَ فَصَلَّى عَلَيْهِ رَسُولُ اللَّهِ صلى الله عليه وسلم وَصَلَّيْنَا مَعَهُ ثُمَّ أَنْزَلَ اللَّهُ عَلَيْهِ {وَلاَ تُصَلِّ عَلَى أَحَدٍ مِنْهُمْ مَاتَ أَبَدًا وَلاَ تَقُمْ عَلَى قَبْرِهِ إِنَّهُمْ كَفَرُوا بِاللَّهِ وَرَسُولِهِ وَمَاتُوا وَهُمْ فَاسِقُونَ}

He frowned and turned away. When the blind man approached him. But how do you know? Perhaps he was seeking to purify himself. Or be reminded, and the message would benefit him. But as for him who was indifferent. You gave him your attention. Though you are not liable if he does not purify himself. But as for him who came to you seeking. In awe. To him you were inattentive. – Surah Abasa 80:1-10

عَبَسَ وَتَوَلَّىٰٓ أَن جَآءَهُ ٱلْأَعْمَىٰ وَمَا يُدْرِيكَ لَعَلَّهُۥ يَزَّكَّىٰٓ أَوْ يَذَّكَّرُ فَتَنفَعَهُ ٱلذِّكْرَىٰٓ أَمَّا مَنِ ٱسْتَغْنَىٰ فَأَنتَ لَهُۥ تَصَدَّىٰ وَمَا عَلَيْكَ أَلَّا يَزَّكَّىٰ وَأَمَّا مَن جَآءَكَ يَسْعَىٰ وَهُوَ يَخْشَىٰ فَأَنتَ عَنْهُ تَلَهَّىٰ

They almost succeeded in tempting you to stray from [the Truth] that We have revealed to you and to declare something else in Our name. In that case, they would have made you their friend. – Surah Al-Isra 17:73

وَإِن كَادُوا۟ لَيَفْتِنُونَكَ عَنِ ٱلَّذِىٓ أَوْحَيْنَآ إِلَيْكَ لِتَفْتَرِىَ عَلَيْنَا غَيْرَهُۥ ۖ وَإِذًا لَّٱتَّخَذُوكَ خَلِيلًا

Abraham said to his father Azar, "Do you take idols for gods? I see that you and your people are in evident error." Thus We showed Abraham the empire of the heavens and the earth, that he might be one of those with certainty. When the night fell over him, he saw a planet. He said, "This is my lord." But when it set, he said, "I do not love those that set." Then, when he saw the moon rising, he said, "This is my lord." But when it set, he said, "If my Lord does not guide me, I will be one of the erring people." Then, when he saw the sun rising, he said,

"This is my lord, this is bigger." But when it set, he said, "O my people, I am innocent of your idolatry. I have directed my attention towards Him Who created the heavens and the earth—a monotheist—and I am not of the idolaters." – Surah Al-An'am 6:74-79

وَإِذْ قَالَ إِبْرَٰهِيمُ لِأَبِيهِ ءَازَرَ أَتَتَّخِذُ أَصْنَامًا ءَالِهَةً إِنِّىٓ أَرَىٰكَ وَقَوْمَكَ فِى ضَلَٰلٍ مُّبِينٍ وَكَذَٰلِكَ نُرِىٓ إِبْرَٰهِيمَ مَلَكُوتَ ٱلسَّمَٰوَٰتِ وَٱلْأَرْضِ وَلِيَكُونَ مِنَ ٱلْمُوقِنِينَ فَلَمَّا جَنَّ عَلَيْهِ ٱلَّيْلُ رَءَا كَوْكَبًا قَالَ هَٰذَا رَبِّى فَلَمَّآ أَفَلَ قَالَ لَآ أُحِبُّ ٱلْءَافِلِينَ فَلَمَّا رَءَا ٱلْقَمَرَ بَازِغًا قَالَ هَٰذَا رَبِّى فَلَمَّآ أَفَلَ قَالَ لَئِن لَّمْ يَهْدِنِى رَبِّى لَأَكُونَنَّ مِنَ ٱلْقَوْمِ ٱلضَّآلِّينَ فَلَمَّا رَءَا ٱلشَّمْسَ بَازِغَةً قَالَ هَٰذَا رَبِّى هَٰذَآ أَكْبَرُ فَلَمَّآ أَفَلَتْ قَالَ يَٰقَوْمِ إِنِّى بَرِىٓءٌ مِّمَّا تُشْرِكُونَ إِنِّى وَجَّهْتُ وَجْهِىَ لِلَّذِى فَطَرَ ٱلسَّمَٰوَٰتِ وَٱلْأَرْضَ حَنِيفًا وَمَآ أَنَا۠ مِنَ ٱلْمُشْرِكِينَ

...... So (do) not ascribe purity (to) yourselves. He knows best (he) who fears. Surah Najm 53:32

....فَلَا تُزَكُّوٓا۟ أَنفُسَكُمْ هُوَ أَعْلَمُ بِمَنِ ٱتَّقَىٰٓ

They were only asked to worship Allah alone, making their faith sincerely His.... Surah Al-Baiyinah 98:5

وَمَآ أُمِرُوٓا۟ إِلَّا لِيَعْبُدُوا۟ ٱللَّهَ مُخْلِصِينَ لَهُ ٱلدِّينَ حُنَفَآءَ

Say, "Do you inform Allah of your faith, when Allah ⌜already⌝ knows whatever is in the heavens and whatever is on the earth? And Allah has ⌜perfect⌝ knowledge of all things." Surah Al-Hujurat 49:16

قُلْ أَتُعَلِّمُونَ ٱللَّهَ بِدِينِكُمْ وَٱللَّهُ يَعْلَمُ مَا فِى ٱلسَّمَٰوَٰتِ وَمَا فِى ٱلْأَرْضِ وَٱللَّهُ بِكُلِّ شَىْءٍ عَلِيمٌ

Say, ⌜O Prophet,⌝ "O People of the Book! Let us come to common terms: that we will worship none but Allah, associate none with Him, nor take one another as lords instead of Allah." But if they turn away, then say, "Bear witness that we have submitted ⌜to Allah alone⌝." – Surah Al-Imran 3:64

قُلْ يَٰٓأَهْلَ ٱلْكِتَٰبِ تَعَالَوْا۟ إِلَىٰ كَلِمَةٍ سَوَآءٍۭ بَيْنَنَا وَبَيْنَكُمْ أَلَّا نَعْبُدَ إِلَّا ٱللَّهَ وَلَا نُشْرِكَ بِهِۦ شَيْـًٔا وَلَا يَتَّخِذَ بَعْضُنَا بَعْضًا أَرْبَابًا مِّن دُونِ ٱللَّهِ فَإِن تَوَلَّوْا۟ فَقُولُوا۟ ٱشْهَدُوا۟ بِأَنَّا مُسْلِمُونَ

Narrated Abu Bakra: A man was mentioned before the Prophet ﷺ and another man praised him greatly The Prophet ﷺ said, "May Allah's Mercy be on you ! You have cut the neck of your friend." The Prophet ﷺ repeated this sentence many times and said, "If it is indispensable for anyone of you to praise someone, then he should say, 'I think that he is so-and-so," if he really thinks that he is such. Allah is the One Who will take his accounts (as He knows his reality) and no-one can sanctify anybody before Allah." (Khalid said, "Woe to you," instead of "Allah's Mercy be on you."). – Sahih al-Bukhari 6061

حَدَّثَنَا آدَمُ، حَدَّثَنَا شُعْبَةُ، عَنْ خَالِدٍ، عَنْ عَبْدِ الرَّحْمَنِ بْنِ أَبِي بَكْرَةَ، عَنْ أَبِيهِ، أَنَّ رَجُلاً، ذُكِرَ عِنْدَ النَّبِيِّ صلى الله عليه وسلم فَأَثْنَى عَلَيْهِ رَجُلٌ خَيْرًا، فَقَالَ النَّبِيُّ صلى الله عليه وسلم " وَيْحَكَ قَطَعْتَ عُنُقَ صَاحِبِكَ - يَقُولُهُ مِرَارًا - إِنْ كَانَ أَحَدُكُمْ مَادِحًا لاَ مَحَالَةَ فَلْيَقُلْ أَحْسِبُ كَذَا وَكَذَا. إِنْ كَانَ يُرَى أَنَّهُ كَذَلِكَ، وَحَسِيبُهُ اللَّهُ، وَلاَ يُزَكِّي عَلَى اللَّهِ أَحَدًا ". قَالَ وُهَيْبٌ عَنْ خَالِدٍ " وَيْلَكَ "

[40]

---

[40] **Imam Abu Haneefah** (may Allah have mercy on him) said:

- "If the hadeeth is saheeh then that is my madhhab."
- "It is not permissible for anyone to follow what we say if they do not know where we got it from."

Narrated Kharija bin Zaid bin Thabit: Um Al-`Ala', an Ansari woman who gave the pledge of allegiance to the Prophet ﷺ said to me, "The emigrants were distributed amongst us by drawing lots and we got in our share `Uthman bin Maz'un. We made him stay with us in our house. Then he suffered from a disease which proved fatal when he died and was given a bath and was shrouded in his clothes, Allah's Messenger ﷺ came I said, 'May Allah be merciful to you, O Abu As-Sa'ib! I testify that Allah has honored you'. The Prophet ﷺ said, 'How do you know that Allah has honored him?' I replied, 'O Allah's Messenger ﷺ ! Let my father be sacrificed for you! On whom else shall Allah bestow His honor?' The Prophet ﷺ said, 'No doubt, death came to him. By Allah, I too wish him good, but by Allah, I do not know what Allah will do with me though I am Allah's Messenger ﷺ . 'By Allah, I never attested the piety of anyone after that." Al-Laith also narrated as above. – Sahih al-Bukhari 1243

حَدَّثَنَا يَحْيَى بْنُ بُكَيْرٍ، حَدَّثَنَا اللَّيْثُ، عَنْ عُقَيْلٍ، عَنِ ابْنِ شِهَابٍ، قَالَ أَخْبَرَنِي خَارِجَةُ بْنُ زَيْدِ بْنِ ثَابِتٍ، أَنَّ أُمَّ الْعَلاَءِ ـ امْرَأَةً مِنَ الأَنْصَارِ ـ بَايَعَتِ النَّبِيَّ صلى الله عليه وسلم أَخْبَرَتْهُ أَنَّهُ اقْتُسِمَ الْمُهَاجِرُونَ قُرْعَةً فَطَارَ لَنَا عُثْمَانُ بْنُ مَظْعُونٍ، فَأَنْزَلْنَاهُ فِي أَبْيَاتِنَا، فَوَجِعَ وَجَعَهُ الَّذِي تُوُفِّيَ فِيهِ، فَلَمَّا تُوُفِّيَ وَغُسِّلَ وَكُفِّنَ فِي أَثْوَابِهِ، دَخَلَ رَسُولُ اللَّهِ صلى الله عليه وسلم فَقُلْتُ رَحْمَةُ اللَّهِ عَلَيْكَ أَبَا السَّائِبِ، فَشَهَادَتِي عَلَيْكَ لَقَدْ أَكْرَمَكَ اللَّهُ. فَقَالَ النَّبِيُّ صلى الله عليه وسلم " وَمَا يُدْرِيكِ أَنَّ اللَّهَ قَدْ أَكْرَمَهُ ". فَقُلْتُ بِأَبِي أَنْتَ يَا رَسُولَ اللَّهِ فَمَنْ يُكْرِمُهُ اللَّهُ فَقَالَ " أَمَّا هُوَ فَقَدْ جَاءَهُ الْيَقِينُ، وَاللَّهِ إِنِّي لأَرْجُو لَهُ الْخَيْرَ، وَاللَّهِ مَا أَدْرِي ـ وَأَنَا رَسُولُ اللَّهِ ـ مَا يُفْعَلُ بِي ". قَالَتْ فَوَاللَّهِ لاَ أُزَكِّي أَحَدًا بَعْدَهُ أَبَدًا. حَدَّثَنَا سَعِيدُ بْنُ عُفَيْرٍ، حَدَّثَنَا اللَّيْثُ، مِثْلَهُ. وَقَالَ نَافِعُ بْنُ يَزِيدَ عَنْ عُقَيْلٍ، مَا يُفْعَلُ بِهِ وَتَابَعَهُ شُعَيْبٌ وَعَمْرُو بْنُ دِينَارٍ وَمَعْمَرٌ

- "It is haraam for the one who does not know my evidence to issue a fatwa based on my words."
- "We are human, we may say something today and retract it tomorrow."
- "If I say something that goes against the Book of Allaah or the report of the Messenger (peace and blessings of Allaah be upon him), then ignore what I say."

Imam Maalik (may Allaah have mercy on him) said:

- "I am only human, sometimes I make mistakes and sometimes I get things right. Look at my opinion and whatever is in accordance with the Qur'aan and Sunnah, take it, and whatever is not in accordance with the Qur'aan and Sunnah, ignore it."
- "There is no one after the Prophet (peace and blessings of Allaah be upon him) whose words cannot be taken or left, apart from the Prophet (peace and blessings of Allaah be upon him)." ("Everyone's statement can be taken or rejected except for the companion of this grave")

Imam al-Shaafa'I (may Allaah have mercy on him) said:

- "There is no one who will not be unaware of some of the Sunnah of the Messenger of Allaah (peace and blessings of Allaah be upon him). Whatever I say or whatever guidelines I establish, if there is a report from the Messenger of Allaah (peace and blessings of Allaah be upon him) which is different to what I said, then what matters is what the Messenger of Allaah (peace and blessings of Allaah be upon him) said, and that is my opinion."

Imam Ahmad (may Allah have mercy on him) said:

- "Do not follow me blindly and do not follow Maalik or al-Shaafa'I or al-Awzaa'I or al-Thawri blindly. Learn from where they learned."
- "The opinion of al-Awzaa'I and the opinion of Maalik and the opinion of Abu Haneefah are all mere conjecture and it is all the same to me. Rather evidence is to be found in the reports – i.e., in the shar'I evidence."

Narrated Abu Huraira: Zainab's original name was "Barrah," but it was said' "By that she is giving herself the prestige of piety." So the Prophetﷺ changed her name to Zainab - Sahih al-Bukhari 6192

حَدَّثَنَا صَدَقَةُ بْنُ الْفَضْلِ، أَخْبَرَنَا مُحَمَّدُ بْنُ جَعْفَرٍ، عَنْ شُعْبَةَ، عَنْ عَطَاءِ بْنِ أَبِي مَيْمُونَةَ، عَنْ أَبِي رَافِعٍ، عَنْ أَبِي هُرَيْرَةَ، أَنَّ زَيْنَبَ، كَانَ اسْمُهَا بَرَّةَ، فَقِيلَ تُزَكِّي نَفْسَهَا. فَسَمَّاهَا رَسُولُ اللَّهِ صلى الله عليه وسلم زَيْنَبَ

"Do you know what is meant by believing in Allah Alone?"
" هَلْ تَدْرُونَ مَا الإِيمَانُ بِاللَّهِ وَحْدَهُ ".

There is no doubt that whatever ˹idols˺ you invite me to ˹worship˺ are not worthy to be invoked either in this world or the Hereafter. ˹Undoubtedly,˺ our return is to Allah, and the transgressors will be the inmates of the Fire. You will remember what I say to you, and I entrust my affairs to Allah. Surely Allah is All-Seeing of all ˹His˺ servants." Surah Al-Ghafir 40:43&44

لَا جَرَمَ أَنَّمَا تَدْعُونَنِىٓ إِلَيْهِ لَيْسَ لَهُۥ دَعْوَةٌ فِى ٱلدُّنْيَا وَلَا فِى ٱلْـَٔاخِرَةِ وَأَنَّ مَرَدَّنَآ إِلَى ٱللَّهِ وَأَنَّ ٱلْمُسْرِفِينَ هُمْ أَصْحَـٰبُ ٱلنَّارِ فَسَتَذْكُرُونَ مَآ أَقُولُ لَكُمْ ۚ وَأُفَوِّضُ أَمْرِىٓ إِلَى ٱللَّهِ ۚ إِنَّ ٱللَّهَ بَصِيرٌۢ بِٱلْعِبَادِ

Yet when Allah alone is mentioned, the hearts of those who disbelieve in the Hereafter are filled with disgust. But as soon as those ˹gods˺ other than Him are mentioned, they are filled with joy. Surah Al-Ghafir 40:12

وَإِذَا ذُكِرَ ٱللَّهُ وَحْدَهُ ٱشْمَأَزَّتْ قُلُوبُ ٱلَّذِينَ لَا يُؤْمِنُونَ بِٱلْـَٔاخِرَةِ ۖ وَإِذَا ذُكِرَ ٱلَّذِينَ مِن دُونِهِۦٓ إِذَا هُمْ يَسْتَبْشِرُونَ

Say, "I have been forbidden to worship those ˹idols˺ you worship besides Allah, since clear proofs have come to me from my Lord. And I have been commanded to ˹fully˺ submit to the Lord of all worlds." Surah Al-Ghafir 40:60

قُلْ إِنِّى نُهِيتُ أَنْ أَعْبُدَ ٱلَّذِينَ تَدْعُونَ مِن دُونِ ٱللَّهِ لَمَّا جَآءَنِىَ ٱلْبَيِّنَـٰتُ مِن رَّبِّى وَأُمِرْتُ أَنْ أُسْلِمَ لِرَبِّ ٱلْعَـٰلَمِينَ

˹They will be told,˺ "˹No!˺ This is because when Allah alone was invoked, you ˹staunchly˺ disbelieved. But when others were associated with Him ˹in worship˺, you ˹readily˺ believed. So judgment belongs to Allah ˹alone˺—the Most High, All-Great." – Surah Az-Zumar 39:45

ذَٰلِكُم بِأَنَّهُۥٓ إِذَا دُعِىَ ٱللَّهُ وَحْدَهُۥ كَفَرْتُمْ ۖ وَإِن يُشْرَكْ بِهِۦ تُؤْمِنُوا۟ ۚ فَٱلْحُكْمُ لِلَّهِ ٱلْعَلِىِّ ٱلْكَبِيرِ

Narrated `Utban bin Malik Al-Ansari :Who was one of the men of the tribe of Bani Salim: Allah's Messengerﷺ came to me and said, "If anybody comes on the Day of Resurrection who has said: La ilaha illal-lah, sincerely, with the intention to win Allah's Pleasure, Allah will make the Hell-Fire forbidden for him – .".Sahih al-Bukhari 6423

قَالَ سَمِعْتُ عِتْبَانَ بْنَ مَالِكٍ الأَنْصَارِيَّ، ثُمَّ أَحَدَ بَنِي سَالِمٍ قَالَ غَدَا عَلَىَّ رَسُولُ اللَّهِ صلى الله عليه وسلم فَقَالَ " لَنْ يُوَافِيَ عَبْدٌ يَوْمَ الْقِيَامَةِ يَقُولُ لاَ إِلَهَ إِلاَّ اللَّهُ. يَبْتَغِي بِهِ وَجْهَ اللَّهِ، إِلاَّ حَرَّمَ اللَّهُ عَلَيْهِ النَّارَ ".

Narrated Abu Jamra: I was an interpreter between the people and Ibn `Abbas. Once Ibn `Abbas said that a delegation of the tribe of `Abdul Qais came to the Prophetﷺ who asked them, "Who are the people (i.e. you)? (Or) who are the delegates?" They replied, "We are from the tribe of Rabi`a." Then the Prophetﷺ said to them, "Welcome, O people (or said, "O delegation (of `Abdul Qais).") Neither will you have disgrace nor will you regret." They said, "We have come to you from a distant place and there is the tribe of the infidels of Mudar intervening between you and us and we cannot come to you except in the sacred month. So please order us to do something good (religious deeds) and that we may also inform our people whom we have left behind (at home) and that we may enter Paradise (by acting on

Them.)" The Prophet ordered them to do four things, and forbade them from four things. He ordered them to believe in Allah Alone, the Honorable the Majestic and said to them, "Do you know what is meant by believing in Allah Alone?" They replied, "Allah and His Apostle know better." Thereupon the Prophet ﷺ said, "(That means to testify that none has the right to be worshipped but Allah and that Muhammad is His Apostle, to offer prayers perfectly, to pay Zakat, to observe fasts during the month of Ramadan, (and) to pay Al-Khumus (one fifth of the booty to be given in Allah's cause)." Then he forbade them four things, namely Ad-Dubba.' Hantam, Muzaffat (and) An-Naqir or Muqaiyar (These were the names of pots in which alcoholic drinks used to be prepared). The Prophet ﷺ further said, "Memorize them (these instructions) and tell them to the people whom you have left behind.". – Sahih al-Bukhari 87

حَدَّثَنَا مُحَمَّدُ بْنُ بَشَّارٍ، قَالَ حَدَّثَنَا غُنْدَرٌ، قَالَ حَدَّثَنَا شُعْبَةُ، عَنْ أَبِي جَمْرَةَ، قَالَ كُنْتُ أُتَرْجِمُ بَيْنَ ابْنِ عَبَّاسٍ وَبَيْنَ النَّاسِ فَقَالَ إِنَّ وَفْدَ عَبْدِ الْقَيْسِ أَتَوُا النَّبِيَّ صلى الله عليه وسلم فَقَالَ " مَنِ الْوَفْدُ ـ أَوْ مَنِ الْقَوْمُ ". قَالُوا رَبِيعَةُ. فَقَالَ " مَرْحَبًا بِالْقَوْمِ ـ أَوْ بِالْوَفْدِ ـ غَيْرَ خَزَايَا وَلاَ نَدَامَى ". قَالُوا إِنَّا نَأْتِيكَ مِنْ شُقَّةٍ بَعِيدَةٍ، وَبَيْنَنَا وَبَيْنَكَ هَذَا الْحَىُّ مِنْ كُفَّارِ مُضَرَ، وَلاَ نَسْتَطِيعُ أَنْ نَأْتِيَكَ إِلاَّ فِي شَهْرٍ حَرَامٍ فَمُرْنَا بِأَمْرٍ نُخْبِرْ بِهِ مَنْ وَرَاءَنَا، نَدْخُلْ بِهِ الْجَنَّةَ. فَأَمَرَهُمْ بِأَرْبَعٍ، وَنَهَاهُمْ عَنْ أَرْبَعٍ أَمَرَهُمْ بِالإِيمَانِ بِاللَّهِ عَزَّ وَجَلَّ وَحْدَهُ. قَالَ " هَلْ تَدْرُونَ مَا الإِيمَانُ بِاللَّهِ وَحْدَهُ ". قَالُوا اللَّهُ وَرَسُولُهُ أَعْلَمُ. قَالَ " شَهَادَةُ أَنْ لاَ إِلَهَ إِلاَّ اللَّهُ وَأَنَّ مُحَمَّدًا رَسُولُ اللَّهِ، وَإِقَامُ الصَّلاَةِ، وَإِيتَاءُ الزَّكَاةِ، وَصَوْمُ رَمَضَانَ، وَتُعْطُوا الْخُمُسَ مِنَ الْمَغْنَمِ ". وَنَهَاهُمْ عَنِ الدُّبَّاءِ وَالْحَنْتَمِ وَالْمُزَفَّتِ. قَالَ شُعْبَةُ رُبَّمَا قَالَ النَّقِيرِ، وَرُبَّمَا قَالَ الْمُقَيَّرِ. قَالَ " احْفَظُوهُ وَأَخْبِرُوهُ مَنْ وَرَاءَكُمْ "

Say, "O you mankind! In case you are in doubt regarding my religion, then I do not worship the ones whom you worship apart from Allah; but I worship Allah Who takes you up to Him, and I am commanded to be of the believers." And keep your (i.e. the prophet's) face up to the religion, unswervingly upright, and definitely do not be of the associators. (Those who associate others with Allah And do not invoke, apart from Allah, that which neither profits nor harms you; then in case you do this, then you will surely be of the unjust (people) Surah Yunus 10:104-106

قُلْ يَـٰٓأَيُّهَا ٱلنَّاسُ إِن كُنتُمْ فِى شَكٍّ مِّن دِينِى فَلَآ أَعْبُدُ ٱلَّذِينَ تَعْبُدُونَ مِن دُونِ ٱللَّهِ وَلَـٰكِنْ أَعْبُدُ ٱللَّهَ ٱلَّذِى يَتَوَفَّىٰكُمْ ۖ وَأُمِرْتُ أَنْ أَكُونَ مِنَ ٱلْمُؤْمِنِينَ وَأَنْ أَقِمْ وَجْهَكَ لِلدِّينِ حَنِيفًا وَلَا تَكُونَنَّ مِنَ ٱلْمُشْرِكِينَ وَلَا تَدْعُ مِن دُونِ ٱللَّهِ مَا لَا يَنفَعُكَ وَلَا يَضُرُّكَ ۖ فَإِن فَعَلْتَ فَإِنَّكَ إِذًا مِّنَ ٱلظَّـٰلِمِينَ

You have already had a fair example in Ibrahim (Abraham) and the ones with him as they said to their people, "Surely we are completely quit of you and whatever you worship apart from Allah. We disbelieve in you, and between you and us enmity has appeared, and abhorrence forever, until you believe in Allah alone."...... Surah Al-Mumtahina 60:4

قَدْ كَانَتْ لَكُمْ أُسْوَةٌ حَسَنَةٌ فِىٓ إِبْرَٰهِيمَ وَٱلَّذِينَ مَعَهُۥٓ إِذْ قَالُوا۟ لِقَوْمِهِمْ إِنَّا بُرَءَٰٓؤُا۟ مِنكُمْ وَمِمَّا تَعْبُدُونَ مِن دُونِ ٱللَّهِ كَفَرْنَا بِكُمْ وَبَدَا بَيْنَنَا وَبَيْنَكُمُ ٱلْعَدَٰوَةُ وَٱلْبَغْضَآءُ أَبَدًا حَتَّىٰ تُؤْمِنُوا۟ بِٱللَّهِ وَحْدَهُۥٓ ...

And in no way did I create the jinn and humankind except to worship Me. – Surah Adh-Dhariyat 51:56

وَمَا خَلَقْتُ ٱلْجِنَّ وَٱلْإِنسَ إِلَّا لِيَعْبُدُونِ

....."we disown you and what you worship besides Allah.... Surah Al-Mumtahinah 60:4

....إِنَّا بُرَءَٰٓؤُا۟ مِنكُمْ وَمِمَّا تَعْبُدُونَ مِن دُونِ ٱللَّهِ

Those who listen to what is said (in the Qur’an) and follow the best of it. These are the ones ˹rightly˺ guided by Allah, and these are ˹truly˺ the people of reason. - Surah Az-Zumar 39:18

ٱلَّذِينَ يَسْتَمِعُونَ ٱلْقَوْلَ فَيَتَّبِعُونَ أَحْسَنَهُۥٓ أُو۟لَـٰٓئِكَ ٱلَّذِينَ هَدَىٰهُمُ ٱللَّهُ ۖ وَأُو۟لَـٰٓئِكَ هُمْ أُو۟لُوا۟ ٱلْأَلْبَـٰبِ

He who is not merciful to others, will not be treated mercifully – Sahih al-Bukhari 6013

مَنْ لاَ يَرْحَمُ لاَ يُرْحَ

Appendix

Umar said, “Be sure of what you say.”. – Sahih al-Bukhari 3221
فَقَالَ عُمَرُ اعْلَمْ مَا تَقُولُ

The Science of Hadith

The Science of Hadith (Arabic: ʿIlm al-Ḥadīth) is a specialized field within Islamic scholarship that focuses on the collection, authentication, classification, and interpretation of hadiths — the sayings, actions, tacit approvals, and characteristics of the Prophet Muhammad ﷺ . This discipline is central to the development of Islamic law (Sharīʿah), ethics, and theology, because the hadith, alongside the Qur’an, serves as one of the two primary sources of Islamic guidance.

Definition and Importance

A hadith consists of two main parts:
Isnād (Chain of Transmission): The sequence of narrators who passed down the report.
Matn (Text): The actual content or wording of the hadith.
Because hadiths were initially transmitted orally, the science of hadith emerged to ensure authenticity, protect against forgery, and preserve the Prophet’s teachings.

Classification of Hadith

Hadiths are classified based on various criteria:
Ṣaḥīḥ (Authentic): Reliable chain, upright and accurate narrators, no flaws.
Ḥasan (Good): Slightly less reliable than ṣaḥīḥ but still acceptable.
Ḍaʿīf (Weak): Chain contains unknown or unreliable narrators.
Mawḍūʿ (Fabricated): Invented; not traceable to the Prophet ﷺ.
By chain continuity:
Mutawātir: Reported by so many people that fabrication is impossible.
Āḥād: Reported by one or a few narrators; may still be authentic.

Major Types of Hadith Based on Authenticity:

Ṣaḥīḥ (Authentic) – meets all five criteria.
Ḥasan (Good) – slightly lesser reliability than ṣaḥīḥ.

Ḍaʿīf (Weak) – fails one or more criteria.
Mawḍūʿ (Fabricated) – falsely attributed to the Prophet.

Branches of Hadith Sciences:

ʿIlm al-Rijāl: Study of narrators' biographies and trustworthiness.
ʿIlm al-Jarḥ wa al-Taʿdīl: Evaluation of narrators' credibility.
ʿIlal al-Ḥadīth: Analysis of hidden defects.
Gharīb and Shādh: Rare and irregular narrations.

Famous Hadith Collections:

Ṣaḥīḥ al-Bukhārī
Ṣaḥīḥ Muslim
Sunan al-Nasāʾī
Sunan Abī Dāwūd
Jāmiʿ al-Tirmidhī
Sunan Ibn Mājah

These six are collectively known as the Kutub al-Sittah (The Six Books).

Purpose of the Science:

The goal is to determine whether a hadith is authentic (ṣaḥīḥ), good (ḥasan), or weak (ḍaʿīf) based on the reliability and memory of the narrators, and the continuity and integrity of the chain.

Key Criteria for Authenticity:

ʿ**Adālah**: Moral integrity and upright character of narrators.
Ḍabt: Precision and strong memory in narration.
Muttaṣil: Unbroken chain of transmission.
Shudhūdh: Absence of contradiction with more reliable sources.
ʿ**Illah**: No hidden defects.

Importance in Islam:

Hadith forms the second primary source of Islamic law and guidance after the Qur'an. It clarifies Qur'anic verses, provides practical examples of the Prophet's life (Sunnah), and offers moral and legal instructions. The science of hadith ensures these teachings are preserved with precision, making it essential for Islamic jurisprudence, theology, and ethics.

Intentions of the Major Hadith Compilers

The compilation of hadith — the sayings, actions, and approvals of the Prophet Muhammad (peace be upon him) — represents one of the most significant scholarly undertakings in Islamic history. In the generations following the Prophet's death, scholars devoted their lives to preserving these narrations with accuracy, sincerity, and intellectual rigor. The motivations of these compilers were rooted in a profound sense of responsibility: to protect the integrity of the Prophet's teachings and to provide reliable sources for Islamic law, theology, and ethics.

What follows is an overview of the major hadith compilers and the primary intentions that guided their monumental efforts. These scholars did not compile hadith arbitrarily; rather, their works were shaped by specific scholarly goals, theological concerns, and legal priorities. While differing in methodology and scope, all were unified by a commitment to preserving the Prophetic legacy for future generations.

Imam al-Bukhari

Imam Muhammad ibn Ismail al-Bukhari (d. 870 CE) is regarded as one of the most distinguished hadith scholars in Islamic history. His Sahih al-Bukhari is often considered the most authentic book in Islam after the Qur'an. Al-Bukhari's primary intention was to create a compilation of hadith that met the strictest criteria for authenticity (ṣaḥīḥ). His goal was not merely preservation but refinement — to filter only the most reliable narrations based on rigorous conditions.

He required not only a trustworthy and precise narrator but also unbroken chains of transmission (isnād) and evidence that the narrators had actually met. Al-Bukhari reportedly reviewed over 600,000 narrations and selected only around 7,000 (with repetitions), demonstrating his extreme precision. His aim was to provide Muslims with a trustworthy legal and moral foundation, free from doubt or fabrication.

Imam Muslim

A student of al-Bukhari, Imam Muslim ibn al-Hajjaj (d. 875 CE) compiled Sahih Muslim with a similarly rigorous standard of authenticity. However, while his criteria were comparable, Muslim often organized hadith differently — grouping together variations of the same narration to allow scholars to compare and analyze them more easily.

His intention was not only to authenticate but to clarify and simplify the understanding of hadith. Sahih Muslim's structure and coherence make it an essential resource for scholars and students alike. Imam Muslim also refrained from inserting personal commentary, allowing the narrations to speak for themselves. His work reflects a scholarly ethic of humility and exactitude, aimed at preserving the Prophetic Sunnah in its clearest form.

Imam an-Nasa'I

Ahmad ibn Shu'ayb an-Nasa'I (d. 915 CE) initially compiled a larger work, Sunan al-Kubra, which included hadith of varying levels of authenticity. However, upon request by the governor of Ramalah, he produced a more refined version, Sunan al-Sughra (also known as Al-Mujtaba), which focused almost exclusively on authentic narrations.

An-Nasa'i's intention was to balance scholarly comprehensiveness with reliability, creating a collection that would be practical for legal scholars while maintaining a high standard of trustworthiness. His careful selection reflects his desire to reduce ambiguity in legal rulings and support the use of sound hadith in judicial and educational contexts.

Imam Abu Dawud

Imam Abu Dawud al-Sijistani (d. 889 CE) focused primarily on hadith relevant to Islamic jurisprudence (fiqh). His Sunan Abi Dawud was designed as a legal reference, gathering narrations used by jurists in issuing fatwas and legal opinions. While not all hadith in the collection are sahih, Abu Dawud often provided commentary on their strength or weakness.

His intention was pragmatic: to furnish scholars with the tools for legal reasoning, even if that meant including narrations of varying reliability — provided their weaknesses were clarified. His work reflects an early form of hadith criticism, where scholarly transparency was prioritized to aid the legal process.

Imam at-Tirmidhi

Imam Muhammad ibn Isa at-Tirmidhi (d. 892 CE) compiled his Sunan with multiple purposes in mind. He included hadith used in legal rulings but also provided evaluations of authenticity, differences of opinion among scholars, and explanations of juristic applications.

At-Tirmidhi's unique contribution was his intention to bridge the gap between hadith scholars and jurists. By including his famous hadith gradings (e.g., sahih, hasan, da'if), along with brief scholarly commentary, he produced an accessible work for both academic and practical use. His Sunan is also notable for highlighting disagreements in interpretation, encouraging scholarly dialogue and respect for differing views.

Imam Ibn Majah

Abu 'Abdullah Ibn Majah (d. 887 CE)[41] sought to expand the scope of hadith available for legal and theological discussion. His Sunan includes many narrations not found in the other five canonical collections (al-Kutub al-Sittah), thus increasing the range of available material for scholars.

His primary intention appears to have been inclusivity — documenting hadith with various levels of authenticity to enrich the legal discourse of his time. As a result, his collection contains a greater proportion of weak (da'if) hadith. Nonetheless, the work holds enduring value for scholars studying the breadth of Prophetic traditions and their transmission.

Ibn Abi Shaybah

Abu Bakr Ibn Abi Shaybah (d. 849 CE) compiled one of the earliest and most expansive hadith collections, the Musannaf, which is organized thematically and includes narrations from the Prophet, his Companions, and early jurists.

His intention was encyclopedic: to preserve a vast array of narrations regardless of legal applicability or authenticity level. The Musannaf includes sahih, mawquf (Companion-attributed), and even munqaṭi' (disconnected) reports, offering valuable insight into early Islamic thought, practice, and legal reasoning

Imam Malik

One of the earliest hadith compilations, the Muwatta' of Imam Malik (d. 795 CE) reflects a unique combination of hadith and the legal opinions of the scholars of Madinah. Imam Malik intended his work to be a practical manual of Islamic law, rooted in the lived practice of the city of the Prophet.

---

[41] Before the formal recognition of the Kutub al-Sittah, Sunni scholars generally treated five major hadith collections as the primary authentic sources, but this changed during the 11th century under the Seljuk Empire, when prominent scholars—most notably Abū'l-Faḍl Muḥammad ibn Ṭāhir al-Maqdisī—advocated for the inclusion of Sunan Ibn Mājah. Their endorsement helped elevate Ibn Mājah's work to canonical status, expanding the established set from five to six books and solidifying the collection now universally known as the Kutub al-Sittah within Sunni Islam.

Unlike later compilers focused solely on isnād verification, Malik emphasized community consensus and legal stability, incorporating the actions of the people of Madinah (ʿamal ahl al-Madīnah) as a source of legal authority. His goal was to preserve not just the sayings of the Prophet, but their correct implementation.

Imam Ahmad

Imam Ahmad ibn Hanbal (d. 855 CE) compiled one of the largest hadith collections, the Musnad, containing over 30,000 narrations. Organized by narrator, not by topic, his work reflects his desire to preserve the Prophetic legacy in its totality.

His primary intention was archival — to compile every hadith he deemed reliable into one collection for posterity. Though not arranged for legal use, the Musnad has served as a foundational source for later hadith scholars and jurists. Imam Ahmad's reverence for the Sunnah and refusal to compromise on authenticity defined his lifelong scholarly mission.

- The compilers of hadith were not mere collectors of texts — they were guardians of a sacred trust. Each scholar approached the task with unique intentions shaped by personal convictions, regional legal traditions, and methodological frameworks. Whether emphasizing strict authenticity, legal utility, or comprehensive documentation, their efforts laid the groundwork for centuries of Islamic scholarship.

By understanding the intentions behind these compilations, modern readers can appreciate not only the technical depth of hadith sciences but also the ethical sincerity that defined early Islamic scholarship.

Hardships endured by our scholars

Imam Bukhari, known for compiling the most authentic collection of hadith, "Sahih al-Bukhari," faced significant opposition from political authorities.

His refusal to accept weak or fabricated narrations, even when they were politically advantageous to rulers, caused tension between him and the ruling elites.

The Trial in Baghdad: In the 9th century, the Abbasid caliphate, under the influence of certain theological factions (notably the Mu'tazila), engaged in a campaign against scholars who upheld the traditionalist views regarding the Hadith and Aqeedah. Imam Bukhari was subjected to suspicion and scrutiny by authorities, particularly when he was accused of supporting certain theological stances that went against the political and doctrinal positions of the caliphs.

His rigorous methodology in Hadith criticism and his refusal to compromise on the authenticity of narrations led to persecution. He was once driven out of Baghdad after a group of scholars, possibly under pressure from the government, accused him of having problematic views.

Imam Nasai, known for his hadith compilation Sunan an-Nasa'I, faced severe opposition during his life. His staunch position on hadith authentication and his bold criticism of certain narrators led to conflict with powerful groups.

Imam Nasai's persecution is most famously associated with the caliphate of the Abbasid rulers. His criticism of certain prominent hadith narrators angered those in power, leading to his expulsion from Baghdad.

Exile to Damascus: Imam Nasai was reportedly attacked for his scholarly positions, particularly his rejection of weak hadiths and his criticism of prominent political figures. Eventually, he was forced into exile, and it is believed that he died in Alexandria, Egypt, possibly as a result of the hardships he endured during this time.

Imam Abu Shayba was one of the prominent scholars of his time, renowned for his knowledge in hadith and fiqh. However, he faced opposition during the period of the Abbasid dynasty, particularly under the influence of the Mu'tazilite movement, which was in conflict with traditionalist scholars like him.

Like Bukhari, Imam Abu Shayba's insistence on adhering strictly to the Quran and Hadith, and his resistance to unverified traditions or innovations, often put him at odds with political authorities.

His views were controversial because they emphasized the importance of authentic traditions over political convenience or doctrinal shifts promoted by the ruling elite.

Imam Abu Hanifa, the founder of the Hanafi school of thought, faced significant political persecution during his lifetime. His relationship with the ruling Abbasid caliphate was particularly strained.

Abu Hanifa's refusal to support the Abbasid caliphate led to his imprisonment. He was an outspoken critic of the oppressive policies of the caliphs, and this ultimately led to his arrest by the authorities.

Imam Abu Hanifa's commitment to justice and his refusal to compromise on his principles led to his imprisonment. He was placed in solitary confinement, where he reportedly suffered a great deal. Despite his difficulties, his scholarship and influence persisted, and the Hanafi school of thought became one of the most widely followed schools in the Islamic world.

Imam Malik, the founder of the Maliki school of jurisprudence, faced significant challenges from both political and theological authorities during his time. He lived in the city of Madinah, where he was respected as a leading scholar.

His views were often in tension with the ruling Umayyad and later Abbasid caliphs. One of the key instances of his persecution was when he was summoned to court by the Umayyad caliph al-Mansur.

The caliph sought to have Malik's views conform to the official government stance, but Imam Malik famously rejected this, maintaining his independence as a scholar. Despite this, Malik was treated with respect, but the tension with political authorities was always present.

Imam Shafi'I, the founder of the Shafi'I school, faced political challenges, particularly from the Umayyad and Abbasid caliphates. However, his persecution was largely intellectual, as he worked to reconcile the different schools of thought and codify the methodology of legal reasoning in Islam.

His rise to prominence coincided with a time of great political instability, and his criticism of various legal and theological ideas earned him enemies in high places. Like other scholars of the time, he was also subjected to suspicion by the authorities who feared the influence of independent scholars.

His legacy, however, remained unshaken, and the Shafi'I school became one of the leading schools of Sunni jurisprudence.

Imam Ahmad ibn Hanbal, the founder of the Hanbali school, is perhaps the most famous for his personal suffering and the persecution he endured. His conflict with the caliph al-Ma'mun, particularly over the Mu'tazilite doctrine of the createdness of the Quran, is one of the most significant episodes in early Islamic history.

The Mi'na Trial (833–835 CE), where Imam Ahmad was tortured and imprisoned for refusing to accept the doctrine of the createdness of the Quran, is a defining moment in his life. Imam Ahmad firmly believed that the Quran was eternal and uncreated, and he refused to accept the theological positions pushed by the ruling caliph.

Imam Ahmad endured beatings and imprisonment for his stance, but he refused to back down. He famously said, "The truth is with the people of Hadith, even if they are beaten with whips."

His resilience in the face of persecution earned him widespread respect, and the Hanbali school became influential in certain regions, though it was always

The persecution faced by these scholars was often tied to their steadfast commitment to preserving the authenticity of Islamic teachings and standing against the political and intellectual pressures of their times. Their opposition to innovations, weak hadiths, or politically motivated theological doctrines made them targets of both government authorities and competing theological factions. Despite the challenges, their legacy endures, and their contributions to Islamic jurisprudence, hadith, and theology have shaped the Muslim world for centuries

Their resilience is seen as an embodiment of the Islamic value of standing up for truth, even in the face of personal hardship, and their perseverance in the pursuit of knowledge is revered throughout the Islamic tradition.

Muhammad ibn Sīrīn said: "They did not use to ask about the chain of narration. But when the fitnah occurred, they said: 'Name your narrators for us.' So the narrations of Ahl al-Sunnah were examined and accepted, And the narrations of the People of Innovation were examined and rejected.". – al-Khaṭīb al-Baghdādī – al-Kifāyah fī 'Ilm al-Riwayah Volume/Page: vol. 1, p. 122

قال محمد بن سيرين : لم يكونوا يسألون عن الإسناد، فلما وقعتِ الفتنةُ قالوا: سَمُّوا لنا رجالكم، فيُنظَرُ إلى أهلِ السُّنَّة فيُؤخذُ حديثُهم، ويُنظَرُ إلى أهلِ البدع فلا يُؤخذُ حديثُهم

The Importance of Reading and Understanding the Qur'an and Hadith

The Qur'an and the Hadith of the Prophet Muhammad ﷺ are the two primary sources of Islamic guidance. They are the light by which Muslims are guided in both their worldly lives and their journey toward the hereafter. The Qur'an is the literal word of Allah, revealed to the Prophet ﷺ as a mercy and guidance for all of humanity. The Hadith, on the other hand, is the record of the sayings, actions, and approvals of the Prophet ﷺ , serving as a practical explanation and application of the Qur'anic teachings.

Reading the Qur'an is not just about reciting its verses; it is a profound act of worship. As the Prophet ﷺ said: "Whoever reads a letter from the Book of Allah will have a reward, and that reward will be multiplied by ten..." (Tirmidhi). However, the higher purpose lies in understanding and reflecting on its meanings. Allah says in the Qur'an: "Do they not reflect upon the Qur'an, or are there locks upon their hearts?" (Surah Muhammad: 24). Deep reflection leads to knowledge, action, spiritual awakening, and increased faith.

As for the Hadith, it clarifies the general meanings of the Qur'an, explains what is ambiguous, and provides details not found in the Qur'an. Without the Hadith, many aspects of Islamic practice—such as prayer, fasting, and ethical conduct—would be incomplete or misunderstood. Thus, understanding the Sunnah of the Prophet ﷺ is essential for practicing Islam correctly and comprehensively.

Moreover, reading and understanding the Qur'an and Hadith strengthens one's relationship with Allah, purifies the soul, shapes moral character, and provides clarity in distinguishing truth from falsehood and right from wrong. They nurture a balanced and principled personality that recognizes the rights of the Creator and the creation and strives to bring goodness and justice to the world.

The Qur'an and Hadith are the heart of a Muslim's life. In them is the life of the heart, happiness in this world, and salvation in the Hereafter. As Allah says: "Whoever follows My guidance will not go astray nor fall into distress." (Surah Taha: 123). Therefore, we must approach the Qur'an and the Sunnah with sincere hearts, thoughtful minds, and a true commitment to live by their teachings—for they are the best provision for this life and the next.

The Importance of Reading the Qur'an in Arabic

The Qur'an, regarded by Muslims as the literal word of God (Allah), was revealed in Arabic over 1,400 years ago to the Prophet Muhammad (peace be upon him). While translations can serve as helpful tools for understanding, they are ultimately interpretations of the original Arabic text. Reading the Qur'an in its original language is essential for a number of profound reasons, both spiritual and intellectual.

Arabic is the precise language chosen by Allah for the final revelation. The Qur'an itself affirms this in several verses, such as: "Indeed, We have sent it down as an Arabic Qur'an so that you may understand." (Qur'an 12:2). The divine choice of Arabic is not incidental; its unique linguistic structure, depth, and eloquence are part of the miracle of the Qur'an. No translation, regardless of the translator's expertise, can fully capture the rhetorical beauty, subtle meanings, or linguistic intricacies of the original

Every translation is inevitably an interpretation. Translators bring their own theological perspectives, cultural assumptions, and limitations of language into their work. Key Arabic terms in the Qur'an—such as taqwa (consciousness of God), rahmah (mercy), or deen (way of life)—carry layered meanings that often get flattened or simplified in translation. As a result, readers relying solely on translations may miss the richness or even misinterpret the intended message

Reading the Qur'an in Arabic fosters a deeper spiritual connection. The rhythmic recitation, the phonetic harmony, and the divine cadence of the Arabic words touch the heart in a way that translations cannot replicate. This is why Qur'anic recitation in prayer and worship is always in Arabic—it preserves the sacred sound and form of divine communication.

While translations are beneficial for learning and accessibility, they should never replace the original Arabic. For anyone seeking a true, unfiltered experience of the Qur'an, learning to read and understand it in its revealed language is not just important—it is essential

Biography of Tadhkir Ad-Deen

Tadhkir Ad-Deen was born in Falls Church, Virginia, and from a young age Allah placed in him a sincere desire to seek knowledge. At fourteen, he began studying the Torah and the Injīl, dedicating several years to understanding the scriptures that came before the Qur'an. During this period, he also faced a significant life test—that reshaped his perspective and humbled his heart. Through that challenge, Allah guided him toward reflection, paving the way for his later commitment to the Qur'an and Sunnah.

At the age of 20, Tadhkir Ad-Deen turned his heart toward the study of Ḥadīth, realizing it to be the key to understanding the Qur'an. He immersed himself in the sayings of the Prophet ﷺ, learning their chains, meanings, and authentic sources. His love for the Qur'an deepened as he labored to recite it in Arabic, completing the full recitation by the age of 34.

Without access to formal universities, he devoted himself to the classical sources of Islam. His curriculum was the library of the early ummah: Ṣaḥīḥ al-Bukhārī, Ṣaḥīḥ Muslim, Sunan al-Nasā'ī, Muwaṭṭa' Mālik, and the Muṣannaf of Ibn Abī Shaybah. In tafsīr, he studied the works of al-Ṭabarī and al-Qurṭubī, seeking to align every understanding with the authentic narrations of the Prophet ﷺ and his Companions.

Years of study led him to compile ʿAqeedatul-Mu'minūn – The Creed of the Believers – a collection of ḥadīth and reflections linking faith to the lived realities of believers. His aim was not authorship for recognition, but understanding for the sake of Allah. He would often remind himself, "Knowledge sought for other than Allah becomes a veil; knowledge sought for His sake becomes light."

Tadhkir Ad-Deen sees himself only as a simple Muslim in need of Allah's mercy. His humility reflects his constant remembrance of his past as a mark of divine mercy and transformation. His words carry sincerity, reminding others that Allah guides whom He wills, from whatever state they may be. He reflects upon the sayings of the early scholars – among them Imām al-Shāfiʿī's saying: "Knowledge is not what is memorized, but what benefits." To him, true knowledge purifies the heart, strengthens faith, and deepens submission to Allah. From poverty, Allah enriched him with the wealth of faith; from solitude, He opened the vastness of understanding.

His life is proof that divine guidance is not confined to scholars of renown, but granted to whoever sincerely seeks the truth.His journey stands as a reminder that through hardship, Allah purifies His servants and draws them nearer to Him. It echoes the Qur'anic promise:"And whoever fears Allah – He will make for him a way out, and provide for him from where he does not expect." (al-Ṭalāq 65:2-3)

Today, the name Tadhkir Ad-Deen – "Reminder of the Faith" – serves not as a title of prestige, but as a symbol of mercy and perseverance. He remains a student of sacred knowledge, a servant of the Qur'an and Sunnah, and a man who knows that all good lies in returning to Allah."Were it not for the grace of my Lord, I would have been among those taken [to Hell]." (al-Ṣāffāt 37:57)

www.ingramcontent.com/pod-product-compliance
Lightning Source LLC
Chambersburg PA
CBHW070045030426
42335CB00016B/1807

* 9 7 9 8 9 9 0 0 1 5 3 1 9 *